Chambers Slang Dictionary

Chambers Slang Dictionary

Jonathon Green

Chambers

CHAMBERS
An imprint of Chambers Harrap Publishers Ltd
7 Hopetoun Crescent, Edinburgh, EH7 4AY

Chambers Harrap is an Hachette UK company

First published by Chambers Harrap Publishers Ltd 2008
Paperback edition published 2009
Folio edition published 2009

A CIP catalogue record for this book is available from the British Library.

ISBN 978 0550 10563 9
ISBN 978 0550 10678 0 (Folio edition)

10 9 8 7 6 5 4 3 2 1

www.chambers.co.uk

Designed by Sharon McTeir
Typeset in Arial, Bliss and Optima by Sharon McTeir
Printed in Great Britain by Clays Ltd, St Ives plc

For SARAH CHATWIN,
with whom I have had the enormous good fortune to work for the
last 15 years, and from whose expertise, dedication and tolerance I
sincerely hope I shall to continue to benefit
for some time to come.

Contents

Contributors

Editor-in-chief
Sarah Chatwin

Researcher
Susie Ford

Editors
Vicky Aldus
Sandra Anderson
Pat Bulhosen
Sheila Ferguson
Lorna Gilmour
Alice Grandison
Andrew Holmes
Michael Munro

Editorial director
Vivian Marr

Publishing manager
Mary O'Neill

Data management
Gerry Breslin
Patrick Gaherty
Ruth O'Donovan

Production controller
Karen Stuart

Introduction

Slang is the language that says 'no'. No to piety, to religion, to ideology and all its permutations, to honour, nobility, patriotism and their kindred infantilisms. It is forever Falstaff, never the Prince. Of humanity it is most resolutely human. Unlike its Standard English 'cousin' – which, like slang, is just one more variety of the greater English language, albeit of an alternative register – its words are coined at society's lower depths, and make their way aloft. With sublime contempt for the prevailing liberalisms, it is sexist, racist, nationalist, prejudiced and welcoming of the crassest stereotyping. It is bawdy, scabrous, scatological, cruel, arrogant, boastful and cowardly. It lacks an iota of caring, sharing or compassion. At any given signpost it opts for the road less approved of, and if it calls a spade a spade, it is only for lack of some less pleasant synonym. It has no comprehension of love, other than as one of the least interesting of four-letter words. It plays no favourites: no one can claim special treatment. In comparison with the Standard English lexis its vocabulary covers a tiny waterfront, but in what depth: 3000 drunks, 1500 copulations, 1000 each of penises and vaginas...a glorious taxonomy of the flesh and its indulgence.

For these and other sins it remains a target: reviled, censored, the repository of sneers, dismissals and condemnations. Slang is unmoved. It just laughs and carries on regardless. It is the great re-inventor: its themes – sex, money, intoxication, insults (racial, national and personal), bodily parts and their functions – may not have changed in half a millennium of its collection, but like the alphabet that underpins it, it is capable of a seeming infinity of variations. 'Slang is a poor man's poetry,' suggested John Moore in *You English Words* (1962). The poor, as the cliché will have it, are always with us. This is to be deplored. That the language that mainly the poor create also shows no signs of vanishing, is not.

Chambers Slang Dictionary

This is not my first dictionary of slang: that was published in 1984 and its entire headword list, around 11,500 words and phrases, would now fit comfortably into those currently assembled under the letter S. This book contains around 85,000 words and phrases, the fruits of researches that have been under way ever since that first publication. But this is not the only change. This is the first of my slang dictionaries to be presented as 'fully nested'. The concept of lexicographical nesting maintains the essential alphabetical order, but rather than offer a succession of headwords offering compounds, derivatives and phrases, and all referring back to and *following* the primary word upon which they are based, the nested system places all those words *within* the basic headword. Thus one no longer looks for the compounds based, say, on *shit*, as a succession of unique entries in the word list, but at *shit* n. itself, where they are now to be found. This saves space, of course, but its main importance is to highlight the relationship of the primary word and its linguistic 'descendants'. The positive effect of nesting can also be seen at those phrases beginning with 'have...', 'put...', 'take...' and the like. Rather than face column upon column of such phrases (all beginning with a word that does not carry the meaning), the dictionary's user can now go straight to the pertinent term in the phrase, often the noun, and find it listed. Other than that, the entries have the features one might expect; each offers a headword, a part of speech, the etymology, variant spellings if found, the dates of use, and a definition. In many cases a term will have multiple definitions and, as noted, will be followed by any relevant nested material in the order of derivatives, compounds, phrases and exclamations.

Slang: the word

Where does the word 'slang' come from? My great predecessor Eric Partridge called it 'that prize-problem word'. But is it? Sir William Craigie, dealing with *slang* in the first edition of the *OED* took that dictionary's usual cautious view on such matters: it was 'a word of cant origin, the ultimate source of which is not apparent'; this refusal to hazard any further guess has not been modified since. Craigie compounded his rejection of possible origins with a further note: 'the date and early associations of the word make it unlikely that there is any connection with certain Norwegian forms in *sleng-* which exhibit some approximation in sense.' This flat declaration ran quite contrary to the views of Walter Skeat, whose *Etymological Dictionary of the English Language* had appeared between 1879 and 1882. Skeat attributed *slang* unequivocally to the Scandinavian languages and offered as evidence such terms as the Norwegian *sleng*: 'a slinging, an invention, device, stratagem [...] a little addition or burthen of a song, in verse and melody'; *slengjenamn*: a nickname; *slengjeord*: an insulting word or allusion and the Swedish *slanger*: to gossip. Other etymologists have tended to agree. Most recently Partridge himself, never one to let caution fetter his deductive skills, modified the Norwegian thesis in his own etymological dictionary. For him *slang* is a dialect past participle of the verb *sling*, which has its roots in Old and Middle English and links to Old Norse, thus giving the concept of 'slung' or 'thrown' language. None of which, unfortunately, appeals to the more contemporary etymologists of *The Chambers Dictionary* who declare (however frustratingly) that the 'connection with *sling* [is] very doubtful' and simply list the term as 'of cant [i.e. underworld jargon] origin'.

Slang: the definition

Slang has elicited a variety of contrasting definitions, both academic and literary, an unresolved variety that doubtless underlines the sheer elusiveness of the term. My own take is to stress its essential opposition, thus my image of the 'nay-saying' language laid out above; elsewhere I have called it a 'counter-language' with a conscious nod to the Sixties 'counterculture' (as much as anything as regards its gloriously unfettered nihilism). I see no reason to alter this. For a general definition, I would suggest *The Chambers Dictionary* (11th Edition), which states as follows: 'Slang: words or usages not forming part of standard language, only used very informally, especially in speech, originally a jargon of thieves and disreputable people; the jargon of any class, profession or set.' Although whether the material that follows all fits into that definition may justifiably be seen as debatable. It is easier to suggest the mood and style of this subset of the English language than it is to render a hard-and-fast statement of what it is and, equally important, is not. The line, for instance, between slang and colloquialism is often opaque, and while one dictionary places a term to one side of that line, another disagrees.

My favourite definition is 150 years old, penned by the lexicographer, publisher and enthusiastic pornographer, John Camden Hotten. For him, 'Slang represents that evanescent, vulgar language, ever changing with fashion and taste, [...] spoken by persons in every grade of life, rich and poor, honest and dishonest [...] Slang is indulged in from a desire to appear familiar with life, gaiety, town-humour and with the transient nick names and street jokes of the day [...] Slang is the language of street humour, of fast, high and low life [...] Slang is as old as speech and the congregating together of people in cities. It is the result of crowding, and excitement, and artificial life.'

Chambers Slang Dictionary: etymologies

Philologists who chase
A panting syllable through time and space
Start it at home, and hunt it in the dark
To Gaul, to Greece, and into Noah's Ark…

William Cowper, 'Retirement' (1782)

The nature of slang, rather than of the themes upon which it concentrates, has often been described as ludic, or playful. This is surely true, and the subject of its play is most consistently the English language of which it forms a part. Thus the etymologies (the 'stories behind the words') that I have offered are often no more than a Standard English word, punned on, rendered figurative, teased away from its fundamental meaning and otherwise played with. For the ultimate etymologies of those words, one must turn to a standard dictionary. There are of course some anecdotal etymologies, and of course much of rhyming slang depends on a name of a popular individual (such as *Britney Spears* for 'beers'). There are also a number of terms that remain widely debated and concomitantly researched, of which *jazz* is perhaps the ultimate example; in such cases I have attempted to offer readers links to more detailed discussions, whether in print or online. Finally dialect, generally seen as a failing force in a world in which globalization has affected language as much as anything else, has an important role. As will be seen, dialect features in many etymologies, and it is my belief that a large amount of slang was generated simply by the arrival of country-dwellers in the new towns and cities of the industrial era. Their local usage came with them but, deprived of its nurturing environment, lost its roots. No longer dialect, an essentially rural phenomenon, and certainly not qualified for Standard English, it became slang, the language of the city. When possible I have identified the source of the given dialect, but where this has not been done, it must be assumed that it was used either all across England (and possibly Scotland, Wales and Ireland too) or in too many and too disparate areas to list them all.

Chambers Slang Dictionary: dating

The lexicographer, once moved from his or her role as a drudge – that period during which the dictionary is being constructed – becomes, dare one suggest, something of a minor deity once it has reached publication. What lies between these covers is meant to be correct. But never was a deity so fallible as when it comes to dating, especially as regards slang. This is not to deny the validity of the dates I offer, but a health warning is in order: these are the dates of use *as currently recorded*; they may change. This book is based on well over half a million citations, examples of slang as written down or otherwise used, whether in movies, TV, lyrics, blogs and anything else that one can scour. It is these citations that provide the dates I use here. However, while the problem for the slang collector was once 'Where do I find examples?', with the advent of the Internet it is 'Where do I dare risk stopping my research?'. I believe that the dates I offer are well grounded, but I am well aware that more research, for instance the publication of another once-lost memoir crammed with slangy usage, can turn everything upside down. But such discoveries are the lexicographer's delight; one can only request the user's tolerance. Until, of course, the entirety of printed, recorded, filmed and other useful examples of the culture are placed online and can there be accessed and searched, the essential serendipity of dating will remain. That may come, but in the meantime the lexicographer – whether of slang or of Standard English – must publish and try as best as possible not be damned.

Chambers Slang Dictionary: geographical labels

This book aims to offer the slang of those countries where English is the primary language, or certainly one of them: the UK, the US and Canada, Australia and New Zealand, Ireland, South

Africa and the Anglophone Caribbean. (India has been excluded, since for all its eccentricities – at least to Western ears – IVE, Indian Vernacular English is not a slang.) Nor has there been an attempt to garner the slangs – and they doubtless exist – of the ever-expanding categories of 'World English'. The bulk of the book, predictably, is British – there were no other Englishes between *c.*1530, when the first slang glossaries appear and the late 18th century, and even those that appeared then – in the US and Australia – would not really develop until the countries themselves had a sufficiency of that vital breeding ground for slang: big cities. As late as 1937 Eric Partridge could call his dictionary one of 'slang and unconventional English' and when he said English, that's what he meant. He admitted the Aussies – colonials, after all, and he was a Kiwi himself – but Yanks? go home! It barely worked then, and certainly has never done since. The 'Yanks' were here to stay. Such discrimination would be absurd in a 21st-century lexicon. It is perhaps hyperbole to suggest that we all speak like black rappers now, but it is undeniably their slang that currently cuts the edge for all, black or white, working class or bourgeois wigga. The days when slang was dominated by Britain's, mainly London's, white working-class, backed up by the underworld coinages of their criminal relations, died somewhere around D-Day. The mass media had been infiltrating US terms long before that, but World War II marks a palpable line.

When checking an entry it should be assumed that I am looking first for the original use and in this the default language and usage area is 'English' English and the UK; thus it bears no label. If I can isolate it elsewhere, I have labelled accordingly. English may be the mother tongue, but many words and phrases remain permanent orphans. Obviously many terms are used in England and America, the Antipodes and so on; I have not, however, attempted to list every relevant country if the default stands. If one needs further clarification, then such labels as 'US Und.[erworld]', 'UK black' and so on are on offer.

Sources

This dictionary draws its authority from my overriding work-in-progress, a database of slang 'on historical principles'. This is not 'historical', i.e. obsolete slang, but a work based on the history of the slang vocabulary. Some words are indeed obsolete, the majority are not, although many 'modern' terms turn out to have been used for a remarkably long time. To amass this material the research has covered several thousand printed works, from the 15th century to the present day, plus examples drawn from whatever other media have become available. I have not listed the bibliography here – without the relevant citations it is hardly useful – but the reader can rest assured that such wide-ranging 'excavation' underpins the material recorded.

Insult and offence

One final area seems to me worthy of consideration. The nature of slang is often, indeed almost invariably, rebarbative. Even its congratulations are mitigated by a certain edge. Its nature is to cause offence, to mock, to scorn, to savage, to dismay. It does not comfort. Whether geared for racial or national insult, describing human interactions, noting intelligence, or more usually lack of it, listing parts of the body, delineating the excesses of drink and drugs, or parading the vocabulary of a criminal underworld, it is often pertinent but rarely complimentary. Thus the nature of the beast. For me, quite frankly, this resulting negation of anything even hinting at political correctness is one of the great pleasures of my work. Others are less happy. Times change and social attitudes change with them. Writing in 1937, and indeed in several subsequent editions, Partridge might have found himself unwilling to spell out such terms as 'fuck', 'cunt' or 'shit', all proscribed by the current standards of 'taste' (and indeed by his own proclaimed squeamishness as regarded such language), but when it came to insults, however vile, he had no problems: a *nigger* was a black person, a *queer*, a homosexual, a *wog*, any brown foreigner. There were also problems when he did attempt auto-censorship. Take his entry for *shit*: *shit* itself (since it was in the *OED*) is spelled out, but the lower-class *s—t-stirrer* and other compounds have a blank vowel. Censorship, it appears, by class origin. It is in this early edition that we also encounter in definitions not the penis, but the *membrum virile*. The 'dirty words' did finally appear in full in the 1970 edition, but the insults, unmodified by any reference as to their possible offensiveness, remained part of his dictionary.

This is not, I stress, to impugn Partridge as a bigot, nor the ranks of his predecessors who similarly found themselves unfazed by racism or sexism but aghast at 'obscenity'. Such an attitude was a given of contemporary culture, and the dictionary-maker's task is to display language, not moralize upon it. To describe, not proscribe. Seventy years on and the social background against which I operate has reversed the situation. I can and do spell out anything, although for racial slurs I prefer to offer some form of label, usually the phrase 'a derog.[atory] term for…'. (The complete omission of such terms, as many US dictionaries are now considering, would be anathema, serving nothing but the diminution of the dictionary.) That said, I see no reason to leave them unadorned and unqualified, even if those who most need reminding of such qualifications are least likely to acknowledge them. So far, then, so good. But if race can be qualified, then why, it might be asked, should other groups – homosexuals, the disabled, the fat, the thin, the tall, the short, the stupid, the sexually active – all of whom get their fair share of invective, not claim equivalent status. Everyone's ass is up for grabs, remarked Lenny Bruce, but in the 'victim culture' of the contemporary world everyone's 'ass' seems up for special treatment. I have chosen, and remain satisfied with my choice, to resist such suggestions. Slang is as it is, and what it is is largely cruel. So be it. It would be easier, were one to succumb to these politically correct sirens, to mark those terms that are not 'derog.' rather than those that are.

In conclusion

So, to conclude, what next for slang? That it will continue to expand, providing work for me and, I trust, whoever succeeds, is in no doubt. Of its nature I can be less positive. More of the same probably, although might I essay one suggestion: taboos cannot be avoided, but they change. Three centuries ago blasphemy was the great taboo, and as such the blasphemies became slang. More recently we have shied from the bodily parts and their functions, especially sexual. Thus the 'dirty words'. These days the dirty words are pretty much wallpaper, especially for the young. They don't have that resonance. It is, might I suggest, the turn of a new taboo, the politically incorrect terms of racism and sexism. Thus a fruitful source of 21st-century slang.

It is the duty of the lexicographer to amass the language and offer it for perusal. It is not a task that can be complete, nor ever completed. The idea of 'fixing' the language was abandoned by Samuel Johnson in 1755, and his submission to the realities of an ever-expanding vocabulary has set the style for all major English dictionaries ever since. The same goes undoubtedly for slang, the creation of which is a non-stop process. The slang lexicographer can chase Cowper's 'panting syllables' and even hope to catch a good proportion, but it remains elusive. I remain open to suggestion.

Jonathon Green, Summer 2008

The major slang dictionaries 1500–2000

This short overview by no means represents a listing of every slang dictionary written since slang collection began in England, *c.*1535. The intention is merely to offer some of the main examples, with emphasis on what might be called the primary 'way-stations' in the development of Anglophone slang lexicography. For those who wish to consult a detailed, scholarly treatment of the subject, I recommend Julie Coleman's *History of Cant and Slang Dictionaries* (OUP, 2004, 2005, 2008 tbc). I have also dealt at much greater length with the topic than is possible here in my own *Chasing the Sun: Dictionary Makers and the Dictionaries They Made* (Cape, 1996).

English slang lexicography falls into three periods. The 'canting' or criminal slang dictionaries of the 16th to 18th centuries, the 'vulgar tongue' works of the late 18th to mid-19th, and the 'modern' productions that have appeared since.

I. Canting

The collection of 'cant', properly the jargon of the mendicant criminal beggars of Tudor and Stuart England, echoes the near-contemporary 'beggar-books' of Europe: designed to alert the law-abiding public to the existence of such beggars – 'the canting crew' – listing their occupational types and offering a small glossary of their language. The word cant comes from Latin *cantare*, to sing, and refers to the sing-song plaints of contemporary beggars. The first such work was Robert Copland's *Hye Way to the Spyttell Hous* (*c.*1535). In the form of a verse dialogue between Copland, a printer who once worked with Caxton, and the Porter of the Spytell House (a charity hospital assumed to be Bart's in London), Copland notes and the Porter describes the various categories of beggars and thieves, as well as their tricks and frauds. There is no glossary as such, but some 36 terms are defined in the text.

Two similar and expanded works followed. In 1561 John Awdeley, another printer, published *The Fraternitye of Vacabondes*. The brief (nine-page) work, offering 48 headwords, falls into three parts: the first deals with rural villains, the second with their urban cousins and the third is Awdeley's list of 'the xxv. Orders of Knaues, otherwyse called a Quartern of Knaues'.

The most influential 16th-century work appears *c.*1566: Thomas Harman's *Caveat for Common Cursetours*. Harman, a magistrate, produced a consciously didactic work, designed to introduce the reader to 'the leud lousey language of these lewtering [loitering] luskes [idlers] and lasy lorrels [blackguards] where with they bye and sell the common people as they pas through the country. Whych language they terme Peddelars Frenche.' There are 24 small essays, each dealing with a different rank of villain, plus a list of some 114 terms. These are very briefly defined, usually with a single synonym. The work concludes with a list of contemporary beggars, e.g. 'Harry Smyth, he drieueleth when he speaketh', and dialogue written in cant and translated into English.

Harman's vocabulary would remain the core of several subsequent glossaries, with a succession of 'rogue pamphlets' appearing over the next two centuries. Among these are *The Bellman of London* and *Lanthorne and Candle Light* (both 1608) by the playwright Thomas Dekker, who also included much canting vocabulary in his 1611 play, *The Roaring Girle*, co-written with Thomas Middleton; and *Martin Mark-all, beadle of Bridewell* by Samuel Rowlands (or Rid), in 1610. Others include Richard Head's *The Canting Academy, or the Devil's Cabinet opened* (1673) and John Shirley's *Triumph of Wit* (1688). Another pair of early 17th-century playwrights, Beaumont and Fletcher, were equally keen to parade their knowledge of cant in their play *Beggar's Bush* (1622).

While Harman can be seen as a sociological researcher, and Dekker (at least in his prose works) and his peers as informative reformers, the 'coney-catching' pamphlets of playwright Robert Greene are nakedly sensational. The first such pamphlet, *A Notable Discouery of Coosnage* [cozenage, or trickery] *Now daily practised by sundry lewd persons called Connie-Catchers* [confidence tricksters] *and Cross-biters* [swindlers] appeared in 1591. Five sequels followed by 1592. Greene gleefully peddles his down-market sensationalism, larded with new canting terms – the vocabularies of the various branches of confidence trickery – and supposedly first-hand anecdote, but carefully quarantined with pious horror. In one pamphlet, *The Defence of Conny Catching* 'by Cuthbert Conny-catcher', he even attacks himself.

With *A New Dictionary of the Terms ancient and modern of the Canting Crew*, by the anonymous B.E., Gent.[leman] (*c*.1698), there emerges the first major development in slang lexicography since Harman. It is the first ever stand-alone 'slang dictionary', rather than an appended glossary. The title emphasizes canting but B.E.'s vocabulary, some 4000 words, adds general slang, colloquialisms, and a variety of non-criminal jargons to the core material. There are other innovations: for some entries, however few, he offers citations and etymologies; there are a number of cross-references and he adopts usage labels.

Like Harman, B.E. would be 'honoured' by his plagiarists. These include Captain Alexander Smith, whose *Thieves' New Canting Dictionary*, in his *History of the Lives and Robberies of the Most Notorious Highwaymen* (1719), is unashamedly derivative. Similarly the anonymously written *New Canting Dictionary* (1725) is no more than an adaptation. The glossary attached to the oft-reprinted *Life of the self-styled gypsy king Bampfylde Moore Carew* (1750 et seq.) is similarly sourced. And it is B.E. (embellished by the *New Canting Dictionary* which it follows almost word-for-word) whose word-list provides the basis of the 'Collection of Canting Words' included in Bailey's *Universal Etymological English Dictionary* (1737).

II. Vulgar tongue

The 18th century did not merely produce adaptations of B.E. Among other works, all offering glossaries, are *Hell Upon Earth* (1703), *The Memoirs of the right villainous John Hall* (1708), *The Amorous Gallant's Tongue*, by 'G.L.' (1710 et seq.), *The Regulator* (1718) by Claude Hitchin, Daniel Defoe's *Street Robberies Considered* (1728), James Dalton's *Genuine Narrative of Street-Robberies Considered* (1728), the confessional *Discoveries of John Poulter* (1753), and George Parker's *View of Society in High and Low Life* (1781) and *Life's Painter of Variegated Characters* (1789). All these trade upon the 'glamour' of criminality and the author's retailing to the innocent but interested consumer of its specialist language, a phenomenon that has by no means vanished in modern use, whether on the printed page or on screen.

In 1785 the next way-station in slang collection arrives: *The Classical Dictionary of the Vulgar Tongue*, by the antiquary and former militia officer Captain Francis Grose, who was both a friend of Robert Burns and an acquaintance of Samuel Johnson. A second, substantially augmented edition appeared in 1788, followed by a third in 1796. The pirated *Lexicon Balatronicum* ('by a member of the Whip Club, assisted by hell-Fire Dick') was effectively the fourth in 1811, and the fifth was edited by the boxing journalist Pierce Egan in 1823. In his 4000 headwords Grose incorporates his main predecessors, but expands much further into general slang, his 'vulgar tongue'. Grose now set the pattern for the next century. One other dictionary appeared in 1823, *Slang, A Dictionary of the Turf, the Ring, the Chase, the Pit, of Bon-Ton, and the Varieties of Life*. Its author was 'Jon Bee' (properly John Badcock), who had already challenged Egan's best-selling chronicle of *Life in London* (1821), in which appear the originals of every subsequent 'Tom and Jerry' (to wit 'Corinthian Tom', the London sophisticate, and his rural friend, up to see the urban sights, Jerry Hawthorn) with his own hugely derivative *Real Life in London* (1821). Badcock's book is far more verbose than Egan's, but lexicographically it is more curiosity than linguistic tool.

Four more noteworthy dictionaries appear by 1900. The first, in 1857, is the brief *Vulgar Tongue* by 'Ducange Anglicus'. It comprises a pair of glossaries, the first collected by the author, the second from a report presented to the Government in 1839. In addition there is 'The Leary Man', a flash song, and a tailor's handbill written in slang, with a translation into standard English on the reverse. It is the first to offer rhyming slang, for all that this style of slanging, even today seen by many as the essence of the whole slang vocabulary, had actually emerged around 1815.

In 1859 appeared the first of the six editions (variously expanded) of John Camden Hotten's *Modern Slang, Cant and Vulgar Words*, latterly *The Slang Dictionary*. Hotten was variously a bookseller/publisher, a pirate of such American 'stars' as Mark Twain, and a cultivator of his 'flower garden', books of flagellant pornography. The dictionary has lists of rhyming slang and of backslang, both prefaced by a brief history and discussion. There is, for the first time, a 'Bibliography of Slang and Cant,' listing some 120 titles, plus his own critical comments on each. Hotten stresses that this is above all a dictionary of 'modern Slang – a list of colloquial words and phrases in present use – whether of ancient or modern formation'. He omits obsolete terms and has opted, unlike Grose, to exclude 'filthy and obscene words' although he acknowledges their prevalence in street-talk. He touches on jargon, without describing it as such, and thus deals with the terminology of the beau monde, politics, the army and navy, the church, the law, literature and the theatre. He has a list of slang terms for money, one of oaths, one for drunkenness and deals with the language of shopkeepers and workmen.

Hotten was the slang dictionary until 1890 (and Chatto & Windus, who bought up his list on his death, continued to publish the book until World War I). His pre-eminence was somewhat breached in 1889 by *The Dictionary of Slang, Jargon and Cant* by Albert Barrère and C.G. Leland. But this two-volume work was barely published when it was displaced by the seven volumes of John Farmer and W.E. Henley's *Slang and Its Analogues* (1890–1904, revised edition of vol. 1 only, 1909). Farmer, who combined slang researches with writings on spiritualism, and Henley, then one of Britain's leading poets, took slang lexicography into a new dimension. The book adopted the same 'historical' method as the contemporaneous *New English Dictionary*. All but a few headwords come with a number of citations, some 100,000 in all, set out as in a standard English dictionary, to illustrate usage and nuance. These quotes take in 'the whole period of English literature from the earliest down to the present time' and are arranged as far as possible from 'first use' to current use. As well as citations, there are, wherever possible, foreign synonyms for the slang words. English synonymy is also paramount: those listed at monosyllable (i.e. the vagina), for instance, run to 13 columns, while those at greens (i.e. sexual intercourse) run to seven. There are errors, typically in the citations, where dates and even the quotes themselves may have fallen foul of the sheer volume of the undertaking (and the fact that a succession of printers, prudishly discomfited by the content, abruptly refused to continue with the work), but the overall achievement of Farmer and Henley far outweighs such slips.

III. Modernity

To list every dictionary of 20th- and 21st-century slang is impossible. The range, from massively researched multi-volume 'historical' dictionaries to fly-by-night glossaries posted on the Internet, defies cataloguing. Nor is it possible to restrict 'English' slang to England. While the last slang lexicographer to dominate his field, Eric Partridge, could entitle his book (based originally on Farmer and Henley, whose rights were owned by his publisher) as the *Dictionary of Slang and Unconventional English* (1937 et seq.) and mean just that, such exclusivity would now be foolhardy. In dictionaries as in the vocabulary, American slang has taken over, and must take equal prominence with its transatlantic forebear. Similarly Australian slang, exemplified in the mid-20th-century work of Sidney J. Baker, has an important presence, even if Baker drew too heavily on such late 19th-century efforts as the *Australian* and the *Sydney Slang Dictionaries*, which themselves drew on both UK and US sources, rather than offering homegrown Australianisms. The mass media, the Internet, the role of English, or certainly Englishes, as a world language mean that its slang is equally multi-headed and its dictionaries reflect the fact.

Partridge, as mentioned, dominated much of the 20th century. As well as his 'pure' slang dictionary, he wrote a *Dictionary of the Underworld* and books on the military slangs of both World Wars. His is perhaps a flawed canon, his lexicographical method was less than wholly scrupulous, his inability to keep personal comment out of his definitions less than useful, his etymologizing sometimes tendentious, but his body of work can be said to have maintained the momentum of slang lexicography through the mid-20th century. He has that rare accolade: like Webster, his name became an eponym. The last edition of the *DSUE* appeared in 1984; the New Partridge, wholly rewritten and expanded with US entries from 1945 onwards, appeared in 2005 edited by Tom Dalzell. Partridge's immediate successor, Jonathon Green, published his single-volume *Cassell's Dictionary of Slang* in 1998; Chambers will be publishing his multi-volume dictionary of slang 'on historical principles' in 2009.

IV. America

Slang is an urban phenomenon. Modern America seems quintessentially urban; 19th-century America was not. Thus the century saw only one major slang dictionary: the *Vocabulum* (1859) by the New York chief of police, G.W. Matsell. (Its only possible predecessor is a short glossary appended by Edward Judson to his *Mysteries and Miseries of New York* in 1848.) Much of his vocabulary seems taken wholesale from Egan's Grose, although there are a number of genuine localisms. Nonetheless, there were no contenders: Matsell remains an American pioneer. The 20th century hosted an explosion of US slang lexica. Many of these, such as Jackson and Hellyer's *Vocabulary of Criminal Slang* (1914), Godfrey Irwin's *American Tramp and Underworld Slang* (1931), Hyman E. Goldin's *Dictionary of American Underworld Lingo* (1950), or the wide-ranging specialist work of David Maurer, published in *American Speech* and elsewhere, point up the wide variety of US criminal slang. More general works include Maurice H. Weseen's *Dictionary of American Slang* (1934), Berrey and Van der Bark's *American Thesaurus of Slang* (1942, 1952), Harold Wentworth and Stuart Berg Flexner's *Dictionary of American Slang* (1960, 1975) and pre-eminently Jonathan Lighter's multi-volume work in progress, *The Historical Dictionary of American Slang* (1994 et seq.). Specialist works abound, especially as regard such sources of slang as the campus, African-American speech, drugs and war. Among these are Connie Eble's series of *Campus Slang* glossaries (1972 et seq.), the works of Edith A. Folb (*Runnin' Down Some Lines*, 1980) and Geneva Smitherman (*Black Talk*, 1994), Richard A. Spears (*The Slang and Jargon of Drink and Drugs*, 1986) and Gregory C. Clark (*Words of the Vietnam War*, 1990).

Today's Anglophone slang is international, English-language rather than English. And its sources, including dictionaries, are increasingly so as the Internet gains influence and online reference searches replace the traditional printed works. The upcoming crop of multi-volume lexica may signify the end of a half-millennium era. The Internet's 'Urban Dictionary' may be inaccurate and puerile, but online is undoubtedly the way ahead. A search for 'slang dictionary' brings up 635,000 hits on Google®: slang collection, one might suggest, has barely begun.

Jonathon Green

Acknowledgements

I have been collecting material for the database where all my researches into slang reside for more than two decades. Many people have helped me and I am profoundly grateful to them all. At this stage, I would like to thank specifically those individuals whose efforts have ensured that this book, *Chambers Slang Dictionary*, has come to life.

At Chambers: Patrick White, managing director and publisher; editorial director Vivian Marr and publishing manager Mary O'Neill; Patrick Gaherty, Ruth O'Donovan and Gerry Breslin in the company's IT department.

Vicky Aldus, Sandra Anderson, Pat Bulhosen, Sheila Ferguson, Lorna Gilmour, Alice Grandison, Andrew Holmes and Michael Munro, who have copy-edited the book.

My agent Julian Alexander.

Susie Ford, whose continuing researches form the very heart of anything I am able to offer as regards the lexicography of slang.

Sarah Chatwin, my colleague and friend, and to whom, as some recompense for her peerless efforts, I dedicate this book.

How to use *Chambers Slang Dictionary*

The following explanations are exemplified in the model of dictionary layout on page xxix.

Order of entries

Entries identical in spelling are ordered according to their part of speech, in the sequence noun, adjective, verb, adverb, phrase, exclamation, suffix, prefix, infix, preposition, pronoun, abbreviation. Where a noun, verb etc have etymologically distinct meanings, these are divided up into separate entries. Within each part of speech, each word is given a superscript number to indicate that they are homographs, i.e. words with the same spelling but different etymology (e.g. **dog** *n.*^{1}, **dog** *n.*^{2} etc followed by **dog** *v.*^{1}, **dog** *v.*^{2} etc). The homographs are arranged in a chronological sequence, according to the first usage of each entry.

All entries are listed alphabetically, on a letter-by-letter basis. Where entries have the same part of speech, a capitalized form will come before one without an initial capital (e.g. **Cam** precedes **cam**); a multiple-word form comes before a hyphenated or otherwise punctuated form; an entry with parentheses is alphabetized on the full term, ignoring the brackets. Abbreviations are ordered as they would be if spelt out, e.g. **&** = *and*, **Mr** = *mister*. Terms beginning with **Mc** are alphabetized as *Mac*.

Where an entry or a distinct homograph has different shades of meaning, these follow sense numbers in bold. Sense numbers are ordered according to chronological first appearance. The numbered senses may have their own dates, usage labels or variant spellings and forms; alternatively, if one or all of these applies to all the senses of the entry, it comes before the first numbered sense.

The entry

Each entry may have the following elements:

(1) Headword
(2) Part of speech label
(3) Alternative forms
(4) Etymology
(5) Date of use
(6) Usage label
(7) Definition(s)

Within an entry there are often subentries – words that are derived from the headword by the addition of a suffix (derivatives), or another word or words (compounds), or phrases or exclamations that include the headword (or one of its derivatives). This grouping of related words within an entry preserves and explains their etymological 'family' link, while at the same time ensuring that space is used as effectively as possible.

Sometimes subentries are not based directly on the main slang senses given at the headword, but rather on a literal or figurative use of the Standard English root word. These subentries will be listed at the headword under a separate heading 'SE in slang uses', e.g. **fruitful vine** or **fruit for the sideboard** under **fruit** *n*.

In some cases, where a related word has derivatives etc of its own, multiple parts of speech or is simply very important in its own right, it is presented as a separate entry, as at **cop a plea** and **arse bandit**, showing their relationships to **cop** *v.* and **arse** *n.* by means of the etymologies.

The elements of an entry are explained in greater detail below:

Headword

The word (in **bold** type) projecting at the head of an entry is referred to as the headword. Some headwords included in the alphabetical order simply contain cross-references to a full entry found elsewhere in the dictionary.

Part of speech label

Following a headword is a label in italic to indicate the part of speech. This label is usually abbreviated, e.g. *adj*. for adjective or *n*. for noun (but note full-out *infix*).

Alternative forms

Words spelt or formed in more than one way, but sharing the same meaning(s), dating and usage, are shown in brackets after the word *also*.

Etymology

An etymology applying to a whole entry is given in square brackets before the definition(s). Those etymologies that apply to only one numbered sense of a word appear in square brackets at the end of the relevant definition.

A word in small capitals in an etymology indicates a cross-reference (*see* below). A question mark indicates a possible link between the headword and the etymology, rather than an established one.

Note also that when part of a word within a definition is given in italics, e.g. *anarch*ist at **anarcho**, it demonstrates the derivation of the slang headword from an abbreviation of the Standard English word.

Date of use

Dates given in square brackets indicate the usage period of the headword or sense. A date in the form [18C] or [19C] indicates that the usage period covers the whole century. The + sign indicates that a term is still in use, e.g. [mid-19C+], as does the label [2000s] which indicates a recent and current slang expression.

The ordering of dates depends primarily on when a term, or the sense of a term, began to be used. If two terms or senses came into use at the same time, then the length of their usage is taken into consideration, e.g. **1** [17C] …; **2** [17C+] …; **3** [18C–19C] ….

Note that a term that is still in use may be listed before one that is not, if it originated earlier or at the same time.

Usage label

A label relating to the usage of a headword or sense appears in italics within brackets, usually following the date label. These indicate either the geographical usage of a term, e.g. *W.I.*, or the social/cultural usage, e.g. *teen*.

Subentries

Subentries are slang terms not listed as separate entries, but instead listed in bold and explained within a larger headword. Subentries may fall into one of four categories:

Derivatives

These are words which are formed by adding a suffix or ending to the headword. They are given, in alphabetical order, immediately after the various senses of the headword.

Compounds

Compound terms (i.e. those made up of two or more words, the first being the headword) follow any direct derivatives. They may be hyphenated, one-word or multi-word compounds. Those multi-word terms which do not begin with the headword are listed under the third category, phrases.

Phrases

Following any direct derivatives and any compound terms, all phrasal items relating to the headword are listed alphabetically. These may be phrases, phrasal verbs or idioms, or multi-word terms which do not begin with the headword or any of its derivatives.

Exclamations

Exclamations are listed alphabetically following the other categories.

Most subentries are assigned parts of speech, to make the usage clear. However, exclamations, phrases other than those used adjectivally, adverbially or as nouns or verbs, or any subentries grouped by part of speech, will not repeat the part of speech label given in the heading.

In most cases, each subentry will have an individual definition, but in exceptional circumstances, where a large number of subentries have the same meaning, these are given an overall definition and not individually defined.

Further categories

Subentries may be grouped under further headings, in addition to the grammatical categories of derivatives, compounds, phrases and exclamations. The most common of these headings is 'SE in slang uses', as explained above. In addition, longer entries may be divided semantically, or occasionally grammatically, e.g. 'pertaining to sycophancy', or 'comparatives'.

Cross-references

A word or expression which appears as a full headword elsewhere in the dictionary will be marked as a cross-reference, in small capital letters. Cross-references occur mainly in the etymologies, in cases where the origin of an expression lies in another slang term. For example, in the etymology for **nabbing cheat**, [NAB *v.*[1] (2) + CHEAT *n.* (1)], the words in small capitals direct the user to other entries, and the bracketed numbers refer to specific sense numbers.

Cross-references to nested subentries also occur. These are displayed in italic small capitals, e.g. *PUT THE ACID ON under* ACID *n.*[2].

Cross-references may also appear in round brackets following 'c.f.', which refers the reader to other entries for comparison.

Cross-references are also used to direct the user from one spelling or form of a particular term to the main spelling or form under which a term is shown, e.g. **altemal** *n. see* ALTAMEL *n.* Some related terms may be listed under both spellings, and in these cases the user is given pointers as to where to look rather than direct cross-references, e.g. **arsehole** *see also under* **asshole** and combs. or **ampster** *see under* AMSTER.

Model of dictionary layout

Headword

Part of speech label

April fools *n.* [rhy. sl.] **1** [late 19C+] tools; usu. implements for burglary. **2** [20C+] stool(s) (for sitting). **3** [1930s+] football pools.

Date of use

April gentleman *n.* [the popularity of spring weddings] [late 16C] a newly married man.

April in Paris *n.* [rhy. sl. = ARRIS *n.*] [2000s] the buttocks, the behind.

April showers *n.* [rhy. sl.] [20C+] flowers.

apron *n.* **1** [1920s] a wife, a woman, esp. when used generically. **2** [1920s–50s] (*US*) a bartender.

Usage label

SE in slang uses

Indicates literal or figurative use(s) of Standard English root word

Derivatives of the headword follow

DERIVATIVES

❑ **aproneer** *n.* [the aristocratic Cavaliers made this contemptuous link between 'trade' (symbolized by a worker's apron) and their parliamentary rivals] **1** [mid-17C] a Roundhead. **2** [mid-17C–early 18C] a shopkeeper. ❑ **aproner** *n.* (*also* **aperner, apron-man**) [his usu. blue SE *apron*] [early–mid-17C] a publican; one who serves alcohol.

Compounds of the headword follow

IN COMPOUNDS

❑ **apron and gaiters** *n.* (*also* **gaiters**) [metonymy, i.e. his vestments] [late 19C–1910s] a bishop, a dean. ❑ **apron husband** *n.* [metonymic use of SE *apron* = woman + *husband*] [early 17C] a man who is seen as involving himself excessively in his wife's business. ❑ **apron preacher** *n.* [mid-17C] a lay preacher. ❑ **apron-rogue** *n.* [a play on SE synon. *apron-man*] [mid-17C] a labourer, an artisan. ❑ **apron squire** *n.* [metonymic use of SE *apron* = woman + SQUIRE *n.* (2)] [late 16C] a pimp. ❑ **apron-stringed** *adj.* [1950s] of a man, henpecked by a woman. ❑ **apron-string hold** *n.* (*also* **apron-string tenure**) [late 17C–early 19C] an estate that a man holds only during the lifetime of his wife. ❑ **apron-up** *adj.* [the use of an apron to hide a pregnancy, also f. the inevitable raising of the apron's profile as the foetus grows] [late 18C–19C] pregnant. ❑ **apron-washings** *n.* [image of a brewery worker wringing out his beer-soaked apron] [1900s] porter.

Cross-reference

Etymology

Phrases that include the headword follow

IN PHRASES

❑ **blue-apron** *n.* (*also* **green apron**) [his 'uniform'] [late 17C–mid-19C] a tradesman. ❑ **green apron** *n.* [female Quaker preachers wore a *green apron*] [mid-17C–mid-18C] a lay preacher. ❑ **have a smell of the barman's apron** *v.* (*also* **have a sniff..., have a whiff..., ...of the barmaid's apron**) [metonymy, i.e. the garment he or she wears] [1920s+] to be drunk. ❑ **tied to someone's apron-strings** *adj.* [earlier use of APRON-STRING HOLD above, property owned by the wife] [mid-18C+] dominated by one's wife, or mother. ❑ **want an apron** *v.* [an era when workmen wore some form of apron – before the modern overall – while at work] [late 19C] to be out of work. ❑ **white apron** *n.* [the SE *white apron* that was recognized as a prostitute's 'uniform'; note D'Urfey, *Pills to Purge Melancholy* (1719): 'And first for those ladies that walk in the Night, / Their Aprons and handkerchiefs they should be White'; the aim was 'the better to be seen'] [late 16C–mid-17C] a prostitute.

Alternative forms

Cross-reference to subentry

Abbreviations

ABBREVIATIONS

adj./adjs.	adjective(s)
adv.	adverb
Afk.	Afrikaans
Anglo-Ind.	Anglo-Indian
Antg.	Antigua/Antiguan
approx.	approximate/approximately
AS	Anglo-Saxon
attrib.	attributive/attributively
Aus.	Australian
backform.	backformation
backsl.	backslang
Baha.	Bahamas/Bahamian
Bdos	Barbados/Barbadian
C	century
camp gay	stereotypically effeminate
Can.	Canada/Canadian
Carib.E.	Caribbean English
colloq.	colloquial
comb./combs.	combination(s)
Da.	Danish
derog.	derogative/derogatory
dial.	dialect
dict.	dictionary
dimin.	diminutive
Dmnca	Dominica
Du.	Dutch
edn	edition
esp.	especially
ety.	etymology
euph.	euphemism/euphemistic
excl.	exclamation
ext.	extension/extended
f.	from
fem.	feminine
fig.	figurative/figuratively
Fr.	French
Ger.	German
Gk	Greek
Gren.	Grenada
Guyn.	Guyana/Guyanese
Heb.	Hebrew
Hind.	Hindustani
Hisp.	Hispanic
Icel.	Icelandic
imper.	imperative
Ind.	Indian
interrog.	interrogative
Ital.	Italian
Jam.	Jamaica/Jamaican
Jap.	Japan/Japanese
joc.	jocular
journ.	journalistic
juv.	juvenile (pre-teenage use)
Lat.	Latin
Ling. Fr.	Lingua Franca
lit.	literally/literal
masc.	masculine
MDu.	Middle Dutch
ME	Middle English
Med.	Medieval

Short forms of reference

Mex.	Mexico/Mexican
MHG	Middle High German
milit.	military
mispron.	mispronunciation
mis-sp.	mis-spelling
MLG	Middle Low German
n.	noun
naut.	nautical
Norw.	Norway/Norwegian
N.Z.	New Zealand
obs.	obsolete
occas.	occasionally
OE	Old English
OF	Old French
OHG	Old High German
ON	Old Norse
onomat.	onomatopoeia/ onomatopoeic
orig.	originally
pej.	pejorative
Pers.	Persian
phr./phrs.	phrase(s)
pfx	prefix
pl.	plural
Port.	Portuguese
poss.	possibly
P.R.	Puerto Rico/Puerto Rican
prev.	previous entry or subentry
prob.	probably
prep.	preposition
pron.	pronunciation
publ.	published
pvb	proverb
RAF	Royal Air Force

redup.	reduplication
ref.	reference
rhy. sl.	rhyming slang
RN	Royal Navy
Rom.	Romany
Rus.	Russian
S.Afr.	South African
S.Afr.E.	South African English
S.Afr.Du.	South African Dutch
St Lu.	St Lucia
SAmE	Standard American English
SAusE	Standard Australian English
Scot.	Scottish
SE	Standard English
SF	science fiction
sfx	suffix
sing.	singular
Skrt	Sanskrit
sl.	slang
SNZE	Standard New Zealand English
society	upper- and middle-class use
Sp.	Spanish
sp.	spelling
spec.	specifically
St	Saint/Street
subseq.	subsequent/subsequently
Sw.	Sweden/Swedish
synon.	synonym/synonymous
Tob.	Tobago
trad.	traditionally/traditional
Trin.	Trinidad
Turk.	Turkish
UKVI	UK Virgin Islands

ult. ultimately
Und. Underworld (criminal cant, *see* Introduction)
US United States
USVI US Virgin Islands
usu. usually
v. verb
var./vars. variation(s)/variant(s)
vol. volume
W.I. West Indies/West Indian
WW1 First World War
WW2 Second World War
Yid. Yiddish
Yorks. Yorkshire

AND W. S. Ramson, ed., *Australian National Dictionary* (1989)
Bee Jon Bee, *A Dictionary of the Turf, the Ring, the Chase, etc* (1823)
B.E. B.E., Gent.[leman], *Dictionary of the Canting Crew* (c.1698)
B&L Albert Barrère & C.G. Leland, *The Dictionary of Slang, Jargon and Cant* (1889–90)
Burley Dan Burley's *Original Handbook of Harlem Jive* (1944)
DARE F. Cassidy, Joan Houston Hall, eds., *Dictionary of American Regional English* (1994 et seq.)
DNZE H.W. Orsman, ed., *Dictionary of New Zealand English* (1997)
DSAE Penny Silva, ed., *Dictionary of South African English* (1996)
DSUE Eric Partridge, *Dictionary of Slang and Unconventional English* (1937–84, 8 edns)
DU Eric Partridge, *Dictionary of the Underworld* (1949, 1961)
EDD Joseph Wright, *English Dialect Dictionary* (1905, 6 vols.)
Egan's Grose Pierce Egan, *Grose's Classical Dictionary of the Vulgar Tongue* (1823)
F&H John Farmer & W.E. Henley, *Slang and Its Analogues* (1890–1904)
Grose Francis Grose, *The Classical Dictionary of the Vulgar Tongue* (1785, 1788, 1796)
Harman Thomas Harman, *Caveat for Common Cursetours* (c.1566)
HDAS Jonathan Lighter, *The Historical Dictionary of American Slang* (1994 et seq.)
Hotten John Camden Hotten, *Modern Slang, Cant and Vulgar Words* (1859, 1860), then as *The Slang Dictionary* (1864, 1867, 1870, 1873)
Lex. Bal. *Lexicon Balatronicum* (1811)
Matsell George W. Matsell, *Vocabulum* (1859)
Nares Robert Nares, *Nares' Glossary* (1822)
OED John Simpson, Edmund Weiner, eds., *The Oxford English Dictionary* (online edition)
Partridge Eric Partridge (see *DSUE* and *DU* above)
Share Bernard Share, *Slanguage: a Dictionary of Irish Slang* (1997)
Vaux Noel Maclachlan, ed., *The Memoirs of James Hardy Vaux* (1812, reprinted 1964)
Ware J. Redding Ware, *Passing English of the Victorian Era* (1909)
Williams Gordon Williams, *Dictionary of Sexual Language and Imagery in Shakespearian and Stuart Literature* (1994, 3 vols.)
Y&B Henry Yule & A.C. Burnell, *Hobson-Jobson, a Glossary of Anglo-Indian Words and Phrases* (1886)

Slang Dictionary

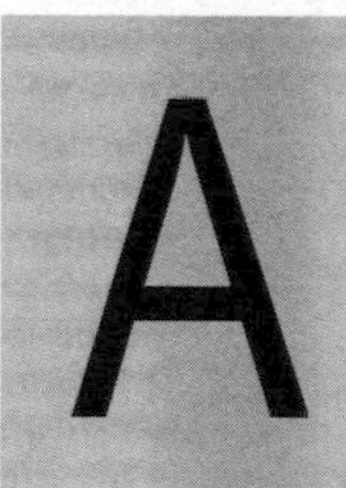

A *n.* [abbr.] [1920s+] (*US*) a Model-*A* Ford automobile.

a *n.*[1] [abbr. ARSE *n.* (1)/ASS *n.*] **1** [20C+] (*W.I., Guyn.*) a general term of dislike. **2** [1940s+] (*US*) a euph. for ASS *n.* (4), e.g. *haul a, bet your fat a.*

a *n.*[2] [abbr.] [1960s+] (*drugs*) **1** LSD, i.e. d-lycergic acid diethylamide-25 [abbr. ACID *n.*[1] (2)]. **2** amphetamine.

-a *sfx* [20C+] used to denote a colloq. or slangy pron. of: (**a**) have, e.g. *coulda, musta, shoulda, woulda.* (**b**) to, e.g. *gonna, gotta, oughta, wanna.* (**c**) of, e.g. CUPPA *n.*, LOTSA *n.*, LOTTA *n.*

aachibombo *n.* [W.I. *aachi*, codfish + BUMBO *n.*[2] (2), lit. 'codfish-arse'] [1940s+] (*W.I.*) a codfish fritter.

aai-aai *n. see* AI-AI *n.*

a. and b. *n.* [abbr.] [1920s] (*US*) assault *and b*attery.

aap *n.* [Afk. *aap*, an ape or monkey; ? derog. ref. to the users] [1940s+] (*S.Afr.*) a cannabis cigarette.

aardvark *n.* [anthropomorphic use of SE; note the character *Aardvark* in Joseph Heller's *Catch-22* (1961), a cheery, bumbling oaf] [1960s+] (*US*) a simpleton, a dullard, an oaf.

aaron, the *n.* [the biblical *Aaron*, Judaism's first high priest] **1** [17C–19C] a criminal, esp. a gang leader. **2** [19C] a cadger.

aaron's rod *n.* [punning on ROD *n.* (1), f. Num. 17:8: 'Behold, the rod of Aaron...was budded, and brought forth buds, and bloomed blossoms and yielded almonds'] [19C; 1980s+] the penis.

aasbed *n.* [? ARSE *n.* (1) + SE *bed*] [1950s] (*W.I.*) a rough bed.

aataclaps *n.* [? SE *clap* of thunder or *collapse*] [1990s+] (*W.I.*) a disaster, a calamity.

A.B. *n.* [abbr.] **1** [1980s] (*N.Z.*) the menstrual period [abbr. Annie Brown, on the model of menstruation = a 'visiting' woman]. **2** [1980s] (*US*) fools as a group, lit. Asshole *Brigade* [ASSHOLE *n.* (3)]. **3** [1990s+] (*US prison*) Aryan Brotherhood, the white supremacist organization that unites many white convicts during (and after) their time in jail. **4** [1990s+] (*Aus. prison*) Aryan *Breed*; the Aus. version of sense 3.

a.b. *n.* (*also* **ab, abb**) [abbr.] [1930s+] (*US drugs*) an *ab*cess that develops after injecting with an unsterile needle or an unsterile water/narcotic solution.

ab *n.* [abbr.] **1** [19C+] (*Aus.*) an *Ab*original; the predecessor of the modern ABO *n.* (1). **2** [1960s+] an *ab*dominal muscle, usu. in the context of a flat stomach; often in pl. **3** [2000s] (*Aus.*) *ab*alone.

abaa *adj.* [ety. unknown; ? 'baaing' of a sheep] [1900s] **1** silly. **2** bad, e.g. *abaa cove*, a bad man.

abactor *n.* (*also* **abacter**) [Lat. *abigere*, to drive away] [mid-17C–early 19C] a dishonest drover or shepherd who connives at stealing the cattle they are guarding.

abaddon *n.* [punning on *a bad 'un/Abaddon*, 'the angel of the bottomless pit', Rev. 9:11] [19C] a thief turned informer.

abaft the wheel-house *phr.* [naval imagery, *abaft*, behind, towards the stern] **1** [late 19C] (*US*) just below the small of the back; thus a euph. for the buttocks. **2** [1900s] crazy.

abandannad *n.* [SE *abandoned* (boy) + *bandanna*] [mid–late 19C] a thief who specializes in stealing bandanna handkerchiefs.

abandoned habits *n.* [pun on their SE *abandoned habits*, i.e. immorality + SE *riding habit*, their costume] [late 19C] the riding dress of the up-market courtesans who frequented Rotten Row in London's Hyde Park.

abareskin *adj.* [joc. mispron. and ref. to SE *bare skin*] [1960s] (*US camp gay*) embarrassing.

abb *n. see* A.B. *n.*

abbess *n.* (*also* **lady abbess, mother abbess**) [ironic use of SE] [late 17C–19C] a brothel-keeper, a madame, 'of the highflyer sort' (Bee).

abbey clogs *n.* [SE *abbey*, as generic for prison] [mid-19C] (*UK Und.*) chains or fetters worn by a criminal.

abbey-croaker *n.* [SE *abbey*, as generic for prison + CROAKER *n.*[1] (2)] [mid-19C] (*UK Und.*) the 'ordinary' or chaplain of Newgate.

abbey-lubber *n.* [SE *abbey* + *lubber*, f. OF *lobeor*, swindler, parasite; the word is the origin of the nautical use] [mid-16C–early 18C] a lazy monk; a reproachful name in regular use after the Reformation.

abbot *n.* **1** [mid-19C] (*UK Und.*) a prison warden [SE *abbey*, as generic for prison]. **2** [late 19C] a brothel-keeper's husband or lover [the male counterpart of the ABBESS *n.*].

abbot on the cross *n.* [the male counterpart of the ABBESS *n.*] [19C] a pimp.

Abbott's Priory *n.* (*also* **Abbott's Lodge, ...Park**) [Sir Charles *Abbott* (1762–1832), Lord Chief Justice (1818–32). The King's Bench prison was generically the Lodge or the *Priory*, and its 'given' name varied according to the current Lord Chief Justice; thus before 1818 'Abbott' had been 'Ellenborough', f. the previous office-holder] [early–mid-19C] the King's Bench prison; thus *Abbott's teeth*, the spikes that topped the prison wall.

ABC *n.*[1] [? play on *ABC* bread company, i.e. one's legs have been toasted] [1920s] (*Irish*) scorch marks on one's legs.

ABC *n.*[2] [abbr.] **1** [1990s+] (*Aus.*) *A*ustralian-*b*orn *C*hinese. **2** *see* AMERICAN BUSINESS COLLEGE *under* AMERICAN *adj.*

a.b.c. *n.*[1] [like *abc*, it is the beginning, although of life rather than the alphabet] [late 17C; 19C] the vagina.

a.b.c. *n.*[2] *see* ACE BOON COON *n.*

abcap *v.* [mid-19C] (*UK Und.*) to get, to obtain; thus phr. *abcapt da snaffle-mitre*, hanged.

abdabs *n.* (*also* **habdabs**) [? echoic of the spluttering, hesitant speech of one who is thus afflicted] [1940s+] **1** nervous anxiety; usu. as *SCREAMING ABDABS* below. **2** empty chatter, nonsense.

IN PHRASES

▫ **come the (old) abdabs** *v.* (*also* **give someone the abdabs**) [COME THE... *v.*] [1940s] to hoax, to fool, to 'tell the tale', often as *don't come/give me the (old) abdabs*, don't try to fool me.
▫ **screaming abdabs** *n.* [SCREAMING *adj.* (3)] [1950s+] **1** the horrors, utter disgust, abhorrence; usu. as *that gives me the screaming abdabs.* **2** delirium tremens.

abdicate *v.* [pun on SE *abdicate the throne* and THRONE *n.*/QUEEN *n.* (2)] [1940s+] (*gay*) to leave a public lavatory in which one is soliciting to avoid interrogation by its attendant or a police officer.

DERIVATIVES

▫ **abdicated** *adj.* ordered out of the public lavatory where one is looking for sex.

Abdul *n.* [stereotypical 'Arab' name] **1** [1910s–20s] (*also* **Abdullah**) a derog. term for an Afghan. **2** [1910s–40s] (*Aus.*) a derog. term for a Turkish soldier. **3** [1980s+] (*US*) a derog. term for an Arab.

Abe *n.*[1] (*also* **abe**) [abbr. of proper name *Abraham*, the biblical patriarch] [19C+] a derog. term for a Jew.

Abe *n.*[2] [ABRAHAM LINCOLN *n.*] **1** [1940s–60s] (*US*) a $5 bill. **2** [1950s+] (*US drugs*) $5 worth of drugs.

abe *n.* [Stephens & O'Brien, *Materials for a Dict. of Aus. Slang* (unpubl. ms. 1900–10), suggest link to ABRAHAM-MAN *n.*] [1900s] (*Aus. Und.*) the last of anything; the only example.

IN PHRASES

❑ **on one's abe** *adj.* impoverished.

abear *v.* [OE *abearan*, to bear, to carry, thence to dial.] [late 19C; 1940s–70s] (*later use US black*) to abide, to tolerate.

Aberdeen cutlet *n.* [the Aberdeen fishing trade] [19C] a dried haddock.

Aberdeen(s) *n.* [rhy. sl.] [20C+] bean(s).

Abergavenny *n.* [rhy. sl.; ult. Welsh town] [19C] a penny.

Abe's cabe *n.* [ABE *n.*[2] (1) + redup.] [1980s+] (*drugs*) a $5 bill.

a.b.f. *n.* [abbr. *a*bsolutely *b*loody *f*inal drink] [1910s+] the last drink of a session.

abfab *adj.* [abbr. of *absolutely fabulous*; the sl. predates the hit UK TV show of the 1990s] [1950s+] (*orig. Aus. teen*) a general term of approval, first-rate, very attractive.

a.b.h. *n.* [abbr. SE *a*ctual *b*odily *h*arm, physical harm deliberately inflicted, but less serious than *grievous bodily harm*] [2000s] a beating up.

Abie *n.* [ABE *n.*[1]] **1** [1910s+] (*also* **Aby**) a Jew. **2** [1940s] (*US black*) a tailor [trad. linking of Jews and tailoring].

Abie Kabibble *n.* [var. on US Yid. *ish kabibble*, who cares, don't worry; prob. ult. synon. Yid. *nish gefidlt*. Adopted by the vaudeville star Fanny Brice (1891–1951), the term was picked up by America's 'dean of cartoonists' Harry Hershfield, who in 1917 launched a character called Abie the Agent, based on one *Abie Kabibble*. Highly successful, the strip lasted until 1932. The term was further popularized by the swing trumpeter Merwyn Bogue (d.1994), who took the name 'Ish Kabibble' and started performing as a comic. Note also the Marx Brothers' character 'Abe Kabiddle', in *The Cocoanuts* (1928)] [1910s–30s] (*US*) a Jew.

abigail *n.*[1] [a character in Francis Beaumont and John Fletcher's play *The Scornful Lady* (1610), although she was poss. so named in allusion to the expression 'thine handmaid' used in the Bible by Abigail the Carmelitess, 1 Sam. 25:24–31] **1** [17C–1900s] a lady's maid. **2** [1950s+] (*camp gay*) an ageing, conservative homosexual.

abigail *n.*[2] [initial letter] [2000s] (*S.Afr. gay*) an abortion.

abigail *adj.* [the image of *abigail* as an 'old-fashioned' name] [2000s] (*S.Afr. gay*) old, ugly, unattractive, a general derog. term.

abishag *n.* [Heb., lit. 'the mother's error'] [19C] the bastard child of a woman who has been seduced and abandoned by a married man.

able and cable *adj.* [SE *able* + redup.] [1950s] (*US black*) ready and willing.

able Grable *n.* [SE *able* + US film star Betty *Grable* (1916–73)] [1940s] (*US teen*) an attractive woman.

Abney Park *n.*

IN PHRASES

❑ **go to Abney Park** [*Abney Park* cemetery in Stoke Newington, north London. Founded in 1840, it succeeded Bunhill Fields as the centre of non-conformist burials. Among those buried there is General William Booth (1829–1912), founder of the Salvation Army] [late 19C–1920s] to die.

abo *n.* (*also* **Abo, Abor**) [? abbr. of the column 'Aboriginalities', launched in the Sydney *Bulletin*, 15 Oct. 1887 (one regular writer for which signed himself 'Abo'); *AND* suggests it was current orally somewhat earlier; the SE *Aborigine* and *Aboriginal* are found in 1829 citations; pl. *Aborigines* is found in 1803] **1** [20C+] (*Aus.*) an *Abo*riginal; also attrib. **2** [1910s–30s] (*Aus.*) an expert on Aborigine and bush customs and folktales.

IN COMPOUNDS

❑ **abo's handbag** *n.* (*also* **handbag**) [2000s] (*Aus.*) any form of boxed (rather than bottled) wine.

IN PHRASES

❑ **dark as an abo's arsehole** *adj.* *see* DARK *adj.*

abo *adj.* [2000s] (*S.Afr. gay*) old.

aboard *adv.* [19C–1940s] (*orig. US*) in one's stomach, esp. of drink; thus *get aboard*, to be drunk.

aboliar *n.* [ABO *n.* (1) + SE *liar;* certainly a coinage and prob. a nonceword of the *Bulletin*] [1900s–30s] (*Aus.*) an expert on Aborigine and bush customs and folktales.

A-bomb *n.* [the supposedly 'expolosive' effects] (*US drugs*) **1** [1960s+] a combination of marijuana or hashish with opium, or another narcotic. **2** [1990s+] phencyclidine mixed with formaldehyde.

IN COMPOUNDS

❑ **A-bomb juice** *n.* [1940s+] (*US*) illicitly distilled alcohol, 'moonshine'.

Abor *n. see* ABO *n.*

abort *v.* [black humour] [1970s+] (*US gay*) to defecate immediately after anal intercourse.

abortion *n.* [late 18C+] an all-purpose derog. term for a person, an object or an enterprise.

about east *adv.* [? sailing use] [mid-19C] (*US*) properly, regularly, as it should be.

about half *adj.* [i.e. halfway between good and bad] [1960s] feeling fine, relatively happy.

about it *adj.* [2000s] (*US black*) totally committed.

about right *adj.*[1] [one of a number of terms implying the positive aspects of drinking: the inference is that the sober state is 'wrong'] [19C+] drunk.

about right *adj.*[2] [ext. of SE; the implication is of a slightly grudging admission] [mid-19C+] correct.

about right *adv.* [mid-19C–1900s] to the best extent possible.

about that *adj.* [1990s+] (*US campus*) in agreement with.

above board *adj.* [the image is of card-players keeping their hands in clear view above the table and thus resisting any temptation to cheat] **1** [17C+] open, honest; thus antonym *under board*. **2** [mid-17C–early 18C] in a sexual context, maintaining an undisguised relationship; thus antonym *under board*.

above board *adv.* [ABOVE BOARD *adj.* (1)] [18C+] openly, honestly.

above oneself *adj.* [late 19C+] over-confident, pushy, esp. of someone who is usu. more self-effacing; often in phr. below.

IN PHRASES

❑ **get above oneself** *v.* **1** [late 19C+] to act in an arrogant manner, to be self-satisfied. **2** [1960s] (*US black*) to brag, to attack verbally.

above par *adj.* [Stock Exchange jargon *par*, face value] **1** [mid-19C] (*UK Und.*) well-off. **2** [late 19C] in good spirits or health. **3** [1930s] mildly drunk.

A-box *n.* [abbr. ATTITUDE *n.* + SE *box*] [1990s+] (*US campus*) someone in an unpleasant mood.

abrac *n.* [? SE *Arabic* or ? abbr. SE *abracadabra*] [early–mid-19C] learning.

abraham *see also under* ABRAM and comb.

abraham *n.*[1] [*Abraham*, the biblical patriarch, i.e. the role of the penis in procreation] [19C] the penis.

abraham *n.*[2] *see* ABRAHAM-MAN *n.*

abraham *adj.* [ABRAHAM-MAN *n.*] [17C] naked.

abraham *v.* [rhy. sl., but note SHAM ABRAM *v.* (1)] [1990s+] to sham, esp. to avoid something by feigning illness.

abraham-cove *n. see* ABRAHAM-MAN *n.*

abrahamer *n.* (*also* **abramer**) [var. on ABRAHAM-MAN *n.*] [late 18C–early 19C] a tramp.

abraham grains *n.* [generic use of proper name *Abraham* + SE *grains*] [late 19C–1900s] a publican who brews his own beer.

Abraham Lincoln *n.* [the face of *Abraham Lincoln* (1809–65), 16th president of the US, is printed on $5 bills] [1940s–60s] (*US, esp. black*) a $5 bill.

abraham-man *n.* (*also* **abraham, abraham-cove**) [? the Abraham Ward of the Hospital of St Mary of Bethlehem, London, in which the insane patients were housed. The hospital, known popularly as Bedlam, allowed certain inmates to go begging on a number of fixed days each year; the *abram-man* posed as one of these licensed beggars. Note the parable of the beggar in Luke 16:19–31; Ribton-Turner, *A History of Vagrants* (1887), suggests Gaelic/Erse *bramanach*, a noisy fellow; + SE *man*/COVE *n.* (1)] [mid-16C–mid-19C; 1930s] a wandering beggar, adopting tattered clothing and posing as a madman.

Abraham Newland *n.* [proper name of *Abraham Newland*, chief cashier of the Bank of England (1778–1807)] [late 18C–early 19C] a banknote.

(IN PHRASES)

❑ **sham Abraham Newland** *v.* to forge banknotes.

abraham's balsam *n.* [SE *Abraham's balm*, the chaste tree (*Vitex agnus-castus*), but presumably punning on *Abraham's bosom*, the abode of the dead (*see* next)] [18C] the gallows.

abraham's bosom *n.* [punning on the biblical use meaning the 'abode of the dead', e.g. at Luke 16:22: 'The beggar died, and was carried by the angels into Abraham's bosom.' In both SE and sl. senses the implication is of 'lying on'] [late 19C] the vagina.

(IN PHRASES)

❑ **be in Abraham's bosom** *v.* to have sexual intercourse.

abraham's willing *n.* [rhy. sl.] [mid-19C–1900s] a shilling (5p).

abram *n.* [abbr. ABRAM-MAN *n.*] [17C–mid-19C] (*UK Und.*) a wandering beggar, adopting tattered clothing and posing as a madman.

(IN COMPOUNDS)

❑ **abram suit** *n.* (*also* **abraham suit**) [SE *suit*, a petition] [19C] working as a writer of begging letters, the pursuit of many small-time 19C confidence tricksters. ❑ **abram work** *n.* (*also* **abraham work**) [late 19C] any form of spurious occupation, esp. some form of confidence trick.

abram *adj.* [ABRAM *n.*] **1** [17C] insane, crazy. **2** [mid-17C–mid-19C] (*UK Und.*) naked.

abram *v.* [? naut. *abram*, a malingerer or rhy. sl. = sham] [mid-19C] to malinger, to fake illness.

abramer *n. see* ABRAHAMER *n.*

abram-man *n.* (*also* **abram-cove, abram-mort**) [var. on ABRAHAM-MAN *n.* + COVE *n.* (1)/MORT *n.*] **1** [17C–19C] a wandering beggar, adopting tattered clothing and posing as a madman. **2** [late 17C–mid-19C] a 'sturdy beggar', i.e. one who could, but rarely does, work for a living. **3** [late 18C–mid-19C] a thief specializing in pocket-books.

abram-sham *n.* [ABRAM SHAM *v.*] [late 19C] the practice of travelling the country posing as a madman.

abram sham *v.* (*also* **abraham sham**) [ABRAM *n.* + SE *sham*] [early–mid-19C] of a beggar, to travel the country posing as a madman, to fake illness.

abridgements *n.* [they are 'abridged' or cut off at the knee] [mid-19C] knee-breeches.

abroad *adj.* **1** [late 18C–mid-19C] of convicts, transported to a penal colony. **2** [19C] in error, confused; thus *all abroad*, wide of the mark. **3** [mid-19C] drunk.

abroaded *adj.* **1** [mid–late 19C] (*UK society*) living in exile somewhere other than the UK. **2** [mid–late 19C] transported to a penal colony. **3** [late 19C–1920s] imprisoned.

abs *prep.* [mid-19C] (*UK Und.*) to, from, out.

abscotchalater *n.* [var. pron. of ABSQUATULATE *v.* (1) + SE sfx *-er*] [late 19C] (*US*) one who runs away.

absentee *n.* [? because he is *absent* from everyday life] [mid-19C+] (*Aus./S.Afr.*) a convict.

absent-minded beggar *n.* [title of poem (1899) by Rudyard Kipling, celebrating the British soldier] [late 19C–1900s] a soldier.

abs-laggy *adj.* [ABS *prep.* + LAG *v.*[2] (1)] [mid-19C] (*UK Und.*) transported.

abs-lushery *adj.* [ABS *prep.* + LUSHERY *n.*] [mid-19C] (*UK Und.*) at a drinking house.

abs-nabbems *adj.* [ABS *prep.* + NAB *v.*[1] (2)] [mid-19C] (*UK Und.*) safe, secure from capture.

abs-nunks *adj.* [ABS *prep.* + SE *nuncle*, an uncle/UNCLE *n.* (1)] [mid-19C] (*UK Und.*) visiting the pawnbroker.

abso *n.* [abbr. SE *absolute*] [1900s] a definite winner, usu. in a sporting context, a CERT *n.* (1).

absoballylutely *adv.* (*also* **absobloominglutely**) [SE *absolutely* + BALLY *adj.*/BLOOMING *adj.*[1]] [1910s+] an intense version of absolutely, very much indeed.

absobloodylutely *adv.* [SE *absolutely* + BLOODY *adv.* (2)] [1910s+] an intensified version of absolutely.

absofuckinglutely *adv.* [SE *absolutely* + FUCKING *adj.* (4), coined by WW1 troops] [1910s+] very much so indeed, without the slightest doubt; also as excl. of affirmation.

absogoddamlutely *adv.* [SE *absolutely* + GOD-DAMN *adj.* (3)] [1960s+] (*US*) an intensified version of absolutely.

absotively *adv.* [comb. of SE *absolutely* + *positively*; inverse of POSILUTELY *adv.*] [1910s+] (*US*) without a doubt, irrefutably.

abs-pad-luck *adj.* [ABS *prep.* + PAD *n.*[1] (1)] [mid-19C] (*UK Und.*) 'gone upon the highway' (Duncombe).

absquattle *v.* [var. on ABSQUATULATE *v.* (1)] [mid-19C] (*orig. US*) of a person or animal, to leave, to run away, to abscond.

absquatulate *v.* (*also* **absquotulate, obsquatulate**) [pig Lat. based on SE *abscond* + *squat* + sfx *-ulate*; note John Mitchell Bonnell, 'A manual of the art of prose composition: for the use of colleges and schools' (1867): 'ABSQUATULATE – to remove one's residence away; as if squat were a Latin root, from which were formed *squatulare* and *absquatulare*'] [19C] (*orig. US*) **1** (*also* **absquat**) of people or animals, to leave, to run away, to abscond. **2** of an object, to separate, to break away from.

abs-smash-rig *n.* [ABS *prep.* + SMASH *v.*[2] (1) + RIG *n.*[2] (1)] [mid-19C] (*UK Und.*) the act of passing counterfeit coin.

abs-spoutems *adj.* [ABS *prep.* + SPOUT *n.*[2] (1)] [mid-19C] (*UK Und.*) gone to the pawnbrokers.

abstain from beans *v.* [Plutarch (AD 46?–AD c.120), *Of the Training of Children*, 'Abstain from beans; that is, keep out of public offices, for anciently the choice of the officers of state was made by beans'] [1920s] to desist from politics.

abstractionist *n.* [SE *abstract*, to remove] [mid-19C] (*US*) a pickpocket.

abstropelous *adj.* [corruption of SE *obstreperous*] [early 18C–mid-19C] aggressively resistant to control or restraint.

a-buck *n.* [1980s+] (*US gay*) lying on one's back with one's legs over one's head to enable both anal intercourse and kissing.

Aby *n. see* ABIE *n.* (1).

abyss *n.* [1980s+] (*US gay*) a large anus that has been frequently used for anal intercourse.

Abyssinia *phr.* [punning on SE phr. *I'll be seeing you*] [1930s+] (*orig. US*) goodbye.

Abyssinian polo *n.* [stereotyping of craps as a black ('Abyssinian') person's favourite game] [1920s+] (*US*) the game of craps.

A.C. *n.* [abbr.; note A.B. *n.* (3) and A.W. *n.*] [2000s] (*US prison*) Aryan Circle, a white supremacist prison gang.

ac *n.* [abbr.] [1990s+] (*US black*) the Acura Legend, a popular automobile.

a.c.a.b. *phr.* [abbr.; a popular tattoo in the UK, esp. among Hell's Angels and other 'outlaw' groups] [1940s+] all coppers are bastards.

academician *n.* [punning use of SE + ACADEMY *n.* (4)/ACADEMY *n.* (1)] **1** [early 19C] a prisoner. **2** [mid–late 19C] a prostitute.

academy *n.* [joc. uses of SE] **1** [early 17C–19C] a brothel, one of a number of contemporary terms based on brothel = school. **2** [early 18C] a casino. **3** [mid-18C] a lunatic asylum. **4** [early 19C–1950s] a prison; used in combs. such as ADKINS'S ACADEMY *n.*; CAMPBELL'S ACADEMY *n.*; FLOATING ACADEMY *n.* **5** [late 19C–1900s] a billiard room.

Acapulco (gold) *n.* [the drug derives in and around Acapulco de Juárez, in Guerrero state on the west coast of Mexico] [1960s+] (*orig. US drugs*) a high-strength grade of marijuana.

entry. [late 19C+] to perform in a given manner; usu. combined with a specific n. or proper name, which defines the 'act' in question. ❑ **do a brown act** *v.* [1980s] (*N.Z.*) to act in a shy manner; to sulk. ❑ **do the — act** *v.* (*also* **play the..., pull the...**) [late 19C+] (*US*) to pretend to a particular (by context) style of behaviour, to assume (often deceitfully) specific characteristics. ❑ **get one's act together** *v.* [1960s+] (*orig. US black*) to calm down, to plan sensibly, to state a goal and aim for it. ❑ **have one's act down** *v.* [1960s+] (*orig. US black*) to be in full control of a situation, whether emotional, social, sexual, financial etc. ❑ **pull an act** *v.* [1930s+] to put on a show with the intention of deceiving or defrauding someone. ❑ **put on an act** *v.* [1930s+] to show off, to talk for display, to behave insincerely. ❑ **queer someone's act** *v.* (*also* **queer the act**) [QUEER *v.* (5)] [1910s+] (*US*) to interfere, to spoil someone's plans.

SE in slang uses

(IN PHRASES)

❑ **on the act** [late 19C] working as an actor.

act-ass *n.* [SE *act* + -ASS *sfx*] [1970s] (*US*) one who sees themselves as cleverer than they really are.

action *n.* [all fig. uses of SE; note Shakespeare's use of *action* (and *activity*) as sexual intercourse] **1** [mid-19C+] sexual ability, lit. the erotic 'action' of the hips or pelvis. **2** [late 19C+] sexual intercourse or similar activity. **3** [late 19C+] (*US*) financial transactions, esp. bets and wagers. **4** [1920s+] (*orig. US black*) what is going on; thus a situation or state of affairs, anything exciting, current, interesting, depending on the context, e.g. the chance for sex, a musical performance, a night's gambling; often used in the greeting, *Where's/what's the action?* **5** [1950s–60s] the potential client for a prostitute, or victim of a confidence trick etc. **6** [1950s–60s] (*US*) one's choice, one's preference. **7** [1960s] the effects of a drug. **8** [1960s] (*US*) a revolver. **9** [1960s–70s] manipulations, activities, esp. when illegal or corrupt. **10** [1960s+] (*drugs*) the current availability of drugs and the best place to obtain them. **11** [1960s+] (*orig. US black*) a woman. **12** [1970s+] (*US black*) a look, a smile, a verbal response. **13** [1990s+] (*Aus. prison*) homosexuality.

(IN COMPOUNDS)

❑ **action piece** *n.* [PIECE *n.* (1)] [1960s] (*US black*) **1** a woman. **2** a pistol, a revolver, a shotgun.

(IN PHRASES)

❑ **action on a solid half traction** (*also* **action on the...**) [sense 4 above + engineering imagery] [1940s–70s] (*US black, mainly Harlem*) ready for anything. ❑ **tighten one's action** *v.* [1970s+] (*US*) to begin behaving in a more effective or positive manner.

-action *sfx* [1960s+] (*US campus*) a comb. form denoting activity, e.g. *dope action, babe action,* GUM ACTION *under* GUM *n.*[1].

active citizens *n.* [play on SE] [early–mid-19C] lice, fleas.

actor *n.* [1940s+] (*US black*) anyone out to deceive or to project a phoney image, a con-man or liar.

actorine *n.* [SE *actor* + fem. sfx *-ine*] [late 19C–1930s] (*US*) an actress.

actress *n.* [camp feminization] [1950s–70s] (*US camp gay*) an egocentric show-off, who is nonetheless amusing and witty.

act the... *v. see also under* the relevant n.

act the angora *v.* [the SE *angora* goat, thus a laboured pun on ACT THE (GIDDY) GOAT *v.*] [20C+] (*Aus./N.Z.*) to play the fool.

act the (giddy) goat *v.* (*also* **play the goat**) [GOAT *n.*[1] (2); the assumption is that the animal is naturally foolish; note Stephens & O'Brien, *Materials for a Dict. of Aus. Slang* (ms. 1900–10): 'No doubt a humorous variation of "caper".'] [late 19C+] to behave foolishly.

act the hog *v.* (*also* **act the monkey, play the monkey, run the hog**) [the assumption is that animals are naturally foolish] **1** [1900s–40s] to play the fool. **2** [1940s] to malfunction.

act the linnet *v.* [SE *linnet*, a song bird] [20C+] (*Irish*) to flirt.

act the wet dog *v.* [the annoyance of a wet dog shaking its fur] [late 19C] (*US*) to make a fuss, to complain.

actual, the *n.* [as in SE, where 'the actual' is opposed to 'the idea', the sense here is of concrete, hard cash] [mid-19C+] money.

act-up *adj.* [ACT UP *v.* (2)] [2000s] (*UK black/teen*) aggressive.

act up *v.* [20C+] **1** to make a fuss in order to attract attention to oneself. **2** to cause (someone) trouble.

a.d. *n.*[1] [used on dance cards to disguise a preference for alcohol over dancing; partners' names were also abbreviated] [late 19C–1900s] (*UK society*) a drink.

a.d. *n.*[2] (*also* **ad, add**) [reversed abbr., in order to avoid confusion with the law's DA, a district attorney; also simple abbr. of SE *addict*] [1930s+] (*US drugs*) a drug addict.

a.d. *n.*[3] [ety. unknown] [1970s+] phencyclidine.

a.d. *n.*[4] *see* ACCIDENTAL DADDY *n.*

a.d. *v.* [abbr. AUDI (5000) *v.*] [1990s+] (*US campus*) to leave.

ad *n.*[1] [abbr.] **1** [mid-19C+] an advertisement. **2** [1970s] (*US gay*) a graffito offering sexual services, as found on a public lavatory wall.

ad *n.*[2] *see* A.D. *n.*[2].

ad *adj.* [abbr.] [20C+] pertaining to advertising; thus *adman, ad exec, ad agency*.

Ada *n.* [2000s] (*S.Afr. gay*) **1** a German homosexual. **2** a homosexual who cannot find a sexual partner. **3** the buttocks [initial letter of ARSE *n.* (1)].

adad! *excl.* [DAD *n.*[1] (1); note ADOD! *excl.*] [mid-17C–mid-18C] God!

Ada from Decatur *n.* (*also* **Decatur, eighter Decatur, eighter from Decatur, little Ada**) [pun on *eighter* + proper name *Decatur*, Alabama or Texas] [1910s+] (*US gambling*) the point of eight in craps dice.

Adam *n.* [use of the first man, *Adam*, as a generic] **1** [late 15C+] used in a variety of phr. indicating a lack of clothing and tools etc. **2** [mid-19C+] used in a variety of phr. indicating a very long time ago.

(IN COMPOUNDS)

❑ **Adam's ale** *n.* (*also* **Adam, Adam's beverage, ...liquor, ...wine**) [late 15C+] water. ❑ **Adam's arm** *n.* [1940s–60s] (*US*) a shovel, a spade. ❑ **Adam's arsenal** *n.* [the biblical *Adam* had no weaponry + SE *arsenal*; it is 'loaded' with semen] [late 19C] the penis. ❑ **Adam's jig** *n. see under* DANCE *v.* (1). ❑ **Adam's off-ox** *n.* [OFF-OX *n.*] [late 19C+] a slow, stubborn person. ❑ **Adam's own (altar)** *n.* [late 19C] the vagina; one of many literary euph., usu. positive. ❑ **Adam's p.j.s** *n.* [gay version of ADAM AND EVE'S P.J.S *n.*] [1970s] (*US gay*) nudity. ❑ **Adam's slippers** *n.* [1900s] (*US*) no shoes, i.e. barefoot. ❑ **Adam's wine** *n. see* ADAM'S ALE above.

(IN PHRASES)

❑ **when Adam was an oakum boy in Brooklyn Navy Yard** (*also* **when Adam was an oakum boy in Chatham**) [mid-19C–1910s] a very long time ago.

adam *n.*[1] [the biblical *Adam*, the first man] **1** [late 16C–early 19C] a bailiff, a sergeant. **2** [late 17C–19C] (*UK Und.*) a fence, a criminal receiver. **3** [mid-19C] (*UK Und.*) a thief's accomplice. **4** [late 19C] a foreman. **5** [1940s] (*US Und.*) a prison warder. **6** [1950s–70s] (*camp gay*) one's first (paid) sexual partner.

adam *n.*[2] [the initial letters + ref. to the primal intensity of the drug experience] [1980s+] MDMA.

adam *v.* [the biblical 'first couple'] [mid–late 18C] to marry.

Adam and Eve *n.*[1] [the similarity is suggested by the fact that there are two eggs, they are alone and 'naked'; note the army use *adam and eve wrecked*, scrambled eggs] [late 19C+] (*orig. US short order*) two poached or fried eggs; thus *adam and eve on a raft*, two poached eggs on toast; *adam and eve on a raft and wreck 'em*, two scrambled eggs on toast.

Adam and Eve *n.*[2] [rhy. sl.] [1980s] (*Aus.*) a sleeve.

Adam (and Eve) *v.* [rhy. sl.] **1** [1910s+] to believe; often in the interrog. phr. *would you Adam and Eve it?* **2** [1930s+] to leave.

Adam and Eve *v.* (*also* **do Adam and Eve**) [the first act thereof in the biblical Garden of Eden] [late 17C+] to have sexual intercourse.

Adam and Eve ball *n.* [at such a time they are fig. ejected from (social) Eden] [1920s+] an early dancing party to which the guests are invited until midnight only.

Adam and Eve's p.j.s *n.* (*also* **Adam and Eve's togs**) [SE *p.j.s*/TOGS *n.* (1); Adam and Eve's initial nakedness in Eden] [late 19C+] nudity; the terms are US and UK respectively.

adam tiler *n.* (*also* **adam tyler**) [? SE *Adam*, generic for man + Ger. *Teile*, a share or slice; note 20C+ US Und. *adam*, a pickpocket's assistant] **1** [late 17C–mid-19C] a pickpocket's assistant. **2** [early 18C–mid-19C] a criminal receiver.

Ada Ross *n.* [var. on ADA FROM DECATUR *n.*] [1940s+] (*US*) the eight point in craps dice; also ext. as *Ada Ross the stable boss/hoss*.

add *n. see* A.D. *n.*[2].

added to the list *phr.* [turf jargon; *the list* was of geldings in training] [late 19C+] castrated.

addition *n.* [an addition to one's natural complexion] [early 18C] make-up, cosmetics.

addle-cove *n.* [SE *addle*, to confuse + COVE *n.* (1); the sl. synon. of SE *addle-pate* or *addle-head*; Partridge claims late 18C but offers no proof; not in Grose, Egan, Hotten] [mid-19C] (*US*) a fool.

addled *adj.* [SE *addle-pated*, stupid] [late 17C+] drunk; one of a number of synons. meaning defective and thus ill or denoting the drunkard's confusion.

addle-plot *n.* [late 17C–early 19C] a spoil-sport who 'addles' the 'plots' or plans of others.

add rabbit!/rot it! *excl. see* OD ROT IT! *under* OD! *excl.*

add up *v.* [1930s+] **1** to make sense, to work out as expected; esp. in phr. *it all adds up*, or *it doesn't add up*. **2** (*also* **add up to**) to amount to, to signify.

Adele *adj.* [ADELE ADDER *n.*] [2000s] (*S.Afr. gay*) vindictive, mean, bitchy.

Adele Adder *n.* [assonant female proper name + image of the stereotypically untrustworthy snake] [2000s] (*S.Afr. gay*) a homosexual person who is vindictive or bitchy.

adept *n.* [Lat. *adeptus*, skilled in; a Med. alchemist who had attained 'the great secret' was entitled *adeptus*, completely skilled (in all the secrets of his art)] [18C] **1** a conjuror. **2** a pickpocket. **3** an alchemist.

adidas *phr.* [abbr.; pun on brandname of sports shoes] [1990s+] a phr. meaning all day *I* dream about sex.

adios amoebas *phr.* [a pun on the more common *adios amigos*, popularized by the 1950s TV series *The Cisco Kid*] [1980s+] (*US campus*) a farewell.

Adirondack steak *n.* [SE *Adirondack* + *steak*; the Adirondacks area is generally regarded as impoverished] [1950s] (*US*) venison.

adjective *adj.* (*also* **adjectival**) [BLOODY *adj.* (1) is so widespread in Aus. it is termed 'the great Australian adjective'] [late 19C–1900s] (*mainly Aus.*) a euph. for BLOODY *adj.* (1).

Adkins's academy *n.* [*Adkins* + ACADEMY *n.* (4)] [early–mid-19C] a London house of correction, named for its governor.

ad lib *n.* [SE *ad lib*, to extemporize; ult. Lat. *ad libitum*, as much as one desires] [1920s+] (*orig. US*) a pointed, provocative or sarcastic comment.

Admiral Browning *n.* [facet. use of SE *admiral* + BROWN *n.* (3)] [20C+] (*orig. naut.*) human excrement.

admiral of… *n.*

IN PHRASES

❑ **admiral of the blue** *n.* [his blue apron] [early 18C–mid-19C] a publican, an innkeeper. ❑ **admiral of the narrow seas** *n.* [facet. use of SE *admiral* + *narrow seas*, the British Channel/the Irish Sea] [mid-17C–mid-19C] a drunkard who vomits over his neighbour at table. ❑ **admiral of the red** *n.* [as well as the colour of wine, the term may also refer to the drunkard's red nose] [mid-19C] a heavy drinker, as borne out by their red face. ❑ **admiral of the red, white and blue** *n.* [the over-elaborate uniforms] [19C] an over-dressed, flashy beadle or other minor, uniformed official. ❑ **admiral of the white** *n.* [white is the colour of cowardice] [mid-19C–1900s] a coward.

adobe *adj.* [Sp. *adobe*, sun-dried mud or clay, widely used as a building material in Mexico] [19C+] (*US*) a generic, and in sl. use derog., term meaning Mexican, hence generic for second-rate, inferior.

IN COMPOUNDS

❑ **adobe dollar** *n.* [20C+] (*US*) a Mexican peso. ❑ **adobe maker** *n.* [1960s] (*US*) a derog. term for a Mexican or Mexican-American.

adod! *excl.* [DOD *n.*[1] (1); note ADAD! *excl.*] [late 17C–18C] God!

adonee *n.* [Heb. *adonai*, the Lord, God] [mid-16C–19C] (*UK Und.*) God.

adonis *n.* [Greek god *Adonis*, known for his outstanding beauty] **1** [early 17C+] a very attractive male. **2** [late 19C–1900s] (*Aus.*) in ironic use, a male admirer, a lover.

adonize *v.* [ADONIS *n.*] [mid-18C–mid-19C] of a man, to adorn oneself, to dress up.

Adrian (Quist) *adj.* [rhy. sl. = PISSED *adj.*[1]; ult. the Aus. tennis player *Adrian Quist* (b.1913)] [1970s+] (*Aus.*) drunk.

adrift *adj.* [SE naut. term; orig. in navy use] **1** [17C] harmless. **2** [late 18C+] missing. **3** [20C+] confused.

ads *n.* [late 17C–mid-19C] God's, used in various excl. oaths, the major ones being listed below (cf. ADZOOKS! *excl.*; ODS *n.*).

IN EXCLAMATIONS

❑ **adsbleed!** (*also* **adsbud!**) God's blood! ❑ **adsheart!** God's heart! ❑ **ad's (heart's) wounds!** God's (heart's) wounds! ❑ **adslife!** (*also* **ads my life!**) God's life! ❑ **adso!** God's oath! ❑ **adsooks!** *see* ADZOOKS! *excl.* ❑ **ads wooks!** *see* ADZOOKS! *excl.*

advertise *v.* [play on SE] **1** [1930s+] (*orig. US*) to show off, to act in an exhibitionist manner (and thus draw un-needed attention to oneself). **2** [1950s+] (*gay*) to dress in a sexually provocative manner. **3** [1970s] (*camp gay*) to pluck and paint one's eybrows.

IN COMPOUNDS

❑ **advertising bar** *n.* [1960s+] (*US gay*) a bar frequented by male prostitutes and their clients. ❑ **advertising club** *n.* [1950s] (*US gay*) a men's washroom.

advertisement conveyancer *n.* [the euph. term (PC long before its time) was coined by W.E. Gladstone (1809–98) and duly mocked by London society] [late 19C] a sandwich-man.

advertising pilgrim *n. see* PILGRIM *n.*[2].

adzooks! *excl.* (*also* **adsooks! ads wooks! adzookers!**) [ADS *n.*; lit. 'God's hooks!'] [late 17C–mid-19C] a mildly blasphemous oath.

aerated *adj.* (*also* **aeriated, airyated**) [1920s+] over-excited, angry.

aerial pingpong *n.* [mainly used in New South Wales to tease the fans, who are mostly from Victoria] [1960s+] (*Aus.*) Australian Rules football.

aeroplane *n.* [? resemblance to a propeller] [1930s+] (*Aus.*) a bow tie.

aeroplane blonde *n.* (*also* **airplane blonde**) [pun on SE *black box*/BOX *n.*[1] (1a), i.e. her pubic hair is still black] [1990s+] a woman with dyed blonde hair.

aeroplane skirt *n.* (*also* **aeroplane dress, airplane dress/skirt**) [it reaches the COCK PIT *under* COCK *n.*[3]] [2000s] a skirt with a long slit reaching the groin.

af *n.* (*also* **aff**) [abbr.] [1960s+] (*S.Afr.*) a derog. term for an African.

IN COMPOUNDS

❑ **aftax** *n.* [SE *taxi*] [1980s] a black-owned taxi (usu. an old, American-made car).

affair *n.*[1] [SE *affair*, a thing] **1** [mid-16C–19C] the penis. **2** [mid-18C+] the vagina.

affair *n.*[2] [SE *affair*, a sexual relationship] [1970s–80s] (*gay*) one's current lover.

affidavit man *n.* [SE *affidavit*, a sworn statement that can be used in evidence] [late 17C–early 19C] a professional witness who, with pay, will swear to anything.

affie *n.*[1] [abbr.] [1990s+] afternoon.

affie *n.*[2] [abbr. SE *African*] [2000s] a derog. term for a black person.

affigraphy *n. see* AFFYGRAPHY *n.*

afflicke *n. see* FLICK *n.*[1].

afflicted *adj.* [late 17C–early 18C] drunk.

afflictions *n.* [mid-19C–1900s] (*orig. drapers*) mourning clothes; thus *mitigated afflictions*, half-mourning.

affygraphy *n.* (*also* **affigraphy**) [SE *autograph* + ? *affidavit*] [mid-19C–1900s] an exact match; usu. as *to an affygraphy*.

afgay *n. see* AGFAY *n.*

Afghan *n.* (*also* **Afghani**) [1960s+] (*drugs*) Afghan hashish.

afghan *n.* [SE *afghan*, a coarse-woven afghan shawl; such a man might need one] [1960s] (*US gay*) a middle-aged gay man, who sometimes cross-dresses.

afkop *n.* [Afk. *afkop*, no head; such women supposedly hide their unalluring faces beneath the bedclothes] [20C+] (*S.Afr.*) an ageing prostitute.

afloat *adj.* [early 19C+] drunk.

a.f.o. *adj.* [abbr. all *f*ucked out, i.e. FUCKED OUT *under* FUCKED *adj.*[1]] [1990s+] exhausted by sexual excess.

Africa *n.* [negative stereotyping] [late 19C–1930s] (*US*) anywhere mainly populated or used by the black community.

IN PHRASES

❑ **go back to Africa** *v.* [20C+] (*W.I., Guyn.*) of a light-skinned man, to marry a woman whose complexion is much darker than his own.

African *n.* [? as smoked by black people] [1940s+] **1** (*Aus.*) (*also* **African nigger**) a 'tailor-made', rather than hand-rolled, cigarette. **2** (*US drugs*) marijuana.

SE in slang uses

IN PHRASES

❑ **get one's African up** *v.* (*also* **get one's North Carolina up**) [racial stereotyping] [mid-19C–1920s] (*US*) to lose control, to lose one's temper.

African *adj.* [20C+] a derog. generic word, used alone or in several combs. below to mean stupid, slow, unskilled or a number of other similar pej. stereotypes attached to black people, whether Africans or Afro-Americans.

IN COMPOUNDS

❑ **African ape** *n.* [1960s] (*US*) a derog. term for a black person. ❑ **African billiards** *n.* [1910s–60s] (*US*) the game of craps. ❑ **African black** *n.* (*also* **black African**) [its origin and colour] [1970s–80s] (*drugs*) marijuana. ❑ **African bush** *n.* [BUSH *n.*[1] (5a)] [1970s] (*drugs*) cannabis. ❑ **African dominoes** *n.* (*also* **African bones**) [BONES *n.*[1] (1)] [1920s–60s] (*US*) craps dice. ❑ **African dust** *n.* [the gold-mines of South Africa; the equation of money = DUST *n.* (1) is presumably coincidental] [1950s] (*US*) gold. ❑ **African engineering** *n.* (*also* **Afro engineering**) [1970s] shoddy, second-rate workmanship. ❑ **African golf** *n.* [1910s+] (*US*) the game of craps; thus *African golfer*, a crap-shooter. ❑ **African golf ball** *n.* **1** [1920s–70s] (*US*) a die; usu. in pl. **2** [1970s+] (*US black*) a watermelon. ❑ **African grape** *n.* [1970s+] (*US black*) a watermelon. ❑ **African harp** *n.* [1930s] (*US*) a banjo. ❑ **African lager** *n.* [apart from its creamy head, the drink is virtually black] [20C+] Guinness stout. ❑ **African nigger** *n. see* AFRICAN *n.* (1). ❑ **African (people's) time** *n.* [racial stereotyping] [1960s+] (*orig. S.Afr.*) unpunctuality, flexible time, a general disregard for time-keeping. ❑ **African pill** *n.* [1910s] (*US*) a craps die; usu. in pl. ❑ **African plum** *n.* [1960s–70s] (*US black*) a watermelon. ❑ **African pool** *n.* [1910s] (*US*) the game of craps. ❑ **African queen** *n.* [QUEEN *n.* (2a)/-QUEEN *sfx*] [1970s] **1** (*gay*) a black homosexual male. **2** a white homosexual male who prefers black partners. ❑ **African salad** *n.* [2000s] (*US drugs*) khat. ❑ **African skyscraper** *n.* [1950s+] (*US*) a giraffe. ❑ **African toothache** *n.* [1950s–60s] (*US*) venereal disease. ❑ **African woodbine** *n.* [Wills' *Woodbines*, popular, cheap UK cigarettes] [1940s+] (*drugs*) marijuana cigarette.

Africa speaks *n.* [? ref. to early S.Afr. documentary film (on the then 'Belgian' Congo) *Africa Speaks* (1930)] [1940s–50s] (*Aus./N.Z.*) strong liquor imported f. South Africa.

Africky *adj.* [the term is descriptive and, unlike AFRICAN *adj.*, there is no specific pej. other than that inevitably pertaining to anything black] [early 17C–1900s] African.

Afriks *n.* (*also* **Afrix**) [abbr.] **1** [1970s+] (*S.Afr. school*) Afrikaans as a school lesson; f. the perspective of English speakers. **2** [2000s] an Afrikaaner.

afro *n.* (*also* **'fro**) [abbr.] **1** [1930s; 1960s+] (*orig. US black*) a black hairstyle in which normally short, curly black hair is allowed to grow out in a bush around the head, supposedly in the style of one's African forebears; also occas. used of white people's hair; thus *afro-style*, having an afro hairstyle. **2** [1930s–70s] an English or American person of African descent, a black.

afro *v.* (*also* **'fro**) [1970s+] (*orig. US*) to grow one's hair into an AFRO *n.* (1) hairstyle; thus adj. *afroed*.

Afro engineering *n. see* AFRICAN ENGINEERING *under* AFRICAN *adj.*

afromobile *n.* [SE *Afro*, AFRICAN *adj.* + *automobile*] **1** [1900s–10s] (*US*) a three-wheeled vehicle used to convey tourists in Palm Beach, Florida; the drivers are invariably black [implies subservience]. **2** [1970s+] (*US black*) any fashionable automobile, e.g. a BMW, Lexus, Mercedes [implies success].

afro set *n.* [SE *Afro* + SET *n.*[1] (1)] [1970s–80s] (*US black*) anywhere that blacks use for talking or acting in furtherance of their own social and political betterment.

aft *n.* [abbr.] [20C+] afternoon.

aftax *n. see under* AF *n.*

after *n.* [abbr.] [1900s–40s] (*Aus./US*) afternoon.

afterbirth *n.* [1960s+] (*US/UK/W.I.*) a general term of abuse.

after-clap *n.* ['an unexpected stroke after the recipient has ceased to be on his guard; a subsequent surprise; an unexpected event happening after an affair is supposed to be at an end' (Johnson, *Dictionary*, 1755)] **1** [late 18C–early 19C] a bill that is presented after the first has already been paid. **2** [early 19C] anything unpleasant that emerges after a situation had been supposedly settled.

after-dark *n.* [rhy. sl.] [late 19C] a (bookmaker's) clerk.

after davy *n.* [mispron.] [mid-19C] an affidavit.

after-dinner man *n. see* AFTERNOON MAN *n.*

after dinner mint *n.* (*also* **minter**) [1980s] (*Aus./N.Z.*) a woman who is willing to swap sex for material favours (but not cash).

After Eight Mint *adj.* [rhy. sl. = SKINT *adj.*; ult. the mint chocolate brand *After Eights*] [1990s+] penniless.

after-hours *n.* [abbr.] [1950s+] (*US*) an *after-hours* bar, club or restaurant; also in comb. as *after-hours joint*, *-place* etc.

afternoon *n.* [? naut. *aft*, the 'behind' of a boat + play on SE *afternoon*] [1990s+] (*W.I., Bdos/Guyn.*) the buttocks, esp. when large and female.

afternoon delight *n.* [1970s+] sex in the afternoon.

afternoon farmer *n.* [they get down to work only in the afternoon] **1** [mid–late 19C] one who wastes time rather than busying themselves with proper work. **2** [1930s] (*US drugs*) one who wastes time and neglects work because they habitually smoke opium.

afternoonified *adj.* [the regular afternoon calls made on each other by society ladies] [late 19C–1900s] smart, chic.

afternoon man *n.* (*also* **after-dinner man**) [note the use for Anthony Powell's book title, *Afternoon Men* (1931)] [early 17C+] a tippler, a drunkard.

afters *n.* **1** [20C+] pudding, dessert. **2** [20C+] in fig. use of sense 1, an extra, a bonus, both negative and positive. **3** [1930s+] after-hours drinking in a public house.

afterthought *n.* [1910s+] the youngest child of a family, conceived long after its siblings.

after you with the po, Jane *phr. see under* PO *n.*

afto *n.* (*also* **arfto**) [abbr. + -O *sfx* (3)] [1930s+] (*Aus./N.Z.*) afternoon.

afty *n.* [abbr.] [1990s+] the *aft*ernoon.

ag *n.*[1] (*also* **aggie**) [abbr.] [1910s+] **1** (*US*) (*also* **ag coll**) an agricultural *coll*ege. **2** an agricultural student. **3** a country bumpkin. **4** agriculture.

ag *n.*[2] see AGG *n.*

ag *adj.* [abbr. SE *aggravated* but note AGG *v.*] [1990s+] (*US campus*) **1** angry, annoyed, irritated. **2** crazy, fun.

ag *v.* see AGG *v.*

ag! *excl.* [Afk. *ach*, a general excl.] [1930s+] (*S.Afr.*) a general excl., esp. of pleasure, irritation or exasperation; usu. with *man* or *sis*; also used to preface a reply to a question one finds hard to answer, e.g. *Ag, I don't really know*, or to denote a sense of resignation, *Ag, I'll have some more pap then*.

agad! *excl.* [GAD *n.*[1]] [mid-18C] a euph. excl. meaning God!

against *adj.* [late 19C–1960s] (*drugs*) addicted to or under the influence of a drug, usu. opium or heroin.

agate *n.* [the carving of tiny figures into SE *agate*, a semi-precious stone] **1** [late 16C–early 17C] a very small person. **2** [1960s+] (*US*) a small penis. **3** *see* GLASSY (ALLEY), THE *n.*

SE in slang uses

(IN PHRASES)

❑ **shoot the agate** *v.* [the extension of the thumb when playing marbles; note nonce sense by Trimble, in *5000 Adult Sex Words & Phrases* (1966): 'SHOOTING THE AGATE [...] Looking for a chance love partner by walking along with hands at the sides and thumbs extended. In hipster code, this means that a man is asking for sexual companionship, and if a hip female is interested, she may respond without a word being spoken'] [1900s–40s] (*US black*) to walk jauntily with one's thumbs extended.

agates *n.* (*also* **aggots**) [SE *agate*, a semi-precious stone] [1940s+] (*US*) the testicles.

Agatha *n.* [AGGIE *n.*[2]] [2000s] (*S.Afr. gay*) a gossip.

ag coll *n.* see AG *n.*[1] (1).

-age *sfx* [adoption of SE sfx, used for abstract nouns, names of people or verbs expressing action] [1940s+] (*mainly US campus*) a sfx forming an abstract n., e.g. *rainage*, a situation in which it is raining; *babage*, attractive young women.

agent *n.* [an agent properly works only for the FBI and is not, as such, a police officer] [1960s] (*US black*) any police officer.

agfay *n.* (*also* **afgay**) [pig Lat. *agfay* = FAG *n.*[5] (1)] [1940s–70s] a male homosexual.

agg *n.* (*also* **ag**) [abbr. SE *aggravation*] [1980s+] problems, trouble, annoyance.

agg *v.* [abbr. SE *aggravate*] [1980s+] to annoy, to upset.

aggerawator *n.* (*also* **haggerawator**) [? the 'aggravation' of the admiring glances it inspires] [mid-19C–1900s] a favoured costermongers' hairstyle, consisting of a well-greased lock of hair twisted and pointing either at the corner of an eye or at an ear.

aggie *n.*[1] (*also* **aggey**) [SE *agricultural implement*] **1** [1960s+] (*US prison*) a long-handled hoe. **2** *see* AG *n.*[1].

aggie *n.*[2] [? generic use of the female name] **1** [1980s+] (*US gay*) a homosexual sailor. **2** [2000s] (*S.Afr. gay*) gossip.

aggie fortis *n.* (*also* **acker fortis, ackie fortis, agur forty**) [Lat. *aqua fortis*, strong water, an alternative name for nitric acid] [mid-19C] (*US*) very strong drink, usu. alcoholic but sometimes coffee.

aggies *n.* [pun on SE aga*panthus*] [2000s] (*N.Z.*) panties.

aggots *n.* see AGATES *n.*

aggranoy *v.* (*also* **agronoy**) [SE *aggravate* + *annoy*] [late 19C+] to irritate, to annoy.

aggravation *n.*[1] [rhy. sl.] [1910s] a station.

aggravation *n.*[2] [1960s+] **1** (*orig. UK police/Und.*) the difficulties that both sides of the professional law make for each other. **2** violence, quarrels, unpleasantness in general.

aggro *n.* (*also* **agro**) [abbr. SE *aggravation* + -O *sfx* (6)] [1960s+] **1** problems, trouble. **2** violence, typically as enjoyed by skinheads, esp. at football matches, beating up Asians etc. **3** an aggressive attitude. **4** any form of problems, difficulties, harassment. **5** (*Aus.*) an aggressive person.

(IN PHRASES)

❑ **go aggro** *v.* [1980s+] (*US campus*) to become aggressive.

aggro *adj.* [AGGRO *n.*] [1990s+] (*orig. US campus*) hot-headed, wild, unpredictable.

aggrovoke *v.* (*also* **agrovoke**) [SE *aggravate* + *provoke*] [1920s+] (*Aus.*) to annoy, to irritate.

agility *n.* [19C] a euph. for the vagina; thus *show one's agility*, of a woman, to reveal one's vagina inadvertently.

aginner *n.* [dial. *agin*, against] [20C+] (*Irish/US*) one who automatically takes an oppositional stance, usu. out of envy or spite.

agitate the gravel *v.* [1940s–60s] (*US*) to leave.

agitator *n.* [mid–late 19C] a bell-pull, a door-knocker.

agnes *n.* [use of female proper name] [1930s+] (*US gay*) a term of address used to one who is presumed to be a fellow homosexual.

agonies *n.* [1970s+] (*drugs*) the pain of withdrawal from narcotic drug use.

agonizer *n.* [late 19C] (*UK society*) one who makes intense efforts to gain a specific effect.

agony *n.* **1** [mid-19C+] problems, difficulties. **2** [1900s–50s] (*orig. US*) style, fashion. **3** [1980s+] (*W.I./UK black teen*) the sensations felt during sex, notably popularized by the reggae singer Pinchers in a dancehall song of the same name. **4** *see* YELLOW AGONY *under* YELLOW *adj.*

SE in slang uses

(IN COMPOUNDS)

❑ **agony aunt** *n.* [the first *OED* citation is 1975, but it refers, in a biog. of the prototype Evelyn Home, to 'the "agony aunties" [of] the 'thirties'; note AGONY COLUMN below dates from 1950s] [1970s+] a problem-solving (usu. female) columnist of newspapers and magazines to whom the lovelorn and generally wretched can write and have their letters answered in print or privately; thus the male equivalent, *agony uncle*. ❑ **agony box** *n.* [the effect these objects supposedly have on listeners] (*US*) **1** [1900s] a piano. **2** [1920s] a record player, a phonograph. **3** [1940s–60s] a radio. **4** [2000s] a ukelele. ❑ **agony column** *n.* **1** [late 19C–1910s] the section of a newspaper dedicated to special advertisements, particularly those for missing relatives or friends, and thus filled with personal agony. **2** [1950s+] a regular newspaper or magazine feature containing readers' questions about personal problems with replies from a (usu. female) columnist. ❑ **agony pipe** *n.* [1930s] (*US*) a clarinet.

(IN PHRASES)

❑ **agony in red** *n.* [a satire on the aesthetic movement of the early 1880s when paintings were described in musical terms, e.g. 'a symphony in amber', 'a nocturne in silver-grey'] [late 19C] a vermilion costume. ❑ **put on the agony** *v.* [late 19C+] to complain, to moan; the implication is that the problems are not wholly genuine, thus to exaggerate.

A-grade *adj.* see GRADE A *adj.*

agreeable rattle *n.* [he 'rattles along'] [late 18C–mid-19C] a chattering, but not unpleasant, young man.

agreeable ruts of life *n.* [pun on SE *rut*, meaning both to have sexual intercourse and a cleft or furrow] [late 19C] the vagina.

agricultural *n.*

(IN PHRASES)

❑ **do an agricultural** *v.* [20C+] **1** to have sex in the open air. **2** to urinate or defecate in the open.

agricultural studies *n.* [1990s+] (*US campus*) the cultivation of home-grown marijuana.

agro *n.* see AGGRO *n.*

agronoy *v.* see AGGRANOY *v.*

aground *adj.* [nautical imagery] [late 18C–19C] ruined, at a loss.

agrovoke *v.* see AGGROVOKE *v.*

alacompain *n.* (*also* **allacompain**) [perversion of rhy. sl. 'all complain'] [mid-19C] rain.

Alan Border *adj.* [rhy. sl. = OUT OF ORDER *adj.*; ult. Aus. cricketer *Alan Border* (b.1955)] [2000s] of events, behaviour or people, unacceptable, excessive, in bad taste.

Alan Ladd *adj.* [rhy. sl.; ult. US film star *Alan Ladd* (1913–64)] [1990s+] sad.

Alan Whickers *n.* (*also* **alans**) [rhy. sl.; ult. *Alan Whicker*, UK journalist and TV personality (b.1925)] [1960s+] knickers.

alarm clock *n.* [a person who keeps one, in real or fig. uses, from 'falling asleep'] **1** [1920s] (*US*) a worrier, a nag. **2** [1920s–40s] (*US campus*) a chaperon. **3** [1940s] (*US black*) a college professor.

Alaska *adj.* with ref. to local stereotypes of the US state.

IN COMPOUNDS

❏ **Alaska time** *n.* [1970s] (*US*) unpunctuality. ❏ **Alaska turkey** *n.* [the local salmon trade] [19C–1940s] (*US*) a salmon.

Albany beef *n.* [the one-time easy availability of sturgeon in the Hudson River near Albany, NY] [late 18C–1900s] (*US*) Hudson River sturgeon.

Albert *n.* see PRINCE ALBERT *n.*

albertine *n.* [the character *Albertine* in Alexander Dumas fils' novel *Un Père Prodigue* (1859)] [late 19C] an adroit, calculating, business-like mistress.

Albertopolis *n.* [proper name of Queen Victoria's husband, Prince *Albert* of Saxe-Coburg-Gotha (1819–61) + sfx *-opolis*] [mid-19C] Kensington Gore, London, site of the Royal Albert Hall and the Albert Memorial.

Alberts *n.* (*also* **Prince Alberts, Prince Alfreds, royal alberts**) [proper name *Prince Albert* (1819–61), consort of Queen Victoria; senses 2 and 3 come from the myth that Albert, before his marriage, was so poor that he was forced to use foot-bindings instead of proper socks] (*Aus.*) **1** [late 19C] dress trousers. **2** [late 19C+] strips of cloth, usu. calico, and rubbed with suet to cut down chafing, used as a substitute for socks, usu. by tramps. **3** [1930s] rough, lace-up boots.

albonized *adj.* [Lat. *alba*, white] [mid-19C] whitened.

Al Capone *n.* [rhy. sl.; ult. the Chicago gang-boss Alphonse *'Al'* Capone (1899–1947)] [1980s+] (*Aus./N.Z.*) the phone, the telephone.

Al Capone ride *n.* [AL CAPONE *n.*] [1970s+] (*US black*) any old car, both the original Capone-era models and more recent ones that lack the most up-to-date gimmicks and accessories and are thus *de facto* 'old fashioned'.

Alcatraz bait *n.* see JAILBAIT *n.* (2).

alchie/alchy *n.* see ALKY *n.*

alco *n.* see ALKO *n.*

alcove *n.* [late 17C] the vagina.

alderman *n.* [the image of a paunchy, pipe-smoking, wealthy administrator of the City of London] **1** [late 18C–mid-19C] a roast turkey. **2** [mid-19C] a long smoking pipe; thus *broken alderman*, a short pipe. **3** [mid–late 19C] half-a-crown, 2s 6d (12½p). **4** [late 19C–1940s] a paunch; thus adj. *aldermanic*, portly. **5** [late 19C–1950s] a large crowbar [on pattern of CITIZEN *n.* (1); GENTLEMAN *n.*; LORD MAYOR *n.*[1]: smaller and larger versions of the tool].

IN COMPOUNDS

❏ **alderman double-slang'd** *n.* [SLANG *v.*[2]] [late 18C] a roast turkey garlanded with sausages. ❏ **alderman in chains** *n.* [SE *chains* (of sausages); 'from the appearance of the City fathers, generally portly – becoming more so when carrying their chains of office over their powerful bust' (Ware); note Jonson, *Masque of the Gipsies* (1621): 'Two roosted Sheriffs came whole to the bord [...] theire Chaines like sausages hung about 'em'] [19C–1900s] a turkey garlanded with sausages. ❏ **alderman's pace** *n.* [17C] a steady, careful pace, as befits an official with a fine sense of his own importance.

Alderman Lushington *n.* [joc. use of a proper name as an embellishment of LUSHINGTON *n.*] [early 19C] a drunkard; thus *Alderman Lushington is concerned*, a phr. meaning that someone is drunk.

alderman's nail *n.* [rhy. sl.] [19C+] an animal's tail.

Aldershot ladies *n.* [pun on 'two fours' = two whores; Aldershot is an 'army town' in the UK] **1** [1940s] the number 44. **2** [1970s+] (*darts*) a double four. **3** [1970s+] (*bingo or lotto*) the number 44.

Aldgate *n.* see BILL ON THE PUMP AT ALDGATE *n.*

ale *n.*

SE in slang uses

IN COMPOUNDS

❏ **alecan** *n.* [late 19C–1910s] a heavy drinker. ❏ **ale-draper** *n.* (*also* **draper**) [SE *draper*, seller] [late 16C–early 19C] an alehouse-keeper; thus *ale-drapery*, a public house. ❏ **ale-knight** *n.* [KNIGHT *n.* (1)] [late 16C–mid-17C] a drunkard, a drinking companion. ❏ **ale-spinner** *n.* [SE *spinner*, in sense of a general manufacturer] [19C] a brewer, a publican.

IN PHRASES

❏ **aled up** *adj.* [1930s+] drunk on beer.

alec *n.* (*also* **aleck**) [abbr. SMART ALECK *n.*] **1** [1900s–30s] (*orig. US*) an unpleasant, conceited, smug person. **2** [1940s+] (*Aus.*) a fool or simpleton, a confidence man's victim [? joc. use].

alecie *n.* (*also* **alecy**) [lit. *ale-cy*, on pattern of SE *luna-cy*] [late 16C] mental aberration, due to ale-drinking; intoxication.

aleck *n.* see ALEC *n.*

Alexander *n.* [? the telephone's inventor *Alexander* Graham Bell (1847–1922)] [2000s] an intercom; a telephone.

alexander *n.* [ALEXANDER HAMILTON *n.* (2); i.e. something one would put one's name to] [1900s] (*US*) a certainty.

alexander *v.* [proper name Sir Jerome *Alexander*, a hanging judge, active in Ireland 1660–74] [early 18C] (*Anglo-Irish*) to hang someone.

Alexander Graham Bell *n.* [rhy. sl.; ult. *Alexander Graham Bell* (1847–1922), Scots-born US inventor of telephone] [1980s+] (*Aus. prison*) a cell.

Alexander Hamilton *n.* [the picture of the US politician, *Alexander Hamilton* (1757–1804), is printed on the note] [1960s] **1** (*US*) a $10 bill. **2** (*US*) one's signature [a confusion with JOHN HANCOCK *n.*].

Alexandra limp *n.* (*also* **Alexandra step**) ['the name given an erstwhile fit of semi-imbecility on the part of...a crowd of limping, petticoated toadies' (F&H)] [late 19C] (*UK society*) a manner of walking taken up by fashionable society as a deliberate tribute to the way in which Princess Alexandra (1844–1925), then Princess of Wales, walked c.1870.

alf *n.* [SE name *Alfred*] **1** [1960s] a conventional person. **2** [1960s+] (*Aus.*) the unsophisticated, nationalistic, basic Aus. male; recently overtaken by OCKER *n.*

alfalfa *n.* [SE *alfalfa*, a form of Lucerne grass, used for fodder] (*US*) **1** [late 19C–1930s] a beard; whiskers. **2** [1900s–30s] the countryside (as opposed to the town/city). **3** [1910s] a bed [f. the mattress stuffing]. **4** [1910s+] money. **5** [1920s–40s] tobacco. **6** [1920s–50s] dried spinach or other dehydrated vegetables. **7** [1930s–60s] nonsense, rubbish. **8** [1990s+] (*US black*) marijuana.

alfalfa *adj.* [ALFALFA *n.*] [1900s–60s] (*US*) of the country; rustic, slow, peasant-like.

alf a mo *n.* (*also* **arf a mo**) [Cockney pron. of SE *half* + MO *n.*[1]] [1910s] **1** a cigarette, esp. when it proves hard to keep alight. **2** (*Aus.*) a small moustache.

Alf Garnett *n.* [rhy. sl. = BARNET (FAIR) *n.*; ult. the character *Alf Garnett* in the 1960s BBC–TV sitcom *Till Death Us Do Part*] [1990s+] the hair.

'alfpenny bumper *n.* [the passengers are bumped up and down] [late 19C–1900s] a halfpenny omnibus fare.

'alfpenny dip *n.* [rhy. sl.] [mid-19C+] a ship.

alfred david *n.* (*also* **alfred davy, alfy**) [mid-19C–1910s] an affidavit.

Alfred (the Great) *n.* [rhy. sl.; ult. *Alfred the Great*, king of Wessex, 849–99] [1990s+] weight.

Algie *n.* (*also* **Algernon, Algy**) [proper name *Algernon*, seen as typically upper-class] [late 19C–1930s] a generic name for any young male aristocrat.

Ali *n.* [story of 'Ali Baba and the 40 Thieves'] [20C+] 'inevitable' nickname for any man surnamed Barber.

aliamba *n.* [ety. unknown; ? Sp.] [1980s+] phencyclidine.

alias *adj.* [ALIAS MAN *n.*] [1950s+] (*W.I.*) dangerous, violent.

alias man *n.* (*also* **alias**) [SE *alias*, another name, an assumed name] [1960s+] (*W.I., orig. Und.*) a cheat, a hypocrite, anyone unethical.

alibi *n.* [weakened form of SE] [1910s+] an excuse.

alibi ike *n.* ['Alibi Ike' (1915), the title of a short story by Ring Lardner (1885–1933), featuring a fictional baseball player] [1910s+] (*US*) one who never takes the blame and invariably has a quick excuse for their faults and failings.

alibi (up) *v.* **1** [1910s+] to provide an excuse for. **2** [1920s+] to make an excuse.

ali-button *v.* [1990s+] (*W.I.*) to be made a fool of by somebody.

alice *n.* [pron. of proper name resembles *L.S.* – i.e. LSD – but note autobiographical novel *Go Ask Alice*, about a 15-year-old's drug habits, and Jefferson Airplane song 'White Rabbit' (1967), with its drug-orientated lyrics, esp. the line 'Go ask Alice, when she's ten feet tall'; both refs. go back to Lewis Carroll's *Alice's Adventures in Wonderland* (1866), which was seized on by the hippies for its supposed drug refs.] [1970s+] (*drugs*) LSD.

Alice, The *n.* [late 19C+] (*Aus.*) the town of Alice Springs.

Alice (Blue Gown) *n.* (*also* **Miss Alice**) [song 'My Sweet Little Alice Blue Gown' by McCarthy & Tierney (1918); thus the ref. is to the uniform] [1930s+] (*US gay*) the police.

Alice B. Toklas (brownie) *n.* [proper name *Alice B. Toklas* (1877–1967), lifetime companion to Gertrude Stein, who in her eponymous cookbook gave a recipe for this drug-based sweetmeat] [1960s+] (*drugs*) a marijuana brownie.

Alice Springs *n.*

IN PHRASES

❑ **from Alice Springs to breakfast time** [1930s+] (*Aus.*) everywhere.

a-licker *n.* [abbr. *ARSE-LICKER under* ARSE-LICK *v.*] [1990s+] (*US*) a toady, a sycophant.

ali oop *n.* [rhy. sl. = POOP *n.*[2] (3)] [1990s+] excrement.

A-(list) gay *n.* [1990s+] the homosexual elite, the class of homosexuals with money and power.

alive *adj.* **1** [mid-19C+] knowledgeable, aware, esp. of a criminal scheme. **2** [1930s–40s] (*US Und.*) well off, wealthy. **3** [1950s] (*UK Und.*) attached to a burglar alarm [SE *alive*, charged with electric current].

aliveo *adj.* [abbr. ALL ALIVO *adj.* (1)] [late 19C–1930s] alert, active.

alive or dead *n.* [rhy. sl.] [20C+] the head.

alkali *n.* [backform. f. ALKALIED *adj.*] [20C+] (*US*) someone who has spent a long time in the American West.

alkalied *adj.* [the alkali-dense streams from which humans and cattle were forced to drink] [mid-19C+] (*US*) experienced at living in the West.

alko *n.* (*also* **alco**) [abbr.] [1960s+] an *alco*holic.

alky *n.* (*also* **alchie, alchy, alki, alkie**) [abbr. + sfx *-y*] (*US*) **1** [mid-19C+] alcohol. **2** [1920s+] an alcoholic, a drunk.

DERIVATIVES

❑ **alkied** *adj.* [1930s+] drunk.

IN COMPOUNDS

❑ **alkie's itch** *n.* [1940s–50s] (*Aus./US*) the twitching and nervousness that are seen in an advanced alcoholic. ❑ **alky-cooker** *n.* [SE *cooker*, a cook/a stove] **1** [1930s+] (*US*) one who is employed in the illegal distillation of 'moonshine' whisky. **2** [1930s+] (*US*) an illegal still. ❑ **alky stiff** *n.* (*also* **alkee stiff, alki stiff**) [STIFF *n.*[1] (4a)] [late 19C–1930s] (*US*) an alcoholic tramp.

IN PHRASES

❑ **alky up** *v.* [1930s] (*US tramp*) to drink, to get drunk.

alky *adj.* [ALKY *n.* (2)] [1930s+] alcoholic.

all *adv.* **1** [mid-19C+] used to intensify an adj., meaning very, completely, e.g. *all fucked-up*. **2** [1920s+] nothing; usu. used in combs. to intensify an oath or obscenity; *see* BUGGER ALL *n.*; DAMN-ALL *n.*; FUCK ALL *n.* **3** [1980s+] (*orig. US campus*) when retelling a story, used with the v. *to be* to denote something said or done, often describing an attitude or pose, something used with an accompanying gesture, e.g. *She was all shouting and I was all 'No way!'*.

all about *phr.* [1980s+] (*US campus*) completely obsessed with, a phr. describing the subject of one's interest or desire, that which matters in a given situation; also used as a general intensifier.

all about trout *phr.* [1960s] on the lookout (for an advantageous opportunity).

all a-cock *adj.* [? *KNOCK INTO A COCKED HAT under* KNOCK INTO *v.* or f. cockfighting jargon *all a-kick*, defeated (the cock's legs kick in its death-agony)] [late 19C–1900s] defeated, overthrown.

allacompain *n. see* ALACOMPAIN *n.*

all afloat *n.* [rhy. sl.] [mid-19C] a coat.

all alive *n.* [rhy. sl.] [1940s] the number five.

all alivo *adj.* (*also* **all alive-o**) [SE *alive* + -O *sfx* (2)] [mid-19C+] alert, active.

all a-mort *adj.* [Fr. *mort*, dead] [late 18C–mid-19C] shocked, surprised and thus rendered motionless.

all and all *n.* [pattern of I AND I *pron.*] [1980s] (*UK black*) everyone.

all-and-all *n.*[1] [SE *and all*, and everything else and everything connected to; ? Scot. phr. 'wooed and married and all'] [1970s] (*US*) one's wife.

all-and-all *n.*[2] [? 'all (dressed up) and all'] [1970s] (*US*) one's best suit of clothes.

all around my hat *phr.* (*also* **all round my hat, all around**) [? ballad 'All around my hat I wears a green willow'] [mid-19C–1920s] all over, completely.

all a-treat *adj.* [SE *a-* + *treat*, something highly enjoyable] [1900s] excellent, wonderful; sometimes used ironically to mean a mild disaster.

all B and B *adj.* [abbr. all *b*osom and *b*ottom] [1940s] of a woman, well built, sexy.

all beer and skittles *phr.* (*also* **all sheoak and quoits, all skittles and beer, all stout and oysters**) [mid-19C+] pleasure, enjoyment, hedonism; also as negative, i.e. *not all…*.

all Betty *adj.* [var. on *all dicky (with)* under DICKY *adj.*[1]] [early 19C] finished, 'done for'.

alleluia lass *n.* [SE *alleluia*, praise the Lord + *lass*] [late 19C–1900s] a young Salvation Army woman.

alleluia stew *n.* [*see* prev.] [1900s–10s] Salvation Army stew.

allergic *adj.* [1930s+] (*orig. US*) sensitive to, usu. with hostile overtones, e.g. *Sorry, but I'm absolutely allergic to religion.*

allerickstix *adv.* [Ger. *alles richtig*, all right] [late 19C; 1980s] (*US*) all right, satisfactorily.

alleviator *n.* (*also* **alleviation**) [ext. use of SE; i.e. it 'alleviates' one's feelings; 20C use is Aus. only] [mid-19C–1940s] a drink, esp. in a 'medicinal' context.

alley *n.*[1] **1** [mid–late 19C] the vagina; one of a number of terms equating the vagina with a road or path. **2** [1920s] (*US Und.*) a place where illicit beer is brewed. **3** [1930s] the anus. **4** [1960s+] (*US black*) a hospital corridor [northeastern urban use; the image is of poor people crowding the hospitals as they do their own slums]. **5** [1990s+] (*US Und.*) the open area outside a row of cells.

SE in slang uses

IN COMPOUNDS

❑ **alley apple** *n.* (*also* **alley lily, alley rifle**) **1** [1910s+] (*US*) a brick or stone when used as a missile [pun on SE *apple*]. **2** [1950s+] (*US*) horse manure, excrement [*HORSE APPLE under* HORSE *n.*]. ❑ **alley bat** *n.* [SE *alley*, the unsavoury area of a town + BAT *n.*[1] (1)] [late 19C–1930s] (*US*) a promiscuous woman, a prostitute; also used as a general term of abuse. ❑ **alley cleaner** *n.* (*also* **street-sweeper**) [the breadth of the shot 'cleans out' those standing across a narrow alley] [1950s] (*US*) a riot gun, usu. a shotgun with a wide blast and thus used to disperse a mob. ❑ **alley rat** *n.* [SE *alley*, the unsavoury area of a town + RAT n.[1] (1a)] (*US*) **1** [1910s–50s] a particularly unpleasant, villainous and impoverished person. **2** [1930s] a pimp, esp. one involved in cheating a prostitute's clients. **3** [1930s–50s] a thief who robs people in alleyways. ▫ **alleyway** *n.* **1** [1910s] (*US*) the throat, in the context of drinking. **2** [1950s] (*US gay*) the anus. ▫ **alley-whipped** *adj.* [image of the hapless worker being taken out into an alley and beaten when money is requested] [2000s] (*US*) unpaid (or robbed of one's pay) despite having done the work required.

IN PHRASES

▫ **big alley** *n.* [1930s] (*orig. US tramp*) the main street.

IN EXCLAMATIONS

▫ **up an alley!** [1900s] (*US*) a general excl. of dismissal. ▫ **up your alley!** [euph. UP YOUR ARSE! *excl.*] [1970s+] a general excl. of rude dismissal.

alley *n.*[2] [? Fr. *aller*, to go] [late 19C–1900s] a go-between.

alley *n.*[3] [SE *alley*, a marble; thus orig. marbles jargon]

SE, meaning marble, in slang uses

IN PHRASES

▫ **alley up** *v.* [1940s] (*Aus.*) to pay one's share. ▫ **make one's alley good** *v.* (*also* **make one's marble good**) [1920s+] (*Aus./N.Z./S.Afr.*) to make a good impression on someone, to ingratiate oneself, to improve one's position. ▫ **off the alley** *adj.* [1900s] (*US*) incorrect, mistaken. ▫ **throw in one's alley** *v.* [1900s–20s] (*Aus.*) **1** (*also* **chuck..., pass..., roll..., sky..., sling...**) to die. **2** to give up, to cease from an action.

alley *adj.* (*also* **ally**) [the negative stereotyping of a racial ghetto] [1990s+] (*US campus*) second-rate.

alley cat *n.* [1930s+] **1** (*US*) a promiscuous woman. **2** (*US*) a prostitute. **3** (*US*) an illegitimate child. **4** (*US*) a street urchin. **5** (*US*) a womanizer. **6** (*UK Und.*) a nightwatchman.

alley cat *v.* [ALLEY CAT *n.* (1)] [1960s+] (*US*) of a woman, to act in an overtly promiscuous manner.

alley-waiter *n.* [play on pron. of SE, with added overtones of the narrowness of an alley and the elevator car, and ref. to SE *dumb waiter*] [late 19C–1950s] (*US*) an elevator or lift.

all-fired *adj.* (*also* **alfired**) [ALL-FIRED *adv.*] [mid-19C+] (*US*) extreme.

all-fired *adv.* (*also* **all-fire**) [euph. for SE *hell-fired*] [mid-19C+] (*US*) extremely, very much so.

DERIVATIVES

▫ **all-firedly** *adv.* [mid-19C+] particularly, excessively.

all forlorn *n.* [rhy. sl. = HORN *n.*[2] (1)] [1960s+] a state of sexual excitement.

all fruits ripe *phr.* [image of a bumper harvest] **1** [1980s+] (*W.I./UK black teen*) everything is fine, OK, all right, fit, all systems are go; popularized by reggae singer Junior Reid in a song of the same name. **2** [1990s+] a phr. meaning all women are potential sexual partners.

all get out *phr.* (*also* **all git-out, get out**) [mid-19C+] (*US*) very much, to a great extent; usu. prefixed by *as* or *like*.

all gong and no dinner *phr.* [in an era when a gong was rung to announce the imminence of dinner] [1970s+] all talk but no action.

all hair oil and no socks *phr.* [2000s] (*N.Z.*) ostentatious but ultimately unimpressive.

All Hallows *n.* [poss. an ironic reflection on orig. meaning of *All Hallows*, all holy men or all martyrs; the martyrs in question being those who are duped] [late 16C] (*UK Und.*) the tolling place, presumably the place where the theft actually takes place, as described by those working as horse-stealers.

all-heeled *adj.* see WELL-HEELED *adj.*[1].

all-hot *n.* [the street cry] [mid-19C] **1** a baked potato, as sold in the street. **2** a seller of baked potatoes.

all hot and bothered *phr.* [ext. of SE use] [1920s+] **1** flustered, maniacally nervous. **2** (*also* **all h. and b.**) sexually excited/frustrated.

all hunched up like a dog on a bag of staples *phr.* [2000s] (*N.Z.*) extremely uncomfortable.

all hunk *adj.* [fig. use of Du. *hunk*, home, e.g. a place of safety or security, as used in juv. games] [mid-19C–1940s] (*US*) satisfactory, fine.

allicholy *adj.* [SE *ale* + *melancholy*; used by Shakespeare in *Two Gentlemen of Verona* (1591)] [late 16C–mid-18C] maudlin, esp. through drink.

Allied Irish *n.* [rhy. sl.; *Allied Irish Bank* = WANK *n.* (1)] [1990s+] (*Irish*) an act of masturbation.

DERIVATIVES

▫ **Allied Irish banker** *n.* [ext. of rhy. sl.] [1990s+] lit. and fig. uses of WANKER *n.*

alligator *n.* [SE *alligator*, based on characteristics of the animal, e.g. gaping jaws, aggressiveness and lack of speed] **1** [early–mid-19C] a singer who opens their mouth wide. **2** [mid–late 19C] a herring. **3** [mid-19C–1940s] a worthless, unpleasant person. **4** [mid-19C+] (*Aus./US*) an old and/or slow horse. **5** [late 19C] a shoe of which the upper and the sole have become separated. **6** [late 19C+] (*US*) a native of Florida [the state's indigenous animal]. **7** [20C+] (*US*) any sexually aggressive male. **8** [1910s] (*Aus.*) an aggressive, tough person. **9** [1910s–70s] (*US*) a chatterbox, a 'big mouth'. **10** [1930s–50s] a person, usu. non-black, who listens to and appreciates jazz, but does not play; orig. dismissive [the jazz musicians' ref. to someone who 'swallowed up' everything on offer, ? coined by Louis Armstrong (1901–71) to describe white musicians who pirated the original ideas created by their black peers; 'We'd call them alligators... because they were the guys who came to swallow everything we had to learn']. **11** [1950s] (*US black*) a white jazz musician [*see* sense 10]. **12** [1950s] (*US teen*) any person, irrespective of musical taste.

IN COMPOUNDS

▫ **alligator bull** *n.* [SE *alligator* (there are none in Aus.) + BULL *n.*[6] (1)] [1940s] (*Aus.*) nonsense, rubbish. ▫ **alligator cigarette** *n.* [1940s] (*US drugs*) a marijuana cigarette. ▫ **alligator (horse)** *n.* [19C] (*US*) a tough man, usu. used of a Kentucky frontiersman. ▫ **Alligatorland** *n.* [sense 4 above: Queensland has a lot of horses] [late 19C] (*Aus.*) Queensland. ▫ **alligator mouth** *n.* [1950s+] (*US*) a boaster, a braggart, someone with an inclination to boast or brag but insufficient courage to back up their words; such a person is usu. described in the extended phr. (*he's got*) *an alligator mouth and a hummingbird/canary ass*.

SE in slang uses

IN COMPOUNDS

▫ **alligator bait** *n.* **1** [1900s–60s] (*US*) any inedible food, esp. liver [the practice in early 20C US construction camps of letting bull's liver rot before cooking it; the meat was thus tenderized, but simultaneously rendered too foul for any human to eat]. **2** [1900s–60s] a black person, usu. a child [image of racist whites lynching blacks and tossing them to the alligators and f. the practice of Southern whites, who found it amusing to threaten such children with 'throwing them to the alligators']. **3** [1910s–50s] (*US*) a worthless, unpleasant person, of any race. **4** [1940s] (*US*) a derog. term for a black native of Florida.

IN PHRASES

▫ **don't let the alligator beat you to the pond** [1930s] (*US black*) don't be slow(witted) or you will be out-done.

alligator *adv.* [rhy. sl., note song 'See You later, Alligator' (1956)] [20C+] later.

alligator! *excl.* [rhy. sl. = LATER *phr.* (1) + abbr. *SEE YA LATER ALLIGATOR under* SEE *v.*] [1950s+] see you later!

alligator skin *n.* see FROG *n.*[3] (1).

all in *adj.* [SE *all in*, everyone (thus every thing/faculty/emotion) included] **1** [late 19C+] exhausted, utterly tired, beaten. **2** [20C+] of an object, run-down, dilapidated. **3** [1900s–20s] penniless. **4** [1920s] (*Aus.*) dead. **5** [1950s] drunk.

all in one *n.* ['person' or 'orifice' is unstated + ? ref. to carnival jargon *ten in one*, a sideshow that offers ten performers, often freaks] [1970s–80s] an orgy.

all in the eye *phr.* [ALL MY EYE *phr.*] [mid–late 19C] nonsense, humbug.

all in the Kool-Aid (and don't even know the flavor) *phr.* [*Kool-Aid*, a popular US soft drink] [1990s+] (*US black teen*) a nosy, inquisitive person.

all keyhole *n.* [pun on pron.] [mid-19C–1930s] alcohol, a drink; also as adj., drunk.

all kinds of *adv.* (*also* **five kinds of**) [ext. of SE use] [late 19C+] (*US*) extremely, a great deal of.

all know *adj.* [late 19C] bookish, like a bookworm.

all my eye *phr.* (*also* **(all) in my eye**) [early 18C+] a phr. meaning utter, absolute nonsense.

(IN PHRASES)

❑ **all my eye and my elbow** [late 19C–1900s] nonsense. ❑ **all my eye and my grandmother** [late 19C] nonsense. ❑ **all my eye and Tommy** [masc. var. on ALL MY EYE AND BETTY MARTIN *phr.*] [19C] nonsense.

all my eye and Betty Martin *phr.* (*also* **all in my eye and Betty, all my eye Betty, that's my eye (and Betty Martin)**) [ext. of ALL MY EYE *phr.*; *Betty Martin* herself continues to be a source of controversy. Partridge suspects that she was a late 18C London character and that no record of her exists other than this catchphrase. Jon Bee (1823) and Hotten (1860) refer to the alleged Lat. prayer, *Ora pro mihi, beate Martine* ('Pray for me blessed Martin'), i.e. St Martin of Tours, the patron saint of publicans and reformed drunkards. It has yet to be found in any version of the liturgy. Writing in 1914, Dr L.A. Waddell suggests another Latinism, *O mihi Britomartis* ('O bring help to me, Britomartis'), referring to the tutelery goddess of Crete. More likely is the idea, proposed in Charles Lee's *Memoirs* (1805), that there had once been 'an abandoned woman called Grace', who, in the late 18C, married a Mr Martin. She became notorious as *Betty Martin*, and *all my eye* was apparently among her favourite phrases. A northern version of the phr. has *Peggy Martin*] [late 18C+] a phr. meaning utter, absolute nonsense.

all nations *n.* [SE phr. *flags of all nations*] **1** [late 18C–early 19C] a mixture of drinks assembled from the dregs of bottles and glasses. **2** [19C] a coat of many colours or covered in patches.

all-nighter *n.* [ext. use of SE] **1** [mid-19C+] anything that lasts all night, e.g. studying, sex, entertainment; thus *all-night house*, a bar which is open all night. **2** [late 19C+] (*also* **all-night man**) a prostitute's client who pays for a whole night's sex. **3** [1930s+] spec. an all-night concert or dance. **4** [1960s+] (*orig. US campus*) working all night before an examination. **5** [1980s+] (*US*) an establishment, e.g. a resturant, that stays open all night.

(IN PHRASES)

❑ **pull an all-nighter** *v.* [1960s+] (*US campus*) to stay up all night, usu. to work.

all-night man *n.* [ext. use of SE, i.e. he is working all night] [early–mid-19C] a body-snatcher, a 'resurrectionist'.

allo *adj.* [pidgin; the *-o* sfx makes up for the lack of a final 'l' in Chinese speech] [mid–late 19C] all.

all of a flare *adv.* [mid–late 19C] in a clumsy, incompetent manner.

all of a tiswas *adj.* (*also* **all of a tizwas, all of a tizzy**) [? SE 'it is, it was', the image is of confusion or TIZZY *n.*[2]; note *Tiswas*, UK TV's children's light entertainment programme in the 1970s] [1940s+] (*orig. RAF*) utterly confused, very excited.

all of it *n.* [1950s–70s] (*US prison*) a life sentence.

all on one side like Lord Thomond's cocks *phr.* [18C anecdote of the Irish cock-feeder of *Lord Thomond* (1769–1855), who foolishly confined a number of his lordship's cocks, due to fight the next day for a considerable sum, all in the same room. Stereotyped for the story as a stupid Irishman, he supposedly believed that since they were all 'on the same side', they would not squabble. He was wrong, and the valuable cocks destroyed each other] [late 18C–early 19C] used of a group of people who appear to be united but are, in fact, more likely to quarrel.

all on top *phr.* [the statement is 'on top' of the facts] [1920s+] that's a lie, that is not so.

all-out *n.* [1960s] (*US campus*) an act of sexual intercourse.

all out *adj.* [20C+] exhausted.

all outdoors *n.* [the 'big skies' and wide prairies of the US West] [early 19C+] (*US*) the whole world, also used fig. to mean a lot; often used as a general intensifier, as in *big as all outdoors, tall as all outdoors*.

all outdoors *adv.* [ALL OUTDOORS *n.*] [1900s] (*US*) completely, absolutely.

all-over *n.* [16C SE *all over*, complete, to the full extent] **1** [mid-19C] a feeling of unease or illness that extends throughout one's body. **2** [1910s] (*US*) a thorough inspection, a lengthy visual assessment.

all over *adj.*[1] [SE *all over*, finished] [19C] dead.

all over *adj.*[2] [SE *all over*, to display great affection] **1** [1920s+] absorbed in, obsessed by. **2** [1950s+] pursuing (in a non-sexual manner); often ext. as *like a cheap suit, like a rash* etc. **3** [1970s+] making physical/sexual advances, often when not desired. **4** [1980s] (*US campus*) in control of. **5** [2000s] attacking verbally.

(IN PHRASES)

❑ **all over oneself** *adj.* [1920s+] (*orig. milit.*) absorbed in oneself, pleased with oneself.

all-over *adv.* [16C SE *all over*, complete, to the full extent] [20C+] (*US*) a generalized intensive for either best or worst, as in *all-over wonderful, all-over crazy*.

all over bar the shouting *phr.* (*also* **all over but the cheering, ...but the shooting, ...but the shouting**) [the 'shouting' being applause] [mid-19C+] a foregone conclusion; often preceded by *it's....*

all-overish *adj.*[1] [ALL OVER *adj.*[1] + sfx *-ish*] [mid-19C+] feeling slightly unwell, usu. as a preliminary to a full-blown attack of some illness; thus *all-overishness*.

all-overish *adj.*[2] (*also* **all over alike**) [ALL OVER *adj.*[2] + sfx *-ish*] [late 19C–1910s] sexually excited.

all-overs *n.* [ALL-OVER *n.*] **1** [late 19C] feelings of irritation. **2** [late 19C–1940s] nervous or apprehensive feelings.

all over the board *phr.* [1960s–70s] eccentric, unstable.

all over the joint *phr. see under* JOINT *n.*

all over the place like a mad woman's shit *phr.* (*also* **all over the place like a mad woman's breakfast, ...knitting, ...lunchbox**) [1950s+] (*Aus.*) confused, extremely messy.

all over the road like Brown's cows *phr.* [1980s] (*N.Z.*) in chaos; out of order.

all over the shop *phr. see under* SHOP *n.*[1].

all pills! *excl. see under* PILL *n.*

all-points *n.* [fig. use of police jargon, *all points bulletin*] [1960s] a general alert, a search for a missing person.

all points bulletin *n.* [fig. use of police jargon, *all points bulletin*] [1960s+] (*US campus*) a plea for help, with work, emotions and so on.

all-powerful *n.* [1900s] (*Aus.*) money.

all quiet *n.* [rhy. sl.; *all quiet on the Western Front* = CUNT *n.* (1); ult. title of novel by Erich Maria Remarque] [1990s+] the vagina.

all ribs and dick like a robber's dog *phr. see under* DICK *n.*[1].

all ricky *adv.* [? SE *all right*] [1940s] (*US*) satisfactorily, easily.

all right *adj.* **1** [late 19C+] an equivocal term of measured praise, acceptable, passing muster. **2** [1900s–50s] in criminal terms, trustworthy. **3** [1920s–30s] sexually amenable.

(IN PHRASES)

❑ **do all right for oneself** *v.* **1** [late 19C] to make money (through betting?). **2** [1930s+] (*Aus.*) (*also* **do a bit of good for oneself, do some good for oneself**) of a man, to seduce, to gain a woman's sexual favours. **3** [1930s+] of a prostitute, to get a client. **4** [1950s+] to improve one's situation. ❑ **this is all right** [late 19C] a phr. of disappointment or complaint that implies quite the opposite.

all right? *phr.* **1** [1960s+] a general phr. of greeting; a question mark is assumed even if not present; often answered by 'all right' or 'not so bad'. **2** [1990s+] a coded query: do you need any drugs?

all right! *excl.* [SE in 20C+] [19C+] yes indeed! I agree!

allrightnik *n.* (*also* **alrightnik, all-rightnick**) [SE *all right* + -NIK *sfx* but the proper ety. is in Yid. *olraytnik*, an upstart, a parvenu; note Ornitz's book retitled 'Allrightnicks Row' in 1990s] [1910s+] (*US*) one who has succeeded, one who has risen from immigrant poverty to material success, esp. of New York Jews; thus *Allrightnik's Row*, Riverside Drive, home at one time of many successful Jews.

all-rounder *n.* **1** [mid-19C] a collar that meets at the front, a style fashionable during the mid-19C. **2** [1930s] (*US Und.*) a clergyman, who wears a 'Roman collar'.

alls *n.* [? ALL NATIONS *n.* / SE *all the dregs/leftovers*; note late 19C wine merchants' *omnes*, i.e. Lat. all mixtures of odds and ends of various wines] [mid-19C–1900s] a drink, consisting of the dregs collected from the overflow from the pouring taps, the ends of spirit bottles and similar leavings, which was sold cheap in gin shops, esp. to women.

all sails set *adj.* [mid-19C] (*US*) drunk.

allsbay *n.* [pig Lat. = BALLS *n.* (4)] [1930s–70s] nonsense, rubbish.

all serene *adj.* (*also* **all sereno, sereno**) [Sp. *sereno*, the 'equivalent to the *English* "all's well", a counter-sign of sentinels, supposed to have been acquired by some filibusters (pirates) who were imprisoned in Cuba, and liberated by the intercession of the British ambassador' (Hotten, 1867); Partridge prefers Gibraltar to Cuba as the passage through which the term entered English] [mid-19C+] all in order, satisfactory; often as a response.

all set *adj.* [ext. of SE use] **1** [late 18C+] of a villain, ready for any criminal undertaking. **2** [mid-19C+] ready, prepared.

IN PHRASES

❑ **you all set?** [1980s+] (*US drugs*) do you need to buy any drugs? the response, if one requires nothing, is 'I'm set (for now)'.

all Sir Garnet *phr.* (*also* **all sigarno, all sigarneo**) [a ref. to the military successes of *Sir Garnet* (later Lord) Wolseley (1833–1923), whose reputation was further enhanced by his efforts to improve the lot of the private soldier; the phr. was popularized through Gilbert & Sullivan's *Pirates of Penzance*, when actor George Grossmith made himself up as Wolseley to sing the song 'I am the very model of a modern Major-General', and the phr. became a slang term of the time for 'all correct'] [late 19C+] all in order, everything as it should be.

all sorts *n.* [ext. of SE use] [early–mid-19C] a drink consisting of the dregs collected from the overflow from the pouring taps, the ends of spirit bottles and similar leavings; it was sold cheaply in gin shops, particularly to women.

allspice *n.* [because they are a purveyor of SE *allspice*, the aromatic spice] [mid-19C–1900s] a grocer.

all stations *n.* [rhy. sl. or joc. mispron.] [2000s] (*Aus.*) an Alsatian dog.

all tan and teeth *phr.* [2000s] (*UK gay*) used of a gay man who is superficially attractive but lacks greater depth.

all that *n.* [abbr. euph. SE *all that sort of thing*] [1920s+] a euph. for physical sex in its various aspects.

all that *adj.* [SE phr. *and all that*, and all the rest of it] **1** [1910s] (*also* **all that and then some**) just as described. **2** [1960s+] of an object, excellent, wonderful. **3** [1980s+] (*orig. US teen*) of a person, in possession of all good qualities; often used sarcastically, thus to describe someone conceited.

IN PHRASES

❑ **all that and a bag of chips** [note that *chips* in the US are *crisps* in the UK] [1990s+] (*US teen*) absolutely excellent. ❑ **give it all that** *v.* [1990s+] to boast, to show off. ❑ **think one is all that** *v.* [1980s+] to overestimate oneself.

all the beans *n.* [Heinz 57 Varieties, of which baked beans are the best known] [20C+] (*bingo*) the number 57.

all the eggs *adj.* [1900s] (*US*) admirable, outstanding.

all there (and a ha'porth over) *adj.* **1** [mid-19C] fashionable, well-dressed. **2** [mid–late 19C] honest, reliable. **3** [late 19C+] as desired, satisfactory. **4** [late 19C+] smart, aware. **5** [late 19C+] sane, in one's right mind.

all there but the most of you *phr.* [*all* is the genitals, the *most* is the rest of the body] [mid-19C–1940s] having sexual intercourse.

all there is *phr.* [1900s] (*US*) reliable, satisfactory.

all the ton *adj.* [late 18C] smart, fashionable.

all the twos *n.* [20C+] (*bingo*) the number 22; thus *all the threes*, 33, *all the fours*, 44, up to *all the nines*, 99.

all the way *n.* [1980s] (*N.Z.*) full sexual intercourse; esp. on a prostitute's 'menu'.

all the way *adv.* **1** [1910s+] completely. **2** [1950s+] (*US*) of a hamburger, occas. hot dog, with a full complement of condiments and garnishes; similarly used of other dishes on a menu, i.e. served as written, without 'holding' or substituting any item.

IN PHRASES

❑ **go all the way** *v.* (*also* **go the whole way**) **1** [1920s+] of a man, to have sexual intercourse; of a woman, to be willing to permit this. **2** [1940s+] to commit oneself completely; to be totally successful. **3** [1960s] of a male prostitute, to take on the 'active' role in oral intercourse. **4** [2000s] (*US gay*) to indulge in anal intercourse, rather than merely fellatio.

all the way live *adj.* [ALL THE WAY *adv.* + LIVE *adj.* (2)] [1970s+] (*US black*) exceptionally lively, exciting, desirable.

all the way there *adj.* [ext. of ALL THERE (AND A HA'PORTH OVER) *adj.*] [mid–late 19C] honest, reliable.

all the world and his wife *n.* (*also* **all the world and his daughter, ...his dog, the world and Garrett Reilly**) [the 'dog' usage is mainly Aus.] [early 18C+] absolutely everyone.

all the world to a china orange *phr.* (*also* **all the world to a penny roll**) [19C] the longest possible odds, an absolute certainty.

all the year round *n.* [1920s+] (*Aus.*) a twelve-month prison sentence.

all-time *adj.* [abbr. SE *in all of time*] [1940s+] (*US*) the very best, the most memorable on record.

all-timer *n.* [ALL-TIME *adj.*] [1970s+] the supreme example of, the greatest version.

all to pieces *adj.* [fig. use of SE; *to* substituted for SE *in*] [early 17C+] exhausted, collapsed, bankrupt.

all to pieces *adv.* (*also* **all to muck, all to flinders, all to sticks**) [late 18C–1940s] completely, utterly, to the furthest extent.

all up *adj.* [SE *up* used to indicate completion, as a synon. with SE *over/finished*] **1** [late 18C+] ruined, finished, defeated. **2** [early 19C+] dead.

IN PHRASES

❑ **all up the country with** [late 19C–1930s] ruinous, being death for. ❑ **all up with** [late 18C+] **1** of a person, doomed, bankrupt, hopeless. **2** of an object or plan, ruined, pointless, destroyed, finished.

all up in *phr.* [1990s+] **1** (*US campus*) sexually involved (with). **2** (*US teen*) interfering, involved in.

all up in here *phr.* [1970s] (*US black*) a phr. indicating the importance of a given place or situation.

all up in the koolaid *phr.* [*Kool-Aid*, a US soft drink] [1990s+] (*US campus/teen*) knowing what is going on; aware of the facts; thus *all up in the koolaid without knowing the flavor*, ignorant, unaware.

all wind (and piss) *phr. see under* PISS *n.*

all woke up *adj.* [1960s] (*US*) aware, knowledgeable.

ally *n.* [abbr. + sfx -*y*] [2000s] an *Al*satian dog.

ally *adj. see* ALLEY *adj.*

ally-beg *n.* [? according to B&L Gaelic *aille*, pleasant + *beg*, little (place); thus a pleasant little place] [18C–19C] a comfortable bed.

ally slope *n.*

IN PHRASES

❑ **do an ally slope** *v.* [the comic character *Ally Sloper*, 'a seedy proletarian loafer', featured in *Alley Sloper's Half-Holiday*, publ. by Dalziel Bros., 1884–1923 and illus. (at first) by W.G. Baxter, an ex-patriate American. Note WW1 milit. use *Alley Sloper's cavalry*,

Army Service Corps; ? underpinned by SE *slope off* + Fr. *aller*, to go] [1920s] to escape, to make off.

alma gray *n.* [rhy. sl. = TRAY *n.*[1] (1); 'Little' *Alma Gray* was a music-hall star *c.*1900] [1940s+] (*Aus.*) a threepenny piece.

almanack *n.* [? it brings one good fortune] [late 19C–1900s] the vagina.

almighty *adj.* [early 19C] mighty, great, exceedingly.

almond *n.*[1] [rhy. sl.; *almond rock* = COCK *n.*[3] (1)] [late 19C+] the penis.

almond *n.*[2] [1910s] (*Aus.*) head, skull.

almond rock *n.* [rhy. sl.] **1** [1910s+] (*also* **almonds**) in pl., socks. **2** [1970s] a frock.

almshouse *adj.* [var./pun on ARMSHOUSE *n.*] [1980s+] (*W.I./UK black*) displaying a negative behaviour or attitude.

IN COMPOUNDS

▫ **almshouse business** *n.* violence.

-alorum *sfx* (*also* **-alorium**) [? on pattern of SE *cockalorum*] [late 19C+] a fake Lat. sfx used to create joc. emphasis from a n., e.g. *scorchalorum, crapalorium*.

alpha and omega *n.* [SE *alpha and omega*, 'the beginning and the end...of the divine being' (*OED*)] [19C] the vagina.

alphabet *n.* [pun on SE *sentence*, i.e. a 'sentence' so long that it cannot be characterized by numbers] [2000s] (*US prison*) an extremely long sentence.

Alphabet City *n.* [the initial letters] [1980s+] (*US*) Avenues A, B, C and D (and the relevant cross-streets) on New York City's Lower East Side.

alphabet-slinger *n.* [on model of HASH-SLINGER *n.* (1); they *sling* the alphabet to the pupils] [1960s] (*US*) a school teacher.

alpha geek *n.* [var. on SE *alpha male*] [1990s+] (*US campus*) one who is exceptionally well versed in (computer) technology.

alpha powder *n.* [1950s] (*US drugs*) any powdered narcotic.

alphonse *n.*[1] [the character in the play *Monsieur Alphonse* (1873) by Alexander Dumas fils] [late 19C] a gigolo.

alphonse *n.*[2] [rhy. sl.; however, note Farmer, *Vocabula Amatoria* (1896): 'ALPHONSE, a prostitute's bully'] [1940s+] (*UK Und.*) a pimp, a ponce.

Alpine mountains *n.* [the shape and the 'snowy' whiteness of the flesh] [mid-19C] (*UK Und.*) the female breasts; thus *crossing the Alpine mountains*, sleeping with one's head pillowed on a woman's breast.

already *adv.* [both terms are ult. rooted in the Ger. *schon*, already, yet, so far; in these uses, sense 1 is Penn. Ger. *schun* and sense 2 Yid. *shoyn*] [19C+] **1** as used by Pennsylvania Germans, previously, before, ago. **2** as used by Yid. speakers and those wishing to indicate Yid. speech rhythms, an intensifier indicating immediacy, even exasperation, e.g. *So tell me, already.*

Alsatia *n.* [named for *Alsace-Lorraine*, the marginal, disputed border area between France and Germany. Higher Alsatia, its earlier manifestation, was once the lands of the Whitefriars Monastery, extending from The Temple to Whitefriars Street and from Fleet Street to the Thames. After the Dissolution of the Monasteries (1536–9), the area went downhill, and, as allowed by Elizabeth I (r.1558–1603) and James I (r.1603–25), its inhabitants claimed exemption from jurisdiction of the City of London. As such, the area became a centre of corruption, a refuge for villains, debtors, cheats and gamesters and a no-man's-land for the law. The privileges were abolished in 1697, but it was decades before the old habits died out] [late 16C–mid-19C] **1** the criminal 'no-man's-land' of 16C London; divided into *Alsatia the Higher* (Whitefriars in the City) and *Alsatia the Lower* (around the Mint in Southwark). **2** in fig. use, any no-man's land.

DERIVATIVES

▫ **Alsatian** *n.* [18C–19C] a member of London's criminal underworld. ▫ **alsatian** *adj.* [late 17C–18C] criminal, roguish.

also-ran *n.* [horseracing use] [late 19C+] (*orig. Aus.*) a useless person, a failure, an irrelevance.

altamel *n.* (*also* **altemal**) [18C Du. *altemal*, wholly, all at once] [late 17C–mid-19C] (*UK Und.*) a financial summary or account produced without detail and demanded as a lump sum.

altar *n.* (*also* **altar room, alter, white altar**) [1920s+] the lavatory.

IN PHRASES

▫ **worship at the white altar** *v.* [2000s] to vomit.

altar of hymen *n.* (*also* **altar of love, ...venus, throne of love**) [SE *altar* + *Hymen*, the Greek god of marriage/*hymen*, the virginal membrane] [late 16C+] the vagina.

altar of pleasure *n.* [a literary euph.] [19C] the vagina.

altemal *n.* *see* ALTAMEL *n.*

alter *n.*[1] [? it 'alters' one's perceptions] [1950s] (*US drugs*) an opium pipe.

alter *n.*[2] *see* ALTAR *n.*

alter kacker *n.* (*also* **alter cocker, ...kocker**) [Yid. *alter kocker*, old shit. A facetious 'bilingual' version is *alter coyote*] [1920s+] (*US*) old fool, old fogey.

alter someone's dial-plate *v. see under* DIAL-PLATE *n.*

altham *n.* [Partridge sees this as ? root of AUTEM *n.*; if so, such a link would require a pun of the ALTAR OF HYMEN *n.* type] [16C] (*UK Und.*) the wife or female companion of a mendicant villain.

altitudes *n.*

IN PHRASES

▫ **in one's altitudes** *adj.* [17C–early 19C] drunk.

altogether, the *n.* ['altogether naked/nude'; coined by George Du Maurier in his novel *Trilby* (1894): 'I have sat for the "altogether" to several other people'] [late 19C+] nudity; esp. in phr. *in the altogether*, naked.

altumal *n.* [Lat. *altum mare*, the deep sea] [early–mid-18C] sailor's slang, nautical jargon.

alum, the *n.* [? phr. *à la mode*] [late 19C] (*US*) the ideal, exactly what one desires.

alvin *n.* [a 'typically' rural name] [1940s+] (*US*) a yokel, an unsophisticated dweller in a small-town or rural settlement.

alvo *adj.* [ety. unknown] [1990s+] (*US campus*) excellent, wonderful.

'Am *n.* [abbr.] [1990s+] (*US*) a Trans-*Am* automobile.

a.m. *n.* (*also* **ayem**) [colloq. version of SE *a.m.*, ante meridiem, used in chronological notation] [late 18C+] the morning; the very early hours after midnight.

amadáin/amadan/amadaun *n. see* OMADHAUN *n.*

amanda *adj.* [initial letter] [2000s] (*S.Afr. gay*) amazing.

-amaroot *sfx see* -EROONIE *sfx.*

amateur *n.* **1** [1910s+] (*also* **E.A., enthusiastic amateur**) a promiscuous young woman; thus [1920s+] (*orig. US*) *lose one's amateur standing/status*, to move into the world of professional, full-time prostitution [the term depends on the assumption that for women any sex before marriage was tantamount to prostitution]. **2** [1930s–40s] (*UK Und.*) a crook who has not been in trouble with the police.

SE in slang uses

IN COMPOUNDS

▫ **amateur hour** *n.* [1950s] (*US Und.*) noon, as a time when banks appear to expect to be robbed. ▫ **amateur night** *n.* [orig. theatrical use, when on special nights amateur hopefuls were encouraged to 'try their stuff' on a real stage] [1930s+] (*orig. US*) an exhibition of more than usual ineptitude, esp. by one who is supposedly more competent.

amazon *n.* **1** [1960s] (*US campus*) an attractive, sexy woman. **2** [1960s] (*US campus*) a very tall or muscular person of either sex. **3** [1990s+] (*US black*) a masculine lesbian.

ambassador *n.* [it 'presents its credentials' to the vagina] [1920s; 2000s] (*US*) the penis.

ambassador of Morocco *n.* [pun on Morocco leather] [early 19C] a shoemaker.

amber *n.* **1** [1910s–30s] (*US*) (*also* **ambeer, ambier**) tobacco juice. **2** [1940s+] (*US/Aus.*) beer; usu. as *the amber.*

amber fluid *n.* (*also* **amber beverage, ...brew, ...eau-de-vie, ...liquid**) [its colour] **1** [mid-19C+] (*Aus.*) beer; thus *amber transfusion*, a drink of beer. **2** [1970s] whisky.

IN PHRASES

□ **old amber** *n.* [1960s–70s] (*Aus.*) beer.

amber-gum *n.* [? the value of *amber-gum*, i.e. ambergris, used in perfumery] [mid-19C] (*UK Und.*) money paid to a perjuror; thus the perjury itself.

ambidexter *n.* [SE *ambidextrous*, in both cases the subject is seen as 'playing with both hands'] **1** [16C–18C] (*gambling*) a house player; one who hedges his bets, backing both sides. **2** [17C–18C] (*also* **ambodexter**) a corrupt lawyer who takes fees from both plaintiff and defendant.

ambidextrous *adj.* [SE *ambidextrous*, capable of using both hands equally well] [1930s+] a euph. for bisexual.

ambier *n. see* AMBER *n.*

ambisextrous *adj.* [pun on AMBIDEXTROUS *adj.* + SE *sex*] [1920s+] (*US*) bisexual.

ambo *n.* [abbr. + -O *sfx* (3)] [1960s+] (*Aus/S.Afr.*) **1** an *amb*ulance. **2** an *amb*ulance officer.

ambodexter *n. see* AMBIDEXTER *n.* (2).

ambs-ace *n.* (*also* **ames-ace**) [SE *ambs-ace*, double ace or both aces; thus the lowest possible throw in dice] **1** [late 14C–18C] nothing, next to nothing. **2** [early 16C–18C] bad luck, misfortune, worthlessness.

IN PHRASES

□ **within ambs-ace of** [late 17C–19C] very close to.

ambulance *n.*

IN EXCLAMATIONS

□ **get the ambulance!** *see* GET THE STRETCHER! *under* STRETCHER *n.*

ambulance-chaser *n.* (*also* **ambulance lawyer**) [late 19C+] a lawyer who specializes in representing the victims of street and other accidents, to whom he offers his services – often appearing at the victim's hospital bed to promise a substantial claim – which are accepted while the victim is still too shocked to make proper and rational arrangements; thus v. *chase ambulances*.

DERIVATIVES

□ **ambulance-chasing** *adj.* [1940s+] of a lawyer, specializing in representing the victims of street and other accidents, by offering one's services; also used of journalists in the context of pursuing stories.

ameche *n.* [proper name of actor Don *Ameche* (1908–93), who portrayed the telephone's inventor, Alexander Graham Bell, in a 1939 biopic] [1930s–50s] (*Can./US*) a telephone.

amen *n.* [18C+] a generic term used in the following combs. pertaining to religion or praying.

IN COMPOUNDS

□ **amen-bawler** *n.* [19C] a parson, a preacher. □ **amen bench** *n.* (*also* **amen corner**) [the seats of the most enthusiastic congregants, who punctuate the prayer and sermon with cries of *Amen!*] [late 19C–1940s] (*US black*) the front seats in a church, on either side of the pulpit; thus those who occupy them, i.e. the most devout members of the congregation. □ **amen-curler** *n.* [? SE *curler*, one who writhes about; thus the clerk, wishing to demonstrate his piety] [18C–early 19C] a parish clerk; thus *queer amen-curler*, a drunken parish clerk. □ **amen-man** *n.* [late 18C] a church clerk. □ **amen-preacher** *n.* [its black plumage, and the dislike felt by many West Indians for the white missionaries who preached at them] [early 19C+] (*W.I.*) the carrion crow. □ **amen-snorter** *n.* [late 19C+] (*mainly Aus.*) a parson. □ **amen theatre royal** *n.* [? the innate theatricality of religious services] [late 19C] a church. □ **amen-wallah** *n.* [WALLAH *n.* (1)] [19C+] the chaplain's clerk.

American *n.* [1980s] a sexual act where the woman rolls on the man to achieve his orgasm, rather than allows penetration, a 'bodyroll'.

American *adj.*

SE in slang uses

IN COMPOUNDS

□ **American business college** *n.* (*also* **ABC**) [initials A.B.C., which are also those of the *A*lcoholic *B*everage *C*ommission] [1940s+] (*US black*) a liquor store. □ **American card** *n.* [1930s] an erotic picture postcard. □ **American culture** *n.* [the supposed blandness of Middle American lifestyles] [1960s+] sexual intercourse in the face-to-face 'missionary position'. □ **American lad** *n.* (*also* **the lad**) [LAD *n.* (1)] [20C+] (*Irish*) unpopular fatty bacon, imported from the US. □ **American trombone** *n.* [1990s+] group sex between one woman and two men; the woman simultaneously fellates one man while being taken from the rear by the other. □ **American workhouse** *n.* [the hotel's many American guests; it is, of course, far from a 'workhouse'] [1910s–30s] Park Lane Hotel, London.

Amerika *n.* (*also* **Amerikka**) [the initials of the *K*u *K*lux *K*lan, although note standard Ger. *Amerika*, America; an identification with Germany, however, still implied fascism or Nazism] [1970s+] (*orig. US*) America, viewed by the revolutionaries of the period as the embodiment and headquarters of a right-wing, establishment-controlled, quasi-fascist conspiracy.

ames-ace *n. see* AMBS-ACE *n.* (1).

amesjay *n.* [backsl. = JAMES *n.* (3)] [1930s] a sovereign.

a.m.f. *phr.* [abbr. *a*dios *m*other*f*ucker; euph. as *a*dios, *m*y *f*riend] [1960s+] a euph. abbr., goodbye, that's it, it's all over.

AM/FM *adj.* [the two varieties of radio frequency] [1980s+] bisexual.

amiable *adj.* [mid-19C] (*US*) stupid.

amidships *adj.* [naut.] [1910s+] in the stomach, in the solar plexus, usu. relating to a blow.

amigo *n.* [Sp. *amigo*, friend] **1** [late 19C] (*US*) an (affectionate) term of address. **2** [1990s+] a friend.

Aminadab *n.* (*also* **Aminidab**) [a 'typical' Quaker name; 'from old comedies' (Hotten, 1867)] [early 17C–early 19C] a Quaker.

Amish golf *n.* [SE *Amish*, a strict sect of the Mennonite church in the US + SE *golf*; the theory is that the Amish are especial fans of the game] [1960s] (*US*) croquet.

ammo *n.* [abbr. + -O *sfx* (6)] **1** [1910s+] ammunition. **2** [1940s] semen [fig. use of sense 1]. **3** [2000s] (*US Und.*) money [fig. use of sense 1].

ammunition *n.* **1** [late 17C–mid-19C] semen. **2** [19C+] lavatory paper. **3** [1910s] alcohol, a drink. **4** [1920s–40s] (*US*) food, esp. as given out by the Salvation Army and similar institutions. **5** [1940s+] a tampon or sanitary towel.

ammunition leg *n.* [SE *ammunition*, as supplied to soldiers] [late 19C] a wooden leg.

ammunition wife *n.* [such a woman, like fired ammunition, was 'hot'] [early–mid-19C] a prostitute.

amoeba-brained *adj.* [the tiny size] [1960s+] (*US*) very stupid.

Amos and Andy *n.*[1] [rhy. sl.; the *Amos and Andy* radio show was highly popular in the US in the 1930s–40s; it featured two white actors, Freeman Gosden (1899–1982) and Charles Correll (1890–1972), faking it as 'dumb but happy darkies', and as such was one of the last interpretations of the old 'minstrel show'] **1** [1940s–50s] brandy. **2** [1990s+] shandy.

Amos and Andy *n.*[2] [see prev. ety.] [1960s] (*US black campus*) a man who takes advantage of a young woman.

amp *n.* [abbr.] **1** [1950s+] (*drugs*) *amp*oule. **2** [1960s+] an *amp*lifier. **3** [1970s+] (*US drugs*) *amp*hetamine. **4** [2000s] (*US drugs*) marijuana dipped in formaldehyde, sometimes laced with PCP.

IN COMPOUNDS

□ **amp joint** *n.* [JOINT *n.* (5c)] [1980s+] (*drugs*) a marijuana cigarette laced with some form of narcotic.

amp down *v.* [AMPED *adj.*] [1990s+] (*US campus*) to calm down, to talk quietly.

amped *adj.* [SE *amplified*; there may also be a subtler link to an AMP *n.* (1) of methedrine] [1970s+] **1** (*US*) high on drugs or caffeine; thus in fig. use, nervous. **2** (*US black*) (*also* **amp**) stirred up, very emotional; ready, enthusiastic.

IN PHRASES

□ **amped-out** *adj.* [AMP *n.* (3)] [1970s+] (*drugs*) suffering exhaustion after using amphetamines.

ampersand *n.* [the fact that in late 19C nursery alphabets the symbol was usu. printed after ('behind') the 26 letters + the suitably curving shape of the &] [mid-18C–19C] the buttocks.

amphets *n.* [abbr.] [1960s+] *amphet*amines.

amp out *v.* (*also* **amp on, amp up**) [AMPED *adj.*] [1990s+] (*US*) to act in a highly neurotic, tense manner; to get angry.

ampster *see under* AMSTER.

amputate one's mahogany *v.* (*also* **amputate one's timber**) [synon. for CUT (ONE'S) STICK(S) *v.* (1)] [mid–late 19C] to run away.

amscray *v.* (*also* **amscra, amscram**) [pig Lat. var. of SCRAM *v.* (1)] [1930s+] (*orig. US*) to leave quickly, to run off.

amster *n.* (*also* **ampster, amsterdam**) [rhy. sl.; *Amsterdam* = RAM *n.*[3] (1)] [1940s+] (*Aus.*) one who works outside a carnival, sideshow, strip club etc, touting the pleasures inside and pulling in the customers.

amster *v.* (*also* **ampster**) [AMSTER *n.*] [1940s+] to work outside a carnival, sideshow, strip club etc, touting the pleasures inside and pulling in the customers.

AMT *n.* [? abbr.] [1960s+] (*US drugs*) dimethytriptamine.

amulet *n.* [SE *amulet*, a charm against evil] [19C] the vagina.

-amundo *sfx* [1970s+] an intensifying sfx, used in comb. with an adj., e.g. *correctamundo*.

amuse *v.* [pun on SE *amuse*, to beguile with entertaining tales or to 'throw dust in one's eyes'] [18C–mid-19C] (*UK Und.*) to fool shopkeepers and other tradesmen in order to cheat or rob them.

(DERIVATIVES)

❑ **amuser** *n.* [mid-18C–mid-19C] (*UK Und.*) one who throws dust (sometimes snuff or pepper) in a victim's eyes and then runs off; a companion then appears and, while ostensibly offering sympathy, picks the victim's pockets.

amy *n.* (*also* **amys**) [abbr.] [1960s–70s] (*drugs*) amyl nitrite.

amy-john *n.* [play on SE *Amazon* + the comb. of male and female names; Wilson (1972) suggests Fr. *amiJean*. i.e. friend John] [1960s–80s] a lesbian.

amyl *n.* [abbr.] [1900s; 1960s+] (*drugs*) *amyl* nitrite.

(IN COMPOUNDS)

❑ **amyl queen** *n.* [-QUEEN *sfx* (3)] [1970s] (*US gay*) a gay man who enjoys sniffing amyl nitrite, which is supposed to enhance orgasm (whether hetero- or homosexual).

amys *n. see* AMY *n.*

ana *adj.* [abbr./pron.] [2000s] (*US teen*) *ano*rexic.

anabaptist *n.* [pun on SE *Anabaptist*, an early 16C German Protestant sect, typified by the re-baptism of all members; ult. f. Gk *anabaptismos*, baptize over again] [late 18C–early 19C] a pickpocket who had been caught in the act and 'baptized' by being placed beneath a pump or dumped into a pond.

anaconda *n.* [1990s+] **1** a mixture of strong beer and rough cider or scrumpy. **2** (*N.Z. teen*) the penis.

(IN PHRASES)

❑ **empty the anaconda** *v.* (*also* **drain the anaconda**) [1990s+] to urinate. ❑ **milk the anaconda** *v. see* MILK THE LIZARD *under* LIZARD *n.*

anal astronaut *n.* [1990s+] a male homosexual.

anal bucaneer *n.* [1980s+] (*US gay*) a male homosexual.

anal crusader *n.* [1990s+] (*UK juv.*) a male homosexual.

anarchists *n.* [they are 'likely to explode'] [1910s–40s] (*Aus.*) non-safety matches.

anarcho *n.* [abbr. + -O *sfx* (6)] [1990s+] an *anarch*ist.

anatomy *n.* [SE *anatomy*, a skeleton; used by Shakespeare in *Comedy of Errors* (1591)] [mid-19C–1900s] a very thin, emaciated person.

anchor *n.* [lit. or fig. resemblances] **1** [mid-19C–1950s] (*orig. US*) a pick-axe. **2** [1910s+] (*US Und.*) a reprieve; a temporary suspension of a sentence. **3** [1930s+] in pl., brakes; thus *drop the anchors, slam on the anchors*, put on the brakes. **4** [1940s–50s] (*US Und.*) a stickpin; thus *anchor and prop*, a stickpin with a safety catch that anchors it to the tie. **5** [1950s] (*US black*) one's home, one's address. **6** [1990s+] (*Aus. juv.*) a younger relation or other small child who 'cramps one's style' and social life.

(IN PHRASES)

❑ **put the anchors on** *v.* [1950s+] to slow down intercourse so as to delay one's orgasm.

SE in slang uses

(IN PHRASES)

❑ **bring oneself to an anchor** *v.* [naut. imagery] [mid-19C] to sit down. ❑ **drag one's anchor** *v.* [1920s+] (*US*) to go slowly, to idle, to dawdle. ❑ **drop anchor** *v.* [1990s+] to defecate. ❑ **drop anchor in bum bay** *v.* [1980s] to have anal intercourse; thus *anchor man*, the subject of the sex. ❑ **swallow the anchor** *v.* [orig. naut. jargon] **1** [late 19C+] (*UK Und.*) to change course, to stop doing something. **2** [1980s] to give oneself up to the police.

anchor *v.* [naut. imagery] **1** [late 19C–1970s] (*US*) to stop for a while, to settle. **2** [1920s–50s] to grant a stay of execution.

anchor (and chain) *n.* [derog. stereotype of a wife as the restraint on male freedoms] [1940s] (*US*) one's wife.

anchored *adj.* [ANCHOR (AND CHAIN) *n.* (1)] [1940s] (*US*) married.

ancient Chinese secret *n.* [appears to have begun with a 1986 TV advert for Calgon washing powder: recalled in email to www.inthe80s.com 23 Apr. 2002: 'The Calgon in the Chinese Laundromat: Woman comes in and asks how the cleaner gets her laundry so fresh. He laughs and says "Ancient Chinese Secret." The woman in the back says "We need more Calgon" and the customer says "Ancient Chinese secret huh????" and the proprieter smiles embarassingly (very cheesy)'] [1980s+] (*US black teen*) a non-committal response when one is asked how one managed a task.

ancient order *n. see* A.O.H. *n.*

and did he marry poor blind Nell? *phr.* [play on the clichéd conventions of popular fiction; allegedly from a late-19C ballad] [1910s+] a phr. used to imply one's disbelief in the previous statement.

and how! *excl.* [synon. Ger. *und wie!*] [mid-19C+] (*orig. US*) a general excl. of agreement or approval, placed at the end of a sentence.

and no flies *phr.* [the image is of flies settling on something that is fig. 'off'] [mid-19C] a general intensifier, meaning 'and no doubt or hesitation about it'.

andramartins *n.* (*also* **andremartins**) [? anecdotal] [20C+] (*Irish*) horseplay, fooling around.

andrew *n.*[1] [? SE merry-*Andrew*, a buffoon, an entertainer] [late 17C–early 18C] a servant, a lazy fellow.

andrew *n.*[2] [proper name of Lieutenant ANDREW MILLAR *n.*, which gave orig. naut. jargon *Andrew Millar's lugger*, a ship of war; note also Shakespeare's *Merchant of Venice* (1596): 'But I should think of shallows and of flats, And see my wealthy Andrew dock'd in sands'; although cited as 'ship, esp. of war' in the *OED*, the capital may simply imply the name of a given ship] [mid-19C+] **1** the Royal Navy. **2** a government department or authority.

Andrew Jackson *n.* [the face of seventh US President *Andrew Jackson* (1767–1845) on the note] [1980s] (*US*) a $20 bill.

Andrew Millar *n.* (*also* **Andrew Millar's lugger, Andrew Miller, Andrew Miller's lugger**) [generally accepted as a ref. to a contemporary RN Lieutenant; a negative alternative suggests the name of a (then) well-known member of a press gang] [19C] a man o'war.

Andrex fart *n.* [the *Andrex* advertising slogan 'soft, strong and very long'] [1990s+] a silent, smelly breaking of wind that lasts for quite some time.

andro *n.* [abbr.] [2000s] (*US drugs*) 4-*andro*stenedione, a natural hormone which is converted to testosterone.

and then some! *excl.* (*also* **and then plenty!**) [Partridge suggests an origin in 18C Scot. *and some*] [20C+] (*orig. US*) rejoinder to the last speaker, that's not all of it, either!

and thing *phr.* [usu. heard as *an' t'ing*] [1970s+] (*UK black*) and so on, used as a non-specific punctuation at the end of a sentence.

andy cain *n.* [rhy. sl.] [20C+] rain.

Andy Capp *n.* [rhy. sl. = CRAP *n.*[1] (2); *Andy Capp* is a well-known strip cartoon character, created in 1956 by Reg Smythe for the *Daily Mirror*] [1960s+] (*Aus.*) an act of defecation.

Andy Gump *n.* [the eponymous cartoon character created by Sidney Smith in 1917; he was virtually chinless; in southwest US the banded sand snake, with its deeply countersunk jaw, is an *andy gump* snake] [1960s–70s] (*US*) a conspicuously receding chin; a notably prominent chin.

Andy Maguire *n.* [rhy. sl.] [20C+] (*Aus.*) a fire.

Andy McGinn *n.* [rhy. sl.] [1930s+] the chin.

Andy McNish *n.* [rhy. sl.] [20C+] fish.

Andy McNoon *n.* [Arab. *inta machnoon* — 'a damned fool'] [1910s] (*Aus.*) an utter fool.

and you! *excl.* (*also* **and you too!**) [i.e. 'and that means you (too)'] [1910s+] a dismissive, antagonistic excl., a general admonition to anyone listening after one has made a pronouncement to someone.

Andy Pandy *n.* [rhy. sl.; ult. the children's puppet *Andy Pandy*, featured on the TV programme *Watch with Mother* (1950s–70s)] [2000s] brandy.

andy up *v. see* ANTE (UP) *v.*

angal shout *n.* [ety. unknown] [mid-19C] (*UK Und.*) the Recorder's report.

angel *n.* **1** [mid-17C–19C] (*also* **fallen angel**) a prostitute [the original, specific coinage applied only to those prostitutes whose beat ran near the Angel public house in Islington, north London]. **2** [mid-19C–1940s] a young woman, esp. a pretty one; also in direct address. **3** [late 19C+] (*US Und.*) the prospective victim of a swindle or confidence trick. **4** [late 19C+] the financial backer of an enterprise or scheme, esp. one who puts up money for a theatrical production. **5** [1920s+] an older homosexual man, usu. one who supports a younger lover. **6** [1930s] a sandwichboard-man. **7** [1930s–60s] a passive homosexual; a tramp's young homosexual companion. **8** [1960s] (*US prison/Und.*) the rich backer of a large-scale crime. **9** [1970s] (*US gay/prison*) a victim of sexual aggression. **10** *see* RABBI *n.*

IN PHRASES

❑ **angel off** *v.* [1960s] to rob a drug dealer's customers immediately after they have bought their supplies. ❑ **angel with a dirty face** *n.* [note film *Angels with Dirty Faces* (1938)] [1930s–60s] a covert, undeclared male homosexual.

SE in slang uses

IN COMPOUNDS

❑ **angel cake and wine** *n.* (*also* **angel food cake and wine**) [1940s+] (*US Und.*) bread and water. ❑ **angel drink** *n.* [it sends the drinker 'to heaven'] [1980s+] a wine made from marijuana. ❑ **angel dust** *n. see* separate entry. ❑ **angel factory** *n.* [the assumption being that its products, priests, are guaranteed entry to heaven] [1930s+] (*US*) a seminary. ❑ **angel food** *n.* [the sermon is the 'price' of the free meal] **1** [1920s–50s] (*US tramp*) preaching, as experienced in a mission. **2** [1960s] (*US gay*) an air force serviceman [as a flier, he reaches heaven; as a potential conquest he is someone one can EAT *v.* (4)]. ❑ **angel hair** *n.* [var. on ANGEL DUST *n.* (4)] [1970s+] (*drugs*) phencyclidine. ❑ **angel kisses** *n.* [the myth that freckles are a sign of angelic affection] [20C+] freckles. ❑ **angel-maker** *n.* [the embryo or the 'farmed' children (who rarely survived the baby-farmer's ministrations) 'join the angels'] **1** [late 19C–1900s] a baby-farmer, a woman who took in (usu. illegitimate) babies on the pretext of bringing them up in return for a fee; thus *angel-making*, the starving to death of such unwanted children. **2** [late 19C+] an abortionist. ❑ **angel puke** *n.* [1970s] (*US drugs*) phencyclidine. ❑ **angel puss** *n.* [PUSS *n.*[2] (1)] [1940s+] (*US*) a pretty young woman, often used as an affectionate term of address. ❑ **angel's food** *n.* [i.e. nectar] [late 16C–early 17C] strong ale. ❑ **angel's oil** *n. see* OIL OF ANGELS *under* OIL OF... *n.* ❑ **angel suit** *n.* [? similar to a one-piece burial shroud in which one 'ascends to heaven'] [late 19C] a 'combination' suit, offering a coat and waistcoat made in one, with the trousers buttoned onto it. ❑ **angel teat** *n.* (*also* **angel's teat**) [stillers' jargon, a mellowed whisky with a rich bouquet] [1940s–70s] (*US*) notably mellow whisky. ❑ **angel tits** *n.* [TIT *n.*[2] (1)] [2000s] (*S.Afr. gay*) a man-to-man term of endearment. ❑ **angel together** *n.* [ety. unknown] [late 19C–1910s] (*mainly W.I.*) a drunkard. ❑ **angel wings** *n.* [it sends the user 'to heaven'] [2000s] (*US drugs*) caladium.

angel *v.* [ANGEL *n.* (4)] [1920s–40s] to use one's money to back an enterprise, esp. a theatrical production.

angela *adj.* [SE *angelic*] [2000s] (*S.Afr. gay*) kind, helpful.

angel dust *n.* (*drugs*) **1** [1960s+] anything smokeable, e.g. tobacco, marijuana, parsley, mixed with phencyclidine. **2** [1970s] a mixture of cocaine, heroin and morphine, which can be smoked or injected. **3** [1970s] finely chopped marijuana. **4** [1970s+] phencyclidine.

IN COMPOUNDS

❑ **angel dust hero** *n.* [1980s+] (*US*) a regular user of cocaine.

angelic *n.* (*also* **angelica**) [SE *angel* + proper name] [early–mid-19C] an unmarried young woman.

angelina *n.* [ANGEL *n.* (7) + sfx *-ina*] **1** [1930s+] (*camp gay*) a young gay man, the partner of an older one. **2** [1950s] an effeminate person, a weakling.

IN COMPOUNDS

❑ **angelina sorority** *n.* [1940s] (*camp gay*) the world of young gay men.

angel liquor *n.* [California use; a pun on SE *angelica*; angelica liquor (angelica mixed with water) was orig. seen as a preventative against poison and the plague] [1940s] (*US black*) a sweet, fortified wine.

angels *n.* [concept of 'flying' HIGH *adj.*[1] (2)] [2000s] (*drugs*) **1** amytal. **2** sodium crystals. **3** alkyl nitrates.

angel's kiss *n.* [rhy. sl. = PISS *n.* (2)] [20C+] (*Aus.*) an act of urination.

angie *n.* [SE *angel* / ? ANGEL *n.* (5)] [1970s] (*US gay*) a general form of address.

angill butter *n.* [? the villain hopes to 'butter up' the angels] [mid-19C] (*UK Und.*) a last-minute repentance or confession on the gallows.

angle *n.* [? the calculation of angles necessary to play a winning game of pool, snooker or billiards] [1910s+] (*orig. US*) any plan that should benefit its maker, an exploitable gimmick, an ulterior motive; thus *get an angle on*, to work out the optimum way of doing something.

IN COMPOUNDS

❑ **angle-shooter** *n.* [1940s+] (*US*) a schemer, a plotter.

IN PHRASES

❑ **play the angles** *v.* [1930s+] (*US*) to scheme, to plot.

angle *v.* [ANGLE *n.*] [20C+] (*US*) to scheme; to obtain by planning.

angled up *adj.* [SE *angled*, skewiff, out of kilter] [1900s–70s] (*US black/Southern*) confused, mixed up.

angle for farthings *v.* [late 18C–early 19C] to dangle a cap, box or other makeshift container from a prison window into the street below in the hope of picking up alms from kind-hearted passers-by.

angler *n.* [fishing imagery] **1** [mid-16C–19C; 1970s+] (*UK Und.*) (*also* **anglero, starrer**) a thief who uses a pole, the *angling stick*, with a hook at one end to 'fish' items from open windows, unguarded market stalls, passing carts etc. **2** [early 18C] (*UK Und.*) a pickpocket. **3** [late 18C–early 19C] (*UK Und.*) a petty thief, working in the street and always on the lookout for opportunities to commit small larcenies. **4** [late 18C–mid-19C] (*UK/US Und.*) a confidence trickster. **5** [mid-19C] (*UK Und.*) a smash-and-grab thief; also ext. as *anglers in troubled water*.

angling-cove *n.* [ANGLER *n.* (1) + COVE *n.* (1), i.e. 'one who fishes in troubled waters'] [late 18C–19C] a receiver of stolen goods; thus *angling*, receiving stolen goods.

anglo *n.* [SE *Anglo-*, English] [1940s+] (*orig. US*) anyone of ostensibly Anglo-Saxon appearance, i.e. a white person.

anglo *adj.* [ANGLO *n.*] [1960s+] (*US*) white, or pertaining to a white lifestyle or culture.

Angola (black) *n.* [its origin] [1980s+] (*drugs*) marijuana.

angora *n.* [backform. f. ACT THE ANGORA *v.*] [1910s–40s] (*Aus./US*) a fool.

IN PHRASES

❑ **get someone's angora** *v.* (*also* **get someone's fur up**) [a pun on *GET SOMEONE'S GOAT under* GOAT *n.*[1]] [1920s–40s] (*US*) to annoy, to irritate.

angry boy *n.* [SE *angry*, troublesome, vexatious, annoying + *boy*] [late 16C–early 17C] a rake, a young man about town.

angury *n.* [ety. unknown] [mid-19C] (*UK Und.*) a psalm sung at an execution.

angus *adj.* [an *Angus* bull] [2000s] (*N.Z.*) angry.

Angus Armanasco *n.* [rhy. sl. = BRASCO *n.*; ult. Aus. racehorse trainer *Angus Armanasco* (1907–2005)] [1980s] (*Aus.*) a lavatory.

animal *n.*[1] **1** [18C+] a general derog. description of a man, esp. a braggart. **2** [late 19C–1900s] a public house, whose sign shows a lion, bull, bear or other creature [the original animal was the elephant at the *Elephant and Castle* in south London]. **3** [1910s] (*US campus*) a young woman, esp. a promiscuous one. **4** [1910s+] a police officer. **5** [1920s+] (*orig. US*) a physically strong man, a 'tough guy', a hired thug. **6** [1940s] (*US black campus*) (*also* **simple animal**) a young college girl. **7** [1940s+] (*orig. US*) a passionate sexual partner. **8** [1950s+] a wild, crazy person. **9** [1950s+] (*orig. Aus.*) an unpleasant person. **10** [1960s] (*US campus*) a male student seen as sexually unsophisticated by his female peers. **11** [1970s] (*US campus*) an athlete. **12** [1970s+] (*drugs*) LSD [? it makes some users behave wildly]. **13** [1990s+] a psychopath.

IN PHRASES

❑ **go animal** *v.* [1960s] (*US*) to lose one's emotional control. ❑ **see the big animal** *v. see SEE THE ELEPHANT under* ELEPHANT *n.*

animal *n.*[2] [var. on HORSE *n.* (5a) or PONY *n.* (3b)] [1900s] (*US*) a word-for-word translation used by US students studying foreign languages.

animal *adj.* [2000s] (*UK teen*) good, excellent.

-animal *sfx* [ANIMAL *n.*[1]] [1980s+] (*US campus*) a combining form indicating one who does something excessively, e.g. *party animal*.

animal cracker *n.* [pun on CRACKERS *adj.* + ref. to Nabisco's *Barnum's Animals*, biscuits first marketed in 1904] [1920s+] (*US*) an eccentric.

animal house *n.* (*also* **animal farm, animal zoo**) [the phr. gained international popularity with the release of the film *Animal House* (1978), starring John Belushi] [1960s+] (*US campus*) a fraternity house that is generally rated the least efficient, the most degenerate and, overall, the one to avoid.

animal tranq *n.* (*also* **animal trank**) [in non-recreational use, an animal tranquillizer] [1970s+] (*drugs*) phencyclidine.

animated cubes/ivories *n. see GALLOPING BONES under* GALLOPING *adj.*

aniseed Robin *n.* (*also* **anniseed Robin**) [one *Robin*, a real-life aniseed-water seller d.1651 (and briefly married to the highwayman John Cottingham, exec. 1685), noted by Pepys as a hermaphrodite and well-known as such in mid-17C literature; a then popular song was entitled 'Aniseed Robin' or 'Cuckolds All in a Row'] [late 17C–mid-18C] a hermaphrodite; latterly generic for a prostitute.

anker of rum *n.* [rhy. sl. = BUM *n.*[1] (1); ult. anker, 'A measure of wine and spirits, used in Holland, North Germany, Denmark, Sweden, and Russia. It varies in different countries; that of Rotterdam, formerly also used in England, contains 10 old wine gallons or 8⅓ imperial gallons.' (*OED*)] [1920s] the buttocks, the posterior.

ankle *n.*

SE in slang uses

IN COMPOUNDS

❑ **ankle-beater** *n.* [he would hit only the animals' ankles, to avoid damaging the flesh] [19C] a boy who drives cattle from the market to the slaughterer. ❑ **ankle-biter** *n.* **1** [1920s] in pl., tight trousers, as worn by hussars. **2** [1960s+] (*orig. US*) (*also* **knee-biter**) a small child [its crawling around at ankle height]. ❑ **ankle express** *n.* [ironic use of SE] [1910s+] (*US*) transportation by foot, walking. ❑ **ankle-grabber** *n.* [1980s+] (*US campus*) a homosexual.

IN PHRASES

❑ **ankle spring warehouse** *n.* [var. on *SPRING ANKLE WAREHOUSE under* SPRING *n.*] [late 18C] (*Anglo-Irish*) the stocks.

ankle *v.* (*also* **ankle around**) (*orig. US*) **1** [1920s] to dance. **2** [1920s+] to walk. **3** [1980s] to leave, to walk away from.

ann *n.* [abbr. *MISS ANN under* MISS *n.*] [1970s+] a derog. term for a white woman; thus by ext. a black woman who apes her white sisters.

anna maria *n.* (*also* **ave Maria**) [rhy. sl.] [late 19C+] a domestic fire.

Anna May Wong *n.* [rhy. sl. = PONG *n.*[1]; ult. Chinese-American film star (1905–61)] [1920s+] a stink, a smell.

Anne's fan *n. see* QUEEN ANNE'S FAN *n.*

annie *n.* [use of female proper name] **1** [1950s–60s] an effeminate male homosexual. **2** [2000s] (*S.Afr. gay*) the anus.

Annie Laurie *n.* [*Annie Laurie* (1682–1764); her grandson Alexander Fergusson of Craigdarroch was the hero of Robert Burns's poem 'The Whistle'; thus *whistler*, another WW2 synon. for a conductress] [1940s] a bus conductress.

annie louise *n.* [rhy. sl.] [20C+] (*Aus.*) cheese.

annie no-rattle *n.* [proper name *Annie* + SE *no* + SE *rattle*] [20C+] (*Ulster*) one who waits until a conversation is over to put in their own opinion.

Annie Oakley *n.* [the markswoman *Annie Oakley* (Phoebe Ann Mozee Butler, 1860–1926); the holes punched in such tickets supposedly resembled the aces out of which Ms Oakley would shoot the pips] **1** [1910s+] (*US*) a free pass, orig. to a circus, but latterly to the theatre. **2** [1940s] (*US Und.*) a pardon or discharge certificate given to a convict.

Annie Oakley *v.* [for ety. *see* prev.] [1910s+] (*US*) to punch an admission ticket, thus rendering it free.

annie's room *phr.* [orig. milit.; used in darts to denote the throw of 'double-one', considered the least attainable double on the board] [1910s+] (*Aus.*) a phr. used in answer to the question 'Where is...?' when the respondent does not actually know.

annie up *v. see* ANTE (UP) *v.*

annihilated *adj.* [1970s+] (*orig. US campus*) extremely drunk or intoxicated by some drug.

anniseed Robin *n. see* ANISEED ROBIN *n.*

anno domini *n.* [Lat. *anno domini*, in the year of Our Lord] [late 19C+] old age and its deleterious effects, esp. on physical prowess.

annual *n.* **1** [late 19C–1900s] an annual holiday. **2** [1900s] (*Aus.*) a year's jail sentence. **3** [1940s] (*Aus.*) a bath.

anodyne *v.* [mid-19C] (*US Und.*) to kill.

anodyne necklace *n.* [ironic use of SE; such a necklace was orig. a form of medicinal amulet and based on the original definition of *anodyne* as soothing pain, in this context that of a misspent life; thus the phrase is a pun on 'painkiller'] [late 18C–early 19C] the hangman's noose.

anointed *adj.* [ext. of SE *anointed*, consecrated king or queen] [mid-18C–19C] used to intensify a n., e.g. *anointed rascal*, a very definite rascal.

anoint (with birchen salve) *v.* [ironic use of SE] [late 16C–1940s] to beat, to thrash.

anonyma *n.* [Lat. *anonyma*, an unknown woman] [mid–late 19C] a courtesan, a high-class prostitute.

anorak *n.* [SE *anorak*, a style of short coat, orig. worn by Greenland Inuits, that is seen as typifying such figures] [1980s+] **1** anyone outside a peer group who thus fails to fit in with 'the gang', esp. a studious individual who eschews drink, drugs and similar teen pleasures. **2** an obsessive, typically as regards computing (in an earlier age his interest would have been trainspotting).

another clean shirt ought to see you out *phr. see under* SHIRT *n.*

another county heard from *phr.* [joc. use of SE phr. usu. used of election results] [1930s+] (*Can.*) a remark made when one of a group breaks wind.

another day, another dollar *phr.* [1910s+] (*orig. US*) **1** a phr. of relief used at the end of the working day. **2** a phr. used to point up the tedium of quotidian existence.

another day up the Queen's arse *phr.* [ARSE *n.* (1)] [1980s+] (*Aus. prison*) a day of one's sentence completed.

another one for the van *phr.* [the 'van' being that which conveys the sufferer to a psychiatric institution] [1920s+] another person's gone mad.

answer the last muster *v.* [milit. imagery] [1930s] to die.

answer the last roll-call *v.* [milit. imagery] [1930s] to die.

answer the last round-up *v.* [Western cowboy imagery] [1930s] to die.

ant-brained *adj.* [1990s+] small-minded, petty.

ante *n.* [Lat. *ante*, before, in this case, before one plays or bets] [late 19C+] (*orig. US*) money in hand, cash.

IN PHRASES

□ **up the ante** *v.* (*also* **raise the ante, whoop...**) [poker imagery] [late 19C+] (*orig. US*) lit. and fig., to increase the amount, to demand a higher price.

anteater *n.* (*also* **corndog**) **1** [1970s] a man with a circumcised penis; a circumcised penis. **2** [1980s+] (*US gay*) an erect penis.

ante-up *n.* [the necessity to *ante up* (place a preliminary bet) to indicate one's playing a round] **1** [late 19C–1950s] (*Aus.*) the game of poker. **2** [1900s–20s] an advance payment, lit. or fig.

ante (up) *v.* (*also* **andy up, annie up**) [poker use, each player must *ante up* (f. Lat. *ante*, before) a specified sum in order to enter each successive hand dealt during the game; the variants are simply folk mispronunciations] [mid-19C+] **1** to pay out money in advance. **2** (*Aus.*) to surrender (something), to hand over, thus to pay one's dues. **3** in fig. use, to explain oneself.

Anthea (Turner) *n.* [rhy. sl. = EARNER *n.*; ult. UK TV presenter *Anthea Turner* (b.1960)] [1990s+] any job or plan that pays well, almost invariably criminal.

anthem cackler *n. see* AUTEM-CACKLER *under* AUTEM *n.*

anthem diver *n. see* AUTEM-DIVER *under* AUTEM *n.*

anthony *n.* (*also* **tantony, tantany**) [SE *St Anthony's pig*; St Anthony is the patron of swine-herds, and is always represented as accompanied by a pig; and Berkshire dial. *t'anthony*, the smallest pig in a litter] [mid-16C–mid-19C] the runt of the litter; the favourite or smallest pig in the litter.

anthony cuffin *n.* [CUFF ANTHONY *under* CUFF *v.*[1]] [19C] a knock-kneed man.

anti *n.* [Lat. *anti*, against; 20C+ use is SE] [late 18C–19C] an objector, a rebel, a dissenter, one who rejects the social status quo.

antidote *n.* [ext. of SE use, i.e. an 'antidote against attraction'] **1** [late 17C–early 18C] a very plain woman. **2** [late 19C] (*US*) a drink.

antifogmatic *n.* (*also* **fog-cutter**) [SE *antidote/ante*, against + *fog* + sfx *-matic*, used to indicate a mechanical device] [late 18C–19C] an alcoholic drink taken (ostensibly) to counteract the effects of cold and damp.

antifreeze *n.* [ext. of SE use, i.e. both refer to their supposed prophylactic powers against cold] **1** [1920s+] alcohol, esp. cheap and as drunk by tramps and alcoholics. **2** [1970s+] (*drugs*) heroin.

anti-lunch *n. see under* LUNCH *n.*

antiman *n. see* AUNTIE-MAN *under* AUNTIE *n.*[2].

antipodean *adj.* [the Antipodes are 'the world turned upside down'] [mid-17C; late 19C–1900s] in a mess, chaotic.

antipodes *n.* [SE *Antipodes*, Australia and thus, f. UK perspective, 'the bottom of the world'] **1** [early 19C] the buttocks. **2** [mid-19C–1920s] the vagina.

antiquated rogue *n.* [ext. of ROGUE *n.*] [late 17C–mid-18C] (*UK Und.*) a retired villain.

antique dealer *n.* [1970s+] (*US gay*) a young man who courts elderly, wealthy men.

ant-killer *n.* (*also* **ants-masher**) [mid-19C; 1960s] (*US*) **1** a large foot, a large, heavy shoe. **2** by metonymy, a man who has or wears one.

Anto *n.* [negative stereotyping of the given name *Anto*] [2000s] (*Irish*) a working-class teenager.

an't please the pigs *phr.* [? SE *pixies*; *Ware* prefers *pyx*, the vessel in which the host or consecrated bread of the sacrament is reserved, thus making it a synon. for 'God willing', or 'please God'; also note *Gentleman's Mag.* 1790: the suggestion is that the 'pigs' were the scholars of St Anthony's School in Threadneedle St, so named by their rivals at St Paul's School, with ref. to the story of St Anthony preaching to pigs and always having a pig at his side; the phr. thus emerged as a derisive ref. to the rival establishment] [late 17C–19C] (*? orig. Irish*) if circumstances permit.

ants *n.* [phr. below prob. predates n.] **1** [1930s–40s] (*US*) restlessness, anxiety. **2** [1950s] (*UK black*) a parasite [SE *ant*, spoken as *ants* in Carib. E].

IN PHRASES

□ **have ants in one's pants** *v.* (*also* **have ants in one's britches, ...up one's ass**) [1930s+] (*orig. US*) to be restless, nervous, twitchy, (sexually) excited.

ants *v.* [ANTS *n.* (2)] [1950s] (*W.I./UK black*) to live as a parasite.

ants-masher *n. see* ANT-KILLER *n.*

ant's pants *n.* **1** [20C+] (*Aus.*) the height of fashion; thus *look like the ant's pants*, to be very smartly dressed. **2** *see* BEE'S KNEES *n.*

antsy *adj.* [ANTS *n.* + sfx *-y*] [1950s+] twitchy, nervous.

anty *n.* [ants were frequently to be found in sugar] [1910s–20s] (*Aus.*) sugar.

A-number-one *n.* [i.e. 'the first'; var. on NUMBER ONE *n.* (1)] [1920s–30s] (*US*) oneself.

A-number-one *adj. see* A-1 *adj.*

anus bandit *n. see* ARSE BANDIT *n.*

anvil chorus *n.* [the 'Anvil Chorus', featured in Verdi's opera *Il Trovatore* (1853)] [late 19C–1970s] (*orig. US*) carping, negative criticism; thus used as a personification.

anxal-bay *n.* [ety. unknown; ? link to SE *anxious*] [mid-19C] (*UK Und.*) the condemned cell.

anxious *adj.* [on bad = good model] [1940s–70s] (*US black*) good, enjoyable, admirable, pleasant.

anxious meeting *n.* [late 19C–1910s] (*orig. US*) the gathering, after a revivalist meeting, of those earnest souls who are 'anxious for salvation'; thus n., *anxious mourner*, a member of such a gathering.

anxup-pasty *n.* [ety. unknown] [mid-19C] (*UK Und.*) the passing of the death sentence; the removing of a prisoner's irons.

any *n.* [CUNT *n.* (1); PUSSY *n.* (1) etc are assumed] [late 19C+] sexual pleasures; esp. in interrog. *getting any?*

any *adv. see* SOME *adv.*

any dog's bottom? *phr.* [ety. unknown; ? canine habit of sniffing at their fellows] [1930s+] (*Aus.*) a phr. used to enquire if someone is any use.

any God's quantity *n.* [late 19C–1930s] many, a good number.

any how *adj.* [late 19C+] disorganized, messy.

any how *adv.* [mid-19C–1920s] indifferently, carelessly.

any old *adj.* [late 19C+] (*orig. US*) anything, whatever, a general term of vagueness, e.g. *any old way, any old job*.

any racket *n.* [rhy. sl.] [mid-19C–1900s] a penny faggot.

anyways! *excl.* [1920s+] (*US campus*) a dismissive excl.

any Wee Georgie? *phr.* [rhy. sl.; *Wee Georgie* Wood = good; Wood was a popular music–hall entertainer in 1920s–30s] [1920s+] any good?

anywhere *adj.* [1940s+] **1** (*drugs*) possessing drugs, as in question *are you anywhere?* **2** psychologically secure.

Anzac *adj.* [the term *Anzac* appears in 1915 (in C.E.W. Bean's diary) as an acronym formed from the initial letters of Australian and New Zealand Army Corps, orig. used as a telegraphic code name for the Corps. In the same year it was used as an abbr. for

'Anzac Cove' at Gallipoli, and then as a term for the 'Gallipoli campaign'. In 1916 it was first used to refer to a member of the Australian and New Zealand Army Corps who served in the Gallipoli campaign. In honour of the fact that they fought at Gallipoli, the Anzacs were commanded in 1919 to attach a small brass 'A' above the colour patch on their sleeve. During the war the term 'Anzac' was used in various compounds: an *Anzac button* was 'a nail used in place of a trouser button', *Anzac soup* was 'shell-hole water polluted by a corpse', *Anzac stew* was 'an urn of hot water and one bacon rind', and an *Anzac wafer* was 'a hard biscuit supplied to the AIF in place of bread'. These terms did not survive their wartime contexts, although the Anzac wafer survives transformed into the *Anzac biscuit* (and, more recently, the *Anzac cookie*)] [1910s+]

IN COMPOUNDS

❑ **Anzac day dinner** *n.* [Anzac Day, a public holiday held on 25 April (the anniversary of the Gallipoli landing in 1915) in Australia and New Zealand in memory of the nations' war dead] (*N.Z.*) a meal, usu. lunch, that is mainly (if not entirely) composed of alcohol. ❑ **Anzac hare** *n.* (*N.Z.*) meat loaf. ❑ **Anzac shandy** *n.* (*N.Z.*) champagne. ❑ **Anzac stew** *n.* (*Aus.*) dirty water, but note orig. wartime use in ety. above.

a.o.h. *n.* (*also* **ancient order**) [abbr.; *a*ncient *o*rder of *h*ibernia] [late 19C] (*US short order*) a potato.

A-OK *adj.* [A-OK *phr.*] [1950s+] satisfactory, fine, good.

A-OK *phr.* (*also* **A-okay**) [A-1 *adj.* (1) + OK *adj.* (1); originated in spaceflight jargon and spread to the wider public after the broadcast of the Mercury flight of Commander Alan Shepard (1923–98) on 5 May 1961] [1950s+] intensifier of OK, all's well, everything's absolutely fine.

A-1 *n.* [A-1 *adj.* (1)] [mid-19C] someone or something of the first class.

A-1 *adj.* (*also* **a-1, a-one, A-number-one, A No.1**) [insurance jargon *A1*, the top rating given to a ship at the insurers Lloyds of London] [early 19C+] **1** (*also* **A1 and no mistake, A1 copper-bottomed, letter A number 1**) excellent, perfect, first class, in prime condition. **2** extreme, supreme, in both negative as well as positive contexts.

DERIVATIVES

❑ **A-1-er** *n.* [late 19C] an exceptional person, an aristocrat.

A-1 *adv.* [A-1 *adj.*] **1** [late 19C+] excellently, in the best way. **2** [2000s] totally, completely.

a over k *phr. see* ARSE OVER KITE *under* ARSE *n.*

a over t *phr. see* ARSE OVER TIT *under* ARSE *n.*

apache *n.* (*also* **Comanche**) [the wearing of 'warpaint' by Apaches and other Native Americans] **1** [1930s+] a lesbian. **2** [1980s] (*US gay*) a man who uses cosmetics. **3** [1990s+] an act of sexual intercourse without the use of a condom [pun on the Apache Indian syle of riding BAREBACK *adv.* (1)]. **4** [2000s] (*Irish*) a joyrider.

apartment to let *n.* (*also* **house to let, tenements to let**) [a widow becomes 'vacant' for new (male) 'occupation'] **1** [mid-17C–early 19C] the vagina. **2** [18C] the widow herself. **3** [18C–19C] a widow's weeds.

apartment to let *phr.* (*also* **attic to let**) [the image is of a certain emptiness in the UPPER STOREY *under* UPPER *adj.*] [mid-19C+] unhinged, insane, crazy.

a.p.b. *n.* [abbr. *a*ll *p*oints *b*ulletin, a general alert broadcast to all officers and vehicles] [1950s+] (*US police*) a general alert, a search for a missing person.

APC *n.* [abbr. *a*rm*p*its and *c*rotch] [1980s] (*Aus.*) a quick wash of 'important' areas of the body.

apcray *n.* [pig Lat. *apcray* = CRAP *n.*[1] (4)] [1930s+] (*US*) nonsense, rubbish.

ape *n.* [SE *ape*; note derog. use of *ape* as fool is found in Chaucer] **1** [mid-16C+] a general pej., the implication being of stupidity and lumbering size. **2** [mid-19C+] (*orig. US*) (*also* **apeman**) a derog. term for a black person. **3** [1920s+] a thug, a hoodlum. **4** [1980s] (*S.Afr.*) a white man.

IN COMPOUNDS

❑ **ape-face** *n.* [1980s] (*US*) an ugly, thuggish person. ❑ **apehangers** *n.* (*also* **monkey-hangers**) [when riding the motorcycle one's arms dangle forward like those of an ape] [1960s+] (*orig. US*) high, extra-long motorcycle handlebars, favoured by outlaw riders such as Hell's Angels. ❑ **apehead** *n.* [-HEAD *sfx* (1)] [mid-19C+] (*US*) a fool, an idiot. ❑ **ape oil** *n.* [? SE *ape* or it makes the drinker GO APE *under* APE *adj.*, although this predates] [1940s] (*US*) liquor.

IN PHRASES

❑ **black ape** *n.* [1920s] (*US*) a derog. term for a black person. ❑ **brush ape** *n. see under* BRUSH *n.*[3]. ❑ **bush ape** *n.* [1940s+] **1** (*Aus./US*) a peasant. **2** (*Aus.*) a rural worker. **3** (*Aus.*) an itinerant fruit-picker, usu. in Queensland. ❑ **cliff ape** *n.* [1910s+] (*US*) a rough, thuggish man. ❑ **like a striped-assed ape** *adv. see* LIKE A BLUE-ARSED BABOON *under* BABOON *n.* ❑ **park ape** *n.* [? ref. to apes in Central Park Zoo, New York City] [1940s+] (*US black*) an extremely unattractive and very dark-skinned person. ❑ **rock ape** *n.* [1970s+] (*Aus.*) **1** a derog. term for a black person. **2** anyone viewed with disfavour, e.g. a teenager.

ape *adj.* **1** [1910s] (*US campus*) drunk. **2** [1920s] a generic term meaning aggressive and dangerous. **3** [1950s+] (*also* **ape wild**) mad, crazy.

DERIVATIVES

❑ **apey** *adj.* [1950s+] (*US*) crazy, unstable.

IN COMPOUNDS

❑ **apeshit** *see* separate entries.

IN PHRASES

❑ **go ape** *v.* [1950s+] (*orig. US*) to lose control, esp. of one's temper. ❑ **go ape for** *v.* (*also* **go ape over**) [1960s+] to be obsessed with.

ape *v.* (*also* **ape out**) [1940s+] (*US*) to lose control, to act in a wild manner.

ape-leader *n.* [SE *lead apes in hell*, to become an old maid] [mid-17C–mid-19C] an old maid.

aperner *n. see* APRONER *under* APRON *n.*

apeshit *n.* [APESHIT *adj.* (1)] [1970s+] (*US*) a psychotic.

apeshit *adj.* [APE *adj.*] **1** [1950s+] (*orig. US black*) berserk, mad, crazy, extremely upset. **2** [1970s+] sexually obsessed; usu. as *apeshit for/over*. **3** [1980s] (*US campus*) drunk.

IN PHRASES

❑ **go apeshit** *v.* [1950s+] (*orig. US*) to lose control, esp. of one's temper.

aphrodisiacal tennis court *n.* [euph. coined by Britain's first translator of Rabelais, the Scot Sir Thomas Urquhart (1611–60)] [17C] the vagina.

Apollo play *n.* [the Apollo Theater, 125 St, Harlem] [1940s–70s] (*US black*) putting on an act.

apostle *n.* [ety. unknown; ? the drug shows the way to a 'better life'] [1930s] (*US Und.*) a pellet of opium prepared for smoking.

Apostle's Grove *n.* [pun; the area was well known for its up-market courtesans and 'kept women'] [mid-19C–1910s] St John's Wood, London NW8.

apostle's pinch *n.* [? fig. link to APOSTLE'S GROVE *n.*] [20C+] a pinch on the buttocks.

apostrophe *n.* [euph.] [1910s] (*Aus.*) an obscenity.

apothecary's bill *n.* [stereotyping of an apothecary as grasping] [late 18C–early 19C] a substantial bill.

appetizer *n.* [1970s+] (*US gay*) the first sexual partner of many encounters in the same day.

appie *n. see* APPY *n.*

applause *n.* [pun on CLAP *n.*] [1990s+] (*US black*) gonorrhoea.

Apple *n.* [abbr. BIG APPLE *n.*] **1** [1930s–40s] (*US black*) Harlem, NYC. **2** [1940s] (*US black*) a large Northern city. **3** [1940s–50s] the earth, the universe. **4** [1940s+] (*orig. US jazz*) usu. *the Apple*, New York City.

apple *n.*[1] **1** [late 19C+] a person. **2** [1920s+] a foolish person, a 'sucker'. **3** (*US*) in uses based on the shape. (**a**) [1920s] a ball. (**b**) [1960s] the head. **4** [1950s] (*US Und.*) (*also* **big apple, top apple**) an important person. **5** [1960s+] (*US black*) the vagina [note 17C *apple*, a woman and/or her virginity (*see* Williams I 28–9), although that APPLES *n.* (1) orig. meant breasts;

an apple is also something to EAT *v.* (4)]. **6** in uses based on the colour green. (**a**) [1960s–70s] (*US black*) money. (**b**) [2000s] (*N.Z.*) NZ$100. **7** in uses based on the colour red. (**a**) [1970s+] a derog. term for a Native American who is condemned as insufficiently nationalistic, i.e. 'red on the outside but white within'. (**b**) [1980s] (*drugs*) any pill capsule coloured red. **8** [1980s] (*drugs*) anyone who does not use drugs.

IN COMPOUNDS

▫ **applehead** *n.* [-HEAD *sfx* (1)] [1910s+] (*US*) a fool. ▫ **apple-monger** *n.* [-MONGER *sfx* + play on SE *apple-monger*, a dealer in fruit, i.e. 'ripe' females] [18C] a pimp.

SE in slang uses

IN COMPOUNDS

▫ **apple-cart** *n.* [pun on the SE, a *cart* for carrying *apples*; there is no connection, despite appearances and a ref. in Bee, to the joc. SE phr. *upset the applecart*, which refers directly to the SE. However, the phr. *down with his apple-cart!* knock or throw him down! (Grose 1788, *Lex. Bal.*, Hotten 1864), seems to suggest a human rather than a vegetable image] [late 18C+] the human body. ▫ **apple-dumpling shop** *n.* [resemblance to SE *apple dumplings*] [late 18C–1920s] the female breasts. ▫ **apple-guard** *n.* [it protects the adam's apple] [late 19C] (*UK Und.*) a scarf and tie. ▫ **apple-john** *n.* [SE *apple-john*, a kind of apple said to keep for two years and to have reached perfection when shrivelled and withered] [late 16C–early 17C] a foolish and prob. impotent old man. ▫ **apple knock/knocker** *see* separate entries. ▫ **apple-picker** *n.* [var. on APPLE-KNOCKER *n.*; their stereotyped occupation] [1910s] (*US*) a fool, an unsophisticated person, a country person. ▫ **apple pie** *see* separate entries. ▫ **apple polish/polisher** *see* separate entries. ▫ **apple sauce** *see* separate entries. ▫ **apple-shaker** *n.* [mid–late 19C] (*US*) a rural, unsophisticated person. ▫ **apple shine/shiner** *see* separate entries. ▫ **apple-squeezer** *n.* [1930s] (*US*) a rural, unsophisticated person. ▫ **apple squire** *n.* [poss. f. APPLES *n.* (1) + SE *squire*, mocking the esquire or the 'country squire'; cf. KNIGHT OF THE... *n.* and its combs.] [16C–19C] **1** a pimp. **2** a kept man. ▫ **apple tart** *see* separate entries.

IN PHRASES

▫ **apples to ashes** *n.* [cognate with 'one rotten apple'] [late 19C–1900s] (*US*) an absolute certainty. ▫ **apple up** *v.* [the image of handing up an apple to teacher] [1960s] (*US*) to toady, to curry favour. ▫ **for sour apples** *adv.* [1910s–60s] (*US*) a general intensifier, meaning 'at all'; usu. in negative, *not for sour apples*, not at all; often *not like for sour apples*, to have no interest in whatsoever. ▫ **get the apple** *v.* [? the fig. 'sourness'] [1970s] (*US*) to blunder, to make mistakes. ▫ **punch the apple** *v.* [1960s+] to masturbate. ▫ **sad apple** *n.* [1910s–40s] **1** (*US*) (*also* **sad bird**) a contemptible person. **2** a pessimist. **3** a pitiable person. ▫ **smart apple** *n.* [20C+] (*US*) a bright, intelligent person. ▫ **square apple** *n.* [SQUARE *adj.* (10)] [1930s–50s] (*US Und.*) an innocent, a naïve, gullible individual. ▫ **wise apple** *n.* [1940s+] (*US*) one who is too clever for their own good.

IN EXCLAMATIONS

▫ **down with his apple-cart!** *see* DOWN *adj.*[1]. ▫ **tough apples!** [? euph. or abbr. *ROAD APPLE under* ROAD *n.*] [1970s+] (*US*) a response indicating a lack of sympathy with the speaker.

apple *n.*[2] [rhy. sl.; *apple core* = SCORE *n.*[2] (1)] [1990s+] **1** (*US black/drugs*) heroin. **2** (*UK prison*) the situation, the 'score'.

apple *n.*[3] [2000s] (*N.Z.*) courage.

apple *n.*[4] *see HORSE APPLE under* HORSE *n.*

apple and pip *v.* [rhy. sl.] **1** [late 19C+] to sip. **2** [1960s+] to urinate [= SIP *v.*[1]].

apple-blossom two-step *n.* [? play on *sour-apple quickstep*; one of many sl. terms for diarrhoea that pun words for dancing/movement (i.e. SE *trot*) on TROTS *n.*] [1960s+] diarrhoea, often contracted on a foreign holiday.

apple core *n.* [rhy. sl. = SCORE *n.*[1]] [1950s+] £20.

apple-core *v.* [rhy. sl. = SCORE *v.* (3)] [2000s] to seduce.

apple cucumber *n.* [1990s+] (*Aus. Und.*) the murder or kidnapping of a target by using a close friend or family member as an unwitting facilitator.

apple fritter *n.* [rhy. sl.] [1920s+] bitter beer.

apple fritter *adj.* [rhy. sl.] [2000s] emotionally bitter.

applejack *n.*[1] [1950s–60s] (*US black*) a generic name for a dance, esp. the current vogue step.

applejack *n.*[2] [ext. of APPLE *n.*[1] (3b)] [1970s] (*US black*) a large-brimmed, oversized hat in 1930s–40s style.

applejack *n.*[3] [rhy. sl. = CRACK *n.*[7] (1)] [1980s+] (*drugs*) crack cocaine.

apple knock *v.* [APPLE-KNOCKER *n.*] [1940s] to act the yokel, to behave in an unsophisticated manner.

apple-knocker *n.* [SAmeE *apple-knocker*, a fruit-picker; ult. origin may be in New York City, referring to the up-state, rural areas with their many apple orchards] **1** [1910s+] (*US*) a rural, unsophisticated person. **2** [1920s+] (*US tramp*) an apple picker. **3** [1930s–40s] a fool.

apple pie *n.*[1] [rhy. sl.] **1** [1930s] (*US Und.*) an eye. **2** [1940s+] the sky.

apple pie *n.*[2] [1950s] (*US prison*) a pretty, young (prison) homosexual.

apple pie *adj.* [abbr. APPLE-PIE ORDER *n.*] [20C+] (*US*) neat, tidy, perfect; in fig. use, in the image of trad., conservative American values embodied by 'Mom's apple-pie'.

apple-pie order *n.* [ety. unknown. Such suggestions that exist include a corruption of Fr. *cap à pie* (head to foot), the arrangement of the ingredients of an apple pie as they are laid neatly in a dish, and a corruption of *alpha-beta*, esp. as in the nursery rhyme that runs 'A ate it, B bit it, C cut it, D divided it...'. Perhaps the most acceptable is that proposed in *Brewer's Dict. of Phrase and Fable* (1995): f. Fr. *nappe plié*, folded linen, which may also give the practical joker's 'apple-pie bed'] [late 18C+] neatness, tidiness.

apple-pips *n.* [rhy. sl.] [20C+] the lips.

apple polish *v.* [backform. f. APPLE-POLISHER *n.*] [1930s+] (*orig. US*) to curry favour, to toady.

apple-polisher *n.* (*also* **apple-pusher, -washer**) [the image suggests that the apple being polished is that presented to the teacher by the class goody-goody] [1920s+] (*orig. US*) a toady, a sycophant.

apples *n.* **1** [17C+] the female breasts [the rounded shape; the term has survived but became more a euph. than sl. by 20C]. **2** [19C+] the testicles.

IN PHRASES

▫ **like two apples in a bag** *adv.* [1950s+] (*orig. US*) a ref. to well-formed buttocks, irrespective of sex. ▫ **love apples** [note Fr. *pomme d'amour*, Ger. *liebesapful*, the fruit of the tomato] [19C; 1980s+] the testicles.

apples *adj.* [APPLE-PIE ORDER *n.* or rhy. sl. APPLES AND SPICE *adj.*; although primarily assoc. with Aus., *apples* is used by the residents of Brooklyn, New York, to mean the same thing] [1940s+] (*Aus./N.Z.*) satisfactory, as required; esp. in phr. *she'll be apples*, it will be fine.

apples (and pears) *n.* (*also* **peaches and pears**) [rhy. sl.; note the children's chorus, sung for a skipping game: 'I don't want your apples, / I don't want your pears, / I don't want your sixpence / To kiss me on the stairs'] **1** [mid-19C+] (*also* **apple and pears**) stairs [apple and pears is mid-19C only]. **2** [1970s] (*UK Und.*) in fig. use, an appearance in court [the stairs here are those of the Old Bailey].

apples and rice *adj.* [rhy. sl.] [1940s+] nice, usu. ironic.

apples and spice *adj.* [rhy. sl. = SE *nice*; note APPLES *adj.*] [1940s+] (*Aus.*) satisfactory.

apple sauce *n.*[1] [old joke, poss. orig. in minstrel shows, based on the problem of dividing equally 11 apples among 12 people/horses: answer, one makes applesauce; hugely popular in 1920s, but note George Rector *The Girl from Rector's* (1927): 'There is an expression today sweeping America which I heard Corse Payton use *twenty-five years ago* [italics added] [...] That expression is apple sauce'] **1** [1920s+] (*US*) nonsense, balderdash; anything banal or out of date. **2** [1960s] (*US*) anything easy.

apple sauce *n.*[2] [the old boarding-house trick of serving an excess of cheaply produced apple sauce to mask the deficiencies in the portions and quality of other food] [1920s+] (*orig. US*) flattery, insincere talk, cheek, impudence.

apple sauce *n.*[3] [rhy. sl.] [2000s] (*Aus.*) a horse.

apple sauce *v.* [APPLE SAUCE *n.*[2]] [1960s] (*US*) to take advantage of, to flatter.

applesauce! *excl.* [APPLE SAUCE *n.*[1]] [late 19C–1970s] (*US*) rubbish! piffle! an excl. of horror.

apple shine *v.* [var. on APPLE POLISH *v.*] [1930s–60s] to toady, to curry favour.

apple shiner *n.* [var. on APPLE-POLISHER *n.*] [1930s–60s] a toady, a sycophant.

apple tart *n.* (*also* **lemon tart**) [rhy. sl. = FART *n.* (1)] [20C+] (*Aus./Irish*) a breaking of wind.

apple tart *v.* [rhy. sl. = FART *v.* (1)] [20C+] (*Aus./Irish*) to break wind.

apply *v.*

SE in slang uses

IN PHRASES

❑ **apply a crimp** *v.* see *PUT A CRIMP IN(TO) under* CRIMP *n.*[1]. ❑ **apply lawyer foot** *v.* [the image is of a foot that, like a lawyer, helps one 'get away'] [1950s] (*W.I.*) to run away. ❑ **apply lip gloss** *v.* [the image of vaginal secretions coating the labia] [1980s+] of a woman, to masturbate. ❑ **apply the acid** *v. see PUT THE ACID ON under* ACID *n.*[2].

appo *n.* [abbr.] [1990s+] an *app*lication form (for a job).

appy *n.* (*also* **appie**) [abbr.] [1980s+] (*S.Afr.*) an *app*rentice.

apricock water *n.* [16C–18C sp. of SE *apricot*] **1** [early 18C] apricot ale. **2** [early–mid-18C] gin.

apricot (and peach) *n.* [rhy. sl.] [1990s+] the beach.

apricots *n.* [the shape] [1960s–80s] (*Aus.*) the testicles.

April fool copper *n.* **1** [1950s] (*US Und.*) a small-town police officer; a private detective; a badly dressed police officer. **2** [1990s+] (*US prison*) a prison guard.

April fools *n.* [rhy. sl.] **1** [late 19C+] tools; usu. implements for burglary. **2** [20C+] stool(s) (for sitting). **3** [1930s+] football pools.

April gentleman *n.* [the popularity of spring weddings] [late 16C] a newly married man.

April in Paris *n.* [rhy. sl. = ARRIS *n.*] [2000s] the buttocks, the behind.

April showers *n.* [rhy. sl.] [20C+] flowers.

apron *n.* **1** [1920s] a wife, a woman, esp. when used generically. **2** [1920s–50s] (*US*) a bartender.

SE in slang uses

DERIVATIVES

❑ **aproneer** *n.* [the aristocratic Cavaliers made this contemptuous link between 'trade' (symbolized by a worker's apron) and their parliamentary rivals] **1** [mid-17C] a Roundhead. **2** [mid-17C–early 18C] a shopkeeper. ❑ **aproner** *n.* (*also* **aperner, apron-man**) [his usu. blue SE *apron*] [early–mid-17C] a publican; one who serves alcohol.

IN COMPOUNDS

❑ **apron and gaiters** *n.* (*also* **gaiters**) [metonymy, i.e. his vestments] [late 19C–1910s] a bishop, a dean. ❑ **apron husband** *n.* [metonymic use of SE *apron* = woman + *husband*] [early 17C] a man who is seen as involving himself excessively in his wife's business. ❑ **apron preacher** *n.* [mid-17C] a lay preacher. ❑ **apron-rogue** *n.* [a play on SE synon. *apron-man*] [mid-17C] a labourer, an artisan. ❑ **apron squire** *n.* [metonymic use of SE *apron* = woman + SQUIRE *n.* (2)] [late 16C] a pimp. ❑ **apron-stringed** *adj.* [1950s] of a man, henpecked by a woman. ❑ **apron-string hold** *n.* (*also* **apron-string tenure**) [late 17C–early 19C] an estate that a man holds only during the lifetime of his wife. ❑ **apron-up** *adj.* [the use of an apron to hide a pregnancy, also f. the inevitable raising of the apron's profile as the foetus grows] [late 18C–19C] pregnant. ❑ **apron-washings** *n.* [image of a brewery worker wringing out his beer-soaked apron] [1900s] porter.

IN PHRASES

❑ **blue-apron** *n.* (*also* **green apron**) [his 'uniform'] [late 17C–mid-19C] a tradesman. ❑ **green apron** *n.* [female Quaker preachers wore a *green apron*] [mid-17C–mid-18C] a lay preacher. ❑ **have a smell of the barman's apron** *v.* (*also* **have a sniff..., have a whiff..., ...of the barmaid's apron**) [metonymy, i.e. the garment he or she wears] [1920s+] to be drunk. ❑ **tied to someone's apron-strings** *adj.* [earlier use of *APRON-STRING HOLD* above, property owned by the wife] [mid-18C+] dominated by one's wife, or mother. ❑ **want an apron** *v.* [an era when workmen wore some form of apron – before the modern overall – while at work] [late 19C] to be out of work. ❑ **white apron** *n.* [the SE *white apron* that was recognized as a prostitute's 'uniform'; note D'Urfey, *Pills to Purge Melancholy* (1719): 'And first for those ladies that walk in the Night, / Their Aprons and handkerchiefs they should be White'; the aim was 'the better to be seen'] [late 16C–mid-17C] a prostitute.

aqua *n.* [Ital. *acqua*, Ling. Fr. *akwa*] [mid-19C–1960s] water.

aqua lung *n.* [SE 'a portable diving apparatus consisting of containers of compressed air...which feed air automatically through a valve and mouthpiece to the diver as he requires it' (*OED*)] [1980s+] (*US drugs*) a long pipe, which is placed in a bucket of water to cool the smoke.

A.R. *n.* [abbr.] [1970s] (*Can. Und.*) an *a*rmed *r*obbery.

A-rab *n. see* AYRAB *n.*

arab *n.* [orig. 'Arab of the streets', 'city Arab' f. the derog. stereotype of Middle Eastern Arabs as nomadic] **1** [mid-19C–1900s] (*US*) any wild or excitable looking person. **2** [mid-19C+] a street urchin. **3** [20C+] (*US*) a derog. term for a Jew [coined by *Variety* magazine writer Jack Conway c.1925]. **4** [1930s–40s] (*US*) a street peddler. **5** [1950s] (*US*) a street bookmaker, an illicit bookmaker.

arab *v.* [ARAB *n.* + negative racial stereotype] **1** [20C+] (*US*) to sell or peddle on the streets. **2** [1950s] to work as a street bookmaker.

arabber *n.* (*also* **ayraba**) [ARAB *n.*] **1** [20C+] a street urchin. **2** [1940s+] a peddler.

arab's knees *n.* [rhy. sl.] [2000s] (*Irish*) keys.

-arama *sfx see* -ORAMA *sfx.*

arbor vitae *n.* [Lat. *arbor vitae*, the tree of life; the SE use refers to various evergreen trees] [18C–19C] the penis.

arbour *n.* [SE *arbour*, a shady retreat] [late 19C] the vagina.

Arby's *adj.* [i.e. *Arby's* fast food franchise, purveyors of roast beef sandwiches, thus play on MEAT *n.* (3)] [2000s] (*US black*) of a woman, sexually experienced, used as a derog.

Arch, the *n.* [abbr.] [1950s+] Marble *Arch*, London, W1.

Archbishop Laud *n.* [rhy. sl.; the term (used in Cook, *The Crust on its Uppers*, 1962) may, like a number of similar citations, be a nonce-word; ult. William *Laud* (1573–1645), *Archbishop* of Canterbury] [1960s] fraud.

arch-duke *n.* [? a specific archduke. *DSUE* suggests the Duke in Shakespeare's *Measure for Measure* (1604), who is 'certainly eccentric enough to serve as an archetype'] [late 18C–19C] a comical or eccentric person.

archer *n.* [a sum of £2000, the disputed payment of which formed the basis of the libel case brought in 1987 against the *Daily Star* newspaper by the writer Jeffrey *Archer* (now Lord Archer, b.1940)] [1990s+] £2,000.

archer up *n.* [the champion jockey Fred *Archer* (1857–86) and thus phr. 'Archer is up in the saddle', which, to betting men, more than likely meant a winning horse] [late 19C] a certainty.

archie *n.* (*also* **archy**) [proper name, seen as upper-class] [late 19C] (*Aus.*) a young station-hand, prob. a well-connected young man out from the UK.

architorture *n.* [perversion of SE] [1990s+] (*US campus*) a course in architecture.

archives *n.* [1990s+] (*US campus*) a thing of the past; usu. in phr. *I'm archives*, goodbye, I'm leaving.

archy *n.* see ARCHIE *n.*

arctic *adj.* [SE *arctic* conditions, extremely cold] [1980s] (*US campus*) of a person, emotionally chilly, very distant.

around the world *n.* (*also* **around the horn, ...universe**) [the tongue 'travels' around the body; usu. used by a prostitute as part of the 'menu' of paid services she can offer] [1930s+] licking and sucking the partner's body, incl. the genitals and sometimes the anus; thus halfway around the world, fellatio and licking of the anus only.

arrest *v.* [SE *arrest*; note 'fashion police', journalists and other style-makers who determine what is and is not fashionable] [1980s] (*US campus*) to accuse another of dressing unfashionably, usu. behind their back.

arrested by the bailiff of marshland *phr.* [ague, a malarial fever, can be caused by damp conditions] [late 17C–19C] stricken with ague.

arrested by the white serjeant *phr.* [late 18C–mid-19C] said of a man who has been fetched out of the tavern by his wife.

'arrico veins *n.* [mispron. + ? a pun on Fr. *haricot verts*, green beans] [late 19C–1900s] varicose veins.

arries *n.*

(IN PHRASES)

❑ **give someone the 'arries** *v.* [? fig. use of ARRIS *n.*] [1980s] to get rid of.

'arriet *n. see* 'ARRY/'ARRIET *n.*

arris *n.* (*also* **ari, aris, arras, arry, harris**) [abbr. of ARISTOTLE *n.*] **1** [late 19C+] a bottle. **2** [1950s+] the buttocks, the behind.

arrive at the end of the sentimental journey *v.* [literary euph.; the conclusion of Laurence Sterne's *Sentimental Journey* (1768), in which the narrator obviously retires to bed with a chambermaid] [late 19C–1910s] of a man, to have sexual intercourse; one of many euph. terms for sexual intercourse.

arrow *n.* [late 19C+] a dart; thus *the arrows game*, darts.

arry *n. see* ARRIS *n.*

'Arry/'Arriet *n.* [popular proper name] [late 19C–1920s] the generic Cockney man or woman.

(DERIVATIVES)

❑ **'Arrydom** *n.* the world of the typical Cockney costermonger. ❑ **'Arryish** *adj.* typical of a coster.

(IN COMPOUNDS)

❑ **'Arry's worrier** *n.* a concertina.

(IN PHRASES)

❑ **go 'arry and 'arrieting** *v.* to go out on an excursion.

arsapeek *adj.* [1910s] (*Aus.*) upside down.

arse *see also under* ASS and its combs.

arse *n.* [note also US spelling ASS *n.* (although this appears increasingly in UK in late 1990s+) is often interchangeable. In combs., both spellings have been included at the same headword, unless usage is nation-specific, where the relevant sp. has been used. The two spellings are synon. but it should be noted that Shakespeare opts for *ass*, often in a punning context, on several occasions. *Arse* was SE at coinage, but it moved gradually into sl. Its sources include a variety of words found in several Teutonic and Scandinavian languages. The nearest relation is the German *arsch*, and there are definite links back to the Greek *orros* and *orsos*. In English it dates at least to 1000, when it is spelt *ars, ears* or *ars*. The modern sp. appears *c.*1300. Once rendered taboo, *arse* was to be resisted in polite conversation and printed only after the exclusion of crucial consonants, typically by Grose, who prefers *a–e* to the full-blown word. It remained off-limits, at least in print, until 1930, when Frederic Manning used it in full in his memoir of World War I, *Her Privates We* (itself a slightly bawdy pun). Since then the word has become relatively acceptable, and such phrs. as *ARSE ABOUT under* ARSE V. or *NOT KNOW ONE'S ARSE FROM ONE'S ELBOW* below, while not yet SE, are as much colloq. as sl. That said, *arse/ass*, remains one of those 'filthy words' cited in 1978 by the US Federal Communications Commission as indecent, if not actually obscene] **1** [late 14C+] the buttocks. **2** in a sexual context. (**a**) [16C+] the vagina; occas. the penis. (**b**) [1990s+] (*orig. US/Aus.*) sexual conquests; thus generic for a woman when viewed purely as a sex object; often as *bit of arse*. **3** [early 17C+] of an object, the rear. **4** [mid-18C+] used generically to mean one's person, one's body. **5** [1930s+] an unpleasant person, esp. a fool, an idiot. **6** [1930s+] (*Aus.*) a worthless, unpleasant place. **7** [1940s+] (*orig. Aus.*) in fig. senses. (**a**) brazen effrontery [punning on SE *cheek*/CHEEK *n.*[2]]. (**b**) luck. (**c**) courage. **8** [1950s+] (*Aus.*) (*also* **big A**) as *the arse*, dismissal, occas. general rejection; usu. in phr. *get/give the arse*, to be dismissed, to dismiss. **9** [1940s+] a comparative intensifier, e.g. *cold as arse*. **10** [1960s+] (*W.I.*) an unspecified thing.

(DERIVATIVES)

❑ **arseness** *n.* [sfx *-ness*, state or condition] [20C+] (*W.I., Trin./Tob.*) wilful stupidity. ❑ **arser** *n.* [20C+] (*orig. hunting/riding*) a fall on one's behind. ❑ **arsewise** *adj.* [SE *wise*; used as a generic negative] [1990s+] absurd, ludicrous, wrong. ❑ **arsewise** *adv.* [SE *wise*; used as a generic negative] [1990s+] back-to-front.

(IN COMPOUNDS)

pertaining to sycophancy

❑ **arse crawl** *v.* (*also* **crawl up someone's arse**) [CRAWL *v.*[1] (1)] [late 19C+] to toady to, to act as a sycophant. ❑ **arse-crawler** *n.* [1990s+] a sycophant. ❑ **arse creep** *v.* (*also* **creep up someone's arse**) [CREEP *v.* (1)] [1940s+] to toady to. ❑ **arse-creeper** *n.* [1990s+] a sycophant.

adjectival or adverbial uses

❑ **arse-high** [early 18C] short. ❑ **arsepants** [1950s] in a suspicious or contemptuous manner. ❑ **arse-splitting** [2000s] a general intensifier: extreme, very great. ❑ **arse up** [20C+] head-over-heels. ❑ **arse upwards** [getting up from a fall in this manner was believed to be lucky] **1** [17C+] lucky, fortunate; often as *rise/raise arse upwards*, to be lucky; thus the punning *Mr R. Suppards*, a very lucky man. **2** [1990s+] easily.

general uses

❑ **arseache** *n.* **1** [1950s+] (*Aus./US*) a general insult. **2** [1990s+] a bad temper. ❑ **arse-alight** *n.* [SE *alight*, i.e. flames come out of its behind] [1940s] a German WW2 V-2 rocket. ❑ **arse bandit** *n. see* separate entry. ❑ **arse-bender** *n. see* ARSE BANDIT *n.* ❑ **arse-bollocks** *n.* [1990s+] a term of abuse. ❑ **arse-cabbage** *n.* [f. the site and the physical appearance] [1990s+] haemorrhoids. ❑ **arse-cooler** *n.* [mid–late 19C] a bustle on a woman's dress. ❑ **arse-end** *n. see* separate entry. ❑ **arse-grapes** *n.* [1990s+] haemorrhoids. ❑ **arsehole** *see* separate entries. ❑ **arse jockey** *n.* [SE *jockey*/JOCKEY *n.*[2] (1)] [1990s+] (*UK juv.*) a male homosexual. ❑ **arse-kicker** *n.* **1** [1960s+] a successful seducer. **2** [1990s+] an aggressive, violent person; also in fig. use, an overbearing, menacing person. ❑ **arse-lick** *see* separate entries. ❑ **arsenuts** *n.* [1990s+] (*UK juv.*) faecal matter found clinging to the anal hairs and buttock cleft. ❑ **arse-opener** *n.* [late 19C+] the penis. ❑ **arse paper** *n.* (*also* **ass paper**) **1** [1930s+] (*N.Z./US*) lavatory paper. **2** [2000s] (*N.Z.*) in fig. use, a despicable individual or object. ❑ **arsepapered** *adj.* [fig. 'thrown away'] [1980s] (*Aus.*) ignored. ❑ **arsepiece** *n.* [1990s+] a general term of derision. ❑ **arse-piss** *n.* [PISS *n.* (1)] [1990s+] diarrhoea. ❑ **arse poker** *n.* [play on SE *poker* = game/phallic implement] [1980s] (*UK gay*) anal intercourse. ❑ **arse rugs** *n.* [SE *rug*, a coarse material used as a cloak] [1900s] trousers. ❑ **arse-shagger** *n.* [SHAGGER *n.*[1] (1)] [1990s+] a male homosexual; a sodomite. ❑ **arse-stabber** *n.* [1990s+] a sodomite. ❑ **arse-strings** *n.* [late 16C] a metaphorical part of the body, holding the buttocks in place. ❑ **arse wedge** *n.* [late 19C] the penis. ❑ **arse-wipe/-wiper** *see* separate entry. ❑ **arse-worm** *n.* [late 17C–early 18C] a diminutive person.

(IN PHRASES)

meaning back-to-front or head-over-heels

❑ **arse about face** [late 19C+] back-to-front, in confusion. ❑ **arse over apex** [1920s+] head-over-heels. ❑ **arse over appetite** (*also* **ass over appetite**) [1930s+] head-over-heels (cf. *END OVER APPETITE under* END *n.*). ❑ **arse over Charlie** [1950s] head-over-heels. ❑ **arse over ears** [1980s+] completely. ❑ **arse over head** [1920s+] head-over-heels. ❑ **arse over kick** [1920s+] (*Irish*) head-over-heels. ❑ **arse over kite** (*also* **a over k**) [northern UK dial. *kite*, the stomach] [1960s+] (*N.Z.*) head-over-heels. ❑ **arse over teakettle** (*also* **arse over kettle, ass over kettle/teakettle, tail over teakettle**) [1940s+] head-over-heels. ❑ **arse over tip** (*also* **ass over tip**) [euph. for TIT *n.*[2] (1)] [1920s+] head-over-heels. ❑ **arse over tit** (*also* **a over t,**

ass over elbow, ass over tit(s) [TIT *n.*^{2} (1)] [1910s+] head-over-heels. ❑ **arse over turkey** [late 19C–1920s] head-over-heels.

comparatives

❑ **arse like a working bullock** [2000s] (*N.Z.*) having large buttocks. ❑ **more arse than a paddock-full of cows** [sense 7a above] [1990s+] (*Aus.*) a phr. used of one who is very cheeky. ❑ **more arse than a toilet seat** (*also* **more arse than a married cow playing snooker**) [1940s+] (*orig. US*) of a man, having an active sex life or conspicuous sexual prowess; usu. as *he gets…* or *he has…* ❑ **more arse than class** [sense 7a above] [1970s+] (*Aus.*) more luck or effrontery than style. ❑ **more arse than Jessie** *see* MORE HIDE THAN JESSIE *under* HIDE *n.*

general adjectival or adverbial phrases

❑ **as arse** (*also* **as ass**) [20C+] (*W.I./US*) a general intensifier, e.g. *cold as arse*. ❑ **in one's arse** [1960s–70s] (*US*) nagging. ❑ **on the back of one's arse** [late 19C+] (*Aus.*) penniless, impoverished. ❑ **on the bones of one's arse** [i.e. one's thinness through lack of food] [1990s+] (*Aus./N.Z.*) very poor, impoverished. ❑ **up someone's arse** [1970s+] (*US*) immediately behind and therefore irritating, bothering. ❑ **up one's own arse** [UP *adv.*, i.e. auto-sodomizing] [2000s] self-important. ❑ **up to the arse** (*also* **up to the ass, up to your arse/ass**) [20C+] (*orig. US*) completely overwhelmed by.

implying stupidity

❑ **not know if one's arse was on fire** *v.* [1940s+] (*orig. N.Z.*) to be very stupid. ❑ **not know one's arse from…** *v.* (*also* **not know one's ass from…**) [mid-19C+] to be particularly stupid or ignorant, in var. combs. other than the main ones below; can be used with any n. that springs to mind, e.g. *…from a hot rock, …from an adding machine, …from an avalanche, …from ice cream, …from third base* etc. ❑ **not know one's arse from a hole in the ground** *v.* (*also* **not know one's ass…**) [1930s+] to be particularly stupid. ❑ **not know one's arse from one's elbow** *v.* (*also* **not know one's ass…, not know whether one is one's arsehole or one's elbow**) [late 19C+] to be ignorant, to be stupid.

general phrases

❑ **can't see someone's arse for dust** [late 19C+] a phr. used to describe a speedy departure. ❑ **mine arse on a bandbox** (*also* **my arse on a bandbox**) [SE *bandbox*, a light cardboard box used to contain millinery etc, which would not make a stable seat] [18C–early 19C] a phr. used when something offered is inadequate for the purposes required, meaning 'that won't do'. ❑ **my arse is a red cabbage** [2000s] (*N.Z.*) a dismissive phr. ❑ **my arse is dragging** [1910s+] (*orig. US*) I am totally exhausted. ❑ **neither one's arse nor one's elbow** [1910s+] (*Irish*) neither one thing nor another. ❑ **not a sixpence to scratch one's arse with** [mid-19C+] absolutely impoverished. ❑ **one's arse, be** (*also* **be one's ass**) [i.e. one's ARSE *n.* (1)/ASS *n.* (2) will get 'kicked'] [1940s+] (*orig. US*) to cause one trouble, to lead to inevitable punishment, e.g. *Do that and it's your ass.* ❑ **one's arse makes buttons** *see under* BUTTON *n.*^{1}.

verbs with *one's/someone's*

❑ **bring one's arse to an anchor** [late 18C–mid-19C] to sit down. ❑ **carry one's arse** (*also* **carry one's ass**) [1970s+] (*US/W.I., Bdos/Trin.*) to leave, to run off. ❑ **crawl up someone's arse** *see* ARSE CRAWL above. ❑ **creep up someone's arse** *see* ARSE CREEP above. ❑ **do one's arse** [sense 4 above] [1990s+] (*Aus.*) to bet heavily and unsuccessfuly; to lose all one's money. ❑ **give one's arse a chance** [20C+] a comment aimed at a talkative person; usu. prefaced by *Why don't you shut up and…* ❑ **give one's arse a salad** [early 18C] to have sexual intercourse outdoors. ❑ **give someone the arse** [? turning one's back, and thus one's buttocks, to someone] [1950s+] (*Aus.*) to treat with contempt, to reject. ❑ **give something the arse** [1950s+] to reject something. ❑ **have one's nose up someone's arse** *see under* NOSE *n.* ❑ **kick someone's arse** (*also* **kick the arse out of**) [1990s+] to surpass, to defeat comprehensively. ❑ **kiss someone's arse** *see* separate entry. ❑ **knock someone's arse in** [1940s–70s] (*N.Z.*) to defeat in an argument or a fight. ❑ **lose one's arse** [late 18C–mid-19C] to be careless; usu. in phr. *they'd lose their arse if it were loose.* ❑ **— one's arse off** [1920s+] a general intensifier implying extreme energy, e.g. TEAR ONE'S ARSE OFF below. ❑ **polish one's arse on the top sheet** [late 19C] of a man, to have sexual intercourse (in the 'missionary' position). ❑ **put someone on the arse** [1970s] (*Aus. Und.*) to attack someone verbally. ❑ **shake one's arse** (*also* **shake one's ass**) [1930s+] **1** (*orig. US*) to hurry up. **2** (*US*) (*also* **shake it like a polaroid**) to move vigorously as in sexual intercourse or dancing. ❑ **shut one's arse** (*also* **shut one's ass**) [1940s+] to be quiet; esp. in imper. *shut your arse!* ❑ **take it up the arse** (*also* **take it in the arse, …in the ass, take it up the arsehole, …up the ass, …up the bum**) (*orig. US*) **1** [1940s+] to submit to anal intercourse, also used as an expression of contempt. **2** [1980s+] to be victimized, treated unfairly or harshly. ❑ **take the foot out of one's arse** [1960s] (*US black*) to rid oneself of ill treatment, of victimization, exploitation. ❑ **tear one's arse off** (*also* **tear one's asshole out, tear one's guts out**) [ASSHOLE *n.* (1)/GUT *n.* (1)] **1** [20C+] to work furiously. **2** [1960s+] to do something fast, to run away.

general verbs

❑ **— the arse off** (*also* **— the ass off**) [1960s+] a general intensifier implying energy, usu. sexual, e.g. SCREW THE ARSE OFF *under* SCREW *v.* ❑ **catch arse** [1950s+] (*W.I.*) to find it hard to make enough money to live. ❑ **die in the arse** [1970s+] (*Aus.*) to be struck rigid, motionless, usu. through terror. ❑ **get the (big) arse** [1950s+] (*Aus.*) to be dismissed from a job. ❑ **hang an arse** **1** [late 16C–early 18C] to hang back, to be afraid to go forwards. **2** [early 17C] to have large buttocks. ❑ **kick the arse out of** *see* KICK SOMEONE'S ARSE above. ❑ **make an arse of** [1960s+] (*Aus.*) to make something or someone look ridiculous. ❑ **play the arse** [1960s+] (*W.I.*) to play the fool, to trick.

IN EXCLAMATIONS

❑ **devil me arse!** [20C+] (*Anglo-Irish*) a general excl. ❑ **dry your arse!** [2000s] (*Irish*) stop whining! stop complaining! ❑ **in your arse!** **1** [20C+] (*W.I.*) an excl. used to add emphasis to what has been said, synon. with 'by God', 'for God's sake'. **2** [2000s] (*US*) an excl. of dismissal. ❑ **lick my arse!** (*also* **lick me! lick my ass!**) [note later LICK SOMEONE'S ARSE *under* LICK *v.*^{2}] [late 19C+] a dismissive, abusive excl. ❑ **me arse and Katty Barry!** [*Katty Barry* was the keeper of a shebeen, an illicit ale house, in Dublin in 1930s] [2000s] (*Irish*) an excl. of disbelief. ❑ **my arse!** (*also* **my ass!**) [late 17C+] a general excl. of disdain, dismissal, arrogant contempt, e.g. *Are you frightened? Frightened, my arse!*; latterly often implying disbelief of the previous statement. ❑ **my arse to…!** (*also* **my arse for/on…! my ass…!**) [late 17C+] a general excl. of contempt or dismissal. ❑ **no arse!** [20C+] (*W.I.*) a general intensifier, like hell! ❑ **not on your arse!** (*also* **not on your ass!**) [1960s+] no way! on no account! ❑ **what the arse!** (*also* **where the arse! why the arse!**) [1950s] (*UK black*) intensified form of *why the hell!* ❑ **your arse!** (*also* **your hairy arse!**) [1920s+] a dismissive excl. meaning, 'I don't believe you'. ❑ **your face and my arse!** *see* YOUR FACE AND MY ASS! *under* FACE *n.*

arse *v.* [ARSE *n.*] **1** [1950s+] to reverse a vehicle. **2** [1980s] to push, to shove. **3** [1990s+] to drink, to consume. **4** [1990s+] (*Aus.*) to dismiss.

IN PHRASES

❑ **arse about** *v.* **1** [mid-17C; 1920s+] to waste time, to idly wander about. **2** [late 18C–early 19C] to turn round. **3** [1940s+] to fool around. ❑ **arse it** *v.* [1970s+] to leave, to exit. ❑ **arse off** *v.* [late 19C+] to leave quickly. ❑ **arse out** *v.* **1** [late 19C+] to leave quickly. **2** [1950s+] to dismiss from a job. ❑ **arse up** *v.* [20C+] to ruin, to make a mess of; thus intensified as *arse up with care*.

-arse *sfx see* -ARSED *sfx.*

arse bandit *n.* (*also* **arse-bender, ass bandit, anus bandit, bandit**) [ARSE *n.* (1) + -BANDIT *sfx* (2)] [1960s+] a homosexual male.

DERIVATIVES

❑ **arse-banditry** *n.* [2000s] homosexuality; homosexual activities.

arsed *adj.* (*also* **assed**) [ARSE *n.* (1)] **1** [1980s+] bothered, concerned. e.g. *I can't be arsed to do it.* **2** [2000s] fed up.

IN PHRASES

□ **arsed up** *adj.* (*also* **assed up**) [1930s+] confused, mixed up; the mildest of such synons. as *BUGGERED UP under* BUGGERED *adj.*[2].

-arsed *sfx* (*also* **-arse**) [ARSE *n.* (1); the initial citation, before any use of arse became sl., is in Abbot Aelfric's *Glossary*, c.1000, as trans. of the Lat. *tergosus*] **1** [mid-16C+] describing someone's ARSE *n.* (1), usu. the shape or size, e.g. BARE-ARSED *adj.*, HOPPER-ARSED *adj.* **2** [late 17C+] in fig. use, describing the type of person, e.g. HOT-ARSED *adj.*, RAGGED-ARSED *adj.*

arse-end *n.* (*also* **ass-end**) [ARSE *n.* (1) + SE *end*] **1** [1930s+] the end, the rear end, the buttocks. **2** [1940s+] the least desirable piece of. **3** [1940s+] a very unappealing place, particularly one far away from 'civilization'; esp. in phr. *arse-end of the universe, arse-end of nowhere.*

arsehole *see also under* ASSHOLE and combs.

arsehole *n.* [ARSE *n.* (1) + SE *hole*; note Wright, *Vol. Vocabs.*, 1857, citing 14C AS/Lat. vocab., *Arce-hoole, podex*; *see also* ASSHOLE *n.*] **1** [mid-16C+] the anus. **2** [1930s+] (*orig. US*) a general derog. term. **3** [1940s+] (*also* **arsehold**) the end, the back of anything. **4** [1940s+] (*orig. US*) the least appetizing, poorest, most run-down and dangerous area of a city or town or place. **5** [2000s] courage.

DERIVATIVES

□ **arseholed** *adj.* [1940s+] very drunk. □ **arseholey** *adj.* **1** [late 19C+] sycophantic [ARSEHOLE CRAWL *v.*]. **2** [1990s+] a general derog. term. □ **arseholishness** *n.* [2000s] acting like an idiot, being annoying, a general derog.

IN COMPOUNDS

□ **arsehole bandit** *n.* [ext. of ARSE BANDIT *n.*] [1960s+] a homosexual male (cf. *ASSHOLE BANDIT under* ASSHOLE *n.*). □ **arsehole lucky** *adj.* [1950s+] extremely fortunate. □ **arsehole perisher** *n.* [SE *perish*, to suffer the cold] [1900s] a short jacket. □ **arsehole polisher** *n.* [1970s] a sycophant, a toady.

IN PHRASES

□ **arsehole of the universe** *n.* (*also* **arsehole of the world, asshole of creation, ...of the world, ...of the universe**) [note description of Holland as 'the Buttock of the world, full of veins and blood, but no bones in't' in *A Brief Character of the Low Countries* (1660) and Primo Levi's ref. to Auschwitz as *anus mundi*, a Lat. synon.] [late 17C; mid-19C+] applied to anywhere considered especially unpleasant on a global or, hyperbolically, local level. □ **dark as an abo's arsehole** *adj.* [1960s] (*Aus.*) very dark. □ **from arsehole to breakfast time** (*also* **from arsehole to breakfast, ...breakfast table, from haircut to breakfast time**) [late 19C+] **1** all the way, all the time, completely. **2** very unsatisfactory, totally confused, very chaotic. □ **give someone the arsehole** *v.* [2000s] to infuriate. □ **give someone arseholes** *v.* [1960s] (*N.Z.*) to harass, to berate. □ **not know if one's arsehole is bored or punched** *v.* [? engineering use] [1920s+] to be an absolute fool. □ **stupid as arseholes** *adj.* [1920s+] extremely stupid. □ **take it up the arsehole** *v. see TAKE IT UP THE ARSE under* ARSE *n.* □ **talk out of one's arsehole** *v.* [talk through...] [1990s+] to talk nonsense. □ **tear one's arsehole out** *v.* (*also* **tear one's asshole out**) [20C+] to work furiously. □ **up arsehole street** (*also* **in arsehole street**) [1950s+] in difficulties, facing problems. □ **white as midnight's arsehole** *adj.* [mid-16C–mid-17C] absolutely dark, totally black.

IN EXCLAMATIONS

□ **arseholes!** [late 19C+] rubbish! nonsense! □ **my arsehole!** [late 17C+] a general excl. of disdain, dismissal, arrogant contempt.

arsehole *adj.* (*also* **arseholing, arsholes, asshole**) [1930s+] a general adj. of derision.

arsehole *v.* [one is fig. 'kicked' in the ARSEHOLE *n.* (1)] [1960s+] (*Aus.*) to dismiss, to get rid of.

DERIVATIVES

□ **arseholed** *adj.* [1960s] (*Aus.*) dismissed.

arsehole crawl *v.* (*also* **arsehole creep**) [ext. of *ARSE CRAWL under* ARSE *n.*] [late 19C+] to grovel unashamedly, to play the sycophant.

IN COMPOUNDS

□ **arsehole-crawler** *n.* (*also* **arsehole-creeper, arsel-creeper**) [late 19C+] a sycophant; thus a general term of abuse.

arse lick *n.* (*also* **ass lick**) [1970s+] (*orig. US*) a toady, a sycophant, a groveller.

arse-lick *v.* (*also* **ass lick**) [1910s+] to toady, to be sycophantic.

DERIVATIVES

□ **arse-licker** *n.* (*also* **ass-licker, licker**) **1** [1930s+] a toady, a sycophant. **2** [1980s+] a person who licks another's anus for sexual pleasure. □ **arse-licking** *n.* [1910s+] sycophancy, grovelling. □ **arse-licking** *adj.* (*also* **ass-licking, arse-lick**) **1** [1930s+] extremely servile, grovelling. **2** [2000s] exaggerated.

arselins coup *n.* [ARSE *n.* + sfx *-ling*, implying direction + SE *coup*, fall; thus lit. 'falling backwards'] [19C] sexual intercourse.

IN PHRASES

□ **get an arselins coup** *v.* of a woman, to have sexual intercourse.

arsenal *n.* [SE *arsenal*] **1** [1950s] (*US drugs*) a supply of narcotics concealed in the rectum (usu. in some form of metal container) [play on ARSE *n.* (1)]. **2** [1950s] any stock of drugs in one's possession. **3** [1990s+] the genitals.

Arsenal are at home *phr.* [the red-and-white strip worn by Arsenal Football Club] [2000s] used by a (N. London) woman to indicate that she is having a period.

arse over header *n.* [rhy. sl. = *varsovienna*; lit. Fr. *Varsovien*, f. *Varsovie*, Warsaw] [20C+] (*Aus.*) the varsovienne, a dance, ? French origin, resembling some of the Polish national dances.

arsewipe *n.* [ARSE *n.* (1) + SE *wipe*] **1** [1950s+] lavatory paper. **2** [1990s+] a general term of abuse; also used affectionately.

arse-wiper *n.* [predates ARSEWIPE *n.* but same idea] [1920s+] a sycophant.

arsey *adj.* (*also* **arsie, arsy**) [TIN-ARSED *adj.*] **1** [1950s+] (*Aus.*) lucky; occas. as n., a lucky person. **2** *see* ARSIE *adj.*[1].

arsey-boo *phr.* [ARSE *n.* + sfx *-y* + ? BUGGERED *adj.*[2]] [1980s] (*N.Z.*) in a state of chaos; wrong.

arsey-tarsey *v.* [ARSE *n.* (1) + sfx *-y* + redup.] [1910s–20s] (*Aus.*) to fall upside down.

arsey-tarsey *phr.* [ARSEY-TARSEY *v.*] [1980s+] (*N.Z.*) in a mess, incoherent.

arsey-varsey *phr.* (*also* **arsey-versey, arsy-versy, assy-turvy**) [ARSE *n.* (1) + sfx *-y* + redup.; on model of SE *vice-versa*; prior use before mid-16C was SE] **1** [mid-16C+] upside down, topsy-turvy, back-to-front. **2** [late 16C+] head-over-heels; usu. in phr. *fall arsey-varsey*, fall head-over-heels. **3** [mid-17C–early 18C] contrary, perverse, preposterous.

arsie *adj.*[1] (*also* **arsey, arsy**) [ARSE *n.* (5)] [2000s] **1** stupid. **2** upper-class.

arsie *adj.*[2] *see* ARSEY *adj.* (1).

ars musica *n.* [pun on Lat. *ars musica*, the musical art + a second pun on BUMFIDDLE *n.* (2)] [late 18C–19C] the anus, esp. when it breaks wind.

arson *v.* [1970s–80s] (*UK black*) to set alight.

arsy *adj.* **1** *see* ARSEY *adj.* (1). **2** *see* ARSIE *adj.*[1].

arsy-versy *adv. see* ARSEY-VARSEY *phr.*

art *n.* [the image is of an 'old master'] [1980s+] (*US campus*) a thing of the past; thus phr. *I'm art*, goodbye, I'm leaving.

artesian *n.* [orig. a very popular beer brewed with water from a well-known artesian well at Sale, Gippsland, Victoria] [late 19C–1910s] (*Aus.*) beer brewed in Australia.

art fag *n.* [FAG *n.*[5] (1); however, there is no need for the target actually to be gay, the term merely reflects the time-honoured, philistine association of the arts with effeminacy] [1990s+] (*US campus*) one who is overly affected, pretentious or 'arty'.

artful as a (whole) wagon-load of monkeys *adj. see* CUNNING AS A (WHOLE) WAGON-LOAD OF MONKEYS *under* CUNNING *adj.*

artful dodger *n.*[1] [the original *Artful Dodger* appears in Charles Dickens's *Oliver Twist* (1838)] [mid-19C] (*US Und.*) a person who dodges the police by never sleeping in the same place twice.

artful dodger *n.*[2] [rhy. sl.; ult. *see* prev.] **1** [mid-19C+] a lodger [the 'artful' here implies the lodger's trad. interest in his landlady]. **2** [2000s] a penis [= TODGER *n.*].

artful fox *n.* [rhy. sl.] [late 19C–1900s] a box in the theatre.

Arthur *n.* [? the masculine name] [2000s] (*S.Afr. gay*) a heterosexual man.

arthur *n.* [rhy. sl. *J. Arthur Rank*; ult. f. J. Arthur, later Lord Rank (1888–1972), the British flour producer turned film magnate who dominated the British film business during the 1930s–40s] [1970s] a bank.

Arthur Bliss *n. see* JOHNNY BLISS *n.*

Arthur Murray *n. see* RUBY MURRAY *n.*

Arthur Power *n.* [rhy. sl.] [2000s] (*Irish*) a shower.

Arthurs *n. see* UNCLE ARTHUR *n.*

artical *adj.* [var. on HORTICAL *adj.*] [1950s+] (*W.I./UK black teen*) bonafide, genuine, sincere, respected.

artichoke *n.* [like the vegetable, such a woman is supposedly spiky on the outside but still tasty within] **1** [17C–19C] a debauched old woman. **2** [1990s+] the vagina.

artichoke (ripe) *v.* [rhy. sl.] [mid–late 19C] to smoke (a pipe).

article *n.* **1** [late 18C–mid-19C] in pl., breeches, trousers. **2** [late 18C+] a person, often ironically, e.g. 'pretty article'. **3** [early 19C] in pl., a brace of pistols. **4** [early 19C+] a woman. **5** [early 19C+] the vagina. **6** [mid-19C] the penis. **7** [mid-19C+] (*Irish/US*) a creature. **8** [late 19C] in pl., the genitals.

article of virtue *n.* [pun on Fr. *objet de vertu*, a curio, an antique] [mid-19C–1910s] a virgin.

artie *n.* [1970s] (*Aus.*) an artistic person, or one who considers themselves to be so.

artillery *n.* **1** [19C+] (*US*) personal weaponry. **2** [1920s] (*US*) (*also* **field artillery**) the female breasts. **3** [1930s+] (*US drugs*) equipment for injecting drugs [plays on SHOT *n.*[1] (6b)]. **4** [1930s+] (*US*) beans [beans, trad. and physiologically, are equated with the breaking of wind and are thus empowered with 'shooting' ability]. **5** [1970s] the attractive female figure. **6** [1980s+] (*Aus. prison*) cutlery, which when metal doubled as weaponry.

IN PHRASES

❑ **light artillery** *n.* [1930s–50s] (*US drugs*) a hypodermic syringe.

artilleryman *n.* [the 'explosiveness' of his talk and actions] [late 19C–1910s] a drunkard.

artist *n.* **1** [mid-19C+] (*US Und./Irish*) an adroit rogue, usu. a pickpocket, sneak thief or confidence trickster. **2** [late 19C] (*US Und.*) a skilful card-sharp.

-artist *sfx* [note ARTIST *n.* (1)] [late 19C+] (*orig. US/Aus./N.Z.*) a generic term for a person, esp. when cited as an expert or devotee of an activity; usu. in combs., e.g. LEGSHAKE ARTIST *n.*; PISS ARTIST *under* PISS *n.*; TRAPEZE ARTIST *n.*

artiste *n.* [the final 'e' reflects both theatrical use and feminization] [1980s+] (*US gay*) an especially competent fellator.

artsy-craftsy *adj.* [the Arts and Crafts Exhibition Society, founded in London in 1888, but more generally an attack on the perceived failings of those condemned as 'artistic'] [1960s] pretentious, humourless, self-opinionated.

artsy-fartsy *n.* [ARTSY-FARTSY *adj.*] [1980s+] a pretentious person.

artsy-fartsy *adj.* (*also* **artsie-fartsie**) [var. on ARTY-FARTY *adj.*] [1960s+] pretentious.

arty *adj.* [20C+] pretentious.

arty-(and-)crafty *adj.* [for ety. *see* ARTSY-CRAFTSY *adj.*] [1950s+] pretentious, humourless.

arty-farty *adj.* (*also* **arty-tarty**) [FART *n.*] [1950s+] pretentious, overly intellectual or artistic, exhibiting superficial form and little positive content etc.

arty rolla *n.* (*also* **arty roller**) [rhy. sl.] [1910s+] (*Aus.*) a collar.

arvie *n.* [abbr.] [1970s+] (*S.Afr.*) the afternoon; often as *this arvie*, this afternoon.

arvo *n.* (*also* **avvo**) [abbr. SE + -O *sfx* (3)] [1930s+] (*mainly Aus.*) **1** afternoon. **2** afternoon tea.

Ascot races *n.* [rhy. sl.; usu. as 'ascots'] [20C+] **1** the horseraces. **2** braces (US: suspenders).

asexual *adj.* [var. on SE *asexual*, sexless] [1980s+] (*US campus*) uninterested in sex.

ash *n.* [London pron. of HASH *n.*[2]] [1990s+] (*UK black*) hashish.

ash *v.* [1930s+] to drop cigarette or cannabis cigarette ash onto the floor.

ash beans and long oats *n.* (*also* **oats**) [SE *ash(plant)*, a walking-stick] [mid-19C] a beating, a flogging.

ashcan *n.* [SE *ashcan*] (*US*) **1** [1910s] an unpleasant person. **2** [1920s+] a small but powerful firecracker, its explosive effects intensified by the layer of tinfoil in which it is wrapped. **3** [1930s] the buttocks [note CAN *n.*[1] (1b)]. **4** [1930s] the vagina [note CAN *n.*[1] (1a)]. **5** [1930s] a shell; a bomb. **6** [1940s] business, affair. **7** [1950s] a car.

ashcan *v.* (*also* **ashtray**) [i.e. to throw in the SAmE *ashcan*] [1930s+] (*US*) to discard, to throw away.

ash-cat *n.* [UK dial. *ashcat*, anyone, usu. a child, who sits near the fire, poking at the ashes] (*US*) **1** [mid–late 19C] (*also* **ash-cat sam**) a dirty, dishevelled child; thus a general insult irrespective of age. **2** [mid-19C–1900s] a thin, wasted, ragged black person [the tendency of black flesh tones, when unhealthy, to seem grey].

ash-faced *adj.* [the 'grey' skin tone] [1900s] (*US*) having a light complexion, applied to light-skinned blacks.

ash-spots *n.* **1** [1970s] goose pimples. **2** [2000s] (*US black*) lighter spots that appear on one's arms and legs when one gets cold.

ashtray *v. see* ASHCAN *v.*

ashy *adj.* [20C+] (*US black*) pale, ashen-faced.

Asia Minor *n.* **1** [late 19C] Belgravia, London [ext. of SE, i.e. the wealthy Jews who bought houses there]. **2** [late 19C–1910s; 2000s] Kensington and Bayswater, London [early use f. the large population of retired Indian civil servants; modern use refers to the Asian population, whether transient or immigrant].

Asian moll *n. see* JAP MOLL *under* JAP *adj.*

asiatic *n.* [ASIATIC *adj.*] [1940s–50s] (*US*) a crazy person.

asiatic *adj.* [coined by the US Marines whose experiences beneath the Asian sun had driven some of them mad] [1940s+] (*US*) insane, crazy; usu. as *go asiatic*, to go crazy.

ask *n.* [abbr.] [1980s+] (*Aus.*) the cost, the asking price.

SE in slang uses

IN PHRASES

❑ **big ask** *n.* [1980s+] something hard to achieve.

ask *v.*

SE in slang uses

IN PHRASES

❑ **ask cheeks near Cunnyborough** *see under* CHEEKS *n.*[1]. ❑ **ask for a piece of wife** *v.* [20C+] (*W.I.*) to ask a woman to whom one is not married for sex; thus *give wife*, to permit such an adulterous affair. ❑ **ask for it** *v.* ['it' being trouble] [20C+] to act in such a manner that unpleasant consequences will (almost) inevitably follow, to 'ask for trouble'. ❑ **ask for the ring** *v. see under* RING *n.* ❑ **ask me one on sport** [a knowledge of sport being seen as the least 'intellectual' of attainments] [1990s+] used to deflect a question to which the speaker does not know the answer.

IN EXCLAMATIONS

❑ **ask bogy!** [SE *bogy/boggard*, a goblin] [late 18C–early 19C] go to hell! ❑ **ask (me) another!** [late 19C+] a riposte to one who has just recited a riddle or a dated or unfunny joke.

asker *n.* [SE *ask*] [mid-19C+] a beggar.

askew *n. see* SKEW *n.*[1] in ety.

ask my...! *excl.* [late 18C+] a coarse and evasive response, implying the speaker's lack of interest in a statement/question, e.g. *ask mine arse/ass!ask my arse/ass!ask my ballocks!ask my left one!ask my sack!ax my arse!ax my foot!ax my pooper!ax my spiff!*

ask-no-questions *n.* [1950s] (*Aus.*) a euph. for ARSE *n.* (1).

asleep at the switch, be *v.* [railroad jargon 'switch', the points lever] [late 19C+] (*US*) to be inattentive, not concentrating on a task.

asleep at the wheel, be *v.* [motoring imagery] [20C+] to be inattentive, not concentrating on a task.

as much use as... *phr.* used in a variety of phrs. meaning no use whatsoever, e.g.

IN PHRASES

❑ **as much use as my arse** [late 19C+] ❑ **as much use as a (sick) headache** [20C+] ❑ **as much use as a chocolate teapot** [1970s+]

as muck *adv.* [late 19C+] extremely, utterly; either succeeding a pej., e.g. *as sick as muck*, or implying one, e.g. *as rich as muck*.

asoc *n.* (*also* **asocial**) [sociological jargon 'antagonistic to society or social order' + SE *asocial*, inconsiderate of or hostile to other people] [1990s+] (*US Und.*) a child molester.

asparagus *n.* [play on racing tips/asparagus *tip*] [1990s+] (*Aus. racing*) one who is full of ideas on the day's races and suggestions as to possible winners.

aspect *n.* [Ital. *aspetto!* look!] [late 19C–1900s] an amorous glance.

asphalt arab *n.* [SE *asphalt* + ARAB *n.* (2)] [1950s] (*US*) a city person, as nicknamed by a country dweller.

aspinall *n.* [*Aspinall*, the inventor and manufacturer of a variety of oxidized enamel paint] [late 19C–1900s] enamel.

aspro *n. see* ASS PRO *under* ASS *n.*

ass *see also under* ARSE and its combs.

ass *n.* [sense 1 SE *ass*, a donkey; subseq. senses *see also* ARSE *n.*] **1** [early 16C+] an unpleasant person, esp. a fool, an idiot. **2** [mid-16C; mid-18C+] (*US*) the buttocks, the anus. **3** [mid-19C+] (*US*) (in a sexual context) the vagina; occas. the penis. **4** [1940s+] (*US*) used generically to mean one's person, one's body. **5** [1940s+] (*orig. US/Aus.*) sexual conquests; thus generic for a woman when viewed purely as a sex object, often as *a bit of ass*. **6** [1960s+] (*US*) sexual intercourse. **7** [1960s+] (*US*) of an object, the rear. **8** [1990s+] (*US*) an unpleasant or disgusting object. **9** [1990s+] (*US drugs*) the last, and thus least potent, puff on a marijuana cigarette or pipe. **10** [2000s] (*US*) mentality, character, personality. **11** [2000s] essence, being.

DERIVATIVES

❑ **assways** *adj.* (*also* **arseways, ass-to and every whichaway**) **1** [20C+] of sexual intercourse, from the rear. **2** [1920s] head-over-heels. **3** [1930s+] (*US*) skew-whiff, back-to-front; rear, as of a pocket. ❑ **assy** *adj.* **1** [1980s+] (*S.Afr./US gay*) malicious, sarcastic. **2** [2000s] (*US black*) insignificant, second-rate, unimportant.

IN COMPOUNDS

adjectival or adverbial uses

❑ **ass-backwards** (*also* **arse-backwards, ass-backward**) [late 19C+] (*US*) back-to-front; thus fig., in a mess, chaotic. ❑ **ass-bad** *see* BAD-ASS *adj.* ❑ **ass deep** [1950s+] (*US*) **1** very deep; usu. in such phrs. as *ass deep to a tall moose*. **2** totally involved with, with an excessive amount of. ❑ **ass-dragging** [1990s+] (*US*) run-down, worn out. ❑ **assed-out** (*US black*) **1** [1980s+] dead, killed. **2** [1990s+] in a bad situation, down on one's luck. ❑ **ass-frontwards** [1960s] head-over-heels. ❑ **ass-grabbing** (*US*) **1** [1960s] irritating. **2** [1970s] good, exciting. ❑ **ass-high** [late 19C+] (*US*) an unspecified measure of height; usu. as *ass-high to a tall Indian*. ❑ **ass-out** [1990s+] (*US*) **1** at the end of one's tether; beyond effort, without luck. **2** straighforward, easy. **3** without money. ❑ **ass-tight** [1960s] (*US*) **1** of things, very tight. **2** in fig. use, very efficient. **3** of friends, very intimate. ❑ **ass-ugly** [1990s+] (*US*) very unattractive.

general uses

❑ **ass-bag** *n.* [1960s+] (*US*) a derog. term of abuse. ❑ **ass bandit** *n.* [-BANDIT *sfx*] **1** [1950s+] a womanizer, a playboy. **2** *see* ARSE BANDIT *n.* ❑ **ass-belly** *n.* [1970s+] (*US*) a grotesquely fat person. ❑ **ass betting** *n.* [BET ONE'S (SWEET) ASS *v.*] [2000s] (*US prison*) gambling without means of paying back one's losses. ❑ **assbone** *n.* [1970s+] (*US*) the buttocks; also as coccyx in phr. *break one's assbone*. ❑ **ass boy** *n.* [1980s] (*US*) a male homosexual. ❑ **ass-breaker** *n.* (*US*) **1** [1950s] a difficult, boring or exasperating job, problem or situation. **2** [1960s] a nag, a dominating woman, one who destroys the self-confidence of a man. **3** [1960s] a dive in which the diver lands stomach down on the water, rather than cutting through it. **4** [2000s] a thug. **5** [2000s] the penis. ❑ **ass-breath** *n.* [1990s+] (*US*) a derog. term of address. ❑ **ass-bucket** *n.* [1950s] (*US black*) an unpopular or unimportant person. ❑ **assbulb** *n.* [2000s] (*US black*) a lazy person. ❑ **ass burglar** *n.* [1970s+] a male homosexual. ❑ **ass business** *n.* [1960s+] (*US gay*) male homosexual prostitution. ❑ **ass-chewing** *n.* [CHEW (ON) SOMEONE'S ASS *under* CHEW *v.*] [1950s+] (*orig. US milit.*) a scolding, a serious reprimand. ❑ **assface** *n.* [1990s+] (*US campus*) an unpleasant, stupid person. ❑ **ass-fault** *n.* [SE *fault*, a crevice] [1990s+] (*US campus*) **1** the crease between one's buttocks. **2** extreme stupidity. ❑ **ass games** *n.* [1980s+] (*US gay*) a variety of homosexual practices, including anal intercourse and sado-masochism. ❑ **ass gasket** *n.* [SE *gasket*, a thin, flat ring used as a seal between two surfaces] [1990s+] (*US campus*) the paper protector that is placed over a lavatory seat to indicate its sanitized state. ❑ **ass hammer** *n.* [the battering one receives from its seat] [1960s+] (*US campus*) a motorcycle. ❑ **asshead** *n.* (*also* **asshat**) [-HEAD *sfx* (1)] [16C–early 17C; 1960s+] (*US*) a fool; thus adj., *ass-headed*. ❑ **ass-hound** *n.* [-HOUND *sfx*] **1** [1940s] (*US*) a womanizer, a 'skirt chaser'. **2** [1980s+] (*US gay*) one who enjoys anal intercourse and is primarily sexually attracted by the buttocks. ❑ **assload** *n.* [mid-19C; 1950s+] an excess. ❑ **ass magazine** *n.* [2000s] (*US*) a pornographic magazine. ❑ **ass-man** *n.* **1** [1950s+] (*also* **arse-man**) a man who finds a woman's buttocks her most alluring feature. **2** [1960s] a pimp. **3** [1960s+] a womanizer, a successful seducer. **4** [1970s+] (*US gay*) a man who is primarily attracted to the buttocks and enjoys anal intercourse. ❑ **ass-master** *n.* [1990s+] (*US campus*) a general term of abuse. ❑ **ass-off** *n.* [1960s+] (*US campus*) a time-waster. ❑ **ass-out** *n.* [2000s] (*US prison*) an inmate who has neither advantages nor respect. ❑ **ass-pack** *n.* [1950s+] (*US*) a small pouch-like bag strapped around the wearer's waist. ❑ **ass peddler** *n.* [1940s+] (*US*) anyone who sells their body as a prostitute, male or female. ❑ **ass pirate** *n.* (*also* **arse pirate**) [var. on ARSE BANDIT *n.*] [1990s+] a male homosexual. ❑ **ass-poots** *n.* [POOT *n.*[2], the propensity of beans to cause an excess of breaking wind] [1960s] (*US*) beans. ❑ **ass pro** *n.* (*also* **aspro**) [abbr. SE *prostitute/professional*; despite the apparent simplicity of the ety., Hancock, 'Shelta and Polari' (1984), suggests Ling. Fr. *aspro*, money] [1960s+] (*Aus./US*) a male homosexual prostitute. ❑ **ass queen** *n.* [-QUEEN *sfx* (3)] [1980s+] (*US gay*) one whose primary area of sexual interest is the buttocks. ❑ **ass raider** *n.* [1980s+] (*US gay*) **1** a male homosexual. **2** the active partner in anal intercourse. ❑ **ass ranger** *n.* [2000s] (*US*) a homosexual. ❑ **ass-ripper** *n.* **1** [1960s] (*US campus*) a difficult course or examination. **2** [1960s+] (*US*) a dive in which a swimmer jumps, holds his nose and hits the water buttocks-first; the aim – and the result – is to make a big splash. ❑ **ass-scratcher** *n.* (*US*) **1** [1930s] a loafer, an idler. **2** [1970s] something that makes one think; thus adj., *ass-scratching*, thoughtful, cleverly executed. ❑ **ass-sucker** *n.* [late 19C; 1960s+] (*US*) a sycophant, a toady. ❑ **ass-tickler** *n.* [1970s] (*US*) something amusing. ❑ **ass watcher** *n.* [1950s–70s] (*gay*) one who walks the streets looking for a potential sexual partner. ❑ **ass waxing** *n.* [1960s+] (*US*) a thrashing, a beating.

IN PHRASES

adjectival or adverbial uses

❑ **ass-end-backwards** (*also* **ass-end up**) [1960s+] in confusion; back-to-front; upside down; thus defeated. ❑ **ass-end-to** [late 19C–1950s] (*US*) in confusion. ❑ **ass on**

backwards [2000s] drunk. ❑ **ass-side-before** [1960s] head-over-heels, in confusion. ❑ **ass-to-elbow** [1980s] (*US*) extremely crowded. ❑ **off one's ass** [1980s+] (*US campus*) to a very great extent, extremely, usu. ref. to drunkenness. ❑ **on one's ass** (*also* **on one's arse**) **1** [1910s+] (*orig. US*) facing serious problems, esp. financial ones. **2** [1960s] (*US campus*) ill, sick. ❑ **on someone's ass** [1940s+] (*US*) in hot pursuit (of someone); persecuting or harassing someone; see *also* GET (ON) SOMEONE'S ASS below. ❑ **on the balls of one's ass** [synon. with SE *balls* of the feet; ext. of ON ONE'S ASS above] [1970s] (*US*) at the nadir of one's fortunes. ❑ **out on one's ass** (*also* **out on one's arse**) [1950s+] (*orig. US*) ejected unceremoniously, thrown out. ❑ **out the ass** [1980s+] (*US*) excessively. ❑ **up the ass** (*also* **up the arse**) [1950s+] (*US*) to excess, in large amounts. ❑ **up to one's ass** (*also* **up to one's arse**) [1960s+] **1** to an extreme extent. **2** totally involved in, overwhelmed by. ❑ **up to one's ass in alligators** [the saying *when you're up to one's ass ears in alligators, you don't worry about draining the swamp*, often used to imply that one has no time for (long-term liberal) social action, when faced by the immediate threat of criminality] [1980s+] (*US*) in very serious troubles, facing overwhelming problems.

general uses

❑ **how's your ass?** [1950s+] (*US*) a general phr. of greeting. ❑ **one's ass is grass** (*also* **one's arse is grass**) [onomat. redup.] [1960s+] (*orig. US*) one is in severe trouble. ❑ **one's ass is mud** [var. on SE phr. *one's name is mud*] [1930s+] (*US*) one is in danger, one's reputation has been destroyed. ❑ **one's ass sucks wind** [1950s+] (*Aus./US*) **1** (*also* **one's ass sucks blue mud**) one is talking (hysterical) nonsense; esp. as a threat, *your ass will suck wind when/unless…* **2** (*also* **one's ass sucks putty**) one is very angry or disgusted.

verbs with *one's/someone's*

❑ **bet one's (sweet) ass** *see* separate entry. ❑ **bust one's ass** *see under* BUST *v.*[1]. ❑ **bust someone's ass** *see under* BUST *v.*[1]. ❑ **carry someone's ass** [1990s+] to beat someone. ❑ **chap someone's ass** [SE *chap*, to crack the skin] [1960s] (*US*) to annoy, to irritate. ❑ **climb up someone's ass** [1980s] (*US*) to subject to pressure. ❑ **eat someone's ass off/out** [1940s+] (*US*) to criticize severely, to punish heavily; thus n., *ass-eating*. ❑ **fan one's ass** [1960s+] (*US black*) **1** to move one's buttocks in an exaggerated manner with the deliberate intention of attracting one's audience sexually; usu. of homosexuals. **2** to move, to walk. ❑ **fix someone's ass** [1940s+] (*US*) to cause trouble for, to attack, to 'do for'. ❑ **get deep in someone's ass** [1980s] (*US black*) to fight; to beat up. ❑ **get in someone's ass** (*also* **put oneself in someone's face**) [1950s+] **1** (*US*) to annoy, to irritate. **2** (*US black*) to hit. ❑ **get one's ass in a crack** (*also* **get one's tail in a crack/trap, have one's tail in a crack**) [1940s+] (*US*) to get into difficulties, esp. in a criminal context. ❑ **get one's ass in an uproar** *see under* UPROAR *n.* ❑ **get one's ass in a sling** *see under* SLING *n.*[2]. ❑ **get one's ass in(to) gear** *see under* GEAR *n.* ❑ **get one's ass on one's shoulders** [the shrugging gesture, which raises one's shoulders and thus, fig. one's posterior + ? ext. of GET ONE'S ASS UP below] [1940s+] (*US*) to become haughty, angry or excited but with no proper cause, to put on airs. ❑ **get one's ass out of joint** [1950s] (*US*) to lose one's temper. ❑ **get one's ass up** [late 19C; 1970s] (*US*) to annoy, to irritate, to infuriate. ❑ **get one's head out (of one's ass)** *see under* HEAD *n.* ❑ **get (on) someone's ass** (*also* **get (on) someone's arse, …tail**) **1** [1930s+] to pressurize, to harass, to nag. **2** [1950s+] to annoy. ❑ **get out of someone's ass** *see* GET OUT OF SOMEONE'S FACE *under* FACE *n.* ❑ **get up in someone's ass** [1990s+] (*US black*) to assault. ❑ **hang one's ass out** (*also* **hang one's fanny out**) [FANNY *n.*[1] (3)] [1940s+] (*US*) **1** to run a risk, to risk one's life (cf. HAVE ONE'S ASS HANGING OUT below). **2** to work hard. ❑ **hang someone's ass** [HANG *v.*[6] (2)] [1960s+] (*US*) to defeat thoroughly, to trounce. ❑ **have a bug up one's ass** (*also* **have a roach up one's ass**) [1970s+] to be in a bad temper. ❑ **have a foot up one's ass** [1960s] (*US black*) to be treated unfairly, to be victimized. ❑ **have a hair on one's ass** *see* HAVE HAIR ON ONE'S CHEST *under* HAIR ON ONE'S CHEST *n.* ❑ **have a stick up one's ass** (*also* **have an oar up one's ass, …pole…**) [1960s+] to be totally and irredeemably boring; such a stick would render one physically, and thus mentally, rigid. ❑ **have a wild hair up one's ass** (*also* **have a hair up one's ass/prat**) [1950s+] **1** to be in a bad temper. **2** to have an obsession. ❑ **have one's ass hanging out** [1940s+] (*US*) to run a risk, to risk one's life (cf. HANG ONE'S ASS OUT above). ❑ **have one's ass in the wind** (*also* **have one's ass out on a wire**) [1960s+] (*US*) to be exposed to trouble or danger. ❑ **have one's ass working buttonholes** [1960s] (*US*) to work extremely hard. ❑ **have one's nose up someone's ass/arse** *see under* NOSE *n.* ❑ **have someone/something by the ass** *v. see* HAVE SOMEONE BY THE BALLS *under* BALLS *n.* ❑ **have someone's ass** (*also* **have someone's arse**) **1** [1950s+] to reprimand severely, to punish. **2** [2000s] to trick, to 'get (someone) going'. ❑ **hold one's ass** [1960s+] (*US*) to be patient. ❑ **jack it up someone's ass** [1960s+] (*US*) to punish or victimize someone. ❑ **jump through one's ass** [1960s+] (*US*) to panic, to lose control, to be terrified. ❑ **jump (up) someone's ass** (*also* **jump up someone's butt**) [1970s+] (*US*) to attack, verbally or physically. ❑ **keep one's foot in someone's ass** [1960s] (*US black*) to pressurize someone, to treat badly. ❑ **kick someone's ass** **1** [1920s+] (*orig. US*) to give someone a beating, to defeat someone. **2** [1970s+] to exhaust, to wear out. **3** [1970s+] (*US black*) to impress, to overwhelm. **4** [1970s+] (*US black*) to defeat intellectually. ❑ **lose one's ass** [1950s+] (*US*) **1** to fight, to brawl, to argue vehemently. **2** in gambling, to lose heavily. **3** to act irrationally, to lose control of one's life (usu. through drug addiction). ❑ **pull something out of one's ass** [1970s+] (*US*) to invent or produce something, apparently 'by magic'. ❑ **put one's ass in one's hand and screw** [pun on SCREW *v.* (2a)/SCREW *v.* (6a)] [1950s–60s] to leave quickly. ❑ **put one's ass on the line** *see under* ON THE LINE *phr.* ❑ **put one's foot in someone's ass** (*also* **put a foot in someone's ass**) [1940s+] (*US black*) to attack someone physically; to treat someone unkindly. ❑ **put someone's ass out** [1960s] to eject, to throw out, to send away. ❑ **run one's ass off** [1960s–70s] to move at high speed, esp. in the context of searching. ❑ **save one's ass** (*also* **save one's arse**) [1960s+] (*orig. US*) to take care of oneself, to save oneself; esp. in phr. *couldn't — to save one's ass.* ❑ **show one's ass** [1950s+] (*US black*) to appear foolish; to show off, to make an exhibition of oneself. ❑ **sit there with one's finger up one's ass** (*also* **sit there with one's thumb up one's ass, stand around with one's finger/thumb up one's ass**) [20C+] (*US*) to be passive, unresponsive, idle and useless. ❑ **stick it up someone's ass** [1980s+] **1** (*US*) to betray, to let down. **2** to humiliate. ❑ **suck someone's ass/arse** [the perceived humiliation of anilingus] [1930s+] (*orig. US black*) to toady to, to be subservient to, to curry favour. ❑ **think the sun shines out of someone's ass** (*also* **…arse**) [1930s+] (*orig. US*) to worship someone, to act extremely sycophantically. ❑ **tuck it up someone's ass** [1980s+] **1** (*US*) to betray, to let down. **2** to humiliate. ❑ **wet someone's ass** [the wetness of blood] [2000s] (*US black*) to shoot someone.

general verbs

❑ **ass about** [SE *ass*, donkey; note ARSE ABOUT *under* ARSE *v.*, although the homonymity with US *ass* and *arse* is coincidental] [late 19C–1930s] to play the fool. ❑ **ass around** [1940s–60s] (*US*) to play around, to wander around (in a foolish manner). ❑ **ass blow** [BLOW *v.*[2] (1c)] [1960s+] (*US gay*) to lick or suck the anus. ❑ **ass out** **1** [1990s+] (*US black*) to rush away. **2** [1990s+] (*US campus*) to make a fool of oneself. **3** [2000s] (*US campus*) to go to sleep. ❑ **ass up** [2000s] (*US black*) to take drugs. ❑ **ass up to** [1970s] (*US*) to toady to, to curry favour. ❑ **bring ass to get ass** [fig. use of sense 2 above] [1950s+] (*US*) to take a risk in order to make a gain. ❑ **bust ass** [1960s+] **1** (*US*) to travel very fast. **2** (*US*) to work very hard. **3** (*US black*) to do well, to succeed. ❑ **bust in the ass** [1950s] (*US*) to kick, to harm; lit. and fig. uses. ❑ **get it in the ass** (*also* **get it in the arse, get it up the arse/ass**) [1940s+] (*orig. US*) to be attacked, victimized, killed; also in fig. use. ❑ **get the ass** [abbr. GET THE RED ASS *under* RED ASS *n.*] [1960s+] (*US black/campus*) to lose one's temper, to become annoyed. ❑ **give up the ass** [1970s+] (*US*) to accede to seduction. ❑ **have a paper ass** *see* HAVE A PAPER ASSHOLE *under* ASSHOLE *n.* ❑ **knock the ass off**

[1960s+] (*orig. US*) to thrash severely, to defeat comprehensively. ❑ **make ass** [MAKE *v.* (1d)] [1980s+] (*US black*) to get going. ❑ **play on ass** [2000s] (*US prison*) gambling without money, but in the knowledge that the loser will earn a beating. ❑ **stack asses** [1970s] (*US*) to defeat heavily, to thrash. ❑ **swing ass** *see* BLOW ASS *under* BLOW *v.*[1]. ❑ **throw some ass** [1950s+] (*US black*) **1** of a woman, to walk in an exaggeratedly or deliberately sexy manner. **2** of a woman, to have sexual intercourse.

IN EXCLAMATIONS

❑ **hang it in your ass!** [1950s+] (*US*) an excl. of contempt, often accompanied by a gesture, the right forefinger is hooked over the left thumb, which in turn makes a circle with the left forefinger. ❑ **it's your ass!** [1960s+] (*US*) a threat. ❑ **jump up my ass!** [1970s] (*US*) a coarse, derisive retort. ❑ **my aching ass!** *see* MY ACHING BACK! *under* BACK *n.*[1]. ❑ **suck my ass!/arse!** [SUCK SOMEONE'S ASS/ARSE above] [1920s+] a general statement of contempt or dismissal. ❑ **your ass is mine!** [1950s+] a general threat, usu. following a conditional, e.g. *if you don't… your ass is mine.* ❑ **your face and my ass!** *see under* FACE *n.*

ass, the *n.* (*also* **arse, the**) [fig. use of ASS *n.* (2)/ abbr. RED ASS *n.* (2)] **1** [1960s+] (*orig. US*) a bad temper. **2** [1980s+] (*US campus/gay*) something unpleasant, a disappointment.

IN PHRASES

❑ **have/get (a case of) the ass** *v.* [1960s+] (*US campus*) to be angry.

ass *v.* [ASS *n.* (3)] [1990s+] to work as a prostitute.

-ass *sfx* [ext. of -ASSED *sfx*/ASS *n.* (2)] [1950s+] (*mainly US black*) used to form generally negative (but increasingly positive too) adjs. and occas. nouns, e.g. BITCH-ASS *adj.*; CANDY-ASS *n.*; DOG-ASS *n.*; DRAG-ASS *adj.*

assassin *n.* **1** [late 19C] (*UK Und.*) a term of abuse. **2** [1900s–10s] an ornamental bow worn at a woman's breast [it 'kills' her admirers].

ass-bite *n.* [ASS *n.* (2) + SE *bite*] [1970s] (*US*) a very unpopular person.

ass bite *v.* [ASS *n.* (2)] [1970s] (*US*) usu. of an employer/employee relationship, to harass, to nag.

ass-buster *n.* [ASS *n.* (2) + BUSTER *n.*[7]] **1** [1950s] (*US*) a dive in which a swimmer jumps, holds their nose and hits the water buttocks-first, the aim, and the result, being to make a big splash. **2** [1970s] an outstanding person. **3** [2000s] a fall. **4** [2000s] something challenging.

ass-busting *adj.* [BUST SOMEONE'S ASS *under* BUST *v.*[1]] (*US*) **1** [1970s] exhausting, tiring. **2** [2000s] remarkable, amazing.

-assed *sfx* [ASS *n.* (2)] **1** [20C+] (*orig. US*) describing someone's ASS *n.* (2), e.g. NARROW-ASSED *adj.* **2** [1950s+] (*orig. US*) a general intensifier, e.g. PANTY-ASSED *adj.* [ext. of -ASS *sfx* but note earlier HALF-ASSED *adj.* (1)].

assed out *adj.* [ASS *n.* (2)] **1** [1980s+] (*US black*) dead, killed. **2** [1990s+] (*US black*) down on one's luck, in a bad situation.

assfuck *n.* [ASS *n.* (2) + FUCK *n.* (1)] (*orig. US*) **1** [1940s+] an act of anal intercourse. **2** [1970s] an instance of cruel victimization. **3** [1990s+] an all-purpose derog. term of address.

assfuck *v.* [ASSFUCK *n.*] [1940s+] (*orig. US*) to have anal intercourse.

ass-fucker *n.* [ASSFUCK *v.* (1)] [1940s+] (*US*) one who has anal sex; the implication is usu. a male homosexual.

assfucking *n.* [ASSFUCK *v.*] [1940s+] anal intercourse.

asshole/arsehole *see also under* ARSEHOLE and combs.

asshole *n.* [ASS *n.* (2) + SE *hole*/HOLE *n.*[1] (1); see also ARSEHOLE *n.*] (*US*) **1** [mid-19C+] the anus. **2** [mid-19C+] the least appetizing, poorest, most run-down and poss. dangerous area of a city or town or place. **3** [1930s+] a fool, a derog. description of a subject. **4** [1970s+] a general term of address. **5** *see* ASSHOLE BUDDY below.

IN COMPOUNDS

❑ **asshole bandit** *n.* [1950s+] **1** (*US gay*) an anilinguist. **2** (*US gay*) in anal intercourse, the active partner. **3** (*US*) a derog. term for a male homosexual (cf. ARSEHOLE BANDIT *under* ARSEHOLE *n.*). ❑ **asshole-breath** *n.* [1960s+] a term of contempt. ❑ **asshole buddy** *n.* [BUDDY *n.*] **1** [1940s+] (*also* **A-hole buddy, asshole**) an extremely close friend. **2** [1950s+] (*US gay*) a normally heterosexual man who, deprived for whatever reason of women, enjoys anal intercourse, whether as an active or passive partner. ❑ **asshole-deep** *adj.* [ext. of ASS DEEP *under* ASS *n.*] [1960s+] (*US*) extremely deep.

IN PHRASES

❑ **break out into assholes** *v.* [1970s+] (*US*) to become terrified. ❑ **fall through one's own asshole** *v.* [1960s–70s] (*US*) to be extremely surprised, utterly shocked. ❑ **from asshole to appetite** [1950s] (*US*) thoroughly, absolutely, totally. ❑ **have an asshole of** *v.* [1920s–50s] (*US black*) to have a great deal of something. ❑ **have a paper asshole** *v.* [1940s+] **1** (*US*) to be a weakling, to be a coward. **2** (*also* **have a paper ass**) to talk excessively, esp. when meaningless; usu. *talk like you have a paper asshole.* **3** to do anything excessively. ❑ **keep a tight asshole** *v.* (*also* **keep a tight hole**) [the propensity of intense fear to loosen one's bowels] [1940s+] (*orig. US milit.*) to maintain emotional control. ❑ **lock assholes** *v.* (*also* **lock, lock asses**) [1950s+] (*US*) to fight. ❑ **not know one's asshole from one's piehole** *v.* [2000s] (*US*) to be stupid. ❑ **out the asshole** *adv.* [i.e. fig. excrement] [1960s+] (*US*) a general intensifier, blatantly, excessively, totally, reprehensibly, in large quantities. ❑ **snap assholes** *v.* [1950s+] (*US*) to fight. ❑ **think one's asshole squirts perfume** *v.* [1940s+] (*US*) to have a high (but unjustifiable) view of one's own abilities. ❑ **up to one's asshole** [1970s+] involved to the greatest extent.

asshole *adj.* [ASSHOLE *n.*] **1** [1930s+] (*US*) a general negative description, unpleasant, worthless, obnoxious etc. **2** [2000s] of a place, run-down.

DERIVATIVES

❑ **assholingest** *adj.* [1970s] (*US*) the notional superlative of sense 1 above.

asshole *v.* [ASSHOLE *n.* (3)] [1940s] to grovel, to beg, to toady.

IN PHRASES

❑ **asshole around** *v.* [1950s+] (*US*) to idle, to loiter, to waste time.

assig *n.* [abbr.] [late 17C–early 19C] an *assig*nation.

assist *n.* [sporting imagery] [1990s+] **1** back-up, usu. in the form of physical power. **2** the person drawn in to provide this back-up.

asskash *n.* [ASS *n.* (2) + SE *cache*] [1950s] (*US drugs*) a supply of narcotics, concealed in the rectum, usu. in a metal container.

ass-keister *v. see* KEISTER *v.*

ass-kick *n.* [fig. use of KICK ASS *v.*] [1970s+] (*US*) **1** a very demanding task. **2** a punishment, a beating.

ass-kicker *n.* [ASS *n.* (2) + SE *kicker*] **1** [1960s+] (*US*) a shoe or boot, esp. a pointed man's shoe. **2** [1960s+] (*orig. US*) an aggressive, domineering person, a bully. **3** [1960s+] an unpleasant place, a challenging situation. **4** [1970s+] (*orig. US*) an amusing, successful, exciting person.

ass-kicking *n.* (*also* **behind-kicking**) [KICK ASS *v.* (1)] [1930s+] (*US*) a beating.

ass-kicking *adj.* [ASS-KICKING *n.*] [1970s+] (*US*) vicious, thuggish.

ass-kicking *adv.* [KICK ASS *v.*] [1960s+] a general intensifier, extremely, very much, powerfully.

ass-kiss *v.* (*also* **arse-kiss**) [backform. f. ASS-KISSER *n.*] [1940s+] (*orig. US*) to toady.

ass-kisser *n.* (*also* **arse-kisser**) [ASS *n.* (2)/ARSE *n.* (1) + SE *kisser*] [1940s+] (*orig. US*) a sycophant, a toady, one who curries favour.

ass-kissing *n.* (*also* **butt-kissing**) [ASS-KISS *v.*] [1940s+] (*orig. US*) sycophancy, toadying.

ass-kissing *adj.* [ASS-KISS *v.*] [1940s+] (*orig. US*) sycophantic, toadying, begging, supplicatory.

associates *n.* [1980s+] (*US black*) friends.

ass-sucker *n.* [ASS *n.* (2) + SE *sucker*] [late 19C; 1960s+] (*US*) a sycophant, a toady.

ass-whipped *adj.* [ASS *n.* (2) + SE *whipped*] [1970s+] (*US*) utterly exhausted.

ass-whipping *n.* (*also* **ass-whooping, ass-whupping**) [ASS *n.* (2) + SE *whipping*] (*US*) **1** [1950s+] a particularly savage beating. **2** [1990s+] in fig. use, any form of non-physical punishment.

ass-wipe *n.* (*also* **ass-wiper, wipe**) [ASS *n.* (2) + SE *wipe*] **1** [mid-16C; 1950s+] lavatory paper. **2** [1950s+] (*also* **bundwipe**) a general term of abuse; thus one who is *not worth wiping one's ass on*. **3** [1980s+] any worthless piece of paper, like a parking ticket; thus by ext. a homophobic newspaper.

ass-wiper *n.* [ASS-WIPE *n.*] **1** [1950s] a sycophant, a toady. **2** [1960s+] something extremely difficult, demanding. **3** [1960s+] (*drugs*) a severe heroin addiction.

assy-fussy *phr.* [var. on ARSEY-VARSEY *phr.*] [1970s] (*US*) back-to-front.

assy-turvy *adv. see* ARSEY-VARSEY *phr.*

astard-ba *n.* [semi-backsl.] [1930s] a bastard.

aste *n.* [? Ital. *asta*, auction] [early 17C] (*UK Und.*) money.

asterisk *n.* [the * that takes the place of the printed letter; on pattern of BLANKY *adj.* or DASHED *adj.*] [1900s] (*Aus.*) a euph. for any unspecified obscenity.

as the actress said to the bishop *phr.* (*also* **as the bishop said to the actress**) [1930s+] a phr. turning what may have been a perfectly innocent comment into a sexual innuendo, e.g. 'Pull it out and we'll see how long it is.' '…As the actress said to the bishop!'; occas. simply as a playful remark.

Aston Villa *n.* [rhy. sl.; Cockney pron. of *Villa*; ult. UK football team *Aston Villa*] [1990s+] **1** a pillow. **2** a pillar.

Astorbilt *n.* (*also* **Mr Astorbilt, Mrs Astorbilt**) [names *Astor* + *Vanderbilt*, two of America's wealthiest families] (*US*) **1** [late 19C+] one who considers themselves a cut above their peers. **2** [20C+] one who dresses ostentatiously. **3** [1920s+] a member of high society.

astorperious *adj.* [*Astor* (*see* prev.) + SE *imperious*] [1920s+] (*US*) arrogant, haughty.

Astor's pet horse *n.* (*also* **Astor's pet poodle**) [joc. use of proper name *Astor* + SE *pet horse*] (*US*) **1** [1930s+] an over-made-up or over-dressed woman. **2** [1960s+] an arrogant, haughty person.

astronomer *n.* [it is always staring at the sky] [mid-19C] a horse that holds its head high.

astro travel *n.* [1970s] (*US drugs*) imaginary space travel while under the influence of a psychedelic or psychotropic drug.

atch *v.* [pig Lat. for SE *catch*] [1920s] (*UK tramp*) to arrest.

atchker *v.* [pig Lat. for SE *catch*] [1910s–20s] to arrest.

ate-the-bolts *n.* [fig. use of SE] [20C+] (*Ulster*) one who is a glutton for work.

ate up *adj. see* EAT UP *adj.*

ate-your-bun *n.* [1990s+] (*Irish*) a general term of abuse.

Athanasian wench *n.* [a pun on the *Athanasian* Creed, which begins with the words 'quicumque vult', thus cf. QUICUMQUE VULT *n.*] [late 18C–early 19C] a promiscuous young woman, a prostitute, 'a forward girl, ready to oblige every man that shall ask her' (Grose, 1785).

atheneum *n.* [? the *Athenaeum* Club, London, which might be seen as the fount of all wisdom] [late 19C–1900s] the penis.

Athenian *n.* [stereotyped link between homosexuality and Greece] [1970s+] (*gay*) a pederast.

-ati *sfx* [on patten of SE *literati*] [1930s+] a sfx used to denote a given group, as defined by the n., e.g. *niggerati*, black community; *gliteratti*, glamorous society.

at it *phr. see under* IT *n.*[1].

atkins *n.* [abbr. TOMMY ATKINS *n.* (1)] [late 19C–1920s] a generic term for a typical private soldier in the British army.

Atlantic ranger *n.* [its breeding grounds] [late 19C] a herring.

atlas *n.* [both ult. f. the mythical *Atlas*, who held up the earth in his hands, though note 20C US strong man Charles *Atlas* (1894–1972)] [1980s] (*US prison*) **1** a very strong prisoner. **2** a prisoner who attempts to carry out everything unaided.

atmos *n.* [abbr.] [1990s+] (*orig. US teen*) *atmos*phere or ambience, used in a positive fashion.

atom bomb *n.* [play on SE *atomic bomb*, intensified by BOMB *n.* (7)] [1960s+] (*US drugs*) **1** a combination of marijuana or hashish with opium or heroin. **2** a combination of cannabis and cocaine.

atom-bombo *n.* [SE *atomic bomb*] [1940s+] (*Aus.*) strong, cheap wine.

atomic *adj.* [1990s+] (*US campus*) exceptionally wonderful.

atomic atmosphere *n.* [1980s+] (*US campus*) the stink created by someone having recently broken wind.

atomized *adj.* [1950s] (*US*) drunk.

atomy *n.* [SE *anatomy/atom*] [16C–19C] a small, thin or deformed person.

A-Town *n. see* BIG A *n.* (2).

atshitshi *n.* [ety. unknown] [1970s+] (*S.Afr. drugs*) marijuana.

attaboy *n.* [ATTABOY! *excl.*] [1930s+] (*US*) a statement of congratulation, e.g. *I'll write you an attaboy*.

attaboy! *excl.* (*also* **attababes! attababy! attagirl! atta kid! thataboy! thatta baby! yattaboy!**) [? phr. 'that's the boy' etc or 'at her, boy' (*DSUE*), where 'her' is neuter. Note US milit./police jargon *attaboy*, a commendation; Fraser & Gibbons, *Soldier & Sailor Words & Phrases* (1925), suggest it is 'American slang used by players and lookers on at Base-ball matches'] [20C+] (*orig. US*) a general excl. of admiration and encouragement.

attack *n.* [early 19C] the moment of starting a meal or dish.

attack *v.* [mid-19C] to begin, to address oneself to, e.g. *attack that beef*.

attack of the week's end *n.* (*also* **attack of the month's end**) [late 19C–1910s] the poverty that comes after one's weekly or monthly wages have run out.

attagirl!/attakid! *excl. see* ATTABOY! *excl.*

attensh *n.* [abbr.] [1930s] *attent*ion.

attic *n.* **1** [early 19C+] (*orig. boxing*) (*also* **top-loft**) the head. **2** [late 19C] the vagina.

IN PHRASES

❑ **have a guest in the attic** *v.* [20C+] **1** (*also* **have toys in the attic**) to be eccentric, to be insane, to be simple, childlike. **2** to be drunk. ❑ **loose in the attic** *adj. see* LOOSE IN THE BEAN *under* BEAN *n.*[1]. ❑ **messy attic** *n.* [1950s+] (*US black*) hair in need of dressing.

attic to let *phr. see* APARTMENT TO LET *phr.*

attitude *n.* (*also* **'tude**) [early use appears to refer to problems between individuals; in modern uses the assumption is that an attitude is hostile to the prevailing establishment status quo, although it may well fit happily into the complementary rebellious teenage standpoint. Thus the rap band NWA, Niggers With Attitude. The meaning shifted slightly f. negative, antisocial in the 1970s–80s, to haughty, pretentious in the 1990s+] [mid-19C+] one's whole posture towards society, its rules and one's own place among them.

IN PHRASES

❑ **cop an attitude** *v.* (*also* **catch an attitude, take an…, cop a 'tude**) [COP *v.* (3e)] [1960s+] (*orig. US black*) to take a negative stance on a given topic, to make one's own position adamant despite prevailing opinions and pressures, to act in an uncooperative or angry manner. ❑ **throw attitude** *v.* (*also* **give attitude, throw 'tude**) [1980s+] (*US campus*) to act in an arrogant, surly, obnoxious manner.

SE in slang uses

IN COMPOUNDS

❑ **attitude adjustment** *n.* [euph.] [2000s] (*US prison*) the administration of mood-altering drugs to a prisoner seen as disruptive; the physical subjugation of such a prisoner.

attitude! *excl.* [ATTITUDE *n.*] [1980s+] a comment made to a person who is seen as displaying ATTITUDE *n.*

Attleborough *n.* [? the town of its manufacture] [mid–late 19C] (*US*) cheap or sham jewellery.

attorney *n.* [legal jargon *devil*, a lawyer working free for another lawyer] [early 19C] a grilled and devilled goose or turkey drumstick.

attract *v.* [ironic euph.] [late 19C–1930s] to steal, to pilfer.

Auckland Park *n.* [by metonymy, *Auckland Park* is the Johannesburg suburb where the SABC headquarters is situated] [1980s+] (*S.Afr.*) the South African Broadcasting Corporation (SABC).

auctioneer *n.* [it 'knocks things down'; the orig. auctioneer was that of prize-fighter Tom Sayers (*fl.*1845–60)] [mid-19C–1920s] (*orig. boxing*) the fist.

Audi (5000) *v.* (*also* **audi**) [pron. of *Audi*, an upscale automobile (the Audi 5000 is a favoured model), as OUTIE *adv.*] [1990s+] (*US teen*) to rush away, to run off, to escape.

Audi (5000) *phr.* (*also* **outtie 5000**) [AUDI (5000) *v.*] [1990s+] (*US black/teen*) a general phr. of farewell; good bye, see you etc.

audition the finger puppets *v.* (*also* **audition the hand puppet**) [1990s+] to masturbate; thus n. *finger puppet audition*, masturbation.

auger *n.* [SE *auger*, a tool for boring] **1** [late 17C; 20C+] the penis; thus *auger-hole*, the vagina. **2** [1980s] (*US campus*) an excessively hard worker.

augur *n.* [a pun on SE *auger*, a bore; note SE *augur*, a prophet] [late 19C] (*US*) a bore, an excessive talker.

August ham *n.* [the month of ripening + the pinkness of both foodstuffs] [1920s–30s] (*US black*) a watermelon.

aunt *n.* [note synon. Yid. *mume*, lit. 'aunt'] **1** [early 17C–1950s] (*also* **auntie**) a procuress, a madame. **2** [early 17C–1970s] a whore. **3** [mid-19C–1940s] (*US*) (*also* **Aunt Dinah, auntie**) an old black woman, used by both blacks and whites. **4** [20C+] (*US*) menstruation; usu. in such phrs. as *Aunt Flo is visiting; my redheaded aunt has arrived; Aunt Jody's come with her suitcase;* (*W.I.*) *auntie coming to town*, menstruation is starting. **5** *see* AUNTIE *n.*² (1).

SE in slang uses

(IN PHRASES)

□ **if my aunt had been a man, she'd have been my uncle** [mid-17C+] a phr. used as a rejoinder to a speaker who has just finished a long and laborious explanation of the obvious. □ **if your aunt had balls she'd be your uncle** [20C+] a phr. used as a rejoinder to a speaker who has just finished a long and laborious explanation of the obvious. □ **live at your aunt** *v.* (*also* **live at your nenne**) [W.I. *nennen*, a godmother] [20C+] (*W.I.*) to find it hard to make enough money to live, to subsist, to suffer great hardship. □ **my aunt** *n.* [euph.] **1** [early 19C] a house of assignation. **2** [early 19C–1930s] (*also* **the Aunt**) the lavatory; thus *visit my aunt, go to see my aunt*, to visit the lavatory.

(IN EXCLAMATIONS)

□ **ask my aunt!** [euph. of ASK MY...! *excl.*] [late 19C] (*US*) go to hell! □ **go and kiss your aunt!** [1920s] a general excl. of contempt or dismissal. □ **my aunt!** (*also* **my Aunt Eliza! my Aunt Jane! my Aunt Nellie! my fat aunt! my giddy aunt! my great aunt! my hairy aunt! my holy aunt! my jumping aunt! my precious aunt! my sacred aunt! my sainted aunt! my sainted hat!**) [late 17C; late 19C+] a mild excl.

Aunt Betsy's cookie store *n.* [initial letters] [1990s+] (*US campus*) Alcoholic Beverage Control store.

Aunt Fanny *n.* [joc. use of proper name + an added emphasis from FANNY *n.*¹] [1930s+] used to express negation or disbelief, e.g. *tell that to my Aunt Fanny*.

(IN EXCLAMATIONS)

□ **my Aunt Fanny!** a mild negating excl., e.g. *Agree? My Aunt Fanny.*

Aunt Flo *n.* (*also* **Flo**) [euph.; AUNT *n.* (4) + pun on SE *flow*] [1950s+] (*US*) menstruation.

Aunt Hagar('s children) *n.* (*also* **Aunt Hagi**) [Gen. 21:9, *Hagar* the Egyptian, the wife of Abraham and the mother of Ishmael] [1930s–40s] (*US black*) the black race.

Aunt Hazel *n.* [the shared initial *H* + the hazel-brown colour of some heroin] [1950s+] (*drugs*) heroin.

Auntie *n.* [in both cases the implication is of prissiness, paternalism, reticence and trad. conservatism] **1** [1940s+] the British Broadcasting Corporation (BBC); orig. used by independent TV companies, but now in general use. **2** [1950s+] (*Aus.*) the Australian Broadcasting Commission (ABC).

auntie *n.*¹ (*also* **aunty**) [euph.] [mid-19C+] the lavatory.

auntie *n.*² **1** [1920s+] (*US gay*) (*also* **aunt, tante**) an ageing male homosexual. **2** [1940s+] an ageing female, occas. male, prostitute. **3** [1960s] a male 'madam'. **4** [1980s+] (*S.Afr.*) a woman who runs a shebeen. **5** *see* AUNT *n.* (1).

(IN COMPOUNDS)

□ **auntie-man** *n.* (*also* **antiman**) [1940s+] (*W.I.*) an effeminate man. □ **auntie queen** *n.* [-QUEEN *sfx*] [1980s+] (*S.Afr. gay*) a young man who chooses older male partners.

SE in slang uses

(IN PHRASES)

□ **don't be auntie** [the stereotyping of foolish (? maiden) aunts] [1920s+] (*Aus.*) don't be foolish. □ **your mal auntie** [Afk. *mal*, mad, crazy] [20C+] (*S.Afr.*) a general phr. of dismissal, disbelief.

auntie *n.*³ [? link to AUNT NORA *n.*] [1950s+] (*drugs*) opium.

Auntie Ella *n.* (*also* **Cousin Ella**) [rhy. sl.] [20C+] an umbrella.

Auntie Emma *n.* (*drugs*) **1** [1970s] morphine [initial *M*]. **2** [1980s+] opium [ext. of sense 1].

Auntie Flora *n.* [partial rhy. sl.] [20C+] (*W.I., Antg./St Lucia*) the floor; *knock/take Auntie Flora*, to sleep on the floor.

Auntie Jane *n.* [AUNT *n.* (4) + proper name] [1970s] (*Irish*) menstruation, a period.

Auntie Meg *n.* [rhy. sl.] [20C+] (*Aus.*) a keg (of beer).

Aunt(ie) Nelly *n.* [rhy. sl.] [1950s+] the belly.

Auntie Poppie *n.* [POPPER *n.*² (4)] [1990s+] (*S.Afr. gay*) amyl nitrate.

Auntie Ruth *n.* [rhy. sl.] [2000s] the truth.

Auntie Willy *n.* *see* UNCLE WILLIE *adj.* (2).

Aunt Jane *n.* **1** [1920s] (*US*) the town of Tijuana, Mexico [lit. translation of Sp. *tía*, aunt + *juana*, Jane]. **2** [1960s–70s] (*US black*) a subservient, obsequious black woman [generic use of proper name]. **3** [1960s–70s] (*US black*) a black woman whose world is defined by spiritual rather than secular values; a regular church-goer and religious believer [generic use of proper name].

Aunt Jemima *n.* [generic use of proper name; 'Aunt Jemima [...] was a stock figure of the black songster tradition [...] and she entered popular iconography and pancake mythology through a song, "Old Aunt Jemima," written and first performed in 1875 by the black minstrel Billy Kersands, who, it has been suggested, adapted it from an actual slave song of the antebellum work-fields [...]. In the fall of 1889 [...] it was heard by Chris Rutt, a man in search of a name for his new self-rising pancake mix. [...] Ruff sold out his Aunt Jemima pancake mix to the R.T. Davis Milling Company; [...] [who] brought Aunt Jemima to life in the person of one Nancy Green [...]. As Aunt Jemima, Green toured the country promoting the pancake flour of that name', Tosches, *Where Dead Voices Gather* (2001)] [1920s+] (*US black*) a subservient, obsequious black woman, the female version of UNCLE TOM *n.* (1); an early fast-food chain, Aunt Jemima's Kitchen, featuring pictures of a stereotyped 'black mammy', existed in the 1960s.

Aunt Lilian is visiting *phr.* (*also* **Aunt Minnie is visiting**) [AUNT *n.* (4)] [1960s] (*US campus*) a phr. meaning that one is menstruating.

Aunt Mame *n.* [the 1958 movie *Auntie Mame*, starring Rosalind Russell as an eccentric, rich aunt] [1970s+] (*US gay*) an older male homosexual.

Aunt Maria *n.*¹ [? AUNT MARIA *n.*², i.e. they get 'hot'] [late 19C–1900s] the female genitals.

Aunt Maria *n.*² [rhy. sl.; note pron. Mar-eye-a] [20C+] a fire.

Aunt Mary *n.*¹ [generic use of proper name] **1** [mid-19C+] a black woman who is a regular church-goer and religious believer. **2** [1970s] a downtrodden, subservient black woman.

Aunt Mary *n.*² [pun/abbr. SE *mar*ijuana] [1950s+] (*drugs*) marijuana.

Aunt Mathilda *n.* [1970s+] (*US gay*) a middle-aged male homosexual.

Aunt Minnie is visiting *phr. see* AUNT LILIAN IS VISITING *phr.*

Aunt Nora *n.* [ety. unknown; ? N of *Nora* and *ne* of cocaine; note that cocaine is a 'feminine drug', *see* GIRL *n.*[2] (1)] [1950s+] (*drugs*) cocaine.

aunt pollys *n.* [ety. unknown] [2000s] (*US black*) very small testicles.

Aunt Rose *n.* [1990s+] (*US*) menstruation.

Aunt Sally *n.* [SE *Aunt Sally*, 'a game much in vogue at fairs and races, in which the figure of a woman's head with a pipe in its mouth is set up, and the player, throwing sticks from a certain distance, aims at breaking the pipe' (*OED*). According to Ware (1909), the original Aunt Sally was a black-faced doll, popular in early 19C London; its face also served as the shop-sign for a second-hand clothiers. The doll, in turn, came from Black Sal, a character created by Pierce Egan in *Life in London* (1821–8)] **1** [early 19C–1960s] (*US black*) (*also* **Sal, Sally**) a subservient black woman, happy to curry favour with whites at the price of her autonomy. **2** [late 19C+] a scapegoat, often unfairly so.

Aunt Thomasina *n.* (*also* **Aunt Tom, Madame Thomasina**) [female var. on UNCLE TOM *n.* (1)] [1960s+] (*orig. US black*) a subservient, obsequious black woman.

aunt tillies *n.* [the image of *Tillie* as an old-fashioned name, accentuated by pfx *Aunt*] [1940s] (*US*) an old-fashioned woman's nightgown.

aunty *n. see* AUNTIE *n.*[1].

aurev *phr.* [abbr. Fr. *au revoir*] [1920s] goodbye.

aurium *n.* [? Lat. *aurius*, an ear, i.e. that which hears confession] [mid-16C] (*UK Und.*) a wandering beggar posing as some type of priest.

aurora borealis *n.* [SE *aurora borealis*, the 'northern lights', lit. northern dawn] [1980s+] (*US drugs*) phencyclidine.

Aussie *n.* [abbr.] **1** [1910s] (*Aus.*) a wound gained during WW1 that was sufficiently incapacitating to ensure one was sent home to Australia from the front. **2** [1910s+] (*also* **Aussieland, aussy**) Australia. **3** [1910s+] an Australian. **4** [2000s] (*UK black*) an ounce of a given drug [play on *oz-ie/Aussie*].

Aussie *adj.* [1910s+] Australian.

IN COMPOUNDS

▫ **Aussie kiss** *n.* [play on *down under*, i.e. the vagina / DOWN UNDER *n.* (1)] [2000s] (*Irish*) cunnilingus.

Australian *n.* [pun on SE *down under* / DOWN UNDER *n.* (1)] [1970s+] (*US gay*) **1** anilinctus. **2** an anilinguist.

Australian *adj.*

IN COMPOUNDS

based on AUSTRALIAN *n.*

▫ **Australian active/passive** *n.* [1980s+] (*US gay*) one who licks or is licked by a sexual partner. ▫ **Australian flag** *n.* [late 19C–1910s] a shirt tail, protruding between the trousers and waistcoat.

based on proper name

▫ **Australian haka** *n.* [HAKA *n.* (1)] [2000s] (*N.Z.*) a blatant attempt to avoid paying one's way, by ostentatiously patting the pockets and claiming to have lost one's wallet. ▫ **Australian salute** *n.* [1970s+] (*Aus.*) brushing away flies from one's face, a characteristic Aus. gesture.

autem *n.* (*also* **autem ken, autum**) [poss. f. SE *anthem*, or poss. f. Yid. *a'tume*, a forbidden church, although the Yid. may be a later coinage. Bee suggests Lat. *auditio*; Partridge opts for ALTHAM *n.* and a further theory suggests Fr. *autel*, an altar (note Fr. Und. *entonne*, church) and the SE *altar* may indeed be the actual root] **1** [mid-16C–mid-19C] (*UK Und.*) a church. **2** *see AUTEM MORT* below.

IN COMPOUNDS

▫ **autem-bawler** *n.* [SE *bawler*, shouter] [early 18C–mid-19C] a parson. ▫ **autem-cackler** *n.* (*also* **anthem cackler, cackler**) [SE *cackle*, to talk] [early 18C–19C] a dissenter, spec. a Puritan. ▫ **autem-cackle-tub** *n.* [*CACKLE TUB under* CACKLE *v.*] [early 18C–mid-19C] a conventicle or dissenters' meeting house. ▫ **autem-cove** *n.* [COVE *n.* (1)] **1** [mid-18C] (*UK Und.*) a married man. **2** [mid-19C] a preacher, a parson. ▫ **autem-croaker ken** *n.* [mid-19C] (*UK Und.*) a church, a pulpit. ▫ **autem-dipper** *n.* [the *dipping* of baptism] [17C–mid-19C] an Anabaptist. ▫ **autem-diver** *n.* (*also* **anthem diver**) [DIVER *n.* (3)] [early 18C–mid-19C] **1** a pickpocket specializing in robbing from church congregations. **2** a churchwarden or other petty official charged with responsibility for distributing alms to the poor; their charges regarded them as little more than licensed robbers. ▫ **autem-gogler** *n.* (*also* **autem-goggler**) [SE *goggle (at)*, to stare (at)] [early 18C–mid-19C] (*UK Und.*) a fortune-teller, a conjuror. ▫ **autem jet** *n.* [SE *jet*, black, i.e. the black clerical gown] [early 18C–mid-19C] a parson. ▫ **autem-mag** *n.* [MAG *n.*[5] (1)] [mid-19C] (*UK Und.*) a church service. ▫ **autem mort** *n.* (*also* **autem, autem mot, autem mott**) [MORT *n.*, lit. a 'married woman', although there may never have been a ceremony. 'Shee is a wyfe married at the church and they be as chaste as a cowe, [which gooeth to bull every month, with what bull she careth not]' (Harman)] **1** [mid-16C–mid-19C] (*UK Und.*) lit. a married woman; a mistress as in a woman who cohabits with a man, or accompanies a mendicant villain on his travels and in his crimes. **2** [mid-19C] a female beggar. ▫ **autem prickear** *n.* [SE *prick-ear*, skullcap] [early 18C–mid-19C] a dissenter, spec. a Puritan. ▫ **autem quaver** *n.* [SE *quaver*, to shiver or tremble; Quakers 'tremble' at the word of the Lord] [early 18C–mid-19C] a Quaker; thus *autem quaver tub, autem quaver's butt*, a Quaker meeting house. ▫ **autem sneak** *n.* [SNEAK *n.*[1] (1a)] [early 19C] the robbery of churches or chapels.

autem *adj.* [AUTEM *n.*] [mid-16C–19C] (*UK Und.*) married.

author *n.* [1980s+] (*US drugs*) an addict or doctor who writes illegal prescriptions for drug users.

auto *n.* [SE *automatic*] [1980s+] (*US drugs*) a device consisting of an aquarium pump and an oxygen mask used to smoke cannabis.

autograph *n.* [which is 'written' in blood] [1950s] (*US drugs*) a narcotic injection.

automobile *n. see* PONY *n.* (3a).

automobubble *n.* (*also* **automobuzzard**) [joc. mispron.] [20C+] (*US*) an automobile.

autum *n. see* AUTEM *n.*

autumn *n.* [play on *GO OFF WITH THE FALL OF THE LEAF under* LEAF *n.*] [mid-19C] death by hanging.

auxiliary *n.* [1970s+] (*US gay*) the male genitals.

av *n.* [abbr.] [late 19C–1910s] (*US*) an avenue.

avachat *n.* [SE *have a chat*] [1980s] (*Aus.*) a chatterer.

avast! *excl.* [naut. jargon *avast*, stop; ult. f. Du. *hou'vast, houd vast*, hold fast] [late 17C–1920s] stop (what one is doing)!

'ave a Jew boy's *n.* [Cockney mispron. of SE *avoirdupois*] [1910s+] a weight.

ave Maria *n. see* ANNA MARIA *n.*

Avenoodles *n.* (*also* **Fifth Avenoodles**) [proper name Fifth Avenue, pron. 'avenoo' + SE *noodle*, a fool] [mid–late 19C] (*US*) the élite residents of New York City.

Avenue, the *n.* [1910s–50s] (*US*) Broadway.

IN PHRASES

▫ **on the avenue** (*US black*) **1** [1930s+] lit. in the street. **2** [1990s+] in general use, from a mass point of view.

avenue-tank *n.* [1940s] (*US black/Harlem*) the double-decker buses on New York's Fifth Avenue route.

average bear, the *n.* [the TV cartoon *Yogi Bear*, whose catchphrase was 'smarter than the average bear'] [1980s+] (*US*) an average person.

avocados *n.* [their shape] **1** [1930s+] (*US*) the female breasts. **2** [2000s] (*S.Afr. gay*) the testicles.

avoirdupois-man *n.* [SE *avoirdupois*, the standard system of weights used in the UK before metrication; it covered all goods except precious metals, precious stones and medicines] [18C–early 19C] a thief of brass weights from shop counters; his profession was known as the *avoirdupois lay*.

avuncular *n.* [play on UNCLE *n.* (1)] [mid-19C–1920s] a pawnbroker; thus *avuncularism*, forced to use a pawnbroker.

avuncular *adj.* [AVUNCULAR *n.*] [mid-19C–1920s] with ref. to a pawnbroker.

avvie *n.* (*also* **avvy**) [abbr.] [2000s] afternoon.

avvo *n. see* ARVO *n.*

A.W. *n.* [abbr.; note A.C. *n.* and A.B. *n.* (3)] [2000s] (*US prison*) Aryan Warrior, a white supremacist prison gang.

awake *v.* [mid-19C] (*UK Und.*) to know; to let (someone) know.

awake, be *v.* (*also* **awake-up**) [early 19C+] to see through or understand a (criminal) scheme.

awash *adj.* [1940s+] drunk.

away *adj.* **1** [late 19C+] in prison; (*London*) in any prison outside London. **2** [late 19C+] (*UK prison/police*) escaped, from prison or police cells. **3** [late 19C+] dead. **4** [1960s+] emotionally satisfied, usu. when intoxicated with drugs or drink. **5** [2000s] successful, as in a seduction.

(IN PHRASES)

❑ **go away** *v.* **1** [20C+] to go to jail. **2** [1910s] to be executed.

SE in slang uses

(IN PHRASES)

❑ **away from home** *adj.* [sports imagery] [1990s+] of a relationship, usu. sexual, illicit, adulterous. ❑ **away to the hills** *adj.* [20C+] (*Irish*) mentally unbalanced. ❑ **away with the fairies** *adj.* [fig. uses of SE] [20C+] (*orig. Irish*) **1** mentally unbalanced. **2** out of this world. ❑ **do away** *v.* [early 19C] (*UK Und.*) to work as a receiver. ❑ **get someone away** *v.* [late 19C] (*Aus. Und.*) to trick, to hoax.

(IN EXCLAMATIONS)

❑ **away to fuck!** (*also* **away to hell!**) [20C+] a general dismissive excl., usu. Scot./Irish.

away *adv.* **1** [mid-19C+] straightaway, forthwith, directly, without hesitation or delay; esp. in imper., e.g. *fire away*; *right away*, at once, immediately. **2** [1900s] (*US*) as an intensifier, exceedingly.

away and claw mould on yourself! *excl.* [20C+] (*Ulster*) a general excl. of dismissal.

awayday girl *n.* [the cheap-rate 'awayday' train fares on which they depended] [1990s+] a prostitute, living outside London, who commutes in to pick up clients in the metropolis.

awerdenty *n.* [Sp. *aguardiente*, strong water, thus brandy (*aguardiente* is more like a Spanish form of Italian *grappa* or French *marc*)] [mid-19C+] (*US*) strong alcohol, often whisky, brandy.

awesome *adj.* [weak use of SE; the term gained a new currency, esp. among the pre-teens, with the popularity *c.*1990 of the cartoon/film heroes Teenage Mutant Ninja Turtles, in whose dialogue it featured heavily] **1** [1920s+] (*also* **awes**) impressive, enormous, frightening. **2** [1970s+] (*orig. US teen*) wonderful, excellent, the best.

awesome! *excl.* [AWESOME *adj.* (2)] [1980s+] an excl. used to indicate that something is very good.

awfu *adj.* [abbr. SE *awful*] [1990s+] (*US campus*) unpleasant.

awful *n.* [mid–late 19C] a 'blood-and-thunder' romance, a 'penny dreadful'.

awful *adj.* [an early version of the bad = good model that underpins such latterday sl. terms as BAD *adj.* (3) and WICKED *adj.* (2)] [late 19C+] excellent, first-rate.

awful *adv.* [SE by late 19C] **1** [19C] a general negative intensifier, orig. frightful, very ugly, monstrous. **2** [mid-19C+] awfully, very, extremely.

awful doom *n.* [rhy. sl.] [1900s] (*Aus.*) room, i.e. space.

awful people *n.* [1940s–60s] (*UK society*) the police.

a-wiper *n.* [abbr. ASS-WIPER *n.* (1)] [1960s] (*US*) a sycophant, a toady.

'Awkins *n. see* HAWKINS *n.*[2].

awkward *adj.* [late 19C–1910s] pregnant.

awkward as a Chow on a bike *phr. see under* CHOW *n.*

a.w.l. *adj. see* A.W.O.L. *adj.*

awl *n.* [17C] the penis.

awning over the toy shop *n.* [the *toy shop* is the genitals] [1990s+] (*Aus.*) a male beer belly.

A.W.O.L. *n.* [A.W.O.L. *adj.* (1)] [1910s+] (*US*) a deserter.

A.W.O.L. *adj.* (*also* **a.w.l.**) [abbr.; coined during US Civil War, *c.*1863] **1** [1910s+] (*orig. milit.*) absent without leave; also in fig. use. **2** [1980s] amour without love, used by habituees of singles bars to denote their brief (strictly sexual) entanglements.

A.W.O.L. *v.* [A.W.O.L. *adj.* (1)] [1950s+] (*US*) to desert; to absent oneself, to leave.

A word *n.* [SE AIDS + -WORD *sfx*] [1980s+] (*US gay*) AIDS.

awright! *excl.* [phonetic trans. of US pron. of *all right* as a greeting or excl.] [1960s+] that's good! I feel great! etc.

awse *adj.* [abbr. AWESOME *adj.* (1)] [1980s+] (*US*) wonderful, perfect, first-rate.

ax and combs. *see under* AXE *n.*

axe *n.* (*also* **ax**) **1** as a weapon. (**a**) [late 19C+] (*US Und./black*) a knife, esp. a switchblade. (**b**) [1980s] (*UK Und.*) a razor. **2** [1910s–70s] (*US*) the penis; thus *axman*, a womanizer, a sexual athlete. **3** [1910s+] as *the axe*, *the ax*, dismissal, an act of dismissal. **4** [1950s+] as an instrument, musical or otherwise [orig. black jazz use, when instrument more likely saxophone or trumpet; the saxophone supposedly resembles an axe]. (**a**) (*US black*) any musical instrument, orig. saxophone, later guitar. (**b**) ext. as any form of 'tool' with which one works, i.e. a typewriter.

(IN COMPOUNDS)

❑ **axman** *n.* (*also* **axe man**) **1** [late 19C+] (*orig. US black*) one who carries or wields a knife. **2** [1920s–40s] (*US prison*) a barber. **3** [1970s+] a musician, esp. a guitarist. ❑ **axe wound** *n.* [note joke cited in Legman, *The Rationale of the Dirty Joke* (1968): '"Mama, what's that?" "That's where Daddy hit me with the axe." "Got you right in the cunt, didn't he?"'; note Cleland, *Memoirs of a Woman of Pleasure* (1748–9): 'His hands convulsively squeez'd, open'd, press'd together again the lips and sides of that deep flesh-wound'] [1990s+] the vagina.

SE in slang uses

(IN COMPOUNDS)

❑ **axe-job** *n.* [1960s+] a severe critique or verbal attack. ❑ **axholder** *n.* [late 19C] (*US*) the hand.

(IN PHRASES)

❑ **axe up** *v.* [1980s] (*Aus.*) to share.

axe *v.* (*also* **ax**) [1920s+] to close down, to terminate; to dismiss, esp. of businesses, jobs.

axis *n.* [19C] the vagina, one of several terms noting the organ's bodily centrality.

axle *n.* [play on ARSEHOLE *n.* (1)] [1930s–50s] the buttocks.

axle grease *n.* **1** [late 19C–1940s] (*orig. Aus.*) (*also* **pin-grease**) butter. **2** [20C+] semen. **3** [1920s+] (*Aus.*) (*also* **axle**) money. **4** [1930s+] a thick application used for one's hair.

ax my...! *excl. see* ASK MY...! *excl.*

ayem *n. see* A.M. *n.*

Aylesbury (Duck) *n.* [rhy. sl. = FUCK *n.* (2a)] [1990s+] a euph. for DAMN *n.*

Aylesbury'ed *adj.* [rhy. sl.; *Aylesbury ducked* = FUCKED *adj.*[1]] [1990s+] exhausted.

a-yo! *excl.* [? YO! *excl.* (2)] [1990s+] a greeting.

Ayrab *n.* (*also* **A-rab**) [deliberate mispron. and popularized in song 'Ahab the Ayrab' (1962) by Ray Stevens. While usu. used of Arabs or Muslim believers, occas. used by European Jews (Ashkenazis) of Eastern and North African Jews (Sephardis)] [1940s+] (*US*) a derog. term for an Arab.

ayraba *n. see* ARABBER *n.*

ayrton (senna) *n.* [rhy. sl. = TENNER *n.* (1); ult. champion racing driver *Ayrton Senna* (1960–94)] [1990s+] £10, a £10 note.

azman *adj.* [mid-19C] (*UK Und.*) pertaining to judicial hanging; as *azman-cable fever*, the state of being hanged; *azman-crick pendans sweater*, the gallows, the hangman, a gibbet.

Aztec *adj.*

(IN COMPOUNDS)

❑ **Aztec hop** *n.* (*also* **Aztec two-step**) [its supposed provenance in Mexico] [1950s+] diarrhoea. ❑ **Aztec revenge** *n.* [2000s] diarrhoea.

azure *adj. see* BLUE *adj.*[3].

B *n.*[1] (*also* **bee**) [abbr.] [1950s+] (*drugs*) Benzedrine; thus *B-head*, a user of Benzedrine.

B *n.*[2] [abbr.] **1** [1960s] (*Aus.*) an M.C.B., the 'B' model of the M.G. sports car. **2** [1970s–80s] (*US black*) a Cadillac Brougham.

B *n.*[3] (*also* **bee**) [abbr. SE *box*] [1960s+] (*drugs*) enough marijuana to fill a matchbox.

B *n.*[4] [abbr. BITCH *n.*[1] (1a)] [1990s+] (*US black*) a woman.

B *n.*[5] [abbr. BLOOD *n.*[2] (3)] [1990s+] (*US black*) a form of address for either sex.

B *n.*[6]

IN PHRASES

❑ **put the B on** *v.* **1** *see* PUT THE BEE ON *under* BAG *n.*[1]. **2** *see* PUT THE BEE ON *under* BEE *n.*[1].

b *n.*[1] [abbr.] **1** [mid-19C] a *bug*. **2** [late 19C] a kiss [SE *buss*]. **3** [1920s+] (*also* **bee**) a bastard.

b *n.*[2] [abbr. BALLOCKS *n.* (3)] [1960s] nonsense, rubbish.

b *n.*[3] *see* BLUNT *n.*[3] (1).

b *n.*[4] *see* BOBBY *n.*

b *adj.* (*also* **bee**) [abbr.] [1910s+] euph. for BLOODY *adj.*; thus also *beeaitch*, bloody hell; *beeeff*, bloody fool.

b.a. *n.*[1] [abbr. SE *big* + ARSE *n.* (5)] [20C+] (*W.I., Guyn.*) a general term of great dislike.

b.a. *n.*[2] **1** *see* BUGGER ALL *n.* **2** *see* BULLSHIT ARTIST *under* BULLSHIT *n.*

IN PHRASES

❑ **sweet b.a.** *n. see under* SWEET *adj.*[1].

b.a. *adj. see* BARE-ASS *adj.*

b.a. *v.* (*also* **hand out the b.a.**) [abbr. BARE-ASS *adj.*] [1970s–80s] (*US campus, Calif.*) to expose one's buttocks for the purpose of evoking shock and/or amusement.

IN PHRASES

❑ **hang a b.a.** *v.* [1990s+] (*US campus*) to expose one's buttocks.

baa cheat *n.* [SE *baa* + CHEAT *n.* (1)] [early 18C] a sheep.

baadjie *n.* [fig. use of Afk. *baadjie*, a jacket/JACKET *n.* (3c)] [2000s] (*S.Afr. prison*) a long sentence.

baa-lamb *n.*[1] [nursery use *baa-lamb*, a lamb] [20C+] anyone mild, pleasing, amicable; often used by women of malleable men.

baa-lamb *n.*[2] [rhy. sl.] [20C+] a tram.

baa-lamb *n.*[3] [assonance] [1910s+] a euph. for BASTARD *n.*

baana *n.* [echoic of the 'bang' as one sits down] [20C+] (*W.I., USVI*) the buttocks.

baarie *n.* (*also* **bari, barry**) [Zulu sl. *ubari*, a bumpkin, an unsophisticated person] [1970s] (*S.Afr.*) a fool; one who has newly arrived at a township from the countryside.

bab *n.*[1] [abbr. BABBLER *n.*, rhy. sl. *babbling brook*] [1910s–60s] a cook.

bab *n.*[2] [abbr. BABYLON *n.*[1] (2)] [1970s+] (*W.I.*) a police officer.

bab *n.*[3] *see* BABE *n.* (1).

baba *v.* [Sp. *baba*, spittle, slaver] [20C+] (*W.I.*) to dribble.

babalaas *n.* (*also* **babalazi, babelaas, bubblejas**) [Zulu *i-babalazi*, the after-effects of a drinking-bout] [1940s+] (*S.Afr.*) a hangover; thus *babalaas*/*babalaased*, suffering from a hangover; *babalaasdop*, a drink taken to alleviate the hangover, the 'hair of the dog'.

babalonian *n. see* BABE-A-LONIAN *under* BABE *n.*

babania *n.* [Sicilian dial. *babonya*, the (bubonic) plague] [2000s] (*US drugs*) heroin.

babaton/babarton *n. see* BARBERTON *n.*

babbie-shop *n.* (*also* **babi-shop, bobbyshop**) [Hind. *babu*, a gentleman, Mr; used derog. in Raj period for an Indian clerk + SE *shop*] [1970s+] (*S.Afr.*) an Indian-owned store.

babbitt *n.* [George F. *Babbitt*, the hero of Sinclair Lewis's novel *Babbitt* (1922); *babbitt* appears itself to be a symbolic concoction of *babble* and *rabbit*, summarizing the character's qualities] [1920s+] (*US*) a self-opinionated, self-satisfied small-town bourgeois, with all the prejudices of such a figure; thus n. *Babbitry*.

-babble *sfx* [on model of the slightly earlier PSYCHOBABBLE *n.*; ult. SE *babble*] [1980s+] used to denote a variety of pretentious or incomprehensible jargon, e.g. *ecobabble, technobabble*.

babbler *n.* (*also* **babbling brook**) [rhy. sl. *babbling brook* = cook, crook] (*Aus./N.Z.*) **1** [20C+] a cook, esp. in an institution, mining camp or farm. **2** [1920s+] a criminal, a villain. **3** [1930s] (*US campus*) a mediocrity.

babbling (brook) *adj.* [rhy. sl. = CROOK *adj.* (3)] [2000s] (*N.Z.*) unwell.

babe *n.* **1** [mid-19C] (*UK Und.*) (*also* **bab**) a man who has recently been initiated into crime; one who has been committed to trial. **2** [mid-19C] (*UK Und.*) a confidence trickster's accomplice [Jim Thompson, *South of Heaven* (1967), has a citation with a 1920s context]. **3** [1910s+] (*orig. US*) a girl, girlfriend or young woman, esp. if attractive; thus *babe alert*, a warning to other men to note the approach of an attractive woman [the term entered sl. *c.*1915, waned somewhat after 1950 but gained a new lease of life, and began to refer to either sex in the late 1980s]. **4** [1910s+] a form of address, irrespective of sex, e.g. *Where you goin', babe?* **5** [1910s+] something excellent, desirable; also as phr. *the babes*. **6** [1980s] (*US campus*) an unpleasant female. **7** [1980s+] used congratulatorily, a person of either sex (though still usu. female).

DERIVATIVES

❑ **babelicious** *adj.* [+ SE de*licious*] [1990s+] of a woman, very beautiful, very sexy. ❑ **babette** *n.* [dimin. sfx *-ette*] [1970s+] (*US gay*) a very youthful-looking homosexual man.

IN COMPOUNDS

❑ **babe-a-lonian** *n.* (*also* **babalonian**) [pun on sense 3 and BABYLON *n.*[2]] [1990s+] (*US campus*) a good-looking woman. ❑ **babe lair** *n.* [SE *lair*; coined in the skit (and later film) 'Wayne's World' on US TV *Saturday Night Live*, the major contemporary popularizer of the word *babe*] [1990s+] (*US*) an apartment used by a man for the seduction of women. ❑ **babe magnet** *n. see under* -MAGNET *sfx.*

IN PHRASES

❑ **real babe** *n.* [SE *real*/REAL *adj.*] [1990s+] (*US teen*) an admirable, attractive person of the opposite (or preferred) sex.

SE in slang uses

IN PHRASES

❑ **babe in the wood** *n.* [SE *babe* + the wooden construction of the stocks/pillory + pun on the title of the folktale] [late 17C–

early 19C] one who is imprisoned in the stocks or pillory. ❑ **babe of grace** *n.* [lit. 'child of grace'] [early–mid-19C] one who looks 'holier-than-thou' but is not; a hypocrite.

babee *n. see* BAUBEE *n.*

babelaas *n. see* BABALAAS *n.*

baberton *n. see* BARBERTON *n.*

Babe Ruth *n.* [rhy. sl.; ult. US baseball star George Herman 'Babe' Ruth (1895–1948)] [1970s–80s] (*N.Z. prison*) the truth.

babes *n.* [BABE *n.* (4)] [1930s+] a term of affection or simply of address between either sex.

babies *n.* [the fertilizing role of semen] [1980s+] (*US gay*) semen.

babi-shop *n. see* BABBIE-SHOP *n.*

babonya *n.* [Sicilian dial. *babonya*, the (bubonic) plague] [1970s] (*US Und.*) drugs.

baboon *n.* [SE; like *ape*/APE *n.* (1), the *baboon* is stereotyped as an aggressive and ugly creature] **1** [early 16C+] a thug, a ruffian; a ne'er-do-well; thus adj. *baboonish*, foolish. **2** [1930s] (*US Und.*) a very hard-working prostitute. **3** [1930s] (*S.Afr.*) an abusive term for a black or coloured person.

IN COMPOUNDS

❑ **baboon-faced** *adj.* (*also* **baboon-visaged**) [1940s+] very ugly.

IN PHRASES

❑ **like a blue-arsed baboon** *adv.* (*also* **like a striped-assed ape**) [1950s+] headlong, very fast; see also *BUZZ AROUND LIKE A BLUE-ARSED FLY under* BUZZ *v.*[1]. ❑ **you are a thief and a murderer and you have killed a baboon and stole his face** [late 18C–early 19C] a general phr. of hostility and contempt.

babu *n.* (*also* **babu-man, baboo**) [Hind. *babu*, a term of respect (Mr, Esquire) or an educated man] [20C+] (*W.I.*) **1** an old East Indian man, usu. bearded and poor. **2** an ugly old man. **3** an imaginary figure, ugly and old, conjured up to frighten children.

baby *n.* **1** [19C] in cards, the jack, i.e. the 'baby' of the king and queen. **2** [mid-19C+] a man. **3** [mid-19C+] a woman. **4** [late 19C+] an object, usu., a person, of one's affection; also of animals. **5** [late 19C+] (*US, usu. black*) a term of affection or general address between men and women or men and men or women and women. **6** as a container. (**a**) [mid-19C+] a bottle or glass of liquor; thus *kiss the baby*, to take a drink; *the baby is born*, there is enough money to buy a bottle. (**b**) [mid-19C+] a small or half-sized bottle, whether of spirits or a non-alcoholic drink, orig. soda water; thus *baby and nurse*, a small bottle of soda water with twopennyworth of spirits. (**c**) [1930s] (*US*) a glass of milk. **7** [20C+] a person, often self-referential as in *this baby*. **8** [1900s–30s] an object of excellence. **9** [1920s+] an otherwise unnamed item or object, esp. used of automobiles, weapons and machinery. **10** [1920s+] one's special interest or responsibility, usu. with the possessive pronoun, e.g. *it's my baby*. **11** [1950s] (*US Und.*) a prostitute's client. **12** [1960s+] (*US gay*) an under-age/teenage boy. **13** [1960s+] (*drugs*) marijuana [as a term of affection for the drug]. **14** [1970s] (*US*) an attractive young woman.

DERIVATIVES

❑ **baby-o** *n.* [-O *sfx* (1)] [1960s] a general term of address, usu. to a woman.

IN PHRASES

❑ **hot baby** *n.* [HOT *adj.* (7)/HOT *adj.* (1a)] [late 19C–1910s] **1** (*US campus*) (*also* **warm-baby**) a student who excels in a certain subject. **2** any person who excels in something. **3** (*US campus*) a promiscuous person, a sexually eager woman.

SE in slang uses

IN COMPOUNDS

❑ **baby-ass** *adj.* [-ASS *sfx*] [1990s+] (*US black*) childish. ❑ **baby batter** *n. see* BATTER *n.*[1] (3). ❑ **baby-blues** *n.* [SE *baby-blue*, a light shade of blue, often associated with a baby's eyes; the implication is of candour and innocence] **1** [1930s+] (*orig. US*) (*also* **icy-blues**) human eyes, irrespective of their actual colour. **2** [1950s] (*US*) a police officer [play on BLUES *n.*[2] (1)]. ❑ **baby bonus** *n.* [1940s+] (*Aus./Can.*) a family allowance. ❑ **baby bouillon** *n. see BABY GRAVY* below. ❑ **baby buggy** *n.* [play on SE] [1970s+] (*US gay*) a convertible sports car. ❑ **baby bumper** *n.* [BUMP *v.*[1] (1a)] [1990s+] (*US*) a child molester. ❑ **baby bumpers** *n.* [SE *bumper*, a railway buffer] [1960s+] the female breasts. ❑ **baby buster** *n.* [on analogy of the *boom* and *bust* of economic jargon] [1980s+] one who was born in the decade 1965–1975, ie the period after the *baby boom* that followed WW2, thus one born during a baby bust. ❑ **baby button** *n.* [the umbilical cord, connecting baby to mother] [1960s+] the navel. ❑ **babycakes** *n.* (*also* **cakes, cakie**) [SE *cake*; so intimate a friend is 'good enough to eat'] [1960s+] (*US*) **1** a term of affection between friends. **2** a (pretty) young woman or handsome man. ❑ **baby-catcher** *n.* (*US*) **1** [1930s–70s] a midwife. **2** [1960s–70s] a doctor. ❑ **baby child** *n.* (*US black*) **1** [1920s+] a baby; a child. **2** [1970s+] a younger, less respected or less experienced individual. **3** [1970s+] an immature person. ❑ **baby chute** *n.* [1990s+] the vagina. ❑ **baby-doll** *n.* [DOLL *n.*[1] (5)] **1** [20C+] (*US*) a young woman, esp. when attractive. **2** [20C+] a direct term of address. **3** [1920s] a success. **4** [1940s] (*US*) in pl., a style of high-heeled woman's shoe. **5** [1980s+] (*US gay*) an attractive male. ❑ **baby factory** *n.* [1990s+] (*US black*) a woman who has had a large number of children. ❑ **baby-farmer** *n.* [play on SE *baby-farmer*, one who reared orphan children, often in atrocious conditions] [20C+] an older person, usu. a woman, who prefers affairs with people much younger than themselves. ❑ **baby-father** *n.* (*also* **baby daddy, ...poppa, child father, pickney...**) [1970s+] (*orig. W.I.*) a boyfriend, esp. the father of one's child although not one's legal husband. ❑ **baby-fetcher** *n.* [1910s+] the penis. ❑ **baby fluid** *n.* [1930s] (*US*) semen. ❑ **baby gravy** *n.* (*also* **baby bouillon**) [SE *gravy*/GRAVY *n.* (1b)] [1990s+] semen. ❑ **baby jesus** *n. see* separate entry. ❑ **baby-kisser** *n.* [the campaigning politician's propensity to believe that the babies encountered enjoy being kissed by a total stranger] [1940s+] (*US black*) a politician. ❑ **baby-maker** *n.* [the procreative function of the organ] **1** [late 19C–1900s] (*also* **lady-maker**) the penis. **2** [late 19C–1900s] the vagina. **3** [1960s] a sexually powerful man. **4** [1970s+] (*S.Afr. gay*) (*also* **BM**) a heterosexual. ❑ **baby-mother** *n.* (*also* **baby mamma, baby momma**) [1980s+] (*orig. UK black*) a girlfriend, spec. the woman who has one's baby but with whom one may not actually live. ❑ **baby paste** *n.* [1970s+] (*US gay*) semen. ❑ **baby poppa** *n. see BABY-FATHER* above. ❑ **baby-rape** *n. see* separate entry. ❑ **baby-raper** *n. see* separate entry. ❑ **baby's arm** *n.* [the supposed resemblance] [1960s+] the penis, esp. when large. ❑ **baby's head** *n.* [the supposed resemblance; presumably that of the smooth suet cover rather than the meat and gravy it contains] [1910s–60s] steak and kidney pudding; a suet dumpling. ❑ **babysit** *v. see* separate entry. ❑ **babysitter** *n. see* separate entry. ❑ **baby-skull** *n.* [the supposed resemblance] [1900s] (*US campus*) an apple dumpling. ❑ **baby's leg** *n.* [the supposed resemblance] [late 19C+] meat loaf, jam-roly-poly. ❑ **baby-snatcher** *n.* [ironic use of SE *baby-snatcher*, a kidnapper] [1920s+] (*US*) an obstetrician. ❑ **baby-snatching** *n.* [1920s+] of either sex, marrying or having an affair with someone much younger than oneself; thus *baby-snatcher*, one who marries a noticeably younger partner.

IN PHRASES

❑ **baby chick farm** *n.* [pun on SE *chick*/CHICK *n.*[1] (2) + SE *farm*] [1950s] (*US black*) 'the locations or towns where the girls look fine from a young age on' (Durst, *The Jives of Dr Hepcat*, 1953). ❑ **baby in the boat** *n.* [1930s] the clitoris; thus *kiss the baby in the boat*, to perform cunnilingus. ❑ **baby in the bushes** *n.* [such a baby is trad. conceived and/or delivered in the bushes] [1970s+] (*US*) an illegitimate child. ❑ **baby's done it** *n.* [a pun on NUMBER TWO *n.* (1)] [1940s+] (*bingo*) the number two. ❑ **baby's public house** *n.* [late 19C–1900s] the female breasts. ❑ **deliver a baby** *v. see* separate entry. ❑ **have a baby** *v.* [var. on *HAVE KITTENS under* KITTEN *n.*] [1930s+] to experience fright, shock or fury. ❑ **hold the baby** *v.* (*also* **carry the baby**) [late 19C+] to be left to clear up a problem, to take an unpleasant responsibility. ❑ **like a baby's arm with an apple/orange in its fist** *adj.* [1930s+] a phr. used to describe an extra-large penis. ❑ **put a baby on** *v.* [1990s+] (*US black*) **1** of a woman, to have a child without the father's knowledge and/

or agreement. **2** to claim a man as one's child's father, even though he is not. ❑ **this won't buy baby a new frock** (*also* **...a new dress**) [20C+] this is useless, this is pointless.

baby *adj.* [late 19C–1940s] small.

IN COMPOUNDS

❑ **baby Benz** *n.* [BENZ *n.*] [1980s+] (*US black*) the Mercedes Benz model 190E, which is small and sporty. ❑ **baby bhang** *n.* [SE *bhang*; the implication is of inferior potency] [1980s] (*drugs*) marijuana. ❑ **baby bio** *n.* [pun on tradename *Baby Bio* + BI *adj.*] [2000s] a heterosexual man or woman who is experimenting with bisexuality. ❑ **baby butch** *n.* [BUTCH *n.*[1] (5)] [1960s+] (*US gay*) a young, boyish lesbian. ❑ **baby crew** *n.* [CREW *n.* (3)] [1980s+] the junior member of a hooligan gang. ❑ **baby crockett** *n. see* separate entry. ❑ **baby dreads** *n.* [DREAD *n.*[2] (5)] [1990s+] (*US black*) a short version of the braided hair worn by Rastafarians. ❑ **baby dyke** *n.* [DYKE *n.*] [1970s+] (*US gay*) a young, inexperienced lesbian. ❑ **baby gangster** *n.* [2000s] (*US black/teen*) a gang member who has yet to commit a murder. ❑ **baby grand** *n.* [GRAND *n.*[1]] [1930s] (*US Und.*) $500. ❑ **Baby Jane** *n. see* separate entry. ❑ **baby life** *n.* [LIFE *n.* (1a)] [1950s+] (*US prison*) the maximum sentence that prisoners must serve (six years, four months) before a parole board is bound to consider their case for the first time. ❑ **baby pro** *n.* [SE *pro*(*stitute*)] [1970s+] (*US*) **1** a prostitute under the age of legal consent. **2** the profession of child prostitution.

baby crockett *n.* [proper name of *Davy Crockett* (1786–1836), the 19C Western hero, whose adventures were fictionalized in the 1950s US TV series] [1970s+] (*camp gay*) a fake cowboy.

Baby Jane *n.* [1990s+] (*US*) a child or underage female prostitute.

baby jesus *n. see* BEJAZUS *n.*

Babylon *n.*[1] [*Babylon*, the ancient capital of Mesopotamia and used fig. to imply sinful luxury, esp. by the Church of Rome. In Rastafarian iconography Babylon is opposed to Zion – the promised land of Africa, esp. Ethiopia] **1** [late 18C+] the hedonistic, exciting world of the city, as opposed to the quietness of the countryside; spec. London, also as *Babylon Town*. **2** [1940s+] (*orig. W.I., then UK/US black*) the police; a prison warder; thus *Babylon House*, a police station. **3** [1950s+] (*also* **Babylon-land**) a generic term for white Western society; by ext. the authorities. **4** [1970s+] any oppression or the forces that oppress the black (esp. Rastafarian) man. **5** [1970s+] anyone perceived as putting material gains before spiritual ones.

Babylon *n.*[2] [BABE *n.* (3); pron. *Babe-y-lon*] [1980s+] anywhere that attractive women are supposed to congregate or, mythically, are supposed to have their origin.

Babylon-land *n. see* BABYLON *n.*[1] (3).

baby paps *n.* [rhy. sl.; ? resemblance of a cap to the breast] [mid-19C–1910s] caps.

baby-rape *n.* [SE *baby-rape*, paedophilia] [1970s+] (*US*) statutory rape.

baby-raper *n.* [BABY-RAPE *n.*] **1** [1950s+] a general derog. term of abuse; thus *baby-raping*, of a person, despicable, disgusting. **2** [1960s+] a man who commits statutory rape.

baby's cries *n.* [rhy. sl.] [1920s+] the eyes.

babysit *v.* **1** [1960s+] (*drugs*) to take care of someone either under the influence of a drug (esp. the hallucinogenic LSD) or, more often, recovering from an unpleasant, drug-induced experience. **2** [1980s+] to monitor progress, to take care of, to watch over.

babysitter *n.* [ironic use of SE] **1** [20C+] (*Can.*) a prison officer. **2** [1980s] (*US drugs*) someone who hides drugs temporarily during importation from one country or area to another.

baby's pram *n.* [rhy. sl.] [20C+] jam.

bacca *n.* (*also* **baccer, bacco, baccy, backee, backer, bakker**) [abbr.] **1** [late 17C+] to*bacco*. **2** [late 19C] by metonymy, a cigar.

IN COMPOUNDS

❑ **bacca-box** *n.* (*also* **baccy-box**) **1** [1900s–20s] the mouth. **2** [1920s] the nose. ❑ **bacca-pipes** *n.* [the similarity to a type of *tobacco-pipe*] [mid–late 19C] whiskers curled in small, close ringlets. ❑ **backer-stick** *n.* [tobacco was orig. sold in short twists a few inches long] [late 19C] (*US*) the human leg.

baccare! *excl.* [pig Lat.] [mid-16C–mid-17C] go back!

bacchus marsh *n.* [*Bacchus Marsh*, a town half-way between Melbourne and Ballarat] [1990s+] (*Aus.*) a semi-erect penis.

bacco/baccy *n. see* BACCA *n.*

baccy-box *n. see* BACCA-BOX *under* BACCA *n.*

bach *n.* (*also* **bache, batch**) [abbr.] **1** [mid-19C–1940s] (*US*) a *bach*elor; thus *old bach*, a confirmed bachelor. **2** [1920s+] (*N.Z.*) a farm-worker's cottage [i.e. a *bach*elor pad]. **3** [1920s+] (*N.Z.*) a weekend cottage [i.e. a *bach*elor pad].

IN PHRASES

❑ **live bache** *v.* [late 19C–1900s] (*UK society*) of a man, to live alone, as a bachelor.

bachelor *n.*

IN COMPOUNDS

❑ **bachelor's baby** *n.* [mid-19C+] an illegitimate child. ❑ **bachelor's buttons** *n.* [? SE phr. *wear bachelor's buttons*, to be unmarried] [late 16C–17C] a foetus, presumably of an illegitimate child. ❑ **bachelor's fare** *n.* (*also* **batchelor's fare**) [late 18C–early 19C] bread and cheese and kisses. ❑ **bachelor's son** *n.* (*also* **batchelor's son**) [euph.] [late 17C–late 18C] an illegitimate child. ❑ **bachelor's wife** *n.* [the implement performs the stereotypically wifely chore] [1950s+] (*US*) a metal plunger with a long wooden handle, used for washing clothes in a tub.

IN PHRASES

❑ **bachelor of arts** *n.* [play on the SE and the equation of a prison to a COLLEGE *n.* (3)] [mid-19C] (*UK prison*) one who has served six months of a prison sentence.

bachie *n.* [abbr. SE *bachelor*] [20C+] (*W.I.*) a room or any small place kept by a man for solo living or for conducting love affairs away from the family home; thus *live bachie*, to live alone.

bach (it) *v. see* BATCH *v.*

back *n.*[1] [note the 17C use of a strong *back* to imply a woman's sexual strength] **1** [1980s] the anus. **2** [1980s] (*US*) back-up. **3** [1990s+] (*US black*) the posterior, the buttocks; thus *baby's got back*, used to remark favourably on a woman's posterior.

IN PHRASES

❑ **take on some backs** *v.* [1970s+] (*US black*) to have anal intercourse.

SE in slang uses

IN COMPOUNDS

❑ **back-and-belly** *n.* [dial. *back and belly*, a two-edged machete, which can cut with either edge and is thus 'two-faced'] [1950s] (*W.I.*) **1** a hypocrite, an untrustworthy person. **2** a very thin person. ❑ **back-and-front** *n.* [1950s] (*W.I.*) a hypocrite. ❑ **back-and-neck** *n.* [the back and neck of a chicken, the cheapest portion available and one that is almost devoid of meat] [20C+] (*W.I., St Kitts*) a very thin person. ❑ **backbiter** *n.* [mid-18C–early 19C] a body louse; a flea. ❑ **back-buster** *n.* [1960s+] (*US*) a dive in which one lands flat on the water. ❑ **back-cheat** *n.* [CHEAT *n.* (1), lit. 'back thing'] [early 18C–early 19C] (*UK Und.*) a cloak. ❑ **backmark** *n.* [the image is of secrecy and deliberate concealment] [1950s+] (*US black/prison*) **1** an undesirable characteristic. **2** an informer, esp. in prison. ❑ **back-out** *n.* [1970s] (*W.I.*) a woman's dress cut very low in the back. ❑ **back-scratcher** *n.* [late 19C+] a sycophant, a toady. ❑ **back-staircase** *n.* [mid–late 19C] a bustle on a dress. ❑ **back-timber** *n.* [mid-17C] clothing. ❑ **back time** *n.* [1950s+] (*US Und.*) time spent in prison awaiting sentencing.

IN PHRASES

❑ **back of my hand (and the sole of my foot)** [the object of the rejection will get a slap or a kick] [late 19C+] (*Irish/Scot.*) phr. implying contempt and rejection. ❑ **back of the hand down** *n.* [BACK-HANDER *n.* (3)] [late 19C–1900s] bribery. ❑ **back of the neck** *n.* [? i.e. unwashed] [1940s] (*Irish*) a distasteful person. ❑ **back-to-back** *adj.* [1980s+] (*US black*) affectionate, friendly, intimate. ❑ **back-to-back** *adv.* [1970s–80s] (*US black*) to the greatest possible extent, comprehensively, fully; of a person, the epitome. ❑ **climb up someone's back** *v. see* CLIMB

SOMEONE'S FRAME *under* FRAME *n.*[1]. ❑ **dust someone's back** *v.* *see* DUST SOMEONE'S JACKET *under* DUST *v.*[1]. ❑ **get off someone's back** *v.* [1940s+] to stop annoying someone, to stop nagging at or otherwise irritating someone; usu. as imper. ❑ **get one's back up** *v.* [the feline habit of bristling the fur when annoyed or frightened] **1** [late 17C+] (*also* **set one's back up**) to become annoyed. **2** [late 18C+] to annoy, to irritate, to infuriate. **3** [1910s] to engender bravery, e.g. by a drink of alcohol. ❑ **get on one's back** *v.* [1930s+] **1** (*UK Und.*) to work as a prostitute. **2** of a female, to have sexual intercourse. ❑ **get on someone's back** *v.* [1920s+] (*orig. Aus.*) **1** to annoy, to harass. **2** to tell off, to scold. ❑ **get someone's back** *v. see* WATCH SOMEONE'S BACK *under* WATCH *v.* ❑ **get up someone's back** *v.* [feline imagery] [1950s+] to annoy. ❑ **have one's back scratched** *v.* [one is *scratched* by the cat-o'-nine-tails] [late 19C+] to suffer a judicial flogging. ❑ **have someone's back** *v.* [the image of guarding one's back from attack] [1980s+] to take care of, to look after. ❑ **knock the back out of** *v.* [ult. euph. for *FUCK THE ARSE OFF SOMEONE under* FUCK *v.*] [1960s+] to express a desire to indulge in a sexual act with a member of the opposite sex, e.g. *I'd knock the back out of that!* ❑ **make a hump in one's back** *v. see under* HUMP *n.*[1]. ❑ **on one's back** *adj.* [late 19C+] penniless, impoverished. ❑ **on someone's back** *adj.* [mid-19C+] causing problems for someone, being irritating. ❑ **set one's back up** *v. see* GET ONE'S BACK UP above. ❑ **take someone's back** *v. see* WATCH SOMEONE'S BACK *under* WATCH *v.*

(IN EXCLAMATIONS)

❑ **my aching back!** (*also* **my aching ass!**) [1940s+] (*US*) a general excl.; there is no actual back pain. ❑ **my back!** [late 17C+] a general excl. of disdain, dismissal, arrogant contempt.

back *n.*[2] [abbr. GREENBACK *n.* (1)] [1960s] a dollar bill.

back *adj.*[1] [abbr. WAY BACK *phr.*] [1930s–50s] (*US black*) well-established, traditional, tried and tested.

back *adj.*[2] [1940s+] (*US*) served and drunk alongside or together with an alcoholic drink, usu. as an order to the barman, e.g. *Scotch with soda back.*

SE in slang uses

(DERIVATIVES)

❑ **backer** *n.* [one is on the 'back seat'] [1990s+] (*UK/Irish juv.*) a lift on the back of a bicycle. ❑ **backsy** *adj.* [1980s] (*US*) reneging on a promise. ❑ **backy** *n.* [abbr. *BACKHOUSE* below] [1900s–60s] (*US*) a privy.

(IN COMPOUNDS)

❑ **back alley** *n. see* separate entry. ❑ **back-alley deal** *n. see* separate entry. ❑ **back-assward** *adj.* (*also* **back-asswards**) [joc. reversal of *ASS-BACKWARDS under* ASS *n.*, emphasizing the meaning] [1950s+] (*US*) confused, muddled, backwards. ❑ **backbeat** *n. see* separate entry. ❑ **back bottie** *n.* [on pattern of *FRONT BOTTOM under* FRONT *adj.*] [1980s] (*Aus.*) the anus. ❑ **backcap** *see* separate entries. ❑ **backchat** *see* separate entries. ❑ **backclap** *v.* [14C SE *clap*, to talk loudly, chatter] [late 19C] to insult someone or disparage something. ❑ **back-door** *see* separate entries. ❑ **backdoor** *v. see* separate entries. ❑ **back double** *n.* [SE *double*, a twist or turn] [late 19C+] a back street. ❑ **back entrance** *n.* (*also* **backgate**) [late 19C+] the anus. ❑ **back eye** *n.* [-EYE *sfx*] [1960s+] **1** the anus. **2** anal intercourse. ❑ **backfall** *n. see* separate entry. ❑ **backfire** *v. see* separate entry. ❑ **backforce** *n. see* separate entry. ❑ **back forty** *n.* [SE *back*, out of the way + *forty*, a plot of 40 acres (16 hectares)] [1950s+] (*US*) an out-of-the-way, usu. barren piece of land. ❑ **back-gate exit** *n.* (*also* **back gate commute, ...discharge, ...parole, south gate discharge**) [dead prisoners are taken out through the back gate of the prison and buried without ceremony] [1920s+] (*US prison*) an inmate's death in prison. ❑ **back gate parole** *n. see* BACK-DOOR PAROLE *under* BACK-DOOR *adj.* ❑ **back-hairing** *n.* [such fights often involve the pulling of the long hair at the back of a woman's head] [1900s] fighting among women. ❑ **backhand** *n. see* BACK-HANDER *n.* (3). ❑ **back-hand** *v. see* separate entries. ❑ **back-hander** *n. see* separate entry. ❑ **backhouse** *n.* [20C+ use is US; its position behind the house] [late 16C; 20C+] a privy. ❑ **back-jaw** *see* separate entries. ❑ **back-jump** *see* separate entries. ❑ **back-land** *n.* [pun on SE] [late 17C–mid-19C] (*W.I.*) the buttocks. ❑ **backlip** *see* separate entries. ❑ **backlog** *n. see* separate entry. ❑ **back number** *n.* [the previous and thus 'dead' editions of newspapers] [late 19C+] an irrelevant person, a 'has been'; used esp. of a former lover, now discarded, or a person or a thing that is behind the times, out of date or useless; also as adj., old fashioned; thus v. *back-number*, to discard; similarly used of objects. ❑ **back-porch** *n.* [1950s+] (*US*) the buttocks. ❑ **back premises** *n. see* BACK-DOOR *n.* ❑ **back roll** *v.* [1980s+] (*drugs*) to roll a joint so that only one layer of paper surrounds the mix. ❑ **backroom boy** *n.* [SE *back room* + *boy*; + play on SE *backroom boys*] [1990s+] (*UK gay*) one who enjoys the semi-public sex of the (often dark) back rooms in gay clubs. ❑ **back-row hopper** *n.* [theatrical imagery] [late 19C–1900s] a scrounger who frequents taverns in the hope of finding someone willing to buy them a drink. ❑ **backsass** *n. see* separate entry. ❑ **back sass** *v. see* separate entry. ❑ **backscull** *v.* [1970s] to have anal intercourse. ❑ **backscuttle** *see* separate entries. ❑ **backseat driver** *n. see* separate entry. ❑ **backshot** *n.* [lit. to shoot in the back] [1950s+] (*UK black*) anal intercourse. ❑ **backside** *n. see* separate entry. ❑ **backslack** *n.* [SLACK *n.*[1] (1)] [1900s–50s] (*Aus./US*) cheek, insolence. ❑ **back slammer cutout** *n.* [SLAMMER *n.*[1] (2b) + CUT OUT *v.*[3] (1); play on *BACK-DOOR PAROLE under* BACK-DOOR *adj.*] [1940s] (*US black*) (premature) death. ❑ **backslice** *n.* [SE *slice*; note SLICE *n.* (1a)] [1980s] of a man or woman, the anus. ❑ **backslider** *n.* [early 17C] a prostitute. ❑ **backsliding** *n.* (*also* **bestial backsliding**) [17C] intercourse in the rear-entry position. ❑ **backslit** *n.* [SLIT *n.* (1a)] [1980s] the anus. ❑ **back slum** *n.* [SLUM *n.*[1] (1)] [19C] (*UK Und.*) the back entrance to a building, the back door or window. ❑ **back slums** *n.* [later SE for very poor slums] [19C] areas or streets known for a high proportion of criminal residents. ❑ **backsman** *n.* [? one who goes in the back way; however, G. A. Thompson (personal correspondence) suggests 'a mistake or typo for "Cracksman"'] [mid-19C] (*US*) a burglar. ❑ **backstage** *adj.* [1970s+] (*US gay*) uncouth, ill-mannered. ❑ **backstall** *n.* [STALL *n.*[1] (2)] (*UK Und.*) **1** [19C] a member of a garrotting gang who keeps watch and provides physical assistance to the actual garrotter if necessary. **2** [19C–1900s] a thief's accomplice. ❑ **backstop** *n.* **1** [1940s+] (*Aus.*) a supporter, accomplice, one on whom one can rely; also as v., to support [cricket jargon *backstop*, a fielder who stands behind the wicket-keeper to stop any balls the keeper may have missed]. **2** [1950s+] (*US Und.*) in a pickpocket team, the one who works directly behind the victim [baseball jargon *backstop*, the catcher]. ❑ **back-street wife** *n.* [1930s] (*US*) a mistress. ❑ **backswing** *n.* [1950s+] (*US gay*) that position of homosexual anal intercourse where the passive partner lies on his stomach, presenting buttocks to his partner. ❑ **back-talk** *see* separate entries. ❑ **back-talking** *n. see* separate entry. ❑ **back tottie** *n.* [TOTTIE *n.*[2] (2)] [1980s] (*Aus. juv.*) of a girl, occas. a boy, the anus. ❑ **backtrack** *v. see* separate entry. ❑ **backwash** *n.* [SE *backwash*, the motion of a receding wave] **1** [1900s–30s] (*US*) insolent talk, cheek, nonsensical talk. **2** [1990s+] liquid that flows back into a bottle, poss. after being in one's mouth when one drinks straight from it. ❑ **back way** *n. see* BACK-DOOR *n.* ❑ **backyard** *see* separate entries.

(IN PHRASES)

❑ **back-end-to** *adj.* [1920s+] (*US*) in confusion. ❑ **backslang it** *v. see* separate entry.

(IN EXCLAMATIONS)

❑ **back-pedal!** [cycling imagery] [1910s–20s] an excl. calling for restraint, steady on! hold it!

back *v.*[1] [SE *back*, to cover or copulate] [mid–late 17C] to have sexual intercourse.

back *v.*[2]

SE in slang uses

(IN COMPOUNDS)

❑ **back out** *n.* [19C] (*US*) cowardice; the act of withdrawal. ❑ **back up** *n. see* separate entries.

(IN PHRASES)

❑ **back and fill** *v. see* separate entry. ❑ **back in one's cart** *v.*

[1910s–20s] (*Aus.*) to butt in; to ask for more. ❑ **back off the boards** *v.* [SE *back*, to push away, to cause to retreat] [1910s+] (*US*) to surpass. ❑ **back one out** *v.* [1990s+] to defecate. ❑ **back one's fist** *v.* [1990s+] (*W.I.*) to masturbate. ❑ **back out** *v.* [horseracing jargon *back out*, to bring a horse backwards out of a stall] [19C–1950s] to retreat. ❑ **back someone out** *v.* [SE *back*, to cause to retreat] [mid-19C+] (*US*) to challenge, to face down. ❑ **back someone's play** *v. see under* PLAY *n.* ❑ **back the barber** *v.* [? like the chatty barber, the speaker talks when there is no actual justification] [1950s] (*Aus.*) to interfere, to butt in. ❑ **back the barrow** *v.* [1910s] (*Aus.*) to interfere, to butt in. ❑ **back the breeze** *v.* [the enthusiasm of one's speech fig. makes the wind reverse direction] [1950s] (*US*) to chatter, to gossip. ❑ **back up** *v. see* separate entries. ❑ **back water** *v.* [nautical jargon *back water*, to reverse a boat] [1950s+] (*US*) to retract a statement, to back down from a position; thus *take back water*, to back down, to accept defeat.

back *adv.* [1940s+] (*US black*) really, very much, completely.

SE in slang uses

IN PHRASES

❑ **back-a-bush** *adj.* [20C+] (*W.I., Jam.*) far away, deep in the countryside, in the 'back of beyond'. ❑ **back-ah-yard** *n.* (*also* **back-o-wall**) [SE *yard*, garden] **1** [1930s] (*US*) a poor area of the city. **2** [1960s+] (*W.I.*) the Caribbean. **3** [1960s+] (*W.I.*) home. ❑ **back in the day** (*also* **back in the days**) [1990s+] (*orig. US black teen*) synon. for 'once upon a time'. ❑ **back in the saddle (again)** *adj.* [SE phr. *back in the saddle*, getting back to a regular routine; ? milit. or cowboy use] [1950s–70s] (*US*) menstruating. ❑ **back in the woods** *adj.* [the stereotype of those who live there] [1960s+] (*US*) unsophisticated, gauche. ❑ **back of beyond** *n.* ['civilization' is implied] [early 19C+] anywhere considered by the speaker as inaccessible, outside the purlieus of acceptable life. ❑ **back of Bourke** (*also* **back of Burke, Back o' Sunset, as far as Bourke, other side of Bourke, out back o' sunset**) [proper name *Bourke*, a town in the extreme west of New South Wales/SE *sunset*] [20C+] a very long way away. ❑ **back of God speed** (*also* **behind God speed**) [SE *God speed*, farewell] [20C+] (*Irish*) very far away. ❑ **back-o-wall** *n. see* BACK-AH-YARD above. ❑ **off the back** *adv.* [1990s+] surreptitiously, on the side.

back alley *n.* [a term of approval, *back alley* is another variety of the black reversal of white values, cf. AWFUL *adj.*] [late 19C+] (*US black*) the main street of an otherwise run-down or 'red-light' area.

back-alley deal *n.* [late 19C+] (*US black*) a deal between one unsuspecting victim and the person who intends and succeeds in cheating them.

back and fill *v.* [SE *back and fill*, to go backwards and forwards; thus the trickster bemuses the victim with a lengthy, convoluted patter] (*Aus./US*) **1** [mid-19C+] to vacillate. **2** [1940s+] to charm a potential victim before subjecting them to a confidence trick.

back-answers *n. see* BACK-TALK *n.*

backasswards *adj. see* BASS-ACKWARDS *adj.*

backbeat *n.* [jazz use *backbeat*, a secondary beat that underlies the main theme] [1970s] (*US black*) **1** an underlying theme or quality. **2** one's heartbeat.

IN PHRASES

❑ **backbeat of the trey thirty** *n.* [TREY *n.*] [1940s] (*US black/Harlem*) the third day of the month. ❑ **on the backbeat** [1940s] (*US black/Harlem*) of time, in the past, ago; before.

backcap *n.* [it 'caps' the previous statement] [late 19C+] (*US*) **1** an insult based on attacking the subject's family. **2** a sharp or witty reply, as offered in the ritual name-calling known as dozens.

backcap *v.* [BACKCAP *n.*] (*US*) **1** [late 19C] (*gambling*) for a bystander to persuade potential victims to avoid a (poss. crooked) gambling game. **2** [late 19C–1900s] to speak evil of someone, so as to spoil their game. **3** [late 19C+] to insult someone by disparaging their family.

backchat *n.*[1] [SE *back* + *chat*; ? orig. milit. use] [20C+] cheek, impudence, malicious gossip.

backchat *n.*[2] [servant girls trad. chatted with delivery boys, policemen etc at the back door] [1930s] (*UK Und.*) the back door.

backchat *v.* [BACKCHAT *n.*[1]] [1910s+] (*Aus./W.I.*) to answer back.

back-door *n.* (*also* **back premises, back way**) [pun on SE] **1** [late 16C+] the anus. **2** [mid-19C] the vagina.

DERIVATIVES

❑ **back-dooring** *n.* [1980s] (*US*) adultery.

IN COMPOUNDS

❑ **backdoor action** *n.* [-ACTION *sfx*] **1** [1940s+] sodomy. **2** [1970s+] (*US*) adultery [the adulterer metaphorically comes in 'through the back door']. ❑ **backdoor bandit** *n.* [-BANDIT *sfx* (2)] [2000s] (*N.Z.*) a male homosexual. ❑ **backdoor commando** *n.* (*also* **backdoor Gentleman, back-door merchant**) [SE *commando/gentleman*/MERCHANT *n.*] [1990s+] a male homosexual. ❑ **backdoor kicker** *n.* [1990s+] a male homosexual. ❑ **back-door man** *n.* **1** [1920s+] (*orig. US black*) an adulterer [the adulterer metaphorically comes in 'through the back door']. **2** [1960s+] one who practises anal intercourse; in homosexual anal sex, the active partner. ❑ **back-door trot** *n.* (*also* **back-door trots**) [SE *back-door* that leads to the privy + SE *trot*/TROTS *n.* (1)] **1** [19C+] diarrhoea. **2** [1950s+] over-frequent urination. ❑ **backdoor work** *n.* [late 19C+] anal intercourse, sodomy.

IN PHRASES

❑ **go up the back door** *v.* (*also* **go in the back door**) [pun on SE] [1930s+] to have heterosexual anal intercourse.

back-door *adj.* [*back door*, while often referring to the anus in white use, almost always means underhand or secretive for blacks] [1920s+] (*US black*) devious, cunning, untrustworthy, usu. in combs.

IN COMPOUNDS

❑ **back-door artist** *n.* [-ARTIST *sfx*] [1940s–60s] (*US black/drugs*) a drug addict who preys on fellow addicts for money or drugs. ❑ **backdoor jive** *n.* [JIVE *n.*[1] (2)] [1940s] (*US black*) (inside) information. ❑ **back-door parole** *n.* [SE *back-door* + *parole*. The remains of those who die in prison are taken out surreptitiously and buried in the prison cemetery] [1930s+] (*US prison*) **1** (*also* **back gate parole**) dying in prison before one's sentence is over. **2** parole.

backdoor *v.*[1] [BACK-DOOR *n.*] **1** [early 18C; 1960s+] to subject to anal intercourse. **2** [1960s] to accuse, to inform.

backdoor *v.*[2] [BACK-DOOR MAN *under* BACK-DOOR *n.*] [1980s+] (*Aus. prison*) for one prisoner – just released – to cuckold one who remains imprisoned.

backed *adj.*[1] [either f. lying on one's *back*, or, according to B.E. and then Grose (1785), f. being supported on the *backs* of those who carry one's coffin; SE *backed*, supported at the back, underpins the latter ety.] [late 17C–early 19C] dead.

backed *adj.*[2] [early 19C] dressed.

backed *adj.*[3] [one is 'knocked back/on one's back' by the strength] [1990s+] (*US campus*) intoxicated by marijuana.

backed-up *adj.* [SE *backed up* (usu. of water or of traffic), to have met an obstruction in the flow] [late 19C+] (*US*) constipated.

backee *n. see* BACCA *n.*

backer *n. see* BACCA *n.*

backfall *n.*

IN PHRASES

❑ **do a backfall** *v.* [late 19C] of a woman, to have sexual intercourse.

backfire *v.* [SE *backfire*, for an internal-combustion engine to ignite prematurely; such ignition causes a loud explosion] [1970s+] to break wind; also in fig. use, to speak abusively.

backforce *n.* [1910s] (*W.I.*) a male lover; esp. one who spends money on his girlfriend.

backgammoner *n.* [pun on SE] [early–mid-19C] a sodomite, one who practises anal intercourse.

IN PHRASES

❑ **bad-ass nigger** *n. see* separate entry. ❑ **bad in the head** *adj.* [1980s+] (*US black*) **1** eccentric, out of control. **2** unhappy. ❑ **bad-to-the-bone** *adj.* [2000s] aggressive, thuggish. ❑ **come on bad** *v.* [1960s–70s] (*US black*) to act aggressively, to threaten; to defeat someone in a contest of words. ❑ **get in bad with** *v.* [1910s+] to earn disfavour, to get into trouble. ❑ **get one's head bad** *v.* [1960s–80s] (*US black*) to get drunk, to become intoxicated by drugs. ❑ **in bad** [note Ger. *schlecht*, bad, orig. meant good; also 19C Aus. convict jargon *bad fellow*, a convict who cooperates with the authorities; *good fellow*, one who maintains intra-convict solidarity; Smitherman, *Black Talk* (1994), suggests Mandingo *a ka nyi ko-jugu*, it is good, badly, i.e. so good that it is bad] [20C+] (*US*) **1** out of favour. **2** in trouble.

SE in slang uses

DERIVATIVES

❑ **badster** *n.* [-STER *sfx*] [1920s+] (*Aus.*) a villain, a morally bad person.

IN COMPOUNDS

❑ **bad actor** *n.* **1** [late 19C+] an unpleasant individual, an aggressive trouble-maker; thus adj. *bad-acting*, troublemaking. **2** [1910s–20s] a vicious or unbroken horse. ❑ **bad-arse** *adj. see* BAD-ASS *adj.* ❑ **bad ass** *see* separate entries. ❑ **bad bongos** *n.* [? assonance] [1970s] (*US campus*) a situation in which things do not go as desired/required. ❑ **bad boy** *n. see* separate entry. ❑ **bad break** *n.* [BREAK *n.*[1] (1)] [late 19C+] (*orig. US*) a stroke of bad luck. ❑ **bad-breath** *v.* [1970s] (*US*) to inform on, to speak ill of. ❑ **bad bundle** *n.* [BUNDLE *n.*[1] (3a)] [1970s+] (*drugs*) inferior quality heroin. ❑ **bad count** *n.* [boxing jargon *bad count*, a count that is too long or too short] [1980s] (*US Und.*) **1** an unfair decision. **2** a short measure of drugs. ❑ **bad crowd** *n.* [as a group, use is SE] [late 19C–1900s] (*US*) an unpleasant, untrustworthy person. ❑ **bad dog** *n.* [unpaid, it won't 'lie down'] [1940s+] (*Aus.*) a bad debt. ❑ **bad dough** *n. see* BAD PAPER below. ❑ **bad egg** *n.* [EGG *n.*[2] (1)] (*orig. US*) **1** [mid-19C+] (*also* **rotten egg**) a rogue, a villain. **2** [mid-19C+] a worthless speculation; a disreputable place. **3** [late 19C] as sense 1, of inanimate objects or ideas. **4** [1920s] a tough man. ❑ **bad-eye** *see* separate entries. ❑ **bad face** *n.* [1960s] (*US black*) an unpleasant, disagreeable person. ❑ **bad fall** *n.* [FALL *n.* (1)] [1910s+] (*US Und.*) an arrest and charge from which one cannot escape, despite attempting to intimidate or bribe the plaintiff or a prosecution witness. ❑ **bad-food** *n.* [20C+] (*W.I.*) food that supposedly contains 'magic' ingredients, which will influence a man to choose a particular woman. ❑ **bad go** *n.* (*drugs*) **1** [1950s–70s] a short or disappointing measure of drugs [GO *n.*[1] (1d)]. **2** [1980s+] a bad reaction to a drug [GO *n.*[1] (3)]. ❑ **bad guy** *n.* [1920s+] (*orig. US*) in film or TV melodramas, the stereotyped villain; also as adj. ❑ **bad halfpenny** *n.* **1** [early 19C] any errand or task that proves pointless. **2** [mid-18C–1910s] an unpleasant, untrustworthy person [note Stephens & O'Brien, *Materials for a Dict. of Aus. Slang* (ms.; 1900–10), include the n. as a headword in one of their three mss. and offer definitions as published by Vaux and B&L, but give none of their own]. ❑ **bad hat** *n. see* separate entry. ❑ **bad-head** *n.* **1** [20C+] (*W.I., Belize*) a tearaway, a young criminal. **2** [1960s] (*US*) a very unattractive face. ❑ **bad iron** *n.* [ety. unknown] [mid-19C–1910s] bad luck, a failure, a disaster. ❑ **bad john** *n.* [JOHN *n.* (1)] **1** [1960s–70s] (*W.I./UK black*) a tearaway, a young criminal; thus *badjohnism*, criminality; *play bad-john*, to act like a hooligan (although not actually to be one). **2** [1970s] (*UK black*) a gangster, an important criminal. ❑ **bad lamps** *n.* [LAMP *n.* (2)] [1960s+] (*US gay*) dark glasses. ❑ **bad land** *n.* [ironic use of SE *badlands*, arid, barren areas of the western US] [late 19C+] (*US*) **1** the slum area of a city (orig. coined for that in Chicago). **2** any dangerous area. ❑ **bad lot** *n.* [auction house jargon *bad lot*, one that will not sell] [mid-19C+] an unpleasant, untrustworthy person. ❑ **Bad Man** *n. see* separate entry. ❑ **bad medicine** *n.* [the SE use of *medicine* to translate terms used in a variety of native American languages meaning a fetish, spell or charm; note use of 'bad juju' and 'juju-man' in the spy novels of John le Carré (b.1931)] [mid-19C+] (*orig. US*) something or someone sinister or ill-fated. ❑ **bad-mind** *see* separate entries. ❑ **badmouth** *see* separate entries. ❑ **bad news** *see* separate entries. ❑ **bad note** *n. see under* NOTE *n.*[2]. ❑ **bad paper** *n.* [PAPER *n.*/DOUGH *n.* (1)] **1** [1910s+] (*also* **bad dough**) any form of fraudulent documents, counterfeit money or similar written or printed frauds or forgeries. **2** [1960s+] an IOU that will not be paid by the debtor. **3** [1990s+] (*US prison*) a negative report on a prisoner. ❑ **bad-pay** *adj.* [20C+] (*W.I.*) extremely slow to pay debts or any money that is owed and expected. ❑ **bad penny** *n.* (*also* **bad shilling**) [mid-19C+] an unpleasant, untrustworthy person. ❑ **bad poker** *n.* [1920s] (*US Und.*) a mistake, a foolish move. ❑ **bad rap** *n. see under* RAP *n.*[1]. ❑ **bad rap** *v. see under* RAP *v.*[1]. ❑ **bad scran** *n.* (*also* **bad scram, ...scrant**) [SCRAN *n.*] [mid-19C+] (*orig. Anglo-Irish*) bad luck, usu. as phr. *bad scran to.* ❑ **bad shag** *n.* [SHAG *n.*[1] (1); note SHAG *n.*[1] (4), used later 20C+ in phrs. like 'a good shag', 'a bad shag'] [late 18C–early 19C] an unsatisfactory lover, usu. in phr. *he is but bad shag.* ❑ **bad shilling** *n.* **1** [late 19C] one's last shilling. **2** *see* BAD PENNY above. **3** (*Aus.*) a remittance man. ❑ **bad shit** *n. see* separate entry. ❑ **bad shot** *n.* [SHOT *n.*[1] (5a)] [mid-19C+] a poor guess. ❑ **bad siddown** *n.* [SE *bad sit-down*; the image is of a prostitute lazing around on a street corner; also note Krio (Sierra Leone Creole) *bad sidom*, a woman sitting so as to expose her genitals] [20C+] (*W.I., Jam.*) poor behaviour in public, disregard of other people's feelings. ❑ **bad smash** *n.* [SMASH *n.*[2] (1)] [20C+] counterfeit coins. ❑ **bad steer** *n. see* BUM STEER *under* BUM *adj.* ❑ **bad time** *n.* [TIME *n.* (1)] [1970s] (*US Und.*) a prison sentence that causes the subject, who cannot acclimatize, a great deal of suffering. ❑ **bad-time** *v.* [1960s] (*US*) to be sexually unfaithful to one's partner. ❑ **bad trip** *n.* [TRIP *n.*[4] (1a)] [1960s+] **1** (*drugs*) a bad or frightening experience while taking psychedelic drugs; also as v. **2** ext. as any sort of unpleasant or unnerving experience. ❑ **bad trot** *n.* [TROT *n.*[2] (4)] (*Aus.*) **1** [20C+] an unfair situation or result. **2** [1920s+] a run of bad luck. ❑ **bad 'un** *n.* [lit. 'a bad one'] **1** [mid–late 19C] (*UK Und.*) a counterfeit coin. **2** [mid-19C+] a rogue, an untrustworthy person; also used of a horse.

IN PHRASES

❑ **bad case of the tins** *n. see under* CASE *n.*[1]. ❑ **badly done** *adj.* [SE *badly* + DO *v.*[1] (2a)] [20C+] (*Ulster*) embarrassed. ❑ **bad place in the road** *n.* (*also* **bad spot in the road, narrow place..., spot...**) [1930s–60s] (*US*) an out-of-the-way, unimportant place or settlement. ❑ **bad up** *v. see* separate entry. ❑ **have it bad** *v.* **1** [late 19C+] to be experiencing something intensely, e.g. illness, sexual obsession, love, delirium tremens. **2** [1960s+] to be sexually frustrated. **3** [1970s] to be heavily addicted to narcotics. ❑ **have them bad** *v.* [late 19C–1910s] to be suffering from delirium tremens. ❑ **in a bad loaf** [var. on IN BAD BREAD *under* BREAD *n.*[1]] [late 18C–early 19C] in trouble, in a difficult situation. ❑ **in bad bread** *see under* BREAD *n.*[1].

IN EXCLAMATIONS

❑ **bad cess to you!** (*also* **good cess to you!**) [? abbr. SE *success* (*OED*); Ware suggests dial. *cess*, a piece of turf; thus 'may you live in a good/bad place'; Partridge prefers *cess*, assessment; thus 'may you suffer a good/bad (tax) assessment'] [mid-19C+] (*orig. Irish*) bad (or good) luck to you! ❑ **bad show!** [20C+] a general excl. of disappointment or disapproval.

bad-ass *n.* [SE *bad* + -ASS *sfx*] **1** [1950s+] (*US*) an unpleasant, aggressive individual. **2** [1970s+] (*US*) on bad = good model, a tough, admirable individual; also occas. metonymic for one's whole body. **3** [1970s+] (*US black*) an untrustworthy male.

bad-ass *adj.* (*also* **ass-bad, bad-arse, bad-assed**) [BAD-ASS *n.*; given the use of *bad*, the term is as much congratulatory as not] (*orig. US black*) **1** [1950s] unpleasant. **2** [1950s+] tough, aggressive, frightening, thus *baddest-ass*. **3** [1970s+] of people, animals, objects: formidable, admirable, first-rate.

bad ass *v.* [BAD-ASS *n.* (1)] [1970s+] (*US*) to bully, to behave like a thug.

bad-ass nigger *n.* [BAD-ASS *adj.* (2) + NIGGER *n.*[1] (1)] [1980s+] (*US black*) **1** (*also* **bad man**) an aggressive, tough black man who rejects the constraints and humiliation of the role the white authorities have selected for him. **2** thus *bad-ass bitch*, the female equivalent.

bad boy *n.* [BAD *adj.* + SE *boy*] **1** [1920s+] (*mainly W.I., Guyn.*) (*also* **bad bwai, bad bwoy**) a tearaway, a young criminal; in positive version, a black who rejects the second-class role offered by the dominant white society. **2** [1950s] (*US black*) a general term of approval, referring both to individuals and to objects. **3** [2000s] (*US*) anything considered impressive.

bad-boy *adj.* [BAD BOY *n.* (2)] [1980s] (*US black*) attractive, well-dressed.

baddie *n.* (*also* **baddy**) [nursery use of SE *bad*] **1** [1900s] (*Aus.*) an immoral person. **2** [1930s+] an unpleasant person; spec. a criminal. **3** [1940s+] in film or TV melodramas, the stereotyped villain who must, and will, be vanquished. **4** [1960s] (*US campus*) a difficult course.

baddiwad *n.* [BADDIE *n.* (2) + sfx -WAD *sfx*; coined by Anthony Burgess in *A Clockwork Orange* (1962)] [1960s+] (*US teen*) something that is bad.

bade *v.* [? BAD *adj.* (4)] [1990s+] (*W.I.*) to make lots of money, usu. in gambling.

Baden-Powell *n.* [rhy. sl.; ult. Robert *Baden-Powell* (1857–1941), the founder of the Boy Scouts] **1** [late 19C–1960s] a trowel. **2** [20C+] (*Aus.*) a towel.

badered *adj.* [LEGLESS *adj.* (1); ult. the RAF's 'legless ace' Sir Douglas *Bader* (1910–82), immortalized in the film *Reach for the Sky* (1956)] [1980s+] drunk.

bad-eye *n.*[1] [? var. on RED-EYE *n.* (1a); + ? it may render the drinker *blind*/BLIND *adj.*[1] (1)] [late 19C] (*US*) cheap, home-distilled whisky.

bad-eye *n.*[2] [? Mandingo *nyejugu*; unlike many black uses of *bad*, this uses the SE *bad*, evil, rather than BAD *adj.* (3) good] [late 19C+] (*orig. US black*) a threatening glance, a threat, the evil eye; the starer; thus adv. *bad-eye*, menacingly.

bad-eye *v.* [BAD-EYE *n.*[2]] [1950s+] (*US black/P.R.*) to stare down.

badge *n.*[1] **1** [18C–mid-19C] (*UK Und.*) in fig. senses. (**a**) a brand used as a judicial punishment. (**b**) one who has been thus branded. **2** [1920s+] from the wearer's badge of office. (**a**) (*US prison*) a warder, a guard, anyone in authority. (**b**) (*US*) a police officer; *private badge*, a private detective.

IN COMPOUNDS

❑ **badge-cove** *n.* [COVE *n.* (1); *badge* in this case meaning an official document or licence; an Und. version of SE *badge-man*, a licensed beggar or almsman] [early 18C–mid-19C] one who draws a pension from their parish; they are distinguished by a special badge. ❑ **badge-man** *n.* **1** [1920s] (*US*) a detective. **2** [1940s–50s] (*US prison*) an inmate who identifies with the authorities rather than his peers [the *badge* of the person in charge].

badge *n.*[2] *see* BADGER *n.*[1] (6).

badge *v.* [1960s+] (*US*) to show one's badge (typically that of a police department) to gain (free) admission.

badger *n.*[1] [SE *badger*, an animal which is nocturnal and carnivorous; the prostitute/thief also 'devours' their victims after dark; senses 9 to 12 are less 'aggressive' versions of sense 7] (*UK Und.*) **1** [early 18C] (*UK Und.*) a pimp. **2** [early 18C–mid-19C] a thief who specializes in robbery on the riverbank, after which he murders the victim and disposes of the corpse in the water. **3** [early 19C+] (*US*) an old man [? the ill-temper of the animal]. **4** [mid-19C+] (*US*) the nickname of the natives or inhabitants of Wisconsin, the *Badger State*; the early Wisconsin lead-miners (*badgers*) lived in subterranean diggings alongside the seams of lead they were mining; for detailed discussion see R.H. Thornton, *An American Glossary*, I 32–3 (1912). **5** [mid-19C+] a thief who rifles the pockets of a man who is currently engaged with his accomplice, a prostitute. **6** [late 19C–1940s] (*US*) (*also* **badge**) a prostitute, esp. one who participates in a scheme to rob her clients. **7** [1930s] (*US Und.*) a man who dresses as a woman in order to exploit other men for money. **8** [1990s+] (*US*) an unattractive woman; thus *badger set*, anywhere that such women can take advantage of a young man. **9** *see* BADGER GAME below.

IN COMPOUNDS

❑ **badger-crib** *n.* [CRIB *n.*[1] (3)] [mid-19C–1900s] a brothel that specializes in robbing its clients. ❑ **badger game** *n.* [SE *game*, scheme, intrigue] [mid-19C+] (*orig. US*) **1** (*also* **badger**) the ensnaring of a client by a woman, often a prostitute, and his subsequent robbery, either by the woman herself or more often by her pimp, posing as an 'outraged boyfriend'; the man often emerged, while the pair were *in flagrante*, from a hidden door or panel in the bedroom wall. **2** in ext. use, to perform a confidence trick based on exploiting the victim's interest in a woman. ❑ **badger house** *n.* [HOUSE *n.*[1] (1)] [mid-19C–1900s] (*US*) an establishment, often a brothel, where the client is robbed. ❑ **badger-man** *n.* [1910s+] (*Aus.*) the accomplice of a prostitute who tricks her clients. ❑ **badger moll** *n.* [MOLL *n.* (1)] [1900s] (*US*) a woman, often a prostitute, who tricks her client. ❑ **badger worker** *n.* (*also* **badger game worker**) [SE *worker*/WORKER *n.*[1] (1)] [late 19C–1940s] (*US*) the accomplice of a prostitute who tricks her clients.

IN PHRASES

❑ **growl at the badger** *v.* [1970s+] to perform cunnilingus.

SE in slang uses

IN COMPOUNDS

❑ **badger-box** *n.* [late 19C] (*Aus.*) 'a roughly-constructed dwelling' (Morris, *Austral English*, 1898). ❑ **badger-gassing** *n.* [1990s+] (*UK juv.*) an especially foul-smelling breaking of wind. ❑ **badger-legged** *adj.* [the erroneous belief that badgers are similarly equipped] [mid-17C–early 18C] used of a person with one leg shorter than the other.

badger *n.*[2] [19C] (*US*) a chamberpot; thus *the badger fight*, *pulling the badger*, a practical joke whereby an innocent is lured into a hoax fight between a dog and a badger but ends up being splashed by the contents of a chamberpot.

badger *v.* [BADGER *n.*[1] (6)] [late 19C+] of a prostitute, to steal from a client; thus n. *badgering*; also used of her male accomplice.

badger-bill *n.* [dial. *badger-bill*, a two-edged machete] [1940s+] (*W.I.*) a hypocrite, a 'two-faced', untrustworthy person.

bad hat *n.* [according to Charles Mackay's *Memoirs of Extraordinary Popular Delusions* (1841) f. a London election in the borough of Southwark, *c.*1838, in which one of the candidates was well known as a hat-maker. As he campaigned he would single out any voter whose hat fell beneath the highest standards and declare: 'What a shocking bad hat you have got, call at my warehouse and you shall have a new one.' On the day of the election, as he gave his final speech, his opponents urged a hostile crowd to drown him out by chanting: 'What a shocking bad hat!' The phr. caught on and, first in its entirety, and subseq. in its abbr. form, entered popular sl. It survived through the 19C and gradually declined through the first half of the 20C+. An alternative ety. attributes the phr. to the Duke of Wellington, who on his first visit to the Peer's Gallery of the House of Commons remarked, on looking down on the members of the Reform Parliament: 'I never saw so many shocking bad hats in my life'; but note Egan, *Book of Sports* (1832): 'I will allow those blackguard little boys again to insult me with the prevailing, foolish, unmeaning phrase of "What a shocking bad hat you have got!" if ever they lay hold of me more'] [early 19C–1950s] a rogue, an untrustworthy person; as adj., *bad-hat*.

badly packed kebab *n.* [2000s] the vagina.

Bad Man *n.* (*also* **Bad Man Below**) [20C+] (*US black*) the Devil.

bad man *n. see* BAD-ASS NIGGER *n.* (1).

bad-mind *n.* [20C+] (*W.I.*) malice, spite, animosity.

IN PHRASES

❑ **play bad-mind** *v.* [20C+] (*W.I.*) to act in a spiteful, malicious way.

bad-mind *adj.* [BAD-MIND *n.*] [20C+] (*W.I.*) envious, malicious, wishing someone ill.

badminton *n.* [the iced cup, made of claret, sugar, spice and cucumber peel, was invented at Badminton, the country seat of the Duke of Beaufort; the term was extended to boxing jargon where it meant blood, as does CLARET *n.*] [mid-19C] **1** claret cup. **2** blood.

badmouth *n.* [SE but note Mandingo *dajugu*, bad mouth] (*orig. US black/W.I.*) **1** [1960s+] a curse, a spell. **2** [1970s+]

malicious gossip. **3** [1980s+] one who talks maliciously or argumentatively.

IN PHRASES

❑ **put the bad mouth on** *v.* [1960s+] to vilify.

badmouth *adj.* [BADMOUTH *n.* (2)] [1970s+] malicious, defamatory.

badmouth *v.* [BADMOUTH *n.*] [1940s+] **1** to attack verbally, to slander. **2** to beat someone in an argument or verbal contest.

bad news *n.* (*orig. US*) **1** [1910s+] the bill, usu. in a café or restaurant. **2** [1910s+] an unattractive, unpleasant person or thing. **3** [1920s+] a shotgun or revolver. **4** [1930s] one's death, usu. in phr. *hear the bad news*, to be killed. **5** [1930s+] the losing throw of three in craps dice. **6** [1940s+] an unpleasant situation, difficulty, trouble. **7** [1940s+] a troublesome, threatening person. **8** [1960s] a pessimist.

IN COMPOUNDS

❑ **bad news wagon** *n.* [1970s] a police car.

bad news *adj.* [BAD NEWS *n.* (2)] [1960s+] (*orig. US*) unpleasant, threatening.

bad shit *n.*[1] [BAD *adj.* (3) + SHIT *n.* (6b)] **1** [1950s] uncured marijuana. **2** [1960s+] better than average marijuana. **3** [1980s+] anything good.

bad shit *n.*[2] [SE *bad* + SHIT *n.* (3c)] [1960s+] worse than average problems.

bad siddown *n.* [SE *bad sit-down*; the image is of a prostitute lazing around on a street corner; also note Krio (Sierra Leone Creole) *bad sidom*, a woman sitting so as to expose her genitals] [20C+] (*W.I.,Jam.*) poor behaviour in public, disregard of other people's feelings.

bad up *v.* [1990s+] (*UK black/drugs*) to render paranoid, to cause trouble.

baduzi *n.* [BOOTY *n.*[2] (1) + DICK *n.*[1] (5) + PUSSY *n.* (1)] [2000s] (*US black*) the smell of sex.

bafan *adj.* [synon. Twi *bafan*] [1950s+] (*W.I. Rasta*) clumsy, awkward; thus *bafang*, a child who has not learned to walk by the age of seven.

baff *n.* [supposedly mimicking the 'sound' of ejaculation] [2000s] (*S.Afr. gay*) semen; thus as v., to ejaculate.

baff *v.* [onomatopoeia] [1980s] (*S.Afr.*) to smell.

baffin *n.* see BIFFIN *n.*[2].

bafflegab *n.* [SE *baffle* + GAB *n.*[2] (2); coined May 1952, by the assistant general counsel of the US Chamber of Commerce, Milton Smith: 'I decided we needed a new and catchy word to describe the utter incomprehensibility, ambiguity, verbosity and complexity of government regulations'] [1950s+] (*US*) (deliberately) unintelligible jargon, esp. as used for the purposes of obfuscation by politicians, civil servants, bureaucrats, businessmen etc.

bafoon *n.* (*also* **puffoon**) [echoic] **1** [20C+] (*W.I.*) a stench, esp. a fart. **2** [2000s] a term of abuse, fool.

bag *n.*[1] **1** as a container or receptacle. (**a**) [mid-16C+] the scrotum [note *double entendre* in D'Urfey, *Pills to Purge Melancholy* (1719): 'But what is this that hangs under his Chin, / [...] / 'Tis the Bag he puts his Provender in']. (**b**) [early 17C] the vagina; one of many terms that refer to the vagina as a receptacle, usu. for sperm or the penis. (**c**) [late 17C+] the womb. (**d**) [mid-19C–1900s] (*UK Und.*) a purse. (**e**) [1920s] (*US prison*) a straitjacket, used for punishment. (**f**) [1920s+] (*US*) a contraceptive sheath. (**g**) [1940s] the stomach. (**h**) [1990s+] (*US campus*) the buttocks. **2** as a lit. or fig. *bag* of money. (**a**) [mid-19C] (*UK Und.*) the act and proceeds of pickpocketing. (**b**) [20C+] (*Aus.*) any form of gain, lit. or fig. (**c**) [1920s+] (*US Und.*) the proceeds of any illegal activity, e.g. unauthorized bookmaking. **3** as an unattractive and/or promiscuous person, usu. a woman. (**a**) [late 19C+] (*US*) a promiscuous woman, a prostitute. (**b**) [1920s+] (*orig. US*) (*also* **old sack**) an unattractive woman, esp. as *old bag*; occas. as adj. (**c**) [1930s+] a homosexual man, esp. an unattractive and/or passive one. **4** [1910s–20s] (*Aus.*) a meal, a 'feed', or a drinking session [a fig. 'bag' of food]. **5** [1940s+] in the context of drinking. (**a**) a state of drunkeness or intoxication. (**b**) a hangover. (**c**) (*US black*) a bottle of beer. **6** [1940s+] (*US campus*) a despised person, an outsider; one who 'brings their lunch in a bag'. **7** (*orig. US drugs*) as a measurement or container of drugs. (**a**) [1950s+] a measure of narcotics, typically sold as a *nickel bag*, $5 worth or a *dime bag*, $10 worth. (**b**) [1950s+] a store of drugs, as carried by a dealer. (**c**) [1960s+] a balloon containg heroin, thus through metonymy, the heroin itself. (**d**) [1980s+] a quarter-ounce (7g) measure of a drug, usu. marijuana. **8** [1960s] a form of bludgeon made from several socks inside each other, filled with sand packed round a solid, ball-shaped object [abbr. SE *sandbag*]. **9** [1960s+] (*US*) a bed, orig. a *bag* of straw or feathers, esp. in phr. *bag it*, *hit the bag*, go to bed, go to sleep.

DERIVATIVES

❑ **bageroo** *n.* [-EROO *sfx*] [1930s] (*US*) a prostitute.

IN COMPOUNDS

❑ **bag bride** *n.* [ironic use of SE *bride*] [1990s+] (*drugs*) a prostitute who is addicted to crack cocaine. ❑ **bag-chasing** *n.* [1970s] obsessed by obtaining narcotic drugs. ❑ **bag dude** *n.* [DUDE *n.*[1] (1)] [1970s] (*US black*) a drug dealer. ❑ **baghead** *n.* [-HEAD *sfx* (4)] [2000s] (*drugs*) a heroin addict. ❑ **bag ho** *n.* [HO *n.* (2)] [2000s] (*US black*) an extremely unattractive woman. ❑ **bagman** *n.* see separate entry. ❑ **bag-thief** *n.* see BAGGER *n.*[1]. ❑ **bag woman** *n.* [the female version of BAGMAN *n.* (5)] [1960s+] (*US*) a female go-between, taking money (usu. bribes or other illicit pay-offs) between two parties.

IN PHRASES

❑ **bagged up** *adj.* wearing a contraceptive. ❑ **big bag** *n.* [SE *big*, important] [1960s+] (*drugs*) **1** heroin. **2** a large wholesale quantity of narcotics. ❑ **bring a bag off** *v.* [mid-19C] (*UK Und.*) to pick pockets (successfully). ❑ **chase the bag** *v.* [1960s+] (*US drugs*) to seek out supplies and/or to be addicted to heroin. ❑ **have a bag on** *v.* **1** [1940s] to have a hangover. **2** [1940s+] to be drunk or intoxicated with a drug. ❑ **have the bag on** *v.* [1900s] to work as a bookmaker. ❑ **hooked through the bag** *adj.* [HOOKED *adj.*[3]] [1950s] (*US drugs*) heavily addicted to narcotics. ❑ **put the bag on** *v.* **1** [20C+] (*Ulster*) to start out as a beggar [a beggar's bag]. **2** [1930s+] (*US*) to enjoy a raucous drinking bout or party. **3** [1970s+] (*Aus./N.Z.*) to breathalyse [the polythene bag that is part of the breathalysing kit]. ❑ **put the bee on** *v.* (*also* **put the B on**) [initial letter of 'bag' in SE *put the bag on*, to halt, to interfere with, to bring to a standstill] [1900s–40s] (*US*) to quash, to bring to an end, to ruin. ❑ **run bag** *v.* [1950s] to work as a go-between, esp. to collect or administer money obtained by various criminal activities.

IN EXCLAMATIONS

❑ **the bag is off!** [mid-19C] (*UK Und.*) the purse, wallet etc has been removed from the victim; as excl., a statement denoting the successful conclusion of a crime: 'we've done it!'.

SE in slang uses

IN COMPOUNDS

❑ **bag and bottle** *n.* [mid–late 17C] food and drink. ❑ **bag-carrier** *n.* [the *bag* in which he keeps his cash] [1900s] (*Aus.*) a bookmaker. ❑ **bag job** *n.* [JOB *n.*[2] (2)] **1** [1960s] (*US campus*) an unpleasant person [i.e. one who deserves a *bag* over their head]. **2** [1970s] (*US*) (*also* **black bag job**) 'an illegal search of a suspect's property by agents of the Federal Bureau of Investigation, esp. for the purpose of copying or stealing incriminating documents etc' (*OED*). ❑ **bag lady** *n.* see separate entry. ❑ **bagpipe(s)/piping** see separate entries. ❑ **bag-puncher** *n.* [PUNCH THE BAG below] [1900s] a gossip. ❑ **bag-slinger** *n.* [the trad. street prostitute carried a large bag] [1930s] (*US*) a street-walker. ❑ **bag-swinger** *n.* [their essential equipment] (*Aus.*) **1** [1930s+] a bookmaker. **2** [1950s–60s] a street-walker, a prostitute.

IN PHRASES

❑ **bag it** *v.* [Yorkshire dial. *bag out*, for a farm-worker to bring their packed lunch to the fields] [1970s] (*US campus/teen*) to bring one's lunch in a paper bag. ❑ **bag of beer** *n.* (*also* **bag o' beer**) [? joc. use of SE; note Fraser & Gibbons *Soldier & Sailor Words & Phrases* (1925): 'Bag Of, A: Sufficiency, Plenty; e.g. A Bag of Beer'] **1** [late 19C] (*Aus.*) a drunk. **2** [late 19C–1900s] a quart pot of beer, holding a mixture of porter and ale. ❑ **bag of bones** *n.*

see separate entries. ❑ **bag of goon** *n. see* GOON *n.*[3]. ❑ **bag of guts** *n.* [late 19C–1970s] (*US*) a fat person. ❑ **bag of hump** *n.* [1930s] a contemptible person. ❑ **bag of jello** *n. see* JELLO-BRAIN *n.* ❑ **bag of mystery** *n.* (*also* **mystery, mystery bag**) [their dubious constituents; note RN use *mystery torpedoes, links of love*; British Army use *spotted mystery*] [late 19C+] a saveloy, a sausage. ❑ **bag of nails** *n.* [joc. pron. of SE *bacchanals* + the disorder of such a bagful] [mid-19C–1940s] (*Aus./US*) chaos, disorder. ❑ **bag of nuts** *n.* (*also* **bag of oats**) [1910s] something, or someone, exceptional. ❑ **bag of pus** *n. see* PUS-BAG *n.* ❑ **bag of shells** *n.* [1950s+] (*Aus.*) a trifle, an unimportant object. ❑ **bag of shit** *n. see under* SHIT *n.* ❑ **bag of smacked twats** *n. see under* TWAT *n.* ❑ **bag of snakes** *n.* **1** [1910s–50s] (*Aus.*) a drooping female breast [such a bag is misshapen, lumpy, soft]. **2** [1950s+] (*Can.*) a lively, sexy young woman [the liveliness of such a bag]. ❑ **bag of tricks** *n.* [SE *bag of tricks*, a clever or dextrous device] **1** [mid–late 19C] the penis. **2** [mid-19C+] whatever one needs. **3** [late 19C] the vagina. ❑ **bag of tripe** *n.* [TRIPE *n.*[2]] [mid-19C+] an unpleasant person. ❑ **bag of wind** *n.* (*also* **sack of wind**) [19C+] a talkative person, a boaster. ❑ **bag o' wank** *n.* [WANK *n.*] [1990s+] a general term of abuse. ❑ **bag-o-wire** *n.* [i.e. if one grasps a bag of (barbed) wire one will get hurt] [1950s+] (*W.I. Rasta*) a betrayer. ❑ **black bag job** *n. see* BAG JOB above. ❑ **doing the bag** *n. see* BAGGING *n.*[3]. ❑ **give someone the bag** *v.* (*also* **give someone the kickout, ...the pike**) [the handing over of a fig. bag of problems, responsibilities etc; SE *bag*, i.e. of possessions/KICKOUT *n.* (1)/SE *pike*; Nares defines phr. as 'to cheat'] [late 16C–19C] **1** to depart suddenly. **2** to dismiss, usu. from a job. **3** to jilt or reject a suitor, to end a relationship. ❑ **have the bags (off)** *v.* [mid–late 19C] to be well-off, to be rich. ❑ **hold the bag** *v. see* separate entry. ❑ **in the bag** (*orig. US*) **1** implying certainty, termination. (**a**) [20C+] secured, made certain. (**b**) [1910s+] of a criminal, arrested, caught. (**c**) [1920s+] of any situation, e.g. a trial or a sporting contest, the outcome has been made certain by the giving of bribes, doping of one or more contestants, horses etc. (**d**) [1980s+] committed. **2** [1910s+] (*also* **in a bag**) in trouble, facing difficulties. **3** [1920s+] (*orig. US*) in debt. **4** [1940s+] (*orig. US*) (*also* **in the wrapper, out of one's bag**) drunk; thus *half in the bag*, beginning to become drunk. **5** [1960s] (*US campus*) feeling ill. ❑ **pull something out of the bag** *v.* [1920s+] to come up with something special or surprising, something held in reserve. ❑ **punch the bag** *v.* [boxing imagery] [1900s–20s] (*US*) **1** to gossip, to chatter. **2** to complain; thus *bag-puncher*, a gossip, a whinger; *bag-punching*, gossiping, complaining. ❑ **suck the bag** *v. see under* SUCK *v.*[1]. ❑ **swing a bag** *v. see under* SWING *v.* ❑ **swing the bag** *v.* [the bookmaker's money *bag*] [1960s+] (*Aus.*) of a bookmaker, to take bets at a racetrack. ❑ **take a bag** *v.* [1960s] (*US campus*) to experience an undesirable situation.

IN EXCLAMATIONS

❑ **put your head in a bag!** [1900s] be quiet! shut up!

bag *n.*[2] [used in 1930s to refer to an actual *bag* used to hold bootleg liquor and in 1940s–50s to that which held narcotics, *bag* took on its abstract (and still current) meaning in the 1960s; Gold, *A Jazz Lexicon* (1964), suggests link to *bag of tricks*] [1960s+] (*orig. US black*) **1** taste, disposition, attitude, occupation, preference, way of life. **2** one's preferred drug.

IN PHRASES

❑ **come out of a bag** *v.* **1** [1930s] (*US black*) to act in an obnoxious manner. **2** [1990s+] to act contrary to expectations, to behave illogically in a given situation. ❑ **get one's own bag going** *v.* [1960s] (*US campus*) to pursue one's own interests. ❑ **have a bag** *v.* [1960s–70s] (*US black*) to have a problem; thus *have a bag and a half*, to have a very great problem.

bag *n.*[3] *see* BAG (OF FRUIT) *n.*

bag *n.*[4] *see* FRATTY-BAGGER *under* FRATTY *adj.*

bag, the *n.* **1** [late 19C+] (*Glasgow*) money. **2** *see* SACK *n.* (2a).

bag *v.* **1** as a lit. or fig. assault. (**a**) [19C+] to shoot (to kill), of animals and humans. (**b**) [1910s+] to hit, to knock out. (**c**) [1960s+] (*US, mainly campus/teen*) of a man, to seduce, to have sexual intercourse with. (**d**) [1970s+] (*US gay*) to have homosexual anal intercourse. (**e**) [1990s+] (*Aus.*) to wound, to beat. **2** fig. to 'place in a bag' for gain. (**a**) [early 19C+] to seize, to catch, to arrest. (**b**) [mid-19C+] to steal; to rob. (**c**) [mid-19C+] to gain, to secure possession of, to win for oneself (esp. after repeated efforts). (**d**) [1910s+] to claim. (**e**) [1990s+] to get something non-material. **3** lit. or fig. to hide or 'throw away' into a bag. (**a**) [mid–late 19C] to dismiss [dial. *bag*, to dismiss, to jilt]. (**b**) [1950s+] (*Aus./US*) to denigrate, to criticize. (**c**) [1960s+] (*US*) to make a mess of, to fail at, to botch. (**d**) [1960s+] (*US campus*) to miss a class or examination; to give up a course of study; often as *bag school, bag it*, see below. (**e**) [1960s+] (*US campus*) to neglect, to stop doing something, to dismiss or disregard an idea or plan. (**f**) [1980s] to break a date, to 'stand someone up'. (**g**) [1980s+] (*US campus*) to throw away; to give up. (**h**) [1980s+] (*US*) to hide something unpleasant from the speaker's sight. (**i**) [1980s+] (*US campus*) to kidnap, esp. as part of a fraternity prank. **4** [1950s+] (*US black*) to swallow semen or vaginal fluid during oral intercourse [SE *bag*, a receptacle, in this case the mouth]. **5** [1960s+] (*drugs*) (*also* **bag up**) to divide bulk purchases of drugs into smaller quantities for dealing. **6** [1960s+] (*US*) to classify, to put into categories. **7** [1960s+] (*US drugs*) to inhale glue or a similarly intoxicating substance, by pouring into a paper or polythene *bag*, from which the fumes are sucked into one's mouth. **8** [1970s] (*US*) to wear.

IN COMPOUNDS

❑ **bag-off** *adj. see* separate entry.

IN PHRASES

❑ **bag it (up)** *v.* (*US*) **1** [late 19C–1930s] to play truant. **2** [1960s] to fake illness to get out of work [note milit. jargon *bag it*, to malinger]. **3** [1960s+] to disregard, to give up. **4** [1960s+] (*US campus*) to be quiet, usu. as imper. **5** [1970s] to go to sleep. ❑ **bag off** *v. see* separate entry. ❑ **bag on** *v.* [1980s+] (*US campus*) **1** to criticize, usu. wittily. **2** to complain. ❑ **bag one's head** *v.* (*also* **bag one's lip**) [lit. 'put one's head in a bag'] [mid–late 19C+] (*US*) to give in, to back off, to admit defeat; usu. as imper. ❑ **bag onto** *v.* [1940s] (*US*) to notice, to pay attention to, often as imper. *bag onto that*, take a look at that. ❑ **bag some rays** *v. see under* RAYS *n.* ❑ **bag up** *v.* **1** *see* sense 5 above. **2** *see also* separate entries. ❑ **bag Z's** *v. see under* Z *n.*[1].

IN EXCLAMATIONS

❑ **bag that!** (*also* **bag it!**) [1960s+] (*US*) forget it! ❑ **bag your face!** (*also* **go bag your head!**) [basically requesting a person to put their face into a rubbish bag and throw it away] [1910s+] (*orig. US*) a general dismissive excl.

-bag *sfx* [SE *bag*/BAG *n.*[1] (1f); the implication is of being a receptacle for something, most usu. sperm; note also BAG *n.*[1] (3)/BAG *n.*[1] (6)] [1910s+] a sfx used in comb. with another term, usu. a n., to describe a contemptible, despised person; when of a woman, often with implications of promiscuity.

bagaga *n.* (*also* **bagada**) [Ital. *baggagio*, baggage] [1970s+] (*Ling. Fr./Polari*) the penis.

bagaga *v.* [BAGAGA *n.*] [1960s] (*US*) of a man, to have sexual intercourse; one of a number of verbs that are backf. from a sl. term for penis or vagina.

bag-blind *adj.* [Bdos. *bag-blind*, a rudimentary window blind made of a jute sack used for sugar, flour etc] [20C+] (*W.I.*) socially contemptible, very low class, slum-dwelling.

bagel *n.* [Yid. *bagel*, a style of doughnut-shaped bread roll popular among Jews] **1** [1950s+] (*US*) (*also* **Jew bagel**) a Jew. **2** [1980s+] (*S.Afr.*) a spoilt, wealthy, upper-class (Jewish) young man.

IN COMPOUNDS

❑ **bagel baby** *n.* (*also* **blintze queen**) [BABY *n.* (3)] [1950s+] (*US*) a young middle-class Jewish woman, active in liberal causes. ❑ **bagel bender** *n.* [1970s+] (*US*) a Jew.

baggage *n.* **1** [16C–17C] a worthless man. **2** [16C–17C] rubbish, nonsense. **3** [late 16C+] a woman, esp. one considered immoral or sexually autonomous [the image of woman as a man's burden or encumbrance; the initial use is often synon. with a camp-follower (a woman who follows the military)

one's intestines] [late 19C+] to refrain from visiting the lavatory, however desperate the need to defecate. ❑ **bake potatoes** *v.* [? the 'warming' of the testicles in conjuction with the buttocks] [1930s+] (*US gay*) to have anal intercourse. ❑ **bake someone's bread** *v.* [fig. use of SE] [late 14C] to kill, to 'do for'.

bake *v.*[2] [play on ROAST *v.* (3)] [1980s+] (*Aus. prison*) to reprimand; to criticize severely.

baked *adj.* **1** [late 18C–1900s] (*also* **baked up**) exhausted. **2** [late 19C; 1980s] (*also* **baked up**) sun-burned or very tanned. **3** [1900s; 1980s+] (*US campus*) drunk. **4** [1980s+] (*US*) under the influence of marijuana.

baked bean *n.* **1** [1990s+] (*Aus.*) a male homosexual [rhy. sl. = QUEEN *n.* (2a)]. **2** [2000s] a sexual encounter [rhy. sl. = SCENE *n.* (6)].

baked dinner *n.* [used to fool new arrivals at a prison who assume such a dinner will be somewhat more extensive] [late 19C–1900s] (*UK Und.*) bread.

baked potato *n. see* FRIED POTATO *n.*

baked up *adj.* **1** *see* BAKED *adj.* (1). **2** *see* BAKED *adj.* (2).

baked wind *n.* [var. on HOT AIR *n.*] [1900s–20s] (*US*) nonsense, rubbish.

baker *n.*[1] [mistranslation by a French author of *loafer*] [mid–late 19C] (*US Und.*) an idler.

baker *n.*[2] [BAKE *v.*[1] (2)] [1950s] (*US Und.*) the electric chair.

baker *n.*[3] [initial letter B] [1960s] (*US campus*) the grade B.

baker-kneed *adj.* (*also* **baker-legged**) [a physical problem that supposedly results from a baker's job; in folk myth knock-knees are one of the 'proofs' of effeminacy] **1** [17C] effeminate. **2** [mid-17C–late 19C] knock kneed.

baker's dozen *n.*[1] [SE post-1800; according to Ware, the term refers to laws of Edward I (r.1272–1307) controlling the sale of bread; so frightened were bakers of being accused of giving short measure that they added one, sometimes two, extra loaves to the dozen ordered] [late 16C+] 13 or occas. 14.

IN PHRASES

❑ **give (someone) a baker's dozen** *v.* [mid-19C] to give someone a beating.

baker's dozen *n.*[2] [rhy. sl.] [20C+] a cousin.

baker's yeast *n.* [rhy.sl.] [1980s] (*Aus.*) a priest.

bakery goods *n.* [the equation of the anus with an 'oven' (although the direct sl. use is restricted to the vagina)] [1960s+] (*US gay*) the buttocks, the anus; thus phr. *the baker's is closed*, sex is not available.

bakgat *adj.* [? Afk. *bak*, fine + *gat*, hole (anus)] [1960s+] (*S.Afr.*) **1** splendid, first-rate, 'posh'. **2** as excl. of approval, pleasure etc.

bakhara *n. see* BUCKAROO *n.*

baking pot *n. see* MELTING POT *n.*

bakker *n. see* BACCA *n.*

bakkie *n.* [Afk. *bak*, a container + dimin. sfx *-ie*] [1960s+] (*S.Afr.*) a light truck, a pick-up, a 4x4 vehicle.

bakore *n.* [Afk. *bak*, a bowl + *ore*, ears] [1970s+] (*S.Afr.*) large, protruding ears.

baksheesh *n.* (*also* **backshee, backsheesh, buckshee, bucksheech, buckshish**) [Pers. *bakhshish*, present, ult. f. *bakhshi-dan*, to give. Given the stereotyping of the 'Oriental merchant' or the Third World beggar, the implication tends to be slightly pej.] **1** [mid-19C+] a gratuity, a tip. **2** [1910s+] something free, a 'perk'.

baksheesh *adj.* [BAKSHEESH *n.* (2)] [1910s] (*Aus.*) convenient, easy, undemanding.

baksheesh *v.* (*also* **buckshish**) [BAKSHEESH *n.* (1)] [late 19C+] to give a tip.

baksheesh *adv.* [BAKSHEESH *n.* (2)] [1910s] (*Aus.*) for free.

bala *n.*[1] [Cornish *bal*, loud talking] [early–mid-19C] coarse or senseless talk.

bala *n.*[2] [abbr.] [1990s+] a *bala*clava.

balaclava *n.* [the beards worn by many soldiers who had returned from the rigours of the Crimean War of 1854–6] [mid-19C] a full beard.

balaclava *v.* [rhy. sl. = CHARVER *v.* (1)] [20C+] to have sexual intercourse.

balahack *n.* (*also* **ballyhack, ballywack, ballywrack**) [? Irish *baile*, a town + HECK *n.*] [mid-19C–1920s] euph. for *Hell*; thus phrs. *all to ballyhack, go to ballyhack*.

balahack *v.* [BALAHACK *n.*] (*US*) **1** [late 19C+] to confuse, to blunder. **2** [1930s+] to impose upon. **3** [1930s+] to beat severely.

balahu *n.* [BALLYHOO *n.*] [1940s+] (*W.I.*) a noisy, boisterous person.

balance *v.* [1910s–50s] (*Aus.*) to swindle; thus *balancer*, a swindling bookmaker.

balangas *n.* [P.R. Sp.] [1980s+] (*US*) the female breasts.

balcony *n.* **1** [1930s] (*Aus.*) a large protruding stomach. **2** [1940s+] (*Aus./US*) the female breasts, esp. as thrust up and forward in the brassieres of the 1940s–50s.

bald *adj.*

SE in slang uses

DERIVATIVES

❑ **baldie** *n.* (*also* **baldy**) [abbr.] **1** [mid-19C+] (*orig. US*) a *bald* man; thus used as a nickname for one who is bald. **2** [late 19C–1940s] an old man. **3** [1940s] (*Aus.*) an Edward VII penny [the king was bald].

IN COMPOUNDS

❑ **bald brigade** *n see* BALD-HEADED ROW *under* BALD-HEADED *adj.* ❑ **baldhead** *n. see* separate entry. ❑ **bald-headed** *see* separate entries. ❑ **bald-rib** *n. see* separate entry. ❑ **bald-tyre bandit** *n.* [SE *bald-tyre* +-BANDIT *sfx* (1); such police are considered less competent or important than their criminal-catching peers] [1970s+] (*UK Und.*) a traffic police officer.

IN PHRASES

❑ **bald man in a boat** *n.* [20C+] the clitoris. ❑ **bury the baldy fella** *v.* (*also* **bury the baldy fellow**) [1980s+] (*Irish*) to achieve vaginal penetration, thus to have sexual intercourse. ❑ **make the bald man puke** *v.* (*also* **make the bald man sick**) [1990s+] of a man, to masturbate. ❑ **not have a baldy** *v.* [abbr. *not have a baldy clue*] [1990s+] to not have any idea. ❑ **snatch bald** *v. see* SNATCH BALD-HEADED *under* BALD-HEADED *adv.*

balderdash *n.* [both senses 1 and 3 and the SE meaning of 'nonsense', which is the sole 20C+ survivor, come f. 16C *balderdash*, frothy water. The origin appears to be Scandinavian, whether in Da. *balder*, noise or clatter, Norw. *bjaldra*, to speak indistinctly, or Icel. *baldras*, to make a clatter. *Dash* comes f. Da. *daske*, to slap or flap; thus *dask*, a slap. The Welsh *baldorddus*, noisy, f. *baldordd*, idle, noisy talk, chatter, may also play a role. An alternative ety. has been suggested (and backed up by a 16C ref. to 'barbers balderdash') as coming from the froth and foam made by barbers in *dashing* their *balls* (spherical pieces of soap) backwards and forwards in hot water] **1** [16C–18C] any adulterated or mixed drink, typically milk and beer, beer and wine, brandy and mineral water, which, while duly consumed, was generally considered unpleasant. **2** [late 17C–18C] obscenity. **3** [early 19C] (*Anglo-Irish*) a fool.

baldface dish *n.* [its lack of ornamentation] [19C] (*US*) a plain white china plate.

baldfaced shirt *n.* [SE *baldfaced cattle*, Herefords, which have white faces; the bald element, pointing up the lack of pattern, may be the root of the *boiled shirt*, another term for a dress shirt, although such starched, formal shirts were literally boiled to achieve the rigid front] [late 19C–1960s] (*US*) a dress shirt with a starched front.

baldfaced stag *n.* [play on SE] [mid-19C] a bald man.

baldface (whisky) *n.* (*also* **baldface juice, ballface, ballface whisky**) [? the *baldfaced hornet*, which has a notable sting + SE *whisky*] [early 19C+] (*US*) cheap, potent whisky.

baldhead *n.* **1** [late 19C+] (*orig. US*) an old man. **2** [1970s+] (*W.I.*) a member of the Rastafarian cult who does not, however, sport the characteristic beard and dreadlocks. **3** [1970s+]

(*W.I.*) (*also* **ballhead**) a white person. **4** [1970s+] (*W.I.*) (*also* **ballhead**) a non-Rastafarian black person.

bald-headed *adj.* **1** [mid-19C+] totally unprepared, utterly spontaneous [the image of one who rushes out without pausing even to put on a hat]. **2** [late 19C+] (*US black*) deliberately deceptive, underhand, e.g. *a bald-headed lie* [one who makes no effort to mask their bald head]. **3** [1930s+] (*US*) bare, hairless, shining white. **4** [1940s] (*US black*) stupid, foolish [such a person has nothing 'on top'].

SE in slang uses

IN COMPOUNDS

❑ **bald-headed bandit** *n.* (*also* **bald-headed bastard**) [1940s] the penis. ❑ **bald-headed butter** *n.* [the pre-industrial era of butter manufacture] [late 19C–1900s] a portion of butter in which there are no hairs. ❑ **bald-headed hermit** *n.* (*also* **bald-headed champ, ...friar, ...sailor, baldpate friar, baldy**) [the *glans penis* which, in uncircumcised men, 'hides away' beneath the foreskin and resembles the monk's bald tonsure] [mid-17C+] the penis, esp. an uncircumcised penis. ❑ **bald-headed lump** *n.* [SE *baldheaded*, i.e. nothing 'on' the food] [1930s] (*US tramp*) a parcel of food containing only the basics, with no 'sweets' such as cake or pie. ❑ **bald-headed mouse** *n.* [1980s+] (*US gay*) the erect penis. ❑ **bald-headed row** *n.* (*also* **bald brigade, baldheaded department, baldheaded seats**) [1900s–20s] the men, stereotyped as old, who take the front row of a burlesque or similar show.

IN PHRASES

❑ **wrestle the bald-headed champion** *v.* [1990s+] to masturbate.

bald-headed *adv.* [mid-19C+] precipitately, esp. in phr. *go (at/in) something bald-headed, go bald-headed for, go bald-headed into*, to put all one's efforts into, to commit oneself wholly, to attack without care or thought – and totally disregard the possible consequences.

IN PHRASES

❑ **snatch bald-headed** *v.* (*also* **jerk bald-headed, snatch bald**) [the idea of being hanged] [mid-19C–1970s] (*US*) **1** to treat roughly, to manhandle. **2** in fig. use, to overwhelm emotionally.

baldober *n.* (*also* **baldover, baldower**) [Ger. Und., ult. Heb. *baal*, a master + *dovor*, a word] [late 19C–1900s] (*UK Und.*) a boss, a leader, a spokesman.

baldpate friar *n. see* BALD-HEADED HERMIT *under* BALD-HEADED *adj.*

bald-rib *n.* [SE *bald-rib*, 'A joint of pork cut from nearer the rump than the spare-rib, so called "because the bones thereof are made bald and bare of flesh" (Minsheu)' (*OED*)] [early 17C] a thin, bony person.

balductum *n.* [SE *balductum*, a posset, hot milk curdled with ale or wine] [late 16C–early 17C] nonsense, rubbish.

balductum *adj.* [BALDUCTUM *n.* (1)] [late 16C–early 17C] nonsensical, rubbish.

baldwin *n.* [the collective fame and attractiveness of the *Baldwin* brothers, all Hollywood actors, namely Alec Baldwin (b.1958), Daniel Baldwin (b.1960), William Baldwin (b.1963) and Stephen Baldwin (b.1966)] [1990s+] (*US campus*) an attractive person.

baldy *n.* **1** *see* BALDIE *under* BALD *adj.* **2** *see* BALD-HEADED HERMIT *under* BALD-HEADED *adj.*

bale *n.* [SE *bale*, a (wrapped) bundle; note Landy, *Underground Dict.* (1971), states 'seventy-five to 500 pounds of marijuana'] [1960s+] (*drugs*) marijuana.

bale *v. see* BAIL *v.* (2).

bale of goods *n. see* PIECE OF GOODS *under* PIECE *n.*

bale of hay *n.* (*also* **bale of straw**) [SE *bale* + *hay*/STRAW *n.* (1)] **1** [late 19C] (*US short order*) corned beef and cabbage. **2** [1920s+] (*orig. US theatre*) a white woman, esp. a blonde. **3** [1930s] (*US*) a strawberry ice-cream.

bale of straw *n.* [rhy. sl. = SE colloq. *in the raw*, naked] [2000s] a state of nakedness.

bale on *v. see* BAIL ON SOMEONE *v.*

bales of briquettes *n.* [resemblance] [1970s+] (*Irish*) platform-soled shoes.

bale up *v. see* BAIL UP *v.*

bale up! *excl. see* BAIL UP! *under* BAIL UP *v.*

Balkan tap *n.* [on pattern of DOOLALLY TAP *n.*; proper name *Balkans* + *tap*, sunstroke; the term evolved to characterize the growing, happy indolence that took over men involved in the Macedonian campaign in WW1] [20C+] madness.

ball *n.*[1] **1** [mid-18C–1910s] (*US*) a bullet [? its circularity]. **2** [mid-19C] (*UK Und.*) a prison ration, 170g (6oz) of meat [? the resemblance of the lump of meat]. **3** [late 19C–1920s] (*US*) a silver dollar; in. pl., money [? its circularity]. **4** [1910s–30s] a small package of a narcotic or other drug [the drug package is rolled into a ball]. **5** [1910s+] (*US*) base*ball* [abbr.]. **6** [1980s+] (*orig. US black*) basket*ball* [abbr.].

SE in slang uses

IN COMPOUNDS

❑ **ball and chain** *n.* [SE *ball and chain*, a device that secured convicts during 19C] **1** [1920s+] (*orig. US black*) one's wife or regular girlfriend; thus *ball-and-chained*, married. **2** [1940s] (*US Und.*) a tramp's younger male companion. ❑ **ballgame** *n. see* separate entry. ❑ **ballhead** *n. see* separate entry. ❑ **ballhop** *n.* [Gaelic sport] [1970s+] (*Irish*) a rumour, an unsupported theory, a lie; thus *ballhopper*, a rumour-monger. ❑ **ball lump** *n.* [resemblance] [1920s–50s] (*US tramp*) a parcel of food given to a tramp. ❑ **ball-park** *adj. see* separate entry. ❑ **ball-up** *n. see* separate entry.

IN PHRASES

❑ **ball of dirt** *n.* [fig. use of SE + ? rhy. sl.] [late 19C] (*US*) the earth. ❑ **ball of fire** *n.* **1** [18C–late 19C] a glass of brandy [the effect of the liquor]. **2** [20C+] an individual known for their energy, resourcefulness or drive. **3** [1920s] an excellent thing, idea. ❑ **ball of muscle** *n.* [1930s+] (*Aus.*) an energetic, lively person. ❑ **ball of wax** *n.* [the wax used in shoe-making] [19C] a shoemaker. ❑ **ball of yarn** *n.* [19C Anglo-Irish bawdy folk-song, e.g. the lyric 'Keep both hands on your little ball of yarn'] [1940s–60s] (*US*) the female genitals. ❑ **ball up** *v. see* separate entry. ❑ **drop the ball** *v.* [sporting imagery] [1940s+] (*orig. US*) to make a mistake at a crucial moment. ❑ **give someone a ball** *v.* [the mythical *trotting ball*, supposedly administered to enliven horses, itself from veterinary use, *ball*, a large pill; Stephens & O'Brien, *Materials for a Dict. of Aus. Slang* (ms.; 1900–10), also state that ball is 'by transference [...] a nip of spirits', but this may be a confusion with older BALL *n.*[2]] [1900s] (*Aus.*) to reprimand, to 'shake up'. ❑ **have one's eye on the ball** *v.* [sporting imagery] [20C+] to be alert and aware. ❑ **loose ball** *n.* [soccer imagery] [1970s+] (*Irish*) an opportunity to pick up free drink. ❑ **run with the ball** *v.* [sporting imagery] [1960s+] to take on a problem and tackle it on one's own initiative, rather than passing the buck. ❑ **something on the ball** *n.* [baseball imagery] [1910s+] (*US*) skill, talent, great ability.

ball *n.*[2] [BALL OF FIRE *under* BALL *n.*[1]] [mid-19C+] (*orig. US*) a shot of liquor; esp. in phr. *a beer and a ball*, a beer and a shot of whisky; *ball joint*, a bar.

ball *n.*[3] **1** [1930s+] (*orig. US black*) a party, a celebration; a riotously, extravagantly good time. **2** [1950s] as *the ball*, an enjoyable time. **3** [1950s] (*US drugs*) a feeling of well-being, a 'high', from a drug. **4** [1960s] an orgy. **5** [1970s+] a delightful person.

IN PHRASES

❑ **have a ball** *v.* [1920s+] to enjoy oneself.

ball *n.*[4] [BALL *v.*[3]] (*orig. US*) **1** [1940s+] sexual intercourse. **2** [1970s] one who has or offers sexual intercourse.

ball *n.*[5] [backform. f. BALLS *n.* (1)] [1990s+] (*US*) a stupid or silly person; used in response to an unintelligent action, as a sarcastic response to a foolish remark or as an observation of another's character (or lack thereof).

ball *v.*[1] (*also* **ball out**) [abbr. BALL THE JACK *v.* (1)] [1930s+] to travel at high speed, to leave.

IN PHRASES

❑ **ball it off** *v. see* separate entry.

ball *v.*^{2} [BALL *n.*^{3} (1)] [1940s+] (*orig. US black*) to have a good time, to enjoy oneself.

IN PHRASES

❑ **ball it** *v. see* separate entry. ❑ **ball it (up)** *v.* [BALL *n.*^{3} (1)] [1950s–60s] (*US*) to celebrate in an uproarious manner. ❑ **ball off** *v. see* separate entry.

ball *v.*^{3} [BALLS *n.* (1); but note SE *ball*, a dance and combs. at DANCE *v.* (1)] [1950s+] to have sexual intercourse.

IN PHRASES

❑ **ball off** *v. see* separate entry.

ball *v.*^{4} [BALL *n.*^{1} (6)] [1980s+] (*US black*) to play basketball.

ball *v.*^{5} *see* BALL OF CHALK *v.*

-ball *sfx* [SE *ball*, i.e. a 'ball of...'] [1910s+] a sfx used in comb. with another term, usu. a n., to describe a contemptible, despised person; when of a woman, often with implications of promiscuity.

balla *n. see* BALLER *n.*

ballad *n.* **1** [1950s] (*W.I./UK black*) a story, usu. long and complicated. **2** [1970s+] (*US gay*) an excuse.

ballad-basket *n.* [mid-18C–late 19C] a street-singer.

ballahoo *adj.* [BALLYHOO *n.* (1)] [20C+] (*W.I.*) noisy, boisterous, obstreperous.

ball and bat *n.* [rhy. sl.] [1900s–20s] a hat.

ball and chalk *see under* BALL OF CHALK.

ballarag *v. see* BALLYRAG *v.*

ballarat *n.*^{1} [rhy. sl. = CAT *n.*^{1} (5)] [1980s+] (*Aus. prison*) a homosexual.

ballarat *n.*^{2} [joc. use of proper name *Ballarat*, the last stop on the railway line from Melbourne] [1990s+] the erect penis; also as v., to have an erection.

ballarat lantern *n.* [proper name *Ballarat* + SE *lantern*; a necessity in pre-electrified days] [late 19C–1940s] (*Aus./N.Z.*) a candle stuck in the neck of a bottle, the bottom of which has been knocked off.

Ballarat passive *n.* [BALLARAT *n.*^{1}] [1980s] (*Aus.*) a male homosexual.

ballast *n.* [SE *ballast*] **1** [early 19C–1930s] heavy food [it fills one up]. **2** [mid-19C–1940s] money [it helps one stay 'afloat' and 'on an even keel']. **3** [1900s] (*US*) a gun.

ball-breaker *n.* [BALLS *n.* (1) + SE *breaker*] (*orig. US*) **1** [1950s+] a difficult, boring or exasperating job, problem or situation. **2** [1950s+] a person who sets difficult work or problems, a hard taskmaster. **3** [1970s] one who likes to tease. **4** [1970s] a thug. **5** [1970s] a weapon. **6** [1970s+] (*Aus.*) (*also* **ballgripper**) something amazing, excellent. **7** [1970s+] (*also* **ball-lopper**) a dominating woman, one who destroys the self-confidence of a man.

ball-breaking *n.* (*also* **ball-busting**) [BALL-BREAKER *n.*/BALL-BUSTER *n.* in all senses] [1940s+] (*orig. US*) harassment.

ball-breaking *adj.* (*also* **ball-busting**) [BALL-BREAKER *n.*/BALL-BUSTER *n.* in all senses] (*orig. US*) **1** [1940s+] acting as a hard taskmaster or dominating woman. **2** [1970s] very irritating. **3** [1980s] physically demanding, exhausting.

ball-buster *n.* [BALLS *n.* (1) + SE *buster*; but note Yid. *baleboosteh*, a bossy woman, lit. 'mistress of the house'] **1** [20C+] (*US Und.*) a thief who grabs his victim by the testicles while his accomplice takes his wallet. **2** [1940s+] (*orig. US*) (*also* **balls buster**) a nagging woman. **3** [1950s–60s] (*US campus*) a notably hard course or examination. **4** [1950s+] any overbearingly unpleasant person or circumstances. **5** [1960s+] any thing or person seen as extraordinary or outstanding. **6** [1980s+] (*also* **buster**) a tease.

ball-busting *n. see* BALL-BREAKING *n.*

ball-busting *adj. see* BALL-BREAKING *adj.*

balled-up *adj.* [BALLS *v.* (1); note Gore, *Student Slang* (1896): 'To come to a standstill after making spasmodic and somewhat erratic efforts — as a horse does when snow gathers in balls upon its hoofs'] [late 19C+] (*US*) confused, mixed up, in a mess.

baller *n.* (*also* **balla, bawla**) [? *HAVE A BALL under* BALL *n.*^{3}; the term is used esp. by the Los Angeles gang the Bloods; *balla/bawla* are consciously 'wrong' spellings, designed to emphasize the 'outlaw' status of such individuals] **1** [1960s] a hedonist. **2** [1990s+] (*US black*) one who is extremely rich, esp. from the profits of criminality. **3** [1990s+] (*US campus*) one who enjoys playing sport, esp. basketball. **4** [1990s+] (*US campus*) an attractive person.

baller blocker *n.* [BALLER *n.* (2) + SE *blocker*] [2000s] (*US black*) a person who stops one from succeeding.

ballface *n.* [? BALLFACE (WHISKY) *n.*] [mid–late 19C] (*US black*) a white person.

ballface (whisky) *n. see* BALDFACE (WHISKY) *n.*

ballgame *n.* [SE *ballgame*, a sporting event, esp. a baseball game] [1930s+] (*orig. US*) a state of affairs, a situation.

IN PHRASES

❑ **end of the ballgame** *n.* [20C+] (*US*) **1** death; one of a number of games-playing/sporting metaphors for life's termination. **2** the definitive conclusion to something. ❑ **that's the ballgame** (*also* **there goes the ballgame**) [1940s+] (*US*) a phr. meaning that's it, no arguments accepted, forget it. ❑ **whole new ballgame** *n.* (*also* **different ballgame**) [1960s+] (*orig. US*) a radically new situation (to which one will be forced to adapt).

ball gown *n.* [1970s+] (*US camp gay*) a man's suit.

ballgripper *n. see* BALL-BREAKER *n.* (6).

ball-gusted *adj.* [BALLY *adj.*+ SE *disgusted*] [mid-19C] (*US*) disgusted, appalled.

ballhead *n.* [SE *ball-head*, a head shaped like a ball; thus the person who has one. In Rastafarian use most whites, however hirsute, may be considered to be *ballheads*, in comparison with the Rastaman and his flowing dreadlocks] **1** [1980s] (*UK black*) a bald person. **2** [1980s+] (*N.Z./Maori*) an outsider. **3** *see* BALDHEAD *n.*

balling *n.* **1** [1930s+] (*orig. US black*) having fun [BALL *v.*^{2}]. **2** [1960s+] (*orig. US black*) having sexual intercourse [BALL *v.*^{3}]. **3** [1990s+] (*US black*) enriching oneself by selling drugs (usu. crack cocaine) [fig. use]. **4** (*US black*) excelling in the playing of basketball [BALL *v.*^{4}]. **5** [2000s] (*US drugs*) carrying a package of contraband cocaine by placing it in the vagina [? f. sense 3 or the BALL *n.*^{1} (4) that is hidden]. **6** [2000s] showing off, flaunting one's possessions [fig. use].

balling *adj.* [BALLING *n.* (1)] [1950s–60s] (*US*) excellent, wonderful, first-rate; usu. in comb. as *balling chick*, an attractive girl or woman.

ballinocack *n.* [? Irish *baile*, a town + CACK *n.*^{2} (1); thus lit. 'shit-town'] [late 18C–early 19C] the anus.

ballistic *adj.*

IN PHRASES

❑ **go ballistic** *v.* [1980s+] (*orig. US*) **1** to lose one's temper. **2** to do very well. **3** of a situation, to escalate out of control.

ball it *v.* [1960s] (*US*) to act, to live, to survive.

ball it off *v.* [the rolling of a ball] [mid-19C] (*US*) to travel at speed.

ball it (up) *v. see under* BALL *v.*^{2}.

ball-lopper *n. see* BALL-BREAKER *n.* (7).

ball naked *adj.* [abbr. SE colloq. *ballock naked*] [20C+] (*US*) utterly naked.

ball o 'chalk *n. see* BALL OF CHALK *n.*

ballock for combs. *see also under* BOLLOCK.

ballock *n.* (*also* **bollock**) [OE *beallucas*, itself Teutonic root *ball-*, thus more immediately ext. of BALLS *n.* (1); *ballock(s)* meant testicle(s) f. 11C but remained SE until late 18C; it appears in Bailey's *Universal Etymological English Dict.* in all editions f. 1721–1800 but was not included in Samuel Johnson's *Dictionary*, which drew heavily on Bailey's word-list, in 1755; one must thus assume that the word was passing then from polite use; it was definitely slang by 1800 and appears as such in Grose (1788, 1796) though, oddly, in neither Grose (1785), Hotten nor F&H; thus *Ballock Hall*, 17C home of Adam & Lucy Loftus, and known for its unsavoury reputation; note single use as a term of affection in Urquhart, *The Complete Works of Rabelais* (1653): 'I must gripe thee, my ballock, till thy back crack with it'] **1** [16C+] a testicle; usu. in pl. (see BALLOCKS *n.* (2)). **2** [1940s+] (*also* **bollicky**) a general term of abuse. **3** [1970s+] (*UK society*) a ball (hunt, charity etc) [pun on BALLS *n.* (1)].

IN COMPOUNDS

❑ **ballock gravy** *n.* [GRAVY *n.* (1b)] [2000s] semen. ❑ **ballock-hair** *n.* [1990s+] a male pubic hair. ❑ **ballock snot** *n.* (*also* **bollock snot**) [SNOT *n.*^{1} (1)] [2000s] semen.

IN PHRASES

❑ **drop a ballock** *v.* (*also* **drop a bollock**) [1920s+] to make a mistake, to blunder.

ballock *v.*^{1} (*also* **bollock, bullock**) [BALLOCK *n.* (1)] **1** [mid-18C–mid-19C] (*US*) to grab by the genitals when fighting. **2** [late 19C] to have sexual intercourse.

IN PHRASES

❑ **go ballocking** *v.* [19C+] to have sexual intercourse.

ballock *v.*^{2} (*also* **ballocks, bollock, bollocks, rollux**) [fig. use of BALLOCK *n.* (1)] [1930s+] to reprimand, to tell off.

ballocking *n.*^{1} [BALLOCK *v.*^{1} (2)] [late 19C] sexual intercourse.

ballocking *n.*^{2} (*also* **bollocking, bolly**) [BALLOCKS *v.*] [1930s+] a severe telling off, a scolding.

ballocks *n.* (*also* **ballyx, bolix, bollix, bollocks, bollox, bollux**) [BALLOCK *n.*] **1** [late 18C–early 19C] a parson. **2** [late 18C+] testicles. **3** [1910s+] (*also* **bollixing**) rubbish, nonsense [? developed f. sense 1 on the premise that sermonizing is, *de facto*, nonsense]. **4** [1910s+] a person in a state of confusion, who is talking *ballocks*. **5** [1910s+] (*also* **bollock, silly-bollocks**) a fool, an incompetent. **6** [1920s+] a person, often used affectionately. **7** [1930s+] (*orig. Irish*) an unpleasant person, esp. as (*right*) *old bollix*. **8** [1940s+] a mess. **9** [1980s+] courage, vigour. **10** [1990s+] used as intensifier in phrs. **11** [1990s+] used as a direct, pej. term of address. **12** *see* DOG'S BALLOCKS *n.*

IN COMPOUNDS

❑ **ballocks worker** *n.* [1950s] any overbearingly unpleasant person or circumstance.

IN PHRASES

❑ **ballocks in brackets** *n.* [visual appearance] [20C+] a bow-legged man. ❑ **big ballocks** *n.* (*also* **big balls**) [1950s] a self-important man. ❑ **do one's ballocks** *v.* (*also* **do one's bollocks**) [1990s+] to make the utmost effort. ❑ **have his brains in his ballocks** *v.* [early 19C] a phr. used to describe a fool. ❑ **have one's ballocks in the right place** *v.* [20C+] to be deserving of praise, commendation, approval by one's fellows. ❑ **have someone/something by the ballocks/bollocks** *v. see* HAVE SOMEONE BY THE BALLS *under* BALLS *n.*

IN EXCLAMATIONS

❑ **my bollocks!** (*also* **my bollix!**) [1990s+] a dismissive excl.

ballocks *v. see* BALLOCK *v.*^{2}.

ballocks! *excl.* (*also* **bollacks! bollicks! bollix! bollocks! bollox!**) [BALLOCKS *n.* (3); ult. BALLOCKS *n.* (2)] **1** [late 17C+] rubbish! nonsense! **2** [1950s+] as an excl. of derision. **3** [1950s+] a general excl. of annoyance, frustration.

ballocks (up) *v.* (*also* **bolix (up), bollix (up), bollocks (up), bollox (up), bollux (up)**) [1950s+] (*orig. Aus.*) to ruin, to make a mess of, also as *make a ballocks of*.

IN PHRASES

❑ **ballocks about** *v.* (*also* **ballocks around, bollocks about, ...around**) **1** [1950s+] to mess about, to play the fool. **2** [1980s+] to infuriate, to waste someone's time, to be indecisive.

ball of chalk *n.* (*also* **ball and chalk, ball o' chalk**) [rhy. sl.] **1** [20C+] a walk. **2** [1990s+] a talk.

ball of chalk *v.* (*also* **ball, ball and chalk, bowl of chalk, lump of chalk**) [rhy. sl.] **1** [20C+] to talk. **2** [2000s] to walk.

ball off *v.*^{1} [BALL *n.*^{2}] [late 19C] (*US*) to treat to a drink.

ball off *v.*^{2} [BALLS *n.* (1) / BALL *v.*^{3}] [20C+] to masturbate; one of many terms of the verb that use 'off'.

ball of lead *n.* [rhy. sl.] [1900s–20s] the head.

ball of twine *n.* [rhy. sl.] [20C+] (*Aus.*) a railway line.

balloon *n.* **1** (*US*) in monetary uses. (**a**) [late 18C] a security certificate issued by the Confederation (the original 13 colonies that seceded from Britain). (**b**) [1970s+] $1. (**c**) [1970s+] (*gambling*) $10. **2** [20C+] (*Scot./Ulster*) a bully, a garrulous person, i.e. 'full of hot air'. **3** [1910s] (*Aus.*) the face, the head. **4** [1920s–30s] (*US*) a bedroll [the supposed resemblance]. **5** [1940s+] in pl., conspicuously large female breasts. **6** [1950s+] a condom. **7** [1960s+] (*drugs*) a condom that is used to carry heroin, cocaine or any other powdered narcotic drug. **8** [2000s] (*drugs*) a heroin supplier.

IN COMPOUNDS

❑ **balloon room** *n. see* separate entry.

IN PHRASES

❑ **balloon it** *v.* [1910s–30s] (*US*) to pack up one's bedroll and set off travelling. ❑ **balloon-knot bandit** *n.* [-BANDIT *sfx* (2); the knotted condom that signifies intercourse] [1990s+] a male homosexual. ❑ **carry the balloon** *v.* [the packing up of one's 'balloon' or bedroll] [1930s] (*US tramp*) to travel around looking for work.

SE in slang uses

IN COMPOUNDS

❑ **balloon-belly** *n.* [1930s] (*US*) an obese person. ❑ **balloon-brain** *n.* [1940s+] (*US*) a fool, a simpleton. ❑ **balloon-head** *n.* [-HEAD *sfx* (1)] [1930s+] (*US*) a fool, a simpleton. ❑ **balloon juice** *n.* **1** [late 19C+] as a drink, usu. fizzy [? gaseous nature of soda-water]. (**a**) soda-water; thus *balloon juice lowerer*, a teetotaller, who only drinks or 'lowers' soda-water. (**b**) (*W.I., Bdos/Guyn.*) any form of sweet, colourful fizzy drink. (**c**) (*US*) any form of alcohol. (**d**) ginger beer. **2** [1900s–60s] (*US*) nonsense, rubbish, empty chatter [play on SE, i.e. HOT AIR *n.*]. ❑ **balloon soup** *n.* [i.e. HOT AIR *n.*] [1920s–30s] (*US*) nonsense, empty chatter.

IN PHRASES

❑ **go up in a balloon** *v.* [mid–late 19C] (*US*) to be ruined, to come to nothing. ❑ **when the balloon goes up** [? raising of an observation *balloon* immediately before an attack] [1910s+] (*orig. milit.*) the start of proceedings, esp. when there is a potential for controversy or argument.

balloon *v.*^{1} [late 18C] (*UK Und.*) for a pickpocket to mingle with the crowds watching the launch of the then new manned balloons.

balloon *v.*^{2} [BALLOON *n.* (7)] [1950s+] (*drugs*) to package narcotic drugs for distribution and sale.

balloon (car) *n.* [rhy. sl. = bar] [20C+] the saloon bar of a public house.

balloon room *n.* [like the SE *balloon*, marijuana smokers get HIGH *adj.*^{1} (2)] [1940s–50s] (*US black*) a place where people gather to smoke marijuana.

IN PHRASES

❑ **balloon room without a parachute** *n.* [1950s–70s] (*US black*) a disappointment, a let-down, esp. a place where one has been promised a smoke of marijuana but which, in fact, offers no supply.

ballot *n. see* BALOT *n.*

ball out *v.* **1** *see* BAWL OUT *v.*^{1}. **2** *see* BALL *v.*^{1}.

ball-park *adj.* [SE *ball-park*, a baseball stadium, i.e. the rough estimate of the number of fans watching the game] [1950s+] (*orig. US*) approximately accurate.

IN COMPOUNDS

❑ **ball-park figure** *n.* [1950s+] (*orig. US*) a round figure for general estimation, assessment.

IN PHRASES

❑ **in the right ball-park** *adj.* (*also* **in the ball-park, within the ball-park**) [1950s+] (*orig. US*) approximately accurate.

balls *n.* [the shape] **1** [16C+] the testicles. **2** [17C; 1950s–60s] (*US*) the female breasts. **3** [late 19C+] courage, bravery; supposedly quintessential male qualities, but now as often applied to women. **4** [20C+] rubbish, nonsense. **5** [1930s–40s] (*orig. US*) nothing, e.g. 'What kind of a tip do I get?' 'Balls.'. **6** [1930s+] (*US*) constr. with *the*, a superlative, either good or bad according to context. **7** [1950s+] substance, power, strength. **8** [1950s+] synon. with ARSE *n.*, e.g. *work one's balls off, put one's balls on the line*. **9** [1960s+] effrontery, gall, audacity. **10** [2000s] (*US black*) something excellent, wonderful; one's preference [on bad = good model]. **11** *see* BALLS-UP *n.*

(DERIVATIVES)

❑ **ball-less** *adj.* [sfx *-less*] [1950s+] weak, emasculated; thus *ball-less wonder*, an especially weak individual. ❑ **ballsy** *adj.* **1** [1930s+] absurd, ridiculous. **2** [1960s+] (*also* **ballsie**) tough, courageous; despite ety., used of either gender.

(IN COMPOUNDS)

❑ **ball-bag** *n.* [SE *bag*/BAG *n.*[1] (1a)] [late 19C+] the scrotum; also as a term of abuse. ❑ **ball-breaker/breaking** *see* separate entries. ❑ **ball-buster/busting** *see* separate entries. ❑ **ball-clanker** *n.* [SE *clanker*] [1960s] (*US*) a man who boasts, prob. groundlessly, of his sexual prowess. ❑ **ball-crusher** *n.* **1** [1970s+] a dominating woman who 'emasculates' her partner, usu. a husband. **2** [1970s+] anything that is excessively hard or frustrating, or impressive; thus adj. *ball-crushing*. **3** [1980s+] a sexually voracious woman who exhausts her partner's virility. ❑ **ball-cutter** *n.* [1960s+] (*US*) a nagging, domineering or demanding woman. ❑ **ball-faced** *adj.* [1990s+] a general term of derision, lit. 'testicle-faced'. ❑ **ball naked** *adj. see* separate entry. ❑ **balls-ache** *v.* [20C+] to nag, to whinge; thus adj. *balls-aching*, nagging, demanding. ❑ **balls-ass** *adj.* [-ASS *sfx*] [1960s+] (*US*) tough, masculine, courageous. ❑ **balls buster** *n. see* BALL-BUSTER *n.* (2). ❑ **ball slap** *v.* [1990s+] of a man, to have sexual intercourse. ❑ **balls naked** *adj. see* separate entry. ❑ **balls out** *adv.* [the implication is that one is willing to risk injuring the genitals] [1940s+] at full tilt, absolutely committed, all out. ❑ **ball-tearer** *n.* **1** [1950s+] (*orig. US*) usu. of a woman, esp. a wife, a nag. **2** [1960s+] (*Aus.*) a physically demanding task. **3** [1970s] (*Aus.*) a violent person. **4** [1970s+] anything spectacular or notably impressive. **5** [1980s] (*Aus.*) a major problem, an exasperation.

(IN PHRASES)

❑ **all balls (and bang-me-arse)** *n.* [1940s+] nonsense. ❑ **as balls** *adv.* [20C+] (*W.I./US*) a general intensifier. ❑ **balls and all** [20C+] (*orig. US*) everything; completely. ❑ **balls it** *v.* [2000s] (*UK drugs*) to hide drugs beneath the scrotum. ❑ **balls-to-the-wall** [seen as a coarse version of SE *back(s) to the wall*; but actually from US Air Force slang: *see* Jesse S at http://www.slate.com/id/2136001] **1** [1960s+] all-out, at maximum speed, with one's greatest effort. **2** [1970s+] (*US campus*) of a situation or period of time, tense or frantic. **3** [2000s] (*US campus*) drinking with the intention of getting drunk. ❑ **balls-to-the-wind** *adv.* [1980s+] (*US*) at top speed. ❑ **bet one's balls** *v.* (*also* **bet one's hairy balls**) [1940s–80s] (*Aus./US*) to be very certain. ❑ **blue balls** *n.* **1** [1910s+] a feeling of intense sexual frustration; thus *have blue balls*, of a man, to be very sexually frustrated. **2** [1920s+] a venereal bubo. **3** [1920s+] (*US*) gonorrhoea. ❑ **break one's balls** *v.* (*also* **bust one's balls**) [1960s+] (*orig. US*) **1** (*also* **bust one's nuts**) to make a great effort; to work very hard, esp. at a physically demanding task. **2** to meet with disaster. ❑ **break someone's balls** *v.* [1960s+] (*orig. US*) **1** to attack verbally, to persecute, to harass. **2** (*also* **bust someone's balls**) to attack physically. **3** to complain to someone, to nag someone. **4** to exhaust sexually. **5** to exhaust physically. ❑ **by the balls** *adv.* [1910s+] (*orig. US*) at one's mercy. ❑ **de-ball** *v.* [SE pfx *de-*] [1950s+] to castrate, lit. and fig. ❑ **do one's balls on** *v.* [late 19C+] of a man, to fall obsessively in love with. ❑ **dry balls** *n.* [1920s–40s] (*US*) an impotent man [i.e. they have 'dried up']. ❑ **get one's balls in an uproar** *v.* (*also* **get one's balls in a knot**) [1910s+] to become excited or agitated. ❑ **get one's balls off** *v.* [1970s+] (*orig. US*) of a man, to achieve orgasm. ❑ **have balls on one like a scoutmaster** *v.* [1930s+] (*Can./N.Z.*) to have large testicles. ❑ **have one's balls in the fire** *v.* [1960s] (*US*) to be in serious trouble. ❑ **have one's balls twisted** *v.* [1970s] to be stupid but outspoken. ❑ **have one's balls under one's chin** *v.* [1930s–60s] (*US*) to be terrified. ❑ **have someone by the balls** *v.* (*also* **have someone/something by the ass, ...by the ballocks, ...by the bollocks, ...by the crotch, ...by the left tit, ...by the leg, ...by the nuts, ...by the screws, ...by the seat of one's pants**) [late 19C+] to have someone at one's mercy, at a complete disadvantage. ❑ **have someone's balls (for a game of pool)** *v.* (*also* **have someone's balls for breakfast, have someone's balls sauteéd, have someone's butt on a biscuit for breakfast**) [1960s+] to treat very harshly, to punish comprehensively. ❑ **have swollen balls for** *v.* [1980s+] (*US prison*) to lust after. ❑ **his balls are bigger than his brains** [1940s+] said of a man who rushes into situations without thinking. ❑ **knock someone's balls off** *v.* [1960s+] to astonish, to amaze. ❑ **man with the fuzzy balls** *n.* [note the theory that FUZZ *n.*[1] derives from this] [1950s–80s] **1** (*US black*) a white man. **2** (*US*) an expert, an accomplished person. ❑ **old balls** *n.* [1940s] a man, not always pej. ❑ **one-ball** *adj.* [1960s] (*US gang*) of a man, weak, worthless. ❑ **put balls on** *v.* (*also* **put hair on**) [1950s+] to make more emphatic, more effective. ❑ **put one's balls in a knot** *v.* [1930s+] (*Aus.*) to discomfit, to embarrass, to irritate. ❑ **put someone's balls in the fire** *v.* [1960s] (*US*) to agitate or excite someone. ❑ **shoot balls** *v.* [20C+] (*W.I.*) to talk nonsense. ❑ **sweat one's balls off** *v. see* SWEAT ONE'S ARSE OFF *under* SWEAT *v.*[2]. ❑ **swing on someone's balls** *v.* [2000s] (*US black*) of a woman, to be sexually obsessed with a man. ❑ **to the balls** *adv.* [1930s+] (*US*) completely, to the utmost. ❑ **wear someone's balls for a necktie** *v.* [1920s+] used as a threat of violence, e.g. *try that again and I'll wear...*

balls *adj.* [BALLS *n.* (3)] [1980s+] (*US*) tough, masculine, courageous.

balls *v.* [BALLS *n.* (1)] **1** [late 19C+] to make a mess of. **2** [1990s+] to secrete near one's genitals.

(IN PHRASES)

❑ **balls up** *v. see* separate entry.

balls! *excl.* [BALLS *n.* (4)] [late 19C+] **1** (*also* **bawls!**) rubbish! nonsense! **2** an excl. of disappointment.

(IN EXCLAMATIONS)

❑ **balls to...!** (*also* **balls with...!**) [BALLS *n.* (1)] [1930s+] a dismissive excl. aimed at people, objects or circumstances; thus *balls to you! balls to that!* ❑ **go to balls!** [1960s] a general excl. of dismissal. ❑ **holy balls!** [1940s+] (*orig. US*) an excl. of shock, surprise, annoyance etc. ❑ **my balls!** [1950s+] (*US*) an excl. of refusal, rejection.

ballsed-up *adj.* [BALLS UP *v.*] [1940s+] in chaos, in a mess, ruined.

balls naked *adj.* (*also* **balls-ass naked**) [BALLS *n.* (1)/-ASS *sfx* + SE *naked*] [1950s–70s] (*Can./US*) stark naked.

balls-up *n.* (*also* **balls**) [synon. with COCK-UP *n.*; FUCK-UP *n.* (1)] [late 19C+] (*orig. milit.*) a blunder, an error.

(IN PHRASES)

❑ **make a balls of** *v.* [late 19C+] to make a mistake, to get into trouble. ❑ **make a barney balls of oneself** *v.* [1940s+] (*Irish*) to make a fool of oneself.

balls up *v.* [BALLS-UP *n.*] [1920s+] to make a mess of, to ruin, to blunder, to make a mistake.

ball the jack *v.* [SAmE phrase *high-ball*, the railway man's hand signal to set a train in motion + (orig. US black) *jack*, a locomotive, abbr. of SE *jackass*, a donkey that, like the locomotive, works very hard; used first in the lumberjack jargon *ball the jack*, of a logging train, to go very fast; thence to general railroad jargon and after that mainstream sl.] **1** [1910s+] (*US*) to drive very fast, to work very hard. **2** [1910s+] (*US black*) to perform an energetic dance to a backing of hand claps. **3** [1910s+] to enjoy a riotous party. **4** [1920s] to risk everything on a single throw. **5** [1920s] to be the last straw. **6** [1920s+] (*US black*) to have sexual intercourse. **7** [1950s] to move in a noticeable manner.

balluba *n. see* BALUBA *n.*

ballum rancum *n.* (*also* **ballum-rankum, ballum ranorum, balum rancum**) [BALLS *n.* (1) + pun on SE *ball*, a dance + *rank*, rancid] [late 17C–late 19C] an orgy, lit. a dance at which all concerned 'dance in their *birthday* suits' (Grose, 1796).

ball-up *n.* [var. on BALLS-UP *n.*] [20C+] (*US*) a mess, a confusion.

ball up *v.* [BALL-UP *n.*] (*US*) **1** [mid-19C+] to become confused, muddled. **2** [late 19C+] to muddle, to err, to blunder, to make a mistake, to entangle oneself with. **3** [1910s+] to ruin, to make a mess of, to clog up, to confuse, to botch.

bally *n. see* BALLYHOO *n.*

bally *adj.* [mid-19C+] a general negative intensifier, very, exceedingly; euph. for BLOODY *adj.*; thus *bally heck*, bloody hell.

bally *v. see* BALLYHOO *v.* (1).

Ballygobackwards *n.* [Irish *baile*, a town + SE *go backwards*] [1990s+] (*Irish*) urban nickname for what is seen as a typical rural town.

ballygog *v.* [? SE *goggle (at)*] [mid-19C] (*US*) to stand around aimlessly.

ballyhack *n. see* BALAHACK *n.*

ballyhoo *n.* (*also* **bally**) [carnival and fairground jargon *ballyhoo*, a barker's speech or a performance given outside the actual attraction, both aimed at touting the attraction itself. The ety. remains obscure; some of the theories, as cited in Mencken, *The American Language* (3rd edn, 1936), include f. Gaelic *bailinghadh*, collect (pron. *ballyhoo*); the predominantly Irish fairground touts of the mid-19C shouted 'Bailinghadh anois!' ('Collection now!) when they passed the hat for payment; f. the cod Arabic cry *b'Allah hoo*, 'through God it is', used by the 'dervishes' in the Oriental Village sited at the Chicago World's Fair of 1893; a comb. of SE *ballet* + *whoop*. Note 19C naut. jargon *ballyhoo of blazes*, a term of contempt for an unpopular vessel] **1** [20C+] rubbish, nonsense, empty praise; a fuss. **2** [1920s] (*US*) an upper-class person.

ballyhoo *v.* [BALLYHOO *n.* (1)] **1** [20C+] (*orig. US*) (*also* **bally**) to publicize to excess, often when the product cannot live up to the manufactured image; thus *ballyhooer*, promoter, publicist. **2** [1920s] to talk nonsense.

ballyhooly *n.* [note music-hall use *Ballyhooly truth*, a lie; the Cork village of *Ballyhooly*, near Fermoy, notable for its faction fights + BALLYHOO *n.* (1)] **1** [late 19C+] (*Irish*) bad trouble. **2** [1910s–20s] rubbish, nonsense. **3** [1940s] noise, commotion, crying.

ballyrag *v.* (*also* **ballarag**) [var. on BULLYRAG *v.*] [mid-19C+] (*orig. Irish*) to bully, to pressurize, to scold.

ballywack/ballywrack *n. see* BALAHACK *n.*

ballyx *n. see* BALLOCKS *n.*

balm *n.* [SE *balm*, 'a healing, soothing, or softly restorative, agency or influence' (*OED*)] [mid-19C+] a lie.

balmedest balm *n.* [SE *balm*] [late 19C–1900s] the ultimate in soothing.

balm of Gilead *n.* [the phrase 'Is there no balm in Gilead?' Jer. 8:22, meaning 'is there no remedy or consolation?'; both money and whisky provide a much-needed consolation for life's problems] [late 19C] (*US*) **1** money. **2** illicitly distilled whisky.

balmy *n.* [BARMY *adj.*; ? nonce-usage] **1** [1940s] a prison wing for disturbed inmates. **2** [1940s–50s] a mad or eccentric person.

balmy, the *n.* [cf. *balmy slumbers* (Shakespeare, *Othello* II.ii)] [mid–late 19C] sleep; thus phr. *have a dose of the balmy*, to sleep; occas. ext. to death.

balmy *adj.* [SE *balm*, soothing but pun on BARMY *adj.*] [mid–late 19C] insane, eccentric; ext. as *balmy in/on the crumpet*.

balmy breeze *n.* [rhy. sl.] [1960s+] cheese.

baloney *n.* (*also* **balogne, bologna, bologney, boloney, bolony**) [? *Bologna* sausage; the *OED* rejects the connection as 'conjectural', but note Adams (*WesternWords*, 1968): 'Bologna bulls, animals of inferior quality whose meat is used to make Bologna sausage'. Partridge offers Rom. *pelonė*, testicles; thus BALLS *n.* (1) or BALLOCKS *n.* (3)] **1** [late 19C+] (*orig. US*) in fig. senses of worthlessness, both of ideas and individuals. (**a**) nonsense, rubbish, humbug; thus *baloney bender*, one who talks nonsense. (**b**) a worthless, stupid person. (**c**) a promiscuous woman. **2** [1940s+] (*orig. US*) (*also* **baloney pony**) the penis.

IN PHRASES

▫ **beat the bologna** *v.* [20C+] to masturbate. ▫ **bop one's baloney** *v.* (*also* **bob one's baloney**) [BOP *v.* (1)] [1970s+] to masturbate. ▫ **have a baloney colonic** *v.* [1980s+] (*US gay*) to have anal intercourse. ▫ **hide one's baloney** *v.* (*also* **hide the baloney**) [1930s+] (*US*) to have sexual intercourse. ▫ **ride the baloney pony** *v. see* RIDE THE WHITE PONY *under* PONY *n.* ▫ **shoot the baloney** *v.* [SHOOT *v.* (5)] [1930s] (*US*) to talk nonsense.

baloney! *excl.* (*also* **boloney!**) [BALONEY *n.* (1a)] [1920s+] (*orig. US*) nonsense!

baloney bender *n.* [SAmE *baloney*, a type of sausage] [1930s] (*US*) an Italian.

balooba *n. see* BALUBA *n.*

baloobas *n. see* BAZOOKAS *n.*

balooey *n.* (*also* **palooey**) [BALONEY *n.* (1a) + SE excl. *pooh!*] [20C+] (*orig. US*) **1** nonsense, rubbish. **2** a worthless, stupid person.

balot *n.* (*also* **ballot**) [Sp. *balota*, a small ball (usu. used in voting, thus a 'ballot'); presumably the shape of pellets of opium] [1970s] (*US drugs*) opium; heroin.

balsam *n.* [SE *balsam*, a soothing, healing unguent; it 'heals' financial pains] [late 17C–1900s] money.

Balt *n.*[1] [abbr.] [1900s] *Balt*imore.

Balt *n.*[2] (*also* **Baltie**) [the mistaken belief that all such people came from the Baltic states] [1940s+] (*Aus.*) any European refugee or immigrant.

baltic *adj.* [the low temperatures of the Baltic Sea] [1990s+] (*US*) cold, usu. in phr. *it's bloody baltic*.

Baltimore steak *n.* [1940s] (*US*) liver.

Balto *n.* [abbr.] [mid-19C+] (*US*) *Balt*imore, Maryland.

baluba *n.* (*also* **balluba, balooba**) [the *Baluba* tribe in Katanga, the former Belgian Congo; coined by Irish soldiers serving with the UN in early 1960s who stereotyped the Baluba as notably savage] [1960s+] (*Irish*) a general term of abuse.

balum rancum *n. see* BALLUM RANCUM *n.*

'Bam *n. see* BAMA *n.* (1).

bam *n.*[1] [BAMBOOZLE *v.* (1)] **1** [18C–late 19C] a hoax. **2** [late 19C] a beggar who fakes physical ills.

bam *n.*[2] [Mex. *bombita*, a little bomb + SE *bam!* echoic of an explosion] (*drugs*) **1** [1950s+] (*also* **bamalam**) low-grade marijuana. **2** [1960s+] amphetamine. **3** [1970s+] a barbiturate/amphetamine mix.

bam *n.*[3] [Ital. *bambina*] [1950s+] (*orig. US black*) a girlfriend, a steady date.

bam *n.*[4] [abbr. BAMPOT *n.*] [1980s+] a violent person.

bam *v.*[1] [BAMBOOZLE *v.* (1)] [mid-18C–late 19C] to hoax; to make fun of.

bam *v.*[2] [echoic] [20C+] to hit.

bam! *excl.* [1910s+] echoic of a sudden sound or action.

IN EXCLAMATIONS

▫ **bam, in yo face!** [IN SOMEONE'S FACE *under* FACE *n.*] [1990s+] (*US teen*) an excl. of triumph, of victory in an argument.

Bama *n.* (*also* **bama, bamma**) [abbr. Ala*bama*, the archetypal southern state] **1** [1930s+] (*also* **'Bam**) Alabama. **2** [1940s+] (*US black*) a generic term for the South and things Southern; thus an implication of rural naïvety. **3** [1960s] as a nickname. **4** [1970s+] (*US black*) (*also* **bammer**) someone or something considered unacceptable or odd.

IN COMPOUNDS

▫ **Bama chukker** *n.* [SAmE *chucker*, one who husks corncobs] [1940s+] (*US black*) a poor southern rural white.

bama *adj.* (*also* **bamma, bammy**) [BAMA *n.*] [1920s+] unsophisticated, out of style, foolish.

bamalam *n. see* BAM *n.*[2] (1).

bamba *n.*[1] [BUM *n.*[1] (2)] [1980s+] (*UK black*) the vagina, used as a general term of abuse; also *bamb(a)claht*, a sanitary towel.

bamba *n.*[2] *see* BAMBALACHA *n.*

bambache *n.* [Sp.] [late 19C–1920s] (*US black*) a riotous, wild party.

bamb(a)claat *n.* (*also* **bambclaht**) [1980s] (*UK black*) a sanitary towel; thus as a term of abuse.

bambalacha *n.* (*also* **bamba**) [Sp.] [1950s+] (*drugs*) marijuana; thus *bambalacha rancher/rambler*, a marijuana smoker.

-bandit *sfx* [ironic use of SE *bandit*] **1** [1950s+] a villain, a thief, often used in combs. as generic for a criminal practising a speciality. **2** [1960s+] in combs., a homosexual, e.g. ARSE BANDIT *n.*, *ARSEHOLE BANDIT under* ARSEHOLE *n.* **3** [1990s+] an obsessive, a user.

bandjax *v. see* BANJAX *v.*

B. and O. [abbr.] [1920s] (*US*) beefsteak with onions.

band of hope *n.* **1** [mid-19C] (*Aus.*) lemonade [the *Band of Hope*, formed 1847, was a temperance society]. **2** [1930s+] (*also* **bander**) soap [rhy. sl.].

bandog *n.* [SE *band*, chain + *dog*. Orig. a large guard-dog, the term re-entered SE in the 1980s to describe a cross-breed of Neapolitan mastiffs and US pit bull terriers; poss. further link to SE *dog*, to pursue, thus note Ned Ward, *Hudibras Redivivus* (1705–07): 'young Drunkards reeling, Bayliffs dogging'] **1** [17C–late 19C] a bailiff or a bailiff's assistant. **2** [late 18C–early 19C] a bandbox. **3** [19C] a policeman. **4** [early 19C] a ruffian.

IN PHRASES

❑ **speak bandog and bedlam** *v.* [*Bedlam* is the Hospital of St Mary of Bethlehem, London, celebrated as the capital's main lunatic asylum] [late 16C–early 17C] to fall into a rage, to act like a madman.

bandook *n.* (*also* **bundook**) ['*Bunduk* was a name applied by the Arabs to filberts (as some allege) because they came from Venice (*Banadik*, ? f. Ger. *Venedig*). The name was transferred to the nut-like pellets shot from crossbows and thence the crossbows or arblasts were called bundooks, f. *kaus al-bundook*, pellet bow. From crossbows the name was transferred again to fire arms' (Y&B)] [late 19C–1940s] (*orig. Anglo-Ind.*) a musket, a rifle, a crossbow.

bandore *n.* (*also* **bandero**) [Fr. *bandeau*] [late 17C–late 18C] a widow's head-dress, worn to signify her mourning state.

bandowzer *n.* [ety. unknown; ? var. on FERRICADOUZER *n.* (1)] [early–mid-19C] a heavy blow.

b & p *n.* [a case involving two such youths, Boulton and Park, known only, so taboo was the thought of homosexuality, by their initials *B and P*] [late 19C–1900s] an effeminate young man.

B-and-Q *n.* [abbr.; ult. punning on the DIY superstore *B&Q*] [1990s+] (*US drugs*) a mixture of *b*onita and *q*uinine sold as counterfeit heroin.

b and s *n.* [abbr.] [mid-19C+] *b*randy *and s*oda; occas. reversed as (late 19C) *s and b*.

bandulu *n.* [ety. unknown; ? link to Fr. *bandeau*, a headscarf, i.e. worn here as a mask] [20C+] (*W.I. Rasta*) a bandit, a criminal, one who lives by guile.

bandy *n.*[1] [SE *bandy*, the easy bending of the thin silver] [19C] a silver sixpence.

bandy *n.*[2] [1990s+] (*US teen/campus*) a dedicated member of a marching band; esp. one whose social life is limited to fellow musicians.

bane, the *n.* [SE *bane*, that which causes ruin; on model of *MOTHER'S RUIN under* MOTHER *n.*] [late 19C–1910s] brandy.

bane *adj. see* BENE *adj.*

bang *n.*[1] **1** as an act of violence. (**a**) [16C+] a blow, a hit, as aimed at and received by a person [ON *banga*, to hammer]. (**b**) [1980s+] (*US*) a murder. **2** in the context of sex. (**a**) [late 17C–18C] a pelvic thrust during intercourse. (**b**) (*also* **bang-bang**) [18C+] an act of sexual intercourse, used in both hetero- and homosexual contexts; thus *dry-bang*, sex without removing one's trousers. (**c**) [1930s+] (*Aus.*) a brothel. (**d**) [1940s+] (*also* **bangee**) a man or woman as a sexual performer, e.g. *he's/she's a great bang*. (**e**) [1990s+] (*US black gang*) a multiple rape, an orgy. (**f**) [2000s] (*US teen*) a party, with overtones of sense 1e. **3** as a fig. 'blow'. (**a**) [1910s+] (*US*) a try, an attempt, usu. in phr. *take a bang at*, to have a try, to make an attempt. (**b**) [1940s+] (*US Und.*) (*also* **banger**) in fig. use, a criminal charge, i.e. something one is 'hit' with. **4** [1920s+] (*drugs*) (*also* **bang in the arm**) a single injection of a narcotic drug, e.g. *a bang of cocaine* [the force used to push the needle into one's flesh + the instantly pleasurable sensation that the drug creates + play on SHOT *n.*[1] (6b). Note the erroneous sp. *bhang*, which is cited in the *OED* (1922) and leads that dict. to assume it is a 'revived' version of the proper use, as a synon. for Indian cannabis]. **5** [1920s+] excitement, stimulation [SE *bang*, a hit. a knock; thus a stimulus]. (**a**) (*orig. US*) a thrill, often in the context of drug use. (**b**) energy. **6** [1930s] (*US*) a handsome man. **7** [1960s] (*US*) luck, fortune, situation; thus a *bad bang*, bad luck, an unfortunate situation.

IN COMPOUNDS

❑ **bang artist** *n.* [-ARTIST *sfx*] [1960s] (*US gay*) an active male homosexual.

IN PHRASES

❑ **bang in the arm** *n. see* sense 4 above. ❑ **dry bang** *n. see DRY RIDE under* DRY *adj.*[1]. ❑ **for bangs** *adv.* [1950s] for fun, for a thrill. ❑ **get a bang out of** *v.* (*also* **get a boot out of**) [1920s+] (*orig. US*) to enjoy, to derive pleasure from, to get a thrill from.

SE in slang uses

IN COMPOUNDS

❑ **bang-stick** *n.* [1970s+] any form of firearm. ❑ **bang wagon** *n.* [it carries those who have 'had a bang'] [1960s] (*US*) an ambulance. ❑ **bang water** *n.* [the sound of a car's engine] [1920s+] (*Can.*) petrol. ❑ **bang word** *n.* [late 19C–1900s] a highly expressive word, a 'swear-word'.

IN PHRASES

❑ **bang of the latch** *n.* [i.e. before the pub door is latched for the night] [20C+] (*Irish*) one final drink after 'time' has been called. ❑ **with a bang** *adv.* [late 19C+] used of something that goes well, successfully.

bang *n.*[2] [weak use of SE] **1** [mid–late 19C] a lie. **2** [1930s] (*US Und.*) information.

bang *n.*[3] [ext. of SHEBANG *n.*] [20C+] (*US*) a crowd of people.

bang *n.*[4] (*also* **bhang**) [Urdu *bhang*, Indian hemp (*Cannabis indica*); the term appears in Eng. in mid-16C but its use (through to mid-20C+) is simply as an exotic foreign word; by the 1930s, as *bang*, it was incorporated, slightly mis-spelt, into popular slang, a process that was accelerated by returnees from the 'Hippie trail' of the 1960s; *bhang* itself remains primarily a technical term, used to describe cannabis as produced and consumed in India and Pakistan] [1930s+] cannabis, esp. in the form of hashish.

bang *n.*[5] [initial letter] [1960s] (*US campus*) a grade of B; thus *bang and a half*, a grade of B+.

bang *adj.*[1] [abbr. BANG-UP *adj.* (2)] **1** [early–mid-19C] smart, alert. **2** [1920s–50s] (*US*) exciting.

bang *adj.*[2] [Afk. *bang*, scared + *broek*, trousers] [mid-19C+] (*S.Afr.*) scared; thus *bangbroek* n., a coward; *bangbroek* adj., cowardly.

bang *v.*[1] **1** [late 16C+] to hit, to thump. **2** in context of sex. (**a**) [18C+] to copulate with; like many sl. terms involving sex, this implies an aggression irrespective of any affection; usu. of men, but occas. of women. (**b**) [1940s] (*US*) to masturbate. (**c**) [1950s+] to have sexual intercourse. **3** (**a**) [mid-18C–1910s] to surpass, esp. as phr. *bang bob-tail*, *bang everything* etc [Cumbrian dial.]. (**b**) [late 19C+] to impress. (**c**) [1960s] to thrill. (**d**) [1990s+] (*US black*) to make an impact. **4** [late 19C] to dismiss from a job. **5** to consume a stimulant [BANG *n.*[1] (5a)]. (**a**) [1920s+] (*drugs*) to inject heroin. (**b**) [1950s+] to throw back a drink. (**c**) [1960s] to inject someone with heroin. **6** [1990s+] (*US*) to inflict, to 'hit with'. **7** [2000s] (*US black*) to play music.

IN COMPOUNDS

❑ **bang-beggar** *n.* [their ill-treatment of tramps] [mid–late 19C] (*mainly Scot.*) a constable. ❑ **bang-bellied** *adj.* [dial. *bang-belly*, a swollen abdomen, whether of a malnourished child or a pregnant woman] [1940s+] (*W.I.*) having a large paunch. ❑ **bang-belly** *n.* [the child hits its stomach to indicate its hunger] [20C+] (*W.I.*) a starving child. ❑ **bang outfit** *n. see* OUTFIT *n.*[1] (3b). ❑ **bang-pitcher** *n.* [SE *pitcher*, the thumping of a tankard on the table] [mid–late 17C] a drunkard. ❑ **bang-straw** *n. see under* STRAW *n.* ❑ **bangtail** *see* separate entries. ❑ **bang-up** *n. see* separate entry.

IN PHRASES

❑ **bang a pitcher** *v.* [SE *pitcher*, one bangs the emptied pitcher on the table] [17C] to empty a pot of beer. ❑ **bang a reefer** *v.*

[REEFER *n.*[1] (1)] [1950s] to smoke marijuana. ❑ **bang around** *v.* [SE *bang around*, to make noise] **1** [20C+] of a person, to make one's presence felt, with little practical result. **2** [1940s–50s] of an item, a situation, to linger, without coming to a conclusion. ❑ **bang back** *v. see* KNOCK BACK *v.* (3). ❑ **bang Banaghan** *v. see* BEAT BANNAGHER *under* BANNAGHER *n.* ❑ **bang heads** *v.* [1960s] (*US*) to fight. ❑ **bang it** *v.* [1970s+] (*US gay*) to achieve orgasm. ❑ **bang like a hammer on a nail** *v.* [1950s+] (*orig. Aus.*) to rate as an enthusiastic sexual performer. ❑ **bang like a/the shithouse door (in a gale)** *v.* (*also* **bang like a dunny door (in a gale), bang like a buggered tappet**) [SHITHOUSE *n.* (2)/ DUNNY *n.*[2]/BUGGERED *adj.*[2] (2)] [1960s+] (*orig. Aus.*) to rate as an enthusiastic sexual performer; usu. said by men of women. ❑ **bang off** *v.* **1** [1950s] (*US*) to murder. **2** [2000s] to ejaculate. **3** *see* BANG *v.*[2]. ❑ **bang out** *v.* **1** [19C+] to rush away, to leave quickly [SE *bang*, to make a noise]. **2** [1950s+] (*US prison*) to murder or beat up. **3** *see* BANG UP *v.*[2] (2). **4** *see* KNOCK OUT *v.* **5** *see* WHACK *v.*[1] (9). ❑ **bang someone's ear** *v.* [1950s+] (*US*) to talk incessantly (and tediously). ❑ **bang the banjo** *v.* [assonance] [1970s] (*US*) to masturbate. ❑ **bang the bishop** *v. see under* BISHOP *n.*[2]. ❑ **bang the bush** *v.* [mid-19C] (*US*) to surpass everything. ❑ **bang the Dutch** *v. see* BEAT THE DUTCH *v.* ❑ **bang the gong** *v. see under* GONG *n.*[2]. ❑ **bang the hoof** *v. see* BEAT THE HOOF *under* HOOF *n.* ❑ **bang the ivories** *v. see* TICKLE THE IVORIES *under* TICKLE *v.* ❑ **bang through the elephant** *v.* [BANG *adv.* + ? ELEPHANT'S (TRUNK) *adj.*] [19C] to plumb the depths of dissipation. ❑ **bang up** *v. see* separate entries. ❑ **bang up to** *v. see* separate entry. ❑ **bang wattle gum** *v. see* BEAT BANNAGHER *under* BANNAGHER *n.*

bang *v.*[2] (*also* **bang off**) [noise of the weapon] [early 19C+] (*US*) to shoot; to kill by shooting.

bang *v.*[3] [1900s] (*US Und.*) to rob; to steal.

IN PHRASES

❑ **bang a hanger** *v.* [HANGER *n.* (5)] [1920s+] to steal a purse.

bang *v.*[4] [1960s+] (*US*) **1** to make a turn while driving, usu. as *bang a U-ie*, to make a U-turn etc. **2** in fig. use, to reverse one's path.

bang *v.*[5] [abbr. GANGBANG *v.* (3)] **1** [1980s+] to be a member of a gang. **2** [1990s+] (*orig. US black*) to fight.

bang *adv.* [SE *bang*, meaning a sudden action or shock] [early 19C+] **1** absolutely, directly, e.g. *bang in trouble, bang up to date.* **2** very, extremely.

IN COMPOUNDS

❑ **bang off** *adv.* [1920s+] immediately. ❑ **bang on** *adv.* [orig. RAF jargon *bang on the target*] [1940s+] exactly right, extremely apposite, excellent. ❑ **bang shoot** *n. see* WHOLE BANG SHOOT *n.* ❑ **bang up** *adv. see* separate entry.

IN PHRASES

❑ **bang to rights** *adv.* (*also* **banged to rights**) [SE *to rights*, fairly, according to the law] [20C+] (*orig. US*) caught in the act, caught red-handed, esp. in Und. use. ❑ **bang up against** *adv. see* separate entry.

bang! *excl.* [late 18C] a euph. for DAMN! *excl.*

bang and biff *n.* [rhy. sl. = SYPH *n.* (1)] [1930s+] syphilis.

bangarang *n.* [BANG *n.*[1] (1a) + echoic redup.] [1970s+] (*W.I.*) hubbub, uproar, disorder.

bangarang *adj.* [BANG *n.*[1] (1a) + echoic redup.] [1940s+] (*W.I.*) worthless; good-for-nothing.

bang-bang *n. see* BANG *n.*[1] (2b).

bange *n.* [dial. *benge*, to lounge, to laze about; note New Eng. dial. *bange*, to idle about, to take advantage of another's hospitality] [mid-19C+] (*Aus.*) a rest, a sleep.

bange *v.* [BANGE *n.*] [late 19C] (*Aus.*) to rest, to sleep.

banged to rights *adv. see* BANG TO RIGHTS *under* BANG *adv.*

banged up *adj.*[1] (*also* **banged**) [BANG *v.*[1] (1)] [20C+] of objects, broken, battered, esp. of a car with notable damage to the panel-work; of people, beaten up, injured, wounded.

banged up *adj.*[2] [SE *bang*; the cell door is literally banged shut] [20C+] **1** (*orig. UK Und.*) (*also* **banged away**) locked up in one's cell; thus, generically, in prison. **2** in fig. use, trapped. **3** of a building or place, locked up.

banged up *adj.*[3] [BANG *n.*[4]] [1920s+] (*drugs*) under the influence of a drug.

banged up *adj.*[4] [BANG *v.*[1] (2a)] [2000s] (*N.Z.*) pregnant.

banged up to the eyes *phr.* [fig. use of BANGED UP *adj.*[1]] [mid-19C–1920s] very drunk.

bangee *n. see* BANG *n.*[1] (2d).

banger *n.*[1] [fig. use of BANG *v.*[1] (1)] **1** [mid-17C–late 19C] a notable lie. **2** [mid-17C–late 19C] a person who lies. **3** [early 19C] something large. **4** [mid-19C] something excellent.

banger *n.*[2] [play on SE *claw-hammer coat*] [late 19C+] (*Aus.*) a morning coat.

banger *n.*[3] **1** [20C+] (*Irish*) an audible breaking of wind. **2** [1910s+] (*orig. Aus.*) a sausage [? its propensity to explode if cooked without initial pricking of the skin]. **3** [1960s+] a dilapidated motorcar [the sound of an ill-tuned, ageing engine]. **4** [1990s+] in fig. use, anything or anyone worn out and run down. **5** [2000s] a cylinder, usu. in comb. *four-banger, six banger.*

IN PHRASES

❑ **bangers and red lead** *n.* [naut. sl. *red lead*, tomato ketchup or tinned tomatoes] [1920s+] tinned sausages and tomato sauce.

banger *n.*[4] [BANG *v.*[1]] **1** pertaining to sex. (**a**) [20C+] the penis [note BANGER *n.*[3] (2); like a sausage it 'spits' when it gets put in the OVEN *n.* (1)]. (**b**) [1960s] one who copulates. **2** pertaining to hitting. (**a**) [1950s+] one who hits (hard). (**b**) [2000s] (*US black/ prison*) any form of knife. **3** [1950s+] pertaining to drugs. (**a**) a hypodermic syringe. (**b**) one who injects narcotics.

banger *n.*[5] [one 'bangs it down' on a counter or table] **1** [1930s–40s] (*US*) $1. **2** [1960s] small change.

banger *n.*[6] [abbr. GANGBANGER *n.* (1)] [1990s+] (*US black*) a gang member.

banger *n.*[7] *see* BANG *n.*[1] (3b).

bangers *n.* [BANG *v.*[1] (1), i.e. they bang together] [1980s+] (*Irish*) the testicles.

bangers (and mash) *n.* [rhy. sl. = SLASH *n.* (2a)] [1970s+] an act of urination.

banging *n.* **1** [1980s+] (*US*) sexual intercourse [BANG *v.*[1] (2a)]. **2** [1980s+] (*US black*) indulging in multiple rape or, if the woman is willing, in an orgy [abbr. GANG-BANGING *n.*[1]]. **3** [1990s+] (*US black*) fighting, living the life of a gangster [abbr. GANG-BANGING *n.*[2]]. **4** [2000s] (*UK black*) a (punishment) beating.

banging *adj.* [BANG *adv.*] **1** [late 18C] big, great in size. **2** [1990s+] (*orig. US black*) popular. **3** [1990s+] a general term of admiration: excellent, first-rate, wonderful.

banging-shop *n.* [BANG *v.*[1] (2a) + SE *shop*; note synon. US milit. jargon *bang house*] [1930s] (*US*) a brothel.

bangle *n.* [1970s] (*S.Afr. prison*) in pl., handcuffs.

bangle *v.* [SE *bangle*, i.e. a handcuff] [1990s+] to arrest.

bango! *excl. see* BINGO! *excl.* (1).

bang on the drum *n.* [rhy. sl.] [1940s+] (*bingo*) the number 71.

bangotcher *n.* [shouts of *Bang! I've got you!*] [1950s+] (*Aus.*) a Western film.

bang out *adj. see* BANG-UP *adj.* (2).

bang-slap *adv. see* SLAP-DAB *adv.*

bangster *n.*[1] [BANG *v.*[1] + -STER *sfx*] **1** [mid-16C–late 18C] a boaster, a braggart. **2** [late 16C] a bully.

bangster *n.*[2] [BANG *v.*[1] (5a) + -STER *sfx*] [1910s+] (*US drugs*) a narcotics addict.

bangtail *n.*[1] [BANG *v.*[1] (2a) + TAIL *n.* (4); a pre-19C term in the UK, it has been sustained through 20C+ US black use] [late 17C+] a prostitute; thus as adj. promiscuous.

bangtail *n.*[2] [SE *bang*, to cut (the front hair) square across, so that it ends abruptly] [mid-19C+] (*Aus./US*) a horse, spec. any animal which has its tail cropped square; thus (*Aus.*) *bang-tail muster*, a round-up of cattle during which the tuft at the end of the tail is cut straight across as the cattle are counted; thus *bang-tailed*, cut square.

bangtail *v.* [SE *bang* + TAIL *n.* (2)] [1940s+] (*US*) to hurry.

bang-up *n.*[1] [BANG-UP *adj.* (2)] **1** [19C] a dandy, a fashionable man. **2** [mid-19C–1940s] (*Anglo-Irish/US*) an overcoat with a cape and high collar.

bang-up *n.*[2] [BANG UP *v.*[2] (2)] [1950s+] (*UK prison*) **1** imprisonment within one's cell, without association or exercise. **2** the shutting of a cell door (at the end of the prison day).

bang-up *adj.* [onomat./BANG *adv.* but note Fr. *bien*, well or good as excl.] **1** [early 19C] drunk. **2** [early 19C+] (*also* **bang out**) first-rate, excellent, fashionable, stylish; often as *bang up to the mark* or *bang up to dick*. **3** [mid-19C] (*US*) impoverished, penniless. **4** [mid-19C] (*US*) finished.

bang up *v.*[1] [BANG *v.*[1] (5a) + SE *up*] [1920s+] to inject a narcotic drug.

bang up *v.*[2] [the banging of the cell door] (*UK prison*) **1** [1930s+] to imprison. **2** [1950s+] (*also* **bang out**) to lock a prisoner in a cell. **3** [1950s+] to be locked up in a cell. **4** [1980s+] (*Aus. prison*) to alert a prison officer by banging on one's cell door.

bang up *v.*[3] [BANG *v.*[1] (1)] [1980s+] to injure.

bang up *adv.* [ext. BANG *adv.*] [early 19C+] completely, very much so, directly.

bang up against *adv.* (*also* **bung up against**) [BANG *adv.* (1) + SE *up against*] [19C+] very close.

bang-up prime *adj.* [BANG UP *adv.* + SE *prime*] [19C] absolutely excellent.

bang up to *v.* [the 'bang' of one's voice] [1950s] (*Aus.*) to speak to.

banjax *v.* (*also* **bandjax**) [usu. in Irish use; f. ? Dublin sl.] [1920s+] to batter, to destroy, to ruin, to get in the way of.

DERIVATIVES

❑ **banjaxed** *adj.* [1930s+] broken, ruined, smashed up.

banjee boy *n.* (*also* **banjy boy**) [? BUM BOY *under* BUM *n.*[1]/BATTY-BOY *under* BATTY *n.*[2]] [1990s+] (*US black*) a gay man who dresses as if he were part of the heterosexual hip-hop culture.

banjo *n.*[1] [the shape] **1** [mid-19C–1900s] a bedpan. **2** [late 19C+] (*orig. Aus.*) a shoulder or leg of mutton. **3** [late 19C+] (*orig. Aus.*) a shovel; thus *banjo and anchor*, a shovel and pick; *banjo-swinger*, manual labourer. **4** [late 19C+] (*Aus./US*) a frying pan. **5** [1990s+] a piece of excrement.

banjo *n.*[2] [backform. f. BANJO-EYES *n.*] [1920s] (*US*) an eye.

banjo *v.* [BANJO *n.*[1] (3)] **1** [1970s+] to force a door or window. **2** [1980s] (*orig. milit.*) to hit, to beat up, to defeat.

banjoey *n.* [SE *banjo* + *joey*, a clown, supposedly coined by the banjo-playing Prince of Wales, later Edward VII (r.1901–10)] [late 19C–1900s] a banjo player.

banjo-eyes *n.* [SE *banjo*; the round, white drumskin on the instrument] [1920s–70s] (*US*) one who has large, wide-open eyes; thus *banjo-eyed*; also in direct address.

banjo (string) *n.* [? resemblance] [1990s+] the frenum, i.e. the ridge of skin connecting the foreskin to the base of the 'bell end' of the penis.

Bank, the *n.* [built according to Jeremy Bentham's ideas on prison reform, outlined in his pamphlet *The Panopticon or Inspection House*, the prison opened in 1821. A gloomy, labyrinthine place, with a reputation for disease and poor conditions, it was shut in 1891] [mid-19C] (*UK Und.*) Millbank Penitentiary.

bank *n.*[1] **1** [19C] the vagina, esp. when seen as a means of making money; one of a number of terms pointing up the commercial potential of the vagina; the man also 'places a deposit in it'. **2** [20C+] (*Aus./US black/campus*) money, one's fortune. **3** [1900s–40s] (*US black*) the lavatory; esp. *visit the bank, take a trip to the bank*.

IN PHRASES

❑ **make bank** *v.* [1990s+] (*US black*) to make money.

SE in slang uses

IN COMPOUNDS

❑ **bank-man** *n.* [1900s] (*US Und.*) a bank robber. ❑ **bank-rag** *n.* [RAG *n.*[1] (1c)] [mid-19C] (*US*) a banknote.

IN PHRASES

❑ **bank of Dunlop** *n.* [brandname *Dunlop*, manufacturer of rubber tyres] [1990s+] a fig. 'bank' on which 'rubber' cheques are drawn. ❑ **bank off** *v.* [similarity of the punishment block to a bank vault] [1930s+] (*US prison*) to place an inmate in the punishment cells. ❑ **bank on** *v.* [gambling jargon *bet the bank*, to commit oneself completely] [late 19C+] to take for granted, to assume as a certainty; thus phr. (*you can*) *take that to the bank*, that's a promise, you can be sure. ❑ **right as a bank** *adj.* (*also* **right as the bank**) [1900s–50s] (*N.Z.*) perfectly satisfactory, perfectly happy.

bank *n.*[2] [BANG *n.*[1] (4) + ? play on pool *bank shot*] [1930s] (*US prison*) a shot of a narcotic.

bank *adj.* [deliberate mispron. SE *bad*] [1990s+] (*US black*) bad, no good.

bank *v.*[1] **1** [19C+] (*UK Und.*) to steal. **2** [19C+] (*UK Und.*) to hide away in a safe place. **3** [19C+] (*UK Und.*) to go fair shares. **4** [20C+] to fail in a task, esp. when it is beyond one's abilities [? SE *bank*, to save up; the image is of saving one's abilities for a task to which one is better suited].

bank *v.*[2] (*also* **bank on**) [BANG *v.*[1] (1)] [1990s+] (*US*) to attack.

bank *v.*[3] *see* BANKROLL *v.*

bank bandit pills *n.* [their calming effect, suitable for use during a robbery] [1960s+] (*drugs*) depressants.

banker *n.* [SE *banker*, one who runs a bank; such figures are supposedly dependable and trustworthy] **1** [early 17C; 1910s+] (*later use is US Und.*) a 'respectable' figure who holds the profits of crime for a thief, one who holds money for a drug dealer (in case of their arrest) etc. **2** [late 19C+] (*orig. gambling*) a sure thing, something or someone on which one can depend, a safe bet (fig. and lit.) [SE *bank on*].

SE in slang uses

IN COMPOUNDS

❑ **banker's bit** *n.* [SE *banker* + BIT *n.*[1] (3b)] [1950s] (*US Und.*) an indeterminate sentence of five to ten years.

banker chapel ho *n.* [cod Ital. *bianca capella*, white chapel + excl. *ho!*] [late 19C–1900s] Whitechapel in East London; by ext. coarse or vulgar language.

bankroll *v.* (*also* **bank**) [SE *bankroll*, a roll of bank notes] **1** [1920s+] (*orig. US*) to provide financial backing for a project, legal or otherwise. **2** [1940s] (*US Und.*) to take a victim's money in a confidence trick where he is allowed to win and lose, but always loses more than he wins.

DERIVATIVES

❑ **bankroller** *n.* [1930s+] (*orig. US*) one who provides financial backing for a project, legal or otherwise.

bankrupt cart *n.* ['said to be so called by a Lord Chief Justice, from their being so frequently used on Sunday jaunts by extravagant shopkeepers and tradesmen' (Grose, 1796)] [late 18C–early 19C] a one-horse chaise.

Bankside lady *n.* [*Bankside*, on the south bank of the Thames at Southwark, the centre of London prostitution during the 17C] [17C] a prostitute.

banna *n.* [ety. unknown] [1990s+] (*W.I. teen, Guyn.*) a young man or woman.

Bannagher *n.*

IN PHRASES

❑ **beat Bannagher** *v.* (*also* **beat Banagher, bang Banaghan, bang wattle gum**) [? name of a real story-teller who is surpassed by the current talker; f. the town of Banagher, a notorious 'rotten borough'. To 'beat it' would be to surpass any extreme] [late 18C+] (*orig. Irish*) to tell fabulous, fantastic tales, often with addition *and Banagher beat the Devil*.

IN EXCLAMATIONS

❑ **go to Bannagher!** [1910s] (*US*) euph. for *GO TO HELL! under* HELL *n.*

banneger *n.* [? link to *BEAT BANNAGHER under* BANNAGHER *n.*/BANGER *n.*[4] (2a)] [1950s] (*US*) a hard blow (with the fist).

banner *n.* [SE *banner*, a flag] **1** [18C] the pubic hair [in this context the 'flag' displayed by the genitals]. **2** [late 19C+] (*US *tramp*) a bedroll [one 'unfurls' it]. **3** [1930s–40s] (*US prison*) a report citing a violation of prison regulations.

IN PHRASES

❑ **carry the banner** *v.* (*also* **pack the banner, carry the stick**) [PACK *v.*[1] (1)] (*US*) **1** [late 19C+] to walk the streets as a tramp; thus n. *banner-carrier*. **2** [1920s–30s] to sleep rough, esp. of the thousands of homeless children who were forced to sleep in the New York streets. **3** [1930s] to live as a tramp. ❑ **flag the banner** *v.* [1940s] (*UK Und./gay*) of a male prostitute, to solicit. ❑ **get oneself a banner** *v.* [1940s–50s] (*US Und.*) to move from the general prison population into protective solitary confinement.

bans *n.* [? SE a *bunch of*] [20C+] (*W.I. Rasta*) a whole lot, a great deal.

bant *v.* [proper name William *Banting* (1797–1878), a fashionable undertaker who reduced his own weight through dieting and a tight-laced corset] [mid-19C–1920s] (*US*) to diet.

bantam *n.* [SE *bantam*, a small variety of domestic fowl; note WW2 US black milit. jargon *banta issue*, a black female soldier] **1** [late 19C–1920s] a lover, a womanizer. **2** [1920s] (*Aus.*) a person with a hot temper. **3** [1920s–30s] (*US*) a young inexperienced man. **4** [1940s–50s] (*US black*) (*also* **banter**) a young woman.

banter *n.* [cited by B.E. *c.*1700, the term was one of those, along with *bamboozle*, *mob*, *kidney* and *country put*, attacked by Swift in *Tatler* no. 230 in 1710 and inspired his proposals to reform the language; despite his condemnation of the term as 'first borrowed from the bullies in White Friars, then fell among the footmen' and as an 'Alsatia phrase' it had joined SE by 1800] [late 17C–late 18C] good-humoured nonsense or teasing.

banter *v.* [BANTER *n.*] **1** [late 17C–early 18C] to tease good-humouredly. **2** [mid-19C+] (*US/Irish*) as ext., to challenge.

bantling *n.* [Ger. *Bänkling*, bastard, ult. SE *bank*, bench; thus 'a child begotten on a bench, and not in the marriage-bed' (Webster, 1864)] **1** [mid-16C–mid-19C] (*also* **bantlin, banty**) a child; also in fig. use, i.e. that which is weak, unformed. **2** [18C; 1980s] an illegitimate child.

banton *v.* [? link to Jam. dancehall star Buju Banton (b.1973)] [1990s+] (*W.I.*) to pose as a superior person.

Bantu beer *n.* [SE *Bantu*, derog. generic for a black African + *beer*] [1960s+] (*S.Afr.*) a drink made from fermented prickly pears and honey.

banty *n. see* BANTLING *n.* (1).

banty *adj.* [northern dial. *banty*, a small conceited person] [late 19C+] saucy, impudent.

Banyan day *n.* [orig. naut. use, a day on which sailors ate no meat; ult. *Banian*, a Hindu merchant (Gujerati *vaniyo*, man of the trading caste), which caste trad. abstained from meat] **1** [mid-18C–1900s] Saturday, or any day of the week without work, and thus money. **2** [1930s–40s] (*Aus.*) Friday.

banzai *n.* [SE *banzai*, 'a reckless attack by Japanese servicemen' (*OED*)] [1900s–30s] a spree.

IN PHRASES

❑ **go banzai** *v.* [2000s] to lose emotional control.

banzai! *excl.* [Jap. *banzai*, hurrah!, lit. 'let him (the Emperor) live ten thousand years!'] [20C+] a general excl. of exultation, excitement.

banzaimobile *n.* [BANZAI! *excl.* + *-mobile* sfx] [1970s] a Japanese-made motorcycle.

b.a.p. *n.* [abbr. *b*lack *A*merican *p*rince/*p*rincess] [1980s+] (*US*) an upwardly mobile black achiever, usu. from the black middle class.

bap *v. see* BOP *v.* (3).

baphead *n.* [? SE *bap*, a soft, flat bread roll + -HEAD *sfx* (1)] [2000s] (*UK teen*) a fool.

bappo *n.* [SE *Bap*(*tist*) + -O *sfx* (3)] [1920s+] (*Aus.*) a Baptist.

baps *n.* [SE *bap*, a small (soft) bread roll] [1980s+] (*orig. Ulster*) the female breasts.

bapsouse *v.* [SE *baptize* + *souse*, immerse] [1900s–50s] (*US*) **1** to baptize. **2** in fig. use, to start off a new machine.

baptist *n.* [pun on SE *Baptists*, who immerse new converts in water] [early–mid-19C] a pickpocket who has been caught and ducked or 'baptized'.

baptize *v.* (*also* **baptise**) [i.e. to 'immerse in water'] [17C+] to dilute wine or alcohol.

DERIVATIVES

❑ **baptized** *adj.* **1** [17C–early 19C] of alcohol, usu. spirits, watered down. **2** [1930s–50s] (*Aus.*) drowned.

baquero *n. see* BUCKAROO *n.*

bar *n.*[1] **1** [mid-16C–mid-17C] (*UK Und.*) a kind of false die, on which certain numbers are prevented from turning up; as v., to use such a die [SE *bar*, a solid object of which one pair of sides is longer than the other]. **2** as a financial unit [SE *bar*, a standard of weight or a denomination of a currency, esp. as used by 18C merchants in trading with Africans who exchanged their goods for a set number of iron bars; or ? Rom. *bauro*, heavy, big]. (**a**) [late 19C+] £1 sterling, orig. a sovereign. (**b**) [1920s+] (*Irish*) a shilling (5p). **3** [20C+] (*also* **bar-up**) the (usu. erect) penis [its rigidity]. **4** (*drugs*) a measure of drugs. (**a**) [1960s+] cannabis, usu. as one ounce of hashish; thus in multiples that refer to ounce-weights, e.g. a *nine-bar*, nine ounces [the shape of a typical lump of the drug]. (**b**) [2000s] an ounce of heroin. **5** [2000s] (*UK Und.*) in pl., prison.

IN PHRASES

❑ **bar up** *v.* [1980s] (*Aus.*) to achieve an erection. ❑ **half a bar** *n.* (*also* **half-bar**) [20C+] a half-sovereign (ten shillings, 50p). ❑ **have a bar on** *v.* [20C+] to have an erection.

SE in slang uses

IN PHRASES

❑ **not stand a bar of** *v.* (*also* **not have a bar of**) [1930s+] (*Aus./N.Z.*) to detest, to reject, to be intolerant of.

bar *n.*[2] [? on the basis of a SE *bar* being a popular site for such activities] [1970s] (*US gay*) any public area, such as a park or beach, that is frequented by gay men looking for sex.

SE in slang uses

IN COMPOUNDS

❑ **bar-bummer** *n.* [BUMMER *n.*[3] (2)] [1900s–20s] (*Aus.*) one who spends their time in bars, a 'barfly'. ❑ **bar-dog** *n.* [*dog*(*sbody*), a worker, a drudge; note SE *sea-dog* for model] [late 19C–1970s] (*US, Western*) a bartender; thus *bardogging*, tending bar. ❑ **bar-fly** *see* separate entries. ❑ **bar golf** *n.* [play on a round of golf/a round of drinks] [1980s+] (*US campus*) the practice of going from bar to bar drinking. ❑ **bar handles** *n.* [HANDLE *n.* (8); the fat has developed after too many trips to the bar] [1960s] an excess of fat around one's stomach, a 'spare tyre' (cf. LOVE HANDLES *under* LOVE *n.*). ❑ **barhound** *n.* [-HOUND *sfx*] [1920s; 1990s+] the habitual occupier of a bar. ❑ **bar-hog** *n. see* separate entries. ❑ **bar-hop** *see* separate entries. ❑ **bar polisher** *n.* [1940s–60s] (*orig. US black*) a hard drinker. ❑ **bar prop** *n. see* separate entry. ❑ **bar steward** *n. see* separate entry.

IN PHRASES

❑ **charter the bar** *v.* (*also* **charter the grocery**) [SE *charter*, to hire] [late 19C–1930s] to buy drinks for everyone in a bar or public house. ❑ **run the bar** *v.* [1940s] to buy drinks for everyone in a bar.

bar *v.*[1] [? 17C *bar*, to take exception to + dicing and two-up jargon *bar*, to declare a throw void] **1** [early 19C+] of actions, to reject unequivocally. **2** [1910s+] (*Aus.*) of people, to dislike intensely.

IN EXCLAMATIONS

❑ **bar that!** [mid-19C] stop! be quiet!

SE in slang uses

IN PHRASES

❑ **bar the bubble** *v.* [SE *bar*, except + play on BUBBLE *n.*[1] (2)] [late 18C–early 19C] to make an exception against the general rule.

bar *v.*[2] *see* IRON BAR *under* IRON *adj.*

Bara *n.* [abbr.] [1970s+] (*S.Afr.*) Baragwanath Hospital, Soweto.

barb *n.*[1] [play on SE *barbarian*, to ancient Greeks, one who is not a Greek] [1900s–20s] (*US campus*) a student who is not a member of a Greek-letter fraternity.

barb *n.*[2] (*also* **barbie**) [abbr.] [1960s+] (*drugs*) any of the hypnotic drugs derived from *barbi*turic acid.

barb *v.* [abbr.; note SE *barb*, to clip, e.g. a hedge or a coin] **1** [mid-19C] (*US*) to *barb*er, to cut hair. **2** *see* BARBER *v.* (1).

barbadoes *v.* [proper name *Barbados*; after the Drogheda massacre of 1655, Oliver Cromwell transported many Irish people as an added punishment] [mid-17C–mid-19C] (*Irish*) to transport to the West Indies.

Barbary Coast *n.* [16C proper name *Barbary Coast*, the countries of the northern coast of Africa; as a sl. term the phr. has applied spec. to the San Francisco waterfront before the 1906 earthquake, Water Street, New York City, and part of Elizabeth Street, Sydney (from Campbell Street to Devonshire Street) during WW2; *DSUE* cites late 17C–early 19C *Little Barbary*, Wapping, home of the Ratcliff Highway, once London's tough port area] [mid-19C–1940s] the 'red-light' area of a city, esp. as frequented by sailors on leave.

barbecue *n.* [? SE *barbecue*, the roasting of a whole animal over an open fire] **1** [1920s] (*US*) a savage fight. **2** [1920s–60s] (*US black*) an attractive woman, esp. one who enjoys or offers oral sex [such a woman is a 'hot piece of meat'; ? a precursor of modern SPIT ROAST *under* SPIT *n.*[1]]. **3** [1990s+] (*US prison*) the murder of a fellow-inmate by tossing a Molotov cocktail or petrol bomb into their cell.

barbecue *v.* **1** [1970s] (*US prison*) to electrocute; also to beat up severely. **2** [2000s] (*US black/drugs*) to smoke marijuana.

barbed wire *n.*[1] (*also* **barbed drink, barbwire**) [it 'tears you up'] [late 19C+] (*US*) strong whisky or brandy.

barbed wire *n.*[2] [the appearance of the XXXX] [1990s+] (*Aus.*) Castlemaine XXXX lager.

barber *n.*[1] **1** [late 16C–mid-17C] a prostitute diseased with syphilis [? plays on the role of a barber as a primitive surgeon (who might treat syphilis), the red-striped (i.e. bloody and phallic) barber's pole/POLE *n.*, and the fact that his shaving water/her vagina is hot/HOT *adj.* (1a), i.e. venereally diseased]. **2** playing on the 'cutting' or 'trimming' functions of the SE *barber*/TRIM *v.* (4). (**a**) [early 19C+] (*Can./US*) a bitterly cold wind. (**b**) [late 19C–1930s] (*Aus.*) a shearer; thus *barber's delight*, a silk shirt; v. *barber*, to shear. (**c**) [1920s+] (*Aus.*) a hotel manager or owner. (**d**) [1930s] (*US Und.*) a pimp. **3** [1920s+] (*US*) a tediously talkative person, a fool, esp. in sports use [the trad. loquacious *barber*, underpinned by US commentator Walter 'Red' Barber (1908–92)].

IN COMPOUNDS

❑ **barber's breakfast** *n.* [sense 2b above] [1960s+] (*N.Z.*) a cough or dry retch, a glass of water and a cigarette.

SE in slang uses

IN COMPOUNDS

❑ **barber's block** *n.* [ext. of SE *barber's block*, the wooden 'head' on which a barber placed a wig] **1** [early 19C+] the head. **2** [late 19C–1920s] an overdressed man. ❑ **barber's cat** *n.* **1** [mid–late 19C] a sickly, malnourished person [the lack of edible scraps at a barber's shop. 'An expression too coarse to print' (Hotten, 1867); Ware suggests corruption of *bare brisket*]. **2** [1910s–50s] a gossip, a chatterer; one who prefers talk to action [phr. *like the barber's cat – all wind and piss*]. **3** [1930s] (*drugs*) an emaciated opium addict. ❑ **barber's clerk** *n.* [mid–late 19C] a shop-boy who attempts to pass himself off as a gentleman; an ignoramus [negative stereotyping]. ❑ **barber's knock** *n.* [early–mid-19C] a double-knock, the first hard, the second far softer. ❑ **barber's pole** *n.* [the red-and-white striped pole that signified a barber's shop + POLE *n.*] [1990s+] a penis streaked with blood after intercourse wih a menstruating woman. ❑ **barber's sign** *n.* [the red-and-white striped pole that signified a barber's shop; 'a standing pole and two wash-balls' (Grose, 1796). Note SE *wash-ball*, a ball of soap, often used for shaving] [late 18C–early 19C] the penis and testicles.

IN PHRASES

❑ **all dolled up like a barber's cat** *see under* DOLLED UP *adj.*

❑ **rob the barber** *v.* [late 19C–1910s] to wear one's hair long and uncut; thus *who robbed the barber?*, a teasing phr. aimed at someone whose hair is seen as too long. ❑ **that's the barber** [ety. unknown, Grose (1785) describes it as 'a ridiculous and unmeaning phrase'] [mid-18C–early 19C] a general term of approbation. ❑ **walk the barber** *v.* [? ref. to the pubic hair or the trad. link between barbers and blood – hence the red-and-white-striped pole – and the blood of a lost virginity] [mid-19C] to seduce a woman.

barber *n.*[2] [? BARBER'S CAT *under* BARBER *n.*[1]; i.e. he is undernourished and thin] [1930s+] (*Aus.*) a tramp.

barber *v.* [a pun on SE *barber*, who gives customers a 'trim'/TRIM *v.* (4)] **1** [late 16C] (*also* **barb**) to clip the edges of gold coins. **2** [mid-19C] (*UK Und.*) to cheat. **3** [mid-19C+] (*orig. UK Und.*) to rob, to steal; thus *hotel barber*, a thief who specializes in robbing hotel guests. **4** [1910s+] (*US*) to gossip, to chatter; thus *barbering*, conversation [ref. to the loquacious SE *barber*, who chatters as he gives customers a 'trim'].

IN PHRASES

❑ **barbered broads** *n.* [SE *barber*, who gives customers a 'trim' + BROADS *n.* (1)] [1950s] (*Aus.*) cards that have been shaved down one side to facilitate cheating.

barberton *n.* (*also* **babaton, babarton, baberton, buckshot**) [proper name *Barberton*, a town in the East Transvaal] (*S.Afr.*) [1940s+] an illicit liquor (blacks were not allowed to buy 'white man's liquor' before 1962) composed of bread, malt, sugar, yeast and warm water; thus *Barberton queen*, a brewer/seller of the drink.

barbie *n. see* BARB *n.*[2].

Barbie (Doll) *n.* [the name of a blue-eyed, blonde-haired designer-labelled plastic doll, created in 1959 for little girls and apparently a role-model for some of their elder sisters] **1** [1970s+] (*orig. US*) a super-conformist, conventionally attractive woman. **2** [1990s+] (*US gay*) a feminine homosexual who prefers to dress in women's clothing.

barbit *n.* [abbr.] [1980s] a *barbit*urate.

barbs *n.* (*drugs*) **1** [1960s+] barbiturates. **2** [1980s+] cocaine [a mis-reading of sense 1].

barbwire *n. see* BARBED WIRE *n.*[1].

barb wire deal *n.* [SE *barbed wire* + *deal*] [1950s] (*US*) a difficult situation.

Barclay (and) Perkins *n.* [the London brewers *Barclay, Perkins & Co.*] [mid-19C–1900s] beer, stout.

Barclay's (bank) *n.* (*also* **Midland bank**) [rhy. sl. = WANK *n.* (1)] [1930s+] masturbation.

Barcoo *n.* **1** [late 19C] (*Aus.*) language heavily peppered with obscenities [proper name *Barcoo*, a region of Queensland where, presumably, such speech was frequent]. **2** [late 19C–1900s] (*Aus.*) bouts of vomiting caused by the ingestion of fly-polluted food [abbr. *Barcoo sickness*].

IN COMPOUNDS

❑ **Barcoo Bill** *n.* [generic use of proper name *Bill*] [1910s] (*Aus.*) generic for a bushman. ❑ **Barcoo rot** *n.* (*also* **Kennedy rot**) [SE *rot*, a putrescent, wasting disease] [late 19C+] (*Aus.*) a form of scurvy. ❑ **Barcoo salute** *n.* (*also* **Queensland salute**) [late 19C+] (*Aus.*) a characteristic gesture in Australia of brushing away flies from one's face. ❑ **Barcoo sandwich** *n.* **1** [1960s] a curlew between two sheets of bark. **2** [1970s] a goanna between two sheets of bark. **3** [1970s] a double rum between two beers. ❑ **Barcoo shout** *n.* [SHOUT *n.* (1a)] [1910s] (*Aus.*) three drinks for half-a-crown (12.5p); a bargain at a time when drinks were usu. a shilling (5p) each. ❑ **Barcoo spew** *n.* (*also* **Barcoo vomit**) [late 19C+] (*Aus.*) severe vomiting brought on by drinking bad water and often accompanied by attacks of dysentery.

bardache *n.* (*also* **bardach, bardash**) [SE *bardash*, a catamite, ult. ? f. Arabic *bardaj*, a slave] [mid-16C–early 18C] a male homosexual; thus v. to sodomize, to bugger.

bardacious *adj.* [var. on BODACIOUS *adj.*] [1900s–30s] excellent, wonderful, the very best.

bardolph *n.* [*Bardolph*, a character in Shakespeare's *Henry V* (1598–9)] [early 19C] a red nose, the result of excessive drinking; thus *Bardolph-faced*, having a red nose.

bare *adj.* (*also* **bere**) [orig. Bdos *bare*, nothing but, i.e. too much of; ult. SE *bare*ly (enough)] [1990s+] (*UK black teen*) many, lots of.

bare-arsed *adj.* (*also* **bare-assed**) [SE *bare* + -ARSED *sfx* (1)/-ASSED *sfx* (1)] [mid-16C+] naked; also fig. use as lacking energy, means or supplies.

bare-ass *adj.* (*also* **b.a., bare-assed**) [SE *bare* + -ASS *sfx*/-ASSED *sfx* (1)] **1** [1930s+] naked; also fig. use; as adv., plainly visible. **2** [1930s+] pertaining to striptease, sex. **3** [1960s] in fig. use, naïve [the image is of a bare-bottomed infant]. **4** [1960s] (*US*) minimal. **5** [1970s] (*US Und.*) of a burglar, not wearing any gloves (to prevent identification).

bare-ass *v.* [BARE-ASS *adj.* (1)] [1980s] to pose naked, to strip.

bare-assed *adj.* **1** *see* BARE-ARSED *adj.* **2** *see* BARE-ASS *adj.*

bareback *adv.* [the nakedness of the penis; note RIDE *v.* (1a)] [1950s+] having sexual intercourse without using a contraceptive sheath; thus *bareback rider*, a man who has sex without a condom.

DERIVATIVES

❑ **barebacking** *n.* (*also* **bareback riding**) [1990s+] hetero- or homosexual intercourse without the use of a condom.

barebones *n.* (*also* **barebone**) [late 16C; 1910s] a thin person.

bare-brisket *n. see under* BRISKET *n.*[1].

bare-bum *n.* [SE *bare* + BUM *n.*[1] (1); the jacket is short, as opposed to a tailcoat] [20C+] (*Aus.*) a dinner jacket.

bared *adj.* [SE *bare*, to denude] [mid-19C–1900s] shaved.

barefoot *adj.* (*also* **barefooted**) (*US*) **1** [mid–late 19C] of an alcoholic drink, undiluted, 'straight'. **2** [mid-19C+] of tea or coffee, without milk/cream or sugar. **3** [1950s] of cornbread, made without eggs or fat.

barelegged *adj.* [early 18C] (*US*) of an alcoholic drink, undiluted.

bares *n.* [abbr.] [1960s–70s] (*US*) the *bare* hands.

barf *n.* [BARF *v.* (1)] [1960s+] **1** (*US*) vomit; thus fig. something disgusting. **2** (*US*) any form of repulsive food. **3** (*US campus*) an ugly young woman.

DERIVATIVES

❑ **barfulous** *adj.* [orig. computing use] [1980s+] (*US campus*) repellent, disgusting. ❑ **barfy** *adj.* (*US campus/teen*) **1** [1950s+] nauseating, repulsive. **2** [1960s] feeling ill.

IN COMPOUNDS

❑ **barfbag** *n.* **1** [1960s+] (*US*) an air-sickness bag, as provided on air flights. **2** [1970s+] (*also* **barf-brain**) used as an insult. ❑ **barf city** *n.* [-CITY *sfx*] [1940s+] (*US teen*) anything particularly unpleasant.

IN PHRASES

❑ **barf on a board** *n.* [note synon. US milit. jargon 'shit on a shingle'] [1960s+] (*US*) chipped creamed beef on toast.

barf *v.* (*also* **barf one's ring**) [echoic/RING *n.* (1b), despite anatomical impossibility] **1** [1940s+] (*mainly US campus*) to vomit. **2** [1960s] (*US campus*) as *barf on*, in fig. use, to treat unfairly.

DERIVATIVES

❑ **barfer** *n.* [1940s] (*US*) a disgusting, worthless person.

IN PHRASES

❑ **barf around** *v.* [1960s] (*US campus*) to waste time. ❑ **barf someone out** *v.* [1980s+] (*US*) to disgust, to revolt; usu. as excl. *barf me out!* an excl. of complete disgust; thus *barfed out*, disgusted.

barf! *excl.* (*also* **barfaroo!**) [BARF *n.*] [1970s+] (*US*) that's disgusting! don't make me sick!

bar-fly *n.* [ext. of SE use, one who 'buzzes around' a bar] **1** [20C+] (*orig. US*) the habitual occupier of a bar, day in, day out. **2** [1950s+] a prostitute who works from a bar; a woman (or gay man) frequenting bars to pick up men.

bar-fly *v.* [BAR-FLY *n.* (1)] [1950s] (*US*) to habitually frequent bars.

bargain basement *n.* [joc. use of SE *bargain basement*, the bargain department of a large store] [1940s–70s] anywhere sex partners can be found easily; thus a cheap prostitute.

barge *n.*[1] [SE *barge*, a flat-bottomed canal- or river-boat, esp. its clumsy motions] **1** [mid-19C] a large (old) woman. **2** [late 19C–1900s] an imitation (padded) breast ['from their likeness to the wide prow of canal-barges' (Ware)]. **3** [1950s+] (*US*) a large foot [note *Dict. Americanisms* (1951): '*barge* N. Eng. a large omnibus or pleasure vehicle']. **4** [1960s+] a particularly large vagina. **5** [1960s+] (*US black*) a large car, esp. a Cadillac. **6** [1990s+] (*US gay*) a large, poss. elderly, male prostitute's client.

IN COMPOUNDS

❑ **barge-arse** *n.* [ARSE *n.* (1)] [mid-19C–1900s; 1990s+] one who has fat buttocks.

IN PHRASES

❑ **barge (in)** *v.* [late 19C+] to interrupt rudely, to push one's way in; thus *barger*, one who pushes in.

barge *n.*[2] [BARGE *v.*] **1** [late 19C–1940s] an argument, a dispute. **2** [20C+] (*Irish*) a cantankerous, argumentative woman.

barge *v.* [? SE *bargee*, a bargeman, an occupation known for its 'colourful' language, or Scot. *bargle*, to squabble; 20C+ use is mainly Irish] [mid-19C+] to abuse, to attack verbally, to 'slang'; thus *barge the point*, to argue, to dispute.

bargee *n.* [stereotyping of SE *bargee*, a bargeman] [late 19C+] **1** a general insult, the inference is a loud-mouthed, objectionable individual. **2** in affectionate use.

bar-hog *n.*[1] [joc. use of SE *hog*] [1930s] (*US*) a heavy drinker who spends most of their time in the bar.

bar-hog *n.*[2] *see under* HOG *n.*

bar-hop *n.* [they 'hop' around the bar] [1900s–30s; 2000s] (*US*) a bartender.

bar-hop *v.* [SE *bar* + HOP *v.*[1] (7)] [1950s+] (*US*) to go from bar to bar, drinking and investigating the social possibilities; thus *barhopper*, one who bar hops; *barhop*, the act of moving from bar to bar.

bari *n. see* BAARIE *n.*

bark *n.*[1] [SE *bark*, the outer surface of a tree; coined *c.*1750 but all 20C+ use is US black] **1** [mid-18C–1940s+] the human skin; thus *take the bark off*, to beat, to thrash. **2** [mid-19C; 1920s] any skin, or animal hide.

SE in slang uses

IN PHRASES

❑ **take the bark off** *v.* [early–mid-19C] to reduce in value. ❑ **with the bark on** *adj.* [mid-19C–1940s] (*US*) of a statement, absolutely unvarnished, totally honest.

bark *n.*[2] (*also* **Bark-islander**) [various northern dials.; ? f. image of a noisy Irish person shouting or 'barking'] [late 18C–19C] an Irish person; thus *Barkshire*, Ireland.

bark *v.*[1] [BARK *n.*[1] (1)] **1** [mid-18C] to flagellate. **2** [late 19C+] to hurt by breaking the skin.

bark *v.*[2] [all fig. uses of SE] **1** [19C] to cough. **2** [early 19C+] to tout a shop or attraction; to work as a costermonger's assistant. **3** [late 19C] (*UK Und.*) to inform. **4** [late 19C–1940s] to make a loud, sudden noise, esp. that of firing a handgun. **5** [1950s+] to hurt. **6** [1960s] (*US*) to boast, to brag. **7** [1990s+] (*Aus./N.Z.*) to vomit. **8** [1990s+] (*US campus*) to lie.

IN EXCLAMATIONS

❑ **go and bark up a tree!** (*also* **go chew on a chitlin!**) [1900s; 1960s] a generally dismissive excl.

bark and growl *n.* [rhy. sl.] **1** [late 19C] a trowel. **2** [20C+] a towel.

barker *n.*[1] [SE *bark*, to shout loudly] **1** [late 15C–late 17C; 19C] a thug, esp. one who offers verbal, but perhaps not physical, aggression [19C use is US]. **2** [late 17C+] a shop tout, esp. the tout who stands outside a second-hand clothes shop attempting to lure customers within [20C+ use is mainly US]. **3** [late 18C+] a pistol. **4** [19C] one who coughs. **5** [mid-19C] a tout who lures victims into mock auctions or corrupt casinos. **6** [mid-19C] a costermonger's assistant. **7** [mid-19C+] an employee of a saloon or similar place of recreational entertainment who

barrack *n.* [late 19C] (*Aus.*) banter, chat.

barrack *v.* [Northern Ireland dial. *barrack*, to brag, to be boastful of one's fighting powers; unlike SE use, no antagonism is implied, other than the usual partisanship; Partridge, via a correspondent in 1944, offers an alternative ety., 'from the rough teams that used to play football on the vacant land near the Victoria barracks (in Melbourne)'; such players were known as *barrackers*] [late 19C+] (*Aus./N.Z.*) **1** to support a team or individual in a sporting context; thus *barracker*, a supporter; thus to support or promote anything or anyone. **2** to back up a confidence trickster. **3** to tease.

barrack hack *n.* [SE *barrack hack*, a horse available to any soldier in a barracks; like the animal, the human is available to anyone who wishes to 'ride'] [late 19C] **1** a prostitute. **2** a woman who regularly attends military balls.

barrack-room lawyer *n.* (*also* **barrack lawyer, guardhouse lawyer**) [1910s+] any amateur, esp. in the services or in prison, who considers themselves more expert in the law, esp. Queen's Regulations or prison rules, than any professional and who will offer services, often to their detriment, to others.

barracks-pork *n.* [mid-19C] (*UK Und.*) prison bread.

barracuda *n.* [SE *barracuda*, a large and voracious fish (*Sphyraena barracuda*) of the perch family] (*US*) **1** [1930s+] a violent, aggressive criminal. **2** [1950s+] a domineering, argumentative person. **3** [1960s] (a predatory homosexual, desperate to obtain a desired partner no matter what it takes. **4** [1970s+] a sexual enthusiast, esp. female. **5** [1980s] (*US campus*) a nasty woman.

barrakin *n. see* BARRIKIN *n.* (1).

barred *adj.* [SE *bar*, a piece of material that is long in proportion to its thickness; although the last *OED* citation is in 1753, when the term has been trimmed to *barr dice*, and Partridge dates it 16C–17C, Aus. use, with the same meaning, persists into mid-20C] [mid-16C–mid-18C; 1950s] (*UK Und.*) referring to a type of false or 'barred' dice, with one of the sides fractionally longer than the others so that they will not easily lie on certain sides; such dice might be *barred sice-aces* (six-aces), *barred cater-treys/trea/tra* (four-threes) etc.

barrel *n.*[1] **1** [late 19C–1900s] (*orig. US*) a large amount, usu. of money [SE *barrel*, pertaining to a large amount]. **2** [1940s+] a fat person [physical shape]. **3** [1970s+] (*drugs*) in pl., LSD [physical shape].

IN PHRASES

❑ **blue barrels** *n.* (*also* **purple barrels**) [packaging] [1970s+] (*drugs*) LSD.

SE in slang uses

DERIVATIVES

❑ **barrelled** *adj.* (*also* **barrelled up**) [1910s–60s] (*US*) drunk.

IN COMPOUNDS

❑ **barrel-ass** *see* separate entries. ❑ **barrel-boarder** *n. see* separate entry. ❑ **barrel fever** *n.* [late 18C+] drunkenness; thus delirium tremens. ❑ **barrelhouse** *see* separate entries. ❑ **barrel stiff** *n. see* BARREL-BOARDER *n.* ❑ **barrel-wash** *n.* [1980s] (*Can.*) illicitly distilled liquor.

IN PHRASES

❑ **barrel of treacle** *n.* [the fig. sticky sweetness thereof] [late 19C–1900s] love, esp. the outward signs of being in love. ❑ **blow one's barrel** *v.* [the barrel is that of a gun] [1940s] (*US*) to lose control. ❑ **have one's barrel full** *v.* [late 19C] (*US*) to be drunk. ❑ **have someone over a barrel** *v.* (*also* **put someone over a barrel**) [? 19C *barrel punishment*, lashing someone across a barrel and whipping them] [late 19C+] to put at a great disadvantage, to inconvenience deliberately. ❑ **in the barrel** (*US*) **1** [1930s+] (*also* **in the bucket**) in debt, bankrupt. **2** [1980s+] dismissed or likely to be dismissed from one's job. ❑ **right up one's barrel** *adj.* (*also* **right into (one's barrel)**) [fitting snugly into a gun barrel] [20C+] (*Aus.*) absolutely perfect, completely to one's taste, exactly what one wants. ❑ **scrape the barrel** *v. see under* SCRAPE *v.*

barrel *n.*[2] [*PORK BARREL under* PORK *n.*] [late 19C–1920s] (*US*) a political 'slush' fund.

barrel *v.*[1] [1930s–60s] (*US tramp*) to drink, usu. to excess.

barrel *v.*[2] [SE *barrel into*, to crash into at speed, like a barrel rolling downhill] **1** [1930s+] (*orig. US*) to charge along, to move swiftly. **2** [1960s+] (*Aus.*) to knock down, to hit, esp. as a result of a tackle in football. **3** [1970s] (*Aus.*) to kill.

barrel-ass *n.* (*also* **barrelarse**) [SE *barrel*/BARREL *n.*[1] (2) + ASS *n.* (2)/ARSE *n.* (1)] [1940s] (*US*) a fat person.

barrel-ass *v.* [SE *barrel into* + ASS *n.* (2)] [1960s+] (*US*) to rush headlong, to charge at; to drive fast.

barrel-boarder *n.* (*also* **barrel dosser, barrel-house stiff, barrel stiff**) [SE *barrel* + SE *boarder*/DOSSER *n.* (1)/BARRELHOUSE *n.*/STIFF *n.*[1] (4a)] [late 19C+] (*US*) an ageing, impoverished, poss. alcoholic tramp who frequents low drinking saloons.

barrelhouse *n.* [the barrels of beer available in such places; thus musical jargon *barrelhouse*, 'swing music played in a "dirty and lowdown" style' (*Downbeat* Year Book of Swing, 1939); thus 1909 WC Handy 'Mr Crump Blues': 'Mister Crump won't 'low no easy riders here, / Mister Crump won't 'low no easy riders here. / I don't care what he don't 'low, / I'm going barrelhouse anyhow'] [late 19C–1940s] (*US*) a brothel or cheap saloon.

barrelhouse *adj.* [BARRELHOUSE *n.*] [late 19C+] (*US, orig. jazz*) of both music and places, rough, tough, unpretentious music that started off in the repertoire of the musicians who played for cheap saloons.

barrelhouse *v.* [BARRELHOUSE *n.*] (*US*) **1** [1910s–40s] to frequent a cheap saloon or brothel. **2** [1910s–60s] (*US black*) to look for sexual partners, to have sexual intercourse. **3** [1950s] to drive very fast. **4** [1990s+] (*US*) to party, to enjoy music.

barrel of fat *n.* [rhy. sl.] [20C+] (*Aus.*) a hat.

barren Joey *n.* [SE *barren* + ? SAusE *joey*, a young kangaroo; she 'jumps around' but has no children] [1940s] (*Aus.*) a prostitute.

barrier *n.* [it stands between the customer and the alcohol] [1910s] (*Aus.*) a bar.

Barrier reef *n.* [rhy. sl.] [1980s] (*Aus.*) teeth.

barrikin *n.* [Fr. *baragouin*, an incomprehensible or alien language, itself f. Breton *bara*, bread + *gwîn*, wine or *gwenn*, white, referring to the astonishment of Breton soldiers at the sight of white bread (Roulin in *Littré Supp.*) and thus transferred to describe bizarre, unintelligible speech] **1** [mid-19C] (*also* **barrakin**) unintelligible language. **2** [mid-19C] a hawker's sales patter. **3** [late 19C] chatter.

barrister's *n.* [the host's name] [late 19C–1900s] (*UK Und.*) the nickname of a thieves' coffeehouse, popular at the time.

barrow *n.* (*Aus.*) **1** [1940s] a police van. **2** [1950s+] a second-hand motorcar.

SE in slang uses

IN COMPOUNDS

❑ **barrow-bunter** *n.* [BUNTER *n.* (1)] [mid-18C] a female costermonger. ❑ **barrow-tram** *n.* [SE *barrow-tram*, the shaft of a barrow] [late 19C] a clumsy, ungainly person.

IN PHRASES

❑ **into one's barrow** (*also* **right up one's barrow**) [20C+] (*Aus.*) absolutely one's business, very much one's concern.

barrow *v.* [mid-19C–1910s] to take home a drunkard who is reclining or passed out in a wheel-barrow.

barrows *n.* [SE *borrows*] [1990s+] (*W.I.*) a loan, esp. of money.

barry *n.*[1] [abbr. SE *embarrassing*; or ? BARRY CROCKER *n.* or ? BARRY WHITE *n.*] [1990s+] an embarassing situation, a disaster, a failure; usu. as *have a barry*, to fail, to have a bad experience.

barry *n.*[2] *see* BAARIE *n.*

barry *adj.* [Rom. *baro*, big, important] [20C+] lovely, sweet, excellent.

Barry Crocker *n.* [rhy. sl.; ult. Aus. entertainer/film actor *Barry Crocker* (b.1935)] [1990s+] (*Aus.*) a shocker, something bad.

Barry White *n.* [rhy. sl. = SHITE *n.* (2); ult. US soul singer *Barry White* (1944–2003)] [2000s] an act of defecation.

barse *n.* [BALLS *n.* (1) + ARSE *n.* (1)] **1** [1960s] (*US campus*) a consistent blunderer. **2** [1990s+] the perineum, i.e. the portion of flesh between the underside of the testes and the anus.

barsterd *n. see* BASTARD *n.* (1).

bar steward *n.* [joc. pron. of SE] [1920s+] euph. for bastard.

bart *n.* (*also* **barty**) [ety. unknown; ? rhy. sl. = TART *n.* (1)] [late 19C–1940s] (*Aus.*) a woman.

barter *n.*

SE in slang uses

IN PHRASES

□ **on the barter** [1950s] (*Aus.*) working as a prostitute.

bartholomew baby *n.* (*also* **bartholomew doll**) [the bright, tawdry dolls sold at the annual Bartholomew Fair, which flourished 1133–1855, when it was suppressed and its grounds replaced by the Smithfield Meat Market] [late–mid-19C] one who is dressed in tawdry finery.

bartholomew (boar) pig *n.* [SE *Bartholomew-pig*, roast pork sold at Bartholomew Fair (see prev.)] [16C–17C] a fat man.

barty *n. see* BART *n.*

bar-up *n. see* BAR *n.*[1] (3).

bas *n.* [abbr.] [1920s+] a *bastard.*

base *n.*[1] [senses 2–4 abbr. FREEBASE *n.* (1), although this itself refers not to crack cocaine, but to base cocaine, the enjoyment of which predated crack cocaine and appealed, through its high price and complex paraphernalia, to a higher social group than the often impoverished crack cocaine users] (*drugs*) **1** [1960s+] morphine base, from which heroin is processed. **2** [1970s+] freebase cocaine. **3** [1970s+] coca paste, from which cocaine is processed. **4** [1980s+] (*also* **base-rock**) a synon. for crack cocaine [ROCK *n.* (4)].

IN COMPOUNDS

□ **base crazies** *n.* [1980s+] (*drugs*) the psychosis that can overtake regular consumers of crack cocaine, typically manifested in a feverish desire to find and consume every last granule of the drug. □ **base freak** *n.* (*also* **base ghost**) [-FREAK *sfx*] [1980s+] (*drugs*) a smoker of crack cocaine. □ **base gallery** *n.* [SE *gallery*; on model of SHOOTING GALLERY *n.* (3)] [1980s+] (*drugs*) a place where users of crack cocaine gather to consume their drug. □ **basehead** *n.* [-HEAD *sfx* (4)] **1** [1970s+] one who smokes cocaine. **2** [1980s+] a regular consumer of crack cocaine. □ **basehouse** *n.* [1980s+] (*drugs*) a place where users gather to consume crack cocaine. □ **base-rock** *n. see* sense 4 above.

IN PHRASES

□ **based out** *adj.* [1990s+] (*drugs*) overcome by the effects of excessive freebasing or smoking crack cocaine.

base *n.*[2]

SE in slang uses

IN PHRASES

□ **first base** *see* separate entries. □ **off base** *adj.* [OFF ONE'S BASE below] [1940s+] (*US*) skewed, incorrect, out of one's depth. □ **off one's base** *adj.* [baseball jargon] (*US*) **1** [late 19C+] insane, crazy, confused, muddled, mistaken. **2** [1930s+] acting in an anti-social or otherwise unacceptable manner, 'out of line', 'out of order'. □ **third base** *n. see under* THIRD *adj.*

base *v.*[1] [SE *debase*] [1980s+] **1** (*orig. US black*) (*also* **base on**) to disparage, criticize or humiliate another person. **2** to argue.

base *v.*[2] [BASE *n.*[1] (4) / abbr. FREEBASE *v.*] [1980s+] (*drugs*) **1** to smoke cocaine. **2** to intensify the effect of cocaine by heating it in combination with ether or other chemicals before inhaling.

DERIVATIVES

□ **baser** *n.* [1980s+] (*US drugs*) one who uses crack cocaine.

baseball *adj.* [the small size of the baseball] [late 19C–1900s] (*US*) small, insignificant.

baseburner *n.* [SE *base-burner*, 'a sheet-iron stove for burning anthracite coal, which is only fed at the top, while the fire is confined to the base, or lower part of the stove' (Bartlett, *Dict. Americanisms*,1877)] [late 19C] (*US*) the buttocks.

basengro *n.* [Rom.] [1900s–10s] (*UK tramp*) a shepherd.

base out *v.* [SE *base*, i.e. the posterior] [20C+] (*W.I.*) to sit around, to hang about with friends or family, watching the passing world and occas. commenting upon it.

bash *n.*[1] [SE *bash*, a heavy blow] **1** [late 19C–1930s] a judicial flogging; thus *nine months and a bash*, a sentence of nine months' prison and a flogging. **2** [1930s+] (*US Und.*) any form of exploit, e.g. a robbery. **3** [1940s] a fight. **4** [1940s+] a party. **5** [1950s] a puff on a cigarette. **6** [1950s] (*Aus.*) brutality, harsh treatment. **7** [1950s+] sexual intercourse. **8** [1950s+] an attempt, a try, esp. as phr. *give it a bash/have a bash at.*

IN PHRASES

□ **put the bash in** *v.* [1940s] (*UK Und.*) to commit a smash-and-grab raid.

SE in slang uses

IN PHRASES

□ **give it a bash** *v. see* BASH *v.* (4). □ **have a bash** *v. see* BASH *v.* (4).

bash *n.*[2] [? misprint for BUSH *n.*[1] (5a)] [1970s+] (*drugs*) marijuana.

bash *n.*[3] *see* BASHER *n.*[2].

bash, the *n.* [BASH *v.* (5)] [1960s] the world of street prostitution.

bash *v.* [ext. of Sw. *basa*, to baste, whip, flog, lash, or Da. *baske*, to beat, strike, cudgel; but poss. onomat.] **1** [late 16C+] (*also* **bash off**) to hit, to batter (with the fist); thus *bash artist*, a violent individual; also fig. use. **2** [mid–late 19C] (*UK prison*) to flog as a judicial punishment. **3** [1910s] (*Aus.*) to dismiss from employment. **4** [1910s+] (*Aus.*) (*also* **bash it, give it a bash, have a bash**) to drink heavily. **5** [1930s+] to work as a prostitute. **6** [1960s+] to have sexual intercourse. **7** [1970s+] (*US*) to berate, to criticize, to abuse; esp. in sfx form *-bashing*, e.g. *gay-bashing*, attacking homosexuals; *Paki-bashing*, attacking Asian immigrants.

IN PHRASES

□ **bash into** *v.* [1920s+] to meet by chance. □ **bash it** *v. see* sense 4 above. □ **bash off** *v. see* sense 1 above. □ **bash on** *v.* [1940s+] (*orig. milit.*) to persist, to keep making an effort. □ **bash out** *v.* [1950s+] **1** to produce with only minimal care, esp. of writing. **2** to do, to perform. □ **bash someone's ear** *v. see* EARBASH *v.* □ **bash the beat** *v. see under* BEAT *n.*[1]. □ **bash the bishop** *v. see* BANG THE BISHOP *under* BISHOP *n.*[2]. □ **bash the candle** *v.* [1990s+] to masturbate [SE *candle* as phallic image]. □ **bash the living Moses out of** *v.* (*also* **give Moses**) [mid-19C+] to beat severely. □ **bash the priest** *v. see* BANG THE BISHOP *under* BISHOP *n.*[2]. □ **bash the shit out of** *v. see* BEAT THE SHIT OUT OF *v.* □ **bash the spine** *v.* [1940s+] (*Aus.*) to idle, to waste time, to loaf around. □ **bash the stick** *v. see under* STICK *n.* □ **bash up** *v.* **1** [1940s–50s] (*mainly juv.*) to beat up, to thrash. **2** [1940s–60s] (*N.Z.*) to make. **3** [1960s] to hurt. □ **on the bash** **1** [1910s+] (*Aus./N.Z.*) drinking, usu. to excess. **2** [1930s+] working the streets as a prostitute. **3** [1940s] (*UK Und.*) fighting, esp. between gangs. **4** [1960s+] having sexual intercourse.

IN EXCLAMATIONS

□ **bash it up you!** [1940s+] (*Aus.*) go away! leave me in peace!

bashed *adj.*[1] [BASH *v.* (4)] [1960s+] (*US campus*) drunk.

bashed *adj.*[2] *see* DASHED *adj.*

basher *n.*[1] [BASH *v.* (1)] **1** [mid-19C+] a professional fighter (and as such used as a professional nickname). **2** [mid-19C+] a thug. **3** [1940s] (*UK Und.*) that member of a smash-and-grab team who breaks the shop window. **4** [1980s+] (*Aus. prison*) a notably violent prison officer.

basher *n.*[2] (*also* **bash**) [milit. jargon *basha*, a shelter made of bamboo and attap (a type of palm frond used for thatching), which was common in Southeast Asia. More recently it has been found among the homeless denizens of London's CARDBOARD CITY *n.* or the protesters at the women's camp at Greenham Common, Berkshire] [1980s+] a makeshift shelter.

-basher *sfx* [1940s+] (*orig. milit.*) a person, usu. in. comb. with a defining n., implying an occupation or job.

bashi-bazouk *n.* [Turk. *Bashi-Bazouk*, lit. 'one whose head is turned'; in 19C a mercenary soldier, fighting for the Turks and known for his blood-thirsty excesses; in WW1 UK sailors' nickname for a Royal Marine] [mid-19C+] a ruffian, a hooligan, a thug.

bashing *n.* **1** [late 19C+] a beating; also in fig. use [BASH v. (1)]. **2** [1920s+] masturbation [fig. use of BASH v. (1)]. **3** [1930s+] prostitution [BASH v. (5)]. **4** [1970s+] verbal aggression, from severe criticism to affectionate teasing [BASH v. (7)].

IN PHRASES

❑ **take a bashing** *v.* [1940s+] (*orig. milit.*) to suffer heavy losses, to do badly.

bashing-in/-out *n.* [BASH v. (2)] [late 19C] the flogging administered to prisoners on their arrival in prison and immediately before their release.

bashment *n.* [fig. use of BASH v. (1)] [1990s+] (*W.I./US black/US campus*) an amazing thing.

bashy *adj.* [fig. use of BASH v. (1)] [1990s+] amazing, wonderful, a general adj. of admiration.

basic *adj.* [1970s+] unexciting, unexceptional, uneventful.

basie *n.* [abbr. + sfx *-ie*] [1990s+] a *base*ball bat.

basil *n.* [? SE *basilisk*, a large cannon, generally made of brass, and throwing a shot weighing about 90kg (200lb)] [late 16C–late 19C] an iron fetter worn on one leg only.

basil-strap *n.* [ety. unknown] [mid-19C] (*UK Und.*) food, esp. tripe.

basinful *n.* [SE *basinful*, the contents of a basin] **1** [1930s] a look (at). **2** [1930s+] an excessive amount, more than enough; usu. as phr. *I've had a basinful of.*

basing *n.* [BASE *n.*[1] (4)] [1980s+] (*drugs*) using crack cocaine.

basing gallery *n.* [BASING *n.* + SE *gallery*, on the model of the heroin-users' SHOOTING GALLERY *n.* (3)] [1980s+] (*drugs*) a place where crack cocaine users gather to consume their drug.

basin of gravy *n.* [rhy. sl.] [1950s+] a baby.

baskerville *n.* [HOUND *n.* (1f); ult. a pun on Arthur Conan Doyle's *The Hound of the Baskervilles*, 1902] [1970s+] (*Aus.*) an informer.

basket *n.*[1] **1** [late 19C+] the stomach. **2** [1940s+] (*gay*) (*also* **basketful of meat, basketwork, picnic basket**) the male genitals; the bulge caused by their display in tight trousers; thus *chicken with a basket*, a 'well-hung' teenager. **3** [2000s] the vagina.

pertaining to heterosexuality

IN COMPOUNDS

❑ **basket-maker** *n.* [late 18C–late 19C] the vagina; thus a woman in a sexual context. ❑ **basket-making** *n.* ['making feet for children's stockings' (Grose, 1785)] [late 17C–early 19C] sexual intercourse, usu. in *the trade of basket-making*, prostitution.

pertaining to homosexuality

DERIVATIVES

❑ **basketeer** *v.* [coined by the homosexual community, like a number of others, e.g. CRUISE v. (4), the term is now occas. applied to women] [1940s–70s] (*gay*) to wander the streets gazing at male genitals; this can provide some men with adequate satisfaction, others may be simply sizing up the available talent for later developments; also as n.

IN COMPOUNDS

❑ **basket days** *n.* [1960s–70s] (*US gay*) a spell of fine weather, permitting one to wear light clothes that reveal one's genitals. ❑ **basket lunch** *n.* [1950s+] (*mainly gay*) fellatio. ❑ **basket party** *n.* [1970s+] (*US gay*) a man with large genitals. ❑ **basket picnic** *n.* [1940s–70s] (*gay*) staring at other men's genitals while wandering the streets. ❑ **basket shopping** *n.* [1970s] (*gay*) staring at passing men, focussing on their genital area. ❑ **basket-watch** *v.* [1940s–70s] (*gay*) to wander the streets gazing at male genitals; thus n. *basket-watcher.* ❑ **basket weaver** *n.* [1960s–70s] (*US gay*) one who wears tight trousers for sexual display; thus *basket-weaving*, wearing tight trousers; *basket-weaves*, tight trousers. ❑ **basketwork** *n. see* sense 2 above.

IN PHRASES

❑ **basketful of meat** *n. see* sense 2 above. ❑ **picnic basket** *n. see* sense 2 above.

SE in slang uses

IN COMPOUNDS

❑ **basket case** *n.* [orig. WW1 milit. use, a quadriplegic, who, bereft of all four limbs, is carried around in a basket] **1** [1910s+] a cripple, either mentally or physically. **2** [1950s+] one who is incapable of tackling a situation. **3** [1960s] in fig. use, something extremely shocking, moving etc. **4** [1970s+] one who behaves in a notably eccentric manner. ❑ **basket cell** *n.* [1910s] (*US prison*) a solitary confinement cell. ❑ **basket man** *n.* [1930s] (*US Und.*) a graft collector for a criminal gang.

IN PHRASES

❑ **basket of oranges** *n.* [fig. use of mining jargon *basket of oranges*, nuggets of gold, as discovered in the gold fields] [late 19C–1900s] (*orig. Aus.*) an attractive woman. ❑ **brought to the basket** [the *alms-basket* on which poor prisoners in the public prisons were mainly dependent for food] [early 17C–early 18C] sent to prison. ❑ **fly the basket** *v.* [late 18C] (*UK Und.*) to steal a parcel or luggage from the basket, or rear part, of a stage coach. ❑ **go to the basket** *v.* [the *alms-basket* on which poor prisoners in the public prisons were mainly dependent for food] [early 17C–early 18C] to go to prison. ❑ **in the basket** [early 19C] confused, nonplussed.

basket *n.*[2] [1930s+] a euph. for BASTARD *n.* (1).

basket! *excl.* [from the practice at 18C cockpits whereby such debtors were placed in a *basket*, suspended above the pit until the fights ended] [late 18C–early 19C] an exclamation directed at those who are unable or unwilling to pay their gambling debts.

basketed *adj.* [BASKET! *excl.*] [late 18C–19C] abandoned, ignored, misunderstood, confused.

bass *n.*[1] [abbr. BASTARD *n.* (1)] [1960s–70s] (*Scot. gang*) a term of abuse.

bass *n.*[2] [the use of sizes of fish to define sizes of glass] [1970s] (*US campus*) a large glass of liquor, a fifth of a gallon.

bass *n.*[3]

SE in slang uses

IN PHRASES

❑ **get the bass out of one's voice** *v.* [one trad. lowers one's voice when one is being verbally threatening] [1990s+] (*US prison*) to stop acting aggressively.

bass *v.* [? the use of a deep, *bass* voice] [1990s+] (*US black*) to be unfriendly; to argue loudly.

bassa-bassa *n.* [Yoruba *basa-basa*, nonsense] [20C+] (*W.I.*) trouble, a fuss, a noisy argument.

bass-ackwards *adj.* (*also* **backasswards**) [a joc. rearrangement of *ASS-BACKWARDS under* ASS *n.*, which emphasizes the overall meaning] [mid-19C; 1930s+] back-to-front; thus fig. messy, chaotic.

bass and flinders *n.* [rhy. sl.; Aus. pron. 'winders'; ult. Aus. explorers George *Bass* (1771–1803) + Matthew *Flinders* (1774–1814)] [1960s+] (*Aus.*) windows.

bastard *n.* **1** [late 16C+] (*also* **barsterd**) a contemptible, objectionable person. **2** [1910s+] (*orig. Aus.*) a general term for a man, a person or any form of creature or thing; not esp. derog.; e.g. *lucky bastard.* **3** [1910s+] (*orig. Aus.*) a term of man-to-man affection. **4** [1920s+] an admirable person, creature or object. **5** [1930s+] (*orig. Aus.*) a situation, a circumstance, usu. a problematic one; also used of a person or situation or place. **6** [1930s+] an object.

DERIVATIVES

❑ **bastarding** *adj.* [1940s+] a general intensifer, a modified version of FUCKING *adj.* (1). ❑ **bastardly** *adj.* [1910s+] a negative intensifier.

IN COMPOUNDS

❑ **bastard-faced** *adj.* [1950s] a general term of abuse. ❑ **bastard-well** *adv.* [1920s–50s] extremely, very much.

IN PHRASES

❑ **as a bastard** *adv.* (*also* **as a beast, as a cunt**) [SE *beast*/CUNT *n.* (4)] [1970s+] a general intensifier, usu. with adj. ❑ **go like a bastard** *v.* [1990s+] (*Aus.*) to commit oneself unrestrainedly. ❑ **it's a bastard** (*also* **it's a proper bastard**) [20C+] (*orig. Aus.*)

a phr. for anything considered unpleasant, excessively challenging etc. ❑ **like a bastard** *adv.* [1910s+] (*orig. US*) a general intensifier; often with *lie* or *work.* ❑ **old bastard** *n.* [late 19C+] a man, often used as a term of affection.

bastard *adj.* **1** [1920s+] a general intensifier, carrying the same pej. imagery as the n. **2** [1950s+] as infix.

bastardly *adj.* [BASTARD *n.* (1)] [1910s+] a negative intensifier.

SE in slang uses

IN COMPOUNDS

❑ **bastardly gullion** *n.* [SE *bastardly* + Lancashire dial. *gullion*, a mean worthless wretch] [late 18C–early 19C] a bastard's bastard.

bastards on a raft *n.* [2000s] (*N.Z.*) poached eggs on toast.

baste *v.* [SE *baste*, to beat, to thrash] **1** [late 19C] of a man, to have sexual intercourse. **2** [1950s+] (*US black*) to attack or ridicule someone behind their back.

SE in slang uses

IN PHRASES

❑ **baste someone's coat** *v.* (*also* **baste someone's jacket**) [ext. of SE *baste*, to beat] [16C–late 18C] to thrash, to beat severely.

basted *adj.* [fig. use of SE *baste*, to beat, to thrash] [1920s+] drunk; one of a number of terms that equate drunkenness with suffering violence; many of the terms can also apply to the effects of drugs.

basteel *n. see* BASTILLE *n.* (2).

baster *n.*[1] [fig. use of SE *baste*, to hit, thrash] [late 19C–1940s] (*Aus./US*) a house thief.

baster *n.*[2] (*also* **baister**) [? BASTARD *n.* (6) or (less likely) f. the large roast that needs substantial *basting* in the oven] [late 19C+] (*US*) something notably large of its type, often as *old baster*.

basticles *n.* [BASTARD *n.* (1) + SE *testicles*] [1990s+] a general term of annoyance, abuse etc.

bastille *n.* [Fr. *bastille*, a fortified tower, and esp. the main Paris prison, built in 14C, the destruction of which in 1789 triggered the French Revolution; note *Bastille by the Bay*, coined by San Francisco columnist Herb Caen for San Quentin prison] **1** [late 18C–early 19C] Coldbath Fields prison in London. **2** [19C] (*also* **basteel**) a workhouse. **3** [mid-19C] a tramps' lodging house. **4** [mid-19C+] (*US*) (*also* **bastile**) any prison. **5** [1960s] a police station.

basuco *n.* (*also* **basuko**) [Colombian Sp., + ? links to Sp. *bazucar*, to shake violently or *basura*, waste, rubbish; a parallel ety. suggests the SE *bazooka*, with a ref. to the drug's 'explosive' effect] [1980s+] (*drugs*) coca paste, part of the process that produces cocaine, mixed with a variety of impure and poss. toxic substances, e.g. leaded gasoline, kerosene, sulphuric acid and potassium permanganate; smoking *basuco* as a 'cigarette' (mixing basuco either with tobacco or marijuana) is common in cocaine-producing countries.

B.A.T. *n.* [*b*usted-*a*ss *t*oes] [2000s] (*US black*) unfashionable footwear.

bat *n.*[1] [SE *bat*, the animal] **1** [early 17C+] (*also* **bat of Venus**) a prostitute or promiscuous woman [like the creatures, they appear at night]. **2** [late 19C+] (*orig. US*) a foolish, worthless person. **3** [1930s+] an unattractive woman, often old. **4** [1930s+] a quarrelsome, unpleasant woman. **5** [1960s+] (*US gay*) a male homosexual.

IN COMPOUNDS

❑ **bat-house** *n.* **1** [20C+] (*Aus.*) a brothel. **2** *see also under* BATS *adj.*

IN PHRASES

❑ **bat of Venus** *n. see* sense 1 above. ❑ **old bat** *n.* [predates sense 3 above] [late 19C+] an unattractive or foolish old woman; occas. of a man. ❑ **on the bat** *adj.* [late 19C+] working as a prostitute (cf. BATTER *v.* (3)).

SE in slang uses

IN COMPOUNDS

❑ **bat-ass** *v. see* separate entry. ❑ **batcave** *see* separate entries. ❑ **batcrap** *n. see under* BATSHIT *n.* ❑ **bat-fowler/fowling** *n. see* separate entries. ❑ **bat hide** *n.* (*also* **batwing**) [? thinness of the paper money; var. on SKIN *n.*[1] (4)] [late 19C–1920s] (*US*) paper money, esp. a $1 bill. ❑ **batmobile** *v. see* separate entry. ❑ **bat's balls** *n.* [var. on CAT'S PYJAMAS *n.* (1)] [1960s] (*US*) the very best, the ultimate. ❑ **batshit** *see* separate entries. ❑ **batwank** *n.* [WANK *n.* (4)] [1990s+] nonsense, rubbish; something that wastes one's time. ❑ **batwing** *see* separate entries.

IN PHRASES

❑ **take off like a bat out of hell** *v. see* TAKE OFF LIKE A BIG-ASSED BIRD *under* TAKE OFF *v.*[2].

IN EXCLAMATIONS

❑ **bat crap!** [1940s] nonsense!

bat *n.*[2] [SE *bat*, a club; to hit] **1** [early 19C+] a hard blow [note 14C–17C *bat*, a hard blow with a club or staff]. **2** [late 19C–1930s] a thug, a 'hard man'. **3** [1920s] (*US*) a complaint or a comment. **4** [1930s] (*US prison*) a whip used for discipline. **5** [1930s+] (*Aus.*) a riding-whip. **6** [1930s+] (*US/Aus.*) the penis; thus (Aus.) *go off the bat*, to masturbate; *bat and balls*, the penis and testicles; *batter*, a man with a large penis; one of a number of terms equating the penis with a stick or rod. **7** [1960s] (*US prison*) a trial.

IN COMPOUNDS

❑ **bat-boy** *n.* [1970s+] (*US gay*) a hitchhiker who allows a homosexual driver to fellate him in exchange for a ride. ❑ **batman** *n.* **1** [1980s] (*Aus.*) a man with a large penis. **2** [1980s+] (*Aus. prison*) an onanist. ❑ **bat material** *n.* [1980s+] (*Aus. prison*) pornography. ❑ **batsucker** *n.* [2000s] (*Aus.*) a fellator or fellatrix.

SE in slang uses, mostly based on baseball/cricket imagery

IN COMPOUNDS

❑ **batbrain** *n.* (*also* **bathead**) [sfx *-brain/*-HEAD *sfx* (1)] [1940s+] (*US*) a fool or a crazy person; thus *batbrained*, stupid, crazy. ❑ **bat carrier** *n.* [1930s+] (*US prison*) a police informer [ety. unknown; ? baseball].

IN PHRASES

❑ **at bat** *adj.* [late 19C+] (*orig. US*) **1** involved in, occupied by. **2** taking one's turn. ❑ **carry one's bat** *v.* [in cricket, a batsman who 'carries his bat' remains undefeated until all his partners have been dismissed and the innings is over] [late 19C+] to outlast one's rivals. ❑ **first crack off the bat** *adv.* [1950s+] at once, immediately, at the first attempt. ❑ **go off the bat** *v.* (*also* **go to bat**) [1980s+] (*Aus. prison*) to masturbate. ❑ **go to bat** *v.* **1** [late 19C+] (*also* **come to bat**) to take action, to involve oneself with a specific task or job, to take a stance. **2** [20C+] to take one's turn. **3** [1920s+] to be prosecuted in court; to receive a jail sentence. ❑ **go to bat for** *v.* [1910s+] (*US*) to act in support of, to back up. ❑ **off one's own bat** *adv.* [SE in 20C+] [mid-19C+] by oneself, without help. ❑ **on one's own bat** *adv.* [mid-19C–1930s] on one's own account. ❑ **on the bat** *adv.* [1930s–40s] (*US black*) in prospect, potentially. ❑ **right off the bat** *adv.* (*also* **hot off the bat**) [late 19C+] (*orig. US*) at once, immediately, from the outset. ❑ **walk out with the bat** *v.* [late 19C] (*UK society*) to emerge a winner.

bat *n.*[3] [dial. *bat*, a stroke, a pace] **1** [mid-19C] (*UK Und.*) a prison sentence. **2** [mid-19C+] (*orig. US*) a spree, a binge. **3** [late 19C+] a pace, a speed, a stroke. **4** [1920s–30s] the price. **5** [1940s] (*US black*) a job.

IN PHRASES

❑ **at full bat** *adv.* [late 19C+] (*Aus.*) at top speed. ❑ **on a bat** [mid-19C+] (*orig. US*) drunk, on a drinking binge. ❑ **on the bat** [note Carew, *The History of Bampfylde Moore Carew* (1750), has *on the battu*, from *battu*, wear and tear] [mid-19C+] out for a drunken, sexy, brawling time (cf. BATTER *n.*[3]).

bat *n.*[4] [Hind. *bat*, speech]

IN PHRASES

❑ **sling the bat** *v.* [SLING *v.* (2a)] [late 19C–1920s] (*orig. milit.*) to speak the local (foreign) language. ❑ **spin the bat** *v.* [late 19C–1900s] (*Anglo-Ind.*) to speak slangily.

bat *n.*[5] [BATTY *adj.*[1], although it could be a result of a BAT *n.*[3] (2)] [20C+] in pl., insanity, esp. manifested in a drinker's delirium tremens.

bat *n.*[6] [pun on STICK *n.* (6d)] [1970s+] a marijuana or hashish cigarette.

bat *n.*[7] *see* GOLDBRICK *n.* (1).

bat *adj.* [BAD *adj.* (3)] [1960s+] (*US campus*) good, attractive.

bat *v.* (*orig. US*) **1** [mid-19C+] to hit; thus ext. as *bat around*, *bat down* etc [SE to mid-19C]. **2** [late 19C–1900s] to overcome, to beat. **3** [late 19C+] (*US*) (*also* **bat around**) to idle, to waste one's time; to wander (aimlessly). **4** [late 19C+] to move, to travel. **5** [1900s] (*US campus*) to earn a grade. **6** [1900s] (*US*) to drink. **7** [1910s–50s] (*US*) to act, to conduct oneself. **8** [1950s] to complain; thus phr. *at the bat*, critical, nagging.

IN PHRASES

□ **bat and bowl** *v. see* separate entry. □ **bat for** *v.* [baseball imagery] **1** [1920s+] to offer one's support. **2** [1930s] to substitute for. □ **bat for the other side** *v.* (*also* **bat for the other team**) [cricket/baseball imagery] [1990s+] to be a homosexual. □ **bat oneself out** *v.* (*also* **bat one's head**) [1940s] **1** (*US*) to work oneself to exhaustion. **2** to be penniless. □ **bat one's gums** *v. see* BEAT ONE'S GUMS *v.* □ **bat one's mouth** *v.* [1920s] (*US*) to talk. □ **bat someone's ear** *v.* [1940s] (*US*) to pester, to nag. □ **bat them out** *v.* [1920s] (*US*) to gossip, to chatter.

bat and ball *n.* [rhy. sl.] [20C+] (*Aus.*) a wall.

bat and ball *v.* [rhy. sl. = STALL *v.*[4] (3)] [1980s+] (*Aus.*) to leave, to depart.

bat and bowl *v.* [cricket imagery, *batting* and *bowling* are the two antithetical positions in the game] [1950s+] to be bisexual.

bat-ass *v.* [(*like a*) *bat* (*out of hell*) + -ASS *sfx* (1)] [1980s+] (*US*) to move at top speed.

bat-bat *n.* [SE *butt*(*ocks*)] [20C+] (*W.I. juv.*) the buttocks, the posterior.

batcave *n.* [senses 2 and 3 underpinned by the *Batman* comics and films, in which the *batcave*, dark, subterranean and mysterious, is the headquarters where Batman (and Robin) keep their car, their hi-tech weapons and other crime-fighting materiel; also note BAT *n.*[2] (6), although this is a primarily heterosexual term] **1** [late 19C] (*US*) a police station and/or its cells [SE *batcave*]. **2** [1970s–80s] (*gay*) the anus. **3** [2000s] the vagina.

batcave *v.* [*see* prev. i.e., Batman's HQ as a place of rest from crime-fighting] [1980s+] (*US campus*) to sleep.

batch *n.*[1] [SE *batch*, a quantity, a number; in this case of bottles or glassfuls] [late 18C–early 19C; 1950s] a quantity of liquor; thus a heavy night's drinking.

SE in slang uses

IN PHRASES

□ **run off a batch by hand** *v.* [1990s+] to masturbate.

batch *n.*[2] *see* BACH *n.*

batch *v.* (*also* **bach (it)**) [SE *bachelor*] [late 19C+] (*Aus./US*) to live by oneself; the inference is obviously of a male, but occas. also a female; of two males, to live together.

DERIVATIVES

□ **batcher** *n.* [20C+] (*Aus./US*) one who lives alone.

batchelor's... *see under* BACHELOR *n.*

batch up *v.* [i.e. the couple make themselves into a SE *batch*, a quantity but note BATCH *v.*] [1960s] (*US*) for a man and woman, to cohabit.

batchy *adj.* [? BATTY *adj.*[1]] [late 19C+] silly, stupid.

bate *n. see* BAIT *n.*[2].

Bates *n. see* MR BATES *under* MR *n.*

Bate's Farm *n.* (*also* **Bate's Garden, Charley Bate's Farm, ...Garden**) [the name of a well-known warder] [mid–late 19C] Cold Bath Fields Prison, in Farringdon, London, *fl.*1794–1877, and known for its severity; thus *feed the chickens on Charley Bate's farm*, to be sentenced to the treadmill.

bate up *n.* [? 16C SE *bate*, an argument] [20C+] an act of sexual intercourse.

batey *n. see* BAIT *n.*[2].

bat-fowler *n.* [SE *bat-fowl*, to catch birds at night by dazzling them with a light and knocking them down or netting them] [late 16C–early 17C] a swindler, a sharper.

bat-fowling *n.* [BAT-FOWLER *n.*] **1** [late 16C–early 17C] (*UK Und.*) swindling, hoaxing. **2** [17C] looking for sex.

Bath *n.*

proper name in slang uses

IN PHRASES

□ **go to Bath** *v.* [the rich pickings that were supposedly to be obtained from Bath's fashionable wealthy population. Bath, with its spas, attracted the mad as well as the rich and their parasites] [mid-17C–19C] to take up life as a beggar; thus excl. *go to Bath* (*and get your head shaved!*) go away, you're insane!

bath *n.* [late 19C] (*Aus.*) a glass of beer.

SE in slang uses

IN PHRASES

□ **go to the baths** *v.* [1980s+] (*US*) to lose badly, esp. in business, sport or gambling. □ **take a bath** *v.* [1930s+] to lose or suffer badly, esp. in business, sport or gambling.

bath bun *n.* [rhy. sl.] **1** [1950s+] a son. **2** [1970s+] the sun.

bathers *n.* [abbr. SE] [20C+] (*orig. Aus.*) a bathing costume.

bath of birth *n.* [literary euph. coined by US writer Walt Whitman (1819–92)] [19C] the vagina.

bathsheba *n.* [SE *baths* + pun on the Biblical queen *Bathsheba*/QUEEN *n.* (2a)] [1970s+] (*US gay*) one who frequents gay bath-houses.

bathtub *n see* TUB *n.*[1].

bathtub hooch *n.* (*also* **bathtub slop**) [SE *bathtub*, the place it was made + HOOCH *n.*[1] (1)] [1930s+] (*US*) illicitly distilled alcohol, esp. in the Prohibition era.

bathtub scum *n. see under* SCUM *n.*

bathtub speed *n. see under* SPEED *n.*

bati *n. see* BATTY *n.*[2].

batmobile *v.* [the Batmobile, in the *Batman* movies, which has a mechanical shield] [1990s+] (*orig. US*) to put up one's defences.

batner *n.* (*also* **battener, battner**) [16C SE *batten*, for an animal to put on weight] [late 17C– early19C] an ox.

bato *n.* [Sp. *bato*, a guy, a bloke, a dude] **1** [20C+] (*US black*) any Mexican, Puerto Rican or other Latin person. **2** [1970s+] (*US Hisp.*) a general term of address.

bato loco *n.* (*also* **vato loco**) [Sp. *bato loco*, crazy dude] [20C+] (*US Hisp.*) an affectionate nickname for a fellow Spanish-American.

bats *n.* [? they are no more comfortable than walking on a pair of flat *bats*] [mid-19C–1920s] a pair of bad boots.

bats *adj.* [SE *have bats in the belfry*] [20C+] crazy, insane, eccentric.

DERIVATIVES

□ **batso** *adj.* [-O *sfx* (5)] [1970s] (*US*) crazy, eccentric.

IN COMPOUNDS

□ **bat house** *n.* [1900s–60s] (*US tramp*) a psychiatric institution. □ **bat house** *adj.* [1940s] mad, crazy, insane.

IN PHRASES

□ **take the bats** *v.* [1920s] to be eccentric or insane.

batshit *n.* (*also* **batcrap**) (*US*) **1** [1940s+] lies, nonsense, rubbish; also as excl. [play on BULLSHIT *n.* (1)/CRAP *n.*[1] (4)]. **2** [1960s–70s] an insane person [BATS *adj.* + APESHIT *adj.* (1)].

batshit *adj.* [BATSHIT *n.* (2) + BATS *adj.*] [1960s+] insane, crazy; often in phr. *go batshit*, to become insane, to act crazily; *drive batshit*, to drive mad.

batshit *v.* [BATSHIT *n.* (1)] [1960s–70s] (*US*) **1** to tell lies, to tease, to confuse with false information. **2** to gossip, to chatter inconsequentially.

batt *n.* [Polari] [mid-19C] a shoe.

batta-foot *n.* [ety. unknown; ? one who 'beats their feet', i.e. walks rather than rides] [1990s+] (*W.I.*) an unexceptional individual.

batted out *adj.* [baseball imagery] [1930s+] (*US Und.*) arrested.

battener *n. see* BATNER *n.*

batter *n.*[1] [SE *batter*, a form of paste] **1** [early 19C+] flattery. **2** [late 19C] (*US*) money [pun on SE *batter*/DOUGH *n.* (1)]. **3** [1940s+] (*also* **baby batter**) semen.

IN PHRASES

❑ **belt one's batter** *v.* [BELT *v.* (1)] **1** [1900s–40s] to copulate with a woman. **2** [1980s] to masturbate. ❑ **splatter one's batter** *v.* [1990s+] to ejaculate.

batter *n.*[2] [SE *batter*, to hit] [mid-19C] wear and tear, stress and strain; thus *can't stand the batter*, not up to the stress.

batter *n.*[3] [ext. of BAT *n.*[3] (2)] [mid-19C+] a drinking spree; thus *on the batter*.

batter *v.* [fig. use of BAT *v.* (1)] **1** [mid-18C+] of a man, to have sexual intercourse. **2** [late 19C+] (*US*) to beg; thus *on the batter*, living as a beggar; *batter the privates*, beg from private citizens [refers to a beggar 'battering' on a door]. **3** [1930s+] of a woman or homosexual man, to work as a (street) prostitute; thus *on the batter*, working as a prostitute.

SE in slang uses

IN PHRASES

❑ **batter the bishop** *v. see* BANG THE BISHOP *under* BISHOP *n.*[2].
❑ **batter the tar out of** *v. see* KICK THE TAR OUT OF *under* TAR *n.*[3].
❑ **batter through** *v. see* separate entry.

battered *adj.* [BATTER *n.*[3]] [mid-19C+] drunk.

battered bully *n.* [SE *battered* + BULLY *n.*[1] (1)] [late 17C–early 18C] 'an old well-cudgell'd and bruis'd huffing fellow' (B.E.).

batter-fang *v.* (*also* **batty-fang**) [SE *batter* + *fang*, to seize, to attack] [mid-17C–late 19C] to hit; as n., a violent person; thus *batty-fanging*, *batty-fagging*, a beating.

batteries *n.* the penis, in phrs. below.

IN PHRASES

❑ **get one's batteries charged** *v.* [1930s+] (*US*) of a man, to have sexual intercourse. ❑ **test one's batteries** *v.* [1990s+] to masturbate.

battering piece *n.* (*also* **battering ram**) [SE *battering piece*, a heavy cannon specially designed for besieging and destroying fortifications] [mid-18C–late 19C] the penis.

battering ram *n.* [1920s–30s] a formidable (older) woman.

Battersea'd *adj.* [the curative herbs that grew in the market-gardens of Battersea] [mid-18C] to have one's penis treated for venereal disease.

batter through *v.* [late 19C+] to struggle on.

battery *n.* [he 'charges his battery'] [1990s+] (*W.I.*) a man who uses a performance-enhancing drug during sexual intercourse.

battery *v.* [Ital. *battere*, to hit] **1** [mid–late 19C] (*Ling. Fr./Polari*) to knock, to strike; thus *battery carsey*, to knock on a door. **2** [1990s+] (*W.I.*) for two or more men to have sex with the same woman.

battery acid *n.* [play on SE] **1** [1940s] (*US milit.*) coffee. **2** [1940s] (*US milit.*) synthetic lemon juice. **3** [1970s+] (*drugs*) LSD [play on ACID *n.*[1] (2)].

battery girl *n.* [SE *battery*, a collection of similar objects grouped together + SE *girl*] [1960s–70s] a prostitute who works as one of a group and who is paid in food and drugs and 'pocket-money'.

batti *n. see* BATTY *n.*[2].

battie-boy *n.* see BATTY-BOY *under* BATTY *n.*[2].

batting practice *n.* [joc. use of baseball jargon] [1990s+] (*US campus*) frequenting a succession of bars with the intention of getting drunk.

battle *n.* **1** [1930s–40s] (*US black/Harlem*) a very unattractive woman [abbr. BATTLE-AXE *n.*[1]]. **2** see BATTLE-CRUISER *n.*[2].

SE in slang uses

IN COMPOUNDS

❑ **battle-axe** *n. see* separate entries. ❑ **battle-cruiser** *n. see* separate entry. ❑ **battle-hammed** *adj.* [SE *hams*, thighs, which 'battle' against each other as one walks] [1930s–40s] (*US black*) misshapen about the hips. ❑ **battle-royal** *n.* [SE *battle-royal*, any battle in which a king leads his forces; also f. cockpit jargon, a cockfight in which a number of cocks fight until only one remains alive] [late 17C–1930s] a serious quarrel, an impassioned argument. ❑ **battleship** *n.* (*US*) **1** [late 19C+] (*black*) a formidable or domineering woman. **2** [1910s–40s] a large, heavy shoe. **3** [1910s+] a tough, physically large and aggressive (older) woman. **4** [1910s+] the foot. **5** [1940s] a pork chop. **6** [1940s+] a shapely young woman; thus *built like a brick battleship*, having a very shapely figure. **7** [1960s+] a large train, truck or car. ❑ **battle wagon** *n.* **1** [1910s+] (*US*) a warship. **2** [1920s–30s] (*US tramp*) a wagon carrying coal. **3** [1920s–40s] (*US Und.*) a police patrol wagon or car [note Liverpool (UK) *battle taxi*, a police Land Rover]. **4** [1940s] (*US*) a homosexual man. **5** [1950s] a large car.

battle *v.* [SE *battle*, to struggle] **1** [late 19C+] (*Aus.*) (*also* **battle around, battle it out, battle through**) to struggle for a livelihood, to work in a low-paid job; both senses imply some self-congratulation. **2** [late 19C+] (*Aus.*) of a tramp, to subsist between periods of employment. **3** [late 19C+] (*Aus.*) to subsist by making small bets at the racetrack. **4** [late 19C+] (*Aus.*) to work as a prostitute. **5** [1970s] (*S.Afr.*) to extract money from. **6** [1990s+] (*W.I./UK black teen*) to compete, usu. in freestyle rapping, sometimes in breakdancing. **7** [2000s] (*N.Z.*) to make pregnant; to make love to.

DERIVATIVES

❑ **battler** *n.* **1** [late 19C+] (*Aus.*) one who uses natural, rather than social or economic, advantages to pursue the struggle for existence and is seen as brave in doing so. **2** [late 19C+] a prostitute. **3** [1900s–40s] a formidable or domineering woman. **4** [1920s] a thug, a violent gangster. **5** [1980s+] a small-time race-course bettor.

IN PHRASES

❑ **battle around** *v. see* sense 1 above. ❑ **battle it out** *v. see* sense 1 above. ❑ **battle the bones** *v. see under* BONES *n.*[1]. ❑ **battle the purple-headed warrior** *v. see* separate entry. ❑ **battle the rattler** *v. see under* RATTLER *n.* ❑ **battle the subs** *v.* [SE *sub*(urb)*s*] [1920s+] (*Aus.*) to sell goods door-to-door in the suburbs. ❑ **battle through** *v. see* sense 1 above. ❑ **on the battle** [20C+] (*Aus.*) working as a prostitute.

battle and cruiser *n. see* BATTLE-CRUISER *n.*[2].

battle-axe *n.*[1] (*also* **battle-ax**) **1** [late 19C+] (*orig. US*) a formidable (older) woman. **2** [1930s] (*US campus*) a fat woman or girl. **3** [1930s] (*US Und.*) a female vagrant. **4** [1980s] (*US campus*) an ex-girlfriend, usu. as *old battle-ax*.

battle-axe *n.*[2] [ext. of AXE *n.* (4a)] [1930s] (*US jazz*) a trumpet.

battle-cruiser *n.*[1] **1** [1910s+] a tough and aggressive (older) woman. **2** [1970s+] as sense 1, applied to a lesbian.

battle-cruiser *n.*[2] (*also* **battle, battle and cruiser, battleship and cruiser**) [rhy. sl. = BOOZER *n.* (2)] [1930s+] a public house.

battle of the Nile *n.* [rhy. sl. = TILE *n.*; in the Battle of the Nile (1 August 1798) Nelson defeated Napoleon's fleet, thus wrecking the French expedition to Egypt] [mid-19C–1900s] a hat.

battle of Waterloo *n.* [rhy. sl.; the actual battle, between Britain and France, took place on 18 June 1815] **1** [early 20C] a stew. **2** [1940s] a queue.

battleship and cruiser *n. see* BATTLE-CRUISER *n.*[2].

battle the purple-helmeted warrior *v.* [1980s+] to masturbate.

battling-stick *n.* [SE *batter*, to beat + *stick*] [mid-19C] (*US black*) **1** a stick used to beat slaves. **2** a stick used for stirring clothes as they boiled in the laundry.

battner *n. see* BATNER *n.*

batts *n. see* BOTS *n.*[1] (3).

batty *n.*[1] [Anglo-Ind. *batta*, an extra allowance given to troops or public servants while serving in the field or on a variety of special postings; also subsistence money given to prisoners, witnesses etc. The payment to soldiers, orig. restricted to field service, became recognized as a regular perk of Indian service, irrespective of the posting; the word comes from Hind. *bhata*, ult. f. *bhat*, an advance without interest made to a ploughman or *bat*, a pack-saddle (as used in the field)] [mid–late 19C] wages, tips.

batty *n.*^{2} (*also* **bati, batti**) [abbr./pron. of SE] **1** [1970s+] (*W.I./UK black*) the buttocks; the anus. **2** [2000s] an effeminate male.

IN COMPOUNDS

▫ **batty-boy** *n.* (*also* **battie-boy, batty bredda, batty-bwoy**) [Carib. pron. of SE *boy/brother*] [1990s+] (*W.I./UK black teen*) a homosexual; a gay person (usu. a man). ▫ **batty-hole** *n.* [20C+] (*W.I.*) the anus. ▫ **battyman** *n.* [1950s+] **1** (*W.I.*) a homosexual. **2** (*UK black*) a term of abuse for an unpopular individual, esp. juv. ▫ **batty monkey** *n.* [1990s+] (*W.I./UK black*) a homosexual man. ▫ **batty paper** *n.* [20C+] (*W.I./UK black*) lavatory paper. ▫ **batty rider** *n.* [1990s+] (*W.I./UK black teen*) a type of skimpy, cut-off shorts worn so tight that they 'ride' up and expose the sides of the wearer's buttocks. ▫ **batty wax** *n.* [SE *wax*, i.e. excrement] [20C+] (*W.I.*) a stupid, gullible person.

batty *adj.*^{1} [either SE colloq. *have bats in the belfry* or (although the chronology militates against it) f. the proper name Fitzherbert *Batty*, a 19C barrister whose certification as mad in 1839 caused much interest] [20C+] insane, crazy, eccentric; as *batty about/for/over*, obsessed (with).

DERIVATIVES

▫ **battiness** *n.* [1900s] madness, eccentricity.

batty *adj.*^{2} [BATTY *n.*^{2}] [2000s] (*UK teen*) homosexual; effeminate.

batty-fang *v. see* BATTER-FANG *v.*

batwing *n.* [resemblance] (*US*) **1** [1930s] (*also* **bat-wing chaps**) cowboy trousers. **2** [1940s] a bow-tie. **3** [1940s–60s] a swinging door, e.g. in a saloon; thus usu. in pl. **4** [1970s] a half-pint flask of liquor, esp. bootleg liquor. **5** [2000s] an upper arm that is flabby or old and so hangs down, usu. in pl. [BATWING *adj.* (2)].

batwing *adj.* [resemblance] [1980s+] **1** of a jumper, with sleeves that hang loose under the upper arm. **2** thus, of a person's upper arms, flabby or old so that the skin hangs loose.

baubee *n.* (*also* **babee, bawbee**) [Scot. *bawbee*, a coin equivalent in value to an Eng. halfpenny; despite the useful similarity to SE *bauble*, a trinket and Fr. *bas billon*, mixed metal, the term appears to come f. the proper name of a 16C mint-master, the laird of *Sillebawby*] **1** [early 17C+] a halfpenny, or penny. **2** [mid-19C–1900s] money in general. **3** [1900s] (*US*) a worthless trifle.

bauble *n.* [SE *bauble*, a plaything/a showy trinket] **1** [late 16C–18C] the penis. **2** [mid-18C–19C] (*also* **bawbels, bawbles, baws**) in pl., the testicles.

baudrons *n.* (*also* **baudrans**) [? Scot. Gaelic *beadrach*, a playful girl] [mid-17C–early 19C] (*Scot.*) a pet name for a cat.

baudy knight *n. see* BAWDY BACHELOR *under* BAWDY *adj.*

b.a.v. *n.* [abbr. *born again virgin*] [1980s] (*US campus*) one who has not had sexual intercourse for a long time.

bawbee *n. see* BAUBEE *n.*

bawbels/bawbles *n. see* BAUBLE *n.* (2).

bawcock *n.* [Fr. *beau coq*, lit. 'a fine cock' although Nares, citing Shakespearian use, prefers *boy cock*, i.e. a young cock; the term was briefly resuscitated by the 19C historical novelist Harrison Ainsworth in *Constable of the Tower* (1862)] [late 16C–early 17C] a fine fellow.

bawd-physic *n.* (*also* **bawdy-physic**) [lit. a lewd, vulgar doctor] [mid–late 16C] an insubordinate servant.

bawdy *adj.*

SE in slang uses

IN COMPOUNDS

▫ **bawdy bachelor** *n.* (*also* **baudy knight**) [late 17C] a bachelor who has no intention of altering his status. ▫ **bawdy banquet** *n.* [sex as food] [mid-16C] whoremongering. ▫ **bawdy-basket** *n.* [one of the 23 ranks of professional mendicant villains, as listed in a number of 16C–18C glossaries] [mid-16C–late 18C] (*UK Und.*) a female beggar who sells obscene literature, as well as pins, ballads and other goods. ▫ **bawdy bush** *n.* [late 16C] a suitable spot outdoors for sexual activity. ▫ **bawdy-house bottle** *n.* [such bottles were designed to be sold at *bawdy houses* (brothels), where they offered the owner yet another means of fleecing clients. Grose (1785) notes that of these frauds this 'is one of the least reprehensible; the less they give a man of their infernal beverages, the kinder they behave'] [late 17C–early 18C] **1** a particularly small bottle. **2** the very last bottle of a drinking session. ▫ **bawdy-house glass** *n.* [early 19C] a small glass. ▫ **bawdy-ken** *n.* (*also* **bodikin**) [KEN *n.*^{1} (1)] [early–mid-19C] a brothel.

bawker *n.* [SE *balker*, one who hinders deliberately] [late 16C] one who cheats at bowls.

bawl *v.*^{1} [SE *bawl*, to cry] [20C+] (*W.I./UK black*) **1** to complain about one's problems, esp. financial. **2** to exclaim from shock, disbelief or surprise. **3** to confess.

bawl *v.*^{2} [ety. unknown] [1930s] to suck; to swallow.

bawl *v.*^{3} *see* BAWL OUT *v.*^{1}.

bawla *n. see* BALLER *n.*

bawling out *n.* [BAWL OUT *v.*^{1}] [20C+] a reprimand, a telling-off.

bawl off *v.* [var. on BAWL OUT *v.*^{1}] [1940s+] (*Irish*) to attack verbally, to scold severely.

bawl-out *n.*^{1} [BAWL OUT *v.*^{1} (1)] **1** [mid-19C] (*UK Und.*) anything that creates suspicions in a watcher/listener. **2** [1910s+] (*US*) a criticism, an accusation, a scolding.

bawl-out *n.*^{2} [it makes one SE *bawl out*] [1990s+] (*W.I.*) something visually exciting.

bawl out *v.*^{1} (*also* **bawl, ball out**) [SE *bawl*, to shout at the top of one's voice, orig. to howl like a dog] [late 19C+] (*orig. US*) **1** to scold, to reprimand, to criticize; all such attacks are delivered in a loud voice. **2** to announce oneself.

bawl out *v.*^{2} *see* BOWL OUT *under* BOWL *v.*

bawls! *excl. see* BALLS! *excl.* (1).

bawly-ike *n.* [SE *bawl* + IKE *n.* (1)] [1930s–50s] (*US*) a complainer, a whinger.

baws *n. see* BAUBLE *n.* (2).

Bay, the *n.* [abbr.] **1** [early–mid-19C] (*Aus.*) Botany *Bay*. **2** [early 19C+] (*S.Afr.*) Port Elizabeth. **3** [mid-19C] (*Can.*) the Hudson's *Bay* Company or one of its stores. **4** [1920s] (*US Und.*) San Quentin Prison, California, overlooking San Francisco *Bay*. **5** [1940s+] (*Aus.*) the State Penitentiary, Long *Bay*, New South Wales. **6** [1950s] (*Aus.*) Sandy *Bay* prison. **7** [2000s] (*N.Z.*) the provinces of the *Bay* of Plenty or Hawkes *Bay*.

IN COMPOUNDS

▫ **Bay fever** *n.* [early–mid-19C] the shamming of illness by convicts, in an attempt to avoid transportation to Botany Bay, New South Wales.

bay *n.*

SE in slang uses

IN PHRASES

▫ **half the bay over** *adj.* [var. on HALF SEAS OVER *adj.* (1)] [late 19C] drunk. ▫ **over the bay** *adj.* (*also* **over the dam**) [var. on HALF THE BAY OVER above] [late 18C–1920s] (*US*) drunk, tipsy.

Bay City *n.* [the San Francisco Bay on which the city stands; however, the fictitious (and massively corrupt) *Bay City* created by Raymond Chandler (1888–1959), is generally seen to be Oakland, California] [1950s] (*US*) the city of San Francisco, California.

bay front *n. see* BAY WINDOW *n.* (1).

bay horse *n.* [1950s–60s] (*US tramp*) bay rum, a hair tonic; thus *bay horse jockey*, a drinker of bay rum.

bayonet *n.* **1** [19C] the penis. **2** [1950s] (*US drugs*) a hypodermic syringe or needle.

bayoo *n.* [? BOYO *n.* (2)] [mid–late 19C] (*US black*) an unpopular, unappealing person, 'a man of whom Quashie thinks very little, "a low down mean cuss"' (Farmer, *Americanisms Old New*, 1889).

Bays, the *n. see* BAZE, THE *n.*

Bay State *n.* [proprietory name] [1930s+] (*US drugs*) a hypodermic syringe.

Bay Street boys *n.* [the business centre of *Bay Street*, Nassau] [20C+] (*W.I., Baha.*) the white mercantile élite who control the Bahamas.

Bayswater captain *n.* [so many of them chose *Bayswater*, London, as a residence. It was cheap but within reasonable distance of the West End and Mayfair] [1900s] a layabout, a sponger.

bay window *n.* **1** [mid–late 19C] (*also* **bay front**) the stomach of a pregnant woman. **2** [mid-19C+] a man's fat stomach; thus the fat man himself.

baz *n.* [ety. unknown] [2000s] (*Irish*) the pubic hair.

bazaar *n.*[1] [Pers. *bāzār*, a market; thence to Hind.] **1** [mid-19C] a shop, a shop counter. **2** [late 19C] the vagina, considered as an economic adjunct.

bazaar *n.*[2] [rhy. sl.] [late 19C–1910s] a bar in a public house.

bazaared *adj.* ['the extortion practised by remorseless, smiling English ladies at bazaars' (Ware)] [late 19C–1900s] (*UK society*) cheated, robbed, over-charged.

Baze, the *n.* (*also* **the Baize, the Bays**) [before the Street Offences Act 1959, Bayswater Road was one of London's centres of street prostitution, seen as slightly less classy than its rivals Piccadilly and, even smarter, Mayfair] [1940s–60s] Bayswater Road, London W2.

bazel *n.* [SE *embezzle*] [early 19C] (*UK Und.*) stolen cloth.

bazongas *n.* (*also* **bazonkas, bazoongas, bazungas**) [SE *bosom*] [1970s+] the female breasts.

bazonkas *adj.* [SE *berserk* + BONKERS *adj.* (2)/BANANAS *adj.* (1)] [1970s+] (*US*) crazy.

bazoo *n.*[1] [Du. *bazu(in)*, a trumpet] (*US*) **1** [late 19C+] mouth; thus talk. **2** [1910s] an orator.

IN PHRASES

❑ **blow (off) one's bazoo** *v.* [late 19C–1940s] (*US*) to boast.

bazoo *n.*[2] (*also* **bazzonus**) [GAZOOK *n.*] [1900s–20s] (*US*) a lout; a fool.

bazooka *n.*[1] [all f. the anti-tank rocket launcher, first used in WW2; like BAZOO *n.*[1] the term may stem f. the Du. *bazu(in)*, a trumpet, in this case f. the shape] **1** [1910s] a metaphorical part of the body. **2** [1950s] the buttocks. **3** [1950s] the head, the mind, with implications of stupidity. **4** [1950s+] the penis. **5** [2000s] (*US black*) an especially large and potent marijuana cigarette, laced with cocaine [note BASUCO *n.*]. **6** [2000s] (*drugs*) cocaine, crack cocaine. **7** [2000s] (*US drugs*) a cigarette that mixes coca paste and tobacco.

IN PHRASES

❑ **up the bazooka** *adv.* [i.e. fig. excrement] [1980s+] (*US*) a general intensifier, blatantly, excessively, totally, reprehensibly, in large quantities.

bazooka *n.*[2] [? BAZOO *n.*[2], but poss. coincidence] [1940s–50s] a fool.

bazooka *v.* [BAZOOKA *n.*[1] (6)] [1990s+] (*US drugs*) to smoke a piece of crack cocaine.

bazookas *n.* (*also* **baloobas**) [play on SE *bosom*] [1960s+] the female breasts; thus *bit of bazooka*, petting, i.e. touching the breasts (and perhaps other parts of the body), but stopping short of penetration.

bazookas *adj.* (*also* **bazooka**) [SE *berserk*] [1970s+] (*US*) crazy.

bazoom *n.* (*also* **bozoom**) [joc. pron. of SE *bosom*] [1920s+] the female breast; usu. pl.

bazoombas *n.* (*also* **bazoomas**) [joc. pron. of SE *bosom*] [1980s+] (*US*) the female breasts.

bazoongas *n. see* BAZONGAS *n.*

bazooz *n.* [? BAZOO *n.*[1] (1)] [1960s] (*US*) the nose.

bazuca *n.* [mis-sp. of BAZOOKA *n.*[1] (5)] [1980s+] (*US black*) a large and potent marijuana cigarette, laced with cocaine.

bazuco *n.* (*also* **bazuca**) [Sp. *bazuco*, base] [1980s+] (*drugs*) the oily substance in freebase cocaine.

bazuko *n. see* BASUCO *n.*

bazungas *n. see* BAZONGAS *n.*

bazz *n.* [Barry '*Bazza*' Mckenzie, created by Aus. comedian, satirist and actor Barry Humphries (b.1934)] [1980s] (*Aus.*) an average, unintelligent male.

bazzer *n.* [? BAZ *n.*] [2000s] (*Irish*) a haircut.

bazzonus *n. see* BAZOO *n.*[2].

B.B. *n. see* BITCH'S BASTARD *n.*

BB *n.* [abbr.] [2000s] (*gay*) in homosexual small ads, a *body-builder*.

b.b. *n.*[1] [abbr. *BUM BOY under* BUM *n.*[1]] [20C+] a male homosexual.

b.b. *n.*[2] [abbr.] [1910s–70s] (*US*) a *bedbug*.

b-ball *n.* [abbr.] [1960s] (*US black*) *basketball*.

b-ball *v.* [B-BALL *n.*] [1990s+] (*US black*) to play basketball.

B.B.B. crop *n.* [abbr. *Bad Borstal Boy* + SE *crop*] [1940s] (*UK prison*) a very short haircut.

b.b.-brained *adj.* [*see* next] [1960s] (*US*) stupid.

b.b. head *n.* [the supposed resemblance to *b.b.* shot, i.e. 'an air gun pellet having a diameter of approximately 0.45 or 0.56 cm (0.177 or 0.22 inches), used esp. by young people' (*OED*)] [1980s] (*US black*) **1** a boy with a tight-curled, 'knotty' head. **2** an unattractive woman, esp. one with short, fuzzy, nappy hair.

b.b.l. *n.* [? abbr. *bloody big lot*] [1920s] (*US*) a great deal.

b-bomb *n.* [the explosive effects, ? var. on A-BOMB *n.*] **1** [1960s+] (*US drugs*) amphetamine [abbr. *Benzedrine*]. **2** [2000s] MDMA.

B-boy *n.* [coined in 1975 to describe those who followed DJ Kool Herc of the Hevalo Club in New York; generally accepted as abbr. *beat-boy*] [1970s+] (*orig. US black*) a black male teenager, focused on rap music and the ghetto street lifestyle; thus the female *B-girl*, *B-boyette*; generic *B people*; as v., to live as a B-boy.

b-boy *n.* [abbr. *bottom-boy*] [1980s+] (*US gay*) a passive male homosexual, poss. a male prostitute.

B-broad *n. see* B-GIRL *n.* (2).

B.B.'s *n.* [*BOVVER BOOTS under* BOVVER *n.*] [1990s+] (*US black*) heavy workman boots worn by fashion-conscious youth.

BB's *n.* [abbr. SE *big brains*] [1940s] (*US black campus*) a clever person, a teacher.

BB stacker *n.* [US army jargon *BB stacker*, one who loads machine-gun belts] [1960s] **1** (*US*) a fool. **2** (*US teen*) a female with large breasts (stereotyped as stupid).

b-bwoy *n.* [abbr. *BATTY-BOY under* BATTY *n.*[2]] [1990s+] (*W.I.*) a male homosexual.

B.C. *adj.* [chronological notation *BC*, before Christ] **1** [late 19C–1900s] extremely old. **2** [2000s] old-fashioned, i.e. before computers.

B.C. *adv.* [abbr.; CRACK *n.*[7] + pun on BC, before Christ] [1990s+] (*US black*) Before Crack.

b.c. *n.* [abbr. *birth control*] [1960s+] (*US black*) contraception; also *b.c.p.*, birth control (i.e. contraceptive) *pills*.

b.d. *n. see* BULL-DYKER *n.*

b/d *n. see* B & D *n.*

b-drink *n.* [B-GIRL *n.* (1); i.e. the sort of drink she consumes] [1930s–60s] (*US*) a drink that resembles whisky (and charged as such) but is in fact cold tea; served to the female companion of a man, or homosexual customer, who has entered a club in the hope of sex; thus *b-drinker/bee-drinker*, the woman, or man, who consumes such drinks.

B-drinker *n. see* B-GIRL *n.* (2).

b.d.t. *n.* (*also* **b.d.t.'s**) [abbr. *BACK-DOOR TROT under* BACK-DOOR *n.*] [20C+] (*US*) **1** diarrhoea. **2** over-frequent urination.

b.d.v. *n.* [abbr. *bend down Virginia*] [1930s] (*UK tramp*) a cigarette stub, picked up in the street.

b-e *v. see* B AND E *v.*

beach *n.*

SE in slang uses

IN COMPOUNDS

❑ **beach bitch** *n.* [BITCH *n.*[1] (3f)] [1970s+] (*US gay*) one who frequents holiday resorts and beaches looking for sex. ❑ **beach bum** *n.* (*also* **beach rat**) [BUM *n.*[3] (1)/-RAT *sfx*] [1950s+] (*Aus./US*) a person, usu. a teenager, who hangs around the beach all day and surfs. ❑ **beach bunny** *n.* [BUNNY *n.*[1] (1b)] [1960s+] a young woman who frequents the world of surfing, but does not herself surf. ❑ **beach-cadger** *n.* [CADGER *n.* (1)] [mid-19C–1910s] a beggar who favours seaside resorts, and poses as a sailor. ❑ **beachcomber** *n. see* separate entry.

IN PHRASES

❑ **on the beach** [naval jargon *on the beach*, discharged from the navy, thus unemployed] [late 19C+] (*US*) out of work, impoverished.

beachcomber *n.* [SE *beachcomber*, a settler in the Pacific islands, living by pearl-fishing and other means] **1** [late 19C] an idler. **2** [1910s–50s] (*Can.*) a white man living with an Inuit woman. **3** [1920s–30s] (*US tramp*) a tramp who frequents docks and waterfront areas. **4** [1950s] (*Aus.*) one who walks the streets in the hope of picking up a woman; thus *beach-combing, combing*.

beached *adj.* **1** [late 19C+] (*orig. RN*) unemployed, impoverished [ext. of SE; one is living as an impoverished beachcomber]. **2** [1990s+] (*US teen*) exhausted; stranded, abandoned [the imagery of a beached whale].

beacon *n.* [late 19C] a red nose.

bead *n.*[1] [SE *bead*, a bubble found in spirits or wine] [19C] a glass of spirits.

bead *n.*[2]

SE, meaning rosary beads, in slang uses

IN COMPOUNDS

❑ **bead-counter** *n.* [early 19C] a clergyman; an overtly religious person; a recluse. ❑ **bead-jiggler** *n.* [1960s] (*US*) a Roman Catholic, esp. a priest. ❑ **bead-puller** *n.* [20C+] (*US*) a Roman Catholic. ❑ **bead-twirler** *n.* [1990s+] a derog. term for a Roman Catholic.

beadie *v. see* BEADY *v.*

beadle *n.* [early 19C] (*UK Und.*) anyone who wears a long, blue overcoat (the uniform of a parish *beadle*).

beadles *n.* [? their serious, beadle-like demeanour] [late 19C–1900s] (*US*) inhabitants of the state of Virginia.

beads *n.*[1] [shape] **1** [1930s] (*US Und.*) morphine tablets. **2** [1940s] (*UK Und.*) diamonds. **3** [1970s] (*US*) the eyes.

beads *n.*[2] [1970s+] (*US gay*) one's inner awareness of being homosexual, a metaphorical string of beads worn by all male homosexuals.

IN PHRASES

❑ **drop one's beads** *v.* [1960s+] (*gay*) **1** accidentally to reveal one's homosexuality by a slip of the tongue or other blunder. **2** to be shocked. ❑ **in the beads** [1970s+] (*US gay*) at the mercy of the fates. ❑ **jump on somebody's beads** *v.* [1970s] to beat up; to belittle. ❑ **rattle one's beads** *v.* [1960s+] **1** (*mainly gay*) to complain. **2** (*US gay*) to gossip, to chatter. ❑ **read someone's beads** *v.* [1960s+] (*orig. gay*) to chastise, to berate, to attack someone verbally. ❑ **wreck someone's beads** *v.* [1970s] (*US gay*) to beat someone up; to shock or startle.

IN EXCLAMATIONS

❑ **my beads!** [1950s–60s] (*US gay*) a camp excl.

beady *n.* [SE phr. *beady* (*little*) *eye*] [1970s+] (*US*) an eye.

beady *v.* (*also* **beadie**) [BEADY *n.*] [1990s+] to see, to look at.

beagle *n.* [fig. use of SE *beagle*, as a dog] **1** [early 17C] a whore [like the dog she 'hunts around']. **2** [mid-19C] (*US*) a native of Virginia [the popularity of fox-hunting in the state]. **3** [1920s–30s] (*US*) a nose [the dog's sniffing abilities]. **4** [1920s+] (*US Und.*) a sausage, esp. a 'hot dog' [pun]. **5** [1940s] (*US*) a journalist [the dog's sniffing abilities]. **6** [1940s–50s] (*US*) a (usu. unattractive) young woman [DOG *n.*[2] (9)].

beagle *v.*[1] [the dog's 'sniffing-out' qualities] [1960s–70s] to pick pockets.

beagle *v.*[2] [? SE *beetle off*] [1990s+] to leave.

beak *n.*[1] [Hotten (1859) + Ware suggest OE *beag*, a necklace worn as a badge of office] **1** [17C+] (*also* **beeks**) a judge, a magistrate; often in phr. *up before the beak*, in the magistrate's court [poss. f. HARMAN *n.*]. **2** [19C] a sheriff's officer, a policeman. **3** [1910s+] a schoolmaster.

IN COMPOUNDS

❑ **beak-gander** *n.* [SE *gander*, a foolish (old) man] [late 19C] a senior judge. ❑ **beak-runner** *n.* [SE *runner*] [late 18C] (*UK Und.*) an officer of the law, lit. 'a runner for the magistrate'. ❑ **beaksman** *n.* [early–mid-19C] a policeman; a police-office clerk.

beak *n.*[2] (*also* **beaker**) [SE *beak* of a bird] **1** [mid-19C+] the nose; thus *beaky*, possessing a large nose; *beaked*, pertinent to the nose. **2** [mid-19C+] (*also* **bake**) the mouth, or face. **3** [late 19C–1900s] the penis. **4** [2000s] (*drugs*) (*also* **beek**) cocaine [f. sense 1].

DERIVATIVES

❑ **beaky** *adj.* [2000s] nosey, inquisitive.

IN COMPOUNDS

❑ **beak-hunter** *n. see* BEAKER-HUNTER *under* BEAKER *n.*[2].

IN PHRASES

❑ **dip one's beak** *v.* (*also* **dip one's nose**) [early 19C+] to have a drink. ❑ **strop one's beak** *v.* [SE *strop*, to sharpen] [19C] of a man, to have sexual intercourse.

IN EXCLAMATIONS

❑ **beak-o!** [i.e. they are 'nosey'] [1980s+] (*Aus. prison*) excl. used to upbraid one who is staring. ❑ **shut your beak!** [20C+] (*W.I.*) shut up! be quiet!

beak *v.*[1] [like a bird, the beggar 'pecks around'] [late 16C–early 17C] to beg.

beak *v.*[2] [BEAK *n.*[1] (1)] [late 19C] to bring an offender before a magistrate.

beaker *n.*[1] [SE *beaker*, a large drinking-vessel with a wide mouth, a goblet] [early 18C–mid-19C] (*UK Und.*) a silver tankard.

beaker *n.*[2] [SE *beak*] [19C] (*UK Und.*) a fowl, a chicken.

IN COMPOUNDS

❑ **beaker-hauler** *n.* [19C] a poultry thief, who hawks booty from door to door. ❑ **beaker-hunter** *n.* (*also* **beak-hunter**) [mid-19C–1900s] a poultry-thief; thus *beak-hunting*, poultry-stealing.

beaker *n.*[3] *see* BEAK *n.*[2].

beak off *v.* [synon. Scot. *bake*] [20C+] (*Ulster*) to truant.

beaky lady/man *n.* [BEAK OFF *v.*] [20C+] (*Ulster*) a truancy officer.

be all... *v.* [1980s+] to take an attitude, to adopt a pose; the phr. is often used with an accompanying gesture, *He was all...*

beals *n.* [ety. unknown; ? slightly pathetic fictional character *Ian Beale* in the BBC TV soap opera *EastEnders*] [1990s+] a fool, an idiot, an unsophisticated person.

beam *n.*[1] [note BEAM-ENDS *n.*] [early 19C+] the buttocks, the hips.

beam *n.*[2] [abbr. SE *sunbeam*; Burley writes 'bean' (see BEAN *n.*[1] (6)) but Major, *Juba to Jive: A Dict. of Afro-American Slang* (1994), suggests it is a misprint for this] [1940s] (*US black*) the sun.

beam *n.*[3]

SE in slang uses

IN PHRASES

❑ **off (the) beam** *adj.* [orig. air force use, referring to radio beams that guide aircraft] [1940s+] (*orig. US*) wholly incorrect; often intensified as *way off beam*. ❑ **on the beam** *adj.* [orig. air force, referring to radio beams that guide aircraft] [1940s+] (*orig. US*) right on course, heading in the right direction; thus *on the beam in short-cut plays*.

beam *v.*[1] (*also* **beam on**) [obs. SE *beam*, to shed light upon] [1940s+] (*US black*) **1** to look at, to stare. **2** in fig. use, to ascertain what is happening.

IN PHRASES

❑ **beam out** *v.* [1980s+] (*US campus*) to daydream [i.e. to stare into the middle distance].

beam *v.*[2] [? play on HEADLIGHT *n.* (4)] [1990s+] (*US juv.*) of a girl's nipples, to be erect.

beamed *adv.* [BEAM *v.*[1] (1)] [1970s] (*US*) staring at, focussed on.

beam-ends *n.* [naut. *beam ends*, the ends of a ship's lateral beams; if these touch the water, the ship is on the verge of capsizing] [early 19C+] the buttocks, often as *on one's beam-ends*, fallen over.

Beamer *n.* (*also* **Bee Em, beemer, bimaz, bimmer**) [more elliptical refs. are found on a variety of rap songs to specific BMW models, e.g. 325i, 735i, 740i, 750iL, 850i] [1980s+] (*orig. US*) a *BMW* motorcar.

beamer *n.*[1] [SE *beam*, to smile broadly] **1** [late 19C+] a smile. **2** [1950s+] a blush.

beamer *n.*[2] [? the triple-beam scales used in weighing drugs and/or spurious *StarTrek* line, BEAM ME UP, SCOTTY! *excl.* (2), i.e. get me HIGH *adj.*[1] (2)] [1980s+] (*drugs*) a user of crack cocaine.

beaming *n.* [BEAMER *n.*[2]] [1980s+] (*US black*) using drugs, esp. crack cocaine.

beamish *adj.* *see* BEAMY *adj.*[2] (2).

beam me up, Scotty *n.* [BEAM ME UP, SCOTTY! *excl.* (2)] [1980s+] (*drugs*) a mixture of phencyclidine and cocaine, thus phrs. *talk to Scotty, high off Scotty, see Scotty*, to be under the influence of the drug.

beam me up, Scotty! *excl.* [the TV series *Star Trek* (from 1966), in which Captain's Kirk's injunction to the chief engineer, *Scotty*, became a trademark catchphrase] **1** [1970s] (*US campus*) an expression of the desire to be elsewhere. **2** [1990s+] (*drugs*) give me some drugs! usu. crack cocaine [i.e. get me HIGH *adj.*[1] (2)].

beam-up *n.* [BEAM UP *v.*] [1980s] (*US black/drugs*) the effects of smoking crack.

beam up *v.* [BEAM ME UP, SCOTTY! *excl.* (2)] [1970s+] (*US black/teen*) to become intoxicated through drug-taking.

beamy *adj.*[1] [naut. jargon *beam*, the width of a ship] [20C+] (*US*) of a person, broad, wide, overweight (cf. *BROAD IN THE BEAM under* BROAD *adj.*).

beamy *adj.*[2] [*OFF (THE) BEAM under* BEAM *n.*[3]] **1** [1950s] (*US black*) wonderful, a play on CRAZY *adj.* (2) [on bad = good model]. **2** [1960s] (*US*) (*also* **beamish**) eccentric, crazy.

bean *n.*[1] **1** as units of money. (**a**) [mid-17C; late 19C+] money, irrespective of the coin (cf. BEANS *n.*[1]). (**b**) [19C] a sovereign, a guinea. (**c**) [20C+] (*also* **green bean**) a dollar. (**d**) [1900s] (*US*) a dollar bill – any denomination. (**e**) [1960s] a small or derisory amount of money. (**f**) [1960s] (*US*) $100. (**g**) [1960s+] a poker chip. **2** the genitals. (**a**) [late 19C+] the penis. (**b**) [1940s–50s] (*US*) the hymen; thus *cop a bean*, to deflower, to have sexual intercourse. (**c**) [1990s+] the clitoris. **3** [20C+] (*also* **beano**) the head. **4** (*US black/drugs*) a drug or tablet. (**a**) [1920s] a package of a drug. (**b**) [1960s+] usu. in pl.; any form of tablet, esp. Benzedrine; thus *beaned up*, under the influence of Benzedrine [resemblance]. **5** [1940s+] (*US*) a Mexican, any Spanish-American [stereotyping of the Mexican diet]. **6** [1940s–70s] (*US black*) (*also* **big bean**) the sun [note comment at BEAM *n.*[2]]. **7** [1950s] (*US*) a minuscule or insignificant amount.

DERIVATIVES

❑ **beanmobile** *n.* [-MOBILE *sfx*] [1980s+] (*US*) a 'lowrider' automobile, as customized and driven by Mexican/Puerto Rican teenagers and gang members.

IN COMPOUNDS

❑ **bean bandit** *n.* [1960s] (*US*) a Mexican. ❑ **beanbag** *n.* [1970s] (*US*) a Mexican. ❑ **bean choker** *n.* [1980s+] (*US*) a Spanish-American. ❑ **bean dip** *n.* [1990s+] (*US*) a derog. term for a Mexican. ❑ **bean-eater** *n.* [the supposed preference of Bostonians and Mexicans for beans] (*US*) **1** [late 19C+] an inhabitant of Boston, Massachusetts; thus *bean-eating*, Bostonian in manner. **2** [1910s+] (*also* **bean and chili eater**) a derog. term for a Mexican. ❑ **bean flicker** *n.* [1990s+] a lesbian. ❑ **bean man** *n.* [1960s] (*drugs*) a seller of any type of drugs in pill form. ❑ **bean oil** *n.* [SE (*hair*) *oil*] [1970s+] (*US gay*) hair oil, esp. when used to lubricate the penis before sex. ❑ **bean queen** *n.* [QUEEN *n.* (2a)/-QUEEN *sfx* (3)] [1970s+] (*US gay*) **1** a non-Hispanic person who prefers Hispanic partners for sex. **2** a Hispanic DRAG QUEEN *n.* (1). ❑ **beanraker** *n.* [RAKE (IT) IN *v.*] [1900s] (*Aus.*) one who is good at amassing money. ❑ **bean-shooter** *n.* *see* separate entries. ❑ **beantown** *n.* **1** [20C+] (*US*) that part of a town in which the poor or the immigrants live; such immigrants are stereotypically, but not invariably, Hispanics. **2** *see also* BEAN TOWN below. ❑ **bean-tosser** *n.* *see* separate entry.

IN PHRASES

❑ **flick the bean** *v.* [1990s+] of a woman, to masturbate. ❑ **flip one's bean** *v.* (*also* **flip one's beanie**) [SE *flip*/FLIP *v.*[3] (2)] [1960s] (*US*) to go crazy, to lose emotional control. ❑ **for beans** *adv.* [1950s+] (*orig. US*) in no way whatsoever. ❑ **half-a-bean** *n.* (*also* **half-bean**) [late 18C–1930s] a half-sovereign, a half-dollar. ❑ **loose in the bean** *adj.* (*also* **loose in the attic, ...canoodle, ...head, ...tiles**) [SE *loose* + ATTIC *n.* (1)SE *head*/? NOODLE *n.*[1] (1)/SE *tiles*] [1920s–70s] (*US*) eccentric, crazy. ❑ **lose one's bean** *v.* [1910s+] to lose one's temper. ❑ **not a bean** *n.* [20C+] nothing at all, esp. of money. ❑ **off one's bean** *adj.* [20C+] **1** insane, eccentric. **2** drunk. ❑ **use one's bean** *v.* [1930s+] to think, to act intelligently, to work things out.

SE in slang uses

IN COMPOUNDS

❑ **beanbelly** *n.* *see* separate entries. ❑ **beanbrain** *n.* [the implication is of minimal size] [1950s+] (*US*) a fool; thus *beanbrained*, foolish. ❑ **bean-count** *v.* [? erect nipples] [1990s+] (*US campus*) to stare at breasts. ❑ **bean counter** *n.* [1970s+] (*orig. US*) anyone who deals with financial matters, esp. an accountant or statistician. ❑ **bean-date** *n.* *see* JELLY-DATE *n.* ❑ **beanfeast** *n.* (*also* **bean feed**) [SE *beanfeast*, an annual dinner given by employers to their workers; in its original form beans were a featured dish] [mid-19C+] any form of festivity or celebration; thus *bean-feaster*; as v., to make merry. ❑ **bean-head** *n.* [-HEAD *sfx* (1)/SE *head*] **1** [1910s+] (*US*) a fool; as adj., stupid. **2** [1950s] someone with a crew-cut hairstyle. ❑ **bean house** *n.* [1970s+] (*US*) a cheap restaurant; as in phr. *bean house bull*, extravagant stories, 'tall tales'. ❑ **bean juice** *n.* [the stereotypical result of eating beans] [1970s+] (*US gay*) oily sweat exuded from the anus or liquid found around the anus of one who constantly breaks wind. ❑ **bean money** *n.* [just enough to buy a meal of beans] [1960s] (*US*) subsistence. ❑ **beanstalk** *n.* *see* separate entry. ❑ **bean time** *n.* *see* BEANS *n.*[3]. ❑ **beanpole** *n.* *see* separate entry. ❑ **Bean Town** *n.* [the supposed local staple] **1** [late 19C+] (*US*) Boston, Massachusetts. **2** *see also* BEANTOWN above. ❑ **bean wagon** *n.* [1940s–50s] (*US*) a cheap restaurant, esp. one that has been converted from a disused railway car.

IN PHRASES

❑ **not worth a bean** *adj.* [15C+] worthless, useless.

bean *n.*[2] [abbr. *beanstalk* or *beanpole* or f. BEAN-TOSSER *n.*] **1** [mid-19C+] a general term of affectionate address. **2** [1910s] (*US*) a foolish or unpleasant person. **3** [1970s] any person.

IN COMPOUNDS

❑ **bean-trap** *n.* [late 19C] (*US Und.*) a high-class confidence man.

IN PHRASES

❑ **old bean** *n.* (*also* **old haricot**) [joc. use of SE *bean*, but ? SE *being*] **1** [1910s+] a fellow, a term of address, usu. to a man. **2** [1940s] an old person, seen affectionately or kindly.

bean *n.*[3] [? corruption of 'bee in one's bonnet'] [late 19C] (*US*) a foolish, silly notion.

bean *v.* [BEAN *n.*[1] (3)] [1910s+] (*orig. US*) to hit on the head.

beanbelly *n.*[1] [that county's production of beans] [mid-17C–19C] a native of Leicestershire.

beanbelly *n.*[2] (*also* **beanie**) [the general 'inflationary' effect of eating lentils etc] [20C+] (*US*) a pot belly.

beaner *n.*[1] [*GIVE SOMEONE BEANS under* BEANS *n.*[2]] [late 19C–1900s] a scolding, a telling-off.

beaner *n.*[2] [? Fr. *bien*] [1910s–70s] (*US*) something excellent.

beaner *n.*[3] [stereotyping; beans are seen as a staple of the Hispanic immigrant diet] [1960s+] (*US*) **1** a Mexican; thus *beaner shoes*, huaraches (leather-thonged sandals, orig. worn by Mexican Indians), *beaner wagon*, an old, dilapidated car typically driven by Mexican immigrants. **2** a Cuban or other Latin-American.

beaner *adj.* [BEANER *n.*[3] (1)] [1990s+] (*US*) Mexican, pertaining to Mexican culture.

beanery *n.* [SE *beans*, seen as part of the staple menu] **1** [late 19C+] (*US*) a cheap restaurant, orig. one that specialized in beans; thus *beanery queen*, a waitress; *beanery-man*, an owner or manager. **2** [1900s–20s] a boarding house. **3** [1940s–60s] (*US prison*) a prison; a prison dining room.

beanery *adj.* [? the size of SE *beans* or the cheapness of a BEANERY *n.* (1)] [1950s] small, insignificant.

beanie *n.*[1] (*also* **beany**) [BEAN *n.*[1] (3) + dimin. sfx *-ie*] **1** [1900s; 1940s+] (*orig. US*) a small, tight-fitting cap, similar to a large skull-cap; thus *propeller-beanie*, such a cap with a small propeller affixed to its top. **2** [1950s] a blackjack, a cosh. **3** [1970s] (*US*) a slingshot. **4** [1970s+] (*also* **Jew beanie**) a yarmulkah, the skullcap worn by religious Jews.

IN PHRASES

❑ **flip one's beanie** *v. see* FLIP ONE'S BEAN *under* BEAN *n.*[1].

beanie *n.*[2] (*also* **beany**) [? she is 'keen as a bean'] [1990s+] (*UK teen*) an attractive young woman.

beanie *n.*[3] *see* BEANBELLY *n.*[2].

bean-jacks *n.* [Irish *bean*, a woman + JAKES *n.*] [1930s+] (*Irish*) a female public convenience.

beano *n.*[1] (*also* **beeno**) [*BEANFEAST under* BEAN *n.*[1]; the abbr. orig. used by printers, who usu. called it a *goose* or *wayzgoose*] **1** [late 19C–1910s] a commotion, a fight. **2** [late 19C+] a party, a celebration.

beano *n.*[2] [BEAN *n.*[1] (5) + -O *sfx* (1)] [1970s+] a derog. term for a Mexican.

beano *n.*[3] *see* BEAN *n.*[1] (3).

beanpea *n.* [a case involving two such youths, known only, so taboo was the thought of homosexuality, by their initials *B and P*, i.e. Boulton and Park] [late 19C–1900s] an effeminate young man.

beanpole *n.* (*also* **telephone pole**) **1** [mid-19C+] a tall, thin person. **2** [1980s] as term of address.

beans *n.*[1] [Fr. *biens*, property; but note BEAN *n.*[1] (1)] [mid-19C+] money.

beans *n.*[2] [SE *bangs*, hits; f. backform. GIVE SOMEONE BEANS below] [late 19C] a disappointment, a punishment.

IN PHRASES

❑ **get beans** *v.* [late 19C–1910s] (*orig. US*) to be punished, to suffer. ❑ **give someone beans** *v.* **1** [mid-19C+] (*orig. US*) to scold; to deal severely with, to punish heavily. **2** [late 19C] to bore. **3** [late 19C+] of a man, to have sexual intercourse. ❑ **sure as beans is beans** *see under* SURE AS... *phr.*

beans *n.*[3] (*also* **bean time**) [1940s+] (*US*) **1** food. **2** a mealtime.

SE in slang uses

IN PHRASES

❑ **full of beans** *adj.* [horseracing jargon, referring to a sprightly horse] **1** [mid-19C+] arrogant, esp. through the sudden or recent acquiring of wealth. **2** [mid-19C+] (*also* **full of oats**) enthusiastic, excited, cheerful. **3** [1930s+] (*US*) nonsensical, rubbishy. ❑ **know beans** *v.* (*also* **know beans when the bag is open, ...untied**) [abbr. KNOW HOW MANY BEANS MAKE FIVE below] [mid-19C–1910s] (*US*) to be well aware, to be knowledgeable; often in negative. ❑ **know how many beans make five** *v.* [late 18C+] to be alert, to be aware of facts or information. ❑ **like beans** *adv.* (*also* **as fast as beans, like beans in Boston**) [mid–late 19C] energetically, very fast. ❑ **like beans and bricks** *adv.* [mid-19C] merrily, gaily, enthusiastically. ❑ **not know beans** *v.* [1960s] to be ignorant. ❑ **put beans up one's nose** *v.* [20C+] (*US*) to do something stupid despite having been warned not to. ❑ **some beans** *adj.* [mid-19C] (*US*) impressive, of some account.

beans! *excl.* **1** [1910s–20s] (*US*) a mild excl. of surprise, disbelief etc. **2** [1950s+] (*US, usu. juv.*) a claim, esp. a claim of first rights to something.

bean-shooter *n.*[1] (*US*) **1** [1910s] a catapult or slingshot. **2** [1930s+] a gun.

bean-shooter *n.*[2] [1920s] (*US*) a native of Boston, Massachusetts.

beanstalk *n.*[1] [1950s–70s] (*US*) a tall person.

beanstalk *n.*[2] [rhy. sl.; ult. the fairy tale *Jack and the beanstalk*] [1980s+] (*Aus. prison*) talk, chatter.

bean-tosser *n.* [? shape] [19C] the penis.

beany *n.*[1] [BEAN-SHOOTER *n.*[1]] [1940s–60s] (*US*) a catapult.

beany *n.*[2] **1** *see* BEANIE *n.*[1]. **2** *see* BEANIE *n.*[2].

beany *adj.* [*OFF ONE'S BEAN under* BEAN *n.*[1]] [1910s] (*US*) eccentric.

bear *n.* **1** stereotyped ursine characteristics. (**a**) [late 17C+] a gruff, irritable person, amplified in phr. *a bear with a sore head*. (**b**) [mid-18C+] the pupil of a private tutor, who is 'led' by his master (like a keeper with a tame bear). (**c**) [1910s+] (*US*) someone who overworks their employees or students, a hard taskmaster/mistress, esp. in phr. *a bear for*, an enthusiast, a devotee. (**d**) [1950s+] (*US black*) (*also* **boggie bear, booga bear**) a particularly ugly person, man or woman [BOOGER *n.*[2] (1)]. (**e**) [1980s] a grasping person, a miser. **2** [early 18C+] a Russian; also as *the Bear*, Russia [the Russian 'national animal']. **3** the bear's strength and power. (**a**) [20C+] an expert, an adept. (**b**) [1900s–20s] an exciting or otherwise exceptional example; an excellent, admirable person. (**c**) [1910s–30s] an attractive (young) woman; usu. in phr. *She's a bear*. (**d**) [1960s] (*US campus*) a well-dressed man. (**e**) [1970s] (*US gay*) sex as a compulsion. **4** in fig. uses, from the animal's negative characteristics. (**a**) [20C+] sunstroke. (**b**) [1920s+] (*US black*) a misfortune, an unfortunate situation, a feeling of depression. (**c**) [1940s–60s] (*US black*) constr. with *the*, poverty, misery. (**d**) [1950s] (*US prison*) solitary confinement. (**e**) [1960s–70s] (*US campus*) any difficult course or circumstance relating to college work. (**f**) [1970s] (*US black*) an unpleasant lifestyle. **5** the bear's furriness. (**a**) [1950s] (*US black*) an overcoat. (**b**) [1960s–70s] (*US*) the vulva. (**c**) [1990s+] (*US*) a hairy, beefy homosexual male; thus adj. *bearish*. **6** [1970s+] (*US*) a policeman; thus *bear in the air*, a police helicopter [f. US Forest Service's mascot *Smokey the Bear*].

SE in slang uses

IN COMPOUNDS

❑ **bear cat** *n.* [SE *bearcat*] (*US*) **1** [1900s–40s] something excellent, first-rate. **2** [1920s+] an aggressive or forceful person; one of great energy or ability; something violent. ❑ **bear-dancer** *n.* [the tutor is seen as 'leading' his pupil, like a keeper with a tame bear] [mid-19C] (*UK Und.*) a young nobleman's travelling tutor. ❑ **bear fight** *n.* [mid-19C] (*UK society*) a play fight, a bit of 'rough-and-tumble'. ❑ **bear-garden** *n.* [late 17C–early 18C] the vagina. ❑ **bear-garden discourse** *n.* (*also* **bear-garden jaw**) [SE *bear garden*, orig. a venue for bear-baiting, latterly any scene of rowdy behaviour + SE *discourse*/JAW *n.* (1)] [late 17C–early 19C] coarse language, vulgarity; sometimes abbr. as *bear-garden*. ❑ **bear-leader** *n.* [the nickname for the tutors of the 18C who ferried their aristocratic pupils around the 'Grand Tour' of Europe] [mid-18C–late 19C] a travelling tutor, thus by ext. an expert who teaches by example. ❑ **bear meat** *n.* [the size of a bear] [1970s] (*US*) an easy target. ❑ **bear party** *n.* [mid-19C] an all-male party, esp. on the night preceding the wedding of one of the men. ❑ **bear's ass** *n.* [ASS *n.* (2)] **1** [1960s] (*US campus*) a fool, an ignoramus. **2** [1990s+] (*US*) a harsh taskmaster. ❑ **bear's breath** *n.* [1940s] a joc./offensive term of address. ❑ **bear sign** *n.* [cowboy/trapper jargon *bear sign*, bear droppings; a doughnut has a similar shape] [1900s] (*US*) a doughnut. ❑ **bearskin** *n.* **1** [late 16C; mid-18C] the pubic hair, orig. hair [resemblance]. **2** [early 18C] (*UK Und*) money [fur as a trading commodity]. ❑ **bear story** *n.* [the wildly overblown stories told by bear-trappers and other woodsmen to credulous listeners] [mid-19C–1950s] (*US*) a 'tall story', an exaggerated story. ❑ **bear trap** *n.* [19C+] (*US*) a difficult situation. ❑ **bear-trapper's hat** *n.* [1990s+] a large, hairy vagina, esp. one that is dark in colour.

IN PHRASES

❑ **bring on your bears** [late 19C] (*US*) a challenge, 'do your worst'. ❑ **can't go no further, like the bear's brother** [1940s] (*US black*) miserable, out of sorts, dejected. ❑ **does a bear shit in the woods? Is the pope a Catholic?** *see* DOES A BEAR SHIT IN THE WOODS? IS THE POPE A CATHOLIC? *phr.* ❑ **do the bear** *v.* [Sp. *hacer el oso*, do the bear; such 'hands-on' courtship was sanctioned in Mexico] [late 19C] (*Mexican-US*) a form of courtship that involves hugging. ❑ **feed the bears** *v.* [1970s+] (*orig. Citizen's Band radio*) to pay a parking fine, to get a parking ticket. ❑ **just like the bear('s daughter), ain't got a quarter** (*also* **just like the bear's brother, Jim, his pickings are slim**) [1920s–40s] (*US black*) miserable, out of sorts, dejected. ❑ **nothing to the bear but his curly hair** [1930s–40s] (*US black*) a phr. implying that a noisy, bragging aggressive person is in fact all show and cowardice. ❑ **show someone where the bear shit in the buckwheat** *v.* (*also* **show someone where the bear came out of the mountains, ...the buckwheat**) [SHIT *v.* (1a)] [19C+] (*US*) to let someone know what's what, to tell someone off; thus *know where the bear...*, to understand a situation. ❑ **stand the bears** *v.* [early 18C] to suffer.

bear a bob *v.* [SE *bear a bob*, join in a chorus] [18C–early 19C] to lend a hand.

bear a hand *v.* [late 18C–1930s] to hurry up, to make haste.

beard *n.* **1** [16C+] female pubic hair; thus BEARDED *adj.* **2** [1920s+] a bearded man; thus, by stereotyping, a beatnik, an intellectual. **3** in the context of disguise [gambling jargon *beard*, a go-between who places bets for another person; thus protecting their identity]. (**a**) [1950s] in betting, one who bets on behalf of a racehorse trainer – who is not supposed to do so on his own runner. (**b**) [1950s+] a friend who acts as a 'cover', usu. for extramarital affairs; thus as v. (**c**) [1960s+] (*US gay/lesbian*) a woman who poses as the wife or lover of a gay man who wishes to hide his real sexual preference. (**d**) [1960s+] (*US gay/lesbian*) a male used as an ostensible lover or even husband, as a disguise for one's real sexual preference; thus as v. (**e**) [1990s+] a disguise; something or someone who encourages misdirection. **4** [1970s] (*US*) a Hasidic Jew.

IN COMPOUNDS

❑ **beard-jammer** *n.* [1920s–60s] (*US*) a pimp. ❑ **beard ride** *n.* [RIDE *n.* (1a)] [1980s] (*US*) cunnilingus. ❑ **beard-splitter** *n.* **1** [late 17C–mid-19C] a seducer, a sexual athlete. **2** [19C] the penis.

IN PHRASES

❑ **go beard-splitting** *v.* [18C] of a man, to have sexual intercourse. ❑ **split the beard** *v.* (*also* **part the whiskers**) [1970s+] of a man, to have sexual intercourse. ❑ **wear the beard** *v.* (*also* **don the beard**) [1990s+] usu. of a man, to perform cunnilingus.

SE in slang uses

IN COMPOUNDS

❑ **beardless wonder** *n.* [1950s] (*US*) an incompetent or foolish person. ❑ **beard-man** *n.* [his appearance] [1960s] (*W.I.*) a Rastafarian.

IN PHRASES

❑ **have a crumb in one's beard** *v.* [18C] to be drunk.

beard! *excl.* [1990s+] (*UK juv.*) an excl. of disbelief, scepticism.

bearded *adj.* [BEARD *n.* (1)]

IN COMPOUNDS

referring to pubic hair

❑ **bearded lady** *n.* (*also* **bearded taco**) [joc. use of SE] [1960s+] the vagina. ❑ **bearded oyster** *n.* [OYSTER *n.* (1a)] [1910s+] the vagina.

bearded clam *n.* [BEARD *n.* (1) + SE *clam*/CLAM *n.*[1] (2)] [1960s+] the vagina; one of several terms linking the organ to fish.

IN PHRASES

❑ **spear the bearded clam** *v.* (*also* **split the bearded clam**) [1960s+] (*Aus.*) to have sexual intercourse with a woman.

beardie *n.* **1** [1900s–10s] (*Aus.*) a member of a body of Southcottians (believers in the teaching of Joanna Southcott (1750–1814), who announced herself as the woman spoken of in Rev. 12), followers of the local prophet John Wroe (1782–1863), who called themselves Christian Israelites [the males' wearing of beards]. **2** [1940s+] (*orig. Aus.*) (*also* **beardo**) a bearded person.

beardo *n.* *see* BEARDIE *n.* (2).

bearer-up *n.* [BEAR UP *v.*; K. Chesney, in *Victorian Underworld* (1970) suggests a 'bully who robs men decoyed by a woman accomplice' but no Dict. supports this definition] **1** [mid–late 19C] a decoy who induces victims to play with card cheats. **2** [late 19C] (*UK Und.*) a pimp who robs his prostitute's client.

be-argured *adj.* (*also* **beargered**) [SE *argumentative*] [mid-19C–1900s] drunk.

bearings *n.* [SE *bearing*, that part of a machine that supports a shaft or axle] [1940s] (*Aus.*) the stomach.

bear's paw *n.* [rhy. sl.] [20C+] a saw.

bear-up *n.* [SE *bear-up*, a hold-up] [late 19C–1900s] (*Aus.*) the pursuit of a woman.

bear up *v.* [SE *bear up*, to support] [early 19C] to help in the commission of a swindle or fraud.

beast *n.* **1** [late 16C+] an unpopular or unpleasant person. **2** [late 19C–1900s] a bicycle [synon. with SE *beast*, a horse]. **3** [1950s] (*US*) a (fast) car. **4** [1950s+] a young woman, usu. unattractive. (**a**) (*US, mainly campus*) a young woman, esp. an unattractive but sexually voracious one. (**b**) (*US, mainly campus*) any unattractive young woman. (**c**) (*US/W.I.*) a girlfriend viewed in a sexual context, esp. when she has another established relationship already. **5** (*drugs*) as a drug [? their unpredictable effects]. (**a**) [1950s+] heroin; thus heroin addiction. (**b**) [1960s+] LSD. **6** also constr. with *the*; an authority figure; coined by black nationalists in the 1960s; it lapsed thereafter but reappeared among rebellious youths in the 1990s. (**a**) [1960s+] (*orig. US black*) a white person. (**b**) [1980s+] the police; a police officer. (**c**) [1980s+] (*Aus. prison*) a prison officer. **7** [1980s+] (*UK prison*) a child molester, a sexual offender [SE *beast*, a brutal, very unpleasant person]. **8** [1980s+] cheap beer.

DERIVATIVES

❑ **beasty** *adj.* (*also* **beastie**) **1** [1980s+] (*US campus*) disgusting, repellent, unattractive. **2** [1990s+] (*UK juv.*) a general term of approbation, congratulation [on bad = good model].

IN COMPOUNDS

❑ **beast-boy** *n.* (*also* **beast-bwoy**) [1990s+] (*UK black*) a policeman. ❑ **beastman** *n.* [1970s+] (*UK black*) a policeman. ❑ **beastmaster** *n.* [SE *master*, note the similarly titled 'sword and sorcery' film of the period] [1980s+] (*US campus*) a man who consistently dates unattractive women. ❑ **beast wagon** *n.* [1980s] (*UK black*) a police van, a BLACK MARIA *n.* (1).

SE in slang uses

IN COMPOUNDS

❑ **beast-lick** *n.* [SE *lick*, a blow] [1940s+] (*W.I.*) a harsh, heavy blow, such as might be given to an animal.

IN PHRASES

❑ **as a beast** *adv.* *see* AS A BASTARD *under* BASTARD *n.* ❑ **beast of a...** *n.* [late 19C+] applied to anything seen as unpleasant. ❑ **food one's beast** *v.* [2000s] to obtain sexual gratification. ❑ **make the beast with two backs** *v.* (*also* **make the two-backed beast, make the double-backed beast**) [the first cited use of the phr. is by Shakespeare, in *Othello* (1604); it also occurs in Fr., where Rabelais uses *faire la bête à deux dos*] [17C+] to have sexual intercourse. ❑ **mark of the beast** *n.* [the popular (male) image of the satanic vagina] [18C–19C] the vagina. ❑ **sit (on) a beast** *v.* (*also* **sit (on) a dago**) [SE *beast*, a monster, i.e. the height of the car/fig. use of DAGO *n.* (1); i.e. a style preferred by Hispanics] [1970s+] (*US black teen/Los Angeles*) to ride in a car that has been mechanically lifted and appears higher off the ground than normal models.

beast *adj.* [survival of schoolboy intensifier *beastly*, very good, very bad] **1** [1950s+] (*W.I.*) a general intensifier, both positive and negative. **2** [1970s+] white; pertaining to white culture. **3** [1990s+] (*US campus*) excellent.

beast *v.* [BEAST *n.* (7)] **1** [1980s+] to molest a child. **2** [2000s] to subject to physical abuse.

beastly *adj.* **1** [late 16C+] unpleasant, distasteful. **2** [1950s] (*US black*) excellent, wonderful, very enjoyable [on bad = good model].

beastly *adv.* [BEASTLY *adj.* (1)] [19C–1920s] (*UK society*) exceedingly, excessively, very.

beastness *n.* [SE *beastliness*] [20C+] (*W.I.*) male promiscuity.

beat *n.*[1] [SE *beat the bounds*; note a police *beat* is SE] **1** [late 18C+] (*orig. UK Und.*) a street or streets as walked by a prostitute. **2** [early 19C+] (*orig. UK Und.*) one's own area of activity, operation. **3** [mid-19C] (*UK Und.*) an area in which a pickpocket works. **4** [mid-19C] (*UK Und.*) the area patrolled by a watchman. **5** [1900s–60s] (*US prison*) that area in which a criminal gang operates, thanks to bribing a local politician/police department. **6** [1930s] an area where drugs are sold on the street. **7** [1940s+] (*Aus.*) the area patrolled by a sheep or cattle musterer.

IN PHRASES

❑ **bash the beat** *v.* (*also* **do the beat**) [1970s+] (*Aus. gay*) to frequent an area in search of a sexual partner. ❑ **off one's beat** (*also* **off the beat**) [1900s–10s] (*mainly Aus.*) drifting away from the subject in hand, out of one's usual routine.

SE in slang uses

IN COMPOUNDS

❑ **beat basher** *n.* [1950s] (*UK juv.*) a police officer. ❑ **beat pounder** *v.* [1940s+] a policeman.

beat *n.*[2] [SE *beat*, to overcome; note WW1 milit. *my beat*, my girlfriend] **1** [mid-19C–1900s] (*US*) an outstanding person, one who defeats all rivals. **2** [mid-19C–1910s] an outstanding object, an incomparable circumstance.

IN PHRASES

❑ **get a beat on** *v.* [mid-19C+] (*US*) to have at a disadvantage.

beat *n.*[3] [i.e. they 'beat' the rules of society] **1** [mid-19C–1910s] a swindler, a confidence trickster. **2** [mid-19C–1930s] (*US*) an unreliable person, esp. one who fails to pay their debts. **3** [mid-19C–1960s] a loafer, a layabout, a sponger. **4** [1930s] (*US Und.*) a swindle. **5** [1950s+] (*also* **beatster**) a beatnik.

IN PHRASES

❑ **on the beat** [late 19C–1960s] (*US*) engaged in a swindle.

beat *n.*[4] [BEAT IT *v.* (1)] [mid-19C–1950s] (*US*) an escape, usu. from prison.

beat *n.*[5] [image of 'beating' rival journalists to a story] [20C+] (*US*) information.

beat *n.*[6] [SE *beat*, to hit] **1** [1970s] a prostitute's client who likes to be beaten, often bringing his own equipment with him. **2** [1970s+] (*US gay*) a homophobic thug.

IN PHRASES

❑ **put the beat down** *v.* [1990s+] to hit, to assault.

beat *adj.* (*also* **beat out, bet**) [SE *beaten*] **1** [late 18C+] of a person, exhausted, tired out, emotionally and physically. **2** [mid-19C–1930s] (*US*) amazed, astonished, at a loss. **3** [1930s+] depressed, emotionally raw; post 1950s esp. in comb. *beat generation*. **4** [1930s+] of a thing, worn out, no longer fashionable. **5** [1930s+] (*orig. US black*) of people, out of funds. **6** [1940s–50s] (*US drugs*) adulterated. **7** [1940s+] (*US*) useless, worthless, boring. **8** [1940s+] (*orig. US*) disillusioned, sad, world-weary. **9** [1950s] (*US drugs*) of an addict, craving for a dose of a drug. **10** [1950s–70s] of objects, shabby, battered, worn-out. **11** [1980s] (*US campus*) bad, depressing. **12** [1980s+] (*US campus*) very ugly. **13** [1980s+] (*US campus*) stupid, weak, ineffectual.

IN PHRASES

❑ **beat for** *v.* **1** [1940s–60s] to be short of, usu. money. **2** [1960s] to be deprived of. ❑ **beat for the yolk** *adj.* [1940s] (*US black/Harlem*) short of cash, temporarily impoverished. ❑ **beat to the ass** *adj.* [ASS *n.* (2)] [1980s] (*US*) extremely exhausted. ❑ **beat to the socks** *adj.* (*also* **beat to the heels**) [1930s–50s] (*US black*) tired out, utterly exhausted.

beat *v.* (*US*) **1** [mid-19C+] to steal from, to defraud, to rob. **2** [mid-19C+] to defeat intellectually, to baffle, to confuse. **3** [late 19C–1930s] to leave quickly. **4** [late 19C+] of a criminal, to get away with a crime; of a lawyer, to defend a client successfully. **5** [20C+] to escape from prison. **6** [1910s+] to escape punishment or duty. **7** [1940s+] (*US black*) (*also* **beat up on**) of a man, to have heterosexual intercourse. **8** *see* BEAT OFF *v.* (1).

IN COMPOUNDS

❑ **beat artist** *n.* [-ARTIST *sfx*] [1980s+] (*US black*) one who sells poor quality or fake drugs.

IN PHRASES

❑ **beat a freight** *v.* [1900s–30s] (*Can.*) to steal a ride on a freight train. ❑ **beat a rap** *v. see under* RAP *n.*[1]. ❑ **beat ass** *v. see* separate entry. ❑ **beat a trick** *v. see under* TRICK *n.*[1]. ❑ **beat cheeks** *v. see under* CHEEKS *n.*[1]. ❑ **beat it** *v. see* separate entry. ❑ **beat off** *v.* [1920s] (*US Und.*) to rob, to break into. ❑ **beat (someone) for** *v.* [1950s+] to take a person's money, whether it is offered or not; to trick someone out of; to rob. ❑ **beat (someone) out of** *v.* [mid-19C+] (*US*) **1** to cheat, to defraud, to steal from. **2** to overcome, to beat a rival. ❑ **beat someone's time** *v.* **1** [mid–late 19C] (*US*) to confuse, to confound. **2** [1930s–50s] (*US black/campus*) to cheat or be cheated in a love affair. ❑ **beat the rap** *v. see under* RAP *n.*[1]. ❑ **beat the road** *v.* [SE (*rail*)*road*] [late 19C] (*US*) to travel by train without paying. ❑ **can you beat it?** (*also* **can you beat that?**) [mid-19C+] (*orig. US*) a phr. used to express surprise or amazement. ❑ **have someone/something beat** *v.* [20C+] (*US*) to defeat intellectually, to get the better of, to baffle, to confuse.

IN EXCLAMATIONS

❑ **beats me!** (*also* **beats all! beats my ass! it beats me!**) [mid-19C+] a general excl. of incomprehension, 'I just can't understand it!'.

SE, meaning to defeat, to surpass, in slang uses

IN COMPOUNDS

❑ **beat-ass** *adj. see* separate entry.

IN PHRASES

❑ **beat akeybo** *v.* [ety. unknown; note Norfolk dial. *acabo*, *akeybo*, used in phr. *that would puzzle acabo*] [mid-19C] to be confusing; thus *he beats akeybo*, he acts in an extreme manner; *akeybo beats the devil*, something is extremely confusing. ❑ **beat all** *v.* (*also* **beat all hell, beat all hollow, beat all holler, beat all nature**) [late 18C+] to surpass in every way, often in phr. *don't that beat all*. ❑ **beat all cockfight** *v.* [20C+] (*W.I.*) to be unbelievable, unheard of, utterly ridiculous. ❑ **beat Bannagher** *v. see under* BANNAGHER *n.* ❑ **beat bobtail** *v.* [? euph. for *beat the devil*, but also ? link to the 'bob-tailed nag' of Stephen Foster's song 'Camptown Races' (1850)] [late 19C–1950s] (*US*) to surpass in every way. ❑ **beat into fits** *v.* (*also* **beat out of fits**) [mid-19C+] to defeat or surpass completely. ❑ **beat someone to the punch** *v.* [boxing imagery] [1960s+] (*orig. US black*) **1** to arrive at a destination sooner than another person. **2** to appreciate or understand something faster than another person. ❑ **beat the bags off** *v. see under* BAGS *n.*[2]. ❑ **beat the band** *v. see under* BAND *n.*[2]. ❑ **beat the bugs** *v.* [mid-19C–1910s] to surpass any contender. ❑ **beat the cars** *v.* [SE *street cars*] [19C] (*US*) to surpass in every way. ❑ **beat the Dutch** *v. see* separate entry. ❑ **beat the gun** *v.* [sporting imagery] [1940s+] (*Aus.*) for an engaged woman to have sex with her fiancé and to get pregnant thereby. ❑ **beat the Jews** *v.* [the stereotype of Jewish ambition/deviousness] [mid-19C–1960s] to surpass any contender. ❑ **beat the little wheel** *v.* (*also* **beat the little dish, beat the wee wheel**) [1920s–40s] (*Irish*) to surpass everything. ❑ **beat the priest** *v.* [negative image of clerical hypocrisy] [20C+] (*W.I., Gren.*) to commit a major crime and act brazenly in acknowledging it without any form of shame or sorrow. ❑ **beat the starter** *v.* (*also* **cheat the starter**) [sporting imagery] [1910s+] to have a child out of wedlock; to become pregnant before the wedding. ❑ **beat to snuff** *v.* [SE *snuff*, powdered tobacco; thus lit. 'to reduce to powder'] [early 19C–1920s] to defeat comprehensively. ❑ **beat to the gun** *v.* (*also* **beat to the wheel**) [the *starting gun* at races]

[1920s–30s] (*US*) to start first. ❑ **couldn't beat a carpet** [late 19C+] a phr. used to indicate weakness. ❑ **that beats cockfighting** (*also* **this beats cockfighting, ...thunder, that beats a hen a-scratchin', ...a-lopin'**) [early 19C–1920s] that is really amazing, that's beyond the bounds of possibility. ❑ **that beats the devil** (*also* **that beats my time**) [late 19C] (*US*) that is really amazing, that's beyond the bounds of possibility. ❑ **to beat four of a kind** *adv.* [poker imagery] [late 19C] (*US campus*) to a very great extent.

SE, meaning to hit, in slang uses

IN COMPOUNDS

❑ **beat-down** *n.* *see* separate entry. ❑ **beat-off** *n.* *see* separate entry. ❑ **beat-up** *see* separate entries.

IN PHRASES

❑ **beat about the bush** *v.* (*also* **beat around the bush, beat the bush, go about the bush**) [hunting imagery] [late 16C+] to avoid a topic, to fail deliberately to come to the point; thus n., *bush-beating*. ❑ **beat a dje** *v.* [Fr. *guerre*, war] [20C+] (*W.I., Gren.*) to be in the mood for a physical fight or verbal confrontation, esp. one that will last for several days. ❑ **beat down** *v.* *see* separate entry. ❑ **beat-'em-up** *n.* *see* separate entry. ❑ **beat foot it** *v.* [1970s+] (*US*) to walk or go quickly. ❑ **beat it on the hoof** *v.* [SE *beat* it, i.e. the ground + HOOF *n.* (1)] [late 17C–mid-18C] to walk on foot. ❑ **beat liquor** *v.* [20C+] (*W.I.*) to drink heavily. ❑ **beat off** *v.* *see* separate entry. ❑ **beat one's bird** *v.* *see under* BIRD *n.*[3]. ❑ **beat one's dummy** *v.* *see under* DUMMY *n.*[3]. ❑ **beat one's gums** *v.* *see* separate entries. ❑ **beat one's hog** *v.* *see under* HOG *n.* ❑ **beat one's little brother** *v.* *see under* LITTLE BROTHER *n.* ❑ **beat one's meat** *v.* *see under* MEAT *n.* ❑ **beat (one's) skin** *v.* [1940s] (*US black/Harlem*) to applaud, to clap. ❑ **beat one's way** *v.* [SE *beat one's way*, to cut a path] [late 19C–1960s] (*US*) to make one's way by employing illegal means, e.g. cheating, swindling, sponging. ❑ **beat someone's ears down** *v.* *see* KNOCK THE EARS OFF *under* EARS *n.* ❑ **beat tar** *v.* (*also* **slap tar**) [SE *tar*, by metonymy the pavement] [20C+] (*W.I., Bdos*) to walk around. ❑ **beat the beaver** *v.* *see under* BEAVER *n.*[1]. ❑ **beat the bishop** *v.* *see* BANG THE BISHOP *under* BISHOP *n.*[2]. ❑ **beat the boards** *v.* [1940s] (*US black*) to (tap)dance. ❑ **beat the booby** *v.* *see under* BOOBY *n.*[1]. ❑ **beat the books** *v.* [1940s+] (*US/W.I.*) to work very hard. ❑ **beat the breeze** *v.* [SE *breeze*/BREEZE *n.*[1] (1d)] [1940s+] (*US*) to chatter, to gossip. ❑ **beat the bull** *v.* *see under* BULL *n.*[6]. ❑ **beat the crap out of** *v.* *see* KNOCK THE CRAP OUT OF *under* CRAP *n.*[1]. ❑ **beat the dog** *v.* *see under* DOG *n.*[2]. ❑ **beat (the) feet** *v.* **1** [1940s+] (*US campus*) to leave, to depart. **2** [1970s] (*US campus*) to hurry. ❑ **beat the gong** *v.* *see under* GONG *n.*[2]. ❑ **beat the goose** *v.* [the movement supposedly resembles a goose in flight] [late 19C] to strike one's hands under the armpits to warm them. ❑ **beat the hay** *v.* *see* HIT THE HAY *under* HAY *n.* ❑ **beat the hoof** *v.* *see under* HOOF *n.* ❑ **beat the hound out of** *v.* [SE *hound*, cussedness, stubbornness] [1940s+] (*US*) to thrash severely. ❑ **beat the lard out of** *v.* *see* LARD *n.* (3). ❑ **beat the (living) daylights out of** *v.* *see under* DAYLIGHTS *n.* ❑ **beat the piss out of** *v.* *see under* PISS *n.* ❑ **beat the rocks** *v.* [esp. used in the context of walking the streets in search of employment] [1940s] (*US black*) to walk the streets. ❑ **beat the rug** *v.* *see* CUT THE RUG *v.* ❑ **beat the sheets** *v.* (*also* **press blankets, press the sheets**) [1950s+] to sleep deeply. ❑ **beat the shit out of** *v.* *see* separate entry. ❑ **beat the stick** *v.* *see under* STICK *n.* ❑ **beat the tracks** *v.* [BEAT IT *v.* (1) + SE *tracks*] [20C+] (*Aus.*) to walk a long way, usu. over rough country. ❑ **beat up** *v.* *see* separate entry.

beat-ass *adj.* [2000s] (*US*) **1** excellent, outstanding [SE *beat* + ASS *n.* (4)]. **2** second-rate [BEAT *adj.* (4) + -ASS *sfx*].

beat ass *v.* [BEAT *v.* (3) + ASS *n.* (4)] [1940s+] (*US*) to leave, to depart.

beatbox *n.* [SE *beat*, rhythm + BOX *n.*[1] (4g)] [1980s+] (*orig. US*) **1** an electronic drum machine. **2** a large, portable tape deck. **3** (*US black*) the making of drumming sounds by mouth; also as v.

beat-down *n.* [BEAT DOWN *v.*] [1980s+] (*US black*) a fight, a beating.

beat down *v.* [ext. of SE] [1980s+] (*US black*) to fight, to beat up; to defeat severely.

beat-'em-up *n.* [1990s+] an action film or computer game.

beaten-out *adj.* [BEAT *adj.* (1)] [mid-19C] impoverished.

beater *n.*[1] [SE *beater*, one who drives game towards the guns] [late 16C–early 17C] (*UK Und.*) one who lures a victim into a crooked game of cards or dice.

beater *n.*[2] **1** [mid–late 19C] (*US*) a person or thing that beats or excels others. **2** [1980s+] a beaten up vehicle.

beater *n.*[3] [DEADBEAT *n.* (7) or BEAT *v.* (1)] [1930s+] one who refuses to pay their debts; a swindler.

beater *n.*[4] [? money 'beats' one's problems] [1940s] (*US black/Harlem*) cash; money.

beater-cases *n.* [DEW-BEATERS *under* DEW *n.* + SE *case*] [18C–mid-19C] (*UK Und.*) shoes.

beaters *n.* [DEW-BEATERS *under* DEW *n.*] [mid–late 19C] (*US*) shoes, boots.

beating *n.*

IN PHRASES

❑ **take a beating** *v.* *see under* BEAT OFF *v.*

beat it *v.* [SE *beat a path*] [20C+] (*US*) **1** (*also* **beat it off, beat it out**) to travel or leave in a hurry. **2** (*also* **beat it off!**) as imper. *beat it!*; also ext. as *beat it while the beating's/going's good.*

IN EXCLAMATIONS

❑ **put an egg in your shoe and beat it!** [1950s] (*US*) go away!

beat-off *n.* [backform. f. BEAT OFF *v.* (1)] [1970s] **1** (*US*) an act of masturbation. **2** (*US campus*) an unpleasant person.

beat off *v.* [SE *beat*/BEAT ONE'S MEAT *under* MEAT *n.* + COME OFF *under* COME *v.*[1]] [1960s+] (*US*) **1** (*also* **beat**) to masturbate. **2** to masturbate another person. **3** in fig. use, to waste time, to loaf around.

IN COMPOUNDS

❑ **beatmeat** *n.* [MEAT *n.* (2)] [1980s] (*US gay*) masturbation; the post-ejaculatory penis. ❑ **beat-nuts** *n.* [NUTS *n.*[2] (1)] [1970s] (*US*) an obsessive masturbator.

IN PHRASES

❑ **have a beat** *v.* [1980s] (*Aus.*) **1** to masturbate. **2** in fig. use, to waste time, to mess about. ❑ **take a beating** *v.* [fig. use of SE] [1960s+] to masturbate.

beat one's gums *v.* (*also* **beat one's chops, ...choppers, ...lips, beat up one's chops, ...choppers, ...gums, bat one's gums, chop one's gums, ...teeth, smack one's gums**) [SE *beat* + CHOPS *n.*[1] (1)/CHOPPERS *n.* (1)/SE *gums*/SE *lips*] [1930s+] (*US*) **1** to chatter, to talk, esp. in an irritating manner. **2** to talk in a melodramatic manner. **3** to eat. **4** to complain.

IN EXCLAMATIONS

❑ **beat your gums!** [1950s+] don't talk rubbish!

beat out *adj.* *see* BEAT *adj.*

beat pad *n.* [SE *beat(nik)* + PAD *n.*[2] (2)] [1930s–50s] (*US drugs*) a place where drugs are consumed.

beatster *n.* *see* BEAT *n.*[3] (5).

beat the Dutch *v.* (*also* **bang the Dutch**) [the Dutch as a national enemy and commercial rival] [mid-18C+] to do something outstanding; thus *that beats the Dutch*, describing something that is otherwise barely credible; *to beat the Dutch*, to the utmost, very much.

beat the shit out of *v.* (*also* **beat the dogshit out of, ...the living shit out of, ...the shite out of, bash the shit out of, pound..., thump..., whack..., stomp the living shit out of, whip the dudu out of**) [DOGSHIT *n.* (1)/SHIT *n.* (5)/SHITE *n.* (6)] [1920s+] (*orig. US*) **1** to beat severely. **2** to improve upon, to be superior to, to surpass. **3** to confuse completely; to be ignorant. **4** in fig. use, e.g., to drink heavily.

beattie and babs *n.* [rhy. sl. = SE colloq. *crabs*] [1930s+] body lice.

beat-up *n.* [1990s+] (*Aus.*) an outrage.

beat-up *adj.* **1** [mid-19C+] (*US*) exhausted. **2** [1910s+] (*US*) of a place or object, dilapidated, run down. **3** [1940s–50s] of a person, ageing, run down, ill. **4** [1980s+] (*US campus*) wrong, bad.

beat up *v.* [fig. use of SE *beat up*, to attack] **1** [20C+] (*orig. US*) to nag, harass. **2** [1910s] to promote, to encourage.

beat up on *v. see* BEAT *v.* (7).

beat up one's chops/choppers/gums *v. see* BEAT ONE'S GUMS *v.*

beat up (the quarters of) *v.* [SE *beat up*, to visit, to tour + SE *quarters*, dwelling-place, home; SE use is to arouse, disturb] [late 19C] (*UK society*) to call upon unceremoniously.

beau *n.*[1] [SE *beau*, a suitor, a sweetheart] [1980s+] (*US campus*) **1** a stupid or clumsy person. **2** a boyfriend.

IN COMPOUNDS

❑ **beauhunk** *n.* [HUNK *n.*[1] (6) + pun on derog. BOHUNK *n.*] [1980s] **1** a boyfriend. **2** a sexy-looking boy.

SE in slang uses

IN COMPOUNDS

❑ **beau-catcher** *n.* [SE *catcher*; such a lock was calculated to ensnare young men. The term did not survive the 19C in the UK but lasted until the 1920s or beyond in the US. 'In olden times this was called a *lovelock*, when it was the mark at which all the Puritan and ranting preachers levelled their pulpit pop-guns, loaded with sharp and virulent abuse' (Hotten, 1867)] [mid-19C–1920s] a lock of hair equivalent to the modern *kiss-curl*. ❑ **beau-dollar** *n.* (*also* **bo-dollar**) [from the presumption that the dandy carried a good supply of such coins. Other suggestions include abbr. HOBO *n.* (2) or SE *boat* or *boar* (the hog seen as a desirable commodity), corruption of SE *Boer* (a supposed lucky piece carried by British soldiers during the Boer Wars (1880–1, 1899–1902)] [1940s+] (*US black*) a silver dollar. ❑ **beau-nasty** *n.* [late 18C–early 19C] a well-dressed, but ill-kempt and grubby dandy. ❑ **beau-trap** *n.* **1** [late 17C–mid-19C] a confidence trickster, esp. a card-sharp. **2** [late 18C–early 19C] a badly laid paving stone that traps water beneath it and, when it is stepped on, squirts that water onto the dandy's finery.

IN PHRASES

❑ **crusty beau** *n.* [SE *crusty*, encrusted] [late 17C–early 19C] a dandy who takes especial care of his (? ageing) complexion, often with cosmetics. ❑ **demi-beau** *n.* [SE *demi*, half] [late 17C–early 18C] a would-be dandy. ❑ **dirty beau** *n.* [late 17C–early 18C] a slovenly man, who poses as a dandy despite his outward appearance. ❑ **sub-beau** *n.* [SE *sub*, secondary] [late 17C–mid-18C] an aspirant dandy.

beau *n.*[2] *see* BO *n.*[1] (1).

beaucoup *n.* (*also* **beaucoups, boocoo, bookoo, boo-koos, booku, buckoo, buku**) [Fr. *beaucoup*, many; used WW1 by Aus./UK/US forces; f. 1920s by blacks in some southern states (Louisiana, Florida, Georgia) but popularized in 1960s–70s by returning US soldiers, who picked it up from the Francophone Vietnamese] [1910s+] (*US*) a large quantity of, a lot of.

beaucoup *adj.* (*also* **beaucoups, boo-koos, booku, boucous**) [BEAUCOUP *n.*] [1920s+] (*US*) excellent, first-rate.

beaucoup *adv.* (*also* **bocoo, bokoo, boocoo, boo-koos, buku**) [Fr. *beaucoup*, very much/BEAUCOUP *n.*] [1910s+] (*US*) very (much), extremely, used as a general intensifier.

beaucoups *see under* BEAUCOUP.

beaulah *adj.* [initial letters plus abbr. SE] [2000s] (*S.Afr. gay*) beautiful.

beauns *n.* [SE *beau* + BUNS *n.* (1)] [1970s+] (*US gay*) the buttocks.

beaut *n.*[1] (*also* **bute**) [abbr. SE *beauty*; coined in US, but most common use is Aus.] [mid-19C+] (*orig. US*) **1** a beautiful person or thing. **2** a splendid example of a type (human or not); also used ironically. **3** ironic uses of senses 1 and 2.

beaut *n.*[2] [1990s+] (*UK juv.*) **1** a cigarette. **2** a magic mushroom.

beaut *adj.* (*also* **beauty**) [abbr.] [1940s+] (*Aus.*) *beautiful*.

beaut *adv.* [abbr.] [1960s+] (*N.Z.*) *beautifully*, very well.

beaut! *excl.* [abbr.] [1950s+] (*Aus./N.Z.*) all-purpose Aus. term of approbation, can equally well be used as adj.; also as *beauty!* (pron. bewdy), *you beaut!*

beautiful *adj.* [mid-19C+] (*orig. US*) **1** pleasing, admirable; as *adv.*, perfectly. **2** happy, satisfied. **3** clever, shrewd, also used iron.

beauty *n.*[1] **1** [19C] the vagina. **2** [early 19C+] an admirable person or creature. **3** [early 19C+] thus ironically, any person, admirable, attractive or, ironically, otherwise. **4** [early 19C+] a thing, usu. with positive overtones. **5** [1960s+] (*US gay*) (*also* **beautocks, beauts**) the buttocks [pron. as well as praise].

IN COMPOUNDS

❑ **beauty spot** *n.* [18C–late 19C] the vagina; one of a number of terms linking the female genital area with nature.

IN PHRASES

❑ **put across a beauty** *v.* [1910s+] (*N.Z.*) to do something smart or clever.

SE in slang uses

IN COMPOUNDS

❑ **beauty mark** *n.* (*also* **beauty spot**) [joc. use of SE] [1920s] a scar.

beauty *n.*[2] [abbr. *BLACK BEAUTY under* BLACK *adj.*] [1960s] the drug Biphetamine, a strong amphetamine.

beauty *adj. see* BEAUT *adj.*

beauty! *excl.* [abbr. SE *that's beautiful!*] [1940s+] (*Aus./UK*) excellent! also in adj. use.

beav *n.* [US TV show *Leave It To Beaver*] [1980s+] (*US campus*) a name that indicates that the referent is acting like a little brother.

beave *n.* [abbr. BEAVER *n.*[1] (5)] [1950s] a prostitute.

beaver *n.*[1] [SE *beaver*] **1** [17C+] a hat of any sort [abbr. SE *beaver hat*; note Ned Ward *The London Spy* (1699): 'What are those Eagle-look'd Fellows, in their Narrow Brim'd White Beavers'; but note SE *beaver/bever*, that part of a helmet which when let down covers the face]. **2** [mid-19C; 1940s] (*US*) money; beaver pelts were orig. a form of exchange. **3** [1910s–60s] a bearded man; thus the early 20C+ street game in which children would compete to be the first to spot a bearded man and signify their success by shouting *Beaver!* **4** [1910s+] a beard; thus *beavered*, bearded. **5** [1920s+] (*orig. US*) the female pubic hair, the vagina, esp. in commercial pornography use; thus *beaver book*, a pornographic book; *beaver film*, a pornographic film; *beaver trader*, a pimp [the supposed similarity between the beaver's coat and the pubic hair]. **6** [1960s+] (*orig. US*) a woman.

IN COMPOUNDS

❑ **beaver cleaver** *n.* [1990s+] the penis. ❑ **beaver palace** *n.* [1970s] (*US*) a brothel. ❑ **beaver patrol** *n. see* separate entry. ❑ **beaver shooter** *n.* [SE *shooter/shoot a glance*] [1960s–70s] a peeping tom. ❑ **beaver shot** *n.* [1970s+] (*US*) **1** a close-up photograph of, or camera-angle on, the female genitals; used in commercial pornography; thus *beaver flick*, a porn movie. **2** a chance glimpse (by a man) of the same area. ❑ **beaver sucker** *n.* [SUCKER *n.*[1] (5)] [1970s] (*US*) a term of abuse.

IN PHRASES

❑ **beat the beaver** *v.* [BEAT OFF *v.* (1)] [1970s+] of a woman, to masturbate. ❑ **brush the beaver** *v.* [1990s+] of a woman, to masturbate. ❑ **shoot a beaver** *v.* (*also* **shoot beaver, shoot the beaver**) [1960s+] **1** of a man, to look under a woman's skirt in the hope of seeing pubic hair or her vagina. **2** of a woman, to display one's genitals, usu. while otherwise dressed. ❑ **split beaver** *n.* (*also* **spread beaver**) [1970s+] the wide-open vagina, esp. as found in hardcore pornography; a striptease artist. ❑ **stroke the beaver** *v.* (*also* **stroke the dog**) [late 17C; 1990s+] (*US*) to have sexual intercourse. ❑ **wager one's beaver** *v. see BET ONE'S BUTTONS under* BET *v.* ❑ **wide-open beaver** *n.* [1970s+] a photograph or film of the inner labia.

SE in slang uses

IN PHRASES

❑ **do beavers piss on flat rocks?** *see* DOES A BEAR SHIT IN THE WOODS? IS THE POPE A CATHOLIC? *phr.*

beaver *n.*[2] [ety. unknown; ? link to dial. *bever*, refreshment, i.e. bread and *butter*] [mid-18C] (*UK Und.*) butter.

beaver patrol *n.*[1] [BEAVER *n.*[1] (5) + SE *patrol*] [1960s+] a group of young men looking for suitable female company.

beaver patrol *n.*[2] [EAGER BEAVER *n.*] [1970s] a group or team of enthusiastic (young) workers.

beavertail *n.* [the similarity in shape] **1** [mid-19C] a hairstyle, popular c.1860–70, whereby middle-class women wore their hair in a net, which then fell onto their shoulders. **2** [1970s+] (*US*) a cosh, a sap.

Beavis *n.* [the TV cartoon *Beavis and Butthead*, featuring a pair of socially inadequate teenagers] [1990s+] (*US campus*) one who fails to prove acceptable to social norms.

beazel *n.* [? SE *besom*] [1920s+] (*US*) a young woman; thus *beasel hound*, a man who pursues girls.

beazle *n.* [? 16C SE *beazler*, a drunkard, a sot] [1930s] (*US campus*) an unappealing person.

be back *adj.* [the idea of 'keeping back' from the danger] [2000s] (*US black*) constituting a warning.

bebee *n.* (*also* **beebee**) [Hind. *bibi*, a lady] **1** [mid-19C] a woman, a lady. **2** [late 19C] a prostitute; a female bed-mate.

be-blowed! *excl.* [euph.] [mid-19C] a general excl. of surprise, annoyance etc, i.e. I'll be damned!

bebop *v.* **1** [1950s–60s] to fight, esp. as one of a street gang [BOP *v.* (1)]. **2** [1970s+] to walk in an arrogant, 'cocky' manner [BOP *v.* (3); pun on SE *bebop*, a style of jazz/dancing].

bebop glasses *n.* (*also* **bop glasses**) [SE *bebop*, the style of jazz played in 1940s by such musicians as Charlie Parker, Kenny Clarke and Bud Powell, as well as Dizzy Gillespie; the glasses were popularized by the jazz stars of the 1940s, esp. Gillespie] [1940s] (*US black*) a then fashionable style of dark glasses, with notably thick frames as well as blackened lenses.

bebopper *n.* [the SE *bebop* jazz craze, new and sophisticated in 1940s, but archaic by 1980s] **1** [1940s+] (*also* **bopper**) one who dances to bebop tunes. **2** [1940s+] (*orig. US black/jazz*) (*also* **bopster**) a musician who plays in the bop style. **3** [1960s] (*US*) a juvenile delinquent [BEBOP *v.* (1)]. **4** [1980s+] (*US black*) (*also* **beebopper, bopper, diddy-bopper**) an inexperienced, naïve and on those grounds unpopular person.

beck *n.*[1] [abbr. HARMAN *n.*] [late 17C–mid-19C] (*UK Und.*) a constable.

beck *n.*[2] [abbr. girl's name *Rebecca*; ? also *Becks* beer, their supposedly favoured drink] [1980s+] a well-off, middle-class Jewish teenager or young person, orig. just girls, usu. from North London, often collectively as *becks*.

bed *n.* [metonymy] [1940s+] the world of sex; sexual intercourse.

DERIVATIVES

❑ **beddies** *n.* (*also* **beddie**) [1960s–70s] bed, in the context of a place for sex. ❑ **beddy** *n.* [SE *bed* + sfx *-y*; but note BETTY *n.* (9)] [1980s+] (*US campus*) an attractive, sexually available young woman.

IN COMPOUNDS

❑ **bed athlete** *n.* (*also* **bed-bounder, bedroom athlete**) [1940s+] (*orig. US*) a promiscuous person. ❑ **bedbait** *n.* [var. on JAILBAIT *n.* (2)] [1930s+] (*US*) an underage sexual partner, who can be of either sex although most often a teenage girl. ❑ **bedbug** *n.* *see* separate entry. ❑ **bed-faggot** *n.* (*also* **bed-fagot**) [FAGGOT *n.*[1] (2)] [mid-19C] a prostitute. ❑ **bed fellow** *n.* [pun] [late 19C] **1** the vagina. **2** the penis. ❑ **bedhop** *v.* [1960s+] to live a sexually promiscuous life; thus n. *bedhopping*. ❑ **bed-house** *n.* [HOUSE *n.*[1] (1)] **1** [mid-19C] (*US*) a 'short-time' hotel. **2** [1920s+] (*US black*) a brothel. ❑ **bed-presser** *n.* **1** [late 16C+] a whoremonger, a womanizer. **2** [late 16C+] a dull and heavy man. **3** [19C] a prostitute. ❑ **bed-sit** *n.* *see* separate entry.

IN PHRASES

❑ **bed and breakfast** *n.* *see* separate entry. ❑ **give bed-service** *v.* [20C+] (*W.I., Bdos*) of a woman, to take part in a sexual relationship in return for material support. ❑ **go bed-pressing** *v.* [19C] to have sexual intercourse. ❑ **wreck a bed** *v.* [1990s+] (*US campus*) to have sexual intercourse.

SE in slang uses

IN PHRASES

❑ **in bed with** *adj.* (*also* **in bed together**) [1970s+] (*orig. US*) allied or associated with, usu. implying nefarious activities. ❑ **put to bed** *v.* **1** [20C+] (*US*) to murder [ironic euph.]. **2** [1900s–50s] (*US*) to trail a subject until they return home and stay there. ❑ **put to bed with a mattock (and tucked up with a spade)** *adj.* [SE *mattock* and *spade*, tools for digging graves] [18C–early 19C] dead and buried. ❑ **put to bed with a shovel** *adj.* (*also* **put to bed with a pickaxe and shovel, put to bed with a spade**) [late 18C–1930s] dead and buried.

bed *v.* [abbr. SE *take to bed*; note mid-16C–mid-18C SE *bed*, to take (a wife) to bed, e.g. in D'Urfey, *Pills to Purge Melancholy* (1719): 'Lastly brought her here, / To court her for his Dear; / To Wed and Bed'; also in non-marital sense: 'Each Hour I long to bed thee: / But if confin'd, / Sould scare believ't a Joy'] [early 16C+] to seduce, to have sexual intercourse with.

bedad! *excl.* (*also* **be the dad!**) [SE *by* + DAD *n.*[1] (1)] [early 18C+] (*Irish*) by God!

bedammit! *excl.* *see* DAMMIT! *excl.*

bedamned *adv.* *see* DAMNED *adv.*

bed and breakfast *n.* [2s 6d (12½p), at one time the going rate for a B & B establishment] [1940s+] (*bingo*) the number 26.

bedbug *n.* [SE *bedbug*] **1** [1920s+] (*drugs*) a drug addict. **2** [1930s–60s] (*US black*) an unpleasant and/or insignificant person [identification]. **3** [1940s] (*US black*) a black Pullman porter [among their other duties the black porters turned back beds for their (mainly white) passengers].

bedbug alley *n.* (*also* **bedbug row**) [the supposed infestation of *bedbugs*] [1920s–50s] (*US*) the poorest area of a town.

bedder *n.* [SE *bed* + -ER *sfx*] [late 19C–1900s] a bedroom.

beddy-bye *n.* [a conscious use of a usu. juv. term] [20C+] bedtime; *go beddy-bye*, to go to sleep.

Bedfordshire *n.* [SE *bed* + sfx *-shire*; ult. the real UK county *Bedfordshire*] [mid-17C+] bed; thus *go up the wooden hill/high road to Bedfordshire*, to go to bed; thus *Bedfordshire woman, n.*, a prostitute.

Bedlam beggar *n.* [the *Bedlam* (Bethlehem) Hospital] [17C–early 19C] a wandering beggar, adopting tattered clothing and posing as a madman.

bedonderd *adj.* (*also* **bedonnerd**) [Du. *bedonderd*, mad] [1960s+] (*S.Afr.*) crazy.

bedoozle *v.* [? SE *bedazzle* + BAMBOOZLE *v.* (1)] [mid–late 19C; 2000s] (*US*) to confuse; thus *bedoozling*, astounding, amazing.

bedroom athlete *n.* *see* BED ATHLETE *under* BED *n.*

bedroom eyes *n.* [1910s+] a look in the eyes that invites the person on whom it is focused towards seduction.

bedroom furniture *n.* *see* PIECE OF FURNITURE *under* PIECE *n.*

bed-sit *n.* (*also* **bed-sitter**) [abbr.] [1960s+] a *bed-sitting* room.

bedstead relation *n.* [SE *bedstead*, occupied by the married couple] [1960s] (*US*) in-laws, relations by marriage.

bee *n.*[1] [the image is of 'stinging', in sense 2 with pain, in senses 1 and 3 as a jolt of inspiration; but note SE phr. *bee in one's bonnet*] **1** [1900s–20s] (*US*) ambition. **2** [1950s–60s] drug addiction. **3** [1950s–60s] (*US black*) an idea.

IN PHRASES

❑ **put the bee on** *v.* (*also* **bee, put on the bee, put the B on**) [play on STING *v.* (1) but note initial letter of BITE *n.*[1]] **1** [1900s–70s] (*US*) to extort, to blackmail, to pressurize, esp. for a loan. **2** [1910s–30s] to air one's obsession [SE *have a bee in one's bonnet*]. **3** [1910s–30s] of a woman, to pursue a man with the intention of marriage. **4** [1920s–50s] (*US*) to swindle, to hoax, to victimize. **5** [1940s] to sue. **6** *see* PUT THE BEE ON *under* BAG *n.*[1].

SE in slang uses

IN COMPOUNDS

❑ **bee's dick** *n.* [DICK *n.*[1] (5)] [2000s] (*N.Z.*) a tiny or insignificant amount. ❑ **bee-stings** *n.* [supposedly comparable size] [1960s+] (*orig. US*) small female breasts.

IN PHRASES

❑ **busy bee** *n.* [ext. of BUSY *n.*] [1950s] (*juv.*) a police officer.

bee *n.*[2] [abbr.] [1990s+] (*US*) a frisbee; a game of frisbee.

bee *n.*[3] **1** *see* B *n.*[1]. **2** *see* B *n.*[3]. **3** *see* B *n.*[1] (3).

bee *adj. see* B *adj.*

beeatch *n. see* BIATCH *n.*

Beeb *n.* [pron. of BB(C)] [1960s+] the British Broadcasting Corporation (BBC).

beebee *n. see* BEBEE *n.*

beebopper *n. see* BEBOPPER *n.* (4).

beece *n.* [? b.c., i.e. *b*iograph *c*inema] [1960s] a cinema.

Beecham's pill *n.* [rhy. sl.] **1** [1920s–30s] a bill; in pl. any form of sign (i.e. a handbill) denoting one's qualifications for begging ('blind', 'ex-soldier' etc). **2** [1950s+] (*Aus.*) a fool, a simpleton [DILL *n.*]. **3** [1950s+] a still (photograph). **4** [1970s+] a will.

Beecham's (Pills) *n.* [despite Partridge, as echoed by *Maledicta* IV (1980), more likely a play on PILL *n.* (1b)/ *Beecham's Pills*, the popular UK medicine, than rhy. sl. (on *testicles*)] **1** [late 19C+] the testicles. **2** [late 19C+] in ext. use, nonsense [i.e. BALLS *n.* (4)].

bee-cup *n.* [play on brassiere size 'B-cup'] [1970s+] (*US gay*) large pectorals.

beedee *adj.* [abbr. *b*ack *d*oor] [1950s] (*S.Afr.*) black-market, illicit.

Bee Em *n. see* BEAMER *n.*

bee-ess *v. see* B.S. *v.*

bee-esser *n. see* B.S.-ER *n.*

beef *n.*[1] **1** [mid-16C–18C] the vagina. **2** [late 16C; 20C+] (*later use W.I., Jam.*) (*also* **piece of beef**) a sexually appealing man or woman. **3** [17C+] (*also* **beef-steak**) the penis. **4** [late 18C+] human flesh. **5** [mid-19C+] (*orig. US*) physical strength, power, muscles. **6** [late 19C] used in Clare Market, a provisions market in London WC2, to describe cat's meat. **7** [1920s+] (*US*) (*also* **piece of beef**) a well-built male; used by both heterosexuals and homosexuals; thus *beef on the hoof*, a number of such men.

DERIVATIVES

❑ **beefo** *adj.* [-O *sfx*] [1950s] well-built, muscled, physically solid. ❑ **beefy** *adj.* **1** [mid-19C] lucky. **2** [mid-19C+] well-built, muscled, stolid. **3** [mid-19C+] thick, usu. of a woman's ankles or wrists. **4** [1910s+] fleshy, overweight.

IN COMPOUNDS

❑ **beef and** *n. see* separate entry. ❑ **beef-a-roni** *n.* [play on BEEFCAKE below + popular US fast-food] [1980s+] (*US campus*) a sexy male. ❑ **beef bag** *n.* [mid-19C–1930s] (*Aus.*) a shirt. ❑ **beef bayonet** *n.* [1960s+] the penis. ❑ **beef bugle** *n. see* separate entry. ❑ **beefcake** *n.* [on model of CHEESECAKE *n.*] (*orig. US*) **1** [1940s+] a male pin-up. **2** [1950s+] any attractive, muscular man. **3** [1970s] male sex-appeal. **4** [1970s] as term of address. ❑ **beef curtains** *n.* (*also* **roast beef curtains**) [1980s+] (*orig. US*) the labia majora. ❑ **beefeater** *n. see* separate entries. ❑ **beef gravy** *n.* [SE *gravy*/GRAVY *n.* (1b)] [1980s+] (*US gay*) semen. ❑ **beefhead** *n.* [-HEAD *sfx* (1)] **1** [mid-17C–early 19C; mid-19C+ in US] a fool, a simpleton; thus *beef-headed, beef-brained*, stupid, foolish. **2** [19C] (*US*) a Texan, a cowboy. **3** [1980s] (*UK black*) a skinhead, usu. synon. with a member of a right-wing/racist party. ❑ **beef injection** *n.* (*also* **hot beef injection**) [1980s+] (*orig. US*) **1** sexual intercourse; sometimes *hot beef incision*; thus *slip one the hot beef*, to have sexual intercourse from the male point of view. **2** a penis. ❑ **beef-steak** *n. see* sense 3 above. ❑ **beef torpedo** *n.* [2000s] (*US*) the penis. ❑ **beef trust** *n.* [ironic use of SE *beef trust*, a conglomerate of beef producers/processors; orig. late 19C carnival use, created by showman W.B. 'Billy' Watson, who thus named his sideshow of grotesquely overweight women] [1940s+] (*US*) an obese person, a group of obese people. ❑ **beef tube** *n.* [1970s] (*orig. US*) the penis. ❑ **beef-tugging** *n. see* separate entry. ❑ **beef-witted** *adj.* [used by Shakespeare in 1606, the term resurfaced briefly in late 19C, describing 'this British bull-neckedness, this British beef-wittedness'] [early 17C] stupid, simple.

IN PHRASES

❑ **aching for a side of beef** *adj.* [1970s+] (*US black*) of a woman, eager to have sex. ❑ **beefsteak eye** *n. see* separate entry. ❑ **beef to the heel** *n.* [late 19C–1920s] a bulky, heavy-set woman, usu. of a countrywoman. ❑ **beef to the heel** *adj.* (*also* **beef to the heels, beef to the ankle**) [20C+] bulky, brawny, stocky, esp. of thick, strong legs or thick female ankles. ❑ **beef up** *v.* [i.e. to add SE *beef* / BEEF *n.*[1] (5)] **1** [1940s+] (*also* **beef**) to strengthen, to improve. **2** [1950s+] to put on weight and/or muscles. ❑ **bludgeon the beefsteak** *v.* [var. on *BEAT ONE'S MEAT under* MEAT *n.*] [1980s+] to masturbate. ❑ **bury one's beef** *v.* [1970s] (*US*) of a man, to have sexual intercourse. ❑ **cream one's beef** *v.* [1990s+] to masturbate. ❑ **cut a side (of beef)** *v.* [1980s+] (*US black*) to have sexual intercourse. ❑ **have a bit of beef** *v.* (*also* **do a bit of beef**) [late 19C] to have sexual intercourse. ❑ **in a man's beef, be** *v.* [late 18C–early 19C] to wound a man with a sword. ❑ **in a woman's beef, be** *v.* [late 18C–mid-19C] to have sexual intercourse with a woman. ❑ **put on beef** *v.* [mid-19C+] to put on weight. ❑ **put some beef into it** *v.* [20C+] to make a physical effort; often as excl. *put some beef into it!* ❑ **save one's beef** *v. see SAVE ONE'S BACON under* BACON *n.*[1]. ❑ **take in beef** *v.* [19C] of women, to have sexual intercourse. ❑ **tame the beef weasel** *v.* (*also* **tame the shrew**) [1990s+] to masturbate.

beef *n.*[2] [BEEF *v.*[1]] **1** [late 19C–1950s] (*US tramp*) an act of betrayal to the authorities. **2** [late 19C+] (*US*) a complaint, a problem; thus *what's one's/the beef?*, what's one's/the problem?; *make a beef*, to complain, to make a fuss; *beefing* complaining. **3** [late 19C+] (*US campus*) a mistake; thus *make a beef*, to err, to blunder. **4** [1910s+] a criminal charge; thus *bum beef*, an unfair (in criminal eyes) charge. **5** [1920s–80s] (*US Und.*) a crime under investigation. **6** [1940s+] (*US black*) a statement, conversation, line of talk. **7** [1940s+] an altercation. **8** [1950s+] (*US Und.*) a discussion; chatter. **9** [1960s] (*US Und.*) an arrest. **10** [1960s] (*US Und.*) a criminal act. **11** [1960s–70s] (*US*) a (usu. hotel or restaurant) bill. **12** [1960s–70s] (*US prison*) a jail sentence. **13** [1960s+] (*US prison*) a disciplinary charge. **14** [1980s] (*US campus*) facts, information. **15** [2000s] (*UK black*) general aggression, atmosphere of violence.

IN COMPOUNDS

❑ **beef baby** *n.* [2000s] (*US black*) a child fathered by a gangster who is living temporarily with a girlfriend or mistress while hiding from the authorities. ❑ **Beef City** *n.* [-CITY *sfx*] [1940s] a situation in which one is complaining.

IN PHRASES

❑ **bogus beef** *n.* [BOGUS *adj.* (2)] [1930s+] (*US black*) a groundless complaint. ❑ **chew the beef** *v.* [1940s] (*US Und.*) to complain. ❑ **chill a beef** *v.* [CHILL *v.*[2] (5)] [1930s–40s] to deal with a problem. ❑ **cool the beef** *v.* [COOL *v.*[2] (1)] [1950s+] to deal with a problem or a complaint. ❑ **put up a beef** *v.* [1950s] to make a fuss. ❑ **square the beef** *v.* [SQUARE *v.* (1)] [1930s] to deal with a problem, typically to escape a criminal charge by paying a bribe. ❑ **squeak beef** *v.* [late 17C–early 19C] to cry 'stop thief!'. ❑ **street beef** *n.* [STREET, THE *n.* (2)] [1990s+] (*US Und.*) crimes committed inside prison by a serving prisoner who is tried in a normal court rather than facing internal prison discipline; such crimes include murder, escape, sex- or drug-related offences; also as v. ❑ **take beef** *v.* [1990s+] (*US black*) to get into arguments, to face criticism. ❑ **where's the beef?** [slogan for Wendy's hamburgers in 1984 + play on SE *beef*] [1980s+] (*US*) what's the real point, importance, inner meaning, content etc?

beef *n.*[3] [? BEEF *n.*[1] (5)] [1940s–50s] (*US*) liquor.

beef *v.*[1] [*CRY (HOT) BEEF under* HOT BEEF! *excl.*] **1** [early–mid-19C] to raise a hue and cry. **2** [mid-19C] to raise an alarm (other than over a crime). **3** [mid-19C–1910s] (*orig. theatre*) to shout. **4** [mid-19C+] to complain. **5** [late 19C] (*US*) to bully. **6** [late 19C–1960s] (*US tramp*) to give someone away, to betray to the authorities; to own up. **7** [late 19C+] (*US*) to argue. **8** [20C+] (*US*) to talk loudly (esp. to no real purpose). **9** [1900s] (*US*) to waste time. **10** [1900s–10s] (*US*) to blunder, to make a mistake. **11** [1910s–50s] to say, to declare. **12** [1970s] (*US prison*) to charge with a crime. **13** [1980s+] to make an official complaint against someone. **14** [2000s] (*US black*) to have a problem with (someone).

(DERIVATIVES)

□ **beefer** *n.* **1** [late 19C–1930s] (*US*) a whinger, a complainer. **2** [late 19C–1940s] (*US tramp*) an informer.

(IN PHRASES)

□ **beef it** *v. see* separate entry. □ **beef (it) out** *v.* [1900s–20s] (*Aus.*) to call or sing, occas. to play, loudly and enthusiastically. □ **make beef** *v.* [19C] to leave, to run off. □ **take beef** *v.* [mid–late 19C] (*UK Und.*) to run away.

beef *v.*^{2} [agricultural jargon *beef*, to slaughter an ox] **1** [late 19C] (*US*) to shoot dead; also fig. use. **2** [1900s–50s] (*orig. US*) to knock (someone) down. **3** [1940s+] to engage in sexual intercourse.

beef *v.*^{3} *see* BEEF UP *under* BEEF *n.*^{1}.

beef! *excl. see* HOT BEEF! *excl.*

beef and *n.* [late 19C] (*US*) an order of corned beef and beans.

beef and ham *n.* (*also* **plate of ham**) [rhy. sl.; note TROLLEY AND TRAM *n.*= SE *ham*] **1** [1940s] a tram. **2** [1950s–70s] a pram.

beef bugle *n.* [2000s] (*Aus./N.Z.*) the penis.

(IN PHRASES)

□ **blow the beef bugle** *v.* [1960s] to fellate.

beefeater *n.*^{1} [stereotype of the beef-eating British + SE *beefeater*, a Yeoman of the Guard, one of London's tourist icons] [17C; 20C+] (*US*) an Englishman or woman.

beefeater *n.*^{2} [his 'appetite' for cattle] [1900s–10s] (*US*) a cattle rustler or poacher.

beef-heart *n.* [rhy. sl.; the true rhyme is sense 2, but sense 1 presumes the effect] **1** [1910s–70s] a bean. **2** [1950s+] a fart.

beef it *v.* [SE *beef*, as symbol of the ultimate in consumption] [19C] to eat heartily.

beefsteak eye *n.* [the practice of putting raw steak on a black eye] [1950s–70s] (*US*) a black eye.

beef-tugging *n.* [SE; the indigestibility of the tough meat served there] [late 19C–1900s] (*London*) eating at City cafés and restaurants.

bee-gum (hat) *n.* [Southern dial. *bee-gum*, a hollow tree or log used as a beehive] **1** [late 19C–1930s] (*US*) a top hat. **2** [1960s] a hairstyle in which a woman piles her hair on the top of her head.

beehive *n.*^{1} [the implication is of honey rather than stings] [late 19C–1930s] the vagina.

beehive *n.*^{2} **1** [1920s+] the number five [rhy. sl.]. **2** [1960s] a five-pound note [rhy. sl.]. **3** [1970s+] a woman's hair style, resembling a hive from excessive back-combing.

beehive sex *n.* [2000s] (*S.Afr. gay*) an orgy.

bee jay *n. see* B.J. *n.*

beejeebers *n. see* BEJABERS *n.*

beek *n. see* BEAK *n.*^{2} (4).

beeks *n. see* BEAK *n.*^{1} (1).

beel *n.* [abbr. SE *automobile*] [1950s+] (*W.I., USVI*) a motorcar.

bee-luther-hatchee *n.* [B. LUTHER HATCHETT *n.*] [1920s–40s] (*US black*) the ultimate in far-away, unpleasant places.

beemer *n. see* BEAMER *n.*

been *adj. see* BENE *adj.*

beenly *adv. see* BENESHIPLY *under* BENESHIP *n.*

beeno *n. see* BEANO *n.*^{1}.

been there *phr.* **1** [mid-19C+] (*orig. US*) dismissive phr. used to imply that one has already experienced the so-called 'novelty' of which another person is speaking. **2** [late 19C+] a remark passed by a man on seeing a passing woman with whom (he claims) he has slept.

been there, done that *phr.* [the phr. was adopted in soft-drink advertising of the mid-1990s; the ref. to *T-shirt* underpins the marketing that accompanies any new cultural phenomenon, esp. mass popular films] [1990s+] used to summarize the assumed youthful ennui of the 1990s; voiced when offered some new stimulus and often appended by the phr. *got the T-shirt*.

been to see Captain Bates? *phr.* [proper name of *Captain Bates*, a well-known London prison governor] [late 19C] a greeting to a person one knows or suspects to have been in prison.

been to three county fairs and a goat-fucking *phr.* (*also* **...and a goat-roping**) [1970s+] (*US, mainly Southern*) phr. implying one's astonishment (one has had many, varied experiences, but never one such as this).

bee-otch *n. see* BIATCH *n.*

beep *v.* [1980s+] (*US black*) to make a call using a pager phone.

beeper *n.* [1980s+] a pager; thus *beep*, a message.

beeper boy *n.* (*also* **beeper-freak**) [from the use of the BEEPER *n.* (personal pager) in the pre-mobile phone era + -FREAK *sfx*] [1980s+] (*US*) a drug dealer.

beer *n.* [1960s+] (*US black/campus*) semen.

SE in slang uses

(DERIVATIVES)

□ **beery** *adj.* **1** [mid-19C+] drunk, tipsy. **2** [late 19C] (*US*) of emotions, songs etc, induced by drink.

(IN COMPOUNDS)

□ **beer barn** *n. see* BOOZE BARN *under* BOOZE *n.* □ **beer barrel** *n.* **1** [19C] the stomach. **2** [1940s] a beer drunkard. **3** [1940s+] (*orig. US*) a (beer-drinker's) paunch. **4** [1950s] a fat person. □ **beer-boep** *n. see* BOEP *n.*^{2}. □ **beer bong** *n.* [BONG *n.*^{1} (1)] [1980s] (*US campus*) a device consisting of a funnel attached to a tube, which facilitates the speedier drinking of beer; thus *do a beer bong*, to drink beer through such a device. □ **beer-bottle** *n.* [metonymy] [late 19C–1900s] a stout, red-faced man. □ **beer bust** *n.* [BUST *n.* (3a)] [1960s+] (*US*) a drinking party that concentrates on beer. □ **beer-buzzer** *n.* [BUZZ *v.*^{1} (1f)] [late 19C] (*US*) one who frequents saloons in the hope of cadging free beer. □ **beer-chewer** *n.* (*also* **beer-guzzler, beer-sparrer, beer-sucker**) [GUZZLE *v.*^{1}/SE *spar*/SUCKER *n.*^{1} (4)] [late 19C+] (*Aus.*) a heavy drinker of beer. □ **Beer City** *n.* (*also* **Beer Town**) [famous for its breweries] [1970s] (*US*) Milwaukee, Wisconsin. □ **beer-crawl** *n.* [CRAWL *n.* (2)] [20C+] a leisurely progress from public house to public house, drinking one or more beers in each. □ **beer-eater** *n.* [note P.G. Wodehouse: 'It was my uncle George who discovered that alcohol was a food well in advance of modern medical thought' (*The Inimitable Jeeves*, 1923)] [late 19C–1910s] a heavy drinker. □ **beer fleas** *n.* [2000s] (*N.Z.*) a tickling sensation in the stomach due to drinking an excess of beer. □ **beer goggle** *v. see* separate entry. □ **beer goggles** *n. see* separate entry. □ **beer goitre** *n.* [1980s] (*N.Z.*) a beer belly. □ **beer-guzzler** *n. see* BEER-CHEWER above. □ **beer gut** *n.* [1950s+] a paunch, a beer belly; thus adj. *beer-gutted*. □ **beerhead** *n.* [-HEAD *sfx* (2)/-HEAD *sfx* (4)] (*US*) **1** [1940s] a German. **2** [1970s] a beer drunkard. □ **beerhound** *n.* [-HOUND *sfx*] [1950s] (*US*) a heavy drinker. □ **beer-jerker** *n.* (*also* **beer-slinger**) **1** [mid-19C] (*also* **beer-yanker**) a bartender who draws beer in a saloon [JERKER *n.*^{1} (3)/SLINGER *n.* (1)/YANK *v.*^{1} (1)]. **2** [mid–late 19C] (*US*) a drunkard [JERKER *n.*^{1} (2)]. □ **beer joint** *n.* [JOINT *n.* (3b)] [1920s+] (*US*) a saloon or bar serving primarily beer. □ **beer-jugger** *n.* [late 19C–1900s] (*US*) a barmaid. □ **beer keg** *n. see* KEG *n.* □ **beer mill** *n.* [on pattern of GIN-MILL *n.* (1)] [late 19C] a saloon that sells beer. □ **beer muscle** *n.* [the 'muscle' is in fact fat] **1** [1930s–40s] (*US*) a pot belly, engendered by excessive beer-drinking. **2** [2000s] in pl., aggressive macho posturing, the result of becoming drunk. □ **beerocracy** *n.* [SE *beer* + *aristocracy*] [late 19C] the world of brewers and publicans. □ **beer-off** *n.* [1930s–70s] an off-licence, a liquor store. □ **beer pot** *n.* [POT *n.*^{1} (3a)] [1980s+] a fat stomach caused by a steady intake of beer. □ **beer sandwich** *n.* [2000s] (*N.Z.*) drinking rather than eating one's lunch. □ **beer scooter** *n.* [1990s+] the process, when very drunk, of making one's way home without knowing what form of transport was employed. □ **beer-slinger** *n. see* BEER-JERKER above. □ **beer-sparrer** *n. see* BEER-CHEWER above. □ **beer street** *n.* [fig. street name; note William Hogarth's celebrated engraving of 1751] [late 19C–1900s] the mouth or throat. □ **beer-sucker** *n. see* BEER-CHEWER above. □ **beer suitcase** *n.* [2000s] a large pack of beers. □ **beer-swiper** *n.* [SWIPE *v.*^{1}] [1910s] (*Aus.*) a drunkard. □ **beer token** *n.* [the assumed primacy of alcohol in making a claim on one's wages] [1990s+] money. □ **Beer Town** *n. see* BEER CITY above. □ **beer trap** *n.* [SE *trap*/TRAP *n.*^{1} (4)] [late 19C–1930s] the mouth. □ **beer-up** *n.* [1910s+] (*Aus.*) a riotous, drunken party. ❑ **beer-yanker** *n. see* BEER-JERKER above.

IN PHRASES

❑ **beer bottle beat** *n.* [1970s] (*US*) a client who likes to be beaten by a prostitute who is wielding a beer bottle. ❑ **beered (up)** *adj.* [1930s+] (*orig. US*) drunk on beer. ❑ **beer up** *v.* [late 19C+] **1** to give someone money for beer. **2** to get drunk. ❑ **have a beer in** *v.* [1900s] (*N.Z.*) to be very drunk. ❑ **in one's beer** *adj.* [late 17C–18C] drunk. ❑ **it's the beer talking** *see under* TALK *v.*

IN EXCLAMATIONS

❑ **beer-o!** [-O *sfx* (7)] [late 19C] a cry raised by workers when one of their number commits a blunder that has to be paid for by buying their fellows a round of drink.

beer *v.* [mid-19C+ use is Aus.] **1** [late 18C+] to get drunk on beer. **2** [late 19C+] to give someone a beer, usu. in imper. *beer me!* **3** [1910s] to spend one's money on beer.

beer and sarse *n.* [rhy. sl. = ARSE *n.* (1); ult. SARSE *n.*] [1980s] (*Aus.*) the buttocks.

beer goggle *v.* [SE *beer* + SE colloq. *goggle* (*at*)] [1990s+] (*US campus*) to find someone attractive because of the influence of alcohol.

beer goggles *n.* [1980s+] (*US campus*) blurred vision that follows an excess of (beer) drinking; such vision has the added effect of making hitherto unexciting individuals appear sexually alluring.

IN PHRASES

❑ **have one's beer goggles on** *v.* [1980s+] (*US campus*) to find someone attractive because of the influence of alcohol.

beery buff *n.* [rhy. sl. = MUFF *n.*[2]] [20C+] a fool.

bees (and honey) *n.* (*also* **beesum**) [rhy. sl.] [late 19C+] money.

bee's knees *n.* (*also* **ants' pants, bee's nuts, clam's garters, duck's quack, frog's eyebrows, owl's bowels, pig's scream, sparrow's chirp, turkey's elbow**) [NUTS *n.*[2] (1)] [20C+] **1** a superior person, or someone who poses as such. **2** the best.

bee'sn *n.* [SE *be*, v.] [2000s] (*US black*) an act of relaxation.

beesum *n. see* BEES (AND HONEY) *n.*

beeswax *n.*[1] **1** [mid-19C] second-rate, soft cheese [it is 'full of holes']. **2** [mid–late 19C] a bore, usu. as *old beeswax* [puns on SE *bore*, a hole].

beeswax *n.*[2] [joc. solipsism] **1** [1930s+] (*US*) business; usu. as *none of your beeswax, mind your own beeswax*. **2** [2000s] flattery, smooth talk.

beeswax! *excl.* [euph. BULLSHIT! *excl.*] [2000s] (*N.Z.*) a dismissive excl.; rubbish!

bees wingers *n.* [rhy. sl.] [1960s+] the fingers.

beetle *n.*[1] [SE; ? precursor of BUG *n.*[4] (3b)] [1910s–60s] (*US*) an eccentric, a madman, an obsessive fan.

SE in slang uses

IN COMPOUNDS

❑ **beetle bait** *n.* [1940s] (*Aus.*) treacle or golden syrup. ❑ **beetle-brain** *n.* (*also* **beetlebrow, gnatbrain**) [SE *beetle*, an instrument used in various industrial applications to drive, wedge, flatten or ram, used in combs. to imply dullness, heaviness or stupidity + sfx *-brain*] [17C+] a fool. ❑ **beetle-case** *n.* [mid–late 19C] a large boot or shoe. ❑ **beetle-crusher** *n.* [mid-19C+] **1** (*also* **beetle-squasher**) the foot. **2** (*also* **grasshopper crusher**) a shoe, esp. a large, heavy boot, often as worn by policemen, labourers or the army. **3** (*juv.*) a police officer. **4** a horse with large feet. ❑ **beetle fat** *n.* [1950s] (*UK juv.*) bubble gum. ❑ **beetle-head** *n.* [-HEAD *sfx* (1); 20C use is US] [late 16C–late 18C; 1940s–50s] a fool; *beetle-headed*, stupid. ❑ **beetle's blood** *n.* [the *beetle*, like the beer, is black] [1920s–30s] (*Anglo-Irish*) stout beer. ❑ **beetle-squasher** *n.* [mid-19C] a shoe. ❑ **beetle-sticker** *n.* [the mounting of specimens] [mid–late 19C] an entomologist.

IN PHRASES

❑ **beetle off** *v.* [the orig. image was of flying directly (as a beetle flies) back to base] [1920s+] (*orig. RAF*) to leave, to wander off; thus *beetle in, beetle up*, to arrive. ❑ **black beetle** *n.* [? his uniform] [mid–late 19C] a constable in the Thames River police. ❑ **black beetles** *n.* [a derog. view of the scurrying, indistinguishable masses] [early–mid-19C] the proletariat. ❑ **have beetles in one's arcade** *v.* [1910s] (*Aus.*) to lose one's senses; be mad.

beetle *n.*[2] [ety. unknown; ? they 'beetle' around] **1** [1910s+] a horse. **2** [1930s–60s] a young woman, esp. one who dresses in flashy clothes. **3** [1950s] (*UK juv.*) a police officer.

beetroot mug *n.* [MUG *n.*[1] (1b); ? coined by Charles Ross, creator, c.1867, of the comic character Ally Sloper, a dissipated looking old man with a red and swollen nose; poss. the orig. of SE phr. *red as a beetroot*] [late 19C–1910s] a red face.

beevos *n.* [BEVVY *n.* (1)] [1970s] (*US campus*) beer.

Beewee *n.* [1970s+] (*W.I.*) pertaining to the British West Indies airline.

beeyatch *n. see* BIATCH *n.*

beeze *n.* [ety. unknown; ? obs. SE *bezel*, a cutting tool] [1940s] the penis.

beezer *n.*[1] [? development of BOWSPRIT *n.* (1)] (*orig. US*) **1** [20C+] (*orig. boxing*) the nose. **2** [1910s+] the head; the face, the mouth.

IN PHRASES

❑ **black beezer** *n.* [20C+] a black person's face.

beezer *n.*[2] [orig. Scot. *beezer*, a smart fellow] [1910s+] something or someone excellent; the best example.

beezer *n.*[3] (*also* **beezo**) [? BUGGER *n.*[1] (1) + GEEZER *n.*[1] (1)] [1920s–40s] (*mainly juv.*) a 'fellow', a 'chap'.

beezer *adj.* [Scot. *beezer*, a smart fellow] [1930s+] very attractive, excellent.

bef *adj.* [? Scot. *beff*, a fool, a stupid person] [1940s+] (*W.I.*) stupid, useless.

be farts and cell partners *n.* [assonance; beans make you fart while frankfurters are their 'partners' in the tin] [2000s] (*US prison*) a meal of beans and frankfurters.

befogged *adj. see* FOGGED *adj.* (2).

befok *adj.* [Afk. *befok*, FUCKED *adj.*[1]] [1970s+] (*S.Afr.*) **1** of people, unhappy, lacking in good sense, crazy, exhausted. **2** of objects, ruined, spoiled, out of order.

befokte *adj.* (*also* **gefoetered**) [Afk. *befok*, FUCKED *adj.*[1]] [1980s] (*S.Afr.*) a general intensifier.

befoozeled *adj. see* FOOZLED *adj.* (3).

before Abe *n.* [for Afro-Americans any time before 1 January 1863, when President *Abraham* Lincoln signed the Emancipation Proclamation] [1940s] **1** (*US black/Harlem*) the era of slavery; the period before Emancipation. **2** fig. work, a regular job [plays on SLAVE *n.* (2)].

IN COMPOUNDS

❑ **before Abe jive** *n.* [JIVE *n.*[1] (4)] [1940s] (*US black/Harlem*) hard, thankless work.

before day creep *n.* [SE *before day*(*break*) + CREEP *v.* (4)] [1920s–40s] (*US black*) a surreptitious late-night or early morning visit to one's lover.

before one can say 'Jump Nigger' *phr.* [1920s–40s] (*US*) very quickly.

beg act *n.* [1940s–60s] (*US black/Harlem*) an attempt to obtain money.

begad! *excl.* (*also* **beged!**) [mid-18C+] a mild, if once blasphemous oath, lit. 'by God!'.

begar!/begarra! *excl. see* BEGORRA! *excl.*

beg for a piece *v. see under* PIECE *n.*

beggar *n.* (*also* **beggarbo**) [mid-19C+] **1** a man, a person, used both negatively, e.g. *a nasty-looking beggar*, and positively or affectionately, e.g. *you're a funny beggar*. **2** a thing, an object, a creature.

SE in slang uses

DERIVATIVES

❑ **beggars** *n.* [they are inferior to the 'court' cards] [19C–1900s] in card-playing, the lower cards, marked two–ten.

IN COMPOUNDS

❑ **beggar for** *n.* (*also* **beggar to**) [they lit. *beg for* the subject] [mid-19C+] an enthusiast, one who is keen on, e.g. *a beggar for work, a beggar to argue.* ❑ **beggar-maker** *n.* [their depriving people of money] [late 18C–early 19C] a publican. ❑ **beggar's benison** *n.* [SE *benison*, blessing] [late 18C–early 19C] a popular toast, 'may your prick and your purse never fail you' (Grose, 1796). ❑ **beggar's bolts** *n.* [SE *bolt*, an arrow; thus a projectile] [late 16C] stones. ❑ **beggar's bullets** *n.* [poverty deprives the beggar of an actual weapon] [late 18C] stones. ❑ **beggar's lagging** *n.* [LAGGING *n.* (2)] [1940s–50s] (*UK prison*) a sentence of 90 days' imprisonment, commonly that meted out for vagrancy. ❑ **beggar's plush** *n.* [SE *plush*, a kind of cloth having a nap longer and softer than that of velvet; used for rich garments, e.g. footmen's liveries] [late 17C] corduroy, cotton velvet. ❑ **beggar's schmaltz** *n.* [1940s] (*US*) chicken fat. ❑ **beggar's velvet** *n.* [SE *beggar's velvet*, ? cotton plush or ? corduroy] [mid-19C] particles of lint and similar household dirt that gather behind or beneath sofas, tables or beds (often following the shaking of an eiderdown).

IN PHRASES

❑ **beggar boy's (ass)** *n.* [note this is the UK SE *ass*, donkey, not ASS *n.* (2) or ARSE *n.* (1)] **1** [late 19C+] money. **2** [1930s+] Bass ale. ❑ **beggar-on-the-coals** *n. see* DEVIL-ON-THE-COALS *under* DEVIL *n.* ❑ **biscuit beggar** *n.* [? their poverty] [1960s] (*US*) a Native American. ❑ **eat like a beggar man and wag one's under jaw** [late 18C–early 19C] 'a jocular reproach to a proud man' (Grose 1785). ❑ **put the beggar on the gentleman** *v.* [mid–late 19C] to drink beer after spirits. ❑ **scratch a beggar's arse** *v.* [ARSE *n.* (1)] [mid-18C] to be impoverished.

beggared *adj.* [mid-19C+] euph. for BUGGERED *adj.*[1]; thus *I'll be beggared if...*

beggar my neighbour *phr.* [rhy. sl. = *on the labour*] [1920s+] visiting the labour exchange/unemployment office to draw unemployment benefit.

begger off *v. see* BUGGER OFF *v.*

begging black *n.* [2000] (*UK black*) aspiring; e.g used of whites attempting to emulate a black lifestyle, also of envy of another's ability, possession, appearance etc.

begging for it *adj.* [SE *beg* + *it*/IT *n.*[1] (1)] [1950s+] a male comment on a woman who, supposedly if not actually, is inflamed with lust.

begin on *v.* (*also* **begin upon**) [early–mid-19C] (*orig. US*) to attack verbally.

begob!/begobs! *excl. see* BEGORRA! *excl.*

begonia *n.* [negative identification of homosexuality with a flower/shrub] [1970s+] (*US black gay*) a derog. term for a black homosexual.

be good! *excl.* [20C+] joc. phr. used on parting; often ext. to *if you can't be good, be careful!*, which in itself can be extended to *if you can't be careful, buy a pram!*

begorra! *excl.* (*also* **begar! begarra! begob! begobs! begor! begorry! by Gorrah!**) [mid-17C+] by God! esp. as the generic expletive of the supposedly 'typical' Irishman.

begosh! *excl. see* BY GOSH! *under* GOSH! *excl.*

beg your pardon *n.* [rhy. sl.] [late 19C] a garden.

behani ghani! *excl. see* BHANI GHANI *phr.*

behave foundry *n.* [1900s] (*US*) a prison.

behave local *v.* [SE *behave* + *local*, rough, of inferior quality] [20C+] (*W.I.*) to act in a crude, unsophisticated manner.

behavish *adj.* [SE *behave* + sfx *-ish*, of the nature or character of] [1980s+] (*US black*) badly behaved.

behind *n.* **1** [mid-16C+] the buttocks, the posterior. **2** [late 19C+] thus used anthropomorphically, the back of an object, e.g. a car, a bus; thus as adv., working as a bus conductor.

DERIVATIVES

❑ **behindativeness** *n.* [SE *behind*/sense 2 above + sfx *-ative*, tending to point out] [late 19C] a large dress-pannier, fashionably affixed to a lady's dress c.1888.

IN COMPOUNDS

❑ **behind-kicking** *n. see* ASS-KICKING *n.*

IN PHRASES

❑ **behind the behind** *n.* [SE *behind* + sense 1 above] [1930s] sodomy. ❑ **behind with the rent** *adj.* [pun on SE *behind*/sense 1 above + RENT *n.* (5) + rhy. sl. BENT *adj.* (5)] [2000s] homosexual. ❑ **not know where one's behind hangs** *v.* [20C+] to be arrogant or to show complete indecision or bewilderment. ❑ **warm someone's behind** *v.* [1970s–80s] (*US black*) to hit or slap someone on the buttocks.

behind *adv.* **1** [1930s+] (*orig. US*) involved with, concerned about, believing in. **2** [1950s+] (*US black*) as a result of, as a consequence of, in reference to. **3** [1960s+] (*orig. US*) in full understanding of. **4** [1970s] (*orig. US*) excited by, obsessed with.

IN PHRASES

❑ **get behind** *v.* [the image of putting one's weight behind] **1** [late 19C] (*US*) to start smoking or drinking. **2** [1900s; 1960s+] to make a commitment to an idea, a job, a person etc. **3** [1970s+] (*also* **groove behind**) to understand, to enjoy, to appreciate [GROOVE *v.* (2)].

SE in slang uses

IN PHRASES

❑ **behind like a slave-driver, be** *v.* (*also* **behind like a tak-tak, be**) [the *tak-tak* or *acoushi ant*, a fierce pest] [20C+] (*W.I.*) to beg, to harass, to pressurize. ❑ **go behind** *v.* [1940s] (*US black*) to argue with, to contradict.

behind *prep.*

SE in slang uses

IN PHRASES

❑ **all behind in Melbourne** *adj.* [pun on BEHIND *n.* (1)/SE *behind*] [1940s+] (*Aus.*) fat, heavy-buttocked. ❑ **all behind like barney's bull** *adj. see under* BARNEY'S BULL *n.* ❑ **all behind like the cow's tail** *adj.* [pun] [20C+] (*Irish*) late. ❑ **behind a dime** *adv.* [SAmE *dime*, the tiny ten-cent coin; i.e. there is no way such a person can 'hide'] [1980s+] (*US*) to any extent, under any circumstances, usu. in phr. *I wouldn't trust (someone) behind a dime.* ❑ **behind of God speed** *see* BACK OF GOD SPEED *under* BACK *adv.* ❑ **behind one's door** [1950s+] (*UK prison*) locked up in solitary confinement; also as an order, *behind your doors!*, 'get into your cell!'. ❑ **behind oneself** *adj.* [SE *behind*, backward] [late 19C] out of date, out of fashion, not up with the latest situation. ❑ **behind the parade** *adj.* [1920s+] (*orig. US black*) old-fashioned, passé. ❑ **behind the ramp** *n.* [the *ramp* implies some form of desk] [1980s] anyone in authority, esp. a police officer or prison warder. ❑ **behind the scales** *n.* (*also* **behind the scale**) [drugs are bought in bulk then weighed out in smaller measures for sale; the image is of a small shopkeeper behind the counter] [1980s+] (*US black*) a drug seller's place of business, thus the weighing and selling of the drug. ❑ **behind the walls** (*also* **inside the walls**) [20C+] (*US Und.*) in prison.

behind the eight ball *phr.* (*also* **back of the fifteen-ball, up against the eight ball**) [pool imagery] [1930s+] (*orig. US*) in trouble, in a difficult situation.

beige *n.* [SE *beige*, yellowish-grey] [1940s+] (*US black*) a light-skinned black person.

IN COMPOUNDS

❑ **beige frame** *n.* [FRAME *n.*[1] (1)] [1950s] (*US black*) 'smooth brown skinned girls, girls with heavy tan' (Durst, *The Jives of Dr Hepcat*, 1953).

beige *adj.* [the perceived blandness of the colour *beige*] [1980s+] (*US*) deeply tedious, very bland.

beiging *n.* [SE *beige* + sfx *-ing*] [1980s+] (*drugs*) a process that alters the colour of cocaine to light brown, thus making it appear purer than it actually is.

Beilby's ball *n.* [ety. unknown. As Grose put it in 1785, 'who Mr Beilby was, or why that ceremony was so called, remains with the quadrature of the circle, the discovery of the philosopher's stone and divers other desiderata as yet undiscovered', but there exist a number of suggestions. The most obvious is that *Beilby* was a well-known sheriff; a second is that *Beilby* is a mispronunciation of *Old Bailey*, the court in which so many villains were sentenced to death. The third, and that espoused by Partridge, is that *Beil* refers to the *bilbo*, a long iron bar, furnished with sliding shackles to confine the ankles of prisoners and a lock by which to fix one end of the bar to the floor or ground. *Bilbo* comes from the Spanish town of Bilbao, where these fetters were invented] the reification of judicial hanging.

IN PHRASES

❑ **dance at Beilby's ball** *v.* [mid-18C–early 19C] to be hanged; also ext. with ...*where the sheriff plays the music* or ...*where the sheriff pays the fiddlers*. ❑ **shake one's trotters at Beilby's ball** *v.* (*also* **shake one's trotters at Bilby's ball, shiver...**) [TROTTER *n.* (1)] [mid-18C–early 19C] to be hanged.

be-in *n.* [play on SE *be in (touch)/being*; taken from the original *Human Be-in* at Golden Gate Park, San Francisco, 1967; the *-in* sfx extended to incl. *fuck-in, smoke-in, love-in, sit-in* etc] [1960s] (*orig. US*) a gathering of young people, usu. hippies, for mutual admiration, smoking cannabis and listening to music.

being poor *n.* [rhy. sl.] [1960s] (*bingo*) the number four.

beitch *n. see* BIATCH *n.*

bejabers *n.* (*also* **beejeebers, bejabbers, bejapers, bejinks**) [1950s+] euph. for HELL, THE *phr.* (3).

IN PHRASES

❑ **scare the bejab(b)ers out of** *v. see SCARE THE BEJAZUS OUT OF under* BEJAZUS *n.*

bejabers! *excl.* (*also* **bejabbers! be japers! be Japes! be javers! bejay! by jagers! by Japers! by the jappers! Jabus!**) [late 18C+] a mild excl., lit. *by Jesus!*

bejaney-mack-tonight! *excl. see* JANEY MACK! *excl.*

bejazus *n.* (*also* **baby jesus, bejasus, bejeesus, bejeezus, bejesus, bejeysus, (bloody) Jesus, plazazus**) **1** [20C+] the life, the essence, the 'daylights'; esp. in phr. *beat/kick/knock the bejazus out of*. **2** a synon. for HELL, THE *phr.*

IN PHRASES

❑ **scare the bejazus out of** *v.* (*also* **scare the bejab(b)ers out of, scare the living (be)Jesus out of**) [1920s+] to terrify completely and utterly.

bejazus! *excl.* (*also* **bejasus! bejeesus! bejesus! b'jasus!**) [late 19C+] a mild excl., lit. *by Jesus!*

bejesus *adj.* [euph. for blasphemous SE *by Jesus!*] [late 19C+] (*US*) a general intensifier, esp. with implications of assurance, arrogance.

bejeysus *n. see* BEJAZUS *n.*

bejinks *n. see* BEJABERS *n.*

belagot *n.* [dial. *belagot*, tripes; lit. *belly-gut*] [1940s+] (*W.I.*) a large iron pot, used for cooking cow-tripes after butchering.

belch *n.* [SE *belch*, an eructation] **1** [late 17C–mid-19C] second-rate beer. **2** [late 17C–mid-19C] malt liquor. **3** [late 19C–1960s] (*US*) a noisy complaint. **4** [1930s] (*US*) a drunken vagrant.

belch *v.* [BELCH *n.* (3)] **1** [20C+] (*US*) to talk; to complain. **2** [20C+] (*US*) to inform on. **3** [1900s] to talk nonsense.

belcher *n.*[1] [the boxer Jim *Belcher* (d.1811), whose preferred adornments these were; since the 19C a *belcher* can be any spotted handkerchief] **1** [early–mid-19C] (*also* **belcher fogle, belcher wipe**) a costermonger's handkerchief, blue with white or occas. yellow spots [FOGLE *n.*]. **2** [mid-19C] a thick ring.

belcher *n.*[2] [BELCH *n.* (1)] [mid–late 19C] (*orig. showmen's*) a dedicated beer-drinker.

belcher *n.*[3] [BELCH *v.*] **1** [1900s–50s] (*US Und.*) an informer. **2** [1930s–60s] a complainant. **3** [1960s] (*S.Afr.*) a garrulous person.

belcher fogle/wipe *n. see* BELCHER *n.*[1] (1).

belfa *n.* (*also* **bellfa, bilfa**) [? Fr. *belle*, beautiful] [late 17C–early 18C] a prostitute.

belfry *n.* [backform. f. SE colloq. *have bats in the belfry*] [late 19C+] the head.

Belgie *n.* [abbr.; note a single early 17C SE use] [1910s+] a *Belgian*.

believer *n.* [1920s+] (*US*) a gullible person, who will believe whatever they are told; thus *make a believer (out of)*, to convince.

bell *n.*[1] **1** [late 16C] the penis. **2** [19C+] o'clock, usu. in pl., e.g. *eight bells*, eight o'clock [naut. use; a bell was struck to indicate the change in the day's watches]. **3** [1960s] (*US black*) personal notoriety, reputation [the image of a *bell* around a cat's neck, announcing its imminent arrival]. **4** [1970s] (*US*) a hotel doorman; a bellboy [? abbr. *bell captain*]. **5** *see* BELL END *n.* **6** *see* BUTTON *n.*[1] (1c).

IN COMPOUNDS

❑ **bell end** *n. see* separate entry. ❑ **bell shiner** *n.* [BELL END *n.* (1) + SE *shine*] [1990s+] homosexual anal intercourse. ❑ **bell topped** *adj.* [BELL END *n.* (1) + SE *topped*] [late 19C+] describing a penis that is larger at the top than it is at the base. ❑ **bell tower** *n.* [play on BELL END *n.* (1)] [1990s+] the shaft of the penis.

SE in slang uses

DERIVATIVES

❑ **beller** *n.* [it 'rings out'] [1970s] (*US*) a loud laugh. ❑ **belling** *n.* [the shape of a bell] [late 19C] the head of the penis.

IN COMPOUNDS

❑ **bell cow** *n. see* separate entry. ❑ **bell-foundered** *adj.* [the tolling of the execution bell at Newgate] [mid-19C] (*UK Und.*) condemned to death. ❑ **bellhop** *n.* (*also* **bellhopper**) [they 'hop to it' when the desk clerk rings the bell] [20C+] (*US*) a hotel doorman, a bell-boy. ❑ **bellman** *n.* [1970s+] (*UK Und.*) the specialist who silences electronic alarm systems. ❑ **bell-ringer** *n.* [the fairground attraction in which one proves one's strength by hammering on a spring and, if successful, ringing a bell] [1930s–60s] (*US*) a great success. ❑ **bell rope** *n.* **1** [mid-19C] a fashionable hairstyle in which men wore their hair twisted into two ropes, on each side of the face [pun, such a hairstyle is designed to 'draw the belles']. **2** [1960s–70s] (*US*) the penis [it gets 'pulled']. ❑ **bell-topper** *n.* [TOPPER *n.*[3] (2)] [mid-19C–1940s] (*Aus./N.Z.*) a top hat. ❑ **bell-wether** *n. see* separate entry.

IN PHRASES

❑ **belled up** *adj.* [1970s] in possession of a burglar alarm. ❑ **bells and whistles** *n.* [1960s+] (*orig. US*) embellishments, gimmicks, esp. used in advertising copy to 'talk up' a product that, bereft of such add-ons, would have little to offer over its peers. ❑ **bell the cat** *v. see* separate entry. ❑ **crack a bell** *v.* [the belief that it is necessary to remain silent while casting a bell; the slightest sound may produce a flaw] [late 19C] to tell a secret, to betray a confidence. ❑ **crack the bell** *v.* [a *cracked* bell is useless as it cannot ring] [late 19C–1900s] to muddle, to ruin, to blunder. ❑ **from the bell** *adv.* [boxing imagery, a bell sounds the beginning of a new round] [1970s] (*orig. US*) from the beginning. ❑ **give someone a bell** *v.* [1930s+] to call on the telephone. ❑ **hop bells** *v.* [backf. f. *BELLHOP* above] [1920s–60s] (*US*) to work as a hotel porter. ❑ **knock seven bells out of** *v.* (*also* **knock thunder out of, scare seven bells out of**) **1** [mid-19C+] to beat viciously. **2** [1940s+] to terrify. ❑ **on the bell** **1** [early 19C] on credit. **2** [1970s+] (*Scot.*) buying (a round of drinks). ❑ **ring a bell** *v.* [1930s+] to remind one of something, to jog one's memory. ❑ **ring someone's bell** *v.* **1** [1910s+] to make a woman orgasm during intercourse. **2** [1930s+] to make a woman pregnant. **3** [1930s+] to appeal to, to impress, to carry any weight with, usu. in negative. **4** [1940s+] (*US*) (*also* **blow someone's horn**) to attract sexually, e.g. *She really rings my bell*. **5** [1960s+] (*orig. US*) (*also* **ring someone's hat**) to concuss, esp. in US football use when this may well follow a clash of helmets. ❑ **ring the bell** *v.* [the 'try-your-strength' machine found at a trad. fairground] [20C+] to carry off the prize; to be the best of a lot; to be acquitted. ❑ **ring the bell on** *v.* (*also* **ring the tinkler on**) [boxing imagery] [1900s–40s] (*US*) to dismiss, to declare useless. ❑ **saved by the bell** *adj.* [boxing imagery; a bell sounds at the end of a round] [1940s+] (*US*) rescued or relieved at the last minute. ❑ **toll the bell on** *v.* [the church bell that tolls the death-knell] [1900s] to put an end to, to forbid. ❑ **with bells on** (*also* **with tits on**) [? the bells that adorned a jester's outfit or the practice in Old West of outfitting the lead animals of a freight-hauling team with bells, to announce their presence and thus minimize accidents] **1** [late 19C+] in a joyous mood, enthusiastic. **2** [20C+] (*US*) (*also* **with bells**) definitely, without doubt; as a negative retort. **3** [1960s+] (*also*

with spangles) with melodramatic, lurid and otherwise exciting embellishments.

bell *n.*[2] [abbr. SE *bellow*] [mid-19C] a song.

bell *v.* (*also* **bell up**) [backform. f. GIVE SOMEONE A BELL *under* BELL *n.*[1]] [1930s+] to call on the telephone.

bella *adj.* [abbr. SE *bellicose*] [2000s] (*S.Afr. gay*) violent; also as v., to assault; thus *bella-bashing*, 'gay-bashing'; *bella queen*, a violent man.

bell-bastard *n.* [? pfx *bel*, indicating relationship, as used in SE *belfader*, *beldame*, grandfather, grandmother] [late 19C] the bastard child of a bastard mother.

bell cow *n.* [rural *bell cow*, the lead cow or ox, which wears a bell and is the herd leader] [19C] (*US*) a leader, a boss.

belle *n.* [Fr. *belle*, a beautiful woman] [1930s+] (*gay*) a good-looking, young homosexual.

belle-chose *n.* [Fr. *belle chose*, a beautiful thing; coined by Geoffrey Chaucer (*c.*1345–1400)] [late 14C] a lit. euph. for the vagina.

bell end *n.* (*also* **bell, bell ender**) [the shape] **1** [1980s+] the tip of the penis. **2** [1990s+] thus, a general term of abuse.

beller-croaker *adj.* [Fr. *belle à croquer*, beautiful enough to command desire] [mid–late 19C] noticeably beautiful, outstandingly attractive.

bellers *n. see* BELLOWS *n.* (1).

bellfa *n. see* BELFA *n.*

bellibone *n.* [Fr. *belle et bonne*, beautiful and good] [1910s–20s] a well-dressed young woman.

bellier *n.* [lit. 'belly-er'] **1** [early 19C] a punch to the belly. **2** [1920s] a 'belly-flop' dive.

bellower *n.* [SE *bellow*, to shout loudly] [late 18C–early 19C] a town crier.

bellows *n.* [SE *bellows*, 'an instrument or machine constructed to furnish a strong blast of air' (*OED*)] **1** [early 17C–1920s] (*also* **bellers**) the lungs [20C use mainly US]. **2** [late 18C] the male genitals. **3** [late 19C] a song.

IN PHRASES

❑ **bellows to mend** *adj.* [late 18C–1910s] used to describe a broken-winded horse or human.

bellowsed *adj.* [mid-19C] **1** out of breath [BELLOWS *n.* (1)]. **2** transported as a convict [? 'blown away' (across the sea) or see BELLOWSER *n.* (2)].

bellowser *n.* **1** [early 19C] a punch in the stomach, a 'blow in the wind'; thus *bellowsing*, n. winding in order to kill [BELLOWS *n.* (1)]. **2** [early–mid-19C] (*Aus./UK Und.*) a sentence of lifetime transportation; thus *knap/nap a bellowser*, to be transported for life [such a sentence 'takes one's breath away'].

bell ringers *n.* [rhy. sl.] [20C+] the fingers.

bells *n.*[1] [abbr.] [1940s+] *bell*-bottomed trousers.

bells *n.*[2] [supposed resemblance] [1970s] the female breasts.

bells! *excl.* [abbr. HELL'S BELLS! *under* HELL *n.*] [1920s+] (*orig. US black*) a general excl. of alarm, anger, surprise.

bellswagger *n.* (*also* **belswagger**) [one who 'swaggers his belly'; Nares cites one 'St. Belswagger of Mims' but cannot offer any information on 'the history of this canonised person'] **1** [late 16C–mid-18C] a womanizer, a pimp. **2** [late 16C–early 19C] a noisy braggart, a bully.

bell the cat *v.* [the nursery tale; SE f. 19C+] [18C] to undertake something dangerous.

bell-wether *n.* [SE *bell-wether*, the leading sheep of a flock, on whose neck a bell is hung] **1** [mid-15C–mid-18C] the leader of a mob. **2** [mid-15C–late 19C] a very noisy man; thus *bell-wetherishness*, noisiness.

belly *n.* **1** [early 19C; 1940s] the vagina. **2** [1920s–60s] (*US*) bravery, courage [var. on GUT *n.* (2a)]. **3** *see* BELLY LAUGH below.

SE in slang uses

DERIVATIVES

❑ **bellyful** *n.* [ext. of SE use; rendered colloq. only because *belly* itself is considered coarse] **1** [late 14C+] (*also* **bellyfull**) a sufficiency (the implication is of 'more than enough'), whether of food or drink or something else of which the subject has lost patience/interest through repetition; often as *have a bellyful of*. **2** [mid-17C–1920s] a thrashing [one has had a *bellyful* of pain].

IN COMPOUNDS

❑ **bellyache** *see* separate entries. ❑ **belly-bachelor** *n.* [a rich wife will help pay the food bills] [20C+] (*Irish*) a man whose amorous pursuits are determined by the income of each potential female. ❑ **belly-band** *n. see under* BAND *n.*[2]. ❑ **belly block** *n.* [mid-19C] (*UK Und.*) food. ❑ **belly-bomber** *n.* [1980s+] (*US*) a hamburger, esp. when particularly greasy. ❑ **belly-bound** *adj.* [SE *bound*, constipated] [17C–19C] usu. of horses, constipated. ❑ **bellybreakers** *n.* [1950s] (*W.I.*) braces. ❑ **belly bristles** *n.* [19C] pubic hair. ❑ **belly bump/-bumper** *see* separate entries. ❑ **belly burglar** *n.* (*also* **belly robber, gut burglar, stomach robber**) [orig. milit. jargon, the trad. meanness of cooks] [20C+] (*Can./US*) a cook or steward. ❑ **belly bust** *v. see* BELLY BUMP *v.* (1). ❑ **belly-buster** *n.* (*also* **belly-smacker**) [BURSTER *n.*[1]] **1** [1940s+] (*Aus./US*) a dive that knocks the wind from the diver [var. on BELLYFLOP *n.*]. **2** [1960s] a belly-laugh. **3** [1980s] (*US*) a large hero sandwich or 'submarine'. **4** [1980s] a very funny joke. ❑ **belly button** *n.* [mid-19C+] (*US*) the navel, esp. in juv. use; thus *my belly button is playing hell with my backbone*, I am very hungry. ❑ **belly cheat** *n.* (*also* **belly chete, belly-chit**) **1** [mid-16C–mid-19C] (*UK Und.*) an apron [CHEAT *n.* (1); lit. 'stomach thing']. **2** [early 17C] food [CHEAT *n.* (1); lit. 'stomach thing']. **3** [early 19C] padding worn by a woman in the hope of counterfeiting pregnancy [SE *cheat*]. ❑ **belly cheater** *n.* [the trad. meanness of cooks] [1910s+] (*US*) a cook. ❑ **belly chere** *n.* (*also* **belly cheer**) [mid-16C–mid-17C] food; thus *belly-cheering*, eating and drinking. ❑ **belly dale** *n.* [SE *dale*, a (river) valley] [late 19C] the vagina. ❑ **belly dingle** *n.* [SE *dingle*, a wooded hollow, a deep narrow cleft between hills] [late 19C] the vagina. ❑ **belly entrance** *n.* [late 19C] the vagina; one of a number of terms relating the vagina to an entrance. ❑ **belly fiddle** *n.* [the normal fiddle or violin is held beneath the chin, while the guitar is strapped across the stomach] [1900s–40s] (*US black*) a guitar. ❑ **bellyflop** *see* separate entries. ❑ **belly-fucker** *n.* [FUCK *v.* (1)] [1970s+] (*US gay*) **1** a homosexual man attracted to men with taut stomachs. **2** a homosexual man who achieves ejaculation by rubbing his penis on his partner's stomach. ❑ **belly furniture** *n.* [SE *furniture*; that with which something is stocked or filled; contents] [mid-17C] food. ❑ **belly grease** *n.* [lit. 'stomach-fat'] [1930s] (*US*) hard liquor. ❑ **belly-grunting** *n.* [one 'grunts' with pain] [1920s+] (*Aus.*) a bad stomach-ache. ❑ **belly gun** *n.* [such a gun can be tucked into one's waistband and/or pressed against the victim's waist] [1920s+] (*orig. US*) a small gun that is most effective when fired at short range, esp. when aimed at a victim's abdomen. ❑ **belly-gut** *n.* [the greediness is implied in the redup., lit. 'stomach-stomach'] [mid-16C–mid-18C] a greedy, lazy person. ❑ **belly habit** *n.* [HABIT *n.* (3)] [1940s+] (*drugs*) pains in the stomach that may accompany withdrawal from continued heroin use. ❑ **belly laugh** *n.* (*also* **belly, belly-shaking laugh**) [it appears to come from deep in the stomach] [1920s+] **1** a deep, sonorous laugh; also as v. **2** a joke. ❑ **belly-patch** *n.* [late 19C] a chef, a cook. ❑ **belly-paunch** *n.* [var. on BELLY-GUT above] [mid-16C–17C] a glutton. ❑ **belly-piece** *n.* [SE *piece*] **1** [17C] a prostitute, a mistress [but note PIECE *n.* (1a)]. **2** [17C–18C] an apron. ❑ **belly plea** *n.* [18C] a plea, offered by a female criminal facing the death sentence, that since she is pregnant, the law should spare her unborn child's life; thus *plead one's belly*, to make such an entreaty. ❑ **belly queen** *n.* [QUEEN *n.* (2a)/-QUEEN *sfx* (3)] [1960s+] (*US gay*) **1** a gay man who enjoys face-to-face intercourse, usu. between the partner's thighs. **2** one who rubs his penis on his partner's stomach to produce ejaculation. **3** one who only likes partners with flat, hard stomachs. ❑ **belly robber** *n. see* BELLY BURGLAR above. ❑ **belly-robbing** *adj.* [the assumption that one's money is needed for food] [1920s] (*US tramp*) cheating, extortionate. ❑ **belly rub** *n.* [BELLY RUB below] [1920s+] (*US*) a dance. ❑ **belly rub** *v.* [1920s+] (*US*) to dance close to one's partner. ❑ **belly ruffian** *n.* (*also* **ruffian**) [affectionate play on SE] [late 17C–19C] the penis. ❑ **belly-smacker** *n. see* BELLY-BUSTER above. ❑ **belly strippers** *n. see* STRIPPERS *n.* ❑ **belly timber** *n.* (*also* **tummy-timber**) [SE *timber*, the 'stuff' of which a person is made; note that *HDAS* adds a single 1970s citation, from

American Speech] [early 17C–19C] food. ❑ **belly vengeance** *n.* [East Anglian dial. *bellywengins*] **1** [mid-19C] weak, sour beer, often the cause of stomach upsets; thus the stomach upset itself. **2** [1930s] spirits. ❑ **belly wash/-washer** *n. see* separate entries. ❑ **belly whiskers** *n.* [late 19C] the female pubic hair. ❑ **belly whopper** *n.* [WHOP! *excl.*] [1910s+] (*US*) a dive, usu. into water, but also onto the ground. ❑ **belly-woman** *n.* [1950s+] (*W.I.*) **1** an unmarried pregnant woman. **2** in fig. use of sense 1, a cutlass with a rounded blade.

IN PHRASES

❑ **bellies in blue** *n. see* BOYS IN BLUE *n.* ❑ **belly-ache belfry** *n. see* separate entry. ❑ **belly and back** *adv.* [lit. 'on both sides'] [20C+] (*W.I., Guyn.*) utterly, completely, ruthlessly. ❑ **belly-bottom concrete** *n.* [its weight and consistency] [1950s+] (*W.I.*) a very large, round boiled dumpling. ❑ **belly full and behind drunk** *adj.* [BEHIND *n.* (1)] [20C+] (*W.I.*) immobile, incapable of movement after a large meal and a good deal to drink. ❑ **belly-go-firster** *n.* (*also* **belly-go-fister, belly-go-fuster**) [early–mid-19C] a blow to the stomach, esp. one given with no warning, or at the start of a fight. ❑ **belly-shaking laugh** *n. see* BELLY LAUGH above. ❑ **belly-to-belly** *adj. see* PLAY AT BELLY-TO-BELLY *under* PLAY (AT)... *v.* ❑ **belly up** *see* separate entries. ❑ **belly up to** *v.* [the pushing forward of one's stomach] [20C+] to move straight towards, to approach directly. ❑ **close to one's belly** *adj.* [1920s–40s] (*US*) almost totally impoverished, very poor. ❑ **dash away belly** *v. see* THROW AWAY BELLY below. ❑ **first belly pain** *n.* [1950s] (*W.I.*) one's first-born child. ❑ **get a belly** *v.* (*also* **grow a belly**) [20C+] (*US/W.I.*) to become noticeably pregnant. ❑ **give a belly** *v.* [mid-17C; 20C+] (*W.I.*) to make a woman pregnant. ❑ **go belly-bumping** *v.* [19C] to have sexual intercourse; thus *get a belly-bumper/belly-buster*, to become pregnant. ❑ **have a belly rash** *v.* [the result of being a 'crawler'] [1990s+] (*Aus.*) to be a sycophant. ❑ **have one's belly boil** *v.* [the rush of adrenaline] [20C+] (*W.I., Gren.*) to be very frightened. ❑ **have one's belly touching one's back** *v.* [20C+] (*W.I.*) to be absolutely starving. ❑ **put a man in one's belly** *v.* [late 16C–early 17C] of a woman, to permit sexual intercourse. ❑ **rub bellies** *v.* **1** [1930s–60s] to have sexual intercourse. **2** [1970s+] (*US gay*) to indulge in an act of frottage. ❑ **rub belly** *n.* [18C–19C] sexual intercourse. ❑ **run belly** *v.* [1990s+] (*W.I.*) to cause diarrhoea. ❑ **throw away belly** *v.* (*also* **dash away belly**) [20C+] (*W.I.*) to procure an abortion, to terminate a pregnancy.

IN EXCLAMATIONS

❑ **belly up!** *see* separate entry.

belly, the *n.* [1990s+] (*W.I.*) a pregnancy.

belly-ache *n.* [SE 16C–early 19C] [mid-16C+] a stomach-ache.

bellyache *n.* [BELLYACHE *v.*; note WW1 Aus. milit. *belly-ache*, a fatal wound] [1930s+] a complaint, a moan, whingeing.

bellyache *v.* [play on SE] [late 19C+] to complain, to moan; thus adj. *belly-aching*, complaining, whingeing.

DERIVATIVES

❑ **belly-acher** *n.* [20C+] a whinger, a whiner. ❑ **bellyaching** *n.* [1920s+] complaining, whingeing.

belly-ache belfry *n.* [BELLYACHE *n.*] [mid-19C] (*UK Und.*) a lawyer's mouth.

belly bump *v.* **1** [late 19C+] (*also* **belly bust**) to have sexual intercourse; one of a number of terms relating to the proximity of stomachs during the act [note the saucily punning ballad 'The Maiden's Choice' (1755): 'And the tune that he plays is called belly pat']. **2** [1910s] (*US*) to slide downhill, face-down on a sledge.

belly bumper *n.* [BELLY BUMP *v.* (1)] [19C] a womanizer, a promiscuous man.

bellyflop *n.* **1** [19C+] (*US*) the act of throwing oneself face-down onto a sledge before coasting downhill; also (US) *belly-bumbo, belly-bumper, belly-flounders, belly-flumps, belly-guts, belly plumper.* **2** [1920s+] (*also* **belly flopper, belly-thumper**) a dive in which one lands flat on the belly (and, in extreme circumstances, winds oneself), rather than cutting through the water; also used fig.

bellyflop *v.* [fig. use of BELLYFLOP *n.*] [1920s+] to throw oneself down; to collapse, to fail badly.

belly up *adj.*[1] [the shape of her stomach] [17C–1900s] of a woman, pregnant.

belly up *adj.*[2] [resembling a dead fish] **1** [1920s+] failed, finished, esp. bankrupt; usu. prefaced by *go.* **2** [1930s+] dead; thus v. *knock belly-up*, to kill. **3** [1970s] drunk.

belly up *v.* [BELLY UP *adj.*[2] (2)] [1980s+] (*US*) to die.

belly up! *excl.* (*also* **belly (up) to the bar boys!**) [*BELLY UP TO under* BELLY *n.*] [1920s–30s] (*Can./US*) the drinks are on the house!

belly wash *n.* [SE *belly* + *wash*, kitchen swill, liquid food for animals] (*US*) **1** [late 19C–1960s] a soft drink. **2** [1900s–30s] a weak or bad alcoholic drink. **3** [1930s–40s] soup. **4** [late 19C+] (*US*) nonsense.

belly-washer *n.*[1] **1** [20C+] (*US*) a soft drink [BELLY WASH *n.* (1)]. **2** [1960s] wine [BELLY WASH *n.* (2)].

belly-washer *n.*[2] [1960s–70s] (*US*) a dive in which one lands flat on the belly (and, in extreme circumstances, winds oneself), rather than cutting through the water.

belonger *n.* [the value of African roots to a perceived sense of blackness] [1990s+] a person of African descent living in the West Indies.

belong to Greater London *v.* [a play on SE *Greater London*, the suburbs immediately surrounding the capital and included with the central districts when assessing its population] [late 19C] to be well known in the metropolis.

below! *excl. see* BILL-O! *excl.*

below Nathaniel *adv.* [*Nathaniel*, Satan (Ware) or f. rhy. sl. = hell (*DSUE*)] [late 19C–1910s] even further 'down' than the supposed situation of hell.

below par *adj.* [Stock Exchange jargon *below par*, at a discount] **1** [19C+] unwell, emotionally low. **2** [1900s] less than successful. **3** [1920s] of less than average intelligence.

below the mahogany *adj. see under* MAHOGANY *n.*

bel-shangle *n.* [? SE *bell-jangler*, a fool capering with cap and bells] [late 16C–early 17C] a fool.

belswagger *n. see* BELLSWAGGER *n.*

belt *n.* [lit. and fig. uses of BELT *v.* (1)] **1** [mid-19C+] a blow, a hit, a punch. **2** [1920s+] a drink of, a swig or swallow of e.g. a *belt of coffee.* **3** [1930s+] (*drugs*) the immediate effect of a drug, usu. one that has been injected. **4** [1930s+] a thrill. **5** [1940s–60s] a measure of marijuana or any other drug. **6** [1940s–60s] an act of sexual intercourse. **7** [1950s] (*Aus.*) a prostitute. **8** [1950s] a sexually appealing woman.

IN PHRASES

❑ **belt of the crozier** *n.* [1990s+] a reprimand from the Church, spec. from a bishop. ❑ **get the belt** *v.* [*see* GIVE SOMEONE THE BELT below] [1920s+] to be rejected, to be jilted. ❑ **give someone the belt** *v.* (*also* **give someone the Lonsdale (belt)**) [the *Lonsdale belt*; thus a pun on BELT *v.* (1); the belt itself, given to a boxing champion, is named for Hugh Cecil Lowther (1857–1944), 5th earl of Lonsdale] [1930s+] (*orig. Aus.*) to get rid of, to throw out, to dismiss, to reject, to jilt.

SE in slang uses

IN PHRASES

❑ **below the belt** *adj.* [boxing use, which declares such blows as foul; 20C+ use is SE] [late 19C] underhand, illegal, cheating. ❑ **belt up** *v.* [one wraps a fig. 'belt' around one's mouth] [1930s+] (*orig. RAF*) to be quiet, esp. in excl. *belt up!* shut up! ❑ **hold the belt** *v.* [boxing imagery] [late 19C–1910s] (*Aus.*) to be the outstanding example, the 'champion'. ❑ **lower one's belt** *v.* [1960s] (*US gay*) to be a promiscuous 'feminine' lesbian. ❑ **take the belt** *v.* [boxing imagery: the belt awarded to a champion] [late 19C] (*US teen*) to be exceptional, to 'take the biscuit'. ❑ **unbelt** *v.* [SE *unbelt*, to remove a sword] [late 19C–1920s] (*US*) to hand over money. ❑ **under one's belt** (*also* **below one's belt**) **1** [late 18C; mid-19C+] in one's stomach, swallowed. **2** [20C+] personally achieved or experienced.

belt *v.* [sense 1: lit. to hit with a belt; senses 2–5 fig. uses of sense 1] **1** [early 19C+] (*also* **belt out, belt up**) to hit (with a fist), to flog, to thrash. **2** [mid-19C+] to drink heavily, esp. straight from the bottle. **3** [late 19C+] (*also* **belt along**) to rush, to hurry. **4** [1960s] to trounce, to defeat soundly. **5** [1960s+] of a man, to have sexual intercourse.

DERIVATIVES

❑ **belter** *n.* **1** [1900s] a prostitute. **2** [1950s+] an admirable, exciting, or exceptional person [northern dial. *belter*, a heavy blow or series of blows]. **3** [1950s+] something exceptional, exciting, amusing etc. **4** [1950s+] a boisterous, energetic singer [*BELT IT OUT* below]. **5** [1950s+] a loud, emotional and melodramatic song [*BELT IT OUT* below]. ❑ **belting** *n.* [19C+] a beating. ❑ **belting** *adj.* [1950s+] excellent, very good of its type.

IN COMPOUNDS

❑ **belt-up** *n.* [1960s] a fight.

IN PHRASES

❑ **at full belt** *adv.* [1960s] at full speed. ❑ **belt along** *v. see* sense 3 above. ❑ **belt down** *v.* **1** [20C+] to rain very hard. **2** [2000s] (*N.Z.*) to drink quickly. ❑ **belt into** *v.* [1960s] to eat heartily. ❑ **belt it** *v.* **1** [1940s+] to masturbate. **2** [1970s] to drive exceptionally fast. ❑ **belt it out** *v.* [1950s+] to sing loudly and enthusiastically. ❑ **belt one on** *v.* [2000s] (*N.Z.*) to get very drunk. ❑ **belt one's batter** *v. see under* BATTER *n.*[1]. ❑ **belt one's hog** *v. see under* HOG *n.* ❑ **belt out** *v.* **1** [1910s] (*Aus.*) to create, to gain, to make. **2** [1910s+] (*orig. Aus.*) to sing lustily; to broadcast noisily. **3** [1930s] (*US*) to eat heartily. **4** [1940s+] (*US*) to knock down, to destroy. **5** [1960s+] (*US*) to murder. **6** *see* sense 1 above. ❑ **belt the bottle** *v.* [1930s+] (*orig. US*) to drink heavily. ❑ **belt the grape** *v.* [1930s+] to drink heavily. ❑ **belt up** *v. see* sense 1 above.

Belteshazzar's off-ox *n.* [see Dan. 4:8–27, in which Daniel, also known as Belteshazzar, foretells Nebuchadnezzar's decline into a state of ox-like stupidity] [mid-19C+] a headstrong person.

beltinker *n.* [? BELT *v.* (1); i.e. a *belting*] [late 19C] a beating, a thrashing.

belty *adv.* [? fig. use of BELT *v.* (1)] [1950s] (*UK prison*) enthusiastically.

beluthahatchie *n.* [elision of B. LUTHER HATCHETT *n.*] [1940s] (*US*) the ultimate in far-away, unpleasant places.

belvidere *n.* [the statue of the *Apollo Belvedere*] [late 19C–1900s] a good-looking man.

belyando spew *n.* [*Belyando* River, in central Queensland + SE *spew*, vomit] [late 19C–1940s] (*Aus.*) a rural sickness, mainly in Queensland.

belyando sprue *n.* [a popular 'home-grown' crop in the *Belyando* River area of Queensland] [1970s+] (*Aus. drugs*) marijuana.

b.e.m. *n.* [abbr.] [1950s+] (*orig. US*) *bug-eyed monster/monsters*; a popular category of SF writing and described as such by fans.

bembe *n.* [? *bam-boy* or Sp. *bemba*, a black person's thick lips or *Bemba*, a Central African people] [20C+] (*W.I.*) a bully, a large, strong person of either sex.

be missing! *excl.* [a phr. first used by Chicago mobster Spike O'Donnell in rejecting the overtures/threats of Al Capone (1899–1947); but note Schele de Vere, *Americanisms* (1872): 'Missing, to be found, denotes, in Western parlance, to be absent, or to run away'] [1920s+] (*US*) go away!

bemused (with beer) *adj.* [mid-18C–late 19C] drunk.

be my guest *phr.* (*also* **be my Georgie Best**) [the rhy. sl. version rhymes on the celebrated UK footballer, *George Best* (1946–2005)] [1950s+] (*orig. US*) a phr. of encouragement (esp. in response to a request to borrow something), go ahead, 'feel free', 'help yourself', 'make yourself at home' etc.

ben *n.*[1] [? link to BENE *adj.*; thus 'good fellow'] [late 17C–mid-19C] (*UK Und.*) a simpleton, a fool.

DERIVATIVES

❑ **benish** *adj.* (*also* **bennish**) [late 17C–18C] foolish.

ben *n.*[2] [abbr.] **1** [early 19C–1900s] (*orig. theatr.*) a benefit, i.e. 'a theatrical performance the receipts from which are given to a particular actor, the playwright, or some other person connected with the theatre' (*OED*). **2** [1900s] *benefit*.

IN PHRASES

❑ **stand ben** *v.* [STAND *v.*[2] (2)] [early 19C] to treat one's companions at an inn or tavern.

ben *n.*[3] [Ital. proverb *se non e vero, e ben trovato*, even if it is not true, it is a happy invention; this was anglicized as *benjamin trovato*, a lie, then shortened to *ben trovato*, *ben tro* and finally *ben*] [late 19C] (*UK society*) a lie.

ben *n.*[4] [abbr. BENJAMIN *n.*[1]] [late 19C–1930s] a coat, a waistcoat.

ben bouse *n. see BENE BOUSE under* BENE *adj.*

ben-bowsy *adj.* [*BENE BOUSE under* BENE *adj.*] [early 17C] drunk.

Ben Cartwright *n.* [rhy. sl.; US TV 'Bonanza' character *Ben Cartwright* = SHITE *n.* (7)] [2000s] nonsense, rubbish.

Bench, the *n.* [abbr.] [early 19C] the King's Bench prison.

bench *n.*

SE in slang uses

DERIVATIVES

❑ **bencher** *n.* **1** [late 19C+] (*US*) any idle or ineffectual person. **2** [1930s] (*US Und.*) one who visits opium dens, but only to observe, not smoke.

IN COMPOUNDS

❑ **bench-legged** *adj.* [legs that could straddle a bench] [1900s] (*US*) of people, but more usu. of dogs, bowlegged. ❑ **bench-man** *n.* (*also* **bench nibs**) [the SE *bench* on which they sit + *man*] [1960s] (*US Und.*) a judge. ❑ **bench-points** *n.* [used of people but f. dog and cat shows where the animals are placed on a bench for judging] [late 19C–1900s] physical advantages. ❑ **bench-warmer** *n.* (*US*) **1** [late 19C+] any idle or ineffectual person. **2** [1910s–40s] (*also* **bench-flopper**) a tramp, a vagrant.

IN PHRASES

❑ **on the anxious bench** *adj.* (*also* **on the anxious seat**) [ecclesiastical jargon *anxious bench/seat*, a seat at the front of the church, near the pulpit, where those particularly concerned about their spiritual status – and willing to admit it – would sit at revival meetings] [19C–1950s] (*US*) worried, nervous.

bench *v.*[1] [1920s] (*US*) to sleep on a public bench.

bench *v.*[2] [1990s+] (*US black*) to criticize.

ben cull *n. see BENE CULL under* BENE *adj.*

bend *n.*[1] [? it 'bends' around the stomach] [late 19C–1910s] a waistcoat.

SE in slang uses

IN PHRASES

❑ **above one's bend** [the image is of an object beyond one's grasp or ? above, i.e. beyond, the bend of river on which one lives] [mid-19C] (*US*) beyond one's abilities. ❑ **bend of the filbert** *n.* [SE *bend* + pun on SE *filbert*, a nut] [18C] a bow of the head, a nod. ❑ **get the bend** *v.* [1940s] (*US*) to be imprisoned. ❑ **on the bend** *adj.* **1** [mid-19C–1940s] crooked, criminal, underhand [predates BENT *adj.* (2) but presumably its derivation]. **2** [1910s] at a disadvantage [the image is one who is bending over and may thus, unaware, be kicked]. **3** *see also ON A BEND under* BEND *n.*[2].

bend *n.*[2] [abbr. BENDER *n.*[2] (1)] [late 19C–1930s] a drunken spree.

IN PHRASES

❑ **on a bend** (*also* **on the bend**) [late 19C+] on a drinking spree.

bend *n.*[3] [? SE *bond/bind*] **1** [20C+] (*Anglo-Irish*) an appointment, a rendezvous [Partridge suggests the bow one gives when one meets]. **2** [1950s] a tip-off, information, as in phr. *give the bend*.

bend *n.*[4] [*BENT OUT OF SHAPE under* BENT *adj.*] [1960s] an experience created by a hallucinogenic drug.

bend *n.*[5] [? *BEND OVER (FOR) under* BEND *v.*[1]] [1990s+] (*rap music*) a prostitute.

bend *v.*[1] [? SE *bend*, i.e. to bend one's arm; or ? SE *bend*, to apply oneself, to pull or strain] [mid-18C] to drink hard; thus n., *bender*, a drinker.

SE in slang uses

IN PHRASES

❑ **bend down for** *v.* [late 19C+] to consent to buggery. ❑ **bend-down plaza** *n.* [the customers have to *bend down* + sarcastic use of *Plaza*, often used as the name of a shopping mall] [20C+] (*W.I., Jam.*) a row of roadside peddlers, specializing in items that are hard to get in shops, because of import restrictions. ❑ **bend one's back** *v.* [1920s–30s] (*Aus./US*) to work hard. ❑ **bend one's elbow** *v.* (*also* **bend the elbow**) [the physical action of tipping up a glass] [20C+] to have a drink, thus *elbow-bending*, drinking. ❑ **bend over (for)** *v.* (*also* **b.o.**) [1950s+] **1** to submit to, to lay oneself open; the image is of submitting to buggery, but the popular use is less specific. **2** to get into difficulties, to be put at a disadvantage; also as an excl. *bend over!* you're bothering me! **3** to make a confession to the police. **4** to sodomize. ❑ **bend over backwards** *v.* (*also* **lean over backwards, fall over backwards**) [1920s+] to go out of one's way to do something, usu. altruistically. ❑ **bend some ham** *v.* [SE *bend* + *hams*, the buttocks] [1980s+] (*US gay*) to have anal intercourse. ❑ **bend up** *v.* [the bending up of the arms behind the back prior to removing the fighters] [1990s+] (*UK prison*) to beat up. ❑ **catch someone bending** *v.* [20C+] to catch someone at a disadvantage.

bend *v.*[2] [ext. of SE; i.e. to *bend* the rules] **1** [1920s+] to allow oneself to be corrupted. **2** [1930s] (*US Und.*) to steal. **3** [1930s+] (*also* **bend backwards**) to pervert, to corrupt, to commit some form of fraudulent manoeuvre, esp. as in losing a race deliberately, bribing a police officer or a sporting competitor. **4** [1980s] (*US*) to kill.

bend *v.*[3] [BENT *adj.* (1)] [1960s] (*US drugs*) to betray the effects of a given drug.

bended knees *n.* [rhy. sl.] [1950s+] cheese.

bender *n.*[1] [SE *bend*] **1** in monetary uses [the ease with which the thin metal could be bent; Bee: 'Bender [...] takes its name from the form, the usual shape of the old coin, which were bent, twice, adversely, presenting the appearance at the edge of the letter (*s*)']. (**a**) [late 18C–1930s] a sixpence (2½p). (**b**) [early–mid-19C] a shilling (5p). **2** as parts of the body [their physical functions as joints]. (**a**) [mid-19C–1940s] the arm. (**b**) [mid-19C–1940s] the elbow; often in phr. *OVER THE BENDER* below. (**c**) [mid-19C+] the leg [lapsed in mainstream sl. by 1900 but adopted by US blacks c.1940]. (**d**) [1940s–50s] the knee. **3** as a homosexual, and related uses [note *Guild Dict.* (1965): '*bender*: A homosexual who submits to passive anal intercourse']. (**a**) [1940s+] a male homosexual. (**b**) [1990s+] a term of abuse for an unpopular individual, esp. juv. (**c**) [2000s] (*N.Z.*) a Catholic [? link to sense 2, i.e. f. a Protestant perspective].

IN PHRASES

❑ **over the bender** ['it is historical in common English that a declaration made over the elbow as distinct from not over it need not be held sacred. Probably from early Christian if not pagan times. The bender is always the left elbow...' (Ware). Note also the Victorian custom of 'over the left', i.e. pointing with one's right thumb over one's left shoulder, implying disbelief] [mid-19C–1900s] a phr. implying that the previous statement is untrue.

bender *n.*[2] [? the image of a drunkard (or drug user) as unsteady on their feet; or ? f. an image of bending a bow or elbow. Note naut. jargon *benjo*, a spree, f. Ital./Lingua Fr. *buengiorno*, a good day] **1** [mid-19C+] a bout of riotous drinking, often lasting several days and including random acts of excess, violence etc; thus *ON A BENDER* below. **2** [late 19C] (*US*) a rampage. **3** [late 19C–1910s] anything exceptional, astounding. **4** [1920s] (*US*) an excessive bout of eating.

IN PHRASES

❑ **on a bender** *adj.* **1** [mid-19C+] on a drinking spree. **2** [20C+] on any other kind of spree. **3** [1930s+] bingeing on drugs.

bender *n.*[3] [BENT *adj.* (4)] **1** [1930s] (*US Und.*) a thief, a cheat. **2** [1930s+] a stolen car. **3** [2000s] a robbery.

bender *n.*[4] [rhy. sl. = *suspender*] [1980s] (*UK Und*) a suspended prison sentence.

bender! *excl.* [ety. unknown; note WW1 RN *bender*, a yarn, a tale] [early 19C] nonsense! humbug! rubbish!

bendigo *n.* [the professional name of William Thompson (1811–89), the Nottingham prize-fighter who fought as *Bendigo* and ended his days as an evangelical preacher] [mid-19C] a rough fur cap.

bending and bowing *phr.* [BENT *adj.* (1)] [1930s–50s] (*US drugs*) experiencing the effects of a drug, esp. heroin.

bending edger *n.* [BENDER *n.*[1] (3a)] [1960s–70s] (*UK prison*) a boy who submits to homosexual advances, esp. from members of staff in an approved school.

bene *adj.* (*also* **bane, ben, been, bien**) [Lat. *bonus* and Fr. *bon*, good] [mid-16C–mid-19C] (*UK Und.*) good; it can be conjugated as *benar*, better and *benat*, best.

IN COMPOUNDS

❑ **bene bouse** *n.* (*also* **ben bouse, bene bowse**) [BOUSE *n.*] [mid-16C–mid-19C] drink, lit. good liquor; thus *bene-bowsy*, tipsy (with good drink). ❑ **bene cove** *n.* [COVE *n.* (1)] (*UK Und.*) **1** [17C–mid-19C] (*also* **bene cofe**) a friend, lit. 'a good fellow'; thus in cant, a fellow criminal. **2** [mid-19C] a tramp. ❑ **bene cull** *n.* (*also* **ben cull**) [CULL *n.*[1] (3)] [19C] a good fellow, a friend. ❑ **bene darkmans** [DARKMANS *n.*; Partridge in *DU* suggests 'ca. 1560 or even earlier. Not dictionaried, however, until 1698 (B.E.)'] [mid-16C–mid-19C] (*UK Und.*) good night. ❑ **bene mort** *n.* (*also* **bien mort**) [BENE *adj.* + MORT *n.* (1)] [17C–mid-19C] a pretty woman.

benedict *n.* (*also* **benedick**) [Shakespeare's character *Benedict* in *Much Ado About Nothing* (1599)] [late 18C–1910s] a married man, esp. a newly married man or a formerly confirmed bachelor who changes his mind.

beneek/beneekte *n.* see BENEUKT *adj.*

bene feaker *n.* (*also* **bene faker, ben faker, benfeaker**) [BENE *adj.* + FAKER *n.* (1); lit. 'good-maker'] [17C–mid-19C] a counterfeiter, initially of documents, later of money.

IN PHRASES

❑ **bene-feaker of gybes** *n.* [GYBE *n.* (1)] [late 17C–mid-19C] (*UK Und.*) a forger of passes and similar documents.

beneship *n.* (*also* **benship**) [BENE *adj.*; the term moved into SE by 18C, when Bailey's *Universal Etymological English Dict.* defined *beenship*, worship, goodness. Note Carew, *The History of Bampfylde Moore Carew* (1850), who defines 'beenship rat' as 'goodnight' in his list of Scot. gypsy terms] [mid-16C–17C] something that is very good.

DERIVATIVES

❑ **beneshiply** *adv.* (*also* **beenly**) **1** [17C] excellently. **2** [late 18C–early 19C] worshipfully.

beneukt *adj.* (*also* **beneek, beneekte**) [Du. *neuk*, to deceive, to push] [1960s+] (*S.Afr.*) **1** contrary, impossible. **2** bad-tempered, insane.

benevolence *n.* ['Ostentation and fear united, with hopes of retaliation in kind hereafter' (Bee)] [early 18C] (*UK society*) doing good for others in the hope that one will receive equal good in return; often as a euph. for sexual intercourse.

ben faker/benfeaker *n.* see BENE FEAKER *n.*

ben-flake *n.* [rhy. sl.] [mid-19C] a cheap beefsteak, 'used at a slap-bang, i.e. a low cook-shop or eating house'.

Ben Franklin *n.* (*also* **benjamin, Benjamin Franklin, Benny, Benny Franklin, franklin, Mr. Franklin, President Franklin**) [the portrait of Franklin printed on the note] [1930s+] (*US*) a $100 bill.

bengal lancers *n.* [pun on SE *Bengal Lancers*, an Indian Army regiment] [1930s–40s] (*Aus.*) razor gangs.

beni *n.* [20C+] (*US black*) human excrement; also fig. use.

benies *n.* (*also* **bennies**) [abbr.] [1940s+] (*US campus*) benefits, spec. those of the GI Bill that puts US service veterans through college for free; thus ext. as food.

benjamin *n.*[1] [? the name of a tailor; according to Hotten (1874), an acknowledgement of the many (Jewish) tailors thus named] [early–mid-19C] a coat.

benjamin *n.*[2] see BEN FRANKLIN *n.*

Benjamin Franklin *n.* see BEN FRANKLIN *n.*

benjamins *n.* [BEN FRANKLIN *n.*] [1990s+] (*US black*) money.

benji *n.* [the picture of *Benjamin* Franklin (1706–90) printed on the bill] [1980s+] a $100 bill.

benjy *n.* (*also* **benjie**) [abbr. BENJAMIN *n.*[1]] [early–mid-19C] a coat.

Bennett! *excl. see* GORDON BENNETT! *excl.*

bennickey bounce *n.* [mid-19C] (*UK Und.*) a swaggerer.

bennie *n.*[1] [? SE *bend down/over*] [1970s] (*US*) a prostitute's term for a client who prefers to give oral sex rather than have sexual intercourse.

bennie *n.*[2] *see* BENNY *n.*[4].

bennies *n.* **1** *see* BENIES *n.* **2** *see* BENNY *n.*[4].

bennish *adj. see* BENISH *under* BEN *n.*[1].

bennit-bound *adj.* [mid-19C] (*UK Und.*) safe.

benny *n.*[1] [black jazz musicians adopted *benny*, which entered mainstream black sl. as BENJAMIN *n.*[1] *c.*1940] **1** [mid-19C–1940s] (*orig. US naut.*) a straw hat. **2** [20C+] (*US*) (*also* **binny**) an overcoat.

IN COMPOUNDS

▫ **benny worker** *n.* [WORKER *n.*[1] (1)] [1920s–40s] (*US Und.*) a pickpocket or shoplifter who disguises their hands under an ovecoat.

benny *n.*[2] [? generic use of proper name] [1920s+] (*US*) a person, a fellow.

benny *n.*[3] [? they *bend over*/BEND OVER (FOR) *under* BEND *v.*[1]] **1** [1930s+] a male homosexual; also attrib. **2** [1970s] (*US gay*) as *steam bath benny*, a male homosexual who frequents steam baths.

IN COMPOUNDS

▫ **benny house** *n.* [note US milit. *benny*, a young male Filipino transvestite] [20C+] a brothel that essentially caters for heterosexuals but that will obtain male prostitutes on request.

benny *n.*[4] (*also* **bennie, bennies**) [abbr.] [1940s+] (*orig. US drugs*) Benzedrine; one pill of Benzedrine; thus *benny-head*, a Benzedrine user; also attrib.

benny *n.*[5] [a derog. ref. derived from an intellectually deficient rural character in the UK TV soap opera *Crossroads*] [1980s] **1** as used by the British Army, an inhabitant of the Falkland Islands. **2** thus, anyone seen as an unsophisicated peasant.

benny *n.*[6] [abbr.] [2000s] (*N.Z.*) one who lives on state *benefits*; thus *benny day*, the day on which such benefits are paid out.

Benny (Franklin) *n. see* BEN FRANKLIN *n.*

Benny Hill *n.* [rhy. sl.; ult. UK comedian *Benny Hill* (1925–92)] [1990s+] **1** a drill. **2** a till, a cash register. **3** a contraceptive pill.

benny mason *n.* (*also* **Mr Mason**) [such marijuana was kept sealed in *Mason* jars] [1990s+] (*US campus*) particularly strong marijuana.

beno *n.* ['there'll *be no* fun'; note WW2 USN *beeno*, there will beeno moving pictures tonight etc] [1950s+] the period of menstruation and thus, for many couples, no sex.

bens *n. see* BENZ *n.*

benship *n. see* BENESHIP *n.*

bent *n.* (*also* **bent-shot**) [BENT *adj.* (5)] [1950s+] a homosexual.

bent *adj.* [all fig. uses of SE + pun on BROKE *adj.*[1]] **1** [mid-19C+] intoxicated by liquor or [1930s+] drugs. **2** [1910s+] criminal; corrupt; thus *ON THE BEND under* BEND *n.*[1]; thus *bent copper*, *bent screw*, corrupt police officer, prison-warder. **3** [1910s] spoiled, ruined. **4** [1930s+] illegal, stolen. **5** [1950s+] sexually eccentric, esp. homosexual. **6** [1960s] impoverished, penniless. **7** [1960s+] (*orig. US*) eccentric, acting oddly, behaving in a strange manner. **8** [1960s+] (*US*) angry, excited; usu. in phr. *BENT OUT OF SHAPE* below. **9** in weak form of sense 5 above, weak, emotional.

IN COMPOUNDS

▫ **bent wrist** *n. see* LIMP WRIST *n.* (1).

IN PHRASES

▫ **bent as a butcher's hook** *adj.* (*also* **bent as a bootlace**) [1950s–70s] extremely corrupt, highly criminal. ▫ **bent as a dog's hind leg** *adj.* [1930s] highly corrupt. ▫ **bent as a nine-bob note** *adj.* (*also* **bent as a forty-eight pence piece**) [1960s+] **1** of a person, dishonest. **2** of an object, stolen. **3** homosexual. ▫ **bent as a two-bob watch** *adj.* [1980s] (*Aus.*) extremely corrupt. ▫ **bent out of shape** *adj.* [1960s+] **1** intoxicated by a drug, esp. cannabis or LSD, or extremely drunk. **2** very angry. **3** socially inept, embarrassing. ▫ **go bent** *v.* [1950s+] (*UK Und./prison*) **1** of a witness, to retract a previous statement (which would have helped the prosecution). **2** to become corrupt. **3** to turn to criminality. **4** of one's girlfriend, to take up with someone else. **5** to let down, to desert.

SE in slang uses

IN PHRASES

▫ **have someone bent** *v.* [2000s] (*US teen*) to misinterpret, to 'read' incorrectly. ▫ **take the bent stick** *v.* [1910s–30s] of a woman who may no longer be easily marriageable, to abandon one's hopes of a perfect partner, substituting instead an elderly but constant admirer.

IN EXCLAMATIONS

▫ **get bent!** [1950s+] (*US campus*) a general excl. of dismissal or contempt.

Benton's mint drops *n.* (*also* **Bentons**) [proper name Thomas Hart *Benton* (1792–1858), campaigner for a gold currency in US; the synon. sweet, a sugar-plum flavoured with peppermint + pun on MINT *n.*[1]] [early–mid-19C] (*US*) gold coin, usu. in pl.; *mint drops*, money.

bent-shot *n. see* BENT *n.*

bent up *adj.* [BENT *adj.* (7); ? pun on MASHED (ON) *adj.* (1)] [late 19C] (*US*) infatuated, obsessively in love.

Benz *n.* (*also* **benzie**) [abbr.] [1950s+] a Mercedes *Benz* automobile.

benz *n.* (*also* **bens, benzie**) [*Benzedrine* + ref. to a Mercedes Benz, which also 'makes one go fast'] **1** [1940s+] (*drugs*) amphetamine. **2** [2000s] MDMA.

DERIVATIVES

▫ **benzed** *adj.* [1950s] under the influence of benzedrine.

benzine *n.* [SE *benzine*, petroleum ether] **1** [mid-19C–1900s] (*US*) cheap 'rotgut' whisky; thus *hit the benzine can*, *maul the benzine*, to drink whisky to excess; *benzinery*, a saloon. **2** [20C+] (*W.I., Guyn./Trin.*) a form of unlicensed and very potent rum distilled secretly in the countryside.

benzine buggy *n.* (*also* **benzine brougham, benzine wagon, gasolene bronc, gasoline buggy, gasoline cart, gasoline go-cart, go-buggy**) [SE *benzine* + BUGGY *n.*[2] (1)] [1900s–20s] (*US*) an automobile.

benzo *n.*[1] [abbr.] [1980s+] (*US black*) a Mercedes *Benz* automobile.

benzo *n.*[2] [abbr.] [1990s+] (*drugs*) *Benzo*diopate.

be off *v.* [var. of SE *come off* or GO OFF *v.* (4)] [1960s] to happen, esp. of a violent incident.

be off (with you)! *excl.* [late 19C+] go away!

beong *n.* [Polari *bianco*, white; the shilling is a 'silver' coin] [mid-19C–1900s] one shilling (5p).

be out! *excl.* [1990s+] (*US black*) a general excl. of encouragement; enjoy yourself! have fun! GO FOR IT! *excl.*

Berdoo *n.* (*also* **San Bardoo, ...Berdoo**) [abbr.] [20C+] (*US*) San Bernardino, California.

bere *adj. see* BARE *adj.*

bereavement lurk *n.* [SE *bereavement* + LURK *n.* (3)] [mid–late 19C] a form of begging that depends on attracting sympathy for the fact that one's wife has supposedly just died.

berg *n. see* BURG *n.*[1].

bergie *n.* [Afk. *berg*, mountain] [1970s] (*S.Afr.*) a vagrant living on the slopes of Table Mountain, Cape Town; also attrib.

bergoo *n. see* BURGOO *n.*

berick *v.* [ety. unknown] [1980s+] (*US drugs*) to smoke an outsized marijuana pipe (2m (6ft) or longer).

berk *n.* (*also* **burk, burke**) [rhy. sl.; *Berkeley hunt* or *Berkshire hunt* = CUNT *n.*] [1930s+] a fool, an incompetent.

berk *adj.* [BERK *n.* (1)] [1980s+] stupid.

Berkeley (hunt) *n.* (*also* **Berkshire Hunt, Burlington Hunt**) [rhy. sl. *Berkeley hunt* or *Berkshire hunt* = CUNT *n.* (1)/CUNT *n.* (4)] **1** [late 19C+] the vagina. **2** [1930s+] a fool, an incompetent. **3** [1930s+] sexual intercourse.

berkeleys *n.* [Rom. *berk*, breast] [late 19C] the female breasts.

berkish *adv.* [1930s] like a BERK *n.*; stupidly.

berko *adj.* (*also* **berkers**) [abbr. SE *beserk* + -O *sfx* (4)] [1960s+] (*Aus./N.Z.*) berserk; in weakened form, temporarily out of control.

Berkshire hog *n.* [SE *Berkshire hog*, a large, dark-skinned pig] [1950s+] (*W.I.*) **1** an ugly person. **2** a very dark-complexioned black man.

Berkshire hunt *n. see* BERKELEY (HUNT) *n.*

berley *n.* (*also* **burley**) [? SE *berley*, ground bait / BURLEY *n.*[1]] (*Aus.*) **1** [1940s+] nonsense, humbug. **2** [2000s] vomit.

Bermondsey banger *n.* [*Bermondsey*, an area of south London + *banger*, one who both 'bangs' his fellows physically, and makes a 'bang' in society; the *Star* was a very popular inn-cum-music-hall] [late 19C–1900s] 'a society leader among the South London tanneries. He must frequent 'the Star', be prepared to hold his own and fight at all times for his social belt' (Ware).

Bermudas *n.* [proper name *Bermuda Islands*, where certain well-connected debtors fled to avoid their creditors. London's *Bermudas* were either the alleys and passageways running near Drury Lane, Covent Garden, and/or the Mint in Southwark] [early 17C–18C] certain areas of London that were considered safe havens for criminals and debtors.

bernice *n.* (*also* **bernies**) ['Possibly the term is based on *burnies*, referring to crystals of cocaine added to a tobacco cigarette and smoked' (Spears, *Slang and Jargon of Drugs and Drink*, 1986); note cocaine is a 'feminine' drug, see GIRL *n.*[2]] [late 19C+] (*US drugs*) cocaine in crystal form.

bernie *n.* [BERNICE *n.*] [late 19C+] (*US drugs*) cocaine.

bernie's flakes *n.* [BERNIE *n.* + SE *flake*] [1950s+] (*drugs*) cocaine.

berries *n.* **1** [1910s] (*US*) beans. **2** [1950s+] the testicles [Williams notes a number of 17C sexual riddles in which a *berry* represents the penis]. **3** [1970s+] (*US black*) wine. **4** *see* BERRY *n.*[1] (2).

berries, the *n.*[1] [fig. use of SE; but note Scot. *to be no the berry*, to be a bad character] [20C+] (*US*) **1** the best, the superlative. **2** as a negative, the ultimate, the last straw.

berries, the *n.*[2]

(IN PHRASES)

▫ **give the berries to** *v.* (*also* **slip the berries to, give someone the berries**) [RASPBERRY *n.*] [1920s–30s] (*US*) to deride, to insult.

berries, the *n.*[3]

(IN PHRASES)

▫ **give it the berries** *v. see* *GIVE IT THE HERBS* *under* HERBS *n.*[1].

berry *n.*[1] **1** [late 19C] (*US*) an easy opponent, anyone seen as 'soft'. **2** [1910s–40s] (*US*) $1, usu. in pl. **3** [1920s] (*US drugs*) a capsule of a powdered drug, e.g. heroin. **4** [1930s] (*US*) a person. **5** [1930s] a £1 note. **6** [1930s] (*US Und.*) an attractive female. **7** [1970s+] (*US black*) a woman's nipple. **8** *see* BERRIES *n.* (2).

berry *n.*[2] [STRAWBERRY *n.* (5)] [1990s+] **1** one who is into bizarre, 'kinky' sex. **2** one who cannot get a partner. **3** (*US black*) a young woman who barters sex for drugs (usu. crack cocaine).

berry picker *n.* [20C+] (*US*) a rural person, a country dweller.

bertha *n.* (*also* **big bertha**) [WW1 Ger. gun, *Big Bertha*, a 42cm (161/2in) mortar; ult. the proper name Frau *Bertha* Krupp von Bohlen und Halbach (1886–1957), the owner of the Krupp steelworks in Germany] **1** [1920s–40s; 1980s+] (*US*) a fat person. **2** [1970s+] (*US camp gay*) nickname for any tall, heavy-set man, esp. if effeminate.

bertiss *n.* [BATTY *n.*[2] (1)] [1940s+] (*W.I.*) the buttocks.

beserko *n.* [SE *beserk* + -O *sfx* (2)] [1980s+] (*US*) an unstable, eccentric person.

beside the lighter *phr.* [? SE *lighter*, a boat used to transport goods/passengers to and from a vessel that has to be moored in deeper water] [late 17C–18C] in a poor condition.

besognio *n.* (*also* **besogno, besonio, bisognio**) [It. *bisogno*, need, want; also a newly levied, untrained and unblooded soldier] [late 16C–early 17C] a greedy beggar, a worthless person.

bespattered *adj.* [1910s–20s] a euph. for BLOODY *adj.* (1).

bess *n.*[1] [BETTY *n.*] **1** [17C–19C] (*UK Und.*) a short iron bar, used to break open doors, force locks etc. **2** [early 19C] a picklock.

bess *n.*[2] [abbr. BROWN BESS *n.*] [early 18C–mid-19C] a firelock or musket.

bessie *n.* **1** [late 19C] (*US*) a blackjack, a club. **2** [1970s] (*US gay*) a male homosexual, esp. when used as a term of address.

Bess of Bedlam *n.* [SE *Bess*, generic female name + *Bedlam* (the Bethlehem Hospital for the insane)] [mid-19C] a lunatic vagrant.

bessy *n.* [dial. *bessy*, an ill-mannered woman or girl; ? linked to BESS OF BEDLAM *n.*] [19C+] (*W.I.*) a busybody, a gossip.

best *n.*[1] [late 17C; late 19C] a popular toast, abbr. of *to the best cunt in Christendom*.

best *n.*[2] [abbr.] [1960s] pornography featuring *best*iality.

best *adj.*

SE in slang uses

(IN COMPOUNDS)

▫ **best boy** *n.* [on model of *BEST GIRL* below] [1900s–10s] (*orig. US*) a sweetheart, a boyfriend, a husband. ▫ **best-built** *adj.* [SE, lit. built in the best way possible; note BUILT *adj.*] [1970s] describing a woman with a voluptuous figure. ▫ **best girl** *n.* [late 19C+] (*orig. US*) a sweetheart, a girlfriend, a wife. ▫ **best part** *n.* [coined by John Donne (1572–1631)] [late 16C–early 17C] the vagina. ▫ **best shot** *n. see* SHOT *n.*[1] (5a).

(IN PHRASES)

▫ **best leg of three** *n. see under* LEG *n.*

best *v.* [orig. dial.] [late 16C; early 19C+] **1** to get the better of. **2** to cheat.

(DERIVATIVES)

▫ **bested** *adj.* [mid-19C+] defeated, defrauded. ▫ **bester** *n.* **1** [mid-19C] a villain who is equally happy to use physical force or verbal deceits to extract money from victims. **2** [mid-19C] (*UK Und.*) a criminal who deceives his peers. **3** [mid-19C+] (*Aus.*) a fraudulent bookmaker.

(IN PHRASES)

▫ **get money at the best** *v.* [19C] to live as a professional criminal.

best friend *n.*

SE in slang uses

(IN PHRASES)

▫ **be your own best friend** *v.* [note Woody Allen's line in his film *Annie Hall* (1977) 'Hey, don't knock masturbation! It's sex with someone I love.'] [1990s+] to masturbate. ▫ **wife's best friend** *n.* [1960s+] the penis.

bestial backsliding *n. see* *BACKSLIDING* *under* BACK *adj.*[2].

best in Christendom *n.* [popularized by John Wilmot, Earl of Rochester (1647–80), who was also responsible for the synon. BULL'S EYE *n.* (1); *CROWN OF SENSE* *under* CROWN *n.*[1]; KENNEL *n.*[1]; TARGET *n.*] [late 17C–18C] the vagina.

best (of it) *n.* [19C+] an advantage.

(IN PHRASES)

▫ **get the best of it** *v.* [19C–1940s] (*Aus./US*) to gain an advantage, typically in a gambling game. ▫ **give someone best** *v.* (*also* **give it best, give something best**) [late 19C–1950s] to leave, to abandon, to acknowledge defeat. ▫ **give someone the best of it** *v.* [late 19C–1940s] (*Aus./US*) to allow someone the advantage, typically in a gambling game.

bet *adj. see* BEAT *adj.*

bet *v.*

(IN PHRASES)

▫ **bet a fat man (against a pile of shit)** *v.* [1930s+] (*US* *black*) to assure or to believe with absolute confidence. ❑ **bet a five pound note to a raspberry** *v.* [1940s] to make what one considers to be a certain bet. ❑ **bet a funky monkey and two old maids** *v.* [1980s] (*US black*) to be certain. ❑ **bet a pound to a piece of shit** *v.* (*also* **bet to a pinch of poop**) [1940s+] a statement denoting the speaker's absolute confidence, whether in a real bet or merely a point of view. ❑ **bet like the Watsons** *v. see* separate entry. ❑ **bet London to a brick** *v.* (*also* **bet to a lump of crap**) [1960s+] (*Scot./Aus.*) to lay long odds. ❑ **bet one's balls** *v. see under* BALLS *n.* ❑ **bet one's (black) arse** *v. see* BET ONE'S (SWEET) ASS *v.* ❑ **bet one's boots** *v.* (*also* **bet one's bootlace, ...braces, ...breeches, ...socks, gamble one's socks**) [mid-19C+] (*orig. US*) to be certain, to wager everything in total confidence. ❑ **bet one's bottom** *v. see* BET ONE'S (SWEET) ASS *v.* ❑ **bet one's bottom dollar** *v.* (*also* **bet one's bottom ace, ...last dollar, stake one's bottom dollar**) [mid-19C+] to be absolutely certain. ❑ **bet one's buns/butt** *v. see* BET ONE'S (SWEET) ASS *v.* ❑ **bet one's buttons** *v.* (*also* **bet one's last button, ...one's hat, ...pants, ...shirt, wager one's beaver**) [mid-17C; mid-19C] to bet all one's money, to go the limit, to commit oneself unreservedly to something. ❑ **bet one's eyes** *v.* [mid–late 19C] (*US gambling*) to watch a game but not get involved in the betting. ❑ **bet one's head to a China orange** *v.* [mid-19C] to be very certain. ❑ **bet one's katookus** *v. see* BET ONE'S (SWEET) ASS *v.* ❑ **bet one's neck** *v.* [1920s] (*US*) to be absolutely sure, to commit oneself unreservedly. ❑ **bet one's socks** *v. see* *BET ONE'S BOOTS* above. ❑ **bet one's (sweet) ass** *v. see* separate entry. ❑ **bet one's (sweet) life** *v.* (*also* **bet one's sweet by-and-by**) [mid-19C+] to be absolutely sure, to commit oneself unreservedly. ❑ **bet on the blue** *v. see under* BLUE *n.*[1]. ❑ **bet on the mary lou** *v. see* *BET ON THE BLUE under* BLUE *n.*[1]. ❑ **bet on the wrong side of the post** *v.* [SE *winning post*] [late 18C–early 19C] to make a losing bet. ❑ **bet the farm** *v. see* separate entry. ❑ **I'll bet** *v.* [late 19C+] a phr. used to imply (depending on context) the speaker's enthusiastic or sceptical response to what they have just heard. ❑ **want to bet?** [1940s+] a challenging refutation of the previous speaker's assertion.

(IN EXCLAMATIONS)

❑ **bet your life!** (*also* **bet your sweet life!**) [mid-19C+] (*orig. US*) an excl., i.e. 'you must be joking'; also found in print as *betcha, betcher*, emphasizing the 'slanginess'. ❑ **you bet!** [mid-19C+] (*orig. US*) a general excl. of affirmation, agreement, certainly, I'll say so, indeed.

bet! *excl.* [*YOU BET! under* BET *v.*] **1** [1980s+] (*US campus*) a response to an event that is totally unexpected but greatly appreciated, e.g. *Class is cancelled today? Bet!* **2** [1990s+] (*US*) a general excl. of affirmation or agreement.

betcha! *excl.* (*also* **betcher!**) [elision of SE *bet you*] [1920s+] (*orig. US*) a general excl. of affirmation or agreement.

bet down *adj.* [2000s] (*Irish*) of a young woman or girl, unattractive.

beteechoot *n. see* BANCHOOT *n.*

be the dad! *excl. see* BEDAD! *excl.*

bethel the city *v.* [proper name of Slingsby *Bethel* (1617–97) who, with Henry Cornish, was elected Sheriff of London in 1680; according to the historian Roger North, Bethel 'used to walk about more like a corncutter than sheriff of London. He kept no house, but lived upon chops, whence it is proverbial for not feasting "to Bethel the city"' (*Examen*, 1740)] [early 18C] **1** to be a poor host. **2** to eat in chop-houses.

be there *v.* **1** [late 19C] (*US*) to be in one's element. **2** [late 19C+] (*US*) to make a definite plan, usu. in form of a statement, *I'm there*, I'm definitely doing that. **3** [1990s+] (*US campus*) to understand. **4** [2000s] of a man, to seduce, to have sexual intercourse.

bethlehemites *n.* [the staple topic of most carols] [late 18C] (*UK Und.*) carol-singers.

Bethlehem steel *n.* [play on name of the US steel manufacturer] [1980s+] (*US black*) a boastful description of the rigidity of one's erect penis.

bet like the Watsons *v.* [the *Watson Brothers* (*fl.*1880s–1910s). They were legendary punters but their background is unknown; poss. b. in Bendigo, Victoria they have been variously cited as Sydney hoteliers and outback shearers in New South Wales] [1940s–70s] (*Aus.*) to bet heavily.

betoger *n.* [Afk. *betoog*, demonstrate] [1970s+] (*S.Afr.*) a political demonstrator.

bet one's (sweet) ass *v.* (*also* **bet one's (black) arse, ...one's bottom, ...buns, ...butt, ...katookus**) [ASS *n.* (2)] [1910s+] a phr. used to imply the certainty of a suggested course of action; usu. as *you bet your ass*.

bets off *phr.* [late 19C] (*Aus.*) a phr. meaning that one will abandon what one is doing.

betsy *n.* (*also* **Betsey Ann, Betsey Jane, old betsy, old Bet**) [abbr. BROWN BESS *n.*] [mid-19C–1960s] (*US*) a gun, thence a pistol.

better *v.* [BETTY *n.* (3)] [early–mid-19C] (*UK Und.*) to relock a door.

better half *n.* (*also* **bitter half, inferior half, other half, worse half**) [late 16C+] one's wife, or partner, usu. joking use.

better than... *phr.* used in comparative phrs. denoting resigned acceptance, i.e. 'it could be worse', it is 'better than nothing'.

(IN PHRASES)

❑ **better than a kick in the ass with a frozen foot** [1960s+] (*Can./US*) ❑ **better than a poke in the eye with a blunt/burnt stick** [late 19C+] ❑ **better than a slap in the belly with a wet fish** [1930s+] (*orig. US*) ❑ **better than a thump on the back with a stone** [late 18C–early 19C] ❑ **better than smashing your leg** [mid-19C]

bet the farm *v.* [1940s+] (*US*) lit. and fig., to bet unreservedly.

betty *n.* **1** [mid-17C–mid-19C] (*UK Und.*) a short iron bar, used to break open doors, force locks etc; the predecessor of the 19C JEMMY *n.*[3] (1). **2** [late 17C–early 19C] a small flask, used to hold wine. **3** [18C+] a skeleton key, a picklock. **4** implying effeminacy [note Scot./US dial. *jenny*(*-woman*) a man who meddles in or assists in a woman's housework; and 17C *Bettyland*, esp. in pamphlet *Erotopolis, The Present State of Betty-Land*, in which the term stands for i) the female body, ii) the lowlife areas of London and iii) human sexuality; in it one finds 'Rutland' and the great city of 'Pego', the 'centre of the whole (i.e. HOLE *n.*[1] (1b) = vagina) Empire']. (**a**) [late 17C+] a homosexual man. (**b**) [19C] a man who takes on a woman's household duties. (**c**) [2000s] (*S.Afr. gay*) the buttocks; thus *Betty called*, to have had anal intercourse; *Betty's house*, the anus. **5** [mid-19C] (*US, Southern*) a cowhide whip. **6** [20C+] a chamberpot. **7** [20C+] (*Irish*) a fireguard. **8** [20C+] a schoolteacher. **9** [1970s+] (*US campus*) a pretty young woman [underpinned by character 'Betty' in TV cartoon *The Flintstones*].

(IN EXCLAMATIONS)

❑ **betty rub!** [1980s+] (*US campus*) an excl. used by one male to another, meaning 'you're going to get lucky with her!'.

betty *v.* [BETTY *n.* (3)] [early 19C] (*UK Und.*) to pick a lock or to relock a lock after committing a robbery so as to avoid detection.

Betty Bangles *n.* [2000s] (*S.Afr. gay*) handcuffs.

Betty Blue *n.* [2000s] (*S.Afr. gay*) a police officer.

Betty Bupe *n.* [play on cartoon character *Betty Boop*] [1990s+] (*US drugs*) Buprenex, Buprenorphine, a narcotic painkiller.

betty coed *n.* [song 'Betty Coed' (Paul Fogarty and Rudy Vallee, 1930) and film *Betty Co-Ed* (1947)] [1960s+] (*US*) a generic for a wholesome, middle-class sorority girl.

Betty Grable *n.* [rhy. sl.; ult. film star and WW2 pin-up *Betty Grable* (1916–73)] [1950s+] **1** a sable fur coar. **2** (*Aus.*) a table.

betty lea *n.* (*also* **betty lee**) [rhy. sl.] [1940s+] tea.

betty swallocks *n.* [1990s+] itching, uncomfortable testicles, lit. 'sweaty bollocks'.

betwattled *adj.* [orig. dial.] [late 18C–early 19C] bewildered, confused.

between jobs *n.* [? analogous with brandname small cigar, Between the Acts (launched 1948); travelling salesmen could smoke them between their calls] [20C+] (*US*) a small cigar.

between the two Ws *phr.* [SHOT BETWEEN WIND AND WATER *under* SHOT *adj.*] [mid-19C] infected with venereal disease.

betwixt and between *adv.* [19C] undecided, uncertain, 'neither one thing nor the other'.

Beulah *n.* [a stereotypical, if old-fashioned black female name] [1970s+] (*US black gay*) a black homosexual.

be up off (me)! *excl.* [2000s] (*US black*) go away! leave me alone!

bev *n.* (*also* **bevarly**) [abbr. SE *beverage* or BEVVY *n.*] [mid-19C+] alcohol, esp. beer; thus a drink.

bever *n.* [late 19C] (*US*) a hasty cold meal.

beverage *n.* [SE, though similar to Fr. *pourboire*, a tip, lit. 'in order to drink'] [late 17C–early 19C] money for drink, demanded of anyone wearing a new suit of clothes; thus in general use to mean a tip.

Beverley *n.* [initial *b* of BOOZE *n.* (1)] [2000s] (*S.Afr. gay*) alcohol; as v. to have had delirium tremens.

bevvy *n.* (*also* **bevy**) [Lat. *bibere*, to drink. Note East Anglia dial. *bever*, a four o'clock halt on the road for drink; Eton/Winchester *bevers*, afternoon tea, Charterhouse *bevor*, a wedge of bread eaten between dinner and supper] **1** [late 19C+] alcohol, esp. beer; thus *bevvy-casey*, *bevvy-ken*, a beer-house, a public house; *bevvy-homey*, a drunkard (lit. 'beer-man'), *on the bevvy*, a drinking session. **2** [1930s+] a drink. **3** [1960s] a (drunken) party.

IN COMPOUNDS

□ **bevvy omee** *n.* [OMEE *n.*] [20C+] (*Ling. Fr./Polari*) a drunkard.

bevvy *v.* [BEVVY *n.* (1)] [late 19C+] to drink.

DERIVATIVES

□ **bevvied (up)** [1960s+] drunk.

IN COMPOUNDS

□ **bevvy-up** *n.* [1960s] a drinking session.

IN PHRASES

□ **bevvy up** *v.* [1940s+] to drink heavily.

beware *n.* [Polari] [mid-19C] anything one can drink.

bewer *n. see* BUER *n.*

bewitched *adj.* [17C–early 18C] drunk.

be with *v.* [20C+] to understand a person's line of thought, to follow their reasoning, e.g. *I'm definitely with you on that.*

Bex *n.*

SE in slang uses

IN PHRASES

□ **have a bex** *v.* [*Bex*, a tranquillizing drug] [1980s+] (*Aus.*) to relax.

bex *adj.* [SE *vex, vexed*] [20C+] (*W.I. Rasta*) angry.

bexandebs *n.* [common Jewish names, *becks*, Rebeccas, *debs*, Deborahs] [18C–late 19C] young Jewish women from the ghetto area of Wentworth Street, London.

Bexley Heath *n.* [rhy. sl.] [late 19C+] the teeth.

beyond the beyonds *n.* [1910s+] (*Anglo-Irish*) the furthest, absolute limit.

beyond the breakers *adj.* [sea imagery] [1900s] (*US*) beyond limits.

bezabor *n.* [SE *bizarre* + SAmE *neighbor*] [mid-19C] (*US*) a strange, eccentric person.

bezark *n.* [? SE *berserk*] [1910s–40s] (*US*) a person, often characterized as eccentric or unpleasant.

bezazz *n. see* PIZZAZZ *n.*

bezesus *n.* (*also* **bezusus**) [BEJAZUS *n.*] [1930s] **1** (*US*) circumstances, situation. **2** a person; thus *Big Bezezus*, an important man.

bezoomy *adj.* [SE *berserk* + *zoom*] [1990s+] (*US teen*) angry.

bezzie *n.* [1990s+] one's *best* friend.

bezzler *n.* [Lancashire dial. *bezzler*, something large] [1900s] (*US*) a self-important person.

B.F. *v. see* BUDDY-FUCK *v.*[1].

b.f. *n.* [abbr.] **1** [late 19C+] (*orig. US*) a *b*loody *f*ool. **2** [1920s] (*US campus*) a *b*oy *f*riend. **3** [1930s] (*US Und.*) a pimp. **4** [1970s+] (*US gay*) in a lesbian couple, the 'male'. **5** [1990s+] (*US campus*) *b*est *f*riend.

b.f. *v. see* BUTTFUCK *v.*

b.f.d. *phr.* [abbr. *big fucking deal*; euph,. as *big fat deal*] [1960s+] (*US*) so what, I should care less.

b.f.e. *n.* (*also* **b.f.a.**) [abbr. *butt fucking Egypt/Africa*; see BUMFUCK, EGYPT *n.*; euph. as *Beyond Far Egypt*] [1980s+] (*US campus*) somewhere very far way.

b flat *n.* [B *n.*[1] (1) + FLAT-BACK *under* FLAT *adj.*[3]] [mid-19C–1900s] a bedbug.

B-40 *n.* [the bomber plane *B-40*, i.e. its effects] [1980s+] (*drugs*) a cigar laced with marijuana and dipped in malt liquor.

b.g. *n.* [abbr.] [1980s+] (*orig. US black/teen*) *b*aby *g*angster, one who is a member of a gang, but has yet to shoot or kill anyone.

B.G.F. *n.* [2000s] (*US prison*) revolutionary black inmate gang, the *B*lack *G*uerilla *F*amily.

b-girl *n.* [abbr. *bar-girl* or (Trimble, 1966) *business-girl*; *RHDAS* suggests ult. ety. in *beading-oil* and/or PUT THE BEE ON *under* BEE *n.*[1]] **1** [1930s–60s] (*US*) a dancehall hostess whose primary job is not to dance but to promote liquor sales to the clientele. **2** [1930s+] (*orig. US*) (*also* **B-broad, B-drinker**) a part-time prostitute, who frequents bars and uses them as a base for soliciting; thus *B-case*, a charge of soliciting. **3** [1960s] (*US gay*) the homosexual equivalent of sense 2. **4** [1980s+] (*US black*) the female equivalent of the B-BOY *n.*

b.h. *n.* [abbr.] [late 19C–1930s] a *b*ank *h*oliday.

bhang *n. see* BANG *n.*[4].

bhangramuffin *n.* [*bhangra*, a form of popular music developed in the UK Asian community and blending Asian folk + Western disco and rock] [1990s+] (*UK Asian*) the Asian equivalent of the W.I./UK black RAGAMUFFIN *n.*

bhani ghani *phr.* (*also* **behani ghani!**) [? Swahili *abarigani*, what's news?] [1980s+] (*US black*) a form of greeting, favoured by supporters of Black Power.

b-head *n.* [1980s] (*drugs*) a barbiturates user.

bhong *n. see* BONG *n.*[1].

bhowji *n.* [Hind. *bhaabii*, one's elder brother's wife] [20C+] (*W.I.*) an elderly East Indian woman.

b'hoy *n.* [Irish pron. of SE *boy*] **1** [mid-19C+] (*orig. US*) a 'lad', a young rowdy, esp. those found around the Bowery, NYC. **2** [late 19C+] an Irishman.

bhuttu *n.* (*also* **bhutto, buhtuh**) [ety. unknown] [20C+] (*W.I. Rasta*) an uncouth, out of fashion, uncultured person.

Bi *n.* [abbr.] [1930s] (*US Und.*) a *Bu*ick.

bi *n.* [BI *adj.*] [1960s+] a bisexual.

bi *adj.* (*also* **by**) [abbr.] [1930s+] *bi*sexual.

bia *n. see* BIATCH *n.*

bianc *n.* (*also* **bionk, bionc**) [Ital. *bianco*, white = silver] [mid–late 19C] a shilling (five pence).

bianca capellas *n.* [a heavy-handed Ital. pun] [late 19C–1900s] White Chapel cigars.

biatch *n.* (*also* **beeatch, beitch, bee-otch, beeyatch, bia**) [deliberately exaggerated pron.] [1990s+] (*US black/teen*) a var. of BITCH *n.*[1]; can be used to refer to a male or a female, a friend or an enemy, as an excl. etc.

bib *n.*

SE in slang uses

IN PHRASES

□ **put on the bib** *v.* [1930s+] (*US*) to eat. □ **stick one's bib in** *v.* (*also* **push one's bib in, put..., poke...**) [1940s+] (*Aus.*) to interfere, to intrude; thus the reverse, *keep one's bib out.*

bib-all-night *n.* [SE *bib*, to drink + *allnight*] [early 17C] a heavy drinker.

bib and bub *n.* [rhy. sl.] [20C+] (*Aus.*) a tub; thus *have a bib and bub*, take a bath.

bibbing *n.* [1970s+] (*US gay*) augmenting sexual activity with extra items or by taking special precautions against discovery.

bibble chunks *n.* [ety. unknown] [1990s+] the female breasts.

bibbling *adj.* [SE *bib*, to drink] [1900s] (*Irish*) drunken.

bibe *n.* [? Irish word] [1930s+] (*Anglo-Irish*) a bringer of bad luck; an unpleasant person.

bible *n.* [lit. and fig. uses of SE] **1** [late 18C] (*UK Und.*) a large piece of lead, stripped from a roof. **2** [mid-19C+] a peddler's box of pins, needles and other items of haberdashery. **3** the myth that religious superstitions offer a superior truth. (**a**) [mid-19C+] absolute authority, the truth; thus *torah*, a 'Judaized' equivalent, based on the Heb. *Torah*, the Old Testament. (**b**) [1940s+] (*US*) any authoritative book, catalogue, reference work, listing, varying as to the context. **4** [mid-19C+] (*US*) a book of cigarette papers.

SE in slang uses

IN COMPOUNDS

❑ **bibleback(ed)** *see* separate entries. ❑ **bible-banger** *n.* **1** [19C] (*also* **bible-sharp**) a clergyman, a preacher; similarly *bible-ranter/-reader/-spouter/-toter*. **2** (*also* **bible-walloper**) [1940s+] (*Aus./N.Z./US campus*) a religious fanatic. ❑ **bible-basher** *n.* (*also* **bible-buster**) [20C+] (*orig. Aus.*) a clergyman; a religious fanatic; thus *bible-bash*, to act in an overly pious fashion, *bible-bashing*, santimonious. ❑ **bible-beater** *n.* [1970s+] (*US campus*) an evangelizing, fundamentalist Christian. ❑ **bible-belter** *n.* [SE *Bible Belt*] [1920s+] a native of those (mainly southern) US states where fundamentalist Christianity dominates social mores. ❑ **bible-carrier** *n.* [mid-19C] a streetseller of songs who offers the sheet-music but does not give a performance to encourage sales. ❑ **bible mill** *n.* [SE *bible* + *mill*, the noise there, reminiscent of a church full of praying congregants] [late 19C–1900s] a public house. ❑ **bible-pounder** *n.* [late 19C+] a clergyman, a preacher. ❑ **bible-puncher** *n.* [20C+] (*orig. milit.*) a religious person, usu. one who wishes to thrust their beliefs on any who will listen and many who would rather not; thus *bible-punching*, giving a sermon. ❑ **bible-ranter** *n.* [1920s–30s] (*US*) a clergyman, a preacher. ❑ **bible salesman** *n.* [1970s] (*US prison*) a Protestant preacher. ❑ **bible-sharp** *n. see* BIBLE-BANGER above. ❑ **bible-thumper** *n.* [one who thumps the bible in order to underline the points they are expounding, often in a sermon] **1** [late 19C+] (*also* **bible-swinger, God-thumper, goodie-book thumper**) a notably religious person; esp. a clergyman; thus *bible-thumping*, *bible-swinging*, fanatical preaching. **2** [1980s+] a street preacher. **3** [1990s+] (*US prison*) an inmate who adopts religious beliefs – whether genuinely or as a way of dealing with prison life – during their sentence. ❑ **bible-walloper** *n.* **1** [20C+] (*US*) a clergyman, a preacher. **2** *see* BIBLE-BANGER above.

IN PHRASES

❑ **devil's bible** *n. see* DEVIL'S (PICTURE) BOOKS *under* DEVIL *n.* ❑ **go to bible class** *v.* [the rowdiness and horseplay of a printer's *chapel* or workshop] [late 19C] (*orig. printing*) to get a pair of black eyes. ❑ **swallow the bible** *v.* [the use of the bible when taking oaths] [1930s] (*US*) to lie. ❑ **that's bible** [19C] that's excellent.

bibleback *n.* [mid-19C+] a sanctimonious, 'holier-than-thou' person; thus a missionary or proselytizer.

DERIVATIVES

❑ **bible-backed** *adj.* (*US*) **1** [mid-19C–1910s] of a person, round-shouldered and hump-backed. **2** [1940s+] sanctimonious, oppressively pious; esp. of a Protestant who is conspicuously anti-Catholic.

bicarb *n.* [abbr.] [1920s+] *bicarb*onate of soda.

biccies *n. see* BIKKIE *n.*

bice *n.* (*also* **byce**) [Fr. *bis*, twice] [20C+] two, thus £2 or a two-year sentence.

bicho *n.* [synon. Sp. sl.] [1960s+] (*US, orig. Hispanic*) the penis.

bickies *n. see* BIKKIES *n.*

bicycle *n.* [all pun on SE *ride*] **1** [1900s] (*US campus*) a lit. translation of a classical text, a 'crib'. **2** [1940s+] a prostitute, a promiscuous woman. **3** [1960s–70s] a bisexual.

bicycle bum *n.* [SE *bicycle* + BUM *n.*[3] (1)] [1920s+] (*Aus.*) a seasonal worker, cycling between jobs.

bid *n.*[1] [abbr. BIDDY *n.*[2]] **1** [1900s] (*US campus*) a young girl. **2** [2000s] an old person.

bid *n.*[2] [var. pron. of BIT *n.*[1] (3b)] [1960s+] (*US black*) a prison sentence.

bidaciously *adv. see* BODACIOUSLY *adv.* (1).

biddie *n.* [BIDDY *n.*[2] (1)] [1940s] (*US black*) a young girl; thus *little biddie/biddie baby*, a small girl, a small woman.

bid-dims *n.* [onomat. *bid-dim*, the sound of a rifle shot; such trousers supposedly resemble a rifle barrel] [20C+] (*W.I.*) a young man's trousers that are too short and narrow.

biddy *n.*[1] [dial.] **1** [17C–19C] a chicken. **2** [1930s+] (*US*) an egg.

IN PHRASES

❑ **neat as a biddy** *adj.* [early 19C] very neat or well turned-out. ❑ **he-biddy** *n.* [early 19C] (*US*) a (fighting) cock.

biddy *n.*[2] [*Biddy*, a nickname for the popular Irish name Bridget] **1** (*also* **bid**) [17C+] any woman, esp. an Irish female servant; thus as term of address. **2** [late 18C+] a young girl. **3** [1900s] (*US*) a policeman. **4** [1940s+] (*US*) an old woman, usu. irritating, interfering; usu. as *old biddy*. **5** [1960s] (*US*) the female breast. **6** [1980s+] (*US black*) a teenage girl.

IN PHRASES

❑ **red biddy** *n.* (*also* **biddy**) [SE *red* + fig. use of *Biddy*, nickname for Bridget] [1920s+] methylated spirits, as a drink, often mixed with red wine.

bidgee *n.* [*Murrumbidgee* River, Australia] [1920s+] (*Aus.*) an alcoholic's drink, consisting primarily of methylated spirits.

Bidgee whaler *n. see* MURRUMBIDGEE WHALER *under* MURRUMBIDGEE *n.*

biding *n.* [SE *bide*, to stay, to spend time] [mid-18C] (*UK Und.*) wherever thieves divide their booty, e.g. a lodging-house.

bidstand *n.* (*also* **bid-stand, bid stand**) [he 'bids' victims 'stand and deliver'] [late 16C–late 17C] a highwayman.

bien *adj. see* BENE *adj.*

bienly *adv.* [Fr. *bien*, well; note WW1 Aus. milit. *beans*, good] [18C–early 19C] very well, excellently.

bien mort *n. see* BENE MORT *under* BENE *adj.*

BIF *n.* [*b*lack *i*gnorant *f*ucker] [1990s+] a derog. term for a black man.

biff *n.*[1] (*also* **biff-bam**) [Scot. *beff*, a blow, a buffet; *HDAS* has one mid-19C citation, but it appears echoic rather than a noun use] (*orig. US*) **1** [late 19C+] a blow, a slap, a punch, also fig.; thus *biffing*, a beating, (*Aus.*) *biff merchant*. **2** [1920s+] (*Aus. school*) in pl., a beating, a caning. **3** [2000s] a fool [? one who has suffered a BIFF *n.*[1] (1) on the head or one who has a *beef* brain or head].

DERIVATIVES

❑ **biffo** *n.* [BIFF *n.*[1] + -O *sfx*] [1990s+] (*Aus.*) a fight; the sport of wrestling.

IN PHRASES

❑ **go the biff** *v.* [1980s+] (*Aus. prison*) to fight.

biff *n.*[2] [? BIFFER *n.*] [1930s+] (*US campus*) an unattractive, stupid and/or promiscuous woman.

biff *v.* (*also* **bif, baff**) [BIFF *n.*[1] (1)] **1** [late 19C] to rebuff, to reject, to leave without an answer. **2** [late 19C+] to hit; thus *biffing*, a beating (up); knocking (e.g. on a door). **3** [late 19C+] to kill, to murder. **4** [late 19C+] (*Aus.*) to throw; to throw out. **5** [1940s] of a weapon, to fire. **6** [1970s+] (*S.Afr. juv*) to ejaculate. **7** [1980s+] (*US campus*) to fail (an examination), to fall causing embarrasment. **8** [1990s+] (*orig. US*) to have sexual intercourse.

DERIVATIVES

❑ **biffed** *adj.* **1** [1920s] (*US*) drunk. **2** [2000s] (*N.Z.*) bothered, esp. in phr. *I couldn't be biffed*.

biff *adv.* [echoic] [20C+] (*orig. US*) used adverbially with *go*, in the sense of 'with a violent blow', e.g. *the brick went biff through the plate-glass window*.

biff! *excl.* [20C+] echoic of a blow.

biffa *n.* **1** *see* BIFFER *n.* **2** [1990s+] (*US juv*) a fat person.

biffa *adj.* [comic character *Biffo* the Bear] [1990s+] (*UK juv.*) ugly.

biffer *n.* (*also* **biff, biffa**) [1930s] (*US black*) an unpleasant, unattractive and/or promiscuous woman.

biffin *n.*[1] [affectionate reverse anthromorphism of dial. *biffin*, a variety of cooking apple, cultivated especially in Norfolk] [late 19C] an intimate friend.

biffin *n.*[2] (*also* **baffin, biffon**) [fig. use of BIFF *v.* (2), i.e. one is *biffing* against it] [1990s+] **1** (*also* **biffin bridge**) the perineum, that area between the scrotum and anus or the vagina and anus. **2** sweat secreted in this area during intercourse.

biffy *n.* [? milit. jargon *bivvy*, a small shelter, ult. SE *bivouac*] **1** [1930s+] (*US*) a privy, an outdoor lavatory. **2** [1940s+] (*Can./US*) an indoor lavatory. **3** [1980s] (*Can./US campus*) a portable lavatory.

IN PHRASES

❑ **go biffy** *v.* [1970s+] (*US gay*) to visit the lavatory.

biffy *adj.* [? BEVVY *n.* or a play on SQUIFFY *adj.* (1)] [20C+] drunk.

biftah *n.* [ety. unknown; ? link to BIFF *n.*[1] (1), i.e. one 'takes' a hit] [1980s+] (*drugs*) cannabis or a cannabis cigarette.

big *n.* [1940s+] (*US*) a superior person or one who claims to be so.

IN PHRASES

❑ **do a big** *v.* [1990s+] (*US black*) to commit a robbery.

big *adj.* **1** in size. (**a**) [late 16C–mid-18C; 1950s] pregnant. (**b**) [late 19C+] (*US*) used of large amounts of money; thus in gambling use multiples of 10,000; high stakes used in poker games where (as in drug) the convention talks of nickels ($500) and dimes ($1000); thus *big nickel* ($5000), *big dime* ($10,000). (**c**) [1980s] large quantities. (**d**) [1990s+] of drugs, large quantities. **2** in fig. uses. (**a**) [late 19C] (*orig. US*) excellent, wonderful. (**b**) [20C+] (*orig. US*) generous, magnanimous, usu. in phr. *that's big of you*. (**c**) [late 19C+] important. (**d**) [1920s+] successful, popular.

SE in slang uses

DERIVATIVES

❑ **big-able** *adj.* [20C+] (*W.I.*) massive, frighteningly huge.

IN COMPOUNDS

❑ **Big...** *see* separate entries. ❑ **big...** *see also* separate entries. ❑ **big auger** *n.* [SE *auger*, a tool that bores holes; thus one who makes 'a big impression'] [mid-19C+] (*US, mainly west*) an important person, a boss. ❑ **big balls** *n. see BIG BALLOCKS under* BALLOCKS *n.* ❑ **big banana** *n.* [on model of BIG CHEESE *n.* + showbiz *top banana*, the star comedian] (*US/Aus.*) **1** [1960s+] a superior person or one who claims to be so. **2** [1980s+] the most important thing, the crux of a matter. ❑ **big bean** *n. see* BEAN *n.*[1] (6). ❑ **big bertha** *n. see* BERTHA *n.* ❑ **big blink** *n.* [1970s–80s] death. ❑ **big blow** *n.* [SAusE *blow*, a storm] [20C+] (*Aus./US*) a hurricane. ❑ **big board** *n.* [SE *board*, a board at the Stock Exchange on which share prices are displayed] [20C+] the New York Stock Exchange. ❑ **big boat** *n. see* BOAT *n.*[1] (1c). ❑ **big bob** *n.* [late 19C] an aristocrat, a notable person. ❑ **big brother** *n.* [1960s] (*US gay*) the penis. ❑ **big Charlie** *n.* [late 19C] (*US*) syphilis. ❑ **big chief** *n.* **1** [1930s+] an important or the most important man. **2** [1960s] (*drugs*) mescaline. **3** *see* BIG BOSS, THE *n.* ❑ **big cigar** *n.* [the stereotyped smoking habits of such figures] [1920s] (*US black*) a self-important person. ❑ **big cog** *n.* [play on *BIG WHEEL* below] [2000s] an important or self-important person. ❑ **big cookie** *n.* [1960s] a nuclear bomb. ❑ **big cough** *n.* [1920s–30s] (*US Und.*) a bomb. ❑ **big day** *n.* [1930s–50s] (*US prison*) visiting day. ❑ **big deuce** *n.* [SE *deuce*, two] [1980s+] (*US teen*) the Second World War. ❑ **big dick** *n.* [generic use of proper name/DICK *n.*[1] (5)] **1** [late 19C+] (*US gambling*) (*also* **big dick from Dixie, big Tom**) the point of ten in craps dice, usu. ext. as *big Dick from Boston*. **2** [1960s+] an important person; also attrib. **3** [1930s] (*US prison*) a ten-year jail sentence. ❑ **big dish** *n.* [1940s] (*Aus.*) a big win; thus *go for the big dish*, to place a large bet, to gamble heavily. ❑ **big ditch** *n.* [joc. deliberate understatement] (*US*) **1** [19C] the Erie Canal. **2** [20C+] the Atlantic Ocean. **3** [1910s–60s] the Panama Canal. ❑ **big do** *n.* [var. on BIG DOING *n.*] [1900–20s] (*US black*) any notable event. ❑ **big dome** *n. see DOUBLE DOME under* DOME *n.* ❑ **big-dome** *adj. see DOUBLE-DOMED under* DOME *n.* ❑ **big dubs** *n.* [Carib.E. *big-dubs*, a large, polished marble] [20C+] (*W.I.*) a large and good-humoured man. ❑ **big E** *n. see under* ELBOW *n.* ❑ **big enchilada** *n.* [coined by White House chief domestic affairs adviser, John F. Erlichman, to describe then Attorney-General John N. Mitchell] [1970s+] (*US*) an important person. ❑ **big fellow** *n. see* BIG BOSS, THE *n.* ❑ **big ferry** *n.* [mid-19C] (*US*) the Atlantic Ocean. ❑ **big figure** *n.* [SE *figure*; a number, a sum] [mid-19C] (*US*) large scale; thus *do something on the big figure, go the big figure*, to do something on a large scale. ❑ **big finger** *n.* [1910s] (*US*) the senior figure, esp. as a prison warden; thus *second finger*, deputy warden. ❑ **big four** *n.* (*also* **big foe**) [the old practice of manning all police vehicles with four officers] [1920s; 1980s+] (*US black*) tough, élite (often physically large) detectives, dealing with organized crime and similar areas; such police officers match their wide powers with indiscriminate physical violence and the general belief (in modern use) that all members of the black community are *de facto* criminals. ❑ **big gates** *n.* [metonymy] [late 19C+] (*UK Und.*) a prison. ❑ **big George** *n.* [generic use of proper name] **1** [1940s] (*US*) a self-important person. **2** [1950s] 25 cents. ❑ **big girl's blouse** *n.* (*also* **blouse, girl's blouse**) [the term, now widespread, originated like the similarly deracinated GOBSMACKED *adj.* in the north of England] [1960s+] a weakling, an ineffectual person; usu. found as a direct statement, *You big girl's blouse!* ❑ **big guy** *n.* (*US*) **1** [20C+] anyone important, or considered as such; e.g. a gang boss. **2** [1980s] a friend; and a joc. form of address. **3** *see* BIG BOSS, THE *n.* ❑ **big hat** *n.* (*US*) **1** [1940s+] an important person. **2** [1960s+] a police officer or state trooper [the headgear worn as part of many US police uniforms]. **3** [1970s] (*US*) a Mexican [the clichéd large Mexican hat]. ❑ **big hen's biddy** *n.* [1930s] (*US black*) a coward, a weakling. ❑ **big huey, the** *n.* [play on SE *long*/Lousiana governor Huey P. *Long* (1893-1935)] [1970s–80s] (*N.Z. prison*) a long sentence. ❑ **big Injun** *n.* [INJUN *n.*, lit. 'big Indian'; thus, note *BIG WHITE CHIEF* below] [late 19C–1900s] (*US*) an important person. ❑ **big J** *n.* [? *big job*] [1970s+] (*US gay*) simultaneously fellating and sodomizing one's partner. ❑ **big jobs** *n.* (*also* **biggies**) [euph.] [1940s+] (*orig. US juv.*) excreta; thus *do big jobs*, to defecate. ❑ **big joint** *n. see* BIG STORE *n.* ❑ **big jump** *n.* [1910s] (*US*) death, usu. in phr. *put someone over the big jump*. ❑ **big leg** *adj.* [LEG *n.* (8c)] [1970s+] (*US*) sexy. ❑ **big legs** *n.* [? who has trousers with big pockets] [1970s–80s] a big spender. ❑ **big lump** *n.* [2000s] (*UK prison*) a long sentence. ❑ **big magilla** *n.* [play on the Magilla Gorilla show/GORILLA *n.*[1] (6); but note Yid. *gantz megillah*, a whole rigmarole] [2000s] (*US*) an important, influential person. ❑ **big man** *n.* **1** [late 19C+] (*also* **big fellow, big honcho**) any form of superior person, esp. in a criminal context; a prison governor. **2** [1900s–30s] (*US Und.*) the Pinkerton Detective Agency. **3** [1910s+] (*drugs*) a dealer, esp. a major dealer, selling bulk quantities of drugs. **4** [1970s] (*US black*) a gallon of wine. **5** *see BIG GUY* above. ❑ **big medicine** *n.* [*BAD MEDICINE under* BAD *adj.*] [late 19C+] (*US*) an important or influential person or thing; by ext. also dangerous. ❑ **big mitt** *n. see* MITT *n.* (2). ❑ **big moment** *n.* [1920s–60s] (*Irish/US*) the person with whom one is infatuated. ❑ **big mucky-muck** *n. see* HIGH MUCK-A-MUCK *n.* ❑ **big nickel** *n.* [1920s+] (*US*) a sum of $500 or $5000. ❑ **big noise** *n.* **1** [mid-19C; 1950s] (*US*) trouble, disturbance. **2** [20C+] (*orig. US*) an important, powerful person. ❑ **big nose** *n.* [20C+] a derog. name for a Jew. ❑ **big — -o, the** *n.* [1980s+] (*orig. US*) used of landmark birthdays, e.g. those that mark another decade, *three-o, four-o* etc. ❑ **big order** *n. see under* ORDER *n.* ❑ **big pappa** *n. see* BIG DADDY *n.* ❑ **big parade** *n.* [the title of the film *The Big Parade* (1925), screenplay by Laurence Stallings, although the term is never used in the film itself] [1920s–50s] (*US*) the First World War. ❑ **big pasture** *n.* [as used by cowboys and other Westerners] [20C+] (*US*) a prison. ❑ **big people** *n.* [mid-19C+] important, influential people. ❑ **big poppa** *n.* [1990s+] (*US black teen*) any influential black man, a power in his own community, aged 30 and over. ❑ **big puddle** *n. see* PUDDLE *n.* ❑ **big rod** *n.* **1** [1920s+] (*US*) an important person. **2** [1940s] (*US Und.*) a machine gun. ❑ **big roller** *n. see* HIGH ROLLER *n.* (1). ❑ **big school** *n. see under* SCHOOL *n.* ❑ **big screech** *n.* [1910s] (*US*) an important person. ❑ **big show** *n.* [SE *show(-off)*.] **1** [20C+] (*US*) an important person. **2** [1910s] an important situation. ❑ **big six** *n.* [? there are six officers; the high number six in dice] [1950s+] (*US prison*) the prison riot squad; thus *big six talk*, empty, if aggressive talk. ❑ **big sleep** *n.* [coined by US writer Raymond Chandler (1888–1959) as the title of his book *The Big Sleep* (1939), although *HDAS* suggests (without confirmatory citations) that he 'gave currency' to the term] [1930s+] (*orig. US*) death. ❑ **big spender** *n.* [usu. slightly derog., the implication being that any such 'spender' will also be a SUCKER *n.*[1] (3a)] [1940s+] a spendthrift, one who flashes their money around, esp. in phr. *last of the big spenders*, used ironically to mock a cheapskate or someone who is spending a great deal of money that they patently cannot afford. ❑ **big spud** *n. see* BIG POTATO *n.*[1]. ❑ **big squash** *n.* [*BIG SQUEEZE* below, ? on pattern of BIG CHEESE *n.*, SE *squash*, the vegetable] [1910s–60s] an important person or someone who think they are so. ❑ **big squeeze** *n.* [SQUEEZE *n.*[1] (11a)] [1910s+] (*US*) an important person. ❑ **big stick** *n. see under* STICK *n.* ❑ **big stir** *n. see* BIG HOUSE *n.* (2). ❑ **big stuff** *n.* [milit. jargon *bigstuff*, heavy artillery shells] **1** [mid-19C+] (*orig. US*) an important or self-important person. **2** [late 19C] a strong, violent person. **3** [late 19C–60s] (*US*) a term of address, usu. slightly derog. **4** [1920s+] (*US*) a major criminal. **5** [1950s–60s] an important situation, esp. with criminal overtones. **6** [1950s+] (*US*) a large amount of money. ❑ **big style** *adv. see* BIG-TIME *adv.* ❑ **big toast** *n.* [1950s] (*US black*) an outstanding person. ❑ **big top** *n.* [1970 reference to Leavenworth Prison, Kansas] [1920s+] (*US Und.*) prison, esp. the main cellblock. ❑ **big toter** *n. see under* TOTE *v.*[1]. ❑ **big twist** *n.* [SE *twist of fate*] [1930s+] (*Aus.*) a cause for celebration, a great success. ❑ **big track** *n. see* FAST TRACK *n.* ❑ **big vegetable** *n.* [1910s] (*orig. US*) an important person, an influential figure, the boss. ❑ **big water** *n. see* WATER, THE *n.* (2). ❑ **big wheel** *n.* (*also* **wheel**) [the image of a smooth-running, powerful machine] [1930s+] (*orig. US*) an important, influential person, esp. in business. ❑ **big wheeze** *n.* [1910s] (*US*) a senior business figure. ❑ **big white chief** *n.* [cod Native American] [1930s+] (*orig. US*) an important or the most important man. ❑ **big white telephone** *n. see under* TELEPHONE *n.* ❑ **big yard** *n.* [SE *yard*, the exercise area of a prison] **1** [1940s+] (*W.I.*) a prison. **2** [1970s] (*US prison*) a prison recreation area.

(IN PHRASES)

❑ **big-and-plenty** *adj.* (*also* **big-and-so-so**) [20C+] (*W.I., Gren.*) fat and clumsy, and of low quality (used of people and things, e.g. vegetables). ❑ **big bout yah** *adj.* [lit. ' big (i.e. important) about you'] [1980s+] (*W.I.*) of a person, important. ❑ **big bull with the brass collar** *n. see* BIG DOG WITH THE BRASS COLLAR *n.* ❑ **big dick from Boston** *n.* **1** [1930s+] (*US gay*) a loudmouth. **2** *see BIG DICK* above. ❑ **big end of** *n.* [late 19C–1940s] (*orig. US*) the majority, the larger share (of loot); thus *big end of a month*, three weeks. ❑ **big enough to choke a bull** *adj.* (*also* **big enough to choke an elephant, ...a horse, ...an ox**) [late 19C+] (*US*) of a bankroll, extremely big. ❑ **big I, little you** *n.* [1960s–70s] (*US*) an important person. ❑ **big juta, little juta, all same price** *adj.* [Hind. *juutaa*, a shoe, and orig. used of shoes] [20C+] (*W.I.*) anything goes, irrespective of size or quality; usu. used of a country person who lacks the city dweller's standards of choice. ❑ **big man with the brass collar** *n. see* BIG DOG WITH THE BRASS COLLAR *n.* ❑ **big nigger in charge** *n. see HEAD NIGGER IN CHARGE under* HEAD *n.* ❑ **big referee in the sky, the** *n. see* BIG BOSS, THE *n.* ❑ **do the big** *v.* [late 19C] (*Irish*) to self-aggrandize.

(IN EXCLAMATIONS)

❑ **big whoop!** [SE *whoop*, a cry (of exultation, triumph)] [1980s+] (*US*) a dismissive, sarcastic excl., 'why bother me?'.

big *v.* [biblical *bigwithchild*] [1930s+] (*US/W.I.*) to make pregnant; thus *bigged*, pregnant.

big *adv.* [orig. US, other than one-off 17C cite in sense 1] **1** [late 17C; mid-19C+] notably, conspicuously, e.g. *win big, go over big*. **2** [mid-19C+] to a great extent.

(IN PHRASES)

❑ **go big** *v.* [1900s–70s] (*US*) **1** to like very much, to enthuse over. **2** to go well. **3** to embark on a major project. ❑ **play big** *v.* [20C+] (*US/W.I.*) to pretend to be more worthy, powerful, important, wealthy etc than one is. ❑ **take it big** *v.* **1** [1930s+] (*US*) to react emotionally, usu. when distressed or angry. **2** [1960s] to fall in love. ❑ **talk big** *v.* (*also* **speak big, talk bigger than a bullock**) [early 17C+] to boast, to exaggerate.

Big A *n.* [abbr.] **1** [1970s+] (*US*) Amarillo, Texas. **2** [1970s+] (*US*) (*also* **A-Town**) Atlanta, Georgia. **3** [1980s+] (*US*) New York [BIG APPLE *n.*]. **4** [1980s+] (*Aus.*) Australia.

big A *n.* [on model of BIG C *n.* (2); BIG H *n.*] **1** [1980s+] (*US*) Acquired Immuno-Deficiency Syndrome (AIDS). **2** *see* ARSE *n.* (8).

bigady *adj. see* BIGGITY *adj.*

big and bulky *n.* [rhy. sl.] [1900s] (*Aus.*) a sulky (a horse-drawn carriage).

Big Apple *n.* [in the *New Yorker* of 6 August 1984 Charles Gillett, the president of the New York Convention & Visitors Bureau, Inc., spoke on the value of the image of New York as the 'Big Apple'. It was his organization that plucked the term from the jazz lingo of the 1920s. The phrase in the jazz world, he said, had been playing 'the Big Stem in the Big Apple, the Big Stem being Broadway. For an exhaustive study of 'big apple' *see* Cohen (ed.) *Studies in Slang* III (1993) and IV (1995); late in 1937 a dance called the Big Apple conquered the country] [1920s+] New York City.

big apple *n.* (*also* **apple**) [? APPLE-KNOCKER *n.*; such a hat being similar to those worn by a farm-worker to keep off the sun or f. the size, fig. resembling that of the BIG APPLE *n.* (1)] **1** [1960s+] (*orig. US black*) a large-brimmed, oversized hat, in 1930s–40s style. **2** *see* APPLE *n.*[1] (4).

big ass *n.* [SE *big* + ASS *n.*] [1950s–60s] (*US*) a superior person or one who claims to be so.

big-ass *adj.* (*also* **big-assed, big-arse**) [SE *big* + ASS *n.*/BIG ASS *n.* (1); the supposed crushing power of such massive buttocks] (*US*) **1** [1940s+] big (in size). **2** [1940s+] important, powerful, self-opinionated.

(DERIVATIVES)

❑ **big-assedly** *adv.* (*US*) aggressively.

big-ass *v.* [SE *big* + *ass*] [1980s+] (*US southwest*) to make a fool of.

Big B *n.* [abbr.] **1** [1970s] (*US*) Baltimore, Maryland. **2** [1970s] (*US*) Birmingham, Alabama.

big-belly *adj.* [1920s+] (*W.I.*) greedy.

big-belly *v.* [1930s+] (*W.I.*) to strut in a pompous manner.

big ben *n.* [rhy. sl.; *Big Ben* is the clock in the tower of the Houses of Parliament] **1** [1910s+] (*US gambling*) the point of ten in craps dice. **2** [1930s+] the number ten. **3** [1950s] ten shillings. **4** [1950s+] £10.

big bloke *n.*[1] [SE *big* + BLOKE *n.* (1)] [1910s] (*Aus.*) a boss, a superior.

big bloke *n.*[2] [rhy. sl. = COKE *n.*[1] (1)] [1930s+] (*drugs*) cocaine.

big boss, the *n.* (*also* **big boy, ...chief, ...fellow, ...guy, ...man, ...referee in the sky**) [joc. cod-intimacy] [20C+] (*US*) God.

big boy *n.* **1** [1910s+] (*US*) a general term of address, sometimes sincere, often ironic. **2** [1920s–40s] (*US black*) a foolish, reckless, devil-may-care young man. **3** [1920s+] (*US*) a superior person or one who claims to be so. **4** [1920s+] (*US Und.*) (*also* **B.B., big fella, big fellow**) the head of an organized crime syndicate, or some equivalent figure. **5** [1940s] (*US*) a 100-dollar bill. **6** [1970s] (*US*) a shotgun. **7** [1990s+] (*W.I.*) a lovable idiot. **8** *see* BIG BOSS, THE *n.*

big buck *n.* [SE big/BIG *adj.* (1) + BUCK *n.*[3] (4)] [1950s–60s] (*US*) a large amount (unspecified) of money.

big-buck *adj.* [BIG BUCK *n.* (1)] [1990s+] (*US black*) expensive.

big bucks *n.* [SE *big*/BIG *adj.* (1) + BUCK *n.*[3] (4)] [1950s+] large sums of money, esp. those earned by performers or stolen by criminals, or as a large, but non-specific price.

Big C *n.* [1970s] (*US*) Chicago.

big C *n.* [abbr.] **1** [1950s+] (*drugs*) cocaine. **2** [1960s+] (*also* **C**) cancer. **3** [2000s] cirrohosis of the liver.

big casino *n.* [the big wins and big losses involved but note LITTLE CASINO *n.*] (*US*) **1** [late 19C+] an important person. **2** [1900s] a large person, thus *little casino*, a small person. **3** [1920s+] the best, the ultimate, the most important. **4** [1930s+] anything terminal, fatal, esp. a disease, e.g. cancer; also syphilis.

IN PHRASES

❑ **give big casino to** *v.* [late 19C+] to take second place.

big casino *adv.* [BIG CASINO *n.* (3)] [1990s+] (*US*) in an important, committed manner.

big cheese *n.* (*also* **big smell, big sugar, cheese, head cheese, main cheese**) **1** [20C+] (*orig. US*) an important person, an influential figure, a boss in a situation or job. **2** [1920s] (*US*) affectionate term of address for a fool.

Big D *n.* [abbr.] (*US*) **1** [1960s+] the nickname of a number of relevantly initialled US cities, i.e. *Dallas*, Texas; *Detroit*, Michigan; *Denver*, Colorado. **2** [1970s+] death. **3** [1980s+] (*drugs*) LSD.

big D *n. see* D *n.*[4] (1).

big daddy *n.* (*also* **big dad, big papa**) [fig. uses of SE] **1** [1940s–50s] (*US black*) any influential black man, a power in his own community, aged 30 and more. **2** [1950s–60s] (*mainly US black*) one's grandfather. **3** [1950s–70s] (*US*) a male lover, a sweetheart. **4** [1960s] (*US*) a pimp. **5** [1960s+] (*orig. US*) an important person. **6** [1960s+] (*US*) the most important of its kind (not necessarily a human being). **7** [1960s+] (*US gay*) the 'masculine' member of a homosexual couple. **8** [1970s] heroin.

IN COMPOUNDS

❑ **big daddy pot** *n.* [1950s+] (*W.I.*) a large iron pot, used for cooking cow-tripes after butchering.

big deal *n.* (*also* **big dealer**) [SE *big* + DEAL *n.*[1]] [1940s+] (*orig. US*) **1** an important (or self-important) person. **2** (*also* **deal, hot deal**) anything that is considered important to the speaker; often ironic.

big deal *adj.* [BIG DEAL *n.* (2)] [1950s+] important, urgent, impressive etc.

big deal *v.* [BIG DEAL *n.*] (*US*) **1** [1940s] to get what one wants by clever, forceful negotiation. **2** [1960s] to aggrandize, to magnify the importance of.

big deal! *excl.* [BIG DEAL *n.*] [1950s+] (*orig. US*) a dismissive, sarcastic excl., 'what's important about that?' 'why bother me?'.

big dealer *n.* BIG DEAL *n.* (1).

big dog *n.* **1** [mid-19C+] (*US*) an important person; thus *Big Dog Upstairs*, God. **2** [late 19C] a thug; a BOUNCER *n.*[1] (9). **3** [1970s] US a greyhound bus. **4** [2000s] as a term of address.

IN PHRASES

❑ **like a big dog** *adv.* (*also* **like a moose**) [1980s+] (*US campus*) having qualities to do with achievement, success, intensity. ❑ **run with the big dogs** *v.* [1980s+] (*US campus*) to do anything anyone else can.

big dog of the tanyard *n.* (*also* **...the meat house**) [fig. use of SE ? a fierce dog kept in a tanyard] [mid–late 19C] an important or the most important person.

big dog with the brass collar *n.* (*also* **big bull with the brass collar, big man with the brass collar**) [mid–late 19C] an important person, esp. in a business context.

big doing *n.* (*also* **big doings**) [SE *big* + *doing*, what is being done] (*US*) **1** [1900s–20s] a boaster, a braggart. **2** [1900s–50s] any notable event, esp. a party or celebration.

big doing *adj.* (*also* **big-doings**) [SE *big* (*things*) + *doing*, performing] [20C+] (*US*) conceited, self-opinionated, snobbish.

Big Easy, the *n.* [? coined by James Conaway as the title of his novel *The Big Easy* (1970), later a popular film (1986); presumably f. the stereotype of its free-and-easy lifestyle] [1970s+] (*US*) New Orleans, Louisiana.

bigeddy *adj. see* BIGGITY *adj.*

big eye *n.* (*US*) **1** [19C+] avarice, greed; thus *have the big eye/eye for*, to covet. **2** [1950s] a stare, esp. when hostile or curious.

big eye *v.* [BIG EYE *n.*] **1** [20C+] to act greedily. **2** [1920s] (*US*) to stare at amorously. **3** [1930s] to look at fixedly, to stare at.

big eyes *n.* [BIG EYE *n.* (2)] [1920s–50s] (*US*) police officers engaged in surveillance duties.

big eyes (for) *n.* [BIG EYE *n.* (1)] (*US black*) a great desire (for).

big-feeler *n.* [BIG-FEELING *adj.*] [1960s–70s] (*US*) an arrogant, self-important person.

big-feeling *adj.* [one who feels themselves *big*] [late 19C+] haughty, conceited.

Big Fog *n.* [play on BIG SMOKE *n.*] [1900s] (*Aus.*) London.

big foot country *n.* [? the population 'walks tall'; note legendary 'Bigfoot', a monstrous creature allegedly found in California] [1940s–70s] (*US black*) the southern United States.

big foot Joe *n.* [? nickname] [1960s] the penis.

bigg *n.* [1990s+] a cigarette.

bigged *adj. see* BIG *v.*

biggedy *adj. see* BIGGITIVE *adj.*

bigger thomas *n.* (*also* **bigger**) [proper name of *Bigger Thomas*, the hero of Richard Wright's novel *Native Son* (1940)] [1960s] (*US black*) a rebellious black man, who refuses to abide by white society's rules and struggles against them.

biggerty *adj. see* BIGGITIVE *adj.*

biggety *adj. see* BIGGITY *adj.*

biggie *n.* (*also* **biggy**) [SE *big* + sfx *-ie/-y*] **1** [1920s+] (*orig. US*) anyone large, important, successful, esp. used in entertainment industries. **2** [1950s+] (*W.I.*) a 750ml (26fl oz) bottle of rum. **3** [1970s] (*US prison*) the prison authorities. **4** [1970s+] something important. **5** [1990s+] £1,000.

biggies *n. see* BIG JOBS *under* BIG *adj.*

biggins *n.* (*also* **biggs**) [big deal] [1990s+] (*UK juv.*) something unimportant, also used as an expression of dismissal.

biggitive *adj.* (*also* **biggerty, biggedy**) [SE *big*] [20C+] (*W.I.*) bumptious, pushy, showing off; thus *biggitive with yourself*, self-satisfied.

biggity *adj.* (*also* **bigaty, bigeddy, biggerty, biggety, bigotty**) [SE *big*] [late 19C+] **1** (*orig. US black*) haughty, conceited, bumptious. **2** as adv.

Big Green *n.* [the college colour] [1930s+] (*US campus*) nickname for Dartmouth College.

biggy *n.*[1] *see* BIGGIE *n.*

biggy *n.*[2] [SE *big*] [1950s+] (*W.I.*) a man who is both tall and lazy.

big H *n.* [initial letter] [1960s+] (*drugs*) heroin.

big Harry *n.* [initial letters] [1960s+] (*drugs*) heroin.

big head *n.*[1] **1** [mid-19C–1900s] (*US*) conceit, self-importance. **2** [mid-19C+] a conceited or arrogant person. **3** [1930s] (*US*) an important person. **4** [1930s–70s] a successful person. **5** [1940s] (*US prison*) the warden. **6** [1970s–80s] (*UK black/drugs*) a large cannabis cigarette. **7** [2000s] an intellectual.

DERIVATIVES

❑ **big-headed** *adj.* (*also* **big-head**) [late 19C+] arrogant, conceited.

IN PHRASES

❑ **get the big head** *v.* [late 19C+] to become arrogant.

big head *n.*[2] *see* FAT-HEAD *n.*[2].

big hit *n.*[1] [rhy. sl. = SHIT *n.* (1b)] [1950s+] (*Aus.*) an act of defecation.

big hit *n.*[2] [ironic use of SE *big* + *hit*, a success] [1970s+] (*US prison*) a long term of imprisonment, usu. three years or more.

big house *n.* **1** [mid-19C] (*also* **large house**) the workhouse. **2** [1900s] a theatre. **3** [1910s+] (*US Und.*) (*also* **big house up the river, big stir**) prison, esp. (*S.Afr. Und.*) Pretoria Central prison or, sometimes ext. as *big house up the river*, San Quentin prison. **4** [1950s+] any large, forbidding institution, esp. a psychiatric institution.

big house nigger *n. see* HOUSE NIGGER *n.*

bigified *adj.* [SE *big* + sfx *-ified*] [1960s+] (*US*) haughty, conceited.

Big L *n.* **1** [1970s] (*US prison*) Leavenworth Prison, Kansas. **2** [1980s+] (*UK prison*) a life sentence.

big L *n.* [abbr. on pattern of BIG C *n.*] [1980s] **1** (*US*) love. **2** (*US campus*) a person who is a failure, a LOSER *n.* (1).

big league *n.* [sporting imagery] [20C+] (*US*) an important or influential situation or position.

big-league *adj.* [BIG LEAGUE *n.*] [1910s+] (*US*) important, substantial, powerful.

big-leaguer *n.* [BIG LEAGUE *n.*] **1** [1910s–40s] an important person; as *v.*, to associate with important people. **2** [1920s] an important thing. **3** [1950s] a resourceful person who can handle any situation. **4** [1950s] a major criminal.

big licks *n.* [SE *big* + *lick*, a blow; note Aus. racing jargon *go for the big lick*, to bet heavily] [mid–late 19C] (*US/Aus.*) hard work.

(IN PHRASES)

❑ **go in/on big licks** *v.* (*also* **put in big licks**) [mid-19C–1940s] to make a great effort. ❑ **give big licks** *v.* [1990s+] to act energetically, e.g. of a rock 'n' roll performance. ❑ **go big licks** *v.* [1950s+] (*Aus.*) to enthuse over, to like very much.

big M *n.* [initial letters] **1** [1950s+] £1 million. **2** [1950s+] (*drugs*) morphine. **3** [1960s] marriage. **4** [1970s] Memphis, Tennessee; Miami, Florida.

big Mac *n.* [1990s+] (*UK Und.*) an Ingram Mac-10 machine pistol.

big mac *n.* [rhy. sl. = SACK *n.* (2)] [1990s+] dismissal from a job.

big mama *n.*[1] [cognate with BIG DADDY *n.* (2)] [1940s+] (*US black*) one's grandmother.

big mama *n.*[2] [euph. for SE *big* + MOTHERFUCKER *n.* (4)] **1** [1970s+] anything notably large, substantial. **2** [1990s+] (*US*) the ocean.

Big Meadow *n.* [1930s] (*US Und.*) prison.

Big Moist *n.* [1940s] (*US black*) the Atlantic Ocean.

bigmouth *n.* [late 19C+] (*orig. US*) **1** a braggart, a boaster. **2** an informer, a tell-tale. **3** empty boasting, showing off.

bigmouth *v.* [BIGMOUTH *n.* (1)] [1960s+] (*US*) to brag (about).

big-mouthed *adj.* (*also* **bigmouth**) **1** [17C+] boastful, self-aggrandizing. **2** [late 19C] noisy.

bignaduo *n.* [lit. 'big as a door'] [1910s+] (*W.I.*) a boaster, a bumptious person, a show-off, one who puts on airs.

big note *n.* [SE *big* + NOTE *n.*[2]] [1990s+] £100.

big-note *v.* (*also* **come the big note**) [SE *big* + *note*, paper money, currency; COME THE... *v.* (1)] [1940s+] (*Aus.*) to boast, usu. as *big-note oneself*, to inflate one's achievements; *big-noting*, boasting.

big note man *n.* [1950s] (*Aus.*) a rich man.

big noter *n.* [BIG-NOTE *v.*] [1960s+] (*Aus.*) a show-off, a braggart.

big number *n.*[1] [the outsize numbers painted on brothel doors in Paris] [mid-19C–1900s] a brothel.

big number *n.*[2] [SE *big* + NUMBER *n.* (1)] **1** [1940s–60s] (*US*) an important person. **2** [1950s] (*US prison*) one who poses as more important in the outside world than is the truth.

big O *n.* [initial letter/zero] **1** [1950s+] (*drugs*) opium. **2** [1960s+] an orgasm. **3** [1980s] (*US campus*) a person with no personality.

big one *n.* **1** as quality or quantity. (**a**) [early 19C+] (*also* **big 'un**) an important person. (**b**) [1900s–10s] (*orig. US*) a tall story, an exaggerated tale. (**c**) [1920s+] anything important. **2** as monetary denominations and amounts. (**a**) [mid-19C+] £20, £100, £1000. (**b**) [mid-19C+] (*US*) $100, $1000. (**c**) [1900s–50s] (*US Und.*) a major and extremely lucrative coup. (**d**) [1960s+] (*US*) $1 million. (**e**) [1970s+] a large – unspecified – amount of money. (**f**) [1970s+] (*US*) one dollar. **3** [1920s–60s] (*US prison*) a year in jail. **4** [1920s+] the penis, esp. a large penis. **5** [1920s+] in pl., large female breasts. **6** [1960s+] (*Aus./US prison/Und.*) (*also* **the big one**) a long sentence; a life sentence. **7** as *the big one*. (**a**) [1930s+] (*US*) death. (**b**) [1950s+] a major operation. (**c**) [1950s+] (*US*) World War I or World War II. (**d**) [1960s] nuclear war. (**e**) [2000s] a very large bomb.

(IN PHRASES)

❑ **bite the big one** *v.* [1970s+] (*US*) **1** to be distasteful, unpleasant, second-rate. **2** to die, to suffer harm. ❑ **buy the big one** *v.* [1980s] (*US*) to die. ❑ **eat the big one** *v.* [2000s] (*US*) to die. ❑ **get the big one** *v.* [1920s] (*US*) to die. ❑ **give it the big one** *v.* [1990s+] **1** to act in a verbally aggressive manner. **2** to celebrate, to act in an excessive manner. ❑ **have the big one** *v.* [1970s] (*US*) to die of a heart attack.

(IN EXCLAMATIONS)

❑ **eat the big one!** [var. on EAT ME! *excl.*] [1980s+] (*US*) to hell with you!

Big Orange *n.* [on model of BIG APPLE *n.*; the ref. is to the state's orange groves] [1980s+] (*US*) Los Angeles, California.

bigotty *adj.* see BIGGITY *adj.*

big pot *n.* (*also* **great pot**) [? SE *potentate*; which was also Oxford jargon in 1850s to mean a don or a prominent undergraduate] [late 19C+] a leader, an important person.

(IN PHRASES)

❑ **put on the pot** *v.* [late 19C–1900s] to put on airs. ❑ **put the pot on** *v.* **1** [mid-19C] to exaggerate. **2** [mid-19C] to bet (too) heavily on a horse. **3** [mid–late 19C] to overcharge. **4** [1910s] (*Aus.*) to inform.

big potato *n.*[1] (*also* **big spud**) [lit. 'big potato'; joc. antonym of SMALL POTATOES *n.* (1)] **1** [late 19C+] an important person. **2** [1930s] a large but stupid man.

big potato *n.*[2] [on model of BIG APPLE *n.*; BIG ORANGE *n.*; potatoes are the main constituent of vodka] [1980s+] (*US*) Moscow.

Big Q. *n.* [2000s] (*US Und.*) San Quentin prison.

Big Red *n.* [the college colour] [1940s+] (*US campus*) Cornell University.

Big Red with the long green stem *n.* [BIG APPLE *n.* + LONG GREEN *n.* + MAIN STEM *n.*] [1940s–50s] (*US black*) Seventh Avenue, between 130th Street and 150th Street, the centre of Harlem nightlife.

Big Rock *n.* see ROCK, THE *n.* (2).

big shit *n.* [SE *big* + SHIT *n.*] (*US*) **1** (*also* **big-shit-shot**) [1930s+] an important person or one who claims to be so. **2** [2000s] serious business.

bigshit *adj.* [BIG SHIT *n.* (1)] [1960s] (*US*) self-important.

bigshit *adv.* [BIG SHIT *n.* (1)] [2000s] (*US*) to a great extent.

big shit! *excl.* [BIG SHIT *n.* (1)] **1** [1910s+] a response to the indicating of someone as a BIG SHOT *n.*, *big shot – big shit!* **2** [1960s+] (*US campus*) an excl. of agreement or a dismissive, sarcastic retort.

big shot *n.* (*also* **top shot, shot, big shout**) [the term began as a positive ref. to a major criminal, but by the 1930s it was mainly used ironically and implied that the individual in question was rather too pleased with themselves. Note dial. *queer shot*, an odd fellow, a strange 'customer', *great shot*, an important person] [1910s+] (*orig. US*) **1** a superior person or one who claims to be. **2** as a term of address.

big-shot *adj.* [BIG SHOT *n.* (1)] [1920s+] superior, important, powerful or posing as such (esp. in the criminal milieu).

big shot *v.* (*also* **bigshot**) [BIG SHOT *n.*] [1930s+] (*US*) to show off, to act like an important person.

big-shot *adv.* [1960s] in an arrogant manner.

Big Smoke *n.* [the pollution and general dirt associated with a major city. *OED* suggests orig. Aus. trans. of Aboriginal *toom-virran*, big-smoke] **1** [late 19C+] London. **2** [late 19C+] any (large) town or city. **3** [late 19C+] (*Aus.*) Sydney. **4** [late 19C+] (*Aus.*) Melbourne. **5** [1930s+] Pittsburgh, Pennsylvania. **6** [1970s+] (*N.Z.*) Auckland. **7** [1980s+] (*Irish*) Dublin.

big smoke *n.* [1900s–30s] (*US*) an important person.

Big Snarl *n.* (*also* **Big Stoush, Great Stoush**) [SE *big* + *snarl*; STOUSH *n.* (1)] [1910s+] (*Aus. ex-soldiers*) the First World War.

big spit *n.* (*also* **long spit**) [1950s+] (*Aus.*) the act of vomiting.

(IN PHRASES)

❑ **go (for) the big spit** *v.* [1950s+] (*Aus.*) to vomit.

big store *n.* (*also* **big joint**) [note Maurer, *The Big Con* (1940): 'The BIG STORE An establishment against which big-con men play their victims. For the wire and the pay-off, it is set up like a poolroom which takes race bets. For the rag, it is set up to resemble a broker's office. Stores are set up with a careful attention to detail which makes them seem bona fide. After each play, the store is taken down and all equipment stored away'] [20C+] (*US Und.*) a fake casino or broker's office, in which victims are subjected to an elaborate large-scale swindle.

Big Stoush *n. see* BIG SNARL *n.*

Big T *n.* [abbr.] [1970s] (*US trucker*) **1** *Tucson, Arizona.* **2** *Tampa, Florida.*

big talk *n.* [mid-19C+] boasting, braggartry, verbal self-aggrandizement.

big talk *v.* [BIG TALK *n.*] [1950s+] (*US*) to show off, to try to impress; thus, n. *big talker*, one who boasts.

big thing *n.* **1** [mid-19C] (*US Und.*) a large amount of plunder. **2** [mid-19C+] anything important, noteworthy; often as a negative phr. (*that's*) *no big thing*; also as *no thing*; *a big thing on*, obsessive about. **3** [1980s] (*US drugs*) a kilo of cocaine.

IN PHRASES

❑ **a big thing on ice** *n.* [mid–late 19C] ext. use of sense 2 above.

big thing, the *n.* [20C+] a generous, magnanimous act, often as *do the big thing*, make a generous gesture.

big-ticket *adj.* [the high-priced ticket placed on expensive retail goods in a shop] [1940s+] (*US*) describing something expensive or requiring a considerable financial outlay.

big ticket (item) *n.* [BIG-TICKET *adj.*] **1** [1940s+] (*US*) something expensive or requiring a considerable financial outlay. **2** (*US*) [1970s] a large female breast. **3** [1980s+] a person that commands considerable respect.

big time *n.*[1] [theatrical use, vaudeville theatres with top-line acts and thus only two (long) shows per day, the opposite of 'small time', which featured shorter acts] **1** [mid-19C–1950s] (*US*) an exciting, enjoyable time. **2** [20C+] success, fame, power; thus *get big time*, to put on airs and graces; *hit/make the big time*, to achieve success. **3** [1920s+] an important person, esp. in ironic use, or a powerful, impressive thing. **4** [1950s+] a form of address, whether or not ironic.

DERIVATIVES

❑ **big-timer** *n.* [1920s+] (*orig. US*) an important person; a major criminal.

IN PHRASES

❑ **on the big time** *adj.* [1930s+] on a spree.

big time *n.*[2] [SE *big* + TIME *n.*] [1930s+] (*US prison*) a lengthy sentence, three years plus.

DERIVATIVES

❑ **big-timer** *n.* [1970s] (*US prison*) one who is serving a long sentence.

big-time *adj.* (*also* **bigtime, big-timey**) [BIG TIME *n.*[1]] **1** [1910s+] (*orig. US*) of a person, important, successful, powerful. **2** [1920s+] of a situation, very great, important. **3** [1930s+] desperate, urgent, forceful.

IN COMPOUNDS

❑ **big-time Charlie** *n.* [1990s+] (*US*) an important person.

big time *v.* [BIG TIME *n.*[1]] [1940s+] (*orig. US*) to act in a self-important manner.

big-time *adv.* (*also* **big style**) [BIG TIME *n.*[1]] [1950s+] (*orig. US black/prison*) very much, completely, absolutely, e.g. *she really loves him big time.*

big town *n.* **1** [20C+] (*US*) New York City, occas. Chicago. **2** [20C+] any city.

bigtown *adj.* [1940s–50s] (*US black*) sophisticated, successful, influential.

big-tree *adj.* [BIG-TREE BOY *n.*] [1940s+] (*W.I.*) violent, bullying, gangsterish.

big-tree boy *n.* (*also* **big-tree man**) [1910s+] (*W.I.*) an idler, a semi-gangster, esp. if idling near a large banyan tree in Victoria Park, Kingston, Jamaica.

Big Two, the *n.* [1950s+] (*US*) World War II.

big-up *n.* [BIG UP *v.* (2)] [1990s+] a promotion of, a reference to.

big up *adj.* [BIG UP *v.*] [1970s+] (*W.I.*) important; of a person, socially or otherwise powerful; of an object, powerful, fashionable.

big up *v.* [1950s+] (*UK black/W.I.*) **1** to act in a proud, self-confident matter. **2** (*UK black*) to promote, to boost, to praise. **3** (*W.I./UK black teen*) to greet friends, to pay tribute to something or someone big or important. e.g. *Big up the dancehall crew dem, seen, come again.*

Big V *n.* [abbr. on model of BIG A *n.*] [1970s] (*US*) Las Vegas, Nevada.

bigwig *n.* (*also* **big wig**) [SE *big* + *wig*] [early 18C+] a powerful, important person, often a politician or bureaucrat; thus v. *bigwig*, to act in a superior manner.

bigwig *adj.* [1960s+] snobbish, superior.

big willie *n.* [SE *big* + generic use of proper name; + ? WILLIE *n.*[4] (1); 'the Big Willie [is] the strong, silent type [...] an old-school romantic (and) a savvy businessman [...] a free thinker, fluent with modern technology. He is fearless, vigilant and innovative.' *Vibe* magazine, September 1996] [1990s+] (*US black*) a sophisticated, successful urban black male.

big willie *adj.* [BIG WILLIE *n.*] [1990s+] (*US black*) important, influential, powerful.

Big Wind *n.* (*also* **Big Windy**) [var. on WINDY CITY *n.*] [1940s+] (*US*) Chicago, Illinois.

big X, the *n.* [marked on a calendar with an X] [1980s+] (*US campus*) one's menstrual period.

bijou *adj.* [Fr.] [1960s+] small and pretty, usu. in combs. with nouns + the sfx *-ette*, e.g. *I'll have just a bijou drinkette*, 'just a little' drink.

bike it *v.* [1980s] to leave.

biker *n.* [SE (*motor*)*bike*] **1** [late 19C] a cyclist. **2** [1960s+] (*orig. US*) a motorcycle rider, usu. a member of an outlaw motorcycle gang. **3** [1980s] a 'biker movie', devoted to the fictionalized exploits of outlaw motorcyclists.

IN COMPOUNDS

❑ **biker's coffee** *n.* [2000s] (*US drugs*) a mix of coffee and methamphetamine.

bikie *n.* (*also* **bikey**) [var. on BIKER *n.* (2)] [1960s+] (*Aus./N.Z.*) an 'outlaw' motorcyclist, e.g. a Hell's Angel.

bikini burger *n.* [SE *bikini* + FURBURGER *n.*] [1990s+] wisps of pubic hair protruding from a bikini.

bikkie *n.* (*also* **biccie, bickie**) [dimin. of SE *biscuit*] [1960s+] **1** a biscuit, often in pl. **2** (*Aus. drugs*) a biscuit cooked with a dose of hashish.

bikkies *n.* (*also* **biccies, bickies**) [dimin. of SE *biscuits* and thus the roundness of coins] [1960s+] (*Aus.*) money; thus *big bikkies*, a large amount of money.

bil *n.* [abbr. of BILBO *n.*] [late 17C–mid-18C] (*UK Und.*) a sword.

bilbo *n.* (*also* **bilboa**) [SE *bilbo*, *bilboa*, a high-quality sword, imported from Bilboa in Spain; Williams (1994) includes *bilbo* among the sword synons. used for penis] **1** [late 17C–mid-19C] (*UK Und.*) a ruffian's sword; thus *bilbo's the word*, it's time for swords, i.e. fighting. **2** [18C–early 19C] iron ankle shackles, also called 'iron-garters'. **3** [late 18C–early 19C] in pl., the stocks.

bilbo *v.* [BILBO *n.* (2)] [mid-18C] (*UK Und.*) to place in shackles or irons.

Bilby's ball *n.*

IN PHRASES

❑ **shake one's trotters at Bilby's ball** *v. see* SHAKE ONE'S TROTTERS AT BEILBY'S BALL *under* BEILBY'S BALL *n.*

biled shirt *n. see* BOILED SHIRT *under* BOILED *adj.*

bilfa *n. see* BELFA *n.*

bilge *n.* [abbr. BILGEWATER *n.*] [20C+] nonsense, rubbish.

IN COMPOUNDS

❑ **bilge artist** *n.* (*also* **bilge-lizard**) [BILGE *n.* + -ARTIST *sfx* (1)] [1920s+] (*Aus.*) a braggart, one given to boasting.

bilgewater *n.* [SE *bilgewater*, the foul water that collects in a vessel's bilges] **1** [late 19C] thin beer; thus any thin, tasteless drink, alcoholic or otherwise. **2** [late 19C+] (*mainly juv.*) nonsense, rubbish, piffle. **3** [1920s] urine.

bilingual *adj.* [pun on SE] **1** [1960s+] (*US*) one who engages in bisexual oral sex. **2** [1980s+] (*orig. US gay*) referring to one who licks and sucks both the anus and penis of his partner.

biljim *n. see* BILLJIM *n.*

bilk *n.* [cribbage jargon *balk*, to spoil an adversary's score in their crib] **1** [mid-17C–mid-18C] an empty, meaningless statement. **2** [late 17C–mid-18C] a hoax; an act of cheating. **3** [late 18C+] (*US Und.*) a swindler or cheat. **4** [mid-19C] (*US*) a disappointment. **5** [1940s] (*US*) a form of swindle worked on a brothel madam.

(IN PHRASES)

❑ **on the bilk** *adj.* [mid-19C] cheating, swindling.

bilk *adj.* [BILK *n.*] [mid-18C] wrong, misleading, meaningless.

bilk *v.* [BILK *n.*] **1** [mid-17C+] (*UK Und.*) to cheat, to swindle. **2** [19C] to evade payments, esp. of a prostitute's client. **3** [1900s–10s] (*Aus. Und.*) of a prostitute, to rob a client; thus *bilking crib*, a house where the woman robs, or has an accomplice rob, her client.

(DERIVATIVES)

❑ **bilker** *n.* [early 18C–1940s] one who habitually cheats, esp. in refusing to pay a bill, e.g. a cabman's fare.

(IN PHRASES)

❑ **bilk the schoolmaster** *v.* [early 19C] to get knowledge without paying for it, e.g. the experience that comes with living one's life.

Bill *n.* **1** [late 19C–1910s] used to address an otherwise unknown male. **2** [1900s] (*Aus.*) generic for an Aus. soldier. **3** [1960s–70s] (*US gay*) generic for a masculine male homosexual or a mannish lesbian.

Bill, the *n.* (*also* **Bill**) [ety. unknown; ? abbr. OLD BILL *n.* (1). There is a poss. semantic link to BEAK *n.*[1] (1), but in reality it is unlikely] [1960s+] the police; thus *Bill from the Hill*, officers serving at Notting Hill police station in London W11.

(IN COMPOUNDS)

❑ **bill shop** *n.* [1960s+] a police station. ❑ **bill-wagon** *n.* [2000s] a police car.

bill *n.*[1] **1** [mid-17C+] the penis. **2** [mid-19C+] (*US*) the nose.

(IN PHRASES)

❑ **bill in** *v.* [1930s] to butt in, to interrupt. ❑ **dip one's/the bill** *v. see under* DIP *v.*[2].

bill *n.*[2] [abbr. SE *bill of divorce*] [1910s] (*US*) a divorce.

bill *n.*[3] [abbr. SE *dollar bill*] [20C+] **1** [1920s+] $10. **2** [1920s+] $20. **3** [1920s+] (*also* **one bill**) $100. **4** [2000s] a pound sterling. **5** [2000s] a euro.

(IN PHRASES)

❑ **big bill** *n.* [1930s] (*US Und.*) $1000. ❑ **half-a-bill** *n.* [1940s–60s] (*US*) fifty dollars, a $50 note.

bill *n.*[4] [BILLY WHIZ *n.* (1)] [2000s] amphetamine (sulphate).

bill *v.* [BILL *n.*[2]] **1** [19C] (*US*) to divorce. **2** [1990s+] (*US black*) to leave.

billabonger *n.* [SE *billabong*, a dry watercourse, in which such men took shelter and slept] [late 19C–1950s] (*Aus.*) a vagrant.

Billejo *n.*

(IN EXCLAMATIONS)

❑ **go to Billejo!** [? small town in Australia] [1950s] (*Aus.*) go to the devil!

billet *n.* [SE *billet*, a place in which a soldier is billeted; a soldier's lodging or quarters; note Stephens & O'Brien, *Materials for a Dict. of Aus. Slang* (ms.; 1900-10): 'Many jobs in Australia are of the board and lodging kind, that is, so much wages and board and lodging, which practically means billet.'] [19C+] an appointment, a job; thus (Aus.) *billet-hunter*, a job-seeker.

billiard ball *n.* **1** [17C] in phr. *billiard balls and stick*, the testicles (and penis). **2** [19C] the head (presumably of a bald person).

billied *adj.* [BILLIE HOKE *n.*] [1950s] (*US drugs*) addicted to cocaine.

billie hoke *n.* [rhy. sl. = COKE *n.*[1] (1)] [1950s+] (*drugs*) cocaine.

billies *n.* (*also* **billys**) [dimin. of BILL *n.*[3] (1)] [1980s] (*US teen*) money.

Billingsgate pheasant *n.* [*Billingsgate*, London's wholesale fish market] [late 19C–1900s] a red herring (the fish).

billjim *n.* (*also* **biljim**) [the proper names *Bill* + *Jim*; the typical Aus. soldier in WW1; a synthetic var., *billzac* (SE *bill* + ANZAC) was created by the Aus. press during WW1, but never spread beyond their own columns] [1900s–10s] (*Aus.*) the typical Australian male; used in WW1 for an Aus. soldier.

bill-o! *excl.* (*also* **below!**) [SE (*watchout*) *below!*] [20C+] (*London school*) a cry of warning.

bill of goods *n.* (*also* **bill**) [SE *bill of goods*, a consignment of merchandise] [20C+] (*orig. US*) false promises, a hoax, theories that are not followed up by practice; thus *sell one a bill of goods*, to persuade (someone) to accept something undesirable, swindle someone.

bill of sale *n.* [? a widow is 'back on the (marriage) market'] **1** [17C] a widow's peak. **2** [18C–mid-19C] a widow's weeds.

bill on the pump at Aldgate *n.* (*also* **Aldgate, draught on the pump at Aldgate**) [proper name *Aldgate Pump*, near junction of Fenchurch Street and Leadenhall Street in London; the pump was a City institution, but hardly a safe financial one] [late 18C–19C] a bad bill of exchange.

bill skinner *n.* [rhy. sl.] [2000s] (*Irish*) dinner.

Bill, Tom and Harry *n. see* TOM, DICK AND HARRY *n.*

bill (up) *v.* [UK black pron. of BUILD *v.* (1)] [1980s+] (*drugs*) to roll up a cannabis cigarette.

Billy *n.* [King William of Orange] **1** [20C+] (*Scot.*) a Protestant. **2** *see* KING BILLY *n.*

billy *n.*[1] [? a play on the *billycock* hat, which is 'felt'] [mid-19C] the vagina.

billy *n.*[2] [mid-19C] (*UK Und.*) a fool.

billy *n.*[3] **1** [mid-19C] a short iron crowbar, used by criminals. **2** [mid–late 19C] (*UK Und.*) stolen metal. **3** [mid-19C+] (*orig. US*) (*also* **bill**) a policeman's wooden club (orig. untanned cowhide, covered in wool), now SE. **4** [mid-19C+] a form of blackjack, usu. 'loaded' with lead. **5** [1960s] (*US*) a police officer; the police as a group. **6** [2000s] (*US prison*) a white man.

(IN COMPOUNDS)

❑ **billy boy** *n.* [1960s] (*US*) a policeman. ❑ **billy-hunting** *n.* [mid-19C] trading in old (poss. stolen) metal. ❑ **billy man** *n.* [1960s] a policeman.

billy *n.*[4] [? King *William* IV, in whose reign (1830–37) the practice began. The silk handkerchief was a central part of costermonger fashion, often apeing that of the prize-ring, where fancy handkerchiefs were an essential trademark of certain fighters. As Mayhew notes, in *London Labour and the London Poor* (1861–62): 'The costermonger [...] prides himself most of all upon his neckerchief and boots. Men, women, boys and girls all have a passion for these articles. The man who does not wear his silk neckerchief/his "King's-man" as it is called – is known to be in desperate circumstances, the implication being that it has gone to supply the morning's stock money'] [mid-19C] a silk handkerchief, worn by London costermongers.

(IN COMPOUNDS)

❑ **billy buzman** *n.* [BUZMAN *under* BUZ *n.*] [19C] a pickpocket who specializes in stealing silk handkerchiefs.

billy *n.*[5] [abbr.] [20C+] (*US*) (*also* **billy-maria**) a hillbilly.

billy *n.*[6] [abbr. BILLY WHIZ *n.*] [1980s+] (*drugs*) amphetamine.

billy *n.*[7] [play on SAusE *billy*, a form of kettle] [1990s+] (*Aus. drugs*) a form of pipe used for smoking cannabis.

billy *n.*[8] [2000s] (*S.Afr. gay*) beer.

billy *n.*[9] *see* BILLYCOCK *n.*

billy, the *n.* [1910s] someone or something excellent, admirable.

Billy Bad-ass *n.* (*also* **Billy Joe Bad-Ass**) [generic name *Billy-Joe* + BAD-ASS *n.* (1)] [1970s+] (*orig. US*) usu. in ironic use, anyone who sets themselves up as tough, aggressive.

billy barlow *n.*[1] [*BillyBarlow*, a real-life street clown, *fl.*1840 around the East End of London. 'Billy was a real person, semi-idiotic, and, though in dirt and rags, fancied himself a swell of the first water. Occasionally he came out with real witticisms [...] and died in Whitechapel Workhouse' (Hotten, 1864)] [mid-19C] a fool.

billy barlow *n.*[2] [? brandname] [20C+] (*US*) a large pocket knife with folding blades.

Billy-be-damned *n.* (*also* **Billy-be-danged, billy b'dam, ...bedam**) [? orig. euph. for the Devil or hell] **1** [mid-19C+] (*US*) comparative phr. used to indicate absoluteness, e.g. *dead as..., cold as...* **2** [1910s] as a term of address.

billy-be-damned *adj.* (*also* **billy-be-blowed**) [? orig. euph. for BLOODY *adj.* (1)] [mid-19C+] (*US*) euph. for the Devil or hell.

billy born drunk *n.* [proper name *Billy* + quasi-nickname *Born-Drunk*] [late 19C–1900s] a drunkard all one's life.

Billy Bunter *n.* [rhy. sl. Billy Bunter = PUNTER *n.* (5); from the fictional schoolboy Billy Bunter, created by 'Frank Richards' (Charles Hamilton 1876-1976)] [2000s] a member of the public, a customer.

billy button *n.*[1] [rhy. sl.] [mid–late 19C] mutton.

billy button *n.*[2] [joc. use of 'proper name' + rhy. sl. = (gets) nothing] [20C+] (*W.I.*) a gullible fool, esp. one who performs a job of work without first making sure that they will be paid.

billy-cart *n.* [abbr. SE *billy-goat cart*] [1950s+] (*Aus./N.Z.*) a child's homemade 'go-kart'.

billycock *n.* (*also* **billy**) [? *bully-cocked*, 'cocked after the fashion of the bullies' (the sp. of the orig. 1721 citation); note Stephens & O'Brien, *Materials for a Dict. of Aus. Slang* (ms.; 1900-10), query as to a possible relationship to Aus. *billy*, 'a can for cooking purposes'] [mid–late 19C] a hat with a low crown; primarily worn by carters, it was also popular among the clergy; thus *billycockgang*, the clergy as a group.

Billy D. juice *n.* [proper name *Billy D* + JUICE *n.*[1] (3)] [1990s+] (*US black/teen*) Colt .45 malt liquor.

billy fencer *n.* [? BILLY *n.*[3] (2) + -FENCER *sfx*] [mid-19C] a marine store owner.

billy-fencing shop *n.* [BILLY FENCER *n.* + SE *shop*] [mid–late 19C] a shop that specializes in buying stolen precious metals.

billy-goat *n.*[1] [the goat's supposed characteristics] **1** [mid-19C–1930s] (*orig. US*) a lecher. **2** [mid-19C+] a boyfriend. **3** [late 19C] a bearded old man. **4** [1910s] (*orig. US*) a bad-tempered man.

billy-goat *n.*[2] [rhy. sl.; var. on NANNY (GOAT) *n.*] [1980s+] **1** a coat. **2** the throat.

billy goat *v.* [BILLY-GOAT *n.*[1] (1)] [1930s–60s] (*orig. US*) to philander.

billy-goat alley *n.* (*also* **billy-goat hill**) [? the denizens keeping goats or, since such areas are associated with various social excesses, f. their 'goatishness'] [1930s+] (*US*) the poorest section of a town.

billy gorman *n.* [rhy. sl.] [late 19C] a foreman or ganger.

Billy Harran' s dog *n.* [anecdotal] [20C+] (*Irish*) a time-server, one who befriends whoever they happen to be with.

billy-jack *adj.* [the title of a 1971 film featuring a raw country-boy] [1980s] (*US black*) unsophisticated, from the back woods.

Billy Joe Bad-Ass *n. see* BILLY BAD-ASS *n.*

Billy Joel *n.* [rhy. sl. = HOLE *n.*[1] (1); ult. f. US singer *Billy Joel* (b. 1949)] [2000s] sexual intercourse.

billy knife *n.* [abbr. BILLY BARLOW *n.*[2]] [20C+] (*US*) a large pocket knife.

billy liar *n.* [rhy. sl.; ult. book *Billy Liar* (1959) by Keith Waterhouse (b. 1929)] [1990s+] a tyre.

billy lid *n.* [rhy. sl. = KID *n.*[1] (1)] [1980s+] (*Aus.*) a child.

billy-maria *n. see* BILLY *n.*[5].

billy muggins *n.* [ext. of MUGGINS *n.*[1]] [1910s+] (*Aus.*) a fool.

billy-my-nag *n. see* BOB-MY-NAG *n.*

billy-noodle *n.* [SE *billy*, generic for a man + NOODLE *n.*[1] (2); US use is 19C; Aus. is 20C] [late 19C+] (*US/Aus.*) a man who firmly believes, all evidence to the contrary notwithstanding, that no woman can resist his charms.

billy-o *n.* [-O *sfx* (2)] **1** [late 19C+] (*also* **billy-oh**) euph. for hell, thus trouble, punishment. **2** [1910s] nonsense, rubbish.

(IN PHRASES)

□ **like billy-o** *adv.* (*also* **like billy-ho, ...billy hell, ...billy-oh, ...billyo**) [dial., euph. for 'bloody hell'] [late 19C+] a general intensifier and expression of energy or effort, most enthusiastically, strenuously, speedily.

billys *n. see* BILLIES *n.*

Billy the Kid *n.* [rhy. sl. = YID *n.*[1]; plus the wearing of large, black, wide-brimmed hat seen as similar to a cowboy hat] [1920s–30s] a very orthodox Jew.

billy turniptop *n.* [generic use of proper name + joc. use of SE; Ware suggests that it is 'probably an outgrowth of TOMMY ATKINS *n.* (1)'] [late 19C–1900s] an agricultural labourer.

Billy Whiz *n.* (*also* **whizz**) [*Billy Whizz*, a character in a children's comic; as his name suggests, he moves fast] [1990s+] (*UK drugs*) **1** amphetamine. **2** a mixture of heroin and cocaine.

Billy Wright *adj.* [rhy. sl. = SHITE *n.*] [1990s+] a general negative: useless, disgusting, repellent.

biltong curtain *n.* [SE *biltong*, salted, wind-dried meat, a S.Afr. national foodstuff + a pun on SE *iron curtain*] [1970s–80s] (*S.Afr.*) a joc. name for the borders of pre-independence South Africa.

bim *n.*[1] [from Igbo *bem*, my house, home, household, folk, fellows + ? Yoruba *ebi mi*, my folk/relative; many Igbo slaves were taken to Barbados] [late 19C+] a Bajan, a native of Barbados; thus *Bimshire*, Barbados.

bim *n.*[2] [ety. unknown; ? abbr. BIMBO *n.*] [1950s–70s] (*US black*) a police officer.

bim *n.*[3] *see* BIMBO *n.*

bim *adv.* [late 18C–mid-19C] echoic of a sudden act, esp. of of one object hitting another.

bimaz *n. see* BEAMER *n.*

bimbette *n.* [BIMBO *n.* (5) + fem. dimin. sfx *-ette*] [1980s+] a junior or aspirant 'good-time girl'.

bimbo *n.* [the earliest use of *himbo* is synon. with 'bozo' to mean a man, prob. unintelligent; overtones of thuggery appear c. 1920. A parallel use was that to mean 'baby', abbr. from the Italian *bambino*. By the 1920s the word also meant young woman, often a prostitute; simultaneously it meant a tramp's companion, poss. gay. The writer Jack Conway (of *Variety* magazine) used it spec. to mean a 'dumb girl'. *Bimbo* gained a new currency during the 1980s when it came to describe a young woman, usu. something of a gold-digger and indulged as such by rich and/or powerful older men and the media to whom they tell or sell their tales. The original 1980s bimbo was a 'model', Fiona Wright, who delighted the press with revelations of her relationship with Sir Ralph Halpern, a millionaire businessman] **1** [1910s–40s] (*orig. US*) (*also* **bim**) a man, usu. young. **2** [1910s+] (*Ling. Fr./Polari*) a dupe, an insignificant person. **3** [1920s–50s] (*US*) (*also* **bim, bombo**) a thug; a large, stupid man. **4** [1920s+] (*also* **bim, bimb, bimby**) (*orig. US*) a woman. **5** [1980s+] an unintelligent, but attractive, young man or woman.

bimbo *adj.* [1960s+] crazy, foolish.

Bimi *n.* [BIM *n.*[1]] [1970s] a West Indian.

Bimi *adj.* [BIMI *n.*] [1970s] (*US*) West Indian.

bimmer *n. see* BEAMER *n.*

bimp *n.* [BEONG *n.*] [1920s] (*UK tramp*) a shilling (five pence).

bimp *v.* [ety. unknown] [1960s+] to spy, esp. as a sexual voyeur.

bimps *n.* [ety. unknown] [1970s] (*US campus*) French fried potatoes.

bin *n.* **1** [mid-19C+] a pocket. **2** [late 19C] an unpleasant or run-down place. **3** [1900s] (*US*) a safe. **4** [1930s+] a psychiatric institution. **5** [1970s–80s] a police or prison cell. **6** [1990s+] prison.

bin *v.* **1** [1940s+] to throw away; to discard [abbr. SE *throw in the bin*]. **2** [1960s+] to commit to a psychiatric institution [BIN *n.* (4)].

binco *n.* [Ital. *bianco*, white] [mid-19C] (*Ling. Fr./Polari*) a kerosene flare.

bind *n.* [such problems 'tie one up'] **1** [colloq.] [mid-19C+] a difficult situation, a predicament. **2** [1930s+] a bore, nuisance.

bind *v.* [orig. RAF use, and poss. the most commonly used of all RAF sl.; thus the celebrated BBC radio comedy programme of the late 1940s, *Much Binding in the Marsh*] **1** [1920s+] to bore intensely, thus *binding*, boring. **2** [1940s–50s] to complain, to scold.

binder *n.*[1] [all f. their 'binding' or costive properties] **1** [mid-19C–1930s] a piece of bread and cheese. **2** [late 19C–1900s] an egg. **3** [late 19C–1950s] a last drink. **4** [late 19C+] (*N.Z.*) a good, filling meal; thus *go a binder*, to eat a meal. **5** [1940s–60s] in pl., brakes; thus *jump on the binders*, to put on the brakes; excl. *hit the binders!* brake! [their tightening on a moving wheel]. **6** [1950s] one who orders a drink in a public house after 'last orders'.

binder *n.*[2] [BIND v.] **1** [1920s+] (*orig. RAF*) a bore. **2** [1920s+] a habitual complainer.

binderjuice *n.* [2000s] (*US black*) vaginal secretions.

binding *adj. see under* BLINDING.

bindle *n.* [Ger. *Büntel*, a package] **1** [late 19C+] (*US*) a bundle containing clothes and possessions, esp. a bedding-roll carried by a tramp. **2** [1920s] as sense 1, other than of clothes etc, a bundle, a package. **3** [1920s+] (*drugs*) a small measure of narcotics, wrapped in a folded square of paper.

IN COMPOUNDS

❑ **bindle boy** *n.* [1930s–50s] (*US gay*) the young companion of a homosexual tramp. ❑ **bindle Kate** *n.* [generic female name] [1950s] (*US drugs*) a female narcotics addict. ❑ **bindle man** *n.* [late 19C+] (*US*) a tramp. ❑ **bindle punk** *n.* [PUNK *n.*[1] (3)] [late 19C+] (*US*) a tramp. ❑ **bindle stiff** *n.* (*also* **bindle bo, bindle bum, bundle stiff, bundle stiff willie**) [STIFF *n.*[1] (4a)/BO *n.*[1]/BUM *n.*[3] (1)] (*US*) **1** [late 19C+] a tramp, spec. one carrying a bedroll; formerly a migrant worker. **2** [1920s–50s] (*US drugs*) (*also* **bindle bum**) a narcotics addict. **3** [1920s+] an unimportant man.

bine *n.* [from the popular cigarette brand, Wills Wood*bines*] (*Aus.*) **1** [20C+] an English immigrant. **2** [1940s] an English soldier.

bines *n.* [BINS *n.*[2] (1)] [1950s] spectacles.

bing *n.*[1] [ety. unknown; image of one being thrown into a cell and landing 'bing!'] [1930s+] (*US prison*) the solitary confinement cell, used for punishment.

bing *n.*[2] [BING *v.*[2]] [1930s+] (*drugs*) enough of a drug for one injection.

IN COMPOUNDS

❑ **bing room** *n.* [1920s–50s] (*US drugs*) a room where narcotics users gather to take drugs, a SHOOTING GALLERY *n.*

bing *n.*[3] [1990s+] (*US black/campus*) money.

bing *v.*[1] (*also* **binge**) [? Rom.; Walter Scott resurrected it for his literary romances of the period in early 19C] [mid-16C+] (*UK Und.*) to go.

bing *v.*[2] [echoic] **1** [20C+] to hit. **2** [1930s] (*US tramp*) to put pressure on, to frighten, as in phr. *put the bing on*. **3** [1990s+] to shoot.

binga *v.* [SE *begone!*] [mid-19C] (*UK Und.*) to send; thus *binga-ridden*, sent away.

bingaloo *adj.* [late 19C–1920s] (*US*) stupid.

bing a waste *v.* (*also* **bing avast**) [the *OED* suggests a poss. Gypsy root but offers no elaboration + SE *waste*, wasteland, desert or f. 16C SE *aways*, away; Carew, in *The History of Bampfylde Moore Carew* (1750), has *bing feck you*, devil take you, and *bing lee ma*, devil miss me, as 'gypsy language'] [mid-16C–late 18C; 1920s] (*UK Und.*) to go away, to depart.

bing-bang *n.* [echoic] [late19C–1930s] a repeated heavy thump or a continued banging noise.

bing-bongs *n.* [the idea of them knocking together] [1990s+] the female breasts.

binge *n.* [dial.] **1** [late 19C+] (*also* **binge-up**) excessive consumption, usu. of drink and (latterly) drugs; thus *binge drinker*, a very heavy drinker; *bingeland*, a notional 'world' of drunken excess. **2** [1920s+] in weak use, any form of party or outing. **3** [1920s+] situation. **4** [1950s] a campaign.

IN PHRASES

❑ **on a binge** (*also* **on the binge**) [1940s+] out on a drunken spree.

binge *v.* [BINGE *n.* (1)] **1** [mid-19C+] to drink heavily; thus as n., *binger*, one who drinks heavily. **2** [1990s+] (*drugs*) to indulge in a continuous period of crack cocaine use; thus *binging*, using crack cocaine for long periods; also used of cocaine.

DERIVATIVES

❑ **binged** *adj.* (*also* **binged up, binjed up**) [20C+] drunk.

IN PHRASES

❑ **binge up** *v.* [1910s] to cheer someone up, to enliven.

bingee *n. see* BINGY *n.* (1).

bingey *n.*[1] [? dial. *bing* n., a heap, a pile or *bing* v., to hit] [late 19C] (*Anglo-Irish*) the penis.

bingey *n.*[2] *see* BINGY *n.*

binghi *n.* (*also* **Binghi**) [Dharuk *binghi*, a brother] [1900s–50s] (*Aus./N.Z.*) an aboriginal or Native Australian.

bingie *n. see* BINGY *n.*

bingle *n.*[1] [? echoic *bing*, the sound of a collision; c. 1900 baseball use *bingle*, a blow, a hit (of the ball)] [1940s+] (*Aus.*) **1** a fight. **2** a collision, a crash.

bingle *n.*[2] [? var. on BINDLE *n.* (3)] [1950s+] (*US drugs*) **1** a large supply of narcotics. **2** a drug seller.

bingo *n.*[1] [? *B* for brandy + Yorks. dial. *stingo*, strong ale (*OED*) or SE *binge* (*DSUE*)] [late 17C–late 19C] brandy or any hard liquor.

DERIVATIVES

❑ **bingoed** *adj.* [1920s+] (*UK society*) drunk.

IN COMPOUNDS

❑ **bingo-boy** *n.* **1** [late 17C–late 19C] a male lover of brandy. **2** [18C] a gin-drinker. **3** [mid-19C; 1940s] (*US gang*) a drunkard. ❑ **bingo-club** *n.* **1** [late 17C–mid-18C] a set of rakes whose favourite tipple is brandy. **2** [18C] a club of gin-drinkers. ❑ **bingo-mort** *n.* (*also* **bingo-mot(t)**) [BINGO *n.*[1] (1) + MORT *n.* (1)] [early 18C–late 19C] a female lover of brandy.

bingo *n.*[2] **1** [1900s–20s] a hard blow. **2** [1950s+] (*Can./US prison*) a riot.

bingo *n.*[3] [? misuse of baseball jargon *bingle*, a hit for a single] **1** [1930s–50s] (*US drugs*) a narcotic injection. **2** [1990s+] (*US black*) a $1 bill.

bingo *n.*[4] [mispron.] **1** [1960s] (*US*) a BIMBO *n.* **2** [2000s] an attractive person.

bingo *adj.* [BINGO *n.*[1]] [early 19C] (*UK Und.*) of a face, red (through alcohol, esp. brandy).

bingo *v.* [BINGO *n.*[3] (1)] [1980s+] (*drugs*) to inject a drug.

bingo! *excl.* [echoic of SE *bing!* a thump; in a flash] **1** [20C+] (*also* **bango! bingorino! zingo!**) used to imply a moment's surprise, excitement, suddenness etc, e.g. *There I was, walking along, then bingo! a cat fell on my head*. **2** [1920s+] used to imply success, esp. of a sighting of something or somebody.

IN PHRASES

❑ **like bingo** *adv.* [1930s–40s] a general intensifier and expression of energy or effort, most enthusiastically, strenuously, speedily.

bingo-bag *n.* [? briefs as opposed to G-strings, thongs etc] [1990s+] (*W.I.*) underwear.

bingo wings *n.* [the image of an old lady waving her arm to signal a 'full house' in a bingo hall; but also var. on BATWING *n.* (5)] [2000s] upper arm flab.

bings *adv.* [1900s] (*Irish*) lots, many.

bingy *n.* (*also* **bingee, bingey, bingie, binjy**) [Dharuk *bingy*, the stomach] [mid-19C–1920s] (*Aus./N.Z.*) the stomach; also corpulence.

binky *n.*[1] **1** [1910s] (*US*) any small mechanical object [? SE *dinky*]. **2** [1950s] (*drugs*) (*also* **bopper**) a needle used for injecting narcotic drugs, most often a disposable needle that is prescribed to a diabetic [BING *n.*[2]].

binky *n.*[2] [? Scot. *bink*, a bench] [1960s] (*US*) the buttocks.

binlid *n.*[1] [fig. use of abbr. SE *dustbin lid*] [1990s+] (*Ulster*) a fool.

binlid *n.*[2] [rhy. sl. = KID *n.*[1] (1)] [2000s] a child.

binned *adj.* [proper name Bartholomew *Binns*, the London hangman in 1883] [late 19C] hanged.

Binnie Hale *n.* [rhy. sl.; ult. UK actress *Binnie Hale* (1899–1984)] [1940s+] a tale, i.e. a 'tall story' or confidence trickster's 'line'.

binnie one/two *n.* [BUSINESS *n.* (3) + NUMBER ONE *n.* (5)/NUMBER TWO *n.* (1)] [1980s] (*Aus. juv.*) urination/defecation.

binns *n. see* BINS *n.*[2] (1).

binny *n. see* BENNY *n.*[1] (2).

binos *n.* [abbr.] [2000s] (*US*) binoculars.

bins *n.*[1] [BIN *n.* (1), i.e. the pockets that they contain] [1930s+] a pair of trousers.

bins *n.*[2] (*also* **binns**) [abbr. SE *binoculars*] [1930s+] **1** glasses, spectacles. **2** binoculars. **3** the eyes.

bint *n.* (*also* **binty**) [Arabic *bint*, daughter; thus a woman who has yet to bear a child; noted in 1855 by the explorer Richard Burton (1821–90), the term gained fuller currency during WW1 and WW2, when it was adopted by Allied servicemen; note WW1 milit. *the bint*, the man who plays a female role in a milit. concert party] **1** [1910s+] a young woman; thus *lush bint*, a very good-looking woman; as v. *go binting*, to go on leave. **2** [1950s] (*Aus.*) a general term of abuse.

bio *n.*[1] [Afk. *bioscope*, a cinema; obs. elsewhere, the term remains current in South Africa] [1910s+] (*S.Afr.*) the cinema.

bio *n.*[2] [abbr.] [1940s+] a *bio*graphy.

biockey *n.* [Ital. *baiocchi*, lit. 'browns', thus cf. BROWN *n.* (2)] [mid–late 19C] (*Anglo-Italian*) money.

biog *n.* [abbr.] [1930s+] (*orig. US*) a *biog*raphy.

biolinging *n.* [SE *bilingual*] [2000s] (*US black/teen*) to write and sing hip-hop lyrics in two languages, i.e. Spanish and English.

bionc *n. see* BIANC *n.*

bionic *adj.* [SE *bionic*, 'having or being an artificial, esp. electromechanical, device that replaces part of the body; having ordinary human capabilities increased (as if) by the aid of such devices' (*OED*); coined 1963 but popularized by the 1970s TV series *Six-Million Dollar Man*, starring actor Lee Majors] [1970s+] **1** exceptional, outstandingly gifted. **2** extreme, beyond the limit.

bionk *n. see* BIANC *n.*

bioscope *n.* [SE *bioscope*, a cinema; the more one drinks the more 'moving pictures' one sees] [1910s] a drink of brandy.

bioscope *adj.* [SE *bioscope*, a cinema] [1960s] (*S.Afr.*) dramatic, exciting.

bip *adv.* [mid-19C+] echoic of the sound of an object hitting/being hit suddenly.

bip-bam-thank-you-ma'am *n.* [BIP *adv.* + BAM! *excl.*] [20C+] quick, spontaneous intercourse, with the implication that only the man will achieve pleasure.

bipe *n.* (*also* **bi**) [? joc. use of SE *bipolar*] [1960s+] (*US*) a bisexual.

bipe *v.* (*also* **bip, scallybip**) [1960s–70s] (*US prison*) to break into and rob houses while the occupants are asleep; thus *bipper, scallybipper*, a thief who specializes in this.

bip (into) *v.* [echoic] [1970s+] (*US campus*) to hit.

bippy *n.* [coined on NBC-TV's *Rowan and Martin's Laugh-In*, c.1967] **1** [1960s+] (*orig. US*) a synon. for ASS *n.*, esp. in phr. *you can bet your (sweet) bippy*. **2** the female breast, as in *bippy top*, a tight top that accentuates a woman's breasts.

birch broom *n.* [rhy. sl.] [mid-19C–1960s] a room.

Birchen/Birchin Lane *n. see* SEND TO BIRCHING LANE *under* SEND *v.*

Birchington hunt *n.* [rhy. sl.; var. on BERKELEY (HUNT) *n.* (1) + ? overtones of sado-masochism] [1930s+] the vagina.

bird *n.*[1] [note first use of sense 1 c.1300, meaning a maiden or girl and not sl. until 1900 when it meant a sweetheart or a prostitute; imagery of sense 2a reflects the world of hunting; in sense 2b note WW1 RN *bird*, a man continually in trouble] **1** as a symbol of feminity or, in men, weakness/effeminacy. (**a**) [mid-16C–17C; 1910s+] a prostitute, a promiscuous woman. (**b**) [mid-19C+] (*also* **bird**) a young woman, a girlfriend. (**c**) [late 19C] (*US*) an attractive (young) woman. (**d**) [1920s+] (*US*) a male homosexual. (**e**) [1950s–70s] (*US black*) an experienced, tough female prostitute. (**f**) [1960s] used in sing. as generic for all women. **2** (*orig. UK Und.*) trapped, controlled, i.e. as a 'bird in a cage'. (**a**) [late 16C+] a confidence trickster's victim. (**b**) [17C+] a prisoner; thus *a bird has flown*, a prisoner has escaped, ext. as *Bridewell bird, penitentiary bird*. **3** in fig. use, a person, esp. a suspect, an outsider, an eccentric. (**a**) [late 16C+] (*also* **birdie**) a person, a man, a 'bloke'. (**b**) [mid-19C] (*US*) a dissolute or degenerate person, 'a fast man, woman or horse' (R.H. Thornton, *An American Glossary*, 1912); often ext. as *perfect bird*. (**c**) [1910s] (*US*) an animal. (**d**) [1920s–70s] (*Aus./US*) an eccentric. (**e**) [1930s–60s] (*orig. US tramp*) an outsider, an unconventional person. **4** [mid–late 19C] (*US*) as a representation of a bird, e.g. an American eagle on the dollar. **5** (*US campus*) representative of good or bad qualities. (**a**) [late 19C] (*US*) something unpleasant. (**b**) [late 19C–1900s] a term of reproach. (**c**) [late 19C+] (*also* **dicky-bird**) something or someone, excellent or admirable. (**d**) [1910s] a failure. **6** [1930s+] (*mainly US*) an aircraft, esp. a helicopter, spacecraft, missile etc. **7** *see* DICKY-BIRD *n.*[1] (5).

IN PHRASES

❑ **bird of the game** *n. see* separate entries. ❑ **bird of the night** *n. see* NIGHTBIRD *under* NIGHT *n.* ❑ **bird (up)** *v.* [2000s] to pursue women for sex. ❑ **catching the bird** *n.* [1930s+] (*Aus.*) picking up a woman while driving one's car and then persuading her to agree to sex.

SE in slang uses

IN COMPOUNDS

❑ **birdbrain** *n.* **1** [1940s+] a fool; thus *bird-brained*, stupid. **2** [1950s+] as term of address. ❑ **birdcage** *see* separate entries. ❑ **bird colonel** *n.* [the silver eagles affixed to the uniform's shoulders denote the rank] [1940s+] (*US*) a full colonel in the US marines; thus *make bird*, to gain this promotion; *light bird*, a lieutenant-colonel. ❑ **birdcrap** *n.* [1970s] (*US*) nonsense, rubbish. ❑ **bird division** *n.* [1950s] (*US*) US Air Force. ❑ **birddog/dogger** *see* separate entries. ❑ **bird eater** *n.* [SE phr. *eat like a bird*] [1960s–70s] (*US*) a finicky eater. ❑ **birdlime** *see* separate entries. ❑ **birdseed** *n. see* separate entries. ❑ **birdshit** *n.* [SE *bird* + SHIT *n.*] **1** [1960s] (*US*) a term of contempt. **2** [1970s] (*US*) nonsense, rubbish. ❑ **bird's nest** *see* separate entries. ❑ **bird turd** *see* separate entries. ❑ **bird-witted** *adj.* **1** [17C–late 18C; 1930s] foolish, scatter-brained, gullible. **2** [late 18C–early 19C] inconsiderate, thoughtless.

IN PHRASES

❑ **bird never flew on one wing, a** [20C+] used as a formula for accepting a second drink (and pretending that one is doing so more from duty than pleasure). ❑ **bird of passage** *n.* [1940s] a tramp, a vagrant. ❑ **birds of a feather** *n.* [pvb *birds of a feather flock together*] [17C–18C] members of the same gang. ❑ **does a bird have wings?** *see* DOES A BEAR SHIT IN THE WOODS? IS THE POPE A CATHOLIC? *phr.* ❑ **for the birds** *adj.* [1940s+] (*orig. US*) trivial, worthless, appealing only to gullible people; ext. as *strictly for the birds* and coarsely as *shit for the birds*. ❑ **go like a bird** *v.* [1920s+] of an automobile, or any vehicle, to go fast and smoothly with no mechanical problems. ❑ **go with the birds** *v.* [1930s] (*US tramp*) to go south for the winter. ❑ **join the bird family** *v.* [to 'fly' away] [1940s] (*US black*) to leave fast, to run away. ❑ **make one's bird** *v.* [from MAKE LIKE (A)… *v.*] [1960s] (*US campus*) to leave.

bird *n.*[2] [echoic of a harsh bird-call] **1** [early 19C+] (*US*) a loud, derisive noise, imitative of a fart, esp. in phr. *give one the bird*. **2** [20C+] one who deserves ridicule. **3** [1900s] (*Aus.*) one who has been dismissed from a job. **4** [1920s+] any form of ridicule or derision. **5** in non-theatrical sense, an act of rejection, e.g. of courtship. **6** [1960s+] (*US*) usu. as *the bird*, an obscene gesture of dismissal, mockery; usu. in phrs.

IN PHRASES

❑ **dead bird** *n. see under* DEAD *adj.* ❑ **flip the bird** *v.* (*also* **bird, flick off, flip off, flip the El Birdo, fly the bird**) [1950s+] **1** to make an obscene gesture by raising the middle finger from the otherwise clenched fist. **2** in fig. use. ❑ **get the (big) bird** *v.* **1** [early 19C+] esp. theatrical use, to be jeered, mocked etc, the image of the hissing noise that geese, and an unappreciative audience, can make. **2** [late 19C+] to be dismissed, usu. from a job. ❑ **give someone the bird** *v.* [late 19C+] **1** to express one's disapproval vocally, esp. by hissing; also in fig. use. **2** to raise the middle finger as a gesture of derision. **3** to reject, to dismiss. ❑ **have a bird** *v.* [1980s] (*US*) to become very angry. ❑ **shoot the bird** *v.* [1970s+] (*orig. US*) to make a mocking, derisory gesture by clenching the fist and raising the middle finger.

bird *n.*[3] **1** [late 19C+] (*mainly US*) the penis; thus *beat/jerk one's bird*, to masturbate, *get one's bird in a splint*, to get into (painful) difficulties; *eat/gobble/swallow one's bird*, to fellate; *how's your bird?* a phrase of greeting, *not on your bird!* in no way! impossible. **2** [1960s–70s] (*US*) the vagina; thus *bird-washing*, mutual cunnilingus. **3** [1970s] (*US gay*) fellatio.

IN COMPOUNDS

❑ **birdbath** *n.* [1970s] the vagina. ❑ **bird circuit** *n. see* separate entry. ❑ **bird taker** *n.* **1** [1930s–40s] a sodomite. **2** [1950s] the vagina. **3** [1970s+] (*US gay*) a male prostitute.

IN PHRASES

❑ **bird in a gilded cage** *n.* [1970s+] (*US gay*) a man's crotch in a pair of expensive trousers. ❑ **cop a bird** *v.* [1930s–40s] (*US*) usu. of a prostitute, to fellate.

bird *n.*[4] [rhy. sl. BIRDLIME *n.*[2] (1) = TIME *n.* (1)] **1** [1920s+] a prison sentence; thus *birded (up)*, imprisoned; *in bird*, in prison; *do bird*, serve a sentence. **2** [1930s–40s] previous convictions. **3** [1950s–60s] in fig. use, any form of constraint, responsibility.

IN COMPOUNDS

❑ **bird-happy** *adj.* [-HAPPY *sfx*] [1970s] (*UK prison*) emotionally affected by a (long) prison sentence. ❑ **birdhouse** *n.* **1** [1940s] (*US*) a prison. **2** [1950s] (*US drugs*) a place where one can purchase narcotics [puns on BIRDSEYE *n.* (2) + SE *house*]. **3** [1950s] a psychiatric institution.

IN PHRASES

❑ **first bird** *n.* [1920s+] (*UK prison*) one's first experience of a prison sentence.

bird *n.*[5] [abbr.] **1** [1960s–70s] (*US*) the Thunder*bird*, a motorcar. **2** [1990s+] (*US black*) Thunderbird wine.

bird *n.*[6] [ety. unknown] [1970s+] the mind, sanity; thus *lose one's bird*, to go mad, *out of one's bird*, crazy, mad.

bird *n.*[7] [1990s+] (*drugs*) a large quantity, e.g., one kilo of cocaine.

bird *n.*[8] [? a 'bird in the hand'] [2000s] (*N.Z.*) success.

IN PHRASES

❑ **make a bird of** *v.* [2000s] to succeed in a project. ❑ **make a dead bird of** *v.* [2000s] to make absolutely sure of what one is doing.

bird *n.*[9] *see* BLACKBIRD *n.*[1] (1).

bird *adj.* [BIRD *n.*[1] (5c)] [late 19C] (*US campus*) wonderful, first-rate, admirable.

bird *v.*[1] [BIRD *n.*[1] (2)] [late 16C–early 17C] to rob, to steal, to search for plunder.

bird *v.*[2] [BIRD TURD *v.*] [1940s–60s] (*US*) to talk nonsense, usu. in phr. *not just birding*.

bird *v.*[3] *see* BIRD *n.*[2] (1).

birdcage *n.* [resemblance; note WW1 milit. *birdcage*, a holding cage near the front lines for prisoners of war, prior to their transfer to a proper prison camp] **1** [mid–late 19C] a bustle on a woman's dress. **2** [mid-19C–1900s] a four-wheeled cab. **3** [late 19C–1950s] (*US*) a prison cell; the condemned cell, into which a prisoner is transferred from DEATH ROW *n.* for the last few days prior to his execution. **4** [1900s–60s] a dormitory for women students. **5** [1920s–40s] (*US*) a brothel. **6** [1930s–60s] (*US*) an elevator with an openwork sliding metal gate. **7** [1940s–50s] a sleeping cubicle in a flophouse, separated from its neighbours by a 'wall' of chicken wire. **8** [1970s–80s] (*N.Z. prison*) the exercise yard.

birdcage hype *n.* [? BIRDCAGE *n.* (7) + HYPE *n.*[2] (2); note Maurer 'Language of the Underworld Narcotic Addict' (1938): 'Probably so-called because this type of addict often lives in a *bird-cage* or *bird-cage joint*, a very cheap lodging house with chicken-wire netting separating the small sleeping compartments. Transients who live in these establishments are called *bird-cage stiffs*. There is also a saying that when an underworld addict is down and out, "he has a bird cage on one foot and a boxing glove on the other" – a humorous variant of "a boot on one foot and a shoe on the other"'] [1930s–50s] (*US drugs*) the lowest class of heroin addict.

bird circuit *n.* [BIRD *n.*[3] (1) + SE *circuit*] [1960s–70s] (*US gay*) touring gay bars in a sucession of cities.

IN PHRASES

❑ **do the bird circuit** *v.* [1950s+] (*US gay*) to visit a succession of bars in order to ascertain the whereabouts of the most attractive men.

bird dog *n.* [SE *bird dog*, a retriever, which fetches things] **1** [20C+] a receiver of stolen goods. **2** [1920s–40s] a persistent, tenacious person. **3** [1930s] (*US Und.*) a contact man for stock and bond thieves. **4** [1930s+] one who lures victims into positions of vulnerability. **5** [1940s–70s] (*US campus/teen*) a young man, bereft of a partner of his own, who attempts to steal a woman from someone else. **6** [1950s+] an assistant, esp. in police or journalism. **7** [1950s+] a watcher, an observer.

bird dog *v.* [BIRD DOG *n.*] [1940s+] **1** (*US, mainly teen*) to steal another person's girlfriend, to break up a school or college romance. **2** to pimp for, to solicit for another person. **3** to hang around in the hope of making a pick-up, either for sex or commercial gain. **4** to spend more time away from home than staying in with one's family. **5** to observe, to lie in wait. **6** to follow. **7** to watch over, to protect. **8** (*US prison*) to eavesdrop.

bird dogger *n.* [SE *bird dog*, a retriever, which is seen as especially keen to please] [1960s] (*US*) one who tries overly hard to gain acceptance or approval.

birder *n.* [abbr. SE *blackbirder*, a slaver] [late 19C] (*Aus.*) a slave-trader.

birdie *n.*[1] [ext. of BIRD *n.*[3] (1)] [20C+] the penis.

birdie *n.*[2] [BIRD *n.*[1] (1); note 14C–16C SE *bird*, a young man] [1930s+] an effeminate male.

birdie *n.*[3] [play on SE *peck*, a perfunctory kiss] [1990s+] (*Irish*) a kiss.

birdie powder *n.* [? BIRDSEYE *n.* (2) or joc. use of SE *birdseed*] [1940s+] (*drugs*) **1** heroin; morphine. **2** cocaine.

birdlime *n.*[1] [SE *bird-lime*, a sticky substance spread on twigs so that birds may be caught; the ref. is to the thief's 'sticky fingers'] [17C–early 19C] stealing; a thief.

birdlime *n.*[2] (*also* **bird's-lime**) [rhy. sl. = TIME *n.* (1)] [mid-19C+] **1** a prison sentence. **2** time.

birdlime *adj.* [BIRDLIME *n.*[1]] [late 18C] larcenous, thieving.

bird of the game *n.*[1] [BIRD *n.*[1] (1) + GAME *n.* (1)] [17C] a prostitute.

bird of the game *n.*[2] [BIRD *n.*[1] (3b) + GAME *n.* (1)] [19C] a womanizer.

birds *n.* [they make one 'fly'] [1980s+] (*drugs*) amobarbitol, Amytal.

birdseed *n.* **1** as food. (**a**) [1910s] chocolates or other sweets [play on the attraction of SE *birdseed* to a BIRD *n.*[1] (1)]. (**b**) [1930s+] any breakfast cereal seen as resembling birdseed. (**c**) [1970s] (*US*) any food. **2** [1930s–60s] (*US*) rubbish, nonsense; thus as adj.

birdseye *n.* [resemblance: a bird's eye is small; senses 2 and 3, note Maurer, *Language of the Underworld Narcotics Addict* (1936): 'Probably so called from the constriction of the pupils and glassy appearance of the addict's eyes immediately after injection'] **1** [mid-19C–1900s] tobacco [also proprietory name]. **2** [1930s+] (*drugs*) a small amount of narcotics. **3** [1950s] (*drugs*) a weak injection of narcotics.

bird's eye *n.* [resemblance of the pattern] [mid-17C–late 19C] a handkerchief.

bird's eye fogle *n.* [BIRD'S EYE *n.* (1) + FOGLE *n.*] [mid-19C] a silk handkerchief with a bird's-eye pattern.

bird's eye wipe *n.* [BIRD'S EYE *n.* (1) + WIPE *n.* (3)] [mid-19C] any spotted silk handkerchief, as sported by fashionable costermongers.

bird's nest *n.*[1] [SE *bird*/BIRD *n.*[1] + SE *nest*/NEST *n.* (1)] **1** [late 16C–mid-18C] (*also* **nest**) the (female) pubic hair. **2** [late 18C] the vagina. **3** [1970s] (*gay*) a hairy chest; of a woman, the breasts. **4** [1970s+] (*US gay*) visible pubic hair extending from the crotch to the navel.

bird's nest *n.*[2] [the image of a nest filled with eggs] [1930s–60s] (*US Und.*) somewhere worth robbing.

bird's-nester *n.* [BIRD'S NEST *n.*^{1} (2)] [late 18C] a promiscuous man, a womanizer.

birdsnies *n. see* PIGSNYES *n.*

bird turd *n.* [1950s–70s] (*US*) **1** nothing, an insignificant amount, foolish talk. **2** an insignificant, worthless person.

(IN PHRASES)

❑ **sweat bird turds** *v. see under* SWEAT *v.*^{2}.

bird turd *v.* [assumed but uncited earlier use of BIRD TURD *n.*] [1940s+] (*US*) to talk nonsense, esp. in phr. *you ain't just (a-) bird-turding*.

birdwood *n.* [ety. unknown] [1940s] (*US*) **1** (*drugs*) marijuana, a marijuana cigarette. **2** a cigarette.

birk *n.* [backsl. = CRIB *n.*^{1} (1)] [mid-19C] a house.

Birkenstock buddy *n.* [the *Birkenstock* shoe, popular among such individuals + BUDDY *n.* (1)] [1990s+] (*US campus*) an environmentalist.

birl *n.*

(IN PHRASES)

❑ **give it a birl** *v. see* GIVE IT A BURL *under* BURL *n.*

Birmingham screwdriver *n.* (*also* **Brummagem screwdriver**) [the supposed oafishness of the Birmingham worker who would rather hammer in a screw than use the correct tool; despite normal racial stereotypes (and their supposed jobs) a US usage *yiddish screwdriver* has been noted c.1939] [20C+] a hammer.

birthday suit *n.* (*also* **birthday coat, ...finery, bodysuit**) [the state in which one emerges from the womb; note also a probable pun by Rochester c.1673: 'Nay looks, and lives, and loves by Rote, / In an old tawdrey Birth-Day-Coat' – in which a 'birthday coat' is properly a coat worn at court on occasion of a royal birthday] [late 17C+] the naked body.

bis *n. see* BISCUIT *n.*^{2}.

biscoe *n. see* BRASCO *n.*

biscuit *n.*^{1} **1** [mid-19C+] a young woman, who is fig. 'sweet' and/or 'good enough to eat'; thus *cold biscuit*, an unappealing woman; *show biscuit*, a very attractive woman; also of a man [Williams (1994) offers examples of *biscuit* as a sexual organ, citing the appearance of biscuits as 17C 'brothel-fare']. **2** the circular shape. (**a**) [late 19C–1930s] (*US*) a watch. (**b**) [1930s–40s] (*US black*) a pillow. (**c**) [1930s+] the face, the head. (**d**) [1940s+] (*orig. US black*) usu. in pl., the buttocks; thus *biscuit-bandit*, an active male homosexual. (**e**) [1950s+] a record. (**f**) [1970s] (*drugs*) a tablet of methadone. (**g**) [1980s+] (*drugs*) 50 rocks of crack cocaine. (**h**) [1990s+] (*drugs*) a tablet of MDMA. **3** [1960s–80s] (*US*) a woman's hairstyle in which the hair is done up in a small knot, usu. favoured by elderly women with thinning hair [a pun on SE *biscuit*, a small bun]. **4** [1980s+] (*US black*) a type of shoe worn for comfort rather than style and favoured by older people.

(IN COMPOUNDS)

❑ **biscuit roller** *n.* [1930s+] (*US black*) a (usu. female) lover.

(IN PHRASES)

❑ **hot in the biscuit** *adj.* [1940s–50s] (*US*) very angry, furious [HOT *adj.* (4a)]. ❑ **reel in the biscuit** *v.* [note Pelecanos, *Big Blowdown* (1996): 'I liked her. But I tried to reel it in too quick'] [1970s+] (*US campus*) to seduce a woman successfully.

SE in slang uses

(IN COMPOUNDS)

❑ **biscuit-arsed** *adj.* [1990s+] (*Scot.*) self-pitying. ❑ **biscuit barrel** *n.* [1910s] (*Aus.*) the stomach. ❑ **biscuit beggar** *n.* [? their poverty] [1960s] (*US*) a Native American. ❑ **biscuit class** *n.* [1980s+] (*N.Z.*) economy class on no-frills internal airlines where no refreshments are offered other than biscuits. ❑ **biscuit-eater** *n.* [such a dog will eat biscuits provided by its owner but will not forage for its own food] (*US*) **1** [1950s–70s] in phr. *son of a biscuit-eater*, a worthless person. **2** [1960s–70s] (*also* **biscuit-hound**) a worthless dog. ❑ **biscuit factory** *n.* [it was sited next to the Huntley & Palmer's biscuit factory; thus the *Biscuit Men*, the Reading football team] [1900s–50s] Reading gaol. ❑ **biscuit-headed** *adj.* [mid-19C] (*US*) foolish. ❑ **biscuit hooks** *n.* [1930s–60s] (*US*) the hands. ❑ **biscuit nibbler** *n.* [mid-19C] a young person. ❑ **biscuit shooter** *n.* [SE *shoot*, to throw violently] **1** [late 19C–1960s] a waiter or waitress. **2** [1900s] (*US milit.*) a female servant working for an army officer. **3** [1910s–30s] (*US*) a cook. ❑ **biscuit snatcher** *n.* [1950s] (*US black*) a hand; in pl. the fingers.

(IN PHRASES)

❑ **biscuit and beer** *v.* [late 19C–1900s] to swindle a gullible dupe by betting them a biscuit against a glass of beer; one will, of course, win. ❑ **build the biscuits** *v.* [1900s] (*US cowboy*) to prepare a meal when travelling. ❑ **chuck one's biscuits** *v.* (*also* **chuck Cheerios, chuck one's cookies**) [SE *chuck* / CHUCK *v.*^{2} (14)] [1970s+] to vomit.

biscuit *n.*^{2} [? one 'snaps' it] **1** [1930s] (*US black*) a penis. **2** [1930s+] (*US*) (*also* **bis**) a pistol, a handgun.

biscuit *n.*^{3} **1** [1980s] (*US campus*) a gullible person. **2** [1990s+] (*US*) a weakling, a coward [euph. for BITCH *n.*^{1} (3a)].

biscuit city *n.* [colloq. phr. *take the biscuit* + -CITY *sfx* (1)] [1980s] something one desires, the absolute best thing or situation.

biscuits and cheese *n.* [rhy. sl.] [1940s+] the knees.

bish *n.* [1950s] (*UK juv.*) a stupid mistake or situation.

bish *v.*^{1} [var. on BIFF *v.* (4)] [1940s] (*Aus./N.Z.*) to throw.

bish *v.*^{2} [BISH *n.*] [1950s] (*UK juv.*) to spoil, to blunder.

bishop *n.*^{1} [BISHOP *v.*^{1}] [late 16C–mid-17C] a fly that is burnt in a candle flame.

bishop *n.*^{2} [SE *bishop*] **1** [early 18C–late 19C] a mixture of wine and water, topped off by a roasted orange, supposedly an episcopal favourite. **2** the size/rotundity of the stereotypically well-fed clergyman. (**a**) [late 18C–early 19C] a large condom. (**b**) [mid-19C] (*US*) ? a form of woman's makeup container. (**c**) [late 19C] a bustle. (**d**) [late 19C–1900s] a chamberpot. (**e**) [late 19C+] (*US black/campus*) the penis. (**f**) [1940s] (*UK Und.*) a folding jemmy. **3** [mid–late 19C] a broken signpost [mild anti-clericalism: it neither points the way nor travels it]. **4** [1950s–70s] a private detective [he 'searches out sin'].

(IN PHRASES)

❑ **bang the bishop** *v.* (*also* **bash the bishop, batter..., beat..., bop..., buff..., capture..., choke..., flip..., flog..., murder..., polish..., bash the priest**) [ety. unknown, although *DSUE* suggests a resemblance of the penis to a bishop's mitre or to the *bishop* in a trad. designed 'Staunton' chess set; however, simple assonance is equally likely] [late 19C+] to masturbate.

bishop *v.*^{1} [proverbial saying 'the bishop hath played the cook' or 'the bishop has put his foot into the pot'] [early 16C–mid-19C] to burn, to let burn.

bishop *v.*^{2} [a man called *Bishop* who specialized in such frauds] [early 18C–late 19C] to use any form of trickery, esp. the burning of marks into the teeth, in order to reduce the appearance of a horse's age.

bishop *v.*^{3} [pun on SE *bishop*, to administer the rite of confirmation] [early 19C] (*UK Und.*) to change the markings on a stolen watch to facilitate its resale.

bishop *v.*^{4} [the murderer *Bishop*, who in Bethnal Green in 1831 drowned a boy in order to sell the body for dissection] [mid-19C] to murder by drowning.

Bishop Barker *n.* [Frederick *Barker* (1808–82), Anglican Bishop of Sydney; the bishop was a teetotaller, but he was extremely tall] [mid-19C–1910s] (*Aus.*) a drinking glass of the largest size.

bishop's bollocks *n.* [1980s] (*UK bingo*) the number 88.

bishop's finger *n.* [SE *bishop* + *finger(-post)*] [mid-19C] a signpost.

bishop's nose *n.* [var. on PARSON'S NOSE *under* PARSON *n.*] [20C+] (*US*) the rump of a chicken, duck, goose or other poultry.

bisognio *n. see* BESOGNIO *n.*

bisom *n.* [SE *besom*, a witch] [20C+] (*Aus.*) an undisciplined child.

bison *v.* [echoic] [1980s+] (*US campus*) to vomit.

bit *n.*^{1} **1** in monetary contexts, esp. a coin of low denomination; as a portion, a share. (**a**) [mid-16C–1960s] money, thus a purse containing money. (**b**) [late 17C–late 19C] the silver coin of the lowest denomination. (**c**) [early 18C–mid-19C] (*UK Und.*) a purse. (**d**) [early 19C+] (*US*) 12.5 cents, but usu. in phrs. TWO BITS *n.*, *FOUR BITS* below, *SIX BITS* below, *LONG BIT* below, *SHORT BIT* below. (**e**) [mid-19C–1960s] any low-denomination coin, e.g. *threepenny bit*, *fourpenny bit*. (**f**) [late 19C–1900s] (*US Und.*) a bribe, e.g., as offered by a thief to a policeman. (**g**) [late 19C–1950s] (*US Und.*) share of the profit from a theft. (**h**) [1910s] a wager, an investment, an insurance premium. **2** lit. or fig. representing a portion, i.e. a *bit* of flesh, a *bit* to eat. (**a**) [17C; mid-19C+] a young woman, usu. seen in a sexual context; also in combs. as below or listed at relevant n. [note D'Urfey, *Pills to Purge Melancholy* (1719): 'Your most Beautiful Bit, that hath all Eyes upon her'; also 'Walter', *My Secret Life* (1888-94): 'That little bit of a girl, Jemmy Smith']. (**b**) [17C–19C] (*also* **the bit**) euph. for the vagina. (**c**) [17C+] sexual intercourse; usu. in combs. as below or at the relevant n. (**d**) [1930s+] (*Ulster*) a worker's or schoolchild's packed lunch, i.e. a *bit* to eat. (**e**) [1950s+] as ext. of sense 3a, in gay use, a young man. **3** as a period of time. (**a**) [mid-19C+] a short time, a brief period, usu. as *for a bit*. (**b**) [mid-19C+] (*UK/US Und.*) a prison sentence of any length; thus *one-year bit*, *two-year bit* etc. (**c**) [1960s] (*US drugs*) the duration of the effect of a given drug. (**d**) [1970s] a period of time in any institution, e.g. a drug rehabilitation hospital. **4** [1950s+] (*orig. US jazz*) in abstract terms [theatrical jargon *bit*, a role]. (**a**) any well-defined action, plan, series of events, or attitudes, usu. but not necessarily, of short duration. (**b**) one's attitude, personality, or way of life. (**c**) the role that one assumes in a situation or in life, e.g. *the college-boy bit*, *the hippie bit*. **5** [2000s] (*UK Und.*) a drug in pill form, e.g. Ecstasy or amphetamine.

(IN PHRASES)

❑ **bit for the finger** *n.* [19C] sexual fondling. ❑ **bit of both** *n.* [play on *a bit of* OTHER, THE *n.*] [1990s+] bisexuality; a taste for sex with men and/or women. ❑ **bit of brown** *n.* **1** [17C] copulation [the *brown* pubic hair]. **2** [mid-19C+] sodomy [BROWN *n.* (3)]. ❑ **bit of cord** *n.* [1940s] an attractive young woman. ❑ **bit of cuff** *n.* [SE *bit* + (*off the*) *cuff*, i.e. spontaneous sex, or SE *cuff*, a blow; thus one of the wide range of terms that equate sex with violence] [late 19C–1900s] a young woman, regarded as a sex object; thus sexual intercourse. ❑ **bit of frock** *n.* [SE *frock*] [late 19C–1910s] an attractive (young) woman. ❑ **bit of fruit** *n.* [FRUIT *n.* (3)] [1940s] sexual intercourse. ❑ **bit of keg** *n.* [abbr. SE *kegmeg* or *cagmag*, rotten meat or a tough old goose] [late 19C] sexual intercourse. ❑ **bit of melon** *n.* [1900s] (*Aus.*) an attractive female. ❑ **bit of muslin** *n.* (*also* **morsel of muslin, piece of muslin, piece of fine linen**) [SE *bit* + *muslin*, a cloth used for dress-making, thus metonymy] [19C–1950s] a young woman, thus young women as a group, the *muslin company*. ❑ **bit of old** *n.* [1990s+] sexual intercourse. ❑ **bit of raspberry** *n.* [20C+] an attractive woman. ❑ **bit of red** *n.* [as opposed to a bit of BROWN *n.* (3)] [late 19C] heterosexual intercourse. ❑ **bit of skate** *n.* [pun on FISH *n.*[1] (1)] [late 19C+] the vagina. ❑ **bit of skin** *n.* [1920s] a woman, a girlfriend; in homosexual context, a young man. ❑ **bit of spare** *n.* *see* SPARE *n.*[2] (3). ❑ **bit of this and that** *n.* [euph.] [1970s–80s] (*N.Z.*) sexual intercourse. ❑ **bit of tickle** *n.* [abbr. SLAP AND TICKLE *n.*[2]] [1920s+] **1** a woman, regarded as a sex object. **2** sexual intercourse. ❑ **bit on a fork** *n.* [pun on SE *fork*, crotch] [mid-19C] the vagina. ❑ **bit, the** *n.* [euph.] [1990s+] (*Irish*) sexual intercourse. ❑ **break a bit off** *v.* [? the equation of sex and violence] [20C+] to have sexual intercourse; the idea that the erect penis 'breaks' following orgasm. ❑ **do a bit** *v.* [mid-19C+] to have sexual intercourse; thus *do a bit of...* in all the combs. that follow. ❑ **do a bit of cock-fighting** *v.* [pun on SE *cock*/COCK *n.*[3] (1)] [19C] to have sexual intercourse. ❑ **do a bit of flat** *v.* [SE *flat*; i.e. she is *flat* on her back] [19C] esp. of a prostitute, to have sexual intercourse. ❑ **do a bit of giblet pie** *v.* (*also* **have a bit of giblet pie**) [GIBLETS *n.*] [19C] to have sexual intercourse. ❑ **do a bit of ladies' tailoring** *v.* [play on NEEDLE *n.* (1)/SEW *v.*] [mid-19C–1920s] to have sexual intercourse. ❑ **do a bit of tailoring** *v.* [play on NEEDLE *n.* (1)/SEW *v.*] [mid-19C–1920s] to impregnate. ❑ **downy bit** *n.* [SE *down*, the first feathering of young birds] **1** [mid-19C] a young prostitute. **2** [late 19C] a young woman, esp. when attractive. **3** [late 19C] the vagina. ❑ **fancy bit** *n.* (*also* **fancy, fancy article**) [mid-17C–19C] the vagina; thus a young woman. ❑ **fresh bit** *n.* (*also* **fresh girl**) [mid–late 19C] a sexually inexperienced woman; a new mistress. ❑ **gay bit** *n.* [GAY *adj.* (1)] [mid–late 19C] a prostitute. ❑ **get a bit** *v.* [20C+] to have sexual intercourse. ❑ **have a bit off the chump end** *v.* [SE *chump-end*, the thick end of a loin of mutton] [late 19C] to have sexual intercourse. ❑ **house-bit** *n.* [mid-19C–1910s] a servant who doubles as a lover. ❑ **merry bit** *n.* (*also* **merry legs**) **1** [early 19C] the vagina. **2** [19C] a prostitute. ❑ **warm bit** *n.* [WARM *adj.* (14)] [late 19C] a promiscuous, sexy woman.

pertaining to money

(IN COMPOUNDS)

❑ **bit cull** *n.* (*also* **bit cove**) [CULL *n.*[1] (3)] [mid-19C] (*UK Und.*) a coiner. ❑ **bit faker** *n.* [FAKER *n.* (2)] [19C] (*UK Und.*) a coiner, a counterfeiter; thus *bit-faking*, counterfeiting, coining. ❑ **bit-maker** *n.* [early–late 19C] (*UK Und.*) a coiner, a counterfeiter. ❑ **bit-queerems** [QUEER *adj.* (2)] [mid-19C] (*UK Und.*) counterfeit coins. ❑ **bit turner-out** *n.* [SE *turn out*, to make] [early–mid-19C] a counterfeiter.

(IN PHRASES)

❑ **blue bit** *n.* **1** [late 18C] (*US Und.*) counterfeit money. **2** [1980s+] (*Aus. prison*) a A$10 note. ❑ **four-bit** *n.* [mid-19C+] (*W.I.*) one shilling and sixpence, post-1969 value 15 cents. ❑ **four-bit** *adj.* [1930s] low-class, insignificant. ❑ **four bits** *n.* **1** [late 19C+] (*US*) 50 cents. **2** *see also* below. ❑ **get a bit** *v.* (*also* **get one's bit**) [late 19C–1900s] to obtain money. ❑ **get/have a bit on** *v.* [late 19C+] to make a bet, to wager money on. ❑ **long bit** *n.* **1** [mid-19C–1950s] (*US*) 12½ or 15 cents, in contrast to a dime or *SHORT BIT* below. **2** *see also* below. ❑ **red bit** *n.* [1980s+] (*Aus. prison*) A$20 note. ❑ **short bit** *n.* **1** [mid-19C–1950s] (*US*) 10 cents, in contrast to 12½ or 15 cents, a *LONG BIT* above. **2** *see also* below. ❑ **six-bit** *adj.* [mid-19C+] (*US*) cheap, worth 75 cents, e.g. *a six-bit sandwich*. ❑ **six bits** *n.* **1** [mid-19C+] (*US*) 75 cents. **2** [1940s] (*US Und.*) $75.00. ❑ **smack the bit** *v.* [mid-19C] (*UK Und.*) to share out booty.

pertaining to prison sentences

(IN PHRASES)

❑ **big bit** *n.* [1940s+] (*US Und.*) a long prison sentence. ❑ **do a bit** *v.* [mid-19C+] (*US prison*) to serve a prison sentence. ❑ **flat bit** *n.* (*also* **flat time**) [SE *flat*, complete, utter] [1940s–90s] (*US Und.*) a sentence served with no remission for good behaviour. ❑ **four bits** *n.* **1** [1970s] (*US prison*) a 50-year prison sentence. **2** *see also* above. ❑ **long bit** *n.* **1** [late 19C+] (*US Und.*) a sentence of ten years or more. **2** any term of imprisonment over 38 months that must be completed before becoming eligible for parole. **3** *see also* above. ❑ **nice bit** *n.* [1930s+] (*US Und.*) a long prison sentence, i.e. ten years or more. ❑ **pull a bit** *v.* [SE *pull through*] [1960s] (*US prison*) to survive one's sentence. ❑ **short bit** *n.* **1** [1910s+] a short prison sentence. **2** *see also* above. ❑ **soft bit** *n.* (*also* **soft time**) [SOFT *adj.* (4) + TIME *n.* (1)] [20C+] (*US Und.*) a system of imprisonment whereby an inmate must serve 50% of the sentence before becoming eligible for parole. ❑ **split bit** *n.* [1950s+] (*US Und.*) an indeterminate sentence, subject the decisions of the parole board. ❑ **telephone number bit** *n.* [1930s] (*US prison*) a sentence of 20 years-plus, but not a life sentence.

other senses

(IN PHRASES)

❑ **do a bit** *v.* *see under* DO *v.*[1]. ❑ **spit-bit** *n.* [1970s] (*US black*) smooth, persuasive talk. ❑ **whole bit** *n.* [1960s+] everything.

SE in slang uses

(IN PHRASES)

❑ **bit of beef** *n.* [? tobacco's use as an appetite suppressant] [late 19C–1900s] a quid of tobacco, less than a pipeful. ❑ **bit of blood** *n.* [SE *bit* + *blood*, pedigree] **1** [late 18C–mid-19C] a spirited, mettlesome horse. **2** [early 19C] a dandy. ❑ **bit of Braille** *n.* [SE *Braille*, the alphabet for the blind; the image of 'feeling something out'] (*Aus.*) **1** [1930s+] a racing tip. **2** [1940s+] a tip-off. **3** [1940s+] sexual groping. ❑ **bit of bull** *n.* [19C] beef. ❑ **bit of cavalry** *n.* [early–mid-19C] a horse. ❑ **bit of corn** *n.* [1960s] (*Aus. Und.*) prison food, thus time in prison. ❑ **bit of fat** *n.* [SE *fat*, of a profitable occupation] [mid-19C+] an unexpected advantage. ❑ **bit of gig** *n.* [SE *gig*, merriment, fun] [early 19C] a spree, a bit of fun. ❑ **bit of goose** *n.* [1930s] a piece of good fortune. ❑ **bit of grey** *n.* [SE *grey* (hair); note 1990s business jargon *grey matter*, an older person recruited to a young firm to give it some gravitas] [late 19C–1900s] an elderly person who is recruited to attend weddings or funerals and by their presence add a degree of solemnity to the proceedings. ❑ **bit of heliotrope** *n.* [1900s] (*Aus.*) a girlfriend. ❑ **bit of hollow** *n.* an item of poultry, e.g. a duck, a turkey. ❑ **bit of mess** *n.* [? affectionate nickname] [1950s+] (*UK Und.*) a prostitute's male lover, who is neither ponce nor client. ❑ **bit of no good** *n.* [1940s+] a good deal of harm, usu. in phr. *do oneself a bit of no good*. ❑ **bit of nonsense** *n.* **1** [20C+] (*UK society*) a mistress. **2** [1950s+] any form of villainy, esp. when easily accomplished. ❑ **bit of prairie** *n.* [SE *prairie*, an open space] [late 19C–1900s] a momentary lull in the flow of traffic down the Strand, then London's busiest street. ❑ **bit of scarlet** *n.* [? the use of the word BLOODY *adj.*] [mid-19C] an oath. ❑ **bit of Spanish** *n.* [? use of long, dark Spanish tresses in wigs] [18C] (*UK Und.*) a natural wig, made from human rather than animal hair. ❑ **bit of stick** *n.* [1980s] £5. ❑ **bit of straw** *n.* [early 19C] a straw hat. ❑ **bit on the side** *n.* [the side of the marital 'straight and narrow'] [1920s+] **1** an affair; a lover other than one's regular partner. **2** an act of sexual intercourse with someone other than your partner. ❑ **bit to go with** *n.* [? parting comment, 'Here's a bit to go with'] [late 19C–1900s] (*orig. US*) generosity. ❑ **give one's bit** *v.* [1900s] (*Aus.*) to do anything in one's power. ❑ **have a bit of someone** *v.* [1900s] (*Aus.*) to assault; to fight with. ❑ **have a bit on** *v.* (*also* **have a bit in**) [SE *bit* (to drink)] [late 19C–1930s] to be drunk. ❑ **in bits over** *adj.* [late 19C+] obsessed with.

bit *n.*[2] [SE *bit*, a biting or cutting tool] [20C+] (*Aus. Und.*) a jemmy, a crowbar.

bit, the *n. see under* BIT *n.*[1].

bit *adj.* **1** [late 17C–late 19C] robbed, cheated, outwitted [BITE *v.* (4)]. **2** [mid-19C] (*US Und.*) arrested, convicted, sentenced. **3** [1990s+] (*US black*) fallen in love.

bit by... *phr.* drunk; in combs. below.

IN PHRASES

❑ **bit by a barn-mouse** (*also* **bit by a barn weasel**) [? the barn-mouse consumes barley, from which beer is brewed] [mid-17C–early 19C] drunk. ❑ **bit by the tavern bitch** (*also* **hit on the head by the tavern bitch**) [17C–18C] drunk. ❑ **bit by the brewer's dog** [1940s] (*US*) drunk.

bitch *n.*[1] [*bitch* as derog. sl. dates to early 17C, before which it had been SE. By 18C it was seen, according to Grose, as 'the most offensive appellation that can be given to an English woman, even more provoking than that of whore', and he cites the 'Billingsgate' rejoinder: 'I may be a whore, but can't be a bitch.' The original use implied disapproval of the woman's sexuality, e.g. *bitch in heat*; today's use focuses on her personality] **1** of women. (**a**) [late 14C+] a derog. term for woman, usu. judged an unpleasant one. (**b**) [18C+] a general derog. term of address to a woman; or female creature. (**c**) [18C+] a prostitute. (**d**) [mid-19C+] the queen in playing cards or in chess. (**e**) [1970s+] (*US black*) a girlfriend. (**f**) [1980s] (*US campus*) the middle seat in a car, i.e. where a woman sits. **2** an object or person, irrespective of gender. (**a**) [18C+] (*orig. US*) something or someone considered extraordinary or surprising. (**b**) [early 19C+] an otherwise unspecified object, or creature. (**c**) [1910s+] (*W.I./UK/US black teen*) a person, neither necessarily negative nor aimed solely at women, nor used solely by men. (**d**) [1920s+] (*orig. US*) an exceptionally skilled person. **3** a weak or effeminate man; a homosexual. (**a**) [mid-18C+] a derog. term for a weak or subservient man; thus as term of address. (**b**) [mid-18C+] (*UK/W.I.*) a general derog. term for a man. (**c**) [early 19C] (*UK campus*) one who plays host at a tea-party. (**d**) [1920s+] (*US gay/prison*) (*also* **bitchy**) an effeminate male, supposedly the 'passive' partner in a homosexual couple; a male prostitute. (**e**) [1950s+] (*US prison*) a homosexual. (**f**) [1960s] (*gay*) a fellow homosexual, usu. a friend. (**g**) [1990s+] (*gay*) a submissive lesbian. (**h**) [1990s+] a subservient person, a servant. **4** a problem, a complaint. (**a**) [mid-18C+] anything unpleasant, difficult, problematic, 'the devil', e.g. *that's the bitch of it; ain't this about a bitch*. (**b**) [1940s+] (*orig. US*) a complaint. (**c**) [1950s+] one, irrespective of gender, who complains or makes (what are perceived as) unfairly negative comments. **5** an exceptionally long prison sentence. (**a**) [1960s+] (*US prison*) as *big bitch*, a conviction under any crime that carries a mandatory life sentence; or a sentence so long that it is an equivalent. (**b**) [1970s+] (*US prison*) as *little bitch*, an exceptionally long prison sentence. **6** [1960s+] (*US gang*) as infix. **7** [1990s+] a large amount of money. **8** [1990s+] (*US black*) a thing.

DERIVATIVES

❑ **bitchery** *n.* [1920s] (*US gay*) a bar frequented by homosexuals. ❑ **Bitchville** *n.* [-VILLE *sfx*[1]] [1990s+] (*US*) a notional state of cowardice.

IN COMPOUNDS

❑ **bitch bath** *n.* [1940s–50s] (*US*) a 'bath' in which the usual water is replaced by an application of cosmetics, masking the dirt rather than removing it. ❑ **bitch booby** *n.* [BOOBY *n.*[1] (1)] [late 18C] a rough, unsophisticated country woman ('military term', Grose). ❑ **bitch-boy** *n.* [1990s+] (*US campus*) **1** an idiot, a general term of abuse. **2** used as a term of affectionate address between friends. ❑ **bitch butter** *n.* [BUTTER *n.*[1] (1)] [1970s] (*US black*) vaginal secretions. ❑ **bitch fight** *n.* [1960s] (*US gay*) an argument between two homosexual men. ❑ **bitch hammer** *n.* [SE *hammer*/HAMMER *n.*[1] (1)] [2000s] the penis. ❑ **bitch-happy** *adj.* [2000s] (*US*) grateful. ❑ **bitch lick** *n.* (*also* **bitch kick**) [? the sort of SE *lick* one gives a BITCH *n.*[1] (1)] [1980s+] (*W.I./UK black*) a hard blow. ❑ **bitch party** *n.* (*also* **bitching party**) **1** ([early 19C] orig. US campus) a tea party. **2** [late 19C+] a party composed solely of women guests. ❑ **bitch's bastard** *n.* [1950s] a term of abuse. ❑ **bitch's blind** *n.* [BLIND *n.*[1] (1)] [1970s+] (*US gay*) a gay or bisexual man's heterosexual wife. ❑ **bitch's Christmas** *n.* [1960s] (*US gay*) Halloween. ❑ **bitch squeak** *n.* [1950s] (*US*) a tell-tale, garrulous female. ❑ **bitch's wine** *n.* [? supposedly preferred by women drinkers] [mid–late 19C] champagne. ❑ **bitch tits** *n.* [2000s] (*US*) a bodybuilder's over-developed pectoral muscles. ❑ **bitch water** *n.* [1940s] (*US*) cologne. ❑ **bitchweed** *n.* [WEED *n.*[1] (4)] [1980s+] (*US drugs*) adulterated, contaminated, inferior or otherwise 'bad' marijuana. ❑ **bitch wheel** *n.* [? BITCH *n.*[1] (1) or W.I. pron. of SE *big* + shape (of a wheel)] [1950s] (*W.I.*) a large, round boiled dumpling.

IN PHRASES

❑ **as a bitch** *adv.* [1950s+] general phr. of intensification. ❑ **bitch-on-wheels** *n.* [sense 2a above] [1940s+] (*US*) an extreme example, somone or something infinitely superior. ❑ **flip a bitch** *v.* (*also* **flip a dick**) [the stereotype of the poor woman driver] [1980s+] (*US campus*) to make an illegal U-turn. ❑ **get the bitch on** *v.* [1990s+] (*US campus*) to yell at someone, to criticize, to nag. ❑ **go bitch** *v.* [1990s+] (*US Und.*) of a man, to act in a cowardly or effeminate manner. ❑ **go bitchcakes** *v.* [2000s] (*US campus*) to be angry, to act aggressively. ❑ **go bitching** *v.* [late 17C–mid-19C] of a man, to have sexual intercourse, esp. with a prostitute. ❑ **kitchen-bitch** *n.* (*also* **kitchen crumb, ...key**) [20C+] (*W.I.*) a man who hangs around the kitchen instead of going out and doing 'man's things'. ❑ **like a bitch** *adv.* [1950s+] a negative intensifier. ❑ **little bitch** *n.* [1970s+] (*US prison*) an exceptionally long prison sentence. ❑ **make a bitch of** *v.* [early 19C+] to bungle, to blunder, to ruin. ❑ **mama bitch** *n.* [1960s] (*US black*) the most reliable and experienced of a pimp's stable of prostitutes. ❑ **nothing-ass bitch** *n.* [1970s] (*US black*) a prostitute who will not work or who will not hand over the money earned to her pimp. ❑ **pitch a bitch** *v.* **1** [1940s+] (*US black*) to complain, to fight, to cause a disturbance. **2** [1990s+] to reject, to leave. ❑ **pull someone's bitch card** *v.* [2000s] (*US black*) to correct someone by using excessive force. ❑ **put the bitch on** *v.* [1960s] to file charges against a criminal as a habitual offender. ❑ **sit bitch** *v.* (*also* **ride bitch, ride the bitch's seat, ride punk, ride pussy**) [1970s+] (*US black/teen*) to ride in the middle of the back seat or pillion on a motorbike, i.e. the supposed 'woman's seat'. ❑ **stamp a bitch** *v.* [2000s] (*US black*) of a man, to hit a woman hard enough to leave the imprint of his rings in her flesh. ❑ **stand bitch** *v.* **1** [late 18C–early 19C] to make tea. **2** [late 18C–mid-19C] (*also* **bitch the pot**) to preside as hostess at a tea party.

IN EXCLAMATIONS

❑ **no bitch!** [*RIDE BITCH under* RIDE *v.*; excl. delivered in response to a claim of *shotgun!*] [1980s+] (*US campus*) an excl. used when choosing seats in a car, 'I won't ride in the middle of the back seat.'

bitch *n.*[2] [ety. unknown] [late 19C–1950s] (*US Western*) an improvised lamp made of a twist of rag in a container of grease.

bitch *n.*[3] [BITCH *n.*[1] (3b) + *BITCHWEED under* BITCH *n.*[1]] **1** [1980s+] (*US drugs*) one who knowingly dispenses unpleasantly adulterated varieties of marijuana. **2** [2000s] the main vein as used by heroin addicts.

bitch *adj.* [BITCH *n.*[1] (3a)] **1** [1970s+] (*US black*) weak, with implications of effeminacy. **2** [2000s] second-rate. **3** [2000s] annoying.

bitch *v.* **1** [late 16C+] to go whoring; thus *bitchery*, working as a whore. **2** [18C; 1950s+] to act in a promiscuous manner. **3** [early 18C; 1910s+] (*orig. US*) to complain. **4** [late 18C–mid-19C] (*UK Und.*) to give in, esp. through cowardice. **5** [early–mid-19C] (*UK campus*) to drink tea. **6** [early 19C+] to spoil, to ruin. **7** [1920s–60s] (*US*) to cheat, to swindle. **8** [1930s+] to treat badly. **9** [1950s+] (*orig. US*) to criticize, to attack verbally, to nag.

DERIVATIVES

❑ **bitcher** *n.* [1960s+] a complainer, a whinger.

IN COMPOUNDS

❑ **bitch-bag** *n.* [BAG *n.*[1] (1a), i.e. to go whoring with them] [2000s] (*Irish*) the testicles. ❑ **bitch box** *n.* [1940s+] **1** (*US*) a small box into which employees of a business can put their complaints/suggestions. **2** a public address system; a loudspeaker. ❑ **bitch session** *n.* (*also* **bitching session**) [1940s+] (*orig. US milit*) a conversation in which one airs one's complaints.

IN PHRASES

❑ **bitch and moan** *v.* [1960s+] to complain all the time. ❑ **bitched off** *adj.* [1950s] (*US*) furious. ❑ **bitched (up)** *adj.* **1** [early 19C+] ruined, spoilt. **2** [1910s+] confused. **3** [1960s] of a woman, very unpleasant. **4** [1960s–70s] (*US*) angry. **5** [1990s+] (*US gay*) dressed up, esp. in a blatant homosexual manner. ❑ **bitch off** *v.* **1** [1950s] (*S.Afr.*) to run away, to escape. **2** [1970s] (*US campus*) to annoy, to irritate. ❑ **bitch out** *v.* [1950s+] (*US campus*) to tell someone off. ❑ **bitch queen** *n.* [BITCH *n.*[1]] [2000s] (*S.Afr. gay*) one who complains constantly.

bitch-ass *adj.* [BITCH *n.*[1] (1) + -ASS *sfx* (1)] [1950s+] (*US black*) a general pej.

bitch-ass nigga *n.* [BITCH-ASS *adj.* + NIGGA *n.* (1)] [1990s+] (*US black teen*) a general term of black-on-black abuse, lit. a black person who complains.

bitchen *adj. see* BITCHING *adj.*

Bitches'-Heaven *n.* [allegedly f. the numerous cheap prostitutes (BITCH *n.*[1] (1d))] [1920s] (*US tramp*) Boston.

bitch-fou *adj.* [lit. 'full as a bitch'] [late 18C] (*Scot.*) very drunk.

bitchin! *excl.* (*also* **bitchen! bitching!**) [BITCHING *adj.*] [1950s+] (*US*) wonderful, great, esp. in surfer use, subseq. adopted by teen girls of 1980s California.

IN PHRASES

❑ **bitchin twitchin!** [1960s+] superlative form of BITCHIN! *excl.*

bitching *n.* [BITCH *v.* (3)] [1920s+] (*US*) arguing, complaining, nagging.

bitching *adj.* (*also* **bitchin**) [BITCH *n.*[1] (1)/BITCH *n.*[1] (4)] **1** [mid-19C+] (*orig. Aus.*) (*also* **bitchly**) an intense pej., euph. for BLOODY *adj.* **2** [1950s+] (*also* **bitchen**) excellent, wonderful; also as adv. [on good = bad model or ? BITCH *n.*[1] (2)].

bitching session *n. see BITCH SESSION under* BITCH *v.*

bitch-kitty *n.* [BITCH *n.*[1] (2a)] [1940s+] (*US*) something extraordinary, esp. extraordinarily hard to achieve.

bitch-kitty *adj.* [BITCH-KITTY *n.*] [1960s] (*US*) extraordinary, exceptional, extreme.

bitchly *adj. see* BITCHING *adj.* (1).

bitch magnet *n. see under* -MAGNET *sfx.*

bitch's bastard *n.* (*also* **B.B.**) [SE *bitch*, i.e. a female dog + BASTARD *n.*] [1950s+] (*UK prison*) a severe, poss. violent, warder; a term of abuse.

bitch slap *n.* [ironic reversal of BITCH SLAP *v.* (1)] [1990s+] **1** (*US black*) the killing of a female. **2** (*US prison*) a slap rather than a punch with the clenched fist; the implication is that the victim isn't 'man enough' to deliver a proper blow.

bitch slap *v.* [BITCH *n.*[1] + SE *slap*] [1990s+] (*US black*) **1** of a woman, to hit, occas. to harangue, one's male partner. **2** of a man, to hit a woman, or a man, in an 'effeminate' way (i.e. with the back of the hand: a 'real man' only uses his fists). **3** to hit, irrespective of gender.

bitch up *v.*[1] [BITCH *v.* (6)] [late 19C+] to make a mess of things, to make a mistake.

bitch up *v.*[2] [BITCH *n.*[1] (3)] [2000s] (*US prison*) to surrender, to act in a cowardly manner.

bitchy *adj.* (*also* **bitch**) [BITCH *n.*[1]] **1** [1920s+] (*orig. US*) sexually provocative, sexually appealing. **2** [1930s+] malicious, sarcastic. **3** [1940s+] (*US*) difficult.

bite *n.*[1] **1** in context of a monetary sum, esp. when begged or borrowed. (**a**) [late 16C] a sum of money. (**b**) [18C+] (*UK Und.*) that which is cadged; thus *a good bite*, a complaisant victim, *on the bite*, cadging, begging. (**c**) [mid-18C+] a cadger. (**d**) [1900s] (*US*) a share of profits. (**e**) [1910s+] (*orig. Aus.*) an attempt to obtain a loan. (**f**) [1930s+] (*Aus.*) an act of begging. (**g**) [1930s+] (*N.Z.*) a miserly authority figure. (**h**) [1950s+] (*US*) the price, the cost, a bill, esp. when the item is expensive. (**i**) [1970s+] a bribe. **2** in context of cheating. (**a**) [late 17C–late 19C] a cheat, a confidence trickster. (**b**) [18C–1920s] a hoax, a confidence trick, a fraud. **3** [1970s] (*US*) an unpleasant surprise or experience, abbr. of *bite in the ass*.

IN PHRASES

❑ **put the bite on** *v.* (*also* **put the bite to, put the bite into**) **1** [1930s+] (*orig. Aus.*) to extort, to blackmail, to force someone to do something they would rather avoid. **2** [1930s+] to solicit a loan or request the repayment of a debt. **3** [1940s–70s] (*US*) to beg. **4** [1960s] (*US*) to put the blame on.

bite *n.*[2] [SE *bite* or Anglo-Saxon *byht*, the fork of the legs; 20C use mainly US black] [17C+] the vagina, 'secreta ( ) mulierum'; one of many words that suggests that vagina is a threat to men.

bite *n.*[3] [abbr. *YORKSHIRE BITE under* YORKSHIRE *adj.*] [late 19C] a Yorkshireman.

bite *n.*[4] [its fig. effect on the drinker] [1910s] (*Aus.*) a measure or 'shot' of hard liquor.

bite *v.* **1** [late 16C–mid-19C] to rob, to steal. **2** [17C+] (*also* **bite on**) to 'fall for', to 'take the bait'. **3** [17C+] to worry, to annoy, to irritate, often ext. as *bite one's ass*, *bite one's britches*; thus *what's biting you?* **4** [mid-17C–1920s] to cheat, to deceive; thus *bitten*, deceived, hoaxed. **5** [late 18C–early 19C] to overreach, to impose. **6** [late 19C+] (*Aus./US*) to cadge or borrow from, usu. money. **7** [1910s+] to be objectionable, distasteful, unpleasant; thus as *n.*, a disparaging person. **8** [1940s] to pressurize, to blackmail. **9** [1940s+] (*US gay*) to fellate. **10** [1970s+] (*rap music*) to plagiarize lyrics; thus *biting*, copying another artist; similarly used by graffiti artists. **11** [1980s+] (*US campus*) (*also* **bite on**) to copy, e.g. a suit of clothes.

IN PHRASES

❑ **bite the blow** *v.* [SE *blow*, a hit] [late 17C–early 18C] to accomplish a major theft. ❑ **bitten out** *adj.* [1930s] (*Aus.*) subjected to as much begging and cadging as a place and its population will tolerate. ❑ **fortune-biter** *n.* [18C] a swindler, a confidence trickster. ❑ **sheep-biter** *n.* **1** [late 16C–18C] a wretched, miserable person; thus *sheep-biting*. **2** [17C–early 18C] a womanizer [plays on MUTTON *n.* (1b)]. **3** [late 17C–18C] a butcher. **4** [mid-18C] a sheep-stealer. ❑ **snaffle biter** *n.* [SE *snaffle*, a bridle] [early 18C] a horse-thief. ❑ **on the bite**

[1940s+] (*Aus.*) demanding money, either as payments, loans or bribes. ❑ **what's biting you?** (*also* **what's itching you?**) [1910s+] what's the matter? what's the problem?

SE in slang uses

DERIVATIVES

❑ **bite-etite** *n.* (*also* **bitytite**) [SE *bite* + *appetite*] [late 19C–1900s] hunger, appetite.

IN COMPOUNDS

❑ **biting dog** *n.* [1950s] (*US gay*) the anal sphincter in the context of intercourse.

IN PHRASES

❑ **bite feathers** *v.* [the image of the passive partner in sodomy biting the pillow] [1960s] (*US gay*) to lie on one's stomach. ❑ **bite it** *v.* [abbr. BITE THE DUST *under* DUST *n.*] (*US*) **1** [1960s+] to die. **2** [2000s] to trip, to fall. ❑ **bite (it) off** *v.* [lit. *bite one's tongue off*] [mid-19C+] (*US*) to restrain oneself, to stop talking. ❑ **bite one's bait** *v.* [16C *bait*, food; the image is of 'chewing over' the topic] [1970s] (*US*) to pause before making too precipitate a decision. ❑ **bite one's grannam** *v.* (*also* **bite one's grandam**) [SE *grannam*, corn, the basic constituent of some spirits] [mid–late 17C] to become very drunk. ❑ **bite one's lips** *v.* [? one's intoxicated state leads to such injury] [1950s+] (*drugs*) to smoke marijuana. ❑ **bite one's nails** *v.* [1960s–70s] (*US gay*) for one homosexual man to use mutually recognizable coded gestures to indicate his interest to another. ❑ **bite one's name in** *v.* [mid-19C] to drink heavily. ❑ **bite one's thumb at** *v.* (*also* **bite one's thumb to**) [the gesturer extends the thumb and clicks its nail forward on the front teeth] [late 16C–1900s] to make a gesture of contempt or of threat. ❑ **bite (on) the bridle** *v.* (*also* **bite on the bit**) [SE *bite on the bridle*, to champ at the bit, like a restless horse] [14C–early 19C] to be in reduced circumstances, to be impoverished. ❑ **bite on the nail** *v.* [1940s] (*US*) to suffer in silence. ❑ **bite shit and die** *v. see under* EAT SHIT *v.* (3). ❑ **bite someone's crank** *v. see under* CRANK *n.*[3]. ❑ **bite someone's ear** *v. see under* EAR *n.*[1]. ❑ **bite someone's name** *v. see under* NAME *n.* ❑ **bite someone's nose off** *v.* [late 19C+] to attack verbally. ❑ **bite the bag** *v.* [? BAG *n.*[1] (1a)] **1** [1950s+] (*US*) to be very unsatisfactory; esp. in imper. *bite/go bite the bag*, an excl. of dismissal, disapproval or contempt. **2** [1970s] (*US campus*) to be quiet, usu. as imper. ❑ **bite the big one** *v. see under* BIG ONE *n.* ❑ **bite the bone** *v. see under* BONE *n.*[1]. ❑ **bite the bullet** *v.* (*also* **bite on the bullet**) [the placing of a bullet between the teeth of wounded soldiers or sailors when undergoing surgery in pre-anaesthesia days] **1** [late 19C+] to suffer in silence. **2** [1910s+] to do what is necessary, however unappealing. ❑ **bite the dust** *v. see under* DUST *n.* ❑ **bite the hairy banana** *v. see under* BANANA *n.* ❑ **bite the hand that feeds one** *v.* [the image is of an ungrateful horse or dog] [20C+] to injure a benefactor, to act ungratefully. ❑ **bite the peter** *v. see under* PETER *n.*[2]. ❑ **bite the roger** *v. see under* ROGER *n.*[3]. ❑ **bite the root** *v.* [image of root as something 'low'] [1980s] to be third-rate. ❑ **nail biter** *n.* [1970s+] (*US*) an anxiety-provoking situation, esp. a close contest. ❑ **tax bite** *n.* [1950s+] (*US*) the amount of tax one has to pay on a sum of money or salary cheque. ❑ **that bites (the big one)** [i.e. that must hurt very much] [1980s+] (*US campus*) an expression of commiseration.

IN EXCLAMATIONS

❑ **bite it!** [SE *bite*, 'it' is the penis or posterior] [1940s+] (*US*) an excl. of aggressive dismissal. ❑ **bite me!** [1980s+] (*US campus*) a general derog./dismissive excl. ❑ **bite moose!** [? euph. of BITE MY ASS! *excl.*] [1980s+] (*US*) an excl. of dismissal. ❑ **bite the ice!** (*also* **make ice!**) [the pain of chewing ice] [1970s+] (*US teen*) an excl. of dismissal, 'go to hell!'. ❑ **bite the weenie!** *see under* WEENIE *n.*[1]. ❑ **bite this!** [1950s+] (*US*) a general derog. excl. ❑ **bite your bum!** *see under* BUM *n.*[1].

bite! *excl.* [BITE *v.* (4)] [early–mid-18C] tricked you! caught you!

bite-and-blow *n.* [dial. *bite-and-blow*, to blow a cool breath on a place before biting it and thus (theoretically) minimizing the pain] [20C+] (*W.I.*) successful deceit, emollient hypocrisy.

bite my ass! *excl.* (*also* **bite my arse! ...bag! ...shite! bite the back of my bollox!**) [1960s+] (*orig. US*) a general excl. of contempt or dismissal.

biter *n.*[1] [BITE *v.*] **1** [late 17C–early 18C] a card-sharp. **2** [late 17C–mid-19C] a confidence trickster. **3** [1950s+] (*Aus.*) a cadger. **4** [1980s+] (*US*) an unpleasant, contemptible person.

biter *n.*[2] [BITE *n.*[2] (1)] [late 18C] a lascivious woman.

biter *n.*[3] [SE] [1940s] (*US*) of an animal, the mouth.

biter *n.*[4] [1980s+] a plagiarist, esp. in rap/hip-hop,.

biter of peters *n.* (*also* **biter of peeters**) [BITE *v.* (1) + PETER *n.*[2] (1)] [late 18C–early 19C] (*UK Und.*) one who specializes in stealing trunks and boxes from the back of stage-coaches or carts.

biters *n.* [1940s] (*US*) teeth.

bites and scratches *n. see* CUTS AND SCRATCHES *n.*

bities *n.* [SE *bite*] [1990s+] (*Aus.*) a general term for biting insects.

bit of (a) *n.* [SE *bit*] **1** [mid-18C+] a good example of, a specimen of, e.g. *bit of a lad, bit of a horseman.* **2** [late 19C+] (*UK/Aus.*) a young person, as in *a bit of a girl* [BIT *n.*[1] (2a)].

IN PHRASES

❑ **bit of a groat** *n.* [early 18C] a woman, seen in a sexual context. ❑ **bit of a lad** *n.* [1930s+] a cheeky, self-possessed youth who 'fancies himself'.

bit of all right, a *phr.* (*also* **little bit of all right**) [late 19C+] **1** an attractive person, usu. a young woman. **2** in abstract use, [late 19C+] anything good and advantageous, e.g., a pleasant surprise, an enjoyable experience; also in ironic use. **3** of objects.

bit of blink *n.* [rhy. sl.] [late 19C–1900s] drink.

bit of drapery *n. see* DRAPERY MISS *n.*

bit of goods *n.* **1** [mid-19C+] a young woman. **2** [1910s+] something exceptional.

bit of pooh *n.* [SE *bit* + excl. *pooh!* nonsense!] [late 19C–1900s] flattery, esp. in the context of courtship.

bit of rough *n.*[1] [its rubbing against the penis] [mid-19C+] the vagina.

IN PHRASES

❑ **have a bit of rough** *v.* [mid-19C+] to have sexual intercourse.

bit of rough *n.*[2] [i.e. a SE *rough* person] [20C+] a lover, orig. female but from mid-20C male, from a lower class and tougher background than their partner.

bit of snug *n. see under* SNUG *v.*[1].

bit of stuff *n.* [SE *bit* + *stuff*, material] **1** [mid-18C+] (*also* **drop of stuff, lump of stuff**) a young woman, usu. attractive and often out enjoying herself. **2** [early 19C] an overdressed man; an over-confident man. **3** [early 19C] a prize-fighter. **4** [mid-19C] an admirable person. **5** [late 19C–1900s] (*Aus.*) a horse. **6** [1940s] (*? Irish*) a tough, aggressive young man.

IN PHRASES

❑ **do a bit of stuff** *v.* [late 19C+] to have sexual intercourse.

bit of the other *n. see* OTHER, THE *n.*

bit of tripe *n.* [? rhy. sl.] [late 19C] one's wife.

bit on the cuff *adj.* [rhy. sl. *bit on the cuff* = a bit rough] [1930s+] (*Aus./N.Z.*) excessive, severe, 'over the top'.

bits *n.* **1** [1940s+] (*Aus.*) the female breasts. **2** [1990s+] the genitals.

bits and bats *n.* [Yorks. dial. *bits and bats*, bits and pieces] [20C+] (*UK Und.*) knick-knacks; items of jewellery.

bits and bobs *n.* [Midlands dial.] **1** [1950s+] bits and pieces. **2** [2000s] the female genitals.

bitser *adj. see* BITZA *n.*

bit smasher *n. see* SMASHER *n.*[1] (1).

bitten *adj. see* JUG-BITTEN *under* JUG *n.*[1].

Bitter Creek *n.*

IN PHRASES

❑ **from Bitter Creek** *adj.* [the image of Bitter Creek, Wyoming, as an outlaw town] [late 19C–1900s] (*US, Western*) very tough.

bitter-ender *n.* [mid-19C+] a diehard, one who does not give up until the *bitter end*.

bitter-gatter *n.* [SE *bitter* (ale) + GATTER *n.*[1] (2)] [late 19C] a mixed drink of beer and gin.

bitter half *n. see* BETTER HALF *n.*

bitter mouth *n.* [rare and mainly southern; talk that 'leaves a bad taste in one's mouth'] [1930s–40s] negative, cynical speech.

bitters *n.*

SE in slang uses

IN PHRASES

□ **get one's bitters** *v.* [SE *bitter end*] [early–mid-19C] (*US*) to get one's deserts.

bitties, the *n.* (*also* **bitty bam-bam**) [2000s] (*W.I.*) diarrhoea.

bitty *n.*[1] [SE *bit*, a small piece (of something mechanical)] [late 19C–1900s] a skeleton key.

bitty *n.*[2] [var. on BIDDY *n.*[2]] [1990s+] (*US black*) a young woman.

bitty *adj.* [dimin. of SE *bit*] [20C+] tiny, small, insignificant, often preceded by 'little'.

Bitumen, the *n. see* TRACK, THE *n.*

bitumen blonde *n.* (*also* **charcoal blonde**) [SE *bitumen*, black asphalt + *blonde*] [1930s–50s] (*Aus.*) a derog. name for an Aborigine woman.

bitytite *n. see* BITE-ETITE N. *under* BITE V.

bitza *n.* (*also* **bitser, bitzer**) [SE *bits and pieces*] (*Aus./N.Z.*) **1** [1920s+] a contraption made of a selection of disparate bits and pieces. **2** [1930s+] a mongrel dog; by ext. any 'mongrel'.

bivvy *n.* [*see* BEVVY *n.*] [mid–late 19C] alcohol, esp. beer.

biz *n.*[1] [abbr.] **1** [mid-19C+] (*orig. US*) (*also* **bis, bizney, bizniz**) business. **2** [late 19C+] as *the biz*, the real thing (and to be respected as such). **3** [1910s+] a situation, with no actual economic 'business' attached.

IN PHRASES

□ **do the biz/bizniz** *v. see* DO THE BUSINESS *under* BUSINESS *n.*
□ **work the biz** *v.* [WORK *v.* (8)] [1990s+] (*Can.*) to work as a prostitute.

IN EXCLAMATIONS

□ **good biz!** [late 19C–1910s] wonderful! excellent!; also as adj.

biz *n.*[2] [abbr. BUSINESS *n.* (9a)] [1930s+] **1** (*drugs*) the kit (eye-dropper, needle, spoon etc) used by a narcotic addict for injections. **2** a bag or portion of drugs.

IN PHRASES

□ **in biz** *adj.* working as a drug dealer.

biza *n.* [2000s] (*S.Afr prison*) a blood brother.

bizalls *n.* [BALLS *n.* (1) + -IZ- *infix*] [2000s] (*US black*) the testicles.

bizarro *n.* [BIZARRO *adj.*] [1980s] a strange, eccentric person; a transvestite.

bizarro *adj.* [SE *bizarre* + -O *sfx* (5), but note *Bizarro*, a character in *Superman* comics] [1970s+] (*US teen*) weird, eccentric.

bizatch *n. see* BIZNATCH *n.*

biznai *n.* (*also* **bizney**) [abbr.] [late 19C–1920s] business, happenings, events, circumstances.

biznatch *n.* (*also* **bizatch**) [BITCH *n.*[1] (2c) + -IZ- *infix*] [1990s+] (*US black*) an unpleasant person, a general negative term.

bizney/bizniz *n. see* BIZ *n.*[1].

bizzaz *n.* [PIZZAZZ *n.* + ? BUSINESS *n.* (5)] [1910s+] (*US*) style, glamour.

bizzie *n. see* BUSY *n.*

bizzo *n.* [abbr. SE *business* + -O *sfx* (3)] [1950s+] (*Aus.*) business.

bizzy *n. see* BUSY *n.*

b.j. *n.* (*also* **b-j, bee jay**) [abbr. BLOW JOB *n.* (1)] [1940s+] (*US*) fellatio.

b'jasus! *excl. see* BEJAZUS! *excl.*

B-job *n.* [BLOW JOB *n.* (1)] [1970s] (*US*) fellatio.

b-joint *n.* [B-GIRL *n.* + JOINT *n.* (3)] [1950s+] (*US*) a bar that employs women whose primary job is not to dance but to promote liquor sales to the clientele.

B.K. *n.* [abbr.] **1** [1990s+] (*US black*) Burger King. **2** [1990s+] (*US*) British Knights, a brand of trainer. **3** [1990s+] (*US prison*) 'Blood Killer': used by the Crips gang to threaten their rival Bloods.

b.k. *n. see* BROWNIE KING *n.*

blab *n.* [*blab* and its v. forms *blab* and, apparently, *blabber* are the first sl. terms relating to speech and can be found as such in the 16C. Their history, however, is somewhat older. There is even, according to the *OED*, a question whether what appears to be an obvious link actually exists. *Blab*, then spelt *blabbe* and meaning a 'chatterer', occurs in Chaucer *c.*1374; *blab*, meaning simply 'chatter' or 'loose talk', can be found in *The Tale of Beryn* (*c.*1400), but then promptly vanishes until the 16C, when it is augmented by a v. form, *blab*, to chatter (1535). This, in turn, creates a n., *blabber*, a chatterer. However, the v. *blabber* predates all these; it occurs in *Piers Ploughman* (1362) and, with its n. *blabberer*, is common in the works of John Wyclif (1330–84). Thus, however tempting it may seem, one cannot simply assume that *blab* is a 14C abbr. of *blabber*. Instead, the *OED* suggests, it is related to the noun *labbe*, a revealer of secrets, in Chaucer, and the verb *labbe* in *Piers Ploughman* and to *labbyng*, open-mouthed. It can also be linked to the Old Dutch *labben*, to chatter. Thus *blab/blabbe* might be a mixture of *labbe* and *blabber*; but might also be simply onomat.] **1** [mid-16C+] a tell-tale. **2** [mid-19C+] talk.

DERIVATIVES

□ **blabfest** *n.* (*also* **talkfest**) [-FEST *sfx*] [late 19C+] (*US*) a gathering where those involved devote themselves to talking, esp. unashamed gossip.

IN COMPOUNDS

□ **blab sheet** *n.* [SHEET *n.* (1)] [1940s–60s] (*orig. US black*) a newspaper.

IN PHRASES

□ **blabs in labs** *n.* [1970s+] (*US campus*) a course in linguistics, the 'labs' are language laboratories.

blab *v.* [BLAB *n.*] **1** [mid-16C+] to talk; thus *blab it out*, to hurry and finish talking. **2** [late 16C+] to inform. **3** [late 17C+] to confess, to tell about.

blabber *n.* [BLAB *n.*] **1** [1920s] a newspaper. **2** [1940s–70s] the mouth.

SE in slang uses

IN COMPOUNDS

□ **blabberguts** *n.* [-GUTS *sfx*] [1910s] (*US*) a gossip.
□ **blabberskite** *n.* [BLATHERSKITE *n.*] [2000s] a voluble, boastful speaker.

blabbermouth *n.* (*also* **blabmouth**) [BLAB *v.* (1) + SE *mouth*] [1920s+] a gossip, an indiscreet talker.

blabbermouth *adj.* (*also* **blab-mouth**) [BLABBERMOUTH *n.*] [1940s] indiscreet, gossiping.

black *n.* **1** representative of the colour. (**a**) [mid–late 17C] (*also* **black parts**) the female genitals. (**b**) [1930s–40s] (*US black*) the night, night-time. (**c**) [1940s] the black market; thus *on the black*, engaged in the black market. (**d**) [1940s+] (*drugs*) opium. (**e**) [1960s+] (*drugs*) a generic term for hashish, esp. varieties that are very dark khaki. (**f**) [2000s] (*drugs*) heroin; esp. black tar heroin. (**g**) [1980s] (*US campus*) incomprehensible course material. **2** abbr. (**a**) [early–mid-19C] a blackguard. (**b**) [1920s+] a blackmailer; thus constr. with *the*, blackmail. (**c**) [1940s+] (*orig. milit.*) a *black mark*, i.e. a mistake, a serious error. (**d**) [1980s+] (*US black*) a form of address, e.g. *Whassup, Black?* i.e. *black man*. (**e**) constr. with *the*, the illegal economy; usu. in phr. *on the black*, working without paying tax, insurance etc.

IN COMPOUNDS

□ **black and blonde** *n.* [1980s+] (*Aus. prison*) hashish.
□ **black domina** *n.* [2000s] (*drugs*) a strong type of marijuana. □ **black gang** *n.* [SE *gang*; such villains blackmail their peers for a share of their profits] [1910s–30s] villains who prey upon other villains, esp. on racecourse confidence tricksters, 'find-the-lady' men, fairground showmen and the like. □ **black oil** *n.* [1970s–80s] (*US drugs*) hashish oil. □ **black Russian** *n.* [? ref. to the supposedly chic cigarette brand] [1980s+] (*drugs*) cannabis resin, hashish, esp. when mixed with opium.

IN PHRASES

❑ **early black** *n.* [the initial darkening of the sky] [1930s–50s] (*US black*) (*also* **early blue**) dusk, nightfall. ❑ **late black** *n.* (*also* **late dark**) [1930s–40s] (*US black*) a very dark night, with neither moon nor stars. **put the black on** *v.* [1920s+] to *black*mail. ❑ **put up a black** *v.* [? the two black balls hauled to the mast of Royal Navy ships when a ship was out of control; but note the general negative imagery of SE *black*] [1940s+] (*orig. RN*) to make a mistake.

SE in slang uses

IN PHRASES

❑ **fast black** *n.* [1960s+] (*UK society*) a black London taxi.

black *adj.* **1** [mid-19C+] depressed, sullen, irritable, thus ext. as *black-looking* [SE in 18C; a *black mood*]. **2** [1970s+] (*Irish*) crowded ['black with people'].

IN COMPOUNDS

❑ **black boogaloo** *n.* [name of a dance popular in 1960s] [1960s–70s] (*US black*) a feeling of depression. ❑ **black Monday** *n.* **1** [mid-18C–early 19C] the first day back at school after the holidays. **2** [mid-19C] the day on which a death sentence is carried out.

IN PHRASES

❑ **in black with** *adj.* [2000s] (*US*) in trouble (with).

SE in slang uses

DERIVATIVES

❑ **blackers** *n.* [*black* velvet + -ER *sfx*] **1** [1930s+] (*also* **blackas**) blackberries. **2** [1940s] champagne and Guinness, mixed. ❑ **blackie** *n.* (*also* **blackee, blackey, blacky**) [SE *black* + sfx *-ie, -y*; the sfx ensures the term's negative, patronizing implication] **1** [18C+] a black person; usu. African but also Indian, Aboriginal. **2** [1950s] (*US gang*) a blackjack.

IN COMPOUNDS

pertaining to race

❑ **black...** *see also* separate entries. ❑ **black ankle** *n.* [var. on DOMINICKER *n.* (2), see for ety] [late 19C–1930s] (*US*) a person of mixed race; usu. black, Indian and white. ❑ **black belly** *n.* [1940s–50s] (*US derog.*) term for a black person. ❑ **black belt** *n.* (*also* **Belt, the**) [SE *belt*, a zone or district] [1920s+] (*US*) that part of a larger urban area in which the black community lives, the black ghetto; also used in larger scale of a geographical area. ❑ **black bottom** *n.* (*also* **bottom**) [such areas were often on low-lying land, near a river] [1910s+] that part of a larger urban area in which the black community lives. ❑ **black cloud** *n.* [1930s] (*US*) a group of black people. ❑ **black dust** *n.* [1980s] (*US black*) an extremely dark-skinned person. ❑ **black fever** *n. see* JUNGLE FEVER *under* JUNGLE *adj.* ❑ **black gin** *n. see* GIN *n.*[1]. ❑ **black head** *n.* [1970s–80s] (*UK black*) a black person. ❑ **black ivory** *n.* [their value] [late 19C] black slaves. ❑ **black plate** *n.* [a pun on the US restaurant dish, the 'blue plate special'] [1940s+] soul food. ❑ **black teapot** *n.* [? his duties include pouring tea] [late 19C] a black footman. ❑ **blacktime** *n.* [negative stereotyping] [1990s+] (*UK/US black*) unpunctuality. ❑ **black town** *n.* [late 19C+] that part of a larger urban area in which the black community lives. ❑ **black trash** *n.* [20C+] (*Aus./UK*) a racist term for black people. ❑ **black velvet** *n.* [fig. use of SE, based on the smoothness, whether of skin or the drink] **1** [late 19C+] (*Aus./N.Z.*) any dark-skinned woman; thus a *bit of black velvet*; occas. of men; by ext., sexual intercourse with someone black. **2** [1960s] (*US*) a black woman's genitals.

general uses

❑ **black...** *see also* separate entries. ❑ **black ape** *n. see under* APE *n.* ❑ **black African** *n. see* AFRICAN BLACK *under* AFRICAN *adj.* ❑ **black annie** *n.* [the colour + generic use of proper name] **1** [20C+] (*also* **black betsy**) a police or prison van. **2** [1930s–70s] (*also* **black aunty**) (*US prison*) a whip, used for punishments. ❑ **black army** *n.* [? their chosen clothing, their sinister image; note Aus. *black army*, a flock of crows] [1920s] the female underworld. ❑ **black arse** *n.* [ARSE *n.*; the kettle and the pot have both been discoloured by the flame; this is the same phr. as the modern one; but these days the final vulgarism has been quietly dropped] [late 17C–early 19C] a kettle, esp. in phr. *the pot calls the kettle black arse*. ❑ **black art** *n.* (*also* **black act**) [SE *black art*, magic or necromancy; thus extended to a criminal activity that required 'devilish ability'] **1** [late 16C–mid-19C] (*UK Und.*) lock-picking. **2** [mid-19C] the profession of undertaking. ❑ **black bag job** *n. see* BAG JOB *under* BAG *n.*[1]. ❑ **black beauty** *n.* [the colour of the capsules] **1** [1960s+] (*US drugs*) biphetamine, a strong amphetamine. **2** [2000s] a depressant. ❑ **black beetle** *n. see under* BEETLE *n.*[1]. ❑ **black beetles** *n. see under* BEETLE *n.*[1]. ❑ **black beezer** *n. see under* BEEZER *n.*[1]. ❑ **black bess** *n.* **1** [early 18C–mid-19C] a firelock or musket. **2** [late 19C] the vagina. **3** [late 19C] (*Aus. Und.*) a prison van. ❑ **black betsy** *n. see* BLACK ANNIE above. ❑ **black betty** *n.* [SE *betty*, a pear-shaped bottle, covered with straw and often used to contain olive oil; properly known as a *Florence flask*] **1** [mid-18C–19C] (*US*) liquor, esp. a bottle that is circulated among the guests at a wedding party; tradition demands that everyone, irrespective of age, must *kiss black betty*, take a swig from the bottle. **2** [1960s+] a police or prison van. ❑ **black bottle** *n.* [SE, the use of *black* carries overtones of death, but presumably the term is also a descendant of 19C 'black drop', a dark-coloured medicine, mainly composed of opium, plus vinegar and spices. It was widely believed by 20C tramps that such a drink was administered to men in charity wards whose resulting death saved the administration the trouble of caring for them] [1910s–60s] (*US*) any poisonous drink, esp. knockout drops. ❑ **black box** *n.* (*also* **black boy, black knob**) [the *black*-painted deed *boxes*] [late 17C–mid-19C] (*UK Und.*) a lawyer. ❑ **black boy** *n.* [his vestments] [mid-19C] a parson, a clergyman. ❑ **black buggy** *n.* [1960s] a hearse. ❑ **black cadillac** *n.* [fig ref. to the quality of the car] [1970s+] (*US drugs*) amphetamine. ❑ **black cap** *n.* [late 19C] (*UK Und.*) a thief who befriends a servant girl in order to gain her trust and access to her master's house. ❑ **black cattle** *n.* [the colour, either of the vestments or of the insects] **1** [18C] clergymen as a group; thus *black cattle show*, a gathering of clergymen. **2** [late 18C–early 19C] lice. ❑ **black coat** *n.* [the trad. clothing] **1** [early 17C–1900s] a clergyman, a parson. **2** [1920s+] (*Aus.*) a waiter. **3** [1930s–60s] (*US*) an undertaker. ❑ **black diamond** *n.* [SE *black diamond*, geological – 'a stone of dubious origin, known for more for its porousity than any endearing quality' (Johannesburg *Mail & Guardian* 23/12/07)] **1** [mid-19C] a person whose tough exterior hides a 'heart of gold'. **2** [2000s] (*S.Afr.*) an affluent, salaried black person. ❑ **black diamonds** *n.* [the value of the mineral, if only to the mine-owners] [mid-19C] **1** (*also* **dusty diamonds**) coal. **2** a coal heaver. ❑ **black drop** *n.* [early 19C] (*Anglo-Irish*) port wine. ❑ **black fly** *n.* (*also* **black slug**) ['the greatest drawback on the farmer is the black fly, i.e. the parson who takes a tithe of the harvest' (Grose)] [late 18C–mid-19C] a parson. ❑ **black gentleman** *n. see* BLACK MAN below. ❑ **black hat** *n.* **1** [mid–late 19C] (*Aus.*) a newly arrived immigrant [he would still wear his black, citified hat in the bush]. **2** [1960s+] (*US*) a villain, a 'baddie' [the traditional means of identifying a villain in films]. ❑ **black hole** *n.* [orig. UK milit.] **1** [early 19C+] (*US prison*) the (underground) punishment cells in a prison. **2** [19C] a police or prison cell. **3** [late 19C] any room set aside for punishment, e.g. in a workhouse or orphanage. **4** [late 19C–1930s] the vagina; one of a number of terms that equate the vagina with hell or any similar dark, threatening place. **5** [2000s] (*S.Afr. gay*) in a bar, a darkened room where anonymous sex may take place. ❑ **black house** *n.* [SE *black*, evil + *house*] [mid-19C] **1** a prison. **2** any place of business where the employees are exploited by long hours and low wages. ❑ **black job** *n.* [mid–late 19C] a funeral. ❑ **black lock** *n.* (*also* **black lockup**) [the blackness of 'the hole'] [1970s+] (*US prison*) solitary confinement for disciplinary reasons; often as *behind the black lock(up)*. ❑ **black machine** *n.* [late 18C] (*UK Und.*) the gallows. ❑ **black man** *n.* (*also* **black gentleman**) [the Devil, personifying evil, is naturally black] [17C+] the Devil. ❑ **black mollies** *n. see under* MOLLY *n.*[2]. ❑ **black mote** *n. see under* MOTA *n.* ❑ **black mummer** *n.* [early 19C] an unshaven person. ❑ **black ointment** *n.* [its use as a cure for black eyes] [mid-19C] (*UK Und.*) a piece of raw meat. ❑ **black pot** *n.* [SE *black pot*, a beer mug] [late 16C–early 19C] a drunkard. ❑ **black Protestant** *n.* (*also* **black Prod**) [SE *black* as generic for

Protestant, on model of 'scarlet' for Catholicism] [1960s+] (*US*) **1** a derog. term used by Catholics to describe a violently anti-Catholic Protestant. **2** a non-practising Protestant. ❑ **black rot, the** *n.* [it 'rots one's brain'] **1** [mid-19C] (*UK Und.*) a death warrant. **2** [mid-19C] (*US*) a fit of intense depression. ❑ **black sal** *n.* (*also* **black sukey**) [SE *black* + *sal*, abbr. Sarah/*sukey*, abbr. Susan; poss. ref. to the nursery rhyme 'Polly Put the Kettle On' ('Sukey take it off again'); but note *DSUE* suggestion Welsh Gipsy *sukar*, to hum, to whisper] [mid-19C–1900s] a kettle. ❑ **blackshanks** *adj. see* BLACKLEG *n.*[1] (2). ❑ **black-shoe** *adj.* [the formality of such footwear] [1950s] (*US campus*) formal, sober. ❑ **blacksock** *v.* [the stereotypical cheap pornographic movie, in which the male actors, otherwise naked, often keep on their socks] [1990s+] (*US*) to perform in a pornographic movie. ❑ **black spy, the** *n.* **1** [late 17C–mid-19C] the Devil; ext. as a derog. term of address. **2** [late 18C–mid-19C] without definite article, a constable; an informer. **3** [early 19C] a blacksmith. ❑ **black stick** *n.* [1930s–60s] (*orig. US black*) a clarinet. ❑ **black strap** *n.* [SE *black strap*, molasses, and thus referring to its excessive sweetness] **1** [late 18C+] poor quality liquor, esp. port wine. **2** [1920s] a variety of chewing tobacco. **3** [1920s–60s] (*US*) very strong black coffee. ❑ **black sukey** *n. see* BLACK SAL above. ❑ **black taxi** *n.* [1980s] (*Aus.*) an official limousine that ferries government members etc to and from houses, appointments and the like. ❑ **black thing** *n.* [euph.] [mid-18C] the vagina. ❑ **blacktop** *n.* **1** [1920s] (*US tramp*) a tent used for the projection of films. **2** [1930s+] (*US*) a minor road, a back road. **3** [1990s+] an asphalt playground. ❑ **black velvet** *n.* [based on the smoothness of the drink] [1930s+] a mixture of stout and champagne. ❑ **black water** *n.* [mid-19C–1960s] (*US West*) weak black coffee. ❑ **black widow** *n.* [the packaging] [1970s] (*drugs*) any black capsule that contains amphetamine. ❑ **black wings** *n.* [the initiate is then given a patch of the appropriate colour and design] [1950s+] usu. of Hell's Angels for whom it is an alleged initiation rite, performing cunnilingus on a black woman. ❑ **black work** *n.* [the pre-eminent role of black in funerary arrangements] [mid-19C] working as an undertaker.

IN PHRASES

❑ **black cat with its throat cut** *n. see under* CAT *n.*[1]. ❑ **black cove dubber** *n. see* DUB *v.*[1]. ❑ **black nigger in charge** *n. see* HEAD NIGGER IN CHARGE *under* HEAD *n.* ❑ **black-on-black** *n.* [1940s+] (*US black*) a car with black paintwork and all-black interior upholstery and fittings. ❑ **black-pepper brain/grains** *n.* [resemblance to black peppercorns] [1960s+] (*W.I.*) very short hair, growing close to the scalp in small balls of fluff. ❑ **black spice racket** *n.* [early 19C] robbing chimney sweeps. ❑ **black 360 degrees** *adj.* [360° describes a complete circle; thus totality] [1960s+] (*US black*) intensely and specifically black in personality and consciousness.

black *v.* [abbr.] **1** [late 19C] (*UK Und.*) to colour one's face *black* with burnt cork, as a 'nigger minstrel'. **2** [1920s+] to *black*mail; thus *put the black on*, to blackmail.

DERIVATIVES

❑ **blacking** *n.* [1960s+] (*UK juv.*) a male initiation ceremony whereby a boy has his genitals covered in black shoe polish.

IN EXCLAMATIONS

❑ **black my soul!** [1920s] (*US black*) an excl. of surprise.

Black and Decker *n.* [rhy. sl. = PECKER *n.*[2] (2)] [1990s+] the penis.

black-and-tan *n.* **1** [mid-19C] (*US black*) the southern states [puns on SE *tan*, to beat, i.e. the violence meted out to the *black* population]. **2** [late 19C] (*US short order*) a cup of coffee. **3** [late 19C–1900s] (*US*) a mulatto, a person of mixed race. **4** [late 19C+] a drink composed of porter or stout and ale. **5** [1930s–40s] a mixture of dark- and light-coloured black people. **6** [1960s] (*drugs*) usu. in pl., capsules of the amphetamine Durophet.

black and tan *adj.* [late 19C+] (*US*) **1** referring to the mixing of blacks and whites, e.g. a nightclub. **2** mixed race.

black and tan club *n.* (*also* **black and tan joint, black and tan parlour, black and tan resort**) [BLACK AND TAN *adj.* (1) + SE *club*] [1920s–60s] (*US*) **1** a place where both blacks and whites can meet and mingle. **2** a place patronized by African Americans [Smitherman, *Black Talk* (1994), suggests on the basis of African American skin tones rather than the greater division between the two races].

black and tans *n. see* BLACK-AND-TAN *n.* (6).

black and white *n.*[1] [SE *down in black and white*, in writing] **1** [mid-19C] (*also* **black and white work**) handwriting; thus written proof. **2** [1920s–30s] (*UK tramp*) tea and sugar. **3** [1950s+] (*US*) (*also* **blackandwhite, black-and-white, b and w, green-and-white**) a police car painted black and white (or other colours where relevant). **4** [1960s–70s] (*US*) a police officer. **5** [1960s+] (*drugs*) a black and white capsule, esp. Biphetamine, Dilantin/Phenobarbitol mix. **6** [1960s+] (*drugs*) a 12.5mg capsule of the amphetamine Durophet. **7** [1970s] a document.

black and white *n.*[2] [rhy. sl.] [late 19C–1900s; 1990s+] (*UK Und.*) night.

black and white minstrel *n. see* MINSTREL *n.*

black and white work *n. see* BLACK AND WHITE *n.*[1] (1).

black as... *adj.*

SE in slang uses

IN PHRASES

❑ **...a bull's backside** (*also* **black as a bear's asshole, black as a cat's ass at midnight, black as a dago's armpits, black as a nigger's hide, black as the inside of a (Taranaki) cow, black as the inside of a dog's guts**) [20C+] (*Aus./N.Z.*) extremely black, usu. of darkness. ❑ **...a musterer's billy** [SE *musterer* + *billy*, a kettle black with use] [1940s] (*N.Z.*) extremely black, usu. of darkness. ❑ **...a yard up a stove-pipe** [1930s] (*US*) extremely black. ❑ **...Natoby's ass** [? anecdotal] [1970s] (*US*) very black, dark-skinned. ❑ **...Newgate** (*also* **dark as Newgate**) [*Newgate*, 19C London's main convict prison and the site of many executions; its reputation was fig. *black*] [early 19C] **1** of an expression, frowning, glowering. **2** of a garment, dirty. ❑ **...Newgate knocker** (*also* **dark as Newgate knocker**) [*see* prev.] **1** [late 19C] of a night, very dark. **2** [1980s] very dirty.

black ass *n.* [SE *black* + ASS *n.* (4)] [1940s–80s] (*US*) a state of depression or disgust; thus *black-assed*, depressed, disgusted.

black-ass *adj.* [SE *black*] **1** intensifying extension of SE black; dark-complexioned [ASS *n.*]. **2** as a negative intensifier [BLACK ASS *n.*].

black-assed peas *n.* [the colouring of the legume] [1940s+] (*US black*) soul food, esp. black-eyed peas.

black bagging *n.*[1] [dynamite was carried in *black bags* and deposited at railway stations and other targets] [late 19C] setting off dynamite bombs.

black bagging *n.*[2] [SE *black* + BAG *n.*[1] (1)] [20C+] (*US*) the genitals of black women, seen collectively, i.e. for sexual exploitation.

blackberry *n.* [pun on the SE fruit] [mid-19C; 1980s+] (*US*) a black person.

blackberry swagger *n.* [? the black colour of the laces + *swagger*, one who carries a 'swag' or pack] [mid-19C–1900s] a hawker of shoelaces, tapes and similar small items.

blackbird *n.*[1] **1** [mid–late 19C] (*also* **bird**) an African slave *en route* from the place of capture to their destination; thus *blackbird-catcher*, a slaver or slave ship, *blackbird-catching*, the slave trade; also as v. **2** [mid-19C–1900s] (*Aus.*) an Aborigine; thus *blackbird shooting*, the killing for 'sport' of Aborigines by white settlers. **3** [mid-19C–1910s] a forced labourer from the Pacific islands, e.g. a Melanesian or Polynesian, thus *blackbird-catching, blackbird-hunting*. **4** [late 19C+] a black person, usu. as in derog. context. **5** [1900s] (*US*) a black child. **6** [1960s+] (*US black*) (*also* **black ball**) a dark-complexioned black person. **7** [1970s+] (*drugs*) strong (20mg) capsules of amphetamine.

blackbird *n.*[2] [var. on BIRD *n.*[3] (1); there is no racial implication] [1940s+] (*US*) a penis.

blackbird and thrush *v.* [rhy. sl. = brush] [late 19C] to clean one's boots or shoes.

blackbirder *n.* [BLACKBIRD *n.*[1] (3)] [late 19C] a man (or ship) working in the Pacific forced labour trade.

blackbirding *n.* [BLACKBIRD *n.*[1] (3)] [late 19C–1930s] the trade in forced labour, esp. between the Pacific Islands and the Queensland sugar plantations in Australia.

black dog *n.*[1] [use of SE *black* as generic negative, evil, sinister, illicit etc + (?) DOG *n.*[3] (1)] [mid-17C–early 18C] a counterfeit silver coin, e.g. a shilling.

black dog *n.*[2] [the most celebrated of such depressions was that suffered by the former prime minister Sir Winston Churchill] **1** [early 19C+] a fit of depression or ill humour. **2** [1930s] delerium tremens.

IN PHRASES

❑ **walk the black dog on** *v.* [late 18C–early 19C] (*UK prison*) to inflict a punishment on a new fellow-prisoner who refuses to pay the automatic fine that is levied on him as a new inmate.

black duck *n.*[1] [SE *black duck*, any dark duck, e.g. mallard, redleg; like the birds, the Native Americans were considered prey by the 18C colonists] [mid-18C–late 19C] a Native American Indian.

black duck *n.*[2] [the logo] [1990s+] (*Aus.*) Swan lager.

black eye *n.* [mid-18C+] a bad reputation;a blow to one's reputation.

IN PHRASES

❑ **give someone/something a black eye** *v.* [late 19C–1940s] to injure someone's or something's reputation.

SE in slang uses

IN PHRASES

❑ **give a bottle a black eye** *v.* [late 18C+] to finish it.

black-eyed susan *n.* [? the black 'eye' of the barrel] [mid–late 19C] (*US, Texas*) a revolver.

black-eye pea soup *n.* [1980s] (*W.I.*) a situation where the majority of the people are white with just a few token blacks.

blackfellows' act *n.* (*also* **dog act**) [SAusE *blackfellow* (now derog.), a Native Australian] [1920s+] (*Aus.*) a government order that can be used by publicans to discipline or bar drunkards.

blackfellow's game *n.* [*see* prev.; its popularity among Native Australians] [1940s] (*Aus.*) the game of euchre.

blackfellow telegraph *n.* *see* BUSH TELEGRAPH *n.* (2).

Blackford-block *n.* (*also* **Blackford swell, ...toff**) [the London clothes-hire firm of *Blackford's* + SE *block*, the wooden head on which wigs were displayed/SWELL *n.*[1] (1)/TOFF *n.* (3)] [late 19C–1900s] a sporadically well-dressed man.

blackfriars! *excl.* [? the black uniform of various authorities, reminiscent of the black-garbed Dominicans] [mid–late 19C] (*US Und.*) a shout of warning, 'someone's coming, let's run for it!'.

black gold *n.* **1** [1960s] black women in general, as sex objects. **2** [1970s] oil. **3** [1980s+] (*drugs*) high potency marijuana [BLACK *n.* (1) + ACAPULCO (GOLD) *n.*].

blackguard *n.* ['a term said to be derived from a number of dirty tattered and roguish boys, who attended at the horse guards [...] in St James's Park, to black the boots and shoes of the soldiers, or to do any other dirty offices, these were nick-named the black guards' (Grose, 1785)] **1** [mid-17C] a shabby dirty individual. **2** [late 18C] (*US*) a foul-mouthed person, a slanderer; thus *blackguarding*, talking obscenely.

blackguard *v.* [BLACKGUARD *n.* (2)] [19C+] to swear at, to curse (someone).

blackguardly *adj.* [BLACKGUARD *n.* (1)] [late 19C] shabbily, dirtily.

Black Hole *n.* [the large number of ex-Indian Army or Indian Civil Service officers who retired there; the ref. is to the *Black Hole* of Calcutta (1756)] [late 19C–1930s] Cheltenham.

Black Indies *n.* [the Indies, whether East or West, were the sources of great mercantile wealth; *black* implies the area's mines] [late 17C–mid-19C] Newcastle upon Tyne, its its role as a centre of coal-mining.

black Irish *n.* [SE *black Irish*, an Irish person with notably Mediterranean features – dark hair and eyes – but with no overtones of ill temper. One theory suggests that the original 'black Irish' were the descendants of mixed marriages between the Irish and the shipwrecked sailors of the Spanish Armada, cast ashore in 1588] [20C+] (*US*) **1** a person with a very bad temper. **2** a lower-class Irish person, typically an unsophisticated new immigrant. **3** an Irish Protestant. **4** a former slave, who took their surname from an Irish owner.

black-is-white *adv.* [i.e. one will argue that 'black is white'] [20C+] (*W.I.*) thoroughly, comprehensively, without restraint.

Black Jack *n.* [the nickname of Sir John Sylvester, the Common Sergeant of London c. 1810] [early 19C] the Recorder of London.

black jack *n.*[1] [SE *black* + *jack*, a vessel for liquor (either for holding it or from drinking from); orig. and usu. of waxed leather coated outside with tar or pitch] **1** [late 16C–mid-19C] a leather jug used for drinking, coated with tar on its exterior. **2** [late 19C] a type of suitcase or portmanteau. **3** [late 19C–1900s] (*Aus.*) a tin pot used for boiling tea.

black jack *n.*[2] [SE *black* + generic use of proper name] [mid-19C+] the ace of spades.

black jack *n.*[3] [? nickname] **1** [1900s] some form of poison. **2** [1930s] (*US tramp*) a purgative.

black jack *n.*[4] [SE *black* + JACK *n.*[3] (3)] [1940s+] **1** (*US gay*) a black man's penis. **2** a black woman's genitals.

blackjack *n.*[1] [SE *black*, the colour of the drinks/treacle + JACK *n.*[13]] **1** [mid–late 19C] (*US*) rum sweetened with molasses. **2** [late 19C+] (*US*) very strong black coffee, usu. sweetened with molasses. **3** [20C+] (*Aus.*) treacle. **4** [20C+] (*US*) illegally distilled whisky.

blackjack *n.*[2] [his weapon] **1** [1920s] (*US*) a thug. **2** [1970s+] (*S.Afr.*) a black municipal police officer.

blackjack *n.*[3] [colour of the capsules] [1960s] (*US drugs*) amphetamine.

black joke *n.* (*also* **coal black joke**) [contemporary popular song, *The Harlot Unmasked* (c.1735), the chorus of which ran, 'Her black joke and belly so white'; Williams notes that 'the C18 saw numerous songs circulating to the tune '*Black Joke*''; Partridge suggests 'something to be cracked'] [mid-18C+] the female genitals.

black label *n.* [play on proprietary Johnny Walker *Black Label* whisky] [1980s+] (*Aus. prison*) illicit home-fermented liquor.

blackleg *n.*[1] [? SE *game-cocks*, which have black legs, or f. the black boots such swindlers always wore; another suggestion notes a pun on ROOK *n.*[1] (1), a bird that also has black legs] **1** [late 18C–1910s] a racecourse swindler; thus adj. *black-legged*. **2** [late 18C–1910s] (*also* **blacklegs, blackshanks**) any swindler; thus *blacklegging, black-leggery*, swindling. **3** [19C] a professional gambler or layer of odds. **4** [late 19C] (*US*) a fashionable dandy. **5** [1930s–50s] (*US Und.*) a professional criminal.

blackleg *n.*[2] [ety. unknown; ? link to Scot. *blackleg*, a go-between (usu. in love-affairs, but fig. between bosses and workers)] [mid-19C+] a strike-breaker.

blackleg *n.*[3] [SE *black* + the idea of its resembling a leg] [20C+] a black man's penis.

blackleg *n.*[4] [1910s] (*US*) strong black coffee.

blackleg *adj.* [BLACKLEG *n.*[1] (5)] [1930s] (*US*) corrupt, underhand.

blackleg *v.* [BLACKLEG *n.*[2]] [late 19C+] to work as a strike-breaker.

black man kissed her *n.* [rhy. sl.] [1910s; 1950s+] a sister.

Black Maria *n.* (*also* **black mariah, Maria, mariar, sable maria**) [SE *black*, the colour of the van, but the ety. of *Maria* is unknown; suggestions include an abbr. of *married*, two or more prisoners chained together; a play on the *-ria* of Queen Victoria's name (which fails in the face of its origins in the US, although *V.R.* was inscribed on the British vans) and Brewer's suggestion in *Dict. of Phrase and Fable* (1894) of a derivation f. one Maria Lee, a Black madam of Boston, Mass. So large and fearsome was Ms Lee that she was regularly called upon by the local police to help them first arrest and then take criminals to prison. According to F&H, themselves citing 'a writer on slang', the term was coined *c.*1838 in Philadelphia, although the *OED* first use is 1847 (usefully for Brewer from a Boston newspaper) and *DSUE* (1984) notes Joseph Neal's story *The Prison Van, or The Black Maria* (1844)] **1** [mid-19C+] (*orig. US*) a prison van for conveying prisoners. **2** [mid-19C+] (*orig. US*) a hearse. **3** [1980s] (*orig. US*) an ambulance.

black maria *n.* [SE *black* + generic use of proper name] **1** [20C+] a black woman's genitals. **2** [1980s] a black prostitute.

black mouth *n.*[1] [SE *black*, malicious, evil + *mouth*] [mid-17C] a slanderer.

black mouth *n.*[2] [20C+] a black woman's genitals.

blackmouth *n.* [20C+] (*Ulster*) a Presbyterian.

black mouth *adj.* [BLACK MOUTH *n.*[1]] [17C–19C] slanderous, malicious.

blackout *n.* [pun on SE] **1** [1940s] (*US black*) a very dark-skinned person. **2** [1940s+] (*S.Afr./US*) black coffee. **3** [1990s+] (*US*) a restaurant or store taken over and controlled by a group of (young) African-Americans (who then leave without paying for the food or goods).

black out *v.* [1940s] (*US Und.*) to murder; to assassinate.

black out with *adj.* [1920s+] (*Irish*) hostile towards.

black people's time *n.* (*also* **colored folks' time, CP (colored people's) time**) [joc. use of derog. racial stereotyping] [1960s+] (*US/UK black*) unpunctuality, lateness.

Black Power dance *n.* (*also* **power dance**) [SE *Black Power*, a political movement created *c.*1966 by Stokely Carmichael (1941–98) and H. Rap Brown (b. 1943). The spirit of Black Power lay behind the 1960s riots, when militant US blacks looted in the big city ghettos] [1960s] (*US black*) **1** looting. **2** fighting back against white oppression.

black sheep *n.* **1** [early 19C] a clergyman. **2** [mid–late 19C] a strike-breaker.

black sheep *v.* [BLACK SHEEP *n.*] [20C+] (*US*) to take advantage of another person's temporary disability or absence to steal their job.

blacksmith *n.* [the hammers, chisels and similar tools common to both occupations] **1** [late 19C+] (*Aus.*) a cook on an outback station, usu. derog. **2** [1900s] (*UK Und.*) a forger. **3** [1920s–40s] (*US Und.*) a safebreaker.

blacksmith *v.* [BLACKSMITH *n.* (3)] [1930s] (*US Und.*) to break into a safe.

blacksmith's daughter *n.* [? ref. to a chastity belt] [mid-19C] a key, a lock and key, a padlock.

blacksmith's shop *n.* [play on SE *shop*/SHOP *n.*[1] (1) + ? HAMMA *n.*/*HAMMER-MAN* *under* HAMMER *n.*[1]] [20C+] a brothel run by a black madam and presumably featuring a number of black prostitutes.

blacksnake *n.* [1930s+] (*US black*) a black penis.

blacksnake *v.* [SE *blacksnake*, a long braided whip, used by mule-drivers and teamsters] [19C] (*US*) to whip, to punish.

blacksploitation *n.* *see* BLAXPLOITATION *n.*

black stuff *n.*[1] (*drugs*) **1** [1930s+] opium. **2** [1960s+] stout, esp. Guinness. **3** [2000s] heroin.

IN PHRASES

❑ **shovelling the black stuff** *adj.* [1950s] (*US drugs*) addicted to opium. [STUFF *n.* (5b); opium is black; the ref. to heroin, usu. brown or white, is based on its relation to opium]

black stuff *n.*[2] [1930s+] (*S.Afr.*) black labourers.

black stump *n.* [SE *black* + *stump*, a free-standing post or pillar] [1950s+] (*Aus.*) a symbolic marker that divides the known or 'civilized' world from the unknown wastelands beyond; usu. in phrs., e.g. *this side of the black stump*.

IN PHRASES

❑ **beyond the black stump** *adj.* eccentric; insane.

blacktracker *n.* [play on SAusE *black-tracker*, a Native Australian used as an auxiliary police officer in the pursuit of criminals] [1900s] (*Aus.*) a nickname for a pious individual who is overly dependent on their spiritual adviser.

black up *v.* [1950s+] (*W.I.*) to get drunk.

black up *adv.* [one is 'blind' drunk] [1940s+] (*W.I.*) in a very drunken manner.

Blackwall Tunnel *n.* [rhy. sl.] [20C+] a ship's funnel.

bladder *n.*[1] (*also* **blatter**) [Ger. *Blatt*, leaf and therefore newspaper] [1900s–60s] (*US*) a newspaper.

bladder *n.*[2] [SE *bladder*, a container, the implication is of diseased matter] [1930s] (*US Und.*) an unattractive and/or ageing prostitute.

bladdered *adj.* [play on SKINFUL *n.* (1)] [1990s+] drunk.

bladder of fat *n.* [rhy. sl.] [1900s–10s] a hat.

bladder of lard *n.*[1] [derog. comparisons] **1** [mid–late 19C] a bald-headed man. **2** [mid-19C+] a fat man.

bladder of lard *n.*[2] [rhy. sl.] **1** [20C+] a playing card. **2** [1910s+] a card as used in the game of bingo. **3** [1920s–50s] Scotland Yard, former headquarters of the Metropolitan Police.

bladdy *adj.* (*also* **bleddy**) [1940s+] (*S.Afr./W.I.*) a general expletive, the local pron. of the UK BLOODY *adj.* (1).

blade *n.* **1** in lit. and fig. uses of an edged weapon. (**a**) [17C–19C] the penis. (**b**) [late 19C+] (*US*) any knife, esp. a switchblade. **2** a man, prob. orig. one who orig. carried an edged weapon. (**a**) [17C+] a gallant, a 'sharp fellow'. (**b**) [17C+] in combs., a style of a man, defined by the adj. (**c**) [17C+] in combs., defined by one's local area. **3** a person who is 'sharp'. (**a**) [1910s] (*Scot./US*) one's wife, usu. *old blade*, or girlfriend. (**b**) [1980s+] (*Ulster*) a showily or bizarrely dressed woman. (**c**) [1980s+] (*Ulster*) a cantankerous, verbally abusive woman. (**d**) [1980s+] a 'difficult' child. (**e**) [1990s+] an expert, a connoisseur, a wise man or one posing as such. **4** [1980s] (*US black*) a Cadillac. **5** [2000s] (*S.Afr. gay*) a young homosexual male. **6** [2000s] (*US black*) in pl., a type of wheel rims, used on a customized automobile.

blade *v.*[1] [BLADE *n.* (2)] [late 18C–early 19C] to act as a roisterer, a 'sharp' man or woman.

blade *v.*[2] [SE *blade*, a sharp weapon] **1** [1980s+] (*US campus*) to get rid of [? the offending item is 'cut out' of one's life]. **2** [1980s+] (*Aus./US Und.*) to stab, to slash with a sharp/bladed weapon.

blades *n.* [1980s+] (*US drugs*) smoking hashish by placing a piece on a knife blade and then exposing it to a flame; e.g. *let's do some blades*.

blades of meat *n.* *see* PLATES (OF MEAT) *n.*

blag *n.* [? SE *blackguard*] **1** [late 19C+] (*also* **blague**) robbery, often with violence, esp. of a bank or post office. **2** [1920s+] bag-snatching, watch-stealing. **3** [1930s+] a wages' snatch. **4** [1940s+] (*orig. Und.*) a persuasive if lying story.

IN COMPOUNDS

❑ **blag-merchant** *n.* [MERCHANT *n.* (1)] [1950s+] a pay-roll robber.

blag *v.* [BLAG *n.*] **1** [late 19C+] (*orig. Und.*) (*also* **blague**) to steal. **2** [1940s+] to deceive, to hoax. **3** [1950s] to be rude or cheeky. **4** [1960s+] to persuade, esp. as in *blag in/into*, to talk one's way in to a party, concert etc. **5** [1970s+] to obtain for free. **6** [1980s+] (*W.I.*) to chat with friends. **7** [2000s] to pretend.

DERIVATIVES

❑ **blagger** *n.* **1** [1930s+] a thief, esp. a bank robber. **2** [1990s+] a smooth talker, a persuasive person. **3** [2000s] a sponger. ❑ **blagging** *n.* [20C+] (*UK Und./police*) **1** a robbery. **2** violence, in the course of a robbery.

blah *n.*[1] (*also* **blaah, blah-blah**) [? Ger. *Blech*, nonsense or onomat.] [1910s+] **1** (*orig. US*) pompous, banal verbosity; also nonsense. **2** a fool, an idiot.

blah *n.*[2] [pron.] [1950s+] (*S.Afr.*) brother.

blah *adj.* [BLAH *v.*] **1** [1920s] (*orig. US*) insincere, verbose, pompous. **2** [1920s] (*US*) insane, crazy. **3** [1920s+] wonky, wrong. **4** [1930s+] blind drunk. **5** [1960s+] (*also* **blasé**) uninterested, non-committal. **6** [1960s+] banal, cliched, undistinguished.

SE in slang uses

IN PHRASES

❑ **go blah** *v.* [SE *blah*, echoic of a nonsensical noise] **1** [20C+] to have one's mind go momentarily blank. **2** [1960s] (*US*) to break down, to fail.

blah *v.* [onomat.] **1** [1920s] to chatter, to gossip. **2** [1960s+] to speak in an insincere, pompous manner; thus intensified as *blah-blah-blah*.

(IN PHRASES)

❑ **blah, blah, blah** **1** [1910s+] (*also* **blahdy blahdy blah**) phr. used to imply that a statement is meaningless, hollow, nonsense, albeit delivered in the most serious of tones. **2** [1940s+] (*Aus./US*) as synon. for etctera, 'and so on'. **3** [1960s] an otherwise unidentified object.

blah! *excl.* [BLAH *n.*[1] (1)] [1940s+] (*US campus*) an excl. of frustration, boredom or resignation.

blahs, the *n.* [1960s+] (*Aus./US*) depression, despondency, low condition.

blaitie bum *n.* (*also* **bummillbaty**) [mid-16C] (*Scot.*) a fool.

blam *v.* [echoic] [1970s+] to do something that generates noise.

blame *adj.* (*also* **blamed, blamedest, blarmed, blimed**) [early 19C+] (*US*) euph. for DAMN *adj.*/DAMNED *adj.*, certain, sure, absolute, complete; thus phr. *I'll be blamed*.

blame *v.* [mid-19C+] (*US*) euph. for *damn*.

blame *adv.* (*also* **blamed**) [BLAME *adj.*] [mid-19C–1900s] confoundedly, exceedingly.

blame it! *excl.* [BLAME *adj.*] [early 19C–1930s] euph. for DAMMIT! *excl.*

blamentation! *excl.* (*also* **blamenation**) [DAMNATION! *excl.*] [mid-19C] (*US*) a mild expletive.

blamps *n.* [? SE *big* + *HEADLAMPS under* HEAD *n.*] [1990s+] large breasts.

blanca *n.* [Sp. *blancas*, whites] [1950s–60s] (*US drugs*) **1** amphetamines. **2** cocaine.

blanched *adj.* (*also* **blanshed**) [pun on SE *blanched*, whitened + *blanch*, to turn white with fear, embarrassment] [1960s+] (*US black*) ruined either physically or socially.

blanco *n.* [Sp. *blanco*, white; some varieties of heroin are white, rather than the usual brown] **1** [1960s+] (*US black*) a white person. **2** [1970s+] (*drugs*) heroin.

blandander *v.* [SE *blandish*/BLETHER... and/or BLARNEY *v.* (1)] **1** [late 19C–1910s] to cajole, to offer blandishments. **2** [late 19C+] to talk nonsense.

blank *n.* **1** [mid-19C+] a euph. for a variety of obscenities, e.g. BUGGER *n.*[1], SHIT *n.*, BASTARD *n.* etc. **2** [1950s] (*US prison*) an aspirin. **3** [1950s–60s] a bad or insignificant, worthless person. **4** [1950s+] (*orig. prison*) a rejection, esp. of a parole application. **5** [1960s] a halt, a stop. **6** [1960s] a fault, a bad characteristic. **7** [1960s+] (*drugs*) any powder sold as a narcotic but absolutely without effect; thus generic for second-rate drugs.

SE in slang uses

(IN PHRASES)

❑ **draw a blank** *v.* (*also* **draw blank(s), draw it blank**) [SE *draw a blank*, ult. drawing a blank ticket in a lottery] [19C+] to fail, to be disappointed, frustrated. ❑ **fire blanks** *v.* [1960s+] **1** of a man, to be infertile, to ejaculate infertile semen. **2** of a man, to have an orgasm without ejaculation. ❑ **pull a blank** *v.* [1920s] (*US*) to be rejected. ❑ **slip someone a blank** *v.* [1900s] to deceive. ❑ **shoot a blank** *v.* **1** [1950s–70s] (*US*) to fail, to have no luck. **2** [1980s+] (*also* **shoot a dud, shoot blanks**) (*US black*) to attempt sophisticated conversation but to fail in so doing; to use words that have no 'target'. ❑ **shoot blanks** *v.* **1** [1950s+] to ejaculate infertile semen; thus *blank shooter*. **2** [1960s+] of a man, to fail to achieve an erection, to be impotent.

blank *adj.* (*also* **blanked, blanking**) [BLANK *n.* (1); lit. the 'blank space' that replaces the unuttered oath] [19C+] euph. for DAMN *adj.*/DAMNED *adj.*

blank *v.*[1] [BLANK *n.* (1)] [late 19C] (*Aus.*) to curse, to swear at.

blank *v.*[2] [SE *blank out*, to erase; note baseball jargon *blank*, to retitre a team without letting them score] **1** [1970s+] to ignore. **2** [1990s+] to wipe out, to reject. **3** [1990s+] to overlook.

(IN PHRASES)

❑ **blank out** *v.* **1** [1950s+] to render unconscious. **2** [2000s] to become (temporarily) unconscious. ❑ **blank up** *v.* [to render one's victim 'blank'] [1980s+] (*US black*) to trick, to murder.

blankard *n.* [BLANK *n.* (1) + SE (*bast*)*ard*] [20C+] (*Aus.*) a bastard.

blanked *adj.* [late 19C+] a negative intensifier, euph. for DAMNED *adj.*

blanker *n.* [BLANK *n.* (1)] [1900s–10s] (*Aus.*) euph. for BUGGER *n.*[1].

blanket *n.* **1** [mid-19C] (*US*) a currency note; thus money in general [it offers its possessor comfort]. **2** [late 19C+] (*S.Afr.*) a peasant, an unsophisticated African; thus in synon. combs. *blanket-boy*, *blanket-kaffir*; and *blanket-vote*, the collective black vote [the trad. blankets that such individuals wear; note 19C US *blanket brave*, *blanket indian*, 'an Indian of a low cultural level [...] a semi-civilized Indian' (Mathews, *Dict. Americanisms*, 1951)]. **3** [1900s–30s] (*US tramp*) a newspaper (which is often used as a makeshift blanket). **4** [1920s–30s] (*US tramp*) an overcoat, which regularly doubles as a blanket. **5** [1920s+] (*US tramp*) a griddlecake or pancake. **6** [1920s+] a cigarette paper; thus *tumblings and blankets*, tobacco and papers. **7** [1930s] (*US Und.*) a bulletproof vest. **8** [1960s] (*US campus*) ext. use of sense 6, a cigarette. **9** [1980s+] (*drugs*) ext. use of sense 6, a marijuana cigarette.

(IN COMPOUNDS)

❑ **blanket-ass** *n.* (*also* **blanket-head**) [ASS *n.* (4)/-HEAD *sfx*] [1950s+] (*US*) a Native American. ❑ **blanket-buck** *n.* [20C+] (*US*) a Native American.

(IN PHRASES)

❑ **wear the blanket** *v.* [mid-19C] (*US*) to have native American blood.

SE in slang uses

(IN COMPOUNDS)

❑ **blanket drill** *n.* [note milit. *blanket drill*, sleep] (*orig. milit.*) **1** [1920s+] masturbation. **2** [1960s] sexual intercourse. ❑ **blanket fair** *n.* [the orig. *Blanket Fair* was the name given to that held on the Thames during the great frost of 1683–84] [late 19C] bed. ❑ **blanket hornpipe** *n.* [19C; 1980s+] sexual intercourse; thus *dance the blanket hornpipe*. ❑ **blanket job** *n.* **1** [1930s–60s] (*US prison*) homosexual gang rape: the victim's head is placed beneath a blanket while he is assaulted. **2** [1980s] (*UK Und*) a form of gangland execution whereby the victim is tricked into hiding beneath a blanket, and then shot dead. **3** [1980s] (*also* **blanket treatment**) a beating given by prison officers. ❑ **blanket muster** *n. see* *TARPAULIN MUSTER under* TARPAULIN *adj.* ❑ **blanket party** *n.* [ironic use of SE] **1** [1930s] (*US*) sexual intercourse. **2** [1970s+] (*US prison*) the murder of a fellow prisoner by tossing a blanket over the head and then bludgeoning or stabbing them to death. **3** [1970s+] an initiation rite whereby a new prisoner is forcibly smothered in a blanket, then beaten up or gang-raped by their fellows; similarly applied to teen gang initiations. **4** [1970s+] (*Aus./N.Z./US prison*) the throwing of a blanket over the head of a prisoner to facilitate a beating or robbery. ❑ **blanket stiff** *n.* [SE *blanket*, a bedroll + STIFF *n.*[1] (4a)] [late 19C+] (*US*) a tramp, esp. a Western tramp.

(IN PHRASES)

❑ **blue blanket** *n.* **1** [late 18C–19C] the sky. **2** [mid-19C] a rough coat made of coarse pilot-cloth (an indigo cloth used for ships' officers' greatcoats). ❑ **close to the blanket** *adj.* (*also* **close to the cushion**) [gambling use, when a poker game would be played on a spread blanket; thus when one's pile of money gets smaller and smaller and 'close to the blanket'] [1900s–10s] (*US, Western*) almost totally impoverished, very poor. ❑ **dance the blanket hornpipe** *v. see under* DANCE *v.* (1). ❑ **fill a blanket** *v.* [1940s–50s] (*US Und.*) to roll a cigarette; thus *filled blanket* a hand-rolled cigarette. ❑ **lawful blanket** *n.* [SE *lawful* + fig. use of *blanket*] [19C] a wife. ❑ **live blanket** *n.* [1990s+] (*W.I./UK black teen*) a human body, particularly when covering another, as in sexual intercourse. ❑ **red blanket** *n.* [the otherwise unmarked red-painted tins in which it was sold] [1920s] (*Aus.*) tinned meat. ❑ **stretch the blanket** *v.* [late 19C+] (*US*) to exaggerate.

Blanket Bay *n.* [late 18C; 19C–1900s] (*Aus./US*) bed.

blanket the headlights *v.* [1940s] (*US short order*) to order fried eggs turned over.

blankety *adj.* [BLANK *adj.* (1)] [mid-19C+] a general term of condemnation.

blankety-blank *phr.* (*also* **blinkety-blankety**) [a euph. in which the words indicate two *blanks*, for presumed obscenities, on the page] [late 19C+] a general term of condemnation, which is found in all parts of speech, e.g. *you blankety-blank!* or *that blankety-blank, no-good,* or *don't you blankety-blank me!*

blanking *adj. see* BLANK *adj.*

blanks *n. see* BLANK *n.* (7).

blanky *adj.* (*also* **blankey**) [BLANK *adj.*] [late 19C] a euph. for BLOODY *adj.* or DAMNED *adj.*, or a similar intensifier.

blanny *n.* [SE *blandishment*/BLARNEY *n.*[1] (1)] [1920s–50s] flattery.

blanny *v.* [BLANNY *n.*] [1960s] (*US*) to flatter.

blanshed *adj. see* BLANCHED *adj.*

blaps *n.* [Afk. *blaps*, a blunder, a howler, a 'blooper'] [1960s+] (*S.Afr.*) a gaucherie, a blunder.

blap up *v.* [echoic of the fast speech] [1980s] (*UK black*) to deceive by talking fast.

blar *v.* [? BLAH *n.*[1]] [1990s+] (*W.I.*) to show off.

blarey-eyed *adj.* [? SE *bleary-eyed*/US Sth *blare-eyed*, heaving bulging eyes] [1970s] (*US black*) a general insult.

blarge *v.* [SE *blunder* + *barge*] [1970s] (*Ulster*) to do anything unceremoniously and loudly.

blaring cheat *n. see* BLEATING CHEAT *under* BLEAT *v.*

blarmed *adj. see* BLAME *adj.*

blarnation! *excl. see* TARNATION! *excl.*

blarney *n.*[1] [*Blarney*, a village near Cork in Ireland. Within the castle is an inscribed stone, which is hard to approach, and the popular belief is that any one who kisses this 'Blarney stone' will ever after be gifted with a persuasive, plausible tongue; note Bartlett, *Dict. of Americanisms*, 1848: 'Dr. Jamieson doubts the Irish origin of this word, and adopts the French etymon *baliverne*, a lie, a fib, gull; also, a babbling, idle discourse'] [late 18C+] nonsense, charming but empty chatter; also as excl.; thus adv. *blarneyish*.

IN COMPOUNDS

❑ **blarney boy** *n.* [1950s] one who is charming, but whose words are nonsensical and empty.

IN PHRASES

❑ **come the blarney (over)** [COME THE… *v.*] [19C+] to flatter. ❑ **put the blarney on** *v.* [19C+] to flatter. ❑ **tip off the blarney** *v.* [TIP OFF *v.*[2]] [late 18C–early 19C] to deceive, to trick by verbal facility.

blarney *n.*[2] [? play on BLARNEY *n.*[1], which will 'get one in anywhere'] [mid-19C] (*US Und.*) a picklock.

blarney *v.* [BLARNEY *n.*[1]] **1** [late 18C+] to flatter, to talk nonsense; thus *blarneyed*, flattered, cajoled, *blarneying*, flattering. **2** [late 19C] (*US Und.*) to pick locks.

blarst! *excl. see* BLAST! *excl.*

blarsted *adj. see* BLASTED *adj.*[1].

blart *n.* [? BLART *v.*] [1990s+] **1** (*also* **blit**) the vagina. **2** a generic for women, considered as sexual objects.

blart *v.* [dial. *blart*, to howl] [late 19C+] to talk wildly, noisily.

blast *n.*[1] [ext. use of SE] **1** [late 19C+] a severe reprimand, a verbal attack. **2** [1920s–50s] an armed (bank) robbery. **3** the consumption of drink or drugs. (**a**) [1940s+] (*drugs*) an injection or inhale of a narcotic drug, and the immediate effect. (**b**) [1950s+] (*US*) a drink of liquor. (**c**) [1950s+] (*orig. US*) marijuana, a puff of a marijuana cigarette; the effect thereof [note early 16C Scot. *blast*, a smoke of tobacco]. (**d**) [1990s+] a smoke of a crack pipe. **4** [1950s–60s] a telephone call. **5** [1950s–70s] (*US prison*) a false rumour. **6** [1950s+] a thrill, a very good time. **7** [1950s+] a wild, uproarious party. **8** [1960s] (*US*) a lie. **9** [1960s] something funny, amusing. **10** [1990s+] an admirable person. **11** [1990s+] (*US black*) a song. **12** [1990s+] a smoke of a crack pipe.

IN COMPOUNDS

❑ **blasting party** *n.* (*also* **blast party**) [1950s–70s] (*orig. US black*) a party where the guests smoke marijuana (in favour of drinking).

IN PHRASES

❑ **put the blast on** *v.* (*US*) **1** [1920s+] (*also* **put one on blast**) to attack verbally, to criticize severely. **2** [1940s] to betray, to inform on. **3** [1940s–50s] to shoot dead.

SE in slang uses

IN PHRASES

❑ **blast from the past** *n.* (*also* **blast from one's past**) [1960s+] (*orig. US*) anything that, or anyone who, causes nostalgia, esp. a piece of music or a popular song.

blast *n.*[2] [BLAST! *excl.*] [1950s–70s] a damn.

blast *v.*[1] [ext. use of SE] **1** [mid-17C] to infect with venereal disease. **2** as a verbal 'explosion'. (**a**) [late 18C+] to swear, to curse. (**b**) [late 18C+] a euph. for *damn*. (**c**) [mid-19C+] to scold, to criticize; to vilify. (**d**) [1940s+] to complain. **3** to use a weapon. (**a**) [1920s+] (*orig. US*) to shoot a gun. (**b**) [1930s–70s] (*orig. US*) (*also* **blast up**) to shoot or kill someone with a gun; thus *blast job*, a murder. **4** [1930s+] (*orig. US*) to defeat heavily. **5** to consume a drug. (**a**) [1940s+] (*drugs*) to smoke a marijuana or hashish cigarette. (**b**) [1950s–60s] (*US*) to go completely mad (esp. under the influence of drugs). (**c**) [1950s+] to take narcotics. (**d**) [1980s] to give someone an injection. (**e**) [1980s+] (*drugs*) to smoke crack cocaine. **6** [1960s] (*US black*) to do something well. **7** [1960s] (*US campus*) to fail an examination or test. **8** in fig. uses. (**a**) [1960s] (*US*) to play music passionately. (**b**) [1970s] (*US*) to drive fast. (**c**) [1990s+] (*orig. US black/teen*) to play a record (loudly). **9** [1980s] (*UK black*) to beat up.

IN PHRASES

❑ **blast a joint** *v. see under* JOINT *n.* ❑ **blast a roach** *v. see under* ROACH *n.* ❑ **blast a stick** *v. see under* STICK *n.*

IN EXCLAMATIONS

❑ **blast my old boots!** (*also* **blast my old slippers!**) [late 18C] an excl. denoting one's astonishment. ❑ **blast (one's) eyes!** *see* DAMN ONE'S EYES! *under* DAMN! *excl.*

blast *v.*[2] [SE *blast off*] **1** [1930s] to leave. **2** [1930s] to give up trying. **3** [1970s+] to move fast.

blast! *excl.* (*also* **blarst!**) [mid-18C+] a mild. excl.; euph. for damn.

blasted *adj.*[1] (*also* **blarsted**) [abbr. SE *God blasted*] **1** [late 17C+] a euph. for damned. **2** [late 19C+] as an infix.

IN COMPOUNDS

❑ **blasted brimstone** *n.* [BRIMSTONE *n.* (1)] [late 18C] (*UK Und.*) a prostitute. ❑ **blasted fellow** *n.* [mid-18C–early 19C] a complete villain.

DERIVATIVES

❑ **blastedly** *adv.* [mid-19C] damnedly.

blasted *adj.*[2] [fig. use of SE *blast*] [1930s+] very drunk or heavily intoxicated by a drug.

blaster *n.*[1] (*US Und.*) **1** [1910s–30s] a safe-blower [SE *blast*]. **2** [1930s–60s] a thug or gangster who is armed [BLAST *v.*[1] (3a)]. **3** [1930s+] a pistol, a revolver, a shotgun [BLAST *v.*[1] (3a)].

blaster *n.*[2] [abbr. *GHETTO BLASTER under* GHETTO *adj.*] [1980s+] a large, portable cassette recorder/player.

blastiferous *adj.* [1900s] (*Aus.*) synon, for BLASTED *adj.*[1].

blast-off *n.* [1960s] (*US*) **1** an orgasm. **2** a thrill, a very good time.

blast off *v.* **1** [1950s+] (*US*) to leave; often as an imper. **2** [1960s] (*US drugs*) to experience a drug and thus get HIGH *adj.*[1] (2). **3** [1990s+] (*US*) to have an orgasm.

blat *n.* [Ger. *Blatt*, leaf; thus newspaper] [1930s+] (*US*) a newspaper.

blat *v.* [SE *blat*, bleating or shrill sound] **1** [late 19C–1960s] (*US*) to talk at length (and with no real importance). **2** [20C+] to talk wildly or loudly.

blatant *adv.* [SE *blatant*, glaringly or defiantly conspicuous] [1990s+] (*UK black*) a general intensifier, definitely, undoubtedly, very much so.

blater *n.* [? SE *bleat*] **1** [18C–mid-19C] a sheep. **2** [18C–19C] a calf.

blather *n.* (*also* **blether**) [ME *blather*, nonsense; thus Scot. *blether*, Irish *bladar*, flattery] [late 18C+] nonsense, also as adj. *blathery*.

blather *v.* (*also* **blather on, blether (on)**) [BLATHER *n.* (1)] [19C+] to talk nonsense, continually and at length, thus n. *blatherer*; adj. *blathering, blethering*.

blathering *n.* (*also* **blething, blethering**) [BLATHER *v.*] [mid-19C+] the talking of nonsense.

blathering *adj.* (*also* **blething, blethering**) [BLATHER *v.*] [late 18C+] absurd, nonsensical.

blatherskite *n.* [BLATHER *v.*, to bluster and SE *skate*, to slide over] **1** [mid-16C; mid-19C+] (*also* **bletherskate, bletherskite**) a voluble, boastful speaker. **2** [early 19C+] (*also* **blatherumskite, bletherumskite**) rubbish, foolish talk.

blatherskite *v.* [BLATHERSKITE *n.*] [late 19C] to boast, to talk nonsense.

blatherskite! *excl.* (*also* **bletherskate! bletherskite!**) [BLATHERSKITE *n.*] [1900s] nonsense!

blatherumskite *n. see* BLATHERSKITE *n.* (2).

-blatt *sfx* [1980s+] (*US campus*) a sfx of familiarity or endearment added to nouns.

blatter *n. see* BLADDER *n.*[1].

blatter *v.* [Scot. *blatter*, to rush with clattering noise] [late 19C+] to hit, to attack; thus n. *blatter*, a blow.

blaw *n.* [Scot. var. on BLOW *n.*[3] (4f)] [1980s+] (*drugs*) cannabis.

blaxican *n.* [SE *Black* + *Mexican*] [2000s] (*US black*) one who is of mixed black and Mexican blood.

blaxploitation *n.* (*also* **blacksploitation**) [SE *black* + *exploitation*] [1970s+] (*orig. US*) the use of black actors in a (usu.) low-budget film featuring a plot filled with sex and violence and peopled by stereotypes (pimps, prostitutes, drug dealers).

blaze *adj.* [1990s+] (*US campus*) admirable and fashionable.

blaze *v.*[1] [SE *blaze the trail*] [1950s+] (*US campus*) to leave.

blaze *v.*[2] (*also* **blaze up**) [1990s+] (*orig. US black/drugs*) **1** to smoke marijuana; as n., marijuana. **2** to light a cannabis cigarette. **3** in fig. use, to 'set on fire'. **4** to have sexual intercourse.

DERIVATIVES

❑ **blazed** *adj.* [1990s+] (*drugs*) intoxicated by drink or drugs.

SE in slang uses

IN PHRASES

❑ **blaze away** *v.* [SE *blaze*, to burn with the fervour of devotion, excitement, or passion + *blaze away*, to fire a weapon rapidly] [mid-19C+] to work at anything with enthusiasm and energy. ❑ **blaze on** *v.* [? SE *blaze away/out*, to fire continuously] [1980s+] (*US black*) to attack or knock down without warning.

blazer *n.* [SE *blazer*, anything that blazes or shines] (*US*) **1** [mid–late 19C] someone or something exceptional of their type. **2** [1900s–30s] a hoax, a lie, a cheating trick [it dazzles the victim].

IN PHRASES

❑ **run a blazer** *v.* [late 19C–1930s] to deceive, to trick.

blazers *n.* [the reflection of the sun in their lenses] [late 19C] spectacles.

blazes *n.* [the trad. fires of hell] **1** [early 19C+] a euph. for hell, esp. in various phrs. below. **2** [mid-19C] the guts, the innards, the 'stuffing'.

IN PHRASES

❑ **all to blazes** *adj.* [late 19C+] completely out of order. ❑ **go to blazes** *v.* [mid-19C+] to decline, to collapse. ❑ **like blazes** *adv.* (*also* **like all blazes**) [early 19C+] energetically, passionately. ❑ **old blazes** *n.* [19C] the Devil. ❑ **raise blazes** *v. see* RAISE HELL *under* HELL *n.*

IN EXCLAMATIONS

❑ **go to blazes!** [mid-19C+] an excl. of dismissal, both of the person and their opinion or statement. ❑ **how the blazes!** (*also* **what the blazes! what the blazing! who the blazes! why the blazes!**) [early 19C+] a general excl.

blazing *adj.* **1** [mid-19C+] (*orig. US*) a general intensifier, esp. in a *blazing row*, a vicious argument. **2** [1930s+] angry. **3** [1980s+] (*US*) first-rate, excellent. **4** [1990s+] (*US black/teen*) of a female, extremely attractive.

blazing *adv.* **1** [mid-19C] (*US*) very well. **2** [late 19C] very, extremely.

bleach *v.* [? play on SE *blank out*] [mid-19C–1900s] (*US campus*) to miss a class or other meeting, e.g. morning chapel.

SE in slang uses

DERIVATIVES

❑ **bleacher** *n.* (*also* **bleecher**) [her job, bleaching clothes] **1** [late 18C–mid-19C] a woman, usu. pej. **2** [1930s] (*Glasgow*) a maidservant. ❑ **bleachification** *n.* [SE *bleach*, a whitening agent; such blocks were often black or Puerto Rican; their new, richer owners will be white] [1990s+] (*US*) the gentrification of former working-class blocks.

IN COMPOUNDS

❑ **bleach-cheat** *n.* [CHEAT *n.* (1)] [late 18C] a sheep.

IN PHRASES

❑ **bleach-bottle blonde** *n. see* BOTTLE BLONDE *under* BOTTLE *n.*[1]. ❑ **bleached mort** *n.* (*also* **bleak mort, bleak mot**) [MORT *n.*] [late 18C] a woman with a pale complexion. ❑ **unbleached American** *n.* [one of the earliest efforts to find a euph. for such derog. terms as NIGGER *n.*[1] (1)] [mid-19C–1940s] an African-American. ❑ **unbleached Australian** *n.* [*see* UNBLEACHED AMERICAN above] [late 19C+] a Native Australian, an Aboriginal.

bleak *adj.* [? SE *bleak*, pale, wan] [mid–late 19C] (*US*) attractive, handsome.

IN COMPOUNDS

❑ **bleak mort** *n.* (*also* **bleak mot**) *see* BLEACHED MORT *under* BLEACH *v.*

bleary *adj.* (*also* **bleary-eyed**) [SE *bleary*, short-sighted] [20C+] drunk.

bleat *n.* [BLEAT *v.*; the weak chance this has of success is underlined by the allusion to the sound of a sheep] **1** [20C+] a (feeble) complaint. **2** [1900s] talk, statements. **3** [1930s–40s] (*US*) an act of informing; a revelation. **4** [1940s] (*US*) a radio message. **5** [1950s] (*UK prison*) a petition to the Home Secretary for reduction or repeal of one's sentence.

bleat *v.* [mid-16C–mid-19C use SE; note mid-19C SC use *bleat*, to propose] **1** [mid-19C+] (*orig. milit.*) to complain, to whinge. **2** [20C+] to inform on someone.

SE, referring to sheep, in slang uses

IN COMPOUNDS

❑ **bleating cheat** *n.* (*also* **bleating chete, blaring cheat**) [CHEAT *n.* (1)] [mid-16C–late 19C] (*UK Und.*) a sheep. ❑ **bleating cull** *n.* (*also* **bleats**) [CULL *n.*[1] (3)] [mid-18C–early 19C] a sheep-stealer. ❑ **bleating prig** *n.* [PRIG *n.*[1] (2); note BLEATING RIG below] [18C–early 19C] sheep-stealing. ❑ **bleating rig** *n.* [RIG *n.*[2] (1)] [18C–early 19C] (*UK Und.*) sheep-stealing.

bleater *n.*[1] [SE *bleat*] **1** [early 17C–early 19C] (*UK Und.*) one who is tricked by a confidence trickster ['a lamb (to the slaughter)']. **2** [mid-17C–mid-19C] a sheep or calf. **3** [early–mid-19C] a sheep-stealer.

bleater *n.*[2] [BLEAT *v.*] **1** [1920s] a weakling, a whinger. **2** [1940s] (*US Und.*) an informer.

bleats *n. see* BLEATING CULL *under* BLEAT *v.*

bleddy *adj. see* BLADDY *adj.*

bleecher *n. see* BLEACHER *under* BLEACH *v.*

bleed *n.* **1** [late 19C–1900s] blood; usu. in phr. *she'll have his bleed*, and used of a woman's forthcoming attack on her husband [SE *blood*]. **2** *see* BLOOD *n.*[2].

bleed *v.*[1] [SE *bleed dry*] **1** [mid-17C+] (*also* **put the bleed on**) to extort money from. **2** [mid-17C+] (*UK Und.*) to part with one's money without complaint, to submit oneself to extortion. **3** [1960s] (*US*) to take advantage of.

IN COMPOUNDS

❑ **bleeding cully** *n.* (*also* **bleeding cull, bleeding gamester**) [CULLY *n.*[1] (1)/CULL *n.*[1] (2)] [mid-17C– early 19C] a gullible victim, who parts cheerfully with their money. ❑ **bleeding dirt** *n.* [DIRT *n.* (5)] [1940s–70s] (*gay*) extorting money from homosexuals.

IN PHRASES

❑ **bleed white** *v.* [the lit. image] [20C+] to submit to excessive extortion, thus draining every drop of money/blood.

SE in slang uses

IN COMPOUNDS

❑ **bleeding new** *adj.* [the image of fish, which bleed only when they are fresh] [late 18C] fresh, new.

IN PHRASES

❑ **bleed like a stuck pig** *v.* [17C+] to bleed heavily, to lose a good deal of blood. ❑ **bleed one's turkey** *v. see under* TURKEY *n.*[1]. ❑ **bleed the liver** *v.* [17C+] to bleed heavily, to lose a good deal of blood. ❑ **bleed the lizard** *v. see under* LIZARD *n.* ❑ **young bleed** *n.* [? she will *bleed* when deflowered] [2000s] (*US black*) a female virgin. ❑ **your nose is bleeding** [late 19C+] advice to a man or boy that his trouser fly is open.

bleed *v.*[2] [1960s–70s] (*US*) to sweat profusely.

bleeder *n.* [SE *bleed*] **1** [early 19C] a spur, usu. pl. **2** [mid-19C] (*US*) a knife, when used as a weapon. **3** [mid-19C] (*UK Und.*) a lie. **4** [late 19C] a sovereign, which is 'bled' to one's creditors. **5** [late 19C–1950s] one who extorts money [BLEED *v.*[1] (1)]. **6** [late 19C+] a person (occas. an animal), usu. but not invariably with derog. implications; also an object. **7** [1900s] generic for a working-class East Ender. **8** [2000s] (*S.Afr. gay*) a heterosexual woman.

bleeding *adj.* **1** [mid-19C+] a euph. for BLOODY *adj.*; also as intensifier, *bleeding hell* etc. **2** [1930s+] as infix.

IN EXCLAMATIONS

❑ **bleeding Nora!** *see* FUCKING NORA! *under* FUCKING *adj.*

bleedy *adj. see* BLOODY *adj.*

bleep *n.* [the electronic 'bleeping' out of supposed obscenities on radio and TV] [1970s+] a euph. substitute for various taboo terms, e.g. SHIT *n.* (1a) in phr. *beat the bleep out of* or FUCK *v.* in phr. *bleeping around*.

bleeping *adj.* [BLEEP *n.*] [1980s+] euph. for various taboo words, e.g. BLEEDING *adj.* (1); FUCKING *adj.* (1).

blem *n.* [abbr. SE *blem*ish] [1960s] (*US campus*) a spot, a pimple.

blemm *v.* [ety. unknown] [1980s+] (*Irish*) to rush, to move at speed.

blemmed up *adj.* [ety. unknown; ? BLEMM *v.*] [1920s] (*Irish*) smartly or fashionably dressed; as v., *blem*, to smarten up.

blench *n. see* HENCH *n.*

blend *n.* [? a mixture of several varieties of the drug] [1990s+] (*drugs*) marijuana.

blend *v.* [20C+] (*US*) **1** to marry. **2** to have sexual intercourse.

blender *n.*[1] [the image of a food *blender* chopping and whirling ingredients together] [1990s+] (*W.I.*) an aggressive person.

blender *n.*[2] [they 'blend' someone else's style into their own] [2000s] (*N.Z. teen*) a copycat.

blenker *v.* [US Brigadier-General Louis *Blenker* (1812–63), whose troops, starving for lack of proper rations, plundered civilian homes near Warrenton, Virginia in April 1862] [mid-19C] (*US*) to plunder.

blenz *n.* [ety. unknown] [2000s] (*US black*) an attractive female.

blerry *adj.* [Afk. pron.] [1920s+] (*S.Afr.*) a general expletive, the local pron. of the UK BLOODY *adj.*

bleskop *n.* [Afk. *bles*, bald + *kop*, head] [1960s+] (*S.Afr.*) a bald-headed person; a bald head.

bless *v.*[1] [ironic reversal of usual SE use] [early 19C] to curse someone, to reprimand, to scold.

IN PHRASES

❑ **bless someone out** *v.* [1990s+] (*US black*) to curse someone.

SE in slang uses

IN PHRASES

❑ **bless in** *v.* [2000s] (*US prison*) to beat up a new member of a gang as an initiation rite. ❑ **bless oneself** *v.* [SE *bless oneself*, to say 'God bless me!'] [17C–late 18C] to curse. ❑ **bless someone's little cotton socks** (*also* **bless someone's garters, bless someone's little bananas**) [1910s+] a general expression of affection. ❑ **bless someone off** *v.* [1990s+] (*US black/drugs*) to give free drugs. ❑ **bless the world with one's heels** *v.* [? the feet twitching in the air could be likened to making the sign of the cross] [mid-16C] to be hanged. ❑ **finger-blessing** *n.* [1990s+] the manual stimulation of a woman's genitals. ❑ **mother-blessing** *n.* [a mix of brandy and tincture of opium, often used to keep children quiet] [19C] a painkiller, esp. laudanum.

IN EXCLAMATIONS

❑ **bless me!** (*also* **bless us!**) [abbr. *Lord bless me!*, but note BLESS ONESELF above] [18C+] a mild excl. ❑ **bless my buttocks!** [1960s] (*US*) a mild euph., poss. for KISS MY ARSE! *excl.* ❑ **bless my heart!** (*also* **bless my eye-balls! ...eyesight! ...(lucky) stars!**) [mid-18C+] a mild excl.

bless *v.*[2] [1960s+] (*US black*) to have sexual intercourse.

blessed *adj.* **1** [19C+] joc. euph. for DAMNED *adj.* (1); thus phrs. *I'm blessed, I'll be blessed*. **2** [1900s] as infix.

blessed *adv.* [joc. euph. for DAMNED *adv.* (1)] [1910s] very.

blessing *n.* [14C SE *blessing*, a present; note Devon dial. *blessing*, an extra handful of produce, thrown in as a bonus to an order, and also the belief, common to many religions, that those who give charity are blessed] **1** [late 18C–mid-19C] a small quantity over and above the stated measure, given to a customer by a stall-holder or shopkeeper. **2** [late 19C] (*Irish*) a tip, a handout.

bless my soul *n.* [rhy. sl.] [1980s] (*Aus.*) the dole.

blether... *see also under* BLATHER...

blether *n.* (*also* **blethers**) [Scot. (*see* BLATHER *n.*)] **1** [late 19C–1920s] one who talks nonsense. **2** [1920s] foolish talkativeness. **3** [2000s] a chat.

blew *v.*[1] [BLOW *v.*[1] (1c)] [mid–late 19C] to inform on, to betray.

IN PHRASES

❑ **blew it** *v.* [mid-19C–1920s] to betray a fellow villain to the police.

blew *v.*[2] *see* BLOW *v.*[2] (2).

blewed *adj. see* BLUED *adj.*[1].

blew in *v.* (*also* **blew, blue, blue in**) [? one 'explodes' or 'blows up' one's finances] **1** [mid-19C] to end a relationship. **2** [mid-19C+] to waste, usu. money; thus *blew one's screw*, to spend all one's wages at once.

IN PHRASES

❑ **all cop and no blue** *see under* COP *v.* (1). ❑ **blew in one's red 'un** *v.* [RED *'UN under* RED *adj.*] [late 19C] to pawn one's watch and spend the money thus realized on drink.

blew out *adj. see* BLOWN (OUT) *adj.*

blick *adj.* [echoic: *blech!*] [2000s] (*UK teen*) unpleasant, unattractive.

blickum *n.* [? development from BLIGGEY! *excl.*] [2000s] (*US prison*) a meaningless word, used when one cannot produce a more pertinent term.

blidiot *n.* [abbr.] [1930s] (*Aus.*) a *bloody idiot*.

bliff *n.* [ety. unknown] [1990s+] the vagina.

IN COMPOUNDS

❑ **bliff mag** *n.* [MAG *n.*[4] (1)] [1990s+] a pornographic magazine.

bliggey! *excl.* (*also* **bliggey-de-bliggey**) [1960s] (*US black, mainly Calif.*) a euph. oath, taking the place of an obscenity.

bligh *n.* [ety. unknown] [1980s+] (*W.I./UK black teen*) a chance, an opportunity, an opening.

bligh! *excl. see* BLIMEY! *excl.*

blighted *adj.* (*also* **blighting**) **1** [late 19C+] a euph. for BLOODY *adj.* **2** [1910s–40s] very drunk or heavily intoxicated by a drug.

blighter *n.* [lit. one who *blights* their surroundings but ? also a euph. for BUGGER *n.*[1] (1); later 20C use is usu. ironic, with images of such actors as Terry-Thomas (1911–90) or Leslie Phillips (b.1924); Ware has theatrical use as 'an actor of evil omen', synon. with *jonah*] [late 19C+] **1** (*also* **blight**) a living creature, usu. human but also animals, usu. derog. **2** an object, usu. dismissive.

Blighty *n.* [Hind. *bilyati* = *wilyati*, foreign, esp. European; ult. f. Arabic *wilayat*, an inhabited country, a foreign country; *bilyati* was used in a variety of contexts, the best known being *bilyati panee*, 'European water', i.e. soda water] [1910s+] (*orig. Ind. Army*) England; thus *Blighty one, Blighty wound*, a wound gained during WW1 that was sufficiently incapacitating to ensure one's being sent home to England from the front; also used for other wars.

Blighty *adj.* [BLIGHTY *n.* (1)] [1910s+] English, pertaining to English lifestyle/culture.

blikkeys *n.* [ety. unknown] [1990s+] (*drugs*) fake crack cocaine that has been manufactured from flakes of soap powder.

Blikkiesdorp *n.* [Afk. *blikkie*, little tin + *dorp*, town] (*S.Afr.*) **1** [1950s+] a fictitious town, used to personify an insignificant, 'one-horse' town, also as *Blikkiesbaai, Blikkiesfontein, Overblikkiesberg*. **2** [1960s+] a slum, a shanty-town.

Blikoor *n.* [Afk. *blik*, tin + *oor*, an ear] [late 19C+] (*S.Afr.*) a derog. term for an inhabitant of the Transvaal or the Orange Free State.

bliksem *n.* [Afk. *bliksem*, lightning] [1970s–80s] (*S.Afr.*) a term of abuse, 'cad', 'bastard'; thus adj. *bliksemse*, despicable.

bliksem *v.* [Afk. *bliksem*, lightning] [1980s] (*S.Afr.*) to hit, to beat up.

bliksem! *excl.* (*also* **bliksom! bluxom!**) [Afk. *bliksem*, lightning] [1950s+] (*S.Afr.*) a general term of abuse, swine! bastard! cad!

blikskottel *n.* [Afk. *bliks*, tin + *skottel*, dish] (*S.Afr.*) **1** [1950s+] a general term of abuse, less hostile than BLIKSEM *n.* **2** [1970s] as excl.

blim *n.* [ety. unknown] [1990s+] (*drugs*) **1** a small piece of hashish, not really sufficient to make a full-strength three-paper cigarette, but enough for perhaps a weak one or a single-skin effort. **2** the residue in a pipe used for smoking hashish.

blimed *adj.* *see* BLAME *adj.*

blimey *n.* [BLIMEY! *excl.*] [1910s–30s] (*US*) a Briton.

blimey! *excl.* (*also* **bligh! bli'me! blime! blimy! bloomey! blue blimey!**) [oath 'God blind me!'] an excl. denoting surprise or disbelief.

IN EXCLAMATIONS

❑ **blimey Charlie!** (*also* **blimey Teddy!**) [20C+] (*Aus./N.Z.*) a general excl., used as sign of the relief of nervous tension.

blimin *adj.* [pron. of BLOOMING *adj.*[1] (1)] [1980s] (*N.Z.*) a mild expletive.

blimp *n.*[1] [the fictitious *Colonel Blimp*, the personification of such emotions, invented by the cartoonist and caricaturist David Low (1891–1963) (his rotund shape echoed the WW1 'blimp', a small airship orig. consisting of a gas-bag – note GASBAG *n.* – with the fuselage of an aeroplane slung underneath). Already widespread, the term and the image became even more popular with the Powell/Pressbuger film *The Life and Death of Col. Blimp* (1943)] **1** [1920s–60s] a promiscuous young woman. **2** [1930s+] a backward-looking, ultra-conservative figure, orig. a military man personified as *Colonel Blimp*, terrified of progress and determined to do anything to prevent it. **3** [1930s+] a very fat person.

DERIVATIVES

❑ **blimpish** *adj.* [1930s+] conservative, hidebound, 'stick-in-the-mud. ❑ **blimpo** *n.* [-O *sfx* (1)] [1990s+] a very fat person. ❑ **blimpy** *adj.* [1990s+] (*US*) fat.

IN COMPOUNDS

❑ **blimp boat** *n.* [1980s+] a very fat person.

IN PHRASES

❑ **blimp out** *v.* [1970s+] (*US black/campus*) **1** to eat voraciously. **2** to become grossly fat.

blimp *n.*[2] [1960s+] a glance, a look; also as v., to glance.

IN PHRASES

❑ **on the blimp** *adj.* [1980s] wandering aimlessly around, looking around.

blimy! *excl.* *see* BLIMEY! *excl.*

blind *n.*[1] [SE *blind*, any means or place of concealment] **1** in the context of deceit. (**a**) [late 18C+] an excuse, a pretence; a person used to fool onlookers, e.g. to disguise a relationship. (**b**) [early 19C; 1950s–70s] (*Und.*) one who distracts from the activities of a criminal, typically a pickpocket's assistant. (**c**) [20C+] (*US Und.*) a supposedly legitimate business which in fact masks a criminal one. **2** [late 19C] night-time; thus *do a blind*, to do a 'moonlight flit'. **3** [2000s] (*US prison*) an area of the prison hidden from the authorities' sight.

IN PHRASES

❑ **on the blind** [20C+] (*Aus.*) at risk, on chance, without any prior information.

blind *n.*[2] [SE *blind*, i.e. it has no windows] **1** [late 19C] an order to leave a town (presumably on the railroad). **2** [late 19C–1960s] (*US tramp*) (*also* **blind baggage, blind car**) a baggage car that has no door at the end leading to the inside; thus it cannot be accessed while the train is in motion; thus *blind baggage tourist*, one who travels on such cars; *beat the blind, jump the blind*, to ride in such a car.

blind *n.*[3] *see* BLINDER *n.*[3].

blind *adj.*[1] (*also* **blinded**) [fig. unable to see; senses 1 and 3 through intoxication] **1** [early 17C+] (*orig. Und.*) extremely drunk; thus phr. *on a blind*, on a drinking spree. **2** [1920s+] (*gay*) uncircumcised [the foreskin renders the penis unable to 'see']. **3** [1950s+] (*orig. Und.*) intoxicated from drug use.

IN COMPOUNDS

❑ **blind cock** *n.* [COCK *n.*[3] (1)] [1980s+] (*US gay*) an uncircumcised penis. ❑ **blind meat** *n.* [MEAT *n.* (2)] [1920s+] (*US gay*) an uncircumcised penis.

IN PHRASES

❑ **blind as Chloe** *adj.* [mainly Aus. use from late 19C] [late 18C+] very drunk. ❑ **make the blind see** *v.* [1960s+] (*US gay*) to fellate an uncircumcised penis.

SE in slang uses

IN COMPOUNDS

❑ **blind alley** *n.* **1** [late 19C] the vagina. **2** [late 19C+] an unlicensed drinking house. ❑ **blind baggage** *n.* *see* BLIND *n.*[2] (2). ❑ **blind boy** *n.* [late 17C] the penis. ❑ **blind buzzard** *n.* [late 18C–early 19C] a partially sighted person. ❑ **blind car** *n.* *see* BLIND *n.*[2] (2). ❑ **blind charley** *n.* *see under* CHARLIE *n.*[1]. ❑ **blind cheeks** *n.* [the shape of the 'nether cheeks'] [early 17C–late 19C] the posteriors; thus *buss blind cheeks*, kiss my arse. ❑ **blind Cupid** *n.* [*Cupid*, the god of love, is often painted as blind] **1** [late 18C–early 19C] an ugly blind man. **2** [early 19C] the buttocks. ❑ **blind date** *n.* *see* separate entry. ❑ **blind dragon** *n.* [SE *dragon*, a fierce old woman; she casts a 'blind eye' on her charge's frolics] [1920s–30s] (*UK society*) a chaperon(e). ❑ **blind eye** *n.* *see* separate entry. ❑ **blind Freddie** *n.* *see* separate entry. ❑ **blind jam** *n.* *see under* JAM *n.*[1]. ❑ **blind harper** *n.* [late 17C–mid-19C] a beggar who fakes blindness, distracting attention from the disguise by playing a harp or fiddle. ❑ **blind hookey** *n.* [proper name *Blind Hookey*, a card-game in which five cards are dealt face down. The dealer takes the centre card and, if that is the highest, wins all the bets; if it is the lowest, the dealer pays all four] [mid-19C–1900s] madness, foolishness, a leap in the dark. ❑ **blind pig/pigger** *n.* *see* separate entries. ❑ **blind robin** *n.* [the red herring and the robin's red breast] [mid-19C+] (*US*) a smoked herring. ❑ **blindside** *v.* *see* separate entry. ❑ **blind staggers** *n.* *see* STAGGERS *n.* ❑ **blind tiger** *n.* *see* separate entry.

IN PHRASES

❑ **Blind Billy's bargain** *n.* *see* separate entry. ❑ **blind both eyes** *adj.* [late 19C] of eggs, fried on both sides, 'turned over'. ❑ **blind cobbler's thumb** *n.* *see* separate entry. ❑ **blind man's holiday** *n.* [once night falls there is nothing – in a pre-street-light world – for a blind man to see] **1** [late 16C–1900s] night-time. **2** [late 17C–early 18C] nightfall, the dusk.

IN EXCLAMATIONS

❑ **blind O'Reilly!** *see under* O'REILLY *n.*

blind *adj.*[2] (*also* **blinded**) **1** [late 19C+] complete, utter. **2** [1930s+] a negative intensifier, e.g. *not a blind bit of use, not a blind word, not take a blind bit of notice*. **3** [1940s+] (*bingo*) the round numbers from 20 to 80 in multiples of 10, e.g. *blind 30, blind 20* [the 0 on the end].

blind *adj.*[3] [1990s+] (*S.Afr. juv.*) unfortunate, unlucky.

blind *v.*[1] [SE *blind*, to conceal] **1** [mid-19C] to cheat. **2** [1900s] (*US campus*) to answer all the questions one is posed by an instructor, esp. when one has done no actual preparation.

blind *v.*[2] [euph. for such words as BLOODY *adj.*; BLEEDING *adj.*] [late 19C+] to swear.

(IN PHRASES)

❑ **put the blind on** *v.* [20C+] (*Irish*) to curse someone.

(IN EXCLAMATIONS)

❑ **blind me!** *see* separate entry.

blind *v.*[3] [? one 'blinds' them with one's own knowledge] [1910s–40s] (*US campus*) to expose another's ignorance.

blind *v.*[4] [1920s–50s] to drive very fast and without noticing anyone else on the road.

blind *adv.*[1] [devoid of any external modification] [late 19C+] utterly, completely.

(IN COMPOUNDS)

❑ **blind drunk** *adj.* [SE in 20C] [mid–late 19C] extremely drunk.

(IN PHRASES)

❑ **go it blind** *v.* [late 19C+] to drink heavily; usu. of alcohol. ❑ **rob blind** *v.* [1930s+] to rob without restraint. ❑ **sell someone blind** *v.* [late 19C] to deceive, to defraud. ❑ **talk someone blind** *v.* [1910s+] (*Aus./N.Z.*) to overwhelm with talk.

blind *adv.*[2] [BLIND *n.*[2] (2)] [1930s] (*US tramp*) in a closed baggage car.

Blind Billy's bargain *n.* [*Blind Billy*, a former Limerick hangman; the soon-to-be-hanged person was in no position to bargain] [late 19C+] a 'bargain' that is, in fact, no bargain at all, since one is unable to impose one's own conditions on the person with whom one is dealing.

blind cobbler's thumb *n.*

(IN PHRASES)

❑ **face like a blind cobbler's thumb** *n.* [? covered in pockmarks, resembling needle-pricks] [1990s+] a derog. description of the face of an unattractive person, usu. a woman.

blind date *n.* [SE colloq. *date*, an appointment made for sexual/social purposes] [1920s+] (*orig. US*) an evening out with someone whom one has never met but who will be introduced by a mutual friend.

(IN PHRASES)

❑ **drag a blind** *v.* [DRAG *v.*[1] (4)] [1920s] (*US campus*) to spend an evening out with someone whom one has never previously met.

blinded *adj.* **1** *see* BLIND *adj.*[1]. **2** *see* BLIND *adj.*[2]. **3** *see* BLINDING *adj.*[2].

blinder *n.*[1] **1** [late 19C] a blow to the eye. **2** [1960s] (*UK Und.*) the act of throwing pepper in someone's eyes to effect a robbery. **3** [1960s+] a hard and exciting sporting encounter, esp. as to *play a blinder* [one is *blinded* by the quality of the game]. **4** [1970s] a severe headache [one is *blinded* by the strength of the pain].

SE in slang uses

(IN PHRASES)

❑ **take a blinder** *v.* [lit. 'take a blind leap' into the next world] [mid-19C–1900s] to die.

blinder *n.*[2] [ext. of SE use; ? the smoke or the smell gets in one's eyes] **1** [20C+] a cheap, bad cigar; mostly in pl. **2** [1930s] a Woodbine cigarette (the cheapest available brand); mostly in pl.

blinder *n.*[3] (*also* **blind**) [BLIND *adj.*[1] (1)] **1** [1910s+] a drunken spree, a binge. **2** [1950s] an intoxicating cocktail.

blind eye *n.* [coarsely joc. use of SE] **1** [late 18C–1900s] the buttocks. **2** [late 19C] the vagina. **3** [1970s] (*US gay*) the anus [-EYE *sfx*].

(IN PHRASES)

❑ **get a shove in the blind eye** *v.* [late 19C–1900s] of a woman, to have sexual intercourse. ❑ **wink at the blind eye** *v.* [late 19C] to have sexual intercourse.

blindfolded lady with the scales *n.* [the trad. image of justice, seen in statues, illustrations etc] [1940s–50s] (*US black*) justice, as a concept rather than as a product of the legal system.

blind Freddie *n.* [some commentators have posited a real-life 'blind Freddie' – a blind beggar in the streets of Sydney in the 1920s – but no one has yet properly identified him; note letter from P.K. Lynch 7/10/00: 'mebbe Sir Frederick Pottinger, Bt, who got into financial trouble in the Coldstream Guards and enlisted as a trooper in the NSW Mounted Police, which hunted bushrangers. Was famed for closing his eyes before loosing off his pistol after miscreants – who more or less inevitably "bounding, rode away". Accidentally shot himself while boarding a coach in Springwood, NSW in 1865.'] [1940s+] (*Aus.*) an imaginary figure seen as representing the lowest denominator of incompetence; thus used in phrs. such as *blind Freddie could see that, wouldn't fool blind Freddie*.

blinding *n. see* EFF AND BLIND *under* EFF *v.*

blinding *adj.*[1] (*also* **binding**) [? so intense as to render one *blind*] [1930s+] wonderful, terrific, perfect etc.

blinding *adj.*[2] (*also* **binding, blinded**) [1940s+] a euph. for BLOODY *adj.*

blindman's buff *n.* [rhy. sl.] [1960s+] snuff.

blind me! *excl.* [mid-19C+] a mild oath.

blind mullet *n.* [supposed resemblance to the fish] [1980s] (*Aus.*) a piece of excrement.

blindo *n.* [BLINDER *n.*[3] (1) + -O *sfx* (6)] [mid-19C–1900s] a drunken spree.

blindo *adj.* (*also* **blindoe**) [BLINDO *n.* / BLIND *adj.*[1] (1) + -O *sfx* (5)] [mid-19C–1920s] tipsy.

blind pig *n.* (*also* **pig**) [? the typical architecture of the earliest of such bars, a blank facade bereft of windows and with only a small peep-hole in its door. Alternatively f. the practice of disguising the bar as an exhibition of natural freaks; G. A. Thompson (personal correspondence) notes a 'widely publicised case' written up in *N.Y. Gazette & General Advertiser*, Sept. 15, and *N.Y. Commercial Advertiser*, 14 Sept. in 1838 where a man in Dedham, Mass. 'took out a regular license for the exhibition of a "striped pig"; he paints a pig appropriately, charges "four pence hapenny" admission, gives a drink of liquor for free'] [late 19C+] (*US*) an unlicensed drinking house, a speakeasy, an 'after-hours' bar.

blind-pigger *n.* [BLIND PIG *n.*] [late 19C+] (*US*) the proprietor of an illicit drinking establishment; thus v. *blind pig*, to run such an establishment.

blinds *n.* [1920s–30s] (*US tramp*) the false door at the end of carriages, thus places between the carriages where a tramp can hide while riding on a passenger train.

(IN PHRASES)

❑ **draw the blinds** *v. see under* DRAW *v.*[4].

blindside *v.* [US football jargon *blindside*, to attack or strike (an opponent) on the side on which the view is obstructed] (*orig. US*) **1** [20C+] to take by surprise. **2** [1920s+] to take advantage of.

blind tiger *n.* (*also* **tiger**) [ety. unknown] (*US*) **1** [late 19C+] an unlicensed drinking house. **2** [1900s] illicit whisky. **3** [1920s] the owner of an illicit bar.

bling *n.* (*also* **bling-bling**) [MTV News (online) 30/4/03: 'The term, which is used to describe diamonds, jewelry and all forms of showy style, was coined by New Orleans rap family Cash Money Millionaires back in the late '90s and started gaining national awareness with a song titled "Bling Bling" by Cash Money artist BG.'] [2000s] money, ostentatious jewellery and personal items.

bling-bling *adj.* (*also* **bling**) [see prev.] [2000s] (*orig. US black*) showy, indicative of conspicuous consumption.

bling-bling *v.* [BLING-BLING *adj.*] [2000s] (*orig. US black*) to demonstrate one's material wealth.

blinged-up *adj.* [BLING *n.*] [2000s] showy in dress and appearance.

blinger *n.* [SE *blink* or echoic *bling*, used for something that hits one with a sudden thump] [1940s–60s] (*US*) the extreme example of a type or situation.

blinging *adj.* [BLING-BLING *adj.*] [2000s] (*US black*) showy, ostentatious.

Blinglish *n.* [BLING *n.* + SE *English*] [2000s] (*UK black/teen*) Jamaican patois as adopted by white English youth.

blink *n.*[1] **1** [early–mid-19C] a light. **2** [late 19C] (*US*) a look, a glance. **3** [late 19C–1930s] (*UK Und.*) a pair of spectacles. **4** [20C+] (*also* **blinkey, blinkie, blinky**) (*orig. US hobo*) a blind person, a one-eyed person. **5** [1900s–30s] (*US*) an eye. **6** [1910s+] (*Aus.*) a cigarette butt [smoking it causes one to blink from the smoke entering the eyes].

IN COMPOUNDS

❑ **blink-fencer** *n.* [-FENCER *sfx*] [mid–late 19C] a seller of spectacles. ❑ **blink-pickings** *n.* [SE *pickings*] [20C+] (*Aus.*) cigarette stubs, picked up from the gutter and either relit or recombined in a new 'roll-your-own'.

SE in slang uses

IN PHRASES

❑ **go blink** *v.* [1910s] to become impoverished. ❑ **like a blink** *adv.* (*also* **like blinko**) [1950s] immediately, very quickly. ❑ **on the blink** *adj.* **1** [late 19C+] (*orig. US*) malfunctioning, working badly, damaged [the blinking of electric lights that signalled a 'short' or similar malfunction]. **2** [1900s–40s] of a person, ill or dead. **3** [1920s–40s] (*US*) impoverished, penniless. **4** [1950s] (*US Und.*) working as a fake 'blind beggar' [the 'blind' man's surreptitious blinking]. ❑ **pabble-blinkers** *n.* [? SE *pebble*] [mid-19C] (*UK Und.*) sore eyes. ❑ **put the blink on** *v.* [the victim blinks nervously] [late 19C] (*US*) to cause problems for. ❑ **two-blink** *adj.* [the equivalent of blinking twice] [20C+] (*US*) extremely small, insignificant. ❑ **under the blinks** *adj.* [late 19C] (*US*) asleep.

blink *n.*[2] [rhy. sl.; abbr. BIT OF BLINK *n.*] [late 19C–1900s] a drink.

blink *v.* **1** [mid-19C] (*US Und.*) to go to sleep. **2** [mid-19C+] to ignore, deny. **3** [late 19C] (*US*) to drink. **4** [late 19C–1920s] (*US*) to see. **5** [1910s] (*Irish*) to bewitch, to spoil.

blinked out *adj.* [ON THE BLINK *under* BLINK *n.*[1]] [20C+] malfunctioning, out of order; of a person, out of touch with reality.

blinker *n.* **1** *see* BLINKERS *n.* (1). **2** [late 18C] (*UK Und.*) a wink. **3** [early 19C] a one-eyed horse. **4** [19C] a hard blow in the eye. **5** [mid-19C+] (*orig. US*) a black eye. **6** [late 19C] a man, a fellow. **7** [1970s] a camera. **8** [1970s+] (*US Und.*) a police surveillance helicopter. **9** [1980s] (*US*) a quadriplegic.

blinkers *n.* **1** [late 18C+] the eyes, occas. sing.; thus *glass-blinkers*, spectacles. **2** [mid-19C–1970s] eyeglasses, spectacles.

blinkety-blankety *phr. see* BLANKETY-BLANK *phr.*

blinkey/blinkie *n. see* BLINK *n.*[1] (4).

blinking *adj.* [euph. for BLOOMING *adj.*[1]] [20C+] a mild pej.

blinko *n.*[1] [? one *blinks* at the mediocrity of it all] [late 19C] an 'amateur night' at the local public house.

blinko *n.*[2]

IN PHRASES

❑ **like blinko** *adv. see* LIKE A BLINK *under* BLINK *n.*[1].

blinko *adv.* [var. on BLIND *adv.*[1] or one *blinks* to clear one's drunken vision] [1950s+] (*US*) of drunkenness, very, to an extreme extent.

blinks *n.* **1** [17C+] a nickname for one who blinks all the time. **2** [mid-19C] the eyes. **3** [mid-19C] a pair of spectacles.

blinky *n. see* BLINK *n.*[1] (4).

blinky *adj.* [1900s] (*US*) obscure, opaque.

blinky bill *n.* [rhy. sl. = DILL *n.*] [1980s] (*Aus.*) a fool.

blintze queen *n. see* BAGEL BABY *under* BAGEL *n.*

blip *n.*[1] [onomat. for a small, short, sharp sound, underpinned by milit. jargon *blip*, a small elongated mark projected on a radar screen, itself ref. to the 'bleeping' noise of radar] **1** [late 19C–1970s] a blow. **2** [20C+] a temporary hiatus. **3** [1930s–50s] (*US black*) a cent, a nickel [fig. links the smallness of the sound and the coin]. **4** [1940s+] (*US black*) a surprise, a sudden disappointment.

blip *n.*[2] [ety. unknown] [1930s–60s] (*US black*) something excellent; also as adj., fine, good.

blip *n.*[3] [ety. unknown] [2000s] (*US black*) one's emotional 'territory'.

blip (off) *v.* [BLIP *n.*[1] (1)] (*orig. US*) **1** [1920s–30s] to hit hard, to shoot. **2** [1920s+] to kill, to murder.

blirt *n.* [Scot. *blirt*, a storm of wind and rain] [1950s+] (*Irish*) a general term of abuse, loudmouth.

bliss *n.* [BLISS OUT *v.* (2)] [1990s+] (*US black/drugs*) any smokeable drug.

bliss out *v.* [coined/introduced by followers of Maharaj Ji, c.1972] [1970s+] **1** to experience a state of (usu. drug- or meditation-induced) ecstasy; thus *blissout*, a state of ecstasy; as adj., *blissed*. **2** by ext., pleasurably intoxicated by narcotic drugs; as adj., *blisted*.

blister *n.*[1] [SE *blister*] **1** from the unpleasantness of the physical *blister*. (**a**) [early 19C–1960s] an offensive or argumentative person, usu. *old blister*; also used affectionately. (**b**) [20C+] an unattractive or promiscuous woman. **2** the role of the blister in adhering to the skin. (**a**) [mid-19C–1940s] a legal summons [the summons results from *scorching*, i.e. exceeding the speed limit (*see* SCORCH *v.* (1))]. (**b**) [1900s–50s] (*Aus.*) a mortgage. (**c**) [2000s] (*Aus./N.Z.*) a written official reprimand. **3** [1930s] (*US Und.*) a tramp who deliberately creates scars and sores on the limbs by the application of acid or alkalis.

blister *n.*[2] *see* SKIN-AND-BLISTER *n.*

blister *v.* [BLISTER *n.*[1] (2a)] **1** [late 19C–1900s] to punish, to hurt; also as excl. *blister them! blister me!* **2** [1900s–30s] to be summoned, fined or punished for an offence. **3** [1940s+] to attack verbally.

blistered *n.* [mid-19C+] euph. for DAMNED *adj.* (1).

blistering *adj.* [the heat of one's language raises blisters] [20C+] a general expletive, used euph. for a variety of taboo synons.

blit *n. see* BLART *n.*

blither *n.* [BLITHER *v.*] [1910s] nonsense.

blither *v.* [BLATHER *v.*] [mid-19C+] to talk nonsense.

blithered *adj.* [BLITHER *v.*, i.e. the inarticulacy of the very drunk] [1910s+] (*Aus.*) very drunk.

blitherer *n.*[1] [BLITHER *v.*] [20C+] a silly fool.

blitherer *n.*[2] [ety. unknown] [1910s] (*Aus.*) an exemplar.

blithering *n.* [BLITHER *v.*] [late 19C+] talking nonsense, babbling on.

blithering *adj.* [BLITHERING *n.*] [late 19C+] absolute, complete, esp. in phrs. *blithering idiot, blithering fool* etc.

blithero *adv.* [BLITHERING *adj.*] [1950s] (*Irish*) extremely.

blitter *v.* [Scot. *blitter*, to rattle] [20C+] (*Ulster*) to break wind; also as n., a fart.

blittered *adj.* [? BLITHERED *adj.*] [2000s] overcome by a given drug.

blitz *n.* [BLITZ *v.*[2]] a burst of energy, a major effort; an attack.

blitz *v.*[1] [1900s] (*US campus*) to absent oneself from a recitation.

blitz *v.*[2] [Ger. *Blitzkrieg*, lightning war] **1** [1940s] to scold. **2** [1940s+] (*orig. US*) to defeat comprehensively, to crush, to overcome, to destroy; also fig. use. **3** [1940s+] to stun, amaze. **4** [1940s+] to arrive or leave quickly; also fig. use. **5** [1960s] to exhaust sexually. **6** [1960s+] to saturate with an advertising campaign or similar form of wide-spectrum information. **7** [1970s+] (*US campus*) to perform well (in an examination). **8** [1980s] (*UK Und.*) to break into a premises for burglary.

blitzed *adj.* [BLITZ *v.*[2] (2)] **1** (*also* **blitzkrieged**) [1960s+] drunk or experiencing the effects of a drug. **2** [1970s] exhausted, emotionally drained; overcome by a situation.

blitz it *v.* [BLITZ *v.*[2] (4)] [1940s] (*S.Afr. campus*) to hurry, to 'get a move on'.

blivet *n.* (*also* **blivit**) ['the expression arose among American flyers in New Guinea and is of Australian origin' (*HDAS*)] [1940s+] (*US, orig. Aus. milit.*) **1** something useless, unnecessary, annoying (popularly defined as 'ten pounds of shit in a five-pound bag'). **2** a fat or unpleasant person or thing. **3** a distasteful or impossible job or situation.

blixen-bus *n.* [Ger. *Blitzen*, lightning + SE *bus*] [1910s–20s] (*US*) an automobile.

blizzard *n.*[1] [dial. *blizzer*, a heavy blow + SE *blizzard*] (*US*) **1** [19C] a hard blow. **2** [19C] a stinging remark, esp. to end an argument or as a parting shot. **3** [mid-19C] a large fire. **4** [mid–

late 19C] a rifle shot or volley of shots. **5** [late 19C] a drink of alcohol, a 'bracer'. **6** [1990s+] (*drugs*) a cloudy white substance seen in a crack pipe.

blizzard *n.*[2] [? play on BLOWHARD *n.*[1]] [1970s] (*US campus*) an unpleasant or unpopular person.

blizzard v. [BLIZZARD *n.*[1] (4)] [mid-19C] (*US*) to let off a volley of shots.

bloak *n.* **1** *see* BLOKE *n.* (3). **2** *see* BLOKE *n.* (7).

bloan *n. see* BLOWEN *n.*

bloat *n.* (*US*) **1** [mid-19C] a worthless, conceited individual. **2** [mid-19C–1920s] a drunkard; thus adj. *bloated*, drunk.

bloater *n.* [senses 2 and 3 abbr. *Yarmouth bloater*, when the fish is first smoked it swells up conspicuously, although it then shrinks as it cools] **1** [late 19C] a general term of affectionate address. **2** [late 19C] a self-opinionated person. **3** [late 19C+] a fat person.

SE in slang uses

(IN PHRASES)

❑ **or my prick's a bloater** (*also* **or my uncle's a bloater**) [SE *bloater*, a type of fish] [1930s+] a phr. used to imply the absolute impossibility or unlikeliness of what has just been said, suggested etc.

blob *n.* **1** [20C+] (*mainly Aus.*) an insignificant person. **2** [1960s] (*US campus*) an ugly or offensive person. **3** [1960s+] a fat person. **4** [1990s+] a condom. **5** [1990s+] menstruation; often as *the blob*.

(IN PHRASES)

❑ **on the blob** [1990s+] menstruating.

blob *v.*[1] [var. on BLAB v. (1)] [mid-19C] **1** to talk indiscreetly. **2** (*Aus./UK Und.*) to beg by delivering some form of speechifying or patter.

(IN PHRASES)

❑ **on the blob** *adv.* [mid–late 19C] by word of mouth; thus *blob*, talk.

blob *v.*[2] [? a *blob* of ink that mars an otherwise faultless piece of handwriting] [1900s–60s] (*US*) to make a mistake.

blobbermouth *n.* [BLOB *v.*[1] (1) + SE *mouth*] [1930s+] an indiscreet talker.

blob off *v.* [the SE *blobs* of semen] [2000s] to ejaculate.

block *n.*[1] **1** [mid-16C–18C] a fool, an idiot. **2** [17C+] the head; 20C+ use mainly in *KNOCK SOMEONE'S BLOCK OFF* below. **3** in drug packaging. (**a**) [1930s–40s] (*US drugs*) a cube of morphine. (**b**) [1970s+] (*drugs*) compressed hashish or marijuana.

(DERIVATIVES)

❑ **blockish** *adj.* [SE *block*, a barrier + sfx *-ish*] [late 16C–mid-19C] stupid; thus *blockishness*, stupidity.

(IN COMPOUNDS)

❑ **blockbuster** *n. see* separate entry.

(IN PHRASES)

❑ **do one's block** *v.* (*also* **do in one's block, do the block, lose one's block**) [20C+] (*Aus.*) **1** to lose emotional control, to lose one's temper; thus *keep one's block*, to remain in control of one's emotions. **2** to go mad, to become irrational. **3** to fall in love. **4** thus antonym *keep the block*, to remain calm. ❑ **knock someone's block off** *v.* (*also* **beat someone's block off, wallop...**) [20C+] to injure someone physically, usu. in the form of a threat, *I'll knock...* ❑ **off one's block** *adj.* [1910s+] (*orig. milit.*) **1** angry. **2** insane. ❑ **use one's block** *v.* [1980s] (*N.Z.*) to act sensibly.

SE in slang uses

(IN COMPOUNDS)

❑ **blockhead/blockheaded** *see* separate entries. ❑ **block ornament** *n.* [SE *block ornament*, a small piece of meat displayed on a butcher's block] [mid–late 19C] an eccentric-looking person.

(IN PHRASES)

❑ **put the blocks to** *v.* **1** [1910s+] (*US*) of a man, to have sexual intercourse. **2** *see also under* BLOCK *n.*[6]. ❑ **up on the blocks** *adj.* [automobile imagery, i.e. 'out of action'] [1990s+] menstruating.

block *n.*[2] [BLOCK *n.*[1] (1) ? or a hard-hearted person] [late 19C–1900s] (*Scot. Und.*) a policeman.

block *n.*[3] [BLOCK *n.*[6]] [20C+] an act of sexual intercourse.

block *n.*[4] [abbr. SE *punishment block*] [20C+] (*UK prison*) the punishment cells; the maximum security cells.

(IN COMPOUNDS)

❑ **blockhouse** *see* separate entries.

block *n.*[5] **1** [1910s+] (*Aus./US Und.*) a watch; thus *block-dealer*, a watch seller, a jeweler [BLOCK AND TACKLE *n.*[1]]. **2** [1970s] (*Can. prison*) a cigarette lighter [resemblance].

(IN COMPOUNDS)

❑ **block and slang** *n.* [SLANG *n.*[2] (2)] [1910s–40s] (*US Und.*) a gold watch and chain. ❑ **block and tackle** *n. see* separate entry.

block *n.*[6] [SE *block*, an impediment]

(IN PHRASES)

❑ **put the block on** *v.* (*also* **put the blockers on, put the blocks to, put the box on**) [1910s+] to interfere with, to stop someone's actions or plans, to defeat, to overcome. ❑ **put the blocks on** *v.* (*also* **put the blocks to**) **1** [late 19C+] to give someone a hard time. **2** [1940s–50s] (*UK prison*) to tighten up regulations that have become temporarily lax.

block *n.*[7] [? a *block* of time] [1930s] (*US Und.*) seven days in jail.

block *n.*[8]

SE, meaning a block of a city street, in slang uses

(IN COMPOUNDS)

❑ **block and tackle** *n. see* separate entry. ❑ **block boy** *n.* [he looks as if he were someone 'off the block'] **1** [1970s] (*US black*) a 'corner-boy'. **2** [1990s+] a gay male who dresses as if he were part of the heterosexual hip-hop culture. ❑ **blockbust/blockbuster/blockbusting** *see* separate entries. ❑ **block game** *n.* (*also* **peeks, the**) [1940s] (*US Und.*) a variety of the 'shell game' employing small boxes.

(IN PHRASES)

❑ **block and fall (joint)** *n. see* separate entries. ❑ **do the block** *v.* [the major blocks are Collins Street between Swanston and Elizabeth Streets in Melbourne, and George Street in Sydney] [mid-19C–1930s] (*Aus.*) **1** (*also* **run the block**) to promenade along a variety of fashionable blocks or stretches of city street; thus *the Block*, Collins Street; *Blockite*, a fashionable individual, given to such a promenade. **2** in fig. use, to show off, to gain acclaim. ❑ **go around the block** *v.* (*also* **go around the wheel**) [1940s+] (*orig. US*) to gain experience, esp. in phr. *X has been around the block* (*a few times*), X is experienced, esp. sexually. ❑ **on the block** *adj.* (*US*) **1** [late 19C+] in business. **2** [1940s+] working as a street prostitute. **3** [1940s+] (*US black campus*) hanging out in a specific meeting place. **4** [1960s] in poverty; among the working-class. ❑ **put someone on the block** *v.* (*also* **put someone on the corner**) **1** [1950s+] (*US*) of a pimp, to launch a woman into a career as a prostitute. **2** [1970s+] (*N.Z.*) to subject a woman (or a homosexual man) to gang rape; thus *go on the block*, to be the subject of such an assault. ❑ **run around the block** *v.* [2000s] to procrastinate.

block *v.*[1] [SE phr. *put one on the block*] [mid-19C] to stand a drink.

block *v.*[2] [SE *block*, to bar the way, to impede] **1** [late 19C–1900s] to loiter, to 'hang around'. **2** [1910s] (*US prison*) to watch. **3** [1930s+] (*Aus.*) to deceive, to get the better of. **4** [1990s+] (*Aus.*) to stop talking as instructed.

block *v.*[3] [abbr. *PUT THE BLOCKS TO under* BLOCK *n.*[1]] **1** [late 19C–1940s] to have sexual intercourse. **2** [1970s+] (*N.Z.*) to gang rape; thus *go on the block*, of a young woman, to be subjected/subject oneself to gang rape.

block *v.*[4] [backform. f. BLOCKED *adj.*] [1960s] (*UK drugs*) to render oneself intoxicated with amphetamines.

block *v.*[5] *see* COCK BLOCK v. (1).

blockade *n.* [the need to defeat the customs blockade to sell it] [mid-19C–1940s] (*US*) illicitly distilled whisky; thus *blockader*, a distiller.

blockade *v.* [SE *blockade*, a barrier, in this case against whisky-runners] [late 19C–1940s] (*US*) to distil illicit liquor.

block a hat *v.* [mid-19C] to knock someone's hat over their eyes.

block-and-block *adj.* [Lincolnshire dial. *blocker*, extreme drunkenness] [early–mid-18C] (*US*) very drunk.

block and fall *n.* [*see* next] [1920s–40s] (*US Und.*) very strong, and prob. adulterated liquor.

block and fall joint *n.* [SE *block* + *fall* + JOINT *n.* (3b); 'you'd get a shock, walk a block and fall in the gutter' (Sante, *Low Life*, 1991)] [late 19C] (*US*) a tavern, catering mainly to black people, in which one would most likely be given some form of knockout drop in one's drink and then be robbed.

block and tackle *n.*[1] [BLOCK *n.*[5] (1)] [1910s+] (*orig. Aus.*) a watch and chain.

block and tackle *n.*[2] [the saying 'you have one, walk one block and you're ready to tackle anyone'] [1930s+] (*US*) a very strong drink.

block and tackle *n.*[3] [rhy. sl. = SE *shackle*] [1930s+] handcuffs.

blockbust *v.* [SE *block* + BUST *v.*[1] (1a)] [1950s+] to be the first black family to move into a formerly all-white inner city area.

blockbuster *n.*[1] [BLOCK *n.*[1] (2) + BUST *v.*[1] (1a)] **1** [1940s+] a very hard blow, literal or fig. use. **2** [1940s+] anything enormous, gigantic; often used of a best-selling novel, film, TV series etc. **3** [1940s+] an intoxicating drink. **4** [1950s+] (*drugs*) barbiturates.

blockbuster *n.*[2] [SE *block* + BUST *v.*[1] (1a)] **1** [1950s] the first black family to move into a formerly all-white inner city area. **2** [1960s+] the first white family to move back into an inner city area, driving out the poor minority tenants and starting the process of gentrification.

blockbusting *n.* [SE *block* + BUST *v.*[1] (1a)] [1980s+] (*US black*) an attack by one gang who move out of their own territory to invade that of another.

blocked *adj.* [rational thought processes/the stomach are impeded] **1** [1950s+] (*also* **block up**) drunk or intoxicated with a drug, usu. cannabis or barbiturates. **2** [2000s] (*N.Z.*) full of food.

blockee *n. see* BLOCKIE *n.*

blocker *n.* [SE *block*, a barrier; such a person will not 'get out of the way'] [1970s] (*US*) a hanger-on.

(IN PHRASES)

❑ **put the blockers on** *v. see* PUT THE BLOCK ON *under* BLOCK *n.*[6].

blockers *n.* [abbr. BLOCKBUSTER *n.*[1] (4)] [1980s+] (*drugs*) barbiturates.

blockhead *n.*[1] [SE *block*, a lump of wood + -HEAD *sfx* (1)] [mid-16C+] a fool, a simpleton, an idiot.

blockhead *n.*[2] [BLOCK *n.*[1] (3b) + -HEAD *sfx* (4); cannabis is manufactured and packaged in blocks] [1980s+] (*drugs*) a dedicated user of cannabis.

blockhead *adj.* [BLOCKHEAD *n.*[1]] [early 18C] stupid, foolish.

blockheaded *adj.* (*also* **blockheadly, chunk-headed**) [BLOCKHEAD *n.*[1]] [early 18C+] stupid.

blockhouse *n.* [SE *blockhouse*, a small fort or defensive wooden enclosure] [17C–late 18C] (*UK Und.*) a prison.

blockhouse *v.* [BLOCKHOUSE *n.*] [mid-19C] (*UK Und.*) to imprison.

blockie *n.* (*also* **blockee, blocky**) [SAusE *block*, a parcel of land on which settlers could build or farm] [1940s+] (*Aus.*) a blocker, one who occupies a small block of rural or semi-rural land.

Block Island turkey *n.* [proper name of *Block Island*, Connecticut] [mid–late 19C] (*US*) salt cod.

Blockite *n. see* DO THE BLOCK *under* BLOCK *n.*[8].

block of ice *n.* [rhy. sl.] [2000s] dice.

block up *adj. see* BLOCKED *adj.* (1).

blocky *n. see* BLOCKIE *n.*

blodger *n. see* BLUDGER *n.*[2] (4).

bloke *n.* (*also* **blokey, blokie**) [either Shelta or Rom., although there is also a case for the Du. *blok*, a fool] **1** [mid-19C] (*UK Und.*) the owner, the master. **2** [mid-19C–1920s] (*UK Und.*) constr. with *the*, a judge; similarly for the Captain in a naval context. **3** [mid-19C+] (*also* **bloak**) a man; thus a *proper bloke*, a man who accords with the cultural standards of the speaker; as adj., *blokeish*; thus *blokette* (Aus.), *blokess* (N.Z.), a woman who fits in with the blokes; also as a term of address. **4** [late 19C] (*US Und.*) a detective, a police-officer, or a minor judge. **5** [late 19C] (*juv.*) a hard worker. **6** [late 19C–1910s] a public house or tavern landlord. **7** [late 19C–1930s] (*US*) (*also* **bloak**) a fool, an unlikeable person. **8** [late 19C+] a lover, a boyfriend. **9** [1900s] as a term of address. **10** [1900s–10s] (*Aus.*) a person in authority or of superior status. **11** [1910s] (*Aus. Und.*) a pimp. **12** [1910s+] constr. with *a*, oneself, e.g. *a bloke ought to get drunk once in a while*.

(DERIVATIVES)

❑ **blokery** *n.* [1950s+] (*N.Z.*) a group of male friends, often bachelors. ❑ **blokey** *adj.* [1990s+] laddish.

(IN COMPOUNDS)

❑ **bloke-buzzer** *n.* [BUZZER *n.*[1] (1)] [mid–late 19C] (*UK Und.*) a pickpocket specializing in stealing from men.

(IN PHRASES)

❑ **blokes in blue** *n. see* BOYS IN BLUE *n.* ❑ **little bloke** *n.* [1970s] (*Aus.*) the penis.

bloker *n.* [BIG BLOKE *n.*[2]] [1950s] (*US drugs*) a cocaine addict.

blokie *n. see* BLOKE *n.*

blonde *n.* [a light-coloured variety] [1970s+] (*drugs*) marijuana.

blonde and sweet *n.* [pun on SE] [1940s+] (*US*) coffee with cream and sugar.

blondie *n.* (*also* **blondy**) [SE *blonde*] [late 19C+] **1** a blond(e) person, usu. a woman. **2** (*US black*) a white woman (irrespective of hair colour). **3** nickname or term of intimate address to anyone with blond(e) hair.

blone *n.* [BLOWEN *n.* (1)] [19C+] (*Irish/Scot.*) a woman.

blonk *n.* [? echoic of a solid object, i.e. the fool's head, hitting something hard] [1980s+] (*Aus. prison*) a fool.

blood *n.*[1] [SE *blood*, either in the sense of the seat of the emotions or in that of breeding] **1** [early 16C–19C] a rake, a roisterer, an aristocratic rowdy. **2** [mid-19C+] a cheap 'blood-and-thunder' magazine, the precursor of 20C+ comics and even the bloodier examples of computer game. **3** from the colour of blood. (**a**) [late 19C–1900s] a wallflower. (**b**) [1910s–40s] (*US*) ketchup, tomato sauce. (**c**) [1950s–70s] (*US black*) wine. **4** [1900s] (*US campus*) a perfect recitation. **5** [1920s] (*US Und.*) a killer.

SE in slang uses

(IN COMPOUNDS)

❑ **blood ball** *n.* [the butchers' sanguineous trade] [late 19C–1900s] an annual butchers' ball. ❑ **blood box** *n.* [1970s+] (*Aus./US*) an ambulance. ❑ **blood bucket** *n.* [var. on *BLOODY BUCKET under* BLOODY *adj.*] [1960s] (*US*) a notably tough saloon or bar. ❑ **blood claat** see separate entries. ❑ **blood factory** *n.* [2000s] a hospital. ❑ **bloodhammer** *n.* [2000s] the penis. ❑ **bloodhole** *n.* [1980s] (*W.I.*) the vagina; used as a negative intensifier. ❑ **bloodhound** *n.* [reverse anthropomorphism] [early 19C+] **1** one who perjures themselves for money. **2** a policeman. ❑ **blood house** *n.* **1** [1910s+] (*Aus./N.Z.*) a public house with a reputation for violence. **2** [2000s] in ext. use, any very tough place. ❑ **blood-red fancy** *n.* [SE *blood-red* + *fancy handkerchief*] [mid-19C] a crimson handkerchief, as worn by costermongers. ❑ **blood sports** *n.* [1990s+] performing cunnilingus on a menstruating woman. ❑ **blood tub** *n.* [the *Blood Tubs*, a Baltimore street gang, who allegedly earned their name from having 'on an election day, dipped an obnoxious German's head in a tub of warm blood, and then sent him running through the town' (Farmer, *Americanisms Old New*, 1889)] [mid–late 19C] **1** a thug, a tough, a street gangster. **2** a theatre presenting lurid melodrama. **3** fig., a dangerous place or situation. ❑ **blood wagon** *n.* [1930s+] an ambulance.

❑ **blood-worm** *n.* [its main ingredient and its appearance] [mid-19C–1900s] a sausage, esp. a black pudding.

IN PHRASES

❑ **blood in, blood out** [1990s+] (*US Und.*) a ritual phr. meaning that to join a prison or street gang you must kill, and you may leave it (other than finishing your sentence) only by being killed yourself. ❑ **blood of the dog** *n. see* HAIR OF THE DOG (THAT BIT ONE) *n.* ❑ **blood's worth bottling** *see* BOTTLING *adj.* ❑ **bucket of blood** *n.* **1** [1940s] (*US Und.*) tomato ketchup. **2** *see BLOODY BUCKET under* BLOODY *adj.* ❑ **in someone's blood** [20C+] (*W.I.*) in hot pursuit. ❑ **spit blood** *v.* [1960s+] to be in a furious temper. ❑ **sweat blood** *v.* [1910s+] **1** to work very hard, esp. in phr. *don't sweat it*, don't worry. **2** to be terrified. ❑ **tired blood** *n.* [an advertising slogan for a tonic, which promised to combat the condition] [1950s+] (*US*) a condition of listlessness.

IN EXCLAMATIONS

❑ **blood and 'ounds!** *see* separate entry. ❑ **blood oath!** *see* separate entry. ❑ **blood or beer!** [late 19C–1900s] a street challenge, albeit usu. jocular, i.e. 'will you fight or buy a round?'.

blood *n.*[2] (*also* **bleed**) [abbr. SE *blood brother*] [1960s+] **1** (*US/UK black*) a (fellow) black person. **2** (*US black*) a young black man. **3** a term of address to a fellow black; by ext. a general term of address, used by any race. **4** (*UK black*) a blood relation. **5** (*US campus*) a friend.

IN PHRASES

❑ **young blood** *n.* [early 19C+] a young man, making his way in the world; thus (*orig. US black*) the up and coming youth who are learning the mores of street life; also as a term of address.

blood *adj.*[1] [BLOOD *n.*[1] (1)] [mid-19C; 1910s] hearty, rakish.

blood *adj.*[2] [BLOOD *n.*[2] (1)] [1980s] (*US black*) black.

blood *v.* **1** [mid-19C–1900s] to deprive of money [BLEED *v.*[1] (1)]. **2** [20C+] (*Aus.*) to cause to bleed [SE *blood*].

blood *adv.* [SE phr. 'blood is thicker than water'] [1990s+] (*Aus./US*) completely, utterly.

blood and 'ounds! *excl.* (*also* **blood and 'ounkers! blood and ouns! blood in ounce! blood and gunpowder! blood and thunder! blood and turf!**) [OONS! *excl.*] [mid-16C–1950s] a mild oath, lit. blood and wounds!, i.e. of Christ.

blood blister *n.* [rhy. sl.] [20C+] (*Aus.*) a sister.

blood claat *n.* (*also* **blood claht, blood clot, blood cloth, bloodklatt**) [Jam. pron. of SE *bloodcloth*, a sanitary towel] [1950s+] (*orig./mainly W.I./UK black*) a highly derog. description of another person.

bloodclaat *adj.* [BLOOD CLAAT *n.*] [1970s+] (*W.I.*) a general derog. intensifier.

blood oath! *excl.* (*also* **bloody oath! blooming oath! my bloody oath!**) [BLOODY *adj.*/BLOOMING *adj.*[1]] [mid-19C+] (*Aus.*) a general expression of agreement.

blood red *n.* [rhy. sl. = HEAD *n.* (2c)] [2000s] fellatio.

bloody *n.* [abbr.] [1980s+] (*US campus*) a *bloody* Mary, a drink of which the chief constituents are vodka and tomato juice.

bloody *adj.* (*also* **bleedy**) [BLOODY *adv.* although a single example vilifiying a 'bloody thief' has been found for 1599, thus predating the adv.; Grose wrote in 1796 of how popular *bloody* was among the contemporary London underworld. There is no doubt that, along with the transported felons of the period, it made its way to the penal colonies of Botany Bay. Fifty years later it was well-established. In his book *Travels in New South Wales* (1847), Alexander Marjoribanks noted the prevalence of the word, claiming that he had heard a bullock-driver use it 27 times in 15 minutes, a rate of speech, he then calculated, that over a 50-year period would produce some 18,200,000 repetitions of the 'disgusting word'. The Sydney *Bulletin* called it 'the Australian adjective' in its edition of 18 August 1894, explaining that 'it is more used, and used more exclusively by Australians, than by any other allegedly civilized nation'. The term gained its final sanctification as the 'Great Australian Adjective' when W.T. Goodge used it as the title for one of the poems he included in his *Hits! Skits! and Jingles!* (1899)] **1** [late 16C; 19C+] a general negative adj., abominable or terrible; esp. in the UK and Aus., where it is so widespread as to be termed 'the great Australian adjective'. **2** [early 19C+] usu. of a person or experience, unpleasant. **3** [mid-19C] rakish.

IN EXCLAMATIONS

❑ **bloody Ada!** *see FUCKING ADA! under* FUCKING *adj.* ❑ **bloody Nora!** *see FUCKING NORA! under* FUCKING *adj.* ❑ **bloody oath!** *see* BLOOD OATH! *excl.*

SE in slang uses

IN COMPOUNDS

❑ **bloody back** *n.* [his scarlet jacket; ? extra ref. to the frequent floggings of army discipline] [late 18C–mid-19C] a soldier. ❑ **bloody bucket** *n.* (*also* **bucket of blood, tub of blood**) [the original 19C *Bucket of Blood*, Shorty Young's tavern in Havre, Montana; its reputation spread and the term became generic for similar establishments; but note ref. to 18C 'a dwelling in Water Lane, off Fleet Street, known as "Blood Bowl house" [...] where there seldom passed a month without the commission of a murder' (in Peter Ackroyd's *London*, 2000); this public house, properly known as the Red Lion, is pictured in plate IX of Hogarth's *Industry & Idleness*] (*US*) **1** [late 19C+] a notably tough saloon or bar. **2** [1960s] a tough area of a town or city, orig. that which surrounded a local rough tavern. ❑ **bloody jemmy** *n.* [JEMMY *n.*[1] (3)] [early 19C–1910s] an uncooked sheep's head. ❑ **bloody mary** *n.* [pun on Mary I of England (1516–58), known popularly as *Bloody Mary* for her vindictive attacks on Protestantism] [1940s+] (*US*) a menstruating woman, used by a woman of herself, e.g. *I'm bloody mary today.* ❑ **bloody Monday** *n.* [thus the episode in Rudyard Kipling's *Stalky and Co.* (1899) when the headmaster canes the entire school before sending them home] [late 17C–late 18C] the last day of the school term, on which holidays begin and on which punishments are trad. given out.

IN PHRASES

❑ **bloody flag is out** [orig. in Shakespeare's *Henry V* (1598–9): 'Stand for your own; unwind your bloody flag'; the aggressiveness that so often accompanies heavy drinking] [late 17C–early 19C] phr. signifying that a person is drunk.

bloody *adv.* [SE *blood.* As Partridge states: 'There is no need for ingenious etymologies, the idea of blood suffices.' There are also no links to theology, nor to the term *'sblood* (God's blood). In addition, declare F&H in their definition: 'In passing it may be mentioned that there is no ground for attributing its derivation to "By'r Our Lady".' Like other so-called 'obscenities' or 'Anglo-Saxon words', *bloody* has experienced a fluctuating position as regards usage. As *OED* put it in 1887, it has been 'in general colloquial use from the Restoration to *c.*175? Now constantly in the mouths of the lowest classes, but by respectable people considered "a horrid word", on a par with obscene or profane language, and usually printed in the newspapers [as b–y.' The latter proscription has largely vanished. When *bloody* does appear in the press it tends to be in direct, quoted speech and is printed in full, but the term, in the UK at least, has yet to enter 'polite' society. As to its etymology, the *OED* links it to the preoccupations of the 'bloods' or aristocratic rowdies of the end of the 17C and beginning of the 18C. Thus the phr. 'bloody drunk' meant 'as drunk as a blood'. Its associations with bloodshed and murder (typically a *bloody battle*) 'have recommended it to the rough classes as a word that appeals to their imagination' and the *OED* goes on to compare its late 19C popularity with other 'impressive or graphic intensives, seen in the use of jolly, awfully, terribly, devilish, deuced, damned, ripping, rattling, thumping, stunning, thundering etc'] **1** [late 17C+] a general negative intensifier, very, exceedingly, abominably or desperately. **2** [20C+] as infix, e.g. ABSOBLOODYLUTELY *adv.*, *not bloody likely* etc.

blooey! *excl.* (*also* **blooie! bluey!**) **1** [1910s+] (*orig. US*) used to mimic the sound of an explosion. **2** [1920s–30s] used to denote failure, collapse.

IN PHRASES

❑ **go blooey** *v.* (*also* **go blooie**) [echoic] [1910s+] to explode suddenly, to go wrong, to fail, to break down.

bloomer *n.*[1] **1** [late 19C] a good-looking woman [SE *bloom*]. **2** [1900s] (*Aus./Can.*) a newly arrived immigrant [they *bloom* in their new environment].

bloomer *n.*[2] [BLOOMING *adj.*[1] + SE *error*] **1** [late 19C+] (*orig. Aus.*) an error, a slip; usu. in phr. *go/make a bloomer, come a bloomer*. **2** [20C+] a complete failure, a disaster. **3** [1910s] (*US*) a fake, a fraud. **4** [1910s] (*US*) a joke; thus *pull a bloomer*, to make a joke. **5** [1910s–50s] (*US Und.*) a safe that proves to be empty. **6** [1920s] (*US*) something or somewhere valueless.

blooming *adj.*[1] [popularized by the music-hall star Alfred 'The Great' Vance in the 1880s] **1** [early 18C+] a euph. for BLOODY *adj.*, e.g. *blooming error*, a major mistake. **2** [20C+] as infix.

IN COMPOUNDS

❑ **blooming shoot** *n.* (*also* **blooming show**) [WHOLE BANG SHOOT *n.*] [late 19C] absolutely everything, 'the lot'.

IN PHRASES

❑ **blooming six foot of tripe** *n.* [pun on TRIPE *n.*[1]/TRIPE *n.*[2]] [late 19C] a large policeman.

IN EXCLAMATIONS

❑ **blooming oath!** *see* BLOOD OATH! *excl.*

blooming *adj.*[2] [SE *bloom*] [late 19C] (*US campus*) excellent.

bloom me! *excl. see* BLOW ME! *excl.*[1].

bloomy! *excl. see* BLIMEY! *excl.*

bloop *n.* [echoic] [1950s+] a euph. substitute for various taboo terms.

bloop *v.*[1] [backform. f. BLOOPER *n.* (1)] (*US*) **1** [1940s] to accelerate a car. **2** [1950s] to hit, to punch.

bloop *v.*[2] [echoic] [1950s] (*US*) to laugh.

blooper *n.* [? BLAB *v.* + SE *oops!* or baseball *blooper*, 'a soggy fly to an unoccupied spot behind the backs of the infielders' (*NY Times*, 1937)] **1** [1940s] (*US*) a swinging blow. **2** [1940s+] (*orig. US*) an embarrassing verbal error, often delivered by a public or authority figure to their own detriment.

blooter *n.* (*also* **bloot**) [Scot. *bluiter*, a rough, clumsy fellow] [late 19C+] (*Ulster/US black*) a coarse, stupid peasant.

blooter *v.* [Scot. *blouter*, a blast of wind] [1980s+] (*Scot.*) to kick.

blootered *adj.* (*also* **bloothered, bluthered**) [Scot. *blout*, of liquids, to boil over] [1970s+] drunk.

blooterer *n.* [? BLOOTER *n.* or Scot. *blouter*, a blast of wind] [20C+] a scourge, a persecutor.

blosh *v.* [echoic] [2000s] to ejaculate.

bloss *n.* [BLOWSE *n.*] **1** [17C–early 19C] a beggar's female companion. **2** [late 17C–early 19C] (*UK Und.*) a thief. **3** [late 17C–early 19C] (*UK Und.*) a prostitute.

blossom *n.*[1] [ety. unknown] [mid–late 19C] a strait-laced or jealous person.

blossom *n.*[2]

SE in slang uses

pertaining to redness

IN COMPOUNDS

❑ **blossom-top** *n.* [mid–late 19C] (*US*) a red-headed or red-faced person.

IN PHRASES

❑ **brandy blossom** *n.* [late 19C] a red-pimpled nose, the result of excessive drinking of brandy. ❑ **cherry blossom kiss** *n.* [the colour of blood] [1990s+] the act of performing oral sex with a woman during her menstrual period. ❑ **gin blossom** *n.* [1930s+] (*US*) a red nose or blotches resulting from drinking alcohol. ❑ **grog blossom** *n.* [GROG *n.*[1] (1) + SE *blossom-faced*, having a red, bloated face; note 1960s US campus *blossom*, a pimple] [late 18C+] a red face caused by the bursting of blood-vessels through excessive, long-term drinking. ❑ **toddy blossom** *n.* [SE *toddy* + *blossom-faced*, having a red, bloated face] [19C] a red face caused by the bursting of blood vessels through excessive long-term drinking.

general uses

IN PHRASES

❑ **put a blossom on it for** *v.* [ety. unknown; ? ref. to the freshness of a SE *blossom* + IT *n.*[1] (2)] [1950s] (*Aus.*) to commit pederasty.

blossom *n.*[3] [positive connotations, esp. child-bearing] [1950s] (*Aus.*) the female genital area.

blot *n.*[1] **1** [1920s–70s] an unpleasant person [a fig. 'blot on the landscape']. **2** [1940s+] (*Aus.*) the anus, the buttocks. **3** [1950s] (*US Und.*) the underworld.

blot *n.*[2] [abbr. BLOTTER *n.*[1] (2c)] [1960s+] (*drugs*) a dose of LSD on paper.

blotch *n.* [1950s+] (*mainly juv.*) blotting-paper.

blotch *v.* [echoic] [1980s+] (*US campus*) to emit a small amount of liquid at the same time as breaking wind.

blotcher *n.* [1980s] (*US campus*) a FART *n.* (1) that also emits a small amount of fecal liquid and stains one's underwear.

blot one's copybook *v.* [1910s+] to make an error, practical or behavioural.

blotter *n.*[1] **1** [1910s–50s] (*US*) a drunkard with a seemingly infinite capacity for alcohol [plays on SOAK *n.*[1] (1)]. **2** in drug contexts. (**a**) [1950s+] a small piece of cotton through which a drug solution is filtered as it is drawn into a needle. (**b**) [1950s+] any drugs that are retrieved by soaking or boiling such a cloth. (**c**) [1960s+] (*also* **blotter cube**) a dose of LSD carried on a small square of blotting-paper; the paper and the drug it has absorbed are consumed together.

IN PHRASES

❑ **make a blue blotter of oneself** *v.* [1900s] (*US*) to drink heavily.

SE in slang uses

IN PHRASES

❑ **on the blotter** [1940s–50s] (*US Und.*) charged with a crime.

blotter *n.*[2] [var. on SHOTTER *n.*] [2000s] (*UK black*) drug dealer.

blot the scrip *v.* [SE *blot* + *scrip*, a scrap of paper, a few lines of writing] [mid-17C–early 19C] (*UK Und.*) to put into writing; thus *blot the scrip and jark it*, to sign a contract.

blotto *n.* [BLOTTO *adj.* (1)] [1950s] (*Aus.*) a drunk.

blotto *adj.* [? one's mind having *blotted out* reality, or one's body *blotted up* the alcohol] (*orig. US*) **1** [1910s+] very drunk. **2** [1920s+] of people, exhausted, confused, dazed, unconscious. **3** [1930s] absolutely forgotten. **4** [1980s+] intoxicated by a drug.

blot up *v.* [1930s] (*US*) to consume, e.g. a drink.

blou *adj.* [DIE BLOU *n.*] [1940s+] (*S.Afr. drugs*) intoxicated by a drug, 'high'.

Standard Afk., meaning blue, in slang uses

IN COMPOUNDS

❑ **bloubaadjie** *n.* [Afk. *baadjie*, badge] [1970s] (*S.Afr.*) **1** a habitual criminal serving an indeterminate sentence; thus the blue jacket he wears; the sentence itself. **2** a provincial traffic officer. ❑ **bloubek** *n.* [Afk. 'blue mouth'] [1960s] (*S.Afr.*) term of abuse. ❑ **blougat** *n.* [Afk. *gat*, anus (arse)] [1960s+] (*S.Afr.*) a national serviceman or woman who has completed half their training; thus, a novice in general. ❑ **bloupak** *n.* [Afk. *pakke*, suit] [1980s+] (*S.Afr.*) an auxiliary police officer (used in those areas where the police wear blue uniforms). ❑ **blouperd** *n. see under* DIE BLOU *n.* ❑ **blourokkie** *n.* [i.e. prison clothes] [1960s] (*S.Afr. Und.*) a prison. ❑ **bloutrein** *n.* (*also* **blue train**) [the *Blue Train*, a luxury passenger train running between Cape Town and Pretoria; those who drink meths take the 'fast train' to death] [1980s+] (*S.Afr.*) methylated spirits; thus *bloutreinryer*, a drinker of methylated spirits.

blouse *n.* [BLOWSE *n.*; the 20C+ use may simply refer to SE *blouse*] **1** [late 16C–early 18C] (*also* **blouze, blowes, blowz**) a slatternly woman, a prostitute. **2** [1930s+] (*also* **blouser**) a derog. term for a woman.

blouse *v.* [? BLOW *v.*[1] (4d)] [1920s] (*US*) to leave.

blouse and skirt! *excl.* [1970s–80s] (*UK black*) a mild excl., usu. as *what the —! who the —!* etc.

blouser *n. see* BLOUSE *n.* (2).

blouser *v.* [Fr. *blouse*, a jacket; thus to cover with one's jacket, to secrete. Ware suggests that the use is xenophobic, such a jacket would 'cover over an honest Englishman's waistcoat'] [late 19C–1900s] to cover up, to hide.

blouwzola *n. see* BLOWSER *n.*[1].

blouzabella *n.* (*also* **blowsabella**) [BLOWSE *n.* + Ital. *bella*, a good-looking slattern] [late 18C–early 19C] a slattern.

blouzalinda *n.* [BLOWSE *n.* + Sp. *linda*, beautiful] [late 18C–mid-19C] a slattern.

blouze *n. see* BLOUSE *n.* (1).

bloviate *v.* [? SE *blow* + sfx *-ate*, to 'blow off steam'] [mid–late 19C] (*US*) to talk loudly or aggressively.

blow *n.*[1] [SE *blow*, to explode] **1** [mid-17C] sexual intercourse [on sex = violence pattern]. **2** [1920s–70s] (*US*) a pistol.

blow *n.*[2] [abbr. BLOWEN *n.* (1)] [early 19C] a prostitute.

blow *n.*[3] [SE *blow*, to breathe] **1** an act of 'blowing off steam' or 'taking a breather'. (**a**) [early 19C–1940s] (*orig. US*) a celebration, a party, a spree. (**b**) [mid-19C] (*US campus*) a reveller, a party-goer. (**c**) [1900s] a treat. (**d**) *see* BLOW-OUT *n.*[1] (2). **2** in the context of speech and/or sound. (**a**) [mid-19C–1900s] (*US*) a betrayal, the passing of information, esp. to the authorities. (**b**) [1910s] (*Aus.*) boasting. (**c**) [1950s+] the act of playing music. (**d**) [1970s] the import or essence of one's conversation. (**e**) *see* BLOW-UP *n.*[1] (4). **3** [mid-19C+] (*Aus./US*) a rest, a period of relaxation. **4** in drug uses, referring to inhalation. (**a**) [late 19C; 1930s] a pipe or a cigarette; a puff on a pipe or a cigarette. (**b**) [1900s] (*US*) a smoke of opium. (**c**) [1950s+] a snort or sniff of cocaine. (**d**) [1960s+] cocaine. (**e**) [1970s] a small portion of heroin, inhaled rather than injected. (**f**) [1970s+] marijuana or hashish. (**g**) [1980s] (*N.Z.*) the act of sniffing glue; usu. in phr. *have a blow*, to sniff glue. (**h**) [1980s+] a puff on a marijuana cigarette or pipe. (**i**) [1990s+] crack cocaine. (**j**) [1990s+] a puff on a crack cocaine pipe. (**k**) [1990s+] a session of smoking cannabis. **5** [1910s+] a breath of fresh air, a rest from work, esp. in phr. *get a blow*.

IN COMPOUNDS

❑ **blow fiend** *n.* [FIEND *n.* (2)] [2000s] (*US drugs*) a cocaine addict. ❑ **blow monkey** *n.* [MONKEY *n.* (11c)] [1990s+] (*drugs*) a regular or excessive user of cocaine.

IN PHRASES

❑ **down blows in someone** *v. see under* DOWN *v.*[2]. ❑ **give someone a blow** *v.* [1930s] to make contact, to communicate. ❑ **make the blow** *v.* [1920s] (*US*) to leave.

blow *n.*[4] [ety. unknown] [late 19C–1900s] a shilling (5p).

blow *n.*[5] [BLOW! *excl.*[1]] [1910s–20s] a damn.

blow *n.*[6] [BLOW *v.*[2] (2f)] [1960s] (*US black*) of a pimp, the loss of one of his prostitutes.

blow *n.*[7] [*BLOW A SHOT under* BLOW *v.*[2]] [1960s+] (*drugs*) a shot of heroin that misses the vein.

blow *n.*[8] *see* BLOWHARD *n.*[2].

blow *n.*[9] *see* BLOW JOB *n.*

blow, the *n.* [1960s] a form of confidence trick in which the victim is convinced that it is possible to raie the denomination on notes, e.g. from $10 to $100.

blow *v.*[1] [lit. and fig. uses of SE *blow*] **1** in terms pertaining to speech. (**a**) [15C; 17C–19C] (*also* **blow upon**) to discredit, to defame; to destroy someone's reputation. (**b**) [15C+] to speak angrily; thus *blow at, blow on*, to chastise, to reprimand. (**c**) [late 16C+] (*also* **blow on, blow upon**) to inform on, to betray, to expose, to reveal (evidence of wrong-doing, espionage etc); ext. as *blow the works*. (**d**) [mid-18C; 1970s+] to sing. (**e**) [late 18C+] (*also* **blow off**) to boast, to brag. (**f**) [mid-19C] to tease aggressively. (**g**) [mid-19C+] to inform, to confess. (**h**) [1910s+] (*US*) to become, e.g. *blow chilly*, to be stand-offish. (**i**) [1920s+] (*US black*) to talk (nonsense); to talk insincerely. (**j**) [1940s+] (*US Und.*) to realize. **2** in terms pertaining to the body. (**a**) [mid-17C] (*also* **blow off**) to break wind. (**b**) [1960s+] to vomit. (**c**) [1970s] to defecate. **3** in terms pertaining to drugs. (**a**) [mid-19C+] to smoke, orig. in a pipe. (**b**) [20C+] to smoke marijuana; thus *blow dope, blow grass*. (**c**) [1910s+] (*US drugs*) to inhale a narcotic, usu. heroin or cocaine. (**d**) [1960s+] (*also* **blow off**) to inject a narcotic. (**e**) [2000s] to smoke crack cocaine. **4** in terms pertaining to movement. (**a**) [late 19C] (*US*) to go round with, to associate with. (**b**) [late 19C] to take a rest. (**c**) [late 19C–1900s] (*US*) to leave someone behind, to depart from. (**d**) [late 19C+] (*US*) (*also* **blow away, blow it, blow off, blow through**) to depart at speed, to walk away quickly; thus imper. *go blow!* go away! *blow yourself!* go to hell! (**e**) [1930s–50s] (*US prison*) to escape from prison. (**f**) [1960s] (*US*) to drive through a red traffic light or similar traffic sign. **5** in terms based on the idea of blowing/playing wind instruments. (**a**) [1920s+] (*orig. US black*) to play music. (**b**) [1950s–60s] (*US*) to create, to 'whip up'. (**c**) [1950s+] (*US black*) to talk enthusiastically and fluently. (**d**) [1950s+] (*US black*) to perform on any 'instrument', e.g. a writer's word processor etc. (**e**) [1960s] (*US campus*) to toady to, to act the sycophant. (**f**) [1980s] (*US campus*) to sing well.

IN PHRASES

❑ **blow...** *v.* **1** *see also under* relevant n. **2** *see also* separate entries.

pertaining to departure

IN PHRASES

❑ **blow ass** *v.* (*also* **swing ass**) [ASS *n.* (4); SWING *v.* (10)] [1980s+] (*US*) to walk fast, to run off. ❑ **blow the joint** *v.* (*also* **blow the scene, ...works, blow town**) [JOINT *n.* (3b)/SCENE *n.* (2)/WORKS, THE *n.* (3)] [20C+] to leave, to run off. ❑ **blow this popsicle stand** *v.* (*also* **blow this garage, ...pop stand, ...taco stand**) [generic use of SE *popsicle stand/garage/taco stand*] [1960s+] (*US campus*) to leave, esp. somewhere one dislikes or pretends to dislike.

pertaining to vomit

IN PHRASES

❑ **blow chunks** *v.* (*also* **blow grits, spew chunks**) [SE *chunks* (of food)/GRITS *n.*[1]] **1** [1930s+] to vomit. **2** [1990s+] thus, of a thing, to be terrible or unpleasant. ❑ **blow dinner** *v. see* LOSE ONE'S LUNCH *under* LOSE *v.* ❑ **blow one's doughnuts** *v.* (*also* **blow donuts, blow one's oats, throw donuts**) [1970s+] (*US campus*) to vomit or regurgitate. ❑ **blow one's groceries** *v.* (*also* **blow g's, lose one's groceries**) [1970s+] (*US campus*) to vomit. ❑ **blow one's lunch** *v. see* LOSE ONE'S LUNCH *under* LOSE *v.*

pertaining to drugs

IN COMPOUNDS

❑ **blowcaine** *n.* [SE *cocaine* + play on SE *procaine, novocaine* etc] [1980s+] crack cocaine diluted with powdered cocaine.

IN PHRASES

❑ **blow jaw** *v.* [stressed pron. of SE (*mari*)*jua*(*na*)] [1980s] (*US*) to smoke marijuana. ❑ **blow smoke** *v. see under* SMOKE *n.*

pertaining to speech and related uses

IN COMPOUNDS

❑ **blowbag** *n.* [WINDBAG *n.* (1)] [1920s+] (*Aus.*) a loud-mouthed braggart.

IN PHRASES

❑ **blow black** *v.* (*also* **blow change**) [SE *black*/(political or social) *change*] [1980s] (*US black*) to talk about and/or initiate black activism, social change, revolution and any similar form of racial advancement. ❑ **blow fire** *v.* [ext. of BLOW *v.*[1] (5a)] [1980s+] (*US black*) to do anything well and keenly, esp. dancing, musicianship. ❑ **blow heavy** *v.* [HEAVY *adv.* (3); jazz imagery] [1980s+] (*US black*) to talk seriously of a contextually vital matter. ❑ **blow one up** *v.* [1910s] (*US prison*) to light or smoke a cigarette. ❑ **blow one's bags (out)** *v.* (*also* **blow one's bag (out)**) [1910s+] (*Aus.*) to boast. ❑ **blow one's horn** *v.* **1** *see under* HORN *n.*[1]. **2** *see also* separate entry. ❑ **blow one's nose** *v.* [pun on SE *blow*/BLOW *v.*[1] (1c), and note NOSE *n.* (1)] [1950s] (*US*) to inform, to talk to. ❑ **blow the gap** *v.* [var. on *BLOW THE GAFF under* GAFF *n.*[1]] [early 19C] to inform on, to betray. ❑ **how are you blowing?** [1900s–20s] (*Irish*) a general term of informal greeting.

SE in slang uses

IN PHRASES

❑ **blow...** *v.* **1** *see also under* relevant n. **2** *see also* separate entries. ❑ **blow foam** *v.* [late 19C] (*US*) to drink beer. ❑ **blow for** *v.* [? heavy breathing] [1950s] (*US*) to be keen on, to be eager for. ❑ **blow hot and cold** *v.* [subseq. use is SE] [mid-16C–late 19C] to vacillate. ❑ **blow in someone's ear** *v. see* BLOW

DOWN SOMEONE'S EAR *under* EAR *n.*[1]. ▫ **blow one out** *v.* ['one' is a RASPBERRY *n.* (1)] [1900s–30s] (*orig. milit.*) to make a rude noise in someone's direction. ▫ **blow one's pipes** *v.* [1970s+] (*US teen*) to make a loud noise through a car's exhaust pipe by suddenly pressing down on the accelerator. ▫ **blow smoke up someone's ass** *v. see under* SMOKE *n.* ▫ **blow the coals** *v.* [fig. use of SE] [late 17C–18C] to stir up trouble between two parties. ▫ **blow the doors off** *v.* (*also* **tear the doors off**) [1960s+] (*orig. US*) to drive at high speed past another car. ▫ **whatever blows your dress up** (*also* **whatever blows your hair back, ...skirt up**) [1980s+] (*N.Z./US*) whatever you like, whatever makes you happy.

blow *v.*[2] [SE *blow*, to explode] **1** in sexual terms. (**a**) [17C] to bring to orgasm. (**b**) [mid-17C+] to reach orgasm. (**c**) [1930s+] (*also* **blow off**) to fellate; occas. to perform cunnilingus. (**d**) [1970s+] (*US campus*) to have sexual intercourse. **2** (*also* **blew, blue**) in fig. uses, meaning to expend. (**a**) [mid-19C] to rob, to steal. (**b**) [mid-19C+] to squander, to waste, esp. of money. (**c**) [late 19C+] (*also* **blow someone off**) to treat to a meal, to food and/or drink; usu. as *blow someone to*. (**d**) [late 19C+] to spend. (**e**) [20C+] to waste an opportunity, a relationship etc. (**f**) [1970s] (*US*) of a pimp, to lose a prostitute from one's STABLE *n.* (2). **3** in terms pertaining to negativity. (**a**) [late 19C+] to ruin, to upset, to destroy, to lose. (**b**) [20C+] to botch, to bungle, to lose (a contest or game); esp. as *blow it*. (**c**) [20C+] to crack under emotional or other pressure, to explode emotionally. (**d**) [20C+] of people, to reject, to abandon. (**e**) [1900s] of a situation, to give up on. (**f**) [1910s] (*US Und.*) to discover that something is missing. (**g**) [1910s+] (*orig. US*) to miss, e.g. a train, an appointment. (**h**) [1920s–60s] (*US*) to dismiss from a job, to break off a love affair. (**i**) [1960s+] (*US*) to fail. (**j**) [1970s+] of a situation or experience, to be unpleasant, pointless, useless. (**k**) *see* BLOW A SHOT below. (**l**) see BLOW (SOMEONE) AWAY *v.* (1).

DERIVATIVES

▫ **blowing** *n.* [1930s] fellatio.

IN COMPOUNDS

▫ **blowboy** *n.* [1930s+] (*US*) a male homosexual. ▫ **blowchoice** *n.* [2000s] (*US campus*) a socially unacceptable person; a stupid, foolish person. ▫ **blowstake** *n.* [1930s] money that one risks on a bet.

IN PHRASES

▫ **blow...** *v.* **1** *see also under* relevant n. **2** *see also* separate entries. ▫ **blow a shot** *v.* (*also* **blow, blow a fix, blow it, blow the vein**) [FIX *n.*[3] (1)] (*drugs*) **1** [1930s+] of an addict, to blunder when injecting oneself or someone else and miss the vein, wasting the narcotic in the skin. **2** [1960s] to waste a shot of a narcotic by missing the vein with the injection. ▫ **blow one's cork** *v.* [1920s+] (*US*) **1** to go mad. **2** to lose one's temper. **3** to become excited. **4** to achieve orgasm. ▫ **blow one's dust** *v.* [1960s–70s] to masturbate; to ejaculate. ▫ **blow oneself out** *v.* [early–mid-19C] to binge. ▫ **blow one's juice** *v. see under* JUICE *n.*[1]. ▫ **blow one's lot** *v.* [1940s+] (*Aus.*) to come to orgasm, to ejaculate. ▫ **blow one's tube** *v.* [the image is of a submarine, but note BLOW *v.*[2] (1b) + TUBE *n.*[1] (1)] [1990s+] of a man, to achieve orgasm. ▫ **blow one's wad** *v.* **1** *see under* WAD *n.*[1]. **2** *see under* WAD *n.*[3]. ▫ **blow someone out of the water** *v. see under* WATER *n.*[1]. ▫ **blow someone's act** *v.* (*also* **blow someone's game, blow the act**) [BLOW *v.*[2] (3a)] [1970s+] (*US*) to ruin, to spoil, to interfere. ▫ **blow someone's back off** *v.* [1980s] of a man, to have sexual intercourse. ▫ **blow some tunes** *v.* [joc. use of BLOW *v.*[2] (1c) + SE *tunes*] **1** [1970s+] (*US*) (*also* **do a tune**) to fellate in hetero- or homosexual contexts. **2** [1980s+] (*US black*) to perform cunnilingus. ▫ **blow the show** *v.* (*also* **blow the scene**) [SHOW *n.* (1)/SCENE *n.* (1)] [1960s+] (*orig. US*) to ruin the entire situation, to miss an opportunity to do or gain something. ▫ **blow the vein** *v. see* BLOW A SHOT above.

SE in slang uses

IN COMPOUNDS

▫ **blowtop** *n.* [BLOW ONE'S TOP *v.*] [1930s+] (*US black*) **1** an excitable or violent, unstable person. **2** a jazz musician, esp. a first-rate performer.

IN PHRASES

▫ **blow...** *v.* **1** *see also under* relevant n. **2** *see also* separate entries. ▫ **blow a cork** *v.* [1950s] (*US*) to lose one's temper; to become over-excited. ▫ **blow a valve** *v.* (*also* **blow a tube**) [1950s+] (*US*) to explode with rage. ▫ **blow a vein** *v.* [1980s] (*US*) to have an apoplectic fit (and die of it). ▫ **blow one's jets** *v.* [2000s] (*orig. US black*) to get angry or annoyed. ▫ **blow one's roof** *v. see under* ROOF *n.* ▫ **blow one's shoes** *v.* [20C+] (*US*) to lose control, to lose one's composure. ▫ **blow the sky** *v.* [1940s] (*US black*) to lose one's mind; to become unconscious, to pass out drunk.

blow! *excl.*[1] **1** [18C+] a dismissive excl.; synon. with *TO HELL WITH...!* *under* HELL *n.* **2** [19C+] euph. for DAMN! *excl.*

blow! *excl.*[2] [BLOW *v.*[1] (4d)] [1930s+] go away!

blow a fuse *v.* **1** [1920s+] to explode (usu. with rage). **2** [1950s–60s] of a plan, to go disastrously wrong.

blow a fuse! *excl.* [1970s] (*Scot.*) go away!

blow along *v. see* BLOW IN *v.*[2].

blowark *adj.* [ety. unknown] [mid-19C] (*UK Und.*) dirty.

blow away *v. see* BLOW *v.*[1] (4d).

blowback *n.* **1** [1980s+] (*drugs*) an exhalation of marijuana/hashish smoke into another's mouth. **2** [2000s] the spray of blood, bones, tissue etc from the victim that follows a shooting.

IN PHRASES

▫ **rising blowback** *n.* [1980s+] (*US drugs*) exhaling cannabis smoke into someone else's mouth, then moving from a crouching position and slowly standing up for an increased sensation.

blow back *v.* [BLOW *v.*[2] (2d)] [1920s–30s] (*US*) to return stolen goods; to pay back money.

blow card *n.* [? BLOW OFF *n.*[2] (1) + SE *card*] (*US Und.*) **1** [1910s–50s] the last card; the final play or thing in any series. **2** [1950s] in fig. use.

blow down *v.* (*US*) **1** [mid-19C+] to kill with a firearm, to shoot dead. **2** [1930s] (*US Und.*) to modify, to soften. **3** [1960s] to defeat comprehensively, to overwhelm. **4** [1980s+] to pass at high speed. **5** *see* BLOW IN *v.*[2].

blowed *adj.*[1] (*also* **busted**) [basically SE, was seen as a profanity from the mid-19C+; today it is accepted and one of the mildest of imprecations] [mid-19C+] used as a euph. for DAMNED *adj.* in general mild oaths of surprise, shock, annoyance, e.g. — *be blowed*.

IN EXCLAMATIONS

▫ **I'll be blowed!** (*also* **blowed! I'm blowed!**) [mid-19C+] a general excl. of surprise, shock etc.

blowed *adj.*[2] *see* BLOWN (OUT) *adj.* (2).

blowed-in-the-bottle/glass *adj. see* BLOWN-IN-THE-GLASS *adj.*

blowed-in-the-glass (stiff) *n.* (*also* **blowed-in-the-bottle**) [BLOWN-IN-THE-GLASS *adj.* + STIFF *n.*[1] (4a)] [late 19C–1940s] (*US tramp*) an elite tramp.

blowee *n.* [BLOW *v.*[2] (1c)] [1970s] one who fellates.

blowen *n.* (*also* **bloan**) [according to George Borrow f. Rom. *beluñi*, 'a sister in debauchery'. Hotten (1867) notes Ger. *Bluhen*, bloom, and *Buhlen*, sweetheart, but adds 'the street term ... may mean one whose reputation has been 'blown on', or damaged'] **1** [late 17C+] a woman, spec. a prostitute. **2** [late 18C] as *blowen of the ken*, a landlady, a 'mistress of the house'. **3** [late 18C–early 19C] (*UK Und.*) the pretended wife of a shoplifter. **4** [mid-19C] a mistress.

blowen spenie *n.* [BLOWEN *n.* (3) + ? link to UK dial. *spean*, the teat of a female animal] [late 18C] (*US Und.*) a thief's female companion.

blower *n.*[1] [var. BLOWEN *n.* (1)] [late 17C–late 19C] (*UK Und.*) a woman, spec. a prostitute; the antonym of JOMER *n.*

blower *n.*[2] **1** [early 19C] a pipe. **2** [mid-19C] (*US*) a liar. **3** [mid-19C–1920s] a braggart [BLOW *v.*[1] (1e)]. **4** [1920s+] a telephone, esp. in phr. *on the blower* [following on f. the earlier 'speaking tubes' down which one had to blow to alert the other person; note bookmaker jargon *blower*, the betting shop public address system that broadcasts races, odds and results].

5 [1950s] (*US*) a broken-down horse. **6** [1990s+] an annoying person.

IN PHRASES

❑ **cop for the blower** *v.* [COP *v.* (1c)] [1960s] to make a phone call.

blower *n.*[3] [SE *blow open/up*] [late 19C–1920s] (*US Und.*) a safe-breaker.

blower *n.*[4] [SE *blow* (one's nose)] [1940s–50s] (*US black*) a handkerchief.

blower *n.*[5] [BLOW *v.*[2] (2b)] [1940s+] (*W.I.*) a spendthrift.

blower *n.*[6] [SE *blow*, to explode, underpinned by BLOW (SOMEONE) AWAY *v.* (1); BLOW DOWN *v.* (1)] [1970s] (*US*) a shotgun.

blower *n.*[7] [BLOW *v.*[2] (2b)] [2000s] (*US black*) a disaster.

blowes *n. see* BLOUSE *n.* (1).

blowey *n. see* BLOWIE *n.*[1].

blowfish *n.* [SE *blowfish*, a puffer, a saltwater fish that is ordinarily thrown away by fishermen] [2000s] an insignificant, unpleasant person.

blowfly *n.* [SE *blowfly* / BLOW *v.*[1] (1e) + SE *fly*] **1** [late 19C+] (*Aus.*) an officious person; thus *blowflyism*, officiousness, 'red tape'. **2** [20C+] (*US*) a boaster.

blow gun *n.* [SE *blow gun*/BLOW (SOMEONE) AWAY *v.* (1)] [1930s–40s] (*US Und.*) a short-barrelled shotgun; a pistol with a large barrel.

blowgun *n.* [SE *blowgun*/BLOW *v.*[1] (1e)] [mid-19C; 1960s] (*US*) a braggart.

blowhard *n.*[1] [BLOW *v.*[1] (1e) + SE *hard*; later 20C use is SE] [early 19C–1920s] (*orig. US*) a boaster, a loud and egocentric talker.

blowhard *n.*[2] (*also* **blow**) [? one's brain 'blows up'] [1990s+] (*Irish*) methylated spirits.

blowhard *adj.* [BLOWHARD *n.*[1]] [1910s+] (*US*) boastful, self-aggrandizing.

blowhole *n.* [pun on SE; but note BLOW *v.*[1] + *CAKEHOLE under* CAKE *n.*[1]] **1** [1920s+] (*Aus.*) a talkative person. **2** [1940s] (*US*) the mouth. **3** [1940s+] (*US*) the anus.

blowie *n.*[1] (*also* **blowey, blowy**) [abbr.] [1910s+] (*Aus./N.Z.*) a blowfly.

blowie *n.*[2] [BLOW *v.*[1] (1e)] [1990s+] a fantasy, a lie.

blow-in *n.* [BLOW IN *v.*[2]] [1920s+] (*Aus./Irish/US*) a stranger, a newcomer, someone who has 'blown in', esp. one who is not yet accepted by the locals.

blow in *v.*[1] [ext. of BLOW *v.*[2] (2b)] **1** [late 19C] (*US*) to obtain. **2** [late 19C+] (*US*) to squander, to waste, usu. of money.

blow in *v.*[2] (*also* **blow along, blow down, blow into, blow out, blow over, blow up**) [image of being wafted by a chance breeze] [late 19C+] to arrive unexpectedly and casually; thus *what's this blown in?* who's this?, a usu. unfriendly reference to a new arrival.

blow in *v.*[3] [SE *blow*] [1960s] (*US*) to hit, to beat up.

blow in a bowl *v.* [synon. with 20C+ HIT *v.* (3b)] [early 16C] to be a habitual drunkard.

blowing *n.*[1] [BLOWEN *n.* (1)] [late 17C–mid-19C] (*UK Und.*) a woman, spec. a prostitute.

blowing *n.*[2] [ety. unknown] [mid-19C] (*US*) a state of drunkenness.

blowing *n.*[3] **1** [mid-19C+] boasting, aggrandizing [BLOW *v.*[1] (1e)]. **2** [late 19C] telling off, reprimanding [BLOW *v.*[1] (1b)].

blowing-up *n.* [BLOW UP *v.*[1] (5)] [early 19C–1900s] a scolding.

blow in one's pipe *v.* [BLOW *v.*[2] (2b) / play on SE] [mid-19C–1910s] to spend one's money.

blow into *v. see* BLOW IN *v.*[2].

blow it *v. see* BLOW *v.*[1] (4d).

blow it! *excl.* (*also* **blow one's sister's wig!**) [early 19C+] a mild excl. of annoyance, euph. for a variety of 'stronger' synons., e.g. FUCK IT! *excl.*

blow it off *v. see* BLOW OFF *v.*[1] (5).

blow it out *v. see* BLOW OUT *v.*[2] (3).

blow it out of one's ass *v.* [BLOW *v.*[2] (2b) + ASS *n.* (2)] **1** [1970s] (*US*) to squander foolishly; to make a foolhardy mistake. **2** [1980s] to boast, to talk emptily.

blow it out your ass! *excl.* (*also* **blow it! blow it out! blow it out your barracks bag! ...B-bag! ...butt! ...footlocker!**) [SE *blow* + ASS *n.* (2)/BUTT *n.*[1] (1a)] [1940s+] (*orig. US milit.*) a general excl. of derision, contempt or dismissal of the previous speaker's statement.

blow job *n.* (*also* **blow**) [BLOW *v.*[2] (1c) + JOB *n.*[2] (2)] (*orig. US*) **1** [1940s+] (*also* **job**) fellatio. **2** [1960s+] (*also* **blow job artist**) a fellator or fellatrix [-ARTIST *sfx*]. **3** [1990s+] (*US black*) cunnilingus.

IN PHRASES

❑ **give someone a blow job** *v.* [1960s] (*US campus*) in fig. use, to toady to.

blow me! *excl.*[1] (*also* **bloom me! blow me up! blow my buttons! feather me!**) [abbr. BLOW ME TIGHT! *excl.*] [late 18C+] an excl. of surprise.

blow me! *excl.*[2] [older use var. BLOW IT! *excl.*; late 20C+ BLOW *v.*[2] (1c)] [mid-19C+] (*orig. US*) a dismissive excl.

blow me down! *excl.* (*also* **blow me backwards!**) [1930s+] a mild expletive.

blow me tight! *excl.* (*also* **blow me pink! blow me up!**) [early 19C–1970s] an excl. expressive of surprise or denial, used as euph. for DAMNED *adj.* in general mild oaths of surprise, shock, annoyance; usu. as *blow me tight if....*

blow my dickey! *excl.* (*also* **blow my bilges! blow my buttons!**) [early 19C–1920s] a general excl. of surprise, amazement etc.

blow-my-skull(-off) *n.* [SE *blow* + *skull*] [mid-19C] (*Aus.*) an alcoholic drink that mixes wine, opium, cayenne pepper and rum, popular at the gold diggings; an alternative recipe mixes boiling water, sugar, lime or lemon juice, porter, rum and brandy.

blow my wig! *excl. see under* WIG *n.*[2].

blown *adj.* (*also* **blown up, blown upon**) [abbr. SE *blown open* / BLOW *v.*[1] (1c)] [late 17C+] revealed.

blown-in-the-glass *adj.* (*also* **blowed-in-the-glass, blown in the bottle, blowed ...**) [early glass-blowing often trapped bubbles in the finished object] [late 19C+] (*orig. US*) genuine, authentic, trustsworthy; also as n.

blown (out) *adj.* (*also* **blew out, blown away**) [SE *blow*, to explode] **1** [mid-19C+] shocked, exhausted, overcome. **2** [1970s+] (*US campus*) (*also* **blowed**) drunk, under the influence of a drug. **3** [1980s+] (*US campus*) crazy, insane. **4** [1990s+] dishevelled. **5** [1990s+] (*Aus.*) delighted.

blown up *adj.* [SE *blow*, to explode + ? image of a bloated drunkard] [1970s+] (*US*) drunk or overindulging in drugs.

blown up/upon *adj. see* BLOWN *adj.*

blow off *n.*[1] [BLOW *v.*[1]] **1** [mid-19C–1950s] (*US*) an emotional outburst, a sudden fight or argument, a sensational piece of news. **2** [late 19C+] a party, a celebration. **3** [1950s+] a braggart. **4** [2000s] (*N.Z.*) boasting.

blow off *n.*[2] [SE *blow*, to explode] **1** [1900s–10s] the end, the climax, esp. a decisive conclusion, an absolute end. **2** [1910s–50s] the very last tolerable happening in a series, 'the last straw'. **3** [1920s] (*US Und.*) the act of commiting a robbery or burglary. **4** [1920s] (*US Und.*) exposure, detection, discovery. **5** [1920s+] (*US Und.*) the final stage of a confidence game, when the victim, now robbed, is quickly sent on his way. **6** [1930s] (*US Und.*) a jail-break. **7** [1930s] (*US black*) a shooting. **8** [2000s] a sudden or casual departure.

blow off *n.*[3] [SE *blow*, to blow something away with a puff of air] **1** [1960s+] (*US campus*) a lazy person, a 'layabout'. **2** [1970s+] (*US teen*) anything considered exceptionally easy.

blow off *v.*[1] [SE *blow*, explode] **1** [mid-19C] (*US*) to stop, to cease. **2** [1910s] (*US*) of events, to develop, to happen. **3** [1940s+] (*US*) to get rid of, esp. (*US Und.*) in the concluding stages of a con-game. **4** [1950s] (*US Und.*) to interrupt criminals during a crime. **5** [1960s+] (*US*) (*also* **blow it off**) to ignore, to make little of. **6** [1960s+] (*US campus*) to fail an examination. **7** [1980s] (*US*) to kill. **8** [1980s+] (*US*) to reject a sexual advance. **9** [1980s+] to terminate a relationship, to jilt someone by not turning up.

blow off *v.*[2] [BLOW OFF *n.*[1] (1) / *BLOW OFF STEAM under* STEAM *n.*] **1** [late 19C+] to release pent-up emotion. **2** [1910s+] to get angry (with). **3** [1970s+] (*US gay*) to achieve orgasm.

IN PHRASES

❑ **blow off at the mouth** *v.* (*also* **blow off at the head**) [BLOW OFF *v.*[2] (1) + SE *mouth/head*] [1940s+] to talk loudly or aggressively, to boast.

blow off *v.*[3] [BLOW *v.*[2] (3g)] [1980s+] (*US campus*) to play truant.

blow off *v.*[4] [1990s+] (*US*) to make a turn.

blow off *v.*[5] **1** *see* BLOW *v.*[1] (1e). **2** *see* BLOW *v.*[1] (2a). **3** *see* BLOW *v.*[1] (3d). **4** *see* BLOW *v.*[1] (4d).

blow off *v.*[6] *see* BLOW *v.*[2] (1c).

blow off! *excl.* [BLOW *v.*[1] (4d)] [1910s+] (*Aus.*) an expression of dismissal.

blow (off) on the groundsills *v.* [SE *blow* + *groundsills*, the foundation or lowest part of any structure, i.e. one's panting breath is exhaled at ground level] [late 17C– late 18C] (*UK Und.*) to have sexual intercourse while lying on the floor.

blow (off) the loose corn(s) *v.* [the image is of sex in a barn; one's panting blows away loose corn] [late 17C–mid-18C] to have sexual intercourse.

blowoh! *excl.* [? BLOW ME! *excl.*[1] + SE *wow!*] [1980s] (*UK black*) a term of surprise and shock, synon. with 'What a lark!' or 'Wow!' or 'Isn't *that* incredible!'.

blow on *v. see* BLOW *v.*[1] (1c).

blow (one's) cookies *v.* **1** [1930s+] to vomit [BLOW *v.*[1] (2b)/ SE *blow* + *cookies* = food consumed]. **2** [2000s] to reach orgasm [BLOW *v.*[2] (1b)].

blow one's head *v.*[1] (*also* **blow one's skull**) [SE *blow*, explode + *head/skull*] [1950s+] (*US, orig. drugs*) to become intoxicated by a drug.

blow one's head *v.*[2] [BLOW *v.*[2] (1b)/BLOW *v.*[2] (1c) + HEAD *n.* (6b)/SE *head*] **1** [1960s] (*US gay*) to ejaculate large quantities of semen while being fellated. **2** [1970s+] (*US*) to fellate.

blow one's head off *v. see* BLOW ONE'S MIND *V.*

blow one's horn *v.* [play on SE/BLOW *v.*[1] (1e)/BLOW *v.*[1] (2a)] (*US*) **1** [mid–late 19C] to speak or sing out of turn. **2** [late 19C+] (*also* **toot one's horn**) to brag, to boast. **3** [20C+] (*US*) to break wind.

blow one's hump *v.* **1** [1950s] (*drugs*) (*also* **go over the hump**) to become intoxicated on a drug, usu. marijuana [BLOW *v.*[1] (3b)]. **2** *see under* HUMP *n.*[1].

blow one's mind *v.* (*also* **blow one's head off**) [SE *blow*, explode + *mind*] [1960s+] (*orig. drugs*) **1** to become intoxicated with a drug or drugs. **2** to become mad. **3** to shock, to surprise, to amaze; thus *mind-blown*, emotionally shattered. **4** to drive mad, to destroy one's powers of reasoning.

IN PHRASES

❑ **blow your mind roulette** *n.* [SE *Russian roulette*] [1960s] (*US black/drugs*) a drug-based game whereby the participants toss a variety of unspecified pills onto a table and then take whatever they fancy and wait to discover what the effects will be.

blow one's roof *v.* (*also* **blow one's top**) [BLOW *v.*[1] (3b) + SE *roof*/ROOF *n.* (2)/TOP *n.* (2)] [1950s+] (*drugs*) to smoke cannabis.

blow one's top *v.* (*also* **blow one's cap, ...lid, ...topper**) [SE *blow*, explode + TOP *n.* (2)/SE *cap*/LID *n.* (2)/TOPPER *n.*[3] (1); the image is of a volcano] (*orig. US*) **1** [1920s+] to lose one's sanity. **2** [1930s] (*US black*) to get drunk. **3** [1930s] (*US tramp*) to commit suicide, esp. by shooting. **4** [1930s+] (*also* **blow gaff**) to lose one's temper, to become violent [GAFF *n.*[2] (4)]. **5** [1930s+] to express intense emotion; to become very excited. **6** [1940s–50s] to talk too much.

blow-out *n.*[1] **1** [early 19C–1930s] (*US*) a brawl, a noisy argument. **2** [early 19C+] (*also* **blow**) a binge of eating, drinking and debauchery, also drug-taking; also fig. use. **3** [early 19C+] a party. **4** [late 19C+] a good time, an exciting event. **5** [1900s] an organized dance, held in a dancehall and frequented by lower-class young people. **6** [1990s+] (*Aus.*) expenditure.

blow-out *n.*[2] [SE *blow out*, i.e. one's hair] [1960s–70s] (*US black/ campus*) a very large 'Afro' hairstyle; a hairstyle in which one's natural tight curls or kinks are blown out with a hairdryer.

blow-out *n.*[3] [BLOW *v.*[1] (5a); orig. jazz use; when two bands staged a competition, the winner was to said to *blow* its rival *out* of the house; thus the defeat itself was a *blow-out*] [1980s+] a comprehensive defeat.

blow out *v.*[1] **1** [early 19C; 1980s] (*US campus*) to tell off, to criticise. **2** [mid-19C+] (*orig. US*) to murder, to kill. **3** [1900s] to spend all one's funds. **4** [1910s+] (*orig. US*) to reject, to break a promise, to neglect a rendezvous etc. **5** [1960s] (*US*) to die, to collapse. **6** [1960s–70s] (*US*) to destroy, to spoil. **7** [1970s] (*orig. US*) to astound, to amaze. **8** [1970s+] to collapse, to malfunction. **9** [1970s+] (*US campus*) to shock, to embarrass.

IN PHRASES

❑ **blow out someone's light(s)** *v.* (*also* **blow someone's light out**) [late 19C+] (*US/Aus.*) to murder, to kill.

blow out *v.*[2] [SE *blow out*, to expand, but note BLOW *v.*[2] (2)] **1** [early 19C+] to eat and/or drink to excess. **2** [mid-19C] to treat. **3** [1970s+] (*US campus*) (*also* **blow it out**) to have a spree.

blow out *v.*[3] [late 19C–1900s] to steal.

blow out *v.*[4] (*also* **blow out of**) [BLOW *v.*[1] (4d)] **1** [20C+] to leave, to depart from a place. **2** [1980s+] to send away, to reject.

blow out *v.*[5] *see* BLOW IN *v.*[2].

blow out of *v. see* BLOW OUT *v.*[4].

blow out the afterglow *v.* [many blacks had moved from candles and oil lamps to electricity only in the 1930s–40s] [1930s–40s] (*US black*) to turn out the lights.

blow over *v. see* BLOW IN *v.*[2].

blowpipe *n.* [1920s+] (*US*) a rifle.

blowsabella *n. see* BLOUZABELLA *n.*

blowse *n.* (*also* **blowz, blowze, blowsy**) [? link to Du. *blos*, blush. Bailey's *Universal Etymological Dict.* (1731) defines it as: 'a fat, red-faced, bloted wench, or one whose head is dressed like a slattern'] [late-16C–1900s] a slatternly a woman, a prostitute.

blowse *v.* [? Northumberland dial. *blow*, to breathe; but note *BIG GIRL'S BLOUSE under* BIG *adj.*; the image is of the stupidity of this form of drug-taking] [1980s+] (*drugs*) to sniff glue; usu. as *blowsing*, glue-sniffing.

blowsed-up *adj.* [BLOWSE *v.*] [1980s+] (*drugs*) intoxicated after sniffing glue.

blowser *n.*[1] (*also* **blouwzola**) [BLOWSE *n.*] [1920s+] a slatternly woman.

blowser *n.*[2] [BLOWSE *v.*] [1980s+] (*drugs*) a glue-sniffer.

blow sky high *v.* (*orig. US*) **1** [mid-19C+] (*also* **give sky-high, sky high**) to scold, to reprimand [ext. BLOW *v.*[1] (1b)]. **2** [1950s+] to destroy, to ruin [SE *blow up*]. **3** [1950s+] to collapse, to come to ruins [SE *blow up*].

blow (someone) away *v.* [ext. of SE use + southern dial. use or jazz use, for two bands to engage in an on-stage competition; the winner was deemed to have *blown away* its rival] **1** [1910s+] (*orig. US black*) (*also* **blow**) to shoot dead. **2** [1960s+] to defeat decisively. **3** [1960s+] to make intoxicated with a drug or drink. **4** [1970s+] (*orig. US teen*) to impress, to bowl over, to astound. **5** [1980s] (*US black*) to defeat verbally. **6** [1980s+] to kill.

blow someone down *v.*[1] [var. on BLOW (SOMEONE) AWAY *v.* (1)] [1930s–40s] to kill, to murder someone.

blow someone down *v.*[2] [1950s] to reject a sexual advance.

blow someone off *v. see* BLOW *v.*[2] (2c).

blow someone out *v.* **1** [1960s+] to exhaust. **2** [1970s] to shock. **3** [1970s+] to ignore, to dismiss, to reject; for one of a couple to abandon the relationship.

blowsy *n. see* BLOWSE *n.*

blowsy *adj.* [BLOW *v.*[1] (1e)] (*US black*) boastful, self-aggrandizing.

blow the froth (off) *v.* [1910s–30s] (*Aus.*) to drink beer; thus ext. to celebrate, to have a good time.

blow the froth off! *excl.* [BLOW THE FROTH (OFF) *v.*; the idea is of removing the superfluous] [1910s] (*Aus.*) a dismissive excl., stop being silly!

blow the socks off *v.* **1** [1960s+] to bring to orgasm. **2** *see* KNOCK THE SOCKS OFF *under* KNOCK *v.*

blow-through *n.* [SE *blow through*, the process of blowing steam through the cylinder of an engine etc, to clear it of air] [1940s–50s] an act of sexual intercourse.

IN PHRASES

▫ **have a blow-through** *v.* [1930s+] to have sexual intercourse.

blow through *v.* see BLOW *v.*[1] (4d).

blowtorch *n.* [1940s] (*US*) the penis.

blow-up *n.*[1] [SE *blow up*, to explode] **1** [late 18C–late 19C] a revelation, a discovery, esp. the embarrassment or confusion that follows such a revelation. **2** [late 18C+] a short-lived but emotional quarrel, a fit of temper. **3** [19C] a financial collapse. **4** [mid-19C–1910s] (*also* **blow**) a scolding, a telling off. **5** [1920s] (*US Und.*) a rumour.

blow-up *n.*[2] [1960s–70s] (*US black*) a natural hairstyle, cut short.

blow-up *n.*[3] [SE *blow up*, to inflate] [1980s+] (*drugs*) crack cocaine cut with lidocaine to increase the size, weight and street value.

blow up *v.*[1] **1** [early 17C–1930s] to ruin, to thrash severely. **2** [late 17C–early 19C] to ruin financially. **3** [mid-18C] to discredit, to betray. **4** [late 18C] to reveal. **5** [late 18C+] to tell off, to reprimand. **6** [early 19C] (*US*) to make pregnant. **7** [early 19C+] to lose control, to lose patience, to become enraged. **8** [late 19C+] (*US*) to overpraise; to aggrandize. **9** [20C+] to break down, of people (usu. athletes), animals (racehorses, greyhounds), schemes and plans, and machinery. **10** [1970s] (*US*) to shoot. **11** [1990s+] (*US black*) to use to excess. **12** [2000s] (*US black*) to raid, to invade.

blow up *v.*[2] **1** [late 19C+] (*orig. US*) to sound a whistle as a signal, e.g. at the end of a working day. **2** [1910s] (*Aus.*) to hail, to call out to. **3** [1930s] to wake up, to start work. **4** [2000s] (*US campus*) of a mobile phone, to ring.

blow up *v.*[3] **1** [1980s] (*US black*) to inherit a legacy. **2** [1980s+] (*rap music*) to achieve great success, esp. after a time of struggle and obscurity; also as adj. **3** [1990s+] (*US black*) to rush around. **4** [1990s+] (*US*) to make money quickly from selling drugs.

blow up *v.*[4] *see* BLOW IN *v.*[2].

blow up a storm *v.* [SE / BLOW *v.*[1] (5) + SE colloq. intensifier *up a storm*] [1950s+] **1** (*orig. US*) to play music with great energy and enthusiasm. **2** (*US drugs*) to get highly intoxicated from smoking a large quantity of marijuana. **3** to make a fuss.

blow upon *v.* **1** *see* BLOW *v.*[1] (1a). **2** *see* BLOW *v.*[1] (1c).

blow with a French faggot-stick *n.* (*also* **blow with a French cowl-staff, ...Naples cowl-staff**) [FRENCH *adj.* (1)] [17C–early 19C] the loss of one's nose through syphilis; thus *knocked with a French faggot-stick*, referring to those who are thus injured.

blowy *n. see* BLOWIE *n.*[1].

blowz *n. see* BLOUSE *n.* (1).

blowz/blowze *n. see* BLOWSE *n.*

blub *v.* [abbr. SE *blubber*] [mid-19C+] (*usu. juv.*) to cry, to burst into tears.

blubber *n.*[1] [BLAB *n.*] [late 18C] (*UK Und.*) the mouth.

IN PHRASES

▫ **stop someone's blubber** *v.* [early 18C] (*UK Und.*) to silence, poss. by murder.

blubber *n.*[2] [ext. of SE] **1** [late 18C] (*orig. Und.*) the female breasts. **2** [late 18C–early 19C] a fool. **3** [late 18C+] fatness, obesity; a fat person. **4** [late 19C] (*Aus.*) a jellyfish.

IN COMPOUNDS

▫ **blubberass** *n.* [ASS *n.* (2)] [1970s+] (*US*) a grossly fat person. ▫ **blubber-belly** *n.* [19C] a very fat person. ▫ **blubber-butt** *n.* [BUTT *n.*[1] (1)] [1950s+] (*orig. US*) a grossly fat person. ▫ **blubber-gut** *n.* (*also* **blubber-guts**) [1940s+] (*US*) a grossly fat person. ▫ **blubber-head** *n.* (*also* **blubber-noddle**) [-HEAD *sfx* (1)/NODDLE *n.* (1)] [late 18C–1950s] a fool; thus *blubber-headed*, foolish.

IN PHRASES

▫ **sport blubber** *v.* [late 18C–early 19C] of a woman, esp. when large and coarse, to expose one's breasts.

blubberation *n.* [BLUB *v.* + SE sfx *-eration*] [1910s] weeping.

blubbered *adj.* [one's muscles turn to *blubber*] [2000s] intoxicated by drink and/or drugs.

blubber-mouth *n.* (*also* **blubber-chops**) [SE *blubber* + *mouth/* CHOPS *n.*[1] (1)] (*US*) **1** [early–mid-19C; 1950s] (*also* **blubber mush**) one whose face has heavy jowls or ugly features [MUSH *n.*[2]]. **2** [1930s] one who cries readily.

blucher *n.* [proper name of Field-Marshal von *Blücher* (1742–1819). According to the Social Science Review (vol. I, 1864), the cabs were 'named after the Prussian Field Marshal who arrived on the field of Waterloo only to do the work that chanced to be undone'] [late 19C–1900s] an 'outsider' cab that is forbidden to enter the London railway termini.

bludge *n.* [BLUDGE *v.*] [1940s+] (*Aus.*) **1** a period of idleness, an undemanding job. **2** an imposition. **3** an act of scrounging. **4** an easy job, a sinecure.

bludge *v.* [backform. f. BLUDGER *n.*[2]] (*Aus.*) **1** [late 19C+] to evade one's responsibilities. **2** [1900s–10s] to live on the earnings of a prostitute. **3** [1940s+] to loaf about, to idle; thus adj. *bludging*. **4** [1940s+] to cadge, to scrounge; also as *bludge in*, to gatecrash.

IN PHRASES

▫ **on the bludge** [1940s+] (*Aus.*) scrounging.

bludgeon *n.* [late 19C] the penis.

bludgeon business *n.* [mid-19C] robbery with violence.

bludgeoner *n.* [mid-19C] **1** a pimp. **2** a tough man employed to keep order at a brothel. **3** (*US Und.*) the man who plays the 'outraged husband' in the BADGER GAME *under* BADGER *n.*[1].

bludgeon the beefsteak *v. see under* BEEF *n.*[1].

bludger *n.*[1] [? SE *bludgeoner*, thus ult. *bludgeon*] [mid-19C+] (*mainly Aus.*) a thief who is as willing to use violence as not.

bludger *n.*[2] [SE *bludgeoner*] (*Aus.*) **1** [late 19C+] a pimp. **2** [20C+] a general term of abuse, usu. implying that the person in question lives off the efforts and money of others. **3** [1910s+] a white-collar worker (from the point of view of a manual labourer, who sees such work as idling). **4** [1940s] (*also* **blodger**) an idler, a lazy person or creature. **5** [1940s+] (*Aus. Und.*) a police officer. **6** [1950s+] one who does not contribute their fair share.

IN PHRASES

▫ **come the bludge on** *v.* [20C+] (*Aus.*) to sponge on.

bludget *n.* [BLUDGER *n.*[1] + SE fem. sfx *-et(te)*] [1920s–40s] (*Aus./US*) a female thief.

blue *n.*[1] **1** a 'blue stocking' [abbr. SE *blue-stocking*, a term that originated *c.*1750 when a coterie of intellectual ladies – Mrs Montague, Mrs Vesey and Mrs Ord – set out to replace London society's trad. post-dinner pursuits – card-playing – with more cerebral amusements. Formal dress was no longer required and among those who attended their soirées was Benjamin Stillingfleet, who habitually wore grey or blue worsted, instead of black silk, stockings. Admiral Boscawen, a staunch traditionalist, labelled these events 'the Blue Stocking Society'; the ladies were called Blue Stockingers, then Blue Stocking Ladies and finally Blue Stockings]. (**a**) [late 18C–late 19C] an intellectual woman. (**b**) [mid–late 19C] (*US campus*) a puritanical, strait-laced student. **2** the colour. (**a**) [19C+] (*US black*) a dark-complexioned black person [note 18C–19C Lousiana dial. *blue*, a mix of Indian, black and white, as well as Allen, *The Language of Ethnic Conflict* 1983): '*Die Blaue*, which Mencken, *The American Language* (3rd edn, 1936), says was used for black servants by German residents of Baltimore in the 1880s; they changed it to *Die Schwarze* when the blacks caught on']. (**b**) [20C+] (*S.Afr.*) methylated spirits. (**c**) [1900s–10s] the sea. (**d**) [1910s+] (*Aus./N.Z.*) a summons; also used in milit. context, a 'write-up' [the colour of the paper on which it is printed; note H. Lawson short story (1899): 'His character was pretty bad just then, so there was a piece of blue paper cut for him']. (**e**) [1930s] (*US*) a blue poker chip. (**f**) [1940s–50s] (*US black*) the sky. (**g**) [1950s+] a £5 note. (**h**) *see* BLUE RUIN *under* BLUE *adj.*^{1}. (**i**) *see* BLUEY *n.*^{1} (3). **3** the colour of a uniform. (**a**) [mid-19C–1900s] a blue-uniformed soldier. (**b**) [mid-19C+] a police officer; the police. (**c**) [1930s+] (*US prison*) a prison inmate. **4** in drug uses [the colour of the pills]. (**a**) [1960s+] (*also* **double blue**) usu. in pl., an amphetamine. (**b**) [1960s+] a barbiturate. (**c**) [1970s] (*UK prison*) (*also* **double blue**) an amphetamine-barbiturate mixture. (**d**) [1980s+] crack cocaine [poss. mis-reading]. (**e**) [1990s+] (*drugs*) an ultra-thin Rizla paper – in a blue pack – used for rolling cannabis cigarettes or to wrap small amounts of cocaine. **5** *see* BLUECOAT *n.* (2). **6** *see* BLUE HEAVEN *under* BLUE *adj.*^{1}. **7** *see* BLUE PIGEON *n.* (2). **8** *see* BLUES *n.*^{1}. **9** *see* BLUEY *n.*^{1} (5).

IN PHRASES

❑ **bet on the blue** *v.* (*also* **bet on the Mary Lou**) [*Mary Lou* is rhy. sl.] [1920s+] (*Aus.*) to bet on credit. ❑ **bilk the blues** *v.* [BILK *v.* (1)] [mid-19C] to evade capture by the police. ❑ **cold on a blue** *adj.* (*also* **cold on the blue**) [COLD *adj.* (11)] [1990s+] (*Aus. Und.*) wrongfully imprisoned or arrested. ❑ **do up blue** *v. see* DO UP BROWN *under* BROWN *adj.*^{2}. ❑ **in the blue** [SE *the wild blue yonder*] [1920s–40s] **1** far away, off in the distance. **2** (*US*) in the clear, not guilty. **3** (*Aus.*) in trouble, in disgrace. ❑ **take a blue** *v.* [1910s] to drink a glass of absinthe.

SE in slang uses

IN PHRASES

❑ **old blue** *n. see* LONG-TAIL BLUE *n.* (1).

blue *n.*^{2} [BLUE *adj.*^{3}] **1** [mid-19C+] a 'smutty' anecdote, a piece of pornography. **2** [late 19C] an obscene or libidinous anecdote.

blue *n.*^{3} [BLUE *v.*^{4}] [1900s–30s] a drinking binge, a spree.

blue *n.*^{4} [abbr. BLOOMER *n.*^{2}] [1940s+] (*Aus./N.Z.*) **1** a blunder, a mistake. **2** a brawl, a quarrel. **3** a serious complaint, an objection.

IN PHRASES

❑ **bung on a blue** *v.* (*also* **put on a blue, stack on a blue**) [BUNG *v.* (3)] [1950s+] (*Aus.*) to make a fuss, to create a disturbance. ❑ **put a blue on** *v.* [1950s+] to make a fuss, to raise an issue. ❑ **send off the blue** *v.* [1970s+] (*N.Z.*) to start a fight. ❑ **smack a blue** *v.* [1930s+] (*Aus.*) to get into trouble. ❑ **wear the blue** *v.* [1990s+] to take the blame, to suffer punishment.

blue *adj.*^{1} [Ware cites a ballad from the reign of George III entitled 'The All-devouring monster. or New Five per C—t', attacking a plan to levy a 5% tax on all imports: 'The effects of the Tax will soon make us look Blue'] **1** [late 17C+] miserable, depressed. **2** [early 18C–1960s] confused, terrified, disappointed. **3** [mid-19C+] (*orig. US*) a general intensifier, e.g. *blue murder, scared blue*. **4** [mid-19C+] unpromising, discouraging. **5** *see* BLUE-NOSED *adj.* (3).

IN COMPOUNDS

❑ **blue boots** *n.* [alliteration] [1950s] (*US*) depression. ❑ **blue brick** *n.* [SE *brick*, i.e. the walls] [1980s] (*UK Und.*) a prison. ❑ **blue fear** *n.* [late 19C] very great fear. ❑ **blue funk** *n.* [FUNK *n.*^{2} (1) + ? the colour of the terrified individual's skin, which turns a leaden blue-grey] [mid-19C+] abject terror, utter cowardice, complete misery; thus *blue-funked*, utterly terrified.

IN PHRASES

❑ **look blue** *v.* [17C+] **1** to be astonished or surprised. **2** to look miserable, to look nervous.

SE in slang uses

IN COMPOUNDS

❑ **blue...** *n. see also under* relevant n.

pertaining to the police

IN COMPOUNDS

❑ **blue-and-white** *n.* [1970s+] (*US*) **1** a police car, painted in those colours (e.g. in New York City, Washington, DC). **2** a police officer in such a police car. ❑ **bluebelly** *n. see* separate entry. ❑ **blue bird** *n. see* separate entry. ❑ **blue bottle** *n. see* separate entry. ❑ **blue box** *n.* [1970s] (*US*) a police wagon. ❑ **blue boy** *n. see* separate entry. ❑ **blue bunnies** *n.* (*also* **blue jeans**) [1990s+] (*US black*) the police. ❑ **blue cap** *n.* [metonymy] **1** [1930s] a police officer. **2** *see also* general uses below. ❑ **blue coat** *n. see* separate entry. ❑ **blue dangers** *n.* [the colour of the vehicle or uniform] [1960s+] (*US Und.*) **1** marked police cars (when painted blue, as in New York). **2** blue-uniformed police officers. ❑ **blue devil** *n. see* separate entry. ❑ **blue heeler** *n.* [SAusE *blue heeler*, a cattle dog] **1** [1990s+] (*Aus.*) a police officer. **2** *see also* general uses below. ❑ **bluejacket** *n. see* separate entry. ❑ **blue lamp boy** *n.* (*also* **blue lamp**) [the blue lamp that hung outside UK police stations; note 1949 movie *The Blue Lamp*] [1900s–50s] (*juv.*) a police officer. ❑ **blue light** *n.* **1** *see* separate entry. **2** *see also* general uses below. ❑ **blue light special** *n. see* separate entry. ❑ **blue meanie** *n.* [*Blue Meanies*, the 'villains' of the animated film *Yellow Submarine* (1968), featuring the Beatles] [1960s–70s] a police officer; thus the establishment in general. ❑ **blue pig** *n.* **1** *see* separate entry. **2** *see also* general uses below. ❑ **blue suit** *n.* [the uniform] [1950s] (*US*) a uniformed police officer. ❑ **bluetop** *n.* [the flashing light on the top] [1990s+] a police car.

pertaining to drugs

IN COMPOUNDS

❑ **blue angel** *n.* [the drugs come in blue capsules] **1** [1970s+] (*drugs*) a barbiturate. **2** *see* BLUE HEAVEN below. ❑ **blue bomber** *n.* [the colour of the pill or capsule] [1970s] (*US drugs*) valium. ❑ **blue boy** *n. see* separate entry. ❑ **blue bullets** *n.* [the packaging] [1960s+] barbiturates. ❑ **blue chairs** *n.* [ety. unknown; ? mispron. of BLUE CHEER below] [1980s+] (*drugs*) LSD. ❑ **blue cheer** *n.* [the laundry detergent *Blue Cheer* and/or the rock band of the same name] [1960s] (*US drugs*) a capsule of LSD cut with methamphetamine or some other form of 'speed'. ❑ **blue clouds** *n.* [packaging] [1970s+] (*drugs*) amobarbital sodium. ❑ **blue devil** *n. see* separate entry. ❑ **blue dolls** *n.* [DOLL *n.*^{2}] [1960s] (*drugs*) barbiturates. ❑ **blue dragons** *n.* [the packaging] [1970s] (*US drugs*) barbiturates. ❑ **blue heaven** *n.* (*also* **blue, blue angel**) [colour of capsule/tablet + play on the popular song 'My Blue Heaven' (1927)] (*drugs*) **1** [1950s+] amytal barbiturate. **2** [1960s+] LSD. **3** [1980s+] alkyl nitrates. ❑ **bluejay** *n.* [the capsule's colour] [1950s] (*US drugs*) a capsule of sodium amytal. ❑ **blue microdot** *n.* (*also* **blue mist**) [MICRODOT *n.*/MIST *n.*] [1960s+] (*drugs*) LSD. ❑ **blue moons** *n. see* separate entry. ❑ **blue mystic** *n.* [2000s] (*US drugs*) a synthetic drug popular in the Ecstasy and club drug scene. ❑ **blue sky** *n.* **1** *see* separate entry. **2** *see also* general terms below. ❑ **blue star** *n.* [1980s+] (*drugs*) a variety of LSD, emblazoned with a blue star symbol. ❑ **blue tips** *n.* [packaging of the capsule] [1970s+] (*drugs*) a depressant. ❑ **blue velvet** *n.* [the 'smoothness' of its effects] [1960s–70s] (*drugs*) a mixture of an antihistamine and paregoric. ❑ **blue vials** *n.* [packaging] [1980s+] (*drugs*) LSD.

IN PHRASES

❑ **blue de hue** *n. see* separate entry. ❑ **blue sky blond** *n. see* separate entry.

general uses

IN COMPOUNDS

❑ **bluebacks** *n.* [its colour] **1** [mid–late 19C] (*US*) money issued by the Confederate States of America. **2** [late 19C] (*S.Afr.*) money issued briefly by the Orange Free State. ❑ **blue-bellied/belly** *see* separate entries. ❑ **blueberry pie** *n. see* separate entry. ❑ **bluebird** *n. see* separate entries. ❑ **blue billy** *n.* **1** [mid–late 19C] a blue handkerchief with white spots, worn and used at prize fights [BILLY *n.*^{4}; 'Before a set to it is common to take it from the neck and tie it round the leg as a garter, or round the waist to "keep it in the wind"' (Hotten, 1867). The *blue billy* made its way to New York where it was defined in a detective manual (*c.*1870) as 'a strange handkerchief']. **2** [late 19C] refuse ammoniacal lime from gas factories [the colour]. ❑ **blue boar** *n.* [? the notorious *Blue Boar* tavern in London, sited on the corner of Oxford Street and Tottenham Court Road, next to the St Giles rookery, and thus a centre of lowlife] [late 18C–late-19C] a venereal bubo. ❑ **blue board** *n.* [ext. of BLUE BOAR above] [20C+] a venereal bubo. ❑ **bluebottle** *n. see* separate entry. ❑ **blue boy** *n.* *see* separate entries. ❑ **blue broadway** *n.* [the *blue* sky + image of *Broadway*, New York, then in its prime, as an earthly version of paradise] [1940s] (*US black/Harlem*) Heaven. ❑ **blue butter** *n.* [the mercury on which it was based] [mid-19C–1900s] an ointment used for the treatment of venereal sores. ❑ **blue cap** *n.* [metonymy] **1** [late 16C–early 18C] a Scotsman. **2** *see also* police terms above. ❑ **blue cent** *n. see* RED CENT *n.* ❑ **blue cheek** *n.* [mid-19C] a style for facial hair whereby all whiskers were shaved off, leaving the cheek 'blue'. ❑ **blue cheese** *n.* [? its consistency] [1950s–70s] (*US drugs*) hashish. ❑ **blue-chin/chinned** *see* separate entries. ❑ **bluecoat** *n. see* separate entry. ❑ **blue devil/devils** *n. see* separate entries. ❑ **blue duck** *n.* [DEAD DUCK *n.* (1)] **1** [late 19C+] (*Aus.*) a lost cause, a failure. **2** [1980s] (*N.Z.*) a (baseless) rumour. ❑ **blue-eyed** *adj. see* separate entry. ❑ **blue-eyed boy/soul/soul brother** *n. see* separate entries. ❑ **blue flag** *n.* [their blue apron] [late 18C–early 19C] a publican. ❑ **bluefoot** *n. see* separate entry. ❑ **blue-foot nigger** *n. see* separate entry. ❑ **blue goose** *see* separate entries. ❑ **bluegown** *n.* [metonymy; prostitutes confined in a house of correction wore a blue dress as their uniform] [late 16C–early 17C] a prostitute. ❑ **bluegrass** *v. see* separate entry. ❑ **blue gum** *n. see* separate entries. ❑ **bluehair** *n.* (*also* **bluehaired**) [the bluish tint that old ladies sometimes have put into their otherwise grey hair] [1980s+] (*US campus*) an old person, usu. female. ❑ **bluehead** *n.* [? it has a bluish tinge] [mid-19C] (*US*) strong and illicitly distilled whisky. ❑ **blue heeler** *n.* [SAusE *blue heeler*, a cattle dog; the Fosters can is predominantly blue] **1** [1980s] (*Aus.*) a can of Fosters lager. **2** *see also* police terms above. ❑ **blue hen's chicken** *n. see* separate entry. ❑ **blue jacket** *n. see* separate entry. ❑ **blue Jews** *n.* [the trad. colour + play on stereotypical Jewish names, i.e. Levi-Strauss] [1970s] (*US gay*) a pair of blue denim Levis, usu. tight. ❑ **blue john** *n.* [such milk has a slightly blue tinge] (*US*) **1** [mid-19C+] skim milk. **2** [1900s] sour or nearly sour milk. ❑ **blue johnny** *n.* [his uniform + generic use of proper name] [mid-19C] (*US*) a Northern, Unionist soldier. ❑ **blue lady** *n.* [2000s] (*N.Z.*) methylated spirits. ❑ **blue light** *n.* **1** *see* separate entries. **2** *see also* police terms above. ❑ **blue-metal** *v.* [SE *blue metal*, small pieces of stone, used in street-fights] [late 19C–1940s] (*Aus.*) to throw pieces of stone, esp. in a street-fight. ❑ **blue Monday** *n. see* separate entry. ❑ **blue moon** *see* separate entries. ❑ **blue mouldies** *n. see* BLUES *n.*[1]. ❑ **blue-nine** *n.* [1970s] (*S.Afr.*) a petty thief or confidence trickster. ❑ **bluenose/bluenosed/bluenoser** *see* separate entries. ❑ **blue ocean** *n.* [1980s+] (*S.Afr.*) methylated spirits. ❑ **blue one** *n.* **1** [1950s] (*Irish*) a ten-pound note. **2** [1990s+] (*Scot.*) a five-pound note. ❑ **blue paper** *n. see* BLUEY *n.*[1] (6). ❑ **blue-pencil** *v. see* separate entry. ❑ **blue pig** *n.* **1** *see* separate entry. **2** *see also* police terms above. ❑ **blue pigeon** *n. see* separate entries. ❑ **blue pill** *n.* [SE *blue*, lead + SE *pill*/PILL *n.* (1e)] [mid–late 19C] (*US*) a bullet. ❑ **blue plum** *n.* (*also* **blue plumb**) [*plumb*, a small piece of lead + pun on the fruit] [late 18C–early 19C] a bullet; thus *give one a taste of plum*, to wound or kill with a bullet; thus *surfeited with a blue plumb*, wounded by gunfire. ❑ **blue ribbon/ribboner** *n. see* separate entries. ❑ **blue room** *n.* [its lack of light + once incarcerated there, one feels BLUE *adj.*[1] (1)] **1** [1920s+] (*US Und.*) a punishment cell. **2** [1950s+] (*Aus.*) an interrogation room in a police station. ❑ **blue ruin** *n.* [*BLUE TAPE* below/BLUE RIBBON *n.* etc + SE *ruin*; i.e. its effects] **1** [19C–1900s] (*also* **blue**) gin, esp. second-rate gin. **2** [mid-19C] (*US*) a strong kind of apple-jack, peach-brandy or whisky. ❑ **blue serge** *n.* [1920s] (*US*) a male sweetheart. ❑ **blueshirt** *n.* **1** [1920s+] (*Aus.*) a farmer or estate owner. **2** [1920s+] (*Aus.*) a lazy worker, a slacker. **3** [1930s] (*Irish*) a member of the Fine Gael party, thus anyone espousing right-wing views [the *Blueshirts*, a 1930s Irish fascist movement, named for their uniform]. ❑ **blueskin** *n. see* separate entry. ❑ **blue sky** **1** *see* separate entries. **2** *see also* drug terms above. ❑ **blue-steel** *n.* [its manufacture] [1940s–60s] (*US*) a pistol. ❑ **blue stocking** *n.* [17C *blue*, used after the Restoration of Charles II in 1660 to denote any diehard Puritan who disapproved of the new moral freedoms] [19C–1920s] (*US*) a puritan, esp. a Presbyterian. ❑ **bluestone** *n.* [SE *bluestone*, copper sulphate or vitriol] [late 19C–1940s] the very lowest quality of gin or whisky. ❑ **blue tape** *n.* [TAPE *n.*] [late 18C–mid-19C] gin, esp. second-rate gin. ❑ **blue-tongue** *n.* [SE *blue-tongue*, an Australian lizard of the genus *Tiliqua*, belonging to the family Scincidae; the ref. is to the sleepiness of such lizards] [1900s–50s] (*Aus.*) a roustabout, an itinerant labourer. ❑ **blue train** *n. see* *BLOUTREIN under* BLOU *adj.* ❑ **Blue 'Un** *n. see* separate entry. ❑ **blue-vein/-veined** *see* separate entries. ❑ **blue whistler** *n.* [the *blue* lead in the bullet and the noise it makes; note the Civil War-era cannon named 'The Blue Whistler', used at the battle of Val Verde, NM] [mid–late 19C] (*US*) a bullet.

IN PHRASES

❑ **get the blue envelope** *v.* [the packaging of a note of dismissal + ? BLUE *adj.*[1] (4)] [1900s–30s] (*US*) to be dismissed from one's job.

IN EXCLAMATIONS

❑ **blue blimey!** *see* BLIMEY! *excl.* ❑ **blue me!** *see* separate entry. ❑ **by all that's blue!** [Fr. *parbleu!* lit. 'by (a) blue (thing)!'] [mid-19C] a mild excl. or oath.

blue *adj.*[2] [? 'blue in the face'] **1** [early 19C+] (*US/Aus.*) drunk.; thus *blue willies*, delirium tremens [appears in the early 19C US, lasts until the mid-century then re-emerges in Australia by the early 20C]. **2** [1940s+] (*S.Afr.*) under the influence of marijuana.

IN COMPOUNDS

❑ **blue-blinded** *adj.* [*BLUE-BLIND (PARALYTIC)* below] [1910s] (*Aus.*) utterly overcome. ❑ **blue-blind (paralytic)** *adj.* [BLIND *adj.*[1] (1)] [1900s–10s] (*Aus.*) extremely drunk. ❑ **blue-eyed** *adj. see* separate entry.

blue *adj.*[3] (*also* **azure, indigo**) [? *BLUEGOWN under* BLUE *adj.*[1], the Fr. *Bibliothèque bleue*, 'a series of books of questionable character' (F&H) or as the opposite of BROWN *adj.*[2] (1); note the *papier bleu* which in 18C covered the pornographic or seditious material on the tray of a *colporteur*, an itinerant Parisian bookseller] [early 19C+] coarse, obscene, pornographic; thus *blue film*, *blue movie*; thus, constr. with *the*, coarseness, obscenity.

IN COMPOUNDS

❑ **blue light** *n. see* separate entry.

IN PHRASES

❑ **burn it blue** *v.* [early 18C] to act outrageously, poss. by speaking very coarsely. ❑ **make the air blue** *v.* (*also* **make the air turn blue, turn the air blue**) [late 19C+] to swear, to use obscenities.

blue *adj.*[4] [BLUE *n.*[1] (1)] [mid-19C] of a woman, intellectual; thus (*US campus*) excessively hard-working, overly dedicated.

blue *adj.*[5] [late 19C+] a euph. for BLOODY *adj.* (1).

IN COMPOUNDS

❑ **blue-blasted** *adj.* [mid-19C] (*US*) euph. for DAMNED *adj.* (1). ❑ **blue blazes** *n.* (*also* **blue blaizes**) [BLAZES *n.* (1)] [19C+] a euph. for *hell*, usu. in phr., e.g. *hot as blue blazes*, *go blue blazes*. ❑ **blue damn** *n.* [SE *damn*] [late 19C–1900s] an oath. ❑ **blue murder** *n. see* separate entry.

IN EXCLAMATIONS

❑ **what the blue blazes!** (*also* **what the blue hell!**) [early 19C+] a general excl. of extreme surprise, absolute confusion etc. ❑ **who in blue!** [1970s] (*US black*) an intensifiying excl. used to underline a question; euph. of HELL *n.* etc.

blue *adj.*[6] [BLUESKIN *n.* (2) + see combs. below for earlier uses] [1920s+] black, as in skin colour.

IN COMPOUNDS

❑ **blue-black** *adj.* [late 19C+] (*US black*) of skin colour, so dark it seems to have tints of blue. ❑ **blue boy** *n. see* separate entry. ❑ **blueskin** *n. see* separate entry.

IN PHRASES

❑ **one of the blue squadron** *n.* [BLUESKIN *n.* (2a)] late 18C–early 19C a mulatto.

blue *adj.*[7] [? BLUE *adj.*[3] or ? the trad. colour of clothing for baby boys] [1990s+] (*US gay*) homosexual.

IN PHRASES

□ **blue-arsed bandit** *n.* [ext. of ARSE BANDIT *n.*] [1990s+] a homosexual male.

blue *v.*^{1} [the colouring (actually dark red) of one's complexion] [early 18C] to blush.

blue *v.*^{2} [BLOW *v.*^{2} (2)] **1** [mid–late 19C] (*also* **blue in**) to pawn. **2** [late 19C] to make a blunder, to be a mistake. **3** *see* BLEW IN *V.*

blue *v.*^{3} [BLUE *n.*^{4} (2)] [1960s+] (*Aus.*) **1** to argue, to fight; thus *blueing*, brawling, fighting. **2** to reprimand, to swear at. **3** to boast.

blue *v.*^{4} *see* BLOW *v.*^{2} (2).

blue-bellied *adj.* [BLUEBELLY *n.*] (*US*) **1** [mid-18C–1920s] of a person, despicable, repellent. **2** [mid-19C–1910s] (*US, Southern*) pertaining to a Northerner, esp. a New Englander.

bluebelly *n.* **1** [early 19C+] (*US, Southern*) a Northerner, a Yankee, esp. a Northern soldier during the Civil War (1861–5) [the uniform of the Northern troops]. **2** [late 19C–1940s] a police officer; thus *blue-bellied*, a derog. adj. for a member of the police [the uniform].

blueberry (hill) *n.* [rhy. sl. = OLD BILL *n.*] [1960s+] the police.

blueberry pie *n.* [the blue uniform + something one can EAT *V.* (4)] [1960s+] (*US gay*) a sailor.

bluebird *n.*^{1} **1** [mid-19C] (*US Southern*) a Northern, Unionist soldier [the colour of the uniform]. **2** [1910s–60s] (*US*) a police officer [the colour of the uniform]. **3** [1930s–70s] (*Aus./US*) a police car, a police wagon [the colour of the Buicks and later Fords that fulfilled the role]. **4** [1960s+] (*drugs*) a blue capsule of sodium amytal [packaging].

bluebird *n.*^{2} [BLUE *adj.*^{1} (4)] [1990s+] (*US black teen*) something annoying or worrying.

bluebird chip *n.* [a pun on the blue packaging of the Bluebird potato chip brand] [2000s] (*N.Z.*) a NZ$10 note.

bluebottle *n.* [Hotten notes a 'singular' pre-dating in Shakespeare's synon. use of *bluebottle* as a beadle in *King Henry IV* Pt. I (1597)] **1** [late 16C–early 17C] a beadle. **2** [mid-19C+] (*also* **bottle**) a police officer; thus *bluebottle mob*, the police force.

blue boy *n.*^{1} [var. on *BLUE BOAR under* BLUE *adj.*^{1}] [18C–19C] a venereal bubo.

blue boy *n.*^{2} (*also* **boy blue**) [colour] **1** [late 19C+] a police officer, a police car. **2** [1960s] (*US prison*) a warder. **3** [2000s] (*drugs*) amphetamine.

blue boy *n.*^{3} [BLUE *adj.*^{6}] [1950s] (*US black*) a black male.

blue-chin *n.* [actors tend to shave for the evening performance rather than in the morning] [20C+] (*Aus.*) an actor.

blue-chinned *adj.* [BLUE-CHIN *n.* and the fact that not shaving can make one's chin look blue] [1900s] unshaven, usu. of actors.

bluecoat *n.* **1** [late 16C–18C] a servant who wore a blue coat; a servant's coat. **2** [late 16C–1930s] (*also* **blue, blue clothes**) a member of the authorities who wears a blue coat, spec. a beadle in the 16C and later a policeman; thus adj. *blue-coated*. **3** [mid-19C] (*US, Southern*) a Northern, Unionist soldier; later any soldier. **4** [1940s+] (*S.Afr.*) (*also* **bluejacket**) a habitual criminal serving an indeterminate sentence; an indeterminate sentence of 9–15 years.

blued *adj.*^{1} (*also* **blewed**) [BLUE *adj.*^{2} (1)] [mid-19C] drunk.

blued *adj.*^{2} [BLUE *adj.*^{1} (1)] [mid–late 19C] depressed.

blue de hue *n.* [internal rhy.; Hue ('Hoo-ay') is a major city in Vietnam] [1970s] (*drugs*) marijuana from Vietnam.

blue devil *n.*^{1} (*also* **devil in blue**) [the blue uniform] [mid-19C] **1** (*US*) a servant. **2** (*UK/US Und.*) a policeman.

blue devil *n.*^{2} [packaging] [1960s–70s] (*drugs*) a depressant, esp. Phenobarbitone (luminal), amobarbital.

blue devils *n.* **1** [18C+] a fit of depression; thus *blue-devilled*, depressed [BLUE *adj.*^{1} (1), feelings that 'bedevil' the sufferer]. **2** [19C+] delirium tremens [the 'blue devils' the drunkard supposedly sees].

IN PHRASES

□ **give someone blue devil** *v.* [1980s+] to be angry with someone.

blue-eyed *adj.*^{1} [BLUE *adj.*^{2} (1)] [mid-19C] (*US campus*) drunk.

blue-eyed *adj.*^{2} [note BLUE *adj.*^{5}] [20C+] (*US*) euph. for DAMNED *adj.*, esp. in phr. *what in the blue-eyed world*.

blue-eyed boy *n.* (*also* **blue eyes**) [SE f. 1930] [1910s–30s] a special favourite.

blue-eyed soul *n.* [SE *blue-eyed*, i.e. shorthand for white + *soul music*] [1960s+] (*US black*) the characteristic of emotional sensitivity (i.e. 'soul') applied to white people.

blue-eyed soul brother *n.* (*also* **blue-eyed soul sister, blue-eyed brother, ...sister**) [SE *blue-eyed* + SOUL BROTHER *under* SOUL *adj.*^{1}/SOUL SISTER *under* SOUL *adj.*^{1}] [1970s+] (*US black*) any white who is accepted as genuinely friendly towards blacks.

blue eyes *n.* *see* BLUE-EYED BOY *n.*

blue foot *n.* [? she is cold from standing in the street] [1970s–80s] (*UK black*) a prostitute.

blue-foot nigger *n.* [? their skin-tone] [1920s+] (*W.I.*) a mulatto, esp. one who is despised.

blue goose *n.* [? *LIKE SHIT THROUGH A GOOSE under* SHIT *n.*] (*US*) **1** [1920s–30s] the general convict cage at a prison camp. **2** [1960s] a small, run-down café or bar. **3** [1960s] an establishment where liquor is sold illegally.

blue goose *v.* [GOOSE *v.*^{3} (5)] [1970s] (*US black*) to engage in sexual affairs.

bluegrass *v.* [the *Bluegrass State*, the nickname of Kentucky] [1950s–60s] (*US drugs*) to commit a drug user to the Lexington Federal Narcotics Hospital in Lexington, Kentucky.

blue gum *n.*^{1} [the bluish gums that many blacks have] (*US*) **1** [mid-19C+] (*also* **bluegum moke, bluegum terror**) a black person, seen by the (white) speaker as especially malevolent; the belief was that their bite is supposedly poisonous [MOKE *n.*^{2} (1)]. **2** [late 19C+] a very dark black person; thus adj. *blue-gummed*. **3** [1970s] a person of mixed Indian, white and black ancestry.

blue gum *n.*^{2} [ety. unknown] [20C+] (*US*) bootleg whisky.

blue hen's chicken *n.* [SE *blue hen*, a hen supposed to breed first-rate fighting cocks; the US state of Delaware is known as 'the Blue Hen State'] **1** [late 18C+] a resident of the state of Delaware. **2** [late 18C+] (*US*) a spirited, plucky person, a good fighter. **3** [early 19C] a dominant, aggressive and esp. short-tempered person, esp. a woman. **4** [20C+] an important person or one who poses as such.

blue in *v.*^{1} *see* BLEW IN *V.*

blue in *v.*^{2} *see* BLUE *v.*^{2} (1).

bluejacket *n.* [the uniform] **1** [19C–1910s] a sailor. **2** [mid-19C] (*US*) an abolitionist. **3** [mid-19C+] a police officer. **4** [late 19C] a coast guard. **5** *see* BLUECOAT *n.* (4).

blue-jeans femme *n.* *see LOW FEMME under* LOW *adj.*

blue light *n.*^{1} [SE *blue laws*, severely puritanical laws enacted in New England; ? the blue light that signifies a police station; note WW1 Aus. milit. *blue light*, 'a prophylactic establishment'; note US *blue light*, one who opposed the War of 1812] **1** [19C] (*US*) a pious, sanctimonious individual. **2** [mid–late 19C] (*US campus*) a student who informs on other students to the authorities.

blue light *n.*^{2} [the rotating/flashing blue lights on top of police cars] **1** [1930s+] a police car. **2** [2000s] (*US*) a police officer.

blue light *n.*^{3} [? BLUE *adj.*^{3}] [1940s+] (*W.I.*) an obscenity, a swearword, a coarse, vulgar expression.

IN PHRASES

□ **drop blue lights** *v.* *see under* DROP *V.*^{1}.

blue-light (clinic) *n.* [its 'signpost'] [20C+] (*Aus.*) a venereal disease clinic.

blue light special *n.* [1990s+] (*US black*) **1** a police officer [SE *blue lights* on police cars + play on *blue-plate special*]. **2** a cheap, low-quality retail item.

blue me! *excl.* [var. on BLOW ME! *excl.*^{1}] [late 19C] (*Aus.*) a general excl. of emphasis.

blue Monday *n.* **1** [mid-19C–1920s] a Monday taken off work and dedicated to self-indulgence [BLUE *adj.*^{2} (1)]. **2** [1960s] a start-of-the-week feeling of depression that follows a weekend of pleasurable excess [BLUE *adj.*^{1} (1)].

blue moon *n.*^{1} [rhy. sl.] [20C+] a spoon.

blue moon *n.*[2] [rhy. sl. = HOON *n.* (2)] [1970s+] (*Aus.*) a pimp.

blue moon *v.* [rhy. sl. = SPOON *v.*[1]] [late 19C–1930s] to romance, to 'chat up'.

blue moons *n.* [its bluish tinge] [1960s+] (*US drugs*) **1** (*also* **blue sage**) a variety of marijuana. **2** LSD.

blue-mouldy *adj. see* MOULDY *adj.*

blue murder *n.* (*also* **bloody murder**) [BLUE *adj.*[5] + SE *murder*] [mid-19C+] cries of terror, horror, alarm; usu. in phrs. below.

IN PHRASES

❑ **like blue murder** *adv.* (*also* **like blue stink**) [mid-19C+] **1** very quickly, at top speed. **2** to a great extent; very much. ❑ **out for blue murder** *adj.* [1950s] very angry. ❑ **screaming blue murder** *adj.* (*also* **hollering blue murder, yelling..., screaming bloody murder**) [mid-19C+] in a state of hysteria, utterly and completely overwrought or terrified.

bluenose *n.*[1] **1** [late 18C+] (*US*) a Canadian, esp. a resident of Nova Scotia [SE *bluenose*, a variety of potato native to Nova Scotia, but note late 17C Scot. *bluenose*, a Scot. Presbyterian and the stereotyped New England Yankee, seen as BLUE-NOSED *adj.* (3), thus the northern nose is *blue* with chilly disapproval]. **2** [mid-19C] (*US*) a Northerner, esp. a New Englander. **3** [late 19C+] (*US*) a dedicated, fanatical puritan, almost invariably a teetotaller [orig. an aristocrat (who had 'blue blood'), *bluenoses* passed the repressive 'blue laws' that restricted the morals of many states ? + the opposite of the drunk, who boasts a conspicuously red nose]. **4** [1930s+] someone who sees themselves as superior to their neighbours.

bluenose *n.*[2] [analogous with BROWN NOSE *n.*] [1960s] (*US*) a sycophant, a toady.

bluenose *v.* [BLUENOSE *n.*[2]] [1960s] (*US campus*) to toady.

blue-nosed *adj.* [BLUENOSE *n.*[1]] (*orig. US*) **1** [early 19C+] pertaining to being a Nova Scotian. **2** [mid-19C+] pertaining to being a New Englander, esp. as *blue-nosed Yankee*. **3** [mid-19C+] (*also* **blue**) rigidly, repressively puritan. **4** [1950s] snobbish.

bluenoser *n.* [BLUENOSE *n.*[1]] (*US*) **1** [mid-19C–1930s] a Canadian. **2** [late 19C] a Nova-Scotian ship. **3** [1970s] a fanatical puritan.

blue o'clock in the morning *n.* [rhy. sl. *two o'clock*] [late 19C–1900s] the last minutes of proper night-time, when darkness is gradually giving way to dawn.

blue-pencil *v.* [the trad. colour of the editor's pencil] **1** [late 19C+] to censor, to edit by cutting; thus as n. *blue pencil*, the act of censorship. **2** [1900s] in ext. use, to bring to a conclusion.

IN PHRASES

❑ **get the blue pencil** *v.* [late 19C] (*US*) to be verbally abused.

blue pig *n.*[1] [BLUE GOOSE *n.* + BLIND PIG *n.*] [1950s+] (*US*) **1** an unlicensed drinking house, a speakeasy, an 'after-hours' bar. **2** the whisky served in such an establishment.

blue pig *n.*[2] [colour of the uniform + PIG *n.* (2a)] [1970s] a police officer.

blue pigeon *n.* [late 18C–late 19C] (*UK Und.*) **1** a thief who specializes in stealing the lead from roofs [like an avian pigeon, the thief 'perches' on a church roof]. **2** (*also* **blue, pigeon**) small off-cuts of lead or similar materials, taken from the job in hand and sold off as perks by plumbers.

IN PHRASES

❑ **fly a blue pigeon** *v.* (*also* **fly the blue pigeon, fly the pigeon**) [late 18C–1900s] to steal the lead from a church roof; thus *pigeon-flying*, conducting such thefts.

blue pigeon flyer *n.* (*also* **blue pigeon flier**) [ext. of BLUE PIGEON *n.* (1)] [mid-19C] a stealer of lead from the roofs of buildings; such a thief poses as a journeyman glazier, plumber or other workman who gets to the roof, strips off the lead and hides it (often by wrapping it round the body) before leaving the house.

bluer *n.* [BLUE *n.*[4] (2)] [2000s] (*Aus.*) a brawler, a fighter.

blue ribbon *n.* [SE *blue ribbon*, a blue ribbon worn as a badge of honour; thus referring to the quality of the best gin] [early 19C] gin.

blue ribboner *n.* (*also* **blue ribbonite, blue ribbon army**) [the *blue ribbons* such individuals wore to proclaim their drink-free status. A Blue Ribbon Army was instituted in 1882, but the Army and its ribbons had virtually vanished by 1896] [late 19C–1900s] a teetotaller, a total abstainer.

blue ribbon fakers *n.* (*also* **blue ribbon army**) [BLUE RIBBONER *n.* + FAKER *n.* (5)] [late 19C–1900s] a teetotaller, a total abstainer.

blues *n.*[1] (*also* **blue, blue mouldies**) [orig. general, white use, despite assumption that the term was created/patented by US blacks. The *OED*'s first citation is from a letter by the actor David Garrick (11 July 1741): 'I am far from being quite well, tho not troubled wth ye Blews as I have been'] **1** [mid-18C+] misery, depression, unhappiness. **2** [1970s] a problem.

IN PHRASES

❑ **cry the blues** *v.* **1** [1930s] (*US*) to complain, to whinge, to bemoan one's lot. **2** [1950s] to mourn, to regret. ❑ **in the blue** [note WW1 milit. *in the blue*, referring to troops who were in difficulties, e.g. from a failed attack] [1920s+] (*Aus.*) **1** in debt, in difficulties. **2** out of control. ❑ **in the blues** **1** [19C] suffering a fit of delirium tremens. [BLUE DEVILS *n.*] **2** [mid-19C] depressed. ❑ **sing the blues** *v.* [1910s+] to complain, to whinge. ❑ **sob the blues** *v.* [1920s–30s] to be very unhappy.

blues *n.*[2] [the colour] **1** [late 19C+] the police. **2** [1910s+] (*Aus./US*) a blue uniform. **3** [1940s] any trousers. **4** [1940s] a police uniform. **5** [1960s+] (*US prison*) a prison uniform. **6** [1960s+] amphetamines. **7** [1970s] (*US*) a sailor's trousers. **8** [1970s+] (*US*) blue jeans. **9** [1980s+] (*Aus. prison*) prison officers; thus used as adj. to refer to staff activity, e.g. *blue talk*, prison officer conversations etc.

blues *n.*[3] [? BLUE *n.*[3]] [1970s+] (*W.I.*) a shebeen, an illegal drinking club or a party where drink is sold without a licence.

blue sage *n. see* BLUE MOONS *n.* (1).

blueskin *n.* **1** from the colour of a uniform. (**a**) [late 18C] (*US*) a keen supporter of the American Revolution. (**b**) [mid-19C] (*US*) a Northern, Unionist soldier. **2** from skin tone. (**a**) [late 18C–early 19C] the offspring of a white man and a black woman, a mulatto. (**b**) [early–mid-19C] a black person. (**c**) [late 19C] the penis. **3** a moralist [on basis of BLUE *n.*[1] (1b) / the repressive 'blue laws' passed in New England; i.e. their demeanour]. (**a**) [late 18C–mid-19C] (*US*) a puritan, a repressive moralist. (**b**) [mid-19C] a Presbyterian.

blue sky *n.*[1] [? the view] [1940s–80s] (*S.Afr.*) the Cinderella Prison in Boksburg.

blue sky *n.*[2] [1950s] (*US*) fig. a 'dream', a fantasy.

blue sky *n.*[3] (*also* **sky**) [? BLUE SKY *v.*; i.e. the dreaminess produced by the drug] [1980s+] (*US drugs*) heroin.

blue-sky *adj.* [BLUE SKY *n.*[2]] [1950s] (*US*) ultimate, as dreamed of.

blue sky *v.* [one is day-dreaming, fig. gazing at the sky] [1950s+] (*US*) to talk unrestrainedly, in a speculative manner; thus [1970s] *blue-skyer*, *blue-sky artist*, one who speculates freely, with little basis in fact.

blue sky blond *n.* [the light colour of the leaves] [1980s+] (*drugs*) high potency marijuana from Columbia.

Bluestone College *n.* [SE *bluestone*, the material of which the prison is constructed + COLLEGE *n.* (3)] [2000s] (*Aus. prison/Und.*) Pentridge prison, Coburg, Victoria.

bluetit *n. see* TIT *n.*[2] (6).

Blue 'Un, the *n.* [so named to distinguish it from the PINK 'UN, THE *n.* (3) and the BROWN 'UN, THE *n.*] [late 19C–1900s] the *Winning Post*, a sporting newspaper.

blue vein *n.* (*also* **blue veiner**) [the vein that runs up the penis] **1** [1970s] an erection. **2** [1980s+] (*Aus. prison/N.Z.*) the penis.

blue-veined *adj.* [BLUE VEIN *n.*] in combs. referring to the penis.

IN COMPOUNDS

❑ **blue-veined custard chucker** *n.* [CUSTARD *n.* (2) + SE *chucker*] [1990s+] the penis. ❑ **blue-veined havana** *n.* [SE *Havana* (cigar) + SMOKE *v.*[3]] [1990s+] penis; thus *smoke the blue-veined havana*, to fellate someone. ❑ **blue-veined junket pump** *n.* (*also* **purple-veined junket gun, ...porridge gun, ...yoghurt gun**) [SE *junket* + *pump*; *porridge/yoghurt* + *gun*]

[1980s+] the penis. ❑ **blue-veined piccolo** *n.* [SE *piccolo*] [1990s+] the penis. ❑ **blue-veined root-on** *n.* [ROOT-ON *n.*] [1990s+] an erection. ❑ **blue-veined steak** *n.* [SE *steak*] [1980s+] the penis. ❑ **blue-veined trumpet** *n.* [SE *trumpet*] [1980s+] the penis.

blue-vein salami *n.* [BLUE VEIN *n.* SE *salami*/SALAMI *n.*] [1990s+] the penis, usu. in the context of fellatio.

bluey *n.*[1] [all SE *blue* + sfx *-y*] **1** [mid-19C] a policeman. **2** [mid-19C+] (*UK Und.*) lead. **3** [late 19C+] (*Aus.*) (*also* **blue**) a pack [f. the trad. blue blanket that covered a pack]. **4** [late 19C+] (*orig. Aus.*) (*also* **blue**) a red-headed person. **5** [20C+] (*Aus./N.Z.*) (*also* **blue paper**) a summons, a traffic ticket. **6** [20C+] a drinker of methylated spirits. **7** [1910s] (*Aus.*) a blue-tongued lizard. **8** [1910s+] (*Aus.*) a blue heeler, an Australian cattle dog. **9** [1970s] (*UK prison/drugs*) any form of amphetamine-barbiturate mixture. **10** [1990s+] a £5 note. **11** [1990s+] (*Aus.*) a can of Foster's lager. **12** [1990s+] (*Aus. prison*) a police warrant.

(IN PHRASES)

❑ **hump one's bluey** *v.* (*also* **hump the bluey**) [HUMP *v.*[1] (1)] [late 19C+] (*Aus.*) to carry a pack.

bluey *n.*[2] [BLUE *adj.*[3]] [1990s+] a pornographic film.

bluey! *excl.* *see* BLOOEY! *excl.*

bluey-cracking *n.* [BLUEY *n.*[1] (2) + CRACK *v.*[2] (2c)] [mid-19C] stealing lead from the roofs of buildings.

bluey-hunter *n.* [BLUEY *n.*[1] (2) + SE *hunter*] [mid-19C] a thief who specializes in stealing lead from the roofs of houses and other buildings.

bluff *n.*[1] [BLUFF *v.*] **1** [mid-19C+] an excuse, a pretence. **2** [late 19C–1910s] deception. **3** [late 19C+] (*US*) an impostor, a deceiver, one who bluffs.

bluff *n.*[2] [BUTCH *n.*[1] (5) + FLUFF *n.*[1] (6)] [1950s+] a female homosexual who can alternate between active/passive roles.

bluff *v.* [20C use is SE poker jargon: 'To impose upon (an opponent) as to the value of one's hand of cards, by betting heavily upon it, speaking or gesticulating or otherwise acting in such a way as to make believe that it is stronger than it is, so as to induce him to "throw up" his cards and lose his stake, rather than run the risk of betting against the bluffer' (*OED*); ult. a late 17C Und. term + ? link to SE *bluff*, a blinker for a horse] [late 18C–late 19C] to confuse, to mislead or deter by a show of confidence or superiority; to fob off.

(IN COMPOUNDS)

❑ **bluff artist** *n.* [-ARTIST *sfx*] [1930s] an insincere person, a confidence trickster. ❑ **bluff stakes** *n.* [1910s] (*Aus.*) a deceitful attempt to influence someone else's conduct.

(IN PHRASES)

❑ **bluff the rats** *v.* [SE *rats*; they will thus 'leave a sinking ship'] [1910s–20s] to spread panic. ❑ **on the bluff** *adj.* [late 19C] (*Aus.*) using influence or persuasive talk to avoid payment (e.g. for a meal).

bluff cuffs with the solid senders *n.* [1940s] (*US black*) trousers with large, ballooning turn-ups.

bluffer *n.*[1] [? their 'bluff' manners, whether using *bluff* as hearty or as in setting out to deceive] [late 17C–mid-19C] (*UK Und.*) an innkeeper; a hotel-keeper.

bluffer *n.*[2] [BLUFF *v.*] **1** [late 18C] (*UK Und.*) a swindler. **2** [20C+] one who relies on an assumed manner to get away with lies.

blug *n.* [SE *blood* + *plug*; the link to the definition remains unresolved] [late 19C] (*US campus*) a stylish, socially admirable individual.

bluggy *adj.* [mid-19C–1920s] (*US*) a deliberate mispron. (as if one were drunk or otherwise verbally impaired) of BLOODY *adj.*

blumpies *n.* [ety. unknown] [2000s] (*US black*) female-to-male fellatio, while the man is seated on the toilet.

blunderbuss *n.*[1] (*also* **blunderbust**) [20C use is US. SE *blunderbuss*, a short gun with a large bore; its unwieldy clumsiness and inaccuracy are transferred to the human version] [late 17C–1960s] a fool, a clumsy, noisy fellow.

blunderbuss *n.*[2] [1930s] (*US prison*) a sawn-off shotgun.

blunderbuss *n.*[3] [pun on SE *blunder bus*] [1940s+] (*US*) any large motor vehicle that handles badly.

blunderbust *n.* *see* BLUNDERBUSS *n.*[1].

blunderhead *n.* (*also* **blunderkin**) [SE *blunder* + -HEAD *sfx* (1)] [late 16C+] a fool.

Blundstones *n.* [the proprietary name] [20C+] (*Aus.*) elastic-sided boots.

blunk *adj.* [? BLOTTO *adj.* (1) / BLIND *adj.*[1] (1) + SE *drunk*] [1960s–70s] (*drugs*) intoxicated.

blunt *n.*[1] [? Fr. *blond*, yellow, using as in other sl. terms the colour of the coin to denote its name; or f. SE *blunt*, referring to the edge of unmilled coins, or, least feasibly, from Mr John *Blunt*, chief architect of the South Sea Bubble financial scandal of 1720] [18C–1910s] money, esp. cash in hand; thus *blunty*, wealthy; *unblunted*, impoverished.

(IN COMPOUNDS)

❑ **blunt-finder** *n.* [SE *finder*] [mid-19C] a money-lender. ❑ **blunt ken** *n.* [KEN *n.*[1] (1)] [mid-19C] (*US Und.*) a bank. ❑ **blunt magazine** *n.* [SE *magazine*, a warehouse] [early–mid-19C] a bank.

(IN PHRASES)

❑ **smart blunt** *n.* [SE *smart*, to feel pain] [mid-19C] (*UK Und.*) forfeit money.

blunt *n.*[2] [1980s] (*US drugs*) a hypodermic needle.

blunt *n.*[3] [note the cigar can be of any brand, and can contain crack cocaine as well as marijuana; one version of the *blunt* is also sealed with a layer of honey] [1980s+] (*orig. US drugs*) **1** (*also* **b, Philly blunt**) a marijuana cigarette made of buds rolled in a tobacco leaf, taken from the wrapper of a Phillies Blunt cigar; thus the cigar itself; latterly used for any marijuana-based cigarette. **2** marijuana. **3** any drug available in a blunt-ended capsule.

blunted *adj.* [BLUNT *n.*[1]] [mid-19C] (*US Und.*) supplied with money.

blunted (up) *adj.* (*also* **blunted out**) [BLUNT *n.*[3]] [1980s+] (*drugs*) under the influence of marijuana.

bluppy *n.* *see* BUPPIE *n.*

blur-an-agers! *excl.* *see* TARE AN' AGES! *excl.*

blur an' ouns! *excl.* *see* TARE AN' OUNS! *excl.*

blurb *n.* [coined 1907 by the US humorist Gelett Burgess (1866–1951), after designing a humorous bookplate (to be given away at a booksellers' dinner), which featured an attractive young woman (lifted from an advertisement for tooth powder or health tonic and suitably embellished by Burgess) whom he christened 'Miss Belinda Blurb'] [20C+] (*orig. US*) **1** a brief piece of promotional material, typically as printed on the back of books; also as v., *blurb*, to promote. **2** promotional talk. **3** a short newspaper story.

blurry *adj.* [late 19C+] slurred mispron. of BLOODY *adj.*

blurt *n.* [? an anatomic var. on BLOT *n.*[1] (2); ? pun on 17C *blurt*, a constable, and CUNT *n.* (1)/CUNT *n.* (4)] [1990s+] the vagina; thus, a general term of abuse.

blurt *v.* [play on SE *blurt out*] [2000s] to ejaculate.

blurt! *excl.* [SE *blurt*, to make a contemptuous puffing gesture with the lips, to puff in scorn] [early 17C] a general excl. of disdain.

blurter *n.* [BLOT *n.*[1] (2) / SE *blurt out*] **1** [1960s+] the anus; the buttocks. **2** [2000s] a fart.

blushing *adj.* **1** [1900s–30s] euph. for BLOODY *adj.* **2** [1990s+] (*US black*) deceitful.

blush like a black dog *v.* (*also* **blush like a blue dog**) [16C–mid-17C = *black*; subseq. is *blue*; a black/blue dog will not turn pink] [late 16C–early 19C] not to blush at all.

blutchel hawk *n.* [ety. unknown] [mid-19C] (*UK Und.*) a wary landlord.

bluthered *adj.* *see* BLOOTERED *adj.*

B. Luther Hatchett *n.* [nonsense words] [1920s–40s] (*US black*) the ultimate in far-away, unpleasant places, the 'back of beyond'.

bluxom! *excl.* *see* BLIKSEM! *excl.*

bly *n.*[1] [SE *blow* + *oxy*] [1930s] (*UK Und.*) an oxy-acetylene blowlamp, as used by safe-crackers.

bly *n.*[2] [? SE (*proba*)*bly*, (*possi*)*bly*] [1950s+] (*W.I. Rasta*) a chance.

bly! *excl.* (*also* **bly me! blymy!**) [var. BLIMEY! *excl.*] [late 19C–1900s] a general excl. of surprise, alarm.

B.M. *n.* [abbr.] [1990s+] a *BMW* car.

BM *n.* see *BABY-MAKER under* BABY *n.*

b.m. *n.*[1] [abbr. *baby maker* / *bloody male* / *bloody masculine*] [1920s–80s] (*gay*) a heterosexual person.

b.m. *n.*[2] [abbr. *bowel movement*] [1960s+] **1** an act of defecation; also as v. *to do a b.m.* **2** a piece of excrement.

b.m.o.c. *n.* (*also* **b.w.o.c.**) [abbr. *big man/woman on campus*] [1930s+] (*US college*) a socially prominent, important person in the context of student life.

b-more ho *n.* [abbr. *block* or *more* + HO *n.* (2)] [2000s] (*US black*) a female who looks attractive from a distance, but not close-up.

b.m.t. *n.* [abbr. *black man's time*, thus negative racial stereotyping] [1990s+] unpunctuality.

b.m.t. *phr.* [abbr. *black man talking*] [1990s+] (*US black*) a phr. designed to affirm one's authority, masculinity etc, and thus reinforce one's argument.

b.m.w. *n.* [abbr.] [1980s+] **1** a nickname for the BMW motorcar, esp. popular as a status symbol and as a target for theft; various 'translations' of *BMW* include 'black man's wheels', 'black man's wagon', 'Bob Marley and the Wailers', 'break my windows'. The actual name comes from that of the German manufacturer, *Bayerische Motor Werke*. **2** [1990s+] (*US black*) black man working [apparently based on the 'luxury' of finding a job if black]. **3** [2000s] (*S.Afr. gay*) *be my wife*, an invitation to have sexual intercourse. **4** [2000s] (*S.Afr.*) black man's wish.

b.n.i.c. *n.* [abbr. *boss/black nigger in charge* (*see* HEAD NIGGER IN CHARGE *under* HEAD *n.*); note H.N.I.C. *n.*] [1970s+] (*US black*) a sarcastic reference to any black authority-figure.

b.o. *n.* [abbr.; invented and widely popularized by the Lifebuoy soap advertising campaign *c.*1930] [1930s+] (*orig. US*) **1** body odour; thus *b.o. juice*. **2** (*US campus*) deodorant.

b.o. *v.* see *BEND OVER (FOR) under* BEND *v.*[1].

b.o. *phr.* [abbr. BUGGER OFF *v.* / SE *beat on*] **1** [1950s+] go away, leave me alone. **2** [1990s+] (*US campus*) used as a threat.

bo *n.*[1] [SE *boy* or abbr. HOBO *n.* (2)] **1** [early 19C+] (*also* **beau, boh**) a fellow, a man, a friend, often as a form of address, e.g. *Hey, bo.* **2** [late 19C+] (*Aus./US*) (*also* **bow**) a vagrant, a tramp. **3** [1910s+] (*US*) a tramp's young homosexual companion; thus a young, effeminate male homosexual.

(IN PHRASES)

❑ **on the bo** [1920s] (*US*) living as a vagrant.

bo *n.*[2] [abbr.] [1950s] (*US campus*) a *bo*hemian.

bo *n.*[3] [abbr. Colom*bo*] [1970s+] (*US drugs*) Colombian marijuana.

bo *v.*[1] [BO *n.*[1] (2)] [1910s–20s] (*US*) to live as a tramp.

bo *v.*[2] [? BO *n.*[1] but note BOING-BOING *n.*] [2000s] (*US black*) to act like a fool.

boag *v.* [BOGUE *n.*[2]] [1980s+] (*US campus*) to vomit.

boak see *under* BOKE.

boang *n.* see BOONG *n.*

boar *n.*[1] [play on HOG *n.* (1a)] [mid-18C] (*UK Und.*) a shilling.

SE in slang uses

(IN COMPOUNDS)

❑ **boar pig** *n.* see BARTHOLOMEW (BOAR) PIG *n.* ❑ **boar pussy** *n.* [SE *boar*, generic for a male animal + PUSSY *n.* (1)] [1950s+] (*US prison*) homosexual anal intercourse. ❑ **boar's nest** *n.* [SE *nest*; note the bar in the TV series *The Dukes of Hazzard*, set in America's bootlegging country, which was named the Boar's Nest, although it appeared to entertain women customers] **1** [late 19C+] (*US*) anywhere, orig. a logging or mining camp, where only men live or only men are admitted. **2** [2000s] an untidy room or house; (*N.Z.*) a mess in general.

boar *n.*[2] [? resemblance to a boar's tusks] [1950s+] (*W.I.*) a straight cutlass with a hooked end.

board *n.*[1] [it is painted on a *board*] [20C+] (*tramp*) a picture sold in the street.

SE in slang uses

(IN COMPOUNDS)

❑ **boardman** *n.* [he augmented his pitch by displaying a board to which were affixed coloured pictures] [mid-19C] 'men who take a stand on the curb of a public thoroughfare, and deliver prepared speeches to effect a sale of any articles they have to vend' (Hotten, 1859). ❑ **board stiff** *n.* see *under* STIFF *n.*[1].

(IN PHRASES)

❑ **board of green cloth** *n.* [the green baize that covers it] **1** [late 18C–mid-19C] a billiard table. **2** [19C] a card-table.

board *n.*[2] [? it gives one support] [1970s] (*US*) the human leg.

board *n.*[3] see BORD *n.*

board *v.*[1] **1** [late 16C–17C] to woo a woman as a preliminary to love-making. **2** [17C–mid-19C] to have sexual intercourse.

(IN PHRASES)

❑ **board a land carrack** *v.* (*also* **board a ship in the bows**) [fig. use of SE *land-carrack*, a coasting vessel] [early 18C; early 19C] of a man, to have sexual intercourse.

board *v.*[2] [SE *board*, a table, esp. one spread with food] [1930s–40s] (*US black*) to eat.

board and plank *n.* [rhy. sl. = YANK *n.*] [20C+] an American.

boardies *n.* [skateboarding/surfboarding?] [1990s+] (*Aus.*) men's shorts.

boarding house *n.* [note *the boarding house*, the old nickname for New York City's Tombs prison] **1** [mid–late 19C] (*US*) a brothel. **2** [mid-19C+] a prison.

boarding-house reach *n.* [the presumed selfishness of boarding-house guests, each of whom attempts to corral the most food for themselves] [1900s–30s] (*US*) **1** reaching rudely across the table to grab what one wants, rather than asking for it to be passed. **2** in fig. use, a grab.

boarding scholar *n.* [ironic use of SE] [late 17C–early 18C] (*UK Und.*) a prisoner.

boarding school *n.* [ironic use of SE] **1** [late 17C–late 19C] a prison, a workhouse; thus *boarding-school gloak*, a prisoner. **2** [late 18C] a brothel.

board lodger *n.* [mid-19C] a prostitute who gives the owner of the brothel a share of her income in exchange for board and lodging.

boards *n.* [the material of which they are made] [1920s+] playing cards.

(IN PHRASES)

❑ **toss the boards** *v.* [1950s] (*US Und.*) **1** to conduct a game of three-card monte. **2** to deal cards, esp. in a crooked or illegal manner.

SE in slang uses

(IN PHRASES)

❑ **off the boards** *adv.* [late 19C–1920s] (*US*) to excess, to a great extent.

boardsman *n.* [BOARDS *n.* + SE *man*] [1970s] (*UK Und.*) one who plays the 'three-card trick'.

boasie *n.* (*also* **boasy**) [BOASIE *adj.*] [1950s+] (*W.I.*) **1** a show-off, a boaster. **2** a flashily dressed person.

boasie *adj.* (*also* **boasify, boasy, bosy**) [SE *boastful* and/or Yoruba *bosi*, proud and ostentatious] [1930s+] (*W.I.*) proud, boastful, showy.

boast *n.*

(IN PHRASES)

❑ **make the boast** *v.* [1910s–20s] (*US Und.*) to obtain a pardon.

boasy *n.* see BOASIE *n.*

boasy-naked *n.* [BOASIE *adj.* + SE *naked*] [1950s+] (*W.I.*) a shameless show-off.

b.o.a.t. *n.* [abbr. *b*ordering *o*n *a* *t*art] [1980s+] a semi-professional prostitute whose clients tend to be wealthy and whose payments are often less obvious than mere cash.

boat *n.*[1] **1** fig. terms based on size or physical resemblance. (**a**) [late 18C+] (*also* **cockboat**) the vagina; hence also a prostitute or mistress [COCK *n.*[3] (1)]. (**b**) [1910s–30s] (*US*) an airplane. (**c**) [1910s+] (*also* **big boat**) a large, trad. American car, esp. a large station wagon. (**d**) [1920s] (*US Und.*) a freight car used to transport bootleg beer. (**e**) [1950s+] (*US*) a large foot. (**f**) [1950s+] (*US*) a large shoe or boot. **2** lit. terms of transportation. (**a**) [late 19C] (*UK tramp*) a jail sentence; a life sentence; thus *get the boat* below. (**b**) [20C+] (*US Und.*) transportation from one prison to another; the mode of transport is irrelevant. (**c**) [1980s+] (*drugs*) a 1,000 tablet shipment of Ecstasy. **3** [1980s+] (*drugs*) fig. ideas of transportation [? one 'sails away']. (**a**) a cannabis cigarette. (**b**) phencyclidine.

IN PHRASES

❑ **get the boat** *v.* [late 19C] to be sentenced to transportation overseas or a severe form of penal servitude.

SE in slang uses

IN COMPOUNDS

❑ **boat-jumper** *n.* [the pej. image of immigrants as stowaways who have to avoid immigration procedures by jumping from boat to dock] [1980s+] (*US*) a recently arrived immigrant. ❑ **boatrace** *n. see* separate entry. ❑ **boat ride** *n.* [one 'sails' through it] [1960s] (*US*) a pleasant, undemanding task. ❑ **boat rider** *n.* [1930s–40s] (*US Und.*) a professional gambler who works the transatlantic liners.

IN PHRASES

❑ **boat it** *v.* [1960s] (*US black*) to walk, to travel. ❑ **boat with** *v.* [mid-19C] (*US Und.*) to become partners with. ❑ **row in the (same) boat** *v.* [late 18C+] to join, to take shares with.

boat *n.*[2] [abbr. rhy. sl. BOATRACE *n.*[2]] [1940s+] the face.

boat, the *n.* [mid-19C] the penal hulks, moored on the Thames.

boat *v.* [the ships that transported the convicts to Australia] (*UK Und.*) **1** [mid–late 19C; 1990s+] to transport a convict. **2** [mid-19C–1900s] to sentence to penal servitude; thus *in the boat*, sentenced to penal servitude.

boat and oar *n.* (*also* **broken oar**) [rhy. sl. *boat and oar* = whore] [1930s+] a prostitute.

boated *adj.* [BOAT *v.* (2)] [mid–late 19C] sentenced to a long term in prison.

boatrace *n.*[1] [orig. horseracing jargon only; the winner 'sails in'] [1910s+] (*US*) any form of 'fixed' sporting contest.

boatrace *n.*[2] [rhy. sl.] [1940s+] the face.

B.O.B. *n.* (*also* **b.o.b.**) [1990s+] (*US black*) a derog. description of an unattractive female, lit. *b*ig *o*ld *b*itch.

Bob *n.*[1] [18C] a generic term for man, on lines of such equally common names as Jack, Tom etc.

Bob *n.*[2] [19C+] euph. for God, esp. in phrs. *s'elp me Bob! no sirree, Bob!*

b.o.b. *n.* see B.O.B. *n.*

bob *n.*[1] **1** [late 16C–late 18C] an act of sexual intercourse [BOB *v.*[2] (1)]. **2** [1990s+] (*US prison*) an effeminate male homosexual [abbr. *b*end *o*ver *b*ackwards].

IN PHRASES

❑ **dry bob** *n. see under* DRY *adj.*[1].

bob *n.*[2] [? 15C–17C SE *give someone the bob*, to cheat, to trick] [late 17C–mid-19C; 1920s–30s] a shoplifter's assistant, to whom the stolen goods are quickly passed by the actual lifter; 20C use refers to any shoplifter.

bob *n.*[3] [BOBSTICK *n.*] **1** [18C] gin, i.e. a shilling's (5p) worth. **2** [late 18C+] a shilling (5p). **3** [mid-19C+] money in general, esp. as *a few bob*. **4** [1930s+] (*US*) $1.

IN COMPOUNDS

❑ **bob hop** *n.* [HOP *n.*[1] (1)] [1980s] (*N.Z.*) a dance. ❑ **bob in** *n.* (*Aus./N.Z.*) **1** [late 19C+] the payment of a shilling (5p) into a common pot, esp. as used for buying drinks. **2** [1940s] (*Aus.*) a dicing game in which all players contribute a shilling (5p); the winner then buys the round of drinks.

IN PHRASES

❑ **bob a nob** *n.* [NOB *n.*[1] (1)] [early 19C+] one shilling each person, used when estimating the cost of meals, outings, tickets etc. ❑ **just the shiny bob** (*also* **just the shiny shilling**) [20C+] (*Aus.*) a general phr. of approval. ❑ **royal bob** *n.* [18C] gin.

bob *n.*[4] [ety. unknown] [mid-19C] (*Aus.*) 50 strokes of the lash.

bob *n.*[5] [abbr. BOBO *n.*[2]] [1980s+] (*drugs*) **1** crack cocaine. **2** (*also* **brown bob**) a marijuana cigarette.

bob *n.*[6] *see* BOBTAIL *n.*[3].

bob *adj.* [abbr. BOBBISH *adj.*] (*UK Und.*) [late 17C–mid-19C] safe; pleasant, satisfactory; usu. in phr. *all is bob*.

IN COMPOUNDS

❑ **bob cull** *n.* [CULL *n.*[1] (3)] [late 17C–late 18C] (*UK Und.*) a pleasant, good-natured person. ❑ **bob ken** *n.* [KEN *n.*[1] (1)] (*UK Und.*) [late 17C–early 19C] **1** a house considered worth robbing. **2** a house occupied by thieves.

bob *v.*[1] [OF *bober*, to deceive. SE to late 17C and found as such in Shakespeare] **1** [early 16C–early 19C] (*UK Und.*) to cheat, to deceive; thus *bobbed*, cheated. **2** [late 18C] to thrash, to beat. **3** [late 19C] to wound or kill.

bob *v.*[2] [SE *bob*, a light, tapping blow or *bob*, to move up and down; there may be a pun on SE *bob*, to cut an animal's tail/TAIL *n.* (4)] **1** [late 16C–late 18C] of a man, to have sexual intercourse; ext. in phr. *play at bob-cherry*. **2** [mid-19C] (*UK Und.*) to work.

bob *v.*[3] [SE *bob* (up and down)] [1940s] to act in a nervous manner.

SE in slang uses

IN PHRASES

❑ **bob and weave** *v.* [boxing imagery] [1920s+] to avoid direct action, either confrontation, explanation, aggression etc. ❑ **bob around** *v.* [note *Dict. Americanisms* (1951): 'The popularity, and possibly the origin of this expression may have been occasioned by a popular song "Bobbing Around" sung by Stephen C. Masseet, a minstrel, in California mining camps during the fifties'] [mid-19C] to move quickly from place to place. ❑ **bob on** *v.* [SE *bob* v.; the image of a cork bobbing on choppy water] [1920s–30s] (*orig. milit.*) to await anxiously. ❑ **bob one's baloney** *v. see* BOP ONE'S BALONEY *under* BALONEY *n.* ❑ **bob up** *v.* [late 19C+] to appear (unexpectedly).

bob *v.*[4] *see* RALPH *V.*

bob! *excl.* [late 19C] (*UK society*) stop! enough! esp. as response to the drink pourer's request 'Say when?'.

bob and dick *n.* [rhy. sl. = PRICK *n.* (1)] [1970s] the penis.

bob and dick *adj.* [rhy. sl.] [1970s+] sick, esp. after drinking.

bob and hit *n.* **1** [late 19C] the vagina [rhy. sl. = PIT *n.* (1)]. **2** [1990s+] excrement [rhy. sl. = SHIT *n.* (1a)].

bob and hit *v.* [rhy. sl. = SHIT *v.* (1a)] [1990s+] to defecate.

bobashilly *n. see* BOBBASHEELY *n.*

bobbasheely *n.* (*also* **bobashilly**) [Choctaw *itibapishili*, my brother] [19C+] (*US*) a friend.

bobbasheely *v.* [BOBBASHEELY *n.*] [1930s+] (*US*) to saunter, to move in a friendly fashion, to mix with.

bobbejaan *n.* [Afk. *bobbejaan*, a baboon] [1980s] (*S.Afr.*) a fool.

bobbe mayse *n. see* BUBBE MAYSE *n.*

bobber *n.*[1] [Shropshire dial. *bobber*, a term of friendly greeting, e.g. 'Hellow bobber'] [mid–late 19C] a friend, a chum, a fellow worker.

bobber *n.*[2] [? BUBBY *n.*[1] or ? it bobs up and down] [1940s–60s] (*Aus.*) a female breast.

bobberous *adj. see* BOBBISH *adj.*

bobbers *n.* [SE *bob* v.; their movement] [1940s+] (*Aus.*) the corks that are worn around the rim of a hat to keep away the flies.

bobbery *n.* (*also* **bobberie**) [Hind. *Bap re!* O father!, a common exclamation of surprise or grief. A popular term, apparently coined c.1816 in the Raj, it had spread to such widely separated areas as East Anglia and Australia by the mid-century. Note Anglo-Ind. hunting use *bobbery pack*, a mongrel, a mixed pack of hounds]

1 [late 18C+] an argument, a disturbance. **2** [1910s] (*also* **bobberee**) a hoax or trick, esp. if illegal.

IN PHRASES

□ **kick up a bobbery** *v.* [late 18C+] to cause trouble, to create a disturbance.

bobbie *n. see* BOBBY *n.*

bobbing *n.* [? the *bobbing* of one's lethargic head] [2000s] (*US black*) a state of inactivity or unconsciousness.

bobbins *n.* [Lancs. dial. *bobbin-winding*, a term of disparagement or ridicule; + ? euph. for BALLOCKS *n.*] [1990s+] nonsense, rubbish; use also extended as a general negative.

bobbish *adj.* (*also* **bobberous, booborous**) [SE *bob* v. + sfx *-ish*; one 'bobs up and down' with good humour and energy] [18C+] of people, healthy, in good spirits, cheery; of situations, prosperous.

bobbishly *adj.* [BOBBISH *adj.*] [19C] healthily, cheerily; thus *tolbobbishly*, elision of *tolerably* + *bobbishly*.

bobble *n.* [SE *bobble*, to shudder up and down] [late 19C–1950s] (*US*) a mess, an error, a confusion.

bobble *v.* **1** [mid-17C–early 18C] to swindle, to cheat [? a misprint or mis-reading for BUBBLE *v.*[1]; Partridge cites a correspondent who found 'an "indignant gentleman captain" writing to the Navy Board' *c.*1688 and using the word, but SE *bobble*, to bob up and down, has not been found until 1812]. **2** [1940s] (*US Und.*) to excite a victim's suspicions, esp. when passing them short change.

bobbles *n.* [SE *baubles*] **1** [late 19C] the testicles. **2** [20C+] (*US black*) gaudy, flashy, ostentatious jewellery.

bobby *n.* (*also* **b, bobbie**) [Sir Robert Peel (1788–1850), who established the force in 19C. 'The term is, however, older. The official square-keeper, who is always armed with a cane to drive away idle and disorderly urchins, has, time out of mind, been called by said urchins *Bobby the Beadle*. Bobby is also an old English word for striking, or hitting, a quality not unknown to policemen' (Hotten, 1860)] **1** [mid-19C+] a British or Australian, occas. US policeman, latterly any police officer. **2** [20C+] (*US*) an Englishman. **3** [1980s+] (*Aus. prison*) a prison officer.

IN COMPOUNDS

□ **bobby peeler** *n. see* separate entry. □ **bobby's helmet** *n.* (*also* **bobby's hat**) [SE *helmet/hat*; the shape of the 'bell end'] [1930s+] the glans penis. □ **bobby's labourers** *n.* [SE *labourer*] [late 19C] volunteers who joined up as special constables during the Fenian scares of the 1860s. □ **bobby twister** *n.* [SE *twist*] [late 19C] a thug who will stop at nothing, even killing a policeman.

bobby atkins *n.* [var. on TOMMY ATKINS *n.*] [1900s–10s] a private soldier.

bobby-dangler *n.* [play on BOBBY-DAZZLER *n.* + SE *dangle*] [1930s+] (*Can.*) the penis.

bobby-dazzler *n.* (*also* **dickey dazzler, mickey dazzler**) [dial. ? f. intensification of dial. *bobby*, smartly dressed, in high spirits (cf. BOBBISH *adj.*) + SE *dazzler*] [late 19C+] anything or anyone seen as exceptional, wonderful.

bobby martin *n.* [rhy. sl.] [20C+] (*Aus.*) a carton.

Bobby Moore *n.* [rhy. sl.; ult. UK footballer Bobby Moore (1941–93)] [1960s+] a door.

bobby peeler *n.* [Sir *Robert Peel* (*see* BOBBY *n.*)] [mid–late 19C] a policeman.

bobby rocks *n.* [rhy. sl.] [20C+] (*Aus.*) a pair of socks.

bobbyshop *n. see* BABBIE-SHOP *n.*

bobby soxer *n.* (*also* **bobby sox**) [orig. describing the fans of Frank Sinatra in 1940s and thus teenage girls of the late 1940s–50s who enjoyed pop music and its ancillary pleasures] [1940s+] (*US*) a teenage girl wearing bobby-socks; also as adj., *bobbysox*, girlish.

Bob Cryer *n.* [rhy. sl.; ult. UK politician *Bob Cryer* (1934–94)] [2000s] a liar.

bob, harry and dick *adj.* [rhy. sl.] [late 19C–1900s] sick, usu. from drinking.

Bob Hope *n.* [rhy. sl.; ult. f. the US comedian *Bob Hope* (1903–2003); senses 1 and 3 = DOPE *n.*[1] (6)] **1** [1960s] (*drugs*) cannabis. **2** [1960s+] (*Aus.*) soap. **3** [1990s+] (*UK drugs*) crack cocaine.

bob it *v.* [BOB! *excl.*] [mid-19C] to abandon; to give up.

bobkhes *n.* (*also* **bubbkis, bubkhes, bubkis, bupkis**) [Yid. *bobkhes*, goat droppings] [20C+] **1** an absurd idea, an insulting sum, price or proposition. **2** nothing (in sense of a return, a reward), esp. in show business use.

Bob Marley *n.* [rhy. sl. = CHARLIE *n.*[8] (1); ult. f. the Jamaican reggae musician (1945–81)] [2000s] cocaine.

bob-my-nag *n.* (*also* **billy-my-nag**) [the image of 'riding' a NAG *n.* (1a)] [late 19C] the penis.

bob my pal *n.* [rhy. sl. = GAL *n.* (1)] [mid–late 19C] a girl or young woman.

bobo *n.*[1] [? Sp. *bobón*, a clumsy simpleton or popular children's entertainer, *Bobo* the Clown] **1** [1940s+] (*US/W.I.*) (*also* **bubu**) a fool. **2** [2000s] a generic insult: an ugly, fat oaf. **3** [2000s] (*US black*) generic for a white man.

bobo *n.*[2] (*drugs*) **1** [1950s+] marijuana [abbr. BOBO BUSH *n.*]. **2** [1990s+] crack cocaine [? BOBO *n.*[1] (3), i.e. its whiteness].

bobo *n.*[3] [abbr.; ult. Fr.] [2000s] a *bo*urgeois *bo*hemian.

bobo *adj.* [? proper name, *Bobo* the Clown / BOBO *n.*[1] (1)] [1980s+] (*US black/campus*) drunk or intoxicated with a drug.

bobo bush *n.* [? BOBO *n.*[1] (1) + BUSH *n.*[1] (5a)] [1930s+] (*drugs*) marijuana.

bo-bo jockey *n.* [BOBO *n.*[2] (1) + JOCKEY *n.*[2] (10)] [1940s] (*US drugs*) a cannabis smoker.

bobo-johnny *n.* [? Yoruba *buburu*, bad, evil + JOHNNY *n.*[1] (2a)] [20C+] (*W.I.*) **1** a bogeyman, an imaginary monster conjured up to frighten naughty children. **2** a peasant, an unsophisticated country person.

bobol *n.* (*also* **bohbohl**) [? Fr. Creole *Vaval*, a masque king of the St Lucia carnival, symbolically thrown into the sea on Ash Wednesday. Orig. 1920s, the term became associated with corrupt 'speculators' trading between Martinique and St Lucia and thence to the larger world of fraud. Note Earl Lovelace's *The Dragon Can't Dance* p.221: 'Bobolee was a sort of effigy of Judas, fellars got an old jacket and old pants and stuffed it up with straw to beat on Good Friday, and all the boys with big sticks beating it and running behind it, crying: 'Beat! Beat! Beat the bobolee!'] [1920s+] (*W.I.*) fraud and corruption, practised by senior figures in government, business or any position of power; thus *make/run a bobol*, to organize a fraud; *bobol(ize)*, to steal a company's or the public's funds; *bobolism*, large-scale corruption; *bobolist*, a fraudster.

bobolition *n.* [early–mid-19C] (*US*) abolition.

bob powell *n.* [rhy. sl.; ? ult. US composer *Bob Powell* (b.1961) or ? US comic book writer *Robert Powell* (b.1916)] [1990s+] (*Aus.*) a towel.

bobsey twins *n.* [the children's adventure story characters created 1904 by 'Laure Lee Hope' (Edward Stratemeyer) + ref. to UK BOBBY *n.* (1)] [1950s–80s] (*US camp gay*) the police, when working as a pair.

bob squash *n.* [rhy. sl.] [20C+] **1** a wash. **2** a public convenience; thus *work the bob*, for a pickpocket to rob jackets and coats that have been hung up while people wash their hands.

bobstay *n.* [naut. jargon *bobstay*, a rope that holds down the bowsprit of a ship, counteracting the upward force of the fore-mast stays] [late 18C–early 19C] the frenum or ligament of the penis.

bobstick *n.* [ety. unknown] [late 18C–mid-19C] **1** a shilling (5p). **2** thus, a shilling's worth.

bob's your uncle *phr.* (*also* **bob's your aunt**) [according to A.J. Langguth, *Saki* (1981), f. the apparently nepotistic choice by Tory leader Robert Cecil of his nephew Arthur Balfour as Chief Secretary for Ireland in 1900, a decision that was both surprising and unpopular; given the apparent gap before adoption, equally posible link to bob = god] [20C+] everything will be absolutely fine, there'll be no worries; sometimes prefixed by *and*.

bobtail *n.*[1] [pun on SE *bobtail*, a horse or dog with its tail cut short] **1** [early 17C] an unpleasant person [a *cur*]. **2** [mid-17C–early

19C] an impotent man, a eunuch. **3** [mid-17C–mid-19C] a prostitute [cf. SE *bob*, go up and down + TAIL *n.* (4); a horse is also good for a RIDE *n.* (1a)].

bobtail *n.*[2] [the wide skirts of his coat] **1** [early 19C] a dandy. **2** [late 19C] a waiter.

bobtail *n.*[3] (*also* **bob**) [fig. use of SE *bobtail*, a horse or dog with its tail cut short] [late 19C–1920s] (*US milit.*) a dishonourable discharge; thus the soldier thus discharged.

bobtail *n.*[4] *see* RAG, TAG AND BOBTAIL *n.*

bobtail *adj.* [poker jargon *bobtail flush*, *bobtail straight*, hands that have only three of the five cards required to make them bettable] (*US*) **1** [19C+] worthless. **2** [1950s] shortened.

bobtail (car) *n.* [SE *bobtail*, a horse's tail that has been docked or cut short] **1** [late 19C] (*US*) 'a small tram-car horsed by a single animal, and on which the only official is a driver, whose office it is to collect fares and generally perform the duties of conductor in addition to his own' (Farmer, *Americanisms Old and New*, 1888). **2** [1920s–30s] (*US tramp*) a short local freight train.

bob-wire *n.* [pron.] [1910s–30s] (*US*) barbed wire.

Boche *n.* (*also* **Bosche**) [post-WW1 use is historical, f. Fr. *caboche*, head, or *Alboche*, a modification of *Allemand*, German; Fraser & Gibbons, *Soldier & Sailor Words & Phrases* (1925), suggest a root 'about 1860, as low-class Parisian slang, meaning "bad lot"'; and that the transfer to a description of Germans came after the Franco-Prussian War of 1870–1 when the enemy was still 'les Prussiens'] [1910s+] a German, esp. a German soldier; thus *Bocheland*, Germany.

bock *n.* [Ger. *Bock*, he-goat, or SE *bock*, a sweetish dark beer, originating in Germany (as *Eimbockbier*), brewed in winter to be drunk in spring] [1960s] (*US*) a Bohemian, a Czech.

bockro *n. see* BACKRA *n.*

boco *n.* [var. on BOKO *n.*] [1940s–50s] (*UK juv.*) the head.

bocoo *adv. see* BEAUCOUP *adv.*

bod *n.* [SE *body*] **1** [1910s+] a person, a 'body'; often in comb. with adj. to denote a job, e.g. *legal bod*, a lawyer [the *OED* offers cites for 1788, 1813 but suggests that while still meaning 'a person' they may in fact abbr. Scot. *bodach*, a peasant, a churl, rather than *body*]. **2** [1930s+] a corpse. **3** [1940s+] the human body, esp. as an object for sexual intercourse, e.g. *give out bod*, make oneself available for sex. **4** [1960s+] (*US campus*) a physically attractive person of the opposite sex. **5** [1980s] the chassis or body of a vehicle.

(IN PHRASES)

❑ **how's your bod?** [1970s+] (*orig. US*) how are you (feeling)?

bod *adj.* [abbr. BODACIOUS *adj.*] [1960s+] (*US campus*) outstanding, exceptional.

bodach *n.* [Irish/Scot. *bodach*, a churl or lout] [1920s] a general term of abuse.

bodacious *adj.* (*also* **bodashes, bowdacious**) [SE *bold* + *audacious.* Coined in the 19C, the term was 'relaunched' on 1970s Citizen's Band radio and with the release of the hit teen film *Bill and Ted's Excellent Adventure* (1989). Major, *Juba to Jive: A Dict. of Afro-American Slang* (1994) suggests earlier US black use, and root in Bantu *botesha*, grand, big] **1** [mid-19C+] (*US*) excellent, wonderful, very enjoyable. **2** [mid-19C+] (*US*) audacious, unceremonious, insolent. **3** [1930s+] (*US campus*) of a young woman, attractive, esp. possessed of large breasts. **4** [1970s+] (*US*) exciting, impressive.

bodaciously *adv.* [BODACIOUS *adj.*] (*US*) **1** [early 19C+] (*also* **bidaciously, bodyaciously**) impressively, entirely. **2** [1930s+] extremely, very.

bodacious tatas *n.* [BODACIOUS *adj.* + TA-TAS *n.*[2]] [1980s+] (*US campus*) large breasts.

bodaggle *n.* [*BULL-DAGGER under* BULL *n.*[1]] [1970s] (*US*) a masculine lesbian.

bodashes *adj. see* BODACIOUS *adj.*

boddy *n.* [abbr. + sfx *-y*] [1980s] (*Aus.*) a bodice.

bodelicious *adj.* [BODACIOUS *adj.* + SE *delicious*] [1990s+] (*US*) excellent, first rate.

boderation *n. see* BOTHERATION *n.*

bodge *n.* **1** *see* BODGER *n.* **2** *see* BODGIE *n.* (1).

bodger *n.* (*also* **bodge**) [SE *bodge*, to mend badly, to patch up] [1940s+] (*Aus.*) anything or anyone second-rate, fake or otherwise worthless.

bodger *adj.* [BODGER *n.*] [1940s+] (*Aus.*) **1** fraudulent, second-rate, worthless. **2** of names, assumed, false.

bodgie *n.* [BODGER *n.*; f. the post-war black market in American-made cloth and attempts by crooked salesmen to pass off inferior cloth as this; when young men started using US accents in order to aggrandize themselves they were termed *bodgies*, a fig. ref. to the cloth; note McGill, *Dict. of Kiwi Slang*, (1988): 'Origins various: English word 'bodge', to patch or mend clumsily; 'bodger', WWII slang for a worthless person; US teen slang 'bodgie' for young male jitterbug with long and curly hair and too large sports jacket; Partridge guesses distortion of 'boysies' for boys'] (*Aus.*) **1** [1950s–60s] (*also* **bodge, bodgie-boy**) the equivalent of a teddy boy. **2** [1960s+] anything worthless; thus *pull a bodgie*, to pose as something one is not. **3** [1980s] a misfit, a person who does not 'fit in'. **4** [1980s] a loafer.

bodgie *adj.* [BODGER *adj.*] **1** [1960s+] (*Aus.*) fake, counterfeit. **2** [1980s] of a job, unprofessional; thus v. *bodgie up*.

bodice-ripper *n.* [the period costumes and their fate] [1980s+] a historical novel (or film), with a greater than usual emphasis on sex, esp. the seduction or even rape of the heroine.

bo-dick *n. see* BO-JACK *n.*

bodikin *n. see BAWDY-KEN under* BAWDY *adj.*

bodini *n.* (*also* **budini**) [Ital. *bodino*, blood sausage] [1960s+] (*US*) the penis.

bodkin *n.*[1] [SE *bodkin*, a large needle or small dagger, esp. a large needle-shaped instrument with a blunt, knobbed point] [17C–19C] the penis.

bodkin *n.*[2] [SE *bodkin*, a long, thin object, usu. a pin; the earliest cognate use is in John Ford's *The Fancies* (1638) when it refers to the person squashed between two others in the same bed] [mid-17C–mid-19C] a person who is wedged between two others, esp. when there is room for only the original couple; thus *sit bodkin* or *ride bodkin*, for a coach passenger to ride wedged between two fellows when there is insufficient room for three abreast.

bo-dollar *n. see BEAU-DOLLAR under* BEAU *n.*[1].

body *n.* **1** [late 17C+] (*UK Und.*) a person, esp. a suspect or wanted criminal, or one who is to be 'framed' for a crime. **2** [mid-19C–1960s] (*US*) generic for women, esp. as sex objects. **3** [1960s] (*US*) sexual intercourse. **4** [1960s] (*US campus*) an athlete.

(IN PHRASES)

❑ **give some body** *v.* [1960s+] to accede to sexual advances. ❑ **give someone a body** *v.* [1960s+] (*UK Und.*) to inform, to betray the names of one's criminal associates, usu. as an exhortation, e.g. *Go on, John, give us a body (and we'll be kinder to you)*. ❑ **old body** *n.* [mid-19C+] an old woman, occas. a man.

SE in slang uses

(IN COMPOUNDS)

❑ **body and breeches** *adv.* [late 19C–1900s] (*US*) completely, wholly. ❑ **body bag** *n.* **1** [early–mid-19C] (*US*) an undershirt. **2** [mid-19C] a shirt. **3** [1990s+] a condom [SE *bag*/BAG *n.*[1] (1f)]. ❑ **body binder** *n.* [early 19C] (*orig. boxing*) a waistcoat or a broad belt. ❑ **body come-down** *n.* [1990s+] (*W.I.*) a dramatic loss in weight or change in one's appearance making one less attractive. ❑ **body companion** *n.* [mid-19C] (*US*) a louse. ❑ **body count** *n.* [Vietnam war jargon *body count*, the number of dead enemy bodies counted after a battle/operation] [1970s+] (*US*) those people who are present. ❑ **body cover** *n.* [mid–late 19C] (*US Und.*) an overcoat. ❑ **body exchange** *n.* [1960s–70s] (*US*) anywhere that people can meet in the hope of finding a new sexual partner, e.g. a singles bar, a party. ❑ **body guard** *n.* [mid-19C] (*US*) a louse. ❑ **body lover** *n.* **1** [1940s–60s] a homosexual who prefers rubbing and fondling a body to anal penetration or fellatio. **2** [1960s] a homosexual who derives sexual pleasure from bodybuilders. ❑ **body popper** *n.* (*also* **popper**) [1980s+] (*orig. US*) a break-dancer; thus v. *bodypop/pop*. ❑ **body queen** *n.* [-QUEEN *sfx* (3)] [1960s+] (*gay*) one who looks primarily for partners who specialize in body-building. ❑ **body slangs** *n.* [SLANG *n.*[2] (1)] [early 19C] body irons. ❑ **body wax** *n.* (*also* **wax**) [? play on SE *ear wax*] [late 19C+] human excrement.

IN PHRASES

❑ **how's the body?** [1940s–50s] (*Irish*) how are you?

body *v.* [early 19C] to hit someone in the body; thus *bodier*, a body-blow.

bodyaciously *adv. see* BODACIOUSLY *adv.* (1).

body of divinity bound in black calf *n.* [a description usu. attached to a Bible] [mid-18C–early 19C] a parson.

body shop *n.*[1] [the implication is that one can 'buy' a new partner] [1970s+] (*US*) anywhere that people can meet in the hope of finding a new sexual partner.

body shop *n.*[2] [a play on the SE] **1** [1970s+] (*US*) a morgue, a cemetery. **2** [1990s+] (*US black*) a hospital [refers to the 'mending' of automobiles].

body-snatcher *n.* [ext. use of SE; note WW1 Aus. milit. *body-snatcher*, a member of a raiding party, the aim of which was to bring back prisoners; UK milit. *body-snatcher*, a sniper] (*orig. US*) **1** [late 18C–mid-19C] a bailiff. **2** [late 18C–mid-19C] a cat-stealer. **3** [early–mid-19C] a resurrectionist [SE after mid-19C]. **4** [mid-19C] a cabman. **5** [mid-19C–1930s] a police officer. **6** [late 19C–1930s] a promiscuous, 'forward' woman, esp. a prostitute. **7** [late 19C+] an undertaker. **8** [1910s] a doctor. **9** [1910s] a sniper. **10** [1910s–20s] a weekly insurance payment collector. **11** [1950s] (*US campus*) one who steals another's date.

bodysuit *n. see* BIRTHDAY SUIT *n.*

boep *n.*[1] (*also* **boop**) [Afk. sl. *boep*, a prison] [1970s] (*S.Afr. prison*) a prison.

IN COMPOUNDS

❑ **boep-chappies** *n.* [2000s] (*S.Afr. prison*) prison tattoos.

boep *n.*[2] (*also* **beer-boep**) [Afk. *boepens*, a paunch] [1970s+] (*S.Afr.*) a paunch, a beer belly.

boer *n.* [Du. *boer*, a farmer, and among various fig. uses a pej. name for an Afrikaner] [1960s+] (*S.Afr. Und.*) any member of the S.Afr. security forces, whether in the services, the police force or the prison department.

boer baroque *n.* [SE *Boer* + *baroque*, 'a florid style of architectural decoration, which arose in Italy in the late Renaissance and became prevalent in Europe during the 18th century' (*OED*)] [1980s] (*S.Afr.*) vulgar, if expensive, interior decoration.

boeretroos *n.* [Afk., lit. 'Boer's solace'] [20C+] (*S.Afr.*) strong, flavoursome black coffee.

boers *n.* [Du. *boer*, a farmer and thus an Afrikaner] [late 19C] (*S.Afr.*) S.Afr. whisky or brandy, distilled in the colony.

boesman *n.* [Afk. *boesman*, bushman] [1950s+] (*S.Afr.*) a derog. term of address to an Indian or Coloured person.

boet *n.* (*also* **boeta, boetie**) [Afk. *boet*, brother] (*S.Afr.*) **1** [mid-19C+] a brother, usu. the eldest/favourite. **2** [20C+] a friendly mode of address between whites. **3** [1970s] a pej. nickname for a black male employee. **4** [1970s] a fellow gang-member. **5** [1970s+] a political fellow-traveller. **6** [1970s+] an Afrikaner or any overly aggressive, macho male.

boetie-boetie *adv.* [BOET *n.* (1)] [1950s–70s] (*S.Afr.*) overly friendly, using flattery with an ulterior motive, sycophantic.

boette *n.* [BO *n.*[1] (2) + SE fem. sfx *-ette*] [1920s] (*US tramp*) a female tramp.

b.o.f. *n.* [abbr. *b*oring *o*ld *f*art] [2000s] a tedious, conventional, killjoy older person.

boff *n.*[1] [SE *buff*, a blow, stroke, buffet] (*orig. US*) **1** [1920s–60s] a strong blow. **2** [1930s+] an act of sexual intercourse. **3** [1990s+] a person seen as an object of sexual intercourse.

boff *n.*[2] [BOFFO *adj.*] [1940s+] (*orig. show business*) a laugh, a joke.

boff *n.*[3] [? SE *boffin*] [1990s+] (*UK juv.*) a child who is considered too keen on work, a 'teacher's pet'.

boff *v.* [BOFF *n.*[1]] (*orig. US*) **1** [1920s+] to hit, to assault. **2** [1930s+] to copulate with; both heterosexual and homosexual. **3** [1930s+] to masturbate. **4** [1950s] to lose out, to lose money, to cause someone to lose their money. **5** [1960s] to fail, to blunder, to make a mistake. **6** [1960s] (*US campus*) to caress sexually, to 'neck'.

IN COMPOUNDS

❑ **boff joint** *n.* [JOINT *n.* (3b)] [1930s] a brothel.

boffer *n.* **1** [1930s+] a masturbator [BOFF *v.* (3)]. **2** [1970s+] (*US*) one who has sexual intercourse [BOFF *v.* (2)].

boffin *n.* (*also* **boff**) [ety. unknown, although according to Robert Watson-Watt (1892–1973), the inventor of radar, the term 'has something to do with an obsolete type of aircraft called the Baffin, something to do with that odd bird, the Puffin' (*Three Steps to Victory*, 1957)] [1940s+] any form of scientific expert, orig. those RAF scientists who were working on radar.

boffo *n.*[1] [ety. unknown] [1920s+] (*US*) $1.00.

boffo *n.*[2] (*also* **boppo**) [? BOFF *v.* (1)/BOP *v.* (1)] [1930s–60s] (*US prison*) a year (in jail).

IN PHRASES

❑ **25 boffos** *n.* [1950s+] (*US Und.*) a 25-year sentence.

boffo *n.*[3] [BOFFO *adj.*] [1950s+] a big laugh, a very funny joke.

boffo *adj.* [fig. use of BOFF *v.* (1) + -O *sfx* (5)] [1940s+] (*US*) superb, magnificent, excellent, usu. show business use.

boffo! *excl.* [BOFFO *adj.*] [1940s+] (*US*) an excl. indicating suddenness, abruptness, agreement.

boffola *n.* [BOFFO *adj.* + -OLA *sfx*] **1** [1910s+] (*orig. US*) a laugh, esp. a loud 'belly laugh', usu. show business use. **2** [1950s] (*US*) a success in show business.

bog *n.*[1] (*also* **bogs**) [abbr. BOGHOUSE *n.*; 'a low word, scarcely found in literature, however common in coarse colloquial language' (*OED*)] [late 18C+] a lavatory.

IN COMPOUNDS

❑ **bogblocker** *n.* [SE *blocker*; the image is of some obstruction, prob. faecal, blocking a lavatory] [1980s+] a general term to denote anything particularly unpleasant. ❑ **bogbrush** *n. see* separate entry. ❑ **bog bumf** *n.* [BUMF *n.* (2)] [20C+] lavatory paper. ❑ **boghouse** *n. see* separate entry. ❑ **bog queen** *n.* [-QUEEN *sfx* (3)] [1960s+] (*UK gay*) a gay man who frequents public toilets for sex. ❑ **bogroll** *n.* [20C+] lavatory paper. ❑ **bog-shop** *n.* [SHOP *n.*[1] (1)] [mid-19C–1900s] an outside lavatory. ❑ **bog wash** *n.* [1990s+] (*UK juv.*) an initiation rite whereby the victim has their head pushed into a lavatory pan which is then flushed.

IN PHRASES

❑ **go to bog** *v.* [early 19C] to use the lavatory.

bog *n.*[2] [? SE *Bulgarian*] **1** [1980s] (*Aus.*) a racist term aimed at any non-Anglo-Saxon individual. **2** *see* BOGAN *n.*

bog *n.*[3]

SE in slang uses

IN COMPOUNDS

❑ **bog Arab** *n.* [ARAB *n.*; racial stereotyping] [1990s+] a derog. term for an Irish person. ❑ **bog-eyed** *adj.* [one's eyes seem 'muddy'] [1940s+] having tired eyes, the result of too little sleep or too much alcohol. ❑ **boghopper** *n.* [20C+] **1** a derog. term for an Irish person; thus adj. *boghopping* [racial stereotyping]. **2** (*US*) a peasant, an unsophisticated rural person. ❑ **bogland** *n.* [2000s] (*Irish*) the countryside. ❑ **boglander** *n.* [late 17C+] an Irishman. ❑ **bogman** *n.* **1** [late 19C] (*UK prison*) a prisoner working outdoors. **2** [1940s+] (*Irish*) (*also* **bog person**) a general term of abuse, presuming rural origins and general backwardness. ❑ **bog oranges** *n.* [*BOGLANDER* above + SE *oranges*; racial stereotyping, the main constituent of the Irish diet is supposedly potatoes] [19C] potatoes. ❑ **bog rat** *n.* [racial stereotyping] [20C+] an Irish person. ❑ **bogtrotter** *n.* [lit. 'one who runs through the bogs'; thus those who live among the peat bogs of Ireland. B.E. states that the orig. use was 'Scotch or North Country Moss-troopers or High-Way Men'. Camden, *Britannia* (1605) used the term to describe the inhabitants of the 'debatable' borders between Scotland and England] **1** [late 17C+] a derog. term for an Irish person; thus adj. *bogtrotting*. **2** [late 18C+] a peasant, a yokel; thus adj. *bogtrotting*. ❑ **bog wog** *n.* [WOG *n.*[1]

(3); racial stereotyping] [1990s+] a derog. term for an Irish person.

bog *v.*[1] [defined by the *OED*, which offers no cites, as '*bog*, intr. to exonerate the bowels; also trans. to defile with excrement' and as 'a low word, scarcely found in literature, however common in coarse colloquial language'; note also SE *bog*, to be enmired in a bog] **1** [16C] to defile with excrement. **2** [16C; late 19C] to defecate. **3** [mid-19C] to urinate. **4** [1960s+] to make a mess of. **5** [1960s+] to wet the end of a cigarette while smoking it. **6** [1990s+] to look dirty, unkempt.

bog *v.*[2] [? SE *boggle* (one's eyes)] [1990s+] (*UK juv.*) to stare at in (what is seen as) an aggressive manner.

bogan *n.* (*also* **bog**) [ety. unknown; ? link to BODGIE *n.* (3)] [1980s+] (*Aus./N.Z.*) **1** an uncouth person. **2** one who is mindlessly conventional. **3** a social misfit, a 'nerd'.

bogart *n.* [Humphrey *Bogart* (1899–1957), whose roles often portrayed a gangster or tough-guy] [1950s+] (*US black*) a bully; thus *pull a bogart*, to act tough; *jump bogart*, to become aggressive.

bogart *v.* (*also* **bogard**) [BOGART *n.*] **1** [1950s+] (*orig. US black*) to act aggressively, in a bullying manner. **2** [1960s–70s] to retain something selfishly, esp. to monopolize or smoke too much of a cannabis cigarette. **3** [1970s+] to waste time, to play around. **4** [1990s+] (*US campus*) to leave. **5** [1990s+] (*US teen*) to steal. **6** [2000s] (*US campus*) to take something with someone else's knowledge but without their approval.

IN PHRASES

□ **bogart a joint** *v.* [JOINT *n.* (5c); based on the idea of Humphrey *Bogart*'s alleged greediness in this area; popularized in the film *Easy Rider* (1969)] **1** [1960s+] to salivate on a marijuana cigarette. **2** [1960s+] (*drugs*) to take more than one's fair share of a cannabis cigarette. **3** [1970s+] (*US campus*) to steal, to take an unfair share.

bogart *adv.* [BOGART *v.* (1)] [1960s] (*US*) aggressively, unrestrainedly.

bogbrush *n.* [BOG *n.*[1] + SE *brush*] [1960s+] a lavatory brush.

IN PHRASES

□ **bog brush upside down** *n.* [1980s] a cropped, spiky haircut, supposedly resembling a lavatory brush.

bogel *v.* [? BOGLE *n.*] [1990s+] (*US campus*) to do nothing.

bogey *n.*[1] (*also* **bogie, bogy**) [f. *bogie*, the devil; play on this devilishness] **1** [mid-19C+] a landlord. **2** [1920s] an informer. **3** [1920s+] a police officer, a detective.

IN COMPOUNDS

□ **straight bogey** *n.* (*also* **straight bogy**) [STRAIGHT *adj.*[1] (8)] [1900s–30s] (*UK Und.*) a corrupt policeman.

bogey *n.*[2] (*also* **bogie**) [? Aborigine] (*Aus.*) **1** [mid-19C+] a bathe, a wash. **2** [1940s] a bathing-place, a bath.

bogey *n.*[3] (*also* **bogie, bogy, loogie**) [1930s+] **1** a piece of dried mucus [? SE *boggy*, soft, spongy; thus the consistency of such pieces of mucus]. **2** a nickname given to a man with prominent, wide nostrils.

bogey *n.*[4]

IN PHRASES

□ **no bogey** [? ext. of SE *bogey*, an evil spirit] [1940s] (*UK Und.*) telling the truth.

bogey *n.*[5] [BOOGIE *n.*[2] (1)] [1940s–50s] (*US*) a black person.

IN PHRASES

□ **faded bogey** *n. see* FADED BOOGIE *under* BOOGIE *n.*[2].

bogey *adj.* [SE *bogey*, an evil spirit] **1** [late 19C; 2000s] (*Irish*) inferior, bad. **2** *see* BOGUS *adj.*

bogey *v.*[1] [BOGEY *n.*[2] (1)] [mid-19C+] (*Aus.*) to bathe; thus *bogying*, bathing.

bogey *v.*[2] [BOGART *v.* (2)] [1980s+] (*US*) to act greedily, esp. in consumption of drugs.

bogey up *v. see* BOGGY UP *v.*

bogger *n.* [SE *bog*, the supposed orig. dwelling-place of many immigrants] [20C+] a derog. term for an Irish person; thus ext. as any stupid country person.

boggeral *n.* (*also* **boggerall, boggerol, bokkerol**) [pron. of BUGGER ALL *n.*] [1960s+] (*S.Afr.*) nothing at all.

boggering *adj. see* BUGGERING *adj.*

bogger off *v. see* BUGGER OFF *v.*

boggie bear *n. see* BEAR *n.* (1d).

boggie up *v. see* BOGGY UP *v.*

bogging *adj.* [BOG *n.*[1]] **1** [1950s+] of a film, X-rated. **2** [1960s+] (*Scot.*) unpleasant, smelly, dirty, filthy, a general negative epithet.

boggins *n.* [*AND* states 'ety. unknown', but ? BOG IN *v.*] [mid-19C–1920s] (*Aus.*) plenty, a great deal.

boggle *n.* [BOGGLE *v.* (1)] [mid-19C] a mess, a mistake, an error.

boggle *v.* [SE *boggle*, to fumble] **1** [mid-17C–1950s] to blunder, to do something very badly. **2** [late 18C+] to amaze, to confuse; to look stunned [1980s+ use popularized by General Alexander Haig's celebrated remark 'It boggles the mind'].

boggled *adj.* [BOGGLE *v.* (2)] [1940s+] confused, disorientated.

boggle-de-botch *n.* (*also* **boggledybotch**) [BOGGLE *n.* + SE *botch*, a mess, an error] [early–mid-19C] a mess, a blunder, a bungling.

boggler *v.* [SE *boggler*, a fumbler] [early 17C; early 19C] a whore, a promiscuous woman.

boggling *n.* [? BOGGLE *v.* (2)] [early 19C] (*US*) hesitating unnecessarily; delaying, finding something difficult.

boggy *n.* [ety. unknown] [mid-19C] (*UK Und.*) a man.

boggy up *v.* (*also* **bogey up, boggie up**) [BOGEY *n.*[1] (2)] [1950s] to turn informer.

boghouse *n.* [BOG *v.*[1] (2) + SE *house*] [mid-17C+] a lavatory, a privy.

bogie *n.*[1] [BOGART *v.* (2)] [2000s] (*US black*) a cigarette.

bogie *n.*[2] *see also under* BOGEY.

bogie house *n.* [BOGEY *n.*[2] + SE *house*] [late 19C+] (*Aus.*) a bathroom.

bog-in *n.* [BOG IN *v.* (1)] [1910s+] (*Aus.*) a heavy meal.

bog in *v.* (*also* **bog into**) [? SE *bog* n., the image is of 'getting stuck in'] (*orig. Aus.*) **1** [late 19C+] to eat heartily. **2** [late 19C+] to work hard, to do anything energetically; thus as imper. **3** [1910s] to interfere in. **4** [1910s+] to get started. **5** [1910s+] to not stand on any ceremony.

bogish *adj.* (*also* **boguish**) [var. on SE] [1930s–40s] (*US black*) bogus.

bog Latin *n.* [the term is found as synon. with SE *shelta*, a form of jargon used by tinkers, which is based on Gaelic and rendered further incomprehensible to non-adepts by the inversion or arbitrary alteration of initial consonants; note SE *pig Latin*, pretend Latin] **1** [late 18C+] fake Latin. **2** [1940s+] tinkers' Gaelic.

bogle *n.* [its main characteristic is the bending backwards of one's body] [1990s+] (*W.I./UK/US black teen*) a dance originated by Jamaican Gerald Levy in 1991 and popularized in songs by artists such as Buju Banton.

bog off *v.* [BOG *n.*[1]; euph. for FUCK OFF! *excl.*] [1940s+] (*orig. RAF*) to go away; usu. as a dismissive excl. *bog off!*

bogs *n. see* BOG *n.*[1].

bog-standard *adj.* (*also* **bog-ordinary**) [despite assumed link to BOG *n.*[1] the *OED* suggests ultimate ety. in *box-standard*, 'motoring, engineering, and other technical contexts: in standard manufactured form, unmodified; (hence) basic, unexceptional'] [1980s+] average.

bogue *n.*[1] [Choctaw *bog*, a stream or creek; thus the swamps that typify the topography of southern Florida] [19C] (*US*) a native of Florida.

bogue *n.*[2] [ety. unknown; ? BOGUS *adj.* (1); Smitherman *Black Talk* (1994), suggests Hausa *boko*, bad, fake] [1960s+] (*US drugs*) the sickness that follows an addict's withdrawal from regular narcotic use.

bogue *n.*[3] [BOGUS *adj.* (1)] [1970s] (*US*) a stupid, unpleasant person.

bogue *adj.* [BOGUS *adj.*] **1** [1950s+] (*US teen*) fake, unsophisticated, naïve. **2** [1960s–70s] (*US drugs*) suffering from narcotic withdrawal symptoms [BOGUE *n.*[2]]. **3** [1960s+]

(*US campus/teen*) disgusting, unappealing. **4** [1970s] (*US black*) inferior, mediocre.

bogue *v.* [BOGUE *n.*[2]] [1980s] (*US campus*) to bring down, to subdue.

boguey *adj.* (*also* **boogy**) [BOGUE *n.*[2]] [1970s] (*US drugs*) suffering from heroin withdrawal.

boguish *adj. see* BOGISH *adj.*

bogus *n.* [note *OED*: 'Dr S. Willard, of Chicago [...] quotes from the Painesville (Ohio) *Telegraph* of July 6 and Nov. 2, 1827, the word bogus as a n. applied to an apparatus for coining false money. Mr Eber D. Howe, who was then editor of that paper, describes in his *Autobiography* (1878) the discovery of such a piece of mechanism in the hands of a gang of coiners at Painesville, in May 1827; it was a mysterious-looking object, and some one in the crowd styled it a "bogus", a designation adopted in the succeeding numbers of the paper. Dr Willard considers this to have been short for "tantrabogus", a word familiar to him from his childhood, and which in his father's time was commonly applied in Vermont to any ill-looking object. He points out that "tantarabobs" is given in Halliwell, *Dict. of Archaic and Provincial Words* (1847), as a Devonshire word for the devil; bogus seems thus to be related to bogy etc.' Farmer, *Americanisms Old New* (1889), posits an Italian swindler called Borghese, working across the southwest US distributing fictitious notes, cheques etc, *c.*1837; this surname was gradually changed to Borges and thence bogus. The writer J.R. Lowell, also cited by Farmer, opted for Fr. *bagasse*, the refuse of sugar cane after the juice was extracted] **1** [early–mid-19C] (*US*) a machine used to produce counterfeit money. **2** [early 19C+] counterfeit money. **3** [20C+] (*US*) a fake, a spurious imitation. **4** [1970s–80s] (*UK black*) a lie, a 'story'.

bogus *adj.* (*also* **bogey**) [BOGUS *n.*] [mid-19C+] **1** a general term of disapproval, unpleasant, undesirable, untrustworthy, unfair. **2** (*also* **bogy**) fake, spurious. **3** (*US campus*) great, excellent. **4** (*US campus*) pretentious, pointless, stupid.

bogus *v.* [BOGUS *adj.* (2)] [1990s+] (*US*) to fool, hoodwink.

bogus beef *n. see under* BEEF *n.*[2].

bogy *n.* **1** *see* BOGEY *n.*[1]. **2** *see* BOGEY *n.*[3].

bogy *adj. see* BOGUS *adj.*

boh *n. see* BO *n.*[1] (1).

bohak/bohawk *n. see* BOHUNK *n.*

bohbohl *n. see* BOBOL *n.*

bohee *n. see* GEORGE BOHEE *n.*

boheize *n.* [ety. unknown; ? BO *n.*[1] (1) + pron. SE *house*] [2000s] (*US black*) a house.

boheme *n.* (*also* **bohem, bohemian, bohim**) [SE *Bohemian*, an artist, literary man or actor, who leads a free, vagabond or irregular life, despising accepted conventions] [1980s+] (*US campus*) one who identifies with the 1960s.

Bohemie *n.* [SE *Bohemian*, i.e. Czechoslovak] [1960s] (*US*) a Czech or Slavic immigrant.

bohn *n.* [*Bohn*'s Classical Library; but reinforced by BONE *v.*[3]] (*US campus*) **1** [mid-19C] a translation, a 'crib'. **2** [late 19C–1900s] a studious person; thus as v., *bohn*, to work hard.

boho *n.*[1] [abbr. SE *Bohemian*, a Czechoslovak] [1920s–30s] (*US*) a Czech immigrant.

boho *n.*[2] [abbr. SE *Bohemian*, a literary/social 'vagabond'] **1** [1960s+] a cultural non-conformist, a bohemian; thus *bohoism*. **2** [1980s+] (*US campus*) in ironic, teasing use, one who identifies with the 1960s.

boho *adj.* [BOHO *n.*[2] (1)] [1960s+] (*orig. US*) bohemian.

bohunk *n.* (*also* **bohak, bohawk**) [SE *Bohemian* + *Hungarian*] **1** [20C+] (*US*) a Slav immigrant from Eastern Europe. **2** [20C+] (*US*) an oafish, dull, if muscular person. **3** [20C+] (*US*) a second-rate person. **4** [20C+] (*US*) an East European language. **5** [20C+] (*US*) as a term of address, the equivalent of 'my boys'. **6** [1990s+] (*US campus*) an attractive-looking man.

bohunk *adj.* [BOHUNK *n.*] [20C+] (*US*) **1** Slavic. **2** mediocre, second-rate.

bohunkus *n.* (*also* **bohunky**) [BOHUNK *n.* (2) + ? echoic of buttocks slapping onto a hard seat] [1920s+] (*US*) the buttocks, thus fig. oneself, e.g. in phr. *get your bohunkus out of here!*

boil *n.* [i.e. things have 'come to the boil'] [17C] the alarm.

SE in slang uses

IN PHRASES

❑ **go off the boil** *v.* [20C+] **1** to lose impetus, to lose enthusiasm. **2** to calm down. **3** of a woman, to lose her enthusiasm for sex.

boil *v.* **1** [late 16C–early 17C] (*UK Und.*) to find out, to unmask, to betray. **2** [mid-19C–1930s] (*US*) to rush along. **3** [late 19C+] to be angry; thus adjs. *boiled up, boiling up*, angry.

SE in slang uses

IN COMPOUNDS

❑ **boil-out** *n.* [1940s–50s] (*US drugs*) total abstention from narcotics in the hope of achieving complete withdrawal. ❑ **boilover** *n.* [late 19C+] (*Aus.*) in sport, spec. horseracing, an upset, the failure of a favourite to win. ❑ **boil-up** *n.* **1** [1920s–30s] (*Aus./US/N.Z. tramp*) a period during which tramps rest from the road, wash and repair clothes, have a meal and do similar 'housekeeping'; also as v. **2** [1940s] (*Aus.*) an argument [one's temper *boils up* (and over)]. **3** [1980s] (*Aus. prison*) the illicit making of tea.

IN PHRASES

❑ **boil down** *v.* [late 19C] (*US black*) to correct or rebuke. ❑ **boil off the stomach** *v.* [1970s] (*US*) to vomit copiously. ❑ **boil one's cabbage twice** *v. see* separate entry. ❑ **boil one's lobster** *v. see under* LOBSTER *n.*[1]. ❑ **boil someone's cabbage** *v. see under* CABBAGE *n.*[6]. ❑ **boil the billy** *v.* [an actual 'billy' (trad. associated with cooking in the open) need not be used; the term can be applied to a kettle] [1950s+] (*Aus.*) to make a cup of tea.

IN EXCLAMATIONS

❑ **go and boil your head!** (*also* **go and boil your can! go boil yourself!**) [late 19C+] a generally dismissive excl., euph. for *go to hell!*

boil and pus *n.* [rhy. sl.] [1980s] (*Aus.*) an omnibus.

boiled *n.* [abbr.] [mid-18C–1910s] *boiled* beef or *boiled* mutton, or *boiled* potatoes.

boiled *adj.* **1** [late 19C+] (*also* **boiled as an owl**) drunk. **2** [1920s+] angry, furious.

IN COMPOUNDS

❑ **boiled-bum** *adj.* [1960s] (*Aus.*) red, from drunkenness.

SE in slang uses

IN COMPOUNDS

❑ **boiled dinner** *n.* [culinary stereotyping] [1940s] (*US*) an Irishman. ❑ **boiled dog** *n.* [? SE *boiled shirt* + PUT ON (THE) DOG *under* DOG *n.*[2]] [1910s+] (*Aus./N.Z.*) snobbery, stand-offishness, 'side'. ❑ **boiled lobster** *n.* [LOBSTER *n.*[1] (1a); cooked lobsters turn red/pink] [late 19C–1900s] a soldier. ❑ **boiled rag** *n.* (*also* **boiled linen**) [joc. var. on *BOILED SHIRT* below] [mid-19C–1910s] (*Aus./US*) a starched dress shirt. ❑ **boiled shirt** *n.* (*also* **biled shirt**) [earlier use can denote, in US, simply a white shirt; such shirts were literally boiled in the wash to remove the starch] **1** [mid-19C+] a starched dress shirt. **2** [1970s] (*US*) a respectably dressed man. ❑ **boiled stuff** *n.* [used by Shakespeare in *Cymbeline* (1610); the ref. is to the sweating tubs, used to treat venereal diseases] [early 17C] prostitutes, viewed collectively.

IN PHRASES

❑ **drunk as a boiled owl** *adj. see* separate entry.

boiler *n.*[1] [the steam or smoke that they all produce] **1** [late 19C–1960s] (*US*) the stomach. **2** [20C+] (*US*) a tobacco pipe. **3** [1910s–50s] (*US*) an automobile. **4** [1920s–30s] (*US Und.*) an illegal still or its minder. **5** [1930s] (*US drugs*) a spoon used to heat the mixture of water and powdered narcotic prior to an injection. **6** [1950s+] (*Aus. prison*) any form of home-made device used to heat water.

IN PHRASES

❑ **on the hot boiler** [1940s] (*US Und.*) stealing automobiles.

SE in slang uses

IN COMPOUNDS

❑ **boiler acid** *n.* (*also* **boiler compound**) [1940s–60s] (*US*) extremely unpleasant tasting coffee. ❑ **boiler factory** *n.*

[1920s] (*US*) an unappealing young person. ❑ **boilermaker** *n.* [? the preferred drink of a SE *boiler-maker*, or strong enough to clean a boiler] **1** [1920s+] a 50/50 mix of mild and brown ale. **2** [1940s–50s] (*US*) (*also* **boilermaker's helper**) beer with a whisky chaser, the US working man's trad. drink [subseq. use is SE]. ❑ **boiler-room** *n.* (*also* **boiler shop**) [1920s+] (*US*) any room full of noisy, energetic activity, e.g. a political campaign headquarters, a newspaper cityroom, a room used by illegal bookmakers, stock swindlers or confidence tricksters.

IN PHRASES

❑ **burst one's boiler** *v.* (*also* **bust one's boiler**) [fig. uses of SE] [early–mid-19C] (*orig. US*) **1** to come to grief, to get into trouble. **2** to lose one's temper. **3** to cause trouble for. **4** (*also* **burst one's boilers**) to overexert oneself physically. **5** to lose emotional control.

boiler *n.*[2] [the old, tough birds (BIRD *n.*[1] (1b)) used for boiling chickens] [1960s+] **1** an old woman, without any remaining sexual appeal; often as *old boiler*. **2** a woman, usu. an unattractive one.

boilerhouse *n.* [rhy. sl. = SE *spouse*] [2000s] one's wife.

boilerplate *n.* [legal and journalistic jargon *boilerplate*, standard practice used by lawyers (the regular clauses in any contract) or the media (the basic syndicated wire-service stories used throughout the US newspaper system)] [20C+] (*US*) clichéd writing; thus ext. to any banal creation.

boiler-plated *adj.* [SE *boiler-plate*, the iron used in the manufacture of boilers] [late 19C+] (*US*) absolutely dependable and consistent.

boilers, the *n.* (*also* **Brompton boilers, the**) [their supposed resemblance to a large boiler, and their being covered in sheet iron] [mid–late 19C] the buildings of the Victoria and Albert Museum (orig. the Kensington Museum and School of Art) in Brompton Road, London (demolished 1898).

boiling *n.*[1] [BOIL *v.* (1)] [early–mid-17C] a betrayal, an unmasking.

boiling *n.*[2] *see* WHOLE BOILING LOT *n.*

boiling *adj.* **1** [mid-19C+] (*US campus*) angry [BOIL *v.* (3)]. **2** [late 19C] (*US*) drunk [BOILED *adj.* (1)]. **3** [late 19C; 1970s] as an intensive.

boiling-out *n.* [BOIL *v.* (3)] [20C+] (*US*) a scolding, a telling-off.

boilo *n.* [SE *boil* + -O *sfx* (1)] [1930s] (*US*) hot, illicit whisky.

boil-pricker *n.* [SE *boil*, a pustule + *pricker*] [1960s–70s] (*US*) a pointed shoe.

boing *v.* [? BONK *v.* (1)] [1990s+] (*US*) to kill, to shoot dead.

boing-boing *n.* (*US*) **1** [1960s+] a tourist [SE *boing*, the sound of elastic snapping back; the image is of the head twanging backwards and forwards as its owner gazes at the big city sights]. **2** [1980s] an embarrassing person [their constant movement and lack of calm].

boingo *n.* [BOING-BOING *n.* (2)] [1990s+] (*US*) a fool.

boink *v.* [BONK *v.* (2)] [1980+] (*US*) to have intercourse with; thus *boinking*, sexual intercourse.

bo-ink-um *n.* [ety. unknown] [19C] guts, stamina, endurance.

boja *n.* [? BUDGE *n.*[1] (1) or BODGER *n.*/SE *botcher*] [1950s] (*W.I.*) an untrustworthy person.

bo-jack *n.* (*also* **bo-dick**) [1970s+] (*US black*) **1** a form of address to a male [BO *n.*[1] (1) + JACK *n.*[2] (3)/DICK *n.*[1] (1)]. **2** the scrotum, the penis [BO *n.*[1] (1) + JACK *n.*[3] (1)/DICK *n.*[1] (5)].

bojangles *n.* [the idea of the testicles 'jangling' against each other; ult. the song 'Mr Bojangles'] [2000s] (*US black*) the testicles.

bojie *n. see* BOOJEE *n.*

bok *n.* [Afk. *bok*, a 'flame', a beau] (*S.Afr.*) **1** [1950s] a young woman, a girlfriend. **2** [1970s+] an enthusiast; thus *bok for*, 'up for', game for. **3** [1970s+] a hero, a masculine or athletic male.

IN PHRASES

❑ **big bok** *n.* [1980s] (*S.Afr.*) someone self-important, a braggart.

bokbaard *n.* [Afk. *bok*, a goat + *baard*, a beard] [1910s+] (*S.Afr.*) a goatee beard.

bokbaardjie *n.* [BOKBAARD *n.*] [1960s+] (*S.Afr.*) a goatee beard.

bokdrol *n.* [Afk. *bok*, goat + *drol*, dropping] [1970s+] (*S.Afr.*) **1** a chocolate-covered peanut. **2** anything, e.g. a hairstyle, that resembles a pile of goat droppings.

boke *n.*[1] [BOKO *n.* (1)] [mid-19C–1960s] (*US*) the nose.

boke *n.*[2] (*also* **boak**) [synon. Scot.; ult. OE *bealcan*, to belch, 'throw up'] [1930s+] (*Ulster*) vomit.

IN PHRASES

❑ **give one the boke** *v.* (*also* **give one the boak**) [1980s+] to make one sick.

boke *v.* (*also* **boak, bowk**) [BOKE *n.*[2]] [late 17C; 1930s+] to vomit.

bokin a smowl *n. see under* BOWL *n.*

bokkerol *n. see* BOGGERAL *n.*

bokkie *n.* [Afk. *bok*, a kid (antelope, goat etc) + dimin. sfx *-ie*] [1950s+] (*S.Afr.*) an affectionate form of address, esp. to a woman; thus a girlfriend.

boko *n.* (*also* **koboko**) **1** [mid-19C+] the nose [? BEAK *n.*[2] (1) and/or COCONUT *n.*[1] (1); Ware suggests an alternative ety., the clown Joseph Grimaldi's (1779–1837) trademark tapping of his nose with the comment, *C'est beaucoup*, that's plenty]. **2** [late 19C] a person. **3** [1900s] (*Aus.*) a person or animal blind in one eye; thus *boko-eyed*, half-blind.

boko *adj.*[1] [Fr. *beaucoup*] [late 19C] too much, excessive.

boko *adj.*[2] [var. on BROKE *adj.*[1] (1)] [1950s] (*UK juv.*) penniless, broke.

bokoo *adv. see* BEAUCOUP *adv.*

boko-smasher *n.* [BOKO *n.* (1) + SE *smasher*, lit. 'nose-smasher'] [late 19C–1900s] a thug.

bokum *n. see* BUNKUM *n.*

bola *adj.* [? college sports cheer *boola-boola*] [1990s+] (*US campus*) general term of approval.

boldacious *adj.* [BODACIOUS *adj.*] [1980s] (*US black*) excessive behaviour (over-aggressive, arrogant, unrestrained, etc) that is inappropriate for a situation.

bold as... *adj.*

IN PHRASES

❑ **bold as a miller's shirt** *adj.* [pvb 'bold as a miller's shirt, which every day takes a rogue by the collar'] [late 18C–early 19C] very bold. ❑ **bold as brass** *adj.* [var. on SE *brazen*] [late 18C+] arrogant, impudent, outspoken, shameless.

boldface *adj.* **1** [late 16C–early 19C] brazen, impudent; used as a term of address. **2** [20C+] (*W.I./UK black*) capable of petty crime.

IN PHRASES

❑ **play boldface** *v.* [1950s] (*W.I./UK black*) to pretend to be braver or more confident than one is; to put on a bold face to mask one's guilt.

boldrumptious *adj.* [SE *bold* + *rumpus*] [late 19C–1900s] presumptuous.

bold thing, the *n.* [1980s+] (*Irish*) sexual intercourse.

IN PHRASES

❑ **do the bold thing** *v.* [2000s] (*Irish*) to have sexual intercourse.

boldyke *n. see* BULL-DYKE *n.*

bolicky *adj. see* BOLLACKING *adj.*

Bolivian marching powder *n.* (*also* **Bolivian brain food, Bolivian flake, marching powder**) [Bolivia, like Colombia, is a major source of cocaine] [1970s+] (*drugs*) cocaine.

bolix *n. see* BALLOCKS *n.*

bolix (up) *v. see* BALLOCKS (UP) *v.*

bollacking *adj.* (*also* **bolicky**) [1970s] (*Irish*) a coarse intensive.

bollacks! *excl. see* BALLOCKS! *excl.*

bollemakiesie *adv.* [Afk. *bollemakiesie*, a somersault] [1920s+] (*S.Afr.*) head-over-heels.

bollicking *adj.* [BALLOCK *n.*] [1920s] (*US*) a general intensifier, e.g. *bollicking great, bollicking awful.*

bollicks! *excl. see* BALLOCKS! *excl.*

bollicky *n. see* BALLOCK *n.* (2).

bollicky *adj.* [BALLOCK *n.*] [1960s+] (*Aus.*) naked.

bollicky bare-ass *adj.* [BOLLICKY *adj.* + BARE-ASS *adj.* (1)] [20C+] absolutely naked.

bollicky bill *adj.* [var. on STARK BALLOCK NAKED *adj.*; *Bollicky Bill (the Sailor)*, a character in a coarse late 19C song] [late 19C+] naked.

bollicky naked *adj. see* BOLLOCKY NAKED *adj.*

bollinger bolshevik *n.* [*Bollinger* champagne] [1980s+] one who preaches socialism but espouses a capitalist lifestyle.

bollix *see under* BALLOCKS and its combs.

bollock *see also under* BALLOCK and its combs.

bollock *n. see* BALLOCKS *n.* (5).

IN COMPOUNDS

❑ **bollock-all** *n.* [var. on FUCK ALL *n.*] [2000s] nothing at all. ❑ **bollockbag** *n.* [SE *bag*/BAG *n.*[1] (1)] [1990s+] the scrotum, container of testicles. ❑ **bollockbrain** *n.* [1960s+] a general term of abuse; thus adj. *bollock-brained*. ❑ **bollockchops** *n.* [CHOPS *n.*[1] (1)] [1990s+] a derog. term of address. ❑ **bollock yoghurt** *n.* [1990s+] semen.

IN PHRASES

❑ **sweat one's bollocks off** *v. see* SWEAT ONE'S ARSE OFF *under* SWEAT *v.*[2].

bollocko *adj.* [SE colloq. phr. *ballock naked*+ -O *sfx* (5)] [1950s+] naked.

bollocky naked *adj.* (*also* **bollicky naked, bollocky, bollocky bare-ass**) [SE colloq. phr. *ballock naked*] [1930s+] (*Aus./US*) stark naked.

bollo-loco *n.* [Sp. 'crazy chick'] [1970s] (*US/P.R.*) a promiscuous woman or girl.

bollox *see also under* BALLOCKS and combs.

bollox *v.* [1930s] (*US*) to go.

bolloxed *adj.* [BALLOCKS (UP) *v.*] [2000s] drunk.

bollux *see also under* BALLOCKS and its combs.

Bolly *n.* [abbr.] [1980s+] *Boll*inger champagne.

bolly *n. see* BALLOCKING *n.*[2].

bolly-eyed *adj.* [? Yorks. dial. *boll*, left-handed] [1990s+] having unfocused eyes.

bolo *n.* **1** [1940s] a shout. **2** [1970s] (*US black*) a punch.

bolo *adj.*[1] [? milit. use *Bolo*, a spy (from one Bolo Pasha, executed for treason in 1918) or abbr. Bolshevik, i.e. fig. something that 'is not straight'; note Vietnam-era US Army *bolo*, to ruin or fail deliberately] [1940s–50s] incorrectly aligned.

bolo *adj.*[2] [1940s+] (*W.I.*) hard.

bologna/bologne *n. see* BALONEY *n.*

boloney/bolony *see under* BALONEY.

bolshie *n.* (*also* **bolshy**) [abbr. Rus. *Bolshevik*, the majority; 'a member of that part of the Russian Social-Democratic Party which took Lenin's side in the split that followed the second Congress of the party in 1903, seized power in the 'October' Revolution of 1917, and was subsequently renamed the (Russian) Communist Party' (*OED*)] [1910s+] **1** a Bolshevik. **2** in weak use of sense 1, a left-winger, a socialist. **3** an unconventional person (judged by a conservative), an opponent of the status quo.

bolshie *adj.* (*also* **bolshy**) [BOLSHIE *n.*] **1** [1910s+] uncooperative, obstructive, subversive. **2** [1920s+] left-wing, spec. communist.

bolshiness *n.* [BOLSHIE *adj.* (1)] [1970s+] rebelliousness, anti-authoritarianism.

bolt *n.*[1] [BOLT *v.* (1)] **1** [19C+] a swift departure. **2** [mid-19C–1900s] (*US campus*) the act of deliberately missing a class or meeting. **3** [mid-19C–1900s] (*US campus*) the cancellation of a class or meeting. **4** [late 19C–1910s] (*Aus./UK*) an act of running away, of absenting oneself, an escape from prison.

bolt *n.*[2] [? SE *bolt*, to swallow hastily, to gulp down whole] [mid-19C] the throat.

bolt *n.*[3] [ety. unknown] [1980s] (*US campus*) a very handsome man.

bolt *n.*[4] [tradename for amyl nitrite] [1980s+] (*drugs*) **1** phencyclidine. **2** isobutyl nitrite. **3** amphetamine.

bolt *v.* [use of SE *bolt*, a missile, as an image of moving at speed] **1** [late 17C+] to leave, to run off [20C use SE]. **2** [early 18C] to rush. **3** [19C+] to leave one's spouse. **4** [mid-19C–1900s] (*US campus*) to cut a class. **5** [mid-19C+] of a man or usu. woman, to run off with a lover. **6** [late 19C+] (*also* **do the bolt**) (*Aus. prison*) to escape from prison. **7** [1990s+] (*US campus*) to defecate in one's pants.

bolter *n.* **1** [late 17C–late 18C] (*UK Und.*) (*also* **bolter of Whitefriars, bolter of the Mint**) 'one that doth but peep out of Whitefriars, and retire again like a rabbit out of his hole' (Shadwell, *The Squire of Alsatia*, 1688) [SE *bolter*, a fugitive from justice. *Whitefriars*, near St Paul's Cathedral, and the *Mint*, near Southwark, were both well-known refuges for 17C–18C villains]. **2** [early 19C+] one who flees their obligations and responsibilities; thus esp. a woman who runs away from her husband, home and family [SE *bolt*, to run off, esp. used of horses and, as such, suitable for the upper/upper-middle class milieu in which it is used. The *locus classicus* is in Nancy Mitford's novel *The Pursuit of Love* (1945), where an errant figure is known simply as 'The Bolter']. **3** [mid-19C] (*Aus.*) a bushranger. **4** [mid-19C–1900s] (*Aus.*) a person once serving a sentence of transportation who absconds and remains free long enough (seven years) to be given an official pardon in the newspaper. **5** [2000s] (*N.Z.*) a horse viewed as an outsider that goes on to win, occas., a competitor who is considered unlikely to win a race.

bolter's chance *n.* [SAusE *bolter*, a fugitive convict, an absconder] [1940s+] (*Aus.*) an outside chance; thus *not have a bolter's chance*, to have no chance at all.

bolt from the blue *n.* [the image is of a thunderbolt; 20C use SE] [late 19C] anything wholly unexpected. usu. unpleasant.

bolt-in-tun *v.* [var. on BOLT *v.*; *Bolt-in-Tun*, a well-known London inn] [early 19C] to run off, to escape; found in such deliberately oblique phrases as *he's gone to bolt-in-tun* or *the bolt-in-tun is concerned*.

B.O.L.T.O.P. *phr.* [abbr.] [1940s+] *b*etter *o*n *l*ips *t*han *o*n *p*aper, written over an 'X' (signifying a kiss).

bolts-and-nuts *adj. see* NUTS-AND-BOLTS *adj.*[1].

boltsprit *n.* [SE *bowsprit*, a large spar extending from the stem of a vessel, to which the foremast stays are fastened] [late 17C–early 18C] the nose.

IN PHRASES

❑ **break one's boltsprit** *v.* [late 17C–early 18C] to lose one's nose as a result of syphilis.

bolt the moon *v. see* SHOOT THE MOON *under* MOON *n.*

bolus *n.* [SE *bolus*, a large pill, part of their stock-in-trade] [late 18C–1960s] an apothecary; a doctor.

bom *n.* [Swahili *boma*, a stockade] [1970s] (*S.Afr. prison*) the solitary confinement block.

bom *v.* [1980s] (*S.Afr.*) to beg; thus *bomming*, begging.

boman *n.* [? Fr. *beau*, good-looking + SE *man*] (*UK Und.*) **1** [17C–18C] a gallant, a sweetheart. **2** [late 18C–early 19C] a thief.

IN PHRASES

❑ **boman-prig** *n. see* BOWMAN-PRIG *under* BOWMAN *adj.*

boman *adj.* [early 18C] (*UK Und.*) safe.

bomb *n.* **1** [1910s+] (*US*) a surprise or unpleasant event, a sensational development. **2** [1930s–40s] (*US prison*) an egg; usu. boiled. **3** [1950s] (*US teen*) verbal aggression. **4** [1950s] (*US*) a very sexy woman. **5** [1950s+] a large sum of money; often in *make a bomb* . **6** as a vehicle or gadget. (**a**) [1950s+] (*orig. Aus./N.Z./US*) a dilapidated, run-down old car. (**b**) [1950s+] (*US*) a fast car or motorcycle. (**c**) [1970s] (*US prison*) toilet paper rolled in a certain way so that it continues to burn for a long time when set alight. (**d**) [1980s+] (*Aus./N.Z. prison*) an illicit gadget used to heat water (for brewing tea etc). (**e**) [2000s] (*S.Afr. prison*) solitary confinement. **7** in the context of drug use. (**a**) [1950s+] a very large and potent cannabis cigarette. (**b**) [1960s] any form of pill containing sleep-inducing or depressant drugs. (**c**) [1960s] (*Aus.*) an illegal stimulant given to a racing animal. (**d**) [1960s–70s] heroin of well-above-average purity. (**e**) [1980s+] crack cocaine. (**f**) [1990s+] (*US*) a package of drugs. (**g**) [2000s] amphetamine, mixed into a drink and swallowed. (**h**) [2000s] swallowing a package of otherwise unpleasantly tasting drugs. **8** [1950s+] (*orig. UK theatrical*) a major success, esp. as phr. *go down a bomb*. **9** [1950s+] (*orig. US theatrical*) a disaster, a flop. **10** [1960s–70s] (*US*) in pl., the female breasts. **11** [1960s+] (*US black/campus*) (*also* **da bomb, bombness**) constr. with *the*, the best. **12** [1960s+] (*US campus*) the grade of B. **13** [1960s+] (*US campus*) a difficult examination. **14** [1970s+] (*US*) a hard blow (with a fist).

IN PHRASES

□ **cost a bomb** *v.* [1950s+] to cost a great deal. □ **go a bomb** *v.* [1960s+] to be very keen on, enthusiastic for. □ **like a bomb** *adv.* **1** [1950s+] very successfully. **2** [1950s+] (*orig. US*) very fast. □ **lower the bomb** *v.* [? mis-reading of *LOWER THE BOOM (ON) under* LOWER *v.*] [1950s–70s] to speak or act in a decisively negative manner. □ **make a bomb** *v.* [1950s+] to make a great deal of money.

SE in slang uses

DERIVATIVES

□ **bombness** *n. see* BOMB *n.* (11).

IN COMPOUNDS

□ **bombhead** *n. see* separate entry. □ **bomb-proof** *adj.* [SE] [mid-19C+] (*orig. US milit.*) untouchable, absolutely secure and safe. □ **bombshell** *n. see* separate entry.

bomb *adj.*[1] (*also* **bomb-ass**) [BOMB *n.* (11)] [1970s+] very good, excellent, the best.

IN COMPOUNDS

□ **bomb-baida** *n.* [ety. unknown] [2000s] (*US black*) extremely potent marijuana. □ **bomb-diggety** *n.* (*also* **bomb-biggity, bombdigadee, bomb-diggidy**) [var. on HOT DIGGETY (DOG)! *excl.*] [1990s+] (*US black*) a general term of approval.

bomb *adj.*[2] [1990s+] (*US campus*) a general pej.

bomb *v.*[1] [fig. uses of SE] **1** [1940s+] (*Aus.*) to dope a horse. **2** [1960s+] (*US*) to hit hard. **3** [1960s+] to move, esp. to drive fast, usu. as *bomb along, bomb down* (the road), *bomb off, bomb around*, to rush around (aimlessly). **4** [1970s] (*US*) to criticize harshly. **5** [1970s] to work hard at something. **6** [1970s+] (*US campus*) to get very drunk. **7** [1980s] to write graffiti. **8** [1980s+] (*orig. US black*) to spray-paint a subway or railway car, a building or similar space with graffiti. **9** [2000s] (*drugs*) to consume a drug, e.g. amphetamine.

DERIVATIVES

□ **bomber** *n.* [1980s+] (*orig. US black*) a graffiti writer. □ **bombing** *n.* [1980s] (*orig. US black*) a piece of graffiti.

bomb *v.*[2] [BOMB *n.* (9)] **1** [1960s] (*US campus*) to get the grade 'B' on a test or examination. **2** [1960s+] (*US*) to fail, to do badly; also BOMB OUT *v.* (1). **3** [1970s] (*US*) (*also* **bomb off**) of machinery or other equipment, to break down, to malfunction. **4** [1990s+] of an experience, to be bad or disappointing.

DERIVATIVES

□ **bombsville** *n.* [sense 2 + -VILLE *sfx*[1] (1)] [1950s–60s] any kind of failure in life.

IN PHRASES

□ **bomb out** *v. see* separate entry.

Bombay *n.*

proper name in slang uses

IN COMPOUNDS

□ **Bombay bloomers** *n.* [? orig. worn by servicemen in India] [1970s] (*Aus.*) baggy shorts. □ **Bombay bottom** *n.* [1990s+] (*Aus.*) an attack of diarrhoea, occasioned by food poisoning. □ **Bombay fornicator** *n.* [presumably long enough to double as a bed] [20C+] (*Anglo-Ind.*) a wickerwork chair with arms and an extended footrest. □ **Bombay Hills** *n.* (*also* **Bombays**) [2000s] (*N.Z.*) a notional dividng line between Auckland and the rest of N.Z., ext. as between urban 'civilization' and peasants; usu. in phr. *north/south of the Bombays/Bombay Hills*.

bombazine *n. see* BUMBAZINE *n.*

bomb bandit *n.* [var. on *BUM BANDIT under* BUM *n.*[1]] [1990s+] a homosexual.

bombed *adj.* **1** [1950s+] (*orig. US*) drunk. **2** [1960s–70s] (*US campus*) marked down on an examination. **3** [1960s+] (*orig. US*) intoxicated by a drug. **4** [1970s] (*US campus*) generally unwell.

bombed out *adj.*[1] [BOMBED *adj.*] **1** [1950s+] overcome by an excess of alcohol or drugs. **2** [1950s+] exhausted. **3** [1960s] driven mad. **4** [1960s] in fig. use.

bombed out *adj.*[2] [1970s+] (*Irish/Scot.*) jilted; sent on one's away, rejected.

bomber *n.*[1] **1** [1940s] (*UK Und.*) a safebreaker who uses explosives. **2** [1940s+] (*drugs*) a very large and potent cannabis cigarette. **3** [1960s+] (*drugs*) a barbiturate or an amphetamine drug. **4** [1980s] (*S.Afr.*) a fast train.

IN PHRASES

□ **black bomber** *n.* [packaging + sense 3] [1960s+] (*drugs*) strong (20mg) capsules of Durophet (amphetamine), coloured black.

bomber *n.*[2] [1980s+] (*US teen*) a loud breaking of wind.

bombers *n.* [1970s] (*US*) the female breasts.

bombhead *n.*[1] [BOMB *v.*[1] (3) + -HEAD *sfx* (1)] [1950s–60s] a happy-go-lucky, eccentric person.

bombhead *n.*[2] [? resemblance to the shape of the explosive] [1990s+] the head of the penis.

bombido *n.* (*also* **bombida**) [Sp. *bombido*, a little bomb] [1960s+] (*drugs*) **1** injectable amphetamine. **2** heroin, esp. when mixed with cocaine. **3** a form of depressant.

bombing *n. see under* BOMB *v.*[1].

bombita *n.* [Sp. *bombita*, a little bomb] [1960s+] (*drugs*) **1** amphetamines. **2** methamphetamine, a compound 'designer drug' made from ingredients easily extracted from over-the-counter drugs. **3** a mix of heroin and cocaine. **4** a depressant.

bombo *n.*[1] [SE *bomb* + -O *sfx* (3); it 'knocks one out'. Note SE *bumbo*, 'A liquor composed of rum, sugar, water and nutmeg' (*OED*)] [1940s+] (*Aus.*) cheap wine, methylated spirits or a combination of the two.

bombo *n.*[2] *see* BUMBO *n.*[2].

bombo-claat *n. see* BUMBO-CLAAT *n.*

bombosity *n.* [BUM *n.*[1] (1).] [1930s–60s] (*US*) the buttocks.

bomb out *v.* [BOMB *v.*[2]] **1** [1960s+] (*Aus./US campus*) to perform poorly, esp. in an examination. **2** [1970s] (*US*) to fail to make an expected appearance. **3** [1970s] to fail a candidate or examinee. **4** [1980s] to die, esp. from a drug overdose. **5** [1990s+] to get rid of, to terminate a relationship. **6** [1990s+] to become extremely intoxicated. **7** [1990s+] (*US*) to render someone intoxicated. **8** [2000s] to have one dismissed or ejected.

bombshell *n.* **1** [late 19C+] a shock, a surprise, usu. unpleasant. **2** [1910s+] (*orig. US*) a very sexy woman, esp. as *blonde bombshell*.

bommy-knocker *n. see* DONGER-KNOCKER *n.*

bona *n.*[1] [Ital. *buona*, a good woman] [mid–late 19C] a woman.

bona *n.*[2] *see* BONEY *n.*[1].

bona *adj.* (*also* **bonar, boner**) [Ital. *buono*, good] [mid-19C+] (*Ling. Fr./Polari*) good, pleasant, agreeable.

IN COMPOUNDS

□ **bona omee** *n.* (*also* **bona homey**) [OMEE *n.* (3)] (*camp gay*) a pleasant person, lit. a 'good man'.

bona fide *n.* [Lat. *bona fide*, in good faith; the act was amended to restrict the drinking to two hours after closing time (10 p.m.) and three miles beyond the city limits; it was abolished on 4 July 1960] [1910s–50s] (*Irish*) **1** a genuine traveller, as defined by the WW1 Defence of the Realm Act, which allowed anyone who had genuinely travelled three miles to be served drink at any hour of the day or night. **2** one who was enjoying such extending drinking time. **3** the premises that provide the drink.

IN PHRASES

□ **do the bona fide** *v.* [1910s–50s] (*Irish*) to travel the requisite distance in order to indulge in after-hours drinking.

bona fide *adj.* [rhy. sl.] [20C+] (*Aus.*) terrified.

bonanza *n.* [Sp. *bonanza*, good weather, prosperity. Orig. applied to wealth taken from the silver mines of the Comstock lode in US] [late 19C+] (*orig. US*) good luck, esp. in quantity and unexpected.

bonar *adj. see* BONA *adj.*

bona roba *n.* [Ital. *bona roba*, a fine dress] [late 16C–late 19C] a prostitute.

bonaroo *adj.* (*also* **bonarue, bonneroo, bonny-roo**) [Cajun; thus Fr. *bon*, good] [1920s+] (*US prison*) excellent, first-rate.

bonarooed *adj.* (*also* **bonerooed**) [BONAROO *adj.*] [1970s+] **1** (*US prison*) dressed in one's best clothes. **2** of a place, smartened up, embellished.

bonaroos *n.* (*also* **bonnaroos**) [BONAROO *adj.*] [1970s+] (*US prison*) one's best clothes.

bonbons *n.* [Fr. *bonbons*, sweets] [1970s+] (*US gay*) **1** erogenous zones on the male body. **2** anal virginity. **3** common sense.

bonce *n.* [SE *bonce*, a large marble] **1** [late 19C+] (*also* **bonse**) the head. **2** [1910s] a hat.

IN PHRASES

❑ **off one's bonce** *adj. see* OFF ONE'S HEAD *adj.*

bondage *n.* [1940s] (*US black/Harlem*) debts.

Bondi *n.*

proper name, *Bondi*, a famous beach in Sydney, in slang uses

IN COMPOUNDS

❑ **Bondi cigar** *n.* [1990s+] (*Aus.*) a piece of human excrement floating in the water.

IN PHRASES

❑ **give bondi** *v.* (*also* **...boondie, ...bundi, ...bundy**) [the obvious link is to SE *bondi*, a heavy Aboriginal club, but *AND* suggests the place name remains the more likely origin] [late 19C–1950s] (*Aus.*) to attack savagely. ❑ **shoot through like a Bondi tram** *v.* (*also* **go Bondi, go through like a Bondi tram**) [*shoot through* + *Bondi tram*, a tram running through a suburb in Sydney] [1940s+] (*Aus.*) to leave very quickly, to run off.

bonds *n.* [since his money has paid for them, this 'binds' the women to him] [1960s+] (*US*) the clothes with which a pimp bedecks his working women.

bone *n.*[1] **1** [mid-17C+] the penis. **2** resemblance in shape and/or colour. (**a**) [late 19C] a thin man. (**b**) [1910s+] (*US black*) a thin woman. (**c**) [1910s+] (*also* **bone-on**) the erect penis. (**d**) [1960s] the figurative bone that makes a penis erect and potent. (**e**) [1970s+] (*US drugs*) a cannabis cigarette. (**f**) [1990s+] (*US black/drugs*) a cigarette that mixes tobacco and crack cocaine. (**g**) [1990s+] (*US black/prison*) a cigarette. (**h**) [1990s+] (*US drugs*) (a $50 piece of) crack cocaine. **3** made of bone. (**a**) [mid-19C] a gambling chip. (**b**) [late 19C+] a domino, usu. in pl. (**c**) *see* BONES *n.*[1] (1). **4** [1980s+] (*W.I./UK/US black teen*) in fig. use, one's core, one's soul.

IN COMPOUNDS

❑ **bone-ache** *n.* **1** [1980s] (*W.I.*) an erection. **2** *see also* SE compounds below. ❑ **bone dance** *n. see* separate entry. ❑ **bone-eater** *n.* [EAT *v.* (4)] [2000s] (*US black*) a male homosexual. ❑ **bone-gobbler** *n. see* GOBBLER *n.*[2]. ❑ **bone hog** *n.* [SE *hog*] [1990s+] (*US*) a dedicated and enthusiastic fellatrix. ❑ **bone-in-a-valley** *n.* [sense 2] [1950s+] (*W.I.*) a thin person. ❑ **bone phone** *n.* [20C+] (*US*) the penis. ❑ **bone queen** *n.* [-QUEEN *sfx*] [1970s+] (*US gay*) a fellator. ❑ **bone-riding** *n.* [RIDE *v.*] [2000s] having sexual intercourse, whether vaginal or anal. ❑ **bone smuggler** *n.* [the 'smuggling' is into the anus] [1990s+] a male homosexual, esp. one who dresses in female clothes; a DRAG QUEEN *n.* (1). ❑ **bone stroker** *n.* [1990s+] **1** a masturbator. **2** a male homosexual.

IN PHRASES

❑ **bite the bone** *v.* [? fig. use of sense 1 above] [1970s+] (*US teen*) to be disgusting, unpleasant, second-rate. ❑ **bone down** *v.* [20C+] (*US*) to have sexual intercourse. ❑ **bone up** *v.* [2000s] of the penis, to become erect. ❑ **buck the bone** *v.* [1990s+] to masturbate. ❑ **bury one's bone** *v.* (*also* **bury one's beef**) [1970s+] (*US black*) of a man, to have sexual intercourse. ❑ **bury one's bone in the back garden** *v.* (*also* **...in the backyard**) [1990s+] to sodomize. ❑ **give someone a bone** *v.* [1990s+] of a man, to have sexual intercourse. ❑ **give the dog a bone** *v.* [1980s+] to have sexual intercourse. ❑ **gnaw the bone** *v.* [1990s+] to perform fellatio. ❑ **knuckle the bone** *v.* [1990s+] to masturbate. ❑ **put the bone to** *v.* [mid-17C+] to have sexual intercourse. ❑ **smoke someone's bone** *v.* [2000s] (*US*) to fellate. ❑ **throw a bone (to)** *v.* [2000s] of a man, to have sexual intercourse.

SE in slang uses

DERIVATIVES

❑ **boned** *adj. see* separate entry.

IN COMPOUNDS

❑ **bone-ache** *n.* (*also* **bone-ague**) [the side-effects of syphilis] **1** [16C–mid-17C] venereal disease. **2** *see also* sl. compounds above. ❑ **bone-bag** *n. see* BAG OF BONES *n.*[1]. ❑ **bone-baster** *n.* [SE *bone* + SE *baste*] [late 16C–mid-17C] a cudgel. ❑ **bone-bender** *n.* (*also* **bone-breaker, bone-butcher, bone-carpenter, bone-chiseller**) **1** [late 19C+] (*US*) a surgeon. **2** *see* BONECRUSHER *n.* (2). ❑ **bone box** *n. see* separate entry. ❑ **bone-breaker** *n.* [the aches it induces in the bones] [late 19C–1910s] fever, ague. ❑ **bone-carrier** *n.* [CARRY A BONE *under* CARRY *v.*] [20C+] (*US*) a gossip, a rumour-monger. ❑ **bone cart** *n.* [1910s] (*Aus.*) an ambulance. ❑ **bone-cleaner** *n.* [SE *bones*, objects made of ivory + *cleaner*] [late 19C–1900s] a domestic servant. ❑ **bone crusher** *n. see* separate entry. ❑ **bone-dome** *n.* [1930s+] a protective helmet, initially for fliers, latterly [1950s] motorcyclists and [1980s] cyclists. ❑ **bone factory** *n.* **1** [1950s] (*US Und.*) a hospital. **2** [2000s] (*US*) an old people's home. ❑ **bone-grubber** *n.* [SE *grubber*] [mid-19C] a scavenger who specializes in collecting old bones and selling them to rag-shops or to the bone-grinders. ❑ **bonehead** *n. see* separate entries. ❑ **bone-heap** *n. see* BAG OF BONES *n.*[1]. ❑ **bone-hider** *n.* [late 19C] (*Aus.*) an undertaker. ❑ **bone-house** *n.* **1** [late 18C–late 19C] a coffin. **2** [early–mid-19C] a house or vault in which the bones of the dead are piled up, a charnel-house. **3** [19C] the human body. **4** [1940s] (*US Und.*) a hospital. ❑ **bone-juggler** *n.* [1970s–80s] (*UK black*) a doctor. ❑ **bone orchard** *n.* (*also* **bone-factory, bone-pile**) [mid-19C+] (*US*) a cemetery. ❑ **bone-picker** *n.* **1** [late 18C–mid-19C] a footman [the poor standard of the meals, often based on leftovers, given to servants]. **2** [mid-19C–1900s] a scavenger, a rag and bone man. ❑ **bone-polisher** *n.* **1** [early–mid-19C] a footman; any servant [the '*bones*' or ivory objects that require cleaning]. **2** [mid-19C] the cat-o'-nine-tails or the man who wields it [the 'polishing' of the malefactor's bones]. **3** [1920s–30s] (*US tramp*) a (vicious) dog [the bones are those of animals, or of the victims the dog attacks]. ❑ **bonerack** *n. see* BAG OF BONES *n.*[1]. ❑ **bone-setter** *n.* [SE *bone-setter*, a surgeon] **1** [early–mid-17C] an impassioned lover [he crushes his partner's *bones* in his passionate embrace]. **2** [mid-18C–early 19C] a horse that gives its rider an uncomfortable journey. **3** [early 19C] (*US*) in fig. use, a surprise, i.e. a jolt. **4** [early–mid-19C] a hackney coach. ❑ **bone-shaker** *n.* **1** [late 19C+] an early model of bicycle, with solid rather than rubber tyres; thus later use implies any old or run-down bicycle. **2** [20C+] a decrepit vehicle with, *inter alia*, inadequate springs, thus jolting its passengers. ❑ **boneshop** *n.* [the paucity of the provisions] [late 19C–1900s] the workhouse. ❑ **bonetop** *n.* [TOP *n.* (2)] [1910s] (*US*) a fool, a dullard.

IN PHRASES

❑ **bag of bones** *n. see* separate entry. ❑ **bundle of bones** *n. see* BAG OF BONES *n.*[1]. ❑ **flag a bone** *v.* (*also* **flag the bone, flip a/the bone, give a/the bone, shoot a/the bone**) [the SE *bones* inside the finger] [1960s+] (*US*) to make a gesture of contempt by raising the middle finger. ❑ **four bones** *n.* [1910s–20s] (*Irish*) the human body. ❑ **keep the bone green** *v.* [20C+] (*Ulster*) **1** to postpone settling an argument. **2** to confront someone. ❑ **make one's bones** *v.* **1** [1950s+] (*US Und.*) to arrange and carry out one's first contracted murder. **2** [1970s+] to achieve a successful course or action, in one's profession or work. ❑ **on bone** *adv.* [2000s] (*US prison*) out of favour among fellow prisoners after committing some form of mistake in terms of inmate standards. ❑ **pick the bones out of that** [1930s+] a phr. of dismissal, retaliation, challenge, now see what you can do with that. ❑ **polish a bone** *v.* [late 18C–early 19C] to eat a meal. ❑ **put a bone in someone's hood** *v.* [ext. of SE phr. *put a bone in someone's hood*, to break or cut off someone's head] [mid–late 16C] to cuckold someone. ❑ **put one's bones up** *v.* (*also* **put up one's forks**) [abbr. SE *knuckle-bones*/FORK *n.*[1] (3)] [late 19C] to get ready to fight. ❑ **stack of bones** *n. see* BAG OF BONES *n.*[1]. ❑ **to the bone** *adv.* [1910s+] (*orig. US black*) to the extreme, to the ultimate extent, usu. in combs.

(IN EXCLAMATIONS)

❑ **give it a bone!** [the silencing of a dog by giving it a bone; 20C+ use mainly N.Z.] [late 19C+] shut up! stop talking!

bone *n.*[2] [Fr. *abonnement*, a subscription. Note the small ivory disc, also called a *bone*, issued by theatre managers to favoured friends and acquaintances] [mid–late 19C] a subscriber's ticket for the opera.

bone *n.*[3] [BONE *v.*[3] + ref. to *Bohn's Classical Library*] [late 19C] (*US campus*) a very hard-working student.

bone *n.*[4] [SE *throw one a bone*] **1** [late 19C] (*Aus.*) a pound sterling. **2** [late 19C] a bribe. **3** [late 19C+] (*US*) $1.

(IN PHRASES)

❑ **bone up** *v.* [1910s] (*US*) to pay off a debt.

bone *n.*[5] [BONEHEADED *adj.*] [1910s–40s] (*US*) a fool, a dullard, a idiot.

bone *n.*[6] [1920s] (*US, West*) a horse.

bone *n.*[7] [BONES *n.*[2]; they are also 'black and white'] **1** [1930s] (*US Und.*) a black person. **2** [1940s] (*US black*) a person of mixed race, esp. Anglo-Irish-black.

bone *n.*[8] [SE *bone in one's throat*] [1940s] (*US*) something annoying or irritating.

bone *n.*[9] [abbr.] [1950s+] (*orig. US black/jazz*) a trom*bone*.

bone *adj.*[1] [Ital. *buono*, Fr. *bon*, good] **1** [mid-19C] good. **2** [1970s] (*US Und.*) complete, absolute.

bone *adj.*[2] [BONE *n.*[5]] (*US*) **1** [1910s] stupid, incompetent. **2** [1990s+] bad, false.

bone *v.*[1] [? the image of a dog finding and/or worrying a bone] **1** [late 17C–19C] (*UK Und.*) to arrest, to seize. **2** [late 17C–1940s] to rob, to steal. **3** [early 19C] (*US*) to trick, to beat with dice. **4** [mid-19C] (*US/UK Und.*) to interrogate, to question. **5** [mid-19C] (*US*) to betray, to inform against. **6** [mid-19C–1920s] (*US*) to beg for; to raise money for a cause. **7** [1900s] (*US campus*) to charge with. **8** [1900s] (*US*) to annoy, to infuriate. **9** [1900s–40s] to nag, to pester, e.g. for an unpaid debt. **10** [1930s] (*US*) to solicit, to proposition. **11** [1980s] (*US teen*) to victimize, to treat unfairly.

(DERIVATIVES)

❑ **boned** *adj.* [late 17C+] (*UK Und.*) arrested, captured.

(IN PHRASES)

❑ **bone the fence** *v.* [late 17C–1940s] to find out where goods have been hidden by a receiver and then steal them.

bone *v.*[2] [BONE *n.*[1] (1)] **1** [late 17C; 1980s+] to have sexual intercourse. **2** [1970s+] to sodomize; also in fig. use.

(IN PHRASES)

❑ **boned out** *adj.* [1990s+] (*US black*) exhausted, esp. of a man who has just had sex.

bone *v.*[3] (*also* **bone up, bone up on**) [? SE *bone*, to polish by the use of a flat bone surface to polish one's boots to a shine or play on *knuckle down*; campus uses are influenced by the *Bohn* translations of the classics, and underpinned by alt. sp. BOHN *n.* in US college *c.*1900] [mid-19C+] (*US, orig. milit.*) to work hard, to study, to revise; also extended as *bone down, bone in, bone through*, etc.

bone *v.*[4] [SAusE *point a bone*, an Aborigine practice] [20C+] (*Aus.*) to jinx, to bring bad luck to.

bone *v.*[5] (*also* **bone-up**) [BONE *adj.*[1]] [1980s+] to drive fast.

bone *adv.* [SE *bone*; i.e. to one's very depths] [1930s+] (*US black*) thoroughly, completely.

bone box *n.* **1** [late 18C–mid-19C] the mouth. **2** [late 19C–1940s] (*US*) a coffin. **3** [1940s] the head. **4** [1970s] (*US*) an ambulance. **5** [1970s+] (*US prison*) a hearse.

(IN PHRASES)

❑ **button one's bonebox** *v.* [mid-19C] (*US*) to be quiet.

bonecrusher *n.* [its effects] **1** [late 19C] (*sporting*) a large-calibre sporting rifle, used on large game. **2** [1940s–60s] (*US*) (*also* **bone-bender, bone-cracker**) a wrestler; a powerful fist. **3** [1960s–70s] (*US*) a person who shakes hands forcefully. **4** [1970s+] (*US prison*) a large knife. **5** [1990s+] in drug contexts. (**a**) a near-overdose in which the user feels as if the injection they have just taken is crushing their bones. (**b**) painful withdrawal symptoms. (**c**) crack cocaine. **6** [2000s] a prison guard who uses physical force.

boned *adj.* **1** [1930s+] tipsy [the image of a *boned* carcass, reduced to flabby, floppy meat]. **2** [1960s–70s] hit hard on the head [the *bone* is that of the battered skull].

bone dance *n.* [BONE *n.*[1] (1)] [1980s+] (*US campus*) sexual intercourse.

(IN PHRASES)

❑ **do the bone (dance)** *v.* [1980s] to have sexual intercourse.

boned out *adj.*[1] [BONE *n.*[4] (3)] [1990s+] (*US black*) out of money.

boned out *adj.*[2] **1** [2000s] (*US gang*) retreated from a confrontation [one lacks SE *backbone*]. **2** *see under* BONE *v.*[2].

boned turkey *n.* [mid-19C] (*US*) a dish of hash.

bonehead *n.*[1] [SE *bone* + -HEAD *sfx* (1); the image is of the hardness of bone; Moore, *Lexicon of Cadet Language* (1993), suggests an alternative link to BONE *n.*[1] (1) on pattern of DICKHEAD *n.*] **1** [20C+] (*orig. US*) a fool, a dullard, an idiot; thus as term of address. **2** [1920s–60s] a stubborn person. **3** [1920s+] a stupid error. **4** [2000s] (*S.Afr.*) an Afrikaaner.

(IN COMPOUNDS)

❑ **bonehead English** *n.* [1920s+] (*US campus*) a remedial course in elementary English composition. ❑ **bonehead play** *n.* [PLAY *n.* (2); note locus classicus the 'bonehead play' committed by Giants 19-year-old Fred Merkle rookie substitute in Giants vs. Cubs game on 23 Sept. 1908; the term was coined by the NY press which headlined 'Merkle's Bonehead Play'] [1910s+] (*US*) an elementary, obvious error or mistake; thus *pull a bonehead play*, to make an elementary error.

(IN PHRASES)

❑ **pull a bonehead** *v. see* PULL A BONER *under* BONER *n.*[3].

bonehead *n.*[2] [the head is shaved to the bone] [1940s+] a bald person.

bonehead *n.*[3] [BONE *n.*[1] (2h) + -HEAD *sfx* (4)] [1990s+] a user of crack cocaine.

boneheaded *adj.* (*also* **bonehead**) [BONEHEAD *n.*[1] (1)] [mid-19C+] stupid.

bone out *v.* [? BONE *v.*[5] + ? *move one's bones*] [1990s+] (*US black*) to run away, to leave fast.

boner *n.*[1] [BONE *v.*[1] (2)] [early–mid-19C] (*UK Und.*) a thief.

boner *n.*[2] [BONE *v.*[3]] [late 19C+] (*US campus*) a hard worker.

boner *n.*[3] [SE *bone of contention*] **1** [1910s+] (*US*) a serious mistake, esp. in phr. PULL A BONER below. **2** [1960s] (*US campus*) a difficult examination.

(IN PHRASES)

❑ **pull a boner** *v.* (*also* **...bone, ...bonehead**) [1910s–80s] (*US*) to make a (serious) mistake.

boner *n.*[4] [BONE *n.*[1] (1)] **1** [1950s+] an erection. **2** [1980s+] the penis. **3** [1990s+] (*Aus.*) of a man, one who has sexual intercourse; thus *mad boner*, an especially keen FUCKER *n.* (1). **4** [1990s+] (*Aus.*) a general term of abuse, on pattern of FUCKER *n.* (3). **5** [2000s] (*US*) in fig. use of sense 1, an obsession.

(IN PHRASES)

❑ **bounce one's boner** *v.* [1990s+] to masturbate.

boner *adj. see* BONA *adj.*

bonerific *adj.* [BONAROO *adj.* (1) + SE *terrific*] [2000s] (*US black*) very attractive.

boner nochy *phr.* [Ital. *buona notte*, good night] [late 19C] (*Ling. Fr./Polari*) good night.

bonerooed *adj.* see BONAROOED *adj.*

boneroos *n.* see BONAROOS *n.* (1).

boners! *excl.* (*also* **boney! bonny!**) [? pidgin *bon eye*, good eye] [late 19C+] (*US teen*) that's mine!

bones *n.*[1] [ext. of SE use; dice were orig. made of bone] **1** [late 14C+] dice, esp. in exhortation *roll them bones!* **2** [19C] the human teeth. **3** [mid-19C] (*US*) gambling chips. **4** [late 19C] a surgeon. **5** [1900s] (*US campus*) a skeleton. **6** [1960s–70s] (*US*) a thin person. **7** [1970s+] dominoes.

(IN PHRASES)

❑ **battle the bones** *v.* [SE *battle*, to fight + sense 1] [mid-19C] to play at dice. ❑ **devil's bones** *n. see under* DEVIL *n.* ❑ **jump (on) someone's bones** *v.* **1** [early 19C+] of a man, to have sexual intercourse. **2** [1980s] to attack. ❑ **roll the bones** *v.* (*also* **shake..., trundle...**) [19C+] (*US*) to play at dice.

bones *n.*[2] [? old vaudeville cross-talk act in which one speaker was Mr *Bones*] [20C+] (*US*) a black person.

bones *n.*[3] [1990s+] (*US prison*) a gang tattoo.

boney *n.*[1] (*also* **bona**) [abbr. SE, ult. *bone-fire*] [20C+] (*Ulster*) a bonfire, esp. one lit on 12 July, Orangeman's Day.

boney *n.*[2] (*also* **bonie**) [*BONE-SHAKER under* BONE *n.*[1]] [1970s+] (*S.Afr.*) **1** a bicycle. **2** a motorcycle.

boney *adj.* [SE *bona fide*] [1990s+] (*UK black*) honest, sincere.

boney! *excl. see* BONERS! *excl.*

boneyard *n.* **1** [19C] a very thin or emaciated person or animal [BONE *n.*[1] (1)]. **2** [mid-19C+] a cemetery [SE *bone*]. **3** [1930s] (*US tramp*) a hospital, esp. in the context of a post-mortem examination [SE *bone*]. **4** [2000s] (*US prison*) the family or conjugal visiting area [BONE *v.*[2] (1)].

bonfire *n.* [post WW1 use is US black] [1910s–40s] (*orig. milit.*) a cigarette, a cigarette stub.

bong *n.*[1] (*also* **bhong, bongo**) [Thai *baung*, lit. 'cylindrical wooden tube'] [1970s+] (*US drugs*) a kind of bowl-shaped water-pipe used for smoking marijuana (the specifics vary as to the maker); thus (*Aus.*) *bongineering, bongology*, the construction of such pipes; *bong hit*, a puff on such a pipe.

bong *n.*[2] [? echoic of the supposed noise of tapping an empty head] [1990s+] (*UK juv*) an eccentric.

bong *adj.* [Fr. *bon*, good] [1960s–70s] (*US*) excellent.

bong *v.*[1] [var. on BONK *v.*] **1** [1940s+] (*US/N.Z.*) to hit. **2** [1960s] (*US campus*) to reject someone for membership in a fraternity, club, etc. **3** [1990s+] to have sexual intercourse.

bong *v.*[2] (*also* **bong on**) [BONG *n.*[1]] [1970s+] (*drugs*) to smoke marijuana through a BONG *n.*[1].

bong! *excl.* [onomat.] [1930s+] term used to suggest the sound of a blow or a sudden noise.

bongo *n.*[1] (*also* **bongo lips, bungo**) [*Bongo*, seen as a stereotypically 'African' name] [1940s+] (*orig. US*) a derog. term for a black person.

(IN PHRASES)

❑ **bongo-bongo land** *n.* [1940s+] (*orig. US*) a Third World/African country.

bongo *n.*[2] *see* BONG *n.*[1] (1).

bongo *adj.* [BONKERS *adj.*] [1950s–70s] (*US*) crazy, eccentric.

bongo lips *n. see* BONGO *n.*[1].

bongos *n.* [they resemble bongo drums or they 'bong' up and down] [1980s+] (*US*) the female breasts.

bong swat *n.* (*also* **bong toke**) [BONG *n.*[1] + SE *swat*, a hit] [1980s+] (*US drugs*) an inhalation of a pipeful of marijuana.

bong tong *n.* [a deliberate deflatory mispron. of Fr. *bonton*, good taste, good breeding] [late 19C–1910s] (*Aus./US*) the social élite and their lifestyle and manners, used ironically, incl. prison use, a prisoner with influence and status.

bongy *adj. see* BUNGY *adj.* (1).

bonie *n. see* BONEY *n.*[2].

boniface *n.* [*Boniface*, the jovial innkeeper in George Farquhar's *The Beaux'Stratagem* (1707); however, the term does not appear in print for nearly a century] **1** [early 18C–1910s] a public house landlord. **2** [early 18C–1910s] (*US*) a hotelier.

bonified *adv.* [? Fr. *bon*, good + sfx *-ified* or pron. of Lat. *bona fide*, genuine, lit. 'in good faith'] [1970s–80s] (*US black*) competent, qualified, the right man for job.

boning *n.* [BONE *v.*[2] (1)] [1960s+] (*US campus*) sexual intercourse.

bonings *n.* [BONE *v.*[1] (2)] [early 19C] (*UK Und.*) stolen goods.

bonita *n.* [Sp., lit. 'good little girl'] **1** [1960s+] (*drugs*) milk sugar, commonly used to adulterate heroin. **2** [2000s] (*drugs*) heroin [may be misreading of sense 1].

bonk *n.* [echoic / BONK *v.*] **1** [1930s+] an abrupt, heavy sound, a thump. **2** [1970s+] sexual intercourse [the theory that this sense is backsl. for KNOB *v.*[1] (2) should be rejected]. **3** [1970s+] a blow, esp. on top of the head. **4** [1980s] an erection. **5** [1990s+] usu. of a woman, one who is available for sex.

(IN COMPOUNDS)

❑ **bonkhole** *n.* [2000s] (*S.Afr. gay*) the anus. ❑ **bonk-on** *n.* [1980s+] an erection.

bonk *adj. see* BONKERS *adj.*

bonk *v.* [echoic + note WW1 milit. use *bonk*, to shell] **1** [1930s+] to hit (esp. on the head). **2** [1970s+] to have sexual intercourse. **3** [1990s+] (*US campus*) to break down, to wear out.

bonk! *excl.* **1** [1980s] (*US campus*) (*also* **bonk it!**) negative expression of disapproval, or disagreement. **2** [1990s+] (*US teen*) used after a statement to emphasize one's feeling that it is unbelievable, fantastic.

bonker *n.* [BONK *v.* (2)] [1980sS] (*S.Afr.*) a copulator, a rapist.

bonkers *adj.* (*also* **bonk, bonker, bonks**) [BONK *n.* (3), i.e. the result of a fig. blow to the head/brain] **1** [1920s] mildly drunk. **2** [1940s+] (*orig. RN*) stupid, insane, eccentric, spec. in phrs. *drive bonkers, go bonkers*.

bonking *n.* [BONK *v.* (2)] [1980s+] sexual intercourse.

bonking *adj.* [BONK *v.* (2), thus euph. for FUCKING *adj.* (1)] [1970s] a general intensifier.

bonk it! *excl. see* BONK! *excl.* (1).

bonks *adj. see* BONKERS *adj.*

bonnaroos *n. see* BONAROOS *n.*

bonne-bouche *n.* [Fr. *bonnebouche*, a 'pleasant taste', anglicized as a 'tasty morsel'] [late 19C] the vagina.

bonneroo *adj. see* BONAROO *adj.*

bonnet *n.*[1] (*also* **bonnetter**) [fig. use of BONNET *v.* (1)] **1** [18C–19C] a gambling cheat, who poses as a normal player, thus luring the victim to join the game, but who, as the play proceeds, begins cheating in favour of the bank or house. **2** [19C] a pretext or pretence, esp. as the legitimate job behind which a thief hides their true occupation, e.g. a newspaper seller or porter. **3** [mid-19C] a sham bidder at auctions who works to drive up the price. **4** [late 19C] one who encourages sales for a street vendor by praising the goods.

(IN PHRASES)

❑ **bonnet for** *v.* [early 19C] to back up someone in their claims, to provide an alibi for someone.

SE in slang uses

(IN COMPOUNDS)

❑ **bonnet-builder** *n.* [mid–late 19C] a milliner. ❑ **bonnet flipper** *n.* [SE *bonnet* as metonymic for the head + FLIP *v.*[3]] [1950s] (*US black*) a person, e.g. a performer, who excites people's emotions.

bonnet *n.*[2] (*also* **cap**) [metonymy] [late 19C] a woman.

bonnet *n.*[3] [BONNET *v.* (2)] [late 19C] a thug.

bonnet *v.* **1** [mid-19C] to cheat. **2** [mid-19C–1930s] to pull or crush a person's hat over their eyes, thus temporarily blinding them.

bonnets so blue *n.* [rhy. sl.] [mid-19C] (*Irish*) stew.

bonnetter *n.* [BONNET *v.*] **1** [mid-19C] a cheat's accomplice, who lures victims into the game. **2** [mid-19C–1900s] a smashing blow on one's hat. **3** [late 19C] (*US*) a stool pigeon.

bonnibel *n.* [Fr. *bonne et belle*, good and beautiful] [early 17C] an attractive woman.

bonnie Brillo *n.* [proper name *Bonnie*, with implications of domestic cheeriness + *Brillo*, the scouring pad] [1980s+] (*US campus*) one who is obsessively neat and tidy.

bonny! *excl. see* BONERS! *excl.*

bonny-baller *n.* [? his pursuit of a BONNIBEL *n.*] [mid–late 17C] a male sexual predator.

bonny-clapper *n.* (*also* **barney clapper, bonny clabbe, bonny clabber, bonnyclaber, bonny clabo, bony-clabber, clabber, clava**) [17C+] sour buttermilk.

bonny fair *n.* [rhy. sl.] [20C+] (*US*) the hair.

bonny lay *n.* [LAY *n.*[3] (1)] [early 19C] (*UK Und.*) highway robbery.

bonny-roo *adj. see* BONAROO *adj.*

bonny-throw *n.* [late 18C] (*US Und.*) the highway.

bono *adj.* [Polari] [mid–late 19C] good.

IN COMPOUNDS

❑ **bono omee** *n.* [OMEE *n.* (3)] [mid-19C–1950s] a husband.

bono Johnny *n.* [Chinese pidgin, 'a good John Bull'] [late 19C–1900s] an Englishman.

bonsa *n. see* BONZER *n.*

bonse *n. see* BONCE *n.* (1).

bonser *see under* BONZER.

bonster *n. see* BONZER *n.*

bont *adj.* [Du. *bonte*, gaudy] [1970s+] (*S.Afr.*) gaudy, lurid, colourful.

bontoger/bontojer *n. see* BONTOSHER *n.*

bon ton *n.* [early 19C] superior prostitutes; courtesans.

bon tosh *adj.* [1910s] (*Aus.*) very good.

bontosher *n.* (*also* **bontoger, bontojer, bontoshter**) [? Fr. *bon toujours*, good all the time; but note F. Ludowyck in *OzWords* May 2003: 'I have a strong suspicion that the French *bon toujours* theory is a bonzer red herring. It is spelt out in the May 1904 *Bulletin* letter, and revived briefly in the 1908 *Australian Magazine* citation, but there is no other evidence for **bontojer**. In any case it is difficult to imagine under what historical circumstances Australian English might have borrowed a French word or expression in the first decade of the twentieth century'; ? link to SE *bonanza* or BONZER *adj.*] [1900s–50s] (*Aus.*) a term of the highest praise, something excellent.

bonus! *excl.* [SE *bonus*, something extra, but cf. BONA *adj.*] [1980s+] (*US campus*) excellent! wonderful! first-class!

bony-clabber *n. see* BONNY-CLAPPER *n.*

bonz *adj. see* BONZER *adj.*

bonza *n. see* BONZER *n.*

bonza *adj. see* BONZER *adj.*

bonzarina *n.* (*also* **bonzerina**) [BONZER *n.* (2) + fem. sfx *-arina*] [1900s–50s] (*Aus.*) a notably beautiful woman.

bonzer *n.* (*also* **bonsa, bonser, bonster, bonza, bonzor**) [BONZER *adj.*] [20C+] (*Aus.*) **1** a good thing. **2** an admirable person; a beautiful woman.

bonzer *adj.* (*also* **bonser, bonz, bonza, bonze, bonzerino**) [mongrel mixture of Fr. *bon*, good + SE *bonanza* + BONTOGER/BONTOJER *n.*] [20C+] (*Aus./N.Z.*) good.

bonzer *adv.* [BONZER *adj.*] [1960s–70s] (*Aus.*) very well.

bonzerina *v. see* BONZARINA *n.* (1).

bonzo *adj.* [? the UK 1920s cartoon puppy *Bonzo* or 1951 film *Bedtime for Bonzo* (a chimp)] **1** [1950s] (*UK Und.*) skilful. **2** [1980s+] eccentric, crazy.

bonzor *n. see* BONZER *n.*

boo *n.*[1] [abbr. BOODLE *n.*[1] (3)] [late 19C] (*US*) money.

boo *n.*[2] [abbr. BOOGER *n.*[1] (1)] [1900s] (*US*) nasal mucus.

boo *n.*[3] **1** [1930s–50s] (*US black*) a bad scare, a serious fright [? JABOOBY *n.* (marijuana), among the effects of which can be temporary paranoia; however, a simpler ety. would be the trad. cry of *boo!* in order to scare someone]. **2** [1970s] a ghostwriter [pun on SE *boo!* + *ghost*(-writer)].

boo *n.*[4] (*also* **bu**) [abbr. JABOOBY *n.*] **1** [1950s+] (*drugs*) marijuana. **2** [2000s] methamphetamine.

boo *n.*[5] [? BABY *n.*] [1990s+] (*US black*) **1** a child. **2** (*also* **boo-piece**) a sweetheart, a loved one; a close friend.

boo *n.*[6] [? abbr. BOOBY *n.*[1]] [1990s+] (*W.I.*) a fool, an idiot.

boo *n.*[7] [1990s+] (*US*) anything.

boo *adj.*[1] [1950s] (*US teen*) excellent.

boo *adj.*[2] *see* BOOGIE *adj.*

boo *v.* [? *boohoo* to weep] [mid-19C] to speak or write in a mawkishly romantic manner.

boo! *excl.* [early 19C] nonsense!

booai *n.* (*also* **booay**) [? Maori *puhoi*, dull, slow or *Puhoi*, a failed mid-19C utopian settlement] [20C+] (*N.Z.*) the backwoods, remote rural areas.

IN PHRASES

❑ **up the boohai** *adv.* [20C+] (*N.Z.*) totally confused, absolutely wrong. ❑ **way to boohai** [1980s] (*N.Z.*) intensifying remoteness or distance; 'way to blazes'.

boob *n.*[1] [BOOBY-HATCH *n.* (1); note WW1 milit. use for detention cells] [20C+] **1** (*orig. Aus.*) orig. milit. use, a prison; thus (all Aus./N.Z.) *boob dot*, a small blue dot tattooed beneath the eye, indicating a spell in borstal or prison, *boob gear*, prison uniform, *boob talk*, prison jargon, *boob tat*, a prison tattoo, *boob tea*, weak, prison-brewed tea, *boob weed*, prison-issue tobacco. **2** (*US*) a police station, esp. the police cells, a local or city prison.

IN COMPOUNDS

❑ **boob blue** *n.* [BLUE *n.*[1] (2b)] [1980s] (*N.Z. prison*) alcohol made from brasso metal polisher. ❑ **boob cat** *n.* [CAT *n.*[1] (5)] [1980s+] (*Aus. prison*) a prisoner who suspends his usual heterosexuality for a homosexual life while in jail. ❑ **boob happy** *adj.* [-HAPPY *sfx* (1)] [1980s+] (*Aus. prison*) institutionalized; no longer able to survive outside the prison environment. ❑ **boobhead** *n.* [-HEAD *sfx* (3)] [1960s+] (*Aus.*) a prisoner, esp. an influential one. ❑ **boob rat** *n.* [RAT *n.*[1] (1)] [1950s] (*Aus. Und.*) a prisoner, esp. a recidivist.

IN PHRASES

❑ **do boob** *v.* [20C+] (*Aus. prison*) to serve time in prison.

boob *n.*[2] [abbr. BOOBY *n.*[1] (1)] **1** [20C+] (*orig. US*) (*also* **boobist**) a fool, an idiot. **2** [1900s–40s] (*US*) an inmate of a psychiatric institution. **3** [1930s] (*US tramp*) an innocent, a potential victim of a thief. **4** [1940s+] an error, a blunder.

DERIVATIVES

❑ **boobish** *adj.* [17C+] stupid, foolish.

IN COMPOUNDS

❑ **boob box** *n.* (*also* **booby box**) [1960s] (*US*) a psychiatric institution. ❑ **boob play** *n.* [PLAY *n.* (2)] [1930s+] a foolish action, an error, a blunder. ❑ **boob trap** *n.* [1920s–60s] (*US*) a nightclub or similar place of entertainment where gullible customers are defrauded of their cash. ❑ **boob tube** *n.* [TUBE *n.*[1] (7)] **1** [1960s+] (*orig. US*) television, thus *boob tuber*, one who watches television a lot. **2** *see also under* BOOB *n.*[3].

boob *n.*[3] [BUB *n.*[4]; since 1970s one of the terms esp. favoured by women] [1940s+] (*orig. US*) **1** the female breast, usu. in pl. **2** the chest of a fat male.

IN COMPOUNDS

❑ **boob job** *n.* (*also* **tit job**) [TIT *n.*[2] (1) + JOB *n.*[2] (2)] [1980s+] cosmetic/plastic surgery on the breast, usu. for enlarging with some form of implant. ❑ **boob tube** *n.* **1** [1970s+] a woman's tight, strapless top, usu. of knitted or elasticated fabric. **2** *see also under* BOOB *n.*[2].

boob *adj.* [BOOB *n.*[2] (1)] [late 19C+] (*Aus.*) inferior, second-rate.

boob *v.* [BOOB *n.*[2] (1) / BOOB *n.*[2] (4)] [1910s+] to make a mistake, to blunder.

IN PHRASES

❑ **boob up** *v.* [1910s+] to make a mess of (something).

boobatch *n.* [? Polish = grandfather] [1930s–40s] (*US*) an old Polish immigrant.

boober *n.* [*BOOB TUBE under* BOOB *n.*[2]] [2000s] (*US*) a television.

booberkin *n.* [BOOBY *n.*[1] + dimin. sfx *-kin*] [late 17C] a fool, a simpleton.

boobery *n.* [BOOB *n.*^{2} (1)] [1920–70s] (*US*) foolishness.

boobie *n. see* BOOBY *n.*^{1}.

boobie hatch *n. see* BOOBY-HATCH *n.*

boobies *n.* [BUB *n.*^{4}] [1930s+] (*orig. US*) the female breasts; occas. sing.

boobish *adj. see* BOOBY *adj.*^{1}.

Boob McNutt *n.* [BOOB *n.*^{2} (1) + NUT *n.*^{2} (1) / NUTCASE *n.*; ult. f. *Boob McNutt*, a strip cartoon character (running 1915–34) created by Rube Goldberg] [1930s–60s] (*US*) a fool, a simpleton.

booboisie *n.* [BOOB *n.*^{2} (1) + *bourgeoisie*. Coined by H.L. Mencken as part of a list of words describing 'the victims of the Depression, then current' and published in the Baltimore *Evening Sun* on 15 February 1922 in a list of 50 similar terms, incl. *boobariat, booberati, boobarian*] [1920s+] (*US*) respectable fools, considered as a class in their own right; a synon. for the modern 'Middle America'.

boo-boo *n.*^{1} [ety. unknown] [1900s] (*US*) a joke.

boo-boo *n.*^{2} [abbr./redup. BOODLE *n.*^{1} (5)] [1900s–20s] (*US*) $1.

boo-boo *n.*^{3} [? Yid. *bulba*, potato. Major, *Juba to Jive: A Dict. of Afro-American Slang* (1994), suggests link to Bantu *mbubu*] **1** [1950s] (*US*) usu. in pl., the testicles. **2** [1970s] (*US gay*) an erection.

boo-boo *n.*^{4} [BOOB *n.*^{2} (4)] **1** [1950s+] (*also* **bubu, booboo**) (*orig. US*) a blunder, usu. embarrassing, esp. in phr. *make a boo-boo*. **2** [2000s] something unpleasant, an unacceptable situation.

boo-boo *n.*^{5} [BOOB *v.* (1) + redup.] [1950s+] (*US*) a minor scar or bruise, an acne spot etc.

boo-boo *n.*^{6} (*also* **booby**) [1980s] (*Aus.*) nasal mucus.

boo-boo *n.*^{7} [abbr. SE *buttocks*] [1990s+] (*US*) the buttocks, the posterior.

boo-boo *adj.* [BOO-BOO *n.*^{4}] **1** [1990s+] (*US campus*) bad, second-rate. **2** [2000s] disgruntled, dissatisfied.

boo-boo *v.* [BOOB *v.* (1) + redup.] [1950s+] (*orig. US*) to blunder, to make a mistake.

booboos *n.* [? BOOB *n.*^{2} (1)] [1990s+] (*US*) a black person.

booborous *adj. see* BOBBISH *adj.*

boobus *n.* [BOOB *n.*^{3} (1)] [1990s+] (*US black/Los Angeles*) small breasts.

booby *n.*^{1} (*also* **boobie**) [? Sp. *bobo*, a fool; phr. also puns on SE *booby*, a large, slow-flying bird] **1** [early 17C+] a fool, an idiot, a peasant. **2** [1990s+] an insane person.

(IN COMPOUNDS)

❑ **booby house** *n.* [late 19C–1940s] (*US*) a lunatic asylum. ❑ **booby wagon** *n.* [1920s–60s] (*US*) the vehicle in which arrested people are transported to the local police station or prison.

(IN PHRASES)

❑ **beat the booby** *v.* [late 18C–early 19C] to beat one's hands against one's sides to get warm on a cold day.

booby *n.*^{2} [BOOBY-HUTCH *n.*] [1910s–50s] (*US*) a cell, a lock-up.

booby *n.*^{3} [BOOB *n.*^{3} (1)] [1910s+] (*orig. US*) the female breast.

booby *n.*^{4} *see* BOO-BOO *n.*^{6}.

booby *adj.*^{1} (*also* **boobish**) [colloq. *booby*, a fool] [late 17C+] stupid, foolish.

booby *adj.*^{2} [BOOB *n.*^{3} (1)] [1990s+] (*US*) having big breasts; thus by stereotyping, promiscuous.

booby-hatch *n.* (*also* **boobie hatch, booby hutch**) [BOOBY *n.*^{1} (1) + SE *hatch*, hutch, underpinned by the well-known asylum at Colney Hatch near London, opened in 1851] **1** [mid-19C–1960s] (*orig. US*) a prison, a police station, a police patrol wagon. **2** [late 19C+] (*also* **booby box, ...cage**) a lunatic asylum. **3** [1910s] a hiding-place, e.g. a dug-out.

booby-hutch *n.* [BOOBY *n.*^{1} (1) + SE *hutch*] [late 18C–early 19C] **1** a one-horse chaise, thus any clumsy carriage. **2** a leather bottle [plays on the idea of the bottle, full of liquor, 'ensnaring' the fool; note milit. use *booby hutch*, a dug out; *boobies' hutch*, a tolerated if unofficial bar in a barracks, which is open after the canteen shuts]. **3** [late 19C] (*US*) a police station.

4 [1920s–30s] (*UK Und.*) a cell, a jail. **5** [1940s] a lunatic asylum.

booch *n.* (*also* **boogh**) [echoic] [20C+] (*Ulster*) a heavy blow, a slap, a punch, a thump.

boochie *n. see* BOOJEE *n.*

boocoo *see under* BEAUCOUP.

boocoodles *n.* (*also* **bookoodles**) [Fr. *beaucoup*, many + OODLES *n.*] [20C+] (*US*) many, a good deal.

booda *n.* [pun on BUDDHA *n.*] [1990s+] (*US black gang*) a large, cannabis-impregnated cookie or biscuit.

boodgeree! *excl.* [Dharuk *bujari*, good] [late 19C+] (*Aus. pidgin*) a general excl. of approval, pleasure.

boodle *n.*^{1} [either Du. *boedel*, household effects, and thus one's personal estate, or Scot. *bodle*, a small coin worth two Scot. pence (or one-sixth of an English one) and as such usu. glossed as 'worthless'. It is in the US that the modern meaning, whether of criminal or political graft (see sense 2), has developed; note West Point *boodle*, contraband edibles, sweets etc] **1** [early 17C–19C] (*orig. US*) a crowd or collection of people or things; usu. in phr. WHOLE BOODLE below. **2** [early 19C–1920s] (*US*) counterfeit money. **3** [mid-19C+] booty, money, esp. money that has been acquired illegally or through corruption. **4** [mid-19C+] (*US Und.*) money used in an elaborate confidence trick; packaged like bundles of bank-wrapped notes, it is usu. comprised of a large note on top and bottom, and $1 bills in the middle. **5** [late 19C–1950s] a large amount of money. **6** [late 19C–1970s] a roll of banknotes. **7** [1900s] (*Aus.*) government contracts which are designed primarily to benefit those involved. **8** [1930s] (*US prison*) bribes extracted from prisoners by the warders or 'trusties'. **9** [1940s] (*US campus*) a parcel of food, usu. sweets or snacks, sent to a student. **10** [1960s] (*US drugs*) a packet of narcotics. **11** [1960s+] (*US Und.*) anything sent to a prisoner from the outside world, not necessarily money. **12** [1970s] working capital. **13** *see* BOODLER *n.* (2).

(IN COMPOUNDS)

❑ **boodle bag** *n.* (*US*) **1** [1920s] loot, as contained in a bag. **2** [1920s+] a purse, a small money-pouch, usu. worn around the neck; later use extends the sense to any small bag. **3** [2000s] a 'goodie bag' with free gifts, promotional material etc given away by a company, e.g. at a press launch. ❑ **boodle buyer** *n.* [1940s] (*UK Und.*) a criminal receiver who specializes in large items.

(IN PHRASES)

❑ **walk the boodle** *v.* [early 19C] (*US Und.*) to distribute counterfeit notes. ❑ **whole boodle** *n.* [mid-19C] (*orig. US*) the lot, everything there is.

boodle *n.*^{2} [? link to NOODLE *n.*^{1} (2); ? Devon dial. *buddled*, drunk] [mid-19C] a fool.

boodle *n.*^{3} [1930s–60s] (*US tramp*) a jail where a tramp lives during the cold winter months.

boodle *n.*^{4} [BOOTY *n.*^{2} (1), but note image of the vagina as a commercially useful commodity, thus BOODLE *n.*^{1} (3)] [1980s] (*US*) the vagina.

boodle *adj.* [BOODLE *n.*^{1}] [late 19C] (*US*) corrupt.

boodle *v.*^{1} [BOODLE *n.*^{1} (3)] [late 19C–1900s] (*US*) to engage in corruption, in graft, to bribe.

boodle *v.*^{2} [SE *bundle*, of an engaged couple, to sleep together, but fully clothed] [1940s–70s] (*US campus*) to pet, to neck.

boodler *n.* [BOODLE *n.*^{1}; US use late 19C; Aus. use 1920s+] (*Aus./US*) **1** [late 19C–1900s] a swindler, specializing in passing counterfeit notes. **2** [late 19C–1960s] (*also* **boodle**) a corrupt politician.

boody *see under* BOOTY and its combs.

booed and hissed *adj.* [rhy. sl. = PISSED *adj.*^{1} (1)] [1980s] drunk.

boof *n.* [unknown] [2000s] (*US prison*) contraband hidden in the rectum.

boofa *n.* (*also* **boofer**) [BOOFHEAD *n.* (1) or BUTTFUCKER *n.*] [1970s+] (*US*) a fool, an incompetent.

boofed (out) *adj.* [SE *bouffant*] [1980s+] (*US campus*) puffed out, usu. of hair.

booferbox *n.* [BOOFA *n.* or *boof*, echoic of the heavy bass notes emerging from the machine + SE *box*/BOX *n.*[1] (4g)] [1980s+] (*orig. US*) a large radio/tape recorder/stereo particularly popular among ghetto youths.

booferish *adj.* [BOOFA *n.*] [2000s] (*US*) a derog. term, pertaining to black people or culture.

boofhead *n.* [Lincolnshire dial.] [1940s+] (*orig. Aus.*) **1** a fool, an idiot, a simpleton. **2** a person or animal having a large head.

boofter *n. see* POOFTER *n.*

boog *n.* [abbr. BOOGIE *n.*[2] (1)] [1940s+] **1** (*US*) (*also* **bug**) a black person. **2** (*Aus.*) an Aborigine.

boog *adj.* [BOOG *n.* (1)] [1930s+] black, of race.

boog *v.*[1] [although logical root is BUG *v.*[2] (3), the term appears to antedate all known cites of the word] [1930s] (*US black*) to irritate, to annoy.

boog *v.*[2] [BOOGIE *v.* (1)] [1940s+] (*US black*) to enjoy oneself, to 'party', to dance.

booga bear *n. see* BEAR *n.* (1d).

boogalee *n. see* BOOGERLEE *n.*

boogaloo *n.* [BOOGIE *n.*[2] (1) + SE *boogaloo*] [1970s–80s] (*US*) a black person.

boogaloo *v.* [SE *boogaloo*, a dance step of the 1960s] [1960s+] (*orig. US black*) **1** to dance. **2** to fool around.

IN PHRASES

❑ **put the boogaloo on** *v.* [1970s] to annoy, to cause trouble (for).

boogar *n. see* BOOGER *n.*[3].

boo-gee *n. see* GEE *n.*[7].

booger *n.*[1] [SE *bugger*] **1** [late 19C+] (*also* **bugger**) (*US*) a piece of nasal mucus. **2** [1970s] (*W.I.*) trainers. **3** [1980s+] (*also* **boogersnot**) as an insult.

booger *n.*[2] [BUGGER *n.*[1]] **1** [20C+] (*US black*) anything unpleasant, burdensome, difficult. **2** [1900s] (*US campus*) an unpleasant person. **3** [1900s] a person, animal or object with no derog. implications. **4** [1930s+] (*US black*) on bad = good model, something excellent, someone admirable. **5** [1950s+] (*US, Southern*) sexual intercourse with a woman. **6** [1960s] the female genitals. **7** [1980s+] (*US campus*) an extremely unattractive woman.

IN COMPOUNDS

❑ **booger bear** *n.* (*also* **buger-bear**) [BEAR *n.* (1d)/US regional use *booger bear*, a hobgoblin used to frighten children] [1970s+] (*US black*) **1** a notably ugly person. **2** any difficult situation or unpleasant thing. ❑ **booger hook** *n.* [2000s] (*US black*) a punch delivered when one's opponent is not expecting it.

booger *n.*[3] (*also* **boogar**) [var. on BOOGIE *n.*[2] (1)] [1970s+] (*US*) a derog. term for a black person.

booger *v.*[1] [such panicking is supposedly the effect of a *booger*, a ghost, a hobgoblin] [late 19C+] (*US West*) to shy, to panic, usu. of an animal.

DERIVATIVES

❑ **boogery** *adj.* [late 19C+] (*US West*) jumpy.

booger *v.*[2] [SE *bugger*] [20C+] (*US*) to sodomize.

boogerboo *n.* [*BOOGER BEAR under* BOOGER *n.*[2]] [1940s–60s] (*US black*) an unpleasant situation or person.

boogerboo *v.* [BOOGERBOO *n.*] [1940s–60s] (*US black*) to behave in an unpleasant manner, to be insincere.

boogering *adj.* (*also* **booging**) [BUGGERING *adj.* (1)] [1960s] (*US*) damned, in the sense of irritating, infuriating.

boogerlee *n.* (*also* **boogalee**) [? BOOGIE *n.*[2] (1) + proper name *Stagolee*] **1** [1960s+] (*US*) a Cajun (a person of French descent in Louisiana). **2** [1960s] a person of mixed black and white ancestry.

boogerman *n.* [SE *bogeyman*] [1940s] (*US*) a police officer.

booger off *v. see* BUGGER OFF *v.*

boogersnot *n. see* BOOGER *n.*[1] (3).

booger wagon *n.* [BOOGERMAN *n.* + SE *wagon*] [1960s] a prison van.

boogery *adj.* (*also* **buggery**) [20C+] **1** (*US*) frightened, frightening [BOOGER *v.*[1] (1)]. **2** unpleasant, malicious [BOOGER *n.*[2] (2)].

IN PHRASES

❑ **boogery-eyed** *adj.* [20C+] (*US*) wide-eyed.

booget *n.* [SE *budget*, a pouch, bag, wallet, usu. of leather] [mid-16C–mid-17C] (*UK Und.*) an itinerant tinker's basket.

boogey *n. see* BOOGIE *n.*[2].

boogh *n. see* BOOCH *n.*

boogie *n.*[1] [BOOGER *n.*[1] (1)] [late 19C+] (*US*) a piece of nasal mucus.

boogie *n.*[2] (*also* **boogey, boogy**) [SE *bogey* or US dial. *boogerman*, bogeyman] [1920s+] **1** a derog. term for a black person. **2** as used by a black person, neutral/non-derog.

IN PHRASES

❑ **bush boogie** *n.* [SE *bush*] [1990s+] (*US*) a black person.
❑ **faded boogie** *n.* (*also* **faded bogey**) [SE *faded*; note Irwin, *American Tramp and Und. Slang* (1931): 'Why the adjective "faded" is applied is hard to say, unless it is felt that the negro who turns informer has still less claim to identity than as a negro, and that he has faded from what small importance he formerly had'] [1920s+] (*US black*) **1** a black informer. **2** a black who apes whites and loses their own ethnicity. **3** a white who imitates blacks.

boogie *n.*[3] [BOOGIE *v.*] (*US black*) **1** [1930s+] the vagina. **2** [1940s–60s] sexual intercourse. **3** [1950s] a sexually promiscuous person. **4** [1960s] syphilis. **5** [1960s+] a good time, a party. **6** [1980s] energy. **7** [1990s+] (*drugs*) marijuana, esp. when more than usu. strong.

boogie *adj.* (*also* **boo**) [BOOGIE *n.*[2] (1)] [1930s+] (*US*) black, Afro-American.

IN COMPOUNDS

❑ **boogie town** *n.* [SE *town*] (*US*) the black section of a town or city. ❑ **boogie weed** *n.* [WEED *n.*[1] (4)] [2000s] (*US drugs*) marijuana.

boogie *v.* [SE *boogie-woogie*, a form of jazz-based dance, or *PITCH A BOOGIE-WOOGIE under* BOOGIE-WOOGIE *n.*] (*orig. US black*) **1** [1940s+] to enjoy oneself, to have a party, a good time, extended in excl. *boogie down!* let's have fun! **2** [1940s+] (*also* **get one's boogies on**) to dance, often energetically. **3** [1940s+] to have sexual intercourse. **4** [1970s+] to go, to move, to do something quickly.

IN COMPOUNDS

❑ **boogie board** *n.* [SE *board*] [1980s+] (*orig. Aus.*) a cut-down, half-sized surfboard. ❑ **boogie box** *n.* [SE *box*/BOX *n.*[1] (4g), but given initial association of such players with African-Americans, note poss. racist implications of BOOGIE *adj.* (1)] [1980s+] a large, portable cassette/tape player. ❑ **boogie joint** *n.* (*also* **boogie joint**) [HOUSE *n.*[1] (1)/JOINT *n.* (3b)] **1** [1920s–40s] (*US prison*) (*also* **boogie**) the prison hospital. **2** [1930s–70s] (*US black*) a brothel.

IN PHRASES

❑ **let's boogie** [1980s+] (*US teen*) let's go, let's be off.

boogie-joogie *n.* (*also* **boogie-joogy**) [BOOGIE *v.* (1) + redup. or JUKE *n.*[2] (1)/JUKE *v.*[1] (2)] (*US black*) **1** [1950s] boogie-woogie music. **2** [1970s–80s] nonsense, trickery, deceit.

boogie-joogie *v.* (*also* **boogie-joogy**) [BOOGIE *v.* (1) + JUKE *v.*[3] (2)] [1960s] to enjoy onself, to have a good time, to lead a hedonistic lifestyle.

boogie-woogie *n.* [fig. uses of SE *boogie-woogie* music] [1940s] **1** (*US*) an emotional outburst. **2** (*US, Southern*) secondary syphilis.

IN PHRASES

❑ **pitch a boogie-woogie** *v.* [1920s+] (*US black*) to make a fuss, to behave in an aggressive manner.

boogie-woogie *v.* [fig. uses of SE *boogie-woogie* music] **1** [1930s] to enjoy onself. **2** [1930s+] (*US black*) to leave, to depart.

booging *adj. see* BOOGERING *adj.*

boogity-boogity *adv.* [? BOOGIE *v.*] [1940s] (*US*) quickly.

boogler *n.* [BOOGIE *v.* (1)] [1960s] (*US black*) a regular party-goer.

boogooyagga *n.* (*also* **buggo-yagga**) [1940s+] (*W.I.*) good-for-nothing person; also as *adj.* worthless.

boogy *n.* *see* BOOGIE *n.*[2].

boogy *adj.*[1] [? *bogie* the devil, or fig. use of BOGUEY *adj.*] [1960s+] suspicious, dubious, untrustworthy.

boogy *adj.*[2] *see* BOGUEY *adj.*

boo-hog *n.* *see* HOG *n.* (5b).

boohonged *adj.* [? *BEER BONG under* BEER *n.*] [1990s+] (*US campus*) drunk.

boo-hoo *n.* [BOOHOO *v.*] **1** [late 19C–1960s] whingeing, complaining. **2** [20C+] a tear; weeping.

boohoo *v.* [echoic] [mid-19C+] (*orig. US*) to whinge, to complain.

DERIVATIVES

❑ **boohooism** *n.* [mid-19c+] (*orig. US*) nagging.

boohoo! *excl.* [1930s–40s] a sarcastic excl. implying that one is shedding (utterly unfelt) tears at a given comment or event.

booitjie *n.* *see* BOYKIE *n.*

boojee *n.* (*also* **bojie, boochie, boojie, boojum, boojy, bourgie, buzhie**) [SE *bourgeois*, middle class] [1970s+] (*orig. US black*) a bourgeois, middle-class, thus law-abiding black (equally applicable to whites).

boojee *adj.* (*also* **boojie, boojum, boojy, bourgie, buji**) [BOOJEE *n.* (1)] [1970s+] bourgeois, middle-class.

boojie *n.*[1] [? BOO *n.*[4] (1)] [1930s] (*US drugs*) a marijuana cigarette.

boojie *n.*[2] *see* BOOJEE *n.*

boojie *adj.* *see* BOOJEE *adj.*

boojum *n.*[1] [from Lewis Carroll's poem 'The Hunting of the Snark' (1876), with its last line 'For the Snark *was* a Boojum, you see.'] [late 19C] a person, esp. a moralist.

boojum *n.*[2] [? var. on BOOTY *n.*[2] (1)] [2000s] (*US*) the vagina, in a sexual context.

boojum/boojy *n.* *see* BOOJEE *n.*

boojum/boojy *adj.* *see* BOOJEE *adj.*

Book, the *n.* [a fig. book of punishment or rules; NB SE phr. *throw the book at*] **1** [1920s–40s] (*US Und.*) a maximum sentence. **2** [1960s+] (*US black*) the oral tradition that forms the basis of black pimping.

book *n.* **1** in lit. use. (**a**) [19C+] a magazine, a periodical; mainly illiterate use. (**b**) [1950s+] (*US black pimp*) a supply of names and addresses of clients; e.g. of a prostitute. **2** in betting, i.e. the 'book' where wagers are entered. (**a**) [mid-19C+] a bet. (**b**) [mid-19C+] a *book*maker's business, usu. in phr. *make a book*. (**c**) [late 19C+] (*Aus./US*) a *book*maker. **3** (*orig. US prison*) a fig. *book* of punishments and/or broken rules. (**a**) [20C+] the maximum sentence for a given crime. (**b**) [1920s–60s] a one-year jail sentence. (**c**) [1920s+] (*also* **book of F.N.O.**) a life sentence; thus *bookman*, one serving a life sentence. (**d**) [1940s] in non-criminal contexts, any form of severe punishment. **4** the context of reading. (**a**) [20C+] (*Irish*) a class in primary school. (**b**) [1960s] (*US campus*) an assiduous, hard worker. (**c**) [1970s] (*US campus*) a study period. **5** (*drugs*) the shape. (**a**) [1950s] a small paper packet of a drug. (**b**) [2000s] (*US drugs*) 100 doses of LSD. **6** [1990s+] (*Irish*) a single parent's allowance [? from the book in which payments are registered].

IN PHRASES

❑ **clear the book** *v.* [1930s–40s] (*US Und.*) of the police, to accuse a criminal, who may have been arrested on another charge, of various unsolved crimes. ❑ **do the book** *v.* [1920s+] (*US Und.*) to serve a life sentence. ❑ **do the book and cover** *v.* [1920s+] (*US Und.*) to be imprisoned for the rest of one's natural life. ❑ **make book (on)** *v.* **1** [mid-19C+] to wager (on), to gamble (on), also fig. **2** [1930s] to conduct a surveillance on someone. **3** [1930s+] to run a bookmaking operation. ❑ **on the book** **1** [20C+] on credit. **2** [2000s] involved. ❑ **on the books** [20C+] (*US*) good for credit. ❑ **throw the book at** *v.* (*also* **chuck the book at, drop the book on, hit with the book, shy the book, toss the book at**) [the 'book of rules' that one has contravened, orig. in legal context, to *throw the book at*, to give someone a maximum sentence] [1910s+] (*orig. US*) to discipline heavily, to reprimand severely. ❑ **throw the book away** *v.* [1940s+] (*orig. US*) to abandon the usual rules and regulations.

SE in slang uses

IN COMPOUNDS

❑ **book-beater** *n.* [*BEAT THE BOOKS under* BEAT *v.*] [1940s] (*US teen*) a hard worker (at school). ❑ **bookbinder's wife** *n.* [play on 'her' occupation: 'manufacturing in sheets'] [late 18C–late 19C] the vagina. ❑ **book bluffing** *n.* [mid-19C] (*US Und.*) a form of swindling whereby one offers an expensive book to the buyer, but actually hands over a cheap one, which has been substituted during the packing process. ❑ **book-keeper** *n.* [pun] [late 18C–early 19C] one who fails to return borrowed books. ❑ **book-pad** *v.* [SE *book*] [late 17C–mid-18C] to plagiarize. ❑ **book rat** *n.* [they 'chew up' books] [late 19C] (*US*) an obsessive reader, a bookworm. ❑ **bookrunner** *n.* [1980s+] (*Aus. prison*) a prisoner who is allowed day release for study purposes. ❑ **book-sharp** *n.* *see under* SHARP *n.*[1]. ❑ **book-smart** *adj.* *see under* SMART *adj.* ❑ **bookworm** *n.* [play on SE] [1940s] (*US Und.*) a shoplifter who specializes in stealing rare books.

IN PHRASES

❑ **beside the book** *adj.* [SE *beside*, in addition, over and above + *book*, in the sense of an authority, a book of rules; 18C+ use is SE] [late 17C] utterly mistaken. ❑ **book of many pages** *n.* [1940s] (*US black*) a dictionary. ❑ **book of the four kings, the** *n.* *see* HISTORY OF THE FOUR KINGS, THE *n.* ❑ **everything in the book** *n.* [1950s] (*US*) whatever is available, whatever is known. ❑ **get the book** *v.* [SE *book*, i.e. the Bible] [1940s+] (*UK prison*) to become religious. ❑ **out of one's books** [late 18C–early 19C] out of favour. ❑ **out of the books** [1920s+] (*Aus.*) exceptional, well above average.

book *v.*[1] **1** to write in a book. (**a**) [mid-19C] to take a private bet, which is written down in one's betting *book*. (**b**) [mid-19C+] to wager outside a sporting context. (**c**) [late 19C] to pay out bets. (**d**) [late 19C+] to work as a bookmaker; to take bets. (**e**) [mid-19C+] to arrest, to write down in a police charge book. **2** to look at a book. (**a**) [1960s] to look at, to examine. (**b**) [1960s+] (*US campus*) (*also* **book ass, book it, book tits, book up**) to study assiduously. (**c**) [1970s] to note, to understand.

IN PHRASES

❑ **book the joint** *v.* *see under* JOINT *n.*

book *v.*[2] (*also* **book it, book out**) [BOOKITY-BOOK *v.*] [1970s+] (*US campus*) to leave, to go fast.

book *v.*[3] [1970s] (*US black*) to fight.

booked *adj.*[1] [? having *booked* one's space in the graveyard or 'set down in the book of history' (Jon Bee)] **1** [19C] (*orig. boxing*) destined, fated, caught, disposed of. **2** [mid-19C] (*US Und.*) arrested. **3** [20C+] (*US*) fatally ill; thus *booked for kingdom come*. **4** [1930s] (*UK Und.*) insane.

booked *adj.*[2] [? BOOG *adj.*] [1990s+] (*US campus*) ugly.

booker *n.*[1] [SE *book*, to reserve, e.g., a ticket] [1930s] (*US Und.*) a person who provides protection, as well as call services, for madams.

booker *n.*[2] [BOOK *v.*[1] (1)] [1960s] (*US campus*) an assiduous worker.

bookful *n.* [BOOK, THE *n.* (1)] [20C+] (*US Und.*) a life sentence.

bookie *n.* [abbr.] **1** [late 19C+] (*also* **booky**) (*orig. Aus.*) a *book*maker. **2** [1920s+] as *bookie's*, a bookmaker's establishment.

bookie joint *n.* (*also* **bookie mill**) [BOOKIE *n.* (1) + SE *mill*, used to mean a place of work/activity] [1940s+] (*US*) a bookmaker's office.

booking *n.* [BOOK *v.*[1] (1e); one's name etc is written into a record book (now a computer)] [1990s+] (*Und./police*) an arrest.

bookity-book *v.* [echoic of the sound of shoes slapping on the ground] [late 19C] (*US black*) to run fast, to move quickly.

bookoo *n.* *see* BEAUCOUP *n.*

bookoo *v.* [Fr. *beaucoup*, very much, thus very much noise] [1930s–60s] (*US black*) to talk loudly and aggressively.

bookoodles *n. see* BOOCOODLES *n.*

boo-koos *see under* BEAUCOUP.

bookra *n.* (*also* **bukra**) [Arabic] [1910s–40s] (*Aus./N.Z.*) tomorrow.

books *n.* [abbr. *DEVIL'S (PICTURE) BOOKS under* DEVIL *n.*; i.e. the pious identification of gambling with sin] [early 18C–1910s] a pack of playing cards.

IN PHRASES

❑ **plant the books** *v.* [early 19C] to stack a deck of cards for the purpose of cheating.

Booksellers' Row *n.* [a deliberate euph. since the 'books' sold in Holywell Street, before it was knocked down for the Aldwych development, were strictly pornographic] [mid-19C] Holywell Street, London, WC.

booku *n. see* BEAUCOUP *n.*

booku *adj. see* BEAUCOUP *adj.*

booky *n. see* BOOKIE *n.* (1).

boola-boola *n.* [college sports cheer *boola-boola*] [1930s+] (*US campus*) **1** college chauvinism; also ext. to any form of in-group self-congratulation. **2** a male college member.

boolhipper *n.* [ety. unknown; ? link to BULLY *n.*[1] (3)] [1970s+] (*US black*) a leather coat.

boom *n.*[1] [BOOM *v.* (2)] [late 19C–1960s] (*US*) a positive endorsement, a piece of favourable publicity.

boom *n.*[2] [Afk. *boom*, a tree / BOO *n.*[4]] **1** [1940s+] (*drugs*) marijuana. **2** [1950s–60s] heroin and/or the sensation thereof.

IN COMPOUNDS

❑ **boom-boy** *n.* [1940s+] (*drugs*) a marijuana smoker. ❑ **boom-skulf** *n.* (*also* **boomstop**) [1940s+] (*S.Afr./drugs*) a marijuana cigarette.

IN PHRASES

❑ **boomed up** *adj.* [1940s+] (*drugs*) intoxicated by marijuana.

boom *adj.* [BOOM *v.* (2)] [1990s+] the very best.

boom *v.* [naut. jargon *boom*, for a sailing ship to reach top speed (the wind-filled sails 'boom' with the movement)] **1** [early 19C] (*US*) to hurry, esp. as *boom along*. **2** [late 19C+] (*US*) to promote, to extol [SE since 1960s]. **3** [20C+] (*US*) to live as a transient worker. **4** *see* BOOM-BOOM *v.* (2).

boom! *excl.* [onomat. sound of an explosion] **1** [1950s+] (*also* **boom-boom!**) an echoic excl. used to imply suddenness, of a statement, an action etc. **2** [1980s+] (*US black*) a general excl. of agreement.

boombah *n.* [1990s+] (*US Und.*) the police.

boom-boom *n.*[1] [the sound of a shot] **1** [1910s+] (*juv.*) a soldier. **2** [1940s+] (*US black*) a pistol, rifle or shotgun. **3** [1940s] (*US black campus*) a cowboy film.

boom-boom *n.*[2] [? echoic of defecation] [1960s+] (*US juv.*) excrement.

boom-boom *n.*[3] [1960s+] (*US*) sexual intercourse.

IN PHRASES

❑ **boom-boom (girl)** *n.* [1960s+] a prostitute. ❑ **boom-boom parlor** *n.* [1990s+] a brothel.

boom-boom *v.* [BOOM-BOOM *n.*[3]] **1** [1930s] to reach orgasm. **2** [1960s+] (*US*) (*also* **boom**) to have sexual intercourse.

boombox *n.* (*also* **boomer**) [ext. of SE; i.e. its reverberating bass] [1980s+] a large, portable cassette/CD/radio player.

boomer *n.*[1] [SAusE *boomah*, a large kangaroo] (*Aus./US*) **1** [mid-19C+] a gross lie. **2** [late 19C+] anything considered exceptionally large or strong. **3** [late 19C+] something considered successful or popular.

boomer *n.*[2] [BOOM *v.* (2)] **1** [late 19C–1950s] a boom town. **2** [late 19C+] (*US*) an enthusiast, esp. one who promotes or pushes a new enterprise, e.g. opening up a new territory or state.

boomer *n.*[3] [SE *boom*, an economic upswing; the US *boomers* moved from one boom oil camp to the next during the 1920s–30s] **1** [late 19C+] (*US*) a transient worker, a migrant; thus *boomer reporter*, a journalist who works on papers all over the country, never keeping one job for too long. **2** [1920s–30s] (*US Und.*) a transient thief, who works in one town for a short while, then moves on.

boomer *n.*[4] [the noise of thunder] **1** [1960s–70s] (*US surf*) a huge wave. **2** [1970s] (*US*) a thunderstorm, a thunder-cloud. **3** [1970s] in fig. use, something impressive.

boomer *n.*[5] [1980s] (*US drugs*) a seller of crack cocaine.

boomer *n.*[6] [1980s+] (*orig. US*) a member of the 'baby-boom' generation (born in the late 1940s).

boomer *n.*[7] *see* BOOMBOX *n.*

boomerang *n.* [SE *boomerang*, which comes back to its thrower] **1** [late 19C+] (*US Und.*) an unpleasant or undesired result, repercussions. **2** [1950s] (*Aus.*) something, esp. a book, that one wishes to have returned.

boomerang *v.* [SE *boomerang* which, after one has thrown it, returns] **1** [1940s] to bring unpleasant consequences. **2** [1990s+] (*US Und.*) to return to prison almost immediately on finishing the last sentence.

boomerang cheque *n.* [SE *boomerang* + *cheque*] [1950s–60s] (*Aus.*) a 'bouncing' cheque, which is not honoured and is 'returned to drawer'.

booming *adj.* [SE *boom*, to advance keenly, to prosper] **1** [mid-19C+] (*Aus.*) large. **2** [late 19C] grand. **3** [late 19C+] successful, flourishing. **4** [1990s+] (*US black*) good-looking. **5** [1990s+] (*US campus*) excellent, worthy of approval.

boom! pow! bam! *excl.* [orig. in comic books] [1990s+] (*US black teen*) an excl. used to place emphasis in one's conversation.

boomskuif *n. see* SKUIF *n.* (2).

boomster *n.* [SE *boom*, an economic upturn] [late 19C] (*orig. US*) a speculator.

boon *n.*[1] [? BONE *n.*[4] (3)] [1950s] (*US black*) $1.

boon *n.*[2] [? SE *boon companion* or Fr. *bon*, good + poss. link to BONE *n.*[7] (1)] [1960s+] (*US black*) **1** a close friend. **2** a black person.

boon *v.* [BOONDOCKS *n.*] [1990s+] to drive cross-country.

boon coon *n.* (*also* **boon-koon**) [SE *boon* (*companion*) + COON *n.* (5)] [1950s+] (*US black*) a close companion.

boondie *n.*

IN PHRASES

❑ **give boondie** *v. see GIVE BONDI under* BONDI *n.*

boondock *adj.* [BOONDOCKS *n.*] [1950s+] (*US*) rural.

boondock *v.* [BOONDOCKS *n.*, a secluded rural spot suitable for love-making] [1960s+] (*US campus*) to neck, to pet or make love in an automobile.

boondocker *n.* [BOONDOCKS *n.*] **1** [1960s+] (*US campus*) (*also* **docker**) a picnic held in the woods where students can drink, play around, neck etc. **2** *see* BOONDOCKS *n.* (1).

boondockers *n.* [BOONDOCKS *n.*] [1940s+] (*US*) a pair of strong shoes suitable for rough use.

boondocks *n.* [Tagalog *bundock*, a mountain; orig. used by US milit. (esp. US Marine Corps) to mean the field, the bush, the jungle, anywhere the troops operate that is not designated a firebase, a basecamp or occupied by civilians] [1940s+] (*US*) rough country, jungle, an isolated or wild region; plus fig. use as an isolated unappealing place; thus *boondocker*, one who comes from such a place.

boondoggle *n.* [according to the term's coiner, Robert Marshall: '"Boon doggles" is simply a term applied back in the pioneer days to what we call gadgets today.' The term also referred to the braided leather lanyard worn by scouts (a *woggle* in the UK) and earlier still to the cowboy term for making saddle trappings out of odds and ends of available leather, something they did when there was no proper work. The 1940s edn of Brewer, *Dict. of Phrase and Fable*, notes the Scot. *boondoggle*, a marble given as gift and for which one has not had to make any effort – that ety. was dropped in subsequent editions.] [1930s+] (*US*) a waste, of time, of money, of energy. esp. used by US government for a project that is considered to waste tax dollars; thus *moondoggle*, any form of lunar exploration judged to be a waste of public money.

boondoggle *v.* [BOONDOGGLE *n.*] [1930s+] to waste time; thus *boondoggler*, a loafer, a time waster, *boondoggling*, time-wasting.

booner *n.* [BOON COON *n.* + ? overtones of BOONDOCKS *n.*, i.e. rural stupidity] [1970s+] (*US*) a black person.

boong *n.* (*also* **boang, bung**) [Wemba *boong*, a human being, a man] [mid-19C+] (*Aus.*) **1** a derog. term for an Aborigine; thus *boongess*, a female Aborigine; *boong-lover*, a white person who is regarded as too friendly towards aborigines. **2** (*also* **boonga, bunga**) a native of Papua New Guinea. **3** any non-white person. **4** attrib. referring to Aborgines or the Aboriginal culture.

boongie *n.* [2000s] (*US prison*) a prison officer.

boong moll *n.* [BOONG *n.* + MOLL *n.* (1)] **1** [1930s+] (*Aus.*) a prostitute who prefers Aborigine clients [refers to sexual exploitation of female Aborigines]. **2** [1960s–70s] a passive male homosexual. **3** [1960s–70s] (*US gay*) a black person.

boongy bungee *n. see* BOUNGIE BUNGEE *n.* (1).

boonie *n.*[1] [BOONDOCKS *n.*] **1** [1950s+] an outdoor lavatory. **2** [1950s+] a peasant, a country person. **3** [1960s–70s] a picnic held in the woods.

IN PHRASES

❑ **go on a boonie** [1980s+] (*US campus use*) to go on a picnic in which sex is likely to be involved.

boonie *n.*[2] *see* BOONER *n.*

boonie *adj.* [BOONDOCKS *n.*] [1960s+] (*US*) pertaining to the countryside or country culture.

boonie rat *n.* [BOONIES *n.* (1) + SE *rat*] [1960s–70s] (*US orig. milit.*) a US combat infantryman in Vietnam.

boonies *n.* [abbr. BOONDOCKS *n.*; HDAS suggests that a 1942 citation may be 'an editiorial intrusion from the 1960s or later'] [1950s+] (*US campus*) rural areas, the countryside (not necessarily rough or unpleasant).

boon-koon *n. see* BOON COON *n.*

boonoonoonoos *adj.* [1940–80s] (*W.I.*) a term of affection, attractive, pleasing.

boop *n. see* BOEP *n.*[1].

boop *v. see* BOP *v.*

boopety *adj.* [UPPITY *adj.*] [20C+] (*US*) arrogant, self-important.

boo-piece *n. see* BOO *n.*[5] (2).

boops *n.* [? POPS *n.* (3)] [1970s+] (*W.I., Jam.*) a wealthy lover.

boopsie *n.* [BOOPS *n.* + sfx *-ie*; note POPSIE *n.*[2] (1)] [1970s+] (*W.I.*) a woman who enjoys the favours (material and otherwise) of her wealthy lover; also in homosexual use.

boose *n. see* BOUSE *n.*

boose *v. see* BOUSE *v.*

boosed *adj. see* BOOZED *adj.*

booser *n. see* BOOZER *n.* (1).

boosey *adj. see* BOOZY *adj.*

booshwa/booshwah *n. see* BUSHWA *n.*

boosing ken *n. see* BOUSING-KEN *n.*

boosle *v. see* BOOZLE *v.*

boost *n.*[1]

IN PHRASES

❑ **get the boost** *v.* [var. on BOOT, THE *n.* (1)] [1900s] (*US*) to be rejected, dismissed.

boost *n.*[2] [BOOST *v.*[2] (1)] (*US Und./police*) **1** [1930s+] a robbery, usu. shoplifting. **2** [2000s] a stolen vehicle.

boost *v.*[1] [early 19C+] (*US*) to praise, to extol, esp. one's own town or city; thus *booster*, one who makes such promotions.

IN PHRASES

❑ **give the boost** *v.* [early 19C+] (*US*) to praise.

boost *v.*[2] [SE *boost*, to lift, to push, to hoist] [20C+] (*US Und.*) to steal, esp. to shoplift.

IN PHRASES

❑ **boost and shoot** *v.* [1960s+] (*drugs*) to steal to support a drug habit. ❑ **on the boost** [1900s–60s] (*US Und.*) **1** working as a pickpocket. **2** working as a shoplifter.

boost *v.*[3] [? BUST *v.*[1] (1), i.e. to hit] [1930s] (*US*) to attack.

boost *v.*[4] [ext. of BOOST *v.*[1] (1)] [1980s+] (*US campus*) to seduce, to have sexual intercourse with.

boost *v.*[5] [1990s+] (*Scot. juv.*) to leave.

booster *n.*[1] [BOOST *v.*[1]] **1** [20C+] (*US*) a house player in a casino who entices genuine players to bet (and usu. lose) their money. **2** [20C+] (*US*) any form of confederate working with a confidence trickster. **3** [1990s+] (*W.I.*) an aphrodisiac.

booster *n.*[2] [BOOST *v.*[2] (1)] **1** [20C+] (*US Und.*) a shoplifter, esp. when on a large and professional scale. **2** [1940s+] a thief.

IN COMPOUNDS

❑ **booster fold** *n.* [20C+] (*US Und.*) a way of carrying stolen goods so as to render them invisible to store detectives, thus *booster bloomers*, *booster skirt*, *booster box*.

IN PHRASES

❑ **snatch-and-grab booster** *n.* (*also* **boot-and-shoe booster**) [1900s–30s] (*US Und.*) an amateur shoplifter, rather than one who works with a professional team.

booster *n.*[3] [BOOST *v.*[1] (1)] [1960s] (*US*) something exceptional of its type.

boosting *n.* [BOOST *v.*[2] (1)] (*US Und.*) **1** shoplifting. **2** general theft.

boosting mob *n.* [BOOST *v.*[2] (1) + MOB *n.*[2] (3)] [1900s–20s] (*US Und.*) a gang of pickpockets.

boost-up boy *n.* [BOOST *v.*[2] (1)] [1960s] (*UK Und.*) a thief.

boosy *n. see* BUZZY *n.*

boosy *adj. see* BOOZY *adj.*

boot *n.*[1] [abbr. BOOTLICKER *n.*] [late 19C–1910s] (*US campus*) a toady, a sycophant.

boot *n.*[2] [SE *boot*, the orig. ref. was to the leggings worn by recruits to the US Navy during training] **1** [1910s+] (*US milit.*) any new recruit in the US armed forces. **2** [1950s+] (*US/UK black*) a fellow black (usu. derog.); also used by whites as derog. term for blacks [*black* boots]. **3** [1950s+] (*US*) a black person; usu. derog. [*black* boots]. **4** [1950s+] a woman, the implication is an unattractive one; thus often as *old boot*. **5** [1950s+] (*US campus*) an automobile tyre. **6** [1970s+] (*US/W.I.*) a condom. **7** [1990s+] (*Can.*) a woman whose overt promiscuity renders her unattractive.

IN COMPOUNDS

❑ **boot camp** *n.* [1910s+] (*US milit.*) basic training camp. ❑ **boothead** *n.* [sense 3 + -HEAD *sfx* (2)] (*US*) a derog. ref. to a black person. ❑ **boot lip** *n.* [sense 3 + SE *lip*] [20C+] (*US*) a black person.

IN PHRASES

❑ **boot second lieutenant** *n.* [1910s+] (*US milit.*) a newly commissioned second lieutenant. ❑ **boot up** *v.* [1970s+] (*US black*) to put on a condom. ❑ **have one's boots on** *v.* [1980s+] (*US black*) to use a condom.

IN EXCLAMATIONS

❑ **in your boot!** [1960s] (*Aus.*) excl. of dismissal, rejection. ❑ **stuff my old boots!** *see* STUFF ME! *under* STUFF *v.*[1].

SE in slang uses

IN COMPOUNDS

❑ **boot boy** *n.* [the heavy boots that make up part of their 'uniform'] [1970s+] a skinhead. ❑ **boot-catcher** *n.* [late 18C–early 19C] the servant whose task it is to help guests off with and to clean their boots on arrival at an inn. ❑ **boot-eater** *n.* [late 19C] a juror who would rather 'eat their boots' than find anyone guilty. ❑ **bootfaced** *adj.* [naut. jargon *have a sea-boot face*, to look unhappy] [1930s+] gloomy, miserable-looking. ❑ **boot kisser** *n.* [1960s] a sycophant, a toady. ❑ **bootheel** *n.* *see* HEELTAP *n.* (1). ❑ **bootstrap** *v.* [phr. *pull oneself up by one's bootstraps*. Note computer jargon *boot*(*strap*), to start the machine] [1950s+] (*orig. US*) to improve one's lot in life by one's own efforts.

IN PHRASES

❑ **are your boots laced?** [1930s–40] (*US black*) a general query as to the state of affairs; is everything in order? are you ready? do you understand? ❑ **boot and shoe** *n.* (*also* **boot and shoe fiend**) [such an addict has pawned even his shoes in order to buy narcotics] [1930s–50s] (*US drugs*) the lowest class of narcotics user. ❑ **boot-and-shoe booster** *n. see* SNATCH-AND-GRAB BOOSTER *under* BOOSTER *n.*^{2}. ❑ **boot in** *v.* [SE *boot*, to kick] [1920s] (*US*) to urge, to force. ❑ **boots and all** *adv.* [mid-19C; 1940s+] (*Aus./N.Z.*) absolutely, completely, with no reservations. ❑ **die in one's boots** *v.* (*also* **die with one's boots on**) *see under* DIE *v.* ❑ **from boots to breakfast** *see* FROM HELL TO BREAKFAST *under* HELL *n.* ❑ **get one's boots on** *v.* [1940s] (*US black*) to come up to date. ❑ **give it the boot** *v.* [one pushes down on the accelerator with a boot or shoe] [1990s+] to accelerate. ❑ **hang up one's boots** *v.* [HANG UP ONE'S... *v.*] [20C+] **1** to die. **2** to retire. ❑ **have one's boots on** *v.* (*also* **...boots laced**) [one is thus ready to confront the world] [1930s–70s] (*US black*) to be wise, sophisticated, intelligent. ❑ **like old boots** *adv.* [mid-19C–1920s] a general intensifier, e.g. *fight like old boots*, to fight enthusiastically. ❑ **put the boot on** *v.* (*also* **...boots on**) [one puts on one's boots before leaving the house] [1920s–40s] (*Irish*) to bring to a close.

boot *n.*^{3} [abbr.] [1920s–40s] (*US*) a *boot*legger.

boot *n.*^{4} [fig. uses of SE *boot*, a kick] **1** [1930s+] (*US*) a thrill; *boot in the ass*, a thrill, a jolt of pleasure. **2** [1990s+] (*drugs*) a dose of a given drug.

IN PHRASES

❑ **get a boot out of** *v. see* GET A BANG OUT OF *under* BANG *n.*^{1}. ❑ **out of one's boots** *adv.* [one has been 'blown' or 'knocked' out of one's boots] [mid-19C–1900s] (*US*) comprehensively, convincingly, totally. ❑ **pull up a boot** *v.* [the adoption of smart boots as a sign of affluence] [late 19C] (*costermonger*) to prosper, to make money.

boot, the *n.* **1** [late 19C+] ejection, dismissal, defeat in all cases, esp. when sudden and ruthless; thus *get the boot*, to be thrown out, both of a place or one's employment. **2** [late 19C+] an act of kicking; usu. in phr. *give someone the boot*.

IN PHRASES

❑ **get the order of the boot** *v.* [late 19C+] to be sacked from work. ❑ **give someone the boot** *v.* [late 19C+] **1** to dismiss from a job, to throw out; to end a relationship. **2** (*also* **...the heel, ...the boots**) to give someone a kicking, also fig. use. ❑ **give someone the order of the boot** *v.* [late 19C+] to dismiss, to reject, usu. from one's job. ❑ **put the boot in** *v.* (*also* **lay in the boot, put in the boot, put the boot to, sock the boot in, stick the boot in**) [1910s+] (*orig. Aus.*) **1** to kick someone during a fight; thus *in with the boot*, no holds barred. **2** (*also* **sock a boot into**) in fig. use. ❑ **put the boots to** *v.* (*also* **throw the boots to**) (*US*) **1** [late 19C+] to give a kicking to; thus *get the boots*, to receive a kicking; also fig. use. **2** [late 19C+] to victimize, to treat harshly. **3** [1920s+] (*also* **get the boots**) to have sexual intercourse with; to rape.

boot *v.*^{1} **1** to use a boot as a lit. or fig. 'weapon'. (**a**) [mid-19C+] (*also* **boot around, boot up**) to kick, usu. in a fight. (**b**) [mid-19C+] (*also* **boot off, boot out**) to eject, to force to leave. (**c**) [1910s] (*US*) to dismiss, to ignore. **2** in the context of movement. (**a**) [20C+] (*US*) (*also* **boot it, boot off**) to walk or run away. (**b**) [1940s–50s] (*US black/teen*) to drive a car (at speed). (**c**) [2000s] (*N.Z.*) to strain to finish. **3** [1940s+] (*US, orig. sports*) to blunder, to make a mistake; lit. to reach for a ball but kick it rather than hold it.

IN PHRASES

❑ **boot out** *v.* [late 19C+] to eject, to dismiss. ❑ **boot the bucket** *v. see* KICK THE BUCKET *v.*

boot *v.*^{2} [BOOT *n.*^{1}] [1900s–10s] (*US campus*) to toady to.

boot *v.*^{3} [BOOT *n.*^{3} (1)] [1920s–30s] (*US*) to bootleg.

boot *v.*^{4} [SE *boot*, to share (booty)] [1920s–50s] (*US black*) to give, to hand over.

boot *v.*^{5} **1** [1940s] (*US black*) to introduce. **2** [1940s–50s] (*US black*) to become aware. **3** [1940s–50s] (*US black*) to inform, to explain. **4** [1960s–70s] (*US*) to disparage, to criticize.

IN PHRASES

❑ **boot-snitch** *n.* [BOOT *v.*^{5} (3) + SNITCH *n.*^{1} (3)] [1900s–40s] (*US black/Harlem*) **1** an informer, a tell-tale. **2** a dictionary.

boot *v.*^{6} [1950s+] (*drugs*) **1** (*also* **kick**) to inject a drug in stages, drawing the heroin/blood mixture up into the syringe/eyedropper, then injecting, then repeating the process several times; usu. as BOOTING *n.*^{3}; thus *booter*, one who performs this [this 'pumping' supposedly intensifies the KICK *n.*^{5} (1) that accompanies the injection; ? thus it 'gives one a kick']. **2** in ext. use, to smoke or sniff heroin or crack cocaine. **3** in weak use of sense 1, to inject a narcotic.

IN PHRASES

❑ **go the boot** *v.* [1950s] (*drugs*) to leave the needle in one's arm after injecting a drug, then jerk the needle so as to draw blood.

boot *v.*^{7} [? echoic] [1970s+] (*US campus*) to vomit.

bootchkey *n.* (*also* **butchski**) [Czech *pockej*, wait, used by Czech youngsters while playing games and thus adopted as generic by early Eastern European immigrants to US] [1920s+] (*US*) a Czech immigrant.

booted *adj.* [BOOT *v.*^{6}] [1940s+] (*drugs*) under the influence of (narcotic) drugs.

booted (on) *adj.* [BOOT *v.*^{5}; Willie Bryant's ety. in *Jive in Hi-Fi* (1958) is spurious; note Burley, *Original Handbook of Harlem Jive* (1944): 'The fellow who is "hipped" or "hepped" is common indeed. But the one who is "booted" is a unique individual [...] To be hipped one has to have his boots on. The tighter the boots are laced, the more hipped the wearer is supposed to be'] [1900s–40s] (*US black*) aware, knowledgeable, smart.

booter *n.*^{1} [BOOT *n.*^{1}] [1900s] (*US campus*) a toady, a sycophant.

booter *n.*^{2} [BOOT *n.*^{3} (1)] [1920s–40s] (*US*) a bootlegger.

booter *n.*^{3} [BOOT *n.*^{4} (2)] [1990s+] (*US drugs*) cocaine.

booth *n.* [late 18C–mid-19C] a thieves' den.

boothale *v.* [SE *booty* + *hale*, haul] [late 16C–early 17C] to rob, to steal.

boot-haler *n.* [BOOTHALE *v.* (1)] [early 17C] a highwayman.

boot hill *n.* [orig. Western *Boot Hill*, in Dodge City, the cemetery set aside for those who died 'with their boots on', i.e. in a gunfight] (*US*) **1** [19C] a cemetery. **2** [20C+] a prison cemetery.

boot-hill two-step *n.* [SE *boot-heel* + *two-step*] [1960s] (*US*) diarrhoea.

bootie *n.* [abbr.] [1920s–30s] (*US*) a *boot*legger.

bootie *adj. see* BOOTSIE *adj.*

bootie-buster *n.* [BOOTY *n.*^{2} (2) + BUST *v.*^{1} (1)] [1980s] (*US*) a male homosexual.

bootilitious *adj. see* BOOTYLICIOUS *adj.*

booting *n.*^{1} [BOOTY *n.*^{2} (1)] [1920s–30s] (*US black*) participation in sexual intercourse.

booting *n.*^{2} [abbr.] [1930s] bootlegging.

booting *n.*^{3} [BOOT *v.*^{6}] [1960s] (*drugs*) enjoying the immediate effects of a narcotic injection by injecting heroin little by little.

bootjack *n.* [SE *bootjack*, an inanimate object used for pulling off boots] [mid-19C] (*US campus*) a fool.

bootjack *adj.* [BOOTJACK *v.*] [1960s] stolen.

bootjack *v.* [SE *bootjack*, the image of removing something, i.e. from its owner] [1930s+] to steal.

bootleg *n.* [the orig. practice of carrying the illicit liquor hidden in one's boot-legs] **1** [late 19C+] (*orig. US*) illicit liquor, usu. whisky (other than during US Prohibition). **2** [1900s–20s] (*US*) adulterated coffee, usu. mixed with chicory. **3** [1920s–30s] (*US black*) a bootlegger. **4** [1950s+] (*orig. US*) a bootleg or pirated record, tape or video etc. **5** [1990s+] (*US teen*) anything or anyone considered pitiful, embarrassing, second-rate etc. **6** [2000s] a song that is a mix of two completely different songs spliced into one.

bootleg *adj.* [BOOTLEG *v.*] (*orig. US*) **1** [late 19C+] of liquor, illegally transported, smuggled or distilled. **2** [late 19C+] fake, counterfeit. **3** [1920s+] illegal in general. **4** [1990s+] (*US teen*) in fig. use, second-rate.

bootleg *v.* [BOOTLEG *n.*] **1** [late 19C+] to smuggle, to transport illegally (generally, but not invariably of liquor). **2** [1920s–30s] to manufacture and sell illegal liquor [later 20C use is SE]. **3** [1940s] to sell cheaply. **4** [1960s+] to make an illegal copy of music, video etc.

bootlegger *n.* [BOOTLEG *v.*; 1940s+ use is SE and covers the pirating of records, tapes, computer games etc] [late 19C–1930s] (*orig. US*) a smuggler or manufacturer of illicit liquor; thus *bootlegger turn*, a handbrake turn (performed to avoid an oncoming car full of revenue officers or police).

bootlick *n.* [BOOTLICK *v.*] [mid-19C+] (*orig. US*) a cowardly, obsequious person, a toady, one who curries favour.

bootlick *v.* [SE] [mid-19C+] (*orig. US*) to toady, to curry favour.

IN COMPOUNDS

❑ **boot-licking** *adj.* [mid-19C+] (*orig. US*) sycophantic.

bootlicker *n.* [ext. of BOOTLICK *n.*] [mid-19C+] (*orig. US*) a cowardly, obsequious person, a toady, one who curries favour.

boots *n.*[1] [? metonymy] [early 17C; mid-19C+] a fellow, a person, usu. in combs. e.g. *CLEVER BOOTS under* CLEVER *adj.*; SMARTY-BOOTS *n.* (1).

boots *n.*[2] [abbr. *BOOT-CATCHER under* BOOT *n.*[2]; late 19C+ use SE; Grose (1785) cites it in military context only] **1** [late 18C–early 19C] the youngest member, i.e. of a regiment, a club etc. **2** [late 18C–late 19C] the servant assigned to the cleaning of boots and other odd jobs. **3** [1990s+] (*US*) a shoeshiner.

boots *n.*[3] [BOOT *n.*[2] (3)/SE *boots*] [1960s] (*US black*) a fellow black person, sometimes derog.

boots *n.*[4]

IN PHRASES

❑ **knock boots with** *v.* [BOOTY *n.*[2]] [1980s+] (*US black/campus*) to have sexual intercourse with.

boots and socks *n.* [rhy. sl. = POX *n.*[1] (3)] [20C+] (*Aus./UK*) venereal disease.

bootsie *adj.* (*also* **bootie, bootsey, bootsy**) [? BOOTLEG *adj.*] [1990s+] (*US black teen*) bad, fake, inferior, second-rate.

boot the gong *v.*[1] (*also* **kick the gong**) [1940s+] (*US*) **1** to fool around. **2** to act energetically. **3** to gossip, to chat.

boot the gong *v.*[2] [marijuana-based development of *KICK THE GONG AROUND under* GONG *n.*[2]] [1950s+] (*drugs*) to smoke marijuana.

boot-up *n.* [BOOT UP *v.*[1] (1)] [1950s] the consumption of drink or drugs to improve one's mood.

boot up *v.*[1] [BOOT *v.*[6]] **1** [1950s–60s] (*US drugs*) to use a drink or drug to improve one's feelings, e.g. inject heroin, drink wine; also as n. **2** [1970s+] (*US black*) to get ready for a fight. **3** [1990s+] (*UK drugs*) to take a narcotic.

boot up *v.*[2] *see under* BOOT *n.*[2].

booty *n.*[1]

IN PHRASES

❑ **play booty** *v.* (*also* **bowl booty, fight booty, ride booty**) [mid-16C–19C] to cheat in cards or dice (occas. bowls), usu. in conspiracy with a confederate. The result of such play is either to gang up on a third party, and share the resulting profits or 'booty', or deliberately to play to lose; also in fig. use; similarly used of horseracing where a jockey deliberately loses.

booty *n.*[2] (*also* **boody**) [SE *body*; note BUTT *n.*[1]] [1920s+] (*US black*) **1** the vagina; thus by metonymy woman, esp. as a sex-object and generic for sex (whether with a man or a woman). **2** the buttocks, the rectum; thus *booty-bandit*, a sodomist, a homosexual rapist; *booty-struck*, obsessively lecherous; *bootyhole*, the anus. **3** generic for the body, thus a person.

IN COMPOUNDS

❑ **booty-buffer** *n.* [SE *buffer*, one who polishes] [1990s+] a male homosexual; a heterosexual who enjoys anal intercourse. ❑ **booty call** *n.* (*also* **boody call**) [sense 1 + SE *call*] [1990s+] (*orig. US black teen*) **1** a late-night rendezvous. **2** a person used for casual sex. ❑ **booty-chokers** *n.* [1990s+] (*US*) extremely tight sweat-pants. ❑ **booty-dooty** *v.* [1980s] (*US black*) to have anal intercourse. ❑ **booty drought** *n.* [sense 1 + SE *drought*/DROUGHT *n.* (2)] [1980s+] (*US black/campus*) a lack of sex. ❑ **booty-funk** *adj.* [sense 2 + FUNK *n.*[1] (3), lit. 'stinky-arse'] [1990s+] (*US campus*) unattractive. ❑ **booty-ho** *n.* [sense 1 + HO *n.*] [2000s] (*US black*) a female one dislikes as a person but finds exciting sexually. ❑ **booty juice** *n.* [sense 1 + JUICE *n.*[1] (2)] [2000s] (*US black*) a mix of sweat and vaginal juices.

IN PHRASES

❑ **bust some booty** *v.* [1980s+] (*US black*) **1** to perform sexual intercourse. **2** to perform anal intercourse. ❑ **get some booty** *v.* (*also* **get some boody**) [1980s+] **1** (*US black*) of a male, to have sexual intercourse. **2** to have homosexual anal intercourse.

booty *adj.* [? fig. use of BOOTY *n.*[2] (3) as a negative in the same way as ARSE *n.* is used] [1990s+] (*US black/W.I./UK black teen*) **1** weak. **2** second-rate, inferior. **3** gullible.

booty *v.* [*PLAY BOOTY under* BOOTY *n.*[1]] [17C–18C] to cheat, to play falsely.

booty bandit *n.* [BOOTY *n.*[2] + -BANDIT *sfx* (2)] **1** [20C+] (*also* **boody bandit, budi-bandit**) (*US*) a homosexual male. **2** [2000s] a heterosexual man who aggressively gropes or rubs up against women.

booty banditry *n.* [BOOTY BANDIT *n.* (1)] [1990s+] (*US*) male homosexual rape.

booty-fellow *n.* [SE *booty* + *fellow*] [mid-16C; 19C] one who takes a share of the booty.

bootylicious *adj.* (*also* **bootilitious**) [1990s+] **1** (*US black*) second-rate, inferior [playing on BOOTY *adj.* to make negative version of BODELICIOUS *adj.*]. **2** (*black*) (*also* **mingelicious**) a general term of approval, wonderful, attractive, sexy [BOOTY *n.*[2] (1)].

booveroo *n.* [? Lincs. dial. *boof*, a clumsy fellow] [1900s] (*Aus.*) a layabout, a LARRIKIN *n.* (1).

boo-ya *adj.* (*also* **booyaka**) [? hip-hop group the *Boo-YaTribe*] [1990s+] (*W.I./UK/US black teen*) totally wonderful, incredibly fine.

booya! *excl.* (*also* **booyah!**) [SE excl. *boo!* + *yah*] [1980s+] (*US black/campus*) **1** a term used to indicate suddenness or surprise. **2** an echoic term used to imitate the sound of a shotgun being fired. **3** an excl. denoting 'I told you so!'. **4** a greeting.

booyaka! *excl.* (*also* **boo-yakka!**) [? echoic] [1990s+] **1** (*W.I./UK black teen*) an excl. of delight, pleasure, made by using the mouth to simulate gun shots fired in celebration or appreciation of something. **2** (*orig. W.I., Jam.*) a gunfight, gunshots.

boozarium *n.* [BOOZE *n.* (1)] [1900s] (*US*) a bar.

booze *n.* [BOUSE *n.*; the orig. spelling is *bouse*, but it has been superseded by *booze* since the late 17C] **1** [late 17C+] (*also* **booz, bues**) alcohol, a drink; for earlier uses *see* BOUSE *n.* **2** [mid-18C+] a drinking spree. **3** [late 19C–1910s] a (glass of) drink.

DERIVATIVES

❑ **booze-fest** *n.* [-FEST *sfx*] [1930s–60s] (*US*) a drunken party.

IN COMPOUNDS

❑ **booze artist** *n.* [-ARTIST *sfx*] [1920s+] (*orig. Aus.*) a drunkard. ❑ **booze balloon** *n.* [1970s+] (*N.Z.*) a fat stomach that has resulted from sustained heavy drinking. ❑ **booze barn** *n.* (*also* **beer barn**) [1970s+] (*N.Z.*) anywhere dedicated to the large-scale and rapid service of alcohol. ❑ **booze bazaar** *n.* [late 19C–1900s] (*US*) a bar. ❑ **booze belly** *n.* [1960s–70s] (*US*) a fat stomach that has resulted from excessive drinking. ❑ **booze bus** *n.* [1990s+] (*Aus.*) a police van used for random breath tests (for excess alcohol). ❑ **booze can** *n.* [1990s+] (*W.I. Rasta*) a drink and dance party, a 'rave'. ❑ **booze-capper** *n.* [CAPPER *n.* (2)] [1900s–10s] a woman who works in a bar to persuade customers to drink more than they wish or should. ❑ **booze casa** *n.* [CASA *n.*[1]] [mid-19C] a public house, a tavern. ❑ **booze clerk** *n.* [late 19C–1920s] (*US*) a bartender. ❑ **booze crib** *n.* (*also* **boozing joint, booze joint, ...mill, ...parlor**) [CRIB *n.*[1] (1)/JOINT *n.* (3b)/SE *mill*, a place of activity, work] [mid-19C–1930s] (*UK/US Und.*) a bar, a tavern, any drinking establishment. ❑ **booze factory** *n.* (*also* **rum factory**) [late 19C–1900s] (*US*) a bar. ❑ **booze-fencer** *n.* [-FENCER *sfx*] [late 19C–1900s] a licensed victualler. ❑ **booze fight** *n.* (*also* **booze killer**) *see* separate entry. ❑ **booze foundry** *n.* [SE *foundry*] [1930s] (*US*) a saloon. ❑ **boozegob** *n.* [GOB *n.*[1] (1)] [1930s] (*US*) a drunkard. ❑ **booze-head** *n.* (*also* **booze freak**) [-HEAD *sfx* (3)] [1960s–70s] (*US*) a drunkard. ❑ **booze-hoister** *n.* **1** [1910s–20s] (*US*) a prodigious drinker, thus *booze-hoisting*, heavy drinking.

2 [1930s] bartender. ❑ **booze-hound** *n.* [-HOUND *sfx*] [1910s+] (*US*) a dedicated drinker. ❑ **booze-pusher** *n.* [late 19C–1900s] a licensed victualler. ❑ **booze rooster** *n.* [play on BOOZEROO *n.*] [1960s] (*N.Z.*) a heavy drinker. ❑ **booze runner** *n.* [RUNNER *n.* (1)] [1920s–30s] (*US Und.*) a transporter/smuggler of illegal alcohol; the vehicle or vessel used for such transport; thus *booze run*, the act of smuggling. ❑ **booze session** *n.* [1960s] a drinking party (usu. in a public house or bar). ❑ **booze shunter** *n.* [coined by railwaymen working for the Southern Region] [late 19C–1900s] a beer drinker. ❑ **booze stupe** *n.* [STUPE *n.*; lit. 'drink-fool'] [1950s] (*US*) an alcoholic.

IN PHRASES

❑ **booze talking** *see IT'S THE BEER TALKING under* TALK *v.* ❑ **booze-up** *n. see* separate entry. ❑ **hit the booze** *v.* [late 19C+] (*orig. US*) to drink heavily. ❑ **on the booze** *adv.* [mid-19C+] drinking heavily. ❑ **sling the booze** *v.* [late 19C] to treat one's companions.

booze *v.* (*also* **booze it**) [BOUSE *v.*] **1** [mid-16C+] to drink. **2** [late 19C+] to drink away, i.e. money.

IN PHRASES

❑ **booze up** *v. see* separate entry.

boozed *adj.* (*also* **boosed, boozed-out, boozed up**) [BOOZE *v.*] [mid-18C+] drunk.

booze emporium *n. see* BOOZORIUM *n.*

booze fight *n.* [BOOZE *n.* (1) + fig. use of SE *fight*] [1940s+] (*orig. US black*) a drinking spree.

booze-fighter *n.* (*also* **booze killer**) [BOOZE *n.* (1) + SE *fighter*] **1** [20C+] (*Aus./US*) a drunkard. **2** [1920s–60s] (*US*) a narcotics addict (in the context of using alcohol to counter withdrawal symptoms).

booze-fighting *adj.* [BOOZE-FIGHTER *n.* (1)] [1900s–40s] rowdy, regularly drinking, drunk.

booze ken *n. see* BOUSING-KEN *n.*

booze killer *n. see* BOOZE-FIGHTER *n.*

boozel-strap *n.* [mid-19C] (*UK Und.*) food, esp. tripe.

boozen-ken *n. see* BOUSING-KEN *n.*

boozeologist *n.* [BOOZE *n.* (1) + sfx *-ologist*, a student of professor of a given 'ology'] [1900s] (*US*) a bartender.

boozer *n.* [BOOZE *n.* (1)] **1** [late 18C+] (*also* **booser, bowser**) a drunkard. **2** [late 19C+] (*also* **oozer**) a public house or bar.

boozeroo *n.* (*also* **boozelum**) [BOOZE *n.* (1) + -EROO *sfx*] [1940s+] (*N.Z.*) **1** a drinking spree. **2** a public house.

boozer's gloom *n.* [BOOZER *n.* (1)] [1970s] (*N.Z.*) a hangover.

boozery *n.* [BOOZER *n.* + sfx *-y*] [1910s–50s] (*US*) a drinking place.

booze-up *n.* [BOOZE *n.* (1)] [late 19C+] a drinking party, a heavy drinking session.

booze up *v.* [BOOZE *v.*] **1** [late 19C–1910s] (*Aus.*) to make someone else drink or drunk. **2** [1910s] (*also* **booze it up**) to drink, to get drunk.

boozey *n.* see BOOZY *adj.*

boozician *n.* [BOOZE *n.* (1) + sfx *-ician*, on pattern of SE *physician, mortician*] [1940s+] (*Aus./US*) a heavy drinker; a drunkard.

boozing *n.* (*also* **bousing, busing**) [BOOZE *v.*] [mid-17C+] drinking, thus combs. *boozing den, boozing club, boozing party.*

boozing-can *n. see* BOUSING-KEN *n.*

boozing-cheat *n.* [BOOZING *n.* + CHEAT *n.* (1)] [mid-19C] (*UK Und.*) a bottle.

boozing crib *n.* [BOOZING *n.* + CRIB *n.*[1] (1)] [mid–late 19C] (*UK Und.*) a public house used by villains.

boozing-cull *n.* (*also* **boozing fellow**) [BOOZING *n.* + CULL *n.*[1] (3)] [mid-18C] (*UK Und.*) a drunkard.

boozing-ken *n. see* BOUSING-KEN *n.*

boozington *n.* (*also* **Mr Boozington**) [BOOZE *n.* (1) + sfx *-ington*] [mid-19C–1910s] (*Aus.*) a drunkard.

boozle *n.* [? fig. use of BAMBOOZLE *v.* (1), i.e. a confusion of bodies] [1940s–60s] sexual intercourse.

boozle *v.* (*also* **boosle**) [abbr. BAMBOOZLE *v.* (1)] [late 18C] to confuse, to outwit.

boozorium *n.* (*also* **booze emporium**) [BOOZE *n.* (1) + sfx *-orium/emporium*] [20C+] (*Can./US*) a bar-room, esp. in a hotel.

boozy *n.* [BOOZE *n.* (1) + sfx *-y*] [1920s+] (*Anglo-Irish*) a drunkard.

boozy *adj.* (*also* **boosey, boosy**) [BOOZE *n.* (1) + sfx *-y*] **1** [mid-16C+] drunk; drunken. **2** [1920s+] redolent of alcohol; in fig. use.

IN PHRASES

❑ **boozy-cock** *n.* [mid-18C] (*UK Und.*) a drunkard.

bop *n.*[1] [BOP *v.*] **1** [1930s+] a blow. **2** [1950s–60s] (*US*) a member of a teen street gang. **3** [1950s–60s] (*US*) a fight between teen street gangs. **4** [1950s+] a dance. **5** [1960s] (*Scot.*) a hairstyle copied from that of Elvis Presley in 1960s. **6** [1960s+] (*drugs*) an injection of a narcotic drug, the immediate effect of any drug, e.g. a puff on a cannabis cigarette. **7** [1990s+] (*US black*) a bouncing style of walking, a stride.

bop *n.*[2] [play on HIT *n.* (3)/BOP *n.*[1] (1)] [1970s] (*US black drugs*) a drug in pill form.

bop *n.*[3] [abbr. REBOP *n.*] [1970s+] (*US black*) foolish talk, prattle, nonsense.

bop *n.*[4] [*Bophuthatswana* lit. 'gathering of the Tswana'] [1980s+] (*S.Afr.*) the former Republic of *Bop*huthatswana, one of the black 'homelands' with its territory surrounded by the Transvaal and Orange Free State.

bop *n.*[5] *see* BOPPER *n.*[3].

bop *v.* (*also* **boop**) [Kentish dial. *bop*, to throw anything down with a resounding noise; ult. onomat.] **1** [1920s+] (*orig. US*) to hit. **2** [1930s+] (*orig. US*) to kill. **3** [1950s+] (*orig. US*) (*also* **bap**) to walk, esp. in a carefree, bouncy way. **4** [1950s+] (*US*) to fight (with a weapon). **5** [1950s+] (*orig. US*) to dance. **6** [1970s+] (*US*) to have sexual intercourse. **7** [1980s] (*orig. US*) to ride, i.e. a bicycle or car. **8** [1990s+] (*orig. US*) to look for someone to seduce.

IN PHRASES

❑ **bop around** *v.* [1960s+] to keep moving, to wander about rather than stay put; to visit briefly. ❑ **bop it up** *v.* [1950s] (*US teen*) to enjoy oneself, to go out on a spree. ❑ **bop one's baloney** *v. see under* BALONEY *n.* ❑ **bop out** *v.* [BOP *v.* (1); the image is of being knocked over] [20C+] (*US*) to faint. ❑ **bop the bishop** *v. see BANG THE BISHOP under* BISHOP *n.*[2]. ❑ **bop up** *v.* [fig. use of BOP *v.* (1), cognate with KNOCK UP *v.* (5), i.e. to make] [1970s–80s] (*N.Z. prison*) to improve the tailoring of prison-issue clothing, thus *bopped-up*, enhanced.

bop! *excl.* [BOP *v.* (1)] [1940s] a general excl. of surprise, suddenness.

bo-peep *n.* [the nursery rhyme of 'Little Bo-Peep'] **1** [early 17C–early 19C] (*UK Und.*) one who hides in order to spy on others. **2** [late 19C+] sleep [strengthened by rhy. sl.]. **3** [1940s+] a look, a 'peep'; also as v.; often in phr. *go for a bo-peep* [strengthened by rhy. sl.]. **4** [1960s+] (*US gay*) the eyes. **5** [1980s+] (*US gay*) dark glasses.

bo-peep *v.* [rhy. sl.] [late 19C+] to sleep.

bop glasses *n. see* BEBOP GLASSES *n.*

bopkes *n. see* BUPKES *n.*

bopper *n.*[1] [BOP *v.* (4)] [1950s–60s] (*US*) a gang fighter.

IN PHRASES

❑ **big bopper** *n.* [note *The Big Bopper*, the nickname of DJ and rock singer J.P. Richardson (1930–59), though his nickname more likely from BEBOPPER *n.* (1)] [1950s+] (*US*) a superior person or one who claims to be.

bopper *n.*[2] [abbr. TEENYBOPPER *n.*] [1970s] a young girl, usu. in very early teens, with a predilection for rock music and the boys who play it.

bopper *n.*[3] (*also* **bop**) [BOP *v.* (6)/BOP *v.* (8)] [1990s+] a person looking for sex all the time.

bopper *n.*[4] **1** *see* BEBOPPER *n.* (1). **2** *see* BEBOPPER *n.* (4).

bopper *n.*[5] *see* BINKY *n.*[1] (2).

boppers *n.* [echoic of the noise of one's footsteps] [1960s–70s] (*US campus*) boots, shoes.

bopping club *n.* [BOP *v.* (4)] [1950s] (*US*) a street gang that has regular fights with opponents.

bopping gang *n.* [BOP *v.* (4)] [1950s] (*US*) a street gang with active fighters.

boppo *n. see* BOFFO *n.*[2].

boppy *adj.* [jazz use, *bop* music] [1940s+] jolly, cheery, upbeat.

bopster *n. see* BEBOPPER *n.* (2).

bora *n.* [? SE *borer*] [1990s+] (*UK black*) a knife.

borachio *n.* (*also* **borarco**) [synon. Ital./Sp.] [late 17C–early 19C] a drunkard.

boracic *see under* BORASS.

boracic (lint) *adj.* (*also* **brass, brassic, brassick, brassic lint**) [rhy. sl. = SKINT *adj.* (1)] [1940s+] out of funds, impoverished, pron. 'brassic'.

borak *n.* (*also* **borac, borack, borax**) [Wathawurung *burag*, no, not, via. Aus. pidgin *borak*, used to express negation] [mid-19C+] (*Aus./N.Z.*) nonsense, humbug, chaff, banter.

IN PHRASES

❑ **poke (the) borak** *v.* (*also* **...borack, ...borax, ...it**) [late 19C+] (*Aus./N.Z.*) to make or poke fun.

borak *v.* [late 19C] (*Aus.*) to mock, to tease.

borarco *n. see* BORACHIO *n.*

borass *n.* (*also* **boress, boracic**) [? fig. use of BORAX *n.*[2] or *bore ass*] [1950s+] (*US campus*) a trick, a prank, a hoax.

borass *v.* (*also* **boress, boracic**) [BORASS *n.*] [1950s–70s] (*US campus*) to hoax, to play tricks.

borax *n.*[1] [SE *borax*, cheap and shoddy material, esp. as peddled by immigrant Jews; supposedly orig. in the practice of a maker of borax (acid borate of sodium) soap offering coupons for cheap furniture] [1920s+] (*US*) **1** rubbish, lies, exaggeration. **2** shoddy, cheap manufactured goods.

borax *n.*[2] *see* BORAK *n.*

bord *n.* (*also* **board, borde**) [SE *bord*, shield] [mid-16C–early 19C] a shilling (5p).

IN PHRASES

❑ **half-(a-)borde** *n.* [late 16C–18C] (*UK Und.*) a sixpence (5p).

bordeaux *n.* [SE *bordeaux*, a variety of red wine] [mid-19C–1900s] blood.

bordello *n.* [SE *bordel*, a brothel; ult. OF *bordel*, cabin, hut, brothel. Post-18C use is SE, if (consciously) archaic] [late 16C–18C] a brothel.

bordens *n.* [the firm *Borden's*, producers of milk and dairy products; *elsie* presumably refers to a 'typical' name for a cow] [1940s–70s] (*US*) the female breasts; also ext. as *borden's and elsie's*, *bordens and bowman*; one of many sl. terms for breasts relating to their role as milk-giving.

border *n.*

SE in slang uses

IN COMPOUNDS

❑ **border brothers** *n.* [cf. BATO *n.*] [2000s] (*US prison*) Mexicans. ❑ **border reds** *n. see* BORDERS *n.* ❑ **border ruffian** *n.* [mid-19C] (*US*) a native of Missouri.

IN PHRASES

❑ **over the border** [2000s] outside Greater London.

border reef *n.* [rhy.sl.] [1980s] (*Aus.*) the teeth.

borders *n.* (*also* **border reds**) [their container, a capsule with a red border] [1970s+] (*drugs*) non-proprietary capsules of barbiturate powder sold on the black market and with implication of having been made up on the US/Mexico border.

borde-timmy *n.* [BORD *n.* (1)+ SE *demi*] [mid-19C] (*UK Und.*) sixpence.

bore *n.*[1] [*OED* states ety. unknown. ? f. SE *bore*, to drill into, but this fails to account for sense 2, from which senses 1 and 3 presumably stem. Partridge suggests poss. link to *boar*, an uncouth, ignorant person, but this still ignores sense 2, which lasted as sl. no later than the 1760s. Grose notes that senses 1 and 3 were very fashionable *c.*1780 and then vanished. 'Not so, burly Grose,' says Hotten in 1859, 'the term is still in favour and as piquant and expressive as ever.' However, although Hotten includes it, the word was by then virtually, if not actually SE] **1** [early 16C; mid-18C–early 19C] a tedious person or thing, a nuisance. **2** [mid-18C] the equivalent of Fr. *ennui*, a feeling of world-weariness, the equivalent of Eng. *spleen*; thus *French bore*, one who feels or at least affects indifference to all things and people. **3** [early 19C] (*US*) a trick, a hoax.

bore *n.*[2] **1** [mid-19C] the penis [SE *bore*, an auger]. **2** [mid-19C–1940s] the vagina [SE *bore*, a hole, a chink, crevice, or cranny].

bore *v.*[1] [SE *bore*, to drill a hole] **1** [early 17C–early 19C] to tease, to mock, to humiliate. **2** [mid-17C+] to have sexual intercourse, either hetero- or homosexual [note 17C SE *bore*, to run through with a sword]. **3** [mid-18C+] to impose one's views, opinions or simply presence upon those who find them tedious and irritating. **4** [mid-19C–1950s] (*US*) to shoot a hole in [note 17C SE *bore*, to run through with a sword].

SE in slang uses

IN PHRASES

❑ **bore a hole in** *v.* [mid-19C] (*US*) to shoot. ❑ **bore for the simples** *v.* [var. on CUT FOR THE SIMPLES *adj.*; SE *bore*, to make a hole + dial. *simples*, simple-mindedness; ? a ref. to trepanning] [1920s–30s] (*US*) a verb used with ref. to a simpleton, e.g. *he ought to be bored for the simples*, he is a fool. ❑ **bore it up** *v.* [SE *bore*, to pierce, stab, run through with a weapon; to wound] [1940s+] (*Aus.*) **1** to attack viciously or energetically. **2** in fig. use. ❑ **bore someone a new one** *v.* ['one' is an ASSHOLE *n.* (1)] [1950s] (*US*) to attack savagely, either physically or verbally. ❑ **bore someone's ear** *v.* [note *OED bore* (*any one's*) *ears*, to consign to perpetual slavery (allusion to Exod. xxi. 6)] [late 18C–late 19C] to bore (as a talker).

bore *v.*[2]

SE, meaning to tire, in slang uses

IN PHRASES

❑ **bore someone rigid** *v.* [1970s+] to bore very much. ❑ **bore stiff** *v. see under* STIFF *adj.*[1]. ❑ **bore the arse off** *v. see* BORE THE PANTS OFF *under* PANTS *n.*

boress *see under* BORASS.

boretto-man *n.* [SE *bore* + Ital. dimin. sfx *-etto*; i.e. 'a little borer'] [late 17C] a male homosexual.

Boris *n.* [1980s] a generic derog. term for a Russian.

boris bold *adj.* [rhy. sl.] [2000s] cold.

born *adj.*

SE in slang uses

IN PHRASES

❑ **born again** *n.* [SE *born* + *again*, after John 3:3: 'Except a man be born again, he cannot see the kingdom of God'] [1990s+] (*US campus*) a fundamentalist Christian. ❑ **born-again virgin** *n. see under* VIRGIN *n.*[2]. ❑ **born on Wednesday looking both ways for Sunday** *adj.* (*also* **born in the middle of the week, looking...**) [mid-19C+] (*US*) cross-eyed. ❑ **born under a threepenny halfpenny planet** *adj.* [17C–19C] being a complete failure, useless; usu. ext. by 'never to be worth a groat'. ❑ **born with burned feet** *adj.* [1970s] (*US*) illegitimate.

born and bred *n.* [rhy. sl.] [2000s] a bed.

'Boro *n.* [abbr.] [1970s+] (*US*) a Marl*boro* cigarette.

boro-onions *n.* [*Boro*(*ugh*)*nians*] [early–mid-19C] (*Cockney*) inhabitants of Southwark.

borrachio *n.* (*also* **borracho**) [Sp. *borracho*, a drunkard, drunk] **1** [17C–19C] (*later use US*) a drunkard. **2** [late 17C] a skin for holding wine.

borrow *v.* [ironic use of SE] [early 19C+] (*US Und.*) to steal.

borrow and beg *n.* [rhy. sl.] [20C+] an egg.

borstal mark *n.* (*also* **borstal spot**) [1990s+] (*UK prison/Und.*) a blue dot tattooed on the face, the mark of a spell in borstal.

b.o.s. *n.* [abbr.] [1990s+] (*US P.R. gangs*) a beating on sight.

bosbefok *adj. see* BOSSIE *adj.*

bosca/boscar *adj. see* BOSKER *adj.*

Bosche *n. see* BOCHE *n.*

bosco *n.* [? BOSKY *adj.* (1) but note ety. for GEEK *n.*[1]] [1920s–70s] (*US*) a foolish, unimportant person.

bosco boulevard *n.* [? SE *bosky*, dark and wooded] [1980s+] (*US gay*) the anus.

bosh *n.*[1] [Turk. *bosh*, empty, worthless. The term gained enormous popularity from the success of James Morier's novel *Ayesha* (1834), a bestseller, esp. in the Standard Novels' edition of 1846] [mid-18C+] nonsense, rubbish.

bosh *n.*[2] [Rom. *bosh*, to fiddle, to crow] [mid-19C–1930s] a fiddle.

IN COMPOUNDS

❑ **bosh-faker** *n.* (*also* **bosh-killer, boshman**) [mid-19C–1930s] a fiddle player.

bosh *n.*[3] [abbr. *bosch butter*, artificial butter manufactured at 'Hertogenbosch' or 'Bosch' (Bois-le-duc) in Holland; ? reinforced by BOSH *n.*[1] (1)] [late 19C–1900s] margarine or any other substitute (e.g. the short-lived *butterine*) for butter.

bosh *v.* (*also* **bosh up**) [BOSH *n.*[1]] [late 19C] **1** to spoil, to render useless. **2** to cause trouble for; to irritate. **3** to apply liberally (used of paint, plaster etc).

IN COMPOUNDS

❑ **bosh-shot** *n.* [SE *shot*] [1930s–50s] a bad shot, an unsuccessful attempt.

IN PHRASES

❑ **bosh up** *v.* [late 19C–1920s] to go bankrupt.

bosh! *excl.*[1] [mid-19C+] rubbish! nonsense!

bosh! *excl.*[2] [1990s+] an echoic term used to imply suddenness of action.

bosher *n.* [BOSH *n.*[1]] [1910s–30s] one who talks nonsense.

boshey *adj. see* BOSHY *adj.*

boshing *n.* [mid-19C] (*US Und.*) a whipping.

boshta *n.* (*also* **boshter**) [BOSHTA *adj.*] [1900s–10s] (*Aus.*) something or someone outstanding.

boshta *adj.* (*also* **boshter, bosker**) [? SE *bonanza*] **1** [20C+] (*Aus.*) good. **2** [1910s] on good terms with, popular. **3** [1910s] extreme, irrespective of quality.

boshta *adv.* [BOSHTA *adj.*] [1910s] (*Aus.*) excellently, very well.

boshter *n. see* BOSHTA *n.*

boshy *adj.* (*also* **boshey**) [BOSH *n.*[1]] [mid-18C+] foolish, nonsensical.

bosie *adj.* [20C+] (*W.I.*) good, smart.

bosie *v.* [W.I. *bosie*, a hunchback; ? link to Aus. cricket jargon *bosie*, a googly or 'wrong 'un'; it 'bends' across the pitch] [1970s+] (*W.I., Trin.*) to beat extremely hard, so as to bend the victim double.

boskage of Venus *n.* [SE *boskage*, a thicket, grove, woody undergrowth] [late 19C] the female pubic hair.

bos-ken *n.* (*also* **bosken**) [Lat. *bos*, ox + KEN *n.*[1] (1)] [19C] a farm house.

bosker *n.* [1920s–60s] (*Aus.*) an admirable person.

bosker *adj.* (*also* **bosca, boscar**) [var. on BONZER *adj.*] [20C+] (*Aus./N.Z.*) good.

boskiness *n.* [BOSKY *adj.* + sfx *-ness*] [late 19C] drunkenness.

bosky *adj.* (*also* **bosko**) [? SE *bosky*, wooded, bushy; thus one's vision is obscured and one's feet may stumble] [early 18C–1930s] drunk.

bos-man *n.* (*also* **bosman**) [Lat. *bos*, ox] [mid-19C] a farmer.

bosom buddy *n.* [1960s] (*US campus*) a male homosexual.

bosom friend *n.* [play on SE *bosom friend*, an especially intimate friend] **1** [18C+] (*also* **bosom chum**) a louse. **2** [19C] alcoholic drink. **3** [20C+] (*US*) a pack of money kept for security inside her brassiere by a woman while she is travelling.

Boss, the *n.* [the use of sl. to 'humanize' the Deity] [20C+] (*orig. US*) God.

boss *n.*[1] [SE *boss*, a swelling or protuberance] [late 16C–mid-17C] a fat woman.

boss *n.*[2] [Du. *baas*, master, in which form it first appeared in the American colonies in mid-17C. The term did not arrive in the UK until the mid-19C and has always been sl. or colloq.] **1** [mid-17C+] (*also* **bosshead**) the master (or mistress), the manager, the person in charge. **2** [mid-19C+] (*US*) an exceptional person. **3** [mid-19C+] (*orig. US*) a term of address, esp. to a man whose name one does not know. **4** [late 19C+] a 'criminal mastermind'. **5** [1930s] (*UK prison*) a prison governor. **6** [1950s] a heroin wholesaler. **7** [1950s+] (*US prison*) a prison warder. **8** [2000s] (*US black*) female-to-male fellatio [the dominant role of the male as 'boss'].

IN COMPOUNDS

❑ **boss-bitch** *n.* [1960s+] (*US black*) the senior member of a pimp's 'stable' of whores. ❑ **boss boy** *n.* [S.Afr. derog. *boy*, an African, usu. a servant or labourer] [20C+] (*S.Afr.*) a black foreman or overseer in charge of subordinate black workers. ❑ **Boss Charlie** *n.* (*also* **...Charley**) [generic use of proper name *Charlie*] [20C+] (*US black*) a white man, esp. in authority. ❑ **boss cocky** *n.* [COCKY *n.*[2] (1)] [late 19C+] **1** (*Aus.*) a farmer who employs labour and still works. **2** (*Aus.*) a person in authority. **3** (*Aus./N.Z.*) the overseer of a shearing-shed. ❑ **boss dog** *n.* [20C+] **1** (*US*) an important person or one who poses as such. **2** (*US prison*) a prison rapist; one who exploits weaker prisoners, esp. sexually. ❑ **boss game** *n.* [1970s] (*US black*) an important person, usu. in ironic use. ❑ **boss lady** *n.* **1** [1920s+] a female superior. **2** [1950s+] (*US*) (*also* **boss-woman**) a wife who dominates her husband. ❑ **boss man** *n.* **1** [19C] (*US*) the overseer, foreman, employer, chief prison guard, anyone in authority; also as term of address. **2** [1960s] a pimp. **3** [1970s+] (*US gay*) the 'masculine' member of a homosexual couple. ❑ **boss's royal** *n. see* ROYAL *n.*[2].

IN PHRASES

❑ **boss nigger in charge** *n.* see *HEAD NIGGER IN CHARGE under* HEAD *n.* ❑ **little boss** *n.* [1980s+] (*Aus. prison*) a middle-level prison officer. ❑ **whip boss** *n.* [he carries a whip] [1940s–50s] (*US prison*) the chief officer on a prison farm.

boss *n.*[3] [? BOSS-EYE *n.*, i.e. a 'squint' at] [late 19C] a view, a sight of.

boss *adj.* [BOSS *n.*[2] (1)] (*orig. US*) **1** [mid-19C+] the best. **2** [mid-19C+] excellent, wonderful; also intensified as *boss like hot sauce*. **3** [mid-19C+] superior, important, influential. **4** [late 19C] of criminals, very dangerous. **5** [late 19C] (*US*) arrogant, overbearing. **6** [1960s] dedicated, obsessed with. **7** [2000s] important, meaningful.

IN COMPOUNDS

❑ **boss player** *n.* [PLAYER *n.* (3)] [1960s] (*US black*) a thoroughly experienced, professional, worldly wise pimp who may even transcend pimping for superior occupations; the term can be applied to any admirable figure outside the pimp milieu.

boss *v.* (*also* **boss about, boss around**) [BOSS *n.*[2] (1)] [mid-19C+] **1** of a person, to domineer, to order about [SE in 20C]. **2** of an object, to dominate, to take control of. **3** to make a mess of, to spoil.

IN PHRASES

❑ **boss the show** *v.* (*also* **...the shebang**) [SHOW *n.* (1)] [late 19C] to take charge of events.

boss *adv.* [BOSS *adj.*] [1970s+] (*US*) splendidly, excellently, perfectly.

bossers *n.* [? BOSS-EYED *adj.*] [late 19C–1900s] spectacles.

boss-eye *n.* [BOSS *v.* (3) + SE *eye*] [late 19C+] a squinting or injured eye, or one who has one.

boss-eyed *adj.* [BOSS-EYE *n.*] **1** [mid-19C+] squinting; also as adv. **2** [1950s] tipsy, drunk.

IN PHRASES

❑ **put on a boss** *v.* [late 19C] to affect a squint in order to make oneself look more threatening.

bosshead *n. see* BOSS *n.*[2] (1).

bossie *adj.* (*also* **bosbefok**) [Afk. *bos*, bush + *befok*, FUCKED *adj.*[1]] [1970s+] (*S.Afr.*) used orig. in army to indicate one has gone mad through exposure to tropical heat and life in the bush, lit. 'bush-fucked'.

bossified *adj. see* BOSSY *adj.*

boss up *v.* [BOSS *v.* (1)] [20C+] (*S.Afr.*) **1** to manage a house, to organize the servants. **2** to work hard.

boss up! *excl.* [calque f. Cape Du. *pas op!* look out!] [late 19C+] (*S.Afr.*) take care! look out!

bossy *n.* [Lat. *bos*, ox] [1930s] (*US tramp*) beef; thus *bossy in a bowl*, beef stew.

bossy *adj.* (*also* **bossified**) [BOSS *n.*[2] (1) + sfx *-y*] [late 19C+] (*orig. US*) officious, domineering.

bossy-boots *n.* [BOSSY *adj.* (1) + BOOTS *n.*[1] (1), on model of SMARTIEPANTS *n.*] [20C+] (*usu. children*) an officious, domineering person.

bosta *n.* [proper name of the populist politician Sir Alexander *Bustamente* (1884–1977), seen as tough] (*W.I.*) **1** [1940s+] a tough, chewy sweet. **2** [1950s] a sandal made from recycled tyres.

bosthoon *n.* (*also* **bostoom, bostoon**) [Irish *bastún*, lout] [mid-19C–1960s] (*Irish*) a fool.

Boston strawberries *n.* [the city's stereotyped dish. The other stereotype is meanness; thus railroad use *Boston quarter*, a nickel or dime tip] [late 19C+] (*US*) baked beans.

Boston woodcock *n.* [analogous with SE *Scotch woodcock*, hard-boiled eggs chopped up, mixed with anchovy sauce, and then laid on slices of hot buttered toast. The foodstuffs here are staples of the Boston area] [1930s+] (*US*) pork and beans.

bostoom/bostoon *n. see* BOSTHOON *n.*

bosy *adj. see* BOASIE *adj.*

bot *n.*[1] [for ety. *see* BOTFLY *n.*] **1** [late 19C] (*Aus.*) a scheme, a plot, a plan. **2** [1910s+] (*Aus./N.Z.*) (*also* **bott**) a cadger, a scrounger, a hanger-on. **3** [1940s+] (*N.Z.*) a germ; thus phr. of greeting, *how are the bots biting?*

IN PHRASES

❑ **have the bot** *v.* [1940s+] (*Aus./N.Z.*) to be ill, to be out of sorts, moody or disagreeable. ❑ **on the bot** [1910s+] (*Aus./N.Z.*) cadging, scrounging.

bot *n.*[2] [abbr.] [late 19C+] a *bot*tle.

bot *n.*[3] (*also* **bott**) [abbr. SE *bottom*] **1** [1920s+] the buttocks. **2** [1990s+] an act of homosexual anal intercourse.

bot *v.* (*Aus./N.Z.*) **1** [1910s] to impose oneself. **2** [1930s+] to scrounge; thus *cold botting*, knocking on a stranger's front door and asking for food [note salesman's jargon *cold call*, to arrive without a prior appointment in the hope of making a sale].

IN PHRASES

❑ **bot about** *v.* [1920s+] (*Aus./N.Z.*) to wander restlessly from place to place.

botanical excursion *n.* [a pun on the penal colony at *Botany Bay*] [early 19C] transportation to New South Wales.

Botany Bay *n.*[1] [the penal colony of *Botany Bay* was 'down under'] [late 19C] the vagina.

Botany Bay *n.*[2] [rhy. sl.] [20C+] (*US*) hay; usu. in context of sleeping, i.e. HAY *n.* (1).

Botany Bay *v.* (*also* **do a Botany**) [rhy. sl.] [20C+] (*Aus.*) to run away.

Botany Bay coat-of-arms *n.* [the violence that was prevalent at the convict settlement] [early–mid-19C] (*Aus.*) a broken nose and black eyes.

Botany Bay dozen *n.* [late 18C–mid-19C] (*Aus. Und.*) a punishment of 25 lashes.

Botany Bay fever *n.* [early–mid-19C] transportation to New South Wales.

Botany beer party *n.* [brandname of *Botany beer*, which was declared after a court case in 1883 not to be real beer] [late 19C] a party at which there is no form of intoxicating liquor.

botch *n.*[1] (*also* **botcher**) [abbr. SE *botcher*, one who repairs or patches; also note SE *bodger* and dial. *botch*, a cobbler] [late 18C–early 19C] a tailor.

botch *n.*[2] [SE *botch*, an eruptive sore, an ulcer, a plague-spot, thus Deut. 28:27 'The Lord will smite thee with the botch of Egypt, and with the emerods, and with the scab, and with the itch, whereof thou canst not be healed.'] [1960s] (*US*) gonorrhoea.

botch *v.* [SE *botch*, to perform work clumsily] [1990s+] (*US campus*) to ignore.

botcher *n. see* BOTCH *n.*[1].

botfly *n.* [SE *botfly*, an insect of the genus *Oestrus*; its eggs produce the parasitical worm or maggot, the bot + BOT *v.* (2)] (*Aus.*) **1** [20C+] an unpleasant, troublesome, interfering person. **2** [1940s+] a scrounger.

both ends of the busk! *excl. see* MILK AND WATER! *under* MILK *n.*

bother *n.* [mid-19C+] trouble, difficulties; thus *in bother*, in trouble.

IN COMPOUNDS

❑ **bother boy** *n.* [BOTHER *n.* + SE *boy*] [1970s] a youth dedicated to fighting, usu. a skinhead.

bother! *excl.* (*also* **bother it!**) [Anglo-Irish but no spec. root found; ? corruption of *pother*, disturbance] [early 19C+] a mild excl. or a euph. synon. for *TO HELL WITH...! under* HELL *n.*

botherate *v.* [SE *bother*, to annoy + sfx *-ate*] [20C+] (*US black/W.I.*) to annoy, to menace, to threaten.

botheration *n.* (*also* **boderation**) [SE *bother*, late 19C+ use is mainly US black] [late 18C+] annoyance, irritation.

botheration! *excl.* [19C+] euph. for DAMNATION! *excl.*; a mild excl. of annoyance that precludes anything more lurid and thus taboo.

bothered up *adj.* [1920s+] flustered, maniacally nervous, sometimes through the suppression of lust.

bothering *n.* [late 18C] a loud fuss, commotion.

botherment *n.* [SE *bother* + sfx *-ment*] [mid-19C] annoyance, irritation.

bother one's soul-case *v. see BURST ONE'S SOUL-CASE under* SOUL-CASE *n.*

both hands *n.* [the *ten* fingers thereon] [1930s–1960s] (*US Und.*) a sentence of ten years.

both-side *adj.* [one who speaks out of 'both sides' of their mouth] [20C+] (*W.I., Trin.*) deceitful, hypocritical.

both ways *adj.* [1960s+] bisexual.

IN PHRASES

❑ **go both ways** *v.* **1** [1960s+] to be a bisexual. **2** [1970s] to take either role in sado-masochistic sex.

both ways from the ace *adv.* (*also* **both ways from the jack**) [playing card imagery] [1910s–20s] (*US*) in every way, completely.

botoss *n.* [? McGill, *Reed Dict. of N.Z. Slang* (2003), suggests poss. contracted from 'boy' and 'tosser' or masturbator] [2000s] (*N.Z.*) a boy.

bots *n.*[1] [SE *bots*, a disease of horses caused by infestation of botfly larvae in the digestive tract] **1** [16C–17C] syphilis. **2** [late 16C–mid-17C] as an oath. **3** [late 18C–19C] (*also* **batts, botts**) a general sense of physical unease. **4** [1900s] (*US*) depression.

bots *n.*[2] [mid-19C] (*US Und.*) boots.

botsie *n.* [SE *bottom*] [20C+] (*W.I.*) the posterior, the buttocks.

bott *n.* **1** *see* BOT *n.*[1] (2). **2** *see* BOT *n.*[3].

bott *v.* [abbr. SE *bottom*] [1990s+] to sodomize.

botter *n.* [BOT *n.*[3]] [1990s+] a male homosexual.

bottie *n.* (*also* **botty**) [abbr. SE *bottom*] [mid-19C+] (*juv.*) a baby's or small child's buttocks.

bottle *n.*[1] **1** [early 18C] the penis [? resemblance]. **2** [1940s] a severe reprimand [abbr. *bottle of acid*]. **3** in drug uses. (**a**) [1990s+] (*US drugs*) a container for a street measurement of crack cocaine; usu. an actual bottle (the coloured stopper is often used to denote the dealer's 'brand') but also tinfoil wraps. (**b**) [2000s] amphetamine. **4** *see* BLUEBOTTLE *n.* (2). **5** *see* BOTTLE (AND GLASS) *n.*

IN COMPOUNDS

❑ **bottle opener** *n.* [sense 1] [1970s] (*US gay*) an active male homosexual.

SE in slang uses

IN COMPOUNDS

❑ **bottle-ache** *n.* [mid-19C–1900s] delirium tremens. ❑ **bottle-arse** *n.* [ARSE *n.* (1); resemblance; note printers' jargon *bottle-arsed*, worn type that is thicker at one end than the other] [mid-16C; late 19C–1910s] a person with notably broad buttocks; thus *bottle-arsed*. ❑ **bottle baby** *n.* [pun on SE *bottle baby*, an infant fed by bottle rather than by breast]

[1920s+] (*orig. US*) an alcoholic tramp who has become insane and whose mental age is that of an infant; thus a heavy drinker. ❑ **bottle blonde** *n.* (*also* **bleach-bottle blonde**) [20C+] a woman with dyed hair. ❑ **bottle-boy** *n.* [1930s–40s] (*US*) a drunkard, an alcoholic. ❑ **bottlebrain** *n.* [1970s] a stupid or intoxicated person. ❑ **bottlehead** *n.* [-HEAD *sfx* (1) / -HEAD *sfx* (4); their brains are fuddled by alcohol, whether actually or figuratively] [mid-17C–mid-19C] **1** a fool; thus *bottle-headed*, foolish. **2** a drunkard. ❑ **bottle-holder** *n.* [boxing use, where the fighter's 'second' holds a bottle of water] [mid-18C–late 19C] a supporter, an assistant; thus *bottle-holding*, assistance, support. ❑ **bottle hound** *n.* [-HOUND *sfx* (1)] [1960s+] (*US*) an alcoholic, a heavy drinker. ❑ **bottle juggler** *n.* [1910s] (*US*) a barperson. ❑ **bottleneck** *n.* [1970s+] (*S.Afr. drugs*) a mixture of tobacco and marijuana (sometimes with other forms of drugs) packed into the neck of a broken bottle, which serves as a pipe and through which it is smoked. ❑ **bottle tipper** *n.* [1940s–60s] (*US*) a drunkard. ❑ **bottle tokes** *n.* [TOKE *n.*^{2}] [1980s+] (*US drugs*) a method of smoking hashish where a small hole is made in a bottle (usu. a beer bottle), then a cigarette with a small chunk of hashish on the tip is inserted in the hole. ❑ **bottle wash** *n.* [i.e. the dregs washed out of a bottle] [late 19C+] nonsense, rubbish. ❑ **bottle washer** *n.* *see* CHIEF COOK AND BOTTLE-WASHER *n.*

IN PHRASES

❑ **and no bottles** [late 19C] without a doubt. ❑ **bottle of...** *n.* *see* separate entries. ❑ **break a bottle in an empty sack** *v.* [a sack that is empty cannot contain a bottle] [late 18C–early 19C] to make a cheating bet. ❑ **drink out of the same bottle** *v.* *see under* DRINK *v.* ❑ **full bottle, the** *n.* [1960s+] (*Aus.*) an expert. ❑ **give a bottle a black eye** *v.* [i.e. to conquer] [late 18C–early 19C] to drink a bottle almost to the bottom. ❑ **no bottle** *see* separate entries.

bottle *n.*^{2} [BOTTLE *v.*^{2}; despite chronological discrepancy, this would appear correct] **1** [late 19C–1930s] a share of money. **2** [1960s+] £2.

bottle *v.*^{1} [20C+] to hit someone (in the face) with a broken bottle.

bottle *v.*^{2} [ext. use of SE *bottle* as a general container] [1920s+] to collect money from a busker's audience.

DERIVATIVES

❑ **bottling** *n.* [1920s+] collecting money from the audience, 'passing round the hat'.

bottle *v.*^{3} [BOTTLE (AND GLASS) *n.* (2)] [1950s+] **1** of a man, to have sexual intercourse. **2** to perform heterosexual anal intercourse. **3** (*gay*) to lick the anus. **4** (*UK prison*) of a prisoner, to hide drugs etc by wrapping in plastic and inserting up the anus.

bottle *v.*^{4} [? rhy. sl.; *bottle of drink* = stink] [1970s] to stink, to smell badly.

bottle (and glass) *n.* [rhy. sl. = ARSE *n.* (1), which, in turn, plays on BOTTOM *n.*^{1} (2)] **1** [1910s–30s] (*UK Und.*) the hip pocket (which is near the buttocks). **2** [1910s+] the buttocks, the anus. **3** [1910s+] courage, bravery, 'spirit'. **4** [2000s] a person, usu. in derog. sense.

IN PHRASES

❑ **bottle it** *v.* [1950s+] to back down, to act in a cowardly manner. ❑ **bottle out** *v.* [1970s+] to be a coward, to run away, to back down from a challenge. ❑ **has your bottle fallen out?** [1940s+] are you afraid? ❑ **have one's bottle fall out** *v.* [1950s] to be frightened, to act in a cowardly manner. ❑ **lose one's bottle** *v.* [20C+] to back down, to turn cowardly. ❑ **on the bottle 1** [20C+] (*later UK black*) working as a pickpocket. **2** [1960s+] working as a male prostitute. **3** [1960s+] (*US*) working in any form of prostitution.

bottle (and stopper) *n.* [rhy. sl. = COPPER *n.* (3)] [1910s+] (*US*) a police officer.

bottled *adj.*^{1} [BOTTLE UP *v.* (1)] **1** [19C] arrested, caught. **2** [late 19C–1910s] stuck in one place, halted [note Ware's suggestion that it refers to the trapping by the US Navy of the Spanish fleet in Santiago in 1898].

bottled *adj.*^{2} (*also* **bottled out**) [1920s–60s] drunk.

bottled earthquake *n.* (*also* **earthquake**) [mid–late 19C] a strong alcoholic drink.

bottled in the barn *n.* [pun on SE *bottled in bond*, bottled and then held in a Customs' warehouse until the appropriate duty is paid] [1940s–50s] (*US*) illicitly distilled whisky.

bottled out *adj.* *see* BOTTLED *adj.*^{2}.

bottled up *adj.* [SE *bottled up*, contained in a bottle] [late 19C] fully occupied, unable to take on any new commitments.

bottlegreen and lousy *adj.* [one's complexion and the state of one's body] [1920s+] (*Aus.*) utterly down-and-out.

bottle-ho *n.* *see* BOTTLE-O *n.*

bottle it *v.*^{1} [SE *bottle it up*] [late 19C+] (*orig. US*) be quiet, shut up.

bottle it *v.*^{2} *see under* BOTTLE (AND GLASS) *n.*

bottle-nose *n.* (*also* **bottlenozzle**) [its shape + the implication of drunkenness] [early 17C; mid-19C–1920s] one who has a large, prominent nose; or a bruised nose.

bottlenosed *adj.* [BOTTLE-NOSE *n.*] **1** [mid-16C+] large-nosed. **2** [18C–mid-19C] drunk. **3** [1920s] thus Jewish, in a derog., stereotyped context.

bottle-o *n.* (*also* **bottle-ho, bottle-oh**) [SE *bottle* + -O *sfx* (3)] **1** [1900s–60s] (*Aus./N.Z.*) a collector and seller of used bottles; also of 'rags and bones'. **2** [1990s+] a liquor store.

bottle of beer *n.* [rhy. sl.] [20C+] the ear.

bottle of cola *n.* (*also* **bottle of Kola**) [rhy. sl.; *Kola* was a bottled drink made by R. White, and sold in London] [1910s–40s] a bowler hat.

bottle of fizz *phr.* [rhy. sl. = *ON THE WHIZ under* WHIZ *v.*^{1}] [1930s+] (*UK Und.*) working as a pickpocket.

bottle of sauce *n.* [rhy. sl.] [late 19C+] a horse.

bottle of scent *adj.* [rhy. sl. = BENT *adj.* (5)] [1990s+] of a man, homosexual, effeminate.

bottle of scotch *n.* [rhy. sl.] [19C] a watch, spec. one of the cheap Waterbury watches, produced since 1884 in Waterbury, Connecticut.

bottle of spruce *n.*^{1} [rhy. sl. = DEUCE *n.*^{1} (2)] [mid-19C–1900s; 1930s–40s] twopence, later usage US gambling, two.

bottle of spruce *n.*^{2} [proper name of *Spruce* Beer, a weak, cheap and thus essentially valueless commodity; its price was 2d.] [late 19C–1900s] zero, nothing; thus *I don't care a bottle of spruce*.

bottle (of water) *n.* [rhy. sl.] **1** [1930s+] a daughter. **2** [1990s+] (*drugs*) a quarter (of an ounce).

bottle of wine *n.* [rhy. sl.] [1990s+] a judicial fine.

bottle out *v.* *see under* BOTTLE (AND GLASS) *n.*

bottler *n.*^{1} [BOTTLE (AND GLASS) *n.*] **1** [mid-19C+] (*Aus./N.Z.*) anyone, or anything, outstanding, either in a positive or negative manner, usu. congratulatory, e.g. *you little bottler*; also as *adj.* [the positive/negative division is between one who has 'bottle' and one who 'bottles out']. **2** [1930s] (*US Und.*) a prostitute. **3** [1930s+] a sodomite. **4** [1940s+] a coward, someone who 'bottles out' [BOTTLE IT *under* BOTTLE (AND) GLASS *n.*]. **5** [1940s+] (*N.Z.*) a 'hard case', a thug; usu. as *bloody bottler*.

bottler *n.*^{2} [BOTTLE *v.*^{2}] [1920s+] one who 'passes round the hat', e.g. after a busker's performance.

bottles of booze *n.* [rhy. sl.] [1940s–50s] (*US*) shoes.

bottletop *n.*^{1} [rhy. sl. = COP *v.*] [20C+] a gain, a benefit, something good.

bottletop *n.*^{2} [resemblance + ref. to BLUEBOTTLE *n.* (2)] [1950s] (*N.Z.*) a police helmet.

bottle up *v.* **1** [17C–19C] to hold back, to keep [SE post-1900]. **2** [19C] to restrain, to exercise control, esp. of one's emotions. **3** [late 19C–1940s] to abandon an argument, to agree to end a dispute by accepting that both sides are evenly matched.

bottle up and go *v.* [BOTTLE IT *v.*^{1}] [1930s–40s] (*US black*) to leave, esp. after an unpleasant disagreement.

bottley *adj.* [BOTTLE OUT *v.* / *LOSE ONE'S BOTTLE under* BOTTLE (AND GLASS) *n.*] [2000s] nervous.

bottling *adj.* [BOTTLER *n.*^{1} (1)] [20C+] (*Aus.*) excellent, first-class; usu. in approving/congratulatory phr. *your blood's worth bottling*.

bottom *n.*[1] [sporting jargon] **1** [mid-17C] capital, (financial) resources. **2** [late 17C–mid-19C] stamina, endurance, pluck; thus *bottom-man*, a courageous fighter; note 17C–18C phr. *stand on one's own bottom*, to act independently, to act for oneself.

bottom *n.*[2] [? SE bottom, 'the part of a boot or shoe below the uppers; the sole, heel, and shank' (*OED*)] [early 19C] (*US*) a (fast) runner.

bottom *n.*[3] (*also* **bottom man**) [metaphorically rather than always physically 'on the bottom'; the anton. of TOP *n.* (4)] [1970s+] in sado-masochistic sex, a passive or masochistic person.

SE in slang uses

IN COMPOUNDS

❑ **bottom bandit** *n.* (*also* **botty burglar**) [1990s+] a male homosexual. ❑ **bottom boy** *n.* [1970s] (*US gay*) one who enjoys anal intercourse. ❑ **bottom burp** *n.* [1980s+] a fart; generally a children's usage, but popularized on BBC TV's 1980s comedy *The Young Ones*. ❑ **bottom dealer** *n.* [card imagery; lit. one who deals from the bottom of the pack] [1930s+] (*US*) a swindler, a cheat. ❑ **bottom feeder** *n.* [SE *bottom-feeder*, a fish that feeds off the sea- or riverbed] [1970s+] (*US teen*) **1** a despicable, unpleasant person. **2** one who has yet to make their mark, an aspirant. **3** a social outcast. **4** a gossip, esp. a trader in malevolent and harmful stories. ❑ **bottom-knocking** *n.* [2000s] (*US black*) having sexual intercourse. ❑ **bottomless pit** *n.* [late 18C–late 19C] the vagina. ❑ **bottom line** see separate entries. ❑ **bottom man** *n.* see separate entry. ❑ **bottom rib** *n.* [supposedly the rib taken from Adam and used in the creation of woman] [1970s] (*US black*) a wife. ❑ **bottom road** *n.* [the 'bottom' of the UK] [1930s] (*tramp*) a road leading from London to the South Coast. ❑ **bottom-wetter** *n.* see separate entry. ❑ **bottom woman** *n.* (*also* **bottom, bottom baby, ...bitch, ...ho, ...lady**) [SE *bottom*, a foundation] [1960s+] (*US black*) **1** the most reliable and experienced of a pimp's stable of prostitutes. **2** one's (attractive) girlfriend.

IN PHRASES

❑ **bet one's bottom** *v.* see BET ONE'S (SWEET) ASS *v.* ❑ **bottom of a woman's tu quoque** *n.* [presumably TU QUOQUE *n.* (1), although anatomically bizarre] [late 18C–early 19C] the crown of a woman's head. ❑ **deal off the bottom of the deck** *v.* (*also* **deal from the bottom of the deck/pack**) see *under* DEAL *v.* ❑ **drop bottom** *v.* see *under* DROP *v.*[4].

bottom *n.*[4] see *BLACK BOTTOM under* BLACK *adj.*

bottom *adj.* [BOTTOM *n.*[1] (2)] [late 18C–mid-19C] courageous, full of stamina and endurance.

bottom *v.* [one reaches the *bottom*] **1** [20C+] (*US campus*) to finish off a drink, to empty a glass. **2** [1900s–30s] (*Aus.*) to bet all one's money. **3** [2000s] to have sexual intercourse.

bottom line *n.* [Yid. *di untershte shure*, the bottom line, in the context of denoting the final profit/loss figure on an account] **1** [1980s+] the end result, the final assessment. **2** [1990s+] something steady, reliable.

bottom line *v.* [BOTTOM LINE *n.*] [1980s+] (*orig. US business*) to sum up, to speak succinctly.

bottoms *n.* [lit. the physically low-lying areas of a town] [20C+] (*US black*) the least pleasant, the poorest part of a ghetto or inner-city area.

bottoms up! *excl.* [the *bottoms* are those of the glasses as the drinks are emptied into the drinkers' mouths] [20C+] (*orig. RN*) a popular toast before drinking.

bottom-wetter *n.* [vaginal secretions and semen] [late 19C+] **1** sexual intercourse, from the point of view of a woman. **2** a penis.

IN PHRASES

❑ **do a bottom-wetter** *v.* (*also* **have..., perform...**) [19C] of a woman, to have sexual intercourse.

botts *n.* see BOTS *n.*[1] (3).

botty *n.* see BOTTIE *n.*

IN PHRASES

❑ **botty burglar** *n.* see *BOTTOM BANDIT under* BOTTOM *n.*[3].

botty *adj.* [orig. stable use] [mid-19C] conceited, swaggering.

botty-basher *n.* (*also* **botty-bandit**) [BOTTIE *n.* + BASH *v.* (6)] [1990s+] (*Aus./UK juv.*) a male homosexual.

botty burp *n.* [BOTTIE *n.* + SE *burp*] [1990s+] the breaking of wind.

boucous *adj.* see BEAUCOUP *adj.*

boudoir bandicoot *n.* [var. on *LOUNGE LIZARD under* LOUNGE *n.*] [1980s] (*Aus.*) a promiscuous male.

boufer *n.* see BUFE *n.*

bouffe *n.* see BUFE *n.*

bought it *adv.* [BUY THE FARM *v.*] [1940s+] killed, usu. in battle.

bougie *adj.* (*also* **bougy**) [SE *bourgeois*] [1970s+] taking on the attitudes and lifestyle of the middle classes.

boulder *n.* **1** [late 19C–1900s] (*US*) a diamond [play on ROCK *n.* (2)]. **2** [1950s+] a woman's breast, in combs. below. **3** [1980s+] (*drugs*) a generic term for crack cocaine; spec. $20 worth of crack cocaine [ROCK *n.* (4d); this is a 'large' rock].

IN COMPOUNDS

❑ **boulder-holder** *n.* (*also* **over-the-shoulder boulder-holder**) **1** [1950s+] (*Aus./US*) a brassiere. **2** [2000s] a tank-top.

IN PHRASES

❑ **shoulder-boulders** *n.* [1990s+] large female breasts.

bouldered *adj.* [pun on STONED *adj.* (2)] [1980s+] (*Aus. drugs*) very heavily intoxicated by a drug, usu. cannabis.

boulevard *n.*

SE in slang uses

IN COMPOUNDS

❑ **boulevard boy** *n.* [1970s+] a Los Angeles male homosexual prostitute who works Sunset or Hollywood Boulevards. ❑ **boulevard cowboy** *n.* (*also* **boulevard westerner**) [1940s+] (*US*) a taxi-driver; esp. a reckless driver whose driving style is uninhibited by the presence of other drivers, let alone pedestrians. ❑ **boulevard junkie** *n.* [1980s] (*US*) a Los Angeles drug user who frequents Sunset or Hollywood Boulevards.

bouman *n.* [ety. unknown; ? BOMAN *n.* (1)] [1910s+] (*Irish*) a friend, a 'pal'.

bounce *n.*[1] **1** as an image of verbal energy, esp. self-promoting. (**a**) [late 17C] a braggart, a swaggerer. (**b**) [18C–1920s] a boast, a self-aggrandizing lie. (**c**) [early 18C–1980s] (*orig. Aus.*) cheek, impudence; arrogance. (**d**) [early–mid-19C] a well-dressed braggart and/or swindler. (**e**) [late 19C+] energy. **2** in criminal contexts. (**a**) [mid-19C] (*UK Und.*) a confidence trick, a swindle. (**b**) [1930s–60s] (*US Und.*) arrest and subsequent trial. (**c**) [1950s+] (*US prison*) a sentence. (**d**) [1970s] (*UK Und.*) fiddling and dishonest practice (adjusting invoices, stealing stock etc) by retail shop employees. **3** [late 19C] cherry brandy. **4** [late 19C] (*US*) a trip, a journey. **5** [late 19C+] (*US*) constr. with *the*, ejection, esp. from a saloon or bar; usu. as *the grand bounce* or *GET THE BOUNCE* below. **6** [1960s+] (*also* **bouncy-bouncy**) an act of sexual intercourse.

IN PHRASES

❑ **come (on) the bounce** *v.* (*also* **come the bouncer**) [1910s–30s] (*Aus.*) to threaten, to intimidate, to suggest blackmail; thus *common bounce(r)*, a man who uses a boy to claim that he has been abused so as to threaten a homosexual with a charge of 'unnatural intercourse'. ❑ **get the bounce** *v.* [late 19C+] to be thrown out, both of a place or one's employment, or to be jilted. ❑ **give someone the bounce** *v.* [late 19C+] (*US*) **1** to jilt. **2** to send away, dismiss from a job. ❑ **great bounce** *n.* [sense 5] [late 19C] (*US*) death. ❑ **on the bounce** *adv.* [the idea 'bounces' into one's brain] [late 19C+] on the spur of the moment, spontaneously. ❑ **put on the bounce** *v.* [1930s+] (*Aus.*) to accost, esp. in pursuit of a loan. ❑ **put the bounce into** *v.* [1950s] (*Aus.*) to threaten, to intimidate.

bounce *n.*[2] [2000s] (*US*) a commission.

bounce *n.*[3] see BUNCE *n.* (1).

bounce *v.*[1] **1** [16C–17C; 1960s+] of a man, to have sexual intercourse [later use is Aus.] **2** [mid-17C–1920s] (*US*) to persuade, to influence by flattery. **3** [late 17C] to boast, to brag, to bully, to scold, to intimidate. **4** [mid-18C–mid-19C] to lie. **5** [early 19C–1900s] to rob, to cheat. **6** [mid-19C+] (*also* **bounce out**) to refuse admission or to throw out of a party, a place of entertainment, etc. **7** [late 19C] to avoid, to get rid of a person. **8** [late 19C+] (*also* **bounce off**) to dismiss, usu. from a job. **9** [late 19C+] (*US*) to reject, esp. of a proposal of marriage. **10** [late 19C+] (*US black/teen*) to leave. **11** [20C+] to escape arrest/prosecution through posing as a respectable person. **12** [1900s–30s] (*US campus*) to be sent down from college, to be sent out of class. **13** [1910s] (*US*) to punch. **14** [1910s] (*Aus.*) to move someone forcibly. **15** [1910s–30s] (*US*) (*also* **bounce off**) to kill. **16** [1920s] (*US*) to attack, esp. from an ambush. **17** [1920s–60s] to beat up. **18** [1930s] (*UK Und.*) to assault, using a piece of lead concealed in a sock. **19** [1930s+] (*US*) to treat, to pay for, to ply with drink. **20** [1950s+] (*US teen/Und.*) to move, to go, to get expelled. **21** [1960s+] to work as a strong-arm man in a bar etc. **22** [1970s] (*US*) as *bounce for*, to agree, to hand over without payment. **23** [1980s] (*US police*) to arrest and interrogate; to pressurize.

(IN COMPOUNDS)

❑ **bounce mutton** *n.* [mid-19C] (*UK Und.*) a female swindler. ❑ **bounce rag** *n.* [mid-19C] (*UK Und.*) a forged cheque.

(IN PHRASES)

❑ **bounce a car** *v.* [2000s] (*US prison*) to borrow a fellow inmate's radio.

SE in slang uses

(IN PHRASES)

❑ **bounce in** *v.* [1940s] (*US*) to appear in an aggressive manner. ❑ **bounce it off** *v.* [mid-17C–mid-18C] to drink heartily. ❑ **bounce refrigerators** *v.* [1990s+] (*US campus*) to have sexual intercourse. ❑ **bounce the ball** *v.* **1** [1910s–20s] (*Aus.*) to assert oneself. **2** [1920s+] (*N.Z.*) to assess public opinion [from the habit of rugby players testing the bounce of a ball prior to drop-kicking it off]. ❑ **how's it bouncing?** [1990s+] (*US*) a general phr. of greeting. ❑ **let's bounce** [2000s] (*US teen*) let's go.

bounce *v.*[2] **1** [early 19C] to put oneself in debt, e.g. making a bet or ordering a drink, knowing that one has no funds. **2** [1900s] (*Aus.*) to lose money. **3** [1920s–50s] to pay a cheque, knowing that one has insufficient funds in one's bank account; thus *bouncer*, one who passes such cheques [SE since 1960s]. **4** [1930s–50s] of a bank, to refuse to honour a cheque, marking it 'return to drawer' [SE since 1960s].

bounceable *adj.* (*also* **bouncible**) [BOUNCE *v.*[1] (3) + sfx *-able*] [mid-19C] prone to boasting or showing off.

bouncefull *adj.* (*also* **bounciful**) [BOUNCE *n.*[1] (1) + sfx *-ful*] [mid-19C] arrogant, domineering.

bouncer *n.*[1] [BOUNCE *v.*[1]] **1** [late 16C; mid-19C] (*US*) something or someone exceptionally large of its kind. **2** [late 17C–early 19C] (*UK Und.*) a swaggerer, a blusterer, a bully. **3** [mid-18C–mid-19C] a liar. **4** [late 18C–1900s] an unashamed lie. **5** [mid-19C] a surprise. **6** [mid–late 19C] (*UK Und.*) a thief who steals from shops, often while distracting the merchant's attention with his argumentative bargaining. **7** [mid–late 19C] an energetic person. **8** [mid–late 19C] (*US*) a social climber. **9** [mid-19C+] (*orig. US*) a large, tough man employed to keep order in premises, often a pub, club, concert hall etc. **10** [late 19C] (*UK Und.*) a sharp, a cheat. **11** [late 19C] (*UK Und.*) a pimp, esp. one who practises the MURPHY (GAME), THE *n.* (1). **12** [late 19C] (*UK Und.*) a thug who, allied with a male street prostitute, blackmails homosexuals. **13** [1950s+] usu. in pl., female breasts.

(IN PHRASES)

❑ **come the bouncer** *v. see* COME (ON) THE BOUNCE *under* BOUNCE *n.*[1].

bouncer *n.*[2] [BOUNCE *v.*[2]] [1930s+] (*US Und.*) a bad cheque.

bounceroo *n.* [BOUNCE *v.*[1] (6) + -EROO *sfx*] [1930s–40s] (*US*) ejection, dismissal.

bouncible *adj. see* BOUNCEABLE *adj.*

bounciful *adj. see* BOUNCEFULL *adj.*

bouncing *n.*[1] [BOUNCE *v.*[1] (3)] [late 19C] a severe scolding; also as *adj.*, scolding.

bouncing *n.*[2] [BOUNCE *v.*[1] (19)] [1980s] (*US*) going out on a spree, to enjoy oneself.

bouncing *adj.* [SE f. 1700] [early 16C–17C] big, lusty, energetic.

bouncing ben *n.* [? a sceptical view of learning, i.e. a BEN *n.*[1] (1), who 'bounces' with their own self-importance] [mid-19C–1920s] an intellectual, a learned person.

bouncing buffer *n.* [London dial. *bouncer*, professional beggar + BUFFER *n.*[4]] [early–mid-19C] a beggar.

bouncing cheat *n.* [SE *bounce* + CHEAT *n.* (1); the bottle 'bounces' as the cork is drawn] [18C] (*UK Und.*) a bottle.

bouncing paper *n.* [BOUNCE *v.*[2] + PAPER *n.* (2)] [1940s] (*US Und.*) bad cheques.

bouncing powder *n.* [the effect it has on its temporarily enlivened users] [1930s+] (*drugs*) cocaine.

bouncy *adj.* [1960] (*US prison*) physically aggressive.

bouncy-bouncy *n. see* BOUNCE *n.*[1] (6).

bouncy in one's deuce of benders *adj.* (*also* **bouncy in one's brace of dukes**) [lit. *bouncing* up and down on one's legs, 'bowing and scraping'] [1900s–40s] (*US black*) subservient to white people.

bounder *n.* **1** [early 19C; 1960s] (*US*) a severe blow [it makes one 'bound', i.e. leap]. **2** [mid-19C] a four-wheeled cab [the 'bounding' motion of the cab]. **3** [late 19C+] one who is considered socially unacceptable or ill-mannered; thus adj. *bounderish* [orig. university use, one who 'bounds' about; but note B&L: 'one who is beyond the boundary of good fellowship.' The individual so branded may not be intrinsically ill-mannered, but has been declared so by the prevailing standards of his fellows; post-1930s use usu. ironic or historic]. **4** [late 19C–1900s] a person with no derog. overtones.

bounder *v.* [SE *bound*, to jump; i.e. the energy expended] [19C] (*US*) to scrub or wash thoroughly.

bounetter *n.* [? BONNETTER *n.* (1)] [mid-19C] a confidence trickster, esp. one who makes a living telling fortunes.

boung *n.* for this and all combs. with *boung*, e.g. *boung-nipper*, *see* BUNG *n.*[1].

boungie bungee *n.* (*also* **boongy bungee**) [var. on BUM *n.*[1] (1)] [20C+] (*W.I.*) the buttocks, the posterior.

bounty (bar) *n.* [the *Bounty Bar*, a popular sweet, made of chocolate-covered flaked coconut, thus CHOCOLATE *n.*[1] (1)] [1970s+] (*UK black*) a black man or woman who is 'black on the outside but white inside'.

bourgie *n. see* BOOJEE *n.*

bourgie *adj. see* BOOJEE *adj.*

Bourke *n. see* BACK OF BOURKE *under* BACK *adv.*

Bourke-street *adj.* [the financial centre of *Bourke Street*, Sydney] [1940s] (*Aus.*) citified.

Bourneville boulevard *n.* [*Bourneville* chocolate, a popular dark chocolate / CHOCOLATE *adj.* (2)] [1990s+] the anus; one of a number of sl. terms relating to the colour of excrement.

bouse *n.* (*also* **boose, bowse**) [Du. *buizen* or Ger. *bausen*, to drink to excess. The *OED*'s first use is *c.*1300, but this may be only the drinking vessel not its contents; the Du. term too is rooted in *buise*, a large drinking vessel. Although *bouse* can be found in ME, its popularity came with its Und. usage] **1** [mid-16C+] (*UK Und.*) drink; thus *ben bouse*, good drink. **2** [late 17C] a toast.

bouse *v.* (*also* **boose, bouze, bowse, bowze**) [BOUSE *n.*] [mid-16C–18C] (*UK Und.*) to drink.

boushwa/boushwah *n. see* BUSHWA *n.*

bousing *n. see* BOOZING *n.*

bousing-ken *n.* (*also* **boosing ken, booze ken, boozen-ken, boozing-can, boozing-ken, bouseing-ken**) [BOUSE *v.* (1) + KEN *n.*[1] (1)] **1** [mid-16C–1930s] (*UK Und.*) an ale-house; latterly a public house. **2** [mid-19C] (*US Und.*) a coffee-house.

bousy *n. see* BOWSIE *n.*

bousy *adj.* (*also* **bowsie**) [BOUSE *n.* + sfx *-y*] [early 17C–late 18C] (*UK Und.*) drunken.

bout it *adj.* [1990s+] an all-purpose phr, covering variously one's knowledge, willingness, sexual availability, self-assuredness, etc.

bout it! *excl.* [SE phr. what do you want/are you going to do *about it?*] [1990s+] (*US juv.*) **1** a verbal challenge, deliberately intended to start a fight. **2** what are you doing?

bouze *v. see* BOUSE *v.*

bouzzie *n. see* BOWSIE *n.*

Bovril *n.* [? a play on BULLSHIT *n.*; in Aus./UK *Bovril* is a beef extract-based spread, often taken as a hot drink] [1930s–50s] (*Aus.*) a general term of dismissal, abuse, rubbish, nonsense, anything unimpressive.

Bovril bypass *n.* [for ety. *see* BOVRIL *n.*; the association of the anus with the colour brown] [1990s+] the anus.

bovver *n.* [Cockney pron. of SE *bother*/BOTHER *n.* (1)] [1960s+] fighting, disturbance, esp. that caused by skinhead youths.

IN COMPOUNDS

❑ **bovver boots** *n.* [1970s+] high-laced boots preferred as footwear by skinhead youths, usu. merchandised under the brandname Dr Martens. ❑ **bovver boy** *n.* [1960s–70s] a hooligan, usu. a SKINHEAD *n.* (3), and quite likely a football fan and member of the right-wing National Front; his female equivalent was a *bovver bird*.

bow *n.*[1] [it shoots 'arrows', presumably of desire] [mid-16C–19C] the penis.

SE in slang uses

IN COMPOUNDS

❑ **bowhead** *n.* [SE *bow* + -HEAD *sfx* (1); lit. a woman with bows in her hair. The image is of a 'nice little girl'] [1980s+] (*US campus*) a young woman who pays a good deal of attention to her looks, dress and general image; she is assumed to be foolish, at best. ❑ **bow-legged** *adj.* [1990s+] (*US prison*) **1** concurrent, referring to a prison sentence. **2** consecutive, of prison sentences. ❑ **bow-window** *n.* [mid–late 19C] a large, protruding stomach; thus adj. *bow-windowed*.

bow *n.*[2] *see* BO *n.*[1] (2).

bow *n.*[3]

IN PHRASES

❑ **on the bow** *see ON THE ELBOW under* ELBOW *n.*

bow *v.* [1990s+] (*W.I.*) to perform oral sex.

IN COMPOUNDS

❑ **bow-cat** *n.* [1990s+] (*W.I.*) a heterosexual male who performs cunnilingus.

SE in slang uses

IN PHRASES

❑ **bow down** *v.* [2000s] (*US black*) to act subserviently, to acknowledge one's inferiority. ❑ **bow low** *v.* [1970s] (*US gay*) to leave, esp. for one's own benefit. ❑ **bow out** *see* separate entries. ❑ **bow to the porcelain god/goddess** *v. see KISS THE PORCELAIN GOD under* PORCELAIN GOD *n.* ❑ **bow to the White God** *v.* [1950s] (*US*) to take heroin.

bow and arrow *n.*[1] [rhy. sl.] [late 19C+] **1** a sparrow [+ ref. to poem 'Who Killed Cock Robin?']. **2** a costermonger's barrow. **3** a *charabanc*, a coach.

bow and arrow *n.*[2] [the stereotypical weaponry] [1930s–40s] (*US*) a Native American.

bow and quiver *n.* [rhy. sl.] [20C+] the liver, as a human organ rather than as edible offal.

bow-catcher *n.* [var. on *BEAU-CATCHER under* BEAU *n.*[1]] [mid-19C] a lock of hair equivalent to the modern kiss-curl.

bowdacious *adj. see* BODACIOUS *adj.*

bowel baby *n.* [1990s+] (*US*) a general term of abuse.

bowel off *v.* [1950s] (*US*) to have an attack of diarrhoea.

bowels *n. see* GUT *n.* (2a).

SE in slang uses

IN PHRASES

❑ **don't get your bowels in an uproar** (*also* **don't get your balls in an uproar**) [20C+] do not make so much (unnecessary) fuss.

bower *n.* [ironic uses of SE *bower*, a shady grove] **1** [mid-19C] (*UK Und.*) as *the Bower*, Newgate prison. **2** [20C+] (*Aus.*) a prison.

bower-bird *n.* [SE *bower-bird*, one of several Aus. birds of the starling family, which build bowers or 'runs' and adorn them with feathers, bones, shells etc] [1920s+] (*Aus.*) **1** a petty thief [reinforced by BOWER *n.* (2)]. **2** a scavenger of waste and similar trifles.

bower bird *v.* [BOWER-BIRD *n.*] [1920s+] (*Aus.*) to hang around, to scavenge.

bower (of bliss) *n.* [SE *bower of bliss*, 'a vague poetic word for an idealized abode, not realized in any actual dwelling' (*OED*)] [late 18C–19C] the vagina.

bowery *adj.* [the Bowery, the downtown section of 3rd Avenue in New York, the trad. home of the city's down-and-outs] [1900s–60s] (*US*) pertaining to tramps, thus impoverished, poor.

bowk *v. see* BOKE *v.*

bowl *n.* (*drugs*) **1** [1930s+] an opium pipe. **2** [1970s+] a pipe used for smoking marijuana; thus a pipeful of marijuana [? imported by veterans of the Vietnam War (1964–75), where pipes, rather than cigarettes were the preferred means of smoking]. **3** [1990s+] a pipe of crack cocaine.

IN PHRASES

❑ **bokin a smowl** *n.* [joc. reversal of 'smoking a bowl'] [1980s+] (*US drugs*) the smoking of a pipe or other container filled with cannabis. ❑ **smoke a bowl** *v.* (*also* **smoke some bowl**) [1970s+] to smoke marijuana.

SE in slang uses

IN PHRASES

❑ **bowl of fruit** *n. see* BAG (OF FRUIT) *n.* ❑ **bowl of jelly** *n. see under* JELLY *n.*[1].

bowl *v.* **1** [1900s] (*UK Und.*) to notice, to find out. **2** [1960s+] (*N.Z.*) to be defeated, to be killed, to seduce.

SE in slang uses

IN PHRASES

❑ **bowl booty** *v. see PLAY BOOTY under* BOOTY *n.*[1]. ❑ **bowl from the pavilion end** *v.* (*also* **play from the pavilion end**) [cricket imagery; no especial gay relevance to the *pavilion end* (the name of the other end will differ as to the ground, e.g. that at Lords is the 'Nursery End' which could be seen as bearing its own poss. paedophile overtones), other than (prob. coincidentally) that the pavilion is likely to contain the lavatories] [1990s+] to be a male homosexual. ❑ **bowl off** *v.* [SE *bowl*, to ride along on wheels] [mid-19C] to die. ❑ **bowl out** *v.* [cricket imagery] **1** [early–mid-19C] to kill. **2** [early 19C+] (*also* **bawl out**) to find out; to be found out. **3** [mid-19C] to be sentenced to death. **4** [mid-19C] to die. **5** [mid-19C+] to defeat, to overcome, to get the better of. ❑ **can I bowl you?** [1900s] (*Aus.*) a phr. used to request that someone buys the speaker a drink.

bowla *n.* [Anglo-Ind. *bowla*, a portmanteau; ult. f. Hind. *baola*] [mid–late 19C] a round tart made of sugar, apple and bread, sold in the streets.

bowldacks *n.* [joc. mispron. BALLOCKS *n.* (3)] [2000s] (*N.Z. teen*) nonsense, rubbish.

bowler *n.*[1] [BOWL *n.* (1)] [1950s] (*US drugs*) an opium smoker.

bowler *n.*[2] [SE *bawl*, i.e. bark] **1** [1970s+] (*Irish*) a dog, usu. a mongrel. **2** [2000s] an ugly person [by ext. of sense 1].

bowler-hatted *adj.* [milit. use *bowler-hatted*, retired from active service (and thus from wearing a uniform) and given a desk job in Whitehall, where the trad. civil service 'uniform' featured a bowler] [1910s+] dismissed, retired.

bowles *n.* [? the shape] [mid-19C–1900s] shoes.

bowling *adj.*

SE in slang uses

IN PHRASES

❑ **do the bowling hold** *v.* (*also* **hold a bowling ball**) *see* TENPIN *v.*

bowl of chalk *n. see* BALL OF CHALK *v.*

bowl-over *n.* [BOWL OVER *v.* (2)] [20C+] (*Aus.*) a fight, a brawl.

bowl over *v.* [cricket imagery] [mid-19C+] **1** to astonish, to surprise. **2** to defeat, also fig. use.

bowl the hoop *n.* [rhy. sl.] [mid-19C] soup.

bowman *n.* [abbr. BOWMAN-PRIG *under* BOWMAN *adj.*] [early 19C] (*UK Und.*) a thief.

bowman *adj.* [? Fr. *beau*, good-looking] [late 17C–early 18C] excellent, first-rate.

IN COMPOUNDS

❑ **bowman ken** *n.* [BOWMAN-PRIG below + KEN *n.*[1] (1)] [late 17C–early 19C] (*UK Und.*) **1** a house considered worth robbing. **2** a house occupied by thieves. ❑ **bowman-prig** *n.* (*also* **boman-prig**) [PRIG *n.*[1]] [early 18C] a first-rate thief.

IN PHRASES

❑ **all's bowman** [late 17C–early 18C] all's safe, everything is in order.

bow-out *n.* [BOW OUT *v.*] [1940s] a resignation.

bow out *v.* [20C+] to retreat or withdraw, to resign.

bowse *n. see* BOUSE *n.*

bowse *v. see* BOUSE *v.*

bowse-ken *n. see* BOWSING-KEN *n.*

bowser *n.*[1] [the once-common dog name] **1** [1940s+] generic for any species of dog. **2** [1970s] (*N.Z.*) a cheerful fellow. **3** [1980s] (*US campus*) an ugly woman. **4** [2000s] (*Irish*) a troublesome character.

bowser *n.*[2] [SE *bowser*, a portable fuel container] [1950s–80s] (*N.Z.*) a petrol pump or garage, esp. one also selling food and drink.

bowser bag *n.* [BOWSER *n.*[1] (1) + SE *bag*] [1960s+] (*US*) a bag provided by some restaurants for customers to take home left-overs, ostensibly for later consumption by a pet dog.

bowsie *n.* (*also* **bousy, bowsey, bowsy, bouzzie**) [Share suggests Ger. *böse*, evil, unpleasant, introduced by the German troops of William III at end of 17C] (*Irish*) **1** [late 19C+] a general term of abuse. **2** [20C+] a street urchin, a lout.

bowsie *adj. see* BOUSY *adj.*

bowsing-ken *n.* (*also* **bowse-ken, bowsing crib, bowsing Inn, bowzing ken**) [BOUSE *n.* + KEN *n.*[1] (1) / CRIB *n.*[1] (1)] [16C–mid-19C] a public house, a tavern, an inn.

bow-sow *n.* [Chinese or 'cod' Chinese] [1930s–50s] (*US drugs*) narcotics.

bowsprit *n.* [SE *bowsprit*, 'a large spar or boom running out from the stem of a vessel, to which (and the jib-boom and flying jib-boom, which extend beyond it) the foremast stays are fastened' (*OED*)] **1** [18C–19C] the nose. **2** [mid-18C+] the penis, esp, when erect.

bowsprit in parenthesis *n.* [BOWSPRIT *n.* (1) + SE *in parenthesis*, a digression, an interlude] [mid-19C] (*US*) a nose that has been pulled, presumably during a fight or argument.

bowsy *n. see* BOWSIE *n.*

bowsy *adj.* [var. on BOOZY *adj.*] [late 17C] drunk, looking drunken.

bow tie *n.* **1** [1940s] (*N.Z.*) a married woman's lover. **2** [1950s] (*US*) a lesbian; thus *bow-tie club, bow-tie party*.

bow-wow *n.* [plays on lit. and sl. uses of SE *dog*] **1** [late 18C–19C] (*US*) a native of Boston, Massachusetts [play on sense 2]. **2** [late 18C+] (*juv.*) a dog. **3** [mid-19C] (*also* **bow-wow coat**) a heavy, shaggy greatcoat, popular among fans of the Prize Ring [play on sense 2]. **4** f. the dog's barking. (**a**) [19C] nonsense. (**b**) [mid–late 19C] (*mainly Ind.*) a lover [who 'yaps']. (**c**) [early 19C; 1940s–60s] (*UK/US black*) a gun [which 'barks']. **5** [1900s–30s] (*US*) a sausage [play on sense 2; note DOG *n.*[2] (7)]. **6** [1960s+] an ugly woman [play on DOG *n.*[2] (9)]. **7** [1990s+] (*Aus.*) an unattractive person [play on DOG *n.*[2] (9)].

IN COMPOUNDS

❑ **bow-wow broth** *n.* [mid-19C] (*UK Und.*) broth made of rotten meat. ❑ **bow-wow mutton** *n.* [late 18C–late 19C] dog's flesh; rotten meat. ❑ **bow-wow shop** *n.* [SE *shop*; 'so called because the servant barks and the master bites' (Grose)] [18C] a second-hand clothes shop in London's Monmouth Street, the city's old-clothes centre through to 19C. ❑ **bow-wow venison** *n.* [mid-19C] (*UK Und.*) second-rate meat.

bowyer *n.* [SE phr. *draw the long bow*, to exaggerate] [late 18C] one who exaggerates, who tells implausible, if grandiose tales.

bowze *v. see* BOUSE *v.*

bowzing ken *n. see* BOWSING-KEN *n.*

box *n.*[1] [uses of SE *box*] **1** as a bodily organ. (**a**) [mid-16C+] (*also* **box of candy, sex-box**) the vagina; thus generic for a woman. (**b**) [1930s–50s] (*US*) the mouth. (**c**) [1940s+] (*US gay*) the male genitals; thus the bulge of genitals in tight trousers. (**d**) [1950s–70s] (*US black*) the buttocks; the anus. (**e**) [1960s] (*US black*) sexual intercourse. (**f**) [1990s+] (*US campus*) an exceptionally attractive female. **2** as a container. (**a**) [early 17C; mid-19C+] a coffin; thus phr. *put to bed in a box, send home in a box*, to bury. (**b**) [19C+] a prison, a prison cell, a prison visiting compartment. (**c**) [late 19C] (*US campus*) a pulpit. (**d**) [20C+] a safe (esp. an old-fashioned model); thus *box-cracker*, a safe-breaker. (**e**) [1910s+] the witness box; thus (*Aus.*) *jump in the box*, to turn Queen's evidence. Also fig. use. (**f**) [1920s] (*US Und.*) a slot machine, a 'one-armed bandit'. (**g**) [1930s] (*US*) a cash till. (**h**) [1960s+] (*US prison*) a measure of marijuana, orig. (1960s) that which filled a matchbox. (**i**) [1970s+] (*US prison*) a carton of cigarettes, the equivalent of $15 in a barter economy. (**j**) [1970s+] (*US*) a refrigerator. **3** as a (small) place [also Fr. *boîte*, lodging house or restaurant]. (**a**) [late 17C] a small drinking house or tavern. (**b**) [mid-18C–mid-19C] a house. (**c**) [20C+] a nightclub. (**d**) [1940s] (*US black*) a room; an apartment. (**e**) [1950s+] (*US Und.*) a punishment cell. **4** as a musical instrument, record player, television, etc. (**a**) [20C+] (*US*) a piano; thus *bang the box*, play the piano. (**b**) [1910s+] a radio, a record-player; a portable radio cassette player. (**c**) [1920s+] (*orig. US black*) a guitar, a fiddle, a banjo. (**d**) [1920s+] (*US*) (*also* **hell-box**) an accordion; a melodeon. (**e**) [1940s+] (*US*) a jukebox. (**f**) [1960s+] television; thus *on the box*, on television. (**g**) [1960s+] a tape-recorder, stereo system, cassette tape deck. (**h**) [1980s] (*UK black*) a speaker-cabinet for a sound system. (**i**) [1990s+] (*US*) a lie-detector.

IN COMPOUNDS

❑ **box-beater** *n.* [sense 4a + SE *beater*] [1910s–40s] (*US*) a piano-player. ❑ **box-biter** *n.* [sense 1a] [2000s] (*S.Afr. gay*) a lesbian. ❑ **box-busting** *n.* [sense 2d + BUST *v.*[1] (1)] [1950s] (*US Und.*) safe-cracking. ❑ **box city** *adj.* [sense 2a + -CITY *sfx*] [1980s+] (*US*) dead. ❑ **box-getter** *n.* [sense 2g + SE *getter*] [1930s] (*UK Und.*) one who steals from tills. ❑ **box job** *n.* [sense 2d + JOB *n.*[2]] [1930s+] (*US Und.*) breaking open a safe. ❑ **box lunch** *n.* [sense 1a + LUNCH *n.* (3)] **1** [1960s] fellatio. **2** [1960s+] cunnilingus. ❑ **box screw** *n.* [sense 2d + SCREW *n.*[1] (2c)] [1930–40s] (*US Und.*) a bank guard. ❑ **box slugger** *n.* [sense 2d + weak form of SLUGGER *n.* (1)] [1970s] (*US Und.*) a safe-breaker. ❑ **box time** *n.* [sense 2b + TIME *n.* (1)] [1990s+] (*US prison*) time spent in solitary confinement. ❑ **box tosser** *n.* [sense 1a + SE *toss*] [1960s–70s] a sexually enthusiastic woman. ❑ **box work** *n.* [sense 2d + WORK *n.* (1)] [1970s] (*US Und.*) the physical act of safe-breaking. ❑ **box worker** *n.* [sense 2d + WORKER *n.*[1] (1)] [1940s–50s] (*US Und.*) a safe-breaker.

IN PHRASES

❑ **hot box** *n.* [HOT *adj.* (1a)] (*US*) **1** [1940s–60s] a sexually promiscuous woman. **2** [1960s+] the female genitals. ❑ **do someone's box in** *v. see* DO SOMEONE'S HEAD IN *under* DO IN *v.* ❑ **lick a box** *v.* [1990s+] (*orig. W.I., Trin.*) to perform cunnilingus. ❑ **shoot a box** *v.* [1940s] (*US Und.*) to blow open a safe.

SE in slang uses

IN COMPOUNDS

❑ **box-ankled** *adj.* [late 19C+] (*US*) having legs so made that the ankle-bones knock together. ❑ **box-bag** *n.* [ext. of BAG *n.*[1] (7)] [1990s+] (*US prison*) the amount of marijuana that can be purchased in exchange for a carton of cigarettes (worth approx. $10). ❑ **box fire** *n.* [1940s] (*US black/Harlem*) a cigarette or cigar (stub). ❑ **box-hat** *n.* [orig. dial.] [late 19C] a silk top-hat. ❑ **boxhead** *n.* [-HEAD *sfx* (1)/-HEAD *sfx* (2)] **1** [20C+] a fool, a simpleton; thus *box-headed*, stupid. **2** [1920s–40s] (*US*) a Scandinavian [var. on SQUAREHEAD *n.*^{2} (2)]. ❑ **box-irons** *n.* [SE *box-iron*, a smoothing iron with a cavity to contain some form of heating] [late 18C–mid-19C] shoes. ❑ **box-it** *n.* [? the use of cheap boxed rather than bottled wine] [1980s] a drink composed of wine and cider, consumed by alcoholics. ❑ **box-rattle** *n.* [mid-19C] (*UK Und.*) a woman's tongue. ❑ **box rustler** *n.* [SE *rustler*, a cattle-thief] [late 19C–1920s] (*US West*) a chorus-girl who followed her performance by mixing with the patrons in their boxes, promoting the sale of drinks and, when desired, offering herself as a part-time prostitute.

IN PHRASES

❑ **box-lobby puppy** *n.* [SE *box lobby*, the area outside a theatre's boxes, patronized by the fashionable and would-be fashionable + SE *puppy*] [late 18C–early 19C] a would-be man of fashion, with ambition, but lacking income; thus the *box-lobby lounger*, one who frequents this area. ❑ **box of...** *n.* see separate entries. ❑ **how's your box?** [1930s] (*US black*) a general phr. of greeting. ❑ **in a box** (*also* **in a bad box**) [late 18C; 20C+] in difficulties, in a confused state of mind, in a quandary. ❑ **in the same box** (*also* **...canoe, ...street**) [late 19C+] (*Aus.*) in the same situation. ❑ **on the box-seat** [coaching imagery] [1950s+] (*N.Z.*) in an advantageous or dominant position, in a secure situation. ❑ **out of the box** *adj.* [1960s+] (*Aus.*) exceptional, well above average. ❑ **take a box** *v.* [1990s+] (*Irish*) to defecate.

box *n.*^{2} [fig. use of farming jargon *box*, to mix up two herds or flocks by mistake] [late 19C–1940s] (*Aus./US*) a blunder, a mix-up, a mess; a predicament.

IN PHRASES

❑ **make a box of** *v.* [1920s+] (*Aus.*) to make a mess of.

box *n.*^{3} [abbr. SE colloq. *brainbox*] [1900s; 1970s+] the brain, the head.

IN PHRASES

❑ **out of one's box** *adj.* **1** [1900s; 1990s+] (*also* **off one's box, out of the box**) mad, eccentric, beyond emotional restraint. **2** [1970s+] (*also* **off one's box, off one's pot**) completely intoxicated, whether by drink or drugs.

box *n.*^{4} [synon. of BAG *n.*^{2}] [1970s] (*US black*) one's personal style.

box *v.*^{1} [BOX *n.*^{2}] [1920s+] (*Aus./N.Z.*) to make a blunder, to mix something up; spec. of cards, to shuffle.

box *v.*^{2}

SE in slang uses

IN PHRASES

❑ **box a charley** *v. see under* CHARLIE *n.*^{1}. ❑ **box clever** *v.* [boxing imagery] [1910s+] to carry out any enterprise smartly and efficiently. ❑ **box Harry** *v.* [northern dial.; thus Lancashire *Boxharry week*, 'the blank week between payweeks when the workmen lived on credit or starved' (*EDD*). Jon Bee suggests that 'confined truants, at school, without fire, fought or boxed an old figure nicknamed 'Harry', which hung up in their prison/to keep heat'. B&L suggest that it means 'box or fight the devil' i.e. OLD HARRY *n.*] [early 19C–1900s] **1** to go without a meal. **2** to take lunch and tea at the same time. **3** to take things as they are. ❑ **box (it) about** *v.* [SE *box*, to fight with the fists; thus to 'hit (the drink) hard'; 19C use is SE] [late 17C–early 18C] to drink briskly. ❑ **box one's mumps** *v.* [early 19C] to walk off, to leave. ❑ **box out of the ring** *v.* [boxing imagery] [1970s+] (*Aus./N.Z.*) to have an affair, to have extra-marital sex. ❑ **box the bozack** *v. see under* BOZACK *n.* ❑ **box the compass** *v.* [naut. jargon *box the compass*, to name the points of the compass, either backwards or in random order] **1** [mid-18C–1940s] to answer all possible questions, to adapt oneself to a wide variety of circumstances. **2** [1920s] (*US*) to order everything on the menu. ❑ **box the Jesuit and get cockroaches** *v.* [pun on SE *cockroaches* + the stereotyping of Jesuits as alien and repellent beings. Like many terms for masturbate this one relies on an image of using violence against the penis, e.g. *box*, to hit] [mid-18C–early 19C; 2000s] to masturbate. ❑ **box the watch** *v.* [mid-19C] to overturn someone, e.g. a watchman, in a sentry or similar box. ❑ **box the wine bin** *v.* [SE *box*, to put in a box] [early–mid-19C] to leave the table after drinking only moderately.

box-about *n.* [SE *box about*, to sail up and down, often changing the direction, ult. ? f. *boxing the compass*] [1950s] (*W.I.*) **1** a man who is an idler, a loafer. **2** a trollop, a promiscuous woman, esp. when she has a number of children, each by a different father.

box about *v.* [to carry one's *boxes*, i.e. possessions, around; but *see* BOX-ABOUT *n.*] [20C+] to move from place to place without any steady job.

box around *v.* [BOX ABOUT *v.*] [1950s] (*W.I.*) to move from place to place without any steady job.

boxcar *n.* [SE *boxcar*, a large closed-in railway goods wagon] **1** [1950s–70s] (*US*) usu. in pl., a large foot or shoe. **2** [1970s] a large, clumsy person. **3** [1970s] (*US Und.*) a prison punishment cell. **4** [1970s+] (*US prison*) a cell.

boxcar number *n.* [1930s–50s] (*US Und.*) a large amount; a long prison sentence.

boxcars *n.* [the resemblance of the two 'sixes', side-by-side to a railway wagon; twelve is a losing throw] [20C+] (*gambling*) **1** the point of twelve in craps dice. **2** thus fig. bad luck.

boxcar sailor *n.* [1940s] (*US Und.*) a hobo who travels on freight trains.

boxed *adj.* **1** [1930s+] (*US*) drunk or overcome by drugs [OUT OF ONE'S BOX *under* BOX *n.*^{3}]. **2** [1960s+] (*US*) dead [? BOX *n.*^{1} (2a)].

boxed-up *adj.* (*also* **boxed**) **1** [mid-19C; 1980s+] in prison [BOX *n.*^{1} (2b)]. **2** [late 19C] (*Aus.*) confused, muddled, upset [BOX *n.*^{2}].

boxer *n.*^{1} [the box-like shape] **1** [late 19C] (*Aus.*) a low-crowned felt hat. **2** [late 19C–1900s] a tall hat, a top-hat. **3** [1920s–30s] (*US tramp*) a boxcar.

boxer *n.*^{2} [SE *box*] [1910s+] (*Aus.*) **1** in the game of two-up the person who takes charge of the apparatus and of the money staked by the main bettors. **2** a commission paid to that person.

boxer *n.*^{3} [BOX *n.*^{1} (2d)] [1930s] (*US Und.*) a safe-cracker.

boxies *n.* [abbr.] [2000s] boxer-shorts.

boxman *n.* [BOX *n.*^{1} (2d) + SE *man*] [mid-19C; 20C] (*US Und.*) a safe-cracker.

box of... *n.*

SE in slang uses

IN PHRASES

❑ **box of dominoes** *n.* [orig. dominoes were made of ivory] **1** [mid-19C] the mouth, the teeth. **2** [late 19C–1920s] a piano. ❑ **box of fives** *n. see* BUNCH OF FIVES *n.* ❑ **box of fruit** *n. see* BAG (OF FRUIT) *n.* ❑ **box of ivories** *n.* [mid-19C] the mouth; the teeth. ❑ **box of minutes** *n.* [mid-19C] a watch; a watchmaker's shop. ❑ **box of rocks** *n.* [phr. *dumb as a box of rocks*] [1980s] (*US*) a fool. ❑ **box of sharks** *n.* [1950s+] (*Can.*) used when one wishes to express surprise, shock, e.g. *she nearly had a box of sharks*. ❑ **box of tricks** *n.* **1** [late 19C+] a tool-box. **2** [1930s] the genitals. **3** [1930s] a crafty person. **4** [1960s] the cinema [rhy. sl. + SE colloq. *flicks*].

box of birds, be a *v.* (*also* **box of fluffy ducks, be a**) [B. Morrison, *Things My Mother Never Told Me* (2002), indicates UK use] [1940s+] (*Aus./N.Z.*) to be very cheerful.

box of glue *n.* [rhy. sl.] [1920s–60s] (*US*) a Jew.

box of toys *n.* [rhy. sl.] [20C+] noise.

box-on *n.* [BOX ON *v.*] 1910s+(*Aus.*) a fight.

box on *v.* [the boxing referee's command *Box on!* after a brief stoppage in the fight] [1910s+] (*Aus.*) to keep going, to persevere.

IN PHRASES

❑ **box on with** *v.* [1910s+] (*Aus.*) to fight with, to punch.

box-up *n.* [farming jargon *box*, the mixing up of different flocks of sheep] [1910s+] a quandary, a state of confusion.

DERIVATIVES

❑ **boxed up** *adj.* [1910s+] lost, confused.

box up *v.* [? BOX *n.*^{1} (2b)] [1950s] to have a relationship with.

boy *n.*[1] [abbr. JINGLEBOY *n.*; *YELLOW BOY under* YELLOW *adj.*] **1** [early 19C] a sovereign, thus latterly £1 sterling. **2** [late 19C+] (*US*) a note, for one dollar, ten dollars etc.

boy *n.*[2] **1** [mid-19C] a hump on a person's back; thus *him and his boy*, a hunchback [the hunchback is seen as carrying a small child]. **2** [late 19C–1910s] champagne [allegedly f. Edward VII's habit of merely saying 'Boy!' to an attendant page who automatically brought him a glass of that wine; note Binstead, *A Pink 'Un and a Pelican* (1898) (the context of the quote is 1879): 'The young bucks of the present day, by the way, generally allude to a bottle of champagne erroneously as "the Boy," in evident ignorance of the origin of the term, which is as follows: At a shooting party of His Royal Highness's, the guns were followed at a distance by a lad who wheeled a barrow-load of champagne, packed in ice. The weather was intensely close and muggy, and whenever anybody felt indined for a drink he called out "Boy!" to the youth in attendance; the frequency with which this happened leading to the adoption of the term. It does not follow, however, that everybody who uses the word nowadays was out shooting that day with the Prince.']. **3** in homosexual senses. (**a**) [1930s+] (*gay*) a male prostitute. (**b**) [1950s+] (*US prison*) a gay prison inmate, esp. when the passive partner in a relationship with an otherwise heterosexual convict. (**c**) [1990s+] (*US gay*) in sado-masochistic sex, the passive or subservient partner. **4** in drug uses. (**a**) [1950s+] heroin [the image of heroin as a 'masculine' drug, i.e. one that 'knocks you down', rather than cocaine or GIRL *n.*[2] (1), the injecting of which gives a sexual thrill (although heroin, too, has that effect on some users)]. (**b**) [1980s+] cocaine [may be a misreading].

IN PHRASES

❑ **do you need a boy?** [1960s+] (*drugs*) a surreptitious request for heroin.

SE in slang uses

IN COMPOUNDS

❑ **boy-ass** *n.* [ASS *n.* (2)] [1940s+] a boy who exists simply as a sex object for his homosexual partners. ❑ **boy bar** *n.* [2000s] (*US*) a bar primarily used by male homosexuals. ❑ **boy blue** *n.* *see* BLUE BOY *n.*[2]. ❑ **boy-buster** *n.* [BUST *v.*[1] (1)] [1940s–50s] (*Aus.*) a man, esp. a prisoner, who specializes in seducing young men. ❑ **boychick** *n.* (*also* **boychik**) [Yid. dimin. sfx -*tschik*] [1950s+] a general term of affection between males; a man who acts like a child. ❑ **boydyke** *n.* [DYKE *n.* (1)] [1990s+] (*US gay*) a boyish 'masculine' lesbian. ❑ **boy-farm** *n.* [late 19C–1900s] a school; thus *boy-farmer*, a school-teacher. ❑ **boyfriend** *n.* **1** [1950s] (*US*) a term of address between men, rarely affectionate. **2** [1990s+] (*US campus*) any attractive man one does not know. ❑ **boy Jones, the** *n.* [one *Jones*, a chimney-sweep, who, *c.*1840, was cleaning the chimneys at Buckingham Palace, fell into an empty hearth and supposedly overheard Queen Victoria and Prince Albert talking of state secrets] [mid-19C–1900s] a teller of secrets. ❑ **boy racer** *n.* [note motorcycle jargon *boy racer*, Model 7R AJS racing motorcycle, manufactured for the mass market in 1948] [1990s+] a daredevil young car-driver; the term implies disdain for such puerile antics. ❑ **boy's favourite** *n.* [16 is the age of consent in the UK] [1950s+] (*bingo*) the number 16. ❑ **boy's gaol** *n.* [1980s+] (*Aus. prison*) a prison which abounds in petty rules. ❑ **boy stuff** *n.* [1990s+] (*US*) gay sex. ❑ **boy toy** *n.* **1** [1950s] (*US gay*) the penis. **2** *see* TOY BOY *under* TOY *n.*[1].

IN PHRASES

❑ **boy in blue** *n.* **1** [1930s–40s] (*Irish*) stew, the food. **2** *see* BOYS IN BLUE *n.* ❑ **boy in the boat** *n.* [1910s+] the clitoris. ❑ **boy of the holy ground** *n.* [HOLY LAND *n.* (2)] [early 19C] a thug, a hoodlum. ❑ **boy of the slang** *n.* *see* SLANG-BOY *under* SLANG *n.*[1]. ❑ **boy with the boots** *n.* [the use of the card as a trump, 'booting' other cards] [late 19C+] (*Anglo-Irish*) the joker in a pack of cards.

IN EXCLAMATIONS

❑ **boy howdy!** [1920s+] (*US*) a mild excl.

boy *n.*[3] [abbr. HOMEBOY *n.* (3)] **1** [1920s] (*US black*) a friend or neighbour, one of one's group or gang. **2** [1940s+] (*Aus./US*) a derogatory term of address to a black man. **3** [1970s] (*US black*) a low-status gang member. **4** [1970s+] a 'character', an eccentric.

boy, the *n.*[1] [its innate masculinity] [mid-19C+] the penis.

boy, the *n.*[2] **1** [mid-19C+] someone important, or posing as such; in phr. *I'm the boy*, I am the right person for the job. **2** [1950s] the accused.

boy *v.* [var. on GUY *v.*[1] (1)] [2000s] (*UK teen*) to tease.

boy! *excl.* (*also* **boyees! boy-oh-boy!**) [late 19C+] (*orig. US*) a general excl. of excitement, pleasure, surprise, amazement.

boy-girl *n.*[1] (*also* **boy-gal**) [1950s+] a homosexual.

boy-girl *n.*[2] [BOY *n.*[2] (1) + GIRL *n.*[2] (1)] [1980s+] (*US drugs*) a mixture of heroin and cocaine, usu. as an injection but sometimes inhaled.

boygul *n.* [Yid. *bagel*, a soft, circular doughnut-like bread + BOY-GIRL *n.*[1]] [1980s+] (*US gay*) an effeminate youth.

boykie *n.* (*also* **booitjie, boytjie**) [SE *boy* + Afk. sfx -*kie*] (*S.Afr.*) **1** [1970s–80s] a male African servant. **2** [1970s+] a generally affectionate term for a male, fellow, chap, 'bloke'. **3** [1970s+] an exceptionally clever person.

boyo *n.* [SE *boy* + -O *sfx* (1)] **1** [mid-19C+] a term of address, usu. Welsh, Irish or clichéd, often as *my boyo*. **2** [late 19C+] (*also* **boyoh**) a man, sometimes used of an object. **3** [late 19C+] the penis.

boy-oh-boy! *excl. see* BOY! *excl.*

boys, the *n.* **1** [early 19C+] (*also* **boyz**) one's (male) social circle; one's companions or 'gang'. **2** [early 19C+] (*orig. US*) a criminal or violent gang, esp. the hangers-on of a corrupt politician. **3** [20C+] (*US*) the police. **4** [20C+] criminals in general, esp. the thieves and swindlers who frequented race-courses or dog-tracks. **5** [1920s+] the employees or hangers-on of a particular world, e.g. *advertising* or *boxing*. **6** [1920s+] (*Irish*) Republican revolutionaries, esp. when fleeing capture. **7** [1930s+] as *the — boys*, individuals conforming to a specific job description, e.g. the *software boys*, the *public relations boys*. **8** [1950s] (*UK/W.I.*) the immigrant West Indian community. **9** [1950s+] the US Mafia. **10** [1960s+] (*US campus*) the male homosexual community.

boys-a-boys! *excl.* (*also* **boys-o-boys!**) [20C+] (*Irish*) a general excl. of amazement, disbelief.

boys and girls *n.* [1920s–40s] (*US*) a general term of address, in fact the audience may be all male.

boysie *n.* [SE *boy* + dimin. sfx -*sie*] [20C+] a general term of address to a male.

boys in blue *n.* (*also* **bellies in blue, blokes in blue, boys blue, men in blue**) [note 1920s UK *boys in blue*, permanently disabled ex-servicemen, some 7000 of whom were inmates of hospitals in Greater London area and wore a blue uniform; early use meant the Royal Navy] **1** [late 19C+] the police; occas. in sing. **2** [1950s] baseball umpires. **3** [1960s] (*US prison*) warders.

boys-o-boys! *excl. see* BOYS-A-BOYS! *excl.*

boys on ice *n.* [rhy. sl.] [late 19C] lice.

Boystown *n.* [pun on *Boys Town*, a celebrated home for delinquent boys] [1960s+] (*gay*) the predominantly homosexual neighbourhood in West Hollywood.

boystown sound *n.* [BOYSTOWN *n.* + SE *sound* + play on popular musical descriptions, e.g. the Liverpool sound, the Motown sound] [1970s–80s] music popular in gay discos.

boytjie *n. see* BOYKIE *n.*

boyz *n. see* BOYS, THE *n.* (1).

bozack *n.* (*also* **'zack**) [ety. unknown; ? black pron. of BALLS *n.* (1) + sfx -*ack*] [1990s+] (*orig. US black teen*) the scrotum, the penis.

IN PHRASES

❑ **box the bozack** *v.* [1990s+] to masturbate.

bozark *n.* [BOZO *n.*[1] (1)] [1920s] (*US*) a stupid girl or woman.

bozie *n.* [ety. unknown] [1980s+] (*S.Afr.*) a black person.

bozo *n.*[1] [? Sp. term meaning the light beard of adolescence or Sp. *bozal*, simple, stupid, or US fairground use BO *n.*[1] (2), or Ital. *bozzo*, a cuckold, a bastard] [1910s+] (*orig. US*) **1** a person, a fellow, a man; there is a slight overtone of clownishness. **2** a form of address. **3** a fool, an idiot. **4** a tough, a thug.

bozo *n.*[2] [abbr. *oz*, an ounce] [1950s+] (*drugs*) one ounce of heroin.

bozo *adj.* [BOZO *n.*[1] (3); BOZO *n.*[1] (4)] **1** [1940s+] crazy, eccentric. **2** [1980s+] stupid, with implications of thuggishness.

bozoom *n. see* BAZOOM *n.*

b.p. *n.* [abbr. *BABY PRO under* BABY *adj.*] [1970s] (*US*) a child prostitute.

b.p.o.m. *n.* [abbr.] [1950s–70s] (*gay*) a *b*ig *p*iece *o*f *m*eat.

b.p.t. *n.* [abbr. BLACK PEOPLE'S TIME *n.*] [1990s+] unpunctuality.

b.q. *n. see* BROWNIE *n.*[1] (5b).

b.r. *n.* [abbr.] [1910s–70s] (*US*) a *b*ank *r*oll.

bra *n.* [abbr. SE *brother*] **1** [1950s+] (*S.Afr./W.I.*) brother, esp. as pfx to a given name, e.g. *Bra Victor*. **2** [1950s+] (*also* **brah**) (*S.Afr./US*) an informal term of address, mate, buddy, pal. **3** [1970s+] an important, influential person, 'one of the boys'. **4** [1980s] 'a Black man who is acknowledged to be particularly STREETWISE and adept at making the most of urban life, while remaining part of working-class Black society' (*DSAE*).

braa *n.* [pron.] [1950s+] (*W.I. Rasta*) brother.

braata *n.* [Mex. Sp. *barata*, cheap] [1910s+] (*W.I.*) a little extra, like the 13th biscuit in a baker's dozen, or an extra helping of food; in musical shows it has come to be the encore.

brace *n.* [SE *bracer*, a nerve tonic] [late 19C] a drink taken as a pick-me-up, a 'bracer'.

(IN PHRASES)

❑ **take a brace** *v.* [and note SE *brace*, used of straps, belts etc that tighten] [late 19C+] (*US*) to pull oneself together, to smarten up.

brace *v.* [? 15C SE *brace*, to bluster, esp. in phr. *face and brace*] **1** [late 19C] (*US gambling*) to cheat. **2** [late 19C–1930s] (*US Und.*) to corrupt, to bribe; to intimidate. **3** [late 19C+] (*US*) to demand, esp. money. **4** [20C+] to question, usu. of police. **5** [20C+] to face up to, to shake up, to grab. **6** [1910s+] to accost, to solicit.

brace and bit *n.* [rhy. sl.] **1** [1980s+] (*Aus. drugs/prison*) the equipment (a needle, a spoon, a dropper) required for injecting narcotics [= FIT *n.*[2]]. **2** [2000s] excrement [= SHIT *n.* (1a)].

brace and bits *n.* [rhy. sl. = tits, + pun on SE *brace*, a pair] [1920s] female breasts.

brace-face *n.* [1990s+] (*UK juv.*) an insult aimed at one who wears a corrective brace on their teeth.

brace game *n.* (*also* **braced game**) [SE *brace*, to bluster, to domineer; see Asbury *Sucker's Progress* (1938) An extraordinary number of the terms, technical and otherwise, which were employed by Faro players in the palmy days of the game have passed into the language [...] and are commonly used by millions who never heard of Faro. Here are some of them: [...] *Brace game* —A crooked Faro bank] **1** [late 19C–1940s] (*US*) any form of gambling game in which there is concealed cheating; thus *brace dealer*, a crooked dealer. **2** [1900s–40s] any fraudulent scheme.

(IN COMPOUNDS)

❑ **brace room** *n.* [BRACE (TAVERN) *n.* + SE *room*] [mid-19C] (*US Und.*) a gambling house where all games are invariably corrupt.

brace house *n. see SKINNING HOUSE under* SKINNING *n.*[2].

bracelets *n.* (*also* **two-hand bracelet**) [mid-17C+] (*orig. UK Und.*) handcuffs.

brace of... *n.*

SE in slang uses

(IN PHRASES)

❑ **brace of broads** *n.* [SE *brace*, a pair + *broad* shoulders] [1940s] (*US black*) one's shoulders. ❑ **brace of hookers** *n.* [SE *brace* + ext. of HOOK *n.*[1] (1a)] [1940s] (*US black*) one's arms. ❑ **brace of horned cows** *n.* [1940s] (*US black*) a pair of aching feet. ❑ **brace of shakes** *n. see TWO SHAKES under* SHAKE *n.*[1].

bracer *n.*[1] [SE *bracer*, a nerve tonic] [early 19C+] (*orig. US*) an alcoholic drink, esp. as a 'pick-me-up'.

bracer *n.*[2] [BRACE *v.*] [1900s] (*US Und.*) a beggar who accosts passers-by with a hard-luck story in hope of alms.

bracers *n.* [1920s–30s] (*US tramp*) the legs.

brace (tavern) *n.* [its 'barmen', a pair or *brace* of brothers surnamed Partridge] [late 18C–early 19C] a room in the King's Bench prison, London, where prisoners can buy beer.

brace up *v.* [? Fr. argot *braser des faffes*, to forge documents] [mid–late 19C] to pawn stolen goods.

brace-up-'tomach *n.* [SE *brace up*, to firm up + *stomach*] [1970s] (*W.I.*) a woman with larger-than-average breasts.

bracket *n.* [the resemblance] [1950s+] an unspecified part of the body, presumably the nose; thus usu. in the phr. *a punch up the bracket*.

bracket-face *n.* [late 17C–1910s] an ugly person; also as adj., *bracket-faced*.

bracket-mug *n.* [SE *bracket* + MUG *n.*[1] (1b)] [mid–late 19C] an ugly face.

bracmard *n.* [Fr. *braquemard*, a short broad sword] [mid-17C] the penis.

Brad *n. see* BRADBURY *n.*

brad *n.*[1] [? SE *brad*, a shoemaker's rivet] **1** [19C] a halfpenny; a cent. **2** [early 19C–1910s] in pl., cash money. **3** [1910s] a cigarette [pun on SE *brad*, a nail/rivet + NAIL *n.*[1] (3a)].

(IN PHRASES)

❑ **tip the brads** *v.* [19C] **1** to be generous. **2** to be a gentleman.

brad *n.*[2] [mid-19C] (*US Und.*) a burglar's tool, a saw.

brad *n.*[3] see BRAD (PITT) *n.*

bradarax! *excl.* (*also* **bragadap! bram! braps! brudum! brugadum! bruggalungdung!**) [1930s+] (*W.I.*) echoic, onomat. words representing the sound of an object or objects crashing to the floor; gunfire, or other sudden noises.

Bradbury *n.* (*also* **Brad, John Bradbury**) [proper name of Sir John *Bradbury*, secretary to the Treasury c.1915] [1910s–50s] a banknote.

brad-faking *n.* [BRAD *n.*[1] (2) + FAKE *v.*[1] (3)] [mid-19C] playing at cards.

Bradford cities *n.* [rhy. sl. = titties] [1990s+] breasts.

Brad (Pitt) *n.* [rhy. sl.; ult. US film star *Brad Pitt* (b.1964)] [1990s+] **1** excrement; lit. and fig. [SHIT *n.* (1a)]. **2** an act of defecation [SHIT *n.* (1b)]. **3** (*Irish*) (*also* **bradleys**) in pl., armpits. **4** (*also* **bradleys**) in pl. the female breast [TIT *n.*[2] (1)].

bradshaw *n.* [*Bradshaw's Railway Guide*, the comprehensive Victorian timetable, founded by George Bradshaw (1801–53) and published 1839–61] [late 19C–1900s] a precise person, one who is good at figures.

bradys *n.* [the type of character portrayed in the 1960s TV series *The Brady Bunch*] [1990s+] (*US black*) young, middle-class, suburban whites; as adj., *brady*, typically conservative.

brag *n.*[1] (*also* **brag-boy, braggadocio**) [abbr. SE; 19C+ use is SE] [late 16C–18C] a swaggering braggart.

brag *n.*[2] [note Egan: 'LOGIC termed these persons *Brags*, in consequence of their repeatedly advertising to render embarrassed individuals assistance, yet making them *pay* well for it'] [early 19C] a money-lender.

brag *adj.* [SE *brag*, to boast; thus worth boasting about] [19C–1900s] (*US*) first-rate, out of the ordinary, notable.

bragadap! *excl. see* BRADARAX! *excl.*

brag-boy *n. see* BRAG *n.*[1].

braggadocio *n.* [SE *braggadocio*, an empty, idle boast or boaster; thus the professional thief's boast that they will never be caught] **1** [mid-19C] a sentence of three months' imprisonment given to a known thief or regular offender. **2** *see* BRAG *n.*[1].

braggadocious *adj.* (*also* **bragga**) [1940s+] (*W.I./US*) arrogant, loud-mouthed; thus *braggadociousness*.

brag it out with a card of ten *v.* (*also* **face it out with a card of ten**) [the image of bluffing in a card game, in which ten is only an average card] [mid-16C] to brazen out a situation.

brah *n.* **1** *see* BRA *n.* (2). **2** *see* BRO *n.*[1].

brahma *n. see* BRAMA *n.*

Brahma bull *n.* [rhy. sl. = pull, i.e. PULL (ONESELF) OFF *under* PULL *v.* etc] [1980s+] (*Aus. prison*) an act of masturbation.

Brahms (and Liszt) *adj.* (*also* **Mozart and Liszt**) [rhy. sl. = PISSED *adj.*[1]] [1920s+] drunk.

brain *n.*[1] **1** [mid-19C+] (*orig. US*) (*also* **brain guy**) a planner, an 'ideas man', a mastermind, often in criminal context, i.e. planning a bank aid but not participating in the actual action; often found in fiction as *The Brain* or *Brains*. **2** [1910s+] (*orig. US*) an intellectual, an intelligent person, esp. as one who is unpleasantly, anti-socially intellectual. **3** [1940s] (*US Und.*) (*also* **brainbox**) the combination of a safe. **4** [1980s] (*US campus*) in ironic reversal, a stupid person.

SE in slang uses

IN COMPOUNDS

❑ **brain box** *n. see* sense 3 above. ❑ **brain bucket** *n.* **1** [mid-19C–1910s] (*US*) (*also* **brain barrel**) the head, the skull. **2** [1950s+] (*UK juv.*) a protective helmet, whatever its use. ❑ **brain-burners** *n.* [1970s] (*US drugs/gay*) amphetamines when taken intravenously. ❑ **brain burp** *n.* [the spontaneity of an explosion of wind] [1990s+] (*US campus*) a random thought. ❑ **brain-canister** *n.* [mid-19C] (*orig. boxing*) the head. ❑ **brain capsule** *n.* [the supposedly stimulating properties of nicotine] [1900s] (*US*) a cigarette. ❑ **brainchild** *n.* [1960s+] (*US*) a very intelligent person. ❑ **brain college** *n.* [ironic use] [late 19C] (*US*) a lunatic asylum. ❑ **brain damage** *n.* [its supposed effects] **1** [1990s+] beer, or any strong intoxicating drink. **2** [2000s] (*drugs*) heroin. ❑ **brain dead** *see* separate entries. ❑ **brain drain** *n.* [1960s+] the emigration of highly qualified people, generally scientists and academics, from Britain in search of more prestigious jobs, better facilities for research and higher salaries. ❑ **brain drainer** *n.* [1960s] (*Aus.*) a university. ❑ **brain fart** *see* separate entries. ❑ **brain guy** *n. see* sense 1 above. ❑ **brainless wonder** *n.* [SE *brainless* + *wonder*, an outstanding specimen of something + ? play on a carnival attraction, the 'Boneless Wonder'] [1910s] (*US*) a fool, a scatter-brained person; a stupid thing. ❑ **brainpan** *n.* [SE *brain-pan*, that which contains the brain, the skull] **1** [late 15C+] the human head. **2** [17C+] the mind. ❑ **brain-pot** *n.* [mid-19C] the skull, the head. ❑ **brain salad** *n.* [pun on HEAD *n.* (3b)] [1990s+] (*US*) drugs. ❑ **brainstem** *n.* [SE *brainstem*, 'the central trunk of the brain upon which the cerebrum and cerebellum are set, and which continues downwards to form the spinal cord' (*OED*)] [1980s] (*US campus*) an eccentric. ❑ **brainstorm** *n.* [ext. of SE use; popularized by the murder trial of society architect Harry Thaw in 1907–8, during which his lawyer claimed he had suffered a 'brain storm'] **1** [20C+] (*orig. US*) a sudden inspiration or bright idea. **2** [1910s+] a nervous breakdown, a physical or emotional collapse. ❑ **brain tablet** *n.* [1930s] (*US*) a cigarette. ❑ **brain ticklers** *n.* [amphetamine accelerates the activity of the central nervous system and thence the brain] [1960s+] (*drugs*) amphetamines. ❑ **brainwave** *n.* [late 19C+] a sudden inspiration or bright idea.

IN PHRASES

❑ **do someone's brain in** *v.* [2000s] to drive mad, to exasperate. ❑ **fuck someone's brains out** *v.* (*also* **ball one's brains out, hump...**) [1950s+] to copulate very strenuously and poss. sadistically, usu. of a man to a woman. ❑ **get up off one's brains** *v.* [1950s] (*Aus.*) to be motivated. ❑ **on the brain** *v.* [late 19C] to be thinking. ❑ **out of one's brain** *adj.* (*also* **off one's brain, out of one's cranium**) **1** [1940s+] intoxicated with drugs, or alcohol; thus *go off one's brain*. **2** [1960s+] mad, crazy; thus *go off one's brain*, to go mad, to lose emotional control. **3** [1990s+] overwhelmed.

brain *n.*[2] [play on HEAD *n.* (2c)] [1990s+] (*US*) fellatio.

brain *v.* [note 14C–19C SE *brain*, to kill by dashing out the brains of] **1** [17C+] to hit on the head (and knock out); thus *brained*, hit very hard on the head; also fig. **2** [1940s–60s] to ponder, to think about.

braindead *n.* [1990s+] (*US*) a complete fool.

brain-dead *adj.* [SE *brain-dead*, used of one who, while still technically alive, is in a persistent vegetative state] [1980s+] utterly stupid, completely inept.

brained *adj.* [1990s+] **1** emotionally exhausted. **2** drunk.

brain fart *n.* [1980s+] (*orig. US campus*) **1** a nonsensical idea. **2** a loss of memory or concentration.

brainfart *v.* [BRAIN FART *n.* (2)] [1990s+] (*US campus*) to have a temporary loss of memory.

brainfart! *excl.* [BRAIN FART *n.* (2)] [1980s] (*orig. US campus*) a general excl. implying that the speaker has lost the thread, forgotten what they were talking about, made a major mental error and all in all lost the power of rational speech and thought.

brainiac *n.* [SE *brain* + *maniac*; note the DC Comics villain *Brainiac*, who first appeared in 1958] [1980s+] a really clever person.

braino *n.* [SE *brain* + -O *sfx* (1)] [1980s+] (*US*) a very clever person.

brains *n.* [note UK/US police jargon *the brains*, the CID or plain-clothes detective department, usu. ironic] **1** [1910s–80s] (*orig. US*) the head of a criminal gang, often as *the brains*; also in non-criminal use. **2** [1930s+] used ironically.

brake lurk *n. see BREAK-LURK under* BREAK *v.*[1].

brakie *n.* (*also* **brakey, braky**) [late 19C+] (*US tramp*) a railroad brakeman.

bram *n.* [echoic; orig. a noisy and disorderly private but open-house party] [1970s] (*W.I.*) a small dance; thus *bram house*, a small dancehall.

bram! *excl. see* BRADARAX! *excl.*

brama *n.* (*also* **bramah, bramma, brahma**) [Skrt *Brahma*, the supreme God of post-Vedic Hindu mythology] [1910s+] **1** a pretty woman. **2** anything good, enjoyable, attractive.

bran *n.* [one of its constituents] [mid-19C] a loaf.

IN COMPOUNDS

❑ **bran-faced** *adj. see* separate entry.

Branch, the *n.* [1970s+] used in the UK and certain one-time Commonwealth countries to denote the Special Branch, that department of the national police force that deals with 'subversion'.

branch out *v.* [SE *branch out*, to expand] [1920s+] (*Aus.*) to become very fat.

brand *v.* [1920s–50s] (*Scot. gang*) to slash with a razor; thus to scar.

brand-fire new *adj.* (*also* **bran fire new**) [19C+] (*US*) absolutely new.

brand X *n.* [joc. play on the drug's illegality] [1970s+] (*US black*) marijuana; a marijuana cigarette.

brandy *n.*

SE in slang uses

IN COMPOUNDS

❑ **brandy and fashoda** *n.* [play on SE based on the *Fashoda Incident* of 1898, when French and British forces clashed in the Sudan following the battle of Omdurman] [late 19C–1900s] (*UK society*) brandy and soda. ❑ **brandy blossom** *n. see under* BLOSSOM *n.*[2]. ❑ **brandy-face** *n.* (*also* **brandy-nose**) [the effects of consistent over-drinking] [late 17C–mid-19C] a drunkard; thus *brandy-faced*, red-faced. ❑ **brandy-pawnee** *n.* [Hind. *pani*, water] [19C] (*Anglo-Ind.*) brandy and water. ❑ **brandy-shunter** *n.* [SE *shunter*, a mover] [late 19C–1900s] a heavy drinker of brandy.

IN PHRASES

❑ **brandy is Latin for pig and goose** [pun on Lat. *anser*, a goose/SE *answer*] [mid-18C–late 19C] used to apologize for drinking brandy after eating either goose or pig.

brandy snap *n.*[1] [its resemblance to SE *brandy-snap*, a very thin gingerbread biscuit] [1920s+] (*Aus.*) a scab on one's face.

brandy snap *n.*[2] [rhy. sl.] [1940s+] (*US*) a slap.

bran-faced *adj.* [SE *bran*, the husk of a cereal after grinding + sfx *-faced*] [late 18C–early 19C] freckled.

brangle *v.* [SE *brangle*, shake, dance] [18C] to have sexual intercourse.

brannigan *n.* (*US*) **1** [late 19C+] a drunken spree. **2** [1940s+] (*also* **branigan**) a fight, a violent argument.

IN PHRASES

❑ **on a brannigan** *adj.* [? proper name, but more likely f.

stereotype of the fighting Irish drunk/ Jim 'Lugs' Brannigan, a popular Dublin policeman renowned for dealing with street fights in a fair manner in 1920s–30s] [late 19C+] (*US*) very drunk.

braps! *excl. see* BRADARAX! *excl.*

brary *n.* [clipping] [1960s+] (*US campus*) the library; thus *brarydog*, someone who studies in the library; *brary*, v. to attend the library.

brasco *n.* (*also* **brascoe, biscoe**) ['where the *brass* knobs *go*'] [1960s+] (*Aus.*) a lavatory.

brass *n.*[1] (*also* **brassey**) **1** as a metal used in coins. (**a**) [16C+] money; esp. as in the UK northern phr. *where there's muck there's brass* and similar homilies. (**b**) [20C+] (*W.I.*) a penny. (**c**) [1920s] genuine jewellery. (**d**) [1920s–60s] (*US Und.*) a fake 'gold' ring. (**e**) [1970s] (*US prison*) currency used in jail. **2** [late 17C+] the image of SE *brass* as a measure of hardness and thus insensibility: audacity, gall, cheek. **3** as a superior figure, usu. in an institution [*BRASS HAT under* BRASS *adj.*[1]]. (**a**) [late 19C+] a senior officer in the police, a prison, or armed services. (**b**) [1940s+] any variety of senior official, e.g. a politician. (**c**) [1950s] a social superior. **4** [1930s+] (*US black*) (*also* **brasses, brassies**) brass knuckles.

IN COMPOUNDS

❑ **brass man** *n.* [1930s+] **1** (*Aus.*) a confidence trickster. **2** (*US Und.*) a politician or one who has influence among politicians. ❑ **brass peddler** *n.* [1920s–40s] (*US tramp*) a person who sells imitation gold jewellery.

IN PHRASES

❑ **brass along** *v.* [1910s+] to go through life cheerfully, without much regard for the feelings of others. ❑ **brass down** *v.* [1900s] to pay money owed. ❑ **brass (it) out** *v.* [1950s+] to bluff, bluster or brazen one's way out of a situation. ❑ **brass up** *v.* **1** [late 19C+] to hand over money; to pay a debt. **2** [1970s] (*W.I. Bdos*) to scold, to reprimand. ❑ **shove the brass** *v.* [1930s] (*US Und.*) to peddle fake or cheap jewellery.

brass *n.*[2] (*also* **brass-nail, brass-nob**) [rhy. sl.; *brass nail* = TAIL *n.* (6)] [1930s+] a prostitute.

IN PHRASES

❑ **half-brass** *n.* [1940s+] a woman who associates with the prostitute milieu but is not a 'working girl' herself.

brass *adj.*[1] [as preferred by the BRASS *n.*[1] (3) or those of similar social status] [1950s–60s] fashionable, chic.

SE in slang uses

IN COMPOUNDS

❑ **brass ankle** *n.* ['My father thinks that the term originated in the neighborhood of Monck's Corner, South Carolina, where the descendants of a Portuguese colony who had intermarried with Negroes and afterwards married largely within their own group were noted for their brass bracelets and anklets.' (*American Speech*, XVIII 1943)] [1920s–60s] a person of mixed race. ❑ **brass ass** *n.* [ASS *n.* (2); cf. SE *brazen*] **1** [1950s–70s] (*US*) a general term of abuse. **2** [1970s+] (*US*) insolence; thus *brass-assed*, insolent. ❑ **Brass Bonce** *n.* [BONCE *n.* (1); ? the helmet] [1950s] (*UK juv.*) a police officer. ❑ **brass buttons** *n.* (*also* **brass button**) [metonymy] **1** [mid-19C–1930s] (*US*) a soldier, esp. an officer. **2** [1900s–60s] (*US*) a police officer. **3** [1940s] a train conductor. ❑ **brass-face** *n.* [SE *brass*/BRASS *n.*[1] (2) + SE *face*] [late 16C; early 19C+] an impudent person, thus adj. *brass-faced*, impudent. ❑ **brass farthing** *n.* (*also* **brass farden, brass fart**) [mid-19C+ use of *brass farthing* is SE] [mid-17C–mid-19C] something of the utmost insignificance, usu. in phr. *I don't give a brass farthing*. ❑ **brass guts** *n.* [1940s] **1** cheek, insolence. **2** (*also* **gold-plated guts**) courage, nerve. ❑ **brass hat** *n.* [the gold braid or similar adornment on their caps, itself known as SCRAMBLED EGGS *n.*[1] (1)] [late 19C+] a senior officer in the police or services; thus *brass-hatted*. ❑ **brass-head** *n.* [1950s] **1** (*US*) a fool [the hardness]. **2** (*W.I.*) a black person who has a reddish tint to their hair – the result of a diet lacking sufficient protein [the colour]. ❑ **brass-house** *n.* [HOUSE *n.*[1] (1)] [2000s] a brothel. ❑ **brass-knocker** *n.* [if a house boasts a brass knocker it is likely that the owners are wealthy enough to give away their leftovers. Note Hobson-Jobson *brass-knocker*. 'a term applied to a *rechauffé* or serving up again of yesterday's dinner or supper; a piece of Anglo-Indian slang it is supposed to be a corruption of (Hind.) *basi khana*, stale food'] [late 19C–1900s] (*UK tramp*) left-over food, scraps. ❑ **brass knucks** *n. see* KNUCK *n.* (3). ❑ **brass monkey** *n. see* separate entry. ❑ **brass-mounted** *adj.* [late 19C] (*US*) a general intensifier, e.g. *I don't give a brass-mounted cuss*. ❑ **brass-nail/-nob** *n. see* BRASS *n.*[2]. ❑ **brass neck** *see* separate entries. ❑ **brass nuts** *n.* [1940s+] (*US prison*) a senior prison officer. ❑ **brass-plater** *n.* [one who advertises their place of work by the *brass plate* placed at its doorway, e.g. a consultant, a lawyer. Note mid-19C coal trade jargon *brass-plate merchant*, a second-rate coal retailer] [1920s] a professional man. ❑ **brass pounder** *n.* [the brass key of the telegraph] [1930s] (*US tramp*) a telegraph operator. ❑ **brass rail** *n.* [metonymy] [1920s–40s] (*US*) a bar; thus as n., *brass railer*, one who frequents bars. ❑ **brass tacks** *n. see* separate entry. ❑ **brass wig** *n.* [var. on *BRASS HAT* above] [1940s] (*US black*) a senior officer of the police or armed services.

IN PHRASES

❑ **brass monkey weather** *n. see* separate entry. ❑ **put the brass hat on** *v. see PUT THE TIN HAT ON under* TIN HAT *n.*[1].

brass *adj.*[2] *see* BORACIC (LINT) *adj.*

brass *v.* [Und. *brass*, a fraudulent betting 'system', ult. BRASS *n.*[1] (1a)] [1930s+] (*Aus.*) to defraud, to trick.

brass balls *n.* (*also* **steel balls**) [SE *brass* + BALLS *n.* (1)] [1960s+] **1** anything severely challenging, esp. in a 'masculine' context. **2** courage, 'guts'; thus *brass-balled*, courageous, tough. **3** cheek, effrontery.

brass balls *adv.* [BRASS BALLS *n.* (2)] [1990s+] in a tough, courageous manner.

brass band *n.* [rhy. sl.] [20C+] the hand.

brass band with/without a leader *n. see under* BAND *n.*[2].

brassed *adj.* (*also* **brassed off**) [BRASS OFF *v.*] [1940s+] irritated, fed up, annoyed.

brasser *n.* [ext. of BRASS *n.*[2]] [1960s+] (*Irish*) a slut, a prostitute; also used affectionately.

brasses *n. see* BRASS *n.*[1] (4).

brassey *n.* [metonymy] [1920s] **1** a police officer. **2** thus an informer. **3** *see* BRASS *n.*[1].

brassic/brassick *adj. see* BORACIC (LINT) *adj.*

brassic lint *adj. see* BORACIC (LINT) *adj.*

brassie *n.* [1960s–70s] (*Aus.*) a brassière.

brassies *n. see* BRASS *n.*[1] (4).

brass monkey *n.* [? brandname] [1980s+] (*US*) an alcoholic concoction available in liquor stores.

brass monkey *adj.* (*also* **brass monkeys**) [COLD ENOUGH TO FREEZE THE BALLS OFF A BRASS MONKEY *phr.*] [mid-19C+] (*orig. US*) extremely cold in temperature; often as *brass monkey weather*.

brass nails *n.*

IN PHRASES

❑ **get down to brass nails** *v. see GET DOWN TO BRASS TACKS under* BRASS TACKS *n.*

brass neck *n.* [the toughness of SE *brass* + *neck*, i.e. able to *STICK ONE'S NECK OUT under* NECK *n.* without risk of hurting it because it's made of brass; but note BRASS *n.*[1] (2) + NECK *n.* (2a)] [20C+] **1** impudence, audacity; often in phr. *have a brass neck*. **2** an impudent, audacious individual.

brass-neck *adj.* (*also* **brass-necked**) [BRASS NECK *n.*] [20C+] (*orig. milit.*) shameless, impudent.

brass off *v.* [? the primary activity of the BRASS *n.*[1] (3a)] [1920s+] (*orig. naut.*) to tell off, to scold, to grumble.

brass tacks *n.* [late 19C+] (*orig. US*) the facts, as in the central issues or heart of a matter,) and as such almost SE.

IN PHRASES

❑ **get down to brass tacks** *v.* (*also* **come down to brass tacks, get/come down to tacks, get down to brass nails**) [mid-19C+] to approach the facts, to deal with the real heart of the matter.

brassy *adj.* [BRASS *n.*[1] (2) + sfx -y] **1** [mid-16C–late 18C] impudent, shameless. **2** [20C+] of a woman, showy, flashy, ostentatious; implies a superficial bright hardness, but also possible prostitution. **3** [1910s] wealthy, rich.

brassy *adv.* [1910s] unashamedly, impudently.

brat *n.* [SE *brat*, a child] [1930s+] (*US prison*) the young partner of a prison homosexual.

SE in slang uses

IN COMPOUNDS

❑ **brat-getter** *n.* [19C] the penis. ❑ **brat-getting place** *n.* [19C] the vagina. ❑ **brat-whacker** *n.* see *KID-WALLOPER under* KID *n.*[1].

brat pack *n.* [on pattern of the Hollywood's *Holmby Hills Rat Pack*, a coterie of film stars and singers led by Humphrey Bogart in the 1950s and boosted by the mid-1980s *brat pack* of youthful Hollywood up-and-comers] [1980s+] any selection of successful young hopefuls, novelists, chefs, black success stories (*black pack*) etc.

brattery *n.* [SE *brat*] [late 18C–mid-19C] a nursery.

bratty *adj.* [1960s+] (*orig. US*) of a child or adolescent: spoiled, badly-behaved; of an adult: immature, given to behaving like a spoiled child.

brave *n.* [BRAVO *n.*] [late 16C–17C] a thug, a hired assassin.

brave and bold *adj.* [rhy. sl.] [20C+] cold.

bravo *n.* [Ital. *bravo*, brave] [late 16C–mid-18C] a hired killer; a thug.

braw *n.* [SE *brother*] [2000s] (*US teen*) a friend or close acquaintance.

brawl *n.* [1920s–50s] a riotous, noisy party.

brawny-buttock *n.* [early 18C] a general epithet of abuse, presumably aimed at a large or fat person.

brawta *n.* (*also* **brawtus**) [compare BRAATA *n.*] [20C+] (*US black/W.I.*) something extra.

Brazilian time *n.* [negative stereotyping] [1960s+] unpunctuality.

breach *n.* [late 16C–19C] the vagina.

breached *adj.* see BREECHED *adj.*

bread *n.*[1] **1** [late 18C–19C] employment, a means of earning money; thus *out of bread*, unemployed [Yid. *broyt*, money, but note Partridge's suggestion rhy. sl. BREAD AND HONEY *n.*]. **2** [1930s+] (*also* **breads**) money [something one might eat but also basic to life, as is bread].

DERIVATIVES

❑ **breadsville** *n.* [-VILLE *sfx*[1]] [1940s–60s] (*US*) a bank.

IN COMPOUNDS

❑ **breadhead** *n.* [-HEAD *sfx* (3); coined by anti-materialist hippies in the 1960s] [1960s+] an individual who is interested primarily in acquiring money. ❑ **bread stasher** *n.* [STASH *v.*[1] (2)] [1940s–60s] (*orig. US black*) a working man.

IN PHRASES

❑ **break some bread** *v.* [2000s] (*US Und.*) of a prostitute, to make some money. ❑ **red bread** *n.* [1960s] (*drugs*) money obtained by blood donation.

SE in slang uses

IN COMPOUNDS

❑ **bread and bread** *n.* [1960s+] a homosexual couple; thus *bread and bread don't make a sandwich*, the reply given by one effeminate gay man when partnered with another, a parallel phrase is 'I'm a pouf, not a lesbian.' ❑ **bread and dripping** *n.* see BREAD AND BUTTER *n.*[1]. ❑ **bread and pullet** *n.* [SE *bread* + pun on SE *pull it*] [late 19C–1910s] bread with no butter, jam or other additive. ❑ **bread and scrape** *n.* (*also* **bread and spit**) [mid-19C+] a piece of bread barely covered in a thin layer or *scrape* of butter or meat dripping. ❑ **bread and skip** *n.* [e.g. 'bread and molasses, and skip the molasses'] [20C+] (*US*) an inadequate meal. ❑ **bread and with it** *n.* [mid-19C] a light meal, e.g. *a loaf of bread and (something else) with it*. ❑ **bread-bag** *n.* [mid-19C] the stomach. ❑ **breadbasket** *n.* [boxing jargon] [mid-18C+] (*orig. boxing*) the stomach. ❑ **bread box** *n.* **1** [1910s–30s] (*US*) the stomach. **2** [1940s] (*US Und.*) a safe that can be opened easily. **3** [1960s] the vagina. **4** [2000s] (*US*) a small car. ❑ **bread-cutter** *n.* (*also* **bread-grinder**) [1960s–70s] (*US*) a tooth. ❑ **breadearner** *n.* [early 19C] (*Irish*) a knife, as used by a shoeblack. ❑ **breadfruit** *n.* [a double EGGPLANT *n.*[1]] [1940s] (*US black*) a ten-dollar bill. ❑ **breadfruit swapper** *n.* [such a person is forced to barter rather than pay for goods] [20C+] (*W.I., Bdos*) a very poor person. ❑ **bread hooks** *n.* **1** [1910s+] (*US*) the hands. **2** [1960s] a fingernail. ❑ **bread room** *n.* [mid-18C–mid-19C] the stomach. ❑ **breadsnapper** *n.* (*also* **breadsnatcher**) [lit. 'a child who can eat their weight in groceries'] [late 19C+] (*Scot., Glasgow/Irish/US*) a child. ❑ **breadsnatchers** *n.* [1960s] (*US*) the hands. ❑ **bread trap** *n.* [SE TRAP *n.*[1] (4)] [late 19C–1920s] (*US*) the mouth. ❑ **breadwinner** *n.* **1** [mid-19C] (*UK Und.*) a knife. **2** [late 19C] the vagina [viewed as a commercial commodity].

IN PHRASES

❑ **in bad bread** [late 18C–early 19C] in trouble, in a difficult situation.

bread *n.*[2] [? the 'staff of life' or, if seen as a generator of money, i.e. BREAD *n.*[1] (1)] (*orig. US black*) **1** [late 19C–1960s] the vagina; esp. in the context of cunnilingus. **2** [1930s] the penis.

IN COMPOUNDS

❑ **bread pan** *n.* [1930s] (*US black*) the vagina.

bread and butter *n.*[1] (*also* **bread and dripping**) [the foodstuffs as staples] **1** [early 18C–19C] business. **2** [mid-18C+] one's basic income and the work that provides it.

IN PHRASES

❑ **no bread and butter of mine** [late 18C–early 19C] no business of mine. ❑ **quarrel with one's bread and butter** *v.* [mid-18C–1910s] to act against one's own best interests.

bread and butter *n.*[2] [rhy. sl.] **1** [late 19C+] the gutter. **2** [1980s] (*Aus.*) a stutter. **3** [1990s+] an eccentric or mad person [NUTTER *n.* (1)]. **4** [1990s+] a golf putter.

bread-and-butter *adj.* [the blandness of the food] **1** [19C] childish, juvenile, esp. schoolgirlish. **2** [mid-19C+] plain. **3** [20C+] basic, fundamental, quotidian.

SE in slang uses

IN PHRASES

❑ **bread and butter fashion** *n.* [the proximity of the *bread* and *butter*, which 'lie on' each other] [late 18C–early 19C] sexual intercourse. ❑ **bread and butter john** *n.* [JOHN *n.*[2] (4)] [1940s] (*US Und.*) a tramp who begs from house to house. ❑ **bread and butter letter** *n.* [note journalistic jargon *bread and nutter column*, a column fuelled in the main by press agent handouts and similar varieties of free publicity for those who send it to the writer; such a column harms no one, 'butters up' a variety of individuals and keeps the writer off the breadline] [20C+] a letter of thanks sent to one's host shortly after having enjoyed their hospitality. ❑ **bread-and-butter teeth** *n.* [large and white, they resemble slices of bread and butter] [20C+] buck teeth. ❑ **bread and butter warehouse** *n.* [? the teas served in its tea rooms or *BREAD AND BUTTER FASHION* above] [late 18C] Ranelagh Gardens in Chelsea, London, which was built as a pleasure garden in 1741, but gradually fell into disrepute and was shut down in 1803; it is now part of the gardens of the Chelsea Hospital.

bread and cheese *n.* [rhy. sl.] **1** [late 19C] the knees. **2** [late 19C–1960s] a sneeze.

bread and cheese *adj.* [the quotidian edibles] [17C–18C; mid-19C–1900s] ordinary, run-of-the-mill, unexceptional.

bread and cheese *v.* [BREAD AND CHEESE *n.* (2)] [late 19C+] to sneeze.

bread and honey *n.* [rhy. sl.] [1950s+] money.

bread and jam *n.* [rhy. sl.] [20C+] a tram.

bread and lard *adj.* [rhy. sl.] [20C+] hard.

bread knife *n.* [rhy. sl.] [2000s] one's wife.

break *n.*[1] **1** [early 19C+] (*orig. US*) a piece of luck, good or bad, usu. in comb. with defining adj. **2** [late 19C–1930s] (*US*) an error, a mistake. **3** [1910s+] (*orig. US/baseball*) in pl. and constr. with *the*, luck, chance, opportunities, either *good breaks* or *bad breaks*. **4** [1920s+] (*orig. US*) a piece of special treatment, kindness, fair treatment.

IN PHRASES

❑ **give someone a break** *v.* (*also* **give something a break, cut**

someone a break) [1920s+] (*orig. US*) to give someone or something a chance, to let off, to excuse, to give an opportunity, esp. in GIVE ME A BREAK! below. ❑ **go for breaks** *v.* [1970s–80s] (*N.Z. prison*) to make excuses; to tell lies.

(IN EXCLAMATIONS)

❑ **give me a break!** [1920s+] (*orig. US*) an ironical excl. of resignation and/or supplication delivered when is faced with a statement or event deemed unacceptable, irritating, etc.

break *n.*[2] **1** [mid-19C+] (*orig. US*) an escape, from prison or custody. **2** [1920s] (*UK Und.*) a building with two entrances/exits, used by con men to disappear from their victim or pursuer.

(IN PHRASES)

❑ **do a break** *v.* [1910s+] (*Aus.*) to run off, to depart. ❑ **get the break** *v.* [1900s] to be dismissed from employment; thus *breaker*, one who has been dismissed. ❑ **make a break** *v.* [mid-19C+] (*orig. US*) to escape or attempt to escape, usu. from prison. ❑ **make a break for** *v.* [mid-19C+] to head towards (not necessarily an escape).

break *n.*[3] [late 19C] (*UK Und.*) a collection taken to give money to a prisoner either awaiting trial or recently discharged.

break *n.*[4] [a play on CRACK *n.*[1] (1b)] [1900s–60s] a remark, poss. in bad taste.

break *n.*[5] [1910s+] (*US*) a break-in, a robbery.

break *v.*[1] **1** [early 18C; late 19C+] to render someone impoverished. **2** [late 18C; 1900s] to become impoverished. **3** [1940s+] (*Aus.*) to cost, e.g. *that'll break for five dollars*.

(IN PHRASES)

❑ **I must break you** [1990s+] (*US black teen*) a general phr. used to threaten an opponent or rival.

SE in slang uses

(IN COMPOUNDS)

❑ **break-ass** *adv.* [-ASS *sfx*] [1960s] (*US*) at top speed. ❑ **break-away** *n.* [late 19C+] (*Aus./N.Z.*) **1** (*also* **break-in, break-out**) a bout of madness or drunkenness. **2** a person who has been 'broken', whether mentally or physically. ❑ **break-lurk** *n.* (*also* **brake lurk**) [LURK *n.* (1)] [mid-19C] (*UK Und.*) a fraudulent begging letter, claiming a broken limb or ribs. ❑ **break-teeth words** *n.* (*also* **crackjaw**) [late 18C–early 19C] words considered hard to pronounce, long and incomprehensible words.

(IN PHRASES)

❑ **break...** *v. see also under* relevant n. ❑ **break a breath** *v. see* BREAK ON below. ❑ **break a pudding** *v.* [the result of one's eating] [20C+] (*Irish*) to belch. ❑ **break camp** *v.* [1970s+] (*US campus*) to hurry; to leave. ❑ **break me off a piece** [1980s+] (*orig. US black*) I want some, give me some. ❑ **break night** *v.* [one 'breaks through' the night + ref. to the SE *break of day*] [1960s+] (*US*) to stay up all night partying, talking, etc. ❑ **break-o'-day drum** *n.* (*also* **break o' day house**) [SE *break-o'-day*, dawn + DRUM *n.*[3] (3)] [late 19C] an all-night tavern. ❑ **break on** *v.* [one 'breaks' their image] [1930s+] (*US black*) **1** to denigrate someone behind their back. **2** (*also* **break a breath**) to humiliate someone in public. ❑ **break one's ankle** *v.* (*also* **sprain one's ankle**) [euph.; orig. 18C–19C UK, 20C+ mainly in US; compare BREAK ONE'S LEG (ABOVE THE KNEE) below] [late 18C+] to be seduced, to be pregnant out of wedlock. ❑ **break one's arrow** *v.* [the 'arrrow', i.e. a rigid penis, is thus 'broken'] [early 17C] of a man, to come to orgasm, to ejaculate. ❑ **break one's ass** *v.* (*also* **break one's arse, ...tail**) [1930s+] to work extremely hard, to put in a great effort. ❑ **break one's back** *v.* **1** [mid-19C+] to stretch beyond one's limits, esp. financially, to become bankrupt. **2** [1900s] (*Aus.*) to become excessively worried or emotional. ❑ **break one's duck** *v.* [cricket imagery] [1980s+] (*W.I.*) to have an initial experience, usu. sexual. ❑ **break oneself** *v.* [2000s] (*US black*) to call oneself to attention. ❑ **break one's gall** *v.* [SE *gall*, bitterness] [late 18C–early 19C] (*UK Und.*) to cheer up, esp. of one who has just arrived in prison and is still suitably dejected. ❑ **break one's hump** *v.* [1930s+] (*US*) to make a special effort. ❑ **break one's leg (above the knee)** *v.* (*also* **break one's toe**) **1** [17C–18C] of a womanizing man, to become father to a child, whether one wishes to or not. **2** [late 17C+] to become pregnant out of wedlock. **3** [late 19C–1940s] of a young woman, to lose one's virginity, to be seduced. ❑ **break one's shins against Covent Garden rails** *v.* [Covent Garden, London, being a centre of prostitution] [late 18C–early 19C] to catch venereal disease. ❑ **break one's shit string** *v.* [1960s+] (*US gay*) to have such vigorous anal intercourse that bleeding results. ❑ **break one's tail** *v. see* BREAK ONE'S ASS above. ❑ **break shins** *v.* [Rus. tradition of beating the shins of those who refuse to pay their debts] [late 17C–19C] to borrow money, esp. during an emergency, when one is forced to run from person to person in the hope of a loan. ❑ **break someone down** *v.* [1990s+] (*US prison*) to turn a fellow inmate into a homosexual. ❑ **break someone in** *v.* **1** [1910s+] (*Aus.*) to deflower. **2** [1950s] to initiate a new prostitute. **3** [1970s+] (*US gay/prison*) to forcibly initiate a new inmate into homosexuality. ❑ **break someone in half** *v.* [2000s] (*UK black*) of a man, to have sexual intercourse in an extremely (and deliberately) violent manner. ❑ **break someone in two** *v.* [20C+] to beat up someone badly, to break their bones. ❑ **break someone off some** *v.* [1990s+] (*US black*) to give, esp. to hand over drugs. ❑ **break someone's ass** *v.* **1** [1950s+] (*orig. US*) to beat up, to attack physically. **2** [1960s+] (*US*) to harass, to nag, to annoy. ❑ **break someone's hump** *v.* [1950s+] (*US*) to harass, to persecute, to cause problems for. ❑ **break the pale** *v.* [SE *pale*, a limit, boundary; a restriction; a defence, safeguard] [late 16C–early 17C] to commit adultery. ❑ **break the sound barrier** *v.* [a pun on SE] [1960s] (*Can.*) to break wind. ❑ **break water** *v.* (*also* **bust water**) [1990s+] (*W.I.*) of a man, to reach orgasm.

break *v.*[2] (*US*) **1** [mid-18C+] (*also* **break for, break it**) of people, to rush off, to leave suddenly; to escape from prison; thus n., *breaker*, one who escapes from prison. **2** [late 19C+] (*also* **break down**) of things, events, to turn out, to transpire, to develop; often qualified by defining adj. **3** [1930s] to conduct oneself. **4** [1930s+] to reveal, to promote, to publicize, usu. in media context. **5** [1970s+] to render successful; to become successful. **6** *see* BREAK UP *v.* (4).

(IN PHRASES)

❑ **break bad** *v.* **1** [1910s] to have a mental breakdown. **2** [1960s+] (*US black*) to become angry or aggressive. **3** [1980s] (*US campus*) to perform well. ❑ **break for tall timber** *v. see* TAKE TO THE TALL TIMBER(S) *under* TALL TIMBERS *n.* ❑ **break hard** *v.* [2000s] to act aggressively. ❑ **break ill** *v.* [ILL *adj.* (2)] [1980s] (*US black*) to make a mistake, to take the wrong course of action. ❑ **break it big** *v.* [1950s] (*Aus.*) to win heavily, esp. when gambling. ❑ **break over** *v. see* BREAK OUT *v.* (4). ❑ **break weak** *v.* [20C+] (*US*) to act in a cowardly manner. ❑ **break wide** *v.* [20C+] (*US black*) **1** to lose interest. **2** to leave in a hurry.

break *v.*[3] [SE *break away (from)*] [late 19C–1900s] to cut, to ignore deliberately, to snub.

break *v.*[4] [late 19C+] to give change for a note or large-denomination coin.

break *v.*[5] [? to make blood 'break out' in a blush] [20C+] (*Ulster*) to embarrass.

break *v.*[6] [BREAK *n.*[1] (1)] [1960s] (*US prison*) to ask for or receive leniency for a violation.

break *v.*[7] [1980s] (*US*) to seize and use a gun.

break a leg *v.* **1** [mid-19C] to seduce. **2** [1900s–30s] (*US*) to be arrested. **3** [1910s–50s] (*orig. US*) to hurry.

break a leg! *excl.* [theatrical superstition outlaws the actual phr. 'good luck'; note Ger. *Hals-und-Bein bruch* (May you break your neck and leg)] [1950s+] usu. to an actor, good luck!

break-down *n.*[1] [a bottle 'breaks down' into several such measures] [mid-18C–1900s] (*Aus.*) a measure of liquor.

break-down *n.*[2] [such weapons can be 'broken' between the barrel and the stock] [1990s+] (*US black*) a shotgun.

breakdown *n.*[1] [BREAK IT DOWN *v.*[1] (1)] [1940s+] (*US Und.*) an explanation.

breakdown *n.*[2] [the dealer 'breaks down' the price] [1990s+] (*drugs*) a $40 piece of crack cocaine sold for $20.

break down *v.*[1] [SE *breakdown*, to dismantle] **1** [20C+] (*Aus./N.Z.*) to make lighter. **2** [1980s] (*US campus*) to relax.

break down *v.*[2] (*orig. US black*) **1** [1930s] to be better than. **2** see BREAK *v.*[2] (2). **3** see BREAK IT DOWN *v.*[1] (1).

breaker *n.*[1] [SE *break in*] **1** [late 19C] (*US Und.*) a safebreaker who relies on picklocks and similar skills rather than on explosives. **2** [1900s–60s] (*Und.*) a burglar.

breaker *n.*[2] [the code-word *breaker*, signifying one's desire to join a conversation] [1970s] a Citizen's Band radio enthusiast; thus used as a term of address to initiate a radio conversation.

breakfast *n.*

SE in slang uses

IN COMPOUNDS

❑ **breakfast pipe** *n.* [mid-19C] (*US*) the gullet. ❑ **breakfast uptown** *n.* [1940s–60s] (*orig. US black*) a night in jail.

IN PHRASES

❑ **breakfast of champions** *n.* [puns on the slogan for US breakfast cereal, Wheaties, long celebrated as the *breakfast of champions*] [1990s+] **1** the labia. **2** mutual oral-genital stimulation. **3** (*US drugs*) crack cocaine. **4** amphetamine. ❑ **have someone for breakfast** *v.* **1** [mid–late 19C] (*US, West*) to discover a murdered body when one wakes in the morning. **2** [20C+] (*also* **eat someone for breakfast**) to be able to achieve a task, defeat a rival etc. ❑ **have a hearty-choke for breakfast** *v.* [pun on SE *artichoke* + *caper*; pun on *hoist*] [early 17C–late 19C] to be hanged, also extended as *have a hearty-choke for breakfast and/with caper sauce*; thus *artichoke and an oyster*, a pre-hanging breakfast. ❑ **out to breakfast** *adj.* [var. on OUT TO LUNCH *adj.*] [1990s+] (*orig. US*) **1** crazy, eccentric, weird. **2** intoxicated by drink or drugs.

breaking *n.*[1] [abbr.] [1900s] *breaking* and entering.

breaking *n.*[2] [one 'breaks out' of the status quo] [1980s] (*US black*) becoming obsessive, going to extremes.

breaking *n.*[3] [abbr. SE *breakdancing*] [1980s+] (*US*) a dance style perfected in New York's South Bronx, in which dancers spin, whirl and twist, pivoting on heads, elbows, knees etc, performed to hip-hop or rap music; also attrib.

breaking up of the spell *n.* [SPELLKEN *n.*] [19C] the end of the nightly performance at the Theatres-Royal, London; as the crowds disperse pickpockets move among them looking for valuables.

break it down *v.*[1] [SE *break down*, to dismantle, either of facts or emotions] **1** [1920s+] (*also* **break down**) to explain, to put the listener right. **2** [1930s+] (*Aus.*) to give in, to desist; to act reasonably. **3** [1980s] to speak unrestrainedly.

break it down *v.*[2] [ext. of SE *break down*, to become distraught] **1** [1930s+] (*US black*) to get excited, to become emotional. **2** [1990s+] (*US campus*) to dance.

break it off *v.* **1** [20C+] (*US*) to wound or hurt verbally. **2** [20C+] (*US black*) to have sexual intercourse. **3** [1940s–60s] (*US black*) to stop talking.

break it off in *v.* [the image is of some form of knife] [late 19C+] (*US*) to treat or hurt badly.

break it up! *excl.* [1930s+] a general admonition to stop what one is doing, e.g. to move on, to break up a meeting, of several people or a couple.

break off *v.*[1] [SE] **1** [1910s] (*US drugs*) to stop taking a narcotic drug. **2** [2000s] (*US black*) to disengage oneself from a confrontation.

break off *v.*[2] [i.e. *breaking off* a small piece of hashish and offering it as a gift] [1990s+] (*US black/campus*) **1** to share, esp. to share one's pleasures. **2** to pay.

break off one's math *v.* [2000s] (*US black*) to give out one's telephone number.

break out *v.* **1** [mid–late 19C] (*US*) to appear. **2** [mid-19C+] to break open a package and remove its contents; to get an article or articles from a place of storage. **3** [late 19C] (*US tramp*) to become a tramp. **4** [1920s+] (*also* **break over**) to become socially or sexually wild. **5** [1940s] to wake someone. **6** [1950s+] (*US black*) to leave. **7** [1960s+] to free, e.g. from prison.

break out with *v.* (*also* **bust out with**) [1980s+] (*US black/campus*) **1** to do, say or wear something surprising or exciting. **2** to produce something unexpected and/or suddenly.

breaks *n.* [1910s] (*US Und.*) any crowded area, e.g. a theatre exit, which offers opportunities to a pickpocket.

break someone's face *v.* (*also* **change someone's face, ...head, rearrange someone's face, ... teeth**) **1** [late 19C+] (*US*) to beat someone up. **2** in fig. uses. (**a**) [1970s] (*US gay*) to surprise someone. (**b**) [1990s+] (*US black*) to hurt someone's feelings.

break-up *n.* [BREAK UP *v.* (2)] [1920s+] (*Aus.*) anyone or anything considered highly amusing or risible.

break up *v.* **1** [late 19C–1930s] (*US*) to make someone very upset, to make one ill with tension, to cause someone to cry. **2** [late 19C+] (*orig. US*) to cause someone to laugh or applaud heartily. **3** [20C+] (*US*) to act hysterically, to act irrationally. **4** [1920s+] (*also* **break**) to collapse in laughter. **5** [1960s] to reduce someone to tears.

breakyleg *n.*[1] (*also* **breaky**) [ety. unknown; ? the price of BREAKYLEG *n.*[2]] [mid-19C] a shilling (5p).

breakyleg *n.*[2] [the concept is an old one. Hotten (1860) notes that 'in the ancient Egyptian language the determinative character in the hieroglyphic verb 'to be drunk' has the significant form of the leg of man being amputated'; also dial. phr. 'been to Bungay fair and broken both his legs', he is drunk] [mid-19C] strong drink, esp. whisky; thus *break one's leg*, to become badly drunk.

bream *n.* [the use of fish to denote varying sizes, as are the fish themselves, of glass; note a similar form of ranking used by British Rail freight wagons, which were labelled *trout*, *perch*, *whale* etc] [1970s] (*US*) a half-pint (300ml) of liquor.

breast fleet *n.* [the beating of their breasts during certain prayers] [late 18C–early 19C] Roman Catholics, seen as a group.

breast-plate *n.* [late 19C] (*US*) a tie that masks a dirty shirt.

breast (up to) *v.* [20C+] (*Aus.*) to accost; thus *breast the bar*, to walk up to a bar to order a drink.

breastworks *n.* [pun on SE] [early 19C+] the female breasts.

breath-and-britches *n.* [breath that smells of liquor and britches that are constantly being dropped at another woman's bedside] **1** [1920s–30s; 2000s] (*US black*) a ne'er-do-well, an untrustworthy, disreputable man. **2** [2000s] a very thin person.

breathe down someone's neck *v. see under* NECK *n.*

breather *n.* **1** [mid-19C] (*US*) something superlative [? it makes one draw a breath in awe]. **2** [1910s] a lung. **3** [1940s+] one who makes a phonecall, saying nothing and merely breathing, usu. for sexual pleasure. **4** [1950s–70s] the nose.

breathe someone's air *v. see under* AIR *n.*

bredren *n.* (*also* **bredrin**) [SE *brethren* + biblical overtones of Rastafarian *bredren*] [1990s+] (*W.I./UK black*) a friend.

bree *n.* [ety. unknown] [1930s–70s] (*US black/Harlem*) a young woman.

breech *n.* [citations are inconsistent as to the front or back pockets, although usage may simply have reversed over time from back to front] [1900s–20s] (*US Und.*) a trouser pocket.

IN COMPOUNDS

❑ **breech hook** *n. see* HOOK *n.*[1] (2a).

breech *v.* [1930s] (*UK Und.*) to steal from someone's trousers.

breeched *adj.* (*also* **breached, britched**) [i.e. having money in one's *breeches*; Egan further defines *well-breeched* as 'a cant phrase for persons who possess all the comforts of life — i.e., who have lots of money'] [19C] (*UK Und.*) financially well-off, materially comfortable.

breeches *n.*

SE in slang uses

IN PHRASES

❑ **don't get your breeches torn** [1960s] (*US*) don't get yourself over-excited. ❑ **have buttered eggs in one's breeches** *v.* [mid-17C–18C] to soil one's trousers through a sudden attack of terror. ❑ **have one's sitting breeches on** *v.* (*also* **wear one's sitting breeches**) [late 18C–early 19C] to outstay one's welcome.

breechloader *n.* [pun on SE *breechloader*, a firearm loaded at the back of the bore + *breech*, the anus] [1910s] one who is sodomized, usu. a male homosexual.

breechy *adj.* [dial. *breachy*, of cattle, liable to break through the pasture fence] [20C+] (*US*) of a woman, immoral.

breed *n.* [abbr.] [late 19C+] (*orig. US*) a half-*breed*, a derog. term for a Native American; also attrib.

breed *v.* **1** [1970s+] (*W.I.*) to impregnate. **2** [1990s+] (*US campus*) to have sex.

breed a black eye (for oneself) *v.* [1960s] (*US*) to stir up trouble for oneself.

breed a scab (on one's nose) *v.* [someone is likely to punch your nose] [20C+] (*US*) to stir up trouble for oneself.

breeded up *adj.* [BREED v.] [2000s] (*UK black*) pregnant.

breeder *n.* [note Shakespeare *III Henry IV* II i: 'You love the breeder (i.e. a child-bearing woman) better than the male'] **1** [1930s] (*US Und*) a master criminal [? they *breed* new crimes]. **2** [1980s] (*US campus*) one who is in a steady relationship. **3** [1980s+] (*gay*) a heterosexual, esp. one who favours child-rearing. **4** [1990s+] (*gay*) a married homosexual who produces children.

breeder-belt *n.* [BREEDER *n.* (3)] [1990s+] (*Aus. gay*) the suburbs.

breeding-cage *n.* [late 19C] a matrimonial bed.

breefs *n. see* BRIEF *n.* (1).

breeker *n. see* BREKER *n.*

breeze *n.*[1] **1** in spoken contexts. (**a**) [late 18C–1940s] an argument, a disturbance, a quarrel; thus *have a breeze in one's breech*, to be disturbed, confused. (**b**) [late 19C–1950s] a rumour, a scandal. (**c**) [1910s] (*US Und.*) a confidence trickster's patter. (**d**) [1930s+] (*US*) empty chatter. **2** referring to the breeze as uncontrollable, insubstantial, offering no barriers. (**a**) [1910s+] (*Aus./W.I.*) freedom; thus *give me breeze, give it a breeze*, leave me in peace, give me some room. (**b**) [1920s+] anything easy, simple, no problems, usu. as phr. *it's a breeze, (go) like a breeze*. **3** [1930s–40s] (*US black*) a great extent, a large amount. **4** [1970s+] (*US black*) a relaxed person; a smart, fashionable person. **5** [2000s] (*US campus*) something of no importance.

IN COMPOUNDS

▫ **breeze-puncher** *n.* [*BAT THE BREEZE* below] [1910s] (*US*) an excessive talker.

IN PHRASES

▫ **back the breeze** *v.* [1950s] (*US*) to chatter, to gossip. ▫ **bat the breeze** *v.* [1930s+] (*orig. Aus./US milit.*) to chatter, to gossip. ▫ **beat the breeze** *v.* [1940s+] (*US*) to chatter, to gossip. ▫ **fan the breeze** *v.* **1** [20C+] (*US*) to chatter, to gossip. **2** *see also under* SE phrs. below. **3** *see* BREEZE *v.*[1] (1). ▫ **kick up a breeze** *v.* (*also* **raise a breeze**) [late 18C+] to make a fuss, to cause trouble. ▫ **not have a breeze** *v.* [2000s] (*Irish*) not have a chance. ▫ **shoot the breeze** *v.* [1930s+] (*orig. US*) to gossip, to talk idly.

SE in slang uses

IN COMPOUNDS

▫ **breeze-up** *n.* [play on *GET THE WIND UP under* WIND *n.*[2]] [1910s] (*Aus.*) fear.

IN PHRASES

▫ **cop a breeze** *v. see* BREEZE *v.*[1] (5). ▫ **fan the breeze** *v.* **1** [late 19C+] (*US*) to go fast, orig. on horseback. **2** *see also under* sl. phrs. above. **3** *see* BREEZE *v.*[1] (1). ▫ **get the breeze up** *v.* (*also* **have the..., put the...**) [1920s+] to worry, to disturb. ▫ **gi' me breeze** *n.* [1950s+] (*W.I.*) ragged, torn, old work clothes (through which the wind blows). ▫ **give someone the breeze** *v.* [var. on *GIVE SOMEONE THE AIR under* AIR *n.*] [1930s+] (*orig. US*) to dismiss, to reject, esp. when ending a love affair. ▫ **hit the breeze** *v.* [late 19C+] (*N.Z./US*) to depart, to travel, to run fast. ▫ **punch the breeze** *v.* [1900s–40s] (*US*) to leave. ▫ **under breeze** *adv.* [sailing imagery] [20C+] (*W.I.*) very fast.

breeze *n.*[2] [ety. unknown; ? it is as insubstantial as a SE *breeze*] [1950s+] (*W.I.*) small change, anything less than a shilling.

breeze *n.*[3] [COOL BREEZE *n.* (1) / COOL BREEZE! *excl.*] **1** [1960s+] (*US black/campus*) a person, esp. as a greeting, 'Breeze!'. **2** [2000s] (*US campus*) a non-commital, sarcastic response; also as *adj.*, silly.

breeze *v.*[1] **1** [late 19C+] (*US*) (*also* **fan the breeze**) to escape from an institution, also as *n.*, an escape. **2** [20C+] (*US*) to appear, to arrive, usu. as *breeze in*. **3** [20C+] (*Aus.*) (*also* **breeze it, breeze through, breeze in**) to do something easily; to remain calm, relax. **4** [1910s+] (*US*) to go fast. **5** [1910s+] (*US*) (*also* **cop a breeze**) to leave, to go away; thus (*US*) *breeze off*, go away, leave me alone, (*W.I.*) *breeze me a bit*, go away, leave me in peace, (*W.I.*) *breeze me ase* (ears), shut up, be quiet.

breeze *v.*[2] [BREEZE *n.*[1] (1d)] **1** [1910s–30s] (*US tramp*) to deceive. **2** [1950s] to chat.

breezer *n.*[1] **1** [1920s–50s] (*US*) an open-topped car. **2** [1970s+] (*Aus.*) the act of breaking wind.

IN PHRASES

▫ **breezer to sneezer** *adv.* (*also* **sneezer to breezer**) [late 19C+] (*Aus.*) from nose to tail.

breezer *n.*[2] [BREEZE *n.*[1] (5)] [2000s] (*US campus*) an unpopular, second-rate person.

breezing *n.* [*BACK THE BREEZE under* BACK *v.*[2]] [mid-19C] (*US*) a scolding, a telling-off.

breezy *n.* [BREEZY *adj.*[1] (5)] [1990s+] (*US juv.*) a girl or young woman, presumably attractive.

breezy *adj.*[1] **1** [mid-19C] (*US*) drunk. **2** [late 19C+] bright and cheery, sometimes too loud and bumptious. **3** [20C+] (*Aus.*) short-tempered. **4** [1990s+] (*UK black*) of a place, smart, fashionable. **5** [2000s] (*US black*) of a woman, attractive.

breezy *adj.*[2] [*GET THE WIND UP under* WIND *n.*[2]] [1910s+] frightened, fearful.

breezy *adj.*[3] [BREEZE *n.*[1] (2b)] [1960s] (*US campus*) easy, simple.

breezy bertie *n.* [BREEZY *adj.*[1] (2) + generic name] [1920s] a brash, self-confident, insensitive young man.

breg *n.* [ety. unknown; poss. misreading of BUG *n.*[5] (2)] [1900s] (*US Und.*) any form of counterfeit scar or wound used to help in begging.

brek *n. see* BREKKIE *n.*

breker *n.* (*also* **breeker**) [Afk. *breek*, to break] [1970s+] (*S.Afr.*) **1** a tough, macho man, a fighter. **2** a motorbike rider dressed in the classic 'leathers', jeans, boots etc.

brekker *n.* (*also* **brekkers**) [SE *break(fast)* + -ER *sfx*] [late 19C+] breakfast.

brekkie *n.* (*also* **brekky, brek**) **1** [1920s+] breakfast. **2** [1980s] (*UK prison*) breakfast as the last meal before release from prison.

brekky bong *v.* [BREKKIE *n.* (1) + BONG *n.*[1]] [1980s+] (*Aus. drugs*) to smoke cannabis as soon as one wakes up.

bremmalow *n.* [ety. unknown] [2000s] (*US black*) an unattractive female.

Brenda *n.* [1980s] (*gay*) a conventional person.

brenda *n.* (*also* **brenda bracelets, Brenda Star**) [joc. assonance, but note BRENDA *n.*] [1980s] (*camp gay*) a police officer, usu. male.

Brenda Bris *n.* [Heb. *bris*, the circumcision ceremony] [2000s] (*S.Afr. gay*) a circumcised man.

Brenda Frickers *n.* [rhy. sl.; ult. Irish movie actress *Brenda Fricker* (1945–)] [1990s+] knickers.

Brenda Star *n. see* BRENDA *n.*

Brenda Starr *n.* [the epon. strip cartoon] [1970s] (*US camp gay*) a journalist.

brer *n.* [SE *brother*] [late 19C+] (*UK black*) a fellow black person.

br'er nancy *n.* [*Br'er*, brother + *Anansie*, the folk-tale hero, who escapes trouble through lying] [20C+] (*W.I.*) an untrustworthy, cunning person.

brethren of the brush *n. see BROTHER OF THE BRUSH under* BROTHER (OF THE)... *n.*

brevet wife *n.* [SE *brevet*, a nominal rank that confers extra authority but no extra pay] [late 19C] a woman with whom a man cohabits, but to whom he is not legally married.

brew *n.*[1] **1** [late 19C–1920s] a meal. **2** [late 19C+] a pot or drink of tea, thus *rush a brew*, make a pot of tea. **3** [1900s] (*US*) any form of home-made concoction. **4** [20C+] (*US*) (*also* **brewster**) beer, ale, esp. in the UK Carlsberg Special Brew, poss. the strongest canned beer on sale in the UK. **5** [1910s+] (*US*) a pot or cup of coffee; thus *cup of brew*, one's preference. **6** [1960s] home-made wine. **7** [1970s+] (*Can./US/ N.Z. prison*) (*also* **homebrew**) illicitly brewed alcohol.

(DERIVATIVES)

❑ **brewski** *n.* (*also* **brewsky**) [-SKI *sfx*] [1980s+] (*US campus*) a can or drink of beer.

(IN COMPOUNDS)

❑ **brew dog** *n.* [DOG *n.*[7] (1)] **1** [1980s+] (*US campus*) (a bottle of) beer. **2** (*also* **brew dogger**) a heavy beer drinker. ❑ **brewhound** *n.* [-HOUND *sfx*] [1980s+] (*US campus*) a regular drunkard (but not an actual alcoholic). ❑ **brew house** *n.* [SE *house*; orig. SE *brewhouse*, a brewery] [1980s] (*US black*) a liquor store.

(IN PHRASES)

❑ **brew up** *see* separate entries. ❑ **crack a brew** *v.* [CRACK *v.*[2] (2b)] [1990s+] to open a beer.

brew *n.*[2] *see* BUROO *n.*

brew *v.* [1950s+] (*drugs*) to prepare heroin for injection by heating with water in a spoon or bottle cap.

(IN PHRASES)

❑ **brew with hops** *v.* [1950s] (*US drugs*) to inject (a solution of) opium into the median cephalic vein.

brewed *adj.* [BREW *n.*[1] (4)] [1980s] (*US campus*) drunk.

brewer's... *n.*

SE in slang uses

(IN COMPOUNDS)

❑ **brewer's asthma** *n.* [play on SE *brewer's asthma*, a disease that is caused by malt contamination] [1950s+] (*Aus./N.Z.*) **1** shortness of breath. **2** (*also* **brewer's croup**) a very bad hangover. ❑ **brewer's droop** *n.* [SE *droop*] [1960s+] (*orig. Aus.*) temporary impotence due to the effects of alcohol on the erectile tissue. ❑ **brewer's fizzle** *n.* [early 18C] beer, ale. ❑ **brewer's goitre** *n.* [SE *goitre*, a swelling on the neck] [1950s+] (*Aus./N.Z.*) a beer belly.

brewer's horse *n.* (*also* **brewer's dog**) [i.e. one who has fig. been 'bitten by the brewer's horse'] [late 16C–17C] a drunkard, a state of drunkeness.

(IN PHRASES)

❑ **drive the brewer's horse** *v.* [late 16C–17C] to be drunk.

brewery *n.* [BREW *v.*] [1950s+] (*drugs*) a place to buy and smoke opium.

brewha *n.* (*also* **brewhaha**) [puns on BREW *n.*[1] (4) + SE *brouhaha*] [1970s+] (*US campus*) a can or drink of beer.

brewising the bed *phr.* (*also* **bruising the bed**) [supposed similarity of the mess to SE *brewis*, a broth made from beef and vegetables or the fat scum from the pot in which salt beef has been boiled] [late 18C] fouling one's bed.

brewster *n. see* BREW *n.*[1] (4).

brewstered *adj.* [BREWSTER'S *n.*] [2000s] very well off.

Brewster's *n.* [the film *Brewster's Millions* (orig. 1914, most recent version 1985)] [2000s] a large amount of money.

brew-up *n.* [BREW *n.*[1]] [1940s+] (*Aus. prison*) illicit liquor, made in prison.

brew up *v.* [SE *brew-up*, the making of tea] [1990s+] (*Aus. prison*) to make illicit liquor.

brian *n. see* BRIAN O'LINN *n.*

Brian Clough *adj.* [rhy. sl.; ult. UK football player and manager *Brian Clough* (1935–2004)] [2000s] rough.

Brian O'Flynn *n.* [rhy. sl.] [20C+] gin.

Brian O'Linn *n.* (*also* **brian, Brian O'Lynn, bryan o' lin**) [rhy. sl.] [mid-19C+] gin.

briar *n.* (*US Und.*) **1** [early–mid-19C] a burglar's tool, a file, a saw. **2** [1920s–50s] a hacksaw blade.

SE in slang uses

(IN COMPOUNDS)

❑ **briar-breaker** *n.* (*also* **briar-hopper, brier-breaker, brier-hopper**) [1930s+] (*US, mainly Midland*) a rustic, a peasant, an unsophisticated person. ❑ **briar patch** *n.* [1960s] (*US*) (female) pubic hair. ❑ **briar-root** *n.* [resemblance to a SE *briar-rootpipe*] [late 19C] an ill-shaped, battered nose.

(IN PHRASES)

❑ **sweet briar** *n. see under* SWEET *adj.*[1].

brick *n.* [the solidity of the object] **1** the lit. or fig. solidity/density of the object. (**a**) [mid-19C] (*Aus.*) in ironic use of sense 1a, a gang member, a wayward young man; thus *brickism*, the philosophy of joining and acting in a gang. (**b**) [mid-19C+] a reliable, kind, selfless person. (**c**) [late 19C] (*US campus*) courage, spirit, 'pluck'. (**d**) [late 19C] as *my brick*, a term of friendly address. (**e**) [1910s] an attractive person. (**f**) [1910s–20s] a fool. (**g**) [1960s+] (*US campus*) a mess, a failure. (**h**) *see* BRICKHOUSE *n.*[2] (1). **2** the shape of the object. (**a**) [mid–late 19C] (*US*) a punishment, performed by bringing someone's knees close up to the chin and lashing the arms tightly to the knees. (**b**) [1950s] (*US prison*) a carton of cigarettes. (**c**) [1960s+] (*drugs*) a block of opium, morphine or marijuana; usu. 1kg (2.2lb). (**d**) [1970s+] 1kg (2.2lb) of heroin. (**e**) [1970s+] (*US drugs*) 1kg (2.2lb) of cocaine or crack cocaine. (**f**) [1990s+] a large piece of excrement. (**g**) [2000s] one gram of heroin. **3** the trad. colour – red – of a brick. (**a**) [1910s+] a £10 or $10 note (which is red). (**b**) [1980s+] (*Aus. prison*) by ext. of sense 3a, a 10lb weight. (**c**) [1990s+] by ext. of sense 3a, a ten-year prison sentence.

SE in slang uses

(DERIVATIVES)

❑ **brickish** *adj.* [mid-19C] a general term of approbation; thus *brickishness*, the quality of being good-hearted or *brickish*.

(IN COMPOUNDS)

❑ **brickfielder** *n.* [orig. a thick cloud of dust brought over Sydney, New South Wales, by a south wind from neighbouring sandhills (called the 'brickfields')] [mid-19C+] (*Aus.*) **1** in Sydney, a sudden squally wind, bringing relief at the end of a hot day although sometimes accompanied by a dust-storm. **2** a hot, dusty wind that blows over parts of northern Australia. **3** a nuisance. ❑ **brick gum** *n.* [GUM *n.*[3]] (*drugs*) **1** [1930s–50s] a block of unprocessed opium. **2** [1980s+] heroin. ❑ **brickhead** *n.* [1970s] a stupid person. ❑ **bricklayer** *n.* [? SE *rubrick layer*, but F&H note, first, the medieval church official the *operarius*, the workman 'on whom devolved the charge of repairing and maintaining the sacred fabric' of a church or cathedral; and, second, the line in Ephesians that compares such early Christians as St Paul to 'master-builders' whose greatest 'building' is the Church] [late 19C] a clergyman. ❑ **brick-presser** *n.* [*HIT THE BRICKS under* BRICKS *n.*] [1920s–30s] (*US black*) a tramp, a vagrant. ❑ **bricktop** *n.* [the redness of 'typical' bricks] [mid-19C+] (*US*) a redhead.

(IN PHRASES)

❑ **have a brick in one's hat** *v.* [one is *top-heavy* (*see TOP-HEAVY under* TOP *n.*)] [mid–late 19C] (*orig. US*) to be extremely drunk. ❑ **like bricks** *adv.* [mid-19C] energetically, noisily. ❑ **sweat bricks** *v. see under* SWEAT *v.*[2].

brick *adj.* [2000s] (*US black*) of weather, cold.

brick *v.*[1] **1** [1920s] (*US Und.*) to throw a brick through a shop window in order to steal the contents. **2** [1960s] (*US*) to throw bricks, esp. at the police, the national guard or any other form of authority against whom one is demonstrating.

brick *v.*[2] (*also* **bricker**) [note bus-drivers' jargon *make a brick*, to defraud London Transport] [1960s–70s] to steal, to filch, to cheat.

brick *v.*[3] [one has 'dropped a brick'] [1980s+] (*US campus*) to fail, to receive a failing grade; to perform badly in one's work.

brick *v.*[4] [one 'builds' the fake case] [1980s+] (*Aus. prison*) to use concocted evidence to have a person imprisoned.

brick *v.*[5] [backform. f. SHIT A BRICK *v.*] [1990s+] to be terrified.

IN PHRASES

❑ **brick it** *v.* [1990s+] to be terrified, to be very nervous.

bricked *adj.* [? SE *breeched*] [late 16C–mid-17C] smartly dressed.

bricker *v. see* BRICK *v.*[2].

brickhouse *n.*[1] ['probably derived from the kind of building in which is housed the general hospital for insane soldiers at Washington, D.C.' (M'Govern, 1906)] [1900s] (*US milit.*) a psychiatric institution.

brickhouse *n.*[2] [*BUILT LIKE A BRICK SHITHOUSE under* BUILT *adj.*] [1970s+] (*US black/campus*) **1** (*also* **brick**) an attractive woman. **2** (*also* **house**) a woman with a large chest.

brickie *n.* (*also* **bricky**) [abbr.] [late 19C+] a *brick*layer.

brickie's bum *n. see* BUILDER'S BUM *n.*

bricking-A *adv. see* FUCKING-A *adv.*

bricks *n.* [1930s+] **1** the city streets, esp. seen from a prison cell. **2** the urban environment in general. **3** a street prostitute's beat.

IN PHRASES

❑ **beat the bricks** *v.* [1920s+] (*US*) to walk the streets, esp. when in search of work. ❑ **hit the bricks** *v.* (*also* **pad the bricks, pound the bricks**) (*orig. US*) **1** [20C+] to exit, to leave for the street, to start walking. **2** [1930s+] to be discharged from a prison sentence. **3** [1940s] to go on strike. **4** [1960s+] to walk the streets all night, through homelessness. ❑ **on the brick** (*also* **on the pavement. on the sidewalk**) **1** [1930s+] (*US*) on the street after being released from prison or hospital. **2** [1960s+] (*drugs*) walking the streets searching for drugs. **3** [1970s+] working as a street prostitute. ❑ **press the bricks** *v.* [20C+] (*US*) **1** to stand around in the street, loafing and gossiping. **2** to walk the streets in search of work. ❑ **to the bricks** *adv.* [1920s+] (*US black*) to the limit, to the furthest extent. ❑ **walk the bricks** *v.* [metonymy] **1** [20C+] to wander around. **2** [1980s+] (*US police*) to patrol on foot.

bricks and mortar *n.*[1] [metonymy] **1** [late 19C+] a house, a building, property in general, esp. as an image of secure investment. **2** [1960s] (*US*) school books.

bricks and mortar *n.*[2] [rhy. sl.] [20C+] a daughter.

Bricky *n.* [2000s] (*UK black*) Brixton, south London.

bricky *adj.*[1] [BRICK *n.* (1b)] [mid–late 19C] plucky, courageous.

bricky *adj.*[2] [*HAVE A BRICK IN ONE'S HAT under* BRICK *n.*] [mid–late 19C] tipsy.

bridal chamber *n.* [1930s] **1** (*US tramp*) a very cheap lodging house. **2** a police station cell.

bridal suite *n.* [it is seen as encouraging prison homosexuality] [1970s+] (*N.Z. prison*) a two-man cell.

briddy *n.* [? proper name *Bridy*, i.e. Bridget, or SE *bride*] [1990s+] (*US black*) a woman.

bride *n.* **1** [late 19C–1930s] a prostitute. **2** [1910s+] a woman, esp. a girlfriend.

bride and groom *n.*[1] [rhy. sl.] **1** [late 19C–1960s] a broom. **2** [20C+] a room.

bride and groom *n.*[2] [1920s+] (*orig. US short-order jargon*) two poached or fried eggs.

bride's nightie *n.*

IN PHRASES

❑ **off like a bride's nightie** *adv.* (*also* **up and down...**) *see under* OFF LIKE A... *phr.*

bridge *n.* [differing senses of SE *bridge a gap*] **1** [1920s+] (*N.Z.*) a glance, a look. **2** [1920s+] (*Aus.*) an introduction. **3** [1930s+] (*Aus.*) a plausible excuse.

SE in slang uses

IN PHRASES

❑ **chuck a bridge** *v.* (*also* **put on a bridge**) [SE *bridge*; i.e. the crotch of her knickers] [1970s+] (*Aus./N.Z.*) of a woman, to reveal her underwear (inadvertently or otherwise). ❑ **make a bridge of someone's nose** *v. see under* NOSE *n.*

bridge *v.*[1] [the image is of two confederates getting together to throw a third party from a (metaphorical) bridge] [19C] (*UK Und.*) **1** to double-cross, to betray (a confidence). **2** in gambling to deceive one's backer by deliberately losing the game.

bridge *v.*[2] (*also* **bring up**) [1930s+] (*drugs*) to ready a vein for injection, by making it swell out of the surrounding flesh.

bridge *v.*[3] **1** [1960s] (*Aus.*) to look at something. **2** [1980s+] (*Aus. prison*) to show off; to gesture as if threatening a fight.

bridge and tunnel (people) *n.* (*also* **bridge and tunnel crowd**) [1980s+] (*US*) used by Manhattanites to describe those who live in the outer boroughs (Queens, Brooklyn, Long Island) or New Jersey and travel to Manhattan via the Holland Tunnel (New Jersey) or over the East Side bridges; ext. to other cities, e.g. San Francisco.

bridget *n.* [proper name *Bridget*, a popular Irish name and thus common among the Irish maids of New York] [mid-19C–1920s] (*Aus./US*) a servant girl.

bridget *v.* [BRIDGET *n.*; Ware notes that the late 19C Fenians commonly used such servants to 'launder' their otherwise illicit funds] [mid-19C–1900s] (*orig. US*) to obtain money from servant girls by false pretences.

bridgewater *n.* [? anecdotal] [1900s–10s] (*Aus. Und.*) a counterfeit banknote or cheque.

bridle-cull *n.* [SE *bridle* + CULL *n.*[1] (3)] [early 18C–mid-19C] (*UK Und.*) a highwayman.

bridle-string *n.* (*also* **bridle**) [it is attached to the 'head' of the penis] [mid-17C–18C] the frenum or ligament of the penis.

brief *n.* [Lat. *breve*, a letter or note; ult. f. *brevis*] **1** [late 17C–mid-19C] (*also* **breefs**) a pack of doctored playing cards; the edges have been carefully trimmed to indicate, to the cheat, which cards are high [Ger. *Briefe*, a playing card (itself f. Lat.)]. **2** [mid-19C] a raffle ticket. **3** [mid-19C–1920s] a pawnbroker's ticket. **4** [mid-19C+] a ticket in general (bus, tube etc); thus *brief-puncher*, ticket collector; *brief jigger*, ticket office. **5** [late 19C] any form of false document, typically a reference or recommendation. **6** [late 19C–1910s] a betting slip. **7** [late 19C+] (*UK Und.*) a note or letter. **8** [late 19C+] a licence. **9** [20C+] (*Anglo-Irish*) a banknote. **10** [1930s] (*UK Und.*) a revoked parole. **11** [1930s+] a barrister, whose legal commissions are their briefs. **12** [1940s+] a (stolen) cheque. **13** [1960s] (*Aus.*) a union card; a letter on official paper. **14** [1960s+] (*UK police*) a warrant to arrest or search.

brief *adj.* [i.e. 'no frills'] [late 19C] (*US black*) elegant, well-dressed, smart.

briefcase brigade *n.* [1980s+] (*Aus. prison*) civilian staff members, with overtones of 'do-gooding'.

brief-snatcher *n.* (*also* **duket-snatching**) [BRIEF *n.* (6) + SE *snatcher*] [late 19C] a pickpocket who specializes in stealing from members of a racecourse crowd.

brier-breaker/-hopper *n. see under* BRIAR *n.*

brierpatch child *n.* [the image of a brierpatch as being secluded and thus safe for an illegitimate delivery; note US dial. *lap child*, the youngest child, still confined to their mother's lap, a spoiled child; *yard child*, a child old enough to play in the yard] [1950s–60s] (*US*) an illegitimate child.

briers *n.*

IN PHRASES

❑ **in the briers** *adj.* [SE *brier*, a thorny, prickly bush, thus implying difficulty] [16C–18C] in trouble, in difficulties.

brig *n.* [orig. sited between the two forward guns on the starboard side of the gun-deck] **1** [mid-19C+] (*orig. US naut.*) a prison; a police station. **2** [1930s] (*US Und.*) a solitary confinement cell.

brig *v.* [BRIG *n.*] [1920s–50s] (*US milit.*) to imprison.

brigade *n.* [mid-19C+] any collection of supposedly like-minded individuals, e.g. the *dirty mac brigade*, middle-aged men with a taste for pornography.

briggity *adj.* (*also* **brigity**) [BIGGITY *adj.*, but ? link to SE *brag*, to boast] [late 19C–1920s] (*US*) arrogant, self-opinionated.

brigg's rest *n.* [rhy. sl.] [20C+] a vest.

brigh *n.* [mid–late 19C] (*UK Und.*) a trouser pocket; thus *brighful*, a pocketful.

Brigham Young *n.* [rhy. sl.; ult. Mormon founder *Brigham Young* (1801–77)] [2000s] the tongue.

bright *n.* [note poetic use of 13C–19C SE *bright*, brightness, light] **1** [20C+] (*US black*) a light-skinned black person. **2** [1930s–70s] (*US black*) a day, daylight, morning. **3** [1960s] (*US*) in pl., headlights. **4** [1970s] (*US black*) in pl., the eyes. **5** *see* BRIGHT BOY *under* BRIGHT *adj.*

IN PHRASES

❑ **late bright** *n.* [1950s] (*US black*) the evening. ❑ **set of seven brights** *n.* [1930s–40s] (*US black*) seven days, a week. ❑ **strike a bright** *v. see under* STRIKE *v.*

bright *adj.* [SE *bright*, clever] [1980s+] (*W.I.*) daring, precocious.

SE in slang uses

IN COMPOUNDS

❑ **bright boy** *n.* (*also* **bright, bright light**) [late 19C+] (*orig. US*) often used ironically, a clever person, a 'know-it-all'. ❑ **bright disease** *n.* [1950s] (*US black*) knowing too much. ❑ **bright eyes** *n.* **1** [1930s–60s] (*US prison*) a lookout. **2** [1960s] (*US campus*) used ironically, an incompetent, a blunder. ❑ **bright-skin** *n.* [ext. BRIGHT *n.* (1)] [1930s+] (*US black*) a light-skinned black or white person. ❑ **bright spark** *n. see under* SPARK *n.* ❑ **bright specimen** *n.* [late 19C] a term, based on irony, for a lively, energetic person.

IN PHRASES

❑ **bright in the eye** *adj.* [late 19C–1920s] tipsy, drunk.

bright and frisky *n.* [rhy. sl.] [1940s–60s] whisky.

brightening *n.* [BRIGHT *n.* (2)] [1940s] (*US black*) dawn.

Brighton line *n.* [rhy. sl.] [20C+] (*bingo*) the number nine.

Brighton pier *adj.* (*also* **Chelsea pier**) [rhy. sl. = *queer*/QUEER *adj.* (4)] **1** [mid-19C+] peculiar, strange. **2** [1950s+] homosexual.

Brighton pier *v.* [rhy. sl. = SE *disappear*] [1990s+] to leave, to run off.

Brighton rock *n.* [rhy. sl.] **1** [1940s+] the penis [COCK *n.*[3] (1)]. **2** [1990s+] a courtoom dock.

brigity *adj. see* BRIGGITY *adj.*

brill *adj.* (*also* **brillo**) [1970s+] wonderful, excellent.

brill! *excl.* (*also* **brillo!**) [SE *brilliant!*] [1980s+] wonderful! excellent!

brilliant *n.* [SE *brilliant*, having showy good qualities] [1940s–60s] (*gay*) an obviously, exaggeratedly homosexual man; thus as adj., *brilli*, effeminately sentimental.

brilliant *adj.* [early 19C; 1940s+] (*US campus*) excellent, worthy of admiration.

brilliant (stark-naked) *n.* [it shines in the glass] [early–mid-19C] raw, undiluted gin.

brillo *n. see* BRILLOHEAD *n.*

brillo *adj. see* BRILL *adj.*

brillo! *excl. see* BRILL! *excl.*

brillohead *n.* (*also* **brillo**) [brandname of *Brillo*, a pan scourer + SE *-head*] [1980s+] **1** a derog. term for a black person. **2** (*orig. US campus*) a person with very coarse hair.

brillo pad *n.* [2000s] (*Irish*) a sanitary towel.

brim *n.*[1] [abbr. SE *brimstone*; in both cases she is 'hot'] **1** [late 17C–1910s] an abandoned or promiscuous woman. **2** [late 18C–19C] (*also* **brimmer**) a termagant.

brim *n.*[2] **1** [1960s–80s] (*US black*) a hat. **2** [1990s+] the flesh at the base of one's glans penis.

brim *v.* [dial. *brim*, of a boar, to have intercourse with a sow] [late 17C–early 18C] of a man, to have sexual intercourse.

brimmer *n.* **1** [mid-17C–early 18C] a broad-brimmed hat. **2** [mid-17C–19C] a brimming glass. **3** *see* BRIM *n.*[1] (2).

brimstone *n.* [SE *brimstone*, sulphur; this brimstone is 'hot stuff'] **1** [late 17C–18C] a prostitute. **2** [mid-19C] a termagant; also attrib.

brimstone buster *n.* (*also* **brimstone peddler**) [SE *brimstone*, hellfire + *buster*, a breaker or smasher] [19C] (*US*) a ranting preacher.

brindle *n.* [SE *brindled*, usu. of an animal, streaked] [1900s–50s] (*Aus.*) a half-caste; also attrib.

brindle *v.* [? SE *bridle*, to draw back resentfully, to exhibit an offended air] [1950s+] (*W.I. Rasta*) to be angry.

brine/briney *n. see* BRINY *n.*

bring *v.* [euph.] **1** [early 19C] to steal. **2** [20C+] (*also* **bring down**) to get or be given a prison sentence. **3** [1970s] to break a prisoner's rebellious nature through punishment.

SE in slang uses

IN COMPOUNDS

❑ **bring-and-carry** *n. see* CARRY-GO-BRING-COME *n.*

IN PHRASES

❑ **bring...** *v. see also under* relevant n. ❑ **bring drama** *v.* [1990s+] (*US campus*) to be very serious. ❑ **bring-go-bring-come** *n. see* CARRY-GO-BRING-COME *n.* ❑ **bring in** *v.* [1990s+] **1** to be included in a proposition or plan. **2** to receive a share of the profits. ❑ **bring it all back home** *v.* [1980s+] (*US campus*) to go out and have a good time. ❑ **bring it away** *v.* ['it' being the foetus] [20C+] to effect an abortion. ❑ **bring (it) off** *v.* [early 18C–mid-19C] (*UK Und.*) to steal; to pickpocket. ❑ **bring off (by hand)** *v. see* separate entries. ❑ **bring on** *v.* [see comment at BRING OFF *v.*] [20C+] to excite sexually. ❑ **bring oneself off** *v. see* separate entry. ❑ **bring one's hogs to a fair market** *v.* (*also* **bring one's pigs..., bring one's hogs to a fine market, ...a bonny market, ...a pretty market, ...a wrong market**) [17C–19C] to be particularly successful in one's business; also fig. and ironic; thus opp. *sell one's pigs in a bad market*, to do badly. ❑ **bring on the china** *v.* [BRING ON above + ? rhy. sl. but with what or ? pun on SE *China root*, a once-popular medicinal plant] [1900s–30s] to bring to orgasm. ❑ **bring out** *v.* **1** [late 19C] (*UK Und.*) for a senior criminal to initiate a young beginner. **2** [1940s–50s] (*US black*) to introduce a hitherto ignorant or naïve person to a faster, more sophisticated lifestyle. **3** [1940s+] (*US gay*) to introduce someone to the gay lifestyle; to recruit a male prostitute. ❑ **bring pinnock to pannock** *v.* [? dial. but none of the extant dial. meanings of *pinnock* – a small bridge or a drain or culvert, the hedge-sparrow or the blue titmouse, a sticky red clay, mixed with small stones – is relevant (*pannock* seems to be redup.); the change from 'i' to 'a' could be said to 'ruin' the word, but seems insufficient] [mid-16C–early 17C] to bring to grief, to cause to be ruined, bring something to nothing. ❑ **bring someone up** *v.* [SE *bring up short* + mid-19C SE *bring up*, to bring into the presence of authority or for examination] [1970s+] (*US black*) **1** to criticize, to tell off. **2** to explain. ❑ **bring the house down** *v.* (*also* **bring down the house**) [theatrical imagery] [mid-18C+] to delight, to gain overall approval. ❑ **bring undone** *v.* [1980s+] (*Aus. prison*) to wreck someone's plans. ❑ **bring up (by hand)** *v. see* separate entries.

bringdown *n.* [SE *bring* + DOWN *adj.*[2] (1); but note US black phr. *bring down my love on me*, make me happy] **1** [1930s+] (*orig. US*) anything depressing, either a person or a circumstance; thus as adj. depressing. **2** [1960s] (*drugs*) as ext. of sense 1 any social forces militating against the drug user's desire to attain nirvana; also attrib.

bring down *v.*[1] [SE *bring* + DOWN *adj.*[2] (1)] **1** [1930s+] (*orig. US black*) to depress. **2** [1940s+] to bring the experience of a drug to an (abrupt) end. **3** [1980s] to calm down.

bring down *v.*[2] **1** [1970s+] (*US*) to have one sent to prison; to arrest. **2** *see* BRING *v.* (2).

bringer *n. see* BRINJER *n.*

bringle *v.* [? SE *burn*/*bristle*] [1990s+] (*W.I.*) to feel annoyed, to demonstrate one's irritation.

bring off *v.* [*DSUE* suggests 'probably since 16C' (as he does for BRING ON *under* BRING *v.*) but offers no citation or further proof; nor is there any ref. in a dict. (sl. or SE) before his own although *HDAS* offers a 1675 citation] [late 17C; late 19C+] to bring to orgasm.

bring off by hand *v.* [BRING OFF *v.*] [early 19C+] to masturbate (someone else).

bring oneself off *v.* [BRING OFF *v.*] [1960s+] to masturbate.

bring up *v.*[1] [i.e. the contents of one's stomach] [early 18C+] to vomit.

bring up *v.*[2] *see* BRIDGE *v.*[2].

bring up by hand *v.* [pun] [late 19C] to achieve an erection.

brinjer *n.* (*also* **bringer**) [? Scot. *breenger*, a formidable foe, ult. f. *breenge*, to rush forward recklessly] [mid-19C–1900s] (*US*) something exceptional.

brink *v.* [1950s–70s] (*US drugs*) to buy narcotics.

brinks *n.* [SE *brings* (the money) or ? the firm of *Brinksmat* Security, used to transport large sums of cash] [1960s+] (*W.I. Rasta*) title given to a man who is supplying a woman with money.

briny *n.* (*also* **briney, brine**) [SE *brine* + sfx *-y*; its saltiness] [late 18C+] the sea; the seaside.

IN PHRASES

❑ **do the briny** *v.* **1** [mid-19C] to burst into tears; to weep. **2** [late 19C] go to the seaside.

briny *adj.* [? play on SALTY *adj.* (3)] [1940s] (*US black*) in a bad mood, angry.

Bris *n.* (*also* **Brissie, Brisso, Brissy, Brizzy**) [abbr.] [1940s+] (*Aus.*) *Bris*bane, the capital of Queensland.

brisby *n.* [SE *brise-bise*, f. Fr. *brise-bise*, windbreaker] [1910s–20s] a net or lace curtain used to cover the lower part of a (sash) window.

brisk *adj.* [SE *brisk*, sharp or smart in regard to movement] [18C–1900s] cheery, sprightly, lively.

brisk about *v.* (*also* **brisk up**) [mid-19C] to enliven, to animate.

brisket *n.*[1] [SE *brisket*, the breast of an animal] **1** [early 19C+] the human chest. **2** [20C+] in pl. the female breasts. **3** [1950s+] the penis, in combs. below.

IN COMPOUNDS

❑ **brisket-beater** *n.* [sense 1 above + SE *beater*] [late 18C–mid-19C] a Roman Catholic. ❑ **brisket-cut** *n.* [SE *cut*, a blow] [early 19C] a blow to the chest.

IN PHRASES

❑ **bare-brisket** *n.* [SE *bare*] [19C–1900s] a thin person. ❑ **bury the brisket** *v.* [1950s+] (*US*) of a man, to have sexual intercourse. ❑ **fuck a brisket** *v.* [1960s] of a man, to have intercourse by rubbing his penis between the woman's breasts.

brisket *n.*[2] [1950s–60s] (*US drugs*) a small pack of narcotics.

brisk up *v. see* BRISK ABOUT *v.*

Brissie/Brisso/Brissy *n. see* BRIS *n.*

bristle *n.*

IN PHRASES

❑ **on the bristle** [late 19C] on a spree.

bristles *n.* [mid-16C–early 19C] (*UK Und.*) dice whose weight has been altered by having bristles forced into them.

Bristol *n.* [SE *Bristol-board*, a type of pasteboard with a smooth surface, popular for printing such cards] [mid-19C–1900s] a visiting card.

proper name in slang uses

IN COMPOUNDS

❑ **Bristol champagne** *n.* [the proliferation of port-shippers based in the city] [early 19C] port. ❑ **Bristol hog** *n.* [late 18C–mid-19C] a native of Bristol. ❑ **Bristol man** *n.* [such figures would often drift towards Bristol, presumably, as a major port, conducive to villainy] [early–mid-19C] a villain, a rogue. ❑ **Bristol milk** *n.* [now a trademark of Harvey's, the Bristol sherry importers] [17C–18C] sherry, esp. rich, sweet sherry. ❑ **Bristol stone** *n.* [SE *Bristol stone*, *Bristol diamonds*, *Bristol gems*, a kind of transparent rock-crystal found in the Clifton limestone near Bristol, Avon, resembling the diamond in brilliancy] [late 17C] sham diamonds.

Bristol bits *n.* (*also* **Bristol Cities, Bristols**) [rhy. sl.; *Bristol bit* = TIT *n.*[2] (1); *Bristol City* = TITTY *n.* (1)] [1960s+] the female breasts.

Brit *n.* [abbr.] [20C+] a *Brit*on.

DERIVATIVES

❑ **Britsville** *n.* [-VILLE *sfx*[1]] [1970s] (*Aus.*) England, esp. London.

IN COMPOUNDS

❑ **Britland** *n.* [2000s] (*N.Z.*) Britain.

Brit, the *n.* [mid-19C–1900s] the Britannia Theatre, Hoxton London E1.

Brit *adj.* [abbr.] [1950s+] British.

britannia *n.* [the engraving of Britannia on the reverse of pre-decimalization pennies] [1950s] (*Aus.*) a double-headed penny used in two-up.

britannia metal *n.* [SE *britannia metal*, an alloy of tin and regulus of antimony, resembling silver in appearance; users of sense 1 ignored the underlying negative implications] **1** [19C] the erect penis. **2** [1980s] something fake, sham.

britched *adj. see* BREECHED *adj.*

britches *n.*

IN EXCLAMATIONS

❑ **keep your britches on!** *see* KEEP YOUR PANTS ON! *under* PANTS *n.*

British champagne *n.* (*also* **British champaigne**) [a tribute to the quality of the beer or a sneer at the lack of homegrown wines] [early 19C] porter, dark ale.

British navy *n.* [rhy. sl.] [1980s] (*Aus.*) gravy.

British roarer *n.* [late 19C–1900s] the lion that appears alongside the unicorn on the British national coat of arms.

Britney Spears *n.* [rhy. sl.; ult. popular singer *Britney Spears* (b.1981)] [2000s] beer(s).

Brixton riot *n.* [rhy. sl.] [2000s] a diet.

Brixton suitcase *n.* (*also* **Brixton briefcase, suitcase**) [the predominantly black area of Brixton, south London] [1970s–90s] (*UK black*) a large stereo tape recorder-cum-radio carried by youths.

Brizzy *n. see* BRIS *n.*

bro *n.*[1] (*also* **broh, brough, bruh**) [note public school use for lit. *brother* only] **1** [mid-18C+] (*orig. US black*) a brother, whether lit. or fig. (cf. BRA *n.*). **2** [1920s+] as a term, of address; esp. between blacks. **3** [1960s] black male, abbr. BROTHER *n.* (2).

bro *n.*[2] [BROGAN *n.*] [1990s+] (*US black*) a heavy, steel toecapped shoe, favoured by street gangs.

bro *n.*[3] *see* BUROO *n.*

broad *n.*[1] **1** [17C–19C] a sovereign, a 20-shilling coin. **2** [1900s] in *broad gang*, *broad joint*, a form of swindling based on betting on which of four cards will be turned over. **3** [1980s] a credit card. **4** *see* BROADS *n.* (1) and combs. for all refs. to playing cards.

IN PHRASES

❑ **beating the broads** [1910s] (*US Und.*) corrupting a conductor on any form of transportation line. ❑ **tipping the broads** [1910s] (*US Und.*) riding on a purchased transportation ticket.

broad *n.*[2] [early black use, *c.*1930s, added to an implication of a shapely, well-built woman (cf. BRACE OF BROADS *under* BRACE OF... *n.*), although this may have been a pun on the mainstream use); Gold, *A Jazz Lexicon* (1964), also suggests link to SE *broad-minded*] **1** [1910s] (*US Und.*) a female confederate. **2** [1910s+] (*mainly US*) a prostitute. **3** [1910s+] (*orig. US*) a woman; the implication is of promiscuity. **4** [1940s+] (*US prison*) (*also* **broad boy, broadski**) an effeminate male homosexual, often a prostitute; thus *broad squad*, a 'team' of homosexuals. **5** [1940s+] (*US campus*) (*also* **brodie**) an attractive woman. **6** [1970s+] (*US gay*) the buttocks.

IN PHRASES

❑ **house broad** *n.* [1940s] (*US*) a prostitute who lives and works in a hotel. ❑ **square broad** *n.* [SQUARE *adj.* (2)] [1940s–70s] (*US black/Und.*) any woman who is not a prostitute.

broad *n.*[3] [1940s] (*US black*) the human shoulder.

broad *adj.* [var. on WIDE *adj.* (1)] **1** [mid-19C–1900s] knowing, alert, 'on the ball'; if not actually criminal then willing and able to bend any rule. **2** [1990s+] (*W.I.*) physically large; socially important.

SE in slang uses

IN COMPOUNDS

❑ **broad-arsed** *adj.* [ARSE *n.* (1)] [late 19C+] having wide hips.
❑ **broadbrim** *adj.* [the broad-brimmed hats adopted by many

members of the Society of Friends] **1** [early 18C–mid-19C] a Quaker; thus *broad-brimmed*, sedate. **2** [mid–late 19C] a quiet, sedate old man, irrespective of religion. ❑ **broadbrow** *adj.* [1920s] a person of wide tastes and interests. ❑ **broad-guage lady** *adj.* [a pun on her breadth, and a ref. to the *broad-gauge* railway tracks, 7ft (1m) wide, which were abandoned when British railways were standardized at 4ft 8½in (44m) in the 1890s] [late 19C] a woman with wide hips.

IN PHRASES

❑ **broad in the beam** *adj.* [naut. jargon] [late 19C+] fat, overweight, esp. around the hips and buttocks. ❑ **broad place in the road** *n. see* WIDE PLACE IN THE ROAD *under* WIDE *adj.*

broad and shallow *n.* [*Broad Church* members of the Church of England, 'who take its formularies and doctrines in a broad or liberal sense and hold that the church should be comprehensive and tolerant' (*OED*)] [mid-19C] the 'Broad Church'.

broad boy *n. see* BROAD *n.*[2] (4).

broadcast *v.* [1920s+] to talk loudly and aggressively; also as n., and adj.

broadie *n.* [BROAD *n.*[2] (2); BROAD *n.*[2] (3)] [1930s+] (*US*) a woman; the inference is of promiscuity if not actual prostitution.

broads *n.* **1** [mid-18C+] playing cards. **2** [late 19C+] the three-card trick. **3** [1920s+] money. **4** [1970s] any form of documentation, e.g. identification papers, rations book, driving licence. **5** [1970s] credit and similar cards.

IN COMPOUNDS

❑ **broad cove** *n.* [COVE *n.* (1)] [early 19C] a card-sharp. ❑ **broad faker** *n.* [FAKER *n.* (1)] [late 19C–1900s] a card-player, usu. a cheat. ❑ **broad-faking** *n.* [*BROAD FAKER* above + sfx *-ing*] **1** [mid-19C] card-playing, esp. with a tinge of illegality/cheating. **2** [late 19C] the three-card trick. ❑ **broad-fencer** *n.* [-FENCER *sfx*] [mid-19C] (*UK Und.*) a peddler of lists of racing tips (known as 'correct cards') at horseraces. ❑ **broad mob** *n.* [MOB *n.*[2] (3)] [late 19C+] a gang of card-sharpers. ❑ **broad pitcher** *n.* [PITCHER *n.*[2] (3)] [mid–late 19C] (*UK Und.*) a street criminal one who works the three-card trick. ❑ **broad-pitching** *n.* [SE *pitch*, to throw] [mid-19C] (*US Und.*) the 'three-card trick'. ❑ **broad-player** *n.* [SE *player*] **1** [early–mid-19C] an expert card-player. **2** [late 19C+] a card-sharp. ❑ **broadsman** *n.* (*also* **broadman**) [SE *man*] [mid-19C+] a card-sharp. ❑ **broad spieler** *n.* [SPIELER *n.* (1)] [1910s] (*US Und.*) the conductor of a THREE-CARD MONTE *n.* game. ❑ **broad tosser** *n.* [SE *tosser*] [1920s+] (*US*) a card-sharp; a THREE-CARD MONTE *n.* dealer. ❑ **broad worker** *n.* [WORKER *n.*[1] (1)] (*UK Und.*) a card-sharp.

IN PHRASES

❑ **fake the broads** *v.* (*also* **work the broads**) [19C] to cheat at cards, to perform the three-card trick. ❑ **spread the broads** *v.* [? the 'breadth' of the piece of card; but note G. Parker (1789), 'who are continually looking out for flats in order to do upon them the broads,' implying a play on FLAT *n.*[2] (1), although note also FLAT *n.*[1] (1), i.e. dice] [mid-19C+] to play cards, esp. to cheat or to play a swindling game such as find the lady; one fans out the cards across the table for the punters to make their choice.

broadski *n. see* BROAD *n.*[2] (4).

Broadway *n.* [2000s] (*US prison*) the ground floor of a prison; it offers more space (sometimes used for overflow housing) than the upper tiers of landings outside the cells.

proper name in slang uses

IN COMPOUNDS

❑ **Broadway battleship** *n.* [1910s] (*orig. US black*) a New York City streetcar. ❑ **Broadway hello** *n.* [1930s] (*US Und.*) a friendly greeting that prefaces a homicidal attack. ❑ **Broadway Joe** *n.* [*Broadway*, New York City's entertainment centre + JOE *n.*[1] (1b)/the proper name] [late 19C+] (*US*) (*also* **Broadway boy**) a well-dressed idler, living off his wits and, when possible, gullible women.

broady *n.* [SE *broadcloth*, 'fine, plain-wove, dressed, double width, black cloth, used chiefly for men's garments' (*OED*)] [mid–late 19C] **1** cloth. **2** (*UK Und.*) anything considered worth stealing.

broady-worker *n.* [BROADY *n.* + SE *worker*/WORKER *n.*[1] (1)] [mid-19C–1910s] (*UK Und.*) a criminal who sells third-rate cloth as the finest material or stolen goods as legitimate.

broccoli *n.* [supposed similarity to the green vegetable] [1980s+] **1** (*drugs*) marijuana. **2** (*US*) pubic hair.

brodie *n.*[1] (*also* **Brodie**) [Steve *Brodie*, a 23-year-old New York saloon-keeper who on 23 July 1886 allegedly leaped some 45m (135ft) from the city's Brooklyn Bridge in order to win a $200 wager. He survived the fall and was scooped out of the East River by a friend in a small boat. He was subseq. charged by the police with attempted suicide. Whether he actually made the jump remains unproven (the witnesses, all of them his friends, claimed that he did, but the general consensus was that a dummy was tossed over the bridge and Brodie, hiding on shore, quickly swam underwater to the point where it had hit the river, in time to be 'rescued'). This scepticism is reflected in theatrical jargon; a *brodie*, a (much touted) flop] **1** [late 19C+] (*US*) a jump, a leap, a dive. **2** [1910s+] (*US*) long odds; a chance. **3** [1930s–50s] (*US drugs*) any form of faked illness, usu. some kind of fit, whereby a user attempts to get narcotics from a doctor. **4** [1930s–60s] (*US*) an error, a failure. **5** [1950s+] a tight turn; a spin made by a skidding vehicle.

IN PHRASES

❑ **pull a Brodie** *v.* **1** [1920s] to jump. **2** [1940s] (*US*) to fail. ❑ **take a Brodie** *v.* (*also* **do a Brodie**) **1** [late 19C+] to attempt a dangerous, foolhardy stunt, esp. a dive or leap and esp. one that ends in failure; in fig. use, to take a chance. **2** [1920s] (*also* **throw a Brodie**) to have a metaphorical fit. **3** [1920s] to fail, to slip back into bad habits. **4** [1920s+] to commit suicide, esp. to throw oneself off a building or bridge or jump out of a window. **5** [1940s] to fall.

brodie *n.*[2] *see* BROAD *n.*[2] (5).

brodie *v.* (*also* **Brodie**) [BRODIE *n.*[1]] **1** [1920s] to take a chance. **2** [1930s+] (*US*) to blunder, to fail. **3** [1960s] (*US*) of a vehicle, to spin, to skid. **4** [1990s+] (*US*) to jump, usu. from a building or bridge, often with the intention of suicide.

brogan *n.* [Irish and Gaelic *brògan*, dimin. of *bròg*, shoe] [mid-19C+] (*US*) a shoe, esp. a stout, coarse shoe (often as issued to US prisoners).

broganeer *n.* (*also* **broganier**) [SE *brogue*, the Irish accent] [late 18C–early 19C] one who has a noticeable Irish accent; also attrib.

broggy *n.* [mis-reading of BRODIE *n.*[1] (5)] [2000s] (*Aus.*) a skid mark on the road, thus *do a broggy*, to skid and produce a mark.

broh *n. see* BRO *n.*[1].

broiler *n.* [pun on SE *broiler* (chicken)] **1** [1900s] any woman. **2** [1900s–20s] (*US*) a small chorus-girl. **3** [2000s] (*N.Z.*) an unattractive, usu. older, woman.

broke *adj.*[1] (*also* **broke-ass, broken, bruk**) [orig. image was of creditors physically 'breaking' a debtor] [mid-16C+] out of funds, impoverished, poor.

IN PHRASES

❑ **broke for** *adj.* [fig. use] [1940s–50s] (*Aus.*) in great need of, desperate for, esp. in the phr. *broke for a feed*, very hungry. ❑ **broke to the wide** *adj.* (*also* **broke to the world**) [20C+] absolutely penniless. ❑ **flat broke** *adj. see* separate entry. ❑ **go for broke** *see* separate entries. ❑ **stone broke** *adj. see* separate entry.

SE in slang uses

IN COMPOUNDS

❑ **broke-dick** *adj.* (*also* **broke-ass**) [DICK *n.*[1] (5), i.e. impotent] [1960s+] (*US*) worthless, useless.

broke *adj.*[2] [1990s+] (*US campus*) **1** intoxicated from marijuana. **2** of an experience, intense, extreme.

broke *adj.*[3] [1990s+] (*US black*) (*also* **broken**) very unattractive.

broke-ass *adj.* [-ASS *sfx* (1)] **1** *see* BROKE *adj.*[1] (1). **2** *see BROKE-DICK under* BROKE *adj.*[1].

broken *adj.* **1** *see* BROKE *adj.*[1]. **2** *see* BROKE *adj.*[3].

SE in slang uses

IN COMPOUNDS

❑ **broken alderman** *n. see* ALDERMAN *n.* (2). ❑ **broken arms** *n.* [? pun on SE *broken victuals*, when *victuals*, usu. food, takes its secondary 17C meaning of weapons or military 'arms'] [1910s] (*US*) leftover food. ❑ **broken arrow** *n.* [1940s] (*US*) a malfunctioning penis; thus an impotent male. ❑ **broken arse** *n.* [ARSE *n.* (1)] [1980s+] (*N.Z. prison*) a prisoner who sides with the authorities and thus ranks lowest in the prisoners' hierarchy. ❑ **broken hill** *n.* [proper name *Broken Hill*, a major Aus. silver mining area] [1940s–50s] (*Aus.*) any silver coin. ❑ **broken-kneed** *adj.* [late 18C] bankrupt. ❑ **broken-legged** *adj.* [BREAK ONE'S LEG (ABOVE THE KNEE) *under* BREAK *v.*[1]] [17C–1910s] seduced, deflowered. ❑ **broken oar** *n. see* BOAT AND OAR *n.* ❑ **broken up** *adj. see* BROKE UP *adj.* ❑ **broken wrist** *n. see* LIMP WRIST *n.* (1).

IN PHRASES

❑ **broken packet of biscuits, be a** *v.* [the crumbs are invisible through the outer wrapping] [1990s+] (*Aus.*) to live a life that looks good to outsiders but is really filled with problems.

broken brigade *n.* [BROKE *adj.*[1] + BRIGADE *n.*] [late 19C–1900s] (*UK society*) aristocratic younger sons, impoverished through the inequalities of primogeniture, who are forced to live on their wits.

broken heart *n.* [rhy. sl. = FART *n.* (1)] [1990s+] breaking wind.

broken mug *n.* [rhy. sl.] [1940s] (*US*) a hug.

broker *n.*[1] (*also* **placket-broaker**) [SE *broker*, a retailer of commodities; a middleman] **1** [mid-17C–18C] a pimp. **2** [1930s+] (*drugs*) a go-between in a drug deal or in any illegal transaction.

broker *n.*[2] [BROKE *adj.*[1] + pun on SE] **1** [late 19C+] (*orig. Aus.*) someone who is usu. having financial problems, a poor person. **2** [2000s] (*drugs*) a heavy drug user [they 'go for broke'].

brokered *adj.* [SE phr. *have the brokers in* + ? pun on BROKE *adj.*[1]] [late 19C] having had one's possessions removed by law.

broke up *adj.* (*also* **broken up**) [suffering from a 'broken heart'] [late 19C+] (*orig. US*) **1** injured, hurt. **2** depressed, badly upset. **3** touched, affected.

brokie *n.* [BROKE *adj.*[1] + sfx *-ie*] [1950s] (*Aus.*) one who has no money.

brolly *n.* [abbr.; note WW2 RAF *brolly*, a parachute] [mid-19C+] (*orig. school/university*) an umbrella.

broly *adj.* [BRO *n.*[1] + *-ly*, i.e. SE *brotherly*] [1990s+] (*US black*) friendly.

Bromagem *adj. see* BRUMMAGEM *adj.*

bromide *n.* [SE *bromide*, a dose of potassium bromide taken as a sedative] [1900s–60s] (*US*) **1** a person whose thoughts and conversation are conventional and commonplace; a dull, boring person. **2** a commonplace saying, a trite remark; a soothing statement; thus *bromidic, bromidically*, commonplace, conventionally.

Bromigham *n. see* BRUMMAGEM *n.*

Bromley (by Bow) *n.* [rhy. sl. = DOUGH *n.* (1)] [1990s+] money.

bromo *n. see* NEXUS *n.*

Brompton boilers *n. see* BOILERS, THE *n.*

Brompton cocktail *n.* (*also* **Brompton's cocktail**) [1960s+] a drug 'cocktail' of a variety of strong painkillers mixed with alcohol, supposedly created for terminally ill patients at the Brompton Hospital, London.

bronco *n.* (*also* **bronc, broncho**) [SE *bronco*, an unbroken horse] **1** [1920s] as term of address. **2** [1920s] (*US Und.*) (*also* **cat's kid**) a spy sent out by safe-blowers to locate potential robberies. **3** [1930s+] a young man, a novice in the gay world and thus somewhat rough; thus *bronco-buster*, an older man who favours sex with young/underage boys. **4** [1950s–60s] (*US prison*) (*also* **bronk**) the effeminate companion/lover of a 'masculine' prison homosexual.

bronco *adj.* (*also* **broncho**) [Sp. *bronco*, rough, esp. as applied to an untamed or half-tamed horse] [mid-19C–1940s] (*US*) wild, untameable.

bronstrops *n.* [SE *bawdstrot*, a pander or procuress] [17C] a procuress.

Bronx *n.* [its reputation as a particularly tough NY borough] [1980s+] (*Aus. prison*) that area of the prison reserved for intractable prisoners.

Bronx cheer *n.* [the uncouth manners of the Bronx, New York] [1920s+] (*orig. US*) a loud, derisive noise, imitative of a fart.

Bronx cheer *v.* [BRONX CHEER *n.*] [1940s+] (*US*) to make a loud derisive noise, as if breaking wind.

Bronx Indian *n.* [the once-large Jewish population of the Bronx; the area, like the rest of the US, was orig. populated by Native Americans] [1940s] (*US*) a Jew.

bronze *n.*[1] [var. on BRASS *n.*[1] (2)] [mid-19C] self-confidence, arrogance, cheek.

bronze *n.*[2] (*also* **bronza, bronzer, bronzo**) [its colour] **1** [1950s+] (*Aus.*) the anus, the posterior. **2** [1980s] excrement.

IN PHRASES

❑ **bronze up** *v.* [1980s+] (*Aus. prison*) to register a 'dirty protest' by smearing one's cell walls with faeces. ❑ **ugly as a hatful of bronzas** *adj.* [1950s] very ugly.

bronze *v.* [play on *DO UP BROWN under* BROWN *adj.*[2]] [early 19C] to impose upon, to cheat.

bronze figure *n.* [rhy. sl.] [20C+] a kipper.

bronze john *n.* [play on *YELLOW JACK under* YELLOW *adj.*] [mid-19C] (*US*) yellow fever.

bronzer *n. see* BRONZE *n.*[2].

bronzewing *n.* [the colour of the *bronzewing* pigeon] **1** [20C+] a member of the lower classes. **2** [1950s] a half-caste Native Australian.

bronzo *n. see* BRONZE *n.*[2].

broo *n. see* BUROO *n.*

broody *adj.* [SE *broody*, of a hen, sitting on her eggs] **1** [late 19C+] contemplative, (sullenly) meditative, feeling depressed or moody, thus adv. *broodily*; comp. *broodier*. **2** [20C+] of a woman, feeling a maternal desire to have a(nother) baby.

Brooklyn Indian *n.* [Brooklyn, New York, home to many Jews + *Indian*, a Native American] [20C+] (*US*) a Jew.

brooks *n.*[1] [Du. *broeks*, breeches] [1900s–10s] (*S.Afr.*) trousers.

brooks *n.*[2] [New York's up-market clothiers *Brooks* Brothers] [1970s] (*US black*) an expensive, esp. silk shirt.

Brooksey boy *n.* [NY up-market clothier *Brooks* Brothers] [1920s] (*US*) a smart dresser.

Brooks of Sheffield *n.* [Charles Dickens's *David Copperfield* (1850) in which the villainous Mr Murdstone initially uses the name instead of David's own] [mid–late 19C] nobody, a nameless person.

broom *n.*[1] [synon. with BRUSH *n.*[3] (2a); note early 17C *broom*, a horse's tail] **1** [late 19C] the pubic hair; of male pubic hair, ext. as *womb broom*. **2** [late 19C] the female genitals. **3** [late 19C] the penis. **4** [1940s] (*US black*) a cigar [resemblance to a small SE *broomstick*].

SE in slang uses

IN COMPOUNDS

❑ **Broomface** *n.* [the figure of a bearded UNCLE SAM *n.*] [1950s] (*US*) the Federal government. ❑ **broom-handle** *n.* [late 19C] the erect penis. ❑ **Broomtown** *n.* [ety. unknown] [1990s+] (*US*) an area of town inhabited mainly by white people only.

IN PHRASES

❑ **collar a broom** *v.* (*also* **cop a broom**) [1930s–40s] (*US black*) to leave quickly, to rush away. ❑ **hang out the broom** *v.* [the tradition of hanging out a broom to announce that one's wife was absent and thus advertise for a temporary housekeeper] [17C] of a man, to admit to one's being cuckolded.

broom *n.*[2] [mispron. of *brum*, abbr. BRUMMAGEM *n.*] [late 19C–1900s] a would-be dandy, who fails in his ambitions.

broom *n.*[3] [BROOM *v.* + ? play on DUST *v.*[2] (1)/BRUSH *v.*[1]] [1940s–70s] (*US black*) an act of walking, of movement.

IN PHRASES

❑ **dust one's broom** *v. see under* DUST *v.*[2]. ❑ **knock a broom** *v.* [1940s] (*US black*) to walk away.

broom *v.* (*also* **broom it**) [synon. with BRUSH *v.*[1]; the image of sweeping away. Orig. UK use faded but was revived by US blacks, esp. in Harlem] [late 18C+] to disappear quickly.

IN PHRASES

❑ **broom to the slammer that fronts the drape crib** *v.* [SLAMMER *n.*[1] (2b) + SE *front* + DRAPE *n.* (1) + CRIB *n.*[1] (1)] [1940s] (*US black*) to walk over to the clothes closet.

broomhilda *n.* [a US comic strip character, itself a pun on the Wagnerian heroine *Brünhilde*] [1980s+] (*US campus*) a short, unattractive woman.

broomie *n.* (*also* **broom-tail**) [SE *broom*, a horse's tail; note N.Z. *broomie*, a sweeper in a shearing-shed] [late 19C+] (*orig. US*) a mustang (esp. a mare) with a short bushy tail.

broomstick *n.* [supposed resemblance] **1** [19C] the penis. **2** [late 19C–1900s] (*Can.*) a gun or rifle [it also 'cleans up'].

broomstick bail *n.* [play on legal jargon *straw bail*, insufficient bail. Broomsticks were often made with straw brushes] [late 17C–early 19C] fraudulent bail; thus *broomstick*, one who puts up such bail.

broomstick marriage *n.* (*also* **broomstick match, broomstick wedding**) [JUMP (OVER) THE BROOMSTICK *v.*] [late 18C–1910s] a common-law marriage, in which the partners have never actually gone through with a civil or religious ceremony.

broom-tail *n. see* BROOMIE *n.*

brooze *v. see* BROWSE *v.*

brophys, the *n.* [joc. nickname for the supposed insects, relations of body lice or crabs, which allegedly carried the disease] [1950s+] (*Irish*) venereal disease.

broseley *n.* [proper name *Broseley*, Salop, famous for its 'churchwarden' pipes] [mid-19C] a pipe, esp. in the phr. *cock a broseley*, to smoke a pipe.

broth *n.* [abbr.] [1970s] (*US campus*) *brother*.

brothel *n.* [fig. use of SE] [1950s+] (*Aus.*) an extremely untidy place or room.

brothel creepers *n.* (*also* **corridor creepers, creepers**) [orig. 1940s service use, referring, first, to officers' suede shoes and then to a form of 'desert boot' issued during WW2] [1950s+] suede shoes, often in lurid colours, with extra thick rubber soles, esp. popular among rock 'n' roll fans of the 1950s (and in 1980s revival).

brothel stompers *n.* [var. on BROTHEL CREEPERS *n.*, although these 'respectable' versions have no great thickness of sole] [1970s+] (*US campus*) suede shoes.

brother *n.* **1** [late 19C+] a general form of address to an unnamed male or self-reflexively. **2** [1910s+] a black male. **3** [1920s+] a form of address to a fellow black male. **4** [1960s+] (*orig. US black*) in pl., constr. with *the*, black people, orig. in 1960s black radical use, now used by both black and white speakers with only residual political overtones. **5** [1960s+] in pl., constr with *the*, one's intimates, one's close friends. **6** [1970s+] a non-black male accepted in the black community.

IN COMPOUNDS

❑ **brotherman** *n.* (*also* **brother man**) [ext.] [1970s+] (*US black*) a form of address from one black man to another; occas. as a n. for a fellow black man.

IN PHRASES

❑ **brother in blackness** *n.* [1930s–40s] (*US black*) a form of address from one black man to another; a black man; thus *sister in black*, n., a black woman.

SE in slang uses

IN COMPOUNDS

❑ **brother bung** *n. see* BROTHER OF THE BUNG *under* BROTHER (OF THE)... *n.* ❑ **brother chip** *n.* [19C] **1** a carpenter. **2** a fellow professional of any sort. ❑ **brother hod** *n. see* HOD *n.* ❑ **brother round-mouth** *n.* [its 'speech' is a fart] [early 19C] the anus. ❑ **brother starling** *n.* (*also* **brother socket**) [SE *brother* + *starling*; ? the characteristics of the bird/SOCKET *n.*] [late 17C–19C] one who shares a friend's mistress.

IN PHRASES

❑ **brother (of the)...** *n. see* separate entry. ❑ **brother-where-are-you?** *n.* (*also* **brother-where-art-thou?**) [his being 'blind' drunk] [1920s] a drunkard.

brother and sister *n.* [rhy. sl.] [1980s+] a blister.

brother-in-law *n.* [1930s–40s] (*US Und.*) a pimp running two street whores.

brother-in-law *v.* [1920s] (*US*) to pursue clandestinely the wife or girlfriend of another man.

brother (of the)... *n.* [mid-17C–19C] a phr. used of members of various professions, a member of, a practitioner of; always constructed with a noun denoting, lit. or fig., the occupation, as listed below.

IN PHRASES

❑ **brother (of the) blade** *n.* **1** [mid-17C–19C] a swordsman, a fellow soldier. **2** [mid-18C–19C] a fellow member of the same profession or occupation. ❑ **brother of the bolus** *n.* [SE *bolus*, a large pill] [mid-19C] (*US*) a physician. ❑ **brother of the brush** *n.* (*also* **brethren of the brush, son of the brush**) [SE *brush*] **1** [late 17C+] an artist. **2** [19C+] a house painter. ❑ **brother of the bunch of fives** *n.* [BUNCH OF FIVES *n.*] [mid-19C] a prize-fighter, a professional boxer. ❑ **brother of the bung** *n.* (*also* **brother bung**) [SE *bung*/BUNG *n.*[2] (2b)] [mid-18C–1900s] a publican, an inn-keeper. ❑ **brother (of the) buskin** *n.* [SE *buskin*] [late 18C] a musician. ❑ **brother of the coif** *n.* [SE *coif*, a coiffed wig, part of his 'uniform'] [late 18C] a barrister. ❑ **brother of the gusset** *n.* (*also* **knight of the gusset, squire of the gusset**) [KNIGHT OF THE... *n.*/SQUIRE *n.* (2) + SE *gusset*] [late 17C–19C] a pimp, a procurer. ❑ **brother of the quill** *n.* [SE *quill*] [late 17C–19C] a writer, an author. ❑ **brother of the string** *n.* [SE *string*] [late 17C–20C] a musician. ❑ **brother of the surplice** *n.* [mid-19C] (*US Und.*) a priest. ❑ **brother (of the) whip** *n.* [SE *whip*] [late 18C–mid-19C] a coachman.

brothers, the *n. see* BROTHER *n.* (4).

brothers and sisters *n.* [rhy. sl.] [1920s–30s] (*US*) whiskers.

broth of a boy *n.* (*also* **broth of a lad**) [the image of broth being the distilled essence and 'goodness' of the meat] [late 17C; 19C+] (*orig. Irish*) the essence of what a boy should be, a downright good fellow.

brough *n. see* BRO *n.*[1].

brougham *n.* [the smart 19C carriages named for Lord Henry *Brougham* (1778–1868)] [1980s+] **1** (*US black*) an elegant, expensive and prized motorcar. **2** a fellow black man.

brought *adj.* [BROUGHT DOWN *adj.*] [1940s] (*US black*) depressed.

brought down *adj.* [BRING DOWN *v.*[1] (1)] [1950s+] (*orig. drugs*) depressed, esp. after a period of elation.

broughtonian *n.* [proper name Jack *Broughton*, 'Captain of the Boxers', inventor of the first prototype 'muffler' or boxing glove, writer of 'Broughton's Rules' (which lasted 1743–1838) and champion of England 1730–5] [late 18C–early 19C] a boxer; thus *Broughton's mark*, the pit of the stomach.

brought out *v.* [*BRING OUT under* BRING *v.*] [1950s+] (*gay*) initiated into the homosexual life.

brought-upsy *n.* [1990s+] (*W.I.*) up-bringing.

brov *n. see* BRUV *n.*

Brow *n.* (*also* **the Brow**) [abbr.] [1970s+] (*S.Afr.*) Hill*brow*, a densely populated, tough, high-rise suburb of Johannesburg.

brow *n. see* HIGHBROW *n.*

brown *n.* **1** as the colour of drinks. (**a**) [19C] porter, stout. (**b**) [mid-19C] brandy. (**c**) [late 19C–1910s] two pennyworth of whisky, esp. as sold in Mooney's Tavern in the Strand, London. (**d**) [1920s–30s] (*US Und.*) whisky. (**e**) [1950s+] brown ale. **2** as the colour of coins or notes. (**a**) [early 19C] (*UK Und.*) counterfeit halfpennies. (**b**) [early 19C–1930s] a halfpenny; a penny; thus *browns*, copper coins. (**c**) [1980s] (*UK black*) a £10 note. **3** pertaining to the anus. (**a**) [late 19C+] (*also* **round**

brown) the anus. (**b**) [late 19C+] sodomy, anal intercourse. (**c**) [1960s+] (*gay*) the dominant partner in anal sex. **4** the colour of drugs, also in pl. *browns*. (**a**) [1900s] (*drugs*) opium. (**b**) [1900s] tobacco. (**c**) [1960s+] (*drugs*) (*also* **brown dope, ...lady**) heroin; also attrib. (**d**) [1960s+] (*drugs*) hashish; also attrib. (**e**) [1960s+] (*US drugs*) usu. in pl., amphetamines. (**f**) [1990s+] (*also* **brown bob**) a cigarette or cigar. **5** [late 19C] (*US*) hot cakes. **6** the colour of one's skin. (**a**) [1910s+] (*US black*) a young, brown-skinned person, esp. as a boy- or girlfriend. (**b**) [1960s] (*S.Afr.*) a black South African. (**c**) [2000s] a Mexican.

pertaining to money

IN PHRASES

❑ **brown paper men** *n. see* separate entry. ❑ **browns and whistlers** *n.* [early 19C] (*UK Und.*) counterfeit halfpence and farthings. ❑ **head browns** *v.* [1910s] (*Aus.*) to play 'two-up'.

pertaining to the anus

IN COMPOUNDS

❑ **brown-dirt cowboy** *n.* [SE *dirt, cowboy*] [1970s+] a male homosexual. ❑ **brown-diver** *n.* [SE *diver*] [2000s] (*US black*) a male homosexual. ❑ **brown job** *n. see* separate entries.

IN PHRASES

❑ **brown out** *v. see* separate entry. ❑ **do a brown** *v. see* BROWN *v.*[3]. ❑ **do it up brown** *v.* [1950s+] (*gay*) to have anal intercourse. ❑ **flash the brown** *v.* [2000s] (*N.Z.*) to expose the buttocks. ❑ **go in the brown** *v.* [1930s] (*US Und.*) to sodomize. ❑ **hawk one's brown** *v.* [1960s+] to work as a male prostitute. ❑ **hit the round brown** *v.* [1970s+] (*US gay*) to sodomize. ❑ **in one's brown** [1980s+] (*Irish*) a phr. of dismissal, contempt, general negation, e.g. *'I mean it, I really do', 'Bollocks!, you do in your brown!'.* ❑ **when the red is over the pink, go for the brown** [snooker imagery] [1990s+] when a woman is menstruating, opt for anal intercourse.

IN EXCLAMATIONS

❑ **up your brown!** (*also* **up your rusty!**) [1910s+] a general excl. of abuse, dismissal; alt. to UP YOUR ARSE! *excl.*

pertaining to drugs

IN COMPOUNDS

❑ **brown dope** *n. see* BROWN *n.* (4c). ❑ **brownhead** [-HEAD *sfx* (4)] [2000s] (*UK drugs*) a heroin user. ❑ **brown lady** *n. see* BROWN *n.* (4c). ❑ **brown rhine** [SE *brown*/BROWN POWDER *under* BROWN *adj.*[2] + *rhine*, abbr./pron. for hero*in*] [1950s] (*drugs*) heroin.

brown *adj.*[1] [BROWN *v.*[1] (1)] [early 19C–1910s] alert, aware, *au fait*.

brown *adj.*[2] **1** [mid-19C; 1950s] worthy, earnest, totally devoid of any *double entendre* or 'smut' [the brown clothes popular among the sedulously pure Quakers]. **2** [1930s+] used in combs. to imply homosexuality [the equation of *brown* and excrement, thus the anus].

IN COMPOUNDS

❑ **brown baby** *n. see* BROWN STUFF *n.* (2). ❑ **brown bucket** *n. see* BUCKET *n.* (4b). ❑ **brown family** *n.* (*also* **browning family**) [1930s+] a generally obsolete generic term for homosexuals, referring to the predilection for anal intercourse. ❑ **brown highway** *n.* [1970s+] the anus. ❑ **brown pipe** *n.* [1990s+] the anus; thus *brown pipe engineer*, a male homosexual, a sodomite. ❑ **brown shower** *n.* [on pattern of GOLDEN SHOWER *n.* (1)] [1990s+] (*US*) an act of defecation for sexual purposes. ❑ **brown star** *n.* (*also* **brown starfish, pink starfish**) [resemblance] [1990s+] the anus. ❑ **brown trout** *n. see* separate entry. ❑ **brown wings** *n.* [the 'wings' awarded to a qualified fighter pilot] [1950s+] (*orig. Hell's Angels*) heterosexual anilingus or anal intercourse.

IN PHRASES

❑ **get a brown dick** *n.* [1990s+] to perform anal intercourse, to sodomize.

SE in slang uses

IN COMPOUNDS

pertaining to currency

❑ **brown abe** *n.* [President *Abraham* Lincoln's head is on the cent, a *buffalo head* is on the nickel] [1930s–60s] (*US black*) a cent; thus *brown Abes and buffalo heads*, small change, cents and nickels. ❑ **brown-back** *n.* [its colour; the brown ten-shilling notes were issued in 1928 and superseded by the 50p piece after decimalization in 1971; from 1940 until 1948 the notes were mauve rather than brown] [1910s–70s] a ten-shilling note.

pertaining to race

❑ **brown Betty** *n.* [SE *brown* plus generic/assonant female name] [1960s] (*US gay*) a black man. ❑ **brown flight** *n.* [1980s+] (*N.Z.*) the removal from predominantly Maori schools of the children of Pacific islanders, fearful of supposedly low standards. ❑ **brown man** *n.* [the belief that light skin is best] [1950s+] (*W.I.*) **1** a light-skinned black man. **2** a prosperous black man. ❑ **brown meat** *n.* [MEAT *n.* (1)] [late 19C+] (*US*) a black woman considered as a sex object. ❑ **brown-out** *n. see* separate entry. ❑ **brownskin** *see* separate entries. ❑ **brown sugar** *n. see* separate entries. ❑ **brown table** *n.* [play on SE *round table*] [1990s+] (*N.Z.*) the Maori Establishment. ❑ **Browntown** *n.* [1950s+] (*US*) the black area of a town or city. ❑ **brown velvet** *n.* [1930s] (*N.Z*) a derog. term for a Maori woman, esp. when seen simply as a sex object.

general uses

❑ **brown ankle** *n.* [he has crawled so far 'up the arse' of the authorities that only his ankles are visible] [1970s+] (*N.Z. prison*) a sycophant, a toady. ❑ **brown bob** *n.* **1** *see* BOB *n.*[5] (2). **2** *see* BROWN *n.* (4f). ❑ **Brown Cow** *n.* [SE *Jersey* cow] [1970s] (*US*) New Jersey. ❑ **brown creatures** *n.* [joc. mispron.; note milit. use *Bill Harris*, bilharzia, *Corporal Forbes*, cholera morbus] [mid-19C–1920s] bronchitis. ❑ **brown dots** *n.* [its packaging] [1970s+] (*drugs*) LSD. ❑ **brown gargle** *n.* [GARGLE *n.*] [1950s+] (*Irish*) stout. ❑ **brown gatter** *n.* [GATTER *n.*[1] (1)] [mid-19C] beer. ❑ **brown george** *n.* [ety. unknown; cf. naut. jargon *negroes' heads*, brown loaves eaten on board ship] **1** [17C–early 19C] bread. **2** [late 17C–18C] a hard, coarse biscuit. **3** [early–mid-19C] a brown wig [ref. to King George IV]. **4** [mid–late 19C] an earthenware jug. ❑ **brown gravy** *n.* [late 18C] (*UK Und.*) melted gold, e.g. golden watch-cases. ❑ **brown madam** *n.* [late 18C–19C] the vagina. ❑ **brown nose/brown-noser** *see* separate entries. ❑ **brown powder** *n.* [Mexican heroin, and some other varieties, is brown rather than the usual white] [1950s+] (*drugs*) heroin. ❑ **brown shell** *n.* [late 19C] an onion. ❑ **brown snout** *n. see* BROWN NOSE *n.* ❑ **brownstone(r)** *see* separate entries. ❑ **brown stuff** *n. see* separate entry. ❑ **brown tommy** *n. see under* TOMMY *n.*[2]. ❑ **brown tongue/tonguer** *see* separate entries.

IN PHRASES

❑ **do brown** *v.* [cooking imagery] **1** [early 17C; 19C+] (*also* **beat brown**) to surpass, to defeat comprehensively, usu. in the phr. *done brown* or *good and brown*. **2** [mid-19C+] to take to extremes, to 'go too far'. ❑ **do it brown** *v.* [cooking imagery] [mid-19C+] to take to the limit, esp. as in prolonging one's enjoyment to the point of excess. ❑ **do up brown** *v.* [positive and negative images in overall sense of action + cooking imagery] **1** [19C+] to beat up thoroughly, also fig. **2** [mid-19C+] (*also* **do up blue**) to do thoroughly, to perform very successfully. **3** [1950s] to deceive, to take in, to surprise. ❑ **on the brown side of** [1940s] (*US*) older than.

IN EXCLAMATIONS

❑ **brown salve!** [ety. unknown] [mid-19C] used as a rejoinder, meaning 'I understand'; the expression combines a degree of surprise at what has been said with, ultimately, comprehension of what it means. ❑ **brown suit!** [? the transgression of some contemporary fashion norm] [mid-19C] no chance!

brown *v.*[1] [DO BROWN *under* BROWN *adj.*[2]] **1** [19C+] (*orig. US*) to understand. **2** [mid-19C] to do perfectly. **3** [mid-19C–1920s] to get the better of, to surpass.

brown *v.*[2] (*also* **brown up, brownie up**) [abbr. BROWN NOSE *n.*] [20C+] to act the toady, to be a sycophant.

brown *v.*[3] (*also* **do a brown**) [BROWN *n.* (3a)] **1** [1920s] (*US*) used in a number of semi-euph. excl. e.g. *I'll be browned! brown me!* [synon. with BUGGERED *adj.*[1] / BUGGER ME! *under* BUGGER *v.*[1]]. **2** [1930s+] (*orig. US*) to perform anal intercourse, to sodomize.

IN COMPOUNDS

□ **brown artist** *n.* [-ARTIST *sfx*] [1950s+] a male homosexual who takes the active role in anal intercourse. □ **brown-hole** *v.* [SE, i.e. the anus; sense 2 above + HOLE *n.*[1] (1a)] [1980s+] (*US gay*) to have anal intercourse.

brownbag *v.* [1960s+] (*US*) **1** to drink liquor from a bottle 'hidden' in the (brown-paper) bag in which it is bought from the liquor store and which is necessary in US states where drinking in the street is illegal; also to take one's own supply of alcohol to a restaurant. **2** to take a packed lunch to work or school.

brownbagger *n.* [BROWNBAG *v.*; note 1950s US Air Force jargon *brown-bagger*, a married man] [1950s+] **1** (*US campus*) an excessively hard-working student [the *brown bag* contains books rather than lunch]. **2** (*US*) one who takes a packed lunch to school or work.

brown berry *n.* [BROWN *n.* (3a) + SE; it is ready to be 'picked'; + var. on CHERRY *n.* (1b)] [1960s] (*US gay*) a virgin anus.

IN PHRASES

□ **have a berry** *v.* [1990s+] to have homosexual anal intercourse.

brown bess *n.* (*also* **brown bessie, brown betsy**) [the brown walnut stock, although there may be links to Du. *bus* or Ger. *Busche*, a gun barrel] [late 18C–1900s] a firelock or musket, otherwise known as the 'soldier's best friend'; thus *hug brown bess*, to carry a firelock, to serve as a private soldier.

IN PHRASES

□ **marry brown bess** *v.* [late 18C–19C] to serve as a soldier.

brown bess *adv.* [rhy. sl.] [mid-19C] yes.

brown bessie *n.* [? a distinguishing *brown* garment + the generic fem. name] **1** [mid-17C] a prostitute. **2** *see* BROWN BESS *n.*

brown bessie *adv.* [rhy. sl.] [mid-19C] yes.

brown betsy *n. see* BROWN BESS *n.*

brown bomber *n.*[1] [the colour] **1** [1940s–70s] (*also* **brown bomb**) a laxative pill. **2** [1950s+] (*Aus., Sydney*) a parking police officer. **3** [1950s+] (*N.Z.*) DB (Dominion Breweries) brown ale. **4** [1960s] (*drugs*) strong (20mg) capsules of amphetamine, usu. coloured brown. **5** [2000s] LSD.

brown bomber *n.*[2] [BROWN *adj.*[2] (2) + play on SE] [1990s+] a male homosexual; a sodomite.

brown bread *adj.*[1] [early 17C] utter, complete.

brown bread *adj.*[2] [rhy. sl.] [1960s+] dead.

browned off *adj.* (*also* **browned**) [accumulation of brown rust on fatigued or worn out metal; but note the various uses of BROWN *v.*[3] (2) / BROWN *adj.*[2] (2) in the context of sodomy] [1930s+] (*orig. milit.*) irritated, annoyed; also as v. to annoy, to irritate.

browned up *adj.* [var. on BROWNED OFF *adj.*] [1930–40s] irritated, annoyed.

browner *n.* [BROWN *n.* (6a)] [1980s] (*Can. teen*) a black person.

brown eye *n.* **1** [1950s+] (*also* **little brown eyeball**) the anus. **2** [1980s+] anal intercourse.

IN PHRASES

□ **do the brown eye express** *v.* [1980s+] (*US*) to sodomize. □ **get some brown eye** *v.* [1980s] (*US*) to sodomize.

brown-eye *v.* [BROWN EYE *n.* (1)] **1** [1940s+] (*US*) to sodomize. **2** [1990s+] (*Aus./N.Z.*) to drop one's trousers and underwear and reveal one's naked buttocks to anyone who is watching, a mainly juv. prank.

brown hat *n.* [rhy. sl.] [late 19C+] a cat.

brown-hatter *n.* (*also* **brown-hat, hatter**) [? a jibe at a long-dead gay fashion or the coarse image of an excrement-coated meatus] [1910s+] (*orig. naval*) a male homosexual who takes the active role in anal intercourse.

brownie *n.*[1] [the colour] **1** as a coin. (**a**) [early 19C–1950s] (*orig. UK Und.*) a penny, a halfpenny. (**b**) [1920s–50s] (*US black*) a cent. **2** [mid-19C+] (*Aus./US*) (*also* **browny**) a brown-skinned person, an Asian; in Aus. an aborgine, a Japanese; in N.Z. a Maori. **3** [late 19C+] (*Aus.*) a cake made of flour, fat and sugar, and filled with raisins or currants; thus (*N.Z.*) *brownie-gorger*, a shearer. **4** [20C+] a shot of whisky. **5** pertaining to the anus. (**a**) [1920s+] (*Aus./US*) the anus, the buttocks. (**b**) [1940s+] (*also* **b.q., brownie queen, browning queen, browning sister**) a homosexual, esp. the passive partner in anal intercourse. (**c**) [1970s] the vagina. (**d**) [1990s+] a piece of excrement. **6** [1960s+] (*US*) a small (usu. chocolate) cake impregnated with hashish or marijuana [*brownie*, a trad. US biscuit].

IN PHRASES

□ **hawk one's brownie** *v.* [1970s] (*US*) to work as a prostitute.

brownie *n.*[2] [the maker's name *Brown's*] [late 19C] usu. pl., small, cheap cigarettes.

brownie *n.*[3] [1920s] (*US Und.*) **1** a child. **2** a machine gun [the *Browning* machine gun].

brownie *v.* [BROWN-NOSE *v.*] [1960s+] to curry favour.

brownie arcade *n.* [the slot-machines that take 1 cent or a BROWNIE *n.*[1] (1b)] [1940s] (*US black/Harlem*) an amusement arcade.

brownie king *n.* (*also* **b.k.**) [BROWNIE *n.*[1] (5a) + play on the passive BROWNIE QUEEN *n.*] [1970s] (*US gay*) a male homosexual who takes the active role in anal intercourse.

brownie point *n.* [ety. unknown; links have been made to the *Brownies*, the junior form of the Girl Guides, and to *brown-nosing*; recent research suggests that its origin may also lie in wartime American food rationing, in which ration points in various colours were required to make food purchases: red and brown ones, for example, referred to meats and fats. There are many references in wartime newspapers to 'brown points'.] [1950s+] a notional 'award', in effect a sarcastic and backhanded form of compliment for anything perceived as sycophancy.

brownie queen *n. see* BROWNIE *n.*[1] (5b).

brownies *n.* (*also* **browns**) [the colour of the pill or capsule] [1960s+] (*US drugs*) amphetamine.

brownie up *v. see* BROWN *v.*[2].

browning *n.*[1] [BROWN *v.*[3] (2)] **1** [late 19C–1930s] anal intercourse. **2** [1920s] a cunnilinguist.

browning *n.*[2] [1980s+] (*W.I.*) a mulatto woman.

browning family *n. see* *BROWN FAMILY under* BROWN *adj.*[2].

browning queen/sister *n. see* BROWNIE *n.*[1] (5b).

browning sisters *n.* [BROWNING *n.*[1] (1) + SE *sisters*] [20C+] homosexuals in general.

brown job *n.*[1] [BROWN NOSE *n.* + JOB *n.*[2] (2)] [1960s+] flattery, empty praise.

brown job *n.*[2] [BROWN *adj.*[2] (2) + JOB *n.*[2] (2)] [1960s+] (*gay*) anilingus.

brown joe *v.* [rhy. sl.] [1940s+] (*Aus.*) to know; thus *brown joe*, in the know.

brown joe *adv.* [rhy. sl.] [mid-19C] no.

brown nose *n.* (*also* **brown snout**) [BROWN-NOSE *v.*] [1930s+] (*orig. US milit.*) a toady, a sycophant; also attrib.

IN PHRASES

□ **have a brown nose** *v.* [1960s+] to be a sycophant. □ **one's nose is always brown** [1930s+] said of a dedicated sycophant.

brown-nose *v.* [SE *brown* + SE *nose*, one achieves this coloration by 'kissing arse'] [1910s+] (*orig. US milit.*) to play the sycophant, to curry favour, to toady, thus n., adj. *brown-nosing*.

brown-noser *n.* [BROWN NOSE *n.*] [1950s+] (*orig. US milit.*) anyone who pays excessive court to authority, at school, in work etc, thus *adj. brown-nosing*.

brown off *v.* **1** [1950s] (*US*) to blunder, to make a mistake. **2** [1960s] (*US campus*) to reject a request for a date.

brown-out *n.* [play on SAmeE *brown-out*, a power outage that dims a city's lights] [1990s+] a boycott organized by US Latino groups.

brown out *v.* [BROWN *v.*[3] (2)] [1980s+] (*US gay*) to lick or suck the anus.

brown paper *n.* [rhy. sl. = caper] [1930s+] a trick, a pursuit, a profession, a 'game'.

brown paper men *n.* [their wagering in pence, i.e. BROWN *n.* (2b)] [mid-19C] the poorest class of gamblers.

brownskin *n.* **1** [mid-19C] a North American Indian. **2** [late 19C+] (*US black*) a light-skinned black person. **3** [1970s–80s] (*US black*) a dark-skinned person who is seen as 'white' by non-blacks, but 'black' by the latter.

brownskin *adj.* [1920s+] (*US black*) used of a light-skinned African American.

brownstone *adj.* [SE *brownstone*, a type of New York City house, built 1850–80, fronted with brownstone and favoured by this section of society] [mid-19C–1900s] (*US*) pertaining to the upper or upper-middle classes.

brownstone front *n.* [their brownstone houses] **1** [mid-19C–1900s] (*US*) meton., an aristocrat, a member of the upper classes who lives in such a building. **2** [late 19C] (*US short-order*) in catering use, as a play on sense 1. (**a**) corned beef hash. (**b**) steak.

brownstoner *n.* [SE *brownstone*, a type of New York City house, built 1850–80, fronted with brownstone and favoured by this section of society] [mid–late 19C] (*US*) a member of the upper-middle or mercantile class; thus *brownstone club*, a private club, *brownstone vote*, the political stance of the upper-middle class.

brown stuff *n.* [STUFF *n.* (5); the colour] **1** as the colour of drink or drugs. (**a**) [1900s] (*Aus./US*) whisky. (**b**) [1930s–40s] (*US drugs*) opium. (**c**) [1970s] (*US drugs*) Mexican heroin. **2** [1950s+] (*also* **brown baby**) excrement, also used fig., i.e. 'the shit'.

brown sugar *n.*[1] [SUGAR *n.*[1] (1)] [mid-19C] (*UK Und.*) a lawyer's fees.

brown sugar *n.*[2] [all colour; the black use of sense 1 crossed over into the white vocabulary with the success in 1971 of the Rolling Stones' song of the same name; the drug use was a spin-off from this] **1** [1920s+] (*orig. US black*) an attractive black woman. **2** [1970s+] (*drugs*) heroin. **3** [1970s+] lowgrade or adulterated heroin. **4** [1980s+] sexual intercourse with a black person.

IN PHRASES

❑ **get some brown sugar** *v.* [BROWN *n.* (3a)/sense 4 above] [1970s+] **1** (*US black*) to have heterosexual intercourse. **2** of a male, whether hetero- or homosexual, to have anal intercourse.

brown tongue *v.* [var. on BROWN NOSE *n.*] [1930s+] to toady, to curry favour.

brown-tonguer *n.* (*also* **brown-tongue**) [BROWN TONGUE *v.*] [20C+] a toady, a sycophant.

brown trout *n.* [it 'swims' in the lavatory bowl] [1990s+] excrement, thus *brown trout pond*, a lavatory bowl.

IN PHRASES

❑ **fish for brown trout** *v.* [1980s+] (*US gay*) to have anal intercourse. ❑ **sling trout** *v.* [1990s+] (*US prison*) to throw excrement or urine over another prisoner.

Brown 'Un, the *n.* [the colour of the newsprint] [late 19C–1900s] the *Sportsman*, a sporting newspaper (cf. PINK 'UN, THE *n.*).

brown up *v.* see BROWN *v.*[2].

browny *n.* see BROWNIE *n.*[1] (2).

browse *v.* (*also* **brooze, bruise, bruze**) [SE *browse*, of cattle, to nibble on twigs or buds, ult. f. 16C *browse*, a bud, a young shoot] [late 19C–1900s] (*Aus./US*) to loaf around, to wander idly, to dawdle.

browsing and sluicing *n.* [coined and most commonly used by P.G. Wodehouse (1881–1975), but echoed by many of his fans] [late 19C; 1920s+] eating and drinking.

broziered *adj.* [ety. unknown] [late 18C] impoverished.

brr rabbit *v.* see *under* RABBIT *n.*[1].

brr-y *adj.* [SE *brr* + sfx *-y*] [1970s] (*US black*) chilly.

bruce *n.* [*Bruce* is seen as a 'typical' gay name; ? its potential, in camp usage, for being lisped; ? the relationship betwen Batman, i.e. *Bruce* Wayne and his 'ward' Robin (Dick Grayson)] **1** [1940s–70s] (*gay*) a term of address among male homosexuals. **2** [1980s+] (*US campus*) a male who thinks he is suave and sophisticated but really is not.

Bruce Lees *n.* [Kung Fu champion and movie star *Bruce Lee* (1941–73), i.e. a SE *hard* + NIP *n.* (1)] [2000s] erect female nipples.

bruck up *v.* [1940s+] (*UK teen*) to beat up.

brudum! *excl.* see BRADARAX! *excl.*

bruffam *n.* [deliberate mispron. of the SE, pretending that the 'gh', as in 'enough', is here pron. 'ff'] [late 19C–1900s] a small, closed carriage, properly known as a *brougham*, pron. 'broom' and named for Lord Brougham.

brugadum! *excl.* see BRADARAX! *excl.*

bruggalungdung! *excl.* see BRADARAX! *excl.*

bruh *n.* see BRO *n.*[1].

bruise *v.* see BROWSE *v.*

bruised *adj.* [euph.] [mid-19C] (*US*) drunk.

bruiser *n.* [SE *bruise*] **1** [mid-18C+] a boxer, a prize-fighter; in fig. use applied to a large person. **2** [early 19C] one who performs strongly (although not necessarily aggressively). **3** [mid-19C+] any form of thug who prefers to express himself with his fists. **4** [late 19C] a pimp. **5** [1960s–70s] (*US*) a black eye.

bruising *n.* [SE *bruise* + sfx *-ing*] [mid-18C–1900s] boxing; thus any form of fighting with the fists; thus *bruising match*, a boxing fight; *bruising shop*, a boxers' training gym.

bruising the bed *phr.* see BREWISING THE BED *phr.*.

bruisy *adj.* [BRUISER *n.* (1)] [1940s+] (*US Und.*) powerfully built, physically aggressive.

bruk *n.* [1990s+] (*W.I./Rasta*) a serious disagreement.

bruk *adj.* see BROKE *adj.*[1].

bruley-squeak *n.* [mid-19C] (*UK Und.*) roast pig.

bruley-wallop *n.* [mid-19C] (*UK Und.*) roast groose.

Brum *n.* [mid-19C+] **1** Birmingham; also attrib. **2** a Birmingham accent. **3** a resident of Birmingham.

brum *n.*[1] [the reputation of Birmingham as a centre of cheap mass-production] **1** [late 18C–1910s] a penny [refers to the copper coins struck in 19C by Boulton & Watt at their works in Birmingham]. **2** [late 18C–1910s] a counterfeit coin. **3** [late 19C+] something inferior. **4** [1910s–20s] (*Aus./US*) cheap goods, esp. showy clothes.

brum *n.*[2] [? BRUM *adj.*; she is an 'inferior' form of woman or var. of BRIM *n.*[1] (1)] [1920s] (*US*) a prostitute.

brum *adj.* [BRUMMAGEM *adj.*] [late 19C+] (*usu. Aus.*) second-rate; fake, counterfeit, of inferior make.

brumbie *adj.* (*also* **brumby, brum**) [SAusE *brumbie*, a wild or half-tamed horse] [late 19C–1930s] (*Aus.*) worn-out, ill-bred, uncouth; also as n.

brumby bull *n.* [BRUMBIE *adj.* + SE *bull*] [late 19C+] (*Aus.*) a remittance man.

Brummagem *n.* (*also* **Bromigham, Brummajum**) [negative stereotyping of Birmingham. Note late 17C citation of *Bromicham*: 'particularly noted a few years ago, for the counterfeit groats made here, and from hence dispersed all over the Kingdom' (G. Miege, *New State of England*, 1691); note fig. use of *Brimigham* to mean an imposter in 1681 ballad 'Ignoramus': 'Old *Tony* plotted, *Brimighams* Voted'] **1** [late 17C–mid-19C] counterfeit coins. **2** [late 17C+] the city of Birmingham, the Birmingham accent, an inhabitant of, or person from, Birmingham; also attrib. **3** [mid-19C] (*also* **Brummagen**) anything fake or inferior in make. **4** [mid-19C] a spur. **5** [late 19C] a second-rate person. **6** [1930s] a Birmingham accent.

Brummagem *adj.* (*also* **Bromagem, Brummigem**) [BRUMMAGEM *n.*] [mid-17C+] cheap, second-rate, fake.

IN COMPOUNDS

❑ **Brummagem button** *n.* [sense 1 above/BRUMMAGEM *n.* (2) + SE *button*] **1** [early–mid-19C] one shilling, poss. a counterfeit one. **2** [mid-19C+] a native of Bimingham. ❑ **Brummagem conscience** *n.* [17C] a very bad conscience. ❑ **Brummagem groats** *n.* [17C] counterfeit coins manufactured in Birmingham. ❑ **Brummagem protestants** *n.* [17C] Whigs or Dissenters. ❑ **Brummagem screwdriver** *n.* see BIRMINGHAM

SCREWDRIVER *n.* ❑ **Brummagem wine** *n.* [17C] any adulterated or mixed drink.

Brummie *see under* BRUMMY.

brummie *n. see* BRUMMY.

Brummigem *adj. see* BRUMMAGEM *adj.*

brummish *adj.* [abbr. BRUMMAGEM *adj.*] [19C] counterfeit, second-rate.

Brummy *n.* (*also* **Brummie**) [mid-19C+] a native of Birmingham, UK.

Brummy *adj.* (*also* **Brummie**) [1940s+] pertaining to Birmingham.

brummy *n.* (*also* **brummie**) [BRUMMAGEM *n.*] [1920s+] a counterfeit coin.

brummy *adj.* (*also* **brummie**) [BRUMMAGEM *n.*] [20C+] second-rate, tawdry, counterfeit.

brunette *n.* (*US*) **1** [late 19C] a Native American woman. **2** [late 19C–1930s] a black person.

Bruno *n.* [proper name *Bruno*, 'brown one'] [1970s+] (*US campus*) Brown University.

brunser *n.* [? BROWN *n.* (3b)] [1930s+] (*US*) (*also* **brunster**) a homosexual, esp. a catamite or tramp's young homosexual companion; by ext., a general derog.

brush $n.^1$ [BRUSH $v.^1$] **1** [late 17C–1920s] a hasty exit. **2** [mid-18C] one who rushes off.

IN PHRASES

❑ **buy a brush** *v.* [late 17C–mid-19C] to run away.

brush $n.^2$ [SE *brush against*, i.e. the vagina, other people] **1** [late 18C–mid-19C] the penis. **2** [late 18C+] (*also* **dab/daub of the brush**) heterosexual, occas. homosexual intercourse. **3** [early–mid-19C] a fight. **4** [1940s+] (*N.Z./Aus.*) a woman who is sexually available.

IN PHRASES

❑ **bit of brush** *n.* [SE *bit*] [1950s] sexual intercourse; thus a young woman, viewed purely sexually. ❑ **brush with a man** *v.* [late 18C–early 19C] to have a fight. ❑ **brush with a woman** *v.* [late 18C–early 19C] to seduce, to have sexual intercourse. ❑ **dab/daub of the brush** *n. see* sense 2 above.

brush $n.^3$ [SE *brush*, undergrowth] **1** [late 18C–19C] a house-painter. **2** pertaining to facial or pubic hair. (**a**) [late 18C; 1930s+] the pubic hair. (**b**) [20C+] (*Aus./N.Z.*) a young woman, a generic term for women. (**c**) [20C+] (*US*) (*also* **brusher**) a moustache or other facial hair. **3** the supposed resemblance of the glass's shape to that of a house-painter's brush. (**a**) [late 19C–1900s] a small glass, made of an inverted cone fixed to a thick stem, which is used for drinking drams of whisky or other spirits. (**b**) [1910s–30s] a drink of whisky.

IN COMPOUNDS

❑ **brush mouth** *n.* [1940s] (*US black*) a sip of whisky.

SE in slang uses

IN COMPOUNDS

❑ **brush ape** *n.* (*also* **brush monkey**) [SE *brush*, undergrowth, small branches] [1920s–60s] (*US*) a hillbilly, a peasant. ❑ **brush colt** *n.* [SE *brush colt*, a horse that has not been deliberately bred] [1940s+] (*US*) an illegitimate child. ❑ **brush hog** *n.* (*also* **brush Yankee**) [1950s] (*US*) a farmer, an unsophisticated rustic.

brush $n.^4$ *see* BRUSH-OFF *n.*

brush $v.^1$ (*also* **brush off, brush the scene**) [SE *brush*, to rush into with force or collision; ult. Fr. *brosser*, to dash through dense underwood] [late 17C–late 19C] (*UK Und.*) to rush off, to run away; as excl. go away!, off with you!

IN PHRASES

❑ **brush and lope** *v.* [late 18C–early 19C] to leave in a hurry.

brush $v.^2$ **1** [mid-19C] (*US Und.*) to flatter. **2** [2000s] (*UK black*) to reprimand. **3** *see* BRUSH OFF *v.*

SE in slang uses

IN COMPOUNDS

❑ **brush-up** *n.* [SE *brush*, a collision] [1910s+] (*US*) a scuffle, a skirmish.

IN PHRASES

❑ **brush someone's coat** *v.* [late 16C–early 18C] to thrash someone, to beat someone up. ❑ **brush someone's teeth** *v.* [pun on SE] [1970s+] **1** (*US*) to hit someone in the face. **2** (*US gay*) to perform fellatio. **3** (*US black*) to perform cunnilingus. ❑ **brush the beaver** *v. see under* BEAVER $n.^1$. ❑ **brush up a flat** *v. see under* FLAT $n.^2$.

IN EXCLAMATIONS

❑ **brush the teatree out of your hair!** [1980s+] (*N.Z.*) a general admonition; don't be a fool! ❑ **brush your brains!** [1920s] (*Aus.*) think! use your intelligence!

brush $v.^3$ [BRUSH OFF *v.*] [1940s–60s] (*US black*) to defeat, to overcome; to beat up.

brush-by *n. see* BRUSH-OFF *n.*

brusher $n.^1$ [? its contents brush against the rim or BRUSH $n.^3$ (3b)] [late 17C–mid-19C] a very full glass.

brusher $n.^2$ [abbr. *BUM-BRUSHER under* BUM $n.^1$] [19C+] a schoolmaster.

brusher $n.^3$ [UK dial. *brusher*, a lively, active boy] [late 19C] (*Aus.*) a 'bloke', a 'chap'.

brusher $n.^4$ [BRUSH-OFF *n.*]

IN PHRASES

❑ **get brusher** *v.* [1900s–30s] (*Aus.*) to be rejected to be snubbed. ❑ **give brusher** *v.* [late 19C+] (*Aus.*) **1** to obtain or borrow something (esp. money) and fail to return it; to fail to pay one's bills. **2** to abandon a task. **3** to run away (from).

brusher $n.^5$ *see* BRUSH $n.^3$ (2c).

brusheroo *n. see* BRUSH-OFF *n.*

brush-off *n.* (*also* **brush, brusheroo, brush-by**) [SE *brush*, to sweep, as with a brush; the image of brushing specks of dirt from one's clothes] [early 18C+] a snub, an act of rejection.

IN PHRASES

❑ **get the brush(-off)** *v.* to be ignored, snubbed. ❑ **give someone the brush(-off)** *v.* [1920s+] (*orig. US*) to ignore, to snub.

brush off *v.* (*also* **brush**) [BRUSH-OFF *n.*] **1** [early 19C+] to ignore, to treat contemptuously, to dismiss. **2** [1940s] (*US Und.*) to murder. **3** *see* BRUSH $v.^1$.

Brussels *n.* [SE *Brussels carpet*/CARPET $n.^2$ (1)] [1920s–30s] a three-month prison sentence.

brussel sprout *n.* [rhy. sl.] **1** [1910s+] a Boy Scout. **2** [1980s+] (*Aus.*) a lout. **3** [2000s] a term of affection [= *OLD SCOUT under* SCOUT *n.*]

brutal *adj.* [ext. of SE use] **1** [mid-19C+] (*Irish*) terrible. **2** [1920s+] (*orig. US*) very good, first-rate [on bad = good model]. **3** [1960s+] (*orig. US campus*) hard, difficult, horrible, a general negative.

brutally *adv.* [BRUTAL *adj.* (2)] [1990s+] (*US teen*) completely, utterly.

brute $n.^1$ [late 17C+] a general term used to imply the size or effect of the object and the distaste of the speaker, usu. in phr. *a brute of a…*

brute $n.^2$ [1980s+] (*Aus. prison*) an erection.

brutus *n.* [SE *brute* 'Latinized' by sfx *-us*] [1980s+] (*US campus*) a mean, ugly person.

bruv *n.* (*also* **brov**) [1980s+] a brother, esp. as a form of address to a friend (or actual sibling).

bruz *n.* (*also* **bruzz**) [SE *brother*] [1950s+] (*US black*) an affectionate term of address.

bruze *v. see* BROWSE *v.*

bry *n.* [BRIAN O'LINN *n.*] [late 19C–1900s] gin.

bryan o' lin *n. see* BRIAN O'LINN *n.*

Bryant and May *n.* [pun on SE *lights*, i.e. the matches produced by the *Bryant and May* company] [1920s+] a light ale.

Bryant and Mays *n.* [rhy. sl. fr. *Bryant and May* match manufacturers] [1900s–10s] stays (a form of light underbodice that preceeded the corset).

Bryant and May's chuckaway *n.* [pun on *CHUCKAWAY under* CHUCK $v.^2$, with a grim ref. to the disposability of those who worked at this dirty, dangerous task] [late 19C–1900s] a woman working at Bryant and May's match factory.

b.s. *n.* [abbr. BULLSHIT *n.*; note synon. WW1 Aus. milit. *beer esses*, based on signalman's pron. of *b.s.*] [late 19C+] (*orig. US*) **1** rubbish, nonsense. **2** in fig. use.

b.s. *v.* (*also* **b.s. around, bee-ess**) [B.S. *n.*] [20C+] (*orig. US*) to talk nonsense, to prevaricate.

b.s.-er *n.* (*also* **bee-esser**) [B.S. *v.*/BULLSHITTER *n.* (1)] [1960s] (*US*) a time-waster.

b.s.h.s *n.* [abbr. the joc. notional administrative measure, *B*ritish *S*tandard *H*and*s*fuls, a pun on the *BSI*, British Standards Institution] [1970s+] the female breasts.

b.t.m. *n.* [euph. abbr. SE *bottom*] [mid-19C; 1910s+] the buttocks.

b.t.o. *n.* [abbr. *b*ig *t*ime *o*perator] [1940s+] (*US campus*) one who schemes successfully to get their own way.

BTs *n.* [1970s] (*US*) barbiturates.

b.u. *n.* [abbr. *b*iological *u*rge] [1930s] (*US campus*) sexual drive or desire.

bu *n.* see BOO *n.*^{4}.

buah *n.* see BUER *n.*

bub *n.*^{1} (*also* **bubb, humming bub**) [Lat. *bibere*, to drink] [mid-17C–19C] drink, esp. strong beer; thus *bub and grub*, drink and food.

IN COMPOUNDS

❑ **bub and grub** *n.* see GRUB AND BUB under GRUB *n.*^{2}.

IN PHRASES

❑ **knock about the bub** *v.* [late 18C–mid-19C] to circulate the bottle, to pass the drink around.

bub *n.*^{2} [BUBBLE *n.*^{1} (2)] [late 17C] the victim of a fraud or hoax.

bub *n.*^{3} [SE *bubby*, a little boy] **1** [early 19C+] (*US*) a boy, esp. when used as derog. form of address, implying youth, insignificance etc. **2** [1980s+] (*US campus*) a person devoid of redeeming qualities.

bub *n.*^{4} (*also* **bubb**) [BUBBY *n.*^{1} (1)] [early 19C+] the female breast, usu. pl.

bub *n.*^{5} **1** see BUBBA *n.* (1). **2** see BUBBA *n.* (4). **3** see BUBBLY *n.*

bub *v.*^{1} [BUB *n.*^{1}] [17C–19C] to drink.

bub *v.*^{2} [BUB *n.*^{2}] [18C–early 19C] **1** to cheat. **2** to bribe.

bubb *n.* **1** see BUB *n.*^{1}. **2** see BUB *n.*^{4}.

bubba *n.* [? pron. by a (younger) sibling] **1** [19C+] (*US*) (*also* **bub**) a brother. **2** [20C+] (*Aus./US black*) (*also* **bubbo**) a young child. **3** [1920s+] (*also* **bub**) a general term of address to an un-named male. **4** [1940s+] (*US*) generic for an uneducated Southern male. **5** [1990s+] a fat man.

bubbalah *n.* see BUBELE *n.*

bubbed *adj.* [BUB *v.*^{1}] [19C] drunk.

bubbeleh *n.* see BUBELE *n.*

bubbelizer *n.* [their 'bu-bu-bu' stammering] [20C+] (*Ulster*) a stammerer.

bubbe mayse *n.* (*also* **bobbe mayse, bubeh miseh**) [Yid. *Bovo Mayse*, the Story of Bovo (or Buovo), an early 16C narrative poem written in Italy and translated into Yid. by the scholar Elijah Bochur. Its unlikely tales, featuring the hero Bovo, were meant as satire. When rewritten in 19C prose it was corrupted as *bubbe mayse*, lit. 'a grandmother's story', since only a gullible old lady was presumed to believe the stories as they stood] [20C+] an old wife's tale.

bubber *n.*^{1} [BUB *v.*^{1}] **1** [mid-17C–early 19C] a heavy drinker. **2** [late 17C–early 19C] a drinking bowl. **3** [late 17C–mid-19C] a thief who steals from taverns.

bubber *n.*^{2} [BUB *n.*^{4}] [mid-19C] (*US*) an old woman with large, pendulous breasts.

bubbery *n.* [BUB *v.*^{1}; i.e. the behaviour of the drinkers] [early 19C] noise, rowdiness.

bubbie *n.* see BUBBY *n.*^{2}.

bubbies *n.* [either f. Lat. *bibere*, to drink, or poss. – in the way that some claim that SE *pap* is onomat., stemming f. the infant's sucking lips – f. the hungry child's cries of 'Bub, bub!'] [late 17C+] the female breasts.

bubbing *n.* [BUB *v.*^{1}] [late 17C] drinking; thus *bubbing-house*, *bubbing-school*, a tavern.

bubbing *v.* [BUB *v.*^{1}] [late 17C] drunken.

bubbkis *n.* see BOBKHES *n.*

bubble *n.*^{1} [the schemes so proposed are as insubstantial, if as superficially shiny, as a soap bubble; the (linguistic) archetype is the *South Sea Bubble* of 1721] **1** [17C–19C] a victim, one who is ripe for being fooled. **2** [18C–1920s] a sham or otherwise dubious company; thus any dubious scheme; also attrib. **3** see BUBBLE-GUM MACHINE *n.* (1).

IN COMPOUNDS

❑ **bubble-man** *n.* [mid-19C] one who promotes fraudulent companies.

SE in slang uses

IN COMPOUNDS

❑ **bubblebrain** *n.* see BUBBLEHEAD *n.* ❑ **bubblebutt** *n.* (*also* **bubbleass**) [BUTT *n.*^{1} (1a)] [1970s+] (*US campus*) **1** large, protruding, rounded buttocks. **2** the person who has such a physique. ❑ **bubble dancing** *n.* [SE *soap bubbles* + pun on SE *bubble-dancer*, a woman who dances, wearing nothing but strategically placed balloons] [1940s] (*US*) washing up; as n., *bubble dancer*, a washer-up. ❑ **bubble gum/gummer** *n.* see see separate entries. ❑ **bubblehead/headed** see see separate entries. ❑ **bubble juice** *n.* see BUBBLY *n.* ❑ **bubble-top** *n.* [1960s+] **1** (*US*) (*also* **bubble**) a police car [the flashing lights on its roof]. **2** an electric sun roof in a car. **3** (*US campus*) a woman with a bouffant hairdo. ❑ **bubble water** *n.* see BUBBLY *n.*

bubble *n.*^{2} [abbr. AUTOMOBUBBLE *n.*] **1** [1900s–70s] (*orig. US*) any automobile. **2** [1960s] a small (three-wheeled) automobile, briefly popular in early 1960s.

bubble *n.*^{3} (*also* **old bubble**) [rhy. sl. = TROUBLE AND STRIFE *n.*] [1930s+] one's wife.

bubble *n.*^{4} [BUB *v.*^{1}] [1940s–60s] (*US*) the female breast.

bubble *n.*^{5} [BUBBLE AND SQUEAK *n.*^{2}; note the intensified *archbubble*, although this is poss. a nonce-coinage in Cook (1962)] [1950s+] a Greek.

bubble *n.*^{6} [1960s] (*drugs*) a small, oval swelling on the skin caused by a careless injection of heroin.

bubble *v.*^{1} [BUBBLE *n.*^{1} (1)] [mid-17C–19C] to cheat, to hoax, to swindle; thus *bubbleable*, gullible.

IN COMPOUNDS

❑ **bubble-bow** *n.* (*also* **bubble buff**) [SE *beau*, lit. a beau-fooler] [early–mid-18C] a woman's tweezer-case.

bubble *v.*^{2} [SE *bubbleup*] **1** [20C+] (*orig. Aus.*) to be in high spirits. **2** [1990s+] (*US black*) to improve one's situation, to make money; thus BUBBLING *n.*^{2}.

SE in slang uses

IN PHRASES

❑ **bubble around** *v.* [fig. use of SE *blow bubbles*] [late 19C] to make a harsh verbal attack on someone.

bubble *v.*^{3} [BUBBLE *n.*^{2}] [1900s–30s] (*US*) to drive a car.

bubble *v.*^{4} [1960s] (*US drugs*) to miss the vein when performing a hypodermic injection; the surrounding skin 'bubbles' up.

bubble and squeak *n.*^{1} (*also* **bubbles-and-squeaks**) [the noise of the cooking; subseq. use is SE] [late 18C–19C; 1930s–40s] (left-over) beef and cabbage and/or potatoes fried up together; occas. fish and potatoes.

bubble and squeak *n.*^{2} [rhy. sl.] **1** [late 19C+] a schoolmaster [BEAK *n.*^{1} (3)]. **2** [late 19C+] a magistrate [BEAK *n.*^{1} (1)]. **3** [20C+] a Greek. **4** [1950s] a creek. **5** [1970s+] a week. **6** [2000s] (*Aus.*) an act of urination [= LEAK *n.* (2)].

bubble (and squeak) *v.* [rhy. sl.] [20C+] to speak, esp. to inform to the police.

IN PHRASES

❑ **put the bubble in** *v.* [1920s+] (*UK Und.*) to inform.

bubble and squeak *adv.* [the noise and action that gives the frying dish its name] [early–mid-19C] vigorously.

bubbled *adv.* [BUBBLE (AND SQUEAK) *v.*] [mid-19C+] betrayed, informed against.

bubble gum *n.*[1] [1960s+] **1** (*orig. music business*) catchy, simplistic pop music aimed spec. at the pre-pubescent and early teenage girl market, all, allegedly, prime consumers of bubble-gum; by ext. anything considered frivolous, banal, unimaginative; also attrib. **2** nonsense.

bubble gum *n.*[2] [1980s] (*US campus*) a police officer.

bubble gum *n.*[3] [rhy. sl. = BUM *n.*[1] (1)] [1990s+] the buttocks, the behind.

bubble-gum machine *n.* [resemblance] (*US*) **1** [1960s+] the flashing lights on top of a police car. **2** [1970s] the vehicle itself. **3** [1970s+] (*US gay*) a condom vending machine, as found in a men's public lavatory.

bubble-gummer *n.* [BUBBLE-GUM *n.*[3] (1)] [1960s+] a girl aged 10–14, also an adolescent boy.

bubblehead *n.* (*also* **bubblebrain**) [SE *bubble* + -HEAD *sfx* (1)] [1950s+] (*US*) a foolish, careless person, with a brain full of air.

bubbleheaded *adj.* [BUBBLEHEAD *n.*] [1940s+] silly, foolish.

bubblejas *n. see* BABALAAS *n.*

bubbler *n.*[1] [BUBBLE *v.*[1]] [18C] a swindler.

bubbler *n.*[2] [1970s+] (*Aus.*) a school drinking fountain.

bubbles *n. see* BUBBLY *n.*

bubbles and squeaks *n.* [BUBBLE *n.*[5] + pun on BUBBLE AND SQUEAK *n.*[1]] [1950s] Greeks and Cypriots seen collectively.

bubble (up) *v.* [abbr. BUBBLE (AND SQUEAK) *v.* or *PUT THE BUBBLE IN under* BUBBLE (AND SQUEAK) *v.*] [1980s+] to inform, to betray.

bubbling *n.*[1] [BUBBLE *v.*[1]] [late 17C–early 18C] (an act of) cheating, hoaxing, swindling.

bubbling *n.*[2] [BUBBLE *v.*[2] (2)] [1990s+] (*US black teen*) rising up, coming up, emerging vigorously.

bubbly *n.* (*also* **bub, bubble juice, bubbles, bubble water, bubbly-wine**) [note WW1 RN *bubbly*, rum] [20C+] champagne.

bubbly jock *n.* [rhy. sl. = turkey cock. Note milit. jargon the *Bubbly Jocks*, the Royal Scots Greys, whose rival regiments equate them with the farmyard bird] **1** [late 18C–1920s] (*also* **bublie-cock**) a turkey. **2** [mid–late 19C] a foolish braggart [implies a turkey's characteristics, strutting and making too much noise]. **3** [late 19C] an excessive talker.

bubbo *n. see* BUBBA *n.* (2).

bubby *n.*[1] *see* BUBBIES *n.*

bubby *n.*[2] (*also* **bubbie**) [BUDDY *n.* + BUBBA *n.* (3)] [19C] a friendly term of address.

bube *n.* (*also* **bubo**) [SE *bubo*, an inflamed swelling or abscess, one of the possible signs of venereal disease] [late 16C–1920s] venereal disease, esp. syphilis.

bubeh miseh *n. see* BUBBE MAYSE *n.*

bubele *n.* (*also* **bubbalah, bubbeleh, bubeleh**) [Yid. *bubele*, little grandmother] [20C+] a general affectionate term of address.

bubkhes/bubkis *n. see* BOBKHES *n.*

bublie-cock *n. see* BUBBLY JOCK *n.* (1).

bubo *n. see* BUBE *n.*

bubonic *adj.* [SE *bubonic plague* which devastated Europe during the 14C Black Death] [1990s+] extreme, notably powerful.

bubs *n.* [SE *babies*] [1960s+] (*Aus.*) kindergarten.

bubu *n.* **1** *see* BOBO *n.*[1] (1). **2** *see* BOO-BOO *n.*[4] (1).

buccaneer *n.* [rhy. sl. = QUEER *n.* (4)] [1990s+] a male homosexual.

buccra *n. see* BACKRA *n.*

buck *n.*[1] [all fig. uses of SE *buck*, a he-goat or male deer] **1** [late 16C–mid-19C] a cuckold. **2** [early 17C–18C] a bold, daring person of either sex [abbr. of *buck-a-dandy*, a fop, but note Ware, who suggests a root in SE *buckram*, a stiffening fabric used by such dandies in the full-skirted coats of the 18C]. **3** [late 17C+] a bold, dashing man, a roisterer. **4** [late 18C–mid-19C] as *my buck*, an affectionate term of address. **5** [early 19C+] (*US/Aus./N.Z.*) a man, esp. used attrib. of a US black, Native American or Aus. Aboriginal; derog. unless used by blacks [the strength and sexuality of the male animal underpins this sense in particular, where buck is often an abbr. of the marginally more opprobrious *buck nigger*, the female equivalent is a *wench*]. **6** [mid-19C–1920s] a dandy [abbr. of BUCKWHEAT *n.* (1)]. **7** [mid-19C–1960s] a small dealer who works for a more powerful master. **8** [1900s–40s] (*Aus.*) a foreman. **9** [1900s–60s] (*US prison*) a priest, esp. as a prison chaplain. **10** [1910s+] (*Aus.*) spirit, energy. **11** [1920s+] (*orig. Liverpool*) (*also* **bucker, buckess**) a tearaway, a young, aggressive criminal. **12** [2000s] (*UK juv.*) an extremely attractive person of either sex.

DERIVATIVES

❑ **buckish** *adj.* [late 18C–early 19C] acting in a dashing manner.

IN COMPOUNDS

❑ **buck bail** *n.* [late 18C–mid-19C] (*orig. UK Und.*) bail put up by one member of a gang for another. ❑ **buckface** *n.* (*also* **buck's face, buck's head**) [17C–early 19C] a cuckold. ❑ **buckload** *n.* [sense 1 above + SE *load* or play on SHOT *n.*[1] (6a), i.e. *buck-shot*] [19C] (*US*) a large measure of liquor. ❑ **buck nation** *n.* [sense 5 above + -NATION *sfx*] [20C+] (*W.I.*) the Amerindian people of Guyana. ❑ **bucknight** *n.* (*also* **buck's night**) [1910s+] (*Aus.*) a party for men only. ❑ **buck nun** *n.* [1930s] (*US*) a batchelor. ❑ **buck party** *n.* [late 19C–1950s] (*Aus./US*) a party for men only. ❑ **bucktown** *n.* [sense 3/5 above; but note US regional (Ohio) *bucktown*, the rough part of town] [1990s+] (*US black*) Brooklyn, New York. ❑ **buck-whyling** *n. see* separate entry. ❑ **buck-wild(ing)** *see* separate entries.

IN PHRASES

❑ **buck of the first head** *n.* [SE *first head*, primacy] [late 18C–early 19C] a celebrated debauchee, whose excesses outpace those of his peers. ❑ **buck up** *v. see* separate entries. ❑ **cut a buck** *v.* [mid-19C] (*US*) to show off. ❑ **old buck** *n.* **1** [late 18C–1920s] a general term of address. **2** [mid-19C–1910s] a man.

SE in slang uses

IN COMPOUNDS

❑ **buck-assed** *adj.* [1940s] (*US*) simple, unadorned, lit. 'naked'. ❑ **buck bathing** *n.* [*BUCK-NAKED* below] [1930s] (*US*) nude bathing. ❑ **buck-eyed** *adj. see* separate entry. ❑ **buck fever** *n.* [hunting jargon *buck fever*, the nerves felt by inexperienced hunters faced by the game they have been pursuing; they get so excited they fail to shoot] [late 19C+] (*S.Afr./US*) nervousness in the face of an unknown or new situation that may render one incapable of action. ❑ **buck fitch** *n.* [SE *buck-fitch*, a male polecat] [late 17C–early 19C] (*UK Und.*) an ageing lecher, an old roué. ❑ **buckhead** *n.* [1990s+] (*UK juv.*) a person with buck teeth. ❑ **buck-naked** *adj.* (*also* **buck, bucked**) [as naked as a SE *buck*; or ? corruption of BUTT *n.*[1] (1a) + SE *naked*] [mid-19C; 1920s+] (*orig. US*) naked. ❑ **buckskin** *n.* [SE *buckskin*, leather (garments) made from the skin of a buck] **1** [late 18C–early 19C] an American soldier, fighting in the Revolutionary War. **2** [19C+] a native of Virginia.

buck *n.*[2] [cabman's jargon *buck*, a fraudulent passenger used by an unlicensed London cabbie, who could get near a theatre or restaurant in the Strand only if he appeared to be bringing a fare; thus a reasonably respectable young man would be picked up, driven a few yards and then dropped] [mid–late 19C] an unlicensed cab-driver.

buck *n.*[3] [orig. abbr. SE *buckskin*, an item used as barter in 19C America] **1** [mid-19C+] (*US*) $1, $10. **2** [late 19C] sixpence, usu. preceded by a number of shillings, e.g. *six and a buck*, 6s 6d. **3** [1920s+] (*US*) money, irrespective of quantity (although the image is usu. of a quantity). **4** [1960s+] (*US*) $100; thus *half-buck*, $50, *buck-and-a-half* $150. **5** [1970s+] (*S.Afr.*) a rand. **6** [1970s+] (*Aus/N.Z.*) A$1.00. **7** [2000s] 100, in non-monetary contexts.

IN COMPOUNDS

❑ **buck-fifty** *n.* [play on sense 4, *buck-fifty*, i.e. $150; the slash requires around 150 stitches to close it] [1990s+] (*US prison*) a razor-slash that runs either over the top of the skull or from ear to ear.

IN PHRASES

❑ **half-a-buck** *n.* [1940s–50s] (*US*) fifty cents. ❑ **in the bucks** *adj.* [1940s–50s] (*US*) well-off, wealthy. ❑ **up in the bucks** *adj.* (*also* **up in the dough**) [1920s–30s] (*US*) wealthy, prospering.

buck *n.*[4] [Hind. *bak*, speech, talk] [late 19C–1940s] talk, conversation, esp. when garrulous or irritating.

IN PHRASES

❑ **put in buck** *v.* [mid-19C] (*UK Und*) to testify (poss. as a perjurer) on someone's behalf.

buck *n.*[5] [1910s] (*US Und.*) a prison.

buck *n.*[6] [SE *buck* v.] **1** [1910s+] (*Aus./N.Z.*) a try, an attempt. **2** [1960s] (*US prison*) a strike.

IN PHRASES

❑ **fair buck** *n.* [sense 1 above] [1940s+] (*N.Z.*) a fair chance, usu. as excl. *fair buck!* ❑ **give it a buck** *v.* (*also* **have a buck at**) [1940s+] to have a try, to make an attempt at.

IN EXCLAMATIONS

❑ **fair buck!** [2000s] (*N.Z.*) be fair! give me a chance!

buck *n.*[7] [? it 'bucks you up'] [1930s+] (*US prison*) homemade alcohol.

buck *n.*[8] [it was a 'galloping' disease] [1940s] (*Irish*) tuberculosis.

buck *adj.*[1] [BUCK *n.*[1]] **1** [late 18C+] tough, virile, aggressive; for attrib. uses as a term of racist abuse *see* BUCK *n.*[1] (5). **2** [mid-19C] (*US campus*) excellent, first-rate. **3** *see BUCK-NAKED under* BUCK *n.*[1].

IN COMPOUNDS

❑ **buck-sick** *adj.* [20C+] (*W.I.*) tired of a boring, but still vital task.

buck *adj.*[2] *see* BUCKSHEE *adj.*

buck *v.*[1] [orig. used of rabbits; late 19C+ use is usu. US] [early 17C+] to have sexual intercourse.

IN PHRASES

❑ **go to buck** *v.* [early 18C] of a woman, to have sexual intercourse.

buck *v.*[2] [SE *buck*, to oppose, to come up against] **1** [mid-19C–1930s] (*US*) to bet (against) in a game of chance. **2** [mid-19C+] to protest, to object, to show irritation. **3** [late-19C–1950s] (*US*) to desire, to work towards, to aim for. **4** [late 19C+] (*also* **buck against**) to avoid, to resist, to oppose oneself to; thus *buck the system*, to fight against the status quo. **5** [1980s] (*US campus*) to miss a class. **6** [1990s+] (*US campus*) to intimidate. **7** [1990s+] (*US black/teen*) to shoot a weapon. **8** [1990s+] (*US black*) (*also* **buck up**) to fight.

IN PHRASES

❑ **buck against** *v. see* sense 3 above. ❑ **buck down** *v.* [1990s+] (*US black*) to challenge, to defeat. ❑ **buck for** *v. see* separate entry. ❑ **buck off** *v.* [1990s+] (*US black*) to murder, to kill. ❑ **buck the horse** *v.* [SE/sense 4 above] [20C+] (*UK Und.*) to deliberately cause trouble in prison by refusing to accept discipline. ❑ **buck the saw** *v.* [sense 3 above + pun on *bucksaw*, a heavy form of frame-saw used with a buck or sawing-frame] [1960s] (*US black*) to overcome a challenge, to triumph despite heavy odds. ❑ **buck the tiger** *v. see under* TIGER *n.* ❑ **buck up** *v. see* sense 8 above.

buck *v.*[3] [synon. Hind. *bakna*, *bukh*] **1** [late 19C–1900s] to talk, to chatter; thus *buck-stick*, a chatterer. **2** [late 19C–1940s] to swagger, to talk big or bumptiously, to brag.

buck *v.*[4] [? SE *buck*, 'Of a horse: to leap vertically from the ground, drawing the feet together like a deer, and arching the back' (*OED*)] **1** [late 19C+] to move, to run. **2** [1910s] (*US*) (*also* **buck in**) to make an effort. **3** [1990s+] (*W.I.*) to meet, to encounter.

SE in slang uses

IN PHRASES

❑ **buck a bull off the bridge** *v.* [1910s–40s] (*US*) to perform wonders, to achieve anything one wants. ❑ **buck into** *v.* (*also* **buck in**) [late 19C–1900s] (*US*) to encounter; to become involved in. ❑ **buck out** *v.* [equine imagery] [1920s–60s] (*US West*) to die, also in fig. use.

buck *v.*[5] **1** [1960s+] (*US*) (*also* **buck-slip**) to pass, to give. **2** [1990s+] (*US*) to shoot, thus *bucked*, shot.

buck *v.*[6] **1** [1970s] (*W.I.*) to stub (one's toe). **2** [1990s+] (*W.I.*) to butt with the forehead.

buck *v.*[7] *see BUCK THE TIGER under* TIGER *n.*

buck *adv.* [BUCK *adj.*[1]] [1990s+] (*US black*) utterly, totally, completely.

buckaroo *n.* (*also* **bakhara, buckayro, buckhara, baquero**) [Sp. *vaquero*, cowboy, cow hand] **1** [early 19C+] a cowboy or cattle-driver; also as v.; also attrib. **2** [1920s+] a lively young man. **3** [1930s+] a man, a fellow. **4** [1940s] (*Aus./N.Z.*) a farmhand; also attrib.

buck-buck! *excl.* [1990s+] (*US black teen*) onomat. noise of a gun being fired.

bucked *adj.*[1] **1** [late 19C] arrested; married. **2** [1980s+] (*Irish*) (*also* **bucked out**) finished, 'done for' [? euph. for FUCKED *adj.*[1]].

bucked *adj.*[2] [BUCK *v.*[3]] [20C+] made to feel better, cheered, encouraged.

bucked *adj.*[3] *see BUCK-NAKED under* BUCK *n.*[1].

buckee *n. see* BUCKY *n.*[1].

buckeen *n.* [Anglo-Irish *buckeen*, a younger son of the impoverished Anglo-Irish aristocracy. The term apes the better-known *squireen*, a petty landowner] [late 18C–early 19C] a bully.

bucker *n.*[1] [*BUCK THE TIGER under* TIGER *n.*] [mid-19C+] (*US*) a gambler.

bucker *n.*[2] [BUCK *v.*[2] (4)] [late 19C–1900s] (*US*) a rebel, one who refuses to follow the party line.

bucker *n.*[3] (*also* **buckeroo**) **1** [1920s–70s] (*US*) a cowboy. **2** [1960s] (*US*) a toady, one who curries favour for self advancement.

bucker *n.*[4] [BUCK *n.*[3] (1)] [1980s] (*US*) $1.

bucker *n.*[5] *see* BUCK *n.*[1] (11).

buckeroo *n.* [BUCK *n.*[3] (1) + -EROO *sfx*] **1** [1940s+] (*US*) $1. **2** *see* BUCKER *n.*[3].

buckeroo *adj. see* PUCKEROO *adj.*

buckess *n. see* BUCK *n.*[1] (11).

bucket *n.* **1** [early 19C] in pl., boots or shoes. **2** [mid–late 19C–1910s] (*UK Und./Aus.*) a glass. **3** [late 19C; 1930s+] (*Can./US Und.*) a county or local prison; later uses underpinned by BUCKET AND PAIL *n.* **4** in sexual contexts. (**a**) [late 19C; 1990s+] (*also* **bucket fanny**) the vagina, esp. when large or loose. (**b**) [1930s+] (*US*) (*also* **brown bucket**) the anus, the buttocks; thus *bucket queen*, a male homosexual who takes the active role in anal intercourse. **5** [1910s] any form of motor vehicle, boat or airplane that has become run down and dilapidated. **6** [1950s–60s] (*US*) a plump woman, an unattractive woman. **7** [1990s+] (*US campus*) an incompetent, clumsy person. **8** [1990s+] (*US*) in basketball, a scoring shot. **9** *see BUCKET BONG* below.

IN COMPOUNDS

❑ **bucket boy** *n.* [1970s+] (*US gay*) a passive partner in anal intercourse. ❑ **bucket broad** *n.* [BROAD *n.*[2] (2)] [1940s–70s] (*US Und.*) a prostitute who permits anal intercourse. ❑ **bucket cunt** *n.* (*also* **bucket fanny**) [coarsely joc. use of SE/sense 4a above + CUNT *n.* (1)/FANNY *n.*[1] (1)] [1990s+] a large vagina.

IN PHRASES

❑ **dropped in the bucket** *adj.* [1990s+] (*US prison*) in prison. ❑ **drop the bucket** *v. see under* DROP *v.*[1]. ❑ **drop the bucket on** *v. see under* DROP *v.*[1]. ❑ **off like a bucket of prawns in the hot sun** *adv. see under* OFF LIKE A... *phr.* ❑ **paint the bucket** *v.* [1950s+] (*US gay*) to have anal intercourse. ❑ **put in the bucket** *v. see* BUCKET *v.* (1). ❑ **toss in the bucket** *v.* [1940s] (*US*) to imprison.

IN EXCLAMATIONS

❑ **up your bucket!** [1960s] (*US*) a general excl. of dismissal.

SE in slang uses

IN COMPOUNDS

❑ **bucket bong** *n.* (*also* **bucket**) [BONG *n.*[1]] [1990s+] (*Aus./US drugs*) a form of gravity pipe for smoking marijuana, made with a 2-litre (3½-pint) plastic bottle and a bucket. ❑ **bucket cheat** *n.* (*also* **bucket-chat**) [? the feeding of lambs from buckets] [mid–late 18C] (*UK Und.*) a sheep. ❑ **buckethead** *n.* [as if poured from a *bucket*] [1920s+] to rain very heavily. ❑ **bucketmouth** *n.* [1970s] (*US*) **1** a chatterer. **2** one who habitually uses 'bad language'.

IN PHRASES

❑ **bucket about** *v.* [? image of a bucket floating on water] [1920s] to move backwards/forwards/from side to side, to oscillate. ❑ **bucket (down)** *v.* [as if poured from a *bucket*] [1920s+] to rain very heavily. ❑ **get off the bucket** *v.* [1970s] a phr. of general dismissal. ❑ **give someone the bucket** *v.* [var. on SACK *v.* (2a)] [mid-19C] to dismiss from a job. ❑ **in the bucket** see *IN THE BARREL under* BARREL *n.*[1].

bucket *v.* ['To *bucket* a person is synonymous with putting him *in the well'* (Vaux)] **1** [19C] (*UK Und.*) (*also* **put in the bucket**) to deceive, to cheat, to swindle, to ruin, esp. to rob an accomplice of their share of a robbery; thus n., *bucketer*. **2** [1970s+] (*Aus.*) to disdain, to denigrate, to despise.

IN COMPOUNDS

❑ **bucket gaff** *n.* (*also* **bucket job**) [GAFF *n.*[1] (12) / SE *job*] [1960s–70s] (*UK Und.*) a fraudulent company.

bucket afloat *n.* (*also* **bucket and float**) [rhy. sl.] [mid–late 19C; 1910s] a coat.

bucket and pail *n.* (*also* **lard and pail, mop and pail**) [rhy. sl. = jail] [1930s+] prison.

bucket house *n. see* BUCKET SHOP *n.* (1).

bucketing *n.* [the effort involved in a laborious task, e.g. filling a bath, using only a bucket] **1** [mid-19C–1910s] a hard task, which one performs only when coerced. **2** [2000s] (*N.Z.*) serious criticism.

bucket of... *n.*

SE in slang uses

IN PHRASES

❑ **bucket of...** *n. see also under* relevant n. ❑ **bucket of bolts** *n.* [1940s+] (*US*) a broken-down vehicle, airplane, etc. ❑ **bucket of lard** *n.* (*also* **bucket of blubber, pail of lard**) [1920s+] a very fat person. ❑ **bucket of puss** *n.* [1990s+] (*US*) a person to be pitied and despised. ❑ **bucket of shit** *n. see* CROCK OF SHIT *n.* ❑ **bucket of smashed crabs** *n.* [1990s+] a general derog. description of an unattractive woman. ❑ **bucket of worms** *n.* [var. on *can of worms*] [1970s+] (*US*) an unpleasant, complex and unappetizing situation.

bucket of dirt *n. see* DICKY (DIRT) *n.*

bucket shop *n.* ['The market authority in Chicago, called the Board of Trade, would not allow a deal in "options" of less than 5,000 bushels of grain. In order to catch men of small means, what was called the "Open Board of Trade" commenced business in an alley under the regular Board of Trade Rooms. There was an elevator to carry the members of the board to their rooms, and occasionally a member, if trade was slack, would call out, "I'll send down and get a bucketful pretty soon," referring to the speculators in the "Open Board of Trade" below' (*Leeds Mercury*, December 1886)] (*orig. US*) **1** [mid-19C–1900s] (*also* **bucket house**) a gin-mill, a low-class liquor-shop. **2** [late 19C+] an unauthorized office used orig. for smaller gambling transactions in grain, and subsequently extended to offices for other descriptions of gambling and betting on the markets, stocks etc. **3** [1980s+] a cut-price travel agent, specializing in long-haul air flights.

bucket shopper *n.* [BUCKET SHOP *n.* (2)] [1920s–30s] (*US Und.*) one who operates (from) an unauthorized office used for gambling and betting on the markets, stocks etc.

buckeye *n.*[1] (*US*) **1** [early 19C+] (*also* **buckey, bucky**) an inhabitant of Ohio [the buckeye tree (*Aesculus glabra*, the American horse chestnut), which flourishes in the state and is featured on its flag]. **2** [early 19C+] a rustic or country person. **3** [mid-19C–1900s] an inferior person or thing, esp. one of no value, poor quality or cheap (but often showy) [the poor quality of the wood of the buckeye tree plus ? poor reputation of Ohians]. **4** [late 19C–1940s] (*US*) a small place of business, esp. one found in a slum area, esp. a cigar factory.

buckeye *n.*[2] [the addition of *buckeye* nuts to the liquor during its production] [mid-19C; 1950s+] (*US*) rotgut whisky.

buck-eyed *adj.* [SE *buck*, to project] [mid-19C+] (*US black*) having eyes considered out of the ordinary, cross-eyed, squinting, protruding etc.

buck for *v.* [SE *buck*, to come up against] [late 19C+] (*orig. milit.*) to struggle towards, to act energetically in one's own interest.

IN COMPOUNDS

❑ **buck private** *n.* (*also* **buck**) [late 19C+] (*US milit.*) a private soldier who is 'bucking for' promotion; thus occas. other ranks in a similar position, e.g. *buck colonel*, who wishes to be a general.

buckhara *n. see* BUCKAROO *n.*

buckhorse *n.* [the pugilist *Buckhorse* (real name John Smith) who, for a small charge, allowed people to hit him hard on the side of the head] [mid–late 19C] a blow on the ear.

Buck House *n.* [abbr.] [1910s+] Buckingham Palace, London home of the British royal family.

buckijit *n.* [BUCK *adj.*[1] + EEJIT *n.*] [20C+] (*Irish*) a very great fool.

bucking *adj.* [BUCK *adj.*[1]] [late 19C+] (*Irish*) a general intensifier.

Buckinger's boot *n.* [proper name of Matthew *Buchinger*, b.1674 in Germany and known as 'The Little man of Nuremberg'. He was only 29" tall and born limbless, 'notwithstanding which he drew coats of arms very neatly and could write the Lord's Prayer within the compass of one shilling, he was married to a tall handsome woman, and traversed the country, shewing himself for money' (Grose). He was also a master dice manipulator. For him, a boot could fit only his *THIRD LEG under* THIRD *adj.*] [late 18C–late 19C] the vagina.

bucking horse *n.* [the image of St George and the Dragon on the coin] [1910s] (*Aus.*) a sovereign (£1).

bucking match *n.* [animal imagery] [late 19C] (*US black*) a fight in which each combatant uses only their head.

buckish *adj.*[1] [late 18C–early 19C] acting like a BUCK *n.*[1] (3).

buckish *adj.*[2] [BUCK UP *v.*[2] (1) + sfx *-ish*] [1900s–10s] in high spirits.

buckle *n.*[1] [ext. of SE use] [early 19C] a fetter, usu. in pl.

buckle *n.*[2] [SE *buckle*, to apply oneself vigorously] [late 19C–1900s] (*Aus.*) a positive or cheerful state, condition, mood.

buckle *n.*[3] *see* BUCKLE MY SHOE *n.*

buckle *v.* [SE *buckle*, to join] **1** [late 16C–mid-19C] to be married. **2** [mid-17C–1900s] to marry, to become a mistress [Partridge suggests 20C Aus. use, but it is in neither *AND* nor *DNZE*]. **3** [mid-19C] to understand. **4** [mid-19C+] to arrest; usu. as *buckled*. **5** [1970s+] (*US*) to argue, to fight.

IN COMPOUNDS

❑ **buckle-beggar** *n.* (*also* **buckle-the-beggars**) [sense 2 above + SE *beggar*] [18C–mid-19C] a clergyman who performs irregular marriages.

SE in slang uses

IN COMPOUNDS

❑ **buckle bosom** *n.* [SE *buckle*, to grapple, to engage/sense 3 above + *bosom*] [early 17C] a constable, a catchpoll. ❑ **buckle-hammed** *adj.* [SE *buckle*, to warp, to bend, to crumple + HAM *n.*[1]] [early 17C] having crooked legs.

IN PHRASES

❑ **buckle down** *v.* (*also* **buckle to**) [ext. of SE *buckle*, to apply oneself vigorously] [18C+] (*orig. US*) to set to work, to apply oneself vigorously.

bucklebury *n.* [play on name of the Berkshire town] [1910s–20s] a euph. for SE *buggery*.

buckled *adj.* [1920s+] (*Irish*) drunk.

buckle my shoe *n.* (*also* **buckle**) [rhy. sl.] **1** [1910s–60s] a Jew. **2** [1940s+] (*bingo*) the number two.

buckler *n.* [SE *buckler*, a small round shield; play on SWORD *n.*] [late 16C–mid-17C] the vagina.

Buckley's *n.* (*also* **Buckley's chance, Buckley's show**) [? proper name of William *Buckley* (1780–1856), an escaped convict who spent 32 years living with Aborigines in South Victoria; or pun on name of defunct firm of *Buckley and Nunn* (founded by Mars Buckley and Crumpton Nunn in 1851) therefore one has two chances 'Buckley and Nunn', i.e. none; see *Ozwords* (Oct. 2000) – journal of the *AND* centre – for an extended discussion] [late 19C+] (*Aus./N.Z.*) no chance at all.

bucko *n.*[1] [BUCK *n.*[1] + -O *sfx* (1), thence naut. jargon *bucko*, an overbearing ship's officer, who enforces his will through (threats of) violence, usu. as *bucko mate*] **1** [late 19C+] a bully, a blustering swaggerer. **2** [late 19C+] a general term of address, e.g. *my bucko*. **3** [1910s+] a (spirited young) man.

bucko *n.*[2] [BUCK *n.*[3] (1)] [1980s+] (*US*) $1.

bucko *adj.* [BUCKO *n.*[1] (1)] [late 19C+] aggressive, overbearing, domineering.

buckoo *n. see* BEAUCOUP *n.*

buckra/buckrah *n. see* BACKRA *n.*

Buck Rogers *n.* [? the idea of a space-ship blasting off] [1980s+] (*Aus. prison*) the ignition of anal wind.

Buck Rogers time *n.* [TIME *n.* (1); note US Army WWII *Buck Rogers gun*, an M-3 light machine gun; the fictional space hero *Buck Rogers* operates several centuries in the future] [2000s] (*US prison*) a prison sentence with a parole date set extremely far in the future.

buckshee *adj.* (*also* **buck**) [Pers. *baksheesh*, a gift, a present; thus a tip; picked up by Middle East and Indian Imperial troops and thus brought to the West] **1** [1910s+] free, gratis. **2** [1930s] (*US Und.*) released from jail. **3** [1940s] obtained irregularly.

buckshee/bucksheech *n. see* BAKSHEESH *n.*

buckshine *n.* [ety. unknown] [mid-19C+] a native of Tennessee.

buckshish *see* BAKSHEESH *n.*

buckshot *n. see* BARBERTON *n.*

buckteen *n.* [ety. unknown] [mid-18C] (*UK Und.*) shoplifting.

buck-up *n.*[1] [late 19C] (*US*) buckwheat cakes.

buck-up *n.*[2] [BUCK UP *v.*[2]] **1** [1900s] (*Aus.*) alcohol, esp. beer. **2** [1910s] encouragement, cheering up. **3** [1950s+] (*W.I.*) a social gathering, for no specific purpose other than enjoyment.

buck up *v.*[1] [BUCK *n.*[1] (3)] [early–mid-19C] to dress oneself up.

buck up *v.*[2] [orig. Winchester Coll. jargon; ult. SE *buck*] **1** [mid-19C+] to encourage, to cheer someone up. **2** [mid-19C+] to cheer (oneself) up. **3** [mid-19C+] to improve. **4** [1910s] to act in an arrogant manner.

buck up! *excl.* [BUCK UP *v.*[2] (1)] [mid-19C+] **1** cheer up! **2** hurry up! **3** come on! improve yourself! put more effort in!

buck up to *v.* [BUCK *v.*[3] (1) / BUCK *v.*[2] (4)] [19C] (*US*) **1** to make advances, to court. **2** to defy, to rebel against, to stand up to.

buck up (with) *v.* (*also* **buck up on**) [BUCK *v.*[2] (4)] [1920s; 1980s+] (*UK black*) to challenge, to encounter; to meet.

buckwheat *n.* [SE *buckwheat*, the cereal grain *Fagopyrum-esculentum*, used as cattle-feed in Europe, but cooked for humans in the US; the foodstuff (and thus the term) was popularized by the black child actor William 'Buckwheat' Thomas, who appeared in the 1930s *Our Gang* series of Saturday morning films] **1** [mid-19C+] (*US*) (*also* **buckwheater**) a naïve peasant, a gullible country person. **2** [1930s+] (*US black*) a light-complexioned black person.

buckwheat crop *n.* [*buckwheat* ripens faster than other grains] [1960s] (*US*) a marriage that takes place when the bride is already pregnant.

buck-whyling *n.* [BUCK *n.*[1] (5) + SE *while away* (time)] [1990s+] (*US black*) chatting, engaging in general conversation.

buck-wild *adj.* [the state of a *buck* during the rutting season] [1940s+] (*US black*) insane, crazy; extreme, intense, desperate.

IN PHRASES

❑ **go buck** *v.* (*also* **get buck**) [1990s+] (*US black*) to act in an outrageous, often destructive and aggressive manner.

buck-wilding *n.* [BUCK-WILD *adj.*] [1990s+] (*US black*) intense activity, usu. sexual or violent.

bucky *n.*[1] (*also* **buckee**) [SE *buck* v. + sfx *-y*] [1990s+] (*W.I. Rasta/UK black*) a gun, usu. homemade.

bucky *n.*[2] *see* BUCKEYE *n.*[1] (1).

bud *n.*[1] [abbr. BUDDY *n.*] **1** [17C; mid-19C+] (*also* **buddie**) a general nickname or term of address for a brother or eldest son, any boy or man, or a close friend. **2** see BUDDY *n.*

bud *n.*[2] **1** in senses of youth, immaturity [SE *bud*, a flower that is yet to be fully opened + phr. *bud of promise*]. (**a**) [late 19C] (*orig. US*) a young, pubescent girl. (**b**) [late 19C–1920s] a debutante. (**c**) [1900s–20s] a young, immature man. (**d**) [1970s+] (*US gay*) a homosexual teenager. **2** [1930s+] (*US*) a nipple, a breast. **3** [1980s+] (*orig. US drugs*) (*also* **buds**) pertaining to cannabis. (**a**) cannabis. (**b**) that part of the cannabis plant that is smoked.

IN COMPOUNDS

❑ **budman** *n.* [1980s+] (*US campus*) a marijuana dealer. ❑ **bud-sack** *n.* [1980s+] (*US*) a container for marijuana.

IN PHRASES

❑ **budded out** *adj.* [1990s+] (*US campus*) intoxicated by marijuana. ❑ **red bud** *n.* [2000s] (*US drugs*) a variety of potent marijuana, containing red hairs from the flower buds.

buda *n. see* BUDDHA *n.*

buddha *n.* (*also* **buda**) [its Asian origins] [1980s+] (*drugs*) **1** heroin. **2** a potent form of marijuana. **3** a mix of marijuana and crack cocaine. **4** marijuana spiked with opium.

IN COMPOUNDS

❑ **buddha monk** *n.* [SE *monk*] [2000s] (*US black*) a habitual marijuana smoker. ❑ **buddha sticks** *n.* [SE *Buddha*/sense 2 above + SE *sticks*] [1970s+] (*drugs*) marijuana grown in Thailand, which is sold wrapped around small, satay sticks.

SE in slang uses

IN COMPOUNDS

❑ **buddha belly** *n.* [the trad. statues of the *Buddha*, resplendent with a huge stomach] [1970s+] (*US*) a very fat person. ❑ **buddhahead** *n.* [-HEAD *sfx* (2)] [1940s+] (*US*) **1** an East Asian or Asian person. **2** a Japanese-American; a Hawaiian [their less assimilated lifestyle, pidgin English and similarly 'unsophisticated' ways].

buddha *adj.* [BUDDHA *n.*; ult. the *Buddha*, *fl.* 5C BC] [1990s+] (*US campus*) excellent, worthy of admiration.

buddhist priest! *excl.* [1970s] (*US*) euph. for *Jesus Christ!*

buddie *n. see* BUD *n.*[1] (1).

buddie *adj. see* BUDDY *adj.*[3].

buddie-buddie *adj. see* BUDDY-BUDDY *n.*

buddley *n.* [Irish *bodalach*, a large, ungainly young person] [20C+] (*Ulster*) **1** a fat person. **2** a sausage.

buddy *n.* [SE *brother* or dial. *butty*; itself ult. obs. SE *booty*, sharing] **1** [mid-19C+] (*orig. US*) (*also* **bud, buddy-buddy**) a friend, an acquaintance. **2** [mid-19C+] (*orig. US*) (*also* **bud**) a form of address. **3** [1970s+] (*W.I./UK black teen*) a sexual partner. **4** [1990s+] (*US/W.I.*) the penis. **5** [1990s+] (*W.I./UK black teen*) the body.

DERIVATIVES

❑ **buddy-o** *n.* (*also* **buddy-roe, buddy-roo**) [-O *sfx* (2)] [1940s+] (*US*) an affectionate or ironic term of address.

IN COMPOUNDS

❑ **buddy boy** *n.* [1950s+] (*orig. US*) a friend, usu. in a negative or ironic use; esp. as a term of address. ❑ **buddy-gee** *n.* (*also* **buddy-ghee**) [GEE *n.*[3] (1)] [1930s–60s] (*US black*) a friend. ❑ **buddy seat** *n.* [1940s–60s] the pillion seat on a motorcycle. ❑ **buddy sex** *n.* [2000s] (*US gay*) hedonistic sexual intercourse without committment.

buddy *adj.*[1] [euph.] [1950s] (*Aus.*) a version of 'bloody'.

buddy *adj.*[2] [BUDDY *n.*] [1950s–60s] (*Aus./US*) friendly.

buddy *adj.*[3] [? *Buddies*, a brand of shoe that looks fashionable but is reputed to fall apart very quickly] [1990s+] (*rap music*) referring to something that appears good at first, but is actually a cheap imitation, esp. when stolen from another artist, e.g. *Get that buddy shit out of here.*

buddy *v.* (*also* **buddy around, buddy with, buddy up**) [BUDDY *n.*] **1** [1910s+] (*orig. US*) to become friendly, to live or travel as friends. **2** [1950s+] (*orig. US*) to ingratiate oneself, to curry favour with someone.

buddy-buddy *n.* [redup. BUDDY *n.*] [1940s+] (*US*) (*also* **buddie-buddie**) close friend.

buddy-buddy *adj.* (*also* **buddy-buddies**) [redup. BUDDY *n.*] [1940s+] exceptionally and overtly friendly, prob. insincerely so.

buddy-buddy *v.* [1940s+] (*orig. US milit.*) to befriend.

buddy-buddy *adv.* [1950s+] (*orig. US*) in a friendly manner.

buddy-fuck *n.* [BUDDY-FUCK *v.*[2]] [2000s] (*US gay*) **1** a sexual partner, but not a steady lover. **2** an act of hedonistic, non-committed sex.

buddy-fuck *v.*[1] (*also* **B.F.**) [FUCK *v.* (2)] [1960s+] (*US, mainly milit./campus*) to impose on, betray or otherwise inconvenience a friend; thus *buddy-fucker, buddy-fucking.*

buddy-fuck *v.*[2] [BUDDY *n.* + FUCK *v.* (1)] [2000s] (*US gay*) to have intercourse with a friend rather than a lover.

budge *n.*[1] (*also* **budgie**) [SE *budge*, a kind of fur, consisting of lamb's skin with the wool dressed outwards] [late 17C–late 19C] **1** a sneak thief, esp. one who specializes in entering houses (occas. shops) and taking furs, cloaks and coats. **2** the criminal speciality of sneak-thieving.

IN COMPOUNDS

❑ **budge and snudge** *n.* [SNUDGE *n.*; note the 1950s British TV sit-com *Bootsie and Snudge*, based on the misadventures of two army friends] [late 17C–mid-18C] (*UK Und.*) a housebreaker and their accomplice.

budge *n.*[2] [BUB *n.*[1] (1)] [19C–1900s] liquor.

IN COMPOUNDS

❑ **budge kain** *n.* [KEN *n.*[1] (1)] [19C] (*Scot.*) a public house, a tavern.

budge *n.*[3] [? abbr. SE *budget*, a pouch, bag, wallet, usu. of leather] [1980s] (*US*) a woman's breasts.

budge *v.*[1] [SE *budge*, to move; in phr. BEAK *n.*[1] (1)] [17C–19C] to leave.

IN PHRASES

❑ **budge a beak** *v.* [early 17C] to run away (from the law).

budge *v.*[2] [BUB *v.*[1]] [early 19C] to drink.

budge *v.*[3] [SE *budge*, to move against, act in hostility to] [mid-19C] to inform.

budger *n.* [BUDGE *v.*[2]] [early 19C] (*UK Und.*) a drunkard.

budget *n.* [SE *budget*, a pouch, bag, wallet, usu. of leather] [late 19C] the vagina.

budget *adj.* [1980s+] (*US campus/UK juv.*) a general negative, applied to people or objects: e.g. inferior, second-rate, stupid.

budgey *adj. see* BUDGY *adj.*

budgie *n.*[1] [abbr.] [1930s+] a *budg*erigar.

budgie *n.*[2] [SE *budgerigar*, a popular cage bird, which can be taught to speak; thus RAF jargon (*paraffin*) *budgie*, a helicopter, presumably the source of the Duchess of York's storybook creation] [1960s+] (*UK Und.*) a talkative person, esp. in police use, a minor informer.

budging ken *n.* (*also* **budging crib**) [BUDGE *v.*[2] + KEN *n.*[1] (1)] [early–mid-19C] a public house, a tavern; thus *cove of the budging-ken*, a landlord.

budgy *adj.* (*also* **budgey**) [BUDGE *n.*[2] (1)] [mid-19C–1910s] drunk.

budhead *n.* [brandname *Budweiser* beer + -HEAD *sfx* (4)] [1970s+] (*US black*) a beer drinker.

budi-bandit *n. see* BOOTY BANDIT *n.* (1).

budini *n. see* BODINI *n.*

budinski *n. see* BUTTINSKI *n.*

budion *n.* [Irish *boidín*, the penis] [20C+] (*Ulster*) a small penis.

budiquette *n.* [BUD *n.*[2] (1) + SE (*et*)*iquette*] [1980s+] (*US drugs*) the etiquette that governs the smoking of marijuana.

budli-budli *n.* [Urdu *badli*, change, used in late 19C as Raj sl. for a *locum tenens* and in 20C Indian vernacular as a temporary employee] [20C+] **1** sodomy. **2** a male homosexual.

budlies *n.* [BUD *n.*[2] (1)] [1980s+] (*drugs*) cannabis or the part of the cannabis that is smoked.

budmash *n.* [Hind. *badmash*, a rascal] [late 19C–1910s] (*orig. Ind. army*) a villain, a rascal.

buds *n.* [ety. unknown; ? link to BUD *n.*[2] (1)] [1980s+] (*drugs*) alkyl nitrates.

buducie *n.* [abbr. of BUTT *n.*[1] (1) + DICK *n.*[1] (5) + PUSSY *n.* (1)] [2000s] (*US black*) a rank, sharp odour, the result of sexual intercourse.

budulars *n.* [BUD *n.*[2] (1)] [1980s+] (*drugs*) cannabis or the part of the cannabis that is smoked.

budup! *excl.* (*also* **budum! bum!**) [20C+] (*W.I.*) echoic, onomat. words representing the sound of an object or objects crashing to the floor.

buel *n.* [SE *body* + *fuel*] [1980s+] (*US campus*) food.

buel *v.* [BUEL *n.*] [1980s+] (*US campus*) to eat voraciously.

Buenos Aires *n.* [the numbers of street prostitutes in that part of Margate; Buenos Aires was seen as a centre of white slavery] [late 19C] Royal Crescent, Margate; thus *go/take the road to Buenos Aires*, to start working as a prostitute.

buer *n.* (*also* **bewer, buah, buor, bure**) [? Shelta] [late 19C+] orig. tramp a woman, esp. one seen as sexually appealing and/or of loose character.

bues *n. see* BOOZE *n.* (1).

buf *adj.* [? SE *beautiful/beautiful fellow* or one who is BUFFED *adj.*] [1980s+] (*US teen*) of a man, attractive.

bufe *n.* (*also* **boufer, bouffe, bufer, buff, buffa, buhar, bugher**) [echoic of a bark; Ribton-Turner, *A History of Vagrants* (1887), suggests Welsh *bwch*, a buck, a male animal] [mid-16C–early 19C] (*UK Und.*) a dog.

IN COMPOUNDS

❑ **bufe nabber** *n.* (*also* **buff-knapper, buffer-nabber, buffer-napper**) [NABBER *n.* (1)] [late 16C–mid-19C] a dog stealer. ❑ **bufe's nab** *n.* [NAB *n.*[1] (1)] [late 17C–mid-19C] (*UK Und.*) a dog's head used as seal.

buff *n.*[1] [the colour of 'white' flesh] [17C+] the bare skin; usu. as *in (the) buff*, naked.

IN COMPOUNDS

❑ **buff-ball** *n.* [guests are soon *in the buff*] [late 19C] a dance attended by prostitutes; thus, *de facto*, an orgy. ❑ **buff-steppered** *adj.* [mid-19C] bare-footed.

buff *n.*[2] [*The Buffs*, men or boys who follow firemen and the fires they fight; f. the buff uniforms worn by volunteer firemen in New York City. The term gradually expanded to take in any (amateur) enthusiast, e.g. *film buff, sports buff*] [1930s+] an enthusiast, a (knowledgeable) fan.

buff *adj.*[1] [17C+] naked.

SE in slang uses

IN COMPOUNDS

❑ **buff-coat** *n.* [the *buff*-coloured uniform; later use SE] [mid–late 17C] a soldier.

IN PHRASES

❑ **buff to one's work** *v.* [coll. *buff*, naked] [early–mid-19C] to strip off preparatory to starting a fist-fight.

buff *adj.*[2] [BUFFED *adj.* (2)] **1** [1970s+] strong, muscular, healthy, good-looking. **2** [1990s+] sexy, attractive.

buff *v.*[1] [? SE *buff*, to 'polish' the truth] **1** [mid-18C] to swear to, to testify; thus, to brazen out; to inform against. **2** [late 18C–mid-19C] to commit perjury, to swear falsely. **3** [1990s+] (*US drugs*) to manipulate, to con, to threaten.

IN PHRASES

❑ **buff to the stuff** *v.* [late 19C] (*UK Und.*) to claim that stolen property is one's own.

SE in slang uses

IN PHRASES

❑ **buff it out** *v.* [? SE *buff up* or the addition of some form of *buffer*] [1970s] (*US drugs*) to adulterate a drug. ❑ **buff the banana** *v. see under* BANANA *n.* ❑ **buff the bishop** *v. see under* BISHOP *n.*[2]. ❑ **buff up** *v.* [SE *buff*, to polish + BUFF *adj.*[2] (1)] [1970s+] (*orig. US*) to work out in the gym to improve one's musculature.

buff *v.*[2] **1** [1970s+] (*US gay*) to have anal intercourse. **2** [1990s+] to perform oral sex.

buffa *n. see* BUFE *n.*

buffalo *n.*[1] **1** [mid-19C] (*US*) during the Civil War, a looter. **2** [mid-19C] (*US*) a Southerner who does not support the Confederacy. **3** [mid-19C+; 1940s+] (*orig. US, then also W.I.*) a large, stupid person. **4** [20C+] (*US Und.*) a black male. **5** [1960s] (*US*) a fat woman. **6** [1970s] (*US*) a male.

SE in slang uses

IN COMPOUNDS

❑ **buffalo navigator** *n.* [1930s–40s] (*Aus.*) a bullock-driver. ❑ **buffalo piss** *n.* [1970s+] (*US*) weak beer. ❑ **buffalo soldier** *n.* [so called by the Native Americans who compared their hair to that of the matted hair between a buffalo's horns] [mid-19C+] (*US*) a black soldier fighting in the US Army.

buffalo *n.*[2] (*also* **buffalohead**) [the picture of a buffalo head on the reverse of the coin] [1920s–70s] (*US*) a nickel (five cents).

buffalo *v.* [the size and strength of the animal] [late 19C+] (*US*) to overawe, to frighten, to confuse, to pressurize, to threaten.

IN PHRASES

❑ **make a buffalo** *v.* [1960s] to push one's way (through). ❑ **put a buffalo on** *v.* [1910s] to pressurize.

buffaloed *adj.* [BUFFALO *v.* (1)] [1900s–50s] (*orig. US*) coerced, fooled, crushed.

buffarilla *n.* (*also* **bufferilla**) [SE *buffalo + gorilla*] [1960s+] (*US campus*) a plump, homely young woman.

buffed *adj.* [SE *buffed up*, polished, in sense 2 via workout sessions at a gymnasium, thus BUFF *adj.*[2] (1)] **1** [19C] drunk. **2** [1950s+] well muscled.

buffer *n.*[1] [? echoic of a dog's bark] **1** [early 19C] a pistol. **2** see BUFE *n.* (1).

IN COMPOUNDS

❑ **buffer-lurking** *n.* (*also* **tike-lurking**) [BUFE *n.*/SE *tike* n. + LURKING *n.* (1)] [mid-19C] (*UK Und.*) stealing dogs. ❑ **buffer-nabber** (*also* **buffer-napper**) [BUFE *n.* + NAB *v.*[1] (1)/NAP *v.*[1] (6)] [18C] a dog stealer.

buffer *n.*[2] [SE *buff*, the skin; see 1821 Jon Bee (Amateur) *Real Life in London* 169: The term Buffer takes it derivation from a custom which at one time prevailed of carrying Bandanas, sarsnets, French stockings, and silk of various kinds, next the shirts of the sellers; so that upon making a sale, they were obliged to undress in order to come at the goods, or in other words, to strip to the skin or *buff* it] (*UK Und.*) **1** [late 17C–mid-19C] a villain who kills healthy horses and sells the skins; also a dog-thief. **2** [mid-18C–mid-19C] a villain.

buffer *n.*[3] (*also* **buffet**) [BUFF *v.*[1]] [mid-18C–mid-19C] one who swears false oaths for a fee; a perjurer.

IN COMPOUNDS

❑ **buffer's nab** *n.* [BUFE *n.* (1) + NAB *n.*[1] (1)] [late 17C–early 18C] (*UK Und.*) **1** a counterfeit seal, shaped like a dog's head, used to give spurious authenticity to counterfeit documents. **2** a fake pass.

buffer *n.*[4] (*also* **buffa**) [Fr. *bouffard*, a fool or clown] **1** [mid-18C+] a genial old fool, a description more affectionate than critical; thus often as *old buffer*. **2** [mid-18C+] a fool, used with a degree of contempt. **3** [late 18C–early 19C] an innkeeper. **4** [mid-19C] a tradesman. **5** [late 19C] as a term of address.

buffer *n.*[5] [SE *buff*, a blow] [late 18C–late 19C] a boxer; a fighter.

buffer *n.*[6] [SE *buffer*, a substance used in the manufacture of CRACK *n.*[7]] [1990s+] (*drugs*) **1** a user of crack cocaine. **2** one who offers oral sex in return for cocaine, thus v. *buff*, to fellate [in its sense of 'polish' cognate with SHINER *n.*[4] (1)].

buffers *n.* [late 19C+] the female breasts.

buffet (flat) *n.* [Fr. *buffet*, a sideboard or corner cupboard; thus the food and drink that is laid out upon it] [1920s–60s] (*US*) an establishment that sells illicitly distilled liquor, esp. a private house that does so.

buffing *n.* [SE *buff*, to polish] [1990s+] female masturbation.

buffing the dog *n.* [BUFF *n.*[1] (1)] [late 18C–mid-19C] killing a stolen dog that has not been advertised for (and that can thus be sold back to its owner). The skin is sold and the flesh used for dog's-meat.

buffity *adj.* [dial. *buffo*, unwieldy; ult. Ewe *bofaa*, broad and thick] [1950s+] (*W.I.*) fat, clumsy and stupid.

buff-knapper *n. see* BUFE NABBER *under* BUFE *n.*

buffle *n.* [Fr. *buffle*, a buffalo] [late 16C–mid-17C] a fool; thus *buffling*, adj., foolish.

buffle *v.* [BUFFLE *n.* (1)] [early 18C] to fool.

bufflehead *n.* [BUFFLE *n.* + -HEAD *sfx* (1). An alternative ety. suggests Du. *buffel*, blockhead] [late 17C–mid-19C] a fool; thus *buffle-headed*, stupid.

buffu-buffu *n.* [1970s] (*W.I./Rasta*) an obese person.

buffugly *adj.* [BUTT *n.*[1] (1) + FUGLY *adj.*] [2000s] (*US black*) extremely unattractive.

buffy *n.*[1] [BUFFER *n.*[4] (1)] [mid-19C] a genial old fool.

buffy *n.*[2] [BUFF *adj.*[2] (1), reinforced by TV show, *Buffy the Vampire Slayer*] [1980s+] a muscular woman or girl.

buffy *adj.* [? BEVVY *n.* (1) or Fr. *bouffé*, bloated] [mid-19C–1920s] drunk.

buft *n.* [SE *buff*, to puff out] [late 16C] (*UK Und.*) **1** a decoy. **2** a thief; thus *buftrap*, a thief-catcher [note Eric Partridge in *DU* prefers 'harlot's protector', although the rest of the list are all synons. for 'thief'].

buftie *n.* (*also* **bufty, buftie-boy, bufty-boy**) [? BUTTFUCKER *n.*] [1990s+] (*Scot.*) a male homosexual.

bufu *n.* [BUTTFUCKER *n.*] [1980s+] (*orig. US*) a male homosexual.

bufu *v.* [BUTTFUCK *v.*] [1980s] (*US*) to have anal intercourse.

bufu-bufu *adj.* [Twi *bufoo*, swollen + Ewa *bofaa*, broad and thick] [1940s+] (*W.I.*) fat, swollen, blubbery, too big, clumsy or lumbering.

bug *n.*[1] [SE *bugaboo*] **1** [mid-16C+] a person, esp. one who puts on airs; thus *bug's words*, boasting language. **2** [1960s] (*US campus*) an insignificant person; an irritating person. **3** *see* BOOG *n.* (1).

IN PHRASES

❑ **big bug** *n.* [19C] (*orig. US*) an important person, an aristocrat; esp. one who considers themselves to be one and acts accordingly; as *adj.*, important.

bug *n.*[2] [? SE *bugger*] [mid-18C] a man who incites homosexuals to join him in illegal pleasures.

bug *n.*[3] [late 18C–mid-19C] (*UK Und.*) a bribe.

bug *n.*[4] [SE *bug*, an insect, usu. a beetle or similar] **1** [late 18C–early 19C] (*Anglo-Irish*) an Englishman [the belief that English settlers imported insects to Ireland in mid-18C]. **2** that which supposedly resembles a SE *bug*, insect or other creature. (**a**) [early 19C–1920s] a breast-pin. (**b**) [late 19C–1930s] (*US gambling*) any device that aids cheating. (**c**) [late 19C+] (*US*) a small object of any kind. (**d**) [1910s–30s] (*Can.*) an old car rebuilt as a hot rod. (**e**) [1910s+] (*US*) a small car, esp. the Volkswagen Beetle. (**f**) [1920s] identification, suspicion; i.e. fig. use of sense 2g or 2h. (**g**) [1920s–40s] (*US*) a telegraph transmission key. (**h**) [1920s–50s] (*US*) a makeshift lantern or flashlight. (**i**) [1920s+] (*US Und.*) a burglar alarm. (**j**) [1930s] (*US Und.*) a time clock. (**k**) [1940s+] (*orig. US*) any form of electronic surveillance gadget. (**l**) [1960s] (*US black*) a trick. (**m**) [1960s+] (*Can./US prison*) a homemade water heater for making coffee. (**n**) [1990s+] (*Aus.*) a Moreton Bay crab. **3** in fig. senses, having a 'bug' in the head. (**a**) [mid-19C] dishonesty; esp. in phr. *put the bug on*, to fool, to tease. (**b**) [mid-19C+] (*orig. US*) an enthusiast, a fan, a devotee; thus *bugess*, a female fan. (**c**) [late 19C+] an obsession, often in combs. e.g. *travel bug*, a desire to go travelling; thus n. *bug*, an obsessive. (**d**) [20C+] an insane, unstable person. (**e**) [20C+] an idea; thus *put a bug in one's ear*, to inspire. (**f**) [1900s] (*US*) a fool. (**g**) [1950s] (*US Und.*) a prostitute's client. (**h**) [1950s] (*US*) a (left-wing) 'soapbox' orator. (**i**) [1960s–70s] a cheat, an unreliable person. (**j**) [1970s+] a lottery ticket. (**k**) [2000s] (*US prison*) a fight. **4** as a problem, difficulty. (**a**) [late 19C+] (*orig. US*) a defect, a problem in any form of machine (inc. computers and their software). (**b**) [1930s+] any form of error or delay.

IN COMPOUNDS

▫ **bug cell** *n.* [1940s] (*US prison*) a padded cell. ▫ **bug doctor** *n.* (*also* **bug doc**) [1930s+] any form of expert dealing with mental problems, a psychoanalyst, a psychologist etc. ▫ **bug fug** *adj.* [1970s] (*US*) crazy. ▫ **bug inspector** *n.* [1900s] (*US*) a psychiatrist. ▫ **bug juice** *n.* [SE *juice*/JUICE *n.*^{1} (3). Orig. the Schlechter whisky drunk by the Pennsylvania Dutch, cheap and second-rate. subseq. generic for any bad whisky; note 1930s Annapolis jargon *bug juice*, meat gravy] **1** [mid-19C+] (*Can./US*) (*also* **bug poison**) illicitly distilled whisky; thus any form of alcohol, esp. cheap and appealing to alcoholics. **2** [late 19C+] (*Can./US*) (*also* **buggy juice**) a soft drink. **3** [1940s–50s] (*US Und.*) knockout drops. **4** [1940s+] (*UK prison*) a sedative drug used for controlling violent or non-cooperative prisoners. **5** [1940s+] (*Can./US*) petrol. **6** [1940s+] (*Can./US*) a mix of saliva and tobacco juice that forms the residue or 'dottle' in a pipe. **7** [1940s+] (*Can./US*) insecticide. ▫ **bugman** *n.* [1960s] one who plants and conducts clandestine surveillance with electronic equipment. ▫ **bug test** *n.* [1930s–50s] (*US prison*) an intelligence test. ▫ **bug ward** *n.* [1900s] (*US*) a psychiatric institution.

IN PHRASES

▫ **bugged on** *adj.* [1940s–50s] (*US black*) obsessed with, very enthusiastic about. ▫ **coke bugs** *n.* (*also* **cocaine bugs, crank bugs, speed bugs**) [1910s+] (*drugs*) a side effect of an excessive consumption of amphetamine, amphetamine-type drugs or cocaine: the sufferer believes insects are living beneath their skin and scratches desperately in order to remove them. ▫ **have a bug on** *v.* (*also* **bug up**) [1930s–70s] (*US*) to be in a bad temper. ▫ **have a bug one's arse/ass** *v.* (*also* **get a bug up one's ass, ...in one's ass, ...up one's behind, ...up one's tail**) [1940s+] (*US*) **1** to be acting nervously, to fidget. **2** to be in a bad mood. **3** to have an obsession. ▫ **have bugs (in the head)** *v.* (*also* **have bugs in one's cotton, ...head, ...wig**) [20C+] (*orig. US*) to be mentally unstable. ▫ **put a bug in someone's ear** *v.* [1900s–50s] (*US*) to confide a secret to someone. ▫ **put a bug on** *v.* [1900s] (*US*) to hit, to silence. ▫ **shoot a bug** *v.* [1900s] (*US prison*) to feign insanity.

SE in slang uses

DERIVATIVES

▫ **bugology** *n.* [-OLOGY *n.*] [mid-19C+] (*US campus*) biology, entomology; thus n., *bugologist*, an entomologist.

IN COMPOUNDS

▫ **bugbear** *n.* [SE *bugbear*, an object of dread; the darkness, both lit. and fig., of the pubic hair] [late 17C] the female pubic area. ▫ **bug bomb** *n.* [1940s+] (*US*) an aerosol insecticide. ▫ **bug-eater** *n.* [ext. uses of SE; the poverty-stricken appearance of the inhabitants; at some stage of the 19C the state was overrun by locusts (i.e. *bugs*) and a serious attempt was made to persuade the impoverished country-people to adopt them as a diet] [19C] (*US*) **1** an inhabitant of Nebraska. **2** a unimportant or worthless person. ▫ **bugfucker** *n.* [SE *bug*, an insect + FUCKER *n.* (1)] [1970s] (*US*) a man with an extremely small penis. ▫ **bug hut** *n.* [var. on FLEAPIT *n.*/BUGHOUSE *n.* (8)] [1930s+] a tawdry, run-down cinema. ▫ **bug hutch** *n.* [1910s] a small hut or sleeping place. ▫ **bug-proof** *adj.* [1910s] (*UK Und.*) in a drunken stupor, i.e. unable to feel the bites of bed bugs. ▫ **bug rake** *n.* [1930s+] a comb. ▫ **bug's age** *n.* [1930s] (*US*) a very long time. ▫ **bug trap** *n.* [SE *(bed)bug* + *trap*] (*US*) **1** [1920s] a verminous lodging house. **2** [1960s] a bed. ▫ **bugturd** *n.* see TURD *n.*^{1} (2). ▫ **bug walk** *n.* [SE *bug* + *walk*. Note milit. jargon *bug-run*, a parting] **1** [mid-19C–early 20C] a bed. **2** [late 19C] the parting of the hair. **3** [late 19C] (*Aus.*) a small road. ▫ **bug wit** *n.* (*also* **bug-wug**) (*Aus./US*) a fool.

IN PHRASES

▫ **bug in one's ear** *n.* [fig. use of SE *bug*] [20C+] (*US*) **1** a friendly warning. **2** rumour, gossip.

bug *n.*^{5} [? SE *bug*, an object of terror; although *OED* questions the link] (*orig. US*) **1** [mid-19C+] a microbe, a germ. **2** [1900s–50s] (*US Und.*) an open sore on the arm which is kept from healing and used to enhance one's efforts at begging; also used by prisoners to get into the prison hospital; thus constr. with *the*, the form of begging that employs such a wound. **3** [1920s+] an illness, a disease. **4** [1940s] as *the bugs*, crabs, body or hair lice. **5** [1940s–50s] (*US*) as *the bug(s)*, tuberculosis. **6** [1950s] malaria. **7** [1990s+] as *the bug*, AIDS.

IN COMPOUNDS

▫ **bug-chaser** *n.* [1990s+] one who aims deliberately to become infected with HIV/AIDS.

IN PHRASES

▫ **put the bug on** *v.* [1930s] (*US Und.*) to burn a young tramp's flesh to improve his appeal when begging.

bug *n.*^{6} [ety. unknown] [late 19C–1900s] a wallflower.

bug *n.*^{7} (*US*) **1** [20C+] a promiscuous woman. **2** [1980s] the vagina.

bug *n.*^{8} [1900s] (*Aus. Und.*) a drunkard.

bug *n.*^{9} [? SE *burglar*] [1910s] (*US prison*) a housebreaker, a burglar.

bug *adj.* [BUG *n.*^{4} (3d)] [1900s–10s] (*US*) mad, crazy, obsessed with.

bug *v.*^{1} **1** [late 18C–late 19C] to bribe (a policeman or, earlier, bailiff) [19C use is mainly US]. **2** [early 19C] to hand over, to give, often as *bug over*. **3** [late 19C] to obtain by underhand or illegal means.

IN PHRASES

▫ **bug over** *v.* [19C] (*UK Und.*) to hand over. ▫ **bug the writ** *v.* [late 17C–19C] of a bailiff or other court officer, to postpone handing out a writ, having been given a suitable bribe.

bug *v.*^{2} [i.e. to act like a SE *bug*, an insect] **1** [mid-19C; 1960s] to ruin, to to destroy. **2** [1930s] (*US Und.*) to conspire. **3** [1940s+] to annoy, to irritate. **4** [1940s+] (*also* **bug up**) to pressurize, to nag. **5** [1950s+] to scare, to unnerve. **6** [1980s+] (*US*) to be tense, nervous, depressed. **7** [2000s] (*US black*) to fight.

IN PHRASES

▫ **bug on** *v.* [1990s+] (*US teen*) to aggravate. ▫ **bug up** *v.* [1930s] (*US tramp*) to take refuge.

bug *v.*^{3} [the pace of the insect] **1** [20C+] (*US*) to walk slowly, lethargically. **2** [1970s] (*US black*) to terminate one's interest in something/someone.

bug *v.*^{4} [although this use antedates BUG *n.*^{4} (1) by 20 years, it remains the logical if anomalous link] [1910s+] to tap a telephone or to install any form of electronic surveillance.

bug *v.*^{5} [BUG *n.*^{5} (2)] [1930s] **1** (*US Und.*) to have an open, unhealed sore on one's arm, to enhance one's efforts at begging. **2** (*US drugs*) to inject one's arm with something that will produce a large and unpleasant-looking swelling; the intention is to obtain a shot of narcotic from a doctor.

bug *v.*^{6} (*orig. US*) **1** [1930s+] (*US prison*) to subject a prisoner to a psychiatric examination. **2** [1930s+] to be insane or to act as if one is. **3** [1930s+] to confine someone in a psychiatric institution. **4** [1960s+] to be shocked, appalled. **5** [1990s+] (*US drugs*) to experience hallucinations from drug use.

IN PHRASES

▫ **bug up** *v.* **1** [1940s] (*US drugs*) to experience the effects of smoking marijuana. **2** [1940s+] to make nervous, to confuse, to excite. **3** [1960s] go crazy.

bug *v.*^{7} [BUG-EYE v.] [1950s] **1** to see, to notice. **2** to enjoy.

bug *v.*^{8} [ext. of BUG *v.*^{6} (2)] [1980s+] (*US*) in rap music, to do something impressive in a performance.

bug *adv.* [BUG *n.*^{4} (3d)] [late 19C–1900s] (*US*) madly, crazily.

buga *n.* [Sp. *buga*/SE *boogieman*] [1970s] (*US gay*) a heterosexual.

bugaboo *n.*^{1} [SE *bugaboo*, a bogeyman, someone or something of whom one is scared] **1** [19C] a bailiff, a sheriff's officer. **2** [early 19C] (*UK Und.*) a debt-collector. **3** [1900s–10s] (*US*) a fuss, a commotion. **4** [20C+] (*US black*) a pesterer, a nuisance, esp. in a sexual context.

bugaboo *n.*^{2} [dial. *boggle+bug*, mucus. Note nursery synon. *bogey*] [1910s+] (*W.I.*) nasal mucus, esp. when dry.

bug and flea *n.* [rhy. sl.] [1960s+] (a cup of) tea.

buger-bear *n.* see BOOGER BEAR *under* BOOGER *n.*^{2}.

bug-eye *n.* [SE *bug*, of eyes, to bulge] [20C+] **1** one who has round or bulging eyes. **2** a round or bulging eye.

bug-eye *v.* [1950s+] (*US*) to stare.

bug-eyed *adj.* **1** [late 19C+] cross-eyed. **2** [20C+] drunk or intoxicated by drugs [one's eyes are popping like those of some insects]. **3** [1920s+] amazed, astounded; also as adv. **4** [1940s+] showing signs of insanity.

bugged *adj.*[1] [abbr. HAVE BUGS (IN THE HEAD) *under* BUG *n.*[4]] **1** [1940s+] infuriated, angry. **2** [1940s+] (*also* **bugged up**) of a person or situation, crazy, insane, mentally unstable. **3** [1960s] frightened. **4** [1990s+] (*US black/drugs*) experiencing a sense of paranoia after smoking strong marijuana or crack cocaine. **5** [2000s] fashionably weird.

bugged *adj.*[2] [BUG *v.*[5] (2)] [1970s+] (*drugs*) covered with sores and abscesses from repeated use of unsterile needles.

bugged on *adj. see under* BUG *n.*[4].

bugged out *adj.* [1950s+] (*US*) bizarre, eccentric.

bugged up *adj.*[1] [BUG *n.*[1] (1) + ? ref. to BUG *n.*[4] (1)] [late 19C–1930s] (*US*) dressed up.

bugged up *adj.*[2] *see* BUGGED *adj.*[1] (2).

bugger *n.*[1] [SE *bugger*, a sodomite; a trans. of 14C Fr. *bougre*, ult. Lat. *Bulgarus*, a Bulgarian, a name given to a sect of heretics who came from Bulgaria in the 11C. The term was transferred to the Albigensian heretics, who it was believed were largely homosexual. Despite appearances, the term remains SE, although the *OED*, c.1900, states that 'in decent use only as a legal term'. Its verbal and comb. uses are, however, sl., as are the n. uses cited here] **1** [early 18C+] (*also* **b., bogger**) a person, usu. a man, a 'bloke', esp. as *silly bugger, daft bugger* etc, none of which is necessarily pej. **2** [mid-19C+] a thing, or creature, with no special connotations. **3** [1910s+] something unpleasant or undesirable, a great nuisance; thus *a bugger to*; *a bugger of.* **4** [1980s+] (*S.Afr.*) a dedicatedly masculine male, whose lack of sensitivity is more than compensated in his enthusiasm for all forms of sport. **5** *see* BOOGER *n.*[1] (1).

(IN COMPOUNDS)

❑ **bugger chick** *n.* [CHICK *n.*[1] (2)] [1980s+] (*S.Afr.*) 'the compliant girlfriend of an aggressively masculine man' (*DSAE*). ❑ **buggers afloat** *n.* [sense 2 above] [1990s+] (*N.Z.*) doughnuts, dumplings or fried scones.

(IN PHRASES)

❑ **buggers-on-the-coals** *n.* [sense 2 above] [mid-19C+] (*Aus./N.Z.*) currant damper. ❑ **it's a fair old bugger** (*also* **it's a proper bugger, ...right bugger, right old bugger**) [mid-19C+] said of anything considered unpleasant, excessively challenging etc. ❑ **play silly buggers** *v.* (*also* **play funny buggers, play silly fannies, play silly fuckers**) [var. on BUGGER ABOUT *v.*] **1** [1960s+] to act uncooperatively, to mess around, to cause a deliberate nuisance. **2** [1990s+] to indulge in sexual relations, both heterosexual and homosexual. ❑ **bugger for 1** [1950s+] a phr. denoting an enthusiast, an obsessive, e.g. a *bugger for work.* **2** [1990s+] someone highly reluctant to do something.

SE in slang uses

(IN COMPOUNDS)

❑ **bugger bandit** *n.* [2000s] a male homosexual. ❑ **bugger's grips** *n.* [note tailor's jargon *bugger-bafflers*, the side vents on a man's jacket] [20C+] (*orig. RN*) the brushed back 'wings' of hair that adorn the temples of many upper class Englishmen. Coarse rumour imputes these as the handholds for those who are positioning such partners ready for anal penetration.

bugger *n.*[2] [BUG *n.*[4] (1)] [mid-19C] (*US Und.*) a pickpocket.

bugger *n.*[3] [1920s+] a semi-euph./synon. for DAMN *n.*

(IN PHRASES)

❑ **not give a bugger** *v.* (*also* **...two buggers, not care a...**) [1920s+] to not care at all.

bugger *n.*[4] [BOOGER *n.*[1] (1); i.e. its texture] [1980s+] (*drugs*) Mexican black tar heroin.

bugger *v.*[1] [late 18C+] a synon. for *damn*; thus to curse.

(IN EXCLAMATIONS)

❑ **bugger me!** [late 19C+] a general excl. of surprise, annoyance, alarm; thus ext. as *bugger my old boots!* (*Aus.*) *bugger me dead!* ❑ **bugger that/this for a game of soldiers!** *see* FUCK THAT/THIS FOR A GAME OF SOLDIERS! *under* FUCK *v.* ❑ **bugger you!** [late 19C+] a vehement excl. expressing personal antagonism.

bugger *v.*[2] [BUGGER UP *v.*] [1910s+] to make a mess of.

bugger! *excl.* (*also* **buggero! buggers!**) [20C+] a synon. for DAMN! *excl.*

bugger about *v.* (*also* **bugger around**) [BUGGER *v.*[2] (1)] [1910s+] **1** to wander around. **2** to mess about with. **3** to waste time, to stall, to be unhelpful. **4** to make someone's life miserable or in some way difficult.

bugger all *n.* (*also* **b.a., blow-all, sweet bugger all**) [1910s+] absolutely nothing; also as *adj., adv.*

buggerama! *excl.* [1980s] (*N.Z.*) excl. of annoyance.

buggeranto *n.* [SE *bugger* + 'Spanish' sfx *-anto*] [late 17C–early 18C] a male homosexual.

bugger around *v. see* BUGGER ABOUT *v.*

bugger around on *v.* [ext. of BUGGER ABOUT *v.*] [1970s+] (*Can.*) to commit adultery, to be unfaithful.

buggered *adj.*[1] [BUGGER! *excl.*] [mid-19C+] a synon. for DAMNED *adj.*; esp. as *I'll be/I'm buggered.*

(IN PHRASES)

❑ **buggered if I know** [1940s+] a phr. in answer to a question, stating one's absolute ignorance.

buggered *adj.*[2] [BUGGER *v.*[2] (1)] [20C+] **1** exhausted. **2** of machinery, not working; of a person, confused, injured. **3** defeated, destroyed.

(IN PHRASES)

❑ **buggered for** *adj.* [1970s+] without, deprived of. ❑ **buggered up** *adj.* **1** [mid-19C+] of objects, broken, out of order. **2** [1910s+] of people, physically beaten or hurt; exhausted. **3** [1940s+] of plans, ideas, schemes, ruined, aborted.

buggering *adj.* (*also* **boggering**) [BUGGER! *excl.*] [late 17C+] a general negative adj.

bugger it! *excl.* (*also* **bugger everything! bugger it all!**) [BUGGER! *excl.*] [late 19C+] an excl. of annoyance, esp. when an inanimate object or a previously determined plan of action fails to function as required.

buggerize about *v.* [BUGGER ABOUT *v.*] [1940s+] (*Aus.*) **1** to wander around. **2** to mess about with. **3** to waste time, to stall, to be unhelpful. **4** to make someone's life miserable or in some way difficult.

buggerlug *v.* [BUGGER ABOUT *v.* + ?] [late 19C] to waste time on trivial activities.

bugger-lugger *n.* [? BUGGERLUG *v.*] **1** [late 19C] one who wastes time on trivial activities. **2** [1920s] in fig. use, a factory hand.

buggerlugs *n.* [SE *bugger* + LUG *n.*[1] (1); lit. 'sodomite ears'] [late 19C+] (*orig. RN*) **1** a general term of (affectionate) address, usu. among men. **2** *see* BUGGER'S GRIPS *under* BUGGER *n.*[1].

buggero! *excl. see* BUGGER! *excl.*

bugger off *v.* (*also* **booger off, begger off, bogger off**) [SE *bugger*, i.e. synon. with FUCK OFF *v.* (1)/FUCK OFF! *excl.* (1)] [1920s+] to go away, esp. in imper. *bugger off* go away.

bugger off! *excl.* [1920s+] a general excl. of disbelief in or dismissal of an idea or statement.

buggeroo *n.* [BUGGER *n.*[1] (1) + -EROO *sfx* + ? pun on BUCKEROO *n.*] [1940s+] an eccentric person, a 'character'.

buggers! *excl. see* BUGGER! *excl.*

bugger's woods *n.* [SAmE *boogerman*, bogeyman; he is supposed to live there] [1970s] an out of the way place, an unimportant place.

bugger-up *n.* [BUGGER UP *v.*] [1990s+] a blunder, a mistake.

bugger up *v.* [BUGGER *v.*[2] note Papua New Guinea Tok Pisin *bagarap*, used as all-purpose negative, e.g. no good, broken] **1** [1920s+] to make a mess of, to blunder. **2** [1920s+] to hurt, to injure. lit. or fig.

buggery *n.* [fig. use of SE *buggery*] [1920s+] (*Aus.*) a difficult time, problems.

IN PHRASES

▫ **all to buggery** *adj.* [20C+] unsatisfactory, mixed up, useless [SE *buggery* + BUGGER UP *v.*]. ▫ **as buggery** *adv.* [1940s+] a general intensifier, e.g. *hot as buggery*. ▫ **gone to buggery** *adj.* [1960s+] of a person, completely defeated; of an object, wrecked beyond repair. ▫ **like buggery** *adv.* (*also* **like a bugger**) [1920s+] a general intensifier, usu. neg. ▫ **out to buggery** *adj.* [1990s+] (*Aus.*) far away or far off the mark. ▫ **play buggery with** *v.* [20C+] to play havoc with. ▫ **to buggery** *adv.* **1** [20C+] synon. with to hell. **2** [1950s+] to the limit, to extremes.

IN EXCLAMATIONS

▫ **go to buggery!** (*also* **go to jiggery!**) [late 19C+] a general excl. of dismissal.

buggery *adj.* *see* BOOGERY *adj.*

buggery! *excl.* [late 19C+] an excl. of annoyance.

bugging *n.*[1] (*also* **buggling**) [? backform. f. *BUG THE WRIT under* BUG *v.*[1]] [late 17C–mid-19C] the taking of bribes by bailiffs and other court officials.

bugging *n.*[2] [BUG *v.*[4] (1)] [1910s+] the tapping of a telephone, or other forms of electronic surveillance.

bugging *n.*[3] [BUG *v.*[2]] [1980s+] (*US*) **1** (*also* **bugging out**) going crazy, suffering mental stress. **2** (*US campus*) relaxing. **3** (*US campus*) acting in a foolish manner. **4** (*US campus*) asking someone to do something silly or foolish. **5** (*US teen*) feeling stupid.

bugging *adj.* **1** [1940s–50s] (*US*) euph. for FUCKING *adj.* **2** [1990s+] (*US campus*) in error, annoyed, upset.

buggins *n.* [generic for a 'foolish' name] [late 19C] a fool.

buggins' turn *n.* [proper name *Buggins*, used as a stereotype for a time-serving mediocrity] [20C+] a sinecure that comes to all members of a committee, board of directors etc, as long as they remain members of that group and, in due course, inevitably take their turn at a task; the antithesis of promotion by merit.

buggle-bo *n.* (*also* **bugle-bow**) [SE *bogle*, a demon, usu. black] [17C] the vagina.

buggling *n.* *see* BUGGING *n.*[1].

buggo *adj.* [BUGS *adj.* (1)] [1970s] (*US*) absurd.

buggo-yagga *n.* *see* BOOGOOYAGGA *n.*

buggy *n.*[1] [mid-19C] (*UK Und.*) a leather bottle.

buggy *n.*[2] [the orig. SE *gasoline buggy*. The earlier *buggy* was a light one-horse (sometimes two-horse) vehicle, for one or two people; it is cited as slang in Grose (1785) and Hotten (1859 et al.)] **1** [20C+] (*also* **gas buggy**) (*orig. US*) a car; thus *buggy bandit*, a car thief or one who uses a a getaway car after a robbery. **2** [1910s–40s] (*US*) a wheelbarrow.

IN PHRASES

▫ **get in the buggy** *v.* (*also* **get in the car**) [SE *buggy*, a coach or carriage/*car*] [1920s] (*US*) to comply with requirements, to act as ordered.

buggy *n.*[3] [? BUG *n.*[5] (2)] [1930s] (*US drugs*) a makeshift 'syringe' used by a narcotics addict.

buggy *adj.*[1] [SE *bug*] [19C+] infested with any sort of bug: lice, bedbugs, etc.

buggy *adj.*[2] [BUG *n.*[4] (3d)] [late 19C] (*US*) lit. or fig., unstable, insane.

IN COMPOUNDS

▫ **buggy bin** *n.* [BUGGY *adj.*[2] (1) + BIN *n.* (4)] [1940s] (*US*) a psychiatric institution.

buggy *adj.*[3] [BUG *n.*[4] (3b)] [1930s] (*US*) pertaining to jazz fans.

bugher *n.* [echoic of its bark] [mid-17C–late 18C] (*UK Und.*) a (little, yelping) dog.

bughouse *n.* [SE *bug*/BUG *n.*[4] + *house*] **1** [mid-19C+] (*US*) a vermin-infested lodging house (latterly hotel). **2** [late 19C+] a hospital, esp. a lunatic asylum; thus *bughouse fable*, an exaggerated story; *bug ward*, *bughouse ward*, a psychiatric ward; thus *bughouser*, an asylum inmate, a mad person. **3** [1900s] (*US*) the brain. **4** [1900s–10s] (*US*) nonsense, rubbish. **5** [1910s] an eccentric. **6** [1920s–30s] (*US*) a prison. **7** [1920s+] (*orig. S.Afr.*) a run-down, dirty, third-rate cinema. **8** [1940s+] any place that drives one crazy.

bughouse *adj.*[1] [BUGHOUSE *n.* (2); Flynt, *Tramping with Tramps* (1900), attributes the coinage to the tramp Boston Mary who believed she had 'bugs' crawling in her brain] [late 19C+] (*US*) insane, crazy.

IN PHRASES

▫ **go bughouse** *v.* [1920s+] to go mad.

bughouse *adj.*[2] [BUGHOUSE *n.* (1)] [1910s–30s] (*Aus.*) second-rate.

bughouse square *n.* [BUGHOUSE *adj.*[1] (1) + SE *square*] [1920s–60s] (*US*) any centre of urban life, typically Union Square, New York City, or Washington Square, Chicago, where tramps, vagrants, the more or less deranged and any other eccentrics gather.

bug-hunter *n.*[1] [SE *bug*] **1** [late 18C–early 19C] an upholsterer [they dislodge the insects as they repair the furniture]. **2** [late 19C+] an entomologist.

bug-hunter *n.*[2] [BUG *n.*[4] (1) + SE *hunter*; also a pun on schoolboy *bug-hunter*, a naturalist] [mid–late 19C] a street thief who specializes in snatching (drunken) men's jewellery; thus *bug-hunting*, robbing or cheating drunks, esp. after dark.

bugle *n.*[1] **1** [early 19C+] the nose; thus *blow one's bugle*, blow one's nose. **2** [late 19C] a loud voice. **3** [1990s+] (*drugs*) cocaine. **4** [2000s] an act of inhaling cocaine.

IN COMPOUNDS

▫ **bugle duster** *n.* [1960s+] a handkerchief.

IN PHRASES

▫ **on the bugle** *adj.* [1930s+] (*Aus.*) smelly, both lit., i.e. no longer edible, and fig., i.e. dishonest, dubious.

bugle *n.*[2] [play on HORN *n.*[2] (1)] [1980s+] (*Irish*) an erection.

IN COMPOUNDS

▫ **bugle boy** *n.* [one *blows*/BLOW *v.*[2] (1) a *bugle*/BUGLE *n.*[2] (1)] [1960s] (*US gay*) a passive male homosexual.

bugle-bow *n.* *see* BUGGLE-BO *n.*

bugly *adj.* *see* *BUTT-UGLY under* BUTT *adv.*

bug off *v.* [BUGGER OFF *v.*] [1960s+] to leave.

bug off! *excl.* [abbr.] [20C+] euph. for BUGGER OFF! *excl.*

bugout *n.* [BUG OUT *v.*[2] (1)] [1990s+] (*US campus*) someone who acts in a silly or comic way.

bug out *v.*[1] [BUG *v.*[3]] [1950s+] **1** (*US*) to leave, to run away. **2** [1950s+] to default on one's duties.

bug out *v.*[2] [BUG *v.*[6]] **1** [1950s+] to go insane, to lose emotional control; thus *bug out on*, to attack in a psychotic rage; *bugged out*, mad. **2** [1950s+] to drive mad, lit. or fig. **3** [1970s+] to subject to psychotherapy. **4** [1990s+] to lose one's temper. **5** [1990s+] (*US drugs*) to experience temporary hallucinations while high from drug use. **6** [1990s+] (*US campus*) to experience pleasure. **7** [1990s+] to act in an excited manner, to be astonished.

IN COMPOUNDS

▫ **bug-out cell** *n.* [1990s+] (*US prison*) a cell for holding emotionally disturbed prisoners.

bug-out juice *n.* [1950s] (*US*) extra-special speed.

bugs *adj.* [*HAVE BUGS (IN THE HEAD) under* BUG *n.*[4]] [20C+] (*orig. US*) crazy, eccentric; also as n., *bugs*, insanity.

IN PHRASES

▫ **bugs on** *adj.* [1910s–50s] crazy about, obsessed by. ▫ **drive (someone) bugs** *v.* [1920s+] to send (someone) mad. ▫ **go bugs** *v.* [20C+] to go mad.

bugs and fleas *n.* [rhy. sl.] [1930s–40s] (*US*) the knees.

Bugs Bunny *n.* [rhy. sl., ult. f. Warner Bros. character *Bugs Bunny*, created 1940] [1950s+] (*orig. Aus.*) money.

bugshit *adj.* [BUGS *adj.* + DIPSHIT *adj.* (1)] [1970s+] (*US*) crazy, eccentric.

bugster *n.* [1920s–50s] (*US Und.*) a night watchman.

bug up *v.*[1] [BUGGER UP *v.*] [1940s] (*US*) to ruin, to spoil.

bug up *v.*[2] *see* BUG *v.*[6] (2).

bug up *v.*[3] *see* BUG *v.*[2] (4).

buguyaga *n.* [SE *bugaboo*/Carib.E. *bugo-bugo*, rough and crusty + Ewe *yakayaka*, slovenly? + Hausa *buguzunzumi*, a big, fat, sloppy person] [1950s+] (*W.I. Rasta*) a sloppy, dirty person, e.g. a vagrant.

buguyaga *adj.* [BUGUYAGA *n.* (1)] [1990s+] (*W.I.*) coarse or common.

buhar *n. see* BUFE *n.*

buhtuh *n. see* BHUTTU *n.*

buick *v.* (*also* **call Buicks, scream Buick**) [echoic] [1970s+] (*US*) to vomit.

IN PHRASES

❑ **ride the buick** *v.* (*also* **sell buicks, sell the buick, go to Europe with Ralph and Earl in a Buick**) [1970s+] (*US*) to vomit.

build *n.* [mid–late 19C] the cut or style of one's clothes.

build *v.* **1** [late 19C+] (*orig. Aus.*) to prepare, food, drink, a marijuana cigarette etc. **2** [1930s] (*US Und.*) to create confidence or apparent friendship, for the sake of enticing a victim.

SE in slang uses

IN PHRASES

❑ **build a sconce** *v. see under* SCONCE OFF *v.* ❑ **build a spliff** *v. see under* SPLIFF *n.* ❑ **build pigpens** *v.* [the practice of woodcutters who pile the wood on their carts in the shape of a pigpen; thus making the pile, which is hollow, appear larger than it is] [1950s] (*US*) to deceive, esp. for a merchant to cheat a customer. ❑ **build the biscuits** *v. see under* BISCUIT *n.*[1]. ❑ **build time** *v. see under* TIME *n.* (1).

builder's bum *n.* (*also* **brickie's bum, builder's crack, plumber's crack, Dagenham cleavage, ...smile**) [SE *builder* + BUM *n.*[1] (1); such a sight is trad. allied to a builder's low-slung trousers] [1990s+] the crevice between the buttocks that is revealed when someone wearing low-cut trousers bends forward.

builder-upper *n.* [1930s+] (*orig. US*) a promoter, a publicity man, a morale booster.

build-up *n.* [1920s+] (*orig. US*) preparation, esp. an accumulation of favourable publicity designed to popularize a person, product etc.

build up *v.* **1** [1900s] (*UK Und.*) to dress up in one's best clothes in order to present a respectable, if fraudulent, image; thus ext. into non-Und. use. **2** [1970s+] (*drugs*) to roll a cannabis cigarette.

built *adj.* **1** [1930s+] (*US*) of a woman, attractive and with a noticeably good figure. **2** [1960s+] (*US campus*) of a man (or woman), well muscled; if a man, poss. referring spec. to his penis.

IN PHRASES

❑ **built for comfort** *adj.* [20C+] of a man, overweight, fat; of a woman, agreeably plump. ❑ **built like a brick shithouse** *adj.* (*also* **built like a brick henhouse, ...outhouse, ...slaughter house, stacked like a brick backhouse**) [1910s+] (*orig. US*) describing a very strong, muscled man or woman, who resembles a squat, four-square, solid edifice, often euphemized as 'schoolhouse', 'outhouse' etc; in (*Aus.*) *built like a brick dunny*. ❑ **built like a tripod** *adj.* [1990s+] (*US*) having a large penis; the image is of a *THIRD LEG under* THIRD *adj.*

buji *adj. see* BOOJEE *adj.*

bujok *adj.* [? Polish] [1930s] a term of disdain.

buke *v.*[1] [abbr. SE *rebuke*, the image is one of punishment] [20C+] (*US*) to sodomize.

buke *v.*[2] [1960s] (*US black*) to deceive, to manipulate.

bukra *n. see* BOOKRA *n.*

buku *see under* BEAUCOUP.

bulchin *n.* (*also* **bulkin, bull chin**) [SE *bulchin*, a bull-calf] **1** [early–mid-17C] a term of contempt to any male. **2** [17C–early 19C] a term of endearment to a child, usu. a chubby one.

bulge *n.* [SE *bulge*, a protuberance] [mid-19C+] (*US*) an advantage.

IN PHRASES

❑ **have the bulge on** *v.* (*also* **get the bulge on**) [mid-19C+] (*US*) to have an advantage over, to be in a superior position.

bulge *v.* [lit. to 'push one out'] [mid-19C] (*US*) to make one rush off.

bulger *n.* [SE *bulge*, a protuberance, i.e. it 'stands out'] [mid-19C] something very important of its type.

bulger *adj.* [mid-19C+] large.

bulk *n.* (*also* **bulker**) [? SE *bulk*, a large lump; thus the image of this human 'lump' pushing one around; *OED* also offers obs. 14C *bulk*, '? to beat'] [mid-17C–mid-19C] (*UK Und.*) a thief's, esp. a pickpocket's accomplice who jostles the victim while their pocket is picked.

IN COMPOUNDS

❑ **bulk and file** *n.* [FILE *n.* (2)] [late 17C–18C] (*UK Und.*) a pickpocket and their assistant (albeit in reverse order – *see* ety.); one jostles the victim, the other picks the pocket. ❑ **bulk-monger** *n.* [sfx *-monger*] [18C] a prostitute who consorts with thieves, esp. pickpockets.

bulk *adj.* [? SE *bulk buying*] [1970s+] (*Aus.*) many, lots.

bulk *v.* [BULK *n.*; BULKER *n.*[1] (1)] **1** [mid-17C–1920s] (*UK Und.*) to push; to jostle when picking a pocket. **2** [late 17C] of a prostitute, to have sexual intercourse.

bulker *n.*[1] [SE *bulk*, a heap, on which she lies] [late 16C–early 19C] **1** (*also* **bulk**) a poor prostitute who is forced to sleep in the streets, esp. on the projecting 'shelf' beneath a shop window. **2** anyone who sleeps in the street. **3** thus phr. *bulk-begotten*, the child of a prostitute.

bulker *n.*[2] *see* BULK *n.* (1).

bulkin *n. see* BULCHIN *n.*

bulky *n.* [SE *bulky*, sizeable + ? 17C sense meaning pompous, self-important] **1** [19C; 1930s] a police officer; thus *bulkie ken*, a police station; a prison guard. **2** [1920s+] (*Ulster*) a member of the Royal Ulster Constabulary; thus the *bulkies*, the RUC.

Bull *n. see* JOHN BULL *n.* (1).

bull *n.*[1] [the images of the animal] **1** in the context of aggressive sexuality. (**a**) [late 16C+] a womanizer, a successful philanderer. (**b**) [1930s+] an aggressively masculine lesbian. (**c**) [1950s+] (*also* **buller, buller-man, bull queer**) (*US/W.I.*) a macho male homosexual. **2** [late 17C–early 19C] false hair, worn by a woman, ? resembling the hair between a bull's horns. **3** in the context of the animal's strength and power. (**a**) [mid-19C] (*US*) a railway locomotive. (**b**) [1950s+] (*Aus.*) a casual wharf labourer who is given preferential treatment by the foreman; thus *bull system*, employment practices on the docks whereby the men line up for work every morning and the foremen pick them for a day's work. (**c**) [1960s–70s] (*US campus*) an academically successful person. (**d**) [1970s+] (*US Und.*) a veteran, long-term convict. (**e**) [1980s] a self-assured, poised person. **4** [mid-19C+] any form of meat as served in an institution, e.g., prison, the US Army. **5** [late 19C] (*US*) an ox. **6** [1920s–30s] (*US*) a buffalo nickel (on which the animal is engraved).

IN COMPOUNDS

❑ **bull-dagger** *n.* (*also* **bull-dag, bull dagger, dagger**) [BULL-DYKE *n.*] **1** [1920s+] a masculine lesbian; thus *bull-dagging*, engaging in lesbian love-making. **2** [1990s+] an effeminate male homosexual. ❑ **bull-dicker** *n.* [sense 1 above + BULL *adj.* (2) + play on BULL-DYKE *n.* (1)] [1970s+] (*US gay*) a lesbian who uses her clitoris to mimic the penis as in face-to-face heterosexual intercourse. ❑ **bull-dike** *n. see* BULL-DYKE *n.* ❑ **bull-dyke** *n. see* separate entries.

SE in slang uses

IN COMPOUNDS

❑ **bull-beef** *see* separate entries. ❑ **bull-bucka** *n.* (*also* **bull-bucker**) [18C US dial. *buck*, to butt; thus one who thinks he is strong enough to butt a bull or ? BULL *adj.* + BACKRA *n.*] [1940s+] (*W.I.*) a thug, a bully, an aggressive man. ❑ **bull butter** *n.* [its innate fakeness + coarse ref. to bull semen] **1** [late 19C–1940s] (*US*) margarine. **2** [1990s+] (*US campus*) nonsense. ❑ **bull camp** *n.* [image of SE *bull* or BULL *adj.* (1)] [late 19C–1930s] (*US*) a camp of outdoor workers. e.g. on an oil pipeline. ❑ **bull calf** *n. see* separate entries. ❑ **bull-catcher** *n.* [1960s] (*S.Afr.*) a mugger. ❑ **bull come** *n.* (*also* **bull gism**) [COME *n.* (2)/JISM *n.*] [1920s] cream gravy. ❑ **bulldog** *see* separate entries. ❑ **bull-dragging** *adj.* [20C+] (*Irish*) tedious, laborious. ❑ **bull-driver** *n.* [1900s] (*US*) a peasant, a farmer. ❑ **bullfighter** *n.* [1930s] (*US tramp*) an empty passenger coach, either when standing in the yards or attached to a freight train. ❑ **bullhead** *n. see* separate entries. ❑ **bull-flesh** *n.* [the innate bulkiness of the animal] [late 19C] swagger, boastfulness, arrogance. ❑ **bull fuck** *n.* [FUCK *n.* (1c), in fig. meaning of semen thus cognate with GRAVY *n.* (1)] [1910s+] (*US/Can.*) **1** cream gravy. **2** custard. ❑ **bull gander** *n.* [mid-19C] (*UK Und.*) a very credulous individual; thus *bull-gander trap*, a cardsharp. ❑ **bull gang** *n.* [SE *bull*, generic for tough, masculine + *gang*] **1** [20C+] (*US*) a team of manual labourers. **2** [1950s+] (*W.I.*) plantation labourers who perform odd jobs. **3** [1970s] (*Can./US prison*) a gang of hardened, dangerous prisoners, used for manual labour. ❑ **bull gism** *n. see* BULL COME above. ❑ **bull-goose** *n.* [SE *bull-goose*, the goose which maintains order among the rest of the flock] [1950s+] (*US*) the leader, the boss; thus *bull goose loony*, the maddest person. ❑ **bull gravy** *n.* [pun on synon. BULL FUCK above] [1940s+] (*US*) cream gravy. ❑ **bull moose** *n. see* separate entries. ❑ **bull party** *n.* [late 19C–1900s] a men-only party. ❑ **bullpen** *n. see* separate entry. ❑ **bull piss** *n.* [PISS *n.* (1)] [1910s+] (*US*) very low quality, cheap liquor. ❑ **bull point** *n.* [the image of a bull's strength] [mid-19C+] (*US*) a point of advantage or superiority. ❑ **bull-puncher** *n.* (*also* **puncher**) [on model of COW-PUNCHER *n.*] [late 19C+] (*Aus./US*) a bullock-driver (Aus.) or the driver of an ox-team (US). ❑ **bull pup** *n.* [it 'barks' or 'growls'] [mid–late 19C] (*US*) a pistol. ❑ **bull-pusher** *n.* [late 19C] (*US*) the driver of an ox-team. ❑ **bull-riding** *n.* [2000s] (*US black*) sexual intercourse in the rear-entry position. ❑ **bull-ring** *n. see* separate entries. ❑ **bull's breakfast** *n.* [20C+] (*Aus.*) a drink of water and an act of urination. ❑ **bull-shiner** *n.* [? the shininess of the wood or the BULL *n.*[5] (1), which gives one a SHINER *n.*[1] (2)] [1920s] (*US*) a police truncheon. ❑ **bull's look** *n.* [1960s] (*Irish*) a hostile glare. ❑ **bull-tour** *n.* [var. on BULL-HEAD *n.*[2] (1)] [early 18C] a mass of curled or frizzled hair worn over the forehead by a woman. ❑ **bull-week** *n. see* CALF WEEK *under* CALF *n.*[1].

IN PHRASES

❑ **bull of the woods** *n.* [logging jargon *bull of the woods*, the foreman] [late 19C+] (*US*) the boss, the leader, or someone who poses as such. ❑ **out where the bull feeds** *adj.* (*also* **out where the bull gets his bleeding breakfast**) [20C+] (*Aus.*) in the Outback.

bull *n.*[2] (*also* **bull-calf**) [Grose (1785) posits an eponym, one Obadiah *Bull*, 'a blundering lawyer of London, who lived in the reign of Henry VII': the *OED* rejects this as having 'no foundation'. The link to Ireland is simply another example of derog. stereotyping; the term's uses predates any such link by many years. Note OF *boul*, *boule*, *bole*, fraud, deceit, trickery, ME *bul*, faslehood] [mid-17C–1940s] a blunder, an error; a self-contradictory proposition, esp. that which is made by an Irishman.

IN PHRASES

❑ **pull a bull** *v.* (*also* **make a bull**) [late 18C+] to blunder.

bull *n.*[3] [abbr. BULL'S EYE *n.*] **1** [late 18C–1910s] five shillings, a crown. **2** [mid-19C] (*Aus.*) 75 strokes of the lash [each number of punitory lashes was named for a different value of coin]. **3** [1910s] a counterfeit coin.

IN PHRASES

❑ **half-a-bull** *n.* (*also* **half-bull, half-bull white**) [late 18C–1900s] half-a-crown, 2s 6d (12½p).

bull *n.*[4] [SE *bull*, a drink made by putting water into an empty spirit cask, or over a sugar-mat, to catch some of the flavour] [late 19C–1940s] a second brew of tea, the once-used leaves are left in the pot and a new kettleful of boiling water poured over them.

bull *n.*[5] [Ger. sl. *Bulle*, police officer or poss. synon. Sp. sl. *bul*; orig. US but Aus./UK black use late 20C] **1** [late 19C+] (*also* **bul**) (*orig. US*) a police officer; thus (*US tramp*) *bull buster*, one who is obsessed with assaulting the police; *fresh bull*, a police officer who cannot be bribed; *wise bull*, a detective. **2** [20C+] (*also* **railroad bull, yard bull**) a railroad security guard. **3** [20C+] (*US prison*) (*also* **night bull**) a prison warder. **4** [1910s+] (*US*) a detective. **5** [1910s+] as *country bull*, a local, small-town police officer. **6** [1930s+] as *narcotic bull*, a Federal narcotic officer. **7** [1930s+] as *motorcycle bull* a motorcycle police officer. **8** [1960s] as *night bull*, a guard who works the night shift. **9** [1970s] as *road bull*, a highway patrolman. **10** [1970s+] (*US Und.*) a veteran, long-term convict.

IN COMPOUNDS

❑ **bull horrors** *n. see* separate entries. ❑ **bull simple** *adj.* [1930s–60s] (*US tramp*) frightened of the police. ❑ **bull trap** *n.* (*also* **bully trap**) **1** [19C] (*US Und.*) one who impersonates an official in order to extort money. **2** [1930s+] (*Aus.*) a villain who impersonates a police officer and preys on couples in lover's lanes, extorting money from those who should not, for whatever reason, be there. ❑ **bullwagon** *n.* [1970s] (*Aus.*) a vehicle carrying suspects or criminals to a police station or prison.

bull *n.*[6] [euph. for BULLSHIT *n.*] **1** [late 19C+] (*orig. US*) lies, flattery, insincere talk of any kind. **2** [1940s+] (*orig. milit.*) unnecessary routine or discipline; thus *bulled-up*, dressed according to the strictest military regulations.

DERIVATIVES

❑ **bullfest** *n.* [-FEST *sfx*] [1910s–40s] a group, usu. of men, sitting around gossiping.

IN COMPOUNDS

❑ **bull artist** *n.* [-ARTIST *sfx*] [1910s+] a braggart, a boaster, one who lies, deceives. ❑ **bull con** *n.* [CON *n.*[1] (7)] [late 19C+] (*US*) specious, deceitful talk. ❑ **bullcorn** *n.* [euph. for BULLSHIT *n.*/BULL CON above] [1960s+] (*US*) nonsense, rubbish. ❑ **bullcrap** *n.* [CRAP *n.*[1] (4)] [1950s+] any form of specious talk, nonsense, rubbish, lies, flattery, also as dismissive excl. ❑ **bull dicky** *n.* (*also* **bull dinky**) [DICKY *n.*[5] (1)/DINGUS *n.* (2)] [1940s+] (*US*) any form of specious talk, nonsense, rubbish, lies, flattery. ❑ **bulldust** *n. see* separate entry. ❑ **bullfeathers** *n.* [SE *feathers*, on pattern of HORSEFEATHERS *n.* (1); note ads for Washington hamburger grill Bullfeathers 'When Teddy Roosevelt was hungry, he'd grumble, "Oh, bullfeathers"'] [20C+] (*US*) rubbish, nonsense. ❑ **bull-fodder** *n.* [euph. for BULLSHIT *n.*] [1910s+] (*orig. Aus.*) rubbish, nonsense, lies. ❑ **bull hockey** *n.* [HOCKIE *n.* (2)] [1960s+] (*US*) any form of specious talk, lies, flattery, insincerity, nonsense etc. ❑ **bull-lobb** *v.* [1930s] (*US*) to gossip or chatter inconsequentially. ❑ **bull merchant** *n.* [MERCHANT *n.*] [1910s–50s] (*Aus./US*) one who speaks insincerely. ❑ **bull muffin** *n.* [MEADOW MUFFIN *n.*] [1980s] (*US*) specious talk, nonsense, rubbish, insincerity. ❑ **bull pucky** *n.* (*also* **bull puckey**) [PUCKEY *n.*] [1970s+] (*US*) any form of specious talk, insincerity, flattery, lies. ❑ **bull roar** *n.* [1970s+] (*US*) any form of specious talk, insincerity, flattery, lies. ❑ **bull scare** *n.* [1940s–60s] (*US black*) an aggressive, menacing manner that is no more than a bluff. ❑ **bull session** *n. see* separate entry. ❑ **bull shooter** *n.* [1920s–60s] (*US*) a braggart, a liar. ❑ **bullskate** *v.* [BULLSHIT *v.* + SKATE *v.*[1]] [1940s–60s] (*US black*) to boast, to brag. ❑ **bull slinger** *n.* [1930s+] (*US*) a braggart, a liar. ❑ **bullstuff** *n.* [euph. for BULLSHIT *n.*] [1980s] (*US*) nonsense. ❑ **bull-sugar** *n.* [SUGAR *n.*[2] (1)] [1960s–70s] nonsense, rubbish. ❑ **bull thrower** *n.* [1910s–60s] (*US*) a braggart, a liar. ❑ **bullwash** *n.* [? BUSHWA *n.*] [1980s] (*US*) any form of specious talk, lies, nonsense, insincerity. ❑ **bullwool** *adj.* [BULL'S WOOL *n.*[1] (1)] [1920s+] (*US campus*) second-rate, inferior.

IN PHRASES

❑ **beat the bull** *v.* [1940s+] (*US*) to chatter, to gossip. ❑ **bung on the bull** *v.* [1940s+] (*Aus.*) to show off, to act in a pretentious manner. ❑ **line of bull** *n.* [1920s+] purportedly persuasive nonsense. ❑ **pull bull** *v.* [fig. use of sense 1; i.e. their illicit service is 'nonsense'] [20C+] (*W.I.*) to run an illegal, unlicensed taxi service, to use one's own car as an unlicensed taxi. ❑ **put the bull on** *v.* [the animal's characteristics] [1960s+] (*US*) to pressurize, to act aggressively towards. ❑ **shoot the bull** *v.* (*also* **peddle the bull, spin the bull**) [20C+] to gossip, to chat;

to talk deliberately deceptive nonsense. ❑ **sling the bull** *v.* [late 19C+] (*US*) to talk nonsense, to chatter about trivialities; thus n. *bullslinging*. ❑ **spread the bull** *v.* [1910s+] to talk boastfully, if inaccurately, of one's prowess. ❑ **tie that bull outside** *v.* (*also* **tie that bull to another ashcan, tie the animal outside**) [1920s] (*US*) stop talking nonsense. ❑ **toss the bull (around)** *v.* (*also* **throw the bull**) [1920s+] (*US*) to chatter, to gossip; to talk nonsense.

bull *n.*[7] [abbr. SE *bulletin*] [1930s–40s] (*US gay/prison*) any form of note, letter, etc.

bull *n.*[8] [BULLET *n.*[2]] **1** [1930s+] in poker, an ace. **2** [1990s+] (*drugs*) one gram of pure cocaine.

bull *adj.* [the image of the animal] **1** [late 19C–1940s] (*US*) large, powerful, authoritative. **2** [1940s+] (*US gay*) of a lesbian or male homosexual, masculine, aggressive.

(IN COMPOUNDS)

❑ **bull bitch** *n. see* separate entries. ❑ **bull dyke/dyker/dyking** *see* separate entries. ❑ **bull fiddle** *n.* [SE *fiddle*] **1** [late 19C; 1930s+] (*US*) the double-bass. **2** [20C+] a stringed instrument made from a tin can; thus *bull-fiddle voice*, a deep bass voice. ❑ **bullgine** *n.* [SE *(en)gine*] [mid-19C] a railway locomotive. ❑ **bull luck** *n.* [SE *luck*] [late 19C–1910s] (*US*) very good luck.

bull *v.*[1] [the aggressive energy of the SE *bull*, reinforced in later uses of sense 1 by abbr. BULLSHIT v.] **1** in the context of aggressive or deceitful speech. (**a**) [16C–17C] to mock, to tease. (**b**) [17C–late 19C] to lie; to cheat, to defraud, to deceive for the purposes of swindling. (**c**) [mid-19C+] (*Aus.*) to brag, to boast; thus *bulldocia*, n., boasting. (**d**) [20C+] (*US*) to chat, to gossip. (**e**) [2000s] (*Irish*) as *bull up*, to promote, to praise. **2** in the context of physical aggression or strength. (**a**) [18C+] of a man, to have sexual intercourse. (**b**) [late 19C+] (*US*) to act violently, aggressively. (**c**) [1900s–50s] to cow, to intimidate. (**d**) [1910s] (*US campus*) to act clumsily. **3** [2000s] (*Irish*) to be angry.

(IN COMPOUNDS)

❑ **bull money** *n.* [late 19C] money handed over to a potentially blackmailing discoverer by someone who has been caught *in flagrante delicto* in the open air.

bull *v.*[2] [note RN jargon *bull the barrel/cask*, to pour water into an empty rum barrel; the resulting (weakly alcoholic) liquid can be drunk] [early 19C+] (*Aus.*) to adulterate, to weaken; thus *bulled grog*, diluted liquor.

(IN PHRASES)

❑ **bull the tea** *v.* [20C+] (*N.Z.*) to add soda to tea, which makes it more potent.

bull *v.*[3] [BULL *n.*[2] (1)] [mid-19C–1930s] (*US campus*) to fail an examination.

bull *v.*[4] [the animal's image as a stud] [1980s+] (*W.I.*) to bugger, to pursue a gay sex-life.

bull! *excl.* [1920s+] abbr. of BULLSHIT! *excl.*

bullabananka *n. see* BULLAMAKANKA *n.*

bulladeen *n.* [BULL *n.*[5] (1)] [1960s] (*US black*) a police officer.

bullamacow *n.* [South Sea Islands pidgin] [1930s+] canned beef.

bullamakanka *n.* (*also* **bullabananka, bullamanka, willamakanka**) [? Fiji *bullamacow*, bullybeef] [1950s+] (*Aus.*) an imaginary place, supposedly far from any civilization.

bull and cow *n.* (*also* **pantomime cow**) [rhy. sl.] **1** [mid-19C–1970s] a row, an argument. **2** [20C+] a loud noise.

bull-ants *n.* [rhy. sl. = pants] [1920s–30s] (*Aus.*) trousers.

bullaphants *adj.* [rhy. sl. var. on ELEPHANT'S (TRUNK) *adj.* (1)] [20C+] (*Irish*) drunk.

bull-beef *n.* **1** [late 16C–late 19C] meat, esp. beef. **2** [17C; early 19C] an arrogant, self-important person.

bull-beef *adj.* [late 18C–early 19C] fierce, intolerant, macho.

bull bitch *n.*[1] [BULL *adj.* (1) + BITCH *n.*[1] (1)] [1930s–50s] (*US*) something or someone unimaginably bad.

bull bitch *n.*[2] [BULL *adj.* (2) + BITCH *n.*[1] (1)] [1960s+] (*US*) a lesbian.

bull-calf *n.*[1] [late 16C–late 19C] a great, hulking, undisciplined oaf.

bull-calf *n.*[2] *see* BULL *n.*[2].

bull chin *adj. see* BULCHIN *n.*

bulldog *n.* **1** from the dog's aggression and strength. (**a**) [late 17C–late 19C] a sheriff's officer. (**b**) [early 19C] (*US*) a watchman [note Oxbridge jargon *bulldog*, an assistant to the Proctors, those dons charged with maintaining university discipline]. (**c**) [late 19C–1940s] (*Aus./US*) a police officer. (**d**) [1970s] (*US prison*) a thug, a bully. **2** [18C–1940s] a pistol, which 'barks'. **3** [early 19C] a sugar-loaf [? its squat, solid shape].

bulldog *adj.* [anthropomorphism] [20C+] **1** large and potentially violent and/or threatening. **2** uncompromising, indomitable.

bulldog *v.* (*US Und.*) **1** [1920s–50s] (*US*) to brag, to exaggerate, to lie. **2** [1930s–60s] to destroy, to wear down. **3** [1960s+] to harass, whether verbally or physically. **4** [2000s] (*N.Z.*) to catch wild deer by dropping on them from helicopters.

bulldogger *n.* [BULLDOG v. (3)] [1990s+] (*US black*) a violent person.

bulldose *n.* (*also* **bulldoze**) [a *dose* of the *bull*-whip] [mid–late 19C] (*US*) a severe flogging.

bulldose *v.* (*also* **bulldoze**) [BULLDOSE *n.* (1)] **1** [late 19C] to flog, to beat severely. **2** [late 19C+] to intimidate, to coerce, to force through violence; thus *bulldozing*, an act of violent coercion.

bulldoser *n.* (*also* **bulldozer**) [BULLDOSE *v.*] **1** [late 19C] (*US*) a large pistol. **2** [late 19C+] (*US*) a bully, a thug. **3** [1950s] (*US*) a domineering woman.

bull durham! *excl.* [brandname of rolling tobacco] [1920s–30s] (*US*) euph. for BULLSHIT! *excl.*

bulldust *n.* (*also* **corral dust**) [note DUST *n.* (3)] [1920s+] (*Aus.*) euph. for BULLSHIT *n./excl.*; thus *bulldust artist*, *bullduster*, BULLSHITTER *n.* Also as v., to lie or fabricate.

bull-dyke *n.* (*also* **bull-dike, boldyke, bulldiker, bulldyker, B.D.**) [SE *bull*/BULL *adj.* + DYKE *n.* (1)] [late 19C+] (*orig. US*) a masculine lesbian. usu. an unpleasant, excessively man-hating one.

bull-dyker *n.* (*also* **bull-dicker, bull-diker, b.d.**) [BULL-DYKE *n.*] [1920s] (*orig. US*) a masculine lesbian.

bull-dyking *n.* (*also* **bull-diking**) [BULL-DYKE *n.* (1)] [1920s+] indulging in lesbian sex.

bullers *n.* [f. a brandname] [2000s] (*N.Z.*) gumboots.

bullet *n.*[1] **1** [late 16C; 19C] in pl. the testicles. **2** [mid-19C+] a notice of dismissal; usu. in phr. (below). **3** [1960s–70s] (*US*) an ejaculation of semen.

(IN PHRASES)

❑ **cop the bullet** *v.* [mid-19C+] to be dismissed from a job. ❑ **get the bullet** *v.* [mid-19C+] to be thrown out of a place or dismissed from one's employment; to lose a relationship. ❑ **give someone the bullet** *v.* **1** [mid-19C+] to dismiss from employment, to throw out of a place. **2** [1930s+] to jilt, to terminate a relationship. ❑ **shake the bullet at** *v.* [mid-19C] to threaten with dismissal, but not actually to dismiss. ❑ **shoot bullets** *v.* [1970s+] (*US gay*) to ejaculate (into a mouth or anus).

bullet *n.*[2] [the image is of a single bullet] **1** [early 19C+] (*also* **bull**) in poker, an ace, esp. in phr. *two bullets and a bragger*, two aces and a knave or a nine; thus (in brag) a winning hand. **2** [late 19C–1970s] (*US*) $1; in pl. money in general. **3** [1950s] a French franc. **4** [1960s+] (*US prison*) a one-year sentence. **5** [1970s+] (*drugs*) (*also* **bullethead**) a single capsule of a drug. **6** [1970s+] (*N.Z. drugs*) a portion of cannabis wrapped in silver foil.

SE in slang uses

(IN COMPOUNDS)

❑ **bullet-head/-headed** *see* separate entries. ❑ **bullet-proof** *adj.* **1** [1920s+] immune, irrefutable. **2** [1940s–60s] (*orig. US black*) very drunk.

(IN PHRASES)

❑ **put it on a bullet (and put it in your brain)** [1990s+] (*US black teen*) remember that, don't forget.

bullet *n.*[3] [late 19C] (*US*) a doughnut.

bullet *n.*[4] [initial letters] [1970s+] (*US campus*) the grade of B.

bullet *n.*[5] [ety. unknown] [1980s+] **1** isobutyl nitrite. **2** (*N.Z. drugs*) cooking foil, as used in heating and smoking heroin. **3** (*US gay*) amyl nitrate. **4** (*N.Z. drugs*) a cannabis cigarette.

(IN COMPOUNDS)

❑ **bullet house** *n.* (*also* **tinny house**) [TINNIE *n.* (3)] [1990s+] (*N.Z. drugs*) a house or flat used for cannabis dealing.

(IN PHRASES)

❑ **red bullet** *n.* [1970s+] (*drugs*) Seconal, a barbiturate.

bullet-head *n.* [SE *bullet* + -HEAD *sfx* (1); the hardness of the projectile] **1** [18C–mid-19C] a fool, a dullard. **2** [1950s–80s] someone with a crew-cut hairstyle.

bullet-headed *adj.* [BULLET-HEAD *n.* (1)] [late 17C+] foolish, stupid.

bullets *n.* [the shape] **1** [20C+] (*US*) beans. **2** [1950s–60s] peas. **3** [1980s] (*US drugs*) (*also* **bulletheads**) Seconal as manufactured by the Eli Lilly Company. **4** [1980s+] (*Aus. drugs/prison*) marijuana that has been compressed around thin sticks.

(IN PHRASES)

❑ **sweat bullets** *v. see under* SWEAT *v.*[2].

bullfinch *n.* **1** [late 16C–mid-17C] a fool, a simpleton [? the bird's willingness to be trained to sing]. **2** [early 19C] a sovereign.

Bullfrog *n. see* FROG *n.* (2).

bull-head *n.*[1] [SE *bull* + -HEAD *sfx* (1); the stolidity of a bull] [late 16C–1940s] a fool.

bull-head *n.*[2] [ext. BULL *n.*[1] (2); the resemblance of the style to a bull's matted 'forelocks'] [late 17C] a mass of curled or frizzled hair worn over the forehead by a woman.

bull-head *n.*[3] [ext. BULL *n.*[1] (6); it carried a bull's head on one face] [1940s] (*US*) a 'buffalo' nickel.

bullhead clap *n.* (*also* **bullheaded clap**) [SE *bullhead* used as an intensifier + CLAP *n.* (1)] [1940s+] (*US*) extremely severe gonorrhoea.

bullheaded *adj.* [BULL-HEAD *n.*[1]] [mid-17C+] very foolish; stubborn.

bullhead luck *n.* [SE *bullhead* used as an intensifier + SE *luck*] [late 19C] very good luck.

bull horrors *n.*[1] [BULL *n.*[5] (1) + HORRORS, THE *n.* (1)] [1920s–30s] (*US tramp*) irrational fear of the police.

bull horrors *n.*[2] [BULL *adj.* + HORRORS, THE *n.* (4)] **1** [1930s–50s] (*US*) severe delirium tremens; usu. caused by drink, sometimes by cocaine. **2** [1970s] (*US drugs*) the aftereffects of excessive cocaine use.

bullicky *n. see* BULLOCKY *n.*

bulling *n.* [? BULL *adj.*] [1910s–60s] (*orig. US black*) something or someone admirable; also as *adj.*

Bulli Pass *n.* [rhy. sl. = ARSE *n.*] [1990s+] (*Aus.*) the anus, the buttocks.

(IN PHRASES)

❑ **got the arse at Bulli Pass** [1990s+] (*Aus.*) a phr. used to denote an unsatisfactory situation.

bullish *adj.* [Stock Exchange jargon *bull*, one who trades on the premise of a rising market] [late 19C+] enthusiastic, keen.

bullissimo *adj.* [BULLY *adj.*[1] (1) + sfx *-issimo*] [mid-19C] (*US*) extremely good, absolutely excellent.

bullivant *n.* [SE *bull* + *elephant*] [late 19C–1930s] a large, clumsy person.

bull-jive *n.* [BULL-JIVE *v.*] [1960s+] (*US*) **1** teasing, abuse. **2** nonsense; empty chatter.

bull-jive *v.* [BULLSHIT *n.* + JIVE *v.*[1] (2)] [1940s+] (*US black*) to tease, to hoax.

Bull Land *n.* [BULL *n.* + SE *land*] [1910s] (*Aus.*) England; Britain.

bull moose *n.*[1] [1920s–50s] (*US*) the leader, the boss.

bull moose *n.*[2] [1960s] (*US*) five cents, a nickel.

bull-moose *n.*[3] *see* MOOSE *n.*[1].

bullo *n.* [BULL *n.*[6] (1) + -O *sfx* (3)] [1930s+] (*Aus./US*) nonsense, rubbish.

bullock *n.* [19C+] (*Aus.*) a bullock-driver.

(IN PHRASES)

❑ **sold like a bullock in Smithfield** *adj. see under* SOLD *adj.*

❑ **talk bullock** *v.* [the typical vocabulary of a *bullock*-driver] [mid–late 19C] (*N.Z.*) to use a good deal of bad language.

SE in slang uses

(IN COMPOUNDS)

❑ **bullock-puncher** *n.* [var. on COW-PUNCHER *n.*] [late 19C+] (*Aus.*) a bullock-driver; thus v. *bullock-punching*. ❑ **bullock's blood** *n.* [1920s–70s] a mixture of strong beer and rum. ❑ **bullock's eye** *n.* [the colour] [19C] port. ❑ **bullock wagon** *n.* [BULLSHIT *n.*] [1920s+] (*Aus.*) nonsense, rubbish.

(IN PHRASES)

❑ **bullock's fart in a thunderstorm** *n.* [1970s] (*Aus.*) something insignificant.

bullock *v.*[1] **1** [early 18C–1900s] to bully, to intimidate. **2** [mid–late 19C+] (*Aus.*) to perform heavy manual labour. **3** [late 19C+] (*Aus.*) to push through.

bullock *v.*[2] *see* BALLOCK *v.*[1].

bullocker *n.* [1920s+] (*Aus.*) **1** a bullock-driver. **2** a foreman, a boss.

bullockese *n. see* BULLOCKY *n.* (2).

bullock's heart *n.* [rhy. sl. = FART *n.*] [late 19C] the breaking of wind.

bullock's (horn) *n.* [rhy. sl.] [late 19C+] pawn.

bullock('s horn) *v.* [rhy. sl.] [mid-19C–1980s] to pawn.

bullock's liver *n.* [rhy. sl.] [late 19C+] a river.

bullocky *n.* (*also* **bullicky**) [late 19C+] (*Aus./N.Z.*) **1** (*also* **bullocky boy**) a bullock-driver. **2** (*also* **bullockese**) the language or jargon of bullock-drivers; the inference being of a preponderance of obscenities and oaths.

bullocky's delight *n.* (*also* **bullocky's joy, cocky's delight, cocky's joy**) [BULLOCKY *n.* + SE *delight/joy*] [20C+] (*Aus.*) treacle, golden syrup.

bullox *n. see* BALLOCKS *n.*

bullpen *n.* **1** [early 19C+] (*orig. UK Und.*) a holding cell surrounded by steel mesh or an open 'cage' made of steel bars (orig. of wooden bars). **2** [mid-19C–1930s] (*US*) a small house or room used by a prostitute; thus a cheap brothel. **3** [late 19C+] (*US police*) the holding cage in a precinct house. **4** [20C+] (*US*) any type of enclosed waiting area. **5** [20C+] (*US*) the dock in a courtroom. **6** [1910s+] (*US*) a prison exercise yard or internal association area. **7** [1920s–30s] (*US prison*) a punishment cell. **8** [1930s+] (*US*) any enclosure (college dormitory, factory changing room etc) where a group of men associate, gossip etc.

bullrag *v. see* BULLYRAG *v.*

bull-ring *n.* [ext. of SE. use; orig. that sited at Étaples, northern France, the British Army training centre during WW1] **1** [mid-19C–1940s] (*US Und.*) severe interrogation of a prisoner, the 'third degree'. **2** [1910s+] a military training ground. **3** [1920s–30s] (*US prison*) a prison excercise yard or an open space used for punishments.

bullring *n.* ['The term comes from a similar ring put on Spanish fighting bulls for the purpose of attaching a lead rope'] [1990s+] (*US campus*) a nasal piercing.

bullring camp *n.* [1950s+] (*US gay*) a male homosexual (or more rarely heterosexual) brothel; in weaker form, anywhere frequented by virile 'masculine' men.

bulls *n.* [euph. for BULLSHIT *n.*] [1940s+] (*Aus./US*) any form of specious talk, insincerity, flattery, lies.

bull's aunts *n.* [rhy. sl. = pants] [1940s] (*US*) trousers.

bull session *n.* (*also* **bullshit session**) [BULLSHIT *n.* + SE *session*] **1** [1910s+] (*US*) usu. of men, a period of sitting around, gossiping. **2** [1940s–50s] (*US black/ teen*) police interrogation [plays on BULL *n.*[5] (1)].

bull's eye *n.* [? the size and shape] **1** [late 17C] the vagina; joc. euph. coined by John Wilmot, Earl of Rochester (1647–80). **2** [late 17C–late 19C] a crown or five-shilling (25p) piece [later use is SE]. **3** [early 19C–1950s] a large, round sweet. **4** [mid-19C] a bull's-eye lantern. **5** [mid–late 19C] a thick, old-fashioned watch. **6** [20C+] £5 [SE *bullseye*, the centre of the darts-board, worth 50 points].

bull's-eye day *n.* [one scores a financial *bull's eye*] [1920s+] (*Irish*) Wednesday, the day on which British Army pensions are disbursed.

bullsh *n.* (*also* **bulsh**) [abbr. BULLSHIT *n.*] [1910s+] (*Aus.*) **1** rubbish. **2** a braggart, a liar.

bullsh *v. see* BULLSHIT *V.*

bullshipper *n.* [euph. for BULLSHITTER *n.*] [1910s+] a braggart, a liar.

bullshit *n.* (*also* **bull**) [fig. use of SE *bull* + SHIT *n.*, i.e. bull dung] **1** [20C+] nonsense, lies. **2** [1910s+] (*also* **bull manure, catshit**) rubbish, anything second-rate or useless. **3** [1920s+] an object or task that is seen as annoying, irritating or 'nonsense'. **4** [1930s+] as *bullshit session*, a pointless conversation. **5** [1970s] an argument. **6** [1970s] (*US drugs*) marijuana. **7** [1970s+] used metonymically to characterize a person.

(IN COMPOUNDS)

❑ **bullshit artist** *n.* (*also* **b.a., b.s. artist, bullshit merchant, ...thrower**) [-ARTIST *sfx*/MERCHANT *n.* (1)] [1940s+] anyone with a good line of persuasive, if insincere patter. ❑ **Bullshit Castle** *n.* [1940s+] (*N.Z.*) Air Force headquarters, then subseq. Parliament.

(IN PHRASES)

❑ **no-bullshit** *adj.* [BULLSHIT *n.* (1)] [1970s] uncompromising.

bullshit *adj.* **1** [1940s+] (*also* **bull**) nonsensical, absurd, pointless. **2** [1960s+] (*also* **bullshitting**) second-rate, inferior. **3** [1960s+] very angry, furious.

bullshit *v.* (*also* **bullsh**) [BULLSHIT *n.*] **1** [1920s+] to gossip, to chatter inconsequentially. **2** [1940s+] (*also* **bullshit on**) to tell lies, to tease, to confuse with false information. **3** [1960s+] (*also* **bullshit around**) to play around, to waste time.

(IN PHRASES)

❑ **don't bullshit a bullshitter** *v. see* DON'T SHIT A SHITTER *under* SHIT *V.*

bullshit! *excl.* (*also* **bull's foot! bull toads!**) [BULLSHIT *n.*] [1940s+] (*orig. US*) rubbish! nonsense!

bullshitter *n.* [BULLSHIT *n.*] **1** [1920s+] a braggart, a liar. **2** [1940s+] the mouth.

bullshitty *adj.* [BULLSHIT *adj.*] [1940s] useless, nonsensical, absurd.

bull's wool *n.*[1] [UK milit. *bull's wool*, coarse woollen cloth or yarn] **1** [1900s–40s] second-hand, cheap or homemade clothes; also attrib. **2** [1930s–60s] (*US black*) stolen clothes. **3** [1950s+] (*Aus.*) a young man with a mop of bushy hair.

bull's wool *n.*[2] [euph. for BULLSHIT *n.*] [1920s+] (*Aus./N.Z.*) any form of specious talk, lies, insincerity, rubbish.

bullwhack *v.* [SE *bull* + WHACK *v.*[1] (1)] [mid–late 19C] (*US*) to drive an ox-team.

bullwhacker *n.* [BULLWHACK *V.* + SAmE *bullwhacker*, the ox-driver's whip] [mid-19C–1950s] (*Aus./US*) an ox-driver.

Bully *n.* [abbr.] [20C+] (*Aus.*) the *Sydney Bulletin*, a popular news magazine.

bully *n.*[1] [? Du. *boel*, a lover of either sex] **1** [late 16C–1930s] a good fellow, a companion. [post-18C use is mainly US] **2** [mid-17C–1900s] a thug hired for purposes of violence or intimidation. **3** [late 17C+] a pimp, a procurer. **4** [late 17C–mid-19C] a braggart, a boaster. **5** [mid-18C] a prostitute's client. **6** [mid-19C] (*US Und.*) a cosh, a 'life preserver'.

(IN COMPOUNDS)

❑ **bully-banco** *n.* [mid-19C] (*UK Und.*) a criminal who, pretending to be drunk, starts a fight with a stranger so that his accomplices can rob the victim. ❑ **bully-buck** *n.* [BUCK *n.*[1] (3)] [18C] a thug who deliberately starts fights between others, so as to rob them in the confusion. ❑ **bully-cock** *n.* [fig. use SE *cock*] [late 18C–early 19C] one who deliberately encourages quarrels so as to rob those who are engaged in the argument. ❑ **bully-fop** *n.* [SE *fop*] [late 17C–18C] a brainless chatterer, a talkative bore. ❑ **bully-hack** *n.* [HACKSTER *n.*] [early 18C] a pimp. ❑ **bully huff** *n.* (*also* **bully huff-cap**) [HUFF *n.* (1)] [late 17C–early 19C] one who poses as a prostitute's husband then defrauds her client of his money by threats of violence or blackmail. ❑ **bully-rock** *n.* (*also* **bully-rook**) [ROOK *n.*[1] (1)] **1** [late 17C–18C] a boon companion. **2** [mid-17C–early 18C] a hired thug, e.g. in a brothel. ❑ **bully-ruffian** *n.* (*also* **bully-ruffin**) [SE *ruffian*] **1** [mid-17C] the penis. **2** [mid-17C–18C] a highwayman who runs contrary to popular fantasies of gentlemanly robbers by shouting and swearing at his victims, in order to intimidate them further. ❑ **bully-swagger** *n.* [SE *swagger*] [early 19C] a ruffianly braggart. ❑ **bully-trap** *n.* [active and passive uses of sense 2 above + SE *trap*] (*UK Und.*) **1** [late 17C–18C] a card-sharp, a cheat. **2** [late 18C–early 19C] a mild looking man, whose lack of overt aggression fools thugs into thinking that they can take advantage of him. **3** *see* separate entry.

(IN PHRASES)

❑ **bully of the blade** *n. see* KNIGHT OF THE BLADE *n.* (1).

bully *n.*[2] [Fr. *boeuf boulli*, boiled beef] [20C+] bully beef (pickled or tinned beef).

bully *n.*[3] [abbr.] [2000s] (*N.Z.*) a bulldozer.

bully *adj.*[1] [BULLY *n.*[1]; the *locus classicus* is Theodore Roosevelt's remark, 'The White House is a bully pulpit', but the term, based in *bully*, a pimp, fits into the street-generated bad = good model seen in BAD *adj.* (3), WICKED *adj.* (2) etc. Note earlier use of *bully*, a good friend, fine fellow; thus Shakespeare *Midsummer Night's Dream* (1590), 'What saist thou, bully Bottom'] [late 17C+] (*orig. UK but usu. US*) excellent, first rate.

(IN EXCLAMATIONS)

❑ **bully for —!** [late 18C+] (*orig. US*) well done! congratulations, usu. ironic/sarcastic use.

bully *adj.*[2] (*also* **bully-headed**) [BULLY *n.*[1] (1)] [18C] aggressive, tough.

bully *v.* [BULLY *n.*[1] (2)] [18C] to act as a hired thug.

bully *adv.* [BULLY *adj.*[1] (1)] [mid-19C–1910s] very well.

bully! *excl.* [BULLY *adj.*[1] (1)] [mid-19C+] excellent!

bully back *n.* [BULLY *n.*[1] (2) + SE *back*, to support, to back up] [early 17C–early 19C] a man hired by a brothel to act as a bouncer, strong-arm man, occasional lover or 'husband' of the madame or one of the prostitutes and a generally intimidating presence.

bully back *v.* [BULLY BACK *n.*] [late 18C] to be employed by a brothel as a bouncer or to be a generally intimidatory presence.

bully beef *n.* [rhy. sl.] [1950s+] (*UK prison*) a chief officer.

bully-fake *n.* [BULLY *adj.*[1] (1) + FAKE *n.*[1] (3)] [late 19C–1910s] a piece of luck.

bully-fake *adj.* [BULLY-FAKE *n.*] [late 19C] lucky, advantageous.

bully-headed *adj. see* BULLY *adj.*[2].

bullying *n.* [BULLY *n.*[1] (3)] [early 18C] pimping.

bullyrag *v.* (*also* **bullrag**) [BULLY *n.*[1] (2) + RAG *V.* (1)] [late 18C+] to bully, to pressurize, to taunt; to cheat out of by intimidation; thus as n.

bullyragging *n.* [BULLYRAG *V.* (1)] [late 19C] scolding.

bully trap *n. see* BULL TRAP *under* BULL *n.*[5].

bully-woolies *n.* [BULL'S WOOL *n.*[1] (1)] [1960s–70s] (*US*) long underwear.

bulrush *n.* [rhy. sl.] [1990s+] a paintbrush.

bulsh *n. see* BULLSH *n.*

bultz *n.* [mid-19C] (*UK Und.*) a purse, pocket-book or note-case; thus *queer bultz*, an empty purse; *rum-bultz*, a full purse; *bultz-niggins*, an empty purse.

bum *n.*[1] [orig. ME; echoic of the smack of one's backside hitting a flat surface, and as such coined as early as 1386. The word is also allied to a variety of terms meaning protuberance or swelling, typically *bump*; a quote c.1650 referring to a cure for syphilis, includes the posterior and genital area] **1** [late 14C+] (*also* **bumbum, bumm, bumb**) the posterior, buttocks, anus, rectum;

thus *bum man*, a heterosexual male who prefers the female buttocks to other parts, e.g. the legs. **2** [17C–late 18C] in a sexual context, the vagina. **3** [late 17C+] in a sexual context, the anus as a target for sodomy; thus *bum-firker*, a sodomite.

DERIVATIVES

▫ **bumfest** *n.* [-FEST *sfx*] [1990s+] a homosexual orgy. ▫ **bumkin** *n.* [dimin. sfx *-kin*] [mid-17C–18C] the buttocks.

IN COMPOUNDS

▫ **bum bacon** *n.* [1990s+] the labia. ▫ **bum bag** *n.* [1950s+] (*orig. skiing*) a small bag or pouch, secured to a belt and worn around the waist. ▫ **bum bags** *n.* [mid-19C–1950s] trousers. ▫ **bum balls** *n.* [19C] the testicles. ▫ **bum bandit** *n.* (*also* **bun bandit**) [-BANDIT *sfx* (2)] [1960s+] a homosexual male. ▫ **bum-banger** *n.* [1940s] (*Aus.*) **1** a short jacket, just covering the buttocks. **2** a male homosexual. ▫ **bum barber** *n.* [2000s] (*N.Z.*) a sheep shearer. ▫ **bum bass** *n.* [late 18C–19C] a cello. ▫ **bum-beating** *n.* [early 17C] jostling. ▫ **bumboat** *n. see* separate entry. ▫ **bum boy** *n.* **1** [19C+] a male homosexual. **2** [20C+] anyone regularly saddled with dirty jobs. **3** [20C+] a toady, a sycophant. **4** [1990s+] (*mainly UK juv.*) on pattern of GAY *adj.* (9), a term of abuse, irrespective of sexuality, for an unpopular individual. ▫ **bum-brusher** *n.* [SE *brush*, to thrash; note WW1 Aus. milit. *bumbrusher*, an officer's servant] [18C–19C] a schoolmaster. ▫ **bumbud** *n.* [1990s+] (*US black teen*) marijuana, a marijuana cigarette. ▫ **bum buddy** *n.* [BUDDY *n.* (1)] [1990s+] a homosexual. ▫ **bum-burn** *n.* [1990s+] (*UK juv.*) pain during defecation, the result of eating an excess of over-spiced food. ▫ **bum card** *n.* [mid-16C–early 17C] (*gaming*) a marked card. ▫ **bumchat** *v.* [1950s+] (*orig. W.I.*) to make statements to a woman with the sole interest being in her seduction. ▫ **bum chum** *n.* [CHUM *n.* (1)] **1** [1970s] (*orig. Aus.*) an intimate friend. **2** [1990s+] a male homosexual. ▫ **Bum Court** *n.* [? BUM *n.*^{1} (1); its members spent much time sitting down] [mid–late 16C] the Ecclesiastical Court. ▫ **bum-crack** *n.* **1** *see* CRACK *n.*^{1} (2a). **2** *see* CRACK *n.*^{3} (4). ▫ **bum-crawler** *n.* [1930s] a toady, a sycophant. ▫ **bum-creeper** *n.* **1** [mid-17C–19C] one who walks with their back noticeably bent. **2** [1910s+] a sycophant, a creeper. ▫ **bum-curtain** *n.* [19C] a jacket. ▫ **bum-drops** *n.* [1930s] hen's eggs. ▫ **bumface/faced** *see* separate entries. ▫ **bumfake/faker** *see* separate entries. ▫ **bum-feague** *v.* (*also* **bumfeagle, bum-feg**) [SE *feague*/FEAGUE *v.* (2)] **1** [late 16C–early 17C] to thrash, to beat severely. **2** [early 18C] to have sexual intercourse. ▫ **bumfiddle** *see* separate entries. ▫ **bum-fighter** *n.* [early 18C] a womanizer, a whoremonger. ▫ **bumfinger** *see* separate entries. ▫ **bum-firking** *n.* [FIRK *v.* (1); sodomy being seen as a stereotypical 'Italian trick' or 'sin'] [late 17C] sodomizing. ▫ **bumfluff** *n. see* separate entries. ▫ **bum-fodder** *n.* **1** [mid-17C–mid-18C] trashy literature [only good for use as sense 2]. **2** [mid-17C+] (*also* **bum fluff, tail fodder**) lavatory paper. **3** [1900s–10s] (*US*) tabloid newspapers. ▫ **bumfoolery** *n.* [SE *tomfoolery*] [2000s] homosexuality, homosexual activity. ▫ **bum freezer** *n.* **1** [1930s+] a short jacket that stops short of covering the buttocks. orig. describing an Eton jacket, latterly the 'Italian' styles of 1950s and thence any short (men's) jacket. **2** [1940s] (*Aus.*) a mean, cheating person. **3** [2000s] used of a very short skirt. ▫ **bum-freezing** *adj.* [2000s] used of a very short skirt. ▫ **bumfuck/fucker** *see* separate entries. ▫ **bum gravy** *n.* [2000s] diarrhoea. ▫ **bum-gut** *n.* [mid-17C; 1920s] the anus; thus *bumgut-shot* a breaking of wind. ▫ **bumhole** *see* separate entries. ▫ **bum-jerker** *n.* [early–mid-19C] a schoolmaster. ▫ **bum juice** *n.* [1990s+] sweat that gathers between the buttocks. ▫ **bum-jumper** *n.* [1980s+] a male homosexual. ▫ **bumkick/kicks** *see* separate entries. ▫ **bum labour** *n.* [early 18C] prostitution. ▫ **bum-licker** *n.* [1930s+] a toady, a sycophant. ▫ **bum man** *n.* [1950s+] a man who finds a woman's buttocks her most alluring feature. ▫ **bum-numbing** *adj.* [SE *numbing*; the image is of sitting so long that one loses sensation in the buttocks] [1970s+] infinitely tedious, usu. applied to work of some sort. ▫ **bum nuts** *n.* [2000s] (*Aus./N.Z.*) eggs. ▫ **bum-perisher** *n.* (*also* **bum-shaver, bum-starver**) [SE *shaver*; the implication is of failing to warm, cover or reach the buttocks, but note PERISHER *n.*^{1}] [late 19C+] a short jacket. ▫ **bum plumber** *n.* (*also* **bumhole plumber**) [SE *plumber*] [1990s+] a male homosexual, a sodomite. ▫ **bum-puncher** *n.* [SE *puncher*] [1980s+] (*Aus.*) a homosexual. ▫ **bum punching** *n.* [1980s+] (*Aus.*) (homosexual) anal intercourse. ▫ **bum-ranger** *n.* [RANGE *v.* (1)] [18C] a womanizer, a promiscuous man. ▫ **bum-robber** *n.* [20C+] a male homosexual. ▫ **bum-roll** *n.* [SE *roll*; the shape] [17C] a bustle. ▫ **bumscrape** *n.* [1990s+] (*Aus.*) an incompetent, a fool. ▫ **bum-shaver** *see* separate entries. ▫ **bumshop** *n.* **1** [mid-19C–1900s] a brothel. **2** the vagina. ▫ **bum-slinger** *n. see* SLINGER *n.* (4). ▫ **bum soup** *n.* [1990s+] diarrhoea. ▫ **bumsuck/sucker** *see* separate entries. ▫ **bum tags** *n.* [20C+] deposits of faecal matter in the hairs around a badly cleaned anus. ▫ **bum-tickler** *n.* **1** [18C] a womanizer, a promiscuous man. **2** [late 19C] the penis. ▫ **bum wad** *n.* [1940s] (*US*) **1** lavatory paper. **2** a newspaper. ▫ **bum-warmer** *n.* [on model of *BUM FREEZER* above] [1940s] a long suit jacket, covering the buttocks. ▫ **bum-worker** *n.* [18C] a womanizer, a promiscuous man.

IN PHRASES

▫ **all bum** *adj.* [mid–late 19C] of a woman, wearing a noticeably large bustle (a stuffed pad that emphasized the rear of the dress). ▫ **bit of bum** *n.* [late 19C+] sexual gratification, whether homo- or heterosexual; thus *have a bit of bum*. ▫ **bum over breakfast** *adv.* [2000s] (*Aus.*) head over heels. ▫ **give one's bum an airing** *v.* [1940s–50s] to visit the lavatory. ▫ **go bum-faking** *v.* [early–mid-18C] to have sexual intercourse. ▫ **go bum-fighting** *v.* (*also* **go bum-tickling, ...-working**) [late 19C–1900s] to have sexual intercourse. ▫ **land with your bum in butter** *v.* [2000s] (*N.Z.*) to experience good luck. ▫ **put the bum on** *v.* [1970] (*US gay*) to offer oneself for homosexual sex. ▫ **talk out of/through one's bum** *v.* [1980s+] to talk nonsense.

IN EXCLAMATIONS

▫ **bite your bum!** (*also* **bite your back! ...backside!**) [1950s+] (*Aus./N.Z.*) an excl. of contemptuous dismissal. ▫ **my bum!** [1930s+] a general excl. of disdain, dismissal, arrogant contempt.

bum *n.*^{2} (*also* **bumb, bum-bailey**) [? SE *bound*, bailiff (Blackstone, *Commentaries*, 1768) or physical proximity of the bailiff to those being arrested (Hotten, 1867); abbr. SE *bum-bailiff*, 'a bailiff of the meanest kind' (Johnson)] [mid-17C–1900s] a bailiff.

IN COMPOUNDS

▫ **bum trap** *n.* [BUM *n.*^{2} (1) + TRAP *n.*^{1} (3)] [mid-18C–early 19C] a bailiff or bailiff's assistant.

bum *n.*^{3} [abbr. BUMMER *n.*^{3} (1); most senses development of sense 1] **1** [mid-19C+] (*US*) a tramp, a vagrant. **2** [20C+] (*US*) a term of abuse for anyone unpleasant. **3** [20C+] (*boxing*) a poor, incompetent fighter; similarly used of a racehorse. **4** [1900s] (*US Und.*) a travelling thief. **5** [1910s] (*US*) a worldly, promiscuous man. **6** [1910s–20s] an incompetent sportsman (other than a boxer). **7** [1920s–50s] something worthless or unsatisfactory. **8** [1920s+] a general term of address, as often affectionate as hostile. **9** [1920s+] (*US*) a promiscuous woman; a prostitute [pun on sense 1, i.e. *tramp* and TRAMP *n.* (2)]. **10** [1920s+] (*US*) a fan or obsessive; usu. of a specified sport, e.g. *scuba bum, surf bum*. **11** [1930s] (*US Und.*) an experienced criminal. **12** [1940s+] a semi-professional athlete who makes a living training others rather than entering high-grade competitions, e.g. *tennis bum, ski bum, surf bum*. **13** [1960s] a thug, a member of a criminal gang. **14** [1970s+] an incompetent.

IN COMPOUNDS

▫ **bum-bitch** *n.* [BITCH *n.*^{1}] [1990s+] (*US black*) a derog. term for a young street girl. ▫ **bum-boozer** *n.* [BOOZER *n.* (1)] [late 19C–1920s] a drunkard. ▫ **bum factory** *n.* [1920s–30s] (*US*) **1** a cheap hostel. **2** a mission. ▫ **bum gang** *n.* [1920s] (*US prison*) the prisoners who perform the most unpleasant tasks. ▫ **bum's rush** *n. see* separate entries. ▫ **bum van** *n.* [1980s+] (*Aus. prison*) the van that transports prisoners to prison.

IN PHRASES

▫ **on the bum** (*US*) **1** [mid-19C+] travelling as a tramp or beggar, scrounging, cadging. **2** [late 19C] looting. **3** [20C+]

penniless. ❑ **make a bum of** *v.* **1** [20C+] to make someone look a fool. **2** [1920s] to make a mess of, to do badly. ❑ **put the bum on** *v.* **1** [1920s+] (*US*) to beg from someone. **2** [1970s] to interfere, to harass.

bum *n.*[4] [BUM *v.*[3] (4)] [late 19C–1930s] a spree.

(IN PHRASES)

❑ **on a bum** *adj.* [late 19C] out on a spree.

bum *adj.* [BUM *n.*[3] (2)] **1** [mid-19C+] (*orig. US*) useless, second-rate, poor, inferior, dirty, ragged. **2** [late 19C+] fake, counterfeit; thus *bum dough, bum paper*, counterfeit notes; *bum paper artist*, a counterfeiter. **3** [20C+] slightly ill, under the weather. **4** [20C+] (*US*) of an individual, injured; malfunctioning. **5** [20C+] (*US*) (*also* **bummin'**) depressed. **6** [20C+] unfair; esp. in *bum beef*, an unfair charge or arrest. **7** [1930s+] of food, stale, bad, 'off'. **8** [1960s] (*US*) aggressive, threatening.

(DERIVATIVES)

❑ **bumsky** *adj.* [-SKI *sfx*] [20C+] (*US*) second-rate, inferior.

(IN COMPOUNDS)

❑ **bum check artist** *n.* (*also* **bum checker**) [SAmE *check* + -ARTIST *sfx*] [1940s–50s] (*US Und.*) one who passes bad cheques. ❑ **bum clink** *n.* [Midlands dial.] [mid–late 19C] bad or second-rate beer. ❑ **bum deal** *n.* [20C+] (*orig. US*) a poor bargain, a mistaken agreement. ❑ **bumrap** *see* separate entries. ❑ **bumrush** *see* separate entries. ❑ **bum steer** *n.* (*also* **bad steer**) [20C+] (*US*) **1** a piece of bad advice or misinformation. **2** a mistake, the wrong direction. ❑ **bum trip** *n.* [1960s+] **1** an unpleasant experience while under the influence of drugs; as a v., to be subjected to an unpleasant and frightening time. **2** any bad situation, experience. **3** (*US campus*) an uninteresting or lazy person.

(IN PHRASES)

❑ **bum for** *adj.* [1920s] (*US*) bad for, e.g. one's health. ❑ **on the bum** *adj.* **1** [late 19C+] broken, out of order; lit. and fig. use. **2** [late 19C+] rubbish, second-rate, inferior, in a bad condition. **3** [1900s] (*US campus*) drunk. **4** [20C+] feeling slightly unwell. ❑ **put (someone/something) on the bum** *v.* (*US*) **1** [late 19C–1930s] to cause trouble for someone or something. **2** [1900s–30s] to hurt someone, to beat someone up.

bum *v.*[1] [BUM *n.*[2] (1)] **1** [late 17C–18C] to arrest. **2** [19C] to serve with a summons.

bum *v.*[2] [Irish *bommanach*, bragging, boastful] **1** [early 19C+] (*Irish/Scot./US*) to set the bailiffs on. **2** [early 19C] to act noisily. **3** [20C+] to boast, to brag, thus *bum up*, to praise, to promote, thus adj. *bumming*, boastful.

bum *v.*[3] [BUM *n.*[3]] **1** [mid-19C+] (*also* **bum off**) to beg (for); thus *bum a fag*, ask for a cigarette. **2** [mid-19C+] (*also* **bum around, be on a bum**) to act lazily, to do nothing positive. **3** [late 19C–1930s] to travel on the railroads as a tramp. **4** [late 19C+] (*also* **bum around, bum out**) to wander around. **5** [1980s] (*US black*) to steal someone's lover. **6** [1980s] (*US black*) to cheat, to rob. **7** [1990s+] to accompany. **8** [2000s] (*US campus*) to dress in a casual manner.

(IN PHRASES)

❑ **bum a ride** *v.* [late 19C+] (*US*) to get a free ride.

bum *v.*[4] [ext. of BUM *v.*[3] (4)] **1** [late 19C–1940s] (*US campus*) to go out on a spree. **2** [1910s–30s] to play truant.

bum *v.*[5] [BUM *n.*[1] (1)] [1970s+] to sodomize.

bum *v.*[6] [BUM *adj.* (5); BUMMER *n.*[4] (2)] [1980s+] (*US campus*) to feel depressed.

bum *adv.* [late 19C] badly, incompetently.

bum! *excl.*[1] [BUM *n.*[1] (1)] [1940s+] an excl. of derision or annoyance.

bum! *excl.*[2] *see* BUDUP! *excl.*

bum and stroke *n.* [rhy. sl.] [2000s] a glass of rum and Coca-Cola (coke).

bumba *n.* (*also* **bumpa**) [BUM *n.*[1] (1); but ? note BUMBO *n.*[2] (2)] [20C+] (*US black*) the buttocks.

bumbaste *v.* [BUM *n.*[1] (1) + SE *baste*, to thrash] **1** [mid-16C–early 18C] to beat hard on the buttocks; also in fig. use. **2** [mid-17C–late 19C] to have sexual intercourse, esp. in the 'rear position'. **3** [18C–19C] to beat, to assault.

bumbazine *n.* (*also* **bombazine**) [? pun on BUM *n.*[1] (1) + SE *bombasine*, 'a twilled or corded dress-material, composed of silk and worsted; sometimes also of cotton and worsted, or of worsted alone. In black the material is much used in mourning' (*OED*); note Walt Kelly's short-lived cartoon strip *Bumbazine and Albert*, featuring a young black boy who talks to animals, created in 1943 and a precursor to *Pogo*] [mid-19C] (*US*) the buttocks.

bum beef *n. see* BEEF *n.*[2] (4).

bum-beefed *adj.* [BUM *adj.* (1) + BEEF *n.*[2] (2)] [1930s–60s] (*US Und.*) arrested on false charges, esp. after evidence (typically drugs) has been planted (*see* PLANT *v.*[1] (3)) on the defendant.

bumbee work *n.* [SE *bumble-bee* and its 'buzz'] [20C+] (*Ulster*) nonsense.

bumbershoot *n.* (*also* **bumberella**) [joc. corruption] [19C+] (*US*) an umbrella.

bumble *n.*[1] [*Mr Bumble* in Charles Dickens's *Oliver Twist* (1838)] [mid-19C] a beadle; thus *bumble-crew, bumbledom* a collective name for corporations, vestries and other official bodies.

bumble *n.*[2] [16C SE *bumble*, a humming noise] [2000s] nonsense, empty chatter.

bumble *v.* [ext. of SE use + ? ref. to 'the birds and the bees' / BUM *n.*[1] (2)] [17C] to have sexual intercourse.

SE in slang uses

(IN COMPOUNDS)

❑ **bumble-footed** *adj.* [mid-19C] club-footed. ❑ **bumblefuck** *n.* [var. on BUMFUCK, EGYPT *n.*] **1** [1980s+] (*US campus*) anywhere categorized as very far away. **2** a fool. ❑ **bumblehead** *n.* [late 18C] (*UK Und.*) a fool.

bumblebee *n.*[1] **1** [1930s+] a male lover. **2** [1960s] (*US black*) the vagina; thus also a female lover.

bumblebee *n.*[2] [1940s] (*US Und.*) a $1 bill.

bumblebee *n.*[3] [rhy. sl.] **1** [1960s+] (*Aus.*) a knee. **2** [1990s+] a tree. **3** [2000s] VD, ie venereal disease.

bumblebee *adj.* [the crop has become so low that the saying has it that the bees can lie on their backs sucking the juice from the flowers or plants] [20C+] (*US*) of a crop that has become dried up and stunted.

bumblebees *n.* [? striped capsules of certain brands of the drug or f. their 'sting'] [1970s+] (*drugs*) amphetamines.

bumblebee whisky *n.* [it 'stings'] [mid-19C+] (*US*) especially potent whisky.

bumble-puppy *n.* [SE *bumble-puppy*, an early form of bagatelle, usu. played in public houses, in which stone balls are rolled down a sloping board, which is pierced with numbered holes. This is based on an older 16C game, usu. played by women, *troule-in-madame* or *troll-madam*] [mid-19C+] amateurish whist, and latterly bridge, the level typically played in family or friendly games.

bumbo *n.*[1] [ety. unknown; *OED* notes Ital. *bombo* 'a child's word for drink'; ? sense 2 underpinned by BUM *n.*[3] (1), its usual drinker] **1** [mid-18C–late 19C] a drink composed of brandy, sugar and water. **2** [1910s+] (*Aus.*) cheap (fortified) wine.

bumbo *n.*[2] (*also* **bombo**) [BUM *n.*[1], but note Efik *mbumbu*, rotten, putrefied, decomposed; orig. W.I. use, where the term is also used to mean SE *alligator*, thus suggesting poss. *vagina dentata* imagery] **1** [late 18C+] (*also* **bombo-red**) the vagina. **2** [1960s] the buttocks, the anus.

bumbo! *excl.* [BUMBO *n.*[2] (2)] [1980s] (*W.I.*) an excl. of surprise, shock, annoyance.

bum-boat *n.* [BUM *n.*[1] (1) + SE *boat*; the original role of such vessels was to collect human and other waste from boats at anchor; they also carried out vegetables etc to sell on board] **1** [late 17C] a scavenger's boat, used to pick up the debris of shipping disasters. **2** [mid-18C–1940s] a boat that brought provisions from land out to larger vessels anchored offshore; thus as a term of affectionate ridicule between sailors; later use, of boat used by hawkers selling goods to passengers on large ships. **3** [1950s+] (*Aus.*) an illegal cargo of alcohol.

bumbo-claat *n.* (*also* **bombo-claat, bumbo-cloth, bumbo-cloth**) [BUMBO *n.*[2] (2) + SE *cloth*] [1950s+] (*W.I.*) **1** a sanitary towel. **2** a highly derog. term of abuse. **3** a euph. for FUCK *n.* in various senses.

bumbole! *excl.* [? BUMHOLE *n.*] [1920s] an expletive; also as general derog. adj.

bumbosity *n.* (*also* **bombosity**) [artificially extended BUM *n.*[1] (1)] [1930s+] (*US*) the buttocks.

bumbum *n. see* BUM *n.*[1] (1).

bum-charter *n.* [ety. unknown] [early 19C] (*UK Und.*) prison bread soaked in hot water.

bumf *n.* [abbr. *BUM-FODDER under* BUM *n.*[1]] [late 19C+] (*also* **bumpf, bumph, bunf**) **1** paperwork, paper. **2** lavatory paper. **3** scrap paper. **4** published material (printed or online) considered as nonsense.

bumface *n.* [BUM *n.*[1] (1) + SE *face*] [1940s+] (*UK/Aus.*) a general term of disdain, usu. only used by children.

bumfaced *adj.* [BUMFACE *n.*] [1940s] stupid, foolish, a general term of abuse.

bum-fake *v.* [BUM *n.*[1] (1) + FAKE *v.*[1] (3)] [late 19C] to have sexual intercourse.

bum-faker *n.* [BUM-FAKE *v.*] **1** [18C] a womanizer, a promiscuous man. **2** [late 19C] a male homosexual.

bumfiddle *n.* [BUM *n.*[1] (1) + SE *fiddle*] **1** [late 17C–early 18C] the vagina. **2** [early 18C] the anus, esp. when it breaks wind.

bum fiddle *v.* [BUM *n.*[1] (1) + SE *fiddle*] **1** [17C] to harm; to attack. **2** [17C–early 18C] to have sexual intercourse.

bum finger *n.* [BUM-FINGER *v.*] [1940s–50s] (*US prison/Und.*) **1** a false accusation. **2** an unfair jail sentence.

bum-finger *v.* [BUM *adj.* + FINGER *v.* (2)] [1960s] (*US Und*) **1** to make a false accusation against someone. **2** to send to jail unfairly.

bum-fluff *n.* (*also* **bum-bluff**) [BUM *n.*[1] (1) + SE *fluff*] **1** [late 19C+] the very light growth of hair on the face of a boy who is on the verge of needing to shave. **2** [1940s+] (*Aus.*) empty talk, nonsense. **3** [1990s+] pubic hair. **4** [2000s] a term of address, whether abuse or affection.

DERIVATIVES

❑ **bumfluffy** *adj.* [2000s] sparse, thin.

bumflummux *v.* [BUM *n.*[1] (1) + FLUMMOX *v.* (4)] [mid-19C] (*US*) to confound, to confuse.

bumfoozle *v. see* BAMBOOZLE *v.*

bumfoozled *adj. see BAMBOOZLED under* BAMBOOZLE *v.*

bumfuck *n.* [BUMFUCK *v.* (1)] **1** [1970s+] (*US*) an extremely unpleasant person. **2** [1970s+] (*Aus.*) an extremely tedious task, i.e. a PAIN IN THE ARSE *n.* (2). **3** [1970s+] (*US gay*) a sexually inadequate partner. **4** [1980s] anal intercourse.

bumfuck *adj.* [BUMFUCK *n.*] [1970s+] third-rate, nondescript.

bumfuck *v.* [BUM *n.*[1] (1) + FUCK *v.* (1)] (*orig. US*) **1** [mid-19C+] to sodomize; thus *bumfucking*, sodomy. **2** [20C+] (*orig. US*) to massage the prostate as a way of diagnosing and treating gonorrhoea.

Bumfuck, Egypt *n.* (*also* **bumfuck, Africa; bumfuck, Texas; buttfucking Egypt; buttfucking Africa; East Buttfuck, Egypt; west Bumfuck; West Buttfuck**) [BUMFUCK *adj.*; orig. US milit. jargon *Bumfuck, Egypt*, a very distant and remote place] [1970s+] (*US milit./campus*) a very distant place.

bumfucker *n.* [BUMFUCK *v.* (1)] [2000s] a sodomite; a pederast.

bumfuddled *adj.* (*also* **bunfungered**) [BAMBOOZLE *v.*] [20C+] (*US*) confused, mixed up.

bumfuzzle *v. see* BAMBOOZLE *v.*

bumfuzzled *adj. see BAMBOOZLED under* BAMBOOZLE *v.*

bumhole *n.* [BUM *n.*[1] (1) + SE *hole*] **1** [mid-19C+] the anus. **2** [1960s+] a despicable person.

bumhole *adj.* [BUMHOLE *n.*] [1950s+] second-rate, inferior.

bum kick *v.* [BUM KICKS *n.*] [1960s+] (*US*) to depress, to annoy; thus *bumkicked*, depressed, irritated.

bum kicks *n.* (*also* **bumkick**) [BUM *adj.* + KICKS *n.*[1]] [1940s–60s] (*US*) an unpleasant experience.

bumly *adj.*[1] [BUM *adj.* (1)] [20C+] (*US*) depressed.

bumly *adj.*[2] [BUM *n.*[3] (1)] [1990s+] pertaining to the world, lifestyle, or image of a tramp or hobo.

bumm *n. see* BUM *n.*[1] (1).

bummage! *excl. see* BUMMER! *excl.*

bummaree *n.* [joc. mispron.] **1** [late 18C–late 19C] a middle-man, esp. at Billingsgate fish market. **2** [late 19C–1900s] a *bain-Marie* or double-boiler.

bummed *adj.* [BUM *n.*[2]] [late 18C] arrested.

bummed (out) *adj.* [BUM *adj.*] [1970s+] **1** suffering from an unpleasant drug experience. **2** drunk. **3** (*also* **bummed**) depressed, miserable. **4** disappointed, feeling 'put upon' by others. **5** (*also* **bummed**) angry. **6** not working, broken, dilapidated. **7** (*US campus*) casually dressed.

bummer *n.*[1] (*also* **bummy**) [BUM *n.*[2] (1)] [mid-17C–early 19C] a bum-bailiff.

bummer *n.*[2] (*also* **bummy**) **1** [mid-19C] (*US campus*) a 'fast' young man [? BUMMER *n.*[3]]. **2** [1960s+] (*gay*) a sodomite [BUM *n.*[1] (1)].

bummer *n.*[3] [the precursor of BUM *n.*[3] (1); note Schele De Vere *Americanisms* (1872) 'he is, far more likely, descended from the German *Bummler*, a man who goes about without aim and purpose, and lives on the fruits of other people's labor.'] (*US/Aus.*) **1** [mid-19C–1940s] a tramp, a vagrant. **2** [mid-19C–1900s] (*orig. US*) a scrounger. **3** [mid-19C+] (*also* **bummy**) an unpleasant or unpopular person. **4** [late 19C] a commercial traveller.

bummer *n.*[4] **1** [1960s+] (*drugs*) an unpleasant drug experience, esp. while using LSD or any other hallucinogenic. **2** [1960s+] (*also* **el bummero**) any unpleasant experience, depressing circumstances. **3** [1960s] a person whose conduct can ruin the enjoyment of a drug. **4** [1960s+] (*US campus*) a hard examination. **5** [1970s+] a failure or bad idea.

IN PHRASES

❑ **ride a bummer** *v.* [orig. Hell's Angels use for a bad crash, see Tom Wolfe *The Electric Kool-Aid Acid Test* (1968): 'Bummer was the Angels' term for a bad trip on a motorcycle and very quckly it became the hip world's term for a bad trip on LSD'; note 19C racing jargon *bummer*, a bad gambling loss] to be depressed.

bummer *adj.* [BUMMER *n.*[4] (2)] [1970s] (*US*) depressing.

bummer *v.* [1970s+] (*drugs*) of LSD, to give the user a bad experience.

bummer! *excl.* (*also* **bummage!**) [BUMMER *n.*[4] (2)] [1960s+] (*orig. US*) excl. of annoyance, disgust, disappointment, commiseration.

bummer(-boy) *n.* [ext. of BUMMER *n.*[2] (2)] [1960s+] a male homosexual.

bummillbaty *n. see* BLAITIE BUM *n.*

bummin' *adj. see* BUM *adj.* (5).

bumming *n.* [BUM *v.*[3] (4)] **1** [mid-19C] (*US campus*) living as an idler or loafer. **2** [mid–late 19C] (*US*) living as a vagrant tramp or hobo. **3** [1990s+] (*US campus*) relaxing. **4** [1990s+] (*US teen*) dressing unfashionably.

bumm-shot *n.* [1990s+] (*W.I.*) something very bad.

bummy *n.*[1] (*also* **bummie**) [BUM *n.*[3] (1) + RUMMY *n.*[1] (2)] [1940s+] (*US*) an alcoholic tramp; thus as nickname.

bummy *n.*[2] *see* BUMMER *n.*[1].

bummy *adj.* [BUM *adj.* (1)/BUM *n.*[3] (1)] **1** [late 19C+] useless second-rate, inferior. **2** [1980s+] ragged, poor, reminiscent of a vagrant.

bum (out) *v.* [BUM *adj.* (1)] [1960s+] (*US*) **1** to disappoint, to depress, to disturb. **2** to be disappointed, to be depressed **3** (*US campus*) to fail a test.

bump *n.*[1] [ext. use of SE *bump*, a blow] (*orig. US*) **1** [1920s+] the action of thrusting forward the abdomen or hips, as in a dance, thus n., *bumper*, a striptease artist who performs this action; esp. as *bump and grind*, the thrusting of the abdomen and gyrating of the hips. **2** [1940s] dismissal, 'the sack'. **3** [1970s+] spontaneous, cursory sexual intercourse.

IN PHRASES

❑ **put the bump on** *v.* [1970s] to deceive someone, to trick someone out of something. ❑ **speed bump** *n.* [1990s+] (*US*) an act of casual sex.

bump *n.*[2] [SE *bump*, a swelling] **1** [1940s–50s] (*US*) a raise, a promotion. **2** [1950s] (*US*) the female breast, usu. in pl. **3** [2000s] (*US*) a bonus.

IN PHRASES

❑ **like a bump on a log** *adv.* [mid-19C–1930s] (*US*) stupidly silent or inarticulate.

bump *n.*[3] [play on HIT *n.* (3)] (*drugs*) **1** [1980s] a draw on a cannabis cigarette. **2** [1990s+] an inhalation of cocaine, usu. small. **3** [1990s+] crack cocaine. **4** [1990s+] fake crack cocaine. **5** [1990s+] one dose ($20) of ketamine. **6** [2000s] a piece of crack, ready for smoking or a crushed up into a 'line' for inhaling.

bump *v.*[1] **1** in sexual contexts. (**a**) [mid-17C–late 18C; 1960s+] (*US campus*) to have sexual intercourse. (**b**) [1930s+] (*US*) to impregnate. (**c**) [1980s] (*W.I., Baha.*) to work as a prostitute. **2** in fig. uses of 'knock' (into, over etc). (**a**) [late 19C] (*US*) to terminate a relationship. (**b**) [late 19C+] (*Aus./US*) (*also* **bump someone's head**) to get the better of, to outdo, to deceive. (**c**) [late 19C+] to meet, to accost. (**d**) [20C+] to dismiss an employee, or someone from a team. **3** in the context of violence. (**a**) [1910s+] to kill; to murder. (**b**) [1910s+] to shoot dead. (**c**) [1910s+] to beat up. (**d**) [1940s] to fight successfully, to defeat. **4** to increase, i.e. 'bump up'. (**a**) [1920s+] to increase, i.e. a prison sentence. (**b**) [1940s+] (*also* **bump up**) to increase wages or, in gambling use, a bet. (**c**) [1940s+] to move someone up or down a queue, appointment calendar, etc. (**d**) [1960s+] to promote. (**e**) [1990s+] to boost one's intoxication (by taking more drugs). **5** [1970s] (*US*) to dance. **6** [1990s+] (*US black*) to create, to produce. **7** [2000s] of music, a record, to play.

IN PHRASES

❑ **bump bellies** *v.* [20C+] (*US*) to have sexual intercourse. ❑ **bump fuzz** *v. see under* FUZZ *n.*[2] (1). ❑ **bump pussies** *v. see under* PUSSY *n.* ❑ **bump titties** *v. see under* TITTY *n.* (1). ❑ **bump uglies** *v.* (*also* **bump nasties**) [SE *bump* + *ugly* (bodies)] [1990s+] (*US black/teen*) to have sexual intercourse.

SE in slang uses

IN COMPOUNDS

❑ **bump-in** *n.* [SE colloq. *bump into*, to meet accidentally] [1990s+] (*US*) a chance meeting. ❑ **bump man** *n.* [he 'bumps into' his victims] [1930s–40s] (*US*) a pickpocket. ❑ **bump stick** *n.* [late 19C–1910s] a police truncheon.

IN PHRASES

❑ **bump across** *v.* [a var. on SE *bump into*] [20C+] (*Aus.*) to meet by accident. ❑ **bump along** *v.* [1900s] (*Aus.*) to appear, to arrive. ❑ **bump and grab** *v.* [on model of SE *smash and grab*] [1990s+] (*US black*) to drive deliberately into someone's car with the intention of stopping and then robbing them. ❑ **bump heads** *v.* [1950s] (*US*) to clash (physically or otherwise), to argue, to debate. ❑ **bump iron** *v. see* PUMP IRON *under* IRON *n.* ❑ **bump one's gums** *v.* (*also* **run one's gums**) [20C+] (*orig. US black*) to argue, to talk excessively. ❑ **how (are) you bumping?** [1900s] (*Aus.*) general phr. of greeting. ❑ **wouldn't that bump you?** [1910s] phr. of disappointment, complaint.

IN EXCLAMATIONS

❑ **bump that!** [1980s] (*US campus*) an excl. of dismissal.

bump *v.*[2] [synon. of CLOUT *v.*[2] (1)/HIT *v.* (1); but ? f. 'bumping' a door to open it] [1980s+] (*US black*) to steal.

bumpa *n. see* BUMBA *n.*

bumper *n.*[1] **1** [late 17C–mid-19C] (*UK Und.*) a pickpocket's assistant who *bumps* into the victim. **2** [1990s+] (*Irish*) an amateur flat race [? contestants may fall off with a *bump* or *bump* each other's horses].

bumper *n.*[2] [the bumping of glasses in the toast or f. SE *bumping*, huge, great. Popular ety. suggests a supposed Fr. toast, *au bon père*, to the good father, *i.e.* the pope] **1** [late 17C–19C] a full glass, esp. when raised in a toast; also as v., to make a toast. **2** [mid-19C+] anything unusually large or plentiful. **3** [20C+] (*W.I.*) a drunkard, a habitual drinker, esp. of rum.

bumper *n.*[3] [ext. of BUM *n.*[1] (1) + echoic of the buttocks hitting a hard surface] **1** [late 19C] (*US*) a trunk. **2** [20C+] (*US/W.I.*) the buttocks [? play on KEISTER *n.* (1)/KEISTER *n.* (6)]. **3** [1940s+] usu. in pl., the female breasts; occas. buttocks. **4** [1970s] (*US*) the vagina.

IN COMPOUNDS

❑ **bumper kit** *n.* [1990s+] (*US black*) a woman's posterior or buttocks.

IN PHRASES

❑ **bumper to bumper** *adv.* [1970s+] (*US lesbian*) of lesbians, vagina to vagina, said of dancing or sexual intercourse.

bumper *n.*[4] [BUTT *n.*[1] (2) + SE *stump*] [late 19C+] (*Aus./N.Z.*) a cigarette butt; thus *bumper-dashing*, *bumper-shooting*, picking up cigarette butts from the street.

IN COMPOUNDS

❑ **bumper-shooter** *n.* [SE *shooter*, note Aus. army sl. *bumper-sniping*, a punishment that requires the defaulter to pick up cigarette-ends] [1940s+] (*Aus.*) a picker-up of discarded cigarette ends; thus *bumper-shooting*, *bumper-sniping*, following this practice.

IN PHRASES

❑ **not worth a bumper** *adj.* [1940s+] (*Aus.*) worthless, useless.

bumper *n.*[5] [1910s] (*Aus.*) a seller.

bumper *n.*[6] [ety. unknown; ? they bump together in the pocket/one bumps it down on the table] [1930s–40s] (*US*) five cents, a nickel.

bumper *n.*[7] [*BUMP PUSSIES under* PUSSY *n.* + ext. of SE use; i.e. her aggressiveness] [1940s+] a masculine lesbian.

bumper *n.*[8] [it 'bumps up' one's energy] [2000s] (*UK drugs*) a portion of a drug, e.g. a 'line' of cocaine.

bumper *adj.* [BUMPER *n.*[2] (3)] [mid-19C+] especially large, especially abundant.

bumper *v.* [BUMPER *n.*[4] (1)] [1960s+] (*Aus.*) to construct a cigarette from cigarette ends.

bumper head *n.* [the head 'bumps' on the partner's body] [1990s+] (*US*) one who performs oral sex.

bumper-jumper *n.* [1970s] (*US*) a driver who stays too close to the vehicle immediately in front, a 'tail-gater'.

bumpers *n.* see BUMPER *n.*[3] (3).

bumper-up *n.* **1** [20C+] a dockyard labourer. **2** [1920s+] (*Aus.*) a pickpocket's assistant. **3** [1920s+] (*Aus.*) a handyman who works for a prostitute. **4** [1920s+] (*Aus.*) a general term for an absolute incompetent.

bumper-upper *n.* [ext. of BUMPER-UP *n.* (3)] [1920s+] (*Aus.*) a handyman who works for a prostitute; thus derog. phr. *he couldn't get a job as a bumper-upper in a brothel*.

bumpf *n. see* BUMF *n.*

bumph *n. see* BUMF *n.*

bumpie *n. see* BUPPIE *n.*

bumping *n.* [the 'bumps' come from the thud of the bass, which will be turned up high] **1** [1980s+] (*US black teen*) the sound of a car stereo. **2** [1990s+] (*US black*) having an uproariously good time.

bumping *adj.* [fig. uses of SE *bump*, to hit, to thump] **1** [late 19C–1900s] large. **2** [1980s] (*US campus*) stylish, attractive. **3** [1980s+] (*US black / campus*) exhilarating.

bump(-off) *n.* **1** [1920s–60s] (*orig. US*) a murder; thus *bump-off guy*, n., a killer. **2** [1930s] the end of something, typically criminal activity.

bump (off) *v.* [SE *bump*, to push] **1** [20C+] (*orig. US*) to murder; thus *the bump*, a murder, *bump oneself off*, to commit suicide. **2** [1910s–50s] to die. **3** [1910s+] (*also* **bump out**) to dismiss, get rid of. **4** [1920s] to wound. **5** [1920s] (*US Und.*) to raid.

bumps *n.*[1] **1** [1900s] (*US*) hard treatment. **2** [1960s–70s] (*US black*) a rash, esp. on the face.

bumps *n.*[2] [? juv. mispron.] [1960s] (*US*) an affectionate name for one's grandfather.

bumpsie *adj.* (*also* **bumpsy, bumsie**) [? liable to 'bump' into people or to fall over with a 'bump'] [early–mid-17C] drunk.

bump start *n.* [BUMP START *v.*] [1970s+] a violent gesture or action (whether physical or metaphorical).

bump start *v.* [SE] [1970s+] to make a violent gesture or action.

bumpsy *n. see* BUMPSIE *adj.*

bumptious *adj.* [SE *bump* + sfx *-ious* on pattern of *fractious, mendacious* etc] **1** [19C+] offensively self-assertive. **2** [late 19C–1920s] (*US black*) short-tempered.

bumpy *n.* [ext. of BUM *n.*[1] (1) + the physical 'bump' of the buttocks] [1960s] (*US*) the buttocks.

bumpy *adj.* [BUMPY *n.*] [1990s+] homosexual.

bum rap *n.* [BUM *adj.* (1) + RAP *n.*[1] (3c)] (*orig. US*) **1** [1920s+] a false accusation or an unfair sentence. **2** [1940s+] a misfortune, an unfair action. **3** [1950s+] harsh (and poss. unfair) criticism. **4** [1970s] a bad reputation.

bum rap *v.* [BUM RAP *n.*] **1** [1940s+] to convict or accuse falsely. **2** [1950s+] to slander, to attack verbally, to catcall.

bumrush *n.* [BUM *adj.* + SE *rush*] [1980s+] (*US black*) **1** a police raid. **2** a stampede, esp. of a crowd wanting to get into a rock concert or film show (usu. without tickets and dependent on force of numbers to overwhelm the security guards).

bumrush *v.* [BUMRUSH *n.*] [1980s+] (*orig. US black*) **1** to attack, to destroy through violence; usu. as part of a gang or group. **2** (*rap music*) to get in (to a concert, a club) without having to pay. **3** to move as a crowd, using numbers to gain access. **4** to pursue. **5** (*US*) to eject. **6** (*US campus*) to be overlooked, rejected. **7** to run off fast; to escape, e.g. from a police raid. **8** to rush someone away.

bum-shaver *n.*[1] [BUM *n.*[1] (2) + SHAVER *n.*[1] (1)/SHAVER *n.*[2] (2)] [18C] a womanizer, a promiscuous man.

bum-shaver *n.*[2] *see* BUM-PERISHER *under* BUM *n.*[1].

bumsie *adj. see* BUMPSIE *adj.*

bumsquabbled *adj.* (*also* **bamsquabbled**) [ety. unknown] [mid-19C] (*US*) discomfited, defeated; confused.

bum's rush *n.* (*also* **rush**) [BUM *n.*[3] (1) + SE *rush*, a sudden onslaught; the origin of the phr. came in the saloons of late 19C New York where vagrants and other hungry people attempted to take advantage of the sometimes sumptuous free lunch counters, which were meant for drinkers only] [20C+] (*orig. US Und.*) **1** a rejection. **2** forcible movement. **3** (*also* **fool's rush, rush**) forcible ejection, esp. from a bar or club, esp. as *get* or *give the bum's rush*. **4** a military defeat.

bumsuck *v.* [BUM *n.*[1] (1) + SE *suck*] [1930s+] to toady to, to act the sycophant.

bum-sucker *n.* [BUMSUCK *v.*] [mid-19C; 1940s+] a sycophant, a crawler.

bumswiggled *adj.* (*also* **bumswizzled**) [ety. unknown; ? BAMBOOZLE *v.*] [19C+] confounded, ruined.

bumy-juice *n.* [mid-19C] (*UK Und.*) porter or beer.

bumzwizzled *adj. see* BUMSWIGGLED *adj.*

bun *n.*[1] [? 16C north. dial. *bun*, the tail of a hare; also abbr. SE *bunny*, the stereotypically 'sexy' rabbit] **1** [late 16C–19C] a squirrel. **2** [late 18C–19C] a rabbit. **3** referring to the stereotyped sexual appetites of sense 2. (**a**) [mid-17C+] pubic hair; thus the vagina. (**b**) [1930s+] (*Scot.*) a prostitute. **4** [late 19C+] an attractive female who is 'good enough to eat'.

IN PHRASES

❑ **butter a bun** *v.* [1950s+] (*US*) to have sexual intercourse. ❑ **touch the bun for luck** *v.* [orig. a RN tradition] [late 18C–early 19C] to touch one's wife's or girlfriend's genital area for luck before leaving on a journey.

bun *n.*[2] [? links to Worcestershire dial. *bun*, a bung or cork or Angus dial. *bun*, a large cask] **1** [late 19C+] a state of drunkenness, esp. as *have a bun, get/have/put/tie a bun on*; occas. a drugged state. **2** [1900s] (*US*) a state of weeping. **3** [1910s] (*US*) a fit of laughter. **4** [1920s+] (*US*) whisky.

bun *n.*[3] [resemblance] **1** [1910s+] (*N.Z.*) (*also* **bun hat**) a bowler hat. **2** [1930s+] the head, fig. one's emotions.

IN PHRASES

❑ **do one's bun** *v.* [1930s+] (*orig. N.Z. milit.*) to lose emotional control.

SE in slang uses

IN COMPOUNDS

❑ **bun-duster** *n.* [SE *bun* + *duster*, he 'dusts off', i.e. finishes, the buns] [1920s] (*US*) an effete young man who attends smart tea parties and charms old ladies. ❑ **bun feast** *n.* [ext. of SE use but ? ironic ref. to *beanfeast*] [late 19C–1900s] a third-rate feast, where even the buns are not enough to make one full. ❑ **bunfight** *n.* [late 19C+] a tea party, esp. with image of children struggling for sticky buns; any party. ❑ **bun-house** *n.* [the distribution of free buns] [1940s] (*UK Und.*) public relief. ❑ **bun-joint** *n.* [JOINT *n.* (3)] [late 19C] (*US*) a coffeehouse. ❑ **bun-puncher** *n.* (*also* **bun-strangler**) [1910s–30s] a teetotaller; thus *bun-punching*, teetotal. ❑ **bunrunner** *n.* [1990s+] (*N.Z.*) a person who delivers lunch and snacks around offices. ❑ **bun-struggle** *n.* (*also* **bun-rush, muffin-struggle, tea-scramble**) [var. on *BUN-WORRY* below; note WW1 milit. *bun-strangler, bun wallah*, a teetotaller] [late 19C–1950s] a tea party. ❑ **bun-trap** *n.* [SE *trap*/TRAP *n.*[1] (4)] [20C+] the mouth. ❑ **bun-worry** *n.* [SE *worry*, to bite at like a dog] **1** [late 19C–1900s] (*orig. milit.*) a tea party. **2** [late 19C+] (*Aus./N.Z.*) a general jollification.

bun *n.*[4] [abbr. of BUNDLE *n.*[1] (3b)] [1980s+] (*drugs*) a quantity of cannabis resin, either 1kg or 5kg.

bun *n.*[5] for combs. pertaining to the buttocks, *see under* BUNS *n.*

bun *v.*[1] [? BUN *n.*[1] (2), i.e. the notoriously sex-driven SE *bunny-rabbit*] [1990s+] (*US black*) to have sexual intercourse.

bun *v.*[2] [pron. of BURN *v.* (5b)] [1990s+] (*orig. UK black*) to smoke cannabis or crack cocaine.

bun-bun *n.* [redup. of BUNS *n.* (1)] [1970s+] (*US gay*) the buttocks.

bunce *n.* (*also* **bunse, bunts**) [costermonger jargon *bunts*, second-rate apples, which were sold off cheap or even given away to market boys, who could in turn sell them at a small profit. Hotten (1867) adds 'money obtained by giving light weight, &c.'. Bunts were further divided into *fair bunts* and *unfair bunts*, depending on whether or not the coster was aware of his boy's tricks] **1** [18C+] (*also* **bounce**) money (esp. for nothing); thus extras, bonuses, profits, whether monetary or otherwise. **2** [1960s+] (*UK Und.*) stolen goods.

IN PHRASES

❑ **bunce in/up** *v.* [20C+] (*Ulster*) to pool resources.

bunce *v.* [BUNCE *n.* (1)] [20C+] (*market*) to overcharge.

buncer *n.* [BUNCE *n.* (1)] **1** [mid-19C+] a salesperson who works for a commission. **2** [20C+] (*market*) one who overcharges the customers.

bunce up *v. see under* BUNCE *n.*

bunch *n.*[1] **1** [late 17C+] a group, usu. in phr. *best of the bunch, best of a bad bunch*. **2** [20C+] a quantity.

bunch *n.*[2] [1970s] (*US gay*) the male genitals.

bunch *n.*[3]

IN PHRASES

❑ **give someone a bunch up** *v. see* GIVE SOMEONE A (CLEAN) LEG UP *under* LEG *n.*

bunch *v.* [BUNK (OFF) *under* BUNK *v.*[1]] [20C+] (*US*) to leave a job, to leave something unfinished.

bunch! *excl.* [? abbr. *bunch of* BULLSHIT *n.*] [1900s] (*US campus*) nonsense! rubbish!

bunched *adj.* [1970s+] (*Irish*) exhausted.

bunch of... *n.*

SE in slang uses

IN PHRASES

❑ **bunch of charms** *n.* [1900s] a pretty young woman ❑ **bunch of dog's meat** *n.* [its fate if it does not stop whinging] [mid-19C] a squalling baby. ❑ **bunch of grapes** *n.* **1** [1910s] (*Aus.*) in cards, the suit of clubs. **2** [1930s] (*US*) jailor's keys ❑ **bunch of onions** *n.* [ONION *n.*[1] (1)] [mid-19C] a watch and seals. ❑ **bunch of rags** *n.* [1910s–60s] (*US*) a young woman esp. a prostitute.

bunch of fives *n.* (*also* **bunch of five, box of fives, bunch of ivories**) [the five fingers] [19C+] the hand, usu. when clenched in a fist; thus a punch.

IN PHRASES

❑ **chuck up the bunch of fives** *v.* [1900s] to die. ❑ **string the fives on** *v.* [1950s] to beat up.

bunch punch *n.* [SE *bunch* + PUNCH *v.* (1)] [1970s+] (*orig. US campus*) group sex in which a number of males have sex with one woman; similarly of male homosexuals.

bunch punch *v.* [BUNCH PUNCH *n.* (1)] [1970s+] (*orig. US campus*) to have group sex, usu. a gang-rape.

bunchy *n.* [BUM *n.*[1] (1) + ? 14C SE *bunchy*, swelling] [1940s+] (*W.I.*) the buttocks.

bunchy *adj.* [14C SE *bunchy*, swelling] (*US*) **1** well-built. **2** [20C+] chubby.

bunco *n.* (*also* **banco, bunko**) [Sp. *banca*, a card-game similar to monte] (*Und., esp. US*) **1** [late 19C–1920s] a swindler. **2** [late 19C+] fraud, a dishonest gambling game. **3** [1910s+] deceit, flattery, empty nonsense. **4** [1960s+] a police squad devoted to combating confidence tricksters.

IN COMPOUNDS

❑ **bunco artist** *n.* (*also* **bunko artist, bunko boy**) [-ARTIST *sfx*] [20C+] (*US*) a confidence trickster. ❑ **bunco game** *n.* (*also* **bunko game, bunk game**) (*US*) **1** [late 19C–1970s] a generic for swindling, confidence trickery. **2** [1900s–20s] any form of 'fixed' gambling game. **3** in fig., i.e. non-criminal, use, any form of duplicity. ❑ **bunco man** *n.* (*also* **banco man, bunk, bunko man**) [Asbury, *The Gangs of Chicago* (1940), differentiates: 'the [confidence man] operated all kinds of swindles, while the bunko man specialized in playing banco, sometimes called bunko, which was an adapatation of the old English game of eight-dice cloth'] [late 19C–1950s] (*US*) a swindler, a confidence trickster. ❑ **bunco squad** *n.* (*also* **bunco people, bunko people**) [1940s+] (*US police/Und.*) a special squad devoted to combating confidence tricksters. ❑ **bunco steerer** *n.* (*also* **bunko-steerer, banco-steerer**) [STEERER *n.* (3)] **1** [late 19C+] (*US Und.*) that member of a confidence trickster gang whose task is to entrap the victim into the current swindle. **2** [late 19C+] as a non-specific term of abuse. ❑ **bunco-steering** *n.* [late 19C–1940s] (*US*) confidence trickery.

bunco *adj.* (*also* **bunko**) [BUNCO *n.*] (*US*) **1** [late 19C+] pertaining to swindlers and confidence tricksters. **2** [20C+] deceptive, fraudulent.

bunco *v.* (*also* **bunko**) [BUNCO *n.* (1)] [late 19C+] (*US*) to swindle, to defraud.

buncombe *n. see* BUNKUM *n.*

buncombe *adj.* [BUNCOMBE *n.*] [mid-19C] (*US*) nonsensical.

bundabust *n.* (*also* **bundobust**) [Hind. *band-o-bast*, tying and binding] [late 19C–1950s] (*orig. Ind. army*) **1** discipline, regulations. **2** arrangements. **3** a revenue settlement.

bunder *n.* [Hind. *band*, an artificial embankment or quay, esp. the Shangai *Bund*, the city's main (pre-revolutionary) commercial centre] [late 19C–1930s] (*Anglo-Chinese*) any supposedly remarkable piece of information that turns out to be no more than a false rumour.

bundi *n.*

IN PHRASES

❑ **give bundi** *v. see GIVE BONDI under* BONDI *n.*

bundie *n.* [BUNS *n.* (1)] [20C+] (*Irish*) a child's buttocks.

bundle *n.*[1] [SE *bundle*] **1** as a (large) quantity. (**a**) [mid-17C+] a large amount. (**b**) [late 19C+] a large amount of money. (**c**) [20C+] loot, plunder. (**d**) [1900s] a wad of money. (**e**) [1930s+] (*US prison*) a long prison sentence. **2** [mid-18C–1950s] cognate with BAGGAGE *n.*: a woman, esp. a fat one; one's wife; thus (*US*) a girlfriend, a female companion [early use is generally derog.; 20C use is neutral]. **3** in drug uses. (**a**) [1960s+] (*drugs*) a package of 25 $5 bags of heroin. (**b**) [1990s+] (*US black/drugs*) a quantity of a drug available for sale. (**c**) [1990s+] (*US drugs*) ten bags of heroin; equiv. of one gram.

IN COMPOUNDS

❑ **bundle connection** *n.* [CONNECTION *n.* (2)] [1990s+] (*US drugs*) a mid-level drug dealer, working between bulk wholesalers and street-level retailers.

IN PHRASES

❑ **bundle that would trip a white wings** *n.* [1900s] (*US*) a very large amount of money. ❑ **go a bundle (on)** *v.* (*also* **go the bundle (on)**) [1930s+] to support whole-heartedly, to be very fond. ❑ **go the bundle** *v.* [20C+] (*orig. US*) **1** to bet heavily, to bet one's entire funds. **2** to be very fond of. **3** to commit oneself completely; fig. use of sense 1.

SE in slang uses

IN COMPOUNDS

❑ **bundle-bum** *n.* [BUM *n.*[3] (1)] [1920s–30s] (*US tramp*) the lowest grade of tramp. ❑ **bundle-tail** *n.* [TAIL *n.* (4)] [late 17C–18C] a short, fat, squat woman.

IN PHRASES

❑ **bundle off** *v.* [fig. use of SE; subseq. use is SE] [19C–1900s] to leave, to send away in a hurry. ❑ **bundle of lard** *n. see TUB OF LARD under* TUB *n.*[1]. ❑ **bundle of ten** *n.* [1910s] a packet of ten cigarettes. ❑ **drop one's bundle** *v.* [note Stephens & O'Brien, *Materials for a Dict. of Aus. Slang* (ms.; 1900-10): 'It has a vulgar derivation from the fact of cowards being said to perform a natural function through fright.'] (*Aus./N.Z.*) **1** [20C+] to panic, to lose (emotional or physical) control, to give up hope. **2** [1980s] to defecate. **3** [1980s] to give birth.

bundle *n.*[2] [the participants have been 'bundled' together] **1** [1930s+] a fight. **2** [1990s+] sexual intercourse [note 18C–19C SE *bundle*, to sleep in one's clothes on the same bed or couch with].

bundle *v.* [SE *bundle* (*together*), i.e. the proximity of the bodies, whether sexual or violent] **1** [late 18C–1940s] to have sexual intercourse. **2** [early 19C] to pass something over. **3** [1930s] (*US tramp*) to steal, esp. when a degree of physical violence is involved. **4** [1930s+] to fight.

bundle! *excl.* [BUNDLE *n.*[2] (1)] [1990s+] (*UK juv.*) a shout that signifies that a fight is taking place.

bundle of socks *n.* [rhy. sl. = *THINKBOX under* THINK *v.*] [late 19C+] (*Aus.*) the head.

bundle stiff *n. see BINDLE STIFF under* BINDLE *n.*

bundobust *n. see* BUNDABUST *n.*

bundook *n. see* BANDOOK *n.*

bundwipe *n. see* ASS-WIPE *n.* (2).

bundy *n.* [the proprietary name of a brand of rum, ult. f. the town in Queensland] [1960s+] (*Aus.*) Bundaberg rum.

IN PHRASES

❑ **give bundy** *v. see GIVE BONDI under* BONDI *n.*

bundy off *v.* [fig. use of and thus synon, with *PUNCH THE BUNDY under* PUNCH *v.*] [1980s+] (*Aus. prison*) to die, esp. of a drug overdose.

bunf *n. see* BUMF *n.*

bunfungered *adj. see* BUMFUDDLED *adj.*

bung *n.*[1] (*also* **boung, bong**) [Frisian *pung*, purse] **1** [mid-16C–mid-19C] (*UK Und.*) a purse. **2** [late 16C–mid-18C] a pocket. **3** [late 16C–mid-19C] a cut-purse. **4** [1950s+] a bribe. **5** [1990s+] a loan.

IN COMPOUNDS

❑ **bung-nip** *v. see NIP A BUNG under* NIP *v.*[1]. ❑ **bung-nipper** *n.* (*also* **boung-nipper, bung napper, boung-napper**) [NIPPER *n.*[1] (1)] [mid-17C–mid-19C] (*UK Und.*) a cut-purse; a pickpocket.

IN PHRASES

❑ **put the bung in** *v.* [1950s] to bribe, to hand over a bribe.

bung *n.*[2] [SE *bung*, the mouth of a cask, the stopper of a barrel of beer; note Welsh *bwng*, an orifice] **1** as a hole, lit. or fig. (**a**) [late 16C+] (*also* **bung head**) a general insult. (**b**) [late 18C+] the anus. (**c**) [1950s–60s] (*US*) in fig. use, the buttocks. (**d**) [1960s] (*US*) the vagina. **2** in the context of brewing. (**a**) [mid-19C–1900s] a brewer; a brewery. (**b**) [late 19C–1950s] beer. (**c**) [mid-19C–1910s] an inn-keeper or publican; thus the *bung ball*, an annual publican's dance. (**d**) [1910s] (*Aus.*) generic for the brewery interest.

IN COMPOUNDS

❑ **bung-juice** *n.* [late 19C] beer, stout. ❑ **bungwad** *n.* [BUNG *n.*^{2} (1) + SE *wad*] (*US*) **1** [1920s] lavatory paper. **2** [1990s+] a general insult.

IN PHRASES

□ **hit the bung** *v.* [1930s] (*US*) to get drunk.

SE in slang uses

IN COMPOUNDS

□ **bung-starter** *n.* [SE *bung-starter*, an implement used to remove the bungs from casks of beer] [late 19C–1930s] (*US*) a bartender.

IN PHRASES

□ **pull the bung out** *v.* [1950s] (*US*) to deflate someone's ego, of an object, to wreck. □ **put a bung in it** *v.* **1** [late 19C] to stop talking, also as imper. **2** [1910s] shut the door!

bung *n.*^{3} [SE *bung up*, to bruise, to beat] [mid-19C+] (*US*) a lump, a swelling.

bung *n.*^{4} [BUNG *v.* (3)] [late 19C] (*Aus.*) eviction.

bung *n.*^{5} [ety. unknown; ? BUNG *v.* (3), i.e. it 'throws away' the truth] [late 19C–1910s] (*juv.*) a lie.

bung *n.*^{6} [dial., ult. echoic] **1** [late 19C+] a blow, esp. in phr. *bung in the eye*, a blow in the eye. **2** [20C+] a black eye.

bung *n.*^{7} (*also* **bungy, bunghole**) [its costive effects, i.e. it 'bungs you up'] [1910s+] (*Aus.*) cheese.

IN PHRASES

□ **draw bungy** *v. see under* DRAW *v.*^{4}.

bung *n.*^{8} [var. on BONG *n.*^{1} (1)] [1980s+] (*US drugs*) a bowl-shaped water-pipe used for smoking marijuana.

bung *adj.*^{1} [fig. use of BUNG *v.* (1)] [mid-18C–19C] (*orig. UK Und.*) drunk.

bung *adj.*^{2} [Abor. *bong*, dead] [1900s] (*Aus.*) impoverished; bankrupt.

IN PHRASES

□ **go bung** *v.* (*Aus./N.Z.*) **1** (*also* **go bong**) [mid-19C+] to die. **2** [late 19C+] to become bankrupt. **3** [late 19C+] to collapse, to break down, to fail.

bung *v.* (*also* **bung out**) [echoic of tossing an article with some violence] **1** [early 19C+] to hit, to punch, esp. in the eye. **2** [mid-19C] to lie, to deceive. **3** [mid-19C+] to pass, to throw, usu. energetically or aggressively. **4** [mid-19C+] to hand over, to give quickly, esp. in imper. e.g. *bung this round to Fred.* **5** [late 19C+] to hand out money, esp. to bet or to bribe. **6** [20C+] to place (inside). **7** [1910s+] to give, as speech. **8** [1940s+] to get rid of, dispose of. **9** [1950s+] (*UK Und./police*) to bribe or to pay protection money.

IN PHRASES

□ **bung it in** *v.* [late 19C] to gamble at a casino. □ **bung it on** *v.* [1940s+] (*Aus.*) **1** to act affectedly, to strike poses, to assume an accent. **2** to overcharge. **3** to assert pressure. **4** (*Aus./N.Z.*) to exaggerate, to act temperamentally. □ **bung off** *v.* [20C+] to leave. □ **bung on** *v.* [1960s+] **1** to put on a garment, to get dressed, usu. in comb. with an article of clothing, e.g. *bung on a jacket*. **2** to organize, to arrange. **3** to perform an action. □ **bung on a blue** *v. see under* BLUE *n.*^{4}. □ **bung one on** *v.* ['one' is a blow or punch] [1950s+] to hit. □ **bung one's eye** *v.* [lit. to drink until one's eyes are *bunged*, closed] **1** [late 18C–19C] to drink a dram, to drink heartily, to get drunk. **2** [1910s] (*US*) a drinking toast. □ **bung on side** *v. see under* SIDE *n.* □ **bung on the bull** *v. see under* BULL *n.*^{6}. □ **bung out** *v.* **1** [mid-19C–1910s] (*US*) to protrude, to stick out. **2** [1900s] (*N.Z.*) to die.

bung *adv.* [BANG *adv.* (1)] [mid-19C+] precisely, accurately, usu. as *bung in*, *bung on*.

bungality *n.* [mid-19C] (*Aus.*) stupidity.

bungalow bill *n.* (*also* **bungalow**) [pun] [late 19C+] a man who is either not very intelligent ('nothing up top') or endowed with large genitals ('it's all down below').

bungaree *n. see* BUNGERY *n.*

bungary *n. see* BUNGERY *n.*

bungdung *n.* [? BANDOOK *n.*] [1920s+] (*Aus.*) a large firecracker.

bunged *adj.* [BUNG *adj.*^{1}] [1930s+] (*S.Afr.*) tipsy.

bunged up *adj.*^{1} [SE *bung*, to enclose] **1** [late 16C; late 19C+] stuffy, blocked, esp. of one's nose during 'flu or a cold, or of constipation. **2** [1900s] (*US*) second-rate; broken down. **3** [1930s] (*Aus.*) in a bad way, hopeless. **4** [1980s] squashed, creased, pushed together uncomfortably.

bunged up *adj.*^{2} [var. on SE *banged up*; + note BUNG *n.*^{6} (2)] **1** [early 19C–1910s] (*also* **bunged**) of the eyes, blackened. **2** [early 19C+] (*Aus./US*) hurt, injured.

bungee *adj.* [? SE *bungee jumping*, an 'extreme sport'] [1990s+] (*US campus*) extremely.

bunger *n.*^{1} [BUNG *v.* (3)/BUNG *n.*^{5} (1)] (*Aus.*) **1** [late 19C] a cannon. **2** [1900s] an outstanding example.

bunger *n.*^{2} [BUNG *n.*^{6} (2)] [1900s–40s] (*US*) a black eye.

bunger *n.*^{3} [BUNGHOLE *n.*^{1} (1)/BUNG *n.*^{2} (1)] [1960s] **1** (*US*) the anus. **2** a male homosexual.

bungery *n.* (*also* **bungaree, bungary**) [BUNG *n.*^{2} (2)] [late 19C–1900s] a tavern, a public house; thus *Bohemian bungery*, a public house frequented by (impecunious) writers and artists.

bung-eye *n.* (*also* **bungy-eye**) [BUNGED UP *adj.*^{2} (2) + SE *eye*] [late 19C+] (*Aus.*) an eye infection caused by flies.

bung-eyed *adj.* [the volume of liquor 'bungs up' one's vision; but note SE *bung*, a stopper (for a cask)] **1** [early–mid-19C] drunk. **2** [1960s+] cross-eyed.

bung eyes *n.* [BUNG *v.* (1) + SE *eyes*] [1960s–70s] (*US*) protruding eyes.

bung-fodder *n.* [BUNG *n.*^{2} (1) + SE *fodder*] [late 19C+] (*US*) **1** lavatory paper. **2** in fig. use, as a derog. description.

bungfoodle *v.* [? BAMBOOZLE *v.* (1)] [1900s] (*Aus.*) to deceive, to 'mess around'.

bungfunger *v.* [? BAMBOOZLE *v.* (1)] [mid-19C] (*US*) to confuse.

bung ho *adj.* [BUNG HO! *excl.*] [1950s] proper, right, good.

bung ho! *excl.* [SE *bung* or BUNG *v.* (3); i.e. one 'throws' the drunk down] **1** [1920s+] a toast when drinking. **2** [1930s–40s] a farewell, goodbye.

bunghole *n.*^{1} [SE *bung* + *hole*] **1** [17C+] the anus, the rectum. **2** [early 17C; late 19C–1900s] (*US*) the vagina. **3** [mid-17C] in fig. use of sense 1, something that stinks. **4** [20C+] (*Aus.*) the mouth. **5** [1960s+] (*US campus*) a term of abuse.

bunghole *n.*^{2} [ext. BUNG *n.*^{7}; ? 'you bung it down your hole'] [1910s+] (*orig. milit.*) cheese.

bunghole *adj.* [2000s] (*Aus.*) a general negative intensifier.

bunghole *v.* **1** [1930s+] to sodomize [BUNGHOLE *n.*^{1} (1)]. **2** (*US drugs*) to inject narcotics [Spears, *Slang and Jargon of Drugs and Drink* (1986), suggests 'probably nonce' but the term plays on the equation of narcotics and excrement, see SHIT *n.* (6)].

bunghole buddy *n.* [BUNGHOLE *n.*^{1} (1) + BUDDY *n.* (1); var. on *ASSHOLE BUDDY under* ASSHOLE *n.*] [1940s] (*US*) a very close friend.

bungi *n.* (*also* **bungie, bungy**) [Hind. *bhang*, cannabis or Ndebele *im-banje*, marijuana. Coined at Rhodes University, Grahamstown] [1980s+] (*S.Afr.*) a 'drop-out', a HIPPIE *n.*^{2} (3).

bungie-bird *n.* [name *Friar Bungay*, as in Robert Greene's's *Friar Bacon and Friar Bungay* (acted 1594)] [late 16C] a Franciscan friar.

bungie-boy *n.* [1990s+] (*US gay*) a homosexual or bisexual male who maintains a heterosexual appearance.

bung it (in) *n.* [rhy. sl.] [1920s+] gin.

bungle *n.* [elided pron. of BUNGHOLE *n.*^{1} (2)] [1990s+] (*W.I.*) someone who performs oral sex on a woman.

bungler *n.* [SE *bungler*, an unskilful worker] [late 16C–early 18C] an impotent husband; *bungling*, adj. sexually inadequate if not actually impotent.

bungo *n.* [? Hausa *bungu*, a nincompoop, a country bumpkin] **1** [20C+] (*W.I., Jam.*) a crude, boorish, ignorant black person, a country bumpkin. **2** *see* BONGO *n.*^{1}.

IN COMPOUNDS

□ **bungo-bessy** *n.* [BESSY *n.*] [1940s+] (*W.I.*) **1** an interfering busybody. **2** a boorish low-class woman. □ **bungo-talk** *n.* [1940s+] (*W.I.*) illiterate speech, the lowest level of uncultivated Jamaican speech. □ **bungo-toughy** *n.* [TOUGHI *n.*] [1940s+] (*W.I., Guyn.*) a little child who eats or behaves like a hooligan.

bungo *v.* [BUNGO *n.* but ? BANJO *v.* (2)/BUNG *v.* (1)] [1980s] (*US campus*) to mistreat severely, to inflict injury on.

bungs up *adj.* [naut. jargon *bungs up*, a vessel that is rolling in a heavy sea to such an extent that the *bungs* in her planking are visible] [1970s] (*US*) very drunk, rolling drunk.

bung-up *n.* [mid-19C+] the act of helping someone mount of horse, climb a wall, etc.

bung up *v.* [SE *bung*; use before 19C use is SE] **1** [late 16C+] to stop up. **2** [early 19C+] to close someone's eye with a punch or for the eye to close after a punch. **3** [late 19C] to impregnate. **4** [1930s+] to spoil.

bung up (against) *adv. see* BANG UP AGAINST *adv.*

bung upwards *adv.* [BUNG *n.*[2] (1)/BUNGHOLE *n.*[1] (1) + SE *upwards*] [late 18C–early 19C] lying on one's stomach.

bungy *n.*[1] *see* BUNG *n.*[7].

bungy *n.*[2] *see* BUNGI *n.*

bungy *adj.* (*also* **bongy**) [BUNG *n.*[2] (2)] [mid-18C–mid-19C] drunk.

bungy-eye *n. see* BUNG-EYE *n.*

bunhouse *n.* [? BUN *n.*[1] (1) + SE *house*] [2000s] ? a brothel.

bunion derby *n.* [SE *bunion* + *The Derby*, a well-known horserace in the UK and as the Kentucky Derby in the US] [1920s; 1990s] (*US*) a cross-country marathon.

bunions *n. see* ONION *n.*[1] (1d).

bunji *n.* [Goreng Goreng *banji*, friend + SE *man*] [1980s+] (*Aus.*) a white man, often old and impoverished, who pursues Aboriginal women for sex.

bunk *n.*[1]

IN PHRASES

□ **do a bunk** *v.* **1** [late 19C+] (*orig. US*) to run off, to escape, to go into hiding. **2** [1910s] (*Aus.*) to move or work fast.

bunk *n.*[2] (*also* **the bunk**) [BUNKUM *n.*] **1** [20C+] (*orig. US*) rubbish, nonsense; thus *bunky*, nonsensical. **2** [20C+] a foolish or otherwise unsatisfactory person. **3** [1920s] (*US tramp*) good manners. **4** as counterfeit drink or drugs. (**a**) [1940s] (*US Und.*) synthetic liquor. (**b**) [1980s+] (*drugs*) fake cocaine.

IN COMPOUNDS

□ **bunk sheet** *n. see under* SHEET *n.* □ **bunkshooter** *n.* [SHOOT *v.* (1)] [1910s–20s] (*US*) a preacher.

IN PHRASES

□ **go to bunk** *v.* [1910s+] (*Aus.*) to fail, to collapse. □ **put the bunk** *v.* [1920s] to talk nonsense.

bunk *n.*[3] [1910s+] (*US*) **1** a Slav immigrant f. Eastern Europe. **2** an oafish, dull, if muscular person.

bunk *n.*[4] [abbr. of BUNKIE *n.* (1)] [1990s+] (*US*) a friend.

bunk *adj.* [BUNK *n.*[2]] [20C+] **1** bad, second-rate, inferior; infuriating. **2** fake, counterfeit. **3** unsophisticated, unfashionable, ugly.

bunk *v.*[1] [Lincolnshire dial. *bunk*, to run away, to make off] **1** [mid-19C+] to escape, to run off (under pressure). **2** [late 19C+] to leave, to be off (of one's own volition). **3** [1900s] to force someone to leave. **4** [1920s] to rush.

IN PHRASES

□ **bunk (off)** *v.* **1** [late 19C+] (*also* **bunk on**) to leave. **2** [1940s+] to play truant, usu. schoolchildren. **3** [1990s+] to avoid one's responsibilities, esp. work. □ **bunk out** *v.* [var. on BUNK (OFF) above] [1970s+] (*Irish*) to play truant. □ **bunk over** *v.* [20C+] to go across.

bunk *v.*[2] (*also* **bunk down, bunk in, bunk up**) [SE *bunk* n.] **1** [mid-19C+] (*orig. US*) to sleep; esp. in the context of a shared prison cell, service dormitory etc. **2** [1900s–40s] to lie down. **3** [1900s–10s] in fig. use, to associate with. **4** [1950s] to give someone a place to sleep. **5** [1970s] to live together.

bunk *v.*[3] [BUNK *n.*[2]] **1** [mid-19C+] to talk nonsense, to fool someone. **2** [1900s] to overcome completely, lit. to reduce to 'nonsense.'.

bunk *v.*[4] [1910s+] (*US*) to hide, to conceal.

bunk *v.*[5] [BUNK UP *v.*[1]] **1** [1950s] (*Aus.*) to carry someone on one's bicycle cross-bar. **2** [1980s+] (*also* **bonk**) to travel without a fare, to get in (e.g. to a cinema) without a ticket.

bunk! *excl.* [BUNK *n.*[2]] [1910s+] (*orig. US*) nonsense!

bunked *adj.* [BUNK *v.*[1] (2)] [1900s] (*US*) abandoned, deserted, esp. by one owing money.

bunker *n.*[1] [? a fig. coal bunker at which one 'fuels up' or Ling. Fr. *bona acqua*, good water] [mid-19C] beer.

bunker *n.*[2] [euph. for SE *bugger*; however, Irwin, *American Tramp and Und. Slang* (1931), suggests a ref. to a sailor's *bunk*, wherein seaboard homosexuality takes place] [1930s] a sodomite.

IN COMPOUNDS

□ **bunker-shy** *adj.* [1920s+] (*orig. US prison/tramp*) of a young man, orig, a prisoner, frightened of being forced into homosexual sex.

bunkered *adj.* [golfing imagery] [late 19C+] in difficulties.

bunk habit *n.* (*also* **bunk yen**) [SE *bunk*, a rudimentary bed as used by a smoker + *yen*, desire/HABIT *n.*] **1** [late 19C–1930s] (*US drugs*) the act of frequenting an opium den, too poor to buy one's own drugs but in the hope that someone else will offer a treat or simply to inhale the airborne fumes. **2** [1930s–60s] (*US drugs*) the desire to sleep excessively, resulting from one's addiction to narcotics.

bunkie *n.* [US army use *bunkie*, a bunkmate; thus a friend] **1** [mid-19C+] (*US milit./campus/prison*) (*also* **bunkey, bunky**) a room-mate, a cell-mate; a friend. **2** [1970s+] (*US*) a general term of address, usu. condescending.

bunk into *v.* [f. SE *bump into*] **1** [20C+] (*US*) to meet by accident. **2** [1950s] to knock against.

bunk it *v.* [SE *bunk*] [mid-19C+] (*US*) **1** to sleep in a bunk (rather than a proper bed). **2** to sleep in any rough, makeshift manner.

bunko *n. see* BUNCO *n.*

bunks *v.* [SE *bounce*] [1950s+] (*W.I. Rasta*) to knock or bump against; thus *bunks mi res*, catch my rest, take a nap.

bunkum *n.* (*also* **buncombe, bokum**) [proper name of *Buncombe County* in North Carolina. The word emerged during the debate on the 'Missouri Question' in 1821 when Felix Walker, the member from this district, rose to speak. Although the debate was due to end and members begged him to sit down, he refused, explaining that his constituents expected it, and that he was bound 'to make a speech for Buncombe'. The term stuck, first as *buncombe*, then *bunkum*, then, as abbr. by the satirist George Ade (1866–1944), *bunk*. An alternative ety. links it to the gambling dice game *banco* or *bunco* , the cheating at which soon made it a synon. for fraud] [19C+] (*orig. US*) nonsense, rubbish, flattery.

bunkum *adj.* [? link to Fr. *bon*, good] [19C] (*US*) excellent, first-rate, esp. of food; thus *the real bunkum*, something first-rate.

bunkum town *n.* (*also* **bunkumville**) [BUNKUM *n.* + SE *town*/-VILLE *sfx*[1]] [1900s] (*US*) that area of the town where the poor live.

bunk up *n.*[1] [lit. a 'lifting up'] [20C+] (*orig. Aus.*) help, assistance.

bunk up *n.*[2] [SE *bunk*] [1930s+] (*orig. UK services*) an act of sexual intercourse.

bunk up *v.*[1] [20C+] to help, esp. in climbing up or over an obstacle, when one person either lets the other stand on their back or links their hands to make a 'stirrup' into which the climber can put one foot and boost themselves upwards.

bunk up *v.*[2] [1930s–40s] (*US gay*) to have male homosexual intercourse.

bunk yen *n. see* BUNK HABIT *n.*

bunk you! *excl.* [1980s+] (*US campus*) euph. for FUCK YOU! *excl.*

bunned *adj.* [BUN *n.*[2] (1)] [1900s–30s] (*US*) drunk.

bunnick (up) *v.* [? BUNKERED *adj.*/BUNK *v.*[1]] [late 19C–1910s] to beat, to ruin, to dispose of, to 'put paid' to.

bunny *n.*[1] [SE *bunny*, an affectionate name for both rabbits and squirrels] **1** in sexual contexts. (**a**) [17C+] the vagina. (**b**) [early 18C; 1940s+] a sexually attractive young woman; also of young homosexual men. (**c**) [20C+] (*US black*) a promiscuous woman, whose habits emulate the preoccupations of rabbits. (**d**) [1920s+] (*US*) a male or female homosexual prostitute. (**e**) [1920s+] a sanitary towel. (**f**) [1930s+] (*US*) the buttocks, the anus. **2** [late 19C] (*US campus*) rarebit. **3** from stereotypes of the animal. (**a**) [1930s+] (*orig. US/Aus.*) a fool, a simpleton. (**b**) [1990s+] a poor player of a sport. (**c**) [2000s] (*US black*) a weakling. **4** [1950s+] rabbit fur, as used for making garments; thus the garments themselves.

IN COMPOUNDS

❑ **bunny basher** *n.* [BASH *v.* (1)] [2000s] (*S.Afr. gay*) a homophobic male who beats up gay men. ❑ **bunny boy** *n.* [1940s+] (*S.Afr.*) a male homosexual.

IN PHRASES

❑ **bush bunny** *n.* [1920s+] (*Aus.*) a gullible fool. ❑ **cuddle bunny** *n.* [1940s–50s] (*US*) an affectionate, passionate or sexually alluring young woman. ❑ **ski bunny** *n.* [1960s+] (*US*) a woman who frequents ski resorts to solicit rather than to ski. ❑ **surf bunny** *n.* (*also* **surf chick**) [1950s+] (*US*) a woman who associates with surfers. ❑ **does your bunny like carrots?** *see under* CARROT *n.*

SE in slang uses

IN COMPOUNDS

❑ **bunny boiler** *n.* [f. a scene in the film *Fatal Attraction* (1987)] [1990s+] an unstable woman. ❑ **bunny hugger** *n.* [1990s+] an environmentalist, esp. an anti-blood sport campaigner.

bunny *n.*[2] [var. on RABBIT *n.*[4] (1)] [1950s+] **1** a chat, a conversation. **2** a talkative person.

bunny *n.*[3] *see* RABBIT *n.*[2] (2).

bunny *v.* [rhy. sl. = RABBIT (AND PORK) *v.* (1)] [1950s+] to talk, to chat with.

buns *n.* [joc. resemblance to the foodstuffs] **1** [20C+] the buttocks. **2** [1950s+] a woman's breasts. **3** [1980s+] fig. one's body. **4** [1980s+] (*US gay*) the buttocks, esp. when attractive.

IN COMPOUNDS

❑ **bun bandit** *n.* [-BANDIT *sfx* (2); var. on *BUM BANDIT under* BUM *n.*[1]] [1960s] (*US gay*) one who performs the active role in anal intercourse. ❑ **bun boy** *n.* [1950s+] a homosexual. ❑ **bun merchant** *n.* [MERCHANT *n.* (1)] [1960s] (*US gay*) a male prostitute specializing in taking a passive role.

IN PHRASES

❑ **bet one's buns** *v. see* BET ONE'S (SWEET) ASS *v.* ❑ **bun over brisket** *adv.* [BUN *n.*[1] (1) + BRISKET *n.*[1] (1)] [1900s] (*Aus.*) head-over-heels. ❑ **bun up** *n.* [1980s+] (*Aus. prison*) homosexual gang rape. ❑ **burn some buns** *v.* [1970s+] (*US gay*) to engage in vigorous sex. ❑ **bust one's buns** *v. see BUST ONE'S ASS under* BUST *v.*[1]. ❑ **hot buns** *n.* [HOT *adj.* (1c)] [1970s] (*US prison*) a prison homosexual. ❑ **split some buns** *v.* [1970s+] (*US gay*) to have anal intercourse. ❑ **strut one's buns** *v.* [1970s] (*US gay*) to walk in an exaggerated way, intended to focus attention on one's tight buttocks.

IN EXCLAMATIONS

❑ **my buns!** [late 17C+] a general excl. of disdain, dismissal, arrogant contempt.

bunse *n. see* BUNCE *n.*

bunsen burner *n.* [rhy. sl. = EARNER *n.*] [1990s+] any job or plan that pays well, almost invariably criminal.

bunser *n.* ['a (little) bun'] [20C+] (*Irish*) a pet name for a child.

bunt *n.* [SE *bunt*, the part of a fishing net that forms a bag or pouch'] **1** [late 17C–early 19C] an apron. **2** [early 19C; 1970s+] (*later use US gay*) the buttocks.

bunt *v.*[1] [dial. *bunt*, to push, to butt] [late 18C] to jostle against, to knock.

bunt *v.*[2] [backform. f. BUNTER *n.* (1)] [mid-19C] to scavenge.

bunt *v.*[3] [1970s+] (*US black/drugs*) to cheat in a drug sale.

bunter *n.* [ety. unknown; ? link to BUNT *n.* (1)] (*UK Und.*) **1** [18C–mid-19C] a woman who scavenges for rags in the street. **2** [18C–mid-19C] (*also* **bunt**) a poor, poss. thieving, prostitute. **3** [mid-19C] a prostitute who hires lodgings, uses them for a short time then leaves without paying her rent. **4** [late 19C–1900s] 'a woman thief of the lowest possible kind' (Ware). **5** [20C+] a man who fails in almost everything he does. **6** [1970s+] (*US gay*) a stereotypically effeminate male homosexual.

IN COMPOUNDS

❑ **bunter's tea** *n.* [early–mid-18C] strong liquor, usu. gin.

bunting sticks *n.* [1930s] legs.

bunting time *n.* [fig. use of BUNT *v.*[1] (1), to have sexual intercourse] [late 17C–18C] summer.

buntling *n.* (*also* **buntlings**) [BUNT *n.* (1), lit. a 'small apron'] [late 17C–mid-19C] (*UK Und.*) a petticoat; thus *hale up the main-buntlings*, to pull up a woman's petticoats.

bunts *n. see* BUNCE *n.*

bunty *n.* [Scot./Irish *bunty*, short and squat] [1920s+] an affectionate term for a small, middle-aged person.

bununus *n.* [? Sp. *bueno*, good; Fr. *bon à nous*, good to us] [1940s] (*W.I.*) a term of endearment applied to a person or object.

bununus *adj.* [BUNUNUS *n.*] [1940s] (*W.I.*) a general term of approval, pretty, wonderful, glorious, fantastic.

bun up *n. see under* BUNS *n.*

bun wagon *n.* [? SE *bun*; or ? BUNS *n.* (1)] [1980s+] (*Aus.*) a police van, a BLACK MARIA *n.* (1).

bunyip *n.* [SE *bunyip*, 'the Aboriginal name of a fabulous monster inhabiting the rushy swamps and lagoons in the interior of Australia' (*OED*)] [mid-19C+] (*Aus./Sydney*) an impostor, a pretender, humbug.

buor *n. see* BUER *n.*

buoyant *adj.* [play on SE; thus phr. 'my teeth are floating'] [20C+] drunk; thus *buoyantly*, drunkenly.

bup *n. see* BUPPER *n.*

bupkes *n.* (*also* **bopkes, bupkis**) [Yid. *bupkes*, beans] [1930s+] nothing (whatsoever).

bupkis *n. see* BOBKHES *n.*

bupper *n.* (*also* **bup, buppie, buppies, bups, bupsie**) [elision/ mispron.] [late 19C–1900s] (*usu. children*) bread and butter.

buppie *n.* (*also* **bluppy, bumpie, buppy**) [SE *black* + YUPPIE *n.*] [1980+] (*orig. US*) a b*l*lack upwardly mobile young professional.

burble *v.* [? linked to Ital. *borbogliare*, to make a rumbling or grumbling noise, Port. *borbulhar* + Sp. *borbollar* but coined by Lewis Carroll in *Through the Looking-Glass* (1872) in which the Jabberwock 'came whiffling through the tulgey wood,/And burbled as it came!'] [late 19C+] to chatter pleasantly; thus *burbler*, a chatty person.

burdetts *n.* [rhy. sl. *Burdett Coutts*, the bankers] [19C] boots.

Burdon's hotel *n.* [proper name of Mr *Burdon*, a one-time governor] [mid-19C] Whitecross Street prison, London.

bure *n. see* BUER *n.*

burerk *n. see* BURICK *n.*

burg *n.*[1] (*also* **berg, burgh**) [Lat. *burgus*, thence Ger. *Burg*, a town (orig. a walled town)] [mid-19C+] (*US*) a town, a city.

IN PHRASES

❑ **big burg** *n.* **1** [1910s–40s] (*US*) (*also* **main burg**) New York City. **2** [1920s] any city.

burg *n.*[2] (*also* **burgie**) [BERK *n.*] **1** [1970s–80s] a person, a fellow. **2** [1980s] (*S.Afr.*) a fool, an idiot, an unpleasant person.

burg *n.*[3] [abbr.] [1980s+] (*Aus./US black gang*) a burglary.

IN COMPOUNDS

❑ **burg merchant** *n.* [MERCHANT *n.*] [1990s+] a specialist burglar.

burgandy *n. see* CLARET *n.*

burger *n.* **1** [2000s] (*N.Z.*) the vagina. **2** *see BURGER WITH CHEESE* below.

SE in slang uses

IN COMPOUNDS

❑ **burger-head** *n.* [-HEAD *sfx* (1)] [1990s+] (*Irish*) a stupid person.

IN PHRASES

❑ **burger with cheese** *n.* (*also* **burger, double burger (with cheese), triple burger with cheese**) [she's 'very good to eat'; a savoury version of the usual identification of pretty women with sweetmeats or cakes] [1980s+] (*US campus*) a sexy/very sexy/ very, very sexy woman.

burgess of the... *n. see* KNIGHT OF THE... *n.*

burgew *n. see* BURGOO *n.*

burgh *n. see* BURG *n.*[1].

burgie *n. see* BURG *n.*[2].

burglar *n.* [play on SE; note WW1 milit. *burglars*, Bulgarians] **1** [late 19C–1960s] (*US*) a swindler, a bribe-taker. **2** [1920s+] a sodomite [euph. for SE *bugger* and implication of 'breaking in']. **3** [1980s+] a security prison officer.

SE in slang uses

IN COMPOUNDS

❑ **burglar cop** *n.* (*also* **burglar copper**) [COP *n.*[1] (1)/COPPER *n.* (3)] [1900s–50s] (*US Und.*) a corrupt police officer. ❑ **burglar hole** *n.* [through which one can espy potential robbers] [1970s+] (*US*) a peephole in a front door.

burglar alarm *n.* [rhy. sl.] [1990s+] the human arm.

burgle *v.* [BURGLAR *n.* (2)] [1960s+] to sodomize.

Burgoo *adj.* [BURGOO *n.*, seen as a Scottish staple] [late 19C] (*Aus.*) pertaining to Scotland or the Scots; by ext. the Presbyterian church.

burgoo *n.* (*also* **bergoo, burgew**) [Arabic *burgul*, cooked, parched and cracked wheat. Orig. an 18C thick oatmeal gruel, consumed by seamen; also known as *loblolly*, a soup or stew made with a variety of meat and vegetables, often eaten at outdoor feasts in the US, esp. in Kentucky] [mid-19C+] stew or porridge.

burick *n.* (*also* **burerk**) [Rom. *burk*, breast or Scot. *bure*, a loose woman] **1** [19C] a prostitute. **2** [mid–late 19C] a wife. **3** [mid–late 19C] a flashily-dressed woman.

buried *adj.* **1** [20C+] (*US Und.*) put in prison for a non-specific length of time. **2** [1920s] (*orig. US black*) extremely drunk. **3** [1930s–40s] (*US Und.*) held incommunicado. **4** [1930s+] (*US Und.*) serving a life sentence or a very long sentence.

burk *n. see* BERK *n.*

burk *v.*[1] [? rhy. sl. *burk* = SE *shirk* or f. SE *burk*, to smother, to 'hush up'. Both are ult. f. *burke*, to strangle (named after the early 19C 'resurrectionists' or grave-robbers *Burke* and Hare; *see* BURKE *v.*)] [late 19C–1910s] (*orig. N.Z.*) to avoid work.

burk *v.*[2] [? onomat.] [1960s] (*US*) **1** to vomit. **2** to break wind.

burke *n. see* BERK *n.*

burke *v.* [proper name of the Edinburgh criminal William *Burke* (1792–1829) who, along with his partner William Hare (1790–*c.*1860), murdered people in order to sell their corpses to the medical school for surgical dissection. Burke was hanged; Hare, who turned King's evidence, escaped the noose] **1** [mid-19C] to murder; thus *burking*, murdering to provide bodies for dissection. **2** [late 19C+] (*also* **burk**) to suppress, to cover up.

burker *n.* [the proper name *Burke*; *see* BURKE *v.*] [early–mid-19C] a 'resurrectionist' or body-snatcher, esp. for the purpose of selling the corpse to a hospital's anatomy department (in an era when the dissection of human corpses was still illegal).

Burketown mosquito net *n.* [proper name of the outback town of *Burketown*, Queensland] [1960s+] (*Aus.*) a bottle of rum and a cow-dung fire.

burl *n.*

IN PHRASES

❑ **give it a burl** *v.* [Scot. *birl*, to spin, to twist] [1910s+] (*Aus.*) **1** (*also* **give it a birl**) to give something a try, to make an attempt. **2** to stop doing something [? misreading]. ❑ **go for a burl** *v.* [play on Scot. *birl*, to spin/SE *go for a spin*; note also SPIN *n.*[3] (2)] [1980s] (*Aus.*) to go out joy-riding in the family car, esp. when one falls foul of the police.

burley *n.*[1] (*also* **burly**) [abbr.] [20C+] (*US*) a *bur*lesque show, a striptease show; usu. in combs.

burley *n.*[2] *see* BERLEY *n.*

burleycue/burley-Q/burley-que *n. see* BURLYCUE *n.*

Burlington Bertie *n.*[1] [the music-hall song 'Burlington Bertie from Bow', sung by Vesta Tilley *c.*1908] [1900s–30s] a dandyish, over-dressed young man, very conscious of (and pleased with) his appearance.

Burlington Bertie *n.*[2] [rhy. sl.] [1910s+] (*bingo*) the number thirty.

Burlington hunt *n. see* BERKELEY (HUNT) *n.*

burly *n.*[1] [SE] [1910s–30s] **1** (*US tramp*) an able-bodied, aggressive tramp or burglar. **2** a large, rough man.

burly *n.*[2] *see* BURLEY *n.*[1].

burlycue *n.* (*also* **burleycue, burley-que, burley-Q**) [abbr./ pron.] [1910s–60s] (*US*) a burlesque show; thus *burleycue house*, a burlesque theater.

B.U.R.M.A. *phr.* [abbr.] [late 19C+] a lover's acronym, *be undressed, ready, my angel*, written on envelopes of love letters.

burn *n.*[1] [lit. and fig. uses of SE] **1** in fig. uses, one 'gets one's fingers burnt'. (**a**) [late 19C+] (*US*) a joke, a prank. (**b**) [1960s+] (*orig. US*) a fraud, a confidence trick; thus the sale of bad or fake drugs. (**c**) [1960s+] (*US*) a major disappointment. (**d**) [1990s+] (*W.I.*) infidelity (usu. by a woman). (**e**) [2000s] (*US campus*) an embarrassing or humiliating situation. **2** [20C+] (*US*) a love-bite [resemblance to a burn scar]. **3** [1940s+] (*orig. Und.*) tobacco; a smoke, a cigarette; thus (*Aus.*) *twist a burn*, roll a cigarette. **4** [1950s] (*US*) a permanent wave hairstyle, which is 'burned' into the hair. **5** [1950s] (*US Und.*) execution in the electric chair [BURN *v.* (6c)]. **6** [1960s] (*US black/gang*) a gun. **7** [1990s+] importance, relevance, pertinence.

IN PHRASES

❑ **put the burn on** *v.* (*US*) **1** [1940s] to pressurize. **2** [1980s] to stare at aggressively. ❑ **take a burn** *v.* [BURN *v.* (4b)] [1950s] to become angry.

burn *n.*[2] (*also* **burnie**) [abbr.] [1970s+] (*US*) a sideburn (US: sideboard).

burn *n.*[3] *see* BURN(-UP) *n.*

burn *v.* **1** [late 14C+] to infect with a venereal disease. **2** to cheat; to rob. (**a**) [17C+] (*also* **burn up**) to cheat (esp. at cards), to defraud. (**b**) [mid-19C] (*US Und.*) to work as a BURNER *n.*[1] (3). (**c**) [1920s+] to rob, to steal. (**d**) [1950s+] to fail to pay a debt or meet an obligation. (**e**) [1950s+] (*drugs*) to sell cut or second-rate drugs, or simply to take a buyer's money and vanish without delivering the promised drugs; as *burn for a stash*, to steal a dealer's cache of drugs. (**f**) [1960s] (*US drugs*) to steal a fellow user's drugs. (**g**) [1960s–70s] to betray sexually. (**h**) [1970s–80s] (*drugs*) to betray a drug user to the authorities. **3** [20C+] (*orig. US*) to fail, to go wrong. **4** in emotional contexts. (**a**) [20C+] to annoy, to infuriate, to embarass. (**b**) [1920s+] to become angry. (**c**) [1940s] to be sexually aroused, to be available. (**d**) [1960s] to experience elation from the effects of an injected drug. (**e**) [1970s–80s] (*US campus*) as *burn for*, to focus on a given goal. **5** to set alight; to use fire. (**a**) [20C+] (*US*) to smoke a cigarette. (**b**) [1960s+] (*drugs*) to smoke a cannabis cigarette. (**c**) [1960s+] (*US black*) to prepare food, to cook, esp. to cook well. (**d**) [1980s] (*Aus.*) to have a barbecue. **6** to overcome, to treat badly, to punish; to have someone punished. (**a**) [1910s+] to be punished, to get into trouble; to punish. (**b**) [1920s+] to punish; ext. as *burn one's ass*. (**c**) [1920s+] to execute or to be executed in the electric chair; thus *burning party*, judicial execution. (**d**) [1930s+] (*also* **burn up**) to shoot dead. (**e**) [1930s+] to kill, to murder. (**f**) [1930s+] (*US black*) to defeat. (**g**) [1960s] (*US campus*) to turn down a request for a date. (**h**) [1960s+] to arrest. (**i**) [1960s+] to write a disciplinary report. (**j**) [1960s+] to attack, verbally or physically. (**k**) [1970s] to dismiss an employee, to jilt a lover. (**l**) [1970s+] (*US campus*) to grade harshly. (**m**) [1980s+] (*US*) to cause trouble for someone. **7** [1960s] (*US police*) to recognize; thus *burned*, exposed. **8** [1960s–70s] (*US black*) to do something well. **9** [1970s] (*US black*) to improvise; orig. in music, but latterly in any context. **10** [1970s+] (*US*) to photocopy [the heating involved in the process]. **11** [1980s] (*drugs*) to overdose. **12** [1990s+] (*US campus*) to play truant. **13** [1990s+] (*UK black/drugs*) to smoke a cigarette laced with crack cocaine. **14** [2000s] (*orig. computer*) to record (information/music) onto a writable CD-Rom, DVD or compact disk [the heating involved in the process]. **15** [2000s] (*UK black*) as synon. for 'to hell with'. **16** *see* BURN (UP) *v.*

IN COMPOUNDS

□ **burn artist** *n.* **1** [1960s] a police informer. **2** [1960s+] a con-man, a cheat, esp. in the drug world where they will either sell second-rate drugs or take a buyer's money and vanish without delivering the goods [BURN *v.* (2e) + -ARTIST *sfx*]. □ **burn-bag** *n.* [BAG *n.*[1] (7)] [1990s+] (*US drugs*) a bag of counterfeit or very weak drugs.

IN PHRASES

□ **burn down** *v.* **1** [1920s–60s] to shoot, to kill. **2** [1950s] to overdo, to use to excess. **3** [1960s+] to attack, verbally or physically. □ **burn on** *v.* [1980s+] (*US*) to insult. □ **burn one's ass** *v.* [1980s] to infuriate. □ **burn the town** *v.* [late 17C–18C] of servicemen, to leave a town without paying for one's board and lodging. □ **burn up** *v. see* separate entry. □ **to burn** *adv.* [the size/dampness of the animal requires a large fire] [late 19C+] (*US*) in very large quantities; often ext. *as to burn a wet dog/mule with*; usu. *money to burn*.

SE in slang uses

IN COMPOUNDS

□ **burn-crust** *n.* [mid-18C–early 19C] a baker.

IN PHRASES

□ **burn bad powder** *v.* [the stench] [1910s–20s] to break wind. □ **burn coal** *v.* (*US*) **1** [1990s+] to have a lesbian or heterosexual relationship. **2** *see under* COAL *n.*[1]. □ **burn it blue** *v. see under* BLUE *adj.*[3]. □ **burn it up/out** *v. see* BURN (UP) *v.* □ **burn leather** *v. see under* LEATHER *n.* □ **burn off** *v.* [var. BURN (UP) *v.* (1)] [1980s+] to accelerate past another driver. □ **burn one** *see* separate entries. □ **burn one's collar** *v.* [SE colloq. *get hot under the collar*] [1940s] (*US*) to get very angry. □ **burn one's foot** *v.* (*US*) **1** [1920s] to hurry. **2** [1960s] to become pregnant [euph.]. □ **burn one's poker** *v.* (*also* **burn one's tail**) [fig. use of SE] [19C–1900s] to catch a venereal disease. □ **burn one's shoulder** *v. see under* SHOULDER *n.* □ **burn one's soles** *v. see* BURN (UP) *v.* □ **burn out** *see* separate entries. □ **burn paper** *v. see under* PAPER *n.* □ **burn powder** *v.* [late 18C; 1920s] (*US*) to fire a gun. □ **burn rubber** *v. see* separate entry. □ **burn smoke** *v.* [1970s] (*US*) to go very fast. □ **burn someone's ears** *v.* (*also* **burn someone's ass**) [ASS *n.* (4)] [1950s–60s] (*US*) to reprimand severely. □ **burn someone's goat** *v. see* GET SOMEONE'S GOAT *under* GOAT *n.*[1]. □ **burn the earth** *v.* (*also* **burn the ground, burn the road (up), burn the street**) [one's acceleration causes the ground to catch fire] [late 19C+] (*orig. US*) to go very fast. □ **burn the grass** *v.* [the destructive effect of urine on grass] [1940s–50s] (*Aus.*) to urinate in the open air. □ **burn the Thames** *v.* [var. on SE colloq. *set the Thames on fire*; note synon. US regional use *burn up someone's millpond*] [late 18C] to accomplish a noteworthy feat. □ **burn the water** *v.* [late 19C+ use is SE] [early–mid-19C] to spear salmon by torchlight. □ **burn the wind** *v.* (*also* **burn the breeze**) [fig. uses of *breeze/wind*] [late 19C+] (*US*) to go fast, orig. on horseback. □ **burn (up)** *see* separate entries. □ **burn wheels** *v.* [one's smoking wheels] [1960s+] to drive a car very fast. □ **burn with a low blue flame** *v.* [the image of lighting the alcohol fumes pouring from one's mouth] [1920s+] to be extremely drunk.

IN EXCLAMATIONS

□ **burn my breeches!** [early 19C] a general excl. □ **burn my clothes!** [1930s] (*US*) a general excl. □ **burn you!** [earlier dial. use; i.e. burn in the fires of hell] [late 19C–1920s] go to hell!

burn! *excl.* [BURN *v.* (4b)] [1980s+] (*US campus*) a triumphant or gloating excl. used after successfully insulting or verbally attacking someone.

burndt *adj. see* BURNT *adj.*[1] (3).

burned *adj.*[1] (*also* **burnt**) [BURN *v.*] **1** [mid-17C–early 19C; 1930s+] infected with venereal disease [note 18C naval joke, *to be sent out a sacrifice and come home a burnt offering*, to be sent off to fight for the Navy, but to return carrying venereal disease; 20C use appears to be US only]. **2** [late 19C; 1930s+] cheated or robbed of any commodity or possession. **3** [1930s+] treated badly, taken advantage of. **4** [1960s+] (*drugs*) sold bad, adulterated or fake drugs. **5** [1960s+] (*US prison*) in trouble, out of luck.

burned *adj.*[2] *see* BURNED OUT *adj.*[2] (1).

burned (at) *adj.* (*also* **burned up, burnt off**) [BURN *v.* (4b)] [1940s+] annoyed (with).

burned out *adj.*[1] (*also* **burnt out**) [var. on BURNED (AT) *adj.*] [20C+] (*Irish*) annoyed, irritated.

burned out *adj.*[2] (*also* **burned up, burnt out**) [SE *burned, burnt,* of a fire, out, extinct, used up] **1** [1920s+] (*also* **burned, fried out**) exhausted, worn out. **2** [1930s+] (*drugs*) used of a vein that has collapsed due to an excess of injections. **3** [1950s+] having had too much drink and/or drugs, which have taken their toll both physically and esp. mentally. **4** [1960s] (*drugs*) used of a drug dealer who has been noted by the police. **5** [1960s+] bored with, tired of, exhausted by; usu. as *burned out on*.

burned up *adj.* [BURN *v.* (4)] **1** [1920s+] (*orig. US*) very excited. **2** [1920s+] (*orig. US*) extremely angry. **3** *see* BURNED (AT) *adj.* **4** *see* BURNED OUT *adj.*[2].

burner *n.*[1] [BURN *v.*] **1** [18C] a card-sharp, a swindler. **2** [early 19C] venereal disease. **3** [mid-19C] (*US Und.*) a confidence trickster who told the victim a story – often simply asking him to change a banknote – that resulted in the production of their wallet; the burner then snatched it and ran off. **4** [late 19C] a sharp blow or punch. **5** [1920s–60s; 1980s+] (*US black*) a pistol. **6** [1950s] an exceptional person. **7** [1970s] (*US black*) a thief. **8** [1990s+] (*US juv.*) fast sexual intercourse. **9** [1990s+] (*US black/teen*) a cellular telephone that is being used illegally.

burner *n.*[2] [SE *burn*] **1** [1940s] (*US*) a cheap cigar. **2** [1940s] (*US*) a pipe. **3** [1940s+] (*UK/US Und.*) an expert in the use of an oxy-acetylene torch. **4** [1950s] an embarrassment [one's cheeks 'burn']. **5** [1970s] (*US gay*) a cigarette. **6** [1990s+] (*US black/teen*) a large piece of graffiti, usu. involving many colours [one 'burns' it onto the wall and/or it glows with colour]. **7** *see* GREASE-BURNER *under* GREASE *n.*[1].

SE in slang uses

IN PHRASES

□ **go off one's burner** *v.* [late 19C–1910s] to go mad.

burners on high *adj.* [SE (*after*)-*burner*, an auxiliary burner fitted to the exhaust-pipe of a jet engine to increase its thrust] [1990s+] (*US campus*) being in a state of sexual excitement.

burnese *n.* (*also* **burneys, crowns**) [BURNIE *n.*[1]/ proprietary name of *Crowns* Catarrh Powder, a patent medicine, which contained cocaine] [1910s+] (*drugs*) cocaine.

burnie *n.*[1] [BERNICE *n.*] [late 19C–1920s] (*US drugs*) cocaine; orig. a proprietary mix of snuff and cocaine, designed as a catarrh medicine and inhaled through a glass and rubber tube.

burnie *n.*[2] [SE *burn*] **1** [1940s] (*US drugs*) a (half-smoked) marijuana cigarette. **2** [1980s] (*US juv.*) a pre-adolescent who smokes, drinks and uses drugs.

burnie *n.*[3] [BURN RUBBER *v.*] [1990s+] a tyre mark.

burnie *n.*[4] *see* BURN *n.*[2].

burnie blower *n.* (*also* **burny blower**) [BURNIE *n.*[1] + BLOW *v.*[1] (3c)] [late 19C] (*US drugs*) a cocaine user.

burning *adj.* **1** [mid-19C+] euph. for BLOODY *adj.* **2** [1960s] (*orig. US black*) a general term of approval: wonderful, excellent.

burning-down habit *n.* [SE *burning down* + HABIT *n.* (1)] [1950s+] an extremely heavy addiction to narcotics.

burning shame *n.* [puns] [late 18C–early 19C] **1** a form of sexual 'game', whereby 'a lighted candle [is] stuck into the parts of a woman, certainly not intended by nature for a candlestick' (Grose, 1796). **2** a nightwatchman placed at the door of a brothel, holding a lantern, even in daylight, to deter people from wandering in and out.

burn one *n.* [1930s] (*US*) a glass of malted milk.

burn one *v.* [BURN *v.* (5b)] [1960s+] (*drugs*) to smoke marijuana.

burnout *n.* [BURN OUT *v.*; orig. 1940s *burnout*, the sudden loss of power in a jet or rocket engine] **1** [1960s+] (*drugs*) a heavy abuser of drugs. **2** [1970s+] the situation of having exhausted one's capabilities (whether through sheer hard work or through drink and/or drugged excess), being no longer able to function efficiently at a job or discipline; thus the 'burned-out' individual. **3** [1980s] a collapse, esp. when sudden. **4** [1980s] (*US*) a burned-out building. **5** [1990s+] an alienated, aimless, poss. suicidal, young person. **6** [1990s+] (*US campus*) LSD. **7** [1990s+] spinning the rear wheels of a car without moving, thus causing a cloud of smoke. **8** [2000s] (*UK prison*) the setting on fire of a despised prisoner's cell.

burn out *v.* [fig. uses of SE] **1** [early 19C] (*US Und.*) to be arrested as a result of a tip-off or an informer. **2** [1910s+] (*also* **burn up**) to become mentally or physically exhausted. **3** [1950s] to die, from over-work, exhaustion. **4** [1960s] (*US*) to suffer a setback or failure. **5** [1960s] to become bored. **6** [1960s] to use up or exhaust a source for stolen goods. **7** [1960s] (*US campus*) to do well. **8** [1990s+] to stop or give up suddenly.

burn rubber *v.* (*also* **get rubber, screech..., smoke..., tear...**) **1** [1930s+] to drive a car very fast, esp. when accelerating from a standing start [the smoking tyres that accompany acceleration]. **2** [1940s–60s] (*orig. US black*) to have sexual intercourse [fig. use of sense 1]. **3** [1990s+] (*US campus*) to go, to leave, esp. quickly [fig. use of sense 1].

burn rubber! *excl.* [2000s] (*US prison*) go away! leave me alone!

burns *n.* [ety. unknown] [2000s] (*S.Afr.*) brandy.

burnt *adj.*[1] [BURN OUT *v.*] (*US campus*) **1** [1960s+] disappointed, betrayed, esp. sexually. **2** [1980s] emotionally drained. **3** [1980s] (*also* **burndt**) embarrassed. **4** [1980s+] (*also* **burnt out**) physically exhausted. **5** [1990s+] mentally impaired from drug use.

burnt *adj.*[2] [BURNED OUT *adj.*[2]] [1980s+] (*US teen*) terrible, hopeless.

burnt *adj.*[3] *see* BURNED *adj.*[1].

burnt (cinder) *n.* (*also* **red hot cinder**) [rhy. sl. (Cockney pron. winder)] [1910s+] a window.

burnt off *adj. see* BURNED (AT) *adj.*

burnt offering *n.* [late 19C+] a joking description of any food that has been burned on the stove.

burnt out *adj.* **1** *see under* BURNED OUT. **2** *see* BURNT *adj.*[1] (4).

burn(-up) *n.* [BURN (UP) *v.* (1)] [1950s+] fast riding of a motorcycle, esp. used by outlaw bike riders, Rockers etc.

burn (up) *v.* (*also* **burn it out, burn it up, burn one's soles**) **1** [1920s+] to ride or drive fast on a motorcycle, car, or other machine; to leave at high speed. **2** [1930s+] to leave (fast). **3** [1970s] to outrun by fast driving. **4** [1970s+] to drive a vehicle, usu. a car or motorbike, fast.

burn up *v.* [BURN *v.*] (*orig. US*) **1** [late 19C] to criticize severely. **2** [late 19C+] to annoy, to irritate, to aggravate; to get a person 'hot under the collar'. **3** [late 19C+] to cut a swathe through. **4** [1920s–60s] to excite. **5** [1920s+] to outdo, to surpass. **6** [1920s+] to become annoyed, esp. underpinned by embarrassment. **7** [1930s] (*US tramp*) to betray one's partner to the police. **8** [1930s+] to be under intense police pressure. **9** [1970s] to draw attention to. **10** *see* BURN *v.* (2a). **11** *see* BURN *v.* (6d). **12** *see* BURN OUT *v.* (2).

burny blower *n. see* BURNIE BLOWER *n.*

buroo *n.* (*also* **brew, bro, broo**) [Scot. pron. of SE *bureau*] [1920s+] (*Ulster/Scot.*) unemployment office, Labour exchange; thus *on the buroo*, unemployed and collecting benefits; an unemployed person.

burp *n.* [echoic] [1930s+] a belch.

burp *v.* [echoic] **1** [1930s+] (*orig. US*) to belch. **2** [1960s+] (*Aus.*) to vomit, also as *burp a rainbow*.

IN COMPOUNDS

❑ **burpgun** *n.* [1950s+] (*US*) an automatic rifle.

IN PHRASES

❑ **burp a chirp** *v.* [assonance] [1950s] (*US black*) to sing. ❑ **burp the worm** *v. see under* WORM *n.*

burr *n.* [SE *burr*, a plant-head that clings to clothes etc] [16C–mid-19C] a hanger-on, one who 'clings'.

burra *adj.* [Hind. *burra*, great] [late 19C] (*Anglo-Ind.*) great, large; thus *burra sahib*, a great man; *burra khana*, a banquet; *burra mem*, a great lady; *burra beebee*, a lady who claims precedence at social gatherings.

burr-gum melter *n.* [ety. unknown] [mid-19C] (*UK Und.*) a swindler who 'sticks' (like a burr) to a victim as long as they have any money left.

burrhead *n.* [20C+] (*US*) **1** a black person [SE *burr*, a rough file + *head*; the tightly curled black hair]. **2** a fool [-HEAD *sfx* (1)].

burrheaded *adj.* [BURRHEAD *n.*] **1** [1920s+] (*US*) having the tight, curly hair typical of black people. **2** [1940s] (*US*) stupid.

burrito *n.* [Mex. *burrito*, a maize-flour tortilla rolled round a savoury filling] **1** [1980s] (*US*) a derog. term for anyone of Latin or Spanish-American descent. **2** [1980s+] (*US campus*) the penis.

IN COMPOUNDS

❑ **Burrito City** *n.* [1970s] (*US*) El Paso, Texas.

burrow *n.* [1960s+] (*Aus.*) a pocket.

Burrowdamp Museum *n.* [? its burrowing rodents and damp cells] [mid-19C] (*UK Und.*) Newgate prison.

burry *n.* [? pron. of Ab*origine*] [1910s+] (*Aus.*) an Aborigine.

burst *n.*[1] (*also* **bust**) [SE *burst*, the act of bursting, breaking open] [mid–late 19C] (*UK Und.*) a burglary.

SE in slang uses

IN PHRASES

❑ **give someone a burst** *v.* [SE *burst of fire*] [1940s+] to complain, to criticize, to remind strongly.

burst *n.*[2] (*also* **bust**) [SE *burst*, a sudden flurry of activity; 20C use is mainly Aus.] [late 19C–1910s] a spree, a party with much eating and excessive drinking.

IN PHRASES

❑ **(go) on the burst** [mid-19C–1940s] (to go) out on a spree, (to go) on a binge of food and drink.

burst *v.*[1] **1** [mid-19C] (*US campus*) to fail an examination. **2** [late 19C–1900s] to spend one's money lavishly, to go out on a spree. **3** [late 19C+] to beat up, usu. as a threat, e.g. *I'll burst him!*

SE in slang uses

IN PHRASES

❑ **burst a blood-vessel** *v.* (*also* **bust a blood-vessel**) [20C+] to lose one's temper, to lose emotional control. ❑ **burst a cheque** *v.* (*also* **bust a cheque**) [late 19C–1900s] (*Aus.*) to go on a spending spree. ❑ **burst in someone's crust** *v. see under* CRUST *n.*[1]. ❑ **burst one's boiler** *v. see under* BOILER *n.*[1]. ❑ **burst one's soul-case** *v. see under* SOUL-CASE *n.* ❑ **burst one's stay-lace** *v.* [SE *stay*, the precursor of the corset] [late 19C] to become over-excited or over-emotional.

IN EXCLAMATIONS

❑ **burst him!** (*also* **burst her!**) [late 19C] an excl. of annoyance, confound him! the hell with her! etc. ❑ **burst me bagpipes!** [1990s+] (*US black teen*) an excl. of surprise, astonishment, annoyance etc.

burst *v.*[2] *see* BUST *v.*[1].

bursted *adj. see* BUSTED *adj.*[1] (2).

burster *n.*[1] (*also* **buster**) [SE *burst*] **1** [19C] a loaf of bread; thus as *twopenny burster*, a twopenny loaf [i.e. it fills one's stomach]. **2** [mid-19C] (*orig. boxing*) a heavy fall that could end a fight [one 'bursts' oneself]. **3** [mid-19C] an exhausting physical effort. **4** [mid-19C] (*UK Und.*) a burglar [BUST *v.*[1] (1a)]. **5** [mid–late 19C] a fall from a horse; thus *come a burster*, to fall from one's horse [one 'bursts' oneself]. **6** [1900s] (*Aus.*) 'a cropper', in fig. uses. **7** *see* BUSTER *n.*[1] (1d).

burster *n.*[2] *see* BUSTER *n.*[2].

burst-up *n. see* BUST-UP *n.* (1).

Burton *n.*

IN PHRASES

❑ **go for a Burton** *v.* [the precise ety. remains unknown but there are a number of suggestions. First is the elision of SE *burnt 'un*, i.e. a burning aircraft (and its pilot). Partridge (*DSUE*, 1970), and Paul Beale (*DSUE*, 1984) suggest: (i) a euph., going for a glass of Burton ale; (ii) *Burton-on-Trent* as rhy. sl. for 'went', as in 'went west' (i.e. GO WEST *under* WEST *adj.*); (iii) Burton ale is heavy, as is a burning aircraft as it crashes to the ground; (iv) the tailors Montague Burton; (v) during WW2 the RAF used a number of billiard halls, invariably sited above Burton shops, as medical centres, and those who attended such centres had 'gone for a Burton'. Other suggestions include the inter-war advertising campaign for Burton ales, bearing the copy line: 'He's gone for a Burton.' Another claim states that Burton's halls were used for Morse aptitude tests, not medical check-ups, thus the phr. meant failing such a test. Finally seafarers' jargon *burton*, the notoriously unsafe stowing of a barrel athwart rather than fore-and-aft; thus *going for a Burton* meant risking death] [1940s+] (*orig. UK milit.*) **1** to die; also in fig. use. **2** to fail, to malfunction.

burton *n.* [rhy. sl. *Burton-on-Trent* = RENT *n.* (5)] [1960s–70s] a male prostitute.

Burton-on-Trent *n.* [rhy. sl.; ult. the UK town] [1930s+] the rent.

bury *v.* [all fig. uses of SE] (*orig. US*) **1** [late 19C–1900s] to eat heartily. **2** [20C+] to condemn to a long spell in prison; ext. as *bury deep*. **3** [1900s–30s] (*US prison*) to betray, to inform on. **4** [1900s–50s] (*US*) to hide. **5** [1930s+] to kill, to murder. **6** [1950s–80s] (*N.Z./US prison*) to place in solitary confinement. **7** [1970s+] to cause serious trouble for. **8** [1990s+] to complain to, to be annoyed with.

SE in slang uses

IN COMPOUNDS

❑ **burying face** *n.* (*also* **churchyard face**) [an expression suitable for a funeral] [late 19C–1900s] a miserable face. ❑ **bury patch** *n. see* separate entry.

IN PHRASES

❑ **bury...** *v. see also under* relevant n. ❑ **bury (it)** *v.* [mid-19C+] of a man, to have sexual intercourse; one of a number of terms relating to the penis in the act. ❑ **bury old fagin** *v. see under* FAGAN *n.* ❑ **bury the hatchet** *v.* (*also* **bury the tomahawk**) [the *hatchet* as a symbol of hostility; 20C+ use is SE] [mid-18C+] to make up one's differences; thus [late 19C] *dig up* or *take up the hatchet* , to renew hostilities. ❑ **bury the landlady** *v.* [late 19C] to leave one's lodgings without paying the rent.

bury patch *n.* (*also* **bury ground**) [dial. *bury*, to be buried] [1960s–70s] (*US*) a cemetery.

bus *n.* [all exts. of SE (*omni*)*bus*] **1** [late 19C–1900s] a dowdy dress, fit only for wearing on public transport. **2** [1910s] a boat. **3** [1910s+] an aeroplane. **4** [1910s+] an automobile, a truck etc, esp. a large one. **5** [1920s–40s] a motorcycle, a motorcycle and side-car. **6** [1930s] (*US*) an elevator, a lift. **7** [1980s] (*US campus*) a fat woman. **8** [1990s+] (*US*) an ambulance.

SE in slang uses

IN COMPOUNDS

❑ **bus driver** *v.* [the player 'takes the opponent to school'] [1990s+] (*US juv.*) a superior player, usu. in 'one-on-one' games, e.g. basketball. ❑ **bus ride** *n.* [2000s] (*US prison*) a court appearance, to which one is conveyed by bus. ❑ **bus therapy** *n.* [2000s] (*US prison*) moving prisoners from one institution to another to ensure their isolation from lawyers, family etc.

IN PHRASES

❑ **bus-bellied ben** *n.* [his stomach has the dimensions of an omnibus; hence the rhyme 'Bus-bellied Ben/Eats enough for ten'] [late 19C–1900s] an alderman. ❑ **drive the (porcelain) bus** *v. see under* DRIVE *v.*[1]. ❑ **on the bus** [coined *c.*1965 by novelist and psychedelic guru Ken Kesey (1935–2001), whose 'Merry Pranksters' drove across America on a bus, named Furthur [*sic*], from San Francisco to Millbrook, New York, where Kesey's opposite number, Timothy Leary (1920–96) held court] [1960s+] used of one who is part of a group, sharing the joint consciousness; thus *off the bus*, abandoning the group and its beliefs and ethos.

bus *v.*[1] (*also* **bus it**) [mid-19C+] to travel by bus; thus similar *tram it*, to travel by tram.

bus *v.*[2] (*also* **bust**) [abbr. *BUST A GUT under* GUT *n.*] [1990s+] (*US black*) to have fun, to enjoy oneself.

bus! *excl.* [Hind. *bas*, stop!] [mid–late 19C] enough! stop!

bus and tram *n.* [rhy. sl.] [20C+] jam.

busby *n.* [SE *busby*, the tall fur cap as worn by various regiments of the British army] [late 19C] **1** the pubic hair. **2** the vagina.

IN PHRASES

❑ **growl in her busby** *v.* (*also* **growl in the busby**) [1930s] to perform cunnilingus.

buse *v. see* BOOZE *v.*

bus'em up *v. see* BUST *v.*[1] (1a).

buser *n. see* BUSSER *n.*[2].

Bush, the *n.*[1]

IN PHRASES

❑ **at the Bush** (*also* **at Staines**) [the *Bush* Inn at Staines, ? a popular refuge for London debtors] [early 19C] in financial difficulties.

Bush, the *n.*[2] [abbr.] [1930s+] Shepherds *Bush*, London, W12.

bush *n.*[1] [SE *bush*] **1** [late 16C–early 17C] (*UK Und.*) the place where thieves defraud their victim [the imagery reflects the world of hunting]. **2** as pubic or facial hair. (**a**) [17C+] the pubic hair of either sex. (**b**) [20C+] (*Aus./US*) a moustache, a beard. (**c**) [1960s–70s] (*Aus.*) in fig. use of sense 2a, a young woman, seen in a purely sexual context. (**d**) [1970s] a hairstyle in which normally short, curly black hair is allowed to grow out around the head. **3** [late 19C] the cat-o'-nine-tails [resemblance]. **4** a distant place. (**a**) [1910s] (*US*) the countryside, the small towns. (**b**) [1930s+] (*Aus.*) the suburbs. **5** in drug contexts, as a plant. (**a**) [1940s+] (*drugs*) marijuana. (**b**) [1980s] (*W.I.*) second-rate marijuana. (**c**) [1980s+] cocaine. (**d**) [2000s] phencyclidine.

IN COMPOUNDS

❑ **bush-beater** *n.* [SE *beater* + pun on SE phr. *beat around the bush*] [mid-17C–late 19C] the penis. ❑ **bush-buzzer** *n.* [SE *buzzer*] [1980s] (*Aus.*) a vibrator. ❑ **bush dinner** *n. see* separate entry. ❑ **bush-faking** *n.* [FAKE *v.*[1] (3)] [late 19C] sexual intercourse. ❑ **bush-head** *n. see* separate entry. ❑ **bush-licker** *n.* [2000s] (*S.Afr. gay*) a lesbian. ❑ **bush patrol** *n.* **1** [1960s] (*US*) sexual foreplay. **2** [1960s] (*US*) sexual intercourse. **3** *see also under* SE compounds below. ❑ **bushwhacker** *n. see* separate entries.

IN PHRASES

❑ **dipping in the bush** *n.* [1970s+] cunnilingus. ❑ **dive in the bushes** *v.* (*also* **go into the bushes**) [1920s+] (*US*) to perform cunnilingus. ❑ **free of the bush** *adj.* [late 19C] sexually intimate with a woman. ❑ **go bush-ranging** *v.* [19C] to have sexual intercourse. ❑ **push in the bush** *n.* [PUSH *n.* (1a)] [1920s+] sexual intercourse. ❑ **shoot in the bush** *v.* [SHOOT *v.* (1b)] [1950s+] to have sexual intercourse.

SE in slang uses

IN COMPOUNDS

❑ **bush ape** *n. see under* APE *n.* ❑ **bush-bashing** *n.* [1960s+] (*Aus.*) travelling in the bush, either on foot or in a four-wheeled off-road vehicle. ❑ **bushbitch** *n.* [BITCH *n.*[1] (1a)] [1980s+] (*US*) an ugly woman. ❑ **bush bunny** *n. see under* BUNNY *n.*[1]. ❑ **bush-cove** *n.* [COVE *n.* (1); their sleeping under hedges] [early 19C] a gypsy. ❑ **bush dinner** *n. see* separate entry. ❑ **bushfire blonde** *n.* [the flames of the bushfire] **1** [1940s+] (*Aus.*) a red-headed woman. **2** [2000s] cherry brandy and lemonade. ❑ **bush hog** *n.* [SE] [1980s] (*US*) a peasant. ❑ **bush parole** *n.* (*also* **bush pass**) [1920s+] (*orig. US prison*) an escape. ❑ **bush patrol** *n.* **1** [1950s+] (*US prison*) an escape. **2** *see also* slang compounds above. ❑ **bushpig** *n.* [1980s+] **1** (*US campus*) an extremely ugly woman [note acronym c. 1986 *T.T.B.B.R.*: 'turn that bush pig round', used when a woman thus described enters a public house]. **2** (*Aus.*) a general insult, irrespective of sex. **3** (*Aus. prison*) a female prison officer. ❑ **bush radio** *n.* (*also* **bush wireless, jail wireless**) [1930s+] (*orig. Aus.*) a network of gossip and rumour that brings news, often inaccurate, before the official sources. ❑ **bushranger** *n.* [weak use of SE *bushranger*, a highwayman] **1** [mid-19C] (*UK Und.*) a low class prostitute. **2** [20C+] (*Aus.*) a petty swindler; one who takes unfair advantage of others. **3** [1950s] (*Aus.*) a dubious business enterprise that exploits rather than serves its customers. ❑ **bush rat** *n.* [1930s–40s] (*US*) a peasant, a hillbilly. ❑ **bush-scrubber** *n.* **1** [late 19C] (*Aus.*) a boor, a bumpkin [SAusE *scrubber*, one who lives in the scrub]. **2** [1940s+] a rural prostitute [SCRUBBER *n.* (5a)]. ❑ **bush-tail** *adj.* [image of an animal vanishing into the bush] [20C+] (*Aus.*) cunning, deceptive. ❑ **bush telegraph** *n.* *see* separate entry. ❑ **bush week** *n.* [the image of the rural 'bush' dwellers coming innocently to town] [1940s+] (*Aus.*) a fig. 'week' when dubious deals may be proposed and confidence tricks carried out; usu. in phr. *What do you think this is? Bush Week?*, used to fend off what is considered a dubious suggestion. ❑ **bush wireless** *n. see* BUSH RADIO above.

(IN PHRASES)

❑ **go about the bush** *v. see* BEAT ABOUT THE BUSH *under* BEAT *v.* ❑ **go bush** *v.* [SE *bush*, uncleared or untilled areas that are still in a state of nature] [20C+] (*Aus.*) **1** to go wild, to go mad. **2** to seek the solitude and privacy of the bush. **3** of farm animals, to run free. **4** to escape from prison and vanish. ❑ **make bush** *v.* [one escapes into the bushes] [20C+] (*US prison*) to escape. ❑ **out of one's bush** *adj. see* OUT OF ONE'S TREE *under* TREE *n.*

bush *n.*[2] [? SE *bourgeois*] [1960s] (*US*) an important person, or one who likes to pose as such.

bush *adj.*[1] [SE *bush*, the rough, uncultivated countryside] **1** [late 19C+] uncivilized, inferior, rough-and-ready, esp. in combs. below; as adv., living or lost in the bush. **2** [1910s+] (*US*) second-rate, unsophisticated, amateur. **3** [1960s] (*US campus*) easy. **4** [1960s] (*US campus*) uninihibited; 'crazy'.

(IN COMPOUNDS)

❑ **bush bacon** *n.* [20C+] (*US*) a rabbit. ❑ **bush baptist** *n.* [20C+] (*mainly Aus./N.Z.*) one who has either no religion or belongs to a dubious sub-cult. ❑ **bush carpenter** *n.* [20C+] (*Aus.*) a second-rate carpenter. ❑ **bush champagne** *n.* [1970s+] (*Aus./N.Z.*) a mixture of methylated spirits and salt. ❑ **bush college** *n.* (*also* **bush university**) [1970s+] (*S.Afr.*) a derog. description (by black students) of a segregated, blacks-only college or university. ❑ **bush fridge** *n.* [2000s] (*N.Z.*) a damp sack or teatowel with its edges soaking in cold water, placed over a tin of food to keep it cool. ❑ **bush-head** *n. see* separate entry. ❑ **bush lawyer** *n.* [early 19C+] (*Aus.*) one who claims to 'lay down the law', but has no real authority to do so. ❑ **bush league** *see* separate entries. ❑ **bush mechanic** *n.* [1980s+] (*N.Z.*) an amateur, untrained mechanic.

bush *adj.*[2] [? SE *bush*] [1990s+] (*W.I.*) of a woman, well-groomed.

bush *v.*[1] [BUSHED *adj.* (2)] [mid-19C+] (*US*) to exhaust, to tire out.

bush *v.*[2] [BUSHWA *n.* (1)] [1930s–70s] to trick, to lie (to).

(IN PHRASES)

❑ **bush up** *v.* [1940s–50s] (*Aus.*) to confuse, to baffle.

bush *v.*[3] [abbr. BUSHWHACK *v.* (1)/SE *ambush*] [1940s+] (*orig. US*) to ambush, to mug.

bush dinner *n.*[1] [SE *bush* + *dinner*] [late 19C+] (*Aus.*) a damper (a form of unleavened cake, baked in the ashes), mutton and tea.

bush dinner *n.*[2] [BUSH *n.*[1] (2a) + SE *dinner*] [1960s+] (*US*) cunnilingus.

bushed *adj.* [SE *bush*] **1** [early–mid-19C] (*UK Und./Aus.*) poor, impoverished. **2** [mid-19C+] (*orig. US*) exhausted, tired out, as if one had been wandering, lost, through the woods. **3** [mid-19C+] (*Aus.*) disorientated, lost (either lit. in the bush or generally so); thus fig. 'lost' (for ideas, words etc). **4** [1910s] (*Aus.*) drunk.

bushel (and peck) *n.* [rhy. sl.] [late 19C+] the neck.

bushel bubby *n.* [SE *bushel*, a dry measure + BUBBIES *n.*] [late 18C–early 19C] a woman with large breasts.

bushel-cunted *adj.* [SE *bushel*, a measure of volume; thus a large quantity + CUNT *n.* (1)] [late 17C–late 19C] having a large vagina.

bushel of coke *n.* [rhy. sl. = BLOKE *n.* (3)] [20C+] a man.

bushel of tits *n. see under* TIT *n.*[2].

busher *n.* [BUSH *adj.*[1] (2)] [20C+] (*US*) an amateur, an unsophisticated person; thus v. *bush*, to act in a second-rate manner.

Bushey Park *n.*[1]

(IN PHRASES)

❑ **in Bushey Park** *adj.* (*also* **at Bushey Park**) [BUSHED *adj.* (1)] [early 19C] poor, impoverished.

Bushey Park *n.*[2] *see under* BUSHY PARK *n.*[1].

bush-head *n.*[1] [1940s] (*US*) a person with bushy hair.

bush-head *n.*[2] [BUSH *adj.*[1] (1) + -HEAD *sfx* (1)] [1950s–70s] (*Aus.*) a naïve, unsophisticated person, a peasant.

bushie *n.*[1] [SE *bush* + sfx *-ie*] [20C+] (*W.I.*) a form of unlicensed and very potent rum distilled secretly in the countryside.

bushie *n.*[2] *see under* BUSHY.

bush league *n.* [baseball imagery] [1910s+] anywhere considered second-rate, out-of-the way.

bush league *adj.* [baseball jargon *bush leagues*, second-rate teams, leagues and thus players] **1** [20C+] (*US*) amateur, unprofessional, unsophisticated; thus n. *bushleaguer*, a person who is a failure. **2** [1980s] (*US campus*) unfair, stupid, inadequate.

bushman's... *n.*

SE in slang uses

(IN COMPOUNDS)

❑ **bushman's bible** *n.* [the magazine always backed the interest of those living outside the big cities] [late 19C+] (*Aus.*) the Sydney *Bulletin*. ❑ **bushman's breakfast** *n.* [the lack of 'civilized' amenities in the bush] [late 19C+] (*Aus.*) a look around and a cough, or any other minimal 'breakfast'. ❑ **bushman's clock** *n.* [its sounds punctuate the day] [mid-19C+] (*Aus.*) a kookaburra or laughing jackass. ❑ **bushman's friend** *n.* **1** [late 19C+] (*S.Afr.*) a large bush-cutting knife. **2** [1980s] (*N.Z.*) any large-leafed plant that can be used as lavatory 'paper'. ❑ **bushman's hot dinner** *n.* [1940s+] (*Aus./N.Z.*) a damper (a form of unleavened cake, baked in the ashes) and mustard. ❑ **bushman's mile** *n.* [2000s] (*N.Z.*) a distance that turns out to be (or seems) far further than expected. ❑ **bushman's tea** *n.* [2000s] (*US drugs*) khat.

bush telegraph *n.* (*also* **bush wire**) [mid-19C] (*orig. Aus.*) **1** a member of a bushranging gang whose task is to keep his colleagues informed of the whereabouts of potential victims or efforts to capture them. **2** (*also* **bush telegram, blackfellow telegraph**) a network of gossip and rumour that brings news, often inaccurate, before the official sources [SAusE *blackfellow* (now derog.), a Native Australian].

bushwa *n.* (*also* **booshwa, booshwah, boushwa, boushwah, bushwah, bushwash**) **1** [20C+] nonsense, euph. for BULLSHIT *n.* (1)[f. BULLSHIT *n.* (1), but ? link to Can. *bois de vache*, buffalo dung]. **2** [1920s] a pretentious, arrogant person [f. Can. *bourgeois*, the head voyageur of a trading post or expedition]. **3** [1940s] a yokel. **4** [1940s] (*US Und.*) an outsider who dislikes criminals.

bushwa! *excl.* (*also* **bushwah!**) [BUSHWA *n.*] [1950s] (*US*) rubbish! nonsense!

bushwhack *n.* [backform. f. BUSHWHACK *v.* (1)] [1930s+] an ambush, a hi-jack; an assassination.

bushwhack *v.* [SE *bushwhack*, to live in the backwoods. Those settlers who did so were doubtless versed in moving quietly through the woods in pursuit of prey; note Schele De Vere, *Americanisms* (1872): 'Originally it was a harmless word, denoting simply the process of propelling a boat by pulling the bushes on the edges of the stream, or of beating them down with a scythe or a cudgel in order to open a way through a thicket'] **1** [19C+] (*orig. US*) to ambush, to attack without warning; lit. and fig.; thus n. *bushwhacking*. **2** [late 19C] (*US*) to seek out, to discover surreptitiously. **3** [late 19C] (*US*) to hide. **4** [1910s] to borrow without permission; the theory is that such items will, eventually be returned, but the term (and the action) is virtually synon. with stealing. **5** [1910s–40s] (*US campus*) to have sexual intercourse in a field or wood. **6** [1920s] (*US*) to beat up. **7** [1950s–70s] (*US campus*) to spy and sneak up on courting couples in automobiles. **8** [1980s] to trick, to deceive.

bushwhacked *adj.* [fig. + lit. uses of BUSHWHACK *v.* (1)] **1** [1960s] (*orig. US*) very drunk. **2** [2000s] ambushed, hijacked.

bushwhacker *n.*[1] [BUSHWHACK *v.* (1)] **1** [19C] (*US*) an illegitimate child. **2** [19C+] (*Aus./US*) one who lives far from urban 'civilization'. **3** [mid-19C] (*orig. US*) an ambusher, an attacker; a street robber.

bushwhacker *n.*[2] [BUSH *n.*[1] (2a) + WHACK *v.*[1] (1)] [late 19C] the penis.

bushwhacker *n.*[3] [BUSH *n.*[1] (1) + fig. use of WHACK *v.*[1] (1)] [1950s] (*US drugs*) a marijuana smoker.

bush wire *n. see* BUSH TELEGRAPH *n.*

bushy *n.*[1] (*also* **bushie**) [SE *bush*] **1** [late 19C+] (*Aus./W.I.*) one who lives in the country. **2** [1980s] (*S.Afr.*) a half-caste.

bushy *n.*[2] (*also* **bushie**) [abbr. *BUSHPIG under* BUSH *n.*[1]] [1980s] (*Aus.*) a very ugly woman.

bushy *adj.* [BUSHY *n.*[1] (1)] [mid-19C+] (*Aus./W.I.*) unsophisticated, countrified.

Bushy Park *n.*[1] (*also* **Bushey Park**) [BUSH *n.*[1] (2a) + pun on proper name *Bushey Park*, Middlesex, UK] [late 18C–late 19C] female pubic hair; thus *take a turn at Bushy Park*, of a man, to have sexual intercourse.

IN PHRASES

❑ **take a turn in Bushey Park** *v.* [19C] to have sexual intercourse.

Bushy Park *n.*[2] (*also* **Bushey Park, in the park**) [rhy. sl.] [mid-19C–1960s] a lark, a joke.

business *n.* **1** [17C; late 19C+] (*UK Und.*) criminal activity. **2** euph. used in sexual contexts. (**a**) [17C+] sexual intercourse, irrespective of sexuality. (**b**) [early 18C; mid-19C+] a prostitute's euphemism for paid intercourse. (**c**) [1900s–60s] (*US*) prostitution as a trade or act. (**d**) [1920s] (*US*) a woman, usu. deemed promiscuous. (**e**) [1940s] the fly buttons or zip. (**f**) [1940s+] (*orig. US*) the male or female genitals. (**g**) [1950s] (*US Und.*) an effeminate/passive male homosexual. **3** [mid-17C+] a euph. term for faeces or urine. **4** [mid-17C+] a (difficult) situation; usu. defined by a n./adj. **5** [late 19C+] constr. with *the*, the best, the peak of excellence; often found as *DO THE BUSINESS* below. **6** [late 19C+] constr. with *the*, cheating, fraud, deception. **7** [20C+] a matter in which one may interfere; thus *mind one's own business*, to keep out of other people's affairs. **8** (*US*) as verbal aggression. (**a**) [1930s–40s] intense interrogation, 'the third degree'. (**b**) [1940s+] complaints, verbal criticism. **9** equipment. (**a**) [1930s+] (*drugs*) the equipment used to take opium and, latterly, heroin. (**b**) [1930s+] (*US prison*) a weapon. (**c**) [1960s] an unspecified mechanical/material object. **10** [1950s] a murder, an assassination; occas. as *get the business*.

IN COMPOUNDS

❑ **business boy** *n.* [1970s+] a homosexual male prostitute. ❑ **business end, the** *n.* [i.e. the end that 'does the business'] **1** [late 19C+] that part (practical or metaphorical) that really matters; thus (*US*) *the business end of a tin tack*, the point. **2** [1970s] the anus. **3** [2000s] the vagina. ❑ **business girl** *n.* (*also* **business woman**) [1920s+] a prostitute.

IN PHRASES

❑ **do a bit of business** *v.* **1** [mid-19C+] to have sexual intercourse; often in the context of prostitution. **2** [1910s] to commit a crime. ❑ **do business** *v.* **1** [late 19C+] to have intercourse with a prostitute. **2** [1990s+] to purchase drugs. ❑ **do one's business** *v.* (*also* **do one's things**) [mid-17C; mid-19C+] a euph. meaning to go to the lavatory, esp. used to children. ❑ **do someone's business** *v. see DO SOMEONE'S JOB FOR THEM under* JOB *n.*[2]. ❑ **do the business** *v.* (*also* **do the biz, ...bizniz**) **1** [17C+] to act in the manner required. **2** [mid-18C+] to hang, to murder, to kill. **3** [late 18C; 1940s+] to have sexual intercourse, irrespective of sexuality. ❑ **get business** *v.* [1980s] (*US black*) to be successful. ❑ **get up in someone's business** *v.* [1990s+] (*US*) to interfere in someone's privacy. ❑ **give someone the business** *v.* [1930s+] (*orig. US*) **1** to kill. **2** to beat up, to assault. **3** to have sexual intercourse with. **4** to tease, to taunt, to put at a disadvantage by one's own actions. **5** to deceive, to bamboozle. **6** to interrogate. **7** to cast flirtatious glances at. **8** to frustrate sexually. **9** to brag to, to boast to. ❑ **in someone's business** *see IN SOMEONE'S FACE under* FACE *n.* ❑ **look like business** *v.* [late 19C+] (*US*) of a person or situation, to look serious or threatening. ❑ **open one's business** *v.* [early 18C] of a woman, to make oneself available for sexual intercourse. ❑ **on the business** *adj. see ON THE GAME under* GAME *n.* ❑ **talk business** *v.* **1** [1950s] (*US Und.*) to offer a bribe to the police or other officials in the hope of securing immunity or leniency. **2** [1960s+] (*US black*) to seduce, to charm.

SE in slang uses

IN PHRASES

❑ **have business on both sides of the way** *v.* [the drunkard meanders from side to side of a street] [18C] to be drunk.

business *v.* [lit. SE *do business* (*with*)] [1930s+] (*orig. US black*) to be concerned with, to be interested in; thus as *got the business*, to be able to put someone down.

busing *n.*[1] [SE *abuse*] [20C+] (*W.I.*) verbal violence, using obscene and aggressive language.

busing *n.*[2] *see* BOOZING *n.*

bus it *v. see* BUS *v.*[1].

busk *n.*

IN PHRASES

❑ **make free with both ends of the busk** *v.* [late 18C–late 19C] of a man, to caress a woman intimately.

IN EXCLAMATIONS

❑ **both ends of the busk!** [SE *busk*, a corset, spec. its stiffening/supporting whalebone or other agent; the top would support the breasts, the bottom be near the vagina, the parts of the body that are being celebrated] [late 18C–early 19C] a toast before drinking.

busk *v.* [? naut. jargon *busk*, to cruise the seas, esp. as a pirate; ult. Ital. *buscare*, to filch, to prowl] **1** [mid-19C] to sell obscene songs and books in the streets and public houses. **2** [mid-19C] to sell goods to a retailer; thus phr. *go on the busk*. **3** [mid-19C+] to work as a street performer.

busker *n.* (*also* **busk**) [BUSK *v.* (3); SE after mid-20C] [mid-19C–1950s] one who sings, plays or otherwise entertains in public houses or, latterly, on the street, typically alongside a cinema queue.

busk it *v.* [fig. use of BUSK *v.* (3)] [2000s] to act or speak in a nonchalant manner.

busman *n. see BUSTMAN under* BUST *n.*

busnacking *n.* (*also* **buznacking, buzznacking**) [dial. *buzz*, to move around in an agitated manner + dial. *knack*, to talk in an affected manner; ? link to SE *nag*; note naut. jargon *busk*, to tack about] **1** [mid-19C] waiting around, wasting time. **2** [late 19C–1900s] prying, interfering, butting in. **3** [1900s] acting in an excessively fussy, officious manner.

bus-napper *n.* (*also* **buz-napper**) [BUZZ *n.* (2b) + NAB *v.*[1]] **1** [late 18C–early 19C] (*UK Und.*) a constable. **2** [late 18C–mid-19C] a young pickpocket. **3** [20C+] (*Aus.*) a police officer.

IN COMPOUNDS

❑ **bus-napper's academy** *n.* (*also* **buz-napper's academy**) [late 18C–mid-19C] a school for thieves. ❑ **bus-napper's kinchin** *n.* [KINCHIN *n.* (1), lit. a 'constable's child'] [18C] a watchman.

buss *v.*[1] [SE *buss*, a kiss] **1** [mid–late 18C] (*UK Und.*) to steal. **2** [mid-19C+] (*US*) to court.

SE in slang uses

IN COMPOUNDS

❑ **buss beggar** *n.* [SE *buss*, a kiss + SE *beggar*; in both cases the subject is 'begging for a kiss'] **1** [17C–19C] an ageing prostitute. **2** [late 18C–early 19C] an aged roué whose enthusiasm for sexual encounters is matched only by the unwillingness of the young and pretty to offer them.

IN EXCLAMATIONS

❑ **buss me rass!** [RAAS *n.* (1)] [late 18C+] (*W.I.*) kiss my arse!

buss *v.*[2] [lit. and fig. uses of W.I. pron. of BUST *v.*[1]] [1960s] (*US black*) to hit.

IN PHRASES

❑ **buss a lime** *v.* [LIME *n.*[2]] [1950s+] (*W.I.*) to enjoy a spontaneous social gathering. ❑ **buss arse** *v.* [ARSE *n.* (1)] [20C+] (*W.I.*) to beat, to thrash. ❑ **buss cunu** *v.* [CUNNY *n.* (1)] [20C+] (*W.I.*) to have sexual intercourse. ❑ **buss dirt** *v.* [20C+] (*W.I.*) to make the fastest possible of exits.

buss-belt *n.* [SE *burst belt*] [1960s+] (*W.I.*) a very fat man.

buss cove *n.* [SE *bus* + COVE *n.* (1)] [mid-19C] a bus ticket collector.

busser *n.*[1] [SE *buss*, to kiss] [mid-19C] (*US*) the mouth.

busser *n.*[2] (*also* **buser**) [late 19C–1900s] a bus horse.

bussie *n.* (*also* **bussy**) [1940s+] (*US*) a bus worker.

bust *n.* [dial. var. on SE *burst*] **1** a 'break' or collapse in one's life or one's affairs; a failure. (**a**) [mid-19C+] (*US*) an inadequate individual; of circumstances, a serious failure, esp. an embarrassing one or a misjudgement. (**b**) [late 19C–1900s; 1960s] (*US campus*) failure in one's examinations; a hard examination. (**c**) [20C+] (*orig. US*) (*also* **busting**) a financial collapse. (**d**) [20C+] a demotion. (**e**) [1930s] (*US tramp*) a serious mistake; a piece of very bad luck. (**f**) [1990s+] (*US black gang*) a coward, a weakling. **2** in the context of crime, a break-in, a raid. (**a**) [mid-19C+] a burglary; late 19C only in UK but extended in Aus. use. (**b**) [1930s+] (*also* **bust-up**) a police raid, esp. on drug-users or dealers. (**c**) [1950s+] (*US black*) by metonymy, the police. (**d**) [1950s+] (*orig. US*) an arrest; a criminal charge. (**e**) [1960s] (*US prison*) as ext. of sense 2d above, a prison sentence. **3** a break or escape from conventional life. (**a**) [mid-19C+] (*orig. US*) a drinking party, a spree, a celebration. (**b**) [1980s] (*US campus*) an exciting, good experience or event. **4** a physical 'explosion'. (**a**) [1920s+] a blow, a punch [BUST *v.*[1] (5b)]. (**b**) [1960s] (*US black*) an orgasm [BUST *v.*[1] (7b)]. **5** [1940s] (*US*) a false piece of information. **6** see BURST *n.*[1]. **7** see BURST *n.*[2].

IN COMPOUNDS

❑ **bustman** *n.* (*also* **busman**) [1940s+] (*Aus.*) a burglar, a house-breaker.

IN PHRASES

❑ **all in a bust** *adj.* [1910s–20s] very excited. ❑ **do a bust** *v.* **1** [late 19C] (*UK Und.*) to break into a house. **2** [1990s+] (*Aus. Und.*) to escape. ❑ **go for a bust** *v.* [1930s] to spend extravagently. ❑ **my bust** [1980s+] (*US campus*) expression of apology: my fault, 'sorry'. ❑ **on a bust** [mid-19C+] **1** (*also* **on a buster**) drinking heavily. **2** failing, doing badly. **3** (*US*) enthusiastically, to a great extent. ❑ **on the bust 1** [late 19C–1930s] (*Aus.*) on a spree. **2** [1920s–30s] facing financial problems, bankruptcy. ❑ **— or bust** [1910s+] an intensifier, suggesting that a failure to accomplish something will lead to disaster. ❑ **stick a bust** *v.* [ext. use of STICK *v.* (3)] [late 19C] (*UK Und.*) to commit a burglary. ❑ **take a bust at** *v.* [1920s+] (*US*) to hit (with the fist).

bust *adj.* [BUST *v.*[1] (4b)] **1** [mid-19C+] bankrupt, subject to financial collapse. **2** [1920s+] impoverished, out of funds.

IN PHRASES

❑ **go bust** *v.* [late 19C+] of an individual firm or company, to lose one's money, to become bankrupt.

bust *v.*[1] **1** to invade, lit. or fig. (**a**) [late 18C+] (*also* **burst, bus'em up, bust into**) to intrude, to break into. (**b**) [late 19C+] to raid. **2** to cause trouble for. (**a**) [early 19C+] (*US*) (*also* **burst**) to cause to go bankrupt, to ruin. (**b**) [mid-19C+] to inform against. (**c**) [late 19C+] to reduce in rank, to demote. (**d**) [1920s] (*US*) to get the better of, to 'put one over on'. (**e**) [1940s+] to arrest, esp. on a drugs charge. (**f**) [1960s] (*US teen*) to tease. (**g**) [1960s–70s] (*US*) to catch someone out. (**h**) [1960s+] of a college professor, to fail a student. (**i**) [1990s+] to discipline, e.g. at work. (**j**) *see* BUST OUT *v.*[5] (1). **3** [mid-19C] to go on a spree. **4** to suffer a lit. or fig. 'break-down'. (**a**) [mid-19C–1970s] (*US campus*) to fail an examination. (**b**) [mid-19C+] (*orig. US*) (*also* **burst, bust up**) to come to financial ruin, to go bankrupt. **5** to attack physically. (**a**) [mid-19C+] (*also* **burst**) to kill, to murder. (**b**) [late 19C+] (*also* **bust up**) to hit. (**c**) [20C+] to fight. (**d**) [1930s–50s] (*also* **bust down**) to defeat. (**e**) [1940s+] to rape, to deflower (forcibly); also homosexual use. **6** [mid-19C+] (*orig. US*) to go very fast; also as *bust along, bust by, bust off.* **7** to 'explode' physically. (**a**) [late 19C+] to explode with rage and pent-up emotion. (**b**) [1960s+] (*US black*) to ejaculate, esp. prematurely. **8** [late 19C+] (*Aus.*) (*also* **bust up**) to waste money, usu. on drink. **9** [1920s] to surpass, e.g. a record. **10** [1920s+] (*orig. US*) to break down in laughter. **11** [1930s] to make someone depressed. **12** [1930s] (*US*) to appear, to arrive. **13** [1950s] to 'break', as in journalistic stories. **14** [1950s+] to do well, esp. in a test, to receive a good grade, e.g. *he busted an A in Math.* **15** [1970s+] (*US black*) an all-purpose term, to do, to happen. **16** [1980s] (*UK black*) to launch, e.g. a new song or artist. **17** [1980s+] (*rap music*) to pay attention, to notice, to listen to, to enjoy. **18** [1980s+] (*US*) to make someone else laugh. **19** [1990s+] (*US campus*) to fall down.

IN PHRASES

❑ **bust...** *v. see also under* relevant n. or adj. ❑ **bust a blood-vessel** *v. see* BURST A BLOOD-VESSEL *under* BURST *v.*[1]. ❑ **bust a cap** *v.* **1** [1970s+] (*US gay*) to have aggressive, fast anal intercourse. **2** *see under* CAP *n.*[2]. **3** *see under* CAP *n.*[4]. ❑ **bust a gun** *v.* [1980s] (*UK black*) to fire a gun. ❑ **bust a light** *v. see* JUMP *v.* (4e). ❑ **bust around** *v.* **1** [1940s] (*US*) to fight with, to attack. **2** [1950s] to arrive, to appear. ❑ **bust a shot** *n.* [1990s+] (*US black*) to shoot someone. ❑ **bust ass** *see* separate entries. ❑ **bust in** *v.* (*also* **bust through**) **1** [late 19C+] (*US*) to enter, with overtones of speed, aggressiveness. **2** [1920s–50s] to interfere, to butt in. **3** [1950s] to gatecrash a party. ❑ **bust it** *v.* [2000s] (*US*) to ejaculate. ❑ **bust on** *v.* **1** [1960s] (*US*) to hit, to attack; as phr. *bust on someone's ass.* **2** [1960s+] (*US*) to criticize. **3** [1990s+] (*US black*) to inform against someone. ❑ **bust one's ass** *v.* (*also* **bust one's arse, ...buns, ...butt, ...pants**) [ASS *n.* (4)/ARSE *n.* (4)/BUNS *n.* (3)/BUTT *n.*[1] (1c)/SE *pants*] **1** [1930s+] to work extremely hard, to put in a great effort. **2** [1940s+] (*orig. US*) to get injured (esp. in a car or similar crash). ❑ **bust out** see separate entries. ❑ **bust out with** *v. see* BREAK OUT WITH *v.* ❑ **bust rhymes** *v.* (*also* **bust a rhyme, bust rhythms**) [1980s+] (*rap music*) to work as a rap musician, DJ or MC. ❑ **bust slugs** *v.* [1990s+] to fire a gun. ❑ **bust someone down** *v.* [1950s] (*US*) to disparage. ❑ **bust someone out** *v.* [1980s+] (*US black*) of a man, to have sexual intercourse with someone, to bring to orgasm. ❑ **bust someone's ass** *v.* [ASS *n.* (4)] **1** [1930s+] (*orig. US*) to beat up, to attack physically. **2** [1960s+] (*US*) to harass, to nag, to annoy. **3** [1970s] (*US*) to arrest. **4** [2000s] (*US*) to sodomize. ❑ **bust someone's horns** *v.* [1980s+] (*US*) to goad, to annoy someone. ❑ **bust someone up** *v.* [mid-19C+] to beat someone up, to hurt someone in a fight. ❑ **bust through** *v. see* BUST IN above. ❑ **bust up** *see* separate entries. ❑ **bust water** *v. see* BREAK WATER *under* BREAK *v.*[1].

IN EXCLAMATIONS

❑ **bust a frog!** [mid-19C–1930s] (*Cockney*) a mild excl. ❑ **bust it! 1** [late 19C+] an excl. of annoyance, frustration. **2** [1920s] (*US*) be quiet! ❑ **bust me!** (*also* **bust him! bust it! bust it all! bustmy! bust you!**) [mid-19C+] a mild oath; an excl. of annoyance, frustration. ❑ **bust my boiler!** (*also* **bust my biler! bust my bob-stay! bust my rifle!**) [20C+] an excl. of surprise or annoyance. ❑ **bust this!** [1980s+] (*orig. US black*) now look here! pay attention!

SE in slang uses

IN COMPOUNDS

❑ **bust-down** *n. see* separate entry. ❑ **busthead** *n.* **1** [mid-19C+] (*US*) strong whisky, or gin, esp. when illegally distilled. **2** [1960s] (*US tramp*) a drunk. ❑ **bustskull** *n.* (*also* **popskull, swell-head, swell-skull**) [mid-19C+] (*US*) strong whisky, esp. when illegally distilled.

IN PHRASES

❑ **bust a grape** *v.* [var. on *BUST A GUT under* GUT *n.*] [1970s+] (*US black/prison*) **1** to engage in any form of hard, productive work. **2** to lose emotional control; to hit someone. ❑ **bust a gusset** *v.* [SE; the straining so hard that the seams of one's clothes split] [20C+] (*US*) to break down with laughter, to lose control, to make a superlative effort. ❑ **bust loose** *v.* [1920s+] (*US*) **1** to commence, to start happening. **2** to break free of constraints. **3** to escape from an institution. ❑ **bust one's buttons** *v.* (*also* **pop one's buttons**) [SE; the real or fig. bursting out of one's clothing] **1** [1950s+] (*US*) to strain oneself physically or emotionally. **2** [1960s+] to swell with pride. ❑ **bust one's vest** *v.* [the image of a chest swelling] [1940s–50s] (*US black*) to be generous, to display one's munificence. ❑ **bust open** *v.* [1950s] (*US*) to distress, to make unhappy.

bust *v.*^{2} *see* BUS *v.*^{2}.

bust! *excl.* [mid-19C–1920s] a mild excl., dash it!; euph. for DAMN! *excl.* or *TO HELL WITH...! under* HELL *n.*

busta *n.* **1** [1990s+] (*US black teen*) an informer, a person who tattle-tales [BUST *v.*^{1} (2b)]. **2** *see* BUSTER *n.*^{1} (1h).

busta backbone *n.* [the effort of chewing it will *bust one's backbone*] [1950s] (*W.I.*) a tough sugar candy, extremely hard to chew.

busta brown *n. see* BUSTER BROWN *n.*

bust-ass *adj.* [SE *bust* + -ASS *sfx*] [1980s+] (*US*) a general derog. term.

bust ass *v. see under* ASS *n.*

bust-down *n.* [SE *bust*] [2000s] (*US black*) a share of a cigarette.

bust down *v. see* BUST *v.*^{1} (5d).

busted *adj.*^{1} (*also* **busted up**) [SE *bust*/BUST *v.*^{1}] **1** [mid-19C+] in fig. use, dead, finished. **2** [20C+] (*also* **bursted**) broken; also fig. use. **3** [20C+] exhausted. **4** [20C+] caught out, in a non-criminal context. **5** [1910s+] (*US*) (*also* **busted out**) expelled, thrown out, esp. from an institutional job; reduced in rank. **6** [1920s+] depressed, in pain. **7** [1940s+] (*orig. US*) arrested, esp. on drug charges. **8** [1950s+] drunk. **9** [1990s+] (*US black*) ugly, unattractive. **10** [2000s] (*US campus*) wrong.

busted *adj.*^{2} *see* BLOWED *adj.*^{1}.

busted down *adj. see* BUSTED (OUT) *adj.*

busted flush *n.* [poker imagery, i.e. a potentially good hand of cards ruined/lost] [20C+] of a person or a situation, a failure, a disappointment.

busted on *adj.* [fig. use of *bust*, in sense of committing oneself] [1920s] (*US*) in love with.

busted (out) *adj.* (*also* **busted down, busted up**) [BUST *v.*^{1} (2a)] **1** [mid-19C+] (*orig. US*) without money, bankrupt. **2** *see* BUSTED *adj.*^{1} (5). **3** *see* BUST-OUT *adj.*^{2} (3).

busted up *adj.* **1** *see* BUSTED *adj.*^{1}. **2** *see* BUSTED (OUT) *adj.*

busted-up shirt *n.* (*also* **buss-up-shot**) [equation of the thin pieces of bread with the remnants of torn-up shirt] [20C+] (*W.I., Trin.*) a type of East Indian bread.

buster *n.*^{1} [BUST *v.*^{1}] **1** in the context of size, energy or (exceptional) character. (**a**) [mid-19C] a 'roistering blade'. (**b**) [mid–late 19C] a dandy. (**c**) [mid-19C+] a large or full-grown child. (**d**) [mid-19C+] (*also* **burster**) something or someone exceptional of its or their type. (**e**) [late 19C] as spec. use of sense 1c above, the teenage Bavarian giantess, who appeared in London music-halls under the name 'Maid Marian' and after a brief but successful career died before she reached the age of 20. (**f**) [late 19C] a substantial meal. (**g**) [1900s–20s] (*US Und.*) one who fights. (**h**) [1990s+] (*US black gang*) (*also* **busta**) a loser, a failure, a coward, a general derog. term. **2** that which breaks. (**a**) [mid–late 19C] a housebreaker. (**b**) [1900s] a thief, usu. with identifying noun. (**c**) [1900s–40s] (*US Und.*) a housebreaker's crowbar. (**d**) [1940s] (*US Und.*) a police truncheon. (**e**) [1950s] (*US Und.*) one who breaks into premises and destroys the contents, while not actually stealing anything – the aim is to persuade the owner to pay 'protection'. (**f**) [1950s+] (*Can.*) a shoplifter. **3** [late 19C+] an exhausting physical effort. (**a**) something difficult. (**b**) a heavy fall. (**c**) a battle, a fight; a blow. **4** [1900s–50s] (*Aus.*) a storm.

buster *n.*^{2} (*also* **burster**) [BUST *n.* (3a)] [mid-19C–1920s] a spree; thus *in for a buster*, keen to go out on a spree; *rare buster*, implying at high speed; in horseracing, a high bet.

IN PHRASES

❑ **go in a buster** *v.* [mid-19C–1920s] to spend regardless of the expense; similarly of unrestrained physical effort.

buster *n.*^{3} [BUSTER *n.*^{1}] **1** [mid-19C+] a person, often an old and cantankerous one; thus *buster, old buster*, a general term of (affectionate) address. **2** [2000s] (*US prison*) 'a term for "Northern Mexicans" used by "Southern Mexicans"' (*Other Side of the Wall*, 2000).

buster *n.*^{4} [abbr. *kidney-buster*] [1970s] (*US*) a motor vehicle that gives one a bumpy and painful ride.

buster *n.*^{5} [BUST *v.*^{1} (2b)] [1990s+] (*US black*) an informer.

buster *n.*^{6} *see* BALL-BUSTER *n.* (6).

buster *n.*^{7} *see* BURSTER *n.*^{1}.

buster *n.*^{8}

IN PHRASES

❑ **on a buster** *adj. see ON A BUST under* BUST *n.*

buster brown *n.* (*also* **busta brown**) [ext. of BUSTER *n.*^{3} (1)] [1990s+] (*US black*) a hanger-on.

buster-in *n.* [*BUST IN under* BUST *v.*^{1}] [1930s] (*US*) a housebreaker.

busters *n.*^{1} [ext. of BUSTER *n.*^{2}] [1960s–70s] (*US black*) pleasure, enjoyment, 'kicks'.

busters *n.*^{2} [BUST *v.*^{1} (2e)] [1990s+] (*US black*) the police.

busting *n.*^{1} [BUST *v.*^{1} (15)] [2000s] (*US teen*) doing something skilfully.

busting *n.*^{2} *see* BUST *n.* (1c).

busting *adj.*^{1} [BUSTER *n.*^{1} (1d)] [mid-19C–1920s] (*US*) very large; thus *busting big*.

busting *adj.*^{2} [SE *bursting*] [1950s+] desperate.

busting out *phr.* [fig. use of BUST *v.*^{1} (15)] (*US black*) **1** [1900s; 1990s+] (*also* **busting loose**) feeling good. **2** [1990s+] looking good, attractive, well-dressed, successful etc.

bust into *v. see* BUST *v.*^{1} (1a).

bustle *n.*^{1} [SE *bustle*, stir, fuss, tumult; 'If a man is worth a thousand pounds, 'tis *blunt*; if as much money be collected in various sums, 'tis *bustle*' Bee] [early–mid-19C] money.

IN PHRASES

❑ **on the bustle** *adj.* [1900s–10s] (*Aus. Und.*) cadging a loan.

bustle *n.*^{2} [SE *bustle*, a 'dress-improver'; i.e. a small pad or wire framework that accentuates the back of the dress] [1920s–70s] (*US*) the buttocks, the posterior.

bustle *v.*^{1} [SE *bustle*, to hurry, to elbow one's way through a crowd] **1** [late 18C] (*UK Und.*) to thieve; thus n., *bustler*, a petty thief. **2** [late 19C] (*UK Und.*) to pickpocket; as n., an act of pickpocketing in which a young woman asks the proposed victim of the crime for the time, then pretends to stumble against him, so that her accomplice can protest to the man, while the woman effects the theft.

bustle *v.*^{2} [ext. use of SE *bustle*, to stir, to rouse] [mid-19C+] to confuse, to perplex.

bustle-punching *n.* (*also* **bustle-pinching, bustle-rubbing**) [SE *bustle*, a 'dress-improver' and out of fashion in the 20C / BUSTLE *n.*^{2} + *punching*] [1960s+] (*UK/US police*) the action of the *frotteur*, using the anonymity of a dense crowd to rub one's penis against the nearby buttocks of defenceless women; thus *bustle-puncher*, a frotteur or one who caresses women's buttocks in a crowd.

bustler *n.* [1910s] (*Aus.*) a notably hard worker in a shearing shed.

bust-maker *n.* [SE *bust*, the female breasts; i.e. the increased size of a pregnant woman's breasts] [late 19C] a seducer, a womanizer.

bust-out *n.*^{1} [BUST *n.* (3a) + SE *out*] [20C+] an enormous feast.

bust-out *n.*^{2} [BUST OUT *v.*^{2}] [1930s+] (*US*) an escape, esp. from prison.

bust-out *n.*^{3} [BUST OUT *v.*^{5} (2)] [1950s–70s] crooked dice.

bust-out *n.*^{4} [BUST *v.*^{1} (4)] [1960s+] (*US*) failure, ruin, a 'smash-up'.

bust-out *adj.*[1] [SE *bust* + *out*] [1950s+] (*US*) an intensifying adj., extreme, tremendous, great, obvious, simple.

bust-out *adj.*[2] [SE *bust*, broken + SE *out*] **1** [1950s+] illegal, esp. of dice. **2** [1950s+] of a place or machine, e.g. a car, rundown. **3** [1970s+] (*US*) (*also* **busted out**) of a person, impoverished.

bust out *v.*[1] [BUST *v.*[1] (2b)] [mid-19C; 1990s+] (*orig. US*) to betray secrets.

bust out *v.*[2] [SE *bust*] **1** [mid-19C+] (*orig. US*) to escape, usu. from prison. **2** [1940s+] (*orig. US*) to run off, to leave. **3** [1960s] to free someone from a problem. **4** [1990s+] (*W.I.*) in fig. use, to be successful. **5** [1990s+] (*US*) to help someone else escape from prison.

bust out *v.*[3] [SE *burst/bust* out laughing] [late 19C; 1990s+] (*US black*) to laugh.

bust out *v.*[4] [late 19C+] to do, to perform, to make happen.

bust out *v.*[5] [BUST *v.*[1] + SE *out*] **1** [1930s+] (*US campus*) (*also* **bust**) to expel a student. **2** [1960s+] (*US*) to ruin financially, esp. through gambling. **3** [1960s+] to ruin, destroy. **4** [1970s] to dismiss from a job. **5** [1990s+] to go bankrupt.

bust out *v.*[6] [ext. of BUST *v.*[1] (5e)] **1** [1960s+] (*US black/P.R.*) to deflower. **2** [1990s+] to rape anally.

bust out *v.*[7] [1990s+] to shout at someone, to tell someone off.

bust-out joint *n.* [BUST-OUT *adj.*[2] (1) + JOINT *n.* (3b)] [1930s–50s] an illegal gambling establishment.

bust-out man *n.* [BUST-OUT *adj.*[2] (1) + SE *man*] [1960s] (*US Und.*) a house gambler who cheats the bettors at a casino.

bustrap *n.* [BUZZ *n.* (2a) + SE *trap*] [mid–late 18C] a thief-catcher.

bust-up *n.* **1** [mid-19C+] (*also* **burst-up**) lit., an explosion; fig., a serious quarrel or argument, a fight [SE *bust*, to break]. **2** [late 19C] a day off [BUST *n.*]. **3** [20C+] a collapse, either emotional or financial [BUST *v.*[1]]. **4** [1930s] a rowdy party [BUST *n.*]. **5** *see* BUST *n.* (2b).

bust up *v.* [SE *bust*, to break up] **1** [late 19C+] to have a major quarrel, to end a love-affair, to divorce. **2** [20C+] to stop something, e.g. a fight, happening. **3** [1920s+] to conclude, e.g. an evening out or a party. **4** *see* BUST *v.*[1] (5b). **5** *see* BUST *v.*[1] (4b). **6** *see* BUST *v.*[1] (8).

busty *n.* [BUSTY *adj.*] [1990s+] (*US campus*) a sexy-looking, large-breasted woman.

busty *adj.* [SE *bust*, the female breasts] **1** [1910s+] of a female, having large breasts; often in comb., e.g. *busty beauty*. **2** [1990s+] (*US campus*) a sexy-looking, large-breasted woman.

busy *n.* (*also* **bizzie, bizzy, busybody**) [SE *busybody*; their rushing around, unlike a uniformed officer, who plods along a set beat] [20C+] a CID officer, a detective, a police officer.

IN PHRASES

❑ **do a busy** *v.* [1970s] to investigate.

busy *adj.* [1970s] interfering, 'nosy'.

SE in slang uses

IN COMPOUNDS

❑ **busy-lickum** *n.* [fig. use of SE *busy* + *lick*, to hit] [1990s+] **1** a gossip, a tattle-tale. **2** gossip.

IN PHRASES

❑ **busy as a one-armed paper-hanger** *adj.* (*also* **busy as a one-armed bill-poster, ...one-armed milker, ...one-legged man in an ass-kicking contest, ...one-legged tap-dancer, ...a bird dog**) [20C+] (*orig. Aus./US*) extremely busy; often ext. by *with hives* or *with an itch*. ❑ **get busy** *v.* **1** [early 19C; 1960s+] (*US black/teen*) to have sexual intercourse [note Nares (1822): '†BUSY. To be busy, to have sexual intercourse', which he links to BRUSH-OFF *n.*]. **2** [mid-19C+] to steal. **3** [1990s+] (*US black/teen*) to eat. **4** [1990s+] (*US black*) to fight. **5** [2000s] to interfere.

busy bee *n.*[1] [rhy. sl. = PCP] [1970s+] (*drugs*) phencyclidine.

busy bee *n.*[2] *see under* BEE *n.*[1].

busybody *n. see* BUSY *n.*

busy-sack *n.* [? SE *business*] [mid-19C–1900s] a carpet-bag.

but *adv.* **1** [mid-19C; 1930s+] (*orig. Aus.*) used (mainly) at the end of sentences to give added emphasis, 'no doubt about it', 'absolutely'; e.g. *He's a nice bloke, but*. **2** [1930s+] (*US*) used as an intensifier, e.g. *but crazy, but cool*.

butch *n.*[1] [abbr. SE *butcher*, seen fig. in senses 2–5 and sense 7 as a 'man of blood', a violent person] **1** [mid-19C] (*US*) a *butcher*'s knife. **2** [1910s] (*Aus.*) a doctor. **3** [1930s+] (*orig. US*) a nickname for a tough man, e.g. the hero of Damon Runyon's short story 'Butch Minds the Baby' (1930); a nickname for a large, tough woman (not a lesbian). **4** [1940s] (*US milit.*) the commanding officer. **5** [1940s+] (*orig. US*) a masculine lesbian. **6** [1940s+] (*orig. US*) a short, 'macho' haircut (used for either gender). **7** [1950s+] (*orig. US*) a masculine male homosexual. **8** [1990s+] (*Aus. teen*) a promiscuous young woman.

IN PHRASES

❑ **butch down (on)** *v.* [1980s] (*US*) to act in a physically aggressive manner. ❑ **butch in** *v.* [2000s] (*US prison*) to force a fellow prisoner to give oral sex in return for favours, protection etc. ❑ **butch it up** *v.* **1** [1950s] to get a military, i.e ultra-short, haircut. **2** [1960s+] (*US gay*) of a homosexual male, to accentuate a spurious masculinity in order to hide one's actual homosexuality; of a lesbian, to accentuate one's 'maleness'. **3** [1980s+] as sense 2 above but in non-homosexual contexts. ❑ **glamour butch** *n.* [1990s+] (*US gay*) a masculine lesbian or homosexual who wears formal clothes. ❑ **soft butch** *n.* [1990s+] (*gay*) a 'masculine' lesbian with a soft side and gentle character.

butch *n.*[2] *see* BUTCHER *n.*[2].

butch *adj.* [BUTCH *n.*[1]] **1** [1930s+] (*orig. US gay*) studiously masculine, of male or female homosexuals. **2** [1940s+] (*orig. US*) heterosexual. **3** [1940s+] of a woman (irrespective of sexuality), masculine, aggressive. **4** [1960s+] (*orig. US*) tough, manly.

DERIVATIVES

❑ **butchly** *adv.* [1980s+] (*gay*) in a macho, masculine manner. ❑ **butchy** *adj.* [1950s+] (*US*) lesbian; masculine-looking.

IN COMPOUNDS

❑ **butch-broad** *n.* [BROAD *n.*[2] (3)] [1960s] a masculine lesbian. ❑ **butch number** *n.* (*also* **butch queen**) [NUMBER *n.* (1c)/QUEEN *n.* (2a)] [1960s+] a 'masculine' male homosexual, usu. in question, e.g. *who's that butch number over there?*

butcha *n.* [Hind. *butcha*, a child] [mid-19C] (*Anglo-Ind.*) a child.

butcher *n.*[1] **1** [19C] the penis. **2** as a (negative) job description. (**a**) [mid-19C+] (*US*) a surgeon, a doctor, esp. an inefficient surgeon. (**b**) [mid-19C+] in playing cards, a king [his warlike image or joc. ref. to the SE occupation]. (**c**) [1910s+] (*Aus./US*) a barber, esp. a second-rate barber, who cuts people when shaving them. (**d**) [1920s–40s] (*US prison*) the chief warder. (**e**) [1940s+] (*US*) a bungler, an incompetent, irrespective of profession. (**f**) [1950s+] one who practises cosmetic work. **3** [late 19C–1900s] stout ale, punning on the SE description of the stereotypically rotund butcher.

IN COMPOUNDS

❑ **butcher knife** *n.* [ext. sense 1 above; note synon. 17C euph. *slaughter-knife*] [1960s+] (*US gay*) the penis. ❑ **butcher's shop** *n.* **1** [19C] the vagina [the image of 'raw meat']. **2** [1900s–10s] (*Aus.*) a wedding [BUTCHER *n.*[1] (1)]. **3** [1930s] the execution shed within a prison. **4** [1960s] (*orig. US black*) a hospital. **5** *see* BUTCHER'S PICNIC below.

SE in slang uses

IN COMPOUNDS

❑ **butcher's canary** *n.* [such insects are often found in butcher's shops] [1930s+] (*Aus.*) a blowfly. ❑ **butcher's cart** *n. see* BUTCHER WAGON below. ❑ **butcher's dog** *n.* [the *butcher's dog* can 'lie by the beef without touching it'] [late 18C–early 19C] a married man. ❑ **butcher's horse** *n.* [early 19C] a poor rider. ❑ **butcher's meat** *n.* [it remains the butcher's property, if only in theory, until fully paid for] [late 18C] meat bought on credit. ❑ **butcher's mourning** *n. see under* MOURNING *n.* ❑ **butcher's picnic** *n.* (*also* **butcher's shop**) [stereotype of the rumbustious butcher] [1960s+] (*Aus.*) a noisy party or other occasion that lacks decorum. ▫ **butcher wagon** *n.* (*also* **butcher's cart**) [late 19C+] (*US prison*) an ambulance.

IN PHRASES

▫ **go in like a butcher's cat** *v.* [the stereotyped aggressiveness of the animal] [2000s] (*N.Z.*) to attack violently. ▫ **talk to the butcher, not the block** *v. see* TALK TO THE ENGINEER, NOT THE OILY RAG *under* TALK TO *v.*

butcher *n.*[2] (*also* **butch**) [ety. unknown; ? *butcher* as generic for a salesman] [late 19C+] (*US*) a seller of sweets, fruit, soft drinks etc, working typically in a cinema or a railway train.

butcher *n.*[3] [? mispron. of Ger. *becher*, a beaker or form of lidded drinking vessel] [late 19C+] (*Aus.*) **1** a glass of beer, orig. two-thirds of a pint, later around half a pint. **2** a 6-ounce (170ml) glass.

butcher *v.*[1] [mid-19C] a euph. for *damn*; used in mild excls.

butcher *v.*[2] [1970s+] (*US gay*) to deflower a young man.

butcher *v.*[3] [BUTCHER'S HOOK *n.*] [1990s+] to look at, to stare.

butcher boy *n.* [ext. of BUTCH *n.*[1] (5)] [1930s] (*US gay*) a male homosexual who has intercourse with a lesbian.

butchering *adj.* [mid-19C+] euph. for BLOODY *adj.*

butcher's *n.*[1] [Polari] [late 19C] noon.

butcher's *n.*[2] *see* BUTCHER'S HOOK *n.*

butchers *adj.* see BUTCHER'S (HOOK) *adj.*

butcher's hoof *n.* [rhy. sl. = POOF *n.* (1)] [1990s+] (*Aus.*) a male homosexual.

butcher's hook *n.* (*also* **butcher's, butcher's look, docker's hook**) [rhy. sl.] [1910s+] a look, a glance.

IN PHRASES

▫ **have a butcher's (at)** *v.* (*also* **grab a butcher's, take a butcher's (at)**) [1930s+] to look at, to inspect.

butcher's (hook) *adj.* [rhy. sl. = CROOK *adj.* (3)] (*Aus.*) [20C+] ill, sick.

IN PHRASES

▫ **go butcher's (hook)** *v.* (*also* **go off butcher's hook**) [CROOK *adj.* (7)] [1910s+] to lose one's temper (with).

butchilinity *n.* [BUTCH *n.*[1] (7) + SE *masculinity*] [1990s+] (*US gay*) of a homosexual, the quality of being masculine.

butchski *n. see* BOOTCHKEY *n.*

bute *n. see* BEAUT *n.*[1].

but good *phr.* [BUT *adv.* (2) + SE *good*] [1950s+] (*orig. US*) very much so, extremely.

but hey! *excl.* [1990s+] (*US*) used as an affectionate acknowledgement or emphasis, esp. when the previous comments have been negative; abbr. 'But hey, what does it really matter…'.

butler's grace *n.* [early 17C] thanks, but no money.

but only! *excl.* [1980s+] (*S.Afr.*) an excl. used to support a statement made by one's companion.

butt *n.*[1] **1** concerning the body. (**a**) [late 17C+] (*also* **butties**) the buttocks; the posterior [SE before 19C]. (**b**) [mid-18C] the vagina. (**c**) [1910s+] generic for one's body, oneself. (**d**) [1970s] (*US campus*) a female. **2** in fig./ext. uses. (**a**) [mid-19C+] a cigarette or cigar end. (**b**) [20C+] a cigarette. (**c**) [1900s] (*US milit.*) in fig. use of sense 2a above, a short time. (**d**) [1940s+] (*US prison/Und.*) the final portion of one's sentence. **3** [late 19C–1950s] (*US*) a fool, an unpleasant person. **4** [1950s] a marijuana cigarette.

IN COMPOUNDS

pertaining to the body or buttocks

▫ **butt-bang** *v. see* BUTTFUCK *v.* ▫ **butt-banger** *n. see* BUTTFUCKER *n.* (1). ▫ **butt boy** *n.* [1980s+] (*US campus*) **1** a homosexual male. **2** thus fig. a weakling, a subservient figure. **3** a stupid, inept youth. ▫ **buttbrain** *n. see* BUTTHEAD below. ▫ **butt breath** *n.* [lit. one whose breath smells like faeces] [1990s+] (*US*) a general term of abuse. ▫ **butt buddy** *n.* [BUDDY *n.* (1)] [1990s+] a very close friend. ▫ **butt cheese** *n.* [1990s+] (*US campus*) anything, or anybody, undesirable, displeasing. ▫ **butt-chuckler** *n.* [pun on SE *chuck*, to toss] [1990s+] a masturbator; thus a general term of abusive address. ▫ **buttcrack** *n. see* CRACK *n.*[3] (4). ▫ **butt darts** *n.* [1990s+] (*UK juv.*) anal intercourse. ▫ **butt-end** *n. see* FAG END *n.* (1) ▫ **buttface** *n.* [1970s+] (*US*) a general term of contempt wit the implication of unattractiveness. ▫ **buttfuck/buttfucker** se separate entries. ▫ **butt-girl** *n.* [? fig. use of BUTT *n.*[1] (1a), i.e. sh has a menial status, or SE *butt*, a target (of derision)] [1980s] (*US* a woman used to run errands, e.g. for a fashion photographer ▫ **butt-grabbing** *adj.* [1970s] (*US*) good, exciting. ▫ **butthea** *n.* (*also* **buttbrain**) [-HEAD *sfx* (1); a term hugely popularized sinc the early 1990s in MTV's semi-animated series *Beavis an Butthead*] [1980s+] (*US*) a stupid or obnoxious person, thu adj. *buttheaded*. ▫ **butthole** *n.* (*US*) **1** [1950s+] the anus **2** [1960s+] a term of contempt. **3** [1990s+] anal intercourse ▫ **butthook** *n.* [? play on SE *buttock*] [1980s] (*US*) a lout. ▫ **butt-kicker/-kicking** *see* separate entries. ▫ **buttlick/-licking** se separate entries. ▫ **buttload** *n.* [fig. use of BUTT *n.*[1] (1a)/BUT *adv.* + SE *load*] [1980s+] (*US campus*) a large quantity, often i pl. ▫ **buttmunch** *n.* [1990s+] a fool. ▫ **butt naked** *n.* [ety unknown; ? it strips away one's inhibitions] [1980s+] (*drugs* phencyclidine. ▫ **buttpack** *n.* [var. on BUM BAG *under* BUM *n.* [1960s+] (*US*) a small pouch-like bag strapped around th wearer's waist. ▫ **butt peddlar** *n.* [1940s] (*US*) anyone wh sells their body as a prostitute, male or female. ▫ **butt pirate** *n* [1980s+] (*US*) a homosexual male. ▫ **butt plug** *n.* (*orig. US* [1980s+] a small dildo, usu. rubber, inserted in the anus durin sexual games. ▫ **butt plunger** *n.* **1** [1970s+] (*US*) a man wh inserts a dildo into his own anus then walks around nake while a prostitute looks on; thus a general insult. **2** [2000s] (*U gay*) the penis. ▫ **butt-puckered** *adj.* [BUTT *n.*[1] (1a) + SE *pucker* the supposed need to tighten the anus in the face of involuntar fear-generated defecation] [1970s] (*US*) scared. ▫ **butt pussy** *n* [PUSSY *n.* (1)] [20C+] (*US*) the anus, usu. in a male homosexua context. ▫ **butt rider** *n.* [RIDE *v.* (1a)] [1990s+] (*US juv.*) a mal homosexual. ▫ **butt-rustler** *n.* [2000s] (*US*) a mal homosexual. ▫ **butt slut** *n.* [1990s+] (*orig. US*) **1** homosexual male, usu. taking a passive role. **2** a woma who prefers anal to vaginal intercourse. ▫ **butt-sprung** *adj* [1930s–40s] (*US black*) of a garment, ill-fitting, esp. around th buttocks. ▫ **butt-suck** *v.* [1970s+] (*US*) to toady. ▫ **butt wa** *n.* [1990s+] (*US*) lavatory paper. ▫ **buttwhip** *v.* [1970s] (*U black*) to spank, usu. a child; thus *buttwhipping*, a spanking ▫ **buttwhipped** *adj.* [fig. use of BUTTWHIP above] [1990s+ drunk. ▫ **butt wipe** *n.* (*US*) **1** [1970s] lavatory paper **2** [1990s+] a term of abuse. ▫ **buttwooping** *n.* [var. o BUTTWHIP above] [1970s] (*US black*) a spanking.

other uses

▫ **butt boy** *n.* [1960s] (*US*) a heavy smoker.

IN PHRASES

▫ **big butt** *n.* [1910s–50s] (*US*) an important person. ▫ **ge more butt than ashtrays** *v.* [pun on senses 1b and 2a above [1990s+] (*US black*) of a man, to lead an active sexual life, t have sexual prowess. ▫ **have someone's butt on a biscu for breakfast** *v. see* HAVE SOMEONE'S BALLS (FOR A GAME OF POOL *under* BALLS *n.* ▫ **jump up someone's butt** *v. see* JUMP (UP SOMEONE'S ASS *under* ASS *n.* ▫ **kick someone's butt** *v* **1** [1950s+] (*orig. US*) to give someone a beating, to defea someone. **2** [1970s+] (*US black*) to impress, to overwhelm **3** [1970s+] (*US black*) to defeat intellectually. ▫ **lick someone's butt** *v.* [2000s] to act as a sycophant towards ▫ **— one's butt off** *adv.* [1950s+] with a v., to do something t an extreme extent. ▫ **on someone's butt** *adj.* [1990s+ harrassing, persecuting. ▫ **out the butt** *adv.* **1** [1980s+] (*US* excessively. **2** *see* UP THE BUTT below. ▫ **peddle one's butt** *v see* PEDDLE ONE'S ASS *under* PEDDLE *v.* ▫ **tear someone's butt** *v.* [1990s+] (*US*) to punish severely. ▫ **up someone's but** [1970s+] (*US*) immediately behind and therefore irritating bothering. ▫ **up the butt** *adv.* (*also* **out the butt**) [1980s+ (*orig. US*) to an excess, to the extreme.

IN EXCLAMATIONS

▫ **butts on!** **1** [1930s+] (*US*) a cry that calls for the right t smoke the last few puffs of another smoker's cigarette **2** [1970s+] (*Irish*) a cry to claim someone's apple core. ▫ **my butt!** [1940s+] a general excl. of disdain, dismissal, arrogan contempt. ▫ **your butt!** [1940s+] a general excl. of disdain dismissal, arrogant contempt. ❑ **your face and my butt!** *see* YOUR FACE AND MY ASS! *under* FACE *n.*

butt *n.*[2] *see* BUTTY *n.*[1].

butt *adj.* [BUTT *n.*[1] (1a)] (*US*) **1** [1990s+] (*rap music*) second-rate, inferior. **2** *see* BUTT-UGLY *under* BUTT *adv.*

butt *v.* [BUTT *n.*[1] (2b)] [1940s–50s] (*US*) **1** to pass someone a cigarette. **2** to crush out a cigarette.

SE in slang uses

IN PHRASES

❑ **butt in** *see* separate entries. ❑ **butt out** *v.* [SE *butt* v.] **1** [20C+] (*W.I., Guyn.*) to ignore, to cut dead, to pass by rudely. **2** *see also* separate entry.

IN EXCLAMATIONS

❑ **butt out!** *see* separate entry.

butt *adv.* [BUTT *n.*[1] (1a), seen as something physically powerful] [1980s+] (*US campus*) a general intensifier, very, very much, extremely, incredibly, truly.

IN COMPOUNDS

❑ **butt-ass** *adj.* [-ASS *sfx*] [1980s+] (*US*) very. ❑ **butt-crazy** *adj.* [1990s+] (*US teen*) utterly, completely. ❑ **butt-ugly** *adj.* (*also* **bugly, butt, buttly**) [BUTT *n.*[1] (1a) + SE *ugly*] [1980s+] (*US*) **1** very ugly. **2** a general derog.

butta/buttah *n. see* BUTTER *n.*[1] (7).

butta/buttah *adj. see* BUTTER *adj.*[2].

butteker *n.* [Ital. *bottega*; Rom. *būtteka*] [late 18C–19C] a shop.

butt-end *n. see* END *n.* (1b).

buttendski *n.* [BUTT *n.*[1] (1a) + SE *end* + -SKI *sfx*] [2000s] (*N.Z.*) the buttocks.

butter *n.*[1] [lit. or fig. characteristics of SE *butter*] **1** [late 17C+] semen; thus *buttery*, semen-filled. **2** [early 19C+] flattery, unctuousness. **3** [1920s] (*US*) nitroglycerine. **4** [1980s+] (*US black*) the vagina. **5** [1980s+] (*US black*) a woman, esp. when sexually active. **6** [1980s+] (*US black*) an attractive man. **7** [1990s+] (*orig. US black/teen*) (*also* **butta, buttah**) a general term of approval, the best, the most fashionable, attractive etc; thus *like butter/butta*, well-executed or performed smoothly or well [underlined by BUTTER *adj.*[2]]. **8** [1990s+] (*W.I.*) a feat which is easily performed.

IN COMPOUNDS

❑ **butter-boat** *n.* [SE *boat* + pun on SE *butter-boat*, a vessel in which one serves melted butter] [19C] the vagina. ❑ **butterbox** *n.* [Nares, perhaps prudishly, prefers the definition 'a woman's breast' ? but Rawson, *Dict. Invective* (1989), notes that F&H also include that definition (although they may be merely echoing Nares)] **1** [early 18C] the vagina. **2** *see also under* SE compounds below.

IN PHRASES

❑ **beat the butter** *v.* [1990s+] to masturbate. ❑ **churn butter** *v.* [1940s] to masturbate. ❑ **in the butter** [1950s] in difficulties. ❑ **make butter with one's tail** *v.* [TAIL *n.* (4)] [mid-17C] of woman, to have sexual intercourse.

SE in slang uses

IN COMPOUNDS

❑ **butter-and-egg** *v. see* separate entry. ❑ **butter baby** *n.* [BABY *n.* (3); one of a variety of sl. terms equating women with food + ? early use of BUTTER *adj.*[2]] [1980s+] (*US black*) **1** a woman, often a mulatto, who is considered sexy. **2** a woman with large breasts and buttocks. ❑ **butterbag** *n.* [stereotype of Dutch as butter-makers] [mid-17C] a Dutchman. ❑ **butterball** *n.* [SE *butter-ball*, a moulded ball of butter] [1940s+] an overweight or plump young person; also as adj. ❑ **butter-bean teeth** *n.* [resemblance of the teeth to the large white beans] [1960s–70s] buck teeth. ❑ **butterbox** *n.* [Dutch butter production and consumption] **1** [early 17C–mid-19C] a Dutchman; the Dutch language. **2** [late 17C] a fop [play on the 'softness' of butter]. **3** [1960s+] an effeminate male; also attrib. [play on the 'softness' of butter]. **4** [mid-19C] a German. **5** *see also under* slang compounds above. ❑ **butterboy** *n.* (*also* **butter-basher**) [orig. (1913) coined for novice taxidrivers; 'butter wouldn't melt in his mouth'] [1970s+] a novice, esp. a young police officer or a newly qualified taxi-driver. ❑ **butterbrain** *n.* [SE *butter* + sfx *-brain*/BUTTERFINGERS below] [1970s+] (*US*) a fool. ❑ **buttercup** *n.* **1** [late 19C–1920s] a pet name for a child. **2** [1920s] (*US*) a young boy. **3** [1930s–40s] an effeminate male homosexual. **4** [1960s] (*US*) a pretty young woman. ❑ **butterfingers** *n.* (*also* **butter-thumbs**) [mid-19C+] (*mainly juv.*) one who lets things slip through their fingers; thus adj. *butter-fingered*. ❑ **butter flower** *n.* [? the smooth cannabis resin] [1970s+] (*drugs*) marijuana. ❑ **butterhead** *n.* [SE or ? BUTTHEAD *under* BUTT *n.*[1]] **1** [1940s] (*US black*) a black person who, for whatever reason, is considered an embarrassment to their race. **2** [1950s+] (*US*) (*also* **butter gills**) a fool; thus *butterheaded*, foolish. ❑ **butterken** *n.* [KEN *n.*[1] (1)] [late 19C] (*US*) a shop. ❑ **butter mouth** *see* separate entries. ❑ **butternut** *n.* [the brown Confederate uniforms (worn in the West and which preceded their grey ones) which were dyed with the juice of the butternut] [mid–late 19C] (*US*) a Northern supporter of the Confederacy during the US Civil War. ❑ **butter pecan** *n.* [SE *butter pecan* ice-cream, which is light brown and sweet] [1990s+] (*US black teen*) an attractive Puerto Rican/Latino woman. ❑ **butter-print** *n.* [fig. use of SE *butter print*, a stamp of carved wood for marking butter-pats; the impression of such a stamp] [17C–early 18C] a baby, a child, esp. when illegitimate. ❑ **butter skin** *n.* [SKIN *n.*[1] (4)] [1930s+] (*US*) money. ❑ **butter teeth** *n.* [var. on BREAD-AND-BUTTER TEETH *under* BREAD-AND-BUTTER *adj.* or BUTTER-BEAN TEETH above] [17C+] (*US*) buck teeth. ❑ **butter-thumbs** *n. see* BUTTERFINGERS above. ❑ **butter tub** *n. see* TUB OF LARD *under* TUB *n.*[1]. ❑ **butter-weight** *n.* [SE *butter-weight*, 18oz (510g) or more to the pound, when the normal equivalent is 16oz (450g)] [early 18C] a good measure. ❑ **butter-whore** *n.* [late 16C–late 18C] an ill-tempered woman who sells butter. ❑ **butter wrapper** *n.* [late 19C] (*Aus.*) a newspaper.

IN PHRASES

❑ **butter-and-egg man** *n. see* separate entry. ❑ **butter-and-eggs trot** *n. see* separate entry. ❑ **have no butter in one's eyes** *v.* [early–mid-19C] to be well aware, to have no illusions.

butter *n.*[2] [BUTT *n.*[1] (1a)] [1980s+] (*US black*) the buttocks.

butter *adj.*[1] (*also* **butters**) [BUTT *n.*[1] (1a) + ? play on CHEESY *adj.*[2] (5); ? note BHUTTU *n.*] **1** [1970s] (*US*) naive, spoilt, foolish. **2** [1980s+] (*orig. US campus*) of an object or person, unfashionable, unsophisticated. **3** [1990s+] of a woman, unattractive.

butter *adj.*[2] (*also* **butta, buttah**) ['smooth as butter'] [1970s+] (*orig. US black/teen*) a general term of approval, attractive, excellent etc.

butter *v.* **1** [late 17C–late 18C] of a gambler, to increase one's wager. **2** [18C+] to flatter; thus to disguise with euphemism, flattery etc. **3** [19C] to whip, to thrash. **4** [1990s+] (*US campus*) to like.

IN PHRASES

❑ **butter up** *v.* (*also* **butter out**) [early 19C+] to flatter, to ingratiate oneself; thus *buttering up*, excessive flattery.

SE in slang uses

IN PHRASES

❑ **butter a bun** *v. see under* BUN *n.*[1]. ❑ **butter the fish** *v.* [ety. unknown; culinary imagery] [1920s] to win at cards. ❑ **butter the muffin** *v. see under* MUFFIN *n.*[2].

butter-and-egg *v.* [BUTTER-AND-EGG MAN *n.*] [1930s] (*US*) to act or pose as a wealthy provincial businessman or farmer.

butter-and-egg man *n.* (*also* **butter-and-egger, butter and egg salesman**) [the dairy products such men often sold. The term was popularized by the nightclub owner Marie Louise 'Texas' Guinan (1884–1933), otherwise celebrated for her invariable greeting, 'Hello sucker!' Columnist Walter Winchell attributed the term to master of ceremonies Harry Richman, while the original 'butter-and-egg man' was supposedly 'Uncle Sam' Balcon, a New York provisioner. The term was further popularized first by Louis Armstrong's song 'The Butter-and-Egg Man' (1924) and George S. Kaufman's similarly named play of 1925] [1920s–60s] (*US*) a prosperous farmer or small-town leading citizen who comes to the big city and poses embarrassingly as a playboy.

butter-and-eggs trot *n.* [based on the way market women make their way, carrying butter and eggs, into the weekly market] [late 18C] a short jog-trot.

buttered *adj.*[1] [BUTTER *v.* (3) and ext. use] **1** [mid–late 19C] (*US*) whipped, flogged. **2** [late 19C] subjected to sexual intercourse.

buttered *adj.*[2] [SE *butter* + sfx *-ed*, i.e. smooth] [1940s+] (*US black*) well-turned-out, elegant.

buttered *adj.*[3] [? fig. use of BUTTER *v.* (3)] [1990s+] drunk.

buttered bread *adj.* [rhy. sl.] [1990s+] dead.

buttered bun *n.*[1] [play on SE + BUTTER *n.*[1] (1) + BUN *n.*[1] (3a)] **1** [mid-17C+] (*also* **buttered scone**) a woman who has had intercourse with one man and is about to repeat this immediately with a new partner; thus *have* or *do* or *go in on the buttered bun/scone*, of a man, to take second place in a bout of serial intercourse. **2** [late 17C+] a mistress, a prostitute.

buttered bun *n.*[2] [early 18C] **1** a country fool, a rustic simpleton. **2** a drunken man.

buttered bun *n.*[3] (*also* **buttered scone**) [rhy. sl.] [1940s+] (*bingo*) the number one.

buttered eggs in one's breeches *n. see under* BREECHES *n.*

buttered scone *n.* **1** *see* BUTTERED BUN *n.*[1] (1). **2** *see* BUTTERED BUN *n.*[3].

butterface *n.* [i.e. *but her face*] [2000s] (*US black*) a female whose body is very attractive, but who has an unattractive face.

butter flap *n.* [rhy. sl.] [mid-19C] **1** a cap. **2** a trap or light carriage.

butterflies (in one's stomach) *n.* [the 'fluttering' sensation of adrenalin] [1940s] nerves, apprehension, tension.

butterfly *n.* [the perceived qualities of the insect] **1** [late 19C–1940s] an effeminate weakling. **2** [20C+] (*US*) an over-dressed, flashy person. **3** [1920s–30s] (*US*) a worthless cheque which 'flutters away'; thus *butterfly man*, one who passed such cheques. **4** [1930s–40s] (*orig. US black*) an attractive young woman [? ref. to black actress Thelma 'Butterfly' McQueen (1911–95) who played a weeping maid in the film *Gone With the Wind* 1939)]. **5** [1940s–60s] (*US campus*) a flirt; thus n. *butterflying*, flirting. **6** [1950s–60s] (*also* **butterfly boy**) an effeminate male homosexual. **7** [1980s] (*US gay*) a black homosexual. **8** [1990s+] (*US Und.*) a new, young and attractive prisoner, characterized as being potentially appealing to prison homosexuals. **9** *see* IRON BUTTERFLY *under* IRON *adj.* **10** *see* FLOATER *n.*[1] (1e).

butterfly *adj.* [BUTTERFLY *n.* (2)] [1900s] of clothes, gaudy, tasteless, flashy.

butterfly kiss *n.* [late 19C+] a 'kiss' made by fluttering one's eyelashes against one's partner's skin to caress it; also as v.

butterinsky *n. see* BUTTINSKI *n.*

buttermilk bottom *n.* [the stereotyped link between *buttermilk* and black appetites; the term was coined for the black section of Atlanta, Georgia, but spread to many towns and cities in the southern states] [1920s+] (*US black*) the black area of town.

buttermouth *n.* [nationalist stereotyping] [mid-16C–19C] a Dutchman.

butter mouth *v.* [BUTTER UP *under* BUTTER *v.*] [1990s+] (*US black*) to flatter.

butters *adj. see* BUTTER *adj.*[1].

buttery *adj.*[1] [BUTTER UP *under* BUTTER *v.*] [mid-19C] susceptible to flattery.

buttery *adj.*[2] [BUTTER *adj.*[1]] [1990s+] (*US campus*) bad.

buttery *adj.*[3] [BUTTER *adj.*[2]] [2000s] (*US black*) the best, first-rate.

buttfuck *n.* [lit. and fig. uses of BUTTFUCK *v.* (1)] **1** [1970s+] an act of anal intercourse. **2** [1980s+] a tedious piece of work, i.e. PAIN IN THE ARSE *n.* (2). **3** [1980s+] a disaster, a piece of victimization.

buttfuck *v.* (*also* **b.f., butt-bang**) [BUTT *n.*[1] (1a) + FUCK *v.* (1)] **1** [1960s+] (*US*) to subject to anal intercourse; thus derog. adj. *buttfucking*. **2** [1970s+] in fig. sense, to treat unfairly, to cheat, to deceive. **3** [1980s] (*US*) to injure.

buttfucker *n.* [BUTTFUCK *v.* (1)] (*US*) **1** [1960s+] (*also* **butt-banger**) one who indulges in anal intercourse. **2** [1970s+] a bully.

buttfucking Egypt *n. see* BUMFUCK, EGYPT *n.*

buttfuck motel *n.* [BUTTFUCK *n.* + SE *motel*; i.e. the frequency of sodomy in US prisons] [1990s+] (*US*) prison.

buttie *n. see* BUTTY *n.*[1].

butties *n. see* BUTT *n.*[1] (1a).

buttiken *n.* [? Fr. *boutique* + KEN *n.*[1] (1)] [mid–late 19C] a shop.

butt-in *n.* [BUTT IN *v.* (1)] [20C+] (*US*) **1** concern, affair, usu. in negative phr. *none of one's butt-in*. **2** a meddler, one who interferes. **3** a gatecrasher.

butt in *v.* (*also* **butt into**) [SE *butt*, to strike or push (with the head or horns)] [20C+] (*orig. US*) **1** to interfere, to make a nuisance of oneself. **2** to arrive.

buttinski *n.* (*also* **budinski, butterinsky, buttinsky**) [BUTT-IN *n.* (2) + -SKI *sfx*] [20C+] (*orig. US*) one who intrudes or interferes.

butt-kicker *n.* [BUTT *n.*[1] (1a) + SE *kicker*] [1980s+] (*US*) an outstanding performer at a pursuit.

butt-kicking *adj.* [BUTT-KICKER *n.*] [1980s+] (*US*) **1** outstanding. **2** strong, powerful, aggressive.

buttlick *n.* [BUTT *n.*[1] (1a) + SE *lick*] [1980s+] (*US campus*) **1** a fool. **2** a toady.

butt-licking *adj.* [BUTTLICK *n.* (2)] [1950s] servile, grovelling.

buttly *adj. see* BUTT-UGLY *under* BUTT *adv.*

buttock *n.* (*also* **buttocks**) [metonymy] [mid-16C–early 19C] (*UK Und.*) a prostitute, esp. one who dispenses her favours for free.

IN COMPOUNDS

❑ **buttock and file** *n.* [FILE *n.* (2); Ware and others define it as 'a shoplifter' but Partridge (*DU*) rejects this as erroneous] [17C–late 19C] a prostitute who doubles as a pickpocket, usu. with the help of her man. ❑ **buttock and tongue** *n.* [17C–early 19C] a shrewish woman. ❑ **buttock and twang** *n.* [TWANG *n.*[1] (2)] **1** [late 17C–early 19C] a prostitute who does not double as a pickpocket. **2** [18C] a robbery executed by a prostitute who lures a customer, picked up in a tavern, into a dark alley where she picks his pocket and her male accomplice knocks down the victim so that both can escape. ❑ **buttock-ball** *n. see* separate entry. ❑ **buttock-banqueting** *n.* [mid-16C–mid-17C] working as a prostitute. ❑ **buttock broker** *n.* [late 17C–early 19C] a brothel-keeper. ❑ **buttock jig** *n. see under* DANCE *v.*

IN PHRASES

❑ **down buttock and sham file** *n. see under* DOWN *adj.*[1].
❑ **go buttock-stirring** *v.* [19C] to have sexual intercourse.

SE in slang uses

IN COMPOUNDS

❑ **buttock and trimmings** *n.* [late 18C–early 19C] an Irish wager, a rump of beef and a dozen of claret. ❑ **buttock penance** *n.* [early 18C] a caning or thrashing at school.

buttock *v.* [BUTTOCK *n.*] [18C] to have sexual intercourse.

IN COMPOUNDS

❑ **buttock mail** *n.* [SE *mail*, payment, tax] [16C–early 19C] a fine imposed for fornication. ❑ **buttocking shop** *n.* [SE *shop*/SHOP *n.*[1] (1)] [early 19C] a brothel.

IN PHRASES

❑ **go buttocking** *v.* [18C] to have sexual intercourse.

buttock-ball *n.* [BUTTOCK *n.* + SE *ball*; the 'Buttock Ball in St Giles', held weekly and described by Ned Ward, *A Compleat and Humorous Account of All the Remarkable Clubs and Societies* (1709) as 'this School of *Venus*' and a '*Diabolical Academy*', is attended by 'a mottl'd Diversity of Rakes, Beaus, grave Hypocrites, and Apprentices; Pimps, Bullies, Stallions, Valets, Butlers, and disguis'd Livery-Men; Thieves, Gamesters, Sweetners, Town Traps and Highwaymen; Procurers, Punks, Cooks, Jades and Chambermaids; damn'd filing Whores, sill Sows and Fireships; lewd Widows, wicked Wives and whorish Daughters; these Larded, by Chance, with here and there, a maid, but the fewest of that Sport of any.' Ward suggests that the first such dance was held 'by the Cole-Yard Gateway into *Drury-Lane*', then a centre of prostitution, c.1670] **1** [late 17C–early 18C] a dance at which the chief aim is to find sexual partners, the 18C equivalent of a MEAT MARKET *n.* (1). **2** [late 18C–early 19C] sexual intercourse.

buttocking *adj.* [BUTTOCK *v.*] [late 17C–mid-18C] promiscuous, whorish.

buttocks *n. see* BUTTOCK *n.*

button *n.*[1] [all f. shape and/or size of SE *button*] **1** fig., as a part of the body. (**a**) [late 17C] the penis. (**b**) [19C+] a baby's penis. (**c**) [20C+] (*also* **bell**) the clitoris. (**d**) [1910s+] the chin, esp. in phr. *on the button*, a blow square on the chin. (**e**) [1920s–70s] (*US*) a man's or woman's nipple; occas. an animal's, e.g. a pig. (**f**) [1930s] a pimple. **2** from the circular shape. (**a**) [late 18C–mid-19C] a counterfeit shilling. (**b**) [19C] a shilling (5p). (**c**) [mid-19C] (*also* **shiny button**) any coin. (**d**) [1940s] (*US black campus*) money. (**e**) [1940s] (*US Und.*) a form of confidence-trick in which a criminal posing as a detective accuses the victim of passing counterfeit money and confiscates it for 'examination'. (**f**) [1950s] (*US Und.*) in pl., derisively small amounts, e.g. of money, stolen goods. **3** [1950s] (*US street gang*) a switchblade knife, which is activated by a button on the handle. **4** in drugs uses. (**a**) [1960s] (*drugs*) a capsule containing heroin or opium. (**b**) [1960s] peyote. (**c**) [1960s+] (*S.Afr. drugs*) a Mandrax (methaqualone) tablet; thus *button-kop* (lit. *button-head*), a regular Mandrax user.

IN COMPOUNDS

❑ **button finger** *n.* [sense 1c + SE *finger*; pun on BUTTERFINGERS *under* BUTTER *n.*[1]] [1990s+] the finger used by a woman to masturbate herself or her partner. ❑ **buttonhole** *n. see* separate entry.

SE in slang uses

IN COMPOUNDS

❑ **button B** *adj.* [the old payphones, where one could push *button B* in the hope of redeeming some other caller's forgotten change] [1930s–50s] penniless. ❑ **button boy** *n.* [his button-adorned uniform] [late 19C+] a (hotel) page. ❑ **button bung** *n.* [BUNG *n.*[1] (3)] [17C] a button thief. ❑ **button-buster** *n.* [1940s–60s] (*orig. US black*) a braggart or boaster, a loudmouth. ❑ **button-down** *adj. see* separate entry. ❑ **button jock** *n.* [JOCK *n.*[2] (3)] [1980s+] anyone who operates a console. ❑ **button lurk** *n.* [LURK *n.* (3)] [1910s] (*Aus.*) a trick played on a naïve woman by a man, bent on intercourse, who removes a button from his coat and promises that it will serve adequately as a contraceptive pessary. ❑ **button music** *n.* [it is played on machines, with buttons, rather than live instruments] [2000s] house music.

IN PHRASES

❑ **button short, a** *adj.* (*also* **a button loose, ...missing**) [var. on NOT ALL THERE *adj.*] [20C+] eccentric, one of many phrs. implying the subject is 'not all there'. ❑ **get off the button** *v.* [1930s] (*US*) to experience orgasm, to relieve sexual tension. ❑ **have all one's buttons on** *v.* (*also* **know one's buttons**) [late 19C–1960s] to be 'sharp', to know what is going on, to be impervious to hoaxers. ❑ **hit the button** *v.* [20C+] of a person, to talk aptly or pertinently; of a thing, to be pertinent. ❑ **loose a button** *v.* [fly buttons] [1940s] (*Irish*) to urinate. ❑ **lost a button** *adj.* [19C+] eccentric, crazy. ❑ **not have all one's buttons** *v.* [mid-19C+] to lack intelligence, to be slightly eccentric or odd. ❑ **not worth a button** *adj.* [mid-17C–19C] worthless, useless. ❑ **one's arse makes buttons** *v.* (*also* **one's ass makes buttons, one's breech..., one's buttocks..., one's tail...**) [SE *buttons*, dung (usu. of animals); the image is of one's involuntarily soiling one's trousers through fear/ARSE *n.* (1)/ASS *n.* (2)/TAIL *n.* (2)] [mid-16C–early 19C; 1980s] one is terrified, or jittery. ❑ **on the button** *adj.* **1** [20C+] right on target, usu. of a blow. **2** [20C+] up to the minute, fully aware. **3** [1920s+] exactly on time, as required. ❑ **pop one's buttons** *v. see* BUST ONE'S BUTTONS *under* BUST *v.*[1]. ❑ **press someone's button** *v.* (*also* **press someone's buttons, press the right buttons, push...**) **1** [1960s+] to make someone feel special, turned on, loved etc. **2** [1970s+] to manipulate someone emotionally, usu. to annoy, to irritate. ❑ **press the button** *v.* **1** [1910s+] to set an event or a chain of circumstances in motion. **2** [1920s] to shoot. ❑ **press the panic button** *v.* (*also* **push the panic button**) [1950s+] (*orig. US*) to panic. ❑ **push the button on** *v.* [1950s] (*US*) to murder. ❑ **sweet as a button** *adj. see* SWEET AS (A) NUT *under* SWEET *adj.*[1]. ❑ **want one's hip buttons** *v.* [20C+] (*Ulster*) to be less than wholly intelligent.

button *n.*[2] **1** [mid-18C–late 19C] any form of illicit decoy; esp. a confederate of those running a game of THREE-CARD MONTE *n.* or THIMBLE-RIG *n.* [? fig. use of SE *button*, something small and worthless]. **2** [1940s+] (*US Und.*) a lookout [? BUTTON MAN *under* BUTTON *n.*[4]].

button *n.*[3] [they are 'bright as a button'] [1910s] (*US*) a bright, cheeky person.

button *n.*[4] [1970s+] (*US Und.*) the status of being in a US Mafia 'family'; usu. as *get one's button*.

IN COMPOUNDS

❑ **button man** *n.* (*also* **button guy**) [1960s+] (*US*) a lower echelon member of a Mafia family; thus *earn a button*, to be made a member of the Mafia.

IN PHRASES

❑ **half a button** *n.* [1970s] (*US Und.*) a criminal who is on the fringe of full membership of the US Mafia.

button *n.*[5] *see* BUTTONS *n.* (1b).

button *v.* **1** [mid-19C+] (*UK Und.*) to act as a confidence trickster's accomplice, a decoy [BUTTON *n.*[2] (1)]. **2** [1910s] of a trick, a ploy, to work [BUTTON *n.*[2] (1)]. **3** [1990s+] (*US prison*) to keep a lookout [BUTTON *n.*[2] (2)].

IN PHRASES

❑ **button it** *v. see* BUTTON ONE'S LIP *v.* ❑ **button one's lip** *v. see* separate entry. ❑ **button on to** *v.* [the grabbing of the jacket buttons] [1900s–10s] to grab hold of someone before forcing oneself on their company, whether they like it or not. ❑ **button up** *v.* [fig. uses of SE; orig. US stockbrocker jargon] **1** [mid-19C+] to be quiet. **2** [20C+] (*US*) to quit work for the day; also as *button up the day*. **3** [1900s] (*Aus.*) of a person, to keep hold of their money. **4** [1930s] (*US prison*) to place in solitary confinement. **5** [1950s–60s] to close, to shut down, to withhold information.

button-down *adj.* (*also* **buttoned-down**) [the button-down collared shirts from Brooks Brothers (New York) that are the uniform of the US business establishment] [1950s+] (*US*) conforming, holding establishment, conservative values.

buttoned up *adj.* [all fig. uses of SE] **1** [1930s+] (*also* **buttoned**) silent. **2** [1940s+] (*also* **buttoned**) all prepared, sorted satisfactorily. **3** [1950s+] (*also* **buttoned down**) repressed.

buttoner *n.* [BUTTON *n.*[2] (1)] (*Aus./UK Und.*) **1** [mid-19C] a decoy. **2** [mid-19C+] the member of a gang running a game of THREE-CARD MONTE *n.* who persuades passers by to bet on the inevitably fraudulent game. **3** [late 19C] in ext. use, referring to any crooked businessman.

buttonhole *n.* **1** [mid-18C–late 19C] the vagina. **2** [1950s] a female.

IN COMPOUNDS

❑ **buttonhole factory** *n.* [19C] a brothel. ❑ **buttonhole worker** *n.* [19C] **1** the penis. **2** a womanizer, a promiscuous man; thus *buttonhole working*, sexual intercourse.

SE in slang uses

IN COMPOUNDS

❑ **buttonhole cousin** *n.* (*also* **buttonhole connection, buttonhole relation**) [ety. unknown; ? one SE *buttonholes* them and claims a relationship] [20C+] (*US*) a distant relation (e.g. a third or fourth cousin), a family friend.

button one's lip *v.* (*also* **button it, button one's chin, ...face, ...flap, ...gabber, ...gob, ...kisser, ...lipper, ...mouth, ...nose, ...trap, ...yap**) [SE *button* + SE *lip/chin/face*/FLAP *n.*[1] (8)/GABBER *n.*[1]/GOB *n.*[1] (1)/SE *lipper/mouth/nose*/TRAP *n.*[1] (4)/YAP *n.*[1] (1a)] **1** [20C+] to be quiet, to stop talking; thus *keep one's lip buttoned*, to keep quiet. **2** [1950s] to make someone keep quiet.

buttons *n.* [their uniforms] **1** as part of a uniform. (**a**) [mid-19C+] a page-boy, a doorman. (**b**) [late 19C+] a police officer, occas. sing. **2** [mid-19C+] in fig. sense, brains, native wit; esp.

as phrs. *not have all one's buttons, not have a full row of buttons, have a few buttons missing, not have (got) all one's buttons on, be a button short, have lost one's buttons*, to not be very intelligent; *have all one's buttons done up*, to be smart, to be aware, 'on the ball'. **3** [1960s+] (*drugs*) mescaline; peyote, which is synthesized from *peyote buttons*. **4** [1990s+] (*US teen*) a television remote control.

(IN EXCLAMATIONS)

❑ **dash my buttons!** (*also* **dang/darn/doggone my buttons!**) *see under* DASH! *excl.*

buttons and bows *n.* [rhy. sl.] [20C+] (*Aus.*) toes.

butt out *v.* [SE *butt* v.] [20C+] **1** to leave; fig., to stop interfering. **2** (*W.I.*) to emerge, to come out of a passage or hidden place.

butt out! *excl.* [BUTT *n.*[1] (1c) + SE *out*] [1910s+] go away! leave me alone!

butty *n.*[1] (*also* **butt, buttie**) [orig. dial.] [mid-19C+] (*mainly UK north*) a friend, a 'mate'.

butty *n.*[2] [SE *butt*(*ered bread*)] [20C+] (*mainly UK north*) a sandwich; thus *jam butty, chip butty* etc.

butty *n.*[3] [? BUTT *n.*[1] (4)] [1980s+] (*Aus. drugs/prison*) hashish.

butty *adj.* **1** [20C+] (*Irish*) short [BUTT *n.*[1] (1a)]. **2** muscular.

buvare *n.* [Polari] [mid–late 19C] a drink.

buxom *n.* [ety. unknown] [mid–late 18C] (*UK Und.*) a sixpence.

Buxton bloaters *n.* [proper name *Buxton*, the popular medicinal springs at Derbyshire + SE *bloat*(*ed*)] [late 19C–1900s] overweight invalids, wheeling around in bath chairs while they take the medicinal waters.

Buxton limp *n.* [the popular medicinal springs at *Buxton*, Derbyshire] [late 19C–1900s] the hobbling walk affected by invalids taking the waters.

buy *n.* [1930s+] (*drugs*) **1** the purchase of a drug. **2** money required to purchase a quantity of drugs.

buy *v.* **1** [1910s+] (*also* **buy into**) to accept, to believe; often in phr. *I'll buy that*, I can accept that, or *do you think he'll buy it?* do you think he'll be persuaded? **2** [1930s+] (*orig. US*) to cause, to make happen, to bring upon oneself.

SE in slang uses

(IN COMPOUNDS)

❑ **buy-up** *n.* [1980s] (*Aus. prison*) a prisoner's weekly allowance and the purchases they make.

(IN PHRASES)

❑ **buy...** *v. see also under* relevant n. ❑ **buy a drink** *v.* [1940s] (*US*) to pour a drink. ❑ **buy a woof ticket** *v.* (*also* **buy a wolf ticket**) [WOOF *v.*[1]] [1980s+] (*US black*) to capitulate to verbal intimidation. ❑ **buy into** *v. see* sense 1 above. ❑ **buy it** *v.* [one prior citation exists for 1825, but nothing follows for a century; WW1 use is abbr. *buy a packet*] **1** [early 19C; 1920s+] to suffer a mishap, esp. to die or be badly hurt. **2** [1920s+] of an inanimate object, to be broken or destroyed. ❑ **buy new shoes** *v. see under* SHOE *n.* ❑ **buy one's boots in Crooked Lane and one's stockings in Bandy-legged Walk** *v.* [late 18C–early 19C] to have bandy legs. ❑ **buy on the never tick** *v. see under* TICK *n.*[3]. ❑ **buy out** *v.* [1950s] (*US*) to escape, to avoid a predicament. ❑ **buy someone a hat** *v.* [euph.] [1910s+] (*US*) to bribe someone. ❑ **buy someone's thirst** *v.* [late 19C] (*orig. US*) to pay for someone's drink. ❑ **buy the baby (new) shoes** *v. see under* SHOE *n.* ❑ **buy the farm** *v. see* separate entry. ❑ **buy the sack** *v.* [SE *sack*, a variety of white wine imported from Spain and the Canaries] [early 18C–early 19C] to get drunk.

buyer *n.* [20C+] (*UK Und./police*) a receiver of stolen goods.

buy the farm *v.* (*also* **buy the mall, ...ranch, ...six-by-three farm, buy a plot**) [orig. US Air Force use: 'Jet pilots say that when a jet crashes on a farm the farmer usually sues the government for damage done to his farm by the crash, and the amount demanded is always more than enough to pay off the mortgage and then buy the farm outright. Since this type of crash (i.e. in a jet fighter) is nearly always fatal to the pilot, the pilot pays for the farm with his life' from 1955 Leo F. Engler 'A Glossary of Air Force Slang' in *American Speech* Vol XXX No 2 116. Note RAF sl. *bought it*, ult. f. WW1 *bought a packet*] [1950s+] to die.

buz *n.* **1** *see* BUZZ *n.* (1a). **2** *see* BUZZ *n.* (2).

(IN COMPOUNDS)

❑ **buz bloak** *n.* [BUZZ *n.* (2c) + BLOKE *n.* (3)] [mid-19C] (*UK Und.*) a pickpocket who specializes in loose cash and purses (as opposed to jewellery or handkerchiefs). ❑ **buz cove** *n.* [BUZZ *n.* (2c) + COVE *n.* (1)] [early 19C] (*UK Und.*) a pickpocket. ❑ **buz-faker** *n.* [BUZZ *n.* (2c) + FAKER *n.*; given the victim is a drunkard, note BOOZE *n.* (1)] [19C] a pickpocket, esp. one who makes the victims drunk before robbing them. ❑ **buz-faking** *n.* (*also* **buzz-faking**) [BUZZ *n.* (2c) + FAKE *v.*[1] (4)] [19C] picking pockets. ❑ **buz-gloak** *n.* (*also* **buzz-gloak**) [BUZZ *n.* (2c) + GLOAK *n.*] [19C] (*UK Und.*) a pickpocket. ❑ **buz-knacker** *n.* (*also* **buzz-knacker**) [BUZZ *n.* (2b) + SE *knacker*, a harness maker and (?) a maker of small (harness-related) articles] [mid-19C] a trainer of young pickpockets. ❑ **buzman** *n.* (*also* **buzzman**) [BUZZ *n.* (2c) + SE *man*] [late 18C–mid-19C] (*UK Und.*) a pickpocket. ❑ **buz-napper** *n. see* BUS-NAPPER *n.* ❑ **buz-napper's academy** *n. see* BUS-NAPPER'S ACADEMY *under* BUS-NAPPER *n.*

buz *v.*[1] (*also* **buzz**) [? BOOZE *v.* (1)] [mid-19C] to share the last bottle of wine equally among all drinkers, when there is not enough for a whole glass each.

buz *v.*[2] *see* BUZZ *v.*[1] (3).

buzhie *n. see* BOOJEE *n.*

buznacking *n. see* BUSNACKING *n.*

buz-wig *n.* [SE *buzz-wig*, a large, bushy wig] [mid-19C] a pompous fool.

buzwuz *n.* [echoic of droning speech] [late 19C] nonsense.

buzz *n.* **1** as speech [BUZZ *v.*[1] (1); note WW1 UK army *buzzer*, a signaller]. (**a**) [17C+] (*also* **buz**) chatter, conversation. (**b**) [1910s+] a rumour. (**c**) [1920s+] a telephone call; usu. as *give someone a buzz* below. (**d**) [1930s] (*US Und.*) an exploratory conversation. (**e**) [1930s] (*US Und.*) a warning. (**f**) [1930s+] (*US*) a call on an intercom. **2** (*also* **buz**) in UK cant; the image is of a 'buzzing' thief that 'stings' their victim. (**a**) [early 18C] a thief. (**b**) [early 18C–mid-19C] a pickpocket. (**c**) [late 18C–mid-19C] the picking of pockets. (**d**) [1950s] (*US Und.*) purse-snatching. **3** as a physical sensation, a 'buzz in the head' [ext. of SE; i.e. a sense of heightened emotion]. (**a**) [late 19C+] (*orig. US*) a thrill, a feeling of excitement. (**b**) [1930s+] (*orig. US*) a (usu.) pleasant sensation from drinking. (**c**) [1930s+] the immediate response to taking a drug, esp. barbiturates or cannabis. (**d**) [1970s] (*drugs*) PCP. (**e**) [1970s+] any form of sensation, good or bad. **4** [1980s+] (*US*) a close haircut, given with electric clippers.

(IN COMPOUNDS)

❑ **buzz...** for combs. pertaining to pickpocketing, *see under* BUZ *n.* ❑ **buzz bomb** *n.* [BOMB *n.* (7a) + pun on SE *buzz-bomb*, a flying bomb] **1** [1940s] (*US*) any sort of strong cocktail. **2** [1980s+] (*US drugs*) nitrous oxide. ❑ **buzz cruncher** *n.* (*also* **buzz crusher, buzz stripper**) [SE *crunch/crush/strip*] [1980s+] (*US campus*) anything that destroys a feeling of euphoria. ❑ **buzzkill** *n. see* separate entry. ❑ **buzzman** *n.* [mid-19C–1950s] (*US Und.*) an informer. ❑ **buzzstomp** *n. see* BUZZKILL *n.*

(IN PHRASES)

❑ **catch a buzz** *v.* [CATCH *v.*[1] (2b)] [1970s] to start experiencing the (pleasurable) effects of alcohol or a given drug. ❑ **cop a buzz** *v.* [COP *v.* (3c)] [1970s+] (*US*) to get drunk, to get 'high' on a drug. ❑ **give someone a buzz** *v.* **1** [1910s] (*US Und.*) to promise, to assure. **2** [1920s+] to call someone on the telephone. **3** [1950s+] to excite, to thrill (usu. sexually). ❑ **give someone the buzz** *v.* [1960s] to run away from, to elude. ❑ **have a buzz on** *v.* (*also* **get a buzz on**) **1** [1930s+] (*orig. US*) to be drinking and mildly intoxicated but not drunk. **2** [1960s+] (*orig. US*) to be slightly intoxicated from drugs. ❑ **kill someone's buzz** *v.* (*also* **stomp someone's buzz**) [1980s+] (*US campus*) to depress someone, to destroy someone's enjoyment or pleasure, to disappoint someone. ❑ **on the buzz** *adj.* [1920s] busy, excited. ❑ **put the buzz on** *v.* [1920s] (*US*) to pressurize, to bribe. ❑ **rape someone's buzz** *v.* [RAPE *v.* (2)] [1980s+] (*US campus*) to put a damper on someone's pleasure.

IN EXCLAMATIONS

❑ **buzzkill!** *see* separate entry. ❑ **buzzstomp!** *see* BUZZKILL! *excl.*

SE in slang uses

IN COMPOUNDS

❑ **buzz-box** *n.* [the sound of the engine] [1920s–30s] an automobile. ❑ **buzz buggy** *n.* [the sound of the engine + BUGGY *n.*[2] (1)] [1910s–40s] (*US*) an automobile, esp. a cheap one. ❑ **buzzwagon** *n.* [the noise] [1900s–60s] an automobile.

buzz *v.*[1] **1** in the context of speech [SE *buzz*, echoic of the bee]. (**a**) [late 16C+] (*also* **buzz it up**) to talk about, to gossip, to promote a rumour; to inform on. (**b**) [mid-19C–1960s] (*US*) to question, to interview; to intimidate. (**c**) [mid-19C+] (*US*) to flirt with. (**d**) [late 19C] (*US*) to scold, to tell off. (**e**) [1900s–20s] to speak. (**f**) [1910s–20s] (*Aus./US tramp*) to solicit handouts, to beg. (**g**) [1910s+] to telephone or to use an intercom. (**h**) [1950s–60s] (*US*) to irritate. **2** [18C+] to make a move: to go, to arrive, to leave, to depart; usu. in comb. with a prep; also as *give the buzz*, to get away from, to lose. **3** (*also* **buz**) in the context of crime [BUZZ *n.* (2)]. (**a**) [late 18C+] to pick pockets. (**b**) [late 19C] in fig. use, to cheat. (**c**) [1950s] (*US Und.*) to work as a purse-snatcher. **4** [1920s+] to happen. **5** [1950s] to make, to prepare, to put on. **6** [1950s+] to become lively, energetic, esp. of the atmosphere at a party or the performance of a rock band. **7** [1960s] (*US black*) to gaze at admiringly. **8** [1960s+] to experience a drug pleasurably [BUZZ *n.* (3)]. **9** [1960s+] to swoop on, in an aircraft or vehicle. **10** [2000s] (*US*) to fail to stop at a red traffic light.

IN PHRASES

❑ **buzz a chariot** *v.* [1930s] (*US Und.*) to pickpocket the passengers on public transport. ❑ **buzz around like a blue-arsed fly** *v.* (*also* **run around like a blue-arsed fly**) [late 19C+] to be excessively busy, often to the detriment of others, to rush around headlong. ❑ **buzz in** *v.* [antonym of BUZZ OFF *v.*] [1930s] to arrive, to enter. ❑ **buzz it** *v.* [BUZZ *n.* (3)] [1950s] (*US*) to relax, to stay calm. ❑ **buzz it up** *v. see* sense 1a above. ❑ **buzz off** *v. see* separate entry. ❑ **what's buzzin' cousin?** (*also* **what's buzzin'?**) [1940s–50s] (*US*) what's happening? how have you been?

IN EXCLAMATIONS

❑ **buzz off!** *see* separate entry.

buzz *v.*[2] [? BOOZE *v.*] [early 18C–19C] to drain a glass or bottle.

buzz *v.*[3] [echoic] [late 19C+] to throw (hard).

buzz *v.*[4] [SE *buss*] [1940s–60s] (*US black*) to kiss.

buzz *v.*[5] *see* BUZ *v.*[1].

buzza *v.* [? BUZZ *v.*[2] + SE *all*] [late 18C] to challenge someone to empty what remains of a bottle into their glass and then to drink it all down.

buzzard *n.* [all fig. uses of SE] **1** [late 16C–late 19C] a weak foolish person, a gullible dupe; thus adj. *buzzardly*. **2** [19C+] an old and unattractive person; often as *old buzzard*. **3** [mid-19C+] (*US*) a native of the state of Georgia. **4** [late 19C] (*US*) a silver dollar [the eagle inscribed on it]. **5** [1900s] (*US*) a filthy child. **6** [1900s] (*US milit.*) an honourable discharge. **7** [1900s–40s] (*US*) a worthless horse. **8** [1910s] (*US Und.*) a police officer. **9** [1910s–30s] (*US tramp*) a second-rate thief; one who preys on women. **10** [1920s] an unpleasant person. **11** [1920s–30s] (*US Und.*) a beggar, the lowest form of tramp. **12** [1930s] (*US*) an aviator. **13** [1940s] (*US army*) chicken. **14** [1950s–60s] an animal, a creature. **15** [1980s] an unattractive woman.

SE in slang uses

IN COMPOUNDS

❑ **buzzard bait** *n.* [mid-19C+] (*US*) **1** a corpse abandoned in the open; by ext. a person fated for death or otherwise doomed. **2** a scraggy old horse. ❑ **buzzard-meat** *n.* [late 19C–1930s] (*US*) **1** a corpse abandoned in the open. **2** a person fated for death or otherwise doomed. ❑ **buzzard roost** *n.* (*also* **buzzard's roost**) [the slaughterhouse area, where buzzards gathered to eat the discarded entrails] **1** [late 19C–1940s] (*US*) a run-down or disreputable place, also as *Buzzard's Row*. **2** [1920s–40s] (*US, Southern*) the top gallery in a theatre, usu. reserved for blacks.

IN PHRASES

❑ **harvest buzzard** *n.* [SE *harvest*] [1920s] (*US tramp*) a thief who robs seasonal workers. ❑ **storm-buzzard** *n.* [1930s–40s] (*US black*) a homeless or unemployed person, a beggar.

buzzed *adj.* [BUZZ *n.* (3)] [1950s+] **1** mildly drunk, tipsy. **2** (*also* **buzzed out**) mildly intoxicated by a drug. **3** excited.

buzzed out *adj.* [BUZZ *n.* (3)] **1** [1980s] tipsy. **2** [1980s+] (*US drugs*) asleep or in a stupor from taking so many drugs, or so much of one drug. **3** *see* BUZZED *adj.* (2).

buzzer *n.*[1] [BUZZ *v.*[1] (3)] **1** [early 19C+] a pickpocket. **2** [late 19C] (*UK Und.*) a confidence trickster, who fools a shopkeeper into parting with a gold sovereign using sleight of hand and some hidden wax.

buzzer *n.*[2] [the noise it makes] [late 19C–1900s] any form of automobile.

buzzer *n.*[3] [the officer SE *buzzes* it in one's face; Irwin, *American Tramp and Und. Slang* (1931), suggests a link to BUZZ *v.*[1] (1d)] [1910s+] (*US*) a police or private detective's badge.

buzzer *n.*[4] [? he *buzzes* around] [1990s+] a male homosexual.

buzzie *n.* [the dilapidated *buses* which some travellers use] [2000s] (*Irish*) a traveller.

buzzimag *n.* [BUZZ *v.*[1] (1a) + MAG *n.*[5] (1)] [mid-19C] (*UK Und.*) evidence against a prisoner, including the charge.

buzzing *n.* (*also* **buzzing lay, fly-buzzing**) [BUZZ *v.*[1] (3a)/LAY *n.*[3] (1)/FLY *n.*[2]] [19C+] stealing, esp. picking pockets.

buzzing *adj.* [BUZZ *v.*[1]] **1** [1920s+] exciting, active. **2** [2000s] (*US campus*) drunk.

buzzkill *n.* (*also* **buzzstomp**) [BUZZ *n.* (1) + SE kill/*stomp*]] [1980s+] (*US campus*) **1** an unpleasant experience or event. **2** an unpleasant person, esp. one who ruins a hitherto enjoyable time.

buzzkill! *excl.* (*also* **buzzstomp!**) [BUZZKILL *n.*] [1980s+] (*US campus*) a general excl. of disappointment and irritation, e.g. too bad! that's awful!

buzzlug lecture rooms *n.* [BUZZ *v.*[1] (1a) + LUG *n.*[1] (1), i.e. the judge's sentence and/or lawyers' pleading] [mid-19C] (*UK Und.*) the Old Bailey.

buzznacking *n. see* BUSNACKING *n.*

buzz off *v.* [BUZZ *v.*[1] (2) + ext. of SE; i.e. image of busy bees] **1** [20C+] to leave, to depart. **2** [1960s] in fig. use, to die.

buzz off! *excl.* [BUZZ OFF *v.*] **1** [20C+] go away! **2** [1910s] in fig. use: don't make me laugh! shut up! don't talk nonsense! **3** [1940s] (*US campus*) be quiet!

buzzy *n.* (*also* **boosy**) [SE *bosom*] [1970s+] the female breasts, usu. in pl. as *buzzies*.

buzzy *adj.*[1] [BOUSY *adj.*] [mid-18C; 2000s] (*US; later use N.Z.*) tipsy.

buzzy *adj.*[2] [? 'bees in one's bonnet'] [late 19C–1930s] crazy, eccentric.

buzzy *adj.*[3] [BUZZ *n.* (3a)] [2000s] thrilling.

buzzy house *n.* [BUZZY *adj.*[2] + SE *house*] [1900s] (*US*) a lunatic asylum.

b.v.d. *n.* [the initial letters of the name of its manufacturers, *Bradley, Voorhees & Day*] [1910s+] (*US*) male underpants.

b.v.h. *n.* [abbr. *b*lue *v*eined *h*ooligan] [1990s+] the penis.

bwai/bway *n. see* BWOY *n.*

B-way *n.* (*also* **B'way**) [abbr.] [mid-19C+] (*US*) *Broadway*, New York City.

bwider-pink *n.* [ety. unknown] [mid-19C] (*UK Und.*) a thief's lookout.

bwiff *v.* [ety. unknown] [mid-19C] (*UK Und.*) to raise the alarm.

b.w.o.c. *n. see* B.M.O.C. *n.*

bwoy *n.* (*also* **bwai, bway**) [W.I. pron. of SE *boy*] (*W.I./UK black*) **1** [late 19C+] a boy. **2** [1940s+] a general excl. of excitement, pleasure. **3** [1980s+] a general excl. of surprise, disdain.

IN PHRASES

❑ **sweet bwai** *n.* [SE *sweet*] [1970s–80s] (*UK black*) a ghetto dandy; a womanizer.

by *adj. see* BI *adj.*

by *prep.* [? Yid. form., e.g. *by me it's OK*] [1920s+] in one's opinion, as far as one is concerned, e.g. *by me, by you, by us.*

by...! *excl. see also under* relevant n. or adj.

by-blow *n.* (*also* **bye-blow, bystart**) [SE *by-blow*, anything that happens, usu. unfortunate, in parallel to the main thrust of one's life or intentions. Ware also suggests Fr. *bibelot*, a rare, precious small *objet d'art*. SE f. 1800] [late 16C–early 19C] a bastard.

byce *n. see* BICE *n.*

by-chop *n.* [var. on BY-BLOW *n.*] [17C; 1990s+] a bastard.

bye *n.*

SE in slang uses

IN COMPOUNDS

❑ **bye-banter** *n.* [mid-19C] (*UK Und.*) a story told while a confederate robs the listener. ❑ **bye-cogger** *n.* [COGGER *n.*] [mid-19C] (*UK Und.*) an old pimp. ❑ **bye-drink** *n.* [SE *bye and/the bye*] [mid-18C–late 19C] an alcoholic drink, taken other than at mealtimes.

IN PHRASES

❑ **bye-baby slum** *n.* [one's tone is reminiscent of singing a lullaby (i.e. 'bye-baby') + SLUM *n.*[2] (1)] [mid-19C] (*UK Und.*) begging in a wheedling manner.

bye-blow *n. see* BY-BLOW *n.*

bye-bye(s) *n.* [earlier nursery use *bye-bye*, sleep] **1** [mid-19C+] sleep, unconsciousness. **2** [1940s] a pain killer.

IN PHRASES

❑ **go to bye-bye(s)** *v.* **1** [mid-19C+] (*also* **go by-by**) to go to sleep. **2** [2000s] to leave. ❑ **put someone to bye-bye** *v.* [1930s] (*UK Und.*) to knock unconscious; to kill.

by-god *adj.* **1** [late 19C+] (*US*) a general intensifier, e.g. *the by-god worst thing ever.* **2** [1970s] as infix.

by Gorrah! *excl. see* BEGORRA! *excl.*

by jagers!/by Japers! *excl. see* BEJABERS! *excl.*

by-jesus *adj.* [1950s] a euph. for DAMN *adj.*

byke *n.* [BI *adj.* + DYKE *n.*] [1990s+] (*US gay*) a lesbian who is also bisexual.

Byker tea-cake *n.* [the *Byker*, a tough area of Newcastle] [1990s+] a head butt.

by korry! *excl. see* PY KORRY! *excl.*

by much *phr. see* NOT MUCH *phr.*

by nails! *excl. see* NAILS! *excl.*

b.y.o. *phr.* [abbr.; the *l* of *b.y.o.l.* has been extended to such usages as bring your own *l*unch, bring your own *l*aptop etc] [1960s+] (*Aus./US*) bring your own, refers to bringing drinks to a party or an unlicensed restaurant; thus in ext. use to refer to anything other than alcohol; var. uses: *b.y.o.b., bring your own bottle or booze*; b.y.o.g., *bring your own grog*; b.y.o.l., *bring your own liquor.*

byr'lakin! *excl. see* BY OUR LAKIN! *under* LAKIN *n.*[1].

by-scape *n.* [SE *by-*, aside + abbr. *escape*] [mid-17C] a bastard.

bystart *n. see* BY-BLOW *n.*

b.y.t. *phr.* [abbr.; the orig. *bright young people/things* flourished in the 1920s–30s] [2000s] *bright young things.*

by the jappers! *excl. see* BEJABERS! *excl.*

b'zillion *n. see* ZILLION *n.*

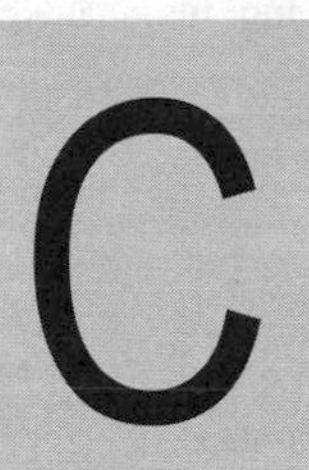

C *n.*[1] [abbr. CUNT *n.* (1)] [19C] the vagina.

C *n.*[2] [SE *century*; Roman numerals] [mid-19C+] (*US*) $100.

IN PHRASES

□ **half-a-C** *n.* (*also* **half-C**) [1930s+] (*orig. US Und.*) a 50-dollar note.

C *n.*[3] (*also* **cee**) [abbr.] **1** [1920s+] (*drugs*) cocaine. **2** [1990s+] as *the C*, methcathinone.

C *n.*[4] **1** *see* BIG C *n.* (2). **2** *see* CHARLIE *n.*

c.a. *n.* [abbr.] [1950s] (*US*) a county attorney.

ca- *pfx see* KER- *pfx* and its combs.

caad *n.*

IN PHRASES

□ **draw caad** *v. see under* DRAW *v.*[4].

caad *v. see* CARD *v.*[1].

cab *n.*[1] [? Sp. *Caballero* or abbr. SE] [mid-17C–early 18C] a Cavalier.

cab *n.*[2] (*also* **cabb**) [abbr.] [18C+] *cabbage*.

cab *n.*[3] [? SE *cabin* or *cabal*, a group that associates secretly and, by implication, for illegal or subversive activities] [early–mid-19C] a brothel.

IN COMPOUNDS

□ **cab mat** *n.* [SE *mat*, i.e. something one 'lies on'] [late 19C] **1** a prostitute. **2** the vagina.

cab *n.*[4] [abbr. CABBAGE *n.*[4] (2)] [mid-19C–1910s] a cheat, a 'crib'.

cab *v.*[1] [SE *cab* n., which, despite Hotten (1860), may 'smack of slang' but is not] **1** [early 19C+] to travel by cab; 20C+ use usu. *cab it*. **2** [1980s+] to drive a cab; thus *cabbing*, working as a cab-driver.

cab *v.*[2] [CAB *n.*[4]] [late 19C] to cheat, to pilfer.

caballo *n.* (*also* **kabayo**) [pun on Sp. *caballo*, a horseman/HORSE *n.* (7)] [1960s+] (*drugs*) heroin.

cabaret *v.* [1950s] (*US drugs*) to get extremely intoxicated.

cabb *n. see* CAB *n.*[2].

cabba-cabba *adj.* [ety. unknown] [1990s+] (*W.I.*) rough, vulgar, badly dressed.

Cabbage, the *n.* [pun on SE *Savoy cabbage*] [late 19C] the Savoy Theatre.

cabbage *n.*[1] [? corruption of 17C SE *garbage/carbage*, shreds and patches used as padding; predated by *hell* or *eye*: 'From the first, when taxed with their knavery, they equivocally swear, that if they have taken any they wish they may find it in *hell*! or, alluding to the second protest, that what they have over and above is not more than they could put in their *eye*. Now generally termed cabbage' (Hindley, *The Old Book Collector's Miscellany*, 1871–3)] **1** [mid-17C–19C] small off-cuts of material, taken from the job in hand and sold off as perks by tailors. **2** [late 17C–19C; 1930s] a tailor.

IN COMPOUNDS

□ **cabbage contractor** *n.* (*also* **cabbage eater, ...monger**) [18C–19C] a tailor.

cabbage *n.*[2] [resemblance] **1** [late 17C–early 18C] a form of hairdressing resembling a chignon, popular at this time. **2** (inferior) smoking materials. (**a**) [mid-19C+] (*also* **spinach**) a cheap, inferior cigar. (**b**) [mid-19C+] (*US*) tobacco. (**c**) [1980s+] (*N.Z. drugs*) low-grade marijuana. **3** in the context of the colour green. (**a**) [20C+] (*orig. US*) (*also* **happy cabbage**) cash, banknotes. (**b**) [1920s] a mortgage. (**c**) [1980s+] (*S.Afr.*) a ten-rand banknote.

IN COMPOUNDS

□ **cabbage leaf** *n.* **1** [mid-19C–1910s] (*US*) (*also* **cabbage roll**) a poor-quality cigar; thus the joc. query *Who's smoking cabbage leaves?* **2** [1930s–60s] (*US*) (*also* **cabbage leaves**) money, banknotes.

SE in slang uses

IN COMPOUNDS

pertaining to nationality

□ **cabbage-eater** *n.* [racial stereotyping: both nationalities are allegedly devoted consumers of cabbage] [20C+] (*US*) **1** a German. **2** a Russian. □ **cabbage garden** *n.* (*also* **cabbage patch, ...state**) [the state crop; note Stephens & O'Brien, *Materials for a Dict. of Aus. Slang* (ms.; 1900–10): 'The phrase is credited to the late Sir John Robertson, a New South politician of more rigour than polish. Sir John Robertson was one of the old Sydney politicians who had a full and bitter contempt for anything Victorian, He was in fact the head and front of the interprovincial jealousy which only received its quietus from the Federal movement. His reason for so calling Victoria was no doubt a retort to somebody who was either extolling Victoria's policy or praising its products.'] [late 19C–1950s] (*Aus.*) Victoria; thus *cabbage gardener*, *cabbage patcher*, *cabbage stater*, a native of Victoria. □ **cabbage-head** *n.* **1** [mid-19C+] (*US*) a Dutch or German person. **2** *see also* separate entry. □ **cabbage town** *n.* [racial stereotyping: the German taste for *Sauerkraut* or pickled cabbage] [20C+] (*US*) **1** the German immigrant section of a town. **2** the poor area of a town.

general uses

□ **cabbage-gelder** *n.* [joc. image of one who gelds or 'castrates', i.e. cuts, the stalks of cabbages] [mid-19C–1900s] a gardener, a greengrocer. □ **cabbage hat** *n. see* CABBAGE-TREE HAT *n.* (1). □ **cabbage John** *n.* (*also* **Ah Cabbage**) [1900s] (*Aus.*) a Chinese vegetable seller. □ **cabbage plant** *n.* [resemblance] [early 19C] an umbrella. □ **cabbage stumps** *n.* [supposedly reminiscent of cut-off cabbage stalks] [late 19C] the legs.

IN PHRASES

□ **boil one's cabbage twice** *v.* (*also* **chew one's cabbage twice, sell one's cabbage twice**) [late 19C+] (*US*) to repeat oneself. □ **summer cabbage** *n.* [the spread of its leaves] [19C] an umbrella.

cabbage *n.*[3] [Fr. *choux*. lit. 'cabbage', used as a term of endearment] [mid-18C; 1930s] a person, a fellow, a chap.

cabbage *n.*[4] [? CABBAGE *n.*[1] (1), tailors' scraps, thus 'padding'; ? OF *cabuse*, imposture, trick; *cabuser*, to deceive, to cheat; also OF *cabas*, cheating, theft; Fr. *cabasser*, to pack up, to cheat, to steal; *cabasseur*, deceiver, thief; 'but evidence is wanting' (*OED*)] **1** [early 19C] deceitful talk. **2** [mid–late 19C] a 'crib' or other form of cheat used by schoolchildren.

cabbage *n.*[5] [CABBAGE GARDEN *under* CABBAGE *n.*[2]] [late 19C] (*Aus.*) a native or inhabitant of Victoria.

cabbage *n.*[6] [? a play on GREENS *n.*[1]] **1** [late 19C+] the vagina; one of a number of terms that equates the vagina with a vegetable. **2** [1940s+] a woman.

IN PHRASES

□ **boil someone's cabbage** *v.* [1920s] (*US*) of a man, to have sexual intercourse. ❑ **have a bit of summer cabbage** *v.* [19C] to have sexual intercourse. ❑ **take a turn among the cabbages** *v.* [19C] to have sexual intercourse.

cabbage *v.*[1] [CABBAGE *n.*[1] (1) + fig. uses] **1** [18C–1940s] to steal, to pilfer, orig. used of tailors stealing offcuts. **2** [19C] to destroy, to defeat. **3** [mid-19C–1930s] to grab. **4** [late 19C] to plagiarize.

cabbage *v.*[2] [CABBAGE *n.*[4] (2)] [mid–late 19C] to use a 'crib'.

cabbage *v.*[3] [CABBAGE *n.*[2] (2c)] **1** [1980s+] (*N.Z. drugs*) to smoke second-rate marijuana. **2** [2000s] to be intoxicated by drugs or drink [CABBAGED *adj.* (3); adds image of the cabbage as a VEGETABLE *adj.*].

cabbaged *adj.* [one has become a SE fig. *vegetable*] [1990s+] **1** absolutely exhausted, metaphorically brain-dead from overwork. **2** rendered imbecilic. **3** drunk or drugged.

cabbage-head *n.* [SE *cabbage* + -HEAD *sfx*; the shape and the supposed 'vegetable' matter of which the person's brain is composed] **1** [late 17C+] a fool, a stupid person. **2** [2000s] (*US drugs*) someone who will try any drug.

cabbage patch *n.*[1] [pun on GREENS *n.*[1] (1)] [late 19C] the vagina.

cabbage patch *n.*[2] [the size of such a patch in one's garden and the commonness of the vegetable] [late 19C–1910s] (*US*) a thing or place of little importance.

cabbage patch *n.*[3] *see* CABBAGE GARDEN *under* CABBAGE *n.*[2].

cabbager *n.*[1] [CABBAGE *n.*[1] (1)] [19C–1900s] a tailor.

cabbager *n.*[2] *see* CABBAGITE *n.*

cabbage tree *v.* [rhy. sl.] [1940s] (*US*) to flee.

cabbage-tree hat *n.* (*also* **cabbage hat**) [rhy. sl. = RAT *n.*[1] (1)] [1940s+] (*Aus./US*) an informer.

cabbage-tree mob *n.* [mid-19C] (*Aus.*) a type of layabout, typified by the wearing of a *cabbage-tree hat* (a hat made of woven cabbage-tree or cabbage-palm leaves).

cabbagio perfumo *n.* [cod Spanish meaning 'a perfumed cabbage'; mocking the Spanish/Cuban origin of the best cigars and their names; note CABBAGE *n.*[2] (2a)] [late 19C+] a cheap cigar.

cabbagite *n.* (*also* **cabbager**) [CABBAGE-TREE MOB *n.*] [mid-19C] (*Aus.*) a layabout.

cabber *n.* [dial. *cab*, to clog with dirt] [20C+] (*Ulster*) a ring of dirt around the neck, a 'tide-mark'.

cabbie *n.* (*also* **cabby**) [SE *cab* + sfx *-ie/-y*] [mid-19C+] a cab-driver.

cabeza *n.* [synon. Sp.] [mid-19C+] (*US, Southwest*) the head.

cabin fever *n.* [coined for those suffering on long sea voyages] [1910s+] lassitude, restlessness or irritability as a result of being confined in too small a space, with no variety in companions or occupations.

cab joint *n.* [SE *cab* + JOINT *n.* (3b) but note CAB *n.*[3]] [1930s+] (*orig. US*) **1** a brothel. **2** a nightclub to which patrons would be steered, were they to request such a place, by a complaisant cab-driver.

cable *n.* **1** [mid-18C; 1990s+] (*US*) the penis. **2** [1990s+] (*US black*) a thick gold chain.

cable-funk *n.* [mid-19C] (*UK Und.*) fear of being hanged; thus *nab the cable-funk*, to be hanged.

cabman's rests *n.* (*also* **rests**) [rhy. sl.] [late 19C–1920s] the female breasts.

cab moll *n.* [SE *cab*/CAB *n.*[3] + MOLL *n.* (2)] [mid–late 19C] (*orig. US*) a prostitute who works either lit. in cabs and trains or poss. from or at a brothel.

caboodle *n.* (*also* **capoodle, kaboodle, kerboodle**) [? KER- *pfx* + BOODLE *n.*[1] (1)] [19C+] a large mixed-up collection of objects or people; usu. in phr. below.

IN PHRASES

❑ **whole caboodle** *n.* (*also* **whole kaboodlum**) [mid-19C+] (*orig. US*) the lot, everything there is.

caboose *n.* [Du. *kabuis*, a cook's galley; briefly used in 18C/19C UK naval jargon to mean a galley, but thereafter appears only in US. Thence SAmE *caboose* as adopted in the American West to mean the cow-hide container stretched across the rear of the chuck wagon, which, when full, hangs down behind the wagon; thence it was used by the railroads to mean a wagon (usu. attached to a freight train) in which the crew could eat, sleep and cook] (*US*) **1** as a small room. (**a**) [mid-19C–1940s] a cubby-hole, a small room. (**b**) [mid-19C+] any form of place or room. (**c**) [mid-19C+] a prison. (**d**) [1950s] in fig. use, penury; i.e. reduced to poor living circumstances. **2** in the context of the rear. (**a**) [19C+] a person who continually follows along behind, a hanger-on. (**b**) [20C+] the buttocks, the behind; occas. the back. (**c**) [1920s] a slow-witted person. (**d**) [1950s] the last child in a family [also puns on SE *papoose*]. (**e**) [1960s] (*US campus*) the last man in a session of group sex.

caboose *v.* (*US*) **1** [late 19C–1930s] to imprison [CABOOSE *n.* (1c)]. **2** [2000s] to sodomize [CABOOSE *n.* (2b)].

cab rank *n.* [rhy. sl.] [1950s+] a bank.

cab-ranker *n.* [punning on SE *cab rank*/CABBAGE *n.*[2] (2a) + *rank*, offensively smelly] [1920s] a cheap cigar.

caca *n.* (*also* **kaka, ka-ka**) [Sp. *caca*, excrement] **1** [late 19C+] excrement; also used fig. **2** [1960s+] (*US drugs*) heroin; esp. when inferior, bogus or adulterated [SHIT *n.* (6a)]. **3** [1970s] (*US*) nonsense, rubbish [SHIT *n.* (4a)].

IN COMPOUNDS

❑ **kaka queen** *n.* [1950s–70s] (*gay*) one whose sexual preferences involve excrement.

IN PHRASES

❑ **go to ca-ca** *v.* [late 19C] to defecate. ❑ **make ca-ca** *v.* (*also* **go ca-ca**) [1980s+] to defecate.

caca *v.* [CACA *n.* (1)] [20C+] to defecate.

caca! *excl.* [CACA *n.*; var. on SHIT! *excl.*] [1970s+] an excl. of negation or anger.

cacada *n.* [CACA *n.* (1) + Fr. *dents*, teeth; either no more food than would slightly dirty the teeth or bits of food that remain between the teeth after eating] [20C+] (*W.I.*) a little food or a very small amount of money, typically used to appease a beggar.

cacafuego *n.* [Port. *cagar*, to excrete + Sp. *fuego*, fire, lit. *shit-fire*; also the name of a Spanish galleon taken by Sir Francis Drake in 1577] [17C–early 19C] a braggart, a noisy bully.

cachunk! *excl. see* KERCHUNK! *under* KER- *pfx*.

cack *n.*[1] [? CACK *n.*[2] or SE *cackle*] [late 19C–1900s] (*US*) a small child.

cack *n.*[2] (*also* **cak**) [15C–16C SE *cack*, to void excrement, itself linked to synon. Lat. *cacare* and OE *cac-hús*, a latrine] **1** [late 19C+] excrement, also used fig. **2** [1920s; 1990s+] nonsense, rubbish [SHIT *n.* (4a)]. **3** [1970s+] (*Irish*) a general term of abuse, a contemptuous term for an individual [SHIT *n.* (2a)]. **4** [1990s+] rubbish, dirt, filth.

IN COMPOUNDS

❑ **cackbag** *n.* [1950s+] a general pej. term, whether of people or things. ❑ **cack-face** *n.* [1990s+] a term of insult. ❑ **cacknacker** *n. see* COCK-KNOCKER *under* COCK *n.*[3].

IN PHRASES

❑ **hot cack** *adj.* [20C+] (*Aus.*) very good [? euph. for SHIT-HOT *adj.*]. ❑ **kick (the) cack out of** *v.* [1970s] to beat up severely.

cack *n.*[3] [CACK *v.*[2] (2)] **1** [1900s–50s] (*US black*) a respected person, an important figure in the community. **2** [1960s] (*US campus*) a good-looking woman.

cack *n.*[4] [SE *cackle*] [1990s+] (*Aus.*) **1** a laugh. **2** someone who has a good sense of humour.

cack *adj.* (*also* **cak**) [CACK *n.*[2]] [1990s+] a general negative, disgusting, loathsome etc.

cack *v.*[1] [16C–early 18C SE *cack*, to excrete] **1** [early 18C+] to defecate; also in fig. use. **2** [1960s+] (*also* **kack it**) in fig. use, to be terrified.

IN PHRASES

❑ **cack on** *v.* [1990s+] (*UK juv.*) to reprimand. ❑ **cack one's pants** *v.* [1990s+] to be absolutely terrified.

cack *v.*[2] [mid-16C+ SE *cackle*, to brag about a petty achievement] **1** [late 19C+] to fall asleep. **2** [1900s–40s] (*US black*) to boast, to brag, esp. of one's good fortune. **3** [1900s–40s] (*US black*) to kill. **4** [1960s] (*US*) to amaze.

(IN COMPOUNDS)

□ **cack-broad** *n.* (*also* **cackle-broad**) [BROAD *n.*[2] (3)] [1940s] (*US black*) a woman who flaunts her wealth, esp. a *nouveau riche* woman.

cack *v.*[3] [CACK *n.*[4] (1)] [1990s+] (*Aus./US*) to joke, to (have a) laugh.

cacked *adj.* [CACK *v.*[1]] [1990s+] (*US teen*) messed up.

cacker *n.* [CACK *v.*[1]] [1990s+] (*US*) a blunderer, one who makes a mess, lit. and fig.

cack-hand *n.* [backform. f. CACK-HANDED *adj.*] [2000s] a clumsy, awkward person.

cack-handed *adj.* [? CACK *v.*[1]; note Fr. *mains de merde*, awkward, butter-fingered, lit. 'shit-hands'; note dial. *cack-handed*, left-handed] [1950s+] clumsy, awkward.

cackie *n. see* CACKY *n.*

cackle *n.* **1** [late 17C+] (*also* **crackle**) empty chatter, foolish talk, esp. in phr. below [CACKLE *v.* (1)]. **2** [1930s–60s] (*US*) an egg [SE *cackle*, the sound made by a hen].

(IN COMPOUNDS)

□ **cackleberry** *n.* [20C+] (*Aus./US*) an egg. □ **cacklebird** *n.* [1960s+] (*US*) a hen. □ **cackle fruit** *n.* (*also* **cackle jelly**) [20C+] an egg.

(IN PHRASES)

□ **cut the cackle** *v.* (*also* **cut the cackle and come to the horses, cut the tackle and get to the horses**) [late 19C+] to come to the point; usu. as an imper.

cackle *v.* [SE *cackle*, the sound made by a hen] **1** [early 16C+] to talk, to chatter, to prattle. **2** [late 17C+] (*UK Und.*) to reveal secrets through indiscreet talk, to inform.

SE in slang uses

(IN COMPOUNDS)

□ **cackle factory** *n.* [1950s] (*US*) a psychiatric institution. □ **cackle tub** *n.* [TUB *n.*[1] (2)] **1** [mid-19C] a preacher. **2** [mid-19C–1900s] a pulpit.

cackle-broad *n. see CACK-BROAD under* CACK *v.*[2].

cackler *n.*[1] [the image, when in a group, of a flock of hens] **1** [15C–19C] a tale-teller, one who talks 'out of turn'. **2** [20C+] (*US*) an office worker, a clerk [note Irwin (1931): 'CACKLER.- […] A white collar worker; this name originated by the I.W.W., who have had a hard time interesting this class of worker in their movement, and who say a clerk or office worker will talk, 'cackle,' all day and do nothing to improve his condition].

cackler *n.*[2] [SE *cackle*, the noise made by a hen] **1** [17C–18C] a hen. **2** [1930s–60s] (*US Und.*) an egg.

(IN COMPOUNDS)

□ **cackler's ken** *n.* [KEN *n.*[1] (1)] [18C–early 19C] (*UK Und.*) a hen roost.

cackling-cheat *n.* (*also* **cackling-chete**) [SE *cackle* + CHEAT *n.* (1)] [mid-16C–early 19C] (*UK Und.*) a cock, a capon.

cackling-cove *n.* [SE *cackle* + COVE *n.* (1); 'The cadger seeing no difference between observing Shakespeare and whining floridly for pence' (Ware)] [mid–late 19C] (*UK tramp*) an actor.

cackling fart *n.* [CACKLER *n.*[2] (1) + FART *n.* (1)] [17C–18C] an egg.

cacko *adj.* [fig. use of CACK *n.*[2] + -O *sfx* (5)] [1960s] (*Aus.*) extremely drunk.

cackpipe *n.* [CACK *n.*[2] (1) + SE *pipe*] [1990s+] the anus, the rectum.

(IN COMPOUNDS)

□ **cackpipe cosmonaut** *n.* [1990s+] a male homosexual.

cacks *n.* [Cumberland dial.] [1920s] children's shoes.

cacky *n.* (*also* **cackie**) [CACK *n.*[2] (1)] [late 19C+] human excrement.

cacky *adj.* [CACK *n.*[2] (1)] **1** [late 19C+] covered in excrement. **2** [1970s+] in fig. use, disgusting, second-rate.

cacky-handed *adj.* [dial. *cack-handed*, left-handed] [1900s–10s] (*Aus.*) left-handed.

cactus *n.* [its origin in the peyote cactus] [1960s+] (*drugs*) mescaline; peyote.

(IN COMPOUNDS)

□ **cactus buttons** *n.* [1960s+] (*drugs*) mescaline. □ **cactus juice** *n.* **1** [1960s+] tequila or mescal [the origin of tequila/mescal in distilling the fermented sap of a maguey (*Agave tequilana*)]. **2** [1970s] (*US*) mescaline [play on SE *mescal/mescaline*, properly the alkaloid 3,4,5-trimethoxyphenethylamine, which is the active ingredient of mescal buttons].

SE in slang uses

(IN PHRASES)

□ **in the cactus** *adj.* [1950s+] (*Aus./N.Z.*) in difficulty.

cactus *adj.* [? pun on CACK *n.*[2] or ? the prickly SE *cactus*] [1940s+] (*Aus.*) ruined, useless, finished, dead.

Cad *n.* [abbr.] **1** [1920s+] (*orig. US*) a *Cad*illac. **2** [1970s–80s] (*US black*) in fig. use, an attractive woman.

cad *n.*[1] [SE *cadee, caddie*, a cadet; thence Eton and Oxford jargon *cad*, a townsman, the implication being that such a figure could not be 'a gentleman', and late 19C *cad-mad*, the excesses of a *nouveau riche* undergraduate; cf. the cognate, but somewhat later BOUNDER *n.* (3)] **1** [late 18C–mid-19C] a passenger taken on board by a coachman for his own profit. **2** (*also* **cad-boy**) [late 18C–mid-19C] a coachman's assistant. **3** [early 19C+] a poorly behaved, ill-mannered lout; thus artists' jargon *cad-catcher*, pictures painted to attract the undiscriminating. **4** [mid-19C] a lowly rated assistant. **5** [mid-19C] a messenger boy. **6** [mid–late 19C] an omnibus conductor. **7** [mid-19C–1910s] (*US campus*) an academy or prep school student.

(DERIVATIVES)

□ **caddish** *adj.* [late 19C+] poorly behaved, ill-mannered, vulgar.

(IN PHRASES)

□ **cads on castors** *n.* [late 19C–1900s] bicyclists.

cad *n.*[2] [abbr. CADILLAC *n.* (1a)] [1930s+] (*drugs*) 28g (1oz) of a narcotic.

cad *n.*[3] *see* CADGER *n.* (1).

cadator *n.* [Lat. *cado*, I fall, thus 'a faller'] [late 17C–early 18C] a confidence trickster, esp. one posing as a 'gentleman fallen on hard times'.

cadaver *n.* [SE *cadaver*, a corpse] [late 19C–1900s] (*orig. US*) a bankrupt.

SE in slang uses

(IN COMPOUNDS)

□ **cadaver cadet** *n.* [1980s+] a necrophile.

(IN EXCLAMATIONS)

□ **by my cadaver!** [late 19C–1900s] (*Cockney*) a mild oath.

cadazy *adj.* [SE *crazy* + infix *mad*] [1980s] (*UK black*) mad, crazy.

Cadbury alley *n.* (*also* **Cadbury canal, ...channel**) [play on *Cadbury*, the major UK chocolate manufacturer/CHOCOLATE *adj.* (2), used in combs. relating to homosexual anal intercourse] [1990s+] the rectal passage.

Cadbury's canal boat cruiser *n.* [for ety. *see* CADBURY ALLEY *n.* + ref. to CRUISE *v.* (1)] [1990s+] a male homosexual.

Cadbury's canal engineer *n.* [for ety. *see* CADBURY ALLEY *n.*] [1990s+] a male homosexual.

Cadbury snack *n.* [rhy. sl.] [2000s] the back.

caddee *n.* [SE *cadee*, a cadet, i.e. a junior] **1** [mid-18C–mid-19C] a person who frequents tavern yards and persuades customers to patronize another inn, for which they are paid by its landlord. **2** [early–mid-19C] a thief's assistant. **3** [early–mid-19C] a passer-on of counterfeit money.

caddie *n.* (*also* **caddy**) [? CADY *n.* (1)] [late 19C+] (*orig. Aus.*) a hat; a slouch hat.

caddock *n.* [ety. unknown] [mid-19C] (*UK Und.*) the stomach.

Caddy *n.* (*also* **Caddie**) [abbr.] [1920s+] (*US*) a *Cad*illac.

cadet *n.* [the essential image of a loafer and an idler persists as the meanings develop] **1** [late 17C–early 18C] a junior in the East India Company. **2** [19C] a street thug. **3** [1900s–40s] (*US*) a pimp. **4** [1940s–70s] (*drugs*) a novice user of drugs. **5** [1960s] (*S.Afr.*) a junior gangster. **6** *see* SPACE CADET *under* SPACE *n.*

cadge, the *n.* [CADGE *v.*] **1** [early–mid-19C] the profession or act of begging. **2** [1930s] (*Glasgow*) a message.

(IN PHRASES)

❑ **do a cadge** *v.* [early 19C] to exist by begging. ❑ **on the cadge** [late 19C+] begging.

cadge *v.* [? SE *cadge*, a pannier, as used by beggars, ult. ? f. Fr. *cacher*, to hide away. By 20C use was more colloq. than sl.] **1** [late 18C+] orig. to wander the country as a beggar; thence to beg (from). **2** [1930s+] (*Ulster*) to hawk. **3** [1980s] to steal.

(IN COMPOUNDS)

❑ **cadge-gloak** *n.* [GLOAK *n.*, lit. 'a wandering fellow'] [mid-18C–early 19C] (*UK Und.*) a beggar.

cadger *n.* [CADGE *v.*] **1** [late 18C+] (*also* **cad**) a beggar. **2** [mid–late 19C] (*UK Und.*) a shoplifter-cum-beggar; also used for the lowest rank of pickpocket. **3** [mid-19C+] a genteel 'sponger'. **4** [late 19C] anyone in a service industry, e.g. a waiter, cab-driver, who solicits for tips. **5** [1930s+] (*Ulster*) a hawker, esp. one who sells poteen or illicit whisky, also as v., to hawk.

cadging *n.* [CADGE *v.*] [early 19C+] begging; thus *grub-cadging*, begging house-to-house for food; *cadging house*, a beggars' dwelling place.

cadgy *adj.* (*also* **cagy**) [18C Scot. *caigie* and Suffolk dial. *kedge*, cheerful, wanton, sportive] [late 19C+] (*US*) sexually adventurous.

Cadillac *n.* [the perceived characteristic of the expensive marque] **1** (*US*) in drug uses. (**a**) [1930s+] a 28g (1oz) packet of a powdered drug. (**b**) [1950s+] any powdered, thus usu. narcotic, drug. (**c**) [1970s+] phencyclidine. **2** [1990s+] (*US*) in prison uses. (**a**) coffee with cream and sugar. (**b**) (*also* **car**) a line used for transferring articles, e.g. a pack of cigarettes, from one cell to another. (**c**) an easy job within the prison. (**d**) something considered the best. (**e**) a vacant cell.
SE in slang uses

(IN COMPOUNDS)

❑ **Cadillac commie** *n.* [the Cadillac is trad. antipathetic to left-wing ideology] [1990s+] (*US*) a liberal, the intensity of whose pronouncements on social problems is in direct proportion to their ability to escape their existence.

cady *n.* (*also* **cadi**) [Scot. *cadie*, a cap; note also KADI *n.*] **1** [mid-19C+] a hat. **2** [1920s+] (*N.Z.*) a straw hat.

cadzo *n. see* CATSO *n.*

Cadzooks! *excl. see* GADZOOKS! *under* GAD *n.*[1].

caemess *n.* [? link to CAGMAG *n.* (1)] [mid-19C] (*UK Und.*) prison porridge.

caesaration! *excl.* [proper name Julius *Caesar* + sfx *-ation*, on pattern of BOTHERATION! *excl.*] [late 19C] (*US*) a mild oath.

caf *n.* (*also* **caff, caffy, kayf**) [corruption of SE *café*] [1920s+] a café, usu. cheap and cheerful.

café au lait *n.* [the beverage; orig. coined to describe the women chosen for the chorus line of Harlem's Cotton Club; thus ? pun on *café*] [1920s+] (*US black*) a light-skinned woman.

café au lait *adj.* [CAFE AU LAIT *n.*] [1940s+] of a black person, light-skinned.

café de move-on *n.* [S.Afr.E. *café*, a convenience store + the need for the canteen to 'move on' when the authorities arrive; the whole phr. is a play on a notional upmarket *Café de...*] [1920s+] (*S.Afr.*) a small mobile canteen catering for workers at their place of work.

cafeteria *n.* **1** [1930s] (*US*) the mouth. **2** [1980s+] (*US gay*) anywhere that plays host to repeated oral sex, e.g. a public lavatory or bath-house [one goes there to EAT *v.* (4)].

caff *n. see* CAF *n.*

caffer *n.* (*also* **kaffir**) [? link to Yorks. dial. *caff*, to break a bargain, to curtail a journey, or *caffle*, to argue] [mid–late 19C] a convict, who has been transported to New South Wales, and subseq. escaped.

caffle *v.* [ety. unknown] [mid-19C] (*UK Und.*) to take, to hold, to secure; thus *caffled*, arrested.

caffler *n.* [dial. *caffler*, a quarrelsome person] [late 19C+] (*Irish*) a contemptible person; often cheeky and foolish.

caffling *n.* [CAFFLER *n.*] [late 19C+] (*Irish*) idle chatter, gossip.

caffrey *n.* [? anecdotal] [mid-19C] (*UK Und.*) a thief-catcher.

caffy *n. see* CAF *n.*

caflugalty *n.* (*also* **cafugelty**) [? SE *kerfuffle*] [1910s–30s] (*US*) a row, an argument.

cafone *n. see* GAVONE *n.*

caf up *v.* [SE *caffeine*] [1980s+] (*US campus*) to ingest caffeine, usu. in the form of coffee, to promote one's energy.

cag *n.* (*also* **kagg**) [dial./RN slang *cag*, an argument] [19C] sulkiness, ill humour.

(IN PHRASES)

❑ **carry the cag** *v.* [early 19C] to be easily irritated, to lack a sense of humour, esp. as regards jokes against oneself.

cag *adj.* [CAG *v.*] [mid-19C] (*US Und.*) sulky, morose.

cag *v.* (*also* **keg**) [dial.] [early–mid-19C] to irritate, to annoy.

(DERIVATIVES)

❑ **cagged** *adj.* irritated, angry.

cage *n.* [all fig. uses of SE] **1** [late 16C+] a lock-up [SE in earlier use; Hindley, *The Life and Times of James Catnach* (1878), glosses as 'the round-house']. **2** [early 19C] (*UK prison*) an exercise cage or yard. **3** [mid-19C] a dress-improver or bustle. **4** [late 19C] a bed. **5** [1900s] (*US*) a hat. **6** [1920s–30s] (*US tramp*) a cubicle within a tramp's lodging house. **7** [1930s+] (*US*) an elevator, a lift. **8** [1930s+] (*US Und.*) a holding cell in a police station or jail; a punishment cell. **9** [1960s+] (*US*) an automobile. **10** [1970s+] (*US gay*) a depressing room or apartment.
SE in slang uses

(IN PHRASES)

❑ **cage of ivories** *n.* [IVORY *n.* (2)] [mid-19C] a set of good teeth.

caged *adj.* [? the drunkard is fit to be SE *caged*] [1940s] (*US*) drunk.

cagey *adj.* [SE *cage*; the image of a caged animal, gazing suspiciously at human onlookers] **1** [late 19C+] (*also* **cagy**) non-committal, reticent, wary. **2** [1910s+] cunning, crafty. **3** [1950s] sexually exciting.

cagmag *n.* [dial. *cag-mag*, an old goose, not fit for eating (according to Grose (1796), such geese were dumped on the undiscriminating London market), an inferior breed of sheep, a disreputable old woman, anything valueless or second-rate. Hotten's (1864) suggestion – a corruption of the Gk *kakos mageiros*, a bad cook, and used as such in university sl. – must be rejected] **1** [late 18C–1920s] refuse, rubbish, odds and ends. **2** [late 19C–1920s] gossip, tittle-tattle.

cagmag *adj.* [CAGMAG *n.* (1)] [mid-19C] second-rate, inferior, 'rubbishy'.

cagy *adj.* **1** *see* CADGY *adj.* **2** *see* CAGEY *adj.* (1).

cahoonas *n. see* KAHOONAS *n.*

cahoot *v.* [backform. f. IN CAHOOTS *phr.*] [mid–late 19C; 1940s] (*US*) to act in partnership.

cahoots *n. see* IN CAHOOTS *phr.*

Cain *n.*

(IN EXCLAMATIONS)

❑ **by Cain!** [early–mid-19C] (*US*) a mild, euph. oath, *by hell!*

Cain and Abel *n.* [rhy. sl.] [mid-19C+] a table.

caine *n.* [abbr.] [1980s+] (*drugs*) **1** cocaine. **2** crack cocaine.

cainsham smoke *n.* [? a lost story pertaining to *Keynsham*, near Bristol] [late 17C–early 18C] the tears of a man who is beaten by his wife.

caj *adj. see* CAS *adj.*

cajooblies *n.* [1990s+] the female breasts.

cajunk! *excl. see* KERCHUNK! *under* KER- *pfx.*

cajuns *n. see* COJONES *n.*

cak *see under* CACK.

cake *n.*[1] (*also* **cakey**) [lit. or fig. characteristics of the foodstuff] **1** lit. or fig. 'softness' of the foodstuff. (**a**) [late 18C–19C] a fool. (**b**) [early 19C; 1920s–30s] (*US/US gang*) a dandy, a fop; youths who wore stylish wide-bottomed trousers. (**c**) [1960s+] (*US campus*) anything easy, simple [underlined by PIECE OF CAKE *under* PIECE *n.*]. (**d**) [1980s+] (*US campus*) a weak person. **2** that which is sweet or 'good enough to eat'. (**a**) [1900s–60s] (*orig. Aus.*) a prostitute. (**b**) [1940s–60s] (*US black*) an attractive woman. (**c**) [1950s+] (*US black*) the vagina. (**d**) [1960s+] (*US*) (*also* **cakes, cakie**) a term of affection between friends. (**e**) [1990s+] (*US campus*) the female posterior.

IN COMPOUNDS

❑ **cake shop** *n.* [1950s–60s] (*Aus.*) a brothel.

IN PHRASES

❑ **cake out** *v.* [1920s–30s] (*US*) to dress in a rakish manner. ❑ **off one's cake** *adj.* (*also* **off one's bap**) [1980s+] crazy, insane.

SE in slang uses

IN COMPOUNDS

❑ **cake and wine** *n.* [1920s] (*US prison*) bread and water. ❑ **cake basket** *n.* [1920s] (*US*) a limousine. ❑ **cake boy** *n.* [one who is both SOFT *adj.* (3) and good enough to EAT *v.* (4)] [1970s+] (*US gay*) a male homosexual; thus *Navy cake*, a homosexual sailor. ❑ **cake cutter** *n.* **1** [1940s+] (*orig. US black*) one who short-changes a customer; thus *cake cutting*, short changing. **2** [1980s] a long-pronged comb. ❑ **cake-date** *n. see* JELLY-DATE *n.* ❑ **cake-eater** *n.* [1910s+] (*US*) **1** a self-indulgent or effeminate young man. **2** an effete young man who attends smart tea parties and charms old ladies. **3** any wealthy young man, a playboy. **4** as a joc./affectionate term of address. ❑ **cakehole** *n.* (*also* **dough-hole**) **1** [1940s+] the mouth; usu. in imper. *shut your cakehole!* **2** [1970s+] (*Aus./Irish*) the anus. ❑ **cakes-and-coffee** *adj.* [1900s–30s] (*US*) basic, fundamental.

IN PHRASES

❑ **cake is dough** [the image is of a cake mixture failing to rise in the oven] [mid-16C+] one's project has failed, one's plans have not worked out. ❑ **hurry up the cakes** *v.* [mid–late 19C] (*US*) to go quickly.

cake *n.*[2] [ext. of BREAD *n.*[1] (2)] **1** [20C+] (*Aus.*) a gold nugget. **2** [1960s+] (*US black*) (*also* **cakes**) money.

cake *n.*[3] [the stereotyped smuggling of a file inside a cake] [1950s] (*US drugs/prison*) drugs smuggled into a prison or hospital.

cake, the *n.* [1900s–20s] (*US*) a (self-appointedly) admirable person.

cake *adj.* [SE *cake*/CAKE *n.*[1] (1c)] **1** [1940s] fine, pleasing. **2** [1980s+] easy, simple.

caked *adj.*[1] [SE *cake*/CAKE *n.*[2]] **1** [1900s] on good (amatory) terms. **2** [1940s+] (*also* **caked up**) well-off; well supplied.

caked *adj.*[2] [? fig. use of CACK *v.*[1] (1)] [1990s+] (*US campus*) drunk.

cakes *n.* [all fig. use of the size and shape of a SE *cake*] **1** [1950s+] (*orig. US*) the female breasts. **2** [1970s+] (*US*) the buttocks. **3** [1980s+] (*US black*) the vagina. **4** [1990s+] (*drugs*) round discs of crack cocaine. **5** *see* CAKE *n.*[1] (2d). **6** *see* CAKE *n.*[2] (2). **7** *see* BABYCAKES *under* BABY *n.*

cakewalk *n.* [SE *cakewalk*, a dance in which the contestants (usu. US black) promenade around a cake placed in the centre of the dance-floor; those who perform the fanciest steps literally 'take the cake'. Orig. as WW1 milit. jargon, an attack or raid that met with little or no opposition] **1** [late 19C+] anything considered very easy. **2** [1900s] (*Aus.*) something excellent.

cakewalk *v.* [CAKEWALK *n.* (1)] [1930s] (*US*) to succeed without problems.

cakey *n. see* CAKE *n.*[1].

cakey *adj.* (*also* **cake**) [CAKE *n.*[1] (1)] [late 19C+] stupid, foolish, 'soft'.

cakey-pannum fencer *n.* [SE *cake* + PANNAM *n.* (1) + -FENCER *sfx*] [mid-19C] a street-seller of pastries.

cakie *n.* **1** *see* CAKE *n.*[1] (2d). **2** *see* BABYCAKES *under* BABY *n.*

cakpants *n.* [CACK *n.*[2] (1) + SE *pants*] [2000s] a general term of abuse; the implication is that the subject is a coward, who soils their underwear through fear.

Cal *n.* [abbr.] **1** [late 19C] (*Anglo-Ind.*) *Cal*cutta. **2** [late 19C+] (*US*) *Cal*ifornia.

cal *n.* [abbr. of proper name Thomas *Cal*craft (*fl.*1860), a hangman] [mid-19C] a hangman.

calabash *n.* [Persian *kharbuz*, or *kharbuza*, meaning melon, or watermelon; ult. Arabic *khirbiz*, melon or *kirbiz*, pumpkin or gourd] **1** [early 18C–19C] the human head. **2** [mid–late 19C] (*Aus.*) (*also* **calibash**) a promissory note or IOU [the image is of the essential worthlessness of such notes, which were no more valid as money than had they been written on a *calabash* or gourd-shell].

IN COMPOUNDS

❑ **calabash cover** *n.* [late 19C] (*US*) a hat.

calaboodle *n. see* CABOODLE *n.*

calaboose *n.* (*also* **calabozo**) [Sp. *calabozo*, gaol] [late 18C+] (*orig. US*) a prison.

calaboose *v.* [CALABOOSE *n.*] [mid-19C] (*US*) to imprison.

calamity *n.*

SE in slang uses

IN COMPOUNDS

❑ **calamity howler** *n.* (*also* **calamity-shouter**) [late 19C–1940s] (*US*) a prophet of doom; thus *calamity howl*, a statement of extreme pessimism. ❑ **calamity jane** *n.* [the markswoman Martha Jane Canary Burke (1852–1903), known as *Calamity Jane* for the effect her six-guns had on those who opposed her] [20C+] (*US*) a nagging woman, a pessimist, a worrier.

calathumpian *n.* [ety. unknown; ? SE *calamity* + *thump* + play on CALLITHUMPIAN *n.*] [1910s+] one who claims an imaginary religion.

calculate *v.* [early–mid-19C] (*US*) to think, to opine.

calcutta *n.* [rhy. sl.] [1990s+] butter.

caldee *v.* (*also* **caldees, chaldee**) [? SE *Chaldee*, an astrologer] [mid–late 17C] to trick, to swindle.

caldron *n.* [SE *cauldron*] [19C] the vagina.

Caleb Quotem *n.* [proper name of a character in George Colman Younger's play *The Wags of Windsor* (1800)] [mid–late 19C] **1** a parish clerk. **2** a jack of all trades.

calebs *n.* [? anecdotal, from an actual robber and his preferred implement] [mid-19C] (*US Und.*) a burglar's device for unlocking doors.

caledonia *n.* [? a book ? play ? song ?] [1920s–80s] (*US black*) a black woman who refuses to accept the trad. role into which her birth is supposed to have thrust her.

calendar *n.* [abbr. SE *calendar year*] (*US Und.*) **1** [1920s+] a year spent in prison. **2** [1940s] a case awaiting trial.

calf *n.*[1] [dial.; note the UK comedian Steve Coogan's 1990s character Paul *Calf*, a loutish, stupid, hedonistic Mancunian] **1** [mid-16C–1920s] (*also* **veal**) a fool, a simpleton. **2** [20C+] (*US*) a coward.

IN COMPOUNDS

❑ **calf-lolly** *n.* [dial. *lolly*, a fool, an idler] [mid–late 17C] an idle simpleton. ❑ **calf's head** *n.* **1** [late 16C–early 19C] a fool. **2** [19C] a white-faced man with a large head. ❑ **calf-sticking** *n.* [STICK *v.* (2a)] [mid-19C–1910s] (*UK Und.*) pretending that perfectly normal goods have supposedly been stolen; a greater price can thus be asked, since some customers like the idea of obtaining stolen goods.

IN PHRASES

❑ **have a calf** *v.* [1970s] (*US*) to lose control, to have an emotional fit.

SE in slang uses

IN COMPOUNDS

❑ **calf-rope** *n. see* HOLLER CALF-ROPE *under* HOLLER *v.* ❑ **calf-slobber** *n.* [dial. *calf-slobber*, the saliva that forms around a calf's mouth] **1** [1920s+] (*US*) a meringue topping for pastry. **2** [2000s] foam on a glass of beer. ❑ **calf week** *n.* (*also* **bull-**

week, cow-week) [the cattle names imply stolid labouring] [mid-19C] the three weeks immediately before Christmas, characterized in shops and factories by an increasingly heavy workload.

calf *n.*[2] [? initial letter] [1940s] (*US black*) a Cadillac.

calf *n.*[3] *see* ESSEX CALF *under* ESSEX *adj.*

calf *v.* [? echoic] [1960s] (*US*) to vomit.

calf-clingers *n.* [mid-19C] very tight-fitting trousers.

calfskin fiddle *n.* [its calfskin head] [late 18C–early 19C] a drum.

Cali *n.* [abbr.] [1930s+] the state of *California*.

Cali *adj.* [1990s+] *Californian*.

calibash *n. see* CALABASH *n.* (2).

calico *n.*[1] (*also* **calic**) [SE *calico*, a cloth, somewhat coarser than muslin, from which women's dresses were often made. There may also be links to Scot. *cailliach*, an old woman, *calik*, a gossip and *callack*, a young woman] [mid-19C+] (*US*) a woman.

IN COMPOUNDS

❑ **callico queen** *n.* [1960s+] (*US*) a prostitute.

IN PHRASES

❑ **bit of calico** *n.* [19C] (*US*) sexual groping.

calico *n.*[2] [the *Calico* M960 sub-machinegun] [1990s+] (*US black*) a fast-firing handgun.

calico *adj.* [the thinness of the cotton cloth] [early 18C–mid-19C; 1950s] thin, wasted.

SE in slang uses

IN COMPOUNDS

❑ **calico ball** *n.* (*also* **calico hop**) [the *calico* (rather than silk or satin) dresses worn by the women] [mid-19C–1930s] (*US*) a cheap, popular public dance. ❑ **calico muster** *n. see* TARPAULIN MUSTER *under* TARPAULIN *adj.*

calico *v.* [CALICO *n.*[1]] [19C] (*US*) to court women, to associate with women.

calicot *n.* [Fr. *calicot*, a draper's assistant, though sl. use is the same] [late 19C–1900s] a 'counter-jumper'.

California *n.* [the *California* Gold Rush of the 1840s] [mid-19C] money, esp. a gold piece.

California *adj.* used in combs., referring to the state or its stereotypes.

IN COMPOUNDS

❑ **California banknote** *n.* (*also* **California shinplaster**) [replaced by coins and notes subsequent to the 1849 Gold Rush] [mid-19C] (*US*) an animal hide, used as money in early 19C California. ❑ **California bankroll** *n.* (*also* **California roll**) [1940s+] (*US black/gambling*) a show bankroll in which one large-denomination note is exhibited on the outside, concealing a quantity of small bills; thus *California roller*, one who carries such a 'bankroll'. ❑ **California bible** *n.* (*also* **California prayerbook**) [the stereotyped sinfulness of California] [mid-19C+] (*US*) a deck of cards. ❑ **California blanket** *n.* (*also* **Tucson blanket**) [SE *blanket*/BLANKET *n.* (3)] [1920s–40s] (*US*) newspapers, when used by tramps as a substitute for blankets. ❑ **California collar** *n.* [the numbers of vigilantes to be found in California, most of whom favoured hanging first and ascertaining guilt later] [19C] (*US*) a noose, used for hangings. ❑ **California cornflakes** *n.* [joc. play on the breakfast cereal's slogan: it's 'good for you each morning'] [1970s+] (*drugs*) cocaine. ❑ **California house** *n.* [? the good weather in California, which permits an outdoor lifestyle] [1970s] (*US*) an outside privy. ❑ **California moccasins** *n.* [as worn by impoverished tramps who travelled to and then in California] [1920s–60s] (*US*) makeshift 'socks' made from sacks or similar rags. ❑ **California overshoes** *n.* [as used by tramps and/or unsuccessful gold prospectors] [19C] (*US*) makeshift 'socks' made by wrapping the feet in sacks, often flour sacks, over which boots can then be put on. ❑ **California prayerbook** *n. see* CALIFORNIA BIBLE above. ❑ **California shinplaster** *n. see* CALIFORNIA BANKNOTE above. ❑ **California socks** *n.* [1900s–60s] (*US*) makeshift 'socks' made from sacks or other rags. ❑ **California stop** *n.* (*also* **Hollywood stop**) [stereotyped Californians are seen as contemptuous of the law] [1970s+] (*US*) of a motorist, running a stop sign. ❑ **California sunshine** *n.* [SUNSHINE *n.* (4)] [1970s+] (*drugs*) LSD. ❑ **California toothpick** *n.* [TOOTHPICK *n.* (2)] [mid-19C] (*US*) a large knife.

Californian *n.* [the association of the red, i.e. gold colour, with the *Californian* Gold Rush] [mid–late 19C] a dried red herring.

caliwampus *adj. see* CATAWAMPUS *adj.*

call *n.*[1] [a pun on the religious use of *call*, a summons to a higher spirituality] [1960s–70s] **1** the first feelings that follow drinking an alcoholic drink. **2** (*drugs*) the immediate response to an injection of a drug.

call *n.*[2] *see* SHOUT *n.*

call *v.* [fig. uses of SE] **1** [mid-18C+] to beg. **2** [late 19C+] to blame. **3** [1920s+] (*US*) to challenge [+ poker imagery]. **4** [1980s] (*Aus.*) to vomit [abbr. of the various phrs. below].

IN PHRASES

meaning to vomit

❑ **call buicks** *v. see under* BUICK *v.* ❑ **call Charles** *v.* (*also* **call dinosaurs, call seals**) [1970s+] (*Aus./US*) ❑ **call (for) Earl** *v. see under* EARL *n.* ❑ **call for Herb** *v.* [1960s+] (*Aus.*) ❑ **call (for) Hughie** *v. see under* HUGHIE *n.* ❑ **call (for) Ralph** *v. see* RALPH *n.* ❑ **call the dogs** *v.* [one's 'barking' noises] [1990s+] (*US campus*)

general uses

❑ **call over the coals** *v.* [mid-19C–1910s] to scold, to tell off. ❑ **call someone out of their name** *v.* [1900s–80s] (*US black*) to insult through name-calling. ❑ **call someone's card** *v.* [poker imagery] [1980s] (*US*) to call someone's bluff. ❑ **call someone's game** *v.* [poker imagery] [1980s+] (*US*) to call someone's bluff, to challenge. ❑ **call someone's hand** *v.* [poker imagery] [mid-19C–1950s] (*US*) to issue a challenge, to call someone's bluff.

SE in slang uses

pertaining to sex

IN COMPOUNDS

❑ **call-boy** *n.* [1960s+] a male prostitute who can be hired on the phone. ❑ **call flat** *n.* (*also* **call apartment**) [var. on CALL HOUSE *n.* (1)] [1910s–40s] (*US*) a brothel. ❑ **call-girl** *n. see* separate entry. ❑ **call house** *n. see* separate entry. ❑ **call joint** *n.* [JOINT *n.* (3b)] [1930s–40s] (*US*) a brothel.

general uses

IN COMPOUNDS

❑ **call-dog** *n.* [one *calls the dog* to eat it] [1940s+] (*W.I.*) a fish too small for human consumption.

IN PHRASES

❑ **call a go** *v.* [mid-19C] **1** of a street-seller, to move on. **2** to give up. ❑ **call a spade a (bloody) shovel** *v. see under* SPADE *n.* ❑ **call down** *v. see* separate entry. ❑ **call full-mouth** *v.* (*also* **call raw**) [*FULLMOUTH under* FULL *adj.*/SE *raw*, i.e. 'uncooked' by good manners] [20C+] (*W.I.*) to address an elder or senior person without using Mr, Mrs or Miss. ❑ **call hogs** *v.* [the noise] [1910s–60s] (*US*) to snore. ❑ **call in one's marker** *v. see under* MARKER *n.*[2]. ❑ **call in someone's chips** *v.* [poker imagery] [late 19C] (*US*) to challenge, to call someone's bluff. ❑ **call it a day** *v.* (*also* **call it a go, ...a night**) [? cribbage jargon *call a go*, to change one's tactics, to give in] [mid-19C+] to stop, to go no further, to express satisfaction with progress or acceptance that one cannot improve a position. ❑ **call it george** *v.* (*also* **call it wally**) [joc. generic use of proper names] [20C+] (*W.I.*) to agree that a matter is concluded, to bring to an end, e.g. a day's work. ❑ **call off all bets** *v.* [poker imagery] [1940s–50s] (*US black*) to die. ❑ **call on the carpet** *v.* [*ON THE CARPET under* CARPET *n.*[1]] **1** [1960s] (*US*) to reprimand, to scold. **2** [1990s+] (*US prison*) to challenge another speaker to justify his remarks, whether hostile, gossiping or whatever. ❑ **call (out)** *v.* [early 19C SE *call out*, to challenge to a duel] **1** [late 19C+] to challenge to a fight. **2** [1920s] (*US Und.*) to use a stolen cheque. **3** [1990s+] (*US campus*) to embarrass. ❑ **call the coin** *v.* [1950s+] (*US*) to call 'heads or tails' when a coin is tossed. ❑ **call the game in** *v.* [lit. to bring a game, e.g. of rugby, to an end] [1910s+] (*Aus./N.Z.*) to abandon one's efforts, to admit defeat. ❑ **call the knock** *v. see under* KNOCK *n.*[1]. ❑ **call the shots** *v.* (*also* **call the plays,**

...punches) [sporting imagery] [1930s+] to dictate a course of action, to say what should happen. ❑ **call the turn** *v.* [gambling use: calling the next turn of the wheel in the game of faro; ? see Asbury *Sucker's Progress* (1938) 15: An extraordinary number of the terms, technical and otherwise, which were employed by Faro players in the palmy days of the game have passed into the language [...] and are commonly used by millions who never heard of Faro. Here are some of them: [...] *Calling the turn*—To guess correctly the order in which the last three cards in the box would appear] [late 19C+] (*US*) to predict accurately.

call a cop *v.* [rhy. sl.] [1990s+] to stop.

Callan Park *n.* [the name of a psychiatric hospital in Sydney, used to represent any such hospital] [20C+] (*Aus.*) a psychiatric institution.

Callard and Bowsers *n.* [rhy. sl.; ult. the confectioners] [1960s+] trousers.

callat *n. see* CALLET *n.*

callawampus *adj.* [CATAWAMPUS *adj.*] [1940s+] (*W.I.*) big, fine, stout, grand.

calldown *n.* [CALL DOWN *v.*] [late 19C–1950s] (*US*) a telling-off, a scolding.

call down *v.* [late 19C+] to scold, to reprimand; thus *calling-down*, a reprimand.

calle *n.* [SE *caul*, a (net) bag, usu. for the hair] [mid-17C–mid-19C] (*UK Und.*) a cloak.

callet *n.* (*also* **callat, callot**) [? Fr. *cailette*, a fool, lit. 'a small quail'; Fr. *calotte*, a skullcap; Gaelic *caille*, a girl; Nares suggests that 'it is more likely to have been derived from the personage of [...] CALLOT, KIT. The fair, or perhaps more properly the brown associate of one Giles Hathr. They are supposed to have been the first couple of English persons who took up the occupation of gipsies'] [early 16C–18C] a whore, a promiscuous woman.

call-girl *n.* (*also* **call girl**) [SE *call*, to make a telephone call + GIRL *n.*[1] (1)] **1** [late 19C+] a woman who works in a brothel. **2** [1920s+] (*orig. US*) a prostitute who advertises her services through an agency, through the (print) media, in telephone kiosks etc and visits a client in his own home or hotel room.

call house *n.* [SE *call* (*on*), to visit + HOUSE *n.*[1] (1)] **1** [early 18C+] (*also* **house of call**) a brothel to which men can come without making any prior appointment. **2** [1910s+] a hetero- or homosexual brothel to which women or men are summoned by telephone after they have been selected, via some form of visual 'menu', by the male clientele; thus *call trade*, prostitution arranged on this basis.

callibisters *n.* [*callistris*, the penis] [16C–17C] the vagina.

callibogus *n.* [ety. unknown] [late 18C–19C] (*US*) a mixture of rum and spruce beer.

callie *n.* **1** *see* CALLY *n.* **2** *see* COLLIE *n.*

calling card *n.* [one leaves one's calling card] **1** [1920s–40s] (*US Und.*) fingerprints. **2** [1980s+] (*Irish*) a euph. for excrement.

callithumpian *n.* (*also* **callithump**) [ety. unknown, ? link to SE *thump*] [mid-19C+] (*US*) a band or member of a band that makes discordant so-called 'music' by playing a number of instruments, either in an unlikely combination or conjured up from unlikely objects, such as washboards, tin kettles etc.

callot *n. see* CALLET *n.*

Cally *n.* [abbr.] [1930s+] (*US*) *Cal*ifornia.

Cally, the *n.* [abbr.] [late 19C+] (*UK/London*) **1** the *Cal*edonian Market, London N1. **2** the *Cal*edonian Road.

cally *n.* (*also* **callie**) [abbr. CALABOOSE *n.*] [1910s–30s] (*US tramp*) **1** a prison. **2** a police station.

calm *n.* [mid-18C] (*UK Und.*) a hat.

Calmuck Tartary *n.* [ref. to the Kalmucks, a Mongolian tribe] [mid-19C] (*UK Und.*) the rookery of St Giles, London WC1.

caló *n.* [SE *California*, to which the sl. is unique] [1940s+] (*US*) Chicano street sl., linked to Mexican and gypsy patois.

calonkus *n.* [? echoic of the 'kalonk' of hitting one's head with a palm or fist] [late 19C+] (*Aus.*) a fool.

caloop *v.* [? KER- *pfx* + SE *loop*, to encircle (with one's arms)] [20C+] (*US*) to go courting, to kiss and cuddle.

calp *n. see* KELP *n.*[1].

calve *v.* [echoic; note CALF *v.*] [mid-19C] (*US*) to vomit.

calves gone to grass *phr.* [a pun] [late 18C–19C] denoting someone who has noticeably thin legs; thus joc. remark: 'veal will be cheap, calves fall' on noticing a man whose calves fall away.

Calvin Klein *n.* [rhy. sl.; ult. US clothes designer *Calvin Klein* (b.1942)] **1** [1990s+] a judicial fine. **2** [1990s+] wine. **3** [2000s] the number nine.

Cam *n.* [abbr.] [1970s+] *Cam*bodian marijuana, usu. very strong.

cam *n.*[1] [ety. unknown; ? abbr. SE *commission*] [late 18C] money.

cam *n.*[2] *see* CAMI *n.*

camac *n.* [two clergymen, named Ryan and *Camac*, hanged for counterfeiting at Wexford in the early 19C] [19C] (*Irish*) anything that is over-complex or over-expensive to achieve its essentially simple purpose.

camarada de aquella *n.* [Sp., lit. 'a good friend is coming'] [1960s+] (*US*) a general term of high praise for an individual, a number one guy.

Camberwell death trap, the *n.* [the drownings that occurred there] [late 19C–1900s] the Surrey Canal.

Cambo *n.* [abbr.] [1990s+] (*US*) a *Camb*odian.

Cambodian red *n.* (*also* **Cam red**) [1960s+] (*drugs*) a slightly reddish variety of marijuana grown in Cambodia.

Cambridge *adj.*

proper name in slang uses

(IN COMPOUNDS)

❑ **Cambridge fortune** *n.* [punning on two staples of the Cambridgeshire countryside, the term is defined by Grose as 'a wind-mill and a water-mill', i.e. she can talk and urinate but that is all] [late 17C–early 19C] a woman who has no fortune of her own and must rely for attraction on her personal charms alone. ❑ **Cambridge nightingale** *n.* (*also* **Cambridgeshire nightingale**) [the large numbers of croaking frogs found in the marshy fens] [late 19C] a frog. ❑ **Cambridge oak** *n.* (*also* **Cambridgeshire oak**) [the frequency of willows in that county] [late 18C–early 19C] a willow. ❑ **Cambridgeshire camel** *n.* [the stilt-walkers once found in the fens] [late 17C–18C] a native or established resident of Cambridgeshire.

Camden Town *n.* [rhy. sl. = BROWN *n.* (2b)] [mid-19C–1910s] a halfpenny.

camel *n.* [various characteristics of the animal, i.e. a long neck, a hump, its supposed dirtiness] **1** [mid-19C–1910s] (*S.Afr.*) a giraffe. **2** [late 19C] (*US*) a bustle or 'dress-improver'. **3** [1990s+] (*Aus. prison*) a prisoner who neglects personal hygiene.

SE in slang uses

(IN COMPOUNDS)

derog. nicknames for inhabitants of the Middle East

❑ **camel-chaser** *n.* [1960s+] (*orig. US*) a derog. term for a Syrian or an Indian (from India) or any form of Arabic Middle Easterner. ❑ **camel-driver** *n.* **1** [1920s] (*US*) a Jew [the inference is of Middle Eastern origins rather than professional stereotyping]. **2** [1970s] an Arab, a native of the Middle East. ❑ **camel-fucker** *n.* [FUCKER *n.* (1)] [2000s] (*US*) a derog. term for an Arabic native of the Middle East. ❑ **camel head** *n.* [-HEAD *sfx* (2)] [2000s] (*US*) a derog. term for an Arabic native of the Middle East. ❑ **camel jockey** *n.* (*also* **camel-jock**) [JOCKEY *n.*[2] (3b)] [1960s+] (*US*) a native of the Middle East; an Arab. ❑ **camel rider** *n.* [? mis-reading] [1930s] (*US Und.*) an Asian.

general uses

❑ **camel-breath** *n.* [1960s] a general derog. description. ❑ **camel dung** *n.* [20C+] a derog. name for unpleasantly tasting cigarettes, orig. using Egyptian tobacco. ❑ **camel-puncher** *n.* [1910s] (*Aus.*) a camel-driver. ❑ **camel's complaint** *n.* [pun on the HUMP *n.*[1] (1)] [late 19C–1920s] depression. ❑ **camel toe** *n.* (*also* **camel toes, camel's foot**) [supposed resemblance] [1990s+] (*orig. US*) the vulva as seen through a tight pair of jeans, shorts etc.

cameo cut *n.* [popularized by Larry Blackmon, lead singer of the band *Cameo*; note *cameo cut*, a technique for decorative glass-cutting] [1980s–90s] (*US black*) short-cropped black hair, pioneered by the hip-hop culture.

camera obscura *n.* [pun on Lat. *camera obscura*, a dark place] [late 19C–1900s] (*US*) the buttocks, the anus.

camerer cuss *n.* [rhy. sl.; the clockmaker's *Camerer Cuss*, founded in 1788] [1910s–30s] a London bus.

camesa *n.* (*also* **cameza, kemesa, smisk**) [Ital. *camisa*, a shirt] [mid-17C–late 19C] a shirt.

cami *n.* (*also* **cam, cammy**) [abbr.] [20C+] **1** a *cami*sole or underbodice. **2** *cami*-knickers.

cami-knicks *n.* [abbr. SE *cami-knickers*] [1930s+] an undergarment that combines *cami*sole and *knickers*.

Camilla Parker (Bowles) *n.* [rhy. sl.; ult. *Camilla Parker Bowles* (b.1949), Duchess of Cornwall, wife of the Prince of Wales] [1990s+] a *Rolls* Royce car.

camisole *n.* [1930s–50s] (*US prison*) a strait-jacket.

camister *n.* [SE *camis*, a surplice + CAMESA *n.*] [mid-19C] (*UK Und.*) a clergyman, a preacher.

cammies *n.* (*also* **camos**) [abbr.] [1970s+] (*orig. US milit.*) *camo*uflage (uniform).

cammy *n. see* CAMI *n.*

camo *adj.* (*also* **cammy**) [abbr.] [1970s+] (*orig. US milit.*) of uniforms, *camo*uflage.

camouflage cocktail *n.* [1930s] (*US black*) a cocktail designed to hide the poor quality liquor of the Prohibition era.

Camp, the *n.* **1** [late 18C–early 19C] (*Aus.*) Sydney. **2** [mid-19C] (*Aus.*) Hobart. **3** [20C+] the area outside Port Stanley in the Falkland Islands.

camp *n.*[1] [mid-19C+] (*Aus.*) a short rest, a lie-down; thus *have a camp, go to camp*, to take a rest.

SE in slang uses

IN COMPOUNDS

❑ **camp candlestick** *n.* [the use of such an empty bottle as a candlestick in army camps etc] [late 18C–early 19C] an empty bottle. ❑ **camp dog** *n.* [1920s–40s] (*US tramp*) one who runs errands and does small jobs for his fellow tramps. ❑ **camp meat** *n.* [i.e. *meat* obtained by those in a *camp*, rather than on a farm] [20C+] (*US*) deer that has been illegally shot by poachers. ❑ **camp strawberries** *n.* [1940s] (*US tramp*) beans, a staple of tramp meals.

camp *n.*[2] [CAMP *adj.*] (*orig. US*) **1** [1920s+] a homosexual male; a homosexual who takes themselves overly seriously; an effeminate male homosexual. **2** [1930s–40s] a gathering place for male homosexuals. **3** [1920s+] (*also* **camping**) flamboyance, overt exhibitionism; thus a flamboyant person (of either sex).

DERIVATIVES

❑ **camposity** *n.* [1950s] the world and culture of male homosexuals.

camp *adj.* ['Actions and gestures of exaggerated emphasis. Probably from the French. Used chiefly by persons of exceptional want of character. "How very camp he is."' (Ware). Anthony Burgess suggests a link to SE *camp*, a military base, mining or railroad camp, in which, as in a prison, a lack of women might lead to homosexuality and where effeminate men would act deliberately in this manner to attract admirers. He also notes the availability, in London, of soldiers from the city barracks, willing to indulge gay men-about-town] [mid-19C+] **1** (*also* **campish, camping**) effeminate, affected, exaggerated; the general image is that of limp-wristed homosexuality. **2** strange, but amusing. **3** stylish.

IN PHRASES

❑ **camp as a row of tents** *adj.* [1950s+] of a male homosexual, extremely, ostentatiously effeminate. ❑ **camp as Chloe** *adj.* [ref. to the same portrait of Chloe that inspired DRUNK AS CHLOE *adj.*] [1950s–60s] of a man or a male homosexual, extremely affected, effeminate.

camp *v.*[1] [CAMP *n.*[1]] (*Aus.*) **1** [mid-19C+] to rest, to lie down. **2** [late 19C] to die.

IN PHRASES

❑ **camp down** *v.* [late 19C] (*Aus.*) **1** to go to bed. **2** to die.

camp *v.*[2] [CAMP *adj.*] **1** [1920s+] to act ostentatiously and outrageously in a homosexual manner, although by no means restricted – verbally or physically – to the gay world. **2** [2000s] (*UK juv.*) to act in an exaggeratedly 'gay' manner in order to humiliate a boy who is, or is believed to be, homosexual. **3** [2000s] (*S.Afr. gay*) to solicit for a sexual partner.

IN PHRASES

❑ **camp about** *v.* (*also* **camp around, camp it up**) **1** [1920s+] of a man, to act in a deliberate and exaggeratedly effeminate manner; used of effeminate male homosexuals and those who, maliciously or otherwise, are attempting to mimic them; thus adj. *camped-up*, ostentatiously effeminate. **2** [1960s–70s] to render something 'camp'. **3** [1970s] to be witty, whimsical, amusing. ❑ **camp it off** *v.* [1970s+] (*US gay*) to shrug off an insult.

camp *adv.* [1970s+] (*US gay*) effeminately, in an affected, exaggerated manner.

campaign coat *n.* [orig. a milit. uniform, then in civilian tailoring a style of coat that resembled military uniform; as worn by a beggar, such a coat was supposed to present the image of an old soldier] [mid-17C–early 18C] a tattered old coat, worn by beggars spec. to excite sympathy in passers-by.

Campbell's academy *n.* [*Campbell*, the name of the first director of such prisons + ACADEMY *n.* (4)] [late 18C–early 19C] the hulks, or floating prisons, sited in ships moored in the Thames Estuary.

camped *adj.* [CAMP *v.*[1] (1)] [late 19C] (*Aus.*) exhausted.

camper *n.*[1] [CAMP *v.*[2] (1)] [1930s+] (*US gay*) a homosexual male, esp. effeminate and young.

camper *n.*[2] [the studied jollity of a holiday *camp*] [1970s+] (*US*) a person, an individual; usu. in (ironic) phr. *happy camper*.

campfire girl *n.* [play on CAMP *adj.* (1)] [1970s+] (*US camp gay*) a soldier.

camphor and moth *n.* [rhy. sl.] [1930s] (*UK tramp*) broth.

camping *n. see* CAMP *n.*[2] (3).

camping/campish *adj. see* CAMP *adj.* (1).

campy *adj.* [CAMP *adj.*] **1** [1940s–60s] ostentatious, affected, effeminate. **2** [1970s] (*US black*) extremely close-knit, happy, cheerful and free-spirited to the point of infuriating one's companions.

Cam red *n. see* CAMBODIAN RED *n.*

can *n.*[1] [SE *can*, a container] **1** as a 'hollow' part of the body. (**a**) [17C+] the vagina. (**b**) [1910s+] (*US*) the buttocks; the anus. (**c**) [1910s+] (*US*) used as a euph. for ASS *n.* (2) in various senses, e.g. *pain in the can, flatter the can off* etc. (**d**) [1910s+] (*Aus./US*) the human head. (**e**) [1910s+] the mouth. **2** [mid-19C; 1910s–20s] (*US*) a bomb; thus *can-maker*, a bomb-maker. **3** [late 19C] by meton., a barman. **4** as a room, place or container. (**a**) [late 19C] a small room, e.g. in a hotel. (**b**) [20C+] (*US*) a water closet, a lavatory. (**c**) [1910s+] a prison, a police station lock-up; as generic *can*, imprisonment. (**d**) [1920s] (*US Und.*) a still. (**e**) [1920s+] (*US Und.*) a safe. (**f**) [1930s] (*US Und.*) a bank. **5** in the context of drugs. (**a**) [late 19C–1920s] a 5oz (140g) container of opium. (**b**) [1930s] a 1oz (28g) container of opium. (**c**) [1930s–50s] 1oz (28g) of morphine. (**d**) [1950s+] approx. 1oz (28g) of marijuana. (**e**) [1980s] (*Aus.*) a phial of morphine, sufficient for a single injection. **6** [1900s–20s] a pocket. **7** as vehicles. (**a**) [1920s+] (*US*) a dilapidated, run-down, malfunctioning vehicle, incl. a ship. (**b**) [1940s] a plane.

IN COMPOUNDS

❑ **can house** *n.* [HOUSE *n.*[1] (1)] [20C+] (*US, mainly Chicago*) a brothel. ❑ **can opener** *n. see* separate entry. ❑ **can shooter** *n. see* CAN OPENER *n.* (4).

IN PHRASES

❑ **crush the can** *v.* [1940s] (*US prison*) to escape from jail. ❑ **get the can** *v.* [sense 1b above; var. on *GET THE (BIG) ARSE under* ARSE *n.*] [1900s] (*US*) to be dismissed from a job. ❑ **go in the can** *v.* [1980s] (*US*) to accept a bribe; to act in a corrupt manner. ❑ **out on one's can** [1930s] (*orig. US*) ejected unceremoniously, thrown out. ❑ **suck someone's can** *v. see* SUCK SOMEONE'S DICK *under* DICK *n.*^{1}. ❑ **swap cans** *v. see under* SWAP *v.* ❑ **sweat one's can off** *v. see under* SWEAT *v.*^{2}.

IN EXCLAMATIONS

❑ **give your can a chance!** [1910s] (*Aus.*) stop talking! ❑ **my can!** [late 17C+] a general excl. of disdain, dismissal, arrogant contempt. ❑ **shut your can!** [1910s] (*US*) shut up! be quiet!

SE in slang uses

IN COMPOUNDS

❑ **can moocher** *n. see* TOMATO-CAN VAG *under* TOMATO CAN *n.* ❑ **can racket** *n.* [RACKET *n.*^{2} (1)] [late 19C] (*US*) a party devoted to drinking beer.

IN PHRASES

❑ **can of piss** *n.* [2000s] (*Irish*) a term of abuse. ❑ **carry the can (for)** *v.* (*also* **carry the can back, carry the shit-can, take the can back, take the can for**) [1920s+] (*orig. naut.*) to take the blame that should be another's, to do the 'dirty work'; esp. as *left carrying the can*. ❑ **chase the can** *v.* [late 19C–1940s] to drink freely at a bar. ❑ **get a can on** *v.* (*also* **pin a can on, tie a can on**) [? SE *can*, a container for beer when taken home from a bar or public house] [1920s–50s] (*US*) to go on a drinking spree. ❑ **hit the can** *v.* [1950s+] (*Aus.*) to pay for a round of drinks. ❑ **hold the can (for)** *v.* [1920s+] to take responsibility, usu. unwanted. ❑ **rattle the can** *v.* [1940s] (*US*) to beg in the street. ❑ **rush the can** *v.* [late 19C+] (*US*) to buy beer from a tavern and bring it home for drinking there. ❑ **tie a can to** *v.* [a child's tying of a can to an animal's tail] **1** [late 19C+] (*US*) to play an unpleasant trick on. **2** [1900s–50s] (*also* **hang a can to, tie a can on**) to reject or dismiss (a person). **3** [1920s+] to stop (an activity). ❑ **tie the can to** *v.* [1910s] to condemn, to reprimand. ❑ **touch the can** *v.* [1950s+] (*Aus.*) to pay for a round of drinks.

can *n.*^{2} [ety. unknown] [mid-19C] (*US*) $1.

can *v.* **1** [20C+] to stop doing something, esp. in imper., e.g. *can that noise!* [fig. 'place it in a can']. **2** [20C+] (*orig. US*) to reject, to abandon, to discard, to dismiss from a job, to throw out, to ignore [toss out on one's CAN *n.*^{1} (1b)]. **3** [1910s+] (*US*) to put in prison; to lock up [CAN *n.*^{1} (4c)]. **4** [1940s–70s] (*US*) to have anal sex with [CAN *n.*^{1} (1b)]. **5** [1960s] (*US black/drugs*) to package heroin for sale [SE *can* or ? link to CAN *n.*^{1} (5)].

IN PHRASES

❑ **can it** *v.* [20C+] (*orig. US*) **1** to stop, esp. to stop talking; usu. in excl. *can it!*, shut up! **2** to reject or give up.

Canadian *adj.* [1970s+] (*US gay*) uncircumcised.

IN COMPOUNDS

❑ **Canadian bacon** *n.* [BACON *n.*^{1} (5)] [1970s+] (*US gay*) an uncircumcised penis.

proper name in slang uses

IN COMPOUNDS

❑ **Canadian black** *n.* [its dark green colouring] [1960s+] (*drugs*) marijuana.

Canadian caper *n.* [rhy. sl.] [1960s] (*Aus.*) a paper.

canadoe *n.* [? SE *can* + Fr. *d'eau*, of water] [early 17C] a drink.

canal boat *n.*^{1} [rhy. sl. = TOTE *n.*] [20C+] the Totalizator.

canal boat *n.*^{2} (*also* **canal-barge**) [supposed resemblance] [1920s–70s] (*US*) a large foot or shoe.

canaller *n.* [mid–late 19C] (*orig. US*) **1** a canal boat. **2** one who lives on a canal boat.

canamo *n.* [Sp. *cañamo*, a reed] [1970s+] (*US drugs*) marijuana.

canappa *n.* [? Sp.] [1930s] (*drugs*) marijuana.

canaries *n.* [SE *canary* yellow] [1930s+] bananas.

Canarsie whitefish *n. see* CONEY ISLAND WHITEFISH *under* CONEY ISLAND *n.*

canary *n.*^{1} **1** (*also* **canary-bird**) synon. with BIRD *n.*^{1}, a woman, underlined by the gaudy colouring of her clothes and/or SE *canary*, a small fluttering bird. (**a**) [17C] the vagina. (**b**) [18C–early 19C] a mistress. (**c**) [18C–early 19C] a prostitute. (**d**) [mid-19C] a thief's female accomplice. (**e**) [late 19C] (*US*) a woman. (**f**) [late 19C–1900s] (*US campus*) a female student at a mixed college. **2** based on the yellow colour of the bird. (**a**) [19C+] (*Aus./S.Afr./US*) a convict [the yellow uniforms that they wore and their being 'caged'; poss. reinforced by earlier CANARY-BIRD *n.*^{1} (2) although that image refers to the cage rather than the colour]. (**b**) [early 19C] a yellow silk handkerchief, as worn by a costermonger, allegedly popularized by the British prize-fighter John Gully (1783–1863). (**c**) [mid-19C–1900s] a guinea; a sovereign; a gold coin. (**d**) [late 19C] a half-sovereign (50p). (**e**) [late 19C] (*UK prison*) a prisoner who has been caught in an escape attempt. (**f**) [late 19C] a convict's yellow jacket. (**g**) [late 19C] (*US*) a mule, usu. in comb. with a geographical name, e.g. ROCKY MOUNTAIN CANARY *n.* (**h**) [late 19C–1900s] a form on which one signs a promise to make a donation to the Salvation Army; a charity subscription [the yellow paper used by the Salvation Army, whose colours were red and yellow (the red paper was more expensive, noted Ware); coined by their founder William Booth (1829–1912)]. (**i**) [late 19C–1910s] (*Aus./N.Z.*) a Chinese immigrant [YELLOW *adj.* (2c)]. (**j**) [1900s] (*US campus*) a cigarette, presumably in a yellow packet or yellow paper. (**k**) [1940s] (*US black*) a mulatto girl [YELLOW *adj.* (2b)]. (**l**) [1980s+] (*Irish*) a fright, i.e. one turns YELLOW *adj.* (4). **3** [mid-19C] (*Aus.*) 100 strokes of the lash [fig. use of sense 2c above: the term plays on the monetary value signifying the number of strokes]. **4** based on the bird's singing. (**a**) [late 19C+] (*US*) a chorus-singer placed in the gallery from where they urge on the rest of the audience. (**b**) [20C+] (*show business*) a female singer, usu. fronting a band. (**c**) [1920s+] (*UK/US/S.Afr. Und.*) an informer. (**d**) [1930s] (*US Und.*) a loquacious person, a chatterer. (**e**) [1930s–50s] a singer, irrespective of gender.

IN COMPOUNDS

❑ **canary cage** *n.* [1910s] (*Aus.*) the locked area inside a prison vehicle. ❑ **canary hatch** *n.* [var. on BOOBY-HATCH *n.* (2)] [1960s] (*US*) a psychiatric institution. ❑ **canary kid** *n.* [i.e. YELLOW *adj.* (4)] [1940s] (*US Und.*) a weakling; a coward. ❑ **canary-talk** *n.* [1910s] (*US*) singing.

IN PHRASES

❑ **have a canary** *v.* **1** [1940s+] (*US*) to be mentally unstable; for one's brain to be injured. **2** [1960s+] (*Irish*) to have an emotional outburst. ❑ **have a hairy canary** *v.* [1950s+] (*US*) to have a temper tantrum, an emotional outburst.

canary *n.*^{2} ['in true descent from the cod-piece, though not so glaring in its declaration' (Ware)] [late 19C–1900s] an ornament worn at the hip.

canary *v.* **1** [1930s+] of a criminal, to confess, to turn state's evidence [CANARY *n.*^{1} (4c)]. **2** [1940s] (*US*) to work as a band vocalist; to sing [CANARY *n.*^{1} (4e)].

canary-bird *n.*^{1} [the cage in which the prisoner is kept or the young villain will end up] **1** [17C–mid-18C] a young villain [with an added inference of smartness of dress]. **2** [late 17C–19C; 1960s] (*later use S.Afr.*) a prisoner.

canary-bird *n.*^{2} [ext. of CANARY *n.*^{1} (2c)] [late 17C–mid-19C] a guinea or gold coin.

canary-bird *n.*^{3} *see* CANARY *n.*^{1} (1).

canasta *n.* [the card-game, ult. f. Sp. *canasta*, a basket; thus pun on BASKET *n.*^{1} (2)] [1950s–70s] the male or female genitals; thus (*US gay*) *play canasta*, to ogle other men's crotches.

canat *n. see* KINAT *n.*

cancelled stamp *n.* [fig. use of SE] [1920s] (*US*) a shy person.

cancelled stick *n.* [? SE *cancel*, i.e. it 'cancels' you out + STICK *n.* (6d); pun on *cancer stick* under CANCER *n.*] [1960s+] (*drugs*) a marijuana cigarette.

cancel someone out *v.* [1990s+] to murder someone.

cancer *n.* [1970s+] (*US*) severe rust on an automobile.

SE in slang uses

IN COMPOUNDS

❑ **cancer alley** *n.* [the polluting factories may well issue carcinogens into the atmosphere] [1980s+] (*US*) the industrial area of a city. ❑ **cancer case** *n.* [1960s] (*Aus.*) an annoying old person. ❑ **cancer stick** *n.* (*also* **cancer pill**) [the proven link between tobacco and lung cancer; note Jap. use of *cancer stick*, a mobile telephone, referring to the belief that the phones can irradiate the user] [1950s+] a cigarette.

C&A *adj.* [rhy. sl. = GAY *adj.* (6); ult. *C&A*, a chain of clothing stores in the UK] [1950s–70s] homosexual.

C and B *v. see* COAT AND BADGE V.

c&b *n. see* C.B. *n.*[1].

C and E man *n.* [Christmas and *Easter*; the two festivals that attract the irregular attender] [1960s] (*US*) someone who attends church only rarely.

C and H *n.* [C *n.*[3] (1) + H *n.* (2); also pun on brandname of *C & H* cane sugar] [1960s+] (*US black*) a mixture of cocaine and heroin.

candle *n.*

SE in slang uses

IN COMPOUNDS

❑ **candle-basher** *n.* [the candle's use as a dildo] [late 19C–1960s] a spinster. ❑ **candle-eater** *n.* [? their poverty] [1920s–30s] (*US tramp*) a Russian. ❑ **candle shop** *n.* [the many candles that burn in one] [late 19C] a Roman Catholic church. ❑ **candlesperm** *n.* [resemblance to drops of semen; Major, *Juba to Jive: A Dict. of Afro-American Slang* (1994), defines it as a 'voodoo term'] [1920s+] (*US black*) melted wax from a candle, which drips down into globular beadlets.

IN PHRASES

❑ **dip the candle** *v. see DIP THE DAGGER under* DAGGER *n.*[1].

candle *v.*[1] [SE *candle*, to test an egg's freshness by holding it to a candle flame] [late 19C] to check carefully.

candle *v.*[2] [BURN UP V. (2)] [1930s] to make angry.

candle (and) sconce *n.* (*also* **candle-sconce**) [rhy. sl. = PONCE *n.* (1)] [1940s+] a pimp.

candlestick *n.*[1] [a place into which the phallic 'candle' is inserted] [mid-17C; late 19C] the vagina.

candlestick *n.*[2] [the running of water or mucus supposedly resembles that of wax] **1** [mid-19C] one of the fountains in Trafalgar Square, London. **2** [20C+] (*Irish*) a drop of mucus running from the nose.

candlesticks *n.* [? the impossibility of getting a clear note when striking a candlestick] [late 18C–early 19C] small, bad or untunable bells.

C and M *n.* [C *n.*[3] (1) + M *n.* (1)] [1950s+] (*drugs*) a cocaine and morphine mixture.

can-do *adj.* [CAN DO *phr.*] [1990s+] (*orig. US*) positive, enthusiastic, aggressive.

can do *phr.* [affirmative phr. *I can do it*] [20C+] it is possible, it is within my power; thus *no can do*, it is impossible.

candy *n.* **1** [20C+] (*US*) something admirable or desirable. **2** [20C+] (*US*) money. **3** [1920s–40s] (*US Und.*) jewellery. **4** something or someone 'sweet'. (**a**) [late 19C+] (*orig. US*) a sexually desirable person of either sex. (**b**) [1920s+] (*orig. US black*) sex as an abstract; thus sexual intercourse. (**c**) [1950s+] (*US gay*) a pretty, young homosexual boy. (**d**) [1950s+] (*US gay*) the passive partner in anal intercourse. (**e**) [1960s] (*US teen*) a weakling. **5** in drug uses. (**a**) [1930s] (*US drugs*) opium. (**b**) [1930s+] (*orig. US drugs*) cocaine. (**c**) [1960s+] (*US drugs*) any drug, esp. in capsule form. (**d**) [1980s+] (*US black/drugs*) heroin. (**e**) [2000s] (*US drugs*) crack cocaine. **6** [2000s] (*US black*) decoration or customization of an automobile.

pertaining to lit./fig. adornment

IN PHRASES

❑ **arm candy** *n.* [1990s+] a pretty young woman whose role is merely to adorn the arm of her male companion. ❑ **brain candy** *n.* [1990s+] anything superficially attractive but intellectually undemanding. ❑ **eye candy** *n.* [1980s+] a sexually attractive looking person.

pertaining to drugs

IN COMPOUNDS

❑ **candy bar** *n.* [1950s] (*US drugs*) a place where cocaine is sold. ❑ **candy C** *n.* [C *n.*[3] (1)] [1950s–70s] (*drugs*) cocaine. ❑ **candy cane** *n.* [SE (*co*)*caine* + play on SE] [1980s+] (*US black*) cocaine, whether as powder or crack. ❑ **candy fiend** *n.* [1950s] (*US drugs*) a cocaine addict. ❑ **candy-flip** *v.* [1990s+] (*US drugs*) to mix or sequence LSD and MDMA; thus n. *candy-flipping*. ❑ **candy rock** *n.* [1990s+] (*Aus. drugs*) cocaine hydrochloride. ❑ **candy stick** *n. see* STICK *n.* (3).

IN PHRASES

❑ **Andes candy** *n.* [the South American origins of cocaine] [1990s+] (*US drugs*) cocaine. ❑ **hard candy** *n.* [HARD *adj.* (5)] [1960s+] (*drugs*) heroin. ❑ **nose candy** *n. see under* NOSE *n.*

general uses

IN COMPOUNDS

❑ **candy-bag** *n.* [1920s+] (*Aus.*) a handyman who works for a prostitute. ❑ **candy boy** *n.* [1900s] (*US*) a boyfriend, a beloved male. ❑ **candy-butt** *n.* [BUTT *n.*[1] (1a)] [1970s+] (*US black*) a young, inexperienced male.

SE in slang uses

IN COMPOUNDS

❑ **candy-ass** *see* separate entries. ❑ **candy-bar punk** *n.* [ext. PUNK *n.*[1] (2); the gifts or payments of candy bars that he receives for his services] [1960s] (*US prison*) a prisoner who has become a passive homosexual while in prison. ❑ **candy cane** *n.* (*also* **candy stick**) [like the synon. sweet, it can be sucked] [late 19C–1970s] (*US*) the penis. ❑ **candy cock** *n.* [1910s] (*US*) a well-behaved, pleasant person; the inference is of softness. ❑ **candy kid** *n. see* separate entry. ❑ **candy-leg** *n.* (*also* **candy boy**) [1920s–40s] (*US campus*) a rich student who is also attractive to women. ❑ **candy-maker** *n.* [1960s] (*US*) a male homosexual who masturbates (but does not fellate) a partner, then swallows the resultant semen. ❑ **candyman** *n. see* separate entry. ❑ **candystriper** *n.* [the usu. red and white striped uniform] [1960s+] (*US*) a volunteer nurse's aide; thus *candystripe*, to work as such an aide. ❑ **candy team** *n.* [1930s] (*US*) the preferred team of mules. ❑ **candy wagon** *n.* **1** [1920s+] (*US*) a buggy. **2** [1940s+] a light truck.

IN PHRASES

❑ **drop one's candy** *v. see under* DROP *v.*[1]. ❑ **rock candy** *n. see under* ROCK *n.*

candy, the *n.* [1900s] (*US*) something excellent, admirable, desirable.

candy *adj.*[1] [ety. unknown; ? link to SE *can*, a container for liquids] [mid-18C–early 19C] (*mainly Anglo-Irish*) drunk.

candy *adj.*[2] [? resemblance to transparent boiled sweets] [late 19C] (*US Und.*) of dice, transparent.

candy *adj.*[3] [CANDY *n.* (1)] **1** [1900s–20s; 1990s+] (*later use US campus*) excellent, worthy of admiration. **2** [1930s+] (*US*) of a job or any other activity, e.g. a crime, easy, undemanding, 'soft'.

candy *adj.*[4] [the perceived link of candy-eating and softness] [1910s+] (*US*) of a person, soft, weak, effeminate.

candy *adv.* [1990s+] (*US black*) in a fashionable manner.

candy-ass *n.* **1** [1960s+] a coward, a weakling, an over-sensitive person [CANDY-ASS *adj.* (1)]. **2** [1960s+] (*US gay*) an attractive young man, thus a term of abuse by non-gays [SAmE *candy* + sfx -ASS *sfx*].

candy-ass *adj.* [SAmE *candy* + sfx -ASS *sfx*] [1950s+] (*US*) **1** of a person, weak, ineffectual. **2** of a job, examination etc, insufficiently challenging, too easy. **3** pathetic, obsessive, dedicated, e.g. *a candy-ass fan*.

candy-assed *adj.* [SAmE *candy* + -ASSED *sfx* (2)] [1950s+] (*US*) weak, ineffectual.

candy kid *n.* [SAmE *candy* + KID *n.*[1] (4)] **1** [1900s–40s] (*US*) a successful womanizer. **2** [1900s–50s] (*US*) a well-behaved, pleasant person. **3** [1900s–50s] (*US*) a weakling, a mother's boy, a favoured child. **4** [1910s–40s] (*US*) a dandy, a fashionably dressed person. **5** [1940s–50s] (*Aus.*) a jack-of-all-trades employed by a brothel.

candyman *n.* [the 'sweetness' of SAmE *candy*] **1** [1910s–30s] (*US*) a dandy. **2** [1920s+] (*US black*) a woman's male partner or (illicit) lover. **3** [1960s+] (*drugs*) a drug dealer. **4** [1980s] (*US black*) a pimp.

cane *n.*[1] [resemblance] **1** [20C+] (*UK Und.*) a short house-breaker's crowbar. **2** [1930s] a bassoon.

SE in slang uses

IN COMPOUNDS

❑ **cane nigger** *n.* [SE (*sugar*)*cane* + NIGGER *n.*[1] (1); i.e. stereotyped image of a cane field worker] [late 19C] a cheerful person. ❑ **cane oil** *n.* [SE *cane oil*, liquor of the sugarcane] [1970s] (*W.I.*) rum. ❑ **cane toad** *n.* [SE *cane toad*, the large toad, *bufo marinus*] [1990s+] (*Aus.*) a rich old man.

IN PHRASES

❑ **varnish the cane** *v.* (*also* **varnish the stick**) [pun on SE/STICK *n.* (1a)] [1900s–60s] (*US*) of a man, to have sexual intercourse.

cane *n.*[2] [var. on CAINE *n.*/abbr. CANDY CANE *under* CANDY *n.*] [1980s+] (*US black*) cocaine, whether as powder or crack.

cane *v.* [fig. uses of SE] **1** [1910s+] to defeat, to treat harshly. **2** [1940s+] (*also* **cane it**) to attack, esp. fig., e.g. to drink heartily, to take a large amount of drugs. **3** [1960s+] to have sexual intercourse. **4** [1990s+] (*also* **cane it**) to hurry, to rush. **5** [1990s+] (*also* **cane it**) to do something in an aggressive, urgent manner, e.g. a robbery. **6** [1990s+] (*also* **cane it**) to make a lot of money. **7** [1990s+] (*UK juv.*) to be seriously reprimanded. **8** [2000s] to cover a wall or other object in graffiti.

caned *adj.* [the equation of the effects of drink/drugs with suffering violence/CANE *v.* (2)] **1** [1980s+] (*drugs*) extremely intoxicated by a drug, usu. cannabis. **2** [2000s] very drunk.

canetta *n.* [CAN *n.*[1] (1b) + sfx *-etta*] [1970s+] (*US gay*) the buttocks.

caning *n.* [CANE *v.* (2)] [1940s+] the act of consuming something enthusiastically.

canister *n.*[1] (*also* **cannister**) [all fig. uses of SE *canister*, a container] **1** [late 18C] the vagina. **2** [late 18C+] the head. **3** [late 19C] a hat. **4** [1900s–30s] (*US*) a watch. **5** [1900s–50s] (*US Und.*) a revolver. **6** [1910s–50s] (*US Und.*) a jail. **7** [1920s] (*US Und.*) a lookout. **8** [1930s–50s] (*US*) a safe or bank vault.

IN COMPOUNDS

❑ **canister cap** *n.* [mid-19C] a hat.

canister *n.*[2] [SE *camis*, a surplice + CAMESA *n.*] [late 19C–1900s] a clergyman.

canister set *n.* [CAN *n.*[1] (1)] [1970s+] (*US gay*) the buttocks.

cank *n.* [? ironic reverse of dial. *cank*, a gossip, a chatterer] [mid-17C–early 19C] (*UK Und.*) a dumb person.

cank *adj.* [CANK *n.*] [mid-17C–early 19C] (*UK Und.*) dumb.

cannabinol *n.* [misreading of SE *cannabinol*, the active constituent of cannabis] [1970s] (*US drugs*) phencyclidine.

cannack ague *phr.* [mid-19C] (*UK Und.*) lacking both money and credit.

cannakin *n. see* CANNIKEN *n.*[1].

canned *adj.* [SE *can*, a container for liquids] **1** [1910s+] (*also* **canned up**) drunk. **2** [1920s] (*US*) of writing, information: rote, pre-packaged, 'boilerplate' [suggests that such writing 'comes in a can'].

IN PHRASES

❑ **half-canned** *adj.* [1920s+] tipsy rather than wholly drunk.

SE in slang uses

IN COMPOUNDS

❑ **canned cattle** *n.* [1930s] (*US prison*) corned beef. ❑ **canned cow** *n.* [COW *n.*[1] (5)] [20C+] (*US*) condensed milk. ❑ **canned goods** *n.* [pun on *can*/CAN *n.*[1] (1a) + the image of a sealed tin] [1910s–70s] (*US*) a virgin of either sex, usu. female; the genitalia of such a person. ❑ **canned mystery** *n. see* MYSTERY MEAT *under* MYSTERY *n.* ❑ **canned sativa** *n.* [pun on Lat. *Cannabis sativa* + ? drug use of sense 1 above] [1980s+] (*drugs*) cannabis. ❑ **canned stuff** *n.* [STUFF *n.* (5b)] [1930s–50s] (*US drugs*) commercially packaged opium. ❑ **canned willie** *n.* [1900s–10s] (*US*) corned beef.

canned heat *n.* [1910s–60s] (*US*) a form of crude alcohol, intended for heating purposes but drunk, as is methylated spirits, by down-and-out alcoholics who can afford nothing better; thus *canned heater, canned-heat stiff*, one who drinks such alcohol.

canner *n.* [late 19C–1910s] (*US*) a scraggy cow or other animal fit only for the lower end of the canned meat market.

cannery *n.* [CAN *n.*[1] (4c)] [1910s+] (*US prison*) a prison.

cannibal *n.*[1] [a pun on SE *cannibal*, one who 'eats' his fellow human beings] [17C] a notably harsh bargainer or grasping tradesman.

cannibal *n.*[2] [pun on SE *eat*/EAT *v.* (4)] **1** [1920s–30s] (*US tramp*) a older homosexual tramp who travels with a young boy. **2** [1960s+] (*US black*) one who indulges in oral sex.

cannie *n.* [abbr.] **1** [1940s] a *canni*bal. **2** [1990s+] (*Scot.*) a *can*teen, usu. institutional.

canniken *n.*[1] (*also* **cannakin, cannikin**) [? SE *canker*] [17C–early 19C] (*UK Und.*) the plague.

canniken *n.*[2] (*also* **cannikin**) [SE *can* + dimin. sfx *-kin*] [late 17C–mid-19C] a small can.

cannis-cove *n.* [Lat. *canis*, a dog + COVE *n.* (1)] [mid-19C] (*US Und.*) a dog-thief, a dog seller.

cannister *n. see* CANISTER *n.*[1].

Cannock *n. see* CANUCK *n.*

cannon *n.*[1] **1** [20C+] (*US*) a gun, esp. a large one; thus a gun barrel. **2** [1910s–30s] (*US*) a hired gunman. **3** [1950s] (*US drugs*) a hypodermic syringe [play on GUN *n.*[1] (5)]. **4** [1960s+] (*US*) the penis [play on GUN *n.*[1] (2)]. **5** [1970s] (*US*) a pimp.

IN PHRASES

❑ **empty the cannon** *v.* [1980s+] to masturbate.

cannon *n.*[2] [? they 'cannon into' or fig. 'shoot at' a victim; note Irwin, *American Tramp and Und. Slang* (1931): 'No doubt from the Yiddish, "gonoph," a thief, which became "gon" and then "gun" and so to its present form. In the argot, "cannon," "rod," "gun," "gat," "heater" and "torch" are all used to designate a revolver or pistol, but cannon is the only word of the group used synonymously with "gun" as a derivative of the root word, "gonov," a thief'] [20C+] **1** a pickpocket; thus *cannon-coppers*, the pickpocket squad. **2** the act of pickpocketing.

IN COMPOUNDS

❑ **cannon mob** *n.* (*also* **cannon gang**) [MOB *n.*[2] (3)] [20C+] a pickpocketing gang.

IN PHRASES

❑ **on the cannon** [20C+] working as a pickpocket.

cannon *adj.* (*also* **canon, cannoned**) [SE *cannon*, i.e. one has been knocked down] [mid-19C–1940s] drunk.

cannon *v.* [CANNON *n.*[2] (1)] [1920s–40s] (*US Und.*) to work as a pickpocket.

cannonball *n.* [the characteristics of the SE *cannonball*, i.e. shape, size, velocity, impact] **1** [late 19C] a testicle. **2** [late 19C] (*US short order*) in pl., crullers. **3** [late 19C–1960s] (*US tramp*) an express train. **4** [1920s–50s] (*US Und.*) a smaller safe that is held within a larger one. **5** [1920s–60s] (*US Und.*) a message sent out of jail by a convict. **6** [1940s–60s] (*US*) a superior person or one who claims to be so. **7** [1950s–70s] (*US drugs*) a mixed injection, e.g of heroin and cocaine or morphine and cocaine.

cannoned *adj. see* CANNON *adj.*

canoe *n.*[1] [rhy. sl.] [20C+] a shoe.

canoe *n.*[2] [supposed physical resemblance] **1** [1930s+] (*US*) a large car. **2** [1960s–80s] the vagina.

IN COMPOUNDS

❑ **canoe inspection** *n.* [1960s–70s] (*US*) a medical inspection of the female genitals.

canoe *n.*[3]

IN PHRASES

❑ **in the same canoe** *see* IN THE SAME BOX *under* BOX *n.*[1].

canoe *v.*[1] (*also* **John Canoe**) [CANOODLE *v.*] [mid-19C; 1920s–50s] to cuddle, to caress sexually.

canoe *v.*[2] [the burned side presumably resembles the hollowed portion of a canoe] [1980s+] of a cigarette or cannabis cigarette, to burn down on top or one side rather than evenly.

canoevre *n.* [? link to SE *manoeuvre*] [early–mid-19C] an attempt at swindling or a similarly dubious enterprise.

can of coke *n.* [rhy. sl.] [1990s+] a joke.

can of oil *n.* (*also* **canov**) [rhy. sl.] [20C+] a boil.

canon *adj. see* CANNON *adj.*

canoneer *n.* [mid–late 17C] an interpreter of ecclesiastical canons, a canonist.

canoodle *n.*

IN PHRASES

❑ **loose in the canoodle** *adj. see* LOOSE IN THE BEAN *under* BEAN *n.*[1].

canoodle *v.* (*also* **conoodle**) [ety. unknown but presumably linked to SE *cuddle*] [mid-19C+] (*orig. US*) to cuddle, to caress sexually; usu. as *canoodling*, cuddling or love-making.

can opener *n.* [SE *can*/CAN *n.*[1] (4e)/SE *can*] **1** [1910s] (*US*) a saber. **2** [1910s–40s] (*US*) a cook. **3** [1910s–60s] (*UK/US Und.*) any tool used for the breaking open of a safe, when explosives would lead to discovery; thus *can-opener artist*, a skilled safe-breaker. **4** [1910s–60s] (*UK/US Und.*) (*also* **can shooter**) a safebreaker; thus *can-opening*, safebreaking.

canov *n. see* CAN OF OIL *n.*

cans *n.* [? cans of milk or just resemblance] [1950s+] (*US*) the female breasts.

cant *n.*[1] [Lat. *cantare*, to sing. The term originates in conventional 12C society as a pej. description of church services that were condemned as substituting rote mouthings for real devotion. It was this use that led to the application of the term to, and adoption by, criminal beggars. SE *cant*, while obviously linked, is generally seen as relating to a pair of 17C Presbyterian ministers, Andrew *Cant* and his son Alexander; in a number of 18C/19C works, e.g. Johnson, *Dictionary* (1755), *cant* is used as a synon. for SE *slang*] [mid-16C+] the language of the world of professional thieves and itinerant criminal beggars; the term echoes the whining tones in which they 'chant' for alms.

cant *n.*[2] (*also* **kant**) [SE *cant*, a throw/to throw] [mid-19C] **1** (*UK tramp*) food [that which one 'cants' down one's throat]. **2** a blow [that which knocks someone down]. **3** a gift [the gift is 'thrown' to the recipient].

IN PHRASES

❑ **cant of togs** *n.* [TOGS *n.* (1)] [mid-19C] a (charitable) gift of clothes.

cant *v.*[1] [CANT *n.*[1]] **1** [mid-16C–19C] (*UK Und.*) to speak, to talk, esp. underworld slang. **2** [early 17C] to beg for alms.

cant *v.*[2] [SE *decant*] [mid-18C–early 19C] to drink, to swallow.

can't... *phr.* in general intensifying phrs. below, usu. suggesting that someone is very stupid or drunk (cf. COULDN'T... *phr.*).

IN PHRASES

❑ **can't find one's arse/ass with both hands** (*also* **...with two hands**) [ARSE *n.* (1)/ASS *n.* (2)] **1** [20C+] very drunk. **2** [1950s+] absolutely confused, totally incompetent. ❑ **can't say 'naval intelligencer'** (*also* **can't say 'national intelligencer'**) [one's trad. inability, when drunk, to pronounce 'difficult' words] [late 19C+] very drunk. ❑ **can't see a hole in a forty-foot ladder** [mid-19C+] very drunk. ❑ **can't see through a ladder** (*also* **too drunk to see through a ladder**) [mid-19C+] **1** extremely drunk. **2** very stupid.

Cantab. *n.* [*Cantab.*, abbr. of Lat. *Cantabrigiensis*, of Cambridge University, given as letters after one's name] **1** [mid-18C–mid-19C] a member (usu. an undergraduate) of Cambridge University. **2** [mid-19C] a member (usu. an undergraduate) of Harvard University in Cambridge, Mass.

cantaloupes *n. see* MELON *n.* (4).

cantankerous *adj.* [20C+ use is SE; ? f. ME *contak*, quarrelling, argument. Grose derives it f. Wilts. dial. and spells it *contankerous*] [late 18C–19C] irritable, ill-tempered, quick to become angry.

can't be bad *phr.* [1960s+] a general phr. of approval.

canter *n.* [CANT *v.*[1] (1)] [mid-16C–19C] a professional thief or criminal mendicant; one who speaks the thieves' language.

Canterbury story *n.* (*also* **Canterbury tale**) [the tales told by pilgrims on the way to Canterbury, and esp. f. the title of Chaucer's *Canterbury Tales* (*c.*1387)] [mid-16C–early 19C] a long, elaborate and ultimately tedious story.

canter gloak *n.* [SE *cant* + GLOAK *n.*] [late 18C–mid-19C] (*UK Und.*) **1** a parson. **2** a liar.

canter's stall *n.* [mid-19C] (*UK Und.*) a pulpit.

canticle *n.* [SE *canticle*, a hymn used during church services; the clerk trad. led the congregation in singing] [late 18C–mid-19C] a parish clerk.

canting *n.* [CANT *v.*[1] (1)] [mid-16C–mid-19C] thieves' jargon.

canting crew *n.* (*also* **canting tribe**) [CANT *v.*[1] (1) + CREW *n.* (1). The 'official' *canting crew*, as delineated by Grose, encompassed 23 orders. Men (in descending order of status): RUFFLER *n.*; UPRIGHT MAN *n.*; HOOKER *n.*[1] (1) or ANGLER *n.* (1); ROGUE *n.*; *WILD ROGUE under* WILD *adj.*; *PRIGGER OF PRANCERS under* PRIGGER *n.*[1]; PALLIARD *n.* (1); FRATER *n.*; JARKMAN *n.* or PATRICO *n.*; *FRESHWATER MARINER under* FRESHWATER *adj.* or *WHIP-JACK under* WHIP *v.*[3]; DOMMERER *n.*; DRUNKEN TINKER *n.*; SWADDER *n.*; ABRAM *n.* Women: DEMANDER FOR GLIMMER *n.*; *BAWDY-BASKET under* BAWDY *adj.*; MORT *n.*; *AUTEM MORT under* AUTEM *n.*; *WALKING MORT under* WALKING *adj.*; DOXY *n.* (1); DELL *n.* (1); *KINCHIN MORT under* KINCHIN *n.* However, such lists vary, e.g. that in the *New Canting Dict.* (1725) runs to 64 'job descriptions'] [mid-16C–19C] the world of professional thieves and criminal mendicants.

can't-keep-still *n. see* NEVER STAND STILL *n.*

cant of dobbin *n.* [SE *cant*, a share, a portion + ? dial. *dobbin*, a form of weaving machine, or *dobbie*, worsted] [late 18C–early 19C] a roll of ribbon.

cantor *v.* [? ext. of SE *cantor*, one who leads the singing in church or synagogue] [mid-19C] (*UK Und.*) to raise, to excite.

canty *adj.*[1] [Low Ger. *kant*, lively, cheerful] [mid-18C+] (*Irish/Scot.*) pleasant, cheerful; neat, thorough.

canty *adj.*[2] [SE *cantankerous*] [1920s+] (*Aus.*) unpleasant, ill-tempered.

Canuck *n.* (*also* **Cannock, Jack Canuck, Kanacka, Kanaka, Kanuck, Kanuk, Knuck**) [Can. Fr. *canaque*, f. Hawaiian *kanaka*, a man or simply *Can*(*ada*) + (*chin*)*ook*. The term supposedly originated in the Maine lumber camps; as regards derog. status, note email, to American Dialect Society List 4/8/99: "Canuck' is not in the least offensive, as Canadian linguists and lay folk have told me. Note the hockey team, the Vancouver Canucks'] [mid-19C+] (*US*) a derog. term for a Canadian, esp. a French Canadian.

Canuck *adj.* [CANUCK *n.*] [mid-19C+] (*US*) Canadian.

canvas *n.* **1** [19C] the human skin. **2** [1940s] (*US Und.*) a strait-jacket.

canvas muster *n. see TARPAULIN MUSTER under* TARPAULIN *adj.*

canyon *n.* **1** [1930s+] the vagina. **2** [1980s+] the anus.

IN PHRASES

❑ **dive in the canyon** *v.* [1960s+] to perform cunnilingus.

cap *n.*[1] [abbr.; Ware cites some UK use but CAP'N *n.* is more common] [mid-19C+] (*orig. mainly US*) captain.

cap *n.*[2] [mid-19C+] (*US*) a bullet, a shot.

IN PHRASES

❑ **bust a cap** *v.* (*also* **bust caps**) [1930s+] (*US*) to fire a bullet. ❑ **pop a cap** *v.* [1900s; 1950s+] to fire a weapon; to shoot someone. ❑ **snap a cap** *v.* [mid-19C–1920s] (*US*) to fire a shot.

cap *n.*[3] [CAPPER *n.* (1)] [late 19C+] (*US Und.*) the act of ensnaring a victim into a confidence game.

cap *n.*[4] [abbr.] **1** [1920s+] (*drugs*) a capsule containing a narcotic, usu. heroin. **2** [1960s+] (*drugs*) a capsule of LSD. **3** [1960s+] (*drugs*) a capsule of any drug. **4** [1960s+] psilocybin/psilocin. **5** [1980s+] (*drugs*) crack cocaine. **6** [1990s+] (*US prison*) a measure of marijuana: as much as can be fitted into a small cap, e.g. of a toothpaste tube or a container of chapstick.

IN PHRASES

❑ **bust a cap** *v.* [1950s–60s] (*drugs*) to inject a shot of heroin (which comes in capsule form). ❑ **cap one's arm** *v.* [1960s] (*US drugs*) to take an injection of a narcotic. ❑ **cap up** *v.* [1960s] (*drugs*) to transfer bulk drugs (in powder form) into capsules for sale.

cap *n.*[5] [CAP *v.*[5]] (*orig. US black*) **1** [1940s+] a rejoinder. **2** [1960s] an insult aimed at someone's family; used as part of a ritualized interchange.

cap *n.*[6] [they 'cap' the body] (*US black*) **1** [1950s+] the mind. **2** [1990s+] the top of the head, the cranium.

(IN PHRASES)

❑ **out of one's cap** [2000s] (*N.Z.*) having lost one's temper.

cap *n.*[7] [strained parallel to HEAD *n.* (2c)] [1960s–70s] (*US black*) the mouth, esp. as used in oral-genital sex; thus in phr. *give (someone) some cap*, to fellate, to perform cunnilingus.

cap *n.*[8] *see* BONNET *n.*[2].

cap *v.*[1] [abbr. SE *capture*] **1** [late 16C–early 17C] to arrest (for debt). **2** [mid-19C] (*UK Und.*) to take, to grab hold of.

cap *v.*[2] (*also* **kap**) [Lat. *capias*, you may take – a term used in a variety of legal writs, e.g. *capias ad respondendum*, to enforce attendance at court, and *capias ad satisfaciendum*, after judgement, to imprison the defendant until the plaintiff's claim is satisfied] [late 17C–early 19C] (*UK Und.*) to swear an oath.

cap *v.*[3] [CAPPER *n.* (1); 20C+ use mainly US] [19C+] (*20C+ use mainly US*) to act as a confederate in a gambling game.

cap *v.*[4] [? abbr. SE *capitulate* or ? doff one's *cap*] [early 19C] (*US Und.*) to give satisfaction.

cap *v.*[5] (*also* **cap on**) [early 19C dial. (later SE) *cap*, to surpass, to outdo] **1** [20C+] to make a smart rejoinder. **2** [20C+] to lie. **3** [1900s] to brag about, to aggrandize. **4** [1950s] to dumbfound, to render silent. **5** [1960s] (*US*) to entice a victim into a swindle. **6** [1960s+] (*US black*) to insult someone, esp. by disparaging their family.

cap *v.*[6] [CAP *n.*[4] (1)] (*drugs*) **1** [1940s+] (*also* **cap up**) to transfer bulk drugs (in powder form) into capsules for sale. **2** [1950s–60s] to be given drugs for free.

cap *v.*[7] [abbr. SE *kneecap*] [1970s] to shoot a person in the knee or leg as a form of punishment.

cap *v.*[8] [CAP *n.*[2] (1)] [1970s+] (*orig. US black*) **1** to fire a gun; thus *capping*, gunfire. **2** to kill, to murder, to shoot dead.

cap *v.*[9] [CAP *n.*[7]] [1990s+] (*US campus*) to punch someone in the face.

cap acquaintance *n.* [a person one knows well enough to raise one's cap when one passes on the street, but not to speak to properly] [late 18C–early 19C] a slight or passing acquaintance.

Cape Ann turkey *n.* [SE *Cape Ann*, a cape in northern Massachusetts] [mid-19C–1940s] (*US*) salt cod.

Cape Cod turkey *n.* [SE *Cape Cod* in Massachusetts] **1** [mid-19C–1960s] (*US*) salt cod; a codfish dinner. **2** [20C+] corned (salt) beef and cabbage.

capeesh! *excl.* (*also* **kapeesh!**) [Ital. *capisce*, from *capito*, I understand] [1950s+] (*US*) do you understand? thus as *v.*, to understand.

Cape Etna *n.* [? misreading of Mount Etna] [mid-19C] (*UK Und.*) the gallows.

cape horn *n.* [pun on HORN *n.*[1]] [late 19C] the vagina.

cape kelly *n.* [rhy. sl. = SE *belly*] [1950s] (*Aus.*) the stomach.

capella *n.* [Lat. *cappella*, little cloak or cape, ult. f. *cappella* or cloak of St Martin, preserved by the Frankish kings as a sacred relic, carried into battle, and used to give sanctity to oaths. The name was then applied to the sanctuary in which the relic was preserved under the care of its *cappellani* (chaplains), and thence to any sanctuary containing holy relics and thus to any place used for worship, other than a church, the earlier name for which was *oratorium*, the oratory] [19C] an overcoat.

cape nightingale *n.* [late 19C+] (*S.Afr.*) a frog.

cape of good hope *n.*[1] [the pleasure it offers plus its position near the 'bottom' of the globe] [19C] the vagina.

cape of good hope *n.*[2] [rhy. sl.] [20C+] soap.

caper *n.*[1] [the SE *cape* that is part of their uniform] [mid-19C] a chorister.

caper *n.*[2] [SE *caper*, a frisky movement] **1** [mid-19C+] a dodge, a trick. **2** [mid-19C+] a situation, an event. **3** [late 19C+] (*mainly US*) an occupation, a job. **4** [late 19C+] the proper course of action; esp. ext. as *the proper caper*, the right thing to do. **5** [1920s+] a large-scale crime, usu. involving a great deal of elaborate planning and aimed at very large sums of money, expensive pieces of jewellery etc; the supposed lack of violence in such enterprises lent them a somewhat 'jokey' air. **6** [1920s+] a crime, irrespective of scale. **7** [1950s] an affair. **8** [1950s+] a scheme. **9** [1960s] (*N.Z.*) a thing, an object.

SE in slang uses

(IN COMPOUNDS)

❑ **caper cove** *n.* [COVE *n.* (1)] [mid-19C] (*US Und.*) a dancing master. ❑ **caper juice** *n.* [a sufficiency or an excess causes one to 'cut capers'] [19C] whisky. ❑ **caper merchant** *n.* [MERCHANT *n.*] [late 18C–mid-19C] a dancing master.

caper *v.*[1] [SE *caper*, to dance or leap in a frolicsome manner] [late 18C–mid-19C] to be hanged.

caper *v.*[2] [CAPER *n.*[2] (6)] [1960s+] to commit a crime, esp. as a professional thief.

caperdewsie *n.* [for ety. *see* CAPPADOCHIO *n.*] [early–mid-17C] stocks.

cape smoke *n.* [Swahili *moshi*, banana liquor, lit. 'smoke, steam, soot, lamp-black'] [early 19C+] whisky or rough, strong brandy distilled in South Africa.

Capey *n.* (*also* **Capie**) **1** [1940s+] (*S.Afr.*) a Cape Coloured, a member of the Coloured population group of the Cape Province, esp. of the Western Province of the Cape. **2** [1960s+] an inhabitant of the Western Cape, or of the city of Cape Town.

(IN COMPOUNDS)

❑ **capeytaal** *n.* [lit. 'capey language'] the argot spoken by some Coloureds, a patois of Afrikaans, English and Xhosa.

capital g's *n.* [? abbr. SE *gonads*] [2000s] (*US black*) the testicles.

capital K *n.* [the approximate shape] [1940s+] (*W.I.*) knock-knees.

capitation drugget *n.* [SE *drugget*, a coarse woollen material used mainly for floor-coverings or tablecloths + SE *capitation*, a tax that was levied on the fabric] [late 17C] cheap, second-rate fabric.

cap'n *n.* [abbr.] [mid-19C+] captain.

cap'n toke *n.* [TOKE *n.*[2] + honorary rank of Captain, a HIPPIE *n.*[2] (3) term used *inter alia* for Jerry Garcia (1942–95) of the Grateful Dead, known as 'Captain Trips'] [1980s+] (*US campus*) a marijuana smoker.

capo *n.* [abbr. Ital. *caporegime*] **1** [1950s+] (*US Und.*) a senior figure in the US Mafia; thus *capo de capo, capo di tutti capi*, the supreme 'boss of bosses'. **2** [1970s+] in fig. use, any authority figure. **3** [2000s] (*UK Und.*) a senior gangster.

capon *n.* [SE *capon*, a castrated cock] **1** [late 16C–early 19C] a eunuch; an impotent man. **2** [mid-17C–early 19C] used for a variety of fish, e.g. a red herring, a sole, a dried haddock [the cheap herring substituted for the more expensive bird]. **3** [1940s–60s] a young homosexual man, sometimes but not invariably a prostitute [the ref. is to CHICKEN *n.* (4d) rather than any implied sexual malfunction].

cap one's arm *v. see under* CAP *n.*[4].

cap one's lucky *v.* [SE *cap*, to protect + *lucky*; i.e. to take advantage of one's opportunity to run away] [20C+] (*Aus.*) to run off, to leave at speed.

capot me! *excl.* [piquet jargon, *capot*, to score a capot against, to win all the tricks from. In this context 'to score off'] [mid-18C] a general excl.

cappadochio *n.* [? the country of *Cappadocia*, the ruler of which, according to Horace (65–8BC), was rich in slaves but lacked cash. That ety., backed by Nares (1822), is dismissed as 'far-fetched' by the *OED*] [early 17C] the stocks; prison.

capped *adj.*[1] [CAP *v.*[5] (1)] [1930s+] outdone, defeated.

capped *adj.*[2] [CAP *v.*[8] (2)] [1970s+] (*US*) shot dead.

capper *n.* [early 19C dial. (later SE) *cap*, to surpass, to outdo] **1** [mid-18C+] a confederate in a gambling game who poses as another gambler but actually works to swindle the genuine participants; similarly used in confidence tricks [such a confederate is always able to *cap* everyone else's bet]. **2** [late

19C+] (*US*) an employee of a casino, brothel, strip-club etc, who points a potential client towards the variety of self-indulgence they seek [ext. use of sense 1 above]. **3** [20C+] anything seen as terminal, 'the last straw'. **4** [1900s–20s] (*US*) a shop tout [ext. use of sense 1 above]. **5** [1960s+] an anecdote that steals the limelight from a previous anecdote, a punchline.

capperclaw *v. see* CLAPPERCLAW *v.*

capping *n.* [CAP *v.*^{5} (6)] [1960s+] (*US black*) the ritual exchange of verbal insults.

capping-cove *n.* [CAP *v.*^{2} + COVE *n.*] [mid-19C] (*UK Und.*) a person who will do anything for money.

capricornified *adj.* [proper name of the astrological constellation of *Capricorn*, the He-Goat; thus one who has been made to 'wear the HORNS *n.*'] [late 18C] cuckolded.

capron hardy *n.* [Fr. *capron hardi*, lit. 'bold hood'] [mid-15C–mid-16C] an impudent fellow.

cap-sick *adj.* [fig. use of SE] [early 17C] drunk, or mentally confused.

capsize *v.* [non-naval uses of SE] **1** [late 18C–early 19C] to fall over when drunk. **2** [late 18C+] to overturn.

captain *n.* **1** [16C–mid-19C] a pimp. **2** [late 16C+] a general term of address. **3** [17C+] in comb., defining a given type of man, usu. energetic and/or aggressive (see below); 20C+ uses are underlined by such comic-book 'superheroes' as *Captain America*. **4** [17C–19C] a successful highwayman. **5** [mid-18C] a thug employed to keep order in a gaming house. **6** [mid-18C–early 19C] money, implying its importance; thus *the captain is not at home*, I have no money. **7** [late 18C–mid-19C; 1930s] the leader of a criminal gang. **8** [mid–late 19C] (*Aus.*) as ext. of sense 4 above, a successful bushranger. **9** [20C+] (*S.Afr.*) the third most important member of a prison gang. **10** [1910s–20s] (*US Und.*) a susceptible person. **11** [1920s+] (*Aus./US*) (*also* **skipper**) someone who has money to spend, and uses it on the assembled company. **12** [1960s] (*US drugs*) a major drug dealer.

IN COMPOUNDS

as a supposed honorific, but usu. a generic derog.

❑ **Captain Armstrong** *n.* (*also* **Johnny Armstrong**) [SE *armstrong*, he uses his 'strong arms' to rein in his horse] [mid-late 19C] a corrupt jockey. ❑ **Captain Bluff** *n.* (*also* **Captain Bluster**) [SE *bluff*, big, surly, blustering] [late 17C–18C] a bully, a braggart. ❑ **Captain Bounce** *n.* [SE *bounce*] [18C] a bully, a braggart. ❑ **Captain Bubble-and Squeak** *n.* [fig. use of SE *bubble*, to foam + *squeak*] [mid-19C] (*UK Und.*) a cowardly blustering man. ❑ **Captain Cash** *n.* [1950s+] (*Aus.*) that member of a group who, recently or temporarily well-off, is expected to buy drinks for the rest. ❑ **Captain Cheddar** *n.* [SE *cheddar*, i.e. CHEESE *n.*[1] (3f)] [1980s+] (*US campus*) an unattractive, old-fashioned male. ❑ **Captain Flashman** *n.* [FLASHMAN *n.*] [mid-19C] (*UK Und.*) a blusterer, a coward. ❑ **Captain Grand** *n.* [18C–19C] a haughty, blustering man. ❑ **Captain Hackum** *n.* [SE *hack them*] [late 17C–early 19C] a bully, a braggart. ❑ **Captain He-man** *n.* [mid-19C] (*US Und.*) a swaggering, blustering bully. ❑ **Captain Huff** *n.* [HUFF *n.* (1)] [late 17C–18C] a braggart, a bully, a thug. ❑ **Captain no prigg** *n.* [late 18C] (*UK Und.*) a penniless, swaggering bully. ❑ **Captain Queer-nabs** *n.* [QUEER *adj.* (1) + NAB *n.*[1]] [late 17C–mid-19C] a shabby, ill-dressed person. ❑ **Captain Quiz** *n.* [SE *quiz*, to mock, to make fun of] [18C] a mocker. ❑ **Captain Save-a-ho** *n.* [HO *n.* (5)] **1** [1990s+] (*US black teen*) a man who lavishes attentions and gifts on a woman; his aim is seduction, but despite his expensive efforts he is rarely successful; also a husband. **2** [2000s] (*US black*) a husband. ❑ **Captain Shaddy** *n.* [SE *shadow*, wherein he lurks] [mid-19C] (*UK Und.*) a prostitute's accomplice, who hides and robs the client. ❑ **Captain Sharp** *n.* [SHARP *n.*[1] (1a)] **1** [early 17C–19C] a cardsharp, a cheat. **2** [late 18C] a hired thug used to police corrupt gambling games. ❑ **Captain Standish** *n.* [SE *stand*, he 'stands erect'] [18C] the penis. ❑ **Captain Tom** *n.* [TOM *n.*[1] (1)] **1** [late 17C–early 19C] the leader of a mob. **2** [late 18C–early 19C] the mob itself.

general uses

❑ **Captain Crank** *n.* [sense 4 above + ? pun SE *crank*, that which is crooked] [18C–early 19C] the leader of a band of highwaymen. ❑ **captain tober** *n.* [sense 4 above + TOBY *n.*^{2} (2)] [mid-19C] (*UK Und.*) a leading highwayman.

SE in slang uses

IN COMPOUNDS

❑ **captain lieutenant** *n.* [i.e. meat that is neither quite veal nor yet proper beef. In milit. jargon a *captain lieutenant* has the rank of the former but remains on the pay of the latter] [late 18C–early 19C] the flesh of an old calf.

IN PHRASES

❑ **captain is at home** (*also* **captain is come**) [play on Gk *catamenia*, monthly + elision of SE *captain* + *home/come*] [late 18C–mid-19C] a euph. phr. used to indicate that a woman is menstruating.

Captain Bligh *n.* [rhy. sl.; ult. *Captain William Bligh* (1754–1817) of HMS *Bounty*] [1990s+] a pie.

Captain Bloods *n.* [rhy. sl. = SPUD *n.*^{3} (1); ult. the Irish adventurer Captain Thomas Blood (1618–80), best-known for a failed attempt to steal the British Crown Jewels in 1671] [20C+] (*Aus.*) potatoes.

Captain Cook *n.* [proper name of *Captain* James *Cook* (1728–79), the explorer who 'discovered' Australia and, inter alia, introduced pigs to New Zealand; other senses are rhy. sl.] **1** [late 19C] (*Aus./N.Z.*) (*also* **Captain cooker, cooker**) a pig, esp. one which is run-down or ill-kempt. **2** [late 19C–1960s] a book. **3** [1940s+] (*Aus./N.Z./US*) a look. **4** [1980s+] (*N.Z. prison*) a hook, i.e. a punch.

Captain Cook *adj.* [rhy. sl. = CROOK *adj.* (3); ult. *Captain* James *Cook* (*see* prev.)] [1950s] (*Aus.*) ill, sick.

Captain Copperthorne's crew *n.* [? the inadequacies of some long-vanished officer] [late 18C] (*orig. naut.*) a group or team without a stated hierarchy, where everyone concerned wishes to lead.

Captain Grimes *n.* [rhy. sl.; ? ult. Evelyn Waugh's *Captain Grimes*, the raffish schoolmaster of *Decline and Fall* (1928)] [1980s] *The Times* newspaper.

Captain Hicks *n.* [rhy. sl.; var. on JIMMY HIX *n.* (1)] [1930s–40s] in craps dice, the point of six made with a pair of threes.

Captain Hook *n.* [rhy. sl.; ult. *Captain Hook*, the villain of *Peter Pan* (1904) by James Barrie (1860–1937)] **1** [1990s+] a look, a glance. **2** [2000s] a book.

Captain Hook *v.* [rhy. sl.; *see* prev.] [1990s+] to look.

Captain Kettle *v.* [rhy. sl.; the character *Captain Kettle*, created by Cutliffe Hyne, appeared in stories published 1893–1938] [late 19C–1930s] to settle (after some energetic dispute).

Captain Kirk *n.* [rhy. sl.; the fictional *Captain* James T. *Kirk*, master of the Starship *Enterprise* in the cult TV series *Star Trek*] [1990s+] a Turk.

Captain Podd *n.* [the proper name of *Captain Podd*, a celebrated puppeteer of the period] [late 18C–early 19C] a puppeteer.

captain's log *n.* [rhy. sl. = BOG *n.*[1]; presumably linked to the cult TV series *Star Trek*, each episode of which began with the intonation 'Captain's Log, Stardate...'] [1990s+] a lavatory.

capture *n.* [1910s+] (*UK Und.*) an arrest and conviction for a crime.

IN PHRASES

❑ **get a capture** *v.* [1950s+] to be arrested.

capture *v.* [1980s+] (*UK Und.*) to arrest.

SE in slang uses

IN PHRASES

❑ **capture the bishop** *v. see* BANG THE BISHOP *under* BISHOP *n.*^{2}. ❑ **capture the crumb** *v. see* TAKE THE CAKE *v.* ❑ **capture the hump** *v. see* GET THE HUMP *under* HUMP *n.*[1]. ❑ **capture the pickled biscuit** *v.* [var. on TAKE THE CAKE *v.* (1)] [late 19C–1940s] (*Aus.*) to beat all rivals, esp. with the implication that the person, announcement, event etc is even more startling or appalling than might have been expected.

capun *n.* [abbr. *cap*ital *pun*ishment] [1990s+] (*US prison*) one who has been sentenced to death.

caput *adj.* [Ger. *kaputt*, done for; also milit. use as 'stolen' during WW1] [1910s+] finished, over, ruined etc.

car *n.* [the image of the prisoners driving/sitting in the same car] **1** [1970s+] (*US prison*) in a prison, a group of inmates who associate to run money-making schemes, dominate other prisoners, and otherwise 'rule' the institution. **2** [1990s+] a group of prisoners who pool their supply of drugs. **3** *see* CADILLAC *n.* (2b).

IN PHRASES

▫ **drive the car** *v.* [1990s+] (*US prison*) of a prisoner, to purchase the day's supply of marijuana for a small group of friends. Members of the group take it in turns to provide for their fellows. Those who are smoking the drugs but not purchasing that day are *hitch-hiking*. ▫ **in the car** [1990s+] (*US prison*) on good terms. ▫ **out of the car** [1990s+] (*US prison*) on bad terms.

SE in slang uses

IN COMPOUNDS

▫ **carhop** *see* separate entries. ▫ **car-jack** *see* separate entries. ▫ **car jockey** *n.* [JOCKEY *n.*[2] (3c)] [1950s+] (*US*) a car-park or garage attendant. ▫ **carnapper** *n.* [play on SE *kidnapper*; modern use, esp. Filipino] [1950s+] (*orig. US*) one who steals a car for joy-riding (rather than for resale), and then dumps it or returns it to the place from where it was taken. ▫ **car-ringing** *n.* [RING *v.* (1k)] [1950s+] the practice of altering a car for the purposes of using it as a getaway vehicle, hold-up van, etc or for reselling it to an unsuspecting customer. ▫ **car surfing** *n.* [2000s] (*N.Z.*) a game based on jumping from one car bonnet to another. ▫ **carwash** *n.* [1970s+] (*US gay*) sexual interaction in a car.

IN PHRASES

▫ **get on the cars** *v.* [SE *streetcar*] [late 19C] (*US campus*) to start. ▫ **to beat the cars** *adv. see* TO BEAT THE BAND *under* BAND *n.*[2].

caramel clone *n.* [2000s] (*US black*) a light-complexioned black person.

caramel sundae *n.* [1990s+] (*US black teen*) an attractive, sexy, medium-to light-complexioned black woman.

caravan *n.* [SE *caravan*, a procession of merchants, travelling together for mutual safety, usu. as found in the Middle or Far East] **1** [late 17C] a type of wagon. **2** [late 17C] a coach travelling from the provinces to London. **3** [late 17C–early 19C] (*UK Und.*) a large sum of money, esp. when seen by thieves as potential booty. **4** [late 17C–early 19C] the victim of financial fraud. **5** [early 19C] a police van for conveying prisoners. **6** [mid-19C] a railway train, esp. when chartered by prize-fight attendees. **7** [mid-19C] a railway 'special' taking London boxing fans to a fight held outside the capital.

caravan *v.*[1] [the SE *caravan* or procession of vehicles that conveys the picnickers] [1910s–20s] to have a picnic.

caravan *v.*[2] [SE *caravan*, a procession of merchants] [1980s+] (*US teen*) to drive (stolen) cars in groups and to perform a variety of elaborate manoeuvres on the street.

caravansera *n.* [SE *caravanserai*, a form of Oriental coaching inn where the merchant caravans could find food and shelter; ult. Per. *karwan*, caravan + *sara*, palace] [mid-19C] a railway station.

carb *n.* [abbr.] [1940s+] (*orig. US*) a *carb*urettor.

carbine *v.* [SE *carbine*, a short musket, presumably used by the villain] [late 19C] (*US Western*) to cheat, to victimize.

carbo *n.* (*also* **carb**) [abbr.] [1970s+] (*orig. US*) *carbo*hydrates, or a meal or food that contains a high percentage of carbohydrate.

carbo-load *v.* [CARBO *n.*] [1990s+] (*US campus*) to ingest carbohydrates; spec. to drink beer.

carbonado *v.* [Sp. *carbonado*, to score meat before grilling or broiling it] [late 16C–19C] to cut, to slash, to hack.

carbon copy *n.* [1990s+] (*US black*) **1** an imitator, someone who yearns to emulate their hero or heroine. **2** someone who resembles their parents.

carbuncle face *n.* [SE *carbuncle*, an inflamed abscess + *face*] [late 17C–18C] a face covered in boils and pimples.

carburettor *n.* [fig. uses of SE] **1** [1910s] the heart. **2** [1980s+] (*drugs*) a water pipe, used for smoking cannabis or crack cocaine.

carby *n.* [abbr.] [1950s+] (*Aus.*) a *carb*urettor.

card *n.*[1] [SURE CARD *under* CARD *n.*[2]] [mid-18C–mid-19C] a device, an expedient; thus *one's best card*, the best plan, the ideal way of acting.

card *n.*[2] **1** [late 18C; 1940s+] a joker, a clown. **2** [mid-19C+] a character, a noticeable person, a likeable eccentric [? one who stands out from the 'pack']. **3** [mid-19C+] an attraction, a 'drawing card'. **4** [1940s] (*US*) an amusing thing or circumstance. **5** [1970s] a fool. **6** (*US*) in drug uses. (**a**) [1900s–40s] pieces of opium weighed out onto a (playing) card; the usual ration of prepared opium used in a single smoking session. (**b**) [1920s–30s] a means of selling opium in which pills of the drug are stuck to the bottom of a playing card.

IN PHRASES

▫ **dead card** *n. see under* DEAD *adj.* ▫ **draw card** *v. see* DRAW CAAD/CARD *under* DRAW *v.*[4]. ▫ **give someone cards and spades** *v.* [card-playing imagery] [late 19C–1930s] to allow someone else an advantage. ▫ **hand in one's cards** *v. see* HAND IN ONE'S CHECKS *under* CHECK *n.*[1]. ▫ **hot card** *n.* [HOT *adj.* (4d)] [late 19C–1920s] (*US*) a provocative, lively person. ▫ **pull someone's card** *v.* **1** [1980s+] to attack, to beat up, to kill. **2** [2000s] (*US prison*) to find out information about another inmate [the image is of file cards; the records are now computerized]. ▫ **sure card** *n.* [note mid-16C SE *sure card*, an expedient to gain a desired object, a person whose name will help one] [early 16C–mid-18C] a safe plan, a trustworthy person.

card, the *n.* [abbr. SE *invitation card/card of admission*] [mid-19C] the correct thing.

card *v.*[1] (*also* **caad**) [Scot. *card*, to scold, to tell off] [20C+] (*W.I./UK black teen*) to jeer jokingly or mock someone about some event, their appearance or situation.

card *v.*[2] [CARD *n.*[2] (5)] [1970s+] (*W.I. Rasta*) to fool someone.

card *v.*[3] [1970s+] (*US campus*) to request proof of age (in a bar) by producing an identification card.

cardboard box *n.* [rhy. sl. = POX *n.*[1] (3)] [1970s+] venereal disease.

cardboard city *n.* (*also* **cardboard condominiums**) [the original *Cardboard City* was situated on the London's South Bank, but increasing homelessness has meant that the term now applies to any such gathering] [1980s+] the cardboard box 'homes' that are used as shelter by the homeless.

card-carrying *adj.* [the orig. application of the phr. to Communists, who carried their Party card] [1950s+] (*US*) genuine, dependable, the 'real thing'.

card-cony-catching *n.* (*also* **card-coney-catching**) [SE *card* + CONY-CATCHING *n.*] [mid-16C–18C] trickery, cheating, usu. with cards.

carder *n.* [early 16C; mid-19C] (*UK Und.*) a professional card player.

cardinal *n.*[1] [ref. to a cardinal's cloak, which is red] **1** [mid-18C–19C] a lady's cloak. **2** [mid-19C+] mulled red wine.

IN PHRASES

▫ **the cardinal is at home** (*also* **the cardinal is come**) [late 18C] a euph. phr. used to indicate that a woman is menstruating.

cardinal *n.*[2] [ety. unknown; ? the use of a red cloth] [late 19C–1910s] a shoeblack.

care! *excl.* [SE excl. *like I care!*] [2000s] (*US campus*) a sarcastic retort, demonstrating a lack of interest.

career boy *n.* [play on SE *career girl*] [1970s+] a male homosexual prostitute.

care factor zero *phr.* [the use of SE *factor* as a measure of sunblock strength] [1990s+] (*US teen*) a phr. indicating indifference, I really couldn't care less.

careless talk *n.* [rhy. sl.; ult. a ref. to the WW2 posters with the legend 'Careless talk costs lives'] [1940s+] a stick of chalk, usu. as used by darts players for scoring.

care package *n.* [SE *care package*, a package of goods distributed by the Co-operative for American Relief Everywhere to the poor citizens of foreign countries] [1960s+] (*US campus/teen*) a package of 'supplies' sent to a student or solo teenager by a parent.

carga *n.* [Sp. = 'charge', i.e. CHARGE *n.*[2]] [1960s+] (*US prison/Hisp.*) heroin.

cargo *n.*[1] [ety. unknown. Despite the apparent logic of relating this to CARGO *n.*[2], i.e. a person as a fig. burden or load, this use precedes the adoption of the Sp. word into SE, and there is no evidence of Sp. *cargo* being used in this way] [early 17C] a person.

cargo *n.*[2] [SE *cargo*, freight carried on a ship; ult. Sp. *cargo*, loading, *carga*, freight] **1** [late 17C–18C] a large sum of money. **2** [mid-18C] a thief's or pickpocket's takings. **3** [1990s+] (*W.I./UK black teen*) a heavy gold chain and medallion sported as an outward (sometimes pretentious) show of wealth.

SE in slang uses

IN PHRASES

❑ **dead cargo** *n. see under* DEAD *adj.* ❑ **take in cargo** *v.* [19C] to get drunk.

cargo! *excl.* [? euph. for CHRIST! *excl.*; ? corruption of Italian *corragio!* courage!] [early 17C] a general excl.

carhop *n.* [i.e. one who *hops* between cars] (*US*) **1** [1920s+] a waiter or waitress who serves customers in their parked cars. **2** [1960s+] a street prostitute (of either sex) who has sex in clients' cars.

carhop *v.* [CARHOP *n.*] (*US*) **1** [1930s+] to work as a waiter or waitress, serving customers in their parked cars. **2** [1960s+] to work as a street prostitute, having sex with clients who drive up in their cars. **3** [1990s+] to steal from parked cars.

Caribee Islands *n.* [SE *Caribbean Islands*, symbolizing far distance from any authority] [late 18C] certain areas of London that were considered safe havens for criminals and debtors.

car-jack *v.* [1990s+] to hijack an automobile or rob its driver.

car-jacker *n.* [CAR-JACK *v.*] [1990s+] (*US*) one who hijacks an automobile or robs its driver.

car-jacking *n.* [CAR-JACK *v.*] [1990s+] (*US*) hijacking an automobile, or robbing its driver.

cark *n.* [COCK *n.*[3] (1)] [1970s] (*US*) the penis.

cark *v.* (*also* **kark**) [dial. *cark* or *kark*, to caw like a crow; thus the association is with a carrion bird] [1970s+] (*orig. Aus.*) **1** to die; often as *cark it*. **2** of machinery, to break down. **3** to vomit. **4** to fall into a drunken sleep.

carked *adj.* [CARK *v.* / dial. *cark*, care, sorrow, anxiety] [1970s] (*Aus.*) ruined, destroyed, exhausted.

carking *adj.* [dial. *cark*, care, sorrow, anxiety] [late 19C] (*Aus.*) anxious, worrying.

carl comedian *n.* [ironic use of SE *comedian* + assonant 'proper' name] [1970s+] (*US campus*) a dismissive term for a raconteur whose jokes and stories fail to have the desired impact.

carler *n.* [mid-19C] (*US Und.*) a clerk.

carleycue *n.* (*also* **carlique**) [ext. of SE *curlicue*] [late 19C–1910s] (*Irish*) anything small or of little value.

carlotta *n.* [the effeminization used by the camp gay world] [1940s–60s] (*camp gay*) **1** a heterosexual who interferes in the gay world, either as a homophobe or as a 'tourist'. **2** a popular 'camp' name.

carl rosa *n.* [rhy. sl.; ult. the popular *Carl Rosa* Operatic Society, founded in London in 1875] [1960s+] a poser, anyone pretending to be something that they are not; thus the *old carl rosa*, a fraud.

carmes *n.* (*also* **carnes**) [Rom.] [mid-19C–1900s] flattery.

carmine *n.* [SE *carmine*, red or crimson pigment obtained from cochineal] [19C] blood.

carn! *excl.* [Antipodean pron. of SE *come on!*] [1980s+] (*N.Z.*) hurry up!

carnal *n.* (*also* **carnales**) [Sp. *carnal*, flesh] [1970s+] (*US Hisp.*) someone from one's own social group, a friend from the same neighbourhood.

carnal-trap *n.* [coined by Sir Thomas Urquhart (1611–60) for his translation of Rabelais] [mid-17C–19C] the vagina.

carnation! *excl. see* TARNATION! *excl.*

carne *n.* [Sp. *carne*, meat; the image is of the drug's strength] [1980s+] (*drugs*) heroin.

carner *n.* [SE *carnal* knowledge] [1970s] (*N.Z.*) someone who has sexual intercourse with an underage person.

carnes *n. see* CARMES *n.*

carney *n.*[1] [Yorks. dial. *carney*, cajolery, flattery. Despite the poss. link to CARNEY *n.*[2], this use precedes it by a century; ult. ety. unknown] [early 19C–1920s] **1** soft, hypocritical talk. **2** a smooth talker; thus *carneying*, smooth talking, flattery.

IN PHRASES

❑ **come the (old) carney** *v.* [1920s] to flatter.

carney *n.*[2] (*also* **carnie, carny**) [1930s+] (*US*) **1** a carnival worker. **2** a carnival (UK: a fair).

carney *adj.* (*also* **carny**) [lit. pertaining to a carnival; thus a negative stereotype] **1** [1910s+] sly, artful. **2** [1930s+] (*US*) pertaining to the carnival or carnival workers.

carney *v.* (*also* **carny**) [CARNEY *n.*[1] (1); there is no link to later US CARNEY *n.*[2], for all that the carney is likely to employ wheedling tones to encourage patrons to spend their money] [early 19C+] to wheedle, to flatter; thus *carneying*, in a wheedling manner.

carnie *n.*[1] (*also* **carny**) [SE *carnal knowledge*] (*N.Z.*) **1** [1960s+] an underage girl seen as a sex object. **2** [1980s+] a young person living on the streets.

carnie *n.*[2] [abbr.] [1990s+] a *carn*ation.

carnie *n.*[3] *see* CARNEY *n.*[2].

carnish *n.* [Ital. *carne*, meat; imported via Ling. Fr.] [mid-19C] (*UK Und.*) meat.

IN COMPOUNDS

❑ **carnish-ken** *n.* [mid-19C] (*UK Und.*) a thieves' eating-house; thus *cove of the carnish-ken*, the owner of such a place.

carny *see also under* CARNEY.

carny *n. see* CARNIE *n.*[1].

carol *n. see* KÊREL *n.*

Carolina nine *n. see* NINA (WITH HER HAIR DOWN) *n.*

Carolina racehorse *n.* [joc. ref. to the prevalence of the animal in North and South Carolina] [mid-19C] (*US*) a razorback hog.

caroline *n.* [? anecdotal; ? ref. to Queen Caroline] [mid–late 19C] (*Irish*) a style of tall hat.

carol singer *n.* [1930s+] (*Aus., Brisbane*) a police car with a loud-speaker.

caroon *n.* (*also* **carroon, crooner**) [Ital. *corona*, a crown] [mid–late 19C] a crown or five shillings (25p).

carousel *n.* [2000s] (*S.Afr. gay*) a public lavatory, frequented by gay men looking for sex.

carp *n.* [SE *carp*, to find fault with, to reprehend, to take exception to] [1900s–30s] (*US*) a whinger, a complainer.

carpark *n.* [rhy. sl. = NARK *n.* (1)] [1950s+] (*UK Und.*) an informer.

carpenter's dream *n.* [pun, i.e. 'flat as a board and easy to screw'] [1970s+] an available woman.

carpet *n.*[1] [early use sporting, e.g. cricket and baseball; also in UK/US air forces] **1** [late 19C+] the grass, the ground. **2** [1980s+] the female pubic hair; used only in combs. relating to cunnilingus (and thus lesbians).

IN COMPOUNDS

❑ **carpet-cleaning** *n.* [1990s+] cunnilingus. ❑ **carpet-muncher** *n.* (*also* **carpet-biter, carpet-licker**) [MUNCH *v.*[1] (2)] [1980s+] (*orig. US campus*) **1** a lesbian. **2** a person who performs cunnilingus. ❑ **carpet-munching** *n.* [1980s+] cunnilingus.

IN PHRASES

❑ **munch the carpet** *v.* (*also* **chew the carpet, lick the carpet**) [MUNCH *v.*[1] (2)] [1980s+] (*US*) to perform cunnilingus.

SE in slang uses

IN COMPOUNDS

❑ **carpet-biter** *n.* [? the myth that Adolf Hitler was prone to such hysterical rages] **1** [1940s+] someone who becomes so enraged that they start chewing the carpet. **2** *see also* CARPET-MUNCHER above. ❑ **carpet bushman** *n.* [1910s] (*Aus.*) a businessman who owns land in the outback but rarely visits. ❑ **carpet champion** *n. see* CARPET KNIGHT *n.* (1). ❑ **carpet dance** *n.* [unlike a larger dance, held in a ballroom with a properly sprung floor, the boards are kept covered] [late 19C–1900s] (*UK society*) a dance for close friends, held in one's drawing room. ❑ **carpet joint** *n.* [JOINT *n.* (3b)] [1930s+] (*US*) an up-market nightclub. ❑ **carpet knight** *n. see* separate entry. ❑ **carpet lecture** *n.* [ON THE CARPET below] [1910s] (*Aus.*) an official reprimand. ❑ **carpet-lover/-monger** *n. see* CARPET KNIGHT *n.* (1). ❑ **carpet patrol** *n.* [1980s+] (*drugs*) smokers of crack cocaine who search the floor for any grains of the drug they may have dropped. ❑ **carpet rat** *n.* (*also* **carpet monkey**) [1970s+] (*US*) a small child. ❑ **carpet road** *n.* [late 17C–early 18C] a smooth, well-maintained road. ❑ **carpet-swab** *n.* [mid-19C] a carpet-bag. ❑ **carpet trade** *n.* [i.e. 'the occupations and amusements of the chamber or boudoir' (*OED*); such rooms would be carpeted] [late 16C] sexual dalliance. ❑ **carpet walker** *n.* [1930s–70s] (*US drugs*) a narcotics addict. ❑ **carpet warrior** *n. see* CARPET KNIGHT *n.* (1).

IN PHRASES

❑ **on the carpet** [the carpet that stands before one's superior's desk] [mid-19C+] (*orig. US*) facing a reprimand, scolding or punishment; thus *toe the carpet, dance on the carpet,* to await and receive such a dressing down (where the image is of a fidgety, nervous person). ❑ **put someone on the carpet** *v.* [1900s] to interrogate.

carpet *n.*[2] [rhy. sl.; *carpet-bag* = DRAG *n.*[1] (5); or f. the earlier assumption that prison workshops took just 90 days to produce a particular type of regulation size carpet. But note No. 77 *Mark of Broad Arrow* (1903): 'Your "Auto-leyne" cares little about a "drag" (three months), a sixer (a "carpet" it is generally called), or a "stretch"'. However, note Michael Quinion (WWW 6/5/00): 'I suspect No 77 made a mistake, since 'carpet' came about as the result of a bit of rhyming slang: 'carpet-bag' = 'drag', implying that the two words have always meant the same thing'] **1** [20C+] (*UK prison*) (*also* **carpeting**) a three-month sentence; thus v. *carpet,* to imprison for three months. **2** [1940s+] £3, £30.

IN PHRASES

❑ **double-carpet** *n.* [1970s+] (*UK prison*) six months' imprisonment.

carpet *n.*[3] [ety. unknown] [1920s+] (*Aus.*) £1.

carpet, the *n.* [1960s] (*US black*) a confidence trick practised by a street criminal.

carpet *v.* (*also* **mat**) [the miscreant is standing on his or her superior's office carpet while receiving a reprimand] [mid-19C+] to reprimand, esp. in the context of a superior telling off an employee; thus *carpeting,* a telling-off.

carpet-bag *n.* [ext. of CARPET *n.*[2] (1)/rhy. sl. = DRAG *n.*[1] (5)] [20C+] (*UK Und.*) a three-month sentence.

carpetbag *v.* [SE *carpetbagger,* a derog. description applied, after the American Civil War (1861–5), to immigrants from the northern into the southern states, whose 'property qualification' consisted merely of the contents of the carpet-bag they had brought with them. Hence, applied to all northerners who went south and tried, by a variety of deceitful tricks, to obtain political influence, esp. by claiming an interest in local areas of which, in fact, they had no real knowledge] [1930s] (*US campus*) **1** to attempt to make a good impression, usu. on one's teachers, by pretending to have an all-consuming interest in a given subject. **2** to deceive.

carpeting *n.* **1** *see* CARPET *n.*[2] (1). **2** *see* CARPET *v.*

carpet knight *n.* [orig. a soldier who was dubbed knight at court (thus kneeling on a carpet) rather than in the chaos of a battlefield] **1** [late 16C–19C] (*also* **carpet-champion, carpet lover, carpet-monger, carpet warrior**) a man whose 'knightly exploits' concentrate on the boudoir rather than the battlefield. **2** [late 19C] a man who frequents drawing rooms rather than places of work.

carpet nap *n.* [rhy. sl.] [1980s] (*Aus.*) a *Japanese* person.

carpy *adj.* [Lat. *carpe diem,* 'make the most of the day'] [1940s–50s] (*UK prison*) locked away in one's cell at night.

carra *n.* (*also* **carrer**) [abbr.] [1920s+] (*Aus.*) a *caravan.*

carren *n. see* CARRION *n.*

carriage drag *n.* [DRAG *n.*[1] (5) + ? image of those who ride in carriages getting an easier life, even in prison] [late 19C] (*UK tramp*) a jail sentence of one week.

carriage trade *n.* [a hangover f. earlier divisions of transport. Note mid-19C SE *carriage company,* those who own their own carriage(s); thus the wealthy or upper classes] [1940s+] the upper classes, usu. used ironically.

carried *adj.* [rhy. sl.] [late 19C–1900s] married.

carried story *n.* [it is *carried* from person to person] [20C+] (*Ulster*) a piece of gossip, a rumour.

carrie (nation) *n.* [proper name *Carrie Nation* (1847–1911), the US temperance campaigner] [1950s+] (*drugs*) cocaine.

carrier *n.* **1** [18C–1910s] that member of a criminal gang who either carries information between gang members or carries away the proceeds of a robbery, of pickpocketing etc. **2** [mid-18C] a thigh. **3** [1950s–70s] (*US drugs*) a distributor of drugs.

carrier-pigeon *n.* **1** [late 18C–mid-19C] one who specializes in swindling lottery office-keepers. **2** [mid-19C] one who places bets on commission.

Carrington *n.*

IN PHRASES

❑ **do a carrington** *v.* [? Right Hon. Charles, Robert, Baron *Carrington,* sometime Governor of New South Wales, whose departure from Australia 'was marked by expressions of regret and esteem, quite without previous parallel in Australian history' (Philip Mennell, *The Dict. of Australian Biography,* 1892)] [1900s] (*Aus.*) to run away.

carrion *n.* (*also* **carren, carrion-hen**) [SE *carrion,* used derog. to denote the body and thus a human being] [17C–mid-18C] a prostitute; thus *carrion-flogger,* a pimp.

IN COMPOUNDS

❑ **carrion-case** *n.* [the shirt's enclosing of the SE *carrion,* the body] [mid-19C] a shirt. ❑ **carrion-crow man** *n.* [SE *carrion-crow,* a species of crow that feeds on dead flesh] [20C+] (*W.I., Guyn.*) a man who canvasses business for an undertaker following a death. ❑ **carrion-flogger** *n.* [late 17C–early 18C] a coachman. ❑ **carrion hen** *n. see* main sense above. ❑ **carrion-hunter** *n.* [late 18C–mid-19C] an undertaker.

SE in slang uses

IN COMPOUNDS

❑ **carrion-row** *n.* [SE *carrion* + *row,* a street + pun on SE *carrion-crow*] [early 18C] a place where one buys second-rate meat.

carriwitchet *n.* [ety. unknown; ? link to SE *witch*] [late 18C–1900s] a hoaxing, puzzling question.

carroon *n. see* CAROON *n.*

carrot *n.* [its shape, also f. the consumption of carrots by rabbits or coneys; also note correspondence from John Geipel (7 June 2000) 'I [have] identified a cluster of obviously related words, many of them vulgar or taboo, all based on the Romani word *kar* (literally, 'thorn', 'spike' or 'prickle' – the original Sanskrit meaning) applied to the penis. The word has long been in circulation in impolite Spanish, as *caralo,* in the original Romani, anatomical sense; this, in turn, has given rise to such expressions as the exclamations: *caray, carape,* the universal Hispanic *caramba* and the euphemistic *caracoles* (literally: 'snails'). Other derivative forms are: *No importa un carajo* (it doesn't matter a bit), *Ni carajo* (nothing at all), the Mexican *Que carajo quieres?* (What the hell do you want?), *caralote* (idiot, nut-case); *de caralo* (splendid) and *vete al caralo* (go to hell). The diminutive *carajillo* (little prick) refers to the mug of coffee with a slug of brandy, taken to kick-start a cold winter's day'] **1** [mid-16C+] the penis. **2** [mid-18C–19C] a large bundle of tobacco. **3** [1980s+] (*drugs*) a very large cannabis cigarette packed to the brim and generally the size of an average garden carrot [note the *Camberwell carrot,* an extra-large cannabis cigarette, coined in the film *Withnail & I* (1986)].

IN PHRASES

❑ **cuff a/the carrot** *v.* **1** [1970s+] (*US gay/prison*) to fellate. **2** [1990s+] to masturbate. ❑ **does your bunny like carrots?** [1900s–20s] a coarse comment made by a man to a passing woman.

IN EXCLAMATIONS

❑ **take a carrot!** [the potential of a *carrot* as a dildo. Note naut. jargon *carrots!* go away!; note correspondence from John Geipel (7/6/2000): 'Partridge records the Victorian expression: "Take a carrot" (piss off), which may stem from the Romani root *kar*. The word *corey* (penis) is certainly known to English Romanies, (even the decorous George Borrow listed it in the two senses, "thorn" and "membrum virile") and John Sampson recorded such derivatives as *koriakeri* ("prick-hungry") applied to a lustful woman by one tribe of Welsh Gypsies'] [mid-19C] an insulting excl., usu. used to women.

SE in slang uses

IN COMPOUNDS

❑ **carrot-cruncher** *n.* [the equation of root vegetables and country-dwellers] [1960s+] a countryman, a peasant, esp. a visitor to London from the provinces and the countryside. ❑ **carrothead** *n.* [mid-19C+] (*US*) a red-headed person. ❑ **carrot-headed** *adj.* (*also* **carrotty-headed**) [mid-19C+] (*US*) having red hair. ❑ **carrot-pated** *adj.* [late 17C–early 19C] having red hair. ❑ **carrot-poled** *adj.* (*also* **carrot-polled**) [POLL *n.*[1] (1)] [mid-19C+] having red hair. ❑ **carrot-top** *n.* [late 19C+] a red-headed person. ❑ **carrot-topped** *adj.* (*also* **carrot-top**) [20C+] having red hair.

carrots *n.* [the colour of the vegetable. Ware declares that 'it has not in origin anything to do with "carrots"', preferring an association with Judas *Iscariot*, trad. seen as a red-head] [late 17C+] a red-headed person; thus red hair; also as a term of address/nickname.

carrotty *adj.* (*also* **carroty**) [18C+] having red hair.

carrucha *n.* [Sp.] [1970s+] (*US*) a broken-down old car.

carry *n.* (*drugs*) **1** [1930s–50s] enough of a certain drug to provide a given period of euphoria. **2** [1960s] the amount of drugs one is carrying at any given moment, esp. when stored for an emergency.

carry *v.* [ext. uses of SE] **1** [1930s] (*US drugs*) of a supply of drugs, to suffice an addict for a given period of time. **2** [1930s+] (*orig. US*) to carry money, to be in the money. **3** [1930s+] (*orig. US*) to carry a weapon, e.g. a gun or knife, thus *carrying*, in possession of a gun. **4** [1940s+] (*orig. US drugs*) to carry drugs, often as *carrying*, being in possession of drugs. **5** [1980s+] (*Aus. prison*) to smuggle or hold contraband.

SE in slang uses

IN COMPOUNDS

❑ **carry-knave** *n.* [Nares, misintepreting the second part of the term and extrapolating backwards for the first, suggests a def. of 'cheap prostitute'; Williams (1994) dismisses this] [mid-17C] a coach. ❑ **carry-over** *n.* [SE *carry-over*, something remaining or transferred from one period to the next] [late 19C–1940s] a hangover that lingers on. ❑ **carry-on** *n. see* separate entry.

IN PHRASES

❑ **carry...** *v. see also under* relevant n. ❑ **carry a bone** *v.* [proverb: a dog that will bring you a bone will carry one away] [1910s] (*US*) to gossip, to spread rumours. ❑ **carry a broom at the masthead** *v.* [the naval tradition of hoisting a broom to signify that a ship has been sold] [early 19C] to work as a prostitute. ❑ **carry a case** *v.* [pun on SE *case*, bag/impending trial] [20C+] (*US Und.*) to be out on bail. ❑ **carry a flag** *v.* [1930s+] (*US tramp*) to travel under an assumed name or alias. ❑ **carry corn** *v.* [Yorks. dial.] [mid-19C–1900s] to behave well when successful, i.e. to be a modest winner, to restrain oneself despite gaining power or money. ❑ **carry in one's heart** *v.* [1940s–50s] (*S.Afr.*) to bear a grudge in the hope of getting eventual revenge. ❑ **carry milk-pails** *v.* [the image of a milkmaid with her yoke and two pails] [mid-19C] of a man, to walk with a woman on each arm. ❑ **carry no coals** *v.* [reverse of SE phr. *carry coals*, to do dirty or degrading work, thus to accept insults] [late 16C–17C] to show oneself proof against swindling or insults. ❑ **carry on** *v. see* separate entry. ❑ **carry one's own weight** *v.* [1950s+] (*US*) **1** to take responsibility for one's actions. **2** to have influence. ❑ **carry the drum** *v.* [? the image of a drummer beating slowly, as in a funeral procession] [1940s] (*Aus.*) to work slowly (in a shearing shed). ❑ **carry the mail** *v.* [the reputation of the US postal service for overcoming any object in order to deliver the mail] **1** [1920s–70s] (*US*) to go fast. **2** [1920s–70s] (*US*) to take responsibility for a difficult task. **3** [1940s–50s] (*Aus.*) to stand a round of drinks [the 'delivery' of the drinks]. ❑ **carry the stockwhip** *v.* [1930s+] (*Aus., Northern Terr.*) of a wife, to dominate her husband. ❑ **carry weight** *v.* [one is bowed beneath one's cares] [1930s+] **1** to be depressed. **2** to take responsibility. ❑ **have all that one can carry** *v.* (*also* **have more than one can carry**) [mid-18C+] to be very drunk.

IN EXCLAMATIONS

❑ **carry me out (and bury me decently)!** [play on Lat. *nunc dimittis*, 'Now let thy servant depart...', the first words of the Song of Simeon in Luke 2:29; bolstered by images of prize- and cockfighting] [late 18C–1930s] a general excl. of disbelief and displeasure. ❑ **carry your hip!** [euph. *hip*, the buttocks, the backside] [20C+] (*W.I.*) get out! go away!

carry-go-bring-come *n.* (*also* **bring and carry, bring-go-bring-come, carry-come-and-bring-come**) [the sequence of events] [1940s+] (*W.I.*) **1** a gossip, a tattle-tale. **2** gossip.

carrying-on *n.* (*also* **carryings on**) [SE *carry on*, to do, to act/ CARRY ON *v.*] [mid-17C; mid-19C+] usu. in pl., any form of conspicuous behaviour, e.g. making a fuss, flirting ostentatiously.

carry-on *n.* [late 19C+] **1** a commotion, an exciting event, a disturbance, fuss, excitement; usu. in phr. *what a carry-on!* or a *right/real carry-on*. **2** activity, with no excesses implied.

carry on *v.* **1** [mid-19C+] to make a fuss. **2** [mid-19C+] to behave in an obstreperous or ostentatious manner. **3** [mid-19C+] (*orig. US*) to flirt. **4** [late 19C+] to have an adulterous or additional (if unmarried) relationship, usu. as *carry on with*.

IN PHRASES

❑ **carry on top-ropes** *v. see* SWAY AWAY ON ALL TOP ROPES *v.*

carsey *n.* [CASE *n.*[3] (1)/Ital. *casa*, house] (*orig. Polari*) **1** [mid-19C+] a brothel. **2** [mid-19C+] a thieves' den. **3** [late 19C–1900s] (*also* **carse**) a public house. **4** [late 19C+] (*also* **carsi, cawsy, karzi, karzie, karzy, kazi, kharzi, khazi**) a lavatory. **5** [late 19C+] (*also* **carse, carser**) a house. **6** [late 19C+] (*also* **karzee, karzi, kazi, khazi**) any messy or otherwise unappealing place.

cart *n.*[1] **1** [late 16C–1900s] the gallows [the *cart* that takes the prisoner from prison to the gallows, esp. from Newgate to Tyburn]. **2** [mid–late 19C] the carapace of a crab [resemblance; orig. Norfolk dial.].

IN PHRASES

❑ **in the cart** **1** [late 19C] aware, in the know. **2** [late 19C+] in trouble, in difficulties; thus *put in the cart*, to trick, to deceive.

SE in slang uses

IN COMPOUNDS

❑ **cart-grease** *n.* **1** [late 19C+] rancid butter. **2** [late 19C+] butter. **3** [20C+] margarine.

IN PHRASES

❑ **keep a cart on the wheel** *v.* [late 19C–1920s] to sustain a situation.

cart *n.*[2] [mid-19C] a racecourse.

cart *n.*[3] [abbr.] [1950s] (*US*) a carton.

cart *v.* **1** [late 16C–early 19C] to expose a whore in a cart, driving her through the streets for public humiliation; thus n. *carting*, 'the punishment formerly indicted on bawds, who were placed in a tumbrel or cart, and led through a town, that their persons might be known' (Grose, 1785). **2** [mid-19C+] to carry, to drag; thus *cart away, cart out* etc. **3** [late 19C–1910s] in fig. use, to punish, to make someone suffer; usu. in passive as *carted*.

cartoon *n.* [metonymy] [1920s+] a fool, an absurd person.

cart out with *v.* [late 19C+] to court, to 'go out with'.

carts *n.*[1] [? echoic of the sound of a labourer's heavy, boot-clad step, or ? CART *n.*[1] (2)] [mid–late 19C] a pair of shoes.

carts *n.*[2] *see* CATSO *n.* (2).

cartso *n. see* CATSO *n.*

cartucho *n.* [? Sp. *cartucho*, a small box] [1950s+] (*drugs*) a package of marijuana cigarettes.

cartwheel *n.*[1] **1** from the circular shape [note used in WW1 Aus. milit. for a five-franc piece]. (**a**) [mid–late 19C] a crown or five-shilling (25p) piece. (**b**) [late 19C+] (*Can./US*) a silver dollar. (**c**) [1900s–40s] (*Aus.*) a round damper marked with a cross. (**d**) [1960s–70s] (*drugs*) a drug in pill form, usu. amphetamine or Benzedrine; often in pl. **2** [late 19C] a broad hint, which, like the cartwheel, is too large to be ignored.

cartwheel *n.*[2] [the supposed sufferer 'turns cartwheels'] [1930s] (*US drugs*) a fake heroin withdrawal spasm.

carty *adj.* [mid–late 19C] of a horse, like a carthorse, whether in build or breed.

carve *v.* [Williams (1994) notes use of *carve*, to enjoy sexually] (*US*) **1** [late 19C+] to attack (and cut) with a bladed weapon. **2** [late 19C+] to destroy, to annihilate completely, esp. in a financial or business context. **3** [1940s] to thrill, to excite; of playing music, to excel, to surpass.
SE in slang uses

IN PHRASES

❑ **carve a slice** *v. see under* SLICE *n.* (1). ❑ **carved out of wood** *adj.* [1950s+] stupid. ❑ **carve someone's knob** *v. see under* KNOB *n.* ❑ **carve up** *see* separate entries. ❑ **carve up scores** *v. see under* SCORE *n.*[2].

carver *n.* [CARVE *v.* (1) + SE *carver*, a carving knife] [1900s–30s] (*US*) a knife when used as a weapon.

carver and gilder *n.* [ironic use of SE; the elite professions are reduced to sl. in the lowly context of match-making] [early 19C] a match-maker.

carve-up *n.* [CARVE UP *v.*] **1** [1930s] a legacy, i.e. one's share of a will. **2** [1930s] a riotous time. **3** [1930s+] any situation in which one feels oneself unfairly deprived of a desired aim or object. **4** [1930s+] a knife or razor-slashing. **5** [1940s] a war. **6** [1940s+] (*UK Und.*) a share-out of loot, profits, etc. **7** [1950s] an upset, a fuss. **8** [1960s] an error, mistake.

carve up *v.* [fig. uses of SE] **1** [late 19C+] (*orig. US*) to destroy, to annihilate completely, esp. in a financial or business context. **2** [1920s+] to attack (and cut) with a razor, a knife or other bladed weapon; also in fig. use. **3** [1930s+] to swindle, to cheat. **4** [1950s+] (*UK Und.*) to share out booty, profits etc. **5** [1970s+] of a driver, to force another out of the way through aggressive (and potentially dangerous) driving. **6** [1990s+] to overwhelm, to 'destroy'.

carvie *n.* (*also* **carving china**) [SE *carve up*/CARVE UP *v.* (4) + CHINA (PLATE) *n.* (1)] [1940s–50s] (*UK prison*) one who helps share or divide up a ration of tobacco; a prisoner may take on a regular 'carvie' for periods of his sentence; thus a trusted friend.

carving knife *n.* [rhy. sl.] [1910s] a wife.

cas *adj.* (*also* **caj, cazh, kasj**) [pron. 'cazz'; abbr. SE *casual*] [1980s+] **1** a term of general approval for anything favoured, e.g. a close friend, an item of clothing, a rock band, a given activity [note 19C use *casual*, not to be depended on, uncertain, 'happy-go-lucky'; thus another e.g. of the bad = good model]. **2** pertaining to a working-class casual style of dress [CASUAL *n.*[2]].

ca-sa *n.* (*also* **ca. sa.**) [abbr.] [late 18C–mid-19C] a writ of *capias ad satisfaciendum*, after judgement, to imprison the defendant until the plaintiff's claim is satisfied.

casa *n.*[1] (*also* **casey**) [Ital./Sp. *casa*, a house] [late 17C+] a house, a brothel.

casa *n.*[2] [abbr. proper name Giovanni *Casa*nova (1725–98), the eponym for a sexually successful man] [1940s+] (*Aus.*) a ladies' man.

casaba *n.*[1] [SE *casaba*, a large fruit] [1930s+] (*US*) in pl., the female breasts.

casaba *n.*[2] [SE *cassava*, 'A plant, called also by its Brazilian name Manioc [...] two varieties (or species) of which are extensively cultivated in the West Indies and tropical America, as also in Africa, for their fleshy tuberous roots, which 'yield the greatest portion of the daily food of the natives of tropical America' (*OED*)] [1950s+] (*US*) the head.

Casbah *n.* [SE *kasbah*, 'the Arab quarter surrounding a castle or fortress in a North African town, esp. that of Algiers' (*OED*)] [1960s] (*S.Afr.*) Sophiatown, Johannesburg.

cascade *n.* [orig. Tasmanian use. f. the *Cascade Brewing Company* of Hobart; ult. f. the *cascade* of water that was used for brewing] [late 19C+] (*Aus.*) beer.

cascade *v.* [from the visual imagery] [mid-18C+] a euph. for to vomit.

case *n.*[1] **1** [17C; mid-19C+] a situation. **2** as personifications. (**a**) [mid-19C] (*US*) a doomed person. (**b**) [mid-19C+] a ne'er-do-well, a dubious character. (**c**) [mid-19C+] a person, irrespective of status, morals, etc, although the usage, usu. denoted by an adj., tends be dismissive. (**d**) [mid-19C+] (*orig. US*) an eccentric or otherwise exceptional person. (**e**) [1980s] (*Aus.*) a nymphomaniac. **3** [mid-19C+] (*orig. US*) an infatuation, a love affair; thus an adulterous affair. **4** [late 19C+] in comb. with a n., implying an example of a given state; usu. as *case of the...*; *see also* phrs. below. **5** [20C+] (*US Und.*) the charge or crime for which one is tried and poss. convicted. **6** [1990s+] (*US prison/Und.*) punishment for breaking prison rules; arrest and charges.

IN PHRASES

❑ **bad case of the tins** *n.* [ety. unknown; ? TIN-CAN *v.*] (*US gay*) **1** [1930s+] a state of fear, esp. of being raped. **2** [1980s+] (temporary) impotence. ❑ **case of the...** *n. see* TOUCH OF THE... *under* TOUCH *n.*[1]. ❑ **case of the brokes** *n.* [BROKE *adj.*[1] (1)] [1920s] a state of being penniless. ❑ **case of the reds** *n.* [? MEAN REDS *under* MEAN *adj.*] [1960s] (*US teen*) a state of irritation at the world. ❑ **get off someone's case** *v.* [1950s+] (*orig. US black*) to stop harassing, to stop annoying; esp. as imper. ❑ **get on someone's case** *v.* (*also* **be on someone's case, get down on someone's case, stay on someone's case**) [1950s+] (*orig. US black*) to pester, to harass. ❑ **get on the case** *v.* [1970s+] to get down to work, to occupy oneself with what needs to be done. ❑ **on someone's case** [1960s+] (*orig. US*) **1** harassing verbally, persecuting. **2** pursuing, following; sexually attracted towards. ❑ **on the case** [1950s+] (*orig. US*) whether in one's personal or professional life, working or acting efficiently, controlling a situation, 'taking care of business'.

case *n.*[2] (*also* **kaze**) [SE *case*, a container (for the penis); note Shakespeare's ext. synon./pun the *genitive case*] [17C–mid-18C] the vagina.

case *n.*[3] [Ital. *casa*, house] **1** [17C–1900s] a house. **2** [late 17C–mid-19C] a shop, a warehouse. **3** [late 17C–1970s] (*also* **caser**) a brothel, esp. those sited in the Haymarket, London, in mid–late 19C. **4** [18C] (*UK Und.*) a house frequented by the underworld, a 'thieves' kitchen'. **5** [mid-19C] a lavatory.

IN COMPOUNDS

❑ **case-fro** *n.* (*also* **case-froe, case-frow, case-vrow**) [Ger. *Frau*/Du. *vrow*, a woman] [late 17C–early 19C] a prostitute, esp. one who works in a brothel. ❑ **case house** *n.* [HOUSE *n.*[1] (1)/SE *house*] [1910s–60s] (*UK Und.*) a brothel. ❑ **case keeper** *n.* [1930s] a brothel-owner. ❑ **case-ranging** *n.* [SE *range*, to look over, to survey] [1920s] (*UK Und.*) the inspection of a property with the intention of robbing it.

IN PHRASES

❑ **crack a case** *v.* [mid–late 19C] (*UK Und.*) to break into a house. ❑ **down to cases** *see under* DOWN *adv.*[2]. ❑ **go case** *v.* **1** [1900s–50s] (*also* **have a case**) to have a semi-permanent relationship with. **2** [1910s+] (*also* **come case, go case-o, have a case going**) to have sexual intercourse with. ❑ **go caso** *v.* [1900s–30s] to work as a genteel prostitute, from a flat, rather than walking the streets. ❑ **keep cases** *v. see under* CASE *v.*[1].

case *n.*[4] [? Fr. *caisse*, cash or CASER *n.*[1]] **1** [mid-19C+] (*US*) (*also* **case note**) $1. **2** [mid–late 19C] a counterfeit crown (5s (25p)); thus *half-a-case*, a counterfeit half-crown (2s 6p (12½p)). **3** [1930s] (*US Und.*) one's last dollar.

IN PHRASES

❑ **half-case** *n.* (*also* **half-a-case**) [late 19C–1950s] (*US*) 50 cents.

case *n.*[5] [CASE *v.*[1] (1)] [1930s+] a surveillance, a look around.

case *adj.* [? SE *suitcase*, i.e. where the money is stored in reserve; ? abbr. SE *just in case*; ? CASE *n.*[4] (1)] [1900s–50s] (*US*) usu. of money, the last available; spare.

IN COMPOUNDS

❑ **case dough** *n.* (*also* **case dollar, case dime, case note**) [DOUGH *n.* (1)] **1** [1900s–60s] (*US prison/gambling*) limited money, one's last available funds. **2** money for use in a confidence trick.

case *v.*[1] [orig. faro jargon *case*, to watch carefully] **1** [1910s+] (*orig. US*) (*also* **case out, case up**) to look over, to appraise, esp. before a robbery. **2** [1950s] to assess a person. **3** [2000s] (*US black*) to steal; to exchange money for a higher denomination.

IN PHRASES

❑ **case it around** *v.* [1980s+] (*US teen*) to check a place or situation. ❑ **case out** *v.* **1** [1940s] (*US*) (*also* **case off**) to leave, to go away. **2** [1940s–60s] (*US*) to join forces for any undertaking. **3** *see* sense 1 above. ❑ **case the joint** *v.* (*also* **case the gaff, ...job**) [JOINT *n.* (3b)/GAFF *n.*[1] (9)/JOB *n.*[2] (1a)] **1** [1910s+] to survey a house, shop etc, with a view to subseq. robbing it. **2** [1950s] to look for employment opportunities. **3** [2000s] (*US black*) to steal; to exchange money for a higher denomination. ❑ **case up** *v. see* sense 1 above. ❑ **keep cases on** *v.* [note Asbury *Sucker's Progress* (1938) 14: An extraordinary number of the terms, technical and otherwise, which were employed by Faro players in the palmy days of the game have passed into the language [...] Case-keeper—A device for keeping a record of the cards as they were drawn. Also, the man who operated the device. *Keeping cases*—Manipulating the *case-keeper*] [late 19C–1930s] (*US*) to watch closely.

case *v.*[2] [? to put aside in a fig. *case*, i.e. container] [1920s–30s] (*UK Und.*) to delay, to spoil, to cause to be postponed.

case *v.*[3] [weak uses of SE criminal *case*] **1** [1950s] (*UK prison*) to discipline, to put on report. **2** [1970s] (*US black*) to joke about. **3** [1970s+] (*US black*) to tell off, to scold.

cased *adj.*[1] [CASE *v.*[3] (1) although this appears to predate, so ? simply SE *(criminal) case*] **1** [1920s] (*UK prison*) subjected to a diet of bread and water. **2** [1940s–50s] (*UK Und.*) charged with an offence.

cased *adj.*[2] [CASE *n.*[1] (3)] [1950s+] (*S.Afr.*) infatuated with, having a relationship with.

cased up *adj.*[1] [CASE *n.*[1] (5)] [1930s] (*US Und.*) imprisoned.

cased up *adj.*[2] [GO CASE *under* CASE *n.*[3]] [1930s+] living with.

caseo *n.* [CASE *n.*[3] (3) + -O *sfx* (7)] [1930s+] **1** a brothel. **2** the hiring of a prostitute for one or more nights. **3** a prostitute who hires out for a whole night. **4** in fig. use of sense 1, any place where women act without constraint.

IN PHRASES

❑ **go case-o** *v. see under* CASE *n.*[3].

case of (the)... *n. see* CASE *n.*[1] (4).

case o' pistles *n.* [lit. a *case of pistols*; ? ref. to SE *pizzle*, a bull's penis] [20C+] (*Ulster*) the buttocks.

caser *n.*[1] [Yid. *kesef*, silver; thus the silver five-shilling piece, and the dollar, then worth five shillings (25p)] **1** [early 19C–1950s] five shillings (25p). **2** [1900s–30s] (*US*) $1. **3** [1940s–50s] (*Aus.*) a five-year prison sentence.

IN PHRASES

❑ **half-a-caser** *n.* (*also* **half-caser, half-a-case**) [late 19C–1950s] (*Aus.*) half-a-crown, 2s 6d (12½ p.). ❑ **half-case** *n.* [late 19C] (*US*) half a dollar.

caser *n.*[2] [presumably CASE *v.*[3] (1) although predates] [1940s–50s] (*UK prison*) a prison officer notorious for excessive discipline.

caser *n.*[3] [CASE *v.*[1] (1)] [1940s+] (*US Und.*) one who assesses a property as a target for burglary.

caser *n.*[4] [one would have to drink a 'case er' (i.e. 'case of') beer before making love to them] [2000s] (*Aus.*) an unattractive woman.

caser *n.*[5] *see* CASE *n.*[3] (3).

cases *n.* [abbr. BEATER-CASES *n.*] [early–mid-19C] shoes.

casey *n.*[1] (*also* **cassey**) [CASSAN *n.*] [19C] cheese.

casey *n.*[2] *see* CASA *n.*[1].

Casey Brown *n.* (*also* **K.C. Brown**) [an artificial proper name *Casey* or *K.C. Brown*] [1930s] (*US black*) a mythical figure endowed with the ability to fight for black rights and against racism.

casey jones *n.* [the legendary locomotive engineer John Luther *Jones* (1864–1900); his nickname came from the town of Cayce, pron. *Casey*, Kentucky; his fame from his death, attempting to avoid the crash that killed him, which event was later immortalized in a poem by Wallace Stevens, an engine wiper] (*US*) **1** [1930s+] a train-driver, a locomotive engineer. **2** [1940s+] a railway train.

cash *n.*[1] [CASSAN *n.*] [late 17C–early 19C] (*UK Und.*) cheese.

cash *n.*[2]

SE in slang uses

IN COMPOUNDS

❑ **cash-ass** *n.* [-ASS *sfx*; a pun on SE *cautious*] [1970s+] (*US gay*) a male prostitute who pretends innocence until promised cash. ❑ **cash carrier** *n.* [late 19C] a pimp. ❑ **cash register** *n.* (*US*) a prostitute's vagina.

IN PHRASES

❑ **cash on delivery** *n.* [play on abbr. *C.O.D.*] [late 19C] (*US*) codfish. ❑ **do one's cash** *v.* [DO IN *v.* (2)] [20C+] (*Aus.*) to spend all one's available funds.

cash *v.*[1] **1** [mid-19C+] (*US*) to lend or give money. **2** [1950s] to pass counterfeit money.

SE in slang uses

IN PHRASES

❑ **cash in** *see* separate entries. ❑ **cash one's pistol** *v.* [joc. image of presenting a pistol at the counter rather than a cheque] [late 19C] (*US Western*) to rob a bank at gunpoint. ❑ **cash out** *v.* [1960s] **1** to die. **2** to kill oneself. **3** to murder, to kill. ❑ **cash up** *v.* **1** [19C] to pay up, to pay over; thus to pay one's debts. **2** [1950s+] (*Aus.*) to earn money. **3** [1970s] (*US campus*) to work out.

cash *v.*[2] [abbr. CASH IN ONE'S CHIPS *under* CHIP *n.*[2]] (*US*) **1** [1900s] to quit, to give up one's efforts. **2** [1930s] to die.

cash and carry *v.* [rhy. sl.; but note that the first *OED* cite of *cash and carry* in purchasing sense is 1917] [late 19C+] to marry; thus *cash and carried*, married.

cashed *adj.* [? CASH IN ONE'S CHIPS *under* CHIP *n.*[2]] **1** [20C+] (*US campus*) (*also* **cashed in**) physically, mentally or economically exhausted. **2** [1940s] (*US*) dead. **3** [1980s+] (*drugs*) used of a marijuana bowl or pipe that contains nothing but ash. **4** [2000s] having had a sufficiency.

cashed up *adj.* [1930s+] (*Aus./N.Z.*) wealthy, well-off, albeit temporarily.

cash-in *n.* [CASH IN *v.* (1)] [1920s] (*US*) the end, i.e. death.

cash in *v.* (*orig. US*) **1** [late 19C+] to die; thus *cashed in*, dead. **2** [late 19C+] to settle up one's accounts or debts, esp. in card-playing. **3** [1910s+] to give up, to accept the situation. **4** [1920s+] to make a profit, to exploit; often as *cash in on*. **5** [1930s] to stop arguing or prevaricating, to confess.

IN PHRASES

❑ **cash in one's checks** *v. see under* CHECK *n.*[1]. ❑ **cash in one's chips** *v. see under* CHIP *n.*[2]. ❑ **cash in the food stamps of love** *v.* [1970s+] (*US black*) to accept a less than ideal sexual partner through one's needs or frustration.

cashish *n.* [SE *cash* + *hashish* (as a desirable/valuable commodity)] [2000s] money.

cashmere *n.* [1960s] (*US black*) a sweater, irrespective of the material.

cashola *n.* [SE *cash* + -OLA *sfx*; on the pattern of PAYOLA *n.*] [1950s+] (*US*) cash.

cashunk! *excl. see* KERCHUNK! *under* KER- *pfx*.

casian *n.* [? pron. of SE *catch* + *man*] [1990s+] (*UK black*) a police officer.

casing *n.* [CASE *v.*[1] (1)] [1920s+] (*orig. US*) the assessment of a place or person to calculate how vulnerable it is or they are to robbery.

cask *n.* [SE *cask*, 'a wooden vessel of cylindrical form' (*OED*)] **1** [mid-19C] 'fashionable Slang for a brougham, or other private carriage' (Hotten, 1859). **2** [1930s] (*US Und.*) a taxi.

casket nail *n.* (*also* **casket tack**) [var. on COFFIN NAIL *n.*[1]] [1960s] (*US*) a cigarette.

Caspar Milquetoast *n.* (*also* **caspar, Casper Milktoast/ Milquetoast, milktoast, milquetoast, Mr Milquetoast**) [the central character in the cartoon 'The Timid Soul' created by H.T. Webster, first publ. in *New York World*, May 1924] [1930s+] a cowardly, weak person; also as adj.

casper *n.* [1950s cartoon character *Casper the Friendly Ghost*, who is white] [1980s] (*US black*) a particularly light-skinned black person.

cassan *n.* (*also* **cass, cassam, cassin, casson, casum, caz, cosan**) [Rom. *cas*, cheese; cf. SE *casein*, the milk ingredient that is the basis of cheese] [mid-16C–mid-19C] (*UK Und.*) cheese.

IN PHRASES

❑ **as good as caz** [early 19C] (*UK Und.*) easy, simple, referring to any projected fraud or robbery, or a person who is to be made a victim of either.

cass-cass *adj.* [Twi *kasakasa*, very thin, *akasakasa*, a dispute] [20C+] (*W.I.*) untidy, disreputable, inferior, low-class.

cassey *n.* *see* CASEY *n.*[1].

cassin *n.* [mid-19C] (*UK Und.*) the neck; thus *cassin-twined*, hanged; *cassin-twiner*, the hangman.

cassin/casson *n.* *see* CASSAN *n.*

cast *adj.* [? pun on SE *cast down*] [1930s–40s] (*Irish/N.Z.*) drunk.

cast *v.*

SE in slang uses

IN PHRASES

❑ **cast accounts** *v.* [late 19C] (*US*) to vomit. ❑ **cast nasturtiums** *v.* [20C+] a joking mispron. of SE *cast aspersions*. ❑ **cast one's skin** *v.* [animal imagery] **1** [mid-19C] to strip oneself naked. **2** [late 19C] (*UK society*) to rejuvenate oneself. ❑ **cast the house out of the windows** *v.* [mid-16C–19C] to make a great deal of noise or disturbance in one's house. ❑ **cast the net** *v.* [1970s+] (*US*) of a pimp, to employ an experienced prostitute to lure a new woman into joining his team. ❑ **cast up** *v.* [abbr./play on SE *cast up accounts*, to make a reckoning] [late 19C+] to bear a grudge, to remind someone of their failings. ❑ **cast up one's accounts** *v.* (*also* **cast up, cast up one's reckoning, discharge one's accounts**) [play on SE *cast up accounts*, to make a reckoning] **1** [late 16C–19C] to vomit. **2** [late 17C–mid-18C] to be drunk, and so likely to vomit.

castell *v.* [? SE *castle*, from the battlements of which one can get a long-range view] [early 17C] (*UK Und.*) to look, to see.

caster *n.*[1] [ety. unknown, but F&H suggest a link to CASTOR *n.*, presumably in a sense of a covering] [mid-16C–mid-19C] (*UK Und.*) a cloak.

caster *n.*[2] [SE *cast off*; note milit. jargon *caster*, a horse considered no longer fit for the cavalry or horse artillery and sold at public auction] [mid-19C+] anything or anyone that has been rejected or cast aside.

caster *n.*[3] [? SE *castor*, a small, round wheel used to make furniture mobile] [late 19C] (*US*) a testicle.

Castieau's hotel *n.* [John Buckley *Castieu*, governor of Melbourne Gaol, inter alia in charge of the hanging of Ned Kelly in 1880] [mid-19C] (*Aus.*) a prison.

casting *n.* [SE *cast*, to form molten metal into a shape with a mould] [mid-19C] (*US*) a coin; thus *castings*, cash.

cast-iron and double-bolted *adj.* [fig. use of engineering terminology] [late 19C+] extremely strong.

cast-iron horrors *n.* [SE *cast-iron*, 'hard-and-fast', unyielding + HORRORS, THE *n.* (2)] [20C+] (*Anglo-Irish*) delirium tremens.

Castle, the *n.* *see* HOLLOWAY CASTLE *n.*

Castle *adj.* [SE Dublin *Castle*, the seat of British rule] [mid-19C–1920s] in comb. meaning Irish, pertaining to pre-Independence British rule.

IN COMPOUNDS

❑ **Castle Catholic** *n.* [1930s–70s] an Irish Catholic who rejected nationalism, preferring to curry favour with and ape the lifestyle of the ruling British. ❑ **Castle hack** *n.* [HACK *n.*[1] (3)] [1910s] an informer.

castle *n.* [the cliché, *an Englishman's home is his castle*] **1** [late 19C] (*US*) a brothel. **2** [1940s+] (*US black*) one's house, one's home.

castle rag *n.* [rhy. sl. = FLAG *n.*[1] (1)] [mid-19C] (*UK Und.*) fourpence.

castor *n.* (*also* **caster**) [14C *castor*, a beaver. Such hats were made of beaver fur or, if as was increasingly the case, of rabbit, disguised to look as if they were beaver] [mid-17C–mid-19C] a hat.

IN PHRASES

❑ **demi-castor** *n.* [mid-17C–mid-19C] 'an inferior quality of beaver's fur, or a mixture of beaver's and other fur' (*OED*).

castor *adj.* [? SE *castor sugar*, thus parallel to SWEET *adj.*[1] (3); Simes, *A Dict. of Australian Underworld Slang* (1993), prefers the old criminal signal of tugging one's hat or CASTOR *n.*, to indicate 'all clear', used fig. in the non-criminal world] [1940s+] (*Aus.*) excellent, admirable, first-rate; thus *be on the castor with*, to be popular with.

Castro clone *n.* [*Castro* Street, San Francisco, known as The Castro, and the centre of the gay community + CLONE *n.* (2)] [1970s+] (*US gay*) a popular variety of post-gay liberation stereotype, often posing as a lumberjack type with checked flannel shirt, Levis, heavy boots etc.

casual *n.*[1] [SE *casual*, non-essential or, in the case of paupers, only temporarily needy] **1** [19C] a casual pauper. **2** [mid-19C+] a part-time labourer or other employee. **3** [late 19C+] the casual ward in a hospital.

casual *n.*[2] [SE *casual clothing*] [1980s+] **1** a working-class youth who dresses in casual clothes, often designer labels, but whose accent and lifestyle remains proletarian. **2** a football hooligan who adopts such a style.

casual *adj.* **1** [1950s+] (*US campus*) acceptable, satisfactory [for ety. *see* CAS *adj.*]. **2** [1980s] not worth becoming upset about. **3** [1980s+] pertaining to a working-class casual style of dress [CASUAL *n.*[2]].

casualty *n.* [late 19C–1900s] a black eye.

casualty *adj.* [mid–late 19C] casual; thus *casualty-boy*, a boy who hires himself out to a costermonger or market greengrocer.

casum *n.* *see* CASSAN *n.*

cat *n.*[1] [lit. and fig. uses of SE *cat*] **1** uses based on the identification of the cat with femininity. (**a**) [15C–18C; 1940s+] (*later use is US black*) (*also* **kat**) a prostitute. (**b**) [17C+] a woman, esp. a spiteful and malicious one; thus *old cat*, an unpleasant, gossiping old woman. (**c**) [18C+] a gossip. (**d**) [1910s+] a sexually attractive woman; in weak use, a girlfriend. (**e**) [1970s+] (*US gay*) a lesbian. **2** uses based on cat's fur. (**a**) [late 17C+] the female pubic hair and genitals. (**b**) [mid-19C] a ladies' muff; thus *free a cat*, to steal a muff. **3** based on other feline characteristics, e.g. quietness, disloyalty. (**a**) [1900s] (*US Und.*) one who researches potential robberies, plans them and poss. works as a lookout. (**b**) [1920s–40s] (*US prison*) an informer. (**c**) [2000s] a narcotics user. **4** [1920s–30s] an animal other than a cat. **5** [1950s+] (*Aus./UK prison*) a passive male homosexual; thus *cats' gaol*, a prison where the majority of inmates are homosexual/ transsexual; *cats' yard*, a segregated area of the prison set aside for homosexuals or otherwise vulnerable prisoners [may also be abbr. SE *catamite*, a boy kept for homosexual purposes; but note PUSSY *n.* (9)].

IN COMPOUNDS

❑ **cat bar** *n.* (*also* **cat's bar**) [1950s–80s] (*N.Z.*) a bar set aside for women and their escorts. ❑ **cat fight** *n.* [1950s+] a fight between two (or more) women. ❑ **cat flat** *n.* [1940s] (*US Und.*) a brothel. ❑ **cat-house** *n.* *see* separate entry. ❑ **cat-lamb** *n.*

[mid-19C] (*UK Und.*) an ageing, worn-out prostitute. ❑ **cat-lapper** *n.* [1960s] (*US*) a (lesbian) cunnilinguist. ❑ **cat o'mountain** *n.* [SE *catamount*, a cougar or panther] **1** [17C] a high-spirited whore or promiscuous woman. **2** [mid–late 19C] (*US*) a shrew. ❑ **cat party** *n.* (*also* **cats' party**) [late 19C+] a party consisting of women only. ❑ **cat-scrap** *n.* [mid-19C] (*UK Und.*) a drunken fighting woman. ❑ **cat shop** *n.* (*also* **cats' nest**) [SHOP *n.*[1] (1)] [1930s–50s] (*US*) a brothel. ❑ **cat wagon** *n.* [found in many US rural areas before the anti-'white slavery' legislation of 1910; the women travelled and worked from a horse-drawn covered wagon, following the cattle trails or visiting cowboys out on the range] (*US*) **1** [19C–1960s] a travelling brothel. **2** [1970s] a van used to take prostitutes to prison.

IN PHRASES

❑ **cat on a testy dodge** *n.* [TESTER *n.*[1] (1) + DODGE *n.* (1)] [late 19C] a genteel female beggar who asks for money at people's houses, often backing her request with a (fake) testimonial from a charity.

SE in slang uses

DERIVATIVES

❑ **catish** *adj.* [the popular idea of the sinuously elegant feline] [19C] (*US*) elegant, stylish.

IN COMPOUNDS

❑ **catbird** *see* separate entries. ❑ **cat-eye** *n. see* separate entries. ❑ **catface** *n.* [fanciful resemblance. Note timber jargon *catface*, a mark in a piece of lumber-wood] [1950s–70s] (*US*) a wrinkle in one's clothing. ❑ **catfish** *see* separate entries. ❑ **cat-fit** *n.* [reverse anthropomorphism] [1900s–30s] (*US*) a tantrum. ❑ **catflap** *n.* [1990s+] **1** the anus. **2** a bisexual person [it swings both ways]. ❑ **catfoot** *see* separate entries. ❑ **catgut** *see* separate entries. ❑ **cathead** *see* separate entries. ❑ **cat-lap** *n.* [LAP *n.*[2]] **1** [late 18C–19C] tea or coffee. **2** [19C] any form of weak drink, incl. watered-down alcohol. **3** [19C] milk. ❑ **cat-lick** *n.* [the phr. is supposedly reminiscent of a cat, although, in fact, cats are punctilious in their self-cleansing] **1** [1930s] a casual, perfunctory wash. **2** *see also* separate entry. ❑ **cat-man** *n.* [1940s–60s] (*US black*) a cat burglar. ❑ **cat-nap** *n.* [SE *cat-nap*, a short sleep] [2000s] (*US prison*) a relatively short sentence. ❑ **catnip** *see* separate entries. ❑ **cat road** *n.* [a cat's nocturnal wanderings] [1930s–40s] (*US*) a back road. ❑ **cat's** *n.* [abbr. CAT'S PYJAMAS *n.*] [1920s] anything exceptional, superlative. ❑ **cat's...** *n. see also* CAT'S PYJAMAS *n.* ❑ **cat's ass** *n. see* separate entry. ❑ **cat's balls** *n.* [BALLS *n.*] [1960s] (*US*) **1** anything exceptional, superlative. **2** a superior person, or someone who poses as such. ❑ **cat sense** *n.* [1930s–40s] (*US black*) common sense, intelligence. ❑ **cat-shag** *v.* [SHAG *v.*[1] (2)] [1940s–70s] (*Aus.*) to fool around. ❑ **cat's head** *n.* **1** [mid-18C] a halfpenny roll of bread. **2** [early 19C] the female breast. ❑ **catshit** *n.* [SHIT *n.*] **1** [1980s+] (*US*) a disgusting, or objectional circumstance or individual. **2** [1990s+] nonsense. ❑ **cat-skin** *n.* **1** [mid-19C] a second-rate silk hat. **2** [1970s+] (*Irish*) the outer crust or end of a loaf of bread. ❑ **cat's kittens** *n.* [var. on CAT'S PYJAMAS *n.*] [1920s] (*US*) anything or anyone exceptional, superlative. ❑ **cat's knee-knuckles** *n. see* CAT'S WHISKERS *n.* ❑ **cat-smellers** *n.* [a cat uses its whiskers as an extra sense] [mid-19C] (*US*) facial hair, whiskers. ❑ **cat's meow** *n. see* separate entry. ❑ **cat's mitts** *n.* [abbr. SE *cat's mittens*; var. on CAT'S PYJAMAS *n.*] [1910s] (*US*) **1** anything exceptional, superlative. **2** a superior person, or someone who poses as such. ❑ **cat's mother** *n.* (*also* **cat's aunt, ...father, ...grandmother**) [? the (middle-class) admonition to a child talking of 'she', when describing a woman, who ought to be 'Mrs X' or 'Miss Y': *'She' is the cat's mother*] [1950s+] a response to the question 'Who are you?' when that question is considered impertinent or over-intrusive. ❑ **cat's nuts** *n.* [NUTS *n.*[2] (1); var. on CAT'S PYJAMAS *n.*] [1910s+] (*US*) **1** anything exceptional, superlative. **2** a superior person, or someone who poses as such. ❑ **cat's pee** *n.* [PEE *n.*[1] (1)] [20C+] any form of weak alcoholic drink. ❑ **cat's piss** *n.* [PISS *n.* (4a)] [1940s+] any form of weak drink. ❑ **cat spraddle** *n.* [dial. *spraddle*, to sprawl + ? SE *spreadeagle*; the image is of a falling cat] [20C+] (*W.I.*) **1** to fall spreadeagled on the ground. **2** to beat severely. ❑ **cat's prick** *n.* [PRICK *n.* (1)] [1990s+] (*UK juv.*) the elongated end of a burning cigarette, caused by its being shared and smoked fast. ❑ **cat's pyjamas** *n. see* separate entry. ❑ **cat sticks** *n.* [SE *catstick*, a stick or bat used in games of tip-cat or trap-ball] [late 18C–19C] very thin legs. ❑ **cat's water** *n.* [19C] gin. ❑ **cat's whiskers** *n. see* separate entry. ❑ **catwanker** *n.* [WANKER *n.*, lit. one who masturbates cats] [1990s+] a general term of derision. ❑ **cat-whipper** *n.* [WHIP THE CAT *v.* (4c)] [20C+] (*Aus.*) one who whinges over their misfortunes. ❑ **cat work/worker** *n. see* CAT-UP *n.* (1).

IN PHRASES

❑ **black cat with its throat cut** *n.* [1950s+] the female pubic hair and vagina. ❑ **cat and dog** *v.* [SE phr. *rain cats and dogs*] [1990s+] (*Aus.*) to rain heavily. ❑ **cat and dog life** *n.* [19C+] an unhappy marriage, in which the partners fight like cat and dog. ❑ **cat couldn't scratch it** (*also* **one a cat couldn't scratch**) [1960s+] (*US*) used of an especially hard penile erection. ❑ **cat-eating-shit grin** *n. see* SHIT-EATING GRIN *n.* ❑ **cat in a sack** *n.* [1960s–70s] (*US*) something to be suspicious or wary about; thus *buy a cat in a sack*, to buy something that one has not actually inspected. ❑ **cat in the pan** *n.* [phr. *turn the cat in the pan*, 'to reverse the order of things so dextrously as to make them appear the very opposite of what they really are' (*OED*) and/or ? *cate* (lit. a culinary 'dainty' and here used as *cake*) *in the pan*, a pancake, which must be turned if it is to be cooked] [mid-16C–mid-19C] a traitor, one who changes sides to advance their self-interest; thus *turn cat in the pan*, to inform, to betray, to change sides. ❑ **cat (out)** *v.* [1940s+] (*US black*) to wander the streets aimlessly, to stay out all night, to hide away. ❑ **cat's head cut open** *n.* [supposed resemblance] [19C] the labia minora. ❑ **cat up** *see* separate entries. ❑ **like a cat up a chimney** [early 19C] very fast. ❑ **like who shot the cat** [1930s] (*US*) a general intensifier, e.g. very fast, very successful. ❑ **live at the sign of the cat's foot** *v.* (*also* **live under the (sign of the) cat's foot**) [? SE *cat's foot*, a fool] [late 17C–19C] of a man, to be dominated by one's wife. ❑ **see which way the cat jumps** *v.* (*also* **see how the cat jumps, ...the pussy jumps, watch which way the cat jumps**) [early 19C+] to wait to see how events turn out before making one's own decision or move. ❑ **something the cat brought/dragged in** *n. see* SOMETHING *n.*

IN EXCLAMATIONS

❑ **my cats!** [1900s] (*US*) a mild oath.

cat *n.*[2] [Ital. *cazzo*, the penis/abbr. CATSO *n.* (2) or the perceived lecherousness of a SE tom*cat*] [17C] the penis; esp. in phr. *a bit for one's cat.*

IN COMPOUNDS

❑ **cat food** *n.* [1960s–70s] (*US black*) sexual intercourse.

IN PHRASES

❑ **skin the cat** *v.* [19C+] to have sexual intercourse.

cat *n.*[3] [abbr.; later use is SE] [late 18C–early 19C] the *cat-o'-nine-tails*; thus *get the cat*, to be given a judicial whipping; note the right-wingers' litany of *bring back the cat.*

IN PHRASES

❑ **comb the cat** *v.* [late 19C] to separate the 'tails' on the whip so that each one inflicts its own welt.

cat *n.*[4] [a double-KITTEN *n.* (1)] [early–mid-19C] a quart pot.

IN COMPOUNDS

❑ **cat and kitten hunter** *n.* [mid-19C] (*UK Und.*) a person who steals pewter quart and pint pots from public houses. ❑ **cat and kitten hunting** *n.* (*also* **cat and kitten sneaking**) [mid-19C] (*UK Und.*) the stealing of pint and quart pots from public houses. ❑ **cat and kitten rig** *n.* [RIG *n.*[2] (1)] [early 19C] (*UK Und.*) the stealing of pint and quart pots from public houses. ❑ **cat sneaking** *n.* [SNEAK *v.* (1)] [late 19C] the stealing of pewter tankards from public houses.

cat *n.*[5] [reverse anthromorphism, poss. playing on its 'going out at night'; however, for jazz/beatnik/hippie uses note Gold, *A Jazz Lexicon* (1964), who suggests 'most. prob. shortened form of general and Negro slang *tomcat*'] **1** [late 19C+] (*orig. US black*) (*also* **kat**) a person. **2** (*orig. US black*) in orig. jazz-orientated uses. (**a**) [1920s+] a jazz musician. (**b**) [1920s+] a smartly dressed, fashion conscious man, thus a 'sharp cat'. (**c**) [1930s] a jazz fan. **3** [1980s+] a user of crack cocaine.

IN COMPOUNDS

❑ **cat clothes** *n.* [1950s] (*orig. US black*) fashionable clothing as favoured by jazz fans. ❑ **cat walk** *n.* [1960s+] (*US black*) a strutting style of walking, intended to emphasize one's pride, independence and masculinity.

IN PHRASES

❑ **cat on the peek port** *n.* [PEEK *n.*] [1940s] (*US black*) a lookout man. ❑ **cat that cracks the whip** *n.* [1940s] (*US black*) a playboy. ❑ **dig the cat** *v. see* DIG *v.*[3]. ❑ **one's kind of cat** [mid-19C] a person as needed in a given situation, usu. in negative.

cat *n.*[6] [abbr.] **1** [1900s] (*Aus.*) a business syndic*ate*. **2** [1910s+] (*orig. US*) *Cat*erpillar tractor; thus a tractor of any make. **3** [1930s+] (*US*) (*also* **cat walker**) a *cat* burglar. **4** [1990s+] (*drugs*) meth*cat*hinone.

cat *n.*[7] [initial letter] [1960s] (*US campus*) the grade C.

cat *n.*[8] **1** *see* GAYCAT *n.* (2). **2** *see* KITTY *n.*[3].

cat *adj.* [Irish *cat marbh*, mischief, calamity or abbr. of SE *catastrophe*] **1** [20C+] (*Irish*) terrible, shocking, unpleasant, rough. **2** [1980s] (*US campus*) likeable, approved of [on the bad = good model].

cat *v.*[1] (*also* **cat around**) [the perceived lecherousness of the SE *tomcat* (cf. TOM CAT *v.*)] (*orig. US*) **1** [20C+] (*also* **go catting**) to search for a sexual partner. **2** [1910s+] to be sexually unfaithful. **3** [1930s+] to wander purposelessly about. **4** [1940s] (*US black*) to ask questions.

IN PHRASES

❑ **on the cat** (*US black*) **1** [1940s] in hiding. **2** [1950s–60s] staying out at night.

cat *v.*[2] [CAT *n.*[1] (1e)] [1940s–70s] (*US gang*) to talk; to gossip; to malign.

cat *v.*[3] [the indolence of the SE *cat*] [1950s–70s] (*US teen/gang*) to loaf about.

cat *v.*[4] *see* CAT (UP) *v.*

catalogue queen *n.* [SE *catalogue* + -QUEEN *sfx* (3)] [1960s+] (*US gay*) a homosexual man who uses physique and body-building magazines as masturbatory pornography.

catamaran *n.* [pun on CAT *n.*[1] (1c) + poss. pun on orig. SE *catamaran*, a fireship or *catamaran*, an ill-tempered person; also note *CAT O'MOUNTAIN under* CAT *n.*[1]] **1** [late 18C–19C] an old scraggy woman, a disagreeable harridan. **2** [mid-19C] a run-down horse.

cat and mouse *n.* [rhy. sl.] [mid-19C+] a house.

cataract *n.* [SE *cataract*, a waterfall; it 'flows' down the wearer's chest] [mid-19C] a large, many-layered black cravat, used to show off one's stick-pin and similar jewellery; such an item was especially favoured by 19C commercial travellers.

catarumpus *n.* [? CATAWAMPUS *adj.* (2)] [mid-19C] (*US*) a riot, a commotion, a rumpus.

catastrophe *n.* [play on upper-class pron. of ARSE *n.* (1)] [mid-19C] (*UK Und.*) the posterior, the buttocks.

catawampus *n.* [CATAWAMPUS *adj.*] **1** [mid–late 19C] a biting, stinging insect. **2** [mid-19C–1930s] (*US*) a peculiar or remarkable thing or person.

catawampus *adj.* (*also* **caliwampus, cattywampus**) [ety. unknown; ? SE *cater-/catty-cornered*, diagonal] (*US*) **1** [mid-19C] fierce, pitiless. **2** [mid-19C; 1930s] ill-tempered, crotchety. **3** [late 19C–1900s] out of order, wrong. **4** [1900s–60s] askew; thus *catawampously, catawamptiously*. **5** [1990s+] (*US campus*) eccentric.

catawampus *v.* [CATAWAMPUS *adj.*] (*US*) **1** [mid-19C–1900s] to confuse, to confound; usu. as *catawampussed*. **2** [mid-19C–1900s] to injure, to harm. **3** [1900s] to move in a diagonal line.

catawampus! *excl.* [SE *catawampus*, a hobgoblin or imaginary demon; in turn ? f. 17C *catamount*, a panther] [19C] (*US*) a general excl., often as *great catawampus!*

catawampusly *adv.* (*also* **catawampus, cattawampously, catawamptiously**) [CATAWAMPUS *adj.*] [mid-19C–1900s] (*US*) fiercely.

catbird *n.* [SE *catbird* (*Dumatella carolinensis*), known for its harassing of fellow birds. The catbird takes up a high, exposed position to deliver its song. The image is of a cat looking down on a targeted bird. Orig. a term used by a poker opponent of the sportscaster Red Barber (1908–92) and popularized first by him and latterly by a James Thurber story, 'The Catbird Seat' (14/11/1942)] **1** [20C+] (*US*) a mischievous or cunning person. **2** [1960s+] (*US*) a person of authority or power. **3** [1990s+] (*US campus*) an admirable person.

IN PHRASES

❑ **in the catbird seat** [1940s+] in a privileged or advantageous position.

catbird *adj.* [ety. unknown; predates CATBIRD *n.* (2)] [mid-19C] (*US*) perfect, ideal.

catch *n.* **1** [mid-18C+] one who is seen as matrimonially desirable, often in phr. *a good catch, no catch*. **2** [mid-19C] (*UK Und.*) a thief's booty, a stolen item. **3** [1900s–10s] anything desirable. **4** [1960s+] (*US black*) a woman, esp. a woman recruited into prostitution; thus *catching*, seducing a woman into prostitution. **5** [1960s+] (*US black*) the number of clients a prostitute has serviced within a given time. **6** *see* CATCHER *n.*[2].

catch *v.*[1] **1** as a mental process. (**a**) [late 19C+] to grasp the meaning, often in negative, e.g. *I didn't quite catch…* (**b**) [late 19C+] to find out, to discover. (**c**) [1960s+] to notice, to appreciate. **2** of a person or object, to come into possession of, to take control of. (**a**) [late 19C+] to ensnare a victim in a confidence trick or crooked gambling game. (**b**) [late 19C+] to obtain, to get, to come into possession of a given item, lit. or fig. (**c**) [1960s] (*US prison*) to make a good impression on. (**d**) [1960s+] to seduce. (**e**) [1960s+] (*US black*) of a pimp, to persuade a woman (whether already a prostitute or not) to start working for him. (**f**) [1970s] (*US black*) of a prostitute, to attract a client. (**g**) [1990s+] (*US black*) to steal. **3** to experience; to encounter. (**a**) [1920s+] of a show or other type of entertainment, to listen to, to watch; to attend. (**b**) [1940s+] (*orig. US*) to have a casual social encounter with. **4** [1930s] to give.

IN COMPOUNDS

❑ **catch-bet** *n.* [mid-19C] a bet made with the intention of ensnaring a gullible punter.

IN PHRASES

❑ **catch…** *v. see also under* relevant n. or adj. ❑ **catch a body** *v.* [1990s+] (*US black*) to kill. ❑ **catch a case** *v.* [1990s+] (*US*) to be arrested. ❑ **catch (a) cold** *v.* **1** [late 18C+] to get into trouble, poss. through impetuousness. **2** [early 19C+] to lose out financially, poss. after purchasing a supposed 'bargain', which proves to be otherwise. ❑ **catch action** *see* separate entries. ❑ **catch a glad** *v.* [SE *glad*(ness)] [20C+] (*W.I.*) to experience an outburst of spontaneous joy. ❑ **catch a pay** *v.* [1990s+] (*US black*) to commit a robbery. ❑ **catch copper** *v.* [ety. unknown] [16C] to come to harm, to suffer grief. ❑ **catch it (hot/warm)** *v.* [euph. for *CATCH HELL under* HELL *n.*] **1** [mid-19C+] to be severely reprimanded, punished or beaten. **2** [1910s–60s] to be shot. ❑ **catch nennen** *v.* (*also* **catch royal, …skin, …tail**) [NENNEN *n.*/ROYAL *n.*[1] (3) n./SE *skin*/TAIL *n.* (2)] [20C+] (*W.I., Trin.*) to find it hard to make enough money to live. ❑ **catch one's lunch** *v.* [1960s+] (*US*) to be killed or to be defeated so comprehensively as to feel physically sick. ❑ **catch vapors** *v.* **1** [1980s+] (*US campus*) to become jealous. **2** [1990s+] to desire sexually. ❑ **catch wreck** *v.* [1990s+] (*US black*) **1** to get into trouble, to be beaten up. **2** to gain respect by one's activity, spec. to rap freestyle.

SE in slang uses

IN COMPOUNDS

❑ **catch-colt** *n.* [dial. *catch colt*, a colt that was bred unintentionally] [20C+] (*US*) an illegitimate child. ❑ **catch-fart** *n.* [var. on *FART-CATCHER under* FART *n.*] [late 17C–19C] a footman.

IN PHRASES

❑ **catch…** *v. see also under* relevant n. ❑ **catch a fox** *v.* [FOX *v.*[1] (1)] [late 17C–18C] to be very drunk; thus *caught a fox*, drunk. ❑ **catch a horse** *v.* [euph.] [20C+] (*Aus.*) to urinate. ❑ **catch**

and kill one's own *v.* [the image of the self-sufficient dweller in the outback] [1970s+] (*Aus.*) to look after oneself, to sort out one's own problems without outside aid. ❑ **catch 'em-alive** *see* separate entries. ❑ **catch on** *v. see* separate entry. ❑ **catch one's length** *v.* [lit., to estimate the size of the problem] [20C+] (*W.I.*) to settle down, to understand what must be done. ❑ **catch on the non-plus** *v.* [SE *nonplussed*] [late 19C] to catch unawares. ❑ **catch out** *v.* [i.e. to *catch* a railroad *out* of town] [1970s+] **1** (*US tramp*) to leave by train; to 'ride the rails'. **2** (*US prison*) to leave, to go out. ❑ **catch rapid** *v.* [1980s+] (*Irish*) to catch in the act. ❑ **catch someone with their pants down** *v.* (*also* **...breeches down, ...britches down, ...trousers down**) [1930s+] (*orig. US*) to find someone in a state of embarrassing unpreparedness, to catch someone 'red-handed'; often used 'literally' of sexual infidelities. ❑ **catch sun(rays)** *v. see under* RAYS *n.* ❑ **catch the chain** *v.* [the chain that links the prisoners together during their journey] [20C+] (*US Und.*) to move from a local jail to a proper prison. ❑ **catch the flavour** *v.* (*also* **get the flavour**) [19C] to get drunk. ❑ **catch the owl** *v.* [late 18C–early 19C] to play a trick on an innocent countryman, who is decoyed into a barn under the pretext of catching an owl; when he enters, a bucket of water is poured upon his head. ❑ **catch up** *see* separate entries. ❑ **catch you later** (*also* **catch you**) [1950s+] (*orig. US black*) goodbye. ❑ **catch you on the flip-flop** [SE *flip-flop*, a reversal, lit. a somersault] [1970s+] (*US campus*) goodbye.

IN EXCLAMATIONS

❑ **catch me!** (*also* **catch me at it!**) [mid-19C–1930s] a defiant excl. implying that one will never be caught.

catch *v.*[2] [late 19C+] to become pregnant.

IN PHRASES

❑ **get catch** *v.* (*also* **get ketch**) [20C+] (*W.I.*) of an unmarried girl or woman, to become pregnant.

catch *v.*[3] [baseball imagery] **1** [1960s+] to take the passive role in (usu. homosexual) sexual intercourse. **2** [1970s] as *catch it*, to fellate.

catch action *n.* [CATCH *n.* (4) + ACTION *n.* (11)] [1960s] (*US black*) young women, typically runaways who have just arrived in the big city and are vulnerable to being recruited as prostitutes.

catch action *v.* [CATCH *v.*[1] (2d) + ACTION *n.* (2)/ACTION *n.* (11)] [1960s+] to seduce.

catchar *n.* [Bhojpuri *khachchar*, lit. 'mule', and used as a term of abuse] [1970s] (*W.I.*) one who attempts to interfere maliciously in a couple's love affair; thus one who talks out of turn, who does not 'mind their own business'.

catch 'em-alive *n.* [mid-19C] **1** a trap. **2** a tooth-comb.

catch 'em alive oh! *excl.* [mid-19C] a popular, if meaningless, catchphrase.

catch 'em (all) alive-o *n.* **1** [mid-19C] the vagina; one of a number of terms equating it with a threat to the penis; thus a prostitute. **2** [mid-19C] a fly-paper. **3** [mid-19C–1900s] a small comb.

catcher *n.*[1] [mid-19C] (*US*) a watchman, a policeman.

catcher *n.*[2] (*also* **catch**) [baseball imagery] [1960s+] one who plays the passive role during sexual intercourse; this can relate to homosexual, sado-masochistic or 'straight' heterosexual intercourse.

catcher *n.*[3] **1** *see* FLAT-CATCHER *n.*[1] (2). **2** *see* STASH CATCHER *under* STASH *n.*[2].

catcher's mitt *n.* [SE *catch*, i.e. semen + baseball imagery] [1980s+] (*US*) a contraceptive diaphragm.

catching harvest *n.* [SE *catching harvest*, unpredictable, unsettled weather + a pun on SE *catch*, implying that the highwayman may get caught] [late 17C–mid-19C] (*UK Und.*) a bad time for highway robbery since heavy traffic is likely to impede a safe getaway.

catch on *v.* (*also* **catch on to**) [late 19C+] (*orig. US*) **1** to attach or fix oneself to, to join on, to catch hold of. **2** to understand, to become aware of. **3** to become popular, fashionable.

IN PHRASES

❑ **catch oneself on** *v.* [1980s+] (*Irish*) to come to one's senses.

catchpenny *n.* [SE *catchpenny* adj., designed for sales rather than quality] **1** [early 19C–1900s] a pamphlet or broadsheet sold in the streets and detailing a lurid, if imaginary, murder. **2** [mid-19C] a cheap theatre or music-hall.

catchpole *n.* [Lat. *cacepollus*, chicken catcher, dating from a period when debts were paid in kind as well as cash] [late 14C; 16C–18C] a sergeant or bailiff, esp. one who arrests for debt.

IN COMPOUNDS

❑ **catchpole rapparee** *n.* [SE *rapparee*, a bandit, a robber] [early 18C] a constable.

catch-up *n.* [fig. use of SE] [1940s] (*US*) a revenge killing.

IN PHRASES

❑ **play catch-up** *v.* [1940s+] (*US*) to recover from a set-back, to make good a disadvantage.

catch up *v.* [one 'catches up' with life; the image of addiction is one of suspended animation] [1930s+] (*drugs*) to withdraw from drug addiction.

catchy *adj.* **1** [early 19C] attractive, esp. when seen as 'cheaply' so. **2** [mid-19C] tending to take an undue advantage.

cat cuff *n.* [rhy. sl.] [20C+] (*US*) a bluff.

caterpillar *n.*[1] [SE *caterpillar*, a rapacious person] **1** [late 16C–18C] a ne'er-do-well, one who lives on his wits and others' gullibility. **2** [mid-18C–early 19C] a soldier.

caterpillar *n.*[2] **1** [mid–late 19C] a girls' school [? the girls will emerge as adult 'butterflies']. **2** [20C+] (*Aus.*) a drunkard [the drunkard crawls, caterpillar-like, from pub to pub or along the floor]. **3** [1930s] a slow horse [its (lack of) speed].

caterpillar *v.* [SE *caterpillar*, the larva of a butterfly or moth, it moves slowly] [mid-19C–1900s] (*US*) to leave quietly.

caterpillar's raincoat *n.* (*also* **caterpillar coat**) [1970s–80s] (*UK black*) a condom.

caterpillar's spats *n. see* CAT'S PYJAMAS *n.*

cater-trey *n.* [*cater*, four + *trey*, three. ult. Fr. *quatre* + *trois*] [mid-16C–early 19C] (*UK Und.*) dice or crooked dice.

caterwaul *v.* [SE *caterwaul*, to make a noise like rutting cats] **1** [mid-16C–19C] to indulge in sexual foreplay; to have sexual intercourse. **2** [mid-16C–early 19C] to wander the streets at night, looking for excitement, esp. sexual conquests.

catever *n.* (*also* **kerteever, kerterver**) [Ital. *cattivo*, bad] [mid–late 19C] **1** a strange affair. **2** an eccentric person.

catever *adj.* (*also* **cateva, kerteever, kerterver**) [mid-19C–1900s] odd, strange; thus bad.

cat-eye *n.*[1] [20C+] (*W.I.*) a black (or other non-European) person with cat-like grey-green irises in their eyes.

cat-eye *n.*[2] [1970s] (*US*) a late-night work shift.

catfish *n.* [the unattractiveness of the SE *catfish*] [mid-19C–1910s] (*US*) an unpleasant person; also a term of address.

Catfish Row *n.* [SE *catfish*, supposedly a staple of a black person's diet] [20C+] (*US*) an area of a town in which the black population live.

cat-foot *v.* [var. on PUSSYFOOT *v.*] [1910s+] (*US*) to move stealthily.

cat-foot *adv.* [CAT-FOOT *v.*] [1900s] stealthily.

cat-footed *adj.* [CAT-FOOT *v.*] [1930s] stealthy.

catgut *n.* [var. on ROTGUT *n.* (4)] [20C+] (*US*) cheap whisky.

catgut-scraper *n.* (*also* **cat-gut squeezer, ...teaser, ...tickler**) [the *catgut* violin strings] [early 17C–1940s] a fiddler or violinist; as *agitate the catgut*, to play the fiddle.

catharpin fashion *n.* [? Gk *kata*, across + *pinein*, to drink; or naut. jargon *cat-harpings*, 'the ropes or (now more generally) iron cramps that serve to brace in the shrouds of the lower-masts behind their respective yards, so as to tighten the shrouds and also give more room to draw the yards in when the ship is close-hauled' (*OED*)] [late 17C–early 19C] 'when People in Company Drink cross, and not round about from the Right to the Left according to the Sun's motion' (*B.E.*).

cathead *n.* [SE *cathead*, a large biscuit eaten in the US; he or she has no more brains than a biscuit] [1950s] (*US*) a fool.

catheads *n.* [SE *cathead*, a large biscuit eaten in the US; thus the breast's roundness reflects that of the foodstuff; however, the term predates US use. Partridge (1984) cites 18C naut. jargon *cathead*, 'a beam projecting almost horizontally at each side of the bows of a ship, for raising the anchor from the surface of the water to the deck without touching the bows, and for carrying the anchor on its stock-end when suspended outside the ship's side' (*OED*). But other than there being a pair of *catheads*, it is hard to see any more concrete a link] [early 19C] the female breasts.

cathedral *adj.* [the antiquity of the great *cathedrals*] [late 17C–18C] antique, ancient, out-of-date.

Catherine Hayes *n.* [proper name; Partridge (1984) suggests an 'Irish singer so popular in Australia', but given slang's love of crime, note *Catherine Hayes* (1690–1725), who murdered her lover following a drinking bout] [mid–late 19C] (*Aus.*) a drink made of claret, sugar and nutmeg/orange.

catherine wheel *n.* [late 19C] the vagina.

cat-house *n.* [CAT *n.*[1] (1) + HOUSE *n.*[1] (1)] [mid-19C+] (*US*) a brothel.

Cat-J *n.* [abbr. *Category J*] [2000s] (*US prison*) a prisoner considered mentally unstable.

cat-licker *n.* (*also* **cat lick**) [mispron. of SE *Catholic*] [1920s+] (*US*) a Roman Catholic; also attrib.

cat melodeon *adj.* (*also* **cat melodium**) [? CAT *adj.* (1) + the supposed tendency of accordion (*melodeon*) players to fluff their notes; ? or the howling of a cat on heat] [20C+] appalling, disastrous.

catnip *n.* [the US name for UK *catmint*; gullible buyers might well be sold bags of catnip (*Nepeta cataria*) or 50% catnip and 50% marijuana; Burroughs, *The Naked Lunch* (1959): 'Catnip smells like marijuana when it burns. Frequently passed on the incautious or uninstructed'] [1960s+] (*drugs*) inferior or fake marijuana.

catnip *v.* [CATNIP *n.*] [1950s–60s] (*US drugs*) to sell second-rate marijuana.

catolla *n.* [ety. unknown; ? Ital./Sp.; note Egan, *Book of Sports* (1832): 'This phrase is a recently *coined* one, and may be termed a new reading for the old *flash* terms of "*a precious sam — a spooney — a muff — a flat — a go-alonger*, &c." or in plain English, a *fool*. The original CATOLLA (the name of a man who was in the habit of using the *Castle* [i.e. the Castle Tavern, Holborn, a celebrated sporting inn] was distinguished for his *mar-plot* qualities and stupid bets. Also in offering wagers, that when called upon to cover, it generally turned out that he had no *blunt* to stake. Catolla, from proving too annoying, was ultimately *laughed out*; but unfortunately his family are very numerous, and still continue to furnish amusement for [...] frequenters of the *Castle Tavern*'] [early 19C] a noisy, foolish person, esp. one who makes foolish bets.

cat o'nine *n.* [SE *cat o'nine tails*] [1950s+] (*W.I.*) severe punishment, a beating.

cats *n.* [? mishearing of CAP *n.*[4] (1)] [1970s] (*US drugs*) barbiturates.

cats and kitties *n.* [rhy. sl. = TITTY *n.* (1)] [1930s+] (*US*) the female breasts.

cats and mice *n.* [rhy. sl.] [20C+] (*Aus.*) dice.

cat's ass *n.*[1] (*also* **cat's arse**) [SE *cat* + ASS *n.* (2)/ARSE *n.* (1)] [1960s+] (*US/Can.*) **1** anything exceptional or superlative. **2** a superior person or someone who poses as such.

(IN PHRASES)

❑ **give a cat's ass** *v.* [1990s+] (*US*) to care about someone or something, usu. in negative.

cat's ass *n.*[2] [SE *cat* + ASS *n.* (2), i.e. supposed resemblance] [1960s+] (*US campus*) the bruise left by a love bite, usu. on the neck.

cat's ass *adj.* [CAT'S ASS *n.*[1]] [1970s+] (*US*) excellent, first-rate.

cat's face *n.* [rhy. sl.] [1940s+] of cards, the ace.

catsing *n.* (*also* **katsing**) [ety. unknown] [18C] (*UK Und.*) a wig.

cat's kid *n. see* BRONCO *n.* (2).

cat's meat *n.* (*also* **catsmeat**) [the lungs and similar animal intestines are used for cat's and dog's meat] **1** [early–mid-19C] the human lungs. **2** [mid–late 19C] the vagina. **3** [late 19C+] (*mainly juv.*) a meat pie. **4** [1920s+] (*N.Z.*) in fig. use, anything insignificant.

(IN COMPOUNDS)

❑ **cat's meat gaff** *n.* [GAFF *n.*[1] (9)] [1960s–80s] a hospital, usu. gynaecological.

SE in slang uses

(IN COMPOUNDS)

❑ **cat's meat pusher** *n.* [late 19C–1900s] a street-seller of cooked horsemeat, presumably as petfood. ❑ **cat's meat shop** *n.* [mid-19C] (*UK Und.*) a restaurant.

cat's meow *n.* (*also* **cat's miaou, ...miaow, ...tonsillitis, cuckoo's chin**) [SE *cat* + *meow*; var. on CAT'S WHISKERS *n.*] [1920s+] (*Aus./US*) **1** anything exceptional or superlative. **2** a superior person or someone who poses as such.

cat's milk *n.* [rhy. sl.] [1940s–60s] (*UK Und.*) silk.

cat's nouns! *excl. see* 'SNOUNS! *excl.*

catso *n.* (*also* **cadzo, cartso, cazzo**) [Ital. *cazzo*, the penis, lit. 'thrust'; it is possible, given similar fig. penis = fool usages, plus CATSO! *excl.*, that sense 2 in fact predates sense 1] **1** [late 16C–early 17C] a rogue or rascal. **2** [17C+] (*also* **carts**) the penis.

catso! *excl.* (*also* **catzo!**) [CATSO *n.* (2)] [late 16C–mid-18C] a general excl. of annoyance, surprise, etc.

cat's pyjamas *n.* (*also* **cat's cuffs, ...lingerie, ...mac, ...nightgown, ...pajamas, ...vest, caterpillar's spats, kitten's vest, lion's bathrobe**) [all constr. with *the*; coined, like many other similar terms, by the US sportwriter T.A. 'Tad' Dorgan (1877–1929)] [1920s+] (*orig. US*) **1** anything exceptional, superlative. **2** used sarcastically, a joke, a 'laugh'. **3** a superior person, or someone who poses as such.

cat's whiskers *n.* (*also* **cat's knee-knuckles, clam's cuticle, elephant's fallen arches, lily's whiskers, owl's bowels, oyster's eye-tooth, pig's whiskers, rat's ass, snail's ankles, snake's eyebrows, ...hips, ...toenails**) [var. on CAT'S PYJAMAS *n.*; all constr. with *the*; later use is mainly Aus.] [1920s+] **1** anything exceptional, superlative. **2** a superior person, or someone who poses as such.

cattawampously *adv. see* CATAWAMPUSLY *adv.*

catter *n.*[1] [mid-19C] (*US Und.*) a crowbar.

catter *n.*[2] [SE *cat*; image of the animal clinging to some perilous perch] [1910s–30s] (*US Und.*) a tramp who rides the platforms of passenger or freight cars, the tender of an engine and similar spaces.

cattie *n.* (*also* **catty**) [abbr.] [late 19C+] (*UK juv.*) a catapult.

catting *n.*[1] [orig. CAT *n.*[1] (1); strengthened in 20C by SE *tomcat*, a stereotypically libidinous animal; obs. in the UK by the early 19C; 20C+ use is US black] [late 17C+] looking for female company and/or conquests.

catting *n.*[2] [abbr. CAT (UP) *v.* (1)] [late 18C+] vomiting.

catting *n.*[3] [CAT *n.*[5] (2b)] [1980s+] (*US black*) a style of walking, characterized by a slight dip in the stride, adopted by young urban black men.

cattle *n.* **1** [late 16C–18C] a collective n. for prostitutes [note SE *cattle*, horses, which are, like prostitutes 'ridden']. **2** [late 16C+] people, sometimes contemptible.

SE in slang uses

(IN COMPOUNDS)

❑ **cattle-banger** *n. see* COW-BANGER *under* COW *n.*[1]. ❑ **cattle-duffer** *see* separate entries. ❑ **cattle-eater** *n.* [late 19C] (*US*) a cattle thief. ❑ **cattle grazier** *n.* [mid-19C] (*UK Und.*) a gaoler. ❑ **cattle-puncher** *n. see* COW-PUNCHER *n.* ❑ **cattle racket** *n.* [originating in a large-scale cattle-rustling racket in New South Wales during the 1840s] [mid–late 19C] (*Aus.*) any form of organized swindle. ❑ **cattle stiff** *n. see under* STIFF *n.*[1]. ❑ **cattle train** *n.* [the name + the size of the car] [1940s–50s] (*US black*) a Cadillac.

cattle *v.* [abbr. CATTLE TRUCK *v.*] [20C+] to copulate.

cattle dog *n.*[1] [joc. pron.] [20C+] (*N.Z., mainly juv.*) a derog. name for a Roman Catholic.

cattle dog *n.*[2] [rhy. sl.] [20C+] (*Aus.*) a catalogue.

cattle-duffer *n.* [SE *cattle* + DUFFER *n.*[1] (7)] [mid-19C+] (*Aus.*) a cattle thief.

cattle-duffing *n.* [CATTLE-DUFFER *n.*] [late 19C+] (*Aus.*) cattle thieving.

cattle ramp *adj.* [rhy. sl. = CAMP *adj.* (1)] [1980s] (*Aus.*) effeminate; homosexual.

cattle ticks *n.* [rhy. sl./joc. pron.] [20C+] (*Aus.*) Catholics.

cattle truck *v.* [rhy. sl. = FUCK *v.* (1)] [20C+] to copulate, also in fig. use; thus *cattled*, ruined, hurt, destroyed, beaten etc.

catty *n.*[1] [abbr.] [1950s+] (*Irish*) a Catholic.

catty *n.*[2] *see* CATTIE *n.*

catty-cat *n.* [redup. of CAT *n.*[1] (2a)] [1970s+] (*US black*) **1** the vagina. **2** sexual intercourse.

cattywampus *adj. see* CATAWAMPUS *adj.*

cat-up *n.* (*also* **cat work**) [? GAT *n.*[1] (1)] [1930s–40s] (*US Und.*) robbery of itinerant workers at gunpoint; thus *cat-up man*, *cat worker*, one who commits such robberies.

cat (up) *v.* [20C+ use mainly US; ? abbr. SE *cataract*, but cf. *JERK THE CAT under* JERK *v.*[2] and WHIP THE CAT *v.* (3)] [late 18C+] to vomit; thus fig. *cat with laughter*, to laugh 'until one is sick'.

cat up *v.* [the elusiveness of a cat] [1950s] (*US*) to hide away, esp. from the police.

catzerie *n.* [CATSO *n.* (1)] [late 16C] roguery.

catzo! *excl. see* CATSO! *excl.*

Cauc *n.* [abbr.] [1980s] (*US*) a *Cauc*asian, i.e. a white person.

caudge-pawed *adj.* [var. on CAW-PAWED *adj.*] [late 17C–18C] left-handed.

caudle-cheat *n.* [SE *caudle*, 'a warm drink consisting of thin gruel, mixed with wine or ale, sweetened and spiced, given chiefly to sick people' (*OED*) + CHEAT *n.* (1)] [mid-19C] (*UK Und.*) an old maid, a spinster.

caudle of hempseed *n.* [pun on SE *caudle*, a gruel spiced with wine or ale and given to the sick, and especially to women in labour; thus the noose is ironically also a form of 'painkiller'] [17C] the hangman's noose.

caught (out) *adj.* [mid-19C+] pregnant.

caught short *adj.* **1** [mid-19C+] (*also* **taken short**) having a desperate desire to visit the lavatory. **2** [1920s+] in an emergency or unforseen situation. **3** [1930s+] of a woman, surprised by menstruation starting, beyond reach of tampons, sanitary towels etc. **4** [1960s] (*US*) a euph. phr. meaning expecting a child out of wedlock.

caught with one's breeches/trousers down *phr. see under* CATCH *v.*[1].

caught with rem-in-re *phr.* [fake legalese, lit. 'caught with thing in thing'; Williams (1994): 'A tr. of the Latin is used in a churchwarden's court testimony to the effect that proof of adultery requires seeing "the thing in the thing".'] [mid-17C] caught having sexual intercourse.

cauldron *n.* [euph.] **1** [mid-17C–early 18C] the vagina. **2** [mid-19C] (*UK Und.*) a brothel.

cauli *n.* (*also* **caulie, collie**) [abbr.] [late 19C+] a *cauli*flower.

cauliflower *n.*[1] [joc. ext. of SE *flower (of)*, the finest example] [late 18C] of a person, the epitome.

cauliflower *n.*[2] [visual resemblance] **1** [late 18C–early 19C] a large white wig 'such as is commonly worn by the dignified clergy, and was formerly by physicians' (Grose, 1785). **2** [early–mid-19C] one who wears powder in their hair. **3** [late 19C+] the foaming top of a newly poured glass of beer. **4** [20C+] a 'cauliflower ear', the sign of a boxer whose ears have taken too many punches to retain their original shape. **5** [1910s] in ext. use of sense 3, the head. **6** [1940s] by metonymy, a boxer.

SE in slang uses

IN COMPOUNDS

❑ **cauliflower cock** *n.* [? the use of vegetables as dildos, although not, presumably, a cauliflower] [2000s] (*US black*) a dildo.

cauliflower *n.*[3] [ult. CAULIFLOWER *n.*[2] (1); 'A woman, who was giving evidence in a case wherein it was necessary to express those parts, made use of the term cauliflower. for which the judge on the bench, a peevish old fellow, reproved her, saying she might as well call it an artichoke. Not so, my lord, replied she, for an artichoke has a bottom, but a **** and a cauliflower have none' (Grose 1785)] **1** [late 18C–19C] the vagina. **2** [19C; 1990s+] sexual intercourse.

IN PHRASES

❑ **do a bit of cauliflower** *v.* (*also* **eat cauliflower**) [late 19C–1910s; 1990s+] to have sexual intercourse. ❑ **have a bit of cauliflower** *v.* [19C] to have sexual intercourse.

cauliflower *n.*[4] [? Fr. *choux*, cabbage, used as a term of affection] [mid-19C] (*US*) a person, a fellow.

cauliflower *n.*[5] [? its white 'heart'; or rhy. sl. *cauliflower ear* = fear] [1970s] (*US*) cowardice, fear.

caulk *v.* [either SE *caulk*, to fill, to stuff, or ME *cauk*, for a male bird to tread the female; note WW1 RN *caulk*, a nap, a short sleep and 1930s Annapolis jargon *caulk off*, to sleep] **1** [mid-19C] to have a surreptitious nap. **2** [late 19C–1930s] as *caulk off*, to idle, to waste time on the job.

caulked *adj.* [naut. jargon *caulk*, to lie down on a soft plank, to sleep with one's clothes on; thus the sailor, rather than the usual pitch or oakum, was fig. 'stopping up the cracks' in the deck] [19C] (*US*) exhausted.

caulker *n.* (*also* **cauker**) [either mis-sp. of CORKER *n.*[2], that which 'puts the cork on'; or naut. jargon *caulk*, to stop up the seams of a ship to 'keep out the wet'] **1** [19C] the last drink of an evening. **2** [mid-19C] an exceptionally amusing story, which 'cannot be topped'. **3** [mid–late 19C] a lie.

cause whore *n.* [1990s+] a voluble proselytizer for modish, leftish causes, often but not necessarily female.

causey *n. see* CARSEY *n.*

caution *n.* [i.e. one with whom caution must be exercised] [mid-19C+] **1** a 'character', an eccentric, a 'difficult' person, sometimes ext. to *a caution to snakes*. **2** anything staggering or alarming.

caution sign *n.* [image of bright red 'Stop' signs] [1970s+] (*US black*) anyone who dresses in an excessively gaudy and vulgar manner, with many clashing bright colours.

cavalier *n.* [the antonym of ROUNDHEAD *n.* (2)] [20C+] (*orig. RN, usu. juv.*) an uncircumcised penis; thus the boy/man who has one.

cavalry curate *n.* [late 19C–1910s] a curate who rides (a horse) rather than walks round his parish.

cavault *v.* [Ling. Fr. *cavolta*, riding] [late 17C–mid-19C] to have sexual intercourse; one of a number of words equating sex with horseriding.

IN COMPOUNDS

❑ **cavaulting school** *n.* [late 17C–early 19C] a brothel.

cave *n.*[1] **1** [1920s–40s] (*US Und.*) a hiding place. **2** [1920s–50s] (*US prison*) a cell. **3** [1930s–40s] (*US black*) one's room, one's home, one's dwelling place.

IN COMPOUNDS

❑ **cave dweller** *n.* **1** [late 19C] (*US*) one who lives in the cellar of a slum tenement. **2** [late 19C–1930s] (*US*) a member of the old New York aristocracy [such aristocrats still lived in the dark, old mansions their families had built earlier in the century].

cave *n.*[2] (*also* **caveboy, cave bitch**) [the belief that the early cave-dwellers were all white, as black Africans lived on the plains] [1990s+] (*US black*) a white person.

cave *v.* [mid-19C+] (*mainly US*) **1** to give in, to yield to pressure from above, to break down, to give way. **2** to die.

IN PHRASES

❑ **cave in** *v.* **1** [early 19C+] (*orig. US*) to give in, to yield to pressure from above, to break down, to give way, to collapse; also as n. **2** [1980s] (*N.Z.*) to defecate. ❑ **cave in someone's crust** *v. see BURST IN SOMEONE'S CRUST under* CRUST *n.*[1]. ❑ **cave out** *v.* [mining jargon *cave out*, the metal casing at the end of a tunnel] [late 19C] (*orig. US*) to come to an end.

cave! *excl.* [Lat. *cave*, beware; pron. 'kay-vee'] [mid-19C+] (*UK schoolboy*) look out!

cave-man *n.* [20C+] an ostentatiously macho male, a 'he-man'; thus *cave-man stuff*, a rough form of wooing or love-making, reminiscent of the clichéd cave-man who (at least in cartoons) drags his woman around by her hair.

Cave of Harmony *n.* [mid-19C] the Cider Cellars or Evans's suppers rooms and singing saloon in London.

cave of harmony *n.* [mid-19C] the vagina.

cavern *n.* [1900s] (*Aus.*) the mouth.

cavey *n. see* CAVY *n.*

cavey *adj.* [? CAVE! *excl.*] [mid-19C] (*UK Und.*) knowing, aware.

cavi *adj.* [fig. use of SE *caviar* as a symbol of luxury and wealth] [1990s+] (*US black*) first-class, excellent, best.

cavite all star *n.* [*Cavite*, a US marshal port in Manila Bay] [1970s] (*drugs*) marijuana.

cavities *n.*

SE in slang uses

IN PHRASES

❑ **give someone cavities** *v. see* GIVE SOMEONE DIABETES *under* DIABETES *n.* ❑ **have cavities** *v.* [1980s+] (*US campus*) to consider something or someone extremely sweet.

cavvy *n.* (*also* **cavi**) [? SE *caviar*, the reference is presumably to its cost and quality rather than to its fishiness] [1990s+] **1** marijuana. **2** crack cocaine.

cavvy *adj.* [fig. use of SE *caviar*, a luxury] [1990s+] (*US black*) materially comfortable.

cavy *n.* (*also* **cavey**) [abbr.] [mid-17C] a Cavalier.

caw! *excl. see* COR! *excl.*

cawallux!/cawhalux! *excl. see* KERWALLUX! *under* KER- *pfx.*

caw-handed *adj.* [Oxon. dial. *caw*, a fool and *cawing*, awkward] [late 17C–early 19C] clumsy, awkward.

cawhump! *excl.* [KER- *pfx*] [20C+] an onomat. term indicating a loud noise.

caw-pawed *adj.* [for ety. *see* CAW-HANDED *adj.*] [late 18C–early 19C] clumsy, awkward.

caws(e)y *n. see* CARSEY *n.*

cawsy *n. see* CARSEY *n.*

caxon *n.* [? from the surname *Caxon*] [late 18C–early 19C] an old, worn-out wig.

cayac *n.* [generic use of *Cayac*, a native of the island of Carriacou] [20C+] (*W.I., Gren.*) a country bumpkin.

cayuse *n.* ['The wild horse of Oregon, named for the Cayuse Indians, an equestrian people.... The name is now commonly used by the northern cowboy to refer to any horse. At first the term was used for the western horse, to set it apart from a horse brought overland from the East. In later years the name came to be applied as a term of contempt to any scrubby, undersized horse.' Francis Haines, *Western Horseman*, II no. 2 (March–April 1937)] (*US*) **1** [mid-19C+] (*also* **cayouse**) an Indian pony. **2** [mid-19C+] any (inferior) horse. **3** [1900s–20s] a worthless person.

caz *n. see* CASSAN *n.*

caze *n.* [? misreading of Ital. *cazzo*, the penis] [late 19C–1910s] the female genitals.

cazh *adj. see* CAS *adj.*

cazzo *n. see* CATSO *n.*

cazzy *n.* [mid-19C] (*UK Und.*) a glass for spirits; thus *cazzy of Dutch drops*, a glass of genever (gin).

c.b. *n.*[1] (*also* **c&b**) [abbr. used in S&M contact advertisements to advertise 'cock and balls torture'] [1970s+] cock and balls.

c.b. *n.*[2] [abbr. SE *clitoris* + BONER *n.*[4] (1)] [1980s+] (*US campus*) of a woman, extreme excitement, usu. sexual.

c.b. *v. see* COCK BLOCK *v.*

C.C. *n.* [SE calling card] [1980s] (*US drugs*) a dealer's sample of cocaine, given away to enlist new customers.

c.c. *n.* [abbr. condemned to capital punishment] **1** [1930s+] (*US prison*) the condemned cells. **2** [1950s] one who is awaiting execution on a capital charge. **3** [1970s] (*US prison*) concurrent sentences.

c.c.m. *phr.* [abbr.] [1990s+] (*US black*) cold cash money.

c.c.w. *phr.* [abbr.] [1980s+] (*US police/Und.*) carrying a concealed weapon.

cease *v.* [abbr. SE *decease*] [1920s–50s] (*US black*) to die.

cecil *n.*[1] [Spears, *Slang and Jargon of Drugs and Drink* (1986), suggests a play on *M. sul.*, morphine sulphate] [1930s–40s] (*US drugs*) morphine.

cecil *n.*[2] [initial letter; note US pron. *seesul*] [1930s+] (*US prison*) cocaine.

Cecil Gee *n.* [rhy. sl.; ult. *Cecil Gee*, the men's outfitters] [1990s+] the human knee.

cedar *n.* [SE *cedar*, i.e. a 'wooden' head] [1930s+] (*Aus.*) a fool.

cedar (pencil) *n.* [the cedar wood of which it is made; such pencils are usu. unpainted and cheap to purchase] [mid-19C+] (*US Und.*) a cheap pencil.

cee *n. see* C *n.*[3].

ceefa *n.* [i.e. '*c for* cat'] [2000s] (*N.Z.*) a cat.

ceiling *n.*

IN PHRASES

❑ **hit the ceiling** *v. see* separate entry.

celeb *n.* [abbr.] [1910s+] (*orig. US*) a *celebrity*.

celebrity fucker *n.* [SE *celebrity* + FUCKER *n.* (1)] [1960s+] (*orig. US*) anyone who courts the famous with the hope of enjoying some proxy fame.

celestial *n.* [CELESTIAL *adj.*[2]] [mid-19C] (*US*) a Chinese person.

celestial *adj.*[1] [SE *celestial*, heavenly, such a nose 'points to the heavens'] [mid–late 19C] used of a turned-up nose.

celestial *adj.*[2] [SE *celestial empire*, a translation of one of the names for China] [mid-19C–1910s] pertaining to Chinese people or culture.

cell *n.*

IN COMPOUNDS

❑ **cell gangster** *n.* (*also* **cell warrior**) [2000s] (*US prison*) one who poses as tough while in their cell, but follows orders elsewhere. ❑ **cell task** *n.* [ironic reference to the official *cell tasks* set prisoners. The pin-up's real-life incarnation would obviously make a preferable 'task' to that set by the authorities] [1940s–50s] (*UK prison*) a pin-up picture.

cell *v.* [the *OED* cites two 16C uses, but they apply to a monk's not a prisoner's cell] [20C+] (*UK/US prison*) **1** (*also* **cell up**) to share a cell with. **2** to have a cell, e.g. *where does he cell?*

cellar *n.* [both occupy a 'low' position on the body] **1** [17C–19C] (*also* **cellarage, cellar-door**) the vagina. **2** [late 19C] a shoe, a boot; usu. in pl.

IN PHRASES

❑ **in the cellar** [note PG Wodehouse (1881–1975) coinage 'down among the wines and spirits'] **1** [mid-18C] drunk. **2** [20C+] in sports, at the bottom of a league or similar points table. **3** [1900s] in trouble. **4** [1950s] miserable, feeling low, 'down in the dumps'.

SE in slang uses

IN COMPOUNDS

❑ **cellar-cordial** *n.* [1900s] (*Aus.*) alcohol. ❑ **cellar-smeller** *n.* (*also* **cellar sniffer**) [1920s] (*US*) **1** a Prohibition agent or Temperance campaigner. **2** a young man who is always on hand for free liquor.

cellar-flap *n.* [rhy. sl.; the image is of a dance performed on a space no larger than the trap-door leading to a cellar] [mid–late 19C] a tap-dance.

cellar-flap *v.* [rhy. sl. = TAP *v.*[2] (3b)] [20C+] to borrow.

cellie *n.* (*also* **celly**) [1970s+] **1** (*US prison*) a cellmate. **2** (*US*) ext. to general, non-prison use, a friend.

cellier *n.* [proper name Elizabeth *Cellier*, implicated, with her partner Thomas Dangerfield, in the Meal Tub Plot of 1679; this plot, which accused various prominent Roman Catholics of treason, hinged on papers supposedly hidden beneath Mrs Cellier's meal tub. It collapsed when Dangerfield was imprisoned for perjury and Cellier was sent to the pillory] [late 17C] an outright lie.

cellies *n.* [abbr.] [1990s+] (*N.Z.*) *celebrations*.

cells *n.* [SE phr. *night(s) in the cells*] [late 19C+] a (brief) term of imprisonment.

celluloid *n.* [it 'burns' easily] [1910s] (*Aus.*) money.

celly *n.* [abbr. SAmE *cell phone*] **1** [1990s+] (*US*) a mobile phone. **2** *see* CELLIE *n.*

cement *n.* **1** [1930s] (*US drugs*) any form of illegally merchandised narcotics. **2** [1970s+] (*Aus.*) any form of diarrhoea cure, such as kaolin (and morphine), which depends for its efficacy on 'hardening' the contents of the stomach.

SE in slang uses

IN COMPOUNDS

❑ **cement city** *n.* [1970s] (*US*) a cemetery. ❑ **cement-head** *n.* [-HEAD *sfx* (1)] [1940s+] (*US teen*) a gullible, conventional person. ❑ **cement kimono** *n.* (*also* **cement cowboy boots, ...overcoat, ...overshoes, ...suit**) [1950s+] (*US Und.*) a method of disposing of a corpse by placing it inside a barrel filled with wet cement and tossing the resultant lump into a river.

cement-mixer *n.* [the movement] (*US*) **1** [1910s+] a rickety, broken-down vehicle. **2** [1930s+] a dance [+ it is a *mixer* that *cements* relationships]. **3** [1950s] a promiscuous woman. **4** [1960s] a striptease artist (or prostitute who offers a strip as part of her services).

cemetery *n.* [1990s+] (*W.I.*) a term of abuse for a woman who has had (or is suspected of having had) an abortion.

cent *n.* (*US black*) **1** [1950s+] $1. **2** [1970s] $100.

centerfield *v.* [the 'centrality' of the vagina to the female body] [1930s] (*US*) to perform cunnilingus.

center lead *n.* [rhy. sl.] [1920s] (*US*) the forehead.

centerman *n.* [prison use *center*, the guards' 'office' in a prison wing] [20C+] (*Can./US prison*) a prisoner who toadies to the guards.

centipees *n.* [synon. milit. use *sancipees*; ult. *sank*, to work as a menial servant in a dining room] [late 18C–early 19C] a tailor of soldiers' clothing.

cent per cent *n.* (*also* **cent-per-center, shent-per-shent(er)**) [his graspingness; he takes back 100% interest for every £100 loaned; the Aus. var. *shent-per-shent*, is supposedly 'Jewish' pronunciation] [late 17C–1910s] a usurer; often as attrib.

-central *sfx* [1990s+] (*US*) a fig. 'place' that acts as an intensifier to a n., e.g. *chick central*.

central furrow *n.* (*also* **central office**) [FURROW *n.*] [mid-18C–19C] the vagina.

centre half *n.* [rhy. sl.] [1990s+] a scarf.

centre of attraction *n.* [mid-18C–19C] the vagina.

centre of bliss *n.* [late 19C] the vagina.

centrique part *n.* [coined by John Donne] [19C] the vagina.

century *n.* (*also* **century note**) [16C SE *century*, a group of 100 things] [mid-19C+] $100 or £100.

IN COMPOUNDS

❑ **century note** *n.* [1900s–50s] (*US*) a $100 bill.

IN PHRASES

❑ **half-century** *n.* (*also* **half-a-century**) [late 19C–1940s] **1** £50. **2** (*US*) a $50 note.

century *v.* [CENTURY *n.* (1)] [1920s] (*US*) **1** to save up $100. **2** to make $100.

cereb *n.* [abbr. SE *cerebral*] [1970s+] (*US campus*) one who works exceptionally hard.

cert *n.* [abbr. SE *certainty*] [late 19C+] **1** a definite winner, usu. in a sporting context. **2** a certainty.

IN PHRASES

❑ **dead cert** *n.* [SE *dead*, complete, utter] [late 19C+] (*orig. racing*) an absolute certainty, esp. in race-course betting. ❑ **on a cert** [1920s] (*Aus.*) certain, guaranteed.

cert *adv.* [late 19C–1930s] certainly.

certificate of birth *n.* [19C] the vagina, one of the few terms that deal with the vagina in its procreative rather than sexual role.

cess *n. see* SESS *n.*

cess! *excl. see* SIS! *excl.*

C file *n.* [abbr.] [2000s] (*US prison*) the central file of information held on each prisoner.

c.f.m. *phr.* [abbr. come fuck me] [1980s+] (*US*) sexually suggestive; thus *c.f.m. shoes*, *c.f.m. dress* etc.

c.h. *n.* [abbr.; the frequent playing, subsequent to the Egyptian War (1882), of the tune 'See the Conquering Hero Comes'] [late 19C] conquering *hero*, usu. used ironically.

c.h.a. *phr. see* C.Y.A. *phr.*

cha *n.*[1] (*also* **chah, chai, char**) [Mandarin *ch'a*, tea] [20C+] tea.

IN COMPOUNDS

❑ **char wallah** *n.* (*also* **lemonade-wallah, pop-wallah**) [WALLAH *n.* (1)] [1910s–30s] a teetotaller.

cha *n.*[2] [abbr. CHARLIE *n.*[8] (1)] [1980s+] (*drugs*) cocaine.

cha! *excl.* (*also* **chaw! cho! chu! tcho!**) [onomat.] [1950s+] (*W.I. Rasta*) a disdainful expletive, a very common, mild excl. of impatience, vexation or disappointment.

chaar ou *n.* (*also* **char ou**) [? Hind. *chaar admi*, people in general + Afk. *ou*, a person] [1970s+] (*S.Afr.*) an Indian.

chaben *n.* (*also* **chabin, shabeen**) [Fr. *chabins*, sheep bred in Bery, with thick, long hair; such sheep were once seen as a sheep/goat cross, and the term, exported to Dominica, was used as a synon. for 'half-breed'] [20C+] (*W.I.*) a person of mixed African/European descent; such people have pale brown skin, coarse reddish hair and, sometimes, freckles and greyish eyes.

chabobs *n.* [? KER- *pfx* + BOOB *n.*[3] (1) n.; note CHORB *n.*] [1960s] (*US*) the female breasts.

cha-cha *n.* [SE *cha-cha*, a popular ballroom dance] [1950s+] (*US black*) sexual intercourse.

SE in slang uses

IN COMPOUNDS

❑ **cha-cha queen** *n.* [SE *cha-cha*, used as a generic for Spanish-American + QUEEN *n.* (2)] [1980s+] (*US gay*) a Hispanic male homosexual.

cha-cha *adj.* [var. on CHICHI *adj.*] [1960s–80s] (*US*) fashionable or smart, when pertaining to homosexuals.

cha-cha *v.* [CHA-CHA *n.*] [1950s+] (*US black*) to have sexual intercourse.

cha-ching! *excl.* [echoic of the sound of a cash register and popularized by the film *Wayne's World* (1992); it can still be used in the context of money, but refers more commonly to general pleasures, esp. a passing pretty woman] [1990s+] (*US teen*) an excl. used to signify that something or someone has made one happy.

chachundar *n.* [Hind. *chhachuudar*, a mole or shrew] [20C+] (*W.I.*) used by those of Indian descent to describe an East Indian woman who has a close friendship or even a child with a black man.

chad *n.* (*also* **Mr Chad**) [proper name] **1** [1940s+] a chalked-up, cartoon-style picture of a rudimentary human head 'looking over' an equally basic brick wall, always depicted with the slogan *Wot, no...* [ety. unknown]. **2** [1990s+] (*US campus*) a derog. term for a male member of a fraternity, usu. in the context of unruly behaviour.

chafe *v.* [SE *chafe*, to warm, to heat] [late 17C–mid-19C] to beat, to thrash; thus *chafed*, beaten.

chafe-litter *n.* [lit. 'rub-bed'] [mid-16C–early 17C] (*UK Und.*) an impudent, cheeky person.

chafer *n. see* COCKCHAFER *n.* (3).

chafer *v.* [var. on CHARVER *v.* (1)] [late 19C–1910s] to have sexual intercourse.

chaff *n.*[1] [mid-17C+] banter, badinage or ridicule; thus *chafflike*, in a teasing manner.

chaff *n.*[2] [SE *chaff*, husks of corn after threshing] [1930s+] (*Aus.*) money.

chaff *v.* [SE *chafe*, to rub] **1** [mid-17C+] to banter, to tease, usu. gently; thus *chaff down a peeler*, to tease a policeman; (university) *chaff a cad*, of an undergraduate, to insult a townsman. **2** [mid-19C] to betray secrets, to gossip. **3** [1960s] (*S.Afr.*) to give someone something. **4** [1960s+] (*S.Afr.*) to say something. **5** [1970s+] (*S.Afr.*) to tell (someone something). **6** [1970s+] (*S.Afr.*) to flirt, to approach sexually, to 'get fresh'. **7** [1980s+] (*S.Afr.*) to ask (someone something).

chaff-cutter *n.*[1] [CHAFF *v.* (1)] [mid-19C] **1** a malicious talker, a slanderer. **2** gossip, slander. **3** a wit. **4** a confidence trickster.

chaff-cutter *n.*[2] [SE *chaff-cutter*, a machine that cuts chaff for fodder; i.e. the noise of the keys] [1940s–50s] (*Aus.*) a typewriter.

chaffer *n.*[1] [? SE *chaffer*, a bargainer, presumably about the price of commercial sex; or ? SE *chaff*, rubbish] [late 16C] a sexual partner; the image is of quasi-prostitution.

chaffer *n.*[2] [CHAFF *v.* (1)] **1** [19C] the throat. **2** [early 19C–1910s] one who banters or teases, a teaser; thus *chaffering*, bantering, chattering. **3** [mid-19C] the tongue; the mouth.

IN PHRASES

❑ **moisten one's chaffer** *v.* (*also* **cool one's chaffer**) [19C] to take a drink, to quench one's thirst.

chaffer *v.*[1] [ext. of CHAFF *v.* (1)] [mid-19C] to banter, to tease; to chatter.

chaffer *v.*[2] *see* CHARVER *v.* (1).

chaffing *n.* [CHAFF *v.* (1)] [early 19C+] teasing, bantering.

IN COMPOUNDS

❑ **chaffing box** *n.* (*also* **chaffing-closet**) [mid-19C] the mouth. ❑ **chaffing crib** *n.* [CRIB *n.*[1] (1)] [19C] a man's private room, where he receives and entertains his friends.

chaffy *adj.* [CHAFF *v.* (1)] [19C] jolly, bantering, light-hearted.

chah *n. see* CHA *n.*[1].

chai *n.*[1] (*also* **chi, chy**) [Rom.] [mid-19C+] (*UK Und./tramp*) a woman.

chai *n.*[2] *see* CHA *n.*[1].

chain *n. see* DAISY CHAIN *n.* (1).

IN COMPOUNDS

❑ **chain gang** *n.* [puns on SE] **1** [late 19C+] the Lord Mayor and Lady Mayoress of London. **2** [late 19C+] married men. **3** [1950s] (*US teen*) a group of students walking to class. **4** [1970s] (*US gay*) a circle of three or more people, hetero- or homosexual, all linked physically in mutual sex acts. ❑ **chain jerk** *n.* [JERK-OFF *n.* (1)] [1930s+] (*US*) joint masturbation, often in competition, by a group of boys, poss. sitting in a circle; also as v. ❑ **chain lightning** *n. see under* LIGHTNING *n.* ❑ **chain man** *n.* [1930s] (*US tramp*) a thief or pickpocket who specializes in taking watches.

IN PHRASES

❑ **off the chain** (*also* **off the string**) [the image of a chained convict or dog] **1** [20C+] (*orig. Aus.*) free, unrestrained or unrestricted. **2** [2000s] excellent, very satisfying.

chain and crank *n.* (*also* **pedal and crank, peddle and crank**) [rhy. sl.] [1990s+] **1** a bank. **2** (*Irish*) an act of masturbation [= WANK *n.* (1)].

chain and locket *n.* [rhy. sl.] [20C+] a pocket.

chains, the *n.* [the chains that closed off a portion of Simmonds Street so that dealers could conduct their business. 'The Chains' lasted from 1887–1902, being replaced by a new Stock Exchange building in 1903] [late 19C–1900s] (*S.Afr.*) the Johannesburg Stock Exchange.

chain up! *excl.* (*also* **chain it up!**) [fig. use of phr. *chain up that dog*] [mid-19C–1920s] shut up! be quiet!

chain up a pup *v.* [var. on DOG *n.*[6] (2)] [1900s–20s] (*Aus.*) to get drinks on credit.

chair *n.*

SE in slang uses

IN COMPOUNDS

❑ **chairbacker** *n.* [the chair that such a preacher carries with him for use as an impromptu pulpit] [1950s+] (*US Southern*) an unprofessional, part-time lay preacher. ❑ **chair days** *n.* [when one is confined to a chair] [late 19C–1900s] (*UK society*) old age. ❑ **chair-pounder** *n.* [he or she spends the day sitting down] [1910s] (*US*) an office worker. ❑ **chair-warmer** *n.* [orig. theatrical jargon *chair-warmer*, 'a lady whose talent is comprised in her physical charms, and who can neither sing, dance, nor act' (Ware)] [late 19C+] a supernumerary, one who is there but does nothing, an observer.

IN PHRASES

❑ **in the chair** [SE *in the chair*, acting as chairperson of a meeting] [1930s+] buying a round of drinks.

chair, the *n.* (*also* **wire chair**) **1** [late 19C+] (*orig. US*) the electric chair. **2** [1950s] the chair in which a prisoner who is condemned to the gas chamber sits.

chair and cross *n. see* CHARING CROSS *n.*

chaka-chaka *adj.* [Ewe *tsáka*, to mix, be mixed] **1** [1950s+] (*W.I. Rasta*) messy, disorderly, untidy. **2** [1980s+] (*W.I./UK black teen*) untidy or unkempt.

chal *n.* [Rom.] [19C+] a man.

chaldee *v. see* CALDEE *v.*

chale! *excl.* [Sp.] [1950s+] (*US*) no.

chalfonts *n.* [rhy. sl.; *Chalfont St Giles* = piles; ult. village in Buckinghamshire, UK] [1970s+] haemorrhoids.

chalice *n.* (*also* **chalewa**) [1950s+] a pipe used for smoking marijuana, which, when used by Rastafarians, takes on a sacred and ritualistic role; thus the 'religious' name.

chalk *n.*[1] **1** [18C] credit. **2** [late 18C–early 19C] (*US*) a quarter dollar, 25 cents. **3** [late 19C] (*US*) money in general.

SE in slang uses

IN COMPOUNDS

❑ **chalk and talk** *n.* (*also* **chalk-and-talker**) [1920s+] (*Aus.*) a schoolteacher, esp. an old-fashioned, trad. teacher; also used of any form of trainer. ❑ **chalk-eater** *n.* [the chalking of odds on a bookmaker's slate] [1930s–60s] (*US gambling*) a gambler who prefers betting on short-priced favourites. ❑ **chalk-head** *n.* [calculation with chalk on a slate] [mid-19C] **1** one who is good at calculating figures. **2** a waiter [ext. of sense 1]. ❑ **Chalk Sunday** *n.* [the backs of those still unmarried on that day were marked with chalk] [20C+] (*Irish*) the first Sunday in Lent.

IN PHRASES

❑ **by a long chalk** (*also* **by long chalks, by many chalks, by two chalks**) [use of *chalk* in scoring points, e.g. in billiards, darts] [mid-19C+] by a long way; often in negative phr. *not by a long chalk*. ❑ **by chalks** [abbr. prev.] [late 19C–1910s] (*Aus.*) by a long way. ❑ **give someone a chalk** *v.* [the scoring of points, written up with SE *chalk*] [mid-19C+] to cheat, to swindle, to get the better of. ❑ **give someone chalks on** *v.* [late 19C+] to acknowledge someone else's superiority. ❑ **one's chalk is up** [SE *chalk up*, to put on account] [late 19C] one's credit at a public house is exhausted.

chalk *n.*[2] [CHALK *v.*[1] (1)] [mid-19C] a scar or scratch.

chalk *n.*[3] [the colour] **1** [1920s+] (*US*) milk or cream. **2** [1940s–80s] (*US black*) a white person; thus *chalkette*, a white woman. **3** US drug uses. (**a**) [1960s+] methamphetamine, Benzedrine, Methedrine. (**b**) [1960s+] cocaine. (**c**) [1970s] Methadone [may be an error, confusing the abbr. 'meth' used for sense 3a]. (**d**) [1990s+] crack cocaine.

chalk *n.*[4] *see* CHALK FARM *n.*[3].

chalk, the *n.* [? the use of *chalk* by a teacher] [mid–late 19C] (*US*) **1** the fashion. **2** the absolute truth.

chalk *v.*[1] [resemblance to a chalk mark] [late 18C–19C] (*UK Und.*) to slash or cut someone's face.

IN PHRASES

❑ **chalk against** *v.* [the chalking up of one's debts on a piece of wood by shopkeepers, publicans etc] [late 19C] to bear a grudge against.

SE in slang uses

IN PHRASES

❑ **chalk one's hat** *v.* [the custom of the conductor placing a white mark or ticket on the headgear of the passenger] [19C] to travel for free, orig. and esp. in railroad use. ❑ **chalk out** *v.* [the drawing of a line with chalk; senses 3 and 4 the chalk line drawn around a corpse] **1** [17C–19C] to describe clearly, to give directions. **2** [mid-19C] (*also* **chalk down**) to plan. **3** [1940s] to die. **4** [1940s+] (*US*) (*also* **chalk off**) to murder, to kill.

IN EXCLAMATIONS

❑ **chalk it up!** [fig. use of *chalk it up*, make a note] [1910s–20s] look at that!

chalk *v.*^{2} [SE *chalk up*] [mid-19C] (*US*) to charge for.

chalk *v.*^{3} **1** [1920s–30s] (*US tramp*) to arrest, albeit without a specific charge. **2** [1940s] (*US*) to assess, to identify. **3** [1950s] (*US black*) to take note of.

chalk *v.*^{4} [1980s+] (*drugs*) **1** to lighten the colour of cocaine in order to make it appear more pure; thus *chalking*, chemically altering the colour of cocaine so it looks white. **2** to cut cocaine into lines for snorting.

chalk boulder *n.* [rhy. sl.] [1920s] (*US*) a shoulder.

chalked up *adj.* [the whiteness of cocaine] (*US drugs*) **1** [1930s] describing a narcotic that has been adulterated with milk of magnesia. **2** [1950s+] under the influence of cocaine.

chalker *n.*^{1} [CHALK *v.*^{1} (1) + ironic use of SE *chalk*, to draw a line] [late 18C] an Irish thug, the equivalent of a London MOHOCK *n.*, who specializes in roaming the streets and slashing the face of any unfortunate victim; thus *chalking*, carrying out this species of urban terrorism or 'amusement' as Grose (1785) grimly notes it.

chalker *n.*^{2} [his supposed watering down of milk with chalky water] [mid-19C] a London milkman.

chalker *n.*^{3} [to measure their girth one has to reach as far round as poss., make a chalk mark, and repeat round the other side to finish the circle] [1990s+] (*US campus*) an extremely obese person.

chalk farm *n.*^{1} [? CHALK *v.*^{1}; or ? a simple ref. to the then isolated place outside London where such duels took place] [early 19C] a duel.

chalk farm *n.*^{2} [SE *chalk*] [mid-19C] credit at a public house.

chalk farm *n.*^{3} (*also* **chalk**) [rhy. sl.; ult. *Chalk Farm*, London NW1] **1** [mid-19C+] an arm; thus of direction, 'hand side'. **2** [1920s+] harm.

chalkies *n.* [the whiteness] [mid-19C] (*US*) the teeth.

chalk off *v.*^{1} [*WALK ONE'S CHALKS under* CHALKS *n.*] [mid-19C] (*US*) to leave.

chalk off *v.*^{2} [one stares at a metaphorical chalk mark] [mid-19C–1910s] to look at closely.

chalks *n.* [ety. unknown; ? resemblance to sticks of *chalk*] [mid-19C] the legs.

(IN PHRASES)

❑ **walk one's chalks** *v.* (*also* **stir one's chalks**) [mid-19C] to leave, to go away; also as imper.

chalky *n.* [one who wields SE *chalk*] **1** [1940s+] (*Aus.*) (*also* **chalkie**) a schoolteacher. **2** [1990s+] (*Irish*) a pavement artist.

chalubbies *n.* [JABONGOES *n.* + BUBBIES *n.*] [1970s] (*US*) the female breasts.

cham *n.*^{1} [mid-19C] (*UK Und.*) money.

cham *n.*^{2} (*also* **chammy**) [abbr.] [mid-19C–1930s] *champagne*.

cham *v.* [CHAM *n.*^{2}] [mid–late 19C] to drink *champagne*.

chamber lye *n.* [play on SE *chamber(pot)* + *lye/lie*; note late 19C–early 20C Southern US black use *chamber lye*, urine sprinkled around a garden to keep wandering deer away] [mid-17C–mid-19C] urine standing in a chamberpot.

chamber music *n.* [pun] [late 19C+] the sound of a chamberpot being used.

chamber of commerce *n.* [SE *chamber*, a lavatory + pun on BUSINESS *n.* (3)] [1900s–40s] (*US black/campus*) a lavatory.

chamber of horrors *n.* **1** [19C] sausages [the supposedly dubious contents]. **2** [late 19C] the Peeresses' gallery at the House of Lords ['its being railed round as if it contained objectionable or repulsive inmates' (B&L)].

chameleon diet *n.* [? SE *chameleon*, an inconstant or variable person] [late 17C–early 18C] a poor diet.

chamming *n.* [CHAM *v.*] [mid–late 19C] drinking champagne (to excess).

chammy *n. see* CHAM *n.*^{2}.

champ *n.*^{1} [SE *champ*, to eat, to chew] [late 19C] appetite.

champ *n.*^{2} [SE *champion*] **1** [1910s+] an excellent, first-rate person, often as a form of address. **2** [1960s–70s] (*drugs*) a drug user who refuses to reveal their sources to the police. **3** [1990s+] (*US campus*) in stronger use of sense 1, a person who does things to excess.

champ *adj.* [CHAMP *n.*^{2} (1)] [1930s+] (*US*) first-rate.

champagne *n.*

(IN COMPOUNDS)

❑ **champagne charlie** *n.* [the song 'Champagne Charlie is My Name' by H.J. Whymark and Alfred Lee was written in 1867 and was a hit on both sides of the Atlantic. The original *Champagne Charlie* was a wine-merchant who was very free with gifts of his stock] **1** [mid–late 19C] a devotee of champagne. **2** [late 19C+] a debauchee, a dissipated man. ❑ **champagne country** *n.* [SE *champagne* as a metaphor for luxury] [early–mid-19C] self-indulgence in eating and drinking. ❑ **champagne coupons** *n.* [1950s] money. ❑ **champagne shoulders** *n.* [resembling a champagne bottle] [late 19C] (*UK society*) sloping shoulders. ❑ **champagne socialist** *n.* (*also* **chardonnay socialist, sushi socialist**) [1980s+] one who preaches socialism but espouses a capitalist lifestyle. ❑ **champagne trick** *n. see under* TRICK *n.*^{1}. ❑ **champagne weather** *n.* [ironic or ? one needs a glass of *champagne* to cheer oneself up] [late 19C] (*UK society*) bad weather.

champagne glass *n.* [rhy. sl. = BRASS *n.*^{2}] [1990s+] a prostitute.

champagner *n.* [her consumption of this expensive drink] [late 19C–1900s] a fashionable prostitute.

champers *n.* (*also* **shampers**) [abbr. SE *champagne* + -ER *sfx*] [1950s+] *champagne*.

champion *n.* **1** [1900s] the penis. **2** [2000s] (*US black*) an attractive, sexy woman.

champion *adj.* [late 19C+] (*mainly northern*) first-rate, excellent.

champion *adv.* [late 19C+] (*mainly northern*) excellently, perfectly.

champion slump of 1897 *n.* [London's motor manufacturers staged a great procession of their products on Lord Mayor's Day, 1897. The aim was to launch the new mode of transport with a great fanfare, as the term implies, it failed – at least initially] [late 19C] the motorcar.

champstack *n.* [SE *champ*, to bite] [mid-19C] (*UK Und.*) the teeth.

champy *n.* [abbr.] [late 19C] (*US*) *champagne*.

chance *v.*

(IN PHRASES)

❑ **chance it** *v.* (*also* **chance her**) [ext. SE *chance*] [mid-19C+] to take risks, to gamble. ❑ **chance one's arm** *v. see under* ARM *n.* ❑ **chance one's mitt** *v. see under* MITT *n.*

chance child *n.* (*also* **come-by-chance child**) [mid-19C] an illegitimate child.

chancer *n.* **1** [late 19C+] anyone who risks their luck, usu. foolishly, although the over-riding image is of their 'getting away with it'; thus adj. *chancing*. **2** [1990s+] a bet, a wager.

chance would be a fine thing *phr.* [20C+] a phr. used of anything that seems absolutely unlikely.

chancey *adv.* [1940s] suspiciously.

chancy *adj.* [SE *chance*, which can be fortunate or otherwise] **1** [19C+] untrustworthy, undependable. **2** [1980s+] (*Irish*) good-looking.

C.H. & D. *phr.* [abbr. *c*old, *h*ungry and *d*ry + play on the initials of the *C*incinnati, *H*amilton and *D*ayton Railroad] [1930s] (*US tramp*) declaration of one's need for food and shelter.

chandelier *n.* [1970s–80s] (*N.Z. prison*) an ear.

chandler-ken *n.* [SE *chandler* + KEN *n.*^{1} (1)] [early 19C] a chandler's shop, selling general provisions, groceries etc.

chandu *n.* [? synon. Malay] [1910s–20s] (*drugs*) Chinese opium prepared for smoking.

chaney-eyed *adj.* [? *chaney* = China, as in china-ware or porcelain; china being the original material used for 'glass' eyes] [late 19C] **1** small-eyed; thus like a china doll. **2** one-eyed; rarely, glassy-eyed.

chang-chang *v.* [? echoic of the sound of the barber's scissors] [20C+] (*W.I., Gren.*) to cut a man or boy's hair in an amateurish, raggedy manner.

change *n.* **1** [early 19C+] something given or taken in return; usu. in phrs. (*see* below). **2** [mid-19C+] (*orig. US black*) money, whether in notes or coins; often as *piece of change*. **3** [1940s+] in fig. use, any insignificant, unquantifiable amount, not necessarily monetary. **4** [1940s+] constr. with *the*, the menopause; also used joc. of a man [euph. SE *the change of life*]. **5** [1950s] (*US black*) a game of dice. **6** [1970s+] (*US prison*) in a jail sentence, any period of time less than a whole year.

IN PHRASES

❑ **give someone change** *v.* [19C] **1** to make a suitable response in verbal badinage. **2** to punish someone. ❑ **let me hold some change** [1960s+] (*US black*) please give me some money. ❑ **make change** *v.* [1940+] (*US black*) to work or otherwise obtain money for staying alive. ❑ **not get any change out of** *v.* (*also* **not get much change out of, get no change out of**) [mid-19C+] to get no return result or satisfaction from; to fail to get the better of (someone). ❑ **take one's change out of** *v.* [early–mid-19C] to take revenge on; esp. in excl. *take your change out of that!*, accompanied by a blow or a rude remark.

SE in slang uses

IN PHRASES

❑ **put the change on** *v.* [one has 'changed' the truth for lies] [mid-17C–19C] to mislead.

change *v.*

SE in slang uses

IN PHRASES

❑ **change black dog for monkey** *v.* [one is still left with a useless animal] [1920s+] (*W.I.*) to get nothing from a deal, to remain as poor as one already was. ❑ **change channels** *v.* (*also* **change the channel**) [TV imagery] **1** [1950s+] (*US*) to change the subject of conversation, or one's line of thought. **2** [1970s] to find a new relationship. ❑ **change one's breath** *v.* [late 19C–1900s] (*US*) to drink alcohol. ❑ **change one's copy** *v.* [early 17C] to alter one's opinions or statements, esp. to go back on what one has previously said. ❑ **change one's luck** *v. see under* LUCK *n.* ❑ **change one's note** *v.* [musical imagery] [late 17C+] to alter one's opinions or statements, esp. to go back on what one has previously said. ❑ **change one's song** *v. see under* SONG *n.* ❑ **change someone's face/head** *v. see* BREAK SOMEONE'S FACE *v.* ❑ **change teams** *v.* [1990s+] to change one's sexuality, usu. from heterosexual to homosexual.

change-machine *n.* (*also* **change-register**) [their role in commercial sex] [1970s+] (*US gay*) the buttocks.

changes *n.* [jazz use *changes*, a chord sequence, thence adopted by hippies/drug users/New Agers in the late 1960s+] [1950s+] (*orig. US black*) any alteration in one's mental or emotional state.

IN PHRASES

❑ **go through changes** *v.* [1950s+] to undergo alterations in one's emotional or mental state or attitudes. ❑ **put through changes** *v.* (*also* **take through changes**) [1960s+] to alter another person's mental or emotional state, opinions or attitudes. ❑ **ring the changes** *v. see* separate entry.

changie *n.* [abbr.] [2000s] a *changing* room.

chank *v.* [? SE *champ* or echoic] [19C] (*US*) to eat noisily, to chew loudly.

channa *n.*

IN PHRASES

❑ **go for channa** *v.* [Hind. *chanaa*, chick-pea; thus the invested money has fig. turned into chick-peas] [20C+] (*W.I., Guyn.*) to be absolutely wasted, esp. of money.

channel *n.* **1** [1930s+] (*drugs*) (*also* **channel line**) the vein into which a drug is injected. **2** [1940s] (*S.Afr. prison*) an inmate courier of illicit and smuggled goods.

IN COMPOUNDS

❑ **channel swimmer** *n.* [1950s–70s] (*drugs*) one who injects heroin.

IN PHRASES

❑ **miss the channel** *v.* [1950s] (*drugs*) to miss the vein, when injecting a narcotic.

channel fleet *n.* [rhy. sl.] [20C+] (*Irish*) a street.

Channel Nine *n.* [rhy. sl.] [1980s] (*Aus.*) wine.

chant *n.* (*also* **chantey, chaunt**) [all fig. uses of SE *chant*, to sing] (*UK Und.*) **1** [late 18C–19C] a song; thus *throw off a rum chant*, to sing a good song. **2** [mid-18C–19C] a newspaper advertisement; an account of a robbery. **3** [early 19C] any form of writing. **4** [early 19C] any form of marking, on silver, linen etc; thus *chanted*, marked. **5** [early–mid-19C] one's name (and address); thus *tip someone a queer chant*, to give a false name, esp. to a tradesman one wishes to defraud. **6** [mid-19C] sheet music, a printed ballad with its lyrics.

IN COMPOUNDS

❑ **chant-cove** *n.* [COVE *n.* (1)] [mid-19C] (*US Und.*) a newspaper reporter. ❑ **chaunt-fencer** *n.* [-FENCER *sfx*] [mid-19C] a seller of sheet music and ballad lyrics, 'last dying speeches' (on the gallows) and similar broadsides.

chant *v.* (*also* **chaunt**) [CHANT *n.*] **1** [mid-17C–1930s] (*orig. UK Und.*) to sing, esp. to sing for money in the street; to sing to sell one's wares. **2** [mid-18C] (*UK Und.*) to count up. **3** [19C] (*UK Und.*) to sell a horse fraudulently. **4** [early 19C] (*UK Und.*) to praise. **5** [early 19C] (*UK Und.*) to publish an account in a newspaper. **6** [early 19C] (*UK Und.*) to mark one's personal possessions with an identifying name. **7** [mid-19C] (*US*) to talk (about), to talk persuasively. **8** [late 19C–1900s] to swear. **9** [1930s] (*UK tramp*) to sing for alms. **10** [1980s] (*UK black*) to speechify in the street.

IN PHRASES

❑ **chant down** *v.* [1980s] (*W.I.*) to criticize. ❑ **chant the can** *v.* [? Ital. *canto*, a song] [1980s] to speak Romany. ❑ **chant the poker** *v.* [? the innate ordinariness of a poker, which cannot be 'chanted' otherwise] [19C] to exaggerate; thus *don't chant the poker*, don't exaggerate. ❑ **chaunt the play** *v.* [PLAY *n.* (2)] [mid–late 19C] (*UK Und.*) to explain the criminal lifestyle and methods. ❑ **chaunt upon the leer** *v.* [LEER *n.*] [late 18C] to advertise, to publicize, to write up in the press.

chanted *adj.* (*also* **chaunted**) [CHANT *v.*] **1** [early 19C] famous, celebrated, lit. 'sung'. **2** [mid-19C] (*UK Und.*) of the theft of a stolen article, announced in public (by a town crier or similar figure).

chanter *n.* [CHANT *v.*] **1** [early 18C–1930s] (*also* **chaunter, chanty man**) a seller and singer of street ballads. **2** [mid-19C–1920s] (*also* **chanterer**) a crooked horse dealer, also of dogs.

IN COMPOUNDS

❑ **chaunter-cove** *n.* [COVE *n.* (1)] [mid–late 19C] a journalist, a reporter. ❑ **chaunter-cull** *n.* (*also* **chanter-cull**) [CULL *n.*[1] (3)] [late 18C–19C] (*UK Und.*) a composer of ballads, broadsides and similar productions for the use of street singers and versifiers.

IN PHRASES

❑ **chaunter upon the leer** *n.* [LEER *n.*] [late 18C–19C] an advertiser.

chanter-pipe *n.* (*also* **chanter**) [SE *chanter* = Irish bagpipes] [mid-18C–mid-19C] the penis.

chanticleer *n.* [a pun on COCK *n.*[3] (1); the cock in the fable of Reynard the Fox is thus named; Williams notes its use as a synon. for a lecher] [mid–late 19C] the penis.

chanting *n.* (*also* **chaunting**) [CHANT *v.*] **1** [late 18C–1930s] street-singing. **2** [19C] the selling of a poor horse by concealing its defects and 'crying up' its good ones.

IN COMPOUNDS

❑ **chanting ken** *n.* [KEN *n.*[1] (1)] [late 19C–1900s] a music-hall. ❑ **chanting slum** *n.* [SLUM *n.*[1] (1)] [mid-19C] a music-hall. ❑ **chaunting-cove** *n.* [COVE *n.* (1)] [19C] a dishonest horse-dealer. ❑ **chaunting-lay** *n.* [LAY *n.*[3] (1)] [mid–late 19C] street-singing.

chanty man *n. see* CHANTER *n.* (1).

chaow *phr. see* CHOW *phr.*

chap *n.* [abbr. of late 16C SE *chapman*, a customer, and as such relates to COVE *n.* An alternative ety., however, links it to the Romany *chavo* or *chavi*, a child, and thus places it as the antecedent of the 19C use. Todd (revised edn of *Johnson's Dict.*, 1818) notes 'it usually designates a person of whom a contemptuous opinion is entertained', but the *OED* adds 'it is now merely familiar and non-dignified, being chiefly applied to a young man'] **1** [18C+] a man, or boy, esp. in sense of 'one of us'. **2** [early 19C] a wife. **3** [mid-19C+] an otherwise unspecified object or animal. **4** [late 19C] a male sweetheart. **5** [late 19C] a sailor. **6** [1910s+] constr. with a, oneself, e.g. *a chap ought to get drunk once in a while*. **7** [1920s+] (*Irish*) the hero, the leading man in a film, the good guy. **8** [1950s+] (*UK Und.*) a member of one's own gang or group; often as *one of the chaps*. **9** [1980s] (*Aus.*) as *the chaps*, the police.

chap *v.*[1] [abbr.] [1920s–30s] to *chap*eron.

chap *v.*[2] [? SE *chap*, to cause (the skin) to crack] [1990s+] to be unsatisfactory, to be bad.

Chapel, the *n.* [abbr.] [mid–late 19C] White*chapel*, London.

chapel *n.*

SE in slang uses

IN COMPOUNDS

❑ **chapel hat-pegs** *n.* [20C+] erect female nipples; usu. in phr. *stand/standing up like chapel hat-pegs*. ❑ **chapel-warmer** *n.* [1930s] (*Aus.*) a church goer.

IN PHRASES

❑ **chapel of ease** *n.* (*also* **chapel**) [play on SE *chapel of ease*, a chapel built for the convenience of parishioners who live far from the parish church] **1** [17C–19C] the vagina. **2** [17C–mid-19C] a privy, a lavatory. ❑ **chapel of little ease** *n.* [SE *little-ease*, 'a place in which there is little ease for him who occupies it. A narrow place of confinement; spec. the name of a dungeon in the Tower of London, and of an ancient place of punishment for unruly apprentices at the Guildhall, London. Also, the pillory or stocks.' (*OED*) + play on prev.] [late 19C] a police station.

chapp *n.* [ety. unknown] [2000s] (*US black*) a child.

chapped *adj.* (*also* **chapt**) [SE *chapped*, cracked, dried out] [late 17C–1900s] thirsty.

chapper *n.*[1] [? SE *chaps*, the mouth] [late 19C] the mouth.

chapper *n.*[2] [? Yid.] [20C+] (*UK Und.*) a police officer.

chapper *v.* [CHAPPER *n.*[1]] [late 19C–1900s] to drink.

chappie *n.* (*also* **chappy**) [CHAP *n.* (1)] **1** [early 19C+] (*orig. Scot.*) a person, esp. a close friend. **2** [mid-19C+] a term of address to a friend. **3** [late 19C] a man about town.

chappy *adj.* [SE *chaps*, the mouth, the jaws] [late 17C–mid-18C] talkative.

chaps *n. see* CHOPS *n.*[1].

chap someone's ass *v. see under* ASS *n.*

chapstick lesbian *n.* [the use of the lip-salve *Chapstick* by sportspeople; play on SE *lipstick lesbian*] [1990s+] (*US gay*) a lesbian who is especially keen on sport.

chapt *adj. see* CHAPPED *adj.*

char *n.*[1] [note orig. 18C *char*, to do odd jobs; B.E.: '*Chare-woman*, Underdrudges, or taskers, assistants to Servantmaids'. The modern synon. *charlady* began as late 19C joc. but now, like *tea-lady*, *cleaning-lady* etc is almost SE; note Nares (1822): 'CHARE or CHARE-WORK. Task-work, or any labour [...] *Chare-woman* is still used, for one hired to work by the day'] [mid-18C+] a charwoman.

char *n.*[2] *see* CHA *n.*[1].

char *v.* [CHAR *n.*[1]] **1** [late 18C] to solicit, to work as a prostitute. **2** [mid-19C+] to work as a cleaner, usu. in a private house.

chara *n.* (*also* **sharrer**) [abbr.] [1920s–60s] a *chara*banc, a coach.

character *n.* **1** [mid-18C+] an eccentric or otherwise distinctive person [abbr. SE *odd character*]. **2** [20C+] (*orig. US*) a person. **3** [1960s+] (*US Und.*) a professional criminal; also attrib.

SE in slang uses

IN COMPOUNDS

❑ **character academy** *n.* [mid-19C] (*UK Und.*) a place where unemployed (and poss. previously dismissed) servants concoct spurious references or 'characters'.

charactered *adj.* [SE *character*, a brand, a stamp] [early 18C–early 19C] (*UK Und.*) branded on the hand.

charas *n.* (*also* **churus**) [Hind. *charas*, hashish] [1920s+] (*drugs*) hashish.

charcoal *n.* [mid-19C+] (*US*) **1** a derog. term for a black person; thus *charcoal blossom*, a young black woman; *charcoal lily*, a very dark black boy; *charcoal bandit*, a black criminal; as adj., black-skinned. **2** as used by a black person, thus not derog.

SE in slang uses

IN COMPOUNDS

❑ **charcoal blonde** *n. see* BITUMEN BLONDE *n.* ❑ **charcoal tart** *n.* [20C+] (*Aus.*) a thin, unleavened loaf baked in the embers.

chardonnay socialist *n. see* CHAMPAGNE SOCIALIST *under* CHAMPAGNE *n.*

charf *v.* [? SE *chaff*, to banter, to tease] [1990s+] (*S.Afr.*) to talk.

charge *n.*[1] [Anglo-Norman *kark*, a burden] [20C+] (*Irish*) **1** a loud-mouthed woman. **2** a lazy, loutish person.

charge *n.*[2] [SE *charge*, an accumulation of electricity, but note 1877 Mrs Frank Leslie *California*: 'The tiny "charge" [of opium] constituting one pipe-full is soon exhausted, and holding the last whiff as long as possible, the smoker prepares another, and another and yet another'] **1** [1920s+] the effect of a given drug. **2** [1920s+] an injection of a narcotic drug. **3** [1940s+] drugs in general, spec. marijuana; thus *charge party*, a party where marijuana is smoked. **4** [1950s+] a thrill, a feeling of excitement or satisfaction; thus *get a charge out of*. **5** [1980s] (*Aus.*) a glass of liquor, esp. spirits. **6** [2000s] a feeling of amusement.

charge *v.*[1] [SE *charge*, to attack] **1** [late 16C–mid-17C; 1960s] of a man, to have sexual intercourse. **2** [late 19C] (*US*) to have a riotously good time. **3** [1930s+] (*US*) to hold up (a bank) at gunpoint. **4** [1960s] (*US*) to arouse sexually.

SE in slang uses

IN PHRASES

❑ **charge like a wounded bull** *v.* [1990s+] (*orig. Aus.*) to ask for a large amount of money; to render a substantial bill. ❑ **charge someone off** *v.* [1960s] (*US*) **1** to end a relationship. **2** to ignore someone one knows well.

charge *v.*[2] [CHARGE *n.*[2]] (*drugs*) **1** [1930s] to use narcotic drugs. **2** [1930s–60s] to smoke marijuana.

charged (up) *adj.* [CHARGE *n.*[2]] [1920s+] **1** intoxicated by alcohol; thus *half-charged*, tipsy. **2** intoxicated by drugs, esp. cannabis. **3** emotionally tense, irrespective of the stimulus.

charger *n.* [1900s] the penis.

charging *n.* [SE *charge*, to command, to exhort authoritatively] [1970s+] (*US black*) an instance of outwitting, insult or verbal humiliation.

charing *adj.* [abbr. *Charing Cross*; thus play on ON THE CROSS *under* CROSS *n.*[1]] [mid-19C] (*UK Und.*) wrong.

Charing Cross *n.* (*also* **chair and cross**) [rhy. sl.; note Cockney pron. 'crorss'] [mid-19C+] a horse.

chariot *n.* **1** [mid–late 19C] an omnibus. **2** [20C+] a motorcar.

IN COMPOUNDS

❑ **chariot-buzzer** *n.* [BUZZER *n.*[1] (1)] [mid-19C] a pickpocket who specializes in the passengers of an omnibus; thus *chariot-buzzing*.

charity *n.* **1** [1970s] (*Aus. gay*) a promiscuous man, who 'gives it away for free'. **2** *see* CHARITY MOLL below.

IN COMPOUNDS

❑ **charity ass** *n.* [ASS *n.* (3)] [1920s–50s] a woman who 'gives it away'; thus sexual intercourse for which no payment is expected. ❑ **charity cunt** *n.* [CUNT *n.* (2)] [1910s; 2000s] (*US*) a promiscuous woman who 'gives it away for free'. ❑ **charity dame** *n.* [DAME *n.*] [1930s+] (*Aus.*) a promiscuous woman who 'gives it away for free'. ❑ **charity girl** *n.* (*also* **charity stuff**) [1920s+] (*US*) a promiscuous woman who 'gives it away for free'. ❑ **charity goods** *n.* (*also* **charity stuff**) [1970s+] (*US gay*) a male prostitute who gives sex but does not get paid. ❑ **charity moll** *n.* (*also* **charity**) [MOLL *n.* (1)] [1940s+] (*Aus.*) an amateur prostitute, or a professional who undercuts her peers. ❑ **charity worker** *n.* [1940s+] (*US*) a promiscuous woman who 'gives it away for free'.

SE in slang uses

IN COMPOUNDS

❑ **charity bob** *n.* [late 19C–1900s] a form of quick curtsy peculiar to charity-school girls. ❑ **charity case** *n.* (*also* **charity stuff**) [1960s+] an older sexual partner whose needs are gratified by a young man or woman out of kindness rather than desire. ❑ **charity fuck** *n.* (*also* **pity fuck**) [FUCK *n.* (1a)] [1960s+] an act of sexual intercourse engaged in out of pity.

Charlene *n.* [fem. dimin. of MR CHARLIE *n.*] [1970s] **1** (*US black*) a white woman, esp. one who is in a position of authority over blacks. **2** (*US gay*) a popular camp nickname for a homosexual man.

Charles *n. see* CHARLIE *n.*

charles *n.*[1] [*BOSS CHARLIE under* BOSS *n.*[2]] [1920s+] (*US black*) a derog. term for a white man.

charles *n.*[2] [initial letter] [1960s+] (*drugs*) cocaine.

Charles Dance *n.* [rhy. sl.; ult. the British actor and film star *Charles Dance* (b. 1946)] [1990s+] a chance.

charles james *n.* [rhy. sl. on 'Fox'; ult. UK politician *Charles James Fox* (1749–1806)] [late 19C+] **1** a theatrical box. **2** (*hunting*) a fox.

Charley *n. see* CHARLIE *n.*

charley *n. see also under* CHARLIE and its combs.

Charley Bate's Farm/Garden *n. see* BATE'S FARM *n.*

charley beck *n.* [rhy. sl.] [1940s] (*US*) a forged check (cheque).

charley brady *n.* (*also* **charles brady**) [rhy. sl. = CADY *n.*] [late 19C–1960s] a hat.

charley chalk *n.* [rhy. sl.] [1940s] (*US*) talk.

Charley Dilke *n.* (*also* **Charlie Dilke**) [rhy. sl.; ult. radical UK politician Sir *Charles Dilke* (1843–1911)] [20C+] milk.

charley frisky *n.* (*also* **charlie frisky**) [rhy. sl.] [mid-19C–1900s] whisky.

charley horse *n.* (*also* **charlie horse, horse**) [orig. baseball use *c.*1886] [late 19C+] (*orig. US*) a cramp or sudden stiffness in the leg; thus *charley-horsed*, suffering from such a problem.

charley howard *n.* [rhy. sl.; poss. based on Tennyson 'The Revenge': 'Then sware Lord Thomas Howard: "'Fore God I am no coward"'; however, note CHARLIE *adj.* (2)] [1930s+] a coward.

charley lancaster *n.* [rhy. sl. = 'handkercher'] [mid-19C] a handkerchief.

charley mason *n.* (*also* **stone mason**) [rhy. sl.] [20C+] a basin, a basinful.

charley-pitcher *n.* (*also* **charlie-pitcher**) [? OE *ceorl* or SE *churl*, a peasant; however, *charley* may simply be a generic term for the peasant to whom he 'pitches the tale', or a euph. for the derisive *churl*] [mid-19C] **1** a cheating gambler. **2** (*UK Und.*) one who runs a 'find the lady' or 'three-card monte' card-game.

charley pope *n.* [rhy. sl.] [1910s] soap.

charley pork *n.* [rhy. sl.] [late 19C] (*Aus.*) cheeky talk, insolence.

charley randy *n.* [rhy. sl.] [mid-19C–1900s] brandy.

Charley rocks *n. see* SIDNEY ROCKS *n.*

charley rollar *n.* [rhy. sl.] [1920s–40s] (*US*) a dollar.

charley roller *n. see* TOMMY ROLLER *n.*

charleys *n. see* CHARLIES *n.*[1].

Charley's aunt! *excl.* [1910s] an excl. of amusement.

charley sheard *n.* [rhy. sl.] [1970s+] a beard.

charley skinner *n.* [rhy. sl.] [mid-19C–1900s] dinner.

charley wag *n.*

IN PHRASES

❑ **play the charley wag** *v.* [var. on *HOP THE WAG under* HOP *v.*[1]] [mid–late 19C] to play truant.

charley-wag *v.* [prev.] [1900s] to play truant.

Charlie *n.* (*also* **Charles, Charley, Mr Charles, the C**) [initial letter; post-1973 use is historical] [1960s–70s] (*US orig. milit.*) a member of the Viet Cong.

charlie *see also under* CHARLEY and its combs.

charlie *n.*[1] (*also* **charley**) **1** [late 17C; 19C] a watchman, a beadle [supposedly linked to the improvement of the London watch system by Charles I, but no recorded use of the word for 150 years afterwards]. **2** [mid-19C] a gold watch [pun on sense 1].

IN COMPOUNDS

❑ **charley-ken** *n.* [KEN *n.*[1] (1)] [early 19C] (*UK Und.*) a watchman's box. ❑ **charley-man** *n.* [early 19C] a watchman, a beadle. ❑ **charley's fiddle** *n.* [early–mid-19C] a watchman's rattle.

IN PHRASES

❑ **blind charley** *n.* [mid-19C] (*US*) a lamp-post. ❑ **box a charlie** *v.* [early–mid-19C] to turn over a watchman in his box. ❑ **get the best of a charlie** *v.* [BEST *v.*] [early 19C] upsetting a watchman in his box, a popular 'game' among upper-class rowdies.

charlie *n.*[2] [fig. use of proper name] **1** [early 19C+] (*orig. US*) a generic term for a person, usu. a man; thus as term of address [generic use of the popular given name]. **2** [mid-19C] a small, pointed beard [that worn by King *Charles I* (r.1625–49)]. **3** [mid-19C+] a hunchback [Lancs. dial.; who supposedly carried his 'little brother Charlie' on his back; note army jargon *charlie*, a pack]. **4** [1920s] (*US*) a moustachioed man [? ext. of sense 2]. **5** [1920s] (*also* **charley**) a chamberpot. **6** [1920s–70s] (*US black*) (*also* **charley, cholly, hard-luck charlie**) a dollar bill. **7** [1960s] (*US campus*) menstruation. **8** [2000s] (*N.Z. juv.*) temporarily deadening someone's leg by driving one's knee into their thigh muscle.

charlie *n.*[3] [abbr. CHARLES JAMES *n.* (2)] [mid–late 19C] a fox.

charlie *n.*[4]

IN PHRASES

❑ **on the charlie** [? CHARLEY WAG *n.*] [1910s] living as a tramp.

charlie *n.*[5] (*also* **charley**) [rhy. sl.; *charlie hunt* = CUNT *n.* (4); given the popularity of the term among otherwise 'clean' radio and TV comedians, one must assume their (and their audiences') ignorance of the ety.] [1920s+] a fool; esp. in phr. *proper charlie, right charlie*.

charlie *n.*[6] [abbr. CHARLIE RONCE *n.*] [1930s+] a ponce, a pimp.

charlie *n.*[7] [the fictional Chinese detective *Charlie Chan*, created in 1925 by Earl Derr Biggers] [1930s+] (*US*) a Chinese man.

charlie *n.*[8] (*also* **charley**) [the same initial letter but note US black use MR CHARLIE *n.* (1) meaning a white man; cocaine, too, is white] (*drugs*) **1** [1930s+] (*also* **charlie cocaine**) cocaine. **2** [1990s+] a heavy user of cocaine.

IN PHRASES

❑ **blow charlie** *v.* [1960s–70s] (*drugs*) to take cocaine.

charlie *n.*[9] [CHARLIE WHEELER *n.*, but Simes, *A Dict. of Australian Underworld Slang* (1993), adds: '"Charlie" was an old Eng. name for nightwatchman: this may be the origin'] [1940s+] (*Aus.*) **1** a woman. **2** a prostitute. **3** a lesbian. **4** a male homosexual.

charlie *n.*[10] (*also* **charley**) [abbr. MR CHARLIE *n.* (1)] [1960s+] (*US black*) a derog. term for a white man.

charlie *n.*[11] (*also* **charley**) [1960s+] (*US*) the penis.

IN PHRASES

❑ **introduce charlie/charley** *v.* [1990s+] to have sexual intercourse.

charlie *n.*[12] (*also* **half-charlie**) [1990s+] (*UK juv.*) a brick or half-brick; usu. as a weapon.

charlie *adj.* **1** [early 19C+] wary [CHARLIE *n.*[1] (1)]. **2** [1930s+] frightened, cowardly; thus *turn charlie*, to become frightened [? CHARLEY HOWARD *n.*].

IN PHRASES

▫ **turn charlie** *v.* [1930s+] to act in a cowardly manner, esp. when one thus lets down one's companions.

Charlie (Big) Potatoes *n.* [CHARLIE *n.*[2] (1) + BIG POTATO *n.*[1] (1)] [2000s] a rich and powerful person.

charlie blow *n.* [CHARLIE *n.*[8] (1) + BLOW *n.*[3] (4d)] [1970s] (*US drugs*) cocaine.

charlie-boy *n.* [CHARLIE *adj.*] [late 19C–1910s] (*US*) an effeminate young man.

charlie britt *n.* [rhy. sl.] [20C+] (*Aus.*) a fit.

IN PHRASES

▫ **chuck a charlie** *v.* (*also* **throw a charlie**) [1940s+] (*Aus.*) to have a fit.

charlie chap *n.* [abbr.; ult. film star *Charlie Chaplin* (1889–1977)] [1910s] (*Aus.*) a moustache resembling that worn (in character) by Charlie Chaplin.

Charlie Chaplain *n.* [pun; *see* prev.] [1980s+] (*Aus. prison*) a prison chaplain.

charlie chase *n.* [rhy. sl.] [20C+] (*Aus.*) a race; thus *not in the charlie*, not worthy of consideration.

Charlie Chester *n.* [rhy. sl.; ult. UK comedian *Charlie Chester* (1914–1997)] [1990s+] (*UK juv.*) a child molester.

Charlie Clore *n.* [rhy. sl.; ult. property developer Sir *Charles Clore* (1904–79)] [1960s] the ground, 'the floor'.

charlie cocaine *n. see* CHARLIE *n.*[8] (1).

charlie coke *n.* [CHARLIE *n.*[8] (1) + COKE *n.*[1] (1)] [1930s+] (*US drugs*) a cocaine addict.

Charlie Cooke *n.* [rhy. sl.; ult. UK footballer *Charlie Cooke* (b.1942)] [1990s+] a look, a glance.

charlie cotton *n. see* COTTON *n.* (1).

charlied *adj.* [CHARLIE *n.*[8] (1)] [2000s] experiencing the effects of cocaine.

Charlie Drake *n.* [rhy. sl.; ult. UK comedian *Charlie Drake* (1925–2006)] **1** [1960s–70s] a brake (on a car). **2** [1990s+] a break (for tea etc).

charlie freer *n.* [rhy. sl.] [late 19C–1980s] beer.

charlie goon *n.* (*also* **charlie goons**) [MR CHARLIE *n.* + GOON *n.*[1] (2)] [1960s] (*US black*) a policeman, the police.

Charlie Horner *n. see* JOHNNY HORNER *n.*

charlie irvine *n.* [? criminal *i*nvestigator] [1970s+] (*US black*) the police.

Charlie Muggins *n. see* MUGGINS *n.*[1].

charlie nebs *n.* [MR CHARLIE *n.* + SE *neb*, a beak, although *neb* may be mispron. for NAB *n.*[2] (1)] [1960s] (*US black*) the police.

charlie-on-the-spot *n.* [var. on JOHNNY-ON-THE-SPOT *n.* (1)] [19C–1940s] (*US*) a reliable or punctual person.

charlie prescott *n.* (*also* **charley prescott, Colonel Prescott, jimmy prescott, john prescott, prescott**) [rhy. sl.; ? anecdotal] [mid-19C+] a waistcoat.

Charlie Pride *n.* [rhy. sl.; ult. US country star *Charley Pride* (b.1938)] [2000s] a ride.

charlie rawler *n.* [rhy. sl.] [1920s–40s] (*US*) a collar.

Charlie Ronce *n.* (*also* **Harry Ronce, Joe Ronce, Johnny Ronce**) [rhy. sl.] [1930s+] a ponce, a pimp.

Charlie Rousers *n. see* JOHNNY ROWSERS *n.*

charlies *n.*[1] (*also* **charleys**) [? CHARLIE WHEELER *n.* = a woman, and thus her distinguishing characteristics. Ware attributes the term to the predilection of King Charles II (r.1660–85) for décolletage, which would seem fanciful but for the date, which well precedes Aus. use. Partridge (1984) suggests Rom. *chara*, to touch, to meddle with] [mid-19C+] the female breasts.

charlies *n.*[2] [? CHARLIES *n.*[1]] [1960s] the testicles.

charlie's dead *phr.* [1940s+] (*UK juv.*) a warning to a woman that her slip is showing.

Charlie Smirke *n.* [rhy. sl. = BERK *n.*; ult. UK jockey *Charlie Smirke* (fl. 1922–53), who claimed three Derbies and the St Leger among other successes] [1970s+] a fool.

charlie taylor *n.* [? anecdotal] [1930s–50s] (*US, Southwest*) syrup or molasses into which bacon or ham fat has been poured.

charlie wheeler *n.* [rhy. sl. = SHEILA *n.*[1] (1); ult. *Charles Wheeler* (1881–1977), a painter specializing in nudes] [1940s+] (*Aus.*) a woman.

charlie whitehouse *n.* [ext. of CHARLIE *n.*[2] (5), f. the whiteness of the porcelain utensil] [1960s+] (*US*) a chamberpot.

Charlie Wood *n. see* MR WOOD *under* MR *n.*

charlotte *n.* ['feminized' version of CHARLIE *n.*[8] (1); note cocaine is a 'feminine' drug, *see* GIRL *n.*[2]] [1960s–70s] (*US drugs*) cocaine.

charm *n.* [it 'charms' locks open] [late 16C–mid-19C] a pick-lock.

charm *v.* [1960s+] (*US black*) to 'chat up'.

charmboat *n. see* DREAMBOAT *n.* (1).

charm bracelet *n.* [1970s+] (*US gay*) a metaphorical list of one's lovers, a 'little black book'.

charmer *n.* **1** [late 17C+] an attractive young woman. **2** [1900s] the penis.

charming! *excl.* [1960s+] an excl. used as a response to a statement that the speaker feels to be rude, crude or otherwise unacceptable, sometimes as *charming, I'm sure!*

charming mottle *n.* [rhy. sl.] [late 19C–1940s] (*Aus.*) a bottle.

charming wife *n.* [rhy. sl.] [1910s+] a knife.

charm-pot *n.* [SE *charm* + -POT *sfx*] [2000s] (*US*) a charmer, also used ironically.

charms *n.* [euph.; prior use is SE] **1** [18C+] the female breasts; esp. in phr. *flash one's charms*, to reveal one's breasts. **2** [early 18C; late 19C+] the male genitals. **3** [late 18C] the vagina. **4** [late 19C] (*US*) money [its efficacy in overcoming problems].

Charon's Ferry-Boat *n.*

IN PHRASES

▫ **ride old Charon's Ferry-Boat** *v. see* GO ACROSS THE RIVER *under* RIVER *n.*

char ou *n. see* CHAAR OU *n.*

charper *v.* [Ital. *cercare*, to seek; for an alternative ety. *see* letter from WS Wilcox at CHARVER *v.*] [mid-19C+] (*Ling. Fr./Polari*) to search.

IN COMPOUNDS

▫ **charpering carsey** *n.* [CARSEY *n.* (5)] [late 19C] (*Ling. Fr./Polari*) a police station. ▫ **charpering omi** *n.* [OMEE *n.* (3)] [late 19C] (*Ling. Fr./Polari*) a policeman.

charra *n.* [CHAAR OU *n.*] [1970s+] (*S.Afr.*) a derog. mode of address to an Indian.

chart *n.* [1900s] (*US*) the face.

chart *v.* [1960s] (*US*) to commit to memory, to comprehend.

charter the bar *v. see under* BAR *n.*[2].

charver *n.*[1] (*also* **charva, charve**) [CHARVER *v.* (1)] **1** [late 19C+] sexual intercourse or a female in a sexual context; thus *bona palone for a charver*, an 'easy lay', a 'good-time girl' (lit., 'a good girl for a fuck'). **2** [1960s+] a friend. **3** [2000s] a term of abuse.

charver *n.*[2] *see* CHAV *n.*

charver *v.* [note Polari etymologist WS Wilcox in a letter 25/11/99: 'Partridge derives *charva* and *charper* from Romany *chava* (touch) and Italian *cercare* respectively, but I think the centuries-old Italian slang word *chiavare* (fuck) and *chiappare* (catch, seize) are far more likely candidates, both in meaning and in form. Compare *scarper* from *scappare*. Regarding the chi- becoming (ts)-, this is the standard reflex in Genoese dialect, where *chiavare* becomes *ciavâ*'] **1** [mid-17C; late 19C+] (*also* **chaffer, chauver**) to have sexual intercourse; thus *charvering*, sexual intercourse. **2** [1930s] (*costermonger*) to ruin, to spoil or interfere in another's business, i.e. to FUCK *v.* (2a).

IN COMPOUNDS

▫ **charvering donna** *n.* (*also* **charvering dona, ...doner, chauvering...**) [DONA *n.* (1)] [mid–late 19C] (*Ling. Fr./Polari*) a prostitute. ▫ **charvering omee** *n.* [OMEE *n.* (3)] [mid-19C] (*Ling. Fr./Polari*) a policeman. ▫ **chauvering cove** *n.* [COVE *n.* (1)] [mid-19C] a womanizer, a promiscuous man. ❑ **chauvering moll** *n.* [MOLL *n.* (1)] [mid–late 19C] a prostitute.

charvered *adj.* [CHARVER *v.* (2)] [1930s+] ruined, wrecked, exhausted.

char wallah *n. see* CHA *n.*[1].

Chas *n.* [abbr. of proper name *Charlie*, thus CHARLIE *n.*[8] (1)] [2000s] cocaine.

chase *n.* [CHASE THE DRAGON *v.* (1)] [1990s+] (*drugs*) the act of smoking heroin.

chase *v.* **1** (*US*) (*also* **chase oneself**) to run off, to leave; as *chase yourself*, 'go away'. **2** [late 19C] (*US tramp*) to escort, to travel with. **3** [20C+] (*US*) (*also* **chase around**) usu. to pursue women, esp. as an adulterer; also of homosexuals, to pursue other men. **4** [1900s] (*US*) to move, to walk. **5** (*US*) in drug contexts [CHASE THE DRAGON *v.* (1); senses 5b and 5c misuses]. (**a**) [1990s+] to smoke heroin. (**b**) [2000s] to smoke cocaine. (**c**) [2000s] to smoke marijuana.

IN PHRASES

❑ **get the chase** *v.* [late 19C–1900s] (*US*) to be ejected, to be chased away.

IN EXCLAMATIONS

❑ **go chase yourself!** (*also* **chase yourself!**) an excl. of aggressive dismissal.

SE in slang uses

IN PHRASES

❑ **chase a piece** *v. see BEG FOR A PIECE under* PIECE *n.* ❑ **chase cheers** *v.* [1930s+] (*Aus.*) to curry favour with the masses; thus *cheer-chaser*, a toady to popular opinion; *cheer-chasing*, taking a deliberately populist stand. ❑ **chase the bag** *v. see under* BAG *n.*[1]. ❑ **chase the can** *v. see under* CAN *n.*[1]. ❑ **chase the (penny)weight** *v.* [1910s–70s] (*Aus.*) to prospect for gold. ❑ **chase the sun(set)** *v.* [1910s–50s] (*Aus.*) to live as a tramp. ❑ **chase (up) a cow** *v. see* CHASE *v.*

chaser *n.*[1] **1** that which accompanies and/or follows, usu. in the context of drinking. (**a**) [late 19C+] (*orig. US*) a glass of water, soda or beer taken after a shot of spirits, usu. to dilute the impact; from late 1980s onwards generally the other way around, a whisky chaser that is taken after drinking a pint of beer to increase the impact [1940s+ use is SE]. (**b**) [20C+] similarly used of foods. (**c**) [1900s] a final touch, e.g. in clothes. (**d**) [1900s] in fig. use. (**e**) [1980s] (*drugs*) a dilutant. **2** a follower. (**a**) [1900s] one who runs errands. (**b**) [1910s+] (*mainly US*) a womanizer. (**c**) [1950s] a promiscuous woman, the equivalent of sense 2b. (**d**) [1960s] a promiscuous homosexual. (**e**) [1990s+] (*US prison*) a prison officer responsible for overseeing prisoners when out of prison, e.g. on a chain gang [the potential for escape].

chaser *n.*[2] [CHASE *v.* (5b)] [1990s+] (*drugs*) a frequent user of crack cocaine.

chase the dragon *v.* [the 'dragon' underlines the Oriental origin of much of the heroin found in the UK] **1** [1960s+] (*drugs*) to smoke heroin, sucking up the smoke of the drug, which is burned on a piece of kitchen foil. The heated heroin liquefies and flows across the paper, gradually giving off smoke, which is sucked into the smoker's lungs by a tube, also usu. made of kitchen foil. **2** [2000s] (*US prison*) looking for a supply of heroin.

chase-up *n.* [1940s–60s] a car chase.

chase up *v.* [1950s+] **1** to pursue (a matter or person) vigorously with a specific intent, esp. after an earlier unsatisfactory response. **2** to make efforts to find or obtain quickly.

chasing *n.* [CHASE THE DRAGON *v.* (1)] [1980s+] (*drugs*) the act of smoking heroin.

chasm *n.* [19C] the vagina.

chasse *n.* [abbr. *chasse-café*, lit. 'chase-coffee'] [mid-19C–1910s] a cup of coffee that accompanies a shot of spirits, usu. whisky; a liqueur taken after or with coffee.

chasse *v.* [SE *chassé*, a gliding step, in a quadrille and other dances; it gives the illusion of walking] [mid-19C] (*UK society*) to dismiss, to send away.

chassis *n.* (*also* **chassy**) [automobile imagery] [1930s+] (*US*) **1** the female figure. **2** the male body.

IN PHRASES

❑ **classy chassis** *n.* [CLASSY *adj.* (1)] [1950s–60s] (*US*) the body of a good-looking, well-built woman.

chat *n.*[1] [Fr. *chat*, cat] **1** [18C] a cat. **2** [19C+] the vagina.

chat *n.*[2] [CHEAT *n.* (1)] **1** [early 19C] (*Scot. Und.*) a seal. **2** [late 19C] a criminal 'job' or undertaking. **3** [late 19C–1930s] a house, incl. one picked for burglary.

chat *n.*[3] [SE *chat*, a conversation, a discussion] **1** [early 19C–1910s] cheek, impudence. **2** [early 19C–1920s] the truth, the apposite thing, the subject under discussion. **3** [1900s–10s] information. **4** [1910s+] verbal skills, fluency, articulacy, the ability to charm a victim with words alone. **5** [1950s+] terminology, a special language, jargon.

chat *n.*[4] [CHATS *n.*[2]] [20C+] (*Aus.*) a general insult, usu. aimed at an old man, esp. an alcoholic.

chat *n.*[5] [its effects, but note CHAT *n.*[4]] [1930s–50s] (*Irish*) methylated spirits, as drunk by alcoholics; thus *chat-shop*, a place where one drinks methylated spirits.

chat *n.*[6] [CHAT-CHAT *v.*] [1950s] (*W.I.*) a male gossip.

chat *v.*[1] (*also* **chat up**) [fig. uses of SE; Williams gives 17C examples of *chat* used euph. for sexual intercourse, e.g. Pepys, *Diary* 11 Aug. 1663: '[the king] hath a chat now and then of Mrs. Stewart.'] **1** [late 19C+] to attempt the first verbal stages of seduction. **2** [20C+] to inform on, to tell on. **3** [1910s+] (*Aus.*) to scold. **4** [1950s] to trick verbally, to 'con', to persuade. **5** [1950s+] thus fig., in non-sexual contexts, to seduce with words. **6** [1960s] (*S.Afr.*) to kick. **7** [1970s+] to interview. **8** [1990s+] to sing rap lyrics. **9** [1990s+] (*UK black*) to speak, to state.

IN PHRASES

❑ **chat down** *v.* [1950s+] (*W.I.*) to make one's first advances to a young woman or man in the hope of eventual sexual conquest. ❑ **chat someone's name** *v.* [1950s+] (*W.I., Jam.*) to gossip maliciously about an absent third party.

chat *v.*[2] [CHATS *n.*[2]] [1910s] to search for lice; thus as n. *chat-up*, a search for lice.

chat-chat *v.* [SE *chat* + redup.] [1950s+] (*W.I.*) to gossip.

chateau cardboard *n.* (*also* **chateau de cask**) [play on Fr. *chateau*; the labels on bottles of Bordeaux wine always indicate the *chateau* at which they are produced] [1980s+] (*Aus./N.Z./S.Afr.*) wine sold in 2.5- or 5-litre (4.5–9-pint) containers, placed in a cardboard box.

chateau collapso *n.* (*also* **chateau collapsio**) [1990s+] (*N.Z.*) cheap wine packaged in a cardboard box rather than a bottle.

chateaued *adj.* [puns on SE *shattered* and Fr. *chateau*] [1980s+] (*UK society*) very drunk on wine.

chateau Taranaki *n.* [TARANAKI *adj.*] [2000s] (*N.Z.*) beer.

chates *n.* **1** *see* CHATS *n.*[1]. **2** *see* CHEATS *n.*[2].

chatham and dover *v.* [rhy. sl. = SE *give over*; ult. towns in Kent, UK] [1900s] to stop, to cease.

chat 'n' chew *n.* [1940s–60s] (*orig. US black*) a restaurant, a café.

chats *n.*[1] (*also* **chates, chattes, cheats**) [CHEAT *n.*] [mid-16C–19C] (*UK Und.*) the gallows.

chats *n.*[2] (*also* **chatts, chits**) [SE *chattels*, moveable property, typically livestock, 'lice being the chief livestock of beggars, gypsies, and the rest of the canting crew' (Grose, 1785)] [late 17C–1910s] (*UK Und.*) lice; thus *chat parade*, a delousing session.

IN COMPOUNDS

❑ **chat-bags** *n.* [BAGS *n.*[2]; the infestation of lice during WW1] [1910s] (*Aus.*) underwear.

chats *n.*[3] [1960s] excessive verbosity, caused by nerves, fear, shock, etc.

chatta *n.* [Skrt *chhatra*, an umbrella] [late 19C] an umbrella.

chatter *n.*

IN COMPOUNDS

❑ **chatter-basket** *n.* [late 18C–1910s] a small, noisy child;

synons. incl. *chatter-bags, chatter-bladder, chatter-cart* and (*US*) *chatter-bones*. ❑ **chatter-broth** *n.* [the stereotypical chattering women supposed to gather around the tea-table] [late 18C–early 19C] tea. ❑ **chattergun** *n.* [its noise] [1930s+] a machinegun or sub-machinegun. ❑ **chattermag** *see* separate entries.

chatterbox *n.* [despite *Grose* & *Lex. Balatronicum, chatterbox*, a habitual chatterer is SE: a 'contemptuous or playful name' (*OED*)] **1** [mid-19C] (*US*) the mouth or tongue. **2** [1930s–40s] a record player. **3** [1940s] a telephone. **4** [1940s] a car radio; thus *chatterbox and fish pole*, a radio and aerial. **5** [1940s–50s] a machinegun. **6** [1950s] (*US Und.*) a typewriter. **7** [1960s] a walkie-talkie.

chatterer *n.* (*also* **chattering**) [fig. use of SE and pun on *shattering*] [early 19C] a blow to the mouth that makes the recipient's teeth chatter.

chatterers *n.* [19C] the teeth.

chattering box *n.* [early 18C] a pulpit.

chattermag *n.* [SE *chatter* + MAG *n.*[2] (1)] **1** [mid–late 19C] a gossip, a chatterbox. **2** [late 19C] chatter, gossip.

chattermag *v.* [CHATTERMAG *n.*] [1900s] to chatter.

chattery *n.* [? CHATS *n.*[2], i.e. they are easily infested by lice] [early 19C] (*UK Und.*) one or more linen articles.

chattes *n. see* CHATS *n.*[1] (1).

chattey *adj. see* CHATTY *adj.*

chattry-feeder *n.* (*also* **chatty-feeder**) [? it *feeds* that which *chatters*, i.e. the mouth] [mid-19C] (*UK prison*) a spoon.

chatts *n.*[1] [they 'chatter' as they hit the table] [mid-19C] dice.

chatts *n.*[2] *see* CHATS *n.*[1].

chatty *n.*[1] [Tamil *shatti*, Telegu *chatti*, a pot; orig. Anglo-Ind. but spread across the British Empire] [mid-18C–1950s] a pot; *chatty-feeder*, a spoon.

chatty *n.*[2] [CHATTY *adj.*; abbr. of *chatty dosser*, a louse-ridden tramp] [19C] a filthy man.

chatty *adj.* (*also* **chattey**) [CHATS *n.*[2]] [mid-18C–1940s] lousy, infested; thus *chatty doss*, a louse-infested bed.

chatty-chatty *n.* [SE *chatty*, talkative + redup.] [1950s+] (*W.I.*) a habitual gossip.

chatty-feeder *n. see* CHATTRY-FEEDER *n.*

chat-up *n.* [CHAT *v.*[1] (1)] [1960s+] the first, verbal stages of seduction; thus *chat-up line*, the words used.

chat up *v. see* CHAT *v.*[1] (1).

chauki *n. see* CHOKEY *n.*

chauncy *adj.* [ety. unknown] [2000s] (*US black*) unattractive.

chaunt *see under* CHANT and its combs.

chauver *v. see* CHARVER *v.* (1) and combs.

chav *n.* (*also* **charver**) [? Rom. *chavi*, a child] [2000s] a working-class youth, esp. if particularly brash, often wearing sportswear and/or designer labels; occas. with implication of petty criminality.

chavala *n.* [Sp. *chava*, a girl] [1970s+] (*US*) **1** (*also* **chava**) a woman. **2** a derog. term for a man, implying he is emasculated.

chavy *n.* (*also* **chavey, chavvie, chavvo, chavvy**) [Rom. *chavi*, a child; note modern Bombay underworld slang *chhava*, a boyfriend] **1** [mid-19C+] (*Polari*) a child. **2** [late 19C+] a form of address to a man, e.g. *wotcher chavvy*.

chaw *n.* [? dial. *chaw*, chew, as in chewing tobacco] **1** [mid–late 19C] a yokel. **2** [mid–late 19C] (*US campus*) a trick, a prank. **3** [late 19C–1920s] a conversation. **4** [1910s–40s] (*US*) an Irish immigrant. **5** [1970s] (*US campus*) a handsome man.

chaw *v.* [fig. uses of dial. *chaw*, to chew] **1** [mid–late 19C] (*US*) (*also* **chaw up**) to mangle, to get the better of, to surpass, to destroy; thus *chawed up*, totally defeated. **2** [mid-19C–1900s] (*US campus*) to trick, to hoax. **3** [late 19C–1900s] (*US*) used in oaths, e.g. *chaw me up if…* **4** [1980s] to arrest; thus *chawry goods*, stolen property.

SE in slang uses

IN PHRASES

❑ **chaw the fat** *v. see* CHEW THE FAT *v.*

chaw! *excl. see* CHA! *excl.*

chaw-bacon *n.* [SE *chew bacon*] [early 19C+] a rustic, a peasant; thus a fool; also attrib.

chawed *adj. see* CHEWED *adj.*

chaw-mouth *n.* [*chaw* = SE *chew* + *mouth*, the noisy talker 'chews on' his words] [late 19C+] (*US*) a talkative person; thus a derog. term for an Irishman [alleged talkativeness of the Irish].

chaws *n.* [? CHARVER *v.* (1); ? or dial. *chaw*, to chew, in a var. on copulation/aggression link] [mid-19C] sexual intercourse.

chay *n.* (*also* **chay-cart, shay**) [pron. 'shay'] [mid-18C–1910s] a chaise or light carriage.

chazerai *n.* [Yid./Heb. *chazer*, a pig] [20C+] **1** a 'pigsty', a mess. **2** junk, rubbish.

chazerai *adj.* [CHAZERAI *n.*] [20C+] cheap, worthless, rubbish, nonsense.

chbye *phr.* [joc. mispron.] [1980s+] (*US campus*) goodbye.

C-head *n.* [C *n.*[3] (1) + -HEAD *sfx* (4)] [1980s+] (*drugs*) a cocaine user.

cheap *adj.* **1** [mid-19C–1920s] out of sorts, feeling ill. **2** [late 19C–1930s] (*US black*) dishonest. **3** [late 19C+] mean, miserly, grasping. **4** [late 19C+] (*also* **cheapshit**) unpleasant, cruel. **5** [2000s] (*US campus*) embarrassed.

IN PHRASES

❑ **feel cheap** *v.* [late 19C–1930s] to feel ill, esp. hungover; often as *feel very cheap*. ❑ **play cheap** *v.* [1940s–60s] (*US black*) to not take seriously; often as *don't play someone cheap*, make sure someone is not underrated.

SE in slang uses

IN COMPOUNDS

❑ **cheap-ass** *adj.* (*also* **cheap-arse**) [-ASS *sfx*] [1960s+] (*US*) cheap, inferior, second-rate. ❑ **cheap charlie** *n.* [CHARLIE *n.*[2] (1)] **1** [late 19C–1900s] (*US*) a candy store. **2** [1960s] one who accepts the second-rate, either through poverty or lack of taste. **3** [1960s+] a mean person. ❑ **cheap john** *n. see* separate entries. ❑ **cheap shot** *see* separate entries. ❑ **cheapskate** *see* separate entries. ❑ **cheap-trick** *adj. see* TRICK *n.*[1]. ❑ **cheapwad** *n.* [-WAD *sfx*] [1970s+] (*US*) a mean, ungenerous person.

IN PHRASES

❑ **cheap as dirt** *adj.* (*also* **dirt-cheap**) [early 19C+] extremely cheap. ❑ **cheap as ticks** *adj.* [1980s] (*US black*) very cheap.

cheap and nasty *n.* [rhy. sl.] [1930s] (*Aus.*) a meat pasty.

cheapie *n.* [SE *cheap* + sfx *-ie*] **1** [1930s+] anything, e.g. a film or play, produced on a low budget. **2** [1940s+] anything or anyone of little value or poor quality. **3** [1970s+] (*orig. US*) a mean person.

cheap john *n.*[1] [SE *cheap* + JOHN *n.* (1)] **1** [mid-19C+] (*US*) a pawnbroker. **2** [mid-19C+] a pawnshop. **3** [mid-19C+] (*also* **cheap jack, cheap johnnye, jack**) a shop, or person, selling cheap goods; thus as *v.*, to sell such goods. **4** [late 19C–1900s] cheap goods, items considered poor taste; also as adj. **5** [1960s] (*US*) a seedy brothel or bar.

cheap john *n.*[2] (*also* **short john**) [CHEAP *adj.* (3) + JOHN *n.* (1)] [mid-19C+] a mean, miserly person.

cheapo *n.* [SE *cheap* + -O *sfx* (7)] **1** [1910s+] a mean person. **2** [1970s+] something that is produced cheaply.

cheapo *adj.* (*also* **cheapo-cheapo**) [SE *cheap* + -O *sfx* (5) (+ redup.)] [1960s+] cheap, produced cheaply; thus often also of inferior quality; also as adv.

cheap shot *n.* [SE *cheap*, in sense of both costing little effort, and being vulgar, in poor taste + SHOT *n.*[1] (3a)] [1960s+] (*US*) a wounding, sneering remark; thus *cheap-shot artist*, one who habitually makes such remarks.

cheap shotter *n.* [CHEAP SHOT *n.*] [1970s+] (*US*) one who makes wounding, cruel remarks.

Cheapside *n.*

IN PHRASES

❑ **by way of Cheapside** [pun on proper name *Cheapside*, a well-known street in the City of London. This name comes from AS *chepe*, a market, a place of buying and selling; although directly linked, the adj. use, meaning low in price, does not emerge until the early 16C] [late 18C–early 19C] on the cheap, at a bargain price; often as *come at it by way of Cheapside* or *come home by way of Cheapside*.

cheapskate *n.* [SE *cheap* + SKATE *n.* (4); orig. 'cheap skate', later use is one word] [late 19C+] (*orig. US*) **1** an unpleasant person. **2** (*also* **short skate**) a mean, ungenerous person.

cheapskate *adj.* [CHEAPSKATE *n.*] **1** [20C+] (*orig. US*) mean, stingy. **2** [1910s–30s] second-rate.

cheat *n.* (*also* **chete**) [AS *chete*, a thing] [mid-16C–mid-18C] **1** a thing, usu. in combs. e.g. GRUNTING-CHEAT *n.*; PRATTLING-CHEAT *n.*; QUACKING CHEAT *n.*; SMELLING-CHEAT *n.* **2** a stolen thing. **3** see CHATS *n.*[1].

cheat *v.*

SE in slang uses

IN COMPOUNDS

❑ **cheat sheet** *n. see* SHEET *n.* ❑ **cheat-stick** *n.* (*also* **cheating-stick**) [1930s–50s] (*US campus*) a slide-rule.

IN PHRASES

❑ **cheat the devil** *n.* [mid-19C] (*UK Und.*) a false shirt-front. ❑ **cheat the starter** *v. see* BEAT THE STARTER *under* BEAT *v.* ❑ **cheat the worms** *v.* [the worms are those encountered in the grave] [mid–late 19C] to recover from a serious illness.

cheater *n.* [fig. uses of SE] **1** [1910s+] an adulterer. **2** [1920s] (*US*) an act of adultery. **3** [1940s] a condom. **4** [1940s+] anything that makes a task simpler, provides safety, gives one advantage, etc. **5** *see* CHEATOR *n.*

cheaters *n.*[1] **1** [mid-16C–early 17C; 1930s] crooked dice. **2** [1930s+] (*US tramp*) marked cards.

cheaters *n.*[2] (*also* **cheeters**) [they help the male genitals, eyes, teeth or female breasts *cheat* their own inadequacies] **1** [20C+] (*also* **eye cheaters**) (*orig. US*) glasses, spectacles, esp. dark glasses; thus *smoke cheaters*, dark glasses. **2** [1910s–70s] close-fitting men's underpants, usu. with elastic legbands. **3** [1940s+] pads which are placed in a brassiere to suggest a fuller breast. **4** [1950s+] (*orig. US*) false teeth.

cheating law *n.* [SE *cheating* + LAW *n.* (1)] [mid-16C–early 17C] (*UK Und.*) crooked dice play or card-sharping.

cheator *n.* (*also* **cheater**) [SE *cheat*] [mid-16C–mid-17C] (*UK Und.*) one who plays with crooked dice.

cheats *n.*[1] [late 16C–early 17C] money won by dice cheats.

cheats *n.*[2] (*also* **chates**) **1** [late 17C] a waistcoat boasting an ostentatious front, but with a cheaply made (and invisible) back. **2** [late 17C–early 19C] sham sleeves, cuffs or wristbands, used to mask an otherwise dirty shirt.

cheats *n.*[3] *see* CHATS *n.*[1].

cheba *n. see* CHEEB *n.*

chebs *n.* [CHABOBS *n.*] [1990s+] the female breasts.

checaco/chechaco *n. see* CHEECHAKO *n.*

che-che *n.* (*also* **chi-chi**) [clipping of FRENCHIE *n.*[1] (5) or RED CHENKE *under* RED *adj.*] [20C+] (*W.I.*) **1** a poor white. **2** a person with a light complexion and freckles. **3** a cowardly, ugly boy.

check *n.*[1] [SE *check*, a token, a ticket; phr. underpinned by gambling imagery; thus Asbury, *Sucker's Progress* (1938) 18: 'An extraordinary number of the terms, technical and otherwise, which were employed by Faro players in the palmy days of the game have passed into the language [...] and are commonly used by millions who never heard of Faro. Here are some of them: [...] *Pass in his checks*—He cashed in.'] (*US*) **1** [mid-19C–1910s] money. **2** [1920s–60s] $1. **3** [1920s–70s] a measure of a drug, usu. 28g (1oz) in a folded packet. **4** [1980s+] one's personal supply of drugs.

IN PHRASES

❑ **cash in one's checks** *v.* (*also* **cash one's last check, cash in one's cheques**) [late 19C+] (*orig. US*) to die. ❑ **get one's checks** *v.* [late 19C] (*US*) to die. ❑ **hand in one's checks** *v.* (*also* **hand in one's cards**) [mid-19C+] (*US*) to die. ❑ **pass in one's checks** *v.* (*also* **pass in one's counters, ...cheque, pass on one's cheque**) **1** [mid-19C+] (*orig. US*) to die. **2** [1900s] to come to one's limit. ❑ **put one's checks in the rack** *v.* [1930s+] (*US*) to die. ❑ **send in one's checks** *v.* [mid-19C+] (*US*) to die.

check *n.*[2] [SE *check*, to restrain] [1970s+] (*US black*) power, influence.

IN PHRASES

❑ **in check** [1990s+] (*US teen*) under control.

check *v.* **1** [1920s+] (*orig. US*) to look over, to inspect. **2** [1970s+] (*orig. US*) to visit, to see. **3** [1970s+] (*orig. US*) to criticize, to attack verbally. **4** [1980s+] (*W.I./UK black teen*) to see someone, to have a (usu. sexual) relationship with someone; thus *checking*, having a relationship. **5** [1990s+] (*US black*) to kill. **6** [1990s+] (*orig. US*) to assess, to envisage. **7** [2000s] (*US prison*) to fight.

IN PHRASES

❑ **check 'em** [2000s] (*US black*) a phr. apologizing or acknowledging a foolish remark or action. ❑ **check for** *v.* [1990s+] (*W.I./UK black teen*) **1** to hate or dislike someone or something, to avoid, to resist becoming involved with. **2** to like, to be involved with. ❑ **check it (to)** *v.* [1930s+] (*US*) to say goodbye. ❑ **check oneself** *v.* [1960s] (*US*) to compose oneself, to 'get a grip'. ❑ **check someone's chin** *v.* [1990s+] (*US black teen*) to hit on the jaw; such a blow is a *chin-check*. ❑ **check you** (*also* **check you later, ...on the flipflop, ...on the flipside**) [1970s+] (*orig. US black/campus*) goodbye, see you later.

SE in slang uses

IN PHRASES

❑ **check it in** *v.* [the idea of checking possessions into a left-luggage locker] [1990s+] (*US black*) as an imper. used by a mugger to his or her victim, to demand that someone hand over their money, valuables, etc. ❑ **check off** *v.* [he checks his name off the general population] [2000s] (*US prison*) to request protective custody. ❑ **check one's bicycle** *v.* a euph. phr. to disguise one's desire/need to visit the lavatory. ❑ **check one's nerves** *v.* [1940s] (*US black*) to take a grip on oneself, to control one's emotions. ❑ **check someone's oil** *v.* [euph. but note OIL *n.* (1)] **1** [1930s+] (*US*) to have sexual intercourse. **2** [1990s+] to masturbate.

check! *excl.* [1920s+] (*orig. US*) a general term of affirmation, OK, that's right, everything's in order.

checker, the *n.* [that which *checks* everything else] [mid-19C–1910s] (*US*) the ideal, the very thing.

checkerboard *n.* **1** [1920s+] (*US*) a work crew or work gang composed of black and white people. **2** [1960s] (*US*) a place or neighbourhood where both black and white people live or congregate.

check in *v.* [SE *check in*, to register (i.e. at a hotel)] **1** [20C+] (*US*) (*also* **cheque in**) to die. **2** [1960s] (*US*) (*also* **check it in**) to go to bed. **3** [1970s+] (*US*) to say hello. **4** [1990s+] (*UK/US Und.*) to move from the general prison population into protective solitary confinement.

check out *n.* [CHECK OUT *v.*[1] (1)] [1990s+] (*US prison*) an inmate who kills themselves while in prison.

checkout *n.* [CHECK OUT *v.*[2] (1)] [1950s+] (*orig. US*) an interrogatory or investigatory glance.

check out *v.*[1] [SE *check out*, to sign out of a hotel, office etc] **1** [1920s+] (*orig. US*) to die. **2** [1920s+] (*orig. US*) to leave. **3** [1970s] to kill.

check out *v.*[2] **1** [1950s+] (*orig. US*) to look over, to sum up; esp. as excl. *check this out!* **2** [1950s+] (*orig. US*) to work out, to fit in. **3** [1970s] (*W.I.*) for a young man, to date a woman regularly and/or visit her home. **4** [1970s+] to visit. **5** [1980s] to believe, to accept. **6** [1980s+] to take note of.

IN PHRASES

❑ **check it out** *v.* [1980s+] (*US campus*) to look for a partner for romance or sex.

check, please *phr.* [1970s] (*US black*) a phr. indicating that a meeting is concluded.

checks! *excl.* [1960s+] (*US, usu. juv.*) a claim, esp. a claim of first rights to something.

cheddar *n.*[1] [CHEESY *adj.*[2] (5)] [1990s+] (*US campus*) someone who is socially unacceptable, who does not fit in.

cheddar *n.*[2] (*also* **chedda**) [CHEESE *n.*[1] (1)] [1990s+] (*US*) money.

cheder *n.* [Yid. *cheder*, a small room, a study; usu. used as a schoolroom for the teaching of religion] [1970s] (*UK Und.*) a prison cell.

cheeb *n.* (*also* **cheba, cheeba, cheebo**) [CHIBA *n.* (2)] [1960s+] (*US drugs*) marijuana.

cheechako *n.* (*also* **checaco, chechaco, cheechaker, cheechalko**) [Chinook jargon *chee*, new + *chako*, to come; thus 'newcomer'] [late 19C–1960s] a newcomer, a novice, esp. a newly arrived immigrant in the mining districts of northwestern North America.

chee-chee *n.* (*also* **chi-chi**) [south Indian excl. *chi!*, fie! or nonsense! or as onomat. representation of the accent. Y&B note, however: 'there are many well-educated East Indians who are quite free from this mincing accent.' Ironically, the accent appears to have been that expressly taught at the convents and Christian Brothers' schools set up by the Raj to educate the children of such unions. Note Du. *lip-lap*, the equivalent term for Dutch-Javans] [mid-19C+] a derog. term for a half-caste or Eurasian (the child of an English father and Indian mother).

chee-chee *adj.* (*also* **chi-chi, shee shee**) [CHEE-CHEE *n.*] [mid-19C–1960s] having the characteristics of the Eurasian stereotype, esp. the supposed mincing pronunciation, thus pretentious, affected or smart, stylish.

cheek *n.*[1] [mid-19C] a share, a portion.

cheek *n.*[2] [the movement of the *cheeks* when speaking] [mid-19C+] **1** verbal insolence. **2** audacity, impudence; esp. in phr. *have the cheek (to)*, to dare, to have the nerve (to do something). **3** an audacious, forward person.

DERIVATIVES

❑ **cheekiness** *n.* [mid-19C+] audacity, effrontery, impudence. ❑ **cheekish** *adj.* [mid-19C] impudent.

IN PHRASES

❑ **to one's own cheek** [metonymic use of SE *cheek*, the side of the face] [early 19C–1900s] **1** to oneself, for one's own private use. **2** a share or portion.

cheek *v.*[1] [CHEEK *n.*[2] (1)] [mid-19C+] to address in an impudent or insolent manner.

IN PHRASES

❑ **cheek it (out)** *v.* [mid–late 19C] to face down, to brazen out. ❑ **cheek it through** *v.* [late 19C] (*US campus*) to assume an air of (spurious) confidence.

cheek *v.*[2] [SE *cheek*, either of the face, or synon. with buttocks] [1990s+] (*drugs*) to smuggle or hide drugs by placing them in the rectum or mouth.

cheeks *n.*[1] [the *OED* cites a one-off use in 1660, the term is then lost (at least from print) until Jon Bee in 1823 and only resurfaces again in James Joyce's *Ulysses* (1922)] [mid-17C+] the posterior, the buttocks.

IN PHRASES

❑ **ask cheeks near Cunnyborough** [mid-18C–mid-19C] a woman-only phr., equivalent to ASK MY…! *excl.* ❑ **beat cheeks** *v.* [var. on BEAT ASS *v.*] [1990s+] (*US*) to leave (at speed). ❑ **powder someone's cheeks** *v.* [1970s+] (*US gay*) to have anal intercourse.

cheeks *n.*[2] [note synon. 19C naut. jargon *Cheeks the Marine*. In both cases the phr. refers to the buttocks and equates with ASK MY…! *excl.*] [mid-19C] an imaginary person, usu. used in a rude reply to an irritating question.

cheeks! *excl.* [mid–late 19C] a coarse and insulting excl.; synon. ASK MY…! *excl.*

cheeks and ears *n.* [? it covered them all] [early 17C] a form of head-dress, briefly in fashion.

cheeky *adj.* [CHEEK *n.*[2] (2)] **1** [mid-19C+] impudent, esp. in the context of a younger person failing to respect their elder. **2** [1950s] (*Aus.*) bad.

IN COMPOUNDS

❑ **cheeky possum** *n.* [POSSUM *n.* (3)] [1930s+] (*Aus.*) an impudent (young) person.

cheena *n.* [? Sp.; coined by Anthony Burgess in *Clockwork Orange* (1962)] [1990s+] (*US teen*) a woman.

cheeo *n.* [SE *chew*] [1970s+] (*drugs*) marijuana seeds, which are chewed.

cheep *n.* [SE *cheep*, a faint, shrill sound, esp. of a young bird] [late 19C+] a sound, a noise, esp. of complaint; usu. in phr. *not a cheep out of*, not a sound from.

cheep *v.* [SE *cheep*, a faint, shrill sound, esp. of a young bird] [late 19C+] to inform on, to complain.

cheer *n.*

IN PHRASES

❑ **give the cheer** *v.* [late 19C] to greet, to welcome.

cheerer *n.* [late 18C Scot. use] [19C] a revivifying glass of alcohol.

cheerful earful *n.* [ironic] [1940s+] (*US*) unpleasant news.

cheerful giver *n.* [rhy. sl.] [20C+] the human liver.

cheer germ *n.* [2000s] (*N.Z.*) a person who is always negative.

cheeri *phr.* [abbr. of colloq. *cheerio*, goodbye] [1930s+] (*N.Z.*) goodbye.

cheerio *n.* [? *cheers*, a toast] [1950s+] (*N.Z.*) a cocktail sausage, like a frankfurter, as served with drinks.

cheerio *adj.* [SE *cheery*, reinforced by *cheers!*, the toast that precedes that drunkenness] **1** [1910s–30s] cheerful, merry. **2** [1930s+] (*S.Afr.*) tipsy, slightly drunk.

cheerioski *phr.* [colloq. *cheerio*, goodbye + -SKI *sfx*] [1920s–30s] goodbye.

cheers! *excl.* [colloq. *cheers!*, a toast before drinking; also 'thank-you'] **1** [1920s+] an excl. of approval. **2** [1940s+] goodbye [? link to Ital. *ciao*, goodbye].

cheery *adj.* **1** [17C] excellent, first rate. **2** [18C+] drunk.

cheese *n.*[1] [resemblance] **1** [mid-19C+] (*US teen*) money [? play on BREAD *n.*[1] (2) or ? the yellow colour]. **2** as bodily fluids and secretions [underpinned by the smell of over-ripe cheese]. (**a**) [mid-19C+] the smegma that accumulates around the uncircumcised penis, occas. the unwashed labia. (**b**) [1920s+] (*US*) (*also* **body cheese**) secretions found between the toes. **3** in fig. uses, usu. negative. (**a**) [late 19C+] an unpleasant, incompetent, stupid person; usu. ext. as *big cheese, old cheese, piece of cheese, plate of cheese, poor cheese* etc. (**b**) [late 19C+] as (3a) but used joc./affectionately. (**c**) [1900s] (*US*) a fool. (**d**) [1950s] (*US*) nonsense; thus phr. *no cheese*, no bad thing, something 'not to be sniffed at'. (**e**) [1980s+] (*US campus*) something out-of-date. (**f**) [1980s+] (*US campus*) someone or something unattractive, unappealing, undesirable. **4** [late 19C–1910s] (*US*) one's affair, one's concern. **5** uses based on the colour. (**a**) [1970s] (*US*) a light-skinned black person. (**b**) [1990s+] (*drugs*) crack cocaine. (**c**) [2000s] (*US drugs*) a combination of heroin and cold medication crushed into a powder.

IN COMPOUNDS

❑ **cheeseball** *n.* [ult. SE *cheeseball*, a recipe/product made from cheese] [1990s+] (*US campus*) someone or something unattractive, unappealing, undesirable or not attuned to group standards. ❑ **cheese champion** *n.* (*also* **cheese champ**) [SE *champion*/CHAMP *n.*[2] (3)] [1920s+] a particularly useless or second-rate person. ❑ **cheesedick** *n.* [DICK *n.*[1] (5)/DICKHEAD *n.* (1)] [1980s+] (*US*) an obnoxious person. ❑ **cheese dong** *n.* [DONG *n.*[1] (2)] [1980s+] (*US campus*) a stupid, unpleasant person. ❑ **cheesehead** *n.* see separate entry. ❑ **cheeseman** *n.* **1** [1980s+] (*US campus*) a socially inept person. **2** a womanizer [CHEESE *n.*[2] (2)]. ❑ **cheese ridge** *n.* [1990s+] the part of the penis between the glans and the shaft. ❑ **cheese tube** *n.* [1990s+] the urethra. ❑ **cheesy head** *n.* [HEAD *n.* (6a)] [1990s+] a penis that has not been cleansed of smegma.

IN PHRASES

❑ **eat cheese** *v.* [1940s+] (*orig. US black*) to have oral sex with a woman. ❑ **on the cheese** [late 19C–1940s] (*US*) unsatisfactory, in a bad way.

SE in slang uses

IN COMPOUNDS

❑ **cheesebox** *n.* **1** [1930s–50s] (*US*) a run-down, dilapidated vehicle. **2** [1960s] a mass-produced suburban house. **3** [1980s] (*US campus*) a computer; thus *cheese*, software. **4** [1990s+] the head, the mind. ❑ **cheesecake** *n. see* separate entry. ❑ **cheese-cutter** *n.* [resemblance to a cheese knife] **1** [mid-19C] an aquiline nose. **2** [mid-19C] in pl., bandy legs. **3** [late 19C+] a large, square peak on a cap; thus a flat cloth cap. **4** [1960s] the penis. ❑ **cheese dagger** *n.* (*also* **...scraper, ...slicer, ...sticker**) [note US milit. use *cheese-knife*, a sword] [1900s–60s] (*US*) a knife. ❑ **cheese-eater** *n.* [equation of *cheese* with RAT *n.*[1] (1); note Urquhart, *The Complete Works of Rabelais* (1653): 'He chargeth the defendant, that he was a botcher, cheese-eater, and trimmer of man's flesh embalmed', where the term is a general derog.] **1** [late 19C+] (*US*) a toady, a sycophant. **2** [1950s+] (*US*) an informer. **3** [2000s] (*US black*) a subservient black person who courts white affection. ❑ **cheese toaster** *n.* [in an era before grills, one skewered the lump of cheese and held it to the fire] **1** [late 18C–1910s] a sword. **2** [1910s] a bayonet.

IN PHRASES

❑ **make the cheese more binding** *v.* [1910s+] (*US*) to make matters worse.

cheese *n.*[2] [abbr. CHEESE AND KISSES *n.*; but US uses may refer to one who is 'good enough to eat'] **1** [1910s+] (*Aus.*) one's girlfriend or wife. **2** [1950s–70s] (*US campus*) a young woman; thus *check the cheese*, watch women pass by. **3** [1960s+] an attractive young man or woman.

cheese *n.*[3] [CHEESE *v.*[3]] [1960s] a smile.

IN PHRASES

❑ **chuck a cheesy** *v.* [1990s+] (*Aus.*) to grin.

cheese, the *n.* [Persian and Urdu *chiz*, thing. 'The expression used to be common among Anglo-Indians, e.g. "My new Arab is the real *chiz*", i.e. the real thing.' (Y&B). Note Charles Kingsley's punning nonce-word *casein*, the real thing, f. SE *casein*, the basic ingredient of cheese] **1** [mid-19C–1920s] (*also* **real cheese**) just what is wanted. **2** [mid-19C+] (*also* **the real cheese**) the best (of a given type or style), the superlative. **3** [late 19C–1920s] an admirable person, esp. as *the real cheese*. **4** [20C+] an important or influential person, the boss. **5** [1990s+] (*US campus*) someone or something that is outdated, in bad taste.

IN PHRASES

❑ **take the cheese** *v.* [var. on TAKE THE CAKE *v.*] [late 19C+] of a negative circumstance or objectionable person, to surpass, to outdo.

cheese *v.*[1] [SE *cease*/CHEESE IT! *excl.* (1)] **1** [early 19C–1960s] to stop, to leave off; thus *cheese on*, as imper., stop (doing something). **2** [early 19C; 1980s] (*US campus*) to go, to wander in a casual manner. **3** [late 19C] (*US*) to disregard, to ignore. **4** [2000s] (*US black*) to treat badly.

cheese *v.*[2] [ety. unknown] [late 19C] (*US*) to pilfer.

cheese *v.*[3] [the photographer's demand that one 'say cheese' to produce a smile] [1930s+] (*orig. UK public school*) to smile.

cheese *v.*[4] **1** [1940s+] to break wind [the smell]. **2** [1950s+] to ejaculate [ext. use of sense 1]. **3** [1980s+] (*US campus*) to vomit [ext. use of sense 1].

cheese *v.*[5] [*CHEESE-EATER under* CHEESE *n.*[1]] [1970s] (*US*) to play up to, to toady to.

cheese! *excl.* (*also* **cheeses! cheesus! cheese and bread! ...and crackers! ...and crust! ...and rice! cheese on! cheese on bread!**) [mid-19C+] (*US*) a euph. for *Jesus!*

cheese and crackers *n.* [rhy. sl. = KNACKERS *n.*] [1990s+] the testicles.

cheese and kisses *n.* [rhy. sl. = SE *Missus*. Now mainly Aus. and usu. abbr. to CHEESE *n.*[2]] [20C+] one's wife.

cheesecake *n.* [fig. uses of SE *chesecake* as something 'tasty', 'soft' or 'white' + common equation of foods with attractive women] **1** [mid–late 17C] a prostitute. **2** [1930s+] (*orig. US*) pin-up pictures; thus *cheese-caker*, a photographer who specializes in pin-up shots. **3** [1930s+] (*orig. US*) a pin-up girl, a sexy woman [? the photographer's call for the woman to 'Say cheese']. **4** [1940s] a fool. **5** [2000s] (*US black*) a white homosexual [the colour but why homosexual?].

cheesed (off) *adj.* [? euph. for PISSED OFF *adj.*; earlier Liverpool excl. *cheese off!*, run away! stop irritating me!] [1940s+] miserable, annoyed, fed up.

cheese grater *n.* [rhy. sl.] [1990s+] a waiter.

cheesehead *n.* **1** [1910s+] (*US*) an idiot, a fool; also attrib. **2** [1960s+] (*US teen*) a general pej. term, esp. directed at an overly emotional or dramatic person.

cheese it! *excl.* [? SE *cease* or f. proverb, *after cheese (at the end of a meal) comes nothing*. Orig. 19C UK, then Aus. Und. but latterly in general use, esp. juv.] **1** [early 19C+] to stop; esp. as excl. *cheese it!* stop it! **2** [early 19C+] be quiet! **3** [mid-19C] (*UK Und.*) be off! run away!

cheese off *v.*[1] [backform. f. CHEESED (OFF) *adj.*] [1940s+] to annoy.

cheese off *v.*[2] [i.e. to get cheese off someone] [1980s+] (*US campus*) to beg from.

cheeser *n.*[1] [all supposedly smell like a ripe cheese] **1** [19C] a burp. **2** [early 19C] a strong-smelling fart. **3** [late 19C] a chestnut. **4** [1960s–70s] a person who has smelly feet.

cheeser *n.*[2] [CHEESE *n.*[1] (3)] **1** [1970s] (*US gang*) a traitor. **2** [1990s+] (*US campus*) one who is not attuned to the prevailing group standards.

cheeses, the *n.* [resemblance to wedges of cheese] [1940s] the 'utility' mark, made of two capital Cs, meaning 'civilian clothing' plus the date of manufacture.

cheesy *n.*

IN PHRASES

❑ **chuck a cheesy** *v. see under* CHEESE *n.*[3].

cheesy *adj.*[1] [CHEESE, THE *n.* (2)] **1** [mid-19C] fine or showy. **2** [1920s] cowardly.

cheesy *adj.*[2] (*also* **cheezy**) [all f. actual or fig. smell given off by ripe cheese] **1** [mid-19C+] outdated, unfashionable, cheap and nasty. **2** [late 19C+] unwell, peaky. **3** [late 19C+] smelly; esp. [1930s+] (*gay*) referring to a smegma-coated foreskin. **4** [1950s] (*US teen*) disloyal. **5** [1970s+] (*also* **cheesey**) socially unacceptable.

IN PHRASES

❑ **cheesy, sleazy, greasy** [SLEAZY *adj.* + SE *greasy*] [1980s+] (*US campus*) used of a woman seen as promiscuous.

cheesy *adj.*[3] [the colour YELLOW *adj.* (4)] [1920s] cowardly.

cheesy kiss *n.* [rhy. sl.] [20C+] (*Aus.*) a miss, esp. a missed catch at cricket.

cheesy quaver *n.* [rhy. sl.; ult. *Quavers*, the tradename of cheese-flavoured savoury snack] [2000s] **1** a favour. **2** a raver.

cheesy rider *n.* [pun on film title *Easy Rider* (1969)] **1** [1960s–70s] a sycophant. **2** [1990s+] (*US prison*) an informer.

cheeters *n. see* CHEATERS *n.*[2].

cheever *n.* (*also* **cheeva**) [CHEEB *n.*] [1990s+] (*drugs*) marijuana.

cheez whiz *n.* [CHEESE *n.*[1] (3a) + pun on the name of a proprietary US cheese spread] [1980s+] (*US campus*) someone who mistakenly thinks that they are impressive.

cheezy *adj. see* CHEESY *adj.*[2].

chef *n.* **1** [1910s–60s] (*drugs*) one who prepares the pipes in an opium den. **2** [1920s] (*US Und.*) one who runs an illicit still. **3** [1930s] (*US prison*) the executioner in charge of the electric chair. **4** [1940s] opium ashes, residue. **5** [1990s+] one who cooks crack cocaine.

chef *v.* [CHEF *n.* (1)] [1910s–50s] (*US drugs*) to prepare opium for smoking.

chefeneer *n.* [Fr. *chiffonier*, 'a piece of furniture with drawers in which women put away their needlework, cuttings of cloth, etc' (Littré, *Dictionnaire* (1863–72)] [20C+] (*Irish*) a small cupboard-cum-sideboard, often used to hold one's best plates, etc.

chello *phr.* [joc. mispron. or ? link to Ital. *ciao*, hello/goodbye] [1980s+] (*US campus*) a greeting.

Chelsea bun *n.* [rhy. sl.] [1990s+] **1** one's son. **2** the sun.

Chelsea college to a sentry-box *phr.* (*also* **Chelsea Hospital to a sentry-box**) [Chelsea College, the second London Polytechnic, was founded in 1891. It orig. contained the Chelsea Art School] [19C] the longest possible odds.

Chelsea pier *adj.* see BRIGHTON PIER *adj.*

Chelsea smile *n.* [such cuts are inflicted on rival supporters by knives wielded by the more violent section of the fans of Chelsea Football Club] [1970s+] a knife slash that runs from the corner of the mouth up and across the cheek.

Cheltenham (gold) *adj.* [rhy. sl.; ult. *Cheltenham Gold (Cup)*] [1950s+] cold.

chemical *n.* [its manufacture] **1** [1930s+] bad or adulterated narcotics. **2** [1950s+] any chemical drug, as opposed to marijuana etc; often as *chemicals*. **3** [1980s+] (*Aus. prison*) toiletries, shampoo etc. **4** [1980s+] (*drugs*) crack cocaine.

SE in slang uses

IN COMPOUNDS

❑ **chemical head** *n.* [1930s+] (*US black*) hair that has been straightened through the application of a special mixture.

chemise-lifter *n.* [? a nonce-coinage by the Australian writer and comedian Barry Humphries (b.1934), playing on the widely used synon. *shirt-lifter* under SHIRT *n.*] **1** [1960s+] a male homosexual. **2** [1990s+] a lesbian [suggests the 'female' chemise vs. the 'male' *shirt*].

chemisery *n.* [play on SE *misery*] [1980s+] (*US campus*) chemistry.

chemist *n.* [20C+] **1** one who runs an illicit distillery. **2** (*W.I.*) an abortionist.

chemist bill *n.* [dial. *chemist's bill*, a two-edged machete, ult. f. an apothecary's knife, which 'cuts on both sides'] [mid-19C+] (*W.I.*) a deceitful, hypocritical person.

chemistry *n.* [CHEMICAL *n.* (2)] [1990s+] (*US drugs*) the manufacture of drugs, e.g. LSD, crack cocaine, PCP (phencyclidine), with common household items and chemicals often stolen from the local hospital or pharmacy.

chemmed-up *adj.* [CHEMICAL *n.* (2)] [2000s] under the influence of drugs.

chemozzle *n.* see SHEMOZZLE *n.*

chepemans *n.* [*Chepe*, Cheapside + -MANS *sfx*; Cheapside market, ult. f. OE *ceap* or *chepe*, was medieval London's main market, flourishing until Henry III (r.1216–72) decided to diversify food-selling into other areas] [16C] (*UK Und.*) Cheapside Market.

chepooka *n.* [coined by Anthony Burgess in *A Clockwork Orange* (1962); ult. Rus. *chyepookha*, nonsense] [1960s+] (*US teen*) nonsense.

cheque see *also under* US sp. CHECK and combs.

cheque *n.*

SE *cheque*, the lump-sum payment given to a rural worker at the end of his season-long contract, in slang uses

IN COMPOUNDS

❑ **cheque busting** *n.* (*also* **cheque bursting**) [1910s–40s] (*Aus.*) going on a spending spree; thus *cheque-buster/burster*, one who does this. ❑ **cheque-man** *n.* [late 19C+] (*Aus.*) a spendthrift, one who spends his season's wages in a single glorious spree. ❑ **cheque-proud** *adj.* (*also* **c.p.**) [late 19C–1910s] (*N.Z.*) recently paid, and keen to start spending.

IN PHRASES

❑ **bust a cheque** *v.* see *BURST A CHEQUE under* BURST *v.*[1]. ❑ **chequed up** *adj.* [20C+] (*Aus.*) well supplied with money.

Chequer Inn in Newgate Street *n.* see KING'S HEAD INN (IN NEWGATE STREET) *n.*

cher *adj.* [CHERRY *adj.* (8); ult. CHERRY *adj.* (1)] [1960s+] (*US campus*) attractive.

cheri *n.* [Madame Montigny, an actress at the Gymnase in Paris who appeared under the stage name of Rose *Cheri*. 'A singularly pure woman and an angelic actress. Used by upper-class gentlemen to describe their mistresses' (Ware)] [mid-19C] a charming woman.

chermozzle *n.* see SHEMOZZLE *n.*

cherrie *n.* see CHERRY *n.* (2).

cherries *n.*[1] [1920s] (*US*) dollars.

cherries *n.*[2] [rhy. sl.; abbr. CHERRY HOG *n.*] [1950s–80s] greyhound racing tracks.

cherries *n.*[3] [resemblance] [1960s+] (*US*) the female nipples.

cherry *n.* [Williams offers examples of *cherry* in sexual contexts, but none refer to virginity, uses tend to the supposed similarity of the black cherry and female pubic hair, or plays on cherry *stones* and *stones*/testicles] **1** as an image of ripeness. (**a**) [1920s+] (*orig. US*) a female virgin. (**b**) [1920s+] (*gay*) an anal virgin; anal virginity. (**c**) [1920s+] a male virgin; thus *harvest the cherries*, to take a youth and deprive him of his virginity. (**d**) [1930s+] (*orig. US*) the hymen, one's virginity; thus *lose one's cherry*, to lose one's virginity; a phr. also used of males. **2** [1950s+] (*S.Afr.*) (*also* **cherrie**) a woman, a girlfriend. **3** [1960s–70s] in fig. use, the state of being without sex for some time. **4** in non-sexual uses of sense 1. (**a**) [1950s+] (*US*) an old car in near-mint condition. (**b**) [1950s+] (*orig. US milit.*) a novice, e.g. a fresh troop, one who has yet to be 'blooded' in combat, or prisoner serving their first jail sentence. (**c**) [1960s] as ext. of sense 4b, an annoying individual. **5** uses based on the colour (i.e. red) and shape. (**a**) [1930s+] a love bite, usu. on the neck. (**b**) [1940s+] (*US*) the still-glowing stub of a cigarette. (**c**) [1960s+] (*US*) the red revolving light on top of a police car; thus *cherrytop*, a police car. (**d**) [1980s+] a blush. (**e**) [1990s+] the (head of the) penis.

IN COMPOUNDS

❑ **cherry-boy** *n.* [1970s+] (*US*) a male virgin. ❑ **cherry-bust** *n.* [*BUST A CHERRY* below] [1970s] (*US*) the act of losing one's virginity, applicable to both sexes. ❑ **cherry-buster** *n.* [*BUST A CHERRY* below] [1950s+] (*US*) a (young) man who specializes in deflowering virgins. ❑ **cherry farm** *n.* [SE *farm*, a prison] [1960s–70s] (*US*) a prison that houses first-offenders. ❑ **cherryhead** *n.* [2000s] (*US black*) a male who pretends to a level of sophistication he does not have. ❑ **cherry pie** *n.* **1** [late 19C+] a virgin. **2** [late 19C+] a woman. **3** [20C+] the vagina, esp. if the woman is menstruating [+ colour]. ❑ **cherry-pop** *v.* [*POP A CHERRY* below] **1** [1950s+] (*orig. US*) to seduce and deflower virgins, usu. women. **2** [2000s] in fig., non-sexual use. ❑ **cherry prick** *n.* [PRICK *n.* (1)] [20C+] a male virgin. ❑ **cherry queen** *n.* [2000s] (*S.Afr. gay*) a man who likes to deflower male virgins. ❑ **cherry splitter** *n.* [19C–1960s] the penis. ❑ **cherry tree** *n.* [TREE *n.* (2)] [1980s+] a very tall virgin.

IN PHRASES

❑ **bust a cherry** *v.* (*also* **break (a) cherry**) [BUST *v.*[1] (1a)] [1940s+] **1** to deflower someone. **2** to be deflowered; to lose one's virginity. **3** in fig. use, to experience something new. ❑ **cop a cherry** *v.* (*also* **get a cherry**) [COP *v.* (2)] [1910s+] to take a woman's, occas. man's, virginity. ❑ **crack a cherry** *v.* (*also* **pick a cherry**) [CRACK *v.*[2] (2a)] [1960s+] **1** to take a woman's virginity. **2** in fig. sense, to become initiated in a given calling. ❑ **get one's cherry busted** *v.* [BUST *v.*[1] (1)] [1950s+] (*US*) to lose one's virginity, both lit. and fig. use. ❑ **lose one's cherry** *v.* (*also* **break one's cherry**) **1** [1920s+] to lose one's virginity. **2** [1970s+] in fig. use, to be initiated into a new experience. ❑ **pop a cherry** *v.* (*also* **pop someone's cherry**) [POP *v.*[1] (1a)] [1950s+] to deflower a girl or woman, occas. a young man.

SE in slang uses

IN COMPOUNDS

❑ **cherry-bounce** *n.* [its effects] **1** [late 17C–19C] cherry brandy. **2** [mid-18C] brandy mixed with sugar. ❑ **cherry-case** *n.* [made of cherry-wood, or stained a (black) cherry colour] [late 19C] (*Aus.*) a coffin. ❑ **cherry-colour** *adj.* [the term is most used in a cheating trick with cards, in which the trickster bets an innocent victim that he can accurately predict the colour of the next card to appear. Since cherries are both red and black, as are cards, he cannot lose] [mid-19C] red or black. ❑ **cherry-coloured** *adj.* [the usual assumption is red, but black cherries are equally common; thus a *cherry-coloured cat*, a black cat (Grose, 1785)] [late 18C–19C] coloured black or red. ❑ **cherry Leb** *n.* [1970s–80s] (*US drugs*) hashish oil. ❑ **cherry-nob** *n.* see REDCAP *n.* (2). ❑ **cherry-nose** *n.* [SE *sherry* + the effect of excess sherry consumption on the complexion] [1940s] (*S.Afr.*) sherry. ❑ **cherry-top** *n.* [1970s+] (*US*) **1** a police car with a red light on its roof. **2** a police officer. **3** the red light itself.

cherry *adj.* [CHERRY *n.*] **1** [1920s+] (*US*) virgin, virginal. **2** [1920s+] of people, in good health. **3** [1950s+] of goods etc, in mint condition, brand-new. **4** [1950s+] (*orig. milit.*) inexperienced, new, untested. **5** [1960s+] innocent, naïve. **6** [1960s+] devoid of any form of recording equipment. **7** [1970s] of a given experience or action, the very first, initiating; thus *cherry kicks*, the first injection after a former drugs user is freed from prison. **8** [1980s+] (*US campus*) very attractive. **9** [2000s] easy, undemanding.

IN PHRASES

❑ **cherry out** *v.* [1980s+] (*US*) to make as good as new.

cherry *v.* [CHERRY *n.* (5d)] [1980s+] to blush.

cherry *adv.* [joc. pron.] [2000s] very.

cherry ace *n.* [rhy. sl.] [1940s–50s] the face.

cherry blossom kiss *n. see under* BLOSSOM *n.*[2].

cherry-bomb muffler *n. see* MEXICAN MUFFLER *under* MEXICAN *adj.*

cherry flips *n.* [rhy. sl.] [1920s] the lips.

cherry hog *n.* [rhy. sl. = DOGS, THE *n.*] [20C+] a dog, usu. greyhound.

cherry-merry *n.* [? given when one is, or rendering one CHERRY-MERRY *adj.*] [mid-19C] a present of money.

cherry-merry *adj.* [? the *cherry-red* colour of wine + SE *merry*] [late 18C] cheerful, merry, esp. after drinking.

cherry-picker *n.*[1] **1** [1920s–40s] a yokel, a peasant [the typical rural occupation]. **2** [1930s] (*Aus./N.Z./US*) a large, hooked nose, supposedly big enough to hang over a branch as a hook while one picks cherries from the tree. **3** [1960s] (*US*) a pointed shoe.

cherry-picker *n.*[2] [CHERRY *n.* (1)] [1960s+] a seducer of virgins.

cherry-picker *n.*[3] [rhy. sl. = NICKER *n.*[2] (1)] [1970s+] £1.

cherry-pipe *n.* [rhy. sl. = CHERRY-RIPE *n.*[2]] [late 19C] a woman.

cherry red *n.* [rhy. sl.] [1990s+] the head.

cherry reds *n.* [the colour of a particular style] [1960s+] Doctor Martens boots, as worn as part of the skinhead uniform.

cherry-ripe *n.*[1] [their uniforms] **1** [late 18C–early 19C] a Bow Street Runner. **2** [mid–late 19C] a footman dressed in red plush.

cherry-ripe *n.*[2] [SE *cherry*/CHERRY *n.* (1) + SE *ripe*, the implication is of virginity, albeit temporary] [mid–late 19C] (*UK Und.*) a woman.

cherry-ripe *n.*[3] [rhy. sl.] [mid-19C+] a pipe.

cherry-ripe *n.*[4] [rhy. sl. = TRIPE *n.*[2]] [20C+] nonsense.

cherry tart *n. see* RASPBERRY TART *n.*

cherubim *n.* [joc. ref. to the line 'To Thee cherubim and seraphim continually do cry' in the *Te Deum*; a similar pun is seen in Ward, *The London Spy* (1699), describing a whore as a 'cherubimical lass'] **1** [late 18C] a whingeing child. **2** [mid-19C] a choirboy [adds the choirboy's supposedly angelic persona].

cheryl *adj.* [? joc. pron.] [2000s] (*S.Afr. gay*) cheerful.

Cheshire, the *n.* [brand-specific var. on CHEESE, THE *n.*] [late 19C–1900s] the best, the ideal.

chesky *n.* [Czech *czezki*, pron. chesky] [20C+] (*US*) a derog. term for a Czech immigrant.

chest *n.*

IN COMPOUNDS

❑ **chest-plaster** *n.* [it 'bandages' the sometimes less than spotless shirt front] [late 19C] a flat cravat that covers the shirt front between the coat and the throat. ❑ **chest-pounder** *n.* [the ritual tapping of the chest that accompanies statements of *Mea culpa*] [1930s] (*US*) a Roman Catholic. ❑ **chest-puppy** *n.* [PUPPIES *n.* (3)] [1990s+] (*Aus.*) the female breast.

chest *adj.* [1900s] of a person, puffed-up, self-satisfied.

IN PHRASES

❑ **get chest** *v.* (*also* **go chest**) [1970s] (*US black*) to look for a fight; to fight. ❑ **I'm chest not breast** [1940s–60s] (*US black/teen*) a statement of one's masculinity used to deny suggestions that one is weak/effeminate.

chester *n.* [? CHESTER (THE) MOLESTER *n.*] **1** [1940s] (*US Und.*) a second-rate criminal. **2** [1990s+] (*US campus*) a socially inept person.

Chester (the) Molester *n.* [note the cartoon 'Chester the Molestor' by Dwayne Tinsley (1945–2000) publ. in Hustler mag] [1980s+] (*US campus/Und.*) a child abuser, a sex criminal.

Chestie *n.* [abbr.] [1980s+] (*S.Afr.*) a Chesterfield cigarette.

chestily *adv.* [CHESTY *adj.* (1)] [1900s–30s] arrogantly, in a conceited way.

chestnut *n.* [the term emerged *c.*1880 but appears to have originated in the play *Broken Sword* (1816) by W. Dimond. The relevant passage reads: 'Zavior: When suddenly from the thick boughs of a cork tree. Pablo: (Jumping up.) A chestnut, Captain, a chestnut. Captain, this is the twenty-seventh time I have heard you relate this story, and you invariably said, a chestnut, till now'] [late 19C+] (*orig. US*) **1** an old, much-repeated joke that has long-since lost any real humour. **2** any anecdote (not necessarily true) that is often repeated. **3** anything once popular, now hackneyed and unfashionable. **4** a scheme, a trick.

chestnut *v.* [CHESTNUT *n.*] [1900s] to come out with an oft-repeated anecdote, homily or joke.

chestnuts *n.* [pun on SE *chest* + *nuts*/NUTS *n.*[2] (1)] [1950s–70s] the female breasts.

chesty *adj.* [SE *chest*; note US military hero 'Chesty' Pullar] **1** [19C+] (*US*) arrogant, conceited; thus *chestiness*, arrogance. **2** [20C+] pugnacious, aggressive. **3** [1910s+] proud. **4** [1950s+] of a woman, having prominent breasts; thus as a term of address.

chesty *adv.* [CHESTY *adj.*] [late 19C+] (*US*) arrogantly, aggressively.

chete *n. see* CHEAT *n.*

'chete *n.* [abbr.] [2000s] (*UK black*) a machete.

chev *see under* CHIV.

chevalier Atkins *n.* [SE *chevalier*, a Knight + TOMMY ATKINS *n.* (1)] [late 19C–1900s] a generic term for the typical private soldier in the British army.

cheveaux *n. see* SHIVOO *n.*

chevie *n. see* CHEVY (CHASE) *n.*

Chevvy *n.* (*also* **Chev, Chevy, Chevvie, Chivy**) [abbr.] [1920s+] (*orig. US*) a Chevrolet automobile.

chevy *see also under* CHIV.

chevy *n.* [? rhy. sl.; *Chevrolet* = gay] [2000s] (*US black*) a homosexual male.

chevy (chase) *n.* (*also* **chevie, chivvy chase**) [rhy. sl.; ult. the proper name *Chevy Chase*, the site of a celebrated 17C border skirmish and thus the subject and title of a popular ballad] [mid-19C+] the face.

chew *n.* **1** [mid-19C+] a quid of chewing tobacco. **2** [20C+] (*S.Afr.*) food. **3** [1910s] (*US*) talk, shouting.

IN PHRASES

❑ **swap chews** *v. see* SWAP SPIT(S) *under* SWAP *v.*

chew *v.* **1** [mid-19C+] (*orig. US*) to eat. **2** [late 19C+] (*US*) (*also* **chew one's cabbage, ...yap**) to talk. **3** [20C+] (*US*) to embarrass. **4** [20C+] (*US*) to argue, to protest. **5** [1920s] to stop, to 'swallow'. **6** [1930s+] (*US*) to fellate. **7** [1940s+] to perfom cunnilingus. **8** [1940s+] (*US black*) to abuse, to attack verbally or physically. **9** [1950s] in fig. use of sense 1, to annoy, to 'eat'. **10** [1990s+] (*US campus*) to be bad, to be disappointing.

SE in slang uses

IN COMPOUNDS

❑ **chew-water** *n.* [dial. *chew-water*, left-over cooking water, thrown out for the pigs] [1940s+] (*W.I.*) thin, tasteless soup.

IN PHRASES

❑ **chew down** *v.* [joc. use of SE + ref. to *jew down* at JEW *v.*] [1930s–60s] (*US*) to cheat financially. ❑ **chew face** *v.* [note 1887 *Bulletin* (Sydney) 15 Oct. 12/1: 'In the absense of her parson-bestowed spouse she gradually evolved a partiality for chewing the radiant hasher's eyebrow, and developed an undue fondness for the encirclement of her waist by his humerus, ulna and radius'] [1930s+] (*US campus*) to kiss. ❑ **chew into dishcloths** *v.* [late 19C–1900s] (*US*) to destroy completely, to annihilate. ❑ **chew (it) over** *v.* (*also* **chew (on)**) [mid-19C+] to discuss, to consider, to ponder. ❑ **chew lead** *v.* [LEAD *n.* (1)] [19C] (*US*) to be shot to death. ❑ **chew nails** *v.* [1970s] (*US campus*) to be enraged. ❑ **chew 'n' spew** *n.* **1** [1960s+] (*Aus./US*) a cheap restaurant. **2** [1980s–90s] (*Aus. prison*) any ready-cooked meal, e.g. hamburgers, fish and chips. **3** [1980s+] (*Aus. prison*) prison food. **4** [1980s+] (*Aus. prison*) prison officers. ❑ **chew on** *v.* **1** [1960s+] (*US*) to nag, to pester. **2** *see* CHEW (IT) OVER above. ❑ **chew one's bit** *v.* [SE *champ at the bit*, (of a horse) to be restive] [20C+] (*US*) **1** to be anxious or upset. **2** to argue or talk loudly. ❑ **chew one's cabbage** *v. see* sense 2 above. ❑ **chew one's cud** *v. see* separate entry. ❑ **chew one's own tobacco** *v.* (*also* **chew one's own meat**) [mid-19C–1900s] (*US*) to rely on oneself. ❑ **chew one's tobacco twice** *v.* [1920s] **1** (*US*) to be mean, to be tight-fisted. **2** to ponder an action or opinion before committing oneself. ❑ **chew one's yap** *v. see* sense 2 above. ❑ **chew (on) someone's ass** *v.* (*also* **chew (on) someone's arse, chew someone's ass (out), ...can off, ...tail**) **1** [1910s+] (*orig. US milit.*) to tell off, to berate, to criticize severely; thus *ass-chewing*, a severe scolding. **2** [1980s] to attack physically. ❑ **chew out** *v. see* separate entry. ❑ **chew over** *v. see* CHEW UP *v.* (1). ❑ **chew someone's balls off** *v.* (*also* **chew someone's ballocks off, ...nackers off, ...the balls off, ...the ballocks off**) [BALLS *n.* (1); BALLOCKS *n.* (2); KNACKERS *n.*] [1920s+] to reprimand severely. ❑ **chew someone's ear** *v. see* separate entry. ❑ **chew the beef** *v. see under* BEEF *n.*[2]. ❑ **chew the boot** *v.* [1940s–50s] (*US*) to converse, to talk something over. ❑ **chew the carpet** *v. see* separate entries. ❑ **chew the cheese** *v.* [1980s+] (*US campus*) to vomit. ❑ **chew the cud** *v. see* separate entry. ❑ **chew the fat** *v. see* separate entry. ❑ **chew (the) fish** *v. see* EAT (THE) FISH *under* FISH *n.*[1]. ❑ **chew the grease** *v.* [var. on CHEW THE FAT *v.*] [1910s–20s] to talk something over. ❑ **chew the Irish bubblegum** *v.* [1980s] to chatter foolishly, to talk nonsense. ❑ **chew the rag** *v. see* separate entry. ❑ **chew the rug** *v.* **1** [late 19C+] to gossip, to chatter. **2** [1970s+] (*US*) to lose emotional control, to suffer a temper tantrum. ❑ **chew up** *v. see* separate entry.

IN EXCLAMATIONS

❑ **chew on this!** (*also* **chew on it! ...that!**) [*this/that/it* is the penis] [1930s+] an obscene retort. ❑ **go chew on a chitlin!** *see* GO AND BARK UP A TREE! *under* BARK *v.*[2].

chewallop *adv.* [var. on KERWHALLOP *v.*] [mid-19C+] when falling or hitting, hard and suddenly, also as *n.*, a fall or dive.

chewed *adj.* (*also* **chawed**) [CHEW *v.*] [19C+] (*US*) **1** embarrassed; overcome by emotion. **2** angry, annoyed, defeated.

chewed-up *adj.* [CHEW *v.*] **1** [mid-19C+] nervous, out of sorts. **2** [1910s+] suffering from a telling-off.

chewers *n.* [1900s–40s] (*US black*) teeth, real or false.

chewie *n.* (*also* **chewy**) [abbr.] [1920s+] (*orig. Aus.*) chewing gum; thus *chewie on your boot*, a phr. used by barrackers at football matches in an attempt to put off a place-kicker by suggesting that he has chewing gum on his boot.

chewing *n.* (*also* **chewings**) [20C+] (*US*) food.

chewing gum *n.* [CHEW *v.* (2)] [1920s] (*US*) empty, meaningless chatter.

chewing gums *n.* [1990s+] (*US teen*) very tight shorts, i.e. they have to 'stretch'.

chewing match *n.* [CHEW *v.* (4)] [20C+] (*US*) an argument.

chewings *n. see* CHEWING *n.*

chew out *v.* [ext. of CHEW *v.* (8)] [1930s+] (*orig. US*) to tell off, to harangue.

chew someone's ear *v.* (*also* **chew someone's lug**) [SE *chew* + *ear*/LUG *n.*[1]] (*Aus.*) **1** [late 19C–1900s] to cadge, to beg. **2** [late 19C+] to talk intensely. **3** [late 19C+] (*also* **chew someone's ear off, ...ear out**) to nag, to talk tediously at someone.

chew the carpet *v.*[1] (*also* **eat the carpet**) [1950s+] (*US*) to lose emotional control, to suffer a temper tantrum.

chew the carpet *v.*[2] *see* MUNCH THE CARPET *under* CARPET *n.*[1].

chew the cud *v.* **1** [17C+] (*also* **chew one's cud**) to ponder, to think something over. **2** [mid-19C–1900s] to chew tobacco; thus *cud-chewer*, one who chews tobacco.

chew the fat *v.* (*also* **chaw the fat, shoot the fat**) [rhy. sl. = *have a chat*] **1** [late 19C+] to converse, to talk something over; as *n.*, a garrulous person. **2** [1910s–30s] to complain; to be resentful.

chew the rag *v.* [RAG *n.*[1] (3a); orig. use held overtones of grumbling and complaining, but this vanished by the 1920s] [late 19C+] (*US*) **1** to gossip, to chatter; thus n. *rag chewing*. **2** to grumble, to complain. **3** to argue, to speak irresponsibly.

chewtobaccy *n.* [cf. synon. Bahamas dial. *chewbaca*] [mid-19C–1940s] (*US black*) chewing tobacco.

chew up *v.* **1** [mid-19C+] (*US*) (*also* **chew over**) to defeat, to overcome; ext. as [1940s+] *chew up and spit out*. **2** [1910s+] (*US*) to scold harshly, to reprimand severely. **3** [1980s] (*S.Afr.*) to upset.

chewy *n.*[1] [? one chews at it as one smokes] [1990s+] (*US black/drugs*) a cigar or marijuana-filled cigar, rolled with cocaine powder (rather than crack).

IN PHRASES

❑ **do the chewy** *v.* [? one gnashes ones teeth/chews one's lips; ? the character Chewbacca or *Chewie* from the *Star Wars* films] [1980s] (*Aus.*) to become angry.

chewy *n.*[2] *see* CHEWIE *n.*

Chi *n.* [abbr.] [late 19C+] (*US*) *Chicago*; also attrib. (cf. CHI-TOWN *n.*).

chi *n.*[1] [abbr. *CHINESE H under* CHINESE *adj.* or *CHINA WHITE under* CHINA *n.*] [1980s+] (*drugs*) heroin.

chi *n.*[2] *see* CHAI *n.*[1].

chiack *see under* CHI-IKE.

chian *n. see* CHRISTACRUTCHIAN *n.*

chib *see also under* CHIV.

chib *n.* [CHIV *n.*[3]] [late 19C] the face.

chiba *n.* (*also* **chiba-chiba**) [? all linked to CHIVA *n.*] **1** [1970s] (*US*) an informer. **2** [1970s+] (*drugs*) high-potency marijuana; spec. from Colombia but used for any powerful marijuana. **3** [1990s+] heroin.

chibe *v. see* CHIV *v.*

chibs *n.* [var. on CHIPS *n.*[2]] [1970s] (*US/P.R.*) the buttocks.

Chic *n.* [abbr.] [1900s–30s] (*US Und.*) *Chicago*.

Chicago *n.*

IN PHRASES

❑ **from Chicago** **1** [1950s] (*US Und.*) of a fellow criminal, acceptable, trustworthy [Chicago's association with gangster Al Capone]. **2** [1980s+] (*US campus*) unaware of what's going on, behaving like an 'air-head' [play on Chicago as the WINDY CITY *n.* (1)].

Chicago *adj.* used in combs., esp. with ref. to Chicago as a centre of 1920s–30s gangsterism.

IN COMPOUNDS

❑ **Chicago atomizer** *n. see* CHICAGO TYPEWRITER below. ❑ **Chicago bankroll** *n.* [1960s+] (*US black/gambling*) a show bankroll, with a large denomination note rolled around lesser ones. ❑ **Chicago black** *n.* (*also* **Chicago green**) [1960s+] (*drugs*) varieties of marijuana, characterized by the colour, popular (and presumably grown) in and around Chicago. ❑ **Chicago chicken** *n.* [the meat-packing industry of the city] [late 19C] (*US Western*) salt pork or bacon. ❑ **Chicago lightning** *n.* [the city's reputation as a centre of gangland warfare] [1920s–30s] gunfire. ❑ **Chicago mowing machine** *n.* [1940s] (*US Und.*) a machinegun. ❑ **Chicago overcoat** *n.* [the practice of sealing corpses in cement prior to disposing of them at sea] [1930s+] (*US*) a coffin; thus fig., death, murder. ❑ **Chicago piano** *n.* [note WW2 RN jargon *Chicago piano*, a multiple pom-pom] [1940s+] a Thompson sub-machinegun, which achieved notoriety as the preferred weapon of Chicago gangsters in the 1920s and later. ❑ **Chicago pills** *n.* [play on SE *pill*/PILL *n.* (1e)] [1940s] (*US Und.*) bullets. ❑ **Chicago typewriter** *n.* (*also* **Chicago atomizer**) [1940s+] a Thompson sub-machinegun.

chicalean *adj.* [ety. unknown; ? SE *chic*] [1990s+] (*US campus*) excellent, stylish, worthy of admiration.

chice *n.* (*also* **chice-am-a-trice, chice-a-trice**) [SHICE *n.* (2)] [19C] (*UK tramp*) nothing, no good.

chicharra *n. see* CHIRA *n.*

chi-chi *see also under* CHEE-CHEE.

chi-chi *n.* [Jap. *chi-chi*, milk, the breast] [1960s+] (*US*) the female breast; usu. in pl.

chichi *adj.* (*also* **shishi**) [Fr. *chi-chi*; ? link to Rom. *chichi*, nothing] **1** [1920s–70s] homosexual; pertaining to homosexuality. **2** [1930s+] affected, pretentious, 'pretty-pretty'.

chichibangas *n.* [CHI-CHI *n.* + BONGOS *n.*] [1960s+] (*US*) the female breasts.

Chi-city *n. see* CHI-TOWN *n.*

chick *n.*[1] [SE *chicken*, lively, perky and 'good enough to eat'; feminine senses underpinned by the perceived vulnerability of SE *chicken*] **1** [17C; 19C] (*US*) a man. **2** [mid-19C+] a young woman. **3** [late 19C] a novice. **4** [1940s+] a girlfriend. **5** [1940s+] a male prostitute. **6** [1950s+] (*also* **chicky**) a term of address to a (young) woman. **7** [1960s] (*US prison*) a young man, or woman, prey for prison homosexuals.

IN COMPOUNDS

❑ **chick bum** *n.* [2000s] a child. ❑ **chick magnet** *n. see under* -MAGNET *sfx.* ❑ **chick man** *n.* [1960s] (*US Und.*) a pimp. ❑ **chickshit** *adj. see* CHICKENSHIT *adj.* (1). ❑ **chick-hearted** *adj. see* CHICKEN-HEARTED *adj.*

chick *n.*[2] [mispron. Fr. *chic*] [late 19C] fashionableness, smartness, *chic*.

chick *adj.* [CHICK *n.*[1] (2)] (*orig. US*) **1** [1950s+] composed of women. **2** [1990s+] of interest to girls or women, e.g. *chick movie, chick lit*.

chickabiddy *n.* [nursery use, ult. rural dial.; note BIDDY *n.*[1] (1)] **1** [late 18C–early 19C] a young woman. **2** [late 18C+] a chicken. **3** [late 19C] a young man, in ironic address.

chickadee *n.* [ext. of CHICK *n.*[1] (2); also SAmE *chickadee*, a type of tit-mouse] (*orig. US*) **1** [late 19C–1940s] (*also* **chickaweewee**) a young man; often ironic address to a man. **2** [20C+] a young woman.

chickaleary *adj.* [? CHEEKY *adj.* (1) + LEERY *adj.* (1) + COVE *n.* (1); popularized by the song 'The Chickaleery Cove' by the music-hall star Alfred 'The Great Vance' Stephens (1839–88)] [mid-19C–1900s] artful, knowing; usu. as *chickaleary cove*, an artful, knowing, 'clever' fellow.

chick-chick *adj.* [CHICKEN *n.* (2a)] [1950s] (*US*) cowardly.

chickee *n. see* CHICKIE *n.* (1).

chickee! *excl.* (*also* **chickie! chicky!**) [CHICKEN *n.* (1), i.e. one is acting in a cowardly manner] [1910s+] (*US*) a warning of the impending approach of authority – whether police officer, parent or teacher – and thus a command to stop whatever one is doing that might cause that authority to act against one (cf. CHIGGERS! *excl.*).

IN PHRASES

❑ **lay chickie** *v.* (*also* **lay chic, ...chick, ...chickee, keep chickie, keep chips, stand chickie**) [1930s+] (*US*) to maintain a lookout (during a crime). ❑ **play chickie** *v.* (*also* **play chicky**) [1940s+] (*US*) to maintain a lookout during a crime.

chicken *n.* [fig. uses of SE *chicken*] **1** as a woman. (**a**) [late 16C; 18C+] a young woman, esp. [late 18C–mid-19C] a prostitute; thus *chicken-chaser, chicken-hustler*, a womanizer; also in direct address. (**b**) [20C+] (*US*) young women considered collectively; thus sexual intercourse with one. (**c**) [1980s] (*US black*) an unattractive (old) woman [on the bad = good model, the direct reverse of the white terms]. (**d**) [1980s] (*US black*) an aggressive woman [on the bad = good model]. **2** the stereotype of the chicken as a cowardly creature. (**a**) [early 17C+] a timid creature, a coward. (**b**) [late 18C+] a weak or naïve person. (**c**) [1930s+] (*US black*) a sheepish, foolish grin. (**d**) [1950s–60s] (*US*) cowardice. (**e**) [1950s+] (*orig. US teen*) a contest of nerve in which two cars drive towards either each other or an obstacle, cliff edge etc – the loser being the driver who turns aside first; thus any form of foolish dare-devilry; also ext. to fig. use. **3** in the context of size. (**a**) [mid-17C+] used as a direct address to a child or young woman. (**b**) [early 18C–1950s] a young man, often as a direct address; as *this chicken*, self-referential. (**c**) [mid-19C] a pint pot, the smaller container of the HEN AND CHICKENS *under* HEN *n.* **4** as an image of sexual vulnerability and/or youth [note 19C US milit. jargon *chicken*, a close friend or young 'buddy']. (**a**) [early 19C+] an underage girl, in a sexual context. (**b**) [mid-19C] anything young, small or insignificant. (**c**) [mid-19C] a novice, esp. a young boxer. (**d**) [late 19C+] (*gay*) an underage boy, or such boys considered collectively. (**e**) [1940s–60s] (*US Und.*) a kidnap victim. (**f**) [1940s+] a young man used as a lure (usu. to blackmail or pressurize gay men) by swindlers. (**g**) [1960s+] a child who is used for paedophiliac sexual exploitation. (**h**) [1960s+] a young lesbian. (**i**) [2000s] a young heterosexual male prostitute, servicing only women. **5** [mid-19C] (*US*) a thing, a phenomenon. **6** [1900s–40s] (*US*) bacon, sausages. **7** [1950s] a person, no cowardice is implied. **8** *see* CHICKENSHIT *n.* (5).

in sexual contexts

IN COMPOUNDS

❑ **chicken-butcher** *n. see* separate entry. ❑ **chicken-chaser** *n.* [1920s] (*US*) a womanizer. ❑ **chicken-chasing** *n.* [2000s] (*US*) pursuing underage boys. ❑ **chicken dinner** *n.* **1** [1940s] (*US black*) an attractive young woman. **2** [1970s–80s] (*US gay*) a young or underage boy, in the context of his being the subject of fellatio; thus *have a chicken dinner*, to fellate an underage boy. ❑ **chicken eyes** *n.* [1940s] a womanizer. ❑ **chicken fancier** *n.* (*US*) **1** [1910s] a womanizer. **2** [1960s] (*also* **chicken-freak**) a male homosexual paedophile. ❑ **chicken-hawk** *n. see* separate entry. ❑ **chicken inspector** *n.* [1920s+] (*US*) a womanizer, a lady-killer. ❑ **chicken man** *n.* **1** [19C] a paedophile. **2** [1980s+] (*Aus. prison*) one who has been jailed for bestiality. ❑ **chicken-pox** *n.* [pun on SE; there is no apparent link to the POX *n.*[1] (1)] [1960s+] (*US gay*) the urge to have sex with underage boys. ❑ **chicken queen** *n.* [-QUEEN *sfx* (3)] [1960s+] (*US gay*) an older homosexual man who prefers sex with teenage boys. ❑ **chicken ranch** *n.* (*also* **chicken-house**) [the original mid-19C *Chicken Ranch* was at Gilbert, Texas. One ety. suggests that the clients, mainly local farmers, paid for their pleasures with chickens, but more likely is a use of sense 3a above] [1960s+] a brothel. ❑ **chicken rustler** *n.* [1970s] (*US gay*) a male homosexual who has been placed in charge of underage boys, e.g. a scoutmaster or choirmaster.

IN PHRASES

❑ **chicken of the sea** *n.* [play on brandname of canned tuna] [1970s+] (*US gay*) a young sailor.

in the context of cowardice or weakness

IN COMPOUNDS

❑ **chicken fight** *n.* [1930s] (*US*) a contest of nerves. ❑ **chicken gizzard** *n.* [mid-19C] (*US*) a coward. ❑ **chicken-gutted** *adj.* [1950s+] (*US*) cowardly. ❑ **chickenheart(ed)** *see* separate entries. ❑ **chicken-liver(ed)** *see* separate entries. ❑ **chicken run** *n.* (*also* **chickie-run**) [1950s+] a teenage virility ritual involving the driving of two cars at high speed towards each other, or towards a dangerous obstacle; the first one to turn aside or brake is 'chicken'.

IN PHRASES

❑ **go chicken** *v. see* CHICKEN (OUT) *v.* ❑ **play chicken** *v.* [1950s+] **1** to challenge another person by attempting to see who 'cracks' first in a given situation. **2** to indulge in dangerous games. **3** [1970s+] (*US black*) to intrude on another (man's) sexual advances. [fig. use of sense 1, i.e. the intruder 'dares' his rival].

general uses

IN COMPOUNDS

❑ **chicken coop** *n.* (*US*) **1** [1900s–10s] any small place. **2** [1940s] (*US Und.*) a women's prison. **3** [1960s] a police car or patrol wagon. **4** [1970s] an outside lavatory. **5** [1970s+] (*US gay*) any place filled with attractive young men, e.g. a basketball game.

IN PHRASES

❑ **dead chicken** *n. see under* DEAD *adj.* ❑ **no chicken** [early

18C+] a phr. describing someone, often a woman, who is no longer young (or attractive). ❑ **that's the chicken** [1910s] (*Aus.*) a general term of approbation.

SE in slang uses

IN COMPOUNDS

❑ **chickenbone special** *n.* [the bags of homemade fried chicken taken by Southern blacks on railroad trips; segregation kept them from using the whites-only dining cars] [1950s] (*US black*) anything second-rate, inferior, cheap and unattractive. ❑ **chicken-breasted** *adj.* [late 18C–early 19C] of a woman, having very small breasts. ❑ **chickenbrain(ed)** *see* separate entries. ❑ **chicken-butcher** *n. see* separate entry. ❑ **chicken butt** *n.* [BUTT *n.*[1] (1a); its innate insignificance] [1960s] (*US black*) nothing, no matter, forget it; used in response to the query *what's up?* ❑ **chicken change** *n. see* CHICKENFEED *n.* (1). ❑ **chicken cock** *n.* [regional AmE *chicken cock*, a cockerel] [1920s–30s] (*US black*) bootleg bourbon. ❑ **chicken crap** *adj. see* CHICKENSHIT *adj.* (1). ❑ **chicken dribble** *n. see* CHICKENFEED *n.* (2). ❑ **chicken-eater** *n.* [members of the congregation would give the preacher roast chicken for his Sunday lunch] (*US*) **1** [1950s+] an unprofessional, part-time lay preacher. **2** [1960s–70s] a Methodist. ❑ **chickenfeed** *n. see* separate entry. ❑ **chicken fixings** *n.* (*also* **chicken fixins**) [the trimmings that accompany a roast chicken] [mid-19C–1910s] (*US*) trifles, small possessions. ❑ **chicken-fucker** *n.* [1950s+] (*US*) a general derog. term; often intensified as *bald-headed chicken-fucker*. ❑ **chicken-hammed** *adj.* [18C–early 19C] bandy-legged. ❑ **chicken hazard** *n.* [early 19C] a gambling table for small-time players. ❑ **chicken hockey** *n.* [HOCKIE *n.* (1)] [1970s] (*US*) one's fig. intestines, innards, i.e. the 'stuffing', the 'daylights'; usu. in phr. *kick/knock the chicken-hockey out of*. ❑ **chicken-lifter** *n.* [LIFT *v.* (1a)] [late 19C–1900s] (*US*) a chicken thief; thus any form of petty thief. ❑ **chicken-lips** *n.* [2000s] (*US black*) a white person. ❑ **chicken money** *n.* [var. on CHICKENFEED *n.*] [19C] (*US*) spending money, small change. ❑ **chicken nabob** *n.* [SE *chicken*, diminutive ('borrowed from the chicken turtle' notes Grose (1796), who defines 'moderate' as £50,000–60,000) + *nabob*, one who has returned from India with great wealth, ult. f. Urdu *nawab*, deputy governor] [late 18C–early 19C] a merchant who has returned from India with a moderate rather than a magnificent fortune. ❑ **chicken-neck** *v.* [the similar action of the fowl] [1990s+] (*US*) to move one's head rapidly from side to side. ❑ **chicken-plucking** *adj. see* separate entry. ❑ **chicken poo-poo** *adj. see* CHICKENSHIT *adj.* (3). ❑ **chicken-preacher** *n.* [abbr. *chicken-eating preacher, see* CHICKEN-EATER above] [20C+] (*US*) an unprofessional, part-time lay preacher. ❑ **chicken scratch(ing)** *see* separate entries. ❑ **chickenshit** *see* separate entries. ❑ **chicken-spanking** *n.* [1950s] (*US*) sexual intercourse with a chicken. ❑ **chicken swoop** *n.* [1980s] (*US Und.*) the act of stealing a vulnerable person's bag or purse. ❑ **chickenstuff** *n. see* CHICKENSHIT *n.* (2). ❑ **chicken thief** *n.* **1** [1910s–40s] (*Aus.*) (*also* **chicken snatcher**) a petty thief. **2** [1920s] a derog. form of address, sometimes used affectionately. ❑ **chicken tracks** *n.* [late 19C+] (*US*) illegible handwriting. ❑ **chicken walk** *n.* (*UK prison*) an exercise yard.

IN PHRASES

❑ **does a chicken have lips?** *see* DOES A BEAR SHIT IN THE WOODS? IS THE POPE A CATHOLIC? *phr.* ❑ **gone chicken** *n.* (*also* **gone chuck**) [GONE *adj.*[1] (2)] [early 19C+] (*US*) a doomed person, a 'lost soul'. ❑ **where the chicken has the axe** [1910s] in the neck.

chicken *adj.* [CHICKEN *n.*] **1** [late 18C+] petty, insignificant. **2** [1930s+] (*also* **chicken-ass**) cowardly, timid. **3** [1960s+] (*gay*) underage, boyish, inexperienced.

chicken *v.* [CHICKEN *n.* (2c)] [1930s] (*US black*) to grin sheepishly.

chicken *adv.* [CHICKEN *n.* (2)] [1940s+] cowardly, scared.

chicken! *excl.* [CHICKEN *n.* (2)] [1950s+] (*orig. US*) a derisive cry, coward!

chicken and rice *adj.* [rhy. sl.] [2000s] nice.

chicken-ass *adj. see* CHICKEN *adj.* (2).

chickenbrain *n.* [CHICKEN-BRAINED *adj.*] [1980s+] (*US*) a fool.

chicken-brained *adj.* [SE *chicken*/CHICKEN *adj.* (1) + sfx *-brain*] [late 17C; 1910s+] stupid.

chicken-butcher *n.*[1] [late 18C+] a poulterer.

chicken-butcher *n.*[2] [CHICKEN *n.* (1a)] [1920s–40s] (*US campus*) a womanizer.

chickenfeed *n.* **1** [mid-19C+] (*also* **chicken change**) small change. **2** [20C+] (*also* **chicken-dribble**) derisorily small amounts of money or anything else. **3** [1930s] (*US*) nonsense, rubbish.

chicken-hawk *n.* [CHICKEN *n.* (4) + SE *hawk*] (*orig. US*) **1** [1960s+] an older male homosexual with a preference for young boys. **2** [1960s+] an older man who prefers teenage girls for sex. **3** [1990s+] in fig. use, a general predator.

chickenhead *n.*[1] (*also* **chicken's head**) [SE *chicken*/CHICKEN *n.*] (*US*) **1** [1910s+] a fool. **2** [1960s+] an aggressive, unpleasant woman. **3** [1980s] a woman with little or no hair. **4** [1980s] a woman with unruly, unkempt hair. **5** [1990s+] a stupid, immature girl. **6** [1990s+] a fellatrix. **7** [1990s+] a promiscuous woman. **8** [1990s+] (*US black*) an unattractive woman.

chickenhead *n.*[2] [the chicken's bobbing head and constant squawking] [1990s+] (*US teen*) **1** one who talks a lot. **2** a crack addict.

chickenheart *n.* [CHICKEN-HEARTED *adj.*] [mid-19C+] a coward.

chicken-hearted *adj.* (*also* **chick-hearted**) [SE *chicken*/CHICKEN *n.* (2) + SE *hearted*] [16C+] cowardly.

chicken-liver *n.* [CHICKEN-LIVERED *adj.*] [1930s–70s] a coward.

chicken-livered *adj.* [CHICKEN *n.* (2) + SE *liver*; note SE *lily-liver(ed)*] [late 19C+] cowardly.

chicken (out) *v.* (*also* **go chicken**) [CHICKEN *n.* (2)] [1930s+] (*orig. US*) to be scared, to be too frightened to act, to back out of something.

chicken-perch *n.* [rhy. sl.] [late 19C+] a church.

chicken-plucking *adj.* [euph. for MOTHERFUCKING *adj.* (1)] [1960s] (*US*) a general term of abuse; second-rate, vulgar, insignificant.

chicken scratch *n.*[1] [resemblance] [1950s+] (*US*) **1** illegible handwriting. **2** short, tightly curled hair.

chicken scratch *n.*[2] [? the small impression it makes on one's expenses; or CHICKEN *adj.* (1) + SCRATCH *n.*[3] (4)] [1950s+] (*US black*) a very small amount of money.

chicken scratch *n.*[3] [visual resemblance] [1980s+] (*drugs*) the searching on hands and knees for grains of crack cocaine that have dropped to the floor.

chicken scratching *n.* [the lack of real impression a chicken's scratching makes on the ground] [1940s–50s] (*US black*) an inadequate effort, a poorly done job, a lack of real commitment to a task.

chicken's hash *n.* [rhy. sl.] [2000s] cash.

chickenshit *n.* [CHICKEN *n.* (1)/SE *chicken* + SHIT *n.* (1a); the cowardice of the person/the essential insignificance of the substance] [1930s+] (*orig. US*) **1** something insignificant, worthless. **2** (*also* **chickenstuff**) a coward. **3** a contemptible, disgusting person. **4** a disgusting, unacceptable action or situation. **5** (*US milit.*) (*also* **chicken**) meaningless, petty discipline.

chickenshit *adj.* [CHICKENSHIT *n.*] [1930s+] (*orig. US*) **1** (*also* **chicken crap, chickshit**) insufficient, inadequate, of poor quality. **2** cowardly, fearful. **3** (*also* **chicken poo-poo**) weak. **4** petty.

chickenshit *v.* [CHICKENSHIT *n.*] [1960s+] (*orig. US*) to act in a cowardly or otherwise distasteful manner.

chickenshit *adv.* [1970s+] in a cowardly manner.

chickenshits, the *n.* [SE *chicken* + SHITS, THE *n.* (1)] [1950s] (*US*) diarrhoea.

chicken's neck *n.* [rhy. sl.] [20C+] a cheque.

chickie *n.* [dimin. of CHICKEN *n.* (1a)/SE *chicken*] **1** [1910s+] (*orig. Aus.*) (*also* **chickee, chicky**) a young woman. **2** [1950s] (*US*) a chicken.

IN COMPOUNDS

❑ **chickie-run** *n. see* CHICKEN RUN *under* CHICKEN *n.*

chickie *adj.* [CHICKEN *adj.* (2)] [1950s–60s] (*US*) cowardly.

chickie! *excl. see* CHICKEE! *excl.*

chickie out *v.* [CHICKIE *adj.*] [1950s] (*US*) to act in a cowardly manner, to back down.

chickle-a-leary chap *n.* [var. or predecessor of CHICKALEARY *adj.*] [early–mid-19C] an artful, knowing fellow.

chicklet *n.* (*also* **chicklette**) [CHICK *n.*[1] (2) + dimin. sfx *-let(te)*] [1920s+] (*orig. US*) a young woman.

chicko *n. see* CHICO *n.*[1].

chick sale *n. see* CHIC SALE *n.*

chickster *n.*[1] [CHICK *n.*[1] (2) + sfx *-ster*] [1990s+] (*US campus*) a female friend.

chickster *n.*[2] *see* SHICKSTER *n.*[1].

chicky *n.* **1** *see* CHICK *n.*[1] (6). **2** *see* CHICKIE *n.* (1).

chicky! *excl. see* CHICKEE! *excl.*

chiclets *n.* [trademark *Chiclets*, a popular chewing gum; the small hard pieces of gum resemble teeth] [1960s+] (*US*) the teeth.

chico *n.*[1] (*also* **chicko**) [SE *chick*] [1950s–60s] a child.

chico *n.*[2] [*Chico*, a popular Mexican name, esp. during ascendancy of baseball stars Chico Cardenas, Chico Fernandez, Chico Salmon and Chico Ruiz] [1960s+] (*US*) **1** a Mexican, esp. one considered lower class or of mixed blood. **2** a Puerto Rican, also a term of address. **3** a Cuban. **4** a Filipino.

chic sale *n.* (*also* **chick sale**) [proper name *Chic Sale*, 'the champion privy builder of Sangamon Co., Ill.' and best known for his book *The Specialist* (1929)] [1910s+] (*US*) a privy, an outside lavatory.

chief *n.* [SE *chief*, the head of a tribe; thus the stereotyping of Native Americans as stupid] **1** [1920s+] a general term of address, often to an unknown person. **2** [1940s+] (*W.I.*) a potential victim of a confidence trickster, a credulous person; the term, common as a form of address, is used ironically by the con-man when he approaches the dupe. **3** [1960s+] (*UK/US black*) a general insult; a fool, a braggart etc. **4** [1960s+] (*drugs*) a hallucinogenic drug, esp. LSD or mescaline [? the association of such drugs with Mexican Indians and Native Americans]. **5** [1970s+] (*S.Afr.*) a form of address, either between those of the same race or (derog.) by whites to a black whose name they do not know.

IN PHRASES

❑ **chief out** *v.* [1990s+] to smoke marijuana.

chief *v.* [CHIEF *n.*[1] (3)] [1990s+] (*UK black*) to insult.

chief cook and bottle-washer *n.* (*also* **bottle-washer, head cook and bottle-washer**) **1** [19C+] a foreman, a person in authority. **2** [20C+] a general factotum who may, in fact, carry out neither of these duties.

chief muck of the crib *n.* [*muck* is synon. with both HIGH MUCK-A-MUCK *n.* and *LORD MUCK under* MUCK *n.*[1] but predates both and must thus be a fig. use of colloq. *muck*, anything filthy, disgusting or abhorrent + CRIB *n.*[1] (1)] [early 19C] an important person, but within only a small field of activity.

chigger *n.*[1] see JIGGER *n.*[3] (1).

chigger *n.*[2] [1990s+] (*US black*) a person of mixed black and Chinese parentage.

chiggers! *excl.* [CHICKEE! *excl.* + JIGGER! *excl.*] [1930s–50s] (*US Und.*) a cry of warning, alerting others to the approach of authority.

chihuahua *n.* [the small size of the dog] [2000s] (*S.Afr. gay*) a small penis.

chi-ike *n.* (*also* **chiack, chi-hike, chi-yike, chyack**) [CHI-IKE *v.*; orig. costermonger use] [mid-19C–1910s] **1** a hearty greeting. **2** (*Aus.*) argument, criticism; teasing, heckling.

chi-ike *v.* (*also* **chiack, chi-hike, chi-yike, chyack**) [echoic] [mid-19C+] (*mainly Aus./N.Z.*) **1** to tease, to fool, to deceive; thus n. *chi-iking*, mockery, teasing. **2** to shout; esp. to shout *chi-ike* as a hearty greeting or salutation.

chikwa *n. see* CHINKER *n.*

child *n.* **1** [early 19C–1930s] a person. **2** [mid-19C+] (*orig. US black*) I, myself, e.g. *this child don't need no more trouble.* **3** [1980s+] (*US campus*) a general term of address to anyone.

SE in slang uses

IN COMPOUNDS

❑ **child father** *n. see BABY-FATHER under* BABY *n.* ❑ **child-getter** *n.* [19C] the penis.

IN PHRASES

❑ **child of darkmans** *n.* [DARKMANS *n.* (1)] [18C] a bellman. ❑ **child of darkness** *n.* [late 17C–early 18C] (*UK Und.*) a bellman or nightwatchman who walked the streets at night calling out the hours. ❑ **child of the horn-thumb** *n.* [*HORN-THUMB under* HORN *n.*[2]] [early 17C] a cut-purse.

children *n.*[1] [rhy. sl.; *boys and girls* = TWIRL *n.* (1), or skeleton keys] [1980s] (*UK Und.*) burglars' tools.

children *n.*[2] [the potential of each individual sperm] [2000s] (*S.Afr. gay*) semen.

children in the wood *n.* [mid–late 19C] dice in a box.

children's shoes *n.*

IN PHRASES

❑ **make children's shoes** *v.* [Norfolk dial.] [17C–19C] to fool, to trifle with, to belittle. ❑ **make feet for children's shoes** *v. see under* FOOT *n.*

chile *n.* (*also* **chile-bean, chili, chili-bean**) [the SE *chile-/chili-pepper*, a stereotypically popular Mexican food] [1910s+] a derog. term for a Mexican.

IN PHRASES

❑ **get one's chili up** *v.* [var. on *GET ONE'S INDIAN UP under* INDIAN *n.*] [1960s] (*US*) to be infuriated.

chile- *pfx* (*also* **chili**) [CHILE *n.*] [1910s+] (*US*) a derog. pfx used to denote a Mexican or anything supposedly Mexican.

IN COMPOUNDS

❑ **chile-bean** *n. see* CHILE *n.* ❑ **chile-belly** *n.* (*also* **chile-gut, chilli-belly, chilli-gut**) [1960s+] (*US*) a Mexican. ❑ **chile-chaser** *n.* (*also* **chili-chaser**) [1950s+] (*US*) a US border patrolman, employed to prevent Mexicans from entering the country illegally. ❑ **chile-choker** *n.* (*also* **chili-choker**) **1** [1950s+] (*US*) a Mexican. **2** (*US black L.A.*) used as a derog. to a fellow black; the premise being one is no better than a Mexican. ❑ **chile-chump** *n.* (*also* **chili-chump**) [CHUMP *n.*[1] (3); the ref. is to the incompetence of small-time Mexican pimps] [1940s+] (*US black*) a pimp who has only one woman working for him, an inexperienced pimp. ❑ **chile-eater** *n.* (*also* **chile-chomper, chile-picker, chili...**) [20C+] (*US*) a Mexican. ❑ **chile-head** *n.* (*also* **chili-head, chilli-head**) [-HEAD *sfx* (2)] [1970s+] (*US*) a Mexican. ❑ **chile joint** *n.* [1930s+] a Mexican restaurant. ❑ **chile pimp** *n.* (*also* **chili pimp, chili-bowl pimp, chile-mack, chili-mack**) [SE *pimp*/MACK *n.*[2] (1)] [1960s+] (*US black*) a pimp who has only one woman working for him; thus a second-rate pimp. ❑ **chili queen** *n.* [2000s] (*US black*) an attractive Latina.

chili *v.* [? *CHILL (FOR) under* CHILL *v.*[2]] [1940s–50s] (*US black*) to ignore, to brush off.

chill *n.* **1** [20C+] (*US*) rejection, 'the cold shoulder'. **2** [1930s+] murder, death, assassination. **3** [1940s] (*US Und.*) a situation where a potential victim of a con trick loses interest in the hoax. **4** [1970s+] (*US campus*) beer. **5** [1980s+] (*US*) a pose of indifference, of coolness.

IN PHRASES

❑ **play the chill (for)** *v.* (*also* **give the chill**) [1920s+] to ignore, to avoid, to act coldly towards. ❑ **put the chill on** *v.* **1** [1920s+] (*US*) to snub, to ignore. **2** [1940s+] (*US prison*) to intimidate, to discourage, to make one uncomfortable. **3** [1940s+] to murder, to kill, to assassinate.

chill *adj.* [CHILL (OUT) *v.*] **1** [1980s+] (*US black*) fashionable, chic, 'with it'. **2** [1980s+] (*US black*) correct, the real thing. **3** [1980s+] (*orig. US black*) calm, untroubled, relaxed. **4** [1990s+] (*US black*) safe. **5** [1990s+] (*US black*) emotionless, withdrawn, detached.

IN COMPOUNDS

❑ **chill pad** *n.* [PAD *n.*[2] (2)] [1990s+] (*US black*) one's home. ❑ **chill pill** *n.* [1980s+] (*US campus*) a metaphorical 'medicine' that acts to calm one down; usu. in phr. *take a chill pill*, to relax.

chill *v.*[1] [abbr. SE *take the chill off*] [mid-19C] to heat up.

chill *v.*[2] [fig. uses of SE] **1** [1930s] (*US Und.*) to knock out or down. **2** [1930s–40s] (*US Und.*) to stack a deck of cards prior to using them in a cheating card-game. **3** [1930s+] to murder, to assassinate. **4** [1930s+] to give up on, to abandon, to ignore. **5** [1930s+] (*US Und.*) to deal with, to nullify, e.g. a criminal charge. **6** [1940s] (*US Und.*) for the victim of a confidence trick to lose interest. **7** [1940s+] (*orig. US*) to become emotionally cold, withdrawn. **8** [1940s+] (*US*) to tolerate, to make no fuss about. **9** [1980s] (*US black*) to undermine someone's plans.

IN PHRASES

❑ **chill (for)** *v.* [1900s–50s] (*US*) to (pretend to) ignore. ❑ **chill (out)** *v. see* separate entry.

chill *adv.*

IN PHRASES

❑ **have (something) down chill** [var. on COLD *adv.*] [1900s–10s] (*US campus*) totally, completely.

chill! *excl.* [CHILL (OUT) *v.* (2)] [1980s+] (*orig. US black*) wait! stop!

chillam *n.* (*also* **chillum**) [Hind. *chilam*, the bowl of a *hugga* pipe or *hookah*] **1** [late 18C+] (*Anglo-Ind.*) a pipeful of tobacco. **2** [1960s+] (*orig. W.I. drugs*) a pipe used for smoking marijuana.

chillax *v.* [CHILL (OUT) *v.* (2) + SE *relax*] [2000s] (*orig. US campus*) to wind down and relax.

chilled *adj.* [CHILL *v.*[2] (7)] **1** [1940s–50s] (*US black/teen*) standoffish, resentful. **2** [1990s+] (*US campus*) informal but sophisticated.

chilled-off *adj.* [CHILL *v.*[2] (3)] [1930s+] (*US*) killed, murdered.

chilled-out *adj.* [CHILL *adj.* (3)] [1980s+] calm, relaxed,'cool'.

chillers *n.* [OE *ceolor*, the throat] [20C+] (*Irish*) **1** jowls. **2** a double chin.

chilling *n.* [CHILL (OUT) *v.* (2)] [1980s+] relaxing; acting in a cool manner.

chilling *adj.* [CHILLING *n.*] [1980s+] good, excellent.

chill-out *adj.* [CHILL (OUT) *v.* (2)] [1980s+] designed to create a relaxed atmosphere; thus *chill-out room*, that part of a nightclub where people can relax and chat rather than dance.

chill (out) *v.* **1** [1950s] (*US Und.*) to get rid of the victim once the confidence game has reached its climax and he has been robbed. **2** [1960s+] (*orig. US*) to calm down, to control one's emotions, to relax, to act 'cool'; often as imper. **3** [1980s+] (*orig. US*) to pass the time of day, to 'hang out'. **4** [1980s+] (*US drugs*) by ext. of prev., of a dealer, to work on a street corner or in a bar. **5** [1990s+] to calm someone down. **6** [1990s+] to take a break, to pause.

chills, the *n.* [1940s+] feelings of unease, scariness.

Chill Town *n.* [CHILL *adj.*] [1990s+] (*US black*) Jersey City, N.J.

chillum *n. see* CHILLAM *n.*

chilly *n.* **1** [1980s+] (*US campus*) a cold beer. **2** [2000s] (*US black*) a mentholated cigarette.

chilly *adj.* [SE *chilly*, cold/CHILL (OUT) *v.*] **1** [late 19C+] emotionless, withdrawn, detached. **2** [1980s+] (*orig. US black/campus*) acceptable, satisfactory, calm. **3** [1980s+] (*US black*) attractive, fine. **4** [1990s+] cold-blooded. **5** [2000s] skilful, competent at a given task or profession.

IN COMPOUNDS

❑ **chilly down** *v.* [CHILL (OUT) *v.* (3)] [1980s+] (*US*) to pass the time of day, to 'hang out'. ❑ **chilly mitt** *n. see under* MITT *n.* ❑ **chilly most** *n.* [MOST, THE *n.*] [1990s+] (*US black*) a relaxed, composed person, an excellent admired person.

IN PHRASES

❑ **lay chilly** *v.* (*also* **sit chilly**) [1970s+] (*US*) to lie low. ❑ **play it chilly** *v.* (*also* **act chilly, hang chilly**) [1950s+] to act in a cool, controlled manner.

SE in slang uses

IN COMPOUNDS

❑ **chilly dog** *n.* [1980s+] (*US campus*) beer.

chime *n.* **1** [mid-19C] (*US*) false praise, empty flattery, esp. when aimed at tricking or defrauding its object [note 17C–18C *chime*, a mere empty 'jingle' of words]. **2** [1930s–40s] (*US black*) one hour. **3** [1940s] (*US black*) the beating of one's heart.

chimer *n.* [17C SE *chimer*, one who rings bells] [1940s] (*US black*) **1** a clock or watch. **2** the heart, which also 'ticks'.

IN PHRASES

❑ **let someone down for their chimer** *v.* [1940s] (*US black*) to steal a watch.

chimes *n.* [the facetious resemblance to a pair of hanging bells] [1960s] (*US*) the testicles.

chimmy *n.*[1] [SE *chemise*] [20C+] (*Aus./W.I.*) a woman's undergarment, essentially synon. with a petticoat.

chimmy *n.*[2] [1950s+] (*W.I.*) a chamberpot.

chimmy *n.*[3] *see under* SHIMMY.

chimney *n.* [SE *chimney*; either its position on top of the house or the smoke issuing from it] **1** [mid-19C+] a heavy smoker. **2** [1920s–40s] (*US black*) a (top) hat. **3** [1940s+] (*US black*) the head.

IN COMPOUNDS

❑ **chimney chops** *n.* [the blackness of a *chimney* + CHOPS *n.*[1] (1); given the continuing arguments vis-a-vis the inclusion of racial abuse in dictionaries, it is interesting, perhaps, to note that Grose (1785), in a relatively rare acknowledgement of such a problem, defines this term as 'an abusive appellation'] [late 18C] a derog. term for a black person. ❑ **chimney-corner** *adj.* [the image of people chatting in a chimney corner] [20C+] (*US*) unofficial, not genuine, on the basis of popular acceptance; thus *chimney-corner law*, popular opinion, saloon-bar opinion. ❑ **chimney-pot** *n.* [resemblance] [mid–late 19C] a cylindrical black silk hat, fashionable during the latter half of the 19C. ❑ **chimney-sweep** *n.* **1** [late 19C] a clergyman [the black clothing]. **2** [mid–late 19C] (*also* **chimney sweeper**) a nickname for an aperient, known as 'the black dose' or 'black drop', composed mainly of opium, mixed with vinegar and spices [colour + the fact that it 'cleans one out'].

chimozzle *n. see* SHEMOZZLE *n.*

chimpung *n.* [supposed imitation of Chinese speech] [1940s+] (*W.I.*) a derog. name for a Chinese person.

chin *n.*[1] [? one counts them by chins] [mid-19C] (*US Und.*) a child.

chin *n.*[2] **1** [mid-19C+] (*also* **chin-chin**) talk, chatter, conversation. **2** [late 19C–1900s] (*US*) cheek, impudence; nagging.

DERIVATIVES

❑ **chinfest** *n.* [-FEST *sfx*] [1940s+] (*US*) any meeting at which there is a good deal of talking and gossip.

IN COMPOUNDS

❑ **chin goods** *n.* [1900s] (*US*) chatter. ❑ **chin jaw** *n.* [JAW *n.* (1)] [1940s] (*US*) idle chatter. ❑ **chin music** *n. see* separate entry. ❑ **chinwork** *n.* [1970s] (*US*) a chat, a conversation.

SE in slang uses

IN COMPOUNDS

❑ **chin check** *n.* [1990s+] (*US campus*) a fight, a blow to the jaw. ❑ **chin curtains** *n. see* LACE CURTAIN *n.*[1] (1). ❑ **chinless wonder** *n. see* separate entry. ❑ **chin-prop** *n.* [PROP *n.*[3] (1)] [19C] a brooch. ❑ **chin pubes** *n.* [1990s+] (*US teen*) a beard. ❑ **chin-rest** *n.* [1990s+] the female perineum, considered in the context of giving a woman oral sex. ❑ **chin-scraper** *n. see* SCRAPER *n.* (2). ❑ **chin-splitter** *n.* [1900s] (*US*) a narrow goatee beard. ❑ **chinstrap** *n. see* separate entries. ❑ **chin-tearer** *n.* [late 19C] a barber. ❑ **chinwag** *see* separate entries.

IN EXCLAMATIONS

❑ **chin up!** *see* separate entry.

chin *n.*[3] [ety. unknown; ? a local language] [1960s–70s] (*S.Afr. township*) money.

chin *v.* **1** [late 19C+] (*US*) (*also* **chin-chin**) to chatter, to talk to/with; thus *chinning*, idle conversation, chatter [CHIN *n.*[2] (1)]. **2** [1910s+] (*orig. Glasgow*) to hit someone (on the chin).

China *n.* [late 19C+] (*UK/Cockney*) anywhere other than England (poss. even other than London) or the place rich people go for their holidays.

proper name in slang uses

IN COMPOUNDS

❑ **China boy** *n.* [mid-19C+] a derog. term for a Chinese man. ❑ **china clippers** *n.* [pun on Pan-American Airlines 'China Clipper' flying-boat service to the Far East] [1950s+] (*US*) false teeth. ❑ **China John** *n. see* JOHN CHINAMAN *n.* ❑ **Chinamat** *n.* [SE (*auto*)*mat*] [1930s–50s] (*US*) a cheap Chinese restaurant. ❑ **China Street** *n. see* separate entry. ❑ **China white** *n.* (*also* **Chinese white**) [1960s+] (*drugs*) **1** heroin, esp. when of above-average strength. **2** fentanyl, a powerful synthetic narcotic.

china *n.*[1] [SE *china*, crockery] (*US*) **1** [1920s+] (*also* **chinaware**) teeth. **2** [1960s] tea, as served at a lunch counter.

china *n.*[2] [ety. unknown] [1940s–50s] (*US*) money.

chinaberry *n.* [SAmE the *chinaberry* tree, common in Southern states] [2000s] (*US black*) sexual intercourse as a highly pleasurable experience.

Chinaman *n.* **1** [late 19C] (*US*) a cup of tea, much of which originated in China. **2** [late 19C+] an Irishman, stereotyped as an immigrant. **3** [1900s] (*Aus.*) in dice, a five [? anecdotal, lost story of five Chinamen]. **4** [1930s+] (*US drugs*) addiction to a narcotic, usu. heroin [the Chinese origin of opium, the base of heroin]. **5** [1940s–50s] (*W.I.*) a farthing, a small coin [like the stereotyped Chinese, the coin is small]. **6** [1970s+] (*US*) a derog. term for one who has political influence [the image of the 'wily Oriental'].

IN COMPOUNDS

❑ **Chinaman's luck** *n.* (*also* **luck of a Chow**) [1900s] (*Aus.*) good luck, with an implication of it being undeserved. ❑ **Chinaman's nightmare** *n.* [racial stereotyping] [1980s] (*US*) bedlam, chaos. ❑ **Chinaman's shout** *n.* [the presumed meanness of the Chinese] [20C+] (*Aus.*) a supposed 'treat' for which everyone involved must pay. ❑ **Chinaman's trot** *n.* [late 19C–1900s] (*Aus.*) a slow and steady jog.

IN PHRASES

❑ **have a Chinaman on one's back** *v.* [1930s–50s] to be addicted to narcotics, esp. heroin. ❑ **I'll be a Chinaman** (*also* **I'll be a cross-eyed Armenian**) [20C+] a mild oath. ❑ **kill a Chinaman** *v.* **1** [late 19C+] (*Aus.*) to experience any form of bad luck [the stereotyping of the Chinese as capable of bringing on ill luck]. **2** [1950s] (*US prison/drugs*) to withdraw from narcotic addiction.

Chinaman's chance *n.* (*also* **Chinese chance**) [orig. gold rush use, when the Chinese worked otherwise abandoned claims] [1910s+] (*US*) **1** no chance whatsoever, no luck. **2** the slightest possible chance; the slightest degree of chance.

china (plate) *n.* (*also* **chiner**) [rhy. sl. = MATE *n.* (1); Powis, *Signs of Crime* (1977), suggests 'particularly used to mean a highly regarded husband or wife'] **1** [late 19C+] one's (best) friend; often as *OLD CHINA* below. **2** [1950s] (*Aus.*) one's wife.

IN PHRASES

❑ **old china** *n.* [1910s+] an old friend.

China Street *n.* [its proximity to Covent Garden, then a market, and thus to 'China oranges'] [early–mid-19C] Bow Street, London.

IN COMPOUNDS

❑ **China Street pig** *n.* [PIG *n.* (2)] [early 19C] a Bow Street officer.

chinch *n.*[1] [Sp. *chinche*, a bedbug] **1** [mid-19C–1950s] a bedbug, thus *chinchy*, adj., infested with bugs. **2** [1960s] a term of affection, usu. aimed at a child.

IN COMPOUNDS

❑ **chinch pad** *n.* [PAD *n.*[2] (2)] [1940s–50s] (*US black tramp*) a very low standard of rooming house or hotel.

chinch *n.*[2] [ME + OF *chiche*, parsimonious, mean; in early 14C–late 16C SE] [1940s–60s] (*US*) **1** a miser. **2** a spoilsport.

chincher *n.* [mid-18C] (*UK Und.*) a crafty person.

chin-chin *see also under* CHIN.

chin-chin! *excl.* [Chinese *ts'ing ts'ing*, a general salutation, and as such picked up by sailors on Far East tours. A response, which has not entered the vocab., is *pa pa*] **1** [late 18C+] a popular toast when drinking, synon. with 'Good health!' or 'Cheers!'. **2** [1910s–50s] goodbye, farewell. **3** [1940s] a greeting.

chinchy *adj.* [14C–16C SE *chinch*, a miser] [1900s–60s] (*US*) miserly, mean, stingy.

chincough *n.* [OE *cincian*, to gasp and cough] [early 18C; 20C+] (*Irish*) **1** whooping cough. **2** a spasm of laughter or tears.

'chine *n.* [abbr.] [1950s–60s] (*US black*) ma*chine*, either a car or a motorcycle.

Chinee *n.* (*also* **Chiney**) [abbr. SE *Chinese*] [mid-19C–1980s] a derog. term for a Chinese person.

Chinee *adj.* (*also* **Chiney, Chinie**) [CHINEE *n.*] [mid-19C+] Chinese.

IN COMPOUNDS

❑ **Chinee nation** *n.* [-NATION *sfx*] [20C+] (*W.I.*) Chinese people.

chinee *n.* (*also* **chinee ducket**) [abbr. *CHINESE DUCKET under* CHINESE *adj.*] [1930s] (*US*) a complimentary ticket.

chiner *n. see* CHINA (PLATE) *n.*

Chinese *adj.* [20C+] one of the racial stereotypes used in many contexts; the Chinese eye-shape, plus the supposed cunning of the 'wily Orientals' always has 'Chinese' implying something slightly out of kilter, physically, ethically or otherwise; thus used in the following combs.

IN COMPOUNDS

❑ **Chinese angle** *n.* [1930s–40s] (*US*) a strange twist. ❑ **Chinese B** *n.* [the preferential treatment given to supposedly disadvantaged East Asian students in an early form of affirmative action] [1950s+] (*US*) a grade that is marked higher than the student's work really deserved. ❑ **Chinese ballast** *n.* [2000s] (*N.Z.*) rice. ❑ **Chinese brown** *n.* [1970s+] (*drugs*) a form of heroin. ❑ **Chinese chance** *n. see* CHINAMAN'S CHANCE *n.* ❑ **Chinese consumption** *n.* [pun on 'wun bung lung', a 'Chinese' name] [1930s+] (*Aus.*) a smoker's cough. ❑ **Chinese copy** *n.* [? the stereotype (usu. ascribed to Japan) of East Asian workmen as taking Western inventions and faithfully copying them in order to sell the cheaper reproductions back to the West] [1930s+] (*US*) any copy that faithfully reproduces not just the accurate work but the mistakes, too. ❑ **Chinese cure** *n.* [1950s–60s] (*drugs*) a form of withdrawing from a narcotic addiction: a mix of heroin and Wampole's Tonic is consumed, with the proportion of narcotic gradually reduced to zero. ❑ **Chinese deal** *n.* [negative stereotype of a Chinese businessman as one who enjoys the minutiae of bargaining but cannot be trusted to deliver the goods] [1970s+] a deal that fails to materialize. ❑ **Chinese ducket** *n.* [DUCKET *n.* (1); the punch-holes in such tickets supposedly resembled Chinese money] [1930s] (*US*) a complimentary ticket to a theatrical or sporting event. ❑ **Chinese fashion** *adv.* [the implication is that such a position accommodates the supposedly transverse Chinese vagina] [1960s+] used to describe having sexual intercourse, with the couple lying on their sides. ❑ **Chinese fire drill** *n.* **1** [1940s+] bedlam, chaos. **2** [1980s] (*US campus*) a student game whereby a car stops at the traffic lights and all those inside jump out, run round and round the car and then jump in again before driving away. ❑ **Chinese flush** *n.* (*also* **Chinese straight**) [1940s–60s] in poker, a worthless hand, i.e. four cards of a flush or a straight – a proper hand requires five. ❑ **Chinese H** *n.* [H *n.* (2)] [1980s+] (*drugs*) heroin. ❑ **Chinese lady** *n.* [2000s] (*N.Z.*) a lavatory. ❑ **Chinese loan** *n.* [late 19C] an unattainably large sum of money. ❑ **Chinese molasses** *n.* [the origin and consistency of opium] [1950s–70s] (*drugs*) opium. ❑ **Chinese needlework** *n.* [the hypodermic *needle* used for injecting heroin and the stereotyped linking of the East to narcotics, orig. opium, subseq. heroin] [1930s–50s] (*US drugs*) **1** the world of drug-dealing. **2** the injection of narcotics. ❑ **Chinese No. 3** *n.* [1970s+] (*drugs*) a variety of heroin, processed in Hong Kong and imported by Chinese smugglers. ❑ **Chinese red** *n.* [1970s+] (*drugs*) heroin.

❑ **Chinese rocks** *n.* [1970s+] (*drugs*) heroin. ❑ **Chinese rot** *n.* [the 'inscrutable' East] [1940s–60s] (*US*) **1** venereal disease. **2** any form of unspecified 'mystery' disease. ❑ **Chinese saxophone** *n. see* SAXOPHONE *n.* ❑ **Chinese screwdriver** *n.* [the supposed inability of the Chinese to perform simple physical tasks] [1950s+] (*Aus.*) a hammer. ❑ **Chinese smoking** *n.* [? reminiscent of opium smoking] [1960s] (*N.Z.*) sucking tobacco smoke through the mouth and exhaling through the nostrils. ❑ **Chinese straight** *n. see* *CHINESE FLUSH* above. ❑ **Chinese take-away** *n.* [pun on SE] [1970s+] (*gay*) a bar where East Asian boys or young men are available for picking up by Western men. ❑ **Chinese tobacco** *n.* [despite the fact that Britain introduced China to opium *c.*1840, the drug and the nation have been inextricably linked ever since] [1920s–50s] opium. ❑ **Chinese white** *n. see* *CHINA WHITE under* CHINA *n.*

IN PHRASES

❑ **get Chinese** *v.* [CHINESE *adj.* (1); the implication is of the 'skewed' aspect of the Chinese stereotype, rather than the effects of a drug] [1980s+] (*US campus*) to succumb heavily to a drug, usu. marijuana.

Chiney *n. see also* under CHINEE.

chiney-brush *n.* [lit. 'China brush'; ? the fineness of a brush used to paint porcelain] [1990s+] (*W.I.*) something used to enhance sexual performance.

Chiney-Royal *n. see* ROYAL *n.*[1] (2).

ching *n.*[1] [common Chinese name] [20C+] (*US*) a derog. term for a Chinese person.

ching *n.*[2] [echoic] **1** [1970s–80s] (*S.Afr*) money. **2** [2000s] £5; a £5 note.

ching *n.*[3] [? on pattern of later BLING *n.*, the sparkle of a cocaine crystal] [1990s+] (*drugs*) cocaine.

chingao! *excl.* [imper. of Sp. sl. *chingar*, FUCK *v.* (1)] [1960s+] (*US*) an excl. of irritation, WHAT THE FUCK! *excl.*

chingazo *n.* (*also* **chingaso**) [Sp. sl. *chingar*, FUCK *v.* (1)] **1** [1970s+] sexual intercourse. **2** [1990s+] the boss, the leader [lit. FUCKER *n.* (3)].

ching-ching *n.* [? the chinking together of glasses] [mid-19C] (*US*) a form of alcohol.

ching-chong *adj.* [1920s+] (*later use is UK black*) Chinese, East Asian.

chingo *n.* [Sp. sl., lit. 'a fuck of a lot'] [1960s+] (*US*) a great deal.

chingoda *n.* [fig. use of Sp. *chingoda*, fucker] [1990s+] (*US prison*) an influential, powerful prison inmate.

chingus *n.* [var. on DINGUS *n.*] (*US*) **1** [1940s+] the penis [note Sp. sl. *chingar*, FUCK *v.* (1)]. **2** [1980s+] any unnamed object.

Chinie *adj. see* CHINEE *adj.*

'chining *n.* ['CHINE *n.*] [1950s–60s] (*US black*) driving an automobile.

Chink *n.* [SE *China* or f. Chinese *ching-ching*, a courteous excl. (*DARE*)] **1** [late 19C+] (*orig. Aus.*) a derog. term for a Chinese person. **2** [1910s+] a nickname for a Chinese person or someone with Chinese features. **3** [1930s] (*orig. US*) the Chinese language. **4** [1950s+] (*orig. US*) a derog. term for any Asian person.

Chink *adj.* [CHINK *n.*] [20C+] Chinese; thus a derog. term for East Asian people in general.

IN COMPOUNDS

❑ **Chink joint** *n.* [JOINT *n.* (3b)] [1930s+] a derog. term for a cheap Chinese restaurant.

chink *n.*[1] [echoic] **1** [late 16C–1950s] money; often in pl. as *chinks*. **2** [mid–late 18C] (*UK Und.*) a tankard.

chink *n.*[2] [17C–19C] the vagina.

IN PHRASES

❑ **chink-stopper** *n.* [late 19C] the penis.

Chinkee *n. see* CHINKY *n.*

chinker *n.* (*also* **chikwa, cinqua, cinque**) [Ital. *cinque*, five] [late 17C+] (*Ling. Fr./Polari*) the number five.

chinkers *n.* [CHINK *n.*[1] (1)] **1** [early–mid-19C] (*UK Und.*) chains, fetters. **2** [mid–late 19C] money, esp. as coins.

chinki-chonks *n.* (*also* **chinky-chonks**) [CHINK *n.* (1) + redup.] [1970s+] a derog. term for East Asians in general.

Chinkie *see under* CHINKY.

chinkie-jog *n.* [CHINKIE (1)] [1930s] (*Aus.*) a slow and steady jog.

chinklops *n.* [echoic] [mid-19C] (*UK Und.*) fetters.

Chinko *n.* [CHINK *n.* (1) + -O *sfx* (3)] [late 19C] (*orig. N.Z.*) a derog. term for a Chinese person.

Chink's *n.* **1** [1900s] (*US*) a Chinese-owned shop. **2** [1930s+] (*orig. US*) a Chinese restaurant; thus a Chinese meal.

chinks *n.* [dial. *chink*, a coughing fit] [1930s+] (*Irish*) the 'creeps', the 'shivers'; esp. in phr. *give someone the chinks*.

chink-stick *n.* [CHINCH *n.*[1] (1), a bedbug, with which such beds are often infested + SE *stick*, a plank of wood] [1950s+] (*W.I.*) a rough board bed.

Chinky *n.* (*also* **Chinkee, Chinkie**) **1** [late 19C+] (*also* **chinky-chap**) a derog. term for a Chinese person. **2** [1980s+] a derog. term for a Chinese restaurant. **3** [2000s] a (take-away) Chinese meal.

Chinky *adj.* (*also* **Chinkie**) [CHINKY *n.*] [late 19C+] Chinese; thus a derog. epithet for East Asians in general.

chinky *adj.*[1] [CHINK *n.*[1] (1)] [late 19C] (*Aus.*) monetary.

chinky *adj.*[2] [CHINCHY *adj.* + ref. to a SE *chink*, i.e. the tightness of one's wallet and pockets] [1970s] (*US campus*) stingy, mean.

chinky-chonks *n. see* CHINKI-CHONKS *n.*

chinless wonder *n.* (*also* **chinless chappie, wingless wonder**) [his stereotyped receding chin; a firm chin supposedly indicates a 'firm' personality] [1910s+] a male scion of the British upper classes; prob. wealthy, certainly well-connected, but essentially devoid of intelligence or 'character'.

chin music *n.* [CHIN *n.*[2] (1) + SE *music*] **1** [early 19C+] conversation, chatter, talk, esp. defiant, aggressive, cheeky talk. **2** [1900s] (*US*) promotional copy; persuasive writing.

IN PHRASES

❑ **jerk chin music** *v.* [late 19C] to gossip, to chatter; to speechify.

chinner *n.* [CHIN *v.* (1) ; lit. a 'talker'] [1900s–10s] (*US*) **1** an actor, a performer. **2** a garrulous, verbose person.

chinny *adj.* [CHIN *n.*[2] (1)] [late 19C] (*US*) talkative, garrulous.

Chino *n.* [abbr. SE *Chinese*] **1** [mid-19C+] a Chinese immigrant [sometimes refers to the Chinese population of the Philippines]. **2** [1930s–50s] (*US drugs*) a Chinese drug dealer.

chinstrap *n.*[1] [20C+] (*Ulster*) a dirty ring around an unwashed neck, a 'tide-mark'.

chinstrap *n.*[2] [SE *chinstrap*, a connecting strap in saddlery, which resembles the buttock crack] [1910s+] the buttocks.

chintz *n.* [CHINCH *n.*[1] (1)] **1** [late 19C+] a bedbug. **2** [late 19C] (*US*) a crop-destroying insect such as a locust.

chintzy *adj.* (*also* **chinzy**) [dial. *chincy*, mean, niggardly/CHINCHY *adj.*; ult. the CHINCH *n.*[1] (1) or *chintz*, an insect that attacks corn or grain and when squashed has an unpleasant smell] **1** [mid-19C+] second-rate, inferior, cheap-looking. **2** [1950s+] stingy, mean.

chin up! *excl.* [1930s+] cheer up! don't worry!

chinwag *n.* **1** [mid-19C] officious impertinence. **2** [late 19C+] a chat, a conversation.

chinwag *v.* [CHINWAG *n.*] [mid-19C+] to chat, to converse.

chinzy *n. see* CHINTZY *adj.*

chip *n.*[1] [SE colloq. phr. *chip off the old block*] [late 17C–1900s] a child.

chip *n.*[2] [? gambling *chips*; note racing jargon *chip*, one shilling; Indian army jargon *chip*, a rupee] **1** [mid-19C–1920s] a dollar. **2** [mid-19C+] (*mainly US*) in pl., money; also in fig. phr. below. **3** [mid-19C+] £1, a sovereign. **4** [1930s–50s] one shilling. **5** [1940s] a rupee.

IN PHRASES

❑ **— and no chips** [late 19C] and no mistake. ❑ **cash in one's chips** *v.* (*also* **throw in one's chips**) (*orig. US*) **1** [late 19C] to change one's way of life. **2** [late 19C] (*US*) to give oneself up. **3** [late 19C+] to die. **4** [late 19C+] to kill someone. **5** [1950s] to be 'over', to be finished. **6** [1960s+] to commit suicide.

❑ **do one's chips** *v.* (*also* **blow one's chips**) [1960s+] (*N.Z.*) to use up or squander one's money. ❑ **hand in one's chips** *v.* [late 19C+] to die. ❑ **have (had) one's chips** *v.* [gambling use] **1** [20C+] to have died; lit. or fig. **2** [1960s+] to have been rejected, dismissed. ❑ **in the chips** [1930s+] (*orig. US*) financially secure, well-off. ❑ **pass in one's chips** *v.* [late 19C+] (*orig. US*) to die. ❑ **when the chips are down** [poker imagery; SE *chip*, a counter used in a game of chance] [1940s+] in the final event, at the denouement, when one has no option.

chip *n.*[3] [CHIPPIE *n.*[1] (1)] [late 19C–1950s] (*US*) **1** a woman. **2** a promiscuous woman, esp. a prostitute.

chip *n.*[4] [CHIP *v.*[1] (3)] [20C+] (*Aus.*) an argument; a reprimand.

chip *n.*[5] [CHIP *n.*[2] (2)] [1910s–50s] (*US Und.*) a cash register.

chip *n.*[6] [SE *chip*, a small amount] [1940s–50s] (*US black*) a sip (of liquor).

chip *n.*[7] [CHIP *v.*[2] (3)] (*drugs*) **1** [1970s+] heroin, esp. that has been diluted or 'cut'. **2** [2000s] any form of cigarette cut with phencyclidine.

chip *n.*[8] [the SE *microchip* that powers it] [1990s+] (*US black teen*) a cellular/portable phone that is stolen and therefore used to make illegal and free phone calls.

chip *adj. see* CHIPPER *adj.*

chip *v.*[1] [dial. *chip*, a tiff, a quarrel] (*mainly Aus./N.Z.*) **1** [late 19C+] (*also* **make chip-chip**) to tease, to banter with; thus *chipping*, teasing. **2** [20C+] to interrupt, to speak impudently. **3** [20C+] (*also* **chip the lips**) to complain, to criticize. **4** [1900s] to hit. **5** [1910s] of a man, to flirt with a woman.

IN PHRASES

❑ **chip at** *v.* [late 19C+] to quarrel with, to criticize. ❑ **have a chip at** *v.* [1910s–20s] to tease, to make fun of.

chip *v.*[2] [SE *chip*, a small amount] **1** [late 19C+] (*US Und.*) to carry out a small crime with only minimal profits. **2** [1950s+] (*drugs*) to dabble in narcotic drug use. **3** [1950s+] to dilute drugs.

chip *v.*[3] [CHIP *n.*[6]] [1940s] (*US black*) to sip one's drink.

chip *v.*[4] [ety. unknown; ? link to UK dial. *chip*, to step down or to SE *ship out*, to leave] **1** [1970s+] (*orig. UK black*) to leave, to depart, to go somewhere. **2** [2000s] (*W.I., Trin.*) to move and sway in time to music.

chip *v.*[5] *see* CHIPPIE *v.*[2] (1).

chiphead *n.* [SE (*silicon*) *chip* + -HEAD *sfx* (3)] [1980s+] a computer enthusiast.

chip in *v.* (*also* **chip into, chuck in**) [poker jargon *chip in*, to put one's gambling chips on the table to signify one's joining in the round of betting] [mid-19C+] (*orig. US*) **1** to contribute. **2** to include in one's speaking. **3** to join in. **4** to butt in, to interrupt.

chipmunks *n.* [rhy. sl.] [2000s] bathing trunks.

chip one's teeth *v. see under* TEETH *n.*

chippens *n.* [? SE *chippings*] [20C+] (*Irish*) money.

chipper *n.*[1] [? CHIPPER *adj.*] **1** [19C] a cheerful, lively young man. **2** [early 19C] a prostitute.

chipper *n.*[2] [SE *chip*, as a v.] [mid-19C] in boxing, a sharp blow, a jab.

chipper *n.*[3] [? CHIP *v.*[2] (1)] [late 19C] (*US Und.*) a cheat, a swindler.

chipper *n.*[4] [SE *chips*] [1910s+] (*Irish/Welsh*) a fish and chip shop.

chipper *n.*[5] [CHIP *v.*[2] (2)] [1980s+] (*drugs*) an occasional user of narcotics.

chipper *adj.* (*also* **chip, chippery**) [dial. *chipper*, a cheery song, amiable chatter] [mid-18C+] (*orig. US*) cheerful, lively, perhaps slightly drunk.

chipper *v.* [CHIPPER *adj.*] [late 19C] (*US*) to cheer (someone) up.

chippery *n.* [CHIP *v.*[1] (1)/SE *chipper*, to twitter, to babble] [1900s–10s] a verbal exchange, an argument.

chippie *n.*[1] (*also* **chippy**) [? SE *cheap* or Fr. *chipie*, a shrewish woman; note Asbury, *The Gangs of Chicago* (1940): 'in the middle of 1860 it was estimated by the [Chicago] Tribune that two thousand "chippies" plied their unholy trade in the retail business district alone'] **1** [mid-19C+] (*orig. US*) a young woman, esp. when promiscuous or a prostitute (often a part-timer or 'amateur'); also as term of address. **2** [1930s–40s] (*US black*) a prostitute's dress. **3** [1940s] (*US black*) a slim, attractive 'glamour girl'. **4** [1960s–70s] (*US gay*) a male prostitute or promiscuous gay man.

IN COMPOUNDS

❑ **chippie-chaser** *n.* (*also* **chippy-chaser**) **1** [late 19C–1930s] a well-dressed loafer who spec. pursues young shopgirls and even schoolgirls. **2** [1920s+] a devotee of prostitutes or promiscuous women; also in homosexual use. ❑ **chippie-chasing** *n.* (*also* **chippy-chasing, chippy-cruising**) [1910s+] pursuing prostitutes or promiscuous women. ❑ **chippie joint** *n.* (*also* **chippie house, chippyhouse, chippy joint**) [HOUSE *n.*[1] (1)/JOINT *n.* (3b)] [1920s+] (*US*) a brothel.

chippie *n.*[2] [SE colloq. phr. *chip off the old block*, or they have only just *chipped in*] **1** [late 19C–1930s] (*US*) a young person. **2** [late 19C–1970s] (*US*) a beginner, an innocent.

chippie *n.*[3] (*also* **chippy**) [SE *chips* of wood. orig. RN jargon *chippy*, the ship's carpenter; *chippy chap*, a carpenter's mate] [20C+] a carpenter.

chippie *n.*[4] (*also* **chippy**) [abbr.] **1** [1910s+] a fish and chip shop. **2** [1980s+] (*N.Z.*) a potato chip (fry). **3** [1990s+] a chip shop owner.

chippie *n.*[5] (*also* **chippy, chippy user**) [CHIPPIE *v.*[1] (1)] **1** [1920s+] (*US drugs*) an occasional user of (usu. narcotic) drugs. **2** [1960s+] a limited drug addiction.

chippie *v.*[1] (*also* **chippy**) [? SE *cheap* or CHIP *v.*[2] (1)] **1** [1920s+] (*drugs*) to use narcotics, esp. heroin, only on an irregular basis rather than to be a habitual addict; thus CHIPPING *n.*[3]. **2** [1970s] in non-drug contexts, to work half-heartedly.

chippie *v.*[2] (*also* **chippy, chippy around, chippy on**) [CHIPPIE *n.*[1]] **1** [1930s+] (*also* **chip**) to be sexually unfaithful; thus n. *chipping*. **2** [1950s] (*US*) to fool, to deceive. **3** [1960s+] (*US black*) to seduce, to be attracted to. **4** [1980s+] to act as a prostitute.

chippie habit *n. see* HABIT *n.* (1).

chippified *adj.* [CHIPPIE *n.*[1] (1)] [1950s] (*US*) of a woman, promiscuous, esp. when acting as an 'amateur' prostitute.

chipping *n.*[1] [CHIP *v.*[1] (1)] [late 19C+] (*Aus.*) the act of being cheeky, impudent.

chipping *n.*[2] [CHIP *n.*[2]] [1920s] the act of tipping.

chipping *n.*[3] (*also* **chippying**) [CHIPPIE *v.*[1]] [1950s+] (*drugs*) the occasional use of drugs.

chip potato *adv.* [rhy. sl.] [1960s+] (*Aus.*) later.

chippy *see also under* CHIPPIE and combs.

chippy *adj.*[1] [CHEAP *adj.* (1)] [late 19C–1930s] **1** hungover. **2** unwell, sick.

chippy *adj.*[2] [*have a chip on one's shoulder*. usu. in middle-class use and often as a means of dismissing genuine complaints, the implication is that such 'chippiness' has no real justification other than class-based resentment] **1** [20C+] cheeky, impudent. **2** [20C+] angry, irritated. **3** [1970s+] resentful, jealous.

chippy *adj.*[3] [CHIRPY *adj.*] [1900s–10s] cheerful, merry.

chippying *n. see* CHIPPING *n.*[3].

chippy's playground *n. see* PLAY *v.*

chips *n.*[1] [late 18C+] a carpenter.

chips *n.*[2] [? SE *chip*, buffalo dung] [1960s+] (*US*) the buttocks.

chips *n.*[3] *see* CHIP *n.*[2] (2).

chips and chase *n.* [rhy. sl.] [1920s] (*US*) the face.

chips (and peas) *n.* [rhy. sl.] [1960s+] the knees.

chipstick *n.* [on the model of DIPSTICK *n.* (2)] [2000s] a fool.

chiquita *n.* (*also* **chiquita banana**) [*Chiquita*, brand of bananas; note BANANA *n.* (3a)] [1960s+] **1** an attractive woman. **2** a woman, usu. term of address.

chira *n.* (*also* **chicharra**) [Sp. *chicharra*, a cicada; thus ? play on ROACH *n.* (2a)] [1970s+] (*drugs*) marijuana.

chirk *adj.* (*also* **chirky**) [SE *chirk*, chirrup; prior use New Eng. dial.] [mid–late 19C] (*US*) cheerful, happy.

chirk (up) *v.* [CHIRK *adj.*] [mid-19C–1930s] (*US*) to cheer up.

chirp *n.* [CHIRP v.] **1** [1920s] (*US Und.*) an act of informing, a betrayal. **2** [1930s–70s] (*US*) a female vocalist. **3** [1940s+] (*UK black*) meaningless chatter. **4** [1990s+] a taunt, a complaint.

IN PHRASES

❑ **on the chirp** [late 19C] singing, singing heartily.

chirp *v.* **1** [early 19C+] (*US*) to talk loudly; thus *chirp in*, to interrupt. **2** [mid-19C+] to inform. **3** [1910s+] (*US*) to sing. **4** [1930s] (*US*) to provide information. **5** [1970s–80s] (*UK black*) to talk glibly and persuasively. **6** [1980s] (*US campus*) to vomit. **7** [1990s+] (*S.Afr.*) to tease, to taunt, to complain, to be cheeky.

chirper *n.*[1] [CHIRPING MERRY *adj.*] [mid-19C] a glass or tankard.

chirper *n.*[2] [CHIRP v.] **1** [late 19C] the mouth. **2** [late 19C–1950s] a singer. **3** [1930s] an informer, a gossip.

SE in slang uses

IN PHRASES

❑ **pull a chirper** *v.* [SE *chirp*] [1970s] (*US*) to accelerate one's car from a standstill so as to make the tyres screech.

chirpiness *n.* [one *chirps* with pleasure] [mid-19C+] happiness, cheerfulness.

chirping merry *adj.* [mid-17C–early 19C] cheerfully drunk; thus *chirping glass*, 'a cheerful glass, that makes the company chirp like birds in spring' (Grose, 1785) and *chirping-cup*, 'a merry cup, or glass; one which makes you chirp' (Nares, 1822); also a *chirping bottle*.

chirpy *adj.* [SE *chirrup*] [mid-19C+] happy, gay, cheerful.

chirrup *v.* **1** [19C] to chat. **2** [late 19C] to cheer or boo a music-hall turn [the response varies as to whether or not the singer has tipped the gallery].

chirrup and titter *n. see* GIGGLE AND TITTER *n.*

chirruper *n.* [its effect will make the drinker CHIRPING MERRY *adj.*] [mid-18C–mid-19C] an extra glass of alcohol.

chirrupy *adj.* [var. on CHIRPY *adj.*] [19C] cheerful.

chis *n.* (*also* **chise**) [var. on CHICE *n.*] [early 19C] (*UK tramp*) nothing, no good.

chise *n.* (*also* **chis**) [var. on CHIV *n.*[1] (1)] [early 19C] a knife.

chisel *n.* **1** [mid–late 19C] a swindler. **2** [1930s+] a swindle, a deception.

IN PHRASES

❑ **on the chisel** [1950s] (*US*) cheating, usu. for financial gain.

SE in slang uses

IN COMPOUNDS

❑ **chisel-chin** *n.* [supposed resemblance] [1950s–60s] (*US*) one whose lower jaw protrudes.

chisel *v.* (*also* **chissel, chizzel, chizzle**) [SE *chisel*, to cut or pare down; thus 'to take a slice off' (Hotten, 1867)] **1** [early 19C+] to cheat; thus *chisel on, chisel out of*, to defraud; *chiseling*, fraudulent. **2** [1920s–60s] (*also* **chisel in**) to butt in, to intrude, to insinuate oneself, e.g. on another man's date [fig. use of sense 1]. **3** [1920s–60s] (*US*) (*also* **chisel out of**) to beg; to pressurize; to obtain by haggling.

chiseler *n.* (*also* **chiseller, chisler**) [CHISEL *v.* (1)] [1910s+] (*orig. US*) a cheat, a swindler; a petty criminal.

chiseller *n.* (*also* **chisler, chisseler, chissler**) [var. on dial. *childer*, a child] [20C+] (*Irish*) a child.

chiselly *adj.* [CHISEL *v.* (1)] [late 19C] (*US campus*) unpleasant.

chiser *n.* (*also* **chiver**) [var. on CHIV *n.*[1]] [early–mid-19C] a knife.

chisler *n.* **1** *see* CHISELER *n.* **2** *see* CHISELLER *n.*

chism *n. see* JISM *n.*

chissel *v. see* CHISEL *v.*

chisseler/chissler *n. see* CHISELLER *n.*

chit *n.* [CHITTY *n.*] [late 18C+] a letter, a note.

chitari *n.* [? Hind.] [1960s+] (*drugs*) a variety of cannabis.

chitchat *n.*[1] [SE *chat* + redup.; SE f. 1800] [late 17C–18C] banter, light talk.

chitchat *n.*[2] [? enough to foster a pleasant CHITCHAT *n.*[1]] [19C] a measure of alcohol.

chit-chat *v.* [CHITCHAT *n.*[1]] [early 19C+] to chatter, to gossip.

chitlin *adj.* [see CHITLINS *n.*] [1960s+] pertaining to the US South.

chitlins *n.* [US black/Southern pron. of SE *chitterlings*, the intestines, usu. of pigs] [mid-19C+] (*US Southern*) the bowels.

IN COMPOUNDS

❑ **chitlins 101** *n.* [self-mockery; the stereotyped black love of soul food, the recipes of which often feature offal or *chitterlings*] [1960s–70s] (*US black campus*) any form of Black Studies course. ❑ **Chitlin Switch** *n.* [1920s+] (*US black*) the stereotypical small Southern town.

Chi-town *n.* (*also* **Chi-city**) [CHI *n.*] [1920s+] Chicago.

chits *n.*[1] [abbr. CHITLINS *n.*] [1940s–50s] (*US black*) pig intestines.

chits *n.*[2] *see* CHATS *n.*[2].

chitterling *n.* (*also* **chitterlin**) [SE *chitterlings*, the small intestines of animals, esp. pigs] **1** [17C–19C] the penis. **2** [late 17C] a flaccid penis.

chitterlings *n.*[1] (*also* **chitterlins**) [for ety. *see* prev.] [late 18C–19C] the human bowels.

chitterlings *n.*[2] (*also* **chitterlins**) [? f. butchers' jargon *frill*, the mesentery veins, suspending the viscera from the backbone] [early–mid-19C] shirt frills, as affected by ageing dandies.

chitty *n.* [Hind. *chitthi*, 'a letter or note. Also, a certificate given to a servant or the like, a pass' (Y&B); ult. Skrt *chitra*, a spot or mark] [late 17C+] (*orig. Anglo-Ind.*) a letter, a note, any small piece of paper inscribed with writing, usu. instructions.

chitty-face *n.* [dial. *chitty*, thin, baby-faced/SE *chit*, a child] [early 17C–18C] a child with a pinched face or a baby-face; a young female prostitute; also adj., *chitty-faced*, baby-faced.

chiv *n.*[1] (*also* **chev, chevy, chib, chieve, chive, chivy, skiv**) [Rom. *chiv, chive*, a knife] **1** [late 17C+] (*UK Und.*) a knife. **2** [2000s] a scar (from a knife slash).

IN COMPOUNDS

❑ **chiv artist** *n.* (*also* **chev man, chiv man**) [-ARTIST *sfx*] [1920s–50s] (*US*) an expert in using a knife. ❑ **chive-fencer** *n.* [-FENCER *sfx*] **1** [mid-19C] a street-seller of knives and cutlery. **2** [1900s] one who harbours murderers. ❑ **chiving-lay** *n.* [LAY *n.*[3] (1)] **1** [18C–early 19C] (*also* **chieving-lay**) cutting the braces of a coach (the strong leather straps that suspend the body of a coach from the springs); the coachman then dismounts and, while his attention is distracted by one robber, an accomplice plunders the boot of its contents; thus *chiving layer*, one who robs in this way. **2** [late 18C–early 19C] (*UK Und.*) cutting open the back of a coach to steal the large wigs worn by the passengers. **3** [mid-18C] the cutting off of a woman's belt, thus stealing any jewellery or watches that might be attached.

chiv *n.*[2] [SE *chivalry*; f. the South's obsession with 'honour' and 'chivalry'] [mid-19C–1910s] (*US Western*) a white Southerner.

chiv *n.*[3] (*also* **shif**) [CHEVY (CHASE) *n.*] [1900s–10s] (*Aus.*) the face.

chiv *v.* (*also* **chev, chib, chive**) [Rom. *chiv*, to stab/CHIV *n.*[1] (1)] **1** [18C–mid-19C] to cut off. **2** [18C–mid-19C] to saw or file. **3** [mid-18C+] to stab. **4** [1930s] to smash a glass in someone's face and slash them with the shards.

IN PHRASES

❑ **chiv the froe** *v.* [mid-18C] (*UK Und.*) to steal from a woman by cutting round the pockets of her outer garment.

chiva *n.* (*also* **shiva**) [synon. in US Hisp. sl. CALÓ *n.*] [1960s+] (*US drugs*) heroin.

chivalry *n.* [mid-19C] sexual intercourse.

chivaria *n.* [CHIVA *n.*] [1970s+] (*US drugs*) anywhere that one can buy heroin.

chive *see also under* CHIV and combs.

chive *n.* [late 19C] (*UK Und.*) the tongue.

chiver *n. see* CHISER *n.*

chivey *n.* [dial. *chevy*, to pursue, to hunt, to tease; ? ult. proper name *Chevy Chase*, the site of a celebrated border skirmish, memorialized in a popular 17C ballad. Also note the game *Chevy Chase*, which depends on the shouting of the word 'chive'] **1** [late 18C–mid-19C] a scolding, a telling off. **2** [mid-19C] a bother, a fuss, a hassle. **3** [mid-19C] (*also* **chive**) a shout.

chivey *v.* [CHIVEY *n.*] **1** [19C+] to chase around, to hunt about, to leave quickly; thus as imper. *chivey!*, hurry up! **2** [mid-19C] (*US Und.*) to scold.

chivoo *n. see* SHIVOO *n.*

chivver *n.* [CHIV *n.*[1]] [1920s+] an expert in using a knife.

chivving *n.* (*also* **chibbing**) [CHIV *v.* (3)] [1990s+] a stabbing.

chivvy *n.* (*also* **chivy**) [CHEVY (CHASE) *n.*] **1** [late 19C–1950s] the face. **2** [1920s] a general term of address, 'old chap'. **3** [1940s–50s] a moustache.

chivvy *v.*[1] [CHIVEY *n.* (1)] **1** [mid–late 19C] to tease, to mock, to make fun of. **2** [late 19C+] to scold, to tell off.

chivvy *v.*[2] [ext. of CHIV *v.* (3)] [1990s+] to slash with a knife.

chivvy chase *n. see* CHEVY (CHASE) *n.*

Chivy *n. see* CHEVVY *n.*

chivy *n.* **1** *see* CHIV *n.*[1]. **2** *see* CHIVVY *n.*

chivy *adj.* [CHIV *n.*[1]] [late 19C] relating to the use of knives; thus *chivy duel*, a knife fight.

chi-yike *see under* CHI-IKE.

chiz *n.* (*also* **chiz-chiz**) [CHISEL *n.* (2)] [1950s] (*UK juv.*) something unpleasant, unfair, disappointing.

chiz *v.* (*also* **chizz**) [CHISEL *v.* (1)] [1940s–50s] (*UK juv.*) to cheat, to swindle.

chizzel *v. see* CHISEL *v.*

chizzer *n.* (*also* **chiz**) [CHISEL *v.*] [1930s] a cheat, a swindler.

chizzle *v. see* CHISEL *v.*

chizzley ken *n.* [CHISEL *v.* (1) + KEN *n.*[1] (1); but note SE *chisel*, an implement that may be required for the break-in] [mid-19C] (*UK Und.*) a house that is difficult to break into.

chizzlin *n.* [CHILLING *n.* + -IZ- *infix*] [2000s] (*US teen*) relaxing.

Chloe *n.*

IN PHRASES

❑ **do a Chloe** *v.* [a nude portrait, entitled *Chloe*, rejected in 1883 by the Melbourne National Gallery and bought by a well-known local hotel; its popularity entered the national stock of idioms (cf. *BLIND AS CHLOE under* BLIND *adj.*[1]; DRUNK AS CHLOE *adj.*; ...*CHLOE under* QUEER AS... *adj.*)] [late 19C+] (*Aus.*) to appear in the nude.

cho! *excl. see* CHA! *excl.*

choad *n.* (*also* **choda, chode**) [? Navajo *chodis*, penis] **1** [1960s+] (*orig. US teen*) the penis; thus *choadsmoker*, a fellator or fellatrix. **2** [1980s+] a piece of excrement. **3** [1990s+] (*also* **chodelick, dickchode**) a fool, an idiot. **4** [1990s+] the perineum.

choak pear *n. see* CHOKE PEAR *under* CHOKE *v.*

choan *n. see* CHONE *n.*

choc *n.*[1] [CHOCOLATE SOLDIER *n.* (2)] [1910s+] (*Aus.*) a soldier who is reluctant to fight.

choc *n.*[2] **1** *see* CHOCTAW *n.* (2). **2** *see* CHOCO *n.*[2] (2).

choc-a-bloc *adj. see* CHOCKABLOCK *adj.* (1).

choc-box *n.* [play on SE/CHOCOLATE *adj.* (2) + BOX *n.*[1] (1)] [1990s+] the anus.

choccy *n.* (*also* **choccy starfish**) [abbr. *CHOCOLATE STARFISH under* CHOCOLATE *adj.*] [1990s+] the anus.

chocha *n.* [Sp. *chocha*, a doddering woman] [1960s+] (*US*) **1** the vagina. **2** sexual intercourse.

cho-cho *n.* [? SE *chocolate*] [2000s] (*US prison*) ice-cream and other sweets purchased from the prison canteen.

choc-ice *n.* [the SE *choc-ice* is black outside but white within] [1990s+] (*US black*) a derog. term for a black person who may be black racially, but whose opinions, attitudes, lifestyle and goals are all taken from white society.

chock *adj. see* CHOCOLATE *adj.* (1).

chocka *adj. see* CHOKKA *adj.*

chockablock *adj.* [naut. jargon *chockablock*, 'said of a tackle with the two blocks run close together so that they touch each other—the limit of hoisting' (*OED*); transferred to people this became naut. sl. and thence sl.] **1** [mid-19C+] (*also* **choc-a-bloc, chock-heaping, chuck-a-block**) crammed full, crammed together; thus *chockablock full*. **2** [1970s+] (*Aus.*) in fig. use, having sexual intercourse.

IN PHRASES

❑ **go chockablock (with)** *v.* [1970s] (*Aus.*) to have sexual intercourse (with.

chocka-block *v.* (*also* **chocka**) [? rhy. sl. = (get a mouthful of) COCK *n.*[3] (1)] [1980s+] (*Aus. prison*) to fellate.

chock and log *n.* [rhy. sl.] [20C+] (*Aus.*) a dog.

chocker *see also under* CHOKKER.

chocker *adj.* [SE *chockablock* (with emotions)] [1940s+] (*orig. naut.*) fed up, disgruntled.

chockers *n.* [ety. unknown; ? rhy. sl.; *chalk* = walk; or ? *chockerblockers* = dockers; ? a type of shoe] [late 19C+] (*costermonger*) the feet, or boots.

chockers (with) *phr.* [1980s+] (*Aus.*) full of.

IN PHRASES

❑ **get chockers** *v.* [1960s] to have sexual intercourse.

chockey *n. see* CHOKEY *n.*

chock-heaping *adj. see* CHOCKABLOCK *adj.* (1).

chocko *n. see under* CHOCO.

chocks away! *excl.* (*also* **pull chocks!**) [the *chocks*, orig. wood, that were positioned as 'brakes' next to aircraft wheels] [1930s+] (*orig. RAF*) let's go! let's be off!

chocky jockey *n.* [CHOCCY *n.* + JOCKEY *n.*[2] (3b)] [1990s+] a male homosexual.

choco *n.*[1] (*also* **chocko**) [CHOCOLATE SOLDIER *n.*] [1930s+] (*Aus.*) **1** a militiaman or conscripted soldier, esp. one who was drafted into the WW2 militia but never left Australia. **2** a conscientious objector.

choco *n.*[2] [abbr. CHOCOLATE *n.*[1] (1)] **1** [1980s+] (*usu. middle/upper class*) (*also* **chokker, chokko**) a derog. term for a black person. **2** [1980s+] (*Aus.*) (*also* **choc, chocko, choko**) a Mediterranean immigrant.

chocolate *n.*[1] [colour; or in racial uses ? f. rhy. sl. *chocolate frog* = WOG *n.*[1] (1). According to *Maledicta* II (1978) 'especially a woman or homosexual'; the gay use has extra connotation of 'eating' or EAT *v.* (4)] **1** [1910s+] a derog. term for a black person. **2** [1920s+] as used by a black person, thus not derog. **3** [1980s+] (*S.Afr. black*) a 20-rand note. **4** [2000s] as black-to-black term of address.

IN PHRASES

❑ **hot chocolate** *n.* (*also* **sweet chocolate**) [1980s] (*US*) a black woman.

chocolate *n.*[2] *see CHOCOLATE (STUFF) under* CHOCOLATE *adj.*

chocolate *adj.* **1** [20C+] (*also* **chock**) used derog. in ref. to a black person, unless used by a black person. **2** [1970s+] pertaining to the anus, to defecation and, by ext., to homosexuality; also as n.

pertaining to race

IN COMPOUNDS

❑ **chocolate baby** *n.* [BABY *n.* (7)] [1900s] (*US*) a derog. term for a black person. ❑ **chocolate bar** *n.* (*also* **chocolate chip, ...malt, ...smartie**) [20C+] (*US*) a derog. term for a black person. ❑ **chocolate bunny** *n.* [SE *bunny* + inference of BUNNY *n.*[1] (3a)] [1970s–80s] (*US*) a derog. term for a black person. ❑ **chocolate city** *n.* [-CITY *sfx*/SE *city*] **1** [1970s+] (*US*) a black ghetto, any place where there is a concentration of blacks [coined by George Clinton, founder of the funk band Parliament-Funkadelic]. **2** [1980s+] (*US black*) Washington D.C. ❑ **chocolate deluxe** *n.* [a popular brand of ice-cream] [1990s+] (*US black teen*) an attractive, sexy, dark-complexioned black woman. ❑ **chocolate drop** *n.* [20C+] a derog. term for a black person. ❑ **chocolate lover** *n.* [1960s+] (*US*) one who prefers black sexual partners, whether hetero- or homosexual. ❑ **chocolate malt** *n. see CHOCOLATE BAR* above. ❑ **chocolate queen** *n.* [2000s] (*S.Afr. gay*) a white homosexual who prefers black sexual partners. ❑ **chocolate sandwich** *n.* [1990s+] three-way sexual intercourse performed by one black man and two white women. ❑ **chocolate smartie** *n. see CHOCOLATE BAR* above. ❑ **chocolate thunder** *n.* [1980s+] (*US black*) any black basketball player.

IN PHRASES

❑ **chocolate to the bone** *adj.* [1920s–50s] (*US black*) very dark-skinned.

pertaining to the anus and/or excrement

IN COMPOUNDS

❑ **chocolate bandit** *n.* [-BANDIT *sfx* (2)] [1980s] a male homosexual. ❑ **chocolate cake** *n.* [2000s] (*US*) homosexual anal intercourse. ❑ **chocolate canyon** *n.* [CANYON *n.* (2)] [1990s+] the anus; thus *ride the chocolate canyon*, to have anal intercourse (usu. in homosexual context. ❑ **chocolate cha-cha** *n.* [1980s+] (*Aus./US*) anal intercourse; thus *dance the chocolate cha-cha*. ❑ **chocolate chimney-sweep** *n.* [1990s+] one who performs anal intercourse. ❑ **chocolate highway** *n.* (*also* **chocolate freeway, ...speedway, ...tunnel, chocolate whizzway**) [1970s+] (*US*) the rectum or anus; thus *cruise the chocolate highway, ride the chocolate freeway*, to have anal intercourse. ❑ **chocolate puncher** *n.* [1970s+] (*Aus.*) a male homosexual. ❑ **chocolate runway** *n.* [1990s+] the anus. ❑ **chocolate starfish** *n.* [1990s+] the anus.

general uses

IN COMPOUNDS

❑ **chocolate chips** *n.* [a variety of LSD packaged in brown capsules/pills] [1970s+] (*drugs*) LSD. ❑ **chocolate rock** *n.* [ROCK *n.* (4d)] [1990s+] (*drugs*) **1** a dark substance that is produced in the pipe during the smoking of crack cocaine. **2** smoking crack cocaine and heroin at the same time. ❑ **chocolate (stuff)** *n.* [STUFF *n.* (5)] (*drugs*) **1** [1950s] opium. **2** [1950s+] heroin, usu. that manufactured in Mexico. **3** [1970s+] hashish.

chocolate frog *n.* [rhy. sl.] [1980s+] (*Aus.*) **1** an informer [= DOG *n.*[2] (6b)]. **2** influenza [= WOG *n.*[2] (2)]. **3** an immigrant from Southern Europe [= WOG *n.*[1] (8)].

chocolates *n.* [as a luxury] [1960s] (*Aus.*) winnings or booty.

chocolate soldier *n.* [SE *chocolate soldier*, a soldier who will not fight] (*Aus.*) **1** [1910s] a member of the 8th Infantry Brigade of the Australian Imperial Forces (A.I.F.) who arrived in Egypt too late to join in the Gallipoli campaign. **2** [1940s] a soldier who was drafted into the WW2 militia but never left Australia.

choco-taco *n.* [CHOCO *n.*[2] (1) + TACO *n.* (1)] [2000s] (*US black*) a Mexican who pretends to or aspires to be black; also a Mexican that interferes with a black person's life in some way.

choctaw *n.* [SE *choctaw*, the language of the Choctaw, a Muskogean North American Indian people, orig. inhabiting Mississippi and Alabama] **1** [mid-19C–1930s] (*orig. US*) an unknown, foreign or otherwise incomprehensible language. **2** [late 19C+] (*US*) (*also* **choc**) home-made beer or whisky [? the stereotypical Native American being satisfied with inferior products].

choda/chode *n. see* CHOAD *n.*

chodelick *n. see* CHOAD *n.* (3).

choff *n.* [CHOW *n.*[1] (1) + SCOFF *n.*; Cape Du. (and orig. European Du.) term meaning a quarter of a day, and thus one of the four meals eaten in a day] [1950s–60s] food.

choice *adj.* **1** [late 19C+] excellent, first-rate. **2** [1980s+] a general intensifier.

choice riot *n.* [late 19C–1900s] an unpleasant noise.

choice spirit *n.* [SE *choice spirit*, a spirit of special excellence, worthy of being chosen; SE was coined by Shakespeare in *Henry VI Pt 1* (1599)] [late 18C–mid-19C] a devil-may-care, selfish, drunken person.

choir bird *n. see* QUEER BIRD *under* QUEER *adj.*

choirboy *n.* **1** [1930s+] (*US Und.*) a novice thief. **2** [1940s+] (*US*) an innocently honest person; a naive and foolish person. **3** [1960s] (*S.Afr.*) an accomplice, a young man who plays a supporting role in a crime. **4** [1970s] (*US gay*) a novice male streetwalker. **5** [1970s+] (*US*) a novice police officer. **6** [1990s+] (*US black*) a derog. term for a black person seen as embracing white values. **7** [2000s] (*S.Afr. gay*) a homosexual male; thus phr. *in the choir*, homosexual.

choir cove *n. see* QUEER COVE *under* QUEER *adj.*

choke *n.*[1] **1** [late 19C–1920s] prison bread, which is hard to swallow and indigestible. **2** [1920s+] (*Aus.*) an act of garrotting. **3** [1940s+] a shock to the nerves; nervousness. **4** [1970s] a cigarette. **5** [1990s+] (*US campus*) marijuana.

choke *n.*[2] [abbr. CHILE-CHOKER *under* CHILE- *pfx*] [1970s+] (*US*) a derog. term for a Mexican.

choke *v.* (*also* **choke in, choke off, choke up**) [fig. uses of SE] **1** [mid-19C+] (*US*) to stop talking; esp. as imper. *choke it!, choke up!* shut up! **2** [1950s+] (*N.Z./US*) to stop doing something; to turn off, e.g. a radio. **3** [1960s] (*US campus*) to reprimand or refuse; to 'shoot down'. **4** [1960s+] (*US black/campus*) orig. sporting, to lose one's nerve when faced by pressure. **5** [1960s+] (*US campus*) to do badly in work that one should have found easy. **6** [1960s+] (*US campus*) to smoke marijuana.

SE in slang uses

IN COMPOUNDS

❑ **choke-dog** *n.* [joc. ref. to the effects] **1** [early 19C] rum, grog. **2** [late 19C–1910s] cheese; unappetizing food. ❑ **choke-me** *n.* [its heavy, cloying consistency] [1950s] (*W.I.*) foofoo, a mixture of yams, plantains and cassava boiled and then pounded into a thick mass. ❑ **choke pear** *n.* (*also* **choak pear**) [SE *choke pear*, an instrument of torture, similar in shape to the rubber gags favoured by today's S&M adepts, made of an iron 'pear', which is forced into the victim's mouth, a key is turned and spikes protrude from the metal into the mouth, rendering it impossible to remove unless the mouth is cut or another key obtained. This object was itself derived f. 16C *choke pear*, an inedible, hard pear, suitable for making the drink *perry*, but rejected as a dessert] [late 16C–early 19C] an unanswerable objection, a reproof. ❑ **choke-rag** *n.* (*also* **choke-strap**) [SE and its supposed effect on the (reluctant) wearer] [1940s–50s] (*US*) a necktie.

IN PHRASES

❑ **choke a brown dog** *v.* [1980s] (*Aus.*) a general negative or dismissive phr. used variously as to context. ❑ **choke a darkie** *v. see under* DARKIE *n.* ❑ **choke and chew** *n.* (*also* **choke and puke**) [the poor quality of the food] [1970s+] (*US*) a roadside café, a truckstop. ❑ **choke Kojak** *v.* (*also* **strangle Kojak**) [proper name *Kojak*, a bald-headed TV detective] [1990s+] to masturbate. ❑ **choke the chicken** *v.* (*also* **feed the chooks (on Master Bates farm)**) [1990s+] **1** to masturbate. **2** to masturbate a partner. ❑ **choke the lizard** *v. see under* LIZARD *n.*

chokebored *adj.* [SE *chokebore*, a shotgun of which the bore narrows towards the muzzle, keeping the shot together and increasing the effective range] [1940s+] (*US*) (of a person) thin; thus *chokebore pants*, trousers that narrow towards the bottom, esp. riding breeches.

choked *adj.* [SE *choke*] **1** [late 19C+] (*also* **choked off, choked up, choky**) upset, annoyed, depressed, having 'a lump in one's throat'. **2** [1940s] overcome with laughter. **3** [1990s+] (*US campus*) drunk.

IN PHRASES

❑ **choked by a hempen quinsy** [SE *quinsey*, inflammation of the throat, tonsillitis; *hempen* refers to the hangman's noose] [late 18C–early 19C] hanged. ❑ **choked down** *adj.* [the collar and tie] [1970s+] (*US black*) well dressed. ❑ **choked up (tight)** *adj.* [the tight collar and tie to which the wearer is unaccustomed] [1960s+] (*US black*) formally dressed, spec. in a buttoned-up shirt; thus as v. to dress up.

chokee *n. see* CHOKEY *n.*

choke off *v.* [SE *choke* v. + the use of a *choke* to force a bulldog to relinquish its grip] **1** [19C+] to silence in mid-flow. **2** [mid-19C] (*UK Und.*) to arrest, to seize. **3** [mid–late 19C] to render someone uninterested (in). **4** [mid-19C+] to get rid of someone, or something. **5** [mid-19C+] to halt a person's activities. **6** [late 19C] to dismiss, to ignore. **7** [late 19C] to stop one's action, speech etc. **8** [1910s–20s] to reprimand.

choker *n.*[1] [lit. or fig. uses of SE *choke*] **1** [early 19C] a rebuff. **2** [early 19C] a large quantity. **3** [mid-19C] an especially amusing story or anecdote, a lie. **4** ext. uses of SE *choker*, that which chokes, esp. as a form of necktie. (**a**) [mid-19C] a garrotter. (**b**) [mid-19C] a cravat; thus *white-choker*, the white cravat worn by tavern waiters or mutes at a funeral and thus the waiter himself. (**c**) [mid–late 19C] (*also* **white-choker**) a clergyman, metonymical use of his collar. (**d**) [mid-19C–1930s] the hangman's noose; thus the hangman. (**e**) [mid-19C–1960s] a high collar. (**f**) [late 19C–1930s] a large neckerchief, which was worn high round the throat. (**g**) [1900s–40s] (*US black*) a tie. **5** [late 19C–1910s] an embarrassing question. **6** [1910s–40s] (*Irish*) a cigarette. **7** [1920s–30s] cheese. **8** [1950s+] a disappointment, an annoyance. **9** [1950s+] (*Irish*) a person who fails to come up to expectations.

IN COMPOUNDS

❑ **choker-hole** *n.* [the fat-saturated dough is likely to choke the eater] [1920s–40s] (*US*) a doughnut.

choker *n.*[2] [var. on CHOKEY *n.* (1)] **1** [mid-19C+] a prison. **2** [1990s+] (*Irish*) a cell for solitary confinement.

chokes *n.* [1980s+] (*US drugs*) an extreme response to taking an extra-large puff on a marijuana cigarette or a pipe.

chokes and croaks *n.* [1960s+] (*US campus*) a course in first aid and safety education.

choke (up) *v.* **1** [mid-18C; 20C+] to speak. **2** [20C+] (*US*) to give unwillingly, esp. to pay a long-standing debt.

chokey *n.* (*also* **chauki, chockey, chokee, choky, chookie**) [Hind. *chauki*, a four-sided building or a shed, esp. a customs house or police station and thus a lock-up] **1** [mid-19C+] a prison; also in fig. use. **2** [mid-19C+] (*UK Und.*) the punishment cells. **3** [late 19C+] imprisonment. **4** [late 19C+] the prison punishment diet of bread and water; thus *chokey merchant*, one who is suffering such a punishment. **5** [1990s+] (*UK black*) physical violence, 'punishment'.

chokey *v.* [CHOKEY *n.* (2)] [1930s–50s] (*UK prison*) to place in the punishment cells.

choking oyster *n.* (*also* **stopping oyster**) [late 15C–16C] a reply that silences one's opponent.

choking pie *n.* (*also* **cold pie**) [17C–early 19C] a heavy-handed practical joke played on someone who falls asleep in company; cotton is wrapped up in a tube of paper, this is then set on fire and the smoke is directed up the sleeper's nostrils.

chokka *n.* (*also* **chocker**) [ety. unknown] [mid-19C+] a man.

chokka *adj.* (*also* **chocka, chocker, chokker**) [SE *choc full* or CHOCKABLOCK *adj.*] **1** [1920s+] full to the brim. **2** [1940s+] extremely dissatisfied, unhappy, 'fed up'. **3** [1990s+] (*UK juv.*) wonderful, fantastic.

chokker/chokko *n. see* CHOCO *n.*[2] (1).

choko *n. see* CHOCO *n.*[2] (2).

choky *n. see* CHOKEY *n.*

choky *adj. see* CHOKED *adj.* (1).

cholita *n.* [fem. version of CHOLO *n.*] [1960s+] (*US*) **1** a derog. term for a Mexican woman, esp. one considered lower class or of mixed blood. **2** (*also* **chola**) a female member of a teen gang.

cholito *n.* [dimin. of CHOLO *n.*] [1990s+] (*US*) a male gang member.

cholly *n.*[1] [? MR CHARLIE *n.*, the source of employment and thus money] [1960s] (*US gay*) a prostitute's client, i.e. one who pays in dollars.

cholly *n.*[2] [CHARLIE *n.*[8] (1)] [1970s+] (*drugs*) cocaine.

cholly *n.*[3] *see* CHARLIE *n.*[2] (6).

cholly (horse) *n. see* HORSE *n.* (3c).

cholo *n.* [*Chololl*á*n*, now *Cholula*, a district of Mexico] (*US*) **1** [mid-19C+] a derog. term for a Mexican or S. American, esp. one considered lower class or of mixed blood. **2** [1950s+] a teenage gang member.

cholo *adj.* [CHOLO *n.* (1)] [1930s+] describing a Mexican or Mexican culture.

chom *n. see* CHOMUS *n.*

chommie *n.* (*also* **tjommie**) [SE *chum*] [1940s+] (*S.Afr.*) a friend, a pal, a mate; also as a form of address.

cho-mo *n.* [abbr.] [1990s+] (*US Und.*) child molester.

chomp *n.* [SE *chomp*, to bite, to chew] [1960s+] a bite, a mouthful.

chomp *v.* [orig. computer jargon] [1980s+] (*US campus*) to be disgusting, unappealing, second-rate.

chomper *n.* [CHOMP *v.*] [1980s+] (*US campus*) anyone or anything inferior, second-rate, unappealing.

chompers *n.* [SE *chomp*, to take a bite] [20C+] (*US*) teeth, either genuine or false.

chomus *n.* (*also* **chom**) [var. on SHAMUS *n.* (2)] [1930s+] (*US*) a (private) detective.

chone *n.* [ety. unknown; ? abbr. ACTION *n.* (2)] [1960s] (*US*) sexual intercourse.

chong *adj.* [ety. unknown] [2000s] (*UK teen*) attractive.

chonga *n.* [ety. unknown] [2000s] (*drugs*) cocaine.

chongo *n.* [stereotypically 'black' name] [1990s+] (*US*) a derog. name for a black person.

chonk *n.* [fig. use of CHONK *v.*] [1990s+] sexual intercourse.

chonk *v.* [echoic] [1930s] (*US Und.*) to hit over the head (with a sap).

chonkeys *n.* [ety. unknown. Partridge, after Ware, suggests the proper name of a long-forgotten pieman, but note Fr. sl. *chancre*, a paunch (lit. 'ulcer') and *manger comme un chancre*, to eat heartily] [mid-19C] a form of meat pasty, sold in the streets.

chooch *n.*[1] [southern Ital. *ciuccio*, lit. a donkey; thus a fool] [1970s+] (*US*) a fool; esp. large and thuggish.

chooch *n.*[2] [? CHINCH *n.*[2] (1)] [1980s+] (*US drugs*) a stingy dealer.

choo choo *n. see* TRAIN *n.*[1].

choof *n.* [? SE *chuff*, to puff] [1980s+] (*Aus. drugs*) cannabis.

choof (off) *v.* (*also* **chuff**) [SE *chuff*, to go, usu. of a locomotive] [1940s+] (*Aus.*) to go, to move, to leave.

choogle *v.* [? *choo-choo* + *chug*] [1960s+] (*US*) **1** to drive around. **2** in fig. use, to continue; to persist.

chook *n.* (*also* **chook-chook, chookey-hen, chookie**) [SE *chicken*] (*usu. Aus./N.Z.*) **1** [late 19C+] a chicken. **2** [1940s+] a woman. **3** [1950s+] (*N.Z.*) a fool.

IN COMPOUNDS

❑ **chook's breakfast** *n. see* DOG'S DINNER *n.* ❑ **chook's bum** *n.* [BUM *n.*[1] (1)] [1980s] (*N.Z.*) the mouth.

IN PHRASES

❑ **may your chooks turn into emus and kick your shithouse down** [1960s+] (*Aus.*) used to convey one's extreme annoyance with another's actions or words.

chook *v. see* JUKE *v.*[2].

chookie *n.*[1] (*also* **chooky**) [CHOOK *n.*] **1** [1940s+] (*Aus.*) a general term of affection. **2** [1980s] (*N.Z.*) a girlfriend; any young woman.

chookie *n.*[2] *see* CHOKEY *n.*

choom *n.* [northern pron. of *chum*, picked up by ANZAC forces in WW1] [1910s+] (*Aus./N.Z.*) **1** an Englishman. **2** a term of address to an Englishman.

choops *n.* [ety. unknown] [2000s] (*US black*) a cigarette.

choor *v.* [CHORE *v.*] [2000s] **1** to steal. **2** to arrest.

choose *v.* [1960s+] (*US black*) of a prostitute, to select the pimp for whom she will work; thus *choosing money*, the voluntary donation of her earnings by the prostitute to signify to her new pimp that she has chosen him.

choose off *v.* (*also* **choose out**) [1930s+] (*US black*) to challenge to a fight; thus imper. *choose off!* let's fight!

choose up *v.* [1960s+] (*US prison*) of an experienced inmate, to select a newcomer as a homosexual partner, whether or not the latter agrees to act as one.

choosing money *n.* [CHOOSE *v.*] [1970s+] money that a new prostitute gives her pimp on joining his STABLE *n.*

chop *n.*[1] **1** [late 18C–early 19C] a blow with the fist, esp. to the face. **2** [late 19C] (*UK Und.*) a bargain based on exchange of goods. **3** [1910s+] (*orig. Aus.*) a share, portion [CHOP *v.*[5]]. **4** [1940s+] (*orig. US*) a cut, usu. in a salary or in a price. **5** [1950s–70s] (*US juv.*) an insult, a cruel remark. **6** [1990s+] (*drugs*) the chopping of cocaine into lines.

IN COMPOUNDS

❑ **chop-up** *n.* [1910s+] (*Aus. Und.*) a division of plunder.

IN PHRASES

❑ **get the chop** *v.* (*also* **get the chopper**) [1940s+] **1** to be killed. **2** to be dismissed from one's job, or from a sports team. **3** to be rejected or dismissed, to have one's relationship ended. ❑ **give someone the chop** *v.* [1940s+] **1** (*also* **give someone the old chop-chop**) to kill or otherwise dispose of a person. **2** to fire from a job. **3** to destroy, to abandon, to stop, to cut off. ❑ **gone for the chop** *adj.* [1970s] finished, defeated, made impossible. ❑ **hop in for one's chop** *v.* [1960s+] (*Aus.*) to seize one's opportunity. ❑ **in for one's chop** [1920s+] (*Aus./N.Z.*) out for oneself, for one's own profit or advantage.

chop *n.*[2] [orig. W.Afr. pidgin, where colonists and Africans alike used it to describe indigenous food. It was further suggested that orig. chop had meant only one dish, *long pig*, human flesh] **1** [early 19C+] food; thus *small chop*, small items of food. **2** [mid-19C] a boat-load of tea. **3** [1900s] (*US Und.*) tobacco.

chop *n.*[3] [? SE *chop*, goods bearing a mark that determines their quality; ult. Hind. *chhāp*, impression, print, stamp, brand etc] **1** [mid-19C+] (*mainly Aus.*) something to be valued or prized. **2** [1980s+] (*UK black*) in pl., gold, as in chains, rings and similar jewellery.

chop *n.*[4] [1990s+] (*US black*) someone unattractive or socially unacceptable.

chop *v.*[1] (*also* **chop up**) [SE *chop*, to thrust or move with force or suddenness] **1** [mid-17C–early 19C] (*UK Und.*) to do something quickly. **2** [late 18C–mid-19C] (*UK Und.*) to speak. **3** [2000s] (*US black*) to drive an automobile.

IN PHRASES

❑ **chop it up** *v.* (*also* **chop mouth**) [1950s–60s] (*US*) to discuss, to talk about. ❑ **chop one's gums** *v.* (*also* **chop one's teeth**) *see* BEAT ONE'S GUMS *v.*

chop *v.*[2] (*also* **chop down**) [ext. of SE *chop*, to cut (off)] **1** [mid-18C+] to kill. **2** [late 19C–1950s] (*US*) to stop what one is doing. **3** [1910s] (*US*) to punch. **4** [1920s+] (*orig. US Und.*) to shoot, esp. with an automatic weapon. **5** [1940s–50s] to hang someone. **6** [1950s] (*US Und.*) to stab. **7** [1950s+] (*orig. US*) to customize a car, or motorcycle, i.e. one 'chops' it down in size. **8** [1960s+] (*drugs*) to adulterate, usu. a drug in powder form by chopping it up with a non-narcotic substance. **9** [1960s+] (*also* **chop it off**) of a man, to have sexual intercourse. **10** [1970s] (*US black*) (*also* **chop low**) to attack someone verbally, to discredit someone, to have the last word. **11** [1970s] (*US black*) to walk. **12** [1980s+] to dismiss from a job.

IN COMPOUNDS

❑ **chop-shop** *n.* [1960s+] a garage where cars or motorbikes can be customized.

IN PHRASES

❑ **chop it** *v.* [1950s] (*US*) as imper., to stop doing something; forget it! ❑ **chop off** *v.* [late 19C–1930s] (*US*) to finish, to bring to a conclusion, e.g. of work.

SE in slang uses

IN COMPOUNDS

❑ **chop-socky** *n.* (*also* **choppy-socky**) [SE *chop*, a martial arts slice + SOCK *v.*[1] (1)] [1970s+] (*orig. US*) used to describe a kung-fu film.

IN PHRASES

❑ **chop cotton** *v.* [1960s] (*US*) to work hard. ❑ **chop no hash** *v. see under* HASH *n.*[1]. ❑ **chop ten** *v. see* COCK TEN *under* COCK *v.*[4]. ❑ **chop (up) the whiners** *v. see under* WHINERS *n.*

chop *v.*[3] [mid–late 19C] to eat a chop.

chop *v.*[4] [CHOP *n.*[2] (1)] [late 19C; 1960s+] to eat.

chop *v.*[5] [late 19C–1920s] (*Aus.*) **1** to share, to divide up, to exchange. **2** to take part in, to interfere.

chop by chance *n.* [late 17C–early 18C] a very rare or extraordinary event.

chop-chop *n.* [CHOP *n.*[2] (1)] [1950s–70s] (*US*) food.

chop-chop *v.* [CHOP-CHOP! *excl.*] [mid-19C+] to hurry.

chop-chop *adv.* [CHOP-CHOP *v.*] [mid-19C+] quickly, fast.

chop-chop! *excl.* [synon. Chinese pidgin, orig. Chinese *k'wâi-k'wâi*] [mid-19C+] hurry up!

chop-church *n.* (*also* **church-chopper**) [SE *chop*, to barter + *church*] [late 18C–early 19C] a corrupt dealer in benefices, the choicest of which could be sold off to the highest bidder.

chopped *adj.* [1990s+] (*US black*) drunk, drugged.

chopped hay *n.* [1910s–20s] imperfectly assimilated knowledge.

chopper *n.*[1] [ext. of SE *chop*, to cut] **1** [late 18C–mid-19C] a blow to the face. **2** [1910s+] (*Aus.*) a blow to the back of the neck, given with the side of the hand. **3** [1940s+] the penis. **4** as weapons. (**a**) [late 19C+] an open, straight-bladed razor. (**b**) [1920s+] a Thompson sub-machinegun, usu. gangster use; also a machinegunner; thus *chopper squad*, a group of men carrying such guns. (**c**) [1930s–60s] one who uses a sub-machinegun. (**d**) [1990s+] (*US prison*) a stabbing weapon. (**e**) [2000s] (*US black*) any form of gun. **5** [late 19C–1900s] (*US*) a ticket-taker, who tears or 'chops' tickets. **6** [1950s+] a helicopter; thus *copper-chopper*, a police helicopter. **7** [1960s+] a cut-down, 'chopped' motorbike, spec. a Harley-Davidson, preferred for speed and style by outlaw motorcycle gangs, e.g. Hell's Angels.

IN PHRASES

❑ **get the chopper** *v. see* GET THE CHOP *under* CHOP *n.*[1].

chopper *n.*[2] [ety. unknown; ? its wagging motion] [late 19C+] a tail.

chopper *n.*[3] *see* ROCKCHOPPER *under* ROCK *n.*

chopper *n.*[4] [? their involvement in the logging industry] [1980s] (*N.Z. campus*) a derog. term for a Malaysian.

chopper *v.* [CHOPPER *n.*[1] (6)] [1960s+] **1** to travel by helicopter. **2** to transport by helicopter.

choppers *n.* **1** [early–mid-19C] the jaw. **2** [1940s+] the teeth, occas. false; thus *china choppers*, *store choppers*, false teeth. **3** [1960s] (*US black*) the legs, esp. the thighs.

chopping *adj.* [SE *chopping*, vigorous, large, strapping] [mid-17C–early 19C] lusty, sexually forward.

chopping high *adj.* [CHOP *v.*[4]] [1950s] (*US black*) living well.

chopping sticks *n. see* CHOPSTICKS *n.*

chops *n.*[1] (*also* **chaps**) [16C SE] **1** [late 16C+] the jaws, the mouth, the lips. **2** [late 19C] (*Aus.*) food, a meal. **3** [20C+] a synon. for ARSE *n.* (4); esp. in phr. *freeze/sweat/work one's chops off*. **4** [1940s+] (*orig. US black*) ability, skill, competence [jazz musicians fig. ref. to the use of one's mouth and lips in playing a wind instrument].

IN PHRASES

❑ **bust one's chops** *v.* [1950s+] (*US*) **1** to talk incessantly. **2** to work very hard. **3** to make a great fuss about something. ❑ **down in the chops** (*also* **down in the gills**) [19C] depressed. ❑ **flap one's chops** *v.* [20C+] to talk incessantly, to gossip. ❑ **flog one's chops** *v.* **1** [1960s+] (*Aus.*) to work very hard. **2** [2000s] (*N.Z.*) to talk incessantly. ❑ **grease one's chops** *v.* [1920s–70s] (*US black*) to eat, esp. to eat highly greasy food. ❑ **lick the chops** *v.* [1930s–40s] (*US black*) of musicians, to tune up before a performance. ❑ **run one's chops out** *v.* [1960s+] (*US black*) to talk, to complain. ❑ **slice one's chops** *v.* [1940s] (*US black*) to talk. ❑ **wag one's chops** *v.* [mid-19C] to chatter, to gossip, to complain.

chops *n.*[2] *see* CHOP *n.*[3] (2).

chops *v.* [CHOPS *n.*[1] (1)] [1990s+] (*UK juv.*) to be cheeky, to be verbose.

chopstick *n.* [the use of chopsticks in eating Asian food] [1940s+] (*usu. US black*) a derog. term for an East Asian person, esp. Chinese; also adj. use.

chopsticks *n.* (*also* **chopping sticks**) [rhy. sl.] [1940s+] (*bingo*) the number six or 26.

chop suey *n.* [SE *chopped up* + *chop suey*, a dish of stir-fried meat and vegetables, created by Chinese chefs for their Western customers. Not part of Asian cuisine, it was seen as adequate for the Western palate. The orig. Chinese is *shap suì*, mixed bits] [1920s+] (*US*) **1** a Chinese person. **2** (*also* **chop suey joint**) a Chinese restaurant, or establishment. **3** a person of mixed ancestry. **4** (*US*) something crazy but appealing.

chorb *n.* [? Bantu *chubaba*, a skin blemish] [1970s+] (*S.Afr. teen*) acne, a spot, a pimple.

chore *v.* (*also* **chorie, chory**) [Rom. *cor*/*chore*, to steal; thus link to costermonger *chordy gear*, stolen goods] [late 19C; 1970s+] to steal (cf. CORE *v.*).

IN PHRASES

□ **on the chorie** [1990s+] (*Scot.*) engaged in thieving (as a regular occupation).

chorie *n.* [CHORE *v.*] [2000s] a thief.

chorrie *n.* (*also* **tjorie, tjorrie**) [Afk. *tjor*, a crock] [1960s+] (*S.Afr.*) a broken-down old car.

chorros *n.* [? Sp.] [1990s+] (*US prison/Hisp.*) a lookout.

chorus and verse *n.* [rhy. sl. = *erse*, i.e. arse] [1990s+] the anus, the rectum.

chorus man *n.* [negative stereotyping] [1920s] (*US*) an effeminate, poss. homosexual man.

chory *v. see* CHORE *v.*

chosen *adj.* [CHOOSE UP *v.*] [1960s+] (*US prison*) selected, like it or not, as the homosexual lover of an older, tougher inmate.

chosen pals *n.* (*also* **chosen pells**) [SE *choose* + Gypsy *pal*, an accomplice in crime] [late 18C] (*UK Und.*) highwaymen who go out robbing in pairs.

chossel *n.* [CHOSSEL *v.*] [20C+] (*W.I.*) a girlfriend.

chossel *v.* [? SE *choose* + HUSTLE *v.* (2)] [20C+] (*W.I.*) to start a romantic or sexual relationship.

chota *n.* [Sp.] [1960s+] (*US*) **1** the police. **2** a police informer.

chotchkie *n. see* TCHOTCHKE *n.*

chote *n.* [CHOTE *v.*] [20C+] (*W.I.*) flattery of another person or boasting about oneself; thus *give someone (a lot of) chote*, to attempt to persuade someone through such talk.

chote *v.* [Sp. *chotear*, to joke, to banter] [20C+] (*W.I.*) to flatter, to persuade through compliments.

chounter *v.* [either earlier form of *chunter* (as suggested by *OED*) or f. Devon dial. *chounting*, taunting, jeering, grumbling] [late 17C–18C] to talk sharply and sometimes aggressively.

chouse *n.* (*also* **chowse**) [Turkish *chiaus*, *chaus*, an official messenger. The link here comes either from the fleecing in 1609 of some Turkish and Persian merchants by an agent or *chiaus* of Sir Robert Shirley (the *OED* rejects this for lack of corroborative evidence), or by the philologist Thomas Henshaw's remark that a Turkish messenger 'is little better than a fool', a dictum that he claimed was sufficient proof of an ety.] **1** [mid-17C] (*also* **chouser**) a cheat, a swindler. **2** [mid-17C–mid-18C] a dupe, a gullible victim. **3** [early–mid-18C] a swindle, a confidence trick.

chouse *v.* (*also* **chowse, chowze**) [CHOUSE *n.*] **1** [mid-17C+] to trick, to defraud; often as *chouse one out of*. **2** [1930s] to leave (in order to hide oneself).

chout *n.* [? SE *shout* or f. East Anglian dial. *chout*, merry-making, a frolic] [mid-19C] (*East London*) a show, an entertainment.

chovey *n.* (*also* **chovy**) [ety. unknown] [late 18C–19C] a shop; thus *ann-chovey* and *man-chovey*, the female and male shop assistant.

IN COMPOUNDS

□ **chovy-bouncing** *n.* [BOUNCE *v.*[1] (5)] [late 19C] (*Aus. Und.*) shoplifting.

Chow *n.* [abbr. pidgin *chow-chow*, food; ult. ? the *chow* dog, eaten in China; note MacGill, *Reed Dict. of N.Z. Slang* (2003): 'Evolved from sailors calling food "chow"; *chowchow* for yellow pickles, from Chinese perceived as yellow in skin pigment. A term of contempt that followed Chinese into market gardening, where a cabbage was known as a chow.'] **1** [late 19C+] (*Aus.*) a derog. term for a Chinese person, esp. an immigrant or descendant of one. **2** [1910s] one who displays the negative characteristics of a stereotyped Chinese person.

IN PHRASES

□ **awkward as a Chow on a bike** [1920s+] extremely clumsy, uncoordinated.

Chow *adj.* [CHOW *n.* (1)] [1910s+] (*Aus.*) Chinese.

IN COMPOUNDS

□ **Chowland** *n.* [1900s] (*Aus.*) Queensland.

chow *n.*[1] [Anglo-Chinese pidgin *chow*, a mixture (of any kind), thus food] **1** [mid-19C+] food, esp. in an institutional setting, i.e. an army mess-hall, prison etc. **2** [late 19C+] (*also* **chowtime**) a mealtime, usu. in some form of institution. **3** [1910s] (*US*) by metonymy, one whose duty it is to wait at table etc. **4** [1920s+] (*Aus.*) cabbage [? Fr. *choux*, cabbage]. **5** [1940s] snuff. **6** [1950s–60s] a meal.

IN COMPOUNDS

□ **chow cart** *n.* [1910s+] (*US prison*) the trolley that carries food from cell to cell; or other vehicle conveying food. □ **chow hall** *n.* [1990s+] the mess-hall. □ **chow hound** *n.* [-HOUND *sfx*] [1910s+] a glutton. □ **chow joint** *n.* [1960s] a restaurant. □ **chow line** *n.* [1910s+] (*US, orig. milit.*) a queue for food. □ **chow wagon** *n.* [1910s+] (*US prison*) a trolley carrying prisoners' meals.

IN PHRASES

□ **blow chow** *v.* [BLOW *v.*[1] (2b)] [1980s+] (*US*) to vomit.

chow *n.*[2] [SE *chew*/? CHEW *v.* (2) / JAW *n.* (1)] **1** [mid-19C] (*UK prison*) a single 'chew' of tobacco. **2** [late 19C–1910s] (*also* **chow-chow**) talk; thus *have plenty of chow*, to be highly loquacious [orig. theatrical use; ult. ety. unknown].

chow *v.*[1] [CHOW *n.*[2] (2); mainly theatrical use] [late 19C+] to chatter, to prattle.

chow *v.*[2] (*also* **chow on**) [CHOW *n.*[1] (1)] [20C+] to eat; thus *chow up*, to prepare food.

IN PHRASES

□ **chow box** *v.* [BOX *n.*[1] (1a)] [1990s+] (*US*) to perform cunnilingus. □ **chow down** *v. see* separate entry. □ **chow out** *v.* [1970s+] (*US campus*) to overeat.

chow *phr.* (*also* **chaow**) [Ital. *ciao* (pron. 'chow'), goodbye] [1960s+] goodbye (cf. CIAO *phr.*).

IN PHRASES

□ **chow for now** [1990s+] (*US campus*) goodbye.

chow-chow *n.*[1] [pidgin *chow-chow*, an edible mixture, typically of pickles or preserves; also a mixed cargo] **1** [mid-19C] a Chinese restaurant. **2** [mid-19C–1940s] (*orig. Anglo-Chinese*) food. **3** [mid-19C–1940s] (*Aus.*) a derog. term for a Chinese person.

chow-chow *n.*[2] *see* CHOW *n.*[2] (2).

chow-chow *v.* [CHOW-CHOW *n.*[1] (2)] [mid-19C+] to eat.

chowdar *n.* (*also* **chowder**) [? Anglo-Chinese, but note CHOWDER-HEAD *n.*] [mid-19C] a fool.

chowder-head *n.* (*also* **chowder-brain**) [SE *chowder*, a fish stew + -HEAD *sfx* (1) but more prob. corruption of JOLTERHEAD *n.* (1)] [mid-19C+] (*US*) a fool, a stupid person.

DERIVATIVES

□ **chowder-headed** *adj.* [slightly predates n.] [early 19C+] foolish.

chow down *v.* [CHOW *v.*[2] (1)] **1** [1940s+] (*US*) to eat voraciously; also as imper. *chow down*, start eating; n. *chow down*, a meal. **2** [1950s+] (*US*) to perform oral sex. **3** [1960s] (*US campus*) to kiss, to pet. **4** [1970s] to provide someone with a meal.

Chowick *n.* [CHOW *n.* (1)] [1990s+] (*N.Z.*) Auckland suburb of Howick, a derog. ref. to its large population of Asian immigrants since 1990s.

chow mein parlor *n.* [standard Chinese dish *chow mein*] [1970s] (*US*) a Chinese restaurant.

chowse *see under* CHOUSE.

chowze *v. see* CHOUSE *v.*

chozz *v.* [play on SE *chew*] [2000s] (*S.Afr.*) to chew, to eat.

chrimbo *n.* [abbr.] [1980s+] Christmas.

Chrissake! *excl. see* FOR CHRIST'S SAKE! *excl.*

chrissie *n.*[1] [*Chrissie*, a character in the play *Liffey Lane* (1951) by Maura Laverty] [1950s+] (*Irish*) a working-class person with delusions of grandeur, esp. as shown in their dress sense.

chrissie *n.*[2] (*also* **chrissy**) [abbr.] [1970s+] *Christmas.*

Christ *n.* (*also* **the Christ**) [1940s+] a general abstract intensifier, implying quantity, strength, essence etc; synon. with HELL, THE *phr.* (3).

IN PHRASES

❑ **bash the Christ out of** *v.* (*also* **belt the Christ out of**) [1970s] (*Aus.*) to beat severely.

proper name in slang uses

DERIVATIVES

❑ **Christless** *adj.* [1910s+] (*US*) lit. 'god-damned' (see GOD-DAMN *adj.*).

IN COMPOUNDS

❑ **Christ-bitten** *adj.* [lit. *bitten by Christ*, i.e. fanatically religious] [1930s+] (*US*) a general derog. description e.g. *these Christ-bitten idiots*. ❑ **Christ-killer** *n.* (*US*) **1** [mid-19C+] a derog. term for a Jew [the teaching by trad. Christianity that the Jews killed Christ]. **2** [1930s] a noisy political orator [the majority of such orators were self-proclaimed atheists]. ❑ **Christ-shouter** *n.* see CHRISTER *n.*

IN PHRASES

❑ **Christ knows what/when** *see* LORD KNOWS HOW *under* LORD *n.* ❑ **to Christ** (*also* **to Christmas**) [1910s+] a general intensifier. ❑ **when Christ was a corporal** [1970s] (*US*) a very long time ago.

IN EXCLAMATIONS

❑ **sweet Christ!** *see* SWEET JESUS! *under* SWEET *adj.*[1].

Christ! *excl.* (*also* **Christes curs! Christ all hell! Holy Christ! my Christ!**) [late 14C+] the main blasphemous oath, which carried a good deal more resonance when religion (and thus potential blasphemy) had greater power.

IN COMPOUNDS

❑ **Christ almighty** *adj.* [20C+] a general intensifier. ❑ **Christ-awful** *adj.* (*also* **Christ-all, Christ all hemlock**) [var. on GOD-AWFUL *adj.*] [1940s+] (*orig. US*) especially appalling; also as excl.

IN EXCLAMATIONS

❑ **Christ almighty!** (*also* **Christamighty! Christ allbloodymighty!**) [20C+] a common blasphemous excl. ❑ **Christ Jesus!** *see* JESUS! *excl.* ❑ **Christ on a bike!** (*also* **Christ on a bicycle! ...bleeding toboggan! ...buckboard! ...Harley! ...fire-engine!**) [1960s+] a mild excl. ❑ **Christ on a crutch!** (*also* **Christ on a raft! ...stretcher!**) [1940s+] a mild excl. ❑ **Christ sake!** *see* FOR CHRIST'S SAKE! *excl.*

christacrutchian *n.* (*also* **chian**) [CHRIST ON A CRUTCH! *under* CHRIST! *excl.*] [1990s+] (*US*) a Bible-thumping, back-sliding hypocrite.

Christchurch! *excl.* (*also* **by Christchurch! oh Christchurch!**) [the towns of Christchurch, found in both countries] [1940s+] (*N.Z./UK*) a euph. oath.

christen *v.* **1** [mid-18C–19C] (*UK Und.*) to change the markings on a stolen watch to facilitate its resale; esp. as *christen a yack*. **2** [late 18C–early 19C] to water down wine or spirits; thus *christened*, adulterated. **3** [late 19C+] to carry out a practical joke in which a chamberpot is emptied over someone's head. **4** [late 19C+] to mark or otherwise damage, esp. of a dog that reveals its lack of house-training. **5** [late 19C+] to use for the first time. **6** [1930s] to hit over the head.

christened by a baker *adj.* (*also* **christened by the baker**) [freckles are reminiscent of spots of brown flour] [late 18C–early 19C] freckle-faced.

christener *n.* [CHRISTEN *v.* (1)] [late 18C–19C] a criminal who fakes the identity marks – the 'christening' – on cheap gold and silver watches.

Christer *n.* (*also* **Christ-shouter**) [SE *Christ*; orig. referring to those who belonged to US college Christian Associations of the 1920s] [1920s+] (*US*) a derog. term for an overly religious person, esp. a proselytizing teetotaller.

Christian *n.*[1] **1** [17C+] an overly religious person. **2** [early–mid-19C] a tradesman who is willing to give credit, i.e. he 'has faith'.

Christian *n.*[2] [1960s] (*US black*) a cigar.

Christian *adj.* [the illusion of Christian beneficence] [19C] of things, 'decent', 'respectable' or 'presentable'.

SE in slang uses

IN COMPOUNDS

❑ **Christian pony** *n.* **1** [late 18C] a chairman of a meeting. **2** [late 18C–early 19C] a sedan chair man. **3** [mid–late 19C] (*Can.*) a handcart man.

christina *n.* (*also* **cris, cristina**) [SE *crystal*] [1970s+] (*drugs*) amphetamine, methamphetamine.

christly *adj.* [abbr. CHRIST ALMIGHTY *under* CHRIST! *excl.*] [1910s+] (*US*) a general intensifier, DAMNED *adj.* (1).

Christmas *n.*

SE in slang uses

IN COMPOUNDS

❑ **Christmas compliments** *n.* [the effects of the winter weather. Grose (1796) includes the synon. entry *Christian compliments* but it is a misprint, as can be seen by the fact that he provides a cross-ref. to 'Christmas' at 'compliment'] [late 18C–early 19C] a cough, 'kibed' (chilblained) heels and a snotty nose. ❑ **Christmas hold** *n.* (*also* **Christmas grip, Father Christmas hold**) [pun on SE 'handful of nuts', a popular Yuletide pleasure and NUTS *n.*[2] (1)] [1950s+] (*Aus./N.Z.*) a squeeze of one's opponent's testicles, usu. in wrestling. ❑ **Christmas rolls** *n.* [1960s–70s] (*drugs*) a mixture of different coloured depressant pills.

IN PHRASES

❑ **from here to Christmas** *see* FROM HELL TO BREAKFAST *under* HELL *n.* ❑ **to Christmas** *see* TO CHRIST *under* CHRIST *n.* ❑ **what is this, Christmas?** [1980s+] a general phr. of pleasurable surprise.

Christmas! *excl.* (*also* **by Christmas! Holy Christmas!**) [20C+] a euph. for CHRIST! *excl.*

christmas *adj.* [1960s] (*N.Z.*) fine, admirable.

Christmas card *n.* [rhy. sl.] [1950s+] a train guard; a military guard.

Christmas crackers *n.* [rhy. sl. = KNACKERS *n.*; *Christmas crackered* = KNACKERED *adj.*] [1970s+] the testicles; thus *Christmas crackered*, utterly exhausted.

Christmas eve *v.* [rhy. sl.] [1930s+] to believe.

Christmas log *n.* [rhy. sl.] [1970s] a dog.

Christmas tree *n.*[1] **1** in drug uses [the multi-coloured pills that are reminiscent of a Christmas tree's lights]. (**a**) [1960s+] a stimulant (deximal spansules). (**b**) [1960s+] a depressant (butabarbital, Tuinal). (**c**) [1980s] LSD. (**d**) [2000s] marijuana. **2** [1980s] (*US*) a heavily over-made-up or over-dressed woman [she is 'lit up like a Christmas tree'].

Christmas tree *n.*[2] [rhy. sl.] [1990s+] the human knee.

Christmas tree *n.*[3] [its triangular shape, plus the serrated edges filed into the knife are supposedly reminiscent of the stereotyped shape of the Christmas pine] [1990s+] (*US prison*) a makeshift, home-made knife.

Christopher! *excl.* (*also* **by Christopher! holy Christopher!**) [mid-19C+] a euph. for CHRIST! *excl.*

Christopher Columbus! *excl.* (*also* **Christopher Hemlock!**) [1940s+] a euph. for CHRIST! *excl.*

Christopher Lee *n.* [rhy. sl. = PEE *n.*[1] (2) / WEE *n.*; ult. UK actor *Christopher Lee* (b.1922)] [1990s+] an act of urination.

chrome *n.* **1** [1970s+] (*US black*) a gun [the *chrome* finish applied to many models of pistol/revolver]. **2** [1990s+] (*US black*) loose change, esp. dimes, quarters and half-dollars [the silvery colour]. **3** [2000s] (*US black*) an automobile (presumably heavily customized).

SE in slang uses

IN COMPOUNDS

❑ **chrome dome** *n.* [DOME *n.* (1)] [1960s+] (*orig. US*) **1** a bald head. **2** a bald-headed person. ❑ **chrome-plated** *adj.* [1950s] (*US gay*) dressed up in one's best or new clothes.

IN PHRASES

❑ **sit on chrome** *v.* [2000s] (*US black*) to possess an automobile that is fitted with chrome rims on the wheels.

chromo *n.* [SE *chromolithograph*, a picture printed in colours from stone. Although the term is uniquely Aus., it originates in the comparison by US writer Francis Brett Harte (1836–1902) of an over-dressed, over-made-up prostitute with a chromolithograph – both are colourful and flashy, but neither resembles natural beauty] [late 19C+] **1** (*also* **cromo**) (*Aus.*) a prostitute. **2** an ugly, distasteful person. **3** (*US campus*) something above average.

chromo *adj.* [abbr. SE *chromolithographic*] [late 19C+] (*US*) spurious, fake, counterfeit.

chroneer *n.* *see* CHRONICKER *n.*

chronic *n.* [SE *chronic*, severe, extreme; thus the drug's effects; an example of the bad = good model + ? CHRONIC *adj.* (1)] **1** [1920s–50s] (*drugs*) a regular narcotics user. **2** [1980s+] (*drugs*) one who smokes cannabis every day. **3** [1990s+] (*US campus*) a cigarette. **4** [1990s+] (*drugs*) extra-strong marijuana. **5** [2000s] (*drugs*) marijuana mixed with crack cocaine.

chronic *adj.* **1** [late 19C+] extreme, usu. in a negative sense and often as phr. *something chronic*. **2** [1990s+] (*orig. US drugs*) of marijuana, first-rate, very strong. **3** [1990s+] (*US campus*) excellent.

chronic *v.* [? one poses as a *chronic* invalid] [1920s–30s] (*US tramp*) to beg; to investigate.

chroniced (out) *adj.* [CHRONIC *n.* (4)] [1990s+] (*US black/drugs*) intoxicated by very strong marijuana.

chronicker *n.* (*also* **chroneer, croniker**) **1** [1910s–30s] (*US tramp*) a tramp who begs food rather than money. **2** [1920s–30s] an ill-natured tramp.

chryssie *n.* [abbr.] [1920s+] (*Aus.*) a *chrys*anthemum.

chu! *excl.* *see* CHA! *excl.*

chub *n.*[1] [SE *chub*, a short, squat fish; thus a pun on 'thick' or 'dense' or being 'easily taken' notes Grose (1785)] **1** [early 16C–early 19C] an inexperienced, naïve person, a fool. **2** [mid-16C–18C] a rustic simpleton; thus adj. *chubbish*. **3** [18C] (*UK Und.*) a sharper. **4** [mid-19C+] a fat person; the fat on their body. **5** [late 19C] (*US campus*) a child; a baby. **6** *see* CHUBBY *n.* (2).

DERIVATIVES

❑ **chubette** *n.* [1950s+] a fat person, usu. a young woman, but in camp gay use a boy.

chub *n.*[2] [ety. unknown; ? ref. to CHUB *n.*[1] (4)] [19C] a Texan.

chubbies *n.* [1960s–70s] (*US*) large and attractive female breasts.

chubbingly *adj.* [late 17C–early 18C] chubby.

chubblies *n.* [SE *chubby*/CHUBBIES *n.*] [1990s+] a fat woman's breasts.

chubbo *n.* (*also* **chub-chub, chubo-twin**) [CHUB *n.*[1] (4)] [1970s+] (*US*) a fat person.

chubbs *n.* [CHUB *n.*[1] (4)] [1990s+] (*US black*) a fat person.

chubb (up) *v.* [the proprietary name of *Chubb* locks] [1940s–80s] (*UK prison*) to lock up a cell for the night; thus *unchubb*, to unlock.

chubby *n.* **1** [1920s] a short, squat umbrella. **2** [1990s+] (*also* **chub**) an erection [play on FAT *n.* (3)].

IN COMPOUNDS

❑ **chubby-chaser** *n.* [1970s+] a man who prefers (unfashionably) plump or fat women or, if gay, men. ❑ **chubbyfat** *adj.* [1940s–50s] (*US black*) very fat, obese.

IN PHRASES

❑ **give someone a chubby** *v.* [1980s+] (*UK juv.*) to pinch and twist someone's nipple, as an aggressive greeting or a punishment.

chub-chub *n.* *see* CHUBBO *n.*

chub off *v.* [? CHUB *n.*[1]] [late 19C–1900s] (*US*) to lose.

chubo-twin *n.* *see* CHUBBO *n.*

chuc *n.* (*also* **chuco**) [abbr. PACHUCO *n.*] [1940s+] (*US*) **1** a Mexican-American, esp. a member of a street gang. **2** a pointed shoe, associated with Mexican youths.

Chuck *n.* (*also* **Mr Chuck**) [colloq. *Chuck*, the nickname derived from Charles; thus CHARLES *n.*[1]/MR CHARLIE *n.* (1)] [1960s+] (*US black*) a white man.

chuck *n.*[1] [dial.; the term also meant a call to fowls (or pigs). It persists in 20C+ northern dial., typified by its use in the TV soap opera *Coronation Street*] [late 16C+] a term of endearment.

chuck *n.*[2] [CHUCK *v.*[2]] **1** [mid-18C+] a toss, a throw. **2** [late 19C+] the act of rejection, usu. as *the chuck* and usu. in the context of terminating a relationship or a term of employment; *see* phrs. below. **3** [late 19C+] a verdict of not guilty. **4** [1960s+] (*Aus.*) vomit. **5** [1960s+] (*Aus.*) an act of vomiting. **6** [1980s] (*Aus.*) a temper tantrum. **7** *see* CHUCK-FARTHING *under* CHUCK *v.*[2].

IN PHRASES

❑ **drop the chuck on** *v.* [1920s–50s] (*US Und.*) to conspire with the police against a fellow criminal. ❑ **get the chuck** *v.* (*also* **sling the chuck**) **1** [late 19C+] to be rejected as a lover. **2** [late 19C+] to be dismissed from employment. **3** [1970s] of a criminal, to be found not guilty in court. ❑ **give someone the chuck** *v.* [late 19C+] to dismiss from a job, to get rid of, to end a relationship. ❑ **give the chuck-up** *v.* [1910s–20s] to abandon, to stop an action, to dismiss, to throw over, to jilt.

chuck *n.*[3] [orig. referring to bread or ship-biscuit only, ult. ? f. *chuck*, a lump or hunk (of food)] **1** [mid-19C–1900s] the act of eating, a mealtime. **2** [mid-19C+] food. **3** [mid-19C+] (*UK prison*) bread.

IN COMPOUNDS

❑ **chuck habit** *n.* [sense 2 above/CHUCK *v.*[2] (16) + HABIT *n.* (1)] [1930s–60s] (*US drugs*) the increase in appetite that accompanies withdrawal from narcotics. ❑ **chuck horrors** *n.* [sense 2 above/CHUCK *v.*[2] (16) + HORRORS, THE *n.* (4)] [1920s–60s] **1** (*US Und.*) a craving for food. **2** (*US drugs*) the craving for food or, paradoxically, the obsessive loathing of food that accompanies one's withdrawal from heroin. ❑ **chuck house** *n.* (*also* **chucktent**) [1930s–60s] (*US tramp*) a restaurant; also used for the canteen in a mine or mill. ❑ **chuck mill** *n.* [late 19C] (*US*) a hotel. ❑ **chuck wagon** *n.* [note cowboy jargon *chuck wagon*, the wagon that carried the provisions and cooking equipment for a ranch] (*US*) **1** [20C+] a buffet. **2** [1950s–60s] a small restaurant or café. ❑ **chuck wagon chicken** *n.* [20C+] (*US*) bacon.

IN PHRASES

❑ **wrestle one's chuck** *v.* [mid–late 19C] (*US*) to dine.

chuck *n.*[4] *see* CHUCK-FARTHING *under* CHUCK *v.*[2].

chuck *adj.* [CHUCK *n.*] [1960s–70s] (*US black*) white.

chuck *v.*[1] [Grose (1796) suggests that the term applies to women only] **1** [mid-16C–18C] to have sexual intercourse. **2** [late 18C–early 19C; 1990s+] (*later use is UK black*) of a woman, to make sexual advances [note CLUCK *v.*[1], for which this may be a mis-reading].

chuck *v.*[2] **1** [mid-17C; late 19C+] to end an affair, to reject a lover. **2** [mid-19C] (*US*) to hit (with the fist). **3** [late 19C] to eject. **4** [late 19C–1910s] to dismiss from employment. **5** [late 19C+] to give up, to abandon. **6** [late 19C+] to spend extravagantly. **7** [late 19C+] (*UK Und.*) to find not guilty. **8** [late 19C+] to throw out, e.g. of a tavern. **9** [1900s] (*Aus.*) to donate money to a charitable collection. **10** [1910s+] to do or perform, usu. with a defining n. (often referring to a fit or similar convulsion). **11** [1920s] to stop doing something. **12** [1930s] (*US*) to throw a party. **13** [1950s+] (*orig. US/Aus.*) (*also* **chuck up**) to vomit. **14** [1990s+] (*W.I.*) to act aggressively, thuggishly. **15** [1990s+] (*drugs*) to withdraw from heroin. **16** [1990s+] (*UK juv.*) to ejaculate.

IN PHRASES

❑ **chuck a charley** *v.* *see under* CHARLIE BRITT *n.* ❑ **chuck a cheesy** *v.* *see under* CHEESE *n.*[3]. ❑ **chuck a chest** *v.* *see* CHUCK THE GAB below. ❑ **chuck a dummy** *v.* (*also* **chuck the dummy**) [SE *dummy*, a fake] [late 19C+] **1** to vomit. **2** to have a fit, esp. when only pretending [orig. milit., to pretend to faint on parade in order to escape duties]. **3** to absent oneself. **4** to lose one's temper. □ **chuck a fit** *v.* **1** [mid–late 19C] to fake a fit. **2** [1920s] to have a fig. fit; to lose emotional control. □ **chuck a jolly** *v.* [orig. used by costermongers to describe their habit of boosting the dubious virtues of some otherwise unappealing item offered on a friend's stall] [mid–late 19C] to praise enthusiastically, to 'talk up' inferior goods. □ **chuck a mag** *v. see under* MAG *n.*^{5}. □ **chuck an Oliver** *v.* (*also* **do an Oliver**) [*Oliver Twist* and his request 'May I have some more?'] [1980s] (*Aus.*) to ask for a second helping of food. □ **chuck a seven** *v.* see separate entry. □ **chuck a shoulder** *v.* [synon. with SE *cold shoulder*] [late 19C–1900s] to ignore, to 'cut'. □ **chuck a sixer** *v.* see separate entry. □ **chuck a slob** *v. see under* SLOBBER *n.* □ **chuck a slug** *v. see under* SLUG *n.*^{1}. □ **chuck a spaz** *v. see under* SPAZ *n.* □ **chuck a stall** *v. see under* STALL *n.*^{1}. □ **chuck a swell** *v. see under* SWELL *n.*^{1}. □ **chuck a tread** *v.* [SE *tread*, of a cock, to have intercourse with a hen] [late 19C–1900s] of a man, to have sexual intercourse. □ **chuck a turd** *v. see under* TURD *n.*^{1}. □ **chuck a willie** *v. see under* WILLIE *n.*^{2}. □ **chuck a wobbly** *v. see under* WOBBLY *n.*^{2}. □ **chuck into** *v. see* THROW (IT) INTO *v.* (2). □ **chuck it** see separate entries. □ **chuck one's ace** *v.* [card-playing imagery] [1900s] (*Aus.*) to pass out. □ **chuck one's biscuits** *v. see under* BISCUIT *n.*^{1}. □ **chuck one's load** *v. see under* LOAD *n.* □ **chuck one's muck** *v. see under* MUCK *n.*^{1}. □ **chuck over** *v.* [late 19C+] to abandon, to dismiss, to throw over, to jilt. □ **chuck the gab** *v.* (*also* **chuck a chest**) [GAB *n.*^{1}/ SE *chest*] [1930s] to 'tell the tale' for the purposes of begging or confidence trickery; to talk eloquently and articulately. □ **chuck up** see separate entries.

SE in slang uses

(IN COMPOUNDS)

□ **chuckaway** *n.* [late 19C–1900s] a lucifer or non-safety match. □ **chuck-bread** *n.* [late 19C–1900s] (*UK tramp*) waste bread that would be thrown away were it not offered to tramps. □ **chuck-farthing** *n.* (*also* **chuck**) [SE *chuck-farthing*, a precursor of 20C pitch and toss, in which coins are first pitched at a mark, and then tossed at a hole by the player who came nearest the mark, and who wins everything that landed in the hole; used as the proper name of a character in the *Satire against Hypocrites*, cited by B.E.] [late 17C–mid-19C] a parish clerk. □ **chuck-office** *n.* (*also* **chuck-hole**) [SE *chuck-farthing*, 'a game of combined skill and chance in which coins were pitched at a mark, and then chucked or tossed at a hole by the player who came nearest the mark, and who won all that alighted in the hole' (*OED*); Priss Fotheringham, the apparent 'champion' had absorbed some 15 half-crowns (£1.87)] [17C] the vagina, esp. in the context of the *half-crown chuck-office*, a prostitute's trick whereby she would stand on her head, exhibiting her spread vulva and clients would throw coins into the vagina.

(IN PHRASES)

□ **chuck in** see separate entries. □ **chuck off (at)** *v.* [20C+] (*Aus./N.Z.*) to sneer at, to speak sarcastically; the addition of *at* implies bantering, teasing. □ **chuck one's fat around** *v.* [late 19C] to talk loudly and stupidly. □ **chuck one's lollies** *v. see* TOSS ONE'S LOLLIES *under* TOSS *v.* □ **chuck one's weight around** *v.* (*also* **chuck one's weight about**) [Ware suggests orig. milit.: of 'one of the household brigades'] [20C+] to act in an arrogant, aggressive manner. □ **chuck out** see separate entries. □ **chuck up at** *v.* [fig. use of sense 1 above] [1900s] (*Aus.*) to tease aggressively.

chuck *v.*^{3} (*also* **chuck up**) [CHUCK *n.*^{3}] [mid-19C–1950s] (*UK/US Und.*) to eat.

chuck-a-block *adj. see* CHOCKABLOCK *adj.* (1).

chuckaboo *n.* [CHUCK *n.*^{1} (1)] [late 19C–1900s] a general endearment.

chuckaby *n.* [CHUCK *n.*^{1} (1)] [early 17C] a general term of endearment.

chuck a seven *v.* (*also* **chuck seven, do a..., throw a..., throw the...**) [? craps dice, where seven, other than in one's initial pass, is a losing throw; Downing, *Digger Dialects* (1919) suggests that this is because it is 'impossible to throw a seven', presumably he means with a single dice, whereas craps uses a pair] (*orig. Aus.*) **1** [late 19C+] (*also* **do the seven**) to die. **2** [late 19C+] to lose emotional control, to become hysterical (cf. CHUCK A SIXER *v.* (1)). **3** [1900s] to suffer misfortune. **4** [1920s] to succeed. **5** [1950s] to faint. **6** [1960s+] to vomit.

chuck a sixer *v.* (*also* **throw a sixer**) [CHUCK *v.*^{2} (11) + fig. use of Aus. rules *sixer*, a scoring kick] **1** [1940s+] (*Aus.*) to become hysterical, to lose one's temper (cf. CHUCK A SEVEN *v.*). **2** [1970s+] (*Aus.*) (*also* **throw sixers**) to vomit.

chucked *adj.*^{1} [CHUCK *v.*^{2}] **1** [late 18C–19C] (*also* **chuck full**) slightly drunk, tipsy. **2** [mid–late 19C] disappointed, tricked. **3** [late 19C+] thrown out; acquitted. **4** [late 19C+] rejected by a lover.

chucked *adj.*^{2} [CHUCK *v.*^{1} (2)] [early 19C] (*UK Und.*) amorous.

chucker *n.* [he 'chucks' barrels around] [late 19C] a public house potman.

chucker-out *n.* [CHUCK OUT *v.* (1)] [late 19C+] a staff member at pubs, dance-halls, concert- halls and similar places of public entertainment who ejects, by force if necessary, rowdy and undesirable people.

chuckey *n. see* CHUCKIE *n.*^{1}.

chuck full *adj. see* CHUCKED *adj.*^{1} (1).

chuckie *n.*^{1} (*also* **chuckey, chucky**) [late 18C–mid-19C] a chicken, a fowl.

chuckie *n.*^{2} [CHUCK *v.*^{2} (15)] [1990s+] (*W.I.*) a thug.

Chuckie Armani *n.* [the IRA slogan *tiocfaidh ár lá*, 'our day will come' + Adams's well-known taste in upmarket tailoring] [1980s+] (*Ulster*) the Sinn Fein leader Gerry Adams (b.1949).

chuckies *n.* [pun on BALLS *n.* (1) / SE *balls*, which one can 'chuck'; note Scot. *chuckies* = stones, thus link to STONE *n.*^{1} (1)] [1960s+] testicles.

chuck-in *n.* [SE *chuck*, to throw] (*Aus.*) **1** [late 19C–1910s] a certainty. **2** [late 19C+] a voluntary subscription.

chuck in *v.* [SE *chuck*, to throw] **1** [late 19C+] to add as a bonus, to throw in. **2** *see* CHIP IN *v.*

(IN PHRASES)

□ **chuck in one's alley** *v. see* THROW IN ONE'S ALLEY *under* ALLEY *n.*^{3}. □ **chuck in one's knife and fork** *v. see* LAY DOWN ONE'S KNIFE AND FORK *under* LAY DOWN *v.* □ **chuck in the towel** *v. see* THROW IN THE TOWEL *under* TOWEL *n.* □ **chuck one's hand in** *v.* [card-playing imagery; note WW1 milit. *chuck one's hand in*, to refuse or stop doing anything] [late 19C+] to die.

chucking-out time *n.* (*also* **chucking time**) [late 19C+] closing time at a public house; this was orig. 12.30 a.m., before the WWI legislation limiting open hours, which made it, according to the time of day, 2.30 p.m. (3 p.m. in London) and 10.30 p.m. (11 p.m. in London). The afternoon closing time has since been abandoned.

chuck it *v.* (*also* **chuck it in, chuck it up**) [CHUCK *v.*^{2} (6)] **1** [late 19C+] to give up, esp. of a job. **2** [1960s] (*US campus*) to commit suicide.

SE in slang uses

(IN PHRASES)

□ **chuck it out** *v.* [20C+] to speak without restraint.

chuck it! *excl.* [CHUCK IT *v.* (1)] [late 19C+] stop it!

(IN PHRASES)

□ **chuck it in!** (*also* **chuck it up!**) [late 19C+] stop it!

chuckle *v.* [1960s+] (*Aus., Queensland*) to vomit.

chucklehead *n.* [18C SE *chuckle*, a clumsy or stupid fellow + -HEAD *sfx* (1)] [early 18C–19C] a dolt, a simpleton, a fool; thus the fool's head.

chuckleheaded *adj.* [CHUCKLEHEAD *n.*] [mid-18C+] foolish.

chuckles *n.* [1950s] (*US*) enjoyment.

chuck me in the gutter *n.* [rhy. sl.] [20C+] (*Aus.*) butter.

chuck-out *n.* [CHUCK OUT *v.*] **1** [late 19C+] (*N.Z.*) a dismissal (from a job). **2** [1920s+] the end of drinking time in a public house, or place of entertainment, when customers are asked to drink up and leave.

chuck out *v.* [SE *chuck*, to throw] **1** [late 19C+] of people, occas. animals, to throw out, to expel physically. **2** [1990s+] of objects, to get rid of, to throw away.

chucks *n.*[1] [abbr. *chuck horrors* under CHUCK *n.*[3]] [1940s+] (*drugs*) the craving for food that affects a heroin addict once they have withdrawn from using the drug, which, on the whole, destroys the appetite during its regular use.

chucks *n.*[2] (*also* **Chuck T's**) [1960s+] Converse All-Star baseball boots, signed by designer *Chuck* Taylor.

chucks *n.*[3] (*also* **chuka sticks**) [1970s+] the *nunchuku*, a martial arts weapon modelled on a Chinese rice flail and made of two hardwood sticks linked by a chain.

chucks! *excl.* [mid–late 19C] (*UK juv.*) look out!

chuck-up *n.* [SE *chuck*; i.e. one 'throws up' the cheer] [1910s–40s] a cheer, encouragement.

chuck-up *adj.* [elision of SE *chunk*, a thick lump] **1** [1940s+] (*W.I.*) short and stout; thus *chuck-up man*, a short, stout person. **2** [1980s+] crowded, full.

chuck up *v.*[1] [abbr. *CHUCK UP THE SPONGE under* SPONGE *n.*] [mid-19C+] to surrender.

chuck up *v.*[2] [CHUCK *v.*[2]] **1** [mid-19C+] to abandon, to stop an action, to dismiss, to throw over, to jilt. **2** [late 19C+] (*UK Und.*) to be released from prison; thus as n., a release.

(IN PHRASES)

❑ **chuck up the sponge** *v. see under* SPONGE *n.*

chucky *n.*[1] [CHUCK *n.*[1]] [18C–mid-19C] a pleasing young woman; a term of endearment.

chucky *n.*[2] *see* CHUCKIE *n.*[1].

chuck you, Farley! *excl.* [1980s+] a joc. euph. expletive, reversing *FUCK YOU, CHARLEY! under* FUCK YOU! *excl.*

chuco *n. see* CHUC *n.*

chud *n.*[1] [? CHAP *n.* (1) + STUD *n.* (1)] [1990s+] (*Aus.*) a tough, virile, well-built man.

chud *n.*[2] *see* CHUTTY *n.*

chud *adj.* [film title *Chud* (1984), *c*annibalistic *h*umanoid *u*nderground *d*wellers] [1980s+] (*US campus*) disgusting, repellent.

chuddy *n. see* CHUTTY *n.*

chud-nuts *n.* [? CHUD *adj.*] [1990s+] (*UK juv.*) faecal matter adhering to the anal hair.

chuff *n.*[1] [dial. *chuff*, surly, ill-tempered] **1** [mid-15C–early 17C] a generally derisive name for anyone seen as boorish, unsophisticated or rude. **2** [mid-16C–mid-19C] a miser.

(DERIVATIVES)

❑ **chuffy** *adj.* [late 19C] surly.

chuff *n.*[2] [dial. *chuff*, fat, plump] **1** [1940s+] the buttocks, the anus. **2** [1940s+] (*mainly Aus./northern UK*) the vagina [ext. of sense 1]. **3** [1960s–70s] (*also* **chuffer**) (*US*) a young, passive homosexual [ext. of sense 1]. **4** [1970s] (*gay*) pubic hair [ext. of sense 1].

(IN COMPOUNDS)

❑ **chuff adder** *n.* [pun on SE snake *puff adder*/POOF *n.* (1)] [1960s] a male homosexual. ❑ **chuff chum** *n.* [CHUM *n.* (1)] [1960s+] a male homosexual. ❑ **chuff chute** *n.* (*also* **chufter chute**) [2000s] the anus. ❑ **chuff muncher** *n.* [MUNCH *v.*[1] (2)] [1990s+] a lesbian.

chuff *n.*[3] [CHUFF *v.*[2]] [1980s+] the act of breaking wind.

chuff *n.*[4] [1990s+] a synon. for FUCK *n.* (2).

chuff *adj.*[1] [dial.] [mid-19C–1900s] happy, cheerful (cf. CHUFFY *adj.* (2)).

chuff *adj.*[2] [CHUFF *n.*[1] (1)] [mid-19C–1900s] rude, impudent.

chuff *v.*[1] [1940s+] a euph. synon. for FUCK *v.* (1), mainly used in the north of England.

(IN COMPOUNDS)

❑ **chuff-box** *n.* [BOX *n.*[1] (1) or dial. *chuff*, to cuff, to hit. The penis 'hits' the vagina during intercourse] [1960s+] the vagina.

chuff *v.*[2] [echoic/CHUFF *n.*[2] (1)] [1940s+] to break wind.

chuff *v.*[3] [SE *chuff*, to go (of a train) or ? SE *puff*] **1** [1990s+] to smoke a drug, esp. marijuana. **2** *see* CHOOF (OFF) *v.*

chuff-chuff *n.* [he/she puffs like a steam-engine or (juv.) *chuff-chuff*] [2000s] (*W.I.*) a pompous old fool.

chuffed *adj.* (*also* **chuft**) [16C SE *chuff*, swollen out or puffed with fat, or the muzzle of an animal] [1950s+] **1** (*orig. milit.*) very pleased, delighted, happy; often *dead chuffed* or ext. to *chuffed to fuck, chuffed to arseholes, chuffed to buggery* etc. **2** annoyed, disgruntled.

chuffer *n. see* CHUFF *n.*[2] (3).

chuffing *adj.* [CHUFF *v.*[1]] [1990s+] a synon. for FUCKING *adj.* (1).

chuff it! *excl.* [? *SHOVE OFF under* SHOVE *v.*] [mid-19C] used to an importuning street-seller or beggar, go away! take it away! get rid of yourself!/it!

chuffy *n. see* CHUTTY *n.*

chuffy *adj.* [dial. *chuffy*, chubby-cheeked, healthy] **1** [late 18C+] chubby, round-faced. **2** [mid-19C] jolly, merry (cf. CHUFF *adj.*[1]). **3** [late 19C] of objects, fat.

(IN COMPOUNDS)

❑ **chuffy badge** *n.* [1990s+] (*UK juv.*) a metaphorical 'badge' worn by one who is exhibiting signs of self-satisfaction.

chuft *adj. see* CHUFFED *adj.*

chufter chute *n. see CHUFF CHUTE under* CHUFF *n.*[2].

chug *n. see* CHUG-A-LUG *n.*

chug *v.*[1] [an Australian toast of the 1950s] [1950s+] **1** to drink down in a single draught, to drink quickly; thus *chugger*, a drinker; (*US campus*) *chugging contest*, a drinking competition in which each contestant has to down a succession of drinks in a single swallow. **2** in fig. use, 'to swallow'.

chug *v.*[2] [1990s+] **1** to masturbate [the arm/hand 'chugs' up and down]. **2** (*US campus*) to throw away [var. on SE *chuck*].

chug-a-lug *n.* (*also* **chug**) [CHUGALUG! *excl.*] [1960s–80s] a drink.

chug-a-lug *v.* (*also* **chuglug**) [1930s+] to down a drink.

chugalug! *excl.* [1950s+] a popular drinking toast.

chugarrow! *excl.* [milit. *chubarrow*, itself adopted f. Hind. *chuprao*, be quiet!] [20C+] shut up!

chuggerhead *n.* (*also* **chugger**) [var. on CHUCKLEHEAD *n.*] [1970s] (*US*) a dolt, a simpleton, a fool.

chuglug *v. see* CHUG-A-LUG *v.*

chugs *n.* [var. on JUG *n.*[1] (7)] [1960s–70s] (*US*) the female breasts.

chugwagon *n.* [SE *chug (along)* + pun on cowboy jargon *chuck wagon*] [1900s–20s] (*US*) a motorcar.

chuka sticks *n. see* CHUCKS *n.*[3].

chul *v.* [? Hind. *chul*, go along, hurry] [mid–late 19C] to succeed.

chulo *n.* [Sp. *chulo*, pimp; note Ana María Eccles, 'Spanish Ethnic Labels: Chulo' (2001): "Estas o vas muy chulo" means smartly dressed (in a lower class fashion). "Eres un chulo" means a boasting, somehow despicable person. "Es un chulo" means "pimp". "Una chulada" means exaggerated, or false bravado. I always think of a "chulo madrileno" as a fellow with tight pants, a scarf around the neck and a visor type beret, dancing, clinging tightly to his partner] [1990s+] (*US*) a Mexican-American teenage gangster.

chum *n.* (*also* **chummie, chummy**) [17C SE *chum*, one who lodges in the same college rooms. Presumably f. *chamber*, poss. abbr. *chamber-fellow* or *chamber-mate*, although no proof has been discovered] **1** [late 17C+] (*also* **chumbuddy**) a close friend, a room-mate, a cell mate [mid-19C+ use is SE, although Hotten (1859) includes it since it is 'in such frequent use with the lower orders that it demanded a place in this glossary']. **2** [late 18C–19C] (*UK Und.*) a fellow-prisoner. **3** [mid-19C+] a term of friendly address. **4** [late 19C] the vagina [, i.e. the 'friend' of the penis]. **5** [1990s+] (*UK juv.*) (*also* **chum boy, chummer**) a male homosexual. **6** *see* NEW CHUM *n.*

(IN PHRASES)

❑ **old chum** *n.* [opposite of NEW CHUM *n.* (2)] [mid-19C+] a veteran.

chum *v.* [CHUM *n.* (1); verb use coined by John Wesley (1703–91) in 1730] **1** [mid-18C–1930s] to put someone in a position of sharing accommodation, esp. in a prison cell. **2** [mid-18C+] (*also* **chum in, chum it**) to live with, to befriend. **3** [mid-19C+] (*also* **chum in**) to join in with.

IN PHRASES

❑ **chum along with** *v.* (*also* **chum around with, ...in with, ...up with**) **1** [late 19C+] to become friendly with. **2** [1910s] (*UK Und.*) to work as an accomplice with.

chummage *n.* [SE *chummage*, the sharing of rooms by a number of people. The rich-to-poor bribe has also been recorded as taking place at mid-19C universities] **1** [late 18C–mid-19C] a sum of money paid by a rich prisoner to a poorer one, for which payment the latter forfeits his part of a shared cell, leaving it all to the rich prisoner and taking up a position in some communal area of the prison. **2** [late 18C–19C] a monetary forfeit, usu. 2s 6d (12.5p), paid by a new prisoner to those who have already established themselves in the prison. **3** [late 19C] in a non-custodial sense, a payment from any newcomer.

chummer *n. see* CHUM *n.* (5).

chummery *n.* [CHUM *n.* (1)] **1** [mid-19C] friendship, friendliness. **2** [late 19C+] the sharing of rooms with a friend.

chummie *n. see* CHUM *n.*

chumming *n.* [CHUM *n.* (1)] [late 19C] making friends.

chumming up *n.* [CHUMMAGE *n.* (2)] [mid-19C] (*UK prison*) the initiatory welcoming of a new prisoner, paid for by a mandatory fee of 2s 6d.

chummo *n.* [CHUM *n.* + -O *sfx* (1)] [1940s] (*US*) a friend; esp. as direct term of address.

chummy *n.*[1] [it was notably comfortable and as such seen as *chummy*, or friendly, to the wearer] [mid-19C] a low-crowned hat.

chummy *n.*[2] [SE *chimney* or his preferred hat, a CHUMMY *n.*[1]] [mid-19C+] a chimney sweep or his assistant.

chummy *n.*[3] [note 1940s+ police use *chummy*, a form of address from anyone to whom the police officer is talking, a suspect] **1** [1910s+] a person. **2** *see* CHUM *n.* **3** *see* NEW CHUM *n.* (1).

chummy *adj.* (*also* **chummy-chummy**) [CHUM *n.*] [late 19C+] friendly.

DERIVATIVES

❑ **chumminess** *n.* [1920s+] friendliness.

chummy *v.* [CHUM THE FISH *v.*] [1980s+] (*US campus*) to vomit.

chummy *adv.* [CHUMMY *adj.*] [late 19C+] in a friendly manner.

chump *n.*[1] [ext. of 18C SE *chump*, a short thick lump of wood chopped or sawn from timber] **1** [mid-19C+] the head, the face. **2** [mid-19C+] a person, esp. a regular working man; thus, in sl. terms, a fool. **3** [late 19C+] (*also* **chumpie**) a fool; anyone gullible or easily taken in. **4** [late 19C+] (*also* **old chump**) a general term of address, either derog. or teasing. **5** [1970s] (*US black*) a second-rate pimp, one who just makes enough money to get by. **6** [1970s+] (*US black*) a disloyal gang member. **7** [1990s+] (*US prison*) a deliberate insult, implying the subject's weakness and/or homosexuality; the spur to a fight.

IN COMPOUNDS

❑ **chump change** *see* separate entries. ❑ **chump job** *n.* [1930s+] (*US*) respectable, low-paying, regular work. ❑ **chump squeeze** *n.* [1950s–60s] (*US black*) a punch on the arm or shoulder, its meaning varying according to context.

IN PHRASES

❑ **chump out** *v.* [1960s] (*US black*) to make a mistake, to blunder. ❑ **get one's chump** *v.* (*also* **provide one's chump**) [Yorks. dial. *chump*, a lump of meat] [mid-19C–1910s] (*UK Und.*) to earn one's living. ❑ **off one's chump** [mid-19C+] mad, eccentric. ❑ **use one's chump** *v.* [20C+] to act intelligently.

chump *n.*[2] [Suffolk dial. *bread and chumps*, bread and cheese; Devon dial. *chump*, to eat noisily] [late 19C] (*UK Und.*) food.

chump *adj.* (*also* **chump-ass, chumpish**) [CHUMP *n.*[1]] [20C+] **1** stupid, gullible. **2** unsophisticated, second-rate, provincial.

chump *v.* [CHUMP *n.*[1] (3)] **1** [1920s] (*also* **chump out**) to trick, to deceive, to make a fool of someone. **2** [1960s] (*US black*) to act like a fool, to be exploited.

IN PHRASES

❑ **chump off** *v.* (*US black*) **1** [1930s+] to act like a fool. **2** [1950s] to lose money irresponsibly. **3** [1970s] to defeat in a verbal battle. **4** [1970s+] to look down on, to disdain. **5** [1970s+] to dupe. ❑ **chump (someone) down** *v.* (*also* **chump (someone) out**) [1970s+] (*US black*) to humiliate someone.

chump change *n.* [CHUMP *n.*[1] + SE *change*] [1950s+] (*US black*) **1** mall change, esp. a sum of money that is too small to buy anything worthwhile. **2** in fig. use, anything insignificant.

chump-change *adj.* [CHUMP CHANGE *n.*] [1970s+] second-rate, inferior, good only for fools.

chumpie *n.*[1] [SE *champion*] [1980s+] (*US campus/black*) **1** something that causes happiness, joy or excitement. **2** something exceptional, outstanding; a large amount.

chumpie *n.*[2] *see* CHUMP *n.*[1] (3).

chump of wood *phr.* [rhy. sl.] [mid-19C] no good.

chumps elizas *n.* [pron.; note 'Five Pounder Tourists' (Ware)] [mid-19C+] the Champs Élysées, Paris.

chumpy *adj.* [CHUMP *n.*[1] (3)] **1** [20C+] naïve, stupid, gullible. **2** [1900s–20s] (*US campus*) mean, contemptible. **3** [1960s] eccentric, odd.

chum the fish *v.* [SE *chum*, to throw ground-bait into the water to attract fish; var. on FEED THE FISHES *under* FEED *v.*] [1980s+] (*US campus*) to vomit.

Chunder *n. see* RAM CHUNDUR *n.*

chunder *n.* [CHUNDER *v.*] [1950s+] (*Aus.*) **1** an act of vomiting; thus *chunderous*, *chundersome*, fit to make one vomit. **2** vomit.

IN COMPOUNDS

❑ **chunder bunny** *n.* [BUNNY *n.*[1] (3a)] [1980s+] (*orig. N.Z.*) one who cannot hold their liquor.

chunder *v.* [according to Barry Humphries (b.1934), the great popularizer of the word in his 'Barry Mackenzie' strip in *Private Eye* and on film, f. naut. shout of warning 'watch under!'; thus Humphries, *Collected Barry Mackenzie* (1988) 'Jeez I'm sorry lady — I forget to yell watch under'. He also offers rhy. sl. f. *Chunder Loo of Akim Foo* = SE *spew*, to vomit. Chunder Loo featured in a long-running series of advertisements for Cobra boot polish (*c.*1910–29), drawn by Norman Lindsay (1879–1969) (and occas by his brother Lionel) featured in the Sydney *Bulletin*. Thence it moved from public school sl. to surf jargon to popular use; Moore, *Lexicon of Cadet Language* (1993), adds ? link to UK dial. *chounter/chunter/chunder*, to grumble] [1950s+] (*orig. Aus.*) to vomit.

chundini *n.* [? on pattern of BODINI *n.*] [1970s+] (*US gay*) the buttocks.

chung *adj.* [ety. unknown] [2000s] (*UK teen*) attractive, sexy.

chunk *n.*[1] [dial. *chuck*, a lump, a large, awkwardly shaped piece] **1** [mid-19C+] (*orig. US*) a large amount, a good deal of, esp. money. **2** [1910s] (*Aus.*) a piece of bread. **3** [1940s] (*US*) (*also* **chunko**) a fat or large person. **4** [1940s–50s] (*US prison*) a long sentence. **5** [1990s+] (*Can./US Und.*) a handgun.

IN PHRASES

❑ **chunk of fanny** *n. see* PIECE OF ASS *under* PIECE *n.* ❑ **in chunks** *see* IN SPADES *under* SPADE *n.*

chunk *n.*[2] [CHUNK *v.*[1] (2)] [1940s–60s] (*US*) sexual intercourse.

chunk *v.*[1] [SE *chuck*, to throw] **1** [late 19C+] (*US black*) to discard, to throw away, to throw. **2** [1940s–60s] (*US*) to ejaculate. **3** [1950s+] (*W.I./US campus*) to batter, to beat up; to fight. **4** [1980s+] (*US campus*) to vomit [+ ref. to BLOW CHUNKS *under* BLOW *v.*[1]].

chunk *v.*[2] [echoic of one's 'hitting the bottom'] [1980s+] (*US campus*) to do badly.

chunka *n.* (*also* **chunker**) [abbr. CHUNK OF BEEF *n.*] [20C+] (*Aus.*) the chief.

chunkery *adj.* (*also* **chunked**) [SE *chunky*] [1970s+] fatness; as n., *chunker*.

chunk-headed *adj. see* BLOCKHEADED *adj.*

chunking *n.* [CHUNK *v.*[1] (1)] [2000s] (*US prison*) throwing water or liquid matter on inmates or staff.

chunko *n. see* CHUNK *n.*[1] (3).

chunk of beef *n.* (*also* **chunka beef**) [rhy. sl.] [20C+] (*Aus.*) the chief, the boss.

chunk of wood *adj.* [rhy. sl.] [mid-19C] good; usu. in negative 'no chunk of wood'.

chunky *n.* [SE *chunk*, the large blocks of hashish] [1970s+] (*US drugs*) hashish.

chunky *adj.* [1950s+] (*US black*) used to describe attractive female buttocks.

chunky shrimp *n.* [supposed resemblance] [2000s] (*UK black*) the clitoris of a fat woman.

chunt *n.* [CHUMP *n.*[1] (3) + CUNT *n.* (4)] [2000s] (*US campus*) an unpleasant, incompetent person.

chupa *n.* [orig. Sp.] [1990s+] (*US campus*) a sucker, often used affectionately.

chupidee *n.* (*also* **chupidie, chupidy, chupiddy, chupit**) [*chupid*, local pron. of stupid] [20C+] (*W.I.*) a gullible, ignorant fool; thus *chupidness*, *trupidness* stupidity; *talk chupidness*, to talk silly nonsense.

church *n.*[1] [? misreading of CHUCK *n.*[1] (1)] [late 19C–1900s] a general term of endearment, e.g. *my church*, my dear.

church *n.*[2] [play on CHRISTEN *v.* (1)] [late 19C–1940s] (*US Und.*) a place where the identity of stolen jewellery is altered.

church *n.*[3] [in the context of a funeral] [1970s] (*US*) the end.

SE in slang uses

IN COMPOUNDS

❑ **church bell** *n.* [late 19C–1900s] (*UK rural*) a talkative woman. ❑ **church-chopper** *n. see* CHOP-CHURCH *n.* ❑ **church key** *n.* [the similarity in shape of the WW2 US forces GI can-opener and an old-fashioned key; presumably some form of opener had been required since beercans were first merchandised in 1937] [1950s+] (*US*) a can-opener; also as v. ❑ **church mouse** *n.* **1** [late 19C+] a regular attender at church. **2** [1940s–70s] (*gay*) a male homosexual who frequents crowded churches in order to fondle any potential sex partners. ❑ **church parade** *n.* [late 19C–1900s] (*UK society*) the regular post-Sunday matins promenading of fashionable people. ❑ **church-piece** *n.* [it was the smallest silver coin and thus the least one could decently place in the collection plate] [late 19C–1900s] (*UK society*) a threepenny piece. ❑ **church work** *n.* [? the time taken to build the great cathedrals or the tedium of religious services] [late 18C] any work that proceeds slowly.

IN PHRASES

❑ **church is out** [i.e. the service is over; one has no further chance to pray] [1950s–60s] (*US*) everything is finished, no alternative is available.

church a yack *v.* (*also* **church a jack**) [play on CHRISTEN *v.* (1) + YACK *n.*[1]] [mid–late 19C] (*UK Und.*) to take the works of one watch and place them in the case of another with the aim of disguising its origins.

church-called *adj.* [1920s–50s] (*US black*) drawn to the vocation of preaching.

churcher *n.* [the Cockney version of society's *church-piece* under CHURCH *n.*[3]] [late 19C] a threepenny piece.

churchwarden *n.* [the supposed predilection of churchwardens for such pipes] **1** [mid-19C] a clay pipe with a very long stem. **2** [1930s] (*US drugs*) a long-stemmed opium pipe.

churchy *adj.* [mid-19C+] pious.

churchyard *n.*

SE in slang uses

IN COMPOUNDS

❑ **churchyard cough** *n.* (*also* **churchyarder, graveyarder**) [both the likelihood of death and burial and the reputation of churchyards as centres of disease] [late 17C+] a particularly bad cough, which is likely to lead to the sufferer's death. ❑ **churchyard face** *n. see* BURYING FACE *under* BURY *v.* ❑ **churchyard luck** *n.* [cruel but pragmatic, the loss of one extra mouth to feed is 'lucky' for the penniless parents] [late 19C–1900s] the death of one child in a large, but impoverished family.

churn *n.* [it makes BUTTER *n.*[1] (1); Williams notes 16C use of *churning*, copulation] [19C] the vagina.

churn butter *v. see under* BUTTER *n.*[1].

churus *n. see* CHARAS *n.*

chury *n.* [Welsh Rom. *chury*, a knife, ult. f. Hind. *chhuri*] [early 19C] a knife.

chute *n.*[1] [the serving and quality of food in such places is compared with the tossing of rubbish down the garbage chute of a tenement block] [late 19C] (*US*) a cheap eating place.

chute *n.*[2] [1970s+] (*US*) the rectum or anus.

IN PHRASES

❑ **go up the chute** *v.* [1970s+] to have anal intercourse. ❑ **up the chute** (*also* **up the shoot**) **1** [1930s+] (*Aus./N.Z.*) useless, worthless, failed, in serious trouble. **2** *see* UP THE POLE *adj.*[2].

chutes *n.* [1930s–50s] (*US Und.*) the subway.

chute the chutes *v. see* GO DOWN THE CHUTES *under* GO DOWN *v.*

chutney *n.* [like CHOCOLATE *adj.* (2), *chutney* is brown and thus generic for matters referring to defecation and sodomy] [1970s+] sodomy.

IN COMPOUNDS

❑ **chutney farmer** *n.* [1990s+] a male homosexual. ❑ **chutney ferret** *n.* **1** [1970s+] the penis. **2** [1980s+] (*also* **ferret**) (*UK juv.*) a male homosexual, a sodomite.

chutney *adj.* [20C+] (*W.I., Trin.*) pertaining to East Indian culture.

chutty *n.* (*also* **chud, chuddy, chuffy**) [? SE *chew*] [1940s+] (*orig. Aus./N.Z.*) chewing gum.

chutzpah *n.* (*also* **chutzpa**) [Heb. *chutzpah*, insolence, audacity] [late 19C+] gall, cheek, outrageousness, audacity, bravado, nerve, courage.

chutzpah *adj.* [CHUTZPAH *n.*] [late 19C] cheeky.

chy *n.* **1** *see* CHAI *n.*[1]. **2** *see* TCHI *v.*

chyack *see under* CHI-IKE.

ci *n.* [abbr.] [2000s] (*US black*) a cigarette.

ciao *phr.* [Ital.] [1960s+] goodbye (cf. CHOW *phr.*).

'cid *n.* [abbr. ACID *n.*[1] (2)] [1970s+] (*drugs*) LSD.

cider-and *n.* [18C] any form of mixed drink in which the basic constituent is cider.

ciel *n.* [? abbr. SAmE *cell phone*] [2000s] (*S.Afr. gay*) a mobile phone.

cig *n.* [abbr.] [late 19C+] a cigarette, a cigar.

cigar *n.* [SE phr. *close but no cigar*] [1930s] (*US*) a beauty, an attractive woman.

cigar box *n.* [the flimsiness of the cigar-box construction] **1** [19C] a violin. **2** [1970s] (*US*) a cheaply built house; thus *cigar box row*, the area of town in which the poor live.

cigar burn *n.* [resemblance] [1990s+] the anus.

cigarette (holder) *n.* [rhy. sl.] [1990s+] a shoulder.

cigarette paper *n.* [a WRAP *n.*[2] (3) or BINDLE *n.* (3) of heroin (or cocaine) is approx. the size of a cigarette paper] [1930s+] (*drugs*) a (small) packet of heroin.

cigarette pimp *n.* [his women make no more than cigarette money] [1950s–60s] (*US black*) a second-rate pimp, esp. a pimp who solicits for his women.

cigarette swag *n.* [resemblance] [1930s–60s] (*Aus.*) a very thin pack or swag, implying poverty.

cigarette with no name *n. see* NO-BRAND CIGARETTE *n.*

cigger *n.* [abbr.] [1910s+] (*Aus.*) a cigarette.

ciggie *n.* (*also* **ciggy, ciggie-butt, cigybutt, siggy**) [abbr.] [20C+] a cigarette.

ciggy-boo *n.* (*also* **ciggy-poo**) [abbr. + sfx *-boo*/*-poo*] [1940s+] (*Aus./US*) a cigarette.

cinch *n.*[1] (*also* **sinch, skinch**) [SE *cinch*, to grip tightly; thus something one can grasp easily. Orig. f. Sp. *cincha*, a saddle girth or bellyband, adopted in US Western use] **1** [late 19C–1900s] (*US*) a fool, one who can be easily overcome [ext. of sense 2]. **2** [late 19C+] (*orig. US*) a simple, easily attained thing, a certainty; thus *cinchy*, easy, easily attained or attainable; *cinch-looking*, apparently easy. **3** [1930s] (*US*) an easily seduced woman.

IN PHRASES

❑ **have the cinch on** *v.* [late 19C–1920s] to place oneself in an unassailable position. ❑ **put the cinch on** *v.* [1910s–60s] (*US*) to ensure, to make something certain.

cinch *n.*[2] (*also* **cinch-notice**) [SE *cinch*, a tight grip] [20C+] (*US campus*) a note sent to a student warning them to work hard and generally 'get a grip'.

cinch *adj.* [CINCH *n.*[1] (2)] [late 19C–1960s] (*US*) definite, guaranteed.

cinch *v.* [fig. use of SE *cinch*, to make tight (orig. of a saddle); underpinned by CINCH *n.*[1] (2)] **1** [late 19C] (*US*) to impose upon. **2** [late 19C–1910s] (*US*) to defeat, to overcome, to trounce. **3** [20C+] (*orig. US*) to guarantee, to make certain, to make conclusive.

Cinci *n.* (*also* **Cincie, Cincy**) [abbr.] [late 19C+] (*US*) *Cinc*innati, Ohio.

Cincinnati *n.* used in combs. suggesting the city's reputation for sharp business practice and/or one-time identification with pig products.

IN COMPOUNDS

❑ **Cincinnati chicken** *n.* (*also* **Cincinnati turkey**) [1900s–70s] salt pork. ❑ **Cincinnati doubloon** *n.* [SE *doubloon*, a coin worth 36/-; the ref. is to the reputation of Cincinnati businessmen as cheats] [mid-19C] (*US*) a penny, a cent. ❑ **Cincinnati olives** *n.* [late 19C] (*US*) pigs. ❑ **Cincinnati oysters** *n.* [late 19C] (*US*) pickled pigs' feet. ❑ **Cincinnati quail** *n.* [late 19C] (*US*) pork or bacon, esp. fat pork.

cinder *n.* [SE *cinder*, an ember or piece of glowing coal; thus it makes the basic drink 'hot'] [mid-19C–1930s] any form of spirit (brandy, whisky etc), taken in tea, soda water or other drink; thus *put a cinder in*, to add liquor to an otherwise non-alcoholic drink.

SE in slang uses

IN COMPOUNDS

❑ **cinder bull** *n.* [BULL *n.*[5] (1)] [1930s+] (*US tramp*) a railroad detective. ❑ **cinder dick** *n.* [DICK *n.*[5] (1)] [1920s+] (*US tramp*) a railroad detective. ❑ **cinder garbler** *n.* [SE *garbler*, a sifter; the servant's morning duty of cleaning out last night's dead fires] [late 18C–early 19C] a servant girl. ❑ **cinder grifter** *n.* [GRIFTER *n.*] [1920s+] (*US*) a tramp, a hobo. ❑ **cinder shifter** *n.* [such tracks are covered with dead cinders] [1920s+] (*Aus.*) a dirt-track motorcycle racer. ❑ **cinder sifter** *n.* [SE *cinder-sifter*, a contrivance for sifting dust or ashes from cinders] **1** [late 19C] a hat with an open-work brim, which supposedly resembles the household tool. **2** [1920s–40s] (*US tramp*) a tramp, esp. one who uses the railroads. ❑ **cinder trail** *n.* [1920s] (*US tramp*) the railroad; the life of tramping, esp. when travelling on railroads.

cinderella *n.* [the fairy-tale of *Cinderella*] **1** [late 19C] (*UK society*) a dance that ends at midnight. **2** [1970s+] (*US gay*) an older homosexual who both looks better by candlelight and has to be home by midnight.

cindy *n.* [the *Sindy* doll] [2000s] (*S.Afr. gay*) a teenager.

cinnamon stick *n.* [resemblance; SE *cinnamon sticks* are brown/ STICK *n.* (1a)] [1940s–60s] (*gay*) the faeces-stained penis after anal intercourse.

cinqua *n. see* CHINKER *n.*

cinquanter *n.*[1] [Fr. *cinquante*, 50, i.e. years of age] [early 17C–mid-18C] an old man.

cinquanter *n.*[2] [Fr. *cinque*, the number five, marked on a die] [early–mid-17C] a gambler.

cinque *n. see* CHINKER *n.*

cinque ports *n.* ['a group of sea-ports (originally five, whence the name) situated on the south-east coast of England' [...] 'the five "Ports" are Hastings, Sandwich, Dover, Romney, Hithe, to which were added in very early times the "Ancient Towns" of Rye and Winchelsea' (*OED*); the genitals are in the 'south' of the body, plus play on *port*, that which is entered] [17C] the female genitals and anus.

cipher *n.* [ety. unknown] [1990s+] (*US black/teen*) **1** knowledge. **2** a circle of black friends.

cipher *v.* (*also* **cypher**) [SE *cipher*, to work out arithmetically] [mid-19C+] to calculate, to think out.

circle *n.* **1** [mid-19C] (*UK Und.*) a form of large drill-bit used to cut into a safe or strong-room. **2** [1930s] (*US jazz*) a gramophone record.

SE in slang uses

IN PHRASES

❑ **give someone a circle** *v.* [the rotating dial of a pre-digital telephone] [2000s] (*N.Z. teen*) to make a telephone call. ❑ **what circle?** [mid-19C] what time is it?

circle jerk *n.* (*also* **ring jerk**) [SE *circle* + JERK OFF *v.* (1)] **1** [1940s+] (*orig. US*) joint masturbation, often in competition, by a group of boys, poss. sitting in a circle. **2** [1970s+] (*US*) in fig. use, chaos, a mess. **3** [1990s+] (*Can.*) in fig. use of sense 1, men who harass prostitutes and their customers for fun. **4** [1970s+] (*orig. US*) in fig. use of sense 1, a pointless or inconclusive discussion by a number of people.

circle-jerk *v.* [CIRCLE JERK *n.* (1)] [1950s+] (*US*) of boys or men, to indulge in group masturbation; thus *circle-jerker*, one who joins a group of masturbators.

circler *n.* [its shape] [1950s] (*W.I.*) a small, round, boiled dumpling.

circle suck *n.* [on pattern of CIRCLE JERK *n.* (1)] [1990s+] (*US*) the forcing of one man or woman to fellate a group of men.

circling boy *n.* [SE *circling*, moving around] [early 17C] (*UK Und.*) a thug who works in a criminal gang and helps lure victims into a position where they might be robbed, with or without violence.

circs *n.* [abbr.] [late 19C+] *circ*umstances.

circuit *n.*

IN PHRASES

❑ **go on circuit** *v.* [1900s] (*Aus.*) of a prostitute, to tour diggings and camps selling her services.

circular file *n.* [note synon. US Army *file seventeen/thirteen*] [1940s+] (*orig. US*) a waste-paper basket.

circumbendibus *n.* [17C pig Lat. *circum* + *bend*, bend around + Lat. ablative pl. *-ibus*] **1** [late 17C–1900s] a long and winding route. **2** [late 18C–1900s] a long and winding story.

circumference *n.* [20C+] a fat person's waist.

circus *n.* [fig. uses of SE] (*US*) **1** [mid-19C+] a commotion, an adventure. **2** [late 19C] a humiliating example. **3** [late 19C–1960s] a live sex show. **4** [1910s] (*Aus.*) one's own affair, one's business. **5** [1930s] a fake fit or seizure, performed in the hope of obtaining an injection of narcotics from a sympathetic doctor. **6** [1930s] a courtroom, a trial. **7** [1940s] a place. **8** [1950s+] a company, group or set of people acting or performing together, esp. in sport or entertainment, e.g. the *Grand Prix circus*. **9** [1960s+] an orgy; sexual excess.

IN COMPOUNDS

pertaining to sex

❑ **circus girl** *n.* [1960s] a woman who is willing to indulge in sex shows or acts of 'perverted' sex. ❑ **circus house** *n.* [HOUSE *n.*[1] (1); such establishments originated in New Orleans and also saw the birth of jazz] [late 19C–1960s] (*US*) a brothel, esp. one featuring sex shows. ❑ **circus love** *n.* [1950s+] sexual intercourse involving as many variations as possible. ❑ **circus queen** *n.* [-QUEEN *sfx* (3)] [1940s+] (*US gay*) one who enjoys watching two other men have sex. ❑ **circus rider** *n.* [1980s+] (*US*) one who participates in orgies.

SE in slang uses

IN COMPOUNDS

❑ **circus bees** *n.* (*also* **circus squirrels**) [1920s–60s] (*US tramp*) fleas, lice, crabs, bedbugs. ❑ **circus try** *n.* [the supposed pluckiness of circus performers] [1940s] (*US*) a determined effort, a good try.

Circus cowboy *n.* [Piccadilly *Circus*, W1] [1960s+] a young male gay prostitute who congregates in and around Piccadilly Circus, London.

cirq *n.* (*also* **kirk**) [abbr.] [1990s+] (*UK juv.*) one who has been circumcised.

cis *n. see* SIS *n.*

cisco *n.* [brandname *Cisco*, a cheap but potent wine] [2000s] (*US black/drugs*) a drink that has been made more potent by adding phencyclidine to it.

Cisco Kid *n.* [rhy. sl. = YID *n.*[1]] [1960s+] a Jew.

cissie/cissy *see under* SISSY.

cit *n.* (*also* **citt**) [the implication is of an urban dweller as opposed to a countryman or of a tradesman or shopkeeper as opposed to a gentleman. 'A pert low tradesman, a pragmatical trader' (Johnson, *Dictionary*, 1755)] **1** [mid-17C+] a citizen, spec. of London. **2** [late 19C] (*US*) a city.

citizen *n.* [SE; note *citizen*, a civilian as opposed to a soldier, used by Shakespeare in *Coriolanus* (1607)] **1** [mid–late 19C] (*UK Und.*) a wedge used for opening safes; thus *citizen's friend*, a smaller form of wedge (cf. ALDERMAN *n.* (5); GENTLEMAN *n.*; LORD MAYOR *n.*[1]). **2** [20C+] (*US*) a person, the implication is of a respectable individual as opposed to a criminal. **3** [1910s+] a rough, poss. criminal person. **4** [1970s] (*US gay*) in specific use of sense 1, a heterosexual.

citron *n. see* LEMON *n.* (1b).

citt *n. see* CIT *n.*

city *n.*

SE in slang uses

IN COMPOUNDS

❑ **city bug** *n.* [BUG *n.*[1] (1)] [20C+] (*US*) a city person, as seen from a farmer's point of view. ❑ **city bulldog** *n.* [BULLDOG *n.* (1a)] [early 18C] a constable. ❑ **city college** *n.* [ironic uses; COLLEGE *n.*] **1** [late 18C–early 19C] Newgate prison. **2** [mid-19C–1940s] (*US*) the Tombs Prison, New York City. **3** [1930s] any prison. ❑ **city minute** *n. see* NEW YORK MINUTE *under* NEW YORK *n.* ❑ **city scales** *n.* [late 18C] the gallows. ❑ **city sherry** *n.* [late 19C] bitter beer. ❑ **city stage** *n.* [the position of Newgate in the City of London; also the condemned villains' 'dance' for their audience] [18C–early 19C] the (Newgate) gallows. ❑ **city wire** *n.* [use of wires in clothing and hair] [17C] a fashionable lady.

IN PHRASES

❑ **city clag blues** *n.* [proprietary name, *Clag* glue] [1980s+] (*Aus. drugs*) the unpleasant sensation in one's mouth following excessive smoking of cannabis.

-city *sfx* (*also* **-town**) [SE *city*; note Gold, *A Jazz Lexicon* (1964): 'according to jazzmen, first used by either Lester Young or Emmett Barry c. 1938'] [1960s+] (*orig. US*) a general sfx meaning place or situation, whether concrete or abstract.

City Hall *n.*

IN PHRASES

❑ **you can't fight City Hall** (*also* **go fight City Hall**) [1940s+] (*US*) you can't win against the establishment.

City Road African *n.* [? the relative exoticism of the City Road, EC1, for those who normally looked for prostitutes in the West End of London] [late 19C–1900s] a prostitute.

City Tote *n.* [rhy. sl.] [1990s+] a coat.

civet *n.* [the musky odour of *civet*, used in perfumes and viewed as overtly erotic; thus *civet-cat*, a general term of abuse for a women seen as too (threateningly) sexy, e.g. as used by Virginia Woolf (1882–1941) of Katherine Mansfield (1888–1923)] [18C–19C] the vagina.

civilian *n.* **1** [1940s+] (*US*) an outsider, one who is not a part of a given group. **2** [1970s] (*US gay*) a heterosexual.

civility money *n.* [late 18C–early 19C] a cash payment claimed by bailiffs for discharging their duty in a courteous manner.

civil rig *n.* [SE *civil* + RIG *n.*[2] (1)] [mid-19C] (*UK Und.*) any means of gaining money through (excessive) politeness.

civvie *n.* (*also* **civvy**) **1** [late 19C+] a civilian; thus termed by members of the forces, the prison service, police etc. **2** [1990s+] (*UK prison*) a commercially sold, 'tailor-made' cigarette.

civvie *adj.* (*also* **civvy**) [late 19C+] civilian.

IN COMPOUNDS

❑ **civvie street** *n.* (*also* **civvy street**) [1940s+] the world of civilian life, usu. service use.

civvies *n.* [CIVVIE *n.*; note Fraser & Gibbons, *Soldier & Sailor Words & Phrases* (1925): '"Civvies" [...] is a Service term at least 70 years old'] **1** [late 19C+] (*also* **civies**) civilian clothing, i.e. neither a uniform nor one's working clothes. **2** [1970s+] (*US gay*) badly designed clothing.

civvy *see under* CIVVIE.

c.j. *n.* [abbr. CRYSTAL JOINT *under* CRYSTAL *n.*] [1970s] (*drugs*) phencyclidine.

C-jag *n.* [C *n.*[3] (1) + JAG *n.*[1] (4)] [1940s] (*US drugs*) a cocaine binge.

C-jam *n.* (*also* **C-jame**) [C *n.*[3] (1) + JAM *n.*[5] (1)] [1960s] (*drugs*) cocaine.

CK-one *n.* [initial letters; a play on the perfume name *CK-one* (i.e. Calvin Klein One)] [2000s] (*UK drugs*) cocaine and ketamine; latterly crack cocaine and ketamine.

clabber *n.* **1** *see* CLOBBER *n.* **2** *see* BONNY-CLAPPER *n.*

clabber jigging *n.* [1920s–30s] (*Scot.*) dancing accompanied by a mouth organ.

clack *n.* [SE *clack*, idle gossip. Grose (1785) links it to the clapper that regulates a water-mill and claims that the term is 'chiefly applied to women'; note WW1 milit. *clack*, gossip, rumor] **1** [late 16C+] (*also* **clack-rattle**) the tongue, usu. a woman's. **2** [late 16C+] a noisy conversation. **3** [late 17C+] whining, whingeing, nagging.

IN COMPOUNDS

❑ **clack-box** *n.* [mid–late 19C] **1** the mouth. **2** a garrulous person. ❑ **clack-loft** *n.* [SE *loft*, a church gallery] [late 18C] a pulpit. ❑ **clack-rattle** *n. see* sense 1 above.

IN PHRASES

❑ **hold one's clack** *v.* [late 16C–early 19C] to stop talking, usu. as imper.

clack *v.* **1** [mid-18C] to fool by deceptive speech. **2** [mid-18C–early 19C] to chatter; to abuse.

IN PHRASES

❑ **clack the doctor** *v.* [mid-18C] (*UK Und.*) to impersonate a doctor in order to rob a surgeon.

clacker *n.*[1] [CLACK *n.* (1); the noise of the teeth rattling together; note WW1 milit. *clacker*, a chatterer, a rumourmonger] **1** [19C] the mouth. **2** [19C] the teeth.

clacker *n.*[2] [? the noise of the coins hitting each other or a solid object] **1** [1900s–20s] (*US*) a dollar. **2** [1920s–30s] a foreign coin of low value.

clacker *n.*[3] [? Lat. *cloaca*, a sewer] [1960s+] (*Aus./UK juv.*) **1** the anus, the rectum; esp. in contemptuous/dismissive phr. *stuff it up your clacker*. **2** a general term of abuse.

clackers *n.* [CLACKER *n.*[1] (2)] [1930s+] false teeth.

clad in Stafford blue *phr.* [SE *clad*, dressed + *Stafford blue*, a type of blue cloth; pun on SE *staff*] [15C] bruised from a beating.

clag *n.* [northern dial. *clag*, a sticky mass] [1980s+] (*Aus. prison*) porridge.

clagnut *n.* [northern dial. *clag*, a sticky mass entangled in hair] [1990s+] a small piece of excrement clinging to the anal hairs.

claim *n.* [20C+] (*Irish*) a woman who is picked up at a dance, usu. to have sexual intercourse.

claim *v.* **1** [late 19C; 1990s+] to steal. **2** [late 19C+] (*UK Und.*) to arrest; thus *claimed*, under arrest. **3** [1970s] (*US black*) of a prostitute, to ally oneself to a pimp by paying him money. **4** [1990s+] (*US black gang*) (*also* **claim the hood**) to claim membership in a gang. **5** [2000s] to choose a victim.

Claire Rayners *n.* (*also* **Claires**) [rhy. sl.; ult. UK agony aunt and novelist *Claire Rayner* (b.1931)] [1990s+] a pair of trainers.

clam *n.*[1] [fig. uses of SE; all open and/or shut like the bivalve] **1** [early 19C–1950s] the mouth. **2** [mid-19C+] (*US*) the vagina, the hymen; thus, by metonymy, a woman. **3** [mid-19C+] (*also* **clam-mouth**) a tight-lipped person. **4** [1900s] (*US*) a mean person; thus *tight as a clamshell*, very close-fisted. **5** [1910s] an untrustworthy person. **6** [1960s+] (*US*) in pl., the hands. **7** [1990s+] (*US*) a Scientologist [note American Dialect Society List 10/5/99: 'I remember reading an explanation of the term years ago, but have forgotten the specifics. It goes *something* like this: in L. Ron Hubbard's sci-fi religion, souls of alien refugees (who were hiding in volcanoes on Earth) were released when their enemies dropped atom bombs on them. These souls came to reside in clams (and early humans?)'].

pertaining to sex

IN COMPOUNDS

□ **clam chowder** *n.* (*also* **clam jam, clam juice**) [1960s+] (*US*) vaginal secretions. □ **clam-diving** *n.* [DIVE *v.* (2)] [2000s] cunnilingus. □ **clam jousting** *n.* [1990s+] lesbian sex. □ **clam jungle** *n.* [2000s] the female genitals and pubic hair. □ **clam smacker** *n.* [SMACK *v.* (1)] [1990s+] (*US*) a lesbian. □ **clam spear** *n.* [1970s+] the penis.

IN PHRASES

□ **club the clam** *v.* [1960s+] of a woman, to masturbate.

pertaining to silence

IN COMPOUNDS

□ **clam act** *n.* [1940s] silence; a refusal to talk. □ **clam-mouth** *n. see* sense 3 above. □ **clamtrap** *n.* [sense 1/3 above, but play on SE *clam* + *trap*; note TRAP *n.*^{1} (4)] [early 19C–1940s] (*US*) the mouth.

IN PHRASES

□ **do the clam** *v. see* CLAM (UP) *v.* (2).

SE in slang uses

IN COMPOUNDS

□ **clambake** *see* separate entries. □ **clam-basket** *n.* [early 19C] (*US*) the stomach. □ **clam-catcher** *n.* (*also* **clam-digger**) [the prevalence of clams off the state's shores] [mid-19C–1900s] (*US*) a native or inhabitant of New Jersey. □ **clam-diggers** *n.* (*US*) **1** [20C+] the hands. **2** [1910s+] the nickname of the inhabitants of various towns in northeast US. **3** [1950s+] trousers cut off at midcalf. □ **clam-headed** *adj.* [late 19C] (*Aus.*) stubborn. □ **clam's cuticle** *n. see* CAT'S WHISKERS *n.* □ **clam's garters** *n. see* BEE'S KNEES *n.* □ **clamshell** *n.* [ext. of sense 1 above + supposed resemblance] **1** [early 19C+] (*US*) the mouth or, in pl., jaws/lips. **2** [1930s] (*US Und.*) the ear.

clam *n.*^{2} (*also* **clamshell**) [ety. unknown; ? link to WAMPUM *n.*, another shell = money term] [late 19C+] (*US*) $1; usu. in pl.

clam *n.*^{3} [punning var. on OYSTER *n.* (2a)] [1970s+] a lump of phlegm.

clam *n.*^{4} [var. on LAM *n.*^{2}] [1980s] a heavy blow.

clam *v.* [one uses one's CLAM *n.*^{1} (1)] [late 19C] (*UK Und.*) to beg.

IN PHRASES

□ **clam (up)** *v. see* separate entry.

clambake *n.* [plays on SE] **1** [late 19C+] a party or get-together. **2** [1930s–60s] (*US black/jazz*) a spontaneous musical session. **3** [1930s+] (*US*) an event, esp. one that fails to live up to the obvious efforts that have been put into its preparation.

clambake *v.* [1980s+] (*US drugs*) to smoke marijuana in an enclosed space.

clammed *adj.* [the mouth is closed like a SE *clam*] [late 17C–1940s] starved.

clammed (up) *adj.* [CLAM (UP) *v.* (2)] [1930s+] silent, discreet, refusing to talk.

clammer *n.* [one is shut up like a SE *clam* + SLAMMER *n.*^{1} (2a)] [1990s+] prison.

clammy *adj.* **1** [late 19C–1900s] (*US*) a general term of abuse. **2** [1920s] (*US*) foolish, stupid.

clamp *v.* [the *clamping* on of handcuffs] [mid-19C–1960s] (*US*) to arrest, to seize.

clampers *n.* (*also* **clamps**) **1** [late 19C+] (*US*) the hands. **2** [1940s] (*US Und.*) handcuffs.

IN PHRASES

□ **put on the clampers** *v.* [20C+] to restrain, to hold back.

clam (up) *v.* [the strength with which the bivalve shuts itself tight] **1** [late 19C] to refuse food. **2** [1910s+] (*also* **do the clam**) to stop talking, to become deliberately secretive; thus as n. *the clam-ups*, silence, a refusal to speak.

clanger *n.*^{1} [the 'noise' of its 'hitting the ground'] [1950s+] **1** a mistake, esp. a social solecism; thus intensified as *clangeroo*. **2** (*Aus.*) a lie, a shock.

IN PHRASES

□ **drop a clanger** *v.* [1940s+] to make a social error, the awfulness of which reverberates around the assembled gathering.

clanger *n.*^{2} [ety. unknown] [2000s] (*N.Z. teen*) a smoke.

clank *n.* (*also* **clanker, clink**) [echoic; i.e. the tankard, plate or dollar hitting a table] **1** [late 17C–mid-19C] (*UK Und.*) a silver tankard; thus *rum clank*, a double tankard. **2** [late 18C] (*UK Und.*) a silver plate. **3** [19C] (*US*) a silver dollar.

IN COMPOUNDS

□ **clank-napper** *n.* (*also* **clanker-napper**) [NAPPER *n.*^{1} (1)] [late 17C–early 19C] a thief who specializes in stealing silver plate.

clanker *n.* [? the fig. 'thump' of the lie as it falls from one's mouth] [late 17C–early 19C] a gross, deliberate lie.

clankers *n.* [they 'clank' together] [1990s+] the testicles.

clanking (for) *adj.* [1990s+] (*UK juv.*) desperate for sex.

clanks *n.* [? aural hallucinations; orig. US Air Force slang *the clanks*, nervousness] [1980s+] (*US*) delirium tremens, nervousness.

clap *n.* (*also* **claps**) [OF *clapoir*, bubo; thus *clapoire* or *clapier*, a place of debauchery and the illness one can contract there. The term appears as SE in late 16C but starts appearing in cant/slang lists in late 17C; Henke, *Gutter Life and Language* (1988) quotes Cotgrave's definition (in *Dict. French and English Tongues*, 1611) of *clapier* as a rabbits' nest (as well as a name for 'old time Baudie houses'); thus a pun on SE *coney*, rabbit/CONY *n.* (2a) – a man might catch the disease from a CONY *n.* (2b) who was working in a *clapoir*] [mid-16C+] venereal disease, esp. gonorrhoea.

IN COMPOUNDS

□ **clap-clinic** *n.* [1970s+] a clinic specializing in venereal diseases. □ **clap-shack** *n.* [1940s] (*US*) a venereal disease clinic or hospital ward. □ **clap-trap** *n. see* separate entry.

SE in slang uses

IN COMPOUNDS

□ **clap-shoulder** *n.* [he *claps a hand on one's shoulder*] [17C] a bailiff or watchman. □ **clap-trap** *n. see* separate entry.

IN PHRASES

□ **clap of thunder** *n.* [play on *FLASH OF LIGHTNING under* LIGHTNING *n.*] [early–mid-19C] a glass of brandy. □ **clap on the shoulder** *n.* [17C–early 19C] an arrest for debt.

clap *v.*^{1} [CLAP *n.*] [17C+] to infect with venereal disease.

clap *v.*^{2} [SE *clap one's hands on*] [mid-19C–1910s] to seize, to arrest.

clap *v.*^{3} [SE *clap*, to strike a hard surface] [1950s+] (*W.I. Rasta*) **1** to hit, to break. **2** to stride. **3** to shoot.

SE in slang uses

IN PHRASES

□ **clap in** *v.* [SE *clap* (*of thunder*); i.e. the energy of one's arrival/departure] [late 17C–early 18C] to rush in vigorously, to push oneself forward, to arrive or leave in a decisive manner. □ **clap it up** *v.* [late 16C–17C] to get married. □ **clap on** *v.* [ext. SE *clap on*, to place with promptness and effect] [mid–late 19C] to commit oneself, to make a determined effort. □ **clap one's clit** *v.* [CLIT *n.*] [1970s+] of a woman, to masturbate.

claperdugion *n. see* CLAPPERDUDGEON *n.*

clapped *adj.* (*also* **clapped-out, clapped-up**) [CLAP *n.*] [mid-17C+] venereally diseased.

clapped-out *adj.* [CLAP *n.* and its deleterious effects, even on things that could not possibly contract it] [1940s+] worn out, useless, esp. of machinery, cars etc.

clapper *n.*^{1} [SE *clapper*, tongue of a bell] **1** [17C+] the tongue, esp. of a talkative person. **2** [1900s–30s] the mouth. **3** [1910s–30s] a sandwich-man; thus the boards he carries.

IN COMPOUNDS

□ **clapper-trap** *n.* [1900s] (*Aus.*) the mouth.

IN EXCLAMATIONS

□ **hold your clapper!** [early 19C–1900s] (*Aus.*) be quiet!

clapper *n.*[2] [CLAP *n.*] **1** [mid-18C] gonorrhoea. **2** [1950s] (*US*) a venereally diseased person.

clapper *n.*[3] [SE *clap*, to strike] [1900s–40s] a hit, a blow.

clapperclaw *v.* (*also* **capperclaw**) [SE *clapper*, tongue + *claw*; the term vanished in the UK but has survived in parts of the USA, where both senses are usu. applied to women] **1** [mid-16C–mid-19C] to claw or scratch with the open hand and nails, to beat, to thrash, to drub. **2** [late 17C–early 19C] to abuse verbally, to revile; thus as n. **3** [late 17C–18C] of a man, to have sexual intercourse, to fondle sexually. **4** [mid-19C] to pickpocket.

clapperdudgeon *n.* (*also* **claperdugion, clapperdogeon, clapperdudgion**) [SE *clapper*, hitter + *dudgeon*, the hilt of a dagger. Its origins remain a mystery, but it has been suggested that it comes from the beggar hitting his clapdish (a wooden dish with a lid, carried by lepers, beggars and mendicants generally, to give warning of their approach and to receive alms) with a dudgeon. *Clapdish* is, in turn, behind the phr. *your tongue goes like a baker's clapdish*] **1** [mid-16C–mid-19C] (*UK Und.*) a beggar who worked with a female companion, posing as man and wife and complete with counterfeit marriage licence; he might deliberately poison himself with ratsbane or spearwort (arsenic) to raise impressive sores. **2** [early 18C] a general term of abuse.

clappers *n.*[1] [their 'clapping together'] [1930s+] (*orig. UK milit.*) the testicles.

clappers *n.*[2] [1960s] (*US black*) an evangelical church, typified by a high degree of participation by the congregation, typically singing, hand-clapping, responding to the prayers and sermon.

clappers *n.*[3]

(IN PHRASES)

❑ **go like the clappers** *v.* [rhy. sl.; *clappers* = *bell* = *hell*; note RAF jargon *like the clappers of hell*, very fast] [1940s+] (*orig. RAF*) to run very fast; a euph. for GO LIKE HELL *under* HELL *n.*; as *like the clappers*, an intensive. ❑ **like the clappers** *adv.* [backform. f. prev.] [1940s+] a general intensive, extremely, a lot.

clapping for credit *n.* [one claps in time to the music] [1970s+] (*US campus*) a music appreciation course.

clappy *adj.* [CLAP *n.*] [1930s+] suffering from venereal disease.

clapster *n.* [CLAP *n.*] **1** [19C+] one who suffers regularly and often from venereal disease. **2** [late 19C+] a promiscuous man.

clap-trap *n.*[1] [play on SE; lit. 'an artifice for attracting applause' *Bartlett* 1848] **1** [19C+] (*also* **clapdish**) idle chatter, meaningless, often positively incorrect or misinformed talk; thus *claptrappy*, nonsensical; also as *adj.* **2** [19C+] any device used to milk an audience for applause. **3** [1960s–70s] (*US black*) the mouth. **4** *see* RATTLETRAP *n.* (2b).

clap-trap *n.*[2] [CLAP *n.* + SE *trap*; ? pun on CLAP-TRAP *n.*[1] (1)] **1** [late 19C] the vagina. **2** [1980s] a brothel where one might contract venereal disease.

clara *adj.* [? initial letter, i.e. SE coarse] [2000s] (*S.Afr. gay*) rude, vulgar.

Clare Market cleavers *n.* [Clare Market, a provisions market in London WC2, was established in 17C, but vanished beneath the Kingsway/Aldwych developments (1900–5)] [late 19C–1900s] butchers working in and around Clare Market, London WC2; thus butchers' jargon *cleavin*, boastful.

Clare Market duck *n.* [for ety. *see* prev.] [late 19C–1900s] a bullock's heart stuffed with sage and onions.

clarence *adj.* [generic/stereotypical use of proper name] [1910s] (*US*) upper-class, or affecting such airs.

claret *n.* (*also* **burgandy**) [OF *claret*, clear, bright, light; orig. used to distinguish yellowish or light red wines from plain red or white wines; used in UK from c.1600 to describe red wines of the Bordeaux vineyards only] [early 17C+] blood; thus (1920s) (boxing jargon) *claret*, to draw blood from an opponent, *claret-christening*, the first blow to draw blood.

(IN COMPOUNDS)

❑ **claret-jug** *n.* (*also* **claret cask, claret-spout**) [mid-19C] the nose.

(IN PHRASES)

❑ **tap someone's claret** *v.* [early 19C–1920s] to cause someone's nose to bleed with a blow.

claret *v.* [CLARET *n.*] [early–mid-19C] (*orig. boxing*) to draw blood, to bleed.

clarinet-player *n.* [pun on SE, the key image is that of *blowing*] [1950s] (*Aus.*) a fellator or fellatrix.

clarissa *adj.* [initial letter] [2000s] (*S.Afr. gay*) clever.

clarity *n.* [its effects] [2000s] (*drugs*) MDMA.

Clark Kent *adj.* [rhy. sl.; ult. *Clark Kent*, the comic book and film character 'Superman'] **1** [1990s+] corrupt [= BENT *adj.* (2)]. **2** [2000s] homosexual [= BENT *adj.* (5)].

clart *n.* [dial. *clart*, viscous sticky mud or filth] **1** [20C+] (*Ulster*) an untidy woman. **2** [1970s+] sticky excrement.

(IN PHRASES)

❑ **in the clarts** [1970s] **1** in trouble, lit. 'in the shit'. **2** suffering from diarrhoea.

clashbag *n.* (*also* **clashbeg**) [dial. *clash*, to gossip] [20C+] (*Ulster*) a gossip, a tattle-tale.

class *n.* [the *upper* class] **1** [mid-19C+] distinction, quality, orig. used of athletes. **2** [20C+] an upper-class or aristocratic person.

(IN PHRASES)

❑ **class up** *v.* [1980s+] (*US*) to make classy; esp. in phr. *class up one's act*, to start living in a more classy manner. ❑ **in the class** *adj.* [1920s–30s] well to do, wealthy.

class *adj.* [late 19C+] (*orig. US*) stylish, impressive, superior.

(IN PHRASES)

❑ **no class** *adj.* [late 19C+] styleless, socially inept, unable to fulfil the group norms.

class A *n.* [1990s+] (*drugs*) any drug, i.e. heroin, cocaine, categorized as 'Class A' under the UK *Dangerous Drugs Act* (1971).

class act *n.* (*also* **classer**) [CLASS *adj.* + SE *act*] [1970s+] (*orig. US*) an impressive performance, example or instance, both lit. and fig., used of things or individuals.

classic *n.* [1960s+] (*orig. US campus*) anyone or anything that is regarded as out of the ordinary, eccentric; the implication is one of ironic appraisal.

classic *adj.* [ext. of SE use, but perhaps, given its use in sl., with a slight ref. to the *classic* horseraces] [1940s+] a general adj. of supreme approval, wonderful, admirable, incomparable, best.

Classo *n.* [*Class*ification + -O *sfx* (3)] [1980s+] (*Aus. prison*) the Classification Committee; the classification a prisoner receives.

classy *adj.* [CLASS *n.* (1)] [late 19C+] of high or superior class, stylish, smart.

(IN COMPOUNDS)

❑ **classy chassis** *n. see under* CHASSIS *n.*

classy *adv.* [CLASSY *adj.*] [late 19C+] (*US*) in a sophisticated manner.

clatter *n.*[1] [the fig. 'explosion' that punctuates each instance of an act] [late 19C–1910s] (*US*) a 'time', an instance.

clatter *n.*[2] [CLATTER *v.*[1]] [20C+] (*orig. Irish*) a blow, a beating, esp. given by a parent to a child.

clatter *n.*[3] [1910s–50s] (*US Und.*) a police patrol wagon.

clatter *n.*[4] [they knock together] [1990s+] (*Irish*) a large number.

clatter *v.*[1] [orig. UK northern dial.] [20C+] to hit, to beat up; thus *clatters*, a smacking.

clatter *v.*[2] [US dial. *clatter*, idle gossip] [20C+] (*Irish*) to gossip.

clatterbrain *n.* (*also* **clatterbox**) [US dial. *clatter*, idle gossip, and earlier UK dial. *clatterbrains*, an idle, lazy gossip] [19C] a gossip.

clatty *adj.* [? CLART *n.* (2)] [1960s+] (*Scot./Irish juv.*) utterly filthy.

clava *n. see* BONNY-CLAPPER *n.*

claven *n.* [ety. unknown] [1990s+] (*US campus*) a know-it-all.

clavo *n.* [Calo *clavo*, a thief] **1** [1970s+] (*US prison*) a hiding place. **2** [1990s+] (*US prison*) a prisoner who is in possession of something valuable, esp. drugs. **3** [1990s+] (*US campus*) drugs.

claw *n.* **1** [mid-16C+] a hand, a finger. **2** [late 19C] (*UK prison*) a blow with a whip. **3** [1910s–50s] (*US Und.*) the member of a pickpocket team who actually steals. **4** [1950s+] (*US Und.*) a police officer.

IN COMPOUNDS

▫ **claw-back** *n.* [he or she metaphorically 'claws' at one's back. Note obs. SE *claw*, to flatter, to wheedle, to cajole] [16C–17C] a sycophant, a toady. ▫ **claw-buttock** *n.* [mid-17C–19C] the penis. ▫ **claw-poll** *n.* [he or she metaphorically 'claws' at one's SE *poll*, hair. Note obs. SE *claw*, to flatter, to wheedle, to cajole] [16C] a sycophant, a toady. ▫ **claw-thumper** *n.* see CRAW-THUMPER *n.* (1).

IN PHRASES

▫ **have the claw** *v.* [1980s] (*Aus.*) to be ruined, to be finished, to be irreparably damaged. ▫ **put the claws on** *v.* [20C+] (*US Und.*) **1** to arrest. **2** to inform on.

claw *v.* **1** [late 16C–18C] to fondle sexually, to masturbate a partner. **2** [1910s] (*US Und.*) to steal; to grab. **3** [1920s–30s] (*US tramp*) to arrest.

IN PHRASES

▫ **clawed off** *adj.* **1** [late 17C–18C] severely beaten or thrashed. **2** [late 17C–19C] suffering from a venereal disease. ▫ **claw me and I'll claw you** (*also* **ka me, ka thee**) [mid-16C–mid-19C] an early version of 20C *scratch my back and I'll scratch yours*. ▫ **claw off** *v.* (*also* **have claws for breakfast**) [SE *claw*, to scratch; but note ? pun on naut. *claw off*, to keep far enough away from the shore to avoid shipwreck] [late 17C–mid-19C] to thrash, to beat severely. ▫ **claw sky** *v.* see GRAB SKY *under* GRAB *v.*

clay *n.* [late 18C–19C] a clay pipe.

IN PHRASES

▫ **moisten the clay** *v.* (*also* **moist the clay, damp the..., soak one's..., wet the...**) [SE *clay*, the human flesh] [early 18C–1950s] to take a drink, to quench one's thirst.

SE in slang uses

IN COMPOUNDS

▫ **clay-assed** *adj.* [1960s–70s] (*US*) stupid, peasant-like. ▫ **clay-brained** *adj.* [late 16C; 1980s+] stupid. ▫ **clay-eater** *n.* [the literal eating of clay by such people in order to supplement their otherwise meagre diet] [mid-19C+] (*US*) a poor white, esp. a native of North or South Carolina or Georgia. ▫ **clay-puncher** *n.* [late 19C] (*Aus.*) a miner. ▫ **clay-punching** *n.* [1900s] (*Aus.*) working as a miner.

clay the jerk *v.* see CLY THE JERK *under* CLY *v.*

clayton's *n.* [the advertising line for *Clayton's* non-alcoholic drink (made from African kola nuts and citrus essences): 'It's the drink I have when I'm not having a drink', written by Noel Delbridge, creative director of ad agency D'Arcy, McManus & Masius] [1980s+] (*Aus.*) a myth, an illusion, a fantasy.

clean *adj.* [fig. uses of SE] **1** [mid-19C+] (*UK Und.*) without any form of incriminating identification. **2** [mid-19C+] (*UK Und.*) skilful, expert. **3** [mid-19C+] honest, not corrupt. **4** [late 19C–1960s] (*US*) penniless, without money. **5** [1910s+] beyond any possible suspicion, guiltless. **6** [1920s–50s] (*US Und.*) peaceful. **7** [1920s+] sober. **8** [1940s] without any conditions. **9** [1940s+] not carrying a weapon. **10** [1940s+] (*drugs*) of a person, not in possession of a drug. **11** [1950s+] (*drugs*) not using any form of drug, not currently addicted. **12** [1950s+] (*US black/prison*) of a person, dressed in the height of current male fashion, perfectly groomed. **13** [1950s+] (*also* **clean-ass**) of an object, fashionable, well-made. **14** [1960s] (*US*) first-class, excellent. **15** [1960s] (*US black/Und.*) of a crime, well-planned. **16** [1970s+] devoid of problems. **17** [1990s+] shaved; bald. **18** [2000s] (*US Und.*) free of surveillance. **19** [2000s] (*S.Afr. gay*) circumcised.

IN COMPOUNDS

▫ **clean-ass** *adj.* see sense 15 above.

IN PHRASES

▫ **clean and ready** *adj.* [1980s] (*US black*) **1** prepared for any eventuality. **2** well-dressed, fashionable. ▫ **clean as a jaybird** *adj.* [1930s–40s] (*US*) penniless, without money. ▫ **cleaner than the board of health** *adj.* **1** [1960s–70s] (*US black*) extremely well turned-out, dressed in the height of fashion. **2** [1980s] free from any criminal suspicion or charges. ▫ **clean to the bone** *adj.* [BONE *n.*[1]] [1970s+] (*US black*) exceptionally well dressed.

SE in slang uses

IN COMPOUNDS

▫ **clean-faced man** *n.* [1960s+] (*W.I.*) a Rastafarian who does not, however, sport the characteristic beard and dreadlocks. ▫ **clean job** *n.* [late 19C+] (*Aus./US*) a thorough or complete job; often used in the context of murder or violence; usu. as *make a clean job of (it)*. ▫ **clean potato** *n.* **1** [mid-19C+] (*Aus.*) anyone who is not a convict. **2** [late 19C–1920s] constr. with *the*, the right thing, the apposite thing; of a person, an honest, honourable one. ▫ **clean queen** *n.* [-QUEEN *sfx* (3)] [1960s+] (*US gay*) a gay man who combines trips to the launderette with picking up partners. ▫ **clean shirt** *n.* see *under* SHIRT *n.* ▫ **clean skin** *n.* see LILYWHITE *n.* (8). ▫ **cleanskin** *n.* see separate entry. ▫ **clean shot** *n.* [SHOT *n.*[1] (5a); fig. use of hunting jargon] [1920s+] a piece of good luck, a favourable opportunity. ▫ **clean sneak** *n.* [SNEAK *n.*[1] (3)] [1930s–40s] (*US*) a getaway (from a robbery, killing or other crime) without leaving incriminating clues. ▫ **clean wheat** *n.* [? wheat that has been threshed and thus free of all impurities] [mid-19C–1900s] the best, the supreme exemplar of a type.

clean *v.* **1** [mid-19C–1960s] (*US tramp*) to rob (of everything). **2** [mid-19C+] to beat, to overcome; thus *cleaning*, a thrashing. **3** [late 19C+] to tell off severely. **4** [late 19C+] (*orig. gambling*) to take all of an opponent's money. **5** [1900s–50s] (*US Und.*) for a pickpocket to rid him- or herself of the stolen object as soon as it has been secured. **6** [1910s+] (*US Und.*) to empty a stolen wallet or purse.

IN PHRASES

▫ **clean out** *v.* see separate entry. ▫ **clean someone's clock** *v.* [fig. use of SE; ? link to US railroad jargon *clean the clock*, to apply the airbrakes and thus bring the train to a sudden stop. The 'clock' in question is the air gauge, which on halting, immediately registers zero and is thus 'clean'] (*orig. US*) **1** [20C+] (*also* **wind someone's clock**) to beat up severely; to destroy. **2** [1980s+] to take all someone's money, esp. during gambling. ▫ **clean someone's greens** *v.* [? assonance] [1960s–70s] (*US*) to beat up severely. ▫ **clean someone's plow** *v.* [20C+] (*US*) to thrash, to beat severely; thus *clean someone's plow off*, to reach the limit of one's patience. ▫ **clean up** see separate entries.

SE in slang uses

IN PHRASES

▫ **clean house** *v.* **1** [20C+] (*US*) to sort things out once and for all, to punish, to beat. **2** [1960s] (*US*) to leave (fast). **3** [1980s+] (*US campus*) to vomit. ▫ **clean one's pipes** *v.* see *under* PIPE *n.*[1]. ▫ **clean one's rifle** *v.* [1990s+] to masturbate. ▫ **clean someone's pipe** *v.* see *under* PIPE *n.*[1]. ▫ **clean someone's rifle** *v.* [play on SE *rifle*/GUN *n.*[1] (2)] [1990s+] (*W.I.*) to fellate. ▫ **clean the floor with** *v.* see WIPE THE FLOOR (WITH) *v.* ▫ **clean the slate** *v.* see *under* SLATE *n.*[1].

clean *adv.* [SE *clean*, completely, entirely] **1** [mid-16C+] honestly. **2** [late 19C–1900s] (*US*) in profit.

SE in slang uses

IN PHRASES

▫ **clean around the bend** *adj.* [AROUND THE BEND *adj.* + pun on advertising slogan for the lavatory cleaner *Harpic*] [1920s+] utterly insane. ▫ **clean broke** *adj.* [BROKE *adj.*[1]] [mid-19C+] absolutely penniless. ▫ **clean gone** *adj.* [GONE *adj.*[1] (1)] [1920s] utterly insane.

cleaned out *adj.* (*also* **cleaned**) [CLEAN OUT *v.* (2)] [early 19C+] bereft of money, either through gambling or through some form of confidence trick or hoax.

cleaner *n.* [CLEAN OUT *v.* (2)] [1920s] (*US*) a successful swindler.

cleaners *n.*

IN PHRASES

▫ **go to the cleaners** *v.* [20C+] (*orig. US*) to lose badly, esp. in sport, gambling or business. ▫ **ready for the cleaners**

1 [1930s] open to being defrauded. **2** [1940s] (*US*) mentally and physically worn out, on the verge of collapse. ❑ **take to the cleaners** *v.* (*also* **send to the cleaners**) **1** [1900s] (*US*) to reduce to penury. **2** [1920s+] to defraud, outwit and otherwise remove all of a victim's assets in a wager, by extortion or by similar legal or illegal means. **3** [1920s+] to defeat thoroughly, to trounce.

cleaning *n.*

IN PHRASES

❑ **make a cleaning** *v. see* MAKE A KILLING *under* KILLING *n.*

clean (it) up *v.* [20C+] (*US Und.*) to explain; to find out information.

clean out *v.* **1** [19C+] to thrash. **2** [19C+] (*also* **clean**) to ruin financially or materially. **3** [mid-19C+] to rob. **4** [mid-19C+] (*US*) to defeat heavily, to trounce, to 'make short work of'. **5** [late 19C–1930s] (*US*) of a place, to smash up. **6** [late 19C+] (*gambling*) to take all of an opponent's money. **7** [1930s–60s] (*US Und.*) of police, to raid.

cleanskin *n.* (*also* **clearskin**) [SE *cleanskin/clearskin*, an unbranded cow] [1940s+] (*Aus./N.Z.*) **1** a person without a criminal record. **2** an honest person, esp. in politics.

clean-up *n.* [CLEAN UP *v.* (1)] **1** [mid-19C+] (*US gambling*) the climactic round of a gambling game in which the successful gambler takes the last of his opponent's money, esp. in cheating contexts. **2** [late 19C+] (*orig. US*) a profit, an exceptional financial success; a betting coup. **3** [1970s] (*US prison*) a story used to avoid a difficult situation, an alibi. **4** [1970s+] (*US*) an excuse, a justification, a way of extricating oneself from a situation.

clean up *v.* (*also* **clean up on**) [fig. uses of SE] **1** [mid-19C+] to do very well out of a project, esp. in gambling use; thus adj. *clean-up*, highly lucrative. **2** [late 19C–1950s] to empty, to empty of contents. **3** [late 19C+] to beat, to overcome. **4** [late 19C+] (*also* **clear up**) to make a large profit. **5** [20C+] to get rid of (hostile or alien elements). **6** to abandon habits. (**a**) [1910s+] to stop drinking alcohol. (**b**) [1950s+] (*drugs*) (*also* **clear up**) to abandon one's drug use, either by oneself or through some form of rehabilitation clinic. **7** [1930s] (*US*) to kill for revenge. **8** [1960s] (*US black*) to make excuses, to create an alibi. **9** [1960s] (*US black*) to confess, esp. to telling lies or to failure.

SE in slang uses

IN PHRASES

❑ **clean up one's act** *v. see under* ACT *n.* ❑ **clean up the kitchen** *n.* (*also* **sweep up the kitchen**) [the (alleged) use of all or any leftovers] [1920s–40s] (*US short-order*) an order for hash or a hamburger. ❑ **clean up the kitchen** *v. see under* KITCHEN *n.*[1].

clear *adj.*[1] (*also* **in the clear**) [? an ironic use of SE *clear*, the drunkard's head is of course far from clear] [late 17C–19C] (*UK Und.*) very drunk.

SE in slang uses

IN COMPOUNDS

❑ **clear crystal** *n.* [mid-19C–1920s] any clear spirit, e.g. gin, but also ext. to brandy or rum. ❑ **clear cut** *n.* [var. on SE *clean cut*] [1980s] (*US black*) **1** stylish clothes. **2** pure drugs. ❑ **clear field** *n.* [sporting imagery] [1960s–70s] (*US*) an unimpeded opportunity, esp. for making contact with or pursuing a member of the opposite sex. ❑ **clear light** *n.* [1970s+] (*drugs*) a variety of LSD. ❑ **clearskin** *n. see* CLEANSKIN *n.* ❑ **clear steer** *n.* [1930s] (*US*) a dismissal, a rejection.

IN PHRASES

❑ **clear as mud** *adj.* [mid-19C+] **1** completely unclear. **2** (*also* **clear as ditchwater**) absolutely clear. ❑ **get clear** *v.* [Scientology jargon *clear*, the ultimate state of those who go on a Scientology course] [1960s+] to work out a situation to its logical conclusion.

clear *adj.*[2] **1** [mid–late 19C] (*US*) pure, unadulterated. **2** [1990s+] (*US gay*) exclusively homosexual.

IN COMPOUNDS

❑ **clear grit** *n.* [GRIT *n.*[1]] [mid–late 19C] the real thing, the genuine article; thus *be the clear grit*, to have genuine spirit or pluck.

clear *v.*

SE in slang uses

IN PHRASES

❑ **clear the coop** *v.* (*also* **clear the fowl-house**) [mid–late 19C] (*US*) to rush off, to vacate. ❑ **clear the custard** *v. see under* CUSTARD *n.* ❑ **clear up** *v. see* CLEAN UP *v.*

cleared (out) *adj.* [CLEAR OUT *v.* (2)] [mid–late 19C] bereft of funds, impoverished.

clear out *v.* **1** [19C+] to take all an opponent's money, to ruin someone financially. **2** [late 19C–1910s] to rob.

cleat *n.* [SE *cleat*, a wedge] [late 19C] the penis; esp. the glans.

cleavage queen *n.* [SE *cleavage* + -QUEEN *sfx* (3)] [1970s] (*gay*) a heterosexual.

cleave *adj. see* CLOVEN *adj.*

cleave *v.* [SE *cleave*, to split; i.e. her legs or her supposed hymen] [mid-17C–18C] of a woman, to behave promiscuously.

cleaver *n.*[1] [his job and his tools] [18C–19C] a butcher.

cleaver *n.*[2] [CLEAVE *v.*] [late 18C–early 19C] a promiscuous woman.

cleave the pin *v.* [archery jargon *cleave the pin*, to score a bull's eye] [late 16C] of a woman, to bring a man to orgasm.

cleek *n.* [jazz use] [1950s] (*orig. US*) a sad, melancholy person, thus one one who spoils a party.

cleety *adj. see* CLUTEY *adj.*

cleft *n. see* CLIFT *n.*

cleft *adj. see* CLOVEN *adj.*

cleft (of flesh) *n.* [mid-18C–19C] the vagina.

clefty *v. see* CLIFTIE *v.*

cleg *n.* [lit. 'a horsefly'] [20C+] (*Ulster*) a parasite, a hanger-on.

clem *n.* [proper name *Clarence* and considered a stereotypical 'country' name] **1** [late 19C+] (*US*) a fight between travelling carnival or circus people and local townspeople. **2** [1960s] (*Irish*) a second-rate thing.

clem *v.* (*also* **do a clem**) [16C+ dial. *clem*, to starve, to waste from hunger; ult. f. various Teut. roots meaning 'pinch' or 'squeeze'] [mid-19C–1930s] (*UK tramp*) to go hungry, to starve.

Clement Freuds *n. see* EMMA FREUDS *n.*

clencher *n. see* CLINCHER *n.*[1].

clenchpoop *n. see* CLINCHPOOP *n.*

clergyman *n.* [the colour of both professions' clothes] [late 18C–19C] a chimney sweep.

clericals *n.* [mid-19C] clerical garments (i.e. those worn by clergymen).

clerked *adj.* [SE *clerk*, such 'learned' figures were automatically distrusted by the illiterate masses] [late 18C–mid-19C] soothed, gulled, imposed upon.

clerk of the kitchen *n.* [mid–late 17C] one who goes to the tavern for food as well as drink.

clerk of the works *n.* [early–mid-19C] a minor functionary.

Cleveland *n.* [the head of US President Grover *Cleveland* (1837–1908), which is printed on the bill] [1920s] (*US*) a $1,000 bill.

clever *n.* (*also* **u-clever**) [SE + Isicamtho *uclever*] [1960s+] (*S.Afr.*) a gangster, a streetwise individual.

clever *adj.* [18C SE *clever*, 'active' rather than 'infirm', healthy] **1** [mid-18C–1900s] (*US*) good-natured, well-disposed, amiable (often too well-disposed for one's own good and thus applied to those whose intelligence is considered somewhat deficient). **2** [19C+] (*orig. Aus./N.Z.*) in good health, in order, working well, etc; thus *not too clever*, a general negative response to 'how are you?'. **3** [19C+] skilful, adroit. **4** [mid-19C; 1970s+] fashionable. **5** [late 19C+] cunning, duplicitous. **6** [1970s+] (*US gay*) good-looking, charming.

SE in slang uses

IN COMPOUNDS

❑ **clever boots** *n.* (*also* **clever-britches**) [1930s+] a clever person, esp. one who is 'too clever for their own good'. ❑ **clever clogs** *n.* [orig. dial.] [mid-19C; 1960s+] a slightly derog. description (usu. used by children) of anyone considered notably clever (often 'too clever for their own good').

clever dick *n.* (*also* **clever dog, cleverguts, cleverpot, clever shins**) [late 19C+] a clever person, esp. when considered suspiciously so.

clever-dick *adj.* [CLEVER DICK *n.*] [1950s+] self-satisfied, too smart for one's own good.

clever Mike *n.* [rhy. sl. = bike] [1950s+] a bicycle.

clevvies *n.* [? SE *cloven/cleft*, i.e. ref. to the vagina] [1970s] (*US black*) a woman, a girl.

clewner *n.* [ety. unknown; Ribton-Turner, *A History of Vagrants* (1887), suggests Gaelic *cluainear*, a cunning fellow, a hypocrite, or Erse *cluanaire*, a seducer, a flatterer, or Manx *cleaynagh*, a tempter] [mid-16C] a senior rank of villain: 'Sir, yet there is another company / Of the same sect, that live more subtily, / And be in manner as master wardens, / To whom these rogers obey as captains / And be named clewners, as I hear say' (Copland, *Hye way to the Spyttel House*, c.1535).

cleyme *n.* (*also* **clyme, cleymans**) [ety. unknown; Partridge suggests a Cockney pron. of SE *claim*, i.e. a 'claim on one's pity'; the *cleyme* is created by 'bruising Crowsfoot, Speerwort, and Salt together, and clapping them on the Place, which frest the Skin, then with a Linnen rag, which sticks close to it, they tear off the Skin, and strew on it a little Powder'd Arsenick, which makes it look angrily...' (B.E.)] [17C–early 19C] (*UK Und.*) an artificial sore or wound, as placed on the body by a variety of mendicant villains.

clica *n.* (*also* **klika**) [Sp. *clica*, a clique] [1960s+] (*US*) a gang.

click *n.*[1] [dial.] [late 18C–mid-19C] (*UK Und.*) a blow.

click *n.*[2] (*also* **clique**) [SE *clique*] [early 19C+] a clique, a gang.

IN PHRASES

❑ **click in** *v.* [1990s+] (*US gang*) to become initiated into a gang. ❑ **click up** *v.* [1980s+] (*US prison*) to form or join a prison gang, usu. one formed on racist lines.

click *n.*[3] [? the SE *click* of a lock] [mid-19C–1900s] a robbery, a theft.

click *n.*[4] [CLICK *v.*[3]] **1** [1920s] (*UK tramp*) money acquired through begging, or trickery; also as v. **2** [1930s–40s] the making of an acquaintance; a flirtation, a pick-up. **3** [1940s–50s] (*US*) a success [appears to be a Winchellism]. **4** *see* KLICK *n.*

click *n.*[5] [1990s+] (*US black*) a gun.

click *adj.* [CLICK *v.*[3] (2)] [1930s–50s] (*US*) successful.

click *v.*[1] [northern dial. *cleek*, to snatch, to clutch eagerly] [late 17C–19C] (*UK Und.*) to snatch, to rob.

click *v.*[2] [CLICKER *n.*[1]] [mid-18C–early 19C] to stand at one's shop doorway and inveigle customers in.

click *v.*[3] [the image of a lock or similar form of machinery working as planned] [1910s+] **1** to get on with, to strike up a friendship with. **2** (*also* **click for**) to become proficient or successful at, to come together. **3** to work out exactly as planned. **4** for something to become clear or comprehensible, esp. after a period of puzzlement, to 'ring a bell'. **5** to be recognized. **6** (*orig. Irish*) to pick up a member of the opposite sex. **7** to be chosen, to be selected.

IN PHRASES

❑ **click onto** *v.* [1990s+] **1** (*US black*) to affiliate oneself with, to associate with. **2** (*US campus*) to understand. ❑ **click with** *v.* [1910s+] to get on with, to strike up a friendship with; thus n. *clicking (with)*, making a successful contact, usu. with a member of the opposite sex (albeit not necessarily sexual).

click *v.*[4] [also used in rural Aus. of a cow] [1930s+] to become pregnant.

click *v.*[5] [CLICK *n.*[2]] [2000s] (*US prison*) to attack in a group.

click! *excl.* [CLICK *v.*[3] (3)] [1930s] a general excl. of satisfaction, indicating the successful conclusion of a plan.

clicker *n.*[1] [orig. shoemaker's jargon *clicker*, a foreman shoemaker who cuts out the leather for boots and shoes, and gives it out to the workmen, or a workman who works at cutting the uppers of boots and shoes] [late 17C–19C] a shopkeeper's (orig. a shoemender's) tout.

clicker *n.*[2] [CLICK *v.*[1]] [late 18C–early 19C] (*UK Und.*) the gang member deputed to divide up the spoils fairly.

clicker *n.*[3] **1** [19C] (*orig. boxing jargon*) a knockout blow; thus also, a professional fighter/boxer, i.e. one who 'clicks' his opponent. **2** [early 19C] a watch. **3** [1920s] (*UK prison*) a warder. **4** [1940s] (*US*) a photographer.

clicker *n.*[4] [CLICK *v.*[1]] [late 19C] (*UK Und.*) a thief.

clickers *n.* [the sound they make] [1990s+] false teeth.

clicket *n.* [SE *clicket*, a latch-key] [late 16C–early 17C] chatter.

clicket *v.* [SE *clicket*, of the fox, to be in heat, to copulate] [early 16C–19C] to copulate; thus *at the clicket*, having intercourse; *clicketing* copulation; *clicket gate*, n., the vagina.

clicketty-clicks *n.* [rhy. sl. = KNICKS *n.* (2)] [1910s+] women's underpants.

clickety-click *n.* [rhy. sl.] **1** [20C+] (*bingo*) the number six or 66. **2** [2000s] (*Aus.*) a stick.

clicking *n.* [? a clock-like jerkiness in one's speech and/or actions] [1990s+] (*US black*) going mad.

click it *v.* [1910s] to die; to be killed.

clickman toad *n.* ['A West-country man, who had never seen a watch, found one on a heath near Pool, which, by the motion of the hand, and the noise of the wheels, he concluded to be a living creature of the toad kind, and, from its clicking, he named it a clickman toad' (Grose, 1785)] [late 18C–mid-19C] **1** a watch. **2** a West Countryman.

clicko *adj.* [CLICK *v.*[3] (2)] [1950s] (*US*) successful.

clicks *n.* [2000s] (*US prison*) minutes spent on the telephone.

cliff ape *n. see under* APE *n.*

cliff-dweller *n.* [SE *cliff dwellers*, a tribe of Native Americans living literally in cliffs in the Southwest] [late 19C–1960s] (*US*) one who lives in a skyscraper apartment block, esp. in New York City.

cliffhanger *n.* [orig. the film description of such silent-era serials as 'The Perils of Pauline' (starring Pearl White) in which the heroine, at an episode's end, was often literally hanging from a cliff] [1930s+] any suspenseful, threatening situation, although usu. one from which one is eventually delivered.

clift *n.* (*also* **cleft**) [? SE *cleave*, i.e. their brain has been cut in several pieces] [late 19C+] (*orig. Irish*) a fool; thus the levels of stupidity, *quarter clift, three-quarter clift, the two ends of a clift*, an utter fool.

clift *v.* [? SE *cleave*, to adhere to or *clift*, to split, to divide (in this case possessions from their owner); *see also* next] [mid-19C–1900s] to steal.

cliftie *v.* (*also* **clefty, clifty**) [CLIFT *v.*, but note Gk *klephtys*, a thief] [20C+] (*Aus.*) to steal.

cligh *see under* CLY.

climb *n.*[1] [20C+] (*UK Und.*) cat burglary; thus *at the climb, climbing*, working as a cat burglar.

climb *n.*[2] [ety. unknown; ? it makes one CLIMB (UP) THE WALLS *under* CLIMB *v.* or play on HIGH *adj.*[1] (2)] [1940s+] (*US drugs*) a marijuana cigarette.

climb *v.* (*also* **climb on**) [Williams has several 16C/17C examples of *climb* in a sexual context, usu. in phr. *climb the tree*] [late 19C+] (*US*) of a man, to have sexual intercourse; to enter a woman and commence intercourse.

SE in slang uses

in the context of judicial hanging

IN PHRASES

❑ **climb the ladder** *v.* [16C+] to be hanged. ❑ **climb the leafless tree** *v. see under* LEAFLESS TREE *n.* ❑ **climb the six-foot ladder** *v.* [the trad. six-foot depth of a grave] [1940s–60s] (*orig. US black*) to die. ❑ **climb the stalk** *v. see under* STALK *n.* ❑ **climb the tree by one's neck** *v.* [1910s] (*Aus.*) to be hanged. ❑ **climb three trees with a ladder** *v.* [the framework of the wooden gallows] [mid-16C–19C] to be hanged.

general uses

IN COMPOUNDS

❑ **climb-a-pole** *n.* [one climbs so as to look down on the world] [mid-19C] (*US*) an arrogant, 'stuck-up' person; also as *adj.*, snobbish.

IN PHRASES

❑ **climb all over** *v.* **1** [late 19C] to trounce, to defeat heavily. **2** [1940s+] (*also* **climb into**) to attack physically. **3** [1940s+] (*also* **climb into**) to attack verbally, to reprimand. **4** [1950s] to maul sexually, usu. spoken by a woman of a man. ❑ **climb in on** *v.* [late 19C] (*US*) to overcome easily, to get the better of, esp. by trickery. ❑ **climb (over) someone's frame** *v. see under* FRAME *n.*[1]. ❑ **climb the golden staircase** *v.* [late 19C] **1** (*US*) to die. **2** to fail badly. ❑ **climb the greasy pole** *v.* [late 19C] to die. ❑ **climb the mountain of piety** *v.* [the world's first government-authorized pawnbrokers, which were established in Rome and sited on the Monte di Pietà ('the mountain of piety')] [late 19C–1900s] to take one's possessions to the pawnshop. ❑ **climb trees to get away from it** *v.* [1940s+] (*Aus. male*) in answer to the query 'getting any?' Allied phrs. are *got to swim underwater to get away from it, so busy I've had to put a man on to help*. ❑ **climb up someone's ass** *v. see under* ASS *n.* ❑ **climb (up) the walls** *v.* (*also* **run up the walls**) **1** [1930s+] to lose one's temper, to run out of patience. **2** [1960s+] to approach insanity through nerves, irritation, tension, etc. **3** [1960s+] to become highly excited.

IN EXCLAMATIONS

❑ **go climb up your thumb!** (*also* **go climb a tree! go climb a wall! go climb the chain!**) [1930s–40s] (*US*) a general excl. of dismissal.

climber *n.* [CLIMB *n.*[1]] [20C+] (*UK Und.*) a cat burglar.

climbing Mary *n.* [1940s] a woman window-cleaner.

clinch *n.* [SE *clinch*/CLINCH *v.*] **1** [mid-19C] a prison cell; thus *get the clinch*, to be locked up; *clinched*, imprisoned. **2** [20C+] a sexual embrace.

clinch *v.* [SE *clinch*] **1** [18C; late 19C–1960s] to embrace sexually. **2** [late 19C] to shake hands.

clinched *adj.* ['in the grip' of alcohol] [20C+] drunk.

clincher *n.*[1] (*also* **clencher**) **1** [18C+] the ultimate solution, the culmination. **2** [mid-19C] an irrefutable lie.

IN PHRASES

❑ **get the clincher** *v.* [mid-19C] (*UK Und.*) to be imprisoned.

clincher *n.*[2] [1950s] (*US prison*) a smokeable cigarette end.

clinchpoop *n.* (*also* **clenchpoop**) [? *clincher*, the workman who clinched the bolts in ship-building] [mid–late 16C] an ill-mannered lout, one who lacks gentlemanly breeding.

cliner *n.* (*also* **clinah**) [ety. unknown; ? Ger. *Kleine*, little one] [late 19C–1940s] (*Aus./US*) a woman, a girlfriend.

clinic *n.* [one visits for 'a bit of what the doctor ordered'] [1950s] a public house.

Clink *n.* [? CLINK *n.*[1] (1)] [16C] a sanctuary for criminals in Southwark; the villains who frequented this area were known as *Clinkers*.

clink *n.*[1] [either SE *clink*, to secure, to fasten securely, or onomat. noise of clinking chains; note WW1 milit. *clink*, guard room] **1** [early 16C+] (*also* **clinker, clinky, klink**) prison. **2** [late 18C+] (*also* **clinkum**) money. **3** [mid–late 19C] (*also* **clinker**) a coin. **4** [late 19C] (*Aus. prison*) a leg-chain. **5** [1900s] (*US*) a police station.

clink *n.*[2] [abbr. *BUM CLINK under* BUM *adj.*] [mid–late 19C] bad or second-rate beer.

clink *n.*[3] [? fig. use of CLINK *n.*[1] (1), so many blacks being imprisoned, or f. *clinker*, a grey-black ash that remains after a fire] [1930s–40s] (*US black*) a black man.

clink *n.*[4] *see* CLANK *n.*

clink *v.* [CLINK *n.*[1] (1)] [early 19C–1910s] (*UK Und.*) to arrest.

clink and clank *n.* [rhy. sl.] [1930s–40s] (*US Und.*) a bank.

clinker *n.*[1] [? CLINKERS *n.*] [late 17C–mid-18C] a crafty person.

clinker *n.*[2] [orig. sporting use f. something that 'rings a (celebratory) bell'] [mid-18C–1940s] anything, or anyone, considered excellent, first-rate.

clinker *n.*[3] [it 'clinks' on its target] [mid-19C–1910s] a sharp blow.

clinker *n.*[4] [? SE *cling* or *clinker*, a hardened mass] **1** [mid-19C+] a piece of excrement adhering to the anus; thus *have clinkers in one's bum*, to act nervously or restlessly. **2** [1990s+] a piece of excrement.

clinker *n.*[5] [SE *clinker*, a very hard brick; ? since its ult. ety. is Du., as imported by Dutch immigrants] [1900s–30s] (*US*) a hard biscuit.

clinker *n.*[6] [orig. baseball use] **1** [1930s–50s] (*US*) a musical discord, a fluffed note. **2** [1950s–60s] a second-rate, worthless person. **3** [1950s+] something second-rate, inferior, esp. a performance. **4** [1960s] (*US*) a problem, a difficulty.

clinker *n.*[7] [1970s] a prison.

clinker *n.*[8] *see* CLINK *n.*[1].

Clinkers *n.* [CLINK *n.*] [16C] a collective term for the villains who inhabited the criminal sanctuary of the CLINK *n.* in Southwark.

clinkers *n.* [the noise] **1** [late 17C–19C; 1950s] chains and fetters worn by imprisoned felons. **2** [1900s] stairs [creaking stairs or the 'clink' of feet]. **3** [1940s] (*US Und.*) handcuffs. **4** [1940s+] (*Ulster*) the testicles [supposedly 'clinking' testicles].

clinkerum *n.* [CLINK *n.*[1] (1)] [19C] a prison.

clinking *adj.* (*also* **hell-clinking**) [mid-19C–1930s] excellent, admirable, first-rate, esp. of racehorses.

clink rig *n.* (*also* **clinking**) [SE *clink*, the noise of tankards hit together + RIG *n.*[2] (1)] [mid-19C] (*UK Und.*) the stealing of tankards from taverns; thus *clink rigger*, one who steals tankards.

clinkum *n. see* CLINK *n.*[1] (2).

clinky *n. see* CLINK *n.*[1] (1).

clip *n.*[1] [fig. use of CLIP *v.*[1] (3)] [19C+] a go, a time.

clip *n.*[2] [CLIP *v.*[1] (3)] [19C+] a sharp blow.

clip *n.*[3] [CLIP *v.*[2]] **1** [mid-19C–1930s] (*US*) a smart, clever or lively young woman or man [ext. of sense 2]. **2** [mid-19C+] a rate of movement, a pace; thus *fair/good clip*, a (reasonably) high speed. **3** [1900s] (*US campus*) a situation.

clip *n.*[4] [CLIP *v.*[1] (4)] **1** [1930s–60s] (*US*) a theft. **2** [1960s] (*US Und.*) a thief or robber.

clip *n.*[5] [abbr. CLIPDICK *n.*] [1940s] a male Jew.

clip *n.*[6] **1** [1990s+] (*drugs*) a bundle of the bottles in which crack cocaine is distributed, tied with a rubber band to facilitate carriage. **2** [2000s] (*US*) a pager [it is clipped to one's belt].

clip *n.*[7] *see* CLIP-JOINT *n.*

clip *v.*[1] [SE *clip*, to cut or snip] **1** [16C–mid-18C] to have sexual intercourse; thus *clipping*, sexual intercourse. **2** [17C] to caress. **3** [late 17C+] to hit, to tap sharply. **4** [late 19C+] (*orig. US*) (*also* **clip in**) to defraud, to steal from, to rob. **5** [1910s+] (*US*) to shoot, usu. dead. **6** [1940s+] (*US*) to place under arrest. **7** [1950s] (*US drugs*) to adulterate a drug. **8** [1950s+] to beat, i.e. in a card game. **9** [1960s+] to esteem as, to reckon.

IN COMPOUNDS

❑ **clip-artist** *n.* [-ARTIST *sfx*] [1940s–60s] (*US Und.*) **1** a petty thief. **2** a swindler. ❑ **clip-joint** *n. see* separate entry. ❑ **clip queen** *n.* [-QUEEN *sfx* (3)] [1940s] (*US gay*) a male prostitute who specializes in robbing clients.

IN PHRASES

❑ **clip a steamer** *v. see under* STEAMER *n.*[1]. ❑ **clip in** *v. see* sense 4 above. ❑ **put the clip on** *v.* [1920s+] (*US*) to overcharge, to defraud; to extort from.

SE in slang uses

IN COMPOUNDS

❑ **clipdick** *n. see* separate entry. ❑ **clip-nit** *n.* [SE *clip*, to grasp + *nit*, a louse egg] [late 17C] a dirty ruffian.

IN PHRASES

❑ **clip the King's English** *v.* [SE *clip*, to mutilate] [late 17C–18C] to slur one's words when drunk; thus, to be drunk. ❑ **clip up** *v.* [1950s] to toss a coin.

clip *v.*[2] [SE *clip*, of a bird, to fly fast] [mid-19C+] to move quickly, to run; often constr. with *across, along, away* etc.

clipdick *n.* [SE *clip* + DICK *n.*[1] (5); his circumcision] [1940s+] **1** a derog. term for a male Jew. **2** a circumcised penis.

clip-joint *n.* (*also* **clip, clip-dive**) [CLIP *v.*^{1} (4) + JOINT *n.* (3b)] [1930s+] (*orig. US*) a club or similar place of entertainment where the customers are deliberately and systematically defrauded under the guise of charging them for their pleasure.

clipped *adj.*^{1} [SE *clip*] [1910s+] (*US*) circumcised.

clipped *adj.*^{2} [CLIP *v.*^{1}] **1** [1930s+] (*US*) shot. **2** [1950s] (*US*) out of funds.

clipped within the ring *n.* [SE *clip* + RING *n.* (1a)] [late 16C–early 17C] deflowered.

clipper *n.*^{1} [senses 3 and 5 CLIP *v.*^{1} (4), but despite the obvious synon., chronology makes other senses fig. uses of SE] **1** [early 18C] (*UK Und.*) a cut-purse. **2** [1940s] a philanderer, a womanizer. **3** [1940s] (*US*) a petty thief or confidence trickster; a prostitute who defrauds her customer. **4** [1960s] (*US Und.*) a thug, a violent person. **5** [1960s+] a professional store thief.

clipper *n.*^{2} [SE *clipper*, a fast-sailing vessel, esp. the raked schooners of America and subseq. the Aus. passenger ships] **1** [mid-19C] an attractive person, esp. a woman. **2** [mid-19C–1920s] an excellent thing.

clipper *n.*^{3} [ety. unknown; ? SE *clipper ship*] [1960s] (*US*) a cigarette.

clipper *n.*^{4} [? Afk. *klippe*, diamonds or the need for a *paper-clip* to keep 100 rands' worth of ten-rand notes together] [1980s+] (*S.Afr.*) a 100-rand note.

clippie *n.*^{1} [1940s+] a bus conductress, who orig. *clipped* tickets.

clippie *n.*^{2} [SE *clip*, i.e. they still cut their hair rather than let it grow into long dreadlocks] [1970s] (*W.I./Rasta*) a young man who identifies with the Rastafarian movement but is not fully committed.

clipping *n.* [CLIP *v.*^{1} (4)] [1970s+] (*UK Und.*) posing as a prostitute, obtaining the money, but absconding before intercourse takes place.

clipping *adj.*^{1} [CLIP *v.*^{2}] [mid–late 19C] of a pace, fast.

clipping *adj.*^{2} [CLIPPER *n.*^{2} (2)] [mid-19C–1920s] excellent, first-rate.

clipping *adv.* [CLIPPING *adj.*^{2}] [late 19C] excellently, ideally.

clippings of tin *n. see under* TIN *n.*

clippy *n.* [1990s+] a (male) hairdresser's shop.

clips, the *adj.* [CLIPPING *adj.*^{2}] [1900s] smart, socially successful.

clip side of big moist *phr.* [CLIP *v.*^{1} (5) + BIG MOIST *n.*; at that time the Western battleground of WW2] [1940s] (*US black, Harlem*) Europe.

clipster *n.* [CLIP *v.*^{1} (4)] [1940s–60s] (*US*) a swindler.

clique *n. see* CLICK *n.*^{2}.

clit *n.* [abbr.] [1950s+] the *clit*oris.

DERIVATIVES

❑ **clitlins** *n.* [play on SE *chitlins*] [2000s] (*UK black*) the vagina.

IN COMPOUNDS

❑ **clit-fight** *n.* [1990s+] (*US*) a sexual game between two women. ❑ **clit-hopper** *n.* [on pattern of *BEDHOP under* BED *n.*, lit. to move or 'hop' from clitoris to clitoris] [1960s+] (*lesbian*) a promiscuous lesbian.

clitty *n.* [abbr.] [1930s+] the *clit*oris.

IN COMPOUNDS

❑ **clitty litter** *n.* [pun on SE *kitty litter*, a cat's 'toilet'] [2000s] (*UK black*) stains on one's underwear produced by vaginal secretions.

clitty *adj. see* CLUTEY *adj.*

cloak *n.* [early 18C] (*UK Und.*) a watch-case.

SE in slang uses

IN COMPOUNDS

❑ **cloak-and-suiter** *n.* [1910s–40s] (*US*) a wealthy individual. ❑ **cloak-twitcher** *n.* [early 18C–early 19C] (*UK Und.*) a thief specializing in the theft of cloaks.

cloaker *n.* [? mis-sp. of *choker*] [mid-19C] (*UK Und.*) execution by hanging.

clob *v. see* CLOBBER *v.*^{2} (1).

clobber *n.* (*also* **clabber, klobber**) [ety. unknown. ? Yid., so claimed by Ware who suggests 'Hebrew KLBR' (the Hebrew has been anglicized without vowels)] **1** [late 19C+] clothes, esp. good quality or conspicuous clothes; thus *clobbered*, well-dressed. **2** [late 19C] (*UK Und.*) ? a shirt. **3** [1930s+] things.

clobber *v.*^{1} (*also* **klobber**) [CLOBBER *n.* (1)] [late 19C–1900s] to dress up.

clobber *v.*^{2} [ety. unknown, ? echoic of the sound of the blow; note US Air Force Academy *clobber in*, to crash] **1** [late 19C+] (*also* **clob**) to hit, to beat up, to kill; also fig.; thus *clobbering*, a beating. **2** [1940s+] to defeat heavily. **3** [1950s+] to criticize, to treat harshly. **4** [1960s+] in fig. use, i.e. to accost. **5** [1990s+] to make a physical effort.

clobbered *adj.* [fig. use of CLOBBER *v.*^{2} (1)] [1940s+] drunk.

clobbo *n.* [? SE *clod*] [1950s] a dull, stupid person.

clock *n.*^{1} [fig. uses of SE referring either to the clock's face or its ticking] **1** [late 19C] a bomb; thus *got a clock*, carrying a handbag (in which a bomb is hidden) [a bomb-carrier who, when stopped during the dynamite scare of the 1880s by an alert policeman, on being asked what was in his bag, replied 'A clock']. **2** [late 19C+] a watch. **3** [20C+] the face; occas. the head. **4** [20C+] a speedometer, taximeter or similar dial that has a 'face'. **5** [1930s] (*US prison*) a life sentence. **6** [1930s–50s] (*also* **clocker**) (*US black*) the heart. **7** [1940s–60s] (*Aus.*) a prison sentence of 12 months; thus synon. phr. *round the clock*. **8** [1950s] (*US prison*) fig. use of sense 6, courage. **9** [1980s] surveillance, observation.

SE in slang uses

IN COMPOUNDS

❑ **clock-weights** *n.* [they supposedly swing backwards and forwards] [19C] the testicles.

IN PHRASES

❑ **clock out** *v. see* separate entries. ❑ **get one's clock cleaned** *v.* (*also* **get one's clock fixed**) [1950s] to be beaten up, to be killed. ❑ **sock the clock** *v. see under* SOCK *v.*^{1}. ❑ **sweet as a clock** *adj. see* SWEET AS (A) NUT *under* SWEET *adj.*^{1}.

clock *n.*^{2} *see* CLOCKER *n.*^{2}.

clock *v.*^{1} [CLOCK *n.*^{1} (3)] **1** [1910s+] to look at. **2** [1920s+] (*orig. Aus./N.Z.*) to hit, usu. in the face. **3** [1920s+] to see, to recognize, to notice, to watch, to understand, to work something out. **4** [1950s] (*US*) to reconnoitre, usu. of a possible crime site. **5** [1980s] (*US*) of a prostitute, to pick up a customer. **6** [1980s+] (*US black gang*) to reconnoitre. **7** [2000s] to defeat, to beat.

IN PHRASES

❑ **clock a daffy** *v. see under* DAFFY *n.*^{3}. ❑ **clock a grip** *v. see under* GRIP *n.* ❑ **clock onto** *v.* [1930s+] to recognize.

clock *v.*^{2} [SE *clock up*] [1980s+] (*US black*) **1** to achieve, to accomplish, to succeed. **2** to earn money.

clock *v.*^{3} [CLOCKER *n.*^{1} (3), but note CLOCK *v.*^{2} (2)] [1980s+] (*US black*) to sell drugs, thus to make money from drug-dealing.

clock *v.*^{4} [CLOCK OUT *v.*^{2}] [2000s] (*US black*) to lose one's temper; to become violent.

clocker *n.*^{1} [SE *clock*, a time piece] **1** [1900s–50s] (*US*) a handicapper, bookmaker or racing tipster who bases their information on timing the horses on their morning exercise. **2** [1940s+] (*UK Und.*) a second-hand car dealer who illegally alters a car's mileage. **3** [1980s+] (*drugs*) a dealer of crack cocaine; thus *clocking*, working as a crack dealer [the need for the drug and the appearances of the dealer both seem to occur at regular intervals, and these dealers are on call 'around the clock', but note CLOCK *v.*^{2} (2)].

clocker *n.*^{2} (*also* **clock**) [orig. UK dial.] [1930s+] (*Irish*) a cockroach or a beetle.

clocker *n.*^{3} *see* CLOCK *n.*^{1} (6).

clockers *n.* [CLOCK *v.*^{1} (1)] [1940s] (*US Und.*) the eyes.

clockey *n. see* CLOCKY *n.*

clocking *n.*^{1} [CLOCK OUT *v.*^{2}] [1980s+] (*US black*) saying inappropriate, tactless things, acting insanely.

clocking *n.*^{2} [CLOCK *v.*^{3}] [1980s+] (*US black*) working as a drug seller.

IN COMPOUNDS

❑ **clocking paper** *n.* [PAPER *n.* (1)] [1980s+] (*drugs*) profits from selling drugs.

clock out *v.*[1] [SE *clock out*, to leave a place of employment] [1980s] to die.

clock out *v.*[2] [WOUND-UP *adj.* (2)] [1980s] to go very crazy, to be 'out of it'.

clockwork *n.* (*US black*) **1** [1940s+] (*also* **clockworks**) the human brain, the mind. **2** [2000s] the female buttocks.

clocky *n.* (*also* **clockey**) [the regularity of his rounds] [late 18C–mid-19C] a watchman.

clod *n.*[1] **1** [late 16C+] (*also* **clod-head**) a stupid person, esp. a dull-witted peasant. **2** [1960s+] a rude, awkward person.

DERIVATIVES

❑ **cloddish** *adj.* **1** [mid-19C+] stupid, dull-witted. **2** [1990s+] clumsy, awkward.

SE in slang uses

IN COMPOUNDS

❑ **clod-brained** *n.* [1940s] (*Irish*) very stupid. ❑ **clod-buster** *n.* [1950s+] (*US*) a rustic, a farmer. ❑ **clod-crusher** *n.* [note also: 'an epithet used by Americans to describe the large feet which they believe to be the characteristics of English women as compared with those of their own country' (B&L)] [early 19C–1910s] (*US*) a rustic, a farmer. ❑ **clod-head** *n. see* sense 1 above. ❑ **clodhopper** *see* separate entries. ❑ **clod-jumper** *n.* [1910s+] (*US*) a rustic, a farmer. ❑ **clod-knocker** *n.* [1940s–70s] (*US*) a rustic, a farmer. ❑ **clod-masher** *n.* (*US/Aus.*) **1** [1910s–40s] a large foot. **2** [1910s–70s] (*also* **clod-smasher**) a heavy shoe. **3** [1940s–70s] a clumsy oaf; a rustic. ❑ **clodpate** *n. see* separate entry. ❑ **clodpoll** *n. see* separate entry. ❑ **clodskipper** *n. see* CLODHOPPER *n.* (3). ❑ **clodskull** *n.* [early 18C] a fool. ❑ **clod-skulled** *adj.* [late 17C–early 18C] stupid. ❑ **clod-smasher** *n. see* CLOD-MASHER above.

IN PHRASES

❑ **clods and stickings** *n.* [mid-19C–1910s] gruel with dumplings. ❑ **punch-clod** *n.* [late 19C–1900s] a peasant, a farm labourer.

clod *n.*[2] [rhy. sl. *clodhopper* = COPPER *n.* (2a)] [1910s] (*UK tramp*) a penny or any copper coin, usu. in pl.

cloddipole *n. see* CLODPOLL *n.*

clodhopper *n.* [SE *clod* + *hopper* lit. one who hops over the clods of earth; note SE *clod-hopper*, a ploughman (cited as slang by B.E. *c.*1698)] **1** [late 17C+] (*orig. UK Und.*) a clumsy oaf, a boor, a dull-witted peasant. **2** [late 19C+] (*US*) a rustic, a farmer. **3** [late 19C+] (*also* **clodskipper**) a heavy work shoe. **4** [1930s] a street dancer, begging for cash. **5** [1960s] a large and clumsy foot. **6** [1960s+] a police officer [rhy. sl. = COPPER *n.* (3)].

clodhopper *adj.* [CLODHOPPER *n.* (2)] [1930s] rural, small-town, rustic.

clodhopping *adj.* [CLODHOPPER *n.*] [mid-19C+] unsophisticated, rustic.

clodpate *n.* (*also* **clotpate**) [CLOD *n.*[1] (1) + SE *pate*, the head; on model of -HEAD *sfx* (1)] [mid-17C–mid-18C] a fool, a dullard; thus adj. *clod-pated*, stupid.

clodpoll *n.* (*also* **cloddipole, clodpole, clotpold**) [CLOD *n.*[1] (1) + SE *poll*, the head] [early 17C+] a fool, an incompetent.

clog *n.* [? the shape; it too is a squat, heavy 'lump'] [1990s+] (*US black*) a gun.

clog clatterer *n.* [the noise their stereotypical *clogs* make] [2000s] (*N.Z.*) a Dutch person.

cloggie *adj.* (*also* **cloggite**) [the stereotyped wearing of *clogs* by the Dutch] [1990s+] Dutch.

clogments *n.* [mid–late 18C] (*UK Und.*) the stocks.

clone *n.* [SE *clone*, a thing produced in imitation of, or closely resembling, another] [1970s+] **1** (*orig. US*) anyone who imitates another person to a slavish extent; thus a tedious, unimportant person. **2** (*orig. US gay*) a general description of a gay man who poses as one of a variety of super-masculine stereotypes, e.g. a truck-driver, military man, cowboy etc, a style epitomized by the members of the 1970s disco group Village People [note Gaymart.com 'Queer Slang in the Gay 90s' (1999): 'In the 70's the look included a mustache, muscle shirt/flannel shirt and Levi's. The late 80's–90's included short hair, long sideburns, white t-shirt, shorts/jeans and Doc boots with gray socks'].

IN COMPOUNDS

❑ **clone zone** *n.* [1990s+] (*US gay*) somewhere that gay 'clones' associate.

clonker *n. see* CLUNKER *n.*[1].

clooge *n. see* KLUDGE *n.*

clootie *adj. see* CLUTEY *adj.*

clop *n.* (*also* **cloop**) [echoic] [1940s+] (*orig. US*) a blow.

clop *v.* [CLOP *n.*] [1940s+] (*orig. US*) to hit hard.

close *adj.* [? from gambling phr. *play close to one's vest*] **1** [1900s] (*Aus.*) well-informed, knowledgeable. **2** [1950s] (*US jazz*) masterful.

SE in slang uses

IN PHRASES

❑ **close as...** *adj. see* separate entry. ❑ **close to one's belly** *adj. see under* BELLY *n.* ❑ **close to the blanket** *adj. see under* BLANKET *n.* ❑ **that's close** [1960s+] (*US campus*) an ironic comment implying that something is far from the truth or excessive.

close *v.*

SE in slang uses

IN PHRASES

❑ **close down** *v.* [1980s] (*US Und.*) to kill someone. ❑ **close one's face** *v. see SHUT ONE'S FACE under* FACE *n.* ❑ **close up** *v.* [late 19C] (*Aus.*) to stop talking.

IN EXCLAMATIONS

❑ **close your head!** [1930s–40s] shut up! be quiet! ❑ **close your shell!** [*CLAMSHELL under* CLAM *n.*[1]] [late 19C] (*US campus*) be quiet!

close as... *adj.*

IN PHRASES

❑ **...God's curse to a whore's arse** [late 18C–early 19C] very close. ❑ **...ninety-nine to one hundred** [1930s–40s] (*US black*) extremely close, as close as possible. ❑ **...shirt and shitten arse** [late 18C–early 19C] extremely close.

close as an oyster *adj. see DUMB AS AN OYSTER under* OYSTER *n.*

closed swinging *n. see* SWINGING *n.*[2].

close file *n.* [SE *close* + FILE *n.* (5)] [18C–mid-19C] a secretive or uncommunicative person.

closer *n.* [mid-19C] (*UK Und.*) a seal.

closet *n.* [euph.] **1** [late 17C] the vagina. **2** [1960s+] (*orig. gay*) a metaphorical 'cupboard' in which a homosexual who is unwilling to reveal his or her sexuality is seen to live; thus adj. *closeted*.

IN PHRASES

❑ **come out of the closet** *v.* [1960s+] (*orig. US*) to reveal one's gay sexuality in public; thus *out of the closet*, acknowledging one's homosexuality. ❑ **in the closet** [1970s+] (*orig. US*) **1** used of a gay man/woman who has yet to reveal their sexuality in public. **2** hidden away. ❑ **open the closet** *v.* [1970s+] to reveal someone to be a homosexual, usu. against their will.

SE in slang uses

IN COMPOUNDS

❑ **closet-man** *n.* [SE *water closet*] [1950s+] (*W.I.*) a sanitary inspector.

IN PHRASES

❑ **closet of ease** *n.* [euph.] [mid-17C] a lavatory or water closet.

closet *adj.* (*also* **closeted**) [CLOSET *n.* (2)] **1** [1960s+] of being homosexual, secret, clandestine, hidden. **2** [1970s+] in non-homosexual contexts.

DERIVATIVES

❑ **closetry** *n.* [1970s] (*gay*) the hiding of one's real sexuality by a homosexual.

IN COMPOUNDS

❑ **closet-case** *n.* **1** [1940s+] (*US campus*) a socially inept, unattractive person; a hard worker. **2** [1960s+] (*gay*) a homosexual who finds it difficult or impossible to admit their sexuality in public. ❑ **closet-queen** *n.* (*also* **closet queer**) [QUEEN *n.* (2)/QUEER *n.* (4); James, *America's Homosexual Underground* (1965), offers a link to (water) *closet* and suggests that the *closet queen* is one who dares not have sex at home, preferring the anonymity of public lavatories, bathhouses, parks etc] [1960s+] (*gay*) a homosexual who finds it difficult to admit his sexuality.

close up *v.* [late 19C] (*Aus.*) to stop talking.

closh *n.* [common Du. proper name *Klaas*, itself abbr. of *Nicolaas*] [late 18C–early 19C] a Dutch seaman.

closhy *adj.* [CLOSH *n.*; thus the derog. stereotype of a slow, stolid Dutchman] [1910s] stupid.

clot *n.*[1] [CLOD *n.*[1] (1)] **1** [1940s] nonsense. **2** [1940s+] a fool, often used affectionately, e.g. *you silly clot*.

clot *n.*[2] [abbr. BLOOD CLAAT *n.*] [1950s+] (*W.I.*) a highly derog. description of another person.

cloth *n.* [? play on theatre use *cloth*, the curtain which stands between the audience and the stage] [late 19C] the vagina.

clothed heavy *adj.* [1970s+] (*US black*) very well-dressed.

clothes *n.* [abbr. SE *plain clothes*] [1970s] (*US*) a detective.

clotheshorse *n.* **1** [mid-19C+] an exquisitely well-dressed, fashionable person, although the implication is that beyond such perfection lies little else. **2** [1930s+] a fashion model.

clothesline *v.* [orig. an illicit tackle in US football] [1980s+] (*US*) to strike someone hard across the throat, usu. using the edge of the hand.

clothes-peg *n.*[1] (*also* **clothes-prop, garment-peg**) [1910s–20s] a fashionably dressed person.

clothes-peg *n.*[2] [rhy. sl.; note Franklyn, *Dict. of Rhyming Slang* (1960) claims this usage is erroneous] [1930s+] an egg.

clothes-pegs *n.*[1] [1940s] (*Aus.*) teeth.

clothes-pegs *n.*[2] [rhy. sl.] [1940s+] the legs.

clothes-prop *n.* [*see* Williams for 17C fig. use of *prop*, penis] **1** [late 19C] the erect penis. **2** [1900s] a silly, empty-headed person. **3** *see* CLOTHES-PEG *n.*[1].

cloth market *n.* [its linen covers] [late 17C–early 19C] a bed.

clotpate *n. see* CLODPATE *n.*

clotpold *n. see* CLODPOLL *n.*

clotty *n.* [ety. unknown; ? link to Yorks. dial. *cloddy*, an awkward, ill-dressed person] [1960s+] (*Irish*) a general term of abuse.

clotzed *adj.* [KLUTZ *n.*] [1960s] (*US campus*) becoming tense and 'freezing' under pressure.

cloud *n.* **1** as a product of smoke. (**a**) [late 17C–early 19C] tobacco, tobacco smoke. (**b**) [1980s+] the smoke that one inhales from a pipe of crack cocaine. (**c**) [1990s+] (*drugs*) the stimulating effect that follows smoking crack cocaine. (**d**) [1990s+] crack cocaine. **2** [late 19C] (*UK Und.*) an attic. **3** [1920s] a derog. term for a black person, esp. a crowd of black people [play on SMOKE *n.* (3a) but note CLOUDY *adj.*[1]].

IN PHRASES

❑ **blow a cloud** *v.* **1** [19C+] to smoke a pipe of tobacco or a cigar. **2** [1930s] (*also* **cock a cloud**) to smoke opium; thus *cloud-blower*, an opium smoker. ❑ **on the cloud** [1950s] intoxicated by marijuana. ❑ **raise a cloud** *v.* [late 17C–mid-18C] to smoke a pipe of tobacco.

SE in slang uses

IN COMPOUNDS

❑ **cloud-chaser** *n.* [1950s] (*US*) a pilot. ❑ **cloud-walker** *n.* [1940s] (*US teen*) a good dancer.

cloud nine *n.* [according to Brewer, *Dict. of Phrase and Fable* (15th edn, 1995), the term stems from the classification of clouds by the US Weather Bureau. There are nine divisions, and number nine is cumulonimbus, a cumulus cloud of great vertical extent, topped with shapes that resemble mountains or towers; *cloud seven/eight/ten* are presumably more/less blissful by degrees, but note seven is trad. a 'lucky' number] **1** [1950s+] (*also* **cloud seven, cloud eight, cloud ten**) a state of bliss, sometimes drug-induced. **2** [1980s+] (*drugs*) crack cocaine.

cloudy *adj.*[1] [late 17C] dark-complexioned.

cloudy *adj.*[2] [SE colloq. phr. *under a cloud*] [late 19C] in disgrace, in trouble, disreputable.

clour *n.* (*also* **clower**) [late 18C–mid-19C] a basket.

clout *n.*[1] [14C SE *clout*, a piece of cloth; a handkerchief] **1** [16C–1920s] (*UK Und.*) (*also* **snoot-cloot**) a cotton handkerchief. **2** [16C+] clothing. **3** [mid-17C–1950s] a sanitary towel or a nappy. **4** [1990s+] the vagina.

IN PHRASES

❑ **top a clout** *v.* [early 19C] (*UK Und.*) to position a handkerchief in a victim's pocket in readiness for removing it at an apposite moment.

clout *n.*[2] [ety. unknown; ? link to SE *clout*, a cloth, thus a 'lump' of material, thus any sort of lump; or link to SE *clod*. Note WW1 Aus. milit. *clout*, a wound. Earlier use of sense 1 was SE] **1** [16C+] a heavy blow; as *the clouts*, a heavy beating. **2** [1960s–70s] aggression, power.

IN PHRASES

❑ **give someone the clouts** *v.* [1910s] to hit, to beat up.

clout *n.*[3] [CLOUT *v.*[2] (1)] **1** [early 19C; 1920s+] (*US Und.*) an act of robbery; a robber. **2** [1930s+] (*US*) a thief, e,g. a pickpocket or shoplifter.

clout *n.*[4] [generally assumed to have been coined *c.*1937 in Chicago and quickly disseminated across the US and thence the English-speaking world, but note mid-19C date based on a single citation. According to William Safire either f. baseball jargon *clout*, a big hit; thus one who 'packs a punch' in government, or CLOUT *v.*[2] (1), to steal (itself orig. f. CLOUTER *n.*[1], a petty thief, lit. a handkerchief thief); thus a thief. In the cynical world of US politics all politicians tend to larceny] [mid-19C; 1930s+] (*orig. US*) influence, esp. in politics.

clout *n.*[5] [SE *clout*, a lump of earth; thus a synon. ety. with CLOD *n.*[1] (1)] [20C+] a stupid, oafish person.

clout *v.*[1] [CLOUT *n.*[2] (1); earlier use was SE] [16C+] to hit, to give heavy blows to; thus *clouting*, a beating.

IN COMPOUNDS

❑ **clout-head** *n.* [1990s+] a thug, a ruffian.

IN PHRASES

❑ **clout one's cookie** *v. see under* COOCHIE *n.*

clout *v.*[2] (*also* **clout on**) [backform. f. CLOUTER *n.*[1] (1)/CLOUT *n.*[1] (1) in the context of handkerchiefs being stolen by 18C pickpockets] **1** [20C+] (*US/Aus.*) to steal; to rob; thus *clouted*, stolen. **2** [1920s–30s] (*US Und.*) to arrest. **3** [1950s] (*Aus.*) to cheat by palming a card or cards. **4** [1950s] to search.

clouted *adj.* [CLOUT *n.*[4]] [1950s+] (*US*) in possession of political influence.

clouted-shoe *n.* (*also* **clout-shoe, clouted shoon**) [SE *clouted shoe*, a shoe tipped with iron and secured with iron nails, the footwear of such individuals] [late 17C–early 19C] a yokel, an unsophisticated peasant.

clouter *n.*[1] [CLOUT *n.*[1] (1)] **1** [early 18C–19C] a pickpocket whose speciality is stealing silk handkerchiefs. **2** [1900s] (*US Und.*) a shoplifter. **3** [1950s] a thief.

clouter *n.*[2] [CLOUT *v.*[1]] [1910s] a heavy blow.

clouting lay *n.* (*also* **clouting**) [CLOUT *n.*[1] (1) + LAY *n.*[3] (1)] [late 18C–19C] (*UK Und.*) the stealing of handkerchiefs.

clout-shoe *n. see* CLOUTED-SHOE *n.*

cloven *adj.* (*also* **cleave, cleft, cliff**) [SE *cloven*, split] [late 16C–early 19C] used to describe a woman, usu. a prostitute, who poses as a virgin but, in reality, is not.

SE in slang uses

IN COMPOUNDS

❑ **cloven spot** *n.* [one of a number of synon. coined by John Cleland for his 1749 novel *Memoirs of a Woman of Pleasure* ('Fanny Hill'), a pornographic work, paradoxically without obscenities] [late 17C–19C] the vagina.

cloven hoofter *n.* [rhy. sl. = POOFTER *n.* (1)] [1990s+] (*Aus.*) a male homosexual.

clover-eater *n.* [the diet of the very poor] [mid-19C] (*US*) an inhabitant of Virginia.

clover-kicker *n.* [play on SE] (*US*) **1** [1910s–60s] a clumsy oaf, a boor, a dull-witted peasant. **2** [1940s–60s] a rustic, a farmer.

clower *n. see* CLOUR *n.*

clowes *n.* (*also* **clows**) [? CLOY *n.*] [late 18C] a rogue, a villain.

clown *n.* **1** [20C+] an irritating person; a troublemaker; a fool; as a term of address. **2** [1920s–50s] (*US Und.*) a police officer. **3** [1950s] (*US black*) a state of having fun, one's frivolous, self-indulgent, partying side; thus *get one's clown down*, to indulge that aspect of one's character. **4** [1950s] (*US black*) a fuss, complaining. **5** *see* TOWN CLOWN *under* TOWN *n.*[2].

IN COMPOUNDS

❑ **clownish** *adj.* [17C] stupid.

IN PHRASES

❑ **clown around** *v.* (*also* **clown about**) [late 19C+] to play the fool.

clown *v.* (*also* **clown on**) [i.e. to make into a fig. clown] **1** [1990s+] (*US black*) to ridicule, to humiliate. **2** [2000s] to defeat in a humiliating manner.

clows *n. see* CLOWES *n.*

cloy *n.* (*also* **cloye**) [CLOY *v.* (2)] **1** [late 18C–early 19C] (*UK Und.*) a thief, a pickpocket. **2** *see* CLY *n.* (2).

cloy *v.* (*also* **cloye**) [CLY *v.*] (*UK Und.*) **1** [16C] to arrest. **2** [early 17C–late 19C] to steal; thus n., *cloyer*, a thief.

cloyer *n.* [poss. CLOY *n.*, or SE *cloyne*, to act deceitfully or fraudulently, to cheat] [17C–18C] a pickpocket or cut-purse, spec. an experienced one who demands a share of their younger peers' profits.

club *n.* **1** [early 17C–19C] the penis. **2** [mid–late 18C] a thick pigtail, shaped like a club and worn by men and subseq. women, which was fashionable in 1750–1800 in the UK; the term has survived in US dials. meaning *bun*.

SE in slang uses

IN COMPOUNDS

❑ **club-fist** *n.* [late 16C–early 17C] a thug. ❑ **clubhouse** *n.* [1900s–40s] a police station.

IN PHRASES

❑ **have a bun in the club** *v. see* HAVE A BUN IN THE OVEN *under* OVEN *n.* ❑ **in the club** *adj.* [abbr. of PUDDING CLUB *n.*] [1940s+] pregnant.

club *v.* [19C+] to have sexual intercourse.

SE in slang uses

IN PHRASES

❑ **club the clam** *v. see under* CLAM *n.*[1].

club and stick *n.* [rhy. sl. = DICK *n.*[5] (2); the implements are, of course, apposite] [1930s–40s] a police officer.

clubbed *adj.* [IN THE CLUB *under* CLUB *n.*] [1990s+] pregnant.

clubber *n.* [1910s] (*US*) a police officer.

clubby *n.* [1900s] (*Aus.*) a member of a club or lodge.

club Fed *n.* [pun on *Club Med*, the holiday firm] [1980s+] (*US*) a low-security Federal penitentiary, usu. for white-collar prisoners and offering them many privileges.

club member *n. see* MEMBER *n.*[2] (2).

club sandwich *n.* [1960s–70s] (*US campus*) sexual activity involving three partners.

cluck *n.*[1] **1** [20C+] (*orig. US*) (*also* **kluck**) a dull, stupid person (with the brains of a chicken). **2** [1940s] a general term of address. **3** [1960s] (*US*) an egg.

cluck *n.*[2] [fig. use of *cluck* as a dud, a second-rate object] **1** [1900s–50s] (*orig. US*) a counterfeit coin. **2** [1970s] (*US*) a tedious situation [? the 'clucking' noise one makes when irritated or bored].

cluck *n.*[3] [ety. unknown] [1940s] (*US*) a derog. term for a person with notably dark skin.

cluck *n.*[4] (*also* **clucker**) [ety. unknown; ? link to CLUCK *v.*[3] (1), i.e. the loquacity engendered by the drug] [1980s+] (*drugs*) a user of crack cocaine.

cluck *v.*[1] [SE *cluck* by a *hen*, i.e. she is noisily and enthusiastically awaiting the *cock*/COCK *n.*[3] (1)] [18C] (*UK Und.*) of a woman, to to be sexually enthusiastic.

cluck *v.*[2] [ety. unknown] [late 19C] (*UK Und.*) to acquit.

cluck *v.*[3] [the noise a chicken makes] (*US*) **1** [1920s+] to speak. **2** [1960s] to be a CHICKEN *n.* (2a) and run away. **3** [2000s] to inform on.

cluck *v.*[4] [CLUCK *n.*[4]] [1990s+] (*UK drugs*) **1** to crave crack cocaine. **2** to suffer withdrawal symptoms from any narcotic.

clucka *n.* [? var. on CLUCK *n.*[4]] [2000s] (*US black/drugs*) a regular user of methamphetamine.

clucker *n. see* CLUCK *n.*[4].

cluckhead *n.*[1] [CLUCK *n.*[1] (1) + -HEAD *sfx* (1)] [1940s+] a fool, an idiot.

cluckhead *n.*[2] [ext. of CLUCK *n.*[4] + -HEAD *sfx* (4)] [1990s+] (*US black gang*) a regular user of crack cocaine.

clucky *adj.* [dial. *clucky*, used of a broody hen] [1940s+] (*Aus./N.Z.*) pregnant.

cludgie *n.* [dial. *cludgy*, sticky, wet and heavy] [1980s+] a lavatory.

clue *n.* [? link to SE *clue*, an aggrandizement of things, thus used euph.] **1** [19C] (*Scot.*) the vagina. **2** [1930s+] (*Aus.*) a woman. **3** [1990s+] (*US campus*) a stupid person.

SE in slang uses

IN PHRASES

❑ **get a clue** *v.* [SE colloq. phr. *not have a clue*] **1** [1960s+] (*US black*) (*also* **find a clue**) to become aware. **2** [1980s+] (*US campus*) to think sensibly or logically, to not be stupid or naïve.

clue *v.* [SE *clue*] [1950s+] (*US*) to inform, to tell; thus *clued*, aware.

IN PHRASES

❑ **clue (someone) in** *v.* (*also* **cue in**) [1950s+] (*orig. US*) to explain, to inform, to make aware. ❑ **clue up** *v.* [1940s+] to explain something to someone; thus *clued up*, well aware, properly informed.

IN EXCLAMATIONS

❑ **clue in!** [1980s] (*US campus*) pay attention!

clueful *adj.* [opposite of CLUELESS *adj.*] [1980s] (*US campus*) aware, intelligent, savvy.

clueless *adj.* [SE colloq. phr. *not have a clue*] [1940s+] stupid, ignorant, incompetent.

cluey *adj.* [CLUE *v.*] [1960s+] (*Aus.*) properly informed.

clumperton *n.* [fig. use of SE *clump*, to hit, on pattern of SE *simpleton*] [mid-16C–early 18C] a fool, a yokel.

clunge *n.* [dial. *clung*, tight shrivelled, ult. SE *cling*] [1990s+] **1** the anus, esp. in abusive, dismissive phr. *up your clunge!* **2** the vagina.

clunk *n.* [LUNK *n.*; LUNKHEAD *n.*] (*Aus./US*) **1** [20C+] a man. **2** [1920s+] a fool.

clunker *n.*[1] (*also* **clonker, clunk, klunker**) [? the noise it makes] **1** [1940s] a worn-out, useless car, occas. aeroplane. **2** [1940s+] anything useless, unattractive, incompetent.

clunker *n.*[2] [colloq. *clunk*] **1** [1950s+] a fool, a dolt, an incompetent. **2** [1970s+] (*US*) a blunder, a mistake.

clunkhead *n.* [colloq. *clunk* + -HEAD *sfx* (1)] [1950s+] (*US*) a fool.

clunk the bucket *v. see* KICK THE BUCKET *v.*

clush *adj.* [ety. unknown] [mid–late 19C] easy, simple.

clusterfuck *n.* **1** [1960s+] (*orig. US*) (*also* **cluster, clutterfuck**) an orgy, irrespective of sexual preference. **2** [1970s+] chaos. **3** [1970s+] a group of indecisive people, unable to decide what to do next. **4** [1980s+] a sharp person.

cluster-fuck *v.* [CLUSTERFUCK *n.* (3)] [2000s] (*US*) to confuse.

cluster-screw *n.* [SE *cluster* + SCREW *n.*[1] (1); a semi-bowdlerized version of CLUSTERFUCK *n.*] [1970s] (*US*) **1** an orgy. **2** in fig. use, a chaotic situation.

clutch *n.* **1** [late 18C] the hand [its action]. **2** [late 19C–1980s] (*UK society*) a dance (the activity, not the event) [the physical proximity of the dancers].

IN PHRASES

❑ **in the clutch** [SE *clutch*, i.e, when one finally 'grasps' and deals with a situation] [1940s–60s] (*US*) in the final assessment, 'when push comes to shove'. ❑ **shove in the clutch** *v.* [1960s] (*S.Afr.*) to get moving.

clutch *adj.* [synon. TIGHT *adj.* (1a)] [1990s+] (*US campus*) attractive, desirable.

clutch *v.* [1950s–60s] (*US campus*) to freeze up under pressure.

DERIVATIVES

❑ **clutched (up)** *adj.* [1950s+] (*US*) frightened, nervous, tense.

clutch-buster *n.* [1940s–60s] (*orig. US black*) one who drives a HOT-ROD *n.* (2).

clutch-butt *n.* [SE *clutch* + BUTT *n.*[1] (1a)] [1960s] (*US*) sexual intercourse.

clutch-fist *n.* [mid-17C] a miser.

DERIVATIVES

❑ **clutch-fisted** *adj.* [late 17C–early 19C] mean, miserly.

clutey *adj.* (*also* **cleety, clitty, clootie**) [dial. *clootie*, a left-handed person] [late 19C+] (*Irish*) awkward.

clutterfuck *n. see* CLUSTERFUCK *n.* (1).

clutz *n. see* KLUTZ *n.*

cly *n.* (*also* **clie, cligh**) [? CLY *v.*] [late 17C–19C] **1** money. **2** (*also* **cloy**) a pocket, also a purse or wallet.

IN COMPOUNDS

❑ **cly-faker** *n.* [early–mid-19C] a pickpocket. ❑ **cly-filer** *n. see* FILER *n.*

cly *v.* (*also* **cligh**) [poss. f. Ger. *kleien* and Du. *kleyen*, to scratch (with the nails), to claw the head; Ribton-Turner, *A History of Vagrants* (1887), suggests Erse *cloib*, a snatch] [mid-16C–mid-19C] to seize, to get, to take; to steal.

IN PHRASES

❑ **cly the jerk** *v.* (*also* **cly the gerke, clay the jerk**) [mid-16C–early 19C] (*UK Und.*) to be whipped.

clyde *n.* [a stereotypical 'peasant' name] **1** [1950s+] (*orig. US black*) an unsophisticated person, a provincial, a yokel. **2** [1960s+] a general term of address.

clydesdale *n.* [? the solid dependability of the *Clydesdale* horse or the attractiveness of the *Clydesdale* terrier] [1980s] (*US*) an attractive man.

clyme *n. see* CLEYME *n.*

clyster-pipe *n.* [SE *clyster-pipe*, a pipe used to administer clysters, or enemas] **1** [early 17C–early 19C] a doctor, an apothecary. **2** [late 17C–mid-19C] (*also* **glister-pipe**) the penis.

C-note *n.* [C *n.*[2]] **1** [20C+] (*US*) a $100 bill. **2** [1970s] (*US prison*) a 100-year jail sentence. **3** [1980s] (*US black*) a one-year sentence.

C.N.R. strawberries *n.* [1970s] (*Can. prison*) prunes.

co *n.*[1] [abbr. COVE *n.* (1)] [mid-16C–18C] a man.

co *n.*[2] [abbr.] [late 19C–1920s] (*UK society*) a *co*-respondent (in a divorce case).

coach *n.* [pun on ROACH *n.* (2c)] [1960s] (*US drugs*) the unsmoked portion of a marijuana cigarette.

coachee/coachie *n. see* COACHY *n.*

coach lay *n.* [late 18C] (*UK Und.*) robbing coaches on the highway.

coachman on the box *n.* [rhy. sl. = POX *n.*[1] (3)] [1940s+] venereal disease.

coachman's seat *n.* [? a coachman is seated behind] [late 19C] (*Aus.*) a bustle or dress imropover.

coach-wheel *n.* [like the SE *coach-wheel*, the crown piece was, by numismatic standards, large and round] **1** [late 18C–1960s] a five-shilling (25p) piece, a crown. **2** [early–mid-19C] (*US*) a silver dollar.

coachy *n.* (*also* **coachee, coachey, coachie**) [on the model of *cabbie*, *bargee*, but note synon. Magyar *kocsi*, Bohemian *koèi*, Ger. *kutsche*] [late 18C–1900s] a coachman.

coads *n. see* COD *n.*[1].

coakie *n. see* COKIE *n.*

coal *n.*[1] **1** [1930+] a derog. term for a dark-skinned black person, esp. a woman. **2** [1930s+] in phr. *load of coal*, a gathering of black people. **3** [1970s] (*US*) the lit end or glowing ash of a cigarette. **4** [1990s+] (*Aus.*) dark 'bags' under the eyes.

IN COMPOUNDS

❑ **coal bin** *n.* [1970s+] (*US black*) a derog. term describing a dark-complexioned black person. ❑ **coal burner** *n.* [1970s+] a white man or woman who enjoys sexual relations with a black man or woman. ❑ **coal mine** *n.* [1940s+] (*US black*) a derog. term for a dark-complexioned black person. ❑ **coal-scuttle blonde** *n.* [1930s–50s] (*US*) a black woman with a blonde wig. ❑ **coal-scuttler** *n.* [1900s] (*US*) a derog. term for a black person. ❑ **coal-shutes** *n.* [note US Navy *coal-chute*, a dirty hammock] [1940s+] (*US*) a very dark-complexioned black person. ❑ **coal tar** *n. see* BLACK TAR *under* TAR *n.*[1].

IN PHRASES

❑ **burn coal** *v.* [1940s+] of a white person, to have sex with a black person. ❑ **deal in coal** *v.* **1** [1930s–40s] (*US black*) to prefer dark-skinned women. **2** [1940s] (*US*) of a white man, to have sex with a black woman.

SE in slang uses

IN COMPOUNDS

❑ **coal bin** *n.* [1930s] (*US black*) the vagina. ❑ **coal-black joke** *n. see* BLACK JOKE *n.* ❑ **coal-box** *n.* [? the noise of a coal-box being shaken] **1** [mid-19C+] the chorus (of a song). **2** [1920s] a music-hall. ❑ **coal-hole** *n.* [early 19C] (*US Und.*) a cell in which drunks are imprisoned. ❑ **coal-pot** *n.* [1940s] (*US black*) a pipe. ❑ **coal-scuttle** *n.* [its chief characteristic was the sides, which projected well beyond those of the face; fashionable *c.*1850] **1** [mid-19C] (*UK Und.*) the punishment cell. **2** [mid–late 19C] a poke bonnet, which it supposedly resembled.

coal *n.*[2] *see* COLE *n.*

coal and coke *adj.* (*also* **coals and coke**) [rhy. sl. = BROKE *adj.*[1]] [1950s+] penniless, impoverished.

coal (heaver) *n.* (*also* **heaver**) [rhy. sl. = STIVER *n.*] [1910s–20s] a coin of small value, usu. a penny.

coalie *n.* (*also* **coaley, coaly**) [SE; post-1840s use is usu. Aus.; note naval jargon *coalie*, a stoker] **1** [early 19C+] a coal heaver. **2** [mid-19C+] a wharf labourer who loads ships with coal.

coaping-cull *n.* [SE *cope*, to barter, to make a bargain, to buy] [mid–late 18C] a jockey.

coarse one *n.* [1930s–40s] (*US Und.*) a large-denomination dollar bill, esp. when used to impress a confidence man's potential victim.

Coast, the *n.* **1** [20C+] the west coast of America, esp. Los Angeles [the Pacific Coast has been thus known since the mid-19C, but the current use refers spec. to Los Angeles, the home of the film and rock industries]. **2** [1960s] the Atlantic coast, to inhabitants of the Pacific seaboard.

coast *v.* [1930s+] (*US*) **1** (*drugs*) to achieve the somnolent, peaceful state that follows an injection of heroin. **2** (*drugs*) the exciting sensation that follows the use of cocaine [Spears, *Slang and Jargon of Drugs and Drink* (1986), suggests 'a slight overdose']. **3** to relax; to act in a relaxed manner.

IN PHRASES

❑ **coast (about)** *v.* [late 19C–1940s] (*Aus.*) to live as a tramp or vagrant. ❑ **coast a lime** *v. see under* LIME *n.*[2]. ❑ **coast home** *v.* [1930s] (*orig. US*) to win easily, usu. in a sporting context.

coaster *n.*[1] [SE *coast*] **1** [late 19C] (*US*) an inhabitant of the Barbary Coast. **2** [1950s+] (*N.Z.*) one who is a native of, or was born in, the west coast of the South Island (cf. COASTIE *n.*).

coaster *n.*[2] [COAST (ABOUT) *under* COAST *v.*] [late 19C–1950s] (*Aus.*) **1** a tramp. **2** a loafer, an idler.

coastie *n.* [2000s] (*N.Z.*) a Maori from the east coast of North Island (cf. COASTER *n.*[1] (2)).

coasts to coasts *n.* [? their use by long-distance truck-drivers] [1960s+] (*US drugs*) amphetamine.

coat *n.* [fig. use of SE *coat* as something one wears] **1** [1940s] constr. with *the*, an arrest. **2** [1970s] (*S.Afr. prison*) a life sentence [note the blue coat orig. worn by prisoners].

SE in slang uses

IN COMPOUNDS

❑ **coat game** *n.* [1940s] (*US Und.*) theft. ❑ **coat party** *n.* [2000s] (*US prison*) throwing a coat over a prisoner's head prior to beating him up. ❑ **coat puller** *n.* [1980s+] (*Aus. prison*) an escapee.

IN PHRASES

❑ **coil someone's coat** *v.* [mid-16C] to beat someone. ❑ **dust someone's coat** *v. see* DUST SOMEONE'S JACKET *under* DUST *v.*[1]. ❑ **tug someone's coat** *v. see* PULL SOMEONE'S COAT *under* PULL *v.* ❑ **tug the coat** *v. see* PULL SOMEONE'S COAT *under* PULL *V.*

coat *v.* [the image of grabbing a lapel; note also the beating that accompanies the *coating* of a miscreant with tar and feathers] **1** [20C+] to reprimand, to scold. **2** [1910s+] to arrest; thus, as n., a suspect. **3** [1930s+] to beat up, to hit. **4** [1940s+] (*Aus.*) to ostracize [in Aus. one tugs one's own lapel as a sign that a given person is not to be trusted]. **5** [1970s] (*US gay*) to have anal intercourse.

IN PHRASES

❑ **give someone a coating** *v.* **1** [1930s+] to beat up, to thrash. **2** [1970s] (*UK Und.*) to give someone a reprimand. ❑ **on the coat** [1940s+] (*Aus.*) out of favour; esp. in phr. *have/put on the coat*, to place someone in a position of disfavour.

coat and badge *v.* (*also* **C and B**) [rhy. sl.; ult. *Doggett's Coat and Badge*, awarded to Thames watermen who, with this prize, had the right to charge higher fares in their mid-19C heyday] [1910s+] to cadge; usu. in phr. *on the coat and badge, on the C & B*, cadging.

coathanger *n.* [the shape] **1** [1930s+] (*Aus.*) the Sydney Harbour Bridge. **2** [2000s] (*N.Z.*) Auckland Harbour Bridge.

coat hangers *n.* [play on CHAPEL HAT-PEGS *under* CHAPEL *n.*] [1990s+] large and erect nipples.

coating *n.* [COAT *v.* (1)] [1950s+] a scolding.

coax *v.* [orig. use of SE *coax*, to fool, to take in; which is apparently linked to 16C *cokes*, a simpleton, a gullible fool] [late 18C] to pull down the soiled or holed part of one's stocking so that it is hidden by the heel of one's shoe.

coaxyorum *n.* [SE *coax* + 'Lat.' sfx] [1990s+] (*Irish*) **1** an opportunist. **2** a cake prepared by a putative mother-in-law to show respect to her daughter's boyfriend.

cob *n.*[1] [B.E. states 'in Ireland'] [late 17C–mid-19C] a Spanish dollar.

cob *n.*[2] [SE *corncob*] **1** [19C] (*US*) a farmer, a rustic [+ ? derog. ref. to supposed use of corncobs in the privy as a substitute for lavatory paper]. **2** [1970s+] (*S.Afr. drugs*) a quantity of marijuana, about the size of a corncob and sometimes packaged in maize leaves.

SE in slang uses

IN PHRASES

❑ **off the cob** *adj.* [SE *corncob*, thus the implication of rustic poverty] [1930s–50s] (*US*) **1** unfashionable, out of style. **2** backward. **3** poor. ❑ **on the cob** *adj.* [play on CORNY *adj.*] [1930s] (*US*) sentimental, simplistic, banal.

cob *n.*[3] [orig. dial. *cob*, a small roundish loaf] (*UK prison*) **1** [late 19C] a punishment cell. **2** [1940s–50s] prison bread.

cob *n.*[4] [orig. dial.] [1920s–60s] (*US*) the penis.

cob *n.*[5]

IN PHRASES

❑ **have a cob on** *v.* [? dial. *cob*, to strike or *cob* a lump, a large piece, thus cf. SE colloq. phr. *have a chip on one's shoulder*] [1930s+] to be in a bad temper, to be annoyed; thus *cobby*, angry.

cob *n.*[6] [abbr. COBBER *n.*[2] (1)] [1950s–70s] (*N.Z.*) a friend, a mate.

cob *v.*[1] [1920s+] (*Aus./juv.*) to forcefully pull down a boy's pants to see his penis.

cob *v.*[2] *see* COP *v.* (1).

Cobar shower *n.* [Cobar is a copper-mining town in New South Wales] [1940s+] (*Aus.*) **1** a flower [rhy. sl.]. **2** a shower of rain [rhy. sl.; other Aus. names can be substituted according to local geography]. **3** a dust storm [pun, i.e. it's very dry].

cobber *n.*[1] [naut. jargon *cob*, to hit on the buttocks with something flat] [19C–1910s] a great lie.

cobber *n.*[2] (*also* **cobba, cobs, kobber**) [? dial. *cob*, to take a liking to someone or Heb./Yid. *chaver*, a 'pal', a 'chum'. Like the other great clichéd Aus. word, BONZER *adj.*, *cobber* is now nearly defunct] **1** [late 19C+] (*Aus./N.Z.*) a friend, a mate. **2** [1950s] an Australian.

IN COMPOUNDS

❑ **cobber-dobber** *n.* [DOBBER *n.*[1]] [1960s–70s] (*Aus.*) one who informs on a friend.

cobber (up) *v.* [COBBER *n.*[2] (1)] [1910s–60s] (*Aus./N.Z.*) to befriend; thus adj. *cobbery*, friendly.

cobble-colter *n.* [*cobble* = gobble] [late 17C–mid-19C] (*UK Und.*) a turkey.

cobbler *n.*[1] [based on an old joke, quoted in *OED*: 'In the harvest field English rustics used to say, when picking up the last sheaf, "This is what the cobbler threw at his wife." "What?" "The last."'] (*Aus./N.Z.*) **1** [late 19C–1950s] a sheep with a hard and dirty fleece, thus difficult to shear; the last and least willing sheep to be sheared. **2** [1900s] in ext. use, the last of anything.

SE in slang uses

IN COMPOUNDS

❑ **cobbler's knot** *n.* [mid-19C] a lock of hair shaped like the figure six and twisted from the temple back towards the ear. ❑ **cobbler's punch** *n.* [late 18C–early 19C] a mixture consisting of treacle, vinegar, gin and water.

cobbler *n.*[2] [? SE *cobble*, to put together or join roughly or clumsily] [20C+] (*US Und.*) a forger, esp. of passports, currency and stocks and bonds.

cobblers *n.*[1] [rhy. sl. on *cobbler's last*] [late 19C] the past.

cobblers *n.*[2] (*also* **cobblers' awls, cobbler's stalls**) [rhy. sl. on *cobbler's awls*] **1** [1930s+] the testicles [= BALLS *n.* (1)]. **2** [1950s+] rubbish, nonsense [= BALLS *n.* (4)].

IN PHRASES

❑ **do one's cobblers** *v.* [fig. use of sense 1 above and/or pun on SE *awls/all*] [1980s] to lose one's money.

cobblers *adj.* [COBBLERS *n.*[2] (2)] [1990s+] stupid, mistaken.

cobblers! *excl.* **1** [1970s+] an excl. of irritation, i.e. BALLS! *excl.* (2). **2** [1990s+] nonsense! rubbish! an excl. of dismissal, i.e. BALLS! *excl.* (1).

cobbler's marbles *n.* [mispron. of *cholera morbus*] [mid-19C] Asiatic cholera.

cobbler's punch *n.* [COBS *n.* (1)] [early–19C] urine with a cinder in it.

cobbles *n.*

IN PHRASES

❑ **on the cobbles** [i.e. 'outside' in the street] [1950s+] looking for a fight.

cobbo *n.* [COBBER *n.*[2] (1) + -O *sfx* (3)] [1920s+] (*Aus.*) a close friend.

cobby *n. see* CUBBY *n.* (2).

co-bim! *excl.* [KER- *pfx* + *bim*] [mid-19C] an onomat. term indicating a sudden blow.

cobitis *n.* [COB *n.*[3] (2) + sfx *-itis*, usu. used in diseases] [1940s–50s] (*UK Und.*) a loathing of invariably unpleasant prison food.

cob o' coal *n.* [rhy. sl. = SE *dole*] [1920s–50s] unemployment benefit.

cobs *n.* [dial.] **1** [20C+] the testicles. **2** *see* COBBER *n.*[2].

cobweb *n.*

SE in slang uses

IN COMPOUNDS

❑ **cobweb-cheat** *n.* [his swindles have no more substance than a cobweb] [late 17C–early 18C] a swindler who can be easily found out. ❑ **cobweb-pretence** *n.* [such ruses are utterly insubstantial] [late 17C–early 18C] an inadequate ruse, a plot that can be detected simply. ❑ **cobweb rig** *n.* [despite prev. which imply incompetence; SE *cobweb*, a subtly woven snare + RIG n.[2] (1)] [late 18C–early 19C] (*UK Und.*) a form of swindle or confidence trick.

(IN PHRASES)

❑ **have cobwebs** *v.* [1980s+] (*US campus*) to have lived a celibate life for a long time.

coc *n. see* COKE *n.*[1] (1).

cocabola *n.* [Arawak *kakabali*, thence Sp. *cocobolo/cocobola*, the timber from any one of several species of tree of the Central American genus *Dalbergia*, or the tree itself, a dark hardwood] [1940s–50s] (*US*) a black person.

Coca-Cola *n.*[1] [rhy. sl.; ult. the soft drink brand *Coca-Cola*] [1950s+] (*Aus.*) a bowler, in cricket.

Coca-Cola *n.*[2] [var. on COKE FRAME *n.*] [1990s+] (*W.I.*) a curvaceous woman.

coch *v.* [ety. unknown] (*UK black*) **1** [1970s–80s] to stay, to hide out. **2** [1970s–80s] to lean on. **3** [2000s] to move without being seen.

coche *n.* [Sp. *coche*, pig; thus PIG *n.* (2d)] [1990s+] (*US prison/Hisp.*) a prison guard.

cochineal *n.* [SE *cochineal*, a scarlet dye] [late 19C–1900s] red wine.

cochore *v.* [? SE *cajole*] [20C+] (*W.I., Guyn.*) **1** to tell tales of others in order to curry favour with a superior. **2** to persuade, to charm, to lull into false confidence.

cochornis *n.* [? Sp.] [1970s+] (*drugs*) marijuana.

cochunk! *excl.* [KER- *pfx* + echoic] [mid-19C] (*US*) an onomat. term indicating the sound of two solid objects colliding.

Cock *n.* [abbr. *Cockney*] [late 19C] (*UK Und.*) a Londoner.

cock *n.*[1] [mispron.] [late 14C–early 19C] a euph. for God.

(IN EXCLAMATIONS)

❑ **cock and pie!** [? SE *pied friar*, a Carmelite or Cistercian] [mid-16C–mid-19C] a mild euph. oath; usu. as *by cock and pie!*

cock *n.*[2] [abbr. SE *Cockney*] [mid-16C+] a general term of address, esp. Cockney use.

cock *n.*[3] [Lat. *cuccus*, the male domestic fowl; thus the term has been used for any object that resembles a cock's head. As far as its use as a sexual term is concerned, *cock* here mixes the basic image of the cock as rooster (itself a 19C US euph.) and the cock's head seen as a tap-like shape, this secondary aspect emphasized by its function in 'pouring' semen (or urine). Tabooed subseq. to Queen Victoria's coronation, it has yet to return to the mainstream. Note *DSUE*: 'always SE but since 1830 a vulgarism' and *OED* (in late 19C) notes 'the current name among the people, but, *pudoris causa*, not admissible in polite speech or literature'] **1** [late 16C+] (*UK/US North*) the penis. **2** [17C] a man as a sexual being. **3** [mid-17C–1900s] a man, spec. a plucky fighter. **4** [late 17C–19C] an expert, an exemplar. **5** [late 18C] (*UK Und.*) one who, being hanged, dies bravely. **6** [1900s] (*also* **cockey**) the clitoris. **7** [1920s+] (*US black*) sexual intercourse. **8** [1960s–70s] (*US black*) an orgasm. **9** [1960s+] a show-off, a self-promoter. **10** [1970s+] (*US campus*) an offensive man. **11** [1970s+] a man who is easy to sponge on, spec. one who buys more than his necessary share in a pub.

(IN COMPOUNDS)

❑ **cock ale** *n.* [SE *cock-ale*, ale mixed with the jelly or minced meat of a boiled cock, besides other ingredients + a pun on sense 1 above] [mid-17C–mid-19C] a variety of beer that supposedly has aphrodisiac properties. ❑ **cock alley** *n.* [late 18C–19C] the female genitals; thus *take a turn in Cock Alley/Lane*, to have sexual intercourse. ❑ **cock-and-breeches** *n.* [early 19C] a small, sturdy boy. ❑ **cock artist** *n.* [-ARTIST *sfx*] [1990s+] a sexually sophisticated man. ❑ **cock-bawd** *n.* [lit. a 'male whore'] **1** [17C–19C] a procurer. **2** [late 17C–early 18C] a superior prostitute. ❑ **cockblock** *see* separate entries. ❑ **cockboat** *n. see* BOAT *n.*[1] (1a). ❑ **cock-brain** *n.* [? a young man's trad. obsession with sex] [mid-16C–17C; mid-19C–1910s] (*later use is US only*) a foolish young man; thus adj., *cockbrained*, foolish. ❑ **cock-breath** *n. see* DICK-BREATH *under* DICK *n.*[1]. ❑ **cockchafer** *n. see* separate entries. ❑ **cock cheese** *n.* (*also* **dick-cheese, knob-cheese, knob yoghurt, prick cheese**) [CHEESE *n.*[1] (2a)/YOGHURT *n.*] **1** [late 19C+] smegma. **2** [2000s] a general term of abuse. ❑ **cock collar** *n.* [1970s] (*US black*) the head of the penis, esp. its base, where it joins the main shaft. ❑ **cock-diesel** *n.* [DIESEL *n.* (2)] [1990s+] **1** (*US black/campus*) a strong, muscular, attractive man. **2** (*US gay*) a muscular male homosexual. ❑ **cock doctor** *n.* [20C+] a venereologist. ❑ **cockface** *n.* [1960s+] (*US*) a general term of abuse. ❑ **cockhead** *n.* [-HEAD *sfx* (1)] [1970s+] (*Aus./US*) a general term of abuse; also used affectionately/intimately. ❑ **cock holder** *n.* [late 19C–1940s] the vagina. ❑ **cock inn** *n.* [a pun on the fictitious public house] [late 19C+] the vagina. ❑ **cock juice** *n. see* JUICE *n.*[1] (2a). ❑ **cock-knocker** *n.* [lit. 'penis-hitter'] **1** [1950s+] (*also* **cacknacker**) (*US*) an unpleasant, worthless person. **2** [1990s+] a male homosexual. ❑ **cock-knob** *see* KNOB *n.* (1b). ❑ **cock-knocking** *adj.* [1980s+] (*US*) a synon. for DAMNED *adj.* (1). ❑ **cock lane** *n.* [The term was reinforced by the real-life *Cock Lane* (in the City), which in the 14C was the only street on which London's prostitutes were licensed to ply their trade in public. The Great Fire was supposed to have stopped at its junction with Giltspur Street, while in February 1762 thousands of the curious (including Dr Johnson, the Duke of York and other grandees) flocked to number 33 Cock Lane to hear the scratchings and knockings of the alleged 'Cock Lane Ghost'] [late 18C+] the vagina. ❑ **cocklicker** *n. see* COCKSUCKER *n.* (3). ❑ **cock manger** *n.* [i.e. the supposed similarity of a urinal to the *manger* from which horses eat] [2000s] (*Irish*) a urinal. ❑ **cock monkey** *n.* **1** [1990s+] (*US campus*) a male homosexual. **2** [1990s+] a general term of abuse, a very unpleasant person. ❑ **cock pit** *n.* **1** [mid-18C+] the vagina. **2** [mid-18C+] the penis. **3** [1980s] (*US*) the clitoris. ❑ **cock puke** *n.* [1990s+] semen. ❑ **cock rock** *n.* [1970s+] heavy metal music with even more than the usual macho strutting and posturing. ❑ **cock-rocker** *n.* [1990s+] a male rock musician, or rock band, whose primary appeal lies in overt sexuality and macho posturing. ❑ **cock-rot** *n.* [1980s+] (*US*) a venereal disease. ❑ **cock-rotted** *adj.* [fig. use of prev.] broken down, useless, lit. rotten. ❑ **cock sauce** *n.* [2000s] (*US*) sperm. ❑ **cock-scratchers** *n.* [1970s] hands. ❑ **cock's eye** *n.* [1900s] (*Aus.*) in dice games, the number one. ❑ **cockshire** *n.* [late 18C+] the vagina. ❑ **cock show** *n.* [1950s] burlesque; striptease. ❑ **cock-shy** *n.* [pun on SE *cockshy*, a fairground game that involved throwing broomsticks at a cock. If the thrower could knock over the cock and grab it before it regained its feet, he would win the bird] [19C] the vagina. ❑ **cock-shy** *adj.* [1990s+] of a woman, uninterested in or frightened of sex. ❑ **cocksman** *n. see* separate entry. ❑ **cocksmoker** *n.* [1990s+] (*Can.*) **1** a fellator; a semi-euph. for COCKSUCKER *n.* **2** any male person. **3** a general term of abuse. ❑ **cock snot** *n.* [SNOT *n.*[1] (5)] [1990s+] semen. ❑ **cock socket** *n.* [2000s] the anus. ❑ **cockstand** *n. see* separate entry. ❑ **cockstrong** *adj.* [1980s+] (*US black/campus*) strong, muscular, masculine. ❑ **cock-struck** *adj.* [late 19C] of a woman, obsessed with sex, or with a particular man; thus used by homosexual men. ❑ **cocksuck(er)** *see* separate entries. ❑ **cock-tail** *n.* **1** [19C–1940s] a prostitute. **2** [1970s+] (*US gay*) a male prostitute. ❑ **cockteas(er)** *see* separate entries. ❑ **cock-trap** *n.* [mid–late 19C] the vagina. ❑ **Cock Tuesday** *n.* [1930s] (*Irish*) the eve of Lent.

(IN PHRASES)

❑ **all cock and ribs like a musterer's dog** [1970s+] (*Aus./N.Z.*) said of a very thin person. ❑ **beat the cock off** *v.* [1990s+] (*US*) to beat severely. ❑ **big-cock** *adj.* [1960s–70s] (*US*) enormous, outsized. ❑ **cock it** *v.* [18C–19C; 1960s+] to have sexual intercourse. ❑ **cock it up** *v.* [1920s+] (*orig. milit.*) to blunder, to make a mess of. ❑ **cop a cock** *v.* [1970s+] (*US gay*) to fellate. ❑ **cream one's cock** *v.* [1990s+] to masturbate. ❑ **get one's cock caught in the zipper** *v.* (*also* **have one's cock caught in a zipper**) [1970s+] to be in very bad trouble, to get into extreme difficulties. ❑ **give someone the cock** *v.* [20C+] (*W.I.*) **1** to outsmart, to outwit by trickery or other unfair means. **2** to cause someone unexpected trouble. ❑ **go cock-fighting** *v.* [19C] to have sexual intercourse. ❑ **have a bit of cock** *v.* [late 19C+] to have sexual intercourse. ❑ **have one's cock on the block** *v.* [1970s+] (*orig. US*) to be facing serious problems, to be prepared to take a risk or a stand that may be dangerous. ❑ **keep one's cock up** *v.* [1970s] (*US*) to stay cheerful, despite possible adversity. ❑ **on half cock** *adj.*

[late 19C] of the penis, semi-erect. ❑ **pull one's cock** *v.* [1960s+] to masturbate. ❑ **pull someone's cock** *v.* (*also* **pull someone's prick**) [1930s] (*US*) to tease, to deceive, to hoax. ❑ **put the cock to** *v.* [1970s] (*US*) to arrest, to discipline, to punish. ❑ **step on one's cock** *v.* (*also* **trip over one's cock**) [1970s+] (*orig. US*) to get oneself into serious trouble, to make a major blunder.

IN EXCLAMATIONS

❑ **cock it!** [euph. for the 'harder' FUCK IT! *excl.*] [1920s] a mild excl. of annoyance, that's it! that's all over! ❑ **suck my cock!** *see under* SUCK *v.*[1].

SE in slang uses

IN COMPOUNDS

❑ **cock-a-brass** *n.* [late 18C] (*UK Und.*) a member of a team of card sharpers who diverts a disgruntled victim from pursuing them. ❑ **cock-and-hen club** *n.* [SE *cock and hen*, a man and wife] [19C] a club that admits both men and women. ❑ **cock-a-wax** *n.* (*also* **cockawax, cockowax**) **1** [early–mid-19C] (*also* **son of wax**) a cobbler, who uses wax in his work. **2** [late 18C–19C] a familiar term of address, esp. as *my old cock-a-wax*. ❑ **cock-broth** *n.* [17C; 1930s] (*UK tramp*) any form of strong, satisfying soup. ❑ **cock-pimp** *n.* [late 17C–18C] a pimp, who poses as his prostitute's husband. ❑ **cock robin** *n.* [nursery rhyme, in which the hapless *Cock Robin* is killed. The original rhyme, first noted *c.*1744, may have concerned the fall in 1742 of Prime Minister Robert Walpole's ministry. It may, on the other hand, have its roots in much earlier events, notably the mythical death of the Norse hero Balder] [late 17C–18C] a complaisant, weak person. ❑ **cock-tail** *n.* [SE *cock*, to lift up + *tail*] [mid–late 19C] a coward; thus *turn cocktail*, to act in a cowardly manner.

IN PHRASES

❑ **cock of the game** *n.* [SE *cock of the game*, a champion; the 'game' in this case is not a sport, but that 'of love'] **1** [mid-16C–mid-19C] a promiscuous man. **2** [19C] (*UK Und.*) a leading villain. ❑ **cock of the walk** *n.* [SE *walk*, a place or enclosure where poultry can exercise] [late 18C+] an important man, occas. any creature. ❑ **that cock won't fight** (*also* **that cat won't fight, that dog won't hunt**) [early 19C–1900s] a phr. used to denigrate the previous statement, 'that won't do', 'you must be joking', 'I'm not having that'.

cock *n.*[4] [Fr. *coquille*, cockleshell or cowrie] **1** [early 19C+] (*US, chiefly black/Southern*) the vagina. **2** [1920s+] sexual intercourse with a woman. **3** [1970s+] (*US Southern*) a woman, viewed solely as a sexual object; thus a *piece of cock*, also the vagina.

IN COMPOUNDS

❑ **cock hammer** *n.* [1960s] (*US campus*) the penis. ❑ **cock hound** *n.* [-HOUND *sfx*] [1940s+] (*US*) a man devoted to sex before all things. ❑ **cock-opener** *n.* [1920s–40s] (*US black*) the penis. ❑ **cock pluck** *n.* [1970s+] (*US black*) to stimulate a woman's genitals manually. ❑ **cocksmith** *n.* [1950s–60s] (*US*) a womanizer, a philanderer. ❑ **cock wagon** *n.* [1970s] (*US*) a car, usu. flashy, new and expensive, that is owned spec. to attract easily impressed young women.

IN PHRASES

❑ **cock it up** *v.* [1960s+] (*Aus.*) of a woman, to offer oneself sexually in an obvious manner. ❑ **get some cock** *v.* [1970s+] (*US black Southern*) of a man, to have sexual intercourse. ❑ **long-cock** *adj.* [1960s–70s] of a woman, possessing a large vagina; thus as an insult.

cock *n.*[5] [SE *cock and bull story* but note COOK UP *v.* (2) + the *Cock Lane ghost*, 'which had a great run, and was a rich harvest to the running stationers' (Hotten, 1867)] **1** [mid-19C] a broadsheet or pamphlet, sold in the streets and relating some form of lurid and sensational incident, typically a fire, a murder or an accident. **2** [1930s+] nonsense, rubbish; also in phr. (*load of*) *old cock*.

IN COMPOUNDS

❑ **cock-catch** *v.* [orig. milit. use] [late 19C–1900s] to obtain money on false pretences.

IN PHRASES

❑ **all to cock** *adj.* [1940s+] unsatisfactory, mixed up, useless. ❑ **hot cock** *n.* [1950s+] (*Aus./US*) nonsense, rubbish. ❑ **talk cock** *v.* [sense 2 above; although the assumed link is to COCK *n.*[3] (1)] [1930s+] to talk nonsense.

cock *n.*[6] [mid-19C] a horse, backed as a favourite by the public, which either fails to run or, if running, fails to race hard.

cock *adj.*[1] [SE *cockerel*] [mid-16C+] chief, top, most important.

cock *adj.*[2] [COCK *n.*[4] (1)] [1960s+] (*US*) pornographic.

IN COMPOUNDS

❑ **cock book** *n.* [1960s+] (*US*) pornography. ❑ **cock movie** *n.* [1960s+] a pornographic film.

cock *v.*[1] [COCK *n.*[3] (1)] **1** [17C; late 19C+] to have sexual intercourse; thus *cocking*, sexual intercourse; *cock in one's eye*, amorous. **2** [mid-18C] to get an erection.

cock *v.*[2] [17C SE *cock*, to place a match in the cock of a matchlock gun] [19C] to smoke.

cock *v.*[3] [abbr. COLD-COCK v.] [1930s] (*US*) to knock out.

cock *v.*[4]

SE in slang uses

IN COMPOUNDS

❑ **cock-my-cap** *n.* [early–mid-18C] gin.

IN PHRASES

❑ **cock a cloud** *v. see* BLOW A CLOUD *under* CLOUD *n.* ❑ **cock a deaf 'un** *v.* [1920s+] to pretend to be deaf, or at least to ignore by 'not hearing' the speaker. ❑ **cock and pinch** *n.* [the hat was *cocked* back and front and *pinched* at the sides, it was made of beaver fur] [mid-19C] an old-fashioned hat, favoured by early 19C dandies. ❑ **cock a snook/snoot (at)** *v. see under* SNOOT *n.* ❑ **cock it over** *v.* [SE *cock*, to behave boastfully or defiantly, to swagger] [mid-19C–1920s] to dominate, to lord it over. ❑ **cock off** *v.* [1970s] (*US*) to blunder, esp. through a display of emotion. ❑ **cock off oneself** *v.* [SE *cock*, to boast, to swagger] [20C+] (*W.I.*) to sit around looking important, esp. with one's feet up. ❑ **cock one's eye** *v.* [thereafter SE, but cf. *have a cocky eye*, to glance sideways] **1** [mid–late 18C] to wink. **2** [1910s] (*Aus.*) to take a look at. ❑ **cock ten** *v.* (*also* **chop ten, cut ten**) [SE *cock/cut* + *ten* (minutes); i.e. to take ten minutes off the working day] [20C+] (*W.I.*) to sit around while others are working. ❑ **cock up one's foot** *v.* (*also* **cock up one's feet**) [ext. of SE use; synon. with SE *put up one's feet*] [20C+] (*W.I.*) **1** to sit around looking important while others work. **2** of a woman, to sit with one's legs sprawled in what is considered an indecent manner. ❑ **cock up one's toes** *v. see under* TOE *n.*

cockadoodle *n.* [SE *cock-a-doodle*, the noise of a cockerel; but note COCK *n.*[5] (2)] [1930s+] (*Aus.*) nonsense, rubbish.

cockaleekie *adj.* [rhy. sl.] [1990s+] cheeky.

cockalize *v.* [COCK *n.*[3] (1)] **1** [1930s+] (*US juv.*) to humiliate/initiate a boy by smearing his penis with some substance, urinating on him, hitting his penis with a knotted handkerchief etc. **2** [1960s] (*US*) to beat, to defeat heavily.

cockamamie *n.* [COCKAMAMIE *adj.*] (*US*) **1** [1920s+] (*also* **cockernannie, kockamamey**) an absurd situation, a 'nonsense'. **2** [1930s+] an absurd, eccentric person.

cockamamie *adj.* (*also* **cockamamy**) [? *decalcomania*, a picture or design left on the skin as a 'transfer', from specially prepared paper, which is wetted and rubbed (popular *c.*1862–4). Rosten, *The Joys of Yiddish* (1968), suggests that the shift came because 'on the Lower East Side...no one knew how to spell "decalcomania"'; thus note Kober, *Thunder over the Bronx* (1935): 'Then there were the "cockamanies" — painted strips of paper which the kids applied to their wrists and rubbed with spit until the image was transferred to their hand'] [1920s+] confused, ludicrous, fake, fraudulent, absurd.

cock and hen *n.* (*also* **cockeren, cockle (and hen)**) [rhy. sl.] **1** [20C+] £10. **2** [20C+] a pen. **3** [1910s+] (*bingo/gambling*) the number ten. **4** [1940s–50s] a ten-year jail sentence.

cockatoo *n.*[1] [SE, punning on COCK *n.*[3] (1)] [mid-17C] the penis.

cockatoo *n.*[2] (*also* **cockatooer**) **1** [mid–late 19C] a convict serving time on Cockatoo Island, Sydney, where criminals were held *c.*1870. **2** [mid-19C+] a lookout for those engaged in some form of illegality [f. sense 1 or f. the noted wariness of the SE *cockatoo* bird]. **3** [mid-19C+] (*Aus./N.Z.*) a small farmer; thus *cockatoo fence*, a fence erected by such a farmer; *cockatoo's weather*, fine by day, wet at night or fine in the week, wet on Sunday [the image of the SE *cockatoo* bird sitting on a fence and staring around + play on sense 1, as the originals of such farmers had come from Sydney to the Port Fairy area].

cockatoo *v.* [COCKATOO *n.*[2]] (*Aus.*) **1** [late 19C] to farm on a small scale. **2** [1940s+] to keep a lookout.

cockatrice *n.* [SE *cockatrice*, a hybrid monster with head, wings and feet of a cock, terminating in a serpent with a barbed tail] **1** [16C–mid-19C] (*also* **cock-trick**) a prostitute [such a monster can kill with a mere glance + pun on COCK *n.*[3] (1) + fem. sfx *-trix*; Halliwell, editor/reviser of Nares, suggests that it 'seems to be applied especially to a captain's concubine']. **2** [18C–19C] a baby [the monster is born from an egg].

cockaty *adj.* [1990s+] (*W.I.*) affected, putting on airs.

cockbite *n.* [? a person who, if permitted, would bite one's penis, i.e. COCK *n.*[3] (1)] [1960s+] (*US*) a repellent, unpopular person.

cock block *n.* [COCK BLOCK *v.*] [2000s] (*US black*) a woman who permits sexual intimacy but refuses intercourse; or anyone who prevents others from pursuing sexual relations.

cock block *v.* (*also* **c.b.**) [COCK *n.*[3] (1)] **1** [1980s+] (*US black*) (*also* **block**) to ruin another man's sexual activities by stealing his woman, interrupting his seduction, etc; thus *cock-blocker*, one who does this. **2** [1990s+] (*US black/campus*) ext. to imply interference in any plans, efforts.

cockchafer *n.* [COCK *n.*[3] (1) + SE *chafer*, that which chafes or rubs painfully] **1** [mid-19C] a woman, occas. a man, who permits or encourages a good deal of sexual intimacy but not intercourse. **2** [mid-19C] a prostitute. **3** [mid–late 19C] (*UK Und./prison*) (*also* **chafer**) a prison treadmill. **4** [late 19C] the vagina. **5** [1920s–40s] a general term of abuse.

cocked *adj.* [SE *cocked*, askew] [mid-18C+] (*US*) drunk.

cocker *n.*[1] [COCK *n.*[2]] [late 19C+] a general term of address, usu. to a man.

cocker *n.*[2] [abbr. + sfx *-er*] [late 19C+] (*orig. Aus.*) a cockroach.

cocker *n.*[3] [? link to SE *cocker*, one who arranges and bets on cockfights] [1920s] (*US*) a racing tipster.

cocker *adj.* [Edward *Cocker* (1631–76), an engraver and teacher, the writer of *Cocker's Arithmetic* (published posthumously in 1678)] [early 19C] calculating.

cockerel *n.* [COCK *n.*[3] (1) + pun on the bird, 'a young cock' (*OED*)] [mid–late 17C] the penis.

cockeren *n. see* COCK AND HEN *n.*

cockernannie *n. see* COCKAMAMIE *n.* (1).

cockers-p *n.* [elision of SE and + -ER *sfx*] [1980s] (*UK society*) a cocktail party.

cockey *n. see* COCK *n.*[3] (6).

cock-eye Bob *n.* (*also* **cock-eye, cock-eyed Bob**) [SE *cock-eye(d)*, topsy-turvy + generic use of *Bob*] [late 19C+] (*W. Aus.*) a cyclone or thunderstorm.

cock-eyed *adj.*[1] [1910s+] used in excl. as a synon. for *confounded*.

cock-eyed *adj.*[2] [1920s+] very drunk.

cockie *n. see* COCKY *n.*[1].

cockies' clip *n.* (*also* **cocky's clip**) [rhy. sl.] [20C+] (*Aus.*) **1** a pickpocket [= DIP *n.*[1] (3)]. **2** a swim [= SE *dip*].

cocking *adj.* [COCK *n.*[3] (1)] [late 17C–early 19C] impudent, cheeky.

cockish *adj.* [SE *cock*, a cockerel + sfx *-ish*] **1** [17C–1930s] esp. of a woman, wanton, sexually forward. **2** [1930s] (*W.I.*) of liquor, strong; usu. made from fermented sugar cane.

cockle *v.*

IN PHRASES

□ **I should cockle** *see I SHOULD COCOA under* COFFEE AND COCOA *v.*

cockle (and hen) *n. see* COCK AND HEN *n.*

cockles *n.* [19C] the labia minora.

IN PHRASES

□ **play at hot cockles** *v.* [SE *hot cockles*, 'A rustic game in which one player lay face downwards, or knelt down with his eyes covered, and being struck on the back by the others in turn, guessed who struck him' (*OED*)] [17C–18C] to caress and stimulate the female or male genitals.

cock linnet *n.*[1] [late 19C] a small but dapper East End youth.

cock linnet *n.*[2] [rhy. sl.] [late 19C+] a minute.

cockloche *n.* (*also* **cockloach**) [? Fr. *coqueluche*] [mid-17C] a term of reproach or contempt.

cockloft *n.* [SE *cockloft*, the room over the garret; COCK *n.*[3] (1)] **1** [mid-17C–18C] the head. **2** [mid-18C–19C] the vagina.

cock lorel *n.* [COCK *adj.*[1] (1) + *losel*, a worthless rogue, a profligate. Usu. as the proper name Cock Lorel, who may poss. have been a genuine person and who features largely in the literature of Elizabethan villainy, orig. as the eponymous anti-hero of *Cock Lorel's Bote* (*c*.1515), a ship-master (Rowlands claims 'a tinker'), whose 'crew' is a group of rogues drawn from the workshops and gutters of London. Together they 'sail' the country, engaging in a variety of villainies. He appears in a number of works, as well as in the glossaries compiled by Awdeley (whose *Fraternity of Vagabonds* (*c*.1561) was 'confirmed by Cock Lorel') and Rowlands (in *Martin-Mark-all*, 1610), who suggests he was a tinker. In all he remains at the head of his marauding beggars, sometimes plotting against the state, on one occasion even entertaining the Devil to dinner. According to Rowlands' generally fictitious 'history' of the canting crew, Cock Lorel's rule supposedly lasted *c*.1511–33] [mid-16C–mid-17C] (*UK Und.*) the chief rogue or rascal.

Cockney *adj.* used in combs. based on Cockney stereotypes.

IN COMPOUNDS

□ **Cockney breakfast** *n.* [mid-19C] (*UK Und.*) gin or brandy and soda water. □ **Cockney counter** *n.* [early 19C] a badly minted guinea. □ **Cockney-shire** *n.* (*also* **Cockneyland**) [19C–1940s] London. □ **Cockney's luxury** *n.* [late 19C–1950s] breakfast in bed and using the pot for defecation, rather than leaving the warm house for a trip to the outdoor privy.

cocko *n.* (*also* **cock-oh**) [COCK *n.*[2]] [1920s–50s] a general term of address.

cockoholic *n.* [COCK *n.*[3] (1) + -AHOLIC *sfx*] [1990s+] a sexually voracious woman.

cock-on *adj.* [1990s+] (*UK juv.*) first-rate, excellent.

cock on! *excl.* [1990s+] (*UK juv.*) fine, good, agreed.

cockpit *n.*[1] [i.e. they are 'fighting' established religion] [late 18C] a Dissenters' meeting-house.

cockpit *n.*[2] [1930s] (*UK Und.*) a prison's punishment cells.

cockquean *n.* [var. on COTQUEAN *n.*] [mid-19C] an effeminate man, who is seen as dealing too keenly with domestic duties that are properly those of his wife.

cockroach *n.*[1] [the cockroach is especially loathed in New York's steam-heated apartments, where it thrives] [mid-19C+] (*US*) a despicable person.

cockroach *n.*[2] [rhy. sl.] [1940s+] a motor (rather than railway) coach.

Cockroach Inn *n.* [1930s+] (*US*) a shabby, run-down apartment or motel.

cockroach killers *n.* [20C+] (*US*) pointed boots or shoes.

cocks *n.* [COG *v.* (1)] [1930s] (*W.I.*) sleight of hand used by a dice cheat to defraud his fellow players.

cocksman *n.* [COCK *n.*[3] (1) + sfx *-man*] **1** [late 19C+] an exceptionally virile man; thus *cocksmanship*, a display of such virility. **2** [1960s] (*US black*) a male prostitute.

cock sparrow *n.* [rhy. sl.] **1** [late 19C+] an arrow. **2** [1920s+] a street trader's barrow. **3** [1960s] a wheelbarrow.

cock-sparrow *adj.* [rhy. sl. *cock-sparrow* (pron. 'sparra') = YARRA *adj.*] [1960s+] (*Aus.*) mad, insane.

cockstand *n.* [COCK *n.*[3] (1) + SE *stand*] [mid-19C+] an erection; thus *this will give you the cockstand*; thus *cockstanding*, sexually arousing.

cocksuck *n.* [backform. f. COCKSUCKER *n.*] (*orig. US*) **1** [1940s+] the act of fellatio. **2** [1960s+] a general term of abuse.

cocksuck *adj. see* COCKSUCKING *adj.*

cocksuck *v.* [backform. f. COCKSUCKER *n.*] [1970s+] (*orig. US*) to fellate.

cocksucker *n.* [COCK *n.*[3] (1) + SUCK *v.*[1] (1)] **1** [late 19C] (*orig. US*) a sycophant, a toady. **2** [late 19C+] a fellator or fellatrix. **3** [1910s+] (*also* **cocklicker**) an abusive term, generally considered to be one of the worst [note SUCKER *n.*[3]]. **4** [1910s] (*Aus.*) a US soldier; spelling in citations (*cark-sucker*) suggests the fooling of Australians by American GIs. **5** [1920s+] a male homosexual; thus his mouth. **6** [1940s+] (*US black/Southern*) one who performs cunnilingus [COCK *n.*[4] (1)]. **7** [1970s+] an object, no pej. implied. **8** [1980s+] (*US*) the mouth. **9** [1980s+] something distasteful, unpopular. **10** [2000s] (*US black*) in pl., the lips.

cocksucking *n.* [COCKSUCKER *n.* (2)] [late 19C+] (*orig. US*) (performing) oral sex.

cocksucking *adj.* (*also* **cocksuck, crotch-sucking, nut-sucking**) [COCKSUCKER *n.* (3)] [1910s+] (*orig. US*) vile, repellent, disgusting; one of the most taboo adj. of abuse.

cocksy fuss *n.* (*also* **coxy fuss**) [COCK *n.*[3] (1)] [early–mid-19C] amatory play, 'billing and cooing'.

cock-tail *n.* [racing use, a horse that tries but is still no thoroughbred] [mid–late 19C] an efficient, energetic, but not quite socially acceptable, person.

cocktail *n.* **1** [1950s+] (*US drugs*) the very last portion of a cannabis cigarette placed on the end of a cigarette. **2** [1980s+] (*drugs*) a cigarette laced with cocaine or crack.

cocktail *v.* [COCKTAIL *n.*] **1** [1950s–60s] (*drugs*) to place the last unsmoked portion of a cannabis cigarette into the end of a regular cigarette so as to make it more easily smokeable. A folded matchbook can be used for the same effect. **2** [1980s+] to lace a tobacco cigarette with cocaine.

cocktail party *n.* [1970s] (*US gang*) using a Molotov cocktail.

cocktails, the *n.* [1920s+] (*Aus.*) diarrhoea.

cocktease *v.* (*also* **tease someone's cock**) [COCKTEASER *n.*] [1920s+] to lead on in a sexual manner but never to permit actual intercourse, usu. of a woman.

cockteaser *n.* (*also* **cocktease, c.t.**) [COCK *n.*[3] (1)] **1** [late 19C+] a woman (or man, if gay) who permits or encourages a good deal of sexual intimacy but not intercourse. **2** [1990s+] in fig. use, a person who strings someone else along.

cock-up *n.* [SE *cock*, to bend at an angle, but with undertones of COCK *n.*[3] (1), on the pattern of FUCK-UP *n.* (1), BALLS-UP *n.*] [1920s+] (*orig. milit.*) an error, a blunder.

cock up *v.* [COCK-UP *n.*] [1920s+] to blunder, to make a mistake.

cocky *n.*[1] (*also* **cockey, cockie**) [COCK *n.*[2] (1)] [late 17C+] a general term of address to a man; occa. to a woman.

cocky *n.*[2] (*also* **cockie, cocky-farmer**) [COCKATOO *n.*[2] (3)] (*Aus.*) **1** [mid-19C+] a small farmer; often modified by the crop in which they specialize, e.g. *spud cocky*, a potato farmer. **2** [1940s+] the rural interest, whether small farmers or large landowners, with the main crop often indicated; thus *cane cocky*, *wheat cocky*, etc. **3** [1950s] a lookout at a two-up game.

(DERIVATIVES)

❑ **cockydom** *n.* [20C+] (*Aus.*) the world of small farmers.

(IN COMPOUNDS)

❑ **cocky's clip** *n.* [rhy. sl.; Baker, *The Australian Language* (1945): 'in rural slang a cocky's clip is given to a sheep when practically every vestige of wool is removed by a shearer'] **1** [1920s+] (*Aus.*) sheep dip. **2** see COCKIES' CLIP *n.* ❑ **cocky's coal** *n.* [1900s–40s] (*Aus.*) dry corncobs used as fuel. ❑ **cocky's crow** *n.* [pun on SE *cock's crow*] [20C+] (*Aus.*) dawn. ❑ **cocky's delight** *n.* (*also* **cocky's joy**) (*Aus.*) **1** [20C+] molasses, treacle or golden syrup. **2** [1970s] wire fencing. ❑ **cocky's friend** *n.* [1930s] (*Aus.*) fencing wire. ❑ **cocky's horror** *n.* [2000s] (*N.Z.*) grease, oil. ❑ **cocky's string** *n.* [20C+] (*Aus.*) fencing wire, which has a variety of everyday uses in addition to marking boundaries.

(IN PHRASES)

❑ **like the cocky on the biscuit tin** [the old tins of Arnott's biscuits had a picture of a cockatoo, which was thus 'on' the tin but not 'in' it] [1980s+] (*Aus.*) useless, impotent, a non-participant. ❑ **sheep-cocky** *n.* [late 19C+] (*Aus./N.Z.*) a small-scale sheep farmer.

cocky *n.*[3] [SE colloq. *cocky*, arrogant] [1950s] an arrogant person, a show-off.

cocky *v.* [COCKY *n.*[2] (1)] [late 19C+] (*Aus.*) to work as a small farmer.

coco *n.*[1] [abbr. SE *coconut*] **1** [mid-19C] (*also* **cocoa**) a hat. **2** [mid-19C+] (*also* **cocoa, cocoa-box, koko**) (*orig. US*) the head. **3** [20C+] (*W.I.*) a bump on the head.

(IN PHRASES)

❑ **give coco for yam** *v.* [mid-19C] (*W.I.*) to give as good as one gets; opposite of *GET TOCO FOR YAM under* TOCO *n.*

coco *n.*[2] *see* COKE *n.*[1] (1) and combs.

coco *v.*

(IN PHRASES)

❑ **I should coco** *see I SHOULD COCOA under* COFFEE AND COCOA *V.*

cocoa *n.*[1] [the colour] [20C+] (*US*) a derog. term for a black person, esp. light-skinned.

SE in slang uses

(IN COMPOUNDS)

❑ **cocoa payol** *n.* (*also* **cocoa pagnol**) [the PAYOL *n.* was mainly employed on cocoa and coffee plantations] [20C+] (*W.I., Trin.*) a mixed-race person who retains traces of Spanish ancestry and culture. ❑ **cocoa press** *n.* [1900s–30s] newspapers, e.g. *The Daily News*, owned by the chocolate-making Cadbury family. ❑ **cocoa puff** *v.* [abbr./redup. *cocaine* + PUFF *v.* (4) + play on *Cocoa Puffs*, the popular breakfast cereal] [1980s+] (*drugs*) to smoke cocaine mixed with marijuana; thus n., *coc(o)a puff*, a marijuana cigarette laced with cocaine. ❑ **cocoa shunter** *n.* [the link of anything 'chocolate'/CHOCOLATE *adj.* (2) to sodomy/the anus] [1990s+] a male homosexual.

cocoa *n.*[2] [backform. f. *COME ONE'S COCOA under* COME *v.*[1]] [1980s+] semen.

cocoa *n.*[3] *see* COCO *n.*[1].

(IN COMPOUNDS)

❑ **cocoa-box** *n. see* COCO *n.*[1] (2).

cocoa *adj.* [1920s] **1** (*US*) a derog. term describing a black person, esp. light-skinned; often ext. as *cocoa-brown*. **2** (*US black*) of a person, black, with no derog. overtones.

cocoa *v.*

(IN PHRASES)

❑ **I should cocoa** *see under* COFFEE AND COCOA *V.*

cocoanut *n. see* COCONUT *n.*[1].

cocobay *adj.* [Twi *kokobé*, leprosy] [20C+] (*W.I.*) having a skin covered in repulsive sores; thus *have cocobay on top of yaws*, to add new troubles to a situation that seemed bad enough already.

cocobola *n.* [Arawak *kakabali*, thence Sp. *cocobolo/cocobola*, the timber from any one of several species of tree of the Central American genus *Dalbergia*, or the tree itself. Nightsticks are made from this timber] [1990s+] (*US*) a police nightstick.

cocola *n.* [? var. on COCABOLA *n.* or Southern US pron. *co-cola* = *Coca-Cola*, which is dark] [1990s+] (*US prison*) a black person.

coconut *n.*[1] (*also* **cocoanut, coker-nut**) **1** [mid-19C+] the head. **2** [late 19C–1900s] in pl., large female breasts. **3** [1920s–40s] (*US*) $1; thus *coconuts*, money. **4** [1970s+] (*W.I./UK/Aus. black teen*) a black person who has 'sold out' to white values; they are 'brown on the outside but white within'. **5** [1980s] (*Aus./N.Z.*) a South Sea Islander. **6** [1990s+] in pl., the testicles.

SE in slang uses

(IN COMPOUNDS)

❑ **coconut-dodger** *n.* [the image of coconut palms shedding their fruit] [1920s] (*US black*) a South American or African black person. ❑ **coconut-head** *n.* [the 'jungle' associations] [20C+]

(*US*) **1** a derog. term for a black person; also as adj., *coconut-headed*. **2** a derog. ref. to a Samoan-American.

IN PHRASES

❑ **go coconuts** *v.* [? one is off/out of one's COCONUT *n.*[1] (1)] [1990s+] to go wild, crazy.

coconut *n.*[2] [play on COKE *n.*[1] (1)] [1940s–70s] (*US drugs*) cocaine.

cocooning *n.* [1970s+] (*US*) staying at home with one's family.

cocum *n.* [Heb. and thence Yid. *kochum*, wisdom] **1** [mid-19C] advantage, luck, resource. **2** [mid-19C] knowledge; thus *fight cocum*, being cunning, artful, usu. in illegal contexts. **3** [mid-19C; 2000s] (*UK Und.*) (*also* **cokum**) sense. **4** [1960s] (*S.Afr. Und.*) (*also* **chochem**) a thief, usu. an intelligent one.

IN PHRASES

❑ **play cocum** *v.* (*also* **play cokum**) [mid-19C–1900s] to act in an artful, cunning manner; to deceive.

cocum *adj.* (*also* **cokum**) [COCUM *n.*] [mid-19C–1900s] **1** resourceful, cunning, thus phr. *fight cocum*, to be wary. **2** sensible. **3** sorted out; arranged satisfactorily.

c.o.d. *n.* [abbr. *c*ock *o*n *d*elivery + a pun on SE *c.o.d.*, cash on delivery] [1950s+] a male prostitute.

co-d. *n.* [abbr.] [1990s+] *co-d*efendant.

cod *n.*[1] (*also* **coads**) [late 16C–mid-19C] a euph. for God; usu. in comb., e.g. *cods so*, God's oath.

cod *n.*[2] [ety. unknown; *cod* has been linked to SE *codger*, and it is found as its abbr., but *cod* is a much earlier word] **1** [mid–late 17C] a friend; thus *honest cod*, a good friend. **2** [late 17C–18C] a fellow. **3** [late 17C+] a fool [? COD'S HEAD *n.*].

cod *n.*[3] [SE *cod*, a bag; thus early 16C SE *cod*, the scrotum, which itself, despite Grose's citations, is only slang in pl., i.e. CODS *n.*[1] (1)] **1** [mid-17C+] (*also* **codshead**) the penis. **2** [late 17C–early 19C] money; thus LUSTY COD *n.* **3** [late 17C–19C] a purse. **4** [1980s+] (*drugs*) a large amount of money.

IN COMPOUNDS

❑ **cod-piece** *n.* [SE *cod-piece*: the flap on breeches which covered the male genitals worn until *c.*1600] [17C] a euph. for the penis. ❑ **cod trench** *n.* [1990s+] the vagina.

IN PHRASES

❑ **jolly/rum cod** *n.* *see* LUSTY COD *n.*

cod *n.*[4] [? COD *n.*[2] (3) or ? like the fish he 'swims' in alcohol] [late 19C+] a drunkard.

cod *n.*[5] [COD *v.* (2)] **1** [late 19C+] deception, deceit, a lie; thus *cod-acting*, foolish behaviour. **2** [20C+] (*orig. Irish*) a joke, a hoax, a leg-pull, a parody.

cod *adj.* [COD *v.* (2) + ? play on FISHY *adj.*[2] (1); note theatrical jargon *cod version*, a burlesque of a well-known play] **1** [1950s+] fake, parodic; usu. in comb., e.g. *cod-Russian*, *cod-typewriter* etc. **2** [1960s–70s] (*also* **codalina, codette, codettareenarone**) a general negative.

cod *v.* [COD *n.*[2] (3)] **1** [18C] to cheat, to defraud. **2** [mid-19C+] (*also* **codd**) to tease, to hoax.

coddam *n.* (*also* **coddem, coddom**) [COD *v.* (2); lit. *cod 'em*, hoax them, fool them. 'The game is "simplicity itself" but requires a great amount of low cunning' (Hotten, 1864)] [mid–late 19C] a public house game played with a button or coin.

codder *n.* [COD *v.* (2)] [mid-19C–1900s] a teaser, a hoaxer.

codding *n.* [COD *v.* (2)] [mid-19C+] teasing, chaffing, hoaxing.

coddom *n.* *see* CODDAM *n.*

codette/codettareenarone *adj.* *see* COD *adj.* (2).

code 21 *n.* [? spec. prison rule] [2000s] (*US prison*) masturbation.

codfish *n.* [COD *n.*[2] (3). Note *codfish aristocracy*, a mocking New England term for those 19C *nouveaux riches* whose fortunes sprang from the Massachusetts cod industry] (*US*) **1** [late 18C–mid-19C] a fool. **2** [early 19C–1910s] one who thinks themselves superior to their peers.

IN COMPOUNDS

❑ **codfish flats** *n.* [1960s] (*US*) the poor area of town.

codge *n.* [Yorks. dial. *cadger*, a beggar, a petty thief] [late 19C–1900s] a vagrant, a tramp.

codie *n.* [ety. unknown] [1980s] a child molester.

cod-on *n.* [COD *v.* (2)] [20C+] (*Irish*) a practical joke.

cods *n.*[1] [SE *cod*, a bag, thus the scrotum; note use – in sing. – as a term of affection in Urquhart, *The Complete Works of Rabelais* (1653): 'Come, my cod, let me coll (i.e. hug) thee till I kill thee'] **1** [17C+] (*also* **cogs**) in pl., the testicles [the term was SE until 19C, when Victorian language prudery rendered it taboo]. **2** [late 18C–early 19C] a curate [play on sense 1; according to Grose (1785, 1796), 'a rude fellow meeting a curate, mistook him for the rector; and accosted him with the vulgar appellation of, Bol—ks the rector, No, Sir, answered he, only Cods the curate, at your service'].

cods *n.*[2] [*OED* suggests abbr. CODSWALLOP *n.* but ? f. CODS *n.*[1] (1), i.e. synon. with BALLS *n.* (4)] [1960s+] **1** a mess. **2** rubbish, nonsense.

cod's head *n.* [dial. ? the 'thickness' of the cod's head; note slightly later COD *n.*[2] (3)] **1** [mid-16C–mid-19C] a dupe, a fool; thus the fool's head; also found in 19C as *cod's head and shoulders*. **2** *see* COD *n.*[3].

cod's roe *n.* [rhy. sl. = DOUGH *n.* (1)] [20C+] money.

codswallop *n.* [ety. unknown; there is an implication of CODS *n.*[1] (1), but no proven link. Linguistically COD *n.*[2] (3) + dial. *wallop*, to chatter, to scold is feasible, but the chronology may militate against it] [1960s+] nonsense, rubbish, drivel.

coe *n.* [COVE *n.* (1)] [16C+] (*UK Und.*) a man.

cofe *n.* [17C Scot. *cofe*, a chapman or pedlar, or, like a number of cant terms, f. Rom. *cova* or *covo*, man] [17C] a man.

coffee *n.* **1** [mid-19C] (*US Und.*) beans. **2** [1940s] (*US*) tobacco. **3** [1960s+] (*US drugs*) LSD.

SE in slang uses

IN COMPOUNDS

❑ **coffee-and-B** *n.* [late 19C–1900s] a coffee and brandy. ❑ **coffee and cakes** *n.* (*also* **two drinks and a sandwich**) [it provides just about enough to buy coffee and cakes/two drinks and a sandwich; note late 19C local New Orleans synon. *ice cream and cakes*] [20C+] (*US*) a very small salary. ❑ **coffee-and-doughnut gun** *n.* **1** [20C+] (*UK Und.*) a small, relatively powerless gun. **2** [1920s] (*US Und.*) a second-rate, unthreatening gangster. ❑ **coffee-bag** *n.* [1910s–40s] (*US black/tramp*) a coat pocket. ❑ **coffee boat** *n.* (*US black*) a wake. ❑ **coffee-break parole** *n.* [so called because it is granted very quickly] [1960s+] (*US prison*) a nickname for a Special Circumstances release. ❑ **coffee-cooler** *n.* [milit. jargon *coffee cooler*, 'one who blows his coffee while the brigade is going by', i.e. a soldier who is constantly searching for a soft job] **1** [mid-19C+] an idler, a shirker; thus v. *cool coffee*, to shirk. **2** [1910s] (*US*) a prospector. **3** [1950–70s] (*US black*) the lips, esp. when large and protuberant [i.e. as used to blow on hot coffee]. ❑ **coffee-grinder** *n.* **1** in sexual contexts, playing on GRIND *v.* (1a). (*US*) (**a**) [late 19C] the vagina. (**b**) [1960s] a striptease artist. (**c**) [1960s] a prostitute. **2** (*also* **coffee pot**) as a machine [its noise, which resembles that of the SE *coffee grinder*]. (**a**) [1910s+] (*orig. US*) any old and unstable machine, typically a veteran propeller-driven aeroplane. (**b**) [1940s] (*US Und.*) a machine gun [orig. milit. use for a Gatling machine gun]. ❑ **coffee-house** *see* separate entries. ❑ **coffee-mill** *n.* [fig. uses of SE *coffee-mill*, a coffee-grinder that works by turning a handle] **1** [early–mid-19C] the mouth. **2** [mid-19C] (*UK Und.*) a watchman's rattle. ❑ **coffee-pot** *n.* [the coffee that is the mainstay of the menu, but note US regional *coffee-pot*, a small-scale operation, esp. a small lumber mill] **1** [1920s+] (*US*) a small lunch-room. **2** [1960s] (*US teen*) the 'life and soul' of a party. ❑ **coffee-pot canyon** *n.* [coined by columnist Walter Winchell (1897–1972); a real Coffee Pot Canyon exists in the San Mateo Mts, New Mexico] [1920s–50s] (*US*) Broadway, New York City. ❑ **coffee-royal** *n.* [1920s] (*US tramp*) coffee with a shot of pure alcohol. ❑ **coffee-shop** *n.* *see* separate entries. ❑ **coffee-spout** *n.* [? use of SE *coffee* to mean semen or vaginal secretions] [1930s+] (*US*) the vagina. ❑ **coffee-strainer** *n.* [1970s] (*US*) a bushy moustache.

IN PHRASES

❑ **— and a coffee** [1970s] (*Can. prison*) the last day of one's sentence: one has breakfast but is released before the other meals.

coffee-and *n.* (*also* **coffee-an'**) [20C+] **1** coffee and cakes or coffee and doughnuts, i.e. the cheapest meal available in a café or diner; thus the reverse, *sinkers and…* **2** just enough money to buy coffee and doughnuts.

coffee-and *adj.* [fig. use of COFFEE-AND *n.* (1)] [1930s+] in context, referring to anything seen as cheap, minimal, second-rate, e.g. (theatre) *coffee-and role*, a small part that will pay for little more than snacks.

IN COMPOUNDS

❑ **coffee-and habit** *n.* [HABIT *n.*] [1930s–50s] (*US drugs*) a small-time heroin habit, adopted either through grim self-control or through simple poverty. ❑ **coffee-and pimp** *n.* (*also* **coffee-and mac**) [1930s–70s] a small-time pimp, whose women barely make him a living, let alone provide the high style to which he would aspire.

coffee and cocoa *v.* [rhy. sl.] [1930s+] say so; usu. as *I SHOULD COCOA* below.

IN PHRASES

❑ **I should cocoa** (*also* **I should coco, I should cockle**) [1930s+] you must be joking, don't make me laugh [esp. popular in BBC Radio's *Billy Cotton Band Show* in the 1950s].

coffee and tea *n.* [rhy. sl.] [2000s] the sea.

coffee-house *n.* [the colour of coffee and of urine and faeces] [late 18C–mid-19C] a privy.

coffee-house *v.* [orig. fox-hunting use, the image is of habitués of an 18C coffee-house] [late 19C; 1970s] (*US*) to chatter, to gossip.

coffee-shop *n.*[1] [the colour of its contents] [late 18C–mid-19C] a privy.

coffee-shop *n.*[2] [? the penis goes 'in and out'] [late 19C] the vagina.

coffee stalls *n.* [rhy. sl. = BALLS *n.* (1)] [1940s–60s] the testicles.

coffin *n.*[1] **1** [early 17C] a piecrust. **2** [mid–late 19C] (*US*) a clumsy, heavy boot or shoe. **3** [1920s–60s] (*US Und.*) a safe. **4** [1930s] (*US Western*) a trunk. **5** [1930s–40s] (*US Und.*) a prison cell.

SE in slang uses

IN COMPOUNDS

❑ **coffin-dodger** *n.* [the image is of being 'one step ahead' of death or, in the case of smokers, mocking death] **1** [1900s–10s] (*US campus*) a heavy smoker. **2** [1980s+] an old person, prob. ill. ❑ **coffin meat** *n.* [mid-19C] (*US*) a corpse. ❑ **coffin varnish** *n.* [joc. use of SE + ref. to its dubious, even fatal, quality] [mid-19C+] (*US*) liquor, esp. that which was sold during the Prohibition era (1920–33).

coffin *n.*[2] [var. on CUFFIN *n.* (1)] [late 17C] a man, a fellow.

coffin nail *n.*[1] [the assumption that drink, esp. in the outposts of the Empire, was a killer. Folk etymology erroneously links this nail with PEG *n.*[4]; *see also* NAIL IN ONE'S COFFIN *under* NAIL *n.*[1]] [19C+] a drink; thus the invitation to drink, *let's put another nail in our coffins, let's drive another nail…*

coffin nail *n.*[2] (*also* **coffin screw, coffin tack**) [? no more than the resemblance of the cigarette to the nail; nicotine's cancerous potential is very much a phenomenon of 1960s+] **1** [late 19C+] a cigarette. **2** [1910s] (*US campus*) one who smokes to excess.

coff's harbour *n. see* SYDNEY HARBOUR *n.*

coflumpux! *excl.* [KER- *pfx* + FLUMMOX *v.* + SE *thump*] [mid-19C] (*US*) an onomat. term indicating the sound of a body falling to the ground with a thump.

cog *n.*[1] [COG *v.* (1)] (*UK Und.*) **1** [mid-16C–mid-19C] a lure, esp. in the form of money, designed to entice a gambler into a game, before cheating him of his own funds. **2** [17C] money. **3** [early 19C] that which is obtained by cheating.

IN PHRASES

❑ **drop a cog** *v.* [late 16C–18C] to drop a coin and thus lure the person who picks it up into a confidence trick.

cog *n.*[2] [early 19C] a tooth.

cog *v.* [ety. unknown; note that while acknowledging it as a 'ruffian's term', the *OED* categorizes the word as SE] (*UK Und.*) **1** [mid-16C–mid-19C] (*also* **cog a dice, cog a die, cog the dice**) to use any form of illicit sleight of hand, spec. to make a surreptitious change of a crooked dice for a legitimate one (or vice versa) during a game. **2** [late 16C–17C] to palm off fraudulently, to put out or utter falsely. **3** [late 16C–early 19C] to deceive, to cheat out of; thus *cog a dinner*, to cheat someone out of a dinner. **4** [17C+] to cheat at cards, or in any other manner, to crib. **5** [late 16C–early 18C] to flatter, to wheedle, to wheedle someone out of (something). **6** [17C] to have sexual intercourse.

IN COMPOUNDS

❑ **cog-foist** *n.* [FOIST *n.*[2] (2)] [early 17C] (*UK Und.*) a cheat. ❑ **cog forth** *v.* [early–mid-17C] to control the fall of dice by sleight of hand.

coge it *v.* [Scot. *cogue*, a small drinking vessel] [mid-18C–mid-19C] (*US*) to drink heavily.

cogger *n.* [COG *v.*] **1** [late 16C+] any form of cheat or schemer. **2** [early 17C] a card-sharp.

cogie *n.* [Scot. *cogue*, (16C) a small pail used for milking cows, or (17C) a drinking vessel] [19C] the vagina.

coglione *n.* [mid-19C] (*US Und.*) a man who is duped by a woman; a fool.

cogniac *n. see* CONEY *n.*[1].

cogs *n.*[1] [such glasses can be seen as 'fooling' other people; ? link to COG *v.* (3)] [1940s] (*US black/Harlem*) sunglasses.

cogs *n.*[2] *see* CODS *n.*[1] (1).

cog-shoulder *n.* [SE *cog*, to place an impediment in front of + *shoulder*] [early 17C] an arrest.

coguey *adj.* [Scot. *cogue*, to drink drams; *cogue*, a small drinking vessel] [19C] drunk.

cog-wheel *n.*

SE in slang uses

IN PHRASES

❑ **have cog-wheels** *v.* [1910s] (*Aus.*) to be demented.

Cohen *n.* (*also* **Kohen**) [1900s–10s] (*Aus.*) a generic term for a Jew, esp. when carrying out a stereotyped job, e.g. banker or bookmaker.

Cohentingent *n.* [COHEN *n.*+ SE *contingent*] [1900s] (*Aus.*) an anti-Semitic slur, aimed at the alleged propensity of Jews to avoid enlisting in the Boer war, while encouraging others to join up; thus *cohentingenter*.

cohones *n. see* COJONES *n.*

coil *n.* [? the circular shape of coins, a roll of banknotes; or fig. ref. to the *mortal coil*, i.e. life and thus money as a basic necessity for life] [1950s+] (*W.I. Rasta*) money.

coiler *n.* [he simply 'coils up' and falls asleep] [20C+] (*Aus.*) a vagrant who sleeps in the open air.

coil one's ropes *v.* (*also* **coil one's cables**) [naut. imagery: a good sailor always coiled his ropes properly at the end of his work] [1910s+] to die.

coil someone's coat *v. see under* COAT *n.*

coin *n.* (*also* **coyne**) **1** [mid-16C+] money. **2** [1900s–50s] (*US black*) in pl., money, whether actual coins or notes.

IN COMPOUNDS

❑ **coin collector** *n.* [1970s] a male homosexual prostitute.

IN PHRASES

❑ **big coin** *n.* [1990s+] (*US teen*) a large amount of money.

SE in slang uses

IN PHRASES

❑ **do a coin slot** *v.* [the supposed resemblance of the crack of the buttocks and a *coin slot*] [2000s] (*Aus.*) for one's low-cut trousers to reveal the top of one's buttocks.

coin (it) *v.* [COIN *n.*] [mid-19C+] to make a great deal of money.

coinkidink *n.* [deliberately 'jokey' mispron.] [1980s+] (*US campus*) coincidence.

coiny *adj.* [COIN *n.*] [late 19C–1910s] rich.

IN COMPOUNDS

❑ **coiny cove** *n.* [COVE *n.* (1)] [1920s+] (*Aus.*) a rich man.

cojones *n.* (*also* **cajuns, cohones**) [synon. Sp.; popularized first by the works of Ernest Hemingway (1899–1961) and latterly by Puerto Rican immigrants to US] [1930s+] testicles, used to mean both the physical organ and metaphorical courage.

coke *n.*[1] (*drugs*) **1** [20C+] (*also* **coc, coco**) cocaine; thus *coked, coked up*, under the influence of cocaine. **2** [1910s–30s] a cocaine user. **3** [1920s+] any injectable opiate drug, usu. morphine or heroin. **4** [1990s+] crack cocaine.

IN COMPOUNDS

❑ **coke-blunt** *n.* [BLUNT *n.*[3] (1)] [1980s+] a mixture of hashish/marijuana and cocaine, made into a cigarette when rolled in a tobacco leaf, taken from the wrapper of a Phillies Blunt cigar. ❑ **coke fiend** *n.* (*also* **coco fiend**) [FIEND *n.* (2)/SE *fiend*; later use tends to be ironic] [20C+] (*drugs*) a cocaine user. ❑ **coke-freak** *n.* [-FREAK *sfx*] [1980s+] (*drugs*) a regular usual of cocaine. ❑ **cokehead** *n.* [-HEAD *sfx* (4)] [1920s+] (*drugs*) a regular cocaine user; thus adj. *coke-headed*. ❑ **coke horrors** *n.* [HORRORS, THE *n.* (4)] [1950s] (*drugs*) paranoid hallucinogenic delusions occasioned by an excessive/long-term use of cocaine. ❑ **cokehound** *n.* [-HOUND *sfx*] [1930s] (*drugs*) a cocaine user. ❑ **coke oven** *n.* [1940s–70s] (*US drugs*) a place where one buys cocaine. ❑ **cokeover** *n.* [play on SE *hangover*] [1980s+] (*drugs*) the after-effects of a cocaine binge. ❑ **coke party** *n.* [1920s–30s] (*drugs*) a party at which the principal aim is to consume cocaine. ❑ **cokeslut** *n.* [SLUT *n.* (3)] [1990s+] a regular cocaine user. ❑ **coke stare** *n.* [SE *stare*; the rigid gaze that may overtake the more paranoid cocaine user] [1970s+] (*US black*) the 'evil eye', a deliberately aggressive and unpleasant look. ❑ **coke-water** *n.* [1930s] (*US prison*) cocaine dissolved in water.

IN PHRASES

❑ **blow coke** *v.* [20C+] (*drugs*) to inhale cocaine; thus *coke-blower*, a cocaine sniffer. ❑ **coke up** *v.* **1** [1930s+] (*drugs*) to take cocaine. **2** [1970s] to consume any drug.

coke *n.*[2] [COCONUT *n.*[1] (1)] **1** [1920s] (*US*) the head. **2** [1930s] in fig. use, an eccentric, a fool.

coke *v.* [COKE *n.*[1] (1)] [1970s] (*drugs*) to take cocaine.

coke bottle eyes *n.* [similar to the effect of one's COKE BOTTLE GLASSES *n.*] [1980s+] (*US campus*) a state achieved by the drunkard when all members of the opposite sex seem far more attractive than they might be when viewed in sobriety.

coke bottle glasses *n.* (*also* **milk-bottle bottoms**) [such glasses supposedly resemble the glass in a trad. Coca-Cola bottle] [1950s+] (*orig. US*) spectacles with very thick lenses, used by those with seriously short sight.

coke-date *n. see* JELLY-DATE *n.*

coked (up) *adj.* [COKE *n.*[1] (1)] **1** [1910s+] (*drugs*) (*also* **coked out, cooked up**) under the influence of cocaine. **2** [1940s] (*US*) drunk.

coke frame *n.* [brandname *Coke*, Coca-Cola + FRAME *n.*[1] (1), i.e. a body curved like the trad. Coca-Cola bottle; + BANTAM *n.* (4)] [1930s–40s] (*US black*) a curvaceous figure; thus *banter play built on a coke frame*, an attractive woman with a good figure.

coker *n.*[1] [CAULKER *n.* (3), but chronology suggests this (or at least this sp.) may have been the orig. term] **1** [late 17C] a liar. **2** [late 17C–mid-19C] a lie.

coker *n.*[2] [COKE *n.*[1] (1) + sfx *-er*] [1980s] (*US*) a cocaine user.

cokernut *n. see* COCONUT *n.*[1].

cokey *n.*[1] *see* COKIE *n.*

cokey *n.*[2] *see* KOKI *n.*

cokey *adj.* (*also* **cokie**) [COKE *n.*[1] (1); although cocaine tends to excite rather than dull the senses, so perhaps senses 1 and 3 both COKE *n.*[1] (3)] (*US*) **1** [1930s–40s] foolish, silly. **2** [1940s+] pertaining to cocaine. **3** [1950s] (*US drugs*) addicted to heroin.

cokey-eye *n.* [SE *cock-eye*] [20C+] (*W.I.*) a squint; thus derog. nickname *cokey*, a squinter.

cokie *n.* (*also* **coakie, cokey**) [COKE *n.*[1], on pattern of JUNKIE *n.*] **1** [1910s+] (*drugs*) a habitual user of heroin or opium. **2** [1920s–60s] (*US Und.*) any form of drug addict. **3** [1920s+] (*drugs*) a habitual user of cocaine; thus [1930s–50s] *Cokie Joe*, a personification of a regular cocaine user. **4** [1940s] (*US gang*) a boy, usu. derog., esp. when referring to a member of another gang.

cokir *n.* [COKER *n.*[1]] [mid-17C–early 18C] a liar.

cokum *see under* COCUM.

cola *n.* [abbr. brandname *Coca-Cola*, thus play on its abbr. *Coke*/COKE *n.*[1] (1)] [1980s+] (*US drugs*) cocaine.

cold *n.* [? it is no longer alight] [1980s+] (*US black*) a cigarette end.

SE in slang uses

IN PHRASES

❑ **have a cold** *v.* [euph.] **1** [19C+] to have a venereal disease. **2** [mid-19C–1910s] to be in debt; thus *have a very bad cold*, to leave one's lodgings without paying the rent.

cold *adj.* [all uses, positive or negative, stem from the unadorned 'iciness' of SE *cold*] **1** [mid-19C+] simple, unadorned. **2** [mid-19C+] unconscious. **3** [late 19C–1930s] (*US campus*) perfect, complete. **4** [late 19C+] sexually unresponsive. **5** [20C+] dead. **6** [20C+] (*US*) of money, the actual sum, i.e. abbr. *cold cash*. **7** [20C+] (*gambling*) unlucky, unfavourable. **8** [1920s+] (*US*) of a cheque, fraudulent, worthless. **9** [1920s+] (*US black/teen*) unpleasant, difficult, unnecessary. **10** [1930s] (*US tramp*) of a safe, wallet, or other target of a crime, empty, worthless, unrewarding. **11** [1950s+] free of suspicion, innocent; of a gun, unlicensed, thus untraceable. **12** [1960s+] (*also* **cold-ass**) (*orig. US*) heartless, ruthless, cruel. **13** [1970s+] (*US black/teen*) on bad = good model, excellent, first-rate, superb. **14** [1980s] (*US black*) confrontational, provocative, conducive to violence.

IN COMPOUNDS

❑ **cold poke** *n.* [POKE *n.*[2] (2)] [1920s–40s] (*US Und.*) a wallet without any money in it; thus a confidence game based on such an empty wallet. ❑ **cold shot** *n.* [sense 12/14 above + SHOT *n.*[1] (5c)] [1960s+] (*US black*) **1** unnecessary and aggressive behaviour. **2** cruel, emotionless behaviour. **3** an unpleasant surprise.

IN PHRASES

❑ **cold as a maggot** *adj.* [1960s+] a phr. suggesting someone is innocent of a police charge. ❑ **cold in hand** (*also* **cold hand**) [gambling jargon, to be *cold* is to have poor cards, unlucky dice etc; however, in poker jargon a *cold deck* for an honest player is a good hand, requiring no change of cards, while for a sharp it is one that has been stacked, guaranteeing a win for the cheat] [1930s–60s] (*US black*) without money, penniless. ❑ **in the cold** [1910s+] (*Aus.*) in prison.

SE in slang uses

IN COMPOUNDS

❑ **cold blood** *n.* [mid-19C] a liquor store or 'off licence' that can sell beer but cannot have it drunk on the premises. ❑ **cold-blooded** *adj.* [1960s+] (*US*) honest, open, candid. ❑ **cold-blooded fish** *n. see* COLD FISH below. ❑ **cold case** *n.* [1980s+] (*US black/Los Angeles*) a very bad situation; a serious scolding. ❑ **cold choke** *n.* [SE *choke*; but note CHOKE *n.*[1] (1)] [mid-19C+] (*W.I.*) cold food, which is hard to swallow. ❑ **cold clay** *n. see* COLD MEAT *n.* (1). ❑ **cold coffee** *n.* [SE *cold coffee*, which is usu. considered an unappetizing drink] **1** [mid–late 19C] bad luck. **2** [late 19C] a snub. **3** [late 19C–1910s] beer [the colour + ? euph.]. ❑ **Cold Country** *n.* [apparently a *Bulletin* nonce-creatiom] [1900s–30s] (*Aus.*) Great Britain. ❑ **cold cream** *n.* [play on SE] [mid–late 19C] gin. ❑ **cold cunt** *v.* [CUNT *n.* (1); pun on SE colloq. *cold-shoulder*] [1970s+] (*lesbian*) to ignore, to brush off. ❑ **cold-deck** *see* separate entries. ❑ **cold-eye** *see* separate entries. ❑ **cold fang** *v.* [FANG *v.*[1] (1)] [1960s+] (*Aus.*) to ask a stranger for money. ❑ **cold-finger man** *n.* [1940s] a pickpocket, esp. one who steals from coatrooms and cloakrooms. ❑ **cold fish** *n.* (*also* **cold-blooded fish**) [FISH *n.*[1] (3)] [1930s+] an unemotional person; also as v., to be sexually unresponsive. ❑ **cold footer** *n.* (*also* **cold-foot**) [1910s–20s] (*orig. Aus.*) a timid, nervous person; thus *cold-footed*, timid, cowardly. ❑ **cold four** *n.* [SE *four-ale*, beer sold at fourpence a quart] [late 19C–1900s] the cheapest variety of beer. ❑ **cold gold** *n.* [advertising slogan for Toohey's KB lager: 'Shake hands with a cold gold'] [1980s+] (*Aus.*) a can of beer. ❑ **cold gruel** *n.* [mid-19C] **1** bad luck. **2** a snub. ❑ **cold Irish** *n. see* FENIAN *n.* ❑ **cold iron** *n.* [late 17C–early 19C] a sword. ❑ **cold meat** *n.* **1** see separate entry. **2** *see* COLD PIE below. ❑ **cold mitt** *n. see under* MITT *n.* ❑ **cold muffin** *n.* [late 19C–1900s] anything mediocre, second-rate. ❑ **cold mutton** *n. see* COLD MEAT *n.* (1). ❑ **cold nantz** *n.* [NANTZ *n.*] [early 18C] brandy. ❑ **cold one** *n. see* separate entries. ❑ **cold pie** *n.* **1** [1900s] (*Aus.*) (*also* **cold meat**) an easy victim. **2** *see* CHOKING PIE *n.* ❑ **cold pig** *n.* [cf. naut. jargon *cold norwester*, a bucket of seawater poured over a new recruit as an initiation ceremony] **1** [late 18C–mid-19C] a punishment or joke in which the bedclothes are stripped off a sleeper or cold water is poured over them; usu. in phr. *give cold pig*. **2** [mid-19C] (*US Und.*) one who has been robbed of their clothes. ❑ **cold pigging** *n.* [? one of the goods sold was cold pork] [20C+] (*Aus./N.Z.*) hawking goods from door to door. ❑ **cold potato** *n. see* separate entries. ❑ **cold prowl** *n.* [1920s] (*US Und.*) breaking into a house while its owners are absent. ❑ **cold pudding** *n.* [late 18C–19C] anything considered worthless, second-rate. ❑ **cold pup** *n. see* COLD ONE *n.*[2]. ❑ **cold quack** *n.* [punning var. on COLD TURKEY *n.* (1)] [1960s] (*drugs*) sudden and total withdrawal from heroin addiction without tapering off or using any assistance from medication. ❑ **cold scran** *n. see under* SCRAN *n.* ❑ **cold shake** *n. see under* SHAKE *n.*[1]. ❑ **cold slaw** *n.* [play on CABBAGE *n.*[1] (1)] [late 19C] (*US*) small off-cuts of material, taken from the job in hand and sold off as perks by tailors. ❑ **cold steel** *n.* [1980s+] (*Aus. drugs/prison*) a hypodermic syringe. ❑ **cold storage** *n. see* separate entries. ❑ **cold tea** *n.* [the colour; note TEA *n.*] **1** [late 17C–18C] brandy. **2** [1900s] (*US*) beer. ❑ **cold turkey** *see* separate entries. ❑ **cold water** *n.* (*also* **cold tea**) [their favourite drink + ? ref. to Salvation Army] **1** [late 19C–1900s] teetotalism, abstinence; thus *cold water army*, the teetotal movement. **2** [1910s] (*Aus.*) a generic term for temperance campaigners.

IN PHRASES

❑ **cold as…** *adj. see* separate entry. ❑ **colder than…** *adj. see* separate entry. ❑ **cold on a blue** *see under* BLUE *n.*[1]. ❑ **do cold with** *v.* [20C+] (*W.I.*) to not be on speaking terms with. ❑ **get someone in the cold** *v.* [1900s] (*orig. US*) to have at one's mercy, to have at a disadvantage. ❑ **go cold at** *v.* [1920s+] (*Aus.*) to scold, to blame, to reprimand.

cold *adv.* **1** [late 19C+] (*US*) absolutely, completely, utterly. **2** [1910s+] unprepared, unannounced. **3** [1960s] (*drugs*) in the context of giving up an addiction, without the aid of any medication. **4** [1980s+] (*orig. rap music*) definitely, indeed, just.

IN COMPOUNDS

❑ **cold-bite** *see* separate entries. ❑ **cold-busted** *adj.* [1980s+] (*US campus*) caught in the act. ❑ **cold chill** *v.* [1980s+] **1** (*US*) to relax. **2** (*US black*) to perturb, to spook. ❑ **cold-cock** *see* separate entries. ❑ **cold-conk** *v.* [CONK *v.*[2] (1); var. on COLD-COCK *v.*] [1960s+] (*US*) to knock unconscious. ❑ **cold-crushing** *adj.* [1980s+] (*US black*) a general term of approval; thus n. *cold crusher*, something outstanding. ❑ **cold lamping** *n.* [LAMP *v.*[2] (2)] [1990s+] (*US black*) explaining hitherto complex, impenetrable matters.

IN PHRASES

❑ **have someone cold** *v.* [1910s+] (*orig. US*) to have at one's mercy, to have at a disadvantage. ❑ **have (something) down cold** *v.* [20C+] (*US*) to know something thoroughly.

cold as… *adj. see also under* COLDER THAN… *adj.*

IN PHRASES

❑ **…a polar bear's behind** (*also* **…backside, cold as a dog's nose, …a penguin's behind, …a snowball's arse, …polar-bear shit**) [1920s+] (*US/Aus.*) of temperature, extremely cold; also in fig. use. ❑ **…a grave-digger's arse** (*also* **…well-digger's arse**) [1950s+] (*US*) of temperature, extremely cold. ❑ **…a step-mother's breath** (*also* **cold as a grandmother's/mother-in-law's kiss**) [1920s+] (*Aus./US*) of the climate or of a person's emotions, very cold. ❑ **…a nun's nasty** (*also* **cold as a nun's crotch**) [1960s+] extremely cold, or sexually frigid. ❑ **…a witch's tit** (*also* **cold as a witch's behind, …witch's teat, …witch's titty, …frog's tit**) **1** [1950s+] (*also* **figid as a witch's tit**) extremely cold, temperature wise. **2** [1950s+] completely without emotions. ❑ **…Kelsey's nuts** *see under* KELSEY'S NUTS *n.*

cold-bite *n.* [COLD-BITE *v.*] [1920s+] (*Aus./N.Z.*) one who will lend money, a 'soft touch'.

cold-bite *v.* [COLD *adv.* (2) + BITE *v.* (6); note commercial jargon *cold-call*, for a salesman to approach a potential client without making a prior appointment] [1920s+] (*Aus./N.Z.*) to ask a stranger for money.

cold cock *n.* [COLD-COCK *v.*] [1940s+] (*orig. US*) a knockout blow.

cold-cock *v.* (*also* **cold-caulk**) [SE (*out*) *cold*, unconscious/*knock cold* under KNOCK *v.*] [1910s+] to knock unconscious; thus n. *cold-cocker*; adj. *cold-cocked*, unconscious.

coldcock *adv.* (*also* **cold-cocked**) [COLD-COCK *v.*] [1980s+] (*US*) completely, utterly.

cold deck *n.* [mid-19C+] (*US Und.*) a stacked deck of cards, used by cheats; lit. and fig.; thus *cold-card artist*, a professional card cheat.

cold-deck *v.*[1] (*also* **give the cold deck**) [COLD DECK *n.*; gambling jargon *cold deck*, of a card-sharp, to introduce a prepared deck of cards into the game; thus guaranteeing his success] [late 19C] (*US Und.*) lit. or fig., to cheat, to deceive.

cold-deck *v.*[2] [SE (*out cold*), unconscious/*knock cold* under KNOCK *v.* + DECK *v.*[2] (1)] [20C+] to knock unconscious; occas. to kill.

cold-decker *n.*[1] [COLD-DECK *v.*[1]] [20C+] (*US Und.*) a cheat.

cold-decker *n.*[2] [COLD-DECK *v.*[2]] [20C+] (*US Und.*) a thug, a hoodlum.

cold enough to freeze the balls off a brass monkey *phr.* (*also* **…to freeze a brass monkey, …the arse off a brass monkey, …the ears off…, …nose…, …tail…, to blow the balls off…, …to freeze the tail off a tin possum, …to make a Jew drop his bundle, snappy enough to freeze the plumbing off a brass elephant**) [mid-19C+] (*US/Aus.*) of temperature, extremely cold; also fig. use.

colder than… *adj. see also under* COLD AS… *adj.*

IN PHRASES

❑ **…a nun's snatch** [1950s+] (*US*) extremely cold. ❑ **…a welldigger's butt** [1950s+] (*US*) very cold. ❑ **…a witch's tit** (*also* **colder than a witch's titty**) **1** [1930s+] of weather, very cold. **2** [1960s] of emotions, very unfriendly. **3** [1960s] sexually frigid. ❑ **…Kelsey's nuts** *see* COLD AS KELSEY'S NUTS *under* KELSEY'S NUTS *n.*

cold-eye *n.* (*also* **icy eye**) [late 19C–1900s] a disdainful stare.

cold-eye *v.* [COLD-EYE *n.*] [1970s] (*US*) to ignore, to reject, to disdain.

coldie *n.* [abbr. COLD ONE *n.*[2] (1)] [1950s+] (*Aus.*) a can or bottle of cold beer.

cold meat *n.* [the first use of the term appears to be that of Grose himself, used as its definition: 'A dead wife is the best *cold meat* in a man's house.' (1796); note WW1 milit. *cold meat ticket*, an identity disc] **1** [late 18C+] (*also* **cold clay, …mutton**) a corpse; thus *cold meat box*, a coffin; *cold meat train*, a funeral procession or a train that serves a cemetery; *cold meat job* (police jargon), any case that involves a corpse; occas. as v. *cold-meat*, to kill. **2** [1910s] one who has been knocked unconscious.

IN COMPOUNDS

❑ **cold meat box** *n.* [mid-19C+] a coffin. ❑ **cold meat cart** *n.* [early 19C+] (*US*) a hearse. ❑ **cold meat party** *n.* [20C+] (*US black*) a funeral, a wake. ❑ **cold meat wagon** *n.* [1940s] a hearse.

cold one *n.*[1] [COLD *adj.* (6)/SE *cold cash*] [1900s] (*US*) $1.

cold one *n.*[2] (*also* **cold pup**) [orig. a conscious euph. for a cold beer, used during Prohibition (1920–33) when it was better not to mention alcohol in any form] [1910s+] (*orig. US*) **1** a bottle (latterly can) of beer. **2** a cold drink.

cold one *n.*[3] [1960s] (*US prison*) an empty container for money, e.g. a safe, a wallet.

cold potato *n.*[1] [late 19C–1940s] (*US*) someone or something judged to be worthless, insignificant or boring.

cold potato *n.*[2] [rhy. sl.; note Cockney pron. 'pertater'] [1950s+] a waiter (cf. HOT POTATO *n.*[2]).

coldrifed *adj.* [dial. *coldrife*, indifferent, spiritless; ult. SE *cold*] [1940s+] (*Irish*) nervous, hesitant, unwilling to take a risk.

cold storage *n.*[1] [20C+] **1** death; thus also a grave or cemetery. **2** a prison.

cold storage *n.*[2] [play on COOL *adj.*] [1910s] (*Aus.*) cheek, impudence.

cold turkey *n.* [? the image of the pallid flesh of a cold, dead, plucked turkey, and a withdrawing addict; *cold turkey* is the 'word of 1922' in David K. Barnhart and Allan A. Metcalf *America in So Many Words* (1999)] [1920s+] (*orig. US drugs*) **1** sudden and total withdrawal from heroin addiction without tapering off or using any assistance from medication; also ext. to other drugs. **2** the fundamental level, the basic situation. **3** an easy target, a vulnerable person.

cold turkey *adj.* [SE/COLD TURKEY *n.* (1)] [1930s–60s] (*US*) **1** dead. **2** emotionless. **3** honest, candid.

cold turkey *v.* [COLD TURKEY *n.* (1)] [1920s+] to subject oneself or another addict (usu. a heroin user) to COLD TURKEY *n.* (1).

cold turkey *adv.* [COLD TURKEY *n.* (1)] **1** [1910s+] (*also* **cold quack**) (*US*) directly, openly, candidly, without any warning. **2** [1920s–50s] (*US*) caught in the act, obviously guilty, without any excuse. **3** [1950s+] (*drugs*) of withdrawal, without any form of medication to modify the pains. **4** [1960s] without any alcohol or narcotics, although not intending withdrawal. **5** [1990s+] in fig. use, denying oneself.

IN PHRASES

❑ **talk cold turkey** *v.* [ext. of SE colloq. phr. *talk turkey*] [1930s+] (*orig. US*) to speak frankly and without reserve, to talk hard facts, to get down to business.

cole *n.* (*also* **cole**) [SE *coal*, the staple, as a heat-provider, of everyday life, as is money. *Cole* had faded by 19C but *post the cole* lasted, increasingly in metaphorical use, until late 19C. Also ? link to SE *cole*, brassica, an earlier play on CABBAGE *n.*[2] (3a)] **1** [late 16C–19C] (*UK Und.*) money. **2** [1930s] a penny.

IN PHRASES

❑ **hard cole** *n.* [mid-19C] (*US Und.*) cash (silver or gold), as opposed to banknotes. ❑ **post the cole** *v.* [late 18C–19C] to pay down money. ❑ **smuggle the cole** *v.* (*also* **smuggle the coal**) [late 17C] to pretend that one has no money when it is time to pay a bill at an inn or tavern. ❑ **tip the cole** *v.* [mid-17C–mid-19C] to pay (a bill).

colfabias *n.* [pig Lat.; coined at Trinity College, Dublin] [mid-19C] a privy.

coli *n. see* COLLIE *n.*

coliander (seed) *n.* [SE *coliander*, the earliest sp. (c.1000) of coriander, which is found as a seed. Seeds provide a form of growth, necessary for life; thus fig. synon. with money] [late 17C–mid-19C] (*UK Und.*) money (cf. CORIANDER (SEED) *n.*).

'colic *n.* [abbr.] [1970s+] (*UK black*) an alcoholic; a drunkard.

colinderies *n.* [abbr.] [late 19C] (*UK society*) the *Col*onial and *Ind*ian Exhibition, South Kensington, London, held in 1886 and visited by more than two million people.

Colisseum curtains *n.* [2000s] (*S.Afr. gay*) a larger than average foreskin.

coll *n.* [CULL *n.*[1] (2)] [mid-17C–early 18C] **1** a dupe, a silly fellow. **2** a man, a fellow, a chap; thus *rum coll*, the king.

collar *n.* [plays on SE *collar*] **1** visual resemblance. (**a**) [early 16C–mid-17C] the hangman's noose. (**b**) [20C+] the foam on a glass of beer. (**c**) [1950s+] (*drugs*) in a makeshift syringe, the strip of paper wrapped around a dropper to ensure a tight fit with the needle. **2** [late 19C–1900s; 1960s+] legitimate work; i.e. that in which one wears a SE *collar*. **3** (*US*) from COLLAR *v.* (**a**) [late 19C] in fig. use of sense 3b, any kind of restraint, e.g. marriage. (**b**) [late 19C+] an arrest; thus phr. *give the collar*. (**c**) [late 19C+] a police officer. (**d**) [1970s+] the person who has been arrested.

IN COMPOUNDS

❑ **collar day** *n.* [late 18C–early 19C] the day of execution.

IN PHRASES

❑ **get one's collar felt** *v.* (*also* **have one's collar felt**) [1940s+] (*UK Und./police*) to be arrested. ❑ **in collar** [mid-19C–1900s] employed. ❑ **put the collar on** *v.* (*also* **put a collar on**) [mid-19C] (*US*) to arrest. ❑ **soft collar** *n.* [1900s–20s] (*Aus.*) an easy job.

SE in slang uses

IN COMPOUNDS

❑ **collar and elbow** *adj.* (*also* **collar and shoulder**) [orig. hobo jargon *collar and shoulder style*, a meal where the food is placed on the table and everyone, sitting shoulder to shoulder, grabs what he or she can from the platters. The idea of struggling for one's share may link the phr. to *collar and elbow*, a style of wrestling practised in Devon and Cornwall] [1920s–30s] (*US*) family style, informal, esp. of a restaurant or café. ❑ **collar and hames** *n.* [1910s] (*US prison*) a collar and tie. ❑ **collar and tie** *n.* [her adoption of men's clothing] [1940s+] a masculine lesbian. ❑ **collar work** *n.* [the image of a horse pulling against its collar] [late 19C] hard, strenuous work.

IN PHRASES

❑ **fill one's collar** *v.* [late 19C] (*US*) to perform adequately, to come up to expectations. ❑ **get in the collar** *v.* [20C+] (*US*) to start working, to work hard. ❑ **go up against the collar** *v.* [19C+] (*US*) to work hard, esp. in a difficult or inconvenient situation. ❑ **have a collar on** *v.* [working-people rarely wore collars on an everyday basis] [late 19C–1900s] to put on airs. ❑ **keep up to the collar** *v.* **1** [mid–late 19C] to stay hard at work, or to make someone else stay hard at work. **2** [1910s–20s] to be overwhelmed by one's work. ❑ **put to the pin of the collar** *v.* [saddlery imagery] [late 19C+] (*20C+ use is Irish*) to put in very great difficulties, to be stretched to the limit.

collar *v.* [SE *collar*, to get hold of] **1** [mid-17C+] to arrest. **2** [early 18C+] to grab, to appropriate. **3** [mid–late 19C] (*orig. UK Und.*) to catch out. **4** [mid-19C+] (*orig. UK Und.*) to understand, to work out. **5** [late 19C] in fig. use, to delight, to overwhelm. **6** [late 19C–1900s] to receive in punishment. **7** [1900s–40s] (*orig. US black*) to get hold of, to obtain. **8** [1910s] (*US*) to master, to deal with.

IN PHRASES

❑ **collar a duster up the ladder** *v.* [1930s–40s] (*US black*) to climb the stairs. ❑ **collar a nod** *v. see under* NOD *n.*[1]. ❑ **collar the jive** *v. see under* JIVE *n.*[1].

collar (and cuff) *n.* [rhy. sl. = PUFF *n.* (3a)] [1930s+] a homosexual.

collar-and-cuffs *adj. see* CUFFS AND COLLAR *under* CUFF *n.*[2].

collar and tie *n.* [rhy. sl.] [1950s+] a lie.

collard greens *n. see* TURNIP GREENS *under* TURNIP *n.*

collared on *adj.* [COLLAR *v.* (2)] [mid-19C–1910s] (*Aus.*) obsessively in love with.

collared up *adj.* [one is unable to remove one's collar, a sign of relaxation] [mid-19C] kept hard at work, closely involved with one's business.

collect *v.* (*Aus.*) **1** [1910s+] to receive one's due deserts. **2** [1960s] to arrest. **3** [1960s+] to be hit by, to collide with, usu. of a car. **4** [1990s+] to be killed.

collector *n.* (*also* **collector of the highways**) [he collects RENT *n.*] [mid-18C–19C] a highwayman.

collect rent *v.* [RENT COLLECTOR *under* RENT *n.*] [late 18C–early 19C] to be a highwayman.

colleen bawn *n.* [rhy. sl. = HORN *n.*[2] (1b); ult. the anglicized version of Irish *cailín bán*, the white or fair woman; Colleen Bawn was the heroine of the opera 'The Lily of Killarney' (Benedict/Oxenford & Dion Boucicault), first produced Feb. 1862 at the Royal English Opera, Covent Garden, London] [mid-19C+] an erection.

college *n.* [ironic uses of SE, the overall ref. is to prison as a 'university of crime'; note mid-17C Oxbridge use *college*, a public house or tavern with a sign of a green garland or painted hoop; WW1 Aus. milit. *college*, 39 General Hospital and No. 2 Stationery

Hospital, primarily treating VD] **1** [early 17C] a brothel. **2** [late 17C–early 19C] (*UK Und.*) Newgate prison. **3** [18C+] (*UK Und.*) any prison; thus [early 18C–mid-19C] *go to college*, to go to prison. **4** [late 18C–mid-19C] (*UK Und.*) King's (or Queen's) Bench or Fleet prison. **5** [mid-19C+] (*US Und.*) a state prison, a penitentiary. **6** [late 19C–1900s] (*UK Und.*) the workhouse.

(IN COMPOUNDS)

❑ **college boy** *n.* [1960s] (*US prison*) an inmate. ❑ **college chum** *n.* [CHUM *n.* (1)] [19C] a prisoner. ❑ **college cove** *n.* [COVE *n.* (1)] [early 19C] (*UK Und.*) the turnkey of Newgate prison.

SE in slang uses

(IN COMPOUNDS)

❑ **college joe** *n.* see *JOE COLLEGE under* JOE *n.*[1]. ❑ **college fuck** *n.* see PRINCETON RUB *n.* ❑ **college try** *n.* [the myth of 'college spirit'] [1910s+] (*US*) a plucky effort, esp. against heavy odds; usu. in phr. *(let's) give it the old college try*. ❑ **college widow** *n.* [coined by the US satirist George Ade] [late 19C–1940s] (*US*) an unmarried woman, in some way associated with a given college, whose advancing age does not deter her from associating with successive generations of students.

(IN PHRASES)

❑ **college of hard knocks** *n.* see SCHOOL OF HARD KNOCKS *n.*

College Street solicitor *n.* [College Street, Sydney, a gay centre since the mid-19C. The street runs into Queen's Square, itself frequented by lawyers visiting the nearby law courts; thus giving puns on QUEEN *n.* (2) and SE *solicitor*] [1940s–60s] (*Aus.*) a male prostitute.

collegian *n.* [COLLEGE *n.* (3)] [mid-17C+] a prisoner.

collegiate *n.* [COLLEGE *n.* (3); ironic use of SE] **1** [mid-17C–early 19C] a prisoner. **2** [late 17C–early 19C] a shopkeeper at the Royal Exchange or Newgate prisons.

collegiate fucking *n.* [SE *collegiate* + FUCKING *n.* (1); for ety. *see* PRINCETON RUB *n.*] [20C+] (*gay*) body-to-body rubbing.

collie *n.* (*also* **callie, coli, colly, collyweed**) [? joc. abbr. SE *broccoli*/BROCCOLI *n.*] **1** [1970s+] (*W.I., Jam.*) marijuana; thus *collie-man*, a marijuana seller. **2** *see* CAULI *n.*

collie knox *n.* [rhy. sl. = POX *n.*[1] (3)] [1960s+] venereal disease.

collies *n.* [abbr. COLLYWOBBLES *n.* (1), i.e. the effects of the drug on one's stomach, or those that accompany withdrawal sickness] [1990s+] (*drugs*) drugs, esp. heroin.

colli-mollie *n.* *see* COLLY-MOLLY *n.*

Collins Street farmer *n.* (*also* **Collins Street grazier**) [*Collins Street*, the financial and social centre of Melbourne; note (*US agricultural*) *suitcase farmer*, 'a term used of farmers on the Great Plains who put in a crop of wheat in the fall and come back to harvest it the next summer, after having spent the winter in their permanent homes elsewhere' (R. Diller, *Farm Ownership, Tenancy, & Land Use* (1941); similarly *sidewalk farmer*, those who live in urban areas and drive to the country to care for their crops and livestock] [1970s+] (*Aus.*) a businessman who owns or shares a farm from which he takes annual profits but rarely visits.

Collins Street squatter *n.* [*Collins Street*, the centre of Melbourne + SAusE *squatter*, a grazier] [1960s] (*Aus.*) a man, usu. a youth, who frequents bars, cafés etc for no other reason than meeting his friends, gossiping and wasting time.

colly *n.* *see* COLLIE *n.*

colly *v.* [? COLLAR *v.* (4) or Fr. *comprendre*, to understand] [1920s–40s] (*US black*) to understand, to comprehend.

colly-molly *n.* (*also* **colli-mollie**) [play on SE] [17C] melancholy.

collyweed *n.* *see* COLLIE *n.*

collywobbles *n.* [SE *colic* + *wobble*] **1** [early 19C+] feelings of tension, fear or sickness, usu. seen as stemming from the stomach. **2** [mid-19C] the stomach. **3** [1980s] diarrhoea.

colney (hatch) *n.* [rhy. sl.; ult. *Colney Hatch* psychiatric hospital] [1930s–70s] a match.

Colombian *n.* (*also* **Colom, Colombo, Columbian**) [the mis-sp. is almost as common as the correct one] [1970s+] (*drugs*) marijuana from Colombia; also ext. as *Colombian green*, *Colombian red*, etc.

(IN COMPOUNDS)

❑ **Colombian necktie** *n.* (*also* **necktie, Sicilian necktie**) [orig. in the drug wars of Colombia] [1980s+] a method of killing whereby the throat is cut and the tongue pulled through the resulting wound; such embellishment is usu. meted out to one who has betrayed the killer or his boss.

colon choker *n.* (*also* **colon commando, ...cowboy, ...crusader**) [SE *colon*, the large intestine, which ends in the rectum] [1990s+] a male homosexual.

Colonel Custer *n.* [rhy.sl.; ult. US soldier George A *Custer* (1839–76)] [1980s] (*Aus.*) **1** a muster. **2** a duster.

colonel of the regiment *n.* (*also* **colonel of horse**) [not necessarily a soldier] [mid-17C–early 18C] one who 'drinks in his boots and jingling spurs'.

Colonel Prescott *n.* *see* CHARLIE PRESCOTT *n.*

Colonel Sanders *n.* [the name, quite poss. libellous, puns on the Colonel's internationally franchised product, *KFC*] [1970s+] (*US gay*) an older male homosexual with a preference for young boys, i.e. CHICKEN *n.* (4d).

colonial *adj.*

SE in slang uses

(IN COMPOUNDS)

❑ **colonial adjective** *n.* [i.e. the 'great Australian adjective'] [1900s] (*N.Z.*) a euph. for BLOODY *adj.* ❑ **colonial duck** *n.* (*also* **colonial goose**) [fig. use of *colonial* to mean second-rate, substitute] [late 19C+] (*Aus.*) a boned roast shoulder (*duck*) or leg (*goose*) of mutton stuffed with sage and onions. ❑ **colonial livery** *n.* [the image of Aus. as a violent country] [19C] (*Aus.*) a bloody nose and a black eye. ❑ **colonial puck** *n.* [rhy. sl. = FUCK *n.* (1a)] [1940s] (*US*) sexual intercourse. ❑ **colonial Robert** *n.* [play on proper name *Bob*/BOB *n.*[3] (2)] [late 19C–1910s] (*Aus./N.Z.*) one shilling.

color *n.*

(IN PHRASES)

❑ **get one's color up** *v.* [1960s] (*US black*) to lose one's temper.

color *v.* [imagery of a children's colouring book] [1960s+] (*US*) to see as, to present as.

colora *n.* [SE *coloured* + fem. sfx *-a*] [1960s+] (*S.Afr. gay*) a mixed-race gay man.

Colorado Kool-Aid *n.* [Coors is brewed in Colorado + the soft-drink mix Kool-Aid] [1970s+] (*US*) Coors beer.

Colorado mockingbird *n.* [the noise of its braying, the antithesis of a mellifluous bird] [20C+] (*US*) a donkey, an ass.

colored people's time *n.* (*also* **colored folks time, c.p.t., c.p.time**) [racist stereotyping] [1930s–60s] (*US black*) unpunctuality.

color guard *n.* [1970s+] (*US black*) a gaudy, unfashionable dresser.

color me gone *phr.* [1980s+] (*US campus*) a phrase indicating one does not wish to be involved or present.

colors *n.* *see* COLOURS *n.*

color-struck *adj.* (*US black*) [1940s+] **1** of a black person, conceited on the grounds of one's light skin colour. **2** of a black person, preferring light-skinned to dark-skinned black people.

colouring *n.* [20C+] (*Irish*) milk as poured into tea.

colours *n.* (*also* **colors**) **1** [mid-19C] (*US*) the colours, signified by a handkerchief, under which rival boxers fight. **2** [1960s+] of 'outlaw' motorcyclists, one's club emblem. Orig. used for the first such outlaws, the Hell's Angels, consisting of an embroidered patch of a winged skull wearing a motorcycle helmet, the name Hell's Angels, the name of the chapter (town etc) and the letters MC (motorcycle club); thus (*N.Z.*) *run for one's colours*, to serve as a probationary member of the club. **3** [1970s+] (*US*) the insignia, e.g. a coloured bandana/headscarf/beads sported by members of the street gangs of Los Angeles, New York etc. **4** [1990s+] (*US prison*) in prison, a gang tattoo.

IN PHRASES

❑ **devil's colours** *n. see under* DEVIL *n.*

colour the meerschaum *v.* [the gradual darkening of the white-clay bowl of a *meerschaum* pipe over years of use] [late 19C] to get a red nose through excessive drinking.

colquarron *n.* (*also* **coloquaron**) [? Fr. *col*, neck + QUARROM *n.*] [late 17C–mid-19C] (*UK Und.*) the neck.

colt *n.*[1] (*also* **coltman**) **1** [17C–mid-19C] (*UK Und.*) anyone, usu. an inn-keeper, who provides and stables horses for a highwayman. **2** [17C–mid-19C] a young man who has just been initiated into crime. **3** [late 17C+] a new apprentice, modern use is usu. in sporting context. **4** [18C] a young girl sold into prostitution. **5** [late 18C–mid-19C] one who serves on a jury for the first time. **6** [1900s–40s] (*US black*) a young man.

SE in slang uses

IN PHRASES

❑ **have a colt's tooth** *v.* [SE *colt's tooth*, the first set of a horse's teeth] [late 14C–19C] to have youthful desires that belie one's real age; thus adj. *coltish*.

colt *n.*[2] [naut. jargon *colt*, a piece of knotted rope, used as a weapon] [mid-19C] a piece of rope with something heavy fastened to the end, used as a weapon or instrument of punishment.

colt *v.*[1] [COLT *n.*[1] (5)] [mid-19C] to 'fine' a first-time server on a jury a sum which is spent on drink for his colleagues; also in other contexts.

colt *v.*[2] [COLT *n.*[2]] [mid–late 19C] to beat with a rope's end.

colting *n.* [COLT *n.*[2]] [mid–late 19C] a thrashing.

colt veal *n.* ['more like the flesh of a colt than that of a calf' (Grose 1785)] [late 17C–mid-19C] very red, coarse-grained veal.

columbered *adj.* [ety. unknown; the *OED* has only this cite and states 'derivation and meaning uncertain'] [early 17C] drunk.

Columbian *n. see* COLOMBIAN *n.*

Columbine *n.* [literary euph. *Columbine*, a character in Italian theatrical tradition *commedia dell'arte*, thence trad. pantomime, the mistress of Harlequin; the original *columbine*, a flower with 'hollow horns' is cited by Williams as a 16C image of cuckoldry] [late 19C] a prostitute.

Columbus black *n.* [marijuana supposedly grown in Columbus, Ohio] [1980s+] (*drugs*) marijuana.

com *n.* [abbr.] **1** [mid-19C+] a *com*mission (in a non-pecuniary sense). **2** [late 19C–1900s] a *com*mercial traveller. **3** [late 19C+] a *com*mission (in a pecuniary sense). **4** [1920s+] (*orig. Aus.*) a *com*munist. **5** [1920s+] (*US Und.*) (*also* **comb**) the *comb*ination of a safe. **6** [1990s+] (*US campus*) *com*munication(s). **7** *see* COMBIE *n.*

coma'd *adj.* (*also* **in a coma**) [1990s+] passed out from an excess of alcohol.

comanche *n.* [proper name *Comanche*; thus Native American use of SE colloq. *warpaint*] [1960s–70s] (*gay*) a man who uses cosmetics.

comate *n. see* MATE *n.* (1).

comatose *adj.* [1980s+] (*US campus*) drunk.

comb *n.*[1] **1** [late 16C] (*UK Und.*) a hooked pole used to extract goods from shop windows. **2** [1930s–50s] (*UK prison*) a carpenter's file.

comb *n.*[2] *see* COM *n.* (5).

comb *v.* [SE *run a fine tooth comb over*] [1940s–50s] to interrogate.

SE in slang uses

IN PHRASES

❑ **comb down** *v.* [late 19C+] (*Aus.*) to thrash, to beat. ❑ **comb out** *see* separate entries. ❑ **comb someone's hair** *v.* (*also* **comb someone's head, ...noddle, ...wool**) **1** [late 16C–19C] to thrash, to beat severely; sometimes ext. by 'with a joint/three-legged stool'. **2** [late 18C–1920s] to tell off, to scold, to reprimand. **3** [1930s–40s] (*US*) to pistol-whip. ❑ **comb the cat** *v. see under* CAT *n.*[3].

comb and brush *n.* [rhy. sl. = LUSH *n.*[1] (1)] [late 19C] a drink.

comb and brush *v.* [COMB AND BRUSH *n.*] [late 19C] to treat to a drink.

combat zone *n.* [1970s+] (*US*) that part of the inner city where racial, social, economic and other tensions are at their height; orig. use in Boston, Mass.

comb-cut *adj.* [COMB-CUT v.] [mid-19C–1900s] disgraced, socially or professionally embarrassed.

comb-cut *v.* (*also* **cut someone's comb**) [cockfighting imagery] [late 16C–19C] to be disgraced.

comber *n.* [COMB *n.*[1] (1)] [late 16C] (*UK Und.*) a thief who operates a hooked pole to extract goods from shop windows.

combie *n.* (*also* **com**) [abbr.] [late 19C+] the all-in-one underwear known as *comb*inations.

combination *n.* [1930s–50s] (*US tramp*) a vegetable stew.

combing law *n.* [COMB *n.*[1] (1) + LAW *n.* (1)] [late 16C] (*UK Und.*) the stealing of goods from shops by using a hooked pole to drag them from windows.

combo *n.*[1] (*also* **kombo**) [abbr. SE *combination* + -O *sfx* (3)] **1** [late 19C+] (*Aus.*) (*also* **comboman**) a white man who cohabits with or marries an Aborigine woman; thus *go combo*, to live with an Aborigine woman; thus *combo-land*, used both for the Northern Territory and for any area where such cohabitation is common. **2** [1910s] a term of address to an Aborigine.

combo *n.*[2] [abbr. SE *combination* + -O *sfx* (6)] **1** [1920s+] a partnership, esp. a group of musicians. **2** [1920s+] (*UK/US Und.*) a combination lock (on a safe). **3** [1920s+] (*US*) any form of combination, whether of people, things, sandwich ingredients, wagers etc. **4** [1950s] a relationship. **5** [1980s+] (*US campus*) a bisexual person.

combobbolate *v. see* CONBOBBOLATE *v.*

combolo *n.* [dial. *combolo*, a companion; ult. Sp. *compañero*, friend or ? *combolo*, an African song-dance] [1940s+] (*W.I.*) **1** an old, trusted machete. **2** a sexual partner.

comboozelated *adj.* [DISCOMBOBULATE V. + BOOZE *n.* (1) + sfx -*ated*] [1970s+] (*US campus*) drunk.

comb-out *n.* [COMB OUT *v.*] [1940s] a sorting-out.

comb out *v.* [late 19C+] to sort out, to put in order.

combs *n.* [abbr.] [late 19C+] *comb*inations, i.e. a woman's or child's garment consisting of combined chemise or undershirt and drawers.

combsome *n.* [1970s] (*W.I./Rasta*) a Rastafarian man who combs his dreadlocks and beard.

come *n.* [COME *v.*[1]] **1** [mid-17C+] an orgasm. **2** [1920s+] semen; thus *comey*, covered in semen. **3** [1940s+] vaginal secretions. **4** [1980s+] energy, spirit; esp. in phr. *young, dumb and full of come*.

IN COMPOUNDS

❑ **come...** *see also under* CUM *n.* ❑ **come-bucket** *n.* (*also* **cum-bucket**) [lit. 'a bucket of ejaculate'] [1970s+] (*US*) a repellent person. ❑ **come-dump** *n.* [1960s] (*US*) a promiscuous woman. ❑ **come-freak** *n.* [-FREAK *sfx*] **1** [1950s+] anyone who is obsessed with physical sex and the delights thereof. **2** [1960s] (*US gay*) a fellator. ❑ **come-juice** *n.* [1990s+] **1** semen. **2** vaginal juices when orgasming. ❑ **come-licking** *adj.* [1970s] (*orig. US*) vile, disgusting. ❑ **come-loving** *adj.* [1950s–70s] (*US black*) obsessed with sex. ❑ **come-pot** *n.* [1940s] a general term of abuse. ❑ **come-stain** *n.* (*also* **cum stain**) [lit. a semen stain] [1990s+] (*US*) a general derog. term.

come *v.*[1] [abbr. SE *cometo a climax*; Williams suggests link to SE *come*, of butter, to form in the churn, and thus a pun on BUTTER *n.*[1] (1)] [late 16C+] to achieve orgasm; of a man to ejaculate.

IN PHRASES

❑ **come a bucket** *v.* [1970s] of a man, to ejaculate copiously. ❑ **come a river** *v.* [1970s] (*US*) of a woman, to experience a very intense orgasm or multiple orgasms. ❑ **come in one's pants** *v.* (*also* **come in one's drawers**) [1960s+] to behave in an exaggerated, over-excited manner; the image is of extremely premature ejaculation. ❑ **come into one's own** *v.* [pun on SE] [1980s+] to masturbate. ❑ **come like a parolee at**

the ho shack *v.* [pun on SE *come*; the image is of a long-term prisoner having the first sex of his freedom] [1970s] (*US black*) to move very fast. ❑ **come off** *v.* [17C; mid-20C+] to experience orgasm. ❑ **come one's cocoa** *v.* **1** [1960s+] to ejaculate. **2** [1970s+] (*UK police/Und.*) to inform or to confess one's crimes. ❑ **come one's fat** *v.* [1970s+] **1** to ejaculate. **2** of a suspect, to confess. ❑ **come one's guts** *v. see under* GUT *n.* ❑ **come one's lot** *v.* [1970s+] **1** to ejaculate. **2** of a suspect, to confess. ❑ **come one's mutton** *v. see under* MUTTON *n.* ❑ **come one's turkey** *v. see under* TURKEY *n.*[1].

SE in slang uses

IN COMPOUNDS

❑ **come-around** *n.* [1990s+] (*W.I.*) an unwanted hanger-on. ❑ **come-in** *n. see* COME-ON *n.* (7).

IN PHRASES

❑ **come...** *v.* **1** *see also* separate entries. **2** *see also under* relevant n. or adj. ❑ **come about** *v.* [late 19C] said by men of women, to have sexual intercourse. ❑ **come all over** *v.* [20C+] (*Aus.*) to thrash, to defeat completely. ❑ **come aloft** *v.* [late 16C–mid-17C] to have an erection. ❑ **come apart** *v. see* FALL APART *under* FALL *v.*[1]. ❑ **come from Liquorpond Street** *v.* [early 19C–1900s] to be drunk. ❑ **come from Tripoli** *v.* [? the troupes of North African dancers who were then popular in London or f. a play on SE *trip*, to tumble] [mid–late 19C] to be a lively, energetic performer, esp. acrobatically. ❑ **come-fuck-me's** *n.* [FUCK *v.* (1)] [1960s+] (*US gay*) very tight trousers. ❑ **come home by rail** *v.* [1930s+] (*Aus.*) to be so drunk that one can only proceed by hanging onto things. ❑ **come home by Spillsbury** *v.* [late 17C–early 18C] to tumble, to fall over, to have a 'spill'; to fail. ❑ **come home by the villages** *v.* [18C] to be reeling drunk. ❑ **come home with your knickers torn and say you found the money** *v. see under* KNICKERS *n.* ❑ **come in Berlin** [? a radio call-sign] [1970s] (*US campus*) an exhortation to pay attention, a greeting. ❑ **come in like Flynn** *v.* [1990s+] (*Aus.*) to 'fall for', to 'swallow' a story. ❑ **come-love tea** *n.* [the phr. *come, love* seen as a mild suggestion] [1930s+] (*Aus.*) weak tea. ❑ **come short home** *v.* [17C] to be imprisoned. ❑ **come-to-bed eyes** *n.* [1920s+] eyes (of either sex) that convey infinite, if not always delivered, sexual promise. ❑ **come together** *v.* [1970s] (*US black*) to dress in high fashion. ❑ **come-to-heaven collar** *n.* [the wings of the collar presumably resemble those of an angel] [20C+] (*US*) a wing collar. ❑ **come to light** *v.* [1910s+] (*Aus.*) to produce, to deliver, esp. money. ❑ **come-too-soon** *n.* [? *too soon* for the parents to get married] [1940s–70s] (*US*) an illegitimate child. ❑ **come to the heath** *v.* [? pun on TIP *n.*[2]/Tiptree Heath, in Essex] [early 19C] to pay out or give money. ❑ **come to the wrong shop** *v. see under* SHOP *n.*[1]. ❑ **come unglued** *v.* [1940s+] to become mentally and emotionally unstable. ❑ **come unscrewed** *v. see under* SCREW *v.* ❑ **come with it** *v.* [1990s+] **1** (*US black/prison*) to dare someone to do something. **2** (*US campus*) to try one's hardest.

come *v.*[2] [one 'comes' forth with the loan] [late 17C–1900s] (*UK Und.*) to lend (money).

IN PHRASES

❑ **come it** *v.* [late 17C–early 19C] to lend money.

come *v.*[3] [abbr. SE *come over*, to become] [late 18C+] to practise some form of dodge, to pose or act in a certain way, e.g. *come the Yorkshire, come the religious dodge*.

IN PHRASES

❑ **come...** *v. see also under* relevant n. or adj. ❑ **come a crash** *v.* [1910s] (*Aus.*) to encounter difficulties. ❑ **come a Kerensky** *v.* [A.F. Kerensky (1881–1970), prime minister of the second Russian provisional govt., deposed in the Bolshevik Revolution of Oct. 1917] [1910s] (*Aus.*) to suffer a humiliation. ❑ **come correct** *v.* [1990s+] (*US black*) to do something the way it should be done. ❑ **come countryman over** *v.* [the gullibility of the country-dweller] [early 19C] to wheedle, to cajole, to trick. ❑ **come good** *v.* [1950s+] (*orig. Aus./N.Z.*) **1** of things, to turn out well. **2** of people, to prove themselves (esp. after an unpromising start), to 'come up trumps'. ❑ **come half-larks with** *v. see under* LARK *n.*[3]. ❑ **come Harry over** *v.* [mid-19C] (*UK Und.*) to cheat. ❑ **come Quaker on** *v.* [1900s] (*US*) to defame. ❑ **come the...** *v. see* separate entries. ❑ **come Vicksburg over** *v.* [GAT: '5 gamblers had been lynched in Vicksburg, Miss. in 1835; reported in *Niles' Weekly Register*, July 25, August 1, August 8'] [mid-19C] (*US*) to break up someone's living quarters.

come *prep.* [1990s+] in (a certain amount of time).

come a clover *v.* [rhy. sl.] [1910s–20s] to fall or trip over.

come across *v.* **1** [late 19C+] (*also* **come up**) to hand something over; to pay up money, esp. reluctantly. **2** [20C+] to acquiesce, to do what is wanted. **3** [1910s+] to deliver. **4** [1920s+] to surrender sexually. **5** [1920s+] to confess (a crime).

come again *v.* [20C+] to repeat oneself; to redo in an improved manner.

come again! *excl.* (*also* **come?**) **1** [20C+] a general phr. indicating either that one has failed to hear a speaker or finds it hard to believe the statement, 'please repeat yourself', 'could you say that again?', 'you must be joking'. **2** [1980s+] (*W.I./UK black teen*) a call to the disc jockey to replay a piece of music.

come-along *n.* **1** [late 19C+] in pl., handcuffs. **2** [1920s–40s] (*US Und.*) (*also* **pullers**) a tool used to pull the lock out of a safe. **3** [1930s] (*US*) a 'hostess' employed by a nightclub to persuade customers to part with their money.

IN PHRASES

❑ **pull the come-along** *v.* [1910s] (*US Und.*) to be arrested.

come at *v.* [20C+] (*Aus./N.Z.*) to undertake, to take on, to get up to, to 'try on'.

comeback *n.*[1] [late 19C+] (*orig. US*) **1** a verbal or other rejoinder. **2** repercussions, results; retaliation; a complaint. **3** a monetary payment.

comeback *n.*[2] [1980s+] (*drugs*) benzocaine and mannitol, chemicals used in the manufacture of crack cocaine.

come back *v.* [COMEBACK *n.*[1]] [late 19C+] to give a verbal rejoinder.

come-by-chance child *n. see* CHANCE CHILD *n.*

come-down *n.* [SE *come down*/COME DOWN *v.*[3]] **1** [mid–late 19C] a fall from grace, a humiliating decline in one's material circumstances [SE in 20C+]. **2** [1950s–70s] (*US black*) a bad situation, esp. an embarrassing one. **3** [1960s+] (*drugs*) the after-effects of drug use, or any highly emotional or stressful situation [not necessarily excessively unpleasant and not spec. applied to addictive drugs]. **4** [1960s+] (*drugs*) withdrawal from drug use [particularly unpleasant and refers to addiction].

come down *v.*[1] [early 18C–1910s] to give or lend money.

IN PHRASES

❑ **come down with** *v.* [early 18C–19C] to hand over money; usu. extended as *come down with the needful/dust/pelf* etc.

come down *v.*[2] **1** [1930s+] to become permanent or established. **2** [1960s] (*US prison*) to go to prison. **3** [1960s+] (*orig. US black*) to occur, to turn out, to develop, to transpire, to happen. **4** [1960s+] (*US*) to talk or behave; usu. in comb., e.g. *she comes down all crazy*.

IN PHRASES

❑ **come down fonky** *v.* [FONKY *adj.*[2]] [1980s+] to belittle, to insult, to talk to severely, to criticize harshly.

SE in slang uses

IN PHRASES

❑ **come down front** *v.* [image of a congregant approaching the front of the church to confess their sins] [1950s–60s] (*US black*) to confess, to tell the truth, to speak openly; usu. as imper. *come down front!* ❑ **come down hard** *v.* [1930s+] (*orig. US black*) to attack, whether physically or verbally. ❑ **come down on** *see* separate entry. ❑ **come down stair-/curtain-rods** *v. see under* STAIR *n.* ❑ **come down the pike** *v. see under* PIKE *n.*[2]. ❑ **come down with the derbies** *v. see under* DARBY *n.*[1].

come down *v.*[3] [one has been HIGH *adj.*[1] (2)] [1940s+] (*drugs*) **1** to experience the ending of a drug's effects (such an experience is often emotionally distressing, although the intoxication may have been pleasurable). **2** in non-drug use, to calm down; to experience the end of an emotional 'high'. **3** to withdraw from habitual narcotic use.

come down *v.*[4] *see* GO DOWN *v.* (8).

come down on *v.* **1** [late 19C+] (*orig. US black*) to belittle, to insult, to talk to severely, to criticize harshly. **2** [late 19C+] to put under pressure. **3** [1940s+] (*orig. US black*) to assault; to harass. **4** [1960s+] (*drugs*) of the pains of withdrawal symptoms, and thus the demands of drug-need, to intensify. **5** [1970s] to move one emotionally in a positive manner. **6** [1990s+] to pressurize emotionally, to depress.

IN PHRASES

❑ **come down on someone like a ton of bricks** *v.* (*also* **...like a thousand of brick**) [mid-19C+] to unleash the full force of one's anger or aggression on someone.

comedy *n.* [1910s–50s] (*US*) irrelevant, impertinent, cheeky talk.

IN PHRASES

❑ **cut the comedy** *v.* [1910s+] to stop doing something considered irritating or foolish; esp. as imper.

come it *v.*[1] **1** [late 18C+] to act, to perform, to behave in a certain manner, usu. constr. with an adv. **2** [early–mid-19C] to show off, to boast. **3** [early 19C+] to act aggressively, often with no grounds for so doing. **4** [mid-19C] to impress as a lover. **5** [mid-19C–1910s] to deceive another for one's own benefit, esp. to avoid an unpleasant task. **6** [1900s–20s] to be cheeky.

IN PHRASES

❑ **come it over** *v.* (*also* **come it on**) [mid-19C+] **1** to compel, to intimidate. **2** (*US*) (*also* **come it on**) to trick, to deceive. ❑ **come it strong** *v.* **1** [early 19C+] (*also* **go it strong**) to act in a challenging, aggressive manner; sometimes intensified by 'as mustard'. **2** [mid-19C] to act, to practise, to perform one's part. **3** [mid-19C] to tell lies. ❑ **come it with** *v.* [late 19C+] to act in a certain way in order to take advantage (of someone).

come it *v.*[2] **1** [early 19C+] to divulge a secret, to confess. **2** [mid-19C+] (*Aus./UK Und.*) to betray, to inform against.

IN PHRASES

❑ **come it as strong as a horse** *v.* [early–mid-19C] (*UK Und.*) to turn King's/Queen's evidence.

come it *v.*[3] [mid-19C] to attain, to reach, to achieve.

come it *v.*[4] *see* COME *v.*[2].

come-off *n.* [earlier use is SE] [mid-19C+] (*US*) a result.

come off *v.*[1] **1** [late 19C–1940s] (*US*) to stop, to refrain from a course of action. **2** [1960s] (*US*) to hand over reluctantly.

IN PHRASES

❑ **come off the bird-lime** [1910s–20s] a general phr. of disbelief, 'you must be joking', 'you don't fool me'. ❑ **come off the (tall) grass** [late 19C] (*orig. US*) stop telling lies, stop exaggerating.

IN EXCLAMATIONS

❑ **come off it!** (*also* **come off! come out of it!**) [late 19C+] stop it! don't keep trying that line!

SE in slang uses

IN PHRASES

❑ **come off one's game** *v. see under* GAME *n.*

IN EXCLAMATIONS

❑ **come off the roof!** [late 19C] used to an equal who is considered to be 'getting above themselves', 'stop acting so superior'.

come off *v.*[2] [one has been 'on' heroin, 'on' cocaine etc] [1930s+] (*drugs*) to stop using a given (addictive) drug.

come off *v.*[3] *see* COME *v.*[1].

come off! *excl.* [COME OFF *v.*[1] (1)] [late 19C+] (*US*) stop it! don't keep trying that line!

come-on *n.* [SE excl. *come on!*] **1** [late 19C–1950s] (*US Und.*) a dupe, a victim of a confidence trickster; a prospective victim; a 'steered' prospect. **2** [20C+] (*US Und.*) (*also* **come-on ghee**) a con-man, a swindler. **3** [20C+] (*US*) a snare, an inducement, a lure. **4** [20C+] (*US*) patter, sales or seduction talk, a line. **5** [1900s] a gullible fool. **6** [1930s] the personification of sense 6, a sexually alluring woman. **7** [1930s+] (*also* **come-in**) a sexual invitation, either through a look or through words. **8** [1950s] a dare.

IN COMPOUNDS

❑ **come-on boy** *n.* [1940s+] a male prostitute who entices a client and then, instead of sex, has him beaten and robbed by a confederate. ❑ **come-on girl** *n.* [late 19C+] (*US*) a promiscuous woman; a prostitute. ❑ **come-on guy** *n.* (*also* **come-on man**) [1920s–30s] **1** (*US*) the member of a confidence trickster team who lures the victim into the circle. **2** (*US tramp*) a hard worker, who encourages others.

come-on *adj.* [COME-ON *n.*] [1910s+] (*orig. US*) alluring, seductive; orig. non-sexual, later sexual.

come on *v.*[1] [late 19C+] (*orig. US*) to seem, to appear, to behave; always modified, usu. by an adj. used adverbially, e.g. *come on tough*, *come on nasty* etc.

IN PHRASES

❑ **come on like a test pilot** *v.* [the test pilot, as a figure of technologically sophisticated derring-do, had a higher profile then than now] [1940s] (*US black/Harlem*) to act in a speedy, efficient manner. ❑ **come on strong** *v.* (*also* **come on, come strong**) **1** [20C+] to speak aggressively, forcefully; to make one's presence and opinions felt; used both positively and negatively, the latter often as *come on too strong*. **2** [1950s+] to be seductive.

come on *v.*[2] [SE *come on*, to begin] **1** [1930s+] (*drugs*) for withdrawal symptoms to start affecting a narcotics addict. **2** [1940s+] (*drugs*) for a drug to begin affecting its user, esp. of a hallucinogen (which takes a short time to enter the bloodstream and hit the brain). **3** [1980s+] of a woman, to start menstruating.

come on *v.*[3] **1** [1930s+] (*also* **come on to**) to approach sexually. **2** [1950s] (*US*) to joke.

IN PHRASES

❑ **come on the bounce** *v. see under* BOUNCE *n.*[1]. ❑ **come on (to)** *v.* [orig. jazz use] **1** [1950s+] (*orig. US*) to approach or speak to aggressively, to solicit. **2** [1990s+] to harass.

come on! *excl.* [20C+] a general excl. of disbelief, disapproval, irritation.

come-out *adj.* [early–mid-19C] disgusting, appalling.

come out *v.* **1** in senses of self-revelation. (**a**) [mid-19C] (*US*) to give up a specific religious denomination, in favour of free opinion on religious matters. (**b**) [mid–late 19C] (*US black*) to declare one's faith in religion, to join the church. (**c**) [20C+] to declare any form of self-revelation. (**d**) [1940s+] (*gay*) to declare oneself openly as a homosexual [sense 2/3 above but note COME OUT OF THE CLOSET *under* CLOSET *n.*]. **2** [20C+] (*W.I.*) to be born in poverty or in some unknown place; esp. in question 'where you come out?'.

IN PHRASES

❑ **come out moldy** *v.* (*also* **come up moldy**) [1980s+] (*US campus*) to be humiliated. ❑ **come out of a bag** *v. see under* BAG *n.*[2]. ❑ **come out of the closet** *v. see under* CLOSET *n.* ❑ **come out of the cupboard** *v.* [late 19C–1900s] to start work on one's first ever job. ❑ **come out of the house** *v.* [1950s+] (*US*) to grow up, lit. to leave one's home life for that of the streets and the larger world. ❑ **come out of the woods** *v.* [1960s] (*US black*) of a Southerner who has moved to a Northern city, to abandon one's rural lifestyle for that of the city. ❑ **come out strong** *v. see under* STRONG *adv.* ❑ **come out with** *v.* (*also* **come right out with**) [20C+] (*orig. US*) to speak openly, candidly, tactlessly.

come over *v.*[1] [ext. use of SE *come over*, to prevail] [17C+] to trick, to cheat; to get the better of.

SE in slang uses

IN PHRASES

❑ **come over on a whelk-stall** *v.* [? the flashy dress preferred by whelk-sellers] [late 19C–1900s] (*costermonger*) to be very flashily dressed.

come over *v.*[2] [var. on COME ON *v.*[1]/COME THE… *v.*] [mid-19C+] **1** as *come the…over*, to act in a given manner, defined by a missing noun. **2** as *come over all…*, to experience certain emotions, usu. with various modifiers, e.g. *come over all queer*, suddenly to feel physically unwell.

comer *n.* [SE *come (on)*, to advance (in one's aims, development)] [late 19C+] **1** (*orig. US*) an ambitious, go-ahead person, 'the coming man'. **2** (*US*) a business, club or project promising success.

comet *n.* [late 19C–1940s] (*US tramp*) the aristocrat of tramps, travelling only on express trains and only for lengthy journeys.

come the... *v.* (*also* **come the old...**) [var. on COME *v.*^{3} (1)] [19C+] in a wide variety of combs. this means to act, to pose as, to attempt to be; it is always constrained by a n., e.g. *come the artful, come the paddy* etc. The word 'old' is often inserted between the phr. and the defining n., e.g. *come the old soldier*; *see* combs. below and at relevant n.

IN PHRASES

❑ **come the...** *v. see also under* relevant n. or adj. ❑ **come the after game** *v.* [image of those who analyse a sporting fixture *after the game*, when they naturally know better than those who actually had to play it] [1920s+] (*Aus.*) to be full of opinions and predictions, after the event. ❑ **come the artful** *v.* [19C+] to hoax, to deceive. ❑ **come the big note** *v. see* BIG-NOTE *v.* ❑ **come the bludge on** *v. see under* BLUDGER *n.*^{2}. ❑ **come the double** *v.* **1** [mid-19C] (*US*) to doublecross. **2** [1910s] (*Aus.*) to take more than one's fair share. ❑ **come the drops** *v.* [mid–late 19C] (*Aus.*) to make a fuss, to burst into tears. ❑ **come the duke** *v. see* COME THE NOB *under* NOB *n.*^{2}. ❑ **come the heavy** *v.* [mid–late 19C] to pose as a member of a superior class to that to which one actually belongs. ❑ **come the (old) bag** *v.* [1920s] (*orig. milit.*) to bluff, to 'try it on'. ❑ **come the old man** *v.* [to pretend to infirm old age, or naut. use of *old man*, the captain] [late 19C] to act in a lazy manner, to shirk one's duties. ❑ **come the old soldier** *v.* (*also* **come the tin soldier, play the old soldier, soldier**) [the skills of a veteran who, supposedly, knows every trick when it comes to avoiding onerous duties. Ware also cites the rash of beggars who proliferated in London after Waterloo (1815), all claiming to have taken part in the battle. Note naut. jargon *soldier*, a poor or lazy seaman, a shirker] [18C+] to deceive another for one's own benefit, esp. to avoid an unpleasant task. ❑ **come the possum over** *v.* [stereotype of the cowardly, dissembling *possum*] [mid-19C+] to pretend to be ill or even dead. ❑ **come the raw prawn** *v.* (*also* **come raw pommie, come the uncooked crustacean, cop the raw prawn**) [1940s+] (*Aus.*) to act resentfully or unpleasantly, to be rude. ❑ **come the roots over** *v.* [mid-19C–1910s] (*US campus*) to defeat by trickery. ❑ **come the Rothschild** *v.* [the proper name *Rothschild*, the epitome of the fabulously wealthy banker, esp. during the reign of the magnate-loving Edward VII] [late 19C–1910s] to pretend to great wealth. ❑ **come the tin man** *v.* [SE *tin*, petty, worthless, counterfeit (as opposed to precious metal) + *man*] [20C+] **1** to deceive, to bluff. **2** to make oneself a nuisance. ❑ **come the Traviata** *v.* [the Verdi opera *La Traviata* (1853), which was based on Dumas *fils*'s *La Dame aux Camélias*, in which the heroine dies of that disease] [mid–late 19C] of a prostitute, to pretend to be suffering from phthisis or pulmonary consumption. ❑ **come the ugly over/with** *v.* [SE *ugly*, unpleasant] [mid–late 19C] to make threats, to menace.

come through *v.* [fig. uses of SE; note late 19C US religious jargon *come through*, to accept conversion] **1** [20C+] of an object, to deliver, to give up. **2** [20C+] to take over in an emergency, to carry out requirements. **3** [1900s] (*US*) to pay one's debts. **4** [1900s–50s] (*US*) to confess, to provide information, to speak out. **5** [1910s+] to act as desired, to do what is wanted. **6** [1920s] to survive, to overcome problems.

come-to-Jesus *adj.* [1920s–30s] (*orig. US tramp*) insincerely pious.

IN COMPOUNDS

❑ **come-to-Jesus coat** *n.* [as worn by, *inter alia*, ministers and preachers] [1930s–40s] (*US*) a frock coat. ❑ **come-to-Jesus collar** *n.* [the preference for such collars among revivalist preachers] [1920s–40s] (*Can./US*) a stiff dress collar.

come up *v.*^{1} **1** [late 19C] (*Aus.*) to exist, to live. **2** [1930s+] (*US black*) to turn out, to happen. **3** [1940s+] to appear, to pose. **4** [1960s+] (*US black*) to grow up. **5** [1990s+] (*US black*) to do well, to prosper. **6** [1990s+] (*drugs*) of a person, for a drug to start taking effect on one.

IN PHRASES

❑ **come up weak** *v.* [1960s] (*US black*) to disappoint, to fail to reach expectations (whether one's own or those of others). ❑ **just come up** *adj.* [20C+] naïve, gauche, inexperienced, stupid.

SE in slang uses

IN PHRASES

❑ **come up moldy** *v. see* COME OUT MOLDY *under* COME OUT *v.* ❑ **come up on** *v.* [1950s+] to succeed at or with. ❑ **come up on the down train** *v.* [2000s] to be stupid. ❑ **come up on the last load** *v.* (*also* **come up the river on a bike**) [1990s+] (*Irish*) to be naive, gullible; usu. in phr. *do you think I came up... / I didn't come up...* ❑ **come up smelling of roses/violets** *v. see under* SMELL *v.* ❑ **come up smiling** *v.* [i.e. when knocked to the canvas one comes up with a (false but brave) smile] [mid-19C+] (*orig. boxing*) to face a difficult circumstance without showing fear or complaining. ❑ **come up tails** *v.* [the tossing of coins] [1970s] (*US*) to find oneself in an unpleasant or problematic situation. ❑ **come up the Foyle in a bubble** *v.* [20C+] (*Ulster*) to be naïve, gullible; usu. in phr. *do you think I came up.../I didn't come up...* ❑ **come up to (the chalk)** *v.* [the chalk mark that indicates the start of a race] [mid-19C] (*US*) to perform as expected, to meet expectations. ❑ **come up to the rack (or jump the fence)** *v.* (*also* **stand up to the rack**) [SE *rack*, racket, i.e. the noise and bustle of a city; thus the image is of entering the urban hustle-bustle, or jumping the fence and heading off for the quiet open spaces of the country] [mid-19C–1900s] (*US*) to make a decision to do one thing or another, to stop dithering, to do what one has to do, to accept one's duty. ❑ **come up trumps** *v.* [card-playing imagery] [mid-19C+] to turn out satisfactorily, esp. when a bad result seems more likely.

come up *v.*^{2} *see* COME ACROSS *v.* (1).

comflogsticate *v.* [ety. unknown, a nonsense word orig. used in the RN] [19C] to astound, to puzzle.

comfoozled *adj.* [used and prob. coined by Charles Dickens (1812–70)] [mid–late 19C] exhausted, overcome.

comfort *n.* [its soothing effects; Partridge also notes the US liquor, *Southern Comfort*] [early–mid-18C] gin.

comfortable *adj.* [mid-19C–1950s] (*US*) a euph. for drunk.

IN COMPOUNDS

❑ **comfortable importance** *n.* [play on SE] **1** [late 17C] a mistress. **2** [late 17C–early 19C] one's wife. ❑ **comfortable impudence** *n.* [play on SE and parody of COMFORTABLE IMPORTANCE above] [18C–19C] a mistress, esp. when posing as one's wife.

comical chris *n.* [rhy. sl. = PISS *n.* (2)] [1970s–80s] an act of urination.

comical farce *n.* [rhy. sl.] [late 19C–1910s] a glass.

comic cuts *n.* (*also* **comics**) [rhy. sl. = lit. and fig. uses of GUT *n.* (1a)] [1940s+] (*Aus.*) **1** the stomach. **2** in two-up, the 'guts', i.e. the centre of the betting circle into which the money bet is tossed. **3** the truth.

comic singer *n.* [rhy. sl.] [20C+] a finger.

coming *adj.* [she is fig. 'coming forward'] **1** [17C–18C] pregnant. **2** [late 17C–early 19C] of a woman, wanton, promiscuous.

coming! *excl.* [late 18C+] 'I'll be with you at once', 'I won't be long'; thus derisive phr., aimed at a slow person, *coming? so is Christmas*.

coming down the hill *phr.* [1940s–50s] (*US prison*) approaching the end of one's sentence.

comings *n.* [COME *n.* (2)] [mid-19C+] semen.

commander of the Fleet *n.* [pun on NAVY OFFICE *n.*] [early–mid-19C] the warden of the Fleet prison.

commando *adv.*

IN PHRASES

❑ **go commando** *v.* [? tough commandos need no such 'soft' apparel] [1970s+] (*US campus*) to go without underwear.

comm-bat *n.* [play on SE *combat/bat*] [2000s] (*US black*) an aluminium baseball bat converted into a stabbing, cutting weapon.

commercial *n.* [abbr./an ironic use of SE *commercial traveller.* Note Und. *commercial*, a thief who travels to pursue his profession] **1** [late 19C–1910s] (*Aus./N.Z.*) an itinerant worker, who travels with his pack on his back while looking for employment. **2** [late 19C+] (*Aus./N.Z.*) a commercial traveller. **3** [1940s+] (*Aus./US gay*) (*also* **commercial queer, commercial trade**) a male prostitute, both homo- and heterosexual. **4** [1970s] (*gay*) either excuses made by male prostitutes to justify their occupation, or actual adverts, based on self-aggrandizement, aimed at attracting clients [play on SE *commercials*, advertisements]. **5** [1980s+] (*US drugs*) (*also* **commersh**) marijuana buds that come in a brick; esp. used of Colombian marijuana (which is packaged in this manner).

IN PHRASES

□ **go commercial** *v.* [1940s–60s] (*orig. US black*) to become a prostitute.

commesse *n.* [Fr. *commerce*, 'business', with implications of illegality, bad behaviour] [1990s+] (*W.I.*) scandal, conflict, illegal behaviour.

commie *n.* (*also* **commy, kommie**) [abbr.] [1930s+] a *comm*unist.

commie *adj.* [COMMIE *n.*] [1940s+] communist, far-left wing.

commish *n.* [abbr./pron.] **1** [mid-19C+] a *commiss*ion (on a financial or other transaction); thus as v., to work as a commission merchant. **2** [1910s+] a *commiss*ioner (usu. in police situations).

commissary department *n.* (*also* **commissariat department, ...region**) [SE *commissary department*, in milit. use the department that deals with the buying, preparing and distribution of food] [late 19C–1900s] (*US*) the stomach.

commission *n.* [Ital. *camisa*, shirt] [mid-16C–mid-19C] (*UK Und.*) a shirt.

commissioner *n.* [? ironic use of next, given the role of Newmarket in racing and the bookmaker's extraction of money from his clients] [mid-19C] the properietor of a gaming house, a bookmaker.

commissioner of Newmarket Heath *n.* [the site of many highway robberies] [late 16C] a footpad.

commister *n.* [his *chemise* or surplice] [mid-19C] (*orig. UK Und.*) a clergyman.

commo *n.* [abbr. + -O *sfx* (3); note Aus. *commie* does not have the same political use as UK/US, but refers to those who live in rural communes] [1940s+] (*Aus.*) a *comm*unist, or one whose views, from hard left to mildly liberal, are seen as deviant from the speaker's (right-wing/conservative) 'norm'; also as adj.

commode-hugging drunk *adj.* [1970s+] (*US campus*) extremely drunk, to the point of hugging the lavatory bowl and vomiting within.

commodity *n.* [SE *commodity*, something available for sale or trade; in both senses the woman and/or her body are seen as no more than pieces of merchandise; thus Ward, *The London Spy* (1698): '*Strumpets* in the Streets were grown a scarce Commodity'] **1** [late 16C–18C] a prostitute. **2** [late 16C–19C] the female genitals.

common *n.* [abbr. SE; note RN jargon *common dog*, common sense] [20C+] **1** common sense; esp. in adjuration *have/use a bit of common*, use your common sense. **2** common decency.

commoner *n.* **1** [mid-19C] an amateur or second-rate boxer. **2** [1970s] (*US gay*) a heterosexual.

Common Garden *n.* [early–mid-19C] Covent Garden, London.

IN COMPOUNDS

□ **Common Garden gout** *n. see* COVENT GARDEN GOUT *under* COVENT GARDEN *adj.*

common law *n.* [late 18C] sexual intercourse.

commons *n.* [abbr. SE *common house*] [17C] a privy, a lavatory.

common sewer *n.* [all plays on SE *common sewer*, into which everything is poured; the *common shore* was that portion of the Thames riverbank where filth could be left and then washed away by the tide] **1** [17C–mid-18C] (*also* **common shore**) a prostitute. **2** [19C] the throat. **3** [19C] a drunkard. **4** [mid-19C] a drink.

communists *n.* [pun on 'the reds'] [1930s] (*US*) menstruation.

commy *n. see* COMMIE *n.*

comp *n.* [abbr.] **1** [mid-19C+] a *comp*ositor. **2** [mid-19C+] (*US*) a *comp*liment. **3** [late 19C+] a *comp*limentary pass or ticket. **4** [20C+] (*US campus*) a course in English *comp*osition. **5** [1930s+] (*US*) a *comp*limentary gift, e.g. as given to 'high-rolling' gamblers by a resort hotel; thus also one who receives such hospitality. **6** [1950s+] *comp*etition. **7** [1950s+] *comp*ensation. **8** [1960s] (*US*) a musical *comp*osition. **9** [1980s+] *comp*rehensive school. **10** [2000s] a *comp*ilation. **11** [2000s] a *comp*arison.

comp *v.* [COMP *n.* (3)] [1960s+] to give free tickets, free board and lodging etc, usu. in the context of show business or casino hotels.

compa *n.* [abbr. Sp. *compadre*, a companion] [1960s+] (*US*) a friend, a fellow gang member.

compadre *n.* (*also* **companero**) [Sp.] [mid-19C+] (*US*) a close male friend.

Company, the *n.* [Sp. *Cia*, abbr. for Company (equivalent of SE *Co.*)] [1960s+] (*US*) the Central Intelligence Agency (CIA).

company man *n.* (*also* **company stiff**) [SE *company* + *man*/ STIFF *n.*[1] (4d)] [1940s–50s] (*US*) a worker who is seen by his peers as loyal to the employers rather than the union.

compellance weed *n.* [under its influence one is supposedly 'compelled' to do something. This hardly fits, however, with the normal image of the marijuana user as a rather comatose figure. Note *compelling oil/powder*, a sweet-smelling oil or powder prepared by an obeahman and used in the hope of winning over or controlling a lover or defeating an evil spirit] [1940s+] (*W.I.*) marijuana.

compo *n.* [abbr. + -O *sfx* (3); note WW1 milit. *compo*, pay; money] [1930s+] (*Aus./N.Z.*) **1** workers' *comp*ensation, payment for time lost after an injury at work. **2** any form of *comp*ensation.

DERIVATIVES

□ **compo-itis** *n.* [1940s+] (*Aus./N.Z.*) the counterfeiting or extension of one's disability in the hope of gaining more compensation payments.

IN COMPOUNDS

□ **compo artist** *n.* (*also* **compo king**) [-ARTIST *sfx*/-KING *sfx* (1)] [1940s+] (*Aus./N.Z.*) one who is a specialist in the extraction of monetary compensation by faking or exaggerating their supposedly work-related injuries.

compos *adj.* [abbr. NON COMPOS *adj.*] **1** [19C+] sane. **2** [1970s] sober.

compositum *n.* [early 18C] (*UK Und.*) a counterfeit coin made from a mixed metal.

comprende? *excl.* (*also* **compree?**) [Sp. Note WW1/WW2 *compree*, understand, f. Fr. *compris*] [1970s+] (*orig. US*) you understand?

compute *v.* [lit. 'add up'. Popularized in 1964 CBS TV series *My Living Doll*. Note mid-17C–18C SE *compute*, to estimate, to reckon, to take account of, to take into consideration] [1960s+] (*orig. US*) to work out, usu. in negative phr. *that doesn't compute*.

compy *v.* [SE *comprehend* or f. Fr. *comprenez?* do you understand?, imported by GIs returning from WW2; note WW1 equivalent *compris*] [1940s] (*US black*) to understand; often as interrog. *compy?* you understand?

Comrade Wobbly *n.*

IN PHRASES

□ **play Comrade Wobbly hides his helmet** (*also* **play Mr Wobbly hides his helmet**) [1990s+] to have sexual intercourse.

con *n.*[1] [abbr.] **1** [early 19C] a *con*fidant. **2** [mid-19C–1910s] a *con*undrum. **3** [late 19C] a *con*tract. **4** [late 19C–1910s] a *con*formist. **5** [late 19C+] a railroad *con*ductor. **6** [late 19C+] a *con*fidence man. **7** [late 19C+] a *con*fidence game or trick;

by ext. deceitful talk. **8** [late 19C+] a *con*vict; thus EX-CON *n.* **9** [1900s–50s] a deceptive speech. **10** [1920s+] a *con*viction. **11** [1940s] *con*fidence.

IN COMPOUNDS

❑ **con-artist** *n. see* separate entry. ❑ **con boss** *n.* (*also* **boss con**) [BOSS *n.*[2] (1)] [1910s+] (*US prison*) an influential convict who runs a gang within a prison. ❑ **con game** *n.* [GAME *n.* (6)] [late 19C+] (*orig. US*) a piece of confidence trickery. ❑ **con job** *n. see* separate entry. ❑ **con-man** *n. see* separate entry. ❑ **con-merchant** *n.* [MERCHANT *n.*] [1930s+] (*US*) a confidence trickster. ❑ **con-mob** *n.* [1930s–40s] (*US Und.*) a team of confidence tricksters. ❑ **con player** *n. see* CON-MAN *n.* ❑ **con talk** *n.* [late 19C–1900s] (*US*) insincerity, lies. ❑ **conwise** [-WISE *sfx* (1)] [1910s+] (*US prison*) **1** well-adjusted to prison life, capable of sustaining one's existence in prison; of officers, experienced. **2** manipulative of the system. ❑ **con woman** *n. see* CON-MAN *n.* ❑ **con work** *n.* [1920s] (*US*) insincerity, lies.

IN PHRASES

❑ **big con** *n.* [1940s+] (*orig. US Und.*) any major confidence trick, the keynote of which is that the victim is persuaded to send for (usu. large sums of) money, rather than merely defrauding them of what they may have in their possession. ❑ **on the con** [20C+] working as a *con*fidence trickster. ❑ **play con** *v.* [1960s–70s] to trick, to hoax, to practice confidence trickery. ❑ **play the con** *v.* [1940s+] (*orig. US Und.*) to pretend, to attempt to swindle or deceive. ❑ **slow con** *n.* [20C+] a fraudulent scheme or confidence trick in which the victim is nurtured slowly and carefully towards their downfall. ❑ **soft con** *n.* [1970s] flattery, persuasion, any form of deceit based on soft words. ❑ **solid con** *n.* [SOLID *adj.* (3)] [20C+] (*US Und.*) a trustworthy fellow criminal or prison inmate. ❑ **sweet con** *n.* [1950s] (*US*) a form of begging in which the beggar uses persuasion and promises rather than threats.

con *n.*[2] [abbr. SE *consumption*] [20C+] (*US*) **1** tuberculosis. **2** a sufferer from tuberculosis.

con *adj.* [CON *n.*[1] (6)] [late 19C+] pertaining to confidence trickery or confidence tricksters; in a weak sense, deceitful.

con *v.* [abbr. SE *confidence trick*] (*orig. US*) **1** [late 19C+] (*also* **con along**) to fool a victim in one or another form of confidence trick. **2** [late 19C+] to persuade, to coax (without criminal intent); usu. as *con someone into*. **3** [1960s+] to tell stories, to fantasize.

IN PHRASES

❑ **con out of** *v.* [1940s+] to trick someone into handing over or giving up something they would prefer to hold on to.

con and coal *n.* [rhy. sl.] [20C+] the dole.

Conan Doyle *n.* (*also* **Jack Doyle**) [rhy. sl.; ult. Sir Arthur *Conan Doyle* (1859–1930), novelist and creator of Sherlock Holmes] [1930s+] a boil (on the neck).

Conan Doyle *v.* [rhy. sl.; for ety. *see* prev.] [late 19C+] to boil (a kettle).

con-artist *n.* (*also* **con artist**) [CON *n.*[1] (7) + ARTIST *n.*] [1930s+] a confidence trickster, a fraud.

conbobberated *adj.* [CONBOBBERATION *n.*] [mid-19C+] (*US*) upset, disconcerted, disturbed.

conbobberation *n.* [SE *con*, with + BOBBERY *n.* (1)] [mid-19C] (*US*) a disturbance, an argument.

conbobbolate *v.* (*also* **combobbolate**) [CONBOBBERATION *n.* + SE *calculate*] [mid-19C+] (*US*) to think, to ponder, to 'calculate'.

concaves and convexes *n.* [the shapes of the doctored cards] [early–mid-19C] 'a pack of cards contrived for cheating, by cutting all the cards from the two to the seven concave, and all from the eight to the king convex. Then by cutting the pack breadthwise a convex card is cut, and by cutting it lengthwise a concave is secured' (Hotten, 1864).

concern *n.* [SE *concern*, a thing, an appurtenance] **1** [19C] the penis. **2** [late 19C] the vagina.

concerned *adj.* **1** [late 17C–mid-19C] a euph. term meaning drunk; thus *concerned with drink, concerned in drink*. **2** *see* CONSARNED *adj.*

concertina *n.*[1] [its shape] [late 19C] (*UK Und.*) a squashed top hat.

concertina *n.*[2] [resemblance] [late 19C+] (*Aus.*) **1** a wrinkly sheep. **2** a side of lamb or mutton. **3** a style of leggings with wrinkles in them.

conch *n.*[1] [SE *conch*, a variety of shellfish for which such people fish] [mid-19C+] **1** (*W.I.*) a native of the Bahamas. **2** (*US*) a poor white native of the Florida Keys. **3** a native of North Carolina.

conch *n.*[2] [abbr. SE *conscientious*] [20C+] (*US campus*) a devotedly hard worker, a taskmaster.

conchie *n.* [abbr.; Brophy & Partridge, *Songs and Slang of the British Soldier* (1930), note that it should be 'properly *Conscie*'] **1** [1910s+] (*also* **concho, conchy, conscie, conshi, conshie**) a *consc*ientious objector. **2** [1960s+] (*Aus.*) (*also* **conch**) a hard worker.

conchie *adj.* [abbr.] [1980s] (*Aus.*) conscientious.

Conchy *n.* [1910s–20s] (*US tramp*) Connecticut.

conchy *n. see* CONCHIE *n.* (1).

conchy Joe *n.* [CONCH *n.*[1] (1) + generic *Joe*] [20C+] (*W.I., Baha.*) **1** a creole white or Caribbean person who has, to all appearances, no black ancestry (although there will be a distant relation). **2** a poor white. **3** a mixed-race Bahamian, who sees themselves as socially superior to blacks.

con-con *n.* [1980s+] (*drugs*) a dark, oily substance that remains in a pipe after crack or FREEBASE *n.* (1) cocaine has been smoked.

concorde *n.* [it 'flies away' very quickly'] [1990s+] (*W.I., Jam.*) a $100 bill.

concosa *n. see* CONGO-SAW *under* CONGO *n.*[2].

concrete *n.*[1] [1940s+] (*W.I.*) any starchy, indigestible food, e.g. dumplings, fufu, usu. with peas (legumes) or beans mixed in.

concrete *n.*[2] [2000s] a city.

concrete overcoat *n.* (*also* **concrete clogs, ...drawers, ...kimono, ...overshoes, ...slippers, ...socks**) [1970s+] a supposed gangland method of murder; the victim's feet are dunked in quick-drying concrete and they are then dumped into a river or overboard from a boat, the irremovable weight ensuring that they drown.

condog *v.* [*condog* is the source of a long-lived lexicographical 'chestnut'. While assembling his dict., the lexicographer Adam Littleton (1627–94) gave the Latin word *concurro* (to meet, to assemble) to his assistant. The assistant, assuming, from the similarity of sounds, that the English followed the Latin, asked Littleton: 'Concur, I suppose, Sir.' Littleton replied tetchily, 'Concur! condog!' Fearing to argue, the assistant listed 'condog' in the manuscript as one of the meanings of *concurro*. It duly appeared in the first edn. Unfortunately the story is marred by chronology, the *OED*'s first citation predates Littleton's work by 86 years] [late 16C–17C] to concur, to agree.

condy *n.* [abbr.; proper name of Henry Bollmann *Condy*, 19C English manufacturer of chemicals] [1920s+] *Condy*'s fluid, a strong solution of sodium manganate or permanganate, used as a disinfectant.

condy's, the *n.* [*Condy's fluid*, which, as a disinfectant, presumably 'deals with any problem'; note Aus. milit. *Abdullah with the Condies*, an Egyptian menial] [1940s] (*Aus.*) advice, usu. in phr. *maleesh/mahlish the condy's*, lit. never mind the condy's, i.e. forget the preliminaries, let's get on with it.

IN COMPOUNDS

❑ **condy boy** *n.* [the use of diluted *Condy's fluid* as a post-intercourse disinfectant] [1940s–50s] (*Aus.*) a jack-of-all-trades employed by a brothel.

cone *n.* [resemblance] **1** [late 19C] (*US*) the head. **2** [1920s] (*Aus.*) the nose. **3** [1980s+] (*Aus. drugs*) a metal cone with a hole in the centre, usu. made of aluminium or brass and used for smoking cannabis. **4** [1980s+] (*US drugs*) a conical cannabis cigarette, which is tapered by rolling with two or more papers glued at an angle.

SE in slang uses

IN PHRASES

❑ **give cone** *v.* [the image of licking an ice-cream cone] [1980s] (*US teen*) to fellate.

conehead *n.* [the *Coneheads*, a bizarre space-dwelling 'family', were created for the TV show *Saturday Night Live* in 1976] [1980s+] (*orig. US*) a strange and foolish person.

coneroo *n.* (*also* **conneroo**) [CON *n.*[1] (6) + sfx -EROO *sfx*] [1940s] (*US*) a confidence trickster.

coney *n.*[1] (*also* **cogniac, coniak, koniack**) [? play upon SE *coin*, money] [19C] (*US Und.*) counterfeit banknotes; thus *coney man*, one who passes counterfeit notes; *coney traffic*, counterfeit money trafficking.

coney *n.*[2] *see also under* CONY and its combs.

coneyacker *n. see* KONIACKER *n.*

Coney Island *n.* [ironic use of the place name, Coney Island, New York's leisure centre] [1930s–40s] (*US prison/Und.*) the room used by police for interrogation.

proper name in slang uses

IN COMPOUNDS

❑ **Coney Island chicken** *n.* [20C+] a spiced, heated sausage or frankfurter, esp. when served in a bun with fried onions, chili sauce and mustard. ❑ **Coney Island (head)** *n.* [the way visitors were defrauded by the bartenders of Coney Island] [late 19C–1960s] (*US*) a beer that has more frothy head than actual beer. ❑ **Coney Island whitefish** *n.* (*also* **Canarsie whitefish**) [the popularity with lovers of the beaches of New York's Coney Island; similarly used of the beachfront at Canarsie, N.Y.] [1930s+] (*US*) a used contraceptive floating at the edge of the beach.

confab *n.* [abbr. SE *confabulation*, a chat, a conversation] [18C+] a conversation, an argument.

confab *v.* [CONFAB *n.*] [1910s+] to converse, to discuss.

confeck *adj.* (*also* **confect**) [SE *confect*, to prepare or mix up ingredients] [17C–early 19C] (*UK Und.*) counterfeit, fake.

confectionery *n. see* SWEET *n.* (1).

confesh *n.* [abbr./pron.] [1910s] (*US Und.*) a *confession*.

confessional *n.* [where a FATHER CONFESSOR *under* FATHER *n.* appears] [late 19C] the vagina.

confess the corn *v.* (*also* **confess the cob**) [for ety. *see* ACKNOWLEDGE THE CORN *v.*] [early 19C–1940s] (*orig. US*) to admit an error; thus *confession*, n., a tutorial.

confetti *n.* [1970s] (*US*) snow.

confidence *v.* [abbr. SE *confidence trick*] [late 17C; late 19C–1940s] (*US*) to defraud, to swindle.

confidence buck *n.* [SE *confidence* + BUCK *v.*[2] (4)] [late 19C] a confidence trick.

confidence-queen *n.* [? in plain-clothes she 'cons' her criminal victims; -QUEEN *sfx*] **1** [late 19C] (*US*) a female detective. **2** [1990s+] (*US campus*) a female confidence trickster.

conflab *n.* [var. on CONFAB *n.*] [mid-19C–1940s] (*US*) a conversation, an argument.

conflab *v.* [CONFLAB *n.*] [2000s] to chat with.

conflabberated *adj.* [ety. unknown; a nonsense word] [mid-19C–1910s] upset, perturbed, un-nerved.

conflabberation *n.* [CONFLABBERATED *adj.*] [mid-19C–1920s] a confused wrangle.

conflobble *v.* [joc. version of SE *confound*] [late 19C] to defeat.

confloption *n.* [nonsense word; ? formed f. SE pfx *con-*, together + *flop* v., to collapse] [late 19C] an unshapely, grotesquely twisted thing.

conflummox *v.* (*also* **conflustercate**) [ext. of FLUMMOX *v.* (4)] [19C+] to fool, to confuse, to overcome by trickery.

confo *n.* [abbr. SE + -O *sfx* (3)] [1930s–50s] (*Aus.*) a *con*ference.

confusion *n.* [euph.] **1** [late 19C+] an argument leading to a fight. **2** [1970s] a street fight, a riot.

conger (eel) *v.* [rhy. sl. = SQUEAL (ON) *v.* (3)] [1990s+] (*UK Und.*) to inform, to betray.

congo *n.*[1] (*also* **congou, kongo**) [Chinese *kung-fu*, work, and workman; thus *kung-fu-ch'a*, tea on which work or labour is expended; *congou, congo* or *kongo* was a type of black tea, imported to England during 18C] [late 18C–mid-19C] tea.

congo *n.*[2] [US slave trade jargon *Congo*, a slave brought from the Congo nation. The term is also used in the W.I. with an additional element of poverty and a rough appearance] [mid-19C+] a derog. term for a black person, esp. one with a notably dark complexion.

IN COMPOUNDS

❑ **congo-saw** *n.* (*also* **concosa**) [SE *saw*, speech, discourse] [early 19C] (*W.I.*) flattery.

congo *n.*[3] [abbr. + -O *sfx* (3)] [1920s+] (*Aus./US*) a Congregationalist.

Congo bush *n.* (*also* **Congo**) [SE *Congo* + BUSH *n.*[1] (5a)] [1960s+] (*drugs*) marijuana from the Congo area of Africa.

Congo croquet *n.* [CONGO *n.*[2]] [20C+] (*US*) the game of craps.

congou *n. see* CONGO *n.*[1].

congrats! *excl.* [abbr. + -ER *sfx*] [late 19C+] *congrat*ulations; thus synon. [1930s] *congraggers*, [20C+] *congratters*.

coniack *n. see* CONEY *n.*[1].

coniacker *n. see* KONIACKER *n.*

coniak *n. see* CONEY *n.*[1].

conish *adj.* [? CONY *n.* (3) on the theory that such a figure may well fall prey to a clever con-man; Partridge suggests perversion of *tonish*, fashionable] [early–late 19C] fashionable, smart, genteel; thus (*Scot.*) *conish cove*, a fashionable gentleman.

coniwobble *n.* [ext. of CONY *n.* (3)] [early 18C] a dupe, a fool.

con job *n.* [CON *n.*[1] (7) + JOB *n.*[2]] [1920s+] (*US*) a confidence trick.

conjobble *v.* [SE pfx *con-*, together + JOB *n.*[2] (2), but note *jabber*, + 17C job, sexual intercourse] **1** [late 17C–mid-18C] to settle, to discuss. **2** [early 18C] to have sexual intercourse.

conjugals *n.* [20C+] sexual intercourse, esp. in a marital context.

conjuror *n.* **1** [early 17C] a pickpocket [the dependence on sleight of hand]. **2** [late 17C–early 19C] (*UK Und.*) a trial judge; *go before the conjuror*, to be tried at the assize [what he 'pulls out of his hat' is a sentence].

conk *n.*[1] (*also* **konk**) [? f. Lat. *concha*, a shell, and Gk *kogcha*, anything hollow] **1** [early 19C+] the nose; thus a nickname for one who has a large nose. **2** [early–mid-19C] (*UK Und.*) an informer, a thief who betrays his accomplices ['sniff things out']. **3** [early 19C–1900s] a policeman ['sniff things out']. **4** [mid-19C+] the head; thus *off one's conk*, crazy, eccentric. **5** [late 19C+] a punch, usu. on the nose. **6** [1940s] intelligence; thinking.

IN COMPOUNDS

❑ **conk-buster** *n.* (*also* **konk-buster**) [BUST *v.*[1] (1); all three meanings imply the straining of one's brain] [1930s–50s] (*US black*) **1** an intellectual. **2** a difficult problem. **3** cheap liquor. ❑ **conkhouse** *n.* [20C+] (*US black*) the head. ❑ **conkpiece** *n.* [1940s] (*US black*) the head.

IN PHRASES

❑ **bust one's conk** *v.* [BUST *v.*[1] (1)] [1930s–40s] (*US black*) **1** to work very hard. **2** to show one's happiness in an emotional outburst. **3** to go mad.

conk *n.*[2] [*Congolene*, a fiery liquid, combining lye, eggs, potatoes and other ingredients, used in the artificial straightening of naturally kinky black (racially) hair] [1930s+] (*US black*) **1** hair that has been straightened through the application of a special mixture. **2** pomade; hair grease.

IN COMPOUNDS

❑ **conk job** *n.* [1960s+] (*US black*) a black hairstyle that has been straightened. ❑ **conkhead** *n.* [1950s] (*US black*) a black person.

conk *v.*[1] [CONK *n.*[1] (1); one 'puts one's nose in'] [early 19C] (*UK Und.*) to inform.

conk *v.*[2] (*also* **konk, kunk**) [CONK *n.*[1] (1) / CONK *n.*[1] (5) + echoic] **1** [early 19C; 1920s+] to hit, esp. on the nose or head, to knock out. **2** [1910s–40s] (*US*) to kill. **3** [1940s] in fig. use, i.e. to burden with, to assail. **4** *see* CONK (OUT) *v.*

IN PHRASES

❑ **conk off** *v.* (*orig. US*) **1** [1940s] to kill. **2** [1940s+] to fall asleep, to sleep. **3** [1950s–60s] to stop work, to skive. **4** [1950s–60s] to die. ❑ **conk out** *v. see* separate entry.

conk *v.*^{3} (*also* **konk**) [CONK *n.*^{2} (1)] [1940s+] (*US black*) to straighten hair with a mixture based on Congolene.

conked *adj.* (*also* **conk-haired, conk-headed, konked**) [CONK *v.*^{3}] [1940s+] (*US black*) having hair that has been straightened; thus *unconked*, hair that is in its natural state.

conked (out) *adj.* (*also* **conked in, conking, konked out**) [CONK (OUT) *v.* (1)] [1910s+] usu. of a machine or engine, broken, no longer working; also in ext. or fig. use, of a person, collapsed, asleep, dead.

conked up *adj.* [CONK *v.*^{2} (1)] [1940s–70s] (*US*) injured, hurt.

conker *n.* (*also* **konker**) [CONK *v.*^{2} (1)] [19C] a very hard blow.

conkers *n.* [resemblance to SE *conker*, a horse chestnut] [1990s+] the testicles.

IN COMPOUNDS

❑ **conkers deep** [1990s+] having the penis fully within the vagina.

conking *adj.* see CONKED (OUT) *adj.*

conk (out) *v.* [CONK *v.*^{2}] **1** [1910s+] usu. of machinery, to collapse, to break down, to malfunction. **2** [1920s+] to lose consciousness. **3** [1940s+] to give up. **4** [1940s+] (*also* **konk out**) to die; thus *conked*, dead. **5** [1940s+] to fall asleep. **6** [1940s+] to knock someone out.

conky *n.* (*also* **konky**) [CONK *n.*^{1} (1); the best known such figure was the Duke of Wellington, widely known as 'Old Conky'] [mid-19C+] a nickname given to anyone with an especially prominent nose.

conky *adj.* [CONK *v.*^{2} (1), i.e. 'knock about', strengthened by CONK (OUT) *v.* (1)] [late 19C+] sub-standard, second-rate.

con-man *n.* (*also* **con player, con-woman**) [CON *v.* (1)] **1** [late 19C] (*US*) a flatterer. **2** [late 19C–1920s] (*orig. US*) a confidence trickster; thus *con-woman* [later use is SE]. **3** [1930s] (*US*) a former convict.

connaught (ranger) *n.* [rhy. sl.; for ult. ety. *see* next] a stranger.

connaught rangers *n.* [the *Connaught Rangers* (disbanded 1922) were also the 88th Regiment of Foot; their army nickname was The Devil's Own] [1940s–50s] (*bingo*) the number eight.

connect *n.* see CONNECTION *n.*

connect *v.* [fig. uses of SE] **1** [mid-19C+] (*US*) to meet; usu. as *connect with*. **2** [1900s–30s] (*US*) to succeed in obtaining something, e.g. the spoils of a burglary. **3** [1920s+] (*drugs*) to obtain drugs, usu. by keeping a specific appointment with the dealer. **4** [1930s] to achieve sexual fulfilment; of a couple, to conceive a child.

connected *adj.* **1** [1920s+] (*orig. US*) having links to someone influential, whether legitimate or otherwise. **2** [1970s+] (*US*) being a member of an organized crime syndicate.

connection *n.* (*also* **connect, connexion**) [CONNECT *v.*] [1920s+] **1** (*orig. US*) a supplier of contraband liquor. **2** (*orig. US*) (*also* **nec**) a supplier of drugs; esp. a wholesaler (rather than a street seller). **3** (*orig. US*) the act of contacting a drug dealer; thus *connection dough*, money for drugs. **4** (*orig. US*) the person with whom one achieves sexual fulfilment; thus the act itself. **5** (*orig. US*) any form of connection or go-between, e.g. one who helps with a crime. **6** (*US prison*) a corrupt guard who helps inmates smuggle contraband into prison; an amenable, friendly guard.

IN PHRASES

❑ **house connect** *n.* [1990s+] (*US drugs*) a drug dealer who works from their home, rather than the street.

connector *n.* [CONNECT *v.* (2)] [1920s] (*US Und.*) a beggar.

conned *adj.* [late 19C+] tricked, hoaxed, fooled.

connexion *n.* see CONNECTION *n.*

Connie *n.* **1** [1950s] a *Con*stellation airliner. **2** [1970s] a Lincoln *Con*tinental.

connie *n.* (*also* **conny**) [abbr.] **1** [1900s] (*US Und.*) a person with tuberculosis, a *con*sumptive. **2** [1900s–70s] (*Aus./US*) a tram or bus *con*ductor. **3** [2000s] (*S.Afr. gay*) a condom.

connie *v.* [CONNIE *n.* (3)] [2000s] (*S.Afr. gay*) to ejaculate.

conny *n.*^{1} see CONNIE *n.*

conny *n.*^{2} *see under* CONY and its combs.

conny wobble *n.* (*also* **conny wabble**) [? CONY *n.* (3) + SE *wobble*; or ? COLLYWOBBLES *n.*] [late 18C–early 19C] a drink made of eggs and brandy beaten up together.

cono *n.* [Sp. sl. *coño*, CUNT *n.* (1)/CUNT *n.* (4)] [1940s+] (*US*) **1** the vagina; thus, women in the context of potential seduction. **2** as a general insult.

coño! *excl.* [Sp. *coño*, CUNT! *excl.*] [1920s+] (*US/P.R.*) a general excl. of fury, shock etc.

conoblin rig *n.* [RIG *n.*^{2} (1)] [late 18C–mid-19C] (*UK Und.*) cutting the strings that attached large pieces of coal to the doorways of coal sheds, i.e. stealing coal.

conoodle *v.* see CANOODLE *v.*

cons *n.* [abbr. tradename] [1960s+] *Con*verse All-Star basketball boots.

con safos *phr.* [Sp.] [1960s+] (*US*) **1** 'nobody can mess with this', a slogan used by the Mexican gangs of Los Angeles, often abbr. as *c/s* and written, as a graffito, after the gang's name. **2** a general term of approval [note latterly used as a magazine title].

consarn *v.* [SE *concern*] [mid–late 19C] (*US*) a euph. for to damn; thus used as a substitute for *damn* in mild oaths, e.g. *consarn it!*

consarned *adj.* (*also* **consarn, concerned**) [CONSARN *v.*] [mid-19C–1900s] (*US*) a euph. for DAMNED *adj.*; ext. as *I'll be consarned, I'm consarned.*

conscie *n.* see CONCHIE *n.* (1).

consent job *n.* (*also* **owner's job**) [JOB *n.*^{2} (1a)] [1950s–60s] (*US Und.*) any form of crime committed with the connivance of the victim; they will be able to collect the insurance.

conshi(e) *n.* see CONCHIE *n.* (1).

consignment *n.* [1990s+] (*W.I.*) the act of cheating on one's partner.

consolation *n.* [mid-19C] (*US*) alcohol, usu. whisky.

constab *n.* [abbr.; note dial. *constab tick*, a cattle tick – its stripes resemble those on the constable's trousers; also *constab-macka*, a large prickle] [20C+] (*W.I.*) a police officer, a constable.

constant *n.* [? abbr. SE *constant attender*] [1990s+] (*US black*) a regular member of a given social scene.

constant screamer *n.* [joc. mispron.] [late 19C–1910s; 2000s] a concertina.

constipated *adj.* [1920s–30s] reluctant to part with money.

constitutional *n.* [SE *constitution*, one's physical and mental state] **1** [1930s+] (*Aus.*) gin and bitters. **2** [1950s] (*US drugs*) the first injection of the day.

consumption stick *n.* [SE *consumption*, tuberculosis, a disease of the lungs] [1910s] (*Aus.*) a cigarette.

contact habit *n.* [SE *contact* + HABIT *n.* (1)] [1950s–60s] (*drugs*) an addiction to associating with drug-users and being around drugs, rather than an addiction to any particular drug; usu. said of drug dealers.

contact high *n.* [SE *contact* + HIGH *n.* (1)] [1960s+] (*drugs*) (*also* **contact**) the marijuana world's equivalent of passive smoking; the sensations that a non-smoker can achieve through the simple act of being in the same room as those who smoke; thus inhaling the drug willy-nilly, as well as picking up on the particular atmosphere generated by a roomful of smokers; similarly ext. to LSD, MDMA etc.

contact lens *n.* [its hallucinatory effects + ? ref. to 'making contact' with one's inner self] [1980s+] (*drugs*) LSD.

continent *n.* [? link to CONTINENTAL *n.*] [late 19C] (*US*) a euph. for hell, e.g. *what the continent do you mean by that?*

continental *n.* [SE *continental*, a coin issued by the Continental Congress during the American War of Independence (1775–83); the coins lost all value with the ending of the war; but note Seal, *The Lingo* (1999): 'his almost obsolete phrase is much more likely to be a polite form of DON'T GIVE A FUCK deriving from the reputation of the Continent for liberated, even excessive sexual behaviour'] [19C+] (*orig. US*) something worthless; usu. used as an adj. in comb., e.g. *continental cuss, continental copper, continental damn*, and phr. *not worth a continental*.

continuando *n.*

IN PHRASES

❑ **with a continuando** [Sp.] [late 17C–early 18C] for a very long time; usu. referring to a drinking bout and thus prefaced by 'drunk...'.

continuations *n.* [orig. gaiters; trousers 'continue' the waistcoat] [mid-19C] **1** trousers. **2** tights.

contract *n.* [late 19C+] a paid assignment usu. to murder someone but also sometimes to get them into a less severe form of difficulty; thus phr. *put/take out a contract on*, to arrange to have someone killed; *contract killer*, a killer for hire.

contract *v.* [CONTRACT *n.*] [1990s+] (*orig. US Und.*) to hire someone to kill a specific individual.

contrapunctum *n.* [Lat. *contrapunctum*, lit. 'counter-point'. The penis is the 'point' in this context] [mid-17C] the vagina.

contraries *n.* [such dice are 'contrary' to those currently in play] [mid-16C–early 19C] any form of false or legitimate dice, to be brought into and withdrawn from a game as the cheater desires.

control *n.*

SE in slang uses

IN COMPOUNDS

❑ **control freak** *n.* [-FREAK *sfx*] [1970s+] (*orig. US*) a person who is never satisfied unless he or she is in absolute control of a situation.

IN PHRASES

❑ **out of control** *adj.* [1980s+] (*US campus*) **1** of inanimate as well as animate objects, extreme, excessive, extremely good or extremely bad. **2** of people, drunk, intoxicated.

control *v.* [1970s+] (*W.I. Rasta/UK black*) **1** to be in charge of, responsible for, to own, to take. **2** to procure, to find, to arrange.

contwisted *adj.* [SE pfx *con-*, together + *twisted*] [mid-19C] (*US*) a euph. for DAMNED *adj.*

conundrum *n.* [SE *conundrum*, 'a whim, crotchet, maggot, conceit'; ? intensified by 19C 'a thing that one is puzzled to name, a "what-d'ye-call-it"' (*OED*)] [mid-17C–19C] the vagina.

convenience *n.* (*also* **place of convenience**) [19C] a euph. for a privy, a chamberpot.

convenient *n.* (*also* **convenience, conveniency**) **1** [late 17C] a wife. **2** [late 17C–early 18C] a prostitute. **3** [late 17C–early 18C] the vagina; thus, by metonymy, its possessor. **4** [late 17C–mid-19C] a mistress. **5** [late 17C–mid-19C] (*also* **convenient house**) a brothel. **6** [late 18C–early 19C] a lavatory.

convent *n.* [ironic use of SE] [mid-17C–mid-18C] a brothel.

conversate *v.* [abbr. SE *conversation*] [1980s+] (*US black*) to talk, usu. in a lively, demonstrative manner.

conversation *n.* [CONVERSATE *v.*; note Shakespearian *conversation*, sexual intimacy] [1990s+] (*US black*) a romantic 'line', used for the purposes of seduction.

SE in slang uses

IN COMPOUNDS

❑ **conversation fluid** *n.* [it 'lubricates' conversation] [20C+] (*US*) illicitly distilled whisky. ❑ **conversation water** *n.* [it 'lubricates' conversation] (*US*) **1** [late 19C] beer. **2** [1900s–20s] champagne.

conversion job *n.* [a healthy body is 'converted' into a seriously injured, even dead one] [1940s+] a severe beating, with or without some form of weapon.

convertible *adj.* [1970s+] (*US gay*) bisexual.

convey *v.* [mid-15C+] to steal; as n. *conveyor*, a thief.

conveyancer *n.* (*also* **conveyance, conveyer**) [CONVEY *v.* + pun on SE; i.e. he 'conveys' one's money etc to his own pocket] **1** [late 16C–mid-19C] a thief. **2** [mid-19C] a pickpocket.

conveyancing *n.* [CONVEY *v.*; the sense is intensified by the pun on SE *conveyancer*, a lawyer who investigates titles to property] [late 16C–19C] theft, stealing.

convictitis *n.* [SE *convict* + sfx *-itis*, usu. used of a disease] [1940s–50s] (*UK prison*) the illusion, fostered by too long a career in the prison service, that every prisoner is about to attack one for no other reason than that one is a warder.

convincer *n.* [SE *convincer*, that which convinces] **1** [1900s–50s] a persuasive action or speech. **2** [1930s–50s] a weapon. **3** [1940s] (*US Und.*) luring a victim into a confidence trick by allowing them to make a large initial profit.

convincing ground *n.* [the fighters attempt to 'convince' each other of the error of their ways] [1940s] (*Aus.*) a place at which prize or grudge fights are held.

convo *n.* [SE *conversation* + -O *sfx* (3)] [1990s+] (*Aus./N.Z.*) a conversation.

cony *n.* (*also* **coney, conny**) [SE *cony*, a rabbit] **1** [mid-16C–mid-17C] a term of affection for a woman. **2** in sexual senses (cf. CUNNY *n.*) [the stereotyped sexuality of rabbits + the pubic hair is supposedly reminiscent of the rabbit's tail + play on CUNT *n.*]. (**a**) [mid-16C–1920s] (*also* **cony-skin**) the vagina. (**b**) [17C] a prostitute. (**c**) [1920s] (*US*) a sexually available woman. **3** [late 16C–19C] (*also* **cunny**) a dupe, the victim of a confidence trick, of card-sharping etc.

IN COMPOUNDS

❑ **cony...** *see also under* CUNNY and its combs. ❑ **cony-burrow** *n.* **1** [late 16C–17C] (*also* **cony-berry**) a brothel. **2** [mid-17C–early 18C] the vagina. ❑ **cony-dog** *n.* [lit. a dog that catches rabbits] [late 17C] one who assists a confidence trickster in CONY-CATCHING *n.* ❑ **cony-skin** *n. see* sense 3a above.

conycatch *v.* (*also* **cony, cunnycatch**) [CONY *n.* (3) / CONY *n.* (2a)] **1** [late 16C–17C; early 19C] to ensnare in a confidence trick. **2** [17C] to go out whoring or womanizing.

cony-catcher *n.*[1] (*also* **coney-catcher, conny-, cunny-**) [CONYCATCH *v.* (1)] **1** [late 16C–mid-17C] a confidence trickster. **2** [late 18C] ext. in non-criminal context, a plausible, smooth-tongued speaker.

cony-catcher *n.*[2] (*also* **coney-catcher, conny-, cunny-**) [CONY *n.* (2)/CUNNY *n.* (1); play on CONY-CATCHER *n.*[1]] **1** [late 16C–early 17C] a prostitute; thus *cony-catching*, prostitution. **2** [17C] the penis. **3** [17C–18C] a prostitute's customer.

cony-catching *n.* [CONYCATCH *v.* (1)] [late 16C–17C] any form of confidence tricking, spec. card-sharping.

cony-catching *adj.* [CONYCATCH *v.* (1)] **1** [late 16C–mid-17C] pertaining to confidence trickery. **2** [mid-17C] in a non-criminal sense, deceitful, mendacious.

cony-fumble *n.* [mispron.] [late 17C–early 18C] a constable.

coo *n.* (*also* **cou, cu**) [abbr./euph. for CUNT *n.* (1)/CUNT *n.* (4)] [late 19C+] **1** the vagina. **2** a woman regarded as a sex object. **3** a derog. term of abuse.

coo *adj.* [2000s] (*US teen*) abbr. COOL *adj.* (9); also as excl.

coo! *excl.* (*also* **coo-er!**) [late 19C+] an excl. expressing surprise or incredulity.

cooch *n.* [abbr./euph. for CUNT *n.* (1); note *Online Dict. Playground Slang* (2001): 'This word raises all sorts of interesting possibilities since the old Welsh word 'cwtch ' (which has a similar pronunciation) is often used to mean a 'place of comfort'. It makes me wonder if the word was carried to the States by Welsh immigrants then mutated and adopted by peoples who would have no idea of its origins'] **1** [1910s+] (*US*) a 'hootchy-kootchy' dance, i.e. belly-dancing; thus *cooch dancer, coocher*, a belly dancer. **2** [1960s+] (*US*) the vagina; thus, by metonymy, a woman. **3** [1970s+] (*US gay*) an effeminate homosexual male.

coochie *n.* (*also* **cookie**) [CUNT *n.* (1), reinforced by SAmE *cookie*/COOKIE *n.*[1] (1)] [1930s+] (*US*) the female genitalia; thus *get some coochie*, to have sexual intercourse.

IN PHRASES

❑ **clout one's cookie** *v.* [1970s] (*US*) of a woman, to masturbate. ❑ **pop coochie** *v.* [1990s+] to have sexual intercourse.

coo-coo *n. see* CUCKOO *n.*[1] (2).

coo-coo *adj.*[1] [abbr./redup. of COOL *adj.*] [1960s] (*US*) sophisticated, aware.

coo-coo *adj.*[2] *see* CUCKOO *adj.*

cooda *n.* see COUTER *n.*^{2}.

coodle *n.* [ety. unknown] [2000s] (*Irish*) excrement.

cook *n.*^{1} [COOK *v.* (5)] (*orig. US drugs*) **1** [late 19C–1950s] an expert who prepares an opium pipe. **2** [1950s] a manufacturer of illicit drugs. **3** [1990s+] a single session of manufacturing heroin.

SE in slang uses

IN COMPOUNDS

❑ **cook-ruffian** *n.* [late 17C–early 19C] (*UK Und.*) a bad or bad-tempered cook. ❑ **cook's own** *n.* [a play on regimental nicknames + the force's supposed affection for the cooks working in the great London mansions] [mid–late 19C] the police force.

cook *n.*^{2} [rhy. sl.; but note Yid. *guck*, a look, a glance, usu. in phr. 'geb a guck', have look] [1940s+] (*Aus.*) a look, a glance.

cook *n.*^{3} see KOOK *n.*

cook *v.* **1** [mid-17C+] to tamper with, to falsify; thus *cook the books, cook the accounts*. **2** [mid-19C–1940s] to ruin, to spoil. **3** [mid-19C+] to suffer from the heat. **4** [late 19C] (*Aus.*) to die by hanging. **5** in the preparation or consumption of drugs; occas. alcohol. (**a**) [late 19C] to manufacture smokeable opium from the crude product. (**b**) [late 19C–1950s] to heat opium before smoking it. (**c**) [1920s+] to prepare a narcotic (esp. heroin) for injection by heating a solution of powder and water for use in a syringe. (**d**) [1930s+] to distil (bootleg) alcohol. (**e**) [1980s] to prepare a non-narcotic drug, e.g. an amphetamine pill, for injection. (**f**) [1980s] to manufacture illicit drugs, e.g. heroin or crack cocaine. (**g**) [1980s+] to heat cocaine until it hardens. **6** [late 19C] to give someone their due deserts. **7** [late 19C–1950s] to overcome. **8** [late 19C+] to bribe, to arrange illicitly. **9** [late 19C+] (*US*) to kill, to murder; lit. and fig. **10** [20C+] used fig. to cover any activity. **11** [1910s] (*US*) to concoct a mendacious story. **12** [1930s+] (*US*) to die or execute in the electric chair. **13** [1930s+] (*US*) to be electrocuted. **14** [1940s+] (*US black*) to do something exceptionally well. **15** [1940s+] (*orig. US black*) of a musician or group of musicians, to be playing in harmony, particularly creatively; to be in mutual understanding. **16** [1960s+] (*Aus.*) to scold; to criticize harshly. **17** [1970s+] to start or rev up a car. **18** [1980s+] to be burnt to death.

IN PHRASES

❑ **cook down** see separate entries. ❑ **cook off** *v. see* separate entry. ❑ **cook on all four** *v.* [1940s+] (*Can./US*) to be very busy, to be working very well. ❑ **cook on the front burner** *v.* [1940s+] (*US*) **1** to do something very well, to act or think correctly. **2** to be currently pertinent. ❑ **cook someone's goose** *v. see* separate entry. ❑ **cook up** *v. see* separate entry. ❑ **cook with gas** *v.* (*also* **cook with electricity, ...radar**) [1940s+] (*orig. US black*) to succeed, to do very well, to tackle a project in the right way, esp. after misdirected efforts have failed; thus usu. in phr. *now we're cooking with gas*. ❑ **what's cooking?** (*also* **what cooks?**) [orig. swing band use] [1930s+] **1** (*orig. US*) a phr. of greeting, 'what's going on?'. **2** lit. 'what's going on?', i.e. what is happening?, thus negative response *nothing cooking*. ❑ **wouldn't that cook you?** [late 19C] (*US campus*) wouldn't that annoy/shock you?

SE in slang uses

IN PHRASES

❑ **cook cucumbers** *v.* [the presumed use of a cucumber as a dildo] [1960s+] of a woman, to masturbate.

cook-down *n.* [COOK DOWN *v.*] [1970s+] (*drugs*) the process whereby users liquefy heroin in order to inhale it.

cook down *v.* [var. on COOK UP *v.* (4c)] [1970s+] to prepare an injection of a narcotic drug, usu. heroin, by heating a measure of the powdered drug plus some water in a teaspoon or bottle cap.

cooked *adj.* [fig. uses of SE + COOK SOMEONE'S GOOSE *v.*] **1** [early 19C+] exhausted, finished, destroyed, in serious trouble. **2** [1920s+] (*US*) drunk. **3** [1930s+] (*US*) intoxicated by a drug.

cooked up *adj. see* COKED (UP) *adj.* (1).

cookee *n.* (*also* **cookie, cooky**) **1** [19C+] (*mainly US*) the head cook. **2** [1910s+] (*US*) a cook's assistant.

cooker *n.*^{1} **1** [mid-19C] that which settles a situation, a clincher, a finisher. **2** [1940s+] anything exciting, e.g. a sexy or sophisticated person, an emotive piece of music.

cooker *n.*^{2} [COOK *v.* (5)] **1** [1910s+] (*US drugs*) an opium addict (who prepares his or her own pipes). **2** [1920s–30s] one who manufactures bootleg alcohol. **3** [1930s+] (*drugs*) a container, usu. a bottle cap, in which the mixture of heroin and water can be heated before drawing it into a syringe and thence injecting it into one's arm. **4** [1940s+] a container used in the illicit manufacture of spirits. **5** [1990s+] one who cooks freebase cocaine. **6** [2000s] one who manufactures amphetamine.

cooker *n.*^{3} **1** [1950s+] (*N.Z.*) a British immigrant to N.Z. who arrived on the TSS *Captain Cook* in the 1950s. **2** *see* CAPTAIN COOK *n.* (1).

cookhouse *n.* [1980s] (*US*) a very hot day (or night).

cookie *n.*^{1} [fig. uses of SE *cookie*, biscuit] **1** [late 19C] the vagina. **2** [1920s+] (*orig. US*) (*also* **cooky**) a man (or woman), often with a qualifying adj., e.g. SMART COOKIE below. **3** [1920s] (*US*) a close friend. **4** [1920s+] (*also* **shop cookie**) an attractive woman. **5** [1920s+] (*Glasgow*) a prostitute. **6** [1920s+] in pl., the contents of one's stomach, lit. things that have been cooked; usu. in phrs. meaning to vomit, e.g. *chuck one's cookies, heave one's cookies, woof one's cookies* (see phrs. below). **7** [1950s] (*US*) $1. **8** [1950s+] (*US black*) a derog. term for a black person who is seen as espousing white values to the detriment of their own background. **9** [1960s] a good example of something, a good one. **10** [1960s] (*US gay*) the penis. **11** [1960s+] (*US black*) in pl., in fig. uses. (**a**) any form of desired object, esp. sex or money. (**b**) emotions, feelings. **12** [1960s+] (*US*) in pl., the male or female genitalia. **13** [1970s] (*US*) a cigarette. **14** [1970s] a lesbian who plays the passive 'feminine' role in sex. **15** [1970s+] (*US gay*) an effeminate male homosexual. **16** [1990s+] (*US*) a lump of expectorated phlegm.

IN COMPOUNDS

❑ **cookies and cream** *n.* [2000s] (*US black*) a mixed-race person of black and white parentage. ❑ **cookies-crashing** *n.* [2000s] (*US black*) slapping a woman's breasts while engaged in sexual intercourse with her.

IN PHRASES

❑ **blow someone's cookies** *v.* [1930s+] to fellate. ❑ **flip one's cookies** *v.* **1** [1950s+] to vomit. **2** [1960s+] to lose emotional control. ❑ **get one's cookies** *v.* [1960s+] **1** to have sexual intercourse; thus *get one's cookies off*, to come to orgasm. **2** fig., to enjoy oneself. ❑ **lose one's cookies** *v.* [1940s+] (*US*) to lose emotional control. ❑ **pop one's cookies** *v.* (*also* **snap one's cookies**) **1** [1920s+] (*US*) to vomit. **2** [1970s+] to reach orgasm. ❑ **shoot one's cookies** *v.* (*also* **drop one's cookies**) [1970s+] (*US campus*) to vomit. ❑ **smart cookie** *n.* (*also* **sharp cookie**) [1940s+] (*orig. US*) a bright, opportunistic person; also ironically. ❑ **throw one's cookies** *v.* [1970s+] (*US*) to vomit. ❑ **toss one's cookies** *v.* (*also* **toss one's tacos**) **1** [1950s+] (*orig. US campus*) to vomit. **2** [1970s] in imper., a derisory retort. **3** [1990s+] to make someone sick.

SE in slang uses

IN COMPOUNDS

❑ **cookie-crumbs** *n.* [1970s+] (*US gay*) semen stains on the trousers. ❑ **cookie-cutter** *n.* [1920s–60s] (*orig. US black*) a police badge. ❑ **cookie-dipper** *n. see* COOKIE-PUSHER *n.* ❑ **cookie-duster** *n.* **1** [1930s+] (*US*) a moustache; thus a moustachioed person. **2** *see* COOKIE-PUSHER *n.* ❑ **cookie-pusher** *n. see* separate entry. ❑ **cookie-shine** *n.* [mid-19C–1930s] a tea-party.

IN PHRASES

❑ **have a cookie in the oven** *v.* [var. on HAVE A BUN IN THE OVEN *under* OVEN *n.*] [1960s] (*US*) to be pregnant. ❑ **shop cookie** *n.* see sense 4 above.

cookie *n.*^{2} **1** [1930s] (*US prison*) cocaine. **2** [1930s–60s] (*US drugs*) (*also* **cookee**) an opium addict. **3** [1990s+] (*drugs*) crack cocaine in its solid, rock form.

cookie *n.*^{3} *see* COOCHIE *n.*

cookie *n.*[4] *see* COOKEE *n.*

cookie-pusher *n.* (*also* **cookie-dipper, -duster**) [SE *cookie* + *pusher*; the cakes that such men are continually passing around such tea parties or that waitresses serve in cafés] (*US*) **1** [1920s+] an ambitious, but lazy, man, esp. a government career man, a sycophant. **2** [1920s+] a young man who errs to the 'feminine side of life' – tea parties, conversation, the niceties of dress and of gossip, art rather than sport etc. **3** [1930s–50s] a waitress.

cookie-truck *n.* [KOOK *n.* (1) + SE *truck*] [1970s+] (*US*) the van that transports patients to a psychiatric institution.

cookie-wagon *n.* [? KOOK *n.* (1)] [1920s] (*US*) a police van, a 'black maria'.

cooking *n.* [COOK *v.* (5f)] [1990s+] (*drugs*) manufacturing illicit drugs, e.g. heroin or crack cocaine; also *cooking house*, a place where these drugs are prepared for consumption; *cooking spoon*, used to prepare the drug.

cooking *adj.*[1] [COOK *v.* (15)] [1940s+] (*orig. US black*) excellent, doing very well, esp. of a performance.

cooking *adj.*[2] [1960s+] **1** (*US drugs*) very intoxicated; feeling the effects. **2** in fig. use, dramatic, aggressive.

cook off *v.* [COOK *v.* (5)] **1** [1910s] (*US Und.*) to satisfy one's addiction by smoking opium. **2** [1960s] in bootlegging, to heat the mix of alcohol and other ingredients preparatory to distilling spirits.

cookoo *adj. see* CUCKOO *adj.*

cook someone's goose *v.* [mid-19C+] **1** to kill; thus *one's goose is cooked*, one is dying; *cooked goose*, one who is doomed. **2** (*also* **cook someone's gruel, do someone's goose**) to spoil someone's chances. **3** to give someone their due deserts.

cook up *v.* [ext. of COOK *v.*] **1** [mid-18C; 1910s] to tamper with, to falsify. **2** [mid-18C+] to invent. **3** [late 18C+] to happen, to develop. **4** to manufacture or prepare drugs. (**a**) [late 19C–1960s] to prepare opium for smoking. (**b**) [1920s–40s] (*US Und.*) to boil nitroglycerine out of dynamite. (**c**) [1920s+] to prepare an injection of a narcotic drug, usu. heroin, by heating a measure of the powdered drug plus some water in a teaspoon or bottle cap. (**d**) [1980s] to turn cocaine into freebase by heating it up [*see* FREEBASE *v.*]. (**e**) [1980s+] to make crack cocaine from cocaine hydrochloride base. (**f**) [1980s+] to manufacture methamphetamine. **5** [1900s] to make. **6** [1930s–50s] (*US black*) to enjoy oneself, to have a good time [COOK *v.* (15)].

IN PHRASES

❑ **cook up a pill** *v.* [20C+] (*drugs*) to prepare a pipe of opium. ❑ **cook up a storm** *v.* [1960s] (*US*) to advocate enthusiastically. ❑ **cook up brown** *v.* [var. on *DO UP BROWN under* BROWN *adj.*[2]] [1950s] (*US*) to defeat comprehensively. ❑ **cook up with** *v.* [? play on HOT *adj.* (1a)] [1980s+] (*US campus*) to 'neck' with, to pet.

cooky *n.*[1] [COOK *n.*[1] (1)] [1920s–50s] (*US drugs*) someone who prepares an opium pipe for use.

cooky *n.*[2] *see* COOKEE *n.*

cool *n.*[1] [ety. unknown; ? his 'coolness' when thieving; or Fr. *cul*, the buttocks, near which the purse hung] [late 16C] (*UK Und.*) a cut-purse.

cool *n.*[2] [COOL *adj.*] **1** [late 19C+] temper, poise, composure, attitude to life and ability to deal with it. **2** [1950s–60s] (*US teen*) a temporary armistice between opposing street gangs. **3** [1960s+] (*orig. US black*) sophistication, the prevailing fashion. **4** [1970s] (*US campus*) a fashionable, drug-taking (or whatever is deemed relevant) young person, as opposed to a straight, conventional person.

IN PHRASES

❑ **blow one's cool** *v.* [1960s+] **1** to lose control, to become nervous or angry. **2** to ruin one's image, to discomfit oneself, to make an exhibition of oneself. ❑ **blow someone's cool** *v.* [1970s] to inform upon. ❑ **hold one's cool** *v.* [1960s] (*US*) to keep calm; to relax. ❑ **keep one's cool** *v.* [1950s+] (*orig. US*) to remain calm, despite circumstances to the contrary. ❑ **lose one's cool** *v.* [1950s+] (*orig. US*) to lose one's dignity or self-possession, to lose one's temper. ❑ **put the cool on** *v. see* COOL *v.*[3] (2).

cool *adj.* [ult. orig. Eton College jargon *cool fish*, a cocky, self-possessed schoolboy; post WW2 use (initially US black) is usu. associated with the cool jazz movement of the 1940s, esp. Charlie Parker's record *Cool Blues* of 1947, but a single citation in *DARE* sets sense 1 at least as early as 1884. Given that the SE 19C use of *cool* meant dispassionate, emotionally withdrawn, and as such is a negative use, its use as a term of approbation gives it some claim to be the first example of the black bad = good sl. model (cf. BAD *adj.* (3); WICKED *adj.* (2))] **1** [19C+] relaxed, calm, self-contained. **2** [mid-19C+] sophisticated, aware. **3** [mid-19C+] insolent, arrogant, impudent. **4** [20C+] (*orig. US black*) (*also* **kool**) calm, self-possessed, aware, sophisticated. **5** [1930s+] (*orig. US black*) good, fine, pleasing. **6** [1940s+] (*orig. US*) fashionable, chic, 'with it'. **7** [1940s+] antonyms of HOT *adj.* (**a**) (*drugs*) not carrying or owning drugs, or believing that one has hidden them well enough to defy any search of one's body or premises. (**b**) (*US Und.*) not suspicious, either of people or objects. (**c**) (*US street gang*) not carrying weapons or acting aggressively. **8** [1950s+] acceptable, satisfactory; esp. in phr. *that's cool*. **9** [1960s+] comfortable, happy, on good terms. **10** [1970s] safe. **11** [1970s+] trustworthy.

IN COMPOUNDS

❑ **cool-brains** *adj.* [1960s+] (*S.Afr.*) relaxed, in control. ❑ **cool breeze** *see* separate entries. ❑ **cool cat** *n.* [1940s+] a sophisticated, competent, unruffled, able person. ❑ **cool hand** *n.* [mid-19C+] (*US*) a cool, calm, controlled and competent individual. ❑ **cool-head** *n.* **1** [mid-19C+] a calm, unflappable person. **2** [1960s] a pleasant person. ❑ **cool jerk** *n.* [1960s–80s] (*US black*) one who deludes himself into a belief that he is COOL *adj.* (3); in fact he is a JERK *n.*[1] (2); thus *do the cool jerk*, to move in an ostentatious manner. ❑ **cool papa** *n.* [1940s] (*US black*) a self-possessed, sophisticated and, as such, alluring man. ❑ **cool whip** *n.* [pun on brandname of the US sweet] [1980s+] (*US campus*) something very new and appealing.

IN PHRASES

❑ **be cool** (*also* **you be cool**) [1980s+] goodbye. ❑ **cool as shit** (*also* **cool as toast**) [1970s+] (*US campus*) an expression of approval. ❑ **cool runnings** [1980s+] (*W.I./UK black teen*) a phr. meaning everything is fine, all is going smoothly. ❑ **on the cool** [2000s] (*US prison*) a general intensifier, usu. meaning truthfully or its opposite. ❑ **that's cool** [1950s+] (*orig. US*) that's satisfactory, that's all right, don't worry. ❑ **too cool for school** *adj.* [1990s+] very fashionable, well-dressed, obsessively so.

IN EXCLAMATIONS

❑ **cool beans!** [1980s+] (*US teen*) excellent! wonderful! ❑ **cool deal!** [DEAL *n.*[1] (4)] [1990s+] (*US campus*) an exclamation of approval, admiration.

SE in slang uses

IN COMPOUNDS

❑ **cool crape** *n.* ['*Cool-crape*, a slight Chequer'd Stuff made in imitation of Scotch Plad' (B.E.)] [late 18C] a shroud; thus *be put into one's cool crape*, to die. ❑ **cool lady** *n.* [ref. to next] [late 17C–early 19C] a female camp follower, specializing in selling brandy to the troops. ❑ **cool nantz** *n.* (*also* **cool nants**) [NANTZ *n.*] [late 17C–early 19C] cognac. ❑ **cool one** *n.* [1950s+] (*orig. US*) a bottle of beer. ❑ **cool smoke** *n.* [1980s+] (*drugs*) a smoke of methamphetamine.

cool *v.*[1] [backsl.; thus *cool him*, look at him, 'a phrase frequently used when one costermonger warns another of the approach of a policeman' (Hotten, 1867)] [mid-19C+] to look at, esp. in *cool esclop!* look, the police!

cool *v.*[2] **1** [1900s; 1950s+] (*orig. US*) to calm down, to deal with a problem in a controlled manner, to resist confrontation. **2** [1950s+] to calm someone or some situation down. **3** [1950s+] to knock out. **4** [1960s] (*US campus*) to turn down a request for a date. **5** [1960s] (*US Und.*) of stolen goods, to remain hidden until police activity quietens. **6** [1960s] to render relaxed, happy. **7** [1960s+] (*US*) to postpone, to put off, to stop. **8** [1960s+] (*US*) of a criminal charge or disciplinary problem, to quash. **9** [1980s+] (*US black/teen*) to lounge around, to 'hang out'. **10** [1980s+] to saunter.

IN PHRASES

❑ **cool in** *v.* [1960s] (*US teen*) to inform. ❑ **cool it** *v. see* separate entry. ❑ **cool off** *see* separate entries. ❑ **cool out** *see* separate entries. ❑ **cool the beef** *v. see under* BEEF *n.*[2].

SE in slang uses

IN PHRASES

❑ **cool-cock** *v.* [var. on COLD-COCK *v.*] [1930s–50s] (*US*) to knock unconscious. ❑ **cool-crack** *v.* [var. on COLD-COCK *v.* (1)] [1940s] (*US black*) to knock unconscious. ❑ **cool one's copper** *v.* (*also* **cool one's coppers**) [HOT COPPERS *n.*] [mid–late 19C] to take a drink to ease the parched throat caused by excessive drinking. ❑ **cool one's jets** *v.* [1970s+] (*orig. US*) to calm down, to relax. ❑ **cool one's role** *v.* [1960s] (*US black/gang*) to calm down.

cool *v.*[3] [the chilliness of the corpse] (*US*) **1** [1920s+] to beat up. **2** [1920s+] (*also* **put the cool on**) to kill, to murder, to assassinate. **3** [1950s+] to die.

cool *v.*[4] [the calming effects of the drug, either as ending withdrawal symptoms or simply removing oneself from 'reality'] [1970s] (*drugs*) to sell heroin; to inject (someone) with heroin.

cool *adv.* **1** [early 19C+] calmly, in an unruffled manner. **2** [late 19C] askance, suspiciously.

IN PHRASES

❑ **play it cool** *v.* (*also* **play cool, pluck it cool**) [1940s+] (*orig. US black*) to act in an uninterested or disinterested manner, to control every emotion. ❑ **play it cool** [1950s–70s] (*US*) a phr. of farewell. ❑ **take it cool** *v.* [mid-19C+] to relax, to remain undisturbed by events.

cool! *excl.* [COOL *v.*[2] (1)] [1950s–60s] (*orig. US*) relax! calm down!

coolarific *adj.* [COOL *adj.* (6)] [1990s+] (*US campus*) fantastic, great.

cool breeze *n.* [COOL-BREEZE *adj.*] (*US black/campus*) **1** [1980s] an admirable and popular person. **2** [1990s+] a person who thinks they are sophisticated when they are not.

cool-breeze *adj.* [joc. use of SE + COOL *adj.* (3)/COOL *adj.* (6)] [1960s+] (*orig. US*) **1** cool, calm. **2** first-rate, wonderful.

cool breeze! *excl.* [COOL-BREEZE *adj.*] [1960s+] excellent! wonderful! first-rate!

cooled out *adj.* [COOL *v.*[2] (1)] [1970s+] (*orig. US black*) **1** calm, unperturbed, in control. **2** under the influence of drugs, usu. narcotics.

cooler *n.* [fig. uses of SE, i.e. things that cool; note SE *cooler*, a fridge] **1** [early 17C–early 19C] a woman, esp. a wife (who 'cools one's passions') as opposed to a mistress or lover (who 'heats them up'). **2** [19C] a glass of porter, taken as a balance to one of spirits. **3** [19C] a 'finisher', a 'clincher', e.g. a knockout punch, a crushing statement. **4** [early 19C] the (female) buttocks; thus phr. *kiss my cooler*. **5** [mid-19C] a glass of beer taken after drinking spirits and water. **6** [late 19C–1900s] (*US campus*) an expert, an outstanding individual. **7** [late 19C+] (*orig. US*) a prison; police cells. **8** [20C+] (*orig. US*) a punishment or solitary confinement cell. **9** [20C+] (*Aus.*) a chilly glance, a snub, a rejection. **10** [1900s] (*Aus.*) a drink of beer. **11** [1900s] (*US campus*) an attractive young woman. **12** [1920s] a deck of doctored cards. **13** [1930s–60s] (*US tramp*) a silencer. **14** [1930s+] (*US black*) a funeral home. **15** [1970s+] (*US gay*) as the homosexual reverse of sense 1, a lover. **16** [1980s+] (*drugs*) a cigarette laced with a drug, usu. crack cocaine.

IN PHRASES

❑ **in the cooler** [late 19C–1900s] (*US*) in reserve.

coolie *n.*[1] (*also* **koelie**) [a variety of Indian languages in all of which the term means lit. a man for hire and thus a (menial) labourer; note Zulu *amakula*, a person of Indian origin] **1** [mid-19C] a private soldier. **2** [mid–late 19C] (*US*) an immigrant Chinese labourer. **3** [mid-19C+] (*S.Afr.*) a derog. term for an Indian; thus *coolie Christmas*, the Islamic festival of Moharram or the Hindu festival of Diwali; *coolie creeper*, in cricket, a ball that stays low without bouncing; *coolie pink*, shocking pink, seen as vulgar and 'typically Indian'; *coolie shop/store*, a shop owned or managed by an Indian. **4** [mid-19C+] (*Aus./S.Afr.*) a derog. term for a black person; esp. as *coolie-boy*, *coolie-girl*. **5** [mid-19C+] (*US*) (*also* **coolie-man**) any East Asian. **6** [20C+] (*W.I.*) the trad. Jamaican epithet for East Indians; usu. in the form *coolie-man* or *coolie-woman*.

IN COMPOUNDS

❑ **coolie mud** *n.* [MUD *n.* (3b)] [1940s–50s] (*US drugs*) inferior opium. ❑ **coolie nation** *n.* [sense 6 above + -NATION *sfx*] [20C+] (*W.I.*) East Indians.

coolie *n.*[2] [SE *cool*, i.e. he remains *cool* towards their approaches] [1950s–60s] (*US teen*) any youth unaffiliated to a street gang.

coolie *n.*[3] [Sp. sl. *culo*, the anus] [1970s+] (*US*) the anus.

coolie *n.*[4] [1970s+] (*US gay*) a blunder, an error; thus *pull a coolie*, to err, to blunder.

coolie *n.*[5] [var. COOLER *n.* (16)] [1980s+] (*drugs*) a cigarette laced with a drug.

coolie Mary *n. see* MARY *n.* (1c).

cooling *n.* [COOL *v.*[2] (9)] [1980s+] (*US*) relaxing.

cool it *v.* [COOL *adj.*/COOL *v.*[2]/COOL *v.*[3]] **1** [1940s] (*US black*) to strike a pose reflecting one's image as a HIPSTER *n.* and to show off the line of one's ZOOT SUIT *n.* **2** [1950s] (*orig. US*) to leave. **3** [1950s] (*US*) to arrange, to fix something, to protect from the authorities. **4** [1950s+] (*orig. US black*) to calm down, to relax; often as imper. *cool it!* **5** [1950s+] (*orig. US black*) to stop, to cease from an action. **6** [1960s] (*US*) to die; thus *cooling board*, the death bed. **7** [1960s] to draw back from, to cease relating to.

cool-off *n.* [COOL OFF *v.*[2] (1)] [1930s–50s] calmness, relaxation; an escape from controversy.

cool off *v.*[1] [COOL *v.*[3]] **1** [mid-19C; 1930s–60s] to kill, to murder. **2** [1930s–60s] to knock out, to subdue with physical force.

cool off *v.*[2] [COOL *v.*[2]] **1** [mid-19C+] (*orig. US*) to calm down. **2** [late 19C–1900s] (*US*) to be imprisoned. **3** [20C+] (*orig. US*) to calm someone down. **4** [1920s+] (*orig. US*) to lose interest in. **5** [1930s+] (*orig. US*) of a criminal, or persons involved in conflict, to lie low until the hue and cry has passed. **6** [1950s] (*orig. US*) to become bored. **7** [1990s+] (*orig. US*) of a gambler, to run out of luck. **8** [1990s+] (*orig. US*) of a stolen object, to be less HOT *adj.* (1d).

IN PHRASES

❑ **cool-off man** *n.* [1930s] (*US Und.*) in a confidence trick, the gang member who calms worried members of the public.

cool-out *n.* [COOL OUT *v.*[2] (3)] [1990s+] relaxation, a rest; also attrib.

cool out *v.*[1] [COOL *v.*[3]] [mid-19C; 1960s+] (*orig. US*) to subdue physically, to kill.

cool out *v.*[2] [COOL *v.*[2]] **1** [1910s+] (*orig. US Und.*) to calm (someone) down; often as imper. *cool out!* also to pacify another. **2** [1950s+] (*W.I.*) to take a rest from work by lying in the shade of a tree. **3** [1950s+] to relax. **4** [1960s] (*US Und.*) of a confidence man, to avoid the victim from whom the money has been extracted. **5** [1960s–70s] to make manageable. **6** [1990s+] (*US drugs*) to abstain from drug use.

IN PHRASES

❑ **cool out on** *v.* [1960s] (*US*) to fail to pay a debt to someone.

cooly *n.* [the drug renders the cigarette 'cool', both to smoke and in terms of image] **1** [1990s+] (*US black/drugs*) a cigarette mixed with cocaine. **2** *see* KALI *n.*

coon *n.* [fig. uses of SE *racoon*, typified as a cunning creature. Used orig. in non-racial senses (emphasizing only cunning), the meaning swiftly became unequivocally racist, and used as such in Aus. too, where it described Aborigines; note American Dialect Society List 17/12/01: 'The daughter of William Lloyd Garrison (the great American abolitionist), while tending to the needs of emancipated slaves on the Gullah Islands, anthologized Negro spirituals. She also made notes on the Gullah dialect. "Coon" was the name that the ex-slaves called each other, and she indicates that it is the word "cousin" as expressed through the dialect. [...] As with many terms that members of ethnic communities call each other, they descend into the pejorative'] **1** [mid-18C–1900s] (*US*) (*also* **cooney**) a sly person, a cunning fellow. **2** [mid-19C] (*US*) a Whig. **3** [mid-19C] (*US*) a Native American. **4** [mid-19C+] (*US*) (*also* **koon**) a person, esp. a rustic, a peasant. **5** [mid-19C+] (*orig. US*) (*also* **coonhead**) a highly derog. term for a black person. **6** [late 19C–1930s] (*US*) a petty thief. **7** [1910s–30s] (*US black*) used non-pejoratively of a fellow black person. **8** [1920s+] a clown, a fool, the image is of a 'chocolate coloured coon'. **9** [1980s+] (*S.Afr.*) a black South African. **10** [2000s] (*Aus.*) an Aborigine.

DERIVATIVES

❑ **coonery** *n.* [1980s+] stupidity, esp. as enacted by black people. ❑ **coonish** *adj.* [mid-19C; 1990s+] (*UK juv.*) stupid.

IN COMPOUNDS

❑ **coon bottom** *n.* (*also* **coon hollow**) [var. on BLACK BOTTOM *under* BLACK *adj.*] [20C+] within a larger urban area, that part recognized as home to the black community. ❑ **coon chaser** *n.* [late 19C] (*US*) a white man who pursues/has sex with black women. ❑ **coon dick** *n.* [DICK *n.*[1] (5), i.e. racist stereotyping] [1920s–30s] (*US*) an illicitly distilled spirit, compounded of 'grapefruit juice, cornmeal mash, beef bones and a few mo' things' (Zora Neale Hurston, *Mules & Men*, 1935). ❑ **coonhead** *n. see* sense 5 above. ❑ **coon juice** *n.* [mid-19C; 1960s+] (*US*) illicitly distilled whisky. ❑ **coon-lover** *n.* [mid-19C+] (*orig. US*) a derog. term, as used by racists, for those who are seen as insufficiently hostile to blacks. ❑ **coon's age** *n.* [mid-19C+] (*US*) a very long time; often as *in a coon's age* [the life-span of a SE *racoon* although the phr. is inevitably seen as linked to sense 5 above]. ❑ **coonshine** *n.* [i.e. racial stereotyping + MOONSHINE *n.* (2)/SE *moonshine*] [late 19C] (*US*) an all-night party. ❑ **Coontown** *n.* (*also* **Coonsville**) [late 19C+] a derog. term for the black section of a town or city.

IN PHRASES

❑ **old coon** *n.* [mid–late 19C] (*US*) a shrewd individual.

coon *adj.*[1] (*also* **cooney, coonful, coony**) [COON *n.* (3)] [mid-19C–1950s] (*US*) sly, cunning; thus *coonfully*, cunningly.

coon *adj.*[2] (*also* **coony**) [mid-19C+] pertaining to a black individual or black culture.

coon *v.* [COON *n.* (3)] (*US*) **1** [mid-19C–1950s] to crawl stealthily (like a racoon). **2** [late 19C+] to pilfer, esp. fruit or other objects of little value.

IN PHRASES

❑ **coon out** *v.* [1960s] (*US*) to leave surreptitiously.

coon-ass *n.* (*also* **coonie**) [Fr. *conasse*, the female genitals; thus *conassière*, sl. for Fr. *femelots*, the gudgeon. The Cajuns known as *coon-asses* were fishers of gudgeon] [1940s+] a Cajun (a person of French descent in Louisiana); also attrib.

IN COMPOUNDS

❑ **coon-ass fruit juice** *n.* [1970s] (*US*) coffee.

coon-assed *adj.* (*also* **coon-bossed**) [COON *n.* (4) + -ASSED *sfx* (1); but note COON-ASS *n.*] [1900s–50s] (*US*) a general term of abuse.

coondie *n. see* COONIE *n.*

cooney/coonful *adj. see* COON *adj.*[1].

coonie *n.* (*also* **coondie, cundy**) [Abor.] [1940s+] (*Aus.*) a small stone suitable for a missile.

coonskin *n.* [? as used in the fur trade, when furs were the barterers' equivalent of cash] [mid-19C] (*US*) a $1 bill.

coony *adj.* **1** *see* COON *adj.*[1]. **2** *see* COON *adj.*[2].

coop *n.*[1] **1** [late 18C+] (*also* **coup**) a prison; a police station. **2** [20C+] (*US Und.*) a hideout. **3** [20C+] (*US police*) a place for a patrolling police officer to take an unauthorized break. **4** [1900s] one's home. **5** [1910s–40s] any form of place, e.g. a nightclub, a bar. **6** [1920s–30s] a particular cell in a prison. **7** [1940s–50s] (*US Und.*) a solitary confinement cell.

IN PHRASES

❑ **fly the coop** *v.* (*also* **clear the coop, flee..., jump...**) **1** [mid-19C+] (*orig. US*) to leave, poss. suddenly. **2** [1940s–50s] (*US Und.*) to escape from prison. **3** [1990s+] (*US*) to lose control, to lose one's temper. ❑ **hop the coop** *v.* [1950s] (*US Und.*) to escape from any form of confinement, not necessarily prison.

coop *n.*[2] [? SE *pigeon coop*, on top of a house; note synon. Ger./Yid. *kopf*] [1900s–20s] (*US*) the head, the mind.

coop *v.* [COOP *n.*[1] (2)/COOP *n.*[1] (3)] **1** [late 19C] (*US*) to stay, to hide. **2** [20C+] (*US/NY police*) to sleep or rest while on duty – in a motel room or similar hideaway.

cooped up *adj.* [SE *coop*, a cage] [late 17C–early 18C] (*UK Und.*) imprisoned.

cooper *n.* (*also* **cooper of crusty**) [the allowance of as much stout and porter as they liked, which was permitted to coopers (barrel-makers) at London breweries] [19C] a mixture composed of equal parts of stout and porter.

cooper *v.*[1] [fig. uses of SE *cooper*, to make casks or barrels; the journeymen coopers or barrel-makers employed on Thames vessels were meant to mend cargo containers; in fact, they often pillaged them and deliberately broke open hogsheads and barrels] **1** [mid-19C] (*UK Und.*) to forge, to counterfeit; thus *cooper*, a forger. **2** [mid–late 19C] to spoil, to ruin. **3** [late 19C] to consume.

cooper *v.*[2] [? SE *comprehend*] [late 19C] (*US*) to understand.

coopered *adj.* [COOPER *v.*[1] (3)] **1** [mid-19C] spoilt, adulterated, tampered with, worn out. **2** [late 19C] drunk.

coose *n. see* COOZE *n.*

coosey *adj.* [COOZE *n.*] [1930s] (*US*) of a woman, sexy.

coosh *adj. see* CUSH *adj.*

cooshie *adj. see* CUSHY *adj.* (1).

coosie *n. see* COOZE *n.*

coot *n.*[1] [proverbial phr. *stupid as a coot*; ? play on Lat. *Fulica*, the species/SE *foolish*; the coot, synon. with the *Foolish Guillemot*, is seen in pvbs as a foolish bird. The popular link with the undoubtedly eccentric Sir Eyre *Coote* (1762–1823) is specious] **1** [mid-18C+] a fool, a simpleton; usu. as *old coot* (below), *silly old coot* etc. **2** [20C+] (*Aus./N.Z./US*) a general derog. description.

IN PHRASES

❑ **old coot** *n.* [mid-18C+] a foolish or cantankerous old person; also used affectionately.

coot *n.*[2] [abbr. COOTIE *n.* (1)] [1910s] a body louse.

coot *n.*[3] [abbr. COOTER *n.*[1]] [1970s] (*US campus*) **1** the vagina. **2** a woman considered solely as a sexual object.

cooter *n.*[1] [US dial. *cooter*, a freshwater turtle] [1970s+] (*US campus*) **1** a female. **2** (*also* **cooder**) the vagina.

cooter *n.*[2] *see* COUTER *n.*[1].

cootie *n.* (*also* **cutey, cutie, koota, kooti, kootie, kuti**) [? Malayan *kutu*, a dog tick; *HDAS* rejects this for lack of any real link] **1** [1910s+] (*US*) a body louse, a bedbug. **2** [1920s] (*US*) a small car. **3** [1930s–60s] (*US*) a general term of abuse. **4** [1950s+] (*US juv.*) an imaginary germ or 'bug'. **5** [1970s+] (*US*) a fig. repellent quality that can be picked up from those one dislikes. **6** [1980s] (*US black*) in fig. use of sense 1, an inexperienced, naïve young person, keen to improve his or her status.

IN COMPOUNDS

❑ **cootie drapes** *n.* [DRAPE *n.* (2)] [1940s] (*US black*) a style of trousers, wide and draped and thus a possible home for lice. ❑ **cootie garage** *n.* [1920s] (*US*) the hair, esp. when styled elaborately. ❑ **cootie heart** *n.* [1920s] (*US*) a contemptuous person; also adj., *cootie-hearted*, despicable.

IN PHRASES

❑ **drunk as a cootie** *adj. see* separate entry.

cootie-loo *n.* [ety. unknown] [1970s] (*US black*) a male homosexual.

cooty *adj.* [COOTIE *n.* (1)] [1920s+] suffering an infestation of body lice or similar vermin.

cooze *n.* (*also* **coose, coosie, cooz, coozey, coozie, coozy**) [var. on CUNT *n.*/COO *n.*] (*mainly US*) **1** [1920s+] the vagina. **2** [1920s+] (*also* **couse**) a woman (usu. promiscuous or unattractive); by ext. a prostitute. **3** [1940s+] a term of abuse aimed at a woman, i.e. a CUNT *n.* (5). **4** [1950s] a passive/effeminate homosexual. **5** [1960s] (*US gay*) a lesbian. **6** [1980s] a term of address to a sexually exciting woman.

7 [1980s+] vaginal secretions. **8** [1990s+] sexual intercourse with a woman.

coozer *n.* [it enters the COOZE *n.* (1)] [2000s] (*N.Z.*) the penis.

cop *n.*[1] [note Cumbrian dial. *cop*, a prison] **1** [mid-19C+] (*orig. US*) a police officer. **2** [late 19C+] (*orig. US*) an arrest; esp. in the old (and prob. fictional) cliché, *It's a fair cop, guv, slap the bracelets on*. **3** [1920s] (*UK prison*) an inmate. **4** [1930s] a sentence. **5** [1970s+] (*US prison*) a warder, a guard.

IN COMPOUNDS

❑ **cop house** *n.* [1920s+] (*US*) a police station. ❑ **cop killer** *n.* [1980s+] (*US*) a Teflon-coated bullet capable of penetrating the body armour worn by police officers; such bullets are outlawed. ❑ **cop magnet** *n. see under* -MAGNET *sfx.* ❑ **cop shop** *n.* [SHOP *n.*[1] (1)] [1940s+] (*orig. Aus.*) a police station.

IN PHRASES

❑ **horse cop** *n.* [1940s+] (*US*) a police officer riding a horse. ❑ **soft cop** *n.* [note the trad. *hard cop/soft cop* interrogation routine] [1980s+] a gullible, well-meaning person, e.g. a community/social worker whose sympathies can be exploited.

IN EXCLAMATIONS

❑ **cop bung!** [fig. use of BUNG *v.* (4)] [late 19C] (*UK Und.*) look out! the police are coming!

cop *n.*[2] [COP *v.* (2)] **1** [late 19C+] a successful bet; thus ext. as any form of 'sure thing' or certainty. **2** [20C+] (*Aus./N.Z.*) a good job obtained by shrewdness or luck; an agreeable proposition; a bit of luck or a trick that leads to large profits; often ext. to *SOFT COP* below. **3** [1910s] (*Aus.*) an experience. **4** [1930s] (*US tramp*) a theft. **5** [1940s] (*US Und.*) the money that confidence men allow a victim to win. **6** [1950s+] (*US*) an acquisition. **7** [1960s] (*US black*) an act of sexual intercourse.

IN PHRASES

❑ **no cop** (*also* **not much cop, any cop**) [late 19C+] of no or little value or use, worthless. ❑ **soft cop** *n.* [1920s+] (*Aus.*) anything seen as easy; esp. in phr. *be on a soft cop*, to have it easy. ❑ **sure cop** *n.* [1940s+] (*Aus.*) an absolute certainty, a 'sure thing', a 'dead cert'.

cop *n.*[3] *see* COPPERHEAD *n.* (3).

cop *adj.* [COP *n.*[1] (1)] [1950s+] pertaining to the police or police culture.

cop *v.* [OF *caper*, to seize] **1** in senses of catching or holding. (**a**) [mid-19C] (*UK Und.*) (*also* **cob**) to imprison. (**b**) [mid-19C] to catch a disease. (**c**) [mid-19C+] (*also* **cob**) of people, to catch, to catch out. (**d**) [mid-19C+] to arrest. (**e**) [mid-19C+] in fig. sense of sense 1c to 'catch' someone with a blow. **2** in senses of obtaining, getting hold of. (**a**) [mid-19C+] (*US*) of objects, to obtain, to purchase, to acquire; 1950s+ use spec. to buy drugs. (**b**) [mid-19C+] (*US*) to grab for oneself, esp. unfairly. (**c**) [late 19C+] to steal. (**d**) [1970s+] (*UK Und.*) to receive bribes, esp. of a police officer. **3** in fig. uses of sense 2. (**a**) [mid-19C+] to experience, to undergo, e.g. *cop a beating*. (**b**) [mid-19C+] (*orig. Aus.*) to notice, to look at; esp. in phr. used by one man to another, indicating an attractive woman, *cop a load of that…* or *cop that lot!* look at them! (**c**) [late 19C+] to take in an abstract sense, usu. in combs. (*see also* COP A… *v.*). (**d**) [1940s–60s] (*US black*) to understand, to 'get'. (**e**) [1940s+] (*US black*) to affect a manner, to pose; esp. in phr. *COP AN ATTITUDE under* ATTITUDE *n.* **4** in senses of lit. or fig. communication. (**a**) [late 19C–1920s] to take in, to persuade. (**b**) [1910s] (*also* **cop out**) to win over. **5** in lit. or fig. senses meaning to overcome, to defeat. (**a**) [20C+] to win, e.g. a bet, a fight. (**b**) [20C+] (*US*) to kill, to shoot dead. (**c**) [1920s+] (*orig. US*) other than of a pimp, to seduce; thus, of a man, to have sexual intercourse. (**d**) [1940s] (*US Und.*) of a confidence man, to win money from a victim. (**e**) [1970s+] (*US black*) of a pimp, to seduce a girl, spec. with the intention of making her into a prostitute. **6** [1960s+] usu. of a prostitute, to fellate; also lesbian use, i.e. cunnilingus. **7** [1990s+] (*Aus.*) to tolerate.

IN COMPOUNDS

❑ **cop money** *n.* [1970s+] (*drugs*) money set aside for the purchase of drugs. ❑ **copping clothes** *n.* [1960s+] (*US*) of a pimp, a particularly smart, legitimate suit of clothes, worn spec. to entice and seduce potential prostitutes. ❑ **copping corner** *n.* [1980s+] (*US drugs*) (*also* **copping zone**) a street corner on which drug dealers collect to sell their wares. ❑ **copping fuck** *n.* [FUCK *n.* (1a)] [1970s] (*US Und.*) the initiatory act of sexual intercourse between a newly recruited whore and her pimp. ❑ **copping zone** *n.* [1980s+] (*drugs*) that area of a town or city where users will find the main drug market.

IN PHRASES

❑ **all cop and no blue** [late 19C] a phr. used to describe a mean person or attitude, lit. 'all take and no give'. ❑ **cop a…** *v. see* separate entry. ❑ **cop and blow** *v.* **1** [1910s–40s] (*US Und.*) of a confidence trickster, to lure in a victim to a dice or card game by playing fair, i.e. by winning and losing as dictated by the law of averages. **2** [1920s+] (*US Und.*) to perform any kind of quick swindle. **3** [1930s+] (*US*) to do something quickly and then leave, e.g. a theft, a quick purchase (of fast food, drugs, prostitutes etc). **4** [1940s–50s] (*US black teen*) to run off. **5** [1950s–60s] (*US black*) to exploit an unsatisfactory prostitute for as much money as possible. ❑ **cop and heel** *v. see COP A HEEL under* HEEL *v.*[1]. ❑ **cop and pass** *n.* [1950s] (*UK prison*) **1** the act of transferring contraband from one prisoner to another. **2** tobacco. ❑ **cop for** *v. see* separate entry. ❑ **cop it** *v. see* separate entry. ❑ **cop, lock and block** *v.* [SE *lock* + COCK BLOCK *v.* (1)] [1970s] (*US black pimp*) to obtain a prostitute, to secure her to one's STABLE *n.* (2) and to ensure that no other pimp is able to lure her away. ❑ **cop low** *v.* [1950s] (*US teen*) to reprimand, to tell off. ❑ **cop off** *v. see* separate entries. ❑ **cop on** *see* separate entries. ❑ **cop one** *v.* [late 19C–1930s] to be hit. ❑ **cop one's doss** *v.* [1910s] (*Aus.*) to get one's deserts. ❑ **cop one's drawers** *v.* [1960s+] (*US*) of a man, to seduce a woman. ❑ **cop on the cross** *v. see under* CROSS *n.*[1]. ❑ **cop out** *see* separate entries. ❑ **cop shit** *v.* [SHIT *n.* (3j)] [1980s] to suffer verbal abuse. ❑ **cop socko** *v.* [SOCK *n.*[3] (1)] [1910s] (*Aus.*) to receive a blow. ❑ **cop (some) Zs** *v. see under* Z *n.*[1]. ❑ **cop the…** *v. see also under* relevant n. ❑ **cop the brewery** *v.* [mid-19C–1900s] to get drunk. ❑ **cop the cake** *v. see* TAKE THE CAKE *v.* ❑ **cop the flick** *v.* [a dismissive *flick* of the fingers] [1990s+] (*Aus.*) to be dismissed from one's employment. ❑ **cop the lot** *v.* [late 19C+] to gain or receive everything, either positively or negatively. ❑ **cop the raw prawn** *v. see COME THE RAW PRAWN under* COME THE… *v.* ❑ **cop to** *v. see* COP FOR *v.* (1). ❑ **cop up** *v.* [1960s+] (*drugs*) to buy drugs. ❑ **on the cop** [1900s] (*Aus.*) engaged in theft.

cop a… *v.*

IN PHRASES

❑ **cop a…** *v. see also under* relevant n. ❑ **cop a bake** *v.* [BAKE *v.*[2]] [1980s+] (*Aus. prison*) to receive a reprimand, a severe criticism. ❑ **cop a beg** *v.* [BEG ACT *n.*] [1960s] (*US black*) to get something (for nothing?) from someone. ❑ **cop a broom** *v. see COLLAR A BROOM under* BROOM *n.*[1]. ❑ **cop a bundle** *v.* [lit./fig. uses of BUNDLE *n.*[1] (1b)] **1** [late 19C+] to earn a good deal of money, to prosper. **2** [1940s] (*Aus.*) in fig. use, to die. ❑ **cop a deaf 'un** *v.* [i.e. a deaf ear] [1950s+] to pretend to be deaf or at least not to hear the last statement; thus ext. to deliberately ignoring any form of wrong-doing (cf. *SLING A DEAF 'UN under* SLING *v.*). ❑ **cop a doodle** *v. see COP A JOINT* below. ❑ **cop a drear** *v.* [SE *drear*, miserable, depressing] [1940s–60s] (*orig. US black*) to die. ❑ **cop a drill** *v.* [SE *drill*; the orderly pace of a military drill] [1940s] (*US black*) **1** to move off at a steady, regular pace. **2** in fig. use, to die. ❑ **cop a final** *v.* [1940s] (*US black/Harlem*) **1** to leave. **2** to get rid of someone who has been used temporarily to help work a confidence trick on a victim. ❑ **cop a flower-pot** *v.* [rhy. sl. = *COP IT HOT under* COP IT *v.*] [1930s–50s] to be severely reprimanded, punished or beaten. ❑ **cop a gander** *v. see TAKE A GANDER AT under* GANDER *n.*[3]. ❑ **cop a joint** *v.* **1** [1930s+] (*US*) (*also* **cop a doodle**) to perform fellatio [JOINT *n.* (1)/DOODLE *n.*[2] (1)]. **2** [1970s] (*US prison*) to smoke a cigarette [JOINT *n.* (5c)]. ❑ **cop an ass** *v.* [ASS *n.* (2)] [1960s] (*US gay*) to sodomize. ❑ **cop a plea** *v. see* separate entries. ❑ **cop a reeler** *v.* [SE *reel*/REELER *n.*[2]] [1930s] to get drunk. ❑ **cop a slew** *v.* [1940s] (*Aus.*) to take a look. ❑ **cop a sneak** *v.* [SNEAK *n.*[1]/SE *sneak*] (*US Und.*) **1** [20C+] to run away or escape surreptitiously. **2** [1920s–50s] to absent oneself from work or duty. **3** [1920s–70s] (*US prison/Und.*) to attack from behind; to ambush. **4** [1930s–40s] to break into and rob, esp. spontaneously. **5** [1930s+] to behave surreptitiously. ❑ **cop a squat** *v.* [SE *squat*] **1** [1940s+] (*US black*) to sit down; also as imper. *cop a squat*, take a seat, make yourself at home. **2** [1950s] (*US gay*) of a man, to sit down when urinating. ❑ **cop a steal** *v.* [1960s] (*US*) to steal. ❑ **cop (a strop)** *v.* [STROP *n.*] [2000s] to lose one's temper. ❑ **cop a Sunday** *v. see under* SUNDAY (PUNCH) *n.* ❑ **cop a tapper** *v.* [SE *tap one's feet*] [1940s] (*US black/Harlem*) to take a walk. ❑ **cop a walk** *v.* [1940s–70s] (*US*) to leave; usu. as imper. *cop a walk*, go away.

copacetic *adj.* (*also* **copa, copasetic, copasetty, copesette, copus, kopasetic, kopasette**) [? Chinook jargon *copasenee*, everything is satisfactory, esp. as orig. used on the waterways of Washington state. Other etys. include: (i) the painfully contrived phr. *the cop is on the settee*, i.e. the cop is not paying attention, which elided into *copacetic* and was supposedly used as such by US hoodlums; (ii) a word presumed to be Ital. but otherwise unknown; (iii) Fr. *coupersetique*, f. *couper*, to strike; thus striking or worth a strike; (iv) the Yid. phr. *hakol b'seder*, all is in order or, earlier, *kol b'tzedek*, all with justice. Note that *HDAS* dismisses all these and states 'ety. unknown'] [1910s+] (*US*) excellent, first-rate; OK, satisfactory.

cop a plea *n.* [COP A PLEA *v.*] [1930s+] (*US Und.*) a lawyer.

cop a plea *adj.* [COP A PLEA *n.*] [1930s] of a lawyer, second-rate.

cop a plea *v.* (*also* **plea-cop**) [COP *v.* (3c) + SE *plea*] **1** [20C+] to make an excuse. **2** [1920s+] (*orig. US*) to plead guilty to a lesser charge in return for the dropping of a greater one, to make a bargain. **3** [1940s–60s] (*US*) to beg, to plead, to implore. **4** [1940s–60s] to give in, to surrender, to compromise. **5** [1950s] (*US Und.*) to plead guilty as charged, and hope by so doing to get a lesser sentence. **6** [1950s] to plead guilty to a criminal charge.

copasetic *adj.* (*also* **copasetty**) *see* COPACETIC *adj.*

copbusy *v.* [COP *n.*[1] (1) + SE *busy*, to busy oneself; i.e. to act fast to elude possible police interference] [mid-19C–1930s] to hand whatever one has just stolen to a confederate or girlfriend.

cop deuces *v.* [rhy. sl. + COP *v.* (3c) + DEUCE *n.*[1] (1); ? ref. to the losing roll of two in craps dice] [20C+] (*US prison*) to make excuses.

cope *v.* [dial. *cope*, a pile] [20C+] (*Ulster*) to defecate.

Copenhagen *n.* [the the pioneering operation undergone in Denmark in 1952 by Christine (formerly George) Jorgensen]

IN COMPOUNDS

❑ **Copenhagen capon** *n.* [a SE *capon* is a gelded cockerel] [1960s+] (*US gay*) a transsexual.

IN PHRASES

❑ **go to Copenhagen** *v.* (*also* **go to Denmark**) [1950s+] (*gay*) to have a sex change operation.

copesette *adj. see* COPACETIC *adj.*

copess *n.* [COP *n.*[1] (1) + fem. sfx -*ess*] [1940s+] a policewoman.

cop for *v.* [COP *v.* (2a)] **1** [1960s+] (*also* **cop to**) to confess, to own up to, to admit. **2** [1970s+] to obtain. **3** [1990s+] to have a relationship with. **4** [1990s+] (*US*) of a pimp, to entice a prostitute to join the group of women under his protection. **5** [1990s+] to make a successful seduction. **6** [1990s+] to claim.

IN PHRASES

❑ **cop for the blower** *v. see under* BLOWER *n.*[2].

co-pilot *n.* [it helps you 'fly'; also poss. the fact that truck drivers use it to stay awake] **1** [1960s+] (*drugs*) an amphetamine; usu. in pl. **2** [1980s+] (*drugs*) two or more people taking LSD together; more usu. the second person is not taking LSD and is there to look after people.

cop it *v.* [COP *v.* (3a) + SE *it*; 'it' being trouble] **1** [late 19C+] to get into trouble, to receive a severe reprimand. **2** [20C+] to be hit, to suffer in a given way, to die. **3** [1980s+] (*Aus. prison*) to be the passive member of a homosexual couple.

IN PHRASES

❑ **cop it hot** *v.* [HOT *adv.*] **1** [late 19C+] to get into trouble, to receive a severe reprimand. **2** [1910s+] to be hit, to suffer, to die. ❑ **cop it in the neck** *v. see* GET IT IN THE NECK *v.* ❑ **cop it sweet** *v.* [SWEET *adv.*[2] (1)] [1960s+] (*Aus.*) **1** to accept problems without complaining, to get one's due deserts. **2** to have a stroke of luck. **3** to relax.

copman *n.*[1] (*also* **copperman**) [COP *n.*[1] (1) + SE *man*] [late 19C–1950s] (*Aus.*) a policeman.

copman *n.*[2] [COP *v.* (2a)] [1960s–80s] (*US drugs*) a drug dealer.

cop off *v.*[1] [var. on COP OUT *v.*[1] (1)/COP OUT *v.*[2] (3)] (*US*) **1** [late 19C] to die. **2** [1920s] to meet someone later. **3** [1940s+] to make an excuse. **4** [1940s+] to inform someone of something.

cop off *v.*[2] [COP *v.* (1)] **1** [1900s–30s] to steal from. **2** [1920s] (*US*) to arrest.

cop off *v.*[3] [orig. northern dial. *cop*, to act saucily or to catch (hold of)] **1** [1920s+] to seduce. **2** [1980s+] to embrace sexually, to indulge in petting; usu. *cop off with*.

cop-on *n.* [COP *v.* (3d)] [1990s+] (*Irish*) common sense, awareness.

cop on *v.* [COP *v.*] **1** [late 19C+] to seduce, to pick up and, poss., to go to bed with. **2** [1930s+] to grab hold of. **3** [1940s+] get a grip on oneself.

cop-out *n.*[1] [COP *v.* (1c)] [1900s] (*US*) a chance or spontaneous meeting, esp. a pick-up by a street prostitute.

cop-out *n.*[2] [COP OUT *v.*[2]] **1** [1910s+] a coward, someone who runs away from problems, a weakling. **2** [1940s+] a flight, an escape, a cowardly compromise or evasion, a retreat from reality.

cop-out *adj.* [COP OUT *v.*[2]] **1** [1950s+] compromised, defeated. **2** [1960s+] evasive.

cop out *v.*[1] [COP *v.*] **1** [mid–late 19C] to get into trouble. **2** [mid-19C–1940s] (*orig. UK Und.*) to arrest. **3** [late 19C–1900s] (*orig. US*) (*also* **cop out on**) to obtain, to take for oneself. **4** [1900s] (*US*) to steal. **5** [1960s] (*US campus*) to fail a test or examination. **6** [1960s] to accept, to understand. **7** *see* COP *v.* (4b).

cop out *v.*[2] [COP A PLEA *v.*] **1** [1930s+] (*US Und.*) to use legal plea-bargaining to plead guilty to a lesser charge in return for having one dropped. **2** [1940s+] to avoid a problem or a difficult situation, to run away, to give up trying. **3** [1940s+] (*US Und.*) (*also* **cop out on**) to confess, to inform. **4** [1950s] (*US black/jazz*) to go to sleep. **5** [1960s+] (*also* **cop out on**) to let down, to betray.

IN PHRASES

❑ **cop (out) to** *v.* [1950s+] (*US*) to admit, to confess, to take responsibility for.

copped *adj.* [COP *v.* (1c)] [mid-19C+] arrested.

copped up *adj.* [1960s] broken, old, run-down.

copper *n.* **1** [late 18C–19C] (*US*) (*also* **copperhide, copperskin**) a Native American. **2** as money. (**a**) [late 18C+] a halfpenny; thus *coppers*, mixed pennies and halfpennies. (**b**) [late 18C+] (*US*) a cent. (**c**) [1930s] in pl., wages. (**d**) [1970s] (*W.I.*) in pl., money in general. **3** [mid-19C+] a police officer [the SE *copper* badges carried by New York City's first police sergeants; patrolmen had brass badges, lieutenants and captains silver ones; strengthened by COP *v.* (1)]. **4** [late 19C+] an informer, whether in or out of prison. **5** [1910s+] (*US prison*) good conduct marks. **6** [1910s+] a prisoner who gains such marks (and who is thus considered to resemble a policeman). **7** [1920s] a private detective. **8** [1940s] (*US Und./police*) ext. of sense 6, parole. **9** *see* COPPERHEAD *n.* (3).

IN COMPOUNDS

❑ **copper-hearted** *adj.* (*US Und.*) **1** [1930s] mean, vicious, adhering to the negative stereotypes of the police. **2** [1930s–60s] being an informer by nature; thus *turn copper-hearted*, to betray one's associates. ❑ **copperhide** *n. see* sense 1 above. ❑ **copper house** *n.* [1930s] a police station. ❑ **copper jitters** *n.* [1950s] (*US drugs/Und.*) excessive fear of the police, verging on obsession. ❑ **copper john** *n.* (*US Und.*) **1** [1910s] a prison warden. **2** [1930s] a prison. **3** [1940s] an informer. ❑ **copperman** *n. see* COPMAN *n.*[1]. ❑ **copper nickel** *n. see* WOODEN NICKEL *under* WOODEN *adj.* ❑ **coppernob** *n.* (*also* **copperknob**) [1910s; 1950s] (*UK juv.*) a police officer. ❑ **copper's helmet** *n. see* HELMET *n.* (1). ❑ **copper shop** *n.*

[SHOP *n.*[1] (1)] [1910s+] a police station. ❑ **coppershy** *adj.* [20C+] (*US Und.*) used of one who is terrified of the police. ❑ **copperskin** *n. see* sense 1 above. ❑ **copper's nark** *n.* [NARK *n.* (1)] [late 19C+] a police informer. ❑ **copper's shanty** *n.* [late 19C] a police station. ❑ **copper-stick** *n.* [note SE *copper-stick*, used to stir a laundry] **1** [19C] a police truncheon. **2** the penis [fig. use of sense 1 + STICK *n.* (1a)].

IN PHRASES

❑ **blow one's copper** *v.* [1930s+] (*US prison*) to lose the reduction in sentence that would otherwise accrue for good conduct; thus *hold one's copper*, to maintain good conduct. ❑ **call copper** *v.* (*also* **scream copper**) [1930s+] (*UK Und.*) to inform the police. ❑ **come the copper** *v.* [1930s+] to become an informer. ❑ **cry copper** *v.* [late 19C+] to raise the alarm. ❑ **give birth to a copper** *v.* (*also* **give birth (to it)**) [fig. use of sense 3 above] [1990s+] (*Aus.*) to defecate. ❑ **half-copper** *n.* [19C] **1** (*N.Z.*) a halfpenny. **2** (*US*) a half-cent. ❑ **holler copper** *v.* (*also* **holler cop, holler police, yell copper, squeal copper**) [HOLLER *v.* (1)/SE *yell*/SQUEAL (ON) *v.* (3)] [1930s+] to inform. ❑ **turn copper** *v.* [late 19C–1950s] (*US*) to become an informer.

copper *adj.*

SE in slang uses

IN COMPOUNDS

❑ **copper captain** *n.* [his 'brass' or cheek in posing in this way] [mid–late 19C] a fraudulent, 'self-promoted' officer. ❑ **copper nickel** *n. see* WOODEN NICKEL *under* WOODEN *adj.* ❑ **copper nob** *n.* (*also* **copper-knob**) [NOB *n.*[1] (1)] [late 19C+] a red-headed person. ❑ **copper-plated** *adj.* [var. on SE *gold-plated*] [late 19C–1920s] (*US*) absolute, certain, definite. ❑ **copper show** *n.* [1900s–10s] (*Aus.*) a copper mine. ❑ **coppertail** *n.* (*also* **coppertop**) [the inferiority of *copper* compared with silver] [late 19C–1950s] (*Aus.*) an unimportant person, a person of little social standing; thus a democrat rather than an aristocrat. ❑ **coppertop** *n.* **1** [1910s–50s] a red-headed person. **2** *see* COPPERTAIL above.

copper *v.*[1] [COP *v.*; + ? faro jargon *copper a bet*, to bet that a given card will lose] (*US*) **1** [mid–late 19C] to steal, to embezzle. **2** [late 19C] to kill. **3** [late 19C–1920s] to outwit, to spoil. **4** [late 19C–1950s] to obtain, to make sure of getting.

copper *v.*[2] [COPPER *n.* (3)] **1** [mid-19C–1920s] to arrest. **2** [1900s] (*US*) to discover. **3** [1920s–60s] to inform. **4** [1920s+] to work as a police officer or detective.

copper-clawing *n.* [? *cap-a-clawing*, the clawing off of each other's cap] [late 19C] a fight between two women.

copperhead *n.* [SE *copperhead*, a venomous snake (*Agkistrodon contortrix*) common in the United States] (*US*) **1** [early–mid-19C] an unpleasant person. **2** [mid-19C] a Native American. **3** [mid-19C] (*also* **cop, copper**) a Northerner who backed the Confederacy.

copping *n.* [COP *v.*] **1** [1960s+] (*UK Und.*) the practice by corrupt policemen of taking bribes from criminals, to turn a blind eye when necessary, to drop charges, to lose evidence etc. **2** [1990s+] (*US teen*) shoplifting.

coppy *n.* [COP *n.*[1] (1)] [1950s–60s] a police officer.

copus *adj. see* COPACETIC *adj.*

copy *n.* [late 19C] (*US*) a go, an instance, an item.

copyhold *n.* [heavily joc. use of the legal terminology *copyhold*, 'the tenure of lands being parcel of a manor, at the will of the lord according to the custom of the manor' in law of King Richard III, 1483] **1** [mid-17C–18C] the vagina. **2** [late 18C] a wife.

copyholder *n.* [for ety. *see* prev.] [mid–late 17C] a drinker who argues about the bill with the landlord.

cor! *excl.* (*also* **caw!**) [1930s+] a euph. for *God!*

IN EXCLAMATIONS

❑ **cor blimey!** *see* GORBLIMEY! *excl.* ❑ **cor, chase me round the gasworks!** (*also* **cor, chase my Aunt Fanny up a gum tree! ...round a mulberry bush!**) [20C+] a general excl. of astonishment or incredulity. ❑ **cor love-a-duck!** *see* GAWD LOVE-A-DUCK! *excl.* ❑ **cor lumme!** [Cockney pron. of SE *love me*] [1910s+] a mild euph. oath, lit. 'God love me!'.

cora *adj.* [shared initial letter] [2000s] (*S.Afr. gay*) common, vulgar.

coral *n.* [mispron.] [1970s+] (*drugs*) chloral hydrate.

coral branch *n.* (*also* **coral head**) [literary euph.] [mid-17C–18C] the penis.

coral stomper *n.* [1980s] (*N.Z.*) a derog. term for a Pacific Islander.

cord *n.* (*also* **corde**) [SE *cord*, a measure of cut wood, usu. 8ft long, 4ft broad and 4ft high (4 x 2 x 2m)] [mid-19C–1900s] (*US*) a great deal, a large amount.

corduroy *n.* [? the brown colour] [mid-19C] (*US*) hash, stew.

cordwood *n.* [SE *cordwood*, lengths of wood cut and stacked for fuel] [20C+] (*US*) a rustic, a farmer.

co-re *n.* [abbr.] [1910s–40s] a *co-respondent* in a divorce case.

core *v.* [Rom. *cor*, to steal] [early–mid-19C; 1990s+] to steal small articles from shops (cf. CHORE *v.*).

coriander (seed) *n.* [for ety. *see* COLIANDER (SEED) *n.*] [mid-18C–early 19C] money.

corie *n.* (*also* **corey**) [Rom. *kori*, a thorn] [20C+] the penis.

coring *n.*[1] (*also* **coring lay**) [CORE *v.* + LAY *n.*[3] (1)] [19C] petty shoplifting.

coring *n.*[2] [Rom. *koor*, to fight] [1930s] boxing.

coring mush *n.* [CORING *n.*[2] + MUSH *n.*[4] (2)] [1930s] a boxer.

corinne *n.* (*also* **corrine**) [initial letters + play on female name; note cocaine is a 'feminine' drug, *see* GIRL *n.*[2]] [1950s+] (*drugs*) cocaine.

corinth *n.* [the Greek city of Corinth, home to the temple of Aphrodite, goddess of love, was renowned for its depraved and licentious lifestyle. The term died out in the UK by the 19C but was perpetuated until the mid-century in the US] [early 17C–mid-19C] a brothel.

corinthian *n.* [SE *Corinth*/CORINTH *n.*; note ancient Gk sl. *corinthianize*, to associate with courtesans. As 19C SE the term came to mean an idealized form of sportsman, this time in the field rather than the bedroom. It was widely popularized with the publication in 1821 of Pierce Egan's *Life in London, The Day and Night Scenes of Jerry Hawthorne and his Elegant Friend, Corinthian Tom*, the original Tom and Jerry and thus fathers to the eponymous Warner Bros. cartoon and the male leads of the 1970s BBC TV series *The Good Life*] **1** [late 16C–mid-19C] a dandy, a rake, one who is 'given to elegant dissipation' (*OED*). **2** [late 18C–early 19C] a regular frequenter of a brothel. **3** [mid-19C] (*US*) a high-class courtesan.

corinthian *adj.* [CORINTHIAN *n.* (1)] [late 16C–early 19C] possessing the qualities of a dandy or rake.

cork *n.*[1] [he bobs up and down like a cork, for lack of pecuniary 'ballast'] [mid–late 19C] a bankrupt.

cork *n.*[2] [one's mouth is stopped with a *cork*] [mid-19C–1900s] (*US campus*) the absolute inability to answer a question in class or to recite a passage from memory.

cork *n.*[3] [it is both a 'stopper' and it 'bobs' up and down] [mid-19C+] (*US*) the penis.

SE in slang uses

IN COMPOUNDS

❑ **cork-brained** *adj.* (*also* **corky-brained, corky-headed**) [play on SE *light-headed*] [mid-17C–early 19C] foolish, stupid. ❑ **corkhead** *n.* [-HEAD *sfx* (1)] [1940s] (*US*) a fool. ❑ **cork-headed** *adj.* [1910s] (*US campus*) arrogant, conceited.

IN EXCLAMATIONS

❑ **put a cork in it!** (*also* **take a cork!**) [1930s+] (*US*) shut up! be quiet!

cork *n.*[4] [proper name *Cork*, a city from whence many immigrants arrived in the US] [1950s–60s] (*US*) an Irish person; thus *corktown, cork hill*, the Irish part of a town or city.

cork *adj. see* CORKED *adj.*

cork *v.*[1] [fig. uses of SE *cork*, a 'stopper'] **1** [late 19C–1900s] (*US campus*) to baffle, to stun into silence. **2** [late 19C–1900s] to hit hard. **3** [late 19C+] to get the better of; thus *wouldn't that cork you?*, doesn't that infuriate or amaze you? **4** [late 19C+] (*also* **cork it, cork it in**) to be quiet, to stop talking.

SE in slang uses

(IN PHRASES)

□ **cork it** *v.* **1** [1980s] to die. **2** *see* sense 4 above. □ **cork off** *v.* [SE *cork off*, to stop up with a cork] (*US*) **1** [1910s–70s] to fall asleep. **2** [1940s] to go mad. **3** [1960s] to produce quickly, easily, to 'knock off'. □ **cork out** *v.* (*US*) **1** [1950s] to collapse exhausted. **2** [1960s] to fall asleep. □ **cork someone's ass** *v.* [1960s] (*US black*) to astound, to stop and make someone think. □ **cork the air** *v.* [1950s] (*drugs*) to inhale cocaine. □ **cork up** *see* separate entries.

(IN EXCLAMATIONS)

□ **cork it!** [1970s] (*US*) be quiet!

cork *v.*[2] [CAULK *v.* + CORK *n.*[3]] **1** [1970s+] of a man, to have sexual intercourse. **2** [1980s] to idle, to waste time.

corked *adj.* [fig. uses of SE *cork*] **1** [late 19C+] drunk. **2** [20C+] constipated. **3** [1930s–40s] exhausted. **4** [1970s–80s] (*UK black*) (*also* **cork**) absolutely full.

corker *n.*[1] [SE *caulk*, to fill up cracks; as a fig. sealant, rum can keep out the cold] **1** [mid-19C] a stiff drink. **2** [20C+] (*W.I.*) alcohol, typically strong rum punch.

corker *n.*[2] [SE *cork*, a stopper; the cork fits the top of the bottle and thus 'tops' or 'corks up' all else] **1** [mid–late 19C] the last word in an argument. **2** [mid-19C–1960s] a knockout punch; similarly in fig. use. **3** [mid-19C+] anything or anyone excellent, superlative, first-rate; sometimes used ironically. **4** [late 19C–1910s] something very difficult. **5** [late 19C+] (*also* **corkerina**) an attractive young woman.

corking *adj.* (*also* **corker**) [CORKER *n.*[2] (3)] [late 19C] excellent, wonderful.

corks *n.*[1] [a cork is something that 'keeps one afloat'] [mid-19C] (*orig. milit.*) money.

corks *n.*[2] [among his jobs is drawing the corks from bottles] [mid-19C] a butler.

corkscrewed *adj.* [fig. use of SE, esp. as a synon. for DUTCH COURAGE *n.*] [1910s] drunk.

cork snorter *n.* [? its use in sniffing wine corks] [mid-19C] (*UK Und.*) the nose.

cork up *adj.* [SE *corked up*] [1950s+] (*W.I. Rasta/UK black*) jammed, filled, crowded.

cork up *v.* [fig. uses of SE *cork* + CORK *v.*[1] (1)] **1** [mid-19C–1950s] (*US*) to be quiet, to stop talking. **2** [late 19C] to make someone be quiet. **3** [1930s+] (*UK/UK black*) to fill up. **4** [1960s] to get drunk.

corky-brained/-headed *adj. see* CORK-BRAINED *under* CORK *n.*[3].

corn *n.*[1] [lit. and fig. uses of SE *corn*] **1** [mid-18C+] (*also* **seed corn**) money; thus *earn one's corn, worth one's corn*, to deserve one's wages [the roles of corn and money as staples of existence]. **2** as an ingredient of alcohol. (**a**) [19C+] (*US*) corn whisky. (**b**) [mid-19C+] (*US*) a drunkard. (**c**) [20C+] (*W.I.*) rum. **3** [1930s+] (*orig. US*) anything unsophisticated, irritatingly or foolishly old-fashioned or sentimental, hackneyed, trite, inferior [such things supposedly appeal to country people, i.e. growers of *corn*]. **4** [1950s+] (*W.I. Rasta*) marijuana.

(IN COMPOUNDS)

□ **corn coffee** *n.* [1940s] (*US*) alcohol. □ **corn juice** *n.* (*also* **corn-moon, ...liquid**) [mid-19C–1930s] (*US*) whisky, whether legally or illicitly distilled. □ **corn mission** *n.* [1980s] (*UK black*) an illegal money-making scheme, e.g. a robbery. □ **corn mule** *n. see under* MULE *n.* □ **corn squeezings** *n.* [1940s+] (*US*) illicitly distilled whisky.

(IN PHRASES)

□ **corn up** *v.* [late 19C] (*US*) to get drunk. □ **on the corn** (*also* **eating corn**) [the hominy diet therein] [1940s–60s] (*Aus. prison*) serving time in prison. □ **put fowl to mind corn** *v.* [a chicken, of course, would eat the corn] [20C+] (*W.I.*) to make a very foolish decision, to trust someone unwisely.

SE in slang uses

(IN COMPOUNDS)

□ **cornball** *see* separate entries. □ **cornbread** *see* separate entries. □ **corncake** *n.* [SAmE *corncake*, a cake made of Indian cornmeal, but why?] [1960s] (*US*) $1. □ **corncob(ber)** *see* separate entries. □ **corncracker** *n.* [? their subsisting on *corn* or maize] [mid-19C+] (*US*) **1** a poor white farmer, a rustic. **2** natives of Florida, Georgia, Kentucky, Tennessee, or Virginia. □ **corndog** *see* separate entries. □ **cornfed** *see* separate entries. □ **cornflake...** *see* separate entries. □ **corn-grinders** *n.* (*also* **corncrackers**) [mid-19C] (*US*) the teeth. □ **corn-haul** *v. see* CORNHOLE *v.* □ **cornhole(r)** *see* separate entries. □ **corn-husker** *n.* [SE *cornhusker*, one who strips the husks from the ears of Indian corn] **1** [20C+] (*US*) a farmer, a peasant. **2** [1960s] a native of Nebraska. □ **cornpone** *n.* [SE *cornpone*, a cornmeal cake or bread made of maize, milk and eggs, formed into ovals and baked or fried] [19C+] (*US black*) a rustic, a peasant, esp. a person obviously from the Southern US. □ **cornpopper** *n.* [? the noise of the exhaust (i.e. like popcorn)] (*US*) **1** [1940s] a large truck. **2** [1970s] a cheap car. □ **cornshucking** *adj.* [mid–late 19C] (*US, Southern*) a euph. for DAMNED *adj.* □ **cornstalk** *see* separate entries. □ **cornstealer** *n.* [mid–late 19C] the human hand. □ **cornthrasher** *n.* (*also* **cornthresher**) [mid-19C] (*US*) a farmer, a rustic.

(IN PHRASES)

□ **acre (of corn)** *n.* [the use of corn is a ref. to hominy, a staple of Aus. prison food; one will eat that much corn during the sentence] [1930s–50s] (*Aus./US*) a prison sentence, cited variously as one month, twelve months or simply 'plenty'. □ **corn in Egypt** *n.* [phr. *corn in Egypt*, a plentiful supply, f. Gen. 42:2] [late 19C] money. □ **corn on the cob** *n.* [1970s+] (*US black*) sexual intercourse in which the partners are partially clad. □ **get one's corn ground** *v.* (*also* **have one's corn ground**) [early 19C] (*US*) to have sexual intercourse. □ **have corn/corns in the head** *v.* [play on SE *corns/corn* as used in brewing] [mid-18C–mid-19C] to be drunk. □ **there's corn growing for some** [ACRE (OF CORN) above] a phr. used of a recidivist.

corn *n.*[2] [CON *v.* (1)] [late 19C–1960s] (*US black*) insincere chatter, flattery, deceit.

corn *n.*[3] [? it resembles a small ear of corn] [1950s+] (*W.I. Rasta*) a bullet.

corn *adj.* [? the golden colour of the crop] [1990s+] (*US campus*) good-looking.

corn *v. see* CORNHOLE *v.*

cornball *n.* [CORNBALL *adj.*] [1950s+] a naïve, unsophisticated person.

cornball *adj.* [CORNY *adj.*] [1940s+] (*US*) naïve, unsophisticated.

cornball *v.* [CORNBALL *adj.*] [1950s] (*US*) to make a bad joke.

cornbread *n.* [SE *cornbread*, a rural staple in southern US] [1950s+] **1** (*US black*) a naïve, unsophisticated Southern person. **2** (*US*) anything old-fashioned, sentimental, hackneyed.

cornbread *adj.* [CORNBREAD *n.*] **1** [20C+] (*US*) plain, simple, down-to-earth. **2** [1950s] (*US black*) conventional, 'square'.

corncob *n.* [his growing and eating of *corncobs*] [late 19C–1910s] (*Aus.*) a countryman, a peasant.

corncobber *n.* [his growing and eating of *corncobs*] [1970s] (*US*) a countryman, a rustic.

corncob (oil) *n.* [mid-19C] (*US*) corn whisky.

corncracker *n.* [? their subsisting on *corn* or maize] [mid-19C+] (*US*) **1** a poor white farmer, a rustic. **2** a native of Florida, Georgia, Kentucky, Tennessee, or Virginia.

corndog *n.* [CORNDOG *n.*; fig. one who has either suffered or enjoys this; thus essentially a homophobic term] **1** [1980s+] (*US campus*) someone who is socially inept or acts bizarrely. **2** *see* ANTEATER *n.*

corndog *v.* [var. on CORNHOLE *v.* (1)] [1980s+] (*US*) to sodomize.

corned *adj.* [the use of SE *corn* in the distillation of spirits; note extended 1885 *Bulletin* (Sydney) 31 Jan. 11/2: '[T]he vehicle was boarded by one of Cobb's boss employés, who, to put it mildly, had evidently anticipated Christmas, and had been where the golden corn was waving'] [late 18C–19C] drunk.

corned beef *n.* [rhy. sl.] **1** [20C+] a thief. **2** [1950s+] (*UK prison*) a chief officer.

corned willie *n.* (*also* **corned bill, …willy, corn willie, …willy**) [1910s–20s] (*US*) canned corned beef.

cornelian tub *n.* [? a pun on Lat. *cornu*, a horn; one's current incapacity is the result of one's HORN *n.*[2] (1b); *see also* ety. at MOTHER CORNELIUS' TUB *n.*] [late 18C] a sweating tub, used in the cure of venereal diseases.

cornel wilder *n.* [the film star *Cornel Wilde* (1915–89)] [1950s] (*Aus.*) a hairstyle once popular among Aus. youth.

corner *n.*[1] **1** [late 19C+] (*orig. US Und.*) a share, usu. in the spoils of a robbery; a commission on a deal. **2** [1970s+] (*US black*) the last mouthful of a bottle of liquor.

corner *n.*[2] [all images of being positioned in the corner or on a corner] **1** pertaining to confidence tricks [+ SE *corner*, to put someone in a difficult position]. (**a**) [1950s+] (*UK Und.*) confidence trickery; thus *at the corner*, working as a confidence trickster. (**b**) [1970s] a confidence trick whereby shoddy goods are sold by pretending they are high-grade stolen property and playing on the 'thrill' some people derive from such a purchase. (**c**) [1970s] arranging to sell stolen goods and then having fake 'policemen' break in, confiscate the goods and threaten the victim with charges of receiving; the charges can, naturally, be dropped in return for a bribe, which is arranged by a fake 'solicitor', who makes sure there is no real police involvement by assuring the victim that he has no rights in law and that paying and shutting up is the best thing to do. **2** [1960s] (*US prison*) the punishment block. **3** [2000s] (*US prison*) one's associates, the group with whom one spends time.

SE in slang uses

IN COMPOUNDS

❑ **corner boy** *n.* (*also* **corner chap**) **1** [mid-19C+] (*orig. US*) an idler, irrespective of age, who whiles away the time hanging around on street corners. **2** [1940s] in general use, an idler. ❑ **corner cove** *n.* [COVE *n.* (1)] [mid-19C] (*orig. US*) an idler who hangs around on street corners. ❑ **corner cowboy** *n.* (*also* **corner wolf, street-corner cowboy**) [COWBOY *n.* (3)/WOLF *n.* (1)] [1950s+] (*orig. US*) a man, usu. young, given to standing around on street corners with his peers, gossiping, fooling around and ogling passing women. ❑ **corner cupboard** *n.* [the 'corner' being the fork of the legs] [19C] the vagina. ❑ **corner man** *n.* (*also* **corner loafer**) **1** [late 19C–1900s] an idler who hangs around on street corners. **2** [1940s] (*UK Und.*) a lookout.

IN PHRASES

❑ **do corners** *v.* [2000s] (*UK black*) to spend time socializing. ❑ **get someone round the corner** *v.* [early–mid-19C] to infuriate on purpose. ❑ **hold one's corner** *v.* [boxing imagery] **1** [mid-19C+] to stay in one's personal space, as opposed to invading someone else's, to hold one's own. **2** [1980s] (*UK black*) to wait. ❑ **put someone on the corner** *v. see* PUT SOMEONE ON THE BLOCK under BLOCK *n.*[8].

corner, the *n.* **1** [mid-19C] Tattersall's horse repository and betting rooms, orig. sited at Hyde Park *Corner*, London. **2** [late 19C+] (*Aus.*) the junction of the states of Queensland, South Australia and New South Wales.

corner *v.* [ext. of SE] [early 19C+] (*orig. US*) to put someone into a difficult or embarrassing position.

cornet player *n.* [play on BLOW *v.*[1] (5a)/BLOW *v.*[1] (3c)] [1970s] (*drugs*) one who sniffs cocaine.

cornfed *n.*[1] [pun on SE *Confed(erate)*] [mid-19C] (*US*) **1** a Confederate soldier. **2** money issued by the Confederacy.

cornfed *n.*[2] [their supposed diet] [1910s–40s] (*US*) a country person.

cornfed *adj.* **1** [late 18C+] plump, chunkily built. **2** [1900s] (*US*) something of high quality. **3** [1910s+] (*orig. US*) banal, provincial, naïve.

cornflake *n.* [CORNY *adj.* + FLAKE *n.*[2] (2)] [1970s+] **1** an eccentric; one who stands outside the group norms. **2** a young male homosexual.

cornflakes in a can *phr.* [use of corn in brewing] [1990s+] (*US campus*) beer.

cornhole *n.* **1** [1910s+] (*orig. US*) the anus, the rectum. **2** [1970s] (*US*) an aggressor, a victimizer. **3** [1970s+] (*orig. US*) anal intercourse; thus *cornhole cowboy*, *cornhole artist*, one who enjoys anal intercourse. **4** [1980s] a rustic, a peasant.

cornhole *v.* (*also* **corn, corn-haul**) [CORNHOLE *n.*] (*US*) **1** [1930s+] to have anal intercourse, to sodomize; thus adj. *cornholing*. **2** [1970s] in fig. use, to defeat, to victimize.

cornholer *n.* [CORNHOLE *v.* (1)] [1950s+] (*US*) a sodomite of men or women.

corniferous *adj.* [lit. 'horn-bearing', thus HORN *n.*[1]] [early 18C] cuckolded.

corniferously *adv.* [CORNIFEROUS *adj.*] [early 18C] in the state of being cuckolded.

Cornish duck *n.* [the local fishing trade] [late 19C] a pilchard.

corns and bunions *n.* [rhy. sl.] [1910s+] onions.

cornstalk *n.* [their characteristic tall slimness, or, like corn, they 'shoot up'] **1** [early–mid-19C] (*US*) a tall, thin person. **2** [early 19C+] (*Aus.*) (*also* **cornstalker**) an Australian, esp. one who originates from Europe and is based in New South Wales; thus *John Cornstalk, Jack Cornstalk*, a generic for such people; *Cornstalkopolis*, Sydney.

cornstalk *adj.* [CORNSTALK *n.* (2)] [late 19C] (*Aus.*) Australian.

cornswoggled *adj. see* HORNSWOGGLED *adj.*

corn willie/willy *n. see* CORNED WILLIE *n.*

corny *adj.* [such characteristics are attributed to country folk, surrounded by *corn*fields] [1930s+] **1** sentimental, naïve, unsophisticated. **2** simple, obvious. **3** rural, socially backward. **4** banal.

corny-faced *adj.* (*also* **corney-faced**) [SE *corn*, a horny lump that appears on the feet] [late 17C–early 19C] acned, heavily pimpled; seen as the badge of a drunkard.

corp *n.*[1] (*also* **corpy**) [abbr.] [20C+] (*orig. milit.*) *corp*oral.

corp *n.*[2] [abbr. SE *corpse*] [20C+] (*Ulster*) a useless person.

corp *adj.* [abbr.] [1990s+] (*US*) *corp*orate.

corpie *n.*[1] [abbr. SE *corporal*] [1940s+] (*W.I.*) a police officer.

corpie *n.*[2] [abbr.] [2000s] the *corp*oration (local government, not business).

corporal (love) *n.* [pun on SE; it 'stands to attention'] [20C+] (*US*) the penis.

corporation *n.* [play on ALDERMAN *n.* (4)] [late 18C–1940s] the body or stomach, esp. when fat.

SE in slang uses

IN COMPOUNDS

❑ **corporation cocktail** *n.* [although in an age of natural gas this drink is redundant] [1970s] coal gas bubbled through milk, a down-and-out alcoholic's tipple. ❑ **corporation hair-oil** *n.* [1950s+] (*Irish*) water, as used in smoothing down the hair.

corpse *n.* **1** [1930s] (*US*) a person. **2** [1990s+] (*US campus*) a boring person.

SE in slang uses

IN COMPOUNDS

❑ **corpse provider** *n.* [cynical assessment of their role] [mid-19C–1920s] a doctor. ❑ **corpse reviver** *n.* [note literal use in 1910 *Bulletin* (Sydney) 22 Dec. 14/4: On a later occasion an old native found a bottle (quart) of medicine known locally as 'corpse reviver,' used in cases of divers' paralysis. Mistaking it for rum, the old nigger took a long, long drink – 'enough to kill four Malay seamen,' said the doctor] [mid-19C–1930s] (*orig. US*) a kind of mixed drink, now esp. a pick-me-up for a hangover.

corpse *v.* [abbr. SE *to make a corpse of*; note theatrical use *corpse*, to cause (intentionally or not) a fellow performer to forget their lines and/or laugh on stage; thus to make him or her 'die'] **1** [mid-19C–1940s] to kill, to murder; also in fig. use; thus *corpsed*, dead. **2** [late 19C; 2000s] (*also* **corpse it**) to die.

corpus delicti *n.* [play on legal Lat. *corpus delicti*, the concrete evidence of a crime] [2000s] (*N.Z.*) an attractive woman.

corpy *n. see* CORP *n.*[1].

corral *n.* [ext. of SE use; var. on STABLE *n.* (2)] [1960s–70s] a group of prostitutes working for a single pimp.

corral *v.* [orig. Sp. *corral*, an enclosed place, yard, courtyard, pen, poultry-yard etc] [mid-19C+] (*orig. US*) to secure, to lay hold of, to seize, to capture, to 'collar'.

corral dust *n. see* BULLDUST *n.*

corredores *n.* [Sp. *corredor*, a broker] [1990s+] (*US drugs*) the people who work for a cocaine dealer, as guards etc.

corridor creepers *n. see* BROTHEL CREEPERS *n.*

corrine *n.* see CORINNE *n.*

corroboree water *n.* [SAusE *corroboree*, a party] [1920s+] (*Aus.*) cheap wine.

corroded *adj.* [1980s+] (*US black*) unappealing, unattractive.

corybungus *n.* [ety. unknown; ? link to SE *bung*, a stopper] [early 19C] (*orig. boxing*) the posterior, the buttocks.

cos *n. see* CUZ *n.*

cosan *n. see* CASSAN *n.*

cosey *n.* [SE *cosy*] [late 19C–1900s] **1** a love affair. **2** 'a small, hilarious public-house, where singing, dancing, drinking etc goes on at all hours' (Ware).

cosh *n.* (*also* **kosh**) [echoic; note dial. *cosh*, stick (of any kind), but it may not predate the sl.] **1** [mid-19C+] a stout stick, bludgeon or truncheon, a 'life-preserver'; thus *cosh-bandit, cosh-boy, cosh-man, the cosh*. **2** [late 19C] an acting of knocking out or down with a cosh. **3** [1980s] in fig. use, anything forceful.

IN COMPOUNDS

❑ **cosh carrier** *n.* [late 19C] one who works with and acts as a bodyguard for a prostitute. ❑ **cosh-poke** *n.* [1950s] (*UK prison*) a club, a bludgeon.

IN PHRASES

❑ **carry the cosh** *v.* [the practice of the pimp ambushing and robbing the whore's client] [late 19C–1940s] (*UK Und.*) working as a pimp. ❑ **under the cosh** **1** [1950s+] in trouble, at a disadvantage; thus *have someone under the cosh*, to have someone at a disadvantage. **2** [2000s] under pressure, usu. at work.

cosh *v.* (*also* **kosh**) [COSH *n.* (1)] [mid-19C+] to hit (with a bludgeon or 'life-preserver').

cosher *n.* (*also* **kosher**) **1** [1900s–10s] (*Aus.*) a police officer. **2** [late 19C] one who carries a COSH *n.*

cosign *n.* [CO-SIGN *v.*] [1970s] (*US black/prison*) an agreement, an act of support.

co-sign *v.* [1970s+] (*US black/prison*) to agree; to underwrite or verify.

coslush! *excl. see* KERSLOSH! *under* KER- *pfx.*

co-smash! *excl. see* KERSMASH! *under* KER- *pfx.*

cosmic *adj.* [SE *cosmic*, i.e. the contemporary interest in psychedelic drugs] [1960s+] excellent, first-rate, perfect, overwhelming.

cosmo *adj.* [abbr. SE *cosmopolitan*] [1980s+] (*US campus*) fashionable, trendy.

cosmoline *n.* [SAmE *cosmoline*, a form of purified solid paraffin] [1940s] (*US milit.*) butter.

cosmopolitan *n.* [late 19C] (*US short order*) Neapolitan ice cream.

cosmos *n.* (*also* **cozmos**) [play on SE *cosmos*, i.e. it gets one HIGH *adj.*[1] (2)] [1970s+] (*drugs*) phencyclidine.

cossack *n.* [proper name *Cossack*, the Turkish tribe living to the north of the Black Sea, who were organized into cavalry and fought for the Polish, then the Russian army; ult. Turki *quzzaq*, adventurer, guerilla] [mid-19C–1930s] a police officer, esp. one used to break a strike.

cosser *n. see* COZZER *n.*

cossie *n.*[1] (*also* **cossy, cozzie**) [abbr.] **1** [1920s+] (*orig. Aus./S.Afr.*) a swimming costume. **2** [1970s+] (*Aus.*) any form of costume, i.e. fancy dress.

cossie *n.*[2] *see* CUZZY *n.*

costa del crime *n.* [coined by tabloid press on model of tourist brochure SE *Costa del Sol*] [1980s+] that part of southeastern Spain where many British criminals have chosen to live.

costard *n.* [SE *costard*, a large apple] [16C–early 19C] the human head.

cost ya! *excl.* (*also* **it'll cost ya!**) [abbr.] [1960s+] it will *cost you* something, i.e. don't ask for favours, but most things can be done – for a price.

cosy *adj.* [early–mid-19C] (*orig. UK*) a euph. for drunk.

cot *n.* [abbr. COTQUEAN *n.*] [late 17C–18C] a man who meddles in 'women's work' around the house.

cotbetty *n.* [orig. Lincolnshire dial., the term survived up to mid-20C in some areas of the US] [mid-19C+] a man who meddles in 'women's work' around the house.

cot-case *n.* [one who is confined to bed] (*Aus./N.Z.*) **1** [1940s+] an invalid. **2** [1960s] an eccentric [fig. use of sense 1]. **3** [1980s] a drunkard; one suffering from a hangover or DTs.

cotch *n.* [COTCH *v.*[1]] [1970s+] (*S.Afr.*) sickness, vomit.

cotch *adj.* [COTCH *v.*[1]] [1970s+] (*S.Afr.*) unpleasant, disgusting.

cotch *v.*[1] (*also* **kotch**) [Afk. *kots*, to vomit] [1970s+] (*S.Afr.*) to vomit.

cotch *v.*[2] (*also* **kotch**) [*cotch*, to lean on; ult. f. SE *scotch*, to wedge or block] [1990s+] (*W.I./UK teen*) to shirk work, to behave lazily; to relax.

cote-si-cote-la *n.* (*also* **kote-si-kote-la**) [Fr. 'on this side and on the other'] [20C+] (*W.I.*) amusing (rather than pointedly malicious) gossip.

cot house *n. see* RAG HOUSE *under* RAG *n.*[1].

'cotics *n.* [abbr.] [1930s+] (*drugs*) narcotics.

cotquean *n.* (*also* **quotquean**) [SE *cotquean*, a peasant housewife] [late 16C–early 19C] an effeminate man, one who is seen as dealing too keenly with domestic duties that are properly those of his wife.

cotso! *excl.* (*also* **cot's flesh! cots-plut!**) [*cot* = God; ? reinforced by CATSO *n.*] [late 17C–early 19C] a general excl. of annoyance, surprise etc; a euph. for 'God's oath!' (cf. COTZOOKS!).

Cotswold lion *n.* [16C–18C] a sheep.

cott *v. see* ENDACOTT *v.*

cottage *n.* [categorized by Ware as a usage of 'fast youths' and attributed to 'the published particulars of an eccentrically worded will in which the testator left a large fortune to be laid out in building "cottages of convenience"'] **1** [mid-19C] an illegal gambling establishment. **2** [late 19C+] a public convenience; thus anywhere male homosexuals gather for sex, often a public lavatory.

IN COMPOUNDS

❑ **cottage queen** *n.* (*also* **cottage cruiser**) [1960s+] a male homosexual who solicits in public conveniences.

cottage *adj.* [? the perceived inadequacy of such a rural dwelling] [1970s+] (*US campus*) bad, second-rate; eccentric.

cottage *v.* (*also* **cottage crawl**) [COTTAGE *n.* (2) + SE *crawl* (on pattern of SE *pub-crawl*)] [1960s+] (*gay*) to frequent public lavatories, parks etc for sex; thus *cottager, cottaging*.

cotterell's salad *n.* [a pun on proper name Sir James *Cotterell*, an Anglo-Irish nobleman, hanged for rape, itself both a crime and a plant, *Brassica napus*] [late 18C] hemp.

cottle-lap *n.* [mid-19C] (*UK Und.*) gin.

cotton *n.* **1** in drug contexts. (**a**) [1930s+] (*also* **charlie cotton**) (*drugs*) a small piece of material through which heroin has been sucked up into a syringe and which can be boiled, when no better supplies exist, to extract one final measure of heroin. (**b**) [1950s–70s] (*US prison/drugs*) the benzedrine-soaked cotton wadding of a nasal inhaler. **2** [1930s+] money; which 'binds' life together. **3** [1960s+] (*US black*) the female pubic hair.

IN COMPOUNDS

❑ **cotton brothers** *n.* [1930s+] (*drugs*) cocaine, heroin and morphine, esp. as saturating the cotton filter used in the injecting process. ❑ **cotton fever** *n.* [1970s+] (*drugs*) a very high temperature that can result from accidentally introducing cotton fibres, impregnated with narcotics, into the bloodstream. ❑ **cotton freak** *n.* [-FREAK *sfx*] [1960s] (*US drugs*) one who breaks open benzedrine inhalers and eats the drug-soaked cotton they contain. ❑ **cotton habit** *n.* [HABIT *n.* (1)] [1930s–60s] (*US drugs*) a poor user's addiction, sustained by boiling cotton filters. ❑ **cotton shooter** *n.* [SHOOTER *n.*[2]] [1930s+] (*US drugs*) one who reduced to begging more prosperous addicts for their used *cotton* in the hope of extracting some narcotic residue from it.

IN PHRASES

❑ **ask for the cotton** *v.* [1930s] (*US drugs*) to ask for another addict's used cotton in the hope of extracting some narcotic residue. ❑ **down at the cotton** [1950s] (*US drugs*) reduced to boiling one's saved-up cottons to extract a last residue of heroin/morphine. ❑ **pound a cotton** *v.* [1990s+] (*US drugs*) to soak a used *cotton* in order to strain out the water/heroin residue.

SE in slang uses

DERIVATIVES

❑ **Cottonopolis** *n.* [its world-dominating 19C cotton industry] [late 19C] Manchester.

IN COMPOUNDS

❑ **cotton-chopper** *n.* [play on SE; the one-time importance of cotton in the economy of the Southern states] [1970s] (*US*) a derog. term for a Southerner. ❑ **cotton curtain** *n.* [for ety. *see* prev. + play on SE phr. the *iron curtain*] [1950s] (*US black*) the Southern states, esp. as seen by those blacks who had moved north during the previous decade. ❑ **cottonmouth** *n. see* separate entry. ❑ **cottonpicker/-picking** *see* separate entries. ❑ **cottontail** *n.* [the common rabbit of the United States (*Lepus sylvaticus*), which has a white fluffy tail + the trad. sexuality of rabbits] [1970s] (*US*) an attractive young woman. ❑ **cottontop** *n. see* separate entries.

IN PHRASES

❑ **have had the cotton** *v.* [? one has come to the end of one's thread] [1970s] (*US*) to be doomed.

cottonhead *n.* [SE *cotton* + -HEAD *sfx* (1)] (*US*) **1** [mid-19C+] a fool. **2** [2000s] a state of forgetfulness.

cotton-headed *adj.* [COTTONHEAD *n.* (1)] [1930s] (*US*) foolish, stupid.

cottonmouth *n.* **1** [20C+] (*also* **desert mouth**) the dry mouth that comes with a hangover. **2** [1940s+] (*US Und.*) a dry mouth caused by fear; thus also as adj., *cotton-mouthed*. **3** [1960s+] (*drugs*) a mouth that has become dry through smoking marijuana.

cotton-picker *n.* [COTTON-PICKING *adj.*/lit. ref. to slavery] (*US*) **1** [1910s+] an unpleasant, unpopular person. **2** [1930s+] a derog. term for a black person. **3** [1950s+] (*US*) in pl., the hands.

cotton-picking *adj.* [the role of the slaves who picked cotton in the American South and as such an implicitly racist term] (*US*) **1** [1930s+] a general term of abuse, second-rate, vulgar, insignificant. **2** [1950s+] a euph. for DAMNED *adj.*

cottontop *n.*[1] [a style of stockings of which the lower, visible portion was silk and the remainder cotton] [mid–late 19C] a 'loose' woman who keeps up quasi-respectable appearances.

cottontop *n.*[2] [equation of white cotton buds with hair] [20C+] (*US*) **1** a person with light-coloured hair, a white blond; thus an old person with gray or white hair. **2** a Swede [stereotypically blond Swedes].

cotton wool *v.* [rhy. sl.] **1** [1980s+] (*Aus. prison*) to masturbate [= PULL *v.* (6)]. **2** [1990s+] to seduce [= PULL *v.* (2e)].

cotzooks! [early 18C] a general oath, lit. 'God's hooks' (cf. COTSO! *excl.*).

cou *n. see* COO *n.*

couch *n.*

SE in slang uses

IN COMPOUNDS

❑ **couch case** *n.* [the trad. analyst's *couch*] [1960s+] an eccentric, a mad person, one in need of psychiatric help. ❑ **couch checkers** *n.* [SAmE *checkers* (UK *draughts*)] [1960s] (*US*) love-making on a couch. ❑ **couch commander** *n.* [1980s+] (*US campus/teen*) **1** a TV remote control unit. **2** (*also* **couch commando**) the person operating the controller. ❑ **couch cootie** *n.* [COOTIE *n.* (1)] [1910s–20s] (*US*) a poor or miserly man who prefers to court a woman in her own house than take her out on the town. ❑ **couch hockey** *n.* [the penis is presumably the 'stick', the vagina the 'goal'] [1990s+] sexual intercourse (on a couch). ❑ **couch hockey for one** *n.* [1990s+] masturbation. ❑ **couch lock** *n.* [2000s] (*US*) a state of inertia induced by excessive drug consumption. ❑ **couch potato** *n.* [coined 1976, allegedly a play on the earlier *boob tuber*] [1970s+] (*orig. US*) one who is addicted to watching TV and who does this while lying on the couch, as inert and brain-dead as a potato.

couch *v.* **1** [early 16C–mid-18C] to lie (down). **2** [1980s+] (*US*) to lounge around on the couch (watching television) [COUCH POTATO *under* COUCH *n.*].

IN PHRASES

❑ **couch a hogshead** *v.* (*also* **couch a cod's head**) [SE *hogshead*, comparing the sleeper to a recumbent pig/COD'S HEAD *n.*; Ribton-Turner, *A History of Vagrants* (1887), suggests Welsh *hepiad, hephun*, a slumber or doze] [early 16C–early 19C] (*UK Und.*) to lie down and sleep. ❑ **couch a porker** *v.* [early 18C] to lie down and sleep.

cougar juice *n.* (*also* **cougar milk**) [note the 1930s–50s US skiers' drink 'Cougar Milk', a blend of condensed milk, rum, nutmeg and boiling water; orig. known as 'moose milk', the recipe was printed on the back labels of then popular Coruba Rum] [1920s–30s] (*US*) rough, illicit whisky, esp. that sold during the Prohibition (1920s).

couge *n.* [ety. unknown] [early 19C] (*US*) the drink, punch.

cough *n.* [COUGH *v.*] **1** [1900s] a payment, the handing over of money. **2** [1920s+] a confession (esp. one that is presumed to be sincere and factual).

IN COMPOUNDS

❑ **cough syrup** *n.* **1** [1920s] (*US Und.*) bribe money. **2** *see* COUGH MEDICINE below.

SE in slang uses

IN COMPOUNDS

❑ **cough drop** *n.* **1** [late 19C+] poison, or anything disagreeable [the slogan of a popular cough lozenge, 'cough no more']. **2** [late 19C+] a disagreeable person. **3** [late 19C+] a 'character', a 'card'. **4** [1940s+] (*S.Afr.*) a pretty woman. ❑ **cough medicine** *n.* (*also* **cough syrup**) [1910s] (*US*) whisky.

cough *v.* [late 19C+] (*orig. US*) **1** (*also* **cough it**) to confess, to inform. **2** (*also* **cough on**) to talk about. **3** to vomit. **4** to hand over, to give, esp. money.

IN PHRASES

❑ **cough up** *v. see* separate entry.

cough and choke *v.* [rhy. sl.] [1990s+] to smoke.

cough and sneeze *n.* [rhy. sl.] [1910s+] cheese.

cough and stutter *n.* [rhy. sl.] [20C+] butter.

cough up *v.* [ext. of COUGH *v.* + SE] **1** [late 19C+] (*also* **cough it up, cough out, cough to**) to confess, to reveal (information). **2** [late 19C+] (*also* **cough over**) to hand over, to give, esp. money. **3** [20C+] to vomit, ext. as *cough up one's guts*. **4** [1920s+] (*Aus.*) to speak.

could it be Satan? *phr.* [the catchphrase of the Church Lady (played by Dana Carvey), in the TV show *Saturday Night Live*] [1980s+] (*US campus*) a reaction to something seen as naughty.

couldn't... *phr.* used in general intensifying phrs. below, suggesting that someone is ineffectual or incompetent (cf. CAN'T... *phr.*).

IN PHRASES

❑ **couldn't brush a bee from a bucket** [1900s] (*Aus.*) a phr. describing someone who is physically weak. ❑ **couldn't catch a cold if they sat naked all night in an icy pond** [2000s] (*N.Z.*) a phr. describing someone who is extremely unlucky. ❑ **couldn't fight their way out of a paper bag** (*also* **...out of a two-bit shirt**) [1910s+] a phr. used to imply that someone is physically weak. ❑ **couldn't fuck a frog trotting** [1980s] (*N.Z.*) a phr. describing someone who is incompetent. ❑ **couldn't get pussy in a cathouse** [play on SE + PUSSY *n.* (1) + CAT-HOUSE *n.* (1)] [1970s] (*US black*) a phr. used to describe someone who is utterly incompetent. ❑ **couldn't hit a bull in the ass** (*also* **couldn't hit a dead bull's bum with a tin can**) [20C+] (*US/N.Z.*) a phr. used of someone clumsy or inept, esp. a poor marksman; often ext. by *...with a bass fiddle*,

...*with a handful of peas*, ...*with a handful of tapioca*, ...*with a shovel*. ❑ **couldn't hit somone in the behind with a red apple** [1990s+] (*US black*) a phr. used of a conceited or arrogant person, a headstrong person or one who believes they are intellectually superior. ❑ **couldn't hit someone with a buggy whip** [1910s] (*US*) of a boxer, completely incompetent. ❑ **couldn't hit the ground with his hat** [20C+] (*US*) **1** a phr. used of a complete incompetent. **2** a phr. used of someone who is extremely drunk. ❑ **couldn't knock a chop off a gridiron** [1900s] (*Aus.*) a phr. meaning someone is physically weak and/or ill. ❑ **couldn't knock the skin off a rice pudding** [1930s+] (*Aus./UK*) a phr. used in contemptuous dismissal of a weakling, an incompetent or other inadequate. ❑ **couldn't lead a parrot to a biscuit factory** [1920s] (*US*) a phr. used to describe someone who is incompetent. ❑ **couldn't organize a fuck in a brothel** [FUCK *n.* (1a)] [1940s+] a phr. used to describe someone who is utterly incompetent. ❑ **couldn't organize a piss-up in a brewery** (*also* **couldn't manage..., couldn't run...**) [1930s+] a phr. used of an individual with such minimal competence that even provided with everything necessary to achieve a given aim, that aim remains beyond him or her. ❑ **couldn't poke a sharp stick up a dead dog's arsehole** [2000s] (*N.Z.*) a phr. describing someone who is totally incompetent. ❑ **couldn't pull a moll off a pisspot** [1950s+] (*Aus.*) a phr. used of a weakling or coward. ❑ **couldn't push an egg off a fence** [1910s] (*Aus.*) a phr. implying weakness and/or incompetence. ❑ **couldn't raffle a chook in a pub** [2000s] (*Aus./N.Z.*) a phr. used to indicate that the subject is very disorganized and incompetent. ❑ **couldn't see the road to the dunny if it had red flags on it** [1980s] (*N.Z.*) a phr. describing someone who is very stupid or drunk. ❑ **couldn't sell a statue to a pigeon** [1980s] (*N.Z.*) a phr. describing someone who is ineffectual.

council gritter *n.* [rhy. sl. = SHITTER *n.*[1] (1)] [1990s+] the anus; usu. in phr. *go up the council*.

council houses *n.* [rhy. sl.] [1930s+] trousers.

councillor of the piepowder court *n.* [SE *Court of Piepowders*, the court of wayfarers or travelling traders; ult. Fr. *pieds poudreux*, dusty feet] [mid-18C–mid-19C] a pettifogging lawyer.

council-of-ten *n.* [proper name *Council of Ten*, a secret tribunal of the Venetian Republic (1310–1797)] [mid-19C] the toes of a man whose feet turn inwards when he walks.

counselling *n.* [ironic] [1980s+] (*Aus. prison*) a beating by a prison officer.

count *n.*[1] [play on SE] [mid-19C] a dandy, a swell.

count *n.*[2] [1970s] (*US drugs*) the quantity of a given drug for sale.

count *n.*[3]

SE in slang uses, based on boxing imagery

IN PHRASES

❑ **down for the count** [1920s–30s] (*orig. US*) as good as defeated, virtually hopeless. ❑ **down for the last count** (*also* **down for the long count**) [20C+] dead; also fig. ❑ **out for the count** *adj.* [late 19C+] ruined, defeated, exhausted, asleep. ❑ **take a count** *v.* [1970s] (*US*) to be shocked [boxing imagery; the number, from one to ten, indicates the intensity]. ❑ **take someone off the count** *v.* [milit./prison imagery: to remove from the roster of personnel or inmates] [1980s] to murder, to kill. ❑ **take the count** *v.* [late 19C–1920s] **1** to die, lit. and fig. **2** to give up, to leave. ❑ **take the last count** *v.* (*also* **...the long count, ...the long rest**) [1930s+] (*US*) to die.

counter-caterpillar *n.* [SE *counter*, a prison attached to a city court or a mayor's office + CATERPILLAR *n.*[1] (1)] [early 18C] a constable.

counterfeit crank *n.* (*also* **counterfeit cranker**) [SE *counterfeit* + Du. or Ger. *krank*, sickness] **1** [mid-16C–early 19C] (*UK Und.*) a mendicant villain who specializes in faking sickness, esp. epilepsy ('the falling sickness'); he would often display convincingly horrific sores and wounds, created by the application of various herbs. **2** [18C–early 19C] a general cheat, with no pretence of medical problems.

counter-hopper *n.* (*also* **counter-spank**) [var. on COUNTER-JUMPER *n.*] [mid-19C–1960s] a store clerk, a male shop assistant, also used as a pej. term.

counter-jumper *n.* (*also* **counter-jump, counter-leaper, counter-skipper**) [play on SE] **1** [early 19C–1950s] a store clerk, a male shop assistant; thus *counter-jumping*, working in such a job; also as adj. **2** [mid-19C+] one who has 'ideas above their station' and who wishes, as it were, to 'jump the counter' to the customers' side.

counter-rat *n.* [SE *counter*, a (debtor's) prison + SE *rat*] **1** [17C–early 18C] an inferior officer of a debtor's prison. **2** [early 18C] a criminal inmate of a debtor's prison.

Countess of Puddle-dock *n.* (*also* **Duchess of Puddle-dock**) [*Puddle Dock* in London, now the site of the Mermaid Theatre, but orig. a large stagnant pool off the River Thames] [mid-17C–mid-18C] a self-appointed but spurious aristocrat.

counting-house *n.*[1] [mid-19C] a lavatory.

counting-house *n.*[2] [mispron. SE *countenance*] [late 19C] the human face.

count lasher *n.* [SE *count* + LASHER *n.*[1]] [1950s] (*W.I.*) a womanizer, a Don Juan.

country *n.*

IN PHRASES

❑ **give someone down the country** *v.* (*also* **give someone down the river**) [ety. unknown] [19C+] (*US*) to scold, to tell off, to reprimand. ❑ **go to the country** *v.* [late 19C] (*Aus. Und.*) to be imprisoned. ❑ **go up-country** *v.* [euph.] (*Aus.*) **1** [1910s–40s] to go to prison. **2** [1920s] to die.

country *adj.* [early 18C+] all-purpose ref. to a lack of sophistication, naïveté, and similar rustic stereotypes, also a direct term of address; usu. in combs., e.g. *country boob, country gook, country hink, country jig, country joker, country peck, country punk, country pumpkin, country rube, country slicker, country squash*; see *also* combs. below.

IN COMPOUNDS

❑ **country bookie** *n.* (*also* **country boo-boo, ...buck**) [20C+] (*W.I.*) an unsophisticated country person. ❑ **country bull** *n.* *see* BULL *n.*[5] (5). ❑ **country chub** *n.* [CHUB *n.*[1] (1)] [early 18C] a fool, a dupe. ❑ **country cokes** *n.* [17C SE *cokes*, a fool] [early 18C] a country fool, a rustic simpleton. ❑ **country cracker** *n.* (*also* **country gawk**) [CRACKER *n.*[3] (1)/colloq. *gawk*, a simpleton or a country bumpkin] [19C] (*US*) an unsophisticated, backward country-dweller. ❑ **country Harry** *n.* [proper name *Harry* as generic] [18C–early 19C] a waggoner. ❑ **country hick** *n.* [HICK *n.*[1] (1)] [early 18C] (*orig. UK Und.*) a country person, a rustic. ❑ **country hotel** *n.* [HOTEL *n.* (2)] [1920s] (*UK Und.*) a prison other than those in London. ❑ **country ike** *n.* *see* IKE *n.* (1). ❑ **country jack** *n.* *see* JACK *n.*[2] (4). ❑ **country jake** *n.* *see* JAKE *n.*[1]. ❑ **country jay** *n.* [JAY *n.*[1] (4)] [late 19C–1950s] a country person, a rustic. ❑ **country jerk** *n.* [JERK *n.*[1] (2)] [20C+] (*US*) a country person, a rustic. ❑ **country johnny** *n.* (*also* **country loper**) [JOHNNY *n.*[1] (7)/? LOPE *v.* (1)] [19C] an unsophisticated country person. ❑ **country put** *n.* [PUT *n.*[1] (1)] [late 17C–18C] a country person, a rustic. ❑ **country work** *n.* [supposed tardiness of rural workers] [early 19C] work that progresses very slowly.

country club *n.* [the supposed luxury of its facilities by prison standards] [1940s+] (*US prison*) a minimum security prison, usu. housing white-collar criminals.

country cousin *n.* (*also* **kissing cousin**) [rhy. sl.] [20C+] a dozen.

count the railings *v.* [mid-19C–1910s] to be hungry.

county *adj.*

SE in slang uses, pertaining to local rather than state jurisdiction

IN COMPOUNDS

❑ **county beef** *n.* [note synon. US regional (Maine) *orchard beef*] [1960s] (*US*) deer that has been illegally shot by poachers. ❑ **county blues** *n.* [1990s+] (*US prison*) a blue prison uniform, worn in a county jail. ❑ **county crop** *n.* (*also* **country crop**) [i.e. the sort of crop given to inmates of local prisons] [mid-19C] a rough haircut, shorn to equal length all round the scalp. ❑ **county hotel** *n.* (*also* **the county**) [HOTEL *n.* (2)] [1940s+] (*US*) a county prison. ❑ **county mountie** *n.* [SE *mountie*, a member of the Royal Canadian Mounted Police] **1** [1970s+] (*US*) a local (rather than state) police officer. **2** [1990s+] any police officer.

county down *n.* [pun on *county*/CUNT *n.* (1) + SE *down*, any substance of a feathery or fluffy nature] [19C] the female pubic hair.

coup *n. see* COOP *n.*[1] (1).

coupe *n.* (*also* **coup**) [abbr.] [1970s+] (*US black*) a Cadillac *Coupe* de Ville.

couple-beggar *n.* [mid-18C–19C] a complaisant clergyman who specializes in solemnizing marriages among the inmates of London's Fleet Prison; also in Ireland.

couple of... *phr.*

IN PHRASES

❑ **couple of bottles short of a six-pack** *see under* ...SHORT OF... *adj.* ❑ **couple of chips short of a fish dinner** *see under* ...SHORT OF... *adj.* ❑ **couple of ducks** [1950s+] (*bingo*) the number 22. ❑ **couple of shakes** *see* TWO SHAKES *under* SHAKE *n.*[1]. ❑ **couple of tinnies short of a slab** *see under* ...SHORT OF... *adj.*

coupon *n.* [1980s+] (*Scot.*) the face; thus *fill in (someone's) coupon*, to hit in the face, esp. with a weapon.

courage *n. see* DUTCH COURAGE *n.*

courage pills *n.* [heroin, which is based on the Gk root meaning *hero*, works to counteract one's fears] (*drugs*) **1** [1930s+] heroin in tablet form. **2** [1960s–70s] any form of anti-depressant.

court *n.*

SE in slang uses

IN COMPOUNDS

❑ **court card** *n.* [note Lincolnshire dial. 'one who has risen very much in social position'] **1** [late 17C–18C] a dandy, a 'gay, fluttering coxcomb' (Grose, 1785). **2** [early 19C] a helpful person. ❑ **court cream** *n.* [the mannered speech of a royal court] [mid-17C–18C] empty speeches, filled only with fake sincerity. ❑ **court element** *n.* (*also* **court holy bread, ...holy water, ...promises, ...water**) [the mannered speech of a royal court] [late 16C–18C] empty speeches, filled only with fake sincerity. ❑ **court noll** *n.* [SE *noll*, a dull, drunken person] [mid-16C–mid-17C] a courtier; thus *courtnold*, courtier-like.

IN PHRASES

❑ **court in** *v.* [the other members fig. 'hold court'] [1980s+] (*US gang*) to subject to a ritual initiation, usu. involving a mild beating from fellow gang members, followed by some form of blooding, typically an armed attack on members of a rival gang. ❑ **court of assistants** *n.* [pun on SE *court of assistants*, senior members of city companies, responsible for managing their affairs] [late 18C–early 19C] the young men with whom young wives, unhappy in their marriages to older men, are likely to seek solace.

courtesy-man *n.* (*also* **courtesy-wife**) [SE *courtesy*] [mid-16C; 1920s] (*UK Und.*) a confidence trickster, well-dressed and well-spoken, and without any visible weapon, who poses as a gentleman down on his luck and tells his 'tale' to the passing victim whom he picks up in the street. They also stay in hostels from which they leave early, paying no bill but taking the bedlinen with them.

cous-cous *n.* [SE *cous-cous*, granulated flour; this can be seen fig. as grains of dirt or specks of dust, and thus stretched further to encompass the sl. meaning] [1950s+] (*W.I.*) old, ragged work clothes.

couse *n. see* COOZE *n.* (2).

cousin *n.*[1] [SE; the implication is of 'country cousin'; + ? pun on SE *cozen*, to cheat, to defraud] [mid-16C] (*UK Und.*) the victim, usu. a rural visitor to London, of a dice-player or a confidence trickster who uses counterfeit gold.

cousin *n.*[2] [senses 1 and 3, the euph. is used when introducing the young man or woman to an acquaintance who might otherwise frown on the relationship] **1** [17C] a prostitute. **2** [late 19C+] (*US*) a friend, usu. a term of address. **3** [1940s+] (*gay*) an older man's younger lover.

cousin betty *n.* **1** [late 18C–early 19C] a (travelling) prostitute. **2** [mid-19C] a foolish woman.

cousin charlie *n.* [ext. of CHARLIE *n.*[8] (1)] [1990s+] (*drugs*) cocaine.

Cousin Ella *n. see* AUNTIE ELLA *n.*

Cousin Jack *n.* (*also* **Cousin Jacky, Cousin Yan, K.G.**) [note dial. *cousin jack/jacky*, a fool, a coward] [mid-19C+] (*Aus./US*) a Cornishman.

cousin john *n. see* CUZ JOHN *n.*

cousin sally ann *n.* (*also* **cousin sal, cousin sally**) [initial letters; Confederate States of America] [mid–late 19C] (*US*) the Confederacy.

cousin sis *n.* [rhy. sl.] [1940s+] **1** urination [= PISS *n.* (2)]. **2** a drinking spree [= PISS *n.* (4)].

cousin tom *n.* [SE *cousin* + TOM OF BEDLAM *n.*] [mid-19C] a madman, esp. a beggar, tramp or similar person.

couter *n.*[1] (*also* **cooter, couta**) [Rom. *kotor*, guinea or Danubian-Gipsy *cuta*, gold coin] [mid–late 19C] a sovereign.

IN PHRASES

❑ **half-couter** *n.* (*also* **half-a-couter**) [mid–late 19C] half a sovereign, 10 shillings.

couter *n.*[2] (*also* **cooda**) [? play on *coup de grace*] [1980s+] (*Aus. prison*) the best.

couthed up *adj.* [backform. f. SE *uncouth*] [1960s+] (*US campus*) neat, tidy, well-behaved.

cove *n.* [either 16C Scot. *cofe*, a chapman or pedlar or, like a number of 16C cant terms, Rom., in this case *cova* or *covo*, man] **1** [mid-16C+] (*orig. UK Und.*) a man. **2** [late 18C–mid-19C] (*UK Und.*) a receiver. **3** [early 19C] the owner or manager of an establishment, esp. (*Aus.*) of a sheep station. **4** [early 19C] a sheriff's officer, a policeman. **5** [mid-19C] an assistant, a shop-boy. **6** [mid-19C] constr. with *a*, oneself, e.g. *a cove ought to get drunk once in a while*. **7** *see* COVE OF THE KEN below.

IN PHRASES

❑ **arch-cove** *n.* [SE pfx *arch-*, principal] [mid–late 19C] (*UK Und.*) the leader of a gang of thieves. ❑ **cove of the dossing-ken** *n.* [DOSS-KEN *under* DOSS *n.*[1]] [19C] the landlord of a lodging house. ❑ **cove of the ken** *n.* (*also* **cove, ken cove**) [KEN *n.*[1] (1)] [early–mid-19C] the master of the house, a landlord; thus *covess of the ken*, a landlady or brothel-keeper. ❑ **square cove** *n.* [SQUARE *adj.* (1)] [19C] an honest man. ❑ **swell cove** *n. see under* SWELL *adj.* (1).

covee *n.* [COVE *n.*] **1** [late 17C] a man. **2** [late 17C–early 19C] a landlord.

Covent Garden *n.* [rhy. sl.; pron. of *farthing* as 'farden'] [mid-19C] a farthing.

Covent Garden *adj.* [late 17C–early 18C] pertaining to sexual excess; usu. in combs. below.

IN COMPOUNDS

❑ **Covent Garden abbess** *n.* [ABBESS *n.*] [late 18C–early 19C] a procuress. ❑ **Covent Garden ague** *n.* [late 17C–early 19C] venereal disease, esp. gonorrhoea. ❑ **Covent Garden gout** *n.* (*also* **common garden gout**) [Williams notes 17C use of unqualified *gout* to mean venereal disease, 'partly through confusion of symptoms, partly as euphemism'] [late 17C–mid-18C] venereal disease. ❑ **Covent Garden nun** *n.* (*also* **Covent Garden lady**) [NUN *n.*/SE *lady*] [mid-17C–early 19C] a prostitute. ❑ **Covent Garden nunnery** *n.* [NUN *n.*] [18C] a brothel.

cover *n.* **1** [early 19C–1950s] (*UK Und.*) (*also* **cover-up man**) a confederate who screens the operations of a thief or pickpocket. **2** [late 19C–1920s] (*US Und.*) an overcoat. **3** [1950s–60s] (*US black/Und.*) 'protection' as supplied by police to criminals.

IN PHRASES

❑ **pull someone's cover** *v.* (*also* **blow someone's cover, pull someone's covers**) [the image of pulling back the bedclothes] [1960s+] (*US black*) to reveal some hidden characteristic or activities, usu. in another but occas. in oneself. ❑ **pull the covers (off)** *v.* [1970s] (*US prison*) to expose a fellow prisoner's sexual preferences.

cover *v.*

SE in slang uses

IN COMPOUNDS

❑ **cover-me-decent** *n.* (*also* **cover-me-decently**) [early–mid-19C] a greatcoat, an overcoat. ❑ **cover-me-properly** *n.* [mid-19C] fashionable, smart clothing. ❑ **cover-me-queerly** *n.* [mid-19C] ragged clothing.

IN PHRASES

❑ **cover (for)** *v.* **1** [mid-19C; 1940s+] to protect a confederate. **2** [1940s+] to conceal wrong-doing. **3** [1940s+] to substitute for, to take over someone else's duties. **4** [1940s+] to provide 'protection'. ❑ **cover one's ass** *v.* (*also* **cover one's arse, cover one's back**) [SE *cover* + ASS *n.* (4)/ARSE *n.* (4)/SE *back*] [1950s+] to look after oneself or someone else.

cover-down *n.* [mid-19C] a coin that has a false cover, which can be used or removed as required and which is used by cheats in games of coin tossing; Hotten (1874) notes: 'This style of cheating is now obsolete. A man who cannot manage to cheat at tossing without machinery is a sorry rogue'.

covered *adj.* [1900s] (*US Und.*) 'protected' from prosecution or arrest.

SE in slang uses

IN PHRASES

❑ **have it covered** *v.* (*also* **have someone covered**) [1950s+] (*orig. US black*) **1** to have a situation well under control. **2** to understand a person and accept their position.

covered-wagon *n.* [1950s+] (*Aus.*) a meat or potato pie or pasty.

covered way *n.* [mid-18C–19C] the vagina.

cover-up *n.* **1** [1920s+] an alibi, concealment, usu. illegal or at least unethical. **2** [1940s] (*US Und.*) a criminal's associate, a confederate.

cover up *v.* [COVER-UP *n.*] [1930s–60s] (*US*) to provide someone with an alibi.

cover-up man *n. see* COVER *n.* (1).

covess *n.* [COVE *n.* (1) + fem. sfx *-ess*] [late 18C–mid-19C] a woman.

covess dinge *n.* [COVESS *n.* + DINGE *n.* (2)] [mid-19C] (*US*) a black woman.

covey *n.* (*also* **covie**) [COVE *n.*] **1** [late 17C–1960s] a fellow, a man. **2** [early 19C] a landlord. **3** [1920s] a child.

covey (of partridge) *n.* [joc. use of SE collective phr.] **1** [late 16C–18C] a group or collection of prostitutes, usu. as found in a brothel. **2** [mid-19C] a group of attractive young women.

coving *n.* [mid-19C] (*US Und.*) shoplifting.

cow *n.*[1] [on model of BITCH *n.*[1] (1a); SOW *n.*[1] (1)] **1** [mid-16C+] a woman, esp. an obese or unattractive one. **2** [17C; mid-19C+] a prostitute. **3** [late 18C; late 19C+] (*Aus./N.Z.*) an objectionable person or thing, a horrendous situation; also in phr. *a cow of a thing* [note 1901 *Bulletin* (Sydney) 7 Dec. 30/2: 'All the cussedness of the bovine race is centred in the cow. In Australia, the most opprobrious epithet one can apply to a man or other object is "cow." In the whole range of a bullock-driver's vocabulary there is no word that expresses his blistering scorn so well as "cow." To a species of feminine perversity a cow adds a fiendish ingenuity in making trouble']. **4** [late 19C–1960s] (*Aus./US*) an awkward or stupid person. **5** [late 19C+] (*US*) milk, cream. **6** [1900s] (*US Und.*) a female beggar. **7** [1910s] a joc. term of address. **8** [1910s–60s] (*US*) beef. **9** [1920s] a tramp's or criminal's female companion. **10** [1950s] (*US gay*) an effeminate male homosexual. **11** [1960s] any animal. **12** [1960s+] (*Aus. teen*) a promiscuous young woman. **13** [1970s–80s] (*UK black*) a double-sized audio speaker box, as used by sound systems. **14** *see* COW JUICE below.

IN COMPOUNDS

❑ **cowbay** *n. see* separate entry. ❑ **cow-crazy** *adj.* [-CRAZY *sfx*] [1920s] (*US*) foolishly obsessed with a woman or with women in general. ❑ **cow-simple** *adj.* [1920s–70s] (*US*) foolishly obsessed with a woman or with women in general; in a homosexual context, heterosexual. ❑ **cowyard** *n. see* separate entry.

IN PHRASES

❑ **black cow** *n.* [1910s–50s] (*US teen/campus*) **1** chocolate milk shake. **2** root beer (and milk). ❑ **cow (it)** *v.* [1970s–80s] to work as a prostitute.

SE in slang uses

IN COMPOUNDS

❑ **cow-banger** *n.* (*also* **cattle-banger**) [SE *bang* or BANG *v.*[1] (1)] **1** [20C+] (*Aus./N.Z./US*) a dairy farmer or any employee of a dairy farm; thus *cowbang*, to run a dairy farm. **2** [20C+] (*Aus.*) a bullock-driver. ❑ **cowboy** *see* separate entries. ❑ **cow cake** *n. see* COW PIE below. ❑ **cowcatcher** *n.* [SE *cowcatcher*, an apparatus fixed in front of a locomotive engine, to remove straying cattle or other obstructions from the rails in front of a train] (*US*) **1** [mid-19C] a full moustache. **2** [1940s–60s] a large bosom. **3** [1950s] a prominent nose. ❑ **cow cocky** *n.* [COCKY *n.*[2] (1)] [20C+] (*Aus./N.Z.*) a dairy farmer or any employee of a dairy farm. ❑ **cow college** *n.* [1910s+] (*US*) an agricultural college. ❑ **cow conductor** *n.* [20C+] (*Aus.*) a bullock-driver. ❑ **cow confetti** *n.* [euph. for BULLSHIT *n.* (1)] [1930s+] nonsense, rubbish. ❑ **cow-cunted** *adj.* [CUNT *n.* (1)] [mid-19C+] having a large vagina. ❑ **cow daisy** *n.* [mid-19C] cow dung. ❑ **cow donick** *n.* [DONICKER *n.*] [1930s] (*US tramp*) cow excrement, used fig. of something unpleasant. ❑ **cow express** *n.* [the *cowhide* provides leather] [1940s] (*US black*) shoe leather. ❑ **cowface** *n.* [1900s] a general term of abuse, aimed at a woman. ❑ **cow gravy** *n.* [2000s] (*N.Z.*) cow manure, when fresh. ❑ **cow grease** *n.* (*also* **cow paste**) [1940s–60s] (*US*) butter. ❑ **cow gun** *n.* [1940s] (*US*) a revolver. ❑ **cowgut** *n.* [? some resemblance] [1940s] (*W.I.*) a tin lamp. ❑ **cow-handed** *adj.* [late 18C–early 19C] clumsy, awkward. ❑ **cow-hearted** *adj.* [mid-17C–early 19C] cowardly. ❑ **cow-hide** *v. see* COW *v.*[1]. ❑ **cow-jerker** *n.* [JERKER *n.*[1] (1)] [20C+] (*N.Z.*) a cow hand, a milker. ❑ **cow jockey** *n.* [JOCKEY *n.*[2] (3b)] [20C+] (*US*) a farmer, a rustic. ❑ **cow juice** *n.* (*also* **cow, juice of the cow**) [late 18C+] milk. ❑ **cow-killer** *n.* [he is barely safe with animals, let alone humans] [late 19C] (*US*) a quack, a poor doctor. ❑ **cow kipper** *n. see* COW PIE below. ❑ **cow-neck** *n.* [ety. unknown; ? play on the *horse's neck*, a mixed drink] [1940s+] (*W.I.*) newly distilled white proof rum. ❑ **cow-paste** *n. see* COW GREASE above. ❑ **cow-persuader** *n.* (*also* **oxen-persuader**) [1900s] (*Aus.*) a cowboy; a herdsman. ❑ **cow pie** *n.* (*also* **cowcake, cow kipper**) [1970s+] (*N.Z./US*) a piece of cow dung. ❑ **cowpoke** *n.* [SE *cow* + *poke*; orig. referred spec. to those men who used long sticks to push cows aboard cattle-trains, bound for the slaughterhouses] [late 19C+] (*US*) a cowboy. ❑ **cow-prod** *n.* (*also* **cow-prodder**) **1** [1900s] (*Aus.*) a dairyman. **2** [1930s] (*US*) a cowboy. ❑ **cow-puncher** *n. see* separate entry. ❑ **cow salve** *n.* [1940s–60s] (*US*) butter. ❑ **cow's baby** *n.* [lit./fig. ext. of SE] **1** [late 17C–mid-19C] a calf. **2** [mid-19C] an awkward, loutish person. ❑ **cow's breakfast** *n.* [1900s] (*Can.*) a large straw hat. ❑ **cow's courant** *n.* [SE *cow* + SE *courant, coranto*, a dance characterized by a running or gliding step] [late 18C–early 19C] diarrhoea. ❑ **cow's grease** *n.* [mid-19C] butter. ❑ **cowshaker** *n.* [1900s] (*Aus.*) a drover; thus used fig. to describe anyone who motivates or drives another. ❑ **cowshit** *n. see* separate entry. ❑ **cowskin** *n. see* separate entry. ❑ **cowson** *n. see* separate entry. ❑ **cow-spanker** *n.* (*also* **cow-squeezer**) **1** [late 19C+] (*Aus./N.Z.*) a dairy farmer or any employee of a dairy farm; thus *cow-spanking*, dairy-farming. **2** [20C+] (*Aus.*) a bullock-driver. ❑ **cow's spouse** *n.* [late 18C] a bull. ❑ **cow town** *n. see* separate entry. ❑ **cow-turd** *n.* [TURD *n.*[1] (1); i.e. a derog. comparison] [mid–late 18C] a cheap cigar. ❑ **cow waddie** *n.* [WADDIE *n.* (2)] [1920s–40s] (*US*) a cowboy, esp. a temporary cowhand. ❑ **cow-week** *n. see* CALF WEEK *under* CALF *n.*[1]. ❑ **cowyard cake/confetti** *n. see under* COWYARD *n.*

IN PHRASES

❑ **chase (up) a cow** *v.* (*also* **hunt up a cow, move a cow**) [the ideal patch would have been literally used by a sleeping cow, and would thus be pre-warmed] [1950s] (*Aus.*) of an amorous couple, to search out a secluded spot in a bush in order to have sexual intercourse. ❑ **cow to cover** *n.* [1940s] (*US*) a portion of butter. ❑ **cow with the iron tail** *n.* [the ref. is to the milkmen's habit, before legislation passed in 1865, of watering the milk] [mid-19C] a water pump. ❑ **have a cow** *v.* [1960s+] (*US*) to lose emotional control, to have a fit. ❑ **I'll be cow-kicked** [20C+] (*US*) a euph. for *I'll be damned!* Often ext. as *cow-kicked by a jackass* or *cow-kicked by a mule*. ❑ **juice of the cow** *n. see* COW JUICE above. ❑ **lay down some cow** *v.* [the leather soles] [1940s+] (*US black*) to walk, esp. to walk so much that one's shoes are worn out. ❑ **like cow buss rope** [Carib.E.; *buss* = SE *burst/bust*] [20C+] (*W.I.*) very angrily, highly enraged. ❑ **who's milking this cow?** [late 19C+] a phr. meaning mind your own business, usu. in response to someone interfering.

cow *n.*[2] [ety. unknown; ? related to PONY *n.* (1b) etc] [mid-19C] £1000 sterling.

cow *n.*[3] [1900s] (*US gambling*) a kitty, a 'pot'.

cow *n.*[4] [SE *milch-cow*, one who can be easily and continually used as a source of money] [1940s] (*W.I.*) a man who is seduced by a woman and abandoned when the money runs out.

cow *adj.* [COW *n.*[1] (3)] [1900s] (*Aus.*) unpleasant, objectionable.

cow *v.*[1] (*also* **cow-hide**) [early–mid-19C; 1930s] to whip or beat; also in fig. use.

cow *v.*[2] [COW *n.*[3]] **1** [1970s] (*US drugs*) to put together one's resources to buy drugs. **2** [2000s] (*US gambling*) to split bets, and thus profits with a fellow-player.

cow! *excl.* **1** [mid-19C–1930s] (*US*) a mild excl., a euph. for God! **2** [1940s–70s] (*UK, mainly northern*) a euph. for FUCK! *excl.* (1).

cowabunga! *excl.* (*also* **kowabunga!**) [the term gained a whole new currency, esp. among the pre-teens, with the popularity (*c.*1990) of the TV programme *The Teenage Mutant Ninja Turtles*, where it featured heavily. Its ultimate origin seems to have been in *Howdy Doody*, a US children's TV programme of the 1950s, in which *Cowabunga!* was the greeting exchanged by Buffalo Bob and Chief Thunderthud] [1950s+] (*orig. surfing*) an excl. of pleasure, victory (over the waves) etc; latterly an excl. of surprise.

co-wallop *adv. see* KERWHALLOP *adv.*

cowan *n.* [ety. unknown; Hotten (1860) offers Gk *kuon*, a dog (as general pej.) or Scot. *cowan* or *kirwan*, a man who builds dry-stone walls without mortar, and thus one who builds but is not a fully qualified mason. Note freemasons' jargon *cowan*, one who has not been initiated into the craft] [mid-19C] a sneak, an eavesdropper.

cow and calf *n.* [rhy. sl.] [1960s+] **1** ten shillings, latterly 50p [i.e. *half* a £1]. **2** (*orig. sporting*) a half-pint (of beer). **3** a laugh.

cow and calf *v.* [rhy. sl.] [mid-19C; 1930s–60s] to laugh.

Cow and Gate *adj.* [rhy. sl] [1990s+] late; esp. in context of a woman missing her period.

cow-and-kisses *n.* [rhy. sl. = MISSUS *n.*] [mid-19C+] a woman; one's wife.

cowbay *n.* [COW *n.*[1] (2); New York City's 'red light area' was known as *Cow Bay*] [mid–late 19C] a cheap brothel, a prostitute's room.

cowboy *n.* [fig. uses of SE; note the earliest *cowboy* (18C–early 19C) was always a black man; his white peers were *cattlemen*] **1** [20C+] (*orig. US*) a reckless man. **2** [1920s] (*US*) a man who appears to lack interest in women. **3** [1920s–30s] (*US*) a man, usu. a youth, who frequents drugstores for no other reason than to meet his friends, to gossip and to waste time. **4** [1920s+] (*orig. US*) a reckless driver. **5** [1920s+] (*US*) a ruthless, unrestrained criminal. **6** [1940s] (*US*) a western sandwich or omelette. **7** [1950s+] a bow-legged man. **8** [1950s+] (*US*) in poker, a king. **9** [1950s+] a police officer. **10** [1960s+] a man; the inference is derog. **11** [1970s] (*US*) (*also* **cowboy killer**) a Marlboro cigarette. **12** [1970s+] an average, run-of-the-mill criminal. **13** [1970s+] a general term of address. **14** [1980s+] (*US black*) an aggressive, tough black man; a thug. **15** [1980s+] a tradesman (esp. of the building and allied trades), who ignores the basic ethics and business standards of his peers and aims only for money; thus *cowboy builder*, *cowboy plumber* etc. **16** [1990s+] (*US prison*) an inmate who has no affiliation with any prison gang or group. **17** [2000s] (*US prison*) a novice officer.

SE in slang uses

(IN COMPOUNDS)

❑ **cowboy bible** *n.* [1970s+] (*US, Western*) a pack of cigarette papers. ❑ **cowboy cadillac** *n.* [1970s+] (*US, Southwest*) any form of open-topped vehicle, e.g. a pick-up truck. ❑ **cowboy cocktail** *n.* [the modern 'cowboy cocktail' blends whisky and cream] [20C+] (*US*) straight whisky. ❑ **cowboy coffee** *n.* [20C+] (*US*) black coffee. ❑ **cowboy killer** *n. see* sense 11 above. ❑ **cowboy question** *n.* [the stereotypical devil-may-care *cowboy*] [1980s+] (*US campus*) a dare.

(IN PHRASES)

❑ **cowboy up** *v.* [the supposed stoicism of cowboys] [1990s+] (*US*) to control one's emotions, to put on a brave, tough face.

cowboy *v.* [COWBOY *n.* (1); the style (or certainly as enshrined by Hollywood) of a classic Wild West hold-up or gunfight] [1940s+] (*US*) **1** to rob in a reckless manner. **2** to murder, to gun down. **3** to act in a reckless manner.

-cowboy *sfx* a sfx denoting one who frequents, regularly if somewhat aimlessly, a given location, e.g. DRUGSTORE COWBOY *n.*; MILK BAR COWBOY *n.*

cowclap *n.* [? rhy. sl. *cowclap* = CRAP *n.*[1] (2)] [1940s–50s] (*Irish*) cow dung.

cowhallop *v. see* KERWHALLOP *v.*

cowhide *adj.* [rhy. sl. = WIDE *adj.* (1)] [1950s–60s] (*Irish*) aware, knowledgeable.

cowing *adj.* [1950s+] (*orig. UK milit.*) a euph. for FUCKING *adj.* (1).

cowollap *v. see* KERWHALLOP *v.*

cow-puncher *n.* (*also* **cattle puncher, cowpunch, puncher**) [late 19C+] a cowboy; thus as v., to work as a cowboy.

cow's (calf) *n.* [rhy. sl. = half (a pound)] **1** [1940s–60s] ten shillings (50p). **2** [1980s] £150 [i.e. *one and a half*].

cowsh *n.* [abbr. COWSHIT *n.* (2)] [1980s+] (*Aus./N.Z.*) nonsense, rubbish.

cowshit *n.* (*US, Western*) **1** [1960s] an unpopular person. **2** [1960s+] nonsense, rubbish.

cowskin *n.* [mid-19C] (*US*) a whip.

(IN COMPOUNDS)

❑ **cowskin hero** *n.* [late 18C] (*W.I.*) a plantation overseer.

cow's lick *n.* [rhy. sl.] **1** [20C+] (*UK Und.*) (*also* **cow's licker**) £1 [= NICKER *n.*[2] (1)]. **2** [1960s+] prison [= NICK *n.*[3] (2a)].

cowson *n.* [on pattern of SE *whoreson*] [1930s–50s] a general pej. description of a person.

cowson *adj.* [1930s–60s] a general pej.

cow town *n.* [its former principal industry] (*US*) **1** [20C+] any town associated with cattle trading; thus anywhere provincial as opposed to a big city. **2** [1960s+] Fort Worth, Texas.

cowyard *n.* [COW *n.*[1] (2) + pun on SE] [late 19C–1910s] (*US*) a cheap brothel.

SE in slang uses

(IN COMPOUNDS)

❑ **cowyard cake** *n.* [it is supposedly reminiscent of a cowpat + attendant flies] [1920s–50s] (*Aus.*) a type of cake or bun that contains sultanas. ❑ **cowyard confetti** *n.* [euph. for BULLSHIT *n.* (1)] [1940s+] (*Aus.*) nonsense, rubbish.

cox *n.* [play on COCK *n.*[3] (1), i.e. one who is 'easily taken in'] [late 16C] a fool.

coxcomb *n.* [SE *coxcomb*, a cock's head; Nares notes: 'The cap of the licensed fool was often terminated at the top with a *cock's* head and *comb*, and some of the feathers'] [late 16C–mid-18C] the head.

cox-nowns! *excl. see* 'SNOUNS! *excl.*

coxy *n.* [ety. unknown] **1** [mid-19C] (*UK Und.*) a fool. **2** [1930s] (*US Und.*) an inexperienced salesman used by a high-pressure salesman for small deals.

coxy fuss *n. see* COCKSY FUSS *n.*

coyne *n. see* COIN *n.*

coynte *n.* [euph. for CUNT *n.* (1)] [19C] the vagina.

coyote *n.* [all fig. uses of SE *coyote*, a prairie dog, generally considered as a 'negative' animal] **1** [late 19C] (*US*) the vagina. **2** [late 19C–1940s] (*US*) a half-breed. **3** [late 19C–1970s] (*US*) a very unpleasant person. **4** [1920s; 1970s+] (*US*) a smuggler of illegal immigrants from Mexico into the US. **5** [1980s+] (*US campus*) (*also* **coyote date**) an ugly woman.

IN COMPOUNDS

❑ **coyote sandwich** *n.* [1990s+] (*US*) a tampon. ❑ **coyote-ugly** *adj.* [1980s+] (*US campus*) extremely ugly.

coyote *v.* [the perceived characteristics of the SE *coyote*] (*US, Western*) **1** [mid-19C+] to run off, esp. in a clandestine manner. **2** [late 19C] to hoax, to deceive. **3** [1920s+] to wander about.

cozies *n.* [? mispron./abbr. COJONES *n.*] [1980s] (*US*) testicles.

cozmos *n. see* COSMOS *n.*

cozo *n. see* COZZER *n.*

cozy *adj.* [1920s+] (*US*) sly, cunning; thus *play it cozy*, to act in a cautious or secretive manner.

cozza *n.* [Yid./Heb. *chazer*, a pig] [mid–late 19C] pork.

cozzer *n.* (*also* **cosser, cozo**) [Yid./Heb. *chazer*, a pig] [1930s+] a police officer.

cozzie *n. see* COSSIE *n.*^{1}.

cozzy *n.* [abbr./var. on COTTAGE *n.* (2)] [1930s] (*UK Und.*) a gentlemen's public convenience.

c.p. *n.* [abbr. CUNT-PENSIONER *under* CUNT *n.*] [mid–late 19C] a kept man, a pimp.

CPT *n.* [abbr.] (*US black*) Compton, Calif.

c.p.t./c.p. time *n. see* COLORED PEOPLE'S TIME *n.*

crab *n.*^{1} [SE *crab-apple*, which is sour; later use is US] **1** [early 19C] a gullible person. **2** [1900s] (*Aus.*) a police officer. **3** [1930s] (*US police*) a police officer who is too conscientious and thus unpopular with local politicians and colleagues. **4** [1940s] (*US black campus*) a freshman. **5** [1980s+] (*Aus. prison*) an individual prisoner who acts in such a way as to provoke a collective punishment. **6** [1990s+] (*US black*) a weakling. **7** [2000s] (*US black*) an impoverished person.

SE in slang uses

pertaining to an ill-tempered person

IN COMPOUNDS

❑ **crab-ass** *n.* [-ASS *sfx*] [1930s–60s] (*US*) an unpleasant person; also as adj. ❑ **crab lanthorn** *n.* [late 18C] a peevish, surly person. ❑ **crab-stick** *n.* [1960s+] a sour, ill-tempered person.

general uses

IN COMPOUNDS

❑ **crab-shells** *n.* [a play on Norfolk dial. *cart*, the carapace or shell of a crab] [late 18C–mid-19C] a pair of shoes; usu. in poor condition.

IN PHRASES

❑ **squeeze-crab** *n.* [late 18C–19C] a morose man, a diminutive man.

crab *n.*^{2} [CRAB *v.*^{1}] **1** [mid-19C] (*UK Und.*) a problem that emerges during an act of theft. **2** [mid-19C] any form of problem; that which places one at a disadvantage. **3** [late 19C–1920s] the act of complaining, of finding fault.

IN PHRASES

❑ **put the crab on** *v. see* CRAB *v.*^{1} (7).

crab *n.*^{3} [supposed resemblance to a SE *crab*, whether the sea creature or the louse] **1** [mid-19C–1950s] (*US*) a horse, usu. second-rate. **2** [1990s+] (*US black gang*) a derog. term for a member of the Crips, as used by a rival Blood.

crab *adj.* [CRAP *adj.*] [1990s+] (*UK juv.*) useless, inadequate.

crab *v.*^{1} [all uses of SE with emphasis on the crab's snapping pincers] **1** [late 17C; mid-19C+] (*also* **crab on**) to tear at, to find fault, to criticize heavily, to complain; thus [early–mid-19C] *throw a crab*, to criticize harshly. **2** [early 19C–1920s] to use offensive language so as to deliberately annoy someone. **3** [mid-19C] to back down, to surrender in a humiliating manner, to run away; esp. as *crab off*. **4** [mid-19C] to inform on. **5** [mid–late 19C] to cheat, to deceive. **6** [mid-19C–1960s] (*mainly US*) to steal. **7** [mid-19C+] (*also* **crab up, put the crab on**) to spoil, to upset, to ruin; thus Aus. phr. *he'd crab on a marble shit house*.

IN PHRASES

❑ **crab someone's act** *v.* (*also* **crab the act, crab someone's game**) [1900s–40s] (*US*) to spoil someone's plans, to interfere.

crab *v.*^{2} [the crustacean's movement] [1950s+] (*W.I. Rasta*) to scratch or claw.

crab *adv. see* CRABS *n.*^{1}.

crab-apple *n.* [SE *crab-apple*, a very sour fruit/SE *crab*, a sour person] [mid-19C–1920s] (*US*) a sour, ill-tempered person.

SE in slang uses

IN COMPOUNDS

❑ **crab-apple two-step** *n.* [the result of eating sour fruit] [1960s] (*US*) diarrhoea.

crabber *n.* **1** [late 19C] (*US*) a small-time gambler [? one who keeps their 'claws' on their cash]. **2** [1910s–30s] a fault-finder, a nag [CRAB *v.*^{1} (1)].

crabby with *adj. see* LOUSY WITH *under* LOUSY *adj.*

crabfish *n.* [play on SE *crabfish*, a crab/SE *crab-louse*] [17C] a cheap whore, likely to be infested with crab-lice.

crab on the rocks *n.* [rhy. sl. = POX *n.*^{1} (1)] [1940s] ? venereal disease.

crabs *n.*^{1} [? the precursor of SE *craps* dice] **1** [mid-18C–19C] in the game of hazard, the lowest throw, a pair of aces; thus fig. in phrs. below. **2** [1950s] (*US Und.*) in the context of a robbery, loot that proves valueless, and thus irritatingly so.

IN PHRASES

❑ **come off crabs** *v.* (*also* **turn up crabs**) [gambling jargon *crabs*, two aces, the lowest throw at hazard] [mid-18C–mid-19C] to turn out to be a failure or disappointment.

crabs *n.*^{2} [abbr. CRAB-SHELLS *under* CRAB *n.*^{1}] **1** [late 18C–1930s] boots, shoes; thus *move one's crabs*, to run off. **2** [mid-19C] the feet.

IN PHRASES

❑ **stamp-crabs** *n.* [late 19C–1900s] one who walks heavily.

crabwalk *n.* [SE *crab*, a pubic louse + SE *walk*] [1970s] (*US*) the perineum.

crack *n.*^{1} **1** in the context of speech. (**a**) [16C–18C] a lie; a boast, an act of bragging, exaggeration. (**b**) [late 19C+] (*orig. US*) a telling, sharp remark. (**c**) [20C+] (*orig. US*) a joke. (**d**) [20C+] (*orig. Irish/Scot.*) a conversation. (**e**) [1970s+] (*US campus*) a funny or witty person. (**f**) [1990s+] boastful talk. (**g**) [2000s] (*Irish*) insulting speech. **2** in the context of a sudden noise. (**a**) [late 16C+] (*also* **bum-crack, cracker**) breaking wind. (**b**) [mid-19C] a pistol. (**c**) [mid-19C] dry wood. (**d**) [late 19C–1930s] a shot from a weapon. **3** in fig. uses. (**a**) [mid-17C+] any person, animal or thing that approaches perfection. (**b**) [late 17C] a fop, a dandy. (**c**) [18C; 1990s+] a jolly, high-spirited party. (**d**) [late 18C+] the current fashion; the fashionable world, the social and sporting élite. **4** [late 17C+] a heavy blow, e.g. *a crack over the head*. **5** in senses of a single instance. (**a**) [early 18C+] an instant, a very brief moment. (**b**) [mid-19C+] an opportunity, a try, a chance. (**c**) [mid-19C+] (*US*) a go, a time, an instance.

IN PHRASES

❑ **get a crack at** *v.* [late 19C+] (*US*) to have a try at, to get a chance to do something. ❑ **have a crack at** *v.* [20C+] (*orig. US*) to attempt, to have a try, to have a go. ❑ **in a crack** [early 18C–19C] very soon, in a moment. ❑ **take a crack at** *v.* **1** [late 19C+] to attack physically, to shoot. **2** [1910s+] to make an attempt, to have a go.

crack *n.*^{2} [one whose brain has a fig. 'crack'] [17C–18C; 1990s+] a fool.

crack *n.*^{3} **1** [late 17C+] (*also* **love crack**) the vagina; thus *crack-shop*, a brothel. **2** [late 17C+] (*also* **town-crack**) a prostitute; a 'fallen woman'; modern use is a woman, but usu. in a derog. sense. **3** [late 19C] (*UK, London*) a narrow passage of houses. **4** [1940s+] (*also* **bumcrack, butt crack**) the cleft between the buttocks. **5** [1970s+] (*gay*) the anus. **6** [1970s+] in fig. use of sense 4, i.e. a generic term for one's body.

DERIVATIVES

❑ **crackish** *adj.* [late 17C–19C] of a woman, wanton, promiscuous.

IN COMPOUNDS

❑ **crack-hunter** *n.* (*also* **crack-haunter**) [late 19C] the penis.

❑ **crack salesman** *n.* **1** [1940s] a pimp. **2** [1960s+] a gay male prostitute. ❑ **crack snaker** *n.* [1990s+] (*US*) a derog. term for a lesbian.

IN PHRASES

❑ **get a shot of crack** *v.* [20C+] (*US*) to have sexual intercourse. ❑ **in someone's crack** [1980s+] (*US campus*) inquisitive, over-involved. ❑ **not on your crack** [1920s] (*US black/W.I.*) in no way at all. ❑ **tickle one's crack** *v.* [19C] of a woman, to masturbate.

crack *n.*[4] [the burglar 'cracks open' his target] **1** [mid-18C–mid-19C] a burglar. **2** [late 18C–19C] a burglary, a break-in.

IN COMPOUNDS

❑ **crack lay** *n.* [LAY *n.*[3] (1)] [late 18C–19C] (*UK Und.*) house-breaking.

IN PHRASES

❑ **do a crack** *v.* [mid-19C–1940s] to commit a burglary. ❑ **(go) on the crack** [late 18C–1930s] (to go) out burgling.

crack *n.*[5] [? perversion of SE *crown*] [1930s–50s] a crown.

IN PHRASES

❑ **half-a-crack** *n.* [1930s–50s] half-a-crown, 2s 6d (12½p).

crack *n.*[6] [? euph. CRAP *n.*[1] (4)] [1960s] (*S.Afr.*) nonsense, rubbish.

crack *n.*[7] [SE by late 1990s. Its strength, alleged addictiveness and destructive popularity have made it a source of social disruption. Unlike its powdered form, cocaine, known as 'the rich man's drug', *crack*, for all that it has many middle-class devotees, is very much a drug of the ghetto and the housing estate, bringing the effects of cocaine to an underclass market] [1980s+] (*drugs*) a purified and potent form of cocaine; a mixture of cocaine, baking powder and water, which is smoked rather than sniffed; crack is heated and the resultant pellets are smoked through a small glass pipe.

IN COMPOUNDS

❑ **crack attack** *n.* [play on McDonald's hamburger's coinage *Mac attack*, a sudden craving for a hamburger; note WW1 Aus. milit. *Bass attack*, a drinking bout, a play on Bass ale] [1980s+] (*drugs*) a sudden craving for crack cocaine. ❑ **crack babe** *n.* [BABE *n.* (3)] [1990s+] (*US*) a girl or woman who swaps sex for crack cocaine. ❑ **crack baby** *n.* **1** [1980s+] the child of an addict of crack cocaine. **2** [1990s+] a general term of abuse; someone irritating. ❑ **crack bitch** *n.* [BITCH *n.*[1] (1a)] [1990s+] (*UK black*) a female crack addict. ❑ **crack diet** *n.* [a minimal diet, high on sugar, that is preferred by regular crack users] [1990s+] (*drugs*) a few sweets and a soft drink. ❑ **crack gallery** *n.* [SHOOTING GALLERY *n.* (3)] [1980s+] (*drugs*) a place where users of crack cocaine congregate to buy and smoke the drug. ❑ **crack head** *n.* [-HEAD *sfx* (4)] **1** [1980s+] (*drugs*) a smoker of crack cocaine. **2** [1990s+] an idiot. ❑ **crack ho** *n.* [HO *n.* (1)] [1990s+] (*US black*) a woman who will offer sex in return for crack cocaine. ❑ **crack house** *n.* (*also* **crack den**) [1980s+] (*drugs*) **1** a room or whole house in which users gather to take crack cocaine. **2** a place where crack is processed from base cocaine. ❑ **crack mama** *n.* [MAMA *n.* (1)] [1990s+] (*US campus*) a crack-addicted black woman; thus, derog., any black woman. ❑ **crack monster** *n.* [-MONSTER *sfx*] [1980s+] **1** (*US drugs*) a habitual user of crack cocaine. **2** a woman who exchanges sexual favours for a dose of crack cocaine. ❑ **crack spot** *n.* [1980s+] (*drugs*) an area where people can purchase crack cocaine, but do not smoke it. ❑ **crack whore** *n.* [SE *crack whore*, a woman who prostitutes herself to sustain a crack cocaine addiction] [2000s] (*US campus*) a general pej., there is no need for drug use to be involved.

IN PHRASES

❑ **crack up** *v.* [1990s+] (*drugs*) to smoke crack cocaine. ❑ **on crack** *adj.* (*US campus*) crazy, ridiculous, of behaviour or a situation.

crack, the *n.* (*also* **craic**) [Irish *craic*; ult. OE *cracian*, a crack] [20C+] (*orig. Irish*) **1** conversation, chatter, gossip. **2** fun, amusement, informal entertainment; thus *cracksome*, jolly, amusing; also of people, amusing, enjoyable.

crack *adj.* [CRACK *n.*[1] (3a)] **1** [late 18C+] (*also* **crack-up**) excellent, first-class. **2** [early 19C–1900s] the best.

IN COMPOUNDS

❑ **crack hand** *n.* [SE *hand*, a person, esp. as regards their working at a job] [mid-19C] an able, competent person.

crack *v.*[1] **1** in senses of speech or communication. (**a**) [mid-15C+] to boast or brag; thus *cracking*, boasting. (**b**) [19C+] to talk; thus *crack on*, to talk at length, to criticize. (**c**) [late 19C+] to make a remark (to someone). (**d**) [1900s] to praise, to promote. (**e**) [1900s–10s] to chatter. (**f**) [1930s+] (*also* **crack on**) to tease, to insult, to make jokes at another's expense. (**g**) [1980s] (*US campus*) to be very funny, to make people laugh. **2** in the context of (sudden) noise and/or action. (**a**) [17C–18C; 1990s+] to break wind. (**b**) [18C+] to hit (with a loud noise), to slap; esp. in threat *I'll crack you one*. (**c**) [mid-18C; mid-19C+] to let off a firearm. (**d**) [mid-19C+] (*US*) to shoot dead.

IN COMPOUNDS

❑ **crackfart** *n.* [FART *n.* (1)] [late 17C–early 18C] a general term of abuse, a blusterer.

IN PHRASES

❑ **crack a bell** *v. see under* BELL *n.*[1]. ❑ **crack a boo** *v.* [? CRACK A BELL *under* BELL *n.*[1]] [1900s–10s] (*Aus.*) to betray a secret, to display one's emotions. ❑ **crack a fart** *v. see under* FART *n.* ❑ **crack a lay** *v.* [? LAY *n.*[3]] **1** [mid-19C; 1940s+] (*orig. UK Und.; later use chiefly Aus.*) to betray, to gossip about, to 'spill the beans'. **2** [mid-19C; 1960s] to speak, to 'say the word'. ❑ **crack a sad** *v.* [1990s+] (*Aus.*) to be upset. ❑ **crack down** *v.* **1** [1930s–40s] to let off a firearm. **2** [1930s–60s] (*US*) to work hard. **3** [1940s+] to repress, to take harsh measures against, esp. used of a campaign against vice or crime. **4** [1960s] (*US*) as imper. to stop talking. ❑ **crack down on** *v.* [20C+] (*Aus.*) to grab and make off with something. ❑ **crack funny** *v.* [1980s+] (*US*) **1** to be cheeky, insolent. **2** to make jokes; to amuse. ❑ **crack off** *v.* [1980s+] (*US*) to make jokes, to make 'smart' comments. ❑ **cracking but facking** [SE *fact*] [1930s–40s] (*US black*) conveying hard factual information in the guise of jokes and humour. ❑ **crack mugs** *v.* [MUG *n.*[1] (2a); the implication is of their worthlessness and the gullibility of the purchasers] [1910s+] (*Aus.*) to sell racing tips. ❑ **crack on** *v. see* separate entries. ❑ **crack one's jaw** *v.* (*also* **crack one's jib**) [1930s–50s] (*US black*) **1** to boast, to brag. **2** to speak. ❑ **crack someone up** *v.* [20C+] to praise, to eulogize. ❑ **crack wise** *v. see under* WISE *adj.* ❑ **what's cracking?** [1990s+] (*orig. US black*) a general excl. of greeting.

crack *v.*[2] **1** in senses of collapse, breakdown. (**a**) [late 16C–18C] to fall into disrepair. (**b**) [1920s+] to collapse, to break down (emotionally). **2** in senses of breaking into, breaking open. (**a**) [late 16C–1930s] to deflower. (**b**) [late 16C+] to open, orig. of a bottle etc, meaning to have a drink, latterly to open anything, e.g. a door etc. (**c**) [late 17C–mid-19C] (*also* **krack**) to break open, to break into; thus *crack a crib*, to break into a house; *cracking*, robbery. (**d**) [late 18C–early 19C] to break, e.g. an opponent's head. (**e**) [late 18C+] to escape from prison. (**f**) [mid-19C+] to work something out, to find a solution. (**g**) [20C+] to change money, to break a note into change. (**h**) [1920s+] to break someone down, e.g. during an interrogation. **3** [1980s] (*S.Afr.*) to arrive at. **4** [1990s+] to break a record, to surpass.

IN PHRASES

❑ **crack it** *v. see* separate entries. ❑ **crack...** *v. see also under* relevant n. ❑ **crack a bottle** *v.* (*also* **crack a quart, ...pint, ... pot**) [late 16C+] to have a drink. ❑ **crack a fat** *v.* [FAT *n.* (3)] [1970s+] to display one's penis. ❑ **crack a ken** *v.* (*also* **crack a swag**) [KEN *n.*[1] (1)/SWAG *n.*[1] (1)] [18C–early 19C] to break into and rob a house. ❑ **crack one's pitcher** *n. see* CRACKED PITCHER *under* CRACKED *adj.*[1]. ❑ **crack the books** *v.* (*also* **crack it**) [1920s–70s] (*US*) to open a book (for the purpose of study). ❑ **crack up** *see* separate entries.

SE in slang uses

IN COMPOUNDS

❑ **crackbrain** *n.* [late 18C+] a fool. ❑ **crack-fencer** *n.* [SE *crack* (of a nut) + -FENCER *sfx*] [mid-19C] a street-seller of nuts. ❑ **crack halter** *n.* (*also* **crack hemp**) [the *halter* is the hangman's noose/*hemp* refers to the hempen noose] [16C–17C] a rogue, a villain. ▫ **crack-rope** *n.* [SE *crack* + *rope*; thus one who might stretch the hangman's rope] [mid-16C–early 19C] a rogue, a villain.

(IN PHRASES)

▫ **crack an egg** *v.* [1980s] (*Aus.*) to have an abortion. ▫ **crack it for a quid** *v.* [SE *crack*, to open, in this case her legs] [1960s+] (*Aus.*) to work as a prostitute. ▫ **crack one's face** *v.* (*also* **crack a grin, ...smile**) [1940s+] to laugh, to smile. ▫ **crack one's ribs** *v.* (*also* **crack one's guts**) [mid-19C+] to laugh uproariously, until one feels actual pain. ▫ **crack one's side** *v.* [mid-19C+] (*US black*) to laugh uproariously, until one feels actual pain. ▫ **crack one's whip** *v.* [1950s–80s] (*N.Z.*) to take one's share or turn, esp. in buying a round of drinks. ▫ **crack someone's face** *v.* [1980s] (*US campus*) to humiliate, to insult. ▫ **crack someone up** *v.* [1960s+] (*orig. US*) to make someone laugh. ▫ **crack the pitch** *v. see* PITCH THE CRACK *under* PITCH *v.*

crack *v.*[3] [SE *crack open*] (*Und.*) **1** [late 19C+] to ask for, to demand; ext. as *crack on*. **2** [20C+] (*US*) (*also* **crack it to**) to pass on a secret, to give information. **3** [1940s+] to arrest.

crack *v.*[4] **1** [20C+] (*orig. Aus.*) to act in a given manner, defined by some form of comb., e.g. CRACK HARDY below. **2** [1900s–10s] (*Aus.*) to pretend, to sham; thus *crack a deaf 'un*, to pretend to be deaf, or not to hear. **3** [2000s] (*US black*) to happen.

(IN PHRASES)

▫ **crack hardy** *v.* [20C+] (*Aus.*) **1** to put up with discomfort, to 'grin and bear it'; thus as adj. *crack-hardy*, resilient. **2** to keep a secret.

crack *adv.* [CRACK *adj.* (1)] **1** [mid-19C] in a first-rate manner. **2** [1920s] incontrovertibly, absolutely.

crack along *v. see* CRACK ON *v.*[1] (2).

cracked *adj.*[1] [fig. uses of SE *cracked*, broken] **1** [mid-16C–early 18C] bankrupt, financially ruined. **2** [late 16C–early 18C] deflowered. **3** [early 17C] of money, counterfeit. **4** [early 17C+] insane, crazy, eccentric; thus *cracked about/on*, obsessed with, infatuated with. **5** [mid-19C; 1970s] at the end of one's tether; emotionally drained (rather than actually insane).

(IN PHRASES)

▫ **half-cracked** *adj.* [late 19C+] slightly insane, not wholly balanced.

SE in slang uses

(IN COMPOUNDS)

▫ **cracked groat** *n.* (*also* **slit groat**) [SE *groat*, a coin worth fourpence; thus of very low value] [17C] something absolutely worthless. ▫ **cracked ice** *n.* [joc. use of SE phr. + ICE *n.*[1] (3)] [late 19C–1960s] (*US*) diamonds. ▫ **cracked pitcher** *n.* [note *double entendre* in D'Urfey, *Pills to Purge Melancholy* (1719): 'Where Wenches sell Glasses and crackt Earthen-ware; / To shew that the World and the Pleasures it brings, / Are made up of Brittle and Slippery things'] **1** [mid-18C–mid-19C] a woman living between respectability and prostitution. **2** [late 18C–early 19C] a recently lost virginity; thus *crack one's pitcher*, to lose one's virginity.

(IN PHRASES)

▫ **cracked in the filbert** *adj. see under* FILBERT *n.* ▫ **cracked in the ring** *adj.* [RING *n.* (1a)] [late 16C–late 19C] deflowered.

cracked *adj.*[2] [CRACK *n.*[7]] [1980s+] (*drugs*) under the influence of or addicted to crack cocaine.

cracked up *adj.*[1] [fig. use of SE] [mid-19C–1900s] impoverished, destitute.

cracked up *adj.*[2] [CRACK *n.*[7]] [1980s+] (*drugs*) under the influence of crack cocaine.

crackee! *excl. see* CRACKY! *excl.*

cracker *n.*[1] [SE *crack*/CRACK *n.*[3] (4)] **1** [late 17C–18C] (*UK Und.*) the backside. **2** [mid-19C+] (*S.Afr.*) sheep-skin trousers.

cracker *n.*[2] [SE *crack*, to make a sharp noise; they all 'go off'] **1** [mid-18C] a pistol. **2** [19C] the penis. **3** [1910s+] (*N.Z.*) a cartridge. **4** *see* CRACK *n.*[1] (2a).

cracker *n.*[3] [CRACK *v.*[1] (1a); for sense 1 note G. Cochrane, letter, 27 June 1766: 'I should explain to your Lordship what is meant by crackers, a name they have got from being great boasters, they are a lawless set of rascalls on the frontiers of Virginia, Maryland, the Carolinas and Georgia, who often change their places of abode'; also Tosches, *Where Dead Voices Gather* (2001): 'The Georgia jurist, educator, and author A.B. Longstreet (1790–1870) wrote endearingly of the poor rural whites known as crackers in Georgia Scenes, an 1835 collection of humorous sketches whose purpose, he said, "was to supply a chasm in history which has always been overlooked—the manners, customs, amusements, wit, dialect, as they appear in all grades of society to an eye and ear witness of them." The term came to be embraced colloquially by Georgians as a source of humor and self-effacing pride; and by the mid-nineteenth century and well into the twentieth, Georgia was known as the Cracker State. In the early 1930's, Erskine Caldwell, another Georgia author, would show a darker and more sordid side of cracker life in his popular novels *Tobacco Road* and *God's Little Acre*; but only later did cracker become the pejorative epithet that it is today, a class slur leveled by other whites or a racial slur cast by blacks'] **1** [mid-18C+] (*US*) a poor Southern US white farmer. **2** [mid-19C] an aphorism. **3** [late 19C–1900s] a lie. **4** [1920s+] (*orig. US black*) (*also* **cracker-man**) a white person, usu. a racist.

(IN COMPOUNDS)

▫ **cracker-ass** *n.* [-ASS *sfx*] [1960s+] (*US black*) a white person. ▫ **crackerbox** *n.* [2000s] (*US black*) a predominantly white neighbourhood. ▫ **cracker-man** *n. see* sense 2 above. ▫ **Cracker State** *n.* [early 19C+] (*US*) Georgia.

cracker *n.*[4] [SE *cracker*, a biscuit; Baker, *Australian Language* (1945), adds *cracker*, a £1 note, and this has been taken up by the *OED*, and in Pulliam, *I Travelled the Lonely Land* (1955), but Wilkes, *A Dict. of Australian Colloquialisms* (1985), rejects it: 'No evidence has been found ...'] **1** [early 19C] (*UK prison*) a small loaf served to prisoners as their daily rations. **2** [mid-19C+] (*Aus./N.Z.*) the smallest feasible amount of money. **3** [1920s+] (*US black*) a very light-coloured black person [biscuit-coloured, or ref. to their similarity to a CRACKER *n.*[3] (4)]. **4** [1930s+] (*US*) $1. **5** [1940s+] (*Aus./N.Z.*) fig. ext. of sense 2, anything worthless, valueless; thus *not have a cracker*, to be penniless.

SE in slang uses

(IN COMPOUNDS)

▫ **cracker-ass** *n.* [-ASS *sfx*] [1960s–70s] (*US*) a skinny person; also as adj. ▫ **crackerbox** *n.* [puns on fragility and size of a SAmE *crackerbox*] **1** [1930s–40s] (*US Und.*) a safe that can be broken into easily [note BOX *n.*[1] (2d)]. **2** [1950s] a second-rate hotel. **3** [1950s+] a small room, e.g. a nightclub, a small house. **4** [1970s] (*US*) a small car.

cracker *n.*[5] [CRACK *v.*[1] (2b)] [mid-19C+] **1** a heavy blow. **2** a fall.

cracker *n.*[6] [CRACK *adj.* (1)] [mid-19C+] someone or something notable, e.g. a fast pace, a dandy, a large sum of money, an exceptional individual.

cracker *n.*[7] [CRACK *v.*[2] (2c)] **1** [1920s] (*US Und.*) a safe. **2** [1970s] a safe-breaker. **3** [2000s] a credit card computer fraudster.

cracker *n.*[8] [CRACKED UP *adj.*[1]] [1940s+] a worn-out sheep, horse or bullock.

cracker *n.*[9] [CRACK *adj.* (1), but note CRACK *n.*[3] (1)] **1** [1950s+] an attractive young woman, usu. as a *little cracker*; occas. a man. **2** [1960s+] (*Aus.*) a prostitute. **3** [1960s+] (*Aus.*) (*also* **cracker joint**) a brothel.

cracker *n.*[10] [CRACK *n.*[7]] [1990s+] a regular user of crack cocaine.

cracker *adj.*[1] [CRACKER *n.*[3]] (*orig. US black*) **1** [mid-19C+] pertaining to the US rural South; ext. to any white person. **2** [1950s+] racist.

cracker *adj.*[2] [CRACKER *n.*[6]] [1980s+] excellent, first-rate.

crackerbarrel *adj.* [CRACKERS *adj.* + SAmE *crackerbarrel*, of a philosophy, plain or unsophisticated] [1980s+] crazy, eccentric.

crackerbox *n.* [CRACKERS *adj.* + SE *box*; pun on SE] [1980s+] (*US*) **1** an eccentric, a madman. **2** a psychiatric institution. **3** *see under* CRACKER *n.*^{3}. **4** *see under* CRACKER *n.*^{4}.

crackerbox *adj.* [CRACKERBOX *under* CRACKER *n.*^{4}] [1940s] (*US Und.*) insecure, vulnerable to theft, rickety.

cracker factory *n.* [CRACKERS *adj.* + SE *factory*; pun on SE] [1980s+] (*US*) a psychiatric institution.

crackerjack *n.* [play on SE colloq. *crackerjack*, exceptional + ? ref. to CRACK *n.*^{7} + JACK *n.*^{2} (1)] [1980s+] (*drugs*) a smoker of crack cocaine.

crackerjack *adj.* [? US sweet *Crackerjack*, which contained toy police badges] [1970s+] fake, make-believe.

crackers *n.*^{1} [CRACK *v.*^{1} (2a)] [1900s–10s] (*US*) beans.

crackers *n.*^{2} [the distribution of LSD by placing a drop on a biscuit] [1960s] (*drugs*) LSD.

crackers *n.*^{3} [SE *crack*] [1970s] the teeth.

crackers *n.*^{4} [SE *crack*, to break open; i.e. one snaps open the vial that contains the drug] [1970s] (*drugs*) amyl nitrite.

crackers *n.*^{5} [they supposedly make a *crack* knocking together] [1990s+] (*Aus.*) the testicles.

crackers *adj.* [CRACKED *adj.*^{1} (4)] [1920s+] mad, crazy; thus *crackers about*, obsessed with.

IN PHRASES

❑ **go crackers** *v.* [1920s+] to go mad, become insane, eccentric.

crackie *n.* [CRACK *n.*^{7}] [2000s] (*US black*) one who is very heavily addicted to crack cocaine.

crackie! *excl. see* CRACKY! *excl.*

cracking *n.* [CRACK *v.*^{2} (2c)] [mid-19C–1920s] (*UK Und.*) housebreaking.

IN COMPOUNDS

❑ **cracking job** *n.* [JOB *n.*^{2} (1a)] [mid-19C] (*UK Und.*) a burglary.

cracking *adj.* [CRACK *adj.*] **1** [early 19C+] vigorous. **2** [mid-19C+] excellent, first-rate. **3** [1950s] a general intensifier, i.e. utter, absolute.

cracking it *n.* [*CRACK IT FOR A QUID under* CRACK *v.*^{2}] [1960s+] (*Aus.*) prostitution.

crackish *adj. see under* CRACK *n.*^{3}.

crack it *v.*^{1} [fig. use of CRACK *v.*^{2} (2c)] [1930s+] (*orig. Aus./N.Z.*) **1** to succeed, to overcome obstacles, esp. to achieve a successful (from the male point of view) seduction or win at gambling. **2** to obtain, to get hold of, poss. by criminal means. **3** to do, to perform; usu. in form *crack it for a...* **4** to seduce a woman.

crack it *v.*^{2} *see CRACK THE BOOKS under* CRACK *v.*^{2}.

crack it to *v. see* CRACK *v.*^{3} (2).

crackjaw *n. see BREAK-TEETH WORDS under* BREAK *v.*^{1}.

crackle *n.* [the noise of the paper] [1940s–50s] (*UK Und.*) a banknote, usu. of £5 and up.

crackling *n.* [SE *crackling*, tasty roast pork fat] [late 19C+] attractive women, used as a generic.

IN PHRASES

❑ **bit of crackling** *n.* [BIT *n.*^{1} (2a)] [20C+] **1** an attractive woman. **2** an attractive man.

crackman *n.* [CRACK *adj.* (1)] [early 19C] a fashionable man.

crackmans *n.* (*also* **cragmans**) [SE *crack*, dry firewood + -MANS *sfx*] [16C–18C] (*UK Und.*) a hedge.

IN PHRASES

❑ **mill a crackmans** *v.* [late 17C–18C] to collect firewood from a hedge, lit. to 'break a hedge'.

cracko *n.* [CRACKED *adj.*^{1} (4) + -O *sfx* (2)] [1980s] a madman, a lunatic.

cracko *adj.* [CRACKO *n.*] [1980s+] eccentric, insane.

crackola *n.* [CRACK *n.*^{7} + -OLA *sfx*] [1990s+] (*US black/drugs*) crack cocaine.

crack on *v.*^{1} **1** [mid-19C] to load up, to 'clap on'. **2** [mid-19C+] (*also* **crack along**) to move along at speed, to bustle about. **3** [1940s+] to get on with one's work.

crack on *v.*^{2} [SE *crack*, to make a loud or sudden noise; Nares notes: 'CRAKE. To boast [...] To *crack*, in the same sense, is of rather more recent usage, and is probably only a corruption of this'] **1** [mid-19C–1900s; 1960s] to inform (against). **2** [late 19C+] to tell tales, to boast. **3** [late 19C+] to pretend. **4** [1960s+] (*US campus*) of a man, to strike up a friendship with a woman in the hope of moving onto a deeper relationship; the alluring factor is not her status or possessions but her personality. **5** [1970s+] (*US black*) to disparage, to attack verbally. **6** [2000s] (*N.Z.*) to bore. **7** *see* CRACK *v.*^{1}. **8** *see* CRACK *v.*^{3} (1).

crackskull *n.* [a melodramatic version of its effects] [mid-19C+] (*US*) whisky.

cracksman *n.*^{1} [CRACK *n.*^{4} (2) + sfx *-man*; the *locus classicus* is in the title of E.W. Hornung's *The Amateur Cracksman* (1899), featuring the exploits of the gentleman-thief A.J. Raffles] **1** [late 18C+] a burglar; thus *swell cracksman*, a superior burglar. **2** [1920s] a safebreaker.

cracksman *n.*^{2} [CRACK *n.*^{3} (1) + sfx *-man*] [19C] the penis.

crack-up *n.*^{1} [SE *crack up*, to break down] [1920s+] (*orig. US*) a truck, motorcar or motorcycle crash.

crack-up *n.*^{2} [SE *crack up*, to laugh out loud] [1960s+] anything considered hilariously funny.

crack-up *adj. see* CRACK *adj.* (1).

crack up *v.*^{1} [the *crack* sound of applauding hands] [early 19C+] to boast or praise.

IN PHRASES

❑ **not all it's cracked up to be** (*also* **not what it's cracked up to be, not the — it/he/she is cracked up to be**) [early 19C+] well below expectations.

crack up *v.*^{2} [SE *crack*, to break] [1920s+] to crash some form of vehicle or conveyance, e.g. a car, an aeroplane.

crack up *v.*^{3} *see under* CRACK *n.*^{7}.

crackwise *n.* [CRACK WISE *v.*] [1940s–60s] (*US black*) one who pretends to a greater sophistication and knowledge of 'the scene' than he or she actually possesses, a poseur.

crack wise *v.* [CRACK *v.*^{1} (1a) + WISE *adj.* (1)] [1920s+] (*orig. US black*) to make a 'clever' comment that impresses no one, to pose as more sophisticated than one actually is.

cracky *n.* [CRACKED *adj.*^{1} (4)] [1900s–40s] a mentally unstable person.

cracky *adj.* [CRACKY *n.*] [1910s+] (*orig. Aus.*) eccentric, mentally unstable.

cracky! *excl.* (*also* **crackee! crackie!**) [mid-19C+] a euph. for *Christ!*; usu. in mild oaths.

IN EXCLAMATIONS

❑ **by cracky!** (*also* **by crackey!**) [late 19C+] a euph. for *by Christ!*

cradle *n.* [late 18C–19C] the vagina.

SE in slang uses

IN COMPOUNDS

❑ **cradle-robber** *n.* **1** [1920s+] (*orig. US*) one who pursues lovers who are younger than themselves. **2** [1940s] (*US*) a child-molester. ❑ **cradle-snatcher** *n.* [20C+] (*orig. US*) an older person, in modern use usu. a woman but also of gay men, who prefers affairs with people substantially younger than they are; thus n. *cradle-snatching*. ❑ **cradle-vanneck** *n.* [ety. unknown; ? 'cradle the neck'] [mid-19C] (*UK Und.*) a gibbet.

craft *n.*^{1} [modern use is UK black/W.I.] [mid-19C+] a woman.

craft *n.*^{2} [SE *craft*, a ship] [late 19C–1900s] a bicycle.

craft rig *n.* [SE *craft* + RIG *n.*^{2} (1)] [late 18C] (*UK Und.*) a form of river robbery.

craftsby *n.* [late 17C] a cheat, a confidence trickster.

crafty butcher *n.* [1990s+] a male homosexual.

crag *n.* **1** [mid-17C–early 19C] the neck, the head. **2** [18C] the stomach, the womb.

craggy *adj.* [1990s+] (*US campus*) good, attractive.

cragmans *n. see* CRACKMANS *n.*

craik v. (*also* **crake**) [dial. *crake*, an ill-natured gossip; ult. SE *crake*, the cry of the corncrake] [20C+] (*Ulster*) to nag, to grumble, to talk without stopping.

Crail capon n. [the local fishery trade of Crail, Fife] [early 19C] a salt herring.

cram *n.* [CRAM *v.*] **1** [mid-19C] (*UK/US campus*) a paper on which material necessary to be learned for a given examination or test is written down. **2** [mid–late 19C] (*orig. Oxon. university*) (*also* **cram-coach**) a tutor. **3** [mid-19C–1900s] a lie; thus *crammer*, a liar; as v., to tell a lie. **4** [mid-19C+] (*UK/US campus*) last-minute work for a specific test or examination; thus *cram-book*, a book used for intensive learning; *cram-paper*, a prepared list of examination answers, to be learned parrot-fashion; *cram-shop*, a school run by a crammer.

(IN COMPOUNDS)

❑ **cram man** *n.* [mid-19C] a person who works extra hard at the last minute before an examination. ❑ **cram session** *n.* [1920s+] (*US*) a burst of study immediately before an examination.

cram v. [SE *cram*, to fill up] **1** [late 18C–mid-19C] to lie, to deceive, to make a person believe false or exaggerated statements [the liar's victim is 'filled up' with untruths]. **2** [19C+] to study hard, esp. at the last minute; thus *crammable*, of work that can be learned by rote; *crammed*, tutored for examinations rather than actual knowledge. **3** [mid-19C] to train up a student for an examination. **4** [mid-19C] to urge a horse on by force. **5** [mid-19C+] of a man, to have sexual intercourse. **6** [late 19C–1920s] to study for a given subject or institution after one has been expelled from a regular school. **7** [1990s+] (*US black*) to be very enthusiastic.

(IN PHRASES)

❑ **cram-o-matic** v. [-O-MATIC *sfx*] [1980s+] (*US campus*) to study hard at the last minute.

(IN EXCLAMATIONS)

❑ **cram it!** [1960s+] (*US*) a general excl. of dismissal, rejection; *the hell with it!shove it!* etc.

crammer *n.* [CRAM *v.*] **1** [19C+] a tutor; thus [late 19C–1920s] *crammer's pup*, a pupil of such a high-pressure tutor. **2** [mid-19C] the stomach [SE *cram*, to fill up]. **3** [mid–late 19C] one who lies. **4** [mid-19C–1920s] a lie. **5** [1910s–60s] a hard worker.

cramming *n.* [CRAM *v.* (2)] [early 19C+] intensive learning aimed purely at passing necessary examinations.

cramp *n.* [? image of one suffering badly from menstrual cramps] [1930s+] (*US black*) an unpleasant, unpopular woman.

cramp v. [fig. uses of SE *cramp*, to compress, to restrict, to limit] (*US*) **1** [mid-19C] to execute by hanging, to kill; thus *cramping-day*, execution-day. **2** [late 19C; 1960s] to annoy.

(IN COMPOUNDS)

❑ **Cramp Abbey** *n.* [mid-19C] (*UK Und.*) orig. Newgate prison; then a generic term for any prison. ❑ **cramping-cull** *n.* [CULL *n.*[1] (3)] [mid-19C] the hangman. ❑ **cramp-jinked** *adj.* [mid-19C] (*UK Und.*) committed to trial. ❑ **cramp words** *n.* [note SE *cramp word*, a long, difficult or unusual word] [18C–mid-19C] (*UK Und.*) a sentence of death.

cramped *adj.*[1] [CRAMP *v.* (1)/SE *cramp*, to torture by compressing or 'cramping' the body] **1** [19C] hanged. **2** [19C] killed.

cramped *adj.*[2] [1990s+] (*US black*) unattractive.

cramp in the hand *n.* [late 19C] meanness.

cramp-rings *n.* (*also* **cramping-rings, queer cramp-ring**) [SE *cramp*: a small iron bar with its ends bent into hooks + ? pun on the orig. 15C SE *cramp-ring*, a ring worn on the finger to ward off cramp, epilepsy etc + QUEER *adj.* (1)] [mid-16C–mid-19C] (*UK Und.*) shackles or fetters.

cranberry eye *n.* [the colour] [late 19C] (*US*) a bloodshot eye (from excessive drinking).

cranberry sauce *n.* [1930s] (*US Und.*) blood.

crane v. [SE *crane one's neck*, to stretch the neck to look around + hunting jargon *crane*, to pull up at a hedge or other obstacle and look over before leaping] [mid–late 19C] to hesitate or balk before an obstacle.

crank *n.*[1] [Ger. *krenk*, sick] **1** [mid-16C–early 19C] the 'falling sickness', epilepsy. **2** [17C–mid-18C] a mendicant villain who specializes in faking sickness, esp. epilepsy, and who often displays convincingly horrific sores and wounds, created by the application of various herbs.

(IN COMPOUNDS)

❑ **crank cuffin** *n.* [CUFFIN *n.* (1)] [late 17C–mid-18C] (*UK Und.*) a tramp who poses as a sufferer from a sympathy-inducing illness.

crank *n.*[2] **1** [late 18C–mid-19C] gin and water. **2** [1960s+] (*drugs*) any form of amphetamine drug. **3** [1970s+] a thrill of excitement, esp. when drug-generated. **4** [1980s+] (*drugs*) crack cocaine. **5** [1990s+] heroin.

(IN COMPOUNDS)

❑ **crank bugs** *n.* *see* BUG *n.*[4]. ❑ **crankhead** *n.* [-HEAD *sfx*] [1980s+] (*US drugs*) a regular user of amphetamines.

(IN PHRASES)

❑ **cranked (out)** *adj.* (*also* **cranked up**) [1980s+] under the influence of amphetamine or crack cocaine.

crank *n.*[3] [resemblance to SE *crank*, a handle] **1** [1960s+] (*orig. US*) the penis. **2** [1990s+] (*Aus.*) (*also* **hand crank**) an act of masturbation performed by a woman.

(IN PHRASES)

❑ **bite someone's crank** v. [1960s+] to fellate.

crank *adj.*[1] [SE *crank*, anything fantastic in behaviour, gesture, or action] **1** [mid-18C+] mad, eccentric. **2** [late 18C] drunk.

crank *adj.*[2] [SE *crank*, exultant, 'cocky'] [mid-19C] (*US*) proud.

crank *v.*[1] [SE *crank* v.] **1** [1920s+] (*also* **crank up**) to start up a mechanical device, esp. a car engine (but not with an actual crank handle); also fig. use. **2** [1920s+] (*also* **crank up**) to turn up the volume of a radio, etc; to talk or sing louder. **3** [1960s+] (*US*) to get, to prepare (oneself). **4** [1960s+] (*drugs*) (*also* **crank up**) to inject narcotics with a hypodermic syringe. **5** [1970s] (*US prison*) to roll a cigarette. **6** [1970s+] (*US teen*) all-purpose word of movement, e.g. *crank oneself together, crank to school.* **7** [1970s+] to intensify, to do something more energetically. **8** [1980s+] (*drugs*) to become intoxicated by amphetamine. **9** *see* CRANK IT UP below.

(IN PHRASES)

❑ **crank it up** v. [1980s+] to intensify, esp. to make louder, to turn up the volume. ❑ **crank off** v. [1960s+] (*US*) to fire a round from a weapon. ❑ **crank on** v. [1980s+] (*US campus*) to work hard and efficiently. ❑ **crank out** v. (*also* **crank**) [1970s] (*US campus*) to produce large amounts, e.g. of work, energy, sound etc. ❑ **crank up** v. *see* senses 1, 2 and 4 above.

SE in slang uses

(IN PHRASES)

❑ **crank it out** v. [SE *crank*, to turn a handle; or sense 6 above] [1970s+] to write (usu. badly) more from duty than pleasure or interest, to be a hack writer. ❑ **crank one's shank** v. (*also* **crank one's shaft, crank the shank**) [SE *crank*, to wind up, to twist + *shank*, a shaft, stem or 'neck'] [1990s+] to masturbate.

crank *v.*[2] [fig. uses of CRANK *v.*[1] (1)] (*drugs*) **1** [1960s+] (*also* **crank up**) to inject narcotics with a hypodermic syringe. **2** [1980s+] to become intoxicated by amphetamine.

cranked *adj.* [CRANK *adj.*[1] (2)] [late 19C–1920s] (*US*) mentally unbalanced.

cranked up *adj.* (*also* **cranked**) [CRANK *v.*[1] (1)] [1950s+] (*US*) excited, 'revved up'.

cranker *n.*[1] [Ger. *krank*, sick] [1930s–40s] (*US*) a doctor.

cranker *n.*[2] [CRANK *n.*[2] (2)] [1970s] (*drugs*) a heavy user of amphetamines.

cranker *n.*[3] [? rhy. sl. link to TANK *n.*[2] (3); or one who uses some form of SE *crank* to open the safe] [1980s+] (*Aus. prison*) a safe-breaker.

cranker *n.*[4] [rhy. sl. = WANKER *n.*; + link to *CRANK ONE'S SHAFT under* CRANK *v.*[1]] [1990s+] (*Aus. prison*) a masturbator.

crank gang *n.* [SE *crank*, an eccentric] [1980s] (*US prison*) a prison work gang composed of eccentric or idle prisoners.

cranking *adj.* [? CRANKED UP *adj.*] [1980s+] (*US campus*) enjoyable, exciting.

crankpot *n.* [SE *cranky*, grumpy + *pot* (*of the head*), the skull, the cranium] [1960s+] (*US*) a mean, ill-tempered individual.

crankpot *adj.* [CRANKPOT *n.*] [2000s] unpleasant, ill-tempered, bigoted.

cranky hatch *n.* [SE *cranky*, eccentric + BOOBY-HATCH *n.* (2)] **1** [20C+] (*US Und.*) a psychiatric institution. **2** [1910s+] (*US prison*) (*also* **crank row**) the prison segregation block.

cranky hutch *n.* [SE *cranky*, eccentric + *hutch*] [mid-19C] (*US*) a lunatic asylum.

cranny *n.* [mid-17C+] the vagina.

IN COMPOUNDS

❑ **cranny-hunter** *n.* (*also* **cranny-haunter**) [late 19C] the penis.

crap *n.*[1] (*also* **crop**) [sense 1: SE *crap*, waste, chaff or Fr. *crape*, dirt, cognate with DIRT *n.* (1); thus linked to sense 2, mix of Du. *krappen*, to pluck off, cut off or separate + OF *crappe*, waste or rejected matter, siftings, particularly 'the grain trodden under feet in the barn, and mingled with the straw and dust'; ult. Med. Lat. *crappa*, *crapinum*, the smaller chaff] **1** [late 17C–mid-19C] money. **2** [mid-19C+] excrement. **3** [mid-19C+] dirt, mess. **4** [1910s+] nonsense. **5** [1910s+] (*US*) insolence, cheek. **6** [1920s+] rubbish, anything useless or unpleasant. **7** [1920s+] an act of defecation. **8** [1930s+] (*orig. US*) the essence, the stuffing; esp. in phrs. below, e.g. *beat the crap out of*, to give a thrashing to. **9** [1930s+] a non-specific descriptor, 'stuff', 'things'. **10** [1940s] (*US gang*) fighting. **11** [1940s+] (*US*) nothing at all. **12** [1940s+] of people, a general derog. term. **13** [1950s–60s] a damn; esp. in phr. (*not*) *give a crap*. **14** [1950s+] (*US*) trouble, problems. **15** [1960s] (*drugs*) marijuana. **16** [1960s+] (*drugs*) (*also* **crop**) low-quality heroin.

DERIVATIVES

❑ **craperoo** *n.* (*also* **crappadooley, crapperoo**) [-EROO *sfx*] [1940s+] (*US*) absolute rubbish, nonsense. ❑ **crapless** *adj.* [1970s+] (*US*) terrified. ❑ **crapola** *n.* [-OLA *sfx*] [1930s+] (*US*) nonsense, rubbish. ❑ **crappapella** *adj.* [1990s+] (*US campus*) very CRAP *adj.*

IN COMPOUNDS

❑ **crap-artist** *n.* (*also* **crap merchant**) [-ARTIST *sfx*/MERCHANT *n.*] [1930s+] (*US*) a liar, an exaggerator, a deceiver. ❑ **crap-bag** *n.* [1960s–70s] (*Scot.*) a coward. ❑ **crapbrain** *n.* [1950s+] a general term of abuse, based on alleged stupidity of the recipient. ❑ **crap can** *n.* [1930s–40s] (*US*) the lavatory. ❑ **crap creek** *n.* [var. on SHIT CREEK *n.*] [1950s+] (*US*) a troublesome, threatening situation. ❑ **crapeating** *adj.* [1950s] (*US*) despicable. ❑ **crap-happy** *adj.* [play on SLAP-HAPPY *adj.*] [1960s+] (*US*) foolishly happy. ❑ **craphead** *n.* (*also* **crapface**) [-HEAD *sfx* (1)] [1950s+] (*orig. US*) a fool, an unpleasant person. ❑ **crapheap** *n.* [1980s] (*Aus.*) a filthy, disgusting place. ❑ **craphole** *n.* [1930s+] a filthy, disgusting place. ❑ **craphouse** *n.* see separate entry. ❑ **crapload** *n.* see SHITLOAD *n.* ❑ **crapmound** *n.* [1950s] a general term of abuse, lit. a 'heap of shit'. ❑ **crap paper** *n.* [1920s] (*US*) lavatory paper. ❑ **crap-pushing** *adj.* [1960s] a general derisory epithet. ❑ **crap-sack** *adj.* [2000s] terrible, of very poor quality. ❑ **crap-scared** *adj.* [1940s] terrified. ❑ **crap shooter** *n.* (*also* **crap-slinger**) [SHOOT THE CRAP below] [1930s–40s] (*US*) one who talks nonsense. ❑ **crap-town** *n.* [1960s] (*US*) the slums. ❑ **crapweasel** *n.* [2000s] (*US campus*) an irritatingly stupid or deceitful person.

IN PHRASES

❑ **cut the crap** *v.* see separate entry. ❑ **drop someone in the crap** *v.* see DROP SOMEONE IN IT under DROP *v.*[1]. ❑ **get one's crap hot** *v.* [1950s] (*US*) to lose one's temper. ❑ **go take a crap** [1970s] a phr. of dismissal, rejection. ❑ **kick the crap out of** *v.* [1950s+] (*orig. US*) to beat up. ❑ **knock the crap out of** *v.* (*also* **beat the crap out of, slap the crap out of**) **1** [1940s+] (*orig. US*) to beat up. **2** [2000s] in fig. sense, to malign. ❑ **know crap from clay** *v.* [1950s] (*Aus.*) to be astute, to not be ignorant. ❑ **like crap through a goose** *adv.* see LIKE SHIT THROUGH A GOOSE under SHIT *n.* ❑ **line of crap** *n.* [1920s–50s] nonsensical talk, usu. intended to persuade. ❑ **scare the (living) crap out of** *v.* [1960s+] to terrify. ❑ **shoot the crap** *v.* (*also* **sling the crap**) [SHOOT *v.* (5)/SLING *v.* (2a)] [1930s–60s] to talk nonsense. ❑ **take a crap** *v.* [1920s+] to defecate. ❑ **take crap** *v.* (*also* **eat crap**) [1930s+] to accept bad behaviour, insulting speech etc; thus as *take no crap*, to stand up for one's rights. ❑ **talk crap** *v.* [1920s+] (*orig. US*) to talk nonsense.

IN EXCLAMATIONS

❑ **no crap!** [1940s–60s] a semi-euph. for NO SHIT! *excl.*

crap *n.*[2] [Du. *krap*, cramp or clasp] [late 18C–mid-19C] the gallows; thus *knock down/up for the crap*, to sentence to be hanged.

IN COMPOUNDS

❑ **crap-merchant** *n.* [MERCHANT *n.*] [late 18C] (*UK Und.*) the hangman.

crap, the *n.* [1940s+] (*orig. US*) used in excl., e.g. *what the crap do you want?*

crap *adj.* [CRAP *n.*[1]] [1930s+] a general negative description; unpleasant, disgusting, repellent, worthless etc.

IN COMPOUNDS

❑ **crap-ass** *adj.* [1970s+] (*US*) second-rate, inferior. ❑ **crap course** *n.* [1950s+] (*US campus*) an easy course.

crap *v.*[1] (*also* **crop**) [CRAP *n.*[2]] [mid-18C–mid-19C] **1** to hang. **2** in excl., e.g. *crap me!, crop me!*

crap *v.*[2] [CRAP *n.*[1]] **1** in the context of defecation. (**a**) [mid-19C+] to visit the lavatory, to defecate. (**b**) [1940s+] to filthy with excrement. (**c**) [1980s] to mess something up. **2** in fig. uses. (**a**) [mid-19C+] to annoy, to irritate. (**b**) [1920s+] to tell deliberate lies (to). (**c**) [1930s+] to complain. (**d**) [1950s] to chatter.

IN PHRASES

❑ **crap around** *v.* **1** [1930s+] to fool about, to waste time. **2** see CRAP SOMEONE AROUND below. ❑ **crap a smoke** *v.* [1940s] (*US*) to smoke surreptitiously in a lavatory. ❑ **crap in the same can** *v.* [1950s] to be intimate, to be together. ❑ **crap it** *v.* [1960s+] to be doomed, to suffer a serious mishap. ❑ **crap off** *v.* [1970s] (*N.Z.*) to stop talking, esp. nonsense. ❑ **crap on** *v.* **1** [1920s+] as imper., 'to hell with'. **2** [1940s+] (*also* **crap over**) to treat contemptuously, to victimize. ❑ **crap on (about)** *v.* [1940s+] **1** to talk lengthily, if irrelevantly (about). **2** to complain (about). ❑ **crap oneself** *v.* see SHIT ONESELF *v.* ❑ **crap one's pants** *v.* [1940s+] to be absolutely terrified. ❑ **crap someone around** *v.* [1970s+] **1** (*also* **crap someone along**) to tell deliberate lies. **2** to annoy, to irritate. ❑ **crap up** *v.* **1** [1940s+] (*orig. US*) to ruin by adding unnecessary or distasteful accessories. **2** [1950s+] (*orig. US*) to make a mess of.

crap! *excl.* (*also* **craps! by craps!**) [late 19C+] a general excl.

IN EXCLAMATIONS

❑ **like crap!** [1940s] (*US*) a general intensifier, usu. negative.

crape-hanger *n.* (*also* **crepe-hanger**) [the hanging of black crape to signify mourning] (*US*) **1** [1910s–60s] a pessimist, a kill-joy. **2** [1920s] a murderer.

craphouse *n.* [CRAP *n.*[1] + SE *house*] **1** [1930s+] (*orig. US*) a lavatory. **2** [1960s+] (*orig. US*) any unpleasant, dirty place; thus (*US show business*) a small, unfashionable venue.

IN COMPOUNDS

❑ **craphouse luck** *n.* [1940s–60s] (*US*) unexpectedly good luck. ❑ **craphouse rat** *n.* [1940s+] (*US*) an image of unpleasantness; in phr. *as cunning as a craphouse rat, as dirty as a craphouse rat.*

crap-out *n.* [CRAP OUT *v.* (1)] [1960s+] (*US*) a defeatist, a quitter.

crap out *v.* [SE *crap out*, to make a losing throw in the game of *craps*. Note COME OFF CRABS under CRABS *n.*[1], taken f. the losing cards, two aces, in the game of hazard; in the dice game *craps* a pair of ones, known as *snake-eyes*, is similarly a losing throw] (*orig. US*) **1** [late 19C+] to back down, to give up, esp. in humiliating circumstances. **2** [20C+] to fail, to go wrong, to blunder. **3** [1910s+] to die. **4** [1940s+] of people, to collapse, to become exhausted, to fall asleep. **5** [1950s–60s] to take a rest.

6 [1950s+] of machinery, to break down. **7** [1960s] to kill. **8** [1980s] (*S.Afr.*) to abuse, to criticize.

crappadooley *n. see* CRAPEROO *under* CRAP *n.*[1].

crappapella *adj. see under* CRAP *n.*[1].

crapped *adj.* (*also* **cropped**) [CRAP *v.*[1] (1)] [late 18C–19C] (*UK Und.*) hanged.

crapped out *adj.* [CRAP OUT *v.*] [1930s+] **1** (*US*) having been defeated in any challenge. **2** (*US*) having hit rock bottom, morally bankrupt. **3** (*US*) asleep, collapsed, comatose. **4** (*orig. US*) (*also* **crapped up**) of machinery, worn out.

crapper *n.*[1] [CRAP *v.*[2]; popular and some scholarly sources (e.g. Seal, *The Lingo*, 1999) attribute the ety. to the eponymously named Thomas Crapper, inventor of the water closet, but this is more likely no more than a fortuitous coincidence, albeit a reinforcement of the actual root] **1** [1900s–60s] (*US campus*) a very unpleasant person. **2** [1920s] (*US Und.*) a prison. **3** [1920s+] a lavatory. **4** [1930s+] a braggart; a liar. **5** [1970s] the anus, the buttocks.

IN COMPOUNDS

❑ **crapper dick** *n.* [DICK *n.*[5] (2)] [1950s–70s] (*US*) a plainclothes policeman who specializes in hanging around public lavatories in the hope of entrapping gay men having sex; thus an extortionist who poses as a policeman to blackmail homosexuals.

IN PHRASES

❑ **down the crapper** *see* DOWN THE PAN *under* DOWN *adv.*[2]. ❑ **go down the crapper** *v. see* GO DOWN THE TOILET *under* TOILET *n.* ❑ **in crapper's ditch** [2000s] (*N.Z.*) in trouble. ❑ **in the crapper** [1940s+] (*US*) finished, failed, rejected, abandoned, rendered useless.

crapper *n.*[2] [? dial. *crap*, settlings of beer at the bottom of a barrel] [1910s+] (*Irish*) a half-glass of whisky.

crapperoo *n. see* CRAPEROO *under* CRAP *n.*[1].

crappers *n.* [1950s] (*US*) dice, as used in shooting craps.

crappery *n.* [CRAP *adj.*] [2000s] any second-rate, mediocre place or venue.

crapping *n.*[1] [CRAP *v.*[1] (1)] [late 18C] (*UK Und.*) hanging.

IN COMPOUNDS

❑ **crapping cull** *n.* [CULL *n.*[1] (3)] [mid-18C–mid-19C] (*UK Und.*) the hangman.

crapping *n.*[2] [CRAP *v.*[2] (1)] defecation, in combs. below.

IN COMPOUNDS

❑ **crapping can** *n.* [SE *can*, but note CAN *n.*[1] (4b)] [1930s+] (*US*) a lavatory. ❑ **crapping casa** *n.* (*also* **crapping case**) [CASA *n.*[1]/CASE *n.*[3] (1)] [mid-19C] a privy or water-closet. ❑ **crapping castle** *n.* [mid-19C] a privy. ❑ **crapping ken** *n.* (*also* **cropping ken, croppin ken**) [KEN *n.*[1] (1)] [late 17C–mid-19C] (*UK Und.*) a privy. ❑ **croppen ken** *n.* [KEN *n.*[1] (1); note CROPPEN *n.*] [late 17C–early 19C] a lavatory.

crapping *adj.* [CRAP *adj.*] [mid-19C; 1920s+] general pej. description, useless, second-rate, disgusting.

crappo *n.* (*also* **croppo, cropoh**) [Fr. *crapaud*, toad] [19C] a Frenchman.

crappo *adj.* [CRAP *adj.* + -O *sfx* (5)] [1970s+] **1** disgusting, appalling. **2** as excl.

crappy *adj.* [CRAP *n.*[1] + sfx *-y*] **1** [mid-19C+] fouled with excrement. **2** [1920s–30s] (*UK, Glasgow*) terrified. **3** [1920s+] (*also* **krappy**) second-rate. **4** [1950s–60s] in colour, reminiscent of excrement. **5** [1950s+] unpleasant, distasteful. **6** [1960s+] unwell.

crappy *adv.* [CRAPPY *adj.* (3)] [1970s+] (*US campus*) badly, in a second-rate manner.

craps *n.* [the dice game SE *craps*] [1920s+] dice.

craps, the *n.* [CRAP *n.*[1]] [1950s] (*US*) diarrhoea.

craps! *excl. see* CRAP! *excl.*

crap-shoot *n.* [SE *shoot craps*; thus an image of random luck] [1970s+] any situation in which luck, not judgement, is of paramount importance.

crash *n.*[1] [SE *crash*] **1** [late 19C–1910s] (*US*) an outstanding success. **2** [20C+] (*Aus.*) an act of defecation. **3** [1900s] (*US campus*) a complete failure in an examination. **4** [1900s–60s] (*US campus*) a crush, an infatuation. **5** [1910s–30s] (*Aus.*) a misfortune. **6** [1930s] (*US Und.*) a police raid. **7** [1960s–70s] (*US Und.*) a break-in. **8** *see* CRASH-OUT *n.*

IN PHRASES

❑ **go a-crash of** *v.* [SE *go* + pfx *a-* (implying motion) + *crash*] [20C+] to assault.

crash *n.*[2] [CRASH (OUT) *v.*] **1** [1940s+] a nap, a sleep. **2** [1960s+] (*drugs*) the return to 'normality' that follows drug-taking. **3** *see* CRASH-PAD *n.*

crash *v.* [dial. *crash*, to break violently into pieces] **1** [mid-17C–early 19C] to kill. **2** [late 17C–mid-18C] to eat. **3** [mid-18C] (*UK Und.*) to steal. **4** [1920s–40s] to steal by smashing a store window and removing the contents. **5** [1920s+] (*orig. US*) (*also* **crash in**) to appear uninvited at a given party or other function. **6** [1920s+] (*US Und.*) to break into; lit. and fig. **7** [1920s+] (*Aus./US*) to hit someone hard. **8** [1930s] (*US Und.*) to be killed. **9** [1930s] (*US Und.*) of a gun, to go off. **10** [1930s] (*US Und.*) of a burglar, to break a shop window prior to plundering the contents. **11** [1930s+] (*US prison*) (*also* **crash out**) to escape. **12** [1990s+] (*UK juv.*) to share out, to distribute. **13** [2000s] (*US black*) to ruin, to make a mess of.

IN PHRASES

❑ **crash out** *see* separate entries. ❑ **crash the ash** *v.* [2000s] to hand round cigarettes. ❑ **crash the gate** *v.* [reverse of SE *gatecrash*; Vernon W. Saul, 'The Vocabulary of Bums', in *American Speech* (IV: 5, 1929), defines it (? implausibly) as 'break into jail'] [1910s–60s] (*US*) to enter uninvited. ❑ **crash up** *v. see* separate entry.

crashed *adj.* [1940s] (*US*) impoverished, without funds.

crasher *n.*[1] [SE *crashing bore*] [mid-19C+] usu. of people, a (very great) bore.

crasher *n.*[2] [CRASH *v.* (5)/abbr. SE *gatecrasher*] [1920s+] an uninvited guest at a party.

crasher *n.*[3] [CRASH (OUT) *v.* (3)] [1960s+] someone who collapses from fatigue, or an excess of alcohol of drugs.

crash-hot *adj.* [fig. use of CRASH *n.*[1] (1) + SE *hot*] [1950s+] (*Aus.*) first-rate, excellent; also used in negative to indicate that one is not feeling well.

crashing *adj.* [SE *crash* + sfx *-ing*] [1910s+] overwhelming, extreme; esp. in phr. *crashing bore*, an extremely boring person.

crashing-cheats *n.* (*also* **crassing cheats**) [SE *crash* + CHEAT *n.* (1), lit. 'crushing or crunching things'] (*UK Und.*) **1** [mid-16C–early 17C] apples, pears or any other fruit [i.e. things that may be crunched]. **2** [mid-16C–mid-19C] the teeth.

crash-out *n.* (*also* **crash**) [CRASH *v.* (11)] [1940s+] an escape from prison.

crash (out) *v.* [orig. from RN sl. *crash the swede*, to sleep; as such it migrated first to Aus. then to US and finally back to UK] **1** [1940s+] (*orig. Aus.*) to sleep, to collapse exhausted; often as *crash out*. **2** [1960s+] to stay, to lodge, to board; thus *crash at*, to stay at; *crash with*, to stay with. **3** [1960s+] (*drugs*) to collapse, esp. after a bout of heavy drug (esp. amphetamine), or alcohol use. **4** [1960s+] (*drugs*) to lose the sensation that follows the use of a given drug. **5** [1970s+] to slip into a state of semi-conscious relaxation after taking a drug. **6** [1980s] (*UK black*) to sit down. **7** [1990s+] to break down emotionally; of an addict, to need more of one's drug.

crash-pad *n.* (*also* **crash**) [CRASH (OUT) *v.* (2) + PAD *n.*[2] (2)] [1960s+] a flat or house in which any passing friends or strangers can find a bed at short notice.

crash up *v.* [1970s–80s] (*N.Z. prison*) to inject oneself with narcotics.

crassing-cheats *n. see* CRASHING-CHEATS *n.*

crate *n.* [SE *crate*, a container; all descriptions of animals/vehicles carry a taint of inferiority and/or the possibility of a physical or mechanical breakdown] **1** [mid–late 19C] (*US*) an old or worthless horse. **2** [1910s+] an aeroplane. **3** [1920s] (*US Und.*) a (wall) safe. **4** [1920s+] an automobile. **5** [1930s–60s] (*US*) a coffin. **6** [1940s–60s] (*US tramp/Und.*) a prison. **7** [1940s–60s] a boat. **8** [1940s+] a lorry; a bus. **9** [1950s] a railway hand car. **10** [1950s] a tank. **11** [1980s] (*Aus.*) a bicycle.

(IN PHRASES)

❑ **hot crate** *n.* [HOT *adj.* (5d)] [1930s+] (*Aus./US*) a stolen car.

crater *n.* **1** [1950s+] (*US campus/teen*) an acne scar; thus *craterface*, a term of abuse used to mock an acne sufferer. **2** [1960s+] (*US drugs*) an abscess that is caused by the long-term injection of narcotics.

crater/crathur/cratur(e) *n. see* CREATURE, THE *n.* (3).

cravat *n. see* TIGHT CRAVAT *under* TIGHT *adj.*

craven *adj.* (*also* **cravicious**) [ext. of SE *crave*, to desire intensely] [1950s+] (*W.I. Rasta*) greedy, gluttonous.

craw *n.*

(IN PHRASES)

❑ **have someone in one's craw** *v.* [SE *craw*, the throat] [20C+] (*W.I.*) to harbour ill-feeling towards someone.

crawfish *n.* [CRAWFISH *v.*] **1** [mid-19C+] (*orig. US*) (*also* **crawdad, crayfish**) a coward, a groveller, one who backs down from a challenge, esp. a physical one. **2** [mid-19C+] (*orig. US*) a political turncoat or rebel. **3** [1960s] (*US*) a French person. **4** [1970s+] (*US campus*) a stingy, mean person.

crawfish *v.* [SE *crawfish*, the US synon. for *crayfish*, a lobster-like crustacean. The term echoes the characteristic backward movement of the fish] [mid-19C+] (*Aus./N.Z./US*) **1** (*also* **crayfish**) in fig. use, to back down, to renege on a previous statement, commitment (the image of is of personal humiliation). **2** in lit. use, to move backwards, to retreat, to run away.

crawl *n.* (*orig. US*) **1** [mid-19C] a promenade, a street used for parading and socializing by the local youth. **2** [late 19C+] visiting a number of public houses, bars etc in succession. **3** [1900s] a walk. **4** [1910s] (*US Und.*) a trick. **5** [1920s] a dance.

crawl *v.*[1] (*also* **crawl to, do a crawl**) **1** [late 18C+] to behave sycophantically, to act the toady; also as n. *crawler*. **2** [late 19C] (*US campus*) to renege on a statement.

(IN PHRASES)

❑ **crawl up someone's arse** *v. see* ARSE CRAWL *under* ARSE *n.*

crawl *v.*[2] **1** [late 19C] (*US*) to leave quietly, stealthily. **2** [late 19C–1930s] (*US*) to mount a horse; thus *crawl off*, to dismount. **3** [late 19C+] to assault. **4** [late 19C+] to spend a night moving from one nightclub, bar or public house to the next. **5** [1930s+] (*US*) to have sexual intercourse.

(IN PHRASES)

❑ **crawl someone's collar** *v.* (*also* **crawl all over**) [orig. US milit.] [late 19C–1910s] (*US campus*) to reprimand, to criticize. ❑ **crawl someone's frame** *v.* [FRAME *n.*[1] (1)] [1900s–40s] (*US*) to give someone a beating or thrashing. ❑ **crawl someone's hump** *v. see under* HUMP *n.*[1].

SE in slang uses

(IN PHRASES)

❑ **could crawl under a snake's belly** *see under* SNAKE *n.*[1]. ❑ **crawl out** *see* separate entries. ❑ **crawl up the wall** *v.* [the inscribing of one's debts on a slate mounted on the wall] [late 18C–early 19C] to run up credit at a public house. ❑ **what's crawling on you?** [ref. is to lice] [1910s+] what's the matter?

crawler *n.* **1** [mid-19C+] a general insult. **2** [late 19C] (*Aus.*) a shepherd, a musterer; one who mends boundary fences. **3** [late 19C+] (*Aus.*) a slow-moving, unexcitable domestic animal, esp. a sheep. **4** [1920s+] (*US*) a legless beggar, usu. moving with the aid of a small wheeled platform.

crawling dandruff *n. see* GALLOPING DANDRUFF *under* GALLOPING *adj.*

crawl-out *n.* [CRAWL OUT *v.*] [1900s–50s] (*US*) an excuse, an evasion.

crawl out *v.* [1900s–50s] (*US*) to make excuses, to evade.

crawly-mawly *adj.* [Norfolk dial.; cf. synon. Sussex dial: *frobly-mobly*] [late 17C–mid-19C] ill, sickly, ailing.

crawsick *adj.* [SE *craw*, the stomach] [late 18C; 1910s+] (*Irish*) suffering from a hangover.

craw-thumper *n.* [SE *craw*, the stomach + SE *thumper*, lit. breast-beater; Catholics were heavily represented among the founders of the colony that became the state of Maryland] **1** [late 18C+] (*also* **claw-thumper**) a Roman Catholic. **2** [mid-19C+] (*US*) a native of Maryland. **3** [20C+] (*Irish*) an overtly pious individual.

craw-thumping *n.* [CRAW-THUMPER *n.*] [late 19C] (*Aus.*) religiosity.

craw-thumping *adj.* [CRAW-THUMPER *n.*] **1** [late 17C; 1910s–60s] overly religious. **2** [1930s+] Roman Catholic.

cray *n.*[1] [abbr.] [1910s] (*Aus.*) a *crayfish*.

cray *n.*[2] [it is coloured red, like the SE *crayfish*] [1980s] (*N.Z.*) a NZ$100 note.

crayfish *see under* CRAWFISH.

crayter/craythur/craytur *see* CREATURE, THE *n.* (3).

crazo *n.* [SE *crazy* + -O *sfx* (2)] [1970s+] (*orig. US*) a mad person, an eccentric.

crazy *n.* **1** [mid-19C+] (*orig. US*) a mad person. **2** [1980s+] (*also* **crazies, the**) a feeling of madness. **3** [2000s] (*drugs*) cocaine.

(IN COMPOUNDS)

❑ **crazy alley** *n.* [1910s+] (*US prison*) a special part of a prison used for insane or uncontrollable prisoners. ❑ **crazy house** *n.* (*also* **crazy farm**) (*US*) **1** [late 19C+] a psychiatric institution. **2** [1960s+] a 'madhouse', somewhere that resembles a lunatic asylum.

crazy *adj.* **1** [mid-19C+] keen on, enthusiastic, esp. as *crazy for, crazy about, crazy to*. **2** [1940s+] (*US black/beatnik*) a general intensifier, wonderful, amazing, weird, bizarre, according to context. **3** [1980s+] (*US black*) a lot, great in quantity, usu. of money.

(IN COMPOUNDS)

❑ **crazy fence boys** *n.* [2000s] (*US prison*) inmates who wish to or are planning to escape.

(IN PHRASES)

❑ **crazy for** *adj.* (*also* **crazy about**) [20C+] extremely enthusiastic, obsessed by.

SE in slang uses

(IN COMPOUNDS)

❑ **crazy-back** *n.* [late 19C] a foolish young woman. ❑ **crazy coke** *n.* [COKE *n.*[1] (1)] [1970s+] (*drugs*) phencyclidine. ❑ **crazyhead** *n.* [-HEAD *sfx* (1)] [1970s] (*US*) a mad person. ❑ **crazy nigger** *n.* [1960s–70s] an independent black man, who refuses to accept an inferior social role. ❑ **crazy rim** *n.* (*also* **crazy brim**) [1960s] (*US black*) a desirable style of hat. ❑ **crazy timbers** *n.* [early 19C] ribs. ❑ **crazy water** *n.* [its effects] [1930s–50s] (*Can./US*) whisky.

(IN PHRASES)

❑ **crazy as a shithouse rat** *adj. see under* SHITHOUSE RAT *n.* ❑ **crazy as a two-bob watch** *adj. see under* SILLY AS… *adj.*

crazy *adv.* [late 19C+] extremely, very much.

crazy! *excl.* [1950s+] (*orig. US*) an excl. of approval, of agreement, of surprise.

-crazy *sfx* (*also* **-screwy**) [1920s+] a sfx used to imply one's enthusiasm for the accompanying n.

crazy-ass *n.* (*also* **crazy-arse**) [CRAZY-ASS *adj.*] [1960s+] (*orig. US*) a fool, one who is out of control.

crazy-ass *adj.* (*also* **crazy-arse**) [SE *crazy* + -ASS *sfx*/-ARSED *sfx* (2)] [1950s+] (*US*) **1** insane, utterly eccentric. **2** bizarre.

creaker *n.* [SE *creak*; the ref. is to one's joints] [1940s–60s] (*US black*) an old person.

c.r.e.a.m. *n.* (*also* **cream**) [abbr. *c*ash *r*ules *e*verything *a*round *m*e] [1990s+] (*orig. US black*) money.

cream *n.*[1] **1** [mid-17C; late 19C+] semen. **2** [1920s+] (*Aus.*) whisky. **3** [1930s+] vaginal secretions.

(IN COMPOUNDS)

❑ **cream jug** *n.* [a receptacle for sense 1 above] [late 19C] the vagina.

IN PHRASES

❑ **take in cream** *v.* [late 19C] of a woman, to have sexual intercourse.

SE in slang uses

IN COMPOUNDS

❑ **cream jugs** *n.* [20C+] the female breasts. ❑ **cream of the valley** *n.* [19C] gin.

cream *n.*[2] [paler than black skin colour] [1980s] (*US black*) a Puerto Rican.

cream *n.*[3] [1990s+] anything simple or very easy.

cream *n.*[4] *see* C.R.E.A.M. *n.*

cream *v.* [CREAM *n.*[1]] **1** lit. or fig. refs. to ejaculation. (**a**) [1910s+] of a man, to ejaculate. (**b**) [1940s–50s] (*US*) to vomit. (**c**) [1940s+] of a woman, for the vagina to become wet. (**d**) [1950s+] in fig. use, i.e to find something extremely exciting; to be very desirous of doing something. **2** in fig. use, the perceived superiority of cream to milk. (**a**) [1920s+] (*orig. US*) to kill, to destroy, to beat up comprehensively, to overcome easily. (**b**) [1930s+] (*also* **cream up**) to win a sporting competition, to pass an examination easily or decisively, thus do anything well. (**c**) [1950s–60s] of a driver, to go fast. (**d**) [1990s+] in fig. use, to do something to excess, e.g. drinking.

IN PHRASES

❑ **cream (in) one's jeans** *v.* (*also* **cream (in) one's pants**) [1950s+] **1** to ejaculate or become vaginally wet while still fully dressed. **2** in fig. use, to become very excited. ❑ **cream one's beef** *v. see under* BEEF *n.*[1]. ❑ **cream the cheese** *v.* [1990s+] to masturbate; to bring to orgasm.

cream billy *n. see* CREAM FANCY *n.*

cream crackered *adj.* (*also* **cream-cracked, Jacob's crackers**) [rhy. sl. = KNACKERED *adj.*; ult. *Jacob's cream crackers*, a brand of savoury biscuit] [1980s+] exhausted, tired out.

cream crackers *n.* [rhy. sl. = KNACKERS *n.*; ult. *see* prev.] [1940s–70s] the testicles.

creamed *adj.* [CREAM *v.* (2a)] **1** [1940s+] utterly defeated, lit. and fig. **2** [1960s+] (*US*) very drunk.

creamer *n.* [lit. fig. ext. CREAM *v.* (1a)] [1950s+] **1** one who lacks control of his emotions, because of excitement or fear. **2** an outstanding example of something. **3** a chronic premature ejaculator. **4** a general term of abuse.

cream fancy *n.* (*also* **cream billy**) [SE *cream* + *fancy (handkerchief)*/BILLY *n.*[4]] [mid-19C] a decorated handkerchief prized by London costermongers; the *cream fancy* had a white or cream background with a variety of patterns.

cream-ice jack *n.* [SE *cream ice* + JACK *n.*[2] (1)] [late 19C–1900s] a street-seller of ice-cream.

creamies *n.* [1960s] (*US*) a gonorrhoeal discharge.

creaming *n.* [fig. 'skimming the cream' from the firm's income] [1960s+] (*UK Und.*) stealing from one's employer, usu. on a small, but protracted scale.

creamo *n.* [SE *cream* + -O *sfx* (2)] [1960s] (*US black*) a white person.

cream puff *n.*[1] [fig. uses of SE] [1910s+] **1** (*US*) an excellent person or object. **2** (*orig. US*) a weakling. **3** a male homosexual; occas. a lesbian [pun on PUFF *n.* (3a)].

cream puff *n.*[2] [rhy. sl. = SE *huff*] [1990s+] a bad temper, a rage.

cream-puff *adj.* [CREAM PUFF *n.*[1] (2)] [1910s+] (*US*) easy, undemanding of physical strength.

creamstick *n.* [CREAM *n.*[1] (1) + SE *stick*/STICK *n.* (1a); 20C+ use mainly US black] [late 19C+] the penis.

IN PHRASES

❑ **have a bit of creamstick** *v.* (*also* **do a bit of creamstick**) [late 19C–1900s] of a woman, to have sexual intercourse. ❑ **have a go at the creamstick** *v.* [late 19C–1900s] to have sexual intercourse.

creamy *n.*[1] [their complexion] [20C+] (*Aus.*) a derog. term for the offspring of white and Aborigine parents.

IN COMPOUNDS

❑ **creamy piece** *n.* [PIECE *n.* (1a)] [1970s] (*Aus.*) a half-Aboriginal woman.

creamy *n.*[2] [CREAMY *adj.* (1)] [1990s+] (*US black/drugs*) premium grade crack cocaine.

creamy *adj.* [the superiority of cream to milk] **1** [mid-19C+] excellent, first-rate. **2** [1910s+] of a woman, very attractive.

IN COMPOUNDS

❑ **creamy do** *n.* [DO *n.* (1)] [1950s+] a piece of exceptionally fortunate luck.

creamy *adv.* [mid–late 19C] secretly.

crease *v.* [orig. hunting use, *crease*, to stun an animal by firing a shot through the cartilege at the back of the neck] **1** [late 19C+] to wound. **2** [20C+] to kill; also in fig. use. **3** [1950s+] to beat severely. **4** [1970s+] to harm, to spoil; also in fig. use.

IN PHRASES

❑ **crease (up)** *v.* **1** [1940s+] to collapse with laughter. **2** [1950s+] to cause someone to collapse with laughter.

creased *adj.* [CREASE *v.*; underpinned by the image of one's body bent double with laughter or tiredness; thus 'creasing' at the waist] **1** [1920s+] exhausted, tired out. **2** [1940s+] collapsing in laughter.

create *v.* [abbr. SE *create a fuss*] [1910s+] to make a fuss, to 'go on about'.

creature *n.* [? the 'creatures' that populate horror films] **1** [20C+] (*W.I.*) an ugly person. **2** [1980s+] (*Aus. prison*) a police or prison officer.

creature, the *n.* [joc. use of SE] **1** [mid-16C–mid-19C] wine. **2** [late 16C; early 19C] porter. **3** [late 17C+] (*also* **crater, crathur, cratur, crature, crayter, craythur, craytur, creater, creatur, cretur**) whisky, esp. Irish whisky. **4** [early–mid-19C] brandy. **5** [early–mid-19C] gin

IN PHRASES

❑ **cup of the creature** *n. see* DROP (OF THE CREATURE) *n.* ❑ **drop (of the creature)** *n. see* separate entry.

crebs *adj.* [ety. unknown] [1990s+] (*W.I.*) low-life, despicable.

cred *n.* [abbr.] [1970s+] lit. *cred*ibility; the term, as used mainly in the 1970s–80s by young people (and those who purvey their material wants), was used to indicate that something had a populist, anti-establishment, 'street' level of acceptability.

cred *adj.* [abbr.] [1970s+] lit. *cred*ible; the term, as used mainly in the 1970s–80s by young people (and those who purvey their material wants), meant acceptable on a populist, anti-establishment, 'street' level, unaffected by puffery, artistic pretentiousness and similar negative trappings.

credentials *n.* **1** [late 19C+] the male genitals. **2** [2000s] the female genitals or underwear.

creech *n.* [? abbr./mispron. SE *creature*] [1920s] (*US*) a person.

creechy *adj.* [? SE *creature* or ? *screechy*] [1990s+] (*US campus*) weird, strange.

creek *n.*

IN PHRASES

❑ **up the creek (without a paddle)** [euph. for *UP SHIT('S) CREEK (WITHOUT A PADDLE) under* SHIT CREEK *n.*] **1** [1920s+] in trouble, facing problems; thus (*Aus.*) pregnant out of wedlock. **2** [1960s+] mad, crazy.

creeme *v.* [? slippery smoothness of SE *cream*] [late 17C–mid-19C] (*UK Und.*) to slip something unobtrusively into another person's hand.

creep *n.* [fig. uses of SE] **1** [1910s+] a stealthy robber, a sneak thief, esp. one who works in a brothel. **2** [1910s+] the profession of sneak-thieving, esp. when pursued in a brothel; the individual who pursues it. **3** [1920s+] an unpleasant person, with poss. implication of some physical peculiarity or of criminality [orig. dial.]. **4** [1930s+] departure, esp. surreptitious. **5** [1960s] (*US black*) a clandestine meeting. **6** [1960s] (*drugs*) an addict who begs or barters services for their narcotics rather than resorting to crime to obtain the funds to buy them. **7** [1970s] (*US*) a spree.

(DERIVATIVES)

❑ **creepazoid** *n.* (*also* **creepaloid**) [quasi SE sfx *-azoid/-aloid*] [1970s+] (*US*) an unpleasant person. ❑ **creepola** *n.* [-OLA *sfx*] [1980s] (*US*) anything or anyone unpleasant.

(IN PHRASES)

❑ **at/on the creep** [1930s+] working as a sneak-thief. ❑ **do a creep** *v.* [1950s] to move quietly, surreptitiously. ❑ **on the creep** *adv.* [late 19C] cheaply; in a second-rate manner.

creep *adj.* [CREEP *n.* (3)] [1940s+] unpleasant, distasteful.

creep *v.* **1** [mid-19C+] to forgo one's pride and beg unashamedly, to curry favour, to 'suck up to'. **2** [1910s+] to rob stealthily, to work as a sneak-thief. **3** [1920s+] (*US*) of a prostitute, to distract one's customer while an accomplice slips into the room and rifles through his wallet; since he always has to pay in advance, he won't check his money until they have parted. **4** [1920s+] (*US black*) to flirt, to make sexual advances, to have a clandestine meeting, usu. that between two adulterous lovers. **5** [1920s+] (*US black*) to sneak up on, to stalk someone with malicious intent. **6** [1930s] to 'walk', to escape punishment; to be let off. **7** [1940s+] to inform. **8** [1960s+] (*US prison*) to escape. **9** [1980s+] (*US black teen*) to go about one's business surreptitiously and quietly. **10** [1980s+] (*US campus*) to go out on the town. **11** [1990s+] (*US black*) to ride slowly in a car. **12** [1990s+] (*US drugs*) to sell marijuana.

(IN COMPOUNDS)

❑ **creep house** *n.* [HOUSE *n.*[1] (1)/SE *house*] [1910s–70s] (*US*) a brothel or unwholesome apartment house, esp. one where patrons are robbed. ❑ **creep joint** *n.* *see* separate entry. ❑ **creep pad** *n.* [PAD *n.*[2] (2)] [1940s] (*US*) a brothel or unwholesome apartment house, esp. where patrons are robbed.

(IN PHRASES)

❑ **creeping and tilling** *n.* [1910s+] (*US black*) diverting a store cashier's attention while a confederate opens and robs the till. ❑ **creep on** *v.* (*US black*) **1** [1920s–40s] to cheat, esp. sexually. **2** [1970s+] to sneak up on someone, with the intention of attacking them physically or robbing them. **3** [1990s+] to follow.

creeped up *adj.* (*also* **creeped, creeped out**) [SE *the creeps*, a feeling of unease] [1940s–80s] (*orig. US black*) apprehensive, worried.

creeper *n.* [fig. uses of SE, they all *creep around*] **1** [17C+] a toady, a sycophant. **2** [17C+] a louse. **3** [early 19C] a penny-a-line hack journalist. **4** [20C+] (*Und./police*) a sneak-thief, esp. when also a prostitute or her accomplice. **5** [1910s+] (*orig. US black*) an adulterous or cheating lover. **6** [1940s–50s] (*US black*) a police officer. **7** [1990s+] a burglary committed when the owners are at home. **8** *see* CREEP JOINT *n.* (3).

(IN COMPOUNDS)

❑ **creeper joint** *n.* [JOINT *n.* (3a)] [1930s] (*US*) an opium den where the semi-conscious sleepers are robbed of their possessions.

creepers *n.* **1** [late 19C–1960s] the feet; the legs. **2** [1900s–80s] (*US*) soft shoes worn by burglars, sneak-thieves and prison guards. **3** *see* BROTHEL CREEPERS *n.*

creeping *n.* [cant use of SE *creep*] [late 16C–early 17C] (*UK Und.*) men and women robbing together.

creeping *adj.* [1960s+] (*US campus*) extremely unpleasant.

creeping law *n.* [SE *creep* (CREEP *v.* (2), while logical, is too late) + LAW *n.*] [late 16C–early 17C] (*UK Und.*) robbery carried out by minor thieves, concentrating on 'suburban' homes (i.e. those outside the City walls).

creep joint *n.* [CREEP *v.* + JOINT *n.* (3b)] **1** [1920s–40s] (*US*) a lowdown dancing club. **2** [1920s+] a brothel or unwholesome apartment house, esp. one where patrons are robbed. **3** [1930s] (*also* **creeper**) a 'floating' gambling game, operating in a different location each night. **4** [1950s] anywhere run by unpleasant or unpopular people [CREEP *n.* (3)].

creepo *n.* [CREEP *n.* (3) + -O *sfx* (1)] [1940s+] an unpleasant person.

creeps *n.* [20C+] (*US black*) the feet.

creepshow *n.* [the horror film *Creepshow* (1982)] [1980s+] a horrifying experience.

creepshow *adj.* [*see* prev.] [1980s+] awful, disgusting.

creep someone out *v.* [SE colloq. *the creeps*, a sense of unease] [1980s+] (*US*) to terrify, to unnerve, to give someone the 'creeps'.

creeps' sake! *excl. see* CRIPES! *excl.*

creepsville *n.* (*also* **creepville**) [CREEP *n.* (3) + -VILLE *sfx*[1]] [1960s+] any unappealing place.

creepy-drawers *n.* [SE *creepy*, sinister + SE *drawers*] [1970s] (*US*) a male homosexual.

creepy pete *n.* [SE *creepy* + SNEAKY PETE *n.* (1), i.e. its effects 'creep up' on the drinker] [1950s] (*US*) cheap, rotgut wine.

cremmie *n.* [abbr.] [1960s+] (*Aus.*) a crematorium.

cremorne *n.* [pun on CREAM *n.*[1] (1) + HORN *n.*[2] (1a) but note *Cremorne* Gardens, Chelsea, the increasingly notorious 'pleasure gardens' (fl. 1832–77)] [19C] the penis.

creped up *adj.* [? wearing shoes with *crepe* soles] [1930s] (*US teen*) dressed up.

crepe-hanger *n. see* CRAPE-HANGER *n.*

crepe sole *n.* [resemblance, texture] [1940s] (*W.I.*) a large, solid cake.

creps *n.* [? orig. trainers had *crepe* soles] [2000s] (*UK teen*) trainers.

crest *v.* [brandname of *Crest* toothpaste] [1990s+] (*US black*) to smile.

cretin *n.* (*also* **cretino, creton**) [ext. SE] [1940s] an obnoxious person; a stupid person.

cretur *n. see* CREATURE, THE *n.* (3).

crevice *n.* [19C] the vagina.

crew *n.* **1** [mid-16C+] any form of gang or group. **2** [1960s+] a gang, usu. of football supporters, who engage in fights with rivals. **3** [1980s+] (*US*) orig. used in US by young blacks to denote a teen gang, spec. of rap singers, break dancers or graffiti, the term has crossed the Atlantic and now, in UK use, both black and white means simply a gang. **4** [1980s+] (*orig. US drugs*) a team of drug sellers.

Cri, the *n.* [abbr.] [late 19C+] the *Cri*terion (bar, restaurant and theatre) at Piccadilly Circus, London, W1, which was ultra-fashionable in the late 19C and revamped in the 1990s.

crib *n.*[1] [16C SE *crib*, a small house or narrow room; the term evolved into 19C cant, and has survived in 20C+ US black use] **1** [late 16C+] (*UK Und.; post WW2 chiefly US black*) a dwelling house, a shop, a public house, apartment. **2** [early 19C] a burial ground. **3** [early 19C+] a small, cheap brothel or 'low' saloon; thus *crib-girl*, a prostitute. **4** [mid-19C] (*UK Und.*) a thieves' hideout. **5** [mid-19C] a cheap theatre. **6** [mid-19C–1900s] a berth, a situation, a job, e.g. a *snug crib*, a safe place. **7** [mid-19C–1960s] (*UK/US Und.*) a casino. **8** [mid-19C+] a bed. **9** [mid-19C+] (*US*) a prison cell. **10** [late 19C–1950s] the room in a brothel where a prostitute services her clients. **11** [1910s–60s] (*Aus./US*) a cheap café or restaurant. **12** [1910s–80s] (*US Und.*) a safe. **13** [1930s+] (*US Und.*) a room kept by a streetwalker to which she could take her clients for sex. **14** [1970s+] (*US gay*) a private cubicle rented out at a gay bath-house.

(IN COMPOUNDS)

❑ **crib-cracker** *n.* [*CRIB-CRACKING* below] [mid-19C–1900s] a house-breaker. ❑ **crib-cracking** *n.* [CRACK *v.*[2] (2c)] [mid-19C–1940s] (*orig. UK Und.*) house-breaking. ❑ **crib-house** *n.* (*also* **crib shack**) [HOUSE *n.*[1] (1)] [1910s–40s] a brothel, esp. a small and dirty one. ❑ **crib joint** *n.* [JOINT *n.* (3b)] [1920s–40s] a brothel, esp. a small and dirty one. ❑ **crib lay** *n.* [LAY *n.*[3] (1)] [mid-19C] (*UK Und.*) a burglary. ❑ **crib man** *n.* [late 19C–1940s] (*US Und.*) **1** one who specializes in breaking into houses and apartments. **2** a safebreaker.

(IN PHRASES)

❑ **crack a crib** *v.* [19C+] (*UK Und.*) to break into a house or shop. ❑ **do a crib** *v.* (*also* **lurk a crib**) [mid-19C+] (*orig. US*

Und.) to break and enter premises for the purpose of robbery. ❑ **square crib** *n.* [early 19C] a respectable house.

crib *n.*[2] [SE *crib*, a container for animal fodder] **1** [mid-17C] the stomach. **2** [18C+] provisions. **3** [late 19C+] (*Aus./N.Z.*) a snack, a light meal, a piece of bread, cake etc; thus *cribtime*.

crib *n.*[3] [CRIB *v.*[2]] **1** [mid-19C+] a translation of a classic or other work in a foreign language, for the illegitimate use of students; thus *crib sheet*. **2** [1980s] (*US campus*) an easy course.

IN COMPOUNDS

❑ **crib course** *n.* [1960s+] (*US campus*) a very easy course. ❑ **crib sheet** *n.* **1** *see* sense 1 above. **2** [2000s] (*US*) a police record.

crib *n.*[4] [abbr.] [mid-19C+] *crib*bage.

crib *n.*[5] [CRIB *v.*[5]] [1940s] a grumble, a complaint.

crib *v.*[1] [? SE *crib*, a small wickerwork container, poss. used by a poacher] **1** [mid-18C–1910s] to indulge in petty theft; to take surreptitiously. **2** [mid-19C] 'to withhold, keep back, pinch, or thieve a part out of money given to lay out for necessaries' (Dyche, *A New General English Dict.*, 1748).

crib *v.*[2] [ext. of CRIB *v.*[1] (1)] [late 18C+] (*orig. campus*) to cheat, to take or copy (a passage, a piece of translation etc) without acknowledgement, to plagiarize.

crib *v.*[3] [the prize-fighter Tom *Cribb* (1781–1848)] [early–mid-19C] to fight, using the fists and in an honourable manner.

crib *v.*[4] [CRIB *n.*[1]] **1** [mid–late 19C] to confine. **2** [1930s+] (*also* **crib out**) to stay in a place. **3** [1960s] to live at home. **4** [1960s+] (*US black*) to live one's uneventful, daily life. **5** [1990s+] to sleep. **6** [2000s] to offer a bed or home to.

crib *v.*[5] [SE *crib-biting*, of a horse, to bite the crib or fodder container] [1910s+] to complain, to grumble (about).

crib *v.*[6] [CRIB *n.*[2] (3)] [1920s] (*Aus./N.Z.*) to eat.

crib *phr.* [CRIB *n.*[1] (1) or ? CRIB *v.*[2]] [2000s] (*US campus*) one's acknowledgement of shared knowledge or of a shared experience.

crib! *excl. see* CRIPES! *excl.*

cribbage-faced *adj.* [the supposed resemblance of such scars to the small holes found in a cribbage board] [late 18C–mid-19C] a face marked with small-pox scars.

cribbage-peg *n.* [rhy. sl.] [late 19C–1920s] a leg.

cribber *n.*[1] [CRIB *v.*[2]] [late 19C] one who uses some form of illicit aid when taking examinations or similar tests.

cribber *n.*[2] [SE *crib-biter*, a horse that bites the metal crib in which its fodder is placed] [late 19C+] a horse that bites parts of its stall, sucking air into its lungs.

Cribbeys *n.* (*also* **Cribbey islands**) [derived f. older nicknames BERMUDAS *n.* and thence CARIBEE ISLANDS *n.*, both of which had been applied to the alleyways of 16C–18C Covent Garden, then a centre of vice and criminality. Grose (1785) offers an alternative ety.: 'perhaps from the houses built there being cribbed (stolen) out of the common way or passage'] [late 18C–early 19C] back alleys, narrow courts and by-ways.

cribbing *n.* [CRIB *n.*[2] (2)] [mid-17C] (*UK Und.*) provisions.

cribbing cove *n.* [CRIB *v.*[1] (1) + COVE *n.* (1)] [early 19C] a thief.

crib-biter *n.* [SE *crib-biter*, a horse that bites the metal crib in which its fodder is placed] [mid-19C] a grumbler.

crib-crust Monday *n. see under* MONDAY *n.*

cricker! *excl. see* CRIKEY! *excl.*

cricket *n.*

SE in slang uses

IN COMPOUNDS

❑ **cricket match** *n.* [it has only *eleven* hairs *a side*] [1910s–20s] (*Aus.*) a small moustache. ❑ **cricket score** *n.* [1980s+] (*Aus. prison*) a very long sentence. ❑ **cricket set** *n.* [i.e. a BAT *n.*[2] (6) and two BALLS *n.* (1)] [1990s+] the male genitals.

cricket bats *n.* [rhy. sl. = TATS *n.* (2)] [20C+] (*Aus.*) the teeth.

crickey(s)! *excl. see* CRIKEY! *excl.*

crick-pendlum *n.* [mid-19C] (*UK Und.*) a hanging.

cries and screeches *n.* [rhy. sl.] [20C+] (*Aus.*) leeches.

crig *n.* [? Irish *creag/creig*, a rock, thus pun on ROCKS *n.* (8)] [1940s+] (*Irish*) a testicle.

crikey! *excl.* (*also* **by crikey! cricker! crickey! crickeys! crikes! crikie jack! for crike's sake! holy crikey! my crikey!**) [mid-19C+] a euph. for CHRIST! *excl.*

crim *n.* [abbr.; one of the three classes in Aus. prison: *screws* (warders and other prison employees), *gigs* (visitors and casual workers) and *crims* (used primarily to denote those with extra-long sentences)] [1950s+] (*orig. US/Aus./N.Z.*) a *crim*inal; also as adj.

crimany! *excl. see* CRIMINY! *excl.*

crimast! *excl.* [late 19C+] (*orig. US*) (*also* **by crimus!**) euph. for CHRIST! *excl.*; usu. in mild oaths.

crimbo *n.* (*also* **chrimbo**) [1980s+] Christmas.

crime *v.* **1** [1940s] to accuse of a crime. **2** [1980s+] to commit crimes.

crimea *n.*[1] [the troops serving in the Crimean War (1854–6) grew their beards long in a small attempt to alleviate the cold] [mid-19C] a full beard.

crimea *n.*[2] [rhy. sl.] [20C+] beer.

crime-buster *n.* [SE *crime* + BUST *v.*[1] (5c)] [1950s+] a detective, a police officer, a melodramatic image, esp. popular in the tabloid press.

crimes! *excl.* (*also* **crimey!**) [mid-19C+] a euph. for CHRIST! *excl.*, usu. in mild oaths.

crimey *n.* [note the association is usu. but need not invariably be criminal] [1960s+] (*US Und.*) a partner in crime, an accomplice, a friend.

criminy! *excl.* (*also* **by criminy! crimany! crimmini! crimine! criminny!**) [the euph. interpretation is the most likely, but the *OED* also suggests ? Ital. *crimine*, a crime, used as a 17C ejaculation] [late 17C+] (*orig. US*) a euph. for CHRIST! *excl.*, usu. in mild oaths.

crimmo *n.* [abbr. + -O *sfx* (3)] [1950s+] (*Aus./N.Z./S.Afr.*) a *crim*inal.

crimp *n.*[1]

SE in slang uses

IN PHRASES

❑ **play crimp** *v.* (*also* **run a crimp**) [SE *crimp*, one who entraps seamen into service, often by violence. Such activities were banned subsequent to the Merchant Shipping Act (1854)] [late 17C–1920s] to cheat, to act criminally, esp. to bet openly on one side and then to cheat in favour of the other, on which one has bet surreptitiously. ❑ **put a crimp in(to)** *v.* (*also* **apply a crimp, put a crimp on, put the crimp into**) [SE *crimp*, to compress] [late 19C+] (*US*) to thwart, to block, to impair, to interfere with. ❑ **run a crimp** *v.* [late 17C–mid-18C] to set up a crooked horserace.

crimp *n.*[2] [*PLAY CRIMP under* CRIMP *n.*[1]] **1** [late 18C–1930s] a swindler, a cheat. **2** [1910s] (*UK Und.*) an opium den owner, a supplier of opium. **3** [1940s–50s] (*US prison*) an informer. **4** [1960s] (*US*) a barely noticeable fold in a card to facilitate cheating.

crimp *v.* [*PUT A CRIMP IN(TO) under* CRIMP *n.*[1]] [1920s+] (*US*) to thwart, to block, to impair, to interfere with.

SE in slang uses

IN PHRASES

❑ **wouldn't that crimp you?** [1900s–20s] (*US*) isn't that amazing?

crimper *n.* [SE *crimp*, to curl] [1960s+] a hairdresser.

crimping fellow *n.* [SE *crimp*, one who 'presses' men into the RN against their will] [late 17C–early 18C] a blackguard, an untrustworthy villain.

crimps *n.* [SE *crimplene*] [2000s] (*S.Afr. gay*) cheap clothes (made from synthetic fibres).

crimps! *excl.* [20C+] (*orig. US*) a euph. for CHRIST! *excl.*, usu. in mild oaths.

crimp up *v.* [SE *crimp*, to pinch] [1950s+] (*US*) to toughen someone up by inflicting verbal and/or physical pain.

crimpy *adj.* [Irwin, *American Tramp and Und. Slang* (1931), suggests that such temperatures encourage *the crimps*, rheumatism] [late 19C–1930s] (*US*) of weather, unpleasant; of a place, cold.

crimson *adj.* [late 19C–1910s] (*Aus.*) a euph. for BLOODY *adj.* (1).

SE in slang uses

IN COMPOUNDS

❑ **crimson chitterling** *n.* [mid-17C–19C] the penis. ❑ **crimson dawn** *n.* [1930s] (*UK, Glasgow*) cheap red wine. ❑ **crimson rambler** *n.* [SE *crimson rambler*, a variety of climbing rose; note cricket jargon *crimson rambler*, the ball] [1900s–60s] (*US*) a bedbug.

crimus! *excl. see* CRIMINY! *excl.*

cringe *n.* [1980s] (*US drugs*) methamphetamine.

crink *n.* [? CRANK *n.*^{2} (2)] [1970s+] (*drugs*) methamphetamine.

crinkle *n.* [1950s] paper money.

crinklepouch *n.* [it makes barely any impact on the shape of one's purse] [late 16C] a sixpence.

crinkler *n.* [ext. CRINKLE *n.*] [20C+] (*Irish*) a currency note.

crinkle top *n.* [1970s] (*US black*) a woman with hair that remains in an unstraightened or otherwise unprocessed style.

crinkum *n.* (*also* **crinkums, grincam, grincom, grincome, grincum, grinkcome, grinkham, grinkum**) [for ety. *see* next, i.e. the sense of twisting pain that accompanies the disease] [early 17C–early 19C] venereal disease.

crinkum-crankum *n.* [SE *crinkum-crankum*, a narrow, twisting passage] [late 17C–19C] the vagina.

crinoline *n.* [metonymy] [mid–late 19C] a woman.

crip *n.* (*also* **crippo**) [abbr. SE *cripple*] **1** [late 19C+] a disabled person. **2** [1920s+] (*orig. US campus*) anything easy; esp. in *crip course*, of a given college course [note CRIB *n.*^{3} (2)]. **3** [1960s] a wounded animal. **4** [1960s+] (*UK juv.*) a general insult; physical deformity is irrelevant.

IN PHRASES

❑ **straight crip** *n.* [1910s–60s] (*US tramp*) a genuinely disabled person; thus *phoney crip*, one who poses as disabled for begging purposes.

crip *v.* [the *Crips* gang, founded in 1969, was orig. called the Cribs, but Crip allegedly arose from a piece in the *LA Sentinel*, which reported on the use of canes by gang members, as if they had been *crippled*; it may alternatively have been a simple typo] [1990s+] (*US black*) to engage in gang activity, usu. but not necessarily as a member of the Crips.

cripes! *excl.* (*also* **by crib! by cripe! by cripes! creeps' sake! cripps! cripus! for cripes' sake! my cripes!**) [19C+] a euph. for CHRIST! *excl.*

crip juice *n.* [1980s] (*US*) any cheap alcoholic beverage drunk by gang members.

cripping *n.* [1980s] (*US*) to participate in gang activity.

cripple *n.*^{1} [play on BENDER *n.*^{1} (1a); its thin metal being susceptible to bending or distortion] [late 18C–19C] a sixpence.

cripple *n.*^{2} [its effect on one's mind] [1950s+] (*drugs*) a marijuana cigarette.

crippo *n. see* CRIP *n.*

cripps! *excl. see* CRIPES! *excl.*

crippy *n.* [SE *cripple*] [1930s] (*US Und.*) a paralysed beggar, or one who poses as such.

cripus! *excl. see* CRIPES! *excl.*

cris *n.* (*also* **Crys**) [abbr.] **1** [2000s] (*US black*) Louis Roederer *Cristal* champagne, the favoured brand of many gangsters, drug dealers and hip-hop stars. **2** *see* CHRISTINA *n.*

cris' *adj.* (*also* **criss**) [CRISP *adj.*^{1} (2)] [1980s+] (*W.I./UK black teen*) used of anything rated as new, fashionable, attractive etc; thus adv. *crissly*.

IN COMPOUNDS

❑ **criss biscuit** *n.* (*also* **crisp biscuit**) [1990s+] (*W.I./UK black*) of people or objects, attractive, fashionable, smart.

Crisco *v.* [proper name *Crisco*, a cooking oil] [1970s+] (*gay*) to lubricate.

crisco frisco *n.* [proper name *Crisco*, a cooking oil + 'FRISCO *n.* (1)] [1950s–60s] (*US gay*) the gay community in San Francisco.

crisp *n.* (*also* **crispy**) [mid-19C–1950s] paper money.

crisp *adj.*^{1} [the crispness of new money] **1** [1920s–30s] new, interesting. **2** [1980s+] (*orig. UK black*) excellent, first-rate, attractive.

IN COMPOUNDS

❑ **crisp biscuit** *n. see* CRISS BISCUIT *under* CRIS' *adj.*

SE in slang uses

IN PHRASES

❑ **make it crisp** *v. see* MAKE IT SNAPPY *under* SNAPPY *adj.*^{1}.

crisp *adj.*^{2} (*also* **crispy**) [play on BURNED OUT *adj.*^{2} (3)] [1970s+] of people, suffering from an excess of drugs, drink, fast living, stress.

crispie *n.*

IN EXCLAMATIONS

❑ **give them a crispie!** [a type of biscuit] [2000s] (*N.Z.*) an excl. meaning that someone has done well, and should be rewarded.

crisp one *n.* [the crisp texture of new notes] [late 19C; 1990s+] a currency note; usu. £1.

crispy *n. see* CRISP *n.*

crispy *adj. see* CRISP *adj.*^{2}.

crispy (critter) *n.* (*also* **crispy batter, krispy kracker**) [lit. 'crispy creature' + play on popular breakfast cereal] **1** [1960s+] (*US, orig. milit./medical*) anyone who has suffered burns or actually burned to death. **2** [1970s] (*US drugs*) one who is under the influence of marijuana.

criss *adj. see* CRIS' *adj.*

Cris sake! *excl. see* FOR CHRIST'S SAKE! *excl.*

crissars *adj.* [fig. use of SE *crisp*] [1950s+] (*W.I. Rasta*) crisp, brand-new, slick-looking.

criss cross *v.* [SE *double-cross*] [1920s+] (*US black*) to deceive or cheat.

crisscross! *excl.* [late 19C] a euph. for *Christ's Cross*, e.g. *so help me crisscross!*

criss-miss *n.* [dial. *kris*, proud, aware (rightly or not) of one's beauty (ult. SE *crisp*) + SE *miss*] [1950s+] (*W.I.*) a pretentious woman who over-estimates her abilities, charms and allure.

cristina *n. see* CHRISTINA *n.*

critical *adj.* [1990s+] (*US campus*) excellent, worthy of admiration.

critter *n.* [regional US pron. of CREATURE, THE *n.* (3)] [mid-19C–1920s] (*US*) whisky.

crivens! *excl.* (*also* **crivvens!**) [? *Christ* + *heavens*] [1910s+] an excl. of astonishment or horror.

cro *n.*^{1} (*also* **cros**) [Fr. *escroc*, a card-sharp. The 's' in *cros* is silent] [early–mid-19C] a professional gambler.

cro *n.*^{2} [CHROMO *n.* (1)/CROW *n.*^{5}] [1950s+] (*Aus.*) **1** a prostitute. **2** a woman.

croacus *n. see* CROCUS (METALLORUM) *n.*

croak *n.* [CROAK *v.*^{2} (1)] **1** [mid-19C] final speeches from the gallows and murderers' confessions, as peddled by street-sellers. **2** [mid–late 19C] a dying speech. **3** [late 19C–1940s] (*also* **croaking**) death. **4** [1910s] (*US*) a boring complainer, a whinger.

IN PHRASES

❑ **do a croak** *v.* (*also* **pull a croak**) [late 19C–1920s] to die. ❑ **do a gun croak** *v.* [1900s–20s] (*US*) to shoot oneself dead. ❑ **on the croak** [late 19C] (*US*) on the verge of death, dying.

croak *v.*^{1} [late 18C–1900s] (*UK Und.*) to talk, irritatingly or pessimistically.

croak *v.*^{2} [the death-rattle] **1** [early 19C+] to die; also in fig. use. **2** [early 19C+] to kill, to murder; thus *croaking*, n., a murder; *croak artist*, n., a murderer. **3** [20C+] as *croak oneself*, to commit suicide. **4** [1900s] (*US campus*) to fail an examination or a course [fig. use of sense 1].

croak *v.*^{3} [mid-19C] (*UK society*) to act in a hypocritical manner.

croak *v.*^{4} [the noise of vomiting] [1920s] (*US*) to vomit.

croaked *adj.* [CROAK *v.*^{2} (1)] **1** [19C+] killed, dead. **2** [late 19C+] very drunk.

croaker *n.*^{1} [? the harsh, miserable croaking of ravens, supposedly ominous birds; + CROAK *v.*^{1}] **1** [mid-17C–1930s] a congenital pessimist. **2** [mid-19C+] a whiner or whinger. **3** [mid–late 19C] a beggar. **4** [20C+] (*US*) one who backs out of undertakings they have promised to perform. **5** [1910s–40s] (*US*) one who talks too lengthily and too loudly. **6** [1940s+] an informer.

croaker *n.*^{2} [? play on CRIPPLE *n.*^{1}] [19C] a silver sixpence.

croaker *n.*^{3} (*also* **croker**) [CROAK *v.*^{2} (1)] **1** [mid-19C] one who has collapsed, i.e. is metaphorically 'dead'. **2** [mid–late 19C] a person who is dying, who cannot be saved, a corpse.

croaker *n.*^{4} [? CROAKER *n.*^{2} i.e. the price; or CROAKER *n.*^{1}] [mid-19C–1940s] (*Aus.*) a newspaper.

croaker *n.*^{5} [CROCUS (METALLORUM) *n.* (1) / CROAK *v.*^{2} (2), i.e. a pessimistic view of the profession] **1** [mid-19C+] (*US*) a doctor, esp. in drug use; thus *croaker joint*, a hospital or a surgery; *nut croaker*, a psychiatrist. **2** [1920s+] (*US prison*) the prison doctor. **3** [1980s+] (*orig. US black*) a murderer.

IN COMPOUNDS

❑ **croaker's chovey** *n.* [CHOVEY *n.*] [19C] a pharmacy.

croaker *n.*^{6} [1920s] (*Anglo-Irish*) a potato; usu. in pl.

IN COMPOUNDS

❑ **croaker sacks** *n.* [1970s+] (*US*) shoes, orig. made of burlap sacks.

croaking *n. see* CROAK *n.* (3).

croaksman *n.* [mid-19C] (*UK Und.*) a murderer for hire.

croakumshire *n.* [the guttural, rolled 'r' that typifies Northumberland speech] [late 18C–early 19C] Northumberland.

croakus *n.* [CROCUS (METALLORUM) *n.* (1)/CROAKER *n.*^{5} (1)] [19C–1920s] a doctor, esp. a quack.

crock *n.*^{1} [fig. use of SE *crock*, a broken-down horse] [mid-19C+] a fool, a foolish idea; a lie.

crock *n.*^{2} [SE *crack*, to break (down); all senses often with pfx *old*; note medical jargon *crock*, a patient whose complaints far outweigh the seriousness of their illness/CROCK *v.* (1)] **1** [late 19C–1900s] (*also* **croc**) an old or broken-down horse. **2** [late 19C–1920s] a bicycle. **3** [late 19C+] a broken-down or physically debilitated person, or thing. **4** [1900s] an invalid, a hypochondriac. **5** [1910s+] a broken-down or mechanically unreliable car, aeroplane or any other vehicle.

IN PHRASES

❑ **crock (up)** *v.* [late 19C–1960s] to break down; of a person or animal, to become disabled, to fall ill.

crock *n.*^{3} [fig. and lit. uses of SE *crock*, a pot] **1** [1920s+] (*US*) the head; esp. in phr. *off one's crock*, out of one's mind, crazy. **2** [1930s–50s] (*US drugs*) an opium pipe. **3** [1930s–60s] (*US*) a bottle of (illicitly distilled) whisky. **4** [1940s–50s] a drunkard.

SE in slang uses

IN PHRASES

❑ **give the crock** *v.* [SE *crock*, a jug, i.e. to award a fig. cup as in a sporting victory] [late 19C] to admit defeat, to award a victory to someone else.

crock *n.*^{4} [CROCK *v.* (2)] [1920s–30s] (*US*) an injury, a blow.

crock *n.*^{5} [abbr. CROCK OF SHIT *n.*] [1940s+] (*orig. US*) a useless, unpleasant event or experience.

DERIVATIVES

❑ **crockful** *n.* [1980s+] (*US*) anything unpleasant, disgusting, repellent.

crock *v.* (*also* **crock up**) [dial.] **1** [late 19C+] to become feeble, to collapse, to give way, to break down; thus *crocked*, injured; *crock off*, to die. **2** [1910s+] (*US*) to hit on the head, to injure.

crocked *adj.* [lit. and fig. uses of CROCK *v.*] [1910s+] **1** drunk; thus n., *crockhead*, a drunk. **2** (*also* **crocked up, crucked**) hurt, damaged, disabled, esp. through a sporting accident. **3** malfunctioning, going wrong.

crocker *n.* [ext. of SE *croak*] [late 17C–early 19C] a shop tout.

crockery *n.* **1** [1910s–40s] (*US*) teeth. **2** [1940s–60s] (*Aus.*) false teeth.

crocko *adj.* [CROCKED *adj.* (1) + -O *sfx* (4)] [1920s+] drunk.

crock of shit *n.* (*also* **bucket of shit, crock of bullshit, ...crap, load of shit**) [SE *crock*, a pot + SHIT *n.* (1a)] [1940s+] a useless, unpleasant event, object or experience; a lying statement.

crocks *n.* [abbr.] **1** [mid-19C] crockery and glass sellers, their wares, their trade. **2** [20C+] crockery, esp. in context of washing it up.

crocky *adj.* [CROCKED *adj.* (2)] [1920s+] (*Aus.*) unwell, shaky, 'under the weather'.

crocodile *n.* [play on CROCK *n.*^{2} (1)] **1** [late 19C+] (*Aus.*) a horse, esp. a broken-down, old horse. **2** [1900s] (*Aus.*) a roustabout [fig. use of sense 1].

Crocodile Dundee *n.* [rhy. sl.] [1990s+] a flea.

crocs *n.* [abbr.] [1980s+] shoes made of *croc*odile skin.

crocus (metallorum) *n.* (*also* **croacus, crockus, crokus**) [? pun on *croak us* (though *croak*, to die or kill is first recorded slightly later), but *OED* suggests 'the Latinized surname of Dr Helkiah Crooke, author of a *Description of the Body of Man*, 1615, *Instruments of Chirurgery*, 1631, etc ...'. The quack implication suggests a further pun on *hocus-pocus*. Note fairground use, *crocus*, a doctor, a herbalist, a miracle-worker; market use, a fair-weather trader who only works during the spring or summer (f. the flower). *Metallorum*, lit. 'of metals' plays on *crocus metallorum* or *crocus antimonii*, which are more or less impure oxysulphides of antimony, obtained by calcination] **1** [late 18C] (*orig. milit.*) a doctor, a surgeon, esp. a quack. **2** [mid–late 19C] a beggar who poses as a doctor.

IN COMPOUNDS

❑ **crocussing (rig)** *n.* [RIG *n.*^{2} (1)] [late 18C–mid-19C] (*UK Und.*) working as a wandering quack doctor. ❑ **crocus-chovey** *n.* [CHOVEY *n.*] **1** [late 18C–mid-19C] a chemist's shop. **2** [mid-19C–1920s] a doctor's consulting room, a surgery. ❑ **crocus-pitcher** *n.* [PITCHER *n.*^{2}] [mid-19C+] (*UK Und.*) an itinerant quack doctor. ❑ **crocus worker** *n.* [SE *worker*/WORKER *n.*^{1} (1)] [late 19C+] a seller of patent medicines.

croker *n.*^{1} [CROAKER *n.*^{2}] [late 17C–early 19C] a groat, fourpence.

croker *n.*^{2} [CROAKER *n.*^{6}] [1930s–40s] a potato.

croker *n.*^{3} *see* CROAKER *n.*^{3}.

cromo *n. see* CHROMO *n.* (1).

croniker *n. see* CHRONICKER *n.*

cronk *n.* [CRONK *adj.*] **1** [late 19C–1910s] (*Aus.*) (*also* **cronck, kronk**) a criminal. **2** [1930s] (*US Und.*) a bad cheque. **3** [1990s+] (*US campus*) something of poor quality. **4** [1990s+] an unattractive woman.

cronk *adj.* [? dial. *cronk*, weak, infirm; note Stephens & O'Brien, *Materials for a Dict. of Aus. Slang* (ms.; 1900–10): 'The word first came into common use in Australia during the prize-fighting and boxing boom of '89, '90, and '91. Its first use was to describe a boxer who lets himself get beat either wilfully or through unfitness.'] **1** [mid-19C] (*US*) drunk. **2** [late 19C+] (*Aus.*) dishonest, illegal, untrustworthy. **3** [late 19C+] (*Aus.*) sick, ill. **4** [1900s] (*Aus.*) of fruit, vegetables etc, rotten. **5** [late 19C–1900s] problematical, 'wrong'.

cronkite *n.* [the newsreader Walter *Cronkite* (b.1916)] [1990s+] news, information.

cronky *adj.* [CRONK *adj.* + sfx *-y*; orig. racing use] [1920s+] **1** unsound, second-rate. **2** (*Aus./US Und.*) corrupt, dishonest, lying.

crony *n.* [SE *crone*, a gnarled old woman + sfx *-y*] **1** [late 17C–early 18C] a tough old hen, a boiling chicken. **2** [mid-19C] an ill-tempered or malicious old woman.

cronz *n.* [ety. unknown] [1990s+] (*US black*) a gun.

crook *n.*^{1} **1** [late 18C] a finger. **2** [1940s] (*US black/Harlem*) an elbow.

crook *n.*^{2} [play on CROAKER *n.*^{2}/abbr. CROOKBACK *n.*] [late 18C–mid-19C] a silver sixpence.

crook *n.*^{3} [SE *crooked*] (*orig. UK Und.*) **1** [mid-19C] the occupation of professional criminality, esp. pickpocketing; thus

ON THE CROOK below. **2** [mid–late 19C] a professional criminal [SE since 20C].

(IN PHRASES)

❑ **on the crook** (*also* **on the crooked**) **1** [mid–late 19C] illicitly, illegally. **2** [late 19C–1950s] working as a professional criminal.

crook *adj.* [SE *crooked*, dishonest, illegal] (*Aus./N.Z.*) **1** [20C+] dishonest, illegal. **2** [20C+] of people and objects, defective, useless, unpleasant; of food, rotten. **3** [20C+] ill, out of sorts. **4** [1900s–10s] suspicious. **5** [1900s–20s] of a woman, promiscuous; venereally diseased. **6** [1910s+] unfair, unacceptable, 'wicked'. **7** [1910s+] annoyed; thus CROOKED ON *adj.* **8** [1950s] drunk.

(IN COMPOUNDS)

❑ **crook house** *n.* [sense 5 above + HOUSE *n.*[1] (1)] [1900s–10s] (*Aus.*) a brothel.

(IN PHRASES)

❑ **come crook** *v.* [1950s] (*Aus.*) to menstruate. ❑ **crook on** *adj.* *see* CROOKED ON *adj.* (2). ❑ **crook up** *v.* [1910s+] (*Aus.*) to fall ill. ❑ **go crook (on)** *v.* (*Aus.*) **1** [20C+] to act dishonestly; of an honest person, to join the underworld. **2** [1910s+] to lose one's temper (with); to assail. **3** [1910s+] of objects, to break down, to stop working, to deteriorate. **4** [1910s+] of people, to experience difficulties. **5** [1910s+] to become ill. ❑ **in crook (with)** [1950s+] (*N.Z.*) in trouble (with). ❑ **put someone crook with** *v.* [1930s+] (*Aus/N.Z.*) to lower someone's standing, to get someone into trouble.

crook *v.*[1] [CROOK *n.*[3] (2)] (*US*) **1** [mid-19C; 1920s–60s] to cheat. **2** [late 19C+] to steal. **3** [1940s] to truant from school.

crook *v.*[2] [CROOK *adj.* (3)] [1900s] (*Aus.*) to ruin, to render useless.

crook *adv.* [CROOK *adj.* (2)] [1910s+] unpleasantly; dishonestly.

crook as Rookwood *adj.* [CROOK *adj.* (3) + *Rookwood* cemetery, Sydney] [1980s] (*Aus.*) on the verge of death.

crookback *n.* [the thin silver sixpence was easily bent or distorted] [late 18C–early 19C] a sixpence.

crooked *n.*

(IN PHRASES)

❑ **on the crooked** *see* ON THE CROOK *under* CROOK *n.*[3].

crooked *adj.* [SE *crooked*, bent] **1** [mid-18C+] drunk. **2** [mid-19C+] wrong, out of order. **3** [20C+] ill, sick, 'under the weather'.

SE in slang uses

(IN COMPOUNDS)

❑ **crooked rib** *n.* [SE (*Adam's*) *rib*, a wife] [late 18C–early 19C] an ill-tempered wife. ❑ **crooked stick** *n.* [play on SE *stick*/STICK *n.* (2c)] [mid-19C+] (*US*) a dishonest person, an untrustworthy person. ❑ **crooked tree** *n.* *see* TREE OF THE TRIPLE CROOK *under* TREE *n.* ❑ **crooked way** *n.* [late 19C] the vagina.

crooked on *adj.* [CROOK *adj.* (7)] [1940s+] (*Aus./N.Z.*) **1** averse to, hostile to. **2** (*also* **crook on**) angry with.

crookie *n.* [CROOK *adj.*] **1** [20C+] a fool, an idiot. **2** [1960s–70s] something unpleasant; of food, 'off'. **3** [2000s] (*N.Z.*) an unpleasant, unreliable or dishonest person.

Crooklyn *n.* [SE *Brooklyn* + *crook*; the borough's associations with (organized) crime] [1990s+] (*US black*) Brooklyn, New York.

crookshanks *n.* [SE *crooked* + *shanks*, legs] [17C–early 19C] a bandy-legged person.

crook the elbow *v.* *see under* ELBOW *n.*

crook up *v.* *see under* CROOK *adj.*

crooky *v.* [the bending of the couple's arms] [mid–late 19C] **1** to walk arm in arm. **2** to court a woman.

crool (the pitch) *v.* *see* CRUEL (THE PITCH) *v.*

crooner *n.* *see* CAROON *n.*

croop *n.* [SE *crop*] [mid-19C–1910s] the stomach.

crooper *n.* *see* CRUPPER *n.*

crop *see also under* CRAP and its combs.

crop *n.*[1] **1** [late 17C–early 18C] a person with very short hair. **2** [late 18C–early 19C] a Presbyterian [the severely cropped haircut favoured by the sect].

crop *n.*[2] [? SE *crop*, the throat or *grape crop*] [1970s] (*US campus*) one-fifth of a gallon of wine.

crop *v.* [? dial. *crop*, the stomach; thus image of anger causing a pain in the stomach] [mid-19C] to annoy, to irritate.

crople on *v.* [? dial. *criple*, to cripple or SE *grapple*] [1920s+] (*Aus.*) to grab, to seize.

cropoh *n.* *see* CRAPPO *n.*

croppen *n.* (*also* **croppin**) [dial. *croppen*, *croppin(g)*, the tail; ult. f. SE *crop*, to cut off the extremity of the ears, tail etc] [18C–early 19C] of an animal or a vehicle, the tail.

(IN COMPOUNDS)

❑ **croppen ken** *n.* *see under* CRAPPING *n.*[2].

croppie *n.* (*also* **croppy**) [note the *croppies* or *croppy-boys*, the Irish rebels of 1798, who wore their hair cut very short as a sign of sympathy with the French Revolution] **1** [mid-19C] anyone who has suffered a prison haircut. **2** [late 19C] a Puritan or Roundhead [as well as their chosen haircuts, they also might have their nose and/or ears cropped in a judicial punishment]. **3** [1930s] (*US Und.*) a prison barber.

croppy *n.* [CROPPY *v.*] [1920s] (*US*) **1** a corpse. **2** a dead fish.

croppy *v.* [SE *crop*, to cut off, to harvest] [1910s] (*US*) to kill.

cropsick *adj.* [SE *crop*, the throat + *sick*] **1** [late 17C–18C] drunk. **2** [late 17C–early 19C] feeling sick after a drinking bout.

crop the conjuror *n.* [it is *cropped*]] [late 18C] a nickname for one who has noticeably short hair.

cros *n.* *see* CRO *n.*[1].

crosbite *n.* *see* CROSSBITE *n.*

croshabell *n.* [north. dial. *crouse*, forward, wanton, vivacious + SE *belle*, beautiful; coined by and only found in the works of George Peele] [late 16C–early 17C] a prostitute.

Cross, the *n.* **1** [1940s+] (*Aus.*) King's *Cross*, Sydney, the 'bohemian' area of the town; thus *crossite*, one who lives there. **2** [2000s] King's *Cross*, London, the area around the mainline railway station.

cross *n.*[1] [abbr. SE *double-cross*] **1** [19C] constr. with *the*, anything deceitful or dishonest. **2** [19C+] a trick, a deception. **3** [mid-19C] in sports, e.g. boxing, the deliberate losing of a fight, a race etc, on payment of a bribe. **4** [mid-19C] (*UK Und.*) the underworld. **5** [1910s] an informer. **6** [1950s+] constr. with *a/the*, a double-cross.

(IN PHRASES)

❑ **cop on the cross** *v.* [late 19C] (*UK Und.*) to discover that someone is cheating, usu. by using cunning or deception oneself. ❑ **in a cross** [1950s–60s] (*US black*) in trouble, at a disadvantage; usu. in the phr. *put in a cross*, to put into a difficult situation. ❑ **on the cross** [early 19C–1910s] **1** surreptitiously, illegally. **2** working as a professional criminal. **3** dishonest. ❑ **pull a cross on** *v.* [1950s] to double-cross. ❑ **put the cross on** *v.* **1** [1900s–40s] to double-cross, to cheat. **2** [1930s] to mark for death [a cross placed, lit. or fig., against the victim's name]. ❑ **shake the cross** *v.* [late 19C] to give up thieving.

cross *n.*[2] [1980s+] (*Aus. prison*) any spring-loaded device, e.g. a safety-pin, held tight by a rubber band and swallowed; the gastric juices dissolve the rubber, and the resultant injury allows the prisoner to get into the hospital ward, as a means of either escaping harassment or obtaining pain-killing drugs.

cross *n.*[3]

(IN PHRASES)

❑ **drink the cross off an ass** *v.* *see* DRINK *v.*

cross *adj.* [fig. uses of SE *cross*, contrary, opposed] **1** [early 19C–1910s] of a person, dishonest; of an object, dishonestly attained. **2** [mid–late 19C] annoying, unkind.

(DERIVATIVES)

❑ **crossways** *adj.* (*also* **crosswise**) [play on SE] [20C+] (*US*) **1** in a bad humour. **2** disagreeing with. **3** lying.

(IN COMPOUNDS)

❑ **cross-boy** *n.* [mid–late 19C] (*Aus./US*) a criminal. ❑ **cross-chap** *n.* [CHAP *n.* (1)] **1** [early 19C] (*US*) a disreputable person. **2** [early 19C–1900s] (*UK Und./costermonger*) a thief. ❑ **cross-**

cove *n.* [COVE *n.* (1)] [19C] a robber, anyone who lives by dishonesty or crime. ❑ **cross-cove and mollisher** *n.* [CROSS-COVE above + MOLLISHER *n.*] [mid-19C] a man and woman who work in tandem as thieves. ❑ **cross-crib** *n.* [CRIB *n.*[1] (1)] [mid-19C] a public house frequented by thieves. ❑ **cross dishonest** *n.* [early 19C] (*UK Und.*) a villain. ❑ **cross-drum** *n.* [DRUM *n.*[3] (3)] [mid-19C] (*UK/US Und.*) a thieves' tavern. ❑ **cross-fight** *n.* [mid-19C] (*UK Und.*) a fixed fight. ❑ **cross-girl** *n.* [mid-19C] a prostitute who specializes in propositioning sailors, taking their money and then vanishing. ❑ **cross-lad** *n.* (*also* **cross-squire**) [mid-19C] (*costermonger*) a thief. ❑ **cross-life man** *n.* [late 19C] (*UK Und.*) a professional thief. ❑ **cross-man** *n.* **1** [mid-19C] a confidence trickster; a thief. **2** [1950s+] (*US black*) anyone who manipulates others for his own advantage. ❑ **cross mollisher** *n.* [MOLLISHER *n.* (1)] [early 19C] a woman who works as a thief or lives in any way dishonestly. ❑ **cross-rattler** *n.* [early 19C] (*UK Und.*) a coach whose coachman aids criminals by taking their booty away from a scene of crime.

(IN PHRASES)

❑ **on the cross-cut** [sawmill imagery] [1900s] (*N.Z.*) angry with, arguing with.

SE in slang uses

(IN COMPOUNDS)

❑ **crossbite** *see* separate entries. ❑ **cross-bones** *n.* [1930s] (*US*) a doctor. ❑ **cross-built** *adj.* [mid-19C] describing a person who moves or stands in an awkward manner. ❑ **cross-buttock** *n.* [wrestling jargon *cross-buttock*, a throw over the hip] [mid-19C–1900s] an unexpected rebuff. ❑ **cross-eye(d)** *see* separate entries. ❑ **cross-kid** *see* separate entries. ❑ **cross-legged** *adj.* [mid-19C] knock-kneed. ❑ **cross-legs** *n.* [the trad. tailoring posture] [19C–1900s] a tailor. ❑ **crossroader/crossroads** *see* separate entries. ❑ **cross-tops** *n.* [the cross cut into the pill] [1970s] (*drugs*) amphetamines.

(IN PHRASES)

❑ **do a cross-country** *n.* [1920s] (*US prison*) to make an escape. ❑ **give the cross-hop** *v.* [late 19C] (*US tramp*) to betray; to double-cross.

cross *v.*[1] [abbr. SE *double-cross*] **1** [18C+] to let down. **2** [19C+] to deceive or mislead; to cheat. **3** [mid-19C+] to betray; thus *crosser*, n., an informer. **4** [1940s+] to oppose.

(IN PHRASES)

❑ **cross up** *v.* **1** [20C+] to betray, to double-cross, to inform against. **2** [1930s+] in fig. use, to let down, to place someone in a negative situation. **3** [1950s+] to go back on one's word, to reverse one's position.

cross *v.*[2] **1** [mid-18C–mid-19C] to sit astride a horse. **2** [mid-19C] to have sexual intercourse [fig. use of sense 1].

SE in slang uses

(IN PHRASES)

❑ **cross-fam** *v.* (*also* **cross-fan**) [FAM *n.*[1]] [19C] (*UK Und.*) to pick a pocket by crossing one's arms in a particular position. ❑ **cross out** *v.* [1980s+] **1** (*US black*) to perform a low-level form of gang warfare, the crossing out of a rival gang's graffiti. **2** (*US prison*) to punish. ❑ **cross the line** *v.* (*US*) **1** [1900s] of a light-coloured black person, to attempt to pass for white. **2** [1960s] of a homosexual man, to abandon his friends and marry a woman.

cross *adv.* [CROSS *adj.* (2)] [early 17C–19C] **1** unfavourably, in an unsatisfactory manner. **2** in a criminal manner.

cross-bar hotel *n.* (*also* **cross-bar Hilton**) [17C SE *cross-bar*, a horizontal bar, as of a window or cell + HOTEL *n.* (2)] [1940s+] (*US Und.*) a prison.

crossbite *n.* (*also* **crosbite**) [CROSSBITE *v.*] [late 16C–early 19C] (*UK Und.*) **1** a swindler. **2** an act of trickery.

crossbite *v.* [SE *cross* + BITE *v.* (1). The image is of fleecing someone who had hoped in their turn to get 'something for nothing', although in the case of the crossbiting law, the client had merely hoped for some illicit, commercial sex] [late 16C–mid-19C] (*UK Und.*) **1** to cheat, usu. in cards or dice, esp. when the victim is another cheat. **2** spec. to practise the CROSSBITING LAW below.

(IN COMPOUNDS)

❑ **crossbiting cully** *n.* [CULLY *n.*[1] (4)] [mid-17C–19C] a swindler, a cheat. ❑ **crossbiting law** *n.* (*also* **crossbiting**) [LAW *n.* (1)] [late 16C–early 17C] (*UK Und.*) the robbery of a prostitute's client by her pimp or other male accomplice, usu. posing as an aggrieved 'husband' or 'lover' (in modern times, the MURPHY (GAME), THE *n.*).

crossbiter *n.* (*also* **crossbite**) [CROSSBITE *v.*] (*UK Und.*) **1** [late 16C] a dice cheat or cardsharp. **2** [late 16C–17C] a man who works with a prostitute to trap and then rob an unfortunate victim; his role was to rob the man and then beat him up – allegedly for his gall in attempting to seduce an innocent 'sister' or 'wife'.

crosses *n.*[1] [1930s] (*US*) the roads.

crosses *n.*[2] [SE phr. *a cross to bear*] [1950s+] (*W.I. Rasta*) problems, vexations, trials, bad luck, misfortunes.

cross-eye *v.* [1920s–50s] (*US*) **1** to look suspiciously, to look askance at. **2** to glance at, to look at furtively, to act in any way suspiciously.

cross-eyed *adj.* [20C+] drunk.

cross-kid *n.* [CROSS-KID *v.*] [late 19C–1910s] irony, teasing, deception.

cross-kid *v.* (*also* **cross-kiddle**) [SE *cross* + KID *v.* (2)] [late 19C] to interrogate, to cross-examine.

cross lots *phr. see* ACROSS LOTS *phr.*

crossroader *n.* [he stands at the crossroads or crosses roads in search of victims] [1960s+] an itinerant card-sharp who travels in search of new victims for his cheating skills; thus *crossroad*, v.

crossroads *n.* [? the cross marked on some amphetamines] [1960s+] (*drugs*) amphetamine.

crot *n.* [? Fr. *crotte*, a small piece of animal excrement] [1970s] (*US*) a term of abuse.

crotch *n.* [SE *crotch*, the fork or bifurcation of the legs; thus the genital area of either sex] [1970s+] a woman, seen purely as an extension of her physical sexuality.

SE in slang uses

(IN COMPOUNDS)

❑ **crotch cheese** *n.* [1960s+] unwashed vaginal secretions. ❑ **crotch cricket** *n.* (*also* **crotch monkey**) [1910s; 1970s+] (*US*) a crab, a pubic louse. ❑ **crotchface** *n.* [play on SE *beard*/BEARD *n.* (1)] [1960s] (*US campus*) a bearded person. ❑ **crotch oil** *n.* [1980s+] (*US*) vaginal secretions that result from sexual foreplay. ❑ **crotch pheasant** *n.* [1960s–70s] (*US*) a body louse. ❑ **crotch rocket** *n.* [1970s+] a motorbike, esp. a dirt bike. ❑ **crotch rot** *n.* [1960s+] (*Can./US*) a fungal infection of the groin. ❑ **crotch-sucking** *adj. see* COCKSUCKING *adj.*

(IN PHRASES)

❑ **have someone/something by the crotch** *v. see* HAVE SOMEONE BY THE BALLS under BALLS *n.*

crotch *adj.* [1960s+] erotic, pornographic; thus *crotch novel*, a pornographic book.

Croton (cocktail) *n.* [the *Croton Reservoir* (now the site of the NY Public Library at 5th Ave. + 42nd St) + SE *cocktail*; the reservoir supplies the bulk of the city's drinking water] [mid-19C–1910s] (*US, New York*) water.

crovey *adj.* [? GROOVY *adj.*[2] (1)] [2000s] (*UK teen*) good, excellent.

crow *n.*[1] [abbr.] [late 17C–mid-19C] (*UK Und.*) a crowbar.

crow *n.*[2] [SE *crow*, whether visual resemblance or alleged characteristics] **1** based on the image of the bird itself, spec. its blackness. (**a**) [late 18C–1900s] a clergyman [his black clothes]. (**b**) [19C+] a derog. term for a black person [underpinned by JIM CROW *n.*]. (**c**) [mid–late 19C] a doctor [? his clothes + the idea of carrion, reflecting his inadequacy as a healer]. (**d**) [20C+] (*Aus.*) a South Australian [the badge of the state features a bird that resembles a crow but note CROW-EATER below]. **2** in criminal uses. (**a**) [early 19C+] that member of a crooked dice or card-game who poses as a stranger, but affirms the supposed honesty of those who run the game. (**b**) [mid-

19C+] a thief's lookout [? the image of crows perched on a fence]. (**c**) [1930s] (*UK tramp*) a man employed by a gang of street singers to protect their territory. (**d**) [1970s+] a lookout in a game of three-card monte. **3** ref. to women or girls. (**a**) [mid-19C–1950s] (*US*) a young woman, esp. a sweetheart. (**b**) [1910s+] (*also* **crow moll**) an unattractive (old) woman; note earlier OLD CROW *under* OLD *adj.* (**c**) [1920s+] (*US*) an attractive woman. (**d**) [1940s–70s] (*N.Z. teen*) a derog. description by a man of a young girl, from her black/navy school uniform. **4** [late 19C] (*US*) a person. **5** [1920s–50s] (*US*) an unpleasant old man. **6** [1940s] (*US milit.*) chicken (as a meal).

IN COMPOUNDS

❑ **crow fair** *n.* [late 18C] a gathering of clergymen. ❑ **crow jane** *n.* [1900s–20s] (*US black*) a very dark-skinned woman. ❑ **crow jim** *n. see* separate entry. ❑ **crow moll** *n. see* sense 3b above.

SE in slang uses

IN COMPOUNDS

❑ **crow-bait** *n. see* separate entry. ❑ **crow-eater** *n.* [the idea that the original settlers of the state ate crow when nothing else was available but note sense 1d above] [late 19C+] **1** (*Aus.*) a white inhabitant of South Australia; thus *crowland*, South Australia. **2** (*Aus./S.Afr.*) a lazy person who will scrounge and otherwise live on his wits rather than do actual work. ❑ **crow's foot** *n.* [mid–late 19C] (*UK prison*) the 'Broad Arrow' that marked all prison property. ❑ **crow's nest** *n. see* separate entry. ❑ **crow's piss** *n.* [mid-17C] dawn; note synon. use by British Army in North Africa during WW2, *crow-pee*. ❑ **crow tracks** *n.* [late 19C+] (*US*) illegible handwriting.

IN PHRASES

❑ **draw the crow** *v. see under* DRAW *v.*[4]. ❑ **give the crow a pudding** *v.* (*also* **make the crow a pudding, yield the crow a pudding, give the crows a pudding**) [SE *crow* + SE *pudding*, entrails, i.e. the crow will eat the entrails of the corpse] [late 16C–early 19C] **1** to hang on a gibbet. **2** to die. ❑ **have a crow's eye** *n.* [1940s] (*Aus.*) to be cunning, underhand. ❑ **when the crow shits** [Aus. var. on US *WHEN THE EAGLE SHITS under* EAGLE *n.*[2]; a bird is engraved on the reverse of an Australian dollar coin] [1970s+] (*Aus.*) payday. ❑ **where the crows fly backwards to keep the dust out of their eyes** [late 19C+] (*Aus.*) of anywhere that is considered beyond the bounds of civilization.

crow *n.*[3] [? one *crows* or exults over it] [mid-19C] an unexpected or fluky piece of luck; usu. in phr. *regular crow*.

crow *n.*[4] [play on/abbr. SE *crowbar*] [late 19C–1910s] a bar counter.

crow *n.*[5] [CHROMO *n.*; note Ital. *cornaccia*, a crow, a loose woman] [1940s+] (*Aus.*) a prostitute; thus *charity crow*, a prostitute who does not charge, esp. to impecunious soldiers during WW2; *society crow*, an upmarket prostitute, a courtesan.

crow *adj.* [? negative stereotype of JIM CROW *n.* (1)] [1910s–40s] (*US Und.*) inferior; worthless; second-rate.

crow *v.* [CROW *n.*[2] (2b)] [late 19C] (*UK Und.*) to keep a lookout.

crow-bait *n.* **1** [mid–late 19C] (*Aus.*) a derog. term for an Aborigine. **2** [mid-19C+] (*US*) a corpse that has been exposed to the elements. **3** [late 19C–1950s] (*US*) an unpleasant, despised person. **4** [late 19C+] (*orig. US*) an emaciated horse. **5** [1930s] (*US Und.*) an old person.

crowbar *n.* [it 'prises open' the vagina] [1920s] (*US*) the penis.

SE in slang uses

IN COMPOUNDS

❑ **crowbar brigade** *n.* [their breaking into houses with the help of a crowbar; the break-in was followed by the eviction of the tenants] [mid–late 19C] (*Irish*) the police; thus *crowbar landlord*, a landlord who enforces his powers through heavy-handed policemen. ❑ **crowbar hotel** *n.* [var. on CROSS-BAR HOTEL *n.* + ? ref. to the need for a SE *crowbar* to escape] [1940s+] a prison.

crowded space *n.* [rhy. sl.] [20C+] a suitcase.

crowd pleaser *n.* [ironic use] [1960s+] (*US police*) the officer's gun.

crowd surf *v.* [1990s+] to leap from the stage at a rock concert, in order to be caught and passed along by the crowd.

crowdy-headed jock *n.* [Scot./northern dial. *crowdy*, a gruel made from milk and meal; thus a porridge + JOCK *n.* (1)] [late 18C–early 19C] a North Country seaman, esp. a collier.

crow jim *n.* [the reverse of anti-black discriminatory JIM CROW *n.* (3) laws] [1950s+] (*US*) anti-white discrimination by blacks; thus *crow jimism*, guilt-induced affection for and fascination with blacks by white liberals.

crow mcgee *adj.* (*also* **crow macgee**) [ety. unknown; ? joc. reversal of REAL MCCOY, THE *n.*] [1930s+] (*US prison*) no good, unreal, false.

crown *n.*[1] **1** [late 19C] the female genital area. **2** [1960s] (*US black*) a hat. **3** [1970s+] (*US gay*) the glans penis.

IN COMPOUNDS

❑ **crown and feathers** *n.* [ext. FEATHER *n.* (1); playing on a typical name for a public house] [mid–late 19C] the pubic hair.

SE in slang uses

IN COMPOUNDS

❑ **crown jewels** *n.* [their importance to the possessor] [1960s+] the male genitals. ❑ **crown office** *n.* [a pun on legal SE] [late 18C–early 19C] the head.

IN PHRASES

❑ **crown of sense** *n.* [late 17C–19C] the vagina. ❑ **in the crown-office** *adj.* [play on SE *crown* (of the head), which suffers] [late 17C–18C] tipsy.

crown *n.*[2] ['a crown was worn on an insignia of rank on the lapel. This practice is now obsolete but the term is still used to denote a prison officer in authority', Tupper & Wortley, *Australian Prison Slang Glossary* (1990)] [1980s+] (*Aus. prison*) the Principal Officer.

crown *adj.* [? SE phr. *crowning glory*] [1920s+] (*Aus.*) very large.

crown *v.* [orig. dial.] **1** [mid-19C+] to hit over the head. **2** [20C+] (*Aus. campus*) to empty a chamberpot over a victim's head. **3** [1910s+] to hit a ball.

crown crap *n.* [? CROWN *adj.* + CRAP *n.*[1] (16)] [1980s+] (*drugs*) heroin.

crowner *n.* [SE *crown*, the top of one's head] [mid–late 19C] a fall (from horseback) onto the top of one's head.

crowns *n. see* BURNESE *n.*

crown sheet *n.* [rhy. sl.] [1930s–50s] (*US tramp*) the seat of one's trousers.

crow's nest *n.* [naut. use *crow's nest*, the platform secured high on a mast that houses a lookout] **1** [late 19C–1900s] (*UK society*) a small bedroom on the higher floors of country houses, reserved for the use of bachelor guests. **2** [20C+] (*US*) a woman's hair when it has been pinned up in a bun. **3** [1960s–70s] (*US*) the upper baclony or 'gods' in a theatre. **4** [1970s+] (*US gay*) a club frequented by older homosexual men.

Croydon facelift *n.* [2000s] a UK female hairstyle which pulls the hair back tightly from the face, supposedly giving the effect of a facelift; stereotyped as that of working-class young women.

croziered abbot *n.* (*also* **abbot on the cross**) [pun SE *croziered*, bearing a crook/*ON THE CROSS under* CROSS *n.*[1] + ABBOT *n.* (2)] [late 19C] a man who runs a brothel designed less for providing sex, and more for robbing or blackmailing the clients.

c.r.s. *adj.* [abbr. *c*an't *r*emember *s*hit] [1980s+] (*US campus*) forgetful.

crub *n.* [1970s–80s] (*UK black*) the rubbing of one's body, esp. the genital area, against one's partner while dancing.

crub *v.* [CRUB *n.*] [1970s–80s] (*UK black*) to rub one's body against one's partner when dancing.

crubber *n.* [? var. GRUBBER *n.*[1] (1)] [1920s] (*US*) one who does not buy their own cigarettes.

crucial *adj.* [1980s+] general term of praise, admiration; serious, important, excellent; thus adv., *crucially*.

crud *n.* (*also* **krud**) [Scot. *crud*, thickened or coagulated milk; note US regional *crud*, curdled milk; note *HDAS* suggests all US uses are backform. f. CRUDDY *adj.*] **1** of foul substances, bodily fluids etc. (**a**) [early 16C+] any filthy and disgusting matter. (**b**) [19C] curds. (**c**) [1930s+] (*orig. US milit.*) any unidentified disease; often as *creeping crud, crawling crud*. (**d**) [1940s+] (*orig. US milit.*) diarrhoea. (**e**) [1950s+] dried semen, whether on the body, clothes or bedlinen. (**f**) [1950s+] dirt, in general. (**g**) [1950s+] (*US*) any venereal disease. (**h**) [1950s+] daylights, guts, stuffing, e.g. *kick the crud out of*. **2** of people. (**a**) [1930s+] anything or anyone worthless or repulsive; also as a generic collective term. (**b**) [1940s+] (*orig. US milit.*) a slovenly, habitually dirty person. **3** [1940s+] (*US*) nonsense, rubbish.

DERIVATIVES

❏ **crudzoid** *n.* [-ZOID *sfx*] [1980s] (*US*) a repellent, disgusting person.

IN COMPOUNDS

❏ **crud-eating grin** *n. see* SHIT-EATING GRIN *n.* ❏ **crudhead** *n.* [-HEAD *sfx* (1)] [1940s+] a fool, an unpleasant person. ❏ **crudman** *n.* [*-man* sfx] [1970s] a term of abuse. ❏ **crud-sucking** *n.* (*also* **crud-eating**) [1950s+] (*US*) a general term of abuse, revolting, disgusting etc. ❏ **crud-work** *n.* [1950s] (*US*) any menial, unpleasant or tedious work.

IN PHRASES

❏ **crud up** *v.* [1960s+] (*orig. US*) to render disgusting, filthy; thus to spoil.

crud *adj. see* CRUDDY *adj.* (1).

crud! *excl.* [CRUD *n.*, i.e. var. on SHIT! *excl.*] [1990s+] (*US campus*) an expresssion of annoyance.

crudball *n.* [CRUD *n.* + sfx *-ball*] [1960s+] (*US*) a filthy or disgusting person or thing.

crudball *adj.* [CRUDBALL *n.*] [1960s+] (*US*) filthy, disgusting.

cruddy *adj.* [CRUD *n.* + sfx *-y*] **1** [1930s+] (*also* **crud, crudding**) useless, no good, second-rate. **2** [1940s+] dirty, unpleasant, unsavoury.

crude *adj.* [1950s+] (*US black*) worthless, excessive and as such useless.

crudget *n.* [ety. unknown] [1920s+] (*Aus.*) the human head.

cruel (the pitch) *v.* (*also* **crool (the pitch)**) [ostensibly rooted in cricket imagery, the phr. does not appear in John Eddowes' *Lang. of Cricket* (1996)] [late 19C+] (*Aus.*) to spoil, to ruin any chance of success with.

cruelty man *n.* [both organizations deal with *cruelty*, to, respectively, children or animals] [1950s+] an officer of the NSPCC or RSPCA.

cruelty-van *n.* [? its discomfort] [mid–late 19C] a four-wheeled chaise.

cruet *n.* [1940s+] (*Aus.*) the human head.

IN PHRASES

❏ **do one's cruet** *v.* [1960s–70s] (*Aus.*) to lose emotional control.

cruff *n.* [? SE *scruffy*; note computer jargon *crufty*, disgusting, distasteful] [1950s+] (*W.I.*) **1** crude, coarse, uncouth manners; also as adj. **2** (*also* **cruffbag**) a crude, uncouth person.

crufty *adj.* [? SE *scruffy*; note computer jargon *crufty*, of a machine or program, poorly constructed, poss. over-complex] [1980s] (*W.I., Jam.*) coarse-looking.

crug *n.* [? SE *crust*; orig. used by boys at Christ's Hospital school to mean bread] [mid-19C] food.

cruise *n.* [CRUISE *v.* (1)] **1** [1950s] (*US Und.*) a male homosexual who picks up partners on the street. **2** [1960s+] (*gay*) a quick glance that assesses a passing individual in sexual terms.

cruise *adj.* [CRUISE *v.* (11)] [1980s+] (*US teen*) easy, simple, useful.

cruise *v.* [fig. uses of SE *cruise*, to sail to and fro with no particular destination; note Ned Ward, *Hudibras Redivivus* (1705–7): 'Now gently cruzing up and down, / T'observe the Follies of the Town'] **1** [late 17C+] to approach someone obviously with sexual intent, both for commercial or non-commercial purposes [Norton, *Mother Clap's Molly House* (2006), claims orig. early 17C synon. Du. *kruisen*]. **2** [mid-18C] (*UK Und.*) to beg. **3** [19C+] to wander along/through. **4** [20C+] (*also* **cruise around**) to drive around, often along a town's main street, surveying the situation, looking for friends, men/women to pick up etc. **5** [1910s+] to search for sexual contacts by walking specific streets, areas etc. **6** [1940s] (*US black*) to walk someone along/around/through. **7** [1940s+] (*US black*) to walk in a strutting manner. **8** [1950s] to find someone attractive. **9** [1950s–60s] (*US*) of a mugger or thief, to search out a potential victim. **10** [1950s+] to walk or drive somewhere. **11** [1960s+] to do something easily, effortlessly. **12** [1970s+] to set off, to leave. **13** [1980s] (*US campus*) to sleep soundly. **14** [1990s+] to drive someone around. **15** [1990s+] to pass, to hand over, to give. **16** [1990s+] of the police, to drive around checking on suspicious activities/individuals.

DERIVATIVES

❏ **cruisemobile** *n.* [-MOBILE *sfx*] [1980s+] (*US teen*) any favoured car. ❏ **cruisy** *adj.* [1940s+] (*gay*) used of the sort of place in which one is likely to make a successful pick-up.

IN PHRASES

❏ **cruising for a bruising** [1940s+] (*orig. US*) **1** looking deliberately to cause trouble. **2** acting in such a manner that will get one into trouble, usu. of a physically harmful nature.

cruiser *n.* [CRUISE *v.*] **1** [late 17C–early 19C] (*UK Und.*) a beggar, esp. one. who passes on information of potential robberies to professional thieves. **2** [mid-19C] (*UK/US Und.*) 'a man who "cruises around" in search of victims and plunder' (Thornton, *An American Glossary*, 1912). **3** [mid-19C; 20C+] (*also* **heavy cruiser**) a prostitute. **4** [1900s] (*Aus.*) a tramp, a vagrant. **5** [1920s+] (*US*) a police patrol car. **6** [1940s+] one who wanders the streets in search of a casual pick-up (usu. a male homosexual but not always).

cruising *n.* [CRUISE *v.* (5)] [1920s+] walking or driving about the streets in search of a casual sexual partner; usu., but not invariably, of a male homosexual, also in a bar, club etc.

Crum, the *n.* [abbr.] [1970s+] (*Ulster*) the *Crum*lin Road prison in Belfast.

crum *n.* (*also* **crumb**) [the diminutive size of the insects, the infestation of the human being] **1** [mid-19C–1920s] a body louse, usu. in pl. **2** [1910s+] a filthy person, an objectionable, worthless or insignificant person. **3** [1970s+] a cruel, vicious person.

IN COMPOUNDS

❏ **crum boss** *n.* (*also* **crumb boss**) [among his duties was delousing the beds] [1920s–30s] (*US tramp/Western*) a janitor in a construction camp or mission. ❏ **crum-catcher** *n.* [1940s] (*US*) a comb. ❏ **Crum Hill** *n.* [1920s–30s] (*US tramp*) Jefferson Park, Chicago. ❏ **crum joint** *n.* [JOINT *n.* (3b)] [1920s–60s] (*US*) a second-rate, dirty dwelling-house, bar or club. ❏ **crum roll** *n.* [i.e. the assumption/slur being that it is infested with lice] [1930s] (*US tramp*) a bedroll.

IN PHRASES

❏ **put on a crumb act** *v.* [1950s] (*Aus.*) to impose on another person.

crum *adj. see* CRUMB *adj.*

crumb *n.*[1] [SE *crumb*, the soft heart of a risen loaf of bread] [19C] **1** a pretty, plumpish woman. **2** plumpness.

IN PHRASES

❏ **bit of crumb** *n.* [BIT *n.*[1] (2a)] [late 19C] a plump, attractive woman.

SE in slang uses

IN COMPOUNDS

❏ **crumb-catcher** *n.* **1** [1940s–50s] (*US*) a hanger-on, one who acts as a parasite on the powerful or influential [the taking of crumbs from the rich man's table]. **2** [1950s+] (*orig. US black*) (*also* **crumb-snatcher**) a baby; usu. one who is just beginning to eat solids. ❏ **crumb-cruncher** *n.* (*orig. US black*) [1940s] in pl., the teeth. ❏ **crumb-crush** *v.* [1940s] (*US black*) to enjoy profoundly, to 'eat up'. ❏ **crumb-crusher** *n.* (*US black*) **1** [1940s–70s] in pl., the teeth. **2** [1970s] in pl., the lips. ❏ **crumb-gobbler** *n.* [1920s] (*US*) a young man who frequents tea-parties. ❏ **crumb-grabber** *n.* [1930s–60s] (*orig. US black*) a baby who is just beginning to eat solids. ❏ **crumb-hall** *n.* [1930s–40s] (*US black*) a dining-room, esp. in an institution. ❏ **crumb-snatcher** *n.* **1** [1970s] the hand. **2** *see* CRUMB-

CATCHER above. ❑ **crumb-stash** *n.* [1930s–40s] (*US black/Harlem*) a kitchen; a dining room.

crumb *n.*[2] [? the shape] **1** [early–mid-19C] (*US*) the head. **2** [1920s] the penis.

crumb *n.*[3] (*also* **crummy**) [CRUM *n.* (1)] [1910s–50s] (*US tramp*) a hobo's bedding.

crumb *n.*[4] *see* CRUM *n.*

crumb *adj.* (*also* **crum**) [abbr. CRUMMY *adj.*[2] (2)] [20C+] (*US*) filthy, dirty, disgusting.

IN COMPOUNDS

❑ **crumb joint** *n.* [JOINT *n.* (3b)] [1930s–50s] (*US*) a filthy lodging house or hostel.

crumb *v.* [i.e. to render CRUMMY *adj.*[2] (3)] **1** [1940s–50s] (*US black/teen*) to ruin, to undermine; usu. as *crumb a/the deal.* **2** [1960s] (*US*) to malign someone. **3** [1980s+] (*US campus*) to feel sad or depressed.

IN PHRASES

❑ **crumb in** *v.* [1960s] (*US*) to interfere, to butt in, esp. to interfere in (and poss. ruin) another confidence man's scheme.

crumb! *excl.* [abbr. CRUMMY *adj.*[2] (3)] [1950s–70s] (*US*) a mild excl. of annoyance.

crumb-bum *n. see* CRUMBUM *n.*

crumbed-up *adj. see* CRUMMY *adj.*[2].

crumbly *n.* (*also* **crumblie**) [such people are fig. 'crumbling away'] [1970s+] (*UK society*) an older person, aged 50–70.

crumbo *n.* [CRUM *n.* (2) + -O *sfx* (1)] [1930s+] (*orig. US*) a filthy, disgusting, despised person.

crumbs *n.* [the diminutive sizes] **1** [1920s–50s] (*US*) very small sums of money. **2** [1980s+] (*drugs*) tiny pieces of crack.

IN PHRASES

❑ **on one's crumbs** [mid-19C] down to one's last few pennies.

crumbs! *excl.* (*also* **crums! by crumbs!**) [late 19C+] (*mainly UK juv.*) a euph. for CHRIST! *excl.*; prob. the mildest of such euph.

crumbum *n.* (*also* **crumb-bum, crumbun**) [CRUM *n.* (2) + BUM *n.*[3] (2)] [1930s+] (*orig. US*) a filthy, disgusting, worthless person.

crumbum *adj.* [CRUMBUM *n.*] [1930s+] (*orig. US*) useless, awful, second-rate, inferior.

crumb up *v.*[1] [CRUMB *adj.*] [1910s+] (*US*) to make filthy, disgusting.

crumb up *v.*[2] *see* CRUM UP *V.*

crumby *adj. see under* CRUMMY.

crummy *n.*[1] [CRUMB *n.*[1] (2) + sfx *-y*] [early 19C] **1** fat. **2** the stomach.

crummy *n.*[2] [CRUM *n.* (1) + sfx *-y*] [mid-19C] (*US*) a louse.

crummy *n.*[3] [CRUMMY *adj.*[2] (1); such coaches or small lockups were trad. infested with lice; logging jargon *crummy*, a pick-up truck that ferries loggers to and from their camps] **1** [1920s–50s] (*US tramp*) (*also* **crumby**) the caboose of a train, i.e. that coach used by railroad workmen or train guards. **2** [1950s] (*US Und.*) a local jail, police station or workhouse. **3** *see* CRUMB *n.*[3].

crummy *adj.*[1] (*also* **crumby**) [SE *crumb*, the soft inner part of a loaf, the antithesis of *crust*; this predates but note CRUMB *n.*[1] (2)] **1** [17C] rich. **2** [mid-18C–19C] fat, fleshy; plump; attractive.

crummy *adj.*[2] (*also* **crumby, crumbed up**) [CRUM *n.* + sfx *-y*] **1** [mid-19C+] infested with lice; thus fig. 'lousy with'. **2** [mid-19C+] generally filthy. **3** [mid-19C+] (*also* **crummy-ass**) second-rate, inferior, unpleasant. **4** [1940s+] a general negative intensifier, synon. with LOUSY *adj.* **5** [1950s+] out of sorts, 'off colour'.

IN COMPOUNDS

❑ **crummy-doss** *n.* [DOSS *n.*[1] (1)] [mid-19C] a lousy or filthy bed.

crummy! *excl.* (*also* **by crummie! by crummit! by crummy!**) [20C+] a mild euph. for CHRIST! *excl.*

crump *n.*[1] [backform. f. phr. *I wish you had, Mrs Crump*: 'a Gloucestershire saying, in answer to a wish for any thing; implying you must not expect any assistance from the speaker. It is said to have originated from the following incident: One Mrs. Crump, the wife of a substantial farmer, dining with the old Lady Coventry, who was extremely deaf, said to one of the footmen, waiting at table, "I wish I had a draught of small beer," her modesty not permitting her to desire so fine a gentleman to bring it: the fellow, conscious that his mistress could not hear either the request or answer, replied, without moving, "I wish you had, Mrs. Crump." These wishes being again repeated by both parties, Mrs. Crump got up from the table to fetch it herself; and being asked by my lady where she was going, related what had passed. The story being told abroad, the expression became proverbial' (Grose, 1785)] [late 17C–mid-19C] a solicitor's assistant, who arranges for false witnesses to perjure themselves as required by a given case.

crump *n.*[2] [early 18C–early 19C] a hunchback.

crump *adj.* [ety. unknown] [1990s+] (*US campus*) good, excellent.

crump *v.* [SE *crump*, the noise of an object hitting the ground] **1** [1950s+] (*US campus*) to pass out through exhaustion, boredom or alcohol; thus *crumped (out)*, adj., passed out drunk. **2** [1950s+] (*US*) of machinery, to break down. **3** [1950s+] (*US*) to die. **4** [1960s] (*US*) to kill. **5** [1980s] (*US*) to destroy.

crump-backed *adj.* [SE *crump*, crooked + *backed*] [late 17C–early 19C] hump-backed.

crump-crusher *n.* [1930s] (*US black*) in pl., the teeth.

crumper *n.* [dial. *crump*, a blow] [mid–late 19C] a hard hit, a blow.

crumpet *n.* [the supposedly similar shapes] **1** [late 19C+] the head; usu. in phrs. below. **2** in sexual contexts. (**a**) [1930s+] women, esp. when viewed as no more than sources of sexual pleasure; thus *get a crumpet*, of a man, to have sexual intercourse. (**b**) [1940s+] (*also* **crump**) sexual intercourse. (**c**) [1960s] (*US gay*) an anal virgin. (**d**) [1960s+] the vagina. (**e**) [1990s+] men viewed as no more than sources of sexual pleasure. **3** [1900s–60s] a term of endearment; often as *old crumpet*. **4** [1920s+] (*Aus.*) a weakling, a fool [the 'softness' of the comestible].

IN COMPOUNDS

❑ **crumpet man** *n.* [1960s+] a womanizer.

IN PHRASES

❑ **barmy on the crumpet** *adj.* [late 19C+] mad, eccentric. ❑ **bow the crumpet** *v.* [1930s+] (*Aus.*) to plead guilty. ❑ **not worth a crumpet** *adj.* [1940s+] (*Aus.*) worthless, useless. ❑ **off one's crumpet** *adj.* [late 19C+] mad, eccentric.

SE in slang uses

IN COMPOUNDS

❑ **crumpet-face** *n.* [similarity to the pocked surface of a crumpet] [mid–late 19C] a face that is covered with smallpox marks. ❑ **crumpet-scramble** *n.* [mid–late 19C] a tea party.

crum up *v.* (*also* **crumb up**) [CRUM *n.* (1)] [1920s–50s] (*US*) to boil one's clothes to get rid of the lice.

crunch *n.* [? 'good enough to eat'] [1970s] (*US campus*) **1** a generic term for women. **2** an infatuation.

crunch *adj.* [SE (*the*) *crunch*] [1970s+] (*orig. Aus.*) critical, decisive, crucial, e.g. *a crunch situation*.

crunch *v.* **1** [mid-19C+] to beat up. **2** [1950s–60s] of a man, to have sexual intercourse.

crunched *adj.* [1990s+] (*US campus*) under intense pressure.

cruncher *n.*[1] (*also* **crunching straight**) [the sound of one's feet] [1940s] (*US*) the street, the pavement.

cruncher *n.*[2] [SE (*the*) *crunch*] [1980s+] the ultimate aspect of a given situation.

crunchers *n.* [echoic: sound of biting or feet hitting the ground] **1** [1920s] (*US tramp*) the teeth. **2** [1940s] (*US*) the feet.

crunchie *n.* [? *mealie cruncher* or f. *krantzie*, abbr. of *krantz-athlete*, milit. sl. for an Afrikaner; the term also reflects their overall image of violence] [1970s+] (*S.Afr.*) a derog. term for an Afrikaner.

crunching straight *n. see* CRUNCHER *n.*[1].

crunchy *adj.*[1] [? the 'crunching up' of one's face/body in embarrassment] [1990s+] (*US campus*) **1** embarrassed. **2** exhausted.

crunchy *adj.*[2] [CRUNCHY (GRANOLA) *n.*] [1990s+] (*US campus*) vegetarian, hippy.

crunchy (granola) *n.* [the popular and supposedly healthy US cereal, *Crunchy Granola*; 'A hiking-boot-wearing, granola-eating, Grateful Dead/Blues Traveler-listening type of person' (Shenk & Silberman, *Skeleton Key*, 1994)] [1980s+] (*US campus*) **1** a vegetarian. **2** a devotee of New Age philosophies. **3** (*also* **earthy-crunchy, hairy crunchy**) someone who identifies with the styles and concerns of the 1960s.

crunk *n.* [CRUNK *adj.*] [1990s+] (*US black*) a state of excitement; a good time.

crunk *adj.* (*also* **crunked up**) [orig. hip-hop use; SE *crazy* + *drunk*] [1990s+] (*US campus/teen*) **1** intoxicated with drink or drugs. **2** excellent, wonderful. **3** (*also* **crunked**) excited, exciting. **4** crazy, obnoxious.

crunk! *excl.* [1960s] (*US campus*) a mild euph. oath.

crunt *n.* [CRUD *n.* (1a)] [1950s–60s] (*US black*) any form of dirt, esp. the (dried) residue of bodily fluids, e.g. blood, semen.

crupper *n.* (*also* **crooper**) [SE *crupper*, the hind-quarters of a horse] **1** [late 16C–mid-19C] the posterior, the buttocks; thus *crupper, ride below the crupper*, to have sexual intercourse. **2** [mid-19C] the penis.

crusader *n.* [1990s+] (*US campus*) an evangelistic, fundamentalist Christian.

crush *n.*[1] [note WW1 Aus. milit. *crush*, a unit] **1** [mid-19C] a crowded social occasion. **2** [1900s–70s] a crowd, a gang.

crush *n.*[2] **1** [late 19C+] a romantic or sexual interest in someone, occas. the person itself [one's emotions 'crush' their object]. **2** [1980s] (*lesbian*) the vagina.

crush *n.*[3] (*also* **crusher**) [note mid-19C UK SE *crush hat*, a soft hat that can be crushed flat, esp. a hat constructed with a spring so that it collapses and becomes flat] [1910s–40s] (*US*) a hat, esp. a soft, felt one.

crush *v.*[1] [? SE *crash*] **1** [mid-19C–1940s] (*UK/US Und.*) to run away, to escape; thus *big crush*, a mass escape. **2** [1900s] (*US*) as *crush in*, to attend an event when uninvited. **3** [1900s–20s] (*US Und.*) to break into.

IN PHRASES

❑ **crush the can** *v. see under* CAN *n.*[1]. ❑ **crush the stir** *v. see under* STIR *n.*[1].

crush *v.*[2] [SE *crush*] **1** [late 19C; 1980s] (*US campus*) to amaze; to do very well. **2** [20C+] (*US campus*) (*also* **crush on**) to be fond of someone [CRUSH *n.*[2] (1)]. **3** (*orig. US black*) to have sexual intercourse.

SE in slang uses

IN PHRASES

❑ **crush a bottle** *v.* (*also* **crush a cup (of wine), crush a pot (of ale)**) [late 16C] to drink.

crushed fruit *n. see* FRUIT *n.* (2).

crushed on *adv.* [CRUSH *n.*[2] (1)] [late 19C–1920s] (*orig. UK society*) infatuated with.

crusher *n.*[1] [sense 1 the stereotype of the policeman's large, booted feet; thus cf. BEETLE-CRUSHER *under* BEETLE *n.*[1]. Note naut. use *crusher*, a ship's corporal; ? link to Irish *Cuir siar ar*, to force upon; an enforcer] **1** [mid–late 19C] something that overwhelms or overpowers. **2** [mid-19C+] a police officer. **3** [20C+] (*US*) a boor, an intruder. **4** [1930s–70s] (*Can.*) a thug. **5** *see* CRUSH *n.*[3].

IN PHRASES

❑ **go a crusher** *v.* [late 19C] to indulge oneself. ❑ **put the crusher on** *v.* [1900s–40s] (*US*) **1** to attack physically. **2** to eject, to throw out. **3** to mount a police raid. **4** to treat harshly.

crusher *n.*[2] [SE *crush*/ CRUSH *v.*[2] (2) + ? MASHER *n.* (3)] [20C+] (*US*) one who persists in making unwanted advances to women.

crushing *adj.* [SE *crushing*, bruising, overwhelming] [mid-19C] excellent, first-rate.

crush me! *excl.* [mid-18C] an excl. of asseveration.

crush out *n.* [CRUSH OUT *v.* (1)] [1920s–50s] (*US prison*) an escape.

crush out *v.* [note Milburn, *The Hobo's Hornbook* (1930), differentiates this from simple CRUSH *v.*[1] (1), which does not involve violence] [1920s+] (*US Und.*) **1** to escape from prison. **2** to obliterate the body and the evidence of a murder by putting the corpse into a car and the car through a junkyard crushing machine. **3** to push through a crowd.

crust *n.*[1] [SE *crust of bread*] **1** [19C+] a living; thus *earn/pick up a crust*, to work for a living. **2** [late 19C+] the head. **3** [1910s–70s] a vagrancy charge, a vagrant [implies that a vagrant has insufficient money to buy a crust].

IN PHRASES

❑ **crack a crust** *v.* [mid-19C] to earn a living; ext. as *crack a tidy crust*, to make a very good living.

SE in slang uses

IN COMPOUNDS

❑ **crust-buster** *n.* [1950s+] (*US black*) a baby who is just learning to eat solids. ❑ **crust-thrower** *n.* (*also* **crust-flopper**) [1900s–20s] (*US Und.*) one who surreptitiously throws a crust into the gutter, then ostentatiously picks it up in the hope of gaining alms for his plight.

IN PHRASES

❑ **burst in someone's crust** *v.* (*also* **bust in someone's crust, cave in someone's crust**) [mid-19C–1910s] (*US*) **1** to hit hard enough to break the skin. **2** to suffer a knock or injury that breaks the skin.

crust *n.*[2] [SE *crust*, an outer covering or shell that is difficult to penetrate] [20C+] cheek, audacity, nerve.

crust *v.* [CRUST *n.*[1] (3)] [1910s–70s] (*orig. Aus./N.Z.*) to charge with vagrancy; thus *do the crust*, to serve a sentence for vagrancy.

SE in slang uses

IN PHRASES

❑ **wouldn't that crust you** [? SE *crush*] [1910s] (*US*) a phr. of disappointment, frustration.

crustafarian *n.* [CRUSTY *n.* + SE *Rastafarian*] [1990s+] a white person who deliberately adopts the lifestyle and image of a Rastafarian.

crusted *adj.* [the *crust* deposited at the bottom of a bottle of vintage port] [mid-19C] drunk.

crust of bread *n.* [rhy. sl.] [1930s+] the head.

crusty *n.* [note 1950s W.I. *crusty*, illiterate, backward, foolish] [1980s+] a member of an underclass who espouse a HIPPIE *n.*[2] (3) lifestyle, although modernized with more of a 'punk' edge; they adopt deliberately filthy clothing (hence their 'crustiness'), live communally (often in squats) or on the streets, enjoy an excess of drink and drugs and generally set out to appal their less extreme peers.

crusty *adj.* [SE *crusty*, encrusted (with something unpleasant) + SE *crusty*, of a person, short-tempered, rebarbative] **1** [mid–late 19C; 1930s+] unpleasant, nasty. **2** [1970s–80s] (*UK black*) of people, well-built, muscled [one is 'encrusted' with muscles]. **3** [1970s–80s] (*UK black*) of objects, large, heavy.

IN COMPOUNDS

❑ **crusty beau** *n. see under* BEAU *n.*[1]. ❑ **crusty gripes** *n.* [SE *gripe*, a complaint] [late 19C] a grumbler.

crut *n.* [CRUD *n.* (1a)] (*US*) **1** [1940s] an unspecifed disease. **2** [1940s–60s] unpleasant, disgusting matter.

crutch *n.*[1] **1** [late 19C] a crutch-handled walking-stick, the badge of the late 19C man-about-town. **2** [20C+] (*bingo*) the number seven; usu. as *one little crutch*; thus *all the crutches*, 77. **3** [1930s+] (*drugs*) a device (a thin piece of cardboard, usu. a matchbook cover, rolled into a cylindrical shape) used to hold the last portion of a marijuana cigarette that has become too hot to hold in the fingers. **4** [1960s] (*US*) any form of (commercially produced) cheating aid used in a test or examination.

IN PHRASES

❑ **crutch-and-toothpick brigade** *n.* [SE *toothpick*; thus the music-hall rhymester's mock solicitous enquiry: 'How do you like the lah-di-dah, the toothpick and the crutch?/How did you get those trousers on, and do they hurt you much?'] [late 19C] a broad group of 'stage door johnnies' and men-about-town whose sartorial badges were a crutch-handled walking-stick and a toothpick (of the dental variety). ▫ **crutch-and-toothpick parade** *n.* [punning on prev.] [late 19C–1900s] a generic term for old and decrepit males.

crutch *n.*[2] [1930s–70s] (*US black*) a car; thus *fly crutch*, an expensive, fashionable car; *P-crutch*, a police car.

crutch *v.* [SE *crotch*] [1990s+] (*UK prison*) to smuggle objects in one's vagina.

cruz *n.* [abbr.] [1980s+] (*drugs*) opium from Veracruz, Mexico.

cry *n.* [precursor of SHOUT *n.* (1b)] [mid-19C+] (*orig. Aus.*) one's turn to order a round of drinks.

cry *v.* [1910s+] (*US*) to complain, to make a fuss.

IN PHRASES

▫ **cry copper** *v. see under* COPPER *n.* ▫ **cry the blues** *v. see under* BLUES *n.*[1]. ▫ **cry uncle** *v. see under* UNCLE *n.* ▫ **I'm not crying** [1960s] (*US black*) used to respond to the greeting: 'how are you', 'how are things', etc.

SE in slang uses

IN PHRASES

▫ **cry (a) crack** *v.* [fig. use SE *crack*] [16C; late 19C–1930s] (*later use Aus./Irish*) to give in, to surrender, to cry 'quits'. ▫ **cry a go** *v.* [cribbage jargon *cry a go*, to pass] [late 19C] to give up, to surrender. ▫ **cry a rope** *v.* [the hangman's rope that awaits those who pay no heed] [late 16C] to shout a warning. ▫ **cry bucket-a-drop** *v.* [the image of filling a bucket with tears] [20C+] (*W.I.*) to make a good deal of fuss (and even cry) about an unimportant matter; to shed 'crocodile tears'. ▫ **cry carrots (and turnips)** *v.* [? onomat. + ironic ref. to the carter's normal cries] [18C] (*UK Und.*) to be whipped at the cart's tail. ▫ **cry champagne** *v.* [1990s+] (*W.I.*) to express oneself in a dramatic fashion. ▫ **cry cockles** *v.* [echoic: *cockles*, the sound made as one chokes] [late 18C–early 19C] to be hanged. ▫ **cry (hot) beef** *v. see under* HOT BEEF! *excl.* ▫ **cry it** *v.* [1910s] (*Aus.*) to name or order a drink. ▫ **cry off** *v.* [1940s–50s] (*US Und.*) **1** to confess. **2** to inform. ▫ **cry pork** *v.* ['a metaphor borrowed from the raven, whose note sounds like the word *pork*. Ravens are said to smell carrion at a distance' (Grose, 1796)] [late 18C–early 19C] to act as an undertaker's tout. ▫ **cry roast meat** *v.* (*also* **cry stinking fish**) [the assumed prosperity of those who eat roast meat. The *OED* suggests that such boasting is foolish] [late 17C–19C] to boast about one's good fortune.

IN EXCLAMATIONS

▫ **cry mapsticks!** [SE play on *mopstick*, mop handle] [early–mid-18C] I beg for mercy!

cry and laugh *n.* [rhy. sl.] [20C+] (*Aus.*) a scarf.

crybaby *v.* [20C+] to collapse in the face of pressure and act like a weeping, pleading child; also in fig. use.

cry-cry *adj.* [20C+] (*W.I.*) of a child, continually or easily tearful, crybabyish.

crying buddy *n.* [? one on whose shoulder one may cry] [1960s] (*US black*) one's best friend.

crying towel *n.* [1920s+] (*US*) a fig. *towel* used to mop the tears of self-pitying people.

crying weed *n.* [SE *crying* + WEED *n.*[1] (4); ? its effects, although the tears are more likely to result from laughter than sorrow] [1950s] (*drugs*) marijuana.

Crys *n. see* CRIS *n.*

crystal *n.* [resemblance] (*drugs*) **1** [1920s+] (*also* **crystal blow**) uncut cocaine. **2** [1960s+] (*also* **crystals**) a term covering a variety of drugs of the amphetamine type, e.g. amphetamine sulphate, powdered methamphetamine, desoxyn. **3** [1970s+] (*also* **crystal flake**) phencyclidine.

IN COMPOUNDS

▫ **crystal joint** *n.* [JOINT *n.* (5c)] [1970s] (*drugs*) phencyclidine. ▫ **crystal lady** *n.* [1970s+] (*US gay*) an amphetamine-using homosexual.

SE in slang uses

IN COMPOUNDS

▫ **crystal bud** *n.* [BUD *n.*[2] (3a)] [1980s+] (*US drugs*) a potent variety of marijuana in which the flowers are covered with tiny crystals. ▫ **crystal-gazer** *n.* [20C+] a person who manages to make successful predictions; thus an intelligent person. ▫ **crystal meth** *n.* [it comes in a crystalline powder] [1960s+] (*drugs*) crystal Methedrine.

c.s. *n.*[1] [abbr. CHICKENSHIT *n.*] [1940s+] (*orig. US*) a coward; a contemptible, disgusting person.

c.s. *n.*[2] [abbr. COCKSUCKING *n.*] [1970s–80s] (*US gay*) fellatio.

c.s.p. *n.* [abbr.] [1980s+] (*US campus*) a casual sex partner.

c.t. *n. see* COCKTEASER *n.*

C-3 *adj.* [play on A-1 *adj.* (1) with the third letter of the alphabet] [1910s–30s] third-rate, inadequate, inferior.

C-town *n.* [initial letter] [1990s+] (*US black*) Cleveland, Ohio.

cu *n.*[1] (*also* **cue, cuke**) [abbr.] [1930s+] a *cu*cumber.

cu *n.*[2] *see* COO *n.*

cub *n.*[1] [*cub* meaning a child, a young person, a novice or a beginner was briefly sl. in early 17C but soon SE] [17C–early 19C] (*UK Und.*) a novice gambler, one who is likely to be cheated of his cash.

cub *n.*[2] [2000s] (*S.Afr. gay*) a young homosexual man who associates with a BEAR *n.* (5c).

cub *n.*[3] *see* CUBBY *n.* (2).

Cubans *n.* (*also* **Cuban pumps**) [1970s+] (*US gay*) heavy work-boots.

Cuba Street Yank *n.* [*Cuba Street*, a central street in Wellington, N.Z., where American GIs would spend time during WW2 + YANK *n.* (1)] [2000s] (*N.Z.*) a brash American.

cubba *n.* (*also* **Miss Cubba**) [in W. African cultures *Cuba*, the day-name of a woman born on a Wednesday] [1940s+] (*W.I.*) **1** a promiscuous woman. **2** an effeminate man.

cubbitch *adj.* [SE *covetous*] [1950s+] (*W.I. Rasta*) covetous, thus both mean and greedy.

cubby *n.* [abbr. SE *cubby-hole*] **1** [mid-19C–1960s] (*US black/ Aus.*) a small room or space. **2** [late 19C+] (*Aus.*) (*also* **cobby, cub**) a child's playhouse, sited in the back garden.

cube *n.*[1] (*also* **cubes**) [shape] **1** [late 18C; 1920s] (*US tramp*) (*also* **cubicles, risk cubes**) in pl., dice. **2** [1910s+] (*drugs*) morphine, esp. 1oz (28g) (or what is sold as 1oz) of morphine [the shape of bulk supplies]. **3** [1960s] (*US campus*) in pl., the testicles. **4** [1960s+] (*drugs*) LSD [early LSD doses were often dripped onto sugar cubes for easy ingestion].

IN COMPOUNDS

▫ **cubehead** *n.* (*also* **cubie**) [-HEAD *sfx* (4)] [1960s–70s] (*drugs*) an LSD user, esp. when ingesting LSD dropped onto a sugar cube.

cube *n.*[2] [an intensified version or 'superlative' of SQUARE *n.* (1c)] [1950s–60s] an extreme conservative, an ultra-respectable person.

DERIVATIVES

▫ **Cubesville** *n.* [-VILLE *sfx*[1]] [1950s–60s] the fig. 'world' or mindset of ultra-conservative, highly respectable people. ▫ **cubistic** *adj.* [SE sfx *-istic*] [1960s] (*US*) extremely conventional.

cubit, the *n.* [William *Cubitt* (1785–1861) who invented the treadmill (albeit for grinding corn), which, from 1818, was introduced into British prisons as a form of punishment] [19C] the treadmill, as employed in prisons; thus *punishment by the cubit*, a spell on the treadmill.

cuck *n.* [abbr.] [mid-16C–early 18C] a cuckold; thus *cuckquean*, a female cuckold.

cuckaboo *n. see* KOOKABOO *n.*

cuckoo *n.*[1] [SE phr. *cuckoo in the nest*, denoting the oddness of such an individual] **1** [late 16C–early 18C] a cuckold [the cuckoo lays its eggs in another bird's nest]. **2** [late 16C+] (*also* **coo-coo**) a fool, an eccentric, a silly person. **3** [1920s] (*US*) something foolish, a failure.

IN COMPOUNDS

▫ **cuckoo academy** *n.* [1960s+] (*US*) a psychiatric institution. ▫ **cuckoo bird** *n.* [BIRD *n.*[1] (3a)] [1940s+] (*US*) an eccentric, a mad person. ▫ **cuckoo farm** *n.* [FARM *n.*[1]] [1960s+] (*US*) a psychiatric institution. ▫ **cuckoo house** *n.* [1930s+] (*US*) a psychiatric institution. □ **cuckoo juice** *n.* [JUICE *n.*[1] (3a); its potency sends one crazy] [1960s–70s] (*US*) strong liquor. □ **cuckoo's nest** *n.* [1960s+] (*US*) a psychiatric institution.

cuckoo *n.*[2] [? COCK *n.*[3] (1)] [late 19C] the penis.

cuckoo *n.*[3] [late 19C] (*US*) a prostitute.

cuckoo *adj.* (*also* **coo-coo, cookoo, cuckoo's nest, koo koo**) [CUCKOO *n.*[1] (2)] [20C+] crazy, eccentric, insane.

IN PHRASES

□ **knock cuckoo** *v.* (*also* **slap cuckoo**) [1920s–30s] (*US*) **1** to knock out. **2** to amaze, to astonish.

cuckoo *v.* [CUCKOO *n.*[1] (2)] [1930s] (*US*) to act foolishly, to mess up.

cuckoos *n.* [ety. unknown; link to dial. *cuckoo-penny*, a penny that if turned in the pocket on hearing the first cuckoo, will guarantee cash for the next year] [17C] money.

cuckoo's nest *n.* [play on SE; note apparently later CUCKOO *n.*[2]] [late 18C–1960s] the female genitals.

cuckoo's nest *adj.* *see* CUCKOO *adj.*

cucumber *n.*[1] [in summer time, when cucumbers ripen, a tailor's best customers, the gentry, are out of London, living on their country estates; thus tailors trad. took their holidays at this time] [late 17C–mid-19C] a tailor.

DERIVATIVES

□ **cucumberish** *adj.* [early 19C] poor, impoverished.

IN COMPOUNDS

□ **cucumber time** *n.* (*also* **cucumber season**) [late 17C] the summer time; thus a slack period in any job.

cucumber *n.*[2] [resemblance] [late 19C+] the penis.

cucumber *n.*[3] [rhy. sl.] [20C+] (*Aus.*) a number.

cud *n. see* UD *n.*

cuddie *n.* [? Devon dial. *cuddy*, a fellow-workman; a little girl] [1920s+] (*US black*) a friend; a lover.

cuddle and kiss *n.* [rhy. sl.] **1** [1910s+] a woman [= SE *miss*]. **2** [1960s+] an act of urination [= PISS *n.* (2)].

cuddle and kissed *adj.* [rhy. sl = PISSED *adj.*[1]] [1960s+] drunk.

cuddle-bunny *n. see under* BUNNY *n.*[1].

cuddy *n.*[1] [? dial. *cuddy*, a sucking lamb or kid] **1** [early 18C–mid-19C] a donkey. **2** [mid–late 19C] a fool. **3** [1900s–60s] (*Aus./Irish*) a (small) horse. **4** [1960s] (*Irish*) a young woman.

cuddy *n.*[2] [UK navy *cuddy*, the captain's cabin] [mid-19C] one's home, a room.

cuds *n.* [17C–mid-18C] used in oaths as a euph. for *God's*, e.g. *cud's bobs!* God's body!

cudsucker *n.* [euph. for COCKSUCKER *n.*] [1950s] (*US*) a general term of abuse.

cue *n.*[1] [? mid-15C *cue* or *q* (Lat. *quadrans*), half a farthing] [1940s–50s] (*US black*) a tip.

cue *n.*[2] *see* CU *n.*[1].

cue *v.* [for ety. *see* GO ON THE LETTER Q *under* Q *n.*[1]] [mid–late 19C] (*UK Und.*) to swindle by abusing one's credit.

cue-ball *n.* [resemblance to a billiards/snooker ball] [1940s] (*US*) a bald-headed person, or one with a crewcut.

cuff *n.*[1] [abbr. CUFFIN *n.* (1)] **1** [early 17C–early 19C] a mean, surly old fellow; often as *old cuff*. **2** [mid–late 17C] a jovial old man.

cuff *n.*[2] [the practice of pencilling debts in shops or bars on a celluloid *cuff*] [late 19C+] (*US*) credit, both lit. and fig.

DERIVATIVES

□ **cufferoo** *adj.* [-EROO *sfx*] [1940s] (*US*) free.

IN PHRASES

□ **on the cuff** (*orig. US*) **1** [1910s+] on account, on credit; thus *put on the cuff*, to give credit, to ask for credit. **2** [1920s+] for free. **3** [1940s+] (*N.Z.*) excessive; usu. as *a bit on the cuff* [? rhy. sl. = SE *rough*]. □ **swing the cuff** *v.* [1910s] to obtain on credit or for free.

SE in slang uses

IN COMPOUNDS

□ **cuffs and collar** *adj.* (*also* **collar-and-cuffs, cuff and collar**) [as opposed to more casual attire] [late 19C–1900s] (*Aus.*) middle-class, prissy, pernickety. □ **cuffs and collars** *n.* (*also* **cuff and collar brigade**) **1** [1900s] (*Aus.*) office workers. **2** [1960s+] pubic hair that matches the colour of the visible hair; thus ostensibly proving that a woman is not dyeing her hair. □ **cuff-shooter** *n.* [his continual 'shooting' of his cuffs] [late 19C–1900s] a clerk.

cuff *n.*[3] *see* CUFFY *n.*

cuff *v.*[1] [SE *cuff*, to strike with the fist; note Rötwelsch (Ger. rogues' cant) *kuffen*, to thrash] **1** [late 19C+] (*US black*) to hit, to fight. **2** [2000s] to defeat (in a competition).

SE in slang uses

IN PHRASES

□ **cuff Anthony** *v.* (*also* **cuff Jonas, knock anthony**) [SE *cuff*, to strike + generic use of *Anthony*/Jonas, a person, oneself] [late 18C–early 19C] **1** of one's knees, to knock together. **2** to strike the hands under the armpits to warm them. □ **cuff a/the carrot** *v. see under* CARROT *n.* □ **cuff one's/the dummy** *v. see* BEAT ONE'S/THE DUMMY *under* DUMMY *n.*[3].

cuff *v.*[2] [NB *OED* 2 edn offers two cites for cuff = to handcuff: 1693, 1851, but neither are listed as sl. and the term is 'rare'] [late 19C+] to handcuff.

cuff *v.*[3] [CUFF *n.*[2]] [1930s+] (*US*) **1** to place on credit. **2** to swindle.

cuff *v.*[4] [one's cuffs help to obscure the cigarette] **1** [1960s+] to hide a (marijuana) cigarette inside the cupped fingers. **2** [1990s+] to hide anything.

cuffa *n. see* CUFFER *n.*

cuff buttons *n.* [late 19C] (*US short order*) fishballs.

cuffee *n. see* CUFFY *n.*

cuffer *n.* (*also* **cuffa**) [dial. *cuff*, to tell a tale] [late 19C–1920s] (*Aus.*) a tale or story.

cuffin *n.* [? COVE *n.*] **1** [late 16C–mid-19C] a man, a fellow. **2** [early 18C] (*UK Und.*) a judge; a magistrate. **3** [mid-19C] (*UK Und.*) a prison warder.

IN COMPOUNDS

□ **cuffin-queer** *n.* (*also* **cuffin-quire, cuffin quier**) [var. on QUEER CUFFIN *under* QUEER *adj.*] [17C–mid-18C] a magistrate.

cuff it *v.* [SE *off the cuff*] [20C+] to extemporize, to respond to a situation spontaneously.

cuff link *n.* [rhy. sl.] [20C+] (*Aus.*) a drink.

cuff-link queen *n.* (*also* **cuff-link faggot, finger-bowl faggot**) [SE *cuff-link* + -QUEEN *sfx* (3)] [1960s] (*US gay*) a wealthy (older) male homosexual.

cuffo *n.* [CUFF *n.*[2] + -O *sfx* (7)] [1970s] (*US*) credit.

cuffo *adj.* [CUFFO *n.*] [1970s] (*US*) free.

cuffs *n.* [abbr.] [mid-19C+] (*orig. UK police/Und.*) hand*cuffs*.

cuffy *n.* (*also* **cuff, cuffee**) [Twi *kofi*, a boy born on a Friday. Like other terms based on name-days, the underlying implication is always that of rural simplicity, even stupidity and backwardness] **1** [early 18C+] (*US*) a black person, usu. in patronizing/derog. use; thus *cuffyism*, black society. **2** [19C] a bear. **3** [mid–late 19C] a young boy. **4** [1940s+] (*W.I.*) a fool, a gullible person.

IN PHRASES

□ **proud as cuffy** *adj.* [19C–1900s] conceited, lit. proud as a black man dressed up in his best clothes.

cuh *n. see* CUZ *n.*

cuirass *n. see* CURE-ARSE *n.*

cuke *n. see* CU *n.*[1].

culch *n.* [southern UK dial. *culch*, rubbish, refuse] **1** [mid-19C] second-rate (odds and ends of) meat. **2** [late 19C] (*US*) a derog. description of a person.

culchie *n.* (*also* **culchy, culshie**) [coined at University College, Galway, to describe agricultural students; ? Irish *Coillte mach* (Kiltimagh) Co. Mayo; Irish *coillte*, woods; Irish *cúl a' tí*, the backdoor of the great house, to which peasants would be directed; note Behan, *Confessions of an Irish Rebel* (1965): 'One night, Culchiemachs, as we call the Irish-speaking people, wished to play a game of pitch and toss'] [1940s+] (*Irish*) a derog. term for a country-dweller, as used by a townsperson.

cule *n.* [abbr. of synon. SE *reticule*] [mid-19C] (*UK Und.*) a small bag, carried on a woman's arm.

culing *n.* (*also* **culling**) [CULE *n.* + sfx *-ing*] [mid-19C] (*UK Und.*) stealing (bags and purses) from carriage seats.

cull *n.*[1] [? CULLY *n.*[1]; ? SE *cullion*, a contemptible person; ? fig. use of CULLS *n.*; in sense 2 Bee (1823) suggests that the cull was orig. 'a prostitute's favourite' before losing status to become merely 'a customer of any sort who pays for "favors secret, sweet, and precious".'] **1** [mid-17C–mid-19C] a prostitute's customer [Bee suggests that the cull was orig. 'a prostitute's favourite' before losing status to become merely 'a customer of any sort who pays for "favors secret, sweet, and precious".']. **2** [mid-17C–1930s] a dupe, a silly fellow, a simpleton, a fool. **3** [18C] a constable. **4** [18C–1930s] a man, a fellow, a chap. **5** [mid–late 19C] a friend.

IN COMPOUNDS

❑ **cull of the bing** *n.* [BINGO *n.*[1]] [mid-19C] (*US*) a tavern-keeper. ❑ **cull of the ken** *n.* [KEN *n.*[1] (1)] [mid-18C] (*UK Und.*) the master of the house.

cull *n.*[2] [SE *cull*, to select weak animals for killing] [1970s] **1** (*US campus*) a socially unacceptable person. **2** (*US campus, spec. fraternity*) anyone rejected for membership in a fraternity or sorority. **3** (*US prison*) a physically weak convict.

IN COMPOUNDS

❑ **cull bird** *n.* [1970s] (*US campus*) any woman considered socially or physically unacceptable.

cullee/culley *n. see* CULLY *n.*[1].

cullibility *n.* (*also* **cullability**) [CULLY *n.*[1] (1) + SE *gullibility*] [mid-18C–mid-19C] a willingness to be fooled.

culling *n. see* CULING *n.*

cullion *n.* (*also* **cullon**) [Fr. *coïon*, *coyon*, a poltroon] [mid-16C–17C] a general term of contempt, a base, despicable person; a rascal; thus *cullionly*, despicably, rascally.

cullions *n.* [Fr. *couillons*, testicles] [17C] the testicles.

cullot *n.* [ety. unknown] [mid-19C] (*US Und.*) a loafer, an idler.

culls *n.* [abbr. CULLIONS *n.*] [17C] the testicles.

cully *n.*[1] (*also* **cullee, culley**) [? as 'fool' there may be links to Ital. *coglione*, a dolt, but as 'man' it may well come from the Sp. Gypsy *chulai* or Turkish Gypsy *khulai*, both meaning man, or poss. fig. use of French *couillon*, testicles] **1** [mid-17C–19C] a simpleton, a victim. **2** [mid-17C–early 19C] a prostitute's customer; thus *cully-catching*, picking up customers. **3** [late 17C–19C] a fop, a dandy. **4** [late 17C–1910s] a man, a fellow, a companion, often a term of address.

IN COMPOUNDS

❑ **cully rumper** *n. see* RUMPER *n.* (1).

IN PHRASES

❑ **dark cully** *n. see under* DARK *adj.*

cully *n.*[2] [COLLIE *n.*] [1970s] (*W.I./Rasta*) top grade marijuana.

cully *v.* [i.e. to render a CULLY *n.*[1] (1)] [mid-17C–18C] to swindle, to cheat.

cully-shangy *n.* [Scot. *collie-shangie*, a disturbance, a noisy argument; ? ult. f. the sound of *collie* dogs fighting or f. Gaelic *callaidh*, wrangling, outcry] [19C] sexual intercourse.

culo *n.* [Sp. sl. *culo*, the anus] [1960s+] (*US*) the buttocks, the behind.

culp *n.* [Fr. *coup*, a blow; ult. Lat. *colaphus*, a box on the ear; however, note SE *culp*, fault, blame] [late 17C–mid-19C] a blow, a buffet.

Culpgill college *n.* [mid-19C] (*UK Und.*) the Giltspur Street prison.

culshie *n. see* CULCHIE *n.*

cultural fruit *n.* (*also* **culture fruit**) [negative racial stereotyping, i.e. *black* cultural fruit] [1960s+] (*US*) a watermelon.

culture *n.* [1950s+] (*W.I. Rasta*) reflecting or pertaining to the values and traditions respected by Rastafarians.

culture-vulture *n.* [derog. SE *culture-vulture*, one who is (affectedly) voracious for culture; thus an intellectual] **1** [1940s+] (*orig. US*) anyone who battens on to the prevailing cultural trends in order to debase and exploit them for economic gain, irrespective of the aesthetic loss involved. **2** [1940s+] (*US campus*) an over-zealous student. **3** [1980s] (*W.I./US black*) a Rastafarian term for white society.

culty-gun *n.* [Lat. *cultellus*, a knife + SE *gun*] [late 19C] the penis.

culver-headed *adj.* [SE *culver*, a dove or young pigeon] [mid–late 19C] foolish, weak-minded; thus *culver-head* a fool, a simpleton.

cum *n.* [CUM *v.*] [1960s+] **1** semen. **2** an ejaculation. **3** an orgasm (for either sex).

DERIVATIVES

❑ **cummy** *adj.* [1960–70s] redolent of semen.

IN COMPOUNDS

❑ **cum...** *see also under* COME *n.* ❑ **cumchugger** *n.* [CHUG *v.*[1]] [1990s+] an enthusiastic fellatrix. ❑ **cum chum** *n.* [CHUM *n.* (1)] [20C+] (*US*) a homosexual male. ❑ **cum drum** *n.* (*also* **come-drum, cundrum**) [1930s+] a condom with a reservoir for semen. ❑ **cum dumpster** *n.* (*also* **cum catcher**) [SAmE *dumpster* = UK *skip*] [1990s+] (*US teen*) a promiscuous young woman or girl. ❑ **cum freak** *n.* [-FREAK *sfx*] [1960s+] a promiscuous man or woman, obsessed with sexual gratification. ❑ **cum queen** *n.* [2000s] (*S.Afr. gay*) a homosexual man who likes semen, whether swallowed during oral sex or ejaculated over his body. ❑ **cum shot** *n.* [1970s+] (*orig. US*) in pornographic film-making, the moment of ejaculation, invariably performed (for the camera) outside the partner's body. ❑ **cum-sucking** *adj.* [1990s+] (*US*) a general insult; lit. 'semen-sucking'.

cum *v.* [often found, e.g. in written pornography, as an alternative to COME *v.*[1]; the sp. enhances the sexual aspect of the otherwise common word] [1950s+] to achieve orgasm.

cummifo *adj.* [mispron. of Fr. *comme il faut*] [late 19C–1900s] satisfactory, correct, lit. 'as things should be'.

cumshaw *n.* [Chinese *kam-sia*, the Amoy pronunciation of the Chinese words *kan*, to be grateful + *hsieh*, thanks; thus 'grateful thanks'] [19C–1960s] a bribe, a tip, a present; also as v.

cundrum *n. see* CUM DRUM *under* CUM *n.*

cundum *n.* [SE *cundum* or *condom*, a contraceptive sheath] [late 18C–early 19C] a false scabbard used to hide a sword.

cundy *n. see* COONIE *n.*

cung *n.* [ety. unknown] [1980s+] (*drugs*) cannabis.

cuniculary warehouse *n.* [joc. elaboration of CUNNY *n.* (1)] [early 18C] a brothel.

cunker *n.* (*also* **kunker**) [CUNT *n.* (1)] [1970s+] (*US gay*) the vagina.

cunnie *n. see* CUNNY *n.*

cunnikin *n.* (*also* **cuntkin, cuntlet**) [dimin. of CUNNY *n.* (1), ult. CUNT *n.* (1)] [18C] the vagina.

cunning *adj.*

SE in slang uses

IN COMPOUNDS

❑ **cunning man** *n.* [note dial. *cunning woman*, a witch] **1** [17C–18C] a confidence trickster who used a (spurious) knowledge of astrology to help to convince his or (more often) her victims; the preferred swindle was the 'miraculous' recovery of stolen goods. **2** [late 18C–early 19C] a trial judge. ❑ **cunning shaver** *n.* [SHAVER *n.*[1] (1), but also one who 'shaves his victims close'] [late 18C] a clever cheat.

IN PHRASES

❑ **cunning as a Maori dog** *adj.* (*also* **cunning as a Maori hen**) [racially derog. comparison] [1920s+] (*N.Z.*) very cunning. ❑ **cunning as a shithouse rat** *adj. see under* SHITHOUSE RAT *n.* ❑ **cunning as a (whole) wagon-load of monkeys** *adj.* (*also* **artful as a (whole) wagon-load of monkeys, cunning as a cartload of monkeys**) [late 19C+] very cunning.

cunningberry *n.* (*also* **cunningbury**) [ironic pun on SE *cunning* + SE *-berry/-bury*, a sfx meaning 'place'] [early–mid-19C] a fool, a gullible person.

cunningham *n.* (*also* **Mr Cunningham**) [ironic pun on SE *cunning* + SE *-ham*, a sfx meaning 'place'] [late 18C–early 19C] a fool, a gullible person.

cunny *n.* (*also* **cunnie**) [SE *coney*, rabbit] **1** [early 17C+] the vagina (cf. CONY *n.* (2)). **2** [2000s] (*UK black*) cunnilingus. **3** *see* CONY *n.* (3).

IN COMPOUNDS

□ **cunny...** *see also under* CONY and its combs. □ **cunny alley** *n.* (*also* **coney court, cony-hall, cunny hall**) [mid-17C–mid-18C] the vagina. □ **cunny-haunted** *adj.* [late 19C] of a man, obsessed with sex. □ **cunny-skin** *n.* [mid-17C–19C] the female pubic hair. □ **cunny-thumbed** *adj.* (*also* **coney-thumbed**) [late 18C–early 19C; 1920s] able to 'double one's fist, with the thumb inwards, like a woman' (Grose, 1785). □ **cunny-thumper** *n.* [lit. 'vagina-hitter'] [1970s] (*US*) a villain, a rascal. □ **cunny warren** *n.* (*also* **coney-warren**) [SE *warren*; the phr. puns on *bunny*, rabbit] **1** [18C] a brothel. **2** [18C] a girls' boarding school. **3** [19C] the vagina.

IN PHRASES

□ **go cunny-catching** *v.* [pun on CONY-CATCHING *n.*] [18C] of a man, to have sexual intercourse.

cunny-burrow *n.* (*also* **cony-berry, cunny-barrow, Cunnyborough**) [CUNNY *n.* (1) + SE *burrow*] [17C–19C] the vagina; thus a woman.

IN COMPOUNDS

□ **cunny-burrow ferret** *n.* [FERRET *n.*[2] (1)] [early 17C–19C] the penis.

cunt *n.* [orig. ME but taboo since 15C. *Cunt* itself, 'a nasty word for a nasty thing', as Grose (1788) dismisses it, appears as 'C–t', although he offers roots in the Gk *konnos* and the Lat. *cunnus*, and lists the Fr. synon. *con*. This reticence was by no means limited to Grose (who, a single entry earlier, was perfectly happy to list *cunny-thumbed* (*see under* CUNNY *n.*)). Not until its supplement of 1972 did the *OED* (albeit unfazed by PRICK *n.* (1) since the late 19C) list the term, and other, lesser dictionaries, on both sides of the Atlantic, showed themselves equally coy. Many otherwise authoritative American tomes, hamstrung either by the religious right or the politically correct left, have yet to break the taboo. Yet, as Partridge, writing in 1931 (six years before the term was included in the *DSUE*), put it: 'To ignore a very frequently used word – one indeed used by a large proportion, though not the majority, of the white population of the British Empire – is to ignore a basic part of the English language.' The first use the *OED* can find for the term appears *c.*1230, when *Gropecuntelane* is listed among the streets that made up the 'stews' (brothel area) of Cheapside. Given the environment, it must be assumed that the term was already in general use. It would also appear from subsequent early citations that the term, while vulgar, was descriptive rather than obscene. Lanfranc, for instance, used it while writing his *Chirurgia Magna* in 1363. But by the end of the 15C cunt was unacceptable and two centuries later it was deemed legally obscene, and to print the word in full rendered one liable to prosecution. Its most notorious appearance in the dock came in 1960 in the trial of *Lady Chatterley's Lover*. It has yet, if ever, to return to grace. As Grose suggested, the word can be traced back to the Gk, although E.P. disputes whether *konnus* – a trinket, a beard, or the wearing of the hair in a tuft – is actually linked to the Lat. *cunnus*, which meant both vagina and, like such English terms as CRACK *n.*[3], SLIT *n.* (1) and PUSSY *n.*, the woman (esp. if seen as promiscuous) who possesses it. More likely Gk roots are *kusos* and *kusthos*, which are both related to the earlier Sanskrit *cushi*, meaning ditch. *Cunnus* itself, setting a pattern for its descendant, was already outlawed as obscene in Rome. Horace used it, Cicero did not. While the French, more heavily influenced by Lat., have *con* (and the Spanish *coño*), with its obvious links to *cunnus*, the English 'cunt' or *cunte*, as found in ME, takes its inspiration from a variety of Ger. (*Kunte*) and Scandinavian (*kunta, kunte*) terms. It would appear, in this form, to be a comb. of the ultimate root *cu* (which also lies at the basis of cow), which appears to imply quintessential femininity and the *nt* of the European synons. Note *val cava*, 'used by Boccaccio for a woman's private parts, a hollow cavity or valley' (Florio, *Worlde of Words*, 1598)] **1** [15C+] (*also* **cuntie**) the vagina. **2** [mid-19C+] a woman considered purely as a sex object. **3** [20C+] copulation with a woman. **4** [20C+] a fool, a dolt, an unpleasant person of either sex; a general term of abuse. **5** [1930s+] a derog. term for a woman; occas. in male homosexual context. **6** [1930s+] an infuriating object, often mechanical. **7** [1940s] (*US gay*) a term of address, used archly as an affectionate derog. term. **8** [1960s+] (*US gay*) the mouth or rectum as a sexual receptacle. **9** [1960s+] (*US gay*) the buttocks. **10** [1960s+] commercial sex; prostitution. **11** [1970s] (*drugs*) the area of a vein into which one injects narcotics; the crease inside the elbow. **12** [1970s] a synon. for *damn* in GIVE A DAMN *v.* **13** [1970s+] a sexually attractive woman. **14** [1970s+] any thing, object or place. **15** [1970s+] a person, usu. male, with no negative implications. **16** [1980s] in fig. use, the essence, the 'daylights'. **17** [1980s+] something very difficult or unpleasant to do or achieve.

DERIVATIVES

□ **cunting** *adj.* [20C+] an intensive term of abuse, derision, dismissal etc. □ **cuntish** *adj.* [1970s] stupid, unpleasant. □ **cuntless** *adj.* [1960s–80s] (*US black*) a general derog. epithet for a woman.

IN COMPOUNDS

□ **cunt-bitten** *adj.* [16C] syphilitic. □ **cunt book** *n.* [1970s] (*US prison*) pornography. □ **cunt-breath** *n. see* DICK-BREATH *under* DICK *n.*[1]. □ **cunt-buster** *n.* [2000s] (*US*) a penis. □ **cunt-chaser** *n.* [1930s] a womanizer. □ **cunt-collar** *n.* [one has been 'arrested' by one's desire] [fig. use of COLLAR *n.* (3b)] [1960s] (*US*) the supposed entrapment of a man by a woman's sexuality. □ **cunt-curtain** *n.* [late 19C] the female pubic hair. □ **cunt-eyed** *adj.* [fig. use of sense 1 above as a 'slit' + sfx *-eyed*] [1910s+] (*US*) used of a person with narrow, squinting eyes. □ **cunt fringe** *n.* [late 19C] the female pubic hair. □ **cunt hair** *n.* (*also* **cunt's hair, pussy hair**) [1950s+] (*US*) an infinitesimally small amount. □ **cunt-hat** *n.* [? pun on 'felt', i.e. 'felt up' + ? shape of the trilby] [1920s] a trilby or felt hat. □ **cunthead** *n.* [-HEAD *sfx* (1)] [1970s+] (*orig. US*) a fool. □ **cunt-hook** *n.* [1990s+] (*UK juv.*) **1** the penis. **2** an insulting term of address. □ **cunt-hooks** *n.* (*also* **twat-hooks**) **1** [early 19C; 1950s+] fingers. **2** [1990s+] a term of endearment, may also be used as a casual greeting. □ **cunt-hound** *n.* (*also* **cunt-hunter**) [-HOUND *sfx*] [1950s+] a man who is obsessed with sex and seduction. □ **cunt juice** *n. see* JUICE *n.*[1] (2a). □ **cunt-lapper/-lapping** *see* separate entries. □ **cunt-lick/-licker/-licking** *see* separate entries. □ **cunt-lips** *n.* [late 19C] the labia. □ **cunt-man** *n.* (*also* **cuntsman**) [1960s+] (*US campus*) a sexual athlete. □ **cunt-muncher** *n.* [MUNCH *v.*[1] (2)] [2000s] (*S.Afr. gay*) a lesbian. □ **cunt pensioner** *n.* [Fr. *pensionaire*, a lodger] [19C] a kept man, a pimp. □ **cunt plugger** *n.* [late 19C] the penis; thus *cunt plugging*, sexual intercourse. □ **cuntprick** *n.* [PRICK *n.* (3)] [1990s+] a general term of abuse. □ **cunt-rag** *n.* [1940s–70s] a sanitary towel. □ **cunt-rammer** *n. see* RAMMER *n.* (1). □ **cunt rug** *n.* [RUG *n.*[1]] [1990s+] the female pubic hair. □ **cunt scratchers** *n.* [1990s+] the hands. □ **cunt's hair** *n. see* CUNT HAIR above. □ **cuntsman** *n. see* CUNT-MAN above. □ **cuntsmith** *n.* [SE sfx *-smith*, on model of SE *blacksmith*] [1960s] (*US*) a gynaecologist. □ **cuntstand** *n.* [STAND *n.* (2)] [19C+] sexual enthusiasm in a woman. □ **cunt-starver** *n.* [the Deserted Wives & Children's Act, known as the *Cunt Act*] [1950s+] (*Aus.*) a man who defaults on his maintenance payments. □ **cunt-stopper** *n.* [late 19C] the penis. □ **cunt-stretcher** *n.* [late 19C] the penis. □ **cunt-struck** *adj.* [mid-19C+] (of a man) obsessed with sex, or with a particular woman. □ **cunt-sucker** *n.* **1** [1940s+] a cunnilinguist. **2** [1960s+] (*orig. US*) a repellent, loathed, unpleasant person. **3** [1990s+] (*US*) a derog. term for a lesbian. □ **cunt-swab** *n.* [late 19C] female underwear. □ **cunt-teaser** *n.* [20C+] a man who excites a woman sexually but refuses to have intercourse. □ **cunt-tickler** *n.* [1960s+] (*US*) a moustache. □ **cunt-wagon** *n.* [1970s+] (*US*) a flashy car seen as an adjunct to the seduction of foolishly impressionable young women. □ **cunt-wig** *n.* [late 19C] the female pubic hair.

IN PHRASES

□ **as a cunt** *adv. see* AS A BASTARD *under* BASTARD *n.* □ **come the (old) cunt** *v.* [20C+] to act in an obnoxious or obstreperous manner; esp. in phr. *don't come the old cunt with me.* □ **cunt** up *adj.* [var. on BELLY UP *adj.*[2] (1)] [2000s] wrong, failed. ▫ **have a bit of cunt** *v.* [late 18C+] to have sexual intercourse. ▫ **like a cunt** [1920s] used as an intensifier. ▫ **make a coffee-house out of a woman's cunt** *v.* (*also* **make a lobster kettle out of one's cunt**) [pun; the popularity of SE *coffeehouses* as social centres, rather than places for eating and drinking] [late 18C] to perform coitus interruptus, i.e. 'to go in and out and spend nothing' (Grose, 1785). ▫ **talk cunt** *v.* [1920s] to talk about sex, to tell smutty jokes. ▫ **that's not cunt, that's peehole** [PEEHOLE *n.*, i.e. THINK IT'S JUST TO PEE THROUGH *under* PEE *v.*] [1970s] (*US*) a phr. used to suggest that a girl is not yet ready for intercourse.

IN EXCLAMATIONS

▫ **stick it up your cunt!** [1930s+] (*Aus.*) a general expression of disdain, dismissal, rejecting the previous speaker's idea, opinion, insult etc.

cunt *adj.* [CUNT *n.* (4)] [1950s+] a general term of abuse, stupid, unpleasant, incompetent etc.

cunt *v.* [fig. use of CUNT *n.* (1)] [1990s+] to destroy, to defeat, whether physically or otherwise.

cunt! *excl.* [CUNT *n.* (1)] [1930s+] a general excl. of annoyance.

cunted *adj.*[1] [CUNT *n.* (1)] [late 19C] of a man, having one's penis in a woman's vagina.

cunted *adj.*[2] [fig. use of CUNT *n.* (1)] [1990s+] extremely drunk.

cuntface *n.* [CUNT *n.* (1) + SE *face*] [late 19C+] a term of address to an unattractive person; a general derog. term.

IN COMPOUNDS

▫ **cuntfaced** *adj.* (*also* **cuntface**) [1940s+] unattractive, a general derog. epithet.

cuntie *n. see* CUNT *n.* (1).

cuntkin *n. see* CUNNIKIN *n.*

cunt-lapper *n.* [CUNT *n.* (1) + SE *lapper*] **1** [1910s+] a cunnilinguist. **2** [1930s] a lesbian. **3** [1950s+] (*also* **cuntlap**) a general term of abuse.

cunt-lapping *n.* [CUNT-LAPPER *n.*] [1910s+] (*orig. US*) cunnilingus.

cunt-lapping *adj.* [CUNT-LAPPER *n.* (3)] [1920s+] (*US*) of a person, despicable, repellent, disgusting.

cuntlet *n. see* CUNNIKIN *n.*

cunt-lick *v.* (*also* **give cunt-licks**) [CUNT *n.* (1)] [late 19C+] to perform cunnilingus.

cunt-licker *n.* [CUNT *n.* (1) + SE *licker*] [1940s+] (*orig. US*) **1** a cunnilinguist. **2** a general term of abuse.

cunt-licking *adj.* [CUNT-LICKER *n.* (2)] [1980s+] (*US*) a general abusive epithet.

cuntocks *n.* [CUNT *n.* (1) + COCK *n.*[3] (1)] [1990s+] the labia.

cup *n.*

SE in slang uses

with ref. to drunkenness

IN COMPOUNDS

▫ **cupman** *n.* [mid–late 19C] a drunkard. ▫ **cup-shaken** *adj.* (*also* **cup-sprung, -stricken**) [early–mid-17C] drunk. ▫ **cupshot** *adj.* [fig. *shot* by one's consumption of *cups*] [mid-16C–mid-19C] drunk. ▫ **cupsweat** *adj.* [mid-19C] (*UK Und.*) drunk.

IN PHRASES

▫ **cup of the creature** *n. see* DROP (OF THE CREATURE) *n.* ▫ **cup too low, a** [the person needs another *cup* to become more loquacious] [late 17C–early 18C] describing someone who remains silent in company.

general uses

IN COMPOUNDS

▫ **cup and can** *n.* [a cup is filled from a can; thus one friend nourishes the other] [mid-16C–mid-19C] great friends. ▫ **cup-tosser** *n.* **1** [mid-19C] a juggler. **2** [mid–late 19C] a fortune-teller who uses tea leaves (occas. coffee grounds) as a medium of prediction.

cup *v.* [SE *cup*] [early 19C] **1** to toast (a person). **2** to imprison [fig. use, one is 'placed in it'].

cupboard *n.* [mid-19C] (*US*) the stomach.

cupcake *n.* [fig. uses of SE *cupcake*, a cake baked from ingredients measured by the cupful, or baked in a small cup] **1** [1930s+] (*US*) an attractive young woman; also as affectionate term of address. **2** [1960s+] (*US*) usu. in pl., the female breasts. **3** [1970s] (*US gay*) a young homosexual man. **4** [1970s+] (*US gay*) in pl., buttocks, esp. when tight, firm and small.

cupcakes *n.* [joc. use of SE] [1980s+] (*US drugs*) LSD.

Cupid *n.* **1** [mid-18C–early 19C] a nickname for an ugly blind man [*Cupid*, as the god of love, is trad. blind]. **2** [late 19C] a pimp who lives with his prostitute [ironic use; the relationship is so rarely affectionate].

proper name in slang uses

IN COMPOUNDS

▫ **Cupid's alley** *n.* [mid–late 19C] the vagina. ▫ **Cupid's anvil** *n.* [late 19C] the vagina. ▫ **Cupid's arbour** *n.* [19C] the vagina. ▫ **Cupid's arms** *n.* [19C] the vagina. ▫ **Cupid's battering ram** *n.* [late 19C] the penis. ▫ **Cupid's cave** *n.* (*also* **Cupid's cloister, ...cupboard, ...feast, ...furrow, ...hotel, ...warehouse**) [19C] the vagina. ▫ **Cupid's itch** *n.* [1920s+] (*US*) gonorrhoea. ▫ **Cupid's kettledrums** *n.* (*also* **kettledrums**) [late 18C–early 19C] the female breasts. ▫ **Cupid's measles** *n.* [1940s+] (*US*) secondary syphilis.

IN PHRASES

▫ **take a turn in Cupid's alley** *v.* (*also* **take a turn in Cupid's corner and hair court**) [19C] to have sexual intercourse.

cupola *n.* [SE *cupola*, a rounded vault or dome forming the roof of any building or part of a building] [late 19C–1950s] (*US*) the head.

cuppa *n.* (*also* **cupper**) [abbr./pron.] [1930s+] (*orig. Aus.*) a cup of tea, occas. coffee.

cups *n.* [the implication being that the sleep is a drunken one] [1930s–50s] (*US black*) sleep.

cura *n.* [Sp. *cura*, a cure] [1960s–70s] (*US drugs*) heroin, esp. when it is injected or smoked when one is suffering from withdrawal symptoms.

curate *n.* [all senses play on the junior, and thus inferior, position of a curate in the local church hierarchy] **1** [late 19C] a small poker, with an iron tip; such a poker is actually used, as opposed to the elaborate brass fire-irons, displayed only for show. **2** [late 19C] a handkerchief that is actually used, rather than one that is worn for fashionable display. **3** [late 19C] the top half of a sliced teacake, which receives less butter. **4** [late 19C–1900s] (*Anglo-Irish*) a grocer's assistant. **5** [late 19C–1940s] (*Irish*) an assistant barman.

curb *n.*[1] [SE *curb*, to bend] [late 16C–early 17C] (*UK Und.*) the pole with a hook on one end that is used to steal items from stall or shop windows.

curb *n.*[2]

SE in slang uses

IN COMPOUNDS

▫ **curb-preach** *v.* [1990s+] (*US black*) to lecture, to give advice. ▫ **curb sailor** *n. see* CURBSTONE SAILOR *under* CURBSTONE *adj.* ▫ **curbstone** *see* separate entries.

IN PHRASES

▫ **put someone to the curb** *v.* [1990s+] (*US*) to dismiss from employment. ▫ **to the curb** (*also* **to the curve**) [1980s+] (*US black/campus*) **1** ugly, distasteful, unpleasant. **2** impoverished [synon. of SE phr. *in the gutter*]. ▫ **to the curb, be** *v.* [the polite person steps off the pavement and carefully vomits into the gutter] [1980s+] (*US campus*) to vomit. ▫ **shoved to the curb** [1910s] overwhelmed, defeated.

curb *v.* [CURB *n.*[1]] [late 16C] (*UK Und.*) to use a hook on a pole to steal from stalls, windows or open shop fronts.

IN COMPOUNDS

▫ **curbing law** *n.* [LAW *n.* (1)] [16C–early 19C] (*UK Und.*) theft accomplished by 'fishing' for objects through open windows, using some form of hooked pole.

curber *n.* (*also* **curb**) [CURB *v.*] [late 16C–mid-17C] (*UK Und.*) a villain who steals by extracting goods from an open window.

curbie *n.* [1990s+] (*US juv.*) lit. a student who smokes between classes on the curb outside the school; thus ext. to mean any school rebel.

curbstone *n.* (*also* **kerbstone**) [1920s–30s] (*US tramp*) a cigarette made from the remains of extinguished cigarettes dropped in the gutter.

curbstone *adj.* (*also* **kerbstone**) [SE *curbstone/kerbstone*; i.e. that which is delivered in the street] [mid-19C+] a general term meaning informal, casual, often quasi-legal.

IN COMPOUNDS

❑ **curbstone broker** *n.* (*also* **curbstoner, kerbstone broker**) [the original *kerbstone brokers* were those brokers of the New York Stock Exchange who were excluded from the reorganization of the institution in 1848 when it left the street, where it had operated, and moved indoors] **1** [mid-19C] anyone who operates an informal and poss. illicit business. **2** [mid-19C–1900s] a street urchin. ❑ **curbstone canary** *n.* (*also* **kerbstone canary**) [ironic use of CANARY *n.*[1] (4c)] [1930s] (*US tramp*) a whinging beggar. ❑ **curbstone chapel** *n.* (*also* **kerbstone chapel**) [late 19C] (*US Und.*) preaching or using religiosity to obtain money. ❑ **curbstone jockey** *n.* (*also* **kerbstone jockey**) [1980s+] (*N.Z.*) a safe job. ❑ **curbstone justice** *n.* (*also* **kerbstone justice**) [mid-19C] (*US*) rough justice, delivered impromptu and without benefit of official warnings of criminal proceedings, typically the policeman's 'clip around the ear' delivered to errant youngsters. ❑ **curbstone language** *n.* (*also* **kerbstone language**) [1900s] (*N.Z.*) coarse language, i.e. that 'of the gutter'. ❑ **curbstone mixture** *n.* (*also* **kerbstone mixture, ...plug, ...twist**) [1930s–50s] tobacco that is extracted from discarded 'fag-ends' and recycled in a pipe or 'roll-up'. ❑ **curbstone philosopher** *n.* (*also* **curbstone orator, kerbstone orator/philosopher**) [1920s] anyone who appoints themselves a purveyor of knowledge and delivers that knowledge from a position on a street corner or outside a store. ❑ **curbstone sailor** *n.* (*also* **curb sailor, kerbstone sailor**) [SE *sailor*; i.e. she 'sails' the streets] [mid-19C+] a prostitute. ❑ **curbstone setter** *n.* (*also* **kerbstone setter**) [1930s+] (*US*) a mongrel.

curby *n.* [SE *curb* + sfx *-y*] [1930s] (*US*) a waiter or waitress who serves customers in their parked car.

curby hocks *n.* [SE *curby hocks*, the hock or other part of a horse's leg which is afflicted by a hard swelling] [mid-19C–1900s] clumsy feet.

curdle *v.* (*also* **sour**) [1930s–40s] **1** (*US Und.*) of a scheme or plan, to go wrong, to misfire. **2** (*US*) to irritate, to cause annoyance.

curds *n.* [17C] vaginal secretions.

cure *n.* [abbr. SE *curiosity* or *curious person*] [mid-19C–1930s] an eccentric person.

cure *v.* [SE *cure*, to improve, applied to a variety of substances including leather, rubber and plastic] **1** [1960s] (*drugs*) to mix two drugs together to create a greater level of enjoyment. **2** [1960s+] (*drugs*) to improve the quality of a batch of marijuana; methods include steeping it in rum or some other spirit, placing it in the deep freeze, mixing it with another variety of marijuana or some other drug and so on. **3** [1980s+] (*US drugs*) to heat hashish so that it is easier to crumble and thus use in a cigarette or pipe.

cure-arse *n.* (*also* **cuirass**) [SE *cure* + ARSE *n.* (1)] [late 18C–early 19C] an absorbent plaster applied to buttocks and thighs that have been chafed by too much riding.

cured of a tympany with two heels, be *v. see* TWO-LEGGED TYMPANY *n.*

curflummux *v. see* KERFLUMMOX *under* KER- *pfx.*

curl *n.* (*also* **curler**) **1** [1970s+] (*US black*) constr. with *the*, a Jheri curl [*Jheri* Redding, who in the 1970s invented this black hairstyle, in which the normal tight curls of black hair are replaced by straighter, softer curls, with a shiny wet look]. **2** [1990s+] a piece of excrement [resemblance].

SE in slang uses

IN COMPOUNDS

❑ **curl paper** *n.* [SE, i.e. its shape; the link to CURL *n.* (2) may be coincidental] [late 19C] lavatory paper.

IN PHRASES

❑ **do twelve-ounce curls** *v.* [play on weight-lifting jargon; the lifting of a 12oz beer can] [1980s+] (*US campus*) to drink beer.

curl *v.*[1] [? the curlicues and flourishes that adorn the handwriting of a good calligrapher. Good students would be assumed to write well as part of their overall excellence] [mid-19C–1910s] (*US campus*) to do well in class, esp. to recite faultlessly; thus *curler*, a first-rate student.

SE in slang uses

IN PHRASES

❑ **curl one off** *v.* (*also* **curl one out**) [note CURL *n.* (2)] [1990s+] to defecate. ❑ **curl someone's hair** *v.* [20C+] (*orig. US*) to scold severely. ❑ **curl someone up** *v.* [late 19C] (*US*) to kill someone. ❑ **curl the mo** *see* separate entries.

curl *v.*[2] [1950s] (*US*) to hit.

curle *n.* (*also* **curl**) [the slivers of metal curled as they were clipped] [late 17C–18C] clippings from money.

curled darlings *n.* [the long beards and curled moustaches such officers sported] [late 19C–1900s] (*UK society*) army officers, esp. those who had returned from fighting in the Crimean War (1854–6); by ext. one who is spoiled.

curler *n.*[1] [CURLE *n.*] [early–mid-19C] (*UK Und.*) one who 'sweats' gold coins by rubbing them together to procure gold dust.

curler *n.*[2] **1** *see* CURL *n.* **2** *see* CURL *v.*[1].

curlicue *n. see* CARLEYCUE *n.*

curlies *n. see* SHORT AND CURLIES *n.*

curls *n.* [early 19C] human teeth, esp. as extracted by body-snatchers.

curl-the-mo *adj.* (*also* **curl-a-mo, kurl-a-mo, kurl-the-mo**) [CURL THE MO *v.*] [1940s+] (*Aus.*) excellent, first-rate, a good deal, e.g. *curl-the-mo mazuma*, a great deal of money.

curl the mo *v.* (*also* **kurl the mo**) [the image of a man curling the tips of his moustache in a self-satisfied manner] [1920s+] (*Aus.*) to succeed brilliantly, to win.

curly *n.* [heavy-handed irony] [1910s+] a nickname for a bald person.

curly *adj.* [SE *curly* hair being seen as attractive] [1930s+] (*N.Z.*) of a person, attractive; of an object or event, first-rate.

SE in slang uses

IN COMPOUNDS

❑ **curly fellas/hairs** *n. see* SHORT AND CURLIES *n.* ❑ **curly one** *n.* [it is not 'straight'] [1950s+] (*mainly Aus./N.Z.*) a tricky problem, a challenge. ❑ **curly wolf** *n.* [qualities of the animal, but note prev.] [1910s+] a tough, tricky individual.

curly locks *n.* [rhy. sl.] [20C+] (*Aus.*) socks.

curly-wurly *n.* [the curled sidelocks or *payess* that are worn by Hasidic Jews] [2000s] a Hasidic, i.e. ultra-orthodox, Jew.

curp *n.* (*also* **kaykirp, kerp**) [backsl. PRICK *n.* (1)] [1970s+] the penis.

currant bread *adj.* [rhy. sl.] [1990s+] dead.

currant bun *n.* [rhy. sl.] **1** [1930s+] the sun. **2** [1940s] the number one. **3** [1960s] (*Aus.*) a German [= HUN *n.* (1)]. **4** [1960s+] one's son. **5** [1980s] (*Aus.*) a nun. **6** [1980s] (*Aus.*) a gun. **7** [1980s+] *The Sun* newspaper.

currant cake *adj.* [rhy. sl.] [1960s–80s] (*Aus.*) awake.

currant-cakey *adj.* [rhy. sl.] [1920s+] shaky.

currants and plums *n.* [rhy. sl. = THRUMS *n.* (1)] [mid-19C] threepence.

curry *n.*

SE in slang uses

IN COMPOUNDS

❑ **curry-bunny** *n.* [S.Afr. colloq. *bunny chow* f. Hind. *bania*, a caste of merchants, thus generic for a Gujerati businessman, who followed a vegetarian diet and for whom a café-owner created the dish] [1950s+] (*S.Afr.*) vegetarian curry sold as a take-away in a hollowed-out half loaf of bread. ❑ **curry-muncher** *n.* (*also* **curry, curry-eater**) [culinary stereotyping] **1** [20C+] (*Aus./N.Z.*) a derog. term for an Indian. **2** [2000s] (*N.Z.*) a man who has sexual intercourse with an Indian woman [MUNCH *v.*[1] (2)]. ❑ **curry nigger** *n.* [NIGGER *n.*[1] (1)] [2000s] (*US black*) an Indian, a Hindu. ❑ **curry queen** *n.* [-QUEEN *sfx* (3)] [1990s+] (*S.Afr./US*) a gay man who is attracted to Indian homosexuals.

IN PHRASES

❑ **give someone curry** *v.* (*also* **give curried hell, give some curry**) [SE *curry* is seen as 'hot', but note mid-19C Aus. pidgin *give someone kurrajong*, to hang with a rope made from kurrajong fibre] [1930s+] (*Aus.*) to attack (verbally or physically), 'to make things hot' for someone.

curry and rice *n.* [rhy. sl.] [1950s+] (*Aus.*) the price.

curry someone's skin-coat *v.* (*also* **curry someone's coat, ...hide, ...jacket**) [SE *curry*, to dress tanned leather; note Grose (1785): 'to curry any one's hide, to beat him'] [mid-17C–1910s] to thrash, to beat.

curse *n. see* CUSS *n.*[1] (1).

curse, the *n.* (*also* **curse of God**) [abbr. SE *the curse of Eve*] [20C+] a euph. for a menstrual period.

cursed-cull *n.* [SE *cursed* + CULL *n.*[1] (2)] [late 17C–18C] an ill-natured person, esp. towards women.

curse of God *n.* **1** [early 19C] a cockade [the cockades worn by the atheistic French revolutionaries]. **2** [1920s–50s] (*Aus.*) (*also* **curse of Cain**) the bundle or pack carried by an itinerant worker or tramp. **3** *see* CURSE, THE *n.*

curse of Scotland *n.* **1** [late 18C–early 19C] the nine of diamonds [diamonds imply royalty, and according to legend every ninth king of Scotland was 'a tyrant and a curse to that country' (Grose, 1785). A further suggestion is that the nine of diamonds resembles the arms of the Duke of Argyll, who was one of the leading proponents of union with England, a move that was not wholly welcomed by his compatriots. Hotten (1860) suggests that this card was that on which 'Butcher' Cumberland wrote the orders for the mopping up of rebels after Culloden (1746), that nine lozenges are the arms of Dalrymple, Earl of Stair 'detested for his share in the Massacre of Glencoe', that the arrangement of diamonds resembles the St Andrew's Cross and adds 'the most probable explanation is, that in the game of Pope Joan the nine of diamonds is the Pope, of whom the Scots have an especial horror']. **2** [20C+] whisky.

cursetor *n.* (*also* **cursitor**) [Lat. *currere*, to run] **1** [mid-16C–early 18C] a tramp, spec. one of the Forty-second Order of Vagabonds [SE *cursitor*, a courier]. **2** [late 18C] one of the 'broken, pettifogging attornies or Newgate solicitors' (Grose, 1785) [ult. SE: 'one of twenty-four officers or clerks of the Court of Chancery, whose office it was to make out all original writs de cursu, i.e. of common official course or routine, each for the particular shire or shires for which he was appointed' (*OED*)].

curtail *n. see* CURTAL *n.*

curtain *n.*

SE in slang uses

IN COMPOUNDS

❑ **curtain climber** *n.* (*also* **curtain puller**) [its habits] [1960s–70s] (*US*) a small child. ❑ **curtain lecture** *n.* (*also* **curtain sermon**) [the curtains in question are those of the four-poster bed] **1** [mid-17C–1900s] a scolding from a wife to her husband, after they have gone to bed (occas. vice versa). **2** [1960s] a telling-off, on the quiet.

curtains *n.*[1] [theatrical imagery i.e. the curtain comes down to signal the end of the play] [20C+] the end, finality; usu. in phr. *It'll be curtains for you.*

curtains *n.*[2] [1970s+] **1** (*US gay*) the foreskin. **2** the labia.

IN PHRASES

❑ **draw the curtains** *v.* [1980s+] to fellate an uncircumcised penis.

curtal *n.* (*also* **curtail, curtall**) [SE *curtal*, anything docked or cut short (orig. a horse's tail)] (*UK Und.*) **1** [mid-16C–18C] a mendicant villain, the 11th rank of the CANTING CREW *n.* and thus marginally less influential than the UPRIGHT MAN *n.*, distinguished by his short cloak, similar to that of the Grey Friars. **2** [late 16C–early 17C] a general insult. **3** [early 17C] a penis. **4** [early 17C–early 18C] a prostitute. **5** [18C] a cut-purse. **6** [18C–early 19C] a thief who cuts off pieces of silk, cloth, linen etc hanging from shop windows.

curve *n.* [baseball imagery] **1** [late 19C–1920s] (*US*) a personal peculiarity. **2** [20C+] an occasion of unfair or surprising treatment; usu. in phr. *THROW A CURVE* below. **3** [1920s+] (*also* **curves**) an attractive young woman.

IN PHRASES

❑ **get a curve on** *v.* [1910s] (*US*) to hurry up, to act at once. ❑ **get on to the curves** *v.* [late 19C–1910s] (*US campus*) to understand. ❑ **throw a curve** *v.* [1930s+] (*orig. US*) to act unpredictably or illegally, to surprise, to trick, to take advantage of someone.

SE in slang uses

IN COMPOUNDS

❑ **curve-buster** *n.* (*also* **curve-killer**) [such grades are above the average curve plotted on a graph] [1960s] (*US campus*) a student whose grades exceed the average.

IN PHRASES

❑ **to the curve** *see TO THE CURB under* CURB *n.*[2].

curveball *n.* [baseball imagery] [1940s+] (*US*) a tricky or unexpected question or action.

cus *n. see* CUZ *n.*

cush *n.*[1] [SE *cushion*] **1** [late 19C+] (*US*) (*also* **cush-cush, koosh, kush**) money. **2** [1900s] (*US Und.*) a bank teller; a cashier. **3** [1920s] (*US*) a tip.

SE in slang uses

IN PHRASES

❑ **on the cush** *see ON THE CUSHIONS under* CUSHION *n.*

cush *n.*[2] (*also* **kush**) [Arabic *cush*, the vagina] [1940s–60s] **1** the vagina; thus a woman seen strictly as a sex object. **2** sexual intercourse with a woman.

cush *n.*[3] [CUSH *adj.* (2)] [1940s] something easy.

cush *adj.* [CUSHY *adj.*] **1** [late 19C+] (*Aus.*) fair, honourable [? another ety. might apply]. **2** [20C+] (*also* **coosh**) easy, comfortable, undemanding.

cushat *n.* [SE *cushat*, a wood pigeon or ring dove] [19C] the vagina.

cush-cush *n. see* CUSH *n.*[1] (1).

cushdi *adj. see* CUSHTY *adj.*

cushiness *n.* [CUSHY *adj.* (1)] [1930s+] soft, comfortable circumstances.

cushion *n.* [fig. uses of SE *cushion*] **1** [1910s–60s] (*US Und.*) in pl., a passenger train; thus a day coach on such a train. **2** [1950s] (*US*) (*also* **cushion money**) bribery. **3** [1950s+] (*drugs*) a vein into which a drug is injected [it is 'plumped up' for the injection]. **4** [1960s] (*US*) physical comforts. **5** [1960s+] (*US gay*) in pl., the buttocks.

SE in slang uses

IN COMPOUNDS

❑ **cushion-cuffer** *n.* [mid-17C–mid-18C] a parson. ❑ **cushion dance** *n. see* DANCE *v.* (1). ❑ **cushion-duster** *n.* ['many of whom, in the fury of their eloquence, heartily belabour their cushions' (Grose, 1796)] [early 18C–early 19C] a parson. ❑ **cushion-smiter** *n.* [mid–late 19C] a parson. ❑ **cushion-thumper** *n.* (*also* **thump-(the-)cushion**) [mid-17C–1930s] a parson.

IN PHRASES

❑ **on the cushions** (*also* **on the cush, on the plush**) [20C+] (*US Und.*) travelling in a passenger coach as opposed to a freight wagon; thus symbolic of any form of luxury/comfort.

cushty *adj.* (*also* **cushdi, cushti, custy**) [Rom. *kushto*, *kushti*, good; widely popularized by the 1980s BBC TV series *Only Fools and Horses*] **1** [1930s+] first-rate, excellent, enjoyable. **2** [2000s] on good terms, involved with sexually. **3** [2000s] physically comfortable.

IN PHRASES

❑ **cushty bok** [1910s+] (*orig. costermonger*) good luck.

cushty *adv.* [CUSHTY *adj.* (1)] [1910s+] easily.

cushy *adj.* [? Rom. *kushto*, good or Hind. *khush*, pleasure] **1** [late 19C+] (*also* **cooshie, kooshy**) soft, comfortable, easy. **2** [1970s] (*US*) of a person, soft-bodied.

cushy *adv.* [CUSHY *adj.* (1)] [1970s] comfortably.

cuss *n.*[1] [joc. use of SE *curse* although no sense is particularly negative] **1** [late 17C+] (*also* **curse, cuss-o'thunder**) a man, a fellow, a person; often as *old cuss*. **2** [mid–late 19C] an animal. **3** [1900s] an object, a thing.

cuss *n.*[2] [SE *curse*] [mid-19C+] a curse.

IN COMPOUNDS

❑ **cuss-word** *n.* (*also* **cuss language**) [late 19C+] (*US*) an obscenity, an oath.

cuss-cuss *n.* [CUSS (DOWN) *v.* (1) + redup.] [1910s+] (*W.I./UK black*) a quarrel or fracas, with lots of cursing.

cuss (down) *v.* (*also* **cuss-cuss, cuss off, cuss up**) [SE *curse*] **1** [late 19C+] to abuse verbally, to insult. **2** [2000s] (*UK teen*) to abuse a person's parents with the direct intent of forcing them to lose their temper; a UK version of the DOZENS *n.*

IN PHRASES

❑ **cuss out** *v.* [late 19C+] to curse, to attack verbally, to criticize.

cussed *adj.* [SE *cursed*] [mid-19C+] cursed, damned; thus *cussedest*.

cussedness *n.* [SE *cursed*] [mid-19C–1930s] (*US*) malignity, perversity, cantankerousness, contrariness.

custard *n.* [resemblance] (*Aus.*) **1** [1920s+] in pl., pimples, acne [the yellow pus such eructations contain]. **2** [1950s+] semen.

IN COMPOUNDS

❑ **custard pie** *n.* [1990s+] (*US teen*) the female genitals.

IN PHRASES

❑ **clear the custard** *v.* [1990s+] to masturbate, after a long period of continence.

custard and jelly *n.* [rhy. sl. = TELLY *n.*] [1960s+] television.

custom *n.*

IN PHRASES

❑ **it's an old — custom** [1930s+] a phr. used to justify a practice, usu. in the workplace, that would otherwise be condemned, abandoned etc had it not been established over a long period; usu. *an old Spanish custom*, earlier *an old Southern custom*.

custom house *n.* [in which punning institution 'Adam made the first entry'] [late 17C–19C] the vagina.

SE in slang uses

IN COMPOUNDS

❑ **custom house goods** *n.* ['the stock in trade of a prostitute, because fairly entered' (Grose, 1796)] [late 18C–19C] the vagina. ❑ **custom house officer** *n.* [pun on permitting 'goods' to 'pass through'] [mid-19C] a laxative pill.

customs officer *n.* [he 'works' in the CUSTOM HOUSE *n.*] [late 18C] the penis.

cut *n.* **1** [17C; late 19C+] a share: of profits, of loot, of the proceeds of a robbery etc. **2** [late 18C] a whore. **3** [late 18C+] an act of ignoring a friend or acquaintance both deliberately and pointedly. **4** [19C+] the female genitals, the vagina. **5** [mid–late 19C] one who deliberately avoids another person. **6** [mid-19C+] (*US*) an insult. **7** [mid-19C+] (*US campus*) the act of absenting oneself from a class. **8** [mid-19C+] (*US campus*) the failure of a class to meet. **9** [late 19C+] a go, an attempt. **10** [20C+] (*Aus./US/UK*) a swing with the fist; thus *take a cut at*, to menace or hit with the fist. **11** uses pertaining to dilution or adulteration. (**a**) [1930s] the dilution of alcohol. (**b**) [1950s+] (*drugs*) an act of diluting a pure drug, usu. heroin or cocaine; thus *two-cut*, dilution with the same amount of an adulterant. (**c**) [1980s] an adulterant. (**d**) [1990s+] a drug that has been thus diluted (the implication is not necessarily of inferiority: narcotics are rarely sold 100% pure). **12** [1950s+] (*orig. US sporting*) a pre-arranged point at which a group of competitors or recruits to a team are reduced by those who fail to achieve a given standard. **13** uses based on being 'cut out' from the surrounding area. (**a**) [1950s–60s] (*US black*) a place or area where young people meet, e.g. a street corner, a drugstore, a house. (**b**) [2000s] (*US prison*) the area immediately surrounding an inmate's bunk. **14** [1940s+] (*US*) a record. **15** [1990s+] a recently received hair*cut*. **16** see CUT-UP *n.*[1].

IN COMPOUNDS

❑ **cut buddy** *n.* [BUDDY *n.* (1)] **1** [1960s] (*US black*) a close friend. **2** [1990s+] (*US drugs*) two or more drug dealers who combine to adulterate a supply of drugs prior to retailing it. ❑ **cut house** *n.* [2000s] (*US drugs*) anywhere that pure drugs are adulterated and packaged prior to street sale. ❑ **cut man** *n.* [2000s] (*US drugs*) one who mixes a pure drug with 'cut' to adulterate it prior to offering it for street sale.

IN PHRASES

❑ **give cuts** *v.* [1980s+] (*US campus*) to let someone into a queue or line; thus *have cuts*, to get into the queue in a favourable position. ❑ **have a cut (at)** *v.* [fig. use of sense 10 above] [late 19C+] (*Aus.*) to try, to make an attempt. ❑ **have one's cut** *v.* [late 19C+] of a man, to have sexual intercourse. ❑ **in the cut** **1** [1960s+] (*US black*) in a location or neighbourhood that is faraway, hidden or removed for some reason; thus *LAY BACK IN THE CUT under* LAY BACK *v.* **2** [1990s+] (*US black*) present, in place, on hand. **3** [2000s] in prison. ❑ **make the cut** *v.* [golf jargon *make the cut*, to score sufficiently well in a preliminary round to proceed to the later stages of a competition; those that fail to make a set figure (the *cut*) are eliminated] [1990s+] to succeed.

cut, the *n.* [SE *cut*, a passage; thus note *The Cut*, London SE1, one of 19C London's best known street markets; also f. the knives wielded in such a place (Major, *Juba to Jive: A Dict. of Afro-American Slang*, 1994)] [1990s+] (*US black*) the ghetto, the poor side of town.

cut *adj.*[1] [abbr. *CUT IN THE BACK under* CUT *v.*[2]] [mid-17C+] drunk; thus HALF-CUT *adj.*[2] (1).

IN PHRASES

❑ **cut over the head** *adj.* [late 18C–early 19C] tipsy, slightly drunk.

cut *adj.*[2] [abbr. CUT UP *adj.*[1] (2)] [mid-19C+] angry, upset about, hurt.

cut *adj.*[3] [CUT *v.*[6] (4)] **1** [1920s+] of drink, adulterated, diluted, weakened. **2** [1960s+] (*drugs*) adulterated, diluted.

IN COMPOUNDS

❑ **cut deck** *n.* [DECK *n.*[4] (1)] [1950s+] (*drugs*) heroin or morphine mixed with powdered milk.

cut *adj.*[4] [SE *cut*] **1** [1970s] having had a vasectomy. **2** [1970s+] (*US gay*) circumcised. **3** [1980s+] (*US*) (*also* **cut up**) of a person, with well-defined or well-developed muscles.

SE in slang uses

IN COMPOUNDS

❑ **cut puss** *n.* [SE *cut*, castrated + SE *puss*/PUSSY *n.* (10)] [1950s] (*W.I.*) an effeminate, fat man.

IN EXCLAMATIONS

❑ **go and get cut!** [20C+] (*Aus.*) a general excl. of dismissal or disdain.

cut *v.*[1] [Partridge suggests abbr. of the past participle of Lat. *loquor, locutus*, spoken] **1** [16C–mid-19C] (*UK Und.*) to speak, to talk. **2** [20C+] (*W.I.*) to speak a language; esp. as *cut...good*. **3** [1950s] to tease. **4** [1960s+] (*US black*) to put someone in their place by a verbal attack, to reprimand, to scold.

IN PHRASES

❑ **cut a joke** *v.* [late 18C–mid-19C] to talk, to tell a joke. ❑ **cut benely** *v.* (*also* **cut bene**) [mid-16C–17C] (*UK Und.*) to speak gently or kindly. ❑ **cut bene whids** *v.* (*also* **cut ben whids, cut benar whids, cut bien whids**) (*UK Und.*) **1** [mid-16C–1900s] to speak kindly. **2** [early 17C] to tell the truth. ❑ **cut queer whids** *v.* (*also* **cut quire whidds**) [16C–mid-19C] (*UK Und.*)

1 to speak unpleasantly or obscenely; thus *queer whidding*, telling off, reprimanding. **2** to tell lies.

cut *v.*[2] [SE *cut*] **1** [mid-16C+] to walk; usu. with prep., e.g. *along, over, through, down*. **2** [mid-17C+] to leave, to desert, to run off, to escape. **3** [mid-19C+] to absent oneself without good reason. **4** [2000s] to turn; thus *cut a left, cut a right*.

(IN PHRASES)

❑ **cut and run** *v. see* separate entry. ❑ **cut ass** *v.* [ASS *n.* (4)] [1950s–60s] (*US*) to leave, to run off. ❑ **cut away** *v.* (*also* **cut by, cut off**) [late 17C+] to leave, to run off. ❑ **cut behind** *v.* [late 19C] (*US*) to steal a ride on a vehicle. ❑ **cut for it** *v.* [late 19C–1920s] to run off, to make an escape. ❑ **cut grit** *v. see* *HIT THE GRIT under* GRIT *n.*[2]. ❑ **cut it (to)** *v.* [mid–late 19C] to run off (to). ❑ **cut one's lucky** *v.* (*also* **make one's lucky**) [? SE *lucky escape*] [early 19C+] to run off. ❑ **cut one's sticks** *v. see* separate entry. ❑ **cut one's wheels** *v.* [1950s] (*US*) to leave, to depart. ❑ **cut quick sticks** *v.* [var. on CUT (ONE'S) STICK(S) *v.* (1)] [mid-19C] to be in a hurry.

SE in slang uses

(IN COMPOUNDS)

❑ **cut and tuck** *n.* [shorthand for the surgery involved] [1980s+] (*Aus. prison*) a male-to-female sex-change operation. ❑ **cut-rate** *see* separate entries. ❑ **cut-throat** *n. see* separate entry.

(IN PHRASES)

❑ **cut...** *v. see also under* relevant n. ❑ **cut a bum card** *v.* [? f. 14C colloq. *bum*, the buttocks, which are 'raised' from the plane of the back; although the meaning is alluring, the use of BUM *adj.* (1), bad, is mid-19C+] [17C] (*UK Und.*) to cheat at cards by using one that has a slightly raised surface. ❑ **cut a cake** *v. see* FROST A CAKE *v.* ❑ **cut a finger** *v.* [euph.] [late 19C–1900s] to break wind. ❑ **cut a gut** *v.* [the butchering of an animal, when a slip of the knife, typically into the gall-bladder, can ruin the meat] [1920s+] (*US*) to make a mistake, esp. an embarrassing one. ❑ **cut a hog** *v.* [20C+] (*US*) **1** to make a mistake. **2** to fail in a task, esp. when it is beyond one's abilities. ❑ **cut a knot** *v.* [2000s] (*US prison*) to assault a fellow inmate. ❑ **cut a rug** *v. see* CUT THE RUG *v.* ❑ **cut a side (of beef)** *v. see under* BEEF *n.*[1]. ❑ **cut a slice (off the joint)** *v. see under* SLICE *n.* ❑ **cut away** *v.* [early 19C] to strike a blow. ❑ **cut dirt** *v.* [the way a horse's hooves cut into the ground as it gallops at speed but note CUT *v.*[2] (2)] [19C] (*US*) to run away, to depart at speed. ❑ **cut down** *see* separate entries. ❑ **cut every which way but loose** *v.* (*also* **turn every which way but loose**) [1920s+] (*US*) to assault comprehensively. ❑ **cut for the simples** *adj. see* separate entry. ❑ **cut gravel** *v.* [the image of a coach's wheels spinning up gravel] [mid-19C] (*US*) to move very fast. ❑ **cut grit** *v. see* *HIT THE GRIT under* GRIT *n.*[2]. ❑ **cut ice (with)** *v. see* separate entry. ❑ **cut in/into** *see* separate entries. ❑ **cut in the back** *adj.* (*also* **cut in the eye, ...leg**) [fig. use of SE] **1** [mid-17C–mid-19C] very drunk. **2** [19C] pregnant [euph.]. ❑ **cut loose** *v. see* separate entry. ❑ **cut on** *v.* [1970s] (*Can. prison*) to sport a prison-made tattoo. ❑ **cut one's cable** *v.* [naut. imagery] **1** [early 19C] to die. **2** [mid-19C] (*also* **cut one's stick**) to run away. ❑ **cut one's eye** *v. see under* EYE *n.* ❑ **cut one's foot** *v.* [mid-19C+] (*US*) **1** to step in excrement [euph.]. **2** thus, to make a stupid blunder. ❑ **cut one's horns** *v. see* *SCRAPE ONE'S HORNS under* HORN *n.*[2]. ❑ **cut one's last fling** *v.* [SE *cut a fling*, to dance, implying DANCE *v.* (2)] [18C] to be hanged. ❑ **cut one's own grass** *v.* [mid–late 19C] to earn one's own living. ❑ **cut out** *see* separate entries. ❑ **cut rug** *v. see* CUT THE RUG *v.* ❑ **cut someone a new ass** *v. see* TEAR SOMEONE A NEW ASS *v.* ❑ **cut someone down** *v.* [1940s+] (*orig. US black*) to challenge, with the intention of proving one's superiority, usu. in the context of verbal, dancing or musical competitions. ❑ **cut someone into** *v.* (*US*) **1** [1910s+] to introduce someone to a scheme, supposedly advantageous. **2** [1930s+] to meet someone. **3** [1950s+] to introduce one person to another. ❑ **cut someone out of** *v.* [mid-19C+] (*US*) to let go, to release someone. ❑ **cut someone's cart** *v.* [mid-19C–1920s] to expose someone's tricks. ❑ **cut someone's comb** *v.* [mid-19C] to humiliate; to disgrace, to 'bring down a peg'. ❑ **cut ten** *v. see* *COCK TEN under* COCK *v.*[4]. ❑ **cut the cheese** *v.* [the pronounced odour of certain cheeses] [1970s+] to break wind; esp. in phr. *who cut the cheese?* ❑ **cut the fool** *v.* [1930s–60s] (*US black*) to act the fool, esp. when dealing with white people, to play tricks. ❑ **cut the gutter** *n.* [20C+] (*Ulster*) an errand boy. ❑ **cut the line** *v.* (*also* **cut the rope, cut the string**) [early 19C] to cut a long story short. ❑ **cut the mustard** *v. see* separate entry. ❑ **cut the painter** *v. see* separate entry. ❑ **cut the rug** *v. see* separate entry. ❑ **cut through the chicken fat** *see* CUT THE CRAP *v.* ❑ **cut under** *v.* **1** [mid-19C] to undersell. **2** [late 19C–1930s] (*US black*) to insult. ❑ **cut up** *see* separate entries. ❑ **cut yai** *v. see* *CUT ONE'S EYES under* EYE *n.* ❑ **cut Z's** *v. see* *BUST SOME Z's under* Z *n.*[1]. ❑ **how's she cutting?** ['she' being some form of agricultural implement] [1970s+] (*Irish*) a general phr. of greeting.

cut *v.*[3] [on model of SE *cut a figure/caper/dash* etc] [late 17C+] to pose as, to act in the manner of.

(IN PHRASES)

❑ **cut...** *v. see also under* relevant n. ❑ **cut a bosh** *v.* [ety. unknown; ? Fr. *ébauche*, outline, a rough-hewn figure] [mid-18C–mid-19C] (*UK Und.*) to cut a figure. ❑ **cut a caper upon nothing** *v.* [late 17C] to be hanged. ❑ **cut a dido** *v. see* CUT UP A DIDO *v.* ❑ **cut a rusty** *v.* [SE *rustic*, a peasant] [mid-19C+] (*US*) to show off, to behave in a silly, unsophisticated manner; to have a tantrum. ❑ **cut a swat** *v.* [SE *cut a swathe*] [late 19C] (*US campus*) to make an impression. ❑ **cut caper-sauce** *v.* [SE *cut a caper*, to dance] [late 18C–mid-19C] to be hanged. ❑ **cut cheese** *v.* [late 19C–1920s] (*US campus*) to impress, to influence, to make a difference. ❑ **cut dicks** *v.* [SE *dignity*] [1950s+] (*W.I.*) to affect an English accent in the hope of impressing people. ❑ **cut didoes** *v. see* CUT UP A DIDO *v.* ❑ **cut Grecian** *v.* [1940s] (*W.I.*) of a woman, to walk in a self-consciously 'stylish' manner, either arrogantly or proudly. ❑ **cut it** *v. see* separate entry. ❑ **cut (old) style** *v.* [20C+] (*W.I.*) to behave in an exhibitionist manner to attract attention. ❑ **cut rough** *v. see* CUT UP ROUGH *v.* ❑ **cut round** *v.* [mid–late 19C] (*US*) to show off, to make a display. ❑ **cut the buck** *v.* [dial. *cut the buck*, to dance vigorously; ult. f. *buck and wing*] [1920s–70s] (*US*) to work hard.

cut *v.*[4] **1** [late 18C+] to ignore a task, rule or obligation, e.g. homework or a college curfew. **2** [early 19C+] to stop doing something; thus *cut that*, be quiet, stop that. **3** [mid-19C] to resign from; to leave a job. **4** [1930s+] to switch off. **5** [1960s] to switch (on).

(IN PHRASES)

❑ **cut it** *v. see* separate entry. ❑ **cut the...** *v. see also under* relevant n. ❑ **cut the bullshit** *v. see* CUT THE CRAP *v.* ❑ **cut the crap** *v. see* separate entry.

cut *v.*[5] **1** [mid-19C] to compete in business. **2** [late 19C+] to manage, to achieve; usu. as CUT IT *v.*[3] (1). **3** [1930s+] (*US black*) to surpass, to outdo. **4** [1960s] (*US campus*) to understand. **5** [1970s] to be convincing, to be as one wishes. **6** *see* *CUT A DEAL under* DEAL *n.*[1].

(IN PHRASES)

❑ **cut someone's arse** *v.* (*also* **cut someone's water off**) [SE/sense 3 above + ARSE *n.* (1)] **1** [20C+] (*W.I., Guyn.*) to thrash severely, to flog; also fig. use. **2** [1970s] (*US*) to defeat, to surpass.

cut *v.*[6] [SE *cut off*] **1** [mid-19C+] of a man, to have sexual intercourse. **2** [late 19C+] (*orig. US*) to stab. **3** [late 19C+] to divide, to receive or take a share, e.g. of a manager who takes a percentage of an artist's or sportsman's earnings or of criminals dividing up loot. **4** to adulterate, to dilute, to weaken. (**a**) [1920s+] to adulterate alcohol, typically of bootleggers making illicit liquor; thus *cutting plant*, a place where the adulteration takes place. (**b**) [1930s+] (*drugs*) to dilute a drug with some adulterant. (**c**) [1980s+] (*orig. US*) to adulterate one's position, to sacrifice one's standards, to equivocate. **5** [1940s–80s] (*Aus./N.Z.*) to finish, e.g. a drink. **6** [1970s+] to give.

cut! *excl.* [CUT *v.*[4] (2)] [mid-19C+] **1** be quiet! **2** go away!

cut and carried *adj.* [rhy. sl.] [1930s+] married.

cut and come again *n.* [fig. and punning use of 'Meat that cries come Eat me' (B.E.)] **1** [late 17C–19C] plenty, abundance. **2** [19C] the vagina.

cut-and-come-again *adj.* [CUT AND COME AGAIN *n.* (1)] [1900s] (*Aus.*) persistent, indomitable.

cut and run *v.* [naut. jargon *cut and run,* to cut the cable and run before the wind; note CUT *v.*^{2} (2)] [19C+] to run off, to escape.

cutback *n.*

IN PHRASES

❑ **on the cutback** [1940s] (*US black*) of time, ago.

cutchie *n.* (*also* **kouchie**) [ety. unknown] [1950s+] (*W.I., Jam.*) a pipe used for smoking marijuana.

cutdown *n.* [1980s] (*US*) a medium-level member of a teen gang.

cut-down *adj.*^{1} [mid-19C+] (*US black*) dejected, miserable.

cut-down *adj.*^{2} [the loser is 'cut down to size'] [1960s] of a confrontation or conflict, important, decisive.

cut down *v.* [CUT *v.*^{1} (1)] [1960s+] (*US campus*) to insult.

cute *n.*^{1} [SE prosecution] [early 18C] (*UK Und.*) a warrant.

cute *n.*^{2} *see* CUTER *n.*^{2}.

cute *adj.* [SE *acute*] **1** [mid-18C+] acute, clever, keen-witted, sharp, often ironically and esp. in phr. [20C+] *don't get cute with me*; thus n. *cuteness* [early 19C adoption in US developed and spread]. **2** [mid-19C+] attractive, charming.

IN PHRASES

❑ **cute as a shithouse rat** *adj.* (*also* **cute as a barrow-load of monkeys, ...as a bug's ear, ...as a cut cat**) [1920s+] extremely devious, very cunning.

cute *adv.* [mid-19C+] cleverly, smartly, esp. with implication of 'too smart for one's own good'.

cuter *n.*^{1} [1910s] (*US Und.*) **1** a surprise. **2** a fool, a victim.

cuter *n.*^{2} (*also* **cute, cutor, kuter, kyuter, quter**) [? pron. SE *quarter*, note hotel jargon *cuter*, one who only tips a quarter] [1910s–60s] (*US*) 25 cents, a quarter.

cuter *n.*^{3} *see* 'CUTOR *n.*

cutes *n.* [CUTE *adj.* (2)] [20C+] (*orig. US*) a pretty young woman, often as a term of address, e.g. *Hey cutes...*

cutes, the *n.* [1940s–50s] (*US*) coy mannerisms.

cutesie *adj.* (*also* **cutesy**) [CUTE *adj.* (2) + sfx *-sie*; later use is SE] [1910s–20s] (*orig. US*) excessively sweet, cloying, esp. in one's behaviour.

cutesie-pie *n.* (*also* **cutie-pie, cutey-pie**) [CUTE *adj.* (2) + SE *pie*] [1920s+] **1** (*also* **cutiepatootie**) an attractive woman, usu. young, poss. a man's girlfriend. **2** a man, as a term of affection or ridicule. **3** a small, admirable object, esp. used ironically. **4** a child. **5** (*gay*) an attractive, feminine man.

cutesie-pie *adj.* (*also* **cutie-pie**) [CUTESIE-PIE *n.*] [1920s+] (*orig. US*) **1** (*also* **cutesy-poo**) excessively sweet, cloying, esp. in one's behaviour. **2** usu. of a woman, very pretty.

cute suit with the loop droop *n.* [CUTE *adj.* (2)] [1940s] (*US black/Harlem*) an ostentatious drape suit, popular at the time.

cutesy *adj. see* CUTESIE *adj.*

cutey *n.* **1** *see* COOTIE *n.* **2** *see* CUTIE *n.*^{1}.

cut-eye *adj.* [CUT EYE *v.*] [1940s] (*US black*) dismissive, hostile.

cut eye *v.* [W.I. *cut*, to dance + *eye*] [19C+] (*W.I., Jam.*) to catch a person's eye then, with the intention of offering a deliberate insult, to turn away.

cutey-pie *n. see* CUTESIE-PIE *n.*

cut for the simples *adj.* [17C Battersea was best known for its market gardens and the medicinal herbs they grew, known as *simples*, basic herbs without any adulterants. The use of *simples* as a cure for physical ailments evolved into one for supposed mental problems once it was absorbed in sl.] [late 17C–19C] cured of one's foolishness; esp. in phr. *go to Battersea to be cut for the simples*.

cuthbert *n.* [stereotype of *Cuthbert* as a slightly 'weak' or foolish name] [1910s–30s] **1** one who deliberately avoids military services, esp. by securing a post in a government office or the civil service. **2** a conscientious objector.

cut ice (with) *v.* **1** [late 19C+] (*orig. US*) to impress, to influence, to make a difference; usu. in negative phr. *cut no ice (with)*, to make no impression, to leave unmoved. **2** [1900s] to chat, to converse.

cutie *n.*^{1} (*also* **cutey**) [CUTE *adj.* + sfx *-y*] **1** [late 18C+] a superficially clever person. **2** [20C+] (*orig. US*) (*also* **cuttie**) a pretty young woman; occas. of a man. **3** [1900s] (*US*) an attractive object. **4** [1910s+] (*US*) someone who is extremely shrewd or adept. **5** [1910s+] a general term of address to a (pretty) woman; also, cynically, to a handsome man. **6** [1940s+] (*US*) a smart, 'clever' move; a cunnning scheme.

cutie *n.*^{2} *see* COOTIE *n.*

cutiepatootie *n. see* CUTESIE-PIE *n.* (1).

cutie-pie *see under* CUTESIE-PIE.

cut-in *n.* [CUT *n.* (1)] **1** [late 19C–1940s] a share: of profits, of loot, of the proceeds of a robbery etc. **2** [1910s] an interruption.

cut in *v.* [CUT-IN *n.*] **1** [19C+] to make a pass at another person's partner. **2** [mid-19C] (*also* **have a cut-in**) to become involved. **3** [late 19C+] to receive a share, to be included in a proposition or plan. **4** [20C+] to give a share. **5** [20C+] (*US Und.*) to introduce oneself to a potential victim. **6** [1970s] to approach.

cut into *v.* (*US*) **1** [20C+] to make oneself known to, to interrupt. **2** [1900s] to take a share of. **3** [1930s+] to meet, to encounter. **4** [1960s–70s] to introduce. **5** [1990s+] (*Aus.*) to attack verbally.

cut it *v.*^{1} (*also* **cut it out**) [19C+] to stop doing something; often as imper.

IN EXCLAMATIONS

❑ **cut it out!** (*also* **cut that out!**) *see* CUT THAT/IT OUT! *under* CUT OUT *v.*^{3}.

cut it *v.*^{2} (*also* **cut it down**) [mid-19C; 1940s+] (*US*) to dance energetically.

cut it *v.*^{3} [ext. CUT *v.*^{5} (2)] **1** [late 19C+] (*orig. US*) to manage, to deal with (difficult) situations; to suffice, to satisfy. **2** [1950s] to accept, to tolerate. **3** [1980s] to surpass.

IN PHRASES

❑ **cut it grand** *v.* [mid-19C] to act in a threatening, domineering manner. ❑ **cut it spicy** *v. see under* SPICY *adj.* ❑ **cut it up** *v.* [20C+] to have an uproarious good time.

SE in slang uses

IN PHRASES

❑ **cut it (too) fat** *v.* [SE *cut (it) fat*, to leave too much fat on a slice of meat when carving/CUT *v.*^{3} + FAT *adv.*] [mid–late 19C] to show off, to make a vulgar display.

cut (it) up *v.* [abbr. *CUT UP (OLD) TOUCHES under* TOUCH *n.*^{1}] [1960s+] (*US*) to reminisce, to talk over.

cutlass *n.* [19C] the penis.

cutlery *n.* **1** [mid-19C] (*UK Und.*) committing murder; thus *Cutler's Alms-house*, the condemned cell. **2** [mid-19C–1910s] (*US*) any form of edged weapon, usu. a knife.

cut loose *v.* [fig. uses of SE] **1** [19C+] to abandon restraints, either in one's action or, in an argument, in one's language and abuse. **2** [mid-19C+] to leave, to walk away [CUT *v.*^{2} (2)]. **3** [20C+] to give out, to release (something). **4** [20C+] to attack; to fire a weapon. **5** [1920s+] (*US*) to escape. **6** [1930s+] (*US black*) to give up something. **7** [1940s+] (*US black*) to jilt; to terminate a relationship. **8** [1950s+] (*US prison*) to release, to be released. **9** [1950s+] to terminate, to let go, to get rid of. **10** [1970s] to launch someone into a situation. **11** [1970s] to give someone drugs.

IN PHRASES

❑ **cut one's dog loose** *v.* (*also* **cut loose one's dog**) [19C+] (*US*) to act spontaneously, without restraint. ❑ **cut one's wolf loose** *v.* [19C+] to act spontaneously, to 'let off steam'.

cut lunch *n.* [i.e. cut from a loaf] [1980s+] (*Aus.*) a meal of sandwiches; thus *cut lunch commando*, a regular employee, i.e. one who takes sandwiches to work.

cut (one's) stick(s) *v.* **1** [19C–1900s] to leave quickly, to run off [Hotten (1859) suggests the rural practice of cutting a notch or tally in a stick to reckon up sheaves of corn; 'CUT YOUR STICK, then, means to make your mark and pass on']. **2** [mid-19C] (*US*) to die. **3** [late 19C–1900s] to travel around looking for work [f. cutting a stick to help one as one walks along].

cutor *n. see* CUTER *n.*^{2}.

'cutor *n.* (*also* **cuter, cutter**) [abbr. SE prose*cutor*] [1920s–60s] (*US*) a prosecuting attorney; thus *big cutor*, a district attorney.

cut-out *n.*[1] [CUT OUT *v.*[3] (1)] [1910s] (*Aus.*) the end of a job.

cut-out *n.*[2] [1960s+] a middleman, esp. in espionage.

cut out *v.*[1] [late 17C; mid-19C] to find (work for someone).

cut out *v.*[2] [ext. of SE use] **1** [late 17C; mid-19C+] (*US*) to do better than, to surpass. **2** [late 18C–1960s] (*US*) to take over as someone's preferred love-object or dance partner.

(IN PHRASES)

❑ **cut out of** *v.* **1** [late 17C+] to deprive of an opportunity. **2** [18C–19C] to cheat.

cut out *v.*[3] [ext. CUT *v.*[2] (2)/CUT *v.*[4] (2)] **1** [mid-19C] to rush away, to leave fast, to escape. **2** [late 19C+] to stop; also as imper. **3** [late 19C+] (*Aus., orig. shearing*) to finish, to complete a job. **4** [1960s+] in fig. use, to die.

(IN PHRASES)

❑ **cut out a cheque** *v.* (*also* **cut (it) out**) [20C+] (*Aus./N.Z.*) to spend all one's earnings in one go. ❑ **cut out on** *v.* [1950s+] to desert, to abandon. ❑ **cut out the crap** *v. see* CUT THE CRAP *v.*

(IN EXCLAMATIONS)

❑ **cut that/it out!** [mid-19C+] stop doing that!

cut out *v.*[4] [SE phr. *cut out from a crowd*] [late 19C] (*US*) to recognize, to identify.

cut out *v.*[5] **1** [1970s–80s] (*N.Z. prison*) to serve a sentence; usu. modified by the pertinent number of years. **2** [1980s+] (*Aus. prison*) to pay off fines by serving time in jail according to an established tariff.

cut-rate *n.* [1930s+] a person considered second-rate.

cut-rate *adj.* [fig. use of SE *cut-rate*, economic, inexpensive] [1930s+] (*US*) second-rate, inferior, unpleasant.

cut-rate *v.* [CUT-RATE *n.*] [1940s] (*US black*) to belittle.

cut-rate *adv.* [CUT-RATE *adj.*] [1930s+] in a cheap, unsatisfactory, limited manner.

cuts *n.*[1] [mid-17C–early 18C] in oaths, a euph. for God's, e.g. *Cuts plutteranails! Cuts bobs!*

cuts *n.*[2] [CUT *n.* (10)] [1910s+] (*Aus./N.Z.*) corporal punishment, esp. of schoolchildren.

cuts *n.*[3] [? SE *cut*, a passageway] [1970s+] (*US gay*) the streets.

cuts *n.*[4] [CUT *adj.*[4] (3)] [1970s+] (*US campus*) well-defined muscles.

cuts and scratches *n.* (*also* **bites and scratches**) [rhy. sl.; ult. cheap imported matches which cut and scratched the box failing to ignite] [late 19C] matches.

cut-tail *n.* [2000s] (*W.I.*) a beating.

cut tail *v. see under* TAIL *n.*

cutter *n.*[1] [CUT *v.*[1] (1)] [mid-16C] a braggart, a boaster, a thug.

cutter *n.*[2] **1** lit. uses of SE *cut*. (**a**) [mid-16C; mid-19C] a pickpocket, a cut-purse. (**b**) [late 16C+] a thug who uses a knife or razor in fights. (**c**) [mid-19C] (*US Und.*) a burglar's implement, used for cutting through sheet iron. (**d**) [1920s] (*US prison*) a needle file. (**e**) [1930s] a robber who enters properties by cutting window bars. (**f**) [1940s] an oxyacetylene blowpipe. (**g**) [1940s] (*US*) one who derives sexual pleasure from stabbing or cutting a woman. (**h**) [1970s] (*US*) a knife. **2** fig. uses of SE *cut*. (**a**) [20C+] (*US*) a revolver, esp. a Colt which 'cuts down' its targets. (**b**) [1900s–60s] (*US*) an attractive or remarkable person. (**c**) [1920s] (*US black*) a pimp. (**d**) [1960s–70s] (*US*) a remarkable occurrence or event.

cutter *n.*[3] **1** [1960s] (*US gambling*) one who takes a percentage from a game of chance [CUT *v.*[6] (3)]. **2** [2000s] (*US drugs*) one who 'cuts' pure drugs prior to sale [CUT *v.*[6] (4b)].

cutter *n.*[4] [? COUTER *n.*[1]] [2000s] money.

cutter *n.*[5] *see* 'CUTOR *n.*

cut the crap *v.* (*also* **cut the bull(shit), ...shit, cut one's crap, cut out the crap, cut through the chicken fat, skip the crap**) [CUT *v.*[4] (2)] [1930s+] (*US*) **1** to stop wasting time or talking or doing something irrelevant. **2** as excl. *cut the crap!* don't try to fool me! stop talking rubbish! etc.

cut the mustard *v.* [the image of the condiment's piquancy] **1** [late 19C+] (*also* **cut the asparagus**) (*orig. US*) to come up to a given standard, to prove satisfactory. **2** [20C+] (*W.I.*) of a man, to satisfy a woman sexually. **3** [20C+] to have sexual intercourse [included in *DSUE* but his citation suggests a journalistic euph. rather than an established sl. phr.]. **4** [1950s] (*US*) to show off. **5** [1980s+] (*US*) to impress, to influence.

cut the painter *v.* [all f. naut. use, the *painter* is the rope that secures a small boat to a larger ship] **1** [mid-17C–mid-19C] to dismiss or send away a person. **2** [mid-19C+] to slip away clandestinely. **3** [mid-19C+] to die. **4** [1900s–10s] to bring something to an irrevocable conclusion.

cut the rug *v.* (*also* **beat the rug, cut a rug, cut rug**) [1920s+] to dance (cf. RUG CUT *v.*).

cut-throat *n.* **1** [late 18C–mid-19C] a dark lantern. **2** [mid-19C] a butcher, a slaughterer. **3** [mid-19C; 1970s+] (*US black*) a tough, aggressive or frightening black man. **4** [late 19C+] an open-bladed, non-safety razor.

cuttie *n.*[1] [SE *cut down*] [1950s+] (*W.I.*) **1** a ten-ounce beer bottle, known as a 'reputed half pint'. **2** a very short man. **3** see CUTIE *n.*[1] (2).

cuttie *n.*[2] *see* CUTIE *n.*[1] (2).

cutting *n.* [CUT *v.*[6]] **1** [mid-19C; 1930s+] a stabbing, a knifing. **2** [1930s+] (*drugs*) the adulteration of drugs to increase the quantity prior to retail sale.

(IN COMPOUNDS)

❑ **cutting gloak** *n.* [GLOAK *n.*] [early–mid-19C] one who is known for using a knife to settle quarrels. ❑ **cutting up** *n.* [the frequent use of blades to assist the suicide] [2000s] (*US prison*) committing suicide.

SE in slang uses

(IN COMPOUNDS)

❑ **cutting Dick** *n.* [SE as predates sense 1 above] [late 16C–early 17C; mid-19C] a ruffian, a braggart. ❑ **cutting shop** *n.* [SE *undercut*] [mid–late 19C] a shop selling cheap, badly made goods.

cutting contest *n.* (*also* **carving contest**) [CUT *v.*[5] (3)] [1940s–50s] (*US black*) a form of musical competition; a musical version of the DOZENS *n.*

cutting ice *n.* [CUT ICE (WITH) *v.*] [1960s–70s] (*US black*) succeeding in a spectacular manner.

cutting man *n. see* CUTTY *n.*

cuttle *n.* [obs. OF *coutel* (mod. Fr. *couteau*); ult. Lat. *cultellum*, a knife] [late 16C–mid-17C] a knife.

cuttle-bung *n.* [CUTTLE *n.* + BUNG *n.*[1] (1)] [late 16C–early 17C] (*UK Und.*) a knife used for cutting purses.

cutty *n.* (*also* **cutting man**) [? dial. *cutty*, small or diminutive; thus used as an affectionate term of address] [1970s+] (*US black*) a friend, a close intimate.

cutty-eye *v.* [SE *cutty*, sharp + *eye*] [late 18C–early 19C] to gaze at in a suspicious manner, to look askance.

(DERIVATIVES)

❑ **cutty-eyed** *adj.* [19C] **1** suspicious (of someone). **2** suspicious-looking.

cutty gun *n.* [Scot./northern UK dial. *cutty-gun*, a short, i.e. 'cut-down' gun; image of the penis as a weapon] [19C] the penis.

cut-up *n.*[1] (*also* **cut**) [CUT UP *v.*[1] (5)] **1** [late 19C+] an amusing person, a joker; also ironically. **2** [1910s] (*US*) a smartly dressed person, or smart thing.

cut-up *n.*[2] **1** [1920s; 1970s] (*US black/prison*) a knife-fight. **2** [2000s] (*US black*) sexual intercourse.

cut up *adj.*[1] [CUT UP *v.*[3] (2)] **1** [early–mid-19C] fallen on hard times. **2** [early 19C+] unhappy, depressed, upset.

cut up *adj.*[2] *see* CUT *adj.*[4] (3).

cut up *v.*[1] [fig. uses of SE] **1** [mid-18C+] to slander, to criticize, esp. behind the victim's back. **2** [early 19C] to box. **3** [mid-19C] to impress. **4** [mid–late 19C] to become, to appear, to show up. **5** [mid-19C+] to show off, to play the clown, to make people laugh; to act eccentrically. **6** [mid-19C+] to behave, to act, usu. with a defining adj. **7** [mid-19C+] (*US*) (*also* **cut up deuced, ...dickens**) to complain, to make a lot of noise; lit. and fig. **8** [20C+] to dance, to have a good time. **9** [1920s+] (*US*) to talk about. **10** [1920s+] (*US*) to cause trouble for. **11** [1950s] to misbehave. **12** [1990s+] (*US black*) to fight.

IN PHRASES

❑ **cut up a dido** *v. see* separate entry. ❑ **cut (up) a shine** *v.* [19C] **1** to play (practical) jokes. **2** to 'cut a caper'. **3** to brag, to boast. ❑ **cut up jack** *v. see* separate entry. ❑ **cut up nasty** *v. see* CUT UP ROUGH *v.* ❑ **cut up old scores** *v. see under* SCORE *n.*[3]. ❑ **cut up (old) touches** *v. see under* TOUCH *n.*[1]. ❑ **cut up rough** *v. see* separate entry. ❑ **cut up rusty** *v.* [RUSTY *adj.*[1] (1)] [early 19C+] to become annoyed. ❑ **cut up savage** *v.* [mid-19C] to become annoyed. ❑ **cut up the score** *v. see under* SCORE *n.*[3]. ❑ **cut up ugly** *v.* [mid-19C+] to become annoyed.

cut up *v.*[2] **1** [late 18C] to defraud, to deprive. **2** [late 18C+] to divide, esp. money, loot. **3** [late 18C+] to leave a fortune; esp. in phrs. *cut up big, cut up large*, to leave a great deal (*see also* phrs. below). **4** [1950s] to achieve, to win.

IN PHRASES

❑ **cut up fat** *v.* [SE *fat*/FAT *adv.* (1) although this is later; note butchers' jargon *cut up fat*, for an animal to be divided into profitably saleable pieces] [18C–19C] to leave a fortune after one's death. ❑ **cut up stiff** *v.* [STIFF *adv.*] [19C] to leave a large estate. ❑ **cut up well** *v.* (*also* **cut up warm**) **1** [late 18C–early 19C] to leave a fortune after one's death. **2** [mid-19C] (*US Und.*) of a robbery, to give all concerned a good share of the loot.

cut up *v.*[3] **1** [19C+] used in the passive, to be in a difficult situation, esp. as regards money. **2** [mid-19C+] to depress, to perturb.

cut up *v.*[4] [early 19C; 1930s+] to overtake another vehicle by driving recklessly in front of it (and forcing it to take some form of evasive action).

cut up a dido *v.* (*also* **cut a dido, cut didoes, cut up didoes**) [CUT UP *v.*[1] (6) + SE *dido*, a prank, a disturbance] **1** [early 19C–1930s] (*orig. US*) to play pranks, to act the fool. **2** [mid-19C+] (*also* **kick up a dido**) to behave outrageously, to cause a fuss or indulge in a row.

cut up jack *v.* (*also* **kick up (high) jack, raise jack, tear up jack, turn up jack**) [ext. of CUT UP *v.*[1] (6) + ? fig. use of JACK *n.*[1]] [mid-19C–1950s] (*US*) to cause a commotion.

cut up rough *v.* (*also* **cut up bad, cut up nasty, cut rough**) [CUT UP *v.*[1] (6) + SE *rough*] **1** [mid-19C+] to react unpleasantly, to become annoyed, to make a fuss. **2** [1900s] to treat harshly.

cut-water *n.* [SE *cut-water*, the prow of a ship] [mid-19C–1900s] the nose.

cuz *n.* (*also* **coz, cuh, cus, cuzz**) [abbr. SE *cousin*, a development of mid-16C–mid-19C *coz*] **1** [1940s+] (*orig. US black*) a form of address between (orig. black) males. **2** [1940s+] (*orig. US black*) a friend. **3** [1970s+] (*US black*) a member of the Crips gang.

cuz john *n.* (*also* **cousin john**) [mid-18C–mid-19C] (*US campus*) a privy.

cuzzy *n.* (*also* **cossie, cuzzie**) [COOZE *n.* (1)] [20C+] (*US*) the vagina.

cuzzy-bro *n.* (*also* **cuzzy**) [SE *cousin* + *brother*, ? coined by Maori comedian Billy T. James (1948–1991)] [1990s+] (*N.Z.*) a friend, a member of one's extended family.

C walk *n.* [abbr.; note Shaw, *Westsiders* (2000): 'Many have speculated that the gang were called Crips as a short version of the word "cripples", because the new gang members copied [its founder Raymond] Washington's habit of walking as if he had a limp and carrying a cane'] [1990s+] (*US gang*) a form of walking — a deliberatelty exaggerated lope — associated with the Crip gang of Los Angeles.

c.y.a. *phr.* (*also* **c.h.a.**) [abbr. cover your/his ass] [1950s+] (*orig. US milit.*) a phr. meaning look after yourself before worrying about anyone else, be it colleagues, customers, the larger world, whatever; the basic admonition to anyone, at any level, working in government or a large corporation.

cycke *n.* [abbr.] [1950s] a bicycle.

cyclone *n.* (*also* **cyline, cyclones**) [abbr.] [1970s+] (*drugs*) phen*cyclidine*.

cyclops *n.* [proper name *Cyclops*, a one-eyed giant who, in Greek mythology, forged thunderbolts for Zeus. A television, too, has 'one eye'] [1960s–70s] (*US black*) a television.

cymbal *n.* [its ticking] [mid-19C] a watch.

cynthia *n.* [play on SE *synthetic/insincere*] [1950s–60s] (*camp gay*) a 'synthetic', insincere person.

cypher *v. see* CIPHER *v.*

cypress hill *n.* [? the rap band of this name] [1990s+] (*US black*) gang rape.

Cyprian *n.* (*also* **Cytherian**) [*Cyprian*, lit. an inhabitant of Cyprus, an island that had once been celebrated for the worship of Aphrodite or Venus; *Cytherian*, f. Gk *kuthereia*, Aphrodite] [late 16C–19C] a prostitute; thus *Cyprian corps*, a collective term for prostitution as a profession.

Cyprian *adj.* (*also* **Cytherian**) [CYPRIAN *n.*] [late 16C–19C] lewd, licentious; latterly used spec. of prostitutes.

IN COMPOUNDS

❑ **Cyprian arbour** *n.* [early 17C] **1** (*also* **Cyprian bower**) the vagina. **2** a brothel. ❑ **Cyprian cave** *n.* [early 17C] the vagina. ❑ **Cyprian sceptre** *n.* [SCEPTRE *n.*] [mid-17C] the penis.

Cyril *n.* [the perceived effeminacy of the male name] [1920s] (*US*) a derog. nickname for an effeminate/homosexual man.

cyrrux *n.* [ety. unknown] [mid-19C] (*UK Und.*) snuff.

cystic grist *n.* [mid-19C] (*UK Und.*) silver plate, gold; thus *cystic-grist smelter*, a receiver who specializes in silver and gold.

Cytherian *see under* CYPRIAN.

czaro *n.* [SE *czar*] [1940s] (*US black*) a general term of address; the implication is that the addressee is superior to oneself.

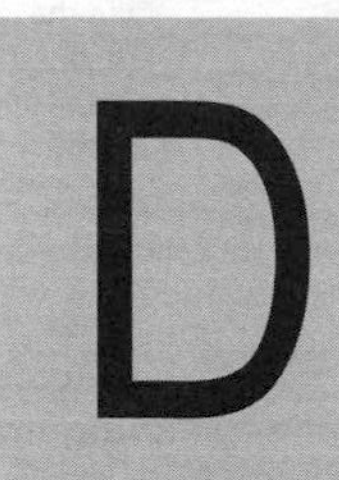

D *n.* [abbr.] [1970s+] (*US*) Detroit.

d *n.*[1] [mid-19C–1930s] abbr. of DAMN *n.*

d *n.*[2] (*also* **D, dee**) [abbr.] [mid-19C+] **1** (*orig. Aus./N.Z.*) a detective; thus *the Dees*, the police in general. **2** (*US Und.*) detention.

d *n.*[3] (*also* **dee**) [abbr.] **1** [mid-19C+] one pre-decimal penny [*£.s.d.*]. **2** [1910s+] (*US*) a dollar.

d *n.*[4] [abbr.] (*drugs*) **1** [1950s+] (*also* **big D**) *d*ilaudid. **2** [1950s+] heroin [DUJI *n.*]. **3** [1970s+] LS*D*. **4** [1970s+] (*drugs*) phencyclidine [ANGEL DUST *n.*]. **5** [1990s+] cannabis [DOPE *n.*[1] (6)].

d *n.*[5] [abbr. DICK *n.*[1] (5)] [1990s+] (*US black*) the penis.

IN PHRASES

❑ **throw the D** *v.* [1990s+] (*US black*) of a man, to have sexual intercourse.

d *n.*[6] [basketball use, *d*, defence] [1990s+] (*US black*) looking after oneself, adopting a defensive posture to potential threats.

d *adj.* [abbr. DANDY *adj.* (1)] [early 19C+] excellent, wonderful, first-rate.

d. *adj.* [abbr. DOWN *adj.*[1] (6)] [1990s+] (*US black*) ready.

d.a. *n.* [abbr.] **1** [1930s–50s] (*US*) a drug addict; dope addict. **2** [1950s+] (*orig. US*) a duck's ass, a style of haircut popular in the 1950s but still found. **3** [1970s] (*US black*) dog's ass, as a term of contempt. **4** [1970s] (*US campus*) a fool, an idiot [DUMB-ASS *n.* (1)].

daag! *excl. see* DAWG! *excl.*

dab *n.*[1] [gaming jargon *dab*, a top-flight gamester; ? orig. schoolboy sl., the obvious ety. is rooted in SE *adept* or *dapper*, but there is no positive proof of either] [17C+] a skilful person, an expert.

dab *n.*[2] [SE *dab*, to pat] **1** [late 18C] in pl., the fingers. **2** [early–mid-19C] (*UK Und.*) a blow. **3** [1920s+] in pl., fingerprints. **4** [1980s+] (*UK drugs*) a small portion of cocaine or other powdered drug, taken by dabbing one's finger into a pile or packet.

dab *n.*[3] [? backsl. Note SE *dab*, a flattish mass of a soft substance, typically butter] [early–mid-19C] a bed.

IN PHRASES

❑ **dab it up (with)** *v.* [early 19C] of a man and woman, to cohabit.

dab *adj.*[1] [DAB *n.*[1] (1)] [18C–1910s] skilled, expert.

dab *adj.*[2] [backsl.] [mid–late 19C] bad.

IN PHRASES

❑ **doing dab** *adj.* [mid-19C] doing badly (in business).

dab *v.* [DAB *n.*[2] (3)] **1** [1940s] (*UK Und./police*) to take a suspect's fingerprints. **2** *see* DUB *v.*[1] (1).

SE in slang uses

IN PHRASES

❑ **dab it up** *v.* [SE *dab*, i.e. the writing down of one's owings] [early–mid-19C] to run up credit at a public house. ❑ **dab out** *v.* [SE *dab*, to strike or cause to strike (usu. with something soft and of broadish surface); thus the slapping of clothes on a washboard etc] [mid–late 19C] to do the laundry; to wash. ❑ **dab the paint** *v.* [mid-19C] in boxing, to jab with the fist.

dabber moll *n.* [DAB *n.*[1] + MOLL *n.* (1)] [mid-19C] (*UK Und.*) a cunning woman; a sharper.

dabble *n.* [ironic use of SE] [late 19C+] (*UK Und.*) stolen property.

dabbler *n.* [SE *dabble*] [mid-19C] (*US Und.*) one who associates with thieves.

dabe *v.* [Lat. *dabo*, I give] [mid-19C] (*UK Und.*) to give.

da bomb *n. see* BOMB *n.* (11).

dabs *n.* [abbr. DABSTER *n.* (1)] [late 19C] an expert.

dabster *n.* [DAB *n.*[1] + -STER *sfx*] **1** [late 19C+] an expert. **2** [1900s] something excellent; also attrib.

dabtros *n.* (*also* **dab tros**) [backsl.; DAB *adj.*[2]] [mid-19C–1900s] a bad sort, an unpleasant person.

dacca *n.* (*also* **dakker**) [var. on S.Afr. *dagga*] [1970s+] (*Aus.*) marijuana.

IN PHRASES

❑ **dack up** *v.* [1990s+] (*N.Z.*) to smoke marijuana.

dace *n.* [SE *deuce*, two] **1** [late 17C–mid-19C] twopence. **2** [mid-19C; 1960s] (*US*) two cents.

dacehead *n.* [SE *dace*, a variety of freshwater fish] [early 19C] a fool.

dacha *n.* (*also* **deger**) [Ital. *deici*, ten] [mid-19C] (*Ling. Fr./Polari*) the number ten.

IN COMPOUNDS

❑ **dacha-one** *n.* [mid-19C] (*Ling. Fr./Polari*) elevenpence.

dacks *n. see* DAKS *n.*

dack up *v. see* DACCA *n.*

dad *n.*[1] (*also* **dads**) [the term flourished, like many similar euph. oaths, in the UK in the late 17C but re-emerged in the 19C in the US, where it remains in many combs., a resurgence poss. helped by the similarity to another taboo word, DAMNED *adj.*] [17C+] a euph. for God; used in a variety of mild verbal oaths (*see* DAD-BURN *v.*) and adjectival oaths (*see* below).

IN COMPOUNDS

❑ **dad-binged** [late 19C+] (*US*) ❑ **dad-blamed** [mid-19C+] (*US*) ❑ **dad-blasted** [mid-19C+] (*US*) ❑ **dad-blistered** [early 19C] ❑ **dad-bob** [1910s] (*US black*) ❑ **dad-fetched** [19C] (*US*) ❑ **dad-gasted** [late 19C–1940s] (*US*) ❑ **dad-rotted** (*also* **dad-ratted**) [mid–late 19C] (*US*) ❑ **dad-snatched** [mid-19C] (*US*) ❑ **dad-swamped** [mid-19C] (*US*)

dad *n.*[2] [mainly in black/beatnik use; thus UK jazz-orientated film of 1960s, *It's Trad, Dad*] [20C+] (*orig. US black*) a term of address by one man to another, esp. when slightly older.

dad *n.*[3]

IN PHRASES

❑ **tip the dad** *v. see* DADDLE *n.*

da-da *n. see* TA-TA *n.* (1).

dada *n.* [20C+] (*W.I. Rasta*) father.

dada-mama *n.* [echoic] [1970s] (*US black*) a drum roll.

Dad and Dave *n.* [*see* DAD AND DAVE *v.*] [1930s+] (*Aus.*) a peasant, an unsophisticated person.

Dad and Dave *v.* [rhy. sl.; ult. the popular 1930s radio serial *Dad and Dave* concerning various aspects of rural Aus. life. The show was based 'somewhat remotely' (Wilkes, *Dict. of Aus. Colloquialisms*, 1985) on characters in the novel *Our Selection* by Steele Rudd (Arthur Hoey Davis, 1868–1935), itself taken from his columns in the *Bulletin*, starting in 1895] [1930s+] (*Aus.*) to shave; also as n.

dad and mum *n.* [rhy. sl.] [20C+] (*Aus.*) rum or the cordial Bonox and rum.

dad at the door *n.* [rhy. sl.] [1960s+] (*bingo*) the number 24.

dad-burn *adj.* (*also* **dad blistered, dad-ratted**) [1930s+] (*US*) a euph. for GOD-DAMN *adj.*

dad-burn *v.* (*also* **dad-blame, dad-bust, dad-fetch, dad-gone, dad-gum**) [DAD *n.*[1]] [mid-19C+] (*US*) a mild oath: 'to hell with'; a euph. for GOD-DAMN *v.*

dad-burned *adj.* (*also* **dad-blamed, dad-blasted**) [euph. for GOD-DAMN *adj.*] [late 19C+] (*US*) a general intensifier.

daddio *n. see* DADDY-O *n.*

daddle *n.* (*also* **dandle, duddle**) [dial.] [late 18C–19C] (*UK Und.*) the hand; in pl., the fists.

IN PHRASES

❑ **sling a daddle** *v. see under* SLING *v.* ❑ **tip a daddle** *v.* (*also* **tip the dad, ...the daddle**) [late 18C–19C] to shake hands.

daddle *v.* [DADDLE *n.*] [19C] to enjoy lesbian sex; the implication is of mutual masturbation.

daddler *n.*[1] [DADDLE *n.*] [late 19C] the hand.

daddler *n.*[2] (*also* **dadla, dadler**) [? SE *tiddler*, something very small] [1900s–30s] a farthing.

daddy *n.* **1** [late 17C+] a general term of address. **2** [mid-19C] (*UK Und.*) 'At mock raffles, lotteries, &c., the Daddy is an accomplice, most commonly the getter up of the swindle, and in all cases the person that has been previously arranged to win the prize' (Hotten, 1864). **3** [mid-19C] the old man, generally an aged pauper, in charge at a tramp's lodging house or casual ward. **4** [mid-19C] the man who gives away the bride at a wedding, trad., but not invariably, her father. **5** [mid-19C+] an influential, powerful person, e.g. a civic leader. **6** [mid-19C+] as *the daddy*, the supreme example, the most important, powerful, the best, the best known etc, often as the *daddy of them/us all*. **7** [1910s+] a boyfriend, a lover; also as a term of address. **8** [1920s+] (*orig. US*) an older man who is willing to provide the various material desires of his younger mistress or, if gay, male lover. **9** [1920s+] (*US black*) a form of address to a black male, esp. by a woman to her lover. **10** [1930s] (*US tramp*) a Cadillac [as a rhyme on CADDY *n.*]. **11** [1930s+] (*US*) a pimp, a prostitute's boyfriend. **12** [1940s+] a masculine lesbian. **13** [1940s+] (*UK prison*) a leader (through intimidation and other influence) of the inmates in a borstal or prison. **14** [1950s+] an older male homosexual; a masculine homosexual. **15** [1960s–70s] (*US prison*) the 'active' or 'masculine' partner of a homosexual couple. **16** [1970s] (*US*) a customer, a client. **17** [1990s+] an unspecified object, a thing.

IN COMPOUNDS

❑ **daddy-one** *n.* [20C+] (*US black*) a lover or any man who provides for a woman.

IN PHRASES

❑ **like daddy-come-to-church** [1950s] (*US*) to a very great extent, very much, a great deal. ❑ **sweet daddy** *n.* **1** [1910s] (*US prison*) a predatory prison homosexual. **2** [1950s+] (*US black*) a lover or any man who provides for a woman; a pimp. ❑ **swing daddy** *n.* [SWING *v.* (8) + sense 7 above] [1970s+] (*US black*) **1** an attractive, well-dressed man. **2** a male lover. **3** a pimp. ❑ **who's your daddy?** [? sense 11 or 14 above, i.e. a mocking statement of the speaker's domination/humiliation of their target] [2000s] (*US black*) a deliberately insulting form of address.

SE in slang uses

IN COMPOUNDS

❑ **daddy-bag** *n.* [their function in procreation] [1990s+] (*US black*) the testes and the scrotum. ❑ **daddy tank** *n. see under* TANK *n.*[1].

daddy! *excl.* [20C+] (*W.I.*) a general expression of surprise and approval.

daddy-o *n.* (*also* **daddio, dadio**) [the jazz-based black use transferred, as did many such terms, to white beatniks in the 1950s and thence HIPPIE *n.*[2] (3) use; modern use is usu. ironic; note Décharné, *Straight from the Fridge Dad* (2000): 'New Orleans DJ Vernon Winslow was broadcasting under the name Doctor Daddy-O in the late 1940s [...] Rock 'n' roll DJ Porky Chadwick of WAMO, Pittsburgh called himself "the Daddy-o of the radio, a porkulatin' platter-pushin' Poppa"'] **1** [1930s+] (*orig. US black*) (*also* **dad-o**) a term of address between males. **2** [1940s+] (*orig. US*) a boyfriend, male lover, husband. **3** [1950s–60s] (*US Und.*) a pimp. **4** [1960s] (*US black*) a thing, an object. **5** [1960s] (*US*) one's father. **6** [1960s] (*US black*) the exemplar. **7** [1970s] a macho, 'butch' male homosexual. **8** [2000s] any male.

dad-fetch/dad-gone *v. see* DAD-BURN *v.*

dad-gum *adj.* (*also* **dad-gummed**) [DAD-GUM *v.*] [1930s+] (*US*) a synon. for GOD-DAMN *adj.*; thus *dadgumit!* an excl. of disappointment.

dad-gum *v. see* DAD-BURN *v.*

dadio *n. see* DADDY-O *n.*

dadla/dadler *n. see* DADDLER *n.*[2].

dad-o *n. see* DADDY-O *n.* (1).

dad-ratted *adj. see* DAD-BURN *adj.* (1).

dads *n.*[1] **1** [18C] an old man. **2** [20C+] one's father. **3** [1950s+] a term of address to anyone somewhat older than oneself. **4** [1990s+] (*W.I.*) a community leader.

dads *n.*[2] *see* DAD *n.*[1].

da-erb *n.* [backsl.] [mid-19C] bread.

daff *n.*[1] (*also* **daffy**) [abbr.] [20C+] a *daffodil*; usu. in pl.

daff *n.*[2] [ety. unknown] [1950s+] (*Irish*) excrement.

daffadown dilly *adj.* (*also* **daffydown dilly**) [rhy. sl. = SE *silly*] [1950s+] foolish, simple.

daffey *adj. see* DAFFY *adj.*

daffier *n.* [DAFFY *n.*[1] (1)] [early 19C] a gin-drinker.

daffing *adj. see* DAFFY *adj.*

daffodil *n.* [the stereotyped linking of flowers to effeminacy] **1** [1920s–80s] (*gay*) an effeminate young man. **2** [1950s–70s] a young male prostitute.

daffy *n.*[1] (*also* **daffy soup**) [proper name *Daffy's Elixir*, a proprietary remedy known as 'the soothing syrup'; gin was commonly added and thus it became sl. for gin itself] **1** [19C] gin. **2** [mid-19C] a small measure, usu. of spirits; thus synon. (*costermonger*) *daffies*.

IN PHRASES

❑ **daffy (it)** *v.* [early–mid-19C] to drink gin.

daffy *n.*[2] [abbr. dial. *daffodil*, a silly, showy woman] [late 19C] (*US*) a promiscuous woman.

daffy *n.*[3] [DAFFY *adj.*] [20C+] (*US*) an eccentric, a mad person; hysteria.

IN PHRASES

❑ **clock a daffy** *v.* [20C+] (*S.Afr.*) to tell a deceitful story with the intention of tricking the hearer.

daffy *n.*[4] [orig. Kent dial.] [1910s] (*UK Und.*) a bunch; a large number.

daffy *n.*[5] *see* DAFF *n.*[1].

daffy *adj.* (*also* **daffey, daffing**) [SE *daft*] [late 19C+] eccentric, foolish; esp. in *daffy about*, *daffy on*, madly in love with.

IN COMPOUNDS

❑ **daffy-headed** *adj.* [1980s+] foolish. ❑ **daffy house** *n.* (*also* **daffy joint**) [JOINT *n.* (3b)] [1900s] (*US*) a psychiatric institution.

daffy-down-dilly *n.* (*also* **daffydill**) [SE *daffydowndilly*, a daffodil] [mid–late 19C] a dandy; a term of affectionate address.

daffydown dilly *adj. see* DAFFADOWN DILLY *adj.*

daffy soup *n. see* DAFFY *n.*[1].

daft and barmy *n.* [rhy. sl.] [1960s+] the army.

daft ha'porth *n. see* SOFT HA'PORTH *under* SOFT *adj.*

dag *n.*[1] [dial. *dag*, a feat of daring] [late 19C–1900s] (*Aus.*) a feat of skill; thus *be a dag at*, to be an expert at.

dag *n.*[2] [dial. *dag*, a piece of matted wool and excrement clinging to a sheep's tail; ? ult. SE *dangle*] (*Aus./N.Z.*) **1** [late 19C+] in affectionate use, an appealingly eccentric person, a 'character', or thing; often ext. as *real dag*, *bit of a dag*. **2** [1950s+] an unenterprising person, a coward. **3** [1990s+] an unfashionable dresser. **4** [2000s] a gauche, socially awkward adolescent.

dag *n.*[3] [late 19C+] a euph. for God, usu. in combs. e.g. *dag on*, *dag gone*, *dag-gum*, *dag nab*.

dag *adj.* [DAG *n.*[1]] [20C+] (*Aus.*) first-rate, excellent.

dag *v.* [SE *dagger*] [1940s] (*US*) to stab.

dagan *n. see* DEGEN *n.* (1).

Dagenham *adj.* [*London Borough of Barking and Dagenham* in East London, thus pun on BARKING *adj.*] [1990s+] mad, eccentric.

Dagenham smile *n. see* BUILDER'S BUM *n.*

dagged *adj.* [Yorks. dial. *dagged*, damp] [late 17C–mid-18C] drunk.

dagger *n.*[1] [mid-19C+] the penis.

IN PHRASES

❑ **dip the dagger** *v.* (*also* **dip the candle**) [1960s–70s] of a man, to have sexual intercourse. ❑ **throw the dagger** *v.* [1980s+] (*US campus*) to have sexual intercourse.

dagger *n.*[2] [*see* DAG *n.*[2] (2)] [1980s] (*Aus.*) a hanger-on, a criminal associate.

dagger *n.*[3] *see BULL-DAGGER under* BULL *n.*[1].

dagger! *excl. see* DAG *n.*[3].

Dagger-ale *n.* [the *Dagger*, a low tavern sited in Holborn; thus such food as *Dagger-pie*, *Dagger-frumety*, sold at the tavern] [late 16C–mid-17C] very cheap ale.

dagger-pointed goldies *n.* [1940s–70s] (*US black*) yellow shoes with sharply pointed toes.

daggle-tail *n.* [ext. of dial. *daggle-tail*, a woman whose skirts drag in the dirt; a slattern] [late 18C–early 19C] a prostitute.

daggone *adj. see* DOGGONE *adj.*

daggy *adj.* [DAG *n.*[2]] [1960s+] (*Aus./N.Z.*) **1** messy, unkempt. **2** unfashionable, lacking grace. **3** amusing, eccentric.

Dago *n.* [pron.] [1940s–70s] (*US*) San Diego, California.

dago *n.* [Sp. proper name *Diego*, James; all uses are derog.; note Nares: '†DIEGO, DON. A popular name for a Spaniard'; John Taylor, 'The Water Poet', *Works* (1630): 'Don Coriat, chiefe Diego of our daies'; note Texas college sl. *dago*, macaroni] **1** [early 19C+] (*orig. US*) an Italian, a Spaniard, a South American; (*Aus.*) a Greek. **2** [late 19C+] the Spanish or Italian language. **3** [20C+] (*orig. US*) a Mexican or Puerto Rican. **4** [1900s] a South American or Spanish ship. **5** [1900s–50s] (*N.Z.*) a Maori. **6** [1910s+] any form of foreigner. **7** [1920s] any man, esp. a sexually attractive man.

dago *adj.*[1] [DAGO *n.* (1)] [mid-19C+] (*orig. US*) pertaining to a Latin, usu. an Italian, a Mexican or a Spaniard; in Aus. Greek; any dark-skinned native.

IN COMPOUNDS

❑ **dagoland** *n.* [1970s+] (*US*) a derog. name for southern Europe, esp. Italy; also Mexico. ❑ **dago red** *n.* [20C+] (*orig. US*) **1** Italian red wine, usu. Chianti; thus the cheap, home-produced red wine made by Italian families and merchandised, during Prohibition, by Italian gangsters. **2** any cheap red wine, usu. drunk by alcoholics. ❑ **dago town** *n.* (*also* **dago center**) [1920s+] (*US*) the Italian, Mexican or Puerto Rican area of a US town or city.

dago *adj.*[2] [non-specific use of DAGO *adj.*[1] as a derog. term] [1940s+] (*W.I.*) bad.

dags *n.*[1] [? OE *daeg*, a task or Scot. *darg*, a job, lit. 'a day's work'] [mid-19C–1920s] a feat, an achievement, a performance; thus *do/set dags*, to do something that the other person cannot do, to show off.

dags *n.*[2] [dial. *dag*, *daglock*, a lock of wool matted with excrement on the tail parts of a sheep; ult. SE *dangle*] [late 19C+] (*Aus.*) pieces of excrement adhering to the anus; thus n. *dagging*, the removal of such pieces; adj., *daggy*.

IN PHRASES

❑ **rattle one's dags** *v.* [1960s+] (*Aus./N.Z.*) to hurry up, to get a move on, esp. as excl.

dagwood *n.* [the favoured food of the character *Dagwood Bumstead* in Chic Young's syndicated cartoon strip *Blondie*, launched in the US in 1930] [1940s+] (*Aus./US*) an extra-large sandwich.

daily *n.* [SE *daily bread*] [1900s–20s] one's wages.

Daily Levy *n.* [its former owner, Joseph Moses *Levy* (1812–88), who took over the newly founded paper from its creator Colonel Sleigh in 1856; it was the first London paper to appear at 1d (½p) a copy] [mid–late 19C] the *Daily Telegraph*.

daily mail *n.* (*also* **daily**) [rhy. sl.] [1920s–70s] **1** the buttocks [= TAIL *n.* (2)]. **2** a tale; thus a lie. **3** ale. **4** bail. **5** sexual enthusiasm [= TAIL *n.* (7)].

IN PHRASES

❑ **on/up someone's daily** [1950s–70s] following someone close behind.

Daily Wail *n.* (*also* **Daily Whale**) [20C+] the *Daily Mail*.

dairy *n.*[1] (*also* **dairies**) [ref. to lactation] [18C+] (*20C+ US black*) the female breasts; sometimes of a man.

IN COMPOUNDS

❑ **dairy arrangements** *n.* [1910s–20s] the female breasts.

IN PHRASES

❑ **air the dairy** *v.* [19C] of a woman, to reveal her naked breasts. ❑ **sport the dairy/dairies** *v.* [late 18C–early 19C] of a woman, to reveal one's breasts.

SE in slang uses

IN COMPOUNDS

❑ **dairy queen** *n.* [pun on *Dairy Queen* chain of restaurants] **1** [1960s+] (*US gay*) a gay milkman. **2** [1960s+] (*US gay*) a gay farmer. **3** [1960s+] (*US gay*) a sexual encounter that takes place in the early morning. **4** [2000s] (*S.Afr. gay*) a man who enjoys sucking on nipples during intercourse. **5** [2000s] a woman with large breasts.

dairy *n.*[2] [? SE *direction*] **1** [1910s+] (*UK prison*) drawing attention to oneself so as to allow a confederate to break prison rules un-noticed. **2** [1910s+] exposure, publicity. **3** [1940s–50s] (*UK prison*) tobacco.

daisies *n. see* DAISY ROOTS *n.*

daisy *n.* **1** [mid-18C] (*UK Und.*) (*also* **dasy**) a diamond. **2** [mid-18C+] anything or anyone particularly appealing, excellent [moved to the US in the 19C, then returned to the UK at end of the century]. **3** [19C] the vagina [euph.]. **4** [late 19C] a term of affection. **5** [late 19C–1900s] (*US campus*) one who is credulous, gullible. **6** [late 19C–1940s] (*US*) a notably attractive young woman. **7** [1900s] (*Aus.*) a perfect blow. **8** [1900s] a person. **9** [1900s] a drunkard. **10** [1940s+] a male homosexual. **11** [1970s+] (*US black*) a housewife. **12** see DAISY CHAIN *n.* (1).

SE in slang uses

IN COMPOUNDS

❑ **daisy-beaters** *n.* **1** [late 19C] feet. **2** [1940s+] (*mainly US black/Harlem*) shoes. ❑ **daisy chain** *n. see* separate entry. ❑ **daisy-cutter** *n.* [? ext. of sense 6 above] [late 19C] an attractive woman. ❑ **daisy-kicker** *n.* [late 18C–mid-19C] **1** a horse. **2** an ostler, working at a coaching inn. ❑ **daisyland** *n.* [1950s] (*US*) the world outside the big cities. ❑ **daisy-picker** *n.* [ext. of SE use, i.e. she picks daisies while the couple attend to more pressing matters] [late 19C–1910s] (*Anglo-Irish*) one who accompanies an engaged couple on their walks, a chaperone; such an individual is invited and even paid.

daisy *adj.* [DAISY *adj.*] [late 19C–1900s] (*US*) pleasant; expert.

daisy *adv.* [DAISY *adj.*] [late 19C] (*US*) **1** admirably, excellently, in a fine manner. **2** very.

daisy beat *v.* [rhy. sl.] [19C+] to cheat; as n., a swindle.

daisy chain *n.* **1** [1910s+] (*also* **chain, daisy**) a spintry, i.e. a circle of three or more people, hetero- or homosexual, all linked physically in mutual sex acts; thus n., *daisy-chainer*, one who participates in such activities; also as v. **2** [1960s] the group of men engaged in a gang-rape or an orgy with a single woman. **3** [1970s–80s] in business use, a situation where a group of three or more companies conspire together at the public's expense. **4** [1990s+] (*US campus*) the connection between people who have had sex with the same person at different times.

daisy dukes *n.* (*also* **dazzey duks**) [the minimal shorts worn by the character *Daisy Duke* in the 1970s TV series *The Dukes of Hazzard*] [1990s+] (*US black teen*) very short shorts, 'hot pants'.

daisy dumpling *n.* [her 'common' name and her shape] [1950s–70s] (*camp gay*) a middle-class, heterosexual housewife.

daisy roots *n.* (*also* **daisies, daisy-trimmers, king canutes, recruits**) [rhy. sl.] [mid-19C+] boots.

daisyville *n. see* DEUSEAVILLE *n.*

dak *n.* [S.Afr. *dagga*] [1980s+] (*N.Z. drugs*) marijuana.

da kine *n.* [Hawaiian surf. sl. *da kine*, anything of which one forgets the precise name] [1960s] (*US*) **1** anything good, e.g. food, drugs, liquor. **2** marijuana.

dakker *n. see* DACCA *n.*

dakma *v.* [ety. unknown] [mid-19C] (*US Und.*) to silence.

daks *n.* (*also* **dacks**) [the proprietary name for a make of clothes, esp. men's trousers with a self-supporting waistband, patented by the London clothiers Simpson's in 1933; supposedly an elision of *dad's slacks*] [1940s+] (*orig. Aus.*) trousers.

dal *n. see* DELL *n.*

da land *n.* [? *da* (i.e. the) *land* of NOD *n.*[1] (1)] [1990s+] (*US black/drugs*) getting intoxicated on a drug while sitting in a car with the windows rolled up, thus intensifying the effects of the ambient smoke.

Dally *n.* (*also* **Dallie**) [abbr.] [1940s+] (*N.Z.*) a *Dal*matian (i.e. Balkan) immigrant; also attrib.

IN COMPOUNDS

❑ **Dally plonk** *n.* [PLONK *n.*[1] (1)] [1950s+] (*N.Z.*) cheap wine manufactured by Dalmatian settlers.

dally *v.* [1970s–80s] (*UK black*) to leave, to go.

Dam, the *n.* [abbr.] [1990s+] Amster*dam*.

dam *n. see* DAMN *n.*

dam *adj. see* DAMN *adj.*

dama blanca *n.* [Sp. *dama blanca*, white lady, i.e. *WHITE LADY under* WHITE *adj.*; note cocaine is a 'feminine' drug, *see* GIRL *n.*[2]] [1980s+] (*drugs*) cocaine.

damage *n.* [late 17C+] the cost; usu. in phr. *what's the damage?* how much is the bill?

damaged *adj.* [late 18C+] (*orig. US*) drunk, or hungover.

damager *n.* [20C+] a joc. corruption of SE *manager*, implying the alleged effect on those whose livelihoods are in his hands.

damber *n.* [? *DAMME-BOY under* DAMME! *excl.*] [mid-17C–early 19C] a rogue, a rascal.

damber-bush *n.* [? SE *dame* + BUSH *n.*[1] (2a)/SE *bush*] [late 19C] the pubic hair.

dambut! *excl. see DAMN-BUT! under* DAMN! *excl.*

dame *n.* [late 16C+] (*mainly US*) a woman, often with the implication of promiscuity or unattractiveness.

dame buzzer *n. see MOLL BUZZER under* MOLL *n.*

Dame Nature's privy seal *see NATURE'S PRIVY SEAL under* NATURE *n.*

damfino! *excl.* (*also* **damfi! damifino!**) [pron.] [late 19C–1910s] (*orig. US*) damned if I know!

damm *adj. see* DAMN *adj.*

damme! *excl.* (*also* **dammy!**) [17C+] a euph. for DAMN! *excl.*

IN COMPOUNDS

❑ **damme-boy** *n.* (*also* **damme, damme-blood, dammee captain, God-dam-me**) [17C–early 19C] a blustering, profane, aggressive thug.

dammit! *excl.* (*also* **bedammit! damnit! damn it all!**) [late 17C+] a mild excl., i.e. *damn it!*

IN EXCLAMATIONS

❑ **dammit to hell (and back)!** [mid-19C+] a mild oath, based on *damn it!*

damn *n.* (*also* **dam, tuppenny damn, twopenny damn**) [the orig. ety. is based on the *dam*, a low value Indian coin, but the widely assumed link is to the oath DAMMIT! *excl.*; the inclusion of 'twopenny' was apparently popularized by the Duke of Wellington (1769–1852)] [late 18C+] a minuscule or virtually non-existent amount; often in NOT GIVE A DAMN *v.*

IN PHRASES

❑ **give a damn** *v. see* separate entry. ❑ **not give a damn** *v. see* separate entry. ❑ **not worth a damn** *see* separate entry.

damn *adj.* (*also* **dam, damm**) [DAMNED *adj.*] **1** [18C+] a strong expression of reprehension or dislike. **2** [18C+] a general intensifier, complete, utter. **3** [1940s+] as an infix, e.g. *anydamnbody*.

damn *adv.* [late 18C+] a general intensifier, very, very much, completely.

damn! *excl.* (*also* **by damn! dom!**) [abbr. SE *damnation!*; the term is not sl. *per se*, but as cited by the *OED* is 'used profanely' and (in late 19C and beyond, still often found as *d–n* or even *d—*); thus it qualifies] [late 16C+] an all-purpose profanity, used in a wide variety of contexts.

IN PHRASES

❑ **damn your eyes** *adj.* [mid-19C–1930s] provocative.

IN EXCLAMATIONS

❑ **damn-but!** (*also* **dambut!**) [1930s+] (*Irish*) an excl. of affirmation. ❑ **damn it (all)!** *see* DAMMIT! *excl.* ❑ **damn me for a horse if I do!** [early 19C] an excl. implying one's absolute refusal to do something. ❑ **damn one's eyes!** (*also* **blast one's eyes! darn one's eyes! ...sight!**) [mid-18C+] an excl. of irritation, impatience, annoyance etc. ❑ **damn Sam!** [assonance] [1950s] (*US black*) an excl. of surprise or annoyance. ❑ **damn straight!** (*also* **damn skipping!**) [STRAIGHT *adj.*[1] (1)] [1970s+] (*orig. US black*) a general excl. of enthusiastic affirmation, absolutely! undoubtedly! ❑ **damn tootin'!** [SE *toot*, to blow a wind instrument, i.e. the fig. 'sound' of the affirmation] [1910s+] (*US*) an intensifying excl., usu. as *you're damn tootin'...*, completely accurate, absolutely right, no doubt at all; also as general excl. of affirmation.

damnable *adj.* [prior use from 16C is SE] [mid-19C+] a general term of dismissal and dislike.

damnably *adv.* [prior use from 16C is SE] [19C+] a general intensifier.

damn-all *n.* [1910s+] nothing; also as excl.

IN PHRASES

❑ **sweet damn-all** *n. see under* SWEET *adj.*[1].

damn all *adj.* [DAMN-ALL *n.*] [1940s] none, no.

damnation! *excl.* [SE *damnation*, condemnation to eternal punishment] [17C+] an oath of annoyance.

damnation bow-wows *n.* [late 19C+] a euph. for SE *hell* [apparently coined by Charles Dickens in *Nicholas Nickleby* (1838–9)].

IN EXCLAMATIONS

❑ **damnation bow-wows!** [20C+] a euph. for DAMN! *excl.*

damned *adj.* (*also* **dammed, dom'd**) **1** [late 16C+] a strong expression of reprehension or dislike. **2** [18C+] a general intensifier.

IN EXCLAMATIONS

❑ **I'll be damned!** (*also* **damned! damnify! I'll be...! I'll be damn! I'll be double damned! I'll be goddamned! I'll go to hell! I'm damned!**) [mid-18C+] an excl. of annoyance, surprise, irritation etc.

damned *adv.* (*also* **bedamned**) **1** [late 16C+] a general intensifier, very, very much, completely. **2** [1920s] (*US*) precisely, exactly.

damned soul *n.* [according to Grose (1796), he 'guards against the crime of perjury, by taking a previous oath, never to swear truly on these occasions'] [late 18C–early 19C] a customs house clerk.

damn well *adv.* [DAMN *adv.*] [late 19C+] certainly, definitely, very much.

Damon (Hill) *n.* [rhy. sl.; ult. racing driver *Damon Hill* (b.1960)] [1990s+] (*drugs*) a pill, esp. an amphetamine.

damp *n.* [the wetness of the drink and of the stimulated vagina] **1** [mid-19C–1900s] a drink; thus *damp bazaar*, a bar.

2 [1950s+] the vagina, one of a number of terms that equate the organ with wetness, whether that of urine, vaginal secretions or the use of the synon. FISH *n.*[1] (1a); thus *slice of damp*. **3** [1970s] (*US*) sexual intercourse with a woman.

damp *adj.* **1** [early 19C] (*US*) tipsy, mildly drunk. **2** [late 19C–1910s] foolish, stupid.

damp *v.*[1] [DAMP *n.* (1)] [mid-19C–1900s] to have a drink.

IN PHRASES

❑ **dampen the dust** *v.* [mid–late 19C] (*US*) to take a drink. ❑ **damp one's mug** *v. see under* MUG *n.*[1].

damp *v.*[2] [1900s] (*US Und.*) to steal, by secreting a small object, a diamond, in the mouth.

damper *n.*[1] [SE *damper*, that which damps down (the appetite) or depresses (the spirits)] **1** [late 18C–early 19C] a snack, eaten between meals. **2** [early 19C–1920s] a glass of porter, used as a balance to a glass of spirits; any drink. **3** [late 19C] (*UK society*) the bill in a restaurant.

damper *n.*[2] [SE *damper*, that which calms or suppresses, i.e. it suppresses the villain's hopes of an easy robbery] **1** [mid-19C–1950s] a till, a cash drawer; thus *draw a damper, tap a damper, turn down the damper*, to rob a till; *damper-drawing*, shoplifting; *damp(er) getter*, a till robber. **2** [1930s] (*US Und.*) a bank; thus *damper pad*, a bank book. **3** [1940s–50s] (*US*) a small safe, a cashbox. **4** [1950s] (*US*) in fig. use of sense 1, somewhere money goes. **5** [1950s+] (*US/Can. prison*) solitary confinement, punishment cells [it damps down the spirits or emotions].

damper *n.*[3] [1990s+] (*UK tramp*) a bed-wetter.

damper *v.* [SE *damp down*] [1970s] (*US black*) to stop, to bring to an end.

damson-pie *n.* (*also* **damson-tart**) [pun on DAMN! *excl.*] [late 19C] obscene language.

damwit *n.* [1940s] (*US*) a fool.

dan *n.*[1] (*also* **dine**) [1900s–40s] dynamite.

dan *n.*[2] [acronym f. dumb-ass nigger] [2000s] (*US black*) a fool.

dance *n.*[1] [mid-16C; 20C+] (*US prison*) a hanging.

IN COMPOUNDS

❑ **dancehall** *n.* (*also* **dancehouse**) [note the term is not limited to hanging] [1920s+] (*US prison*) **1** the execution chamber [Goldin et al., *Dict. of American Und. Lingo* (1950), suggests this is 'erroneously used']. **2** the cell in which a prisoner is placed before being executed.

IN PHRASES

❑ **do the dance** *v.* [1920s] (*US*) to be hanged.

SE in slang uses

IN PHRASES

❑ **do the — dance** *v.* [late 19C] to act in a given manner, presumably active, defined by the n.

dance *n.*[2] [abbr. DANCERS *n.*] [mid-19C] a flight of stairs.

dance *v.* **1** [16C+] to have sexual intercourse, used in a variety of phrs., *see* below. **2** [17C+] to be hanged, used in a variety of phrs., *see* below. **3** [mid-19C+] (*also* **dance the stairs**) to steal from first or higher floors, usu. in the daytime when residents are downstairs and not in bed.

IN PHRASES

pertaining to sexual intercourse

❑ **dance Adam's jig** *v.* [18C] ❑ **dance Barnaby** *v.* [17C phr. *dance barnaby*, to enjoy oneself; ult. presumably a lost country dance] [17C] ❑ **dance bobb in-jo** *v.* [the old dance 'Bobbing Joan'; Williams suggests that *Bobbing Joan* might also have been generic for a prostitute and cites a similar use of *Bobbing Bess* in 1654] [17C] ❑ **dance on the mattress** *v.* [late 19C–1920s] ❑ **dance Sallinger's round** *v.* (*also* **dance Sallenger's dance, ...Sallenger's round, ...Sellinger's round**) [*Sallenger*, St Leger. 'St Leger's Round' was a popular ballad *c.*1600, according to Nares 'of an indelicate character'] [mid-17C–mid-18C] ❑ **dance the blanket hornpipe** *v. see BLANKET HORNPIPE under* BLANKET *n.* ❑ **dance the buttock jig** *v.* [19C] ❑ **dance the cushion dance** *v.* [late 19C] ❑ **dance the goat's jig** *v. see GOAT'S JIG under* GOAT *n.*[1]. ❑ **dance the Irish jig** *v.* [18C] ❑ **dance the kipples** *v.* [Scot. *kipple*, couple] [19C] ❑ **dance the married man's cotillion** *v.* [19C] ❑ **dance the matrimonial polka** *v.* [19C] ❑ **dance the miller's reel** *v.* [19C] ❑ **dance the reel(s) of bogie** *v.* [? ref. to river *Bogie*, Aberdeenshire] [18C] ❑ **dance the reels of stumpie** *v.* [dial. *stumpy*, something stump-like, i.e. the penis] [late 18C–19C] ❑ **dance to the tune/time of shaking the sheets (without music)** *v.* [SE *shaking of the sheets*, 'an old country dance, often alluded to, but seldom without an indecent intimation' (Nares)] [19C] ❑ **dance with one's arse to the ceiling** *v.* [19C] ❑ **do a bit of (bum) dancing** *v.* [mid–late 19C]

pertaining to judicial hanging

❑ **dance at Beilby's ball** *v. see under* BEILBY'S BALL *n.* ❑ **dance at the sheriff's ball** *v.* (*also* **dance at the sheriff's ball and loll one's tongue out at the comany**) [late 18C–early 19C] ❑ **dance at tuck 'em fair** *v. see under* TUCK 'EM FAIR *n.* ❑ **dance in/on a rope** *v.* [mid-17C–1940s] ❑ **dance off** *v.* [1930s] (*US*) ❑ **dance on air** *v.* (*also* **kick the air**) [late 18C–1940s] to hang; also as n. *dance in the air*. ❑ **dance on nothing** *v.* (*also* **dance on nothing at the sheriff's door, ...in a hempen cravat, ...at the tolling of a bell**) [the sheriff has jurisdiction over the hanging, thus the *sheriff's door* is that of a prison, outside which the hanging took place; *HEMPEN CRAVAT under* HEMPEN *adj.*] [18C–1930s] to hang; also as n., a judicial hanging. ❑ **dance the Newgate hornpipe** *v.* [*Newgate*, the site of London's major prison and public executions] [late 18C–mid-19C] ❑ **dance the Paddington frisk** *v.* (*also* **do the Paddington frisk, go in the road to Paddington**) [Tyburn, the site of London's main 18C gallows, was in the then village of *Paddington*, near the modern Marble Arch] [mid-18C–early 19C] ❑ **dance the Tyburn hornpipe on nothing** *v.* [the role of *Tyburn* as an execution ground] [late 18C–mid-19C] ❑ **dance the Tyburn jig** *v.* (*also* **do the Tyburn jig**) [*Tyburn*, the site of London's main 18C gallows, was in the then village of Paddington, near the modern Marble Arch] [late 17C–mid-19C] ❑ **dance upon nothing** *v.* [late 18C–mid-19C]

SE in slang uses

IN PHRASES

❑ **dance a haka** *v.* [Maori *haka*, a posture dance, accompanied by chants; a war-dance] [1940s–50s] (*N.Z.*) to express one's pleasure. ❑ **dance in the hog trough** *v.* (*also* **...pig trough**) [? to have no suitors and have, therefore, to dance with the swine] [mid-19C] (*US*) **1** of an older sister, to be left unmarried when a younger sister has already found a husband. **2** to be the last child in a family to be married. ❑ **dance in the sandbox** *v.* [var. on SE *throw sand in one's eyes*] [1960s] (*US black*) to scheme, to deceive. ❑ **dance on someone's lips** *v.* (*also* **dance on someone's face**) [1980s+] (*US black*) **1** to hit in the face. **2** to kick in the face. ❑ **dance someone around** *v.* (*US*) **1** [1970s] to deceive, to 'mess around'. **2** [1980s] to harass, to pressurize. ❑ **dance the chocolate cha-cha** *v. see CHOCOLATE CHA-CHA under* CHOCOLATE *adj.* ❑ **dance the stairs** *v. see* sense 3 above.

dancer *n.* [SE *dance*, later strengthened DANCE *v.* (3)] [mid-19C+] a cat burglar who 'dances' along the roof and in through a convenient window, or a thief entering a house to rob the upstairs, when the residents are not in bed, or are out; thus usu. a daylight robbery; 20C use also refers to those who steal from empty offices.

dancers *n.* [one *dances* down the stairs or on one's feet] **1** [mid-17C+] (*orig. UK Und.*) a flight of stairs. **2** [1950s+] the feet.

IN PHRASES

❑ **have it on one's dancers** *v.* [1970s] to run off, to escape. ❑ **track up the dancers** *v.* (*also* **lope..., pike...**) [SE *track*, to make one's way] [late 17C–mid-19C] to rush quickly up the stairs; also with *down*.

dancing academy *n.* (*also* **dancing school**) [DANCE *v.* (1) + ACADEMY *n.* (1)/SE *school*] [late 16C–early 18C] a brothel.

dancing dog *n.* [SE *dancing* + SE *dog*/DOG *n.*[2] (1b); the term was used in a period when dancing was no longer seen as fashionable] [late 19C–1900s] a man who enjoys dancing.

dancing master *n.* **1** [17C] the hangman [DANCE *v.* (2)]. **2** [mid-17C–early 18C] an upper-class rowdy who found his amusement in making his victims 'dance' by stabbing at their legs with his sword [SE *dance*]. **3** [mid-19C] a cat burglar [SE *dance*].

dancing school *n. see* DANCING ACADEMY *n.*

dand *n.* [abbr.] [late 19C] a *dandy*.

Dan Dares *n.* [rhy. sl.; ult. SF character *Dan Dare*, who appeared in the *Eagle* comic from 1950] [1990s+] flared trousers, flares.

d and d *n.* [late 19C+] the criminal charge of *d*runk and *d*isorderly.

d & d *adj.* [abbr.] **1** [20C+] *d*runk and *d*isorderly. **2** [1930s+] *d*eaf and *d*umb.

dandeprat *n. see* DANDIPRAT *n.*

dandered *adj.* (*also* **dander**) [SE *get one's dander up*] [mid–late 19C] angry.

dandery *adj.* [SE *get one's dander up*] [early 19C] (*US*) irritated, angry, alarmed.

d. and i. *n.* [1970s+] the criminal charge of *d*runk and *i*ncapable.

dandiprat *n.* (*also* **dandeprat, dandprat, dandyprat**) [16C–17C SE *dandiprat*, a small coin worth 1½ old pence. F&H says 'half a farthing' in late 15C; Cotgrave, *Dict. French and English Tongues* (1611), defines it as 'a slender little fellow or dwarf'] [mid-16C–19C] an insignificant, contemptible person.

dandisette/dandizette *n. see* DANDYSETTE *n.*

dandle *n. see* DADDLE *n.*

d & m *n.* [abbr.] [1990s+] (*orig. US teen*) a *d*eep *and m*eaningful conversation.

dandruff *n.* **1** [1950s–80s] a head butt. **2** [1970s] (*US*) light snow.

SE in slang uses

IN PHRASES

❑ **get one's dandruff up** *v.* [joc. corruption of the colloq. *get one's dander up* + image of flecks of dandruff rising as one gesticulates with rage] [20C+] (*US*) to lose one's temper.
❑ **swap dandruff** *v. see under* SWAP *v.*

dandy *n.*[1] [Hind. *dandi*, a staff or oar] (*Anglo-Ind.*) **1** [late 17C–19C] a Ganges boatman. **2** [late 19C] 'a kind of vehicle used in the Himalaya, consisting of a strong cloth slung like a hammock to a bamboo staff, and carried by two (or more) men [dandy-wallahs]' (Y&B).

dandy *n.*[2] [SE *dandy*] [late 18C+] **1** a first-rate, admirable thing; an extreme example, negative as well as positive. **2** an admirable person, a skilful person.

IN COMPOUNDS

❑ **dandy boy** *n.* [1940s+] (*W.I.*) a well-dressed young man.
❑ **dandy dude** *n.* [DUDE *n.*[1] (2)] [1940s] (*W.I.*) a dandy.

dandy *n.*[3] [? fig. use of DANDY *adj.*] [mid-19C+] (*orig. Irish*) **1** a small drink, usu. of whisky. **2** the glass in which it is served.

dandy *n.*[4] [late 19C] (*UK Und.*) an imitation gold coin, a fake sovereign; also *dandy-master*, a forger of gold coins.

dandy *adj.* [SE *dandy*, i.e. something of which the fashionable dandy would approve] [late 18C+] attractive, first-rate, excellent, a general term of approbation; thus *the dandy*, the correct thing, 'the ticket'.

dandy *adv.* [DANDY *adj.*] [20C+] (*orig. US*) excellently, wonderfully.

dandyfunk *n.* (*also* **dundefunk, dunderfunk**) [? SE *dandy*, a sloop, a cutter + *funk*, a smell] [mid-19C–1900s] (*US*) a mixture of powdered biscuit, molasses and fat.

dandyprat *n. see* DANDIPRAT *n.*

dandysette *n.* (*also* **dandisette, dandizette**) [SE *dandy* + fem. sfx -(*s*)*ette*] **1** [early–mid-19C] a female dandy. **2** [1960s+] (*US*) a lesbian.

dang *n.*[1] [orig. UK dial., but 20C+ use is US] [late 18C+] a euph. for DAMN *n.*

dang *n.*[2] *see* DONG *n.*[1] (1).

dang *adj.* (*also* **dang-bang, dang-burn, dang-gum, dangy**) [? euph.; DAMN *adj.* + SE *hang*] [mid-19C+] damned.

dang *v.* [orig. dial.] **1** [early 19C+] a euph. for SE *damn*. **2** [mid-19C] to curse, to abuse.

dang! *excl.* [late 18C+] a euph. for DAMN! *excl.* and used in similar combs., e.g. *dang it!by dang!dang my buttons!*

dang-bang *adj. see* DANG *adj.*

dangbatted *adj.* [DINGBAT *n.*[7] (1)] [1960s] (*US*) crazy.

dang-burn *adj. see* DANG *adj.*

dange *n. see* DONG *n.*[1] (1).

danged *adj.* [DANG *adj.*] [mid-19C+] (*US*) a euph. for DAMNED *adj.*

danger *n.* [1920s+] a chance, a possibility, a likelihood.

IN PHRASES

❑ **no danger** [1920s+] a general phr. of affirmation, no problem, absolutely, truthfully.

dangermuff *n.* [SE *danger* + MUFF *n.*[1] (4)] [1990s+] an extremely attractive, sexy woman.

danger signal *n.* [late 19C] (*UK Und.*) a policeman.

IN PHRASES

❑ **danger signal is up** *see* FLAG IS UP, THE *under* FLAG *n.*[2].

dang-gum *adj. see* DANG *adj.*

dangle *n.* [1910s+] the penis.

IN COMPOUNDS

❑ **dangle queen** *n.* [-QUEEN *sfx* (3)] [1980s+] (*US gay*) one who wears clothes that deliberately emphasize the penis, or who exposes the genitals.

IN PHRASES

❑ **on the dangle** *adj.* [1970s] (*US campus*) of the penis, flaccid; of a person, sexually unexcited.

dangle *v.* **1** [late 17C–18C] to hang. **2** [18C+] to follow a woman, without actually addressing her. **3** [early–mid-18C] to pursue. **4** [mid-18C] to be in attendance, e.g. as a servant. **5** [1920s–60s] to go, to travel, to move. **6** [1930s] (*US*) to go away, esp. in imper. *dangle!* go away! **7** [1960s+] to keep waiting, lit. or fig.

IN PHRASES

❑ **dangle in a Tyburn string** *v.* [*Tyburn*, the site of the gallows] [late 18C] to be hanged. ❑ **dangle in the sheriff's picture-frame** *v.* [late 18C–early 19C] to be hanged.

SE in slang uses

IN PHRASES

❑ **dangle one's donger** *v. see under* DONGER *n.*[1].

dangler *n.* **1** [18C+] a hanger-on; a suitor [DANGLE *v.* (2)]. **2** [mid-18C–mid-19C] one who follows women in the street but does not actually speak to them; a roué; a womanizer [DANGLE *v.* (2)]. **3** [late 18C] an effeminate male who prefers female company; the inference is of homosexuality. **4** [mid-19C+] (*UK Und.*) any form of pendant jewellery, e.g. a watch fob, an earring. **5** [1910s–30s] (*US tramp*) a tramp who travels via hanging on to the rails and similar handgrips beneath a passenger coach. **6** [1920s+] (*Aus./US*) an exhibitionist [SE *dangle*, v./DANGLE *n.*]. **7** [1920s+] (*US*) a thief [? he keeps one *dangling* in expectation of money]. **8** [1930s–50s] (*US tramp*) a freight train [the wagons 'dangle' behind the locomotive]. **9** [1970s+] (*US gay/Aus.*) a (large) penis. **10** [1990s+] (*US black*) a businessman [? he keeps one *dangling* in expectation of money].

dangle roll *n.* [DANGLE *v.* (5), i.e. one must leave the game] [1990s+] (*US black*) a losing throw of the dice in craps.

danglers *n.* **1** [mid-19C] a bunch of seals (hanging from a watch chain). **2** [mid-19C+] the testicles.

dangling modifier *n.* [pun on the grammatical term] [1980s+] (*US campus*) a single, long, flashy earring.

dangy *adj. see* DANG *adj.*

daniel *n.*[1] [? corruption of SE *dangle*] [1930s–40s] (*US black*) the buttocks.

daniel *n.*[2] [1990s+] (*Aus. teen*) a rowdy person.

Danish *n.* [1980s] (*US*) conventional penetrative heterosexual sexual intercourse.

Danish pastry *n.* [the ref. is to the pioneering operation undergone in Denmark in 1952 by Christine (formerly George) Jorgensen] [1950s–60s] (*gay*) a transsexual.

dank *n.* [DANK NUGS *under* DANK *adj.*] [1980s+] (*US black/drugs*) extremely strong marijuana.

dank *adj.* [SE *dank*, which is always negative and usu. refers to swamps and marshes] [1980s+] (*orig. US campus*) **1** bad, unpleasant. **2** (*also* **diggity dank**) excellent, first-rate [presumably on the bad = good model].

IN COMPOUNDS

❑ **dank nugs** *n.* (*also* **dark nuggets**) [1990s+] (*US drugs*) the very best marijuana.

danna *n.* [DUNNAKEN *n.*] [late 18C–mid-19C] human or other excrement; thus *danna drag*, a nightman's or dustman's cart.

dannie *n.* [ext. of DANDY *n.*[3] (1)] [20C+] a drink of liquor.

Danny boy *n.* [the picture on the pre-Euro note was of Irish politician *Daniel O'Connell* (1775–1847)] [2000s] (*Irish*) £20.

Danny La Rue *n.* [rhy. sl.; ult. *Danny La Rue*, stage name of British entertainer and female impersonator *Daniel Patrick Carroll* (b.1927)] **1** [1980s] (*Aus.*) an act of defecation [= POO *n.*[1] (2)]. **2** [2000s] a clue, an idea, suspicion. **3** [2000s] (*bingo*) the number 52.

Danny Marr *n.* [rhy. sl.] [2000s] a car.

dant *n.* [synon. Du. *dante*] [early–mid-16C] a promiscuous woman.

dan tucker *n.* (*also* **danny rucker**) [rhy. sl.; ? anecdotal] [mid–late 19C; 1930s+] **1** butter. **2** by ext., breakfast.

dap *n.*[1] [SE *dab*, to strike] [1970s+] (*US black*) a ritualistic handshake, differing from area to area, involving much slapping of palms, snapping of fingers etc; thus v.

dap *n.*[2] [abbr. *d*ignity *a*nd *p*ride] [1970s+] (*US black*) credit, acknowledgement, respect, self-awareness.

dap *adj.* (*also* **dapt**) [SE *dapper*, spruce, neat] [1950s+] **1** (*US black/P.R.*) alert, aware, knowledgeable, sophisticated. **2** (*US black/P.R.*) well-dressed. **3** (*US black*) of a person, pleasant, generous.

IN COMPOUNDS

❑ **dap daddy** *n.* (*also* **doogie daddy**) [DADDY *n.* (7); *doogie* = do good] [1950s+] (*US black*) a well-dressed man.

IN PHRASES

❑ **dapped down** *adj.* [1950s+] (*US black*) very well dressed. ❑ **dapped to a T** *adj.* (*also* **dapped to a tee**) [1950s+] (*US black*) very well dressed.

dap *v.* [? SE *dab*, to touch lightly] [20C+] to pick up, to steal, esp. luggage.

daphne *n.* [initial letters] **1** [1980s] (*Aus.*) a foolish woman [SE *daft*]. **2** [2000s] (*S.Afr. gay*) a deaf person; thus as adj., deaf.

dapper *n.* [SE *dapper* + DAP *adj.* (1)] [1990s+] (*UK black*) a general term of congratulation, an admirable person.

dapper *adj.* [ext. of SE + DAP *adj.* (1)] [1960s+] (*US black*) admirable, excellent.

dappy *adj. see* DIPPY *adj.*

daps *n.* [? dial. *dap*, the bounce of a ball, a hop, i.e. the image of bouncing along in one's rubber-soled shoes] **1** [1920s–30s] slippers. **2** [1940s+] gym shoes, tennis shoes.

dapt *adj. see* DAP *adj.*

dapto *n.* [the *Dapto* Dog Races, held in NSW; thus a DOG *n.*[2] (1b)] [1970s] (*Aus. teen*) a general insult.

Dapto dog *n.* [rhy. sl. = WOG *n.*[1] (1)] [1970s] (*Aus.*) a derog. term for a black or Asian person.

d.a.r. *n.* [play on abbr. of *d*amned *a*verage *r*aiser and *D*aughters of the *A*merican *R*evolution] [1930s–40s] (*US campus*) an academically successful student.

darb *n.*[1] [? DAB *n.*[1] (1) or fig. ext. of DARB *n.*[2]] **1** [20C+] anything or anyone seen as first-rate; as *the darb*, 'the thing'. **2** [1910s–40s] (*US tramp*) an attractive woman. **3** [1920s–40s] a fool.

DERIVATIVES

❑ **darberoo** *n.* [-EROO *sfx*] [1930s] a good thing.

darb *n.*[2] [? DARBY *n.*[1] (1)] [1900s–40s] (*US Und.*) money, usu. stolen.

darb *adj.* [DARB *n.*[1] (1)] [1930s–60s] (*US Und.*) highly competent.

darbies *n.* [16C SE *Father Darby's bands*, a moneylender's bond of particular severity, which effectively bound the borrower to the lender while the debt remained outstanding] **1** [late 17C+] shackles, fetters, handcuffs; thus *darbies and joans*, fetters linking a pair of prisoners; *darby-ringer*, a villain [for *darbies and joans, see* DARBY AND JOAN *n.*]. **2** [early 19C; 1980s+] in fig. use, anything that shackles one. **3** [mid-19C] sausages.

IN COMPOUNDS

❑ **darby-cove** *n.* [COVE *n.* (1)] [mid-19C] (*UK Und.*) a blacksmith; thus *darby crib*, *darby ken*, a smithy. ❑ **darby roll** *n.* [early 19C] a style of walking that betrays an individual's experience of fetters and thus time spent in prison. ❑ **darby's fair** *n.* [mid-19C] the day on which a prisoner is moved from one prison to another, and must thus be fettered.

darble *n.* [mangled pron. of Fr. *diable*] [mid-19C] the devil.

darbs *n.* [? backsl., the pips on a card resembles the *brads* or shoemakers' rivets in the sole of a boot] [1930s] playing cards.

darby *n.*[1] (*also* **derby**) [for ety. *see* DARBIES *n.*] **1** [late 17C–1920s] (*UK Und.*) money. **2** [mid-19C+] (*UK Und.*) a haul of stolen goods. **3** [1920s] (*US*) a wealthy person who will usu. pay the bill in a restaurant/bar etc.

IN PHRASES

❑ **come down with the derbies** *v.* [late 18C–early 19C] to pay a bill or a debt.

darby *n.*[2] [ety. unknown; ? anecdotal] [19C] (*Irish*) a glass of whisky; usu. as *small darby*.

darby *adj.* [DARB *n.*[1] (1)] [1910s–30s] (*US*) wonderful, excellent, first-rate.

darby *v.* [DARBIES *n.* (1)] [late 19C] (*Aus. prison*) to handcuff, to shackle.

darby and joan *n.* [rhy. sl.; the phr. *Darby and Joan*, a synon. for an elderly, poss. impoverished, long-married couple, first appeared in the *Gentleman's Magazine* (V, 1735) in a verse titled 'The joys of love never forgot, a song'. The third verse runs: 'Old Darby, with Joan by his side,/You've often regarded with wonder,/He's dropsical, she is sore-eyed,/Yet they're never happy asunder.' Whether the names refer to real-life characters (*Darby* is not a common UK name) or are taken from some earlier fiction remains unknown] **1** [1920s+] the telephone. **2** [1940s+] (*Aus.*) a loan.

darby and joan *adj.* [rhy. sl.; ult. *see* prev.] [1940s–70s] alone; thus in phr. *on one's Darby*, by oneself.

darby kelly *n.* (*also* **darby kell, derby kel**) [rhy. sl. = SE *belly*] [20C+] the stomach.

dard *n.* [Fr. *dard*, a dart; note synon. Fr. sl. *dard* + *darder*, 'to fuck'] [17C–18C] the penis.

dargie *n. see* DOGGY *n.* (1).

dark *n.* **1** [mid–late 19C] (*Aus.*) Australian-distilled, dark, very strong brandy [the dark red colour]. **2** [mid-19C+] (*US*) a derog. term for a black person [abbr. DARKIE *n.* (1)/SE *dark*]. **3** [late 19C–1900s] (*Aus./US prison*) solitary confinement in a dark cell. **4** [1910s] (*Aus.*) a nickname for those with dark hair or complexion. **5** [1960s] (*US campus*) a fool, a dullard [DARK *adj.* (1)]. **6** [1980s+] (*Aus. prison*) tobacco [the dark red colour].

IN COMPOUNDS

❑ **darktown** *n.* (*also* **darkytown**) [DARKIE *n.* (1)] [late 19C+] (*US*) the black area of a town or city.

SE in slang uses

IN COMPOUNDS

❑ **darkman** *n.* **1** [early–mid-18C] a nightwatchman. **2** *see* DARKMANS *n.* (1).

IN PHRASES

❑ **in the dark** *adj.* [the colour of the coffee] [late 19C–1940s] (*US*) of coffee, black.

dark *adj.* **1** [mid-17C–early 18C; 1940s+] (*later use W.I.*) stupid, ignorant [SE *dark*, unenlightened, uninformed, as in *dark ages*]. **2** [mid-19C+] (*20C+ use Irish/W.I.*) weak-sighted, nearly or actually blind. **3** [late 19C+] a derog. term meaning pertaining to black people; usu. in combs. below [DARK *n.* (2)]. **4** [1980s+] (*Aus. prison*) angry (with). **5** [1990s+] (*UK black*) aggressive, very serious. **6** [1990s+] (*UK teen*) a general negative, bad, unpleasant, second-rate etc.

(IN COMPOUNDS)

❑ **Dark City** *n.* [1950s–60s] (*S.Afr.*) the township of Alexandra, near Johannesburg. ❑ **dark cloud** *n.* [1900s–50s] (*usu. Aus./US*) a derog. term for a black person, a Native Australian. ❑ **dark man** *n.* [1970s] (*Aus.*) a derog. term for an Aborigine. ❑ **dark meat** *n.* see separate entry. ❑ **dark-sambo** *n.* [SAMBO *n.*[1] (2)] [1950s+] (*W.I.*) a person of mixed race, with one-quarter white to three-quarters black. ❑ **dark stuff** *n.* [1960s] (*US*) a black person, usu. a woman, in a sexual context.

SE in slang uses

(IN COMPOUNDS)

❑ **dark cell** *n.* [its lack of amenities] [20C+] (*US Und.*) a prison punishment cell. ❑ **dark cully** *n.* [CULLY *n.*[1] (2)] [18C–mid-19C] (*UK Und.*) one who keeps a mistress and only dares visit her surreptitiously at night. ❑ **dark engineer** *n.* [SE *engineer*, to manipulate, to perform] [late 17C] a villain. ❑ **dark glim** *n.* [mid–late 18C] (*UK Und.*) a dark lanthorn. ❑ **dark (hole)** *n.* **1** [late 19C] the vagina. **2** [2000s] (*S.Afr. gay*) the anus. ❑ **dark house** *n.* **1** [early 17C–mid-19C] a room used to confine the insane. **2** [late 17C] a tavern offering bedrooms for the night. ❑ **dark lantern** *n.* [mid-19C] a thief's candle or light, made so as to shut out the light when not needed. ❑ **dark lanthorn** *n.* (*also* **dark lantern**) [he metaphorically diverts the light of his lantern from the robbery] [late 17C–mid-19C] a servant or agent who takes and transmits a bribe offered to his master.

(IN PHRASES)

❑ **dark as an abo's arsehole** *adj.* [1960s] (*Aus.*) very dark. ❑ **dark as a nigger's pocket** *adj.* [mid-19C–1910s] (*Aus.*) very dark. ❑ **dark as Newgate** *adj.* see ...NEWGATE *under* BLACK AS... *adj.* ❑ **dark as the inside of a cow** *adj.* [UK use is naut. only] [late 19C+] (*Can./US*) very dark. ❑ **dark it** *v.* [late 19C] to say nothing; esp. as imper. *dark it!* be quiet! keep quiet! ❑ **dark out** *v.* [1990s+] (*UK black*) to kill.

dark and dim *n.* [rhy. sl.] [20C+] (*Aus.*) a swim.

dark and dim *v.* [rhy. sl.] [1900s] (*Aus.*) to swim.

darkee *n.* see DARKEY *n.*

darken someone's daylights *v.* see *under* DAYLIGHTS *n.*

darkers *n.* [SE *dark* (*glasses*)] [1950s+] (*W.I. Rasta*) sunglasses.

darkey *n.* (*also* **darkee, darky**) [DARKMANS *n.*] **1** [mid-18C–19C] night-time. **2** [19C] a 'dark', i.e. shuttered, lantern. **3** [early 19C] (*US Und.*) a cloudy sky. **4** [mid-19C] twilight. **5** [late 19C] a night watchman. **6** see DARKIE *n.*

darkey *adj.* see DARKIE *adj.*

dark felt *n.* [rhy. sl.] [20C+] (*Aus.*) a belt.

darkie *n.* (*also* **darkey, darky**) [coined in the UK, the term has spread to all English-language slangs, denoting Afro-Americans, Aborigines, Maoris and others] **1** [late 18C+] a derog., patronizing description of a black person; also used ironically by blacks as a self-description. **2** [mid-19C] a derog. term of address to a black person. **3** [mid-19C] (*UK Und.*) a beggar who feigns blindness. **4** [mid–late 19C] in pl., a collective term for a variety of late-night music-halls and bars on or near the Strand, London, usu. situated below ground level, e.g. the Shades, the Cider Cellars and the Coal Hole. **5** [1930s] a person with dark hair. **6** [1980s] a dark-skinned person, e.g. a Latino.

(IN PHRASES)

❑ **choke a darkie** *v.* (*also* **park a darkie, sink..., strangle...**) [SE *choke* + pun on SE *dark* + sfx *-y*/DARKIE *n.*] [1960s+] (*Aus.*) to defecate.

darkie *adj.* (*also* **darkey, darky**) [mid-19C+] (*US*) a derog. ref.; pertaining to black people or culture.

darkie *adv.* [DARKIE *n.* (1)] [1920s] (*US*) in a stereotypically black manner.

darkmans *n.* [SE *dark* + -MANS *sfx*] **1** [mid-16C–19C] (*UK Und.*) (*also* **darkman, darkum**) the night. **2** [early 19C] (*UK Und.*) a covered 'dark' lantern.

(IN COMPOUNDS)

❑ **darkmans budge** *n.* [BUDGE *n.*[1] (1)] [late 17C–early 19C] (*UK Und.*) a thief's accomplice, who climbs into a house through a window and opens a door to admit the rest of the gang.

dark meat *n.* **1** [late 19C; 1930s+] (*also* **dark shanks, dark-skinned meat**) black people, esp. as sex objects. **2** [1940s] the 'black sheep'. **3** [1940s+] (*US*) the black penis or vagina.

darks, the *n.* **1** [late 18C] the night. **2** [mid-19C] (*UK prison*) the punishment cell, solitary confinement. **3** [2000s] depression.

darkum *n.* see DARKMANS *n.* (1).

darky *n.*[1] see DARKEY *n.*

darky *n.*[2] see DARKIE *n.*

darky *adj.* see DARKIE *adj.*

darl *n.* [abbr. SE *darling*] **1** [1930s+] (*mainly Aus.*) (*also* **darls**) a general term of endearment. **2** [2000s] (*N.Z.*) a lesbian.

darling it hurts *n.* [rhy. sl.] [20C+] (*Aus.*) Darlinghurst, a rough inner-city area of Sydney.

darling pea *n.* [SAusE *Darling pea*, a variety of *Swainsona*, a herb that can cause cattle to suffer from stiffness of limbs, muscle tremor and uncoordination] [late 19C–1910s] (*Aus.*) madness, eccentricity; usu. as *have/get the darling pea*, to act eccentrically.

Darlo *n.* [abbr. + -O *sfx* (3)] [1930s+] (*Aus.*) *Darl*inghurst.

(IN COMPOUNDS)

❑ **Darlo drop** *n.* [1990s+] (*Aus. police/Und.*) police brutality towards a victim in custody.

darn *n.* (*also* **dern**) [mid-19C+] a euph. for DAMN *n.*

darn *adj.* (*also* **dern, durn**) [late 18C+] a euph. for DAMN *adj.*

darn *v.* [mid-19C+] a euph. for SE *damn*.

darn *adv.* (*also* **darnation, durn**) [19C+] a euph. for DAMN *adv.*, i.e. very or very much.

darn! *excl.* (*also* **darn my whiskers! dern! dern my skin!**) [mid-19C+] (*US*) a euph. for DAMN! *excl.*

darnation *adj.* (*also* **dernation**) [DARNATION! *excl.*] [late 18C+] (*US*) a euph. for DAMNED *adj.*

darnation! *excl.* (*also* **durnation!**) [19C+] a euph. for DAMNATION! *excl.*

darned *adj.* (*also* **derned, durned**) [19C+] a euph. for DAMNED *adj.*; thus *darnedest*, very damned.

(IN PHRASES)

❑ **do one's darnedest** *v.* [20C+] (*orig. US*) to do one's very best.

(IN EXCLAMATIONS)

❑ **I'll be darned!** (*also* **I'll be durned! ...goll darned! ...gosh-darned! ...gosh-dashed! I'm darned!**) [19C+] a mild oath, a euph. for *I'LL BE DAMNED! under* DAMNED *adj.*

darned *adv.* [mid-19C+] a euph. for DAMNED *adv.*

darrel lea *n.* [rhy. sl.; ult. a well-known brand of chocolate] [1980s+] (*Aus. prison*) tea.

Darren Gough *n.* [rhy. sl.] [1990s+] a cough.

darry *n.* [? DERREY *n.*] [1940s–50s] (*UK prison*) a look.

darryl *n.* [? negative stereotyping of the proper name] [1990s+] a general term of abuse.

dart *n.*[1] [SE *dart* used fig. to describe the target as much as the missile] (*Aus.*) **1** [late 19C] one's fancy or favourite. **2** [late 19C] an illicit activity, a 'racket'. **3** [late 19C–1910] a plan, an aim, a scheme. **4** [late 19C+] a try, a 'go'. **5** [20C+] a good idea.

dart *n.*[2] [2000s] (*US drugs*) a hypodermic syringe.

dart accent *n.* (*also* **dortspeak, Roadwatch accent**) [DART, *D*ublin *A*rea *R*apid *T*ransit, i.e. those areas served by the system. The accent was orig. identified among radio/TV presenters (thus the ref. to the programme *Roadwatch*) and is typified by the use of the phoneme 'ou' in such words as 'cow'] [1990s+] (*Irish*) an affectedly quasi-British accent, adopted by the middle class in and around Dublin.

daru *n.* [Bhojpuri *daaruu*, liquor] [20C+] (*W.I.*) rum.

Darwin blonde *n.* [proper name *Darwin* + SE *blonde*; the ref. is to the Aborigine population of Northern Territory, of which Darwin is the capital] [1940s] (*Aus.*) a mixed-race woman.

Darwin stubby *n.* [proper name *Darwin* + STUBBIE *n.* (1)] [1970s+] (*Aus.*) an extra-large beer bottle: introduced in 1958 at 80 fl.oz (2.25 litres).

d.a.'s *n.* [*d*omestic *a*fflictions] [mid-19C–1920s] the menstrual flow.

dash *n.*[1] [SE *dash*, to rush about or, n., style, flair] [late 17C–19C] a tavern waiter.

SE in slang uses

IN PHRASES

❑ **dash in the bloomers** *n.* [1960s+] sexual intercourse, usu. quick and adulterous. ❑ **dash of the tarbrush** *n. see* TOUCH OF THE TARBRUSH *under* TOUCH *n.*[1]. ❑ **do one's dash** *v.* (*also* **lose one's dash**) [1910s+] (*Aus.*) to reach one's limit, to exhaust one's energies, to lose one's opportunity – and suffer accordingly.

dash *n.*[2] [SE *dashee*, a gift, present, gratuity; a 'Negrish word' used on the Guinea Coast] [late 18C+] a tip, bribery, the money paid as a bribe.

dash *n.*[3] [SE *dash*, style] [early 19C] (*US*) an attractive young woman.

dash *n.*[4] [fig. use of SE *dash*, a short run] [early 19C+] an attempt.

IN PHRASES

❑ **do one's dash** *v.* [1910s] (*Aus.*) to become infatuated, to fall in love. ❑ **have a dash** *v.* **1** [early 19C+] to try, to make an attempt. **2** [late 19C] to make a bet.

dash *n.*[5] [backform. f. HAVE A DASH OF LAVENDER *under* LAVENDER *adj.*] [1970s+] (*US gay*) a latent homosexual.

dash *adj. see* DASHED *adj.*

dash *v.* [DASH! *excl.*] [1990s+] (*UK black*) to become enraged with.

dash! *excl.* [from the dash that replaces the 'am' in *damn!*, i.e. *d–n!*, and subseq. in other 'obscenities'; note Captain Alexander Smith, *History of the Lives of the Most Noted Highwaymen* (5th edn, 1719): 'If we have here and there brought in some of these wicked offenders venting a profane oath or curse, which is dashed, it is to paint them in their proper colours'] [early 19C+] a general euph. for excls. using taboo obscenities.

IN EXCLAMATIONS

❑ **dash it (all)!** [19C+] a general euph. excl. ❑ **dash my buttons!** (*also* **dang my buttons! darn...! dash my rags! ...skin! ...timbers! doggone my buttons!**) [19C–1910s] a mild oath. ❑ **dash my wig(s)!** (*also* **burn my old wig! dash my jasey!**) [late 18C–19C] a mild oath. ❑ **double-dash!** (*also* **double damn!**) [mid-19C; 1970s] a more emphatic version of DASH! *excl.*

dash away belly *v. see* THROW AWAY BELLY *under* BELLY *n.*

dashed *adj.* (*also* **bashed, dash, dished**) [DASH! *excl.*] [mid-19C+] a general adj. of annoyance or irritation; lit. the use of a dash when printing DAMNED *adj.*

dasher *n.* [ext. use of SE *cut a dash*] **1** [mid-18C–19C] a flashy prostitute. **2** [late 18C–1950s] a smart young person, keen on parties and socializing. **3** [early 19C+] a 'fast' young woman. **4** [late 19C] a dashing attempt. **5** [late 19C+] (*W.I.*) a dandy. **6** [late 19C+] (*W.I.*) a womanizer.

dashing *adj.* [SE *cut a dash*; SE in 20C+] [19C] showy, given to excess, esp. in dress.

dasted *adj.* [late 19C] (*US*) a euph. mix of DAMNED *adj.* and BLASTED *adj.*[1].

dasy *n. see* DAISY *n.* (1).

date *n.*[1] **1** [late 19C+] (*orig. US*) a person with whom one makes or has made an appointment or engagement, usu. for social/sexual purposes; thus *double date*, for two couples to join each other on the same engagement; *dated*, 'booked' for an engagement or meeting; *dating*, going on dates. **2** [late 19C+] (*orig. US*) the appointment that has been made. **3** [1930s+] (*US*) a prostitute's client. **4** [1950s+] (*US*) a paid encounter with a prostitute.

IN COMPOUNDS

❑ **date bait** *n.* **1** [1940s+] (*US campus*) someone with whom one would like to form a relationship. **2** [1950s] (*US black*) a boy- or girlfriend. **3** [1980s+] something that will persuade a member of the opposite sex to accept the offer of a date.

IN PHRASES

❑ **dry date** *n. see under* DRY *adj.*[1].

date *n.*[2] [the common use of fruit to indicate stupidity] [1900s–50s] a foolish or comic person; thus (*UK juv.*) *soppy date*, an affectionate term of abuse.

date *n.*[3] [rhy. sl.; *date and plum* = BUM *n.*[1] (1); note 17C *dog-date*, dog excrement, from supposed resemblance] **1** [1910s] (*Aus.*) a term of abuse [f. sense 2]. **2** [1910s+] (*Aus./N.Z./UK*) the anus, the backside as a whole.

IN COMPOUNDS

❑ **date-puncher** *n.* (*also* **date driller, ...packer**) [1980s+] (*Aus.*) a male homosexual.

date *v.*[1] (*also* **date up**) [DATE *n.*[1] (2)] [20C+] (*orig. US*) to have an affair with someone, to be going out together on a number of pre-arranged days.

IN PHRASES

❑ **date Rosy Palm and her (five) sisters** *v. see* HAVE A BIG DATE WITH ROSY PALM *under* ROSY PALM AND HER FIVE (LITTLE) SISTERS *n.*

date *v.*[2] [DATE *n.*[3] (2)] [1910s+] (*Aus./N.Z.*) to caress the buttocks; to 'goose', i.e to stick a thumb or finger into someone's anus.

date *v.*[3] [1990s+] to have sexual intercourse.

datty *adj.* [? DOTTY *adj.* (2) + BATTY *adj.*[1]] [2000s] (*UK teen*) mad.

daub *n.*[1] (*also* **dawb**) [DAUB v.] **1** [18C] a bribe. **2** [1960s] a spot of grease used to mark a card.

daub *n.*[2] [mid-19C] (*US Und.*) a ribbon.

daub *n.*[3] [SE *daub*, a second-rate painting] [mid-19C–1900s] an artist.

daub *v.* (*also* **dawb**) [? SE *daub*, to lay on thick; dial. *daub*, to flatter, to 'butter up', cf. SE phr. *grease one's palm*] [16C–mid-19C] to bribe.

dauber *n.* (*also* **dobber**) [? link to dial. *dobber*, a 'wonder'] [1910s+] (*US*) spirit, morale.

daughter *n.* **1** [1940s–70s] a male homosexual brought into the gay world by a homosexual friend. **2** [1990s+] (*UK black/W.I.*) any young woman, irrespective of relationship.

SE in slang uses

IN PHRASES

❑ **daughter of pleasure** *n. see* LADY OF PLEASURE *under* LADY *n.* ❑ **daughters of the game** *n. see* GAME *n.* (1a).

dave *adj.* [? orig. anecdotal] [1990s+] a general positive term, friendly, excellent.

Davey's locker *n. see* DAVY JONES'S LOCKER *n.*

David Gower *n.* [rhy. sl.; ult. UK cricketer *David Gower* (1957–)] [1990s+] a shower (of rain).

David Jones *n.* [rhy. sl. + DAVY JONES'S LOCKER *n.*] [1980s] (*Aus.*) bones.

David Joneses *n. see* DAVY JONES'S LOCKER *n.*

davy *n.* [abbr. SE *affidavit*] **1** [late 18C–1950s] an oath; thus *on my davy*, on my oath, on my honour; *take one's davy*, to swear an oath. **2** [19C] God, usu. in phrs., e.g. *so help my Davy*.

Davy Crockett *n.*[1] [proper name *Davy Crockett* (1786–1836), frontiersman, trapper, US Congressman and one of those who died defending the Alamo; in this context he was seen as 'trapping' men for the services] [1940s] (*US black/Harlem*) a draft board official during WW2.

Davy Crockett *n.*[2] [rhy. sl.] [1950s+] a pocket.

Davy Jones's locker *n.* (*also* **Davey's locker, David Joneses, Davy Jones, Davy Jones's chest-lid, Davy Jones's dock-yard, Davy's locker, Jones's locker, old Davey**) [at best *Davy Jones* represents the spirit of the sea, at worst he is the ocean's own devil (thus Dickens, *Bleak House*, 1853: 'If you only have to swab a plank, you should swab it as if Davy Jones were after you'); either way it is in his 'locker' that drowned seamen are stowed. The identification was first printed by Tobias Smollett in *Peregrine Pickle* (1751). The ety. remains obscure, but *DSUE* suggests that *Jones* refers to Jonah whose own 'locker' was the belly of the whale. *Davy*, it is proposed, may have been added by Welsh sailors] [18C+] a watery grave; thus death in general.

IN PHRASES

❑ **go to Davy Jones's locker** *v.* [mid-19C] to die.

IN EXCLAMATIONS

❑ **by the bones of Davy Jones!** [1910s] (*Aus.*) a mild oath.

davy large *n.* [rhy. sl.] [late 19C] a barge.

Davy's dust *n.* [mid-19C] (*UK Und.*) gunpowder.

Davy's locker *n. see* DAVY JONES'S LOCKER *n.*

daw *n. see* GOBDAW *n.*

dawamesk *n.* [Arabic; *dawamesc*, a form of 'cannabis jam', mixing hashish with oil, vanilla, pistachio, almonds and musk; plus sometimes Cantharides] [1960s+] (*drugs*) marijuana; orig. a mixture of hashish and a variety of spices and other ingredients.

dawb *n. see* DAUB *n.*[1].

dawb *v. see* DAUB *v.*

dawg *n. see* DOG *n.*[2].

dawg! *excl.* (*also* **daag!**) [joc. pron. of SE *dog*; thus cf. HOT DOG! *excl.*] [1980s+] (*US campus/teen*) an expression of approval or surprise and disbelief.

dawner *n.* [1980s] (*US*) a meeting that lasts all night; lit. until dawn.

Dawn Frazer *n.* (*also* **Malcolm Fraser**) [rhy. sl.; ult. the 1960s Aus. swimming star *Dawn Fraser* (b.1937) or Aus. prime minister 1975–83 *Malcolm Fraser* (b.1930)] [1960s+] (*Aus.*) a razor.

day *n.*

SE in slang uses

IN COMPOUNDS

❑ **day dot** *n. see* YEAR DOT *under* DOT *n.*[2]. ❑ **day lizard** *n. see under* -LIZARD *sfx.* ❑ **daylight** *see* separate entries. ❑ **daylights** *n. see* separate entry. ❑ **day one** *n.* [lit. the first-ever day] [1970s+] (*orig. US*) the beginning; long ago. ❑ **day opener** *n.* [mid–late 19C] (*orig. boxing*) an eye.

IN PHRASES

❑ **all day** *n.* **1** [late 19C] the end of one's life. **2** [1970s+] (*US Und.*) a life sentence. ❑ **all day, all night, just like New York** [1930s] (*US black*) fashionable, sophisticated. ❑ **all day and a night** *n.* [ext. of *ALL DAY* above] [2000s] (*US prison*) a life sentence without the opportunity of parole. ❑ **all day from a quarter** [*ALL DAY* above + QUARTER *n.* (3b)] [1970s+] (*US Und.*) a sentence of 25 years to life. ❑ **day-day** [the daytime equivalent of SE *night-night*, goodnight, and similarly used to children or in a consciously joc. manner] [1900s–30s] (*US*) goodbye, farewell. ❑ **day for a/the king** *n.* (*also* **day for a/the queen, day on...**) [SE phr. *a day* (*fit*) *for a king*, a very pleasant day + the idea of the king/queen, as ruler, paying for the day] [1940s+] (*N.Z.*) a day off, orig. when outdoor work was impossible, but used generally to cover any unofficial day off, e.g. one that follows a night of over-enthusiastic enjoyment. ❑ **dig a day under the skin** *v. see under* DIG *v.*[1]. ❑ **sure as the day is long** *see under* SURE AS... *phr.*

IN EXCLAMATIONS

❑ **for days!** [the orig. implication was of having sex continually, for day after day] [1950s+] **1** (*gay*) an excl. implying shock or amazement. **2** (*orig. US black*) (*also* **days!**) a general intensifier implying an extreme, for a very long time, absolutely truthfully.

day and martin *n.* [*Day and Martin's* shoe blacking] [19C–1900s] a derog. term for a black person.

day and night *n.* [rhy. sl.] [1950s+] light ale.

daylight *n.*[1] [late 18C–mid-19C] the space left in a glass between the top of the liquid and the rim; such a space is not allowed when drinking bumpers, thus the toast *no daylight!*

SE in slang uses

IN PHRASES

❑ **let the daylight into/through** *v.* (*also* **let moonlight into, let sunshine through, put daylight through**) [late 18C+] to shoot, to stab; often ext. as *let the daylight into the victualling department, let the daylight into the luncheon reservoir.*

daylight *n.*[2] [20C+] (*Ulster*) the minimum, anything, e.g. *don't belive daylight out of him.*

daylight *v.* [SE *let in some daylight*] [1970s] (*US black*) to enlighten, to explain.

daylights *n.* **1** [mid-18C+] the eyes. **2** [mid-19C+] the insides; the essence; usu. in combs. involving fear and/or violence, *see* phrs. below.

IN PHRASES

❑ **beat the (living) daylights out of** *v.* (*also* **kick..., knock..., shake..., thrash...**) [mid-18C+] to beat severely. ❑ **darken someone's daylights** *v.* [mid-18C–1900s] to black someone's eye. ❑ **frighten the (living) daylights out of** *v.* (*also* **scare...**) [late 19C+] to terrify. ❑ **send the daylights out of** *v.* [20C+] (*W.I.*) to beat severely, to hit an animal hard enough to kill it.

day's dawning *n.* (*also* **day's a-dawning**) [rhy. sl.] [20C+] morning.

daze *v.* [1970s+] (*US campus*) to daydream.

dazzey duks *n. see* DAISY DUKES *n.*

dazzler *n.* **1** [19C] esp. of an ostentatious woman, one who dazzles. **2** [late 19C] a dazzling blow.

d.b. *n. see* DOUCHEBAG *n.*

d-boy *n.* [abbr. SE *drugs* + *boy*] [1990s+] (*US black teen*) a drug dealer.

D.C. *n.* [abbr.] [1980s+] (*US*) Washington, *D.C.*

d.c. *n.* [abbr.] **1** [1900s] (*Aus.*) the *d*ress *c*ircle of the theatre. **2** [1930s] (*US Und.*) a *d*angerous *c*haracter. **3** [1980s] (*UK Und.*) detention centre. **4** [1990s+] (*US prison*) the death cell.

d.c.m. *n.*

IN PHRASES

❑ **get a d.c.m.** *v.* [abbr. *d*on't *c*ome *M*onday] [1990s+] (*Aus.*) to be dismissed from one's job.

d.d.f.m.g. *n.* [*d*rop *d*ead *f*uck *m*e *g*orgeous, i.e. DROP-DEAD *adv.* + FUCK-ME *adj.*] [1990s+] (*US campus*) an exceptionally attractive member of the opposite sex.

D.D.G. *adj.* [abbr. *DROP-DEAD GORGEOUS under* DROP-DEAD *adv.*] [2000s] extremely attractive.

d.d.t.! **1** [1940s–50s] (*US campus*) a general excl. of dismissal, contempt [abbr. DROP DEAD! *excl.* + SE *twice*]. **2** [1970s] (*US*) a command to stop doing something [abbr. *d*on't *d*o *t*hat].

de *n.* [abbr.] [1970s] (*US Und.*) **1** a *de*ceased person. **2** a *de*fendant.

deacon *n. see* JOEY *n.*[1] (4).

deacon's nose *n. see* PARSON'S NOSE *under* PARSON *n.*

dead *n.*[1] [19C] (*US campus*) a class recitation that is judged to be a total failure.

IN PHRASES

❑ **take a dead** *v.* [19C] (*US campus*) to fail one's recitation.

dead *n.*[2]

IN PHRASES

❑ **on the dead** [abbr. *ON THE DEAD LEVEL under* DEAD *adj.*] [late 19C–1960s] (*US*) in earnest, sincerely, straightforwardly, honestly.

dead *n.*[3] [20C+] (*W.I., Bdos*) problems, trouble.

dead *adj.* **1** [mid-18C+] of a bottle, finished, empty. **2** [mid-19C+] (*US black*) of people, forgotten; of things, ideas, unfashionable, out of style. **3** [late 19C–1920s] of a house or place, uninhabited, empty, deserted. **4** [late 19C–1940s] (*US tramp*) reformed. **5** [1900s–30s] having no knowledge. **6** [1930s+] of a place, esp. a club, a party, boring, unexciting. **7** [1950s+] finished, lost, spec. arrested, captured. **8** [1960s] (*US black*) penniless. **9** [1990s+] (*US campus*) facing trouble.

IN PHRASES

❑ **have someone/something dead** *v.* [predates sense 7 above; var. on *KNOCK COLD under* KNOCK *v.*] [1900s] (*Aus./US*) to have at one's mercy; to dominate completely, to astound.

SE, meaning not alive, in slang uses

IN COMPOUNDS

❑ **dead alive** *n. see* MAN ALIVE *n.* ❑ **dead alive** *adj.* (*also* **dead and alive**) **1** [mid-19C] stupid, dull. **2** [mid-19C+] miserable, down in the mouth. ❑ **dead ass** *see* separate entries. ❑ **dead bird** *n.* [like the bird, it cannot 'move'; note Stephens & O'Brien, *Materials for a Dict. of Aus. Sl.* (ms.; 1900–10): 'derived from pigeon shooting [...] the prowess of any champion shot that "anything he aims at is a 'dead bird'".'] **1** [late 19C+] (*Aus.*) a certain bet, a sure thing. **2** [1900s–10s] (*US*) a hopeless case or situation. ❑ **dead book** *v.* [lit. to inscribe in the 'book of the dead'] [early 19C] (*UK Und.*) to kill, to hang. ❑ **dead-broker** *n.* [*DEAD BROKE under* DEAD *adv.*] [late 19C+] (*Aus.*) a down-and-out. ❑ **dead butt** *n. see* DEAD ASS *n.* ❑ **dead butt** *adj. see* DEAD-ASS *adj.* ❑ **dead card** *n.* [SE *dead card*, a card that has been discarded in a game and is no longer to be used by the players] [late 19C–1900s] (*US*) something that is unlucky, unfashionable or unpopular. ❑ **dead cargo** *n.* [late 17C–19C] (*UK Und.*) the proceeds of a robbery that have turned out to be less valuable than hoped. ❑ **dead chicken** *n.* [1960s+] (*US*) a doomed person, a lost soul. ❑ **dead duck** *n. see* separate entry. ❑ **dead-end street** *n.* [synon. for cul-de-sac; there is in *dead* an extra implication of passivity on the woman's part] [19C; 1990s+] the vagina. ❑ **deadeye** *see* separate entries. ❑ **dead fall** *n.* [the drunks 'fall down dead' + ? pun on SE *deadfall*, a trap for large game] **1** [mid–late 19C] a cheap, poss. corrupt casino. **2** [mid-19C–1950s] (*US*) a rough saloon. ❑ **dead fink** *n.* [ety. unknown] [20C+] (*Irish*) an attractive young woman. ❑ **dead-fly cake** *n. see* SQUASHED FLIES *n.* ❑ **dead game** *adj.* [late 19C–1950s] (*US campus*) dissolute, ostentatious. ❑ **deadhead** *see* separate entries. ❑ **dead heat** *n.* [pun on SE (neck)*tie/tie* (dead heat or draw)] [1980s] (*Aus.*) a necktie. ❑ **dead horse** *n. see* separate entries. ❑ **dead house** *n.* **1** [mid-19C–1940s] (*Aus.*) a room in an outback public house set aside for those who are incapably drunk. **2** [late 19C–1920s] (*US*) a particularly unappealing bar or saloon. ❑ **dead Indian** *n.* [the negative stereotype of allegedly alcoholic Native Americans] [1960s] (*US*) an empty bottle. ❑ **dead knowledge** *n.* [1900s] (*Aus.*) deceit, cunning; thus *dead-knowledge man*, a cunning or deceitful man. ❑ **dead lag** *n.* [LAG *n.*[2] (2)] [mid-19C] (*UK Und.*) one who is certain to be imprisoned. ❑ **dead leg** *n.* [1960s–70s] a down-and-out, a failure. ❑ **deadlights** *n.* [var. on DAYLIGHTS *n.* (1)] [19C] the eyes. ❑ **dead line** *n. see under* LINE *n.*[1]. ❑ **deadlock/locker** *see* separate entries. ❑ **deadlurk/lurker** *see* separate entries. ❑ **deadman** *see* separate entry. ❑ **dead marine** *n.* (*also* **marine, marine officer, marine recruit**) [orig. naut. jargon, now mainly Aus. use; Fraser & Gibbons, *Soldier & Sailor Words & Phrases* (1925): 'William IV., when Duke of Clarence and Lord High Admiral, at an official dinner, is related to have said to a waiter, pointing to some empty bottles, "Take away those marines!" An elderly major of Marines present rose and said: "May I respectfully ask why your Royal Highness applies the name of the corps to which I have the honour to belong to an empty bottle?" The Duke, with the unfailing tact of his family, saved the situation. "I call them marines because they are good fellows who have done their duty and are ready to do it again!"'] [late 18C+] an empty bottle. ❑ **deadmeat** *n. see* separate entry. ❑ **dead nail** *n. see* NAIL *n.*[1] (1). ❑ **dead neck** *n.* [i.e. one who is *dead from the neck up*] [1910s–60s] a very stupid person. ❑ **dead one** *n. see* separate entry. ❑ **deadpan** *see* separate entries. ❑ **dead pecker** *n.* [PECKER *n.*[2] (2)] [1970s] (*US*) an impotent old man. ❑ **deadpicker** *n.* **1** [1930s–40s] (*US tramp*) one who robs passed-out drunks. **2** [1940s] (*US*) a general term of abuse. ❑ **dead pickles** *n. see* PICKLE *n.* (2). ❑ **dead pigeon** *n.* [1910s–50s] **1** (*US*) a guaranteed and absolute failure, often in the context of a forthcoming election. **2** one who is doomed. **3** one who is unconscious. ❑ **dead pork** *n. see* PORK *n.* (1c). ❑ **dead president** *n.* (*also* **dead man, dead one, president**) [the pictures of US presidents that are printed on the various denominations] [1940s+] (*US*) a $1 bill; thus in pl. money. ❑ **dead pudding** *n.* [late 19C] (*US campus*) something easy. ❑ **dead rabbit** *n.* **1** [mid–late 19C] (*US*) a street thug, a hoodlum [the New York City street gang, known as the Dead Rabbits, who would parade brandishing such a corpse, the symbol of their defeated rivals, as their standard; ? link to Irish *ráibéad*, a big, hulking person, a rowdy]. **2** [1900s–40s] a hopeless person, one who has absolutely no chance. **3** [1960s–70s] an impotent penis, incapable of erection. ❑ **dead rag** *n.* [the DO-RAC *n.* (2) or bandanna handkerchief, worn by gang members to indicate their affiliation] [1980s+] (*US black gang*) a dead gang member. ❑ **dead recruit** *n.* [var. on *DEAD SOLDIER under* SOLDIER *n.*] [20C+] an empty bottle. ❑ **dead shot** *n.* [SE *dead shot*, an expert marksman] **1** [mid-19C] (*US*) very poor quality or adulterated whisky [it 'kills' the drinker]. **2** [1970s+] (*US black*) sexual intercourse, whether vaginal or anal. ❑ **dead soldier** *n. see under* SOLDIER *n.* ❑ **dead stock** *n.* [Carib. *stock*, animals bred for slaughter] [1990s+] (*W.I.*) a 'non-event'. ❑ **dead swag** *n. see* SWAG *n.*[1]. ❑ **dead time** *n.* [TIME *n.* (1)] [1970s+] (*US prison*) **1** any time spent in prison that does not actually diminish one's sentence. **2** any period of one's prison sentence when one is prohibited from associating with other prisoners. ❑ **dead turkey** *n.* [1940s+] a hopeless person, a person or thing that has absolutely no chance. ❑ **dead 'un** *n. see* separate entry. ❑ **dead whiteboy** *n.* [play on *DEAD PRESIDENT* above: there has as yet been no black president of the USA] [1990s+] (*US black*) a dollar bill of any denomination. ❑ **deadwood** *see* separate entries.

IN PHRASES

❑ **dead as...** *see* separate entry. ❑ **dead for** *adj.* [var. on SE *dying for*] [late 19C–1960s] (*Aus./US*) desperate for, in great need of. ❑ **dead on** *adj. see* separate entry. ❑ **give someone the dead hand** *v.* **1** [late 19C] (*US campus*) to betray. **2** [1970s] (*US*) to grope a woman in a crowd, e.g. on a tube train. ❑ **kill/knock dead** *v. see KNOCK COLD under* KNOCK *v.* ❑ **wouldn't be seen dead with (someone) in a 40-acre paddock** [late 19C+] (*orig. Aus.*) an expression of extreme dislike.

IN EXCLAMATIONS

❑ **play dead!** [1950s] (*US teen*) be quiet!

SE, meaning complete, utter, in slang uses

IN COMPOUNDS

❑ **dead cop** *n.* [COP *n.*[1] (2)] [1900s] (*Aus.*) a sure winner. ❑ **dead-copper** *n.* [COPPER *n.* (3)] [1920s+] (*Aus.*) a police informer. ❑ **dead cunt** *n.* [CUNT *n.* (4)] [1990s+] (*Aus.*) a strong term of abuse. ❑ **dead finish** *n.* **1** [late 19C] an outback drinking saloon. **2** [late 19C–1900s] (*Aus.*) the absolute, the complete; the end. ❑ **dead hand** *n.* [SE *hand*, an expert + pun on SE] [19C+] (*20C+ Aus.*) an expert. ❑ **dead nap** *n.* [NAPPER *n.*[1] (1)] [late 19C] an absolute villain. ❑ **dead nark** *n.* [NARK *n.* (4)] [20C+] (*Aus.*) **1** a spoilsport. **2** a very bad temper. ❑ **dead nip** *n.* [? SE *nip*, a fragment, a small portion] [late 19C] an unimportant project that turns out to be a failure. ❑ **dead oodles** *n.* [ety. unknown, but Cohen, *Studies in Slang* (1985), suggests progression from *scadoodles* by mispron. of first syllable] [mid-19C+] (*orig. US*) a large quantity, many. ❑ **dead ringer** *n. see* separate entry. ❑ **dead shit** *n.* [1980s+] (*Aus.*) a general term of abuse. ❑ **dead tumble** *n.* [TUMBLE *n.* (1a)] [1930s–50s] (*US Und.*) an obvious give-away, discovery in the act of a crime.

IN PHRASES

❑ **dead ring of** [1910s+] (*Aus./N.Z.*) the absolute image of. ❑ **on the dead level** [ext. of SE phr. *on the level*] [late 19C+] in earnest, sincerely, straightforwardly, honestly.

dead *v.* **1** [mid-19C] (*US campus*) of a student, to fail completely in one's recitation. **2** [mid–late 19C] (*US campus*) of a teacher, to make a student botch the recitation. **3** [20C+] (*US*) to loaf around, to idle. **4** [2000s] (*US prison*) to remove, to steal. **5** [2000s] (*UK black*) to die.

dead *adv.* (*also* **dead-ahead**) [17C+] a general intensifier, very, extremely, absolutely, completely.

IN COMPOUNDS

❑ **dead-bang** *see* separate entry. ❑ **deadbeat** *see* separate entries.

IN PHRASES

❑ **dead broke** *adj.* [BROKE *adj.*[1] (1)] [mid-19C+] (*orig. US*) completely without funds; also as v. to impoverish. ❑ **dead chocker** *adj.* (*also* **dead chokka**) [CHOCKER *adj.*] [1950s] (*orig. milit.*) very bored. ❑ **dead chuffed** *adj. see* CHUFFED *adj.* (1). ❑ **dead loads** *n.* [LOADS OF *n.*] [mid-19C+] (*US*) many, a great quantity. ❑ **dead nuts** *adj.* [NUTS *adj.* (1)] **1** [late 19C+] (*US*) completely, absolutely, keenly for or against something. **2** [1970s] constr. with *the*, for certain. ❑ **dead on** *adj. see* separate entry. ❑ **dead-right** *adj.* [RIGHT *adj.* (1)] [20C+] (*US*) unassailable. ❑ **dead set** *see* separate entries. ❑ **dead thick** *adj.* [ironic reversal of THICK *adj.* (1a)] [late 19C+] (*Glasgow*) very clever. ❑ **dead to rights** *adv. see* separate entry. ❑ **dead to the curb** *adv.* [1950s] (*US black*) completely, utterly, comprehensively.

deadas *n.* [1990s+] (*W.I.*) meat.

dead as... *adj.* [20C+] used in a variety of phrs. meaning absolutely dead (*see also* combs. below).

IN PHRASES

❑ **...a doornail** (*also* **dead as a coffin nail, ...hangnail, ...nail**) [SE *doornail*, the large-headed nails with which doors were studded for extra strength and protection; 17C+ use is SE] [mid-14C–16C] ❑ **...dogshit** *see under* DOGSHIT *n.* ❑ **...Kelsey's nuts** *see under* KELSEY'S NUTS *n.* ❑ **...mutton** *see under* MUTTON *n.*

dead ass *n.* (*also* **dead butt**) [SE *dead* + -ASS *sfx*/BUTT *n.*[1] (1c)] [1950s+] (*US*) **1** the seated rump, usu. as symbolic of laziness. **2** an idler, a lazy person. **3** one who is effectively dead. **4** a listless, de-energized person. **5** an utterly boring, useless person.

dead-ass *adj.* (*also* **dead-butt**) [DEAD ASS *n.*] [1950s+] (*US*) **1** lacking energy, listless, lifeless. **2** of a place, inactive, boring. **3** (*W.I.*) a general negative intensifier.

dead-ass *adv.*[1] (*also* **dead-assed**) [DEAD-ASS *adj.* (1)] [1970s+] (*US*) lifelessly, listlessly.

dead-ass *adv.*[2] [DEAD *adv.* + -ASS *sfx*] [1970s+] (*US*) very, completely, wholly, utterly.

dead-bang *adj.* [DEAD *adv.* + BANG TO RIGHTS *under* BANG *adv.*] **1** [1930s] certain. **2** [1930s+] (*US*) of a criminal prosecution, lacking any possibility of defence or argument because the case is watertight.

dead-bang *adv.* [DEAD *adv.* + BANG *adv.* (1)] [1910s+] completely, utterly, totally, absolutely.

deadbeat *n.* [backform. f. DEADBEAT *adj.*] **1** [early 19C] a state of exhaustion. **2** [mid-19C] of things, a failure, a deception. **3** [mid-19C+] of people, a failure, a down-and-out. **4** [mid-19C+] a malingerer, an idler, a wastrel. **5** [mid-19C+] a cadger, a sponge. **6** [late 19C] (*US*) a form of alcohol. **7** [1910s+] one who reneges on their debts.

deadbeat *adj.* [DEAD *adv.* + SE *beaten*] **1** [early–mid-19C] absolutely defeated. **2** [early 19C+] worn out, exhausted [note Egan, *Life in London* (1821): '"Dead beat!" or "beat to a stand still!" Common phrases in the Sporting World, when a man or horse is so completely exhausted from over-exertion, or the constitution breaking down, as to give up the object in view, not being able to pursue it any further']. **3** [mid-19C] lazy, idle. **4** [late 19C+] useless, ne'er-do-well, impoverished.

deadbeat *v.* [DEADBEAT *n.*] [late 19C+] (*US*) **1** to waste time, to idle around. **2** to sponge on. **3** to cheat.

dead duck *n.* [fig. use of SE + pvb 'never waste powder on a dead duck'] (*orig. US*) **1** [mid-19C+] a complete, irredeemable failure. **2** [1910s+] a hopeless person, one who has absolutely no chance.

deadener *n.* [SE *deaden*] **1** [mid–late 19C] (*US*) a very attractive woman. **2** [1930s+] (*Aus.*) a bully, one who prefers to settle arguments through violence.

deader *n.* (*orig. US*) **1** [late 19C] an exhausted person. **2** [20C+] a dead person, a corpse; thus *be a deader*, to be recently dead.

deaders *n.* [SE *dead*; the implication is that such foods are unpalatable] [1980s+] (*W.I./UK black teen*) animal flesh, meat by-products eaten as food.

deadeye *n.*[1] **1** [mid-19C] a term of abuse. **2** [mid-19C] a blank wall. **3** [1970s+] the anus [SE *dead* + -EYE *sfx*].

deadeye *n.*[2] *see* DEADY *n.*

deadeye *v.* [1960s+] (*US*) to stare at in a chilly manner; also as adv.

dead-eye dick *n.* [nickname for a superlative marksman + pun on DICK *n.*[1] (5)] [1930s+] (*gay*) one who performs anal intercourse.

deadhead *n.* [orig. theatre jargon *deadhead*, one who does not pay for their ticket] **1** [mid-19C+] one who receives goods or services without paying. **2** [mid-19C+] a non-participant, one who does not contribute; a stranger. **3** [late 19C–1950s] (*US tramp*) (*also* **deadheader**) an empty freight car or freight train; one who rides it. **4** [late 19C+] a lazy worthless person. **5** [1930s+] a drunk. **6** [1940s+] a fool. **7** [2000s] a state of non-communication.

deadhead *adj.* (*also* **deadheaded**) [DEADHEAD *n.*] [mid-19C+] (*US*) **1** free of charge. **2** useless, spec. non-participant.

deadhead *v.* [DEADHEAD *n.* (1)] (*orig. US*) **1** [mid-19C+] to obtain services or things without paying. **2** [mid-19C+] to ride for free; also allow someone to ride for free; also in fig. use. **3** [1920s+] to drive a cab, aeroplane etc without its usual load or passengers. **4** [2000s] to ignore.

deadhead *adv.* **1** [mid-19C+] for free. **2** [late 19C+] of a cab, aeroplane etc, being driven without its usual load or passengers.

deadheaded *adj. see* DEADHEAD *adj.*

deadheader *n. see* DEADHEAD *n.* (3).

dead horse *n.*[1] **1** [mid-17C+] work that has been already paid for but is yet to be done; thus *play a dead horse, pull a dead horse, work for a dead horse*, to perform such work. **2** [19C+] (*US/Aus./N.Z.*) a debt that has been incurred by accepting an advance on one's wages, it must now be worked off; thus *ride the dead horse, work off the dead horse, bury the dead horse*. **3** [19C+] any form of debt. **4** [mid-19C] any form of useless job, which doesn't bring in any profits but still must be done; thus *draw the dead horse*, to work at such a job.

dead horse *n.*[2] [the disparaging comparison] [20C+] stew.

dead horse *n.*[3] [rhy. sl.] [1940s+] (*Aus.*) tomato sauce.

deadie *n.* [SE *dead* + sfx *-ie*] [1970s] a dead person.

deadlock *n.* [1930s+] (*US prison*) solitary confinement; forfeiture of privileges; also as *v.*

deadlocker *n.* [DEADLOCK *n.*] [1940s] (*US prison*) one who is in solitary confinement or deprived of privileges.

dead lurk *n.* [SE *dead*, abandoned, unused + LURK *n.* (3)] **1** [mid-19C] (*UK Und.*) breaking into houses while the occupiers are at church. **2** [mid–late 19C] empty premises.

dead-lurk *v.* [DEAD LURK *n.* (1)] [late 19C] (*UK Und.*) to break into a house when the occupants are away, esp. when they are at church on a Sunday.

dead lurker *n.* [DEAD LURK *n.* (1)] [mid-19C] (*UK Und.*) a thief specializing in theft from quiet or semi-dark places.

deadly *adj.* [on bad = good model] [1940s+] (*orig. US black/campus*) excellent, first-rate.

deadly-lively *adj.* [19C] offering false joviality.

deadly nevergreen *n.* [pun on SE *evergreen*] [late 18C–early 19C] the gallows.

deadly nightshade *n.* [pun on the SE plant] [mid-19C–1920s] the lowest grade of prostitute.

deadly suspense *n.*

IN PHRASES

❑ **in deadly suspense** [pun] [late 18C–early 19C] hanged.

dead man *n.* **1** [late 17C+] (*orig. milit.*) an empty bottle. **2** [late 18C–19C] a baker; 'Properly speaking, it is an extra loaf smuggled into the basket by the man who carries it out, to the loss of the master. Sometimes the dead man is charged to a customer, though never delivered' (Hotten, 1864). **3** [late 19C] a scarecrow, esp. when made in the trad. manner of old clothes stuffed with straw. **4** [1930s] (*Irish*) a weekly insurance collector, whose policy pays off when one is dead. **5** [1980s] (*N.Z.*) any large object (a baulk of timber, a steel stanchion, a lump of concrete etc) used as an anchor for hawsers, guy-ropes etc. **6** *see* DEAD PRESIDENT *under* DEAD *adj.*

IN PHRASES

❑ **down among the dead men** [mid-19C] very drunk.

SE in slang uses

IN COMPOUNDS

❑ **deadman choppers** *n.* (*also* **deadman teeth**) [CHOPPERS *n.*

(2)] [1960s–70s] (*US black*) false teeth. ❑ **dead man's arm** *n.* [1980s+] (*N.Z.*) steamed (currant) roll pudding. ❑ **dead man's ears** *n.* [1980s+] (*N.Z.*) stewed dried apricots. ❑ **dead man's hand** *n.* [the lawman Wild Bill Hickok (1837–76) was allegedly holding a hand of aces and eights when he was gunned down] **1** [mid-19C+] a poker hand of mixed aces and eights or jacks and (red) sevens or eights. **2** [1960s] bad luck. ❑ **dead man's head** *n.* [1980s+] (*N.Z.*) a round, steamed plum pudding, eaten hot or cold. ❑ **dead man's leg** *n.* [1980s] (*Aus.*) meatloaf. ❑ **deadman teeth** *n. see* DEADMAN CHOPPERS above.

dead meat *n.* [lit. or fig. uses of SE] **1** [mid-19C+] someone who is facing certain death; also in fig. use. **2** [late 19C+] a corpse. **3** [late 19C+] a prostitute, esp. an older woman. **4** [20C+] a horse that has no chance of winning a race. **5** [1960s] the flaccid penis. **6** [1980s+] a stupid, dull person.

IN COMPOUNDS

❑ **dead-meat ticket** *n.* (*also* **meat ticket**) [SE *ticket*; orig. milit. use, such tags identified the corpses of otherwise anonymous soldiers] [1910s+] (*Aus./N.Z.*) an identity tag.

deado *n.* [SE *dead* + -O *sfx* (2)] [1910s+] a corpse.

deado *adj.* (*also* **deadoh**) [SE *dead drunk* + -O *sfx* (5)] **1** [late 19C–1910s] dead. **2** [late 19C+] very drunk.

deado *adv.* [1900s–10s] (*US*) completely.

dead on *adj.* [DEAD *adv.* (1) + SE *on*] **1** [mid–late 19C] very fond of; determined (to do something). **2** [late 19C+] (*orig. US*) dealing very strictly and severely with a situation or person. **3** [late 19C+] (*orig. US*) absolutely right, utterly correct, exact [modern use is SE; abbr. SE *dead on target*].

dead one *n.* **1** [mid-19C+] (*also* **dead 'un**) a second-rate racehorse. **2** [late 19C–1900s] (*US*) a fool. **3** [late 19C+] (*US*) a useless, unsociable, impoverished or mean person. **4** [1900s–50s] (*US*) someone or something that is doomed, on the verge of death or actually dead. **5** [1900s–60s] (*US Und.*) a reformed or retired tramp or criminal. **6** [1930s] (*US tramp*) a drunk. **7** *see* DEAD PRESIDENT *under* DEAD *adj.*

IN PHRASES

❑ **play a dead one** *v.* [late 19C] (*US*) to waste time; to act mistakenly.

deadpan *n.* [DEADPAN *adj.*] [1930s+] (*orig. US*) an expressionless stare.

deadpan *adj.* (*also* **deadpanned**) [SE *dead* + PAN *n.*[1] (4); *deadpan* (as n., adj., adv.) is cited as SE in *OED*, though *pan* is acknowledged to be 'orig. US slang'; it would thus seem likely to have been sl. at its coinage] [1920s+] (*US*) expressionlesss.

deadpan *v.* [DEADPAN *adj.*] [1930s+] (*orig. US*) to speak without expression, esp. in a situation that would normally demand some emotion.

deadpan *adv.* [DEADPAN *adj.*] [1930s+] (*US*) in an expressionless, emotionless manner.

dead ringer *n.* [SE *dead*, complete, utter + RINGER *n.* (2b)] [late 19C+] (*orig. US*) usu. of people, an absolute replica (of); thus *to be a dead ringer/a ringer for*, to resemble completely.

dead set *n.* [DEAD *adv.* + SE *set*, the act of a dog in setting game; orig. used by thief-catchers referring to their imminent arrest of a villain] **1** [18C–early 19C; 1910s] (*UK Und.*) (*also* **set**) a scheme aimed at defrauding a victim through crooked gambling. **2** [late 18C–1940s] a pointed attack on or approach to another person, often in the context of wooing. **3** [19C] (*US campus*) a complete failure to learn and recite the lesson.

dead set *adj.* [DEAD *adv.* + SE *set*, positioned] **1** [mid-19C+] fully committed. **2** [1940s+] (*Aus./US*) superlative, in both positive and negative uses.

IN PHRASES

❑ **dead set against** *adj.* [early 19C+] totally hostile towards. ❑ **dead set on** *adj.* [late 19C+] fascinated by, obsessed with, in love with, determined.

dead-set *adv.* [DEAD SET *adj.*] [1970s] (*Aus.*) definitely, certainly; also as excl.

dead set *phr.* [DEAD SET *adj.*] [1970s] (*Aus.*) **1** a phr. denoting acquiescence, 'that's fine'. **2** a general negative phr.

dead spotted ling of *phr.* [rhy. sl. = *DEAD RING OF under* DEAD *adj.*] [1930s+] (*Aus.*) the absolute image of.

dead 'un *n.*[1] [? DEAD MAN *n.* (2)] [late 19C] a half-quartern loaf.

dead 'un *n.*[2] [lit. a 'dead one'] **1** [late 19C] a bankrupt company. **2** [late 19C] (*UK Und.*) an uninhabited house. **3** [20C+] an empty bottle. **4** *see* DEAD ONE *n.* (1).

deadwood *n.* [pun] [mid-19C] (*US*) a coffin.

SE in slang uses

IN PHRASES

❑ **have the deadwood on** *v.* (*also* **get the deadwood on, have the wood on**) [logging use, where a skilled axeman would cut a tree in such a way that he spared himself work by ensuring that any dead wood broke off by itself when the tree fell; alternate ety. suggests the shooting in the back of Marshall James Butler 'Wild Bill' Hickok in the town of Deadwood, South Dakota on 2 August 1876; ? or in ten-pin bowling, if a single pin is left lying in front of those that have not been knocked down, hitting that 'dead wood' will knock it into the others, successfully knocking them all down] [mid-19C+] (*US*) to have at a disadvantage, to control, esp. through the possession of incriminating information.

deadwood *adj.*[1] [i.e. there is no possibility of further 'growth'] [mid-19C] (*US*) absolute, complete, unequivocal, e.g. *deadwood agreement*.

deadwood *adj.*[2] [fig. use of DEADWOOD *n.*/SE *dead wood*] [late 19C+] (*US Und.*) caught in the act.

dead wowsers *n.* [rhy. sl.] [20C+] (*Aus.*) trousers.

deady *n.* (*also* **deadeye, deady's fluid**) [name of the distiller D. *Deady*, listed in the London Directory (1812) as 'Distiller and Brandy-merchant, Sol's Row, Tottenham Court Rd'] [early–mid-19C] gin, or a particular quality of gin.

deaf and dumb *n.*[1] [rhy. sl. = DRUM *n.*[6] (1)] [1910s+] (*Aus.*) inside information, e.g. *I'll give you the deaf and dumb*.

deaf and dumb *n.*[2] [rhy. sl. = BUM *n.*[1] (1)] [1980s] (*Aus.*) the buttocks; the anus.

deafy *n.* (*also* **deafey**) [1930s] (*US Und.*) a deaf beggar (or one who poses as such).

deal *n.*[1] [ult. SE *deal*, the act or system of dividing into parts for distribution; note Asbury, *Sucker's Progress* (1938) 16: An extraordinary number of the terms, technical and otherwise, which were employed by Faro players in the palmy days of the game have passed into the language [...] and are commonly used by millions who never heard of Faro. Here are some of them: [...] *Deal*—Twenty-five turns] **1** [mid–late 19C] any form of financial or commercial transaction [20C+ use is SE]. **2** [late 19C+] (*orig. US*) an idea, plan, scheme, arrangement, current situation, esp. with the implication of illegality or subterfuge. **3** [late 19C+] the treatment one has received, whether good or bad; thus *square deal*, fair treatment. **4** [late 19C+] (*orig. US*) the situation, the state of affairs, e.g. *that's the deal*. **5** [1910s+] (*drugs*) a purchase or sale of drugs, esp. cannabis; thus *quid deal*, one pound's worth etc. **6** [1920s+] (*US*) a turn of events, a development. **7** [1940s+] (*orig. US*) (*also* **dealie**) an individual or thing. **8** [1950s] one's concern or business, e.g. *that's my deal*, that's my business. **9** [1990s+] (*US campus*) a problem, a conflict. **10** *see* DEALER *n.*

IN PHRASES

❑ **cut a deal** *v.* (*also* **cut**) [1970s+] (*orig. US*) to compromise; to make an arrangement, to make a deal.

deal *n.*[2] [despite commercial overtones, not a prostitute] (*US black*) **1** [1960s–70s] a woman. **2** [1970s] a sports star.

deal, the *n.* (*US campus*) **1** [1980s] the best. **2** [1990s+] the facts, the situation.

deal *v.* [DEAL *n.*[1]/SE *deal*, to hand out] **1** [20C+] (*US*) to make a bargain, to conduct business. **2** [1920s] (*US*) to give, to hand over. **3** [1920s+] (*US black*) to cause trouble for, to treat harshly. **4** [1950s+] to sell drugs, esp. marijuana. **5** [1960s+] (*US black*) to manage a situation or circumstance. **6** [1970s–80s] (*UK black*) to have sexual intercourse with. **7** [1980s] (*US prison*) to play the active role in a homosexual couple. **8** [1980s] (*US campus*) to make dates frequently.

IN PHRASES

❑ **deal in coal** *v. see under* COAL *n.*[1]. ❑ **deal (in) dirt** *v. see under* DIRT *n.* ❑ **deal in zeroes** *v.* [1960s] (*US black*) to achieve nothing, to fail completely, to draw a blank. ❑ **deal it out** *v.* [20C+] (*Aus.*) to attack, esp. verbally, to punish. ❑ **deal on** *v.* [1970s] (*US black*) to trick, to deceive, to take advantage. ❑ **deal someone one** *v. see under* ONE *n.*[1]. ❑ **deal to** *v.* [1980s+] (*N.Z.*) **1** to beat up. **2** to treat roughly.

SE card-playing imagery, in slang uses

IN PHRASES

❑ **deal off the bottom of the deck** *v.* (*also* **deal from the bottom of the deck/pack**) [a classic method of cheating in cards] [late 19C+] (*orig. US*) to cheat, to defraud, to swindle. ❑ **deal one off the top** *v.* [1960s] (*US*) to give someone a piece of good luck. ❑ **deal someone in** *v.* [1940s+] (*orig. US*) to include in an undertaking, often a criminal one, to give someone a share; thus the reverse, *deal someone out*. ❑ **deal them off the arm** *v. see under* ARM *n.*

IN EXCLAMATIONS

❑ **deal me out!** [1950s] (*US*) a general excl. of rejection: I'm not interested! leave me out!

dealer *n.* (*also* **deal, John Deal**) [a specific use of an 11C SE word meaning trafficker, in whatever he or she happened to deal; note Maurer, 'Lang. of the Underworld Narcotic Addict' Pt.1 (1936): 'Often restricted to a druggist who is amenable to persuasion'; *Current Slang* III:2 (1968) suggests 'a dealer, unlike a pusher, sells marijuana to his friends as a favor and not for a profit'] **1** [early 19C–1920s] (*US Und.*) a wholesaler of counterfeit money. **2** [1920s+] (*drugs*) a drug seller, one with a wholesale role, as opposed to the less important PUSHER *n.* (3a).

dealie *n. see* DEAL *n.*[1] (7).

deals *n.* [DEAL *v.* (6)] [2000s] (*US black*) a successful seduction.

deal suit *n.* [SE *deal*, a form of pine wood from which cheap coffins are constructed] [mid–late 19C] a cheap coffin, as supplied by the parish (rather than purchased through an undertaker).

dean *n.* [play on academic title: the *dean* is responsible for campus discipline] [2000s] (*US black*) a police officer.

deaner *n.* (*also* **dena, denar, denare, denari, dener, diener, dienner**) [Ital. *dinero*, ult. f. Lat. *denarius*] [mid-19C–1960s] (*orig. Ling. Fr./Polari; later Aus.*) a shilling (5p).

dean maitland *n.* [title *The Silence of Dean Maitland*, a film (1934) based on the novel (1914) by Maxwell Grey] [1940s–60s] (*Aus.*) a silent person, one who does not talk.

Dear Jane *n.* [feminized version of DEAR JOHN *n.*] [1980s+] a letter concluding a relationship.

Dear John *n.* [its fig. salutation, *Dear John...*] [1940s+] a letter concluding a relationship, usu. sent by the woman and received by the man, often in prison or serving in the forces; also a verbal rejection.

dear joy *n.* (*also* **dear honey**) [SE *dear joy!* a supposedly favourite Irish expression] [late 17C–early 19C] an Irishman.

dear-stalker *n.* [pun on SE *deer-stalker*, i.e. one who stalks deer, and on 'the little dears'] [1910s–30s] a wealthy idler who likes to follow and/or ogle attractive shopgirls or secretaries.

deasyville *n. see* DEUSEAVILLE *n.*

death *n.* **1** [1960s] (*US campus*) an unattractive woman. **2** [1960s+] (*US black*) something excellent, something outstanding. **3** [1980s] (*US campus*) a terrible situation or event.

IN PHRASES

❑ **at the death** *adv.* [SE *death*, termination, finality] [20C+] in the end, in conclusion. ❑ **in the death** *adv.* [1950s–60s] in the end. ❑ **like death to a...** [19C+] (*US*) a phr. used of someone who is holding on without the slightest weakening, e.g. *he's holding on like death to a...*

SE in slang uses

IN COMPOUNDS

❑ **death-head** *n.* [-HEAD *sfx* (3)] [1990s+] a fan of Goth music. ❑ **death house** *n.* [20C+] (*US*) the execution chamber in a prison. ❑ **death-hunter** *n.* [note Grose (1785): 'DEATH HUNTER, an undertaker, one who furnishes the necessary articles for funerals'] **1** [early 18C–mid-19C] an undertaker. **2** [mid-18C–mid-19C] one who sells stories of interesting deaths to the press. **3** [early 19C] one who visits battlefields in order to scavenge for clothes and other saleable items. **4** [mid–late 19C] a seller of the printed versions of dying speeches, usu. of those made on the gallows. ❑ **death seat** *n.* [note trotting jargon *death seat*, the position outside the leader, from which it is difficult to win] [1960s+] the passenger seat in a motorcar, shown statistically to be the seat most likely to bring death to its occupier when the car crashes. ❑ **death's head** *n.* [image of a skull mounted on a pole] [late 18C–19C] a miserable, impoverished, emaciated person; often ext. with *on/upon a mopstick*. ❑ **death-wish** *n.* [its potentially dangerous effects] [1970s–80s] (*drugs*) phencyclidine.

IN PHRASES

❑ **death o' day** *n.* [1900s] (*Aus.*) a place that is extremely far away. ❑ **die the death of a trooper's horse** *v. see under* DIE *v.*

death! *excl.* **1** [mid-17C+] (*also* **death and furies!**) a general excl. **2** [1980s+] (*US campus*) an excl. of approval or admiration [on bad = good model].

death on *adj.* [var. on DEAD ON *adj.*] **1** [mid-19C+] very fond of. **2** [mid-19C+] (*orig. US*) (*also* **murder on**) dealing very strictly and severely with a situation or person; very good at dealing with. **3** [20C+] (*US*) finding abhorrent or being opposed to.

Death Row *n.* (*also* **death row, the row**) [mid-19C+] (*US prison*) the condemned cells.

deausavilla-stampers *n. see* DEUSEAVILLE STAMPERS *under* DEUSEAVILLE *n.*

deausaville *n. see* DEUSEAVILLE *n.*

deb *n.*[1] [backsl.] [mid-19C] a bed.

deb *n.*[2] (*also* **girl-deb**) [SE *debutante*, itself commonly abbr. as *deb*] [1940s+] (*US teen*) a female member of a street gang.

de-bag *v.* [SE pfx *de-* + BAGS *n.*[2] (1)] [late 19C+] **1** to remove someone's trousers, either as a joke or as a form of punishment [post-1960s only in rare (public) school use]. **2** [1990s+] in fig. use, to reveal the sexual underside.

debbie *n.* [abbr.] [1920s+] a *debutante*.

debblish *n.* [ety. unknown] [late 19C] (*S.Afr.*) a penny.

de-bollock *v.* [SE pfx *de-* + BALLOCK *n.* (1)] [1960s+] to castrate, usu. in fig. sense of hurting or punishing severely.

debra *adj.* [initial letter] [2000s] (*S.Afr. gay*) depressed, depressing.

debs *n.* (*US drugs*) **1** [1970s] depressants, tranquillizers, barbiturates. **2** [2000s] MDMA. **3** [2000s] amphetamine.

debut *n.* [play on SE *debut*, pun on COME OUT *v.* (1d)/SE *come out*, i.e. of a debutante] [1950s+] a first homosexual experience.

debutante *n.* **1** [1930s] (*US Und.*) a woman serving ber first jail sentence. **2** [1950s+] someone new to the gay lifestyle.

Decatur *n. see* ADA FROM DECATUR *n.*

decco *n. see* DEKKO *v.*

decent *adv.* [mid–late 19C] acceptably.

decent shake *n. see* FAIR SHAKE *n.*

deck *n.*[1] [orig. naut. use] **1** [mid-19C; 20C+] (*orig. US*) the floor, the ground. **2** [mid-19C–1950s] the roof of a train or stagecoach. **3** [1950s] (*US black*) the street.

IN PHRASES

❑ **hit the deck** *v.* **1** [1910s+] to get up from one's bed. **2** [1920s+] to fall down, to throw oneself down. **3** [1920s+] to go to bed. **4** [1930s+] to be poor. **5** [1950s+] (*Aus.*) to pay for a round of drinks.

SE/sense 1 above, in slang uses

IN PHRASES

❑ **on deck** [naut. imagery] (*US*) **1** [late 19C–1910s] on the schedule, scheduled. **2** [late 19C–1910s] alive; conscious. **3** [late 19C+] available, prepared. **4** [1940s] present. ❑ **on the**

deck [milit. use *on the deck*, at ground level] [1920s+] bankrupt, without funds.

deck *n.*[2] (*also* **dekk**) [Hind. *dekha*, sight] [mid-19C+] a look, a glance.

deck *n.*[3] [SE *deck*, but note DECK *n.*[2] as the convergence of seven roads means one can look in many directions; Seven Dials, near Covent Garden, was a criminal ROOKERY *n.* (2) of 19C London; Monmouth Street, one of the seven streets that gave it its name, was a noted centre for second-hand clothes dealing] [late 19C] Seven Dials, London, WC2; thus *decker*, an inhabitant of Seven Dials; *on the deck*, living in Seven Dials.

deck *n.*[4] [SAmE *deck*, a pack of cards; ult. 16C SE, then dial.] **1** [1910s+] (*US drugs*) a packet of heroin, cocaine or similar narcotic. **2** [1920s+] (*US prison*) a pack of cigarettes.

IN PHRASES

❑ **deck up** *v.* [1960s] (*drugs*) to portion out large measures of heroin into small portions. ❑ **not play with a full deck** *v.* [1960s+] to be aware, intelligent, 'all there'. ❑ **play with a full deck** *v.* [1960s+] to be aware, intelligent, 'all there'.

deck *v.*[1] [DECK *n.*[1] (2)] **1** [late 19C–1930s] (*US tramp*) to ride on the roof of a freight car. **2** [1920s] (*US Und.*) to drill through the top of a safe. **3** [1990s+] (*orig. US teen*) to ride a skateboard.

deck *v.*[2] [DECK *n.*[1] (1)] **1** [1940s+] to knock down. **2** [1960s] to press down the accelerator pedal of a car; thus to go fast. **3** [1960s] of a man, to have sexual intercourse.

deck *v.*[3] (*also* **dekk**) [DECK *v.*[1] (1)] [20C+] to see, to look at.

decked *adj.* (*also* **decked to death**) [SE *decked out*] [1960s+] (*US black*) well-dressed.

decked (out) *adj.* [fig. use of DECK *v.*[2] (1)] [1960s–70s] (*US*) intoxicated by drink or drugs.

decker *n.*[1] [SE *deck*] **1** [early–mid-19C] a deckhand. **2** [mid-19C+] a deck passenger. **3** [1930s+] (*Aus.*) the top deck of a double-decker bus.

decker *n.*[2] [DECK *n.*[1] (2)] [20C+] (*Aus.*) a (peaked) cap or hat.

decker *n.*[3] [DECK *v.*[3]] **1** [20C+] (*US Und.*) in a pickpocketing gang, the member who surveys the street for approaching policemen; any form of lookout. **2** [1940s+] (*Aus.*) a glance.

deckhand *n.* [1900s–40s] (*US*) a menial labourer, a domestic servant.

deckie *n.* [abbr.] [1960s+] (*Aus.*) a *deck*hand.

decko *see under* DEKKO.

decks-awash *adj.* [1930s–60s] drunk.

deck up *v. see* DECK *n.*[4].

declare off *v.* [horseracing use] [mid-18C–19C] to withdraw from an undertaking, e.g. an engagement to be married.

Decomposition Row *n.* [a pun on *Rotten Row*, itself ult. *route du roi*, the royal road, from Kensington Palace and St James's] [mid-19C] Rotten Row, the track in Hyde Park frequented by fashionable horseriders.

decorate *v.* (*also* **ornament**) [1910s–50s] (*US*) to injure, esp. to give a black eye.

decorate the mahogany *v. see* MAHOGANY *n.*

decunt *v. see* UNCUNT *V.*

decus *n.* [from the Lat. motto *decus et tutamen*, 'an ornament and a safeguard', from Virgil, *Aeneid*, Bk V, and orig. describing a breast-plate. It was subseq. engraved on coins (where it referred both to the inscription and to its helping to prevent their being clipped) and has reappeared on the English version of the modern £1 coin] [late 17C–early 19C] a crown piece, five shillings (25p).

dee *n.*[1] [orig. Rom.] [mid-19C] a purse, a pocket-book.

dee *n.*[2] **1** *see* D *n.*[2]. **2** *see* D *n.*[3].

deeache *n.* [backsl.] [mid-19C+] the head.

dee-bo *v.* [2000s] (*orig. US black*) **1** to steal. **2** to beat up, to knock down.

dee-bo *phr.* [DEE-BO *v.* (2)] [2000s] a phr. used to acknowledge someone else's wit or rudeness, i.e. *touché*.

dee-boed *adj.* [DEE-BO *v.* (2)] [2000s] (*US black*) muscular.

deece *n.* [Fr. *dix*, ten] [1940s] (*US black/Harlem*) a dime, ten cents.

deed *n.*

IN PHRASES

❑ **do the dealy deed** *v.* [1980s+] (*US campus*) to have sexual intercourse without using a contraceptive. ❑ **do the deed (of darkness)** *v.* [late 16C–17C; late 19C+] to have sexual intercourse.

deeda *n.* [1960s–70s] (*US black/Harlem/drugs*) LSD.

deedee *n.* [abbr.] **1** [1920s–40s] (*US tramp*) one who poses as a deaf mute or deaf and dumb. **2** [1990s+] (*UK drugs*) a drug dealer.

dee-dee *adj.* [DEEDEE *n.* (1)] [1920s] (*US tramp*) deaf and dumb.

dee-dee *v.* [Viet. *didi-mau*, go away] [1980s] (*US*) to run away.

dee-donk *n.* [Fr. *dis donc*, so tell me. Note antecedents in the synon. *didones* (used in Spain after the Peninsular War (1808–14), a century earlier), *dido* (as used in Ling. Fr.) as well as, somewhat later, the Javanese *orang deedonc*, 'the dis donc people'] [mid-19C] a Frenchman.

dee horn *n. see* DEHORN *n.*

Dee-Jay *n.* [Department of Justice] [1940s] (*US Und.*) an agent of the Federal Bureau of Investigation.

deejay *see under* DJ.

deek *n.*[1] [pron.] [1930s+] (*US*) a detective.

deek *n.*[2] (*also* **deeks**) [DEKKO *n.*] [1990s+] a look, a glance.

deek *v.* [DEKKO *v.*] [mid-19C+] to look at.

deeker *n.* [DEEK *v.*] [19C–1930s] (*Scot. Und.*) a thief who also acts as a police informer.

deeks *n. see* DEEK *n.*[2].

deelo *adj.* (*also* **delo, dillo**) [backsl.] [mid-19C+] old.

IN COMPOUNDS

❑ **de(e)lo diam** *n.* [late 19C+] an old maid. ❑ **de(e)lo nam of the barrack** *n.* [NAM *n.* (1) + SE *barrack*] [late 19C] the master of the house. ❑ **deelo nammo** *n.* (*also* **delonammon, delo nammow, dillo namo, dillo nemo**) [NAMMO *n.*] [mid-19C+] an old woman; thus one's wife.

deemer *n.* (*US*) **1** [1920s–60s] (*also* **deem, demier, dimer**) a dime. **2** [1930s] the number ten. **3** [1930s–60s] one who tips a dime; a small tip.

deener *n.* (*also* **deena, deenir, deiner**) [DEANER *n.*] **1** [mid-19C+] (*Aus./N.Z./UK*) one shilling, money in general. **2** [1950s+] (*US*) ten cents; also attrib.

deep *adj.* [ext. use of SE] **1** [late 17C+] sly, artful. **2** [late 18C] fast. **3** [1980s+] (*US black*) extreme, amazing.

IN COMPOUNDS

❑ **deep file** *n.* [FILE *n.* (5)] [19C] an artful, cunning or shrewd person. ❑ **deep sugar** *n. see under* SUGAR *n.*[4].

SE in slang uses

IN COMPOUNDS

❑ **deep freeze** *n.* (*US*) **1** [1950s] a place of imprisonment, a prison. **2** [1960s+] ostracism. ❑ **deep noser** *n.* [one has to push one's nose deep into the glass] [1940s–50s] (*Aus.*) a deep glass of beer. ❑ **deep sea** *see* separate entries. ❑ **deep shit** *n.* [SHIT *n.* (3c)] [1970s+] a serious situation, a difficult problem; usu. as *in deep shit*. ❑ **deep sinker** *n.* [supposed resemblance to a deep mine-shaft] [late 19C–1950s] (*Aus.*) **1** a drinking-glass of the largest size. **2** the drink served in such a glass. ❑ **deep six** *see* separate entries. ❑ **deep throat** *see* separate entries. ❑ **deep yellow** *n. see* HIGH YELLOW *n.*

deep *adv.* **1** [1970s+] (*US black*) (*also* **deep-down**) a general intensifier. **2** [1990s+] (*US black gang*) well-supplied with members. **3** [1990s+] (*US black gang*) in number.

IN PHRASES

❑ **get deep in someone's ass** *v.* [1980s] (*US black*) to fight; to beat up.

deep sea *n. see* ALL AT SEA *under* SEA *n.*

SE in slang uses

IN COMPOUNDS

❑ **deep sea chef** [1920s] (*US*) a dishwasher. ❑ **deep sea fisherman** (*also* **deep sea gambler**) [1940s–70s] a confidence trickster working the transatlantic liners. ❑ **deep sea turkey**

[20C+] (*US*) **1** salt cod; a codfish (dinner). **2** (*also* **submarine turkey**) salmon.

deep sea dive *n.* [rhy. sl.] [1980s] (*Aus.*) the number five.

deep-sea diver *n.*[1] [DIVE *v.* (2)] [1920s] (*US black*) a cunnilinguist; thus *deep-sea diving*, cunnilingus.

deep-sea diver *n.*[2] [rhy. sl. = FIVER *n.* (1)] [1940s+] a £5 note.

deep six *n.* [SE phr. *six feet under*, dead] **1** [1920s–40s] a grave. **2** [1930s+] suicide. **3** [1950s+] death. **4** [1960s] a dismissal from work.

IN PHRASES

▫ **give someone the deep six** *v.* [1920s+] (*US*) to kill, to murder. ▫ **hit the deep six** *v.* [1960s] to die. ▫ **take the deep six** *v.* [1930s+] to die; also in fig. use.

deep six *v.* [naut. use *deep six*, to throw overboard; ult. SE phr. *six feet under*, dead] **1** [1940s+] (*orig. US*) to get rid of, to abandon. **2** [1950s+] (*orig. US*) to ruin, to destroy. **3** [1950s+] (*US*) to kill, to die. **4** [1960s+] (*US campus*) to expel from a college. **5** [1980s+] (*US campus*) to finish a six-pack of beer.

deep throat *n.* [the term was popularized by the 'art porn' film *Deep Throat* (1973) starring Linda Lovelace; it was also used as the nickname of the otherwise anonymous source who helped journalists investigate the Watergate Affair (1972–4)] [1970s+] deep fellatio, in which the penis is taken not simply into the mouth, but down the throat.

deep throat *v.* [DEEP THROAT *n.*] [1970s+] **1** to take the entire length of the penis into one's mouth, and thus down one's throat, during fellatio. **2** in a non-sexual or semi-sexual sense, e.g. to suck suggestively on a straw.

deer *n.* [abbr. WHETSTONE PARK DEER *n.*; note Shakespearian use of *deer*, a man or woman in the context of sexual activity] **1** [17C; mid-19C–1960s] a (promiscuous) young woman. **2** [late 17C] a dupe.

IN COMPOUNDS

▫ **deer-stalking** *n.* [1920s] chasing after women.

Dees, the *n. see* D *n.*[2] (1).

deez (nuts) *n.* [SE *these* + NUTS *n.*[2] (1)] [1990s+] (*US black*) the testicles; the male genitals.

def *adj.* [? black pron. of SE *death*; or ? abbr. SE *definitive*. Note 1907 citation in Cassidy & LePage, *Dict. of Jam. English* (1967, 1992): 'I never do him one def ting', where *def* means 'single'] [1970s+] (*orig. US black*) perfect, excellent, first-rate.

IN PHRASES

▫ **do to def** *v.* [1980s+] (*US*) to do something as well as possible.

def *adv.* [abbr.] [1940s+] *definitely.*

de facto *n.* [Lat. *de facto*, in fact, as opposed to *de jure*, in law] [1990s+] (*Aus.*) one of the two partners in an unmarried but steady relationship.

deffo *adv.* (*also* **defo**) [abbr. + -O *sfx* (7)] [1960s+] (*orig. Irish*) *definitely.*

defi *n.* [abbr. SE act of *defiance*] [late 19C–1960s] (*orig. Aus.*) a challenge.

def jam *n.* [DEF *adj.* + JAM *n.*[1] (5)] [1980s+] an outstanding record or track.

defo *adv. see* DEFFO *adv.*

def O.J. *n.* ['In "Rapper's Delight" the term "Death OJ" is used. In current slang "death" means something good, while "OJ" is a ref. to a big car. Erstwhile football star and all-around adman O.J. Simpson does Hertz commercials featuring Ford and Lincoln Mercury cars. If we add "death" to Ford and Lincoln Mercury cars [...] we come up with the "Rapper's Delight" character driving off in a Lincoln Continental' (Nelson George, *Buppies, B-Boys, Baps and Bohos*, 1992)] [1970s+] an extremely smart, fashionable automobile.

dege *adj.* (*also* **dege-dege**) [Ewe *deká*, single, solitary] [1950s+] (*W.I. Rasta*) little, skimpy, small; both in size and number.

degen *n.* [Ger. *Degen*, a sword] **1** [late 17C–mid-19C] (*also* **dagan**) a sword. **2** [19C] an artful person [suggests play on *knowing blade*].

deger *n. see* DACHA *n.*

dehorn *n.* (*also* **dee horn**) [pun on SE *dehorn*, to deprive an animal of its horns] [1920s–50s] (*US*) **1** denatured or adulterated alcohol, as drunk by alcoholics, tramps etc. **2** a person who becomes ill through drinking such liquor.

dehorned *adj.* [SE *dehorn*, to deprive an animal of its horns] [20C+] (*US*) demoted, deprived of a position of power or authority.

deiner *n. see* DEENER *n.*

deke *n.* (*also* **deak**) [late 19C+] (*US campus*) a member of the Delta Kappa Epsilon fraternity.

deke *v.* [DUCK *v.*[1] (2)] [1990s+] (*Can. teen*) to dodge, to avoid.

dekk *n. see* DECK *n.*[2].

dekk *v. see* DECK *v.*[3].

dekko *n.* (*also* **decco, decko, dekker**) [DEKKO *v.*] [late 19C+] a look, a view.

IN PHRASES

▫ **keep dekko** *v.* (*also* **keep decko**) (*US Und.*) to keep a lookout.

dekko *v.* (*also* **decko**) [Hindi *dekh-nā*, to look/Rom. *dik*, to look] [late 19C+] to look.

del *n. see* DELL *n.*

delf *n.* [SE *deadself*] [1990s+] oneself; thus *go for delf*, *release your delf.*

Delhi belly *n.* (*also* **New Delhi belly**) [*Delhi*, capital of India + SE *belly*] [1940s+] food poisoning, epitomized by diarrhoea suffered by tourists in India.

delicate *n.* [? the need for *delicacy* in pursuing these tricks] **1** [mid-19C] a fake subscription list carried by one who poses as an alms collector. **2** [late 19C] a begging-letter.

delinko *n.* (*also* **delink**) [abbr./pron.] [1950s+] (*Aus./US*) a juvenile *delinquent.*

deliver a baby *v.* [1970s] (*US gay*) to remove one's trousers in order to expose one's erect penis.

deliver the goods *v. see under* GOODS *n.*

dell *n.* (*also* **dal, del, dill**) [poss. SE name *Doll* or, in the way that CUNT *n.* is linked to Welsh *cwm*, a valley, then a pun on SE *dell*, also meaning valley; Ribton-Turner, *A History of Vagrants* (1887), notes Welsh *del*, pert, smart; Lowland Scot. *dilp*, a trollop] **1** [17C–early 19C] a young woman on the tramp, spec. a young or virgin prostitute; thus *wild dell*, such a young woman conceived or born under a hedge. **2** [late 18C] a prostitute.

IN PHRASES

▫ **arch-dell** *n.* [early 18C–mid-19C] (*UK Und.*) the woman accomplice of a criminal gang-leader.

delo *adj. see* DEELO *adj.*

delog *n.* (*also* **dilog, dlog**) [backsl.] [mid-19C] gold.

delonammon/delo nammow *n. see* DEELO NAMMO *under* DEELO *adj.*

delosis *n.* [? SE *delicious*] [1950s] (*US black*) a pretty young woman.

Delphi *n.* [abbr.] [mid–late 19C] the *Adelphi* Theatre, the Strand, London WC2.

delphinium *n.* [? the phallic plant] [2000s] (*S.Afr. gay*) **1** the penis. **2** an active homosexual man.

del. trem. *n.* [abbr.] [mid–late 19C] *delirium tremens.*

dem *n. see* DEMO *n.*[1] (3).

dem! *excl. see* DAMN! *excl.*

demander for glimmer *n.* [SE *demand* + GLIMMER *n.* (1)] [16C] (*UK Und.*) a female beggar who poses as the victim of a fire (complete with fake documents to prove it) and begs alms on that basis.

demento *n.* [SE *demented* + ? the 1970s US radio show *Dr Demento*] [1970s+] (*US*) a crazy, eccentric person.

demi-bar *n. see* DEMY *n.*

demi-beau *n. see under* BEAU *n.*[1].

demi-castor *n. see under* CASTOR *n.*

demi-doss *n.* [SE *demi*, half + DOSS *n.*[1] (1); ? one gets only half a bed or the comfort is substandard] [late 19C–1910s] (*UK tramp*) a penny bed.

demier *n. see* DEEMER *n.*

demi-rep *n.* (*also* **demi-rip, demy-rep**) [SE *demi*, half + abbr. *reputation* or *reprobate*. Note synon. SE *demi-mondaine*] [mid-18C+] a woman of doubtful reputation; ext. as a relatively classy prostitute, and a figure defined by Henry Fielding in *Tom Jones* (1749) as one 'whom everybody knows to be what nobody calls her'.

demis *n.* (*also* **demmies**) [abbr.] [1950s–80s] (*US drugs*) tablets/capsules of *dem*erol.

demmie *n.* [abbr.] [2000s] (*US drugs*) *dem*erol.

demnition *adj.* [pron. of SE *damnation*, used as an adj.] [mid-19C–1920s] a var. on DAMNED *adj.*

demo *n.*[1] [abbr.] **1** [late 18C] (*US*) a *demo*crat. **2** [1900s; 1930s+] (*orig. Aus.*) demonstration (of a political or pressure-group nature). **3** [1940s+] (*also* **dem**) a *dem*onstration, e.g. of a specific skill or action. **4** [1940s+] *demo*lition. **5** [1950s+] a *demo*nstration record or tape, used to promote a band's or individual musician's work [SE *demonstration (disc/record/tape)*].

demo *n.*[2] [pron.] [1920s+] (*US*) a dime.

demob *n.* [abbr.] [1940s+] *demob*ilization from the armed forces.

IN COMPOUNDS

❑ **demob-happy** *adj.* [-HAPPY *sfx* (1); orig. milit. use, the sense of the nervous happiness that overtakes men nearing demobilization and whose milit. service is nearing its end. Note prison use *gate-happy*, the sense of nervous excitement that takes over those whose sentence is almost up] [1940s+] excited at the prospect of being released from a long-term, usu. tedious job. ❑ **demob suit** *n.* [1940s+] the suit issued to discharged men on their quitting the services.

demob *v.* [abbr.] [1920s+] of a soldier, to be demobilized.

demon *n.*[1] [proper name *Van Dieman's Land*, modern Tasmania, where bushranging was supposed to have been inaugurated] (*Aus.*) **1** [early–mid-19C] a convict. **2** [late 19C] a veteran bushranger. **3** [late 19C+] often as pl.; a detective or police officer [SE/D *n.*[2] (1) + *men*].

demon *n.*[2] [SE/D *n.*[2] (1) + *man*] [late 19C+] a detective or police officer; often in pl.

demon *n.*[3] [pron.] [1940s] (*US black/Harlem*) a dime.

dempstered *adj.* [Scot. *dempster*, the official who, until 1773, had the duty of repeating the judge's sentence in open court] [mid–late 17C] hanged.

demy *n.* (*also* **demi-bar**) [lit. half a BARRED *adj.* (1) dice; post-17C listings are historical] [16C–early 19C] a type of crooked dice.

demy-rep *n. see* DEMI-REP *n.*

Den, the *n.* **1** [late 18C–19C] a public house frequented by a regular group of cronies and thus named by them. **2** [early–mid-19C] the Stock Exchange. **3** [20C+] New Cross, London; thus *The Den*, the nickname for the Millwall Football Club ground.

den *n.* **1** [late 18C+] a small room, usu. occupied by a single man [SE f. 1900]. **2** [late 18C+] (*US Und.*) one's home, an establishment. **3** [1920s–50s] (*US Und.*) a single prison cell.

dena/denar/denare/denari/dener *n. see* DEANER *n.*

Denmark *n.*

IN PHRASES

❑ **go to Denmark** *v. see GO TO* COPENHAGEN *under* COPENHAGEN *n.*

dennis *n.* [? its manufacturer] [early 19C] a small walking-stick.

IN PHRASES

❑ **one's name is Dennis** [whaling jargon *dennis*, a whale that has been harpooned and is on the verge of death] [mid-19C–1920s] (*US*) a phr. indicating failure, one has no chance, one is finished, 'done for'; also abbr. as *Dennis*.

Dennis the Menace *n.* [the middle letters] [1990s+] MDMA.

dennyaiser *n. see* DINNYHAZER *n.*

denso *n.* [SE *dense* + -O *sfx* (2)] [1980s+] (*US*) a very unintelligent person.

dent *v.* [1990s+] (*US black*) to shoot.

dentals *n.* (*also* **dent**) [1960s] (*US*) teeth, false teeth.

de-nut *v.* [SE pfx *de-* + NUTS *n.*[2] (1)] [1950s+] to castrate.

dep *n.* [abbr. SE *deputy*] **1** [mid-19C] a porter at a cheap lodging house. **2** [late 19C+] a deputy, e.g. a prison's deputy governor.

dep *v.* [DEP *n.* (2)] [20C+] to act as deputy.

departer *n.* [late 19C] a last drink prior to leaving on a journey.

depresh *n.* [abbr./pron.] [1930s–40s] (*orig. US*) the *Depression*, the financial and industrial slump of 1929 and subseq. years.

depressed area *n.* [i.e. when hungry] [1940s] the stomach.

depresso *n.* [SE *depressed* + -O *sfx* (2)] [1970s+] (*US*) a deeply depressed individual.

depresso *adj.* [DEPRESSO *n.*] [1960s–70s] (*US teen*) depressing; depressed.

depth charge *n.* **1** [1940s–50s] (*orig. milit./prison*) any form of stodgy food. **2** [1960s] (*US*) an ejaculation.

deputy do-right *n.* (*also* **do-right**) [1970s+] (*US black*) the police.

derail *n.* **1** [1920s–30s] (*US campus*) an unpopular student [*HDAS*, citing Weseen, *Dict. of American Sl.* (1934), suggests that this may be a mis-reading, but it may equally be be a separate or fig./ext. use of sense 2]. **2** [1920s–50s] (*US/N.Z.*) denatured or adulterated alcohol, as drunk by alcoholics, tramps etc. **3** [1930s] a person who becomes ill through drinking such liquor.

derailed *adj.* [DERAIL *n.* (2)] [2000s] (*US campus*) drunk.

derb queen *n.* [DERBY *n.* (2) + -QUEEN *sfx* (2)] [2000s] (*US black*) an enthusiastic fellatrix.

derby *n.* **1** [1930s+] the head [? the *Derby hat*, which sits on the SE *head*]. **2** [1960s–70s] (*US black*) an act of oral sex [? the *Derby hat*, which sits on the SE *head*/HEAD *n.* (2C); ? the bobbing/jolting action of a jockey on horseback]. **3** *see* DARBY *n.*[1].

derby kelly *n. see* DARBY KELLY *n.*

derby winner *n.* [rhy. sl.] [20C+] (*Aus.*) a dinner.

derelict *n.* [1970s] (*US campus*) a boring person.

deri *n.* (*also* **derry**) [abbr.] [1960s+] *der*elict house or other dwelling.

derm *n.* [fig. use of Afk. *derm*, intestines] [1970s+] (*S.Afr.*) 'guts', both lit. and fig., i.e. courage, bravery, staying power.

dermo *n.* [abbr. + -O *sfx* (3)] [1940s] (*Aus.*) *derm*atitis.

dern *n. see under* DARN.

dernation *adj. see* DARNATION *adj.*

derned *adj. see* DARNED *adj.*

dero *n.* (*also* **derro**) [abbr. + -O *sfx* (3)] [1970s+] (*Aus./N.Z.*) a *der*elict person, a down-and-out; also as general term of insult.

derrey *n.* [? play on SE *derry down*, one 'looks down'] [mid–late 19C] (*UK/US Und.*) an eyeglass.

derrick *n.*[1] **1** [17C] the gallows, the hangman, the hanging [*Derrick*, a well-known hangman at Tyburn, c.1600; he appears, *inter alia*, in Thomas Dekker's *The Bellman of London* (1608); *see* Grose (1785): 'DERRICK, the name of the finisher of the law, or hangman, about the year 1608']. **2** [19C] the penis [ext. of sense 1, i.e. with the idea of 'lifting up']. **3** [1910s–40s] (*US*) a shoplifter, esp. a proficient one; also attrib. [ext. of sense 1, i.e. 'lifting'].

IN PHRASES

❑ **clout/root on the derrick** *v.* [1930s] (*US drugs*) to support a drug addiction by thieving.

derrick *n.*[2] [the masculine name] [1960s] (*US gay*) a lesbian.

derrick *v.* [DERRICK *n.*[1]] **1** [mid-18C] to leave; to go. **2** [mid-19C] (*UK Und.*) to embark on an adventure. **3** [20C+] (*US*) to execute someone or to kill oneself. **4** [1930s] (*US*) to shoplift. **5** [1970s] (*US*) to take, to remove.

derro *n. see* DERO *n.*

derry *n.*[1] [abbr. SE refrain *derry down*, i.e. DOWN ON *under* DOWN *adj.*[1]] [mid-19C+] (*orig. UK Und., late 19C+ mainly Aus./N.Z.*) **1** an aversion towards. **2** a feud.

IN PHRASES

❑ **have a derry on** *v.* (*also* **get a derry on**) [mid-19C+] (*orig. UK Und., later use Aus./N.Z.*) to be prejudiced against.

❑ **without dip or derry** *adv.* [note dial. *deray*, an uproar, ult. Fr. *derroi*, confusion] [mid-19C] (*UK Und.*) without any problems.

derry *n.*[2] [ety. unknown] [1900s] (*Aus. Und.*) an eyeglass.

derry *n.*[3] *see* DERI *n.*

derwenter *n.* [a veteran of the prison at the *River Derwent*, Tasmania] [late 19C] (*Aus.*) a released convict.

des *adj.* [abbr.] [1990s+] (*W.I.*) desperate.

desert *n.* [i.e. the relative absence of members] [late 19C] (*UK society*) a ladies-only club.

SE in slang uses

IN COMPOUNDS

❑ **desert canary** *n.* [20C+] (*US*) a mule, a donkey. ❑ **desert mouth** *n. see* COTTONMOUTH *n.* (1). ❑ **desert rat** *n.* (*also* **desert-head**) [SE *desert rat*, the jerboa] [20C+] (*US*) **1** one who lives in the desert, esp. a prospector working there. **2** a native of the southwestern states.

desi (boy) *n.* [Urdu *deysi*, local] [2000s] (*UK teen*) a young man of immigrant Pakistani descent.

desk *n.*

SE in slang uses

IN COMPOUNDS

❑ **desk jockey** *n.* [JOCKEY *n.*[2] (3b)] [1950s+] (*US*) a clerk. ❑ **desk piano** *n.* [1940s] (*US black/Harlem*) a typewriter. ❑ **desk-polisher** *n.* [1930s] a non-combatant.

deskie *n.* (*also* **deskateer**) [SE *desk* + sfx *-ie/-ateer*, the latter hinting at the spurious romance of *musketeer*] [1980s] (*US*) a desk clerk.

Desmond (Tutu) *n.* [rhy. sl. *Tutu* = '2:2; ult. *Desmond Tutu*, South African clergyman and political activist (b.1931)] [1990s+] a lower second university degree.

despatcher(s) *n. see* DISPATCHER *n.*

despatches *n.* **1** *see* DISPATCHER *n.* **2** *see* DISPATCHES *n.* (1).

despatch one's cargo *v.* [1910s–20s] to defecate.

desperado *n.* [SE *desperado*, a despairing, reckless man] [1950s+] a gambler who bets heavily but cannot pay off when he loses.

desperation hour *n.* (*also* **d.h.**) [2000s] (*S.Afr. gay*) the final hour before a bar closes when one becomes less selective in the choice of a sexual partner.

de-stat *v.* [SE pfx *de-* + *stat*(*utory tenant*)] [1950s–60s] of a landlord or owner, to evict sitting tenants so as to gain possession of a valuable property, which can then be sold for a high profit.

destroy *v.* [2000s] to cover a wall or other object in graffiti.

destroyed *adj.* [1950s+] **1** exhausted. **2** (*drugs*) under the influence of either drugs or drink.

destroyer *n.* [1950s] (*W.I.*) a deceitful man.

d.e.t. *n.* [abbr.] [1960s+] (*drugs*) dimethyltryptamine.

det *adj.* (*also* **dett**) [var. on DEF *adj.*] [1990s+] first-rate, excellent, wonderful.

detec *n.* [abbr.] [late 19C] a *detec*tive.

dethroned *adj.* [punning use of SE] [1940s–70s] (*gay*) of a gay man, ejected from the public lavatory where he is looking for sex.

detox *n.* [abbr.] [1970s+] *detox*ification after a period of drink or drug addiction; thus *Detox*, any hospital or similar establishment that specializes in detoxification of drink or drug addicts; also attrib.

detox *v.* [DETOX *n.*] [1970s+] to enter a period of voluntary withdrawal from narcotic or alcohol addiction; to render someone free of alcohol or drug addiction.

detrimental *n.* **1** [mid-19C] (*UK society*) a younger brother of the heir of an estate [note primogeniture rendered such younger sons ineligible to inherit]. **2** [mid-19C] a male flirt. **3** [mid–late 19C] (*UK society*) an ineligible suitor. **4** [20C+] a male homosexual.

Detroit disaster *n.* (*also* **Detroit iron, ...junk**) [presumably in bad condition] [1910s–60s] (*orig. US black*) a car.

Detroit pink *n.* [? local packaging] [1980s+] (*drugs*) phencyclidine.

dett *adj. see* DET *adj.*

detweed *v.* [SE *de-* + TWEEDS *n.*] [1980s] (*Aus.*) to take off one's clothes.

Deuce, the *n.* **1** [1960s+] the main street of downtown (less fashionable) Las Vegas. **2** [1980s+] New York's 42nd Street, between Seventh and Eighth Avenues [until the shutting down of many cinemas and bookstores specializing in pornography in the early 1990s, this was the centre of mid-town vice].

deuce *n.*[1] (*also* **deucie, duce**) [SE *deuce*, the two in dice or cards] **1** [16C+] two, a pair, of objects and occas. individuals. **2** [late 17C–1960s] twopence. **3** [mid-19C] two cents. **4** [late 19C–1960s] a useless gambler, a worthless individual [the deuce is the lowest card in the deck]. **5** [20C+] (*Aus.*) (*also* **deucer**) a champion shearer capable of shearing 200 sheep in a day. **6** [1910s+] (*also* **deucer, deuce spot**) (*US*) $2; a two-dollar bill. **7** [1920s+] (*US prison*) (*also* **deuce-burger**) a two-year sentence. **8** in drug uses. (**a**) [1930s] (*drugs*) two marijuana cigarettes, sold together. (**b**) [1960s–70s] (*US drugs*) a $2 package of heroin. (**c**) [1970s] (*US drugs*) two pills. (**d**) [1990s+] a $2 vial of crack cocaine. **9** [1940s] (*Aus.*) two shillings (10p). **10** [1950s] £2. **11** [1960s] (*Scot. prison*) a two-month prison sentence. **12** [1970s] (*also* **deucer**) a two-hour shift. **13** [1990s+] (*US black*) an unattractive young woman, i.e. one considered second-rate.

IN COMPOUNDS

❑ **deuce-burger** *n. see* sense 7 above. ❑ **deuce-deuce** *n.* **1** [1980s+] a .22 revolver or pistol. **2** [1990s+] a 22fl.oz beer. ❑ **deuce-five** *n.* [1980s+] a .25 pistol. ❑ **deuce wins** *n.* (*also* **deux wins, dews wins**) [WIN *n.*] [late 17C–mid-19C] (*UK Und.*) twopence.

IN PHRASES

❑ **deuce and a quarter** *n.* **1** [1960s+] (*US black/teen*) a Buick Electra 225. **2** [1980s] (*US black*) (*also* **deuce-25**) any car with a 225 h.p. engine. **3** [1990s+] (*US prison*) a sentence of 2 to 25 years. ❑ **deuce of benders** *n.* [BENDER *n.*[2] (1)] [1930s–40s] (*US black/Harlem*) the knees. ❑ **deuce of boxcars** *n.* [BOXCARS *n.* (1)] [1940s] (*US black*) one day, i.e. 24 hours. ❑ **deuce of clubs** *n.* [pun on cards/weapons] [1940s] (*US*) the fists, used for violent assaults; thus *play the deuce of clubs*, to beat someone up. ❑ **deuce of grabbers** *n.* [GRABBER *n.* (4)] [1940s] (*US black*) the hands. ❑ **deuce of haircuts** *n.* [a fortnightly haircut] [1940s] (*US black/Harlem*) two weeks. ❑ **deuce of nods on the backbeat** *n.* [NOD *n.*[1] + SE *backbeat*] [1940s] (*US black/Harlem*) two days ago. ❑ **deuce of peekers** *n.* [PEEKER *n.*] [1940s] (*US black/Harlem*) a pair of eyes. ❑ **deuce of ruffs** *n.* [RUFF *n.*] [1940s] (*US black/Harlem*) 20 cents. ❑ **deuce of ticks** *n.* [TICK *n.*[4] (2)] [1940s] (*US black/Harlem*) two minutes. ❑ **deuce (out)** *v.* [the weakness of the *deuce* in a pack of cards] [1940s+] (*US*) to back down, to act the coward. ❑ **double-deuce** *n.* [1990s+] (*US black*) a .22 calibre handgun.

deuce *n.*[2] [? SE *deuce*, the lowest, and thus the least lucky throw in dice] **1** [mid–late 17C] a synon. for syphilis or the plague, e.g. *deuce on him, the deuce on it*. **2** [late 17C+] (*also* **dooce, doose, duce**) used in phrs. as a euph. for 'the devil', e.g. *the deuce! what the deuce! so/who/how/where/when the deuce? (the) deuce take it! the deuce is in it!* thus *play the deuce (with)*, to cause trouble for; *the deuce and all/much; the deuce to pay, a deuce of a mess*; also. lit. the devil. **3** [1900s–10s] an inferior person, a 'devil'.

IN PHRASES

❑ **raise the deuce** *v. see* RAISE HELL *under* HELL *n.*

deuce *adj.* [DEUCE *n.*[1] (1)] [1920s+] second in sequence, order or rank.

deuce *v.* [DEUCE *n.*[1] (5)/DEUCE *n.*[1] (8a)] **1** [20C+] (*Aus.*) to shear approximately 200 sheep in one day. **2** [1940s] (*US drugs*) to sell two marijuana cigarettes.

deuce and ace *n.* [rhy. sl.] [1910s+] the face.

deuced *adj.* (*also* **dooced, doosid, duced**) [DEUCE *n.*[2] (2)] [late 18C+] a euph. for DAMNED *adj.*

deuced *adv.* [19C+] a euph. for DAMNED *adv.*; thus *deuced infernal*, very unpleasant.

deucedly *adv.* [DEUCED *adj.*] [early 19C+] a synon./euph. for *devilishly, damnably*.

deucer *n.* see DEUCE *n.*[1].

deuceways *n.* [1940s–50s] **1** (*US black*) a pair. **2** (*US drugs*) two dollars' worth of narcotics.

IN PHRASES

❑ **cop a deuceways** *v.* [DEUCE *n.*[1] (6)] [1940s–50s] (*US black*) to obtain two dollars' worth of something.

deucie *n.* see DEUCE *n.*[1].

deuseaville *n.* (*also* **daisyville, deasyville, deausaville, dewsavell, dewse-a-vill, duceavil**) [-VILLE *sfx*[1]. *DSUE* suggests a corruption of *daisy-ville* but *dewse*= deuce = the devil and thus a generic negative; given that London, the big city, is RUM VILLE *n.* (1), lit. 'good town', might not the country, its opposite, be 'bad town'?] [mid-16C–mid-19C] (*UK Und.*) the countryside.

IN COMPOUNDS

❑ **deuseaville stampers** *n.* (*also* **deausavilla-stampers**) [SE *stamp*/STAMPERS *n.* (1)] [mid-16C–18C] (*UK Und.*) members of a criminal gang who wander the country roads and frequent country inns in the hope of picking up information about possible robberies.

deux wins *n.* see *DEUCE WINS under* DEUCE *n.*[1].

devil *n.* [the role of the white race in black Muslim iconography] [1960s+] (*US black, esp. black Muslim*) a white person.

SE in slang uses

IN COMPOUNDS

as a clergyman or preacher

❑ **devil-catcher** *n.* [late 18C] a parson. ❑ **devil-chaser** *n.* [20C+] (*US*) a volunteer preacher, without proper qualifications but capable of earnestly quoting what he/she has read in the Bible. ❑ **devil-dodger** *n.* **1** [late 18C+] a clergyman, a preacher. **2** [mid-19C] one who sometimes attends an Anglican church and sometimes a Quaker meeting. ❑ **devil-driver** *n.* [late 18C–early 19C] a parson. ❑ **devil-pitcher** *n.* [late 18C–19C] a clergyman. ❑ **devil-scolder** *n.* [mid-19C] a clergyman. ❑ **devil-teaser** *n.* [1910s] (*US*) a clergyman.

in the context of gambling

❑ **devil's bedpost** *n.* (*also* **devil's bedposts**) [note whist jargon *devil's bedstead*, the 13th card of whichever suit has been led] [mid–late 19C] the four of clubs, considered to be unlucky. ❑ **devil's bones** *n.* (*also* **devil's ribs**) [mid-17C–mid-18C] dice. ❑ **devil's dozen** *n.* [a supposedly unlucky number: the number of witches supposed to attend a sabbath] [early 17C–19C] the number 13. ❑ **devil's four-poster** *n.* [clubs, being black, are characterized as 'devilish'] [mid-19C] the four of clubs. ❑ **devil's (picture) books** *n.* (*also* **devil's bible, ...prayer books**) [early 18C+] a pack of playing cards. ❑ **devil's picture-gallery** *n.* [1920s] a pack of playing cards. ❑ **devil's pictures** *n.* [1910s] a pack of playing cards. ❑ **devil's playthings** *n.* [19C] a pack of playing cards. ❑ **devil's ribs** *n.* see *DEVIL'S BONES* above. ❑ **devil's teeth** *n.* [mid-19C] dice.

in the context of alcohol

❑ **devil's brew** *n.* [1940s+] (*US*) whisky. ❑ **devil's dye** *n.* [mid-19C] (*US*) whisky. ❑ **devil's eyewater** *n.* see *EYEWATER under* EYE *n.* ❑ **devil's nobbler** *n.* [NOBBLER *n.*[3]] [late 19C] (*Aus.*) a variety of alcoholic drink. ❑ **devil soup** *n.* [1980s] (*W.I.*) white rum. ❑ **devil's tail** *n.* [mid-19C] (*UK Und.*) brandy.

in the context of drugs

❑ **devil's dandruff** *n.* [1980s+] (*drugs*) crack cocaine. ❑ **devil's dick** *n.* [DICK *n.*[1] (5)] [1980s+] (*US black*) a pipe for smoking crack cocaine. ❑ **devil's dust** *n.* see separate entry.

general uses

❑ **devil dogs** *n.* [1910s+] the US Marines. ❑ **devil's bite** *n.* [mid-19C] the contraction of the vaginal muscles around the penis during intercourse. ❑ **devil's box** *n.* [the supposed sinfulness of music] [20C+] (*US*) a violin. ❑ **devil's claws** *n.* [late 19C] (*UK prison*) the 'broad arrow' marking on convict clothes. ❑ **devil's colours** *n.* (*also* **devil's livery**) [the use of *black* to denote mourning and *yellow* for quarantine] [mid-19C] black and yellow. ❑ **devil's delight** *n.* [mid-19C+] a row, a fuss; thus *kick up the devil's delight*, to have a rowdy argument or make a disturbance. ❑ **devil's dinner-hour** *n.* [late 19C] midnight. ❑ **devil's dung** *n.* [i.e. Pers. *aza*, mastic + Lat. *foetida*, stinking; the substance is used both in medicine and in cooking] [17C–mid-19C] asafoetida (*Ferula assa-foetida*). ❑ **devil's dust** *n.* see separate entry. ❑ **devil's front porch** *n.* see *HELL'S FRONT PORCH under* HELL *n.* ❑ **devil's guts** *n.* ['so called by farmers, who do not like their land should be measured by their landlords' (Grose, 1785)] [mid-17C–early 19C] a surveyor's chain. ❑ **devil's half-acre** *n.* [1950s+] (*US*) **1** a rough or unworkable piece of land. **2** the rough area of a town. ❑ **devil's livery** *n.* see *DEVIL'S COLOURS* above. ❑ **devil's neckerchief** *n.* [18C] the hangman's noose; often ext. with *...on the way to Redriffe*. ❑ **devil's necklace** *n.* [1900s] (*Aus.*) a snake. ❑ **devil's regiment** *n.* (*also* **devil's regiment of the line**) [coined by Thomas Carlyle (1795–1881)] [mid-19C] prisoners. ❑ **devil's smiles** *n.* [19C] spring weather, esp. the alternating sun and showers of a 'typical' April. ❑ **devil's tattoo** *n.* (*also* **tattoo**) [? pvb 'The devil finds work for idle hands'] [late 18C–1930s] the tapping of one's fingers or feet, often through boredom or irritation.

IN PHRASES

❑ **devil among the tailors** *n.* [according to F&H (and backed by *OED*) 'Originating in a riot at the Haymarket when Dowton announced the performance for his benefit, of a burlesque entitled "The Tailors: a Tragedy for Warm Weather". Many thousands of journeymen tailors congregated, and interrupted the performances. Thirty-three were brought up at Bow Street next day.'] [mid-19C] an argument, a row. ❑ **devil beating tanbark** see *HELL BEATING TANBARK under* HELL *n.* ❑ **devil in blue** *n.* see BLUE DEVIL *n.*[1]. ❑ **devil-on-the-coals** *n.* (*also* **beggar-on-the-coals**) [mid-19C–1900s] (*Aus.*) a small unleavened loaf hastily baked in hot ashes. ❑ **go like the devil** *v.* see *GO LIKE HELL under* HELL *n.* ❑ **marry the devil's daughter (and live with the old folks)** *v.* see *under* MARRY *v.* ❑ **sure as the devil's in London** *adv.* see *under* SURE AS... *phr.*

IN EXCLAMATIONS

❑ **devil me arse!** see *under* ARSE *n.* ❑ **devil's cure!** [1920s–50s] (*Irish*) a mild excl. ❑ **get to the devil out of it!** see *GET TO FUCK! under* FUCK *n.*

devil's dust *n.*[1] [SE *devil*, the machine that shreds the old rags + *dust*, refuse] [mid-19C–1900s] shoddy, i.e. yarn made from reprocessed woollen rags.

devil's dust *n.*[2] [SE *devil* + ANGEL DUST *n.* (1)] [1980s+] (*drugs*) phencyclidine.

devious *adj.* [ext. of SE use] [1990s+] (*US teen*) extreme.

devo *n.* [abbr.] [1970s+] a sexual *deviant*.

devotional habits *n.* [pun on SE] [mid-19C] used of a horse that persists in falling to its knees.

dew *n.* **1** [mid-19C+] (*also* **dew-bowl**) (*Anglo-Irish/US*) whisky, usu. illicitly distilled. **2** [1970s+] (*US drugs*) marijuana [depends on illegality rather than on any image of wetness]. **3** [1970s+] (*US gay*) oily sweat exuded by the anus.

SE in slang uses

IN COMPOUNDS

❑ **dewbaby** *n.* [1970s] (*US black*) a very dark-skinned male. ❑ **dew-beaters** *n.* [note Norfolk dial. *dew-beaters*, heavy, waterproof shoes] **1** [17C–early 19C] those who get up early, i.e. before the dew has evaporated. **2** [mid-18C–19C] (*UK Und.*) the feet. ❑ **dew-drink** *n.* [mid-19C] a drink served to farm labourers before they start work. ❑ **dew-drop** see separate entries. ❑ **dew-dusters** *n.* [19C] the feet. ❑ **dew-flaps** *n.* [var. on *PISSFLAPS under* PISS *n.*] [1990s+] the labia. ❑ **dew-treaders** *n.* [19C] the feet.

dewdrop *n.*[1] **1** [late 18C+] a drop of mucus lodged at the opening of a nostril and hanging there before removal. **2** [1900s–10s] the lock on a gas-meter [it also 'hangs down'].

dewdrop *n.*[2] [ety. unknown] [late 19C] (*US campus*) a grudging compliment.

dewdrop *v.* [fig. use equating a stone to a SE *dewdrop*] [1900s–30s] (*US tramp*) to throw a rock or stone.

dewey *n.* [Ital. *due*, two] [mid-19C+] (*Polari*) two.

dew rag *n. see* DO-RAG *n.*

dews *n.* **1** [mid-19C] (*UK Und.*) a crown piece. **2** [1970s+] (*drugs*) $10 worth of drugs [DEUCE *n.*[1] (1), i.e. two $5 bags].

dewsavell/dewse-a-vill *n. see* DEUSEAVILLE *n.*

dewskitch *n.* [? 'catch one's due'] [mid-19C] a severe beating, a good thrashing.

dews wins *n. see* DEUCE WINS *under* DEUCE *n.*[1].

dex *n.* [abbr.] **1** [1950s+] dexedrine, a form of amphetamine. **2** [1990s+] dextromethorphan (DXM); also as v., to take the drug. **3** [2000s] MDMA [methylene*dioxy*methamphetamine].

dex *v.* [DEX *n.* (1)] [1950s+] (*drugs*) to take dexedrine.

dexed *adj.* (*also* **dexed out, ...up**) [DEX *n.*] [1970s+] intoxicated on dexedrine.

dexies *n.* (*also* **dexy**) [abbr.] [1950s+] (*drugs*) dexedrine.

dexo *n.* [abbr. + -O *sfx* (6)] [1940s+] (*Aus. drugs*) dexedrine.

dexter *n.* [Lat. *dexter*, right] [early 19C+] the right hand.

dexy *n. see* DEXIES *n.*

DF *n.* [1970s+] (*drugs*) *DF*118, a painkiller mainly made of synthetic codeine.

d.f. *n.* [abbr.] [1910s–30s] (*US*) a *d*amned *f*ool.

d.f. and l. *phr.* [abbr.] [1930s] (*US drugs*) *d*irty, *f*ilthy, and *l*ousy.

d.f.f.l. *phr.* [abbr.] [1950s+] *d*ope *f*orever, *f*orever *l*oaded, a popular patch worn by Hell's Angels, hippies, and other 'outlaws'.

d.h. *n. see* DESPERATION HOUR *n.*

d.h.c. *n.* [*d*eep *h*eavy *c*onversation] [1980s+] (*US campus*) a very intense conversation.

dhobe *n. see* DOBE *n.*[2].

dhobi *n.* (*also* **dhoby, dobee**) [Hind. *dhob*, washing] (*orig. Anglo-Ind.*) **1** [mid-19C+] a washerwoman. **2** [1910s+] the laundry; thus *dhobi dust*, washing powder. **3** [1980s] (*Aus.*) (*also* **dobie**) a bathe or wash.

diabetes *n.*

IN PHRASES

❑ **give someone diabetes** *v.* (*also* **give someone cavities**) [SE *diabetes* results from an excess of sugar in the blood; tooth *cavities* from eating too many sweet things] [1980s+] (*US campus*) to be excessively sweet.

diabolical *adj.* [SE *diabolical*, pertaining to the devil] [1950s+] outrageous, disgraceful, disgracefully bad; esp. in phr. *diabolical liberty*.

Diagonal Street *n.* [its address] [1980s+] (*S.Afr.*) the Johannesburg Stock Exchange.

dial *n.* [SE *dial*, a clock-face; note earlier DIAL-PLATE *n.*] [early 19C+] the human face.

IN PHRASES

❑ **turn the hands on someone's dial** *v.* [mid-19C–1900s] to scar or otherwise disfigure someone's face, usu. in a fight.

dialogue *n.* [1980s+] (*US teen*) a conversation. esp. one person's monologue; also as v., to chat to.

dial out on *v.* [1940s] to cut off; to ignore.

dial-plate *n.* (*also* **dial-piece**) [SE *dial-plate*, the face plate of a clock] [19C] the human face.

IN PHRASES

❑ **alter someone's dial-plate** *v.* [early 19C] to disfigure someone's face.

Dials, the *n.* [in its 18C–19C prime one of London's best-known criminal enclaves] [early 19C+] Seven Dials, London WC; thus *Dialler, Dialonian*, a (criminal) frequenter of Seven Dials.

dialtone *n.* [? play on DINGALING *n.*[1] (2)] [1980s+] (*US*) a fool.

diambista *n.* [Sp.] [1950s+] (*drugs*) marijuana.

diamond *n.* **1** [late 19C] (*US short order*) a meat pie. **2** [1960s] (*US gay*) in pl., the testicles [play on CROWN JEWELS *under* CROWN *n.*[1]].

SE in slang uses

IN COMPOUNDS

❑ **diamond-cracking** *n.* [late 19C–1910s] (*Aus.*) breaking rocks as part of one's prison sentence; thus *diamond-cracker*, one who is working off such a sentence. ❑ **diamond-cutter** *n.* [1970s+] the erect penis. ❑ **diamond-squad** *n.* [their jewellery] [mid-19C] (*UK Und.*) rich, powerful individuals.

IN PHRASES

❑ **diamond a horn** *v.* [fig. use of a SE *diamond* for a stone + ? *horn* as the shape of one's lame leg] [mid-19C] (*UK Und.*) to place a stone in one's shoe to counterfeit lameness.

diamond *adj.* [the value of the precious stone] [1910s+] of people or objects, first-rate, excellent.

Diana Dors *n.* [rhy. sl.; ult. UK actress and personality *Diana Dors* (1931–84)] **1** [1960s+] (*bingo*) the number 44, i.e. 'all the fours'. **2** [1990s+] drawers, (female) underwear.

diaper *n.* [16C SE, but now SAmE *diaper*, a nappy] **1** [1930s–40s] in pl., clothes; thus *pin one's diapers on*, to get dressed. **2** [1980s] (*US black*) a sanitary napkin.

SE in slang uses

IN EXCLAMATIONS

❑ **keep your diaper on!** *see* KEEP YOUR PANTS ON! *under* PANTS *n.*

diaper the baby *v.* [DIAPER *n.* (2)] [1980s] (*US black*) to put on a sanitary towel.

diarrhoea *n.*

SE in slang uses

IN COMPOUNDS

❑ **diarrhoea bags** *n.* [1980s] (*N.Z.*) knickerbockers. ❑ **diarrhoea clips** *n.* [2000s] (*N.Z.*) bicycle clips. ❑ **diarrhoea-mouth** *n.* [1960s+] (*US*) a very talkative individual.

IN PHRASES

❑ **diarrhoea of the mouth** *n.* (*also* **diarrhoea of the jawbone, ...jib**) [1940s+] (*US*) excessive loquacity.

diasticutis *n.* (*also* **diasticurious**) [pig Lat. formation based on ASS *n.* (2)] [1930s–60s] (*US black*) the buttocks, the posterior.

diazzy *n.* [abbr.] [1990s+] (*UK drugs*) diazepam.

dib *n.* [a corruption of SE *division* or *divide*] [early 19C+] a share.

dibb *n. see* DIBBLE *n.*[3].

dibber-dobber *n.* [DOB (IN) *v.* (2)] [1980s+] (*Aus.*) a tell-tale; a 'whistleblower'.

dibbi dibbi *n.* [DIBBI DIBBI *adj.*] **1** [1980s+] (*W.I./UK black teen*) a small and insignificant thing or person. **2** [1990s+] a promiscuous woman.

dibbi dibbi *adj.* [? pron. of SE *little*] [1980s+] (*W.I./UK black teen*) stupid, useless, not resourceful, worthless.

dibble *n.*[1] [ety. unknown] [early 17C] a moustache.

dibble *n.*[2] [SE *dibbler*, a gardening implement with which one drills holes for planting] **1** [late 19C–1920s] the penis. **2** [1960s] (*US campus*) a fool, a social inadequate.

dibble *n.*[3] (*also* **dibb**) [proper name of *Officer Dibble*, a character in the TV cartoon series *Top Cat*] [1980s+] a police officer.

dibbs *n.* (*also* **dibs**) [*dibs* or *dibstones*, a children's game played with the knuckle-bones of sheep] **1** [early 19C+] money. **2** [1930s–50s] $1.

IN PHRASES

❑ **flash the dibbs** *v.* [mid-19C–1920s] to spend one's money.

dibs *n.* [var. on DIDDIES *n.*] [1900s] (*Aus.*) the female breasts.

dibs and dabs *n.* [rhy. sl.] [1960s+] (*Aus.*) crabs (body lice).

dibs (on)! *excl.* [DIB *n.*] [1930s+] (*orig. US*) that's mine! I want to do that! I want a share! A child's term used to claim the whole or an equal part of an object; the negative response to the cry is *fen dibs*.

dic *n.* (*also* **dick, dicky**) [abbr.] [mid-19C+] **1** a *dic*tionary. **2** 'jaw-breaking', pretentious language [fig. use of sense 1].

dice *n.*[1] [craps imagery] [1950s] (*US*) luck.

SE in slang uses

IN PHRASES

□ **swing the dice** *v. see under* SWING *v.*

dice *n.*[2] [ety. unknown] (*US drugs*) **1** [1970s] Desoxyn. **2** [2000s] crack cocaine.

dice *v.* [an image of tossing a die and losing] [1940s–50s] (*Aus.*) **1** to reject, to throw away, to dismiss. **2** of a lover or friend, to abandon.

dicer *n.*[1] [its resemblance to a dice-box] [late 19C–1960s] a hat.

dicer *n.*[2] [vagrant travellers in the boxcars feel like dice being shaken in a cup] [1920s–30s] (*US tramp*) a fast freight train.

dicey *adj.* [gambling imagery] [1950s+] (*orig. RAF jargon*) risky, dangerous, dubious.

dichty *see under* DICTY.

dick *n.*[1] [generic use of proper name] **1** [mid-16C+] a man, a fellow. **2** [mid-17C; 1960s+] a victim; a simpleton. **3** [mid-17C–early 18C] a man as a sexual partner. **4** [early 18C] a countryman. **5** [mid-19C+] the penis [*see* Williams I:382 for discussion of possible 16C uses]. **6** [1910s+] nothing, e.g. *we ain't got dick; not worth dick* [fig. use of sense 5, as with FUCK *n.* (2a)/SHIT *n.* (3i)]. **7** [1930s–40s; 1980s+] (*US black*) a term of address between males. **8** [1950s+] sexual intercourse. **9** [1960s+] (*US teen*) an unattractive man, esp. one who has an overly high self-image. **10** [1960s+] (*US*) a mean or offensive person. **11** [1960s+] a fool. **12** [1990s+] in fig. use, courage, 'guts', virility, ambition.

DERIVATIVES

□ **dickless** *adj. see* separate entry.

IN COMPOUNDS

□ **dick-bitch** *n.* [BITCH *n.*[1] (1a)] [2000s] (*US black*) an over-emotional man, esp. as regards women. □ **dickbrain** *n.* [sfx *-brain*] [1970s+] (*US*) a fool; thus a general derog. term. □ **dick-breath** *n.* **1** [1970s+] (*US*) (*also* **cock-breath, cunt-breath**) an unpleasant person. **2** [1990s+] anyone, esp. a superior, who has foul breath. □ **dick-cheese** *n. see* COCK CHEESE *under* COCK *n.*[3]. □ **dick-chewer** *n.* [1970s] (*US*) a fellator. □ **dick curd** *n.* [2000s] (*US black*) one who enjoys storing up rivalry between others. □ **dick-do** *n.* [2000s] (*US*) a large, drooping stomach. □ **dick drink** *n.* [1980s+] (*US gay*) semen. □ **dick-eating** *adj.* [1990s+] (*US*) a general insult, lit. 'fellating'; thus as n. *dick-eater*. □ **dickface** *n.* (*also* **dick features**) [1970s+] (*orig. US campus*) a general term of derision. □ **dick-fingered** *adj.* [1980s+] (*US*) maladroit. □ **dick-fuck** *n.* [1990s+] (*Aus.*) a general term of abuse. □ **dickhead** *see* separate entries. □ **dick-hound** *n.* [-HOUND *sfx*] **1** [1980s+] (*US black*) a promiscuous woman. **2** [2000s] (*US gay*) a promiscuous male homosexual. □ **dick-knob** *n. see* DICKWIT below. □ **dicklick/licker** *see* separate entries. □ **dick mac** *n.* [SE *mac(intosh)*] [1970s–80s] (*UK black*) a condom. □ **dick-nailer** *n.* [NAIL *v.* (14)] [19C+] (*US*) something outstanding, exceptional of its type. □ **dicknose** *n.* [1970s+] (*orig. US*) a general term of derision. □ **dick peddler** *n.* (*also* **prick peddler**) [PRICK *n.* (1)] [1940s+] a male prostitute who takes only active roles with his clients. □ **dick sack** *n.* [2000s] (*US*) **1** a contraceptive sheath. **2** the scrotum. □ **dickshaft** *n.* [1990s+] a general derog. description. □ **dick shit** *n.* [1980s+] (*orig. US*) absolutely nothing; always used with a qualifying negative v., e.g. *you don't know dick shit about…* etc. □ **dick-shriveler** *n.* [1980s+] (*US*) an unpleasant person. □ **dick-skinners** *n.* [1980s] (*US*) hands. □ **dicksplash** *n.* [1990s+] a semen stain; thus, an incompetent, unpleasant, unpopular person. □ **dickstring** *n.* [SE *string*, i.e. lit. the frenum] **1** [1960s+] (*US black*) the notional governor of a man's ability to attain an erection. **2** [2000s] (*US*) a general insult. □ **dicksucker/sucking** *see* separate entries. □ **dicktease/teaser** *see* separate entries. □ **dick thang** *n.* [joc. pron. of SE *thing*; lit. 'a penis thing'] [1990s+] (*US campus*) something characteristically associated with men. □ **dick thing** *n.* [1990s+] (*US campus*) something that concerns men and/or masculinity. □ **dickwad** *n.* [-WAD *sfx*/WAD *n.*[3]; lit. an ejaculation] [1980s+] (*orig. US campus*) a fool, an idiot, an unpleasant person; also attrib. □ **dickweed** *n.* (*US*) **1** [1980s+] a fool. **2** [1990s+] the pubic hair. □ **dickwhacker** *n.* [2000s] (*N.Z.*) a fool, lit. a masturbator. □ **dick-whupped** *adj.* (*also* **d-whupped**) [1990s+] (*US black*) of a woman, so besotted with her lover that she allows herself to be exploited and generally treated badly. □ **dickwipe** *n.* [1990s+] (*US*) a general term of abuse. □ **dickwit** *n.* (*also* **dick-knob**) [1990s+] (*Aus. teen*) a general insult.

IN PHRASES

□ **all ribs and dick like a robber's dog** [1990s+] (*Aus.*) **1** very thin. **2** in fig. use, impoverished. □ **buy the dick** *v.* [1960s–70s] (*US*) to get into trouble; to die. □ **caught holding one's dick** [20C+] (*US*) to be caught in an embarrassing or generally disadvantageous situation. □ **devil's dick** *n. see under* DEVIL *n.* □ **dick-for-brains** *n. see* SHIT-FOR-BRAINS *n.* □ **dip one's dick** *v. see* DIP ONE'S WICK *under* WICK *n.*[1]. □ **do something on one's dick** *v.* (*also* **do something on one's prick**) [var. on DO SOMETHING STANDING ON ONE'S HEAD *under* STAND *v.*[2]] [1960s+] to do with ease, esp. to endure any challenging situation, e.g. a prison sentence, with no difficulty. □ **eat a dick** [1990s+] (*US black teen*) a general phr. of dislike or dismissal. □ **get one's dick away** *v. see* GET ONE'S END AWAY *under* END *n.* □ **give some dick** *v.* [1960s+] to accede to sexual advances. □ **grab one's dick** *v.* (*also* **grab one's balls**) [1980s+] (*US black*) to boast, to brag. □ **have a woman on one's dick** *v.* [1980s+] (*US*) of a man, to be sexually successful. □ **have one's dick in the dirt** *v.* [2000s] (*US*) to be in serious trouble. □ **have the dick** *v. see* HAVE THE RICHARD *under* RICHARD *n.* □ **keep one's dick in one's pants** *v.* (*also* **keep it in one's pants**) [1980s+] to act calmly, in sexual contexts or otherwise; often as imper. *keep your dick in your pants!* □ **keep someone's dick in the dirt** *v.* (*also* **put someone's dick in the dirt**) [1970s+] (*US*) **1** to knock down. **2** to defeat, to punish. **3** (*US gay*) to share good marijuana with a friend. □ **kiss someone's dick** *v. see* SUCK SOMEONE'S DICK below. □ **knock the dick off** *v.* [1970s] to defeat comprehensively, to beat up. □ **led by (the head of) one's dick** [1990s+] (*US black*) of a man, blinded by sexual desire. □ **like a spare dick on a honeymoon** *adv. see* LIKE A SPARE PRICK AT A WEDDING *under* PRICK *n.* □ **on someone's dick** [1980s+] (*US black*) **1** keen on, supporting. **2** oppressing, nagging, harassing. □ **on the dick** [1990s+] (*US black*) of a woman, to be ready for sexual activity. □ **pull one's dick** *v.* [1960s+] (*Aus./US*) **1** to masturbate. **2** in fig. use, to talk nonsense. □ **step on one's dick** *v.* (*also* **step on one's foreskin, …prick, step over one's whang**) [PRICK *n.* (1)/WHANG *n.*[1] (4)] [1950s+] to make a fool of oneself; to blunder badly. □ **suck dick** *v.* (*also* **suck-a-butt**) [mid-17C+] to perform fellatio or cunnilingus. □ **suck someone's dick** *v.* (*also* **kiss someone's dick**) [1930s+] (*orig. US*) to flatter, to toady to, to congratulate effusively. □ **swinging dick** *n. see under* SWINGING *adj.*[2]. □ **take the hard out of the dick** *v.* [lit. to detumesce someone's erection] [1960s] (*US black*) to take an unfair share (of profits). □ **think one has sugar on one's dick** *v.* [1960s] (*US*) to have a high (but unjustifiable) view of one's own physical attractiveness.

IN EXCLAMATIONS

□ **my dick!** [1970s+] (*US*) an excl. of disdain, disbelief. □ **suck my dick!** *see under* SUCK *v.*[1].

dick *n.*[2] [? link to a celebrated contemporary coachman Walter Dickson, nicknamed 'Dickie the Driver'] [mid–late 19C] a riding whip.

dick *n.*[3] [abbr. SE *declaration*] [mid–late 19C] an oath, a statement, an affidavit; thus to *take one's dick*, to take one's declaration.

IN PHRASES

□ **up to dick** (*also* **up to door**) [late 19C–1910s] up to standard, as required; thus in negative, unwell, sick, wretched.

dick *n.*[4] [? Sheffield dial. a leather apron worn by children + link to Du. *dek*, a cover] [1910s] a perambulator.

dick *n.*[5] [? gypsy use *dicked*, being watched (cf. DEKKO *n.*), DICK *v.*[1] or abbr. SE *detective*; the link to the fictional *Dick Tracy* (created 1931) is chronologically impossible] [1910s+] (*US*) **1** a detective; thus *house dick*, the security officer in a hotel, office; *store-dick* a store detective etc. **2** a police officer, usu. male.

dick *n.*^{6} [play on COCK *n.*^{4} (1); the clitoris, being phallic, is linked to US black use of *dick* for penis, *cock* being used for vagina] [1960s] (*US*) the clitoris.

IN PHRASES

❑ **stick (the) dick to** *v.* [synon. for FUCK OVER *v.* (1)] [1960s] to treat badly, to exploit.

dick *n.*^{7} *see* DIC *n.*

dick *v.*^{1} [Rom. *dik*, to look, ult. Hindi *dekh-nā*, to look] [mid-19C] (*UK Und.*) to look at.

IN PHRASES

❑ **keep dick** *v.* [20C+] (*Ulster*) to keep a lookout.

dick *v.*^{2} [lit. and fig. uses of DICK *n.*^{1} (5)] **1** [1940s+] (*mainly US black*) of a man, to have sexual intercourse. **2** [1950s+] (*US*) (*also* **dick up**) to ruin, to botch, to make a mess of. **3** [1960s+] (*Aus./US*) a synon. for FUCK WITH *v.*: to trick or deceive, to be unfair to, to treat meanly, to victimize. **4** [1970s+] (*US gay*) to sodomize. **5** [2000s] (*N.Z.*) to beat, to defeat. **6** *see* DICK (AROUND) below.

IN PHRASES

❑ **dick (about/around) with** *v.* [1970s+] (*US*) to mess someone around, to fool around with; thus *dicked-up*, messed up. ❑ **dick (around)** *v.* **1** [1920s+] to waste time, to dither [SE colloq. phr. *dicker (around)*, but with overtones of acting like a DICK *n.*^{1} (11)]. **2** [1960s+] to be sexually promiscuous, to be a womanizer [sense 1 above]. ❑ **dick off** *v.* [DICK (AROUND) above + SE *off*] [1940s–60s] (*US*) to waste time, to shirk, to avoid work. ❑ **dick out** *v.* [fig. use of DICK *n.*^{1} (5)] [1970s+] (*US*) to persevere, to endure. ❑ **dick someone around** *v.* [1980s+] (*US*) to harass, to impose on, to irritate, to 'mess someone about'. ❑ **long dick** *v.* [2000s] (*US black*) of a man, to make love very enthusiastically.

Dick and Harry *n. see* TOM, DICK AND HARRY *n.*

dickchode *n. see* CHOAD *n.* (3).

dicked *adj.*^{1} [DICK *v.*^{2} (2)/DICK *v.*^{2} (3)] [1960s+] **1** defeated, destroyed, out of luck. **2** in a mess.

dicked *adj.*^{2} [fig. use of DICK *v.*^{2} (1); thus image of potency] [1970s+] (*US*) assured of success; completely in control (of).

dicked in the nob *phr.* [ety. unknown; the sexual use of DICK *v.*^{2} (1), which would work in fig. use, is too late + NOB *n.*^{1} (1)] [early 19C] insane.

dicked up *adj.* [2000s] (*Aus.*) dressed up.

dicken *v.* [DICKEN! *excl.*] [1900s] (*Aus.*) to pretend.

dicken! *excl.* (*also* **dickens! dickin! dickon!**) [late 19C+] (*Aus./N.Z.*) a mild oath; esp. as *dicken on/to that!* enough of that! the hell with that! stop it!

dickens *n.* (*also* **dickings, dickins, dickons**) **1** [late 16C+] a euph. for the devil, most commonly in phr. *what the dickens?* **2** [1990s+] a euph. for sexual intercourse or other activity.

IN PHRASES

❑ **raise the dickens** *v. see* RAISE HELL *under* HELL *n.*

dicker *n.*^{1} (*also* **dikker**) [abbr. SE *dictionary* + -ER *sfx*] [1920s] a dictionary.

dicker *n.*^{2} [DICK *v.*^{2} (1)] [1960s] (*US black*) a sexually powerful man.

dickery (dock) *n. see* DICKORY DOCK *n.*

dickey *see also under* DICKY and combs.

dickey bow *n.* (*also* **dickie bow, dicky bow**) [1970s+] a detachable bow tie.

dickey dazzler *n. see* BOBBY-DAZZLER *n.*

dickey-eye *n.* [KEEP DICK *under* DICK *v.*^{1}] [1950s] (*UK juv.*) a lookout.

dickey suit *n.* [? DICK *v.*^{1}] [1950s] the naked body.

dickhead *n.* [DICK *n.*^{1} (5) + -HEAD *sfx* (1)] [1960s+] **1** a fool, an incompetent. **2** a general term of abuse. **3** something problematic.

dickhead *adj.* (*also* **dickheaded**) [DICKHEAD *n.* (1)] [1990s+] stupid, foolish.

dickie *see also under* DICKY and combs.

dickie bow *n. see* DICKEY BOW *n.*

dickies *n.* [? brandname] [1950s+] (*US*) baggy trousers, favoured by teenage gang members.

dickin! *excl. see* DICKEN! *excl.*

dickins *n. see* DICKENS *n.*

dick in the green *adj. see* DICKY *adj.*^{1} (2).

dickless *adj.* [DICK *n.*^{1} (5)] [1980s+] (*orig. US*) a general term of abuse; lit. without a penis.

IN COMPOUNDS

❑ **dickless tracy** *n.* [puns on DICK *n.*^{1} (5) + DICK TRACY *n.* + common female name *Tracey*] [1960s+] (*mainly US Und.*) a woman police officer; occas. security guard.

dicklick *n.* [backform. f. DICKLICKER *n.*] [1980s+] **1** (*US*) a fool, an idiot, an unpleasant person. **2** (*US gay*) fellatio.

dicklicker *n.* [DICK *n.*^{1} (5) + SE *licker*] [1960s+] a fellator or fellatrix; thus an unpleasant person; adj. *dicklicking*.

dickon! *excl. see* DICKEN! *excl.*

dickon pitch *n.* [DICKEN! *excl.*] [late 19C–1930s] (*Aus.*) a lie.

dickons *n. see* DICKENS *n.*

dickory dock *n.* (*also* **dickery (dock)**) [rhy. sl. = COCK *n.*^{3} (1). The nursery rhyme from which this comes is itself a Romany creation. According to Gerald Denley: 'Hickory is derived from the Romany "Ek Ore" meaning one o'clock. The word for one in Romany varies according to the tribe, so it is either "ek", "yek" or "ik". The stress is on the first vowel, so that "ek ore" is pronounced as one word. Dickory Dock is often described as London rhyming slang. But it could mean the *dock* where the *dick* puts you when you are caught *choring* or stealing.'] **1** [late 19C+] (*also* **dicky**) a clock. **2** [1960s+] the penis [COCK *n.*^{3} (1)]. **3** [1960s+] a sock.

Dick's hatband *n.* [the orig. *hatband* was a narrow strip of material wrapped around the hat, esp. as a badge of mourning. The identity of Dick is not known – 'some local character or half-wit' (*OED*) – but his hatband was presumably an improvised and absurd object; however, Brewer, *Dict. of Phrase and Fable* (1894), suggests *Dick* = Richard Cromwell (1626–1712) and *hatband* = a crown, which as a republican he could not wear] [early 19C+] (*US*) anything makeshift; also in *odd as Dick's hatband*.

dick smith *n.* [logger jargon; ? *Richard Penn Smith* (1790–1854), a US playwright celebrated for his unsociability – and his plagiarism of others] [19C+] (*US*) **1** a solitary drinker or drug-taker. **2** in ext. use, a mean, sponging or reclusive person.

dicksucker *n.* [DICK *n.*^{1} (5) + SE *sucker*] [1970s+] (*US*) **1** a fellator. **2** a general derog. term.

dicksucking *n.* [DICKSUCKER *n.* (1)] [1970s+] fellatio.

dicksucking *adj.* [DICKSUCKER *n.* (2)] [1970s+] unpleasant, disgusting, a general term of abuse.

dicktease *v.* [DICK *n.*^{1} (5) + SE *tease*] [1960s+] (*orig. US*) **1** usu. of a woman, to appear to be offering unrestrained sexual favours but stopping short of intercourse, leaving the man frustrated. **2** in fig. use, to be frustrating, teasing, unfulfilling.

dickteaser *n.* (*also* **dicktease**) [DICKTEASE *v.*] [1960s+] one who provokes their partner sexually but stops short of intercourse.

Dick, Tom and Joe *n. see* TOM, DICK AND HARRY *n.*

Dick Tracy *n.* [the cartoon strip created by Chester Gould in 1931 for the Chicago *Tribune*/New York *News* syndicate; ult. DICK *n.*^{5} (1) + SE *trace*] [1930s+] a police officer (usu. male), esp. a detective.

dickty *see under* DICTY.

dickup! *excl.* [1990s+] (*UK juv.*) a cry of alarm/warning: put out your cigarette – a teacher is coming!

Dick Van Dyke *n.* [rhy. sl.; ult. US actor *Dick Van Dyke* (b.1925)] [2000s] (*Irish*) a bike.

dicky *n.*^{1} (*also* **dickey, dickie**) [? link to dial. *dick*, a leather apron] **1** [mid-18C–19C] a woman's under-petticoat. **2** [late 18C–mid-19C] a worn-out shirt. **3** [early 19C+] a detachable shirt-front. **4** [mid-19C–1910s] a shirt-collar. **5** [late 19C] a detachable nameplate, used on a tradesman's van.

IN PHRASES

❑ **flash the dickey** *v.* [mid-19C] to expose one's shirt-front.

dicky *n.*^{2} (*also* **dickey**) [DICKY *adj.*^{2}] [late 18C–19C] a dandy, a 'swell'.

dicky *n.*^{3} (*also* **dickey**) [? *Dicky*, used as a generic name for a coachman] **1** [19C] (*also* **dicky-box**) the seat in a carriage on which the driver sits. **2** [19C] (*also* **dickey-box**) a seat at the back of a carriage for servants etc, or of a mail-coach for the guard. **3** [1910s–30s] (*also* **dickie**) an extra seat at the back of a two-seater motorcar, which can be closed down when not in use; also of a boat.

dicky *n.*^{4} (*also* **dickey**) [East Anglian dial.; the habit of using proper names as sl. terms for donkeys] [19C] a donkey.

dicky *n.*^{5} [ext. of DICK *n.*^{1} (5)] [19C+] the penis.

IN COMPOUNDS

❑ **dicky check** *n.* [1990s+] (*US Und.*) a search of the genital area, usu. for drugs. ❑ **dicky diaper** *n.* [early 19C] a linen-draper. ❑ **dicky-doodle** *n.* [DOODLE *n.*^{2} (1)] [1990s+] the penis. ❑ **dicky-licker** *n.* [var. on DICKLICKER *n.*] [1930s+] (*orig. US*) **1** a homosexual, esp. a fellator. **2** a fellatrix. ❑ **dicky-waver** *n.* (*also* **dickie-waver**) [1970s+] (*US*) an exhibitionist.

dicky *n.*^{6} [SE *declaration*] [mid-19C–1920s] an affidavit.

dicky *n.*^{7} (*also* **dickie, dickey**) [DICKY-BIRD *n.*^{2}] [late 19C+] a word.

dicky *n.*^{8} **1** *see* DIC *n.* **2** *see* DICKORY DOCK *n.* (1).

dicky *adj.*^{1} (*also* **dickey**) [dial.] **1** [late 18C+] of people or animals, sickly, unhealthy; also in fig. use. **2** [19C+] (*also* **dick in the green**) of things, and people, second-rate, of poor quality, weak, sub-standard, not working as they should. **3** [late 19C] (*UK Und.*) suspicious, odd. **4** [1940s+] (*Aus./N.Z.*) stupid. **5** [1960s+] of plans, risky, ill-advised, overly complex.

IN PHRASES

❑ **all dicky with** (*also* **all dickey (with)**) [late 18C–mid-19C] all over, ruined, finished, 'all up with'.

dicky *adj.*^{2} (*also* **dickey**) [mid-19C–1900s] smart, fashionable.

dicky-bird *n.*^{1} (*also* **dickey-bird, dickie, dickie bird**) **1** [mid-19C] a prostitute; esp. as *naughty dicky-bird*. **2** [mid-19C; 1990s+] a louse. **3** [mid-19C+] a small bird; a chicken or goose. **4** [late 19C] a professional singer. **5** [1900s–40s] (*US*) (*also* **bird**) an informer, a betrayer. **6** [1950s] the penis [BIRD *n.*^{3} (1)].

dicky-bird *n.*^{2} (*also* **dickey-bird, dickie-bird**) [rhy. sl.] [1930s+] a word; thus *not a dicky-bird*, lit. 'not a word', i.e. nothing at all.

dicky-bird *n.*^{3} *see* BIRD *n.*^{1} (5c).

dicky bow *n. see* DICKEY BOW *n.*

dicky diddle *n.* [DICKY DIDDLE *v.*] [1960s+] (*UK juv.*) an act of urination.

dicky diddle *v.* [rhy. sl. = PIDDLE *v.* (1)] [1960s+] to urinate.

dicky-dido *n.* **1** [mid–late 19C] (*also* **dicky-dout**) a fool. **2** [20C+] the vagina. **3** [2000s] (*N.Z.*) the penis.

dicky (dirt) *n.* (*also* **dickey, bucket of dirt**) [rhy. sl.; despite obvious links to DICKY *n.*^{1} (3), this appears to be a discrete coinage] [late 19C+] a shirt.

dicky fit *n.* [ety. unknown; ? var. on *hissy fit* at HISSY *n.*] [1990s+] (*UK juv.*) a temper tantrum.

dicky lee *n.* [rhy. sl.] [20C+] (*Aus.*) tea.

dicky-man *n.* [late 19C] (*UK Und.*) a husband or common-law partner.

dictee *see under* DICTY.

dictionary *n.* [ety. unknown] [2000s] (*US prison*) a hacksaw blade.

dictionary *adv.* [mid-19C] (*US*) of speech, elaborately, in a complex, long-winded manner.

dicty *n.* (*also* **dichty, dickty, dictee**) [? SE *decked*, dressed (lit. 'covered')] [1920s+] (*orig. US black*) a stuck-up, conceited, snobbish person.

dicty *adj.* (*also* **dichty, dickty, dictee, dikty**) [? SE *decked*, dressed (lit. 'covered')] [1920s+] (*US black*) **1** arrogant, haughty, snobbish, conceited. **2** elegant, high-class, sophisticated. **3** of clothes, elegant, chic, smart.

diddicoi *n.* (*also* **diddik(a)i, didek(e)i, didicai**) [Rom.] [mid-19C+] a gypsy, esp. a half-breed gypsy.

diddies *n.* (*also* **diddeys, diddly, diddys**) [dial. *diddy*, the female breast, usu. when feeding a baby; also used of animals. Note. mispron. of TITTY *n.* (1)] [late 18C+] the female breasts, the chest, occas. in sing.

IN PHRASES

❑ **up to one's diddies** *see* UP TO ONE'S ARMPITS *under* ARMPIT *n.*

diddle *n.*^{1} [SE *diddle*, to walk unsteadily; i.e. the effects of the liquor] **1** [18C–19C] gin or genever. **2** [19C] liquor in general.

IN COMPOUNDS

❑ **diddle-cove** *n.* [late 18C–mid-19C] (*UK Und.*) a keeper of a gin or liquor tavern. ❑ **diddle-shop** *n.* [early 18C] a gin-shop. ❑ **diddle-spinner** *n.* [mid-19C] (*UK Und.*) a gin-shop keeper.

diddle *n.*^{2} [early 19C] the sound of a fiddle.

diddle *n.*^{3} [DIDDLE *v.*^{1} (1)] **1** [mid-19C+] the penis. **2** [mid-19C+] the vagina. **3** [1930s+] (*also* **diddling**) sexual intercourse. **4** [1930s+] masturbation.

IN COMPOUNDS

❑ **diddlehead** *n.* [sense 1 above + -HEAD *sfx* (1)] [1970s] (*US campus*) a fool.

diddle *n.*^{4} [DIDDLE *v.*^{2} (2)] [late 19C+] a swindle.

diddle *v.*^{1} [SE *diddle*, to jerk from side to side + *didder*, to shake, to quiver] **1** [mid-17C+] to have sexual intercourse; thus *diddling*, sexual intercourse. **2** [1930s+] (*also* **didle**) to molest sexually. **3** [1930s+] (*orig. US*) (*also* **diddle-fuck**) to masturbate oneself or another.

IN PHRASES

❑ **diddle the dinky** *v. see under* DINKY *n.*^{4}. ❑ **how are you diddling?** [poss. only play on SE *do*] [1970s] a general term of informal greeting.

IN EXCLAMATIONS

❑ **go diddle yourself!** *see* GO FUCK YOURSELF! *under* FUCK *v.*

diddle *v.*^{2} **1** [early 19C; 20C+] to waste time; thus *diddle away*, to waste time [fig. use of SE *diddle*, to jerk from side to side, to quiver]. **2** [early 19C+] to cheat or swindle, to victimize, to 'do'; ext. to *diddle out of* [? *diddler*, a swindler, fraud, itself f. Jeremy Diddler, the chief character in James Kenney's farce *Raising the Wind* (1803) and ult. f. DIDDLE *v.*^{1} or OE *didrian, dydrian*, to deceive, delude]. **3** [mid-19C] to fail. **4** [20C+] to do for, to ruin, to kill.

diddle! *excl.* [FIDDLEDEEDEE! *excl.*] [1960s] nonsense! rubbish!

diddlebop *n.* [1950s] (*US gang*) a gangfight.

diddle-dumb *adj.* [1970s] (*US*) stupid.

diddle-fuck *v. see* DIDDLE *v.*^{1} (3).

diddler *n.*^{1} [DIDDLE *n.*^{3} (1)/DIDDLE *v.*^{1} (3)/DIDDLE *v.*^{1} (2)] **1** [19C] a small boy's penis. **2** [mid-19C] a male homosexual. **3** [1930s–50s] a masturbator. **4** [1930s+] (*US/Can.Und.*) a child molester.

diddler *n.*^{2} (*also* **jeremy diddler**) [the character Jeremy Diddler in James Kenney's farce *Raising the Wind* (1803)] [early 19C+] a cheat, a confidence trickster.

IN COMPOUNDS

❑ **diddler (machine)** *n.* [1930s–40s] (*UK Und.*) a gambling fruit machine.

diddleums *n.* [note Baker, *The Aus. Language* (1945), attributes Henry Kingsley with the coinage] [mid-19C+] (*Aus.*) delirium tremens.

diddley *n.* (*also* **diddly**) **1** [1920s+] (*Irish*) a small monetary payment; thus the *diddley club*, a savings club, used by the poor, to which one could contribute as little as one halfpenny a week. **2** [1960s+] nothing whatsoever. **3** [1970s+] (*orig. US black*) anything unimportant or insignificant; usu. in phr. *not give a diddley*, couldn't care less.

IN COMPOUNDS

❑ **diddley-damn** *adj.* (*also* **diddly-damn**) [DIDDLEY *adj.* + DAMN *adj.*] [1920s–70s] (*US*) insignificant, irritating; also as n. something insignificant. ❑ **diddley-dick** *n.* (*also* **diddly-dick**) [var. on DIDDLY-SHIT *n.* + DICK *n.*^{1} (6)] [1970s] (*US*) something of no value. ❑ **diddley-poo** *n. see* separate entry.

diddley *adj.* (*also* **diddly**) [DIDDLEY *n.* (2)] [1960s+] (*US*) **1** crazy, eccentric. **2** insignificant, unimportant, worthless.

diddley-bop *see under* DIDDY-BOP.

diddley-poo *n.* (*also* **diddly-poop**) [DIDDLEY *n.* (3) + POO *n.*^{1} (2)] **1** [1950s+] (*usu. US juv.*) excreta. **2** [1980s] anything insignificant.

diddley-pout *n.* [? DIDDLE *n.*^{3} (2) for which, when stimulated, it 'pouts'] [19C] the vagina.

diddley-shit *see under* DIDDLY-SHIT.

diddling *n.*^{1} [DIDDLE *v.*^{2} (2)] [early 19C+] petty criminality, cheating, constant borrowing.

diddling *n.*^{2} *see* DIDDLE *n.*^{3} (3).

diddlum *adj.* [pron. of DIDDLE *v.*^{2} (2) + SE *them*] [1930s] illicit, crooked, swindling.

diddly *see also under* DIDDLEY.

diddly *n.* **1** *see* DIDDIES *n.* **2** *see* DIDDLY-SQUAT *n.*^{1}.

diddly-bop *see under* DIDDY-BOP.

diddly-shit *n.* (*also* **diddley-shit**) [DIDDLEY *n.* (3) + SHIT *n.* (3i)] [1960s+] (*US*) anything or anyone insignificant, unimportant.

IN PHRASES

❑ **not worth diddley-shit** *adj.* (*also* **...diddly doo, ...diddly-shot, ...doodley-shit, ...doodly-shit**) [1960s+] (*US*) worthless, useless.

diddly-shit *adj.* (*also* **diddley-shit**) [DIDDLY-SHIT *n.*] [1960s+] (*US*) worthless; insignificant.

diddly-squat *n.*^{1} (*also* **diddly, diddly doo, piddly-squat**) [DIDDLEY *n.* (2)] [1950s+] (*orig. US*) nothing, zero; thus *it don't mean diddly-squat*, it is totally irrelevant, unimportant.

diddly-squat *n.*^{2} [pun on DIDDLY-SQUAT *n.*^{1} + SE *squat*] [1990s+] (*US juv.*) faeces or urine.

diddlywhacker *n.* [DIDDLE *n.*^{3} (1) + SE *whacker*] [1960s] (*US*) the penis.

diddy *n.*^{1} [dimin. of DIDDICOI *n.*] [late 19C+] a gypsy.

diddy *n.*^{2} (*also* **didee**) [? DUNNY *n.*^{2} (1) but *see* DIDDY *adj.*, i.e. the 'little room'] [1950s+] (*Aus. juv.*) a lavatory.

diddy *n.*^{3} [? DIDDLE *n.*^{3} (1)] [1980s+] (*Irish/UK juv.*) a penis.

diddy *n.*^{4} *see* DIDDIES *n.* (1).

diddy *adj.* [nursery pron. of SE *little* + the popularity of the Diddy Men created by the UK comedian Ken Dodd (b.1927)] [1930s+] small, diminutive.

diddy-bop *n.* (*also* **diddly-bop, ditty bop**) [1940s+] (*US black*) **1** a pretentious black person, pretending or trying to identify with whites; thus a worthless person. **2** a juvenile delinquent, street gang member. **3** a style of walking typified by an exaggerated rolling gait and swinging arms, hips and shoulders, plus the locking of one knee.

diddy-bop *adj.* (*also* **diddley-bop**) **1** [1960s+] (*US black*) immature, unpleasant, stupid, bland. **2** [1960s+] (*US campus*) unattractive. **3** [1980s] stylish, sophisticated.

diddy-bop *v.* (*also* **diddley-bop, diddly-bop, dirty-bop, ditty-bop**) [? the *didd(l)y-bop, didd(l)y-bop* rhythm used in bebop jazz] [1950s+] (*orig. US black*) **1** to swagger, to saunter. **2** to be a street hoodlum.

diddy-bopper *n.* (*US black*) **1** [1980s+] an upwardly mobile, pretentious or snobbish black person. **2** *see* BEBOPPER *n.* (4).

diddy-bopping *n.* (*also* **diddly-bopping**) [DIDDY-BOP *v.*] [1960s+] (*US, orig. milit./black*) **1** walking carelessly. **2** walking in a swaggering or strutting manner. **3** living as a teen hoodlum.

diddys *n. see* DIDDIES *n.*

diddywaddle *adj.* [ety. unknown; ? DIDDY-BOP *adj.* (1)] [1970s] (*US*) insignificant, unimportant.

diddy-wah-diddy *n. see* DOO-WAH-DIDDY *n.*

didee *n. see* DIDDY *n.*^{2}.

didek(e)i *n. see* DIDDICOI *n.*

didgy *adj.* [? var. on SE colloq. *dodgy*] [2000s] crazy, insane.

did I...! *excl.* (*also* **will I...!**) [20C+] an excl. of negation, e.g. *Did I steal that car, did I fuck!* similarly *will I fuck!* no, I certainly won't!

didicai *n. see* DIDDICOI *n.*

didies *n.* [? DIDDY *adj.*, i.e. a play on 'smalls'] [1980s] underpants, occas. a nappy/diaper.

did I ever! *excl.* [early 19C+] a general excl. of intensification, i.e. I certainly did! usu. in answer to a question, also with other personal pronouns or 'anyone'.

didle *v. see* DIDDLE *v.*^{1} (2).

didn't ought *n.* [rhy. sl.] [late 19C–1940s] port (wine).

didn't oughter *n.* [rhy. sl.] **1** [1940s+] water. **2** [1970s+] a daughter.

dido *n.* [ety. unknown; *DSUE* suggests the Greek *Dido*, 'the tragic queen', perhaps weeping for her distant lover, Aeneas] **1** [19C+] (*US*) something fancy or frivolous. **2** [mid-19C+] usu. in pl., a caper, a prank, a trick, an antic. **3** [1910s+] (*Irish*) an overdressed woman.

IN PHRASES

❑ **kick up a dido** *v.* [1930s] to make a noisy fuss.

dido *v.* [? DIDO *n.* (2)] [20C+] (*Aus.*) to steal from carts in the street.

die *n.*^{1} [mid-19C] **1** a last dying speech, usu. that delivered on the gallows, or the account of an especially gruesome trial. **2** a capital trial for which the condemned man may be executed.

die *n.*^{2} [? it 'stamps out' coins] [mid-19C] (*US Und.*) a pocket-book.

die *v.* **1** [early 19C; 1910s+] to fail utterly, to have a difficult time. **2** [1960s+] to collapse with laughter.

SE in slang uses

IN COMPOUNDS

❑ **die-devil rasp** *n.* [mid-19C] (*UK Und.*) a desperate villain, undeterred by any form of opposition.

IN PHRASES

❑ **die dog (or shite the licence)** *v.* (*also* **die dog or eat the meat-axe/hatchet, ...for them that pats me**) [mid-19C+] (*Aus/Irish*) to commit oneself unreservedly. ❑ **die dungill** *v.* [DUNGHILL *n.*^{1}] [18C] to die in a cowardly manner, repenting or showing any act of contrition on the gallows, where a plucky villain was supposed to display bravado. ❑ **die in a horse's nightcap** *v.* (*also* **go to rest in a horse's nightcap**) [a *horse's nightcap* is a halter, thus a noose] [late 18C–mid-19C] to be hanged. ❑ **die in one's boots** *v.* (*also* **die with one's boots on**) **1** [late 17C–early 19C] to be hanged. **2** [mid-19C–1910s] (*US*) to die by violence, esp. in a gunfight. ❑ **die in one's shoes** *v. see under* SHOE *n.* ❑ **die in the arse** *v. see under* ARSE *n.* ❑ **die in the furrow** *v. see under* FURROW *n.* ❑ **die like a dog (in a string)** *v.* [late 17C–early 18C] to be hanged. ❑ **die like Jenkin's hen** *v.* [mid-18C–early 19C] to die unmarried. ❑ **die of acceleration** *v. see* ACCELERATION *n.* ❑ **die of a hempen fever** *v.* [HEMPEN FEVER *under* HEMPEN *adj.*] [18C–early 19C] to be hanged. ❑ **die on a fish day** *v.* [? hangings taking place on Catholic 'fish-days', i.e. Wednesdays and Fridays] [late 17C–early 18C] to be hanged. ❑ **die on it** *v.* [1910s+] (*Aus.*) to break one's promise, to fail to finish something one has undertaken to do. ❑ **die the death of a trooper's horse** *v.* [like the horse, the villain dies 'with his shoes on'] [late 18C–early 19C] to be hanged. ❑ **die with a hard-on** *v.* [HARD-ON *n.* (1); the victim's penis becomes erect during a hanging] [1960s+] (*US*) to die violently, esp. by hanging. ❑ **die with cotton in one's ears** *v.* [proper name Rev. *Cotton*, the early 19C Newgate 'ordinary' or chaplain, 'an able and indefatigable man' who would preach a last sermon to the condemned man] [early 19C] to be hanged. ❑ **die with one's boots on** *v. see* DIE IN ONE'S BOOTS above.

die blou *n.* [Afk. *die*, the + *blou*, blue, the colour of meths] [20C+] (*S.Afr.*) methylated spirits, as used by alcoholics.

IN COMPOUNDS

❑ **blouperd** *n.* [Afk. *perd*, horse; one who 'rides' it] [1980s+] (*S.Afr.*) methylated spirits.

diener *n.* (*also* **diender**) [Afk. *dienaaren*, lit. one who serves; note Afk. sl. *dienaars*, prison warders known for their brutality] [1940s+] (*S.Afr.*) a police officer.

diener/dienner *n. see* DEANER *n.*

diesel *n.* [SE *diesel*, a locomotive driven by a diesel engine] **1** [1970s+] (*UK prison*) prison tea [its taste, supposedly reminiscent of diesel fuel]. **2** [1980s+] (*US*) one who has a muscular, well-developed physique. **3** *see* DIESEL-DYKE *n.*

IN COMPOUNDS

❑ **diesel-queen** *n.* [-QUEEN *sfx* (3)] [2000s] (*S.Afr. gay*) a male homosexual who dresses like a stereotypical lesbian.

SE in slang uses

IN COMPOUNDS

❑ **diesel therapy** *n.* [the diesel engine of the bus that transports the prisoners; the circuit of prisons around which they are taken] [2000s] (*US prison*) the constant movement of an inmate between prisons.

IN PHRASES

❑ **suck diesel** *v. see under* SUCK *v.*[1].

diesel *adj.* [DIESEL *n.* (2)] [1990s+] strong, tough, muscular.

diesel-dyke *n.* (*also* **diesel, dieseler**) [SE *diesel* + DYKE *n.*] [1950s+] (*orig. US*) a conspicuously masculine lesbian; also attrib.

diet of worms *n.*

IN PHRASES

❑ **go to the diet of worms** *v.* [pun on the proper name *Diet of Worms*, the meeting (1521) between Emperor Charles V and Martin Luther that effectively launched the Protestant Reformation + the action of worms on the dead body] [late 18C–early 19C] to die.

diet pills *n.* [their appetite-reducing effects] [1970s+] (*drugs*) amphetamines.

dif *n.* (*also* **diff**) [abbr; ? orig. Stock Exchange use] **1** [late 19C] in pl., *dificulties*, usu. financial ones. **2** [late 19C+] the *difference*, e.g. *that's the dif; what's the dif?* **3** [1940s+] (*Aus./N.Z.*) the *diferential* gear on a motorcar.

diff *n.* [? Scot. *dowf*, a dull blow] [late 19C] (*US*) a blow.

differ *n.* [abbr.] [20C+] (*Aus./Irish/N.Z.*) the *difference*.

difference, the *n.* [20C+] (*US*) a telling advantage, e.g. a hidden weapon.

differs *n.* [abbr.] [1950s] (*Anglo-Irish*) *difference*.

diffs *n.* see DIF *n.* (1).

diffy *adj.* [abbr.] [1940s–50s] (*UK society*) *difficult*.

dig *n.*[1] [SE *dig*, a thrust, a sharp poke, as with the elbow, fist, or other part of the body] **1** [early 19C+] a punch. **2** [late 19C–1910s] in fig. use, a verbal attack. **3** [1990s+] (*US black*) a verbal risposte.

dig *n.*[2] **1** [mid-19C–1900s] (*US campus*) a diligent or over-dedicated student, one who studies hard [DIG *v.*[1] (1), i.e. they *dig* for knowledge. The term also flourished briefly in UK schools in the late 19C]. **2** [1920s–30s] (*US tramp*) a hiding place for stolen goods [? one *digs* a hole for the cache]. **3** [1950s] (*US Und.*) a pickpocket. **4** [1990s+] (*drugs*) an injection of a narcotic [the needle 'digs into' the vein].

dig *n.*[3] (*also* **otium dig**) [Lat. *otium cum dignitate*, the dignity of leisure, popularized in Cicero, *Ad Familiares*, I.xi.21] [late 19C–1910s] dignity.

dig *n.*[4] [abbr. DIGGER *n.*[1] (2)] [1920s+] (*Aus./N.Z.*) **1** an Australian or New Zealander. **2** a friend. **3** a general form of address.

IN PHRASES

❑ **old dig** *n.* [1940s+] (*Aus./N.Z.*) a veteran soldier.

dig *n.*[5] [? DIG *v.*[3], i.e. something one studies closely or enjoys] [1930s–70s] (*US*) a sex show.

dig *v.*[1] **1** [early 19C–1900s] (*US campus*) to work extremely hard. **2** [1900s] (*US*) (*also* **dig it out**) to leave quickly, to run off [one *digs* oneself out of the current situation or one *digs* one's heels into the ground as one runs]. **3** [1900s–50s] (*US*) (*also* **dig up**) to search in one's pockets for money; sometimes refers to tobacco, used in prison for barter. **4** [1910s] (*US prison*) to stab. **5** [1920s] in fig. use of sense 3, to pay for, i.e. to dig in one's pocket. **6** [1920s–30s] (*US Und.*) to pick pockets (incompetently). **7** [2000s] (*UK drugs*) to inject a drug intravenously.

IN PHRASES

❑ **at full dig** *adv.* [mid-19C] speedily. ❑ **dig dirt** *v.* [1950s] as an imper., get moving fast. ❑ **dig down** *v.* (*also* **dig deep**) [1940s–50s] (*US/Aus.*) to pay out of one's own pocket. ❑ **dig foot** *v.* [1930s+] (*W.I.*) to run away fast. ❑ **dig it out** *v. see* sense 2 above. ❑ **dig out** *v. see* separate entry. ❑ **dig up** *v. see* separate entries. ❑ **in full dig** [mid-19C–1900s] earning one's full pay.

SE in slang uses

IN COMPOUNDS

❑ **dig-out** *n. see* separate entry.

IN PHRASES

❑ **dig a day under the skin** *v.* [late 19C] to shave on alternate days. ❑ **dig a ditch** *v.* [1970s+] (*US gay*) to have anal intercourse. ❑ **dig a hole in the road** *v.* [1950s] (*US*) to drive fast. ❑ **dig for gold** *v.* [backform. f. GOLD-DIGGER *n.*[1] (2)] **1** [1930s–60s] to sleep with or marry a man for his money. **2** [2000s] (*US campus*) to pick one's nose. ❑ **dig gravel** *v. see* SCRATCH GRAVEL *under* SCRATCH *v.* ❑ **dig horrors** *v. see* separate entry. ❑ **dig into** *v.* [1920s] (*US Und.*) to rob (a bank), to break into a safe. ❑ **dig up** *v. see* separate entry. ❑ **dig with both feet** *v.* [play on DIG WITH THE…FOOT *v.*] [20C+] (*Ulster*) to be duplicitous, cunning; in positive sense, to be very clever. ❑ **dig with the…foot** *v. see* separate entry.

dig *v.*[2] [DIGS *n.*[1]] [1910s] to share lodgings or DIGGINGS *n.* with.

dig *v.*[3] [all orig. jazz musician use, thence adopted by the fans; ? ult. Wolof *dega*, to understand (Smitherman, *Black Talk*, 1994), although *DARE* remarks 'questionable' and *HDAS* 'not been substantiated'); or ? SE *dig*, to excavate; or ? TWIG *v.*[2]] **1** [1930s–60s] (*orig. US black*) to get together, to meet. **2** [1930s–60s] (*US black*) to visit. **3** [1930s+] (*orig. US black*) to appreciate, to enjoy, to love. **4** [1930s+] (*orig. US black*) (*also* **dig it**) to understand. **5** [1930s+] (*orig. US black*) to pay close attention to; also ext. as *dig it* or *dig up*. **6** [1940s–50s] (*US black*) (*also* **dig the cat**) to discuss, to converse. **7** [1940s+] (*orig. US black*) to find out, to discover; to interrogate. **8** [1950s+] to believe. **9** [1950s+] to see, to recognize. **10** [1960s] (*orig. US black*) to imagine.

IN PHRASES

❑ **can you dig it?** [1960s+] (*US black*) a rhetorical phr. seeking affirmation as a response. ❑ **dig horrors** *v. see* separate entry. ❑ **dig it** *v. see* sense 5 above. ❑ **dig on** *v.* [1980s+] (*orig. US black*) **1** to observe, to pay attention to, to watch. **2** to find (sexually) attractive. **3** to like, to appreciate. ❑ **dig the cat** *v. see* sense 6 above. ❑ **dig the dip on the two and four** *v.* [SE *two and four*, six, i.e. the sixth (day)] [1940s] (*US black/Harlem*) to take a bath every Saturday night. ❑ **dig you later** [1940s+] see you later, goodbye. ❑ **plant you now, dig you later** [1940s–50s] (*US black*) goodbye for now, and see you later.

dig *v.*[4] [1970s] (*US black*) to borrow.

dig? *phr.* [DIG *v.*[3] (4)] [1950s+] (*orig. US black*) understand? know what I mean?

dig a grave *v.* [rhy. sl.] [20C+] (*Aus.*) to have a shave.

dig and dirt *n.* [rhy. sl.] [1920s] (*US*) a shirt.

Digby chicken *n.* [the fishing trade of *Digby*, Nova Scotia] [late 19C] a herring; when smoked it is known as a *Digby duck*.

digest *v.* [1990s+] (*US campus*) to tolerate.

digger *n.*[1] **1** based on the shape of a spade or shovel. (**a**) [mid-18C–19C] a spur; usu. in pl. (**b**) [mid–late 19C] a finger-nail. (**c**) [mid-19C+] a card of the spade suit; thus *big digger*, the ace of spades. **2** [mid-19C+] any Australian or New Zealander, although orig. a soldier [form of address used by miners in the 19C Aus./N.Z. gold-fields; it spread after Aus./N.Z. participation in WW1; note Fraser & Gibbons, *Soldier & Sailor Words & Phrases* (1925): 'Australians specially claimed it […] for their trench work at Gallipoli, and New Zealanders for the work of the N.Z. Tunnelling Company on the Western front']. **3** [1910s+] a term of (affectionate) address.

digger *n.*^{2} [DIG *v.*^{1}] **1** [early 19C–1900s] a diligent student. **2** [1930s+] (*US Und.*) a pickpocket. **3** [2000s] (*UK drugs*) (*also* **dirty digger**) an intravenous drug user.

digger *n.*^{3} [orig. late 19C UK army use *digger*, a guardroom, in which defaulters were 'buried'] (*Can./N.Z./US Und.*) **1** [1920s] a county or city prison. **2** [1980s+] a solitary confinement cell.

digger *n.*^{4} [abbr. GOLD-DIGGER *n.*^{1}] [1920s+] (*US*) a young woman, orig. typically from the chorus line, who swaps sexual favours for the monetary and material gifts of a (usu.) older lover.

digger *n.*^{5} [initial letters] [1960s] (*US campus*) the grade D.

digger, the *n.* [1960s] (*US*) a superior figure; the government.

digger *adj.* [mid–late 19C] (*Aus.*) used as a qualifier to indicate the ostentation of the newly rich *diggers*, i.e. gold miners.

Diggerland *n.* [DIGGER *n.*^{1} (2) + SE *land*] [1910s] (*N.Z.*) New Zealand.

diggermania *n.* (*also* **diggerphobia**) [SE *digger*/DIGGER *n.*^{1} (2) + *-mania/-phobia*] [mid–late 19C] (*Aus./N.Z.*) an obsession with digging in the Antipodean goldfields, usu. fostered by one's failure to find anything.

digger's delight *n.* [DIGGER *n.*^{1} (2) + SE *delight*] [late 19C] (*N.Z.*) a wide-brimmed felt hat.

diggings *n.* (*also* **diggins**) [one *digs* oneself in] [mid-19C+] lodgings, temporary accommodation.

diggities *n.* [? HOT DIGGETY (DOG)! *excl.*] [2000s] (*US black*) the best quality marijuana.

diggity dank *adj.* *see* DANK *adj.* (2).

diggity dank! *excl.* *see* HOT DIGGETY (DOG)! *excl.*

diggums *n.* [var. on DIGGER *n.*^{1} (1c); resemblance to a spade or shovel] [late 19C] cards in the spade suit.

diggy *adj.* [DIG *v.*^{3} (3)] [1990s+] (*US black*) admirable, aware, 'hip'; lit. one who 'digs'.

dig horrors *v.*^{1} (*also* **get horrors**) [DIG *v.*^{3} (7) + HORRORS, THE *n.* (1)] [1950s+] (*W.I.*) to be emotionally troubled.

dig horrors *v.*^{2} (*also* **get horrors**) [DIG *v.*^{2} + HORRORS, THE *n.* (1)] [1950s+] (*W.I.*) to live in material squalor.

dig in the grave *n.* [rhy. sl.] [1910s+] (*orig. Aus.*) a shave.

dig in the grave *v.* [1980s+] (*Aus. prison*) to divide up spoils.

digital *adj.* [1990s+] (*US black*) new, sophisticated, excellent.

digithead *n.* [SE *digits*, numbers + -HEAD *sfx* (3)] [1980s+] (*orig. US*) an obsessive computer user.

digits *n.* **1** [1930s+] (*US Und.*) the numbers racket. **2** [1990s+] (*US black*) a telephone number (and address). **3** [1990s+] (*US black*) the amount written on a cheque, usu. pay cheque. **4** [1990s+] (*US black*) welfare benefits.

(IN COMPOUNDS)

❑ **digits baron** *n.* [BARON *n.* (1)] [1930s] (*US Und.*) the head of a numbers betting syndicate. ❑ **digits dealer** *n.* [1950s+] (*US Und.*) a numbers racketeer.

dig-out *n.* **1** [1900s] (*N.Z. Und.*) a pit into which recalcitrant prisoners are placed for punishment; a solitary confinement cell. **2** [1990s+] (*Irish*) a loan. **3** [2000s] an act of support.

dig out *v.* [DIG *v.*^{1} (2)] **1** [mid-19C–1940s] (*US*) to leave, to depart. **2** [1980s] (*Irish*) to separate from.

(IN PHRASES)

❑ **dig out after** *v.* **1** [1910s+] to attempt to get something one desires. **2** [1990s+] (*US black*) to have sexual intercourse.

SE in slang uses

(IN PHRASES)

❑ **dig out someone's eye** *v.* [1950s+] (*W.I.*) to cheat in a business deal.

digs *n.*^{1} [SE *diggings*, the mining districts of Australia and California, first adopted in lodgings sense by UK actors/DIGGINGS *n.*] [mid-19C+] (*orig. Aus.*) temporary rented accommodation.

digs *n.*^{2} (*US black*) **1** [1960s–70s] food [SE colloq. *dig in*]. **2** [2000s] new clothes or footwear [DIG *v.*^{3} (3)].

digs *n.*^{3} [DIG *v.*^{3} (7)] [1970s+] (*US*) the facts, information.

dig up *v.*^{1} **1** [mid-19C+] to discover, to unearth, to find. **2** [late 19C+] to obtain, to provide. **3** [1930s] to disturb, to awaken. **4** [1930s–50s] to look for.

dig up *v.*^{2} [DIG *v.*^{1} (2)] [1920s+] to leave.

dig up *v.*^{3} *see* DIG *v.*^{1} (3).

dig with the...foot *v.* [in the Republic of Ireland (Catholic), people usu. press on the spade with the right foot; in Northern Ireland (largely Protestant), it is the reverse] [20C+] (*Ulster*) used in various combs. below to denote one's religious persuasion.

(IN PHRASES)

❑ **dig with the left foot** *v.* to be a Protestant. ❑ **dig with the right foot** *v.* to be a Roman Catholic. ❑ **dig with the other foot** *v.* (*also* **...wrong foot**) to be of another religion. ❑ **dig with the same foot** *v.* to share a religion.

dik *n.* [fig. use of Afk. *dik*, dense, thick] [1970s+] (*S.Afr.*) a fool.

dik *adj.*^{1} [fig. use of Afk. *dik*, dense, thick] [1970s+] (*S.Afr.*) **1** stupid. **2** sated, full; thus *dik of*, tired of. **3** fat.

dik *adj.*^{2} [2000s] (*US black*) agreeing with.

dikbek *n.* (*also* **diklip**) [Afk. *dik*, thick + Afk. *bek*, mouth or SE *lip*] [1970s+] (*S.Afr.*) a sour-faced or sulky person.

dikbek *adj.* (*also* **diklip**) [DIKBEK *n.*] [1970s+] (*S.Afr.*) sulky, pouting.

dik dik *phr.* [DIK *adj.*^{2} + redup.] [2000s] (*US black*) a statement implying that one is in absolute agreement.

dike *see also under* DYKE.

dike *n.*^{1} (*also* **dyke**) [SE *dike*, a pit] [mid-19C; 1920s+] (*Aus.*) a lavatory, esp. a communal urinal used by schoolboys, soldiers etc.

dike *n.*^{2} [? SE *decked out*] [mid-19C+] (*US*) someone who is dressed up; thus *out on a dike*, dressed up specially for a particular event or visit.

dike *n.*^{3} [abbr./pron.] [1980s+] (*drugs*) *Diconal*.

dike down *v.* (*also* **dike out, dike up, dyke down**) [SE *decked out* + ? 13C SE *dight*, to put or place in order, to array, to arrange] [19C+] (*US*) to dress smartly; thus *diked/dyked down*, smartly dressed.

diked up *adj.*^{1} (*also* **diked (out), dyked up**) [DIKE DOWN *v.*] [mid-19C+] (*US*) well-dressed.

diked up *adj.*^{2} (*also* **dyked up**) [? SE *dike/dyke*, a water-course or channel, in this case for alcohol] [1900s] drunk.

dikey *adj.* *see* DYKEY *adj.*

dikker *n.* *see* DICKER *n.*^{1}.

diklip *see under* DIKBEK.

dil *n.*^{1} [1990s+] (*US black*) a dollar bill.

dil *n.*^{2} *see* DILL *n.*

dilberry *n.* **1** [early 19C+] (*also* **dill-ball**) a small piece of excrement or semen clinging to the hairs around the anus or the female pubic hair; usu. in pl. **2** [20C+] (*also* **dillberry**) a stupid, dull or obnoxious person. **3** [1910s] a piece of nasal mucus dripping from the bottom of the nostril.

(IN COMPOUNDS)

❑ **dilberry bush** *n.* [BUSH *n.*^{1} (2a)/SE *bush*] [mid–late 19C] the pubic hair. ❑ **dilberry creek** *n.* [mid–late 19C] the anus. ❑ **dilberry-maker** *n.* [early 19C] the anus.

Dil-Dil *n.* [abbr.] [1990s+] (*US drugs*) *Dil*audid.

dildo *n.* [SE *dildo*, an artificial penis; itself ? Ital. *diletto*, a (lady's) delight; thus fig. the lack of autonomous competence of the sexual aid so named; thus Grose (1785): 'DILDO, an implement resembling the virile member, for which it is said to be substituted, by nuns, boarding school misses, and others obliged to celibacy, or fearful of pregnancy'] **1** [1960s+] a general term of abuse: a fool, an incompetent. **2** [1990s+] (*Irish*) a promiscuous woman.

(IN COMPOUNDS)

❑ **dildohead** *n.* (*also* **dildobrain**) [-HEAD *sfx* (1)] [1970s+] (*US*) a general term of abuse.

dildock *n.* [derog. implications of SE *dildo*] [1910s+] (*US*) a fool.

dill *n.*^{1} (*also* **dil**) [? DILLYPOT *n.* (2)/backform. f. DILLY *adj.*^{1} (1); the late 20C UK use may also be attributed to an abbr. of the comic name *Dilbert* (slightly transformed by the comedian Lenny Henry into his bumptious character Delbert Wilkins); also note DILDO *n.* (1)] [1940s+] (*Aus./N.Z./US*) a fool; also as adj., foolish.

IN COMPOUNDS

▫ **dillbrain** *n.* [1950s+] (*Aus./N.Z.*) a fool.

dill *n.*[2] *see* DELL *n.*

dillack *adj.* [mid-19C] (*UK Und.*) cowardly.

dillberry *n. see* DILBERRY *n.* (2).

dillecky *adj.* [mid-19C] (*UK Und.*) slow.

diller *n.* [var. on DIDDLYWHACKER *n.* or DILLYWHACKER *n.*] [1960s] (*US*) the penis.

dill-hole *n.* [? SE *dildo*] [1990s+] (*US teen*) the urethra, thus used as an insult.

dilli *n.* (*also* **dilly**) [abbr.] [mid–late 18C] a *dil*ettante.

dillidakey *adj.* [mid-19C] (*UK Und.*) mentally slow, stupid.

dillied *adj.* [DILLY *n.*[2]] [1910s] (*Aus.*) confused, disorientated.

dillies *n.* [abbr.] [1960s+] (*US drugs*) *Dil*audid.

dillio *adj.* [ety. unknown] [1990s+] (*US teen*) ugly, esp. of a young woman.

dillo *adj. see* DEELO *adj.*

dillo namo/nemo *n. see* DEELO NAMMO *under* DEELO *adj.*

dill pickle *n.* [despite appearances, the ref. is to the apparent absurdity of a gherkin (? its phallic resemblance) thus cf. WALLY *n.*[2] (1), and not to the later Aus./N.Z. DILL *n.*] [1900s] (*US*) a fool.

dillweed *n.* [ext. of DILDO *n.* (1)] [1990s+] (*US campus*) a fool.

Dilly, the *n.* [abbr.] **1** [mid-19C] the Picca*dilly* Saloon. **2** [1920s+] (*UK Und./police*) Picca*dilly*, esp. as a favoured area for prostitutes; also attrib.

IN COMPOUNDS

▫ **Dilly boy** *n.* [1950s+] (*UK gay*) a teenage male prostitute.

dilly *n.*[1] [SE *diligence*, a public stage-coach] [late 18C–early 19C] **1** a coach. **2** a night-soil cart.

dilly *n.*[2] [ext. of DILL *n.*] [20C+] (*Aus./US*) a fool; a lunatic.

dilly *n.*[3] [? SE *delightful* and/or *delicious*] [20C+] (*US*) anything or anyone outstanding or remarkable, often used ironically.

dilly *n.*[4] [abbr. DILLYWHACKER *n.*] [1940s–60s] (*US*) a penis.

dilly *n.*[5] *see* DILLI *n.*

dilly *n.*[6] *see* DILLY-BAG *n.*

dilly *adj.*[1] [orig. Gloucestershire dial. *dilly*, cranky, odd; ? ult. SE *silly*] [20C+] (*orig. Aus.*) **1** foolish. **2** mad.

IN COMPOUNDS

▫ **dilly dude** *n.* [orig. Ohio use] [1960s] (*US black*) an eccentric, an outsider.

dilly *adj.*[2] [abbr./pron. + sfx *-y*] [1900s–20s] *del*ightful.

dilly-bag *n.* (*also* **dilly**) [synon. SE *ditty-bag*] [mid-19C+] (*orig. Aus.*) a small sack or similar container in which articles are carried; thus *dilly-bags of*.

dilly-dad *n.* [joc. pron.] [1960s] (*US drugs*) Dilaudid, synthetic morphine.

dillypot *n.* [rhy. sl. = TWAT *n.*] [1940s–60s] (*Aus.*) **1** the vagina. **2** a fool.

dillywhacker *n.* (*also* **tillywhacker**) [1920s] (*US*) the penis.

dilog *n. see* DELOG *n.*

dilsnick *n.* [ext. DICK *n.*[1] (5)] [1990s+] (*US black*) a (large) penis.

dilsy *n.* [ety. unknown] [20C+] (*Ulster*) **1** a foolish, usu. female, person. **2** an overdressed, showy woman. **3** a social climber.

dim *n.* [note 15C SE *dim*, the dusk] [1940s–50s] (*US black*) the evening, the night.

dimba *n.* [used synon. in various west African languages] [1980s+] (*drugs*) marijuana from West Africa.

dimber *adj.* **1** [mid-17C–1930s] (*UK Und.*) pretty. **2** [mid-19C] smart, active, adroit.

IN COMPOUNDS

▫ **dimber cove** *n.* [COVE *n.* (1)] [late 18C–mid-19C] (*UK Und.*) a handsome man. ▫ **dimber mort** *n.* [MORT *n.* (1)] [late 17C–mid-19C] a pretty young woman.

dimber-damber *n.* [DIMBER *adj.* (1) + DAMBER *n.*, lit. a 'handsome rascal'] [17C–19C] (*UK Und.*) a gang leader.

dimber-damber *adj.* [adjectival use of the lit. meaning of DIMBER-DAMBER *n.*] [17C–19C] smart, neat.

dimbo *n.* [SE *dim* + sfx *-bo*] [1970s+] a fool of either sex.

dimbox *n.* [? its 'for hire' light] [1920s] (*US*) a taxi.

dim bulb *n.* [1920s+] (*US/Can.*) a fool, a dullard.

dime *n.* [SAmE *dime*, ten cents] **1** (*US*) in drug uses. (**a**) [20C+] $10 worth of a given drug. (**b**) [1980s+] crack cocaine. (**c**) [1980s+] $10 worth of crack cocaine, $10 worth of marijuana. **2** [1930s+] (*US prison*) a ten-year prison sentence; a period of ten years. **3** [1940s+] (*US*) the number ten, often as $10. **4** [1950s+] (*gambling*) $1,000, $10,000. **5** [1990s+] (*US black/campus*) (*also* **dime piece**) a very attractive person [they score 'a perfect ten' i.e. out of ten].

IN COMPOUNDS

▫ **dime bag** *n.* [BAG *n.*[1] (7a)] **1** [1960s+] (*US drugs*) $10 worth of a drug. **2** [1990s+] attrib., of a dealer, low in the drug-selling hierarchy. ▫ **dime note** *n.* [1930s–60s] (*US black*) a $10 bill. ▫ **Dimetown, USA** *n.* [sense 1 above/*DIME BAG* above; there is an added implication of the poverty of this fig. world] [1990s+] the world of street drug addicts.

IN PHRASES

▫ **double dime** *n.* [1960s–70s] (*US*) **1** $20. **2** 20 years.

SE in slang uses

IN COMPOUNDS

▫ **dime-ass** *adj.* [1960s–70s] (*US black*) worthless, contemptible. ▫ **dime dropper** *n.* [*DROP A DIME* below] [1960s+] (*US*) an informer. ▫ **dime-grind palace** *n.* [GRIND *n.* (2d)] [1930s] (*US jazz*) a cheap dancehall.

IN PHRASES

▫ **don't take any rubber dimes** [1920s] (*US*) be careful, watch your step. ▫ **drop a dime** *v.* (*also* **drop a dime on, drop (the) dime, put a dime on**) [the act of making a call from a public telephone, which in the 1970s cost ten cents. Note basketball jargon *drop a dime*, to shoot a three-point basket] (*US*) **1** [1930s] to leave a tip. **2** [1960s+] to inform, to inform against; thus *dime-dropping*. **3** [1960s+] to explain, to recount, to pass on information (in a non-criminal context). ▫ **on the dime** *adv.* [1940s] (*US black*) by chance, spontaneously.

dime *v.* [DIME *n.*] [2000s] (*US drugs*) to divide bulk drugs into measures worth $10 each.

dime a pop *n.* [rhy. sl. = COP *n.*[1] (1)] [1930s–40s] (*US Und.*) a police officer.

dime on *v.* [*DROP A DIME under* DIME *n.*] [1970s] (*US black*) to inform against.

dimer *n. see* DEEMER *n.*

dimes, the *n.* [generic use of SAmE *dime*] [mid-19C] (*US*) money.

dime store *n.* [ext. DIME *n.* (2)] [1930s] (*US Und.*) a five- to ten-year sentence.

dime-store *adj.* [ext. of SE use; i.e. the poor quality of the goods sold in such stores] [1940s+] (*US*) cheap, second-rate.

dimey *n.* [SAmE *dime*] [1960s+] (*US*) a glass of beer costing ten cents.

dimmer *n.*[1] [1920s–30s] (*US*) a dime, ten cents.

dimmer *n.*[2] **1** [1930s–50s] (*US prison*) an electric light. **2** [1950s] (*US*) in pl., the eyes. **3** [2000s] (*UK juv.*) a stupid person.

dimmick *n.* [var. on DIMMOCK *n.*[1]] [mid–late 19C] counterfeit coins.

Dimmie *n.* [abbr./pron.] [1900s] a *Dem*ocrat.

dimmo *n.*[1] (*also* **dimo**) [SAmE *dime* + -O *sfx* (1)] [20C+] (*US*) a dime, ten cents.

dimmo *n.*[2] (*also* **dimo**) [SE *dim* + -O *sfx* (2)] [1970s+] a fool.

dimmock *n.*[1] [dial.; but note 14C *dime*, a tithe or tenth + US *dime*, ten cents] [early–mid-19C] money.

dimmock *n.*[2] [SE *dim*; ? on pattern of DILDOCK *n.*; *OnLine Dict. Playground Slang* (2001) defines it as 'a person whose behaviour suggested some sort of mental imbalance'] [1990s+] an unpleasant person.

dimmy *n.* [DIMMOCK *n.*[1]/SAmE *dime*] [mid-19C] (*US*) money.

dimo *n. see* DIMMO *n.*[2].

dimp *n.* [SE *dimple*, the indentation that is put in the cigarette when one pinches it out for further use] [1930s+] (*orig. milit.*) a cigarette end, esp. one that is large enough to be relit.

dimp *v.* [DIMP *n.*] [1930s+] to stub out a cigarette; to extinguish a cigarette leaving a still-smokeable stub.

dimper mot *n.* [var. or mis-sp. *DIMBER MORT under* DIMBER *adj.*] [mid-19C] a delightful young woman.

dimple *n.* [SE *dimple*, a depression in the flesh] [late 17C–19C] the vagina.

dims and brights *n.* [DIM *n.* + BRIGHT *n.* (2)] [1920s–40s] (*US black*) nights and days.

dim sim *n.*[1] [SE *dim*+ abbr. SE *simple*, but ? pun on Chinese *dim sum*, a lunchtime snack, i.e. 'I could eat him for lunch'] [1950s+] (*Aus.*) the victim of a confidence trickster.

dim sim *n.*[2] [rhy. sl. = CRIM *n.*] [1980s+] (*Aus. prison*) a criminal.

dina *n. see* DINO *n.*[2].

dinah *n.*[1] [? var. on DONA *n.*] [late 19C–1930s] one's favourite female companion.

dinah *n.*[2] (*also* **dina, dine**) [abbr. SE *dynamite*] [1920s+] nitroglycerine; *dynamite*.

dinarly *n.* (*also* **dinali, dinaly, dinarla**) [Lat. *denarius*. The word is part of Ling. Fr. and cognate with Sp. *dinero*] [mid–late 19C] (*Polari*) a shilling (5p); money in general.

dinch *n.* (*also* **dincher, dintch**) [DIMP *n.* + SE *pinch*] [1920s–30s] (*US Und.*) a cigar or cigarette end.

dinch *v.* [DINCH *n.*] [1920s–30s] (*US*) to pinch out a cigarette for later use.

din-din *n.* (*also* **din-dins**) [the pl. use is 1960s+] [20C+] (*mainly UK juv.*) dinner.

dine *n.*[1] [ety. unknown] [17C–18C] spite.

dine *n.*[2] *see* DAN *n.*[1].

dine *n.*[3] **1** *see* DINAH *n.*[2]. **2** *see* DINO *n.*[2].

dine *v.*

SE in slang uses

IN PHRASES

❑ **dine at the downstairs restaurant** *v.* [2000s] to have homosexual oral intercourse. ❑ **dine at the Y** *v.* [play on EAT *v.* (4); Y = the conjunction of the thighs, plus a pun on the YMCA/YWCA] [1940s+] (*orig. US*) to perform cunnilingus. ❑ **dine out** *v.* **1** [mid–late 19C] to go without a meal. **2** [1970s+] (*US gay*) (*also* **dine in**) to invite someone home for sex (as opposed to picking up a partner for alfresco coupling). ❑ **dine with Duke Humphrey** *v.* (*also* **drink a health to Duke Humphrey**) [Duke Humphrey's Walk at Old St Paul's Cathedral. The real Duke Humphrey of Gloucester was actually buried in St Albans, but a statue of Sir John Beauchamp, which stood in one of the cathedral aisles, was popularly supposed to be the duke; thus to *dine with Duke Humphrey* meant to frequent this aisle, in the hope, often vain, of being invited to dinner. The Scottish equivalent was *DINE WITH ST GILES AND THE EARL OF MURRAY* below] [late 16C–mid-19C] to go without one's meal. ❑ **dine with Sir Thomas Gresham** *v.* (*also* **sup with Sir Thomas Gresham**) [*Sir Thomas Gresham* (1519–79) founder of the Royal Society and a well-known philanthropist; the image is of a poor person forced to appeal to Gresham for charity] [early–mid-17C] to go without one's dinner. ❑ **dine with St Giles and the Earl of Murray** *v.* [18C] to go without one's dinner.

dinero *n.* [Sp.] [19C+] (*orig. US*) money.

ding *n.*[1] [DING *v.*[1]] **1** [late 18C] (*UK Und.*) the passing of stolen goods to a confederate. **2** [1950s+] a notice of rejection, a negative assessment. **3** [1950s+] (*Aus.*) a hole in the bottom of anything. **4** [1950s+] (*Aus.*) the anus. **5** [1960s+] of an object, a small knock or dent. **6** [1960s+] (*orig. US*) of a person, a minor injury, a bruise.

ding *n.*[2] [DINGBAT *n.*[7] (1)/DING *v.*[2] (2)] **1** [late 19C; 1920s–40s] a beggar, a tramp, a worthless person. **2** [1940s+] (*Aus.*) a derog. term for foreigners, esp. Italians and Greeks. **3** [1950s+] (*US*) (*also* **ding-ding, dinglame**) a fool, a mentally unstable person; also attrib. **4** [1960s] (*US prison*) an outsider.

IN COMPOUNDS

❑ **ding farm** *n.* [2000s] (*US*) a psychiatric institution.

ding *n.*[3] [abbr. DINGUS *n.* (2)] [1920s–70s] the penis.

ding *n.*[4] **1** [1940s] (*US Und.*) a doorbell. **2** [1990s+] (*W.I.*) a telephone call.

ding *n.*[5] [ety. unknown; the *ding* of pleasure it creates] [1950s] (*US drugs*) marijuana.

ding *n.*[6] [WING-DING *n.*] **1** [1950s+] (*Aus.*) a party. **2** [1960s] (*US*) a drinking spree. **3** [1980s] a sudden feeling of pleasure, a thrill.

ding *v.*[1] [fig. uses of 14C SE *ding*, to beat heavily] **1** [17C+] to knock down. **2** [late 17C–early 18C] to act in an arrogant manner. **3** [late 18C–1930s] to throw away, esp. to get rid of contraband when threatened by arrest. **4** [early 19C] to steal by snatching, e.g. a hat. **5** [early 19C] (*UK Und.*) to pass to a confederate. **6** [early 19C+] to break off relations with, to abandon a person. **7** [1930s] to stub out. **8** [1930s+] (*US campus*) to turn (someone) down, to blackball. **9** [1930s+] to dent, to scratch; thus *dinged*, scratched, dented. **10** [1960s] (*US campus*) to reject a request for a date; to blackball a candidate for a fraternity or club. **11** [1960s+] to kill, to shoot, to be shot dead; in weak use, to be wounded. **12** [1970s] in fig. use of sense 1, to astonish, to amaze. **13** [1990s+] to smash into.

DERIVATIVES

❑ **dingable** *adj.* [early 19C] of persons or objects, worthless, to be discarded.

IN COMPOUNDS

❑ **ding boy** *n.* [late 17C–mid-19C] (*UK Und.*) a thug, esp. when he acts as a bodyguard or accomplice, providing the 'muscle' for a more skilful villain.

IN PHRASES

❑ **ding it in one's ears** *v.* [late 18C] to criticize; to pass on information the hearer does not wish to hear.

ding *v.*[2] [SE *ding*, to nag, to bore with repetitious speech] **1** [1910s+] (*US*) to nag, to harass. **2** [1920s–60s] (*US tramp*) to beg money; also as *hit the ding, put the ding on*. **3** [1940s+] (*US*) in business, to come to a negative assessment.

ding *v.*[3] [1970s+] to telephone.

ding! *excl.* (*also* **dingy!**) [mid-19C+] a euph. for DAMN! *excl.*

IN EXCLAMATIONS

❑ **by ding!** (*also* **by dinkey!**) [1920s–30s] (*US*) a euph. excl.

dingaling *n.*[1] (*also* **ding-a-ling**) [the ringing in the sufferer's head] **1** [1930s+] (*UK/US prison*) a prisoner whose confinement has driven him mad. **2** [1930s+] (*US*) a fool, an eccentric, a mad person. **3** [1960s+] (*US*) an effeminate man [seen as SE *queer*, i.e. eccentric].

dingaling *n.*[2] (*also* **ding-a-ling, ding-a-thing, thing-a-ling**) [SE *dangle* + image of the testicles as bells] [1930s+] (*orig. US black*) the penis.

dingaling *n.*[3] (*also* **ding-a-ling**) [rhy. sl.] [1990s+] (*Aus.*) the king.

dingaling *adj.* [1910s+] crazy, insane, eccentric.

dingaloo *n.* [1960s] (*S.Afr. Und.*) a beggar, a petty criminal.

ding-a-thing *n. see* DINGALING *n.*[2].

dingbat *n.*[1] [? a specific bartender's name] [mid-19C] (*US*) a strong drink.

dingbat *n.*[2] [mid–late 19C] **1** a ball of dung on the buttocks of sheep or cattle. **2** (*US*) a cannon-ball, a bullet, a flying missile.

IN PHRASES

❑ **go like a dingbat** *v.* [1940s] to go very fast.

dingbat *n.*[3] **1** [mid-19C–1900s] (*US*) a coin, a banknote; thus in pl. money. **2** [late 19C] a blow or slap on the buttocks. **3** [late 19C] (*US*) verbal squabbling, physical pushing. **4** [late 19C] (*US*) an affectionate embrace, esp. mothers hugging and kissing their children. **5** [1910s–40s] the penis.

dingbat *n.*[4] [late 19C] (*US campus*) one of various types of muffin or biscuit.

dingbat *n.*[5] [late 19C+] a term of admiration.

dingbat *n.*^{6} [late 19C+] anything for which one cannot specify the proper name.

dingbat *n.*^{7} [popularized by George Herriman's carton *The Dingbat Family*, created in 1909 and revived c.1971 in the TV sitcom *All in the Family*] (*orig. US*) **1** [20C+] a fool, an idiot. **2** [1910s] (*Aus. milit.*) a batman, an officer's servant. **3** [1910s–40s] a tramp, a vagrant. **4** [1940s] (*US*) a woman. **5** [1940s–60s] (*US*) a derog. term for an Italian. **6** [1960s] (*US*) a derog. term for a Chinese person.

dingbat *adj.* [DINGBAT *n.*^{7} (1)] [1930s+] foolish, stupid, idiotic.

dingbatisis *n.* [DINGBATS *n.*] **1** [1920s] (*N.Z.*) drunkenness, very heavy drinking. **2** [1990s+] (*US*) nervousness; neurosis.

dingbats *n.* [DINGBAT *n.*^{7} (1)] [1910s+] (*Aus./N.Z.*) **1** madness. **2** delirium tremens. **3** an eccentric, a mad person.

IN PHRASES

❑ **give someone the dingbats** *v.* [1930s+] to make someone feel nervous.

dingbats *adj.* [DINGBATS *n.*] [1910s+] (*Aus.*) eccentric, crazy.

ding-batty *adj.* [DINGBAT *adj.*] [1910s–30s] mad, crazy.

ding blasted *adj. see* DINGBUSTED *adj.*

dingbust *v.* (*also* **dingblastit**) [euph. for DAMN! *excl.*] [late 19C+] (*US*) used in oaths or excls.

dingbusted *adj.* (*also* **ding blasted**) [euph. for DAMNED *adj.*] [late 19C+] (*US*) used in oaths or excl.

ding-ding *n.* [redup. DING *n.*^{2} (3)] [1970s–80s] (*US prison*) a mad person.

ding-dong *n.*^{1} **1** [mid-19C] an alcoholic drink. **2** [late 19C] (*US campus*) in pl., side whiskers. **3** [1920s] (*US*) the head.

ding-dong *n.*^{2} [rhy. sl.] **1** [mid-19C+] a song; a (domestic) sing-song. **2** [1920s+] (*US*) a bell, a gong. **3** [1920s+] a serious argument, a fight; esp. in phr. *a right old ding-dong* [may be more echoic]. **4** [1920s+] a noisy party or other gathering [may be more echoic].

ding-dong *n.*^{3} [1920s; 1970s+] (*US*) a stupid, dull person.

ding-dong *n.*^{4} [1940s+] (*US*) the penis.

ding-dong *n.*^{5} *see* DINGDONGER *n.* (1).

ding-dong *adj.*^{1} [the ringing of bells in celebration] [late 19C–1920s] (*US*) exciting, smart.

ding-dong *adj.*^{2} [20C+] (*US*) a euph. for DAMNED *adj.*, e.g. *I feel like a ding-dong fool.*

ding-dong *adj.*^{3} [DING-DONG *n.*^{3}; the supposed ringing bells heard by the sufferer] [1960s+] eccentric, insane.

ding-dong *v.* [? the ringing of house bells prior to asking for money] [1920s–50s] (*US tramp*) to beg door to door.

ding-dong *adv.* [late 18C+] in an energetic, if chaotic, manner.

ding-dong bell *n.* [rhy. sl.] [1940s+] a euph. for HELL, THE *phr.*

dingdonger *n.* **1** [1940s] (*US Und.*) (*also* **ding-dong**) a house-to-house beggar [DING-DONG *v.*]. **2** [1990s+] (*US*) one who enjoys hedonistic pleasures to excess [DING-DONG *n.*^{2} (4)].

ding-dong pants *n.* (*also* **ding-dongs**) [pun] [1920s–70s] (*US*) bell-bottomed trousers.

ding-dongs *n.* [DING-DONG *n.*^{2} (2), i.e. they supposedly knock together, 'like bells'] [1950s+] (*US*) the testicles.

ding-dust *n.* [ON *denja*, to thrash] [20C+] (*Ulster*) a noise.

ding-dust *adv.* [ext. of DING *v.*^{1} (1)] [20C+] (*Ulster*) very fast.

dinge *n.* (*also* **dingy**) [SE *dingy*, grimy, shabby; ? Mandingo *denke*, black; now seen as pej.] **1** [early 19C] (*US Und.*) a moonless night. **2** [mid-19C+] (*also* **dinghe, dingy**) a black person.

dinge *adj.* (*also* **dingo**) [DINGE *n.*] [mid-19C+] (*US*) black.

IN COMPOUNDS

❑ **dinge blowen** *n.* [BLOWEN *n.* (1)] [mid-19C+] (*US*) a black woman. ❑ **dinge joint** *n.* (*also* **dinge palace**) [JOINT *n.* (3b)/SE *palace*] [1940s+] (*US*) a nightclub or similar place patronized by black people only. ❑ **dinge kinch** *n.* [KINCHIN *n.*] [19C] (*US*) a black child. ❑ **dinge queen** *n.* [-QUEEN *sfx* (3)] [1960s+] (*US gay*) a male homosexual who prefers black partners; used of both whites and blacks.

dinged *adj.* (*also* **ding-whanged**) [mid-19C–1910s] (*US*) a euph. for DAMNED *adj.*

dinged out *adj.* [fig. use of DING *v.*^{1} (1)] (*US*) **1** [1960s] drunk. **2** [1970s+] insane, mentally unbalanced.

dingelberry *n. see* DINGLEBERRY *n.* (2).

dinger *n.*^{1} [DING *v.*^{1}] (*UK Und.*) **1** [late 18C–19C] a thief who throws away anything he possesses that might be incriminating, e.g. a pistol, a coat. **2** [late 18C–mid-19C] a pickpocket. **3** [late 19C+] (*Aus./Irish/US*) something exceptional, something striking; also as adj., *dingery*. **4** [1940s+] (*Aus.*) the anus, the buttocks.

dinger *n.*^{2} [abbr.] [mid-19C+] (*Aus.*) a *dingo*.

dinger *n.*^{3} [echoic] **1** [1910s] (*US Und.*) a till. **2** [1930s] (*US*) a bell. **3** [1930s+] a telephone. **4** [1940s] a railroad conductor.

dinger *n.*^{4} [DING *n.*^{2} (1)] **1** [1920s] (*US*) a beggar or tramp, esp. one who pretends to have some sort of injury or throws fake 'fits'. **2** [1930s] a fit.

dinger *n.*^{5} [DINGUS *n.* (2)] [1950s] (*US*) the penis.

dinges *n.* [var. on DINGUS *n.* (1)] [1990s+] (*S.Afr.*) anything for which one cannot recall the proper name; also ext. to people.

dingey Christian *n.* (*also* **dingy Christian**) ['anyone who has, as the West Indian term is, a lick of the tar-brush' (Grose, 1785); the presumption that a 'real' Christian is white] [late 18C] a mulatto or anyone with a degree of mixed blood.

dinghe *n. see* DINGE *n.* (2).

dinghizen *n.* [ety. unknown] [1930s–50s] (*US drugs*) a hypodermic syringe, or an improvised syringe based on a medicine dropper attached to a hollow needle.

dinglame *n. see* DING *n.*^{2} (3).

dingle *n.*^{1} [? DINGUS *n.* (2), SE *dangle*] [1910s+] (*US*) the penis.

dingle *n.*^{2} [? fig. use of SE *dingle*, to ring as a bell] [1930s] (*US campus*) the regard of one's seniors; thus *get/have a dingle with*, to be in favour; *pluck a dingle*, to toady to.

dingle *adj.* [ety. unknown] [late 18C] banal, clichéd, used up.

dingleberry *n.* **1** [1910s+] a testicle. **2** [1920s+] (*US*) (*also* **dingelberry, dingledork**) someone, or something, stupid, dull, obnoxious. **3** [1950s+] a piece of excrement clinging to the hairs around an inadequately cleansed anus. **4** [1970s] the vagina, the clitoris. **5** [1970s+] in pl., the female breasts.

dingleberry *adj.* [DINGLEBERRY *n.* (2)] [1970s] (*US*) stupid, dull, obnoxious.

dinglebody *n.* [var. DINGLEBERRY *n.* (2)] [1950s] (*US*) someone stupid.

dingle-dangle *n.* (*also* **dingle-doodle, doodle-dasher**) [SE *dingle-dangle*, a dangling appendage] [late 19C+] the penis.

dingledork *n. see* DINGLEBERRY *n.* (2).

dingnation *adj. see* TARNATION *adj.*

dingo *n.* [SE *dingo*, Lat. *Canis dingo*, the wild, or semi-domesticated dog of Australia] **1** [late 19C+] (*Aus.*) a cheat, a scoundrel, a traitor, a coward. **2** [1920s–30s] (*US*) a tramp who refuses to work, a minor confidence trickster. **3** [1950s+] (*US*) an eccentric. **4** [1980s+] (*Aus. prison*) a boy who has escaped from a boys' home. **5** [2000s] (*N.Z.*) a derog. term for an Australian.

SE in slang uses

IN COMPOUNDS

❑ **dingo's breakfast** *n.* [1960s+] (*Aus.*) 'a piss and a look around'.

dingo *adj.*^{1} [? Aus. *dingo dog* or DINGALING *adj.*/DINGBATS *adj.* + -O *sfx* (4); Brophy & Partridge, *Songs & Slang of the British Soldier* (1930), suggest Fr. slang *dingot*, mad] [late 19C–1950s] (*US*) crazy, eccentric.

dingo *adj.*^{2} *see* DINGE *adj.*

dingo *v.* [DINGO *n.* (1)] [1910s+] (*Aus.*) to act in a particularly cowardly and treacherous manner, to exhibit the mannerisms of the dingo, the native Aus. dog, a despised creature.

dingswizzled *adj.* [late 19C] (*US*) a general excl., e.g. *I'll be dingswizzled!*

dingus *n.* [Du. *ding*, a thing] **1** [late 19C+] anything for which one cannot recall the proper name. **2** [late 19C+] a euph. for the penis. **3** [1930s–50s] (*US drugs*) an improvised hypodermic syringe, made from an eye-dropper and a pin. **4** [1950s–70s] a dildo.

dingus *adj.* [1960s] (*S.Afr.*) excited, angry.

dingwallace *n.* [ety. unknown; ext. of DINGUS *n.* (2) but ? *wallace*] [1920s] (*US*) the penis.

ding-whanged *adj. see* DINGED *adj.*

dingy *n.*[1] [DING *v.*[1] (1); note *HDAS*, using same citation, has alternative sense 'a beggar', based on ety. DING *n.*[2] (1)] **1** [1950s] (*US*) one who has been beaten up. **2** *see* DINGY *adj.*[2].

dingy *n.*[2] *see* DINGE *n.* (2).

dingy *adj.*[1] [SE *dingy* + DINGE *n.* (2)] [19C+] (*US*) pertaining to the black community, or a black person.

dingy *adj.*[2] [DING *n.*[2] (3)] [1910s+] (*US*) silly, foolish, crazy; thus as n., a mad person.

dingy *adj.*[3] [DING *v.*[2] (2)] [1960s] (*US black*) very mean; impoverished, penniless.

dingy! *excl. see* DING! *excl.*

dingy Christian *n. see* DINGEY CHRISTIAN *n.*

dining room *n.* [early 19C] the mouth.

IN COMPOUNDS

❑ **dining room chairs** *n.* [early 19C] the teeth. ❑ **dining room furniture** *n.* [1930s] the teeth.

SE in slang uses

IN COMPOUNDS

❑ **dining room jump** *n.* [late 18C–early 19C] (*UK Und.*) a species of robbery whereby one man poses as a lamplighter, leaning his ladder against the house that is to be robbed. The thief mounts it and makes an entry at a first-floor window. If the police appear and the 'lamplighter' runs, his partner has no means of leaving the house other than to jump. ❑ **dining room post** *n.* [late 18C–early 19C] (*UK Und.*) a method of robbery in which the villain poses as a postman, sends up a sham letter to a resident of a lodging house and, while waiting for the postage to be brought down, robs the first open and empty room they encounter.

dink *n.*[1] [? DINGE *n.* (2)] [late 19C–1940s] (*US*) a black American.

dink *n.*[2] (*also* **dinkle**) [? SE *dinky*, small] **1** [late 19C+] (*US*) the penis, esp. of a small boy or, if small, of an adult. **2** [1900s] (*US*) a flashy dresser. **3** [1920s+] any small person. **4** [1930s+] (*also* **rinky dink**) a derog. term for an Asian person. **5** [1960s+] a derog. term for a Vietnamese. **6** [1960s+] (*also* **dinkweed**) a fool, a laughable or obnoxious figure. **7** [1980s] the Vietnamese language.

dink *n.*[3] [1900s] (*US campus*) failure to pass an examination.

IN PHRASES

❑ **on the dink** [? var. of *ON THE BLINK under* BLINK *n.*[1]] [1900s–10s] in trouble, facing problems.

dink *n.*[4] [? DINKY *adj.*[1]] [1910s] (*US campus*) a small skullcap worn by freshmen.

dink *n.*[5] [ety. unknown] [1930s+] (*Aus.*) a lift on the crossbar of a bicycle.

dink *n.*[6] (*also* **dinky**) [1980s+] *d*ual *i*ncome *n*o *k*ids (yet), a social acronym created to describe the ideal couple of the booming 1980s.

dink *n.*[7] *see* DINKUM OIL *n.*

dink *adj.*[1] [abbr. DINKUM *adj.*] [1900s–30s] (*Aus.*) honest, genuine, trustworthy.

dink *adj.*[2] [DINK *n.*[2] (4)] [1970s] (*US*) pertaining to an Asian person.

dink *adj.*[3] *see* DINKY *adj.*[1] (2).

dink *v.* (*also* **double-dink**) [DINK *n.*[5]] [1940s+] (*Aus. juv.*) to give someone a lift on the crossbar of your bicycle.

dinker *n.* [DINKY *adj.*[1]] [2000s] (*US*) something small, esp. when neat, trim or dainty.

dinker *adj.* [DINKUM *adj.*] [1920s+] (*Aus.*) honest, genuine, trustworthy.

dinker *v.* [? SE *dicker*] [late 19C] (*US*) to cheat, to swindle.

dinkey! *excl.*

IN EXCLAMATIONS

❑ **by dinkey!** *see BY DING! under* DING! *excl.*

dinkie *adj. see* DINKY *adj.*[2].

dinkie dow *n.* [play on US milit. pidgin *dinky dau*, crazy (orig. Viet. *dien cai dau*, he is mad); imported by US troops in Vietnam (1964–75)] [1960s+] (*drugs*) marijuana.

dinkle *n. see* DINK *n.*[2].

Dinktown *n.* [DINK *n.*[1]] [1920s] (*US*) a derog. term for the black section of a town or city.

dinkum *n.* [dial. *dinkum*, a fair share of work] **1** [late 19C+] (*Aus.*) work, esp. hard work, a due share of work. **2** [1910s] an Australian, spec. an Australian soldier in WW1. **3** [1910s+] the truth.

dinkum *adj.* [DINKUM *n.* (3)] [20C+] (*Aus.*) honest, genuine; esp. as FAIR DINKUM *adj.*; thus *dinkumest*.

dinkum *adv.* [DINKUM *adj.*] [1910s+] (*Aus.*) honestly, genuinely; thus *dinkum?* really? is that so?

dinkum! *excl. see* FAIR DINKUM! *excl.*

dinkum oil *n.* (*also* **dink**) [DINKUM *adj.* + OIL *n.* (2c)] [1910s+] (*Aus.*) the honest truth, true facts.

dinkus *n.*[1] [DINGUS *n.*] [1920s] (*US*) a small child.

dinkus *n.*[2] *see* DOODINKUS *n.*

dinkweed *n. see* DINK *n.*[2] (6).

dinky *n.*[1] [1920s] **1** (*US black*) a second-rate, inferior person; used as insult. **2** (*US*) a black person, usu. derog.

dinky *n.*[2] [abbr. DINKUM *n.*] [1940s] (*Aus.*) the truth.

dinky *n.*[3] [deliberate understatement + ref. to *Dinky Toys*, defunct brand of toy cars] [1980s] (*UK society*) a large car.

dinky *n.*[4] [DINK *n.*[2] (1) or DINGUS *n.* (2)] [1970s+] the penis.

IN PHRASES

❑ **diddle the dinky** *v.* [DIDDLE *v.*[1] (3)] [1980s+] to masturbate.

dinky *n.*[5] *see* DINK *n.*[6].

dinky *adj.*[1] [Scot. *dink*, smartly dressed, neat and trim; note 1920s US journ. jargon *dinky*, a 300-word, i.e. small, piece] **1** [mid-19C] (*UK Und.*) alert, sharp-sighted. **2** [late 19C+] (*also* **dink**) neat, trim, dainty. **3** [late 19C+] tiny, trifling. **4** [1920s] attractive.

dinky *adj.*[2] (*also* **dinkie**) [RINKY-DINK *adj.*[2] (1)] [1910s+] (*US*) second-rate, poor-quality.

dinky-di *adj.* (*also* **dinky, dinky-dao, dinky-die, dinky-dy**) [DINKY *adj.*[1] (2) + SE *di*(*amond*)] **1** [20C+] (*Aus./N.Z.*) excellent, first-rate, the best of its type; also ext. to *dinky-di-do*. **2** [1950s+] true, honest, genuine.

dinky-di *adv.* (*also* **dinky-die**) [DINKY-DI *adj.* (1)] [1910s+] (*Aus./N.Z.*) truly, certainly.

dinky-dink *n.*

IN PHRASES

❑ **give someone the dinky-dink** *v.* [late 19C] to reject; to dismiss.

dinky dirt *n.* [rhy. sl.; var. on DICKY (DIRT) *n.*] [1930s+] (*Aus./US*) a shirt.

dinky-doo *n.* [1910s+] (*bingo*) the number 22.

dinky-dy *adj. see* DINKY-DI *adj.*

dinky dyke *n.* [DINKY *adj.*[1] (3) + DYKE *n.* (1)] [1980s+] (*US gay*) a feminine or boyish lesbian.

dinky one's slinky *v.* [assonance, but note DINK *n.*[2] (1)] [1960s+] to masturbate.

dinner *n.* [abbr. *CHICKEN DINNER under* CHICKEN *n.*; + she is 'good enough to eat'] [1940s–60s] (*US black*) an attractive young woman.

SE in slang uses

IN COMPOUNDS

❑ **dinner buckets** *n.* (*also* **dinners**) [their role as milk carriers] [20C+] (*US*) the female breasts. ❑ **dinner masher** *n.* [MASHER *n.*] [1980s+] a male homosexual. ❑ **dinner pailer** *n.* [SE *dinner pail*; lit. one who carries a dinner pail] [1940s–50s] (*US*) a regular working man or woman; also as v. *dinner-pail*, to work at a regular job. ❑ **dinner-set** *n.* [late 19C] the teeth.

IN PHRASES

❑ **be dinner for tea** *v.* [late 19C+] to be very easy and pleasant. ❑ **dive for a dinner** *v. see* DIVE *v.* ❑ **have had more — than one has had hot dinners** *v.* [1930s+] a general phr. used to imply the expertise of the named person in a certain area of life, esp. of sexual experience.

dinny *n.* [abbr.] [1900s] (*US Und.*) dynamite.

dinnyhazer *n.* (*also* **dennyaiser**) [*DSUE* suggests the Aus. boxer *Dinny Hayes*, but note that *AND* and *DNZE* claim 'of unknown origin'] [20C+] (*Aus.*) **1** a knockout blow. **2** a strenuous attempt. **3** something large, outstanding, exceptional (depending on context).

dino *n.*[1] **1** [1910s] (*US*) (*also* **dyno**) a tramp, a layabout, esp. an old one [DINGBAT *n.*[7] (3)]. **2** [1910s–40s] (*US*) an Italian or Hispanic labourer [the 'typical' Mediterranean name, *Dino*].

IN COMPOUNDS

❑ **dyno (rouster)** *n.* [1920s–30s] (*US tramp*) one who robs drunks.

dino *n.*[2] (*also* **dina, dine, dyno**) [abbr. SE *dynamite*] [1920s–30s] (*US*) a worker who handles dynamite.

dinosaur *n.* [male bravado + supposed resemblance to a dinosaur's neck] [1980s+] (*US black*) the penis.

dintch *n. see* DINCH *n.*

d.i.o. *phr.* [abbr.; the phr. satirizes the various forms of polite initials left on visiting cards] [late 18C–mid-19C] *damn! I'm off.*

Dip, the *n.* **1** [late 18C–early 19C] a cookshop under Furnival's Inn, London, popular among legal clerks. **2** [20C+] (*UK gay*) a stretch of Piccadilly adjoining Green Park, where gay prostitutes solicit wealthy clients.

dip *n.*[1] **1** [late 18C–mid-19C] a dip-candle or tallow-chandler. **2** foods that are dipped or have something dipped into them. (**a**) [mid-19C] (*Aus.*) a boiled flour dumpling. (**b**) [20C+] (*Ulster*) fried bread. (**c**) [20C+] (*Ulster*) hot gravy or an egg to dip in. **3** [mid-19C+] (*Und.*) a pickpocket. **4** [mid-19C+] (*Und.*) an act of pickpocketing. **5** [late 19C] (*US Und.*) a burglary. **6** [1900s–40s] (*US*) a hat.

DERIVATIVES

❑ **dipology** *n.* [mid-19C] (*UK Und.*) a faux-academic term for the world of pickpocketing.

IN COMPOUNDS

❑ **dip lay** *n.* [LAY *n.*[3] (1)] [mid-19C] (*UK Und.*) pickpocketing.

IN PHRASES

❑ **on the dip** [mid-19C+] (*UK Und.*) working as a pickpocket; resulting from pickpocketing.

SE in slang uses

IN PHRASES

❑ **dig the dip on the two and four** *v. see under* DIG *v.*[3]. ❑ **off one's dip** *adj.* (*also* **off one's dipper**) [SE *dip*, a sauce] [late 19C–1920s] mad, eccentric.

dip *n.*[2] [ext. use of SE *dip*, to plunge in] **1** [19C+] (*US*) a blow, a hit. **2** [1940s+] a bout of quick sexual intercourse. **3** [1970s] (*US prison*) one who participates in anal intercourse.

dip *n.*[3] [? the sideshow game, *lucky dip*] [late 19C] a wager.

dip *n.*[4] [abbr.] **1** [late 19C] (*US campus*) a *dip*loma. **2** [1930s] (*Aus./UK/US*) *dip*htheria. **3** [1940s+] a member of the *Dip*lomatic Service.

dip *n.*[5] **1** [late 19C+] (*orig. Aus.*) a fool. **2** [1960s+] (*US campus*) (*also* **dippo**) a bore, a dullard; something tedious.

IN COMPOUNDS

❑ **diphead** *n.* [-HEAD *sfx* (1)] [1970s+] a fool, an unpleasant person. ❑ **dipshit** *see* separate entries. ❑ **dipwad** *n.* [-WAD *sfx*] [1970s+] (*US*) a general term of abuse.

dip *n.*[6] [SE *dip*(*somaniac*)] [1910s–60s] (*US*) a drunkard.

dip *n.*[7] [SE *dip*, a pinch of snuff] (*drugs*) **1** [1940s+] a drug addict; a drug user. **2** [1950s] a dose or portion of a drug. **3** [1980s+] crack cocaine. **4** [2000s] a cigarette dipped into SHERM *n.*, i.e. formaldehyde.

dip *n.*[8] [the *Beale Street Dip*, a popular jazz dance of early 20C] [1960s] (*US black*) a party, a get-together, esp. of those in their teens or twenties.

dip *adj.* [ety. unknown] [1990s+] (*US black*) stylish, fashionable.

dip *v.*[1] [SE *dip*, to mortgage] [late 17C–19C] to pawn, to mortgage; thus *dipped*, in debt, mortgaged; *dip one's rigging*, to pawn one's clothes.

dip *v.*[2] **1** [early 19C+] (*also* **dip on**) to pick a pocket. **2** [late 19C+] to rob a till. **3** [1940s+] to steal, to take away, e.g. a prostitute's clients.

IN PHRASES

❑ **dip into** *v.* **1** [early 19C] to pick a pocket. **2** [mid-19C] (*US*) to attack physically. **3** [1950s–70s] to have sexual intercourse.

SE in slang uses

IN COMPOUNDS

❑ **dip-around** *n.* [1960s–70s] (*Aus.*) an act of urination. ❑ **dip-dunk** *n.* [1990s+] (*US*) an insignificant or dull person. ❑ **dipstick** *see* separate entries.

IN PHRASES

❑ **dip in the fudgepot** *v.* [FUDGEPOT *under* FUDGE *n.*] [1970s+] (*US gay*) to have anal intercourse. ❑ **dip it** *v.* [abbr. DIP ONE'S WICK *under* WICK *n.*[1]] [20C+] to have sexual intercourse. ❑ **dip one's beak/nose** *v. see under* BEAK *n.*[2]. ❑ **dip one's bill** *v.* (*also* **dip the bill**) **1** [late 17C–mid-18C] to be mildly tipsy, to be nearly drunk. **2** [1930s–60s] to take a drink. ❑ **dip one's lid** *v. see under* LID *n.* ❑ **dip one's mouth/nose in someone's business** *v.* [var. on SE *poke one's nose in*] [20C+] (*W.I.*) to interfere where one's interest is not required. ❑ **dip one's wick** *v. see under* WICK *n.*[1]. ❑ **dip south** *v. see under* SOUTH *adv.* ❑ **dip the bill** *v. see* DIP ONE'S BILL above. ❑ **dip the dagger** *v. see under* DAGGER *n.*[1]. ❑ **dip the fly** *v.* [the 'dipping' or lowering of the trouser fly before intercourse] [1980s+] (*US black*) of a man, to have sexual intercourse. ❑ **dip the schnitzel** *v. see under* SCHNITZEL *n.* ❑ **dip the weenie** *v. see under* WEENIE *n.*[1].

IN EXCLAMATIONS

❑ **dip your eye!** [1950s] (*Aus.*) a dismissive retort.

dip *v.*[3] [20C+] (*Irish*) to work.

dip *v.*[4] [ety. unknown] **1** [1910s–60s] (*Aus.*) to go. **2** [1990s+] (*US black teen*) to leave.

IN PHRASES

❑ **dip out** *v.* [1990s+] (*US teen*) to leave. ❑ **dip out on** *v.* [1950s+] (*Aus.*) **1** to fail, to miss an opportunity. **2** to refuse to join in.

dip *v.*[5] [1940s–70s] (*Aus. Und.*) to fail in an endeavour, e.g. an act of shoplifting.

dip *v.*[6] [SE *dip in* or DIP ONE'S MOUTH/NOSE IN SOMEONE'S BUSINESS *under* DIP *v.*[2]] [1970s+] to eavesdrop, to butt into another's conversation, to pay more attention to other people's business than to one's own.

dip *v.*[7] [1980s] (*US drugs*) to mix together cocaine and heroin.

dip and chuck it *n.* (*also* **dip and duck it**) [rhy. sl.] [20C+] (*Aus.*) a bucket.

dipe-ducat *n.* [DUCAT *n.* (3)] [1920s] (*US*) a subway ticket.

dipped *adj.*[1] [? DIPPY *adj.* (1)] **1** [late 19C–1910s] (*Aus.*) mad. **2** [1950s–70s] (*US drugs*) addicted to narcotics.

dipped *adj.*[2] [2000s] (*US black*) smart, well-dressed.

dipped in the Shannon *adj.* [those who are dipped in the Irish River Shannon are supposedly rendered free of any self-effacement] [late 18C–early 19C] shameless, devoid of shyness.

dipper *n.*[1] (*also* **dipping denomination**) [SE *dip*, to plunge into water, thus the practice of baptism by total immersion; note Nares: 'ADOPER or DOPPER. An anabaptist; that is, a dipper'] [mid-17C+] a Baptist; an Anabaptist.

SE in slang uses

IN PHRASES

❑ **get one's dipper wet** *v.* [1980s+] (*US*) of a man, to have sexual intercourse.

dipper *n.*[2] [DIP *v.*[2] (1)] [late 19C+] a pickpocket.

dipper *n.*[3] [1940s] (*US black*) a barman.

dipper *n.*^{4} [? the dipping of the YEN HOCK *under* YEN *n.*^{1} into the bowl of the pipe prior to lighting the opium] [1940s–50s] (*US drugs*) an opium pipe.

dipper *n.*^{5} [DIP *n.*^{7}] [1980s+] (*drugs*) a marijuana cigarette mixed with phencyclidine.

dipper *n.*^{6}

(IN PHRASES)

□ **off one's dipper** *adj. see* OFF ONE'S DIP *under* DIP *n.*^{1}.

dippiness *n.* [DIPPY *adj.* (1)] [1960s] eccentricity, craziness.

dipping *n.* [DIP *v.*^{2} (1) + sfx *-ing*] [mid-19C+] the world and practice of pickpocketing; thus *dipping-bloke*, a pickpocket; *dipping gag*, pickpocketing.

dipping denomination *n. see* DIPPER *n.*^{1}.

dipping duke *n.* [DIP *v.*^{2} (1) + DUKE *n.*^{3} (1)] [mid-19C] (*UK Und.*) the hand with which a pickpocket works.

dipping in the bush *n. see* BUSH *n.*^{1}.

dippo *n.* **1** *see* DIP *n.*^{5} (2). **2** *see* DIPSO *n.*

dippy *n.* **1** [1930s] a nickname for a stupid person. **2** [1990s+] (*W.I.*) a deportee from the UK.

dippy *adj.* (*also* **dappy, dippit**) [? the image of a head that is 'not screwed on' and thus moves up and down like a bird dipping its beak] **1** [late 19C+] crazy, eccentric, mildly insane; thus *dippy about*, *dippy over*, obsessed with, usu. a person with whom one is in love; *dippy department*, the psychiatric ward. **2** [1970s] (*US campus*) unexciting. **3** [1980s+] mildly drunk.

dips *n.* [the grocer dipped into various sacks or boxes of goods to measure out a customer's wants] [19C] a grocer.

dipshit *n.* **1** [1960s+] (*orig. US*) a fool [DIP *n.*^{5} (1)]. **2** [1960s+] (*orig. US*) a form of derog. address [DIP *n.*^{5} (1)]. **3** [1990s+] (*Aus.*) a male homosexual [SE *dip* + SHIT *n.* (1a)].

dipshit *adj.* [DIPSHIT *n.* (1)] [1960s+] (*orig. US*) **1** stupid. **2** second-rate, inferior; thus *dipshitting*, horrible, vile.

dipso *n.* (*also* **dippo**) [abbr. SE *dipsomaniac*] [late 19C+] an alcoholic; also attrib.

dipstick *n.* [play on SE; widely popularized by the BBC TV series *Only Fools and Horses* (from 1981), whose star, David Jason, refused to use obscenities, but *dipstick* fits neatly in the range of words that mean both penis and fool, e.g. DICKHEAD *n.*, DORK *n.*; also popularized by the character 'Boss Hogg' in US TV show *The Dukes of Hazzard*] [1960s+] **1** the penis. **2** (*orig. US*) a fool, an incompetent.

dipstick *adj.* [DIPSTICK *n.* (2)] [1980s+] (*US*) stupid.

dipsy *n.*^{1} [? abbr. SE *dipsomaniac*, i.e. a drunkard will receive a relatively short sentence] [1920s–50s] (*US tramp*) a sentence to time in the workhouse.

dipsy *n.*^{2} [? DIPSO *n.* / DIPSTICK *n.* (2)] [1990s+] (*US*) a mentally retarded person.

dipsy *adj.*^{1} [SE *dipsomaniac*] [1970s] (*US*) drunk.

dipsy *adj.*^{2} [DIPPY *adj.* (1) / DIPSY *n.*^{2}] [1980s] (*US*) eccentric.

dipsy-doo *n.* [? euph.] [1980s] (*US*) the anus.

dipsy-doodle *n.* (*also* **dipsy-do**) [baseball jargon *dipsy-do*, a deceptive sinking curveball, associated with pitcher Carl Hubbell; ult. SE *dip*] [1940s] (*US*) trickery, scheming.

dipsy-doodle *v.* [DIPSY-DOODLE *n.*] (*US*) **1** [1940s–50s] to trick, to plot. **2** [1970s–80s] to wander along.

dirk *n.*^{1} [proper name] [late 18C+] the penis.

dirk *n.*^{2} [var. on JERK *n.*^{1} (2)] [1960s+] a fool, an idiot, a failure.

dirt *n.* **1** [mid-17C; 19C+] money. **2** [late 19C+] (*Aus./N.Z.*) a mean action or a malicious remark. **3** [late 19C+] (*orig. US*) information, not necessarily, but often, scurrilous; often as [1930s+] *what's the dirt (on)...?* **4** [20C+] (*orig. US*) an unpleasant individual. **5** [1920s–60s] (*US*) a male or female prostitute who steals from clients. **6** [1920s+] (*orig. US*) gossip, malicious chatter. **7** [1920s+] (*US gay*) one who professes homosexuality in order to practise blackmail. **8** [1930s–40s] (*US prison*) sugar. **9** [1940s–70s] (*US gay*) a homophobic thug. **10** in drug uses. (**a**) [1970s+] (*US drugs*) (*also* **dirt grass**) marijuana, usu. very poor quality. (**b**) [1970s+] heroin. **11** [1990s+] (*US*) an alienated drug-taking youth, sometimes one who enjoys 'Goth' music and the associated lifestyle.

(IN COMPOUNDS)

□ **dirt devil** *n.* [1980s+] (*US drugs*) an individual who has low quality marijuana. □ **dirt farm** *n.* [pun on SE] [1970s+] (*US black*) any centre for (malicious) gossip.

(IN PHRASES)

□ **blow some dirt** *v.* [1970s+] (*US gay*) to gossip maliciously. □ **deal (in) dirt** *v.* (*also* **do dirt**) [1970s+] (*US black*) to gossip, to malign. □ **dish (out) the dirt** *v.* (*also* **dish the dope/joint**) [1920s+] to gossip maliciously, to slander; thus *dirt disher*, a gossip. □ **do dirt to someone** *v.* (*also* **do dirt by someone, do someone dirt**) **1** [late 19C+] to harm, to injure deliberately, often verbally; also ext. to a place. **2** [late 19C+] to act in a deliberately immoral or unethical manner. **3** [1970s+] (*US gay*) to pass on gossip. □ **do the dirt** *v. see* DO THE DIRTIES *under* DIRTY *n.* □ **sling the dirt (at)** *v.* (*also* **sling (the) shit**) [SLING *v.* (2a)] [1930s] (*Aus./N.Z.*) to malign, to slander. □ **throw some dirt on** *v.* [1970s+] (*US black*) to malign, to slander.

SE in slang uses

(IN COMPOUNDS)

□ **dirtbag** *see* separate entries. □ **dirtball** *see* separate entries. □ **dirtbird** *n.* [? dial. *dirt bird*, the skua but prob. SE *dirt* + BIRD *n.*^{1} (3a)] [1940s+] (*Irish*) a general term of abuse. □ **dirt-box** *n.* [BOX *n.*^{1} (1d)] [20C+] the anus. □ **dirt chute** *n.* **1** [1940s+] (*US*) the anus. **2** [2000s] an insult. □ **dirt-dobber** *n.* (*also* **dirt-scratcher**) [SE *dob*, to dab, to pat/*scratcher*, also US, a kind of wasp] [1940s–60s] **1** (*US, South/West*) a poor farmer. **2** (*US, South/West*) a worthless person. **3** (*US campus*) a sandal. □ **dirt-eater** *n.* [CLAY-EATER *under* CLAY *n.*] [mid-19C–1950s] (*US*) a poor white; thus derog. adj. *dirt-eating*. □ **dirthead** *n. see* DIRTBAG *n.* □ **dirtnap** *see* separate entries. □ **dirt road** *n. see* separate entry. □ **dirt surfer** *n.* [SE *surfer* used as explorer, e.g. *Net surfer*] [1980s+] (*US*) one who has abandoned most if not all the normal standards of hygiene and cleanliness. □ **dirt tamper** *n.* [SE *tamp*, to ram down hard] [1940s–70s] a male homosexual, a sodomite. □ **dirt track** *n. see* separate entry.

(IN PHRASES)

□ **hit the dirt** *v.* (*also* **dig the dirt**) **1** [20C+] (*US*) to throw oneself to the ground. **2** [1930s+] to run away, to leave quickly.

dirt *adv.* [1910s] (*Aus.*) a general intensifier, e.g. *dirt mean*.

dirtbag *n.* (*also* **dirthead**) [SE *dirt* + -BAG *sfx*] **1** [1940s+] (*orig. US*) a general term of abuse, irrespective of sex. **2** [1990s+] a promiscuous woman.

dirtbag *adj.* [DIRTBAG *n.*] [1980s+] repellent, disgusting, despicable.

dirtball *n.* (*also* **dirtbomb, dirt merchant**) [SE *dirt* + -BALL *sfx*] [1970s+] (*US*) a dirty or generally unpleasant person; a promiscuous young woman.

dirtball *adj.* [DIRTBALL *n.*] [1990s+] (*US*) unpleasant, disgusting.

dirt, grime and dust *n.* [rhy. sl.] [20C+] (*Aus.*) a crust (on a pie).

dirt nap *n.* [1980s+] (*US black*) death.

(IN PHRASES)

□ **take a dirt nap** *v.* [1980s+] (*US black*) **1** to be buried. **2** to die. **3** to be knocked out.

dirt-nap *v.* [DIRT NAP *n.*] [1990s+] (*US black*) to be dead.

dirt road *n.* (*also* **dirt run, old dirt road**) [1910s+] the anus.

(IN PHRASES)

□ **go up the old dirt road** *v.* (*also* **go down the dirt road, ...up the dirt route**) [fig. use of colloq. *dirt road*, the highway] [1930s+] to perform anal intercourse. □ **take it up the dirt road** *v.* [1950s+] to be sodomized.

dirt track *n.* [1960s+] the anus; thus *dirt track rider/specialist*, a sodomite.

(IN PHRASES)

□ **when the road runs red, hit the dirt track** [SE *road*/ROAD *n.* (1b)] [1990s+] when a woman is menstruating, opt for anal intercourse.

dirty *n.*

SE in slang uses

IN PHRASES

❑ **do one's dirty** *v.* [1970s] (*US*) to defecate. ❑ **do someone the dirty** *v.* (*also* **do the dirty on someone**) [1910s+] to cheat, to betray, to inform against, to treat harshly. ❑ **do the dirties** *v.* (*also* **do the dirt, do the dirty, do the dirty deed, do the dirty thing**) [note synon. Shakespearian *do the deed of darkness*] [1960s+] (*orig. US teen/campus*) to have sexual intercourse; *Current Slang* (1970) suggests 'applies only to girls'. ❑ **do the dirty** *v.* **1** [1990s+] (*US*) to commit a crime; to murder. **2** [2000s] to vomit. ❑ **ring a dirty** *v.* [1940s] (*S.Afr. prison*) to make a false charge.

dirty *adj.* **1** [early 19C+] corrupt; morally unsound. **2** [late 19C–1960s] having money, funds. **3** [20C+] (*usu. US black*) good, wonderful, excellent (on bad = good model). **4** [20C+] (*UK/US Und.*) dubious, unsafe, to be avoided. **5** [1900s–20s] (*US*) in possession of a large quantity. **6** [1910s+] of money, acquired through crime. **7** [1920s+] holding incriminating evidence. **8** [1960s+] (*drugs*) currently addicted to drugs. **9** [1960s+] (*drugs*) in possession of drugs. **10** [1970s+] (*US Und.*) in possession of or carrying a weapon. **11** [1970s+] (*N.Z. prison*) angry, embittered. **12** [1990s+] (*US prison*) showing evidence of recent drug use in a urine test. **13** [1990s+] (*US campus*) unattractive.

IN PHRASES

❑ **give the dirty sign** *v.* [sense 4 above] [1940s] (*US Und.*) to warn.

SE in slang uses

IN COMPOUNDS

❑ **dirty acres** *n.* [late 17C–mid-19C] a landed estate. ❑ **dirty-arsed** *adj.* [-ARSED *sfx*] [1990s+] a general pej. ❑ **dirty barrel** *n.* [1960s–70s] (*US*) the male or female genitals when suffering a venereal disease. ❑ **dirty beau** *n. see under* BEAU *n.*[1]. ❑ **dirty bird** *n. see* separate entries. ❑ **dirty bundle** *n.* (*also* **old bundle**) [1940s+] (*W.I.*) an untidy person. ❑ **dirty digger** *n. see* DIGGER *n.*[2] (3). ❑ **dirty dog** *n.* [DOG *n.*[2] (1b)/DOG *n.*[2] (1d)] **1** [mid-19C+] a generally unpleasant person, often with overtones of womanizing. **2** [1940s–50s] (*US black*) a man who habitually mistreats women. ❑ **dirty dowager** *n.* [SE *dowager*, orig. the widow of a dead king, i.e. a QUEEN *n.* (2a)] [1940s–70s] (*gay*) an unkempt, ill-preserved, older, gay man. ❑ **dirty dozens** *n. see* DOZENS *n.* ❑ **dirtyfoot** *n.* [? ext. of *DIRTY LEG* below] [2000s] (*US black*) a fellatrix. ❑ **dirty gertie** *n.* [redup. Note that *Gertie* is a 'typically' vulgar name] **1** [1920s–40s] (*US*) a promiscuous or sexually enthusiastic woman. **2** [2000s] (*bingo*) the number 30. ❑ **dirty laundry** *n.* (*also* **dirty linen, ...washing**) [20C+] unpleasant, embarrassing or revelatory information; thus *air one's dirty laundry in public*. ❑ **dirty left/right** *n.* [1900s–10s] (*Aus.*) a powerful fist, of the left or right hand. ❑ **dirty leg** *n.* [LEG *n.* (8a)] [1960s+] (*US*) **1** a promiscuous woman. **2** sexual intercourse. ❑ **dirty-livered** *adj.* [1950s] (*Aus.*) a general term of abuse: grumpy, objectionable; thus *in a dirty liver*, in a bad mood. ❑ **dirty name** *v.* [1920s] (*US*) to abuse, to slander. ❑ **dirty neck** *n.* [coined by US troops in WW1 to describe French women] [1910s–60s] (*US*) a promiscuous woman; a general term of abuse. ❑ **dirty old man** *n. see* separate entry. ❑ **dirty pool** *n.* [1940s+] (*orig. US*) unfair, duplicitous activity; thus *play dirty pool*, to behave in an underhand manner. ❑ **dirty right** *n. see* *DIRTY LEFT/RIGHT* above. ❑ **dirty sanchez** *n.* [1980s+] (*US black*) the act of sticking one's finger up someone's anus and then wiping their top lip with one's finger, to give them a dirty moustache; usu. by a man to a woman. ❑ **dirty shirt** *n. see* separate entries. ❑ **dirty spoon** *n. see* GREASY SPOON *n.*[1]. ❑ **dirty towel** *n.* [1960s] (*US prison*) the prison barber shop. ❑ **dirty washing** *n. see* *DIRTY LAUNDRY* above.

IN PHRASES

❑ **dirty end (of the stick)** *n. see* *SHORT END (OF THE STICK)* under STICK *n.* ❑ **the dirty half-mile** *n.* [both areas are/were known for roughness, decadence and excess] (*Aus.*) **1** [1920s+] Kings Cross Road, Sydney. **2** [1930s+] William Street, Sydney. ❑ **dirty night at sea** *n. see under* SEA *n.* ❑ **dirty (on)** *adj.* [1960s+] (*Aus.*) resentful (of).

IN EXCLAMATIONS

❑ **I'll be a dirty word!** (*also* **I'll be a dirty name!**) [lit. + fig. use of SE *dirty word*] [20C+] a mild oath.

dirty *adv.* **1** [mid-19C+] a general intensifier, extremely, very, exceedingly; esp. in *dirty big, dirty great*. **2** [1980s+] (*US*) illegally, in a criminal manner.

SE in slang uses

IN PHRASES

❑ **play dirty** *v. see under* PLAY *v.*

dirty a plate (with) *v. see under* PLATE *n.*[1].

dirty bird *n.*[1] [the black bird on its label] [1940s–50s] (*US black*) Old Crow whisky.

dirty bird *n.*[2] [coined by comedian George Gobel on his 1954 TV show] [1950s–70s] an unappealing individual.

IN EXCLAMATIONS

❑ **I'll be a dirty bird!** [1950s+] (*US*) a mild excl.

dirty-bop *v. see* DIDDY-BOP *v.*

dirty daughter *n.* [rhy. sl. Note lyrics of the once-popular song 'Wash me in the water/In which you wash your dirty daughter'] [20C+] water.

dirty dish *n.* [rhy. sl.] [20C+] (*Aus.*) fish.

dirty drawers *n.* [rhy. sl.] [1980s+] (*UK bingo*) the number 44.

dirty face *n.* [rhy. sl.] [1990s+] a shoelace.

dirty old Jew *n.* [rhy. sl.] [1910s+] (*bingo*) the number two.

dirty old man *n.* [1930s+] an older man whose sexual tastes (whether or not fulfilled) err towards much younger lovers, esp. when under the legal age of consent.

dirty 'ore *n. see* DIRTY WHORE *n.*

dirty shirt *n.*[1] [a *bulla cake* is a flat cake, sometimes with a central hole, made of flour and brown sugar and cooked by country people and the urban poor (wearers of SE *dirty shirts*); also known as a *cartman's hymn-book*] [1940s+] (*W.I.*) a bulla cake.

dirty shirt *n.*[2] [1960s] (*US Und.*) an incompetent lawyer who is given clients by court or jail officials; he has no substantial legal knowledge, charges minimal fees, and usu. loses.

dirty whore *n.* (*also* **dirty 'ore**) [rhy. sl.] [1910s+] (*bingo*) the number 34.

dis *n.* (*also* **diss**) [abbr.] **1** [1920s; 1980s+] an act of *dis*paragement or of *dis*respect [the earlier UK use seems to have faded before its resurrection by US blacks in the 1980s]. **2** [1980s] a *dis*appointment.

dis *adj.* [orig. naut. use; ult. telegraphist's jargon *dis*, disconnected] [1920s+] eccentric, mentally unstable.

dis *v.* (*also* **diss**) [1980s+] (*orig. US black/campus*) **1** to disrespect. **2** to disparage, to attack verbally. **3** to denigrate someone in public to the extent that it makes that person feel bad. **4** to deliberately break an appointment or date without consulting the second party. **5** to inform on.

IN PHRASES

❑ **dis di program** *v.* [sense 1 above + abbr. SE *dis*(*rupt*) + SAmE *program* (UK *programme*)] [1980s+] (*W.I./UK black teen*) to put a planned thing on hold, to delay something, to disrupt a schedule.

disabilly *n. see* DISHABILLY *n.*

disappearing act *n.*

IN PHRASES

❑ **do a/the disappearing act** *v.* [SE *disappear* + mock theatricality] [1910s+] (*orig. US*) to vanish suddenly. ❑ **pull a disappearing act** *v.* [1950s+] (*US*) of a spouse or lover, to run off without warning and without leaving any message.

disc *n.* [the shape] [1910s+] (*US*) a $1 coin.

discharge one's accounts *v. see* *CAST UP ONE'S ACCOUNTS* under CAST *v.*

disco *n.*

SE in slang uses

IN COMPOUNDS

❑ **disco biscuit** *n.* (*also* **disco burger**) [its shape and the environment in which it is often consumed] [1990s+] (*drugs*)

MDMA. ❑ **disco danny** *n.* [1980s] (*US*) a male fan and frequenter of nightclubs. ❑ **disco powder** *n.* [2000s] amphetamine sulphate.

disco *adj.* [the innate superficiality of a SE *disco*] [1980s] (*US*) applied to activities or people who are playing at being serious about something.

disco dancer *n.* [rhy. sl.] [1980s] (*Aus.*) cancer.

discombobberate *v.* [mid-19C+] (*US*) to discomfit, to perplex, to confuse.

discombobulate *v.* (*also* **discombobligate, discombooble, discumfuddle**) [a nonsense word, playing on SE *discomfit* and/or *discompose* + ? BOBBERY *n.*] [mid-19C+] to discomfit; also as n., *discombobulation*.

discombobulated *adj.* (*also* **discomboomerated**) [1950s+] unsettled, out of sorts.

discomboobelate *v.* [1940s–60s] (*US*) to discomfit.

discombooberate *v. see* DISCONBOOBERATE *v.*

discombooble *v. see* DISCOMBOBULATE *v.*

discomfoozled *adj. see* FOOZLED *adj.* (3).

disconbooberate *v.* (*also* **discombooberate, discomfolidate**) [mid-19C+] to discomfit.

discount *v.* [lit. use, i.e. *dis-* + *count*; SE *discount*, to make a deduction in estimating the worth of] [late 19C–1940s] (*US black*) to disparage, to hold in very low regard.

discouraged *adj.* [mid-19C] (*US*) a euph. for drunk.

discover one's gender *v.* [1940s+] (*gay*) to accept or acknowledge one's homosexuality.

discumfuddle *v. see* DISCOMBOBULATE *v.*

discuss *v.* [early 19C–1900s] to sample or enjoy one's food and drink; thus [mid-19C] *discussion*, the sampling of a commodity's quality.

dise *n.* [abbr. SE (*merchan*)*dise*] [1910s–20s] (*US*) goods, commodities.

disease of France *n. see* FRENCH DISEASE *under* FRENCH *adj.*

disguise *v.* [SE *disguise in liquor*] [mid-16C–early 19C] to intoxicate, to make drunk.

disguised *adj.* [DISGUISE *v.*] [early 17C–1900s] drunk.

dish *n.*[1] [SE *dish*, an item of food; *dish* was used in 16C–17C to mean a sexually attractive person, e.g. Shakespeare, *Antony & Cleopatra* (1607): 'A woman is a dish for the gods, if the devil dress her not'] **1** [17C] the female genitals. **2** [20C+] something one likes, something suited to one's taste. **3** [1930s+] (*orig. US*) an attractive woman. **4** [1930s+] an attractive person of either sex. **5** [1950s+] (*gay*) the buttocks.

SE in slang uses

IN COMPOUNDS

❑ **dish-down** *n.* [1920s] a disappointment. ❑ **dish-faced** *adj. see* PIE-FACED *adj.* ❑ **dishlicker** *n.* [1990s+] (*Aus.*) a dog. ❑ **dishrag** *n.* [1940s+] a person who is exploited, treated poorly. ❑ **dish-walloper** *n.* [1900s] (*Aus.*) a dishwasher in a restaurant. ❑ **dish-walloping** *n.* [late 19C] (*Aus.*) dish-washing. ❑ **dishwater blonde** *n.* [1950s] (*US*) a woman, or man, with ash-blonde hair. ❑ **dish-wrestler** *n.* [1920s–30s] a restaurant dish-washer.

IN PHRASES

❑ **dish of chat** *n.* [mid-19C] (*US*) a talk, a conversation. ❑ **dish of rails** *n.* [SE *rail*, an act of railing or reviling] [late 18C–early 19C] a scolding from a wife to her husband. ❑ **dish of red rag** *n.* [pun on SE *dish* + RED RAG *n.* (1), but note DISH *v.* (3)] [early 19C–1910s] verbal abuse.

dish *n.*[2] [DISH *v.* (1)/DISH *v.* (3)] **1** [late 19C] the act of abusing, cheating. **2** [1960s+] an embarrassing story about a subject's life.

IN PHRASES

❑ **know the dish** *v.* [1980s+] (*US black*) to be aware of the, usu. embarrassing, truth.

dish *v.* [the image of food, which having been 'done' is 'dished up'] **1** [late 18C+] to hurt, to stop another's plans, to frustrate, to cheat. **2** [mid-19C–1950s] to stop, to suppress, to do away with. **3** [20C+] (*orig. US gay*) to gossip maliciously, to tell tales. **4** [1940s+] to speak, to say. **5** [1960s+] (*US gay*) to hurt verbally.

IN COMPOUNDS

❑ **dish queen** *n.* [-QUEEN *sfx* (3)] [1950s+] a homosexual who enjoys slandering his peers.

IN PHRASES

❑ **dish one's gravy** *v.* [1920s] (*US*) to cause trouble for oneself. ❑ **dish (out) the dirt** *v. see under* DIRT *n.* ❑ **dish the dope/joint** *v. see* DISH (OUT) THE DIRT *under* DIRT *n.*

SE in slang uses

IN PHRASES

❑ **dish it** *v.* [1920s–30s] (*US*) to vomit. ❑ **dish it out** *v.* [20C+] (*orig. US*) to hand out, usu. punishment, blows, abuse etc. ❑ **dish (oneself) off** *v.* [late 18C] to go, to leave, esp. as a command. ❑ **dish out** *v. see* separate entry. ❑ **dish up** *v.* **1** [late 18C+] to beat, to defeat. **2** *see* DISH OUT *v.*

dishabells *n.* (*also* **dizybells**) [Fr. *déshabillé*, undressed] [20C+] (*Irish*) a state of undress.

dishabilly *n.* (*also* **disabilly**) [Fr. *déshabillé*, undressed] [18C+] a state of undress.

dishclout *n.* [metonyny; SE *dishclout*, a kitchen rag] [early 16C–early 19C] a dirty, greasy woman.

IN PHRASES

❑ **make a napkin out of a dischclout** *v.* [late 18C–early 19C] to marry a kitchen servant.

dished *adj.* [DISH *v.* (1); 'a correspondent suggests that meat is usually *done brown* [*see* DO BROWN *under* BROWN *adj.*[2]] before being *dished* and conceives that the latter term may have arisen as the natural sequence of the former' (Hotten, 1867)] **1** [late 18C+] (*also* **dished up**) ruined, beaten, silenced. **2** *see* DASHED *adj.*

IN EXCLAMATIONS

❑ **I'll be dished!** [late 19C] a euph. for *I'LL BE DAMNED! under* DAMNED *adj.*

dished out *adj.* [food imagery] [late 16C–mid-17C] dressed up (flashily).

dished up *adj.* [ext. of DISHED *adj.* (1)] **1** [1930s+] (*Aus.*) exhausted, tired out. **2** *see* DISHED *adj.* (1).

dish out *v.* (*also* **dish up**) [early 18C; mid-19C+] to give out, to apportion.

IN PHRASES

❑ **dish out the gravy/porridge** *v.* [puns + ironic use of GRAVY *n.* (2b)/ PORRIDGE *n.* (1)] [1940s–50s] of a judge, to hand out a heavy sentence.

dish ran away with the spoon *n.* [rhy. sl. = HOON *n.* (2)] [1970s+] (*Aus.*) a pimp.

dishy *adj.*[1] [DISH *n.*[1] (4); i.e. 'good enough to eat'] [1960s+] attractive, pretty.

dishy *adj.*[2] [DISH *v.* (3)] [1970s+] (*US gay*) verbally cruel, negative.

dishybilly *adj.* [Fr. *déshabillé*, undressed] [20C+] undressed, not fully dressed, dishevelled.

dismal ditty *n.* [SE *dismal*, dreary, cheerless + *ditty*] [late 17C–early 19C] a psalm recited on the gallows by a criminal who is about to die.

dismal jimmy *n.* (*also* **dismal jemmy**) [mid-19C–1940s] a miserable, gloomy person.

dismiss *v.* **1** [mid-19C] (*US*) to leave. **2** [1980s+] (*US campus*) to end a relationship.

Disneyland *n.* [note 1960s+ US milit. use *Disneyland East*, the Pentagon, the US Air Force Academy and similar headquarters] [20C+] (*US Und.*) a prison known for its liberal regime, or sarcastically, the opposite.

dispatcher *n.* (*also* **despatcher(s), despatches, dispatchers dispatches**) [late 18C–19C] a form of false dice, on which the pips are arranged in wrong numbers; a *high dispatcher* cannot throw less than two, while a *low dispatcher* cannot throw higher than three.

dispatches *n.* [late 18C–early 19C] (*also* **despatches**) a justice of the peace's warrant for the commitment of a criminal.

diss *see under* DIS.

dissolver *n.* [rhy. sl.] [1910s] (*Aus.*) a revolver.

distance *n.*

IN PHRASES

❑ **go the distance** *v.* [boxing/horseracing imagery] [1910s+] to commit oneself wholeheartedly.

distiller *n.* [abbr. WALKING DISTILLER *under* WALKING *adj.*] [late 19C] (*Aus.*) one who cannot take a joke.

distress *v.* [1980s] (*UK black*) of a gang, to carry out a robbery of a collection of people, as on the underground.

District, the *n.* [1940s–50s] (*US black/jazz*) the Storyville area of New Orleans, centre of the city's jazz community.

disturbance *n.* [its effects] [late 19C] (*US*) alcohol.

Ditch, the *n.*[1] [the *Mahratta Ditch*, built by the East India Company in 1742 to protect Calcutta from the Mahratta tribesmen, it ran for 8km (3 miles) but the work was never finished] **1** [late 19C] Calcutta; thus *ditcher*, an inhabitant of Calcutta. **2** [1980s] the Suez Canal. **3** [2000s] (*N.Z.*) the Tasman Sea, which divides New Zealand from Australia.

Ditch, the *n.*[2] [abbr.] [late 19C–1920s] **1** Shore*ditch*, East London; thus *Ditch and Chapel*, Shoreditch and Whitechapel. **2** Hounds*ditch*.

ditch *n.* **1** [17C+] the vagina; also a term of abuse to a woman. **2** [mid-19C–1910s] the Atlantic Ocean. **3** [late 19C+] (*US*) a canal, e.g. Panama, Suez, Erie. **4** [1910s+] the sea, esp. the English Channel or the North Sea. **5** [1960s–70s] (*drugs*) the inside of the elbow, used for injections of narcotics. **6** [1970s+] (*US gay*) the anus.

IN PHRASES

❑ **dig a ditch** *v. see under* DIG *v.*[1]. ❑ **in the ditch** *adj.* (*US*) **1** [1970s+] impoverished, at the bottom of the social ladder. **2** [1980s+] extremely drunk [the image of a drunk driver steering off the road and into a ditch].

SE in slang uses

IN COMPOUNDS

❑ **ditch pig** *n.* [1990s+] a derog. term for an unattractive, fat woman. ❑ **ditchweed** *n.* [such plants grow lit. or fig. in the ditch] [1980s+] (*US drugs*) **1** wild marijuana, which is usu. less powerful than cultivated varieties. **2** any inferior quality marijuana, often from Mexico.

IN PHRASES

❑ **give the ditch** *v. see* DITCH *v.*[1] (3). ❑ **keep it between the ditches** [1990s+] (*US*) a phr. of farewell; 'it' being a metaphorical vehicle.

ditch *v.*[1] **1** [late 19C–1920s] (*US tramp*) to throw off a moving train. **2** [late 19C–1920s] to ruin, to stand in the way of a plan. **3** [late 19C+] (*also* **give the ditch**) of people and objects, to throw away, to dispense with, to abandon; to end a relationship. **4** [1900s] (*US*) to drink. **5** [1920s–30s] (*US Und*) to be sent to prison. **6** [1920s–30s] (*US tramp*) to hide (something). **7** [1920s+] (*US*) to leave in a hurry. **8** [1930s+] (*US teen/campus*) to play truant from school.

IN PHRASES

❑ **ditch out** *v.* [1920s+] (*US*) to leave quickly or clandestinely.

ditch *v.*[2] [DITCH *n.* (4)] [1940s+] (*orig. RAF*) to land one's aircraft in the sea.

ditched *adj.* [fig. use of DITCH *v.*[1]] **1** [late 19C–1900s] nonplussed, at a loss. **2** [late 19C+] (*US*) in difficulties, in trouble.

dithered *adj.* [1920s+] (*Aus.*) mildly drunk, tipsy.

dits *n. see* DITZ *n.*[2].

dits *adj. see* DITZY *adj.*[2] (3).

ditso *adj.* [DITZ *n.*[2]] [1970s+] (*US*) useless, second-rate, no good.

ditsoon *n.* [Ital. dial. *titsune*, an ember, something burnt] [2000s] (*US*) a black person.

ditsy *adj.* [DITZ *n.*[1]] [1970s+] (*US*) **1** wonderful, outstanding. **2** fussy, intricate. **3** *see* DITZY *adj.*[2].

ditties *n.* [DIDDIES *n.*] [1990s+] the female breasts.

ditto *n.* (*also* **dittoes**) [SE *ditto*, the same. The style is common today, but less so when the sl. was coined] [late 18C–19C] a suit of clothes (jacket, waistcoat, trousers) all the same colour.

ditty *n.*[1] **1** [late 19C+] (*Aus./N.Z.*) a lie; a 'shaggy-dog story'. **2** [1950s] (*US black*) an anecdote, an experience.

ditty *n.*[2] [1990s+] (*US campus*) a small object; a penis.

ditty-bop *see under* DIDDY-BOP.

ditz *n.*[1] [ety. unknown] [1920s–70s] (*US*) something excellent.

ditz *n.*[2] (*also* **dits**) [SE *dizzy*] [1970s+] (*US*) a scatterbrained person, usu. a woman, a fool, an idiot.

ditz *v.* [DITZ *n.*[2]] [1970s+] to treat like a fool.

ditzo *n.* [DITZ *n.*[2]] [1980s+] (*US*) a scatterbrained person; also as a term of address.

ditzy *adj.*[1] [DITZ *n.*[1]] [1970s+] (*US*) first-rate, excellent, exceptional.

ditzy *adj.*[2] (*also* **ditsy**) [DITZ *n.*[2]] **1** [1970s+] (*US*) eccentric. **2** [1980s+] nervous, edgy. **3** [1980s+] (*orig. US*) (*also* **dits**) esp. of women, scatterbrained, silly; also as n.

div *n.*[1] [SE *dividend*] [1900s] (*Aus.*) a sum of money, esp. money won from a bookmaker.

div *n.*[2] [ety. unknown; ? link to echoic DUH *n.*] [1970s+] a weakling, a fool.

diva *n.* [SE *diva*, a distinguished female singer; ult. Ital. *diva*, goddess] [1990s+] **1** (*US black*) a stately woman, not invariably beautiful, but always of a certain grandeur. **2** any accomplished woman in any occupation. **3** (*US black/gay*) an arrogant black man, who indicates his feelings by elaborate finger-snaps.

diva *adj.* [DIVA *n.*] **1** [1990s+] (*US campus*) excellent, worthy of admiration. **2** [2000s] (*S.Afr. gay*) sexually sophisticated.

dive *n.*[1] (*UK Und.*) **1** [early 17C–19C] (*also* **diver**) a pickpocket; an act of pickpocketing [DIVE *v.* (1)]. **2** [late 18C–early 19C] a thief who stands outside a house or shop, inside which is a small boy who throws out goods that have been stolen [? he dives to catch the falling goods/the goods 'dive' from the window]. **3** [1910s+] (*orig. US*) (*also* **diveroo**) the voluntary losing of a fight by a boxer, presumably at the behest of a criminal bettor [he 'dives' to the canvas].

IN PHRASES

❑ **take a dive** *v.* [one lit. + fig. *dives* to the canvas] (*orig. US*) **1** [1910s+] (*also* **high-dive**) in boxing, or any competition, for a fighter deliberately to lose a fight (cf. GO IN THE TANK *under* TANK *n.*[1]). **2** [1900s] to make a bet. **3** [1950s] to faint. **4** [1980s+] to compromise oneself. **5** [1980s+] to fail.

SE in slang uses

IN PHRASES

❑ **do a dive into the dark** *v.* [late 19C+] to have sexual intercourse.

dive *n.*[2] [SE *dive*. The implication is of both physical and social 'lowness'; such places were usu. situated in a basement, cellar or other slightly clandestine place into which patrons could 'dive' without being noticed. *Dive* reached its heyday with US Prohibition (1920–33) but the term *dive bar* has persisted, lending an air of spurious romance to otherwise unexceptional drinking places] **1** [mid-19C+] (*orig. US*) an illicit drinking establishment or any similarly down-market place of entertainment, a brothel. **2** [1910s] (*drugs*) an opium den. **3** [1920s+] any unappealing place; a slum, any form of run-down housing.

dive *v.* **1** [early 17C–19C] to pick a pocket; thus *diving hooks*, the hands in the context of pickpocketing [the plunging of one's hand into another's pocket or purse; thus the name of the celebrated pickpocket *Jenny Diver*]. **2** [1930s+] (*orig. US*) (*also* **dive into it**) to perform cunnilingus.

IN PHRASES

❑ **dive a muff** *v.* [1940s+] (*orig. US*) to perform cunnilingus. ❑ **dive for black pearls** *v.* [1970s] (*US*) to perform cunnilingus on a black woman. ❑ **dive in the bushes** *v. see under* BUSH *n.*[1]. ❑ **dive in the canyon** *v. see under* CANYON *n.*

SE in slang uses

IN PHRASES

❑ **dive for a meal** *v.* (*also* **dive for a dinner**) [late 18C–early 19C] to eat in a cellar. ❑ **dive for pearls** *v.* [1920s–40s] (*US*) to work as a dishwasher. ❑ **dive into one's sky** *v. see under* SKY (ROCKET) *n.* ❑ **dive into the sack** *v. see under* SACK *n.* ❑ **dive into the sky** *v.* [1970s+] to penetrate the anus with one's penis.

dive-bomber *n.* [1940s–60s] a tramp who picks up cigarette ends.

divebombing *n.* [DIVE-BOMBER *n.*] [1970s+] picking up cigarette ends from the pavement.

diver *n.* [DIVE *v.* (1)/SE *dive*] **1** [16C–early 17C] a small boy who, like Oliver Twist in Charles Dickens's novel (1837–9), is put in through an otherwise impassably small window; once inside the house, he either lets in the gang or passes booty out to them. **2** [17C–mid-18C] a man in the context of having sexual intercourse. **3** [17C–1940s] a pickpocket. **4** [late 18C–early 19C] one who lives in a cellar. **5** [mid-19C] in pl., the fingers. **6** [1940s+] (*US*) a beggar who forages in garbage cans for food.

diveroo *n. see* DIVE *n.*[1] (3).

divi *n. see* DIVVY *n.*[1] (1).

dividends *n.* [1990s+] (*US campus*) money.

divine line, the *n. see* HAPPY TRAIL *under* HAPPY *adj.*

divine rights *n.* (*also* **divine right**) [SE *Divine Right of Kings*, the concept that monarchs are answerable only to God for their actions] [1980s] (*US black*) the police.

diving-bell *n.* [? general use of the proper name of a well-known rough tavern in mid-19C New York's gang-infested Fourth Ward] [late 19C] a basement or cellar tavern; 'a rum-shop in a basement' (Matsell).

diving-suit *n.* [1940s+] (*Aus.*) a condom.

divorce *n.* [1970s] (*S.Afr.*) alcohol, beer.

divot *n.*[1] [perceived resemblance] **1** [1930s] a toupee. **2** [1990s+] the female genitals, when heavily covered in pubic hair.

divot *n.*[2] [play on SE *divot*, a clod of earth/CLOD *n.*[1] (1)] [1990s+] (*UK juv.*) a fool.

divvie *n.* [? SE *diviner*] [1970s+] one who can sense the right answer even when they have no facts or expertise on which to base their opinion.

divvy *n.*[1] [abbr.] **1** [late 19C+] (*also* **divi**) *dividend*, the annual financial share-out by a cooperative society; thus *divvy-hunter*, one who joins the society purely to benefit from the dividend. **2** [late 19C+] (a share of) profits, usu. illicit. **3** [late 19C+] a share. **4** [1900s–40s] a share-out, a division (of criminal spoils). **5** [1910s] a fig. dividend, an advantage. **6** [1990s+] any free sample, free trip, esp. press tours, promotions etc.

IN COMPOUNDS

❑ **divvy-van** *n.* [1990s+] (*Aus.*) a police *divisional van*; esp. in sports chant 'You're going home in the back of a divvy van!'.

divvy *n.*[2] [? SE a *division* (of time)] [20C+] (*Aus.*) a very short time.

divvy *n.*[3] [ext. of DIV *n.*[2]] [1970s+] a fool, a socially unacceptable person.

divvy *adj.* [DIVVY *n.*[1] (2)] [late 19C] profitable, esp. in a criminal context.

divvy *v.* (*also* **divy, divvy up**) [SE *divide*] **1** [late 19C+] to divide up, usu. illicit profits; also *divvy man*, one who blackmails criminals for a share of their profits. **2** [1930s–40s] (*US*) to separate.

Dixie *n.* [20C use is SE. The song 'Dixie's Land' was written and first performed by the 'blackface minstrel' Daniel D Emmett (1815–1904) on 4 April 1859. The term 'Dixie Land' had appeared two months earlier in another Emmett song, 'Jonny Roach'. Of the various poss. etys. the preferred choice is an abbr. of the Mason–Dixon line (which divided the North and South in 1763–7). 'Dixie's land' was also a common term in 19C children's games of tag; note Asbury, *Sucker's Progress* (1938): 'A few years after the Louisiana Purchase one of the New Orleans banks issued ten dollar notes, on one side of which was the French word for ten, *dix*. To the flatboatmen one of the notes was a dix, and collectively they were dixies, while New Orleans was known as "the town of the dixies," and, later, simply as Dixie. The word does not appear to have been used to designate the entire South until after 1859, when D. D. Emmett wrote his famous song.' Schele de Vere, who opts for Mason-Dixon, adds another ref. to a supposed slaveholder, one *Dixey*, who had allegedly treated his slaves very well, thus leading to the 'minstrel' song] [mid–late 19C] (*US*) the American South, esp. those states that formed the Confederacy in the Civil War (1861–5).

IN PHRASES

❑ **do dixie** *v.* [*Dixieland* jazz and the energetic dancing it inspired] [20C+] (*W.I.*) to make an exciting, successful show (of what is being done); to make events work out as one wishes. ❑ **get on Dixie** *v.* [the energy and noise associated with *Dixieland* jazz] [20C+] (*W.I.*) to quarrel noisily, to become very angry. ❑ **whistle Dixie** *v.* [20C+] (*US*) **1** to engage in wishful fantasies. **2** to pursue without hope of success. **3** to boast, to brag without substance. ❑ **you ain't just whistling Dixie** [20C+] (*US*) you really mean what you're saying, you're not just being flippant.

dixie cup *n.*[1] [DIXIE *n.* + CUPCAKE *n.* (1)] [1970s+] an attractive Southern woman.

dixie cup *n.*[2] [the brandname of America's best known disposable cup] [1990s+] (*US*) anyone seen as disposable.

dixie lid *n.* [rhy. sl. = KID *n.*[1] (1)] [1990s+] a child.

diz *n. see* DIZZ *n.*

dizankster *n.* [a nonsense-word blending DOWN *adj.*[1] (1) + -IZ- *infix* + GANGSTER *adj.* (1)] [2000s] (*US black*) someone or something superlative.

dizybells *n. see* DISHABELLS *n.*

dizz *n.* (*also* **diz**) [abbr. SE *dizzy*] [1960s+] (*US*) an eccentric.

dizzie *adj.* [1990s+] dyslexic.

dizzy *n.*[1] [*Dizzy*, the popular nickname of British prime minister Benjamin *Disraeli*, Lord Beaconsfield (1804–81)] [mid-19C–1910s] a clever man; esp. in phr. *quite a dizzy*.

dizzy *n.*[2] [DIZZY *adj.* (3)] [1910s] (*US*) a madman.

dizzy *n.*[3] [mispron. of *dirham*] [1910s] (*Aus.*) an Egyptian coin.

dizzy *adj.* **1** [late 18C; 1900s] drunk; thus *dizzy ward*, the alcoholic ward. **2** [mid-19C–1900s] (*US*) startling, astonishing, vivid. **3** [late 19C+] eccentric, mad, stupid. **4** [1920s+] obsessed by; thus *dizzy with a dame*, to be obsessed with a woman.

IN COMPOUNDS

❑ **dizzy-ass** *adj.* [-ASS *sfx*] [1970s] foolish, stupid. ❑ **dizzy flat** *n.* [FLAT *n.*[2] (1) + the image of stupidity so great that it makes witnesses giddy] [late 19C] (*US*) a complete fool. ❑ **dizzy limit** *n.* (*also* **lurid limit**) [1910s+] (*Aus.*) the absolute limit.

IN PHRASES

❑ **do the dizzy** *v.* [1900s] (*Aus.*) to act in an uninhibited manner.

dizzy-wizzy *n.* [1900s] (*US*) any small thing, e.g. a pill.

DJ *n.* (*also* **deejay, dj, d.j.**) [abbr.] [1950s+] a *disc jockey*; also attrib.

DJ *v.* (*also* **deejay, dj, d.j.**) [DJ *n.*] [1980s+] (*orig. US*) to work as a disc jockey.

d.j. *n.* [abbr.] [1950s+] *dinner jacket*.

djamba *n.* [used synon. in various west African languages, e.g Mende] [1930s+] (*drugs*) marijuana.

d.l. *n.* [DOWN LOW *n.*] **1** [1990s+] (*US black*) a state of secrecy. **2** [2000s] (*US black*) ostensibly heterosexual, married men who enjoy sex with homosexual men.

IN PHRASES

❑ **on the d.l.** *adj.* [1990s+] (*US black*) depressed, out of sorts.

d.l. *adj.* [abbr. DOWN LOW *adj.*] [1990s+] secret.

d.l. *v.* [D.L. *n.*] [1990s+] (*US teen*) to keep secret or hidden.

d.l. *adv.* [D.L. *n.*] [1990s+] (*US black*) in a clandestine, sneaky manner.

d.l.c. *n.* [abbr. *d*own *l*ow *c*onversation] [1980s+] (*US campus*) a deep or heavy conversation.

dlog *n.* *see* DELOG *n.*

DMs *n.* [abbr. brand *Doc Martens* (*see* DOCS *n.*)] [1980s+] heavy boots favoured first by working men, then by skinheads and latterly by fashionable teenagers.

d.m.t. *n.* [abbr.] [1960s+] (*drugs*) *d*i*m*ethyl*t*ryptamine.

do *n.* [note 1910s milit. jargon *do*, an offensive] **1** [mid–late 17C; 20C+] (*also* **doo**) a success; esp. in phr. *make a do (of)*. **2** [19C+] a fraud, a swindle; a (practical) joke. **3** [early 19C+] a party, a celebration, a dinner etc, often reasonably formal. **4** [mid-19C] a confidence trickster. **5** [mid-19C] (*US*) noise, confusion. **6** [late 19C] a cup of coffee. **7** [late 19C+] a period of suffering, usu. physical, e.g. *I've had a rotten do today*. **8** [1900s] (*Aus.*) any criminal activity. **9** [1910s+] an attack, a gang fight; in weak use, an argument. **10** [1930s+] excrement, usu. animal. **11** [1940s+] murder. **12** [1960s–70s] (*drugs*) a shot or measure of a narcotic drug. **13** [1960s+] (*US black/campus*) a haircut. **14** [1960s+] (*US black*) straightened hair; as v., to straighten. **15** [1970s] (*US black*) an Afro hairstyle. **16** [1990s+] (*US*) a business, an organization.

IN PHRASES

❑ **do one's do** *v.* [20C+] (*US*) to do what is necessary, to do what one must do. ❑ **do the do** *v.* **1** [1950s+] (*US black/campus*) to have sexual intercourse. **2** [1990s+] to pass time. **3** [1990s+] (*US campus*) to do a necessary task. ❑ **have a bit of a do** *v.* [1940s] (*Aus.*) to suffer a bout of veneral disease. ❑ **make a do out of** *v.* [20C+] (*Aus/N.Z.*) to succeed at, to 'make a go' of.

do *v.*[1] **1** to attack, lit. or fig. (**a**) [16C+] (*also* **do with**) of a man, to copulate with a woman; occas. vice versa. (**b**) [late 18C+] to defeat. (**c**) [late 18C+] to murder, to kill. (**d**) [late 18C+] to prosecute; usu. *do for* burglary, rape etc. (**e**) [mid-19C+] of people, to assault, to beat up; of things, places, to break up, to destroy. (**f**) [20C+] to arrest, to capture. (**g**) [1900s] to make the butt of a joke. (**h**) [1900s–40s] (*US*) to betray, to inform on. (**i**) [1910s–40s] (*US*) to search, to raid. (**j**) [1930s+] to sue, to take to court, to charge with a crime; thus *X was done for taking and driving away*. (**k**) [1940s+] of a man, to have homosexual intercourse. (**l**) [1940s+] to attack in a non-physical sense. (**m**) [1940s+] (*US gay*) to perform fellatio. (**n**) [1970s+] to irritate, to mess around. (**o**) [1990s+] to injure (other than through violence). **2** in criminal senses. (**a**) [mid-17C+] (*also* **do for**) to cheat, to defraud, to swindle. (**b**) [late 18C+] to rob. (**c**) [early 19C] (*UK Und.*) to counterfeit, to forge; thus *do a queer half-quid*, to counterfeit a half-guinea coin; *do a queer screen*, to counterfeit a banknote. **3** to offer or consume. (**a**) [mid-19C+] to eat or drink, usu. with the relevant food or drink attached, e.g. *do a couple of pints*, *do a burger*. (**b**) [late 19C+] to serve, to make available, e.g. of accommodation, food and/or drink. (**c**) [1940s] (*US drugs*) to effect. (**d**) [1960s+] (*drugs*) to consume a given drug, e.g. *do a line*. (**e**) [1970s+] of a sport or hobby, to engage in; thus ext. to any experience. **4** to spend time. (**a**) [mid-19C+] to serve a sentence in prison; usu. in phrs., e.g. *do life*, *do five years*. (**b**) [1920s+] to pass a period of time, other than in prison. **5** to spend, dispose of, waste. (**a**) [mid-19C+] to dispose of, to squander, to waste, to destroy. (**b**) [late 19C] to honour a promissory note. (**c**) [late 19C+] to squander one's money; usu. with *...one's cheque/dough*. (**d**) [1950s] to hand over, usu. money. **6** [1900s] to place a bet. **7** [1950s] (*US*) to defecate. **8** [1960s+] to conduct business, usu. as a drug dealer.

IN COMPOUNDS

❑ **do-room** *n.* [1970s] (*US black/drugs*) a room in which drug addicts gather to inject themselves.

IN PHRASES

❑ **do...** *v. see also under* relevant n. ❑ **do a bit** *v.* [1900s] (*Aus. Und.*) to rob, to break in. ❑ **do for** *v. see* separate entry. ❑ **do in** *v. see* separate entry. ❑ **do in the eye** *v.* **1** [20C+] (*also* **do in the eyeball**) to cheat. **2** [1910s] to beat squarely. ❑ **do oneself** *v.* [1980s+] (*US*) to make a fool of oneself, to embarrass oneself. ❑ **do oneself off** *v.* [1960s+] to masturbate. ❑ **do over** *v. see* separate entry. ❑ **do the lot** *v.* [20C+] to spend all one's available money. ❑ **do under** *v.* [play on DO OVER *v.*] [1960s+] (*US black/P.R.*) to defeat, to ruin, to kill. ❑ **do up** *v. see* separate entries. ❑ **do (up) like a kipper** *v.* [1980s+] **1** to beat up severely. **2** to take advantage of, to manipulate for one's own ends. ❑ **do with** *v. see* sense 1a above.

IN EXCLAMATIONS

❑ **do me!** [late 19C] (*Aus.*) an excl. of surprise.

SE in slang uses

IN COMPOUNDS

❑ **do-right** *adj. see* separate entries.

IN PHRASES

❑ **do a/an...** *v. see under* ACT *n.* ❑ **do it** *v. see* separate entries. ❑ **do how?** [20C+] (*US*) what did you say? please repeat the question. ❑ **do social work** *v.* [1970s+] (*US gay*) to go out of one's way to have an inter-racial sexual partner; thus exhibiting one's liberal credentials. ❑ **do something standing on one's head** *v. see under* STAND *v.*[2]. ❑ **do the...** *v.* [mid-19C+] to act in a given manner, qualified by a pertinent n. or adj.; for combs. *see* relevant n. or adj. ❑ **do the...act** *v. see under* ACT *n.* ❑ **do well** *v.* [20C+] (*W.I.*) to be inconsiderate of others or thoughtless of oneself; usu. in ironic phr. *you do well*. ❑ **do what?** [1960s+] (*US*) what did you say? please repeat the question. ❑ **do which?** [20C+] what did you say?

do *v.*[2] **1** [early 19C+] to inspect as a tourist, to visit, e.g. *do London*. **2** [late 19C] to travel, to journey. **3** [late 19C–1910s] to report on. **4** [20C+] to attend an entertainment, e.g. *do a show*.

do... *v.* (*also* **have...**) [17C+] in addition to the many synons. for sexual intercourse with individual entries, other vars. include *do/have...a back scuttle, ...a ballocking, ...a beanfeast in bed, ...a bedward bit, ...a belly warmer, ...a bit of rabbit-pie, ...a blindfold bit, ...a bout, ...a brush with the cue, ...a buttered bun, ...a dash in the bloomers, ...a dash up the channel, ...a dog's marriage, ...a double fight, ...a drop in, ...a four-legged frolic, ...a fuck, ...a futter, ...a game in the cock loft, ...a goose and duck, ...a grind, ...a hoist-in, ...a jottle, ...a jumble giblets, ...a jumble up, ...a knee trembler, ...a lassie's by-job, ...a leap (up the ladder), ...a little of one with the other, ...a mount, ...a mow, ...an inside worry, ...a plaster of warm guts, ...a poke, ...a put, ...a rasp, ...a ride, ...a roger, ...a rootle, ...a rush up the straight, ...a St George, ...a shag, ...a shot at the bull's eye, ...a slide up the board, ...a squirt and a squeeze, ...a touch off, ...a tumble in, ...a wallop in, ...a wet 'un, ...a wipe at the place*. *See also* BIT *n.*[1].

-do *sfx* [? link to earlier *dues*, e.g. as in NARKING DUES *under* NARK *v.*[1] or LAGGING DUES *under* LAGGING *n.*] [mid-19C] (*UK Und.*) used with various present participles to denote a given action, e.g. FRISKING-DO *n.*

d.o.a. *n.* [orig. police jargon *d*ead *o*n *a*rrival, i.e. the potentially fatal effects] (*drugs*) **1** [1970s+] phencyclidine. **2** [1980s+] crack cocaine. **3** [1980s+] a street name for a variety of heroin.

d.o.a. *v.* [orig. police jargon *d*ead *o*n *a*rrival] [1940s+] to die before one arrives at a hospital.

doady *n.* [ety. unknown; ? Yorks. dial. *doady*, the penis] [2000s] (*Scot.*) the penis.

do and dare *n.* [rhy. sl.] [1920s] (*US*) underwear.

doash *n.* [ety. unknown] [late 17C–early 19C] (*UK Und.*) a cloak.

do as you like *n.* [rhy. sl. = SE *bike*] [late 19C+] a bicycle.

DOB *n.* (*also* **DOM**) [1990s+] (*drugs*) a far stronger form of MDMA.

dob *n.*[1] [dial.] [20C+] a small portion, a dab, pat or dollop.

dob *n.*[2] [SE *dob*, a dab, i.e. the blow or thrust of penetration; also note Scot. *dob*, a prick] [1970s] (*US*) the penis.

dob *v.*[1] [ety. unknown] [20C+] (*Ulster*) usu. of boys, to play truant.

dob *v.*[2] *see* DOB (IN) *v.*

dobber *n.*[1] (*also* **dobber-in**) [DOB (IN) *v.*] [1950s+] (*Aus./N.Z.*) an informer, a tale-teller.

dobber *n.*^{2} [DOB *n.*^{2}] [1970s] **1** (*US*) the penis. **2** (*Aus.*) a semi-erect penis.

dobber *n.*^{3} *see* DAUBER *n.*

dobbin *n.* [? link to weaving jargon *dobby*, an attachment to a loom for weaving small figures, though this presumably relates back to colloq. *dobbin*, a farmhorse (dial. *dobby* = dimin. of Robert + a hobby-*horse*) or dial. *dobbin-wheels*, the large rear wheels of a cart, similar to spools on which ribbon was wound] [late 18C–early 19C] a ribbon.

dobbin-lay *n.* [DOBBIN *n.* + LAY *n.*^{3} (1)] [mid-19C] (*US Und.*) to rob a shop as soon as it opens, by one person distracting the store porter and the other making the robbery.

dobbin rig *n.* (*also* **dobin rig**) [DOBBIN *n.* + RIG *n.*^{2} (1)] [late 18C–early 19C] (*UK Und.*) the stealing of ribbons from haberdashers, usu. performed by women.

dobe *n.*^{1} [ety. unknown] [20C+] (*US*) **1** a cigarette or cigar butt. **2** (*also* **dobie**) a Doberman dog.

dobe *n.*^{2} (*also* **dhobe**) [? SE *do*llar *b*ill] [1900s–30s] (*US Und.*) a dollar.

dobee *n. see* DHOBI *n.*

doberman *n.* [? the character *Doberman*, in the US TV comedy *The Phil Silvers Show* (1955–9)] [1960s] (*US black*) a dishonest, cowardly or deceitful person.

dobe-wall *v.* [SE *adobe wall*] [late 19C–1930s] (*US*) to put up against a wall and shoot.

dobie *n. see* DOBE *n.*^{1} (2).

dobie *adj.* [abbr. ADOBE *adj.*] [19C+] (*US*) inferior, second-rate.

dob (in) *v.* [dial. *dob*, to put down with a sharp, abrupt motion] (*Aus./N.Z.*) **1** [1930s+] (*also* **dob down**) to contribute (financially). **2** [1950s+] (*also* **dob on**) to betray, to inform against. **3** [1960s] (*also* **dob it on**) to impose a responsibility on. **4** [1980s] to cause trouble for someone.

IN PHRASES

❑ **dob oneself in** *v.* [1950s+] (*Aus.*) to let oneself in for problems.

dobin rig *n. see* DOBBIN RIG *n.*

dob out *v.* [antonym of DOB (IN) *v.*] [1960s–70s] (*Aus.*) to miss out on, to absent oneself from, to reject an offer.

doc *n.* [mid-19C+] **1** (*orig. US*) abbr. of SE *doctor*. **2** (*US*) an all-purpose form of address for a man whose real name is unknown.

doc and doris *n. see* DOCK AND DORIS *n.*

doccy *n. see* DOXY *n.*

doch and doris *n. see* DOCK AND DORIS *n.*

dock *n.*^{1} [SE *dock*, the hindquarters of an animal; the buttocks of a human] [mid-16C–18C] the vagina.

dock *n.*^{2}

SE in slang uses

IN COMPOUNDS

❑ **dock rat** *n.* [mid-19C–1930s] (*US/Aus.*) a vagrant that hangs around the docks. ❑ **dock-shanker** *n.* [SE *dock*, a port, in this case a hospital + *shanker*, mis-sp. of SE *chancre*, a venereal ulcer; note SE colloq. *in dock*, in hospital, esp. if suffering from venereal disease] [early 19C] a fellow sufferer in a venereal ward. ❑ **dock-walloper** *n.* (*US*) **1** [mid-19C–1910s] an idler who frequents the waterfront. **2** [mid-19C+] a dock-worker, a longshoreman. ❑ **dock-walloping** *adj.* [1930s] lazy. ❑ **dock-yarder** *n.* [mid-19C] (*UK Und.*) a skulker.

IN PHRASES

❑ **in dock** *adj.* [SE colloq. *in dock*, in hospital; itself fig. use of naval term] [1950s] ill, out of commission.

dock *v.* [SE *dock*, to cut (esp. as in a SE *tail*/TAIL *n.* (4)); or Rom. *dukker*, to rape + DELL *n.* (1)] [mid-16C–19C] (*UK Und.*) to have sexual intercourse; thus *dock the dell*, to deflower a young woman.

dock and doris *n.* (*also* **doc and doris, doch and doris, dock-and-doris, dockin doris**) [Scot. *deoch-an-doris*, a parting drink or stirrup cup, which, by ancient custom, must be taken standing and need not be paid for] [mid-19C+] a drink, usu. of whisky.

dock asthma *n.* [1970s+] (*UK Und.*) ironic description of the gasps of alleged 'surprise' from the accused when the police produce their evidence in court.

docker *n.*^{1} [Scot. *docker*, to work (hard)] [1920s+] (*Aus.*) a large sum of money; thus *go a docker*, to spend extravagantly.

docker *n.*^{2} [SE *dock*, to cut the tail off] [1970s] a half-smoked cigarette, put out for later re-ignition.

docker *n.*^{3} *see* BOONDOCKER *n.* (1).

docker's hook *n.* (*also* **left hook**) [rhy. sl.] **1** [20C+] (*Aus.*) a book, a reading book, or as a 'bookie;' thus phr. *make a docker's hook*, to lay the odds or make a book. **2** *see* BUTCHER'S HOOK *n.*

docket *n.* [1900s] (*US Und.*) a piece of paper that facilitates begging (cf. SCREEVE *n.*).

dockie *n.* [post 1930s use is mainly Aus.] [late 19C+] a dock labourer.

dockin doris *n. see* DOCK AND DORIS *n.*

docking *n.*^{1} **1** [early 18C–mid-19C] 'A punishment inflicted by sailors on the prostitutes who have infected them with the venereal disease, it consists in cutting off all their clothes, petticoat, shift and all, close to their stays, and then turning them out into the street' (Grose, 1785). **2** [early 19C] bettering the condition of the run-down horse in order to improve the chances of selling it.

docking *n.*^{2} [the image of docking spacecraft] [1980s+] (*US gay*) a form of mutual masturbation, involving one partner with an exceptionally long foreskin, which is drawn over the glans of the other partner before commencing masturbation.

docs *n.* (*also* **Doc Martens**) [brandname *Dr. Martens*, patented in Germany in 1965 by Herbert Funck and Klaus Maertens. The original boots were for work use only, but the firm diversified during the 1980s and their product, esp. in the form of a Dr. Martens sole attached to one of a variety of uppers, became a leading fashion staple for both sexes] [1980s+] Dr. Martens boots.

doctor *n.* **1** in the context of food or drink [SE *doctor*, to mix, to adulterate]. (**a**) [late 18C–early 19C] milk and water with rum and nutmeg. (**b**) [late 18C–early 19C] an adulterant, e.g. alum, used in food or drink. (**c**) [19C+] brown sherry [brown sherry is a mix of sherry and wine, which gives it the darker 'brown' tint]. (**d**) [1980s+] (*US campus*) any form of alcoholic drink. **2** [early 19C] the last throw in a game, e.g. dice or ninepins [? the doctor at one's end/death]. **3** [mid-19C+] (*Aus.*) the cook on a sheep station [ext. of naut. use *doctor*, a shipboard cook or 19C N.Z. whalers' *doctor*, a Maori slave used as a cook]. **4** [1910s+] (*bingo*) doctor's shop, the number nine [milit. jargon *doctor*, pill number nine, the most frequently prescribed medicine in the Field Medical Chest + ref. to the nine months of pregnancy, after which one 'calls for the doctor']. **5** [1940s–70s] (*US gay*) a man with a large penis [? he gives you an 'injection'].

IN PHRASES

❑ **keep the doctor** *v.* [late 19C–1930s] to sell adulterated alcohol.

SE in slang uses

IN COMPOUNDS

❑ **doctor's curse** *n.* [early 19C] a dose of calomel. ❑ **doctor's favourite** *n.* [the ubiquity, in the army, of the number nine pill as a general cure-all] [20C+] (*bingo*) the number nine. ❑ **doctor's loss** *n.* [? the price of a doctor's visit] [late 18C] £1 sterling. ❑ **doctor's orders** *n.* [the army's number nine pills, or the nine months of pregnancy] [20C+] (*bingo*) the number nine.

IN PHRASES

❑ **go (through) for the doctor** *v.* (*also* **look for the doctor**) [the image of rushing for (and paying a large fee to) a doctor] [1940s+] (*Aus. orig. racing*) **1** for one rider and his mount to move significantly ahead of the field. **2** (*Aus. gambling*) to bet all one's money. **3** to go full tilt at something, to commit oneself wholeheartedly. ❑ **go to (see) the doctor** *v.* (*also* **have a doctor's appointment**) [the supposedly restorative effects of alcohol] [1980s+] (*US campus*) to drink alcohol.

doctor, the *n. see* DOCTORS *n.*

doctor and nurse *n.* [rhy. sl.] [1990s+] a purse.

doctorate in applied chemistry *n.* see BIG JAB *under* JAB *n.*

Dr Bates *n.* [devel. of BEEN TO SEE CAPTAIN BATES? *phr.*] [1920s] (*US Und.*) a dangerous ex-convict.

Dr Cotton *adj.* [rhy. sl.] [1930s–60s] rotten.

Dr Crippen *n.* [rhy. sl.; ult. Dr Hawley Harvey *Crippen* (1862–1910), a celebrated murderer] [1910s+] dripping, rendered fat, occas. bread and dripping.

Dr Death *n.* [the negative image of prison doctors] [1980s+] (*Aus. prison*) a prison doctor.

Dr Draw-fart *n.* [19C] an itinerant quack doctor.

Dr Feelgood *n.* [the phr. was coined by the blues pianist Piano Red (William Perryman) in his record 'Dr Feelgood and the Interns' (1962); the drug ref. is a slightly later addition] **1** [1960s+] a doctor who obliges patients, often showbusiness or entertainment celebrities, with amphetamines or narcotics, which, although the user has no real medical need for them, guarantee 'good feelings'. **2** [2000s] heroin.

Dr Green *n.*[1] ['a physician, or rather medicine, found very successful in curing most disorders to which horses are liable' (Grose, 1788)] [late 18C–19C] grass; thus *send to Dr Green*, to put a horse out to grass.

Dr Green *n.*[2] [SE *green*, innocent; note 20C medical jargon *Dr Green*, a hospital tannoy announcement that will not alarm patients and visitors but that signifies the 'all clear' to staff after the termination of an emergency] [mid-19C] (*US*) a naïve, gullible young person.

Dr Hall *n.* [? a brandname or rhy. sl.] [1920s–30s] (*US tramp*) grain alcohol and water.

Dr Jim *n.* (*also* **jimkwim, jimmunt**) [Dr *Jameson*, whose Jameson Raid (1895) brought him much notoriety, sported such a hat; the vars. are (*Dr*) *Jim* + QUIM *n.* (1) / CUNT *n.* (1) and are thus origins of *CUNT-HAT under* CUNT *n.*] [late 19C] a soft felt hat with a wide brim.

Dr Johnson *n.* [ext. of JOHNSON *n.* (1); Partridge's suggestion that 'there was no one Dr Johnson was not prepared to stand up to' is unlikely] [19C] the penis.

Dr Legg *n.* [rhy. sl.; ult. *Dr Legg*, a fictional doctor on the UK soap opera *EastEnders*] [1990s+] an egg.

doctors *n.* (*also* **the doctor**) [mid-16C–19C] **1** false or loaded dice. **2** counterfeit coins.

IN PHRASES

❑ **load the doctors** *v.* [SE *doctor*, to adulterate + DOCTOR *n.* (2)] to prepare the loaded dice. ❑ **put the doctor(s) on** *v.* to cheat with loaded dice.

Dr Shop-knife *n.* [Carib.E. *doctor shop*, a chemist + SE *knife*; for explanation of ety. *see* CHEMIST BILL *n.*] [late 19C+] (*W.I.*) a deceitful, hypocritical person.

Dr Thomas *n.* see UNCLE TOM *n.*

Dr White *n.* [WHITE *n.* (3)] [1930s–50s] (*US drugs*) narcotics; narcotic addiction.

Dr Who *n.* [rhy. sl.; ult. BBC TV programme] [1970s+] (*bingo*) the number two.

docxy *n. see* DOXY *n.*

DOD *n.* [? pun on phr. *d*eath *o*n *d*elivery/*d*ick *o*f *d*eath] **1** [1920s] (*US Und.*) very strong liquor. **2** [2000s] (*US black*) a very large penis.

dod *n.*[1] (*also* **dodd**) [late 17C–1910s] a euph. for God, usu. in combs., as below.

IN COMPOUNDS

❑ **dod-bimmed** *adj.* (*also* **dod binged**) [1900s] (*Aus./US*) a euph. for GOD-DAMN *adj.* ❑ **dod-gasted** *adj.* [late 19C–1920s] a euph. for GOD-DAMN *adj.*

IN EXCLAMATIONS

❑ **dodgast!** [SE *gast*, to terrify] [early 19C–1910s] (*US*) a general imprecation, curse, e.g. DAMN! *excl.* ❑ **dod rabbit it!** [mid–late 19C] (*US*) a mild oath, euph. of 16C *God rebate it!* ❑ **dod rot it!** (*also* **dod drot!**) [mid-19C] a mild oath of exasperation.

dod *n.*[2] [abbr. SE *dodderer*] [1940s] (*US*) an old, poss. infirm person.

do-dad *n.* (*also* **doodad**) [20C+] any object or gadget without a specific name.

dodaddle *n.* [1920s] (*US*) something trivial.

dodd *n. see* DOD *n.*[1].

dodder *n.* [SE *dottle*, the residue of ash remaining in the bottom of a pipe after smoking] [mid–late 19C] burnt tobacco that is taken from a dead pipe and placed on a fresh plug in order to strengthen the flavour.

doddies *n.* [the proletarian version of society's *do-ut-des*, from Lat. *do ut des*, I give in order that you may give back] [late 19C] a selfish person.

doddipool *n. see* DODDYPOLL *n.*

doddle *n.* [? Scot. *doddle*, a small lump of homemade toffee, hence something attractive and easily obtained, or SE *dawdle/toddle*] [1920s+] (*orig. racing*) anything absolutely simple or easy to achieve.

doddle *v.* [DODDLE *n.*] [1930s+] to accomplish something easily, e.g. win a race.

doddypoll *n.* (*also* **doddipool, doddy(pate), dodipol**) [SE *dote*, to be foolish or silly + SE *poll*, a head] [early 16C–mid-18C] a fool.

dode *n.* [? DORK *n.* + DUDE *n.*[1] (3) or SE *dodo*, a simpleton, a silly old man; note Scot. dial. *dode*, a slow person] [1980s+] (*orig. US teen*) **1** the penis. **2** thus, an unappealing person, a fool.

dodelheimer *n.* (*also* **dodenheimer**) [? DO-DAD *n.* + 'German' sfx *-enheimer*] [1910s+] any nameless small object, typically some form of gadget.

Dodge *n.*

IN PHRASES

❑ **get the hell out of Dodge** *v.* (*also* **get the heck out of Dodge, get the fuck...**) [the clichéd dialogue of a variety of Western films/TV series in which the 'baddie' is ordered, *Get the hell...*] [1960s+] to leave, usu. at speed; thus as imper. *get the hell out of Dodge!* go away now!

dodge *n.* [other than in date, it is hard to differ between the orig. 16C SE *dodge*, 'a shifty trick, an artifice to elude or cheat' (*OED*) and this sl. 'a clever or adroit expedient or contrivance' (*OED*)] [mid-17C+] **1** a trick, a gimmick, a means of avoiding problems, esp. those encountered in work. **2** a job, an occupation, a profession.

IN PHRASES

❑ **do the — dodge (over)** *v.* [1930s+] to take on a pose – e.g. a clergyman, an ex-soldier – for the purposes of fraud. ❑ **on the dodge** [20C+] **1** involved in something illegal or underhand. **2** hiding from or avoiding the authorities. ❑ **up to the dodge** [mid-19C–1910s] (*US*) aware, shrewd, knowledgeable.

dodge *adj.* [2000s] dubious, untrustworthy.

dodge *v.* [SE *dodge*, to act in a dubious, untrustworthy manner] **1** [late 18C–19C] to follow someone surreptitiously. **2** [1910s+] (*Aus.*) to steal, usu. cattle.

IN PHRASES

❑ **dodge pompey** *v.* [naut. jargon *dodge pompey*, to skulk around, to avoid work by the use of any semi-legitimate excuse] [1930s] (*Aus.*) to steal grass, rather than to grow and harvest one's own crop.

dodge and shirk *n.* [rhy. sl.] [20C+] (*Aus.*) work.

dodger *n.*[1] [note Kent dial. *dodger*, a nightcap, the last drink of the day] [mid-19C] one dram of spirits or the glass that holds it.

dodger *n.*[2] [? Northumberland dial. *dodge*, a lump, a chunk] [mid-19C; 1910s+] (*Aus./US*) bread, a sandwich, food in general; thus *hunk of dodger*, a slice of bread.

dodger *n.*[3] [*DEVIL-DODGER under* DEVIL *n.*] [mid–late 19C] a clergyman.

dodger *n.*[4] [SE *dodger*, a handbill] **1** [late 19C+] (*Aus./US*) an advertising leaflet, a flyer. **2** [1930s–40s] (*US Und.*) a 'wanted' flyer distributed to law enforcement agencies, post offices etc.

dodger *n.*[5] [1920s] a threepenny bit coin.

dodger *n.*[6] [? the cockroach, like the clergyman (DODGER *n.*[3]), has a black 'coat' or the insect's dodging of its human enemies] [1990s+] (*US black*) a cockroach.

dodger *adj.* [? DODGER *n.*[2]; i.e. the innate goodness of bread] [1940s–50s] (*Aus.*) excellent, first-rate.

dodinkus *n. see* DOODINKUS *n.*

dodipol *n. see* DODDYPOLL *n.*

do-do *n.*[1] (*also* **doo-doo, du-du**) [DO *n.* (10) + redup.] [1930s+] **1** excrement, usu. animal; thus *dodo-head*, a term of abuse. **2** fig. use of sense 1, trouble, difficulties; esp. as *deep doo-doo*, serious trouble. **3** (*US black*) something utterly insignificant; usu. in phr. *don't mean do-do* (*to me*). **4** (*US black*) rubbish; also attrib.

IN PHRASES

▫ **whip the dudu out of** *v. see* BEAT THE SHIT OUT OF *V.*

do-do *n.*[2] [redup. abbr. of DOPE *n.*[1] (6); but note DO-DO *n.*[1] (1), i.e. a play on SHIT *n.* (6b)] [2000s] (*US black/drugs*) cannabis, usu. marijuana.

dodo *n.* [SE *dodo*, the bird famous for being extinct] **1** [late 19C+] an idiot, a dullard, esp. an old one. **2** [late 19C+] a conservative, one who refuses to change with the times. **3** [1930s–50s] (*US drugs*) a drug addict.

do-do *v.* [DO-DO *n.*[1] (1)] [1930s+] to defecate.

dodsey *n.* [? DOXY *n.* (2)] [18C–mid-19C] (*UK Und.*) a woman.

dodunk *n.* [? DODO *n.* (1) + BOHUNK *n.* (2)] [19C+] (*US*) a fool, a simpleton.

doe *n.*[1] [SE *doe*, a female deer] **1** [late 16C–early 17C] a girl or young woman. **2** [late 17C–early 18C] a prostitute. **3** [1900s] (*US Und.*) a baby. **4** [1900s–70s] a woman. **5** [1950s–60s] (*US black*) a gullible person, a fool, a potential victim. **6** [1960s] (*US*) an unaccompanied young woman.

doe *n.*[2] *see* DOUGH *n.*

doe-boy *n. see* DOUGHBOY *n.*[1].

doedie *n.* [Afk. sl. *doedie*, 'chick'] [1950s+] (*S.Afr.*) an attractive and sexually available woman.

doee *n. see* DOOE(E) *n.*

doer *n.*[1] [DO *v.*[1] (1a)] [early 17C] a womanizer.

doer *n.*[2] [DO *v.*[1] (2a)/SE *do*] **1** [mid-19C] a cheat, one who defrauds another. **2** [20C+] (*Aus.*) a character, an eccentric, one who never gives up despite any circumstances; often intensified as *HARD DOER under* HARD *adj.* **3** [1990s+] (*US*) a criminal.

doer and gone *phr.* [Afk. *doer*, far away] [1970s+] (*S.Afr.*) very far away, out of one's reach.

does a bear shit in the woods? Is the pope a Catholic? *phr.* (*also* **do beavers piss on flat rocks? does a bird have wings? does a chicken have lips? do I know my grandmother? do sheep wear sweaters? has a dog a nose? is the pope a guinea?**) [*see Maledicta* I:1 (Summer 1977) pp.77–82 for discussion of these 'sarcastic interrogative affirmatives and negatives'] [1910s+] (*orig. US*) a rhetorical phr. of which the implication is, 'Don't ask me stupid questions. Of course… .' The phr. is also found reversed, 'Does the pope shit in the woods? Is a bear a Catholic?' (cf. *CAN A DUCK SWIM? under* DUCK *n.*[1]).

doeskin *n.* [var. on FROGSKIN *n.*[2]; *see* FROG *n.*[3]] [1960s] (*US*) money.

does she? *phr.* [late 19C+] a comment passed by men on an adjacent women, the implication being, *does she fuck?*

does your bunny like carrots? *phr. see under* CARROT *n.*

dof *adj.* [Afk. *dof*, stupid] [1970s+] (*S.Afr.*) stupid, simple, dim; thus *doffie*, a fool, a simpleton.

IN COMPOUNDS

▫ **dof-brain** *n.* [1980s+] (*S.Afr.*) a fool. ▫ **dofburger** *n.* [1980s+] (*S.Afr.*) a fool.

doff *v. see* DUFF *v.*[1] (3).

doflickety *n. see* DOOFLICKER *n.* (1).

do for *v.* [DO *v.*[1] (1)/abbr. SE phr. *do a bad turn for*] [mid-18C+] **1** to beat up, to injure, to murder. **2** to ruin, to destroy, to harm. **3** to wear out completely.

dofous *n. see* DUFUS *n.* (1).

dofunny *n. see* DOOFUNNY *n.*

dog *n.*[1] [var. on DAD *n.*[1] (1); DAG *n.*[3]; DOD *n.*[1]; despite possibility, coinage is too early for backsl.] [16C; late 19C+] (*orig. UK, latterly US*) a euph. for God, used in a variety of mild, semi-blasphemous oaths.

IN COMPOUNDS

▫ **dog-durned** *adj.* (*also* **dog blasted**) [late 19C] (*US*) a euph. for GOD-DAMN *adj.*

IN EXCLAMATIONS

▫ **dog bite 'em!** (*also* **dog bite me! dog bite my ear! …my onions!**) [16C; 20C+] (*orig. UK, latterly US*) a mild, semi-blasphemous oath. ▫ **dog bline me!** [1920s] a euph. for GORBLIMEY! *excl.* ▫ **dogdamn it!** [1960s] (*US*) an excl. of surprise, annoyance; a semi-euph. for GOD-DAMN IT! *excl.*

dog *n.*[2] **1** of humans or animals, based on negative characteristics. (**a**) [16C+] an untrustworthy, treacherous, completely venal man. (**b**) [17C+] an unpleasant woman or man. (**c**) [mid-19C+] a horse that is slow, difficult to handle etc; also attrib. (**d**) [1930s+] (*US black*) (*also* **doggie**) an offensive or abusive man. **2** of humans, based on positive or neutral characteristics. (**a**) [late 16C+] (*also* **dogg**) a person, irrespective of moral/social status. (**b**) [late 17C+] a clever, cheery, hearty person; esp. in affectionate phr. *you old dog*. (**c**) [1990s+] (*also* **dawg, dogg**) a close friend. (**d**) [1990s+] (*also* **dawg, dogg**) a general term of address, usu. between men. (**e**) [1990s+] constr. with *the*, an admirable person. **3** senses based on sexuality. (**a**) [17C; 20C+] (*US*) (*also* **doggy**) the penis. (**b**) [late 17C] the vagina [early 17C nonce use: *a dog with a hole in its head*]. (**c**) [late 19C+] (*orig. US*) a promiscuous man or woman. (**d**) [1930s+] (*US black*) a prostitute, esp. when ageing and/or run-down. (**e**) [1960s+] (*US black*) lust, sexual desire. **4** of inanimate objects, based on negative characteristics. (**a**) [mid-18C; 1950s+] a general negative description, something useless, worthless, broken down etc; a second-rate product or one that is hard to sell; a mediocre performance. (**b**) [mid-19C; 1960s+] unpleasantness, bad characteristics, meanness. (**c**) [1910s+] (*US*) a disappointment, a failure. (**d**) [1950s+] weakness, cowardice, e.g. in a boxer. **5** [19C+] ostentation, showiness, style, esp. if affected or pretentious. **6** Und. uses. (**a**) [mid-19C; 1940s+] (*UK Und.; later use US*) a police officer. (**b**) [mid-19C+] (*Aus./US*) an informer, a 'stool pigeon', a traitor; esp. one who betrays fellow criminals; thus *underdogs*. (**c**) [1920s+] (*Aus.*) a plain-clothes detective working on the railways. (**d**) [1950s–60s] (*US black*) a notably brutal police officer or prison officer. (**e**) [1960s] (*US prison*) in a women's prison, an inmate who turns temporarily to homosexuality. (**f**) [1970s] (*US prison*) an older or tougher prisoner who exploits younger, weaker men as homosexual partners. (**g**) [1970s] (*US prison*) a guard. **7** [late 19C+] a sausage; thus *dog roll*, a hot dog. **8** [1920s+] (*US black*) something or someone unusual or surprising. **9** [1920s+] an unattractive woman or man. **10** [1930s–40s] (*US black campus*) a freshman. **11** *see* DOG (END) below. **12** *see* DOG JOINT below. **13** *see* DOG-LEG below. **14** *see* DOG'S DISEASE below.

DERIVATIVES

▫ **doggish** *adj.* **1** [1920s] (*US*) second-rate. **2** [1960s+] (*US black*) obsessed with sex, lecherous; also adv. *doggishly*.

IN COMPOUNDS

▫ **dog nigger** *n.* [NIGGER *n.*[1] (1)] [1970s] (*US black*) **1** a black person who rejects the second-class role offered by the dominant white society. **2** an unpleasant, aggressive person.

IN PHRASES

▫ **beat the dog** *v.* [1930s+] to masturbate. ▫ **carry dog** *v. see* PUT ON (THE) DOG below. ▫ **clapping the dog** *n.* [1990s+] stimulating a woman's genitals with one's fingers. ▫ **dog-eat-dog** *n.* [1970s] (*Aus.*) an abusive term for a young woman. ▫ **do the dog** *v.* **1** [1920s+] (*US*) to show off, to strut about. **2** *see* DOG *v.*[1] (3b). ▫ **dog (up)** *v. see* PUT ON (THE) DOG below. ▫ **go dog** *v.* **1** [late 19C–1950s] (*Aus.*) to let down; to betray, to inform against. **2** [2000s] (*US*) to be a coward. ▫ **let the dog see the rabbit** *v.* [1930s+] to give someone a chance to get on with a task. ▫ **lose one's dog** *v.* [1910s] (*US*) to lose control of a situation. ▫ **on the dog** [1980s+] (*Aus. prison*) branded as an informer and thereafter ostracized. ▫ **play the dog** *v.* [1960s] (*US*) to display oneself sexually, to act in an ostentatiously promiscuous manner. ▫ **put on (the) dog** *v.* (*also* **carry dog, dog (up), pile on dog, throw on dog**) (*orig. US*) **1** [mid-19C+] to show off, to put on airs; to do something energetically, noisily. **2** [1970s] to have sexual intercourse. ▫ **stroke the dog** *v. see* STROKE THE BEAVER *under* BEAVER *n.*[1]. ▫ **suck a big dog's dick** *v. see* SUCK *v.*[1] (5). ▫ **suck a dog's dick** *v. see under* SUCK *v.*[1]. ▫ **turn dog** *v.* (*Aus.*) **1** [mid-19C–1940s] to become an informer, to inform on. **2** [1900s] to become unkind (and treat someone cuelly). **3** [1910s] to let down, to 'bite the hand that feeds you'. **4** [1910s] to betray; to take a bribe. ▫ **walk one's dog** *v.* (*also* **take the dog for a walk, water the dog**) [the euph. excuse one makes when leaving the room] [1960s+] (*US*) to urinate or to defecate.

SE in slang uses

DERIVATIVES

▫ **dogways** *adv.* [late 19C] having sexual intercourse in the rear-entry position.

IN COMPOUNDS

▫ **dog act** *n. see* BLACKFELLOWS' ACT *n.* ▫ **dog-ass/-assed** *see* separate entries. ▫ **dog-booby** *n.* [SE *dog* adj., male + BOOBY *n.*[1] (1)] [late 18C] a country lout, a male peasant. ▫ **dogbox** *n. see* separate entry. ▫ **dog-breath** *n.* (*orig. US*) **1** [1940s+] bad breath. **2** [1980s+] one who has bad breath; thus an offensive person. ▫ **dog buffer** *n.* [BUFFER *n.*[2] (1)] [late 18C–early 19C] a dog stealer. ▫ **dogcart** *n.* [1920s+] (*Aus.*) a police car. ▫ **dogcock** *n.* [2000s] (*N.Z.*) a form of sausage. ▫ **dog-collar** *n.* **1** [mid-19C+] the reversed collar worn by clergymen. **2** [late 19C+] a choker necklace. ▫ **dog-days** *n.* [SE *dog-day*, an evil time, a period in which malignant influences prevail; lit. the rising of the Dog Star] [1910s+] a menstrual period. ▫ **dog-driver** *n.* [the term sneers at the police officer, giving him the lowly task of driving off stray dogs] [1910s+] (*W.I.*) a police officer. ▫ **dog (end)** *n.* [? SE *docked end*] [1930s+] **1** the last fraction of a cigarette; thus phr. *dog-ends on*, please give me the last fraction of your cigarette. **2** [1940s] in fig. use, anything small or insignificant. ▫ **dogface** *n.* **1** [late 19C+] (*US*) an unpleasant person; a term of abuse; as adj., *dogfaced*, stupid-looking, ugly [prior use from mid-19C in nicknames for specific individuals (see *HDAS*)]. **2** [1930s+] (*US*) a soldier, an infantryman; thus adj. *dogfaced* [coined as an insult by members of the US Marine Corps, who look down on infantrymen. Allegedly from the old Cheyenne War Society in the Plains Wars, who called themselves Dog Soldiers; the Cavalry took it from them]. ▫ **dog fashion** *adv. see* DOGGY FASHION *adv.* ▫ **dog-fever** *n.* [1910s+] (*Aus.*) influenza. ▫ **dog-fight** *n.* (*US*) **1** [late 19C] a fistfight, a brawl. **2** [1970s] any event considered coarse or vulgar. ▫ **dogfood** *n. see* separate entries. ▫ **dogfuck/fucker/fucking** *see* separate entries. ▫ **dog-heart** *n.* [20C+] (*W.I. Rasta*) a person who is especially cold and cruel. ▫ **dog hours** *n.* [1920s–30s] (*US*) a late-night/early-morning shift. ▫ **doghouse** *n. see* separate entry. ▫ **dog joint** *n.* [SE *hot dog* + JOINT *n.* (3b)] [1920s] (*US*) (*also* **dog**) a cheap restaurant, a hot dog stand. ▫ **dog juice** *n.* [JUICE *n.*[1] (3a), i.e. only good enough for an animal or common *dog*] [1970s+] (*US black*) cheap liquor or wine. ▫ **dog kennels** *n. see under* KENNEL *n.*[2]. ▫ **dog-knotted** *adj.* [1950s+] for two lovers to be locked together during intercourse because of a vaginal muscle spasm brought on by a sudden shock. ▫ **dog-leg** *n.* (*also* **dog**) [the twists in which the tobacco was sold, which resembled a dog's leg] [mid–late 19C] (*US*) second-rate tobacco. ▫ **dog licence** *n.* [1940s+] (*Aus.*) a certificate of exemption from the prohibition of alcohol to Native Australians (under the Aborigines Protection Act 1909–43) that permits them to buy a drink in a hotel. ▫ **dog meat** *n.* [20C+] (*US*) a worthless, despicable person. ▫ **dog-mouth** *v.* [1980s] (*US black*) to abuse verbally. ▫ **dog music** *n.* [1900s] (*Aus.*) howling (of a wounded person). ▫ **dog nuts** *n.* [NUTS *n.*[2] (1)] **1** [1960s+] a term of contempt. **2** [1990s+] a friend, a general term of address. ▫ **dogpaddle** *v.* [1960s] (*US*) to have anal intercourse. ▫ **dogpatch** *n.* [*Dogpatch*, the hillbilly settlement in which the syndicated cartoon strip by Al Capp, *L'il Abner* (1934–77), takes place] [1970s+] (*US*) a small town or hamlet. ▫ **dogpile** *v.* [1940s+] (*US*) for a group of people to leap on a single individual. ▫ **dogpiss** *see* separate entries. ▫ **dog-robber** *n. see* separate entry. ▫ **dog's...** *n. see also* separate entries. ▫ **dog's abuse** *n.* [1920s+] (*Irish*) harsh verbal criticism. ▫ **dog's age** *n.* [mid-19C+] (*US*) a very long time. ▫ **dog-salmon aristocracy** *n.* [late 19C] (*US*) one who thinks they are superior to their peers. ▫ **dog's bottom** *n.* [1930s+] a joc. form of address. ▫ **dog's breakfast** *n. see* DOG'S DINNER *n.* ▫ **dog's chance** *n.* [mid-19C+] the smallest posible chance; use in negative uses. ▫ **dog's dinner** *n. see* separate entry. ▫ **dog's disease** *n.* (*also* **dog**) [late 19C+] (*Aus.*) one of a variety of illnesses, e.g. influenza, malaria, a hangover. ▫ **dog's dram** *n.* [mid-18C–early 19C] the act of spitting in someone's mouth and hitting them on the back. ▫ **dog's head** *n.* [late 19C–1900s] (*US*) a variety of beer. ▫ **dogshit** *see* separate entries. ▫ **dog's lady** *n.* [late 18C] a euph. for BITCH *n.*[1] (1a). ▫ **dog's licence** *n.* [a dog's licence cost 7s 6d (37½p)] [1930s+] the sum of seven shillings and sixpence. ▫ **dog's marriage** *n.* [1990s+] sexual intercourse in the rear-entry position. ▫ **dog's match** *n.* [the brevity of the intercourse and the lack of privacy of mating dogs] [19C+] sex in the open air, spec. by the wayside; thus to *make a dog's match of it*, to have sex in the open air, to have spontaneous sex. ▫ **dog's mouth** *n.* [1960s] (*US*) a tight vagina. ▫ **dog's paste** *n.* [mid–late 19C] sausagemeat or mincemeat. ▫ **dog's paw** *n.* [2000s] (*US gang*) a tattoo comprising a triangle of three dots, indicating gang membership. ▫ **dog's portion** *n.* [lit. 'a lick and a smell' (Grose, 1785)] [late 18C–19C] virtually nothing; esp. of a man who pursues a woman and gets only very little for his pains. ▫ **dog's rig** *n.* [SE *rig*, a romp; i.e. the observation of dogs mating] [late 18C–early 19C] sexual intercourse taken to exhaustion, followed by mutual disinterest. ▫ **dog's shelf** *n.* [1950s+] the floor. ▫ **dog's show** *n.* [DOG'S CHANCE above] [late 19C–1900s] (*Aus.*) no chance at all. ▫ **dog's soup** *n.* [post-19C use is US] **1** [late 18C+] rainwater. **2** [mid-19C–1930s] water (for drinking). ▫ **dog-stiffener** *n.* (*also* **stiffener**) [STIFFEN *v.*[1] (3)] [20C+] (*Aus.*) a professional dingo-killer. ▫ **dog style** *adv. see* DOGGY STYLE *adv.* ▫ **dogsucker/sucking** *see* separate entries. ▫ **dog's wife** *n.* [late 18C] a euph. for BITCH *n.*[1] (1a). ▫ **dog tag** *n.* [for a dog to be 'legal' (not a stray) in the US it must have a labelled collar] **1** [1910s+] (*orig. US*) an identification disk. **2** [1950s+] (*US drugs*) a legitimate prescription for otherwise illegal narcotics. ▫ **dogtown** *n. see* separate entries. ▫ **dog trick** *n.* [mid-16C–early 18C] a treacherous or spiteful act, an ill-turn, a mean, cruel trick. ▫ **dog turd** *see* separate entries. ▫ **dog wagon** *n.* [play on SE *dog wagon*, used by the dog-catcher] **1** [20C+] (*US*) a small café or restaurant sited in a converted vehicle, a diner [the quality of food is generally poor]. **2** [1960s–70s] (*US*) a prison van for conveying prisoners. ▫ **dog water** *n.* [1960s+] (*US*) **1** semen. **2** urine. ▫ **dog work** *n.* [1980s+] (*US*) tedious, menial tasks.

IN PHRASES

▫ **die like a dog (in a string)** *v. see under* DIE *v.* ▫ **dog and goanna rules** *n.* [the image of a fight between a dog and a goanna lizard] [1960s+] (*Aus.*) no rules at all. ▫ **dog and pony show** *n.* (*also* **horse and dog show**) [the orig. dog and pony shows were small circuses, where they were the sole animal performers; thus the image is of an event which boasts much presentation but little substance] [1950s+] (*US*) any elaborately formal occasion, used for official briefings, public relations etc. ▫ **dog in a doublet** *n.* [the custom in Germany and Flanders to dress the dogs used to hunt wild boar in a form of buff doublet] [late 17C–early 19C] a daring, bold person; thus *proud as a dog in a doublet*, very proud; *a mere dog in a doublet*, a pitiful figure, one who shows off to no avail. ▫ **the dogs are barking** [1980s] (*Aus.*) used to imply that one has a 'hot tip' on a racehorse. ▫ **dogs have not dined** [late 18C–early 19C] a phr. used to alert someone whose shirt is hanging out. ▫ **dogs in the grass** *n.* (*also* **puppies in a haystack**) [1930s] (*US*) frankfurters and sauerkraut. ▫ **dogs in the street** *n.* [dogs on the street] [20C+] (*Irish*) everyone, the whole world. ▫ **do like a dog** *v. see* DOG OUT *under* DOG *v.*[1]. ▫ **fuck the dog (and sell the pups)** *v.* (*also* **feed the dog, finger..., fug..., screw..., walk..., f.t.d.**) [fig. use of SE *dog*] [1910s+] (*US*) **1** to idle, to waste time, to loaf on the job. **2** to bungle, to blunder. ▫ **get**

in(to) a dog corn-piece *v.* [*dog* is synon. with a guard or watchman, and if he catches you in his *corn-piece* or corn-field you are in trouble] [1910s+] (*W.I.*) to get into difficulties. ❑ **has a dog a nose?** *see* DOES A BEAR SHIT IN THE WOODS? IS THE POPE A CATHOLIC? *phr.* ❑ **have a dog tied up** *v.* [the image of having left one's dog while moving on elsewhere] [1910s–40s] (*Aus./N.Z.*) to be indebted, esp. at a hotel. ❑ **keep dog** *v.* [SE *watchdog*] [1980s+] to keep a lookout.

IN EXCLAMATIONS

❑ **to the dogs with!** [1900s] a dismissive excl.

dog *n.*[3] (*also* **doggie**) [ety. unknown] [late 18C] (*W.I.*) a small copper or silver coin.

dog *n.*[4] [? the animal's inability to speak] [early 19C+] (*US*) nothing; usu. in phr. *never say dog*, to stay silent.

dog *n.*[5] [pun on BARKER *n.*[1] (3)] [mid-19C] (*US*) a pistol.

dog *n.*[6] **1** [20C+] (*Aus.*) food. **2** [20C+] (*Aus.*) a drinking debt. **3** [1920s] (*US*) a state of drunkenness.

IN PHRASES

❑ **kill one's dog** *v.* **1** [mid-18C] to be drunk, to drink heavily. **2** [1900s] (*Aus.*) as *let's kill a dog*, an invitation to drink. ❑ **on the dog list** [ety. unknown] [1920s+] (*Aus.*) barred from drinking.

dog *n.*[7] [? Yorks. dial. *dog*, a small pitcher] **1** [20C+] (*US*) a pint bottle (470ml) of liquor; thus *short dog*, a half-pint bottle. **2** *see* FORTY DOG *under* FORTY *n.*

dog *n.*[8] **1** [20C+] a beggar who searches for cigarette ends. **2** [1930s–60s] (*drugs*) the residue of poor-quality opium or heroin.

dog *n.*[9] [abbr. SALESMAN'S DOG *n.*] [1910s] (*Aus.*) a tout.

dog *n.*[10] [rhy. sl.; abbr. DOG (AND BONE) *n.*] [1940s+] the telephone.

dog *n.*[11] [once done all that is left is the 'tail'] [1950s–60s] (*US*) the hardest part of the job.

dog *n.*[12] [initial letters] [1960s+] (*US campus use*) the grade D.

dog *n.*[13] see DOGS *n.*[1] (2).

dog, the *n.*[1] [play on proper name] [1970s+] (*US*) a Greyhound bus.

dog, the *n.*[2] *see* OLD DOG *n.* (3).

dog *adj.* [1980s] (*US black*) cruel, coldhearted.

dog *v.*[1] **1** to act antagonistically. (**a**) [late 16C+] to pursue, to hunt down (often with sexual intent). (**b**) [mid-19C] (*US Und.*) to follow; thus *dog on*, to make someone follow someone else. (**c**) [late 19C] (*US*) to stare at, to glance unpleasantly at. **2** in negative verbal contexts. (**a**) [early 17C; 20C+] (*Und.*) (*also* **dog in**) to betray, to inform against. (**b**) [late 19C+] (*US*) to nag, to criticize, to harass, to mistreat. (**c**) [late 19C+] (*US black*) to abuse, to curse, to despise. (**d**) [20C+] to pester, to irritate. (**e**) [20C+] (*US*) to cheat. (**f**) [20C+] (*US*) to lie, to deceive. (**g**) [1970s+] (*US/W.I.*) to taunt, to tease, to mock, to be rude. (**h**) [1990s+] (*US black teen*) to insult someone in front of their friends. **3** in sexual contexts. (**a**) [18C+] to have sexual intercourse with. (**b**) [late 19C+] (*also* **doggy, do the dog**) to engage in sexual intercourse with the male using a rear-entry position. (**c**) [1980s+] (*US*) to rape. **4** to be inadequate; to fail, to disappoint. (**a**) [20C+] to act in a menial capacity. (**b**) [1910s–50s] to idle, to shirk work. (**c**) [1980s+] (*UK juv.*) to absent onself from school. (**d**) [1980s+] to break an appointment, to stand someone up. (**e**) [1990s+] (*US black*) to end a relationship. (**f**) [2000s] (*Aus.*) to abandon one friend for a new one. **5** *see* DOG IT *v.*[1] (1).

IN PHRASES

❑ **dog along** *v.* [? SE *dogged*] [20C+] (*Can.*) to manage, to subsist. ❑ **dog around** *v. see* separate entry. ❑ **dog away one's time** *v.* [late 19C] to waste time, to idle about. ❑ **dog back** *v.* [20C+] (*W.I.*) to swallow one's pride in the hope of regaining a formerly positive relationship. ❑ **dog behind** *v.* [20C+] (*W.I.*) to act in a servile manner, to toady to. ❑ **dog-eye** *see* separate entries. ❑ **dog it** *v. see* separate entries. ❑ **dog on** *v.* **1** [late 19C–1910s] (*Aus.*) to treat badly. **2** [1980s+] (*US campus*) to criticize, usu. in the victim's absence. ❑ **dog out** *v.* **1** [1940s+] to keep a lookout. **2** [1980s] (*US black*) to approach sexually. **3** [1980s+] (*US campus*) (*also* **do someone like a dog**) to betray, to neglect, to treat with disrespect. **4** [1980s+] (*US black/prison*) to intimidate; to abuse, to criticize.

dog *v.*[2] [abbr. BIRD DOG *v.* (1)] [1980s+] (*US*) to filch, to steal.

dog *v.*[3] [DOG *n.*[12]] [1980s+] (*US campus*) to get a grade D in an examination.

dog *v.*[4] [DOG (END) *under* DOG *n.*[2]] [1980s+] to put out a cigarette.

dog *v.*[5] [1980s+] (*US campus*) to do something fast, hard or well.

dog *v.*[6] [1990s+] (*US black teen*) **1** to tear something up in the manner of a dog, to worry. **2** to defeat.

dog *v.*[7] *see* DOG (UP) *under* DOG *n.*[2].

dog *adv.* [mid-19C+] (*US*) utterly, completely.

IN COMPOUNDS

❑ **dog-drunk** *adj.* [early 17C; mid-19C+] very drunk. ❑ **dog-poor** *adj.* [late 19C–1900s] (*Aus./US*) extremely poor, financially or of condition. ❑ **dog-sick** *adj. see* …A DOG *under* SICK AS… *adj.* ❑ **dog-wallop** *v.* [WALLOP *v.* (3)] [1900s] (*Aus.*) to beat comprehensively.

dog! *excl.* (*also* **by doggies! dog it!**) [late 19C+] (*US*) a euph. for DAMN! *excl.*

IN EXCLAMATIONS

❑ **dog my cats/hide/melts!** [mid-19C+] (*US*) a general excl. of amazement, annoyance, surprise. ❑ **dog on it!** [mid–late 19C] a mild expletive. ❑ **the dog's foot!** [20C+] (*US*) a mild excl.

dogan *n.* (*also* **dogun**) [? Irish surname *Duggan* or f. TAIG *n.* (1)] [mid-19C–1930s] an Irish Roman Catholic.

dog (and bone) *n.* [rhy. sl.] [1940s+] telephone.

dog and cat *n.* [rhy. sl.] [1950s+] a mat.

dog around *v.* [DOG *v.*[1]] **1** [20C+] to live a promiscuous life. **2** [1910s+] (*US campus*) to neglect one's academic work. **3** [1920s–40s] (*orig. US*) to follow. **4** [1920s–70s] (*US black*) to nag, to abuse verbally.

dog-ass *n.* (*also* **dog-arse**) [DOG-ASSED *adj.*] [1960s+] (*orig. US*) an objectionable, unpleasant person; also oneself.

dog-assed *adj.* (*also* **dog-arse(d), dog-ass**) [SE *dog* + -ASS *sfx*/-ARSE *sfx*/-ARSED *sfx* (2)/-ASSED *sfx* (2)] [1950s+] (*orig. US*) inferior, second-rate, unpleasant.

dogbox *n.* **1** [20C+] (*Aus.*) a railway compartment with no access to other compartments, usu. on a rural railway line. **2** [20C+] (*Aus.*) a substandard railway carriage. **3** [20C+] (*Aus./N.Z.*) any small, cramped room or house. **4** [1980s] (*Aus. prison*) a cubicle.

IN PHRASES

❑ **in the dogbox** [1950s+] (*N.Z.*) out of favour, in disgrace.

dog-eye *n.* [DOG *v.*[1] (1a) + SE *eye*] **1** [1910s+] (*US, mainly prison*) a sidelong glance, usu. aggressive or unfriendly. **2** [1950s+] (*UK juv./Und.*) a lookout, esp. for a team of three-card monte players.

dog-eye *v.* [DOG-EYE *n.*] **1** [1910s+] (*US, mainly prison*) to cast a sidelong glance at someone. **2** [1960s] (*US prison*) to inspect, to scrutinize.

dog food *n.*[1] **1** [1940s–60s] (*US*) any form of canned meat. **2** [1970s] any food considered disgusting.

dog food *n.*[2] [DOG *n.*[2] (6a) + ironic use of SE *food*] [1960s] (*US black*) a bribe paid to a corrupt police officer.

dog food *n.*[3] [*DOGFACE under* DOG *n.*[2] + SE *food*, i.e. something one can EAT *v.* (4)] [1970s+] (*US gay*) a soldier, viewed as a potential sexual partner.

dog food *n.*[4] [ext. of SE use; ? its colour (brown) or the low status of its users] [1980s+] (*drugs*) heroin.

dog-foolish *adj.* [backsl. *dog* = *good*, thus 'good and foolish'] [mid-19C] very stupid.

dogfuck *n.* [DOGFUCK *v.*] **1** [1970s] (*US*) trouble; usu. in phr. *in the dogfuck*. **2** [1970s+] sexual intercourse in which entry is made from the rear.

dogfuck *v.* (*also* **doggy, doggy-fuck**) [SE *dog* + FUCK *v.* (1)] [1970s+] to have rear-entry or anal intercourse.

dogfucker *n.* [SE *dog* + FUCKER *n.* (1)] [1990s+] (*US*) a general term of abuse, lit. one who has sex with dogs.

dogfucking *adj.* [DOGFUCKER *n.*] [1990s+] (*US black*) a term of extreme contempt.

dogg *n.* see DOG *n.*[2] (2).

dogged *adj.* **1** [17C; mid-19C+] a euph. for DAMNED *adj.* **2** [mid-19C] amazed.

dogged out *adj.* (*also* **dogged up**) [*PUT ON (THE) DOG under* DOG *n.*[2]] [1910s+] (*orig. US*) dressed up.

dogger *n.*[1] [*DOG (END) under* DOG *n.*[2]] [1940s+] one who collects cigarette ends, cleans out the tobacco and resells it.

dogger *n.*[2] [the excuse, 'I'm just walking my dog' used by the voyeur] [1990s+] a peeping tom who spies on couples in 'lovers' lanes' and similar places.

dogger out *n.* [DOG *v.*[1] (1c)] [1930s] (*UK Und.*) a lookout man.

doggery *n.*[1] [negative image of SE *dog*] [early 19C+] (*US*) a low drinking house.

doggery *n.*[2] [SE *doggery*, dog-like behaviour or practice; mean and contemptible action] **1** [mid-19C] cheating. **2** [late 19C] nonsense.

doggie *n.*[1] [SE *dog-collar*] [late 19C] an all-round stand-up collar.

doggie *n.*[2] [abbr. *DOGFACE under* DOG *n.*[2]] [1930s+] (*US*) a soldier, an infantryman.

doggie *n.*[3] see DOG *n.*[2] (1d).

doggie *n.*[4] see DOG *n.*[3].

doggies *n.*[1] [1990s+] sexual intercourse 'dog-fashion', i.e. from the rear.

doggies *n.*[2]

(IN EXCLAMATIONS)

❑ **by doggies!** see DOG! *excl.*

doggies *n.*[3] **1** see DOGS *n.*[1]. **2** see DOGS, THE *n.*

doggie style *adv.* see DOGGY STYLE *adv.*

doggin *n.* (*also* **doggins**) [*DOG (END) under* DOG *n.*[2]] [1930s+] (*N.Z.*) a cigarette end.

dogging *n.* [DOG *v.*[1] (3a)] [1990s+] **1** spying on others having sex in public spaces, usu. parked cars. **2** having sex with strangers in public spaces, often parked cars. **3** (*US*) offering sex in return for drugs. **4** (*US campus*) obtaining maximum sexual pleasure from a member of the opposite sex. **5** (*US*) philandering.

doggo *n.* [DOG *n.*[2] (2b)] [1920s] (*US*) a fellow, a man.

doggo *v.* see *LIE DOGGO under* LIE *v.*[1].

doggone *adj.* (*also* **daggone, dog(g)ondest, dog-goned, doggoned, dog-hanged, dog on, doll-goned**) [mid-19C+] (*US*) a euph. for GOD-DAMN *adj.*

(IN EXCLAMATIONS)

❑ **I'll be doggoned!** (*also* **I'll be daggoned! ...dog! ...dogdamned! ...doggarnded!!, ...dogged!**) [mid-19C+] (*US*) a general excl. of surprise, amazement.

doggone *adv.* (*also* **daggone**) [mid-19C+] extremely, very.

doggone! *excl.* (*also* **daggone, dog-garn, pleggone it**) [SE *god-damned*] [mid-19C+] (*orig. US*) a general excl.; a euph. for GOD-DAMN! *excl.*

doggoned *adj.* see DOGGONE *adj.*

doggy *n.* [abbr. + sfx -y] **1** [1940s+] (*Aus.*) (*also* **dargie**) a hot *dog*. **2** [1980s+] (*Aus. prison*) one who is accused of bestiality. **3** see DOG *n.*[2] (3a).

doggy *adj.*[1] [*PUT ON (THE)… under* PUT ON *v.*] [late 19C+] fashionable, esp. when showy, over-ornate.

doggy *adj.*[2] [DOG *n.*[2] (1); negative images of the animal] **1** [20C+] (*US black*) hard, mean, thoughtless. **2** [20C+] obsessed with sex, lecherous. **3** [1930s] somewhat overly enthusiastic.

doggy *v.* see DOGFUCK *v.*

doggy *adv.* see DOGGY STYLE *adv.*

doggy-do *n.* [SE *doggy* + DO *n.* (10)] [1960s+] **1** a euph. for canine excrement. **2** thus by ext. anything, e.g. food, that is disgusting.

doggy-dog *adj.* [SE *dog-eat-dog*] [1990s+] (*US black*) competitive, ruthless, lacking in compassion.

doggy fashion *adv.* (*also* **dog fashion**) [late 19C+] a way of having sexual intercourse in which entry is made from the rear.

doggy-fuck *v.* see DOGFUCK *v.*

doggy's dinner *n.* see DOG'S DINNER *n.*

doggy style *adv.* (*also* **doggie style, doggy, dog style**) [1940s+] used to describe sexual intercourse in the rear-entry position.

dog-hanged *adj.* see DOGGONE *adj.*

doghouse *n.* (*also* **doghole**) **1** [late 19C–1930s] (*US Und.*) prison; a solitary-confinement cell. **2** [late 19C+] any small structure that seems to resemble a dog kennel. **3** [1920s–50s] (*orig. US*) a double-bass; a bass-player. **4** [1930s] (*US prison*) a watchtower. **5** [1930s+] in fig. use, a place of disgrace or punishment; sometimes spec. of marriage. **6** [1940s+] (*US prison*) the protective custody unit in a prison. **7** [1990s+] (*US campus*) a romantic relationship.

(IN PHRASES)

❑ **in the doghouse** [SAmE *doghouse*, a dog kennel; i.e. in disgrace and so consigned to the dog's kennel rather than one's own home] [1930s+] (*orig. US*) in trouble, out of favour.

dogi *n.* [Bambara *dogo*, small, short] [1940s+] (*W.I.*) a short, stocky person.

dogie *n.* see DUJI *n.*

dog it *v.*[1] [DOG *v.*[1] (3a)] **1** [20C+] (*orig. gambling*) (*also* **dog**) to act weakly, to be a loser, to lack winning spirit. **2** [20C+] (*US*) to shirk, to waste time, to hang back. **3** [1920s+] (*US*) to dawdle, to go slowly. **4** [1920s+] (*US*) to malinger, to act lazily. **5** in sexual contexts. (**a**) [1920s] (*US black*) to dance in a provocative manner. (**b**) [1940s+] to have sexual intercourse from the rear. (**c**) [1980s+] (*US campus*) of a woman, to make oneself sexually available. **6** [1930s+] (*US*) to run off. **7** [1990s+] (*US prison*) to betray, to inform against. **8** [1990s+] (*US drugs*) to spoil, thus make no longer suitable or safe.

dog it *v.*[2] [*PUT ON (THE) DOG under* DOG *n.*[2]] [1930s+] **1** to dress up, to show off. **2** (*N.Z.*) to lord it over someone.

dog it *v.*[3] [DOGS *n.*[1] (1)] [1970s+] (*US gay*) to work as a part-time male homosexual prostitute.

dog it *v.*[4] [DOGHOUSE *n.* (2)] [2000s] (*US tramp*) to travel on freight trains.

Dogleg *n.*

(IN PHRASES)

❑ **from Dogleg to the Day of Judgment** [1900s] (*Aus.*) anywhere; everywhere.

dog on *adj.* see DOGGONE *adj.*

dogpiss *n.* [1990s+] any weak or diluted drink.

dog-piss *adj.* [1970s–80s] (*N.Z.*) despicable.

dog-robber *n.* [milit. jargon *dog-robber*, an officer's servant, who gained his unflattering nickname from his post-mealtime habit of grabbing any edible left-overs from the mess tables before they could be tossed out to the dogs] **1** [mid-19C+] (*orig. milit.*) a subservient person, a menial; as adj. *dog-robbing*, a term of abuse. **2** [late 19C+] the tweed suit customarily worn by off-duty British officers.

dogs *n.*[1] (*also* **doggers, doggies**) [coined by US sportswriter T.A. 'Tad' Dorgan (1877–1929) in the New York *Evening Journal*] **1** [1910s+] (*US*) the feet; occas. sing. **2** [1910s+] (*W.I./US*) shoes. **3** [1990s+] (*US black*) gym shoes, trainers.

(IN COMPOUNDS)

❑ **dog-stiffeners** *n.* [20C+] (*Aus.*) leather leggings.

(IN PHRASES)

❑ **pedal one's dogs** *v.* [1920s+] (*US*) to leave, to go away; esp. as excl. *pedal your dogs!*

dogs *n.*[2] [1940s] (*US Und.*) the tumblers of a safe's combination lock.

dogs, the *n.* (*also* **doggies**) [1920s+] the greyhound races, greyhound racing.

dog's ballocks *n.* (*also* **ballocks, bollocks, dog's bollocks, mutt's nuts**) [orig. in phr. *sticks out like a dog's ballocks*] **1** [1920s+] anything obvious. **2** [1980s+] anything excellent, admirable, first-rate. **3** [1990s+] a derisive retort.

dogsbody *n.* [19C–1930s] a stew, esp. pease pudding; also bully-beef.

dog's dinner *n.* (*also* **chook's breakfast, doggy's dinner, dog's breakfast, pig's breakfast**) **1** [1920s+] a distasteful mess; usu. as *make a dog's dinner out of* [but note colloq. *dressed up like a dog's dinner*, dressed in the height of chic and fashion]. **2** [1950s] an unpleasant person. **3** [1960s] (*US gay*) fellatio (the implication being that the fellator is a BITCH *n.*[1] (3f)).

IN PHRASES

❑ **done like a dog's dinner** *adj.* [cooking imagery] **1** [mid-19C+] (*Aus./N.Z*) 'done to a turn', i.e. utterly defeated. **2** [1980s–90s] (*US campus*) drunk.

dog's eye *n.* [rhy. sl.] [1960s] (*Aus.*) a meat pie.

dogshit *n.* **1** [1950s+] (*orig. US*) the essence, the spirit. **2** [1960s+] anything or anyone considered objectionable, unpleasant, disgusting. **3** [1970s+] nonsense.

IN PHRASES

❑ **dead as dogshit** *adj.* [1970s+] absolutely dead. ❑ **knock (the) dogshit out of** *v.* [1990s+] to beat severely. ❑ **not worth dogshit** *adj.* [1960s+] worthless, useless.

IN EXCLAMATIONS

❑ **dogshit!** [1980s+] an excl. of anger, despair.

dogshit *adj.* [DOGSHIT *n.* (2)] **1** [1960s+] (*US*) insignificant, second-rate. **2** [1980s] (*US*) crazy.

dog's meat *n.*[1] [late 16C–19C] anything considered worthless, e.g. a badly written book, a poorly executed painting etc.

dog's meat *n.*[2] [otherwise good enough only for the dogs] [1960s+] (*S.Afr.*) domestic workers, lit. cheap cuts of meat which are cooked for the servants' meals.

dog's nose *n.*[1] (*also* **dogsnose**) [like the animal's nose, alcohol is cold and wet] **1** [19C–1900s] beer warmed nearly to boiling, mixed with gin or wormwood (the basis of absinthe), sugar and ginger; an alternative version substitutes brandy for the wormwood. **2** [mid–late 19C] an alcoholic whose preferred tipple is whisky.

dog's nose *n.*[2] [DOG *n.*[2] (6b)] [1960s] (*US Und.*) a paid informer.

dogsucker *n.* [1990s+] (*US black*) a general term of abuse.

dogsucking *adv.* [1980s] (*US*) extremely.

dogtown *n.*[1] [orig. theatrical jargon *dogtown*, an out-of-town (i.e. out of New York City) theatre used to try out a new show before 'bringing it in'] [late 19C+] (*US*) an out-of-the-way or small place; thus *dogtowner*, a native of such a town.

dogtown *n.*[2] [? its fig. population of 'one man and a dog'] [1910s] (*N.Z.*) a derog. nickname for Port Chalmers.

dog turd *n.* (*also* **turd**) [lit./fig. resemblance] (*US*) **1** [20C+] a large cigar. **2** [1980s+] an obnoxious person.

dogturd *adj.* [1980s+] (*US*) obnoxious.

dogun *n. see* DOGAN *n.*

dohickey *n.*[1] (*also* **do'hickey, do-hinky, doohickey**) [ety. unknown; ? DO-DAD *n.* + ? HICKEY *n.*[1]] [1910s+] (*orig. US*) **1** any nameless small object, typically some form of gadget. **2** something small, used for decoration.

dohickey *n.*[2] [HICKEY *n.*[2]] [1960s+] a love-bite or a pimple.

do how? *excl.* [20C+] (*US*) what did you say? please repeat the question.

do I fuck! *excl. see* FUCK! *excl.*

do in *v.* [all ext. uses of DO *v.*[1]] **1** [late 19C–1900s] to steal; to rob. **2** [late 19C+] (*orig. Aus./N.Z.*) to spend one's entire funds. **3** [20C+] to kill, to murder. **4** [20C+] (*Aus.*) to defeat. **5** [20C+] in fig. use, to kill off; of food, to finish. **6** [1900s] to break off, to abandon. **7** [1900s–50s] to make an error, to fail in some way. **8** [1910s+] to wear out, to exhaust. **9** [1920s+] to beat up. **10** [1930s+] of machinery, objects, to break or damage. **11** [1950s+] (*drugs*) to inject a narcotic drug. **12** [1960s] (*drugs*) to consume. **13** [1990s+] (*US black/teen*) to gang rape.

IN PHRASES

❑ **do oneself in** *v.* **1** [20C+] to commit suicide. **2** [1930s] to put oneself in a deliberately unpleasant situation or position. ❑ **do someone's head in** *v.* **1** [1950s+] (*also* **do someone's box in**) to upset, to disconcert. **2** [1970s+] (*orig. US campus*) to take a preferred drug.

doing *n.* [DO *v.*[1]] **1** [mid–late 17C; 1920s] sexual intercourse. **2** [early 19C] (*UK Und.*) a crime, such as a robbery. **3** [late 19C+] (*also* **doing down**) a thrashing, a beating; lit. or fig.

doings *n.*[1] [ext. of SE *doing*, an act, a piece of business, a transaction] **1** [late 16C+] the circumstances, the event. **2** [late 18C; 1910s+] (*orig. milit.*) anything for which the precise name cannot be recalled at the moment of speaking. **3** [mid-19C–1910s] (*US*) the trimming or ornaments that enhance a dress. **4** [mid-19C+] the components, e.g. of a meal, of a piece of engineering. **5** [late 19C–1940s] the testicles; the male genitals. **6** [1990s+] a condom.

doings *n.*[2] **1** [1950s+] (*Aus.*) excrement. **2** [1980s+] animal excrement.

doink *n.* [echoic of their solidity/dullness] [1960s+] (*US campus*) **1** a clumsy, inept person. **2** an overly hard worker, a 'grind'.

do it *v.*[1] [euph.] **1** [mid-16C] to have sexual intercourse. **2** [late 19C+] of a man, to ejaculate; of a woman, to reach orgasm.

IN COMPOUNDS

❑ **do-it fluid** *n.* [1970s+] (*US black*) liquor, usu. gin, usu. as an enhancer of sexual potency.

SE in slang uses

IN PHRASES

❑ **do it all** *v.* (*also* **get it all**) [1910s+] (*US prison*) to serve a life sentence; to serve the whole of a sentence, with no time off for good behaviour. ❑ **do-it-easies** *n.* [they help make being in prison easier] [1970s–80s] (*N.Z. prison*) tranquilizers. ❑ **do it on the rush** *v.* [mid-19C] to run away, to escape. ❑ **do it up** *v.* [early–mid-19C; 2000s] to accomplish one's object, to have success; thus *do it up in good twig*, to live a constantly enjoyable (and ever-improving) life. ❑ **do it with one hand tied behind one's back** *v.* (*also* **do it on one leg, ...with one's shoes on, ...on one's head**) [20C+] (*orig. US*) to do very easily, with minimal effort. ❑ **do-it-yourself** *n.* (*also* **do it yourself kit**) [1950s+] masturbation.

do it *v.*[2] [1910s+] to defecate or urinate.

do it *v.*[3] [1970s+] to leave, to start going; esp. in phr. *let's do it*.

dojigger *n.* (*also* **doojigger**) [ety. unknown; ? link to SE *jiggle*] **1** [20C+] an indefinite expression used to describe a nameless object; also as *dojiggie, dojiggum, dojiggus, dojiggy, dojimmie, dojinnie, dojisser, dojohn, dojohnnie*. **2** [1960s+] (*also* **modigger**) a euph. for the penis.

dokus *n. see* TOCHES *n.*

dol *n.* (*also* **doll**) [abbr.] [mid-19C–1900s] a *dol*lar.

do-lally *adj. see* DOOLALLY *adj.*

dolan's ass *n.* [proper name Dolan + SE *ass*; it goes 'a bit of the way with everyone'; ? anecdotal origins] [20C+] (*Irish*) a time-server.

dole-bludger *n.* [SE *dole* + BLUDGER *n.*[2] (2)] [1930s; 1970s+] (*Aus.*) (*also* **dole bug**) one who claims unemployment benefit either when work is available or while actually employed in the Black Economy, the Aus. equivalent to a UK 'dole-scrounger'; thus *dole-bludgery, dole-bludging*.

dolhja *n.* [2000s] (*US black/drugs*) high-quality marijuana.

dolie *n.* (*also* **doley**) [SE *dole*] [1940s+] (*orig. Aus.*) **1** anyone drawing unemployment benefit. **2** someone who illegally draws unemployment benefit while working.

doll *n.*[1] **1** [mid-16C–mid-18C; 1930s] (*also* **doll common**) a prostitute. **2** [early 17C+] a woman. **3** [mid-19C+] (*US*) anything, or anyone, excellent, first-rate; also as adj. **4** [mid-19C+] (*US*) a conceited or self-satisfied person. **5** [1910s+] a conventionally attractive young woman; occas. used of (homosexual) young men. **6** [1950s+] a general term of affection. **7** [1960s] (*US*) a person, a man. **8** [1990s+] (*S.Afr.*) a term of affection.

IN COMPOUNDS

❑ **doll baby** *n.* [BABY *n.* (3)] [mid-19C+] (*US*) an attractive young woman; also attrib. ❑ **doll-boy** *n. see* DOLLY-BOY *under* DOLLY *n.*[1]. ❑ **doll city** *n.* [-CITY *sfx*] [1980s+] (*US teen*) a conventionally pretty woman. ❑ **doll common** *n. see* sense 1 above. ❑ **doll house** *n.* [HOUSE *n.*[1] (1)] [1920s–50s] (*US*) a brothel; thus *doll woman*, a prostitute. ❑ **doll shop** *n.* [SHOP *n.*[1] (1)] [1990s+] (*US*) a brothel.

SE in slang uses

IN COMPOUNDS

❑ **doll-rags** *n.* [SE *doll* + *rags*, clothes; thus pieces small enough to make a doll's wardrobe] [1900s] (*US*) small pieces.

doll *n.*[2] [popularized and apparently coined by the book/film *Valley of the Dolls* (1968) by Jacqueline Susann] [1960s–70s] (*drugs*) any drug in pill form, e.g. amphetamines, barbiturates.

doll *n.*[3] *see* DOL *n.*

doll *n.*[4] *see* DOLLY *n.*[3].

doll *v. see* DOLL UP *v.*

dollar *n.*[1] **1** [early 19C+] five shillings (25p); obs. outside films, books etc of a pre-metric era; thus *half a dollar*, 2s 6d [the contemporary exchange rate was US$4 to £1 sterling]. **2** [late 19C] (*S.Afr.*) 1s 6d. **3** [1960s+] (*US black/Und.*) $100; $100 worth of drugs. **4** [1980s+] money; often in pl.

SE in slang uses

IN COMPOUNDS

❑ **dollar-an-inch man** *n.* [? play on SAmE *dollar-a-year man*, one who works for the government at a nominal salary] [1960s+] (*US gay*) a male prostitute who claims that his penis is so large that even charging by the inch he could still get rich. ❑ **dollar store** *n.* [late 19C] (*US Und.*) 'The dollar store displayed valuable articles priced at one dollar in order to bring in marks, who were played for with short-con games' (Maurer, *The Big Con*, 1940). ❑ **dollar-woman** *n.* [her price] [1930s–40s] (*US*) a cheap prostitute.

dollar *n.*[2] [? $ sign on the pill] [1990s+] (*drugs*) MDMA.

dolled out *adj.* [var. DOLLED UP *adj.*] [1920s+] (*US campus*) dressed up, esp. for a night out.

dolled up *adj.* (*also* **dolled, dollied up**) [20C+] (*orig. US*) dressed up, esp. for a night out.

IN PHRASES

❑ **all dolled up like a barber's cat** [DOLL *n.*[1] (5); why the barber's cat should be especially decorated is unknown] [mid–late 19C] (*Can.*) dressed in the height of fashion. ❑ **dolled up like a sore finger/thumb/toe** *see* DRESSED UP LIKE A SORE FINGER/THUMB/TOE *under* DRESSED *adj.*

dollface *n.* [DOLL *n.*[1] (5) + SE *face*] [20C+] an attractive woman or boy; often used as a form of address *Hey, dollface!*

doll-faced *adj.* [? DOLLFACE *n.* or SE] [late 19C] of a young woman, attractive.

doll-goned *adj. see* DOGGONE *adj.*

dollied up *adj. see* DOLLED UP *adj.*

dollies *n.*[1] (*also* **dolly**) [brandname *Dolophine*, a type of synthetic opiate slightly stronger than morphine] [1950s+] (*drugs*) synthetic morphine.

dollies *n.*[2] [one sucks them] [1960s+] (*Irish*) the female breasts.

dollop *n.* [note East Anglian dial. *dollop*, untidy woman, a slattern, a trollop] **1** [early 19C+] a lump; thus the *whole dollop*, the whole lot; *dollops of*, lots of. **2** [mid-19C] a large sum of money. **3** [mid-19C] a three-month sentence, i.e. a small 'lump' of time.

dollop *v.* **1** [mid-19C] to give up a share, lit. 'dole up'. **2** [20C+] (*Irish*) to adulterate.

doll up *v.* (*also* **doll**) [DOLL *n.*[1] (5)] [20C+] to dress up a person or an object; esp. as *doll oneself up*, to smarten oneself up, put on one's best clothes; the implication is often of excess or flashiness.

dolly *n.*[1] [DOLL *n.*[1] + sfx *-y*, but note Hancock, 'Shelta and Polari' (1984), who suggests Ital. *dolce*, sweet and thus claims the word for Polari] **1** [17C] a female pet or favourite. **2** [mid-17C–mid-19C] a mistress, a prostitute. **3** [mid-19C] a slattern, a dull, unattractive woman. **4** [late 19C] a servant girl. **5** [20C+] (*also* **dolly-girl**) any girl or woman, esp. when attractive; also as a term of affection; also attrib. **6** [1960s+] a teenage girl or young woman, usu. associated with the 1960s and 'swinging London', usu. a young secretary or similar, dressed in the latest fashions, obsessed by the current 'in' rock group and other accoutrements of popular culture; post-1960s use usu. historic/ironic. **7** [1970s] (*US*) a term of address, synon. with SE *darling*. **8** [2000s] (*N.Z. prison*) the younger lover of a 'butch' lesbian.

IN COMPOUNDS

❑ **dollybird** *n.* [sense 6 above + BIRD *n.*[1] (1b); post-1960s use is historical] [1960s] an attractive young woman, typically a secretary or shopgirl in her late teens or early twenties and found in such centres of 'swinging London' as Carnaby Street or the King's Road. ❑ **dolly-boy** *n.* (*also* **doll-boy**) [1970s+] (*orig. gay*) a homosexual, a young male prostitute. ❑ **dolly-girl** *n. see* sense 5 above. ❑ **dolly sweetness** *n.* [1940s] (*US black campus*) a hitherto unknown young woman.

IN PHRASES

❑ **dolly in** *v.* [1960s] to behave in a effeminate provocative manner.

SE in slang uses

IN COMPOUNDS

❑ **dolly gray** *n.* [? Boer War song 'Goodbye, Dolly Gray'] [1900s] (*US*) a woman, a housewife. ❑ **dolly sisters** *n.* [the singers Janszieka (1893–1941) and Roszika (1893–1970) Deutsch, better known as Jenny and Rosie *Dolly*] [1950s–70s] (*US*) a pair of patrolmen. ❑ **dolly-worship** *n.* [the use of statues and religious images in Catholic churches] [late 19C–1900s] a derog. term for Roman Catholicism.

IN PHRASES

❑ **up to dolly's eyeweights** [1960s] (*N.Z.*) completely. ❑ **up to dolly's wax** (*also* **up to pussy's bow**) [nursery use, dolls used to have solid bodies surmounted with carefully modelled wax heads] [1940s+] (*Aus.*) absolutely full of food.

dolly *n.*[2] [? they have as much sense as a child's doll] [mid-19C] anyone who has committed a *faux pas* or social solecism.

dolly *n.*[3] (*also* **doll**) [f. a variety of jokes in which a supposedly innocent girl plays with a man's 'dolly', which then spits at her, vomits etc] [late 19C+] the penis.

dolly *n.*[4] [ety. unknown; ? link to SE *tallow*, of which candles were made; or school sl. *tolly*, a candle] [20C+] (*UK tramp*) a candle.

IN PHRASES

❑ **dolly up** *v.* [20C+] (*UK tramp*) to heat water or tea with a candle.

dolly *n.*[5] *see* DOLLIES *n.*[1].

dolly *n.*[6] *see* DOLLYSHOP *n.*

dolly *adj.* [note Dickens, *Bleak House* (1853): 'A dolly sort of beauty, perhaps [...] but in its way, perfect; such bloom I never saw'] (*orig. Polari*) **1** [mid-19C–1900s] silly, foolish. **2** [1960s+] nice or pleasant; attractive, fashionable.

dolly *v.* [fig. use of a v. form of gold-mining *dolly*, an implement for crushing quartz; ult. UK dial. *dolly*, a wooden implement for beating clothes in the wash] [1930s+] (*Aus.*) **1** to treat harshly. **2** to interrogate.

Dolly Cotton *adj. see* JOHNNY COTTON *adj.*

dolly-man *n.* (*also* **pitchy-man**) [? DOLLYSHOP *n.*, SE *trader's pitch*] **1** [mid-19C] the keeper of an unlicensed pawnbroker's. **2** [late 19C] a Jew.

dolly mixtures *n.* [rhy. sl. = SE *pictures*] [1980s+] the cinema.

dollymop *n.* [DOLLY *n.*[1] (7) + the equation of women and fish, in this case the SE *mop*, a young whiting or gurnard, thus a young woman. Note obs. Ger. sl. *Backfisch*, a teenage girl, lit. a 'fish for baking'] [mid-19C–1900s] **1** a part-time prostitute, often a servant or shopgirl, esp. a milliner, who occas. sold her body to supplement her otherwise meagre income. **2** (*US*) a prostitute specializing in sailors. **3** a slovenly, ill-kempt servant girl. **4** (*Aus.*) a term of abuse.

dollymopper *n.* [DOLLYMOP *n.*] [mid–late 19C] a womanizer, esp. a soldier.

dollypot *n.* [rhy. sl. = TWAT *n.* (3)] [1920s+] (*Aus.*) a fool.

dollyshop *n.* (*also* **dolly**) [orig. a marine store, signified by the black doll hanging outside as a sign] [mid-19C–1930s] a low or illegal pawnshop, whose owner may also act as a receiver.

dolly varden *n.* [rhy. sl.; ult. *Dolly Varden*, a character in Charles Dickens's *Barnaby Rudge* (1841)] [late 19C+] the garden.

dolo *adv.* [ety. unknown] [1990s+] **1** (*US black*) on one's own, solo. **2** (*US campus*) secret.

dolomite *n.* [SE *dolomite*, a form of rock, composed of lime and magnesia; thus a pun on ROCK *n.* (4c); + ? ref. to blaxploitation film *Dolemite*(1975)] [1980s+] (*US campus*) cocaine.

d.o.m. *n.* [abbr.] [1950s+] a *d*irty *o*ld *m*an; poss. an actual or alleged child molester but usu. any older man who makes obvious his preference for women younger than he might be expected to pursue.

DOM *n. see* DOB *n.*

dom *n.* [abbr.] **1** [1960s+] a *dom*inatrix. **2** [1980s+] *Dom* Perignon champgane, a premier brand.

dom *adj.* [1980s+] in sado-masochistic sex, *dom*inant, pertaining to a *dom*inatrix.

dom! *excl. see* DAMN! *excl.*

-dom *sfx* [17C+] a sfx added to a n. to imply 'the domain of'.

domain cocktail *n.* [proper name of the *Domain*, a park in Sydney, Australia, popular for speech-making and frequented by the unemployed and the alcoholic] [late 19C–1930s] (*Aus.*) 'a lethal concoction of petrol and pepper which reputedly once had a vogue among deadbeat drinkers in the Sydney Domain' (Baker, *Aus. Sl.*, 1941); thus *domain dosser*, a loafer or down-and-out who frequents the Sydney Domain.

dome *n.* **1** [mid-18C+] (*orig. US*) the head. **2** [1900s] (*US*) a hat.

IN COMPOUNDS

❑ **domelights** *n.* [1990s+] (*US*) the eyes. ❑ **domepiece** *n.* **1** [1970s+] (*US*) the head. **2** [1990s+] (*US black*) a hat. ❑ **dome-shot** *n.* [play on HEAD *n.* (2c)] [2000s] (*US black*) to request or receive fellatio. ❑ **domework** *n.* [1910s] (*US*) brainwork.

IN PHRASES

❑ **blow domes** *v.* [1990s+] (*US*) to amaze, to astound. ❑ **double dome** *n.* (*also* **big dome**) [1930s+] an intellectual, a scholar, esp. one who seems to hold eccentric or impractical opinions. ❑ **double-domed** *adj.* (*also* **big-dome**) [1950s+] intellectual. ❑ **off the top of the dome** [1980s+] (*US black*) of rap lyrics, spontaneous, composing lyrics as you go along; usu. as *coming…* or *going…*

do me a favour *n.* [rhy. sl.] [1990s+] a neighbour.

do me a favour *phr.* (*also* **do us a favour**) [ironic uses of SE] [1950s+] **1** a synon. for 'you must be joking' or 'who do you think you're fooling?'. **2** a phr. meaning stop harassing me, go away, be off.

do-me-dag *n.* [rhy. sl. = FAG *n.*[4] (2); ult. *do my dags*, a children's game synon. with 'follow my leader'; the image is of children encouraging each other to smoke] [late 19C+] a cigarette.

do me good *n.* [rhy. sl.] **1** [late 19C+] a Woodbine cigarette. **2** [20C+] wood; (*Aus.*) firewood. **3** [1910s] food.

doment *n.* [orig. dial; DO *n.* (3) + sfx *-ment*] [mid-19C] a performance, a show.

domes *n.* [? the shape of a capsule or the effect on one's head, i.e. DOME *n.* (1)] [1970s+] (*drugs*) LSD.

domestic *n.* [1970s+] **1** any problems accruing to one's home (rather than criminal / professional) life. **2** an argument or fight between a couple who live together.

domie *n.* (*also* **domi, dommie, dommy**) [abbr. SE *domicile*; ult. Lat. *domus*, home] [1930s] (*US black*) one's house, one's home.

domine do-little *n.* (*also* **domini, domini do-little, dominie do-little**) [SE *dominie*, a schoolmaster + *do-little*] [late 18C–early 19C] an impotent old man.

dominicker *n.* (*also* **dommernecker**) [SE *dominicker*, the Dominique fowl or any other chicken with mottled or barred plumage. The dominicker rooster was believed always to back down when challenged by another rooster] [20C+] (*W.I.*) **1** a coward. **2** a person of mixed race, esp. of black, Indian and white ancestry.

domino *n.*[1] **1** [early 19C–1910s] a tooth; usu. in pl., esp. when yellow and rotten. **2** [late 19C] piano, or street organ, keys. **3** [1920s] (*US*) a die; usu. in pl.; thus *jumping dominoes*, crooked dice; *domino boy*, a dice player. **4** [1960s+] (*drugs*) a capsule containing a combination of an amphetamine and a sedative.

IN COMPOUNDS

❑ **domino-box** *n. see* BOX OF DOMINOES *under* BOX OF… *n.* ❑ **domino-thumper** *n.* [late 19C–1920s] a pianist.

domino *n.*[2] [DOMINO! *excl.*] [mid-19C; 1970s+] (*UK Und.*) a knockout blow.

domino *n.*[3] [SLAM *n.*[1] (1), i.e. one 'slams' her down] [1990s+] (*UK black*) a woman seen as a sex object.

domino *v.* [the knocking down of a row of SE *dominoes*] **1** [1910s] (*Aus.*) to kill. **2** [1950s] (*US black*) to stop.

domino! *excl.* [the game of *dominoes*, in which the winner is the player who gets rid of all their pieces first] [mid–late 19C] a general excl. to signify the end of or last of a situation: that's it, that's done, all over etc; esp. among soldiers and sailors, to signify the last blow of a thrashing; thus *it is domino with…*, it is finished, it is all over, it is hopeless.

dommerer *n.* (*also* **dommerar, drommerar**) [SE *dumb*] [mid-16C–early 19C] (*UK Und.*) a mendicant villain who feigned dumbness, often claiming to have suffered at the hands of the infidel Turk who, on capturing him during a sea voyage, had torn out his tongue for denying Muhammad.

dommernecker *n. see* DOMINICKER *n.*

dommie *n.* **1** [1990s+] (*S.Afr.*) a dumb person. **2** *see* DOMIE *n.*

dommy *n.* [abbr.] **1** [2000s] (*US black*) con*dom*. **2** *see* DOMIE *n.*

dommy *v.* [DOMIE *n.*] [1940s] (*US*) to live, to stay.

dommy-knocker *n. see* DONGER-KNOCKER *n.*

dompas *n.* (*also* **dompass**) [Afk. *dom*, stupid + *pas*, pass] [1950s+] (*S.Afr. black*) a pass book, i.e. the mandatory identity document formerly carried by all blacks.

doms *n.* [abbr.] **1** [20C+] (*Aus.*) *Dom*inicans. **2** [1990s+] *dom*inoes.

don *n.* [the original use comes from the Sp. honorific *Don*. The term has been re-invented, with much the same meaning, in the late 20C, mainly by teen gangs, with a ref. to the Italian Mafia's use of *Don* to refer to a senior Mafioso, a use that was spread with the popularity of the film *The Godfather* (1972), the story of the fictitious *Don* Corleone] **1** [17C–mid-19C; 1910s–20s] a Spaniard. **2** [17C+] a clever or outstanding person, a distinguished individual, a leader. **3** [1970s+] (*W.I./UK black teen*) (*also* **donette, don man, donna**) a respected boss or leader, the master or mistress of a situation.

IN COMPOUNDS

❑ **don dada** *n.* [SE *dada*; lit. 'don father'] [1980s+] (*W.I./UK black teen*) the highest ranking leader, Don of Dons. ❑ **don gorgon** *n.* [the mythical *Gorgon*, whose 'hair' was actually writhing snakes] [1980s+] (*W.I./Rasta*) **1** outstanding dreadlocks; thus a person who is respected. **2** an enforcer.

don *adj.* [DON *n.*] [mid-19C; 1990s+] the ultimate example, the very best.

dona *n.* (*also* **donah, done, doner, doney, donie, donna, donner, donny, dony**) [Polari *donah*; ult. Ital. *donna*, a woman] **1** [mid-19C+] (*Ling. Fr./Polari*) a woman, often attractive. **2** [late 19C–1940s] a wife or girlfriend. **3** [1920s] a landlady. **4** [1970s] (*UK Und.*) the 'lady', the queen in a game of three-card monte. **5** [1990s+] (*W.I.*) an attractive woman.

IN COMPOUNDS

❑ **dona jack** *n.* [JACK *n.*[2]] [late 19C–1900s] a pimp.

IN PHRASES

❑ **old donah** *n.* [19C+] one's mother. ❑ **swell dona** *n. see under* SWELL *adj.*

donagher *n.* [DANNA *n.*] [early 19C–1920s] (*20C use mainly US*) a privy.

dona highland-flinger *n.* [rhy. sl.] [late 19C–1900s] a music-hall singer.

dona juanita *n.* [lit. 'lady Jane'; play on Mex. *marijuana*, i.e. Mary Jane] [1930s+] (*drugs*) marijuana.

donaker *n.* see DUNAKER *n.*

Donald (Duck) *n.* [rhy. sl.] **1** [1960s+] (*orig. Aus.*) sexual intercourse; also fig. in phr. *not give a donald* [= FUCK *n.* (1a)]. **2** [1960s+] (*Aus.*) a truck. **3** [1970s+] luck.

Donald Trump *n.* [rhy. sl. = DUMP *n.*[4] (3); ult. US millionaire property developer *Donald Trump* (b.1946)] [2000s] an act of defecation.

Don Cheech *n.* (*also* **Don Cheechero**) [generic 'Italian' name] [1930s+] (*US Und.*) a senior member of the US Mafia.

Don Cypriano *n.* [play on Sp. honorific *Don* + CYPRIAN *adj.*; coined by Sir Thomas Urquhart for his translation of *Rabelais* (1653–93)] [17C] the penis.

donder *n.* [DONDER *v.*] [late 19C+] (*S.Afr.*) 'a blighter, a bastard' (*DSAE*).

IN COMPOUNDS

❑ **donderkop** *n.* [late 19C+] (*S.Afr.*) a fool.

donder *v.* (*also* **donner**) [synon. Afk. *donder*] **1** [mid-19C+] (*S.Afr.*) to beat up, to thrash. **2** [1970s–80s] to beat, to overcome, to defeat (someone or something).

done *n.*[1] [DONA *n.*; Asbury, *The Gangs of Chicago* (1940), cites: 'Belle Jones's den in Clark Street which in 1871 could boast of harboring "the oldest dones in the world" — Nellie Welch and Mollie Moore'] **1** [mid–late 19C] (*US Und.*) a prostitute. **2** see DONA *n.*

done *n.*[2]

IN PHRASES

❑ **get the done** *v.* [20C+] (*W.I. teen*) to be 'dropped' by a boy- or girlfriend; thus *give the done*, to end a relationship, to drop one's partner.

done *adj.* [DO *v.*[1]] **1** [late 16C+] dead; killed. **2** [late 16C+] exhausted, worn out. **3** [late 16C+] impoverished. **4** [mid-18C+] cheated, swindled. **5** [late 18C–early 19C] hanged. **6** [early 19C+] arrested (on a given charge); punished. **7** [mid-19C+] in fig. senses, badly defeated, 'finished'. **8** [mid-19C+] of a commodity, finished. **9** [1930s+] beaten up, assaulted. **10** [1960s] (*US*) (*also* **done in**) raped. **11** [1980s+] (*UK juv.*) reprimanded, told off.

IN PHRASES

❑ **done like a dog's dinner** *adj.* see *under* DOG'S DINNER *n.* ❑ **done to the wide world** *adj.* [20C+] defeated, beaten, utterly vanquished.

done for *adj.* [DO FOR *v.*/ext. of DONE *adj.*] **1** [late 18C+] of people, badly defeated, 'finished'. **2** [mid–late 19C] of objects, destroyed. **3** [mid-19C+] exhausted, used up. **4** [mid-19C+] dead, killed. **5** [mid-19C+] without a chance, hopeless, defeated, lost, abandoned.

donegan *n.* see DONIGAN *n.*

donegan worker *n.* see *DUNNIGAN WORKER under* DUNNAKEN *n.*

done in *adj.* (*also* **done out**) [DONE *adj.*] [20C+] **1** very tired, exhausted. **2** beyond further effort. **3** see DONE *adj.* (10).

done-over *adj.* [DO *v.*[1]] **1** [18C–19C] of a woman, having been used for sexual purposes. **2** [19C+] drunk. **3** [mid-19C] worsted, put at a disadvantage, forced to lose out in a disagreement or struggle. **4** see DO OVER *v.* (4).

done promote *n.* [? joking allusion, *I see you done promote* (have been promoted, i.e. from bare feet)] [1940s+] (*W.I.*) sandals or shoes made from old automobile tyres.

doner *n.*[1] [DONE *adj.* + ? pun on GONER *n.*[1]] [mid-19C–1930s] one who is ruined, on the verge of death or collapse.

doner *n.*[2] see DONA *n.*

donette *n.* see DON *n.* (3).

done up *adj.*[1] **1** [late 18C–1910s] (*US*) ruined (by gambling or other forms of speculation). **2** [early 19C] (*orig. US*) beaten up. **3** [early 19C+] exhausted, worn out, fed up. **4** [mid-19C] extremely drunk. **5** [mid-19C+] worsted, put at a disadvantage, forced to lose out in a disagreement or struggle. **6** [20C+] ill, whether mildly or extremely. **7** [1910s] out of order, not working.

IN PHRASES

❑ **done up like a kipper** [DONE *adj.*; Grose (1785) labels it a 'modern term'] [20C+] **1** beaten up. **2** caught red-handed by the police, ambushed during a crime. **3** utterly defeated.

done up *adj.*[2] [SE *do up*, to decorate, renovate a building or room] [late 19C+] dressed up; esp. as *done up to the nines*.

IN PHRASES

❑ **done up like a pox doctor's clerk** see POX-DOCTOR'S CLERK *n.* ❑ **done up like a sore finger/thumb/toe** [20C+] (*Aus./N.Z./US*) overdressed, flashily dressed.

doney *n.* see DONA *n.*

dong *n.*[1] [abbr. DING-DONG *n.*[4], which predates general regional sl. use] (*orig. US*) **1** [late 19C+] (*also* **dang, dange**) the penis. **2** [1950s+] a general derog. term: a fool. **3** [2000s] a dildo.

IN PHRASES

❑ **dong and gongs** *n.* [1980s] (*US gay*) the male genitalia. ❑ **doubledong(er)** *n.* [1990s+] (*US*) a dildo with two penis-shaped ends which can be used simultaneously by two people, usu. women. ❑ **flog one's dong** *v.* [20C+] to masturbate.

dong *n.*[2] (*also* **donger**) [echoic] **1** [20C+] a blow, esp. with the fist [post-1930s use is mainly Aus.]. **2** [1990s+] a phonecall.

dong *v.* [DONG *n.*[2]] **1** [20C+] to hit. **2** [1990s+] (*US campus*) to have sexual intercourse.

donged-up *adj.* [ext. use of DONG *v.* (1)] [20C+] tense, anxious.

donger *n.*[1] (*also* **dunga, dunger**) [ext. of DONG *n.*[1] (1), but note *donger*, a fisherman's club] [1960s+] (*orig. Aus.*) **1** (*also* **doniger**) the penis. **2** a general term of abuse.

IN PHRASES

❑ **dangle one's donger** *v.* [1970s] to urinate. ❑ **in the donger** [2000s] (*N.Z.*) in trouble.

donger *n.*[2] see DONG *n.*[2].

donger-knocker *n.* (*also* **bommy-knocker, dommy-knocker, dongy-knocker**) [DONG *v.* (1)/SE *bomb* + *knocker*] [1930s+] (*N.Z., mainly juv.*) a club, a bludgeon.

donicker *n.* (*also* **doniker, donneker, donnicker**) [DUNNAKEN *n.* (1)] [18C–19C] a privy.

donigan *n.* (*also* **donegan**) [DUNNAKEN *n.* (1)] [1910s–40s] a privy.

doniger *n.* see DONGER *n.*[1] (1).

doniker *n.* see DONICKER *n.*

don jem *n.* [var. on DJAMBA *n.*] [1950s+] (*drugs*) marijuana.

donk *n.*[1] [abbr. SE] **1** [1910s+] a *donkey*. **2** [1910s+] (*Aus.*) a car or boat engine, a motorcycle. **3** [1940s+] (*Aus.*) a lift on the crossbar of a bicycle. **4** [1950s] (*N.Z.*) a racehorse; thus *on the donks*, on the horses. **5** [1990s+] (*US campus*) excrement. **6** [2000s] (*US campus*) large, protruding buttocks.

donk *n.*[2] [? both have 'a kick like a mule'] **1** [1920s] illicit 'moonshine' whisky. **2** [2000s] (*US drugs*) marijuana and PCP.

donkey *n.* [the donkey is used as a working animal, plus supposedly has a large appendage] **1** [mid-19C] (*US campus*) a notably religious student. **2** [1920s+] (*US*) a working-class Irish person; also attrib. **3** [1940s] a manual labourer. **4** [1960s+] a (large) penis; usu. in combs. below.

IN COMPOUNDS

❑ **donkey-hung** *adj.* [late 19C] possessing a very large penis. ❑ **donkey-rigged** *adj.* [late 19C+] in possession of a notably large penis. ❑ **donkey prick** *n.* [PRICK *n.* (1)] [late 19C] a notably large penis. ❑ **donkey's knob** *n.* [KNOB *n.* (1c)] [1990s+] **1** anything obvious. **2** anything excellent, admirable, first-rate.

IN PHRASES

❑ **flog one's donkey** *v.* [1960s+] to masturbate. ❑ **pull one's donkey** *v.* [1990s+] to masturbate.

SE in slang uses

IN COMPOUNDS

❑ **donkey dipper** *n.* [1910s] (*Aus.*) a pickpocket. ❑ **donkey dust** *n.* [SE *dust*, rubbish] [1950s+] a euph. for BULLSHIT *n.* ❑ **donkey lick** see separate entries. ❑ **donkey price** *n.*

[1950s+] (*W.I.*) an inflated price, one only a fool would pay. ▫ **donkey roast** *n.* [? link to the US Democratic Party's mascot, the donkey] [1960s] (*US*) a formal banquet. ▫ **donkey's breakfast** *n.* **1** [late 19C–1960s] a straw hat. **2** [1910s+] (*Aus./US*) a straw palliasse. ▫ **donkey's ears** *n.* [mid-19C] a false collar; a detachable shirt-collar with long points. ▫ **donkey show** *n.* [? a sex show involving a donkey and a woman] [1990s+] (*US black*) a complete mess, a farcical situation. ▫ **donkey wallop** *v.* [var. on DONKEY LICK *v.*] [1980s] (*Aus.*) to defeat easily. ▫ **donkey yawn** *n.* [1990s+] a large vagina.

IN PHRASES

▫ **donkey-deep in** [lit. or fig.] [1910s–20s] (*N.Z.*) immersed in, up to one's neck in. ▫ **who stole the donkey?** [certainly anecdotal, but Hotten (1864) is 'unable to explain the phrase'] [mid–late 19C] a phr. shouted after anyone wearing a white hat, and the reply is 'The man in the white hat'.

donkey dick *n.*[1] [note late 18C–mid-19C *donkey* (? f. proper name *Duncan*) itself was orig. sl.] [late 18C–early 19C] an ass.

donkey dick *n.*[2] (*also* **donkey-cock**) [DONKEY *n.* (5) + DICK *n.*[1] (5)] [1960s+] **1** (*US*) a notably large penis; usu. as adj. *donkey-dicked*, having a large penis [US successor to *DONKEY PRICK under* DONKEY *n.*]. **2** (*US prison*) a hot dog. **3** (*US milit./prison*) sliced cold cuts. **4** (*US*) in fig. use, a problematic situation.

donkey lick *n.* [? its appeal to the animal] [1940s–50s] (*Aus.*) treacle or golden syrup.

donkey lick *v.* [SE *donkey* + LICK *v.*[1] (2)] [late 19C–1940s] (*Aus./N.Z.*) to defeat easily.

donko *n.* [? synon. N.Z. SE *donkey room*, orig. (1920s) the enclosure on the Wellington docks where a donkey engine was kept and at the time was the only warm shelter available] [1970s+] (*N.Z.*) a room set aside in the workplace for smoking, relaxation etc.

donks *n.* [colloq. *donkey's years*] [1990s+] a very long time.

don man *n. see* DON *n.* (3).

donna *n.*[1] *see* DONA *n.*

donna *n.*[2] *see* DON *n.* (3).

donna and feeles *n.* [Ital. or Ling. Fr. *donna e figlie*, a woman and children] [mid-19C] a woman and children.

donneker *n. see* DONICKER *n.*

donnelly *n.* [the prize-fighter Daniel *Donnelly* (1788–1820)] [mid-19C] (*US*) a heavy blow or punch.

donner *v.* [Afk. *donner*, to thrash] (*S.Afr.*) **1** [mid-19C+] to beat up, to thrash. **2** [1960s+] in fig. use, to defeat, to overcome; to reprimand severely; thus n. *donnering*.

donnicker *n. see* DONICKER *n.*

donnie *n.* (*also* **donny**) [abbr. SE *donnybrook*, a fight, a riot, a noisy brawl] [1950s–60s] (*N.Z.*) a fight, a disturbance.

donny *n. see* DONA *n.*

donor *n.* [1980s+] (*US campus*) one who makes themselves available for sexual intercourse.

do-nothing stool *n.* [used when one is sitting down idly] [late 19C; 1980s] (*US black*) the buttocks, the posterior.

donovan *n.*[1] [the commonness of the Irish surname and the stereotyping of the Irish appetite for potatoes] **1** [mid-19C] a nickname for an Irishman. **2** [mid-19C+] a potato.

donovan *n.*[2] [a pej. based on the HIPPIE *adj.* singer *Donovan* (b.1946)] [1990s+] (*W.I.*) an aspirant DON *n.* (3).

Don Pego *n. see* PEGO *n.*

Don Revie *n.* [rhy. sl. = BEVVY *n.*; ult. UK football manager *Don Revie* (1928–89)] [1990s+] alcohol, a drink.

don't... *phr. see under* relevant n. or v.

don't be funny *n.* [rhy. sl. = DUNNY *n.*[2] (1)] [20C+] (*Aus.*) a lavatory.

don't forget her *n.* [rhy. sl.] [1900s] (*Aus.*) a letter.

don't-know-what-to-call-'ems *n.* (*also* **don't name 'ems, don't-speak-of-'ems**) [euph.; the image of trousers, so close to the genitals and legs, as 'obscene' or taboo] [mid-19C–1900s] (*US*) trousers.

don't make a fuss *n.* [rhy. sl.] [1960s] a bus.

donut *n. see under* DOUGHNUT.

doo *n. see* DO *n.* (1).

doob *n.*[1] [ety. unknown] [1950s+] (*Aus.*) the penis.

doob *n.*[2] [ety. unknown; originated with the UK Mods of the early 1960s and then spread among other users] [1960s+] (*UK drugs*) amphetamine.

dooberry *n. see* DOOBRIE *n.*

doobie *n.*[1] (*also* **doob, doober, dubbe, dube, dubee, duby**) [ety. unknown; poss. same ety. as DOOBIE *n.*[2]] **1** [1960s+] (*orig. US drugs*) cannabis; thus adj., *doobious*, intoxicated from cannabis. **2** [1960s+] (*drugs*) a cannabis cigarette. **3** [1970s] (*US prison*) a cigarette.

DERIVATIVES

▫ **doobage** *n.* [-AGE *sfx*] [1980s+] (*US campus*) marijuana.

doobie *n.*[2] [Scot. *dobie*, a dull, stupid fellow; ult. f. *Dobie*, Robert] [1980s+] (*US*) an unimportant, worthless or stupid person.

doobob *n.* (*also* **doobobbis, doobobbus**) [ety. unknown] [1910s+] (*orig. US*) any nameless small object, typically some form of gadget.

doobrie *n.* (*also* **dooberry, doobry, dubry**) [orig. in the army, the term gained a new lease of life thanks to the DJ and TV performer Kenny Everett, who used it frequently in the 1970s–80s] [1950s+] (*orig. milit.*) anything for which one cannot recall the name.

doobs *adj.* [SE *dubious*] [1990s+] second-rate, unpopular, a general negative term.

dooby *adj.* [SE *dowdy* + ? BOOBY *n.*[1] (1)] [1950s+] (*Aus.*) old-fashioned.

dooce *n. see* DEUCE *n.*[2] (2).

dooced *adj. see* DEUCED *adj.*

dood *n.* [Irish *dudeen*, a short clay pipe] **1** [1910s+] (*Aus.*) a pipe. **2** [1920s–50s] (*US*) the penis.

doo-da *n. see* DOODAH *n.*[1].

doodackie *n.* [ety. unknown] [1940s+] (*N.Z.*) any nameless small object, typically some form of gadget; the *doodackied up*, dressed up.

doodad *n.* (*also* **doodab(bus), doogood, dudaddle, dudedad**) [ety. unknown; the many synon. terms for the word may represent the stammering efforts of one who is struggling to recall the correct name] (*orig. US*) **1** [late 19C+] any nameless small object, typically some form of gadget. **2** [1920s+] (*also* **doodah**) something small, used as a decoration. **3** [1920s+] nonsense, foolish chatter.

doodads *n.* [DOODAD *n.*] [late 19C+] (*orig. US*) morsels, pieces, odds and ends.

doodah *n.*[1] (*also* **doo-da**) [the refrain *doo-da(h)* of the plantation song 'Camptown Races' (1850)] [1910s+] an emotional crisis, a nervous, tense state.

IN PHRASES

▫ **all of a doodah** (*also* **all of a doo-da**) [1910s+] in a fluster, in a state, very agitated.

doodah *n.*[2] [DOODAD *n.*] **1** [1920s+] anything or anyone for which one cannot remember the name. **2** [2000s] the genitals.

doodah *n.*[3] *see* DOODAD *n.* (2).

doo-dah up *v.* [DOODAH *n.*[2] (1)] [1980s] to decorate or dress up showily.

doodey-squat *n. see* DOODY-SQUAT *n.*

doodgooi *n.* [Afk. *doodgooier*, a dumpling, lit. a 'dead-thrower', i.e. dough that has not risen] [1910s+] (*S.Afr.*) a lethal weapon.

doodibbie *n.* [ety. unknown] [1910s+] any nameless small object, typically some form of gadget.

doodinkus *n.* (*also* **dinkus, dodinkus, dudinkus**) [ety. unknown] [1910s+] any nameless small object, typically some form of gadget.

doodle *n.*[1] [var. on SE *noodle*, a fool; ? link to Low Ger. *Dudeltopf*, a simpleton, lit. a 'nightcap'] [early 17C–mid-19C] a fool, a dull person.

doodle *n.*[2] [20C+ use of all senses is US] **1** [late 18C+] the penis, esp. a child's penis. **2** [late 19C+] the vagina. **3** [1910s] any nameless small object, typically some form of gadget.

pertaining to the penis

(IN COMPOUNDS)

❑ **doodle-case** *n.* **1** [19C] a masturbator. **2** [late 19C] the vagina. ❑ **doodle-dandler** *n.* [19C] a masturbator. ❑ **doodle-dasher** *n.* [SE *dash*, to strike, to hit] **1** [late 19C] a masturbator. **2** *see* DINGLE-DANGLE *n.* ❑ **doodleflap** *n.* [late 19C] the flaccid penis. ❑ **doodle-head** *n.* (*also* **doodlebrain**) [-HEAD *sfx* (1)] [1990s+] (*Aus. teen*) a general insult. ❑ **doodle-sack** *n. see* separate entry.

(IN PHRASES)

❑ **dash one's doodle** *v.* [19C] of a man, to masturbate. ❑ **do a doodle-dandler** *v.* [SE *dandle*, to fondle, to stroke] [19C] to masturbate. ❑ **whack one's doodle** *v.* [1970s] of a man, to masturbate.

pertaining to nameless objects

(IN COMPOUNDS)

❑ **doodlebug** *n.* [? southeastern dial. *doodle-bug*, a booming cockchafer] **1** [1930s+] a small cheap car, any small vehicle or a machine or gadget. **2** [1940s+] a German V-1 flying bomb [post-WW2 use is historical]. ❑ **doodlebum** *n.* [1910s] any nameless small object, typically some form of gadget. ❑ **doodlefagit** *n.* [1910s] any nameless small object, typically some form of gadget. ❑ **doodleflap** *n. see* FLAPDOODLE *n.*[2]. ❑ **doodleflicker** *n.* (*also* **doodleflickus, doodlegadget**) [1910s] any nameless small object, typically some form of gadget.

doodle *n.*[3] [var. on DODDLE *n.* (1)] **1** [1910s] (*US*) something or someone attractive. **2** [1990s+] (*US*) anything completely simple or easy to achieve.

doodle *adj.* [DOODLE *n.*[1]] [18C] foolish.

doodle *v.*[1] [DOODLE *n.*[1]] [19C] to make a fool of, to cheat.

(IN COMPOUNDS)

❑ **doodle-em-buck** *n.* [late 19C] (*Aus.*) confidence trickery.

doodle *v.*[2] [DOODLE *n.*[2] (1)] **1** [late 19C–1950s] (*US*) of a man, to have sexual intercourse. **2** [1990s+] to masturbate.

(IN PHRASES)

❑ **go doodling** *v.* [late 19C–1900s] to have sexual intercourse.

doodle-do(o) *n.* (*also* **doodly-do**) [1960s+] (*US*) **1** nothing at all, e.g. *I can't do doodle-do about it* [the trad. phonetic version of the cock's crowing, *cock-a-doodle-do*]. **2** the vagina or penis, i.e. THING *n.* (2) [ext. DOODLE *n.*[2] (1)].

doodle-doo man *n.* [SE *cock-a-doodle-doo*] [early 19C] one who breeds or fights cocks.

doodler *n.* [SE *doodle*, to draw idle patterns] [20C+] a lazy person, an idler.

doodle-sack *n.*[1] [Ger. *Dudelsack* bagpipes; ? ult. SE *tootle*] [late 18C–early 19C] (*Scot.*) a bagpipe.

doodle-sack *n.*[2] **1** [late 18C–early 19C] a pocket. **2** [late 18C–19C] the vagina [DOODLE *n.*[2] (1)].

doodley *n.* (*also* **doodly**) [abbr. DOODLEY-SQUAT *n.*] [1930s+] (*US*) nothing, with inference that the subject is additionally worthless.

doodley-shit *n.* (*also* **doodly-shit**) [var. on DOODLEY-SQUAT *n.*] **1** [1950s+] (*orig. US*) worthless rubbish, trash. **2** [1980s] nothing, anything.

doodley-squat *n.* (*also* **doodly-squat**) [1930s+] nothing, zero.

doodley-squat *adv.* (*also* **doodly-squat**) [DOODLEY-SQUAT *n.*] [1930s+] (*US*) in no way at all.

doodly *see also under* DOODLEY.

doodly-do *n. see* DOODLE-DO(O) *n.*

doodlyfuck *n.* [2000s] (*US*) a fool.

doo-doo *n. see* DO-DO *n.*[1].

doo-doo *adj.* [DO-DO *n.*[1] (1), i.e. SHIT *adj.* (3)] [2000s] (*US black*) excellent, first-rate; thus *doodoofetic*, arrogant.

doody-squat *n.* (*also* **doodey-squat**) [var. DIDDLY-SQUAT *n.*[1]] [1950s+] nothing; something of insignificance.

dooe(e) *n.* (*also* **doee, due, duey**) [Ital. *due*, two] [mid-19C+] (*Ling. Fr./Polari*) the number two.

doof *n.*[1] [abbr. DOOFLUS *n.*, but note Scot. *doof*, a dull, stupid person; ? ult. Ger. *doof*, dense, stupid, dull-witted] [1970s+] (*US*) a fool, a simpleton.

doof *n.*[2] [echoic of the sound of the kick drum used in such music] [1990s+] (*Aus.*) rhythmic dance music, as played in clubs.

doofer *n.* [SE *do for*] **1** [20C+] a partially smoked cigarette. **2** [1970s+] (*Irish*) any otherwise unnamed object.

doofis *adj. see* DOOFUS *adj.*

doofless *adj.* [DOOFLUS *n.*] [1970s+] (*US*) idiotic, stupid, dull.

dooflicker *n.* [abbr. DOODLEFLICKER *under* DOODLE *n.*[2]; note West Point use *duflicket*, derog. term for a plebe or first-year cadet] **1** [1900s–40s] (*orig. Can. milit.*) (*also* **doflickety, dooflinkus, duflickerty**) any nameless small object, typically some form of gadget. **2** [1950s] the foreskin.

dooflop *n.* [ety. unknown] [1950s+] any nameless small object, typically some form of gadget.

dooflus *n.* (*also* **duflus**) [? Ger. *doof*, stupid] [1930s+] (*US black/teen*) a bizarre, eccentric individual.

doofunny *n.* (*also* **dofunny, doojumfunny, dufunny**) [ety. unknown] [1900s–40s] any nameless small object, typically some form of gadget.

doofus *n.* (*also* **doufas, doufus, duffus**) [see DOOF *n.*[1]; note also the character *Dufus*, in the cartoon strip *Popeye*, a foolish, bumbling individual] [1950s+] (*orig. US black*) an odd person, an eccentric; a fool.

doofus *adj.* (*also* **doofis**) [DOOFUS *n.*] [1960s+] odd, strange, eccentric.

doofy *adj.* [DOOF *n.*[1] + sfx *-y*] [1980s] (*US, usu. juv.*) foolish, silly, eccentric.

doog *adj.* [backsl.] [mid-19C+] good.

(IN COMPOUNDS)

❑ **doog eno** *n.* (*also* **doogheno**) [ENO *n.*] [mid-19C+] good one, esp. when referring to the state of the day's market. ❑ **doog gels** *n.* [mid-19C+] of a passing woman, good legs. ❑ **doogheo hit** *n.* [mid-19C] a good or profitable market.

(IN PHRASES)

❑ **on doog** [ON *adv.*] [mid-19C+] no good.

doogie *n. see* DUJI *n.*

doogie daddy *n. see* DAP DADDY *under* DAP *adj.*

doogood *n. see* DOODAD *n.*

doohickey *n. see* DOHICKEY *n.*[1].

dooie *n.* [1980s+] (*US campus*) an echoic equivalent of the sound of a punch or slap; thus v. *dooie*, to hit.

doojee *n. see* DUJI *n.*

doojie *n.* [ety. unknown] [1950s] (*US black*) the vagina.

doojigger *n. see* DOJIGGER *n.*

doojumfunny *n. see* DOOFUNNY *n.*

dook *n.*[1] **1** [mid–late 19C] a notably large nose [mispron. of *duke* = Duke of Wellington (1769–1852), known for his large nose and thus nicknamed *Conky*]. **2** [mid-19C+] a hand [var. of DUKE *n.*[3] (1)].

(IN PHRASES)

❑ **have dook on it** *v.* [20C+] (*Aus.*) to shake hands in order to seal a bargain. ❑ **put up the dooks** *v.* [1900s] (*UK Und.*) to thieve, esp. to pickpocket.

dook *n.*[2] [DUKIE *n.*[2] (1)] [1980s+] (*US campus*) something unpleasant or worthless.

dook *v.*[1] [DUKIE *n.*[2] (1)] [1990s+] to defecate.

dook *v.*[2] *see* DUKE *v.*[1].

dooker *n. see* DUKER *n.*[1].

dookering *n.* (*also* **dookin', duckering**) [Rom. *dukker*, to tell fortunes] [mid-19C+] (*gypsy and tramp*) fortune-telling.

(IN COMPOUNDS)

❑ **dookin cove** *n.* [COVE *n.* (1)] [mid–late 19C] a fortune-teller.

dookey *see also under* DUKIE.

dookey *n.* (*also* **dookie, dooky, dukie**) [DUKIE *n.*[2]] **1** [1960s+] rubbish, nonsense. **2** [1980s] the stuffing, the 'daylights'.

IN PHRASES

❑ **scare the dookey out of** *v.* [1960s+] (*US*) to terrify.

dookie *see also under* DUKIE.

dookie *adj.* (*also* **dookey, dooky**) [DOOKEY *n.*] **1** [1920s+] dirty. **2** [1980s+] (*US campus*) unpleasant, distasteful, disgusting.

dookin' *n. see* DOOKERING *n.*

dooks *n.* [DOOK *n.*[1] (2)/DUKE *n.*[3]] [mid-19C+] the fists.

dooky *n. see* DOOKEY *n.*

dooky *adj. see* DOOKIE *adj.*

doola *n.* [ety. unknown] [1990s+] (*US black*) a son.

doolally *adj.* (*also* **doolaley, do-lally**) [the Deolalie milit. sanatorium in Bombay, to which mentally ill troops were sent. However, according to the veteran Frank Richards, writing in his memoir *Old Soldier Sahib* (1936), the illness came not before one arrived at Deolalie but during one's stay there. Time-expired troops were sent to the sanatorium to await the next troop-ship home. It was during the long hot days of tedium that men, formerly first-class soldiers, might gradually go to pieces] [late 19C+] (*orig. milit.*) **1** mad, eccentric. **2** very drunk. **3** malfunctioning, out of order.

doolally tap *n.* [DOOLALLY *adj.* + SE *tap*, malarial fever; ult. Skt *tapa*, heat, pain, torment] [late 19C+] madness, eccentricity, orig. a form of madness that afflicted soldiers stationed in India, and spec. at Deolalie.

doolan *n.* (*also* **doolie, doolin**) [the common Irish surname] [1930s+] **1** (*N.Z*) a Catholic, usu. an Irish Catholic. **2** (*Aus.*) a police officer [stereotyped link between the Irish and the police]. **3** attrib.

dooley *n.* [? DUJI *n.*] [1980s+] (*drugs*) heroin.

doolittle *n.* [mid-18C] a euph. for a penis; the implication is of impotence.

doololly *n.* [var. on DOHICKEY *n.*[1]; DOJIGGER *n.* etc] [20C+] any nameless small object, typically some form of gadget.

doom *adj.* [1960s+] (*US*) of drugs, very strong.

doomie *n.* [? they are 'doomed'] [1950s] (*Aus.*) a criminally inclined teenage rebel.

doom (out) *v.* [1970s+] (*US*) to kill, to murder.

doondoos *n. see* DUNDUS *n.*

doonup *n.* (*also* **dunop**) [backsl.] [mid-19C] £1 sterling.

door *n.* **1** [1920s+] (*Aus.*) a brothel [euph.; note similar imagery in 17C *door*, the vulva]. **2** [2000s] (*US prison*) the end of one's sentence.

SE in slang uses

IN COMPOUNDS

❑ **door and hinge** *n.* [the way in which the joint bends] [late 19C] the neck and breast of mutton. ❑ **doorknob** *n. see* separate entries. ❑ **door-knock/-knocker** *n. see* separate entries. ❑ **doormat** *n. see* separate entry. ❑ **door shaker** *n.* [patrolling police or security guards shake doors to check that they are locked] [1940s–70s] (*US*) **1** a police officer. **2** a security guard. ❑ **doorstep** *n. see* separate entry.

IN PHRASES

❑ **from the door** [1960s] (*US*) from the very beginning. ❑ **live up to the door** *v. see* LIVE UP TO THE KNOCKER *under* KNOCKER *n.*[1]. ❑ **out the door** [the situation is so bad one has to leave the room] [1980s+] (*US*) an intensifer. ❑ **up to door** *see* UP TO DICK *under* DICK *n.*[3]. ❑ **you make a better door than a window** [20C+] a phr. used to someone who is blocking one's view.

doo rag *n. see* DO-RAG *n.*

doorknob *n.*[1] [rhy. sl.] **1** [late 19C–1970s] one shilling (5p) [= BOB *n.*[3] (2)]. **2** [20C+] a job.

doorknob *n.*[2] [SE, strengthened by later KNOB *n.* (1g)] [1930s+] a fool.

doorknob *n.*[3] [resemblance] [1960s] (*US*) **1** a doughnut. **2** the head. **3** the female breast.

door-knock *n.* [1950s+] (*Aus.*) a door-to-door appeal for charity or similar collection.

door-knocker *n.* [supposed similarities] **1** [mid–late 19C] a beard that runs along and just beneath the jaw line; when linking up with a moustache it was seen as resembling a door-knocker. **2** [late 19C–1900s] a female hairstyle consisting of two plaits bunched on top of the head. **3** [1990s+] (*US black*) a large hoop ear-ring.

doormat *n.* (*also* **mat**) [the heavy beards that veterans of the Crimean War (1854–6) wore against the Russian cold. These were cropped short when the soldiers returned to the UK] **1** [mid–late 19C] a short cropped beard. **2** [1900s] a moustache.

SE in slang uses

IN COMPOUNDS

❑ **doormat thief** *n.* (*also* **doormat grafter, doormatter**) [1900s–50s] a petty or incompetent thief.

doorstep *n.* (*also* **flight of steps, step**) [note WW1 milit. *couple o' doorsteps*, a sandwich] [late 19C+] a thickly cut slice of bread, or cake; sometimes ext. to a *couple of doorsteps*.

SE in slang uses

IN COMPOUNDS

❑ **doorstep child** *n.* [such a child is trad. abandoned on a, it is hoped, welcoming doorstep] [20C+] an illegitimate child.

door-to-door *n.* [20C+] (*bingo*) the number four or, if the context makes this obvious, any combination ending in four.

doos *n.* [Afk. *doos*, box; thus BOX *n.*[1] (1a)] [20C+] (*S.Afr.*) **1** the vagina. **2** a general term of strong abuse.

doose *n. see* DEUCE *n.*[2] (2).

doosid *adj. see* DEUCED *adj.*

doosie *n. see* DOOZIE *n.*

doosy *adj. see* DOOZIE *adj.*

dooteroomus *n.* (*also* **doot**) [? SE *duty* + *Deuteronomy*, the book of the Pentateuch that dictates the rules of society] [mid–late 19C] (*US*) money.

dooty *n.* [? DOOKEY *n.* or SE *dirty*] [1960s+] (*US juv.*) excrement.

do out *v.* **1** [mid-19C–1950s] to kill, to murder. **2** [1930s–50s] (*US*) to knock out. **3** [1950s+] (*US prison*) to behave; usu. in phr. *don't do out like that*, don't behave in a way likely to debase oneself in the eyes of one's fellow convicts.

doovah *n.* (*also* **doovah-dah**) [var. on DOOVER *n.*] [1930s] a cigarette end, preserved for later use.

doover *n.* [? Heb. *davar*, a word or thing, but orig. use was as a shelter or rough dug-out] (*Aus.*) **1** [1930s+] (*also* **dooverlackey**) any nameless object or gadget or task. **2** [1940s] a hospital urine bottle; thus *doover-joey*, a hospital orderly (among whose jobs is the emptying of such bottles). **3** [1940s] (*Aus. milit.*) a dug-out. **4** [1960s] the penis.

do over *v.* [DO *v.*[1] + SE *over*] **1** [late 18C–early 19C] in fig. use, to cause harm. **2** [late 18C–1900s] to disable, to wear out, to tire out. **3** [late 18C+] to cheat, to defraud. **4** [late 18C+] (*? orig. Aus./N.Z.*) to beat up. **5** [late 18C+] of a man, to seduce, to have intercourse with. **6** [mid-19C] to rob. **7** [1950s] to search thoroughly. **8** [1950s+] to ransack (a building).

doo-wah-diddy *n.* (*also* **diddy-wah-diddy**) [nonsense word derived f. musical rhythms] [1920s–60s] (*US*) **1** used as an all-purpose substitute for a word or phr. one does not wish to use properly. **2** an imaginary place, a very distant place, a place one dislikes.

doowhacker *n.* [ety. unknown] [20C+] any nameless small object, typically some form of gadget.

doowhanger *n.* [ety. unknown] [1920s] (*US*) any nameless small object, typically some form of gadget.

doozer *n.* [var. on DOOZIE *n.*] [1950s+] (*Can.*) anything notably large or outstanding.

doozie *n.* (*also* **doosie, dooze, doozey, duzy**) [DOOZIE *adj.*] **1** [1910s+] (*US*) a thing or person deemed to be extraordinary, remarkable or otherwise noteworthy. **2** [1960s] (*US campus*) a hard examination.

doozie *adj.* (*also* **doosy, doozy**) [? DAISY *n.* (2) + actress Eleanora *Duse* (1859–1924)] [1900s–20s] (*US*) splendid, wonderful.

dop *n.*[1] [Afk. *dop*, brandy] (*S.Afr.*) **1** [late 19C+] brandy; thus *dop and dam*, brandy and water. **2** [1940s] whisky. **3** [1950s+] a drink, a tot; thus *doppie*, a little drink, a small one.

dop *n.*[2] [Du. *dop*, a husk, a shell, used generally for any bowl-shaped or spherical object] [1970s] (*S.Afr.*) **1** one's head or brain. **2** a motorcycle crash helmet.

dop *v.*[1] [Afk. *dop*, to fail] (*S.Afr.*) **1** [1950s+] to fail (an examination). **2** [1970s+] to fail (at something).

dop *v.*[2] [DOP *n.*[1]] [1980s] (*S.Afr.*) to drink.

dopalicious *adj.* [DOPE *n.*[1] (6) + SE *delicious*] [2000s] (*US black*) wonderful.

dope *n.*[1] [? SE *daub*, the axle grease used on wagons or Du. *doop*, sauce] **1** [early 19C+] (*US*) (*also* **doup**) sauce, gravy. **2** [mid-19C+] any preparation, mixture or drug that is not spec. named. **3** [late 19C] (*US*) butter. **4** [late 19C–1940s] (*US*) coffee. **5** [late 19C+] any form of grease, lubricant, coolant etc. **6** [late 19C+] (*orig. US drugs*) any form of illicit drug; orig. opium, but taking in all popular 'recreational' drugs, esp. marijuana. **7** [20C+] (*orig. US*) any form of medicine or medicinal preparation; thus *sleep dope*, a sleeping draught or injection. **8** [1900s–10s] (*US*) constr. with *the*, the suitable or ideal thing. **9** [1900s–20s] (*Aus./US*) flattery, foolishness, nonsense. **10** [1900s–30s] (*Aus./US*) alcohol, esp. whisky. **11** [1900s–40s] unspecified and wide-ranging 'stuff', varying as to context. **12** [1900s–50s] a drug addict. **13** [1910s–20s] (*US*) an otherwise unspecified poison or adulterant. **14** [1910s–20s] (*US drugs*) a state of drugged intoxication. **15** [1910s–20s] (*US*) a cigarette. **16** [1910s+] Coca-Cola or any other carbonated drink. **17** [1910s+] molasses, treacle, syrup.

IN COMPOUNDS

❑ **dope addict** *n.* [1930s+] (*orig. US*) a drug addict, orig. the drug was opium. ❑ **dope booster** *n.* [var. use of BOOSTER *n.*[1] (1)] [1940s–50s] (*US drugs*) a drug seller, esp. when proselytizing new customers/users. ❑ **dope-boy** *n.* [1990s+] a drug dealer. ❑ **dope city** *n.* [-CITY *sfx*] [1950s+] (*drugs*) any area of a town known for its high level of drug sales/consumption. ❑ **dope crew** *n.* [CREW *n.* (3)] [1980s+] (*drugs*) a group of drug dealers who divide up, package and then retail the bulk purchases of the drug (usu. crack cocaine). ❑ **dope daddy** *n.* [1930s–50s] (*US drugs*) a drug dealer. ❑ **dope doctor** *n.* **1** [1920s–40s] (*US*) a general practitioner known for his/her (over-)prescribing of narcotics. **2** [2000s] a doctor who administers painkillers. ❑ **dope fiend** *n.* [FIEND *n.* (2)/SE *fiend*; the original use, popularized in the US tabloid press of late 19C, referred to opium; the current incarnation refers to crack cocaine] [late 19C+] (*drugs*) a user of drugs, in modern use often used ironically; also attrib. ❑ **dope fiend move** *n.* [1990s+] (*US black*) a wild, bizarre move, an extreme action taken out of desperation. ❑ **dope gun** *n.* [GUN *n.*[1] (5)] [1940s] (*US drugs*) a hypodermic syringe. ❑ **dopehead** *n.* [-HEAD *sfx* (4)] [1920s+] (*drugs*) a drug user; also attrib. ❑ **dope hop** *n.* (*also* **dope-pop**) **1** [1930s–70s] (*US drugs/prison*) a drug addict. **2** [1950s] (*US drugs*) the euphoric effect of a drug. ❑ **dope house** *n.* [1910s+] (*drugs*) any room or apartment in which drugs are on sale; a drug clinic. ❑ **dopeman** *n.* [SE *man*, but note MAN *n.*[1] (4d)] [1960s+] a drug dealer. ❑ **dope pad** *n.* [PAD *n.*[2] (2)] [1960s+] (*US drugs*) anywhere, e.g. a house, room or apartment, where drug addicts congregate to use drugs. ❑ **dope peddler** *n.* *see* PEDDLER *n.* (3). ❑ **dope rope** *n.* [1980s+] (*US*) the gold chains sported by well-off drug dealers. ❑ **dope shop** *n.* [1910s–20s] (*US drugs*) a place where one can buy illicit drugs. ❑ **dopeslinger** *n.* [SLING *v.* (1h)] [1990s+] (*US*) a drug seller. ❑ **dope stick** *n.* [STICK *n.* (6d)] **1** [20C+] a cigarette. **2** [1900s] a marijuana cigarette. ❑ **dope trap** *n.* [TRAP *n.*[1] (5)] [1960s] (*drugs*) any room or apartment in which drugs are on sale.

IN PHRASES

❑ **dope out** *v.* [1970s] (*US*) to take drugs; to render oneself intoxicated. ❑ **dope up** *v.* **1** [1910s] (*US*) to administer medicines or recreational drugs; also in fig. use. **2** [1920s] (*US Und.*) to tie mustard-oil soaked rags to one's shoes in order to put dogs off one's scent. **3** [1950s] (*US drugs*) to obtain one's supply of drugs.

dope *n.*[2] [orig. Cumberland dial.] **1** [mid-19C+] an ignoramus, a fool, a simpleton. **2** [1940s+] a term of address.

DERIVATIVES

❑ **dopish** *adj.* [1930s] (*US*) foolish.

IN COMPOUNDS

❑ **dopehead** *n.* [1910s–60s] (*US*) a fool.

dope *n.*[3] [20C+] (*orig. US*) **1** any information. **2** fraudulent information. **3** horseracing tips. **4** nonsense. **5** (*Aus.*) behaviour. **6** a plan, a scheme, an idea. **7** (*US*) the right thing.

IN COMPOUNDS

❑ **dope artist** *n.* [1910s] a prescient person. ❑ **dope book** *n.* (*also* **dope sheet**) [late 19C+] (*orig. US*) a book of information on any subject, although mainly horseracing. ❑ **dope sheet** *n.* **1** [1900s] any information. **2** [1920s] a menu.

IN PHRASES

❑ **get the dope on** *v.* [1930s] to find out about someone or something. ❑ **spin the dope** *v.* [1920s+] (*Aus.*) to tell a good story, to 'read the cards,' as a fortune-teller.

dope *adj.*[1] [lit. and fig. uses of DOPE *n.*[1] (6)] **1** [1930s+] pertaining to drugs. **2** [1980s+] (*US black*) (*also* **dope-ass**) very good, excellent [note DOPE *n.*[1] (8)].

dope *adj.*[2] [DOPE *n.*[2]] [1930s+] (*US*) foolish, stupid.

dope *v.*[1] [DOPE *n.*[1]] (*US*) **1** [mid-19C–1930s] to apply a lubricant or salve. **2** [mid-19C+] to poison, to put drugs into food or drink. **3** [late 19C–1930s] to adulterate. **4** [late 19C+] (*also* **dope up**) to administer drugs (occas. drink) to a person, either to excite them or, usu., to knock them out. **5** [20C+] to use 'recreational' drugs. **6** [20C+] to stimulate or undermine the performance of a racehorse, or racing. **7** [1900s–20s] to give or take medicine. **8** [1910s] (*US*) to administer medicines or recreational drugs; also in fig. use. **9** [1910s] in fig. use, e.g. to undermine morale. **10** [1910s] to drink to excess. **11** [1920s+] (*US Und.*) to tamper with a gambling machine to ensure the house wins.

IN PHRASES

❑ **dope off** *v.* **1** [1910s+] (*US*) to fall asleep, to doze off; thus *doped off*, asleep. **2** [1920s+] (*US, mainly milit.*) to be inattentive, to malinger.

dope *v.*[2] (*also* **dope it, dope out, dope up**) [DOPE *n.*[3]] **1** [20C+] (*orig. US*) to work (something) out, to assess, esp. in working out possible winners in a horserace. **2** [1930s+] to feed biased or inaccurate information to someone. **3** [1960s] (*US*) constr. with *in*, to explain, to inform, to recount.

dope *v.*[3] [DOPE *n.*[2]] [20C+] to idle, to loaf about.

IN PHRASES

❑ **dope off** *v.* **1** [1910s+] (*US*) to fall asleep, to doze off; thus *doped off*, asleep. **2** [1920s+] (*US, mainly milit.*) to be inattentive, to malinger.

dope-ass *adj.* *see* DOPE *adj.*[1] (2).

doped *adj.* [DOPE *v.*[1]] **1** [20C+] (*US*) drunk. **2** [20C+] (*orig. US*) (*also* **doped off, ...out, ...up**) under the influence of drugs; also in fig. use. **3** [1910s] addicted to a drug. **4** [1910s+] adulterated with a drug.

dopeless *adj.* [DOPEY *adj.*[2] + SE *hopeless*] [1920s] (*US*) a general negative: useless, foolish, socially inadequate.

doper *n.*[1] [DOPE *n.*[1] (6)] [1910s+] a drug user.

doper *n.*[2] *see* DOPEY *n.*[1].

doper *adj.* [DOPER *n.*[1]] [1970s+] pertaining to drug use/users.

dopester *n.*[1] [DOPE *v.*[2] + -STER *sfx*] [20C+] (*orig. US*) one who collects information on, and forecasts the result of, sporting events, elections etc.

dopester *n.*[2] [DOPE *n.*[1] + -STER *sfx*] **1** [1910s] a poisoner. **2** [1920s+] a drug user or seller.

dopey *n.*[1] (*also* **doper, dopye**) [poss., as suggested by Partridge and Williams, a misprint for DOXY *n.* (1) and used interchangeably by Dekker; however, note Henke, *Gutter Life and Language* (1988), who sees a link to SE *didapper/dydapper*, often abbr. as *doppe/dopper*, a small diving waterfowl which exhibits its hindquarters when it dives for food] [17C–early 19C] a female beggar, often a prostitute.

dopey *n.*[2] [ety. unknown; ? link to SE *didapper/dydapper* (*see* prev.)] [late 18C] the buttocks, the rump.

dopey *n.*[3] (*also* **dopie, mopey**) [DOPE *n.*[2]] [1920s+] a fool, usu. as a term of derog. address.

dopey *n.*[4] *see* DOPIE *n.*[1].

dopey *adj.*[1] [DOPE *n.*[1] (6) + sfx *-y*] **1** [late 19C–1900s] (*US*) rendering one sleepy or comatose. **2** [late 19C+] mildly ill; comatose. **3** [late 19C+] drunk. **4** [late 19C+] drugged, sedated; used as a nickname for a habitual drug user. **5** [1900s] sleepy.

dopey *adj.*[2] (*also* **dopy**) [DOPE *n.*[2] (1) + sfx *-y*] [late 19C+] dull, stupid, vapid.

IN COMPOUNDS

❑ **dopey dilbert** *n.* [the foolish perception of the proper name *Dilbert*] [1960s] a fool.

dopie *n.*[1] (*also* **dopey**) [DOPE *n.*[1] (6) + sfx *-ie/-y*] [1920s–30s] a drug user.

dopie *n.*[2] *see* DOPEY *n.*[3].

dopo *n.* [DOPE *n.*[2] (1) + -O *sfx* (1)] [1940s–70s] a sycophant, a toady.

do-pop *n.* [ety. unknown] [1970s] (*US prison*) a semi-trusty.

Dopper *n.* (*also* **Dorper**) [? Du. *domper*, an extinguisher, implying the Church's desire to extinguish any form of what it saw as 'progressive' or 'liberal' thinking, theological or otherwise. Or f. *dorp*, a village, implying the rural backgrounds of most of its members. A final theory is f. *dop*, a shell, referring to the sect's haircuts, which resembled an inverted calabash] [mid-19C+] (*S.Afr.*) a member of the strictly Calvinist Dutch Reformed Church (Gereformeerde Kerk in Suid-Afrika).

dopper *n.* [DOP *n.*[1] (2)] [1990s+] (*S.Afr.*) a drinker.

doppess *n.* [? Yid. *tipesh*, a fool; ult. Ger. *Täppisch*, fool. The term ult. is not European Yid. but an American word that merely seems Yid.] [20C+] (*US*) **1** a fool; a layabout. **2** an ineffectual observer who in a crisis offers no practical help, merely sympathetic banalities.

doppie *n.* [Du. *dop*, a shell, thus a container] [1940s+] (*S.Afr. Und.*) a measure of tobacco, about one-40th of an ounce.

dopy *adj. see* DOPEY *adj.*[2].

dora *adj.* [initial letter] [2000s] (*S.Afr. gay*) drunk.

doradilla *n.* [Sp. term for a kind of fern, ? resembling marijuana] [1970s+] (*drugs*) marijuana.

do-rag *n.* (*also* **dew rag, doo rag, durag, rag**) [DO *n.* (13) + SE *rag*] [1950s+] (*US black*) **1** the scarf or similar cloth that is used to bind up one's newly straightened hair. **2** a bandanna used as part of one's gang insignia.

dora (gray) *n.* [rhy. sl. = TRAY *n.*[1] (1)] [20C+] (*Aus.*) a threepenny-bit.

do-ray-me *n. see* DO-RE-MI *n.*

dorc *n. see* DORK *n.* (2).

dorcas *n.* [the sewing woman mentioned in the Bible, Acts 9:36; cf. Lincolnshire dial. *dorcas*, an overdressed woman] [late 19C] a seamstress, esp. one who works for a charity.

do-re-mi *n.* (*also* **do-ray-me, do-re-me, dough-ray-mi, dough-re-mi**) [a pun on DOUGH *n.* (1)/SE *do-re-mi* the first three notes of a musical scale] [20C+] money.

dorf *n.* (*also* **dorfy**) [var. on DORK *n.* (2), but note UK dial. *dorfer*, an impudent fellow] [1960s+] (*US campus*) a fool, an eccentric.

do-right *adj.* [1910s+] (*US*) law-abiding, honest, socially concerned.

IN COMPOUNDS

❑ **do-right boys** *n.* [1970s+] (*US*) the police, esp. the Highway Patrol. ❑ **do-right man** *n.* [1930s+] (*US*) a conformist, esp. one who follows rules within an institution. ❑ **do-right people** *n.* **1** [1930s–40s] (*US drugs*) (*also* **do-right johns**) those who are not addicted to narcotics. **2** [1930s+] (*US*) (*also* **do-right daddies**) honest citizens.

IN PHRASES

❑ **deputy do-right** *n. see* separate entry.

do-righter *n.* (*also* **do-rightie**) [i.e. others must do what is 'right'] [1950s] (*US*) a law-maker, one who lays down the law for others.

Doris *n.* [stereotype of Doris as an 'old-fashioned' name] [1990s+] an older woman.

doris *adj.* [? initial letter of *d*aft] [2000s] (*S.Afr. gay*) mad; eccentric.

dork *n.* [1950s+] (*orig. US*) **1** (*also* **dorque**) the penis. **2** (*also* **dorc, dorko**) a fool.

IN COMPOUNDS

❑ **dorkbinder** *n.* [2000s] (*US black*) a sexual athlete, of indiscriminate appetites. ❑ **dorkbrain** *n.* [1970s+] (*orig. US*) a fool; also attrib. ❑ **dorkbreath** *n.* [1970s+] an unpleasant person. ❑ **dorkface** *n.* [1970s+] (*US campus/teen*) an unpleasant person; thus an insulting term of address. ❑ **dorkhead** *n.* [-HEAD *sfx* (1)] [1980s+] (*orig. US teen/ campus*) a fool. ❑ **dorkoff** *n. see* separate entry. ❑ **dorkmunder** *n.* [? link to *Dortmünder Union Pils*, a beer: those who get drunk also get foolish] [1980s+] (*US campus*) a fool, an idiot.

IN PHRASES

❑ **dork around** *v.* [1980s+] (*orig. US*) **1** to play around, to mess about. **2** to waste time; to act pointlessly. ❑ **dork off** *v. see* separate entry.

dork *adj.* [DORK *n.* (2)] [1980s+] stupid.

dork *v.* [DORK *n.* (1)] [1970s+] (*orig. US*) of a man, to have sexual intercourse.

Dorklander *n.* [2000s] (*N.Z.*) an inhabitant of Auckland; thus *Dorkalofa*, Auckland.

dorkoff *n.* [1990s+] (*Aus.*) a term of abuse.

dork off *v.* [DORK *n.* (2)] [1980s+] (*US campus*) **1** to fool around, to mess about. **2** to disobey orders.

dorkum *n.* [? DORK *n.*] [1920s+] (*Aus.*) a damper.

dorkus (pretentious) *n.* [DORK *n.* (2)] [1990s+] (*US campus*) a pretentious fool.

dorky *adj.* [DORK *n.* (2) + sfx *-y*] [1970s+] (*orig. US campus*) odd, weird, bizarre, stupid.

dormie *n.* (*also* **dorm frog/rat**) [SE *dorm*, abbr. of *dormitory* + sfx *-ie*] [1960s+] (*US campus*) a student living in (and rarely leaving) a college dormitory.

dormouse *n.* [? resemblance] [19C] the female genitals.

dornick *n.*[1] [Irish *dornog*, a pebble, a stone] **1** [mid-19C] (*US*) a coin. **2** [1930s] a (half) brick, as thrown during riots. **3** [1940s] a precious stone, a piece of jewellery.

dornick *n.*[2] [1920s–50s] (*US*) the penis.

dorothy *n.* [an opera, *Dorothy* (1886), by Alfred Cellier, which featured such activity] [late 19C] simple, naïve love-making.

Dorothy Dix *n.* [rhy. sl.; ult. US journalist *Dorothy Dix* (pseudonym for E.M. Gilmer, 1870–1951), who wrote a popular question-and-answer column] [1970s+] (*Aus. sporting*) a six in cricket.

Dorothy's friend *n.* (*also* **friend of Dorothy('s)**) [Dorothy, the character played by Judy Garland (1922–69), an icon for much of the gay world, in the film *The Wizard of Oz* (1939)] [1960s+] a homosexual.

Dorper *n. see* DOPPER *n.*

dorque *n. see* DORK *n.* (1).

dors and 4s *n.* (*also* **dors 'n' fours**) [abbr.] [1980s+] (*drugs*) a combination of Doriden and Tylenol 4 or Codeine 4.

dorse *n.* [var. on DOSS *n.*[1] (1)] [late 18C–mid-19C] **1** a bed, a lodging. **2** sleep.

dorse *v.*[1] [DOSS *v.* (1)] [late 18C–19C] to sleep (with).

dorse *v.*[2] [Lat. *dorsum*, the back, onto which one is knocked] [early 19C] to knock down.

dors 'n' fours *n. see* DORS AND 4S *n.*

dortspeak *n. see* DART ACCENT *n.*

dos *n. see* DOSS *n.*[1].

dos a reno *n.* [backsl.] [mid-19C] a sod.

doscus *n.* (*also* **dosc**) [ety. unknown; ? link to DOSS *v.*, to sleep, thus one who is sleepy] [1970s+] (*US campus*) a fool, an idiot.

dose *n.*[1] **1** [late 17C–18C; 1920s] an act of copulation; the ejaculation of semen. **2** [mid-18C+] as much alcohol as one can hold (and prob. more); thus *take a grown man's dose*, to drink very heavily. **3** a physical problem, usu. an illness, a disease. (**a**) [late 18C+] venereal disease. (**b**) [late 19C+] a bad attack of an illness, or some unpleasant physical feeling. (**c**) [20C+] 'a sight'. (**d**) [1930s] (*US Und.*) a bullet, a gun shot. (**e**) [1980s] (*Aus.*) a distasteful sensation [SE *dose*, an unpleasant experience]. **4** [mid-19C] (*UK Und.*) in fig. use of sense 2, as much money as is offered. **5** [mid-19C+] a punishment, usu. judicial. (**a**) a three-month sentence with hard labour. (**b**) a short sentence. (**c**) any length of sentence. (**d**) a punishment one deserves. **6** [20C+] (*Ulster*) a crowd of people.

DERIVATIVES

❑ **dosed** *adj.* [1900s] drunk.

IN PHRASES

❑ **cop a dose** *v.* [1940s+] to catch a venereal disease. ❑ **give someone a dose** *v.* **1** [19C] (*UK Und.*) (*also* **dose**) to kill, to beat up. **2** [1930s] (*US*) to shoot.

dose *n.*[2] [DOASH *n.*] **1** [late 17C–mid-19C] (*UK Und.*) burglary. **2** [early 18C] (*UK Und.*) a cloak.

dose *n.*[3] [1960s+] (*UK juv.*) a fool.

dose *v.* [DOSE *n.*[1] (3a)/SE *dose*] **1** [late 19C+] to infect with venereal disease. **2** [2000s] (*US teen*) to give someone a dose of LSD. **3** *see* GIVE SOMEONE A DOSE *under* DOSE *n.*[1].

dosed *adj.* [? one is responding as if energized by a SE *dose of salts*] [20C+] (*Irish*) impressed.

dosed (up) *adj.* [DOSE *v.* (1)] [late 19C+] suffering from venereal disease.

dose of locust *n.* [the *locust* or locust-wood club carried by New York policemen; however, this would seem to negate the use of fists] [late 19C] (*US/New York*) a thrashing with the fists.

doser *n.* [mid-19C] in boxing, a violent or knockout blow.

dosh *n.* (*also* **dush**) [? DOSS *n.*[1] (1) (note in UK dial. *dosh* is synon. for *doss*); thus, by ext., the money needed for accommodation; the term appeared in US *c.*1850, then vanished, to re-emerge in the UK in the 1950s] [mid-19C; 1950s+] (*orig. US*) money.

dosh *v.* [DOSH *n.*] **1** [1980s+] to pay. **2** [2000s] to hand, to give.

dosha *n.* (*also* **dozier**) (*US black*) a marijuana cigarette.

dosh-burned *adj.* [late 19C–1900s] (*US*) a euph. for GOD-DAMNED/-DAMNEDEST *adj.*

doss *n.*[1] (*also* **dos**) [Lat. *dorsus*, the back, on which the sleeper lies] **1** [mid-19C+] a place to sleep, a bed, a lodging. **2** [mid-19C+] a sleep. **3** [late 19C; 1940s–50s] (*orig. UK Und.*) one month, as part of a jail sentence. **4** [1920s] (*US*) a rest. **5** in fig. uses. (**a**) [1960s] (*US black*) an attractive woman. (**b**) [1980s+] something easy to accomplish. (**c**) [2000s] any form of aimless, pleasurable activity. **6** *see* DOSSHOUSE *n.*

IN COMPOUNDS

❑ **doss-bag** *n.* [1990s+] (*UK juv.*) an extremely idle person. ❑ **doss-down** *n.* [late 19C+] **1** a cheap lodging-house. **2** a sleep. **3** (*N.Z.*) a makeshift bed. ❑ **dosshead** *n.* [-HEAD *sfx* (1); lit. 'sleep head'] [20C+] a fool, an idiot, a simpleton. ❑ **doss-hole** *n.* [2000s] a filthy room or lodging place. ❑ **dosshouse** *n. see* separate entry. ❑ **dossing crib** *n.* [CRIB *n.*[1] (3)] [mid-19C] a brothel. ❑ **dossing moll** *n.* [MOLL *n.* (2)] [mid-19C] (*UK Und.*) a prostitute. ❑ **doss-ken** *n.* (*also* **dossing drum, dossing-ken**) [KEN *n.*[1] (1)/DRUM *n.*[3] (5)] [mid-19C] a lodging house. ❑ **doss-man** *n.* [19C] the keeper of a lodging house. ❑ **doss money** *n.* [late 19C] the price of a night's lodging. ❑ **doss ticket** *n.* [late 19C] (*UK tramp*) a ticket giving one the right to a night's lodging.

IN PHRASES

❑ **do a doss** *v.* **1** [mid-19C+] to go to sleep. **2** [late 19C] to go to bed (when ill). ❑ **on the doss** [1900s] homeless, living as a tramp.

doss *n.*[2] [? link to Scot. *doss*, a tobacco-pouch] [1990s+] (*UK juv.*) the last few puffs of a cigarette.

doss *adj.* [DOSS *n.*[1] (5b)] [1980s+] easy, simple, undemanding; thus a general pej.

doss *v.* [DOSS *n.*[1]] **1** [late 18C+] to sleep. **2** [late 19C–1900s] (*US*) to lean against. **3** [1970s+] to do nothing, to relax. **4** [1990s+] (*Irish*) to play truant.

IN PHRASES

❑ **doss down** *v.* **1** [18C+] to fall asleep, usu. on the floor or similar temporary accommodation. **2** [1930s+] (*drugs*) to fall asleep after injecting heroin. ❑ **doss out** *v.* [1910s–20s] to sleep in the open air.

dosser *n.* [DOSS *v.* (1)] **1** [mid-19C+] (*also* **dosser-out**) a tramp, a vagrant, a homeless person. **2** [late 19C] the head of a household [he is the person who pays for/provides the place to sleep]. **3** [20C+] someone who exists without working.

IN COMPOUNDS

❑ **dossers' hotel** *n.* [20C+] a workhouse or any form of lodging for homeless people.

dosshouse *n.* (*also* **doss**) [DOSS *v.* (1) + SE *house*] [late 19C+] a lodging house, night shelter or similar refuge for homeless people.

dossie *n.* (*also* **dossy**) [DOXY *n.* (1) + DOSS *v.* (1)] [late 19C–1920s] a tramp's female companion.

doss (out) *v.* [SE *dash*] [1990s+] (*black*) to leave, to run off.

dossy *adj.*[1] [the proletarian pron. of the *Count D'Orsay* (1805–52), a well-known dandy] [mid-19C–1900s] excellent, first-rate; smart, stylish.

dossy *adj.*[2] [? one who would DOSS *v.* (3) rather than act] [1940s–50s] ineffectual, weak, 'soft'.

dossy *adj.*[3] [DOSS *n.*[1] (5b) + sfx *-y*] [1980s+] easy, effortless.

dot *n.*[1] [? Du. *dot*, a twirled knot of silk or thread] [early 19C] a ribbon; thus *dot-drag*, a watch ribbon.

dot *n.*[2] [lit. or fig. resemblance] **1** [mid-19C] (*US Und.*) a useless person. **2** [late 19C] (*Aus.*) the face. **3** [late 19C] (*US*) an attractive young woman. **4** [1950s+] (*Aus.*) the anus. **5** [1960s+] (*lesbian*) the clitoris.

SE in slang uses

IN COMPOUNDS

❑ **dothead** *n.* [the Hindu *bindi* or caste mark worn by married women] [1980s+] (*US*) a derog. term for an Indian.

IN PHRASES

❑ **dot on the card** *n.* [image of making a form of notation, e.g. on a register] **1** [1950s–60s] (*UK Und.*) a well-known person, usu. meaning too well-known for a criminal. **2** [1960s] a certainty. ❑ **put the dot on** *v.* [1950s] (*US*) to murder. ❑ **spot your dot** *v.* [billiards jargon *spot*, to place a ball] [1990s+] (*Aus.*) an invitation to sit down. ❑ **year dot** *n.* (*also* **day dot, year one**) [late 19C+] a very long time ago; usu. *from the year dot*, for ever.

dot *n.*[3] [? shape of coins] **1** [mid-19C+] in pl., money. **2** [1910s–20s] (*UK Und.*) in pl., piano keys.

dot *n.*[4] [abbr. MICRODOT *n.*] [1960s+] (*drugs*) LSD.

dot *n.*[5]

IN PHRASES

❑ **go off one's dot** *v. see* DOTTY *adj.*

dot *v.* [SE *dot*, a mark, a spot] [late 19C+] to punch someone, esp. in the eye.

SE in slang uses

IN PHRASES

❑ **dot the 'i'** *v.* [the anus is the DOT *n.*[2] (4), the penis the *eye* (although this is different from the usual use of EYE *n.* (4) or -EYE *sfx* to mean anus)] [1970s+] (*US gay*) to have anal intercourse.

dot and carried *adj.* [rhy. sl.] [20C+] married.

dot and carry one *n.* (*also* **dot and go one**) **1** [late 18C–early 19C] a derog. term for a second-rate teacher of writing or mathematics. **2** [late 18C+] a person with a wooden leg or a club foot [the dot is the impression made by the bottom of the wooden leg, in an era before properly moulded 'feet' were available, while the good leg is 'carried'].

dot and dash *n.* [rhy. sl.] **1** [1920s–40s] (*US*) a moustache. **2** [1950s+] money [= SE *cash*].

dot and go one *v.* [DOT AND CARRY ONE *n.*] [late 18C+] to waddle or hobble, esp. of those who have lost a leg.

dot and go one! *excl.* [early 19C] a general excl. of dismissal.

dotey *adj.* (*also* **doty**) [dial. *doty*, a general term of affection, usu. of a child; ult. SE *dote (upon)*] [1920s+] (*Irish*) cute, charming; thus also as n., *dote*, a cute person or thing.

dotted *adj.* [DOT *v.*] [late 19C] having a black eye.

dotties man *n.* [DOT *n.*[3] (1)] [late 19C] a greedy, grasping person.

dotty *adj.* [orig. dial; phr. *dotty on one's pins*, unsteady on one's legs and thence in one's brain + ? link to DOT AND CARRY ONE *n.*] [late 19C+] **1** unstable, unsteady on one's feet. **2** (*also* **dotty in the dome**) eccentric, odd; thus *dottiness*, eccentricity; *dotty homestead*, a pyschiatric institution. **3** usu. constr. with preps. *on/over*, in love with, desirous of.

IN PHRASES

▫ **go off one's dot** *v.* [late 19C–1920s] to go mad. ▫ **off one's dotty** (*also* **off one's dot**) [late 19C–1920s] mad, eccentric.

doty *adj. see* DOTEY *adj.*

doub *v. see* DOUBLE-BANK *v.* (6).

double *n.*[1] [abbr. SE *doublecross*] [late 18C–19C] a trick.

IN PHRASES

▫ **come the double (on)** *v.* [mid-19C–1920s] (*Aus.*) to double-cross. ▫ **give someone the double** *v.* [to trace a winding, tortuous path; to evade] [19C] to give the slip, to evade by stratagem. ▫ **put the double on** *v.* [late 19C] to double-cross. ▫ **tip the double** *v.* [late 18C–mid-19C] **1** to run off, from a creditor or from the authorities; thus *tip the double to sherry*, to elude the sheriff. **2** to jilt.

double *n.*[2] [abbr. *DOUBLE SAWBUCK under* SAWBUCK *n.*] [20C+] (*US*) a $20 bill.

double *n.*[3] [Williams has 17C *double*, 'allusive of copulation'] [1920s+] **1** a pornographic picture that offers both the male and female genitals. **2** a sex show involving two women.

double *adj.*

SE in slang uses

IN COMPOUNDS

▫ **double adaptor** *n.* [2000s] (*S.Afr. gay*) a bisexual. ▫ **double-bagger** *n.* (*also* **two-bagger**) [either based on the need to place not just one but two bags over her before having sex or the need for each participant to be covered with a bag] [1980s+] (*US*) an intensely unappealing person, usu. used of an unattractive woman. ▫ **double-banger** *n.* [SE *double* + *bang*, i.e. the 'explosion' of the orgasm] [1980s+] (*N.Z.*) a multi-orgasmic woman. ▫ **double-bank** *v. see* separate entry. ▫ **double-barrel/-barrelled** *see* separate entries. ▫ **double black dog** *v. see DOUBLE-DOG* below. ▫ **double blue** *n. see* BLUE *n.*[1] (4). ▫ **double-bottomed** *adj.* [? one 'bottom' is false] [late 19C–1900s] insincere, hypocritical. ▫ **double-breasted** *adj.* [mid-19C–1930s] excellent, admirable, impressive; an intensive. ▫ **double-breasters** *n.* (*also* **double-breasted feet**) [late 19C] the feet, esp. when one or both is a club foot. ▫ **double bubble** *n.* **1** [1950s] (*US*) a very attractive young woman. **2** [1980s+] a double portion, an extra helping. ▫ **double bubblegum** *n.* [ety. unknown] [1990s+] (*drugs*) a variety of potent marijuana. ▫ **double-bunked** *adj.* [1990s+] (*US Und.*) of two men, sharing a cell. ▫ **double burger** *n. see BURGER WITH CHEESE under* BURGER *n.* ▫ **double-carpet** *n. see under* CARPET *n.*[2]. ▫ **double-clutch/-clutcher/-clutching** *see* separate entries. ▫ **double-cross** *n.* [the crosses stamped into the pill] [1970s+] (*drugs*) amphetamine. ▫ **double-decker** *n.* **1** [early 19C] a form of shackles. **2** [late 19C] (*US*) a double-strength cocktail, used as a pick-me-up. **3** [1980s] (*N.Z.*) a sheep with two seasons' wool. ▫ **double deuce** *n. see under* DEUCE *n.*[1]. ▫ **double dime** *n. see under* DIME *n.* ▫ **double-dink** *v. see* DINK *v.* ▫ **double-distilled** *adj.* **1** [19C+] the worst. **2** [late 19C+] (*Aus.*) excellent, the very best. ▫ **double-dog** *v.* (*also* **double black dog, double darse, double nigger (dare)**) [20C+] (*US*) to challenge defiantly. ▫ **doubledong(er)** *n. see under* DONG *n.*[1]. ▫ **double dreads** *n.* [1980s+] (*drugs*) a mixture of amphetamine and LSD. ▫ **double-ender** *n.* [mid–late 19C] (*UK Und.*) **1** a type of purse. **2** a skeleton key. **3** a fist.

▫ **double fin** *n.* (*also* **double finn, double finnif, double finnup**) *see* separate entry. ▫ **double-fucking** *adj. see under* FUCKING *adj.* ▫ **double-gaited** *adj.* [SE *gait*, a manner of walking] [1920s+] (*US*) bisexual. ▫ **double-glazing** *n.* [1990s+] (*UK juv.*) insult aimed at a spectacles-wearer. ▫ **double-gutted** *adj.* [19C] very fat. ▫ **double harness** *n.* [coaching imagery] [mid-19C+] (*US*) marriage; usu. as *jump in a double harness, take on a double harness*, to get married; *run in double harness*, to dance with a partner. ▫ **double-headed** *adj.* [the idea of having two brains; the orig. use comes f. hoodoo, a var. form of voodoo] [20C+] (*US black*) very clever, exceptionally intelligent. ▫ **double-header** *n.* **1** [late 19C–1940s] (*Aus.*) a double measure of a drink. **2** [1920s+] (*US*) a second act of intercourse with a prostitute in one session. **3** [1970s] mutual oral-genital stimulation, a SIXTY-NINE *n.* (1). **4** [1950s+] a double measure or occurrence of anything. ▫ **double jugg(s)** *n.* [late 17C–19C] the buttocks. ▫ **double-life man** *n.* [1940s–60s] a bisexual. ▫ **double master-blaster** *n.* [1980s] (*drugs*) an orgasm reached through fellatio at the same time as one is smoking a pipe of crack cocaine. ▫ **double maw** *n.* [dial. pron. *maw*, ma, i.e. mother] [1920s–60s] (*US black*) a grandmother. ▫ **double-narky** *n.* [SE *narcotic*] [1950s] (*US drugs*) a double dose of one's preferred drug. ▫ **double nickel** *n.* [SAmE *nickel*, five (cents)/NICKEL *n.* (3)] **1** [1970s+] (*US*) the 55mph (88.5kph) speed limit, introduced nationally in 1974; thus the road itself. **2** [1990s+] (*US prison*) a ten-year sentence. ▫ **double nigger (dare)** *n. see DOUBLE-DOG* above. ▫ **double-O/-Os** *n. see* separate entries. ▫ **double pay** *n.* [the area's inflated prices and the incomes of those who live there] [1980s+] (*Aus.*) the upmarket Sydney suburb of Double Bay. ▫ **double-punch** *v.* [1980s] (*US black*) to assault in a group. ▫ **double rough** *see* separate entries. ▫ **double-scotched** *adj. see* SCOTCHED UP *adj.* ▫ **double-shooted** *adj.* [milit. use *double-shotted*, loaded with two cannon balls] [mid–late 19C] of a mixed drink, containing a double measure of alcohol. ▫ **double-shot** *n. see under* SHOT *n.*[1]. ▫ **double-shuffle** *n. see* separate entry. ▫ **double-six** *n.* [1940s] (*US black*) one year, i.e. twelve months. ▫ **double-slagging** *n.* [1980s+] (*Aus. prison*) a 20-year jail sentence. ▫ **double slangs** *n. see under* SLANG *n.*[2]. ▫ **double sticker** *n.* [late 19C] the *labia minora*, esp. when prominent. ▫ **double-thumper** *n. see under* THUMPER *n.* ▫ **double time** *n.* [TWO-TIME *v.*] [1950s] an act of betrayal, esp. adultery. ▫ **double-tongued squib** *n. see* SQUIB *n.*[2] (1). ▫ **double tripe** *n. see* separate entries. ▫ **double trouble** *n.* [Tuinal is a mixture of Seconal and Amytal] [1960s+] (*drugs*) Tuinal. ▫ **double-ups** *n.* [1990s+] (*drugs*) a $20 piece of crack cocaine that can be broken into two pieces, each of which is then sold for $20. ▫ **double whammy** *n. see under* WHAMMY *n.* ▫ **double-X** *n. see* separate entries. ▫ **double-yolker** *n. see* EGG *n.*[2] (3). ▫ **double zero** *n.* **1** [1990s+] (*drugs*) prime grade hashish. **2** *see* ZERO *n.* (1).

IN PHRASES

▫ **double bag and stumper** *n.* [ext. *DOUBLE-BAGGER* above; she is so ugly that one would have to place paper bags over both participants' heads in order to face up to intercourse, and one would, in any case, rather cut off all one's limbs than have sex with her] [1990s+] a very unattractive young woman. ▫ **double-click one's mouse** *v.* [1990s+] (*Aus. teen*) of a woman, to masturbate.

IN EXCLAMATIONS

▫ **double-dash!** *see under* DASH! *excl.*

double *v.*[1] [SE *double*, to turn sharply and suddenly in running, to turn back on one's course] **1** [early 19C] to run off, to escape. **2** [early 19C] to avoid, to elude, to give the slip to.

SE in slang uses

IN PHRASES

▫ **double in brass** *v.* [circus/vaudeville jargon *double in brass*, to perform one's own speciality as well as play in the orchestra] [1910s+] (*orig. US*) to have a wide range of abilities; to perform more than one's primary job. ▫ **double one's milt** *v. see under* MILT *n.* ▫ **double up** *v. see* separate entries.

double *v.*[2] [abbr.] **1** [mid–late 19C] to *double*-cross. **2** [1900s] (*US campus*) to go out on a date. **3** [1930s] (*US tramp*) to sleep with someone; to have sexual intercourse. **4** [1930s+] (*US*) to *double*-date, i.e. for two couples to go out together. **5** [1960s+] to act as a *double*-agent. **6** [1990s+] to *double*-park.

double *adv.* [mid-19C+] a qualifying adv. that intensifies a v. or adj.

IN PHRASES

❑ **play (someone) double** *v.* [1910s] to trick, to betray sexually.

double-bank *v.* [SAusE *double-bank*, to yoke together two oxen] **1** [late 19C–1940s] (*US*) to trick, to doublecross. **2** [late 19C+] (*US*) to attack as a gang. **3** [late 19C+] (*Aus./N.Z.*) to carry two people on a single horse. **4** [1900s–10s] (*Aus.*) to work something extra hard. **5** [1930s] to have two drinks in front of one. **6** [1940s+] (*Aus./N.Z.*) (*also* **doub, dub, dubb**) to carry two people on one bicycle.

double-barrel *n.*[1] [SE *double-barrel*, a double-barrelled gun] [late 19C] field-glasses, opera-glasses.

double-barrel *n.*[2] [note Cleland, *Memoirs of a Woman of Pleasure* (1748–9): 'My hot-mettled spark [...] loaded for a double-fire, recontinu'd the sweet battery with undying vigour'] [1990s+] of a man, more than one orgasm in a single session of sex.

double-barrelled *adj.* **1** [mid-19C–1960s] (*US*) extreme, utter, complete. **2** [late 19C] used of a woman, enjoying simultaneous vaginal and anal intercourse. **3** [late 19C+] used of a lesbian, e.g. *double-barrelled broad*.

IN COMPOUNDS

❑ **double-barrelled ghee** *n.* [GHEE *n.*[1]; his mouth and anus] [1960s–70s] (*gay*) a male homosexual.

double-clutch *v.* [trucker jargon *double-clutch*, to change gears by changing first to neutral, then selecting the desired, usu. lower, gear. The clutch is disengaged at each stage. The link to the drug use is the idea of doing something twice] **1** [1960s] (*US*) to have sexual intercourse. **2** [1980s+] (*US drugs*) to take more than one's share of a communally smoked marijuana cigarette. US smokers ritually take only one puff before passing on their cigarette.

double-clutcher *n.* [1960s+] (*US*) a euph. term for MOTHERFUCKER *n.*

double-clutching *adj.* [1960s+] (*US*) a euph. term for MOTHERFUCKING *adj.*

double fin *n.* (*also* **double finn, double finnif, double finnup**) [SE *double* + FIN *n.*[1]/FIN *n.*[2]] **1** [mid–late 19C] a UK £10 note. **2** [1940s+] (*US*) a $10 bill. **3** [1940s] (*US Und.*) a ten-year jail sentence.

double-O *n.*[1] [the resemblance to a pair of eyes or glasses] [1910s–60s] a hard look; a serious, studious look.

double-O *n.*[2] [DOUBLE-O *v.* (2)] [1920s–30s] (*US Und.*) an act of betrayal.

double-O *n.*[3] [1940s] (*US*) nothing, zero.

double-O *n.*[4] [1990s+] (*US prison*) prison-issue bread.

double-O *v.* [DOUBLE-O *n.*[1]] **1** [1910s–50s] (*US*) to stare at; to survey. **2** [1920s] to doublecross. **3** [1950s] to reject, to deny.

double-Os *n.* [the 'double-o' of the spelling] [1970s+] (*US prison*) Kool brand cigarettes.

doubler *n.*[1] **1** [mid-19C] (*N.Z.*) a double portion of a drink, two shots of a spirit in the same glass. **2** [late 19C+] (*UK Und.*) a corrupt police officer who not only takes the offered bribe but still arrests one for the crime. **3** [1950s+] (*Aus.*) a lift on a bicycle crossbar.

doubler *n.*[2] [it causes the recipient to DOUBLE UP *v.*[2] (1)] [early 19C] an extremely severe blow.

double rough *n.* [1970s] (*US prison/Und.*) a 50-year jail sentence.

double rough *adj.* [1970s] serious, hard.

double shuffle *n.* [farming jargon *double shuffle*, a sudden shift of bucking style by a bronco, intended to throw an unwanted rider. Note also UK *double shuffle*, a shuffling, noisy dance, once popular among costermongers] **1** [mid-19C–1960s] (*US*) a doublecross. **2** [late 19C] (*UK Und.*) the act of repeatedly walking up and down one's prison cell. **3** [1930s] (*US*) a quick get-away.

IN PHRASES

❑ **come the double shuffle** *v.* [mid-19C] to double-cross.

double tripe *n.*[1] (*also* **Mr Double Tripes**) [TRIPE *n.*[1]] [late 17C–early 19C] an exceptionally fat man.

double tripe *n.*[2] [? its resemblance to thick sheets of *tripe*] [early 19C] (*UK Und.*) lead, as used on roofs etc.

double up *v.*[1] **1** [19C+] (*US*) to get married, to become engaged, to live together. **2** [mid-19C+] to share quarters. **3** [1920s] (*US Und.*) to work as a team. **4** [1980s+] of a man, to have sexual intercourse with two women together.

double up *v.*[2] [a blow that forces the recipient to bend double] [19C] (*orig. boxing*) **1** to cause to collapse, to beat up; also as n. **2** to die. **3** to defeat, to stop someone in their tracks.

double up *v.*[3] (*also* **double-up halves, dub**) [1980s+] (*US drugs*) of a crack cocaine dealer, to offer 'two for the price of one'.

double-X *n.*[1] [racetrack jargon *double-X*, the horse most likely to win; thus the optimum bet] **1** [early 19C] (*US*) something superlative, outstanding. **2** [mid-19C] strong beer.

double-X *n.*[2] (*also* **XX**) (*US*) **1** [mid-19C–1910s] $20, a $20 bill [*X* as Roman numeral for ten]. **2** [1930s+] an act of doublecrossing; thus v. to doublecross [*X* as the mark of a cross].

doubloon *n.* [SE *doubloon*, a Spanish coin orig. worth a half-pistole, i.e. 33–36 shillings] [late 19C+] money.

doucer *n.* [orig. Fr.; SE *douceur*, 'A conciliatory present or gift; a gratuity or 'tip'; a bribe' (*OED*)] [mid-19C–1920s] (*UK Und.*) a bribe, a 'sweetener'; one who takes money with false promises.

douche *n.*

IN PHRASES

❑ **take a douche** *v.* [1960s+] (*US teen*) to leave hurriedly, esp. as imper. *take a douche!* go away!

douchebag *n.* (*also* **d.b., douch, doucher**) [SE *douchebag*] **1** [1950s+] (*US*) a term of general abuse, directed esp. at women. **2** [1990s+] a lesbian.

IN PHRASES

❑ **have a face like a douchebag** *v.* [1970s] (*US*) to be very ugly.

douche can alley *n.* [the use of douches by the street's prostitutes + pun on music's *Tin Pan Alley*] [1910s–50s] (*Aus.*) Palmer Street, Sydney – the city's 'red-light' area.

doudon *n.* [? SE *dowdy*] [late 17C; 1910s–20s] a short, fat woman.

doufas/doufus *n.* see DOOFUS *n.*

dough *n.* (*also* **doe**) [the idea of bread as an essential constituent of life] **1** [mid-19C+] (*orig. US*) money; thus *dough up*, *dough over*, to pay. **2** [1940s] (*UK Und.*) counterfeit coins. **3** see DOUGHBOY *n.*[1].

IN COMPOUNDS

❑ **dough stacks** *n.* [STACKS *n.*[1] (1)] [2000s] (*US black*) large quantities of money.

IN PHRASES

❑ **cook dough** *v.* [1940s] (*UK Und.*) to manufacture counterfeit money. ❑ **do one's dough** *v.* [1910s+] (*orig. Aus.*) to lose one's money, to spend up. ❑ **in the dough** (*also* **doughy**) [1910s+] well off, prospering, rich.

SE in slang uses

IN COMPOUNDS

❑ **dough-baked** *adj.* (*also* **dow-baked**) [late 16C] stupid, dull. ❑ **doughbanger** *n.* [late 19C+] (*Aus.*) a cook; thus *dough-banging*, cooking. ❑ **doughbelly** *n.* (*also* **dough-ring**) [1940s+] (*US*) a very fat person, a large stomach; thus *doughbellied*, fat. ❑ **dough boxer** *n.* see DOUGH-ROLLER below. ❑ **doughboy** *n.* see separate entries. ❑ **dough-brain** *n.* [1980s+] (*US campus*) someone who acts foolishly or as if they have not been thinking. ❑ **doughface** *n.* [SE *doughface*, a whiteface mask made orig. of flour and water and used for fancy dress; a *doughface* and a white sheet rendered the wearer a 'ghost'; coined by John Randolph of Roanoke] **1** [mid-19C] (*US*) a malleable person, esp. a Northern politician who accepts slavery. **2** [20C+] (*US*) a woman who wears an excess of cosmetics. ▫ **doughfoot** *n.* [var. on DOUGHBOY *n.*[1]] [1940s+] (*US*) an infantryman. ▫ **dough-god(s)** *n. see* DOUGH-JEHOVAHS below. ▫ **doughguts** *n.* [mid-19C] (*US*) an extremely fat person. ▫ **dough-head** *n.* [-HEAD *sfx* (1)] **1** [19C+] (*US*) a very silly or stupid person. **2** [1920s–60s] (*US tramp*) a baker. ▫ **dough-hole** *n. see* CAKEHOLE *under* CAKE *n.*[1]. ▫ **dough-Jehovahs** *n.* (*also* **dough-god(s)**) [ety. unknown] [late 19C–1910s] a biscuit or pastry. ▫ **doughnut** *see* separate entries. ▫ **dough-pop** *v.* [POP *v.*[1] (1c); ? link to DOUGHBOY *n.*[1]] [1970s] **1** to hit hard. **2** to defeat completely. ▫ **dough-ring** *n. see* DOUGHBELLY above. ▫ **dough-roller** *n.* (*also* **dough boxer, ...pounder, ...puncher**) [navy jargon *dough roller*, the ship's cook] [20C+] (*US*) a cook, often spec. a baker.

dough *adj.* [DOUGH *n.* (1)] [20C+] (*US campus*) excellent, first-rate.

doughboy *n.*[1] (*also* **doe-boy, dough**) [? the large round buttons worn by Civil War soldiers, reminiscent of the doughnuts or the boiled dumplings, based on flour and rice and known as *doughboys*, that were a military staple; or f. the *dough* or pipeclay used to clean US soldiers' belts in mid-19C; note Mencken, *The American Language* (3rd edn, 1936): '*Doughboy* is an old English navy term for dumpling. It was formerly applied to the infantry only, and its use is said to have originated in the fact that the infantrymen once pipe-clayed parts of their uniforms, with the result that they became covered with a doughy mass when it rained'] [mid-19C+] (*orig. US milit.*) a US soldier, orig. those serving in the Mexican War *c.*1847; subseq. replaced by BOONIE RAT *n.*, *GI* etc.

doughboy *n.*[2] [1910s+] a punch in the face; usu. in phr. *give someone a doughboy*, to punch someone in the face.

doughnut *n.*[1] (*also* **donut**) **1** [late 19C] (*US*) a baker. **2** [1920s+] a rubber tyre. **3** [1930s] (*US black*) the vagina. **4** [1980s] of a woman, a state of sexual excitement, supposedly the vaginal equivalent of the penile erection. **5** [1980s] (*Aus.*) the anus. **6** [2000s] (*N.Z.*) a single round tyre track created by driving on one wheel. **7** *see* DOUGHNUT (HOLE) below.

SE in slang uses

IN COMPOUNDS

▫ **doughnut bumper** *n.* (*also* **donut bumper**) [BUMPER *n.*[7]] [20C+] (*US*) a lesbian. ▫ **doughnut dolly** *n.* (*also* **donut dolly**) [among other things she offered coffee and doughnuts to the troops] [1960s–70s] (*US milit.*) a Red cross recreation girl. ▫ **doughnut foundry** *n.* (*also* **doughnut factory**) [1920s–60s] (*US*) a very cheap restaurant or café. ▫ **doughnut head** *n.* [-HEAD *sfx* (1)] [1970s+] (*US*) a fool. ▫ **doughnut (hole)** *n.* (*also* **donut (hole)**) [the emptiness of the hole in a SAmE *donut*. Note US milit. use *donut hole*, a female volunteer worker with the US Red Cross, although the ref. is to sexuality, i.e. the HOLE *n.*[1] (1b), rather than stupidity] [1990s+] (*US campus*) someone with no social skills. ▫ **doughnut maker** *n.* [1980s] (*Aus.*) a male homosexual. ▫ **doughnut poker** *n.* [1980s] (*US*) a male homosexual. ▫ **doughnut puncher** *n.* (*also* **donut puncher**) [1980s+] (*Aus./US*) a male homosexual.

doughnut *n.*[2] **1** [1920s] a rich fool [they are surrounded by money]. **2** [2000s] a person [? the emptiness at the doughnut's centre].

doughnut *v.* (*also* **donut**) [the circularity of the doughnut and the spin] [1970s+] (*Aus./US teen*) to make an automobile spin by pulling on the hand-brake. The vehicle in question is usu. stolen.

dough-re-mi *n. see* DO-RE-MI *n.*

doughy *n.*[1] **1** [19C] a baker. **2** [1950s] (*Aus.*) a cook.

doughy *n.*[2] (*Aus.*) **1** [1950s] the buttocks [resemblance of plump, pale buttocks to dough]. **2** [1960s] a cigarette end [ext. of sense 1, with its 'end' imagery].

doughy *adj.* [the 'thickness' of dough] **1** [20C+] (*Aus.*) stupid; thus *doughy over*, in love with, 'mooning over'. **2** *see* IN THE DOUGH *under* DOUGH *n.*

dougla *n.* [Hindi, a person with one Afro-Trinidadian parent and one Indo-Trinidadian] [1960s+] (*W.I.*) a person of mixed race, typically African/Indian.

Douglas *n.* [brandname of the *Douglas* Axe Manufacturing Co., East Douglas, Massachusetts] [20C+] (*Aus.*) an axe; thus *swing Douglas*, to swing an axe.

Douglas Hurd *n.* [rhy. sl.; ult. *Douglas*, Lord *Hurd*, British Conservative M.P. (b.1930)] [1990s+] **1** a piece of excrement [= TURD *n.*[1]]. **2** a third class degree.

doul *n.* [ety. unknown] [1960s–70s] (*US gay*) a very young homosexual man.

doup *n.*[1] *see* DOPE *n.*[1] (1).

doup *n.*[2] *see* DUCK *n.*[7].

do up *v.*[1] [DO *v.*[1]] **1** [late 18C] to ruin. **2** [late 18C+] to rob, to cheat. **3** [late 18C+] to exhaust, to tire out. **4** [19C+] of people, to beat up; of objects, to smash. **5** [mid-19C+] to deal with. **6** [late 19C] to unnerve. **7** [late 19C] (*Aus.*) to squander all one's money. **8** [20C+] to kill. **9** [20C+] to cause trouble for. **10** [1950s+] (*US black*) to have sexual intercourse. **11** in drug uses. (**a**) [1950s+] to inject a narcotic. (**b**) [1950s+] to consume in non-drug context. (**c**) [1950s+] to take a non-narcotic drug. (**d**) [1980s] to give someone else an injection.

do up *v.*[2] [SE *do*, to act, to perform] [1940s–70s] (*US black*) to make something happen, to make things change.

do us a favour *phr. see* DO ME A FAVOUR *phr.*

douse *v.* [SE *douse*, to turn off, to put out] **1** [late 18C] (*Irish*) to pawn. **2** [late 18C–mid-19C] to take off; thus *douse the dog vane*, take the cockade out of one's hat. **3** [mid-19C] to hit.

douser *n.* (*also* **douse, dowse, dowser**) [SE *douse*, to strike, to punch; ult. Du. *doesen*, to beat with force and noise] [18C–mid 19C] a heavy blow; esp. as *douse/dowse on the chops*.

douse the glim *v. see under* GLIM *n.*

dove *n.* [1990s+] (*drugs*) **1** a variety of MDMA [usu. has a picture of a dove on the pill]. **2** a $35 piece of crack cocaine.

dove of the roost *n. see* SOILED DOVE *n.*

dover *n.*[1] [proprietary name] [late 19C–1910s] (*Aus.*) a clasp-knife; thus *flash one's dover*, to use one's clasp-knife to cut up one's food.

IN PHRASES

▫ **run of one's Dover** *n.* [development of orig. mid-19C phr. *run of one's knife*] [late 19C] (*Aus.*) board and lodging.

dover *n.*[2] [ext. of DOVER *n.*[1]] [1900s–10s] (*Aus.*) food, provisions.

Dover boat *n.* [rhy. sl.] [1970s+] a coat.

Dover Castle boarder *n.* [a legally specified area around the Queen's Bench Prison in Southwark Bridge Road within which debtors, while not actually confined in the prison, were ordered to live during the period of their sentence. The nickname came from the prominent local landmark, the *Dover Castle* tavern] [19C] a debtor.

Dover harbour *n. see* SYDNEY HARBOUR *n.*

dover's powder *n.* (*also* **dover's deck**) [proper name Thomas *Dover* (1660–1742), an English physician whose patented preparation of opium and ipecacuanha (*Pulvis doveri*) was used as a pain-killing medicine] [20C+] (*drugs*) opium.

dowager *n.* [SE *dowager*, orig. the widow of a dead king, i.e. a QUEEN *n.* (2)] [1940s+] (*gay*) an elegant, older, gay man.

dow-baked *adj. see* DOUGH-BAKED *under* DOUGH *n.*

dowdy *v.* [the sound *dow de dow*, the basic lyric of a song chanted by one Pearce who, according to Grose (1785), was the first to play this 'joke'] [late 18C] to play a practical joke based on one's pretending to be mad, esp. to have just escaped from one's keeper or from a psychiatric institution.

dowlas *n.* [*Doulas*, near Brest, in Brittany, the eponymous name of a coarse kind of linen, much used in the 16C and 17C, and later a strong calico made in imitation of this; the sl. is more immediately linked to the character Daniel *Dowlas*, in George Colman's play *The Heir at Law* (1797)] [late 18C–mid-19C] a linen-draper.

down *n.*[1] [DOWN *adj.*[2] (1)] [mid-18C+] something depressing.

down *n.*[2] **1** [early–mid-19C] (*UK Und.*) a suspicion, a degree of illegality; thus *take down off*, to render a (stolen) object less suspicious; *there is no down*, there is no risk. **2** [mid-19C+] (*orig. Aus.*) a prejudice against, a suspicion of; a tendency to be unkind towards; usu. as *have a down on*.

IN PHRASES

❑ **put a down (up)on** *v.* [19C] to inform against someone. ❑ **raise the down** *v.* [early 19C] (*Scot. Und.*) to give the alarm.

down *n.*[3] [SE *down*, under weight] [late 19C+] (*US*) a diluted or even alcohol-free drink, as consumed by a 'hostess' who is persuading her client to buy hugely overpriced 'champagne' etc.

down *n.*[4] [abbr.] [1940s] (*US*) a *down*-payment.

down *n.*[5] [the calming, slowing down effect of the drugs] (*drugs*) **1** [1960s+] a barbiturate. **2** [1980s+] codeine-based cough syrup. **3** [1990s+] (*US prison*) heroin.

IN COMPOUNDS

❑ **down freak** *n.* (*also* **downs freak**) [-FREAK *sfx*] [1970s+] (*drugs*) a regular user of depressant drugs. ❑ **down-head** *n.* [-HEAD *sfx* (4)] [1960s+] (*drugs*) a regular user of depressant drugs.

down *adj.*[1] [orig. Und. *down cove*, a potential victim of a robbery who is aware of being targeted. Originating among late-18C London criminals, the term survives mainly among US blacks] **1** [17C; late 18C+] (*also* **downish**) aware, conscious of, knowledgeable; thus *be down upon*, to be aware, to be knowledgeable; in 1940s+ use, to be part of the current (youth) fads and fashions. **2** [mid-18C] suspicious. **3** [mid-19C+] first-rate, excellent. **4** [1940s+] (*US black*) alert, keen to get on, tough, challenging in a fight. **5** [1950s] (*US black*) loyal, trustworthy. **6** [1950s+] willing (to do something), enthusiastic. **7** [1950s+] (*US black*) fashionably dressed, chic. **8** [1960s] (*US black*) interesting, current. **9** [1990s+] worked out in a satisfactory manner. **10** [1990s+] (*US*) in a relationship. **11** [2000s] (*US black*) feeling well, happy, at one with the world.

DERIVATIVES

❑ **downish** *adj. see* sense 1 above.

IN COMPOUNDS

❑ **down...** *see also* separate entries. ❑ **down-ass** *adj.* [-ASS *sfx*] [1980s+] (*US black*) a general term of approval. ❑ **downmouth** *v.* [sense 2 above/DOWN *n.*[2] (2) + SE *mouth*] [1980s] (*US*) to attack verbally, to slander.

IN PHRASES

❑ **ain't down with** [1980s+] (*US black/campus*) used when referring to a situation one does not particularly like, e.g. *I ain't down with this idea!* ❑ **down as a hammer/nail/trippet** [early–mid-19C] very well aware. ❑ **down by law** [1980s+] (*orig. US black*) **1** expert, professional (within one's occupation). **2** describing a wholly admirable person, object or idea. ❑ **down for** [1950s+] (*US black*) loyal to, committed to, in favour of. ❑ **down for mine** [MINE *n.*] [1950s+] (*orig. US black*) able to look after oneself. ❑ **down on** [sense 2 above/DOWN *n.*[2] (2)] **1** [18C–19C] attacking physically. **2** [mid-19C+] annoyed with, disappointed in, holding a negative opinion of. ❑ **down on the case** [1970s] (*US black*) fully aware, completely knowledgeable. ❑ **down upon** [late 18C+] aware, knowledgeable. ❑ **down with** (*orig. US black*) **1** [1930s–40s] through with. **2** [1940s+] involved with, agreeable to. **3** [1940s+] empathetic, emotionally responsive; enjoying, appreciating. **4** [1990s+] (*US*) friendly with. ❑ **have something down** *v.* [1910s+] to be aware of the situation, to know what is going on. ❑ **put down** *v.* [early 19C; 1970s] (*UK / US Und.*) to convey information to someone, to explain, to make someone aware; thus (*UK Und.*) *put a swell down*, to alert one's target (typically the target of a pickpocket) that one is about to rob them.

SE in slang uses

IN COMPOUNDS

❑ **downblow** *n.* [1940s] (*Irish*) a disaster. ❑ **downface** *v.* [1900s–40s] to assert something in order to make someone look foolish. ❑ **down-hills** *n.* [late 17C–early 19C] doctored dice that will always show low numbers.

IN PHRASES

❑ **down buttock and sham file** *n.* (*also* **downright buttock and sham file**) [SE *down*(*right*) + BUTTOCK AND FILE *under* BUTTOCK *n.*, modified by SE *sham*, fake] [19C] a prostitute who does not resort to thieving.

down *adj.*[2] [the lowering of one's spirits] **1** [mid-17C+] (*also* **down on it**) depressed. **2** [1950s+] depressing. **3** [1960s] in a state unassisted by any drug.

IN COMPOUNDS

❑ **down pin** *adj.* [skittles imagery] [late 19C–1900s] depressed, indisposed. ❑ **down-yonders** *n.* [1930s] (*US black*) depression, feelings of misery.

IN PHRASES

❑ **down in the chops** *see under* CHOPS *n.*[1]. ❑ **drop down on oneself** *v.* [early–mid-19C] to feel depressed, esp. at the prospect of prison or judicially sanctioned death, to sink beneath one's problems. ❑ **get someone down** *v.* [late 19C+] to make someone depressed.

down *adj.*[3] [abbr. *GO DOWN THE RIVER under* RIVER *n.* or *DOWN THE RIVER under* RIVER *n.*] [mid-19C; 1930s+] (*US Und.*) serving time in prison.

down *adj.*[4] [lit. *fallen down*] **1** [20C+] (*US*) collapsed, seriously ill. **2** [1950s+] (*US*) dead.

IN PHRASES

❑ **down as a dab** [? a dead *dab* lying flat on a fishmonger's slab] [late 19C] very ill. ❑ **down for the count** *see under* COUNT *n.*[3].

down *adj.*[5] [SE *down*, under weight] [1920s+] (*US black*) owing, deficient in.

IN PHRASES

❑ **down in** [mid–late 19C] lacking in, short of.

down *v.*[1] [late 18C–mid-19C] (*UK Und.*) to understand.

down *v.*[2] [abbr. SE *knock down*] (*US*) **1** [mid-19C+] to beat up; to assault. **2** [late 19C+] to defeat. **3** [1930s] to shoot dead.

IN PHRASES

❑ **down blows in someone** *v.* (*also* **down a cuff/lash in someone**) [20C+] (*W.I., Guyn.*) to beat up severely. ❑ **down hand on someone** *v.* [20C+] (*W.I.*) to seize firmly.

down *v.*[3] (*also* **down on**) [abbr. PUT DOWN *v.*[1] (2a)] [late 19C+] to denigrate.

down *v.*[4] [1960s] **1** to dispose of, to sell, to get rid of. **2** of a pimp, to situate a whore on the street.

down *adv.*[1] [DOWN *adj.*[1] (3)] **1** [late 19C–1940s] very much so, exceedingly. **2** [1920s+] (*orig. US black*) to the limit.

down *adv.*[2] [1960s+] (*US*) happening, going on.

IN COMPOUNDS

❑ **down front** *adj.* [var. on UP FRONT *adj.* (1)] [1950s+] (*US black*) open, honest, candid.

IN PHRASES

❑ **down among the dead men** *see under* DEAD MAN *n.* ❑ **down...** *see also* separate entries. ❑ **down the banks** *n.* [the steep banks found in peat bogs; those who fell off them rolled down into the deep, peaty water] [late 19C+] (*Irish*) **1** a reprimand. **2** a state of failure. ❑ **down the chute** [SE *chute*, a narrow passage through which animals are driven for branding, shearing etc] [1920s+] (*Aus.*) in prison. ❑ **down the gurgler** [SE *gurgler*, echoic nickname for plughole] [1930s+] (*Aus.*) used of something that has not worked out. ❑ **down the pan** (*also* **down the crapper/shitter**) [i.e. the lavatory *pan* /CRAPPER *n.*[1] (3)/ SHITTER *n.*[1] (4)] [1930s+] wasted, lost, abandoned. ❑ **down there** (*also* **down low**) [euph.] [20C+] a coy ref. to the vagina; occas. the penis. ❑ **down to cases** **1** [late 19C+] (*US*) down to the hard facts. **2** [1940s] (*US Und.*) down to one's last pennies. ❑ **down to one's seams** *see under* SEAM *n.* ❑ **down to the short strokes** *see ON THE SHORT STROKES under* SHORT STROKES *n.* ❑ **give someone down the banks** *v.* [late 19C; 1960s+] (*orig. Irish*) to scold, to reprimand.

IN EXCLAMATIONS

❑ **down with his apple-cart!** [northern dial.; SE phr. *down with* + APPLE *n.*[1]] [mid-19C] knock him down!

down-and-out *n.* [*down* in the gutter and *out* of luck] [late 19C+] (*orig. US*) a homeless or destitute person, a tramp.

down-and-out *adj.* (*also* **in the downs, out and down**) [20C+] homeless or destitute; living as a tramp.

down-and-outer *n.* [ext. DOWN-AND-OUT *n.*] [1910s+] (*US*) a vagrant, a tramp.

down and up *n.* [rhy. sl.] [20C+] (*Aus.*) a cup.

down below *n.*[1] [euph.] [mid-19C+] a coy ref. to the vagina.

down below *n.*[2] **1** [1900s] (*US Und.*) prison. **2** [1910s] (*Aus.*) Sydney; any southern city, which is 'down below' the outback.

Down-easter *n.* [mid-19C+] (*US*) **1** a 'Yankee', i.e. an inhabitant or native of the north-eastern states. **2** an inhabitant or native of Maine.

downer *n.*[1] [Rom. *tawno*, a little one] **1** [mid-19C] (*US*) a nickel, five cents. **2** [mid–late 19C] a sixpence (2½p.).

downer *n.*[2] [DOWN *adj.*[2] (1)] **1** [mid-19C; 1960s+] a depressing, worrying situation. **2** [1970s+] a depressing person. **3** [1970s+] a state of depression; often as *on a downer*; also attrib.

downer *n.*[3] [DOWN *n.*[2] (2)] [20C+] a grudge; esp. in phr. *have a downer on*.

downer *n.*[4] [on which one lies down] [1920s–30s] (*UK tramp*) a bed.

downer *n.*[5] [DOWN *n.*[5] (1)] **1** [1960s+] a barbiturate, a tranquillizer. **2** [1990s+] any drug used to reduce the unpleasant experiences that can accompany the end of using a given 'up' drug, e.g. crack cocaine. **3** [1990s+] heroin, as opposed to cocaine. **4** [2000s] methadone.

downey *n. see* DOWNY *n.*[2].

down-home *n.* [1920s+] (*usu. US black*) one's home, esp. among black speakers, the South.

down-home *adj.* [note early 19C *go down-home*, to visit one's home] [1920s+] (*usu. US black*) reminiscent or characteristic of one's home, esp. among black speakers, of the South; thus *talk down-home*, to speak black English; also adv., and fig. use.

downie *n.* [DOWNER *n.*[2]] [1960s+] (*drugs*) a depressant.

Downing Street *n.* [the residence of UK prime ministers at 10 Downing Street, London SW1] [20C+] (*bingo*) the number ten.

down low *n.* **1** [1990s+] (*US black*) a state of secrecy. **2** [2000s] (*US black*) ostensibly heterosexual, married men who enjoy sex with homosexual men.

IN PHRASES

❑ **on the down low** (*also* **on the d.l./low**) [1990s+] (*orig. US black*) **1** in the background; in a clandestine manner. **2** of a (married) man, having homosexual relations despite parading an ostensibly heterosexual lifestyle. **3** being a fan of hip-hop/rap music.

down low *adj.* [i.e. keeping a *low* profile] [1990s+] (*US black*) covert, secret.

downpressor *n.* [1950s+] (*W.I. Rasta*) a preferred term for SE *oppressor*.

downright *n.* [late 19C–1930s] (*UK tramp*) begging, tramping; esp. in phr. *on the downright*, wandering the country as a beggar.

downright buttock and sham file *n. see* DOWN BUTTOCK AND SHAM FILE *under* DOWN *adj.*[1].

downrighter *n.* [DOWNRIGHT *n.*] [1900s] a beggar, a tramp.

Downs, the *n.* [the site of the prison in the fields that surrounded and were geographically lower than Tothill] [mid-19C] (*UK Und.*) Tothill Fields Prison.

downs *n.* [one puts it *down* as a payment] [2000s] (*US black*) money.

downshire *n.* [pun] [19C] the female pubic hair.

downstairs *n.* **1** [19C] hell. **2** [late 19C+] the urino-genital area. **3** [1910s+] the guts, the belly.

IN PHRASES

❑ **dine at the downstairs restaurant** *v. see under* DINE *v.*
❑ **go downstairs for breakfast** *v.* [ext. of GO DOWN *v.* (6) + play on EAT *v.* (4)] [1970s] (*Aus.*) to perform cunnilingus.

down to *adj.*[1] (*also* **down upon**) [DOWN *adj.*[1] (1)] [19C+] alert to, aware of, 'fly'.

down to *adj.*[2] [fig. use of abbr. of SE *written down to*] **1** [late 19C] to the account of. **2** [1960s+] the responsibility of.

down to *adj.*[3] [1950s+] for the sake of.

downtown *n.* **1** [1920s+] (*US black*) the female genital area, in the context of cunnilingus. **2** [1930s+] (*US police/Und.*) police headquarters. **3** [1940s–50s] (*US black*) the area where the black community lives. **4** [1980s+] (*US*) a generic for the city government, the police department and similar authorities.

IN PHRASES

❑ **go downtown** *v.* [play on DOWN *n.*[5]] [1990s+] (*US drugs*) to use heroin, i.e. a depressant which sends one 'down'. ❑ **just like downtown** [1990s+] (*US teen*) a phr. of satisfaction when a plan works out as required.

downtown *adj.* [20C+] (*US*) sophisticated; smart; well-dressed.

downtown *v.* [newly prosperous Harlemites signified their new status by leaving the ghetto and moving *downtown*, i.e. to more prosperous parts of New York] [1920s+] (*US black*) to improve one's lot in society, to go 'up in the world'.

down under *n.* [late 19C+] **1** Australia; supposedly sited 'underneath' the UK on the globe. **2** (*Aus.*) the United Kingdom. **3** (*also* **way down under**) New Zealand.

Downy *n.* [2000s] one who has Down's Syndrome.

downy *n.*[1] [DOWN *adj.*[1] (1) + sfx *-y*] [19C] a knowledgeable, artful, aware person.

downy *n.*[2] (*also* **downey**) [SE *down* mattress + *lie down*] [mid-19C–1900s] a bed.

IN PHRASES

❑ **do the downy** *v.* [mid-19C] to lie in bed.

downy *adj.*[1] [DOWN *adj.*[1] (1) + sfx *-y*] **1** [19C] aware, knowledgeable. **2** [mid-19C] fashionable. **3** [late 19C] as sense 1, with overtones of criminality.

IN COMPOUNDS

❑ **downy bird** *n.* [BIRD *n.*[1] (3a)] [19C] a knowledgeable, artful, aware person. ❑ **downy bit** *n. see under* BIT *n.*[1]. ❑ **downy cove** *n.* (*also* **downey cove**) [COVE *n.* (1)] [early–mid-19C] a knowledgeable, artful, aware, 'fly' person. ❑ **downy earwig** *n.* [EARWIG *n.* (3)] [1920s–30s] (*UK tramp*) a sympathetic listener.

downy *adj.*[2] [1950s] (*drugs*) in a state that follows the climactic euphoria of a drug experience.

dowry *n.* [SE *dowry*, money given with a bride; ult. Ital. *dare*, to give] [mid-19C] (*Ling. Fr./Polari*) a great deal, very much, plenty of.

dowse/dowser *n. see* DOUSER *n.*

doxey/doxie *n. see* DOXY *n.*

doxology dumper *n.* [SE *doxology*, the praising of God] [late 19C] (*Aus.*) a preacher, a clergyman.

doxology-works *n.* [SE *doxology*, the praising of God] [late 19C] a place of Christian worship.

doxy *n.* (*also* **doccy, docxy, doxey, doxie, doxsy**) [? Du. *docke*, a doll or SE *dock*, an animal's tail; Ribton-Turner, *A History of Vagrants* (1887), suggests Lowland Scot. *doxie*, lazy] (*UK Und.*) **1** [early 16C–mid-19C] the female companion of a variety of mendicant villains. **2** [early 16C+] a general term, usu. derog., for a woman or girl, esp. a mistress. **3** [late 17C+] a prostitute.

IN COMPOUNDS

❑ **doxy-dell** *n.* [DELL *n.* (1)] [mid-17C] a whore.

IN PHRASES

❑ **arch-doxy** *n.* [early 18C–early 19C] (*UK Und.*) the woman accomplice of a gang-leader.

doxy *adj.* **1** [early 17C–mid-18C] of a woman, corrupt, amoral, whorish. **2** [2000s] with ref. other than to a woman, flashy, 'tarted up'.

D'Oyly Carte *n.* [rhy. sl.; ult. Sir Richard *D'Oyly Carte* (1844–1901), late 19C producer of many Gilbert and Sullivan operas] [1970s+] a fart.

dozed *adj.* [fig. use of dial. *dozed*, of wood, rotten] **1** [mid-18C; 20C+] (*Ulster*) very drunk. **2** [1950s] (*US drugs*) intoxicated.

dozen *n.* [backform. f. DOZENS *n.*] [1920s+] (*US black*) a ritual insult.

dozens *n.* (*also* **dirty dozens, dozen, snagging**) [f. the throw of twelve in craps, the worst possible throw, or f. its folk origins as a set of ritualized verses, usu. in rhymed couplets, which ran through twelve specific sexual acts, each rhyming with the numbers one to twelve; dozens can be 'dirty' or 'clean', depending on the level of obscenity involved; otherwise unsupported, Legman, *The Rationale of the Dirty Joke* (1968), suggests 'possibly from the Saxon word "doze", to stun or overwhelm, as in bulldozer'; for a discussion of ety. *see American Speech* XXV:3 (1950) pp.230–33] [1910s+] (*US black*) a ritual game of testing a rival's emotional strength by insulting his various relatives, esp. his mother, in twelve 'rounds' of attack and taking similar insults in return; the insults are usu. sexual and/or scatological; thus the common addition of the adj. *dirty*.

IN PHRASES

❑ **play the dozens** *v.* (*also* **play dozen, shoot the dozens, slip (in) the dozens, slip in the twelves**) [1910s+] (*US black*) **1** to compete in ritualized mutual insults, often about one's family. **2** to take advantage of, to deceive. ❑ **play the dozens with one's uncle's cousin** *v.* [1940s] (*US black*) to go about things in quite the wrong way, to make a mess of things. ❑ **put someone in the dozens** *v.* [1920s+] (*US*) to put somone in a negative situation.

dozer *n.* [SE *doze*] [1970s+] (*Irish*) a slow-witted person; usu. as *no dozer*.

dozey-arsed *adj.* [colloq. *dozy* + -ARSED *sfx* (2)] [1990s+] stupid, 'slow'.

dozier *n. see* DOSHA *n.*

dozing-crib *n.* [SE *doze* + CRIB *n.*[1] (1)] [mid–late 19C] a bedroom.

dozo *n.* [colloq. *dozy* + -O *sfx* (2)] [1980s] (*N.Z.*) a fool.

D.P. *n. see* DURBAN POISON *n.*

d.ph. *n.* [abbr./pron. + pun on the degree of Ph.D.] [1910s+] (*US*) a damned fool.

d.q. *n.*

IN PHRASES

❑ **on the d.q.** *adv.* [abbr. *d*ead *q*uiet] [late 19C] (*US*) quietly, surreptitiously, privately.

drab *n.* [Rom. *drab*, poison; thus *drabengro*, doctor, lit. 'poison-man'] [mid-19C] poison.

drabbit! *excl.* [16C–19C] a mild excl., i.e. *(Go)d rabbit!*, *(Go)d rat it!*

drabble-tail *n.* [? DRAGGLE-TAIL *n.*] [mid-19C–1920s] a term of abuse; as adj., *drabbled*.

drab-driver *n.* [SE *drab*, a slattern] [early 17C] a pimp.

drack *n.*[1] (*also* **drac**) [DRACK *adj.*] [1930s+] (*Aus.*) rubbishy, worthless goods.

drack *n.*[2] (*also* **drac**) [proper name *Dracula* but *see* DRACK *n.*[1]] [1960s+] (*Aus.*) **1** an unattractive woman. **2** a police officer.

drack *adj.* [? Yid. *dreck*, rubbish, dirt] [1930s+] (*Aus.*) (*also* **drac**) second-rate, inferior, unattractive.

IN COMPOUNDS

❑ **drack sort** *n.* [SE *sort*, a type (of person)] [1930s+] (*Aus.*) an unattractive person of either sex.

dracs *n.* (*also* **duracs**) [backsl.] [1930s–40s] playing cards.

Dracula *n.* [a cruel comparison to the well-known vampire] **1** [1950s+] (*Aus.*) an unattractive woman. **2** [1970s] (*US teen*) an unpleasant, severe father, or person.

draft *n.* [SAmE *draft*, the selecting of a smaller group from a larger body, usu. in milit. context] [1940s–50s] (*US Und.*) the transportation of a convict from one prison to another.

draft on the pump at Aldgate *n.* (*also* **draught on the pump at Aldgate**) [SE *draft*, a written order for the payment of money] [late 18C–early 19C] a bad bill of exchange.

draftpak *n.* [Scot. *draftpak*, take-away packs of draft beer available over the bar in Scottish public houses] [1990s+] (*Scot.*) a lowlife, an eccentric; a habitual drunkard.

draft up *n.* (*also* **draft vertical, wind vertical**) [play on WIND *n.*[2]] [1910s] (*Aus.*) a state of nervousness.

drag *n.*[1] **1** (*UK Und.*) in the context of theft. (**a**) [18C; 1900s–20s] a form of 'rod', whereby robbers 'fish' items from a shop window; then a tool for breaking the lock of a safe. (**b**) [late 18C+] the robbery of vehicles, initially horse-drawn, subseq. motorized; thus *go on the drag*, to pursue this as a profession; *done/lagged for a drag*, convicted of robbing a wagon or cart. (**c**) [19C] (*US Und.*) a theft. **2** as a vehicle, i.e. that which is *dragged* (by horses or an engine). (**a**) [mid-18C] a ferryboat. (**b**) [late 18C–1910s] a one- or two-horse wagon or cart. (**c**) [19C] a type of stagecoach, drawn by four horses, with seats on top. (**d**) [1900s] a prison van, a Black Maria. (**e**) [1910s+] a motorcar, thus vehicles in general. (**f**) [1920s–30s] (*US tramp*) a (slow) freight-train. (**g**) [1930s+] a van. **3** [early 19C] (*US Und.*) a prisoner. **4** [early 19C] (*Scot. Und.*) a watch chain. **5** [mid-19C+] a period of imprisonment lasting three months. **6** something along which one is 'dragged' or 'drags oneself'. (**a**) [mid-19C+] a street; thus MAIN DRAG *n.* (1), the main street; *back drag*, back street. (**b**) [1920s+] a long distance, which will make for tedious travelling. (**c**) [1930s] (*US tramp*) a railroad line. **7** any person or object that fig. impedes progress. (**a**) [mid-19C+] a disappointment, a pity, a nuisance, a task that one has no desire to perform; a bore. (**b**) [20C+] of a person, a disappointment, a hanger-on, a pest. (**c**) [1940s] (*US black campus*) an old-fashioned person. (**d**) [1950s–60s] a depressing atmosphere. (**e**) [1980s] of drugs, second-rate. **8** in the context of clothing, which 'drags along' the ground, and ext. uses [orig. theatrical use, which stressed the *drag* of a long dress along the floor, as opposed to tight-fitting trousers. The first *OED* citations (1870) imply fancy dress; gay refs. not overt until 20C]. (**a**) [late 19C+] female dress as worn by men, but not in a homosexual context, e.g. on stage. (**b**) [20C+] female dress as worn by homosexual males or female impersonators; also male dress as worn by lesbians. (**c**) [1910s+] (*also* **drag ball**) a party held *en travesti*. (**d**) [1920s–70s] (*US/Aus.*) a party (with no specific gay overtones). (**e**) [1920s+] (*US gay*) a homosexual man dressed in female clothing, a DRAG QUEEN *n.* (1). (**f**) [1930s–40s] (*US*) a bar that caters primarily to a gay clientele. (**g**) [1950s+] clothing in general; a costume, a disguise. **9** [late 19C+] influence. **10** a draw, puff or drink. (**a**) [20C+] a puff of a marijuana cigarette; hence *give a drag*, to pass a marijuana cigarette; *take a drag*, to take a puff on the cigarette. (**b**) [1910s+] a puff of a cigarette; thus the cigarette itself; thus v. *drag*, to smoke. (**c**) [1950s] a gulp or mouthful of alcohol. (**d**) [1950s+] (*UK prison*) a cannabis or cannabis/tobacco cigarette. **11** [20C+] (*US*) what one 'drags down/in'. (**a**) a share of money. (**b**) wages. **12** one who 'drags' or is fig. 'dragged along'. (**a**) [1900s] (*US campus*) a toady, a parasite, a flatterer. (**b**) [1920s+] (*US*) a young woman who is being taken to a party. (**c**) [1950s] (*US*) a girlfriend, a young woman. **13** pertaining to dancing. (**a**) [1910s+] a slow dance or the music that accompanies it. (**b**) [1950s] a dance, a party.

pertaining to transvestism

IN COMPOUNDS

❑ **drag-dyke** *n.* [DYKE *n.*] [1960s+] a 'masculine' lesbian who chooses to dress in male clothing. ❑ **drag joint** *n.* [JOINT *n.* (3b)] [1930s+] (*US gay*) a bar or club that caters predominantly to transvestites. ❑ **drag-king** *n.* (*also* **drag-butch**) [SE *king*/BUTCH *n.*[1] (5)] [1990s+] (*gay*) a woman who dresses as a man. ❑ **drag queen** *n. see* separate entry.

IN PHRASES

❑ **drag up** *v.* **1** [1960s+] to get dressed (up). **2** [1970s] of a homosexual man, to put on women's clothing and appear *en travesti*. ❑ **flash the drag** *v.* [late 19C] (*UK Und.*) of a man, to wear female clothes for criminal purposes. ❑ **play drag** *v.* [1960s] (*US black*) of a female prostitute, to dress as a man in order to attract clients.

general uses

IN COMPOUNDS

❑ **drag-cove** *n.* [COVE *n.* (1)] [early 19C] a cart-driver. ❑ **drag lay** *n.* [LAY *n.*[3] (1)] [late 18C–early 19C] the robbery of vehicles. ❑ **dragsman** *n.* **1** [19C] a coachman; a cart or wagon driver; thus *swell dragsman*, a gentleman who drives a coach [20C+ use is SE]. **2** [19C–1930s] a thief who robs goods or trunks from the back of vans or carts. ❑ **drag-sneak** *n.* [SNEAK *n.*[1] (1b)] [mid-19C] a thief who specializes in the robbery of vehicles. ❑ **drag-weed** *n.* [1940s–50s] (*US drugs*) marijuana.

IN PHRASES

❑ **do the drag** *v.* [1940s] (*US Und.*) to wander around or loiter in a town. ❑ **go on the drag** *v.* [late 18C] to follow a cart or wagon in order to rob it. ❑ **put the drags on** *v.* [SE *drag*, in the sense of dragging on someone's sleeve; + poss. link to DRAG *n.*[1] (1)] [1910s+] (*Aus.*) to ask someone for a loan. ❑ **run a drag on** *v.* [1980s+] (*US black*) to deceive, to trick, to hoax. ❑ **work the drag** *v.* [1940s] (*US Und.*) to beg on the street.

drag *n.*[2] [note this version of the DOZENS *n.* is characterized by its extreme vulgarity and coarseness] [20C+] (*US black*) a ritual game of testing a rival's emotional strength by insulting his various relatives.

drag *n.*[3] [ety. unknown] [1900s] (*US campus*) a joke.

drag *n.*[4] [16C SE *draggle-tail*, an unkempt, slatternly woman, whose skirts drag along the ground] [1920s+] (*US*) an unkempt or immoral woman, a slattern.

drag *n.*[5] [abbr.] [1930s–60s] (*US Und.*) a police *drag*net, i.e. the systematic searching of a large area, even a whole town or city.

drag *adj.*[1] (*also* **draggy**) [DRAG *n.*[1] (8)] **1** [late 19C+] pertaining to female impersonation (not invariably by homosexuals), usu. in a theatrical context. **2** [1920s+] relevant to the gay lifestyle.

drag *adj.*[2] [1960s+] (*US*) boring.

drag *v.*[1] **1** in the context of theft. (**a**) [early 19C–1950s] (*UK Und.*) to rob from vehicles; thus n. *dragging*. (**b**) [mid-19C] (*US Und.*) to steal goods deposited in shop doorways. (**c**) [1900s] (*Aus. Und.*) to rob on the street. to 'mug'. (**d**) [1970s] (*UK Und.*) to steal a car. **2** [mid-19C] (*UK Und.*) to sentence to three months' imprisonment. **3** [late 19C] (*US*) to search for contraband. **4** [late 19C+] (*US campus*) to escort to a dance. **5** to move, to 'drag oneself away'. (**a**) [20C+] (*US*) to leave something unfinished. (**b**) [20C+] to leave quickly. (**c**) [1920s+] (*US*) (*also* **drag it**) to resign from a job, or participation in a betting game. **6** [1900s] (*US campus*) to toady to, to curry favour with a superior. **7** to 'drag along'. (**a**) [1920s+] to force someone to go to a place against their will; often as *drag along*. (**b**) [1950s+] (*US black/prison*) to lead someone on, to persuade, to trick. **8** [1940s–70s] (*US*) to irritate, to bore, to 'bring down'. **9** [1950s+] to use the *drag*, i.e. street. (**a**) to drive up and down, chatting to one's friends and displaying one's car. (**b**) (*US campus*) to race a car. **10** [1960s+] to waste time, to idle, to move slowly. **11** [2000s] (*Aus. drugs*) to inhale a powdered drug.

IN PHRASES

❑ **drag it** *v. see* sense 5c above. ❑ **drag the gut** *v.* [GUT *n.* (5)] [1960s+] (*US teen*) to drive up and down the main street. ❑ **drag up** *v.* [1920s] (*US*) to leave one's job, to resign.

SE in slang uses

IN COMPOUNDS

❑ **drag-out** *n. see* separate entry.

IN PHRASES

❑ **drag a blind** *v. see under* BLIND DATE *n.* ❑ **drag-ass** *see* separate entries. ❑ **drag down** *v.* [note DRAG *n.*[1] (11a)] [1920s+] (*US*) to earn a salary, wages. ❑ **drag in** *v.* [20C+] (*US*) to arrive, to appear. ❑ **drag it** *v. see* DRAG ONE'S ASS *v.* ❑ **drag it through the garden** *v.* [1970s+] (*US*) to add salad etc to a portion of meat/fish. ❑ **drag on** *v.* [1910s+] (*Aus.*) **1** to marry a woman. **2** to perform a task. ❑ **drag one's anchor** *v. see under* ANCHOR *n.* ❑ **drag one's ass** *v. see* separate entry. ❑ **drag one's heels** *v.* [1970s] (*US campus*) to walk, to stroll. ❑ **drag one's hook** *v.* [naut. *hook*, an anchor] [1960s] (*N.Z.*) to leave. ❑ **drag tail** *v. see* DRAG ASS *v.* ❑ **drag the chain** *v.* [sheep-shearing jargon] [1930s+] (*Aus./N.Z.*) to be slow, to be inferior, to be last in any work or contest, to be the slowest drinker of a group. ❑ **drag through the sheet** *v.* [late 18C] to rescue someone from financial difficulties, spec. to loan money.

drag *v.*[2] [? SE *drag*, i.e. into one's brain] [1900s] (*US campus*) to understand.

drag *v.*[3] [DRAG *n.*[3]] [1900s] (*US campus*) to joke, to jest.

drag-ass *adj.* [DRAG ASS *v.*] (*US*) **1** [1930s+] annoying, irritating. **2** [1950s] of a person, lazy, bedraggled. **3** [1950s+] of a thing or person, tedious. **4** [1990s+] tired.

drag ass *v.* [SE *drag* + ASS *n.* (4)] [1930s+] (*US*) **1** to go, to travel (the subtext is often of reluctance). **2** (*also* **drag tail**) to act slowly, lazily [note DRAG ONE'S TAIL *under* TAIL *n.*]. **3** to do badly.

drag-ass *adv.* [DRAG-ASS *adj.* (2)] [1990s+] (*US*) lazily, hesitantly.

dragged (out) *adj.* **1** [mid-19C+] (*orig. US*) (*also* **dragging**) exhausted, sickly. **2** [1950s] angry. **3** [1960s] suffering adverse reactions after smoking cannabis. **4** [1990s+] drunk.

dragger *n.*[1] (*also* **rum dragger**) [DRAG *v.*[1] (1a)] [late 18C; 20C+] one who robs vehicles.

dragger *n.*[2] [SE] [1990s+] (*US campus*) one who is so drunk that they have to be *dragged* back to their room.

dragging *n.*[1] [DRAG *v.*[1] (1a) + sfx *-ing*] [mid-19C+] stealing from carts and vans.

IN COMPOUNDS

❑ **dragging lark** *n.* (*also* **dragging game**) [1910s–30s] stealing from automobiles.

dragging *n.*[2] [DRAG ONE'S ASS *v.* (2)] [1980s+] (*US campus*) the state of feeling ill or lethargic.

dragging *adj. see* DRAGGED (OUT) *adj.* (1).

dragging time *n.* [mid-19C] the evening of a country fair, when everyone has been drinking and the men begin to make robust physical advances towards the women.

draggin' wagon *n.* [SE *drag racing*] [1950s] (*US teen*) a fast car.

draggle-tail *n.* [16C SE *draggle-tail*, an unkempt, slatternly woman, whose skirts drag along the ground] **1** [late 16C+] a prostitute. **2** [1900s] (*Aus.*) a female servant.

draggle-tailed *adj.* (*also* **draggled-skirted, draggle-skirted, draggle-tail**) **1** [mid-17C+] (*also* **draggled**) promiscuous, pertaining to prostitution; also general term of abuse. **2** [late 17C+] impoverished.

draggy *adj.*[1] (*also* **draggly**) [DRAGGED (OUT) *adj.* (1)] [late 19C+] (*orig. US*) unwell, sickly-looking.

draggy *adj.*[2] [DRAG *n.*[1] (7a)] [1920s+] of people or events, boring.

draggy *adj.*[3] *see* DRAG *adj.*[1].

dragon *n.*[1] **1** [17C–early 18C] a slattern, a promiscuous woman. **2** [1950s–60s] an old prostitute. **3** [1960s] (*N.Z.*) a wife.

dragon *n.*[2] [the image of St George and the dragon engraved on the obverse of the coin] [19C] a sovereign.

dragon *n.*[3] [backform. f. CHASE THE DRAGON *v.*] [1980s+] (*drugs*) heroin.

dragon *n.*[4] [1980s+] (*US*) a (large) penis.

IN PHRASES

❑ **drain the dragon** *v. see under* DRAIN *v.*

dragon *n.*[5] [abbr. DRAGON BREATH *n.*; i.e. such a person 'breathes fire'] [1980s+] (*US campus*) a person with particularly bad breath.

dragon breath *n.* [the image of one who 'breathes fire'] [1970s+] (*US*) bad halitosis, or any bad smell.

drag one's ass *v.* (*also* **drag it, drag one's butt**) [SE *drag* + ASS *n.* (2)/BUTT *n.*[1] (1a)] (*US*) **1** [1920s+] to leave, to go, to move. **2** [1930s+] to be fatigued, run down, miserable. **3** [1940s] to be slow, lazy.

dragon upon St George *n.* [the female *dragon* is on top of a male *St George*] [late 17C–18C] a position of sexual intercourse in which the woman is on top of the man.

dragoon (it) *v.* [SE *dragoon*, orig. a horse soldier, i.e. one who rode to battle on horseback but dismounted to fight like infantry] [late 18C–19C] to work at two jobs simultaneously.

drag-out *n.* [the loser, knocked unconscious, is *dragged out* of the way/room] (*US*) **1** [early 19C+] a rough party, a brawl; also attrib. **2** [mid-19C] one who indulges in a fierce fight. **3** [late 19C] a dance.

drag queen *n.* (*also* **queen drag**) [DRAG *n.*[1] (8a) + -QUEEN *sfx* (3)] **1** [1930s+] an effeminate homosexual who prefers to dress as a woman; sometimes as a professional female impersonator. **2** [1960s+] a female impersonator. **3** [1990s+] in fig. use, as a general insult.

d-railed *adj.* [SE *derailed*, but note DERAIL *n.* (2)] [2000s] (*US campus*) drunk.

drain *n.*[1] [SE *drain a glass*] **1** [early–mid-19C] gin. **2** [early 19C+] a drink; thus *do a drain*, to have a drink (with a friend); *drain of pale*, a glass of brandy.

drain *n.*[2] **1** [late 19C] the vagina. **2** [1930s] the throat.

drain *n.*[3] [1930s] an act of urination.

drain *v.* (*also* **drain off**) [19C+] to urinate; usu. in combs. below.

IN COMPOUNDS

❑ **drain-off** *n.* [2000s] an act of urination.

IN PHRASES

❑ **drain the anaconda** *v. see* EMPTY THE ANACONDA *under* ANACONDA *n.* ❑ **drain the dragon/snake** *v.* [DRAGON *n.*[4]/SNAKE *n.*[3]] [1960s+] to urinate. ❑ **drain the lily** *v. see under* LILY *n.* ❑ **drain the (main) vein** *v.* [1940s+] (*orig. Aus.*) to urinate.

drainies *n.* [1970s+] very narrow 'drainpipe' trousers.

drake *v.* [play on SE *duck*] [early 19C] to duck in a pond, a punishment sometimes meted out to pickpockets captured at fairs or races.

drake and duck *n.* [rhy. sl. = FUCK *n.* (1a)] [1940s] sexual intercourse.

drama queen *n.* (*also* **d.q.**) [SE *drama* + QUEEN *n.* (2b)] [1960s+] (*orig. gay*) anyone considered to be making an excessive fuss or 'making a mountain out of a molehill'.

drammed up *adj.* [1940s] (*US*) drunk.

drank *n.* (*also* **drink, purple drank**) (*US drugs*) prescription cough syrup, containing codeine.

dranka *n.* [ety. unknown] [2000s] (*US black*) a close friend, esp. a fellow gang member.

drap *n.* [var. on colloq. *drab*] [late 18C] a 'nasty, sluttish whore' (Egan's Grose).

drape *n.* [after its rejection by US blacks, the *drape* suit was taken up by Teddy Boys in the UK in the 1950s] **1** [1930s–60s] (*orig. US black*) a suit, typified by its generously cut, long, draped jacket with padded shoulders and high-waisted, tapering trousers. **2** [1930s+] (*orig. US black*) in pl., clothes, a suit. **3** [1950s+] (*orig. US black*) those who wear such suits. **4** [1990s+] (*W.I.*) 'the act of grabbing someone in the waist and hoisting him onto his toes' (Francis-Jackson, *Official Dancehall Dict.*, 1995).

IN COMPOUNDS

❑ **drape crib** *n.* [CRIB *n.*[1] (1)] [1940s] (*US black*) a wardrobe. ❑ **drape shape** *n.* [1940s–50s] a style of man's suit, typified by its generously cut, long, draped jacket with padded shoulders and high-waisted, tapering trousers.

drape *v.* [DRAPE *n.* (1)] **1** [1940s–50s] (*US black*) to dress (up). **2** [1990s+] (*W.I.*) to beat.

IN PHRASES

❑ **drape up** *v.* [1990s+] (*W.I. Rasta*) to beat, to thrash.

drape ape *n. see* RUG APE *under* RUG *n.*[1].

draped *adj.*[1] [? one is *draped* across the bar or around another's shoulders] [1940s] (*orig. milit.*) drunk.

draped *adj.*[2] [SE *draped* (*in*), covered in] **1** [1970s+] (*US gay*) uncircumcised. **2** [1970s+] (*US gay*) having a large penis. **3** [1990s+] (*US black*) wearing large amounts of gold jewellery.

draped down *adj.* [DRAPE *v.* (1)] [1940s] (*US black*) dressed in the height of urban fashion.

draper *n. see* ALE-DRAPER *under* ALE *n.*

drapers *n.* [1990s+] (*W.I.*) braces (UK), suspenders (US).

drapery miss *n.* (*also* **bit of drapery**) [orig. cited by Lord Byron c.1811 as 'a pretty, a high-born, a fashionable young female, well-instructed by her friends, and furnished by her milliner with a wardrobe upon credit, to be repaid, when *married*, by her *husband*'] [late 19C–1900s] a woman who is considered sexually forward and who emphasizes her appeal by a flashy style of dress.

drapes *n. see* DRAPE *n.* (2).

drapes *v.* [1970s–80s] (*UK black*) **1** to mug, to rob with violence. **2** to beat up.

drat! *excl.* (*also* **drats! drot!**) [19C+] a mild oath; a euph. for *God rot it!*; usu. as v. *drat* —! damn —!

dratsab *n.* [backsl.] [mid-19C+] a bastard.

dratted *adj.* [mid-19C+] irritating, infuriating.

draught-board suit *n.* [1910s] a dinner jacket.

draught on the pump at Aldgate *n. see* DRAFT ON THE PUMP AT ALDGATE *n.*

draw *n.*[1] [19C] **1** any device (or person) used to extract information from a third party. **2** the person from whom the information may be extracted.

draw *n.*[2] [one *draws* upon it] **1** [1920s–30s] (*also* **long draw**) a pipeload of opium. **2** [1940s+] (*Aus.*) a cigarette. **3** [1980s+] (*drugs*) cannabis, a portion of cannabis, esp. as an ounce or multiples thereof, e.g. *five-draw, seven-draw* etc. **4** [1990s+] a cannabis cigarette.

draw *n.*[3] [SE *draw*, a match in which both sides are equal] [1940s–50s] (*US prison*) a suspended sentence.

draw *v.*[1] [abbr. SE *withdraw*] [late 16C–19C] to pick a pocket.

IN PHRASES

❑ **on the draw** [early 19C] working as a pickpocket.

draw *v.*[2] [SE *drawn*] [20C+] (*W.I.*) to be born with a skin-colour noticeably different from that of the rest of one's family.

draw *v.*[3] [1930s; 1990s+] (*drugs*) to take a drug, e.g. cocaine or cannabis.

draw *v.*[4]

SE in slang uses

based on SE *draw*, to extract, to withdraw

IN COMPOUNDS

❑ **drawback** [the recipient *draws back* some money for themselves] [20C+] (*W.I.*) a small bribe.

IN PHRASES

❑ **draw a blank** *v. see under* BLANK *n.* ❑ **draw a cork** *v. see* separate entries. ❑ **draw blank(s)** *v. see* DRAW A BLANK *under* BLANK *n.* ❑ **draw bungy** *v.* [? the sound of a bung being withdrawn from a cask] [1950s+] (*W.I.*) to snore. ❑ **draw caad/card** *v.* [1950s+] (*W.I./UK black teen*) to trick or connive, to mislead, to 'pull a fast one' on someone. ❑ **draw down** *v.* [1990s+] (*W.I.*) to make an advance of some sort, usu. sexual. ❑ **draw iron** *v.* [SHOOTING IRON *n.* (1)] [mid–late 19C] (*US*) to draw a pistol. ❑ **draw it blank** *v. see* DRAW A BLANK *under* BLANK *n.* ❑ **draw it mild** *v. see* separate entries. ❑ **draw it strong** *v. see under* STRONG *adv.* ❑ **draw off** *v.* [SE *draw off*, to divert one's attention] [late 19C] of a woman, to calm a man's passion by consenting to sleep with him. ❑ **draw one** [late 19C–1940s] (*US short order*) a phr. meaning pour me a cup of coffee; thus ext. as *draw one in the dark*, pour me a black coffee; also n., a cup of coffee. ❑ **draw someone for** *v.* [19C] to borrow money from someone. ❑ **draw straws** *v. see under* STRAW *n.* ❑ **draw teeth** *v. see under* TEETH *n.* ❑ **draw the crabs** *v.* [1930s+] (*Aus.*) to attract unwelcome attention, to draw enemy fire (actual or metaphorical). ❑ **draw the crow** *v.* [an anecdote in which a number of game birds and one crow were on offer and one hapless person *drew the crow*] [1940s+] (*Aus.*) to come off worst, usu. in a share-out or division of spoils, labour, prizes etc. ❑ **draw the twine** *v.* [? the twine used in bricklaying] [1990s+] (*Irish*) to pursue a profitable activity. ❑ **draw water** *v.* [naut. jargon, a large ship draws more water than a smaller one] [20C+] to have influence.

IN EXCLAMATIONS

❑ **draw it easy!** [mid-19C] (*US*) a general excl. expressing incredulity or derision.

based on other SE senses

IN COMPOUNDS

❑ **draw drapes** *n.* [1970s] (*US gay*) the foreskin.

IN PHRASES

▫ **draw the blinds** *v.* (*also* **draw the veil**) [the foreskin represents the *blinds* that cover the penis] (*US gay*) **1** [1920s] to engage in homosexual activity. **2** [1970s+] to pull back the foreskin. **3** [1980s+] to fellate an uncircumcised penis. ▫ **draw the king's/queen's picture** *v.* [UK banknotes always carry the current monarch's head] [late 18C–19C] (*UK Und.*) to create counterfeit banknotes.

draw a cork *v.*[1] [19C] (*UK Und.*) to give someone a bleeding nose.

draw a cork *v.*[2] [the image is of an exhausted, post-coital male] [late 19C] of a woman, to have sexual intercourse.

drawers *n.* [? their being drawn on and off; the subseq. colloq. use to mean underpants does not materialize until 17C] [mid-16C–18C] (*UK Und.*) stockings.

SE in slang uses

IN PHRASES

▫ **drag one's drawers** *v.* [1920s+] (*US*) to go slowly, to idle, to dawdle. ▫ **drop one's drawers** *v. see under* DROP *v.*[1]. ▫ **get into someone's drawers** *v. see* GET INTO SOMEONE'S PANTS *under* PANTS *n.* ▫ **get to the drawers** *v.* [abbr. *get the drawers off*] [20C+] (*US black*) to have sexual intercourse.

IN EXCLAMATIONS

▫ **keep your drawers on!** *see* KEEP YOUR PANTS ON! *under* PANTS *n.*

draw it mild *v.* **1** [mid-19C] to amaze, to impress. **2** [mid-19C+] to restrain oneself, usu. in speech.

draw it mild! *excl.* [public house imagery, i.e. the *drawing* of pints of beer] [mid-19C+] a general excl. expressing incredulity or derision, i.e. don't exaggerate!

draw-latch *n.* (*also* **draw-lock**) [SE *draw-latch*, a string hanging on the outside of a door by which a latch is drawn or raised] **1** [early 16C–mid-19C] a thief who enters a house by lifting the latch. **2** [mid-19C] a loiterer.

dray *n.* see TRAY *n.*[1].

drayman bible *n.* [the *bulla cake* is a food of the poor; thus a drayman would rely on it for sustenance] [1940s+] (*W.I.*) a bulla cake.

dread *n.*[1] [1940s–60s] (*Irish*) an object of pity, or distaste.

dread *n.*[2] [Exod 15:16: 'Fear and dread shall fall upon them; by the greatness of thy arm they shall be as still as a stone'] [1950s+] (*W.I. Rasta/UK black*) **1** a Rastafarian. **2** one who wears dreadlocks but follows no other Rastafarian teachings. **3** the beliefs, practice or expression of Rastafarianism. **4** a youngster, usu. a male teenager, who shows off by taking dangerous risks. **5** (*also* **dred**) dreadlocks; usu. in pl. **6** as a term of address; the person addressed need not be a Rastafarian or wear dreadlocks.

dread *adj.* [DREAD *n.*[2]] [1960s+] (*W.I./Rasta*) of a situation, serious, important, amazing, whether positively or negatively.

dreadful *n.* [abbr. PENNY DREADFUL *under* PENNY *n.*] [late 19C] a sensationally written 'true crime' story, sold for one penny.

dreadie *n. see* DREADY *n.*

dreadnought *n.*[1] [all plays on SE] **1** [mid-19C] an overcoat. **2** [1900s] a male pessary or suppository. **3** [1900s–10s] a high, stiff corset. **4** [1910s] (*Aus. milit.*) a prophylactic kit.

dreadnought *n.*[2] [fig. uses of SE *dreadnought*, a large battleship, the first of which, HMS *Dreadnought*, was launched on 18 February 1906 and became the world's greatest armaments platform] (*Aus.*) **1** [1910s–30s] a long, deep glass of beer. **2** [1980s+] a shearer who can shear 300 sheep in a day.

dready *n.* (*also* **dreadie**) [DREAD *n.*[2] (1) + sfx *-y*] [1950s+] (*W.I. Rasta*) a friendly term for a fellow Rastafarian.

dream *n.*[1] **1** [late 19C+] a very attractive, charming, personable individual. **2** [late 19C+] someone or something exceptional, remarkable; often in ironic use. **3** [1910s] an expert.

SE in slang uses

IN COMPOUNDS

▫ **dreambox** *n.* [1910s–40s] (*US black*) the head. ▫ **dream puss** *n.* [PUSS *n.*[2] (1)] [1940s] (*US campus*) the idealized young woman.

dream *n.*[2] [? one can do it in one's sleep] [late 19C+] (*Aus.*) a six-month prison sentence.

dream *n.*[3] [? a brandname] [1910s] (*US*) a hand-rolled cigarette.

dream *n.*[4] [the effects on one's brain] (*drugs*) **1** [1920s+] opium, morphine; thus *dream beads*, pellets of opium. **2** [1940s] marijuana. **3** [1980s+] cocaine.

IN COMPOUNDS

▫ **dream dust** *n.* (*also* **dream powder**) [1950s+] (*drugs*) any narcotic in a powdered form; also attrib. ▫ **dream gum** *n.* [GUM *n.*[3] (1)] [1930s–50s] (*drugs*) opium. ▫ **dream stick** *n.* [STICK *n.* (6c)] (*US drugs*) **1** [1930s–50s] an opium pipe. **2** [1940s–50s] (*also* **dream stuff**) a marijuana cigarette. ▫ **dream wax** *n.* [its effects and its consistency] [1920s–50s] (*US drugs*) opium.

IN PHRASES

▫ **sweet dreams** *n. see under* SWEET *adj.*[1].

dreamboat *n.* [1940s+] (*orig. US*) **1** (*also* **charmboat, dream bait**) a particularly attractive man or woman, the fuel of one's fantasies. **2** something particularly attractive, esp. a car. **3** a general term of admiration or affection (also used ironically); also attrib.

dreamer *n.* [DREAM *n.*[4] (1)] [1960s+] (*drugs*) morphine.

dreamers *n.* [SE *dream*; one dreams between them] [1930s–40s] (*US black*) sheets and blankets.

dream off *v.* (*US*) **1** [late 19C] to have a nocturnal emission of semen, a 'wet dream.'. **2** [1930s–40s] to fall asleep on the job, to drift off.

dream on! *excl.* [i.e. your theory is, at best, a daydream] [1980s+] a dismissive excl.: don't you wish!

Dream Street *n.* [the term was coined by the short story writer and chronicler of Broadway, Damon Runyon (1880–1946); the block was the site of the stage door to B.F. Keith's Palace Theater, 1913–2, the headquarters of American vaudeville] [1930s+] 47th Street, New York City, between Sixth and Seventh Avenues.

dreamy *adj.* [DREAM *n.*[1]] [1940s+] (*orig. US teen*) perfect, ideal, delightful, beautiful.

dreck *n.* (*also* **drek**) [Yid. *drek*, thence Ger. *dreck*, excrement, dung] (*US*) **1** [1920s+] excrement, filth. **2** [1920s+] anything worthless, second-rate, rubbishy. **3** [1970s+] (*drugs*) heroin.

drecky *adj.* [DRECK *n.* (2)] [1950s+] second-rate, trashy, rubbishy, dirty.

dred *n. see* DREAD *n.*[2] (5).

dredge-head *n.* [SE *dredge* + -HEAD *sfx* (4)] [1970s+] a habitual drinker, who drinks up the dregs in each glass.

dreg *n.* [SE *dreg*] [1980s] (*Aus.*) a term of abuse, esp. by women towards men.

dreggy *n.* [colloq. *dregged*, tired and lethargic after smoking canabis] [1980s+] (*Aus./US drugs*) cannabis that causes one to become tired and lethargic.

drek *n. see* DRECK *n.*

drenched *adj.* [ME *drench*, drink] [1920s–60s] (*US*) very drunk.

dress *n.*

SE in slang uses

IN COMPOUNDS

▫ **dress house** *n.* [mid-19C] (*UK Und.*) a brothel where each prostitute is a DRESS-LODGER below. ▫ **dress-lodger** *n.* (*also* **dress-lady, dress-woman**) [Bee notes *dress house*, a dress-hire shop where smart outfits were rented by the night, but suggests no Und. overtones] [mid-19C] a prostitute who is dressed in finery by her landlady and repays the favour by walking the streets and turning over her profits. ▫ **dress-puss** *n.* [SE *dress* + PUSSY *n.* (10)] [1940s+] (*W.I.*) an overdressed or fashionably dressed person, a provocatively dressed woman; also as phr. *dressed up to puss-foot*. ▫ **dress-suit burglar** *n.* [1910s] (*US Und.*) a lobbyist.

IN PHRASES

▫ **whatever blows your dress up** *see under* BLOW *v.*[1].

dress *v.* [ironic use of SE *dress*, to treat a person properly] **1** [late 18C–early 19C] to beat, to thrash. **2** [early–mid-19C] to tell off, to reprimand, to criticize. **3** [mid-19C] (*UK Und.*) to subject to robbery.

SE in slang uses

IN COMPOUNDS

❑ **dress-and-breath** *n.* [the most effort she makes is to get dressed and breathe] [1920s–30s] (*US black*) a very lazy woman. ❑ **dress-up** *n.* **1** [1930s] (*US Und.*) an outfit of one's best clothes. **2** [1970s] a prostitute's client who enjoys dressing up, usu. in her clothes and make-up, although some prefer to provide their own wardrobe.

IN PHRASES

❑ **dress a hat** *v.* ['Most likely from the fact that a hat receives the attention of three or four people before it is properly fit for wear' (*Slang Dict.*, 1873)] [mid-19C] to carry out various methods of robbery contrived by two or more servants or shopmen, either exchanging their master's goods (e.g. shoes for a hat) or pooling them (the butcher's boy steals steaks, the potboy steals beer etc) and all is sold to a third party. ❑ **dress and res** *v.* [1990s+] (*US black*) to dress smartly, fashionably. ❑ **dress it in mourning** *v. see under* MOURNING *n.*

dressed *adj.* [SE *dressed up*] [1910s+] (*US black*) of a car, filled with every conceivable decoration, gimmick and similar flashy adornment.

SE in slang uses

IN PHRASES

❑ **dressed down** *adj.* (*also* **dressed tight**) [but note recent 'dress-down Friday', a day on which office workers are allowed to dress casually] [1970s+] (*US black*) very well dressed. ❑ **dressed in** *n.* [i.e. *dressed in* newly issued clothes] [20C+] (*US prison*) a new inmate. ❑ **dressed up like a lighthouse** [1920s–30s] (*US*) flashily, ostentatiously dressed. ❑ **dressed up like a pox-doctor's clerk** *see* DONE UP LIKE A POX DOCTOR'S CLERK *under* DONE UP *adj.*[2]. ❑ **dressed up like a sore finger/thumb/toe** (*also* **dolled up like a sore finger/thumb/toe**) [20C+] (*Aus./N.Z./US*) overdressed, flashily dressed. ❑ **dressed up to the knocker** *see under* KNOCKER *n.*[1].

dressed (up) to the nines *phr.* (*also* **dressed out...**) [UP TO THE NINES *phr.*] **1** [mid-19C+] dressed up to the height of fashion. **2** [1910s–20s] occas. intensified as *dressed to the tens*.

dresser *n.* [abbr. SE *cross-dresser*] [1990s+] (*gay*) a transvestite.

dreykop *n.* [Yid. *dreykop*, lit. 'twisted head'] [1960s–70s] a trickster, a fraudsman.

drib *v.* [SE *drib*, to fall drop by drop] [late 17C] (*UK Und.*) to crop, to cut off.

dribble *n.* [late 19C+] meaningless chatter.

IN COMPOUNDS

❑ **dribble-lipped** *adj.* [1980s+] (*US black*) having a notably pendulous bottom lip. ❑ **dribble-puss** *n.* [PUSS *n.*[2] (1)] [1940s+] (*US*) a person, usu. a child, with a runny nose.

dribble *v.* **1** [late 18C–early 19C] to throw dice in such a way that they 'dribble' slowly from the cup, thus facilitating manipulation by a cheat. **2** [1930s–40s] (*US black*) to stutter.

dribbling shits *n.* (*also* **dribbles**) [SE *dribble* + SHITS, THE *n.* (1)] [20C+] incontinence, diarrhoea.

dribs and drabs *n.* [rhy. sl. = colloq. *crabs*] [20C+] (*Aus.*) body lice.

dried-barkers *n.* [SE *dried* + *barker*, a dog, thus any furred animal] [1940s] (*US black*) furs.

dried salmon *n. see* SALMON *n.*[1].

drift *v.* [the overtone is of moving slowly and aimlessly, although the imper. dispenses with it] (*orig. US*) **1** [mid-19C; 20C+] to leave, to depart; esp. as imper. *drift!* go away! **2** [1920s+] to arrive.

IN PHRASES

❑ **on the drift** [1950s] (*Aus.*) travelling as a tramp.

drill *n.* **1** [late 17C] a gigolo. **2** [1910s–20s; 1970s] (*US*) the penis.

drill, the *n.* [ext. of milit. use] [1940s+] the proper way of doing things, the recognized procedure; esp. in phrs. *what's the drill?* how are things done (round here)?; *know the drill*, to understand the way things are done.

drill *v.*[1] **1** [early 17C+] to have sexual intercourse, usu. of a male. **2** [late 18C+] to shoot (dead). **3** [1990s+] to punch, to beat. **4** [1990s+] to finish a drink. **5** [2000s] (*Aus.*) to interrogate.

IN PHRASES

❑ **drill for Marmite** *v. see under* MARMITE *n.* ❑ **drill for oil** *v.* [1940s] (*orig. US black*) **1** of a man, to have sexual intercourse. **2** of a woman, to masturbate. ❑ **drill for Vegemite** *v.* [1980s+] (*Aus.*) to perform homosexual anal intercourse; thus to be a male homosexual.

drill *v.*[2] [the slow progress of a *drill* as it penetrates wood] **1** [late 17C–18C] to lure, to entice slowly. **2** [1960s] (*US*) to stare.

drill *v.*[3] [SE *drill*, to perform military exercises on a parade ground] [late 19C+] (*US*) to walk, esp. of a hobo who would normally ride in a boxcar.

drillions *n.* [1940s+] an enormous unspecified amount.

driman *n.* [SE *dram/drink*] [mid–late 18C] a *dram* of spirits.

dring *n.* [pron.] [1960s] (*S.Afr.*) a drink.

drink *n.*[1] [joc. deliberate understatement] **1** [mid-19C] (*US*) a river. **2** [mid-19C+] the ocean, the sea, a lake. **3** [1930s+] the River Thames. **4** *see* DRANK *n.*

IN COMPOUNDS

❑ **drink wagon** *n.* [1940s] (*US black*) a ship.

IN PHRASES

❑ **big drink** *n.* [mid-19C+] (*US*) **1** the Mississippi River. **2** the ocean, esp. the Atlantic or Pacific Ocean.

SE in slang uses

IN COMPOUNDS

❑ **drink link** *n.* [the 'link' to one's cash before one goes out drinking] [2000s] an ATM. ❑ **drink-slinger** *n.* [1910s] (*US*) a bartender.

IN PHRASES

❑ **drink of water** *n.* [20C+] (*Ulster*) **1** an irritating person. **2** a weakling, a bore. ❑ **drink's talking** *see* IT'S THE BEER TALKING *under* TALK *v.*

drink *n.*[2] [Scot. *drink*, a lanky, overgrown person] [late 19C+] one who is too tall for their age.

drink *n.*[3] [i.e. a drink of SOUP *n.* (2)] [1930s] (*US prison*) nitroglycerine.

drink *n.*[4] [1970s+] **1** a bribe, a sum of money that would supposedly purchase 'a drink' but is usu. much larger. **2** a tip, a commission, a bonus.

drink *v.* [DRINK *n.*[4] (1)] [1970s+] (*UK Und.*) to be susceptible to bribery; thus code between newly arrested criminal and police officer *Do you drink, officer?*

SE in slang uses

DERIVATIVES

❑ **drinkage** *n.* [-AGE *sfx* (1)] [1980s+] (*US campus*) alcohol, esp. beer.

IN PHRASES

❑ **drink a health to Duke Humphrey** *v. see* DINE WITH DUKE HUMPHREY *under* DINE *v.* ❑ **drink all out** *v.* [mid-16C–early 17C] to empty one's glass. ❑ **drink at Freeman's Quay** *v.* (*also* **lush at Freeman's Quay**) [SE *drink*/LUSH *v.*[1] (2); the free drinks distributed at this quay near London Bridge to porters and carmen in 1810–80; the RN amplified it to *Harry Freemans* (and used it for anything, not merely drink, that was free), while the British Army shortened it to *Freemans*] [19C] to drink at another's expense. ❑ **drink at St Patrick's well** *v.* [*St Patrick*, patron saint of Ireland] [mid-17C] to drink (Irish) whisky. ❑ **drink at the fuzzy cup** *v.* [1970s+] (*US black*) to engage in cunnilingus. ❑ **drink by word of mouth** *v.* [late 18C–early 19C] to drink straight from the bottle. ❑ **drink from both taps** *v.* [1990s+] to be bisexual. ❑ **drink like a fish** *v.* (*also* **...like a sieve, ...a well**) [SE in 20C+] [mid-17C–19C] to drink heavily. ❑ **drink of sauce's**

cup *v.* (*also* **eat sauce**) [SE *saucy*, insolent] [late 15C–16C] to be abusive or insolent. ❑ **drink on the whip** *v.* (*also* **lick on the whip**) [15C–16C] to receive a thrashing. ❑ **drink out of the island** *v.* [the *island* is the inverted glass 'hillock' in the base of a wine bottle] [late 18C–19C] to drink to the bottom of a wine bottle. ❑ **drink out of the same bottle** *v.* [mid-19C; 1930s+] (*orig. UK Und., later use US*) to be close friends. ❑ **drink soup off** *v.* see TAKE THE SOUP *under* SOUP *n.* ❑ **drink the cross off an ass** *v.* [20C+] (*Irish*) to have a substantial capacity for alcohol. ❑ **drink the Dolphin waters** *v.* [the notorious laxity of the prison's regime: prisoners could easily obtain alcohol; there may be a further ref. to a nearby Dolphin public house] [mid-19C] to be imprisoned for debt. ❑ **drink with the flies** *v.* [a situation in which there are no companions other than the flies – whose presence is, of course, unwelcome] [20C+] (*Aus.*) to drink by oneself. ❑ **he would drink the piss from a brewer's horse** [2000s] (*N.Z.*) a phr. used of a dedicated drinker.

drinker *n.* [1970s+] **1** an after-hours or unlicensed drinking club. **2** a public house.

drinkery *n.* [mid-19C–1910s] (*orig. US*) a liquor store, a bar, anywhere where alcohol is sold.

drinkie *n. see* DRINKY-POO *n.*

drinkitite *n.* [pun on SE *appetite* + TIGHT *adj.* (7)] [late 19C] thirst; thus *on the drinkitite*, on a drunken spree.

drinky *adj.* [1900s] (*Aus./US*) mildly drunk, tipsy.

drinky-poo *n.* (*also* **drinkie, drinkle, drinky-winky**) [1950s+] a drink, rendered facetious by this arch baby-talk.

drip *n.* **1** in verbal senses [the words drip from one's mouth; note RN *dripper*, a habitual whinger]. (**a**) [1910s–40s] (*US*) nonsense, flattery, sentimental drivel. (**b**) [1940s+] complaints, grumbling. **2** [1930s+] a weakling, a spineless person [a weak drip of water, rather than a full gush]. **3** [1940s+] (*also* **drips, dripsy**) venereal disease, esp. gonorrhoea.

IN PHRASES

❑ **on the drip** [1950s+] bought on hire purchase.

drip-dry lover *n.* [the joke is that he has to let it drip dry – it's too short to shake] [1970s] (*US gay*) a gay man with a small penis.

dripper *n.*[1] [SE *drip*, a falling drop; the pus-like discharge is a primary symptom of gonorrhoea] **1** [late 17C–early 19C] venereal disease, esp. gonorrhoea; the discharge that accompanies it. **2** [1930s+] an ageing prostitute. **3** [1970s+] a prostitute, a promiscuous woman; the implication is of her *de facto* carrying a venereal disease.

dripper *n.*[2] [1920s+] (*drugs*) an eye-dropper, used to make a makeshift syringe or to drop LSD on to sugar-cubes, blotting-paper or some other medium of delivery.

IN PHRASES

❑ **lip the dripper** *v.* [1930s–50s] (*drugs*) to use suction to remove all traces of air from the medicine dropper that is used as a makeshift hypodermic syringe.

dripping *n.*[1] [SE *dripping*, rendered animal fat] [mid-19C] a cook.

dripping *n.*[2] **1** [1900s–40s] (*Aus.*) nagging; also as v., to complain. **2** [1940s] sentimental nonsense.

dripping *n.*[3]

IN PHRASES

❑ **in the dripping** *see* IN THE GREASE *under* GREASE *n.*[1].

dripping for it (like a butcher's daughter) *phr.* (*also* **dripping like a fucked fridge**) [pun on *dripping*, fat/*dripping*, sexually excited; the image is of uncontrollable vaginal secretions] [1910s+] (*orig. Aus.*) sexually voracious; sometimes abbr. to *like a butcher's daughter*.

dripping pan *n.* [colloq. *drippings*, vaginal secretions + SE *pan*] [17C; 19C] the vagina.

dripping (toast) *n.* [rhy. sl. = (mine) host] [1960s+] a publican.

drippy *adj.* [DRIP *n.* (2)] [1950s+] weak, ineffectual.

drippy tummy *n.* [the watery stools thus engendered] [1960s] (*US*) diarrhoea.

drips(y) *n. see* DRIP *n.* (3).

drit *v.* [? mis-reading of SE *dirt*, to foul, to pollute] [mid-18C] (*UK Und.*) to defecate.

drive *n.* [SE *drive*, energy, intensity] [1920s–60s] (*US drugs*) a thrill, a feeling of excitement, esp. after using narcotics.

IN PHRASES

❑ **get a drive on** *v.* [late 19C] (*US campus*) to make a joke at someone else's expense.

drive *v.*[1] [late 17C–18C; 1920s+] (*US black*) of a man, to have sexual intercourse.

SE in slang uses

IN PHRASES

❑ **drive bananas** *v. see under* BANANAS *adj.* ❑ **drive iron** *v. see* PUMP IRON *under* IRON *n.* ❑ **drive licks in someone's skin/tail** *v.* [SE *drive* + LICKS *n.* (1) + TAIL *n.* (2)] [20C+] (*W.I.*) to beat severely. ❑ **drive on** *v.* **1** [1950s+] (*orig. US black*) to hit hard and without warning. **2** [1960s+] (*US*) to trick, to deceive. ❑ **drive one's hogs (to market)** *v.* [early 18C–19C] to snore. ❑ **drive (one's) pigs to market** *v.* (*also* **drive the pigs home**) [18C+] to snore. ❑ **drive on the other side of the road** *v.* [1990s+] to be homosexual. ❑ **drive tab** *v.* [late 18C–early 19C] to go out for a drive with one's family. ❑ **drive the brewer's horse** *v. see under* BREWER'S HORSE *n.* ❑ **drive the car** *v. see under* CAR *n.* ❑ **drive the (porcelain) bus** *v.* [1970s+] (*US campus*) to vomit, spec. when hugging the circular (i.e. steering-wheel-shaped) lavatory bowl and vomiting therein. ❑ **drive turkeys to market** *v. see under* TURKEY *n.*[1].

drive *v.*[2] [abbr. SE *drive mad, drive crazy* etc] [1940s+] (*orig. Aus.*) to infuriate.

drive-by *n.* [the subjects 'drive by' the victim/place] [1980s+] **1** (*also* **ride-by**) a shooting that is carried out by gunmen firing from a moving car. **2** a slow drive past a given place; no violence is involved. **3** surveillance from a moving car.

drive-by *v.* [DRIVE-BY *n.* (1)] [1990s+] (*US*) to shoot at or be shot at from a moving car.

drive-me-silly *n.* [rhy. sl.] [1950s] (*Aus.*) a *billy*, the container used for boiling water.

driver *n.* [abbr. SE *slave-driver*] [mid-19C] a manager or foreman who forces employees to work much harder than their wages demand.

drivers *n.* [they 'drive one along'] **1** [1970s] (*US campus*) legs. **2** [1970s+] (*US drugs*) amphetamine. **3** [2000s] (*US drugs*) MDMA.

driz *n.* [Rom. *doriez*, thread, lace] [early–mid-19C] lace; thus *driz fencer*, one who sells lace; *driz camesa/kemesa*, a lace-adorned shirt.

drizzle *n.* **1** [late 18C] tears. **2** [1920s] (*US*) nonsense, empty chatter. **3** [1930s–60s] (*US campus*) a weakling, a whinger; thus as adj., *drizzly*.

drizzlepuss *n.* [PUSS *n.*[2] (1)] [1930s–50s] (*US*) a sour-faced person, a grumbler, a killjoy.

drizzlies, the *n.* [1960s–70s] (*US*) diarrhoea.

drizzunk *adj.* [SE + infix -IZ- *infix*] [2000s] (*US campus*) drunk.

drol *n.* [Afk. *drol(letjies)*, animal droppings] [1960s+] (*S.Afr.*) a general term of abuse.

dromaky *n.* [abbr. *Andromache*, wife of the Trojan hero Hector, referring to the poor reputation of the travelling actresses who played her in Euripedes' play (5C BC)] [19C] (*mainly northern*) a prostitute.

drome *n.* (*also* **'drome**) [abbr.] [1900s–40s] an aero*drome*.

dromedary *n.* (*also* **purple dromedary**) [SE *dromedary*, a bungling fellow (although the dromedary or Arabian single-humped camel is, according to the *OED*, 'a light and fleet breed')] [late 17C–18C] (*UK Und.*) a thief, esp. an incompetent or novice one.

drone *n.* [SE *drone*, a parasite] **1** [early 19C; 1940s+] (*US campus*) a tedious, unpleasant person. **2** [1990s+] a low-echelon drug dealer.

droned *adj.* [1970s+] (*US drugs*) both *drunk* and *stoned*.

drongo *n.* [orig. used of a recruit to the RAAF. Baker links the term to 'Drongo [...] the name of a horse [...] which won a certain claim to fame by consistently finishing last or near last'. The *OED* dismisses this as 'highly speculative', while the *AND* suggests that the horse's name might have 'influenced' the earlier use; thus ? f. *drongo cuckoo*, the cuckoo genus *Surniculus*; this relates to CUCKOO *n.*[1] (2), thus cf. BOOBY *n.*[1] (1); however, note Seal, *The Lingo* (1999): 'drongo, a very Australian insult, was the name of a racehorse of the mid-1920s. Named after an Australian bird (*Chibea bracteatus*), commonly known as the DRONGO, the four-legged version was totally unable to win a race. This prolonged ineptitude was so spectacular that punters began to refer to any horses that failed to win (rather a lot) as a DRONGO. The term spread very quickly from this racegoers' little lingo into the Great Australian Lingo'; *see also* Bruce Moore (ed. *AND*), in *Ozwords* Oct. 1996, who maintains the centrality of the horse] [1940s+] (*orig. Aus.*) a simpleton, a stupid person.

drongo *adj.* [DRONGO *n.*] [1940s+] silly, foolish.

dronkie *n.* [Afk. *dronk*, drunk] [1930s+] (*S.Afr.*) a drunkard, an alcoholic.

dronklap *n.* [Afk. *dronk*, drunk + *lap*, clout] [1950s+] (*S.Afr.*) a drunkard; also adv.

droob *n.* (*also* **drube**) [? link to RUBE *n.*[1] (2)] [1930s+] (*Aus.*) a useless, foolish, depressing person.

droog *n.* (*also* **droogie**) [coined by Anthony Burgess for *A Clockwork Orange* (1962); ult. Rus. *drug*, friend] **1** [1970s] a thug, a gangster. **2** [1990s+] (*US campus/teen*) a good friend. **3** [1990s+] a dull person. **4** [1990s+] a young man, esp. working class.

drool *n.* [SE *drivel*] (*orig. US*) **1** [mid-19C+] spittle. **2** [20C+] (*also* **drule**) nonsense, rubbish. **3** [1930s] vaginal secretions. **4** [1940s+] a socially unacceptable person.

IN COMPOUNDS

❑ **drool farm** *n.* [2000s] a psychiatric institution.

drool *v.* [DROOL *n.* (2)] **1** [1900s–20s] to talk nonsense. **2** [1920s+] (*orig. Aus.*) to waste time, to idle around.

drooly *n.* [DROOL *n.* (2) + sfx *-y*] [1940s–60s] (*US*) a stupid, unpopular person; also as adj.

drooly *adj.* [one who causes admirers to SE *drool*] **1** [1950s] of an object or place, very attractive. **2** [1990s+] (*US*) sexy.

droop *n.* [1920s–60s] (*US campus*) an unpleasant, esp. boring, person.

droopy *adj.* [DROOP *n.*/SE] **1** [20C+] unpleasant, dull, weak. **2** [1940s+] depressed.

droopy-drawers *n.* [1910s+] an untidy, sloppy or depressing person; thus adj. *droopy-drawered*.

drop *n.*[1] **1** [late 18C+] (*UK/US Und.*) a confidence trick, spec. ring-dropping. **2** [mid-19C] (*UK Und.*) a confidence trickster.

drop *n.*[2] **1** [mid-19C+] an advantage. **2** [1960s] (*Aus.*) a good thing.

IN PHRASES

❑ **get the drop(s) on** *v.* [mid-19C+] (*orig. US*) to obtain an (unfair) advantage over someone; orig. spec. with a gun. ❑ **give someone the drop** *v.* [late 19C] (*US tramp*) to pass on information. ❑ **have the drop on** *v.* [mid-19C+] to place someone else at a disadvantage, in any confrontation, physical, mental, financial etc. ❑ **take a drop on** *v.* [late 19C] (*US*) to take control, to get a grip.

drop *n.*[3] **1** [late 19C] a financial loss. **2** [late 19C] (*UK Und.*) a share of stolen goods or money. **3** [1910s+] a receiver of stolen goods. **4** [1910s+] a delivery, usu. of stolen goods, drugs, contraband etc. **5** [1920s+] a hiding-place for stolen, smuggled or illicit goods. **6** [1930s+] (*drugs*) a delivery point for drugs. **7** [1930s+] a payment or delivery of money. **8** [1950s+] a place where letters, papers and similar material (usu. secret) can be left for subseq. collection by another person. **9** [1970s] one who temporarily stores stolen goods immediately after a robbery, but who does not actually buy them from the thief. **10** [2000s] (*drugs*) the consumption of a pill or drug, taken orally.

IN COMPOUNDS

❑ **drop car** *n.* [2000s] (*US Und.*) a vehicle parked at some distance from a crime scene, which the perpetrators pick up after abandoning the one in which they actually committed the crime (and which might thus be identifiable). ❑ **drop joint** *n.* (*also* **drop house**) [JOINT *n.* (3b)] (*US Und.*) **1** [1920s] a suitable place for conducting a confidence game based on dropped articles. **2** [1930s–50s] a place used for storing and hiding stolen goods.

SE in slang uses

IN COMPOUNDS

❑ **drop lullaby** *n.* [SE *drop*, the gallows] [1950s] (*Aus.*) execution by hanging.

IN PHRASES

❑ **from the drop** [1960s] (*US*) from the very beginning. ❑ **give (someone) the drop** *v.* [mid-18C] (*UK Und.*) to slip away. ❑ **take a drop** *v.* [one *drops* out of sight] [late 19C+] to run off. ❑ **take a drop to** *v.* [play on TUMBLE TO *under* TUMBLE *v.*[2]] [late 19C+] to realize, to understand.

drop *n.*[4] [farming jargon *drop*, an animal bred by accident] [20C+] (*US black*) an orphan, esp. one whose parents are unknown.

drop *n.*[5] [1900s] (*US campus*) an unexpected examination.

drop *n.*[6] [one *drops* off the money] **1** [1910s+] a bribe. **2** [1910s+] the money used for a bribe. **3** [1930s] the money paid to a street beggar. **4** [1960s] (*Aus. Und.*) an informer.

IN PHRASES

❑ **cop a/the drop** *v.* [1910s+] (*UK Und.*) of police, to accept a bribe.

drop *n.*[7] [? DROPPING MEMBER *n.*] [1950s] (*Aus.*) the penis.

drop *n.*[8] [1950s+] (*W.I.*) a free ride in a car or cart, at the end of which one is *dropped off*.

drop *n.*[9] [1960s] (*Aus.*) a young woman.

drop *n.*[10] [1980s] (*US drugs*) the physical discomfort that accompanies withdrawal from crack cocaine.

drop *n.*[11] *see* DROP (OF THE CREATURE) *n.*

IN PHRASES

❑ **drop in one's eye** *n. see* separate entry. ❑ **drop of something/the necessary/the other** *n. see* DROP (OF THE CREATURE) *n.* ❑ **drop of the old author** *n. see* LEAF OF THE OLD AUTHOR *n.*

drop, the *n.* (*also* **the long drop**) **1** [mid-19C+] (*Aus./UK prison*) execution by hanging. **2** *see* KNOCKOUT DROPS *n.*

drop *v.*[1] **1** [early 17C+] to abandon a friendship or relationship; to snub. **2** [early 19C+] of an idea or train of thought, to overlook, to ignore, to give up on. **3** [mid-19C–1950s] to quit, to turn aside, e.g. on a road. **4** [1940s+] to evade.

SE in slang uses

IN COMPOUNDS

❑ **drop-case** *n.* [1970s] (*US*) a fool. ❑ **drop cove** *n. see* DROP GAME *n.* ❑ **drop game** *n. see* separate entry. ❑ **drophead** *n.* [2000s] (*N.Z.*) a fool. ❑ **drop-in** *n.* [the image of a gullible victim who may sometimes *drop in* to a confidence game without having to be steered there first] [1930s–40s] (*US*) **1** something that is easy; easy money. **2** a victim, a sucker. ❑ **drop-shoulder** *n.* [the contorted form of Dr Frankenstein's deformed assistant Igor] [2000s] (*N.Z.*) a fool.

IN PHRASES

❑ **drop...** *v. see also under* relevant n. ❑ **drop a net on** *v.* [1940s+] (*US*) to commit to a psychiatric institution. ❑ **drop a spanner** *v.* [2000s] (*S.Afr. gay*) to indicate that one is a lesbian. ❑ **drop away** *v.* [late 17C] to give, lose or part with something, usu. money. ❑ **drop blue lights** *v.* [1960s] to swear, to use obscenities. ❑ **drop-dead** *see* separate entries. ❑ **drop down on** *v.* [late 19C] to visit. ❑ **drop down on oneself** *v. see under* DOWN *adj.*[2]. ❑ **drop 'em** *v.* ['*em* are her knickers] [1940s+] of a woman, to have sexual intercourse. ❑ **drop foot** *v.* [1950s+] (*W.I., Jam.*) to dance energetically. ❑ **drop hairpins** *v. see* separate entry. ❑ **drop hand** *v.* (*also* **drop a hand in**) [1950s+] (*W.I.*) to hit with the clenched fist. ❑ **drop into** *v.* [the whip or fist is *dropped into* the victim] [mid–late 19C] to beat, to thrash. ❑ **drop it** *v.* [1990s+] (*W.I.*) to display street style. ❑ **drop it across** *v.* [1910s] to reject someone. ❑ **drop off** *v. see* separate entries. ❑ **drop on** *v.* **1** [mid-19C–1910s] to accuse, to rebuke. **2** [late 19C] to encounter. ❑ **drop one** *v.*

1 [1990s+] (*Aus.*) to break wind. **2** *see* DROP ONE'S LOAD *under* LOAD *n.* ❑ **drop one's bait-can** *v.* [the most serious mistake an angler can make is to drop his bait-can] [late 19C] (*US black*) to make a serious mistake. ❑ **drop one's candy** *v.* (*also* **drop one's watermelon**) [1900s–30s] (*US*) to make a serious mistake. ❑ **drop one's cock and grab one's socks** *v. see* HANDS OFF (YOUR) COCKS, FEET IN (YOUR) SOCKS *under* HAND *n.*[1]. ❑ **drop one's drawers** *v.* [1970s+] of a woman, to allow intercourse; to lead a promiscuous sex life. ❑ **drop one's ears** *v.* [equine imagery] [mid-19C] to give up, to be discouraged. ❑ **drop one's lunch** *v. see* LOSE ONE'S LUNCH *under* LOSE *v.* ❑ **drop one's ovaries** *v.* [2000s] (*S.Afr. camp gay*) **1** to be completely in love with someone. **2** to have a shock or fright. ❑ **drop onto/upon** *v.* [the image of a bird of prey plummeting onto a victim] [mid–late 19C] **1** to become aware of. **2** to accuse, to turn on someone suddenly. ❑ **drop out** *see* separate entries. ❑ **dropped in the bucket** *see under* BUCKET *n.* ❑ **drop someone in it** *v.* (*also* **drop someone in the crap, ...the shit**) [*it* is trouble, but the implication is also of excrement] [1930s+] to put someone deliberately into difficulties. ❑ **drop the arm on** *v.* [the physical action + the fig. SE *arm of the law*] [1920+] (*US*) to arrest. ❑ **drop the bucket** *v.* [1940s+] (*Aus.*) to 'leave in the lurch'. ❑ **drop the bucket on** *v.* (*also* **tip/turn the bucket on**) [1950s+] (*Aus.*) to make damaging revelations about, esp. in a political context. ❑ **drop the hook on** *v.* [1930s] to become involved with, to take advantage of. ❑ **drop the pill on** *v.* [the gas is triggered by breaking open a pill of cyanide] [1990s+] (*US Und.*) to execute in the gas chamber. ❑ **drop the rag** *v.* [RAG *n.*[1] (2a); the dropping of a flag to signal the start] [late 19C+] (*US*) to give a signal, to set events in motion. ❑ **drop the soap** *v. see* separate entry. ❑ **drop trou** *v.* [a supposedly more sophisticated version of MOON *v.* (2)] (*US campus*) **1** [1950s] (*also* **down trou**) to drop one's trousers (in public). **2** [1960s+] in fig. use, to be amazed, astonished. **3** [1990s+] to urinate. ❑ **drop up** *v.* [1940s–50s] to visit. ❑ **drop upon** *v.* [late 19C] to treat badly, to victimize.

IN EXCLAMATIONS

❑ **drop dead!** *see* separate entry. ❑ **drop it!** [mid-19C+] change the subject! stop talking that way! stop what you are doing! ❑ **drop off!** *see* separate entry.

drop *v.*[2] [the money is *dropped* on the table] **1** [late 17C+] to pay over money, to spend money. **2** [19C+] to lose money. **3** [mid-19C; 1920s+] (*US Und.*) to sell stolen property to a receiver. **4** [mid-19C; 1960s] (*US Und.*) to sell something inferior for more than it is worth. **5** [1920s+] (*orig. US*) to pass dud cheques or counterfeit money. **6** [1930s] to hand over drugs. **7** [1950s] to bribe. **8** [2000s] to give.

IN PHRASES

❑ **drop man** *n.* [1960s] (*drugs*) a wholesale drug dealer's runner, who delivers bulk supplies to less important dealers.

drop *v.*[3] [SE *drop*, to fall or make another fall to the ground] **1** [early 18C+] to shoot down, to kill. **2** [late 18C+] to die. **3** [early 19C+] to knock down; also in fig. use. **4** [20C+] (*US Und.*) to arrest. **5** [1920s+] (*US*) to be convicted of a crime. **6** [2000s] to fire a bullet.

IN PHRASES

❑ **drop someone one** *v.* [ONE *n.*[1] (1a)] [1920s+] to hit, to knock down.

drop *v.*[4] [one *drops* or *drops onto* information] **1** [late 18C–1920s] to get to know about, to become aware of. **2** [late 19C–1900s] to understand. **3** [20C+] (*US*) to reveal. **4** [1940s+] (*jazz/rap music*) to produce, to deliver. **5** [1960s+] (*US black*) to explain, to enlighten.

IN PHRASES

❑ **drop bottom** *v.* [1990s+] (*orig. US black*) to drive around in one's car playing loud (hip-hop) music with a heavy bass-line. ❑ **drop down to** *v.* [early 19C] to find out about someone's character or plans. ❑ **drop knowledge** *v.* [1980s+] (*US black*) to demonstrate wisdom or skill. ❑ **drop science** *v. see under* SCIENCE *n.* ❑ **drop to** *v.* (*also* **drop on**) **1** [mid-19C+] to become aware of, to work out, to recognize. **2** [20C+] (*US Und.*) to obtain, to gain. ❑ **drop word(s)** *v.* (*also* **throw words**) [20C+] (*W.I.*) to utter veiled insults, to make sarcastic comments.

drop *v.*[5] [SE *drop*, usu. of a sheep, to give birth] [20C+] to give birth.

drop *v.*[6] [one *drops* them down one's throat] **1** [1960s+] (*drugs*) to consume pills or any drug that can be taken orally. **2** [1980s] to drink (beer).

IN PHRASES

❑ **drop a roll** *v.* [ROLL *n.* (4b)] [1980s] (*US drugs*) to take three to five pills, of various types of drug.

drop-dead *adj.* [DROP-DEAD *adv.*] [1970s+] wonderful, first-rate, exceptional.

drop-dead *adv.* [so beautiful, striking etc as to cause the onlooker to *drop dead*] [1970s+] (*orig. US*) extremely.

IN COMPOUNDS

❑ **drop-dead gorgeous** *adj.* extremely attractive.

drop dead! *excl.* [1920s+] (*orig. US*) a general excl. of dismissal.

IN COMPOUNDS

❑ **drop-dead money** *n.* [1980s+] money, the possession of which enables one to tell the world, *drop dead!* i.e. bestows freedom on its possessor.

drop game *n.* **1** [mid-19C+] (*UK Und.*) a confidence trick whereby the victim is persuaded to pay money for a wallet, ring or some valuable, supposedly found on the ground but actually planted by the con man. **2** [late 19C] in gambling, a trick whereby a gambler substitutes a note of higher value than that which was apparently bet, then reveals its worth and demands to be paid the correspondingly greater winnings.

IN COMPOUNDS

❑ **drop cove** *n.* [COVE *n.* (1)] [early 19C+] (*UK Und.*) a confidence trickster, specializing in RING DROPPING *n.* (1). ❑ **drop gamester** *n.* [mid-19C] (*US Und.*) a confidence trickster who performs the *drop game*.

drop hairpins *v.* (*also* **drop the hairpin**) [SE *hairpins* are seen as a quintessentially feminine possession] [1960s+] (*gay*) to reveal one's sexual preferences by dropping broad hints; thus *keep your hairpins up*, maintain a 'normal' mask.

drop in one's eye *n.* [? SE *drop* of liquor, or one is on the verge of drunken tears] [late 17C–18C] a state of (near) drunkenness.

IN PHRASES

❑ **have a drop in the eye** *v.* [late 17C–mid-19C] to be tipsy. ❑ **take a drop in the eye** *v.* [late 17C–early 18C] to have a drink.

dropkick *n.* [rhy. sl. = PRICK *n.* (3)] [1980s+] (*Aus./N.Z.*) a general term of abuse.

dropkick and punt *n.* [rhy. sl. = CUNT *n.*] [1980s+] (*Aus.*) the vagina; thus a general insult.

drop off *v.*[1] [fig. use of SE] **1** [late 18C+] to die. **2** [mid-19C] to retire. **3** [1930s] to kill.

SE in slang uses

IN PHRASES

❑ **drop off a style** *v.* [1990s+] (*W.I.*) to lose one's sex appeal. ❑ **drop off the hook(s)** *v.* [mid-19C–1930s] to die. ❑ **drop off the shopping** *v.* [2000s] to defecate.

drop off *v.*[2] [1990s+] (*Aus. Und.*) to reject, to abandon.

drop off! *excl.* [1960s] (*Aus.*) a dismissive retort.

drop (of the creature) *n.* (*also* **cup of the creature, drop of something, drop of the necessary, ...the other**) [SE *drop* + CREATURE, THE *n.* (3)] [late 18C+] a drink.

dropout *n.* [SE *dropout*, one who abandons their education] [20C+] (*orig. US*) a dull, boring person.

drop out *v.* **1** [20C+] to die. **2** [1970s+] to dismiss, to get rid of someone.

dropped *adj.*[1] [DROP *v.*[3] (4)] [20C+] arrested.

dropped *adj.*[2] [the trad. gift by the man of a pendant or *drop*, bearing his initials] [1970s] (*US campus*) unofficially but dedicatedly engaged to be married.

dropper *n.*[1] [DROP *v.*[2] (5)] [mid-19C+] one who passes counterfeit money, whether cheques or notes.

dropper *n.*[2] [DROP *v.*[3] (1)] (*US*) **1** [late 19C] a gun, a pistol. **2** [1920s+] a paid killer. **3** [1930s] (*US prison*) one who carries a knife. **4** [1930s+] (*US Und.*) a violent robber.

dropper *n.*[3] [abbr. *shop-dropper*] (*Aus./N.Z.*) **1** [1910s+] one who delivers supplies of contraband liquor. **2** [1940s–50s] one who makes deliveries of goods to retailers.

dropper *n.*[4] [1930s+] (*drugs*) an *eye-dropper* used by narcotics addicts as a makeshift syringe when proper hypodermics are unavailable.

dropper *n.*[5] [1960s] (*US prison*) a device for heating drinks.

dropper *n.*[6] **1** *see* GOLD-DROPPER *n.* **2** *see* RUM DROPPER *under* RUM *adj.*

dropping member *n. see under* MEMBER *n.*[1].

droppings *n.* [mid-19C] (*UK Und.*) beer.

drops *n.*[1] [late 18C–mid-19C] (*UK Und.*) confidence tricksters, specializing in defrauding country vistors to London/New York.

drops *n.*[2] [early 19C] (*UK Und.*) alcoholic drinks, usu. gin.

IN PHRASES

❑ **fond of their drops** [late 19C] a phr. used of a heavy drinker. ❑ **take one's drops** *v.* [18C–19C] to drink heavily.

dropsy *n.*[1] [pun on SE *dropsy*, the falling sickness] **1** [mid-19C] one who 'drops off' to sleep. **2** [1930s+] the habit of dropping things; usu. as *the dropsy* [SE *drop off*]. **3** [1990s+] (*W.I.*) an illness whereby the sufferer is prone to sudden sleepiness.

dropsy *n.*[2] (*also* **dropsey**) [SE *drop*/DROP *v.*[2] (1); the giver *drops* the money in someone's pocket or hand; a single nonce-use 'the silver dropsie' has been cited for 1616] [1930s+] **1** a bribe. **2** a tip. **3** money.

drop the soap *v.* [orig. gay use, but also as a semi-joc. warning from one self-proclaimedly heterosexual young man to another, *I wouldn't drop the soap while he was around*] [1960s+] to make oneself available for anal penetration.

IN PHRASES

❑ **play drop the soap** *v.* (*also* **play pick up the soap**) [1950s–70s] (*US*) to indulge in homosexual activity.

dross *n.* [the trad. (if high-minded) equation of money and rubbish] [mid-18C–early 19C] (*Scot. Und.*) gold coins, money; also as adj., gold.

drot! *excl. see* DRAT! *excl.*

drought *n.* **1** [1960s+] (*drugs*) a period when drugs are in very short supply or even non-existent. **2** [1980s+] (*orig. US campus*) a period without sex or even dates.

drove *adj.* [SE *driven*] **1** [1960s+] (*US*) very angry, infuriated. **2** [1970s] exhausted.

drover *n.*

SE in slang uses

IN COMPOUNDS

❑ **drover's breakfast** *n.* [SE *drover*, a shepherd; either the lack of 'civilized' amenities in the bush or his lack of desire for anything more] [1940s+] (*Aus.*) a look around and a cough. ❑ **drover's dog** *n.* [the *drover's dog* never stops working] [1970s+] (*Aus.*) a useless or insignificant person, a drudge. ❑ **drover's guide** *n.* [1920s+] (*Aus.*) gossip and rumour, reified as an imaginary newspaper.

drove up *adj.* [DRIVE ON *under* DRIVE *v.*[1]] [1970s] **1** (*US black*) excited. **2** (*US prison*) frightened.

drowned in the mercer's book *adj.* [late 16C] deeply indebted, i.e. 'over head and ears in debt'.

drowse *n.* [late 19C] (*UK Und.*) a knockout drug made from laudanam; used by brothel keepers to initiate young girls into the trade.

drozel *n.* [Yorks. dial. *drasil*, 'a dirty slut, a draggle-tailed person' (*EDD*)] **1** [early 18C] a young woman. **2** [early 19C] (*US*) a slattern.

drube *n. see* DROOB *n.*

drudge *n.* [ety. unknown; ? link to SE *draught*] [mid–late 19C] (*US*) whisky.

drudge *v.* [SE *drudge*, a menial job; the implication is that the wearer has to wear shoes in their job] [1940s+] (*W.I.*) to wear shoes or boots regularly (rather than go barefoot); shoes would normally have been worn only on special occasions.

drug *n.* [abbr.] [1980s+] (*US*) a *drug*store.

SE in slang uses

IN COMPOUNDS

❑ **drughead** *n.* [-HEAD *sfx* (4)] [1960s+] (*US*) a consumer of illicit recreational drugs. ❑ **drugsman** *n.* [2000s] a drug dealer.

drug *adj.* (*also* **drugg, drugged, drugger**) [DRAG *v.*[1] (8)] [1940s+] (*US black*) exhausted, disinclined, bored, e.g. *I'm too drug to go out tonight.*

drug *v.* **1** [late 19C+] to take drugs. **2** [1990s+] (*US campus*) to beat decisively.

drugged *adj.* [ext. DRUG *adj.*] [1960s] (*US*) annoyed, irritated.

drugger *n.* [1940s+] a drug user.

drugger *adj. see* DRUG *adj.*

druggist *n.* [1990s+] (*W.I.*) a general term of address.

druggy *n.* (*also* **druggie, druggo**) [SE *drug*] (*US*) **1** [20C+] a drugstore owner, a druggist. **2** [1960s+] a drug user; rarely used by anyone involved with drugs; also attrib.

druggy *adj.* (*also* **druggie**) [1970s+] (*orig. US*) **1** of, pertaining to, or characteristic of recreational drugs or their users. **2** consisting of drug-takers.

drugola *n.* [SE *drug* + -OLA *sfx*] [1970s+] (*orig. US*) bribery in which the pay-off comes not in money but in drugs.

drugstore cowboy *n.* [1920s+] (*US*) a man, usu. a youth, who frequents drugstores for no other reason than meeting his friends, gossiping and wasting time.

drugstore stuff *n.* [STUFF *n.* (5b)] [1960s+] (*US drugs*) painkillers, synthetic opiates, available from drugstores but less effective than heroin.

drukkie *n.* [Afk. *druk*, squeeze] [20C+] (*S.Afr.*) a hug, an affectionate squeeze.

drule *n. see* DROOL *n.* (2).

drum *n.*[1] **1** [mid–late 17C] the penis. **2** [late 18C] (*also* **drummers**) the testicles.

drum *n.*[2] [Gk *dromos*, thence Rom. *drom*] [late 18C–19C] the road, the street.

drum *n.*[3] [ety. unknown; ? the image of the hollow drum resembling a hollow house or room or the use of DRUM *n.*[2] as a fig. house for wandering gypsies and tinkers] (*orig. UK Und.*) **1** [late 18C–19C] a social gathering, a party. **2** [mid-19C] a casino. **3** [mid-19C–1950s] a saloon, a drinking house, a speakeasy, a nightclub. **4** [mid-19C+] a brothel. **5** [mid-19C+] a house, a home. **6** [late 19C] a travelling salesman's stall. **7** [20C+] a prison cell, a prison. **8** [1900s; 1980s] (*Aus./US*) a room. **9** [1920s] (*US*) a place, a town. **10** [1930s] (*US tramp*) a safe. **11** [1960s] (*US prison*) a criminal's hide-out.

IN PHRASES

❑ **break a drum** *v.* [mid-19C] (*UK Und.*) to burgle a house. ❑ **drum up** *v.* [1950s] to rob; thus *drummer-up*, a housebreaker. ❑ **speel (on) the drum** *v.* [mid–late 19C] to go off with stolen property. ❑ **square drum** *n.* [SQUARE *adj.* (1)] [mid-19C] (*UK Und.*) a public house (mainly) frequented by non-criminal customers.

drum *n.*[4] [mid-19C] (*orig. boxing*) the ear.

drum *n.*[5] [the shape] **1** [mid-19C+] (*Aus.*) a pack. **2** [late 19C] (*US*) any hat but a silk one. **3** [1910s+] a tin or can in which tea etc is made. **4** [1950s] (*UK prison*) a primitive and illicitly constructed cooking stove, using a small tin bowl, a basic adjustment lever and as a wick a hospital bandage, rubbed with mutton fat.

IN PHRASES

❑ **hump one's drum** *v.* [HUMP *v.*[1] (2d)] [mid-19C–1900s] to carry a pack.

drum *n.*[6] [the image of drummers beating out information for transmission through jungles etc] [1940s+] (*Aus.*) a piece of information, esp. a racing tip.

drum, the *n.* [1940s+] (*Aus.*) true or reliable information.

drum *v.*[1] [DRUM *n.*[3] (5)] [1910s+] **1** to knock on a front door to ascertain whether or not the home owner is in; if they are not, the house is broken into and robbed. **2** to steal from an empty or unoccupied house.

drum *v.*[2] [DRUM *n.*[6] (1)] [1910s+] (*Aus.*) to inform, to 'tip off'.

drum *v.*[3] [DRUMMER *n.*[2] (1)] [1940s+] (*US*) to work as a commercial traveller.

drum and fife *n.* [rhy. sl.] [20C+] **1** (*also* **Duke of Fife**) a knife. **2** (*also* **duchess, Duchess of Fife**) a wife.

drum-arsed *adj.* [SE *drum* + -ARSED *sfx* (1)] [mid-17C] having large buttocks.

drumbelo *n.* [late 17C–mid-19C] 'a dull heavy Fellow' (B.E.).

drummer *n.*[1] [? the 'beating' he administered] [mid-19C] a thug who robbed drunks, often after helping them to oblivion with a knockout draught.

SE in slang uses

IN PHRASES

❑ **give the drummer some** *v.* [the drumming of one hand upon another] [1950s+] (*US black*) ritual palm slapping that forms a greeting between blacks or between blacks and knowledgeable whites.

drummer *n.*[2] [SE *drum up trade* + DRUM *n.*[3] (5)] [mid-19C+] (*US*) a commercial traveller, a salesman.

drummer *n.*[3] [DRUM *n.*[2]] [late 19C] (*Aus./N.Z.*) an itinerant.

drummer *n.*[4] [? DRUMMER *n.*[2]; i.e. a commercial traveller is not a *real* workman] [late 19C+] (*Aus./N.Z.*) the laziest and therefore the slowest shearer in a shed.

drummer *n.*[5] [DRUM *v.*[1] (1)] [1930s+] a thief who specializes in robbing houses while their occupants are out, usu. for a short time.

drummer *n.*[6] [DRUM *n.*[6] (1)] [1990s+] (*Aus.*) a racecourse tipster.

drummers *n. see* DRUM *n.*[1] (2).

drumming *n.* [DRUMMER *n.*[2]] [1920s+] (*UK Und.*) posing as a door-to-door salesman to tour houses and thus identify empty ones, ripe for robbery.

drummond *n.* [the fabled stability of the bankers *Drummond & Co.*] [early 19C] (*UK Und.*) a supposedly infallible scheme or project.

drummond and roce *n.* [rhy. sl.; *drummond* = drum = DRUM AND FIFE *n.* (1) + *roce* = roast = ROAST PORK *n.*[1] (2)] [1940s–70s] a knife and fork.

drum out *v.* [1930s] (*US Und.*) to shoot dead.

drumstick *n.* **1** [mid-17C; late 19C+] the penis. **2** [late 18C–1940s] in pl., the legs. **3** [mid-19C] (*US Und.*) a cosh. **4** [mid-19C] in pl., the arms. **5** [1970s+] (*US black*) in pl., the well-rounded thighs of an attractive woman.

IN COMPOUNDS

❑ **drumstick case** *n.* [SE *case*, a legal proceeding] [1970s+] (*US black*) rape. ❑ **drumstick cases** *n.* [mid-19C] trousers.

drum-up *n.* [DRUM *n.*[5] (3)] [1910s+] the preparation of a cup of tea, or meal.

drum up *v.* [SE *drum*/DRUM *n.*[5] (3)] **1** [1910s+] to make tea in a billy-can or similar container. **2** [1930s] to prepare a meal under rough conditions (typically on a battlefield or out of doors).

drunk *n.* (*also* **drunk up**) **1** [mid-19C+] (*orig. US*) a bout of drinking, usu. to excess or oblivion. **2** [late 19C] a session of opium smoking.

IN COMPOUNDS

❑ **drunk-on** *n.* [mid-19C–1920s] (*US*) the state of being drunk; also attrib.

IN PHRASES

❑ **dry drunk** *n. see under* DRY *adj.*[1].

SE in slang uses

IN COMPOUNDS

❑ **drunk farm** *n. see* DRY-OUT FARM *under* DRY OUT *v.* ❑ **drunk's lagging** *n.* [LAGGING *n.* (2)] [1960s] (*Aus.*) a short prison sentence, as given to one convicted of being drunk and disorderly. ❑ **drunk tank** *n. see* TANK *n.*[2] (2).

IN PHRASES

❑ **drunk with a bad cold** *n.* [play on OYSTER *n.* (2a)/SE *oyster*] [1940s] (*US*) oyster stew.

drunk as (a)... *adj.* [early 16C+] the images of drunkenness are many and varied, for all that some comparisons seem somewhat far-fetched. As well as the following phrs. and the major entries separated out, all the following nouns have been allied with drunk: *drunk as a ...bastard, ...bat, ...beggar, ...besom, ...big owl, ...bowdow, ...brewer's fart, ...cook, ...coon, ...dog, ...emperor, ...fiddler, ...fiddler's bitch, ...fish, ...fly, ...fowl, ...forty, ...Gosport fiddler, ...hog, ...jaybird, ...little red wagon, ...log, ...loon, ...lord, ...monkey, ...mouse, ...peep, ...Perraner, ...pig, ...piper, ...poet, ...rolling fart, ...sailor, ...skunk in a trunk, ...sow, ...swine, ...tapster, ...tick, ...top, ...wheelbarrow.*

IN PHRASES

❑ **...a duck** [1910s+] drunk; often ext. by *and don't give a fuck/quack.* ❑ **...a polony** [? Fr. phr. *soul comme un Polonnais*, drunk as a Pole (supposedly mocking the Polish-French Maréchal de Saxe, a great tippler), although the phr. might simply mean drunk as a POLONY *n.*[1] (1) or sausage, which cannot stand upright] [late 19C] extremely drunk. ❑ **...floey** [? misuse of DRUNK AS CHLOE *adj.*] [late 19C–1900s] very drunk.

drunk as a boiled owl *adj.* (*also* **drunk as a biled owl, ...a fresh-boiled owl, ...an owl, ...two hoot owls, full as a boiled owl, lushy as..., tight as..., stewed as an owl, tight as...**) [late 18C+] (*orig. US*) very drunk; intensified as *drunker than a boiled owl*; thus *boiled owl*, a drunk person.

drunk as a cootie *adj.* (*also* **coot-drunk, drunk as a coot(er), tight as a coot**) [COOTIE *n.* (1)] [early 19C+] very drunk.

drunk as a rat *adj.* (*also* **drunk as a mouse**) [mid-16C+] very drunk.

drunk as Chloe *adj.* (*also* **tight as Chloe**) [20C+ use mainly Aus; Jon Bee (1823), noted: 'she must have been an uproarious lass'; poss. popularized in Aus. by the picture, *Chloe*, rejected in 1883 by the Melbourne National Gallery and bought by a well-known local hotel, where it became a point of attraction for many visitors; but note ref. in Parker's 1789 poem to one 'dust-cart Chloe' as a guest at the christening – the orig. ref. may thus be to a 'real' person in the foregoing narrative] [late 18C+] very drunk.

drunk as cooter brown *adj.* (*also* **drunk as kooter brown**) [? anecdotal, supposedly one Cooter Brown who avoided the US Civil War by staying drunk for its duration; but note DRUNK AS A COOTIE *adj.*] [1900s–40s; 1980s] (*orig. US black*) very drunk.

drunk as David's sow *adj.* (*also* **drunk as Davy's sow, tipsy as David's sow**) [late 17C+] very drunk.

drunked up *adj.* (*also* **drunked out**) [1940s+] (*US*) drunk.

drunken piece *n.* [1910s–20s] a drunkard.

drunken tinker *n.* [mid-16C–19C] a ne'er-do-well who, accompanied by his woman, wanders the country, mixing villainy and legitimate work, pursuing neither, it appears, with particular enthusiasm.

drunkery *n.* [SE *drunk* + sfx *-ery*] [19C] a cheap saloon.

drunkie *n.* (*also* **drunker, drunkman**) [mid-19C; 1950s+] (*orig. W.I.*) a heavy drinker, a drunkard.

drunkie *adj.* (*also* **drunky**) [mid-19C+] (*US*) drunken; esp. with a name, e.g. *drunkie John*.

drunking *adj.* (*also* **drunkin**) [pron. of SE *drunken*] [1950s+] (*W.I.*) extremely drunk.

drunkman *n. see* DRUNKIE *n.*

drunky *adj. see* DRUNKIE *adj.*

Drury Lane ague *n.* [the reputation of *Drury Lane* as a centre of prostitution] [mid-18C–early 19C] venereal disease, esp. gonorrhoea.

Drury Lane vestal *n.* (*also* **Drury**) [for ety. *see* prev.; note 'Foreigners in England' (in Hindley, *Curiosities of Street Literature*, 1871): 'If he wants some wives for the Ottoman plains/He can have all the women in Drury Lane'] [mid-18C–early 19C] a prostitute.

druthers *n.* (*also* **rathers, ruthers**) [pron. of SE *I'd rather*] [late 19C+] (*orig. US*) an alternative choice, a preference; esp. in phr. *have one's druthers*, to gain one's preference.

dry *n.*[1] [the term was appropriated under Margaret Thatcher's leadership of the UK Conservative party to define those who opposed policies dedicated to free-ranging, deregulated market forces (and the resulting mass-unemployment, false economic booms etc)] [late 19C+] (*US*) a Prohibitionist, dedicated to the cause of eradicating alcohol; also attrib.

dry *n.*[2] [1930s] (*US prison*) the bread and water diet given as a punishment.

dry, the *n.* [mid-19C+] (*Aus.*) the dry season.

dry *adj.*[1] **1** [18C+] abstaining from alcohol; teetotal. **2** [19C+] bereft of alcohol. **3** [20C+] without supplies. **4** [1920s+] (*US*) without money. **5** [1970s+] (*drugs*) bereft of drugs.

IN COMPOUNDS

pertaining to alcohol or drugs

❑ **dry drunk** *n.* [1960s] the state of being intoxicated by drugs, not alcohol. ❑ **dry Dutch courage** *n.* [a modern play on the trad. 'wet' DUTCH COURAGE *n.* (1), which refers to alcohol] [1940s+] narcotics, esp. as a fig. 'killer of pain'. ❑ **dry gin** *n.* [GANJA *n.* + pun on SE] [1930s] (*W.I.*) marijuana. ❑ **dry grog** *n.* [drugs have a similar effect to 'wet' GROG *n.*[1] (1)] [1940s–50s] (*US drugs*) narcotics. ❑ **dry horrors** *n.* [HORRORS, THE *n.* (4)] **1** [1900s] (*Aus.*) delirium tremens. **2** [1900s] a negative reaction to alcohol, due to one's having been without drink for a long period. **3** [1970s+] (*Aus. drugs*) a dry mouth and throat after smoking marijuana. ❑ **dry jag** *n.* [JAG *n.*[1] (1)] [20C+] (*US*) a sense of brief excitement similar to that produced by alcohol, but without any drinking.

SE in slang uses

IN COMPOUNDS

pertaining to sexual activity without fulfiment

❑ **dry bob** *n.* [late 16C–19C] sex without ejaculation by the man; thus v. *dry-bob*. ❑ **dry date** *n.* [1970s+] (*US gay*) a platonic date; any appointment other than a sexual one; pornography. ❑ **dry fuck** see separate entries. ❑ **dry hump** see separate entries. ❑ **dry ride** *n.* (*also* **dry bang**) [RIDE *n.* (1a)/BANG *n.*[1] (2b)] [1930s+] a simulated act of sexual intercourse, without penetration and usu. without removing the clothes. ❑ **dry root** *n.* [ROOT *n.*[1] (1d)] [1970s] (*Aus.*) a simulated act of sexual intercourse, without penetration and usu. without removing the clothes. ❑ **dry root** *v. see* DRY HUMP *v.* (1). ❑ **dry rub** *n. see* DRY FUCK *n.* (1). ❑ **dry-rub** *v. see* separate entry. ❑ **dry run** *n.* **1** [1950s] an act of sexual intercourse using a contraceptive. **2** [1950s+] (*US gay*) sex without ejaculation; frottage; also as v. ❑ **dry run** *v. see* DRY HUMP *v.* (1). ❑ **dry screw** *see* separate entries.

general uses

❑ **dryback** *v.* [play on WETBACK *n.*] [1950s] (*US*) to smuggle (oneself) across the US border from Mexico in a vehicle. ❑ **dryball** *see* separate entries. ❑ **dry bath** *n.* [1920s+] (*UK Und.*) the search of a prisoner who has been first stripped naked; or a prison cell. ❑ **dry-bone(s)** *n.* [mid-17C–mid-19C] 'a contemptuous or familiar term for a thin or withered person, who has little flesh on his bones' (*OED*). ❑ **dry boots** *n.* [late 18C–early 19C] 'a sly, humorous fellow' (Grose, 1785). ❑ **dry combo** *n.* [1950s] (*US tramp*) a piece of cake and a sandwich, i.e. no drink. ❑ **dry-eye** *adj.* [1990s+] (*W.I.*) daring, dauntless. ❑ **dry goods** *n. see* separate entries. ❑ **dry gulch** *n.* [Western outlaws often ambushed and shot their victim as he passed through the narrow confines of a SE *dry gulch*, or f. the rustlers' killing of stolen animals by driving them over the edge of such a gulch] [1930s+] (*US*) **1** to murder; thus n., *dry-gulcher*, a murderer. **2** to assault. ❑ **dry hash** *n.* [late 19C–1910s] (*Aus.*) dullness, ill-temper. ❑ **dry head** *see* separate entries. ❑ **dry house** *n.* [mid-19C] (*US Und.*) a dungeon. ❑ **dry land...** *see* separate entries. ❑ **dry lodging** *n.* [mid-19C] lodging without inclusive board. ❑ **dry malice** *v.* [1990s+] (*W.I.*) to ignore someone deliberately, even to the extent of communicating through a third party. ❑ **dry money** *n.* [1900s] (*Irish*) cash, ready money. ❑ **dry-nursing** *adj.* [mid-19C] (*UK Und.*) committed for trial. ❑ **dry room** *n.* [irony] **1** [19C] a prison; the inference is that its cells are damp. **2** [1930s] an interrogation room. ❑ **dry salter** *n.* [mid-19C] (*UK Und.*) a Jew who sells second-hand clothes. ❑ **dry shave** *v. see* separate entries. ❑ **dry shite** *n.* [SHITE *n.* (4)] [2000s] (*Irish*) a boring, unpopular person. ❑ **dry skull** *n.* [1950s] (*W.I.*) a completely bald person. ❑ **dry snitch** *see* separate entries. ❑ **dry stick** *n. see under* STICK *n.*

dry *adj.*[2] [play on SE *dry*, thirsty] [mid-18C–19C] drunk.

dry *adj.*[3] [SE *drunk* + HIGH *adj.*[1] (2)] [1990s+] (*US black*) simultaneously drunk and intoxicated by drugs.

dry *adj.*[4] [2000s] substandard, second-rate.

dry *v.* [1940s+] to deprive a person of everything they possess.

SE in slang uses

IN PHRASES

❑ **dry out** *see* separate entries. ❑ **dry straight** *v. see under* STRAIGHT *adj.*[1].

IN EXCLAMATIONS

❑ **dry your arse!** *see under* ARSE *n.* ❑ **dry your eyes!** [lit. 'stop crying'] [1940s+] (*Aus.*) stop complaining! stop whingeing!

dry along so *adj. see* DRYLONGSO *adj.*

dry as (a)... *adj.* (*Aus./N.Z.*) in a variety of adj. phrs. used to denote the intensity of one's thirst; also of the weather.

IN PHRASES

❑ **...a sack of gum-dust** [late 19C] ❑ **...a cocky's selection after a long drought** [*cocky's selection*, a small farm] [1900s] ❑ **...a wooden god** [1950s+] ❑ **...the rim of a lime-burner's hat** [1910s]

dryball *n.* [he refuses to 'get wet', i.e. to drink and enjoy himself] [1920s] (*US campus*) a student who does nothing but study.

dryball *v.* [DRYBALL *n.*] [1930s] to study hard.

dry fuck *n.* [SE *dry* + FUCK *n.* (1a)] (*orig. US*) **1** [1930s+] (*also* **dry rub**) a simulated act of sexual intercourse, without penetration and usu. without removing the clothes. **2** [1930s+] an unsatisfactory act of intercourse, esp. one that does not result in ejaculation or orgasm. **3** [1940s] in fig. use, something tedious or disappointing. **4** [1950s+] (*gay*) anal intercourse without any form of lubricant.

dry fuck *v.* [DRY FUCK *n.*] **1** [1920s+] to simulate intercourse by rubbing one's clothed body against that of one's partner. **2** [1960s–70s] to have lesbian sex, rubbing the vaginas together. **3** [2000s] to have (anal) intercourse without any form of lubrication.

dryfucking *adj.* [DRY FUCK *n.* (3)] [1950s] (*orig. US*) infuriating, disappointing and other negatives, relevant to context.

dry goods *n.*[1] [*see* prev.] [mid–late 19C] (*US*) a derog. term for a woman.

dry goods *n.*[2] [retail jargon *dry goods*, items of drapery, haberdashery etc, as opposed to groceries] (*US*) **1** [mid-19C–1960s] (outer) clothing. **2** [1920s–40s] (*US black*) a style of suit characterized by a long draped jacket with padded shoulders and high-waisted, tapering trousers.

IN PHRASES

❑ **kick into dry goods** *v.* [late 19C] (*US*) to get dressed.

dry head *n.* [1940s+] (*W.I.*) a bald person.

dry-head *adj.* (*also* **dry-headed**) [1930s+] (*W.I.*) bald; when used of women it is an insult.

dry hump *n.* [DRY HUMP *v.*] [1960s+] **1** simulated or mutually unsatisfying intercourse. **2** in fig. use, a failure, a disappointment.

dry hump *v.* [SE *dry* + HUMP *v.*[1] (1)] [1960s+] **1** (*also* **dry root, dry run**) to simulate intercourse. **2** in fig. use, to exploit, to do something that inevitably fails.

dry land *n.* [one has fig. reached *dry land*] [1970s] (*US black*) a situation of safety; thus *dry land!* all clear!

dry land? *phr.* [rhy. sl.] [mid–late 19C] you understand?

dry-land sailor *n.* (*also* **dry-land Jack**) [mid–late 19C] a criminal beggar who claims to have suffered shipwreck or piracy and requests alms to return home; or one who claims his goods are smuggled and thus sells them at an exorbitant rate.

drylongso *adj.* (*also* **dry along so**) [ety. unknown] [20C+] (*US black*) ordinary, customary.

dry out *n.* [DRY OUT *v.* (2)] [1960s+] (*US drugs*) a period in jail, in order to withdraw compulsorily from drug addiction.

dry out *v.* (*orig. US*) **1** [1950s+] to stop drinking alcohol; usu. to recover from alcoholism or from a bout of excessive drinking. **2** [1960s+] to withdraw from narcotics addiction.

IN COMPOUNDS

❑ **dry-out farm** *n.* (*also* **drunk farm**) [1950s] rehabilitation clinic.

dry-rub *v.* **1** [late 19C] to beat severely. **2** [1950s+] (*US gay*) wrestling or simlar 'horseplay' with strong homosexual overtones.

dry screw *n.* [SCREW *n.*[1] (1b); var. on DRY FUCK *n.* (1)] [1920s+] an act of simulated sexual intercourse, usu. with clothes on.

dry screw *v.* [SCREW *v.* (2a); var. on DRY FUCK *v.* (1)] [1920s] (*US*) to simulate intercourse.

dry shave *n.*

IN PHRASES

❑ **give someone a dry shave** *v.* [DRY SHAVE *v.*[1]] [1930s] (*US*) to defraud, to hoax.

dry shave *v.*[1] [? idea of being 'cheated' of the water required for a proper shave] [17C–18C] to deceive, to defraud, to rob.

dry shave *v.*[2] [orig. a milit. punishment; men who had failed to shave adequately were roughly shaved on the parade-ground without benefit of soap or water] [19C+] to carry out an act of 'effrontery' (F&H) whereby one rubs the knuckles hard across one's victim's skull or chin.

dry snitch *n.* [SE *dry* + SNITCH *n.*[1] (3)] [1990s+] (*US prison*) **1** an act of informing committed by innuendo, or even error, rather than by direct accusation. **2** an individual who passes on information in this manner.

dry snitch *v.* [SE *dry* + SNITCH *v.* (1)] [1950s+] (*US prison*) to inform by innuendo, or even error, rather than by direct accusation.

dry up *v.* **1** [mid-19C] to cover up, to keep quiet about. **2** [mid-19C+] to stop talking. **3** [mid-19C+] as imper., be quiet. **4** [1980s] (*US Und.*) to refuse to give information (to the police).

D. S., the *n.* [abbr.] [1960s+] *Drug Squad*.

DSL *n.* [*d*ick *s*uckin' *l*ips] [2000s] (*US black*) a mouth seen as well-suited for the performance of fellatio.

'dswounds! *excl. see* 'SWOUNDS! *excl.*

DT *n. see* DTs *n.*

d.t. *n.* [abbr.] [1920s+] (*US*) a *d*e*t*ective, in later 20C esp. a member of the drug squad.

d/t *n.* [abbr.] [1970s+] in sex contact advertisements, *d*irty *t*alk; dominance training.

d.t. centre *n.* [DTs *n.* (1) and thus a ref. to the enthusiastic drinking that takes place] [late 19C–1900s] a small literary club.

D-town *n.* [initial letter] [1970s] (*US*) Dallas, Texas.

d.t.r. *phr.* [abbr.; used of a conversation, often between the partners] [1990s+] (*US campus*) *d*efining *t*he *r*elationship.

DTs *n.* (*also* **DT**) [abbr.] **1** [mid-19C+] *d*elirium *t*remens. **2** [1940s+] a general malaise, not based on alcohol; also attrib.

Dub *n.* [abbr.] [1920s+] (*Irish*) **1** *Dub*lin. **2** (*also* **Dubbo**) a *Dub*liner.

dub *n.*[1] [DUB *v.*[1]] **1** [late 17C–mid-19C] a key, a picklock; thus *dubs*, a bunch of keys. **2** [18C] (*UK Und.*) opening a door with a skeleton key or picklock. **3** [early 18C] a picklock boy. **4** [early 19C] a toll collector. **5** [late 19C] a prison warder.

IN COMPOUNDS

❑ **dub-cove** *n.* [COVE *n.* (1)] [mid-18C–mid-19C] a turnkey. ❑ **dub-cull** *n.* (*also* **quad-cull**) [mid–late 18C] (*UK Und.*) a turnkey, a gaoler. ❑ **dub-lay** *n.* [LAY *n.*[3] (1)] (*UK Und.*) **1** [18C] picking pockets [given the ety., this may be a misinterpretation by *The Tyburn Chronicle*'s author – there are no refs. in any other dict.]. **2** [late 18C–19C] robbery of a house by picking the lock.

IN PHRASES

❑ **go on the dub** *v.* [late 17C–18C] (*UK Und.*) to break into a house using a picklock or skeleton key.

dub *n.*[2] [dial. *dub*, a pond, a small pool of water] [mid-19C] (*UK Und.*) the sea.

dub *n.*[3] [mid-19C] (*UK Und.*) a blow; usu. as *dub o' the hick*, a blow on the head.

dub *n.*[4] [Scot. *dub*, filth, a dirty puddle] **1** [mid-19C] filth; thus a piece of excrement. **2** [1940s+] (*also* **dubs**) (*Aus./N.Z.*) a lavatory [+ abbr. of *double-you see*, i.e. W.C.].

dub *n.*[5] [? SE *dubbed*, blunted, without a point] [late 19C+] (*orig. US*) **1** a failure, an incompetent, a novice, an oaf. **2** something that fails, a disaster.

IN PHRASES

❑ **dub along** *v.* (*also* **dub around**) [late 19C–1960s] (*US*) to idle, to loaf, to fool about, to spend time with; thus *dubber*, a time waster.

dub *n.*[6] [abbr./pron.] **1** [1940s+] (*US*) a $20 bill [*doub*le ten]. **2** [1950s] (*N.Z.*) a *doub*le-decker tram. **3** [2000s] the number 20 [*doub*le ten].

dub *n.*[7] (*US black*) **1** [1960s] a friend. **2** [2000s] one's local neighbourhood.

dub *n.*[8] [? link to DUB *v.*[1], i.e. it 'shuts up' one's mouth or northern dial. *tab*, a cigarette] **1** [1970s] (*US*) a cigarette. **2** [1990s+] (*US drugs*) a marijuana cigarette.

dub *n.*[9] [1970s+] (*W.I./UK black*) music with or without vocals, invariably spiced up with snatches of echo and similar special effects, created by skilful, artistic re-engineering of recorded tracks.

dub *n.*[10] [SE *dub*, to smear, but given the lifestyle of the artists note DUB *n.*[1]] [1990s+] a piece of graffito, painted on a wall or train.

dub, the *n.* [northern dial. *dub*, a deep, dark pool] [1910s] the Atlantic Ocean.

dub *v.*[1] [dial. *dup*, to open; ult. SE *do up*] [17C–19C] (*also* **dab**) to work the lock of a door, found both as to lock and to unlock, the latter esp. in prison use.

IN PHRASES

❑ **black cove dubber** *n.* [COVE *n.* (1)] [early–mid-19C] (*UK Und.*) a gaoler, a turnkey. ❑ **dub in** *v.* [? fig. use, i.e. to 'unlock' one's pocket or purse] [early 19C+] to pay a share of money, to contribute. ❑ **dub one's mummer** *v.* [fig. use, i.e. to 'shut' + MUMMER *n.* (1)] [early 19C] to be quiet, esp. as imper. ❑ **dub the gig(ger)** *v.* (*also* **dub the jigger**) [GIGGER *n.*[1]] [17C–late 18C] to open a door, to unlock a door; occas. to shut or lock up a door.

dub *v.*[2] [SE *dub*, to thrust, to poke] [1990s+] (*W.I.*) to make sexual advances.

dub *v.*[3] **1** *see* DOUBLE-BANK *v.* (6). **2** *see* DOUBLE UP *v.*[3].

dubbe *n. see* DOOBIE *n.*[1].

dubber *n.*[1] [DUB *v.*[1]] **1** [late 17C–mid-19C] (*UK Und.*) a thief who specializes in picking locks. **2** [early 19C] a turnkey, a gaoler.

dubber *n.*[2] [DUB *n.*[1]; i.e. something that opens and shuts] [18C–19C] the mouth.

IN PHRASES

❑ **dubber-mumed** *adj.* [MUM *adj.*] [late 18C] silent.

dubber *n.*[3] *see* DUB *n.*[8] (1).

dubbies *n.* [var. on BUBBIES *n.*] [1960s+] the female breasts.

Dubbo *n. see* DUB *n.* (2).

dubbo *n.* [DUB *n.*[5] (1)] [1970s] (*Aus.*) a fool, a general term of abuse.

dubbo *adj.* [DUBBO *n.*] [late 19C+] (*Aus.*) stupid; senile.

dubbs *n. see* DUBS *n.*[1] (1).

dube(e) *n. see* DOOBIE *n.*[1].

Dublin *n.* [*Dublin*, the capital of the Republic of Ireland] [20C+] (*US*) the Irish area of a town or city.

proper name in slang uses

IN COMPOUNDS

❑ **Dublin jackeen** *n. see* JACKEEN *n.* ❑ **Dublin rules** *n.* [stereotyping the Irish as rough-and-ready brawlers] [1900s] (*Aus.*) no rules at all. ❑ **Dublin University graduate** *n.* [the clichéd condemnation of the Irish as fools] [1950s+] a particularly stupid person.

IN PHRASES

❑ **take the Dublin packet** *v.* [? SE *double*, to evade escape, to run off; or ? the image of a lit. escape from the UK to Ireland by the SE *packet-boat*, e.g. by a debtor or criminal] [mid-19C–1900s] to run round the corner. ❑ **tip the Dublin packet** *v.* [TIP *v.*[3]; *see* prev.] [early 19C] (*UK Und.*) to run off, to escape.

Dublin fair *n.* [rhy. sl.] [20C+] (*Aus.*) the hair.

Dublin trick *n.* [rhy. sl.; the identification of Irishmen with the building trade] [late 19C] a brick.

dub off *v.* [? SE *dub*, to beat blunt] [1910s] (*US*) to masturbate.

dubry *n. see* DOOBRIE *n.*

dubs *n.*[1] (*also* **dubbs**) [ety. unknown; ? link to Essex dial. *dubs*, money, itself f. DIBBS *n.* (1)] **1** [early 19C–1910s] money. **2** *see* DUB *n.*[1] (1).

dubs *n.*[2] [abbr. SE *doubles*] [1910s+] (*Aus.*) marbles.

dubs *n.*[3] [2000s] (*US black/campus*) 20-inch tyre rims.

IN PHRASES

❑ **sit on dubs** *v.* of a car, to have 20-inch tyre rims.

dubs *n.*[4] *see* DUB *n.*[4] (2).

dubsman *n.* [DUB *n.*[1] (1) + *-man* sfx] [mid-19C] a prison warder or turnkey.

dub up *v.*[1] [DUBS *n.*[1]] [early 19C+] to pay over money, to pay on demand.

dub up *v.*[2] [DUB *v.*[1]] [early 19C+] to lock up, e.g. in a cell or in handcuffs.

dub up *v.*[3] [SE *dub*, to thrust, to poke] [mid-19C] of a man, to ejaculate.

duby *n. see* DOOBIE *n.*[1].

ducat *n.* [SE *ducat*. 'A gold coin of varying value, formerly in use in most European countries. That current in Holland, Russia, Austria and Sweden being equivalent to about 9s 4d. Also applied to a silver coin of Italy, value about 3s 6d' (*OED*)] **1** [late 18C; mid-19C+] usu. in pl., money, cash. **2** [mid-19C+] (*US*) (*also* **duc**) $1. **3** [mid-19C+] (*also* **ducket, duket**) a ticket for the theatre, a sporting event etc. **4** [1920s] a (businesss) card. **5** [1920s–30s] (*US tramp*) a counterfeited letter identifying one as some form of victim, used to facilitate begging. **6** [1920s+] (*US prison*) any form of document. **7** [1940s] (*US Und.*) as *the ducats*, a form of confidence trick involving marked cards.

IN PHRASES

❑ **give a ducat to chapel** *v.* [2000s] (*US prison*) to set up a victim to be killed.

ducat *v.* [DUCAT *n.* (6)] [1970s+] (*US prison*) to single out, to place on a list.

duce *n.* **1** *see* DEUCE *n.*[1]. **2** *see* DEUCE *n.*[2] (2).

duceavil *n. see* DEUSEAVILLE *n.*

duced *adj. see* DEUCED *adj.*

ducey *n.* [ety. unknown; ? link to SE *juicy* or DOOZIE *n.* (1)] [1900s–50s] (*US*) the penis.

duchess *n.*[1] [play on SE] **1** [late 17C–18C] a woman, esp. when good-looking, even showy [the image of a *duchess* as an imposing figure]. **2** [early 18C] an old woman. **3** [late 18C] a prostitute. **4** [19C+] a general term of address to a woman. **5** [late 19C–1900s] one's mother. **6** [1920s+] a woman who is making money in films. **7** [1970s] an ageing, affected male homosexual.

IN COMPOUNDS

❑ **Duchess of Puddle-dock** *see* COUNTESS OF PUDDLE-DOCK *n.*

duchess *n.*[2] [? the diary of Sarah, *Duchess* of Marlborough (1660–1744), who, following the return of her husband, wrote: 'Today my Lord returned from the wars and pleasured me twice in his top-boots'] [late 18C–early 19C] **1** a woman who has intercourse while still half-dressed. **2** a man who has intercourse without removing his boots; thus *make a duchess*, to have intercourse in this spontaneous manner.

duchess *n.*[3] *see* DRUM AND FIFE *n.* (2).

duchess *v.* [note letter from Paul Kunino Lynch 12/9/00: Duchess is 'widely understood here as meaning what happens when an Australian or other provincial goes to the UK, and British power figures try to sap the visitor's will & judgment by overpowering them with experiences such as weekends in the luxurious homes of the mighty, duchesses and such. Presumably this used to work once upon a time, and it was at its peak during WWI. Verb both transitive & intransitive. I was duchessed, they duchessed or tried to duchess me. Stupid bastard went to London and let them duchess him [...] So the central meaning of the word is "treated by (generic) duchesses", rather than like them'] [1950s+] (*Aus.*) to treat in a patronizing manner, in the image of a stereotyped duchess; trad. attributed to the treatment by certain Britons of visiting Australians.

Duchess of Fife *n. see* DRUM AND FIFE *n.* (2).

duck *n.*[1] **1** [mid-16C+] a lover, a sweetheart; a general term of affection; thus adj. *duckheaded*, romantic, sentimental. **2** [17C] a prostitute. **3** [early 19C+] a fine example of; usu. in phr. (a) *duck of a…* **4** [early 19C+] a fellow, a person. **5** [mid-19C+] (*orig. US Und.*) a gullible fool. **6** [late 19C+] (*US campus*) a misfit, an unappealing person. **7** *see* DUCKS *n.*[1].

SE in slang uses

IN COMPOUNDS

❑ **duck-arsed** *adj.* [-ARSED *sfx* (1)] [1940s–60s] **1** (*Irish*) short and squat, with large buttocks. **2** a general derog. ❑ **duckass** *n. see* DUCK'S ARSE *n.* ❑ **duckbutt** *n.* [BUTT *n.*[1] (1a)] [1930s+] (*US*) a short person. ❑ **duck butter** *n.* [the smell, reminiscent of duck droppings + the colour of butter] [1930s+] (*US*) **1** semen. **2** smegma. ❑ **duck-fanny** *n. see* DUCK'S ARSE *n.* ❑ **duck fart** *n.* [1940s–60s] (*N.Z. juv.*) the 'plop' of a stone falling into water. ❑ **duck fit** *n. see* separate entry. ❑ **duck-fucker** *n.* (*also* **duck plucker**) [FUCKER *n.* (3)/PLUCK *v.* (1); note Grose (1785): '*Duck f-ck-r*, The man who has care of the poultry on board a ship of war'] [1970s+] (*US*) an unpleasant, unpopular person. ❑ **duckhead** *n.* [? resemblance] **1** [1970s+] (*US black*) a woman with short, nappy hair. **2** [1980s] a fool. ❑ **duck-house door** *n.* [20C+] (*Ulster*) a very thick slice of bread (and butter). ❑ **duck legs** *n.* [late 18C] short legs; thus *duck-legged*, short. ❑ **duckpond** *n.* **1** [mid-17C; late 19C] the vagina. **2** [1920s] a joc. name for the Atlantic Ocean. ❑ **duck's arse** *n. see* separate entry. ❑ **duck's breakfast** *n.* [1900s–10s] (*Aus.*) a drink of water and a wash. ❑ **duck's bum** *n. see* DUCK'S ARSE *n.* ❑ **duck's butt** *n.* [BUTT *n.*[1] (1a); ? resemblance; presumably it sticks up at the back] **1** [1970s] (*US black*) a woman with unkempt hair. **2** *see* DUCK'S ARSE *n.* ❑ **duck's dinner** *n.* [1990s+] (*Aus.*) a drink of water, but no food to accompany it. ❑ **duck's disease** *n.* [like a duck, one waddles around with one's buttocks close to the ground] [1910s+] having short legs. ❑ **duck's guts, the** *n.* **1** [1970s] (*W.I.*) in trouble. **2** [1990s+] (*Aus.*) something superlative. ❑ **duck shoot** *n.* ['like shooting ducks on a pond'] [1940s+] (*orig. milit.*) a simple operation. ❑ **duck-shoving** *n.* [19C cabman's jargon *duck-shoving*, touting for passengers rather than waiting one's turn in line; ult. image is of the farmyard; note WW1 milit. *duck shoving*, evading duty] [1910s+] (*Aus./N.Z.*) fighting for status, rank, position, esp. in political terms; thus *duck-shover*, one who uses unfair business methods; gambling use, manipulating, using sleight of hand. ❑ **duck's meat** *n.* [1990s+] (*Ulster*) mucus produced in the eye. ❑ **duck soup** *n. see* separate entry. ❑ **duck's quack** *n. see* BEE'S KNEES *n.* ❑ **ducktail** *n.* [the preferred hairstyle of the teen sub-culture] **1** [1940s] (*also* **duck's tail**) a type of hairstyle in which the back of the hair is turned upwards in a manner similar to a duck's tail. **2** [1950s+] (*S.Afr.*) a teddyboy; also attrib.

IN PHRASES

❑ **be in duck's guts** *v.* [20C+] (*W.I.*) to be in a hopeless situation, to be in irretrievable difficulties. ❑ **can a duck swim?** (*also* **does a duck like water? …know water? does a fish swim? will a duck swim? …fish swim?**) [forerunner of DOES A BEAR SHIT IN THE WOODS? IS THE POPE A CATHOLIC? *phr.*] [mid-19C+] used to emphasize one's absolute agreement; thus phr. *can a duck whistle?*, a sarcastic rejoinder. ❑ **for ducks** [ety. unknown] [1900s–60s] (*US*) for no special reason, 'for the hell of it'. ❑ **have one's ducks in a row** *v.* [? image of the mother duck and her attendant ducklings] [1930s+] (*US*) to have one's affairs in order. ❑ **like a duck on a June bug** *adv.* (*also* **…a dough-pile**) [late 19C] (*US*) heavily, solidly; thus *landed like a duck…*

IN EXCLAMATIONS

▫ **go milk a duck!** [20C+] (*US campus*) an excl. of dismissal; a euph. for *GO FUCK A DUCK! under* FUCK *v.*

duck *n.*^{2} [Yorks. dial.] [mid-19C] a faggot, a parcel of meat scraps sold cheaply to the poor.

duck *n.*^{3} [the Bombay *duck*, the bummalo (*Harpodon nehereus*), a small local fish, usu. eaten dried as a relish] [mid–late 19C] (*Anglo-Ind.*) a nickname for soldiers of the Bombay Presidency.

duck *n.*^{4} [late 19C] a type of watch.

duck *n.*^{5} [? its spout resembles a duck's neck] [late 19C–1940s] (*US*) a container used to bring back beer from the saloon.

IN PHRASES

▫ **rush the duck** *v.* (*also* **chase the duck**) to bring home beer in a bucket or pail.

duck *n.*^{6} [late 19C–1950s] an evasion.

IN PHRASES

▫ **cop a duck** *v.* [1970s] (*US*) to hide, to stay out of the way. ▫ **do a/the duck** *v.* [1910s] to escape, to run off. ▫ **do a duck in** *v.* [1910s] (*Aus.*) to make an appearance. ▫ **play the duck** *v.* **1** [mid-17C] to behave in a cowardly manner. **2** [1920s+] to avoid.

duck *n.*^{7} (*also* **ducks, doup**) [20C+] (*US*) a cigarette or cigar end; thus *shoot ducks*, to relight a cigar or cigarette end.

IN COMPOUNDS

▫ **duck buddy** *n.* [BUDDY *n.* (1)] [1910s] (*US*) one who, bereft of a cigarette himself, is given the last few puffs on a friend's.

duck *n.*^{8} [DEUCE *n.*^{1} (1)] **1** [1910s+] (*US*) in gambling, two. **2** [1970s] (*US prison*) a two-year prison sentence.

duck *n.*^{9} [abbr. DUCAT *n.* (3)] [1940s–50s] (*US*) a ticket, e.g. for the theatre, a sporting event.

duck *n.*^{10} [DUCK'S ARSE *n.*] [1950s–60s] a type of hairstyle in which the back turns up.

duck *n.*^{11} [1980s+] (*US prison*) **1** a weakling; an inferior. **2** an officer who passes on information to the inmates.

duck *n.*^{12} [? SE *duchess*] [1980s+] (*US campus*) **1** a snob, a conceited, stuck-up young woman. **2** an unpleasant or ugly person. **3** (*US campus*) a silly person.

duck *v.*^{1} [SE *duck* (one's head)/DUCK *n.*^{6} (1)] **1** [late 19C–1920s] to travel, to go. **2** [late 19C+] (*also* **duck on, duck the nut**) to avoid, to escape from. **3** [20C+] to hide. **4** [1910s] to avoid an activity. **5** [1950s] to get rid of.

IN COMPOUNDS

▫ **duck-arse** *n.* [ARSE *n.* (3)] [1980s+] (*Aus. prison*) a lazy prison officer. ▫ **duckhole** *n.* [2000s] a hideout. ▫ **duck-out** *n. see* separate entry.

IN PHRASES

▫ **duck out** *v. see* separate entry. ▫ **duck the scone** *v. see under* SCONE *n.*^{2}. ▫ **duck Uncle** *v. see under* UNCLE *n.*

duck *v.*^{2} [1930s–40s] (*US*) a euph. for FUCK *v.* (1) / FUCK *v.* (3).

duck *v.*^{3} [1940s+] to bend over in preparation for anal intercourse; usu. in phr. *fuck, suck and duck*.

Ducker *n.* [play on DUCK *v.*^{1} (1)] [1930s–50s] (*US tramp*) a Dodge automobile.

duckering *n. see* DOOKERING *n.*

ducket *n.* [var. on DUCAT *n.*] **1** [mid–late 19C] a ticket; thus fig. in phr. *that's the ducket*. **2** [mid–late 19C] a hawker's licence. **3** [1920s–30s] (*US*) a union card. **4** [1920s–30s] (*US tramp*) a cripple's begging letter. **5** [1940s] (*US Und.*) a pardon. **6** [1990s+] (*US black/teen*) (*also* **duckettes**) in pl., money, cash.

duck fit *n.* [the noise of a duck] **1** [20C+] (*US*) a temper tantrum; usu. in phr. below. **2** [1900s] laughter, hysterics.

IN PHRASES

▫ **throw a duck fit** *v.* [one resembles an angry duck] [20C+] (*US*) to become hysterical, to lose one's temper, to become extremely excited.

duckie *n.* **1** *see* DUCKS *n.*^{1}. **2** *see* DUCKY *n.*

duckie *adj. see* DUCKY *adj.*

duckies *n.* [DUCAT *n.* (1)] [1970s+] (*US black/campus*) money.

ducking and diving *n.* [rhy. sl.; *duck and dive* = SKIVE *v.*] [1960s+] living a life on the (criminal) margins; avoiding organized jobs, society, etc.

duck-out *n.* [DUCK OUT *v.* (3)] **1** [1940s] (*US*) an escape, a withdrawal. **2** [2000s] a failure, something that fails a test.

duck out *v.* (*also* **duck, duck on, duck out of**) [DUCK *v.*^{1}] **1** [late 19C+] to make off, to leave, to abscond. **2** [20C+] to back out, to withdraw. **3** [1970s+] to default on, to avoid.

ducks *n.*^{1} (*also* **duck, duckie, ducksey**) [DUCK *n.*^{1} (1)] [mid-17C+] a term of address, generally affectionate or friendly.

ducks *n.*^{2} *see* DUCK *n.*^{7}.

ducks! *excl.* [1930s+] (*US, usu. juv.*) a claim, esp. a claim of first rights to something.

ducks and drakes *n.*^{1} [fig. use of SE, i.e. a crowd of poultry] **1** [early 19C+] a mess. **2** [1990s+] (*N.Z.*) a difficult or frustrating person or situation.

ducks and drakes *n.*^{2} [rhy. sl. = SHAKES, THE *n.* (1)] [1960s+] (*Aus.*) delirium tremens, or excessive anxiety causing 'the shakes'.

ducks and geese *n.* [rhy. sl.] [20C+] (*Aus.*) the police.

duck's arse *n.* (*also* **duckass, duck-fanny, duck's ass, ...bum, ...butt**) [SE *duck* + ARSE *n.* (1)/ASS *n.* (2)/FANNY *n.*^{1} (3)/ BUM *n.*^{1} (1)/BUTT *n.*^{1} (1a)] **1** [1950s+] (*orig. US*) a type of hairstyle, esp. as adopted by teddyboys and rockers, in which the back of the hair is turned upwards in a manner similar to a duck's tail. **2** [1990s+] (*Irish*) a soggy cigarette butt; also attrib.

ducksey *n. see* DUCKS *n.*^{1}.

duck's neck *n.* [rhy. sl.] [20C+] (*Aus.*) a cheque.

duck soup *n.* (*US*) **1** [late 19C+] the total destruction of; usu. as *make duck soup of*. **2** [late 19C+] anything simple, easy. **3** [1900s] a guaranteed success. **4** [1910s–50s] something that suits one perfectly. **5** [1920s–30s] of a person, easily persuaded or victimized. **6** [1940s] something strange; as in phr. *queer as duck soup*.

ducky *n.* (*also* **duckie**) **1** [early 19C+] a term of address; used between men there is an implication of effeminacy. **2** [1990s+] a person.

IN PHRASES

▫ **do duckie** *v.* [1910s] (*Aus.*) to flirt, to pet with.

ducky *adj.* (*also* **duckie**) [DUCK *n.*^{1} (3); an example of the supposed charm of farmyard animals; late 20C use generally ironic] [mid-19C+] sweet, delightful, charming.

dud *n.*^{1} (*also* **dudde**) [ety. unknown] [mid-15C+] an article of clothing, esp. a cloak, made from rough, coarse cloth.

IN COMPOUNDS

▫ **dud-dropper** *n. see* separate entry.

dud *n.*^{2} [? DUD *n.*^{1}, thence rags and thus one who dresses in them, esp. a *dudman*, a scarecrow] **1** [early 19C; 20C+] of a person, a failure, an incompetent, a weakling, a bore. **2** [20C+] anything that lit. or fig. 'does not work'. **3** [20C+] of a thing or event, a failure, a disappointment, a 'flop'.

IN COMPOUNDS

▫ **dudhead** *n.* [-HEAD *sfx* (1)] [1960s+] (*US*) an idiot.

dud *adj.* [DUD *n.*^{2}] [20C+] **1** fake, false, counterfeit. **2** second-rate, unsuccessful. **3** broken.

dud *v.*^{1} [DUDS *n.*^{1} (1)] [20C+] (*US*) (*also* **dud up**) to dress up, to dress smartly.

dud *v.*^{2} [1970s+] (*Aus. Und.*) to misrepresent the origin, quality and value of goods; thus n. *dudding*.

IN PHRASES

▫ **dud up** *v.* [1930s+] (*Aus.*) to misinform, to cheat, to swindle; thus *dudder(-upper)*, one who fraudulently misrepresents the price and/or value of the goods he is selling, e.g. selling dyed aspirins as 'purple hearts', or claiming that perfectly legitimately purchased goods are actually 'off the back of a lorry' (and thus more glamorous).

dudaddle *n. see* DOODAD *n.*

dudde *n. see* DUD *n.*^{1}.

dudder *n.*[1] (*also* **whispering dudder**) [DUD *n.*[1]] [18C–mid-19C] a criminal beggar who wanders the country, selling goods that have supposedly been smuggled through the customs; thus capitalizing on the greed and gullibility of their provincial customers. The clandestine style of their encounter with a customer gives the synon. *whispering dudder*.

dudder *n.*[2] [synon. Rom.] [late 19C] (*UK Und.*) money.

duddering rake *n.* (*also* **dundering rake**) [late 17C–early 19C] 'a thundering rake, a buck of the first head, one extremely lewd' (Grose, 1785).

duddies *n. see* DUDS *n.*[1].

dudding *n. see* DUD *v.*[2].

duddle *n. see* DADDLE *n.*

dud-dropper *n.* [DUD *n.*[1]/DUD *v.*[2] + DROPPER *n.*[3] (2)] [1940s+] (*Aus.*) **1** a seller of stolen or inferior clothes. **2** a confidence trickster specializing in selling otherwise second-rate goods to those who believe that they have 'fallen off the back of a lorry'.

dudds *n. see* DUDS *n.*[1].

duddy *adj.* [DUD *adj.* (2)] [1950s] (*Aus.*) useless, incompetent.

dude *n.*[1] (*also* **dood**) [DUDS *n.*[1] (1) or abbr. SE *attitude*. The term gained a whole new currency, esp. among the pre-teens, with the popularity *c.*1990 of the cartoon characters Teenage Mutant Ninja Turtles, where it featured heavily; note also in *Comments on Etymology* Apr. 1997, Gerald Cohen has posited an orig. pron. of *doo-dee* and suggested an origin in Yankee *Dood*le + SE dandy] **1** [late 19C+] (*orig. US*) (*also* **dudelet**) a man, a fellow; post 1980s, a person, irrespective of gender. **2** [late 19C+] (*orig. US*) an overdressed, showy person, a fop or dandy; as *dudine*, *dudess*, a similarly showy woman. **3** [1900s] (*US campus*) a fool. **4** [1910s] (*US*) an expert. **5** [1920s] an excellent example. **6** [1950s+] (*US*) a thing. **7** [1960s+] a form of address.

(DERIVATIVES)

❑ **dudester** *n.* [-STER *sfx*] [1980s] (*US*) a person, irrespective of gender. ❑ **dudette** *n.* (*also* **dudinette**) [fem. sfx *-ette*] [late 19C+] (*US*) a girl, a woman. ❑ **dudish** *adj.* (*also* **dudeish**) [late 19C+] smart, dandyish.

(IN PHRASES)

❑ **big dude** *n.* [1960s] (*US*) an important person. ❑ **dude up** *v.* [late 19C+] (*US*) to dress (oneself) up.

dude *n.*[2] [1980s] (*US drugs*) heroin.

dude *adj.* [DUDE *n.*[1]] **1** [late 19C+] (*also* **dudy**) showy, smart. **2** [late 19C+] a general term of approbation. **3** [1930s+] of one who is posing as a cowboy.

dude! *excl.* [1980s+] (*US campus*) a mild excl., synon. with SE *wow!*, GEE! *excl.*, SHIT! *excl.* (3) etc and generally implying agreement or approval.

dudedad *n. see* DOODAD *n.*

duded up *adj.* (*also* **dudied up**) [*DUDE UP under* DUDE *n.*[1]] [late 19C+] (*US*) dressed up, esp. for a party or night out.

dudinkus *n. see* DOODINKUS *n.*

duds *n.*[1] (*also* **duddies, dudds**) [DUD *n.*[1]] **1** [16C+] clothing [Vaux glosses 'women's apparel in general']. **2** [mid-17C+] one's possessions, one's things in general. **3** [late 17C–mid-18C] (*UK Und.*) stolen articles. **4** [1900s] imitation jewels. **5** [1960s+] (*Aus./UK juv.*) trousers.

(IN COMPOUNDS)

❑ **duds-cheat** *adj.* [CHEAT *n.* (1)] [late 18C–mid-19C] (*UK Und.*) poor, ragged.

(IN PHRASES)

❑ **sweat duds** *v.* [SWEAT *v.*[1] (3)] [19C] to pawn one's clothes.

duds *n.*[2] [? BUB *n.*[4] (1)] [1960s] (*N.Z.*) the female breasts.

dudsman *n.* [var. DUDDER *n.*[1] (1)] [18C–mid-19C] a criminal beggar, often dressed as a sailor, who wanders the country, selling goods that they claim fraudulently to have been smuggled.

du-du *n. see* DO-DO *n.*[1].

dudy *adj. see* DUDE *adj.* (1).

due *n.* [abbr. SE *residue*] [1980s+] (*drugs*) the cocaine oil that remains in a pipe after freebasing.

dues *n.* [19C] **1** money. **2** a term used in phrs. meaning the business, concern or affair; *see LAGGING DUES under* LAGGING *n.*; *NARKING DUES under* NARK *v.*[1]; *QUODDING DUES ARE CONCERNED under* QUOD *v.*; *SLANGING DUES CONCERNED under* SLANG *v.*[1]; WEEDING DUES *n.*

SE in slang uses

(IN PHRASES)

❑ **pay one's dues** *v.* [1940s+] (*orig. US*) to undergo usu. undesirable experiences before one attains a desirable goal.

duey *n. see* DOOE(E) *n.*

duff *n.*[1] [? Yorks. dial. *duff*, to avoid, to dodge] **1** [late 18C+] counterfeit money, smuggled goods. **2** [late 19C] (*UK Und.*) constr. with *the*, the passing off of false jewellery. **3** [1920s] a fake. **4** [1950s+] (*UK prison*) tobacco that is contraband.

(IN PHRASES)

❑ **at the duff** [1900s–10s] (*Aus. Und.*) dealing in counterfeit jewellery.

duff *n.*[2] [west Yorks. dial. *duff*, the posterior] **1** [mid-19C+] the buttocks. **2** [late 19C] the vagina.

(IN COMPOUNDS)

❑ **duff-flogger** *n.* [1930s] (*US*) a male masturbator.

(IN PHRASES)

❑ **duff around** *v.* [20C+] to sit about, to act lazily. ❑ **fluff the duff** *v.* **1** [1950s] to shirk, to act lazily. **2** [1980s+] (*US gay*) to have anal intercourse.

duff *n.*[3]

(IN PHRASES)

❑ **up the duff** *adj.* [SE *duff*, a pudding, same imagery as *HAVE A BUN IN THE OVEN under* OVEN *n.*; PUDDING CLUB *n.*] [1940s+] (*orig. Aus.*) pregnant; thus rhy. sl. *up the Damien* (*duff*).

duff *n.*[4] [abbr.] [1950s] (*US*) a *duff*el bag.

duff *adj.* (*also* **duffed**) [DUFF *n.*[1]] **1** [late 19C+] fake, spurious. **2** [1920s+] of objects, useless, broken down, inferior. **3** [1930s+] of people, inadequate, incompetent.

(IN COMPOUNDS)

❑ **duffman** *adj.* [1910s–20s] (*UK Und.*) inferior, bad.

duff *v.*[1] [DUFF *adj.*] **1** [late 18C–19C] to sell ordinary goods that are touted as smuggled contraband. **2** [mid-19C] to make old goods look like new. **3** [mid-19C] (*also* **doff**) to make poor quality new goods look old, and thus of better quality. **4** [mid-19C] to cheat out of, to defraud. **5** [mid-19C+] (*Aus.*) to alter the brands on (stolen) cattle. **6** [mid-19C+] (*Aus.*) to steal (cattle or horses). **7** [late 19C+] to blunder, to make a mess of. **8** [1900s–10s] (*Aus.*) in weakened use, to use (a possession, a place) without the owner's permission; spec. to pasture cattle on someone else's land. **9** [1940s] to smuggle. **10** *see* DUFF UP *v.*

(IN COMPOUNDS)

❑ **duffing-yard** *n.* [late 19C] (*Aus.*) an isolated place where cattle-stealers can hide rustled cattle, rebrand them etc.

duff *v.*[2] [DUFF *n.*[2] (2) or fig. use of DUFF UP *v.*] **1** [1960s] (*Aus./US*) to have sexual intercourse with. **2** [1960s+] (*Aus./N.Z.*) to impregnate.

duffed *adj. see* DUFF *adj.*

duffer *n.*[1] [DUFF *v.*[1]] (*UK Und.*) **1** [mid-18C–19C] a crooked salesman who pretends to deal in smuggled goods but whose stock is actually cheap, mass-produced items, sold at a substantial mark-up, and who targets especially provincials up in London, mainly from a site at St Clement's Church in the Strand. **2** [mid-18C+] a hawker or pedlar. **3** [mid-19C] an inferior prostitute. **4** [mid–late 19C] a counterfeit coin or article; any spurious article. **5** [mid–late 19C] a petty swindler. **6** [mid-19C+] (*Aus.*) a cattle-stealer. **7** [late 19C–1920s] (*US*) a liar, a trickster; a general pej.

duffer *n.*[2] [DUFF *n.*[1] (1); i.e. the item is 'no good' and so is the person, or Scot. *duffar*, a blunt, stupid person, or *dofart*, *doofart*, *dowfart*, a dull, heavy-headed, inactive fellow. Note 1920s angling jargon *duffers' fortnight*, a fortnight of the angling season during which trout are supposed to be caught easily] [mid-19C+] **1** an incompetent, foolish person. **2** (*Aus.*) an unproductive mine or goldfield. **3** a failure.

duffer *n.*^{3} [SE *dough*] [1900s–40s] (*UK prison*) food, esp. pudding.

duffer *n.*^{4} *see* DUFF UP *v.*

duffer (out) *v.* [DUFFER *n.*^{2} (2)] [mid-19C+] (*Aus.*) **1** of a mine or goldfield, to prove unproductive. **2** of a miner or prospector, to fail in one's searches.

duffing *n.* [DUFF *v.*^{1}] [mid-19C] passing off a worthless article as valuable.

duffing *adj.* [DUFF *adj.* (1)] **1** [mid-19C] worthless, false, esp. of goods sold as more valuable than they really are. **2** [late 19C] foolish, incompetent.

duffis *n. see* DUFUS *n.* (1).

duffle-headed *adj.* [? var. on BUFFLEHEAD *n.*] [mid-19C] stupid, dull-witted.

duff-trap *v.* [SE *duff*, a form of pudding + TRAP *n.*^{1} (4)] [1900s] (*Aus.*) the mouth.

duff up *v.* (*also* **duff, duff over**) [orig. RAF jargon; ? Scot. *duff*, to hit, to strike] [1940s+] to beat up; thus as n. *duffer*, a violent thug.

duffus *n. see* DOOFUS *n.*

duffy *n.*^{1} [? a brandname; var. on DAFFY *n.*^{1} (1)] [early 19C] a quarter-pint of gin.

duffy *n.*^{2} [var. on DUFFER *n.*^{3}] [1900s] (*US*) bread.

duffy *n.*^{3} [? its popularity among Irish wearers, f. the common surname *Duffy*] [1920s–30s] (*US*) a derby hat.

duffy *n.*^{4} [a 'tribute' to former San Quentin warden Clinton *Duffy*] [1930s] (*US prison*) state issue tobacco.

duflickerty *n. see* DOOFLICKER *n.* (1).

duflus *n. see* DOOFLUS *n.*

dufunny *n. see* DOOFUNNY *n.*

dufus *n.* [var. on DOOFUS *n.*] [1970s+] **1** (*also* **duffis, dofous**) an eccentric, foolish or gauche person. **2** an unnamed object.

dufus *adj.* [DUFUS *n.*] [1970s+] (*US*) strange, foolish.

dugee/dugie *n. see* DUJI *n.*

dug-out *n.*^{1} [SE *dugout*, a roofed shelter used in trench warfare; note Fraser & Gibbons (1925) suggest: 'It first came in apparently during the South African War of 1899–1902 for pensioned or retired officers who came back to service in consequence of the depleting of the active establishment through casualties in the field', however, first citation in the *OED* is 1912] [1910s+] an old-fashioned person, either in ideas or appearance, esp. a retired officer etc, recalled for temporary military service.

dug-out *n.*^{2} [the image of digging a hole, either in one's arm or in a pile of food] **1** [1930s–50s] (*US drugs*) the lowest class of addict. **2** [1930s–70s] (*US prison*) a voracious eater.

dugu-dugu *n.* [? play on SE *dig*] [1990s+] (*W.I.*) sexual intercourse.

dug-up *adj.* [1970s] (*US*) out of sorts, unwell.

duh *n.* [DUH! *excl.*; echoic of a stupid person's uncomprehending grunt] [1950s+] (*S.Afr.*) a fool.

duh! *excl.* [echoic] [1950s+] a grunt of incomprehension; often used as a rejoinder, implying that the first speaker is stupid; often in positive or negative phrs. *well, duh!* or *no, duh!*

duh-brain *n. see* DUR-BRAIN *n.*

duibb *v. see* DOUBLE-BANK *v.* (6).

duji *n.* (*also* **d, dogie, doogie, doogy, doojee, dugee, dugie, dujie**) [ety. unknown] [1930s+] (*drugs*) heroin.

duji *v.* [DUJI *n.*] [1970s] (*US drugs*) to render oneself impotent through heroin use.

duke *n.*^{1} [abbr. *RUM DUKE under* RUM *adj.*; 20C+ use is US although its root may lie in the more recent DUDE *n.*^{1} (2)] **1** [late 16C] (*UK Und.*) a lookout. **2** [late 17C+] a showy, ostentatious man.

duke *n.*^{2} [used by servants in upper-class houses] [mid-19C] gin.

duke *n.*^{3} (*also* **dook, duke of york**) [? rhy. sl. *duke of york* = FORK *n.*^{1} (3); or ? Rom, *dukkering*, palm-reading] **1** [mid-19C+] (*US*) (*also* **juke**) a hand, usu. in pl.; also in fig. use; thus *dukefull*, a handful; occas. an arm. **2** [mid-19C+] (*also* **dooks**) in pl., the fists. **3** [1900s–40s] (*US Und.*) a form of confidence game. **4** [1910s–50s] a hand of cards. **5** [1930s–70s] in boxing, a decision [the referee raises the winning boxer's hand]. **6** [1940s] (*US black*) in pl., knees. **7** [1950s] the bill, usu. in a restaurant. **8** [1970s] in fig. use, a plan, i.e a hand of cards that one deals or is dealt.

IN COMPOUNDS

❑ **duke city** *n. see FIST CITY under* FIST *n.* ❑ **duke player** *n.* [1930s] (*US Und.*) a gambler who cheats at cards.

IN PHRASES

❑ **blow the duke** *v.* [fig. use of sense 3 above] [1960s–70s] to make a complete mess of something. ❑ **crop someone's duke** *v.* [1910s] (*US Und.*) to read an opponent's cards by some form of fraud. ❑ **get some duke** *v.* **1** [1970s+] of a male homosexual, to have someone's fingers or fist pushed into one's anus. **2** [1980s] (*US black*) of a man, to have sexual intercourse with a male-to-female transvestite. ❑ **give the duke** *v.* [1960s+] to slow hand-clap as a sign of disapproval of a sporting event. ❑ **grease someone's duke** *v.* [late 19C] **1** to hand over money. **2** to give a bribe. ❑ **hot duke** *v.* [1970s+] (*Aus.*) to fool, to take advantage by trickery. ❑ **put up one's dukes** *v.* [late 19C+] to (prepare to) fight. ❑ **read the dukes** *v.* [1910s] (*US Und.*) working as a palm-reader. ❑ **ring the dukes** *v. see* DUKE *v.*^{1} (1). ❑ **tip one's duke** *v.* [1910s] (*US Und.*) to reveal one's intentions.

duke *n.*^{4} **1** [1920s] a champion, one of the best. **2** [1930s+] a tough, dominant individual, a leader or boss, esp. in the criminal world. **3** [1940s] (*US prison*) the warden. **4** [1970s+] (*US gay/prison*) a predatory prison homosexual.

IN PHRASES

❑ **get some duke** *v.* [1980s+] (*US black*) to have sexual intercourse.

duke *v.*^{1} [DUKE *n.*^{3} (1); note WW1 Aus. milit. *dook 'im one*, to salute] **1** [mid-19C–1920s] (*also* **dook (it), duke it, ring the dukes**) to shake hands, to welcome. **2** [1920s+] (*also* **dook (it), duke it, ...on**) to give out, to hand over; to bribe. **3** [1930s+] (*also* **duck**) to fight with the fists. **4** [1960s+] to inform. **5** [1980s+] (*US gay*) to push one or more fingers or even the whole fist into one's partner's anus. **6** [1990s+] (*US black*) to have sexual intercourse.

IN PHRASES

❑ **duke in** *v.* [handshaking in both duplicitous and sincere contexts] (*US*) **1** [1930s+] to introduce, to bring in to a plan or group; also as n. **2** [1950s+] to fool, to trick. **3** [1960s] to give a share. ❑ **duke it** *v.* **1** *see* sense 1 above. **2** *see* sense 2 above. ❑ **duke it out** *v.* (*also* **duck it out**) **1** [1930s+] (*US*) to fight with fists. **2** [1990s+] to argue, to dispute; to challenge. ❑ **duke on** *v. see* sense 2 above. ❑ **duke out** *see* separate entries.

duke *v.*^{2} [ety. unknown; ? link to DUDE *n.*^{1} (2)] [1980s+] to get dressed.

duked out *adj.* (*also* **duked up**) [DUKE *v.*^{2} (1)] [1930s–50s] (*US*) dressed up.

dukee *n.* [1920s–50s] (*US tramp*) a handout of cold food, e.g. a sandwich.

duke of Cork *n. see* EARL OF CORK *n.*^{2}.

Duke of Fife *n. see* DRUM AND FIFE *n.* (1).

duke (of Kent) *n.* [rhy. sl.] **1** [1930s+] the rent. **2** [1960s+] (*Aus.*) (*also* **dukers**) a cent. **3** [1970s+] a homosexual [= BENT *n.* (1)]. **4** [1980s] (*Aus.*) a tent.

duke of limbs *n.* [mid-18C–mid-19C] an awkward, ungainly person.

Duke of Teck *n.* [rhy. sl.] [20C+] the neck.

Duke of York *n.* [rhy. sl.] **1** [mid–late 19C] a walk. **2** [late 19C] talk. **3** [late 19C+] a fork. **4** [late 19C+] in pl., fingers [= FORK *n.*^{1} (3)]. **5** [1930s+] chalk. **6** [1950s] a cork. **7** [1960s] pork.

Duke of York *v.* [rhy. sl.] **1** [mid-19C+] to walk. **2** [late 19C+] to talk.

duke-out *n.* [DUKE OUT *v.* (2)] [1970s+] (*US*) an argument, a fight.

duke out *v.* [DUKE *v.*^{1} (3)] **1** [1950s] (*US Und.*) to throw out; to get rid of. **2** [1970s+] (*US*) to knock out.

duker *n.*[1] (*also* **dooker**) [1920s–50s] (*US Und.*) the member of a team of cheats, con men or similar group who pretends to be an 'innocent bystander' to lure in genuine victims.

duker *n.*[2] [DUKE *n.*[3] (1)/DUKE *v.*[1] (3)] **1** [1940s] (*US carnival*) a fortune teller. **2** [1970s] (*US*) a boxer, a fist-fighter.

duket *n. see* DUCAT *n.* (3).

duket-snatching *n. see* BRIEF-SNATCHER *n.*

dukey *see also under* DUKIE.

dukey *n.* [a particular theatre whose Jewish proprietor had a large nose, i.e. a DOOK *n.*[1] (1)] [mid–late 19C] a cheap theatre or music-hall.

dukey rope *n.* [1990s+] (*US black/teen*) a large, heavy gold chain, worn as jewellery.

dukie *n.*[1] (*also* **dookey, dukey**) [DUKE *n.*[3] (1); thus something one can carry or ? dial. *docky*, a light meal taken in the fields] **1** [1910s] (*US Und.*) a meal (of scraps/leftovers) given to a tramp. **2** [1920s–40s] (*US carnival*) a meal ticket. **3** [1920s–60s] (*US*) a light meal, esp. that carried to work by a labourer or factory worker. **4** [1960s] (*US prison*) a sandwich.

dukie *n.*[2] (*also* **dookey, dookie**) [? Scot. *dook*, the bung of a cask] **1** [1960s+] excrement. **2** [1970s+] (*US black*) an act of defecation; thus *dukie hole*, the anus. **3** [1980s] nothing. **4** [1990s+] (*US campus*) an unpleasant, obnoxious person.

IN COMPOUNDS

❑ **dookie love** *n.* [2000s] (*US black*) anal intercourse.

IN PHRASES

❑ **drop a dookie** *v.* (*also* **blast a dookie, do dukie, take a dookie**) [1980s+] (*US*) to defecate.

dukie *n.*[3] *see* DOOKEY *n.*

dukie *v.* (*also* **dookie**) [DUKIE *n.*[2] (1)] [1990s+] to defecate.

dull *adj.*

SE in slang uses

DERIVATIVES

❑ **dullsville** *n.* [-VILLE *sfx*[1]] [1950s+] an imaginary town, characterized by extreme dullness or boredom; thus a state, environment or situation of extreme dullness. ❑ **dullsville** *adj.* [*DULLSVILLE* above] [1960s+] (*orig. US*) tedious.

IN COMPOUNDS

❑ **dullhead** *n.* [-HEAD *sfx* (1)] [mid-19C+] (*US*) a dullard. ❑ **dull-pickle** *n.* [PICKLE *n.* (1)] [late 17C–18C] a fool, a dullard. ❑ **dull swift** *n. see under* SWIFT *n.*

dum *adj.* (*also* **dumb**) [DUM *adv.*; ult. euph. for DAMN *adj.*] [late 19C–1920s] a general intensifier, great.

dum *adv.* (*also* **dumb**) [euph. for DAMN *adv.*] [late 18C+] (*US black*) extremely, very.

dum-ass *n. see* DUMB-ASS *n.*

dumb *n.* **1** [1920s+] (*orig. US*) a fool, a stupid person. **2** [1990s+] stupidity.

dumb *adj.*[1] **1** [1920s] (*US*) boring, dull. **2** [1920s–50s] (*US campus*) unattractive.

SE in slang uses

based on SE *dumb*, stupid

DERIVATIVES

❑ **dumbski** *n.* [-SKI *sfx*] [20C+] (*US*) a fool.

IN COMPOUNDS

❑ **dumb-arsed** *adj. see* DUMB-ASS *adj.* ❑ **dumb-ass/-assed** *see* separate entries. ❑ **dumb-bum** *n. see* DUMB-ASS *n.* ❑ **dumb bunny** *n.* (*also* **dumb rabbit**) [1920s+] (*US*) a fool; also attrib. ❑ **dumb cluck** *n.* [CLUCK *n.*[1] (1)] [1930s+] (*orig. US*) a fool; also attrib. ❑ **dumb cunt** *n. see* DUMBFUCK *n.* ❑ **dumb dora** *n.* [allegedly coined *c.*1890 by Anita Pines, the first woman manager of a burlesque theatre but popularized in 1920s via Chic Young's eponymous comic strip] [1920s+] (*US*) **1** (*also* **dumb Mabel**) a pretty, but empty-headed woman, often a member of the chorus line. **2** a stupid person; also attrib. ❑ **dumbfuck** *see* separate entries. ❑ **dumb isaac** *n.* [play on SMART ALECK *n.*] [1900s–20s] (*US*) a fool. ❑ **dumbnuts** *n.* [play on *NUMBNUTS under* NUMB *adj.*] [1970s+] (*US*) a fool. ❑ **dumb rabbit** *n. see* *DUMB BUNNY* above. ❑ **dumbshit** *see* separate entries. ❑ **dumb smack** *n.* [? the smacking of the forehead in perplexity] [1950s+] (*US*) a fool. ❑ **dumb sock** *n.* [? SOCK *n.*[3] (1)] [1930s+] (*US*) **1** a fool. **2** a Swede or any Scandinavian immigrant. ❑ **dumbsquat** *n.* [? DIDDLY-SQUAT *n.*[1]] [1960s+] (*US*) a fool. ❑ **dumbum** *n.* [BUM *n.*[3] (2)/BUM *n.*[1] (1)] [1990s+] (*UK juv./N.Z.*) a fool. ❑ **dumbwad** *n.* [-WAD *sfx*] [1960s+] (*US campus*) a fool. ❑ **dumbwit** *n.* [SE *wit*, on pattern of *FUCKWIT under* FUCK *n.*] [1930s+] (*US*) a fool.

based on SE *dumb*, mute

IN COMPOUNDS

❑ **dumb glutton** *n. see* separate entries. ❑ **dumbhead** *n.* [lit. translation of Ger. *Dummkopf*, a dumbhead] [late 19C+] (*orig. US*) a fool; also attrib. ❑ **dumb oracle** *n.* [18C] the vagina; thus *work the dumb oracle*, to have sexual intercourse. ❑ **dumb squint** *n.* [18C] the vagina. ❑ **dumbstick** *n.* [1990s+] (*US campus*) the penis. ❑ **dumb watch** *n.* [? SE *watch*, a sentinel; such a sentinel is looking out for any further sexual misadventures] [late 18C–early 19C] a venereal bubo in the groin.

IN PHRASES

❑ **dumb as an oyster** *adj. see under* OYSTER *n.* ❑ **dumb it** *v.* [mid-19C] of a beggar, to pose as a mute in order to extract money.

dumb *adj.*[2] *see* DUM *adj.*

dumb *adv. see* DUM *adv.*

dumbarton *n.* (*also* **dumby**) [joc. use of proper name, but note *dounby*, buttocks, used by Sir Thomas Urquhart (*c.*1611–60) in his translation of Rabelais] [1910s] (*W.I.*) the buttocks.

dumb-ass *n.* (*also* **dum-ass, dumb-arse, dumb-bum**) [SE *dumb*, stupid + -ARSE *sfx*/-ASS *sfx*] **1** [1950s+] (*orig. US*) a fool. **2** [1980s+] a state of stupidity.

dumb-ass *adj.* (*also* **dumb-arsed, dumb-assed**) [DUMB-ASS *n.*] [1930s+] (*orig. US*) stupid, unintelligent.

dumb-bell *n.* [SE *dumb*, mute + SE *bell*, i.e. lit. a bell that will not ring; or ? SE *dumb-bell*, a weight, which dates to late 18C] [mid-19C+] an idiot, a fool.

dumb-bell *adj.* [DUMB-BELL *n.*] [1920s] stupid, foolish.

dumb-dumb *n. see under* DUM-DUM .

dumb-dumb *adj. see* DUMB-ASS *n.*

dumbellina *n.* [DUMB-BELL *n.* + fem. sfx *-ina* + pun on Disney character *Thumbelina*] [1950s+] (*camp gay*) a fool.

dumbfuck *n.* (*also* **dumbcunt**) [SE *dumb*, stupid + FUCK *n.* (4)] [1940s+] (*orig. US*) a fool, an idiot; thus *dumbfuckery*, behaviour typical of such an individual.

dumb-fuck *adj.* (*also* **dumb-fucker**) [DUMBFUCK *n.*] [1960s+] absurd, stupid, with undertones of unpleasantness.

dumb glutton *n.* [late 18C] the vagina.

IN PHRASES

❑ **feed the dumb glutton** *v.* [it 'eats' the penis; note *double entendre* in D'Urfey, *Pills to Purge Melancholy* (1719); he is referring to a girl's 'kitty' and says 'I play'd with its Whiskers and would have had discourse,/But, ah! it was dumb and blind'] [mid-18C–19C] to have sexual intercourse.

dumbie *n.* [DUMMY *n.*[2]] [early 19C] (*Scot. Und.*) a pocket book.

dumbo *n.* [SE *dumb*, stupid/DUMB *n.* (1) + -O *sfx* (2). Note the Walt Disney cartoon *Dumbo* (1941), although the elephant in question was naïve rather than stupid] (*orig. US*) **1** [1930s+] a fool, a dullard; also a term of address. **2** [1950s] a foolish blunder.

dumbo *adj.* [DUMBO *n.* (1)] [1960s+] (*Aus.*) stupid, senile.

dumbshit *n.* [SE *dumb*, stupid + SHIT *n.* (2a)] [1960s+] (*US*) a fool; thus as term of address.

dumbshit *adj.* (*also* **dumshit**) [DUMBSHIT *n.*] [1960s+] (*US*) stupid.

dumby *n. see* DUMBARTON *n.*

dum-dum *n.*[1] (*also* **dumb-dumb**) [redup. DUMB *n.* (1)] (*orig. US*) **1** [1930s+] a fool, an idiot, a general term of abuse; also as adj. **2** [1970s] the penis.

dum-dum *n.*[2] (*also* **dumb-dumb**) [SE *dumb* + redup.] [1940s+] (*orig. US*) a deaf mute.

dumfoozled *adj. see* BAMBOOZLED *under* BAMBOOZLE *v.*

dumfound *v.* [late 17C–mid-19C] (*UK Und.*) to beat, to thrash.

dummacker *n.* [? development of DUNAKER *n.*] [mid-19C–1900s] a knowing, aware person.

dummee *n. see* DUMMY *n.*[2].

dummerer *n.* (*also* **dummerar**) [DOMMERER *n.*] [17C–mid-18C; 1920s] a beggar who fakes dumbness in order to gain alms.

dummie *n.*[1] *see* DUMMY *n.*[1] (6).

dummie *n.*[2] *see* DUMMY *n.*[2].

dummied up *adj.* [DUMMY UP *v.*[1] (2)] [1920s+] (*US Und.*) silent, e.g. under interrogation.

dummo *n.* (*also* **dummox**) [var. DUMBO *n.* (1)] [1970s] (*US*) a fool.

dummock *n.* [Yorks. dial. + ? Rom. *dummock*, back] [late 19C] the buttocks.

dummy *n.*[1] [SE *dumb*; note Egan, *Life in London* (1821): 'A cant phrase for a stupid fellow; a man who has not a word to say for himself. The family of the *dummies* is very numerous'] **1** [late 16C+] a dumb (i.e. mute) person. **2** [19C+] a fool, an idiot. **3** [mid-19C; 1910s+] a deaf mute, or a tramp or beggar who pretends to be deaf and dumb. **4** [1920s] (*US Und.*) a detective. **5** [1930s] (*UK Und.*) one who poses as the law-abiding owner of an establishment, e.g. a nightclub, to shield the criminal who is the actual owner. **6** [1930s+] (*also* **dummie**) a retarded person; also attrib. **7** [1950s+] (*N.Z. Und.*) solitary confinement; the solitary confinement/punishment cell in a prison (the inmate is forced to be silent).

IN COMPOUNDS

❑ **dummy dust** *n.* [a drug that appeals to or creates a *dummy* (i.e. sense 2 above) + DUST *n.* (6e)] [1970s+] (*drugs*) phencyclidine.

IN PHRASES

❑ **catch a dummy** *v.* [1970s] (*US prison*) to refuse to talk. ❑ **dummy out** *v.* [1970s] (*drugs*) to lose awareness and coordination through drug use. ❑ **go on the dummy** *v.* [1930s–70s] (*US*) to stop talking, to be quiet.

dummy *n.*[2] (*also* **dummee, dummie**) [Hotten (1864) suggests that money in a pocket-book or wallet makes no noise, while coins in a purse chink together] [early 19C+] a pocket-book, a wallet.

IN COMPOUNDS

❑ **dummy-hunter** *n.* [late 19C–1900s] a pickpocket specializing in stealing wallets.

IN PHRASES

❑ **hunt the dummy** *v.* [19C] to steal pocket-books.

dummy *n.*[3] [its silence or its use for sucking on] [mid-19C+] the penis.

IN PHRASES

❑ **beat one's/the dummy** *v.* (*also* **cuff one's dummy, flog..., whip...**) [1930s+] to masturbate; thus *dummy flogger*, a masturbator.

dummy *n.*[4] [SE *dummy*, i.e. both being suckable] **1** [late 19C+] (*Can./UK/US Und.*) bread. **2** [20C+] an empty bottle.

dummy *n.*[5] [they are effectively SE *dummy*, or fake] **1** [1920s] (*UK Und.*) a mannequin, garbed in a coat hung with bells, used to train pickpockets. **2** [1930s–60s] (*US Und.*) a roll of counterfeit money. **3** [1960s+] (*drugs*) poor-quality or fake drugs.

dummy *v.* [1960s] (*US Und.*) to disguise.

dummy-chucker *n.* [CHUCK A DUMMY *under* CHUCK *v.*[2]] **1** [1910s–30s] (*US*) one who throws fake fits. **2** [2000s] in fig. use, an attention-grabber.

dummy up *v.*[1] [DUMMY *n.*[1] (3)] (*orig. US*) **1** [1920s] to pose as a mute. **2** [1920s+] to stop talking, to keep quiet. **3** [1950s] to keep something secret.

dummy up *v.*[2] [SE *dummy*, a sham] [1950s+] (*US*) to concoct a fraud, to fake something up.

dump *n.*[1] [SE *dump*, a coin worth 1s 3d (6½p), formerly current in Australia, made by punching a disc out of the middle of a Spanish dollar and milling the edge] (*Aus./US*) **1** [19C+] a small coin or small sum of money. **2** [mid-19C–1900s] a button, often as sold by a street-hawker; thus *not care a dump*, not care at all. **3** [1950s] a marble. **4** [1960s+] a bill or fare.

IN COMPOUNDS

❑ **dump-fencer** *n.* [-FENCER *sfx*] [mid-19C] a button-seller.

IN PHRASES

❑ **not worth a dump** *adj.* [1910s] (*Aus.*) utterly worthless.

dump *n.*[2] [? abbr. SE *dumpling*] [mid–late 19C; 1960s] (*US*) a short, fat person.

dump *n.*[3] [SE *dump*, a pile or heap of refuse or other matter 'dumped' or thrown down] (*orig. US*) **1** [late 19C–1960s] (*US tramp*) a lodging house or criminal rendezvous. **2** [late 19C+] an unpleasant, disgusting and unappealing place. **3** [20C+] a place in general. **4** [1900s–30s] (*US Und.*) a prison. **5** [1910s] (*US Und.*) a restaurant. **6** [1920s+] one's home, irrespective of its appearance. **7** [1960s] (*Aus.*) a rest, a sleep.

SE in slang uses

IN PHRASES

❑ **get the dump** *v.* [1910s] to be thrown out, ejected. ❑ **take a dump** *v. see* DUMP *v.* (7).

dump *n.*[4] [SE *dump*, a heap] **1** [1940s+] (*orig. US*) an act of defecation. **2** [1950s+] (*drugs*) the vomiting that may follow an injection of heroin. **3** [1970s+] (*orig. US*) a piece of excrement.

IN PHRASES

❑ **take a dump** *v.* [1940s+] (*orig. US*) to defecate, usu. in sense of incontinence.

dump *n.*[5] [DUMP *v.* (1)] [1990s+] (*US prison*) a rejection of parole.

dump *v.* [SE *dump*, to throw down in a lump or mass] **1** [late 18C+] (*orig. US*) to get rid of, to dispose of. **2** [mid-19C+] (*US*) to injure or kill by gunfire. **3** [20C+] to beat up; to knock down. **4** [1940s] (*US*) to confess, to betray. **5** [1940s–70s] to murder. **6** [1940s+] to jilt, to terminate a relationship. **7** [1950s+] (*also* **take a dump**) to lose a game, esp. on purpose. **8** [1950s+] (*orig. US campus*) (*also* **dump it out**) to defecate. **9** [1950s+] (*drugs*) to vomit through drug withdrawal sickness, or on first taking a drug. **10** [1960s] to dismiss from a job. **11** [1960s] (*US prison*) to reject a parole application. **12** [1960s] (*US*) to leave. **13** [1970s] to defeat, to ruin. **14** [1980s] (*US black*) to attack verbally.

IN PHRASES

❑ **dump one's change** *v.* [2000s] (*US black/drugs*) to excrete bags of drugs after swallowing them when facing a police search. ❑ **dump one's load** *v. see* DUMP A/ONE'S LOAD *under* LOAD *n.*

SE in slang uses

IN PHRASES

❑ **dump on** *v. see* separate entries. ❑ **dump someone in it** *v. see* LAND SOMEONE IN THE SHIT *under* SHIT *n.*

dumper *n.*[1] [DUMP *v.* (3)] [1950s] (*US*) a sexual sadist (poss. with an obsession with excrement/defecation), usu. as encountered by prostitutes.

dumper *n.*[2] [ety. unknown] [1960s+] (*N.Z. Und.*) a racecourse detective.

dumper *n.*[3] [one who should be thrown into a SE *dumpster*, a large rubbish container or skip] [1970s] (*US*) an ageing prostitute, i.e. over 40.

SE in slang uses

IN PHRASES

❑ **in the dumper** [1980s+] **1** out of favour, rejected, thrown away. **2** lost, ruined, good for nothing.

dumpie *n.* (*also* **dumpy**) [1960s+] (*S.Afr.*) a non-returnable 340ml (12fl oz) beer bottle.

dumpling *n.* **1** [early 18C+] in pl., the female breasts; thus [20C+] (*Aus.*) *her dumplings are boiling over*, her breasts are falling out of a low-cut dress. **2** [late 19C] a native of Norfolk [such individuals are supposed to be excessively fond of *dumplings*].

SE in slang uses

IN COMPOUNDS

❑ **dumpling depot** *n.* [boxing jargon] [mid-19C] the stomach.

dump on *v.*[1] (*also* **dump all over**) [SE *dump*] (*orig. US*) **1** [1940s+] to criticize, to abuse. **2** [1950s–70s] to better in an argument; thus *dumped on*, abused, out-argued. **3** [1960s–70s] to reject, e.g. a lover, an application to join a club or fraternity etc. **4** [1970s+] to impose oneself or one's emotions on another person. **5** [1980s] to shoot dead, to wound.

dump on *v.*[2] [ext. DUMP *v.* (8)] [1970s+] (*US*) to defecate.

dumptruck *n.*[1] [the perceived 'masculinity' of the SAmE *dump truck*] [1970s] (*US gay*) **1** a car full of lesbians. **2** a masculine lesbian.

SE in slang uses

IN COMPOUNDS

❑ **dumptruck date** *n.* [1980s+] (*US campus*) an overweight woman.

dumptruck *n.*[2] [? one can DUMP *v.* (1) all one's troubles on them or their incompetence *dumps* one in jail] [1970s+] (*US Und.*) a public defender.

dumptruck *v.* [DUMP *v.* (8); the image of losing control of one's bowels + pun] [1960s+] (*US prison*) to fail through a lack of nerve and courage, rather than through actual physical inadequacy.

dumpty *n.* (*also* **dumpty-doo, dumpy**) [? DUNNY *n.*[2] (1), but note DUMP *v.* (8)] [1960s+] (*Aus./N.Z.*) an outside privy.

dumpy *n. see* DUMPIE *n.*

dumpy *adj.* [DUMP *n.*[3] (2)] [1930s–80s] of a place, dirty, run-down, squalid.

dumshit *n. see* DUMBSHIT *n.*

dunaker *n.* (*also* **donaker**) [DUNNOCK *n.*] [late 17C–18C] a cow-stealer.

Dunbar wether *n.* [the fishing trade of *Dunbar*, Scotland + SE *wether*, a castrated ram] [late 19C] a red herring.

duncarring *n.* [? a proper name or corruption of DUNNAKEN *n.*] [late 17C–18C] the practice of male homosexuality.

dunced out *adj.* [SE *dunce*] [1960s–70s] (*US*) dumbfounded, stupid.

duncehead *n.* [SE *dunce* + -HEAD *sfx* (1)] **1** [mid-19C+] (*US*) (*also* **dunce-cap**) a fool, a simpleton. **2** [1980s] (*US black*) one who shows off, 'acts the fool'.

dundee *adj.* [? SE *done*] [1950s] (*US*) exhausted.

dunde(r)funk *n. see* DANDYFUNK *n.*

dundus *n.* (*also* **doondoos**) [Kongo *ndundu*, an albino] [1940s+] (*W.I.*) **1** an albino. **2** a freak.

dune coon *n.* [SE (*sand-*)*dune* + COON *n.* (5)] [1990s+] an Arab.

dunegan *n. see* DUNNAKEN *n.*

dung *n.* [mid-18C tailors' jargon *dung*, a tailor who accepts the master's terms without argument, or who works when his fellows are striking; the *dung* is 'soft' (and disgusting), while the union man, the *flint*, is 'hard' (and admirable)] [late 18C–19C] a workman who accepts less than union wages; thus a strike-breaker.

SE in slang uses

IN COMPOUNDS

❑ **dung-puncher** *n.* (*also* **dung-pusher**) [1960s+] (*Aus.*) a derog. term for a male homosexual. ❑ **dung-stabber** *n.* [1990s+] the penetrative partner in anal sex.

dunga *n.*[1] (*also* **dunger**) [? 'combining "donger" and "punga", the tree fern with the suggestive penis shape' (McGill, *Dict. of Kiwi Sl.*, 1988)] [1980s+] (*N.Z.*) **1** the penis. **2** a general term of abuse.

dunga *n.*[2] *see* DUNGER *n.*[1].

dungaree *adj.* [Hind. *dungrī*, a coarse calico; also name of a disreputable Bombay suburb] [mid-19C] (*Anglo-Ind.*) low, common, vulgar.

dungeon *n.* **1** [1930s] (*US black*) a gun. **2** [1990s+] (*UK prison*) an open area on the floor of a wing used for recreation, association etc. **3** [2000s] a prison.

dungeon head *n.* [1960s] (*US*) a fool.

dunger *n.*[1] (*also* **dunga**) [echoic of the engine noises] [1980s+] (*Aus./N.Z.*) anything, usu. mechanical, that is worn out or malfunctioning, e.g. an old car.

dunger *n.*[2] *see* DUNGA *n.*[1].

dunghead *n. see* DUNHEAD *n.*

dunghill *n.*[1] [cock-fighting jargon *dunghill*, any cock but a fighting cock] [mid-18C–early 19C] a coward.

IN PHRASES

❑ **die dunghill** *v. see under* DIE *v.*

dunghill *n.*[2]

SE in slang uses

IN PHRASES

❑ **moving dunghill** *n.* [late 18C–early 19C] a notably filthy man or woman.

dungle *n.* [ety. unknown] [1960s+] (*W.I.*) ordinary, second-rate, insignificant; also as n.

dunhead *n.* (*also* **dunghead**) [? colloq. *dunderhead*, but note DUNNY *n.*[2] (2), i.e. synon. with SHITHEAD *n.* (1)] [1950s] (*Aus.*) a general term of abuse.

dunk *v.* [baseball use *dunk*, to push (the ball) down through the basket, esp. by jumping so that the hand is above the level of the ring] **1** [1970s+] (*US gay*) to charge, to use a credit card. **2** [1990s+] (*US campus*) to humiliate someone. **3** [1990s+] (*US black*) to outwit, to overcome an opponent by an unorthodox move.

dunker *n.* [? one *dunks* the penis in the vagina] [1960s] a condom.

dunkie *n.* [var. DUNKER *n.*] [1990s+] a condom.

Dunkirk *n.* [rhy. sl.] [2000s] work.

Dunlop cheque *n.* [the *Dunlop* Rubber Company, i.e. a RUBBER CHEQUE *n.*] [1980s+] (*Aus.*) a cheque that has 'bounced', i.e. been marked 'return to drawer' by the bank.

Dunlop overcoat *n. see* OVERCOAT *n.* (3).

Dunlop tyre *n.* [rhy. sl.] [1960s+] a liar.

dunnage *n.* [naut. use *dunnage*, material such as brushwood or mats, used to protect valuable or easily broken cargo; ult. Low Ger. *dün*, thin, and *dünne Twige*, brushwood] [mid-19C+] **1** baggage, esp. carried by a tramp or a sailor. **2** clothes.

dunnaken *n.* (*also* **dunegan, dunnakin, dunnick, dunnigan, dunnikan, dunniken, dunyken**) [DANNA *n.* + KEN *n.*[1] (1); note synon. US carnival use *donniker*] **1** [late 18C–19C] a lavatory. **2** [1960s] a term of abuse.

IN COMPOUNDS

❑ **dunnigan worker** *n.* (*also* **donegan worker**) [WORKER *n.*[1] (1)] [1930s] (*US Und.*) a thief who hangs around public lavatories, hoping to steal from discarded coats or take parcels etc that have been put down.

dunnee *n. see* DUNNY *n.*[2].

dunnock *n.* (*also* **dunney**) [SE *dun*, brown, the colour of many cows] [18C–mid-19C] (*UK Und.*) a cow.

dunny *n.*[1] [? SE *dung*] [mid–late 18C] a bullock.

dunny *n.*[2] (*also* **dunnee**) [DUNNAKEN *n.*] [1930s+] (*Aus./N.Z.*) **1** any lavatory; thus *dunny cart*, a vehicle used to remove excrement; *dunny man*, a night-soil cleaner; *dunny roll*, lavatory paper. **2** an outside lavatory or privy.

IN COMPOUNDS

❑ **dunny-brush** *n.* [1980s+] (*Aus.*) a term of abuse. ❑ **dunny budgie** *n.* [facet. use of BUDGIE *n.*[2]; i.e. the size of noisiness of the flies is reminiscent of the bird] [1990s+] (*Aus.*) a fly. ❑ **dunny rat** *n.* [2000s] (*N.Z.*) a cunning person.

IN PHRASES

❑ **down the dunny** [2000s] (*N.Z.*) failed, disastrous. ❑ **flap like a dunny door in a high wind** *v.* [2000s] (*N.Z.*) to act in a panicky, nervous manner.

dunny *n.*[3] [1980s] (*W.I.*) money.

dunnyken *n. see* DUNNAKEN *n.* (1).

dunop *n. see* DOONUP *n.*

duns *n.* (*also* **dunsa, dunsie**) [SE *dun*] [1950s+] (*W.I. Rasta*) money.

dunsy *adj.* [SE *dunce*] [20C+] (*Ulster*) foolish, 'slow'.

dunt *n.* [DICK *n.*[1] (5) + CUNT *n.* (1)] [1980s+] (*US campus*) a person of ambivalent sexuality.

dunyken *n. see* DUNNAKEN *n.*

d-up *v.* [D *n.*[6]] [1990s+] **1** (*US black*) to protect oneself in those areas of one's life where one might be vulnerable. **2** to defecate [pun on sense 1 + initial letter of SE *defecate*].

dup *v.* [DUB *v.*[1] or SE *do up*, although this would imply closing, unless the image is of fastening the door] [17C–mid-19C] (*UK Und.*) to open (a door).

IN PHRASES

❑ **dup the jigger** *v.* (*also* **dup the giger, ...gigger**) [JIGGER *n.*[1] (1)] [mid-16C–mid-19C] (*UK Und.*) to open a door. ❑ **dup the ken** *v.* [KEN *n.*[1] (1)] [late 17C–18C] to enter a house.

dupa *n.* [Polish *dupa*, little ass] [20C+] (*US*) the buttocks, the posterior, often used as an affectionate term, esp. among Polish speakers or the families of Polish immigrants.

dupe *n.* [abbr.] [late 19C+] a *dup*licate, e.g. key, identification card.

dupe *v.* [1980s+] (*US campus*) to abuse, to do wrong to.

dupey-dupe *n.* [1970s+] a foolishly naïve (young) police officer.

duppy *v.* [2000s] (*UK black*) to kill, to murder.

duracs *n. see* DRACS *n.*

durag *n. see* DO-RAG *n.*

Durban poison *n.* (*also* **Durban, D.P.**) [similarity in pron. between Afk. *gif*, poison and KIF *n.*/KIF *adj.*] [1960s+] (*orig. S.Afr.*) an exceptionally well-regarded variety of marijuana, grown near Durban, Natal.

dur-brain *n.* (*also* **duh-brain**) [echoic of the stupid person's grunt DUH! *excl.* or *dur*] [1990s+] (*UK juv.*) a fool.

dur-brained *adj.* (*also* **durr-brained**) [DUR-BRAIN *n.*] [2000s] stupid, idiotic.

Durbs *n.* [abbr.] [1970s+] (*S.Afr.*) *Durb*an.

durgen *n.* [ety. unknown] [late 17C–early 19C] an insignificant person.

Durham man *n.* [proper name *Durham*, home of high-quality mustard, which was ground between two stones] [late 18C–early 19C] one whose knees knock or rub together.

duria *n.* [ety. unknown] [mid-19C] (*UK Und.*) fire.

durn *n.* [19C+] a euph. for DAMN *n.*; usu. found in phrs., e.g. *I don't give a durn*, I couldn't care less.

durn *adj. see* DARN *adj.*

durnation! *excl. see* DARNATION! *excl.*

durned *adj. see* DARNED *adj.*

durog *n.* [poss. misreading of DUROS *n.*] [1970s+] (*drugs*) marijuana.

duros *n.* [Sp. *duros*, hard, i.e. tough] [1970s] (*drugs*) marijuana.

durr-brained *adj. see* DUR-BRAINED *adj.*

durry *n.* [? Ulster *durrie*, anything small; ? link to rolling tobacco Bull *Dur*ham] [1940s+] (*Aus./N.Z.*) **1** a cigarette butt. **2** a cigarette, esp. when hand-rolled.

durry *v.* [DURRY *n.* (2)] [1960s+] (*N.Z.*) usu. of adolescents, to smoke illicitly.

durrynacker *n.* [Rom. *dukker*, to tell fortunes] [mid-19C] a female lace-hawker, who may also tell fortunes to her customers.

durrynacking *n.* (*also* **durynacking, duryking**) [DURRYNACKER *n.*] [mid-19C] **1** begging. **2** fortune-telling, under the guise of lace-selling, usu. practised by gypsy women.

dush *n. see* DOSH *n.*

dusky *adj.* [early 19C+] used to describe a black person; also *dusk*, spec. describing an Indian.

dust *n.* [lit. and fig. uses of SE *dust*] **1** [17C–19C] money [? SE *gold-dust*, but note the religious equation of money with dirt; note Egan, *Book of Sports* (1832): 'Sovereigns were golden dust, which blew about in the breath of his opinion']. **2** [mid-18C–1920s] a fight, an argument, a disturbance [the dust kicked up]. **3** [late 18C–19C] excrement. **4** [late 18C–19C] in fig. use, nothing, a worthless object. **5** as powdery substances. (**a**) [mid–late 19C] (*Aus.*) gunpowder. (**b**) [late 19C–1930s] (*Aus.*) flour; thus as v. *dust*, to fill (a bag) with flour [note S. & O'B.: 'Overground flour is said to be killed and known as dust [...] No doubt unscrupulous squatters were not above buying and keeping inferior flour for travellers, who gave it the nicknames of dust, and by transference it has become general for all flour']. (**c**) [1900s–80s] (*Aus./US*) tobacco. (**d**) [1910s] (*US Navy*) salt. (**e**) [1930s+] (*US*) rolling tobacco. **6** in drug uses [all these drugs (except marijuana) come in powdered form]. (**a**) [1910s+] (*also* **Jesus dust**) heroin. (**b**) [1910s+] cocaine. (**c**) [1940s–50s] morphine. (**d**) [1950s] marijuana. (**e**) [1970s+] phencyclidine. (**f**) [1980s+] marijuana mixed with phencyclidine, cocaine or any other powdered drug.

IN COMPOUNDS

❑ **dustbag** *n.* [late 19C–1900s] (*US*) a wallet. ❑ **dust bunny** *n.* [2000s] (*US drugs*) a user of phencyclidine. ❑ **dusthead** *n.* [-HEAD *sfx* (4)] [1970s+] a phencyclidine user or addict. ❑ **dust joint** *n.* [JOINT *n.* (5c)] [1970s+] (*drugs*) a cigarette made with phencyclidine.

IN PHRASES

❑ **down with one's dust** *v.* [mid-17C–mid-19C] to lay down one's money, esp. as imper. ❑ **kick up a dust** *v.* **1** [mid-18C+] (*also* **raise a dust**) to cause a commotion. **2** [19C] to die.

SE in slang uses

IN COMPOUNDS

❑ **dust-bin** *n.* [1940s] (*US black*) a grave. ❑ **dust-cutter** *n.* [late 19C–1950s] (*US*) a drink, esp. as a 'pick-me-up' or 'reviver'.

IN PHRASES

❑ **bite the dust** *v.* (*also* **chew dust, lick the dust**) [US Wild West cliché] **1** [mid-18C+] to die. **2** [mid–late 19C] to fall over. **3** [late 19C+] (*Aus./US*) to be defeated or prevailed over. ❑ **dampen the dust** *v. see under* DAMP *v.*[1]. ❑ **dust it away** *v.* [late 17C–early 19C] 'to drink about' (Grose, 1785). ❑ **no dust on** [the image of dust gathering on a conservative or old-fashioned person] [late 19C] (*US*) up to the minute, highly fashionable. ❑ **take the dust** *v.* (*also* **chew dust**) [the *dust* emanating from the passing vehicle] [late 19C–1950s] (*US*) to be overtaken in a car.

dust *adj.* [SE *dust*, the condition of human decay] [1980s+] (*US campus*) ruined, utterly exhausted; in serious trouble.

dust *v.*[1] [image of knocking the dust from someone's coat or jacket] **1** [early 17C; 19C+] to thrash, to beat up, to hit hard. **2** [1960s+] (*US*) to defeat. **3** [1970s+] to kill, to murder. **4** [1980s+] (*US campus*) to humiliate, to insult.

IN PHRASES

❑ **dust off** *v.* **1** [1930s+] to finish off. **2** [1930s+] (*US*) to beat up. **3** [1940s+] (*US*) (*also* **give someone the dust off**) to reject, to snub. **4** [1980s] to kill. ❑ **dust someone's jacket** *v.* (*also* **dust someone's back/coat/drabs/linen**) [late 17C–1910s] to thrash, to beat someone up. ❑ **dust the floor/furniture with** *v. see* WIPE THE FLOOR (WITH) *v.* ❑ **dust the sidewalk** *v.* [late 19C–1900s] to beat up thoroughly, to defeat comprehensively.

dust *v.*[2] (*also* **dust along/it/off/out**) [all reflect an image of the dust raised by one's speedy movement] **1** [mid-17C; mid-19C+] (*orig. US*) to rush off, to leave fast. **2** [late 19C+] (*US*) (*also* **dust out**) to overtake, to pass on the road. **3** [1930s+] (*US*) (*also* **dust off**) to get rid of, to jilt. **4** [1950s] to pursue.

IN PHRASES

❑ **dust one's broom** *v.* [1930s–50s] (*US black*) to leave. ❑ **get up and dust** *v.* [mid-19C–1910s] (*US*) to act energetically; to run off quickly.

dust *v.*[3] ['throw dust in one's eyes'] **1** [early 19C] (*also* **dust down**) to deceive, to mislead. **2** [1950s] (*US*) to tease, to hoax.

dustbin (lid) *n.* **1** [20C+] a child [= KID *n.*[1] (1)]. **2** [1990s+] (*UK juv.*) a handicapped person, esp. one suffering the after-effects of Thalidomide [= FLID *n.* (1)].

dusted *adj.*[1] [DUST *v.*[1] (1)] **1** [1930s+] beaten, defeated, killed. **2** [1980s+] shamed, humiliated.

dusted *adj.*[2] [SE *dust*, to clean up] **1** [1950s–70s] (*drugs*) having consumed and finished off a drug. **2** [1960s] (*US campus*) drunk.

dusted *adj.*[3] [DUST *n.* (6e)] [1970s+] (*drugs*) under the influence of phencyclidine.

duster *n.*[1] [abbr.] [1910s] (*Aus.*) a knuckle*duster*.

duster *n.*[2] [DUST *v.*[2]] [1930s] (*US tramp*) one who steals from freight trains or box cars.

duster *n.*[3] [DUST *v.*[2] (1)] [1940s] (*US black*) the act of moving; usu. in phrs. *dig a duster, collar a duster*.

duster *n.*[4] [RUSTY-DUSTY *n.*] [1940s+] (*US black*) the buttocks, the posterior.

(IN PHRASES)

❑ **on someone's duster** [1970s] harassing, persecuting someone.

duster *n.*[5] [DUST *v.*[1] (1) + ? late 19C NYC gang the Hudson *Dusters*] [1950s] (*US Und.*) a thug.

duster *n.*[6] [DUST *n.* (6)] **1** [1960s–70s] a cigarette laced with heroin. **2** [1970s+] (*drugs*) a user of phencyclidine.

dusters *n.* [? boastful image of testicles that hang so low as to 'dust' the floor] [1950s+] (*orig. milit.*) the testicles.

dustie *n.*[1] [DUST *n.* (6) + sfx *-ie*] [1950s] (*US drugs*) a narcotics user.

dustie *n.*[2] *see* DUSTY *n.*[1].

dusting *n.*[1] [DUST *v.*[1] (1) + sfx *-ing*] [late 18C+] a beating or thrashing.

dusting *n.*[2] [DUST *n.* (6) + sfx *-ing*] [1960s] (*drugs*) adding phencyclidine, heroin or another drug to marijuana.

dustman *n.*[1] [the line in the Church of England burial service: 'ashes to ashes and dust to dust'] [late 18C–early 19C] a corpse.

dustman *n.*[2] [he throws *sleep-dust* (or sand) into sleepy eyes] [19C] (*usu. nursery*) sleep personified; thus soothing phr. *the dustman's coming*.

(IN COMPOUNDS)

❑ **dustman's bell** *n.* [Victorian dustman rang a bell] [late 19C] (*nursery*) bedtime.

dustman *n.*[3] [DUST *v.*[1]; he thumps the pulpit as he preaches] [mid–late 19C] an energetic, fanatical preacher.

dusty *n.*[1] (*also* **dustie**) [abbr. + sfx *-y*] [mid–late 19C] a *dust*man.

dusty *n.*[2] [one of a set of words implying the physical disintegration of the body as one ages] **1** [1970s] (*US black*) an old record. **2** [1980s+] (*UK society*) a very old person, 70 years old and onwards.

dusty *adj.*[1] [17C SE *dusty*, worthless, distasteful; ult. *dust*, rubbish, garbage] **1** [mid-19C] (*US*) tough, dangerous. **2** [mid-19C+] of a person, uncouth, unattractive; of a thing, bad. **3** [1980s+] (*US campus*) tetchy, irritable, out of sorts.

(IN COMPOUNDS)

❑ **dusty pup** *n.* [1950s] (*Aus.*) an unpleasant person, a synon. for 'dirty dog'.

(IN PHRASES)

❑ **not so dusty** *adj.* [mid-19C+] surprisingly good, not as bad as expected or advertised.

SE in slang uses

(IN COMPOUNDS)

❑ **dusty bob** *n.* [early 19C] a chimney sweep. ❑ **dusty bread** *n.* [? the poor quality of everyday bread] [1970s] (*US black*) a conventional, conservative woman. ❑ **dusty butt** *n.* [BUTT *n.*[1] (1a)] **1** [1900s–50s] (*US black*) a low-grade, unattractive prostitute. **2** [1960s] (*US*) a short person [joc. ref. to their proximity to the ground]. ❑ **dusty diamonds** *n. see* BLACK DIAMONDS *under* BLACK *adj.* ❑ **dusty line** *n. see under* LINE *n.*[1].

dusty *adj.*[2] [there is *dust* in one's eyes] [1970s] (*US black*) unclear, unable to predict the future.

dusty *adj.*[3] [DUST *n.* (6)] [1990s+] (*US drugs*) pertaining to narcotic use.

Dutch *n.*[1] [Ger. *Deutsch*] **1** [late 14C–mid-17C; mid-19C–1950s] (*US*) the German language. **2** [mid-19C+] (*US*) a German. **3** [1900s–50s] a nickname for a German.

SE in slang uses

(IN PHRASES)

❑ **do a Dutch** *v.* [late 19C] (*orig. US*) **1** to leave without paying. **2** to remove one's possessions (and oneself) from a rented apartment or house without paying one's rent. ❑ **in Dutch** [one who has fig. succumbed to the DUTCH ACT *n.*] [20C+] (*US*) in trouble, out of favour.

Dutch *n.*[2] [abbr. colloq. *double Dutch*] [mid-19C+] (*US*) nonsense, incomprehensible rubbish.

Dutch *n.*[3] (*US*) **1** [mid-19C+] bad temper, irascibility [stereotyping]. **2** [1960s+] a crewcut haircut [confusion between Dutch and *Deutsch*, German].

Dutch *n.*[4] [1990s+] (*US*) intercourse between the breasts.

Dutch *adj.*[1] [17C+] a derog. racial stereotype, meaning stolid, miserly, dour and bad-tempered, and used as such in the combs. below.

(IN COMPOUNDS)

❑ **Dutch act** *n. see* separate entry. ❑ **Dutch almanac** *n.* [late 17C] gibberish. ❑ **Dutch auction** *n.* [mid-19C+] a mock auction or sale in which the much-touted 'reductions' have no bearing in commercial fact. ❑ **Dutch bargain** *n.* [17C] **1** a one-sided bargain. **2** a deal concluded over drinks. ❑ **Dutch bath** *n.* [20C+] (*US*) a very cursory wash. ❑ **Dutch boy** *n.* [play on the story of the 'little Dutch boy' who 'put his finger in the dyke'] [1990s+] (*US gay*) a man, irrespective of sexuality, who enjoys the company of lesbians. ❑ **Dutch build** *n.* [19C] a stocky, thickset individual. ❑ **Dutch-buttocked** *adj.* [SE *Dutch-buttocked*, of cattle, having large hind-quarters] [late 17C] fat, 'broad in the beam'. ❑ **Dutch cheese** *n.* [the Dutch Edam cheese, which is round, red and shiny] [19C] a bald person. ❑ **Dutch clock** *n.* **1** [late 19C] the vagina [f. sense 2]. **2** [late 19C–1910s] a woman [resemblance of a woman's face to a clockface]. ❑ **Dutch comfort** *n.* [late 18C–early 19C] a style of comforting in which the speaker intones 'Thank God it is no worse'. ❑ **Dutch concert** *n.* (*also* **Dutch medley**) [late 18C–19C] any performance in which each musician plays a different tune; thus a general pej. for a bad performance, musical or metaphorical. ❑ **Dutch consolation** *n.* [mid–late 19C] a style of comforting in which the speaker intones 'Thank God it is no worse'. ❑ **Dutch courage** *n. see* separate entry. ❑ **Dutch daub** *n.* (*also* **Dutch dab**) [orig. the second-rate Dutch still-lifes that were imported in bulk into the US during the 1880s, an influx that was slowed only by the imposition of a 35% duty on such pictures] [late 19C] (*US*) a badly executed picture. ❑ **Dutch distemper** *n.* [the disproportionately large number of Dutch (or Germans) in the prison population] [early–mid-19C] (*US*) gaol fever. ❑ **Dutch doggery** *n.* [DOGGERY *n.*[1], reinforced by the stereotypical surliness of the Dutch] [mid-19C] a grog-shop. ❑ **Dutch doll** *n.* [mid-19C] a woman's silk scarf. ❑ **Dutch door** *n.* [she 'swings both ways'] [1990s+] a bisexual woman. ❑ **Dutch drops** *n.* [mid-19C] Hollands gin, genever. ❑ **Dutch dumplings** *n.* [1950s–70s] (*gay*) the buttocks. ❑ **Dutch fair** *n.* [mid-19C] a warehouse fire. ❑ **Dutch father** *n. see* DUTCH UNCLE *n.* ❑ **Dutch feast** *n.* [the assumption is that he has monopolized the supply of alcohol] [late 18C–19C] any meal where the host gets drunk before his friends. ❑ **Dutch fit** *n.* [stereotype of the grumpy Dutch] [mid-19C] (*US*) a fit of temper, an explosion of rage. ❑ **Dutch foil** *n.* (*also* **Dutch gilding, ...gold, ...leaf, ...metal**) [late 18C; 1970s] (*US*) an alloy of 11 parts copper and two parts zinc, used as a substitute for gold leaf – and presumably passed off as such to the unwary. ❑ **Dutch fuck** *n.* [the implication in both is of meanness] **1** [1950s+] the lighting of one cigarette from another, thus saving matches. **2** [1990s+] (*US*) intercourse between the breasts; also as v. ❑ **Dutch fustian** *n.* [SE *fustian*, lofty or turgid language, accentuated by ref. to *HIGH DUTCH under* HIGH *adj.*[1]; note late 16C *fustian*, Und. or thieves' jargon] [late 16C–early 17C] nonsense. ❑ **Dutch girl** *n.* [pun on SE *dike* (i.e. the dikes that form the basis of Holland's coast defences)/DYKE *n.* (1)] [1930s+] a lesbian. ❑ **Dutch gleek** *n.* [derog. use of *Dutch* (implying generic drunkenness) + SE *gleek*, 'a game at cards, played by three persons; forty-four cards were used, twelve being dealt to each player, while the remaining eight formed a common "stock"' (*OED*)] [17C] any form of drinks. ❑ **Dutch guts** *n.* [GUT

n. (2a)] [1990s+] (*Aus.*) courage created by alcoholic intake. ▫ **Dutch leaf** *n. see* DUTCH FOIL above. ▫ **Dutch leave** *n.* [late 19C] (*US*) taking time off without permission, absenting oneself illegally. ▫ **Dutch lunch** *n. see* DUTCH TREAT *n.* ▫ **Dutchman** *n. see* separate entries. ▫ **Dutch medley** *n. see* DUTCH CONCERT above. ▫ **Dutch metal** *n. see* DUTCH FOIL above. ▫ **Dutch milk** *n.* [the stereotyping of Germans as beer-drinkers] [1900s–40s] (*orig. US black*) beer. ▫ **Dutch nerve** *n. see* DUTCH COURAGE *n.* ▫ **Dutch nightingale** *n.* [the implied inability of the Dutch to sing] [late 18C–mid-19C] a frog. ▫ **Dutch oven** *n.* [SE *Dutch oven*, a large pot that gains heat from coals placed around and on top of it] **1** [1920s] the mouth. **2** [1980s+] (*also* **Greek sauna**) the smell of a bed in which someone has just broken wind. **3** [1980s+] (*Aus. drugs*) an enclosed area or room filled with cannabis smoke [underpinned by Holland's liberal understanding of the harmless uses of cannabis]. ▫ **Dutch parliament** *n. see* DUTCH ROW below. ▫ **Dutch party** *n. see* DUTCH TREAT *n.* ▫ **Dutch pink** *n.* (*also* **pink**) [SE *Dutch pink*, a yellow lake pigment] [early–mid-19C] blood. ▫ **Dutch reckoning** *n.* [the poor image of Dutch businessmen] **1** [17C] a bill presented as a lump sum, with no details attached. **2** [17C] a bill that, if disputed, only gets higher. **3** [19C] (*naval*) a bad day's work. ▫ **Dutch rod** *n.* [ROD *n.* (2)] [1940s] (*US Und.*) a Luger pistol. ▫ **Dutch route** *n. see* DUTCH ACT *n.* ▫ **Dutch row** *n.* (*also* **Dutch parliament**) [note Fr. synon. *une querelle d'Allemand*, lit. a 'German argument'] [late 19C–1910s] a spurious argument, generating far more sound than any real fury. ▫ **Dutch rub** *n.* [1930s+] the act of rubbing one's knuckles hard across one's victim's skull. ▫ **Dutch salute** *n. see* IRISH TOOTHACHE *under* IRISH *adj.* ▫ **Dutch spunk** *n. see* DUTCH COURAGE *n.* ▫ **Dutch supper** *n. see* DUTCH TREAT *n.* ▫ **Dutch town** *n. see* separate entry. ▫ **Dutch treat** *n. see* separate entry. ▫ **Dutch uncle** *n. see* separate entry. ▫ **Dutch widow** *n.* [early 17C] a prostitute. ▫ **Dutch wife** *n.* [late 19C+] a bolster, otherwise defined as a 'masturbation machine'; in modern use, a blow-up sex doll.

IN PHRASES

▫ **Dutch by injection** [1920s+] of a woman, living with a foreigner. ▫ **Dutch it** *v.* [1910s+] to share expenses, usu. of a meal. ▫ **Dutch oneself out** *v.* [DUTCH ACT *n.*] [1950s] to commit suicide. ▫ **Dutch out** *v.* [mid-19C] (*US*) to give up, to let go of, as in a hold-up. ▫ **go Dutch** *v.* [1910s+] (*orig. US*) **1** to share expenses, esp. of a meal. **2** *see* DO THE DUTCH (ACT) *under* DUTCH ACT *n.* ▫ **take the Dutch route** *v.* [20C+] (*US prison*) to commit suicide.

Dutch *adj.*[2] [Eng. pron. of Ger. *Deutsch*, German, as 'Dutch'; popularized in the US by the growth of German settlements, notably in Pennsylvania] [early 17C+] German.

dutch *n.* [the precise origins of this term remain debatable. Either the term is an abbr. of SE *duchess*, strengthened by 17C RUM DUCHESS *under* RUM *adj.* and the rhy. sl. DUCHESS OF FIFE *n.*, or, according to the 19C music-hall star Albert Chevalier (1861–1923), whose signature song was entitled 'My Old Dutch', the term was semantically linked to another piece of sl., DIAL *n.*, face. In Chevalier's version, the original term was 'my old Dutch clock', whose face, i.e. dial, resembled that of his wife. Partridge, formerly a partisan of the Duchess, claimed to have changed his mind in the later editions of the *DSUE*. The *OED*, however, while citing Chevalier's song in 1893, has a previous citation, dated four years earlier, and states unequivocally that in this context *dutch* is 'an abbr. of duchess'] [late 19C+] a wife.

IN PHRASES

▫ **old dutch** *n.* [late 19C] a woman.

dutch *v.* [all racial stereotypes of Dutch] (*US*) **1** [1910s+] to ruin another's business, social standing, enjoyment etc with deliberate malice. **2** [1970s] to bet in such a way that the bank is broken. **3** [1970s] to speak emphatically. **4** *see* DO THE DUTCH (ACT) *under* DUTCH ACT *n.*

Dutch act *n.* (*also* **Dutch route**) [late 19C+] (*Can./US Und.*) suicide.

IN PHRASES

▫ **do the Dutch (act)** *v.* **1** [20C+] (*Can./US Und.*) (*also* **dutch, go Dutch**) to commit suicide. **2** [1970s] to run away, to flee.

Dutch courage *n.* (*also* **courage, Dutch nerve, ...spunk**) [coined as a propagandist measure during various Anglo-Dutch wars of 18C] **1** [19C+] cowardice that, fortified by generous quantities of alcohol, becomes (temporary) bravery; also as fortified by drugs. **2** [mid-19C] in fig. use, courage that is obtained through some form of non-alcoholic extra-personal aid, e.g. a weapon.

IN PHRASES

▫ **dry Dutch courage** *n. see under* DRY *adj.*[1].

Dutchman *n.* [Ger. *Deutsch*, German] **1** [17C+] (*US*) anyone of German (occas. Scandinavian) origin. **2** [1910s–30s] (*orig. US*) a foreigner, one who does not speak English well. **3** [1930s] a bar- or saloon-keeper [Germans were trad. linked to the brewing industry].

IN COMPOUNDS

▫ **Dutchman's drink** *n.* [19C] a drink that empties the pot or drains some form of communal drinking vessel. ▫ **Dutchman's headache** *n.* [19C] a state of drunkenness.

IN PHRASES

▫ **big Dutchman** *n.* [late 19C+] (*US*) a general term of disparagement. ▫ **I'm a Dutchman** *see* separate entry.

Dutchman, the *n.* [late 19C] Deutz and Gelderman champagne.

dutchmasta *n.* [brandname *Dutchmaster*] [1990s+] (*US black*) a cigar, esp. when its tobacco is removed and replaced by marijuana.

Dutch pegs *n.* [rhy. sl.] [20C+] legs.

Dutch (plate) *n.* [rhy. sl. = MATE *n.* (1)] [1960s+] a friend.

Dutch town *n.* [Ger. *Deutsch*, German + SE *town*] [20C+] (*US*) that area of a town predominantly populated by German immigrants or their descendants.

Dutch treat *n.* (*also* **Dutch lunch, ...party, ...supper**) [late 19C+] an outing, a visit to a restaurant etc, in which costs are shared equally, i.e. there is no 'treat' at all in the sense of one party being entertained at the other's expense; occas. as v.

Dutch uncle *n.* (*also* **Dutch father, uncle**) [mid-19C+] one who talks severely and critically, who lays down the law; usu. in phr. *talk like a Dutch uncle*; also attrib.

Dutchy *n.* **1** [late 18C+] a German; a nickname for a German. **2** [late 19C–1920s] a Dutchman.

Dutchy *adj.* [DUTCH *adj.*[2] + sfx *-y*] (*US*) **1** [mid-19C–1900s] typically German, esp. of recent immigrants who have yet to adapt to America and still retain their old-country crudities. **2** [1900s–10s] low-class, dowdy, slovenly [SE *Dutch*]. **3** [1940s] typically Dutch.

dutchy *n.* [20C+] (*W.I. Rasta*) **1** a Dutch cooking pot, a low, round-bottomed heavy pot. **2** a pipe or bowl used for smoking marijuana.

duty *n.*

IN PHRASES

▫ **do one's duty** *v.* [euph.] [20C+] to urinate, to defecate.

duzey *n. see* DOOZIE *n.*

D.V. *n.* [abbr.] [1970s+] (*US black*) Cadillac Coupe *De Ville*.

d.v. *n.* [the initials, but also a cynical ref. to Lat. *deo volente*, God willing] [late 19C] (*UK society*) divorce.

D.V.D.A. *n.* [1990s+] a variety of pornographic film that features double-vaginal and double-anal penetration.

dwaal *n.* [Afk. *dwaal*, to wander, to lose one's way] [1960s–70s] (*S.Afr.*) a daze, a confusion; esp. in phr. *in a dwaal*, in a daze.

dwang *n.*

IN PHRASES

▫ **in the dwang** [Afk. *dwing*, to force; but note dial. Scot. *dwang*, to struggle, to oppress] [1990s+] (*S.Afr.*) in trouble, in difficulties, constrained.

dweeb *n.* (*also* **dweeber, dweebie, dweeble**) [ety. unknown; ? the name of a lost SF alien] [1960s+] (*orig. US teen*) an idiot, one lacking social qualities; thus fem. as *dweebette*.

dweeb *adj.* [DWEEB *n.*] [1980s+] (*US*) stupid, foolish, ineffectual.

dweezle *n.* (*also* **dweasal**) [ety. unknown; ? a development of DWEEB *n.*] [1980s+] (*US campus*) a socially inept person.

-dweller *sfx* [1980s+] (*US campus*) a comb. form to indicate someone who frequents a particular place.

dwelling dancer *n.* [SE *dwelling* + DANCER *n.*] [1940s] (*Aus.*) a thief.

dwell in the box *v.* [1930s–50s] (*UK Und.*) to pickpocket at a racecourse.

d-whupped *adj. see* DICK-WHUPPED *under* DICK *n.*^{1}.

dyestuffs *n.* [a pun on SE + the metal *dies* used for printing notes] [mid–late 19C] (*US*) money.

dyke *see also under* DIKE and its combs.

dyke *n.* (*also* **dike**) [ety. unknown; ? f. *dyked down*, dressed up; certainly some lesbians have always dressed as men. Another theory suggests the gradual corruption of SE *hermaphrodite* to *morphodite* to *dike* and *dyke* and thence, with the masc. generic *bull*, to BULL-DYKE *n.* and *BULL-DAGGER under* BULL *n.*^{1}; however, the first use of BULL-DYKE *n.* appears to predate dyke, which may thus be an abbr.] [1930s+] a lesbian.

IN COMPOUNDS

❑ **dykeface** *n.* [1990s+] a general term of abuse, aimed at a woman; lit. 'lesbian-face'. ❑ **dyke-hag** *n.* [on pattern of FAG-HAG *n.*^{2} (1)] [2000s] (*S.Afr. gay*) a man, usu. heterosexual, whose friends are lesbians.

dyke *adj.* (*also* **dike**) [DYKE *n.*] [1930s+] pertaining to lesbians or lesbianism.

dyke *v.* (*also* **dike**) [DYKE *n.*] **1** [1940s] to engage in lesbian sex. **2** [1960s] to live as a lesbian.

dykey *adj.* (*also* **dikey, dykey-ass, dykish**) [DYKE *n.* + sfx *-y*] [1960s+] having the appearance or characteristics of a lesbian.

dykon *n.* [DYKE *n.* + SE *icon*] [1990s+] (*US gay*) a lesbian icon, such as Ellen Degeneres.

Dyna *n.* [abbr.] [1950s] (*US*) a Buick *Dyna*flow automobile.

dyna *n.*^{1} [abbr.] [1920s] *dyna*mite.

dyna *n.*^{2} [rhy. sl.; *dynamite* = SE *catamite*] [1960s] a male homosexual.

dynamite *n.*^{1} [the use of 'tea' as a codeword for *dynamite* as revealed during a trial of 1888; but note SE *gunpowder*, a fine, green-leafed tea, popular in the UK from the 1770s] [late 19C] tea.

dynamite *n.*^{2} [the strength and effect] (*drugs*) **1** [late 19C+] whisky. **2** [1920s+] heroin, morphine, esp. good-quality, highly potent drugs. **3** [1930s] cocaine. **4** [1930s] (*US prison*) a form of ersatz 'snuff' used by convicts; it is made of tobacco, soda, salt and sugar. **5** [1940s+] (*Aus.*) baking powder [it makes things 'blow up']. **6** [1940s+] (*also* **dynamiter**) hashish or marijuana; and as a prepared 'joint'. **7** [1950s+] a mixture of cocaine and morphine/heroin. **8** [1960s] (*US short order*) buttermilk. **9** [1960s+] any pure, undiluted drugs.

dynamite *adj.* **1** [20C+] very strong; intense. **2** [1920s+] (*also* **dynamo**) excellent, wonderful, first-rate; often as *dynamite!* wonderful! **3** [1930s+] very important, extremely effective; used both positively and negatively.

dynamite *v.* [i.e. to 'go off with a bang'] (*US*) **1** [1920s] to talk loudly, to complain, to make a fuss. **2** [1920s–50s] to talk in an aggressive manner, esp. when trying to sell something or seduce someone. **3** [1930s] to push something through, to make it happen fast.

dynamiter *n.* [DYNAMITE *v.*/DYNAMITE *n.*^{2} (3)] **1** [1910s–30s] (*US*) a sponger, a cadger. **2** [1920s–40s] (*US*) a very aggressive salesman. **3** [1930s–60s] (*US*) a very ambitious person, a trouble-maker. **4** [1950s] (*US drugs*) a cocaine user. **5** [1950s–60s] (*UK Und.*) a drug pusher.

dynamo *adj. see* DYNAMITE *adj.* (2).

dyno *n.*^{1} [DYNAMITE *n.*^{2}] **1** [1920s–60s] (*US prison*) a manual labourer. **2** [1940s–60s] (*drugs*) (*also* **dyno-pure**) heroin. **3** [1960s] (*US prison*) liquor. **4** *see* DINO *n.*^{2}.

dyno *n.*^{2} *see* DINO *n.*^{1} (1).

dyno *adj.*^{1} [DYNAMITE *n.*^{2} (2)] [1960s] (*drugs*) uncut, therefore stronger than usual; of heroin or any other drug.

dyno *adj.*^{2} [DYNAMITE *adj.* (2)] [1980s] (*US campus*) **1** pretty. **2** excellent, first-rate.

dyno-pure *n. see* DYNO *n.*^{1} (2).

dyno rouster *n. see under* DINO *n.*^{1}.

dyspepsia in a snow storm *n.* [late 19C] (*US*) an order of pie topped with powdered sugar.

d.y.w.y.k. *phr.* [abbr. *d*on't *y*ou *w*ish *y*ou *k*new] [late 19C] (*US campus*) a phr. of mocking dismissal and exclusion.

E *n.* (*also* **E-ball**) [abbr. ECSTASY *n.*] [1980s+] the popular nickname of the hallucinogenic drug MDMA (methylene dioxymethamphetamine).

E.A. *n. see* AMATEUR *n.* (1).

eager beaver *n.* [the ever-industrious beaver] [1940s+] (*orig. US*) an excessively earnest, keen person whose efforts are sometimes more notable for their sound and fury than their actual usefulness.

eager beaver *adj.* [EAGER BEAVER *n.*] [1940s+] earnest, usu. excessively so.

eagers, the *n.* [SE *eager*] [1920s–60s] (*US*) anxiety, apprehension or excessive keenness.

eager up *v.* [1960s] (*US*) to excite.

eagle *n.*[1] [? the strength of the predatory bird] [early 17C–early 18C] (*UK Und.*) a gambler, presumably a cheat, who wins.

eagle *n.*[2] [the eagle that appears on the coin or note] **1** [late 18C+] a $10 coin; thus *half-eagle*, a $5 coin, *double-eagle*, a $20 coin. **2** [mid–late 19C] a silver dollar. **3** [1920s+] a dollar bill.

IN COMPOUNDS

▫ **eagle day** *n.* (*also* **eagle's day**) [1940s+] (*US*) payday.

IN PHRASES

▫ **when the eagle shits** *n.* (*also* **when the eagle flies, ... screams, ...walks, ...the eagle's bowels move**) [the eagle engraved on the US silver dollar coin] [1940s+] (*orig. US milit./Aus.*) payday.

SE in slang uses

IN COMPOUNDS

▫ **eagle-beak** *n.* [the stereotypically large-nosed Jew] [1920s–50s] (*US*) a derog. term for a Jew. ▫ **eagle-hawking** *n.* [? shearing jargon *tomahawk*, to shear sheep badly] [1900s–10s] (*Aus.*) the shearing of dead or dying sheep in the bush in times of drought.

eagle *n.*[3] [the initial letter] [1960s] (*US campus*) the grade of E.

eagle eye *n.* [EYE *n.* (2) + SE *eagle-eyed*, keen-sighted] [1910s–30s] (*US Und.*) a detective.

eagle eye *v.* [EAGLE-EYED *adj.*] [1960s] (*US*) to look closely, to scrutinize.

eagle-eyed *adj.* [the visual acuity of the bird; note SE *eagle-eyed*, keen-sighted] [1900s] scrutinizing, paying close attention, watching.

ear *n.*[1] [resemblance] [mid-19C] (*US black*) a tuning peg on a guitar or fiddle.

SE in slang uses

DERIVATIVES

▫ **earful** *n. see* separate entry.

IN COMPOUNDS

▫ **earbash/basher/bashing** *see* separate entries. ▫ **earbiter/biting** *see* separate entries. ▫ **earflap** *n.* (*also* **earblock**) [mid-19C; 1930s] (*US*) an ear. ▫ **earguard** *n.* [SE *earguard*, a small flap attached to a cap and covering the ear] [1940s] (*Aus.*) short side-whiskers or sideboards. ▫ **earhole** *see* separate entries. ▫ **earhustle/hustler** *see* separate entries. ▫ **ear job** *n.* [JOB *n.*[2] (2)] **1** [1960s] (*US*) a kissing and caressing of someone's ear with the tongue. **2** [1970s] a phone call to a sexual phone service, sexually stimulating talk on the phone. ▫ **ear-lugger** *n.* [LUG *v.*[2] (1)] [20C+] (*Aus.*) a cadger, a scrounger. ▫ **ear man** *n.* [he picks it up *by ear*] [1970s] (*US black*) an individual expressing a natural ability to excel at an endeavour, a virtuoso. ▫ **ear music** *n.* [1970s] (*US black*) improvised music. ▫ **ear-piece** *n.* [1980s] (*UK black*) an ear. ▫ **ear sex** *n.* [1980s+] (*US*) an instance of sexually stimulating talk on the phone. ▫ **earwag** *v.* [1980s] (*N.Z.*) to gossip.

IN PHRASES

▫ **bend someone's ear** *v.* (*orig. US*) **1** [1930s+] to chatter on interminably and prob. tediously. **2** [1950s] to speak privately, to whisper. ▫ **bite someone's ear** *v.* [mid-19C+] **1** (*also* **beat someone's ears**) to nag, to importune. **2** to borrow money. ▫ **blow down someone's ear** *v.* (*also* **blow in someone's ear**) [1930s+] to whisper, esp. to whisper information (accurate or otherwise) that is intended to persuade the hearer to do what one wishes. ▫ **do on one's ear** *v.* [1940s+] (*Aus.*) to accomplish something easily. ▫ **ear between the legs** *n.* [resemblance] [19C] the labia minora. ▫ **ear of corn** *n.* [1910s–30s] (*US*) a country person. ▫ **from ears to crupper** *adv.* [horse imagery] [1900s] (*Aus.*) to the fullest extent. ▫ **get in someone's ear** *v.* [1970s] (*Aus.*) to ask questions. ▫ **get one's ears back** *v.* [1930s] (*US*) to get excited. ▫ **get on one's ear** *v.* [1920s] (*US*) to shout, to talk loudly and effusively. ▫ **get (up) on one's ear** *v.* (*also* **go off on one's ear, spin round on one's ear**) [late 19C+] (*US*) to lose one's temper, to become violently angry, to get embarrassed; thus excl. *get off my ear!* leave me alone! ▫ **have ears** *v.* [1940s+] (*orig. US black*) to listen; to be aware. ▫ **live in someone's ear** *v.* [20C+] (*Irish*) to live on very intimate terms. ▫ **on one's ear** **1** [late 19C+] (*US campus*) in a state of offended dignity, angry. **2** [late 19C+] (*orig. US*) in disgrace. **3** [1900s–40s] (*Aus.*) drunk. **4** [1920s+] amazed, overwhelmed. **5** [1930s+] (*US*) easily, with little effort; usu. in phr. *(one) could do that on one's ear* [var. on *DO SOMETHING STANDING ON ONE'S HEAD under* STAND *v.*[2]]. ▫ **on one's (pink) ear** [1910s–30s] (*Aus.*) down and out, homeless. ▫ **pin back one's ears** *v.* **1** [1920s+] to shock, to surprise. **2** [1940s+] (*orig. US*) to defeat, to punish verbally or physically, to reprimand. **3** [1950s+] to give one's full attention, esp. as *pin your ears back!* ▫ **pull down someone's ear** *v.* [late 19C–1920s] to extract money from someone. ▫ **pull in one's ear** *v.* [1910s–30s] (*US*) to mind one's own business. ▫ **pull in one's ears** *v.* [var. on SE phr. *pull in one's horns*] [1910s+] (*US*) to act cautiously, to minimize one's aggression. ▫ **put one's ears out** *v.* [1990s+] to listen for news, to gather information. ▫ **put on someone's ear** *v.* [the victim is knocked down, 'on their ear'] [late 19C–1900s] to set on, to attack. ▫ **spin round on one's ear** *v. see GET (UP) ON ONE'S EAR* above. ▫ **take it in the ear** *v.* [1960s+] (*US campus*) to be severely criticized. ▫ **take someone's ear off** *v.* [1930s+] (*orig. US*) to talk incessantly at someone. ▫ **with ears** *adv.* (*also* **with earflaps, with earlaps**) [the creation of fig. 'noise'] [1970s+] (*US*) to an extreme and insufferable degree.

IN EXCLAMATIONS

▫ **go soap your ear!** *see GO SOAK YOUR HEAD! under* SOAK *v.*[1].

ear *n.*[2] [mid-19C] (*US campus*) self-importance, dignity.

earbash *v.* (*also* **bash someone's ear**) [SE *ear* + BASH *v.* (1); lit. to 'hit one's ear'] [1940s+] (*orig. Aus./N.Z.*) **1** (*also* **earbang**) to talk incessantly; thus *ear-bash*, a chat. **2** to subject to one's opinions, grievances etc.

ear-basher *n.* (*also* **ear banger**) [EARBASH *v.* + sfx *-er*] [1940s+] (*orig. Aus./N.Z.*) a bore, a loudmouth who refuses to stop talking.

earbashing *n.* [EARBASH *v.* + sfx *-ing*] **1** [1940s+] (*orig. Aus.*) nagging, non-stop chatter. **2** [1990s+] (*UK black*) reprimands, scoldings.

ear-biter *n.* **1** [mid-19C] (*US*) a special agent of the US Post Office ['so-called because one of the agents about 1845 chewed off the ear of an opponent in a fight' (Craigie, *Dict. of American English*, 1944)]. **2** [1930s–50s] a cadger, one who seeks constantly to borrow money [*BITE SOMEONE'S EAR under* EAR *n.*[1]].

ear-biting *n.* [*BITE SOMEONE'S EAR under* EAR *n.*[1]] [1900s] (*Aus.*) cadging, begging.

earful *n.* **1** [20C+] (*US*) a forceful expression of opinion, esp. a complaint or rebuke. **2** [1910s–30s] information, the implication being that it is illicitly overheard.

IN PHRASES

❑ **get an earful** *v.* [1910s+] to listen to, usu. in the context of a scolding or criticism. ❑ **give an earful** *v.* [1910s+] to assail verbally. ❑ **say an earful** *v.* [1930s] to make things clear.

earhole *n.* **1** [mid-19C+] the ear. **2** [20C+] a toady, a sycophant. **3** [1960s] an act of listening, of eavesdropping.

IN PHRASES

❑ **on the earhole** (*also* **on the Happy New 'Ear**) [one is talking into a victim's *earhole*] [1910s+] (*UK Und.*) on the scrounge.

earhole *v.* [1950s+] to listen, to overhear, to eavesdrop.

ear hustle *v.* [1990s+] (*US black/prison*) to eavesdrop.

ear hustler *n.* [EAR HUSTLE *v.*] [1990s+] (*US black*) a gossip, an eavesdropper.

Earl *n.* [echoic] used in phr. pertaining to vomiting.

IN PHRASES

❑ **call Earl** *v.* [1980s+] (*Aus./US*) to vomit.

earl *v.* [echoic] [1960s+] (*US*) to vomit; thus *call earl, go to see earl, earl's knocking at the door.*

earl of Cork *n.*[1] ['the worst ace and the poorest card in the pack', so called from the contemporary earl, who was the poorest nobleman in Ireland] [mid-19C] (*Anglo-Irish*) the ace of diamonds.

earl of Cork *n.*[2] (*also* **duke of Cork**) [rhy. sl.] [1940s] **1** a talk. **2** a walk.

early *adj.* [1980s+] (*US black*) up-to-date.

SE in slang uses

IN COMPOUNDS

❑ **early Battersea** *n.* [the stereotyping of Battersea (south London) taste as vulgar] [mid-20C] vulgar, tasteless decor. ❑ **early beam** *n.* [the first sunbeams] [1930s–40s] (*US black*) dawn, the early morning. ❑ **early black** *n. see under* BLACK *n.* ❑ **early bright** *n.* [1940s–70s] (*US black*) the early morning. ❑ **early eclectic** *n.* [mid-20C] vulgar, tasteless decor. ❑ **early Halloween** *n.* [1970s+] vulgar, tasteless decor. ❑ **early homosexual** *n.* [1970s+] vulgar, tasteless decor. ❑ **early morn** *n. see* SUNDAY MORN *n.* ❑ **early parole** *n.* [1990s+] (*Aus. prison*) suicide. ❑ **early purl** *n.* [PURL *n.*[1]] [late 19C–1900s] a drink made of hot beer and gin.

early bird *n.*[1] **1** [mid-19C+] one who habitually gets up or arrives early. **2** [1930s] one who goes to bed early.

early bird *n.*[2] [rhy. sl.] [20C+] a word.

early-bird *adj.* [EARLY BIRD *n.*[1] (1)] [20C+] first of the day, e.g. *early-bird matinee.*

early door *n.* [rhy. sl.] [late 19C] a whore.

early doors *n.* [rhy. sl. = SE *drawers*] [20C+] underwear.

early doors *adv.* [1970s+] **1** early on, prematurely, as n., something that happens prematurely. **2** early.

early hour *n. see* HAPPY HOUR *n.* (1).

early riser *n.*[1] [1900s] (*Aus. tramp*) an old, worn or thin blanket or rag, used as a substitute blanket, carried in a swag.

early riser *n.*[2] [1960s+] (*US prison*) an inmate who is granted an early parole.

earn *n. see* EARNER *n.*

earn *v.* [1950s+] (*UK Und.*) **1** to work as a prostitute. **2** of a police officer, to take bribes. **3** to make a dishonest profit from a crime.

SE in slang uses

IN PHRASES

❑ **earn one's peasoup** *v. see EARN ONE'S TUCKER under* TUCKER *n.* ❑ **earn one's stripes** *v.* [military imagery] [1990s+] (*US black/teen*) for a young gang member to commit a crime to advance their status. ❑ **earn one's tucker** *v. see under* TUCKER *n.*

earner *n.* (*also* **earn**) [1960s+] **1** (*orig. UK Und.*) any job or plan that pays well, almost invariably criminal; often as *nice little earner*. **2** (*UK police*) a bribe, esp. one paid as regularly as more legitimate wages.

IN PHRASES

❑ **on the earn** *adj.* [1940s] intending to make money by illicit means.

earnest *n.* [SE *earnest*, money, esp. as paid as a pledge for securing a contract] [mid-17C–mid-18C] (*UK Und.*) a share (of the booty); thus *tip one their earnest*, to hand out a share.

ears *n.* **1** [1920s–30s] euph. for ARSE *n.* (1). **2** [1970s] (*orig. US*) a citizens' band radio, its antenna or the vehicle carrying it; thus *have one's ears on*, to be tuned into one's CB transceiver.

IN PHRASES

❑ **ding it in one's ears** *v. see under* DING *v.*[1]. ❑ **drop one's ears** *v. see under* DROP *v.*[1]. ❑ **knock the ears off** *v.* (*also* **beat someone's ears down**) [1930s] (*US*) to beat up comprehensively. ❑ **...to the ears** [1950s] intensifying phr., usu. referring to drunkenness or drug intoxication.

earth *n.*[1] (*also* **erth, eerth**) [backsl.] [mid-19C+] three; thus *earth/erth sis noms*, a three-month prison term.

earth *n.*[2] [? its organic (rather than chemical) origins] [1980s+] (*drugs*) a marijuana cigarette.

earth *n.*[3]

SE in slang uses

IN COMPOUNDS

❑ **earth bath** *n.* [SE *earth bath*, 'a kind of medical treatment in which the patient was buried up to the shoulders in the ground' *OED*] [early–mid-19C] a grave. ❑ **earth biscuit** *n.* [the *save the earth* attitudes of the period + the 'whole-grain' image of the *biscuit*] [1990s+] (*US campus*) someone who identifies with the styles and concerns of the 1960s. ❑ **earth daddy** *n.* [play on a classic figure of the 1960s, the *earth mother*] [1980s+] (*US campus*) older than average college male who professes the values of the 1960s. ❑ **earth muffin** *n.* [SE *earth*, i.e. one who espouses the values of the sixties + MUFFIN *n.*[1] (8)] [1980s+] (*US campus*) older than average college male; used derog. to indicate one who pursues a 'Sixties' lifestyle. ❑ **earth pads** *n.* (*US black/campus*) **1** [1940s] feet. **2** [1960s] shoes. ❑ **earthquake** *n.* [its effects] [mid–late 19C] (*US*) an alcoholic mixed drink. ❑ **earth-stopper** *n.* [SE *earth stopper*, 'one who is employed to stop up the 'earths' or holes of foxes' *OED*] [mid-19C] a horse's foot. ❑ **earthworm** *n.* [1990s+] the penis.

IN PHRASES

❑ **earth to...** [the image is of their day-dreaming, 'out in space'] [1970s+] (*US*) used to call someone's attention, also to tease.

earth, the *n.* [late 19C+] everything, a large amount or quantity, e.g. *cost the earth, pay the earth, want the earth.*

eartha (kitt) *n.* [rhy. sl.; ult. US singer *Eartha Kitt* (b.1928)] [1950s+] **1** excrement; also in fig. use [SHIT *n.* (1a)]. **2** an act of defecation; also as in phr. *not give an Eartha Kitt* [SHIT *n.* (1b)]. **3** in pl. diarrhoea [SHITS, THE *n.* (1)]. **4** in pl. breasts [TIT *n.*[2] (1)].

earth gens *n.* (*also* **erth gens**) [backsl.; EARTH *n.*[1] + GEN *n.*[1]] [mid-19C] three shillings.

earthly *n.* [SE *earthly*, emphatic epithet meaning 'on earth'] **1** [late 19C+] a chance, usu. in negative phr. meaning no chance, e.g. NO EARTHLY *phr.* **2** [1920s+] an idea [f. sense 1].

earth-pu *n.* (*also* **erth-pu**) [backsl.; EARTH *n.*[1]] [mid-19C] three-up, a street gambling game based on coin-tossing.

earthquake *n. see* BOTTLED EARTHQUAKE *n.*

earth yannops *n.* (*also* **earth yenneps, erth yannops, erth yenneps**) [backsl.; EARTH *n.*[1] + YENNEP *n.*] [mid-19C] three pence.

earthy-crunchy *n. see* CRUNCHY (GRANOLA) *n.* (3).

earwig *n.* [play on SE *ear*] **1** [mid-17C–late 19C] a malicious gossip or flatterer. **2** [mid-19C] a clergyman. **3** [mid-19C] a close, intimate friend. **4** [mid-19C] (*UK Und.*) information. **5** [late 19C] an inquisitive person. **6** [mid-19C; 1930s+] (*also* **ear-wigger, wiggins**) an eavesdropper; and thus poss. an informer. **7** [1940s+] a lookout, one who listens for approaching steps then checks the owner before admitting them.

IN PHRASES

❑ **do the wig** *v.* [mid-19C] to eavesdrop.

earwig *v.*[1] [EARWIG *n.*] **1** [19C] to gossip, esp. maliciously, to feed another with unpleasant rumours. **2** [mid-19C] to address surreptitiously. **3** [mid–late 19C] to lecture, to sermonize. **4** [mid-19C+] (*also* **ear-wag**) to eavesdrop.

IN PHRASES

❑ **on the earwig** *adj.* [2000s] eavesdropping.

earwig *v.*[2] [rhy. sl. = TWIG *v.*[2] (2)] [1910s+] to understand.

earwigger *n.* [EARWIG *v.*[1] (4)] [mid-19C; 1920s+] an eavesdropper.

earwigging *n.* [EARWIG *v.*[1] (3); EARWIG *v.*[1] (4)] **1** [mid-19C] whispering, gossiping secretively. **2** [mid-19C] a private rebuke. **3** [mid-19C+] eavesdropping.

ease *v.*[1] [SE *ease*, to deprive, to despoil] [early 17C–late 19C] **1** to have sexual intercourse, esp. to deflower. **2** to rob, to steal.

ease *v.*[2] (*also* **ease in, ease off, ease out**) [1920s+] (*US*) **1** to leave, esp. quietly and discreetly; usu. in phr. *ease out*. **2** to get rid of, to leave behind. **3** to move quietly. **4** to move, to travel.

IN PHRASES

❑ **ease on** *v.* [1950s] (*US black*) to go, to make one's way. ❑ **ease over** *v.* [1930s] (*orig. US*) to move towards.

ease it *v.* [1940s+] (*UK prison*) to relax, to let up on some form of crime or rule-breaking.

easeman *n. see* EASTMAN *n.*

ease-up *n.* [orig. dial.] [20C+] (*W.I.*) assistance, esp. in a difficult situation; thus *give one an ease-up*, to help.

ease up *v.* **1** [mid-19C+] to relax, to 'lighten up'. **2** [1920s+] as imper.

easies *n.* [1950s+] (*N.Z.*) a woman's elasticated foundation garment.

easily *adv.* [1940s+] at least, more than, e.g. *easily twenty*.

easing powder *n.* [SE *ease*, to relieve pain + *powder*] [20C+] (*drugs*) opium.

eason *v.* [? abbr. SE *reason*] [mid-19C] (*US Und.*) to tell, to inform.

east and south *n.* [rhy. sl.] [mid–late 19C] the mouth.

east and west *n.*[1] [rhy. sl.] **1** [late 19C] the male chest. **2** [1920s+] a vest [note SE *vest* is an undergarment; SAmE *vest* is a waistcoat]. **3** [1970s+] the female breast.

east and west *n.*[2]

IN PHRASES

❑ **give somone the east and west** *v.* [1910s] (*US*) to look someone over, to appraise.

east and west *phr.* (*also* **east, west and crooked**) [20C+] (*US*) disorderly, confused.

East Buttfuck *n. see* BUMFUCK, EGYPT *n.*

Easter bunny *n.* [rhy. sl.] [1990s+] money.

easter bunny *n.* [the Easter bunny is a beneficent creature] [1990s+] (*US campus*) a benefactor, someone who does a favour.

Easter egg *n.*[1] [the trad. painted Easter eggs created annually in some cultures] [20C+] (*US*) a woman wearing too much make-up.

Easter egg *n.*[2] [rhy. sl.] [1990s+] the human leg.

easter queen *n.* [SE *easter* (*bunny*), i.e. he 'comes quick as a rabbit' + -QUEEN *sfx* (3)] [1960s+] (*US gay*) one who ejaculates prematurely.

East Hell *n. see* WEST HELL *under* WEST *adj.*

East India docks *n.* [rhy. sl.] [1990s+] socks.

East Jesus *n.* (*also* **East Jesus, Kansas**) [1950s+] an out-of-the-way place, a small town.

Eastman *n.* (*also* **easeman**) [black pron. of *yeast* as *east*; thus the image of yeast as expanding and thus making a 'big man'; or *yeast* = BREAD *n.*[1] (2) = DOUGH *n.* (1)] [1910s–40s] (*US black*) a kept man, one who lives on money earned by a woman; a pimp.

Eastside O *n.* [1990s+] (*US black teen*) East Oakland, California.

east, west and crooked *phr. see* EAST AND WEST *phr.*

easy *n.* (*US*) **1** [1900s] a gullible person [*EASY MARK under* MARK *n.*[1]]. **2** [1970s+] New Orleans, Louisiana [abbr. of BIG EASY, THE *n.*].

SE in slang uses

IN PHRASES

❑ **on the easy** *adv.* [1990s+] (*US*) without effort; easily.

easy *adj.* **1** [late 17C–early 19C; 20C+] of a woman, sexually promiscuous; thus *easy lady*, *easy piece*. **2** [late 17C+] innocent, gullible. **3** [18C–mid-19C] (*UK Und.*) dead; silent. **4** [late 19C] (*UK/US Und.*) amenable to bribery. **5** [20C+] (*Can./US*) kind-hearted, easily imposed upon.

IN COMPOUNDS

❑ **easy game** *n.* [late 19C+] a sexually available woman. ❑ **easy lay** *n.* [LAY *n.*[2] (2)] [1920s+] **1** (*also* **lay-easy**) usu. of a woman, one who can be easily seduced. **2** in fig. use, anything easily achieved. ❑ **easy make** *n.* [MAKE *n.*[2] (3)] [1940s+] (*US*) a promiscuous or easily seducible woman, also in homosexual use. ❑ **easy mort** *n.* [MORT *n.* (1)] [mid-17C–early 18C] a promiscuous, 'forward' woman. ❑ **easy ride** *n.* [RIDE *n.* (1b)] [1980s+] (*US*) a sexually available woman. ❑ **easy stuff** *n.* [STUFF *n.* (8b)] [1950s+] (*US*) a sexually available woman. ❑ **easy virtue** *n.* [late 18C–early 19C] a prostitute.

SE in slang uses

IN COMPOUNDS

❑ **easy digging** *n.* [ety. unknown; ? the ease with which one can spoon this sugar into a cup] [1930s] (*US*) granulated sugar. ❑ **easy-doer** *n.* [1940s] (*US prison*) one who copes well with prison life. ❑ **easy meat** *n.* [MEAT *n.* (5)] [late 19C+] someone who is easily fooled or seduced. ❑ **easy rider** *n. see* separate entries. ❑ **easy six** *n.* [it is *easy* because of the number of combinations that equal six] [20C+] (*US gambling*) the point of six in craps dice. ❑ **easy street** *n. see* separate entry. ❑ **easy walkers** *n.* [ety. unknown; ? the ease with which one can spoon this sugar into a cup] [1930s] (*US*) granulated sugar.

IN PHRASES

❑ **easy does it** [late 19C+] a phr. used as a warning, go easy, take your time, careful. ❑ **easy on the eye** *adj.* [note 1900s synon. *easy to look at*] [1920s+] (*orig. US*) attractive, esp. of women. ❑ **easy over** [1960s] (*US*) no problems, don't worry. ❑ **make easy** *v.* [ironic use of SE *easy*, free of care and discomfort] [late 18C] to kill.

easy! *excl.* [abbr. phr. *take it easy*] [late 18C+] an exhortation to relax, e.g. don't get flustered! stay calm!

easy as... *adj.* [17C+] used in a variety of combs. as follows, to mean very simple indeed, sometimes almost criminally so; *see also* separate entries.

IN PHRASES

❑ **...ABC** ❑ **...a gum shoe** ❑ **...an old glove** ❑ **...a pig would eat a daisy** ❑ **...apple pie** (*also* **...apple tart**) (*Aus.*) ❑ **...cake (and ice-cream)** ❑ **...damn it** ❑ **...drinking beer** (*Aus.*) ❑ **...eating a mango** ❑ **...go and be blowed** ❑ **...kiss my eye** (*also* **...kiss my arm, ...arse, ...your hand**) ❑ **...ninepence** ❑ **...peas** ❑ **...pie** (*orig. US*) ❑ **...pissing the bed** (*also* **...pissing backwards**) ❑ **...pulling a cork** (*Aus.*) ❑ **...shelling peas** ❑ **...shit** ❑ **...shitting in bed** (*Aus.*) ❑ **...stirring a foot** ❑ **...taking candy from a baby** (*also* **...taking money from a child**) ❑ **...tilly** ❑ **...wink** (*also* **...winking**)

easy as falling off a log *adj.* (*also* **easy as falling off a horse, easy as rolling off a log, easy as tumbling off a log, like falling off a log, simple as falling off a log, ...a greased pig**) [late 19C+] very easy indeed.

easy as piss *adj.* [note local Aus. use *easy as pee-the-bed-awake*] [1990s+] extremely easy.

easy as pushing shit uphill (with a pointed stick) *adj.* (*also* **...with a rubber fork, ...carrying a kerosene tin full of cowshit uphill on your head, ...hooking an eel with a blunt pin, ...shoving a pound of butter up a cow's bum (with a size five knitting needle on a hot day)**) [1990s+] (*N.Z.*) not very easy, difficult and unpleasant.

easy on! *excl.* [1920s+] a general excl. go easy! stop it! be sensible!

easy rider *n.*[1] [SE *easy* + RIDE *n.* (1b); the term crossed briefly into white vocabulary with the release of the hit film *Easy Rider* (1969)] [20C+] (*US black*) **1** a male sexual athlete; a promiscuous woman. **2** a pimp, a kept man.

easy rider *n.*[2] [from the film of that name (1969)] [1960s] any 'outlaw' motorcyclist.

easy rider *n.*[3] [1970s] a calm, unruffled person.

easy street *n.* **1** [late 19C] euph. for a town's 'red-light' area. **2** [late 19C+] a secure, comfortable life; a situation free of problems, esp. material ones, usu. in phr. *on easy street*.

eat *n. see* EATS *n.*

eat *v.* **1** [early 19C–1920s] (*US*) to provide with food. **2** [mid-19C+] to defeat or destroy; thus *I'll eat him alive*. **3** [mid-19C+] (*also* **eat off**) to annoy, bother; thus *What's eating you?* **4** [late-19C+] to perform hetero- or homosexual fellatio or, more usu. cunnilingus. **5** [1920s+] (*US Und.*) to take a profit from criminality. **6** [1960s+] to strike face-first or be hit by (e.g. a bullet). **7** [1980s] (*S.Afr.*) to have sexual intercourse. **8** [1990s+] (*US*) to dispose of; to forget. **9** [2000s] to perform anilingus. **10** *see* EAT UP *v.* (3). **11** *see* EAT UP *v.* (5).

IN PHRASES

❑ **eat a dick** *v. see under* DICK *n.*[1]. ❑ **eat a furburger** *v. see under* FURBURGER *n.* ❑ **eat at the Y** *v.* (*also* **eat box lunch at the Y**) [Y *n.*/SE *Y*, referring to the spread legs; *box* plays on BOX *n.*[1] (1a)] [1950s+] (*US*) to perform cunnilingus. ❑ **eat hair pie** *v.* (*also* **eat fur pie**) [*HAIR PIE under* HAIR *n.*/*FUR PIE under* FUR *n.*] [1940s+] to perform cunnilingus. ❑ **eat out** *v.* [1960s+] (*US*) to perform cunnilingus or fellatio, or occas. anilingus. ❑ **eat pie** *v.* [*HAIR PIE under* HAIR *n.*] [1980s+] to perform cunnilingus. ❑ **eat poundcake** *v.* [pun on SE + POUND *v.*[2] (1)] **1** [1940s+] (*UK gay*) to suck a partner's anus. **2** [1970s] to indulge in coprophilia. **3** [1970s+] (*US black*) to have sexual intercourse. ❑ **eat pussy** *v.* [PUSSY *n.* (1)] [1930s+] to perform cunnilingus. ❑ **eat someone's meat** *v.* [MEAT *n.* (2)] [1920s+] to perform oral intercourse. ❑ **eat taffey** *v.* [fig. use of SAmE *taffey*, toffee, based on colour] [1980s] (*US black*) to perform cunnilingus. ❑ **eat-unda-table** *n.* [1990s+] (*W.I.*) a man who indulges in oral sex.

SE in slang uses

IN COMPOUNDS

❑ **eat-house** *n.* [2000s] (*US*) a café or restaurant. ❑ **eat joint** *n.* [JOINT *n.* (3b)] [1920s] (*US*) a restaurant, a café. ❑ **eat shop** *n.* [1960s] (*US*) a café, a restaurant.

IN PHRASES

❑ **eat a child** *v.* [the price for the commutation (registering as legitimate) of a bastard child was 'ten pounds and a greasy chin' (Grose 1785), i.e. a good meal] [late 18C–19C] to share in a treat given to the parish officers. ❑ **eat acorns** *v.* [a peasant might eat acorns when deprived of a more nutritious source of food] [1930s] (*US black*) to suffer humiliation, to accept defeat. ❑ **eat alone** *v.* [1990s+] (*US Und.*) to be greedy. ❑ **eat an apple/pumpkin through a knothole, be able to** *v.* **1** [20C+] (*US*) to have buck teeth. **2** (*also* **eat a baby's arse through the bars of a cot, be able to**) [2000s] (*Irish*) to be very hungry. ❑ **eat (boiled) crow** *v.* (*also* **eat the blackbird**) [the mid-19C story of a man who bet that he was able to eat a cooked crow, and duly did so, but remarked as he chewed the bird: 'Yes, I can eat a crow, but I'll be darned if I hanker after it!'] [mid-19C+] to suffer humiliations and insults without responding in kind. ❑ **eat bull beef** *v.* [the image of *bull beef* as tough meat] [late 16C–19C] to become strong, to become fierce. ❑ **eat cauliflower** *v. see DO A BIT OF CAULIFLOWER under* CAULIFLOWER *n.*[3]. ❑ **eat cheese** *v. see* separate entries. ❑ **eat concrete** *v.* [1970s] (*US*) to drive fast, esp. a truck, down a highway. ❑ **eat corn-a-the-cob through a picket fence, be able to** *v.* [20C+] (*US*) to have buck teeth. ❑ **eat crap** *v.* [CRAP *n.*[1] (2)] [1930s+] (*orig. US*) to suffer and accept humiliation, to humble oneself, usu. in order to attain a desired goal. ❑ **eat dirt** *v.* [proverb, 'Every man must *eat a peck of dirt* (i.e. retract a number of errors) before he dies'] [mid-19C+] **1** (*also* **eat dirt pie, eat dust**) to retract a previous statement, usu. incurring humiliation and embarrassment by so doing. **2** to act in a demeaning, humiliating manner. ❑ **eat dog** *v.* [19C+] to suffer humiliation and insult without reciprocating. ❑ **eat dong** *v.* [DONG *n.*[1]] [1970s] (*US*) to suffer humiliation. ❑ **eat dried apples** *v.* (*also* **eat pumpkin seeds**) [the way in which dried fruit swells up when placed in water] [1960s–70s] (*US*) to become pregnant. ❑ **eat dust** *v.* (*US*) **1** [late 19C] to be killed. **2** [late 19C+] to leave, to travel. ❑ **eat face** *v.* [1960s+] (*US campus*) to kiss passionately on the mouth and face. ❑ **eat fist-meat** *v.* [mid-16C] to receive a punch in the mouth. ❑ **eat gravel** *v.* (*also* **eat dirt, eat grass**) [20C+] (*US*) to be thrown or to fall on one's face. ❑ **eat hempseed** *v.* [the rope is made from *hemp*] [early 17C] to be hanged. ❑ **eat in Dutch street** [DUTCH *adj.*[1], i.e. stereotyping] [1910s+] to share expenses. ❑ **eat it** *v. see* separate entry. ❑ **eat jam** *v. see under* JAM *n.*[2]. ❑ **eat like a beggar man and wag one's under jaw** *v. see under* BEGGAR *n.* ❑ **eat one's boots** *v. see* EAT ONE'S HAT *v.* ❑ **eat one's gun** *v.* (*also* **eat the gun**) [1970s+] (*US*) to commit suicide by shooting oneself in the mouth. ❑ **eat one's hat** *v. see* separate entry. ❑ **eat one's head** *v.* [mid-19C+] to go back on one's words, esp. to admit that a public statement was, in fact, wrong. ❑ **eat one's head off** *v.* **1** [18C+] (*also* **eat its head off**) to cost more than a person/thing is worth. **2** [1930s+] (*also* **eat, eat the face off**) to verbally abuse. ❑ **eat one's shorts** *v.* [1960s+] (*US*) to suffer, to die. ❑ **eat one's tutu** *v.* (*also* **eat one's toot**) [Maori *tutu*, a New Zealand shrub yielding shining black juicy berries which can be eaten, but also containing poisonous seeds] [mid–late 19C] (*N.Z.*) to become acclimatized, esp. to colonial life. ❑ **eat out** *v.* [var. on CHEW OUT *v.*] [1940s] (*US*) to tell off, to reprimand. ❑ **eat popcorn** *v.* [1960s] (*US drugs*) to take some form of pill. ❑ **eat razor soup** *v.* [1930s] (*US*) to say something cheeky or impertinent. ❑ **eat sauce** *v. see DRINK OF SAUCE'S CUP under* DRINK *v.* ❑ **eat shit** *v. see* separate entry. ❑ **eat someone's cookies** *v.* [1970s] (*US*) to defeat someone. ❑ **eat someone's lunch** *v. see under* LUNCH *n.* ❑ **eat supper before you say grace** *v.* [20C+] (*US*) to conceive a child before one gets married. ❑ **eat the big one** *v. see under* BIG ONE *n.* ❑ **eat the carpet** *v. see* CHEW THE CARPET *v.*[1]. ❑ **eat the cookie** *v.* (*also* **eat the porridge**) [1970s] (*US/Aus.?*) to be defeated. ❑ **eat the greaser** *v.* [dial. *greaser*, a lump of salt pork used to grease the bars of a griddle] [20C+] (*US*) to swallow one's words, to recant. ❑ **eat the green weenie** *v.* [? the grass; thus cf. *BITE THE DUST under* DUST *n.*] [1970s+] (*US, orig. milit.*) to get killed. ❑ **eat the gun** *v. see EAT ONE'S GUN* above. ❑ **eat the leek** *v.* [the 'sharpness' of the SE *leek*] [late 19C] to be forced to address unpleasant consequences. ❑ **eat turkey** *v. see under* TURKEY *n.*[1]. ❑ **eat up** *see* separate entries. ❑ **eat vinegar with a fork** *v.* [late 19C–1900s] to have a sharp tongue. ❑ **I could eat a horse** (*also* **...and chase the jockey/rider**) [20C+] (*Aus./US*) I am extremely hungry. ❑ **I could eat the hind leg off a donkey** (*also* **...off a boudie, I could eat a farmer's arse (through a hedge)**) [20C+] **1** I am extremely hungry. **2** an emphatic expression. ❑ **I'd eat my chips out of her knickers** [var. on *I COULD USE USE HER SHIT FOR TOOTHPASTE under* SHIT *n.*] [1970s+] a statement of absolute (sexual) devotion.

IN EXCLAMATIONS

❑ **eat it!** *see* separate entry. ❑ **eat me!** *see* separate entry. ❑ **eat shit!** *see* separate entry. ❑ **eat my shorts!** [SAmE *shorts* = SE underpants; the phrase moved into the mainstream with the success of television's cartoon family, *The Simpsons*, whose renegade son Bart took it as his personal catchphrase] [1970s+] (*US*) a dismissive excl., drop dead! go to hell! etc.

eat a fig *v.* [rhy. sl. = CRACK A CRIB *under* CRIB *n.*[1]] [mid-19C] to commit burglary, to rob a house.

eat cheese *v.*[1] [SE *eat* + SE *cheesy*; i.e. the quality of one's smiles] **1** [1940s+] (*orig. US black*) to toady to, to ingratiate oneself with. **2** [1950s+] (*US*) to inform on, to betray; thus n. *cheese-eating*. **3** [1970s] (*US black*) to be in love.

eat cheese *v.*[2] *see under* CHEESE *n.*[1].

eater *n.* [1990s+] a café, a restaurant.

eaters *n.* [1910s] (*Aus.*) false teeth.

eatery *n.* (*also* **eaterie**) [20C+] (*US*) a restaurant.

eat hay with a horse *v. see* EAT ONE'S HAT *v.*

eating irons *n.* [1940s+] utensils, knives and forks.

eating match *n.* [mid-19C] (*W.I.*) a feast.

eatings *n.* [1900s–30s] food.

eating tackle *n.* [20C+] teeth.

eating tobacco *n.* [1900s–60s] (*US*) chewing tobacco.

eating tool *n.* [1920s–60s] (*US*) an eating utensil.

eat it *v.* [EAT *v.*] **1** [1910s+] to perform oral sex. **2** [1930s+] to suffer humiliation, esp. in attaining a desired goal. **3** [1960s+] (*US campus*) to do poorly, to achieve low marks. **4** [1960s+] to die. **5** [1970s] (*US*) to be unpleasant. **6** [1990s+] to take responsibility.

eat it! *excl.* (*also* **eat this!**) [EAT *v.* (4); *it/this* is the penis] [20C+] a general term of dismissal, disdain.

eat me! *excl.* (*also* **eat my meat!**) [EAT *v.* (4)] [1960s+] (*US*) shut up! you make me sick! the hell with you! go away!

eat one's hat *v.* (*also* **eat one's, eat one's bonnet, ...boots, ... cap, ...pants, ...shirt, eat hay with a horse**) [late 18C+] to go back on one's words, esp. to admit that a public statement was, in fact, wrong.

eats *n.* (*also* **eat**) [orig. UK but in 20C US only] [mid-19C+] food; a meal.

eat shit *v.* **1** [1930s+] to humble oneself, usu. to attain a desired goal. **2** [1940s+] to be utterly contemptible. **3** [1940s+] (*also* **bite/eat shit and die**) to suffer and accept humiliation.

eat shit! *excl.* (*also* **eat shit and die!**) [EAT SHIT *v.*] [1960s+] (*US*) a general dismissive, derog. expression; it has no specific meaning.

eat this! *excl. see* EAT IT! *excl.*

eat-up *n.* [1910s] (*Aus.*) a meal; thus *eat-up joint*, a restaurant.

eat up *adj.* (*also* **ate up**) [SE *eaten up*/EAT UP *v.*] **1** [1970s] (*US campus*) tired out, exhausted. **2** [1990s+] disorganized, messy, all over the place. **3** [1990s+] strange, unusual, crazy. **4** [1990s+] keen on, obsessed with.

eat up *v.* **1** [mid-19C–1950s] to scold or rebuke. **2** [mid-19C+] to defeat or destroy. **3** [late 19C+] (*also* **eat**) to believe unquestioningly. **4** [1900s–10s] to do well; to act competently; to deal with efficiently. **5** [1910s+] (*orig. theatre*) (*also* **eat**) to enjoy immensely, to acclaim. **6** [1930s+] to take control of, to 'consume'.

eau-de-Cologne *n.* [rhy. sl.] **1** [1960s+] (*Aus.*) the telephone. **2** [1990s+] a woman [= POLONE *n.* (1)].

E-ball *n. see* E *n.*

ebb-water *n.* [late 17C–18C] (*UK Und.*) a lack of money.

ebenezer *n.* (*also* **ebeneser**) [Heb. *eben ha-ezer*, the stone of help, the memorial stone set up by Samuel after the victory of Mizpeh (1 Sam. 7:12); a misreading of Samuel's 'raising' of a memorial] [mid-19C] (*US*) temper, passion.

ebony *n.* (*also* **ebon, son of ebony**) **1** [19C+] (*US*) a black person. **2** [20C+] (*US black*) the quintessence of black sensibility.

IN PHRASES

❑ **bit of ebony** *n.* [BIT *n.*[1] (2a)] [mid-19C+] a black woman, viewed as a sex object.

ebony *adj.* [mid-19C+] a general ref. to any black person; thus *ebony chick*, *ebony pidgeon*, a black woman.

E-boy *n.* [E *n.* + SE *boy*] [1980s+] a devotee of MDMA.

ecaf *n. see* EEK *n.*

eccer *n.* (*also* **eccker, ecker, ekker**) [SE *exercise* + -ER *sfx*] **1** [late 19C] physical exercise. **2** [1910s+] (*Aus./Irish*) homework.

ecckie *n. see* ECKY *n.*

eccy *n.* (*also* **ec**) [abbr.] [1920s+] (*US campus*) economics.

echohead *n.* [SE *echo* + -HEAD *sfx* (1); thoughts 'echo' around the empty skull] [1990s+] a foolish person, usu. female.

ecker *n. see* ECCER *n.*

eckied (up) *adj.* [ECKY *n.*] [1980s+] (*drugs*) under the influence of MDMA.

ecky *n.* (*also* **eckie**) [abbr. ECSTASY *n.*] [1980s+] (*drugs*) MDMA.

IN PHRASES

❑ **ecky (up)** *v.* [1980s+] (*drugs*) to take MDMA.

ecky-becky *n.* [? redup. of Ijo *beke*, a European; or ironic use of Ijo *ekee*, God + *beke*] [20C+] (*W.I., Bdos*) a poor white.

E class *n.* [Mercedes *E class*; although the sl. term can mean any luxury brand] [2000s] (*US teen*) a very expensive car.

ecnop *n.* [backsl.] [1950s–80s] a ponce.

eco *n.* [abbr. *economy/economics*] [2000s] (*US black*) money.

ecod *n.* [late 18C–mid-19C] God, as used in a variety of oaths.

ecod! *excl.* (*also* **i'cod!**) [18C–19C] God! as used in a variety of oaths.

ecofreak *n.* [SE *ecology* + -FREAK *sfx*] [1970s+] an extremist in the cause of environmentalism.

econut *n.* [SE *ecology* + NUT *n.*[2] (3)] [1970s+] (*US*) an extremist in the cause of environmentalism.

ecstasy *n.* [*ecstasy* existed in the 1960s as one of many synthetic hallucinogens (although it is more amphetamine than a 'real' hallucinogen) from a group known as 'Schulgin's compounds'; it only reached its apotheosis in the late 1980s. Its nickname comes from the indiscriminate affection that its ingestion promotes, and the earlier popular name of 'love-drug'; virtually SE by late 1990s] [1980s+] a name for the drug known officially as methylene dioxymethamphetamine (MDMA).

EC women *n.* [the London postal code *East Central*; a snobbish usage by those who despise 'trade'] [late 19C] (*UK society*) the wives of City businessmen.

E'd *adj. see* E'ED *adj.*

edad! *excl. see* EGAD! *excl.*

Eddie *n.* [abbr. *MR EDDIE under* MR *n.*] [1920s] (*US black*) a white male.

eddie *n.* [ety. unknown; ? anecdotal or link to EDDIE *n.*] (*US campus*) [1980s+] **1** an ugly man. **2** anything stupid.

Eddie Grundys *n.* [rhy. sl. = undies; ult. a character from the BBC radio drama series *The Archers*] [2000s] underwear.

eddress *n.* [abbr. + pun on SE *address*] [1990s+] (*US teen*) an email *address*.

e.d. *adj.* (*also* **'ed**) [SE exhausted] [1920s] finished, worn out.

edgabac *n.* (*also* **egabac**) [backsl.] [mid-19C] cabbage.

edgar allan *n.* [rhy. sl. = PO *n.* (1); ult. US author Edgar Allan *Poe* (1809–49)] [1970s] a chamberpot.

Edgar Britt *n.* [rhy. sl.; ult. Aus. jockey *Edgar Britt* (b.1913)] [1960s+] (*Aus.*) **1** excrement, an act of defecation [SHIT *n.*]. **2** in pl. diarrhoea [SHITS, THE *n.* (1)].

Edgar Wallace *v.* [the British thriller writer *Edgar Wallace* (1875–1932)] [1970s] to thrill.

edge *n.*[1] **1** [late 19C–1960s] a state of mild intoxication; often as *have an edge on*, *get on edge on* [one is at the *edge* of inebriation]. **2** [late 19C+] an advantage. **3** [1930s+] (*also* **edgies**) drug-created stress; or symptoms of withdrawal from a drug. **4** [1940s+] tension, usu. creative.

IN COMPOUNDS

❑ **edge city** *n.* [-CITY *sfx* (1)] [1960s+] the extremes of experience, whether spiritual, physical, drug induced etc; usu. with overtones of fear and challenge.

SE in slang uses

IN COMPOUNDS

❑ **edge-work** *n.* [1930s–50s] (*US Und.*) barely perceptible markings on the edges of cards, used by cheats.

edge *n.*[2] [1960s+] (*US black*) a knife; thus phr. *pack an edge*, carry a knife.

edge *v.* **1** [late 19C–1960s] (*UK Und.*) to escape, to run away, esp. as excl. *edge!*, run for it!, called out by a lookout; to avoid or keep away; thus also phr., *keep the edge up*, act as lookout. **2** [1910s–20s] (*Aus.*) to discontinue. **3** [1950s] (*Aus.*) to be unreasonable.

edged *adj.*[1] [EDGE *n.*[1] (1)] [late 19C–1930s] (*US*) tipsy.

edged *adj.*[2] [EDGE *n.*[1] (4)] [1980s+] (*US*) angry.

edge it! *excl.* [1930s] (*Aus.*) be quiet! shut up!

edgenaro *n.* [backsl.] [mid-19C] an orange.

edge-up *adj.* [the image is of physically moving overly close] [20C+] (*W.I.*) used of one who is trying excessively hard to become friends.

edgies *n. see* EDGE *n.*[1] (3).

edie *n.* [the image of *Edie* as a poor person's name] [1940s–50s] a prostitute (working Piccadilly, Bayswater Road and other 'cheap' streets in London).

edison *v.* [the inventor of the electric light, Thomas Alva *Edison* (1847–1931): it is presumably 'shone' on the interrogatee] [1920s] (*US*) to interrogate.

Edison medicine *n.* [*see* EDISON *v.* + SE *medicine*] [1990s+] (*US*) electro-shock therapy.

Edison special *n.* [*see* EDISON *v.* + SE *special*] [1970s] (*US prison*) death in the electric chair.

edmundo *n.* [rhy. sl. = boss; ult. *Edmundo Ros* (b.1910), a popular Latin American band leader] [1960s+] the leader, the most important person.

edna! *excl.* (*also* **Edna May!**) [rhy. sl. *Edna May* = on your way!] [20C+] (*UK Und.*) a general excl. of dismissal: be off!, go away!

-ed out *sfx* [1970s+] glutted with, full of; both lit. and fig. uses.

educated *adj.* [ironic use of SE] **1** [20C+] (*US*) fraudulent, esp. of a card deck that has been fixed. **2** [1940s+] clever but criminal.

SE in slang uses

IN COMPOUNDS

❑ **educated fool** *n.* [1950s+] (*orig. US black*) one who is academic but not very sophisticated or worldly-wise. ❑ **educated ignorant** *n.* [1950s+] (*US black*) one who is academic but not very sophisticated or worldly-wise. ❑ **educated pussy** *n.* [PUSSY *n.* (10); the image is of one who is 'not a real man'] [1950s–60s] (*US black*) a weakling, an inadequate.

-ed up *sfx* [1990s+] wearing a specific (designer) brand of clothing, eg *Guccied up*.

edward *n.* [proper name for Ted] [1960s] a Teddy-boy.

Edward Heath *n.* see HAMPSTEAD(S) *n.*

E'ed *adj.* (*also* **E'd**) [E *n.*] [1980s+] under the influence of MDMA; usu. as *E'd up*.

eejit *n.* (*also* **eedjit, eegot, eejut, ejot, idjeet, idjet, idjit, idjut, ijet, ijit, ijjit, ijut**) [mispron. of SE *idiot*] [mid-19C+] (*usu. Irish*) a fool, also as adj. *eejity*, foolish.

eek *n.* (*also* **ecaf**) [backsl.] [1960s+] (*Ling. Fr./Polari*) the face.

eekcher *n.* [pig Lat.] [late 19C–1900s] cheek, audacity.

eeks *n.* [Polari] [1950s+] the eyes.

eel *n.*[1] [resemblance] **1** [17C; mid-19C+] the penis. **2** [1920s] a very thin person.

IN COMPOUNDS

❑ **eelpot** *n.* (*also* **eel trap**) [late 18C–early 19C] the vagina.

eel *n.*[2] [SE *eel*, seen anthropomorphically as an untrustworthy creature] **1** [mid-19C] (*US, Western*) a native of New England. **2** [mid-19C+] (*orig. US*) anyone who possesses the 'slippery' qualities of the fish, e.g. an accomplished escaper from prison, a spy, a confidence trickster.

SE in slang uses

IN COMPOUNDS

❑ **eel juice** *n.* [? it makes one wriggle like an eel; note SE *liquor*, the green sauce that is served with eels at pie and mash shops] [20C+] liquor. ❑ **eel's ankle** *n.* (*also* **eel's hips, snake's hips, trout's ankles**) [all on pattern of CAT'S PYJAMAS *n.*] [1920s] (*US*) something extraordinary or very special. ❑ **eel's eyebrows** *n.* [1920s] something utterly repellent.

IN PHRASES

❑ **eel out** *v.* [1920s] (*US*) to avoid a problem, esp. in a deceitful, self-serving way.

eelerspee *n.* (*also* **eeler-spieler**) [backsl. *eelerspee* = SPIELER *n.* (1)] [1910s+] (*Aus. Und.*) a confidence trickster.

eel skin *n.*[1] [? its greenness] [mid-19C] a banknote.

eel skin *n.*[2] [EEL *n.*[2] (1)] [mid-19C] a New Englander.

eel skin *n.*[3] [it fits the wearer like an eel's skin] [late 19C] a tight skirt, fashionable c.1881.

eel skin *n.*[4] [resemblance] [late 19C] a cosh, made from a canvas tube filled with sand.

eel-skinner *n.* [EEL *n.*[1] (1)] [late 18C–early 19C] the vagina.

eel skins *n.* [mid-19C] extremely tight trousers.

eel trap *n. see* EELPOT *under* EEL *n.*[1].

eely *n.* [the 'slippery' characteristic of an eel] [1980s] (*Aus.*) a confidence trick.

eemosh *n.* [backsl.] [mid-19C+] home.

eenin *n. see* ENIN *n.*

eenque *n.* [backsl.] [late 19C] the queen.

eensie-teensie *adj. see* TEENSIE-WEENSIE *adj.*

eensy-beensy/weensy *adj. see* TEENSIE-WEENSIE *adj.*

eentsy-weentsy *adj. see* TEENSIE-WEENSIE *adj.*

eerht *n.* [backsl.] [mid-19C] the number three.

eerquay *n.* [pig Lat. = QUEER *n.* (4)/QUEER *adj.* (4)] [1930s–40s] (*US*) a male homosexual; also adj.

eerth *n. see* EARTH *n.*[1].

eeson *n.* [backsl.] [mid-19C+] nose.

eetswe *adj.* [backsl. = *SWEET ON under* SWEET *adj.*[1]] [late 19C] fond of.

eevach a kool *v.* [backsl.] [late 19C] to have a look.

eevige *v.* [backsl.] [late 19C] to give.

eff *n.* **1** [1930s] a euph. for FUCKER *n.* (3). **2** [1970s+] a euph. for FUCK *n.* in various uses.

eff *v.* (*also* **f**) [1910s+] euph. for FUCK *v.*; thus *effing* adj. euph. for FUCKING *adj.* (1); *eff off* v. euph. for FUCK OFF *v.* (1).

IN PHRASES

❑ **eff and blind** *v.* (*also* **eff, effing, F-ing and blinding, fuck and blind**) [BLIND *v.*[2] (1)] [1920s+] to swear intensely; thus *effing and blinding*, using obscenities. ❑ **sweet eff-ay** *n. see SWEET FUCK ALL under* SWEET *adj.*[1].

IN EXCLAMATIONS

❑ **eff off!** [1950s+] euph. for FUCK OFF! *excl.*

eff, in the *n. see* FUCK *n.* (3a).

effags! *excl. see* FAGS! *excl.*

effer *n.* [EFF *v.*] **1** [1970s] (*Irish*) a term of abuse, a 'fucker'. **2** [1980s] a user of obscenity.

effie *n.* [generic use of female proper name; or abbr. SE *effeminate*] [1930s+] (*US gay*) an effeminate male homosexual.

effing *adj.* see *EFF AND BLIND under* EFF *v.*

e-fink *n.* [backsl.] [mid-19C] a knife.

e-flat *adj.* [1970s] (*US black*) small.

efter *n.* [? SE *after*, he is *after* the valuables; or backsl. *thief*] [mid-19C] a thief (who specializes in theatre audiences).

egabac *n.* see EDGABAC *n.*

egad! *excl.* (*also* **agad! edad! 'gad! i'gad! ivads!**) [? A God!] [late 17C+] used in mild oaths as a euph. for *God!*

egg *n.*[1] **1** [mid-15C+] in pl., the testicles. **2** [1900s–30s] the head or skull. **3** [1910s–40s] a grenade, a bomb, thus *lay an egg*, to drop a bomb. **4** [1940s] (*US*) a baseball. **5** [1950s–60s] in fig. use of sense 1, courage, virility. **6** in drug uses. (**a**) [1970s+] usu. pl., a capsule of a drug. (**b**) [1970s+] any drug in capsule/tablet form. (**c**) [1980s+] temazepam, a tranquillizer. (**d**) [1980s+] crack cocaine. (**e**) [1990s+] (*Aus.*) MDMA tablets.

IN PHRASES

❑ **eggs in the basket** *n.* [BASKET *n.*[1] (2)] [1940s–70s] (*US gay*) the testicles. ▫ **out of one's egg** *adj.* [1900s] (*Aus.*) insane.

SE in slang uses

IN COMPOUNDS

▫ **eggbeater** *n.* **1** [1930s+] (*US*) an autogiro or helicopter. **2** [1970s+] an old car. ▫ **egg-boiler** *n.* [in hot weather it 'boils' one's EGG *n.*[1] (2)] [1930s] (*Aus.*) a bowler hat. ▫ **egg-crate** *n.* [resemblance] **1** [1920s–50s] (*US*) an old car or aeroplane. **2** [1930s] an old elevator. ▫ **egghead/headed** *see* separate entries. ▫ **eggnog** *n.* [1920s] (*US*) a foolish or unpleasant person. ▫ **egg roll** *n.* [the foodstuff] **1** [1970s–80s] (*N.Z. prison*) a general term of abuse. **2** [1980s] (*US*) a derog. term for a Korean immigrant. **3** [1980s+] (*US gay*) a Chinese man's penis. ▫ **eggshell blond** *n.* [1950s+] (*Aus./N.Z.*) a bald person. ▫ **eggsuck/sucker/sucking** *see* separate entries. ▫ **egg-white** *n.* [1910s+] semen, thus *egg-white cannon*, the penis.

IN PHRASES

▫ **egg-for-fuck** *n.* [FUCK *v.* (1); joc. var. on SHIT-FOR-BRAINS *adj.*] [1990s+] (*US campus*) a fool, a simpleton, an obnoxious person. ▫ **egg in your beer** *n.* [1930s+] (*US*) something for nothing, used as an ironical retort. ▫ **eggs in the coffee** *adj.* [1920s–30s] (*US*) **1** excellent, wonderful, ideal. **2** (*also* **eggs and the coffee**) trustworthy. ▫ **have an egg in the nest** *v.* [20C+] (*US black*) to be pregnant. ▫ **sure as eggs ain't chicken** (*also* **sure as eggs is eggs, true as eggs is bacon**) *see* SURE AS HOGS ARE MADE OF BACON *under* SURE AS… *phr.*

IN EXCLAMATIONS

▫ **egg-a-muffin!** [SE *egg on* + McDonald's *egg McMuffin*] [1980s+] (*US campus*) enthusiastic response of agreement. ▫ **egg on!** [1950s] (*Aus.*) hurry up! ▫ **eggs are cooked!, the** (*also* **one's potato is cooked!**) [WW1 *eggs a-cook*, hard-boiled Egyptian eggs] [late 19C+] (*N.Z.*) that's it! that's all! it's over! etc. ▫ **go lay an egg!** [1920s–30s] (*US campus*) excl. of dismissal.

egg *n.*[2] **1** [mid-19C+] a person, usu. qualified by adj., esp. as GOOD EGG *n.* (2), *OLD EGG* below etc. **2** [1900s] (*US*) an important person. **3** [1910s+] (*also* **double-yolker**) a fool or obnoxious person. **4** [1940s] (*US Und.*) the victim of a confidence trick.

IN PHRASES

▫ **old egg** *n.* [20C+] a man or woman, esp. as a term of affectionate address.

egg *n.*[3] [abbr. EGGHEAD *n.*[1] (1)] [20C+] (*US campus*) a conspicuously studious and intellectual student.

egg *n.*[4] [pun on SE *egg*, thus *hen*] [20C+] (*US*) a henpecked husband.

egg *n.*[5] [? abbr. SE *nest-egg*] [1910s] (*US*) $1.

egg *n.*[6] *see* GOOSE EGG *n.*

egg *v.*[1] [phr. *walk on eggshells*, to tread delicately] [late 19C+] (*US*) to move carefully, quietly.

egg *v.*[2] [SE *egg on*] [1930s+] to make fun of someone; to make a fool of oneself.

egg and spoon *n.* [rhy. sl.] **1** [1960s+] a black person [COON *n.* (5)]. **2** [1970s+] (*Aus.*) a fool, a silly person [GOON *n.*[1] (1)]. **3** [1970s+] (*Aus.*) a pimp [HOON *n.* (2)].

egg flip *n.* [rhy. sl.] [20C+] (*Aus.*) a tip, information, usu. in horseracing.

egghead *n.*[1] [20C+] (*orig. US*) **1** an intellectual, anyone considered to work with brain rather than brawn. **2** a pretentiously intellectual type.

egghead *n.*[2] [resemblance] [20C+] **1** (*US*) a fool. **2** a bald person. **3** a bald head.

egghead *adj.* (*also* **egg-heady**) [1950s+] (*orig. US*) intellectual, or pretentiously so.

eggheaded *adj.*[1] [EGGHEAD *n.*[1] (1)] [1910s+] intellectual, or posing as such.

eggheaded *adj.*[2] [EGGHEAD *n.*[2] (3)] [1930s+] (*US*) bald.

eggo *n.* [? EGG *n.*[2] (3)] [1980s+] (*US campus*) a fool, a misfit, a social anachronism.

eggplant *n.*[1] [1940s] (*US black*) a five-dollar bill.

eggplant *n.*[2] [SE *eggplant* or aubergine, the vegetable has a shiny purple-black skin; 'translation' of MULENYAM *n.*] [1970s] (*US*) a black person.

egg suck *v.* [SUCK UP *v.* (1)/obs. SE *suck-egg*, a foolish person] [1970s+] (*US*) to curry favour; as adj., fawning.

egg-sucker *n.* [dial. *egg-sucker*, a worthless animal, esp. a dog] **1** [19C+] (*US*) a worthless and unpleasant person. **2** [1950s+] (*US gay*) an ageing or old homosexual [the pun is on the *egg*, i.e. an unformed youth, who is the target of the older man's desires].

egg-sucking *adj.* [EGG-SUCKER *n.* (1)] [19C+] (*US*) worthless, contemptible, unpleasant.

eggy *adj.* [EGG *v.*[2]] [1920s+] (*US*) angry, irritated.

eggy! *excl.* [1990s+] (*UK juv.*) excellent!, wonderful!

eggy-peggy *n.* [ety. unknown] [1960s] an exchange, e.g. of glances.

Egon (Ronay) *n.* [rhy. sl.; *pony* fr. PONY (AND TRAP) *n.* = CRAP *n.*[1] (2); ult. food guidebook pioneer *Egon Ronay* (b. 1920)] [1990s+] an act of defecation.

ego-surfing *n.* [2000s] surfing the Internet in search of one's own name.

ego trip *n.* [SE *ego* + TRIP *n.*[4] (1c)] [1960s+] (*orig. US*) self-aggrandizement, boastfulness, egocentricity.

ego trip *v.* [EGO TRIP *n.*] [1970s+] (*orig. US*) to act in an egocentric, self-aggrandizing manner.

E.G.Y.P.T. *phr.* [abbr.] [20C+] eager to grab your pretty tits, written on envelopes of love letters.

Egypt *n.* [image of *Egypt* as a far distant and/or exotic place] (*US*) **1** [19C+] an outside lavatory. **2** [20C+] the black section of a town or city [the dark complexions of US blacks and Egyptians]. **3** *see* BUMFUCK, EGYPT *n.*

Egyptian *adj.*

proper name in slang uses

IN COMPOUNDS

▫ **Egyptian charger** *n.* [the association of this animal with the gypsies or *Egyptians*] [early 19C] a donkey. ▫ **Egyptian flu** *n.* [i.e. one is going to be a *mummy*] [1980s+] (*US*) a pregnancy. ▫ **Egyptian queen** *n.* [the well-known picture of Queen Nefertiti + -QUEEN *sfx* (3)] [1960s+] (*gay*) 'a homosexual black man, particularly if he is stately and proud' (Rodgers, *Queens' Vernacular*, 1972).

Egyptian hall *n.* [rhy. sl.; the *Egyptian Hall* was the popular name for the London Museum, established at today's 170 Piccadilly *c.*1812, holding 'upwards of Fifteen Thousand Natural and Foreign Curiosities, Antiques and Productions of the Fine Arts'. It featured an 'Egyptian' façade, and among the many visitors was, in 1844, General Tom Thumb. The hall was demolished in 1905] [mid-19C] a ball.

eh? *phr.* [mid-19C+] used interrogatively, as a request for the repetition or explanation of something that has just been said, i.e. 'What did you say?'.

E-head *n.* [E *n.* + -HEAD *sfx* (4)] [1990s+] (*UK drugs*) a regular user of MDMA.

eh-eh *n.* [Yid. *eh-eh* = baby's word for faeces] [1960s+] (*US gay*) the anus; thus used of anything seen as tasteless/unpleasant.

eh, what! *excl. see* WHAT? *phr.* (3).

eicespie *n.* [backsl. = *pieces* (of gold)] [late 19C] money.

Eiffel Tower *n.* [rhy. sl.] **1** [20C+] (*Aus.*) a shower. **2** [1980s] a flower.

eight *n.* [1970s–80s] (*US drugs*) **1** heroin [*H* is the eighth letter of the alphabet]. **2** an eighth of an ounce of a narcotic, usu. heroin.

IN COMPOUNDS

▫ **eight track** *n.* [? partial rhy. sl. = CRACK *n.*[7]] [1990s+] (*US black*) 5g of crack cocaine.

eight *adj.*

SE in slang uses

IN COMPOUNDS

▫ **eight-pager** *n.* (*also* **sixteener**) [1930s+] a small, illustrated eight-page pornographic booklet in which popular cartoon characters (Popeye, Mickey Mouse, Blondie etc) are crudely pastiched in erotic scenarios far removed from their everyday antics. ❑ **eight-piece** *n.* [PIECE *n.* (7a)] [1990s+] US drugs an eighth of a kilo of crack cocaine. ❑ **eight rock** *n.* [EIGHTBALL *n.* (1a)] [1930s–50s] (*US black*) a very dark-skinned person. ❑ **eight wheeler** *n.* [the wagon has eight wheels] [1930s–50s] (*US tramp*) a person who robs trains whether en route or stationary.

eightball *n.* [pool imagery; the eight ball is black] (*US*) **1** the colour, black, of the ball in pool. (**a**) [1910s+] a derog. term for an Afro-American, a black person. (**b**) [1990s+] excrement, a turd. **2** [1930s+] (*also* **eightball holder**) an incompetent; a fool [sinking the eight ball out of turn will lose the game]. **3** [1950s] a conventional, law-abiding person. **4** (*US drugs*) in drug uses. (**a**) [1980s+] an eighth of an ounce (3.5g) of a drug. (**b**) [2000s] a 'cocktail' of crack cocaine and heroin. **5** [1980s+] (*US black*) (*also* **eight**) Olde English 800, a popular beer in black neighbourhoods. **6** [2000s] (*US prison*) a clique of prisoners, or an eight-year term.

eightball *adj.* [EIGHTBALL *n.* (1a)] (*US*) a derog. ref. to a black person.

IN COMPOUNDS

❑ **eightball chick** *n.* [1990s+] a female gang member.

eight ball *v.* [pool imagery] [1940s+] (*US*) to ruin or frustrate, esp. by cheating; as n., an overpowering experience, e.g. a hangover from drink or drugs.

eight-day clock *n.* [rhy. sl. = COCK *n.*[3] (1)] [1980s] (*Aus.*) the penis.

eighteen *n.* [1910s+] (*Aus.*) an 18-gallon (82-litre) keg of beer.

eighteen-carat *adj.* (*also* **fourteen-carat, nineteen-carat, seventeen-carat, sixteen-karat**) [note in assessment of gold, the best is not 18 but 22 carat] [late 19C–1910s] (*US*) **1** first-class. **2** absolute, complete.

eighteen-holer *n.* [1990s+] (*UK teen*) the highest-lacing version of Dr. Marten's boots.

eighteen pence *n.* [rhy. sl.] **1** [1910s+] sense. **2** [1950s+] (*Aus.*) a (garden) fence. **3** [1950s+] (*Aus./UK*) a receiver of stolen goods [FENCE *n.*[1] (1)].

8–8–16 *n.* [the dimensions in inches of a single one of the concrete blocks that make up the cell walls] [1990s+] (*US Und.*) a prison cell.

eighter Decatur/eighter from Decatur *n. see* ADA FROM DECATUR *n.*

eighth *n.* (*also* **one-eight**) [1930s+] (*drugs*) one-eighth of an ounce or gram of a drug, usu. a narcotic.

808 *n.* [the Roland 808 drum machine] [1990s+] (*rap music*) the bassdrum from a Roland TR-808 drum machine, which is now a popular make.

eight-six *v. see* EIGHTY-SIX *v.*

eighty days *n.* (*also* **eighty miles**) [1900s–10s] (*US*) the point of eight in craps.

eighty-eight *n.*[1] (*also* **eighty-eighty**) [? number of keys or 8:8 time] [1930s–50s] (*US black*) a piano.

eighty-eight *n.*[2] (*also* **88**) [1950s] (*US*) an Oldsmobile 88, a.k.a. *Rocket 88.*

eighty-eighter *n.* [EIGHTY-EIGHT *n.*[1] + sfx *-er*] [1940s+] (*US*) a pianist.

eighty-eights *n.* [orig. used by telegraph operators] [1930s–70s] (*US*) love and kisses.

eighty-eighty *n. see* EIGHTY-EIGHT *n.*[1].

85% *n.* [for full ety. *see* 5% NATION *n.*] [1990s+] (*US black*) the great uneducated mass of (black) people, who are destined to be taught and led by the knowledgeable 5%.

eighty miles *n. see* EIGHTY DAYS *n.*

eighty-six *adj.* (*also* **86**) [EIGHTY-SIX *v.* (1)] [1940s–80s] (*US*) unwelcome, esp. as at a bar.

eighty-six *v.* (*also* **eight-six, 86**) [rhy. sl. = NIX *v.* (1); orig. restaurant and bar use, indicating that the supply of an item is exhausted or that a customer is not to be served] **1** [1940s+] (*US*) to throw out, to get rid of; as *n.*, an unwanted item. **2** [1970s+] (*US*) to kill, murder; to execute judicially. **3** [1980s+] (*US campus*) to be finished, to be ready to leave.

eighty-six! *excl.* [EIGHTY-SIX *v.*] [1960s+] **1** get out! go away! **2** (*US campus*) no!

einstein *n.* [the crinkly grey hair/genius of the scientist Albert *Einstein* (1879–1955)] **1** [1960s] (*US campus*) an intellectual. **2** [1980s+] (*US campus*) pubic hair. **3** [1990s+] brains.

einstein *v.* [the scientist Albert *Einstein* (1879–1955)] [1950s] to think.

ejot *n. see* EEJIT *n.*

ekame *n.* [backsl. = MAKE *n.*[2] (1)] [mid-19C] a swindle.

eke *n.* [EEK *n.*] [1970s] (*gay*) make-up, cosmetics.

Ekka, the *n.* [abbr. SE *exhibition*] [1970s+] (*Aus.*) the annual Exhibition held at the Brisbane Exhibition Grounds.

ekker *n. see* ECCER *n.*

ekom *n.* [backsl. = MOKE *n.*[1] (3)] [mid-19C] a donkey.

ek se! *excl.* [Afk. phr. *ek sê vir jou*, I'm telling you] [1980s+] (*S.Afr.*) general intensifying excl.; 'I'm telling you!', 'you know what I mean!' etc.

El, the *n.* [1940s] (*US prison/Und.*) Elmira Prison, New York.

el *n.*[1] (*also* **L, El**) [abbr./pron.] **1** [late 19C+] (*US*) the *el*evated railway, usu. that of New York (opened in 1879), but also in other cities, e.g. Chicago, where such transport systems existed. **2** *see* L *n.* (3b).

el *n.*[2] [1980s] (*US black*) a limousine.

el- *pfx* [1920s+] (*orig. US*) a cod Sp. pfx used to decry a given n./adj.; usu. the object is also 'Spanished' with an *-o* sfx, e.g. EL CHEAPO *adj.*; EL DORKO *n.*; also as a derog. personal ref.

elakazoo *n.* [ety. unknown] [1900s] (*US*) money.

el-bee *n. see* L.B. *n.*

elbow *n.* **1** [late 19C–1900s] (*US*) a detective, a policeman [pun on the 'long arm of the law'; note Casey, *The Gay-cat* (1921): '"Elbow" comes from the detective's way of elbowing through a crowd']. **2** [1920s–30s] (*UK Und.*) a pickpocket's assistant [he *elbows* the victim to distract their attention from the pickpocketing]. **3** [1940s] (*US Und.*) a general term of abuse [the victim is *elbowed* out of the way]. **4** [1970s+] (*also* **el bow**) rejection, dismissal.

SE in slang uses

IN COMPOUNDS

❑ **elbow-bender** *n.* (*also* **arm bender, elbow crooker**) [20C+] **1** a heavy drinker; thus *elbow-bending*, drinking. **2** a drinking party. ❑ **elbow exercise** *n.* [1910s] (*US*) drinking. ❑ **elbow grease** *n. see* separate entry. ❑ **elbow-jigger** *n.* (*also* **elbow-scraper**) [mid-19C] a fiddle-player. ❑ **elbow-quaker** *n.* [mid-19C] (*UK Und.*) a violinist. ❑ **elbow-shaker** *n.* **1** [18C–mid-19C] a dice-player [the action of shaking the dice cup]. **2** [1950s+] (*US black*) one who reminds others of a forgotten or overlooked fact or event by (fig.) digging them in the ribs. ❑ **elbow-titting** *n.* [1960s] (*US*) a game whereby a man accosts an unknown woman and rubs his elbows against her breasts before running off – or getting hit or shouted at.

IN PHRASES

❑ **big E** *n.* [initial letter] **1** [1980s+] a brush-off, a rejection. **2** [1990s+] dismissal from a job. ❑ **crook the elbow** *v.* [late18C–1940s] to drink; thus *elbow-crooking*, drinking. ❑ **get on one's elbows** *v.* [1940s] (*US*) to get angry. ❑ **get the elbow** *v.* [1970s+] to be rejected, to be dismissed. ❑ **keep one's elbow down** *v.* to resist drinking alcohol. ❑ **more power to your elbow** *see under* POWER *n.* ❑ **on the elbow** (*also* **on the bow, on the bow-wow**) [the scrounger nudges or tugs one's elbow] [late 19C+] on the scrounge. ❑ **shake one's elbow** *v.* [the shaking of the dice-box] **1** [17C–19C] to play dice, to gamble, hence n. *elbow-shaking*. **2** [mid–late 19C] to play cards. ❑ **up to one's elbows** *see* UP TO ONE'S ARMPITS *under* ARMPIT *n.*

IN EXCLAMATIONS

❑ **me elbow!** [euph. var. on *MY ARSE! under* ARSE *n.*] [1910s+] (*Irish*) a general excl. of incredulity, dismissal. ❑ **my elbow!** [euph. var. on *MY ARSE! under* ARSE *n.*] [20C+] (*N.Z.*) excl. of surprise or disbelief.

elbow *v.*[1] [ELBOW *n.* (1); + ? one nudges the person with an *elbow*] [mid-19C–1930s] (*US Und.*) to warn an accomplice to get out of sight when police appear, usu. as excl. *elbow!*

elbow *v.*[2] [ELBOW *n.* (4)] [1970s+] to reject, to dismiss.

elbow grease *n.* [the movement of one's *elbow*] **1** [late 17C+] physical effort. **2** [mid-19C] fiddle-playing.

el bummero *n. see* BUMMER *n.*[4] (2).

el cheapo *adj.* [cod Sp.; EL- *pfx*] [1960s+] (*US*) cheap.

El D *n.* (*also* **eldo**) [abbr.] [1970s+] (*US*) a Cadillac *El Dorado*.

elderberry *n.* [pun on SE *elder* and FRUIT *n.* (2)] [1950s–60s] (*gay*) an ageing or old homosexual.

elderly jam *n. see under* JAM *n.*[3].

elders *n.* [SE *udders*] [1960s+] (*Irish*) **1** the female breasts. **2** a term of abuse, as in *dirty elders*.

el diablito *n.* (*also* **el diablo**) [Sp. 'the little devil'] [2000s] (*drugs*) a mixture of marijuana, cocaine, heroin and phencyclidine.

el dingo *adj.* [cod Sp.; EL- *pfx* + DINGY *adj.*[2]] [1980s] (*US*) crazy.

eldo *n. see* EL D *n.*

el dorko *n.* [cod Sp.; EL- *pfx* + DORK *n.* (2)] [1980s+] (*US*) a fool, an incompetent.

eldpineer *n.* [SE *elder* + ? *pin*] [mid-19C] (*UK Und.*) a veteran pickpocket.

electric *adj.* **1** [1960s–70s] containing LSD. **2** [1970s] weird and wonderful, marvellous.

IN COMPOUNDS

❑ **electric lettuce** *n.* [1990s+] (*drugs*) very potent cannabis. ❑ **electric machine** *n. see under* MACHINE *n.* ❑ **electric puha** *n.* [NZE *puha*, a form of sowthistle] [2000s] (*N.Z.*) marijuana, usu. homegrown. ❑ **electric queen** *n.* [-QUEEN *sfx*] [1960s–70s] (*US gay*) a gay HIPPIE *n.*[2] (3). ❑ **electric soup** *n. see* LUNATIC SOUP *n.* (2).

SE in slang uses

IN COMPOUNDS

❑ **electric cure** *n.* [1920s+] (*US prison*) the electric chair.

electrician *n.* [his appearance gives debtors 'a shock'] [early 19C] a sheriff's officer, dealing with bankrupts.

electrified *adj.* [late 19C] drunk.

elegant *n.* [1950s] (*US Und.*) an escape from prison.

elegant *adj.* [mid-18C+] excellent, first-rate.

elegantifferously *adv.* [SE *elegant* + SPLENDIFEROUS *adj.*] [mid-19C] (*US*) outstandingly.

element *n.* [mid-18C–mid-19C] (*US*) an alcoholic drink; thus *in one's element*, intoxicated.

elephant *n.* **1** [mid-19C] (*US Und.*) a thief who has stolen more than he can carry and then hide. **2** [mid-19C+] an extraordinary sight or remarkable situation and the experience of such that leads to gaining knowledge or the loss of innocence. **3** [late 19C+] the Elephant and Castle, London SE. **4** [20C+] (*US*) a clumsy, awkward person. **5** [1980s] (*US gay*) a fat person.

IN COMPOUNDS

❑ **elephant business** *n.* [late 19C] (*US*) sightseeing.

IN PHRASES

❑ **see the elephant** *v.* (*also* **get a look at the elephant, hunt the elephant**) (*orig. US*) **1** [mid-19C+] (*also* **see the big animal**) to see the world or something spectacular within it; usu. to have become bored and jaded by doing so; to be disappointed in one's optimistic expectations [the exoticism of the creature; despite US origin, phr. poss. popularized in the UK by the appearance in London in 1867 of the original Jumbo, a major and much-loved attraction who was controversially sold to Barnum and Bailey's Circus in 1882]. **2** [mid-19C+] to seek out excitement, esp. in the context of going slumming in poor and/or dangerous urban areas. **3** [late 19C] to be seduced, to be fooled. ❑ **show the elephant** *v.* [var. on *SEE THE ELEPHANT* above] [mid–late 19C] (*US*) to show someone the sights, used esp. of town-dwellers thus regaling their 'country cousins'.

SE in slang uses

IN COMPOUNDS

❑ **elephant ears** *n.* [1920s–50s] (*US Und.*) a detective or police officer. ❑ **elephant's fallen arches** *n. see* CAT'S WHISKERS *n.* ❑ **elephant teeth** *n.* [the ivory keys] [1950s] (*US black*) piano keys. ❑ **elephant (tranquillizer)** *n.* [such drugs could 'knock out an elephant'] [1980s+] (*drugs*) **1** heroin. **2** phencyclidine.

elephant and castle *n.* [rhy. sl.] **1** [20C+] the anus [ARSEHOLE *n.* (1) (pron. 'arssle')]. **2** [1920s+] a parcel.

elephant's trunk *n.* [quasi-rhy. sl. TRONK *n.*] (*S.Afr.*) prison.

elephant's (trunk) *adj.* (*also* **Jumbo's trunk**) [rhy. sl.] [mid-19C+] drunk.

elevate *v.*[1] [late 19C–1920s] (*US*) in poker, to raise an opponent.

elevate *v.*[2] [pun on HOLD UP *v.*[1] (1)] [1920s–50s] (*UK/US Und.*) **1** to rob at gunpoint. **2** to hold someone up (other than for robbery). **3** to put up one's hands in a hold up; thus used as imper.

elevated *adj.* [pun on SE] [mid-17C+] drunk, one of a number of words and phrases that equate drunkenness with 'getting high'; thus *elevation*, a state of drunkenness.

elevator *n.* **1** [late 19C] a crinolette or bustle used for distending the back of a woman's skirt [it raises or 'elevates' the back of the skirt]. **2** [1910s–20s] (*UK Und.*) a hold-up man, a robber; a shoplifter [pun on SE *hold up*/HOLD UP *v.*[1] (1)].

SE in slang uses

IN COMPOUNDS

❑ **elevator jockey** *n.* (*also* **elevator pilot**) [JOCKEY *n.*[2] (3b)] [1960s–70s] (*US*) a lift operator.

IN PHRASES

❑ **elevator doesn't reach the top floor** [1980s+] a phr. describing a fool; one of several implying that one is 'not all there'.

eleven forty-fiver *n.* [the trad. time –11.45 a.m. – of the pre-show parade that passed through a town where the minstrels were performing] [1940s] (*US*) a blackface minstrel.

eleven steps *n. see under* STEP *n.*[1].

eleven, twenty-nine, twenty-three *n.* [1920s] (*US Und.*) a jail sentence of one hour less than a whole year, thus avoiding the mandatory loss of citizenship that in some states comes with a one-year sentence.

eleventy-eleven *n.* (*also* **eleventeen, leventy-leven**) [late 19C+] (*US black*) a very large or infinite number.

elffinger *n.* [SE *elder*, i.e. veteran (*see* ELDPINEER *n.*) + FINGER *v.* (1b)] [mid-19C] (*UK Und.*) an expert thief.

el foldo *n.* (*also* **el floppo**) [cod Sp.; EL- *pfx* + FOLD *v.* (3)] [1930s+] (*US*) a failure, esp. in sport or a feigned knockout in boxing.

IN PHRASES

❑ **pull an el-foldo** *v.* [1950s+] (*US*) to collapse, to give in.

Eli *n.* [*Eli*hu Yale (1649–1721) founder of the original college at Saybrook before it moved to New Haven] [19C+] (*US campus*) Yale University; thus *Elis*, alumni of Yale.

elick *n. see* ELLICK *n.*

Elijah two *n.* [Dr John Alexander Dowie (1847–1907), a US evangelist, who was thus satirically christened in memory of the original, biblical *Elijah*; his son, in time, became Elijah three] [late 19C] (*US*) a false prophet.

elk *v.* [ety. unknown] [mid-19C] (*UK Und.*) to loan.

Elkie Clark *n. see* L.K. CLARK *n.*

ell *n.* [play on SE *ell*, 45 inches (a Flemish ell was 27 inches) + therefore link to YARD *n.*[1] + Fr. *elle*, she] [late 16C–18C] the vagina.

Ellen *n.* [ult. US lesbian actress *Ellen* Degeneres (b. 1958)] [1990s+] (*US campus*) a lesbian.

Ellenborough's lodge *n.* (*also* **Ellenborough's park, Ellenborough's spike**) [Lord *Ellenborough* (1750–1818) Lord Chief Justice 1802–17] [early 19C] the King's Bench prison.

Ellenborough's teeth *n.* [Lord *Ellenborough* (see ELLENBOROUGH'S LODGE *n.*) + SE *teeth*] [early 19C] the spiked *chevaux-de-frise* that top the walls of the King's Bench prison.

Ellen Terry *n.* [rhy. sl. = JERRY *n.*[5] (1); ult. Shakespearian actress Ellen Terry (1847–1928)] [1920s+] a chamberpot.

ellersby *n.* [abbr. (LSB). Note printers' use *Ellessea*, London Society of Compositors (LSC)] [late 19C] the London School Board.

ellick *n.* (*also* **elick**) [ety. unknown; ? proper name *Alec*] [1900s–20s] (*US*) the penis.

elly-bay *n.* [pig Lat.] [mid-19C+] the belly.

el magnifico *adj.* [cod Sp.; EL- *pfx*] [1990s+] wonderful, excellent, magnificent.

elmer *n.* [the use of *Elmer* as a 'typical' country name] [1920s–60s] (*US*) a rural or unsophisticated man.

elmer fudge *n.* [rhy. sl.; ult. cartoon character *Elmer Fudd*] [1980s] (*Aus.*) a judge.

el paso *n.* [cod Sp.; EL- *pfx* + SE *pass* + pun on *El Paso*, Texas] [1990s+] (*US*) an act of rejection, ignoring.

el pee *n.* [abbr./pron.] [1990s+] (*US black*) an *El* Producto cigar.

el primo *adj.* [Sp. *primo*, the best] [1980s+] (*US*) first class.

elrig *n.* [backsl.] [mid-19C+] girl.

el ropo *n.* (*also* **el ropo stinkadoro, el stinko**) [cod Sp.; EL- *pfx*; note Rudyard Kipling, *Stalky & Co.* (1899), '*pomposo stinkadoro*, a large, malodorous cigar'] [1940s+] (*US*) a cheap, strong cigar.

Elsie Tanner *n.* [rhy. sl.; ult, fictional character *Elsie Tanner* in UK TV's soap opera *Coronation Street*] [2000s] a hammer.

elsin *n.* [dial. *elsin*, a shoemaker's awl; ult. MDu. *elssene*, an awl] [late 19C+] (*Ulster*) a 'sharp' individual.

el sleazo *n.* *see* SLEAZO *under* SLEAZE *n.*

el stinko *n.* *see* EL ROPO *n.*

el stinkola *n.* [cod Sp.; EL- *pfx* + STINK *v.*] [1940s] (*US*) anything or anyone considered worthless, useless.

Elton (John) *n.* [rhy. sl.; ult. UK singer/songwriter *Elton John* (b. 1947)] [1990s+] a confidence trick.

elvis *v.* [a play on the SAmE *sideburns* (UK *side-boards*), which adorned the cheeks of the singer *Elvis* Presley (1935–77)] [1990s+] (*drugs*) of a cannabis cigarette, to burn unevenly, proceding faster down one side than the other.

Elvis year *n.*

SE in slang uses

IN PHRASES

❑ **have an Elvis year** *v.* [2000s] (*orig. US*) to be successful.

el zilch-o *n.* [cod Sp.; EL- *pfx* + ZILCH *n.*[1]] [1970s] (*US*) nothing.

elzoo *n.* [1920s] (*US Und.*) a surveillance preparatory to committing a crime.

em *n.* *see* M *n.*

emag *n.* [backsl.] [late 19C+] a game, usu. as a term of disgust or disappointment meaning 'what's your game?' etc.

embalmed *adj.* [play on SE + EMBALMING FLUID *n.* (1)] [20C+] very drunk.

SE in slang uses

IN COMPOUNDS

❑ **embalmed horse** *n.* *see* HORSE *n.* (4).

embalmer *n.* [EMBALMING FLUID *n.* (1)] [1920s–30s] (*orig. US black*) a bootlegger.

embalming fluid *n.* **1** [1920s+] second-rate whisky. **2** [1920s+] (*US tramp*) coffee. **3** [1980s] (*drugs*) phencyclidine. **4** [1980s] marijuana mixed with cocaine.

embarrassed *adj.* [1960s] (*W.I.*) of a woman, pregnant; of a man, castrated; thus as the major insult, *embarrassed sow, embarrassed hog*.

emboosticated *adj.* [1970s] (*US campus*) embarrassed.

embroidery *n.* *see* CHINESE NEEDLEWORK *under* CHINESE *adj.*

emcee *n.* *see* M.C. *n.*

em-eff *n.* (*also* **emm-eff**) [pron. of initial letters; M.F. *n.*] [1960s+] (*orig. US*) euph. for MOTHERFUCKER *n.*

em-eff *adj.* (*also* **emeffing, emm-eff**) [pron. of initial letters; M.F. *adj.*] [1950s+] (*orig. US*) euph. for MOTHERFUCKING *adj.*

emergency gun *n.* [SE *emergency* + GUN *n.*[1] (5)] [1930s] (*drugs*) any makeshift instrument used to inject when one does not have a syringe.

emigrate *v.* [mid-19C] (*US*) to leave.

emily post *n.* [rhy. sl. = GHOST *n.* (6); ult. author of popular etiquette manual *Emily Post* (1872/3–1960)] [1980s] (*Aus.*) a creditor.

Emma Freuds *n.* (*also* **Clement Freud(s), emmas**) [rhy. sl.; ult. *Emma Freud* (b. 1962), UK TV presenter, *Clement Freud* (b. 1924), UK food writer and broadcaster] [1990s+] haemorrhoids.

emm-eff *see* EM-EFF.

Emmerdale (Farm) *n.* [rhy. sl.; ult. UK soap opera *Emmerdale Farm*, now renamed *Emmerdale*] [1990s+] an arm.

emok nye *phr.* [backsl.] [late 19C] come in.

empty *n.*[1] [20C+] any container or vessel that has been emptied, esp. a bottle once containing alcohol.

IN PHRASES

❑ **get the empty** *v.* [play on SACK *n.* (2a), which is seen as empty of contents] [late 19C] to be dismissed from one's job.

empty *n.*[2] [1980s] (*Aus.*) an ejaculation of semen; thus *have an empty*, to masturbate.

empty *adj.* **1** [18C] (*UK Und.*) of a person or place, not worth robbing. **2** [1940s–50s] (*US*) penniless, broke.

SE in slang uses

IN COMPOUNDS

❑ **empty bottle** *n.* [early–mid-19C] (*UK campus*) at Cambridge University, a fellow-commoner, i.e. a rich or aristocratic undergraduate, with special privileges and a reputation for self-indulgent laziness. ❑ **empty suit** *n.* [1980s+] (*US*) a useless or insincere person.

IN PHRASES

❑ **empty house is better than a bad tenant** [1930s+] (*N.Z.*) a phr. used after breaking wind in public.

empty *v.* **1** [late 19C] (*UK Und.*) to trick, to swindle. **2** [1980s+] (*Aus. prison*) to be transferred suddenly to another prison. **3** [1990s+] (*Aus. Und.*) to dismiss from a job.

SE in slang uses

IN PHRASES

❑ **empty one's trash** *v.* *see under* TRASH *n.* ❑ **empty the anaconda** *v.* *see under* ANACONDA *n.*

emsel *n.* [medical *M.sel*, morphine] [1950s–70s] (*US drugs*) morphine.

emu *n.* [the image of an *emu* pecking at the ground; note Ozwords Oct. 1996: 'The term appears to have its origin in the early twentieth century when it was used to describe people picking up pieces of timber after clearing or burning (and bobbing up and down in emu-fashion). It was also used of people picking up litter.'] [1960s+] (*Aus.*) a racecourse idler who picks up discarded tote tickets in the hope of finding one that has not been cashed.

emu-bobber *n.* [for ety. *see* EMU *n.*] [1920s+] (*Aus.*) a man employed to pick up the remnants after clearing or burning off in the bush.

enamel *n.* [1940s] (*US black*) skin.

enamel god/goddess *n.* *see* PORCELAIN GOD *n.*

enchilada *n.* [resemblance] [1970s] (*US*) the penis.

encore *n.* [20C+] sexual intercourse for the second time, usu. soon after one has just had the initial bout.

end *n.* [note milit. use *ends away*, having intercourse] **1** as a part of the body. (**a**) [late 16C–mid-17C; 1920s+] the penis; esp. in phr. *get one's end away*. (**b**) [17C–18C] (*also* **butt-end, lower end**) the vagina, the female genitals. (**c**) [late 18C+] the buttocks, the posterior. **2** in fig. uses. (**a**) [late 19C+] a share, usu. of criminal profits or responsibility. (**b**) [1940s] that proportion of one's illicit gains that is used to bribe the police. **3** in geographical uses. (**a**) [20C+] that area of a football stadium, behind the respective goals, trad. reserved for the hardcore supporters of home and away teams and the scene of most fighting. (**b**) [1990s+] (*UK black/teen*) an area of a city.

IN PHRASES

❑ **end over appetite** *adj.* [20C+] (*US*) head over heels (cf. ARSE OVER APPETITE *under* ARSE *n.*). ❑ **get one's end away** *v.* (*also* **get one's dick away**) [1910s+] to have sexual intercourse; thus *end-away*, an act of intercourse. ❑ **get one's end in** *v.* [1930s+] to have sexual intercourse. ❑ **take one's end** *v.* [1940s] (*US Und.*) to accept bribe money.

SE in slang uses

IN PHRASES

❑ **end of the ballgame** *n. see under* BALLGAME *n.* ❑ **end of the line** *n.* (*also* **end of the road**) [railway imagery] [1940s+] (*orig. US*) the very end, the ultimate. ❑ **get the hard end** *v.* [1900s–30s] (*US*) to suffer, to be victimized, to be placed in an invidious position. ❑ **get the sticky end** *v.* [1920s] (*US*) to do badly, to be treated unfairly. ❑ **knock the end in** *v.* (*also* **knock the end of**) [late 19C–1920s] to ruin a situation. ❑ **long end** *n.* **1** [1900s–10s] in betting, the favourite. **2** [1900s–40s] (*US*) the majority, the bulk.

end, the *n.* **1** [1910s+] the absolute limit that the speaker will tolerate, 'the last straw'. **2** [1940s+] (*orig. US black*) perfection, absolute excellence, the best possible.

endacott *v.* (*also* **cott, endicott**) [a Constable *Endacott* who, in 1887, was tried and acquitted for the arrest on these grounds of a respectable dressmaker; the term, poss. coined by Annie Besant (1847–1933), was abbr. to *cott*] [late 19C] to arrest on false pretences, spec. those of being a prostitute.

endjie *n. see* ENTJIE *n.*

endo *n.* [var. INDO *n.* (2)] [1980s+] (*drugs*) marijuana.

ends *n.*[1] [SE phr. *make ends meet*; US SE *dividends*] [1950s+] (*US black*) money; living expenses.

IN PHRASES

❑ **loose ends** *n.* [1970s+] (*US black*) spare money available for loans.

ends *n.*[2] [1960s] (*US black*) shoes.

endsville *n.* [END, THE *n.* + -VILLE *sfx*[1] (1)] [1950s+] (*US*) **1** the best, the ultimate. **2** the limit, the end, as far as one can go, death. **3** absolute, irretrievable failure. **4** of a place, out-of-the-way, without quality, thus ext. *east of Endsville*.

endways *adv.* [SE *endways*, end on, with the end facing] [1900s–40s] (*US black*) backwards, back-to-front.

enemy *n.* **1** [mid-19C–1930s] time; thus *kill the enemy*, to pass time; *how's the enemy?, what says the enemy?*, what time is it? **2** [late 19C] the penis. **3** [late 19C] the vagina.

energizer *n.* (*drugs*) **1** [1980s+] phencyclidine. **2** [1990s+] MDMA.

enforcer *n.* **1** [1920s+] a person, usu. a thug, used to enforce his (or another's) will through violence or threats of violence. **2** [1950s+] (*gay*) a lesbian who keeps the other women in line.

engabachado *n.* [Mex. Sp. *engabachado*, rendered white] [1960s+] (*US*) a Mexican who attempts to 'pass' as white.

engage in three to one (and bound to lose) *v.* [the image is of a conflict between the penis and two testicles and the vagina; the 'loss' is of semen] [late 18C–late 19C] to have sexual intercourse.

engagement *n. see* NAVAL ENGAGEMENT *n.*

Engelbert (Humperdinck) *n.* [rhy. sl.; ult. UK pop star *Engelbert Humperdinck*, real name Arnold George Dorsey (b. 1936)] [1990s+] a drink.

engine *n.* **1** [early 17C–late 19C] the penis. **2** [late 17C–mid-18C; 1910s] the vagina. **3** [1930s–50s] (*US drugs*) the equipment used by an opium smoker.

engineer *n.*

IN PHRASES

❑ **talk to the engineer, not the oily rag** *v. see under* TALK TO *v.* ❑ **dark engineer** *n. see under* DARK *adj.*

engka *v.* [ety. unknown] [1990s+] (*W.I.*) to associate with someone in the hope of begging a loan.

English *n.*[1] [the national drink] [17C] ale.

English *n.*[2] [billiards jargon *English*, spin imparted to one or other side of the ball] [mid-19C+] (*orig. US*) deceptiveness, duplicity, 'spin'.

IN PHRASES

❑ **use the English** *v.* [snooker jargon *English*, a swerving shot] [1940s+] (*US gay*) to wriggle one's buttocks while being penetrated anally.

English *n.*[3] [abbr.] [1990s+] (*US*) Olde *English* Malt Liquor.

English *adj.* [the national stereotype of the English as enjoying beatings] [1960s–70s] (*US*) sado-masochistic.

IN COMPOUNDS

❑ **English culture** *n.* [ironic use of SE *culture*] [1960s+] sex advertisements for bondage and discipline. ❑ **English guidance** *n.* [the popular assumption that the English enjoy such activities] [1960s+] bondage and discipline.

SE in slang uses

IN COMPOUNDS

❑ **English burgundy** *n.* [the real *Burgundy* is a variety of French wine] [late 18C–mid-19C] porter (a type of dark beer brewed from malt). ❑ **English cane** *n.* [late 17C–early 18C] a cudgel. ❑ **English cold** *n.* (*also* **English winter**) [tea is seen as a quintessential English pleasure] [20C+] (*US*) iced tea. ❑ **English disease** *n.* **1** [18C–19C] melancholy, depression. **2** [1960s+] a propensity for industrial action and strikes. **3** [1960s+] erotic flagellation. ❑ **English manufacture** *n.* (*also* **manufacture**) [SE; all these are native drinks, as opposed to wine or brandy] [late 17C–early 19C] ale, beer or cider. ❑ **English martini** *n.* [1960s+] (*US gay*) tea; esp. when spiked with gin. ❑ **English method** *n.* [1960s+] (*US gay*) intercrural homosexual intercourse, i.e. non-penetrative rubbing between closed thighs. ❑ **English muffins** *n.* [the sexual image of the *English* + MUFFIN *n.*[1] (6)] [1960s+] (*US gay*) a boy's buttocks. ❑ **English sentry** *n.* [it 'stands to attention' + ? reputation of Guardsmen for gay prostitution] [1960s+] (*US gay*) the erect penis. ❑ **English shower** *n. see* POLISH SHOWER *under* POLISH *adj.* ❑ **English sunbathing** *n.* [the foolishness of recent immigrants from the UK] [1970s+] (*N.Z.*) sitting fully-clothed in the sun. ❑ **English winter** *n. see* ENGLISH COLD above.

English channel *n.*[1] [rhy. sl. = SE *panel* (of doctors)] [1950s–70s] the National Health Service.

English channel *n.*[2] [1970s] (*US campus*) bloodshot or drooping eyes, the effect of smoking cannabis.

Englishified *adj.* [20C+] (*W.I.*) **1** said of one who has returned from a stay in England with an English accent and a generally more sophisticated persona. **2** of East Indians, generally urbanized or Westernized (there need have been no visit to the UK).

enif *n.* [backsl.] [mid–late 19C] fine.

enin *n.* (*also* **eenin**) [backsl.] [mid-19C+] the number nine.

enin gens *n.* [ENIN *n.* + GEN *n.*[1]] [mid-19C] nine shillings (45p).

enin yeneps *n.* (*also* **enine yenep, enin yannops, enin yenneps**) [backsl.; ENIN *n.* + YENNEP *n.*] [mid-19C] nine pence.

enlightened *adj.* [2000s] (*US black*) intoxicated by marijuana.

ennit! *excl. see* INNIT! *excl.*

eno *n.* [backsl.] [mid-19C+] one.

enob *n.* [backsl.] **1** [late 19C+] a bone. **2** [1980s] the penis.

enoch *n.*[1] [stereotyped 'rural' name] [1950s] (*US*) a peasant.

enoch *n.*[2] [rhy. sl.; ult. *Enoch Powell* (1912–98), UK right-wing politician] [1990s+] a towel.

enormous *adj.* [late 19C] (*US*) splendid.

enough to… *phr.*

SE in slang uses

IN PHRASES

❑ **…gag a maggot** *see under* MAGGOT *n.* ❑ **…make a black man choke** [negative stereotyping, on the basis that blacks have a less refined palate] [20C+] a phr. indicating that something (usu. food and medicines but also of abstract objects, emotions etc) is unpalatable. ❑ **…make a cat laugh** (*also* **enough to make a cat sick, enough to make a cow satirical, enough to make a dog/mouse/rat laugh, it would make a cat laugh**) [early

17C; mid-19C+] utterly hilarious, devastatingly funny. ❑ **...split the grain** [1900s] enough to render one very drunk.

ensign-bearer *n.* [the colours of the face resemble those of the Union Jack] [mid-17C–early 19C] a red-faced drunkard.

entered *adj.* [early 18C] (*US*) intoxicated.

enter for the gelding stakes *v.* [joc. use of racing imagery] [late 19C] to castrate someone; thus *entered...* to be a eunuch.

entertain the general *v.* [? his red coat] [20C+] (*US*) to menstruate.

enthroned *adj.* [THRONE *n.*] (*US*) **1** [1940s] using the lavatory. **2** [1950s–60s] (*gay*) searching for sex in public lavatories [+ a pun on QUEEN *n.* (2)].

enthusiastic amateur *n. see* AMATEUR *n.* (1).

enthuzimuzzy *n.* [late 19C] enthusiasm.

entire *adj.* [also in Lincolnshire dial.] [late 19C+] (*Ulster*) financially independent; retired from business.

SE in slang uses

(IN COMPOUNDS)

❑ **entire shoot** *n. see* WHOLE BANG SHOOT *n.*

entire animal *n.* (*also* **extreme animal**) [semi-euph. for WHOLE HOG *n.*] [mid-19C] absolutely everything, 'the lot'.

entjie *n.* (*also* **endjie**) [Afk. *end*, end + dimin. sfx *-ie*] [1980s+] (*S.Afr.*) a cigarette end.

entrance *n.* [late 17C; late 19C–1900s] the vagina.

entry *n.* [? entered on a marriage certificate] [1930s] a couple.

enzed *n.* [abbr.] [1910s+] (*Aus./ N.Z.*) New Zealand; thus *enzedder*, a New Zealander.

ep *n.*[1] [abbr. SE *ep*isode] [2000s] event, situation.

ep *n.*[2] *see* EPPY *n.*

epar! *excl.* [reverse of SE *rape!* used fig.] [1950s–70s] (*US campus*) a cry of distress used ironically.

Eph *n.* [? abbr. popular black proper name *Ephraim*] [1910s] (*US*) a black servant: a porter, a waiter.

ephus *n.* [ety. unknown] **1** [1930s–50s] (*US*) the truth. **2** [1950s] a trick or gimmick.

eppes *n.* (*also* **eppis, eppus**) [Ger. *etwas*, something, thence Yid. *eppes*; like many Yid. terms *eppes* is capable of many uses, often ironic, and all dependent on context. It entered the sl. vocabulary via the underworld, which used it to mean low-class or worthless. Subseq. meanings have developed since] [20C+] **1** something, a little. **2** a somebody. **3** nothing.

eppes *adj.* (*also* **eppis, eppus**) [20C+] debatable, worthless, unsatisfactory.

eppes *adv.* (*also* **eppis, eppus**) [20C+] quite, perhaps, maybe, for some inexplicable reason.

eppo *n.* [2000s] (*Irish*) a fit, lit. an epileptic fit.

eppy *n.* (*also* **ep**) [1980s+] **1** an *ep*ileptic. **2** an *ep*ileptic fit; a temper tantrum. **3** a very stupid or unpopular person.

Epsom races *n.* [rhy. sl.] **1** [mid-19C] a pair of braces. **2** [mid-19C] faces.

equalizer *n.* [it reduces all before it to the same abject level; note McCall *Makes Me Wanna Holler* (1994) 'For me guns were life's great equalizer'] [late 19C+] (*US*) **1** a gun. **2** any weapon, a cosh, a knife, a bomb.

equipment *n.* [euph.] **1** [late 19C+] the male genitals. **2** [1940s+] the female breasts.

equipped *adj.* **1** [late 17C–early 19C] rich. **2** [late 17C–early 19C; 1960s] well-turned out, well-dressed [20C use mainly US black]. **3** [1970s] (*US black*) emotionally and socially poised. **4** [1990s+] carrying a weapon of one sort or another.

-er *sfx* [the 'Oxford -er' sfx appeared 'early in the Queen's [sc. Victoria] reign' (Ware) or was 'introduced from Rugby School into Oxford University slang, orig. at University College, in Michaelmas Term, 1875' (*OED*). The absence of any such terms from the seminal (and slang-laden) Oxford novel *The Adventures of Mr Verdant Green* (1853, by 'Cuthbert Bede') makes the later date far more likely. Strictly jargon, given its use at Oxford, it has moved into wider areas, typically *fresher*, a university freshman, *footer*, football, *soccer*, football and *rugger*, rugby. The extreme uses, e.g. *pragger-wagger*, the Prince of Wales and *wagger-pagger-bagger*, a waste-paper basket remain strictly Oxford and 1900s–20s Oxford at that. For a fuller discussion *see* M. Marples, *University Slang* (1950); *inter alia* he suggests the importation came not from Rugby but from Harrow] [late 19C+] used to create slangy formations of nouns by shortening the original noun and replacing the missing letters with *-er*. When the word is a monosyllable, this can be extended by the sfxs *-agger* or *-ugger*.

-erama *sfx see* -ORAMA *sfx*.

erase *v.* [1930s+] to murder, to kill.

erb *n.* [abbr. proper name Herbert, which is seen to be 'funny'] **1** [1910s+] a wag, a humourist. **2** [1920s] anyone whose real name is unknown.

erection section *n.* [2000s] (*Irish*) a slow set at a disco.

-ereenie *sfx see* -EROONIE *sfx*.

erica *n.* [2000s] (*S.Afr. gay*) an erection.

erie *n.* [SE *ear*]

(IN COMPOUNDS)

❑ **erie canal** *n.* [pun on SE *ear* + *Erie Canal*, a canal in New York State between the Hudson River and Lake Erie] [1930s] an eavesdropper.

(IN PHRASES)

❑ **on the erie** (*also* **on the ear-ie**) **1** [1910s+] (*orig. UK Und.*) on the scrounge [var. on *ON THE EARHOLE under* EARHOLE *n.*]. **2** [1920s+] (*US Und./prison*) (*also* **on the earie, ...eary**) eavesdropping.

(IN EXCLAMATIONS)

❑ **on the erie!** (*also* **on the earie!**) [1920s+] (*US prison*) be quiet, someone is listening!

erie *v.* [*ON THE ERIE under* ERIE *n.*] [1940s] (*US Und.*) to overhear.

erif *n.* [backsl.] [mid-19C] fire.

eriff *n.* [SE *eriff*, a two-year-old canary; the term migrated to the US during the 19C] [late 17C–19C] a young or novice criminal.

-erino *sfx* (*also* **-erama, -erina, -erine**) [late 19C+] (*US*) an intensifier applicable to various words, generally implying further excellence, appeal etc, e.g. *PEACHERINO under* PEACH *n.*[1], very wonderful indeed.

erk *n.* [orig. WW1 milit. use, either RN *erk*, a lower deck rating, or RAF *erk*/urk, aircraftsman, second class] [1940s+] a general term of contempt, an insignificant person.

erk *v.* [? *JERK AROUND under* JERK *v.*[2] or SE *irk*] [2000s] (*US black*) to annoy, to irritate.

erky *adj.* [ERK *n.* + sfx *-y*, but note *yuck*, a grunt of distaste] [1950s–60s] (*Aus.*) unpleasant, distasteful.

ernie marsh *n.* [rhy. sl.] [1960s+] the grass.

-eroo *sfx* (*also* **-aroo**) [late 19C; 1930s+] (*orig. US*) a general intensifier, implying a greater flamboyance or exaggeration; allied to a variety of terms, e.g. BOOZEROO *n.*; SMACKEROOS *n.*; STINKEROO *n.*

-eroonie *sfx* (*also* **-amaroot, -aroon, -aroonie, -arooney, -arootie, -ereenie, -eroon, -ooney, -oroonie**) [var. on -ERINO *sfx*] [1910s+] (*US*) an intensifier, usu. positive and added to various words, e.g. *smackeroonie*.

Eros and Cupid *adj.* [rhy. sl.] [1990s+] stupid.

Errol Flynn *n.* [rhy. sl.; ult. Hollywood star *Errol Flynn* (1909–59)] [1940s+] the chin.

error *n.*

(IN PHRASES)

❑ **and no error** [var. on *AND NO MISTAKE under* MISTAKE *n.*] a general intensifier, certainly, without any doubt.

erth *n. see under* EARTH *n.*[1] and its combs.

ervine *n.* [? the *E* on number-plates in L.A. signifies a police vehicle] [1960s] (*US black, LA*) a police officer.

esaff *n.* [backsl.] [late 19C] the face.

escamado *adj.* [Sp. sl. *escamado*, 'losing it'] [1960s+] (*US*) nervous, shaken up.

escape *n.*

SE in slang uses

(IN PHRASES)

❑ **go up the escape** *v.* [1900s] (*US*) to die.

escape out *v.* [SE *escape*, to let a word out inadvertently] [mid-19C] (*US*) to speak, to request.

escargot *n.* [Fr. *escargot*, a snail; such couples appear curled up as tightly as a snail in its shell; Eble, *Slang & Sociability* (1996), prefers play on *his cargo*, i.e. the woman is the man's cargo] [1980s] (*US campus*) a man walking arm in arm with his date.

esclop *n.* (*also* **esilop, eslop**) [backsl., neither the *e* nor the *c* are pronounced] [mid-19C+] the police.

ése *n.* (*also* **essay**) [Sp.] [1960s+] **1** (*US/Hispanic*) a fellow Hispanic, esp. in the context of a street gang. **2** (*US black*) a congratulatory term for a Hispanic; the inference is that such a person is effectively black; qualified as *ése bato, ése vato, ése vacho, cool ése, okay ése, righteous ése*. **3** a term of address, irrespective of ethnicity.

esel *n.* (*also* **ezel**) [Afk. *ezel*, a donkey, an ass] [1910s] (*S.Afr.*) a fool, a simpleton.

esilop *n. see* ESCLOP *n.*

eska *n.* [1990s+] (*US*) marijuana.

Eskimo Nell *n.* [rhy. sl. = SE *bell*] [1990s+] a call on the telephone.

Eskimo pie *n.* [i.e. COLD *adj.* (4)] [1970s] (*US*) a frigid woman.

esky *n.*[1] [abbr. SE *Eskimo*] [1910s+] (*US*) a derog. term for an Inuit, an Eskimo person or an Eskimo dog.

esky *n.*[2] (*also* **eski, eskie**) [SE *Eskimo* and thus chilliness] [1950s+] (*Aus.*) a portable drinks cooler, popularly filled with beer for cricket watching etc.

eslop *n. see* ESCLOP *n.*

Esprit chick *n.* [the fashionable dress shop chain *Esprit* + CHICK *n.*[1] (2)] [1990s+] (*US teen*) a young woman who wears only designer clothing and looks down on others who dress differently.

espysay *n.* [initials SPCA, 'secretive in its nature, being created by people about horses and cattle, many of whom go about in savage fear of this valuable society' (Ware)] [late 19C] the Society for the Prevention of Cruelty to Animals.

esra *n.* (*also* **esrar**) [Turkish *esrar*, cannabis] [1930s+] (*drugs*) marijuana.

es-roph *n.* (*also* **es-roch**) [backsl.] [mid-19C] a horse.

essay *n. see* ÉSE *n.*

essedartus *n.* [Lat. *essedarius*, a fighter in a Gaulish war-chariot] [early 18C] a coachman.

essence *n.*[1] [SE *essence*, an extract obtained by distillation or otherwise from a plant] [mid-19C] (*US*) whisky.

SE in slang uses

IN COMPOUNDS

❑ **essence of hickory** *n.* [mid-19C] (*US*) a whipping with a hickory switch. ❑ **essence-peddler** *n.* [the skunk's notoriety as a smelly animal] [mid-19C–1970s] (*US*) a skunk.

essence *n.*[2] [ECSTASY *n.*] [1980s+] (*drugs*) MDMA.

Essex *adj.*

proper name in slang uses

IN COMPOUNDS

❑ **Essex calf** *n.* (*also* **calf**) [17C–late 19C] a native of Essex, as used by those of Suffolk, who look down on their southern neighbours. ❑ **Essex lion** *n.* [Essex was a popular source of cattle for the London meat markets] **1** [mid-17C–19C] a calf. **2** [late 19C–1900s] a pej. term for a native of Essex, as used by those of Kent. ❑ **Essex stile** *n.* [Essex being a low, marshy county, there are more ditches than stiles] [late 18C–mid-19C] a ditch.

Establishment, the *n.* [SE *establishment*, an institution] [mid–late 19C] (*Aus.*) the Fremantle Gaol.

esther (the queen) *n.* [joc. ref. to the biblical *Esther*, who was a SE *queen*, thus pun on QUEEN *n.* (2)] [1950s–60s] (*camp gay*) a Jewish homosexual male.

estuffa *n.* [Sp.] [1980s+] (*drugs*) heroin.

esuch *n.* [backsl. CASA *n.*[1]] [mid-19C] (*UK Und.*) a house.

etarnal *adj. see* TARNAL *adj.*

et-caetera *n.* (*also* **etcetera**) [euph.] **1** [late 16C–early 17C] the vagina. **2** [mid-17C] venereal disease. **3** [late 17C–mid-18C] sexual intercourse.

etcetera *n.* [early 18C] a bookseller.

etching rig *n.* [mid-19C] (*UK Und.*) the cutting off of women's pockets.

eternity box *n.* [late 18C+] a coffin.

ethel *n.* [the female name] [1920s+] a male homosexual.

ether *n.* [1920s+] fig. use for communication through the radio or the wireless.

Ethiopian paradise *n.* (*also* **Ethiopian heaven**) [poor black theatre-goers could usu. afford only the cheapest seats] [20C+] (*US*) the top gallery in a theatre.

ethno *n.* [SE *ethnic* + -O *sfx* (3)] [1970s] (*Aus.*) immigrants to Australia, of various ethnic persuasions.

ethy meat *n.* [SE *Ethiopian* + MEAT *n.* (1)] [20C+] a black woman.

etter *n.* [fig. use of Du. *etter*, pus] [1990s+] (*S.Afr.*) a general abusive term.

euchre *v.* [for ety. *see* EUCHRED *adj.*] **1** [mid-19C+] (*US*) to swindle, trick or cheat. **2** [1970s+] to destroy.

euchred *adj.* [the card-game *euchre* (orig. US) in which, if a player chooses to play a round and fails to take three tricks, they are 'euchred' (*OED*)] [late 19C+] (*Aus.*) exhausted, destitute, faulty.

euphoria *n. see* U4EUH *n.*

European accentuation *n.* [? body-building use] [1950s+] (*gay*) a tapered body with jutting buttocks.

evaporate *v.* **1** [early 19C] to die. **2** [mid-19C+] to leave, to vanish, to escape.

evatch *v.* [backsl.] [mid–late 19C] to have.

eve *n.*[1] ['Som.(erset) slang' (*EDD*)] [early 18C–early 19C] a hen-roost.

eve *n.*[2] [play on ADAM *n.*[2]] [2000s] (*drugs*) MDEA, a synthetic hallucinogen similar to MDMA.

even *adv.* [1980s+] (*US*) at all, used as a negative emphasis.

even break *n.* [SE *even* + BREAK *n.*[1] (1)] [20C+] (*orig. US*) a fair chance.

even-even *adj.* [20C+] (*US*) equal.

evening *adj.*

SE in slang uses

IN COMPOUNDS

❑ **evening sneak** *n.* [SE *evening* + SNEAK *n.*[1] (1b)] [mid-18C–early 19C] (*UK Und.*) (*also* **night sneak**) a thief who works after dark. ❑ **evening socket** *n.* [the male 'plugs in' at night] [1990s+] the female genitalia. ❑ **evening star** *n.* (*also* **lady of the evening**) [mid–late 19C] (*US*) a prostitute. ❑ **evening wheeze** *n.* [WHEEZE *n.*; the exciting but implausible stories used to sell evening papers] [late 19C] false news, rumours.

evening! *excl.* [abbr.] [late 19C+] good *evening*!

evens *n.* [1910s] (*US*) revenge, a person as an object of revenge.

even shake *n. see under* SHAKE *n.*[1].

even-up *n.* [1990s+] (*W.I.*) presumptuousness.

everfucking *adj. see* EVER-LOVING *adj.*

evergreen *n.* [its colour] [1900s] (*US*) money.

evergreens *n.* [SE *ever* + GREENS *n.*[1]] [19C] the vagina.

everlasting *adj.* [mid-19C–1940s] (*US*) general intensifier, very, exceeding, excessive.

SE in slang uses

IN COMPOUNDS

❑ **everlasting shoes** *n. see under* SHOE *n.* ❑ **everlasting staircase** *n.* (*also* **everlasting stairs**) [invented by the builder William Cubitt (1785–1861) for use in prisons; it was improved by Colonel Chesterton, thus its expanded name *Colonel Chesterton's everlasting staircase*] [mid–late 19C] the prison treadmill ❑ **everlasting wound** *n.* [late 17C; mid–late 19C] the vagina

everlastingly *adv.* [mid–late 19C] (*US*) beyond measure immeasurably, excessively.

ever-loving *n.* [apparently coined and primarily used by US writer Damon Runyon (1884–1946)] [1930s+] one's wife.

ever-loving *adj.* (*also* **everfucking**) [1910s+] (*US*) an intensifier.

ever so *phr.* [late 19C+] much, e.g. *thanks ever so*.

Everton toffee *n.* [rhy. sl.; like white coffee, this toffee is also made with cream or (later) evaporated milk. Note nickname for the British football club Everton, 'the Toffees'] [mid-19C] coffee.

every *adj.*

SE in slang uses

IN PHRASES

❑ **every dog and devil** *n.* [20C+] (*Irish*) everyone. ❑ **every last (one)** *n.* [late 19C+] (*orig. US*) every one without exception. ❑ **every living ass** *n.* [play on SE + ASS *n.* (4)] [1940s+] (*US*) every single person. ❑ **every man jack** *n.* (*also* **every man jag, ...john, every jack man, every woman jill**) [JACK *n.*[2] (1) as generic for a man] [early 19C+] every single one; thus *not a man jack*, not a single one. ❑ **every postman on his beat** *n.* [1930s–40s] (*US black*) kinky hair that stands up in odd strands or areas of the head.

IN EXCLAMATIONS

❑ **every time!** [1920s+] (*US*) a general affirmative excl.

everybody and his cousin *n.* (*also* **everybody and his aunt, ...mother, ...their mamas, ...their mothers-in-law, everybody/one and his brother**) [mid-19C+] (*US*) absolutely everybody.

every mother's son *n.* (*also* **every daddy's babby, every mother's child, ...babe, every woman's son, each mother's son**) [late 16C+] of people, each and every one; of objects, everything.

everything *n.*

SE in slang uses

IN PHRASES

❑ **everything but the kitchen sink** *n.* (*also* **everything but the cat's blanket**) [1910s+] used of an undertaking that requires whatever is available, no matter what it is, relevant or not. ❑ **everything cook and curry** [culinary imagery] [1950s+] (*W.I. Rasta*) all is well, all is taken care of. ❑ **everything is everything** [1960s+] (*US teen/W.I.*) everything is fine.

everywheres *n.* [mid-19C+] (*US*) everywhere.

Eve's custom house *n.* [ext. of CUSTOM HOUSE *n.*] [late 18C–early 19C] the vagina.

evesdropper *n.* [pun on SE *eaves* + *eavesdropper*] **1** [mid-17C] the penis. **2** [18C–mid-19C] a robber of hen-houses. **3** [18C–late 19C] a burglar who lurks outside a house waiting for the chance to break in while the owners are absent; thus a petty thief.

eve with the lid on *n.* [the Garden of Eden story] [1930s–40s] (*US*) apple pie.

evif *n.* (*also* **ewif**) [backsl.] [mid-19C] the number five.

evif-gens *n. see* EWIF GENS *n.*

evif yenneps *n. see* EWIF YENEPS *n.*

evil *n.*[1] [dial. *evil*, a swelling on the neck] [18C–early 19C] a halter.

evil *n.*[2] [sl.'s usu. negative image of marriage] **1** [early–mid-19C] one's wife, 'an admirable synonyme' (*Egan's Grose* 1823). **2** [mid-19C] marriage.

evil *adj.* [ext. of SE] **1** [1920s–70s] excellent, wonderful, the best [on bad = good model]. **2** [1930s+] unpleasant, neurotic, cruel. **3** [1930s+] in a bad mood.

evilling *n.* [SE *evil*/EVIL *adj.* (2) + sfx *-ing*] [1930s+] (*US black*) acting in a deliberately negative manner, e.g. riotously, argumentatively, criminally.

evils, the *n.* [2000s] (*N.Z.*) malicious looks.

evlenet gens *n.* [backsl.; GEN *n.*[1]] [mid-19C] twelve shillings.

evlenet sith-noms *n.* [backsl.; SITH-NOM *n.*] [mid-19C] twelve months, usu. as a prison sentence.

evo *n.* [SE *evening* + -O *sfx* (3); var. on ARVO *n.*] [1950s+] (*Aus.*) evening.

ewe *n.* **1** [late 17C–late 18C] (*UK Und.*) a young and beautiful female member of a criminal gang. **2** [2000s] (*N.Z.*) a female.

ewe-mutton *n.* [SE *ewe* + MUTTON *n.* (1a)] [late 19C] **1** an ageing prostitute. **2** an amateur prostitute.

ewif *n. see* EVIF *n.*

ewif gens *n.* (*also* **evif-gens**) [backsl.; EVIF *n.* + GEN *n.*[1]] [mid-19C] five shillings, a crown.

ewif yeneps *n.* (*also* **evif yenneps, ewif yenneps**) [backsl.; EVIF *n.* + YENNEP *n.*] [mid-19C] five pence.

ewscray *v.* [pig Lat. = SCREW *v.* (6a)] [1930s–40s] (*US*) to go away, used as a command.

ex *n.*[1] (*also* **X**) [SE pfx *ex-*, former, previous] **1** [early 19C+] an ex-husband, ex-wife, ex-lover, the other half of a lapsed relationship. **2** [1900s–60s] (*US prison*) an ex-convict.

ex *n.*[2] [SE *execution*] [2000s] (*US Und.*) a murder, an assassination.

ex *adj.*[1] [abbr. SE *excellent*] [20C+] superlative, first-rate.

ex *adj.*[2] *see* X *adj.*

ex *v.* [abbr. SE *execute*] **1** (*US Und.*) to murder, to assassinate. **2** *see* X *v.*[1].

ex! *excl.* [abbr.; used in preparatory schools] [1920s; 1980s+] (*juv.*) excellent!

exalted *adj.* [mid-17C–mid-18C] slightly drunk.

excavator *n.* [mid-19C] (*UK Und.*) a thief who burgles a wine-merchant's cellar.

excellent *adj.* [popularized by the film *Bill and Ted's Excellent Adventure* (1989)] [1980s+] (*US campus*) extremely good or exciting.

excess baggage *n.* [play on SE] [1940s+] (*US Und.*) a second-rate confidence man.

exchange spit *v. see under* SPIT *n.*[3].

exchequer *n.* [into which one makes a 'deposit', or the image of the vagina as a commodity] [early–mid-16C] the vagina.

ex-con *n.* [SE pfx *ex-*, former + CON *n.*[1] (8)] [20C+] (*orig. US*) a former convict.

excremental *adj.* [1960s+] euph. for SHITTY *adj.*[1].

excused, be *v.* [1950s+] (*mainly school*) euph. for to be allowed to visit the lavatory, usu. in interrog. phr. *may I be excused?*

excuse-me *n.* [their good manners] [1960s+] (*S.Afr.*) a member of the educated middle class.

excuse my/the French *phr. see under* FRENCH *n.*

exec *n.* [abbr.] [late 19C+] an executive (of a firm or business).

execution day *n.* **1** [late 18C] washing day [the washing is 'hanged' out to dry]. **2** [20C+] (*US*) Monday; also the trad. washday.

exercise me *phr.* [1990s+] (*W.I.*) a request to dance.

exercise the ferret *v.* (*also* **exercise one's pecker, exercise the armadillo**) [SE *exercise* + CHUTNEY FERRET *under* CHUTNEY *n.*/ PECKER *n.*[2] (2)/fig. use of SE *armadillo*] [1950s+] to copulate.

exes *n.* (*also* **ex's, exies**) [abbr.] **1** [mid-19C+] expenses. **2** *see* EXIS *n.*

Exeter hall *n.* [a teasing allusion to Exeter Hall, best known for its temperance sermons and, later, as the first London site of a YMCA] [19C] the vagina.

exflunct *v.* [? SE *fling*] [mid-19C–1970s] (*US*) to destroy or overwhelm; usu. as adj. *exflunctified*, overwhelmed, destroyed.

exhaust pipe *n.* [1970s+] (*US gay*) the anus.

exhibition meal *n.* [1920s–30s] (*US tramp*) food left for a beggar outside the door.

exies *n. see* EXES *n.*

exis *n.* (*also* **exes, xis**) [backsl.] **1** [mid-19C] sixpence. **2** [mid-19C+] the number six. **3** [1930s+] six pounds sterling. **4** [1980s] (*UK Und.*) a six-month prison sentence.

exis-evif yeneps *n.* [backsl.; EXIS *n.* + EVIF *n.* + YENNEP *n.* (lit. 'six plus five pence')] [mid-19C] elevenpence.

exis-ewif gens *n.* [backsl.; EXIS *n.* + EVIF *n.* + GEN *n.*[1] (lit. 'six times five shillings')] [mid-19C] 30 shillings, £1 10s (£1.50).

exis gens *n.* [backsl.; EXIS *n.* + GEN *n.*[1]] [mid-19C] six shillings (30p).

exis sith-noms *n.* [backsl.; EXIS *n.* + SITH-NOM *n.*] [mid-19C] six months, usu. as a prison sentence.

exis yeneps *n.* (*also* **exis-yenneps**) [backsl.; EXIS *n.* + YENNEP *n.*] [mid-19C] sixpence (2½p).

expat *n.* [abbr.] [1960s+] **1** an *expatriate*, any citizen of one country living abroad. **2** (*W.I.*) an immigrant, esp. a white foreigner, working in a local job.

expecting *adj.* [abbr. SE *expecting a baby*] [late 19C+] pregnant.

expense *n.* [the cost of bringing up a child] [1940s] (*US black*) a baby.

explore me! *excl.* [1910s] (*US*) used to express lack of knowledge.

explorers' club *n.* [they go on a TRIP *n.*[4] (1)] [1970s+] (*drugs*) group of LSD users.

exsie *adj.* [1990s+] (*Aus.*) expensive.

extensive *adj.* [euph.] [mid-19C] showy, vulgar.

extensive *adv.* [EXTENSIVE *adj.*] [late 19C] to a great extent, unreservedly, ostentatiously.

extortion *n.* [hyperbole] [late 19C] (*US*) the cost.

extra *n.* [1990s+] (*W.I.*) a show-off; also as adj.

extra *adj.* **1** [1940s–60s] (*Aus./US*) extraordinarily good. **2** [1980s] (*N.Z.*) as an intensifier.

extract the Michael *v.* (*also* **take the Michael**) [1950s+] a consciously 'genteel' version of TAKE THE MICKEY (OUT OF) *v.*

extract the urine *v.* [1930s+] (*orig. milit.*) euph. for *TAKE THE PISS (OUT OF) under* PISS *n.*

extreme animal *n. see* ENTIRE ANIMAL *n.*

e ya later *phr.* [var. on *see you later* + joc. ref. to the drug ECSTASY *n.* or E *n.*] [1990s+] (*US teen*) goodbye; spec. on the Internet, an electronic version of *see you later*.

eye *n.* **1** [late 16C; mid-19C] the vagina [the eye is similarly shaped, is surrounded by hair, and can 'water']. **2** [20C+] detective, a private eye. **3** [20C+] (*also* **the Eye**) (*US Und.*) Pinkerton's Detective Agency, the logo of which is an eye. **4** [1930s+] (*US gay/prison*) the rectum, the anus; usu. in comb. [note -EYE *sfx*]. **5** [1940s] a warning. **6** [1950s] a lookout. **7** [1950s–70s] (*US campus*) (*also* **eyeball**) a television set. **8** [1950s+] (*US black*) a hole.

IN COMPOUNDS

▫ **eye doctor** *n.* [1930s+] (*gay*) a male homosexual, i.e. one who practises anal intercourse.

IN PHRASES

▫ **eye of one's arse** *n.* [ARSE *n.* (1)] [1950s+] (*Irish*) the anus. ▫ **eye that weeps most when pleased** *n.* [the secretions that indicate excitement] [19C] the vagina.

IN EXCLAMATIONS

▫ **in your eye!** [late 19C+] (*US*) an excl. of general derision, dismissal, contempt. ▫ **your other eye!** [20C+] (*Irish*) an excl. of disbelief, rubbish! nonsense!

SE in slang uses

DERIVATIVES

▫ **eyeful** *n. see* separate entry.

IN COMPOUNDS

▫ **eye ache** *n.* [i.e. a pain in the EYE *n.* (4)] [1990s+] a bore, a nuisance, an irritation. ▫ **eyeball/baller/balling** *see* separate entries. ▫ **eye booger** *n.* [BOOGER *n.*[1] (1)] [1980s+] (*US campus*) the small pieces of 'sleep' or mucus that collect in the corners of the eyes. ▫ **eye bunger** *n.* [BUNG *v.* (1)] [late 19C] a setback, lit. something that 'blacks one's eye'. ▫ **eye cheaters** *n. see* CHEATERS *n.*[2] (1). ▫ **eye drops** *n.* [1960s] (*US*) tears. ▫ **eyefuck** *see* separate entries. ▫ **eye-game** *v.* [1960s] (*W.I.*) to stare at and ogle women. ▫ **eyeglass weather** *n.* [one requires an *eyeglass*] [late 19C] foggy weather, in which one cannot see clearly. ▫ **eyelid movies** *n.* [1970s+] (*US*) daydreams, fantasies enjoyed with the eyes closed, often as stimulated by a hallucinogenic drug; often of masturbation fantasies, esp. in phr. *watch eyelid movies*, to masturbate. ▫ **eye-limpet** *n.* [its sticks to one's eye socket] [late 19C] an artificial eye. ▫ **eye-opener** *n. see* separate entries. ▫ **eye-popper** *n.* [one's eyes *pop out of one's head*] [1940s+] (*US*) something sensational. ▫ **eye-shoot** *v.* [2000s] (*US*) to stare at aggressively. ▫ **eye-trouble** *n.* [1980s+] (*N.Z. prison*) a propensity (real or imagined) for staring at other prisoners or at warders, usu. in challenging phr. *have you got eye-trouble?*, often the start of a fight. ▫ **eyewash** *n.* [the army use meant anything, e.g. washing the eyes, that is done for effect rather than for any practical purpose] **1** [late 19C+] (*orig. milit.*) rubbish, nonsense, humbug, anything done for appearance rather than effect. **2** [1910s–70s] cheap liquor. ▫ **eyewater** *n.* **1** [19C] gin. **2** [early 19C] (*also* **devil's eyewater**) brandy. **3** [1940s+] (*US*) illicitly distilled whisky.

IN PHRASES

▫ **all my eye (and Betty Martin)** *see* separate entries. ▫ **cut one's eyes** *v.* (*also* **cut yai**) [dial. *cut-eye*, a scornful gesture made with the eyes] [mid-19C+] to glance (suspiciously) at, to look at furtively; to look askance at. ▫ **dig out someone's eye** *v. see under* DIG OUT *v.* ▫ **do in the eye** *v. see under* DO *v.*[1]. ▫ **eye in the sky** *n.* (*orig. US*) **1** [1960s+] a two-way mirror used for security in a casino. **2** [1970s+] a police or traffic helicopter. ▫ **eyes like pissholes in the snow** *n.* (*also* **...in a snowbank, ...like two burnt holes in a blanket**) [poss. the result of an excess of alcohol] [1920s+] (*orig. milit.*) deeply sunken eyes, often bloodshot. ▫ **eyes set at eight in the morning** *adj.* [one's eyes are staring in different directions] [early 17C] drunk. ▫ **eyes set in one's head** *adj.* [early 17C] drunk. ▫ **eyes out** *adv.* [1980s] (*N.Z.*) as fast as possible. ▫ **get in someone's eye** *v.* [1970s+] (*US black*) **1** to beat up. **2** to crowd, to encroach on someone's personal space. **3** to shout at someone from close quarters. **4** to hit someone in the face or eye; also fig. use, to throw or pass something. ▫ **get the eye** *v.* [1990s+] to be stared at. ▫ **give someone an eye** *v.* [abbr. SE *black eye*] [1900s] (*Aus.*) to blacken someone's eye. ▫ **give someone one in the eye** *v.* (*also* **give someone one on the nose**) [late 19C+] to hit, to reprimand, also in fig. use. ▫ **give someone the eye** *v.* (*also* **give someone the eyes, ...the eyeball, give the eye to**) **1** [late 19C+] to stare at. **2** [20C+] to appraise sexually. **3** [1940s–50s] to give a signal, to 'tip the wink'. ▫ **have a sore eye** *v. see under* SORE *adj.*[1]. ▫ **have eyes for** *v.* **1** [20C+] (*US*) to desire, wish for, usu. sexually. **2** [1960s+] to see what is happening. ▫ **have eyes like cod's ballocks** *v.* [20C+] to have popping eyes. ▫ **have long eyes for** *v.* (*also* **have raw eyes for**) [20C+] (*W.I.*) to be covetous for. ▫ **have one's eye in a sling** *v. see under* SLING *n.*[2]. ▫ **have one's eye on the ball** *v. see* BALL *n.*[1]. ▫ **have one's eyes opened** *v.* [one's wild, unfocused stare] [20C+] to be drunk. ▫ **I'll knock out your eight eyes** ['a common Billingsgate threat from one fish nymph to another: every woman, according to the naturalists of that society, having eight eyes, viz. two seeing eyes, two bub-eyes (cf. BUBBIES *n.*), a bell-eye (SE *belly*), two popes-eyes (SE *pope's eye*: the lymphatic gland in a leg of mutton regarded as a delicacy; here presumably the urinal and anal orifices), and a ***-eye' (Grose 1796) (the censored term remains mysterious, it is, presumably, a ref. to the vagina)] [late 18C–early 19C] a threat, commonly used by Billingsgate fishwives. ▫ **knock someone's eye out** *v.* (*also* **knock someone's eyes out**) **1** [late 19C] (*US campus*) to perform one's work well. **2** [20C+] (*US*) of a person, usu. a woman, to be stunningly attractive. **3** [20C+] (*orig. US*) of an object, to delight, to impress. ▫ **make four eyes** *v.* [1940s] (*W.I.*) of two people, to gaze at one another. ▫ **make one's eyes pass somebody** *v.* (*also* **take one's eye(s) pass somebody**) [20C+] (*W.I., Guyn.*) to speak disrespectfully to one who ought to be treated respectfully. ▫ **nice pair of eyes** *n.* [1960s+] a euph. for attractive breasts, usu. in phr. *she's got a ...* ▫ **pick the eyes out of** *v.* [orig. referring spec. to a system whereby a squatter chose the best bits of a tract of land (a 'run') so as to render the remainder useless to a rival] [20C+] (*Aus.*) to get the best bits for oneself. ▫ **put a finger in one's eye** *v.* [the implication is of forced, and thus insincere, tears] [18C–early 19C] to weep. ▫ **put one's eye on** *v.* [20C+] (*W.I.*) to become obsessed with at first sight and thus to desire to possess immediately. ▫ **put the eye on** *v.* [1930s+] (*orig. US*) **1** to look at seductively. **2** to examine, to stare at. **3** to place under surveillance.

(IN EXCLAMATIONS)

❑ **dip your eye!** *see under* DIP *v.*[2]. ❑ **mind your eye!** [mid-19C+] be careful! look out! ❑ **there he goes with his eye out!** (*also* **there she goes with her eye out!**) [mid-19C] an all-purpose excl. aimed at passers-by.

eye *adj.* [EYE *n.* (3)] [1900s–40s] (*US Und.*) pertaining to the Pinkerton Detective Agency.

-eye *sfx* [20C+] used in combs. meaning anus; cf. *BACK EYE under* BACK *adj.*[2]; BLIND EYE *n.* (3); DEADEYE *n.*[1] (3); HOG-EYE *n.* (5); RED-EYE *n.* (2); ROUNDEYE *n.* (1); note also words like *THIRD EYE under* THIRD *adj.*; note also EYE *n.* (4).

eyeball *n.*[1] [play on SE *the apple of one's eye*] [20C+] (*W.I.*) the most beloved child in a family.

eyeball *n.*[2] [EYEBALL *v.* (2)] **1** [1960s+] a look or glance; an inspection. **2** [1970s] a headlamp. **3** [1990s+] a careful person. **4** *see* EYE *n.* (7).

(IN PHRASES)

❑ **do in the eyeball** *v. see DO IN THE EYE under* DO *v.*[1]. ❑ **give someone the dirty eyeball** *v.* [1990s+] (*Aus.*) to stare at aggressively. ❑ **to the eyeballs** *adv.* [1950s+] an intensifying phr. implying to an extreme extent.

eyeball *adj.* [EYEBALL *v.* (2)] [1950s+] (*US*) used of a personal inspection or eyewitness account.

eyeball *v.* **1** [mid-19C; 20C+] (*orig. Aus.*) to stare at, to ogle. **2** [1940s+] (*orig. US*) to inspect or examine. **3** [1970s] (*US*) to meet or experience in person.

(IN COMPOUNDS)

❑ **eyeball queen** *n.* [-QUEEN *sfx*] [1960s] (*US gay*) one who stares rather than talks.

eyeballer *n.* [EYEBALL *v.*] [1920s+] (*US*) a know-it-all, esp. one who takes it upon him- or herself to tell others what to do.

eyeballing *n.* [EYEBALL *v.* (1)] [mid-19C; 1940s+] staring, esp. by a man at a woman.

eyeberry plant *n.* [they stand as anonymous as 'plants' around the pub and 'eye' the goings-on] [mid-19C] (*UK Und.*) a villain who frequents public houses used by servants in order to ascertain details of their employers' lives and possessions.

eye-eye! *excl.* [1940s+] look at that! what's all this! take a look around! etc.

eyefuck *n.* [EYEFUCK *v.* (3)] [1990s+] (*US*) an aggressive, challenging stare.

eyefuck *v.* [SE *eye* + FUCK *v.* (1)] [1910s; 1970s+] (*US*) **1** to stare pointedly and lustfully at a sexually desirable person; thus n. *eyefucking*. **2** to stare, without sexual overtones. **3** to stare with deliberate, challenging aggressiveness.

eyeful *n.* **1** [late 19C+] a good look at. **2** [1930s+] (*also* **eye filler**) an attractive woman.

(IN PHRASES)

❑ **get an eyeful** *v.* [1910s+] to have a good look at, to stare; often in the challenging phr. *got your eyeful?* aimed at one who is seen to be gazing over-intently at oneself or a (female) companion; a follow-up is 'Want a picture?'.

eye-opener *n.*[1] [all 'wake you up'] **1** [early 19C+] (*orig. US*) the first drink of the day; also as a name of a given whisky. **2** [mid-19C+] a surprise, a shock, not necessarily unpleasant. **3** [1910s] an attractive woman. **4** [1930s+] (*drugs*) the day's first dose of a drug. **5** [1970s+] (*drugs*) amphetamine. **6** [2000s] (*drugs*) crack cocaine.

eye-opener *n.*[2] **1** [late 19C] the penis [cf. *ARSE-OPENER under* ARSE *n.*]. **2** [1920s+] (*US Und.*) a tramp who has homosexual sex with a young companion.

eyes *n.*[1] [resemblance] **1** [1930s+] the nipples or female breasts. **2** [1990s+] (*US black*) sunglasses.

SE in slang uses

(IN PHRASES)

❑ **get one's eyes together** *v.* [20C+] (*Ulster*) to have a nap.

(IN EXCLAMATIONS)

❑ **damn one's eyes!** (*also* **blast/darn one's eyes!**) *see under* DAMN! *excl.* ❑ **dry your eyes!** *see under* DRY *v.*

eyes *n.*[2] [the mirror extends the range of one's eyesight] [1990s+] (*US prison*) mirrors held through the bars of one's cell and used to survey the outer world.

Eyetie *n.* (*also* **Eyetalian, eyetallyano, eye-tye, eytie, Ite, I-Tie, Itie**) [exaggerated pron. of *Italian*] [1910s+] (*orig. US*) **1** a derog. term for an Italian. **2** the Italian language.

Eyetie *adj.* (*also* **Itie**) [EYETIE *n.*] [1910s+] Italian, or pertaining to Italian culture or language.

eyeto *n.* (*also* **Eyetoe**) [EYETIE *n.* + -O *sfx* (3)] [1940s–50s] (*Aus.*) **1** an Italian. **2** the Italian language.

ezel *n.* see ESEL *n.*

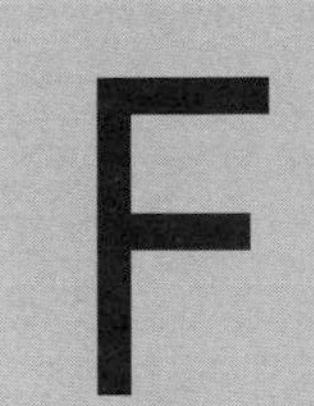

F *n.* [abbr. SE *fifty*] [1980s] (*US*) a $50 bill.

F! *excl.* [1920s+] a euph. for FUCK! *excl.*; thus *f-ing*, FUCKING *n./* FUCKING *adj.* ; thus v. *F*, to swear.

f. *n.* [abbr.] [1990s+] (*US black*) a felony; thus phr. *catch an f*, to be arrested for a felony.

F.A./f.a. *n. see* FANNY ADAMS *n.*[2].

faas *v.* (*also* **fass**) [SE *fuss*] [1930s+] (*W.I.*) to be nosy, inquisitive; as n., impudence, cheek.

faastie *adj.* (*also* **fasty**) [? Surinam Creole *fiesti*, nasty, or FEISTY *adj.* (1); but note SE *fuss* and thus FAAS *v.*] [1950s+] (*W.I., Jam.*) rude, impertinent, impudent.

faastiness *n.* [FAASTIE *adj.*] [1980s] (*W.I.*) rudeness.

FAB *n.* [FAT-ASS *adj.* (1)/*fake-ass* under FAKE *adj.* + BITCH *n.*[1] (1a)] [2000s] (*US black*) a derog. term for a woman.

fab *adj.* (*also* **fabbo, fabby, faboo**) [abbr. SE *fabulous*, but Hancock, 'Shelta and Polari' (1984), suggests Sp. *fabulosa*, and sees it as orig. Polari] [1960s+] a general term of approbation, first popularized by the Beatles *c.*1963 but still used, often with an ironic intonation.

fab! *excl.* [FAB *adj.*] [1960s+] a general excl. of approbation.

fabbo/fabby/faboo *adj. see* FAB *adj.*

fabric *n.* [1970s] (*US black*) clothes.

fabu *adj.* [fabulous] [1990s+] (*US*) excellent.

fabuloso *adj.* [cod Ital. version of SE *fabulous*] [1990s+] (*orig. gay*) wonderful.

fabulous drop *n.* [the comparison is with a good drink, 'a good drop' (of liquor)] [1940s+] (*Aus.*) an attractive young woman.

faburrific *adj.* [SE *fabulous* + *terrific*] [2000s] (*US*) excellent.

face *n.* **1** [16C–18C] a coin. **2** [late 16C–early 17C] a grimace. **3** [17C+] (*also* **facial area**) (*US*) audacity, impudence. **4** [mid-18C–mid-19C] credit at a public house. **5** [mid-19C+] (*US*) the mouth, as a source of speech, usu. in phr. SHUT ONE'S FACE below. **6** [late 19C–1950s] (*US*) interference, nosiness; thus *stick one's face in*. **7** [late 19C+] a general term of address, e.g. *Hello, face*. **8** [1920s+] (*Aus.*) one's personal appearance. **9** [1930s–40s] (*US black*) a stranger, esp. a white stranger. **10** [1930s+] (*US*) fellatio or cunnilingus; usu. as *get face* or *give face*. **11** [1930s+] (*US Und.*) a respectable image, a 'front'. **12** [1940s] (*US black*) a white person. **13** [1940s+] (*US*) a cosmetics kit, thus make-up. **14** [1940s+] a person; esp. in police use, a known criminal. **15** [1960s+] a recognizable person. **16** [1960s+] a fellow member of a mod gang, esp. one who is considered particularly fashionable. **17** [1960s+] (*UK Und.*) a professional criminal, usu. an armed robber with no territorial ambitions.

pertaining to oral sex

IN COMPOUNDS

❑ **face artist** *n.* [-ARTIST *sfx*] [1920s+] (*US Und.*) a fellator or fellatrix. ❑ **face cream** *n.* [CREAM *n.*[1] (1)] [1970s+] (*US gay*) semen, esp. when ejaculated onto a fellator's face. ❑ **face job** *n.* [late 19C–1930s] (*US*) cunnilingus. ❑ **face-painting** *n.* [1990s+] the ejaculation of semen over one's female partner's face. ❑ **face-pussy** *n.* [PUSSY *n.* (1)] [1980s+] (*US gay*) fellatio.

IN PHRASES

❑ **face the nation** *v.* [1970s+] (*US black*) to perform cunnilingus. ❑ **give up one's face** *v.* [FACE *n.* (10)] [1960s+] to permit oneself to indulge in oral intercourse at the insistence of a partner.

pertaining to the mouth

IN PHRASES

❑ **open one's face** *v.* [late 19C+] (*US*) to speak, esp. to speak rudely. ❑ **shut one's face** *v.* (*also* **close one's face, shut one's face up**) [late 19C+] to be quiet; esp. as imper. *shut your face!* thus *open one's face*, to talk.

SE in slang uses

IN COMPOUNDS

❑ **face-ache** *n.* [despite the apparent rudeness of the phr., the *ache* presumably comes f. laughter] **1** [1930s+] a joc. form of address. **2** [1970s] a beating-up. ❑ **face-card** *n.* [1990s+] (*US black*) $100 bill. ❑ **face fannies** *n.* [FANNY *n.*[1] (1)] [1990s+] sideboards; sideburns (US). ❑ **face fart** *n.* **1** [2000s] (*N.Z.*) a belch. **2** [2000s] (*N.Z.*) a general term of abuse. ❑ **face-feeder/-feeding** *see* FEED ONE'S FACE *v.* (1). ❑ **face fins** *n.* [20C+] a moustache, presumably a large one that protrudes on either side of the cheeks. ❑ **face fittings** *n.* [20C+] (*Aus.*) a beard and/or moustache. ❑ **face fungus** *n.* (*also* **fungus**) [20C+] male facial hair, i.e. a beard and/or moustache; occas. as a term of address. ❑ **face-lace** *n.* [1920s–40s] whiskers; a beard. ❑ **face-maker** *n.* [early 19C] a father of an illegitimate child; thus *face-making*, to conceive a child illegitimately. ❑ **face-man** *n.* [note the character *Faceman* in the 1980s US TV series *The A-Team*] [1960s–80s] an attractive man, a 'pretty boy'. ❑ **face-plaster** *n.* [it 'bandages up' a miserable face] [1940s+] (*Aus.*) an alcoholic drink. ❑ **face-prickle** *n.* [1990s+] (*Aus.*) facial hair. ❑ **face stretcher** *n.* [1920s] (*US*) an old woman who attempts to look young.

IN PHRASES

❑ **as many faces as a churchyard clock** [church clocks can have faces on all four sides of a rectangular tower] [20C+] used of anyone seen as duplicitous or unreliable. ❑ **get one's face in a knot** *v.* [20C+] (*Aus.*) to get angry, excited or over emotional. ❑ **go off one's face** *v.* [1960s] to be extremely enthusiastic; to collapse with laughter. ❑ **have ne'er a face but one's own** *v.* (*also* **have never a face but one's own**) [the 'faces' are those on coins] [late 17C–early 18C] to be penniless. ❑ **in someone's face** (*also* **in someone's business**) [basketball use, when a defensive player crowds his opposite number. The term, while ostensibly unappealing, is considered positive by its primary users, the young; note also FACE *v.* (2)] [1950s+] (*orig. US black*) in a confrontational manner, used of one who forces their attentions on another; thus *get in someone's face*, to confront, to provoke. ❑ **in-your-face** *adj.* [IN SOMEONE'S FACE above] [1970s+] (*orig. US*) **1** aggressive, intense, confrontational. **2** unashamed. ❑ **get out of someone's face** *v.* (*also* **get out of someone's ass**) [1920s+] (*orig. US black*) to stop pestering, to leave alone, esp. as imper. ❑ **get up in someone's face** *v.* [1990s+] (*orig. US black*) to argue, to confront face-to-face. ❑ **go on one's face** *v. see* RUN (ON) ONE'S FACE (FOR) below. ❑ **have a face on one** *v.* **1** [20C+] to be ugly, e.g. *she's got a face on her…* **2** [1980s+] to be in a troubled, nervous mood. ❑ **have one's face at half-past eight** *v.* (*also* **have a face like half-past six**) [the corners of the mouth point down, as would the hands of the clock] [late 19C+] to look miserable. ❑ **have one's face made of a fiddle** *v.* [late 18C] to be irresistibly charming. ❑ **make faces** *v.* [late 18C early 19C] to father children; thus *face-making*, sexual intercourse. ❑ **off one's face** *adj.* [1960s+] **1** under the influence of drink or drugs. **2** in fig. use, extremely enthusiastic about. **3** crazy. ❑ **on one's face** *adv.* [late 19C–1910s] (*US*) on credit, for free. ❑ **out of one's face** *adj.* [1970s+] under the influence of drink or drugs. ❑ **out of someone's face** *adj.* [1980s] (*UK black*) absent, away. ❑ **push one's face** *v.* [ext. use of SE *push one's face forward*] [mid-18C] to obtain credit through deceit or bravado. ❑ **run (on) one's face (for)** *v.* (*also* **go on one's face, run one's shape for**) [SE *run*, to enter into a race, i.e. to bet one's *face* or *shape*, i.e. body, as the agent of obtaining credit] [mid-19C+] (*orig. US*) to obtain credit. ❑ **soak one's/the face** *v. see under* SOAK *v.*[1]. ❑ **suck face** *v. see under* SUCK *v.*[1]. ❑ **suck one's face** *v. see under* SUCK *v.*[1].

IN EXCLAMATIONS

❑ **in your face!** (*also* **in your gob!**) [1950s+] a dismissive rejoinder. ❑ **your face and my ass!** (*also* **your face and my arse! ...butt!**) [the implication is KISS MY ARSE! *excl.*] [1970s+] a general dismissive excl., often following a real or imagined request for a match.

face *adj. see* FACEY *adj.*

face *v.* [15C SE *face*, 'to show a bold face, look big; to brag, boast, swagger' (*OED*)] **1** [1920s+] (*Irish*) of a man, to pay court to a woman. **2** [1950s+] (*US campus*) to outperform, to correct, to show up, to humiliate, to insult.

SE in slang uses

IN PHRASES

❑ **face and brace** *v.* [16C] to bluster, to defy, to bully verbally. ❑ **face it out with a card of ten** *v. see* BRAG IT OUT WITH A CARD OF TEN *v.* ❑ **face the music** *v. see under* MUSIC *n.* ❑ **face rape** *v.* [on model of SE *date rape*] [1980s+] (*US campus*) to kiss passionately.

face! *excl.* [FACE *v.* (2)] [1980s] (*US campus*) an excl. delivered to a person whom one has just insulted or humiliated.

faced *adj.*[1] [abbr. SHITFACED *adj.*] **1** [1960s+] (*US teen*) extremely drunk. **2** [1980s] (*drugs*) stunned by the potency of a drug, usu. cannabis.

faced *adj.*[2] [FACE *v.* (2)] [1980s+] (*US campus*) humiliated, embarrassed.

face-fuck *v.* [FUCK *v.* (1)] [1970s+] to be the active partner in an act of fellatio.

face-fucked *adj.* [FUCKED *adj.*[1] (5)/FUCKED *adj.*[1] (3)] [1990s+] (*drugs*) so intoxicated by drugs that one is incapable of controlling one's facial movements.

face-fucking *n.* [FUCKING *n.* (1)] [1970s+] fellatio in which one partner lies on their back with an opened mouth.

face like... *n.*

IN PHRASES

❑ **...a bull's bum** [2000s] (*N.Z.*) a phr. used to describe a very ugly face. ❑ **...a festering pickle** [2000s] (*N.Z.*) a phr. describing a face that is covered in severe acne. ❑ **...an abandoned quarry** [2000s] (*N.Z.*) a phr. used to describe a very ugly face. ❑ **...a smacked arse** [2000s] a phr. used to describe someone who looks very depressed. ❑ **...a stopped clock** [1980s] (*UK/Aus.*) a phr. used to describe a very unattractive (usu. female) face; also of one who is momentarily stunned. ❑ **...a stripper's clit** [1990s+] a derog. description of the face of an unattractive woman. ❑ **...a twisted sandshoe** [2000s] (*N.Z.*) a phr. used to describe someone who is exhibiting great disgust. ❑ **...a yard of tripe** [2000s] (*N.Z.*) a phr. used to describe someone looking very depressed. ❑ **...yesterday** [1900s–10s] a phr. decribing a very miserable-looking face.

facer *n.*[1] [all are poured into the face] **1** [late 17C–mid-19C] a brimming glass. **2** [mid-19C] a glass that holds a single dram of spirits. **3** [mid-19C] a glass of whisky punch.

facer *n.*[2] **1** [early–mid-19C] a blow in the face; thus as v., to hit in the face. **2** [mid-19C] (*US Und.*) a criminal who stalls those in pursuit of their accomplices [SE *face off*]. **3** [mid-19C+] an unexpected problem or obstacle, anything to which one must face up.

facety *adj.* [SE *feisty* but ? note Surinam Creole *fiesti*, dirty, nasty; and SE *fist*, a fart] [1940s+] (*W.I./UK black*) cheeky, impudent; thus *facetyness*, impudence.

face-up *n.* [var. on SE *face-off*] [1950s–60s] (*US*) a gang-fight, incl. single-person combat.

facey *adj.* (*also* **face, facy**) [SE *face*, effrontery] [early 17C+] (*20C+ use is W.I.*) cheeky, rude, impudent.

facial *n.*[1] [? FACE *v.* (2)] [1970s] (*US campus*) an insult, a rebuff.

facial *n.*[2] [SE *facial*, cosmetic treatment for the face] [1970s+] **1** a prostitute's client who likes the woman to sit on his face, sometimes after she has inserted a suppository or even when she is having intercourse with another man. **2** ejaculation in one's partner's face.

facial area *n. see* FACE *n.* (3).

facialist *n.* [1990s+] (*W.I.*) a woman who likes fellatio.

facker *n. see* FUCKER *n.*

facking *adj. see* FUCKING *adj.*

fack off *v. see* FUCK OFF *v.*

facquing *adj. see* FUCKING *adj.*

factor *n. see* FATER *n.*

-factor *sfx* [1970s+] (*US campus*) in comb. with a relevant noun, a quantity of, a degree of, e.g. *dork-factor*, the number of fools; *dog-factor*, the number of ugly women.

factory *n.*[1] [resemblance to the architecture of 19C factories + ? allusion to the 'manufacturing' of evidence] **1** [mid-19C] (*Aus.*) a prison. **2** [mid-19C+] (*UK Und.*) a large, forbidding Victorian police station in the London Metropolitan area.

factory *n.*[2] [1930s+] (*drugs*) **1** the kit used by a narcotics addict for injections. **2** a place where drugs are packaged, diluted or manufactured.

factotum *n.* [SE *factotum*, a man of all work; a servant who has the entire management of his master's affairs] [late 19C] the vagina.

facy *adj. see* FACEY *adj.*

fadangle *v.* [FINAGLE *v.* (1)] [2000s] (*US black*) to cheat, to do wrong.

fad-cattle *n.* [dial. *faddle*, to make much of (a child) + SE *cattle*] [19C] a generic term for sexually available women.

faddle *n.* [Midlands dial. *faddle*, an over-particular, fussy person] **1** [19C] a trifling person; a busybody. **2** [1930s] an affected and/or homosexual man.

fade *n.*[1] [SE; note SE phr. *faded glory*] **1** [late 19C] (*US*) a former dandy, now fallen on hard times and thus less resplendent. **2** [20C+] (*US black*) a derog. term for a white person. **3** [1970s+] (*US black*) a black person who becomes immersed in the white world and thus 'fades away'. **4** [1980s+] (*US black*) short-cropped black hair, pioneered by the hip-hop culture, usu. featuring patterns delineated through an even closer shave [it fades into the skull]. **5** [1990s+] (*US campus*) a badly dressed person.

fade *n.*[2] (*also* **fadeaway**) [FADE *v.*[2] (1)] [1900s–60s] (*US*) a departure, an escape.

IN PHRASES

❑ **do a fade** *v.* [1900s–60s] to leave.

fade *v.*[1] **1** [late 19C+] (*gambling*) in dice games, to bet against the player holding the dice; or, in poker, to match the previous bet; thus *fader*, the person who covers the bet. **2** [late 19C+] (*US*) to put at a disadvantage, to cause problems for someone; esp. in phr. *don't fade me*; thus *have someone faded*, to have someone at a disadvantage. **3** [1920s–30s] fig. use of sense 1, to respond, to counter. **4** [1920s–40s] (*US Und.*) to hold up with a gun. **5** [1960s] (*US*) to put up with, to manage something. **6** [1990s+] (*US black teen*) to fool around or tinker with something or someone.

fade *v.*[2] (*also* **fade away**) [SE *fade*, to grow dim, faint or pale] **1** [20C+] to leave, to vanish. **2** [1940s] (*US black campus*) to stop talking. **3** [1940s–70s] (*US*) to die. **4** [1960s] (*US campus*) to miss a class; to waste time rather than work. **5** [1960s] (*US Und.*) to withstand interrogation. **6** [1960s] (*US Und.*) to obtain a verdict of 'not guilty'. **7** [1980s] (*US black*) to drop a topic of conversation, to change an unpalatable subject. **8** [1980s] (*US *black*) to remain sufficiently silent not to be noticed. **9** [1980s] (*US campus*) to become tired, to feel increasingly exhausted. **10** [1990s+] (*US*) to let down, to renege.

fade *v.*^{3} [SE *fader*, a slider on the mixing board; if one pulls the fader down it gradually reduces the volume; note also FADE *v.*^{1} (2)] [1990s+] (*US black*) **1** to ignore, to erase, to get rid of. **2** to shoot dead.

fadeaway *n. see* FADE *n.*^{2}.

fade away *v. see* FADE *v.*^{2}.

faded *adj.* [SE *fade*, to grow pale] [1980s+] (*US black/campus*) **1** drunk, under the influence of drugs. **2** unfashionable. **3** used to excess.

fade-out *n.* [film imagery + FADE *v.*^{2} (1)] (*US*) **1** [1910s–60s] a disappearance, a departure, an escape. **2** [1920s–50s] death.

IN PHRASES

❑ **on the fade-out** [1950s+] (*Aus.*) evading the police, on the run. ❑ **pull a fadeout** *v.* (*also* **do a fade-out**) [1910s–60s] (*US*) to vanish, to escape, to depart.

fade out *v.* [film imagery] [1920s–50s] (*orig. US*) **1** to die. **2** to leave.

fadge *n.*^{1} [pron.] [late 18C–1900s] a farthing.

fadge *n.*^{2} [? FADGE *v.*] [mid-19C] (*UK Und.*) a trick.

fadge *v.* [ety. unknown] [late 16C–mid-19C] to suit, to work out, to 'do'.

fadger *n.* [FADGE *n.*^{1}] [late 19C–1910s] a farthing.

fadoodle *n.* [cited in Manchon, *Le Slang* (2001); *OED* has one SE citation for 1670] [mid-17C; 1920s+] a nothing, a trifle.

fadoodling *n.* [SE *fadoodle*, nothing, nonsense, a foolish trifle; the *OED* first and only use is 1670, but the term is used in Thomas Middleton's *The Roaring Girl* (1611) V.i, when, midway through a scene in which the whole canting vocabulary is paraded and properly translated, the authors back away from explaining *wapping* (*see* WAP *n.*) and *niggling* (*see* NIGGLE *v.*), dismissing them as 'fadoodling, if it please you'] [17C] a euph. for sexual intercourse.

faff *n.* [FAFF *v.*] [2000s] a nuisance.

faff *v.* (*also* **faff about/around**) [orig. dial. *faff*, to fuss (about); note echoic dial. *faffle*, to stutter or stammer, to utter incoherent sounds] [1950s+] to play around, to mess about, a euph. for FUCK ABOUT *v.* (1).

fag *n.*^{1} [school use *fag*, a junior boy who performs (menial) tasks for his elders; ult. SE *fag*] **1** [late 18C–mid-19C] a young female fish seller. **2** [early–mid-19C] (*US*) an errand boy or clerk. **3** [mid-19C+] (*US/Aus.*) a lawyer's clerk.

fag *n.*^{2} [SE *fag*, to tire, to perform a wearisome task; ? ult. *flag* v., to droop, to tire] **1** [late 18C+] a bore, a chore, an unpleasant, tedious task [usu. considered UK; note Thompson, *Now and On Earth* (1942), has it in a US setting in the 1920s]. **2** [mid-19C; 1960s] (*US campus*) a hard worker.

IN PHRASES

❑ **stand a good fag** *v.* [late 18C–mid-19C] to resist tiredness, to persevere.

fag *n.*^{3} (*also* **fish-fag**) [? SE *fag-end*, the way a pickpocket tugs at handkerchiefs, watch-chains etc; or ? dial. *fag*, to cut corn with a sickle] [mid-19C] a pickpocket.

fag *n.*^{4} [abbr. FAG END *n.* (4)] [late 19C+] **1** a cheap cigarette, usu. as issued to troops in WW1. **2** any cigarette; thus *fag-ash*, cigarette ash; *Fag-Ash Lil*, a nickname for a woman who smokes heavily; *fag-card*, a cigarette card.

IN COMPOUNDS

❑ **fag-butt** *n.* [1930s+] a cigarette end. ❑ **fag-hag** *n. see* separate entry. ❑ **fag-hole** *n.* [1940s+] the mouth. ❑ **fag-paper** *n.* [1910s+] a cigarette paper. ❑ **fag-topper** *n.* [1900s] a cigarette end.

fag *n.*^{5} (*also* **faggio**) [abbr. FAGGOT *n.*^{1} but note comments in ety. there] **1** [1920s+] (*orig. US*) a male homosexual; thus *fag-bait*, one who is an object of homosexual desire. **2** [1970s+] (*US campus/teen*) an offensive person.

DERIVATIVES

❑ **faggish** *adj.* [1950s] (*US*) homosexual in manner. ❑ **faglish** *n.* [abbr. SE *English*] [1980s+] (*US gay*) gay slang. ❑ **fagola** *n.* [-OLA *sfx*; but note FAYGELE *n.*] [1970s+] (*US*) a male homosexual.

IN COMPOUNDS

❑ **fag-bagging** *n.* [BAG *v.* (1)] [1970s] (*US*) to beat up and rob a homosexual. ❑ **fag-basher** *n.* [1980s+] (*orig. US gay*) **1** an ostensibly heterosexual man who specializes in beating and terrorizing gay men. **2** any anti-gay spokesperson. ❑ **fag-bashing** *n.* [1980s+] the beating up of male homosexuals. ❑ **faggamuffin** *n.* [RAGAMUFFIN *n.*] [1980s+] (*US/UK black*) a black homosexual person, usu. male. ❑ **fag-hag** *see* separate entries. ❑ **fag hots** *n.* [? HOT STUFF *n.*^{2} (3) + play on FAGGOT *n.*^{1} (3)] [1960s+] (*gay*) cheap pornography aimed at the male homosexual readership. ❑ **fag rags** *n.* [1980s] (*US black*) smart casual clothing. ❑ **fag show** *n.* [1940s] (*US carnival*) a carnival show featuring men in women's dress. ❑ **fag stag** *n.* [STAG *n.*^{4} (1); var. on FAG-HAG *n.*^{2}] [1990s+] (*US*) a heterosexual male who enjoys the company of homosexual men. ❑ **fag tag** *n.* [1980s+] (*US campus*) the small loop (ostensibly for hanging the shirt when no hanger is available) on the upper back of many shirts; such a loop, supposedly, can be used to hold a victim ready for buggery. ❑ **fag water** *n.* [1980s] (*US*) cologne.

IN PHRASES

❑ **play the fag role** *v.* [2000s] (*US prison*) pretending sexual interest in another inmate; the aim is to annoy a third party.

fag *adj.* [FAG *n.*^{5} (1)] **1** [1930s+] homosexual; pertaining to homosexuality. **2** [1950s] in fig. use, effeminate, although also used of objects, i.e. lacking power.

fag *v.*^{1} [SE *feague*, to beat, to whip; ult. Ger. *fegen*, to polish] [late 17C–19C] (*UK Und.*) to beat; thus *fagging*, a beating.

fag *v.*^{2} [FAG *n.*^{2} (2)] **1** [late 18C–mid-19C] to make someone work hard. **2** [late 18C–1910s] to work hard academically. **3** [mid-19C] to work hard (in other than academic contexts).

fag *v.*^{3} (*also* **fag along**) [20C+] (*US*) **1** to move quickly, to leave in a hurry. **2** to move when it requires an effort.

fag *v.*^{4} [FAG *n.*^{4}] [1920s–50s] to supply with a cigarette, to smoke a cigarette.

fag *v.*^{5} [FAG *n.*^{5} (1)] [1960s+] (*US*) a derog. term, meaning to engage in or subject another to homosexual practices.

IN PHRASES

❑ **fag around** *v.* [1960s+] (*US*) of a heterosexual man, to play at acting in a 'homosexual' manner.

fagan *n.* (*also* **fagin**) [the character *Fagin* from Charles Dickens's *Oliver Twist* (1837–9); despite Fagin's poss. homosexual paedophilia and the use of 'fag', no specific gay context is implied] [1940s+] the penis.

IN PHRASES

❑ **bury old Fagin** *v.* [1950s] of a man, to have sexual intercourse. ❑ **introduce her to Fagan** *v.* [1950s+] of a man, to have sexual intercourse.

fag end *n.* [SE *fag*, to droop, to decline, to flag] **1** [17C+] (*also* **butt-end**) the last part or remnant of anything. **2** [early 18C+] of ropes, the end of, a part near the end of. **3** [19C+] a fragmentary part of a speech or conversation that one might overhear, just as it tails off. **4** [mid-19C+] the butt of a cigarette or cigar.

IN COMPOUNDS

❑ **fag-end man** *n.* [1910s–20s] a man who collects cigarette ends from the pavement.

IN PHRASES

❑ **pick up fag-ends** *v.* [1910s+] to listen in to other people's conversations and attempt to comment upon them or join in; esp. as *don't pick up fag-ends*.

fagged (out) *adj.* [SE *fag* + ? corruption of SE *fatigued*] **1** [late 18C+] exhausted. **2** [1900s] shocked, mentally destroyed.

fagger *n.*^{1} (*also* **figger, figure**) [SE *fag*, to work (for another)] [17C–18C] a small boy used by robbers to enter a house through a window that would be too small to allow a man to climb through it.

fagger *n.*^{2} [FAG *v.*^{4}] [1920s–50s] a person who smokes.

fagging *n. see* FAG *v.*^{1} (1).

fagging *adj.* [SE *fag*] [late 19C] exhausting.

fagging law *n. see* FIGGING LAW *n.*

faggio *n. see* FAG *n.*[5].

faggot *n.*[1] (*also* **fagot**) [the 'homosexual' use at sense 3 (plus extensions at senses 4 and 6) is usu. seen as a US coinage, but *faggot* has an older, if debatable, UK etymology. One, somewhat fanciful, version suggests that a *faggot* was used in the burning of heretics, and thus became transferred to the name of an embroidered patch (like the pink triangles of the Nazi concentration camps) worn by unburned heretics; homosexuals are certainly considered as fig. heretics, therefore *faggot* means homosexual. More feasible is the descent from the 18C use of *faggot* as a pej. for a woman in sense 1 (thus playing on homosexual effeminacy), esp. in the derog. form of a 'baggage', which stems from the faggots that one had to haul to the fire. The abbr. *fag* may be linked independently to the British public school use *fag*, a junior boy performing menial tasks and poss. conducting homosexual affairs with the seniors. Rodgers, *The Queen's Vernacular* (1972), acknowledges all these and adds 'fr WW I sl *fag* = cigarette, because cigarettes were considered effeminate by cigar-smoking he-men.' Finally, there is the Yid. FAYGELE *n.*, orig. meaning little bird (thus the synon. *birdie*), and thence homosexual] **1** [late 16C; early 18C+] a general term of abuse, usu. of women or children. **2** [late 18C] a prostitute. **3** [1910s+] (*US*) a homosexual man; in general use the term covers any gay man, in gay use the implication is of overt effeminacy. **4** [1950s] (*US*) a lesbian. **5** [1950s+] (*US*) a general term of abuse, irrespective of sex. **6** [1970s] (*US gay*) (*also* **faggotina**) a heterosexual woman who associates with male homosexual men. **7** [1970s+] (*US teen/campus*) an unattractive young woman. **8** [1970s+] a coward, a weakling.

(IN COMPOUNDS)

▫ **faggot-ass** *n.* [-ASS *sfx*] [2000s] (*US black*) weak, cowardly, contemptible. ▫ **faggot-lover** *n.* [1960s+] (*Aus./US*) one who has no feelings of homophobia. ▫ **faggot-master** *n.* (*also* **faggoteer**) [19C] a pimp, a lecher. ▫ **faggot's lunchbox** *n.* [1960s] (*US gay*) an athletic supporter.

faggot *n.*[2] [SE *faggot*, a bundle (usu. of sticks) bound together] [late 17C–early 19C] a man mustered for duty in the army (and thus 'bound' to service) but not yet formally enlisted.

faggot *n.*[3] [? supposed resemblance to SE *faggot*, a stick] [late 18C] the penis.

faggot *adj.* [FAGGOT *n.*[1] (3)] **1** [1940s+] (*US*) pertaining to homosexuality or homosexuals. **2** [1960s+] in fig. use, weak, ineffectual.

faggot *v.* [SE *faggot*, to tie up bundles of wood] [late 18C–early 19C] (*UK Und.*) to bind, to tie up.

(IN PHRASES)

▫ **faggot and stall** *n.* (*also* **faggot and storm**) [SE *stall*, to confine/*storm* (one's way in)] [early 18C] (*UK Und.*) the act of breaking into a house, tying up the residents and robbing them.

faggoter *n.* [FAGGOT *n.*[1] (3) but note *fagoteer* at *faggot-master* under FAGGOT *n.*[1]] [1960s+] (*US black*) a pimp who specializes in selling the services of male homosexual prostitutes.

faggotina *n. see* FAGGOT *n.*[1] (6).

faggotry *n.* [1940s+] (*US*) homosexuality.

faggoty *adj.* [FAGGOT *n.*[1]] (*US*) **1** [1920s+] (*also* **faggoty-assed**) effeminate, homosexual [+ -ASSED *sfx* (2)]. **2** [1960s+] cowardly, useless, second-rate.

faggy *adj.* [FAG *n.*[5] (1)] [20C+] (*orig. US*) effeminate, homosexual.

fag-hag *n.*[1] [FAG *n.*[4] (2) + SE *hag*] [1940s–50s] (*Can.*) a woman who smokes excessively.

fag-hag *n.*[2] [FAG *n.*[5] (1) + SE *hag*] [1960s+] (*orig. US*) **1** a woman, prob. heterosexual, poss. ageing, who courts and indulges the company of male homosexuals. **2** a heterosexual man, irrespective of age, who prefers the company of homosexuals to that of his peers.

fag-hag *v.* [FAG-HAG *n.*[2] (1)] [1960s+] of a woman, to associate with and choose one's close friends from homosexual men.

fagin *n. see* FAGAN *n.*

fagingy-fagade *n.* [pig Lat. version of FADE *n.*[1] (2)] [1920s–30s] (*US black*) a white person.

fagola *n.* [FAG *n.*[5] (1) + sfx *-ola* on model of SE *payola*, but note FAYGELE *n.*] [1960s] (*US*) a male homosexual.

fagot *n. see* FAGGOT *n.*[1].

fagoteer *n. see* FAGGOT-MASTER *under* FAGGOT *n.*[1].

fags! *excl.* (*also* **effags!**) [? SE *faith!*] [mid-17C–18C; 1920s+] a mild excl.

faguen *n.* [? Dickens's character *Fagin*, from *Oliver Twist* (1838); or ? SE *vagrant*] [mid-19C] (*UK Und.*) a villain, a depraved character.

faigelah *n. see* FAYGELE *n.*

faike *n.* [? FAKE *n.*[1] (1)] [late 19C] (*UK Und.*) an experienced, senior criminal.

fail *v.* [1980s+] (*US campus*) to fail to understand, to be unable to understand.

SE in slang uses

(IN PHRASES)

▫ **fail in the furrow** *v. see* DIE IN THE FURROW *under* FURROW *n.*

fains! *excl.* (*also* **fain I! fainits! fainlights! fains I! faix!**) [SE *fen*, to forbid; ? ult. f. *fend*, forbid] [mid-19C+] (*juv.*) a call for a truce during a game, or a statement that one is ineligible for a given duty or command.

faint *adj.* [mid-19C] (*US*) a euph. for drunk.

fainting fits *n.* [rhy. sl. = TIT *n.*[2] (1)] [1940s+] the female breasts.

fair *n.* (*also* **fair-skin**) [20C+] (*US black*) a light-complexioned individual.

fair *adj.* [late 19C+] (*orig. Aus.*) absolute, complete, usu. in comb., *see* below and under relevant n.

(IN COMPOUNDS)

▫ **fair cow** *n.* [20C+] **1** (*Aus./N.Z.*) (*also* **fair lizard**) a general negative, applied to persons or things to which the speaker takes great exception, e.g. *fair cow of a day, he's a fair cow*; often in phr. *it's a fair cow.* **2** (*N.Z.*) a call for fair treatment. ▫ **fair cuss** *n.* [1950s] (*Aus.*) an unreasonable person. ▫ **fair dink** *adj. see* FAIR DINKUM *adj.* ▫ **fair dinkum** *see* separate entries. ▫ **fair go** *see* separate entries. ▫ **fair nark** *n.* [NARK *n.* (6)] [20C+] (*Aus./N.Z.*) something or someone inexpressibly tedious or baffling. ▫ **fair treat, a** *adv.* **1** [1940s+] (*Aus./N.Z.*) to a great extent. **2** *see also* SE compounds below. ▫ **fair whack** *n.* [WHACK *n.*[1] (4)] [20C+] (*N.Z.*) an appeal for equable treatment.

(IN PHRASES)

▫ **fair suck of the sauce bottle** *n.* (*also* **fair suck of the sauce stick**) [1960s+] (*Aus.*) an equal opportunity, a fair chance. ▫ **fair suck of the sav** *n.* (*also* **fair suck of the pineapple, ... sausage**) [SE *sav*, a saveloy] [1960s+] (*Aus./N.Z.*) a fair or equal chance.

(IN EXCLAMATIONS)

▫ **fair dos!** (*also* **fair do! fair doos! fair dues!**) [SE *fair* + *do*, dealing, treatment] [mid-19C+] (*Aus./N.Z.*) a general statement of agreement, acceptance; as n., decent treatment.

SE in slang uses

(IN COMPOUNDS)

▫ **fair cop** *n. see* separate entry. ▫ **fair deal** *n.* [DEAL *n.*[1] (1)] [1910s+] (*orig. US*) an honest transaction, a fair bargain. ▫ **fair itch** *n.* [late 19C–1930s] an absolute imitation. ▫ **fair one** *n.* [1950s+] (*UK/US gang*) a (street gang) fight conducted under some sort of mutually recognized rules and poss. preceded by a verbal argument. ▫ **fair-play artist** *n.* [SE *fair play* + -ARTIST *sfx*] [1950s] a trustworthy, honest person. ▫ **fair pop** *n.* [POP *n.*[1] (3a)] [late 19C+] a good opportunity, a fair chance. ▫ **fair shake** *n. see* separate entries. ▫ **fair trade** *n. see* TRADE, THE *n.* (1). ▫ **fair treat** *n.* **1** [late 19C+] something or someone highly enjoyable or satisfactory; also used ironically to describe something or someone quite the opposite. **2** *see also* slang compounds above.

(IN PHRASES)

▫ **fair crack of the whip** *n. see* separate entries. ▫ **fair fucks**

to [1980s+] (*Irish*) good luck (to). ❑ **fair trod on** *adj.* [late 19C] abused, treated very badly. ❑ **that's fair** [1970s+] (*US campus*) an ironic comment that something is not fair.

fair *adv.* [mid-19C+] very, absolutely, really, e.g. *fair tasty, fair gorgeous*.

fair cop *n.* [SE *fair* + COP *n.*[1] (2)] [late 19C+] (*orig. UK Und.*) **1** a justifiable arrest; usu. in the tongue-in-cheek phr. *it's a fair cop guvnor, put the bracelets on…* **2** any situation seen as fair and about which there is no complaint.

fair crack of the whip *n.* [1920s+] (*Aus.*) an equitable opportunity, a reasonable chance.

fair crack of the whip! *excl.* [1960s+] (*Aus./N.Z.*) be fair! give someone a chance!

fair dinkum *adj.* (*also* **fair dink, square dinkum**) [FAIR DINKUM! *excl.*] [20C+] (*Aus.*) completely honest.

fair dinkum! *excl.* (*also* **dinkum! fair dink! square dinkum! straight dinkum!**) [FAIR *adj.*/FAIR *adv.* + DINKUM *adj.*] [late 19C+] (*usu. Aus.*) honest! really! on the level!

fair gang *n.* [? their regular appearances at fairs; or ? f. *Faa*, the Scot. gypsy equivalent of Smith] [19C] the gypsies.

fair go *n.* (*also* **open go**) [a call in a game of 'two-up' that indicates all relevant rules were satisfied and that the coins could be spun] [20C+] (*usu. Aus.*) **1** any situation that meets a basic requirement of impartiality to all without fear of favour or prejudice. **2** a fair fight.

fair go! *excl.* [20C+] **1** (*Aus.*) be reasonable! be fair! **2** (*N.Z.*) interrog.: really?

fairground *n.*

SE in slang uses

(IN PHRASES)

❑ **up the fairground** [? the fairground's gambling sideshows] [1980s] likely to be lucky.

fairish *adj.* [late 19C+] considerable in amount.

fair roebuck *n.* [SE *fair roebuck*, a roebuck in its fifth year] [early 18C] a woman at the peak of her beauty.

fair shake *n.* (*also* **decent shake, shake**) [the image of an honest throw or 'shake' of a dice cup] [mid-19C+] **1** a fair or acceptable situation; thus antonym *rough shake*, an unfair or difficult situation. **2** equable treatment.

fair shake of the dice! *excl.* [1920s+] (*Aus.*) be fair!

fair shakes! *excl.* [mid-19C+] (*Aus.*) a general statement of agreement, acceptance.

fair-skin *n. see* FAIR *n.*

fair-weather drink *n.* [one toasts actual and fig. *fair weather*] [1970s] a small celebration before initiating some project or journey.

fairy *n.*[1] [SE] **1** [mid–late 17C; late 18C+] (*later use US*) a young woman, with a poss. implication of promiscuity. **2** [19C] a drunken old hag. **3** [late 19C+] (*orig. US*) a homosexual man. **4** [20C+] (*N.Z.*) a blonde-haired woman. **5** [1920s–30s] a young boy tramp who accompanies an older homosexual tramp.

(IN COMPOUNDS)

❑ **fairy hawk** *n.* [SE *hawk*, an aggressive person] [1960s+] (*US gay*) one who attacks (and robs) homosexuals. ❑ **fairy house** *n.* (*also* **fairy joint**) [HOUSE *n.*[1] (1)/JOINT *n.* (3b)] [late 19C–1930s] (*US gay*) a male brothel for homosexuals. ❑ **fairy lady** *n.* [1940s–60s] (*US*) a lesbian, esp. a 'feminine' one. ❑ **fairy loop** *n.* [despite the link to homosexuality implicit in *fairy*, the term is sometimes capable of more fanciful interpretation, i.e. the practice cited in *DARE* as regards a Utah high school where 'a group of girls…will run a contest. They were to pick a boy, usually in their class. The girl who gets the most of his "fairy loops"…would be the one to marry him'] [1990s+] (*US*) the small loop on the upper back of many shirts; such a loop, supposedly, can be used to hold a victim ready for buggery. ❑ **fairy-shaking** *n.* [SHAKE DOWN *v.* (1)] [1990s+] (*US*) blackmailing married men who frequent gay bars and similar centres. ❑ **fairy's phonebooth** *n.* [SE *phonebooth*, but note TELEPHONE *n.* (2) and *BONE PHONE under* BONE *n.*[1]] [1960s+] (*US gay*) a public lavatory cubicle. ❑ **fairy's wand** *n.* [1960s+] (*US gay*) any phallic object carried by a cruising gay man, e.g. a cigarette holder, a rolled umbrella (on a dry day), a long-stemmed rose.

SE in slang uses

(IN COMPOUNDS)

❑ **fairy dust** *n.* [synon. ANGEL DUST *n.*] [1970s+] (*drugs*) phencyclidine. ❑ **fairy powder** *n.* [1950s–70s] (*drugs*) any form of powdered narcotic. ❑ **fairy-story** *n.* (*also* **fairy pipe, fairy-tale, fairy yarn**) [late 19C+] (*orig. US*) a fanciful, mendacious tale, often in aid of obtaining money or favours (cf. FAIRY *n.*[3]).

(IN PHRASES)

❑ **go a fairy** *v.* [SE *fairy*, very small] [late 19C] to toss coins to see who buys a round of halfpennyworths of gin.

fairy *n.*[2] [late 19C] (*US drugs*) a lamp for preparing opium.

fairy *n.*[3] [SE *fairy-tale*; note *fairy-story* under FAIRY *n.*[1]] [1900s–20s] (*Aus.*) **1** a fanciful tale, a 'tall story'. **2** the teller of fanciful tales.

(IN PHRASES)

❑ **pitch a fairy** *v.* to tell a 'tall story'.

fairy *adj.* [FAIRY *n.*[1] (3)] [1920s+] effeminate, homosexual.

fairy bower *n.* [rhy. sl.] [20C+] (*Aus.*) **1** a shower of rain. **2** a shower for washing. **3** an hour.

fairydiddle *n.* [SE *fadoodle*, nonsense] [20C+] (*US*) nonsense, rubbish.

fairy snuff *phr.* [20C+] a joke corruption of SE colloq. phr. *fair enough*.

faix! *excl. see* FAINS! *excl.*

fake *n.*[1] [FAKE *v.*[1]] **1** [19C–1940s] a dodge, a swindle, some form of fraudulent money-making scheme. **2** [mid-19C–1910s] (*US*) an invented newspaper story or false rumour. **3** [mid-19C+] any form of action, often a trick, varying as to context. **4** [late 19C] in fig. use, any situation (the underlying image is of trickery or deception). **5** [late 19C] (*US*) a patent medicine. **6** [late 19C] (*US*) cheap, esp. worthless, merchandise sold by street vendors. **7** [late 19C+] (*US*) an impostor or insincere person. **8** [late 19C+] (*US*) a confidence trickster. **9** [1930s+] (*US drugs*) (*also* **fake-a-loo**) any form of substitute for a hypodermic syringe.

fake *n.*[2] [dial. *fake*, to hurt; *fakement*, pain] [20C+] (*Ulster*) cancer.

fake *adj.* [1990s+] (*US campus*) bad, disappointing, negative.

SE in slang uses

(IN COMPOUNDS)

❑ **fake-ass** *adj.* [-ASS *sfx*] [1990s+] (*US*) fraudulent. ❑ **fake bandager** *n.* [1900s] (*US Und.*) a beggar who poses as a cripple to elicit sympathy. ❑ **fake boodle** *n.* [BOODLE *n.*[1] (3)] [late 19C] (*US*) a roll of money in which small bills (or even paper cut to the right size) are surrounded, for ostentation's sake, by one large one.

fake *v.*[1] [prob. fig. uses of SE *feague* + Ger. *fegen*, to furbish up, to clean, to sweep; or Ital. *faccio*, I make] **1** [early 18C; mid-19C+] to cheat, to deceive, to swindle, to counterfeit; thus *faked (up)*, counterfeit, spurious. **2** [19C] to shoot, to wound, to hit or cut; to poison. **3** [early 19C–1940s] (*Ling. Fr./Polari*) to make, to do. **4** [early 19C+] to steal, to rob. **5** [late 19C–1900s] to dress the hair, to make up the face. **6** [late 19C+] to pretend. **7** [late 19C+] (*US*) to malinger by feigning illness. **8** [1990s+] to fail to meet someone.

(IN COMPOUNDS)

❑ **fake-man** *n.* [1900s] (*Aus.*) a confidence trickster. ❑ **fake-bake** see separate entries.

(IN PHRASES)

❑ **fake a cly** *v.* [CLY *n.* (2)] [19C] to pick or search a pocket. ❑ **fake a pin** *v.* [PIN *n.* (2)] [early 19C] (*UK Und.*) to create a sore leg or to cut it, as if accidentally, in the hope of getting onto the doctor's list. ❑ **fake a poke** *v.* [POKE *n.*[2] (2)] [late 19C] (*UK Und.*) to pick a pocket. ❑ **fake a screeve** *v. see under* SCREEVE *n.* (4). ❑ **fake a screw** *v. see under* SCREW *n.*[1]. ❑ **fake down** *v.* [mid-19C] (*N.Z.*) to carry out a crime. ❑ **fake it** *v.* [1930s+] to pretend. ❑ **fake oneself** *v.* [19C] to inflict wounds upon or otherwise disfigure oneself for a criminal purpose. ❑ **fake one's slangs** *v.* [SLANG *n.*[2] (1)] [19C] to cut off one's chains or irons to make an escape from prison. ❑ **fake on someone** *v.* [1970s+] **1** (*US black, west coast*) to ignore. **2** (*US black, east coast*) to humiliate, to deceive. ❑ **fake out** see separate entries. ❑ **fake the broads** *v. see under* BROADS *n.* ❑ **fake the duck** *v.* [SE (*decoy*) *duck*] [mid–late 19C] to adulterate drink, to cheat, to swindle. ❑ **fake the funk** *v.* [FUNK *n.*[1] (5)] [1970s+] (*US black*) to pose as more sophisticated than one actually is. ❑ **fake the rubber** *v.* [RUBBER *n.*[1] (2)] [mid-19C] to stand treat. ❑ **fake the sweeteners** *v.* [SWEETENER *n.*[2] (4)] [mid–late 19C] to kiss.

(IN EXCLAMATIONS)

❑ **fake away (there's no down)!** [19C] carry on! don't stop!

fake *v.*[2] [dial. *fake*, to hurt] [early 19C] to hurt, e.g. *this shoe fakes my foot*, this shoe pinches my foot.

fake! *excl.* [1980s+] (*US campus*) an expression used by the trickster to underline that someone has been tricked or duped.

fake-a-loo *n. see* FAKE *n.*[1] (9).

fake-bake *n.* [FAKE-BAKE *v.*] [1980s+] (*US campus*) **1** a tanning salon. **2** a fake tan.

fake-bake *v.* (*also* **fake and bake**) [FAKE *v.*[1] (6) + SE *bake*] [1980s+] (*US campus*) to get a tan in a tanning booth.

fakeloo *n.* [1920s+] (*US*) a spurious tale, a 'fairy story'.

fakement *n.* [FAKE *v.*[1] (1) + sfx *-ment*] **1** [19C] any act of robbery or swindling. **2** [19C] a forged signature. **3** [early 19C] a letter, a note. **4** [mid-19C] scraps. **5** [mid-19C] any form of printed material. **6** [mid-19C] an object, whether or not uncommon. **7** [mid–late 19C] a false begging petition, a begging letter. **8** [late 19C] any action or problem. **9** [late 19C–1900s] a trimming, a superfluous thing. **10** [1910s] (*UK Und.*) burglar's tools.

(IN COMPOUNDS)

❑ **fakement charley** *n.* (*also* **fakeman charley, fakement-chorley**) [CHARLIE *n.*[2] (1)] [early–mid-19C] a private sign or mark. ❑ **fakement dodge** *n.* [DODGE *n.* (1)] [mid-19C–1900s] the writing of spurious begging letters; thus *fakement dodger*, the individual who does so.

fake out *n.* [FAKE OUT *v.*[1] (1)] [1950s+] (*US*) a bluff, a deception, an unpleasant surprise.

fake out *v.*[1] **1** [late 19C; 1940s+] to fool, to get the better of. **2** [1950s] to sneak away.

fake out *v.*[2] [var. on *FAKE ON SOMEONE under* FAKE *v.*[1]] [1990s+] (*US black*) **1** to ignore. **2** to humiliate, to deceive.

fake out and out *v.* [FAKE *v.*[1] (2) + SE *out and out*, complete, extreme] [19C] to kill, to murder.

faker *n.* [Fr. *faire*, to make, ult. Lat. *faceo*] **1** [late 17C–19C] a maker. **2** [19C+] a forger. **3** [mid-19C–1910s] (*US*) a thief. **4** [mid-19C–1920s] a street salesman of cheap goods. **5** [mid-19C–1920s] (*also* **fakir**) a confidence trickster, a fraudster. **6** [late 19C] a pimp. **7** [1910s–50s] (*US*) (*also* **fakir**) a person feigning illness or injury. **8** [1990s+] (*US campus*) one who poses falsely in order to gain status.

(IN PHRASES)

❑ **faker of loges** *n.* (*also* **feaker of loges**) [LOGES *n.*] [17C] a beggar, esp. one who backs up his fraudulent tales with especially created fake documents.

faking *n.* [FAKE *v.*[1]] **1** (*UK Und.*) thieving. **2** (*UK Und.*) cheating (e. g. at a card game). **3** (*UK prison*) counterfeiting illness.

(IN COMPOUNDS)

❑ **faking-boy** *n.* (*also* **faking kid**) [mid-19C] (*UK Und.*) a thief.

fakir *n.*[1] [FAKER *n.* (4); note the additional exotic tinge of SE *fakir*, a Muslim or Hindu holy mendicant] **1** [mid-19C–1930s] a street salesman of cheap goods, an itinerant repairman etc. **2** [late 19C] (*US*) an actor. **3** [1900s] a street cardsharp.

fakir *n.*[2] *see* FAKER *n.*

fakus *n.* [? FAKE *n.*[1] (3)] **1** [1910s] (*Aus.*) something, without a specific name, that has been 'thrown together' or 'knocked up'. **2** [1960s] deceptive acts that contribute to a confidence trick.

fal *n.* [rhy. sl. = GAL *n.* (1)] [late 19C] a young woman.

falairy *adj.* [SE *floury*] [20C+] (*Ulster*) unpleasant.

falconer *n.* [17C] (*UK Und.*) a confidence trickster, spec. one who poses as a poor scholar and thus persuades his victims to put up money in order to back the printing of some spurious learned pamphlet.

Falkirk *n.*

(IN EXCLAMATIONS)

❑ **get to Falkirk!** *see* *GET TO FUCK! under* FUCK *n.*

fall *n.* (*UK/US Und.*) **1** [late 19C+] an arrest. **2** [1910s+] problems, difficulties, a 'fall from grace'. **3** [1920s+] the consequences, esp. blame taken on behalf of another; *see TAKE THE FALL* below. **4** [1930s+] a conviction and the concomitant spell of imprisonment.

(IN COMPOUNDS)

❑ **fall bitch** *n. see* FALL GUY *n.* ❑ **fall dough** *n.* [DOUGH *n.* (1)] [1910s–50s] (*US Und.*) money set aside by a criminal for bribing policemen or obtaining bail if he is arrested. ❑ **fall-gink** *n. see* FALL GUY *n.* (2). ❑ **fall guy** *n. see* separate entry. ❑ **fall money** *n.* [late 19C+] (*US Und.*) bail and legal fees, just in case one is arrested. ❑ **fall partner** *n.* [1950s+] (*US Und.*) one of two or more people who are arrested or sentenced to prison at the same time for the same crime; also one of a pair of thieves working together. ❑ **fall scratch** *n.* [SCRATCH *n.*[3] (4)] [1960s] (*US Und.*) money that is held ready for use as bail, e.g. by a pimp for one of his whores. ❑ **fall togs** *n.* [TOGS *n.* (1)] [1920s–40s] (*US Und.*) respectable/smart clothing worn for a court appearance.

(IN PHRASES)

❑ **make a good/bad fall** *v.* [late 19C–1920s] to have a piece of good or bad luck. ❑ **take a fall** *v.* (*also* **get a fall**) **1** [1920s+] (*US Und.*) to be arrested, to be imprisoned. **2** [1920s+] (*US*) to fall in love. **3** [1950s+] (*US*) to tumble, to slip over. **4** [1970s+] (*US*) to find oneself in difficulties, to come to grief. ❑ **take a fall out of** *v.* (*also* **get a fall out of**) [late 19C–1910s] (*US/Aus.*) **1** to get the better of someone. **2** to involve oneself with something. **3** to reprimand someone. ❑ **take the fall** *v.* [1920s+] (*US*) **1** to volunteer oneself as a victim, usu. as the alleged perpetrator of a crime, in the place of the real villain. **2** to be accused (and condemned) unfairly of a crime.

SE in slang uses

(IN PHRASES)

❑ **dead fall** *n. see* DEAD *adj.* ❑ **give someone a fall** *v.* [mid-17C–18C] of a man, to lie a woman down prior to sexual intercourse.

fall *v.*[1] **1** [mid-19C+] (*orig. UK, mainly US since 1930s*) to be caught in illegal activities and subseq. arrested, tried and convicted. **2** [1990s+] to lose status, to be deprived of a comfortable situation.

SE in slang uses

(IN COMPOUNDS)

❑ **fall-downs** *n.* [late 19C] fragments of a pie that fall from the larger piece or slice when it is being cut up; plates of such fragments were sold at a halfpenny a plate in cookshops.

(IN PHRASES)

❑ **fall about** *v.* [1940s+] (*orig. US*) to collapse in laughter. ❑ **fall all over oneself** *v.* [late 19C+] to make extreme, if chaotic, efforts to achieve what one or another wants. ❑ **fall apart** *v.* (*also* **come apart**) [1930s+] to collapse emotionally, to lose control of one's feelings. ❑ **fall back** *v.* [early 19C] (*US*) to run off. ❑ **fall down (on)** *v.* **1** [mid-19C+] (*US*) to fail, to blunder, to 'come to grief'. **2** [1960s] (*US gang/black*) to attack. **3** [1960s] (*US*) to experience, to enjoy. ❑ **fall downstairs** *v.* [Ger. *die Treppe herunterfallen*, to fall downstairs; the sl. is found in Ger. areas of the US] [20C+] (*US*) to get a haircut. ❑ **fall for** *v. see* separate entry. ❑ **fall in the furrow** *v. see under* FURROW *n.* ❑ **fall in the shit** *v. see under* SHIT *n.* ❑ **fall in the thick** *v. see under* THICK *n.* ❑ **fall into** *v. see* separate entries. ❑ **fall off the Christmas tree** *v.* [late 19C] (*US campus*) to be amazed. ❑ **fall off the roof** *v. see under* ROOF *n.* ❑ **fall off the (water) wagon** *v.* [play on *water wagon* under WATER *n.*[1]] [late 19C+] **1** to drink heavily, usu. in the context of resuming drinking after a period of abstinence. **2** in ext. use, to abandon any good resolution. ❑ **fall of the leaf** *n. see under* LEAF *n.* ❑ **fall on the wrong side of the hedge** *v. see under* HEDGE *n.*[2]. ❑ **fall out** *see* separate entries. ❑ **fall over backwards** *v. see* BEND OVER BACKWARDS *under* BEND *v.*[1]. ❑ **fall over oneself** *v.* [20C+] to go out of one's way to do something (usu. altruistic). ❑ **fall through one's (own) asshole** *v. see under* ASSHOLE *n.* ❑ **fall to** *v.* [1900s] (*US Und.*) to notice. ❑ **fall to pieces** *v.* [19C Leicester dial.; 1940s+ use is Aus.] [late 19C+] to go into labour, to give birth.

IN EXCLAMATIONS

❑ **go fall on yourself!** [late 19C] (*US*) a dismissive excl.

fall *v.*[2] **1** [late 19C–1920s] to commit oneself. **2** [1910s] to get married. **3** [1910s+] to fall in love.

fall *v.*[3] **1** [1920s–50s] (*US black*) to leave. **2** [1940s+] (*Aus.*) to arrive suddenly, usu. of the police.

IN PHRASES

❑ **fall by** *v.* (*also* **fall over to**) [1950s+] (*orig. US black*) to visit without prior warning, to drop in. ❑ **fall in** *v.* (*also* **fall on, fall out, fall over**) **1** [late 19C+] (*orig. US black*) to arrive, to go to, to visit; thus *fall-in*, an entrance. **2** [mid-19C–1910s] (*also* **fall to**) in fig. use, to become involved. **3** [20C+] (*US*) to go to bed. ❑ **fall into** *v. see* separate entries. ❑ **fall out** *see* separate entries. ❑ **fall up** *v.* [late 19C+] (*US black*) to arrive, to turn up.

fall *v.*[4] (*also* **fall for**) [abbr. SE *fall pregnant*] [1930s+] to become pregnant.

fallen angel *n. see* ANGEL *n.* (1).

fallen on *adj.* [FALL *v.*[4]] [1930s+] pregnant.

fallen soldier *n. see* DEAD SOLDIER *under* SOLDIER *n.*

fall for *v.* [20C+] **1** to fall in love with a person or an idea or plan. **2** to be fooled by a plan or trick.

fall guy *n.* (*also* **fall bitch**) [according to Bentley & Corbett, *Prison Slang* (1992), there was a real-life *fall guy*, Albert Bacon *Fall* (1861–1944), who in 1922 took upon himself the entire blame for the Teapot Dome Scandal; despite the involvement of many top government officials, Fall was the only one to serve time, a sentence of one year and one day; this, however, does not match available and earlier citations] [20C+] **1** one who bears the punishment for another's wrong-doing. **2** (*also* **fall-gink**) a person who is easily duped, a victim.

falling *n.* [2000s] (*US black*) acting insanely.

falling den *n.* [*fall in* under FALL *v.*[3]] [1920s] (*US black*) a bed.

falling sickness *n.* [SE *falling sickness*, epilepsy] [17C–early 18C] sexual intercourse.

fall into *v.*[1] [1930s] to come upon, to obtain.

fall into *v.*[2] [1940s–60s] (*US*) **1** to stay. **2** to visit.

fall-out *n.* **1** [1950s+] (*Aus.*) the threat of pieces falling from an old, unsafe automobile. **2** [1960s+] (*orig. Aus.*) of a woman's breasts, their falling out of a badly secured or overly low-cut bikini or swimsuit. **3** [1970s] (*US black*) a fainting fit.

fall out *v.* **1** [1930s+] to leave. **2** [1930s+] to enthuse, to be delighted by. **3** [1940s+] (*US black*) to faint; to collapse, to fall asleep; often when overcome by drug consumption or excessive drinking. **4** [1940s+] to be overcome with laughter. **5** [1940s+] to lose control of a situation. **6** [1940s+] (*US black*) to be surprised. **7** [1950s] to relax.

SE in slang uses

IN PHRASES

❑ **fall out of one's standing** *v.* [1990s+] (*Irish*) **1** to collapse from exhaustion. **2** to be surprised, stunned.

faloose/falouse *n. see* FELOOSE *n.*

false *n.* [SE *falsehood*; note 16C–18C SE *false*, a lie, a deception] [1920s–30s] (*US black*) a lie.

false *adj.*

SE in slang uses

IN COMPOUNDS

❑ **false face** *n.* [1970s+] (*US campus*) a hypocrite, an insincere person. ❑ **false gig** *v.* [GIG *v.*[4]] [1940s+] (*Aus.*) to pretend to be what one is not, to act under false pretences; thus *falsing*, shamming, malingering. ❑ **false hereafter** *n.* [pun] [late 19C] (*US society*) a bustle.

false *v.* [obs. SE *false*, to cheat, to betray, to defraud, to break one's word] [1930s+] (*Aus.*) to lie, to deceive.

false! *excl.* [SE but note *true/false* answers required in various forms of examination] [1980s+] (*US campus*) no! impossible! that's not true!

false alarm *n.*[1] [play on SE] [1900s–50s] **1** a braggart, a boaster. **2** something or someone that does not live up to expectations.

false alarm *n.*[2] [rhy. sl.] [1910s+] (*orig. milit.*) the arm.

falsies *n.* **1** [1940s+] pads placed in a brassiere that accentuate the shape and dimensions of otherwise diminutive female breasts. **2** [1940s+] anything fake added to a body, e.g. false eyelashes. **3** [1950s–60s] padding inserted in the trousers to resemble large genitals. **4** [1980s+] false teeth.

fam *n.*[1] (*also* **famm, fem, feme**) [abbr. FAMBLE *n.* (1)] **1** [late 17C–1910s] a hand. **2** [18C–mid-19C] a ring.

IN COMPOUNDS

❑ **fam-cheat** *n. see* FAMBLING-CHEAT *n.* ❑ **fam-cloth** *n.* [late 17C–18C] a handkerchief. ❑ **fam-grasp** *v.* [late 17C–18C] to shake hands (and make up one's differences). ❑ **fam-lay** *n.* [LAY *n.*[3] (1)] [18C–19C] shoplifting; thus *fam-layer*, a shoplifter. ❑ **fam-rust** *n.* [fig. use of SE *rust*] [mid-19C] (*UK Und.*) a lack of practice at thieving (esp. pickpocketing). ❑ **fam-snatcher** *n.* [early 19C] a glove. ❑ **fam-squeeze** *n.* [early 19C] throttling. ❑ **fam-sticks** *n.* [late 18C] (*UK Und.*) gloves. ❑ **fam-strings** *n.* [18C] (*UK Und.*) gloves.

fam *n.*[2] [abbr.] [1970s+] **1** (*US black/gay/teen*) the *family*. **2** (*US gay*) a large number [ext. of sense 1 above].

fam *v.* [abbr. FAMBLE *n.* (1)] [mid-18C–early 19C] to feel, to handle; to grope a woman.

IN PHRASES

❑ **fam a dona** *v.* (*also* **fam a donna**) [DONA *n.* (1)] [19C] to take liberties with a woman.

famble *n.* [? SE *fumble*] **1** [mid-16C–1900s] a hand. **2** [late 17C–mid-19C] (*UK Und.*) a ring.

IN COMPOUNDS

❑ **famble-cheat** *n. see* FAMBLING-CHEAT *n.*

fambler *n.* (*also* **famble**) [FAMBLE *n.* (2)] [late 17C–early 18C] a dealer in fake 'gold' rings.

famblers *n.* [FAMBLE *n.* (1)] [17C] a pair of gloves.

fambling-cheat *n.* (*also* **famble-cheat, fam cheat**) [FAMBLE *n.* (1) + CHEAT *n.* (1), lit. 'hand thing'] [16C] (*UK Und.*) a ring; a glove.

familiars *n.* [19C] lice.

family *n.*[1] **1** [mid-18C+] the criminal fraternity. **2** [1910s+] an intimate, whether related by blood or ties of friendship; usu. in phr. *he/she's family* etc. **3** [1950s+] the American Mafia. **4** [1970s] (*US black*) a pimp and the women who work for him. **5** [1970s+] (*US gay*) the world of homosexuality.

IN COMPOUNDS

❑ **family hotel** *n.* [HOTEL *n.* (2)] [mid–late 19C] a prison. ❑ **family man** *n.* **1** [late 18C–1930s] a member of the criminal fraternity; a thief. **2** [early 19C] a receiver of stolen goods. ❑ **family people** *n.* [Vaux glosses this as 'persons living by fraud and depredation'] [late 18C–early 19C] thieves, robbers.

IN PHRASES

❑ **play in the family** *v.* (*also* **play in someone's family**) [1920s–30s] (*US black*) to indulge in a bout of ritualized name-calling, based on insulting each other's mother.

SE in slang uses

IN COMPOUNDS

❑ **family disturbance** *n.* [the supposedly deleterious effects of alcohol on family life] [19C] (*US, Western*) whisky. ❑ **family-style** *adv.* [it supposedly mimics 'missionary position' heterosexual intercourse] [1970s+] (*US prison*) describing a style of anal intercourse, where the passive partner's legs are thrown over the head. ❑ **family jewels** *n. see* separate entry. ❑ **family organ** *n.* [pun] [1920s–50s] (*US*) the penis. ❑ **family plate** *n.* [SE (*silver*) *plate*, silver coins] [19C] silver coins.

❑ **family pound** *n.* [SE *pound*, an enclosure] [late 19C] a family grave. ❑ **family ram** *n.* [SE *ram*/RAM *n.*[1] (2)] [1990s+] (*W.I.*) an incestuous male; a man who sleeps with two or more female members of the same family.

(IN PHRASES)

❑ **family of love** *n.* [SE *family of love*, a 16C–17C religious sect, based in Holland, and very popular in England; its main tenets were that religion could best be realized through sex and that all governments, however tyrannical, must be obeyed] [late 17C–early 19C] prostitutes, considered as a group or occupation.

family *n.*[2] [note the prostitute's phr.: 'Sleep with that pig and you'll end up with a family to feed'] [1940s+] (*US*) crab lice.

family jewels *n.* **1** [1910s+] the male genitalia. **2** [1950s] wealth, ready money. **3** [1960s] in fig. use, something very valuable.

(IN PHRASES)

❑ **organize the family jewels** *v.* [1990s+] to masturbate.

famm *n. see* FAM *n.*[1].

fan *n.*[1] [? FANCY, THE *n.* (1) who sported such garments, or its fan-like expanse across the frame] [mid–late 19C] (*Aus./UK Und.*) a waistcoat.

fan *n.*[2] [FANNY *n.*[1] (1)] [mid-19C+] the vagina.

fan *v.*[1] [SE *fan*, to wave a fan] **1** [late 18C+] (*US 20C+*) to beat; also in fig. use, as in excl. *fan my jawbone!* [underpinned by SE *fan*, to winnow or thresh corn]. **2** [mid-19C+] to run one's hands over a potential victim's clothes to see if they have anything in their pockets that can be stolen; thus *fan out of*, to steal while 'fanning' [poss. link to FAM *v.*]. **3** [1910s+] (*orig. US*) to conduct a search of a suspect's clothes, possessions or premises [poss. link to FAM *v.*]. **4** [1920s+] (*also* **give the fan**) to pick pockets [poss. link to FAM *v.*]. **5** [1930s] to shoot.

SE in slang uses

(IN PHRASES)

❑ **fan the breeze** *v. see under* BREEZE *n.*[1]. ❑ **fan the hammer** *v.* [the action of fanning the hammer of a pistol or revolver in order to fire more speedily] [late 19C] (*US*) to act in a brilliant but unscrupulous manner.

fan *v.*[2] **1** [late 19C+] (*US*) to move around quickly, to run, to escape. **2** [20C+] (*US*) to flaunt oneself deliberately to gain sexual interest. **3** [1980s] (*US campus*) to play truant, to miss a class.

fan *v.*[3] [SE *fan*, a supporter; ult. *fanatic*] [1900s–50s] (*US*) to converse, to chat, usu. about sport.

fan *v.*[4] [1970s+] (*US*) to calm someone down.

fanciness *n.* [1990s+] (*W.I.*) items of clothing or jewellery that are expensive or flashy.

Fancy, the *n.* [orig. used of any adherents of a given amusement, thus J. Moore, *Columbarium* (1735) 40: 'These Pigeons by their Flight afford an admirable Satisfaction, to those Gentlemen of the Fancy that have time to attend them'] **1** [19C] the sporting fraternity; thus *fancy house*, a public house where 'the Fancy' gather. **2** [mid–late 19C] (*Aus./US*) the underworld. **3** [mid-19C–1940s] (*US*) the aristocracy, the wealthy and powerful. **4** [mid-19C+] (*US*) the world of professional boxers.

(IN COMPOUNDS)

❑ **fancy lay** *n.* [LAY *n.*[3] (1)] **1** [19C] the sport of boxing, prize-fighting. **2** [1910s] (*UK Und.*) any form of swindling or robbery. ❑ **fancy ring** *n.* [mid-19C] (*UK Und.*) a boxing arena.

fancy *n.* **1** [mid-17C–early 18C] the vagina. **2** [early 19C+] a girlfriend; a mistress. **3** [late 19C] (*US*) a prostitute. **4** *see* FANCY MAN *n.*[2].

(IN COMPOUNDS)

❑ **fancy-bit** *n. see under* BIT *n.*[1]. ❑ **fancy house** *n.* [HOUSE *n.*[1] (1)] [19C] a whore-house, a house of ill-repute, a brothel. ❑ **fancy work** *n.* [play on SEW *v.* (1)] **1** [late 19C] prostitution; thus *take in fancy work*, to work secretly as a prostitute. **2** [late 19C] sexual intercourse. **3** [20C+] the (usu. male) genitals and pubic hair.

fancy *adj.* [FANCY, THE *n.*] [early 19C] pertaining to boxing or prize-fighting.

(IN COMPOUNDS)

pertaining to the sporting world or prostitution; often underpinned by SE *fancy*

❑ **fancy bloke** *n.* [BLOKE *n.* (3)] **1** [mid–late 19C] a member of the sporting world. **2** [mid-19C+] orig. a prostitute's boyfriend; then a male lover, not always adulterous, but the relationship usu. refers to a married or older woman. ❑ **fancy cove** *n.* [COVE *n.* (1)] **1** [19C] a pimp, a procurer. **2** [mid-19C–1910s] a thief. ❑ **fancy joseph** *n.* [generic use of Joseph or ? link to JOSEPH *n.* (2)] [19C] a boy or young man who is a favourite of prostitutes (but not a customer or a pimp). ❑ **fancy lady** *n. see* FANCY WOMAN *n.* ❑ **fancy man** *n. see* separate entries. ❑ **fancy piece** *n.* [PIECE *n.* (1)] **1** [early 19C] a prostitute, a mistress [note Egan, *Life In London* (1821): 'A sporting phrase for a "bit of *nice* GAME" kept in a *preserve* in the suburbs. A sort of BIRD OF PARADISE!']. **2** [1920s+] a girlfriend, a 'best girl'. ❑ **fancy woman** *n. see* separate entry.

SE in slang uses

(IN COMPOUNDS)

❑ **fancy-ass** *adj.* (*also* **fancy-assed**) [1980s+] showy, smart. ❑ **fancy crib** *n.* [20C+] (*US black*) a fashionable, chic, well-designed home. ❑ **fancy Dan** *n. see* separate entry. ❑ **fancy girl** *n. see* separate entry. ❑ **fancy pants** *see* separate entries. ❑ **fancy smile** *n. see* SMILE *n.*[1]. ❑ **fancy stroll** *n.* [STROLL *n.* (1)] [1980s+] (*US black*) the main street on which the high life happens.

fancy *v.* [SE *fancy*, to take a liking to] **1** [late 17C; late 19C+] to find attractive; esp. in phr. *I could fancy that*, used of a passing attractive member of the opposite sex; also in phr. *fancy the knickers/pants off*. **2** [1920s+] of a gambler, to select as worthy of a bet, usu. of a horse or dog.

(IN PHRASES)

❑ **don't fancy yours (much)** [20C+] a joking reflex comment when two young men see two women, irrespective of their real charms.

SE in slang uses

(IN PHRASES)

❑ **fancy one's chances** *v.* [20C+] to feel confident of success. ❑ **fancy oneself** *v.* [late 19C+] to have a (smugly) good opinion of oneself.

fancy *adv.* [1940s–50s] fancily, affectedly.

fancy! *excl.* [abbr. of SE *fancy me!/fancy that!*] [mid-19C+] an excl. of surprise.

fancy Dan *n.* [SE *fancy* + *Dan* as a generic for a man] [1930s+] (*orig. US*) **1** a flashily dressed man, a dandy. **2** a showy but ineffective sportsman or worker. **3** (*also* **fancy damn**) anything showy.

fancy girl *n.* [SE *fancy* + *girl*; note US use pre-Civil War *fancy girl*, a slave girl or woman used for the sexual enjoyment of her master] **1** [early 19C+] a man's girlfriend. **2** [early 19C+] the woman with whom a married man is having an affair. **3** [19C+] (*US*) a prostitute. **4** [1990s+] (*W.I.*) a materialistic woman.

fancy man *n.*[1] [FANCY, THE *n.* (1) + SE *man*] [early–mid-19C] a member of the fashionable sporting world.

fancy man *n.*[2] [SE *fancy* + *man*, lit. one who is fancied] [early 19C+] **1** (*also* **fancy**) a man who lives on the earnings of a prostitute. **2** (*also* **fancy**) a male lover, not always adulterous, but the relationship usu. refers to a married or older woman; occas. used of male homosexuals. **3** in weak form of sense 2 above, a (younger) man who is befriended by a (older) woman. **4** a sexually attractive man.

fancy man *n.*[3] [SE *fancy*, over-adorned, ornamental + *man*] [1970s+] (*US*) a male homosexual or transvestite.

fancy pants *n.* [SE *fancy* adj. + *pants*] **1** [1910s+] an overdressed man, erring towards the effeminate in this preoccupation. **2** [1930s+] (*orig. US*) the social elite, the aristocracy; thus, someone who puts on airs.

fancy pants *adj.* [FANCY PANTS *n.*] [1940s+] smart, pretentious.

fancy pants *v.* [FANCY PANTS *n.*] [1940s+] **1** to act in an arrogant or supercilious manner. **2** to play around, to 'mess about'.

fancy sash *v.* [rhy. sl. = BASH *v.*] [20C+] (*Aus.*) to hit.

fancy woman *n.* (*also* **fancy lady**) [SE *fancy* + *woman*] [early 19C+] **1** a man's favourite girl or woman. **2** a prostitute. **3** a mistress, a 'bit on the side'.

fandangle *n.* **1** [late 19C] nonsense, excessively ornate speech. **2** [1940s+] (*W.I.*) any form of fussy ornamentation, whether of clothes, buildings, automobiles etc. **3** [1940s+] (*W.I.*) stupidity, foolishness.

fandango girl *n.* [SE *fandango*, a boisterous, energetic Spanish/Spanish-American dance, which was associated with dancehalls, which, in turn, were seen by their critics as quasi-brothels] [mid-19C] (*US*) a prostitute.

fanfoot *n.* [FAN-FOOT *v.*] [1940s+] (*US black*) a promiscuous woman, one who openly seeks sex; thus *fan-foot*, to play around.

fan-foot *v.* [FAN *v.*[2] (2) + SE *foot*] [1930s] (*US black*) to openly seek sex, to play around.

fanfuckingtastic *adj.* [SE *fantastic* + FUCKING *adj.* (4)] [1980s+] extremely fantastic, an intensified form of SE.

fang *n.* [SE *fang*, an animal tooth; the pointed tapering part of anything which is embedded in something else] **1** [early 18C+] a tooth. **2** [1950s–60s] (*US black/jazz*) in pl., the lips; thus, in fig. use, the equivalent of CHOPS *n.*[1] (4). **3** [1950s+] the penis; thus *bury the fang*, to have sexual intercourse.

IN COMPOUNDS

▫ **fang artist** *n. see* separate entries. ▫ **fang bandit** *n.* (*also* **fang carpenter**) [-BANDIT *sfx* (3)] [1950s+] (*Aus.*) a dentist. ▫ **fang chovey** *n.* [CHOVEY *n.*] [mid–late 19C] a dental surgery. ▫ **fang factory** *n.* [1970s+] a dental surgery. ▫ **fang job** *n.* [1960s] criticism, esp. a critical article. ▫ **fang faker** *n.* [FAKER *n.* (5); cf. 20C milit. jargon *fang-farrier*, a dentist] [late 19C] a dentist. ▫ **fang-lifter** *n.* [1930s] (*US Und.*) a dentist.

IN PHRASES

▫ **put the fangs into** *v.* [var. on *PUT THE BITE ON under* BITE *n.*[1]] [1910s+] (*Aus.*) **1** to pressurize, to blackmail. **2** to demand a loan or favour.

fang *v.*[1] [FANG *n.* (1); note SE *fang*, to tear or seize with the teeth] [1910s+] (*Aus.*) **1** to demand money, to cadge, to beg for a loan; thus *fanging for*, desperate for. **2** to eat.

fang *v.*[2] [abbr. of proper name of the Argentine racing driver Juan *Fangio* (1911–95)] [1960s+] (*Aus.*) **1** to drive fast; also as n. **2** to do something fast, to send something quickly.

fang artist *n.*[1] [FANG *v.*[1] + -ARTIST *sfx*] [1970s+] (*Aus.*) **1** one who is particularly adept at obtaining loans. **2** a glutton.

fang artist *n.*[2] [FANG *n.* (3) + -ARTIST *sfx*] [1970s+] (*Aus.*) a lecher, a womanizer.

fanning *n.* [FAN *v.*[1] (1)] **1** [mid-19C–1940s] a beating, a thrashing. **2** [1900s–40s] (*US Und.*) a pickpocket's preliminary running of their hands over a victim to find a wallet or bankroll. **3** [1930s] a search of a person, usu. for weapons.

fanny *n.*[1] [ety. unknown. *DSUE* suggests link to *Fanny* Hill, the heroine of John Cleland's *Memoirs of a Woman of Pleasure* (1749)] **1** [mid-19C+] (*UK only*) the vagina. **2** [1910s] (*US*) an old(er) woman. **3** [1910s+] (*US*) (*also* **fannie, fannyolo**) the buttocks; thus *fanny-shaker*, a bellydancer. **4** [1920s+] (*US*) one's self. **5** [1990s+] women, considered simply as sex objects. **6** [2000s] a fool, an idiot, a general term of abuse.

IN COMPOUNDS

▫ **fanny-artful** *n.* (*also* **fanny-fair**) [19C] the vagina. ▫ **fanny batter** *n.* [1990s+] vaginal secretions. ▫ **fanny flap** *n.* [1990s+] the labia. ▫ **fanny hat** *n.* [the dent in its crown; euph. for *CUNT-HAT under* CUNT *n.*] [1930s–60s] a trilby. ▫ **fanny magnet** *n. see under* -MAGNET *sfx.* ▫ **fanny nosher** *n.* [NOSH *v.* (2)] [1990s+] a lesbian. ▫ **fanny nudger** *n.* [1990s+] a vibrator. ▫ **fanny pack** *n.* (*also* **fanny flask**) [1950s+] (*US*) a small pouch-like bag strapped around the wearer's waist. ▫ **fanny rag** *n.* [1940s+] (*Aus.*) a sanitary towel. ▫ **fanny rat** *n.* **1** [1940s–50s] a pubic louse. **2** [1990s+] the penis. **3** [1990s+] a promiscuous man. **4** [1990s+] a general term of abuse. **5** [2000s] a womanizer.

IN PHRASES

▫ **hang one's fanny out** *v. see HANG ONE'S ASS OUT under* ASS *n.* ▫ **pin in the fanny** *v.* [1970s] (*US*) a tedious and troublesome situation. ▫ **shake one's fanny** *v.* [1930s] (*orig. US*) to hurry up.

IN EXCLAMATIONS

▫ **my (old) fanny!** [late 17C+] a general excl. of disdain, dismissal, arrogant contempt.

fanny *n.*[2] [? fig. use of FANNY *n.*[1] (3) on model of BALLOCKS *n.* (3)] **1** [1910s+] verbal effusiveness, usu. nonsensical. **2** [1920s+] any form of story (poss. mendacious) designed to elicit money or sympathy, to provide excuses etc. **3** [2000s] a fit of temper.

IN COMPOUNDS

▫ **fanny merchant** *n.* [MERCHANT *n.* (1)] [1990s+] one who offers only empty boasts and promises. ▫ **fanny mob** *n.* [MOB *n.*[2] (3)] [1970s] (*UK Und.*) confidence tricksters.

IN PHRASES

▫ **spin a fanny** *v.* [1930s–50s] to tell a deceitful story.

fanny *n.*[3] [1950s+] (*camp gay*) a proper name, with its sl. allusions, used for a variety of camp nicknames, e.g. *Fanny Fed*, the FBI.

fanny *v.* [FANNY *n.*[2] (2)] [1930s+] to deceive or persuade by glib talk.

fanny about *v.* (*also* **fanny around**) [euph. FUCK ABOUT *v.* (1)] [1960s+] to waste time, to act aimlessly.

fanny adams *n.*[1] [the brutal murder and dismemberment of eight-year-old *Fanny Adams*, at Alton, Hampshire, on 24 August 1867; the murderer, one Frederick Baker, was hanged at Winchester on Christmas Eve; 5000 people watched the execution] [late 19C–1910s] (*orig. Royal Navy*) tinned mutton.

fanny adams *n.*[2] (*also* **F.A., f.a.**) [for ety. *see* prev.] [1910s+] a euph. for FUCK ALL *n.*, i.e. absolutely nothing.

fanny blair *n.* [rhy. sl.] [mid-19C–1960s] the hair.

fannyolo *n. see* FANNY *n.*[1] (3).

fanqui *n.* [lit. 'foreign devil'] [mid-19C] (*Anglo-Chinese*) a European.

fantabulosa *adj.* [Polari; SE *fantastic* + *fabulous*] [1950s+] excellent, perfect.

fantabulous *adj.* [SE *fantastic* + *fabulous*] [1950s+] incredibly wonderful.

fantadlins *n.* [SE *tantoblin*, a sweet tart] [mid-19C] a pastry.

fantail *n.*[1] [naut. jargon *fantail*, 'the projecting part of the stern of a yacht or other small vessel when it extends unusually far over the water abaft the stern post' (*Century Dict.*, 1889)] **1** [19C] a coal-heaver's or dustman's hat, resembling a sou'wester; thus *fantail gentleman*, a coal-heaver. **2** [19C] the buttocks; only found in combs. below.

DERIVATIVES

▫ **fantailer** *n.* [sense 2 above] [early 19C] a person whose tail coat is excessively long.

IN COMPOUNDS

▫ **fantail-banger** *n.* [sense 2 above + BANGER *n.*[2]] [late 19C] (*Aus.*) a morning coat. ▫ **fantail-boy** *n.* [i.e. the sou'wester that was part of his 'uniform'] [early 19C] a dustman.

fantail *n.*[2] [*FAN ONE'S ASS under* ASS *n.* + TAIL *n.* (2)] [1960s+] (*US prison*) a highly promiscuous prison homosexual.

fantasia *n.* [the hallucinogenic effects] [1980s+] (*drugs*) **1** MDMA. **2** mescaline. **3** dimethyltryptamine.

fantastic *adj.* [loose use of the SE] [1930s+] excellent, good beyond expectation.

fantastic plastic *n.* [1990s+] (*Aus.*) a contraceptive sheath, a condom.

fanti *adj.* (*also* **fantee**) [SE *go fanti*, to 'go native', to adopt the habits of a native tribe; ult. W. African *Fantee*, a tribe in Ghana] [late 19C–1930s] crazy, insane; usu. as *go fanti*, to go crazy, to run amok.

fantod *n.* (*also* **fantods, fant-tods**) [SE *fantod*, a crotchety way of acting; ? ult. f. SE *fantasy, fantastic*] [19C+] (*US*) **1** a feeling of uneasiness, a feeling of depression. **2** a feeling of excitement. **3** a minor or imaginary disease. **4** diarrhoea.

fap *adj.* [ety. unknown] [late 16C; early 19C] drunk.

far and near *n.* [rhy. sl.] [late 19C–1980s] (*US*) beer.

far away *adv.* [the hymn 'There is a happy land,/Far, far away', which was often parodied in such lines as 'Where are my Sunday clothes?/far, far away'] [late 19C] in pawn; also as v.

far away! *excl. see* FAR OUT! *excl.*

farblondjet *adj.* [Yid. *farblondzhen*, to lose one's way, to go astray] [20C+] (*US*) confused, lost, astray.

farchadet *adj.* [Yid. *fartschadat*, confused; ult. Slavic, *chad*, smoke, daze] [1960s+] (*US*) confused, befuddled.

farcing *n.* (*also* **farsing**) [SE *force*] [late 16C–early 17C] (*UK Und.*) the picking of a lock.

fardel *n.* [OE *féora dæ'l*, fourth part] [late 19C+] (*Irish*) a farthing.

farden *n.* [pron.] [mid-18C+] a farthing.

far-down *n.* [County *Down*, one of the six counties of Northern Ireland] **1** [mid–late 19C] (*US*) an Irish-American Catholic whose forebears come from Northern Ireland; thus *fardownianism*. **2** [late 19C] (*Aus.*) Ulster.

fare *n.* [someone who 'pays for a ride'] [1930s+] a male or female prostitute's client.

IN PHRASES

❑ **pick fares** *v.* [20C+] (*W.I., Bdos*) to work as a prostitute.

Far East Two-step *n.* [1960s] (*US*) diarrhoea; dysentery.

farger *n.* [play on SE *forger*] [late 16C–early 17C] (*UK Und.*) a false die.

far gone *adj.* [mid-19C+] **1** exhausted, worn out. **2** mad, eccentric, insane. **3** far along drunk or otherwise intoxicated.

farkakte *adj.* [synon. Yid.] [1930s+] (*US*) unpleasant, disgusting.

farking *adj. see* FUCKING *adj.*

Farm, the *n.* [Monash, which opened in 1961 with 363 students, was orig. set on a rural campus where cows still grazed and wildlife was a common sight] [1960s+] (*Aus.*) Monash University, Melbourne.

farm *n.*[1] [SE *farm*, an institution for poor children] **1** [late 19C–1930s] a prison infirmary; thus *fetch the farm*, to have oneself admitted to the infirmary. **2** [1950s–70s] a clinic for alcholics to take 'the cure'.

farm *n.*[2] [abbr. SE *work farm*] [20C+] (*US*) a prison; thus *junk farm*, a Federal rehabilitation institution.

farm *n.*[3] [abbr. FUNNY FARM *under* FUNNY *adj.*[1]] [1940s+] (*US*) a psychiatric institution.

farm *v.* [one 'harvests' the CROP *n.*[2]] [1970s+] (*US campus*) to drink alcohol; thus *farmed*, drunk.

farmer *n.*[1] [SE *farm*, to lease or let the proceeds or profits of customs, taxes etc for a fixed payment] [mid-19C] **1** an alderman. **2** a churchwarden.

farmer *n.*[2] **1** [mid-19C+] (*US*) a derog. term for a peasant, an unsophisticated country person, whether an actual farmer or not. **2** [mid-19C+] a stupid or unsophisticated person. **3** [1940s+] (*US black*) recently arrived Southern farm workers who persist in their country ways despite the pressing sophistication of the Northern cities.

SE in slang uses

IN COMPOUNDS

❑ **farmer's alliance** *n.* [late 19C] (*US*) pumpkin pie. ❑ **farmer's beef** *n.* [20C+] (*US*) illegally shot deer, butchered and eaten by its hunter. ❑ **farmer's haircut** *n.* [the farmer's outdoor life gives the tan] [20C+] (*US*) a short haircut that leaves a white strip of skin showing between the bottom of the hair and the tanned portion of the neck. ❑ **farmer's time** *n.* [20C+] (*US*) 30 minutes fast. ❑ **farmer's wine** *n.* (*also* **farm liquor**) [joc. euph.] [20C+] (*US*) illicitly distilled whisky.

farmer Giles *n.* (*also* **farmers**) [rhy. sl. = piles] [1950s+] (*UK/Aus.*) haemorrhoids.

farmisht *adj.* [Yid. *farmisht*, confused] [20C+] (*US*) confused, mixed up.

farm liquor *n. see* FARMER'S WINE *under* FARMER *n.*[2].

Farms, the *n.* [1950s] (*US Und.*) The New York City Reformatory.

farmyard confetti *n.* [euph. for BULLSHIT *n.* (1)] [1960s+] (*Aus.*) nonsense, rubbish.

faro-bank *v.* [mid-19C; 1940s–50s] (*US Und.*) a form of cheating whereby the victim is allowed to win, but never as much as he loses.

far out *adj.*[1] **1** [1920s+] bizarre, eccentric, strange. **2** [1950s+] extreme.

far out *adj.*[2] [with its implication of 'other-worldliness' – and thus hallucinogenic drugs – the term became a staple of the white HIPPIE *n.*[2] (3) vocabulary of the 1960s and faded, other than in ironic use, by the 1970s] [1950s+] (*orig. US black*) excellent, wonderful, first-rate.

far out! *excl.* (*also* **far away!**) [the mental 'space' entered under the influence of hallucinogens] [1960s+] amazing! remarkable! wonderful!

farputst *adj.* [Yid. *farpotshket*, sloppy, messy; ult. Ger. *Patsche*, a slap] [20C+] (*US*) dressed up to excess.

Farringdon hotel *n.* [ironic euph.] [mid-19C] the Fleet prison, in Farringdon Road, London EC4.

farshtinkener *adj.* [Yid.; ult. Ger. *verstinken*, stink up] [1940s+] (*US*) stinking.

farsing *n. see* FARCING *n.*

fart *n.* [FART *v.* (1)] **1** [late 14C+] an act of breaking wind. **2** [mid-18C; 1930s+] a fool, an unpleasant person, often older than the speaker; thus synon. *old fart*. **3** [1930s+] as sense 2 above, but used affectionately. **4** [1940s] something worthless. **5** [1970s] something important, worthwhile.

IN COMPOUNDS

❑ **fart-arse(d)** *see* separate entries. ❑ **fart-box** *n.* [SE *box*/BOX *n.*[1] (1)] [1960s+] (*US*) the anus or rectum. ❑ **fartbreath** *n. see* FART-FACE *n.* ❑ **fart-catcher** *n.* [the job requires walking closely behind his master or mistress] [late 18C–early 19C; 1970s+] a footman. ❑ **fart-daniel** *n.* [? misprint for dial. *fare-daniel*, a suckling pig that is the youngest of a litter] [19C] the vagina. ❑ **fart-face(d)** *see* separate entries. ❑ **fart-hammer** *n. see* FART-FACE *n.* ❑ **fart-head** *n.* (*also* **farthook**) [-HEAD *sfx* (1) + play on FAT-HEAD *n.*[1]] **1** [1960s+] (*US*) a contemptible person. **2** [1990s+] a conservative, trad. old person. ❑ **fart-knocker** *n.* [SE *knocker*, i.e. one who *knocks* or makes *farts*; created or at least popularized in the 1990s TV cartoon *Beavis and Butthead*] (*US*) **1** [1950s+] an obscure person. **2** [1990s+] someone who does not know what they are talking about. ❑ **fart off** *see* separate entries. ❑ **fart-sack** *n.* [1940s+] **1** (*also* **farter**) a bed. **2** a sleeping-bag. **3** (*US*) a sheet, bedding. **4** a term of abuse. ❑ **fart's end** *n.* [early 18C] a term of abuse. ❑ **fart-sucker** *n.* [late 19C; 1970s] a toady, a parasite.

IN PHRASES

❑ **crack a fart** *v.* [late 17C; 1980s+] (*US campus*) to break wind. ❑ **give a fart** *v.* [1980s+] to care. ❑ **give the farts out of one's ass** *v.* [1970s] to treat with contempt. ❑ **go like a strangled fart** *v.* [2000s] (*N.Z.*) to go very slowly. ❑ **I dare not trust my arse with a fart** [late 18C–early 19C] I have diarrhoea. ❑ **last as long as a fart in a windstorm** *v.* (*also* **... whirlwind**) [1930s+] (*Can./US*) to give up quickly, to be defeated quickly. ❑ **like a fart in a bottle** (*also* **like a fart in a colander, ...in a fit**) [late 19C+] twitchy, nervous, agitated. ❑ **like a fart in a phonebox** [1980s] persistently. ❑ **like a fart on a curtain-pole** [2000s] (*N.Z.*) in a great hurry. ❑ **like an Irishman's fart** [1970s] (*US*) of a family, always making a STINK *n.* (1). ❑ **not a fart's chance in a windstorm** (*also* **... whirlwind**) [1950s+] (*Can./US*) no chance at all. ❑ **scared fartless** *adj. see* SCARED SHITLESS *under* SCARE *v.*

fart, a *n.* [mid-16C–mid-18C] a dismissive excl., usu. as *a fart for...*

fart *v.* [cognate with various words in Teutonic and Indo-Germanic languages, e.g. Skrt *pard*, MHG *verzen*, ON *freta*, Lith. *pérdzu*, Rus. *perdet*] **1** [late 14C+] to break wind; thus in fig. use.

2 [1970s–80s] (*UK black*) to suffer.

IN PHRASES

❑ **fart about** *v.* (*also* **fart around**) **1** [1910s+] to dawdle, to mess around. **2** [1980s] to irritate. ❑ **fart along** *v.* [1990s+] (*US*) to do something very slowly, without conviction. ❑ **fart sparks** *v.* [1990s+] (*Aus.*) to be very angry. ❑ **fart through silk** *v.* [1920s+] (*US*) to live prosperously, to feel happy, to be important.

fart-arse *n.* [fig. use of FART *v.* (1) + ARSE *n.* (1)] [1940s+] a general term of contempt, e.g. a fool, an incompetent.

fart-arse *v.* (*also* **fart-arse about/around**) [FART-ARSE *n.*] [1940s+] to dawdle, to mess around, to waste time.

fart-arsed *adj.* (*also* **fart-arse, fart-arseing**) [FART-ARSE *n.*] [1940s+] useless, incompetent, 'half-baked'.

IN COMPOUNDS

❑ **fart-arsed mechanic** *n.* [MECHANIC *n.* (1)] [1920s–30s] a clumsy incompetent.

farteen *n.* [FART *n.* (4) + Irish dimin. sfx *-een*] [1960s] (*Irish*) anything totally insignificant.

farter *n.* [FART *v.* (1)] **1** [mid-17C; 20C+] someone who breaks wind (in a noticeable and even ostentatious manner). **2** [1920s–40s] anus. **3** *see* FART-SACK *under* FART *n.*

fart-face *n.* (*also* **fartbreath, fart-hammer**) [FART *n.* (1)] [1930s+] a general term of abuse.

fart-faced *adj.* [FART-FACE *n.*] [1970s+] a general epithet of abuse.

fartfu *n.* [FART *n.* (1)] [1970s] a very small or insignificant amount.

farthing *n.* [SE *farthing*; thus the minimal value of the coin] [mid–late 19C] worthlessness.

IN COMPOUNDS

❑ **farthing-face** *n.* ['as insignificant as a farthing' (Ware)] [late 19C+] mean-faced, pinched features.

SE in slang uses

IN COMPOUNDS

❑ **farthing taster** *n.* [late 19C] the smallest available portion of ice-cream as sold by street vendors.

fartick *n.* (*also* **fartkin**) [FART *n.* (1)] [late 19C] a small act of breaking wind.

farting *adj.* [FART *v.* (1) + sfx *-ing*] [1930s+] a general pej., piffling, trivial, irrelevant.

SE in slang uses

IN COMPOUNDS

❑ **farting-crackers** *n.* [CRACKER *n.*[1] (1)] [late 17C–18C] (*UK Und.*) breeches, trousers. ❑ **farting strings** *n.* (*also* **puckering string**) [1910s+] a fig. part of the body, which can be damaged by some form of excess, usu. laughter, e.g. *If you don't stop that, I'll bust my farting strings!* ❑ **farting-trap** *n.* [late 19C–1910s] (*Anglo-Irish*) a jaunting car, a light two-wheeled vehicle carrying four people, seated two on each side, back to back.

fartleberried *adj.* [FARTLEBERRIES *n.*] [1940s] a term of disdain.

fartleberries *n.* [FART *n.* (1) + joc. use of SE *berries*] [late 18C+] pieces of excrement clinging to the anal hairs.

fart-off *n.* [fig. use of FART *n.* (1)] [1940s+] (*US*) someone who shirks responsibilities, a loafer.

fart off *v.* [FART-OFF *n.*] [1960s+] (*US*) to idle, to avoid responsibilities.

fas' *v.* [FAASTIE *adj.*] [1950s+] (*W.I. Rasta*) to be rude or impertinent, to meddle in somebody's business, to be forward.

fascio *n.* [? abbr. of 'fuck ass' or link to Jamaican *fas, fassy*, dirty] [2000s] (*UK black/teen*) a derog. term for a homosexual, used as a general insult.

fash *v.* [Scot. *fash*, to concern oneself, to worry about] [late 18C+] (*orig. UK Und*) to trouble, to bother.

fa' sheezy! *excl. see* FO' SHO! *excl.*

fashion arrest *n.* [1980s+] (*orig. US campus*) a fig. 'arrest' (most likely heavy verbal criticism) of one whose style is considered unacceptably unfashionable; usu. as *make a fashion arrest*.

fashion criminal *n.* (*also* **fashion mutant**) [1980s+] (*US campus*) one whose style is considered outside the bounds of acceptable fashion.

fass *n. see* FAAS *v.*

fast *n.* [1980s+] (*drugs*) amphetamine.

fast *adj.*[1] ['A *fast* man – a person who, by late hours, gaiety and continual rounds of pleasure, lives too fast, and wears himself out [...] a *fast* young lady is one who affects mannish habits, or makes herself conspicuous by some unfeminine accomplishment, – talks Slang, drives about in London, smokes cigarettes, is knowing in dogs, horses, &c.' (Hotten, 1859); the *Saturday Review* (28 July 1860) defines a *fast* woman as 'a woman who has lost her respect for men, and for whom men have lost their respect also'] **1** [mid–late 19C] of a woman, acting in a 'masculine' and thus socially unacceptable/unnerving manner. **2** [mid-19C+] immoral, illegal, corrupt; hedonistic. **3** [mid-19C+] of a man or woman, promiscuous. **4** [1960s+] (*US black*) illegal, obtained through crime, spec. of money.

IN COMPOUNDS

❑ **fast dollar boy** *n.* [1940s] (*US*) one who is unscrupulous as to the source of their income. ❑ **fast house** *n.* [HOUSE *n.*[1] (1)] [mid-19C+] (*US*) a brothel. ❑ **fast life** *n.* [1960s+] (*US*) the worlds of gambling, drug-dealing, prostitution etc. ❑ **fast stuff** *n.* [1930s] cheating, swindling.

IN PHRASES

❑ **get fast** *v.* [1980s+] to act in an illegal or unsanctioned manner, to 'play fast and loose'.

SE in slang uses

IN COMPOUNDS

❑ **fast alec** *n.* (*also* **fast aleck**) [var. on SMART ALECK *n.*] [1930s] (*US black*) anyone who moves fast. ❑ **fast-ass** *adj.* [-ASS *sfx*] [1930s+] (*US*) **1** peremptory. **2** fast, quick. ❑ **fast black** *n. see under* BLACK *n.* ❑ **fast buck** *see* separate entries. ❑ **fast fast** *adj.* [redup.] [20C+] (*W.I.*) very fast. ❑ **fast food sex** *n.* [1980s+] (*US gay*) spontaneous, short-term sex, e.g. that enjoyed in lavatories, bath-houses and similar places of anonymous assignation. ❑ **fast freddie** *n.* [1980s] (*US drugs*) phencyclidine. ❑ **fast fuck** *n.* [FUCK *n.* (1)] [20C+] **1** sexual intercourse that, through various circumstances, has to be hurried and brief. **2** of a man, one who is unable to delay his own orgasm until his partner is satisfied too; a premature ejaculator. ❑ **fast lane(r)** *see* separate entries. ❑ **fast mouth** *adj.* (*also* **fast-fast mouth**) [FAASTIE *adj.*] [1940s+] (*W.I.*) cheeky, impertinent. ❑ **fast one** *n. see* separate entry. ❑ **fast quid** *n. see* FAST BUCK *n.* ❑ **fast-rod** *n.* [ROD *n.* (2)] [1960s] (*US*) someone who is quick to use a gun. ❑ **fast-sheet hotel** *n.* (*also* **fast-sheet joint, ...set-up**) [the pillows (and beds) are always in use] [1940s+] (*US*) a cheap hotel that rents out its rooms by the hour to prostitutes and their clients or to illicit lovers. ❑ **fast talker** *n.* [1930s+] a confidence trickster. ❑ **fast-talking Charlie** *n. see under* MR CHARLIE *n.* ❑ **fast track** *n. see* separate entry. ❑ **fast worker** *n.* (*also* **quick worker**) [1910s+] a successful womanizer, one who achieves his seductions quickly; occas. of a woman.

IN PHRASES

❑ **fast as beans** *adj. see* LIKE BEANS *under* BEANS *n.*[3]. ❑ **fast as greased titties** *adj.* [1960s] very fast.

fast *adj.*[2] [mid–late 19C] in financial difficulties.

fast *adj.*[3] [FAASTIE *adj.*] [1940s+] (*US/W.I.*) **1** interfering, meddlesome. **2** cheeky, rude, impertinent.

fast *v.*[1] [FAST *adj.*[2]] [mid-19C] to be out of pocket.

fast *v.*[2] [FAST *adj.*[3]] [20C+] (*W.I.*) to interfere, to meddle.

fast and loose *n.* [late 16C; early 19C] a gambling and cheating game, often practised by thimbleriggers, in which a garter is folded and held out to the punter who bets that by pricking with a pin they can hit the place where the material is folded. Almost inevitably they fail and lose their money.

fast buck *n.* (*also* **fast quid, quick buck**) [SE *fast* + BUCK *n.*[3] (1)] [1940s+] (*orig. US*) money that is earned quickly, and poss. illicitly.

(IN COMPOUNDS)

❑ **fast-buck artist** *n.* (*also* **fast-buck guy**) [-ARTIST *sfx*/GUY *n.*[2] (1)] [1970s+] (*US*) anyone keen on (and successful in) making a great deal of money.

fast-buck *adj.* [FAST BUCK *n.*] [1960s+] (*US*) greedy, 'get rich quick'.

fastener *n.* *see* FASTNER *n.*

fastidious cove *n.* [ironic use of SE *fastidious* + COVE *n.* (1)] [late 19C] a fashionable swindler, who poses as a member of the class he deceives.

fast lane *n.* [1970s+] the active, competitive and ruthless world fought over by those of ambition and intent.

fast lane *v.* [FAST LANE *n.*] [1980s+] (*Aus. prison*) to indulge in a crime spree.

fast laner *n.* [? to live in the FAST LANE *n.*] [1990s+] (*US campus*) one who takes illegal hard drugs.

fastner *n.* (*also* **fastener**) [late 17C–mid-19C] a warrant (of arrest).

fast one *n.* [orig. milit. use, to malinger] [1920s] any scheme seen as amoral, corrupt, underhand.

(IN PHRASES)

❑ **pull a fast one** *v.* (*also* **get over a fast one, put over..., spring..., work..., pull a fast switch/shuffle**) **1** [1920s+] to get away with something, usu. a slightly nefarious scheme. **2** [1930s] to stage a crime, e.g. a hold-up. **3** [1930s] to make an escape, to run away. ❑ **slip a fast one over** *v.* (*also* **slip over a fast one**) [1920s+] to take advantage of someone by trickery, to hoodwink.

fast-sheet hotel *n.* (*also* **fast-sheet joint, fast sheet set-up**) [the pillows (and beds) are always in use] [1940s+] (*US*) a cheap hotel that rents out its rooms by the hour to prostitutes and their clients or to illicit lovers.

fast track *n.* (*also* **big track**) [TRACK *n.*[2] (1)] [1960s+] (*orig. US*) **1** those streets or blocks in a city where prostitutes work; esp., in US, differentiating the East Coast cities from the slower world of the West, esp. California. **2** the lifestyle pursued by the ambitious and successful.

fasty *adj.* *see* FAASTIE *adj.*

fat *n.* **1** [mid-19C; 1960s] (*Aus./US*) money. **2** [late 19C–1950s] (*Aus./N.Z.*) (*also* **fatman, Harry Fat, Mr Fat**) a generic term for the business elite, the wealthiest members of the community. **3** [1930s+] (*Aus./N.Z.*) an erection; esp. in phr. *CRACK A FAT* below. **4** [1940s+] (*usu. gay*) a fat person, esp. as used in small ads.

(IN COMPOUNDS)

❑ **fats and fems** *n.* [1970s+] (*gay*) fat or effeminate male homosexuals, as described in gay advertisements.

(IN PHRASES)

❑ **crack a fat** *v.* [1940s+] (*Aus.*) to achieve an erection.

SE in slang uses

(IN PHRASES)

❑ **fat is in the fire, (all) the** *see* separate entry. ❑ **fat scraps and glorious bits** *n.* [17C] (*UK Und.*) a sound beating.

(IN EXCLAMATIONS)

❑ **fat's a-running!** [late 19C–1930s] (*UK Und.*) a phr. used to indicate that a loaded van is passing along the street and may be robbed, to the greatest possible extent, by opportunists.

fat *adj.* **1** in fig. senses of positive assessment. (**a**) [17C; mid-19C+] good. (**b**) [1950s] a general intensifier, e.g *a fat damn*. (**c**) [1960s+] a general term of approval, first-rate, excellent. **2** in senses of possession. (**a**) [early 17C; late 18C+] substantial; wealthy, rich; thus *fat cull*, a rich man. (**b**) [1970s+] well supplied with drugs. **3** [20C+] self-obsessed, smug. **4** [1950s+] (*US black*) pregnant.

(DERIVATIVES)

❑ **fatness** *n.* [19C] wealth.

(IN COMPOUNDS)

❑ **fat tape** *n.* *see PHAT TAPE under* PHAT *adj.*

(IN PHRASES)

❑ **cut it fat** *v.* *see CUT IT SPICY under* SPICY *adj.* ❑ **get fat** *v.* [1990s+] (*US black*) to become rich. ❑ **go fat** *v.* [1960s] (*S.Afr.*) to go wild, to 'let off steam'. ❑ **sit fat** *v.* [1990s+] (*US*) to be successful and powerful.

SE in slang uses

(IN COMPOUNDS)

❑ **fat ale** *n.* [mid-19C] strong beer. ❑ **fatarm** *n. see under* ARM *n.* ❑ **fat-arse/-ass** *see* separate entries. ❑ **fatboy** *n.* [2000s] (*US*) the penis. ❑ **fat-brain** *n.* *see* FAT-HEAD *n.*[1]. ❑ **fat-brained** *adj.* *see* FAT-HEADED *adj.* ❑ **fat cat** *see* separate entries. ❑ **fat chance** *n.* *see* separate entry. ❑ **fat city** *see* separate entries. ❑ **fat cock** *n.* *see* separate entries. ❑ **fat-face** *n.* [mid-18C] a general term of opprobrium. ❑ **fat-fancier** *n.* (*also* **fat-monger**) [19C] a man who prefers plump women. ❑ **fat farm** *n.* [1960s+] (*orig. US*) a slimming clinic. ❑ **fatgut** *n.* [1950s] a derog. name for a fat person; also attrib. ❑ **fatguts** *n.* (*also* **gutfatty**) [GUT *n.*] [late 16C+] a term of abuse, used of one who has a fat stomach. ❑ **fat-head(ed)** *see* separate entries. ❑ **fat knacker** *n.* [KNACKER *n.* (1)] [1990s+] (*UK juv.*) an unattractive, promiscuous woman. ❑ **fat knot** *n.* [1970s+] (*US black*) a substantial roll of dollar bills. ❑ **fat lip** *n.* [1940s+] a bruised and swollen mouth, the result of a blow. ❑ **fat lot** *n.* [an ironic reversal] [mid-19C+] not very much, if anything at all; often as phr. *a fat lot of good (that will do)*. ❑ **fatman** *n.* *see* FAT *n.* (2). ❑ **fat meat** *n.* [phr. *fat meat is greasy*] [1940s–60s] (*US black*) the truth. ❑ **fat-monger** *n.* *see FAT-FANCIER* above. ❑ **fatmouth** *see* separate entries. ❑ **fat one** *n.* **1** [19C] (*also* **fat 'un**) an especially noisy breaking of wind. **2** [1950s–60s] (*US*) a $100 bill. **3** [1960s+] (*US drugs*) (*also* **fattie, fatty**) a marijuana cigarette, esp. a large one. **4** [1990s+] (*US*) a large cigar. ❑ **fat-tailed** *adj.* [1950s] (*US*) overweight. ❑ **fatwad** *n.* [1910s] (*US*) an aristocrat, a wealthy person.

(IN PHRASES)

❑ **fat around the heart** *adj.* [fat around the heart clogs the arteries and makes one's blood, fig. courage, flow more slowly] [1930s] (*US black*) cowardly. ❑ **fat as a buggy-whip** *adj.* [19C+] (*US*) very thin. ❑ **fat as a match** *adj.* [late 19C+] (*US*) very thin. ❑ **fat as Sir Roger** *adj.* [the weighty Arthur Orton (1834–98), self-styled *Sir Roger* Tichborne, 'star' of the 1871 'Tichborne claimant' case] [late 19C] extremely fat. ❑ **fat on top** *adj.* [1970s+] (*US gay*) **1** intellectual. **2** drunk.

(IN EXCLAMATIONS)

❑ **fat show!** [1930s+] (*N.Z.*) no chance at all!

fat *adv.* **1** [late 19C+] (*US campus*) successfully. **2** [1900s] comfortably. **3** [1960s] very, extremely.

(IN PHRASES)

❑ **do it fat** *v.* [1910s–20s] to pose as a gentleman.

fatal tree *n.* *see* TRIPLE TREE *n.*

fat and wide *n.* [rhy. sl.] [20C+] a bride.

fat-arse *n.* (*also* **fat-ass**) [FAT-ARSE *adj.*] [1920s+] a very fat person; also as a term of address.

fat-arse *adj.* (*also* **fat-arsed**) [SE *fat* + ARSE *n.* (1)/-ARSED *sfx* (1)] [18C+] fat, large-buttocked; also of objects, large.

fat-ass *adj.* (*also* **fat-assed, fat-assing**) [SE *fat* + ASS *n.* (2)/-ASS *sfx*/-ASSED *sfx*] (*US*) **1** [1930s+] of people, fat; of objects, large. **2** [1950s–60s] a general intensifying adj. **3** [1960s+] in fig. use, comfortably off. **4** [2000s] money grabbing, superficial, fake.

fat ass *v.* [FAT-ARSE *n.*] [1960s+] (*US*) to loaf, to idle.

fat cat *n.* [1920s+] (*orig. US*) any successful, wealthy, influential person; recent UK use has tended to imply a degree of self-serving corruption to such individuals.

fat-cat *adj.* [FAT CAT *n.*] [1950s+] (*orig. US*) prosperous; esp. when the implication is that such prosperity has been gained by corruption.

fatcha *n.* [Ital. *faccia*, face] [20C+] (*Ling. Fr./Polari*) the human face; thus *fake the fatcha*, to shave, to put on make-up.

fat chance *n.* (*also* **hot chance**) [mid-19C+] no chance at all; also as excl.

fat city *n.*[1] [SE *fat*, abundant, stimulating + -CITY *sfx* (1)] [1960s+] success, wealth, often from criminal activities.

fat city *n.*[2] [SE *fat*, overweight + -CITY *sfx* (1)] [1970s+] (*US*) the process of gaining weight or the state of being fat.

fat city *adj.* [FAT CITY *n.*[1]] [1960s+] excellent, splendid.

fat cock *n.*[1] [SE *fat* + COCK *n.*[3] (3)] [mid-19C] a fat old man.

fat cock *n.*[2] [SE *fat* + COCK *n.*[4] (1)] [late 19C] the labia minora, esp. when prominent.

fater *n.* (*also* **factor, fayter**) [Fr. *faiteur*, maker; 'the Second (old) Rank of the Canting Crew' (B.E.)] [16C–early 19C] (*UK Und.*) a cheat or impostor; a fraudulent fortune-teller.

fat head *n.* [HEAD *n.* (4)] [1910s+] **1** a hangover. **2** a headache.

fat-head *n.*[1] (*also* **fat-brain**) [FAT-HEADED *adj.*/SE *fat* + -HEAD *sfx* (1)] [late 16C; mid-19C+] a fool, an idiot; often used affectionately as well as derog.

fat-head *n.*[2] (*also* **big-head**) [2000s] (*UK black*) a marijuana cigarette.

fat-headed *adj.* (*also* **fat-brained, fathead**) [17C+] foolish, stupid.

father *n.* **1** [mid-19C] the owner of a common lodging house. **2** [mid–late 19C] a receiver of stolen goods [play on UNCLE *n.* (1)]. **3** [1950s] (*US prison*) the dominant lesbian of a small 'family' group. **4** [1960s] (*US drugs*) a large-scale drug dealer.

SE in slang uses

(IN COMPOUNDS)

❑ **father abraham** *n.* [19C] the penis. ❑ **father confessor** *n.* [play on SE + ? ref. to popular image of the venal priest] [19C] the penis. ❑ **father-fucker/-fucking** *see* separate entries. ❑ **father-grabber** *see* MOTHER-GRABBER *under* MOTHER- *n.* ❑ **father-grabbing** *see* MOTHER-GRABBING *under* MOTHER- *n.* ❑ **father-mucker** *n. see* FATHER-FUCKER *n.* ❑ **father-of-all** *n. see* FATHER-FUCKER *n.* ❑ **father time** *n.* **1** [1920s] (*US campus*) an older man (but poss. still attractive). **2** [1940s] (*US prison*) the warden [play on TIME *n.* (1)].

father (and mother) of... *phr.* (*also* **mama and papa of..., mother and father of...**) [mid-19C+] a general intensifier; usu. *...of a thrashing, ...of a row.*

Father Christmas hold *n. see* CHRISTMAS HOLD *under* CHRISTMAS *n.*

father-fucker *n.* (*also* **fathermucker, furthermucker**) **1** [1960s] (*US gay*) a synon. for MOTHERFUCKER *n.* **2** [1980s] (*US black*) a positive epithet.

father-fucking *adj.* [1960s] (*US gay*) a synon. for MOTHERFUCKING *adj.*

Father O'Flynn *n.* [rhy. sl.] [1960s+] the chin.

father something on someone *v. see under* SOMETHING *n.*

fatima *adj.* [ext. of SE] [2000s] (*S.Afr. gay*) fat.

fat is in the fire, (all) the *phr.* **1** [mid-16C–mid-19C] a phr. used to indicate that a plan has failed. **2** [late 19C+] a phr. used to indicate that the result of an action will be to provoke anger. **3** [1950s] a phr. used to describe an energetic situation, but with no negative overtones.

fatmouth *n.* [fig. use of SE or lit. trans. of Mandingo *da-ba*, big, fat mouth; thus fig. excessive talking] **1** [1920s+] (*US black*) a braggart, a boaster; the quality of being one. **2** [1990s+] (*US*) verbosity.

fatmouth *adj.* (*also* **fat-mouthed**) [FATMOUTH *n.*] [1960s+] (*orig. US black*) boastful, noisy, verbose.

fatmouth *v.* [FATMOUTH *n.* (1)] [1960s+] (*orig. US black*) to argue, to answer back, to be cheeky, to talk excessively, to boast.

fats *n.* (*also* **fatstuff**) **1** [1910s–30s] (*orig. US black*) a generic term for jazz musicians. **2** [1930s+] (*US*) a nickname for anyone seen as overweight.

fatso *n.* [1930s+] (*orig. US*) **1** a general derog. term addressed to a fat person. **2** a fat person.

fatten frogs for snakes *v. see under* SNAKE *n.*[1].

fattie *n. see* FAT ONE *under* FAT *adj.*

fattoon *n.* [SE *fat* + sfx *-oon*; on model of *octaron, quadroon* etc] [1950s] (*W.I.*) a very fat person.

fatty *n.*[1] [early 19C+] a fat person, esp. as a nickname.

(IN COMPOUNDS)

❑ **fatty bum-bum** *n.* [redup. BUM *n.*[1] (1)] [1950s+] (*W.I. Gren./Trin.*) a fat person, esp. a woman with large buttocks. ❑ **fattycake** *n.* [1940s] (*US black campus*) a plump woman.

fatty *n.*[2] [FAT ONE *under* FAT *adj.*] [1990s+] (*US drugs*) a drug dealer.

fatty *n.*[3] *see* FAT ONE *under* FAT *adj.*

fatymus *n.* (*also* **fatyma, fattyma, fattymus**) [pig Lat.] [mid–late 19C] a fat man or woman.

faucet *n.* [mid-18C; 1980s] (*US*) a penis.

SE in slang uses

(IN PHRASES)

❑ **turn off the faucet** *v. see* TURN ON THE WATERWORKS *under* WATERWORKS *n.*

faugh! *excl.* (*also* **faw! fogh! foh! fough! fugh! hough! paugh! pho(h)! pogh! pough! pugh! wagh!**) [early uses are no more than aggressive throat-clearing, but later uses (perhaps mid-19C+) seem likely to be a euph. for FUCK! *excl.*] [late 17C+] an excl. of dismissal, derision, anger or surprise.

faulkener *n.* (*also* **faulkner**) [? SE *faulconer*, who lures his hawks onto his hand or into a cage] (*UK Und.*) **1** [late 17C–18C] one who lures an innocent player into a crooked gambling game. **2** [late 17C–mid-19C] a juggler, a tumbler.

faulties *n.* [SE *faulty*] [1990s+] (*US black teen*) a cellular telephone that is being used illegally.

Fauntleroy *v.* [Henry *Fauntleroy*, British criminal, hanged for forgery in 1824] [early 19C] (*US*) to act as a forger.

fauny shop *n. see* FAWNEY-SHOP *under* FAWNEY *n.*

faust *n.* [? the fictional *Dr Faustus*] [1930s–50s] (*US black*) **1** an ugly person of either sex. **2** a blind date.

faux *n.* [abbr. Fr. *faux pas*, a blunder] [1980s+] (*US campus*) a mistake.

faux *v.* [FAUX *n.*] [1980s+] (*US campus*) to make a mistake.

fave *n.* (*also* **fav**) [abbr.] [1930s+] (*orig. US*) a favourite.

fave *adj.* (*also* **fav**) [abbr.] [1930s+] (*orig. US*) favourite.

(IN COMPOUNDS)

❑ **fave rave** *n.* [1960s+] (*UK teen*) most favoured person, most enjoyable experience, preferred food etc.

favour *n.*

(IN PHRASES)

❑ **I could do her a favour** (*also* **I could do that a favour**) [the *favour* would, of course, be sexual] [1930s+] a remark made by a man of a passing woman.

favourite vice *n.* [late 19C–1910s] one's preferred drink; usu. in phr. *what's your favourite vice?* what would you like to drink?

faw! *excl. see* FAUGH! *excl.*

fawney *n.* (*also* **fawny, forney, forny**) [Irish *fáin(n)e*, a ring] **1** [late 18C–1900s] a ring. **2** [late 18C–1930s] one who practises fraud involving bogus jewellery.

(IN COMPOUNDS)

❑ **fawney-bouncing** *n.* [mid-19C] selling a ring to a victim; the justification for the sale is a supposed wager, which the seller can win only by selling the ring. ❑ **fawney-dropper** *n.* [mid–late 19C] (*UK Und.*) one who practises the FAWNEY-RIG below. ❑ **fawney-man** *n.* [late 19C–1930s] a seller of bogus jewellery. ❑ **fawney-rig** *n.* (*also* **fawney-dropping**) [RIG *n.*[2] (1)] [late 18C–mid-19C] 'A common fraud thus practised. A fellow drops a brass ring, double gilt, which he picks up before the party meant to be cheated, and to whom he disposes of it for less than its supposed, and ten times more than its real, value' (Grose, 1796). ❑ **fawney-shop** *n.* (*also* **fauny shop**) [1900s] (*US Und.*) a shop selling fake or cheap jewellery.

(IN PHRASES)

❑ **flash a fawney** *v.* [19C] to wear a counterfeit ring. ❑ **go**

upon the fawney *v.* [late 18C] to perform acts of fraud involving bogus jewellery.

fawnied *adj.* (*also* **fawney-fam'd**) [FAWNEY *n.* (1)] [late 18C–mid-19C] wearing more than one ring on a single finger.

fay *see all parts of speech for* OFAY.

fay broad *n.* [OFAY *adj.* + BROAD *n.*[2] (3)] [20C+] (*US black*) a light-skinned black woman or a white woman.

faygele *n.* (*also* **fagola, faigelah, fegala, feigele**) [Yid. *feygele*, little bird + FAG *n.*[5] (1); Yid. *Feygel* is also a woman's proper name] [20C+] (*US*) a male homosexual.

fayter *n. see* FATER *n.*

fazzey *n.* [ety. unknown] [mid-19C] (*UK Und.*) luck.

fazzled *adj.* [1920s] (*US*) disconcerted, worried.

f.b.i. *adj.* [abbr.] [1970s] (*US black*) fat, black and ignorant.

f.b.i.! *excl.* [abbr.] [1990s+] a general term of abuse, fucking bloody idiot!

f.d.a. *v.* [*f*uck *d*at *a*ss] [2000s] (*US black*) to have sexual intercourse.

f.d.r. *n.* (*also* **roosevelt**) [abbr. *F*ranklin *D*elano *R*oosevelt (1882–1945); one of the projects of Roosevelt's New Deal WPA programme was the building in deprived rural areas of new outdoor toilets] [1930s–60s] (*US*) an outdoor toilet.

f'd up *adj. see* FUCKED UP *adj.* (2).

f.e. *n.* [abbr. *F*rench *e*nvelope] [1990s+] (*S.Afr.*) a condom.

feague *v.* [SE *feague*, to beat, to whip; ult. Ger. *fegen*, to polish] **1** [mid–late 17C] to have sexual intercourse. **2** [late 18C–early 19C] to enliven, usu. of a horse.

feak *n.* [? link to FEAGUE *v.*] [early 19C] the posterior, the buttocks.

feaker of loges *n. see* FAKER OF LOGES *under* FAKER *n.*

fear! *excl.* [1980s+] (*US campus*) a response to anything the speaker finds either distasteful or admirable.

fearful *adj.* [early 17C; late 18C+] a general intensifier.

fearful frights *n.* [late 19C] a kick in the posterior.

fearfully *adv.* [mid-17C; early 19C+] a general intensifying adv.

Feargal Sharkey *n.* [rhy. sl. = DARKIE *n.*; ult. Northern Irish pop star *Feargal Sharkey* (b.1958)] [1990s+] a derog. term for a black person.

fearnought *n.* [late 19C] a drink to boost one's morale.

feast of St Lubbock *n. see* ST LUBBOCK'S DAY *under* ST LUBBOCK *n.*

feather *n.* **1** [late 17C+] the pubic hair. **2** [mid-19C] (*UK Und.*) the hair. **3** [late 19C–1920s] (*UK tramp*) a bed.

SE in slang uses

IN COMPOUNDS

❑ **feather bed(ding)** *see* separate entries. ❑ **featherbrain** *n. see* FEATHERHEAD *n.* ❑ **featherbrained** *adj. see* FEATHER-HEADED *adj.* ❑ **feather driver** *n.* [his quill pens] [late 16C–early 17C] a clerk. ❑ **feather-eyed** *adj. see* FEATHER-HEADED *adj.* ❑ **feather duster** *n.* [resemblance] **1** [1920s] (*US*) a style of facial whisker. **2** [1930s] (*US*) an American Indian [ref. to the head-dress]. ❑ **feather-legged** *adj.* [i.e. one's legs are shaking like feathers in the wind] [1930s+] (*US*) terrified, extremely frightened. ❑ **feather merchant** *n.* [he cannot or does not 'pull his weight'] [1930s+] (*orig. US milit.*) **1** a physical weakling. **2** a foolish, silly person. **3** a shirker. ❑ **feather plucker** *n.* [rhy. euph. for FUCKER *n.* (3)] [1940s+] a general term of abuse, usu. used to refer to someone unpleasant. ❑ **featherweight** *see under* LIGHTWEIGHT. ❑ **featherwood** *n.* [play on PECKERWOOD *n.*; ? she 'flies in and out' of the jail or is clad in metaphorical feminine feathers] [1990s+] (*US prison*) **1** a white prisoner's wife or girlfriend. **2** a white female inmate.

IN PHRASES

❑ **feather up** *v.* [the action of birds] [1930s–50s] (*US*) to prepare to fight. ❑ **in full feather** (*also* **in feather**) **1** [late 18C–19C] (*US*) (*also* **in full puff**) in one's best clothes. **2** [19C] rich. **3** [early 19C+] in top condition, very cheerful. ❑ **in high feather** [early 19C–1920s] rich, very cheerful; thus *out of feather*, penniless. ❑ **in the feathers** [1900s] (*US*) in bed. ❑ **moult one's feathers** *v.* [17C] to lose one's hair through syphilis. ❑ **not a feather to fly with** [orig. university use, where to be *plucked* was to have failed one's examinations] [mid-19C–1900s] ruined, penniless. ❑ **take a feather out of** *v.* [the pulling out of a *feather* will make a bird jump] [20C+] (*Irish*) to confuse, to surprise, to astonish.

feather *v.* [SE phr. *feather one's own nest*] [20C+] (*US*) to curry favour with, to toady to.

feather (and flip) *n.* [rhy. sl. = KIP *n.*[1] (2)/KIP *n.*[1] (4)] [1930s+] a sleep or a bed.

feather-bed *n.* (*also* **feather-bed and pillows**) [resemblance] [late 19C; 1950s] (*US*) an extremely fat person.

SE in slang uses

IN COMPOUNDS

❑ **feather-bed jig** *n.* [late 18C–19C] sexual intercourse. ❑ **feather-bed lane** *n.* ['particularly that betwixt Dunchurch and Daintrie' (B.E.)] [late 17C–18C] a notably rough road or track. ❑ **feather-bed soldier** *n.* **1** [late 19C] (*US*) a soldier who avoids hard tasks. **2** [1910s] a womanizer, a lecher.

feather bed *v.* [fig. use of the softness of the bed] [1920s+] to make things (unfairly) easy for a friend, relation or confederate.

feather-bedding *n.* [FEATHER BED *v.*] [20C+] the practice of making things easy for one's associates, handing out easy 'jobs for the boys'.

feathered oof-bird *n.* [OOF *n.* (1)] [late 19C–1920s] a source or supplier of a large amount of money.

featherhead *n.* (*also* **featherbrain**) [SE *feather* + SE *head*/-HEAD *sfx* (1)] **1** [mid-19C+] (*US*) a Native American. **2** [mid-19C+] a scatterbrain. **3** [20C+] one who takes foolish chances.

feather-headed *adj.* (*also* **feather-brained, feather-eyed**) [FEATHERHEAD *n.* (2)] [17C+] scatterbrained.

feather me! *excl. see* BLOW ME! *excl.*[1].

feathers *n.*[1] [SE phr. *feather one's nest*; ? they help you fly] **1** [early 17C; mid-19C] wealth, money. **2** [late 19C+] (*US*) fancy clothes; thus *fine feathers*.

IN PHRASES

❑ **his feathers** *n.* [1900s] (*US*) an important or self-important person.

feathers *n.*[2] **1** [mid-19C+] (*US*) a bed or pillow. **2** [1940s+] facial or body hair.

Featherston Street farmer *n.* [*Featherstone Street* in Wellington] [2000s] (*N.Z.*) an absentee farm owner.

feature *n.* [*FEATURE WITH under* FEATURE *v.*] [1960s–70s] (*Aus.*) an act of sexual intercourse.

feature *v.* **1** [1920s+] (*US*) to note, to pay attention to, to understand; often as phr. *feature this*. **2** [1950s+] to like, to appreciate.

IN PHRASES

❑ **feature with** *v.* [coined by the Australian comedian and writer Barry Humphries (b.1934) for his strip character Barry Mackenzie] [1960s+] (*orig. Aus.*) to seduce a compliant woman.

features *n.* [late 19C–1900s] a term of address, e.g. *Hello, features*.

feaze *v. see* FEEZE *v.*

February *adj.* [1990s+] unfashionable.

February face *n. see FRIDAY FACE under* FRIDAY *n.*

feck *v.*[1] [? OE *feccan*, to fetch; Ger. *fegen*, to plunder] (*Irish/Scot.*) **1** [late 18C–mid-19C] (*UK Und.*) to ascertain the best method of committing a robbery. **2** [late 19C+] to steal.

feck *v.*[2] [1950s+] (*mainly Irish*) a euph. for FUCK *v.* in various senses.

feck! *excl.* [1920s+] (*mainly Irish*) a euph. for FUCK! *excl.*

feck-all *n.* [1970s+] (*Irish*) nothing at all; a euph. for FUCK ALL *n.*

fecker *n. see* FUCKER *n.*

fecking *adj.* [1920s+] (*mainly Irish*) **1** a euph. for FUCKING *adj.* **2** as infix *-fucking-*.

Fecky the Ninth *n.* [FECK *v.*[2]] [2000s] (*Irish*) an utter fool.

Fed *n.* (*also* **fed**) [abbr.] **1** [late 18C–early 19C] (*US*) a *Fed*eralist. **2** [mid-19C] (*US*) a supporter of the Northern cause in the US

Civil War, fighting for *fed*eral rather than states' rights. **3** [1910s+] (*US*) (*also* **Federales**) a member of the *Fed*eral Bureau of Investigation; often in pl. **4** [1950s+] (*US*) the *Fed*eral government. **5** [1960s+] (*Aus.*) a *fed*eral police officer. **6** [1970s+] (*Aus.*) a member of the *Fed*eral government. **7** [1990s+] (*US campus*) money, i.e. *Fed*eral dollar bills. **8** [1990s+] (*Irish/UK black/teen*) a police officer.

Fed *adj.* [FED *n.* (4)] [1950s+] (*US*) pertaining to the Federal government.

fed *adj. see* FED UP *adj.*

feddy *n.* [FED *n.* (7)] [2000s] (*US black*) money.

federal *adj.* [SE *federal*, pertaining to the federal, i.e. national rather than state (local) government] **1** [1990s+] used of something of exceptional quality or of an extreme nature. **2** [2000s] (*US teen*) criminal.

SE in slang uses

IN COMPOUNDS

□ **federal building** *n.* [1940s–60s] (*US*) an outdoor toilet. □ **federal joint** *n.* [JOINT *n.* (3i)] [1950s+] (*US Und.*) a federal, rather than a state, prison.

federating *n.* [SE *federate*, to join together] [1900s–50s] (*Aus.*) having sexual intercourse.

fedex *n.* [popular abbr. for the *Fed*eral *Ex*press courier company] [1990s+] (*US black teen*) an individual who pays debts quickly.

feds *n.* [1990s+] (*US prison*) a federal, rather than a state prison.

fed up *adj.* (*also* **fed**) [20C+] irritated, annoyed, bored; intensified as *fed up to the back teeth, fed to the teeth* and (orig. milit.) *fed up, fucked up and far from home*.

fed up *v.* [FED UP *adj.* (1)] [1910s–30s] (*Aus./US*) to annoy.

fed with a fire-shovel *phr.* [late 18C–19C] a phr. used of someone who has a notably wide mouth.

fedy *adj.* [FEDERAL *adj.* (1); ult. abbr. *Federal* (Bureau of Investigation)] [1990s+] (*US black*) aggressive.

Feeb *n.* (*also* **Feebee, Feebie, Phoebe**) [1920s+] (*US*) the FBI; thus an agent of the FBI.

feeb *n.* [FEEB *adj.* (1)] [1910s+] a feeble, useless person.

feeb *adj.* (*also* **feebly**) [abbr.] [1910s+] *feeble*.

Feebee/Feebie *n.* see FEEB *n.*

feeblo *n.* [SE *feeble* + -O *sfx* (4)] [1930s–50s] (*US prison*) **1** one who is mentally impaired. **2** a drug addict.

fee-chaser *n.* [their supposed primary interest] [20C+] (*US derog.*) a lawyer.

feed *n.* **1** [early 19C+] food and drink, usu. as served in a meal, esp. a substantial one. **2** [1940s–50s] (*US drugs*) drugs.

IN COMPOUNDS

□ **feed bag** *n. see* separate entry. □ **feed-box** *n.* [horseracing imagery] [20C+] **1** the mouth; usu. in *STRAIGHT FROM THE FEED BOX under* STRAIGHT *adv.* **2** food, a meal. □ **feed joint** *n.* [JOINT *n.* (3b)] [1900s–10s] (*US*) a café or restaurant.

IN PHRASES

□ **off one's feed** [horse stable jargon] **1** [mid-19C+] depressed, miserable, nervous. **2** [1900s] incompetent, unskilled.

feed *v.*

IN PHRASES

□ **feed a line** *v. see under* LINE *n.*[1]. □ **feed from home** *v.* [late 16C–early 17C] to commit adultery. □ **feed (hot) lead** *v. see under* LEAD *n.* □ **feed one's face** *v. see* separate entry. □ **feed one's habit** *v. see under* HABIT *n.* □ **feed one's pussy** *v. see under* PUSSY *n.* □ **feed pap** *v.* (*also* **give pap**) [late 18C] (*UK Und.*) to trick with the intention of causing harm. □ **feed pap with a hatchet** *v.* (*also* **give pap with a hatchet**) [SE *pap*, baby food; thus one feeds the baby (a kindness) with a hatchet (a cruelty)] [late 16C–early 18C] to perform a kind act in an unkind manner, to be 'cruel to be kind'. □ **feed someone chunks** *v.* [late 19C] (*US campus*) to attempt verbal deception. □ **feed someone stuff** *v.* [1970s+] (*US black*) to deceive, to pass on false (and self-serving) information. □ **feed the bears** *v. see under* BEAR *n.* □ **feed the chooks** *v. see CHOKE THE CHICKEN under* CHOKE *v.* □ **feed the dog** *v. see FUCK THE DOG (AND SELL THE PUPS) under* DOG *n.*[2]. □ **feed the ducks** *v.* [the similarity in hand motions] [1990s+] (*US*) to masturbate. □ **feed the dumb glutton** *v. see under* DUMB GLUTTON *n.* □ **feed the dummy** *v.* [var. on *FEED THE DUMB GLUTTON under* DUMB GLUTTON *n.*] [19C] to have sexual intercourse. □ **feed the fishes** *v.* **1** [19C+] to die by drowning. **2** [late 19C+] (*US*) to vomit, esp. over the side of a ship. □ **feed the goldfish** *v.* (*also* **feed the kippers**) [20C+] (*US*) to vomit, esp. over the side of a ship. □ **feed the pigeons** *v.* [the image of a hand shaking out breadcrumbs] [2000s] to masturbate. □ **feed the pony** *v. see under* PONY *n.* □ **feed the roots of daisies** *v.* [var. on PUSH UP (THE) DAISIES *v.* (1)] [1930s] to die. □ **feed the worms** *v.* [although the image dates to the early 17C, the sl. use is modern] [mid-19C+] to die. □ **feed with a spoon** *v.* [1910s–20s] to bribe.

feedback *n.* [1970s] (*US*) cheek, insolence.

feed bag *n.* **1** [1900s] (*Aus.*) the face; the mouth. **2** [1960s+] (*drugs*) a container for narcotics or marijuana. **3** [1990s+] (*US campus*) an appetite.

IN PHRASES

□ **put on the feed bag** *v.* (*also* **put on the bag, tie on the feedbag, strap on a feedbag**) [1910s+] to eat.

feedelo *n.* [FEEDER *n.* (1)] [mid-19C] (*UK Und.*) a silver punch-ladle.

feeder *n.* **1** [18C–19C] (*UK Und.*) a (silver) spoon. **2** [1900s–20s] (*US*) the mouth or throat. **3** [1950s–70s] (*US drugs*) a hypodermic syringe.

IN COMPOUNDS

□ **feeder-prigger** *n.* [PRIGGER *n.*[1] (1)] [late 18C–19C] (*UK Und.*) a thief specializing in silver spoons.

feeding *n.* [20C+] (*W.I.*) **1** sexual intercourse. **2** a woman with whom a man wishes to have sex.

SE in slang uses

IN COMPOUNDS

□ **feeding birk** *n.* [? SE *barrack*] [late 19C] (*UK Und.*) a cookshop. □ **feeding bottles** *n.* [20C+] the female breasts.

feed one's face *v.* **1** [late 19C+] to eat, esp. to stuff oneself with food; thus *face-feeding*, over-eating; *face-feeder*, an (over-)eater. **2** [1930s+] to feed someone else. **3** [1980s+] to indulge in oral intercourse.

fee-faw-fum *n.* [the favoured phrase of the Giant in the nursery tale of Jack the Giant-Killer] [19C] nonsense, spec. bloodthirsty, threatening nonsense.

feel *n.* [FEEL *v.* (1)] [late 19C+] an act of sexual groping.

IN COMPOUNDS

□ **feel day** *n.* [pun on SE *field day*] [1910s+] (*Can.*) heavy petting.

IN PHRASES

□ **cop a feel** *v.* [20C+] (*US*) to indulge in some form of petting or sexual groping, but not intercourse. □ **put the feel on** *v.* [1930s] (*US*) to sound out, to assess.

feel *v.* **1** [mid-17C+] to caress sexually, whether or not the advance is desired. **2** [1960s+] (*US black*) to empathize with; thus affirmatory phr. *I feel you.* **3** [1990s+] to arrest.

SE in slang uses

IN PHRASES

□ **feel a draught** *v.* (*also* **feel a draft**) [the phr. is generally credited to the jazz musician Lester Young (1909–59)] **1** [1920s+] to feel insecure, esp. financially. **2** [1930s–40s] (*US black*) to sense racial antagonism in one's conversation or dealings with whites; thus *drafty*, unfriendly to blacks. **3** [1930s–40s] (*US black*) to warn one's friends that a white person has entered the room. □ **feel all (a)round my hat** *v.* [? ballad 'all round my hat I wears a green willow'; thus ? ref. to the green pallor of an ill complexion] [mid-19C–1910s] to feel unwell. □ **feel as if a cat had kittened in one's mouth** *v.* [late 19C+] to feel the nauseous after-effects of drinking on 'the morning after'. □ **feel cheap** *v. see under* CHEAP *adj.* □ **feel froggy** *v. see under* FROGGY *adj.*[2]. □ **feel funny** *v.* **1** [early 19C+] to feel (unpleasantly) drunk. **2** [mid-19C+] to feel very emotional. **3** [20C+] to feel ill. ❑ **feel good** *v.* (*orig. US*) **1** [mid-19C+] to feel in good spirits or health. **2** [late 19C+] to feel mildly drunk, experiencing a drug. ❑ **feel like a ball of string** *v.* (*also* **feel like a bag of string**) [pun on Aus. phr. *ball of muscle*, an energetic person + poss. pun on phr. *all wound up*, emotional, tense] [1950s] (*Aus.*) to feel exhausted. ❑ **feel like a boiled rag** *v.* (*also* **feel like a piece of chewed rag/string**) [20C+] to feel ill. ❑ **feel like a (fresh-)boiled owl** *v.* (*also* **feel like a stewed witch**) [mid-19C–1900s] (*US*) to be extremely hungover, to be very exhausted, run down. ❑ **feel like death warmed up** *v.* (*also* **feel like a warmed-up corpse, feel like death on a bun/cracker**) [1910s+] to feel absolutely appalling, often used by those suffering from hangovers (cf. LOOK LIKE DEATH WARMED UP *under* LOOK LIKE… *v.*). ❑ **feel (like) shit** *v.* (*also* **feel shitty**) *see under* SHIT *n.* ❑ **feel moldy** *v.* [SE *mouldy*] [1980s+] (*US campus*) to feel humiliated, embarrassed. ❑ **feel no way** [1950s+] (*W.I., Rasta*) don't take offence, don't be sorry, don't worry. ❑ **feel off** *v.* [SE *off* used to imply agency as in JERK OFF *v.* (3) etc] [1970s+] to manipulate a sexual partner to orgasm. ❑ **feel one's piss** *v. see* PISS *n.* (1). ❑ **feel someone's collar** *v.* [the physical act of grabbing a villain] [1950s+] (*UK Und.*) to arrest, to place under suspicion. ❑ **feel the draught** *v.* **1** [1920s] to be inconvenienced, suffering the consequences of something. **2** [1940s+] to have serious money problems. ❑ **feel the physics** *v.* [1990s+] (*US black*) to get hurt. ❑ **feel the steel** *v.* [i.e. the *steel* syringe] [1980s+] (*Aus. prison*) to inject heroin. ❑ **feel up** *see* separate entries. ❑ **go feel around** [late 19C] (*US*) a dismissive phr.

feele *n.* (*also* **feelia, feelier**) [Ital. *figlie*, children] [mid-19C] (*Ling. Fr./Polari*) a child; thus *donah and feeles*, a woman and (her) children; *feele omi*, a young (and poss. underage) man.

feeler *n.*[1] [the victim *feels* the point] [mid-19C] (*US*) a knife or other pointed weapon.

feeler *n.*[2] **1** [mid-19C] (*US Und.*) a small boy who pilfers small items, then hands them over to his elders in a gang for sale to a junk-shop. **2** [late 19C+] a hand. **3** [1910s+] a finger, usu. in pl.

feel fine *n.* [rhy. sl.] [1980s] £9.

feelia/feelier *n. see* FEELE *n.*

feelies *n.* [FEEL *n.* (1)] [1980s–90s] sexual petting (and intercourse).

feelies, the *n.* [FEEL *n.* (1)] [1940s+] (*Aus.*) petting in a darkened cinema.

feeling no pain *phr.* [i.e. anaesthetized by liquor] **1** [1920s+] drunk. **2** [1950s+] unconcerned, casual; a state achieved with or without drugs.

feeling right royal *phr.* [SE *feeling* + RIGHT *adv.* (1) + SE *royal*] [late 19C+] drunk.

feel up *n.* [FEEL UP *v.*] [1980s+] an intimate caress, usu. of a woman by a man.

feel up *v.* [20C+] to caress (usu. a woman) sexually.

feero *n.* [? pron. of SE *fire*] [1930s] (*US prison*) an arsonist.

feese *see under* FEEZE.

feet-casements *n.* [SE *feet* + *casement*, a frame] [mid-19C–1910s] boots, shoes.

feet uppermost *adj.* [19C+] used to describe a woman lying supine, in the sexual 'missionary position'.

feevee *n.* [pron. of SE] [1910s] (*US*) $15.

feeze *n.* (*also* **feese, pheeze**) [SE *feeze*, to frighten, to put into a state of alarm] [mid-19C] (*US*) a state of worry or alarm.

feeze *v.* (*also* **feaze, feese, feize, pheeze**) [SE *feeze*, to beat, to flog; ult. OE *fesian*, to drive] [17C; late 19C] to have sexual intercourse.

fegala *n. see* FAYGELE *n.*

fegs! *excl. see* I'FECKS! *excl.*

feigele *n. see* FAYGELE *n.*

feint *n.* [mid-19C] (*UK Und.*) a pawnbroker.

feist *n.* [FEISTY *adj.* (1)] [20C+] (*US*) a truculent, short-tempered person or animal.

feisty *adj.* [SE *fist*, a small dog; thus having the characteristics of such a yappy, snappy, energetic creature; the dog shares an ety. with 15C *fist*, a foul smell, the breaking of wind, but whether, as Wentworth & Flexner suggest in *Dict. American Slang* (1960, 1975), the dog was so named because one's own smells could be blamed upon it remains debatable. Equally feasible is the 19C suggestion that such dogs were not much bigger than a man's *fist*. Note dial. *feist*, to strut about, to flirt or show off] **1** [late 19C+] (*orig. US*) truculent, irascible, impertinent. **2** [20C+] (*orig. US*) (*also* **fisty**) of a young woman, flirtatious (to a greater extent than the speaker sees as proper), showing off, putting on airs, of dubious morality; 1980s+ use tends to perceive this in a more positive light.

feize *v. see* FEEZE *v.*

feke *n.* [*feke* = *fake*, i.e. fake alcohol] [1910s–30s] methylated spirits; thus *feke-drinker*, a drinker of 'meths'.

fel *n.* [mid-19C] (*US*) abbr. *fel*low, as a term of address.

felch *v.* [? echoic; but note this suggestion by the linguist Laura Wright (in personal correspondence), '"Filch" orig. meant to hook something out of something with a stick according to the OED and in the Bridewell it always involves the hooking of something with a stick covered in sticky lime, so when I heard about modern 'felch' [...] I figured that the two variants have a common source, and the usual P-DE meaning has lost the sense of hooking and kept the sense of stealing, whereas the homosexual sense has kept the sense of hooking and lost the sense of stealing'] [1970s+] (*usu. gay*) to lick out the semen from the anus of someone who has just enjoyed anal intercourse; the semen is then spat into the partner's mouth.

IN COMPOUNDS

❑ **felch queen** *n.* [-QUEEN *sfx* (3)] [1970s+] a male homosexual who indulges in *felching*.

felcher *n.* [FELCH *v.*] [1970s] (*gay*) a man who ejaculates into another man's rectum and then eats all of what he has deposited there.

felicia *n.* [SE *fellatio* + ? ref. to FELIX *n.*[1]] [1970s+] (*US gay*) a fellator.

Felipe *n.* [the common Latino name] [1980s] (*US black*) a familiar name for a Chicano or Latino.

felix *n.*[1] [ety. unknown; ? a nonce-word coined by Colin MacInnes in his novel *Absolute Beginners* (1959)] [1950s] the penis.

felix *n.*[2] [? the cartoon character *Felix* the Cat (1931), known for his toughness, or onomat., the dumpling makes a noise like 'flix' when one bites it] [1950s+] (*W.I.*) a very large, tough dumpling.

fellow *n.* **1** [early 19C+] constr. with *a*, oneself, e.g. *a fellow ought to get drunk once in a while*. **2** [mid-19C] a person, male or female. **3** [late 19C+] (*also* **felly**) one's husband or regular male partner. **4** [1960s+] (*US gay*) a lesbian. **5** [1970s+] (*US gay*) an effeminate homosexual.

fellow commoner *n.* [orig. Cambridge Univ. use, as opposed to scholars, commoners were 'not in general considered as over-full of learning' (Grose, 1785)] [late 18C] an empty bottle.

fellow-feeling *n.* [rhy. sl.] [late 19C–1950s] a ceiling.

felly *n. see* FELLOW *n.* (3).

felon fodder *n.* [2000s] (*US prison*) prison inmates (seen as an indistinguishable mass).

felon swell *n.* [SE *felon* + SWELL *n.*[1] (1)] [early–mid-19C] (*Aus.*) a gentleman convict.

felony shoes *n.* (*also* **felony flyers**) [the term is implicitly racist, suggesting that the (orig. black) teenagers who particularly favour such footwear are automatically up to no good] [1980s+] (*US*) any brand of the high-priced trainers (Nike, Adidas etc) worn by teenagers (cf. LARCENY SHOES *under* LARCENY *n.*).

feloose *n.* (*also* **faloose, falouse, feloos, filoose, fils**) [Arabic for money] [1910s–40s] (*N.Z.*) money.

fem *n.*[1] *see* FAM *n.*[1].

fem *n.*[2] *see* FEMME *n.*

female of the game *n. see* LADY OF THE GAME *under* LADY *n.*

fembo *n.* [SE *female* + BIMBO *n.* (1); ? or proper name of the 1980s macho film hero *Rambo*] [1980s+] (*US campus*) a homosexual man.

feme *n. see* FAM *n.*[1].

fem fatale *n.* [adopted SE *femme fatale*] [1990s+] (*US gay*) an overtly effeminate male homosexual.

femme *n.* (*also* **fem**) [Fr. *femme*, a woman; note West Point jargon *femme*, a young woman] (*orig. US*) **1** [late 19C+] a young woman [note synon. use in Kendall, *Flowers of Epigrammes* (1577): 'Which are three ills that mischief men [...] The fem, the flud, the fire']. **2** [1930s+] (*also* **femmie**) an effeminate homosexual man. **3** [1940s+] a feminine lesbian. **4** [1960s+] the 'female' partner of a couple whether hetero- or homosexual.

IN COMPOUNDS

❑ **fem sem** *n.* [1900s] (*US campus*) a female-only college.

femme *adj.* (*also* **fem**) [FEMME *n.*] **1** [20C+] female. **2** [1930s+] (*gay*) used of an effeminate male homosexual. **3** [1940s+] (*gay*) used of a 'female' lesbian.

femo *n.* [SE *feminist* + -O *sfx* (3)] [2000s] (*Aus.*) a feminist.

fen *n.* [SE *fen*, a marshy bog; the image is of the 'dirtiness' of the prostitute or the receiver] (*UK Und.*) **1** [late 17C–early 19C] a prostitute; thus *fag the fen*, beat the prostitute. **2** [18C–early 19C] a madame, a procuress. **3** [late 18C] a receiver of stolen goods.

fen *v. see* FEND *v.*

fen! *excl.* [*fen*, to forbid; ? ult. SE *fend*, forbid] [mid–late 19C] a call for a truce during a game, a statement that one is ineligible for a given duty or command.

fenagle *v. see* FINAGLE *v.*

fence *n.*[1] [? as a middleman he provides a *fence* between the thief and the buyer of the goods] **1** [17C+] a receiver and seller of stolen property. **2** [mid-19C–1960s] (*US Und.*) the place where stolen goods are received, kept and sold. **3** [2000s] (*Aus.*) a procurer of the sexually complaisant for customers who prefer something 'out of the ordinary'.

IN COMPOUNDS

❑ **fence-ken** *n.* [KEN *n.*[1] (1)] [late 18C–mid-19C] (*UK Und.*) a house where stolen property is received. ❑ **fence-master** *n.* [early 17C–18C] (*UK Und.*) a receiver and seller of stolen goods. ❑ **fence-shop** *n.* [late 18C] a shop where stolen property is on sale.

SE in slang uses

IN COMPOUNDS

❑ **fence con** *n.* [CON *n.*[1] (8)] [20C+] (*US prison*) an escapee, a prisoner who is planning an escape. ❑ **fence-corner** *adj.* [20C+] (*US*) illegitimate. ❑ **fence-jumping** *n.* [farmyard imagery, i.e. an animal jumping the *fence* that separates different breeds] [1990s+] (*N.Z.*) race mixing. ❑ **fence parole** *n.* [1990s+] (*US prison*) the attempt to make an escape by climbing the prison fence or wall; such efforts, inevitably, lead to death.

IN PHRASES

❑ **give the fence a run** *v.* [the image of a bull smashing through or jumping over a fence on the way to a cow] [1970s+] (*N.Z.*) to fulfil one's sexual urges. ❑ **on the fence** (*also* **jump over the fence**) [1940s+] (*gay*) turning to heterosexuality. ❑ **over the fence** **1** [1910s] (*Aus.*) out of trouble. **2** [1910s+] (*Aus./N.Z.*) extreme, beyond the bounds of taste. ❑ **sweat the fence** *v. see under* SWEAT *v.*[2].

fence *n.*[2] [i.e. the collar provides a *fence* around the neck] [1910s] (*US*) a man's detachable collar.

fence *v.* [FENCE *n.*[1] (1)] **1** [17C+] to buy and sell stolen property. **2** [late 17C–early 18C] to spend money. **3** [early 19C] (*UK Und.*) to pawn goods with a receiver.

fencer *n.* [FENCE *n.*[1] (1)] [17C–19C] a receiver and seller of stolen property.

IN COMPOUNDS

❑ **fencer's wharf** *n.* [mid-19C] (*UK Und.*) a receiver's warehouse.

-fencer *sfx* [weak use of FENCER *n.* (1)] [19C] a (street) seller of various commodities, e.g. BILLY FENCER *n.*; CAKEY-PANNUM FENCER *n.*

fencing *n.* [FENCE *v.* (1) + sfx *-ing*] [late 18C+] receiving or dealing in stolen goods.

IN COMPOUNDS

❑ **fencing crib** *n.* [CRIB *n.*[1] (1)] [19C–1900s] the shop, house or room from which a receiver operates. ❑ **fencing cully** *n.* [CULLY *n.*[1] (4)] [mid-17C–18C] a receiver and seller of stolen goods. ❑ **fencing ken** *n.* [KEN *n.*[1] (1)] [late 17C–19C] the shop, house or room from which a receiver operates.

fend *v.* (*also* **fen**) [abbr.] [1920s–30s] (*US black*) to *defend*.

fender-bender *n.* [SAmE *fender* (UK bumper) + *bender*] **1** [1960s+] (*US*) a minor automobile accident. **2** [1970s+] (*drugs*) in fig. use, a barbiturate capsule.

fenderhead *n.* [1970s] a fool.

fend off *v.* [one *fends off* the object from its owner so that one may keep it oneself] [1930s] (*N.Z.*) to take, to steal.

feng *v.* [Anglo-Saxon *feng*, a grasp, a hug] [mid-16C] (*UK Und.*) to steal.

Fenian *n.* (*also* **cold Irish, three cold Irish**) [a pun on 'three cold Irish', itself referring to the hanging of the Fenians Allen, Larkin and O'Brien for the 'Manchester Murder' of PC Brett in 1867 or for three men, also Fenians, hanged for the Phoenix Park murders of Lord Frederick Cavendish and Thomas Henry Burke, Under-Secretary for Ireland, on 6 May 1882] [late 19C] threepenny-worth of whisky and water; thus generic for any quantity of whisky.

fenky-fenky *adj.* [? SE *finicky* + redup.] [1940s+] (*W.I.*) **1** cowardly, effeminate, 'crybabyish'. **2** ordinary.

fenneh *v.* [Twi *fene*, to vomit; Fante *fena*, to be troubled; Lumba *feno*, to faint] [1950s+] (*W.I. Rasta*) to feel physical distress or pain.

feral *n.* [1990s+] (*Aus.*) a New Age hippie or environmentalist.

feral *adj.* [SE *feral*, savage, untamed] [2000s] (*Aus.*) disgusting.

ferculate *v.* [1990s+] (*W.I.*) a mild obscenity.

fergle *v. see* FURGLE *v.*

feria *n.* [SE *fare* + Hisp. sfx *-ia*] [1960s+] (*US*) money.

ferk *v.* [SE *firk/ferk*, to move about briskly; to dance, to frisk about; note D'Urfey, *Pills to Purge Melancholy* (1719): 'Oh, how they did jerk it, / Caper and ferk it, / Under the Green-wood Tree'] [17C; 1920s+] lit. to dance about, but used as euph. for FUCK *v.* (1).

ferme *n.* [Fr. *fermer*, to shut, to close] [early 17C–early 19C] (*UK Und.*) a hole; thus a prison, a cave.

fermedy beggars *n.* (*also* **fermerly beggars**) [? Fr. *fermer*, to close; i.e. their skin is 'closed' or 'shut'] [late 17C–early 18C] (*UK Und.*) beggars in general, other than those who parade their (faked) open sores.

fern *n.*[1] [? ref. to SE *maidenhair fern*] [1950s+] **1** (*US*) the female genitals and pubic hair. **2** (*US campus*) the buttocks. **3** (*US campus*) a homosexual.

fern *n.*[2] [image of flowers and 'love'] [1980s+] (*US campus*) someone who clings to the styles of the 1960s; an environmentalist.

fernleaf *n.* [the SE *silver fern*, adopted as a national emblem, also seen on the uniforms of some representative N.Z. sporting teams] [1910s+] (*N.Z.*) a New Zealander, usu. a soldier.

fernrooter *n.* [*see* prev.] [2000s] (*N.Z.*) a New Zealander.

ferny *adj.* [FERN *n.*[2]] [1980s+] (*US campus*) clinging to the styles of the 1960s.

ferret *n.*[1] [SE *ferret*, a thief; ult. Lat. *fur*, a thief + image of a SE *ferret*, a predator used in the hunting of rabbits] **1** [17C–early 18C] a tradesman who entices the young and naïve to spend money on credit, then promptly duns them for his bill. **2** [early 17C] a low class pimp. **3** [early 18C–mid-19C] a pawnbroker. **4** [late 19C] a young thief who gets into a coal barge and throws coal over the side to his confederates.

ferret *n.*[2] [SE *ferret*; like the animal, it burrows into holes] **1** [17C+] the penis. **2** *see* CHUTNEY FERRET *under* CHUTNEY *n.*

IN PHRASES

❑ **walk one's ferret** *v.* [1940s] (*N.Z.*) to masturbate.

ferret *n.*[3] [SE *ferret (out)*, to search] **1** [late 19C–1920s] (*US*) a detective. **2** [1940s] (*UK Und.*) an informer.

ferret *v.* [FERRET *n.*[1] (1)] [late 17C–18C] to cheat, to defraud.

ferreting *n.*[1] [FERRET *n.*[1] (1) + sfx *-ing*] [16C–17C] (*UK Und.*) a confidence trick that involves the offering of spurious credit and the subsequent profitable dunning of the victim who has taken it.

ferreting *n.*[2] [FERRET *n.*[2]] [19C] sexual intercourse.

ferricadouzer *n.* [Ital. *fare cadere*, to knock down + *dosso*, back, or Lat. *ferri*, iron + intensifier *ca* + *douse*, a heavy blow. Hancock, 'Shelta and Polari' (1984), suggests an origin in Polari] [mid-19C+] **1** a knockout blow. **2** also in fig. use, anything outstanding or overwhelming.

Ferris Bueller *n.*

(IN PHRASES)

❑ **pull a Ferris Bueller** *v.* [movie *Ferris Bueller's Day Off* (1986)] [1980s+] (*US campus*) to cut class, to take time away from studies.

ferry *n.* [many men get to 'ride on her'] **1** [1940s] (*US black*) a homosexual. **2** [1960s+] (*Aus./US*) a prostitute.

ferryboat *n.* [1900s] (*US*) **1** a large, clumsy shoe. **2** a large automobile.

ferry dust *n.* [? var. on FAIRY DUST *under* FAIRY *n.*[1]] [1980s+] (*drugs*) heroin.

ferschlugginer *adj.* (*also* **furschlugginer**) [Yid. *farshlogn*, worried, careworn] [1950s+] (*US*) confounded, darned, wretched.

fescue *n.* [SE *fescue*, 'a small stick, pin, etc. used for pointing out the letters to children learning to read; a pointer' (*OED*)] [17C–mid-18C] the penis.

fess *v.* [abbr. SE *confess*] **1** [19C+] to admit, to confess, esp. in phr. *fess up (to)*. **2** [19C+] (*US campus*) to fail in one's recitation, to admit that one has not prepared the lesson's work. **3** [1980s+] (*US black*) to back down or decline. **4** [1990s+] to annoy or irritate someone [suggesting an image of insincere or excessive confession, i.e. verbal manipulation]. **5** [2000s] to complain, to whinge [suggesting an image of insincere or excessive confession, i.e. verbal manipulation].

fessor *n.* [abbr.] [20C+] (*US black*) **1** a professor, i.e. male teacher. **2** in fig. use, any intelligent man.

-fest *sfx* [abbr. SE *festival*] [20C+] (*orig. US*) used in comb. with a relevant n. to indicate a gathering or get-together.

festive *adj.* [mid-19C–1930s] 'loud, fast, a kind of general utility word' (F&H).

fetch *n.*[1] (*UK Und.*) **1** [mid-16C–early 19C] a trick, a fraud. **2** [early 19C] the act of eliciting secrets from a victim.

fetch *n.*[2] [northern dial. *fetch*, an apparition, a double of a living person] [19C] **1** a success; one who appeals. **2** a likeness; thus *the very fetch of*, the image of.

fetch *n.*[3] [SE *fetch*, to draw forth] [19C] semen.

fetch *n.*[4] [20C+] (*US black*) an illegitimate or abandoned child.

fetch *v.*[1] **1** [late 16C+] to attract, to interest. **2** [late 19C] to excite sexually. **3** [late 19C+] to gain access to, to go to (esp. prison).

(IN PHRASES)

❑ **fetch a Tyburn stretch** *v. see under* TYBURN *n.* ❑ **fetch the brewer** *v.* [mid-19C] to become drunk.

SE in slang uses

(IN PHRASES)

❑ **fetch away** *v.* [mid–late 19C] to divide, to separate, to take away (something) from. ❑ **fetch mettle** *v.* [METTLE *n.*] [17C–early 19C] to masturbate. ❑ **fetch one's pennyworth out of** *v.* [late 17C–early 18C] to ensure that a person works hard for their wages, to get one's money's worth out of. ❑ **fetch over the coals** *v.* [the burning of heretics at the stake] [late 16C–early 18C] to reprimand.

fetch *v.*[2] [13C SE *fetch*, to give a blow] **1** [18C+] to hit; esp. as *fetch someone one*. **2** [late 19C] of a man, to ejaculate, to come to orgasm. **3** [late 19C] to give one's partner an orgasm.

fetched *adj.* [mid-19C] (*US*) a euph. for DAMNED *adj.*

fetch up *v.* [orig. naut.] **1** [mid–late 19C] to recuperate from an illness, to recover one's health. **2** [mid-19C+] (*orig. US naut.*) to arrive at a destination, intentionally or otherwise.

fete down *v.* [SE *fête*, a party] [20C+] (*W.I.*) to go on a (lengthy) spree.

fete up *v.* [SE *fête*, a party] [20C+] (*W.I.*) to take out and entertain in the hope of persuading one's guest to agree with one's plans, esp. in a political or business context.

fettled *adj.* [SE phr. *in fine fettle* + note Cheshire dial. *fettled ale*, ale mulled with ginger and sugar] [19C] tipsy, drunk.

fever *n.* (*also* **fever in the South**) [i.e. FIVER *n.*] **1** [late 19C+] (*US gambling*) the point of five in craps dice. **2** [1970s] (*US prison*) a five-year sentence.

fever cart *n.* [1900s] (*UK Und.*) an ambulance.

feverish *adj.* [mid-19C] (*US*) a euph. for drunk.

fevvers *n.* [Cockney pron. of SE *feathers*, which adorn her hat] [1910s] (*Aus.*) a Cockney woman.

few, a *n.* **1** [mid-19C] someone extreme in manner. **2** [late 19C+] a number, unspecified, of drinks. **3** [1900s–50s] (*US prison*) a short prison sentence. **4** [2000s] a short time, i.e. a few minutes.

(IN PHRASES)

❑ **have a few** *v.* (*also* **have a few in, have one or two in**) [20C+] (*orig. Aus.*) to have a few drinks; thus *have a few too many*, to be drunk. ❑ **put a few back** *v.* (*also* **put a few down**) [20C+] to have a few drinks.

SE in slang uses

(IN COMPOUNDS)

❑ **few tickers** *n.* [TICK *n.*[4] (2)] [1940s] (*US black*) a few minutes.

few, a *adv.* [mid-18C–1910s] a good deal.

(IN PHRASES)

❑ **a few sheets in the wind** *see* THREE SHEETS IN THE WIND *phr.*

few!, a *excl.* [late 18C–1950s] a deliberately down-played rejoinder to a suggestion that an event is worth noticing.

few pence short in the shilling, a *phr.* [var. on NOT ALL THERE *adj.*] [20C+] unintelligent, eccentric.

fews and twos *n.* [1930s–40s] (*US black*) a very small amount of money.

few...short of a... *phr. see under* ...SHORT OF... *adj.*

fey *n. see* OFAY *n.*

f.f. *n. see* FIST-FUCKING *n.*

f.f.f. *phr.* [abbr. *f*rigged, *f*ucked, and *f*ar from home or *f*orlorn, *f*amished, and *f*ar from home] [1910s] (*Aus.*) utterly miserable (on account of the war).

F-40 *n.* [the pharmaceutical identification stamped on the capsule] [1980s+] (*drugs*) a Seconal capsule.

fhawkner *n.* [? SE *hawk*] [mid-19C] (*UK Und.*) a thief who steals poultry from shops.

fiasco *n.* [joc. mispron.] [20C+] a fiancé; occas. fiancée.

fib *n.* [FIB *v.*] [early 19C] a blow, a punch; thus *fibbery*, n., boxing.

fib *v.* [Lancs. dial.; note Egan, *Book of Sports*, (1832): '*Technical*, in the P.R., to *hammer* your opponent repeatedly in close quarters; and to get no return for the compliment you are bestowing on him'] [mid-17C–mid-19C] to beat, to thrash; to box; thus *fibber*, a prizefighter.

fibbing *n.* [FIB *v.*] [19C] prize-fighting, boxing.

(IN COMPOUNDS)

❑ **fibbing gloak** *n.* [GLOAK *n.*] [early 19C] a boxer.

fibre *n.* [SE *wood fibre*] [1940s] (*S.Afr.*) a matchbox.

fice *n.* (*also* **fico, foyse**) [FOIST *n.*[1]; note 19C US dial. *fice*, a small dog] [late 18C–early 19C] a silent breaking of wind, 'more obvious to the nose than to the ears; frequently by old ladies charged on their lapdogs' (Grose, 1796).

ficky-fick *n.* (*also* **ficky boom-boom, ficky-ficky**) [pidgin var. of FUCK *n.* (1) + redup.] [20C+] sexual intercourse.

fico, a *n. see* FIG, A *n.*

fid *n.* [abbr. SE *fiddle*] [late 19C–1900s] (*US*) a violin.

fidas *n. see* FIETAS *n.*

fiddle *n.*[1] [SE *fiddle*, a violin, i.e. resemblance or sound or one 'plays' on it] **1** [16C–early 18C] the penis. **2** [17C+] the vagina. **3** [19C] a watchman's rattle (the precursor of the policeman's whistle). **4** [late 19C] (*UK prison*) a primitive 'machine' used in prison to 'pick' oakum. **5** [20C+] (*Aus.*) a maize grater. **6** [1930s] (*N.Z.*) a dressed hindquarter of mutton. **7** [2000s] (*N.Z.*) a car radio.

IN COMPOUNDS

❑ **fiddle-bow** *n.* [it 'plays' sense 2 above] [19C] the penis. ❑ **fiddle-diddle** *n.* [DIDDLE *n.*[3] (1)] [19C] the penis.

SE in slang uses

IN COMPOUNDS

❑ **fiddlecases** *n.* [resemblance] [1940s] (*US black*) shoes, esp. large ones. ❑ **fiddleface** *n.* [the long face resembles the shape of a violin] [mid–late 19C; 1950s] **1** one who has a wizened, drawn face. **2** one who has a miserable, 'long' face; thus *fiddle-faced*, wizened, miserable; foolish, empty-headed.

fiddle *n.*[2] [the victim must 'face the music'] [late 17C–18C] a writ of arrest.

fiddle *n.*[3] [FIDDLE *v.*[2]] **1** [mid-19C] a swindler, a card-sharp. **2** [late 19C+] (*orig. US*) a swindle, a fraud. **3** [1910s–20s] an unrewarding, annoying job of work.

IN PHRASES

❑ **on the fiddle** (*also* **at the fiddle**) [1910s+] cheating, committing fraud, swindling.

fiddle *n.*[4] [abbr. SE *fiddlestick*] [mid-19C] a whip.

fiddle *n.*[5] [abbr. FIDDLER *n.*[3] (2)] [late 19C] a sixpence.

fiddle *n.*[6] see FIDDLE (AND FLUTE) *n.*

fiddle *v.*[1] **1** [early 17C+] to take liberties with a woman. **2** [20C+] to abuse sexually, usu. a child.

IN EXCLAMATIONS

❑ **go fiddle yourself!** *see* GO FUCK YOURSELF! *under* FUCK *v.*

fiddle *v.*[2] [SE *fiddle*, to swindle; the swindler can 'make people dance to his tune'] **1** [mid-19C–1920s] to make one's living taking small jobs on the street, e.g. unloading a cart. **2** [mid-19C+] to cheat, to swindle [prior use from 17C is SE]. **3** [late 19C] to drug liquor. **4** [1930s] (*UK tramp*) to beg. **5** [1940s+] to cheat on one's expenses. **6** [1960s] to work as a petty thief.

fiddle (and flute) *n.* [rhy. sl.] [1910s+] (*US*) a suit.

fiddle-arse *v.* (*also* **fiddle-arse about/around, fiddle-fart (about/around)**) [SE *fiddle* + *ARSE ABOUT under* ARSE *v.*/*FART ABOUT under* FART *v.*; note *fiddlefoot*, for a horse to make jumpy, skittish movements; thus *fiddlefoot*, to wander aimlessly] [20C+] (*Aus.*) to mess around, to waste time.

fiddle-britches *n.* [20C+] (*US*) anyone who is too clever for their own good.

fiddle-come-faddle *n.* [early 18C] an indecisive person.

fiddled *adj. see* JIGGERED *adj.*[1] (1).

fiddledeedee *n.* (*also* **fiddlededee**) [FIDDLEDEEDEE! *excl.*] [late 19C–1950s] nonsense.

fiddledeedee! *excl.* [SE *fiddle* + a nonsense sfx] [late 18C+] a mild excl. denying the validity of the other speaker's remark.

fiddle-fart (around) *v. see* FIDDLE-ARSE *v.* (1).

fiddle-fuck *n.* [FIDDLE-FUCK (AROUND) *v.*] [1960s–80s] (*US*) an unpleasant situation.

fiddle-fuck (around) *v.* (*also* **play fiddly-fuck**) [SE *fiddle* + FUCK ABOUT *v.* (1)] [20C+] to waste time, to shirk one's duties, to change something.

fiddle-fucked *adj.* [SE *fiddle* + FUCKED *adj.*[2]] [1970s+] (*US*) a var. on DAMNED *adj.*; esp. in phr. *I'll be fiddle-fucked*.

fiddle-fucking *adj.* [1970s] a var. on FUCKING *adj.*

fiddler *n.*[1] [FIDDLE *v.*[2] (2)] **1** [late 18C] a ne'er do well. **2** [mid-19C+] a cheat, a swindler.

fiddler *n.*[2] [early 19C] a coachman.

fiddler *n.*[3] [? the old custom of each couple at a dance paying the fiddler a farthing, and later sixpence] [mid–late 19C] **1** a farthing. **2** a sixpence.

SE in slang uses

IN COMPOUNDS

❑ **fiddler's curse** *n. see under* NOT WORTH A CURSE *phr.* ❑ **fiddler's damn** *n. see under* NOT CARE A TINKER'S (CURSE) *v.* ❑ **fiddler's fare** *n.* [SE *fare*, the wages paid to an itinerant fiddler] [mid-17C–early 19C] meat, drink and money. ❑ **fiddler's fuck** *n.* [1930s+] (*US*) anything considered utterly insignificant, a 'damn'; usu. in phr. *not worth a fiddler's fuck* or NOT GIVE A FIDDLER'S FUCK below. ❑ **fiddler's green** *n.* [19C–1910s] (*orig. naut.*) paradise, a place of unlimited rum, women and tobacco, i.e. 'nine miles this side (or the other side) of hell'. ❑ **fiddler's money** *n.* [the paucity or actual lack of fiddlers' pay] [late 18C–mid-19C] small change. ❑ **fiddler's pay** *n.* [i.e. no actual money] [late 17C–early 19C] wine and thanks. ❑ **fiddler's wages** *n.* [late 16C] no wages at all, but simply a thank-you.

IN PHRASES

❑ **not give a fiddler's fuck** *v.* (*also* **...a flying fiddler's mickey, ...a fiddler's screw in hell, not care a...**) [1930s+] (*orig. US*) to not care at all.

fiddles and flutes *n.* [rhy. sl.] [20C+] (*Aus.*) boots.

fiddlestick *n.* [resemblance] **1** [late 16C–early 17C] a sword. **2** [18C+] the penis [note Jonson, *Bartholomew Fair* (1614): 'My Fiddle-stick does fiddle in and out too much']. **3** [early 19C] (*Scot. Und.*) a spring saw.

SE in slang uses

IN COMPOUNDS

❑ **fiddlestick's end** *n.* [a SE *fiddlestick* ends in a point] [late 18C–1900s] nothing; thus as excl., a dismissive retort.

fiddley(-did) *n.* (*also* **fiddlie**) [rhy. sl. = QUID *n.* (3)] [1920s+] (*Aus.*) £1; often in pl.

fiddling *n.*[1] [FIDDLE *v.*[2] (2)] [mid-19C] gambling.

fiddling *n.*[2] [FIDDLE *v.*[2] (1)] **1** [mid-19C] picking up a variety of odd jobs in the streets, holding horses, carrying parcels etc. **2** [1910s] buying cheap and selling dear. **3** [1920s–30s] (*UK tramp*) selling matches.

fiddling-stick *n.* [var. on FIDDLESTICK *n.* (2)] [19C] the penis.

fiddly-fuck *n.* [var. on *FIDDLER'S FUCK under* FIDDLER *n.*[3]] [1960s+] (*US*) anything considered utterly insignificant.

IN PHRASES

❑ **play fiddly-fuck** *v. see* FIDDLE-FUCK (AROUND) *v.*

fidlum-ben *n.* (*also* **fidlam-ben, fidlam-cove**) [FIDDLE *v.*[2] (2) + abbr. *'em* + *BENE COVE under* BENE *adj.*] [late 18C–mid-19C] (*UK Und.*) a petty thief, who will grab anything, irrespective of its value.

f.i.d.o. *phr.* [1980s+] a term of emotional resignation: *fuck it, drive on.*

fido *n.* [Lat. *fidus*, faithful; as *Fido*, a dog's name] [1930s–40s] (*US prison*) a trusty.

fi-do-nie *n.* [ety. unknown] [1950s] (*drugs*) opium.

fie-fie *adj.* [SE excl. *fie!*, intended to express disgust or elicit shame] [19C] improper, of improper character.

fie-fie *v.* (*also* **put on the fie-fie**) [SE *fie!*] [late 19C] to make a fuss, to upbraid.

fie for shame *n.* [all are things seen as shameful] **1** [mid-19C] breeches. **2** [late 19C] the vagina [note the common use, e.g. throughout *DSUE*, of the euph. Lat. *pudendum* (lit. 'that of which one ought to be ashamed'), as the definition for the many sl. terms for the female genitals]. **3** [late 19C] tights.

field *n.*

SE in slang uses

IN COMPOUNDS

❑ **field artillery** *n. see* ARTILLERY *n.* (2). ❑ **field turnup** *n.* [mid-19C] (*UK Und.*) a back-street robbery, a mugging. ❑ **field whiskey** *n.* [1950s] (*US*) illicitly distilled whisky.

Field Lane duck *n.* [*Field Lane*, which once linked Holborn to Clerkenwell; '*Field Lane* is a low London thoroughfare, leading from the foot of Holborn Hill to the purlieus of Clerkenwell. It was formerly the market for stolen pocket-handkerchiefs' (Hotten, 1864)] [late 18C–19C] a baked sheep's head.

field nigger *n.* [SAmE *field negro/nigger*, a black slave who worked in the fields; slavery distinguished between the rougher, less refined field workers and those who worked as 'house' servants] **1** [20C+] (*W.I.*) a term of abuse for a deferential black, who curries favour with whites [this use is a paradox, or an erroneous sense, since the usu. meanings are senses 2 and 3]. **2** [1960s+] (*US black*) working-class, street blacks, as opposed to black bourgeoisie. **3** [1960s+] (*US black*) blacks from the rural, Southern states rather than the Northern cities.

field of wheat *n.* [rhy. sl.] [late 19C+] a street.

fiemies *n.* [Afk. *fiemies*, whims] [20C+] (*S.Afr.*) whims, fads; thus *full of fiemies*, capricious, pernickety.

fiend *n.* **1** [late 19C–1910s] (*US campus*) a fool [fig. use of sense 2 below]. **2** [late 19C+] (*orig. US drugs*) an addict, esp. of opium; usu. comb. with drug name [contemporary use tends to be ironic]. **3** [late 19C+] an addict, an obsessive, other than of drugs. **4** on bad = good model. (**a**) [1900s] (*US campus*) a clever student. (**b**) [1960s] (*US black*) a general term of praise for any person or thing. **5** [2000s] someone who smokes marijuana alone (since smoking is usu. a communal experience).

IN PHRASES

❑ **hoosier fiend** *n.* [HOOSIER *n.* (5)] [1930s–50s] (*US drugs*) an inexperienced or naïve drug user, one who is in the early days of their addiction to narcotics.

fiend v. [fig. use of FIEND *n.*] **1** [1980s] (*US black*) to steal, esp. in the street. **2** [1990s+] (*US drugs*) to be addicted to narcotics. **3** [1990s+] (*US prison*) to need intensely; to be addicted to. **4** [1990s+] (*US black*) to act aggressively.

IN PHRASES

❑ **fiend (on)** v. [1960s+] (*US black*) **1** to show off, to outdo a rival. **2** to covet, to lust after, to become obsessed with.

fiendish(-back) *adj.* [on bad = good model] [1900s; 1960s+] (*US black*) excellent, wonderful, admirable.

fiendishly *adv.* [1980s] (*US black*) especially, very much so.

fierce *adj.* [late 19C+] (*orig. US*) **1** very bad or unpleasant. **2** great, large, fast. **3** a general adj. of approval: excellent, wonderful, first-rate [on bad = good model].

fierce *adv.* (*also* **fiercely**) [mid-18C; late 19C+] a general intensifier, whether positive or negative.

fieri facias *n.*

IN PHRASES

❑ **served with a writ of fieri facias** [legal jargon *fieri facias*, 'a writ wherein the sheriff is commanded that he cause to be made out of the goods and chattels of the defendant the sum for which judgement was given' (Blackstone, *Laws of England* 1765–9); for sl. use this is punningly mispronounced as 'fiery face'] [late 16C–18C] having a red face.

fiery lot *n.* [var. on HOT STUFF *n.*[2] (1)] [late 19C] a 'fast', 'sporting' man.

fietas *n.* (*also* **fidas, vietas**) [Afk. *fiela*, a backward, slovenly person + Du. *vielt*, a scoundrel ? and/or Zulu *i-vila*, a loafer] [1980s] (*S.Afr.*) Vredeorp/Pageview, i.e. Soweto District Six, an area from which the occupants were removed compulsorily under the Group Areas Act.

fiezle *n.* see FIZZLE *n.*[1].

fife and drum *n.* [rhy. sl. = BUM *n.*[1] (1)] [1930s+] the buttocks, the posterior.

f.i.f.i. *phr.* [1980s] (*US campus*) an expression of frustration, anger; *fuck it, fuck it.*

fifi *n.* [? *Fifi*, the clichéd name of the stereotyped sexy French maid of farce and fantasy; note Hotten (1864–70): 'Fi-Fi, Mr Thackeray's term for Paul de Kock's novels, and similar modern French literature'] **1** [1900s] (*also* **fiff**) an effeminate or 'aesthetic' man. **2** [1940s] (*US gay*) one who enjoys oral sex. **3** [1940s–50s] a French prostitute working in London. **4** [1980s+] (*US campus*) an attractive, sexy young woman, who dresses to match but is, in the end, considered superficial.

IN COMPOUNDS

❑ **fifi bag** *n.* (*also* **fifi**) [sense 1 above] [1960s+] (*US prison*) a substitute 'vagina' for masturbation; one version uses a container stuffed with a towel soaked in warm water. ❑ **fifi water** *n.* [sense 1 above, the presumed effeminacy of those who use it] [1970s+] (*US prison*) aftershave.

fifi *adj.* [for ety. *see* FIFI *n.*] [1900s; 1960s+] (*orig. US prison*) effeminate.

fifteen and two *n.* (*also* **fifteen-two**) [rhy. sl.] [1930s+] (*US*) a Jew.

fifth, the *n.*

IN PHRASES

❑ **plead the fifth** *v.* (*also* **take the fifth**) [the Fifth Amendment (1791) to the US Constitution states that no person 'shall be compelled in any criminal case to be a witness against himself'] [1950s+] (*US*) to avoid committing oneself, to refuse to take an action or make a statement.

Fifth Avenoodles *n. see* AVENOODLES *n.*

fifth gear *n.* [rhy. sl.] [1990s+] ear.

fifty *n.* **1** [1970s+] (*Aus.*) a pint of beer composed of 50% old beer and 50% new. **2** [1980s] (*US drugs*) a packet of a drug worth $50. **3** [1990s+] (*US black*) the police [FIVE-OH *n.*].

IN PHRASES

❑ **get a fifty** *v.* [Gaelic football, a form of penalty] [20C+] (*Irish*) to be rebuffed, rejected or 'stood up' by a woman. ❑ **fifty ways from the jack** *adv. see* FORTY WAYS FROM THE JACK under FORTY *adj.*[1].

fifty and a ten *n.* [the charge is $50 for services plus $10 per hour for a room] [2000s] (*US Und.*) an act of intercourse with a prostitute (cf. FIVE AND TWO *n.*).

fifty cent bag *n.* [CENT *n.* (1) + BAG *n.*[1] (7)] [1960s+] (*US drugs*) $50 worth of marijuana.

fifty cents *n.* [CENT *n.* (1)] [1990s+] (*US prison*) $50 worth of drugs.

fifty-cent word *n.* (*also* **twenty-five cent word**) [1930s+] (*US*) a polysyllabic or supposedly 'difficult' word.

fifty-eleven *n.* (*also* **fifty-'leven**) [late 19C–1950s] (*US black*) a large or infinite quantity.

fifty-fifty *n.* [SE adv. *fifty-fifty*, half and half] [1930s+] (*gay*) a sexual act in which the two partners alternately perform fellatio and sodomy on each other.

fifty-one *n.* [ety. unknown] **1** [1960s] (*US short order*) hot chocolate. **2** [1990s+] (*drugs*) crack cocaine. **3** [1990s+] (*drugs*) a cigarette made from a mix of marijuana and crack cocaine.

5150 *n.* [police code, an insane person is annoying the public] [1990s+] (*US black/prison*) someone in need of mental health treatment; an eccentric, a crazy person.

5150 *adj.* (*also* **fifty-one fifty**) [5150 *n.*] [1990s+] (*US black/prison*) psychotic; eccentric.

52-20 Club *n.* [1960s] (*US*) a notional club that took advantage of the US government's payment to ex-GIs of $20/week for one year (52 weeks) or until they could find a job.

52-26 Club *n.* [? 52 weeks, i.e. 1 year, at ? $26 per week] [1960s] (*US*) unemployment insurance.

fig *n.*[1] [Ital. sl. *fica*, the vagina (lit. a fig)] [late 16C–17C; late 19C] the vagina.

fig *n.*[2] (*also* **figthing**) [phr. *not worth a fig*] [late 18C–19C] a counterfeit coin.

fig *n.*[3]

IN PHRASES

❑ **in full fig** [SE *fig out*, to dress up; but note FEAGUE v. (2)/FIG (A HORSE) v.] [mid-19C+] dressed up.

fig *n.*[4] [SNZE *fig*, tobacco, used as a unit of barter between settlers and Maoris in the mid-19C; note also Clarke, *For the Term of His Natural Life* (1874): 'You may flog, and welcome, master [...] if you'll give me a fig o' tibbacky'; Warung, *Tales of the Early Days* (1894): 'Distribute that tobacco – half a fig to a man'] [1970s+] (*N.Z. prison*) a 1oz (28g) packet of prison-issue tobacco.

fig *n.*[5]

IN EXCLAMATIONS

❑ **by fig!** see FIGGINS *n.*[1].

fig, a *n.* (*also* **a fico**) [Ital. *fico*, a fig] [late 16C+] a dismissive excl.; usu. as *a fig for...*

fig v. [SE *feague*, to overcome by trickery, to beat] [mid-16C–early 19C] to pick pockets.

IN COMPOUNDS

❑ **fig-boy** *n.* [mid-16C–early 17C] (*UK Und.*) a pickpocket or cut-purse.

fig (a horse) *v.* (*also* **fig a nag**) [FEAGUE *v.*] [late 18C–19C] 'to play improper tricks with [a horse] in order to make him lively' (Hotten, 1860).

figaro *n.* [Beaumarchais' story *Le Mariage de Figaro* (1784) and Mozart's opera *Le Nozze di Figaro* (1786)] [mid-19C–1920s] a barber.

figary *n.* [lit. 'a fig garden', i.e. FIG *n.*[1]] [mid-17C] the vagina.

figdean *v.* [? Fr. *figer*, to freeze] [early 19C] to kill.

figger *n.* **1** [mid-16C] (*UK Und.*) a pickpocket. **2** *see* FAGGER *n.*[1].

figger *v. see* FIGURE *v.*

figging law *n.* (*also* **fagging law**) [FIG *v.* + LAW *n.* (1)] [16C–early 19C] (*UK Und.*) the art of picking pockets.

figgins *n.*[1]

IN EXCLAMATIONS

❑ **by my figgins!** (*also* **by my fig!**) [? SE *faith* + dimin. sfx *-kins*] [mid-17C–mid-18C] a general excl. of astonishment or emphasis.

figgins *n.*[2] *see* FIGS *n.*

fight *n.* [abbr. *BUNFIGHT under* BUN *n.*[3]] [late 19C–1950s] (*US*) a party, a brawl.

fight *v.*

SE in slang uses

IN COMPOUNDS

❑ **fight-water** *n.* [the effect] [late 19C–1900s] (*Can.*) a spirit.

IN PHRASES

❑ **fight at the leg** *v. see under* LEG *n.* ❑ **fight booty** *v. see PLAY BOOTY under* BOOTY *n.*[1]. ❑ **fight in armour** *v. see IN ONE'S ARMOUR under* ARMOUR *n.* ❑ **fight nob work** *v.* [? to act like a NOB *n.*[2] (1)] [early 19C] (*UK Und.*) to succeed without working in the respectable world. ❑ **fight off** *v.* (*also* **fight up with**) [20C+] (*W.I.*) to attack with unexpected aggression. ❑ **fight the tiger** *v. see BUCK THE TIGER under* TIGER *n.* ❑ **fight up oneself/with** *v.* [20C+] (*W.I.*) to struggle for survival. ❑ **fight with the nails on your toes** *v.* (*also* **fight with your own toenails**) [1990s+] (*Irish*) to be obsessively, continually aggressive.

fighting Irish *n.* [racial stereotyping] [20C+] (*US*) a boast.

fightist *n.* [SE *fight* + sfx *-ist*] [late 19C] a prize-fighter, a boxer.

fighty *adj.* [late 19C] aggressive.

fig-leaf *n.* [18C–19C] an apron.

fig me! *excl.* [late 17C] a euph. synon. for FUCK ME! *excl.*

f.i.g.m.o. *phr.* [abbr.] [1960s+] fuck *it*, got *my* orders; sometimes bowdlerized as finally *I…* or forget *it…*

fig (of Spain) *n.* [late 16C–19C] a coarse gesture of dismissal whereby one sticks one's thumb up between two forefingers.

IN PHRASES

❑ **give the fig** *v.* [late 16C–early 19C] to stick one's thumb up between two forefingers as a gesture of derision.

fig-picker *n.* [2000s] (*US black*) a cadger.

figs *n.* (*also* **figgins**) [his stock] [late 19C] a grocer.

figthing *n. see* FIG *n.*[2].

fig-trap *n.* [mid-19C] (*UK Und.*) watch-stealers.

fig up *v.* [fig. use of FIG (A HORSE) *v.* (1)] [early 19C] to invigorate, to cheer up, to improve morale.

figure *n.*[1] [SE *figure*, a number] [mid–late 19C] a sum of money, esp. a bill.

SE in slang uses

IN COMPOUNDS

❑ **figure-dancer** *n.* [they make the 'figures dance' + pun on SE *figure-dancer*, one who performs in a figure-dance; i.e. a dance that offers representations of famous historical events] [late 18C–early 19C] a forger who specializes in altering the figures on banknotes, usu. adding a zero to make 10 into 100. ❑ **figure-eight** *n.* [? the twisting of the body] [1930s–50s] (*US drugs*) a fake fit or similar spasm, used by an addict attempting to persuade a doctor to give out drugs. ❑ **figure-fancier** *n.* [19C] a man who prefers plump women. ❑ **figure-maker** *n.* [late 19C] a womanizer. ❑ **figure-waltzing** *n.* [mid-19C] (*UK Und.*) the writhings of one who is being publicly whipped as a judicial punishment.

IN PHRASES

❑ **figure on** *v.* [late 18C] to total up (a bill or account) against. ❑ **miss one's figure** *v.* [late 19C] to miss a chance.

figure *n.*[2] *see* FAGGER *n.*[1].

figure *v.* (*also* **figger**) [SE *figure*, to calculate, to ascertain, to understand] (*orig. US*) **1** [mid-19C+] to consider, to feel, to estimate. **2** [1920s+] to think of a person or object in a given way; usu. *figure him/her for…* **3** [1930s+] (*also* **figure on**) to intend, to plan. **4** [1940s+] (*orig. US*) to work out as expected; esp. as *THAT FIGURES* below. **5** [1990s+] to understand.

IN PHRASES

❑ **that figures** [1940s+] (*orig. Aus.*) that's right, that adds up as it should.

figure out *v.* [mid-19C+] (*orig. US*) **1** to work out, to understand. **2** to assess (a person's character). **3** to make a plan. **4** to seem, to appear.

figuring *n.* [FIGURE *v.* (4)] [1950s] calculation, assumption, assessment.

fi-heath *n.* [backsl.] [mid-19C] a thief.

Fiji uncle *n.* (*also* **uncle from/in Fiji**) [one's refs. to 'when my uncle in Fiji…'] [1900s–20s] (*Aus.*) a mythical figure whose supposed wealth is ready and waiting to bail one out of any problems.

filbert *n.* [SE *filbert*, a hazelnut, which in France trad. ripened on or near St Philibert's day, 22 August (Old Style)] **1** [late 19C–1930s] the human head [play on NUT *n.*[1] (1)]. **2** [1900s–10s] a fashionable dandy [pun on KNUT *n.*; esp. in song 'Gilbert the Filbert/Colonel of the Knuts', by Arthur Wimperis (1874–1953) featured in a 1914 version of *The Passing Show*]. **3** [1910s–50s] (*US*) a crazy person; a clownish person [play on NUT *n.*[2] (1)].

IN PHRASES

❑ **cracked in the filbert** *adj.* [late 19C] eccentric, slightly crazy. ❑ **filberts on** *adj.* [late 19C] keen on, enthusiastic about.

filch *n.* [a cant word of no certain origin; it is poss. that sense 1 here may have been the source of FILCH *v.*; Ribton-Turner, *A History of Vagrants* (1887), suggests Welsh *yspeilio*, to steal, with a 'common' change from p/sp to f plus Lowland Scot. *pilk*, to pilfer] **1** [mid-16C–mid-19C] a short pole with a hook on one end, used to steal small, portable items from windows, stalls etc. **2** [late 16C+] a thief. **3** [late 17C–18C] that which is stolen, the booty of a theft.

filch *v.* **1** [mid-16C–early 18C] to beat, to strike. **2** [mid-16C+] (*orig. UK Und.*) to steal; to rob. **3** [mid-19C] (*US*) to defraud, to cheat.

IN COMPOUNDS

❑ **filching cove** *n.* [COVE *n.* (1)] [17C–early 19C] a thief. ❑ **filching mort** *n.* [MORT *n.* (1)] [17C–early 19C] a female thief. ❑ **filchman** *n.* [mid-16C–17C] a cudgel or staff.

IN PHRASES

❑ **on the filch** [late 19C] working as a thief.

filcher *n.* [FILCH *v.* (2)] [16C–18C; 1990s+] a thief, orig. one who uses a FILCH *n.*

file *n.* [ety. unknown; despite chronology *OED* suggests abbr. FOIL-CLOY *n.*, thence *FILE-CLOY under* FILE *v.*[1]. Weekley, *Etymological Dict. of Modern English* (1921), offers link to Fr. *filou*, a pickpocket; *DSUE* suggests SE *file*, a metal tool used to cut through things, and *file*, a rascal; 18C Fr. argot also has *filer doux*, to flatter, wheedle, 'play the sleeping dog', i.e. lie in wait] (*UK Und.*) **1** [early 17C–early 18C] an act of pickpocketing. **2** [mid-17C–19C] a pickpocket. **3** [mid-18C] a shoplifter. **4** [early–mid-19C] (*also* **old file upon the town**) an experienced fraudster or confidence trickster. **5** [early 19C–1900s] an artful, cunning or shrewd person, a man, a 'fellow'; thus *old file*, an old and/or experienced person. **6** [mid-19C] a pickpocket's assistant.

IN COMPOUNDS

❑ **file-lifter** *n.* [late 17C–18C] a pickpocket.

IN PHRASES

❑ **deep file** *n. see under* DEEP *adj.*

file *v.*[1] [FILE *n.*] **1** [17C–early 19C] to pick a pocket. **2** [mid-17C–early 19C] (*UK Und.*) to cheat, to rob. **3** [early 18C] to break into.

IN COMPOUNDS

□ **file-cloy** *n.* (*also* **file-cly, file coy**) [CLY *n.* (2)] [18C–mid-19C] a pickpocket. □ **file-lay** *n.* (*also* **filing lay**) [LAY *n.*[3] (1)] [18C] (*UK Und.*) pickpocketing.

IN PHRASES

□ **file a cly** *v.* [CLY *n.* (2)] [mid-17C–early 19C] (*UK Und.*) to pick a pocket. □ **file onto** *v.* [1920s–30s] (*Can.*) to grab hold of, to seize.

SE in slang uses

IN PHRASES

□ **file on** *v.* [1960s] (*US Und.*) to arrest; to charge.

file *v.*[2] [1930s+] (*US campus*) to throw away into a wastepaper bin.

file *v.*[3] [? 13C SE *file*, defile or f. SE *vile*] [1960s] (*US black*) to act in a brutal, cruel manner.

file *v.*[4] [abbr. of PROFILE *v.*] [1970s+] (*US campus*) to show off, dress up.

filer *n.* (*also* **cly-filer**) [FILE *v.*[1] (1)] [mid-17C–mid-18C] a pickpocket.

filet *n.* [Fr. *filet de boeuf*, fillet steak + ? joc. ref. to LAY *n.*[2] (1)] [1980s+] (*US campus*) a very attractive young woman.

filiome *n.* [FEELE *n.* + OMEE *n.* (3), lit. 'child-man'] [mid-19C+] (*Ling. Fr./Polari*) a child that is under the age of consent.

filipinyock *n.* [*Filipino* + ? HUNYAK *n.*] [1940s] (*US*) a derog. term for a Filipino.

fill *n.*

IN PHRASES

□ **give someone a fill** *v.* [1900s] (*UK Und.*) to deceive.

fill *v.*

SE in slang uses

IN PHRASES

□ **fill a blanket** *v. see under* BLANKET *n.* □ **fill an eye** *v.* [1910s–30s] (*Aus.*) to punch in the eye. □ **fill a woman's pannier** *v.* [17C] to impregnate a woman. □ **fill in** *see* separate entries. □ **fill one's boots** *v.* [1970s–80s] **1** to take as much of something as one can. **2** as a drinking toast. □ **fill one's collar** *v. see under* COLLAR *n.* □ **fill one's pipe** *v.* [one can lie back and smoke] [early 19C] to attain a comfortable lifestyle, to amass wealth; thus ext. by *...leave others to enjoy it*. □ **fill one's shirt** *v. see under* SHIRT *n.* □ **fill someone up** *v.* [1970s+] (*US black*) to gratify and satisfy completely; with obvious sexual overtones, although sex need not invariably be involved. □ **fill the funnel** *v.* [1960s] (*US*) to attain a target, e.g. a given monetary sum.

fillaloo *n.* (*also* **phililoo**) [SE *hullaballo*] [19C–1920s] a commotion, a row.

filled *adj.* [1990s+] (*US campus*) of a woman, attractive.

filled up *adj.* [one's eyes are filled with tears] [1960s+] (*Ulster*) on the verge of tears.

fillet of cod *n.* [rhy. sl. = SOD *n.*[1] (1)] [1970s] a mild pej.

fillet of veal *n.* [rhy. sl.] **1** [mid-19C] the treadmill [= SE *wheel*]. **2** [mid-19C] a prison, i.e. the site of sense 1 above [= STEEL, THE *n.* (2)]. **3** [1940s] (*US*) a wheel.

fillibrush *v.* [? SE *filibuster*] [mid-19C] to flatter, to praise ironically.

fill-in *n.* [FILL IN (ON) *v.* (1)] [1950s] information.

fill in *v.*[1] [1900s–50s] (*US Und.*) **1** to join a criminal gang. **2** to recruit into a criminal gang.

fill in *v.*[2] [the image is of 'filling' one's victim's face with a fist, to give them a black eye] [1920s+] (*orig. naut.*) to beat up.

fill in *v.*[3] [1950s+] (*Aus.*) to make pregnant; thus *filled in*, pregnant.

filling station *n.* [lit. or punning use of SE *filling station*, a petrol or gas station] (*US*) **1** [1920s–40s] an urban description of a small town [apart from its filling station, such a town holds no use or appeal to a passing city-dweller]. **2** [1930s–40s] a place to eat or drink, esp. a nightclub. **3** [1970s+] (*US black*) a liquor store.

fill in (on) *v.* [i.e. to fill in blank spaces] [1940s+] (*orig. US*) to inform, to explain.

fillmill *n.* [SE *fill* + *mill*, a building characterized by the task performed within it, in this case 'filling'] [1940s] (*orig. US black*) a bar, a saloon.

filly *n.* [SE *filly*, a young woman] [1970s+] (*US gay*) **1** an effeminate male homosexual. **2** a passive lesbian.

film for your brownie *n.* [pun on the Brownie (camera) + BROWNIE *n.*[1] (5a)] [1970s+] toilet paper.

filoose/fils *n. see* FELOOSE *n.*

filter *v.* **1** [late 19C] (*US*) to catch on (to a story or joke). **2** [1980s] to desert.

f.i.l.t.h. *phr.* [abbr. *f*ailed *i*n *L*ondon, *t*ry *H*ong Kong] [1980s+] used of one who is attempting to resuscitate their career, stalled in London, in the Far East.

filth *n.* [SE] **1** [late 16C–early 17C] a prostitute. **2** [1960s] (*Aus.*) an objectionable, rude person. **3** [1960s+] (*UK Und.*) the police, esp. the CID (Criminal Investigation Department).

filth *adj.* [1980s+] (*Aus.*) excellent, first-rate.

filthy *n.* [2000s] (*Irish*) a disapproving glare, a 'dirty look'.

filthy, the *n.* [abbr. SE *filthy lucre*] [19C+] money.

filthy *adj.* [synon. DIRTY *adj.* (9)] **1** [1960s] (*US Und.*) in possession of incriminating items, esp. drugs. **2** [1990s+] (*US campus*) amazing, excellent [on bad = good model].

IN COMPOUNDS

□ **Filthy MacNasty** *n.* [1930s] a nickname for an unpleasant man, esp. a 'peeping tom' or 'dirty old man'. □ **filthy pillows** *n.* [1990s+] the female breasts.

IN PHRASES

□ **filthy on** [1990s+] (*Aus. Und.*) furious with. □ **filthy with** [phr. *filthy rich*, but note FILTHY, THE *n.* (1)] [20C+] full with, overloaded with, usu. money.

fimble-famble *n.* [the image is of fumbling weakly for the excuse] [mid-19C] a lame, prevaricating excuse.

fimpted *adj.* [ety. unknown] [20C+] (*US black*) very ugly.

fi'muth *n.* [1900s] (*US*) a $5 bill.

fin *n.*[1] [SE refers only to fish; Grose (1785) defines it as 'a sea phrase'] **1** [late 18C+] the hand and sometimes the arm. **2** [1980s] (*US black*) a female hip that resembles in its opulent curve the fins of a 1950s model automobile.

fin *n.*[2] (*also* **finn**) [abbr. FINNIF *n.*/FINNIP *n.*] **1** [mid–late 19C] £5, a £5 note. **2** [1920s+] (*US*) (*also* **fin-spot, pfinif**) a $1 or, more commonly, $5 bill. **3** [1930s+] (*Can./US Und.*) a prison sentence of five years. **4** [2000s] (*US*) a throw of five in craps dice.

IN PHRASES

□ **fin up** *n.* [1930s+] (*US Und.*) a sentence of five years to life.

fina *adj.* [abbr. SE *finished*] [2000s] (*S.Afr. gay*) astounded, amazed.

finagle *v.* (*also* **fenagle, phenagle**) **1** [1920s+] (*orig. US*) to use dishonest or devious methods to bring something about; to fiddle; to 'wangle', to scheme, to get (something) by trickery. **2** [1930s] to ask questions. **3** [1930s–60s] to associate with (for hedonistic purposes).

finagler *n.* (*also* **phenogler**) [FINAGLE *v.* (1)] **1** [1920s] (*US*) one who plays for time until a fellow-diner or drinker picks up a bill. **2** [1930s+] a trickster.

final *n.* [1930s] the fourth round of a pub drinking session.

final *v.* [1920s–40s] (*US black*) to move, to go, to travel.

finale *n.* [1940s] (*US black*) death.

finale hopper *n.* [1920s] (*US*) one who arrives at the end of any situation, e.g. the paying of a bill, in time for the last dance.

final trill *n.* [SE *final* + TRILL *n.*[2] (1)] [1940s] (*US black*) death.

finance *n.* [joc. mispron.] [1900s–10s] a (rich) fiancé(e).

financial *adj.* [late 19C+] (*Aus./N.Z.*) in credit, solvent, 'in the black'.

financier *n. see* SPONSOR *n.* (4).

find *v.* [mid-19C–1940s] a self-serving euph. for to steal.

SE in slang uses

IN PHRASES

❑ **find a clue** *v. see* GET A CLUE *under* CLUE *n.* ❑ **find a home** *v.* [1940s–50s] (*US prison*) of a prisoner, to be completely dependent on the prison system for stability. ❑ **find a stump to fit your rump** *see under* STUMP *n.* ❑ **find cold weather** *v.* [late 19C] to be thrown out of a public house. ❑ **find fish on one's fingers** *v.* [i.e. 'something smells'] [late 16C] to make up an excuse. ❑ **find one's sex and size** *v.* [shopping imagery] [20C+] (*W.I.*) to mix with people of one's own age and class; thus *not be sex and size with*, not to fit in with on an age or social level.

IN EXCLAMATIONS

❑ **find where you live!** (*also* **find your hole! ...place! ...yard!**) [20C+] (*W.I.*) an aggressive command; go home! go away! ❑ **find your bound-place!** (*also* **go back to your bound-place!**) [*bound-place*, that part of a sugar estate in which indentured labourers were confined on their arrival; thus the image is of poverty and lowly origins] [20C+] (*W.I.*) go back to where you came from!

finder *n.* [FIND *v.*] **1** [mid-19C] one who gathers the scraps from the floors of a meat-market. **2** [mid-19C–1940s] a thief. **3** [1920s] (*US Und.*) that member of a safe-blowing team who actually blows the safe.

find the lady *n.* [late 19C+] (*Und./gambling*) the 'three-card trick', usu. played on the street, the 'lady' being a solitary queen alongside two nondescript cards.

find the lady *v.* [FIND THE LADY *n.*] [late 19C–1930s] **1** (*Und./gambling*) to play the 'three-card trick'. **2** in fig. use, to catch a culprit.

fine *n.* [early–mid-19C] (*UK Und.*) one who has been imprisoned for any offence; thus a sentence.

fine *adj.* **1** [early 17C] smart, clever. **2** [early–mid-19C] (*orig. US*) drunk. **3** [1930s+] (*orig. US black*) (*also* **foine**) attractive, good-looking. **4** [1940s+] (*US black*) first-rate, satisfactory.

IN COMPOUNDS

❑ **fine-ass** *adj.* [-ASS *sfx*] [1960s+] (*US black*) first-rate, excellent. ❑ **fine banana** *n. see under* BANANA *n.* ❑ **fine brown frame** *n.* [FRAME *n.*[1] (2)] [1930s–60s] (*US black*) (the figure of) an attractive black woman. ❑ **fine dinner** *n.* (*also* **fine fryer**) [she is 'good enough to eat'] [1930s–40s] (*US black*) a good-looking black woman. ❑ **fine-fine** *adv.* [redup.] [20C+] (*W.I., Guyn.*) in infinite and thus irritating detail. ❑ **fine-haired** *adj.* [late 19C–1910s] (*US*) **1** arrogant, conceited. **2** over-fastidious, pernickety. ❑ **fine people** *n. see* GOOD PEOPLE *under* PEOPLE *n.* ❑ **fine Scot** *n. see* SCOT *n.* (1). ❑ **fine stuff** *n.* [STUFF *n.* (5b)] [1980s+] (*drugs*) marijuana. ❑ **fine thing** *n.* [1940s+] (*Irish/US black*) an attractive woman. ❑ **fine weather** *n.* [1940s] (*US black/Southern campus*) an attractive woman. ❑ **fine wirer** *n. see under* WIRE *n.*[2]. ❑ **fine worker** *n. see under* WIRE *n.*[2] (1).

IN PHRASES

❑ **fine as frog hair** *adj.* [pun on SE *fine*, thin/*fine*, well] **1** [20C+] (*US*) feeling very well or very cheerful. **2** [1990s+] (*US*) of a person, very attractive; of a place, first-class. ❑ **fine as wine** *adj.* [1940s+] (*US black*) **1** of an object or idea, satisfactory, pleasing; of a person, pleasant, amusing, decent. **2** referring to any particularly attractive man or woman.

fine *v.* [early 19C] (*UK Und.*) to sentence.

fine *adv.* **1** [late 19C+] very well. **2** [1930s+] (*orig. US black*) attractively.

fine and dandy *n.* [rhy. sl.] [1930s+] brandy.

finger *n.* **1** in senses of the shape. (**a**) [17C] the penis. (**b**) [19C+] (*orig. US*) a measure of alcohol; thus *three fingers of rye* etc; abbr. to *three* [the width of a finger, measured against the side of the glass]. **2** an individual, esp. in authority. (**a**) [late 19C] (*Aus.*) the manager or boss in a shearing shed. (**b**) [1910s] (*Aus.*) an amusing person. (**c**) [1910s+] a person. (**d**) [1920s] (*N.Z.*) one's father; often ext. as *old finger*. (**e**) [1930s+] an unpopular person. **3** in the context of police work [SE phr. *point the finger at*]. (**a**) [late 19C–1940s] a policeman [note P. & T. Casey, *The Gay-Cat* (1921): 'Fingers – policemen. From the policeman's method of fingering and frisking the arrested hobo']. (**b**) [1910s+] a police informer. (**c**) [1930s+] (*US police*) an identified suspect. (**d**) [1940s–50s] an identification. **4** [late 19C+] (*orig. US*) usu. constr. with *the*, an obscene gesture of contempt created by extending the middle finger vertically while holding the others curled tight, esp. in phr. GIVE SOMEONE THE FINGER below. **5** in drug uses. (**a**) [1930s–60s] (*US drugs*) a quantity of drugs smuggled into prison in a rubber finger. (**b**) [1960s] (*US drugs*) a finger-shaped piece of hashish. (**c**) [1970s+] (*S.Afr. drugs*) a measure of marijuana sold 'retail'. (**d**) [2000s] (*US drugs*) a marijuana cigarette. **6** [1970s] (*UK Und.*) a thief. **7** [1970s] (*Aus.*) the manual stimulation of the vagina and clitoris [FINGER *v.* (1)]. **8** *see* FINGER AND THUMB *n.* (1). **9** *see* FINGER MAN *n.* (1).

pertaining to police work

IN COMPOUNDS

❑ **finger egg** *n.* [EGG *n.*[2] (1)] [1940s] (*US Und.*) an informer. ❑ **finger guy** *n. see* FINGER MAN *n.* (1). ❑ **finger man** *n. see* separate entry. ❑ **finger map** *n.* [MAP *n.* (1)] [1940s] (*US Und.*) a fingerprint. ❑ **finger merchant** *n. see* FINGER MAN *n.* (1). ❑ **finger mob** *n.* [MOB *n.*[2] (3)] [1930s–40s] (*US Und.*) a criminal gang who have paid off the police; they may also inform on rival gangs.

IN PHRASES

❑ **put a finger on** *v.* [1930s+] **1** (*US*) to betray, esp. to the police. **2** (*also* **have the finger on**) to work out, to identify. **3** to identify someone; esp. as someone about to die. ❑ **put the finger on** *v.* [1920s+] (*orig. US*) **1** to betray, to inform against. **2** to identify a target or possible victim. **3** to murder.

pertaining to genital stimulation

IN COMPOUNDS

❑ **finger artist** *n.* [-ARTIST *sfx*] [1940s–70s] (*US black*) a lesbian. ❑ **finger-bang** *n.* [BANG *v.*[1] (1)] [1970s+] to stimulate the vagina with one's fingers. ❑ **finger-banging** *n.* [prev.] [1970s+] the stimulation of a woman's genitals with the fingers. ❑ **finger-blasting** *n.* [1990s+] masturbation. ❑ **finger fuck(ing)** *see* separate entries. ❑ **finger job** *n.* [JOB *n.*[2] (2)] [1960s] (*US*) a young woman who allows her vagina to be penetrated by fingers only. ❑ **finger pie** *n.* [1950s+] the manual stimulation of the female genitals. ❑ **finger puppet audition** *n. see* AUDITION THE FINGER PUPPETS *v.* ❑ **finger-stink** *see* separate entries.

other uses

IN PHRASES

❑ **give someone the finger** *v.* (*also* **do the finger, finger, flip the finger, get the..., make a..., shoot the..., whip the...**) [late 19C+] (*orig. US*) to make a manual gesture (the raised middle finger in the US, the V-sign in the UK) to imply derision and disdain; also in fig. use.

SE in slang uses

IN COMPOUNDS

❑ **finger-bowl faggot** *n. see* CUFF-LINK QUEEN *n.* ❑ **finger-popping** *adj. see* separate entry. ❑ **finger-post** *n.* [he points the way (that one should live one's life) but does not follow his own directions; 'like the finger post he points out a way he has never been, and probably will never go, i.e. the way to heaven' (Grose, 1785)] [late 18C] a parson. ❑ **finger-smith** *n.* [SE *finger* + sfx *-smith*, an adept, an expert] **1** [19C] a midwife. **2** [19C+] a pickpocket; a thief. ❑ **finger wave** *n.* [1980s] (*UK Und./police*) an anal examination for drugs.

IN PHRASES

❑ **fingers are made of lime-twigs** [lime-twigs are sticky] [late 16C–mid-18C] a phr. used to describe a thief. ❑ **get one's finger out** *v.* (*also* **get one's thumb out of one's ass, have one's finger out**) [ASS *n.* (2) is implied] [1940s+] to stop dawdling or lazing about and begin some constructive activity. ❑ **get one's fingers nipped** *v.* (*also* **get one's fingers burned**) [late 19C+] to get into trouble. ❑ **have one's finger up one's ass** *v.* [ASS *n.* (2)] [1940s+] to idle, to loiter, to stand around doing nothing. ❑ **letting the finger ride the thumb too often** [? FINGER AND THUMB *n.* (1) or ? SUPERNACULUM *n.* (1)] [19C] getting drunk. ❑ **pull one's finger out** *v.* (*also* **get one's finger out, take one's..., remove one's digit, pull finger, pull it out**) [it is withdrawn, presumably, from the anus] [1910s+] (*orig. Aus.*) to get on with something, to stop malingering and commit oneself to positive action; esp. as command *pull your finger out*. ❑ **sit there with one's finger up one's ass** *v.* (*also* **stand around with one's finger up one's ass**) *see under* ASS *n.*

finger *v.* **1** in senses of manipulating the fingers. (**a**) [late 16C+] to indulge in sexual foreplay; usu. stimulation of the female genitals. (**b**) [late 18C+] to steal; to rob. (**c**) [late 19C+] (*US Und.*) to arrest. **2** in senses of pointing the fingers. (**a**) [1920s+] to identify a target or possible victim, to incriminate. (**b**) [1930s+] (*orig. US*) to inform on, to tip off. (**c**) [1940s] to put a curse on. (**d**) [1950s+] to point out. **3** *see* GIVE SOMEONE THE FINGER *under* FINGER *n.*

IN PHRASES

❑ **finger the dog** *v. see* FUCK THE DOG (AND SELL THE PUPS) *under* DOG *n.*[2].

finger and thumb *n.* [rhy. sl.] **1** [mid-19C–1960s] (*also* **finger**) rum. **2** [20C+] a road [= DRUM *n.*[2]]. **3** [1930s+] a friend [= CHUM *n.* (1)]. **4** [2000s] one's mother; also as *'keep mum'*, keep quiet [SE *mum*]. **5** [2000s] a drum.

fingerer *n.* [SE *finger* or Lat. *fingere*, to feign, to cheat] [16C] (*UK Und.*) **1** a pilferer, one who uses his fingers to remove small objects. **2** the accomplice of a team of card-sharps, the fingerer appears as an old, poor man and dresses accordingly; he then allows himself to be lured into some form of gaming by a group of young confederates, and, through his apparent inability to win, persuades their victim to bet and, inevitably, lose heavily.

finger fuck *n.* [FINGER FUCK *v.* (1)] [1960s+] the manual stimulation of the female genitals or of the anus (usu. male).

finger fuck *v.* [SE *finger* + FUCK *v.* (1)] **1** [late 17C+] to stimulate the vagina with one's fingers; occas. of the anus. **2** [1960s+] of a woman, to masturbate. **3** [2000s] (*S.Afr. prison*) to make an anal examination.

finger fucking *n.* [FINGER FUCK *v.* (1)] [mid-19C+] the use of one or more fingers to stimulate the clitoris or penetrate the vagina.

finger man *n.* [criminal var. on FINGER *n.* (3b)] **1** [1910s+] (*orig. US*) (*also* **finger, finger guy, finger merchant**) a traitor, an informer; in criminal terms one who helps with a robbery 'from the inside'. **2** [1930s] a safebreaker. **3** [1950s] an assassin.

finger-popping *adj.* [the 'popping' or snapping of one's fingers in time to the beat] **1** [1950s–60s] (*US*) enjoying music intensely. **2** [1960s+] dedicated.

IN COMPOUNDS

❑ **finger-popping daddy** *n.* [1950s] one who affects to enjoy music but lacks any real knowledge/understanding.

finger-stink *n.* [FINGER-STINK *v.*] [late 19C] the manipulation of the vagina with a (male) finger.

finger-stink *v.* [late 19C] usu. of a man, to manipulate the vagina with the finger.

fingy *n.* [on pattern of WINGY *n.*] [1910s+] (*orig. US Und.*) a person lacking one or more fingers.

finif/finiph *n. see* FINNIF *n.*

Finish, the *n.* [a place where one *finishes* one's night out] **1** [18C–19C] Carpenter's late-night coffee shop, sited in Covent Garden opposite Russell Street and ostensibly catering to the market porters, which closed only when the last customer had gone home into the dawn [Bee notes that the owner, Carpenter, 'was a lecher, his handy bar-maid Mrs. Gibson, a travelled dame']. **2** [19C] any late-night or early-morning café.

finish *n.* [? it *finishes* one off] [1930s] (*tramp*) methylated spirits; thus *finish-drinker*.

finisher *n.* **1** [18C–19C] (*also* **finisher of the law**) the hangman. **2** [early 18C+] something that puts an end to, discomfits or 'does for' someone; in boxing, a knockout blow. **3** [late 18C–mid-19C] something that settles a dispute.

finishing academy *n.* (*also* **finishing school**) [? pun on SE *finish*, to end a girl's education/to reach orgasm + ACADEMY *n.* (1)] [18C] a brothel.

finishing school *n.* [1930s–40s] (*US Und.*) a women's prison.

finito *adj.* [FINITO! *excl.*] [1970s+] over, finished, completed.

finito! *excl.* [Ital. *finito*, finished] [1950s+] an excl. used to signify the end, a completion.

fink *n.* [ety. unknown; although the *American Mercury* (Jan. 1926) claimed that 'dating from the famous Homestead strike of 1892 is the odious *fink*. [It] according to one version was originally Pink, a contraction of Pinkerton, and referred to the army of strike-breakers recruited by the detective agency', that popular ety. is considered to be most likely spurious, since no citations of fink = strikebreaker have been found prior to 1914; for an alternative theory note *HDAS*: 'G *Fink* "student not belonging to the students association [...] hence, not one of the guys"; [...] or G. *Schmierfink* "a low dirty hack"'] [20C+] **1** an unpleasant or contemptible person, one who cannot be trusted. **2** a strike-breaker, a company policeman. **3** a contemptible object or thing. **4** an informer. **5** (*US Und.*) a confidence trickster's victim. **6** (*US*) (*also* **fink-out**) an act of backing down.

IN PHRASES

❑ **dead fink** *n. see under* DEAD *adj.*

fink *v.* (*also* **fink on, fink out**) [FINK *n.*] (*US*) **1** [1920s+] to inform, to inform on. **2** [1950s+] to back down, to let down. **3** [1960s] to brand as an informer.

finky *adj.* (*also* **fink**) [FINK *n.*] [1940s+] (*US Und.*) given to acting as an informer, untrustworthy.

finn *n. see* FIN *n.*[2].

finna *v.* (*also* **funna**) [elision of SE *fixing to*] [1990s+] (*US black*) to get oneself ready, to prepare.

finnif *n.* (*also* **finif, finiph, finnuff, finuf**) [Yid. *fünf*, five] **1** [mid–late 19C] (*UK Und.*) £5; a £5 note; thus *half a finnuff*, £2.10s. **2** [mid-19C+] (*US*) $5. **3** [1900s–40s] (*US Und.*) a five-year jail sentence.

finnip *n.* (*also* **finnep, finnio, finnup**) [Yid. *fünf*, five] [mid-19C+] a £5 note; thus *cross-finnep*, a forged note; note DOUBLE FIN *n.*

finny *n.*[1] (*also* **phinney**) [? abbr.] [18C] (*UK Und.*) a funeral.

finny *n.*[2] [FIN *n.*[2] (1)] [mid–late 19C] a £5 note.

fin-spot *n. see* FIN *n.*[2] (2).

finuf *n. see* FINNIF *n.*

fip *n.* [elision of SE *fivepence*] **1** [19C] any very small amount of money. **2** [early 19C] (*US*) a fivepenny bit, the nickname for the Spanish *half-real*, worth about 4½ cents or 6 cents in some states. **3** *see* FIPPENCE *n.*

fi'penny *n.* [? its original price] [early 19C–1910s] (*Aus.*) a clasp-knife.

fipp *n.* [ety. unknown] [1900s] (*US*) a general derog. term.

fippence *n.* (*also* **fip, fipance**) [the earliest example of *fip* is found in US in 1822 and represents a coin worth 4.5 cents; poss. considered the contemporary equivalent of 3d] [mid–late 19C] a threepenny bit.

fip-pound *n.* [elision of SE] [mid–late 19C] five-pound (of money).

fir *n.* [? resemblance to fir leaves] [1980s+] (*drugs*) marijuana.

fire *n.* **1** [16C–19C] venereal disease [the pain it causes]. **2** [late 17C; 19C] the vagina. **3** [mid-19C+] (*US Und.*) danger, esp. from the police; thus *on fire*, very dangerous. **4** pertaining to smoking. (**a**) [1940s] (*US black*) a cigarette. (**b**) [1940s] (*US black*) a marijuana cigarette. (**c**) [1940s+] (*US*) matches or a cigarette lighter. (**d**) [1980s+] a mixture of crack cocaine and methamphetamine. (**e**) [1980s+] bad or weak crack cocaine [it burns the throat or play on BURN *v.* (1)]. (**f**) [1990s+] (*US black/drugs*) potent marijuana. **5** [1990s+] (*US Und.*) a firearm.

IN COMPOUNDS

❑ **firelock** *n.* (*also* **fireplace, firework, tinder-box**) [late 17C–19C] the vagina. ❑ **fireship** *n. see* separate entry.

IN PHRASES

❑ **go up in that fire** *v.* [2000s] (*US prison*) to have AIDS. ❑ **pass through the fire** *v.* [19C] to catch a venereal disease, i.e. to be BURNED *adj.*[1] (1). ❑ **set on fire** *v.* [18C] to give someone a venereal disease.

IN EXCLAMATIONS

□ **fire on the line!** (*also* **fire on the walk!**) [2000s] (*US prison*) a warning that there is an officer in the vicinity.

SE in slang uses

IN COMPOUNDS

□ **fire-alarm** *n.* [1920s] (*US*) a divorceé. □ **fire-burn(er)** *see* separate entries. □ **fire-catcher** *n.* [such clothes are worth using only to light a fire] [1950s] (*W.I.*) old, ragged, workclothes. □ **fire-eater/-eating** *see* separate entries. □ **fire-escape** *n.* **1** [mid–late 19C] a clergyman [the *fire* is that of hell; 20C+ use is naut. jargon]. **2** [1900s] (*US*) in pl., a style of side whiskers [visual resemblance]. □ **fire fluid** *n.* [late 19C] (*Aus.*) strong liquor; spirits. □ **fire-plug** *n. see* separate entries. □ **fire power** *n.* [1980s] (*US black*) physical strength and ability. □ **fire prigger** *n.* [PRIGGER *n.*[1] (1)] [late 18C–early 19C] one who robs those who are otherwise preoccupied with watching their, or someone else's, home burn down. □ **fireproof** *adj.* [mid-19C+] (*orig. US*) invulnerable, guaranteed against failure. □ **fire queen** *n.* [-QUEEN *sfx* (3); they wish to 'set the world on fire'] [1980s+] (*US gay*) a militant gay activist. □ **fire rage** *n.* [20C+] (*W.I.*) **1** intense anger, uncontrolled fury; thus *pick up someone's fire-rage*, to take someone's side in a quarrel as energetically as if it were one's own. **2** of a man, one who loses his temper easily, who 'flies off the handle'. □ **fire-tail** *n.* [20C+] (*W.I., Guyn.*) of a woman, one who loses her temper easily. □ **fireworks** *n. see* separate entry.

IN PHRASES

□ **give someone the fire** *v. see* FIRE *v.*[2] (3).

fire *v.*[1] [FIRE *n.* (1)] [early 16C–mid-18C] to give someone a venereal disease.

fire *v.*[2] [pun on SE *fire*, discharge (a weapon)] **1** [18C+] to ejaculate semen. **2** [late 19C–1920s] (*Aus./US*) to eject, in a non-institutional context. **3** [late 19C+] (*orig. US*) (*also* **fire out, give someone the fire**) to dismiss from a job, to throw out or expel. **4** [1910s+] (*drugs*) to inject a drug. **5** [1940s+] (*US*) to light a cigarette or marijuana cigarette. **6** [1950s+] (*US black*) to strike a blow. **7** [1980s] (*Aus.*) to excel. **8** [1990s+] (*UK black*) to prosper, to do well. **9** [1990s+] (*US*) to have sexual intercourse.

IN PHRASES

□ **fire a shot** *v.* [SHOT *n.*[1] (2)] [late 19C+] of a man, to ejaculate. □ **fire blanks** *v. see under* BLANK *n.* □ **fire in** *v.* **1** [1910s] to send in. **2** [2000s] to fight, to throw a punch. □ **fire into** *v.* [20C+] to approach sexually, to pick up, to seduce. □ **fire on** *v.* [1960s+] (*US black/campus*) **1** to disparage, to ridicule. **2** to hit, to assault, usu. with a weapon. □ **fire out** *v. see* sense 3 above.

SE in slang uses

IN PHRASES

□ **fire a gun** *v.* [the firing of a warning gun + the suddenness of the explosion] [late 18C–early 19C] to push a topic unsubtly into the conversation. □ **fire a warmer into the bank** *v.* [? orig. milit, the imagery is of the shooting range] [2000s] (*N.Z.*) to take the first beer of a session. □ **fire up** *v. see* separate entry. □ **firing to** *adj.* [1960s] (*US black*) eager (to), keen (to).

IN EXCLAMATIONS

□ **fire your tail!** [TAIL *n.* (2)] [20C+] (*W.I.*) get out! go away!

fire *v.*[3] [SE *fire*, to stimulate, to inflame with passion] [20C+] (*W.I.*) used in several phr. to denote aggressive or decisive action; thus *fire a blow/box/chop/cuff/hand/kick/lash*, to hit hard; *fire yourself/your skin*, hurry up.

fire *v.*[4] [20C+] (*orig. W.I.*) **1** to obtain a drink, esp. of a barman, e.g. *fire me a rum*. **2** to drink strong liquor; thus *fire a booze/drink/few/rum/the grog*, to take a drink.

IN PHRASES

□ **fire a slug** *v. see under* SLUG *n.*[1]. □ **fire the acid** *v. see under* ACID *n.*[1].

fi real *adv.* [pron. of FOR REAL *adv.*] [1970s+] (*W.I./UK black teen*) precisely or genuinely.

fire-alarms *n.* [rhy. sl.] [1910s] the arms.

fire-burn *n.* [such a person might, when enjoying themselves, start a fire] [20C+] (*W.I.*) a rowdy, riotous person.

fire-burn *v.* [2000s] (*UK black*) to attack verbally.

IN EXCLAMATIONS

□ **fire burn me hand!** (*also* **fire bur' me hand!**) [20C+] (*W.I.*) an excl. indicating that a major fight is in the offing.

fire-burner *n.* [1960s] (*US Und.*) a very enthusiastic, passionate lawyer.

fired up *adj.* **1** [mid-19C] drunk. **2** [1950s+] (*US*) angry. **3** [1960s+] (*also* **fired**) energized; thus *unfired*, unenthusiastic.

fire-eater *n.* **1** [late 18C+] a braggart, an aggressive person always spoiling for a fight. **2** [mid-19C+] a noticeably courageous person, with the supposed daring of the performer. **3** [1920s+] (*US*) a firefighter.

fire-eating *adj.* [FIRE-EATER *n.* (1)] [mid-19C; 1930s+] of a person, being aggressive and spoiling for a fight.

fireman's hose *n. see* GARDEN HOSE *n.*

fireplug *n.*[1] [FIRE *n.* (1) + pun] [19C] a man who is suffering from a venereal disease.

fireplug *n.*[2] [supposed resemblance] **1** [20C+] (*US*) a short, squat person. **2** [1930s–40s] (*US drugs*) a large piece of opium.

fireship *n.* [FIRE *n.* (1) + pun] [mid-17C–late 18C] a diseased prostitute.

fire up *v.* (*US*) **1** to commence, to set in motion. (**a**) [mid-19C+] to begin, to get ready. (**b**) [1950s+] to start up a mechanical device, e.g. a car. **2** in emotional senses. (**a**) [late 19C] to become emotional, angry. (**b**) [20C+] to anger, to arouse emotionally. (**c**) [1960s+] to excite in general. (**d**) [1970s] (*US campus*) to drink with the intention of boosting one's spirits. (**e**) [1970s+] (*orig. US black/campus*) to excite sexually; to have sexual intercourse. (**f**) [1980s] (*US campus*) to get excited, to dedicate oneself; to be happy. **3** to apply a flame. (**a**) [late 19C+] to light a pipe, cigarette or cigar. (**b**) [1940s+] (*drugs*) by ext., to pump the blood and heroin mixture out of the hypodermic into the vein or muscle, to inject a narcotic. (**c**) [1960s+] to light a marijuana cigarette. (**d**) [1990s+] to heat up crack cocaine. **4** [1970s+] to hit; to shoot or kill.

fireworks *n.* **1** [17C; late 19C+] an emotional outburst, a state of intense excitement. **2** [mid-19C] (*US*) guns. **3** [late 19C] (*US*) matches. **4** [1920s+] (*US Und.*) gunplay, shooting; in the context of war, a bombing raid. **5** [1970s] a police vehicle with flashing lights.

firk *v.* [SE *firk*, to move about briskly; to whip, to beat + euph. FUCK *v.* (1)] [late 16C–early 18C] to have sexual intercourse; thus *firking school*, a brothel or any place of unrestrained sexual frolics.

firking *adj.* [FIRK *v.*] [1970s+] a euph. for FUCKING *adj.*

firkin of foul stuff *n.* [late 17C–early 18C] a very plain, fat, coarse woman.

firkytoodle *v.* [FIRK *v.* + SE *toodle/tootle*, to play upon] [late 19C] to indulge in foreplay.

firm *n.* **1** [early 19C; 20C+] a criminal gang, large or small. **2** [1910s+] any form of gang, e.g. of football hooligans. **3** [1970s] an influential group.

IN PHRASES

□ **get on the firm** *v.* [1980s] to charm, to please, to seduce. □ **odd-mark firm** *n.* [1990s+] (*UK Und.*) a group or gang that includes various different types of minor criminals, and even a few non-criminal types.

firme *adj.* [Sp.] [1960s+] (*US*) a general term of high approval; also used as a magazine name in 1970s–80s.

firming *n.* [FIRM *n.* (1)] [1980s] (*UK Und.*) an assault or beating by a gang.

first, the *n.* [1960s] (*orig. US*) nothing, not a single one, usu. in negative.

first *adj.*

SE in slang uses

IN COMPOUNDS

□ **first and fifteenth** *n.* [2000s] (*US black*) those days in a month on which welfare cheques are distributed. ❑ **first base** *see* separate entries. ❑ **first belly-pain** *n. see under* BELLY *n.* ❑ **first chop** *see* separate entries. ❑ **first feel** *n.* [1950s+] (*W.I.*) the first chance, the earliest opportunity. ❑ **first go-off, the** *n. see* GO-OFF *n.* (1). ❑ **first line** *n. see under* LINE *n.*[1]. ❑ **first national bank** *n.* [the resentment of the farming community towards the banks, which regularly repossessed their land when times became hard] [20C+] (*US*) an outside lavatory. ❑ **first-nighter** *n.* [1970s+] (*US black*) a one-time sexual encounter, unlikely to be repeated. ❑ **first-timer** *n.* [late 19C+] (*Aus. Und.*) one who is serving their first sentence in prison; thus *second-timer.*

IN PHRASES

❑ **first cab off the rank** *n.* (*also* **next cab off the rank**) (*Aus.*) **1** [1950s+] a prime suspect. **2** [1960s+] the speediest one to react, the first one off the mark. **3** [1980s] one's primary interest. **4** [2000s] the first to do something. ❑ **first crack off the bat** *adv. see under* BAT *n.*[2]. ❑ **first crack out of the box** *adv.* (*also* **first bang out of the box, first cat..., ...dash..., ... flop..., ...pop..., ...rattle..., ...shot..., ...throw..., ...shot out of the locker**) [20C+] at once, immediately, at the first attempt. ❑ **first off** *adv.* [late 19C+] (*orig. US*) at the outset, to start with. ❑ **first-rate** *adv.* [adj. use is SE] [mid-19C+] excellently, very well. ❑ **first thing smoking** *n.* [1940s] (*US black*) a railroad train. ❑ **first-up** *adv.* [20C+] (*Aus.*) for the first time, at the first try.

first base *n.* [baseball jargon] [1920s+] (*orig. US*) **1** a man's initial advances on a young woman, usu. implying just kissing, but sometimes also caressing some part of the body or even the removal of some clothing; such a 'base' is always above the waist; thus *SECOND BASE under* SECOND *adj.*; *THIRD BASE under* THIRD *adj.*; HOME RUN *n.* **2** the start of something, e.g. a relationship, usu. applied in terms of failure, e.g. *he couldn't even get to first base.*

first base *v.* [FIRST BASE *n.* (2)] [1930s+] (*US*) to take one's first steps towards an objective.

first chop *n.* [1910s] the first opportunity.

first chop *adj.* [from Hind. *chhaap* meaning a print, and thus a seal, notably that which is placed on first-rate merchandise; Schele de Vere, *Americanisms* (1872), however, cites it as 'Canton-jargon of the Anglo-Chinese'] [early 19C+] excellent, first-rate; thus *second chop*, inferior.

first of May *n.*[1] [rhy. sl. = SE *say*] [mid–late 19C; 1970s] the tongue; ext. to firm speech as in 'have one's say'.

first of May *n.*[2] [1930s–50s] (*US tramp*) a novice; also in ext. use as anyone who does not stay the course.

firsts *n.* **1** [20C+] (*US black*) any blacks who are the first to take on a specific job in a formerly all-white world. **2** [1950s+] the first chance, the first opportunity; often as excl. *firsts!* I want to do something first!

fisgig *n.* (*also* **fizgig**) [SE *fizz*, animal spirits + *gig*, a frivolous person] [early–mid-19C] amusement gained at the expense of others.

fish *n.*[1] [fig. uses of SE *fish*] **1** pertaining to sex [sense 1a is derog. ref. to the supposed odour; senses 1b–i are ext. uses]. (**a**) [mid-16C+] the vagina. (**b**) [late 16C–early 17C; 1970s+] a woman. (**c**) [19C+] a prostitute; a promiscuous woman. (**d**) [1920s+] (*US gay*) a heterosexual woman, sometimes derog. (**e**) [1930s–40s] (*US gay*) one who masturbates while performing oral intercourse. (**f**) [1930s–50s] (*US gay*) an effeminate male homosexual. (**g**) [1950s] sexual intercourse. (**h**) [1960s+] (*US*) a feminine lesbian. (**i**) [1970s+] (*US gay*) semen. **2** as money or a monetary token. (**a**) [early 18C–19C] a gambling chip. (**b**) [late 19C+] (*US*) a dollar. (**c**) [1940s] a pound sterling [may exist only in the works of P.G. Wodehouse, living in the US and using its sl., but usu. in a UK context]. **3** [early 18C+] a man, a person, esp. one who is easily fooled or duped; *see also* sense 5c below. **4** [late 18C–mid-19C] a sailor; thus *scaly fish*, a rough, blunt sailor. **5** [late 18C+] a person, as qualified, esp. in various comb. below. **6** as a novice, i.e. a *fresh fish* [abbr. SE *fresh fish*]. (**a**) [mid-19C+] (*Can./US prison*) a new inmate; thus prison jargon *fish number*, the number issued to each prisoner by the US Department of Corrections; *fish gallery, fish row*, a segregated area of the prison where new inmates are housed. (**b**) [late 19C–1940s] (*US campus*) a freshman. (**c**) [late 19C+] (*US*) any form of novice, esp. a gullible innocent [note Greene, *The Blacke Bookes Messenger* (1592): 'He that drawes the fish to the bait, *the Beater*']. (**d**) [1970s] (*US campus*) a socially inexperienced boy. (**e**) [1990s+] a virgin or someone who has not even been kissed. **7** [1910s+] (*US*) a heavy drinker, one who *drinks like a fish*. **8** [1950s+] (*US*) a Roman Catholic [the Catholic tradition of abstaining from meat on Fridays]. **9** [1970s+] (*US*) a derog. term for a Newfoundlander [the staple industry]. **10** [1990s+] (*UK juv.*) a very unpopular person.

pertaining to prison

IN COMPOUNDS

❑ **fish bowl** *n. see* separate entry. ❑ **fish line** *n.* (*US prison*) **1** [1960s] a bus that brings in new inmates. **2** [2000s] a line used to pull items from one cell to another. ❑ **fish queen** *n. see* separate entry. ❑ **fish roll** *n.* [1990s+] (*US prison*) the clothing and other necessities issued to a new inmate. ❑ **fish tank** *n. see* FISH-BOWL *n.*

IN PHRASES

❑ **new fish** *n.* [1910s+] (*US prison*) a new inmate.

pertaining to female sexuality

IN COMPOUNDS

❑ **fishcunt** *n.* [1990s+] a general term of abuse, aimed at a female. ❑ **fish dinner** *n.* [1970s+] (*US gay*) sexual intercourse with a woman; thus a woman. ❑ **fish-fanny** *n.* (*also* **fishy-fanny**) [FANNY *n.*[1] (1)] [2000s] a general insult aimed at a woman; the implication is that her vagina smells. ❑ **fish fingers** *n.* [play on SE] [1990s+] (*UK juv.*) a general insult, implying that someone has placed his finger(s) in a woman's vagina and then failed to wash them, so his fingers supposedly smell of fish. ❑ **fish market** *n.* **1** [mid-19C–1900s] the vagina. **2** [mid-19C–1900s] a brothel. **3** [1960s] (*US campus*) a women's dormitory. ❑ **fishmonger** *n.* **1** [17C] a womanizer, a promiscuous man. **2** [mid-17C] a madame, a bawd. ❑ **fishmonger's daughter** *n.* [late 16C–early 17C] a prostitute. ❑ **fishpond** *n.* [17C–18C] the vagina. ❑ **fish queen** *see* separate entries. ❑ **fish supper** *n.* [1990s+] sexual intercourse, esp. in the context of a conjugal right. ❑ **fish tank** *n.* [1980s+] (*US gay*) the vagina of a heterosexual woman.

IN PHRASES

❑ **eat (the) fish** *v.* (*also* **chew (the) fish**) [1940s+] (*US*) to perform cunnilingus. ❑ **go fish** *n.* (*gay*) **1** [1940s+] for an effeminate gay man to take the 'feminine', passive role during sex. **2** [1960s+] of a male homosexual or lesbian, to give cunnilingus. **3** [1970s+] (*US gay*) to become coy or flirtatious, i.e. to react like a teenage girl. ❑ **go fishing** *v.* [mid-19C+] to go out looking for a sexually obliging woman; also in gay use, to seek a sexual partner. ❑ **slip the fish** [1990s+] of a man, to have sexual intercourse.

general uses

IN COMPOUNDS

❑ **fish-sticks** *n.* [2000s] (*US black*) money.

IN PHRASES

❑ **big fish** *n.* (*US*) **1** [early 19C+] an important, powerful person. **2** [mid-19C–1950s] an important event, undertaking etc. ❑ **bit of fish** *n.* [late 19C] **1** the vagina. **2** sexual intercourse; thus *have a bit of fish (on a fork)*, to have sexual intercourse. ❑ **cold fish** *n. see under* COLD *adj.* ❑ **little fish** *n.* [reverse of *BIG FISH* above] [early 19C+] (*US*) an unimportant person. ❑ **loose fish** *n.* [note whaling jargon *loose fish*, a whale that is fair game for anybody who can catch it] **1** [19C] a promiscuous woman. **2** [early 19C] a prostitute. **3** [early 19C–1940s] one who has no settled way of life. ❑ **odd fish** *n.* [late 18C+] an eccentric person. ❑ **poor fish** *n.* [late 18C+] a sorry person, a pathetic figure. ❑ **queer fish** *n.* [late 18C+] an odd or eccentric person. ❑ **timid fish** *n.* [1980s] (*Aus.*) a shirker. ❑ **mind your own fish** [20C+] (*Aus.*) mind your own business. ❑ **not give a fish's tit** *v. see under* TIT *n.*[2].

SE in slang uses

IN COMPOUNDS

❑ **fishbagger** *n.* [they use their supposedly important briefcase to take home food, esp. cheap fish] [late 19C] a suburbanite who works in the City. ❑ **fishbelly** *n.* [the colour of the stomachs of some fish] [1960s] (*US black*) a derog. term for a white person. ❑ **fish bits** *n.* [1980s+] (*UK juv.*) that portion of the hair that hangs down at the back of a MULLET *n.*[2] haircut. ❑ **fish-black** *n.* [the Catholic tradition of eating fish on Friday + the *black*ness of night] [1940s] (*US black*) Friday night. ❑ **fish-brained** *adj.* [1910s–40s] (*UK juv.*) stupid. ❑ **fish broth** *n.* [late 16C–early 17C] water, esp. when salted. ❑ **fish-eater** *n.* [1930s+] **1** a Roman Catholic. **2** (*Can.*) an inhabitant of Nova Scotia. ❑ **fish-eye** *n. see* separate entries. ❑ **fishfag** *n.* **1** [mid-19C] a fishwife, both lit, i.e a fish seller, and as pej. **2** *see* FAG *n.*[3]. ❑ **fish-fry** *n.* [1920s+] (*US black*) a party to which guests bring refreshment, or pay to attend, c.f. *rent party*; thus as adj., well supplied with money. ❑ **fish-head** *n. see* separate entries. ❑ **fish-hook** *n.* **1** [late 16C+] in pl., the fingers [the term, derived f. 19C naut. use, was UK and then moved to US black use by 1930s]. **2** [mid-19C+] a hand. **3** [1980s] (*N.Z.*) a problem. ❑ **fish-horn** *n.* **1** [mid-19C–1900s] (*US*) a wind instrument. **2** [1930s+] (*US, chiefly black*) a saxophone. ❑ **fish-pond, the** *n.* **1** [early 19C] (*Anglo-Irish*) the Irish Sea; thus *over the fish-pond*, England. **2** *see* POND, THE *n.* (1). ❑ **fish scales** *n.* [? resemblance to the flakes of crack cocaine] [1980s+] (*drugs*) crack cocaine. ❑ **fish-skin** *n. see* FROG *n.*[3] (1). ❑ **fish tank** *n. see* separate entry. ❑ **fish-wrapper** *n.* (*also* **fried fish wrapper, meat wrapper**) [the assumption that newspapers were good only for wrapping fish] [late 19C+] (*orig. US*) a newspaper.

IN PHRASES

❑ **die on a fish day** *v. see under* DIE *v.* ❑ **do fish swim?** *see* CAN A DUCK SWIM? *under* DUCK *n.*[1]. ❑ **drink like a fish** *v. see under* DRINK *v.* ❑ **fish 'n' chip mob** *n.* [note Sandhurst jargon *fish 'n' chip mob*, unfashionable regiments] [1970s+] (*UK society*) anyone considered socially unacceptable. ❑ **give someone the fish** *v. see* GIVE SOMEONE THE FISH-EYE *under* FISH-EYE *n.*[1]. ❑ **will a fish swim?** *see* CAN A DUCK SWIM? *under* DUCK *n.*[1].

fish *n.*[2] (*also* **fisher**) [FISH *v.*[1] (1)] [19C] (*US campus*) a toady, a sycophant.

fish *n.*[3] [1950s+] (*W.I.*) any form of sauce that accompanies the staple, some form of starch, which need not contain fish.

fish *adj.*[1] [FISH *n.*[1] (1)] [mid-19C+] (*Can./US prison*) fresh, uninitiated, new, esp. of a prisoner.

fish *adj.*[2] *see* FISHY *adj.*[2] (1).

fish *v.*[1] [? SE *fish* for compliments] **1** [late 18C+] (*US campus*) to toady, to ingratiate oneself. **2** [late 19C] to interrogate.

SE in slang uses

IN PHRASES

❑ **fish for food** *v.* [FOOD *n.* (1)] [1940s] (*US black*) to gossip. ❑ **fish or cut bait** [mid-19C+] either carry out what you're doing to the fullest extent or let someone else more competent get on with it while you take a secondary role. ❑ **fish out** *v.* (*also* **fish up**) **1** [late 19C+] to obtain, to produce. **2** [1930s] (*US Und.*) to rob.

fish *v.*[2] [SE] [1940s–60s] to shoplift, to steal.

fish *v.*[3] [1960s] (*US*) to regard with scorn, dislike.

fish *v.*[4] [FISH *n.*[1] (1)] [1970s+] (*US gay*) to practise cunnilingus.

fish! *excl.* [late 19C; 1990s+] a general excl. of dismissal; a euph. for FUCK! *excl.* (1).

fish and shrimp *n.* [rhy. sl.] [1930s+] a procurer, a pimp.

fish and tank *n.* [rhy. sl.] [1990s+] (*UK Und.*) a bank.

fish-bowl *n.* **1** [1930s+] (*US Und.*) (*also* **fish tank**) a holding cell in a police station [play on SE, the visibility of the prisoners]. **2** [1940s+] (*US prison*) (*also* **fish tank**) the processing unit for new arrivals at a prison [FISH *n.*[1] (6a)]. **3** [1960s] (*US*) steam baths frequented by homosexual men. **4** [1970s] (*S.Afr.*) a sleek car, e.g. a Cadillac.

fished *adj.* [1980s] (*US campus*) drunk.

fisher *n.*[1] [proper name of Sir Warren *Fisher*, secretary to the Treasury c.1919–33] [1910s–30s] a banknote.

fisher *n.*[2] *see* FISH *n.*[2].

Fisheries *n.* [late 19C] the Fisheries Exhibition, London 1883.

fisherman's daughter *n.* [rhy. sl.] [late 19C+] water (usu. as a drink).

fisherman's luck *n.* [popularly defined as 'a wet ass and a hungry gut'] [19C+] (*Aus./US*) no luck at all, bad luck.

fisher's flimsies *n.* [1910s–30s] (*Aus.*) currency notes issued during the government of Prime Minister Andrew *Fisher* (1862–1928).

fishery *n.* [they are 'fishing' for souls] [1930s] (*US tramp*) a mission hall.

fish-eye *n.*[1]

IN PHRASES

❑ **give someone the fish-eye** *v.* (*also* **...the fish, ...the fishy eye, ...the frozen eye, fish-eye**) [the wide, round eyes of a fish] [20C+] (*US*) to stare at (in a hostile manner).

fish-eye *n.*[2] [supposed resemblance] **1** [1910s] (*US Und.*) a diamond. **2** [1940s] (*US milit./prison*) in pl., tapioca (pudding).

fish-face *n.* [early 17C; 1910s+] a stupid or ugly looking person; also used as a derog. term of address.

fish-faced *adj.* [FISH-FACE *n.*] [1920s+] stupid- or ugly-looking.

fish-head *n.*[1] [all uses are derog.; their consumption of and/or occupation with fish] **1** [20C+] (*US*) a native of the west Florida coast. **2** [20C+] anyone who lives alongside a river. **3** [20C+] a West Indian. **4** [20C+] a worker in a fish cannery. **5** [1970s+] an East Asian.

fish-head *n.*[2] [among the poor a fish-head was considered a treat or delicacy] [1950s] (*W.I.*) a bribe, a tip.

fisho *n.* [SE *fish* + -O *sfx* (3)] [1920s+] (*Aus.*) a professional fisherman; a fish-seller.

fisho *v.* [FISHO *n.* (1)] [1960s] to fish professionally.

fish queen *n.*[1] [FISH *n.*[1] (1d) + -QUEEN *sfx*] **1** [1940s] a male homosexual who openly associates with women, with the supposed aim of appearing to be bisexual. **2** [1940s+] (*US gay*) any man, homo- or heterosexual, who enjoys cunnilingus. **3** [1970s] (*US gay*) a heterosexual man.

fish queen *n.*[2] [FISH *n.*[1] (6a) + QUEEN *n.* (2a)] [1970s+] (*US prison*) a gay inmate who has newly arrived at the prison.

fish-queen *v.* [FISH QUEEN *n.*[1] (2)] [1940s–50s] (*US*) to perform cunnilingus.

fishy *adj.*[1] [one's eyes resemble those of a dead fish] [mid-18C–mid-19C] looking ill, esp. around the eyes, after a drinking session.

IN PHRASES

❑ **fishy about the gills** [GILLS *n.* (1)] [late 19C] hungover.

fishy *adj.*[2] [the smell of rotting fish or the slipperiness of fresh fish] **1** [mid-19C+] (*also* **fish**) suspect, dubious, unreliable, questionable; thus adv. *fishily*. **2** [1910s] (*US*) supercilious.

SE in slang uses

IN COMPOUNDS

❑ **fishy fanny** *n. see* FISH-FANNY *under* FISH *n.*[1].

IN PHRASES

❑ **give someone the fishy eye** *v. see* GIVE SOMEONE THE FISH-EYE *under* FISH-EYE *n.*[1].

fisk *n.* [ety. unknown] [mid-19C] (*UK Und.*) a lie; thus *fisk-smith*, a notorious liar.

fisk *v. see* FRISK *v.*[2] (1).

fisle *v. see* FIZZLE *v.*[1] (2).

fisno *n.* [backsl. = OFFICE *n.* (3)] [late 19C] (*tramp*) a warning.

fist *n.*

SE in slang uses

pertaining to violence

IN COMPOUNDS

❑ **fist-burger** *n.* [1970s] (*US*) a punch. ❑ **fist city** *n.* (*also* **duke city, fist holler**) [SE *fist*/ DUKE *n.*[3] (2) + -CITY *sfx*/SE *hollow*; an imaginary place where quarrels are settled with the fists] [1930s+] (*US*) a fist fight. ❑ **fist junction** *n.* [1970s+] (*US black*) that point in a confrontation when a physical fight takes over from mere words. ❑ **fist oil** *n.* [mid-18C] (*US*) physical violence, to be administered by the fists. ❑ **fist sandwich** *n. see* KNUCKLE SANDWICH *under* KNUCKLE *n.*

IN PHRASES

❑ **fist up** *v.* [1990s+] to clench one's fingers into a fist, preparatory to fighting or hitting.

general uses

IN COMPOUNDS

❑ **fist queen** *n.* [-QUEEN *sfx* (3)] [2000s] (*S.Afr. gay*) one who enjoys FISTING *n.*

IN PHRASES

❑ **fist in** *v.* [1990s+] to interrupt. ❑ **fist it** *v.* **1** [19C] of a woman, to caress a man's penis. **2** [mid–late 19C] (*Aus./N.Z.*) to eat with one's hands. ❑ **fist one's mister** *v.* [20C+] to masturbate.

fist-fuck *n.* (*also* **fist**) [FIST-FUCK *v.*] **1** [1970s+] the insertion of the hand (and forearm) into the vagina or anus. **2** [1940s+] an act of masturbation.

fist-fuck *v.* (*also* **fist**) [FIST-FUCKING *n.*] **1** [1970s+] (*gay*) to insert one's hand (and forearm) into someone's anus or vagina. **2** *see* FUCK ONE'S FIST *under* FUCK *v.*

fist-fucker *n.* [FIST-FUCK *v.*] **1** [1960s] (*US*) a habitual masturbator. **2** [1970s+] (*usu. gay*) one who practises FIST-FUCKING *n.* **3** [1990s+] (*US*) a generally unpleasant person.

fist-fucking *n.* (*also* **f.f.**) [FIST-FUCK *v.*] **1** [1960s+] male masturbation. **2** [1970s+] (*gay*) the insertion of the hand (and sometimes forearm) into the anus of one's partner for purposes of sexual stimulation [popular in the 1970s but latterly in decline through fears of injury and hence the possibility of spreading AIDS; also found in heterosexual and lesbian sex, where the orifice is the vagina].

fistful *n.* [the five fingers] [1930s] (*US Und.*) a five-year jail sentence.

fisting *n.* [FIST-FUCKING *n.* (2)] [1970s+] (*usu. gay*) the insertion of the hand and poss. forearm into the anus or vagina of one's partner.

fisty *adj. see* FEISTY *adj.* (2).

fisty palmer *n.*

IN PHRASES

❑ **have a date with fisty palmer** *v.* [play on SE *fist* + *palm*] [1990s+] to masturbate.

fit *n.*[1] [abbr. SE *outfit*] [1950s–60s] (*US black*) a suit of clothes, esp. a well-cut garment.

fit *n.*[2] [abbr. OUTFIT *n.*[1] (3b)] [1950s+] (*US drugs*) the equipment (a needle, a spoon, a dropper) required for injecting narcotics.

IN PHRASES

❑ **have a fit** *v.* (*also* **fit up**) (*US prison*) to inject heroin.

fit *n.*[3]

SE in slang uses

IN COMPOUNDS

❑ **fit house** *n.* [1920s] (*US Und.*) a hospital for the criminally insane.

IN PHRASES

❑ **fit in the arm** *n.* ['In June 1897 one Tom Kelly was given into custody by a woman for striking her. His defence was that "a fit had seized him in the arm", and for months afterwards backstreet frequenters called a blow a fit' (Ware)]] [late 19C–1900s] a blow, a punch; thus *have a fit in the arm*, to aim a punch or blow. ❑ **fit of the mazes** *n.* [late 19C] (*US black*) a trance. ❑ **forty fits** *n.* [FORTY *adj.*[1]] [late 19C+] an extreme loss of emotional control; thus *have forty fits*, to lose all control. ❑ **get fits** *v.* [late 19C–1900s] **1** to become angered by defeat. **2** to be criticized harshly; to be humiliated. ❑ **give someone fits** *v.* (*orig. US*) **1** [mid-19C–1900s] to inflict a humiliating defeat on, to crush. **2** [mid-19C–1920s] to scold vigorously, to reprimand. **3** [20C+] to frighten. ❑ **throw a fit** *v.* (*also* **throw forty fits**) [late 19C+] to lose all emotional control.

fit *adj.* [note agricultural use *fit*, of fruits and vegetables, ready to pick, full-grown, though not necessarily fully ripe; note Shakespearian use *fit*, of a woman, having an aptitude for love-making] **1** [late 19C] very well, healthy, usu. in response to the query 'How are you?'. **2** [late 19C+] (*later 20C+ use is UK black*) good-looking.

IN COMPOUNDS

❑ **fit-batty** *adj.* [2000s] (*UK black*) very attractive.

SE in slang uses

IN COMPOUNDS

❑ **fit-me-tight** *n.* [1960s] (*Irish*) a journeyman tailor.

IN PHRASES

❑ **fit as a buck rat** *adj.* [1940s+] (*N.Z.*) extremely healthy. ❑ **fit as a fiddle** *adj.* [20C+] (*Aus.*) extremely healthy. ❑ **fit as a trout** *adj.* [1960s–80s] (*Aus./N.Z.*) very healthy.

fit *v.* **1** [late 19C+] to identify someone as the perpetrator of a crime. **2** [1910s] to characterize; to identify. **3** *see* FIT UP *v.*[1].

SE in slang uses

IN PHRASES

❑ **fit end to end** *v.* (*also* **fit ends to end**) [late 19C–1900s] to have sexual intercourse. ❑ **fit someone for a jacket** *v. see* JACKET *v.*[2] (2b).

fit! *excl.* [1950s+] (*orig. W.I.*) a general excl. of approval, excellent! first-rate! very good!

fitch *n.* [SE *fitch*, the hair of a polecat] [1920s] (*US Und.*) fur, as worn in a coat.

fitness *n.* [FIT *adj.* (2)] [1970s+] (*UK black*) attractiveness; an attractive (young) woman.

fitshaced *adj.* [play on SHITFACED *adj.*; the idea being that one is too drunk to be able to say the word properly] [1990s+] drunk.

fitted *adj.* [1990s+] well-dressed.

fitter *n.* **1** [mid-19C] (*US Und.*) a maker of skeleton keys. **2** [1940s] (*UK Und.*) a corrupt supplier who provides criminals with disguises, weapons, transport etc.

fit to... *phr.*

IN PHRASES

❑ **fit to be tied** [the image of one so hysterically furious that they need to be tied down] [late 19C+] furious, enraged and in need, therefore, of restraint. ❑ **fit to bust** (*also* **fit to burst, ...split**) [mid-19C+] **1** emotionally moved, either to rage or ecstasy depending on context. **2** to a very great extent. ❑ **fit to kill** [mid-19C+] (*orig. US*) a phr. used of something done to excess, esp. of one's dress.

fit-up *n.*[1] [orig. theatre use] [mid-19C+] any temporary structure, esp. a stage, boxing ring etc, which can be assembled, then knocked down for assembly at another venue.

fit-up *n.*[2] [FIT UP *v.*[1] (2)] [1930s+] (*UK Und.*) a false accusation or perjured evidence used to have an innocent suspect (albeit one who has a criminal record) arrested and found guilty.

fit up *v.*[1] (*also* **fit, fix up**) **1** [mid-19C–1910s] (*UK Und.*) to prepare. **2** [20C+] to incriminate by using false evidence, both physical and verbal. **3** [1970s] to make responsible (for).

fit up *v.*[2] *see* HAVE A FIT *under* FIT *n.*[2].

fitz *n.* [? a brandname] [20C+] (*Aus./S.Afr.*) a large sausage used for cutting into slices for sandwiches or to eat with salad.

Fitzroy cocktail *n.* [*Fitzroy* is a suburb of Melbourne] [1920s+] (*Aus./Melbourne*) a drink based on methylated spirits with some form of mixer to mediate the taste.

Fitzroy Yank *n.* [for ety. *see* FITZROY COCKTAIL *n.* + YANK *n.* (1)] [1940s+] (*Aus.*) a relatively unsophisticated person who attempts to ape the supposedly smart style of an American.

five *n.*[1] [abbr.] **1** [20C+] a five-year prison sentence. **2** [1970s+] five minutes.

five *n.*[2] [BUNCH OF FIVES *n.*] **1** [1930s+] (*US*) a blow with the fist. **2** [1940s] (*US black*) the five fingers, thus the hand.

IN PHRASES

❑ **give five** *v.* (*also* **give someone five**) [the *five* fingers] [1910s+] (*orig. US*) to slap hands in order to seal a bargain or to greet a friend; occas. ext. as *give ten*, to slap both hands; *give five on the sly*, to slap hands behind one's back so as not to alert onlookers; *give five on the black-hand side/the soul side*, to slap hands on the back (darker) side or the palm side of the hand. ▫ **have five on** *v.* [the lit./fig. use of one's *five* fingers] [1990s+] (*US campus*) to help. ▫ **slap five** *v.* (*also* **five-slap, lay five, slip five**) [1910s+] (*US*) to indulge in a mutual hand-slapping ritual used by blacks (and some whites) for greeting, emphasis, congratulation etc.

IN EXCLAMATIONS

▫ **give me five!** (*also* **gimme five! hand me five! slip me five!**) [1910s+] (*orig. US black*) imper., let's slap hands to seal the deal or bargain!

five *adj.*

SE in slang uses

IN COMPOUNDS

▫ **five-acre Tory** *n.* [1980s+] (*N.Z.*) a very conservative small farmer. ▫ **five-alarm** *adj.* [1960s] (*Aus.*) best, most impressive. ▫ **five alls** *n.* [late 18C–mid-19C] a public house sign. ▫ **five-and-dime(r)** *see* separate entries. ▫ **five-barred gate** *n.* [the majority of policemen were recruited from the countryside, home of such gates] [late 19C] a policeman. ▫ **five-bucker** *n.* [BUCK *n.*[3] (1)] [1940s] (*US*) a $5 bill. ▫ **five-cent bag** *n.* (*also* **five-cent balloon, ...paper**) [BAG *n.*[1] (7a)/BALLOON *n.* (7)/PAPER *n.* (13b)] [1960s] (*US drugs*) a small amount of heroin, less than 28g (1oz), sold for $5. ▫ **five-center** *n.* (*also* **five cent word**) [1990s+] (*US*) a long and supposedly 'difficult' word. ▫ **five-dollar** *n. see* separate entry. ▫ **five-finger(ed)** *see* separate entries. ▫ **five-fingers** *see* separate entries. ▫ **five-Fs** *n. see* FOUR-FS *n.* ▫ **five hundred** *n.* [a specific model number, the series 500] [1990s+] (*US black*) a BMW automobile. ▫ **five-knuckle shuffle** *n. see* separate entry. ▫ **five-letter woman** *n.* [1920s+] a prostitute, i.e. *w-h-o-r-e* or *b-i-t-c-h*; see also FOUR-LETTER MAN *n.* ▫ **five pennyworth** *n.* [late 19C] (*UK tramp*) a jail sentence of five years. ▫ **5% Nation/Five Percenter** *n. see* separate entry. ▫ **five-pot piece** *n.* [orig. medical student use, f. the contemporary price of a quart or *pot* of mixed mild and bitter beer] [mid-19C] two shillings and sixpence (2s 6d; 12½p). ▫ **five-seven** *n.* [1980s] (*US Und.*) a .357 magnum handgun. ▫ **five specker** *n.* [1920s–30s] (*US Und.*) a five-year sentence. ▫ **five-spot** *n. see under* -SPOT *sfx.*

IN PHRASES

▫ **five against one** *n.* (*also* **five on one**) [five fingers v. one penis or vagina] [1990s+] masturbation. ▫ **five annas short of the rupee** *n. see under* ...SHORT OF... *adj.* ▫ **five by five** *see* separate entries. ▫ **five by two** *n. see* FIVE TO TWO *n.* (2). ▫ **five in the south** *n.* [20C+] (*US gambling*) the point of five in craps dice. ▫ **five miles of bad road** *n. see TEN MILES OF BAD ROAD under* TEN *adj.* ▫ **five of clubs** *n.* [1940s] (*US*) the fist. ▫ **five on one** *n. see FIVE AGAINST ONE* above. ▫ **five or seven** *n.* [the popular sentence, a five-shilling fine or seven days in prison] [late 19C] a drunkard. ▫ **five to six rush** *n.* (*also* **five to six swill**) [SE *five/six o'clock + rush/swill*] [1950s–70s] (*N.Z.*) the nightly rush to the public house, caused by severely restricted licensing laws. ▫ **five twenty-nine** *n.* [1950s] (*US Und.*) the sentence of five months and 29 days for 'jostling' a drunk, i.e. robbing them.

five-acre farm *n.* [rhy. sl.] [mid-19C] an arm.

five and dime *n.* (*also* **five and ten**) [the original such store was that opened (1879) by F.W. Woolworth (1852–1919)] [late 19C+] (*US*) a small store where articles are all priced at five or ten cents.

five and dime *adj.* (*also* **five-and-ten-cent**) [FIVE AND DIME *n.*] [1930s+] (*US black*) **1** insignificant, paltry. **2** badly dressed, cheap, unattractive, sleazy.

five-and-dimer *n.* [FIVE AND DIME *adj.* (1)] [1940s] (*US*) an insignificant person.

five and two *n.* (*also* **seven and a three, twenty and a ten**) [at 1970s rates he charges $5.00 for his services plus $2.00 for a room; such figures have been subject to inflation or perhaps imply the 'quality' of the prostitute] [1970s] (*gay*) a male homosexual prostitute (cf. FIFTY AND A TEN *n.*).

five by five *n.* [their girth presumably equals their height] [1940s+] (*Can./US black*) a short fat person.

five-by-five *adj.* [five x five = SQUARE *adj.* (1)] [2000s] (*US*) good, in order.

five-dollar *n.* [2000s] (*US black*) fellatio for which the woman charges $5.

SE in slang uses

IN COMPOUNDS

▫ **five-dollar bag** *n.* [BAG *n.*[1] (7)] [1960s+] (*US drugs*) a bag of heroin costing $5 or $50. ▫ **five-dollar expression** *n.* (*also* **... words**) *see TWO-DOLLAR WORDS under* TWO-DOLLAR *adj.*

five-eight *n.* [rhy. sl. = MATE *n.* (1); ult. a position in the game of rugby] [1980s+] (*Aus. prison*) a friend.

five-finger *v.* [1910s; 2000s] (*US black*) to steal.

five-finger(ed) *adj.*

IN COMPOUNDS

▫ **five-finger discount** *n.* [1960s+] (*orig. Aus./N.Z./US*) the act and proceeds of shoplifting, stealing. ▫ **five-fingered exercise** *n.* [1960s+] masturbation. ▫ **five-finger(ed) Mary** *n.* (*also* **five-fingered Annie**) [1940s+] the hand, as used for masturbation. ▫ **five-fingered salute** *n.* [1940s] (*US*) a gesture of derision, placing the thumb on the tip of the nose and fanning out and wriggling the four fingers. ▫ **five-fingered widow** *n.* (*also* **widow five-finger**) [1970s+] masturbation. ▫ **five-finger sandwich** *n.* [1990s+] (*Aus.*) a punch. ▫ **five-finger shuffle** *n. see* FIVE-KNUCKLE SHUFFLE *n.*

IN PHRASES

▫ **use the five-fingered chequebook** *v.* [1980s+] (*N.Z.*) to shoplift.

five fingers *n.* [ety. unknown] **1** [late 16C–late 17C; mid-19C] in card-games, the five of trumps. **2** [1930s] (*US Und.*) a five-year jail sentence.

five fingers *adj.* [*five fingers* make a fig. whole hand] [20C+] (*Irish*) first-rate, excellent.

five-knuckle shuffle *n.* (*also* **five-finger shuffle**) [1980s+] masturbation.

IN PHRASES

▫ **do the five-knuckle shuffle** *v.* [1980s+] to masturbate.

five-oh *n.* (*also* **5-0, five-o, Hawaii 5-0**) [1960s TV police show *Hawaii 5-0*] [1980s+] (*US black/teen*) **1** the police. **2** a 50-litre Ford Mustang (used as a police vehicle in some areas). **3** (*US drugs*) a $50-rock of cocaine. **4** (*US prison*) a prison officer.

502 *n.* [California police code for the offence] [1970s+] (*US black/teen*) drink-driving.

502 *v.* [502 *n.*] [1990s+] (*US black/teen*) to get arrested for drink-driving.

5% Nation *n.* [the Nation of Islam teaches that any large group of people, and more spec., the African-American nation, can be divided into three groups, the 85%, basically the ignorant masses that need to be led, the 5%, the people with true knowledge of self whose job it is to lead the masses and fight against the 10%, the people who have partial knowledge of self and use it to gain power and wealth by exploiting the 85%, also referred to as 'bloodsuckers of the poor'. The chosen percentages are those they feel are the percentages within the black community. These numbers are neither universal (although these groups do exist within any large group) nor unchangeable] [1990s+] (*US black*) a black radical group, an offshoot of the Nation of Islam; thus *Five Percenter*, a member of the group.

fiver *n.* **1** [mid-19C+] a £5 note, £5. **2** [mid-19C+] (*US*) a $5 bill. **3** [late 19C–1920s] (*Aus./UK/US*) a five-year prison sentence; one serving such. **4** [20C+] £500. **5** [1970s] (*US drugs*) a quantity of heroin costing $5.

fives *n.* **1** [17C] a foot. **2** [late 18C+] the hand, usu. when clenched in a fist; thus *the fives*, prizefighting; *man of fives*, a professional fighter. **3** [mid-19C+] a street fight. **4** [1960s] (*drugs*) 5mg Benzedrine or amphetamine tablets. **5** [1990s+] masturbation.

IN PHRASES

▫ **break fives** *v.* [1970s] (*W.I.*) to shake hands. ▫ **tip someone the fives** *v.* [late 18C] to shake hands.

5000 *phr.* ['I'm outta here', which evolved to 'I'm Audi', and to *5000* after the Audi *5000* car] [1990s+] (*US black/teen*) goodbye, I'm off.

five-time *v. see* TWO-TIME *v.* (1).

five to four *n. see* TWO BY FOUR *n.*[2].

five to two *n.* [rhy. sl.; ult. ref. to racing bets] **1** [1930s] a shoe. **2** [1930s+] (*also* **five by two**) a Jew.

fix *n.*[1] [FIX *v.*[1] (4)] **1** [mid-19C] (*US*) an outfit. **2** [1900s] (*Aus.*) fitness, condition.

fix *n.*[2] [1910s+] (*orig. US Und.*) **1** any corrupt deal, a bribe, a favour. **2** the person who makes such deals.

IN PHRASES

❑ **put the fix in/on** *v.* (*also* **have the fix in**) to ensure a plan or event favours whoever has paid the bribe, arranged the deal etc.

fix *n.*[3] [it 'fixes' one's emotional and/or physical state] **1** [1930s+] (*drugs*) an injection of a narcotic which 'fixes one up' when one is 'sick'; the usual presumption being that the drug is heroin. **2** [1960s–70s] (*drugs*) a small amount of cocaine or heroin. **3** [1960s+] an ingestion of any drug. **4** [1960s+] (*US*) a compulsive desire or thrill. **5** [1980s+] anything that satisfies a craving, e.g. for food.

fix *n.*[4] [FIX *v.*[1]] [1950s] (*US*) a meeting.

fix *v.*[1] **1** [late 17C; mid-19C+] to prepare some form of trick. **2** [late 18C+] to bribe, to suborn, esp. in the context of sports or politics. **3** [late 18C+] to take revenge upon, to get even with, to foil an antagonist's plans. **4** [mid-19C+] (*orig. US*) to arrange, to prepare, to get ready. **5** [mid-19C+] to prepare food or a meal. **6** [mid-19C+] (*also* **fix off**) to kill, to murder. **7** [late 19C] (*US*) to look after. **8** [late 19C+] to intend. **9** [late 19C+] to attack, to beat up; also in fig. use. **10** [late 19C+] to sort out. **11** [1900s] to pay.

IN PHRASES

❑ **fix oneself** *v.* [1920s] to get oneself into trouble. ❑ **fix one's hash** *v. see* SETTLE THE HASH *under* HASH *n.*[1]. ❑ **fix someone's clock** *v.* [ironic use of SE *fix* + *clock*; the image is that the clock will indeed be 'fixed', but not in the way its owner desires] [20C+] (*US*) to thwart another's plans, to cause trouble for an enemy, to get even with. ❑ **fix someone's flint** *v.* [ironic use of SE *fix* + *flint*, the flint of a matchlock or musket] [mid-19C–1910s] (*US*) to thwart another's plans, to cause trouble for an enemy, to get even with. ❑ **fix someone's wagon** *v.* (*also* **fix someone's little red wagon**) [1930s+] to thwart someone's plans. ❑ **fix the old gum-tree** *v.* [20C+] (*Aus.*) of a former wanderer, to settle down at last.

fix *v.*[2] **1** [mid-19C; 1930s+] to have sexual intercourse. **2** [1960s] to make pregnant.

IN PHRASES

❑ **get fixed** *v.* [the image of 'fixing' or curing one's sexual frustration] [1940s–50s] (*US*) to have sexual intercourse.

fix *v.*[3] [the over-riding image is of 'fixing' a problem, i.e. the pain of withdrawal; note William Burroughs, *Junkie* (1953): 'If you have any habit at all it takes two papers to fix you, and I mean just fix'] (*drugs*) **1** [1930s+] to inject oneself with narcotics. **2** [1940s+] to give someone else an injection. **3** [1960s] (*US prison*) in ext. use, to eat heavily. **4** [1990s+] in fig. use, to excite.

IN PHRASES

❑ **fix one's bones** *v.* [sense 1 above/SE *fix*, to mend; the aching bones that are part of the symptoms of heroin withdrawal] [1990s+] (*drugs*) to take some heroin in order to ward off the pains of an unsatisfied heroin addiction.

fixed *adj.*[1] [FIX *v.*[1]] **1** [mid-19C+] (*also* **fixed-up**) sorted out, arranged, satisfied, often financially. **2** [mid-19C+] situated materially or financially, e.g. *how are you fixed for…?* have you got any/enough…? **3** [late 19C+] in funds. **4** [late 19C+] (*orig. US*) corrupted, bribed, 'squared', tampered with. **5** [20C+] of a sporting contest, having had the result pre-arranged (to favour a group of gamblers). **6** [1910s] of alcohol, drugged.

fixed *adj.*[2] [late 19C] (*US*) armed; carrying a weapon.

fixed *adj.*[3] [SE *in a fix*] [1910s] (*Aus.*) dispirited, unwell.

fixed *adj.*[4] [FIX *v.*[3] (1)] [1950s+] (*drugs*) using or under the influence of injectable narcotics.

fixed bayonet *n.* **1** [19C] an erect penis. **2** [1910s] (*Aus. milit.*) red wine. **3** [1940s] (*N.Z. milit.*) methylated spirits.

fixed up *adj.* **1** [mid-19C] (*also* **fixed off**) appearing well provided with material goods. **2** [late 19C] (*US*) (*also* **fixed out**) dressed up. **3** [1920s+] fine, good, worked out, happy, content. **4** [1940s] married.

fixed up! *excl.* [FIXED UP *adj.* (3)] [1990s+] (*S.Afr.*) an excl. of approval.

fixer *n.*[1] [SE *fix*/FIX *v.*[1] (2)] [late 19C+] (*orig. US*) one who arranges or adjusts matters, a go-between, esp. in an illegal context.

fixer *n.*[2] [FIX *v.*[3]] **1** [1940s+] (*US drugs*) a drug dealer. **2** [1970s+] (*US drugs*) a narcotics user, a person who injects narcotics.

fixing *n.* [it *fixes* one up] [late 19C] (*Aus.*) strong drink.

fixings *n.*[1] [SE *fixing*, the garnishing of food] [19C+] (*US*) **1** equipment. **2** food. **3** clothes. **4** anything used to dilute or mix with alcohol, e.g. tonic water. **5** the tobacco and matches required to light a pipe.

fixings *n.*[2] [it is *fixed* in the house] [late 19C–1910s] **1** furniture. **2** in ext. use, the trappings of luxury.

fixings *n.*[3] [the couple are *fixed* together] [1930s–60s] (*US*) sexual intercourse.

fix-up *n.*[1] [FIX UP *v.*[2]] **1** [mid–late 19C] (*US*) an alcoholic drink. **2** [1930s] (*drugs*) an injection of a narcotic drug.

fix-up *n.*[2] [FIX UP *v.*[1] (3)] [1990s+] a blind date arranged by a third party.

fix up *v.*[1] **1** [mid-19C+] to set up a meeting (usu. for someone else), e.g. with a prostitute or a date; thus *fixed up*, having such an appointment arranged. **2** [late 19C+] to provide someone with food, clothing, accommodation, a job etc. **3** [1930s+] to initiate a relationship or bring two people together for sex; to marry. **4** [1940s] (*US gay*) to fellate. **5** [1940s–70s] to have sexual intercourse. **6** [1950s] to pay someone. **7** [1970s] (*US*) to beat, to defeat.

fix up *v.*[2] [ext. of FIX *n.*[3] (1)] **1** [20C+] (*US drugs*) to inject heroin or morphine. **2** [20C+] (*US drugs*) to sniff cocaine. **3** [1950s] to give someone, usu. an alcoholic, a drink. **4** [1950s+] to give (or sell) someone some narcotics.

fix up *v.*[3] *see* FIT UP *v.*[1].

fix up! *excl.* [FIT UP *v.*[1]] [1990s+] a general excl. of admonition.

fiz *n.*[1] [abbr./pron. SE *physiognomy*] [early 18C] the face.

fiz *n.*[2] *see* FIZZ *n.*[1] (3).

fizgig *n.*[1] [ext. of SE *gig*, a flighty young woman; despite logical imagery of FIZZ *n.*[1] (2), i.e. one who fizzes (with animal spirits) the chronology renders this impossible] [16C; mid-19C] a promiscuous woman.

fizgig *n.*[2] (*also* **fizzer, fizzgig, phizgig**) [ety. unknown; *AND* suggests an ext. use of FIZGIG *n.*[1], i.e. one who runs around and chatters indiscreetly] [20C+] (*Aus.*) a police informer.

fizgig *n.*[3] *see* FISGIG *n.*

fizz *n.*[1] **1** [mid-18C+] a fuss, a commotion. **2** [mid-19C+] animal spirits, raw energy. **3** [mid-19C+] (*also* **fiz, fizzly, pfiz, phiz, phizz water**) champagne; occas. lemonade and ginger beer mixed. **4** [1910s+] (*also* **fizz water**) sparkling water; soda water. **5** [1970s] sherbet.

SE in slang uses

IN COMPOUNDS

❑ **fizzboat** *n.* [2000s] (*N.Z.*) a small noisy speedboat. ❑ **fizz water** *n. see* sense 4 above.

fizz *n.*[2] [abbr. FIZGIG *n.*[2] (1)] [1940s+] (*Aus.*) an informer.

fizz *v.*[1] [FIZGIG *n.*[2] (1)] [1900s] (*Aus.*) to be an informer.

fizz *v.*[2] [1960s] (*US teen*) to lose one's temper.

SE in slang uses

IN PHRASES

❑ **fizz out (on)** *v.* [SE + FIZZLE *v.*[2] (3)] [1940s+] (*Aus.*) to let down, to fail in a promise.

IN EXCLAMATIONS

❑ **fizz off!** [1960s] (*N.Z.*) leave! go away!

fizzer *n.*[1] [FIZZ *n.*[1] (2)] [mid-19C–1920s] anything or anyone excellent or first-rate.

fizzer *n.*[2] [FIZZLE *v.*[2] (3)] **1** [1910s+] (*US*) a firecracker that fails to go off. **2** [1940s+] (*Aus./N.Z.*) a disappointing failure, a fiasco, a 'wash-out'. **3** [1960s] a form of contraceptive.

fizzer *n.*[3] (*also* **phizzer**) [FIZGIG *n.*[2] (1)] [1950s+] (*Aus.*) an informer.

fizzer/fizzgig *n. see* FIZGIG *n.*[2].

fizzical culturalist *n.* [puns on SE *fizzy/physical*] [1940s+] (*US black*) a bartender.

fizzing *adj.* (*also* **phizzing**) [ref. to the effervescence of champagne, i.e. FIZZ *n.*[1] (3)] **1** [mid-19C+] wonderful, excellent, first-rate. **2** [1950s+] a general negative [euph. for FUCKING *adj.* (1)].

fizzle *n.*[1] (*also* **fiezle**) [FIZZLE *v.*[1] (2)] [mid-17C–1900s] a breaking of wind.

fizzle *n.*[2] [FIZZLE *v.*[2]] [mid-19C+] **1** (*US campus*) a (partial) failure in a recitation or examination. **2** (*orig. US*) a failure. **3** (*US*) a minor quarrel. **4** (*US Und.*) an escape.

fizzle *v.*[1] [echoic] **1** [late 16C–early 18C] to defecate. **2** [mid-17C–mid-18C] (*also* **fisle**) to break wind.

fizzle *v.*[2] **1** [mid-19C] (*US campus*) to fail someone in an examination. **2** [mid-19C–1920s] (*US campus*) to fail in an examination. **3** [mid-19C+] to fail, to make a mess of.

fizzle-fart *n.* [1930s] (*US teen*) a term of abuse.

fizzle (out) *v.* [the sound of escaping air + FIZZLE *v.*[2] (3)] **1** [mid-19C] to kill. **2** [mid-19C+] (*orig. US*) to peter out, to fail gradually but surely.

fizzler *n.* [FIZZ *n.*[1] (3)] [mid-19C] a champagne bottle.

fizzly *n. see* FIZZ *n.*[1] (3).

fizzog *n. see* PHIZ *n.*[1].

fizzy *n.* [ext. FIZZ *n.*[1] (3)] **1** [1910s] (*Aus.*) beer. **2** [1920s–30s] champagne.

fizzy *adj.* [FIZZ *n.*[1] (2)] **1** [1930s–50s] energetic, excitable. **2** [1960s] (*S.Afr. drugs*) of a cigarette, containing marijuana.

fla/flaa *see under* FLAH.

flaaitaal *n. see* *FLY TAAL under* FLY *adj.*

flab *n.* [onomat. for something hanging down; now virtually SE] [1920s+] **1** fat, fatness. **2** (*juv.*) a fat person.

flaba-flaba *adj.* [SE *flabby* + redup.] [1950s] (*W.I.*) **1** worthless, good-for-nothing. **2** stocky, short and thickset.

flab-stabbing *n.* [FLAB *n.* (1) + STAB *v.* (1)] [2000s] (*US black*) having sexual intercourse with a fat woman.

flach *n. see* FLATCH *n.*

flack *n. see* FLAK *n.*

flack *v.* [FLAK *n.*] [1960s+] (*US*) to publicize; to work as a press agent.

fladge *n.* (*also* **flage, fladge and padge**) [abbr./pron.] [1950s+] *fla*gellation, only when used in a sexual context; thus in comb. below.

IN COMPOUNDS

❑ **fladge queen** *n.* (*also* **fladge fiend, ...freak**) [-QUEEN *sfx* (3)/FIEND *n.* (3)/-FREAK *sfx*] [1970s] (*US gay*) a homosexual who enjoys flagellation.

flag *n.*[1] (*also* **flagg**) **1** [mid-16C–mid-19C] (*UK Und.*) a groat, four pence[? f. MLG *vleger*, 'a coin worth somewhat more than a Bremer groat']. **2** [20C+] (*US*) a $1 note [var. on sense 1 above or abbr. *JEWISH FLAG under* JEWISH *adj.*]. **3** [1940s–60s] (*Aus.*) a £1 note.

flag *n.*[2] [fig. uses of SE] **1** [mid–late 19C] an apron; thus *flag-flasher*, one who wears an apron when not actually working. **2** [mid–late 19C] in pl., clothes drying in the open air. **3** [mid-19C+] a sanitary towel. **4** [late 19C] the labia. **5** [1930s–60s] (*US Und.*) an assumed name, an alias, i.e. 'a flag of convenience'. **6** [1960s] (*US*) an erect penis; thus *grow a flag*, to have an erection. **7** [1960s] (*US*) the act of avoiding looking at one's partner's face during sexual intercourse; thus *using the flag*, doing this. **8** [1960s] (*US prison*) a warning. **9** [1970s] (*US*) an instinct, a personal standard or belief. **10** [1970s+] (*drugs*) the flow of blood from the vein into the syringe, where it blends with the narcotic/water mixture before being pumped back into the vein [the blood 'waves' as it enters the syringe; note 19C whaling jargon *flag*, the blood spouted by a harpooned whale].

IN COMPOUNDS

❑ **flag-day** *n.* [1960s] (*US campus*) the menstrual period.

IN PHRASES

❑ **flag is up, the** (*also* **danger signal is up, flag is in port, the flag is out**) [late 19C+] used of a woman who is menstruating. ❑ **fly a flag** *v.* [1990s+] **1** (*US prison*) to betray one's personality, esp. in a situation, e.g. prison, where such honesty may be foolish. **2** (*US black teen*) to wear gang colours. ❑ **have the flags out** *v.* (*also* **put the flags out**) [20C+] of a woman, to be menstruating. ❑ **have the flag up** *v.* [1980s] (*drugs*) to have the needle in a vein. ❑ **one's flag is at half-mast** *see* *THE BARN DOOR IS OPEN under* BARN *n.*[2].

SE in slang uses

IN COMPOUNDS

❑ **flag-flapper** *n.* [late 19C+] one whose noisy patriotism is surpassed only by the care with which they ensure their ineligibility for active service. ❑ **flagpole** *n.* [2000s] (*S.Afr.*) an erect penis. ❑ **flag-spot** *n.* (*also* **flag stop**) [SE *flag down*] [1930s–40s] (*US black*) a bus stop. ❑ **flag-wagger** *n.* (*also* **flag-waver**) [note jazz use *flagwaver*, 'a spectacular piece of music or part of a musical performance intended to excite the listeners and win their applause' (Gold, *A Jazz Lexicon*, 1964)] **1** [late 19C+] an overt and excessive patriot, esp. as found during the Anglo-Boer Wars. **2** [1920s+] (*US*) a song, film or oration which arouses patriotic fervour.

IN PHRASES

❑ **flag of defiance is out, the** [the aggressiveness that so often accompanies heavy drinking] [late 17C–early 19C] used of someone who is drunk. ❑ **flag of distress** *n. see* separate entry. ❑ **flag the banner** *v. see under* BANNER *n.* ❑ **fly a flag** *v. see* FLAG *v.*[2] (3). ❑ **put up the flag** *n.* [ety. unknown] [1900s] (*US*) a plate of macaroni.

flag *n.*[3] [? one waves it or misreading of FAG *n.*[4] (2)] [1960s] a cigarette.

flag *n.*[4] [initial letter] [1980s] (*US campus*) the grade of F (fail).

flag *n.*[5] [SE *flagstone*] [1990s+] (*US Und.*) the bottom row of cells in a prison block.

SE in slang uses

IN COMPOUNDS

❑ **flag-about** *n.* [she walks on *flag*stones or ? waves her fig. flag to attract customers] [mid-19C] a street-walking prostitute. ❑ **flag-hopper** *n.* [she 'hops' along the *flag*stones/pavement] [mid-19C] a street prostitute; thus adj. *flaghopping*.

flag *v.*[1] **1** [late 19C–1950s] (*gay*) to attract a stranger with the eyes or with a slight gesture of the head. **2** [late 19C+] (*US*) to signal an interest in someone in anticipation of romantic or sexual involvement; to accost; thus as n. the gesture that signifies attraction. **3** [late 19C+] (*US*) to allow someone to pass by, esp. the intended victim of a pickpocket, to avoid. **4** [late 19C+] to refuse service to in a bar, to stop someone drinking; often as *flagging*, refusing service. **5** [20C+] (*US tramp*) to reject, to turn someone away. **6** [1900s–60s] to attract someone's attention. **7** [1910s] to stop doing something, to be quiet. **8** [1920s] (*US tramp*) to beg. **9** [1930s] to leave.

flag *v.*[2] [? SE *wave the white flag*, to surrender + initial letters] **1** [1920s] (*US Und.*) to release from custody. **2** [1920s–60s] (*US Und.*) to arrest. **3** [1950s+] (*US campus*) (*also* **fly a flag**) to fail a test or examination; thus to get a grade F in an examination. **4** [1990s+] (*US campus*) to fail to attend a class. **5** [2000s] (*N.Z.*) (*also* **flag away**) to give something up, to abandon.

flagg *n. see* FLAG *n.*[1].

flagger *n.* [SE *flag*, a paving stone, upon which she walks; + ? her *showing the flag*/FLAG-ABOUT *under* FLAG *n.*[5]] [mid-19C] a street prostitute.

flagging *n.*[1] [FLAG *n.*[2] (3)] [1930s] (*US*) menstruation.

flagging *n.*[2] [1990s+] (*US gay*) wearing a handkerchief, in a back trouser pocket, to indicate a sexual preference.

(IN PHRASES)

❑ **flaggin', saggin' and braggin'** [such activities are often spec. prohibited in prisons in the (vain) hope of minimizing inter-gang tensions] [1990s+] (*US black gang*) a phr. describing the means of identifying oneself as a member of a gang, esp. in prison; spec. wearing the gang colours, wearing one's trousers low on the hips and boasting about one's exploits in the free world.

flaggings *n.* [? the *flagging down* by the tramp of a passing citizen, in the hope of getting a hand-out] [20C+] (*orig. US tramp*) meat or any other foodstuff, usu. cold.

flaggot *n.* [*fl*aming f*aggot*] [1990s+] (*US gay*) an overt and ostentatious effeminate gay man.

flag of distress *n.* [mid–late 19C] **1** an advertisement or similar statement of charges for board and lodging. **2** thus a generic term for poverty. **3** the end of a person's shirt protruding through a hole in their trousers.

(IN PHRASES)

❑ **hang out the flag of distress** *v.* [mid–late 19C] **1** to advertise charges for board and lodging. **2** to be in poverty. **3** to have one's shirt hanging out. **4** to live in furnished accommodation. **5** to be a street prostitute.

flagon-wagon *n.* [1960s+] (*N.Z.*) a beer truck.

flag unfurled *n.* [rhy. sl.] [mid–late 19C] a man of the world.

flah *n.* (*also* **fla, flaa**) [FLAH *v.*] [1990s+] (*Irish*) a sexually attractive/active young person, usu. a woman.

flah *v.* (*also* **fla, flaa**) [Irish *fleadh*, a party (pron. 'flah')] [1990s+] (*Irish*) to have sexual intercourse.

flahoola *n.* [Irish] [late 19C–1900s] (*Irish*) a fat, noisy, extremely vulgar woman.

flail *v.* [SE *fluster* + *fail*; SE *flail*, to act energetically but without direction] [1980s+] (*US campus*) to fail a test through being flustered or over-pressured.

flailing *adj.* [SE *flail*/FLAIL *v.*] [1990s+] very intoxicated, usu. with marijuana.

flak *n.* (*also* **flack**) [SE *flak*, anti-aircraft fire, ult. the initials of the elements of Ger. *fliegerabwehrkanone* 'pilot-defence-gun'] (*orig. US*) **1** [1930s+] (*also* **flak-artist, flak merchant**) a publicity man/woman, a press agent [apparently f. Gene *Flack*, a contemporary US publicist for films]. **2** [1940s] interference, annoyance, problems. **3** [1960s+] cheek, negative criticism, verbal attacks. **4** [1970s+] publicity material.

(IN COMPOUNDS)

❑ **flak catcher** *n.* [1970s+] a civil servant or similar figure in private industry whose task is to intercept complaints, queries etc from the public, before such problems reach their superiors.

(IN PHRASES)

❑ **catch flak** *v.* (*also* **catch flack, get flack/flak**) [1960s+] (*US*) to receive criticism, to face verbal attacks.

flake *n.*[1] [SE *flake*, a thin broad piece peeled or split off from the surface of something] **1** [1920s+] (*drugs*) cocaine, spec. pieces that are smaller than average. **2** [1950s] (*drugs*) heroin. **3** [1970s+] (*drugs*) in pl., phencyclidine. **4** [1980s] (*drugs*) crack cocaine. **5** [1980s] (*Aus.*) shark meat, esp. as sold in fish 'n' chip shops.

flake *n.*[2] [FLAKY *adj.*] **1** [1950s+] (*orig. US*) (*also* **flakeout, flako**) a boring, unappealing, incompetent, undesirable person. **2** [1950s+] (*US*) an eccentric, crazy person. **3** [1960s+] (*US*) a disappointment or failure. **4** [1990s+] a worthless or second-rate type.

flake *n.*[3] [FLAKE *v.*[2]] [1980s] (*US Und.*) planted evidence.

flake *v.*[1] [mid-19C+] (*Aus./Irish*) to beat, to thrash.

flake *v.*[2] [FLAKE *n.*[2] (1), i.e. to act in that way] [1970s+] (*US Und.*) of police, to plant evidence; thus n. *flake*, planted evidence.

flake *v.*[3] **1** *see* FLAKE OFF *v.* (4). **2** *see* FLAKE (OUT) *v.*

flaked out *adj.* [? SE *flag*, to grow weak, to become exhausted, or US commercial fishing jargon *on the flakes*, dead, laid out for burial; this refers to the laying out of split fish on wooden racks or *flakes*] **1** [1940s+] (*orig. US*) exhausted, unconscious, asleep, lying down, resting. **2** [1950s] (*US campus*) drunk.

flake off *v.* **1** [1950s+] (*US campus*) to depart, to go away; to leave someone in peace; also as imper. **2** [1960s] (*US campus*) to irritate. **3** [1970s] (*US black*) to break off one's line of thought. **4** [1990s+] (*US*) (*also* **flake**) to back down in an argument or fight.

flakeout *n.* [FLAKE (OUT) *v.* (1)] **1** [1970s] (*US*) a person who has collapsed from exhaustion, drink or drugs. **2** *see* FLAKE *n.*[2] (1).

flake (out) *v.* [for ety. *see* FLAKED OUT *adj.*] **1** [1940s+] to collapse, from exhaustion, or an excess of drink or drugs. **2** [1940s+] (*US*) to recline or lie down, to sleep. **3** [1950s+] to go mad. **4** [1960s] (*US*) to die. **5** [1970s+] (*US campus*) to astound. **6** [1980s+] to fail, to let down. **7** [1980s+] (*US campus*) to fail to keep an appointment or other commitment; usu. as *flake out on*.

(IN PHRASES)

❑ **on flake** [1970s–80s] (*US black*) passed out, unconscious, esp. as a result of drug-taking.

flaker *n.* [1910s] (*Aus.*) a fall; a crash.

flakers *adj.* [FLAKE (OUT) *v.* (1) + -ER *sfx*] [1950s+] (*orig. naut.*) collapsed drunk.

flakey *adj. see* FLAKY *adj.*

flako *n. see* FLAKE *n.*[2] (1).

flako *adj.* [FLAKED OUT *adj.*] **1** [1950s+] drunk. **2** *see* FLAKY *adj.*

flaky *adj.* (*also* **flakey, flako**) [orig. baseball use. 'It's an insider's word...It does not mean anything so crude as "crazy", but it's well beyond "screwball" and far off to the side of "eccentric"' *New York Times*, 26 April 1964; ? SE *fall/crumble into flakes*, i.e. to come apart] [1960s+] (*orig. US*) **1** of a person, second-rate, unreliable, distasteful, eccentric, crazy. **2** of an object, eccentric, crazy, outrageous, unusual, unreliable or erratic.

flam *n.*[1] [FLAM *v.*; but note FLIM-FLAM *n.* (1) + Scot. *flamfew*, a trifle, a trinket] [late 17C–1910s] **1** a lie, a deception. **2** an idle tale, a piece of nonsense.

flam *n.*[2] [? FAMBLE *n.* (2)] [mid-19C] a ring.

flam *v.* [SE *flam*, to deceive by a sham story or trick or by flattery] **1** [17C–19C; 1980s+] (*also* **flam off**) to hoodwink, to deceive. **2** [mid-19C] (*US campus*) to be attentive to a woman. **3** [1900s] (*US campus*) to fail. **4** [1970s] (*US*) to flirt with or be aggressively forceful towards someone.

flam-blam *n. see* FLIM-FLAM *n.* (1).

flamboast *v.* [FLAM *v.* + SE *boast*] [1990s+] (*US teen*) to show off or flaunt material items.

flamdoodle *see under* FLAPDOODLE.

flame *n.* **1** [18C] venereal disease; thus *flaming*, diseased. **2** [mid-18C+] a (female) lover; the (male) object of much romantic adoration. **3** [early 19C] a redhead. **4** [1930s] (*US*) an infatuation. **5** *see* FLAMER *n.*[1] (4).

(IN COMPOUNDS)

❑ **flame artist/thrower** *n. see* FLAMER *n.*[1] (4).

flame *v.*[1] **1** [late 18C] to spend extravagantly. **2** [1940s+] to rant in an unacceptable manner, esp. to insult a specific individual, via a communications network, e.g. the Internet. **3** [1950s+] to talk nonsense about an otherwise interesting subject. **4** [1960s] (*US campus*) to be sexually aroused, to flirt, esp. when drunk. **5** [1960s] to exaggerate, to bore.

flame *v.*[2] (*also* **flame it up**) [FLAMER *n.*[1] (4)] [1960s+] **1** (*US gay/campus*) of a man (whether actually homosexual or not), to look exaggeratedly 'feminine' in dress and style; thus *flaming*, acting in an obviously homosexual manner. **2** (*US gay*) to wear make-up.

flame! *excl.* (*also* **flames! flaming hell!**) [1910s+] a general excl.

flame cooking *n.* [1980s+] (*drugs*) smoking freebase cocaine by placing the pipe over the gas burner of a domestic stove.

flamer *n.*[1] [they all fig. 'burn brightly'] **1** [late 17C+] an admirer, a lover, a promiscuous woman. **2** [early–mid-19C] a conspicuous, ostentatious person who 'burns brightly'. **3** [late 19C; 1960s–70s] an enthusiast; a success with the female sex, a ladies' man. **4** [1940s+] (*US*) (*also* **flame, flame artist, flame thrower**) a blatantly homosexual man; also attrib [underpinned by abbr. of *flaming faggot*].

flamer *n.*[2] **1** [early 19C] a redhead. **2** [late 19C] a safety match burning with notably bright flame. **3** [1990s+] (*US black*) a gun.

flamer *n.*[3] [such blunders mean that one 'goes down in flames'] (*US campus*) **1** [1930s+] a clumsy, embarrassing or highly unpleasant person. **2** [1960s+] anyone who commits a major social error; thus the error itself.

flames! *excl. see* FLAME! *excl.*

flaming *n.* [FLAME *v.*[1] (2)] **1** [1950s+] speaking incessantly and obsessively on a particular topic of little interest to anyone but oneself. **2** [1980s+] using computer 'bulletin boards' and other communications links to circulate obscene messages, pictures etc.

flaming *adj.*[1] [SE *flaming*, burning brightly] **1** [mid-18C–19C; 1990s+] excessively noticeable, flagrant, monstrous. **2** [1960s+] (*US gay*) ostentatiously homosexual; thus comb. as *flaming faggot*, *flaming queen*. **3** [1990s+] (*US campus*) sexy. **4** [2000s] (*Irish*) drunk.

SE in slang uses

IN COMPOUNDS

❑ **flaming fury** *n.* [1960s+] (*Aus.*) an outside lavatory, the contents of which were periodically burned off.

flaming *adj.*[2] [synon. SE *hellish* or euph. FUCKING *adj.* (1)] (*orig. Aus.*) **1** [late 19C+] a mild pej. **2** [1940s+] as a congratulatory epithet. **3** [1960s+] as infix.

flaming hell! *excl. see* FLAME! *excl.*

flanderkin *n.* [proper name *Flanders* + sfx *-kin*] [late 17C–early 19C] a notably fat man or horse.

Flanders *n.* used in combs. stereotyping the Dutch as mean, hypocritical or deceitful.

IN COMPOUNDS

❑ **Flanders fortune** *n.* [late 17C–18C] a relatively small fortune or inheritance. ❑ **Flanders piece** *n.* [late 17C–18C] a painting that looks good from a distance but not so good close to. ❑ **Flanders reckoning** *n.* [early 17C] spending money in a place that has no links to the place where one received the money.

flange *n.* [SE *flange*, that which stands out from the surface, esp. a collar] **1** [1960s+] the head of the penis. **2** [1990s+] (*orig. US*) the vagina.

flangehead *n.* [derog. use of SE] [1930s–60s] a derog. term for an East Asian; as a nickname.

flank *v.* [SE *flank*, to go around the side] [mid–late 19C] (*US, orig. milit.*) **1** to dodge, to evade. **2** to trick out of.

flankard *n.* [hunting jargon *flankard*, a wound in a deer's flank or side] [16C–17C] a venereal sore.

flanker *n.* [FLANK *v.*/SE *flank*, to go around the side; note WW1 milit. *flanker*, a shirker] **1** [mid-19C–1900s] a blow or punch. **2** [mid-19C–1900s] a verbal response. **3** [1920s+] (*orig. milit.*) a trick, a swindle, a hoax; thus *do/pull/work a flanker*, to trick, to swindle.

flankey *n.* [SE *flank*, 'the fleshy or muscular part of the side of an animal or a man between the ribs and the hip' (*OED*)] [mid-19C] (*UK Und.*) the buttocks.

flannel *n.*[1] [SE *flannel*, a form of woollen cloth; the drink 'keeps one warm'] [early–mid-19C] grog, punch or gin-twist, with a dash of beer.

SE in slang uses

IN COMPOUNDS

❑ **flannel-jacket** *n.* (*also* **flannel back**) [late 19C] a navvy, who wears such a garment.

flannel *n.*[2] [? 19C tradesmen's jargon *flannel*, the ornate, scroll-ridden letterheads with which tradesmen garlanded the invoices they sent to their aristocratic clients. There is no proof, however, that this is linked to the 20C use, albeit a similar one] [20C+] rubbish, nonsense, albeit plausible rubbish.

flannel *v.* [FLANNEL *n.*[2]] [1940s+] to flatter, to curry favour, to talk nonsense in a soothing, plausible manner, esp. for the purposes of charming a woman one wishes to seduce.

flannel mouth *n.* (*also* **flannel face**) [FLANNEL-MOUTHED *adj.*; senses 2–4 are considered derog] **1** [late 19C–1960s] (*US*) an Irishman. **2** [late 19C+] (*US*) a loudmouth, a braggart, one who talks too much and with too little sense; also as term of address. **3** [20C+] (*Can.*) a well-spoken person. **4** [1940s] (*US*) a Pole.

flannel-mouthed *adj.* (*also* **flannel-tongued**) [predates FLANNEL *n.*[2]; note SAmE *flannelmouth*, a very large catfish] (*orig. US*) **1** [late 19C] having a large mouth. **2** [late 19C+] loud-mouthed. **3** [1930s] talking thickly or with a brogue [the idea of talking with a SE *flannel* in one's mouth].

flap *n.*[1] **1** [early 17C] a cap. **2** [mid-17C; 1910s+] a promiscuous woman; a prostitute. **3** [late 18C–1920s] any garment that has a pendant flap or flaps. **4** [late 19C] (*UK Und.*) strips of lead used on roofs. **5** [late 19C–1910s] the vagina. **6** [late 19C+] (*also* **hearing flap, side-flap**) an ear, usu. large. **7** [late 19C+] in pl., the labia majora. **8** [1950s+] (*US*) the mouth. **9** [1950s+] (*Aus.*) a cheque.

IN COMPOUNDS

❑ **flap-cap** *n.* [early 18C] a whore. ❑ **flap shot** *n.* [SE *shot*, a picture] [1970s+] in pornographic still or moving pictures, a close-up shot of the labia and open vagina. ❑ **flap snot** *n.* [SNOT *n.*[1] (5)] [1990s+] vaginal secretions. ❑ **flaptabs** *n.* [TAB *n.*[1]] [1950s+] the ears. ❑ **flap-trap** *n.* [ext. TRAP *n.*[1] (4)] [1940s] (*US*) the mouth.

IN PHRASES

❑ **flap for sore eyes** *n. see* SIGHT FOR SORE EYES *under* SIGHT *n.*[1].

SE in slang uses

IN PHRASES

❑ **chuck a flap** *v. see* FLAP *v.*[1].

flap *n.*[2] [abbr. FLAPDOODLE *n.*[2]] [1950s–60s] (*US*) nonsense, rubbish.

flap *v.*[1] (*also* **chuck a flap**) [? SE *flop*] [mid-17C–mid-19C] to fall or throw oneself down suddenly; to throw down.

flap *v.*[2] [late 19C] to rob, to swindle; thus *flap the dimmock*, to pay (money).

IN PHRASES

❑ **flap a jay** *v.* [JAY *n.*[1] (4)] [late 19C+] (*UK Und.*) to trick a simpleton, to swindle an innocent victim.

flap *v.*[3] [FLAP *n.*[1] (5)] [late 19C] of a man, to have sexual intercourse.

flap *v.*[4] [SE *flap*, to fuss, to panic] **1** [1910s] to chatter. **2** [1970s+] (*US gay*) to act in an exaggeratedly effeminate manner.

SE in slang uses

IN PHRASES

❑ **flap at the jibs** *v. see under* JIB *n.*[1]. ❑ **flap like a dunny door in a high wind** *v. see under* DUNNY *n.*[2]. ❑ **flap one's chops** *v. see under* CHOPS *n.*[1]. ❑ **flap one's ears** *v.* [1920s+] (*US*) to listen (hard). ❑ **flap one's horns** *v.* [1960s] (*US black*) to listen. ❑ **flap one's jaw** *v. see under* JAW *n.* ❑ **flap one's mouth** *v.* (*also* **flap one's lips, ...tongue**) [now mainly W.I. use] [1910s+] to chatter, to say more than is sensible or proper.

flapdash *adj.* [? confusion of the two parts of *slapdash*, assuming the imagery to be of dusting] [1910s–20s] very clean, shiny.

flapdoodle *n.*[1] [SE *flap*, something hanging down + DOODLE *n.*[2] (1) although this predates] **1** [17C] the penis. **2** [late 19C] the vagina. **3** [late 19C] a sexually incompetent man, either one who is still too young to have had sex or one who is now too old to attempt it.

flapdoodle *n.*[2] (*also* **doodleflap, flamdoodle**) [ety. unknown; the image is of flapping lips] **1** [mid-19C+] nonsense, rubbish; thus *flapdoodler*, a charlatan, a politician, a speaker of portentous but empty words; also as v. **2** [20C+] (*US black*) mischief, malicious behaviour. **3** [1920s] (*US*) any thing. **4** [1950s] a fuss, an uproar.

flapdoodle *adj.* (*also* **flamdoodle**) [FLAPDOODLE *n.*[2] (1)] [late 19C+] absurd, nonsensical.

flapdragon *n.* [imagery drawn on SE *flapdragon/snapdragon*, a game 'in which they catch raisins out of burning brandy and, extinguishing them by closing the mouth, eat them' (Johnson, *Dictionary*, 1755)] **1** [17C] a derog. term for a German or Dutchman [supposes an image of the German or Dutchman as all display but no substance and as races that, for all their external show, can be 'eaten up' by an Englishman]. **2** [late 17C–early 19C] venereal disease [the 'heat' affects the penis].

flapjack *n.* [1940s+] (*Aus.*) a powder compact.

flapjaw *n.* [SE *flap* + *jaw*] **1** [1950s–60s] (*US*) a noisy talker, a braggart; one who talks too much. **2** [2000s] verbosity; also attrib.

flapper *n.*[1] **1** [17C] the (flaccid) penis. **2** [19C] an impotent old man. **3** [19C] the hand. **4** [late 19C] in pl., the labia majora. **5** [late 19C] in pl., exaggeratedly long, pointed shoes. **6** [1930s] (*tramp*) in pl., the boards carried by a 'sandwich-man'. **7** [1930s–40s] in pl., the arms. **8** [1930s+] (*US*) in pl., the ears. **9** [1940s+] (*US black*) the mouth; thus in pl. the lips.

IN COMPOUNDS

❑ **flapper-shaker** *n.* [19C] the hand; thus *flapper-shaking*, hand-shaking. ❑ **flapper steaks** *n.* [1940s] (*US black*) pigs' ears (eaten as a 'soul food' dish).

flapper *n.*[2] [various etys. have been offered, each of which may have some claim to accuracy: the Northumbrian dial. *flap*, an unsteady young woman; SE *flapper*, a young wild duck or partridge (which flaps its wings as it experiments with flying); SE *flap*, to act in an emotional manner, supposedly typical of such young women] **1** [late 19C–1910s] a very young prostitute (usu. in her early teens). **2** [late 19C+] (*orig. US*) (*also* **flapp**) a flighty girl or young woman, usu. middle-class, in her late teens or very early 20s, who sported short, bobbed hair, lipstick and skimpy dresses and generally led a lifestyle as far as possible removed from that desired by her parents; thus *flapper-seat*, a seat at the back of a bicycle to accommodate a young woman; *flapper vote*, a contemptuous expression for the parliamentary vote, which was granted to women over 21 years in 1928 (the over-30s having been enfranchised in 1918).

IN COMPOUNDS

❑ **flapper bracket** *n.* [1920s] a motorcycle pillion. ❑ **flapper pirate** *n.* [1910s] (*Aus.*) a cardsharper.

flapping *n.* (*also* **flappers**) [1910s+] any form of racing, e.g. horses or dogs, that is not subject to Jockey Club or National Hunt Committee regulations or, in greyhound racing, to those of the National Greyhound Racing Club.

IN COMPOUNDS

❑ **flapping track** *n.* (*also* **flapper**) [1910s+] a small, unlicensed racetrack for horses or dogs.

flare *v.* [mid-19C] **1** to swagger. **2** to behave excessively, thus in poor taste. **3** to steal by sleight of hand.

flare-up *n.*[1] (*also* **flare-out**) [mid-19C–1900s] **1** an argument, a fight. **2** a jovial social gathering. **3** one who seeks a good time. **4** one who is socially adept. **5** an orgy.

flare-up *n.*[2] [its flammability] [1900s–10s] brandy.

flare up *v.* [mid-19C+] to lose one's temper (suddenly), to speak forcefully.

flare up! *excl.* [coined at the burnings that accompanied Reform Riots of 1832, esp. in Bristol] [mid-19C] a cry of delight, triumph or defiance.

flash *n.*[1] **1** in senses of display, ostentation. (**a**) [17C] an ostentatious swindler, a loud-mouthed bully (**b**) [early 17C–mid-19C] a nouveau riche, ostentatious person. (**c**) [early 19C] fashion. (**d**) [mid-19C+] ostentation, showiness, vulgarity. (**e**) [1920s–50s] (*US Und.*) a suit of clothes. (**f**) [1920s+] (*Aus.*) one's personal appearance. **2** [late 17C–18C] a periwig; thus *rum flash*, a long, full, expensive wig; *queer flash*, an old, raggedy wig [? its being worn by an ostentatious person, i.e. sense 1b above]. **3** in the context of the criminal and/or sporting worlds. (**a**) [mid-18C+] cant or criminal slang. (**b**) [19C] a generic term for the criminal underworld. (**c**) [early 19C] sporting jargon. **4** with ref. to money or commodities (often counterfeit). (**a**) [mid-19C+] (*UK Und.*) a large bundle of notes, esp. when used in a game of three-card monte to entice victims; thus phr. *make a flash*, to exhibit a large bundle of notes. (**b**) [late 19C+] (*UK Und.*) imitation gold coins or banknotes. (**c**) [1920s+] (*UK/US Und.*) cheap but alluring items, e.g. cheap jewellery, used to lure players into carnival games, confidence tricks etc. (**d**) [1960s] anything counterfeit. (**e**) [1970s+] (*US gay*) cheap jewellery worn by homosexual males. **5** in senses of brevity. (**a**) [late 19C–1950s] (*orig. US*) a quick look around. (**b**) [20C+] (*orig. US*) a brief glimpse [initially a ref. to the conscious 'flashing' by striptease/burlesque artists]. (**c**) [1930s+] a brief glimpse when offered to a man by a woman inadvertently revealing her thighs, breasts or genitals; or vice versa, of a penis. (**d**) [1980s] a sign of flirtatious behaviour. **6** in senses of suddenness. (**a**) [late 19C–1970s] (*US*) a surprising piece of news or a rumour. (**b**) [1920s+] (*US*) a burst of inspiration, a sudden idea. (**c**) [1920s+] a flashback. **7** [1940s] a success. **8** in the context of drugs. (**a**) [1940s+] the instantaneous effect that follows the injection of a narcotic or other drug; also in non-drug use. (**b**) [1960s] a flashback to a previous psychotropic drug experience. (**c**) [1960s+] the effect of LSD. (**d**) [1970s+] LSD. **9** [1970s] a cigarette lighter. **10** [1970s] a general term of address.

IN PHRASES

❑ **cut a flash** *v.* [late 18C–mid-19C] to act in a vulgar manner, to show off. ❑ **cut the flash** *v.* [20C+] (*Aus.*) to show off, to be very well known or successful, to cut a 'fine figure'. ❑ **out of flash** [early 19C] in an attempt to show off; 'a person who affects any particular habit, as swearing, dressing...taking snuff..., merely to be taken notice of, is said to do it "out of flash"' (Vaux). ❑ **patter the flash** *v.* [19C] (*UK Und.*) to talk, usu. slang or underworld cant. ❑ **scoff the flash** *v.* [1960s] (*US Und.*) to consume or otherwise use anything that is being displayed as a lure in a confidence trick. ❑ **stam flash** *v.* (*also* **stam flesh, stamp-flash**) [? Ger. *stimmen*, to make one's voice heard, to sing] [late 17C–mid-19C] (*UK Und.*) to talk in thieves' cant.

SE in slang uses

IN COMPOUNDS

❑ **flash in the pan** *n.* see separate entries. ❑ **flash of light** *n.* **1** [late 19C] a gaudily dressed woman ['upon the model of a rainbow' (Ware)]. **2** [1970s+] a sight [rhy. sl.]. ❑ **flash of lightning** *n.* see *under* LIGHTNING *n.*

flash *n.*[2] [initial letter] [1960s] (*US campus*) the grade of F.

flash *adj.* **1** senses based on display, ostentation. (**a**) [mid-17C+] of a person or thing, ostentatious, showy. (**b**) [mid-19C] fashionable, smart, chic. (**c**) [1910s+] cheeky; arrogant, boastful. **2** in the context of the criminal and/or sporting worlds. (**a**) [late 17C+] belonging to or connected with the underworld. (**b**) [18C+] expert, understanding what someone else means, 'knowing the ropes', esp. of the underworld. (**c**) [early 19C–1910s] belonging to, connected with or resembling the world of 'sportsmen', esp. the patrons of the prize-fight 'ring'. **3** [19C–1900s] (*UK Und.*) counterfeit; thus *flash note*, a counterfeit banknote. **4** [mid-19C] amoral, promiscuous.

based on ostentation, display

DERIVATIVES

❑ **flashness** *n.* [mid–late 19C] ostentation, showing-off.

IN COMPOUNDS

❑ **flash girl** *n.* [late 19C] a showy dresser. ❑ **flash harry** *n.* [generic *Harry*; best known as the nickname of the conductor Sir Malcolm Sargeant (1895–1967) and as the SPIV *n.* character played by George Cole (b.1925) in the 'St Trinian's' films in the 1950s] [1910s+] an ostentatious, loudly dressed and usu. ill-mannered man. ❑ **flash jack** *n.* [generic *Jack*] [late 19C–1960s] (*Aus.*) a dandy, a swell, esp. in the context of a sheep station; thus *flash jane*, a showy woman. ❑ **flashman** *n.* see separate entry. ❑ **flash piece** *n.* [1990s+] a promiscuous young woman. ❑ **flash sport** *n.* [SPORT *n.* (2)] [1950s] (*US black*) a notably stylish man. ❑ **flash toggery** *n.* (*also* **flash togs**) [TOGGERY *n.* (1)/TOGS *n.* (1)] [mid–late 19C] smart clothes. ❑ **flash yad** *n.* [mid-19C–1900s] a pleasant day out.

IN PHRASES

❑ **flash as a rat with a gold tooth** *adj.* (*also* **flash as a chinky's horse, flash as a Chow on a red bike**) [20C+] (*Aus.*) extremely ostentatious. ❑ **flash up** *v.* (*US*) **1** [late 19C] to produce, to hand over. **2** [1930s] of a woman, to dress showily, to use an excess of cosmetics. **3** [1980s] to act in an exhibitionist manner. ❑ **half-flash and half-foolish** [early 19C] (*UK Und.*) one who exists on the fringes of the underworld and pretends to a far greater involvement than they actually have. ❑ **quarter flash and three parts stupid** (*also* **quarter flash and three parts foolish**) [early 19C] a phr. describing a fool who claims to have a small degree of fashionable worldliness.

based on criminality

IN COMPOUNDS

❑ **flash blowen** *n.* (*also* **flash blone**) [BLOWEN *n.* (1)/BLONE *n.*] [mid-19C] (*UK Und.*) a dishonest woman; spec. a receiver of stolen goods. ❑ **flash boy** *n.* [late 19C] (*UK Und.*) a swindler. ❑ **flash cane** *n. see* FLASH KEN below. ❑ **flash captain** *n.* [CAPTAIN *n.* (5)] [mid-18C] a thug employed by a casino to ensure order. ❑ **flash case** *n.* **1** [early 18C–19C] (*also* **flash crib**) a public house frequented mainly by criminals [CASE *n.*[3] (1)/CRIB *n.*[1] (3)]. **2** [1930s+] (*US black*) a satchel or bag that contains illegal drugs or any other contraband [SE *case*]. ❑ **flash chant** *n.* (*also* **flash chaunt**) [CHANT *n.* (1)] [early 19C] a song filled with criminal slang. ❑ **flash chap** *n. see* FLASHMAN *n.* (3). ❑ **flash cove** *n.* (*also* **flash covess**) [COVE *n.* (1)/COVESS *n.*] [19C] **1** a thief. **2** a landlord or landlady, esp. of a criminal public house. **3** a receiver of stolen goods. ❑ **flash cracker** *n.* (*also* **flash burster**) [despite link, appears to predate use of CRACKER *n.*[7]] [late 18C] (*UK Und.*) a burglar. ❑ **flash cull** *n.* [CULL *n.*[1] (3)] [early 18C] (*UK Und.*) one who enjoys the society of the underworld. ❑ **flash dona** *n.* [DONA *n.* (1)] [late 19C] a showy, working-class woman. ❑ **flash dough** *n.* [DOUGH *n.* (1)] [1940s] (*US Und.*) counterfeit money, used in a confidence trick. ❑ **flash drum** *n.* [DRUM *n.*[3]] [mid-19C] **1** a criminal lodging house; a tavern frequented by thieves. **2** a brothel. ❑ **flash gentry** *n.* [18C–19C] thieves as a group. ❑ **flash girl** *n.* (*also* **flash hen, flash madam**) [late 18C–19C] a prostitute. ❑ **flash house** *n.* [SE *house*/HOUSE *n.*[1] (1)] **1** [mid-18C–19C] a public house frequented mainly by the underworld. **2** [mid-19C–1920s] a brothel. ❑ **flash-Jack** *n.* [JACK *n.*[9] (1)] [mid-19C] (*UK Und.*) a woman with connections to the underworld. ❑ **flash ken** *n.* [KEN *n.*[1] (1)] **1** [late 17C–19C] (*also* **flash cane, ...kane**) a criminal lodging house. **2** [mid-19C–1940s] a brothel. ❑ **flash kiddy** *n.* [KIDDY *n.* (1)] [19C] a dandified young thief. ❑ **flash lady** *n.* [mid-19C] (*UK Und.*) a prostitute. ❑ **flash lingo** *n.* [late 18C–19C] the jargon of the criminal underworld. ❑ **flash madam** *n. see* FLASH GIRL above. ❑ **flashman** *n. see* separate entry. ❑ **flash mob** *n.* [MOB *n.*[2] (3)] [1940s] (*US Und.*) a gang of thieves or confidence tricksters. ❑ **flash moll** *n.* [MOLL *n.* (3)] [19C] a thief's female companion. ❑ **flash mollisher** *n.* [MOLLISHER *n.*] [early 19C] a female criminal or habitué of the underworld; a prostitute. ❑ **flash notes** *n.* (*also* **flash 'un**) [mid–late 19C] pieces of paper that at first glance look like banknotes; forged notes of any sort, e.g. licences, certificates. ❑ **flash panny** *n.* (*also* **flash panney**) [PANNEY *n.*[2] (1)] **1** [early 19C] a public house used primarily by criminals. **2** [mid-19C] a brothel. ❑ **flash roll** *n.* (*also* **flash money**) [ROLL *n.* (2)] [1940s+] a sum of money that is revealed as proof that a person, esp. a narcotics dealer or other criminal, is willing to do business; the money is 'flashed' before the client. ❑ **flash screen** *n.* see SCREEN *n.*[1] (2). ❑ **flash song** *n.* [early 19C] a song filled with criminal slang. ❑ **flashtail** *n.* [TAIL *n.* (6)] **1** [19C] a prostitute; esp. one seeking wealthy customers who will be robbed by her pimp. **2** [1970s+] (*US black*) any prostitute. ❑ **flash 'un** *n. see* FLASH NOTES above. ❑ **flash woman** *n.* [19C] a prostitute.

IN PHRASES

❑ **on the flash lay** [LAY *n.*[3] (1)] [mid-19C] (*UK Und.*) involved in some form of criminality. ❑ **put flash to** *v.* [19C] (*UK Und.*) to inform, to put on guard, to pass on information.

flash *v.*[1] [FLASH *adj.* (1a)] **1** [mid-18C+] to 'cut a figure', to show off, usu. one's material possessions and gross self-esteem. **2** [mid-18C+] to display, e.g. a gun; also in non-material use, e.g. to display an idea. **3** [mid-19C+] (*orig. US*) to expose a part of the body in a quick or provocative manner. **4** [late 19C+] to expose one's genitals, esp. in a public place. **5** [1920s–30s] (*US tramp*) to turn State's evidence. **6** [2000s] (*US teen*) to shout at, while others are watching.

IN PHRASES

❑ **flash...** *v. see also under* relevant n. ❑ **flash a bit** *v.* [mid–late 19C] of a woman, to behave immodestly. ❑ **flash it** *v.* (*also* **flash it about, ...away**) **1** [late 18C–mid-19C] to show off. **2** [mid-19C+] to reveal one's genitals. **3** [1960s+] to show off one's money or wealth in an ostentatious manner. ❑ **flash one's hand** *v.* [card-playing imagery] [1960s] (*US*) to let down one's guard; to reveal one's secrets, plans etc. ❑ **flash the ash** *v.* [20C+] to hand around one's pack of cigarettes. ❑ **flash the gallery** *v. see* FLASH THE RANGE *under* RANGE *n.* ❑ **flash the gnarl** *v.* (*also* **flash the narl**) [SE *gnarl*, a snarl] [early 19C] to complain aggressively, to take exception (to). ❑ **flash the hash** *v.* (*also* **flash one's hash, hash**) [SE *hash*, stew] [late 18C+] (*orig. UK Und.; 20C+ US*) to vomit. ❑ **flash the muzzle** *v.* [19C] to draw a pistol. ❑ **flash the tongue** *v.* [19C] to talk fast and, usu., meaninglessly.

flash *v.*[2] **1** [early 19C] (*UK Und.*) to buy and sell stolen property. **2** [1900s] (*US Und.*) to acquire through pickpocketing.

flash *v.*[3] [compounded by drug imagery] **1** [1920s+] to notice. **2** [1960s–70s] to amaze, to impress. **3** [1960s+] to realize, to think, usu. suddenly or spontaneously.

IN PHRASES

❑ **flash on** *v.* **1** [late 19C+] to have a sudden inspiration, memory, moment of absolute comprehension etc. **2** [1920s+] (*US*) to catch sight of.

flash *v.*[4] [SE phr. *quick as a flash*] [1950s+] (*UK black*) to rush, to run away.

IN PHRASES

❑ **flash off** *v.* [1990s+] (*W.I./Rasta*) to push away.

flash *v.*[5] [echoic; but note FLASH THE HASH *under* FLASH *v.*[1]] [1950s+] (*US campus*) to vomit.

flash *v.*[6] [FLASH *n.*[2]] [1960s] (*US campus*) to do badly in a test or examination.

flash *v.*[7] [1960s+] (*US*) to experience the effects of taking a drug, esp. hallucinatory.

flash *adv.* [FLASH *adj.* (1)] [1950s+] boastfully, arrogantly, in a showing-off manner.

flashback *n.* [1970s+] (*drugs*) the repetition after the event, typically without the presence of any drug, of the emotions, sensations or hallucinations of a previous LSD experience.

flashed-up *adj.* [FLASH *adj.* (1)] [20C+] dressed up in one's best clothes.

flasher *n.*[1] [FLASH *v.*[1]] **1** [18C] one who lures players into a corrupt casino, by stressing how often the bank there has been broken. **2** [late 19C; 1960s+] an exhibitionist.

flasher *n.*[2] [FLASH *v.*[1] (1)] [20C+] (*US*) a spendthrift, one who shops ostentatiously.

flashes *n.* [1910s–30s] used as an intensifier, e.g *swearing flashes, cursing flashes.*

flashing *n.* [FLASH *v.*[1] (4)] [1960s+] indecent exposure.

flash in the pan *n.* [SE phr. *flash in the pan*, an explosion of gunpowder without any communication beyond the touch-hole, thus the gun fails to fire] **1** [late 17C–18C; 1980s+] sex without ejaculation. **2** [18C+] an incompetent, useless person. **3** [18C+] an abortive effort or outburst.

flash in the pan *v.* [FLASH IN THE PAN *n.*] **1** [18C–mid-19C] to be incompetent. **2** [mid-19C] to have sex without ejaculation.

flashly *adv.* [FLASH *adj.*] [early–mid-19C] **1** in an ostentatious, showy manner. **2** using the language of the criminal underworld.

flashman *n.* [FLASH *adj.* + SE *man*] **1** [late 18C] a highwayman; a robber. **2** [late 18C] a thug employed by a brothel to deal with undesirables and drunks. **3** [late 18C–mid-19C] (*also* **flash chap**) a pimp. **4** [late 18C–19C] anyone conversant with the criminal world and thus its vocabulary. **5** [mid-19C] (*US*) a man-about-town, a loafer with no visible means of support but an endless appetite for good clothes, parties and places of entertainment; such a man lived by his wits and often off foolish women. **6** [mid-19C] an intinerant hawker.

flashy *adj.* [FLASH *adj.* (2)] [late 18C+] pertaining to the sporting and criminal worlds.

flashy blade *n.* (*also* **flashy fop, ...spark**) [FLASH *adj.* (1a) + BLADE *n.* (2a)/SE *spark*, a dandy] [18C–19C] a dandy.

flat *n.*[1] **1** [mid-16C–18C; 1930s] (*UK Und.*) a type of false die, in which one side is fractionally shorter than the others. **2** [late 18C–19C] in pl., counterfeit coinage. **3** [late 18C+] in pl., playing cards. **4** [late 19C] (*Aus.*) a third-rate painting. **5** [1900s–40s] (*US black*) five cents, a nickel. **6** [1940s+] a *flat* tyre. **7** [1950s] (*US drugs*) a thin packet of heroin. **8** [1970s+] a plastic credit card.

flat *n.*[2] **1** [mid-18C+] a peasant, a rustic and, as such, considered a fool or innocent; antonym of SHARP *n.*[1]; thus (*UK Und.*) *it's a good flat that's never down*, even the most naïve of dupes must realize what's happening eventually. **2** [mid-19C] ext. of sense 1 above, a prostitute's customer. **3** [late 19C–1900s] (*also* **flatite**) ext. as a common person, one who is not a member of an elite, i.e. a minor criminal.

IN COMPOUNDS

❑ **flat-catcher/-catching** *see* separate entries.

IN PHRASES

❑ **brush up a flat** *v.* [mid-19C] to flatter a gullible person. ❑ **prime flat** *n.* [PRIME *adj.*] [early 19C] (*UK Und.*) an extremely susceptible person, the ideal victim for a confidence trickster. ❑ **strike a flat** *v.* [mid-19C] (*US*) to encounter a gullible victim.

flat *n.*[3] [FLAT *v.*] [mid-19C] (*US*) a rejection.

IN PHRASES

❑ **give someone the flat** *v.* [mid-19C] (*US*) to turn down a suitor.

flat *n.*[4] *see* FLATFOOT *n.* (3).

flat *adj.*[1] [opposite of SHARP *adj.* (1)] [early 17C; late 18C–mid-19C] naïve, unsophisticated.

IN COMPOUNDS

❑ **flat fish** *n.* (*also* **regular flat fish**) [FISH *n.*[1] (3); or ? just a simple joc. use of SE] **1** [late 18C–1900s] a fool, a dullard. **2** [19C] a beggar's or confidence trickster's prey.

flat *adj.*[2] [abbr. *flat broke*; SE *flat*, completely + BROKE *adj.*[1] (1)] [mid-19C+] without any money.

flat *adj.*[3] [SE *flat*/FLAT OUT *adj.*[2] (1)] [20C+] **1** emotionally crippled. **2** exhausted, worn out.

SE in slang uses

IN COMPOUNDS

❑ **flat-back** *n.* [mid-19C] a bedbug. ❑ **flatback/-backer/-backing** *see* separate entries. ❑ **flat bit** *n. see* BIT *n.*[1]. ❑ **flat blues** *n.* [packaging] [1970s+] (*drugs*) LSD. ❑ **flat-cap** *n. see* separate entry. ❑ **flat-car** *n.* [1920s–30s] (*US tramp*) a pancake. ❑ **flat-car tourist** *n.* [late 19C–1900s] (*US*) an itinerant who travels in freight-cars. ❑ **flat chicken** *n.* [? the taste, the consistency, the look] [late 19C] stewed tripe. ❑ **flat-cock/-cocking** *see* separate entries. ❑ **flat dog** *n.* [1960s–70s] (*US prison*) bologna sausage. ❑ **flatfoot/-footed** *see* separate entries. ❑ **flatfuck** *see* separate entries. ❑ **flathead(ed)** *see* separate entries. ❑ **flatheel** *n. see* FLATFOOT *n.* (3). ❑ **flat joint** *n.* [SE *flat* + JOINT *n.* (3b); the flat surface that is vital to the playing of the sort of games, e.g. three-card monte, the shell game, featured at such places] [20C+] (*US Und.*) a crooked gambling game or casino; orig. fair/carnival use, when a flat was a crooked or doctored 'wheel of fortune'; also as v. ❑ **flatline** *v. see* separate entry. ❑ **flat-move** *n.* [SE *flat*, i.e. lifeless, disappointing + MOVE *n.* (2)] [early 19C] (*orig. UK Und.*) any plan – criminal or otherwise – that fails. ❑ **flat top** *n.* **1** [1950s+] a style of haircut. **2** [1960s] a style of hat. ❑ **flat tyre** *n.* (*also* **flat tire**) [1920s–60s] **1** (*US campus*) an unattractive young woman. **2** (*US*) a woman who has been thrown over by a lover; a prostitute who has been rejected by her pimp. **3** (*orig. US black*) a disappointment, an illusion. **4** (*US*) a failure, an inadequate. **5** (*US*) an impotent man. ❑ **flat-stick** *adv.* (*also* **flat stick, ...strap, ...tack, ...tap**) [1970s+] (*Aus./N.Z.*) at top speed, at the limit of one's abilities or resources. ❑ **flat tack** *adv. see* FLAT AS A TACK *phr.*[1]. ❑ **flat-wheel(er)** *see* separate entries. ❑ **flat-wig** *v.* [2000s] (*US prison*) to knock down violently.

IN PHRASES

❑ **flat as a tack** *adj. see* separate entry. ❑ **flat as a witch's tit** *adj.* [1970s] (*Aus.*) of beer, very flat. ❑ **flat on one's ass** *adj.* (*also* **flat on one's can, flat on the dead-end**) [ASS *n.* (2)/CAN *n.*[1] (1)] [1940s+] (*US*) out of work, without money.

flat *v.* [SE *turn down flat* / a *flat refusal*] [19C] (*US*) to reject a suitor.

flat *adv.*

SE, meaning completely, utterly, in slang uses

IN COMPOUNDS

❑ **flat broke** *adj. see* separate entry. ❑ **flat out** *see* separate entries.

flat as a tack *phr.*[1] (*also* **flat tack**) [SE *flat*, i.e. with the car's accelerator pressed to the floor] [1950s+] (*Aus./N.Z.*) at full speed.

flat as a tack *phr.*[2] [FLAT *adj.*[3] (1)] [1960s+] (*Aus.*) very depressed.

flatback *n.* [2000s] (*US*) **1** an act of conventional heterosexual intercourse, usu. as offered by a prostitute, who lays 'flat on her back'. **2** a promiscuous woman; a prostitute.

flatback *v.* [1950s+] (*US*) **1** to work as a prostitute, the image is a whore working from a given place, rather than walking the streets. **2** to have sex in the missionary position.

flatbacker *n.* [FLATBACK *v.* (1); she does no more than lie *flat on her back*] [1960s+] (*US black pimp*) a prostitute, esp. one who specializes in quantity rather than quality; also an honest prostitute (i.e. who delivers the promised sex and neither tricks nor robs her client).

flatbacking *n.* [the trad. 'missionary position'] [1960s+] (*US black*) working as a prostitute.

flat broke *adj.* (*also* **flat**) [SE *flat*, completely, utterly + BROKE *adj.*[1] (1)] [mid-19C] totally impoverished.

flat-cap *n.* [the headgear; thus Jonson, *Every Man in his Humour* (1598): 'Mock me all over From my flat-cap unto my shining shoes'; or Dekker, *Honest Whore* (1630): 'Flat caps as proper are to Citty Gownes / As to armour helmets, or to kings their Crownes'] **1** [late 16C–early 18C] a citizen of London; thus a tradesman. **2** [late 17C–early 18C] a Billingsgate fishwife.

flat-catcher *n.*[1] [FLAT *n.*[2] (1) + SE *catcher*] **1** [19C] anything that will serve to dupe the public. **2** [19C+] (*also* **catcher**) a confidence trickster, one who indulges in 'sharp practice'.

flat-catcher *n.*[2] [it is always caught and passed *in the flat*] [mid-19C–1920s] a horse that looks good but fails to win races.

flat-catching *n.* [FLAT-CATCHER *n.*[1] (2)] [19C–1910s] confidence trickery, fraud.

flatch *n.* (*also* **flach**) [backsl.] [mid-19C+] **1** a half. **2** a halfpenny.

flatch *adj.* [backsl.] [mid–late 19C] half, usu. in comb. below.

IN COMPOUNDS

❑ **flatch-enorc/-yennork/-ynork** *n. see* HALF-YENNORK *under* YENORK *n.* ❑ **flatch-kennurd** *adj.* [KENNURD *adj.*; lit. 'half-drunk'] [mid–late 19C] tipsy, mildly drunk. ❑ **flatch yenep** *n.* (*also* **flatch yennep, flatch yennop**) [YENNEP *n.*] [mid-19C] a halfpenny.

flat-cock *n.* [the anatomical difference] [late 18C–19C] a woman.

IN PHRASES

❑ **play at flatcock** *v.* [late 19C] of two lesbians, to enjoy intercourse by rubbing one's genital areas together.

flat-cocking *n.* (*also* **flat cocks**) [FLAT-COCK *n.*] [late 19C] of two women, rubbing their bodies together for sexual stimulation.

flatfoot *n.* [all refer to marching or to walking in menial jobs] **1** [mid-19C] a sailor. **2** [mid-19C–1940s] an infantryman. **3** [mid-19C+] (*also* **flat, flat heel**) a police officer, a (private) detective. **4** [late 19C] (*US*) a man who stands firmly for one political party, come what may. **5** [1910s–20s] a person who has flat feet. **6** [1920s] (*US*) a fool. **7** [1960s] (*US*) an Irish immigrant.

flatfoot *v.*[1] [FLATFOOT *n.* (3)] [1920s+] (*US*) to walk like a police officer.

flatfoot *v.*[2] [? after drinking one slaps the glass *flat* on the table or bar] [1960s] (*US*) to down a glass of liquor in one gulp.

flat-footed *adj.*[1] [early 19C+] downright, positive, undeviating, straightforward.

flat-footed *adj.*[2] [SE *flat*, complete, utter + pun on SE] [mid-19C] (*US*) destitute, penniless.

flat-footed *adj.*[3] [sporting imagery] [20C+] (*US*) **1** of food, plain, devoid of any further cooking or mixing. **2** insipid, maladroit. **3** unprepared, caught unawares; thus *catch flat-footed*, to catch unawares.

flat-footed *adj.*[4] [FLATFOOT *n.* (3)] [1920s–30s] used to describe a police officer.

flat fuck *n.* [FLAT FUCK *v.*] [1980s+] (*gay*) sexual relations between two women, rubbing their bodies together.

flat fuck *v.* [SE *flat* + FUCK *v.* (1)] [late 19C; 1960s+] of lesbians, to rub their bodies together for sexual stimulation.

flathead *n.*[1] [all uses are derog.] **1** [late 18C+] a foolish, stupid person. **2** [1910s] (*US prison*) a police officer. **3** [1930s–40s] a Lithuanian. **4** [1950s] a Jew. **5** [1960s] an inhabitant of the Illinois-Ohio lowlands. **6** [1960s] a German settler in Dakota or Wisconsin.

flathead *n.*[2] [1980s] (*US drugs*) a barbiturate as sold by a dealer (rather than by a pharmacy).

flatheaded *adj.* [FLATHEAD *n.*[1] (1)] [20C+] foolish, stupid.

flatite *n.* [SE *flat* + sfx *-ite*, connected with or belonging to] **1** [1940s+] (*Aus.*) a flat-dweller. **2** *see* FLAT *n.*[2] (3).

flatline *v.* (*also* **catch a flatline**) [the flattening of the electronic line on the medical equipment, indicating that the patient's heart has stopped] [1980s+] (*US*) **1** of a person, to die. **2** of an inanimate object, to fail, to collapse.

flat out *adj.*[1] [late 19C+] straightforward, unadorned, blunt, esp. of speech.

flat out *adj.*[2] [1910s+] (*orig. Aus.*) **1** exhausted. **2** busy. **3** hard put.

flat-out *adv.* [1940s+] (*US*) **1** completely, utterly, totally. **2** openly.

(IN PHRASES)

❑ **come flat out with** [1940s+] (*orig. US*) to state unequivocally, to make one's point without hesitation.

flats *n.*[1] [mid-17C–18C] lesbian sexual intercourse.

flats *n.*[2] [1920s–30s] (*US tramp*) griddlecakes or pancakes.

flats *n.*[3] [19C SE *flat*, a floor or storey in a house] [1950s+] (*US Und.*) the bottom row of cells in a prison block.

(IN PHRASES)

❑ **walk the flats** *v.* [1950s+] (*US prison*) to clean the area outside the cells.

flats and sharps *n.* [late 18C–early 19C] edged weapons.

flatten *v.* [late 19C+] **1** to get the better of. **2** (*also* **flatten out**) to knock down. **3** fig. use of sense 2 above, to defeat. **4** to kill, to murder.

flattener *n.* [late 19C] **1** a hard blow. **2** in fig. use, something defeating.

flatter *n.* [FLATFOOT *n.* (3)] [late 19C] a police officer.

flatter-trap *n.* [SE *flatter* + TRAP *n.*[1] (4)] [mid-19C] the mouth, esp. that of a sycophant or toady.

flattie *n.*[1] (*also* **flatty**) [FLAT *n.*[2] (1)] [mid–late 19C] a dupe, a naïve countryman.

(IN COMPOUNDS)

❑ **flatty-cop** *n.* [COP *n.*[1] (1)] [mid-19C] (*UK Und.*) a policeman who lacks sophistication in dealing with the underworld; a country policeman. ❑ **flatty-ken** *n.* [KEN *n.*[1] (1)] [mid-19C] a public house that is frequented by members of the underworld but where the landlord remains oblivious of their activities.

flattie *n.*[2] (*also* **flatty**) [abbr.] **1** [mid-19C+] a small, flat-bottomed sailing boat. **2** [1980s+] (*N.Z.*) a *flat* tyre.

flattie *n.*[3] (*also* **flatty**) [abbr. FLATFOOT *n.* (3)] **1** [late 19C+] a police officer. **2** [1920s] (*US tramp*) a railroad police officer.

flattie *n.*[4] [2000s] (*N.Z.*) a flat-dweller.

flattie *n.*[5] [SE phr. *in a flat spin*] [2000s] (*N.Z.*) a state of confusion.

flattie *adj.* (*also* **flatty**) [FLATTIE *n.*[1] (1)] [mid-19C] (*UK Und.*) gullible, naïve.

flat time *n. see* FLAT BIT *under* BIT *n.*[1].

flatty *see also under* FLATTIE.

flatty *n.* [he operates a *flat store* or *flat-joint*, any kind of carnival or circus concession designed to fleece the public] [1950s+] (*US*) a confidence trickster; a crooked carnival game operator.

flatty-gory *n.* [FLAT *n.*[1] (2)/ FLATTIE *n.*[1] (1) + GOREE *n.*] [early 19C] **1** a counterfeit coin. **2** the potential victim of a confidence trickster.

flat-wheel *n.* [railroad jargon *flat wheel*, a car wheel that has worn flat spots on its tread and thus rolls slightly askew] (*US*) **1** [1920s] a dull, boring person. **2** [1930s–50s] one who walks with a limp.

flat-wheel *v.* [FLAT-WHEEL *n.*] [1950s] of a person or object, to fail.

flat-wheeler *n.* [FLAT-WHEEL *n.* (1)] [1920s] (*US*) one who is mean or impoverished.

flat worker *n.* [SE *flat* + WORKER *n.*[1] (1)] [1900s–70s] (*US Und.*) a burglar.

flava *n.* [deliberate mis-sp. of FLAVOR *n.* (2)] [1990s+] (*orig. US black*) style.

flave *adj.* [FLAVA *n.*] [1990s+] (*US black*) stylish.

flavor *n.* [abbr. colloq. *flavor of the month*] **1** [1980s+] (*US drugs*) top quality cocaine. **2** [1990s+] (*US black*) style. **3** [1990s+] (*US black*) attractiveness; thus an attractive young woman. **4** [2000s] (*US prison*) a branded cigarette.

flaw *v.* [late 17C–early 18C] to make drunk.

flawed *adj.* **1** [mid-17C–19C] drunk. **2** [mid-19C] (*US*) bad-tempered. **3** [mid-19C] (*US*) not wholly honest (but not actually criminal). **4** [late 19C] of a woman, deflowered but still unmarried.

flaxation! *excl.* [ety. unknown; ? link to *flax*, humbug, which is cited with an 1857 use in Thornton, *American Gloss.* (1912), and there labelled as 'rarely met with'] [late 19C] (*US*) a euph. version of *damnation!*

flaxie *n.* [abbr.] [1910s–20s] (*N.Z.*) a *flax*-cutter.

flaxstick *n.* [New Zealand's cultivation of flax] [1900s] (*Aus.*) a derog. term for a New Zealander.

flaybottomist *n.* (*also* **flaybottom**) [late 18C–19C] a schoolmaster.

flay the fox *v.* (*also* **flea the fox**) [lit. trans. of Fr. sl. *écorcher le renard*] [mid-17C–early 19C] to vomit.

flea *n.*

SE in slang uses

(IN COMPOUNDS)

❑ **fleabag** *see* separate entries. ❑ **flea-bed** *n. see* FLEABAG *n.* (3). ❑ **fleabox** *n.* [1930s–40s] a cheap hotel or lodging house. ❑ **flea-catcher** *n.* [early 19C] a tailor. ❑ **flea circus** *n.* [1920s+] (*Aus.*) a cheap, tawdry, run-down cinema. ❑ **flea house** *n. see* FLEAPIT *n.* (3). ❑ **flea joint/palace** *n. see* FLEAPIT *n.* (1). ❑ **flea-park** *n. see* FLEABAG *n.* (1). ❑ **fleapit** *n. see* separate entry. ❑ **flea powder** *n.* [1950s+] (*drugs*) second-rate or poor quality drugs. ❑ **flea powder habit** *n.* [*FLEA POWDER* above + HABIT *n.* (1)] [1950s] (*drugs*) a low-level narcotics addiction or an addiction to weak heroin. ❑ **flea taxi** *n.* [1980s] (*N.Z.*) a sheepdog pup. ❑ **flea track** *n.* [2000s] (*N.Z.*) the parting in one's hair. ❑ **flea trap** *n.* **1** [1930s] (*US*) a bed. **2** [1930s+] (*US*) an ageing, ill dog. **3** [1940s+] a cheap and dirty hotel.

flea and louse *n.* [rhy. sl.] [mid-19C; 1930s+] a house, esp. a house with a bad reputation.

fleabag *n.* [c.1910 there was an actual *Fleabag* in New York City, a cheap saloon at 241 Bowery; note WW1 Aus. milit. *fleabag*, an officer's valise] **1** [late 18C+] (*orig. milit.*) (*also* **flea-park**) a sleeping bag or bed; a bedroll, a mattress. **2** [20C+] a cheap hotel or lodging house. **3** [20C+] (*US*) (*also* **flea-bed**) an ageing, ill dog. **4** [1930s+] (*US*) an old, worn-out prostitute who is forced to seek equally run-down clients, often on Skid Row, in cheap hotels etc. **5** [1940s+] a general pej. **6** [1950s+] (*US black*) a troublesome, difficult person who tends, like fleas, to follow around and irritate the individual who has been made subject to their woes. **7** [2000s] a smelly person, usu. a tramp, a vagrant.

fleabag *adj.* [FLEABAG *n.*] **1** [1950s+] (*US*) of a hotel, or anything, cheap, run-down, second-rate. **2** [1980s] of an animal, mangy.

fleapit *n.* **1** [20C+] (*also* **flea joint, ...palace**) a cheap, tawdry, run-down hotel, motel or club, or any place. **2** [1910s] a (run-down) flat. **3** [1930s+] (*also* **fleahouse**) a cheap, tawdry, run-down cinema; also attrib.

fleas and ants *n.* [rhy. sl.] [1930s–50s] (*US*) pants, trousers.

fleas and itches *n.* (*also* **flies and itchers**) [rhy. sl. = SE *pictures*] [1940s+] (*Aus.*) the cinema; also occas. paintings.

fleas and scratches *n.* [rhy. sl.] [20C+] (*Aus.*) matches.

flea the fox *v. see* FLAY THE FOX *v.*

flee *n.* [FLEA POWDER *under* FLEA *n.*] [1970s] (*drugs*) second-rate narcotics.

fleece *n.*[1] [Williams offers examples of synon. plays on *golden fleece*] **1** [mid-19C] hair of the head. **2** [late 19C] a generic term for women as sex objects; esp. in *fleece-hunter*, *fleece-monger*, a womanizer. **3** [late 19C+] pubic hair of either sex.

fleece *n.*[2] [? FLEE *n.* (1) or SE *fleece*, to cheat] [2000s] (*US black*) second-rate drugs.

fleecer *n.* [SE *fleece*, to plunder, to rob heartlessly, to victimize] [20C+] a confidence trickster.

fleecy-claiming *n.* [late 19C] sheep-stealing.

Fleet *n.* [abbr.] [1990s+] (*US black*) a *Fleet*wood Cadillac.

fleet *adj.* [? the *Fleet* Prison] [early 19C] counterfeit.

Fleet-ditch *n.* [the Fleet prison was situated on the banks of the Fleet Ditch in London (now covered over as Farringdon St)] [late 18C] the Fleet prison (*fl.* *c.*1170–1842).

fleet of blows *n.* (*also* **fleet of licks**) [20C+] (*W.I., Guyn./Trin.*) a painful thrashing.

Fleet Street dove *n.* (*also* **Fleet Street houri**) [proper name *Fleet Street*, London EC4, the late 19C–1980s centre of London journalism, also celebrated for its population of prostitutes + SE *dove/houri*, a nymph of the Muslim paradise, thus a beautiful woman; note T. Brown, *Amusements Serious & Comical*, (1707): 'A country client pick'd up by a Fleet street stroller at nine'] [19C] a prostitute.

Fleet-Streeter *n.* [*Fleet-Street* 'the estate of journalism, especially journalism of the baser sort' (F&H)] [late 19C] 'a journalist of the baser sort, a spunging prophet; a sharking dramatic critic; a spicy paragraphist; and so on' (F&H); thus *Fleet-Streetese*, 'the so-called English, written to sell by the Fleet-Streeter, a mixture of sesquipedelians and slang, of phrases worn threadbare and phrases sprung from the kennel; of bad grammar and worse manners; the like of which is impossible outside Fleet Street, but which in Fleet Street commands a price, and enables not a few to live' (F&H).

fleggy *n.* [SE *phlegm*] [1970s+] (*UK juv.*) a gob of spit.

Flemington confetti *n.* [? *Flemington* racecourse, covered in torn-up betting slips etc at the end of a major meeting; or *Flemington* saleyards in Sydney and Melbourne] [1920s+] (*Aus.*) rubbish, nonsense, 'tripe'.

Flemington races *n.* [rhy. sl.; ult. *see* prev.] [1920s+] (*Aus.*) braces.

Flemish account *n.* [successor to FLANDERS RECKONING *under* FLANDERS *n.*; the Flemish *livre* or pound was worth only 12 rather than 20 shillings; the main implication, however, is of the grasping stereotype attributed to any native of the Low Countries] [late 17C–mid-19C] a badly prepared account or books that do not balance.

Flemo *n.* [abbr. + -O *sfx* (3)] [20C+] (*Aus.*) the suburb of *Flem*ington, northwest of Melbourne.

flesh *n.*

SE in slang uses

(IN COMPOUNDS)

□ **flesh-and-blood** *n.* [a loose approx. of the colours of the drinks] [mid–late 19C] a drink composed of equal measures of port and brandy. □ **fleshbag** *n.* [late 18C–19C] a shirt. □ **flesh-broker** *n.* [17C–mid-19C] a madame, a procuress; a match-maker. □ **flesh-dresser** *n.* [SE *flesh-dresser*, a butcher] [17C] an official who punishes prostitutes with flogging. □ **flesh-fly** *n.* **1** [mid-16C–mid-17C] a lecher, a womanizer. **2** [early 17C] a prostitute. **3** [early–mid-17C] a madame, a bawd; occas. a pander. □ **flesh hooks** *n.* [mid-16C–early 17C] the hands. □ **flesh hound** *n.* [-HOUND *sfx*] [1980s] (*US black*) an obsessive womanizer. □ **flesh market** *n.* **1** [mid-18C–early 19C] any street or urban area, e.g. Cheapside, the Strand, Covent Garden, that is home to parading prostitutes. **2** [mid-19C] a brothel. □ **fleshpot** *n.* **1** [late 19C] the vagina. **2** [1910s+] a brothel. **3** [1930s+] (*US black*) a woman, viewed strictly (and thus offensively) as a sex object. □ **flesh-presser** *n.* **1** [1920s+] (*orig. US*) a politician who attempts to curry favour with the voters by shaking as many hands, kissing as many babies and patting as many backs as possible during a campaign. **2** [2000s] (*US*) a porn star. □ **flesh shambles** *n.* [SE *shambles*, a slaughterhouse] [early 17C] a brothel. □ **flesh tailor** *n.* [mid-17C] a surgeon.

(IN PHRASES)

□ **flesh (it)** *v.* (*also* **flesh one's will**) [SE *flesh*, to plunge one's weapon into flesh, to gratify one's lusts] [late 16C–early 17C; 1990s+] of a man, to have sexual intercourse; modern use is by both sexes. □ **give some flesh** *n.* [20C+] (*W.I.*) ritual palm slapping that forms greeting between blacks, or between blacks and knowledgeable whites.

flesh! *excl.* (*also* **flesh and eels! flesh and fire! flesh and nouns!**) [abbr. of SE *God's flesh/? eyes/wounds*] [late 17C–early 18C] a blasphemous excl.

flewzie *n. see* FLOOZY *n.*

flex *n.* [FLEX *v.*] [1990s+] **1** (*US black*) guts, courage, integrity, energy. **2** (*W.I./UK black teen*) a person's mannerism, idiosyncrasies etc.

flex *v.* [SE *flex one's muscles*] [1980s+] **1** (*US prison*) to get emotionally prepared for a (gang) fight. **2** (*US black*) to make others aware of one's potential for violence and willingness to use it; thus *on the flex*, acting in an excessively macho manner in the hope of impressing onlookers. **3** (*US black*) to show off generally. **4** (*US teen*) to hit, to intimidate someone. **5** (*UK black*) to go well, to work out. **6** (*UK black*) to scratch records, i.e. to move the record backwards and forwards so the needle scratches across the record, thus repeating or distorting a chosen section [in this case it is the wrist that is flexed]. **7** (*US black*) to rap well. **8** (*UK black*) to display, to show off.

(IN PHRASES)

□ **flex (one's sex)** *v.* [1990s+] (*US black teen*) to have an erection. □ **flex with** *v.* [1990s+] (*UK black*) to associate with.

flex *adv.* [1990s+] (*UK black*) quickly, at high speed.

flick *n.*[1] [the word orig. appeared as *afflicke* (albeit at F in the A–Z listing in Rowlands' *Martin-Mark-all*, 1610) and has always been assumed, by the *OED* and others, to have been a misprint of *a flick*. That said, it has no proven ety. and may indeed be one, equally incomprehensible word] [early 17C] a thief.

flick *n.*[2] [mid-19C–1930s] an amusing person; esp. as *old flick*.

flick *n.*[3] [abbr. SE *flick-knife*] **1** [1950s+] a knife with a spring-loaded blade. **2** [1980s] a razor blade with one side taped so that it can be held as a weapon.

SE in slang uses

(IN PHRASES)

□ **get the flick** *v.* [a dismissive flick of the fingers] [1980s] (*Aus.*) to be dismissed from one's job. □ **give it the flick** *v.* [1990s+]

(*Aus.*) to throw something away, to ignore. ▫ **give someone the flick** *v.* [1990s+] (*Aus./UK teen*) to reject someone, to end a relationship.

flick *adj.* [mid-19C] (*UK Und.*) **1** sly. **2** old-fashioned.

flick *v.*[1] [late 17C–mid-19C] (*UK Und.*) **1** to cut. **2** to cut off.

SE in slang uses

IN PHRASES

▫ **flick off** *see* separate entries. ▫ **flick one's/someone's bic** *v.* [brandname *Bic*, whose popular disposable lighter was orig. marketed with the slogan 'Flick your bic'] [1970s+] to stimulate the genitals with a hand (whether one's own or that of a partner). ▫ **flick one's wick** *v.* [the flicking of a cigarette lighter] [1950s] (*N.Z.*) to hurry up. ▫ **flick the bean** *v. see under* BEAN *n.*[1]. ▫ **flick the switch** *v.* [1980s+] (*Aus.*) of a woman, to masturbate. ▫ **flick the vee** *v.* (*also* **flick the vees, ...vick**) [1990s+] (*UK juv.*) to make the 'V-sign' gesture. ▫ **flick up** *v.* [2000s] (*US prison*) to take a photo.

flick *v.*[2] [1970s+] (*US black*) to fail deliberately to turn up for work or school.

flicker *n.*[1] [ety. unknown; ? one 'flicks' the contents down one's throat] [late 17C–mid-19C] (*UK Und.*) a glassful of alcohol; thus *rum flicker*, a large glass; *queer flicker*, an ordinary glass.

flicker *n.*[2] (*also* **flickers**) [FLICKER *v.*[2] (2)] [late 19C–1960s] (*US tramp*) a fainting fit, esp. if faked.

flicker *v.*[1] [? the SE *flick* of the tongue or fingers] [early 17C] to kiss or caress a woman.

flicker *v.*[2] **1** [late 17C–early 19C] to grin, to laugh in someone's face. **2** [late 19C–1960s] (*US tramp*) to faint or pretend to faint, to die.

flicker *v.*[3] [FLICKER *n.*[1]] [mid-19C] to drink.

flickerbox *n.* [1970s] (*Aus.*) television.

flickers *n. see* FLICKER *n.*[2].

flickertail *n.* [dial. *flickertail*, the ground squirrel, the state's best known native animal] [20C+] (*US*) a native of North Dakota.

flicking *adj.* [1940s+] a euph. for FUCKING *adj.*

flick-off *n.* [FLICK OFF *v.* (1)] [1950s+] an act of rejection, a snub.

flick off *v.* [a dismissive *flick* of the fingers] **1** [1950s+] to snub, to reject, to ignore. **2** *see* FLIP THE BIRD *under* BIRD *n.*[2].

flick (pass), the *n.* [rhy. sl.] [1980s+] (*Aus.*) dismissal.

flid *n.* [elision of *Thalid*(omide) as '*flid*omide'] [1990s+] **1** (*UK juv.*) a handicapped person, esp. one suffering the after-effects of Thalidomide, which drug, erroneously distributed to pregnant women in 1960s as a counter to morning sickness, caused widespread physical disabilities in the babies. **2** a general term of abuse.

flier *n.*[1] [they are always HIGH *adj.*[1] (2)] [1940s–50s] (*US drugs*) a drug addict.

flier *n.*[2] *see also under* FLYER.

flier *n.*[3] *see* HIGH-FLYER *n.*

Flies *n.* [1970s] (*UK Und.*) the Flying Squad.

flies and itchers *n. see* FLEAS AND ITCHES *n.*

flies' skating rink *n. see* SKATING RINK *n.*

flight *n.* [FLY *v.* (3)] [1950s] an experience of a drug.

flight deck *n.* [? nonce-word created by UK cartoonist Posy Simmonds for her raffish character Edmund Heap] [1980s] the female breasts.

flight of steps *n. see* DOORSTEP *n.*

flim *n.*[1] [FLIMSY *n.* (1)] **1** [mid-19C+] a £5 note. **2** [1940s–50s] a five-year prison sentence [fig. use of sense 1 above].

flim *n.*[2] [abbr. FLIM-FLAM *n.* (2)] [1910s+] a swindle, a fraud, a confidence trick.

flim *v.* [abbr. FLIM-FLAM *v.* (1)] [late 19C–1920s] to swindle, to defraud, to trick.

flim-flam *n.* [? ON *flim*, a lampoon; *flimska*, mockery] **1** [mid-16C+] (*also* **flam-blam**) an idle tale, a piece of nonsense. **2** [late 19C+] (*orig. US*) a confidence trick, a criminal hoax, orig. a short-change swindle. **3** [1900s–30s] (*US*) a deceptive, untrustworthy person. **4** [1990s+] (*US*) a confidence trickster; also attrib.

IN COMPOUNDS

▫ **flim-flam artist/man** *n. see* FLIM-FLAMMER *n.*

flim-flam *adj.* [FLIM-FLAM *n.* (1)] **1** [mid-17C; late 19C] nonsensical. **2** [1900s–50s] tricky, cheating.

flim-flam *v.* [FLIM-FLAM *n.*] **1** [late 19C+] (*US*) to perpetrate a confidence trick or hoax, orig. to practise a short-change swindle. **2** [1900s] to perform a task inadequately. **3** [1930s] (*US Und.*) to scold, to berate.

flim-flammer *n.* (*also* **flim-flam artist, flim-flam man**) [FLIM-FLAM *v.* (1)] [late 19C+] (*US*) a confidence trickster.

flimmer *n.* [FLIM *v.*] [late 19C] (*US campus*) a cheat.

flimp *v.* [western Flemish *flimpe*, to hit in the face; *flimping* is equivalent to two-man mugging, one person pushes the victim from behind, the other robs him] **1** [mid–late 19C] (*US Und.*) to wrestle. **2** [mid-19C–1900s] to steal, esp. watches, by snatching items from their owners (rather than carefully picking a pocket), often using violent means, e.g. garrotting. **3** [mid-19C+] to have sexual intercourse. **4** [1910s–50s] to swindle, to cheat.

IN PHRASES

▫ **put the flimp on** *v.* [mid-19C–1900s] to rob on the highway, to rob and garrotte.

flimper *n.* (*also* **flimp**) [FLIMP *v.* (2)] [mid–late 19C] a mugger or thief, esp. of watches, working in a team; one man grabs the victim from behind, while the *flimper* steals his watch.

flimping *n.* [FLIMP *v.* (2)] **1** [mid-19C] (*US Und.*) garrotting. **2** [mid-19C–1900s] stealing by snatching items, usu. watches, rather than carefully and surreptitiously removing them.

flimsy *n.* [the *flimsy* paper on which it is printed or written] **1** [early 19C+] a banknote, esp. a £5 note. **2** [mid-19C] (*US*) a $100 note. **3** [mid-19C] (*UK Und.*) a counterfeit banknote or cheque. **4** [mid-19C–1910s] multi-leaved copy paper used by journalists. **5** [late 19C] (*Aus.*) a cheque. **6** [1940s–70s] in pl., papers, a report.

flindereens *n. see* SMITHEREENS *n.*

fling *v.* [SE *fling*, i.e. to fling money out of] **1** [early 18C] to snatch. **2** [mid-18C–mid-19C] to get the better of, to cheat, to deceive; esp. as *fling out of*; *fling for*, to be caught out. **3** [1960s] to move, to walk.

SE in slang uses

IN COMPOUNDS

▫ **fling-down** *n.* [early 19C] (*Anglo-Irish*) a fight. ▫ **fling-dust** *n.* (*also* **fling-stink**) [the dirt or dust that she stirs on her walk] [17C] a street-walking prostitute.

IN PHRASES

▫ **fling it up** *v.* [1990s+] (*W.I.*) to behave in a wild manner, without restraints, usu. of dancing or sexual intercourse. ▫ **fling the hatchet** *v. see* THROW THE HATCHET *under* HATCHET *n.* ▫ **fling the house out of the windows** *v.* [early 17C] to make a great deal of noise or disturbance in one's house.

fling of a cow's tail *phr. see* TWO SHAKES OF A LAMB'S TAIL *phr.*

flink *v.* [? SE *flinch*, to slink off, to sneak away] (*US*) **1** [late 19C] to act like a coward, to shirk one's duties. **2** [1960s] to play truant from school. **3** [1970s+] (*UK gay*) of a male homosexual, to have a relationship with a woman in order to appear heterosexual.

flint *n.*[1] [the hardness of SE *flint*] [late 18C–mid-19C] a worker who refuses to accept anything but full, union-negotiated wages.

flint *n.*[2] [the flint that it contains] [1970s] (*US black*) a cigarette lighter.

flint *n.*[3] *see* SKINFLINT *n.*

Flip *n.* [abbr.] [1930s+] (*US*) a derog. name for a *Filipino*.

IN COMPOUNDS

▫ **Fliptown** *n.* [1950s] (*US*) Manila.

Flip *adj.* (*also* **flip**) [abbr.] [1950s] (*US*) Filipino.

flip *n.*[1] (*also* **phlip**) [SE *flip*, to whip up] [late 17C–19C] a mixture of beer and spirit sweetened with sugar and heated with a hot iron.

flip *n.*[2] [one 'flips' the recipient a coin] [late 19C+] a bribe or tip.

flip *n.*[3] **1** [late 19C+] a triviality, an irrelevance; a tiny amount. **2** [1910s+] an impudent, flippant, 'lightweight' person. **3** [1940s–60s] (*Aus.*) an act of sexual intercourse. **4** [1940s+] (*US*) an eccentric, a madman. **5** [1950s+] (*US*) a state of high excitement, delight or craziness, esp. as produced by drug use.

IN PHRASES

❑ **go flip** *v.* [1980s] (*US*) to lose control, to go mad.

flip *n.*[4] [SE *fillip*] [1910s+] a short trip, orig. in an aeroplane, but also in other forms of conveyance.

flip *n.*[5] [FLIP *v.*[4] (2a)] **1** [1960s] (*US Und.*) an informer. **2** [1970s+] (*US black*) a passive male homosexual.

flip *n.*[6] [euph. for FUCK *n.* (2a)] [1960s+] (*US*) a jot, an iota, nothing at all; thus *couldn't give a flip*.

flip *adj.*[1] [Devon dial. *flip*, glib, flippant] [1920s+] (*orig. US*) **1** nonchalant, unconcerned, in control. **2** exciting, excitable, eccentric, crazy.

flip *adj.*[2] *see* FLIP *adj.*

flip *v.*[1] [SE *flip*, to strike at sharply] **1** [19C] to shoot with a pistol or revolver. **2** [20C+] (*US*) to steal a ride, esp. on a freight train. **3** [1930s] (*US drugs*) to make another addict unconscious in order to steal their drugs. **4** [1940s] (*US black*) to reject someone.

flip *v.*[2] [SE *flip*, to give a flip with (the finger)] **1** [late 19C+] (*orig. Aus.*) to masturbate. **2** [1930s+] (*US*) to hand over, to give. **3** [1950s+] to make a sign, usu. in *FLIP THE BIRD under* BIRD *n.*[2]. **4** [1990s+] (*US black*) to make, to create, e.g. a marijuana cigarette, or a rap song.

IN PHRASES

❑ **flip off** *v. see* separate entries. ❑ **flip the bird** *v. see under* BIRD *n.*[2]. ❑ **flip the bishop** *v. see BANG THE BISHOP under* BISHOP *n.*[2].

flip *v.*[3] [abbr. *FLIP ONE'S WIG under* WIG *n.*[2]; and ext. uses] **1** [1950s] (*US drugs*) to become unconscious through an overdose of a drug. **2** [1950s+] (*orig. US*) (*also* **flit, pliff**) to lose control, to get over-excited or very worried; often ext. in phr. *flip one's cork/frijoles/noodle/raspberry/stack*. **3** [1950s+] to excite (sexually). **4** [1960s] to be sexually excited. **5** [1960s] to become drunk. **6** [2000s] (*US black*) to start an argument, to fight, esp. with an intimate.

IN PHRASES

❑ **flip for** *v.* [1950s+] (*orig. US*) to become fascinated, obsessed by. ❑ **flip off at the jibs** *v. see under* JIB *n.*[1]. ❑ **flip one's bananas** *v. see under* BANANAS *adj.* ❑ **flip one's bean** *v. see under* BEAN *n.*[1]. ❑ **flip one's cookies** *v. see under* COOKIE *n.*[1]. ❑ **flip one's cork** *v.* [1950s–60s] (*US*) to lose one's temper; to go mad. ❑ **flip one's gourd** *v. see BLOW ONE'S GOURD under* GOURD *n.* ❑ **flip one's lid** *v. see under* LID *n.* ❑ **flip one's top** *v.* [1940s–60s] (*US black*) to go crazy, to lose one's temper; thus *fliptop*, adj., crazy; as n., a crazy person. ❑ **flip one's wig** *v. see under* WIG *n.*[2]. ❑ **flip out** *see* separate entries.

flip *v.*[4] [SE *flip*, i.e. to turn someone over] **1** in the context of sexuality. (**a**) [1960s] (*US*) to 'come out' as a homosexual. (**b**) [1970s+] (*US gay*) to reverse one's primary sexual activity, i.e. for a masculine lesbian to turn 'femme' or a sadist to play masochist; thus adj. *flippy*, describing a homosexual who will take the active or passive role in intercourse. (**c**) [1990s+] (*US prison*) to convert a fellow inmate to homosexuality. **2** in the context of informing. (**a**) [1960s+] (*US Und.*) (*also* **flip on**) to inform (against). (**b**) [1980s+] to turn state's evidence. (**c**) [1990s+] to tell a story. (**d**) [2000s] to make someone into an informer.

SE in slang uses

IN PHRASES

❑ **flip a bitch** *v. see under* BITCH *n.*[1]. ❑ **flip a lip** *v.* (*also* **flip one's mouth**) [1930s–60s] (*US*) to speak, to talk to. ❑ **flip on** *v. see* sense 2a above. ❑ **flip over** *v.* [1960s+] (*gay*) to make oneself/a partner available for anal intercourse. ❑ **flip the scrip** *v.* [SE *script*] [1990s+] (*US black teen*) to change completely, to take an utterly fresh direction. ❑ **flip the switch** *v.* [1950s] to cease some activity; as imper.

flip *v.*[5] [2000s] (*US black*) to increase, e.g. money or stocks of drugs.

flip! *excl.* [20C+] a euph. for FUCK! *excl.* (1).

flip-flap *n.* **1** [mid-17C] the penis [it 'flaps' around]. **2** [18C] copulation. **3** [late 19C] a broad fringe of hair falling across the forehead, esp. as used by street boys [it 'flaps' around].

flip-flop *n.*[1] [SE *flip-flop*, a somersault/FLIP-FLOP *v.*] **1** [20C+] (*US prison*) an individual who first gains parole and then returns to the same prison after breaking the terms of that parole or committing a new crime. **2** [1960s+] mutual oral-genital stimulation. **3** [1970s] (*also* **flippy**) a homosexual who takes either the active or passive role in sex. **4** [1990s+] (*US campus*) a bisexual.

flip-flop *n.*[2] [the non-protective footwear worn by Albanians on Saudi construction sites] [2000s] an Albanian.

flipflop *n.* [1910s–20s] (*US*) a trick, a gimmick.

flip-flop *v.* (*also* **turn flip-flops**) [SE *flip-flop*, to turn over, in this case for anal sex] **1** [1960s+] (*US prison*) to indulge in gay sex. **2** [1970s+] to change direction. **3** [1990s+] (*US prison*) of a male homosexual, to take either the active or passive role in intercourse. **4** [1990s+] (*US prison*) to practise bisexuality.

flip off *v.*[1] [ext. FLIP *v.*[2] (1)] [1930s+] to masturbate.

IN PHRASES

❑ **flip oneself off** *v.* [1930s+] (*Aus.*) to masturbate.

flip off *v.*[2] *see FLIP THE BIRD under* BIRD *n.*[2].

flip off! *excl.* [euph. FUCK OFF! *excl.* (1)] [1950s+] go away!

flip-out *n.* [FLIP OUT *v.*] [1960s+] (*US*) **1** an eccentric, a madman. **2** a crazy, uncontrolled reaction to a drug or a situation.

flip out *v.* [FLIP *v.*[3] (2)] [1960s+] (*orig. US*) **1** to lose emotional control, to go mad. **2** to be intoxicated. **3** to be overjoyed. **4** to amaze someone, to delight. **5** to cause someone emotional problems.

flipped-out *adj.* (*also* **flipped**) [FLIP OUT *v.*] (*orig. US*) **1** [1940s+] crazy, over-reacting; fascinated. **2** [1990s+] intoxicated with drink or drugs.

flipper *n.*[1] [reverse anthropomorphism] **1** [late 18C–1910s] (*US*) a leg. **2** [19C+] the hand or arm. **3** [mid-19C] (*UK Und.*) a whip. **4** [1900s–40s] (*US black*) an ear.

flipper *n.*[2] [SE *flip*; one flips it over in the pan] [mid-19C+] (*Aus./US*) a pancake.

flipper *n.*[3] **1** [late 19C–1910s] (*orig. US*) a very young prostitute. **2** [1920s] (*US*) a male FLAPPER *n.*[2] (2). **3** [1950s] a euph. for FUCKER *n.* (3). **4** [1960s] a friend; in general, a man. **5** [1980s] (*Aus.*) a fool.

flipper *n.*[4] [? he 'flips' things around/SE *flippant*] **1** [20C+] (*Irish*) a messy, untidy man. **2** [1980s] (*US campus*) an impulsive person.

flipper *n.*[5] [FLIP *v.*[1] (2)] [1930s] (*US tramp*) a tramp who rides the railroads, rather than travels by road.

flipping *adj.* **1** [1910s+] a euph. for FUCKING *adj.* (1); esp. in *flipping heck!* fucking hell! **2** [1960s+] (*US campus*) splendid.

flippy *n. see* FLIP-FLOP *n.*[1] (3).

flippy *adj.* [FLIP *n.*[3] (2)/FLIP *n.*[3] (4)] **1** [1920s] (*US*) flippant, insignificant. **2** [1950s–70s] crazy, eccentric.

flipside *n.* [rock music use, the 'other side' of a record, the B-side] **1** [1960s+] the reverse, the alternative. **2** [1980s+] (*US gay*) the anus; the buttocks [the man 'flips over' to offer his anus for sex].

IN PHRASES

❑ **on the flipside** [1960s+] on the other side, on the reverse, 'on the other hand'.

flipside *adj.* [i.e. the FLIPSIDE *n.* (1) of respectable society] [1990s+] (*US*) pertaining to the world of criminality.

flipwreck *n.* [FLIP *v.*[2] (1); pun on SE *shipwreck*] [1910s+] (*Aus.*) **1** a person who has (supposedly) masturbated themselves into physical and mental decline. **2** a fool, an idiot.

flirt *n.* (*also* **flurt**) [SE *flirt*] [late 16C–17C] a prostitute.

IN COMPOUNDS

❑ **flirt-gill** *n.* [SE *gill*, a lass, a wench] [late 16C–early 18C] a prostitute; a promiscuous woman (cf. GILL-FLIRT *n.*).

flirtina cop-all *n.* [play on SE *flirt* + fem. sfx *-ina* + COP *v.* (1c) + SE *all*] [mid–late 19C] a woman, esp. when considered 'too fond of men' (B&L).

flit *n.*[1] [brandname *Flit*, an insect repellent spray] [1920s+] (*US prison*) prison-made coffee.

flit *n.*[2] [SE *flit*, a flutter, a light movement; the stereotypical effeminacy of male homosexuals] [1930s+] (*US*) **1** (*also* **flitty**) a male homosexual. **2** a foolish person.

flit *n.*[3] [SE *flit*, a sudden movement] [1940s+] (*US*) drunkenness.

flit *n.*[4] *see* MOONLIGHT FLIT *n.*

flit *v.*[1] [FLIT *n.*[2] (1)] [1980s+] to be a homosexual.

flit *v.*[2] *see* FLIP *v.*[3] (2).

flitter *n.* [dial. *flitter*, a pancake] [19C] (*US*) the vagina.

flitter *v.* [dial. *flitter*, to fluster] [mid-19C; 1920s+] (*Irish*) to reduce to rags and tatters, both lit. and fig., thus n. *flitters*, bits and pieces.

flitty *n.* *see* FLIT *n.*[2] (1).

flitty *adj.* (*also* **flitting**) [FLIT *n.*[2] (1)] [1930s+] effeminate.

flivver *n.* [ety. unknown; note US Navy 1920s use, 'a destroyer of 750 tons or less'] (*US*) **1** [1900s–60s] (*also* **fliv**) a failure, disappointment or something cheap and inferior. **2** [1910s] something or someone that has a negative influence on others. **3** [1910s+] (*also* **fliv, fliver**) a cheap automobile, spec. a Model T Ford.

IN COMPOUNDS

❑ **flivver tramp** *n.* [1930s] (*US tramp*) a tramp who travels in an old car.

flivver *v.* [FLIVVER *n.*] **1** [1910s–20s] to fail, to falter. **2** [1920s] of a car, to go fast.

Flo/flo *n.* *see* AUNT FLO *n.*

float *n.* [SE *float*, a sum of money in a shop used to provide change etc at the start of business] **1** [1950s] an error. **2** [1960s+] a small loan.

float *v.*[1] **1** [late 19C+] (*US*) to leave; also of objects, *do a float*. **2** [late 19C+] (*orig. US*) to wander around; to travel. **3** [1910s–60s] (*Aus.*) to die. **4** [1920s–60s] to eject, to send away. **5** [1930s–50s] to be drunk. **6** [1930s+] (*drugs*) to experience the 'other-worldliness' that can accompany the use of certain drugs, typically cannabis and the hallucinogens.

IN PHRASES

❑ **float around** *v.* [20C+] to wander aimlessly. ❑ **float up** *see* separate entries.

SE in slang uses

IN PHRASES

❑ **float an air biscuit** *v.* *see* AIR BISCUIT *n.* ❑ **float one's boat** *v.* [1980s+] to satisfy, to be to one's liking. ❑ **whatever floats your boat** [1980s+] (*US*) a general phr. of acquiescence: whatever you like, whatever 'turns you on'.

float *v.*[2] [FLOAT *n.* (2)] [1960s+] (*US campus*) to pay for, to lend money.

floater *n.*[1] **1** of inanimate objects. (**a**) [mid-19C–1910s] a suet dumpling. (**b**) [late 19C] the (flaccid) penis. (**c**) [late 19C+] (*orig. US*) a dead body found floating in water. (**d**) [1910s+] (*also* **pie floater**) (*Aus./N.Z.*) a meat pie floating in pea soup. (**e**) [1940s+] (*Aus./N.Z.*) (*also* **butterfly**) in two-up, a coin that fails to spin. (**f**) [1980s] (*US Und.*) a stolen gun which is used in various crimes by different criminals. (**g**) [1980s+] a large piece of excrement that cannot be flushed away. (**h**) [1990s+] (*N.Z.*) a fried scone. **2** in fig. uses, of humans. (**a**) [mid-19C+] (*Aus./US*) a wanderer; a person of no fixed occupation, living on their wits. (**b**) [late 19C+] (*US*) a migratory worker. (**c**) [1930s+] (*UK prison*) an old magazine, book or newspaper that is smuggled irregularly from cell to cell. (**d**) [1940s+] (*gay*) a homosexual prostitute who works only in towns where he is unknown and in which he does not live. (**e**) [1970s] a prisoner on a short-term sentence.

floater *n.*[2] [orig. Oxbridge use; ? corruption of Fr./SE *faux pas* as 'foper', thence 'floater'; SE *float*, to circulate a rumour] [1910s+] an error, a faux pas.

floater *n.*[3] [FLOAT *v.*[1] (1)] [1910s+] (*US*) **1** an official order to leave a town or district. **2** a sentence suspended on condition that the offender leaves the area.

floating academy *n.* [SE *floating* + ACADEMY *n.* (4); run-down or part-derelict ships, no longer seaworthy, were recycled as prison ships, moored in the Thames estuary] [late 18C–mid-19C] the prison hulks.

floating boat *n.* [? resemblance] [1950s] (*W.I.*) cooked breadfruit.

floating bullet *n.* [? resemblance] [1940s+] (*W.I.*) a large, spherical cooked breadfruit.

floating buoy *n.* [? resemblance] [1950s] (*W.I.*) a dumpling made of flour and baking soda; it rises to the surface when cooking.

float-up *n.* [FLOAT UP *v.*] [20C+] (*N.Z.*) a casual approach to someone.

float up *v.* [FLOAT *v.*[1] (2)] [20C+] (*N.Z.*) to approach casually, to stroll up.

flob *n.* [FLOB *v.*] [1990s+] (*UK juv.*) saliva, in the context of spitting.

flob *v.* [note Yorks. dial. *flob*, to puff, to cause to swell, i.e. the puffing of the cheeks that accompanies the action of spitting] [1930s+] (*mainly juv.*) **1** to spit. **2** to vomit.

flock *n.* [1980s] (*US*) those women currently working for a pimp.

flock of sparrows flying out of one's backside *phr.* *see under* SPARROW *n.*

flog *v.* **1** [late 17C–18C] (*UK Und.*) to whip [SE from 1800]. **2** [early 18C; 20C+] to have sexual intercourse. **3** [late 18C+] (*also* **flog on**) to proceed by violent or painful effort. **4** [late 18C+] to obtain, usu. by violent effort. **5** [19C] to beat, to surpass. **6** [mid-19C] (*UK Und.*) to drink heavily; thus *flogger*, a heavy drinker. **7** [20C+] to masturbate; thus *flogger*, a masturbator. **8** [1910s] (*Aus.*) to worry. **9** [1910s+] (*also* **flog off**) to sell, currently non-specific, but orig. with criminal overtones. **10** [1970s+] (*US*) to hurry; thus *flog it*. **11** [1980s+] (*Aus. prison*) to beat up. **12** [1990s+] of an idea, a complaint, to belabour.

IN PHRASES

❑ **flogged at the tumbler** (*also* **flogged at the cart's arse, ... tail**) [late 17C] whipped at the cart's end, a judicial punishment. ❑ **flog off** *v.* **1** [1950s+] (*N.Z.*) to leave. **2** *see* sense 9 above. ❑ **flog on** *v.* *see* sense 3 above. ❑ **flog one's/the...** *v.* *see also under* relevant n. ❑ **flog the (finless) dolphin** *v.* (*also* **stroke the dolphin, swing the dolphin**) [1920s+] (*orig. naut.*) to masturbate. ❑ **nap the flog** *v.* [mid-18C] (*UK Und.*) to receive a judicial flogging.

IN EXCLAMATIONS

❑ **go flog yourself!** *see* GO FUCK YOURSELF! *under* FUCK *v.*

flogged *adj.* [fig. use FLOG *v.* (1)] **1** [1940s–50s] (*US drugs*) overcome by a drug. **2** [1960s–70s] exhausted.

flogger *n.* [FLOG *v.* (1)] **1** [mid-18C–1900s] (*UK Und.*) a whip. **2** [1900s–10s] (*Aus.*) (*also* **flogger coat, flogger tail**) a morning coat [fig. use of sense 1 above: like a whip, esp. a cat-o-nine-tails, it has 'tails']. **3** [1900s–40s] (*Aus./US*) an overcoat [fig. use of sense 1 above: like a whip, esp. a cat-o-nine-tails, it has 'tails'].

flogging *n.* [? ext. use of FLOG *v.* (7)] [2000s] (*US black*) acting eccentrically.

flogging *adj.* [1920s+] (*Aus.*) a euph. for FUCKING *adj.*

flogging-cheat *n.* [FLOG *v.* (1) + CHEAT *n.* (1)] [mid-18C] (*UK Und.*) a whipping post.

flogging-cove *n.* (*also* **flogging cull**) [FLOG *v.* (1) + COVE *n.* (1)] **1** [late 17C–early 19C] one who gives out corporal punishment as authorized by the courts; often synon. with a beadle. **2** [early 18C] a hangman.

flogging cully *n.* (*also* **flogging cull**) [FLOG *v.* (1) + CULLY *n.*[1] (2)/CULL *n.*[1] (1)] [late 17C–early 19C] one who enjoys receiving a whipping as sexual stimulation.

flogster *n.* [FLOG *v.* (1) + sfx *-ster*] [19C] one who enjoys flagellation for sexual purposes.

flood *v.* (*US black*) **1** [1920s–30s] to have a menstrual period. **2** [1970s+] to have an erection, for the penis to 'flood' with blood.

flood-pants *n.* [such trousers are ideal for walking through a flood – the legs are too short to get wet] [20C+] (*orig. W.I.*) trousers that are too short and narrow.

flooey! *excl.* [20C+] (*orig. US*) an echoic excl. designed to resemble the sound of an explosion.

IN PHRASES

❑ **go flooey** *v.* [1910s+] (*US*) to go wrong.

floor *n.*

IN COMPOUNDS

❑ **floorburners** *n.* [1950s–70s] (*US black*) shoes. ❑ **floor-polish** *n. see* SHOE-POLISH *under* POLISH *n.*

IN PHRASES

❑ **dust the floor with** *v. see* DUST *v.*[1]. ❑ **on the floor** [20C+] **1** drunk. **2** beaten. **3** poor [rhy. sl.].

floor *v.* [pressing the accelerator pedal down to the floor] **1** [1950s+] (*orig. US*) to accelerate, to drive extremely fast. **2** [1970s+] (*US*) in fig. use of sense 1 above, to hurry, get a move on.

floored *adj.* [SE colloq. *floor*, to drink alcohol with intensity] [early 19C; 1930s+] very drunk.

floorer *n.* [SE *floor*, to knock down] [mid-19C] (*UK Und.*) a judge in the act of passing the sentence of death.

IN PHRASES

❑ **old floorer** *n.* [fig. use of SE *floorer*, i.e. he 'knocks you down'] [mid-19C–1920s] a fig. name for death.

flooze up *v.* [? euph. FUCK UP *v.* (1)] [1930s] (*US*) to make a mess, to bungle.

floozled *adj.* [1990s+] drunk.

floozy *n.* (*also* **flewzie, floosie, flooze, flusie, fluzie, he-fluesy**) [dial. *floosy*, flossy; thus soft. Note Irish *Floozie in the Jacuzzi*, the monument in O'Connell Street, Dublin, representing the spirit of the River Liffey] [20C+] (*orig. US*) a promiscuous young woman; also of homosexual men.

floozy *adj.* (*also* **floosie, floosy**) [FLOOZY *n.*] [1910s+] **1** (*US*) showy, stylish. **2** (*US*) over-dressed, over-made-up. **3** (*US*) silly or light-headed. **4** (*US Und.*) immoral, corrupt, dissipated. **5** (*US campus*) sexy.

flop *n.*[1] [SE *flop*, i.e. one fig. lets something fall on the person one is cheating] [mid-19C–1910s] (*orig. US campus*) **1** any action by which someone else is deceived. **2** any form of cheating in an examination that leads to scoring high marks.

flop *n.*[2] [Ware notes the synon. *cretin* and *poodle* style] [late 19C] **1** a male hairstyle, in which the hair is worn low over the brow. **2** a similar female hairstyle.

flop *n.*[3] [abbr. SE *flip-flop*] [late 19C–1920s] (*US*) a sudden political change of policy.

flop *n.*[4] **1** [late 19C+] a failure, esp. of a film or stage play; also attrib. **2** [1900s–30s] a fat, ungainly, slovenly person, esp. a woman. **3** [1900s–50s] (*US Und.*) an arrest. **4** [1920s+] a dull, unpleasant person, a misfit, a failure. **5** [1930s+] (*US prison*) the rejection of one's application for parole.

flop *n.*[5] [SE *flop*, to fall down in a heap] **1** [1910s–50s] (*US*) a sleep. **2** [1910s+] (*US*) a cheap room or bed. **3** [1920s–50s] (*US Und.*) a legless beggar. **4** [1920s–60s] (*US*) an act of sexual intercourse. **5** [1930s] a blow. **6** [1940s–60s] (*US*) a seat. **7** [1950s] (*US*) a drunk who has passed out and as such is a possible victim for a robber. **8** [1950s+] (*US prison*) one's last morning in jail. **9** [1960s+] (*UK Und.*) anywhere a thief or gang can leave the loot so as to avoid detection during the immediate aftermath of a crime. **10** *see* FLOPHOUSE *n.*

DERIVATIVES

❑ **floperoo** *n.* [-EROO *sfx*] [1930s+] (*orig. US*) an extreme failure, esp. in a show business context.

IN COMPOUNDS

❑ **flop-and-slop** *n.* [SLOP *n.*[1] (1c)] [1990s+] a hostel, a cheap lodging. ❑ **flop dough** *n.* [DOUGH *n.* (1)] [1930s–40s] (*US Und.*) money set aside for lodging. ❑ **flophouse** *n. see* separate entry. ❑ **flop joint** *n.* [JOINT *n.* (3b)] [late 19C+] (*US*) a tramp's lodging, a cheap hotel. ❑ **flop racket** *n. see* FLOPPER *n.* (2). ❑ **flop worker** *n.* [WORKER *n.*[1] (1)] [1930s] (*US tramp*) one who robs sleepers, usu. fellow tramps.

IN PHRASES

❑ **do a flop** *v.* [20C+] **1** to sit or fall down. **2** of a woman, to prostrate oneself for intercourse. **3** to faint. ❑ **hit the flop** *v.* [1940s] (*US Und.*) to go to bed. ❑ **take a flop** *v.* [1950s] to get into bed.

flop *n.*[6] [Wilts. dial. *flop*, thick liquid] **1** [1930s+] (*US*) excrement, esp. *cow-flop*; thus as a dimissive retort. **2** [1980s] in fig. use, nonsense.

flop, the *n.* [FLOP *v.* (7)] [1920s–40s] (*US Und.*) a form of confidence trick.

flop *v.* **1** [mid-19C] (*US campus*) to cheat in an examination, esp. by faking sickness. **2** [mid-19C–1910s] to hit. **3** [late 19C–1910s] (*US*) to knock down an opponent; also in fig. use. **4** [20C+] to fall asleep, to go to bed. **5** [20C+] to lodge, i.e. in a hotel. **6** [1910s] (*US prison*) to inform. **7** [1910s] (*US Und.*) to short-change. **8** [1910s] to move, to walk; often ext. as *flop around*, *flop in* etc. **9** [1910s–30s] (*US*) to become enamoured of someone. **10** [1910s+] (*also* **go flop**) to collapse, to fail, esp. of a stage entertainment or similar undertaking. **11** [1920s] to murder. **12** [1920s] to lose a fight deliberately, to 'take a dive'. **13** [1930s] (*US*) to fall to the ground for protection. **14** [1930s–40s] (*US*) to copulate; to offer oneself for sex. **15** [1930s+] (*Aus.*) to die. **16** [1940s–50s] (*US prison*) to deny a parole appeal; to be denied parole. **17** [1960s] constr. with *for*, to favour, to 'fall for'. **18** [1970s+] (*US*) to demote. **19** [2000s] (*UK black*) to forget, to let down.

IN PHRASES

❑ **flop a judy** *v. see under* JUDY *n.*[1]. ❑ **flop off** *v.* [1950s] to lose control emotionally. ❑ **flop one** *v.* [1990s+] (*US teen*) to masturbate. ❑ **flop out** *v.* [Yorks. dial. *flop*, to strike with a sudden blow] **1** [late 19C–1910s] to jump out. **2** [1930s–60s] to collapse; occas. as n., a failure.

flop-ear *n. see* LOP-EAR *n.*

flop-eared *adj. see* LOP-EARED *adj.*

flophouse *n.* (*also* **flop**) [FLOP *n.*[5] (2) + SE *house*] [20C+] (*mainly US*) **1** a lodging house or night shelter for tramps, down-and-outs, alcoholics etc; also attrib. **2** a cheap hotel. **3** a brothel. **4** a cheap restaurant or café. **5** a prison.

flopper *n.* [FLOP *v.*] **1** [late 19C–1910s] (*US Und.*) a petty swindler. **2** [late 19C+] (*UK Und.*) a criminal who pretends to have 'slipped' on a shop floor or 'been knocked down' by a slow-moving automobile; they then claim damages, usu. offering to take a quick cash payment rather than go to an insurance company; thus *flop racket*, performing such frauds. **3** [1910s–20s] a weakling, a spineless person. **4** [1910s+] (*US Und.*) a beggar who pretends to be crippled.

flopping *n.* [FLOP *n.*[5] (2)] [1900s–20s] (*US tramp*) a sleeping bag or similar covering; in pl, a place where one sleeps.

flopping *adj.* [1910s–40s] (*Aus./N.Z.*) a euph. for FUCKING *adj.*

floppy *n.* [orig. Rhodesian milit. use, one who 'flops down dead' when hit by bullets; the targets of such bullets were invariably black] [1970s+] (*S.Afr.*) a derog. term for a black person.

floral arrangement *n.* [pun on DAISY CHAIN *n.*] [1960s+] (*US gay*) a spintry, i.e. a circle of three or more people, hetero- or homosexual, all linked physically in mutual sex acts.

flor di cabbagio *n.* [CABBAGIO PERFUMO *n.*] [1900s–10s] a cheap cigar.

florence *n.* [Northants. dial. *florence*, one who dresses untidily; whether this comes from the proper name and thus memorializes a long-forgotten woman is unknown; Williams prefers a link to the prostitutes of *Florence*, Italy, and their speciality, the *Florentine kiss*, synon. with a French kiss] [late 17C–18C] an untidily dressed young woman.

Florida *n.* [the siting of such cells in the warmest areas of the prison, often underground] [20C+] (*US prison*) the solitary confinement/punishment block.

floss *n.* [ety. unknown] [1990s+] (*US*) money.

floss *v.* [fig. uses of SE *floss*, to clean one's teeth with dental floss, or elision of SE *flourish*] [1990s+] (*US black*) **1** to relax. **2** to pose, to present a false image of oneself. **3** to appear stylish and attractive. **4** to harass.

flossed up *adj.* see FLOSSY (UP) *v.*

flossie *n.* (*also* **flossy**) [FLOOZY *n.*] **1** [late 19C+] (*Aus./N.Z./S.Afr.*) a prostitute; thus *flossiedom*, the world of prostitution. **2** [1900s] an overdressed, over-affectionate woman. **3** [1900s] a barmaid. **4** [1910s–20s] a girlfriend, esp. one who is older than her partner.

flossy *adj.* [SE *floss*, silk used for embroidery] **1** [late 19C+] (*US*) showy, slick, saucy, impertinent, ostentatious, attractive. **2** [1960s–70s] of homosexuals, flagrant, ostentatious.

flossy *adv.* [FLOSSY *adj.* (1)] [1910s] attractively, smartly.

flossy (up) *v.* [? FLOOZY *n.* or FLOSSIE *n.*] [1940s+] (*Aus.*) to dress oneself up, esp. in a showy, excessive manner; thus adj. *flossed up*.

flounder *n.*[1] [pun] [mid–late 19C] a drowned man, his corpse.

flounder *n.*[2] [SE *flounder*, i.e. the fishing industry] [1910s] (*US*) a Newfoundlander.

flounder (and dab) *n.* [rhy. sl.] [mid-19C+] a taxi-cab.

flounder mouth *n.* [SE *flounder*, a fish with a large mouth] [mid-17C–mid-18C; 1950s+] (*US*) a person with a notably large mouth.

flourbags *n.* [1910s] (*Aus.*) a bush cook.

flour mixer *n.* [rhy. sl. = SHIKSA *n.* (1)] [20C+] **1** a non-Jewish woman. **2** an inoffensive man, a clerk [ext. of sense 1 above; note orig. Yid. *shikse* means non-Jewish woman or a female servant].

flous *v.* [Ger. *Flause*, deceit] [1900s–10s] (*S.Afr.*) to cheat, to trick, to put at a disadvantage.

floush *v.* (*also* **go flouch**) [echoic] [early 19C] to collapse.

flow *n.*[1] [1990s+] (*US black*) in rap music, one's delivery.

flow *n.*[2] [abbr. SE *cash flow*] [2000s] (*US black*) money.

flow *v.* [1990s+] **1** (*orig. US black*) to perform music, esp. rap music well; to create rap lyrics very well. **2** (*US campus*) to speak eloquently.

flower *n.* [the 'feminine' image of flowers] [1910s–70s] an effeminate male homosexual.

SE in slang uses

IN COMPOUNDS

❑ **flower-fancier** *n.* [late 19C–1900s] a womanizer, a lecher, presumably specializing in 'flowers', i.e. virgins. ❑ **flower patch** *n.* [1980s] (*US*) the female genital area. ❑ **flower-pot** *n.* [19C; 2000s] the vagina.

IN PHRASES

❑ **flower in a wet spot** *n.* [2000s] (*N.Z.*) a sexually aroused female. ❑ **flowers-on-his-grave** *n.* [1910s] (*Aus.*) fastidiousness.

flowers *n.* **1** [late 17C–1950s] a euph. for menstruation [prior use is SE since 15C]. **2** [1980s+] (*orig. US*) the vulva; thus *eat someone's flowers*, to perform cunnilingus.

flowers and frolics *n.* see FUN AND FROLICS *n.*

flowery (dell) *n.* [pedlars' Ling. Fr., thence rhy. sl.] **1** [mid-19C] a room, esp. a room in an inn. **2** [20C+] a cell.

flub *n.* (*also* **flubdub, flubdubbery**) [FLUB *v.*] [1910s–30s] nonsense, or one who talks nonsense.

flub *v.* [? link to FLUFF *v.*[1]] [1920s+] (*US*) **1** (*also* **flub up**) to botch, to bungle, to make a mess of. **2** to confuse. **3** to waste time, to fool around.

flubdub *v.* [FLUB *v.* (3) + redup. or ? DUB *n.*[5] (1)] [1990s+] (*US*) to mess around, to waste time.

flub the dub *v.* [FLUBDUB *v.*] **1** [1940s+] (*orig. US milit.*) to shirk, to evade one's duties. **2** [1940s+] (*US*) to masturbate. **3** [1950s+] (*US*) to blunder, to fail in a task.

flue *n.*[1] [SE *flue*, a chimney, thus any form of passage for conveying heat] **1** [17C+] (*US*) the vagina. **2** [early–mid-19C] a lift formerly in use in pawnbrokers' shops, in which the articles pawned were taken up for storage; thus phr. *put up the flue*, to pawn. **3** [1900s–60s] the stomach; usu. in phr. LINE ONE'S FLUE below. **4** [1920s+] the anus. **5** [1940s] (*US Und.*) the envelope supposedly containing money in a swindle. **6** [1970s] (*US black*) a room, as used by a prostitute for work.

IN PHRASES

❑ **go up the flue** *v.* [late 19C] (*US campus*) to die. ❑ **in the flue** (*also* **up the flue**) **1** [19C–1900s] in pawn. **2** [mid-19C] in trouble. **3** [mid-19C–1900s] dead. **4** [1920s] physically or mentally run down. **5** [2000s] pregnant. ❑ **line one's flue** *v.* [1900s–60s] (*orig. US Western, mainly black*) to eat. ❑ **overheat one's flues** *v.* [late 19C] to get drunk.

IN EXCLAMATIONS

❑ **up your flue!** [1970s] a coarse excl. of dismissal.

SE in slang uses

IN COMPOUNDS

❑ **flue-faker** *n.* [FAKER *n.* (1)] [19C] **1** a chimney-sweep. **2** (*racing*) 'low sporting characters, who are so termed from their chiefly betting on the Great Sweeps' (sweepstakes) (Hotten, 1860).

flue *n.*[2] [rhy. sl. = SCREW *n.*[1] (2c)] [1940s–50s] (*UK prison*) a warder.

flue *v.* [FLUE *n.*[1] (2)] [late 19C] to put in pawn.

fluff *n.*[1] **1** [mid-19C] the pubic hair of either gender. **2** [mid-19C+] (*Aus.*) rubbish, nonsense, something superficial. **3** [20C+] a young, attractive, but empty-headed woman; esp. in phr. BIT OF FLUFF below; also attrib. **4** [1900s–60s] (*US*) (*also* **fluffbrain**) a foolish person. **5** [1940s+] anything – writing, music – considered lightweight. **6** [1940s+] the passive, 'feminine' partner in a lesbian couple. **7** [1960s+] (*gay*) an effeminate male homosexual. **8** [1970s+] (*US black*) the vagina. **9** [1970s+] (*US gay*) the male genitals, esp. the anus.

IN COMPOUNDS

❑ **fluffhead** *n.* [-HEAD *sfx* (1)] [1980s+] an insubstantial, superficial person.

IN PHRASES

❑ **bit of fluff** *n.* (*also* **piece of fluff**) [BIT *n.*[1] (2a)] **1** [20C+] an attractive, but otherwise unexceptional woman, esp. a girlfriend; occas. a young man. **2** [1980s] any thing or person considered insignificant, ineffectual.

fluff *n.*[2] [ety. unknown; ? link to FLUFF *v.*[1] (2)] [1920s+] (*Aus.*) a railway ticket.

fluff *adj.* [FLUFF *n.*[1] (2)/FLUFF *n.*[1] (5)] [1930s+] of writing, lightweight, nonsensical, meaningless; of courses, easy.

fluff *v.*[1] **1** [late 19C–1950s] to disconcert or put off a public speaker. **2** [late 19C+] (*orig. theatrical*) to make a mistake, to bungle. **3** [1900s–50s] to bluff, to lie. **4** [1900s–50s] to falsify (accounts etc).

IN PHRASES

❑ **fluff in** *v.* [late 19C] to deceive by smooth talk. ❑ **fluff in the pan** *n.* [var. on FLASH IN THE PAN *n.* (3)] [mid–late 19C] a failure.

SE in slang uses

IN PHRASES

❑ **fluff about** *v.* [2000s] (*N.Z.*) to waste time, to mess about. ❑ **fluff it up** *v.* [1970s+] (*US gay*) to make the penis erect prior to appearing on the street in tight trousers. ❑ **fluff off** *v.* see separate entries. ❑ **fluff up** *v.* **1** [1970s+] (*US drugs*) to adulterate a drug to bulk it out. **2** [1990s+] to get drunk, to become intoxicated by drugs.

IN EXCLAMATIONS

❑ **fluff it!** see separate entry.

fluff *v.*[2] [ety. unknown] **1** [1930s–40s] to realize, to work out. **2** [1950s] to understand.

fluff *v.*[3] [echoic + SE *fluff*, a puff, an explosion] [1960s+] (*N.Z. juv./US campus*) to break wind.

fluffed *adj.* [SE *fluff*/fig. use of FLUFF *v.*[1] (2)] **1** [late 19C–1930s] drunk. **2** [20C+] intoxicated by drugs.

fluffer *n.*[1] [FLUFFED *adj.*] [late 19C] a drunkard.

fluffer *n.*[2] [FLUFF IT UP *under* FLUFF *v.*[1]] **1** [1980s+] (*US*) a person employed on a film set to arouse an actor physically before filming a sexual episode. **2** [2000s] an erection.

fluffiness *n.* [FLUFFED *adj.*] [late 19C] drunkenness.

fluff it! *excl.* [? euph. for FUCK IT! *excl.*] [mid–late 19C] take it away! I don't want it!

fluff off *v.*[1] [SE *fluff*, to blow, to puff] [1940s+] (*US*) to dismiss or reject; also as imper.

fluff off *v.*[2] [? euph. for FUCK OFF *v.* (2)] [1950s+] to avoid work, to shirk.

fluffy *adj.* [SE *fluffy*, soft, covered in down] **1** [late 19C] drunk and incapable [link to FLUFF *v.*[1] (2)]. **2** [1920s] gentle, unaggressive, sympathetic. **3** [1980s] (*US campus*) an intensifier. **4** [1990s+] (*US gay*) of a lesbian, sexually excited. **5** [1990s+] (*US gay*) among leather-wearing homosexual men, refusing to accept the dress-code.

fluffy duck *n.* [rhy. sl. = FUCK *n.* (1)] [1980s] (*Aus.*) an act of sexual intercourse.

flugens! *excl.* [ety. unknown; ? link to Ger.] [mid-19C–1950s] a general, mild oath.

fluke *n.*[1] [SE *fluke*, a flat fish; thus ? play on FLAT *n.*[2] (1)] [early 19C; 1930s–60s] a gullible victim.

fluke *n.*[2] [? billiards jargon *fluke*, to succeed in a given shot more through luck than judgement; thus a player who wins through flukes cannot be judged as capable as one who wins through skill alone; ult. ety. unknown; ? link to dial. *fluke*, a guess] **1** [mid-19C+] an unforeseen success, a piece of unexpected good luck; thus *flukiness*, fortuitous good fortune. **2** [late 19C] (*orig. US campus*) a failure, a worthless person or thing. **3** [1990s+] (*Aus.*) a lucky person.

fluke *v.*[1] [ety. unknown] **1** [mid-19C–1940s] to fail; as *fluke up*, to do badly. **2** [20C+] to steal. **3** [20C+] to back out, to renege on a promise. **4** [1950s] (*US*) to die; thus *fluke out*.

(IN PHRASES)

❑ **to go up the fluke** *v.* [1900s] (*US campus*) to fail in a recitation or examination.

fluke *v.*[2] [FLUKE *n.*[2] (1); the implication is always of some degree of unfairness in such luck] [late 19C+] to get a piece of good luck.

fluked out *adj.* [1940s–50s] intoxicated with a drug.

fluker *n.* [logically FLUKE *n.*[2] (1) but this is earlier than available cites] [early 19C] a lucky blow.

flukum *n.* [? FLUKE *n.*[2] (1), i.e. it's a *fluke* that any of it gets sold] [1930s] (*US tramp*) cheap, nickel-plated goods sold as 'silver-plate'.

fluky *adj.* (*also* **flukey**) [FLUKE *n.*[2] (1) + sfx *-y*] [late 19C+] **1** lucky; thus adv. *flukily*. **2** (*US*) peculiar, bizarre.

flumdiddle *n.* [var. on FLUMMADIDDLE *n.*] [1910s–20s] empty flattery, humbug.

flumdoodle *n.* [FLUMDOODLE *v.*] [1910s+] (*Aus.*) a trick, a hoax.

flumdoodle *v.* [FLUMDIDDLE *n.*] [1910s+] (*Aus.*) to cheat, to trick, to hoax (someone).

flume *n.*

(IN PHRASES)

❑ **go up the flume** *v.* [mining jargon *flume*, an artificial stream that brings water to a mine] [mid–late 19C] (*US*) **1** to suffer a disaster. **2** to be exhausted, to be worn out, to be dead.

flummadiddle *n.* (*also* **flummydiddle**) [? SE *flummery*, nonsense + DIDDLE *n.*[4]; *Flummery* was also a variety of sweet dish; thus note *flummadiddle*, 'stale bread, pork-fat, molasses, cinnamon, allspice, from which a kind of mush is made, which is baked in the oven and brought to the table hot and brown' (Schele de Vere, *Americanisms*, 1872)] [mid-19C+] (*US*) **1** nonsense, empty flattery, humbug. **2** something trivial or ridiculous.

flummer *v.* [backform. SE *flummery*, empty flattery, nonsense] [mid-18C] to flatter, to charm for a particular purpose.

flummox *n.* (*also* **flummux**) [FLUMMOX *v.* (2)] [mid-19C–1900s] (*mainly US*) **1** a failure. **2** a stupid person. **3** confusion, 'a state'.

flummox *v.* (*also* **flummix, flummux**) [? dial. *flummocks*, to maul, to mangle; *flummock* n., a slovenly person or *flummock* v., to make untidy, to disorder, to confuse, to bewilder + onomat. element based on throwing down roughly and untidily. As such, the term is reminiscent of *flump*, a hummock, and *slommock*, a sloven] **1** [mid-19C] to move in a clumsy manner. **2** [mid-19C–1910s] (*US*) to blunder, to fail; to die. **3** [mid-19C–1910s] to back down, to back out of a promise; to disappoint; to opt out of a round of betting. **4** [mid-19C+] to fool, to confuse, to overcome (by trickery).

flummoxed *adj.*[1] (*also* **flummuxed**) [FLUMMUT *n.* + fig. use of FLUMMOX *v.*; in tramp jargon *flummoxed* refers to a place that is unsafe to visit, the owners or guardians are likely to have one imprisoned] [mid-19C] (*UK Und.*) imprisoned for one month.

flummoxed *adj.*[2] (*also* **flummuxed**) [FLUMMOX *v.*] [mid-19C+] **1** (*also* **flummoxed up**) confused, let down, outwitted. **2** ruined. **3** dangerous, to be avoided. **4** drunk.

flummut *n.* [tramp/tinker use, *flummut*, a mark placed on a door to indicate a house that will be unfriendly; ult. FLUMMOX *v.*] [mid–late 19C] a one-month prison sentence.

flummux *see under* FLUMMOX.

flummydiddle *n. see* FLUMMADIDDLE *n.*

flunk *n.*[1] [FLUNK *v.* (1)] **1** [mid-19C+] (*US campus*) a total failure in academic work, a grade F; thus a student who has failed. **2** [mid-19C+] (*US*) a failure. **3** [late 19C–1910s] (*US*) an idler, a loafer.

flunk *n.*[2] [ety. unknown] [1920s–50s] (*US Und.*) the strongbox within a safe.

flunk *v.* [? US dial. *flink*, ult. SE *flinch*, to act in a cowardly way, to shrink from one's duties; + 18C Oxford jargon (later sl.) *funk*, to exhibit a state of complete fear or panic] **1** [early 19C+] (*US campus*) (*also* **flunk out**) to fail an examination or course. **2** [mid-19C] (*US gambling*) to 'fold' one's cards. **3** [mid-19C+] (*US campus*) to be dismissed or to dismiss on the grounds of academic failure. **4** [mid-19C+] (*US*) to give in, to back down or renege in a cowardly manner. **5** [late 19C+] to fail a student; to give a fail mark. **6** [late 19C+] (*US*) to fail (in a non-academic context), to blunder, to make a mistake. **7** [late 19C+] to embarrass someone (by an indiscreet remark). **8** [late 19C+] (*orig. US*) to do a skimpy, inadequate job.

flunker *n.* [FLUNK *v.*] [late 19C–1900s] (*US campus*) **1** one who regularly fails their examinations or recitations. **2** a teacher who often fails students.

flunky *n.*[1] (*also* **flunkee, flunkey**) [FLUNK *v.* (1)] [mid-19C+] (*US campus*) one who fails an examination; thus one who is expelled as a result of this.

flunky *n.*[2] (*also* **flunkey**) [SE *flunkey*, servant] **1** [20C+] a menial, a stooge. **2** [20C+] (*US*) an assistant cook in a mining or lumber camp. **3** [1960s+] (*US black*) an undistinguished person.

flunky *n.*[3] [? joc. use of FLUNK *n.*[1] (1)] [1990s+] a condom.

flunky *adj.* [FLUNK *n.*[1] (3)] [late 19C–1910s] (*US*) ignorant, second-rate.

flurgle *v. see* FURGLE *v.*

flurry *n.* [McDonald's *McFlurry* ice cream] [2000s] (*Aus.*) a promiscuous young woman.

flurt *n.*[1] [SE *flurt/flirt*, a smart rap or tap] [early 18C] an act of copulation.

flurt *n.*[2] *see* FLIRT *n.*

flush *n.*[1] [ety. unknown] [1940s+] (*W.I.*) a six-month prison sentence.

flush *n.*[2] [1960s+] (*US*) the lavatory.

flush *n.*[3] [pun on poker *flush*, five consecutive cards of the same suit] [2000s] (*S.Afr. gay*) a group of homosexual men.

flush *adj.* (*also* **flushed**) [the level of the liquid that is *flush* with the rim of the glass] [18C+] drunk.

flush *v.*[1] [some punitive whipping was still carried out in public; the *horse* is a wooden frame to which the victim is secured] [mid-19C] to whip; thus *flushed on the horse*, privately whipped in prison.

flush *v.*[2] [SE *flush*, to empty/refill a lavatory bowl] [1950s+] (*US*) to reject, to cancel, to discard.

flushed *adj. see* FLUSH *adj.*

flushing *n.* [1970s+] (*UK drugs*) the act of drawing blood into the syringe when injecting a narcotic.

flusie *n. see* FLOOZY *n.*

flustered *adj.* [17C SE *fluster*, to make half-tipsy] [mid-17C–mid-19C] drunk.

flusticate *v.* [SE *fluster*] [mid–late 19C] to confuse.

flute *n.*^{1} [note *double entendre* in D'Urfey, *Pills to Purge Melancholy* (1719): '*Sawney*'s Flute can only do't, / And Pipe a Tune to please me'] **1** [late 17C–mid-19C] the Recorder of London [pun on SE *recorder*, a flute-like instrument]. **2** [late 17C+] (*also* **silent flute**) the penis. **3** [mid-19C] a pistol. **4** [late 19C] (*US drugs*) an opium pipe; thus *hit the flute*, to smoke opium. **5** [1900s–10s] (*Aus.*) a jockey's whip; thus phr. *put the flute on*, to whip a horse. **6** [1900s–50s] a police whistle. **7** [1930s] a male homosexual.

IN COMPOUNDS

❑ **flute-player** *n.* [1950s+] (*US*) a fellator or fellatrix.

IN PHRASES

❑ **play a tune on the one-holed flute** *v.* [1970s+] (*US gay*) to fellate. ❑ **play the flute** *v.* **1** [late 19C+] (*US*) to perform fellatio. **2** in drugs use. (**a**) [1940s] to smoke opium. (**b**) [1980s+] to smoke crack cocaine.

flute *n.*^{2} (*also* **highland flute**) [abbr.] [1910s+] suit.

flute *v.*^{1} [SE *flute* v.] [late 19C+] (*Aus.*) to talk incessantly.

IN PHRASES

❑ **hold the flute** *v.* [1900s] (*Aus.*) to monopolize the conversation. ❑ **on the flute** [1920s] (*Aus.*) talking continually. ❑ **pass the flute** *v.* [1900s–10s] (*Aus.*) to let someone else speak. ❑ **put your flute away** [1900s] (*Aus.*) stop talking, shut up.

flute *v.*^{2} [FLUTE *n.*^{1} (2)] [1930s] (*US gay*) to fellate.

flute! *excl.* [? euph. for FUCK! *excl.*] [20C+] (*Irish*) a general excl. of surprise, annoyance.

fluter *n.*^{1} [FLUTE *v.*^{1}] [late 19C–1950s] (*Aus.*) an incessant talker.

fluter *n.*^{2} [FLUTE *n.*^{1} (2)] [20C+] a fellator (thus generic for a male homosexual) or fellatrix.

fluthered *adj.* [? SE *fluttered*] [1940s+] (*Irish*) very drunk.

flutter *n.*^{1} [the excitement that flutters one's heart or the punter fluttering their money at the bookmaker] **1** [mid–late 19C] a small, swift trip. **2** [late 19C–1900s] a spree, an adventure; thus *on the flutter*, out on a spree. **3** [late 19C–1950s] an attempt, a try. **4** [late 19C+] a bet, often presumed to be small, unless used ironically; usu. in phr. *have a flutter*.

IN PHRASES

❑ **do a flutter** *v.* (*also* **have a flutter**) [late 19C+] to make a wager, to gamble (usu. for small stakes). ❑ **have a flutter for** *v.* [late 19C] to attempt, to try to obtain something.

flutter *n.*^{2} **1** [late 19C–1930s] any form of sexual experience; thus *be on the flutter*, to be a sexual sophisticate; *do/have a flutter*, to enjoy hedonistic rather than procreative intercourse; *have had a flutter*, to have lost one's virginity. **2** [1930s–40s] (*US*) (*also* **flutterer**) a male homosexual.

IN PHRASES

❑ **do a flutter** *v.* (*also* **have a flutter**) [mid–late 19C] to have sexual intercourse.

flutter *v.*^{1} [mid–late 19C] to have sexual intercourse; thus *flutter a judy*, to pursue and/or seduce a woman.

SE in slang uses

IN PHRASES

❑ **flutter a judy** *v.* [mid–late 19C] to pursue and/or seduce a woman. ❑ **flutter a skirt** *v.* [late 19C–1900s] to work as a prostitute.

flutter *v.*^{2} [FLUTTER *n.*^{1}] [late 19C–1900s] **1** to enjoy oneself. **2** to gamble, to wager.

flutterbudget *n.* (*also* **flutter-guts**) [20C+] (*US*) a particularly fussy person.

flux *v.*^{1} [SE *flux*, to confuse] [18C–mid-19C] to cheat, to deceive.

flux *v.*^{2} [SE *flux*, to make salivate, to purge] [late 18C–early 19C] to salivate.

flux me! *excl.* [18C] an excl. of asseveration; I'll be damned!

fluxy *adj.* [orig. used of under-ripe or blemished mangoes] [1970s+] (*W.I.*) superficially impressive.

fluzie *n. see* FLOOZY *n.*

fuzzy-duzzy *n.* [? play on LEZZIE *n.* + redup.] [1980s] (*US black*) a lesbian.

fly *n.*^{1} [SE *fly*, a fast carriage, a stage-coach] [18C–early 19C] (*UK Und.*) a wagon.

SE in slang uses

IN PHRASES

❑ **catch on the fly** *v.* [1920s–30s] (*US tramp*) to board a moving (freight) train. ❑ **on the fly** [SE *fly*, to move quickly] [mid-19C+] (*US*) in a hurry, on the move, spontaneously.

fly *n.*^{2} [SE *fly*, i.e. one is 'flying a kite'] [mid–late 19C] a trick, a dodge.

IN PHRASES

❑ **on the fly** **1** [mid-19C] begging by following passers-by and asking for cash, rather than standing in one place. **2** [mid-19C–1930s] getting one's living by theft, prostitution or some other form of crime.

fly *n.*^{3} [pun on BLUEBOTTLE *n.* (2)] **1** [mid–late 19C; 1950s] a police officer. **2** *see* FLY COP *n.* (1).

SE in slang uses

IN COMPOUNDS

❑ **fly-blister** *n.* [? its minimal impact] [late 19C] (*Aus.*) a minor newspaper. ❑ **flybog** *n.* [flies that land on jam tend to get stuck] [1910s+] (*Aus.*) treacle, jam. ❑ **fly-cage** *n.* (*also* **flytrap**) [joc. use of SE + ? ref. to the FLY *adj.* (1) young gentleman it ensnares] [late 19C] the vagina. ❑ **fly-catcher** *n.* **1** [mid-17C–19C] a gawping fool [his open mouth]. **2** [19C] the vagina [*see* prev.]. ❑ **fly cemetery** *n.* [joc. 'resemblance'] **1** [1930s+] (*N.Z.*) a pastry square filled with mincemeat. **2** [1930s+] (*N.Z.*) a raisin biscuit. **3** [1950s–60s] steamed pudding with currants. **4** [2000s] (*Irish*) a currant bun. ❑ **fly-dusters** *n.* [late 19C–1900s] the fists. ❑ **fly flapper** *n.* [mid-19C–1920s] a heavy club. ❑ **fly jerks** *n.* [late 19C+] (*Aus.*) the small pieces of cork suspended from a hat to ward off flies. ❑ **fly machine** *n.* [? the effect of the drink makes one 'fly'] [1980s] (*S.Afr. black*) methylated spirits. ❑ **flypaper** *n.* [1920s] (*US*) a contemptible person. ❑ **fly pies** *n. see* SQUASHED FLIES *n.* ❑ **fly rink** *n.* [late 19C] a bald head. ❑ **fly slicer** *n.* ['from their sitting on horse-back, under an arch, where they are frequently observed to drive away flies with their swords' (Grose, 1785)] **1** [late 18C–early 19C] a member of the Life Guards. **2** [19C] a cavalryman. ❑ **flyspeck** *adj. see* separate entry. ❑ **fly-swisher stew** *n.* [the function of the ox's tail] [1910s+] (*Aus.*) oxtail stew. ❑ **flytrap** *n.* **1** [late 18C+] the mouth, esp. a large one [note TRAP *n.*^{1} (4)]. **2** [20C+] a run-down hotel or similar establishment. **3** *see* FLY-CAGE above. ❑ **fly-up-the-creek** *n.* [regional use *fly-up-the-creek*, a popular name of the small green heron (*Butorides virescens*), a native of Florida] [late 19C+] (*US*) **1** an inhabitant of Florida. **2** a capricious person. **3** an immoral woman.

IN PHRASES

❑ **drink with the flies** *v. see* DRINK *v.*

fly *n.*^{4} [fig. uses of SE *on the fly*, on the wing] [late 19C] a spree, a 'lark'.

IN PHRASES

❑ **on the fly** [mid-19C] out on a spree; drunk.

fly *n.*^{5} [SE *fly*, a throw, a toss] [late 19C+] (*Aus.*) **1** the act of tossing a coin; esp. in a game of 'two-up'. **2** in fig. use, a try, a 'go'.

IN PHRASES

❑ **give it a fly** *v.* [1910s+] (*Aus.*) to give something a try. ❑ **have a fly at** *v.* [1910s+] (*Aus.*) to have a try, to make an attempt.

fly *n.*^{6} [? FLY *adj.* (10)] [1980s] (*US black*) a perm or processed hair.

fly *n.*^{7}

IN PHRASES

❑ **dip the fly** *v. see* DIP *v.*^{2}.

fly *n.*[8] **1** *see* fly *adj.* (1). **2** *see* fly cop *n.* (1).

fly *adj.* [Scot. *flee*, aware] **1** [early 18C+] aware, knowledgeable. **2** [mid-18C–early 19C; 1950s+] fashionable. **3** [mid-18C+] smart, sharp, perspicacious; thus *flyness*, perspicacity. **4** [mid-19C–1910s] dextrous, agile. **5** [late 19C] enjoying a run of good luck. **6** [late 19C+] of a woman, occas. a man, promiscuous, flirtatious. **7** [late 19C+] (*US*) sophisticated. **8** [20C+] (*US*) rebellious, uninhibited in behaviour. **9** [1940s] (*orig. US*) insolent, brash. **10** [1950s+] (*US black/campus*) of a woman, attractive, pretty, stylish. **11** [1990s+] (*US*) terrific.

IN COMPOUNDS

□ **fly-ass** *n.* [-ass *sfx*] [1990s+] sophisticated, up-to-the-minute. □ **fly-boy** *n. see* separate entry. □ **fly bull** *n. see* fly cop *n.* (1). □ **fly card** *n.* [card *n.*[2] (2)] [late 19C] a knowledgeable, aware, cunning person. □ **fly chick** *n.* [chick *n.*[1] (2)] [1930s–40s] (*US black*) a hedonistic young woman who enjoys parties and her social life. □ **fly cop** *n. see* separate entry. □ **fly crutch** *n.* [crutch *n.*[2]] [1970s+] (*US*) any fashionable automobile. □ **fly dick** *n. see* fly cop *n.* (1). □ **fly-dipping** *n.* [mid-19C] (*UK Und.*) pickpocketing; ? without a supporting gang. □ **fly flat** *n.* [flat *n.*[2] (1)] **1** [late 19C–1940s] (*also* **fly gee**) a con-man's victim who believes himself to be cleverer than he actually is [gee *n.*[3] (1)]. **2** [1910s] in ext. use, anyone gullible. **3** [1940s] (*US*) a gun. □ **fly girl** *n.* **1** [late 19C] a prostitute. **2** [1980s+] (*US/UK black*) (*also* **fly**) a smart, attractive woman. □ **fly jay** *n.* [jay *n.*[1] (2)] [1970s+] (*US black*) an attractive woman. □ **fly man** *n.* **1** [mid 19C–1910s] a private or plainclothes detective. **2** [late 19C–1950s] a shrewd, cunning, usu. criminal man. **3** [1920s] an expert thief. □ **fly mobsman** *n.* [mobsman *n.* (1)] [1930s] (*UK Und.*) a confidence trickster who poses as a gentleman. □ **fly mug** *n.* [1930s] **1** (*US prison*) a railroad detective. **2** a detective. □ **fly peeler** *n.* [peeler *n.*[2] (1)] [mid-19C] (*UK Und.*) a detective, a plainclothes policeman. □ **fly sleuth** *n. see* fly cop *n.* (1). □ **fly taal** *n.* (*also* **flaaitaal**) [Afk. *taal*, language] [1950s+] (*S.Afr. black*) a form of urban slang used by streetwise young people. □ **flytime** *adj.* [1950s] (*US black*) fashionable, sophisticated.

IN PHRASES

□ **on fly time** *adj.* [1950s] (*US black*) sophisticated. □ **on the fly** **1** [20C+] cunningly, clandestinely. **2** [1970s] by mistake. **3** [1970s+] (*US black*) living in an expensive, fashionable, self-indulgent manner. □ **on the fly tip** [1990s+] (*US black*) devoted to fashion. □ **poke someone fly** *v.* [mid-19C] (*UK Und.*) to explain a situation to someone; to make things clear. □ **put fly** *v.* [19C] (*Aus./UK Und.*) to make (someone) aware.

fly *v.* [fig. uses of SE *fly*] **1** [mid-19C] (*UK Und.*) to lift, to raise; thus *fly a window*, to open a (sash) window for the purpose of breaking into a house [note theatre jargon *fly*, to suspend scenery or lights from above the stage]. **2** [late 19C+] of an idea, a plan, to work out, usu. in negative [the same metaphorical 'flag' as found in the SE phr. *run it up the flagpole and we'll see who salutes*]. **3** [1930s+] (*US drugs*) to take or to be intoxicated by psychotropic drugs [one gets high *adj.*[1] (2)]. **4** [1970s+] to be drunk [one gets high *adj.*[1] (1)].

IN PHRASES

□ **fly a/the blue pigeon** *v. see under* blue pigeon *n.*

SE, meaning to rush away, in slang uses

IN COMPOUNDS

□ **fly-away** *n.* **1** [late 19C] a tricycle. **2** [1910s–30s] (*US*) a deserter. **3** [1940s] (*US prison*) a fugitive. □ **fly-boy** *n. see* separate entry. □ **fly-pitch** *n.* [i.e. they run off when a police officer approaches] [20C+] any form of street stall or other place where goods are sold in the open air; thus *fly-pitcher*, a street-seller.

IN PHRASES

□ **fly a line** *v.* [SE *line*, a short letter or note] [mid-19C] to send a letter. □ **fly a tile** *v. see under* tile *n.* □ **fly one's mouth** *v. see under* mouth *n.* □ **fly the basket** *v. see under* basket *n.*[1]. □ **fly the coop** *v. see under* coop *n.*[1]. □ **fly the mags** *v. see under* mag *n.*[3].

SE, meaning to travel through the air, in slang uses

IN COMPOUNDS

□ **flyball** *n.* [? the image is of a ball that travels far and fast; or ? pun on baseball jargon *flyball*, a ball that can be caught 'on the fly'] **1** [1920s–30s] (*US tramp*) a city detective. **2** [1960s–70s] (*US*) a male homosexual. □ **flykite** *adj. see under* kite *n.* □ **fly-over people** *n.* [1990s+] (*US*) inhabitants of those states of the US over which one passes in an aeroplane flying from coast to coast; 'middle America'.

IN PHRASES

□ **fly a flag** *v.* **1** *see under* flag *n.*[2]. **2** *see* flag *v.*[2] (3). □ **fly a kite** *v. see under* kite *n.* □ **fly-by-night** *see* separate entries. □ **fly by the seat of one's pants** *v.* (*also* **drive by the seat of one's pants, fly with one's ass**) [1940s+] to fly an aircraft using natural ability and daring rather than instruments and technology; thus fig. to gamble with one's life, to take extravagant risks. □ **fly-flapped** *adj.* [SE *fly-flap*, to beat, to whip, orig. to hit flies with a swatter] [late 18C] whipped at the cart's tail or in the stocks. □ **fly hot** *v.* [SE *fly*, to become + hot *adj.* (4a)] [1900s–40s] (*US black*) to lose one's temper suddenly. □ **flying high** *adj.* [fig. use of SE, but cf. flying *adj.* and high *adj.*[1]] [20C+] drunk. □ **flying light** *adj.* [Irwin, *American Tramp and Underworld Slang* (1931): 'From the railroads, where a "light engine" is one travelling over the line without a train, and so able to move swiftly and without needless delay'] [1930s–60s] (*US tramp*) hungry; unencumbered by a pack or similar possessions. □ **flying low** *adj.* [pun] [1960s+] (*Irish*) having one's flies open. □ **flying porter** *n.* [late 18C–early 19C] a cheat who approaches the victim of robbery, tells him that he can regain the stolen goods for him and demands a payment for fetching them. □ **flying stationer** *n.* [SE *stationer*, a bookseller] [late 18C–19C] a street seller of cheap ballads, criminal 'confessions' and similar popular material. □ **fly low** *v.* [1900s] (*US*) to economize. □ **fly Mexican airlines** *v.* [the easy access to marijuana in Mexico + flying 'high'] [1960s+] (*drugs*) to smoke marijuana. □ **fly off in one's face** *v.* (*also* **fly up...**) [20C+] (*W.I.*) to lose control, to become extremely angry. □ **fly out of one's skin** *v.* [20C+] (*W.I.*) to become violently excited. □ **fly salty** *v. see* *jump salty under* jump *v.* □ **fly the flag** *v. see* separate entries. □ **fly the kite** *v. see* *fly a kite under* kite *n.* □ **fly the red flag** *v.* [1940s+] to be menstruating. □ **fly (up) in one's head** *v.* [20C+] (*W.I.*) of alcohol, to go to one's head, to make one extremely and thus dangerously drunk. □ **fly up in the air** *v. see under* air *n.*

fly *adv.* [fly *adj.* (2)] [1950s] (*US black*) smartly, fashionably.

fly-blow *n.* [by-blow *n.* + ? SE *fly-blown*] [mid–late 19C] an illegitimate child.

fly-blow *v.* [SE *flyblow*, the egg of a fly, which turns into a maggot that will, in this context, figuratively devour the victim's reputation or money] **1** [19C–1900s] (*US*) to gossip maliciously about an absent third party, to attack behind one's back. **2** [20C+] (*Aus.*) to take money from someone, often by chicanery.

fly-blown *adj.* (*also* **fly-blowed, sun-blown**) [fig. uses of SE] **1** [17C–19C] deflowered; no longer virgin, thus, of a whore, thought to be used by many men. **2** [19C] drunk. **3** [mid-19C–1950s] (*Aus./N.Z.*) ruined, penniless, without funds. **4** [late 19C] suspected of carrying venereal disease. **5** [late 19C] tired out, exhausted.

fly-boy *n.*[1] [fly *adj.*] **1** [late 19C; 1980s+] (*latterly US black*) (*also* **fly guy**) a sophisticated, intelligent, stylish young man. **2** [1940s+] a 'wide boy', a spiv *n.*

fly-boy *n.*[2] [joc. uses of SE *fly* + *boy*] **1** [1910s] (*Anglo-Irish*) a British citizen who escaped to Ireland to avoid conscription in WW1. **2** [1930s+] (*US*) a pilot, civil or milit.; usu. with slight implication of disdain or dislike.

fly-buzzing *n. see* buzzing *n.*

fly-by-night *n.* [lit. one who 'flies by night'. Grose (1796) adds his punning joke: 'an ancient term of reproach to an old woman, signifying that she was a witch'] **1** [19C+] (*also* **fly-by-nighter**) one who defrauds the landlord by leaving his lodgings in the middle of the night, having failed to pay the rent. **2** [early–mid-

19C] a sedan chair on wheels. **3** [late 19C] (*US*) a small touring theatrical company. **4** [20C+] (*also* **fly-by-nighter**) anyone dubious, crooked, criminal, esp. of a businessman who takes one's money but fails to provide any or at least adequate recompense. **5** [1930s] (*UK Und.*) itinerant casinos, moving every night to avoid the detection of illegal gambling.

fly-by-night *adj.* [FLY-BY-NIGHT *n.* (4)] [20C+] **1** dubious, untrustworthy, undependable. **2** crooked, criminal.

fly-by-night, pitch-by-day *n.* [1950s] (*W.I.*) an idle, worthless person with no home.

fly-by-nights *n.* [rhy. sl.] [1970s+] tights.

fly cop *n.* [FLY *adj.* (1) + COP *n.*[1] (1)] (*US*) **1** [19C+] (*also* **fly, fly bull, fly dick, fly sleuth**) a plainclothes police officer. **2** [mid–late 19C] an alert or experienced police officer. **3** [late 19C+] a detective.

flyer *n.*[1] (*also* **flier**) [? play on 'flying away' in one's footwear] **1** [late 17C–19C] a shoe. **2** [mid-19C] a shoe that has been soled without having been welted.

flyer *n.*[2] (*also* **flier**) [early 19C+] (*US*) **1** a wager or investment; thus *take a flyer*, to take a gamble, a risk. **2** a game, a 'lark'. **3** a try; attempt.

(IN PHRASES)

❑ **take a flier** *v.* (*also* **take a flyer**) [SE *take a flying leap*] **1** [late 18C–19C] to have quick and spontaneous sexual intercourse with both parties fully or partially dressed. **2** [mid-19C+] to go out on a spree. **3** [late 19C+] (*US*) to take a chance, to gamble, esp. financially. **4** [20C+] (*US prison*) to escape from prison. **5** [1920s+] to fall heavily. **6** [1950s] to escape, to run away from.

flyer *n.*[3] (*also* **flier**) [SE *fly*, to go fast] **1** [mid–late 19C] a racehorse; a fast horse. **2** [late 19C] in ext. use of sense 1 above, an attractive young woman. **3** [late 19C] in ext. use of sense 1 above, a successful person. **4** [late 19C] a fast vehicle.

flyer *n.*[4] (*also* **flier**) [1940s+] (*US prison*) suicide by throwing oneself from an upper gallery in a cell-block.

(IN PHRASES)

❑ **take a flier** *v.* [1940s] (*US prison*) to kill oneself by leaping from an upper gallery.

flyer *n.*[5] (*also* **flier**) [*FLY A KITE under* KITE *n.*] [1960s] (*US campus*) an idiotic or obnoxious person.

flying *n.* (*also* **flying favour**) [synon, with SE *fling*] [late 18C–mid-19C] (*UK Und.*) a bout of hedonistic enjoyment; a brief act of intercourse.

flying *adj.* [FLY *v.*] [1950s+] (*drugs*) under the influence of drink or drugs.

SE in slang uses

(IN COMPOUNDS)

❑ **flying baker** *n. see* separate entry. ❑ **flying bedstead** *n.* [note WW1 milit. *flying bedstead*, a military bicycle or mortobike] [19C] a cart/stall used by a bric-a-brac dealer. ❑ **flying camps** *n.* [SE *flying camp*, 'a little army of horse and foot, that keeps the field, and is continually in motion' (Phillips, *The New World of Words*, 1671)] [late 17C–early 19C] a group of beggars who work as a team at funerals. ❑ **flying cat** *n.* [its predilection for mice and other small rodents] [late 17C–early 18C] (*UK Und.*) an owl. ❑ **flying cove** *n.* [COVE *n.* (1)] [mid-19C] (*US Und.*) a type of confidence trickster. ❑ **flying dustman** *n.* [pun on the *Flying Dutchman*] [early 19C] a 'pirate' dustman, who collects garbage before the contracted dustman can arrive. ❑ **flying fornicator** *n.* [the image of drunken couples necking on their way home] **1** [1900s–30s] the last express train from London to a provincial town. **2** [1970s] (*Aus.*) the last train from Sydney to Wollongong on Saturday night, primarily patronized by young people. ❑ **flying fuck** *n. see* separate entry. ❑ **flying giggers** *n.* (*also* **flying jiggers**) [GIGGER *n.*[1] (1)] [late 18C–early 19C] turnpike gates. ❑ **flying handicap** *n.* [1950s] (*Aus.*) diarrhoea. ❑ **flying horse** *n.* [the person who sits on it 'flies'] [1950s] (*W.I.*) a bent pin or similar sharp object placed on a chair. ❑ **flying jib** *n. see* JIB *n.*[1] (5). ❑ **flying lessons** *n.* [1990s+] (*UK/US prison*) the throwing of a guard or fellow inmate off the balcony of a cell tier. ❑ **flying pasty** *n.* **1** [late 18C–early 19C] a packet of excrement wrapped in paper and flung over a neighbour's wall. **2** [19C] (*US prison*) a similar package wrapped in newspaper and tossed out of one's cell window. ❑ **flying saucer** *n. see* separate entry. ❑ **flying shit** *n. see* FLYING FUCK *n.* ❑ **flying sixty-nine** *n.* [SIXTY-NINE *n.*] [1990s+] mutual oral-genital stimulation.

flying baker *n.* [naut. jargon *baker* = B; the flag signifying the second letter of the alphabet is red] [20C+] menstruation.

flying fuck *n.* (*also* **flying shit**) [1950s+] an all-purpose negative expression; usu. in comb., e.g. (*not*) *give a flying fuck*.

(IN PHRASES)

❑ **take a flying fuck** *v.* (*also* **take a flying frig, ...jump, ...leap**) [FUCK *n.* (2a)/FRIG *n.* (3)] **1** [20C+] (*orig. US*) a derisory, dismissive phr.; also ext. by *...at a galloping goose!*; *...at a rolling doughnut!*; *...at a rubber duck!*; *...at the moon!*; *... at yourself!* **2** [1960s] (*US black*) to leave, to travel.

flying saucer *n.* [f. their shape and/or their effect on the user] **1** [1950s+] (*orig. US*) a diaphragm. **2** [1960s+] (*drugs*) the seeds of the plant *Ipomoea*, popularly known as morning glory. **3** [1970s–80s] (*N.Z. prison*) one capsule of the strong tranquilizer, Largactil. **4** [1990s+] (*W.I.*) a motorcycle police officer. **5** [2000s] (*N.Z.*) a fried slice of luncheon sausage.

flying sixty-six *n.* [rhy. sl. = *FRENCH TRICKS under* FRENCH *adj.* but note *FLYING SIXTY-NINE under* FLYING *adj.*] [20C+] oral sex.

flying trapeze *n.* [rhy. sl.] [late 19C+] cheese.

flymy *adj.* [FLY *adj.* (1) + SE *slimy*] [mid–late 19C] sly, roguish, cunning.

fly my kite *n.* [rhy. sl.] [mid-19C] a light.

flyspeck *adj.* [1970s] (*US*) small, insignificant.

(IN COMPOUNDS)

❑ **fly speck (isle)** *n.* [its relative size compared to Australia] [20C+] (*Aus.*) Tasmania; thus *fly-specker*, *flyspeck*, an inhabitant of Tasmania; *fly-speck*, Tasmanian.

fly the flag *v.*[1] **1** [mid-19C] of a prostitute, to walk the streets looking for trade. **2** [1940s+] to be menstruating [var. on *FLY THE RED FLAG under* FLY *v.*].

fly the flag *v.*[2] **1** [1970s+] (*Aus. Und.*) (*also* **raise the flag**) to appeal to a higher court. **2** [1990s+] to make a fuss for form's sake.

fly (tipper) *n.* [rhy. sl. = NIPPER *n.*[3] (1)] [1990s+] a child.

flyweight *n.* [boxing imagery] [1940s–70s] (*US*) a person, usu. criminal, of little or no importance or influence.

FM boots *n. see FUCK-ME BOOTS under* FUCK-ME *adj.*

f.n.g. *n.* [*f*ucking *n*ew *g*uy] [1960s+] (*orig. US milit.*) an innocent, a novice.

f.o. *v. see* FUCK OFF *v.* (2).

f.o.! *excl.* [abbr. FUCK OFF! *excl.*] [1940s+] (*US*) go away! leave me alone!

f.o.a.d.! *excl.* [abbr.] [1980s+] *f*uck *o*ff *a*nd *d*ie!

foam *n.* [20C+] (*US black*) beer.

foamin' at the gash *phr.* [SE *foam* + GASH *n.*[1] (1)] [1990s+] of a woman, becoming damp with sexual arousal.

foaming *adj.* [1960s] an intensifier; a euph. for FUCKING *adj.*

foaming (at the mouth) *phr.* **1** [20C+] absolutely furious. **2** [1960s+] (*US*) of a penis, on the verge of ejaculation.

foamy *n.* [FOAM *n.*] [1950s] a bottle, can or glass of beer.

f.o.b. *n.* (*also* **fob**) [abbr. *f*resh *o*ff the *b*oat] [1930s] (*Aus./N.Z./US*) a newly arrived Asian immigrant; ext. as derog. term for any minority group.

fob *n.* [the term was SE in 1622 (*OED* first citation) but sl. by late 17C; thus SE use *fob off*, to sidetrack, to put off with a lie or deceit] [late 17C–early 19C] a trick, a deceit.

(IN PHRASES)

❑ **come the fob on** *v.* [mid-19C] (*US*) to cheat, to trick.

fob *v.* [FOB *n.*] **1** [late 17C–mid-19C] to trick, to deceive, to steal from. **2** [mid-19C–1900s] to place in one's fob pocket. **3** [late 19C–1940s] (*US Und.*) to steal from a fob pocket.

(IN PHRASES)

❑ **fob someone off** *v.* (*also* **fob someone out of**) [late 17C+] to deceive, to pacify.

fobber *n.* [SE *fob*] [late 19C–1940s] (*US Und.*) a pickpocket who specializes in removing small change from the victim's fob pocket; Irwin, *American Tramp and Und. Slang* (1931), suggests that such a pickpocket has lost his skills, and can no longer attempt less accessible pockets.

fob-diver *n.* [SE *fob* (pocket) + DIVER *n.* (3)] [late 19C–1900s] a pickpocket.

fobus *n.*[1] [ety. unknown; ? link to dial. *fobey*, an eccentric] [late 17C] a general term of dislike.

fobus *n.*[2] [ety. unknown; ? link to SE *fob*, a small pocket] [late 19C] the vagina.

focking *adj. see* FUCKING *adj.*

focus *n. see* FOGUS *n.*

focus *v.* [1930s–40s] (*US black*) to look; to see.

fodder *n.*[1] [although it covered all forms of food in 11C–14C the SE is now only used for animal food] [mid-19C; 1910s+] food, often metaphorical.

SE in slang uses

(IN COMPOUNDS)

❑ **fodder-forker** *n.* [his usual task] [20C+] (*US*) a derog. term for a farmer, as seen by cowboys.

fodder *n.*[2] [abbr. *BUM-FODDER under* BUM *n.*[1]] [late 19C+] lavatory paper.

foe shizzy! *excl. see* FO' SHO! *excl.*

fofi-eye *n.* [ety. unknown; ? link to *fufu*, a plantain dough, which is white] [20C+] (*W.I., Bdos/Guyn.*) an eye with a discoloured, whitish eyeball.

fog *n.* **1** [18C–mid-19C] (*UK Und.*) smoke. **2** [1940s] (*US Und.*) shooting.

SE in slang uses

(DERIVATIVES)

❑ **fogmatic** *see* separate entries.

(IN COMPOUNDS)

❑ **fog-bound** *adj.* **1** [1920s–30s] slightly drunk. **2** [1920s–40s] (*US*) confused, dazed, infatuated. ❑ **fog-cutter** *n. see* ANTIFOGMATIC *n.* ❑ **foghorn** *n. see* separate entry. ❑ **Fogland** *n. see* separate entry.

(IN PHRASES)

❑ **fog in** *v.* [late 19C] (*UK society*) to see a place by accident; to achieve one's object by accident. ❑ **fog out** *v. see* separate entries. ❑ **in the fog** *adj. see* FOGGY *adj.*

fog *v.*[1] [early 17C; mid-19C–1910s] (*also* **fogify**) to perplex, to confuse, to mystify.

fog *v.*[2] [play on SE] **1** [18C–early 19C; 1920s] to smoke a pipe. **2** [late 19C–1930s] (*US*) to go fast, to rush around, to chase. **3** [1900s–60s] (*US*) to fire a gun rapidly. **4** [1920s–40s] (*US*) to attack; to kill. **5** [1930s] (*US*) to scold, to complain. **6** [1990s+] (*US prison*) to delouse a new prisoner.

fog *v.*[3] *see* FUG *v.*

fog! *excl.* [1940s–50s] (*Aus.*) a euph. for FUCK! *excl.*

fogare *n. see* FOGUS *n.*

fogey *n.* [Fr. *fourgeaux*, fierce, fiery or Scot. dial. *foggy*, fat, bloated. Note SE *fogram/fogrum*, an old-fashioned, out-of-date person] **1** [late 18C] (*also* **foggy**) an invalid soldier [thence the SE use, usu. with pfx *old*]. **2** [late 19C] an old maid.

fogey *adj.* (*also* **fogy**) [SE *fogey*] [mid-19C+] (*orig. Scot.*) old-fashioned, 'stuck-in-the-mud'.

fogged *adj.* [SE *fog*, to confuse] **1** [mid-19C+] confused, bewildered. **2** [mid-19C+] (*also* **befogged**) drunk, tipsy. **3** [1930s] exhausted. **4** [1940s] under the influence of a drug.

fogging *adj.* [1940s–50s] a euph. for FUCKING *adj.*

foggy *n. see* FOGEY *n.* (1).

foggy *adj.* [play on SE] **1** [late 16C+] (*also* **in the fog**) drunk, tipsy. **2** [late 18C+] confused, not very intelligent.

Foggy Bottom *n.* (*also* **Foggy Butts**) [derived both f. the name of an area of Washington, D.C., and f. the 'foggy' obfuscations produced by its bureaucrats] [1940s+] (*US*) the US State Department.

fogh! *excl. see* FAUGH! *excl.*

foghorn *n.* [the noise it makes] (*US*) **1** [1910s–30s] a tuba or saxophone. **2** [1940s+] the nose. **3** [1960s] one who talks too loudly; thus the mouth.

fogie *n.* [var. pron.of FORTY *n.* (4)] [2000s] (*US black*) a 40oz bottle of malt liquor.

Fogland *n.* [the weather and the contemporary smogs in London] [1910s] (*Aus.*) Britain; thus *Fogtown*, *Fogville-on-Thames*, London.

fogle *n.* [? Ital. *foglia*, leaf; thus handkerchief or Fr. sl. *fouille*, a pocket; less likely is Ger. *vogel*, bird, and thus the 'bird's eye' pattern of some handkerchiefs] [19C] (*orig. Ling. Fr./Polari*) a silk handkerchief; thus *draw a fogle*, to steal a silk handkerchief.

(IN COMPOUNDS)

❑ **fogle-hunter** *n.* (*also* **fogle-drawer**) [early–mid-19C] a pickpocket who specializes in stealing silk handerchiefs. ❑ **fogle-hunting** *n.* (*also* **fogle-drawing**) [early–mid-19C] (*orig. Ling. Fr./Polari*) the stealing of silk handkerchiefs.

fogmatic *n.* [ANTIFOGMATIC *n.*] [mid-19C] (*US campus*) a bracing drink of alcohol.

fogmatic *adj.* [FOGMATIC *n.*] [mid-19C] (*US campus*) drunk.

fogo *n.* [? SE *fog* + *hogo*, f. Fr. *haut gout*, high taste, i.e. a high or putrescent flavour, an offensive taste or smell, or *foh!*, an excl. of disgust] [mid-19C] a stench, esp. of breaking wind.

fog out *v.*[1] [1980s+] (*US drugs*) to fill a room or car with smoke.

fog out *v.*[2] [1990s+] (*US*) to daydream.

fogue *v.* [FOGO *n.*] [1920s–30s] (*Aus./N.Z.*) to stink.

fogus *n.* (*also* **focus, fogare**) [? SE *fog*, in this case that produced by a pipe] [mid-17C–mid-19C] tobacco.

(IN PHRASES)

❑ **blow a fogus** *v.* [mid-19C] (*UK Und.*) to smoke a pipe.

fogy *adj. see* FOGEY *adj.*

foh! *excl. see* FAUGH! *excl.*

foil *n.* [1960s+] (*drugs*) a quantity of drugs, e.g. amphetamine, heroin or cannabis, wrapped in foil ready for sale.

(IN COMPOUNDS)

❑ **foil-face** *n.* [2000s] (*UK drugs*) a heroin addict whose preferred method of ingestion is to inhale the fumes when the drug is heated on a piece of silver foil.

(IN PHRASES)

❑ **put on the foil** *n.* [1970s] to inhale fumes from heroin heated on a piece of foil.

foil *v.* [1990s+] (*UK Und.*) to wrap a copper coin in silver foil to create a silver one, which can be used in slot or gaming machines.

foil-cloy *n.* (*also* **foyl-cloy, foyler**) [FILE *v.*[1] (1) + CLY *n.* (2)] [late 17C–early 18C] (*UK Und.*) a pickpocket; also as v. *foyl someone's cloy*.

foily *n.* [1990s+] (*Aus. drugs*) a foil-wrapped package of heroin.

foin *n.* [SE *foin*, a thrust with a pointed weapon] [late 16C] (*UK Und.*) a cut-purse or pickpocket.

foin *v.* [SE *foin*, to make a thrust with pointed weapon] [14C–17C] of a man, to have sexual intercourse; thus *foining*, having sexual intercourse.

foine *adj. see* FINE *adj.* (3).

fois *adj.* [? Fr. *fois*, time, i.e. the perceived antiquity of such styles] [1980s+] (*US campus*) reminiscent of European style.

foist *n.*[1] (*also* **foyst, fyst**) [FOIST *v.*[2] (1)] [late 16C–early 18C] a silent breaking of wind.

foist *n.*[2] (*also* **foyst, fyst**) [FOIST *v.*[1]] **1** [late 16C–early 19C] (*UK Und.*) a pickpocket or cut-purse. **2** [late 16C–mid-19C] (*UK Und.*) a card-sharp, a cheat. **3** [17C] a trick, a hoax.

(IN PHRASES)

❑ **skirt-foist** *n.* [mid–late 17C] a female cheat.

foist *v.*[1] (*also* **foyst, fyst**) [prob. Du. dial. *vuisten*, to take in the hand, f. *vuist*, fist; the Du. means to play at a game in which one player holds some coins in his hand, and the others guess their number] **1** [mid-16C–early 17C] to palm a false die so as to be able to introduce it into the game when required. **2** [mid-16C–early 17C] to cheat by this means; thus *foist in*, to introduce a false die surreptitiously when palmed. **3** [late 16C–19C] to steal, esp. to pick a pocket.

foist *v.*^{2} (*also* **fyst**) [15C SE *fist*, to break wind; 16C SE *foist*, to smell or grow musty] [late 16C–early 18C] to break wind silently.

foister *n.* [FOIST *v.*^{1} (3)] [mid-19C] (*US Und.*) a pickpocket.

fold *n.*^{1} [powdered narcotic drugs are sold in folds of paper] [1990s+] (*US drugs*) a piece of paper folded to contain a measure of a given drug; the standard price is $25 per fold.

fold *n.*^{2} [2000s] a collapse into laughter.

fold *v.* [poker imagery] (*US*) **1** [1930s+] to become exhausted, to tire, to fall asleep. **2** [1930s+] to shut down, esp. in show business use. **3** [1950s+] to collapse, to fail, e.g. in the context of a town becoming useless for criminal activities. **4** [1950s+] to give up. **5** [1970s] of a shop, club etc, to shut. **6** [1990s+] (*US Und.*) to collapse under pressure, e.g. police interrogation.

SE in slang uses

IN PHRASES

▫ **fold out** *v.* [the unfolding of one's bedroll] **1** [20C+] (*US*) to go to bed. **2** *see* FOLD UP *v.* (5). ▫ **fold someone's ears** *v.* [1960s–70s] (*US black*) to lecture or advise someone at great and serious length.

folder *n.* [FOLD *v.* (1)] [1980s+] (*US campus*) one who tires easily; thus a poor companion for partying.

folding *n.* (*also* **folding dough, ...money, ...stuff**) [1930s+] (*orig. US*) paper money.

folding green *n.* (*also* **green folding**) [SE *folding*/FOLDING *n.* + GREEN *n.*^{2} (1)] [1940s+] (*US black*) paper money, dollar bills.

fold up *v.* [poker use, *fold* (*up*), to withdraw from a round of betting] **1** [1910s+] to collapse or to surrender, both under unbearable pressure; to cause to knock out. **2** [1930s–50s] (*drugs*) to withdraw from drug use. **3** [1930s–50s] to terminate an activity. **4** [1950s] to knock down, to defeat. **5** [1960s] (*also* **fold out**) to leave. **6** [1970s] to shut down someone's business or other activity.

folks *n.* [SAmE *folks*, one's family] **1** [late 19C] (*US Und.*) fellow criminals; also in sing. **2** [late 19C+] (*US teen*) one's group of friends. **3** [1990s+] (*US black teen*) fellow gang members, esp. used in prison where gang membership is, where possible, hidden from the authorities.

IN PHRASES

▫ **real folks** *n.* [1920s] (*US Und.*) people who have been in prison or live by crime.

follies *n.* (*also* **fullies**) [ironic use] [1940s–50s] (*UK prison*) the Quarter Sessions.

follow *v.*

SE in slang uses

IN PHRASES

▫ **follow a whereas** *v.* (*also* **march in the rear of a whereas**) [notices of bankruptcy in the *London Gazette* invariably began with the word *Whereas...*] [late 18C–mid-19C] to become bankrupt. ▫ **follow-me-home-and-fuck-me shoes** *n. see* FUCK-ME SHOES *under* FUCK-ME *adj.* ▫ **follow-me-lads** *n.* [the apparent sexual invitation implicit in the hairstyle] [mid-19C–1900s] curls that hang over a woman's shoulder. ▫ **follow one's nose** *v.* [play on SE *follow one's nose*, to go (lit.) straight] [1980s] (*US black*) to lead a law-abiding life, whatever temptations may exist to the contrary. ▫ **follow through** *v.* **1** [20C+] to ejaculate twice without withdrawal. **2** [1920s+] to soil one's underwear by mistake.

follower-upper *n.* (*also* **follyer-upper, follyinupper, folly-up**) [SE *follow-up*] [1940s–50s] (*Irish*) a weekly cinema serial, usu. screened on Saturday mornings.

follow-foot monkey *n.* [20C+] (*W.I.*) someone, often a young person, who 'apes' (as far as they can) the famous.

follow-foot monkey *v.* [FOLLOW-FOOT MONKEY *n.*] [20C+] (*W.I.*) to 'ape' the famous.

follyer-upper/follyinupper/folly-up *n. see* FOLLOWER-UPPER *n.*

fondle *v.* [19C] to have sexual intercourse.

fond of one's drops *phr. see under* DROP (OF THE CREATURE) *n.*

fonfen *n.* [Yid. *fonfer*, a cheat, one who deceives, fails to deliver on their promises] [1960s–70s] the verbal trickery created by con-men to further a given fraud or trick.

fong *n.*^{1} (*also* **fong-eye**) [1940s+] (*N.Z.*) **1** strong liquor. **2** methylated spirits as drunk by alcoholics. **3** a very heavy drinker.

fong *n.*^{2} [? echoic] [1960s] (*Irish*) a kick.

fonged (up) *adj.* (*also* **half-fonged**) [FONG *n.*^{1}] [1940s+] (*N.Z.*) drunk, tipsy.

fonk *n.* [1990s+] a euph. for FUCK *n.* (3a).

fonked out heavy *adj.* [FUNKED OUT *adj.* (2) + HEAVY *adv.* (1)] [1960s+] (*US black*) very well dressed.

fonk (out) *v.* [FONKY *adj.*^{1}] (*US black*) **1** [1960s+] to show off; to upstage. **2** [1980s+] to praise.

fonky *adj.*^{1} (*also* **fonk**) [FUNKY *adj.*^{1} (1) / FUNKY *adj.*^{3} (1)] [1960s+] (*US black*) a positive or negative intensifier depending on context; thus exceptionally good or bad, smelling sweet or vile etc.

IN COMPOUNDS

▫ **fonky-fresh** *adj. see* FUNKY-FRESH *under* FUNKY *adj.*^{3}.

IN PHRASES

▫ **fonky to the bone** *adj.* [BONE *n.*^{1}] [1940s+] (*US black*) **1** exceptionally well dressed. **2** handsome.

fonky *adj.*^{2} [FUNKY *adj.*^{3} (1)] [1980s] (*US black*) aggressive.

foo *n. see* FOOL *n.*

foo *adj.* [? SE *foolish* or FOO-FOO *adj.* (1)] [1910s] (*Aus.*) drunk.

foob *adj. see* F.U.B.A.R. *adj.* (4).

food *n.* [something one 'chews' over or 'eats up'] **1** [1940s] (*US black*) gossip. **2** [1970s+] (*US gang/gay*) a victim, prey; a sex object.

SE in slang uses

IN COMPOUNDS

▫ **food boat** *n.* [2000s] a group of prisoners who cook their own food. ▫ **foodbox** *n.* [1990s+] (*US black*) the stomach. ▫ **food grinder** *n.* [1910s] the jaw. ▫ **food inspector** *n.* [his 'inspection' of whatever food he can obtain] [1900s–50s] (*Aus.*) a tramp.

IN PHRASES

▫ **food one's beast** *v. see under* BEAST *n.*

fooey! *excl. see* PHOOEY! *excl.*

foof *n.* [? echoic of an insubstantial puff of wind] [1960s+] (*US campus*) a superficial person; as adj. *foofy*, silly.

foo-foo *n.* [SE *fool* + redup.] **1** [mid-19C] (*orig. US*) an effeminate or weak man. **2** [mid-19C+] (*US/W.I.*) a naïve, gullible, foolish person.

IN COMPOUNDS

▫ **foo-foo dust** *n.* [orig. naut. jargon *foo-foo*, cologne] **1** [1910s+] (*US*) (*also* **foo-foo, foo-foo powder**) talcum powder, baby powder, anti-louse powder etc. **2** [1940s+] (*drugs*) (*also* **foo-foo stuff**) any form of powdered narcotic [ext. of sense 1 above].

foo-foo *adj.* (*also* **foo-fool, fool-fool**) [FOO-FOO *n.*] **1** [mid-19C+] simple-minded, stupid, oafish. **2** [1950s] credulous, gullible.

foo-foo *v.* [FOO-FOO *adj.* (1)] [1970s] to act stupidly, to mess around.

fool *n.* **1** [late 19C] a stupid or foolish thing. **2** [late 19C–1900s] an easy thing, in comparison; usu. in phr. *a fool to it.* **3** [late 19C+] anyone excessively enthusiastic about a given activity or topic; thus *dancing fool, singing fool*; often found as a *fool for...* **4** [1960s+] a person, irrespective of their actual intelligence. **5** [1960s+] (*also* **foo**) a general term of address. **6** [1990s+] (*also* **foo**) a stupid person.

SE in slang uses

IN COMPOUNDS

▫ **fool-ass** *n.* [-ASS *sfx*] [1960s–70s] a general term of disparagement; the inference is of stupidity. ▫ **fool-finder** *n.* [? because only fools are available when he comes to call] [late

18C–early 19C] a bailiff. ❑ **foolhead** *n.* [-HEAD *sfx* (1)] [20C+] a fool; thus *foolheaded*, stupid, foolish. ❑ **fool-monger** *n.* [SE sfx *-monger*] [late 16C–early 18C] **1** one who 'trades on' the credulity of fools, a swindler. **2** a gambler. ❑ **fool-taker** *n.* [late 16C–early 17C] (*UK Und.*) a dice- or card-sharp; thus *fool-taking*, the swindling of gamblers. ❑ **fool trap** *n.* **1** [late 16C–early 18C] one who 'trades on' the credulity of fools, a swindler. **2** [19C] the vagina. **3** [19C] a high-class prostitute.

IN PHRASES

❑ **fool up** *v.* [1950s] (*W.I.*) to deceive, to trick.

fool around *v.* **1** [1920s+] to conduct a promiscuous sex life; thus the invitation *let's fool around*, a suggestion by one of a couple that they should abandon speech for (sexual) action. **2** [1930s+] to enjoy sexual activity short of intercourse. **3** [1950s] to tease. **4** [1970s] to have a sexual relationship.

fooley *n.*

IN PHRASES

❑ **pull a fooley** *v.* [2000s] (*US black*) to act very stupidly; to act in an exceptional manner.

fool-fool *adj. see* FOO-FOO *adj.*

fool-fool house *n.* [FOOL-FOOL *adj.* + SE *house*] [1970s–80s] (*UK black*) a psychiatric institution.

foolish *adj.* **1** [late 18C–early 19C] used by prostitutes to distinguish a casual customer from a more sophisticated client; thus the query, *Is he foolish or* FLASH *adj.* (2b)? **2** [1990s+] (*US black*) excellent.

SE in slang uses

IN COMPOUNDS

❑ **foolish house** *n.* (*also* **foolish factory**) [1900s–30s] (*US*) a psychiatric institution. ❑ **foolish powder** *n.* [their effects] [1930s+] (*drugs*) any powdered narcotic, i.e. heroin, cocaine, morphine. ❑ **foolish water** *n.* [1900s] (*US*) alcohol.

fool's rush *n. see* BUM'S RUSH *n.* (3).

foon *n.* (*also* **fun**) [Chinese measurement] [1920s–50s] (*US drugs*) a pellet of prepared opium.

foont *n. see* FUNT *n.*

foop *n.* [backsl. POOF *n.*] [1900s–10s] a homosexual man.

foop *v.* [FOOP *n.*] **1** [1920s] (*US black*) to dance uninhibitedly. **2** [1970s] (*US campus*) to engage in homosexual acts.

fooper *n.* [FOOP *v.* (2)] [1970s] (*US campus*) a homosexual.

foostie-minged *adj.* [Scot. *foost*, a stench + MINGE *n.* (2)] [1990s+] (*Scot.*) a general term of abuse aimed at a woman; lit. 'smelly cunted'.

foot *n.*

SE in slang uses

DERIVATIVES

❑ **footmobile** *n.* [-MOBILE *sfx*] [1960s+] (*US*) transportation by foot.

IN COMPOUNDS

❑ **footback (it)** *see* separate entries. ❑ **football(er)** *see* separate entries. ❑ **foot juice** *n.* [1920s] (*US tramp*) cheap red wine. ❑ **foot land-raker** *n.* [late 16C–early 17C] a highway robber. ❑ **foot-rot** *n.* [? link to dial. *foot-ale*, in mining communities a miner uses his first day's pay to 'stand his foot-ale', i.e. buy drinks for his fellows] [late 19C] cheap (fourpenny) ale. ❑ **foot-rotting** *n.* [SAusE *footrot*, to treat a sheep's foot for rot] [1930s+] (*Aus.*) idling away one's time in boredom. ❑ **foot scamp/scamper/scamperer** *n. see under* SCAMP *n.* ❑ **foot-shaker** *n.* [1900s] (*US*) an infantryman. ❑ **foot soldier** *n.* [1970s+] (*US gay*) a male street prostitute. ❑ **foot-wabbler** *n.* (*also* **foot-wobbler, wabbler**) [late 18C–mid-19C] an infantryman, esp. as described by a cavalryman. ❑ **footwasher** *n.* [the religious rite whereby Primitive Baptists wash each other's feet, as commanded in John 13:14, 'If I then, your Lord and Master, have washed your feet, ye also ought to wash one another's feet'] [19C+] (*US*) a trad., fundamentalist Baptist.

IN PHRASES

❑ **foot is hot** [20C+] (*W.I., Trin.*) a phr. used of one who is restless, esp. a woman. ❑ **foot is too short** [20C+] (*W.I.*) a phr. said of one who has missed their chance or has arrived too late, esp. for a meal. ❑ **foot up** *v.* [the placing of the final result at the foot of a column of figures] [mid–late 19C] (*US*) to work out, to sum up a person. ❑ **foot-walk it** *v.* [1940s+] (*Aus.*) to travel by foot. ❑ **get on the good foot** *v.* [1970s+] (*US black*) **1** to correct what needs improving. **2** to do one's best, to 'put one's best foot forward'. ❑ **get there with both feet** *v.* [late 19C+] (*US*) to do something well, to succeed in a notable manner. ❑ **give someone the foot** *v.* [20C+] (*US*) **1** to throw out, to oust, to reject. **2** to kick. ❑ **have a foot up one's ass** *v. see under* ASS *n.* ❑ **have foot** *v.* [1930s] to have an advantage in a chase. ❑ **have one's foot on the rail** *v.* [the 'rail' is that of a bar] [20C+] (*US*) to drink heavily. ❑ **how are your poor feet?** [mid–late 19C] a general interrog. aimed at a passing person. ❑ **keep one's foot in someone's ass** *v. see under* ASS *n.* ❑ **make feet for children's shoes** *v.* (*also* **make feet for children's socks, ...stockings**) **1** [late 18C–19C] to have sexual intercourse. **2** [1930s+] (*US black*) to be pregnant. ❑ **make foot** *v.* (*also* **pick up one's foot, put one's foot in one's hand, take foot, take up one's foot and run**) [late 19C+] (*US*) to leave; to flee in panic. ❑ **my feet are staying** [a play on the pron. of the Ger. *auf Wiedersehen*, goodbye] [1980s+] (*US campus*) a farewell. ❑ **pull foot** *v.* [20C+ use mainly W.I.] [19C+] (*US/W.I.*) to run away. ❑ **put one's/a foot in someone's ass** *v. see under* ASS *n.* ❑ **put one's foot on the floor** *v.* [the pressing down of the accelerator pedal] [1920s+] to accelerate a motorcar. ❑ **throw one's feet** *v.* (*also* **throw one's legs**) [SE *throw the feet*, of a horse, to move its feet well, esp. when crossing rough ground] [late 19C–1930s] (*US*) to beg, to 'hustle', usu. for money. ❑ **throw the feet** *v.* [i.e. walking the streets, knocking on doors, in order to beg] [late 19C–1930s] (*orig. US*) **1** to beg. **2** to hurry off.

foot *v.* (*also* **footer, footy**) [Fr. *foutre*, to fuck] [17C] a euph. for FUCK *v.*

foot! *excl.* (*also* **foot! foot!**) [Fr. *foutre*, to fuck; usu. addressed to 'the respectably dressed person who wanders into strange and doubtful bye-ways' (Ware)] [late 19C–1900s] go away!

footback *n.* [pun on SE *horseback*] [late 16C; 19C+] travelling on foot; also as adv.

footback it *v.* (*also* **footpack it**) [FOOTBACK *n.*] [1930s] (*Aus.*) to travel by foot, with a pack on one's back.

football *n.* [1960s+] (*drugs*) **1** a measure of one half grain of a narcotic. **2** a capsule of a psychotropic drug. **3** in pl., amphetamine.

footballer *n.* [the use of the feet as an agent of violence] [1910s–20s] **1** (*Aus. prison*) a prison warder, who disciplines through kicking the prisoners. **2** (*Aus.*) anyone who fights with their feet.

footer *n.*[1] [Fr. *foutre*, to fuck; thus cf. FUCKER *n.* (3)] [mid-18C–mid-19C] a general term of contempt, a 'scurvy fellow', a 'low fellow'.

footer *n.*[2] [SE *football* + -ER *sfx*] **1** [mid-19C+] football, a football. **2** [1910s+] (*Aus.*) Australian Rules football. **3** [1920s] (*US*) a footstep.

footer *v.*[1] [FOOTER *n.*[1]] [mid-19C] to idle around.

footer *v.*[2] *see* FOOT *v.*

footie *n.* (*also* **footey, footy**) [1910s+] **1** (*Aus./N.Z.*) Australian Rules football. **2** (*Aus./N.Z.*) an Australian rules football. **3** rugby. **4** football (soccer).

footie-footie *v. see* FOOTSIE-FOOTSIE *n.*

footle *v.* [*OED* has 'of obscure origin' and suggests link to FOOTER *v.*[1], but *EDD* offers Nottingham dial. *footle*, to do anything in a feeble, ineffectual manner] **1** [late 18C] to titivate, to enhance. **2** [late 19C+] to act or talk foolishly. **3** [1920s–30s] to potter around.

footman's inn *n.* [the poor status and negative image of the SE *footman*] [early–mid-17C] very poor lodgings.

footman's mawnd *n.* [SE *footman* + MAUND *n.*] [late 17C–early 19C] a sore that counterfeits a kick or bite from a horse.

footsack! *excl.* [anglicized version of VOETSAK! *excl.*] [mid-19C+] (*orig. S.Afr.*) a general excl. of dismissal, go away! be off! get out!

footsie-footsie *n.* (*also* **footie-footie, footy-footy**) [1930s+] (*orig. US*) the surreptitious nudging of someone's foot out of sight of anyone else, typically beneath a table; the contact is usu. a prelude to greater intimacy; usu. with *play*...

IN PHRASES

❑ **play footsie** *v.* (*also* **play footie-footie, ...footies, ...footy-footy**) [1930s+] **1** to nudge someone's foot with one's own – out of sight of companions – as a possible prelude to further intimacy. **2** to indulge in the cautious sounding out of any relationship, economic, political etc, to curry favour. **3** to waste time; to prevaricate.

footy *n. see* FOOTIE *n.*

footy *adj.* [Fr. *foutu*, fucked or SE *futile*] **1** [18C+] (*US 19C+*) insignificant, worthless, despicable, futile. **2** [19C+] (*US*) foolish, simple.

footy *v. see* FOOT *v.*

footy-footy *n. see* FOOTSIE-FOOTSIE *n.*

fooy! *excl. see* PHOOEY! *excl.*

foozle *n.* [FOOZLE *v.* (1)] **1** [mid–late 19C] a conservative, one who is behind the times; a gullible fool [note SE *fossil*]. **2** [20C+] (*orig. sporting*) a miss, a blunder.

foozle *v.* [Ger. *fuseln*, to work too fast and thus badly] **1** [19C+] to perform clumsily, to bungle, to make a mess of. **2** [20C+] (*sporting*) to miss a shot.

IN PHRASES

❑ **foozle about (with)** *v.* **1** [mid-19C] to have sex on a casual basis. **2** [mid-19C+] (*also* **camfoozle, fuzzle**) to fool around (with).

foozled *adj.* (*also* **foozlified, foozly**) [FOOZLE *v.* (1)] **1** [17C–1900s] (*also* **fusled**) drunk. **2** [mid-19C+] (*also* **fuzzled**) blurred, spoilt. **3** [mid-19C+] (*also* **befoozeled, discomfoozled**) confused.

foozler *n.* [FOOZLE *v.* (1)] [late 19C] a bungler, one who does things clumsily.

fopdoodle *n.* [15C SE *fop*, a fool + DOODLE *n.*[1]] [17C] a fool, a simpleton.

fopdoodle *v.* [FOPDOODLE *n.*] [17C] **1** to have sexual intercourse. **2** to deceive, to cheat.

fop fops *v.* [echoic] [2000s] (*US prison*) to have a fistfight.

foplin *n.* (*also* **fopling**) [late 17C–18C] a young fop.

fopper *n.* [mispron. Fr. *faux pas*] [late 19C] a blunder, a mistake.

f.o.q.! *excl.* [SE *fly off*/FUCK OFF! *excl. quickly*] [1900s] (*Aus.*) leave! go away!

for Africa *phr.* [1970s+] (*S.Afr.*) a lot, a great many, a great deal.

forakers *n.* [orig. Winchester School jargon; ? synon. Lat. *forica* or SE *four acres*, i.e. a field (cf. BOG *n.*[1])] [mid-19C] the lavatory.

forbidden fruit *n.* [the biblical myth] **1** [1930s–40s] (*Irish*) the 'Adam's apple' in the throat. **2** [1940s–60s] an underage sexual partner of either sex.

for cat's sake *phr.* [1920s] (*US*) a euph. for FOR CHRIST'S SAKE! *excl.* (1).

forced landing *n.* [1980s] (*S.Afr.*) an unplanned pregnancy, esp. one that results in marriage.

force-meat ball *n.* [early 19C] anything essentially unpleasant, endured whether one likes it or not.

force-ripe *adj.* [the image of 'forced' (i.e. grown at abnormal speed) fruit or vegetables] [1950s+] (*W.I.*) precocious.

force the voucher *v.* [mid-19C] (*UK Und.*) to perform a specific swindle, whereby a 'firm' offers to place 'guaranteed winning' bets for a victim who has to forward the money in advance; the firm has, of course, vanished when it is time to pay off.

force-up *adj.* [for ety. *see* FORCE-RIPE *adj.*] [1990s+] (*W.I.*) socially ambitious.

for Christ's sake! *excl.* (*also* **Chrissake! Christ sake! Cris sake! for Chrissakes! for Christ sake! for crissake! for Crizzakes! for krissake!**) [20C+] a now mildly blasphemous excl. of rage, annoyance, surprise, amazement.

for crap's sake! *excl.* (*also* **for shit sake!**) [euph. for FOR CHRIST'S SAKE! *excl.* (1)] [1930s+] (*orig. US*) a general excl. of annoyance, surprise etc.

for crazy *phr.* [1960s] (*US*) for fun, for pleasure.

for cripes' sake! *excl.* (*also* **for cripe sake! for creep sake!**) [euph. for FOR CHRIST'S SAKE! *excl.* (1)] [1920s+] a general excl. of annoyance, surprise etc.

for crissake!/crizzakes! *excl. see* FOR CHRIST'S SAKE! *excl.*

for crying in a cemetery! *excl.* (*also* **for crying in the beer!**) [20C+] (*orig. US*) a euph. for FOR CHRIST'S SAKE! *excl.*

for crying out loud! *excl.* [1920s+] a euph. for FOR CHRIST'S SAKE! *excl.*

ford *n.* [fig. use of the perceived inferiority of a Ford automobile] [1960s+] (*US prison*) any generally antagonistic or unhelpful doctor.

Ford car salesman *n.* [1980s+] (*Aus. prison*) a prison superintendant who promises reforms but never carries them out.

fore/aft *adj.* [1970s+] (*US gay*) of a homosexual male, active or passive.

fore and aft *adj.* [rhy. sl.] [2000s] daft, foolish.

fore and after *n.* [19C] a woman, usu. a prostitute, who is agreeable to group sex, involving vaginal (*fore*) and anal (*aft*) intercourse.

forecaster *n.* [it is the *fore*, i.e. front of the body] [19C] the vagina.

forecastle *n.* [SE *forecastle*, the forward area of a ship] [19C] the vagina.

fore coach-wheel *n.* [the fore or front coach-wheels were smaller than those at the rear] [late 18C–19C] a half-a-crown (12.5p).

fore-court *n.* [19C] the vagina.

foredeck *n.* [SE *foredeck*, the forward deck of a boat] [17C] the vagina.

forefoot *n.* (*also* **forepaw**) [late 16C–early 19C] the human hand.

foregather *v.* [SE *foregather*, to meet together, to associate with] [18C] to have sexual intercourse.

foregut *n.* [SE *fore*, front + *gut*] [19C] the vagina.

fore-hatch *n.* [19C] the vagina.

foreign *adj.* [the automatic xenophobia that attaches itself to fantasies about 'foreign' sexual practices] [1900s–40s] (*US black*) referring to any form of sexual activity considered 'unnatural'; thus *foreigner*, one deemed a sexual 'pervert'.

foreigneering cove *n.* [SE *foreign* + COVE *n.* (1)] [mid–late 19C] a foreigner; also adj. *foreigneering*.

foreigner *n.* **1** [1930s] (*US Und.*) any convict who is not a professional thief. **2** [1970s+] (*US black*) a homosexual; thus *speak in a foreign tongue*, to have oral sex [the 'foreign tongue' is FRENCH *n.* (4)].

SE in slang uses

IN PHRASES

❑ **do a foreigner** *v.* [SE *foreign*; i.e. somewhere 'away from home'] [1970s+] for a worker contracted to one job to take time off illegally to tackle another, more lucrative, one.

foreign parts *n.*

SE in slang uses

IN PHRASES

❑ **go to foreign parts** *v.* [euph.] [early 19C] to be transported as a convict.

foreman *n.*[1] [*OED* marks this as '? slang ? goose'; the definition is assumed f. one use in Beaumont & Fletcher's *Philaster* (1622); Michaelmas (29 Sept.) is a trad. goose-eating day; ? a foreman precedes an alderman in a procession as Michaelmas precedes Christmas when one eats an ALDERMAN *n.* (1), i.e. turkey] [early 17C] ? a goose.

foreman *n.*[2] [it stands at the *fore*front of the body] [19C] the penis (cf. FOREWOMAN *n.*).

foreman of the jury *n.* [a specific 'tavern term' drawn from the anonymous *The English Liberal Science, or a new-found Art and*

Order of Drinking (1650)] [mid-17C–early 19C] one who takes over the conversation.

forenoon *n.* [19C] an alcoholic drink taken before breakfast.

fore-paw *n. see* FOREFOOT *n.*

fore-pokers *n.* [late 18C–early 19C] in cards, aces and kings.

fore-room *n.* [19C] the vagina.

foreskin hunter *n.* [19C] a prostitute.

forest *n.* [17C+] the female pubic hair.

forewoman *n.* [antonym of FOREMAN *n.*[2]] [mid-19C] the vagina.

for fair *adv.* [late 19C+] (*US*) completely, absolutely, altogether.

for-free *n.* [she effectively 'gives it away for free'] [1940s] (*orig. US*) a prostitute who undercuts the going price, an amateur.

for freezies *phr.* [SE *free* + -IZ- *infix*] [1960s] (*US black/teen*) without rules or restrictions.

for fuck's sake! *excl.* (*also* **for fuck's sakes! for fuck sake! fuck's sake!**) [1920s+] a general excl. of exasperation.

forge *n.* [where the male 'rod' is softened] [18C–19C] the vagina.

forgers *n.* [late 16C] crooked dice.

forgive and forget *n.* [rhy. sl.] [20C+] (*Aus.*) a cigarette.

for gosh sake! *excl.* [20C+] (*US*) a euph. version of *for God's sake!*

for grins *phr. see* GRIN *n.*[3] (1).

fo' rilla *adv. see* FOR REAL *adv.*

fork *n.*[1] **1** [late 17C–18C] a spendthrift, a wastrel. **2** [late 17C–mid-19C; 1940s] (*UK Und.; 1940s US*) a pickpocket. **3** [early 19C+] (*orig. UK; US black*) usu. in pl., the fingers, esp. the middle and forefingers. **4** [mid-19C+] usu. in pl., the hands. **5** [late 19C+] the crotch; thus ext. as the penis. **6** [1980s] (*Aus.*) a jockey.

IN PHRASES

❑ **hawk one's fork** *v.* [1970s+] (*Aus.*) to work as a prostitute; the 'fork' is the juncture of the legs and thus the vagina. ❑ **put up one's forks** *v. see* PUT ONE'S BONES UP *under* BONE *n.*[1].

fork *n.*[2] *see* FORK AND KNIFE *n.* (1).

fork *v.*[1] **1** [late 17C–early 19C] to pick pockets, using the fore and middle fingers, extended like the tines of a fork, which are thrust into the pocket, then closed tight on any object within; this is then withdrawn between the 'fork'. **2** [mid–late 19C] to lay a woman down with spread legs preparatory to intercourse; also as *fork out*. **3** [late 19C+] (*US*) (*also* **fork leather**) to mount a horse. **4** [20C+] (*Aus.*) to ride a horse.

IN PHRASES

❑ **fork out** *see* separate entries. ❑ **fork over** *v. see* separate entry.

fork *v.*[2] [1950s] a euph. for FUCK *v.*

fork and knife *n.* [rhy. sl.] [20C+] **1** (*also* **fork**) life. **2** a wife.

fork and spoon *n.*[1] [the shape] [1930s] (*US*) mutual oral-genital stimulation.

fork and spoon *n.*[2] [rhy. sl. = HOON *n.* (1)] [1980s+] (*Aus. prison*) a lout, a hooligan.

fork-out *n.* [FORK OUT *v.*] [mid-19C] a price, a payment.

fork out *v.* (*also* **fork, fork up**) [FORK *n.*[1] (4)] [early 19C+] **1** to pay, to donate. **2** to hand over.

fork over *v.* [FORK *n.*[1] (4)] [mid-19C+] to hand over, to give out.

for krissake! *excl. see* FOR CHRIST'S SAKE! *excl.*

forlorn hope *n.* [Du. *verloren hoop*, a lost troop (of soldiers); the orig. 16C use described a band of skirmishers or assault troops who were sent ahead of the main force; this mutates into a desperate band of men and thence a desperate enterprise] **1** [17C] the losers at a gaming table. **2** [late 18C–early 19C] a gambler's last, despairing bet.

form *n.*[1] [horseracing use] **1** [mid-19C+] character, style. **2** [late 19C+] the accepted way of doing things. **3** [1950s+] (*UK Und.*) previous convictions.

form *n.*[2] [abbr. SE *reformatory*] [late 19C+] (*S.Afr.*) a prison.

for Mike's sake! *excl. see* FOR PETE'S SAKE! *excl.*

formula *n.* [? SAmE *formula*, baby food, pap] [1980s] (*drugs*) fake cannabis.

forney *n. see* FAWNEY *n.*

fornicating *adj.* [20C+] a lit. euph. for FUCKING *adj.*

SE in slang uses

IN COMPOUNDS

❑ **fornicating engine** *n.* (*also* **fornicating member, ...tool**) [ENGINE *n.*/MEMBER *n.*[1]/TOOL *n.*[1] (1a)] [19C] the penis.

fornicator *n.* **1** [19C] the penis; thus *fornicator's hall*, the vagina. **2** [late 19C] in pl., trousers with a flap front rather than the modern fly.

forny *n. see* FAWNEY *n.*

for Pete's sake! *excl.* (*also* **for Mike's sake! for Pat's sake! for Pete Almighty's sake!**) [20C+] (*orig. US*) a euph. excl., usu. used to indicate one's mild annoyance.

for real *adj.* (*also* **4-real**) [1950s+] (*US*) genuine.

for real *adv.* (*also* **fo' rilla**) [1940s+] (*orig. US black*) genuinely, honestly, sincerely, to be taken at face value.

IN PHRASES

❑ **on the furilla** [1980s+] (*US black*) acting honestly, honourably.

for real? *phr.* (*also* **for reals?**) [1930s+] (*US teen*) used as a question to ask whether someone is teasing or telling the truth.

for real! *excl.* [FOR REAL *adv.*] [1970s+] **1** an affirmative excl. absolutely! genuinely! **2** as a negative excl., implying alarm or threat.

for shit sake! *excl. see* FOR CRAP'S SAKE! *excl.*

for sure *adj.* [FOR SURE *adv.*] **1** [1960s] absolute, certain. **2** [1990s+] reliable, trustworthy.

for sure *adv.* (*also* **fo' sho, real-for-sure**) [20C+] (*US*) definitely, certainly, absolutely.

for sure! *excl.* [the phr. gained a new lease of life as part of the Valley Girl vocab. of the early 1980s+; and then was taken over by US black usage, *see* FO' SHO! *excl.*] [20C+] certainly! definitely! absolutely!

Forsyte Saga *n.* [rhy. sl.; ult. John Galsworthy's early 20C literary saga of British business/social life] [1970s+] lager.

fort *n.* (*also* **fortress**) [lit. euph.] [mid-16C–19C] the vagina; thus fig. the state of chastity or honour.

IN COMPOUNDS

❑ **fort bushy** *n.* [BUSH *n.*[1] (1)] **1** [20C+] the vagina. **2** [1970s+] (*gay*) the pubic hair.

for the fuck of it *phr.* [FUCK *n.* (2a)] [20C+] for the fun of it.

for the good of the loo *phr.* [SE *loo*, a card-game resembling whist; the ref. to the game extends to its players and thence, fig., to the whole community] [late 18C–early 19C] for the good of all, for the benefit of the community.

Forties *n.*[1] *see* FORTY *n.* (3).

Forties *n.*[2] *see* ROARING FORTIES *n.*

fortnighter *n.* [1950s–70s] (*US drugs*) an occasional, notionally fortnightly, use of narcotics.

Fortnum and Mason *n.* [rhy. sl.] [1990s+] **1** a basin. **2** a pudding-basin haircut, a 'short back and sides'.

fortress *n. see* FORT *n.*

fortune-biter *n. see* BITE *v.*

fortune-teller *n.* [he tells you your *fortune*, i.e. your sentence] [late 17C–early 19C] a trial judge.

forty *n.* **1** [early 19C] a reward of £40. **2** [19C] (*US Und.*) a gang, properly the 'Forty Thieves' based in New York's Five Points area. **3** [late 19C+] (*Aus.*) a crook, a confidence trickster, a rascal, a layabout youth; often in pl. [a Sydney gang of the mid-19C; poss. called the *Forty Thieves*, although that name may have been a subsequent journalistic invention]. **4** [1980s+] (*US black*) (*also* **40, forty ounce, four-oh**) a 40oz. (1-litre) bottle of beer.

IN COMPOUNDS

❑ **forty dog** *n.* (*also* **dog**) [DOG *n.*[7]] [1980s+] (*US black*) a 40oz (1-litre) bottle of beer.

forty *adj.*[1] [thus orig. *OED* citation: 'I could beat forty of them' (Shakespeare, *Coriolanus*, 1607)] [17C+] many.

IN COMPOUNDS

❑ **forty-eleven** *n.* (*also* **forty-leven**) [mid-19C+] (*US black/W.I.*) too many, an infinite number. ❑ **forty-guts** *n.* [mid-19C] a fat man. ❑ **forty-jawed** *adj.* [1910s] loquacious, talkative.

SE in slang uses

IN COMPOUNDS

❑ **forty acres** *n.* [their supposed dimensions] [20C+] (*US*) extremely large feet. ❑ **forty-faced** *adj.* [? one has 'forty faces', none of them trustworthy, but note FORTY *adj.*[1] + dial. *forty-legs*, a millipede, where *forty* is generic for 'many'] [late 19C–1950s] shameless; thus combs. *forty-faced liar, forty-faced flirt*. ❑ **forty fits** *n. see under* FIT *n.*[3]. ❑ **forty-foot** *n.* [mid-19C] a short person. ❑ **forty h.p.** *adj.* [lit. 40 *h*orse *p*ower, a high speed for the period] [late 19C] (*Aus.*) substantial, very great. ❑ **forty ounce** *n. see* FORTY *n.* (4). ❑ **forty-pounder** *n.* [the £40 cash bonus awarded to any policeman who secured a 'Tyburn ticket', i.e. captured a murderer] [19C] a policeman. ❑ **forty-rod (lightning)** *n.* [its strength; such whisky was jokingly said to be powerful enough to kill at a distance of 40 rods (about 17km/11 miles). Alternatively, its strength empowered the drinker to run at top speed for a similar distance, or the drinker is guaranteed to collapse if he attempts to walk much further than this; note LIGHTNING *n.* (2)] [mid-19C–1930s] cheap, strong whisky. ❑ **forty-shilling word** *n.* [1960s] (*W.I.*) an obscene word, for the use of which one can be fined 40 shillings or £2.

IN PHRASES

❑ **forty miles of bad road** *n.* [1920s+] (*US*) **1** a very unattractive person, sight or situation; the number can differ. **2** one who is completely exhausted. ❑ **forty ways from the jack** *adv.* (*also* **fifty ways from the jack, forty ways, two ways from the jack**) [20C+] (*US, orig. gambling*) in every way possible. ❑ **forty weeks favour** *adv.* [SE *forty weeks*, the approx. period of gestation + *favour*, something given as a mark of favour, e.g. a gift to a lover such as a handkerchief] [early 17C] the state of pregnancy, often in the context of an illegitimate child.

forty *adj.*[2] (*also* **four-oh, four-point-oh, thirty-eight and two, thirty-eight plus two, twice twenty**) [1930s–70s] (*orig. US black*) exceptionally pleasing, very fine.

Forty-Deuce *n.* [ext. DEUCE, THE *n.* (2)] [1980s+] (*US*) 42nd Street from Eighth Avenue to Times Square; orig. the centre of New York's tourism, nightlife and underworld.

forty-eight carat *adj. see* TWENTY-FOUR CARAT *adj.*

forty-five *n.* [the popular Colt .45 revolver] **1** [20C+] a .45 calibre pistol. **2** [1930s] (*US tramp*) in pl., beans [? the (.45) pistol-shot like explosion of bean-induced breaking wind].

forty-five minute psychosis *n.* [the short duration and intensity of the drug experience] [1970s+] (*drugs*) dimethyltryptarine (DMT).

forty-four *n.* [rhy. sl.] **1** [1930s+] a whore. **2** [1950s+] a door-to-door salesman.

forty-four *adv.* [rhy. sl.] [20C+] door-to-door.

forty-niner *n.* [the image is of cocaine as GOLD DUST *n.* (1) due to the Californian Gold Rush of 1849] [1950s–70s] (*US drugs*) a cocaine user.

forty-one *n.* [? a menu number; ? orig. short order] [1930s] (*US*) orangeade.

forty to the dozen *adv.* (*also* **fourteen to the dozen, thirteen to the dozen**) [SE phr. *nineteen to the dozen*] [mid-19C+] extremely fast; often as *talk forty to the dozen*.

forward *adj.* [late 18C] drunk.

forward *v.* [1980s] (*UK black*) to go to.

forward (pass) *n.* [rhy. sl.] [1990s+] (*Aus.*) a beer or wine glass.

forwards *n.* [it impels its users to action] [1960s+] (*drugs*) amphetamine.

fo' sheezy! *excl. see* FO' SHO! *excl.*

fo' shizzle (my nizzle)! *excl. see* FO' SHO! *excl.*

fo' sho *adv. see* FOR SURE *adv.*

fo' sho! *excl.* (*also* **fa' sheezy! foe shizzy! fo' sheezy! fo' shizzle! fo' shizzle my nizzle!**) [FOR SURE! *excl.* + -IZ- *infix*] [1990s+] (*US black*) certainly! definitely! absolutely!

foss *n. see* PHOS *n.*

fossil farming *n.* [1980s+] (*Aus. prison*) snatching purses from old women.

fotie *n. see* PHOTIE *n.*

fotog *n. see* PHOTOG *n.*

fotz up *v. see* FUTZ UP *under* FUTZ *v.*

fou *adj.*[1] (*also* **fu**) [Scot. pron. of SE *full*] [late 17C–1910s] drunk.

fou *adj.*[2] [Fr. *fou*, mad] [20C+] (*W.I.*) crazy, mad.

fough! *excl. see* FAUGH! *excl.*

foul *adj.* **1** [20C+] a general negative, revolting, disgusting. **2** [1960s+] (*US black*) of talk, deliberately belligerent. **3** [1960s+] (*US black*) of a person, aggressive.

IN PHRASES

❑ **not too foul** [2000s] (*N.Z.*) acceptable, tolerable.

foul *adv.* [14C–17C SE *foul*, 'guilty of a charge or accusation; criminally implicated' *OED*] [mid-19C–1920s] (*US Und.*) guilty, 'red-handed'; usu. in phr. *caught foul*, caught in the act.

foul a plate with *v. see under* PLATE *n.*[1].

foul ball *n.* [baseball jargon *foul ball*, a ball struck so that it falls outside the lines drawn from the home base through the first and third bases] (*US*) **1** [1920s+] an unpleasant, poss. criminal character. **2** [1990s+] a distasteful statement.

foulcher *n.* [? SE *full*] [late 19C] (*UK Und.*) a purse.

foul out *v.* [baseball imagery] [1940s+] (*US*) to go wrong, to fail.

found on *adj.* [police charge sheet, *found on licensed premises...*] [20C+] (*Irish*) arrested for drinking in a public house after licensing hours.

foundry *n.* **1** [late 19C] a shop, esp. a pork butcher's shop because of the noise of the sausage machine. **2** [1900s] (*US*) a restaurant.

fountain of love *n.* [late 16C–19C] the vagina.

four *n.* [mid-19C–1910s] fourpenny-worth of a given drink, as sold in a public house.

SE in slang uses

IN COMPOUNDS

❑ **four and nine (penny)** *n.* [the 1844 advertisement, which declared 'Whene'er to slumber you incline/Take a *short nap* at 4 and 9'] [mid-19C] a cheap hat. ❑ **four and one** *n.* [1940s] (*US black*) the fifth day of the working week, i.e. payday, which is Friday. ❑ **four-and-twenty (steps)** *n.* [ety. unknown; ? the number of steps from a particular courtroom to the cells] [1950s] (*W.I.*) an arrest, a trial. ❑ **four-and-two** *n.* [? of the four sides of bread, only two are buttered] [1930s] a sandwich. ❑ **four-by** *n.* [abbr. SE *four-by-four* or 4X4] [1990s+] a four-wheel-drive vehicle, usu. a form of Jeep, popular among drug dealers, rappers and their fans.

IN PHRASES

❑ **four of one suit** *n. see* FOUR-FLUSHER *n.*

four *adj.*

SE in slang uses

DERIVATIVES

❑ **foursome** *n.* [1940s+] (*US*) four people involved in sex together; it can involve any combination of genders.

IN COMPOUNDS

❑ **four bars** *n.* [1930s] (*US black*) a short time. ❑ **four bit(s)** *see under* BIT *n.*[1]. ❑ **four bones** *n. see under* BONE *n.*[1]. ❑ **four cautions, the** *n.* [late 18C–early 19C] 'I. Beware of a woman before. – II. Beware of a horse behind. – III. Beware of a cart sideways. – IV. Beware of a priest every way' (Grose, 1785). ❑ **four-cornered** *adj.* [elaboration of SE *cornered*] [20C+] (*US prison*) caught in the act. ❑ **four corners** *n.* [*four-corners*, a crossroads and thus a small settlement that might grow up around it] [19C+] (*US*) a small, out-of-the-way place. ❑ **four decker** *n.* [1980s] group sex, involving two heterosexual couples. ❑ **four-eye/-eyed/-eyes** *see* separate entries. ❑ **four-fifth** *n.* [1990s+] (*US black*) a.45 pistol. ❑ **four-fingered shuffle** *n.*

[1980s+] masturbation. ❑ **four-flush/-flusher** *see* separate entries. ❑ **four-foot amelia** *n.* [1930s] (*W.I.*) a flimsy or roughly constructed bed. ❑ **four-Fs** *n. see* separate entry. ❑ **four-half** *n.* [late 19C–1920s] a mix of ale and porter, sold at fourpence a quart. ❑ **four-headed** *adj.* [1930s] (*US black*) very clever, exceptionally intelligent. ❑ **four-letter man/word** *n. see* separate entries. ❑ **four-minute job** *n.* [2000s] (*US prison*) a shower. ❑ **four piece** *n.* [2000s] a full set of restraints, comprising four pieces: cuffs, leg irons, waist, and security cover. ❑ **four pound** *n.* (*also* **4-pound**) [1990s+] (*US black*) a gun. ❑ **four prices** *adj.* [? it costs fig. 'four times as much' as a normal item] [20C+] (*Ulster*) very expensive. ❑ **fours up** *n.* [1990s+] sexual intercourse involving two couples. ❑ **four thick** *n.* [late 19C] beer sold at fourpence a quart. ❑ **four-wheeler** *n.* [? the cow's four legs] [19C] a beefsteak.

IN PHRASES

❑ **four sisters on thumb street** *n.* [1970s+] (*US black*) masturbation. ❑ **go four** *v.* [card-playing imagery] [1910s] (*Aus.*) to support, to back up.

four-by-four *n.* [2000s] **1** (*UK black*) a very pretty young woman [? the rectilinearity of her features]. **2** a whore [rhy. sl.].

four by two *n.* (*also* **fourby**) [rhy. sl.] **1** [1910s+] (*also* **three be two**) a Jew. **2** [1970s+] (*usu. Aus./N.Z.*) a prison warder [= SCREW *n.*[1] (2c)].

four by two *adj.* [? standard sizing, thus idea of jobsworth] [2000s] (*N.Z.*) aggressive, tactless.

four-eleven *n.* (*also* **411, four-one-one**) [the US phone number for information] [1980s+] (*US black/campus*) information.

IN PHRASES

❑ **give the four-eleven/411** *v.* [1990s+] (*US black*) to give out information, to instruct; also as excl.

four-eleven-forty-four *n.* (*also* **4-11-44**) [a 'lucky number' popularized by NUMBERS, THE *n.* or POLICY *n.* bettors from late 19C+, and known in numbers' jargon as the *fancy gal roll* or the *Washerwoman's Number*; note 1872 *The Galaxy* (NY) 495: 'Sometimes a mania seizes the entire fraternity of colored players to play some particular "flat gig," which is generally 4—11—44, and the numbers being sure to be drawn only after everybody has been tired out and quit betting on them, their appearance evokes a storm that is comical in its intensity when its occasion is remembered.'] [1960s] (*US black*) the penis.

four-eyed *adj.* (*also* **four-eyes**) [late 19C+] a derog. epithet aimed at those who wear spectacles.

IN COMPOUNDS

❑ **four-eye puss** *n.* [PUSS *n.*[2] (1)] [1940s] (*W.I.*) one who wears glasses.

four-eyes *n.* **1** [early 19C] spectacles. **2** [mid-19C+] one who wears glasses; also with overtones of distrust of anyone 'intellectual'.

IN PHRASES

❑ **make four eyes** *v.* [1940s] (*W.I.*) of two people, to gaze at one another, to meet.

4F *n.* [4-F *adj.*] [1940s–50s] (*US*) a weak and generally inferior man.

4-F *adj.* (*also* **four-eff, Four-F**) [milit. specification for anyone unfit to serve] [1940s+] (*US*) useless, inferior, weak.

4-F club *n.* [note Mae West in *I'm No Angel* (1933) tells her maid to 'find 'em, fool 'em and forget 'em' when it comes to men; the rap group NWA used 'find 'em, fuck 'em and flee' in 1991] [1950s+] (*US*) a metaphorical 'club' based on the slogan 'find 'em, feel 'em, fuck 'em (or euph. as *fool 'em*) and forget 'em', the axiom for macho US youth in its dealings with women.

459 *n.* [1980s+] (*US Und.*) a burglary; also as v. *459*, to steal.

four-flush *n.* [FOUR-FLUSH *v.*] **1** [1900s] an act of deception. **2** *see* FOUR-FLUSHER *n.*

four-flush *adj.* [FOUR-FLUSHER *n.*] [late 19C+] (*US*) cheating, crooked, untrustworthy.

four-flush *v.* [FOUR-FLUSHER *n.*] [late 19C+] (*US*) to cheat or bluff; thus n. *four-flushing*.

four-flusher *n.* (*also* **four-flush, four of one suit**) [poker jargon; a real flush requires five cards of the same suit, four is merely a bluff] (*US*) **1** [late 19C+] a cheat, a bluffer. **2** [20C+] a braggart, a boaster. **3** [1910s] something worthless. **4** [1910s+] a scrounger, one who fails to pay due debts.

four-flushing *adj.* [FOUR-FLUSH *v.*] [20C+] lying, cheating, bragging.

four-Fs *n.* [1940s+] (*US*) a young man's guide to sexual ethics, 'find 'em, feel 'em, fuck 'em and forget 'em', sometimes amplified to *five Fs* by adding 'feed 'em' after 'find 'em'.

four-letter man *n.* **1** [1920s+] (*UK society*) an unpleasant person; the four letters are perhaps *s-h-i-t* (as suggested by Manchon, *Le Slang*, 1923) or *c-u-n-t* (cf. *FIVE-LETTER WOMAN under* FIVE *adj.* **2** [1940s+] (*US*) a male homosexual: both as sense 1 above and as *h-o-m-o*.

four-letter word *n.* [euph.] [20C+] an obscenity, notably CUNT *n.*, FUCK *n.*, SHIT *n.* etc; thus *six-letter word*: BUGGER *n.*[1]; and *ten-letter word*: COCKSUCKER *n.* etc.

four-oh *n. see* FORTY *n.* (4).

four-oh *adj. see* FORTY *adj.*[2].

four-oh-four *n.* (*also* **404**) [computer use *404*, 'File Not Found' message on the Web] [1990s+] (*US teen*) a fool.

four-one-one/411 *n. see* FOUR-ELEVEN *n.*

fourpenny *n.* [the price of the various commodities] **1** [mid-19C] beer costing fourpence a pint. **2** [late 19C–1900s] an ugly, worn-out old prostitute. **3** [late 19C–1900s] (*also* **fourpenny touch**) a short, commercial act of intercourse. **4** [1950s] (*UK Und.*) a cheap lodging house.

fourpenny *adj.*

IN COMPOUNDS

❑ **fourpenny cannon** *n.* [its shape and/or its consistency resembles a cannon ball + the cost] [late 19C] a steak and kidney pie. ❑ **fourpenny dark** *n.* [1950s+] (*Aus.*) cheap red wine. ❑ **fourpenny (one)** *n.* [ult. rhy. sl. *fourpenny bit* = hit] [late 19C+] 'a clip round the ear-hole'; usu. as *get a…* or *give a…* ❑ **fourpenny pit** *n.* [late 19C] a fourpenny bit or groat, the predecessor of the threepenny bit.

four-point-oh *adj. see* FORTY *adj.*[2].

14 *n.* [1990s+] (*US prison*) N, the 14th letter of the alphabet; the ref. is to gangs from North California.

fourteen-carat *adj. see* EIGHTEEN-CARAT *adj.*

fourteen penn'orth *n.* [early 19C] a sentence of 14 years' transportation.

fourteen to the dozen *adv. see* FORTY TO THE DOZEN *adv.*

four-twenty *n.* (*also* **4:20**) [email on American Dialect Society List 10/5/2001: '[The term] originated at San Rafael High School in San Rafael, CA, in the early 1970s as a code for smoking marijuana at 4:20 pm (70 minutes after school dismissal). The Grateful Dead were long based out of San Rafael, and the phrase was used on a flyer at Grateful Dead shows in 1990, leading to its wider use.'] [1970s+] (*US black/drugs*) marijuana.

four-twenty *v.* (*also* **4:20**) [FOUR-TWENTY *n.*] [1990s+] (*US black/drugs*) to smoke marijuana.

four-wheel skid *n. see* FRONT-WHEEL SKID *n.* (1).

foutra *v.* (*also* **foutre**) [Fr. *foutre*] [17C] to have sexual intercourse.

foutre, a *n.* [Fr. *foutre*; note 19C US regional (Pennsylvania) *fouty*, trifling] [late 16C–mid-17C] a synon. for FUCK *n.* (2a).

foutre! *excl.* [Fr. *foutre*] [late 16C–mid-17C; mid-19C] a general oath of dismissal; synon. with FUCK! *excl.*

f.o.w.b. *phr.* [1920s–60s] (*US black/teen*) a phr. used to a young woman who has been taken out in a car: *fuck or walk back*.

fowling piece *n. see* PIECE *n.* (3b).

fox *n.*[1] [stereotypical positive/negative characteristics of the animal] **1** [late 16C+] (*also* **Mr. Fox**) a cunning, duplicitous person. **2** [mid-19C] an artificial sore. **3** [1900s] (*Aus.*) a lie, nonsense. **4** [1910s–30s] (*US Und.*) a tramp who rides on passenger trains by tricking the conductor as to his/her legitimacy. **5** [1930s] (*US Und.*) an escape, either from the police or prison. **6** [1940s+] (*orig. US black*) a girl, a woman, esp. an attractive and sexually active one; thus *superfox*, an extreme example [backform. f. FOXY *adj.* (3)]. **7** [1940s+] a womanizer. **8** [1960s] (*US prison*) the passive partner in a lesbian relationship. **9** [1970s+] (*US campus*) a sexually attractive person of the opposite sex. **10** [1970s+] (*orig. US*) a drinker who slips out of the bar when it is his turn to pay for a round.

IN COMPOUNDS

❑ **fox-drunk** *adj.* [late 16C] drunk but still cunning.

IN PHRASES

❑ **fox around** *v.* [1930s] (*US*) to sneak about, to act in a surreptitious manner. ❑ **fox in the bush** *n.* [the negative stereotype of Jewish cunning] [1900s–20s] (*US*) a derog. term for a Jew. ❑ **play the fox** *v.* **1** [late 19C] to cheat, to sham, to dissemble. **2** [1930s] to vomit [var. on FLAY THE FOX *v.*].

SE in slang uses

IN COMPOUNDS

❑ **fox's sleep** *n.* (*also* **foxing**) [the belief that a fox sleeps with one eye open] [mid-19C] an air of indifference to what is going on.

fox *n.*[2] [backform. f. FOXED *adj.* (1)] [late 17C–early 18C] a state of drunkenness.

IN PHRASES

❑ **catch a fox** *v.* [late 17C] to be drunk.

fox *n.*[3] [? the preponderance of foxes; ? their cunning characteristics] [mid-19C+] (*US*) an inhabitant of Maine.

fox *v.*[1] [SE *fox*, to confuse] **1** [mid-17C] to make drunk. **2** [late 18C] (*UK Und.*) of prisoners, to practise a trick on a visitor to the jail.

IN PHRASES

❑ **on the fox** [late 19C] (*Aus.*) behaving in a duplicitous manner.

fox *v.*[2] **1** [mid-19C–1900s] to observe surreptitiously. **2** [late 19C–1900s] (*Aus./N.Z.*) to be a voyeur, esp. when spying on couples in the open air.

fox *v.*[3] [mid-19C+] to feign sleep or (*Aus.*) to feign unconsciousness.

foxed *adj.* (*also* **foxified**) [FOX *v.*[1] (1)] [17C+] drunk; thus *unfoxed*, sober.

foxer *n.*[1] [FOX *v.*[2] (2)] [1900s] (*Aus./N.Z.*) a voyeur, esp. one who spies on couples in the open air.

foxer *n.*[2] *see* NIXER *n.*

foxhead *n.* [SE *fox*, to confuse + *head*] [20C+] (*US*) illicitly distilled whisky.

foxified *adj. see* FOXED *adj.*

foxiness *n.* [FOXY *adj.* (3)] [1990s+] (*US*) flirtatiousness.

foxing *n. see* FOX'S SLEEP *under* FOX *n.*[1].

fox's paw *n.* [Fr. *faux pas*] [late 18C–early 19C] a mistake, a blunder.

foxy *n.* (*also* **foxy methoxy**) [rhyme on drug name] [2000s] (*US drugs*) the drug 5-methoxy-N, N-diisopropyltryptamine.

foxy *adj.* [FOX *n.*[1] (1) + sfx -*y*] **1** [mid-19C–1900s] (*UK Und.*) avoiding trouble. **2** [late 19C] (*US campus*) artistic, neat. **3** [late 19C+] (*orig. US*) attractive, sexy; also fig. use. **4** [1900s–50s] (*US black*) splendid, good. **5** [1900s–60s] clever, intellectual.

IN COMPOUNDS

❑ **foxy grandpa** *n.* [the cartoon character *Foxy Granpa*, by C.E. Schultze (1866–1939), which appeared *c.*1900 and featured an adult who, in a reverse of the usual cartoon situation, played tricks on children] [20C+] (*US*) a sly person, neither necessarily old nor a grandfather.

foy *n.* [abbr. FOIST *n.*[2] (2)] [late 16C–early 17C] a swindler.

foy! *excl. see* PHOOEY! *excl.*

foyl-cloy/foyler *n. see* FOIL-CLOY *n.*

foyse *n. see* FICE *n.*

foyst *see under* FOIST.

f.p. *n.* [abbr.] [20C+] (*UK Und.*) false pretences, thus fraud.

fraai *v. see* VRY *v.*

frabbajabba *n.* [SE *jabber*, to talk unrestrainedly + redup.] [1950s] (*US*) nonsensical chatter.

fracture *v.* **1** [1930s–70s] (*US*) to beat up, to trounce. **2** [1940s–70s] (*US*) to astonish, to disconcert. **3** [1950s–70s] to make one laugh, to amuse greatly, e.g. *that fractures me*, that's an amusing joke.

fractured *adj.* [1950s+] **1** very drunk. **2** emotionally overcome. **3** divorced.

fraggle *n.* [the 1980s TV series *Fraggle Rock*] [2000s] (*UK prison*) someone who is mentally disturbed.

fraho *n.* (*also* **frajo**) [Sp.] **1** [1950s+] (*US drugs*) marijuana. **2** [1990s+] (*US prison*) a cigarette.

fraidy *adj.* (*also* **fraidy-fraidy**) [SE *afraid*; note SE *fraidy-cat*, a timid person] [1950s] (*W.I.*) timid, fearful.

frail *n.*[1] [the image of women as weaklings] **1** [early 19C–1930s] (*also* **frail one**) a prostitute, a mistress. **2** [20C+] (*orig. US*) a girl, a woman. **3** [1950s] (*US prison*) a passive partner in a lesbian relationship.

IN COMPOUNDS

❑ **frail sisterhood** *n.* (*also* **frailty**) [late 18C–mid-19C] a collective term for prostitutes as a class.

frail *n.*[2] [? its insubstantiality] [1940s] (*US Und.*) a stolen cheque.

frail eel *n.* [FRAIL *n.*[1] (2) + SE *eel*, an elusive creature which is hard to hold on to; ? poss. Zora-Neale Hurston nonce-word] [1930s–40s] (*US black*) an attractive woman.

frajo *n. see* FRAHO *n.*

frame *n.*[1] **1** [17C+] the body. **2** [20C+] (*US black*) a person. **3** [1900s] a skeleton. **4** [1940s] (*US black*) a suit of clothes.

IN PHRASES

❑ **climb someone's frame** *v.* (*US*) **1** [late 19C+] (*also* **climb over someone's frame, climb up someone's back**) to harass or criticize verbally. **2** [1930s–60s] (*US*) (*also* **jar someone's frame, rock...**) to assault physically. ❑ **hop one's frame** *v.* [1910s–40s] (*N.Z.*) to move, to make a sudden journey.

frame *n.*[2] (*UK/US Und.*) **1** [mid-19C; 1910s+] circumstances that combine to place an individual in a disadvantageous position, usu. leading to their arrest. **2** [1910s] corruption, malpractice. **3** [1930s+] the general situation, esp. that surrounding the suspects in a given crime.

IN PHRASES

❑ **out of the frame** *adj.* [1990s+] (*US black/campus*) **1** very ugly. **2** drunk. ❑ **put in the frame** *v.* [1960s+] (*UK Und./police*) to concoct evidence against a criminal, whether or not guilty of the crime under investigation.

frame *v.* [SE *frame*, to put in a frame] **1** [20C+] (*US Und.*) to create the environment – a fake bookmaker's, a fake stock dealer's – in which an elaborate confidence trick can take place; to arrange a 'fixed' boxing match. **2** [1900s] (*US Und.*) to place in a Rogues' Gallery. **3** [1900s] (*US*) to dress [i.e. to frame a picture]. **4** [1910s–50s] to fake. **5** [1910s+] (*orig. US*) (*also* **frame on, frame up**) to concoct a false charge or accusation against, to devise a scheme or plot with regard to, by creating false evidence, witnesses etc. **6** [1910s+] in ext. use, to arrange, to prepare. **7** [1920s–40s] (*US*) to trick or hoodwink.

IN PHRASES

❑ **frame the gaff/joint** *v. see under* GAFF *n.*[1].

frame in *v.* [1900s] (*US Und.*) to join up with.

framer *n.*[1] [mid-19C] (*US Und.*) a shawl.

framer *n.*[2] [FRAME *v.*] [1940s] one who accuses another person unfairly, and/or through the provision of faked evidence.

frames *n.* [1950s] (*US black*) spectacles, glasses.

frame-up *n.* [FRAME UP *v.*] [20C+] (*orig. US*) **1** a plot, a plan. **2** the concoction of criminal guilt or charges. **3** a 'fixed' sporting encounter. **4** a character assessment.

IN PHRASES

❑ **in the frame** [20C+] (*UK Und./police*) **1** under suspicion, usu. with some grounds, of having committed a crime [note also racetrack use, the *frame* holds the numbers of the winning horses in a race]. **2** involved in a situation.

frame-up *adj.* [FRAME UP *v.*] [1910s] (*US*) counterfeit.

frame up *v.* [ext. of FRAME *v.* (1)] (*orig. US*) **1** [1900s] (*US*) to explain. **2** [1900s–30s] to form a plan of action, esp. in secret. **3** [1910s] to link together, e.g. of a couple. **4** *see* FRAME *v.* (5).

frammagem *v. see* FRUMMAGEM *v.*

frammis *n.* [? FRAME *n.*[2] (1)] [1950s+] (*US*) **1** (*also* **frammiss**) any form of confidence trick. **2** any unspecified object.

France *n.* [the orig. use, *France!*, is as an oath, and refers to the horrors of WW1, when many West Indians fought and died in the trenches of Flanders. Thereafter, the uses can all be paralleled by *fuck* and/or *hell*, and usu. in phr. below. These uses may also have some background in the Du. *Loop naar de Franschen*, run to the French, i.e. go to the devil] [1920s+] (*W.I.*) a euph. for FUCK *n.* or *hell*.

(IN PHRASES)

❑ **catch France** *v.* [20C+] (*W.I.*) to find it hard to make enough money to live. ❑ **give France** *v.* [20C+] (*W.I.*) **1** to quarrel very bitterly. **2** to cause a good deal of trouble for someone. ❑ **put France on** *v.* [20C+] (*W.I.*) to scold severely, to give a tongue-lashing.

(IN EXCLAMATIONS)

❑ **go to France!** [20C+] (*W.I.*) a general excl. of dismissal; a euph. for *GO TO HELL! under* HELL *n.*

France and Spain *n.* [rhy. sl.] [late 19C+] rain.

frances *n.* (*also* **francesca**) [FANNY *n.*[1] (1), which is a nickname derived f. this proper name] [1930s–60s] (*US*) the buttocks.

franger *n.* [? FRENCH LETTER *n.*] [1970s+] (*Aus.*) a condom.

Frank Bough *adj.* [rhy. sl. = SE *off*, stale; ult. UK sportscaster and TV personality *Frank Bough* (b.1933), pron. 'Boff'] [1990s+] of food or drink, off, stale, sour.

Frankie Fraser *n.* [rhy. sl.; ult. London gangster 'Mad' Frankie Fraser (b.1923)] [1990s+] a razor.

franklin *n. see* BEN FRANKLIN *n.*

franklin teeth *n.* [the protruding grille of the Franklin automobile] [1920s–30s] (*Can.*) projecting or 'buck' teeth.

frank thring *n.* [rhy. sl.] [1970s+] (*Aus.*) a (wedding) ring.

Frank Zappa *n.* [rhy. sl. = CRAPPER *n.*[1] (3); ult. US rock star and experimental musician *Frank Zappa* (1940–93)] [1990s+] a lavatory.

fransman *n.* (*also* **franse, Frenchman**) [Afk. *fransman*, Frenchman, thus fig. a foreigner] [1970s+] (*S.Afr. Und.*) an outsider, a convict who is not affiliated to a prison gang; thus as adj., *frans(e)*, outsider.

frantic *n.* [1950s] (*US black*) a lively, remarkable person.

frantic *adj.* **1** [late 19C–1950s] a general intensifier, terrific, awful. **2** [1920s–60s] exciting, amusing, enjoyable. **3** [1940s–60s] of people or things, good looking, fashionable.

frantically *adv.* [FRANTIC *adj.*] **1** [1900s] a general intensifier, terrifically, awfully. **2** [1950s] of a party, lively, frenetically. **3** [1950s–60s] excitingly, amusingly, enjoyably.

franzy house *n.* [dial. *franzy*, SE *frenzy*, craziness, madness + HOUSE *n.*[1] (1)/SE *house* as in *madhouse*] [20C+] (*US*) **1** a brothel. **2** a psychiatric institution.

frap *n.* [note dial *frap*, to strike, to beat] [1990s+] a euph. for FUCK *n.* in all uses.

frapping *n.* [Fr. *frapper*, to beat] [mid-19C] a beating.

frapping *adj.* [1990s+] a euph. for FUCKING *adj.*

frat *n.* [abbr.] [late 19C+] (*US*) **1** a college *fraternity*; also attrib., *frat house*, *frat-pin* etc. **2** (*also* **frat boy, ...brother, ...bull, ... head, ...man**) a member of a *fraternity*; thus *non-frat*.

(DERIVATIVES)

❑ **fratdom** *n.* [sfx *-dom*] [1980s+] (*US campus*) the world of fraternities.

(IN COMPOUNDS)

❑ **frat dick** *n.* (*also* **frat fag**) [DICK *n.*[1] (11)/FAG *n.*[5] (2)] [1980s] (*US campus*) a derog. description of a typical fraternity member. ❑ **frat rat** *n.* (*also* **frat brat, ...star**) [FRAT *n.* (1) + SE *rat/boy/star*] [1960s+] (*US campus*) a member of a fraternity.

(IN PHRASES)

❑ **frat out** *v.* [1970s] (*US campus*) to dress and act like a fraternity member.

frat *v.* [SE *fraternize*; orig. US milit. at end of WW2/ FRAT *n.* (2)] [1980s] **1** to associate with. **2** (*US campus*) to participate in fraternity parties, events, in order to pick up girls.

fratastic *adj. see* FRATTY *adj.*

frater *n.* [Lat. *frater*, brother] [mid-16C–early 18C] (*UK Und.*) a mendicant villain who poses as a friar and claims, as such, to beg alms for a hospital or charitable institution; he specializes in poor, gullible women.

fratosoralingoid *n.* (*also* **fratosororalingoid**) [SE *fraternity* + *sorority* = SF sfx *-lingoid*] [1990s+] (*US campus*) an obnoxious fraternity or sorority member.

fratstar *adj. see* FRATTY *adj.*

fratting *n.* [essentially abbr. of SE *fraternizing*] [1940s+] a euph. for FUCKING *n.* (1).

fratty *adj.* (*also* **fratastic, fratstar**) [FRAT *n.* (1) + sfx *-y*/SE *fra*ternity + fan*tastic/star*] [1970s] (*US campus*) pertaining to fraternity life.

(IN COMPOUNDS)

❑ **fratty-bagger** *n.* (*also* **bag, bagger**) [BAGS *n.*[2] (1), i.e. the style of baggy trousers worn] [1970s+] (*US campus*) a stereotypical fraternity member.

frau *n.* [synon. Ger. *frau*] [1900s–40s] (*US*) a wife.

fraughty issue *n.* [1930s–40s] an unacceptable or unpleasant situation.

fray *v. see* VRY *v.*

fray bentos *adj.* [pun on pron. Fr. *tres bien*; ult. *Fray Bentos*, a brand of meat pies] [1900s] (*Aus. milit.*) very good.

frazer nash *n.* [rhy. sl. = SLASH *n.* (2a); ult. *Frazer-Nash*, the sports car manufactured before 1940] [1970s] an act of urination.

frazzle *n.* [SE *frazzle*, a frayed end, a fragment] [mid-19C+] (*orig. US*) a state of emotional and/or physical exhaustion; usu. as *to a frazzle*, completely, utterly; esp. in phrs. below.

(IN COMPOUNDS)

❑ **frazzle-headed** *adj.* [1980s] wild, crazy, unkempt.

(IN PHRASES)

❑ **beat to a frazzle** *v.* (*also* **lick to a frazzle**) [late 19C+] (*orig. US*) to destroy completely, to defeat or exhaust. ❑ **wear to a frazzle** *v.* [late 19C+] (*orig. US*) to tire someone out; usu. as *worn to a frazzle*, completely exhausted.

frazzle *v.* [East Anglia dial. *frazzle*, to wear away, to unravel; ult. SE *fray*] **1** [19C+] to fray, to become unravelled, often used of a whip's end. **2** [20C+] (*Aus.*) to rob. **3** [1900s] (*US*) to whip. **4** [1960s] (*US*) to excite, to render upset. **5** [2000s] to defeat, to overcome.

frazzled *adj.* [fig. use of FRAZZLE *v.*] **1** [19C+] (*orig. US*) (*also* **frazzle-assed, frazzled out**) emotionally drained, physically exhausted. **2** [19C+] (*orig. US*) drunk. **3** [1970s+] (*US drugs*) under the influence of a drug, e.g. cocaine or marijuana.

frazzling *adj.* [1900s–40s] (*US*) a general intensifier; a euph. for FUCKING *adj.*

freak *n.*[1] [note 16C *freke*, a man, often derog./SE *freak*, a monstrosity (of nature), often as exhibited in a show] **1** [late 19C] (*US campus*) a student who is exceptionally proficient in a subject. **2** [late 19C+] (*US*) (*also* **freako, freke**) an offensively eccentric or crazy person. **3** [20C+] an obsession. **4** [20C+] an obsessive. **5** [1900s] (*US campus*) a fool. **6** [1900s] a person. **7** [1920s+] one who enjoys non-standard sexual practices. **8** [1940s] an impotent man. **9** [1950s+] (*orig. US black*) an effeminate man, a male homosexual. **10** [1950s+] (*US black*) (*also* **freakette**) a woman, usu. sexually aggressive and adventurous. **11** [1960s] a piece of bad luck. **12** [1960s+] (*orig. US*) a young person devoted to the 'counter-culture' or 'alternative society'; by extension, a drug user [like many parallel usages on the bad = good model, the young people in question adopted the name; synon. with 'extreme HIPPIE *n.*[2] (3)', after they had been branded as 'freaks' by their critics]. **13** [1960s+] (*US campus*) an unattractive person. **14** [1970s+] a lesbian; a prostitute who deals with lesbian clients. **15** [1980s+] (*US campus*) an extremely beautiful, good-looking woman, usu. but not always a member of one's own peer group.

(DERIVATIVES)

❑ **freak-a-zoid** *n.* [SF sfx *-azoid*] [1990s+] (*US black teen*) an eccentric, an obsessive, a freak. ❑ **freaksome** *adj.* [coined in late 1990s US TV show *Buffy the Vampire Slayer*] [1990s+] eccentric, bizarre.

(IN COMPOUNDS)

❑ **freak book** *n.* [1960s] (*US prison*) a pornographic book. ❑ **freak daddy** *n.* [DADDY *n.* (7)] [1980s+] (*US campus*) an attractive man. ❑ **freak fuck** *see* separate entries. ❑ **freak magazine** *n.* [1990s+] (*US black*) a pornographic magazine. ❑ **freak mama** *n.* [MAMA *n.* (1)] [1980s+] (*US campus*) an attractive woman, with overtones of sluttishness. ❑ **freaknasty** *adj.* [NASTY *adj.* (2)] [2000s] (*US*) sexually exciting and poss. perverse. ❑ **freak party** *n.* [1960s+] perverted or otherwise out of the ordinary sex. ❑ **freak rock** *n. see* ACID ROCK *under* ACID *n.*[1]. ❑ **freak show** *n.* [1960s+] a sexual display or performance, usu. of unorthodox sex. ❑ **freak trick** *n. see under* TRICK *n.*[1].

(IN PHRASES)

❑ **get one's freak on** *v.* **1** [1990s+] (*US*) to get into a particular mood, usu. with ref. to sex. **2** to enjoy sexual eccentricities.

freak *n.*[2] [1990s+] used as a euph. for FUCK *n.* in various contexts.

freak *n.*[3] *see* FREAK-OUT *n.*

freak *adj.* [FREAK *n.*[1]] [1910s; 1960s+] (*US black*) **1** obsessive, crazy. **2** promiscuous. **3** pertaining to the world of hippies. **4** (*US campus*) good. **5** sexually eccentric.

freak *v.*[1] [1950s+] a euph. for FUCK *v.* in various senses.

(IN PHRASES)

❑ **freak around** *v.* [euph. FUCK ABOUT *v.* (1)] [1970s+] (*US gay*) to waste time; to window shop.

freak *v.*[2] [FREAK *n.*[1] (7)] **1** [1960s+] to have adventurous sex; to have anal intercourse. **2** [1980s+] (*US campus*) (*also* **freak all over, freak on**) to dance in a highly sexual manner, to simulate sex on the dance-floor. **3** [1990s+] to have sexual intercourse, usu. forced. **4** [2000s] to excite (sexually).

(IN PHRASES)

❑ **freak it up** *v.* [1970s] (*US gay*) to behave extravagantly, whether sexually, socially or on a dance-floor.

freak *v.*[3] [abbr. FREAK OUT *v.*] [1960s+] (*orig. drug/hippie*) **1** to lose psychological control, whether enjoyably or otherwise, as the result of drugs, usu. hallucinogens; usu. as *freaking*. **2** to worry, to disturb, to cause severe anxiety (the extent of the disturbance varies totally as to context). **3** (*also* **freak one's mind**) to be worried, to be severely anxious. **4** to act in an emotional, melodramatic manner; thus adj. *freaked*, emotionally overwhelmed. **5** (*US gay*) to be uninhibited, esp. at a party. **6** (*US black*) to perform.

(IN COMPOUNDS)

❑ **freak attack** *n.* [1990s+] (*US teen*) a state of extreme tension.

-freak *sfx* [20C+] (*orig. US campus*) a comb. form that indicates an obsessive, one who is extremely interested in or overly fond of something, e.g. *health-freak*, *dope-freak* etc.

Freakeries, the *n.* [SE *freak*, a monstrosity + sfx *-eries*] [late 19C] Barnum's freak and acrobat shows, put on at Olympia.

freakette *n. see* FREAK *n.*[1] (10).

freak fuck *n.* [FREAK FUCK *v.*] [1960s+] **1** any variation on 'straight' heterosexual intercourse, esp. anal intercourse. **2** (*orig. US black*) a client who demands unusual or poss. physically dangerous services from a prostitute.

freak fuck *v.* [FREAK *n.*[1] (7) + FUCK *v.* (1)] [1970s+] (*orig. US black*) **1** to engage in anal intercourse with a woman. **2** to engage in cunnilingus.

freaking *n. see* FREAK *v.*[3] (1).

freaking *adj.*[1] **1** [1920s+] (*US*) a euph. for FUCKING *adj.*; thus ext. *freakin'-A!* **2** [1980s+] (*US campus*) extraordinary, good. **3** [2000s] as infix.

freaking *adj.*[2] [1970s+] sexually perverse.

freakish *adj.* [FREAK *n.*[1]] [1920s+] (*US black*) **1** homosexual, of either gender. **2** sexually deviant or lustful. **3** (*US black*) exciting, wonderful. **4** bizarre.

freako *n. see* FREAK *n.*[1] (2).

freak-off *n.* [FREAK OFF *v.*] [1960s] (*US black*) an act of sexual intercourse.

freak off *v.* [FREAK *n.*[1] (7)] **1** [1950s+] (*US black*) to masturbate. **2** [1950s+] (*US black*) to engage in unrestrained or unorthodox sexual activity. **3** [1960s] to flirt, to attempt to pick up. **4** [1960s–70s] (*US black*) to express one's enjoyment. **5** [1960s–80s] to decorate, esp. to create something beautiful. **6** [1970s+] (*US black*) to have homosexual sex.

freak-out *n.* (*also* **freak**) [FREAK OUT *v.*] [1960s+] (*orig. US drugs*) **1** any unpleasant experience caused by drug use, esp. with LSD. **2** anxiety, ranging from twinges of fear to a full nervous breakdown, varying as to context. **3** a gathering of young people, esp. hippies, to enjoy music and take drugs together. **4** an orgy. **5** an explosion of temper.

freak out *v.* [FREAK *v.*[3] (1)] [1960s+] (*orig. US drugs*) **1** to experience an altered state of consciousness from the effects of a hallucinogenic drug; usu. an unpleasant effect; thus n. *freaker-out*. **2** to worry, to disturb, to horrify – the level of trauma depends on context. **3** to engage in unorthodox or unrestrained sexual activity. **4** to go crazy, wild or out of control from fear or instability. **5** to experience intense emotional pleasure; thus *freak someone out*, to engender such pleasure. **6** to be upset, worried; thus to back down, retreat.

freaky *adj.*[1] [FREAK *n.*[1] (2) + sfx *-y*] **1** [late 19C+] odd, bizarre, unnerving. **2** [1960s+] (*drugs*) hallucinogenic, psychedelic. **3** [1970s] (*drugs*) strong, powerful. **4** [1980s] nervous.

(IN COMPOUNDS)

❑ **freaky-deaky** *adj.* [1980s+] (*US*) weird, bizarre. ❑ **freaky deal** *v.* [2000s] (*US*) to cheat, to deceive. ❑ **freaky-freak** *n.* [FREAK *n.*[1] (2)] [1990s+] an eccentric; also used as a term of affection. ❑ **freaky-straight** *n.* [STRAIGHT *n.*[2] (2)] [1960s] 'either ordinary-looking people with fanatical ideas on one particular theme, [...] or people whose appearance is very weird but whose minds are channelled into one usual line of thought and on all other subjects their thinking is just as stereotyped as 'Mr. Average'' (*Gandalf's Garden*, 1969).

freaky *adj.*[2] [FREAK *n.*[1] (7)] [1960s+] **1** sexually aroused. **2** sexually deviant. **3** sexually exciting.

freckle *n.* [1960s+] (*Aus.*) the anus.

(IN COMPOUNDS)

❑ **freckle-puncher** *n.* [1960s+] a male homosexual.

freckle-nature *n.* [1950s] (*W.I.*) an albino.

fred *n.* [the common name, underpinned in US by the character *Fred Flintstone* in *The Flintstones* cartoon and film (1994)] [1970s+] **1** (*US campus*) a socially unacceptable person, a freeloader. **2** (*US campus*) a fool, a loser. **3** (*US campus*) (*also* **freddie**) a term of address to a friend. **4** (*Aus.*) the average Australian.

fred *v.* [echoic] [1980s+] (*US campus*) to vomit.

Fred Astaire *n.* [rhy. sl.; ult. film star and dancer *Fred Astaire* (1899–1987)] [1960s+] (*Aus.*) **1** a chair. **2** the hair. **3** a dandy [= LAIR *n.*].

Fred Astaire *adj.* [his style; for full ety. *see* prev.] [1940s] (*US campus*) stylish.

fred astaires *n.* [rhy. sl.; ult. *see* FRED ASTAIRE *n.*] [1940s] stairs.

freddie *n. see* FRED *n.* (3).

Freddy *n.* [abbr./pron.] [1960s] (*UK drugs*) ephidrine.

Fred Karno's army *n.* (*also* **Fred Karno's mob**) [the popular comedian *Fred Karno* (1866–1941), who fronted a series of slapstick mini-shows, often burlesquing music-hall. Orig. milit. use in WW1 for the 'New', i.e. conscripted, army and in WW2 for any platoon or section seen as inept] [1910s–50s] a group of people considered incompetent.

Fred McMurrays *n.* [rhy. sl.; ult. Hollywood film star *Fred McMurray* (1908–91)] [2000s] worries.

fred nerk *n.* [1990s+] (*Aus.*) an imaginary person, esp. one on whom the blame can be placed, e.g. in phr. *I suppose it was Fred Nerk* (who did it).

Fred's out *phr.* [1970s] (*US campus*) an expression used to admit to breaking wind.

free *n.* [1960s+] (*US prison*) the free world, i.e. the world outside prison.

free *adj.*

SE in slang uses

IN COMPOUNDS

❑ **free-and-easy** *v. see* separate entry. ❑ **freeball** *v.* [2000s] (*US*) of a man, to wear no underwear. ❑ **freebase/freebasing** *see* separate entries. ❑ **free-fuck** *v.* [FUCK *v.* (1)] [late 19C+] of a woman, esp. a potential prostitute, to have sexual intercourse without charging. ❑ **free hotel** *n.* (*also* **free motel**) [i.e. one pays nothing for one's accommodation] [20C+] (*US*) a prison. ❑ **freeload/loader/loading** *see* separate entries. ❑ **free ride** *n.* **1** [1910s] (*US*) an arrest. **2** [1950s+] an easy time. **3** [1970s] a prostitute. **4** [1990s+] an unpaid sexual encounter with a prostitute. ❑ **free shot** *n.* [SHOT *n.*[1] (5a)] [1970s+] the unpaid-for services of a prostitute. ❑ **free show** *n.* [1960s+] the inadvertent revelation by a woman of her body, in all or part, glimpsed by a passing man. ❑ **free side** *n.* [1960s+] the world outside prison. ❑ **freestyle** *see* separate entries. ❑ **free trade** *n. see* TRADE, THE *n.* (1). ❑ **free traders** *n.* [the freedom of access to the vagina] [late 19C–1930s] women's knickers, open at the crotch. ❑ **free world** *see* separate entries.

IN PHRASES

❑ **free of fumbler's hall** [*FUMBLER'S HALL under* FUMBLER *n.*] [late 17C–early 19C] a phr. describing an impotent husband. ❑ **free of the bush** *see under* BUSH *n.*[1].

free *v.* [ironic use of SE] [mid-19C] to steal, usu. a horse; thus *free a cat*, to steal a muff.

free-and-easy *n.* **1** [late 18C–19C] a cheap brothel. **2** [19C–1900s] a convivial gathering for singing, at which one may drink, smoke etc. **3** [early 19C] a prostitute. **4** [late 19C] a burlesque or 'tableau' show.

freebase *n.* [FREEBASE *v.*] [1980s+] (*drugs*) **1** cocaine base, purified by ether and smoked rather than sniffed or injected. **2** crack cocaine.

freebase *v.* [SE *free*, to set free, to separate from + BASE *v.*[2] (2)] [1980s+] (*drugs*) to intensify the effect of cocaine by heating it in combination with ether or other chemicals before inhaling.

freebasing *n.* [FREEBASE *v.*] [1980s+] (*drugs*) intensifying the effect of cocaine by heating it in combination with ether or other chemicals before inhaling it.

freebie *n.* **1** [1920s+] (*orig. US*) (*also* **freebee, freeby, freebye**) any free sample, free trip, esp. press tours, promotions etc. **2** [1940s+] (*US*) one who gives their services for free, esp. a prostitute. **3** [1970s+] (*drugs*) a free sample. **4** [1990s+] something, e.g. food, given away for free (in a non-promotional context).

freebie *adj.* [FREEBIE *n.*] [1940s+] (*orig. US*) used of anything or anyone free or of obtaining something without paying.

freebie *v.* [FREEBIE *n.* (2)] [1940s+] (*orig. US*) of a prostitute, to provide sexual services without making a charge.

freeholder *n.* [? pun on SE *freeholder*, one who has land worth 40s (£2) a year; presumably one needed such income to buy one's wife a drink or ? one had such an income f. the prostitute] **1** [late 17C–18C] a man whose wife accompanies him to the tavern [note: a specific 'tavern term' drawn f. *The English Liberal Science, or a new-found Art and Order of Drinking*]. **2** [late 19C–1900s] a prostitute's companion.

freelance *n.* [19C] a habitual adulteress, although not a professional prostitute.

freelance *v.* [1960s+] of a woman, to work as a prostitute without informing her pimp or without a pimp at all.

freeload *v.* [backform. f. FREELOADER *n.*] [1940s+] to enjoy for free the pleasures that are primarily made available to a celebrity or laid on at an important event but become equally available to anyone who cares to struggle hard enough to grab them; in general use, to define the taking of any benefits that one has not made due efforts to deserve.

freeloader *n.* [SE *free* + *load up*, to fill (oneself) up] [1940s+] (*orig. US*) a parasite, one who eats and drinks without spending any money; more recently those who form a celebrity's entourage and enjoy the crumbs from their various tables.

freeloading *adj.* [FREELOAD *v.*] [1960s+] describing one who is enjoying pleasures for free; taking benefits that one has not earned.

freeman *n.* [19C] an adulterer.

freeman of a corporation's work *n.* [SE *corporation*, the magistrates of a provincial town] [late 18C] an unattractive, weak man.

freeman of bucks *n.* [FREEMAN *n.* + pun on BUCK *n.*[1] (1)] [19C] an adulterer.

freeman's *n.* (*also* **harry freeman's**) [for ety. *see* DRINK AT FREEMAN'S QUAY *under* DRINK *v.*] [1910s+] anything obtained for free, esp. as a bribe given to a corrupt police officer.

freeman's key *n.* [corruption of/var. on *DRINK AT FREEMAN'S QUAY under* DRINK *v.*] [late 19C–1910s] (*Aus.*) any situation in which payment, esp. for alcohol, can be put off.

freesies *adv.* [1970s+] for free.

Free State coal *n.* [late 19C] (*S.Afr.*) dried cow-dung, used as fuel.

freestyle *n.* [1990s+] (*US black/teen*) unwritten rap lyrics (occas. used of other forms of music), using whatever comes to mind at the spur of the moment.

freestyle *v.* [1990s+] (*US black/teen*) **1** to create spontaneous rap rhymes, without prior preparation. **2** to act in a spontaneous manner, to live by one's own rules, to wear one's own styles of clothes etc.

freeway Freddie *n.* [California use] [1970s+] (*US black*) a highway patrolman.

free world *n.* [1970s+] (*US prison*) **1** the world outside prison. **2** (*also* **world**) a tailormade cigarette [as opposed to the hand-rolled ones mostly found inside prisons].

free-world *adj.* [FREE WORLD *n.*] [1960s+] (*US prison*) pertaining to the non-prison environment.

IN COMPOUNDS

❑ **free-world girl** *n.* (*also* **free-world gal, ...punk**) [SE *girl*/GAL *n.* (1)/PUNK *n.*[1] (2)] [1960s] (*US prison*) a jail homosexual who has also been a homosexual in 'civilian' life.

freeze *n.* [FREEZE *v.*[2]] **1** [1930s+] (*Aus.*) a wife's deliberate withholding of sexual favours. **2** [1940s+] (*orig. US*) a snub, a rejection. **3** [1970s+] in drug uses. (**a**) cocaine. (**b**) the 'freezing' sensation that results from using cocaine. (**c**) a taste, a pinch of cocaine.

IN PHRASES

❑ **do a freeze** *v.* (*also* **play a freeze**) [1940s+] (*Aus./N.Z.*) to ignore, to overlook. ❑ **do the freeze** *v. see* FREEZE *v.*[2] (1e). ❑ **put a/the freeze on** *v.* **1** [1950s] to snub, to ignore, to reject. **2** [1970s+] (*US*) to stop.

freeze *v.*[1] [FREEZE ON *v.*] **1** [19C] (*also* **freeze on to**) to steal. **2** [mid–late 19C] (*US*) to yearn for; thus *froze for*, desirous of.

IN PHRASES

❑ **freeze to** *v.* [mid–late 19C] (*orig. US*) of people or objects, to be very keen on, to fancy greatly.

freeze *v.*[2] **1** in transitive uses. (**a**) [mid–late 19C] to exclude from society, business etc by intimidating, snubbing behaviour. (**b**) [20C+] (*US*) to intimidate. (**c**) [20C+] (*US*) to snub, to ignore. (**d**) [1930s] (*US*) to end a relationship; to obtain a divorce. (**e**) [1930s+] (*also* **do the freeze**) (*Aus.*) of a woman, to refuse sexual favours. (**f**) [1960s+] (*drugs*) to renege on an agreement, esp. on a drug deal. **2** (*also* **freeze up**) in intransitive uses. (**a**) [mid-19C] to stay where one is. (**b**) [mid-19C; 20C+] to stand absolutely still, to remain motionless. (**c**) [1920s+] to become silent, to quieten down, to refuse to answer questions or make conversation. (**d**) [1920s+] to stop what one is doing. (**e**) [1960s+] to act calmly, to 'play it cool'.

(IN PHRASES)

❑ **freeze off** *v.* [1900s–30s] to kill; also in fig. use, to curtail someone's activity. ❑ **freeze out** *see* separate entries.

SE in slang uses

(IN PHRASES)

❑ **freeze one's nose** *v.* [from the effects of the drug when inhaled or rubbed on the gums] [1960s] to inhale cocaine.

freeze! *excl.* [FREEZE *v.*[2] (1)] [1910s+] don't move! stay where you are!

freeze-a! *n.* ['corruption of "for he's a jolly good fellow!"'] [1910s] (*Aus.*) 'a catch word satirically applied to a popularity-hunter' (Downing, *Digger Dialects*, 1919).

freeze on *v.* **1** [mid-19C+] (*orig. US/Aus.*) to take a tight grip of, to grasp, e.g. to refuse to leave someone alone or to get behind someone. **2** [late 19C+] (*also* **freeze up on**) to ignore, to snub, to reject.

(IN PHRASES)

❑ **freeze on to** *v. see* FREEZE *v.*[1] (1).

freeze-out *n.* [FREEZE OUT *v.*] **1** [mid-19C+] (*orig. US*) the act of deliberately excluding someone; sometimes the person excluded. **2** [1940s] (*US*) a situation that offers no opportunities, e.g. for theft.

(IN COMPOUNDS)

❑ **freeze-out game** *n.* [mid-19C+] (*orig. US*) the act of deliberately excluding someone; sometimes the person excluded.

freeze out *v.* [mid-19C+] (*orig. US*) to snub, to render socially unacceptable, to exclude from a (business) deal.

freezer *n.*[1] [play on SE] **1** [late 18C+] a rebuff, a snub. **2** [mid–late 19C] a chilly look, a dismissive remark.

freezer *n.*[2] [1920s–50s] (*Aus./US*) a prison.

freezing weather *n.* [1930s–40s] (*US black*) an unattractive woman.

freight *n.* [1920s+] (*US*) payment, cost, e.g. rent or a subway fare; a bribe.

(IN PHRASES)

❑ **pull one's freight** *v.* (*also* **drag one's freight**) **1** [mid-19C–1960s] (*US*) to rush off, to leave in a hurry. **2** *see* PULL ONE'S LOAD *under* LOAD *n.*

freight (it) *v.* **1** [late 19C] to travel a long distance. **2** [1910s–40s] (*US tramp*) to travel on a freight rain.

freke *n. see* FREAK *n.*[1] (2).

French *n.* **1** [late 16C+] syphilis. **2** [18C–19C] brandy. **3** [late 19C+] taboo language. **4** [1910s+] (*also* **French art, Frenching, full French**) fellatio.

(IN PHRASES)

❑ **excuse my French** (*also* **excuse the French, pardon my French**) [late 19C+] a genteel euph. automatically offered after the speaker has sworn in public. ❑ **learn French** *v.* [17C] to become infected with syphilis. ❑ **speak French** *v.* [20C+] to indulge in unconventional sexual play. ❑ **talk French** *v.* [1940s] (*US*) to fellate.

French *adj.* **1** [late 16C–mid-18C] in combs. meaning syphilis (see also below). **2** [late 16C+] a racial stereotype used in various contexts; the Anglo-Saxon belief in 'gay Paree' and its supposedly sex-obsessed denizens has long equated 'French' with sexy or, pej., pornographic and 'dirty'. **3** [mid-19C–1900s] (*US*) unfashionable, vulgar, distasteful. **4** [20C+] used in comb. meaning fellatio/fellate (see also below); thus, by ext., denoting homosexuality. **5** [1930s+] used by a prostitute, willing to give oral sex.

pertaining to oral sex (usu. male-to-male)

(IN COMPOUNDS)

❑ **French active** *n.* [1950s+] (*gay*) the passive (sucked) partner in fellatio. ❑ **French art** *n. see* FRENCH *n.* (4). ❑ **French artist** *n.* [1970s+] (*US gay*) a fellator. ❑ **French bath** *n.* [1930s] (*US*) fellatio. ❑ **French culture** *n.* [1960s+] fellatio, obs. except in homosexual contact advertisements. ❑ **French date** *n.* **1** [1930s] (*US Und.*) a prostitute's client who enjoys fellatio. **2** [1960s] a paid-for act of fellatio. ❑ **French dressing** *n.* [1950s+] (*US gay*) semen, in the context of fellatio. ❑ **French embassy** *n.* [1960s] (*US gay*) any location, esp. a gym or YMCA, where homosexual activity is extensive and unchecked. ❑ **French-fried ice-cream** *n.* [1950s+] (*gay*) semen. ❑ **French-fried ice water** *n.* [1960s] (*US gay*) lumpy semen. ❑ **French girl** *n.* [1930s] (*US Und.*) a prostitute who offers fellatio. ❑ **French (head) job** *n.* [JOB *n.*[2] (2)] [1960s+] (*US gay*) fellatio. ❑ **French lady** *n.* [1980s] (*US*) a fellator. ❑ **French language expert** *n.* [1950s+] (*gay*) a fellator. ❑ **French language training** *n.* [1970s+] (*gay*) the teaching of fellatio to another person. ❑ **French love** *n.* [20C+] fellatio. ❑ **French passive** *n.* [1950s+] (*gay*) the fellator. ❑ **French photographer** *n.* [1950s+] (*gay*) a homosexual photographer. ❑ **French polishing** *n.* [1980s] fellatio; thus *French polisher*, a fellatrix. ❑ **French revolution** *n.* [1950s–60s] (*gay*) the movement for homosexual rights. ❑ **French style** *adv.* [1970s] of sex, with the mouth, i.e. fellatio. ❑ **French tricks** *n.* [Williams cites 17C use of *French tricks* as a general euph. for degeneracy/debauchery] [1960s+] oral sex, of a man or a woman. ❑ **French way** *n.* [1960s+] fellatio.

(IN PHRASES)

❑ **French by injection** *n.* **1** [1950s–60s] (*US gay*) said of anyone considered particularly well-versed in fellatio. **2** [1960s] (*US*) any American prostitute who opts for foreign customers. ❑ **tell a French joke** *v.* [1960s+] (*gay*) to stimulate the anus orally.

pertaining to sex in general

(IN COMPOUNDS)

❑ **French cap** *n.* [var. on SE *Dutch cap*] [1920s] (*US*) a condom. ❑ **French deck** *n.* [1960s+] (*US*) a pack of playing cards decorated with erotic pictures. ❑ **French dip** *n.* [1950s+] (*gay*) vaginal juices. ❑ **French fuck** *n.* [FUCK *n.* (1)] [1930s+] (*US*) the rubbing of a man's penis between a woman's breasts. ❑ **French handshake** *n.* [1970s] (*US teen*) a form of handshake signifying a sexual interest or invitation. ❑ **French kiss** *see* separate entries. ❑ **French letter** *n. see* separate entry. ❑ **French postcard** *n.* **1** [1910s+] (*orig. US*) (*also* **French picture**) an erotic picture postcard. **2** [1950s+] (*gay*) an exciting prospective sexual partner. ❑ **French prints** *n.* **1** [mid-19C+] pornographic pictures and engravings. **2** [1950s+] (*gay*) unusual heterosexual pornography. ❑ **French safe** *n.* [SAFE *n.* (1)] [late 19C+] (*Can./US*) a condom. ❑ **French stuff** *n.* [1970s] (*gay*) **1** pornography. **2** any unusual sexual activity. ❑ **French tickler** *n.* (*also* **tickler**) [1910s+] a contraceptive sheath with extra protrusions for added stimulation.

pertaining to venereal disease

(IN COMPOUNDS)

❑ **French chillblains** *n.* [17C] venereal disease. ❑ **French crown** *n.* (*also* **French goods, French gout**) [aka *Corona Veneris*; joc. uses of SE *crown*, the ring of spots around the forehead/*goods*/*gout*] [late 17C–19C] venereal disease. ❑ **French disease** *n.* (*also* **disease/malady of France**) [late 16C–18C] venereal disease, esp. syphilis. ❑ **French marbles** *n.* [late 16C] venereal disease, esp. syphilis. ❑ **French measles** *n.* (*also* **French cannibal, French mole, French morbus**) [early 17C–18C] venereal disease, esp. syphilis. ❑ **French pig** *n.* [late 19C–1900s] syphilis, esp. the syphilitic pustule or bubo. ❑ **French pox** *n.* [early 16C–18C] venereal disease, esp. syphilis. ❑ **French razor** *n.* [early 17C] syphilis. ❑ **French welcome** *n.* [17C] a dose of syphilis.

(IN PHRASES)

❑ **take French lessons** *v.* [20C+] to contract venereal disease.

SE in slang uses

(IN COMPOUNDS)

pertaining to brandy

❑ **French article** *n.* [18C] brandy. ❑ **French cream** *n.* [SE; France as the home of brandy; 'so called by the old tabbies and dowagers when they drink their tea' (Grose, 1796)] [18C] brandy. ❑ **French elixir** *n.* [19C] brandy. ❑ **French lace** *n.* [early 19C] brandy.

general uses

❑ **French article** *n.* [ARTICLE *n.* (4)] [mid-19C+] a French prostitute. ❑ **French bathe** *see* separate entries. ❑ **French blue** *n.* [manufacturers Smith, Kline and *French* + BLUE *n.*[1] (4a)] [1960s+] **1** (*UK drugs*) a mix of barbiturate and amphetamine. **2** (*US drugs*) amphetamine. ❑ **French fits** *n.* [? a link to insanity attendant on syphilis, i.e. the *FRENCH DISEASE* above; or ? pertaining to brandy, see combs. above] [1940s–50s] (*US*) delirium tremens. ❑ **French inhale** *v.* [the supposed sophistication of the French] **1** [1950s+] (*US*) to blow out cigarette smoke through the nose. **2** [1970s] (*US black/drugs*) to deeply inhale cannabis smoke. ❑ **French leave** *n. see* separate entry. ❑ **French peasoup** *n.* [19C+] (*US/Can.*) a French immigrant. ❑ **French poodle** *n. see* POODLE *n.* (2). ❑ **French screwdriver** *n.* [supposed French inability to perform simple manual tasks] [20C+] a hammer. ❑ **french toast** *adj. see* TOAST *adj.*[2] (2). ❑ **French vanilla** *n.* [play on popular variety of ice cream] [1990s+] (*US black teen*) **1** a sexy white woman. **2** a light-coloured black woman. ❑ **French walk** *n.* [a pun on FROG *n.* (2) + SE *walk*; unwelcome or obstreperous drinkers would be grasped by a couple of bouncers, held up with all four limbs spread out (like a frog) and tossed into the street] [late 19C] (*US*) the posture assumed by those being thrown bodily out of a saloon. ❑ **Frenchwoman** *n.* [fig. use of *French* to mean strange, mysterious] [1920s+] (*W.I.*) a fortune-teller.

French *v.* [oral sex was generally seen as a French 'perversion'] **1** [1910s+] (*also* **french it, french off**) to fellate. **2** [1950s+] to deep kiss.

French bathe *n.* [stereotyping of the French as physically as well as morally dirty] [1950s+] (*gay*) the use of perfumes as a deodorant in lieu of bathing.

French bathe *v.* [FRENCH BATHE *n.*] [1950s+] (*gay*) to use perfumes as a deodorant in lieu of bathing.

Frencher *n.* [FRENCH *v.* (1)] [1960s+] one who enjoys oral sex, usu. a man.

Frenchery *n.* [FRENCH *adj.* (2) + sfx *-ery*] [mid-19C+] a brothel.

Frenchie *n.*[1] (*also* **Frenchy**) [SE *French* + sfx *-ie*] **1** [mid-19C+] (*US*) a Frenchman, a person of French descent, a French-Canadian; one who is assumed to be French. **2** [late 19C] anyone seen in the street and classified as foreign. **3** [late 19C+] as a term of direct address or a nickname. **4** [20C+] (*US*) a Cajun. **5** [20C+] (*W.I., St Kitts*) a poor white, a descendant of the original French settlers on St Kitts who, as Roman Catholics, lost their status when the island was taken over by the Protestant British in 1690. **6** [1910s–30s] something French, e.g. a play, a boat.

Frenchie *n.*[2] (*also* **Frenchy**) [stereotyping / FRENCH *adj.* (4)] **1** [20C+] (*US*) a foolish man. **2** [1930s] a flighty woman. **3** [1950s+] (*US Und.*) an act of fellatio, usu. as offered by a prostitute. **4** [1960s+] (*US gay*) a fellator. **5** [1970s+] a French kiss.

Frenchie *n.*[3] (*also* **Frenchy**) [SE *French fry*] [1990s+] (*N.Z.*) a potato chip.

Frenchie *adj.* (*also* **Frenchy**) [FRENCHIE *n.*[1]] **1** [1910s–40s] lightheaded, frivolous. **2** [1910s+] French. **3** [1970s] smartly dressed.

frenchie *n.* (*also* **frenchy**) [FRENCH LETTER *n.* + sfx *-ie*] [20C+] a contraceptive sheath.

Frenchified *adj.* [FRENCH *adj.* (1) + sfx *-ified*] **1** [late 17C–early 19C] having venereal disease. **2** [1980s] usu. of a woman, sexually talented.

Frenching *n. see* FRENCH *n.* (4).

French kiss *n.* [FRENCH KISS *v.*] [1930s+] a deep kiss, using the tongue as well as the lips; thus *French kissing*.

IN COMPOUNDS

❑ **French kiss filter** *n.* [1950s+] (*gay*) any filter-tipped cigarette.

French kiss *v.* [FRENCH *adj.* (2) + SE *kiss*] [1910s+] to kiss with the tongue.

French leave *n.* [negative national stereotyping] [mid-18C+] absenting oneself from a job or duty without prior permission.

IN PHRASES

❑ **take French leave** *v.* [late 19C+] to do something without requesting permission.

French letter *n.* (*also* **letter**) [FRENCH *adj.* (2) + SE *letter*; accepted as SE since 1950s] [mid-19C+] a contraceptive sheath; rare alts. are *American/Italian/Spanish letter*.

Frenchman *n.* **1** [mid-17C–early 19C] a scholar of French. **2** *see* FRANSMAN *n.*

SE in slang uses

IN COMPOUNDS

❑ **Frenchman's parole** *n.* [play on FRENCH LEAVE *n.* (1)] [1950s] an escape from prison.

Frenchy/frenchy *see under* FRENCHIE/FRENCHIE.

freney *n.* [the 18C highwayman James *Freney*, who had one eye] [late 18C–early 19C] (*Irish*) a one-eyed person.

fresh *n.*[1] [ety. unknown; poss. a misprint for PUSH *n.* (2a)] [mid-19C] (*UK Und.*) a gathering.

fresh *n.*[2] *see* FRESHER *n.*

fresh *adj.*[1] (*also* **freshish**) [SE *fresh wind*, a light wind that is noticeable but that wouldn't blow one over; Egan, *Life in London* (1821), defines it as 'a country phrase altogether'] [19C] tipsy, slightly drunk.

fresh *adj.*[2] **1** [20C+] (*W.I.*) sexually aggressive, making open advances to the opposite sex. **2** [1980s+] (*US black/campus*) smart, 'on the ball', aware, attractive; a general term of approval, varying as to context and applying to objects and events as well as people.

IN COMPOUNDS

❑ **fresh cut** *n.* [1980s+] (*US black*) a short, neat haircut.

IN PHRASES

❑ **bust fresh** *v.* [1980s+] (*US teen*) to look one's best, usu. coupled to a specific event, such as a party, an anniversary, a festival. ❑ **fresh and fast** *adj.* (*also* **fresh and forward**) [20C+] (*W.I.*) **1** cheeky and impertinent. **2** sexually promiscuous. **3** of meat, smelling raw (although not stale). **4** of fish, smelling 'off'. **5** of popular music, in the latest style. ❑ **fresh-up** *adj.* [20C+] (*W.I.*) **1** precocious. **2** sexually cheeky, suggestive.

SE in slang uses

IN COMPOUNDS

❑ **fresh bit** *n. see under* BIT *n.*[1]. ❑ **fresh cat** *n.* [1900s–30s] (*US tramp*) a new, inexperienced tramp. ❑ **fresh cow** *n.* [1920s–30s] (*US tramp*) one who has just developed a venereal disease. ❑ **fresh fish** *n.* [FISH *n.*[1] (6)] [mid-19C+] **1** (*US prison*) a new inmate in a prison; thus *fresh fish special*, the prison crop given to a new inmate. **2** any novice, e.g. a new recruit. **3** a new young prostitute. ❑ **fresh hide** *n.* [HIDE *n.* (1)] [1980s+] (*US black*) a new lover or sexual partner. ❑ **fresh lamb** *n. see under* LAMB *n.*[1]. ❑ **freshman** *n.* [1950s] (*US drugs*) a novice drug user. ❑ **fresh meat** *n. see* separate entry. ❑ **fresh union** *adj.* [? SAmE *union suit*, a suit of one-piece underwear] [1980s+] (*US*) clean, healthy. ❑ **fresh vegetable** *n.* [1990s+] (*W.I.*) from the perspective of an older woman, the young man one is having a relationship with. ❑ **fresh-whites** *n.* [late 19C] a pallid complexion.

IN PHRASES

❑ **fresh as paint** *adj.* [play on SE *fresh as paint*, blooming, healthy] [1910s] (*Aus.*) naïve.

fresh *v.* [i.e. calling someone FRESH *adj.*[2] (2)] [1980s] (*US black*) to compliment.

fresher *n.* (*also* **fresh, freshie**) [one of the last survivors of the -ER *sfx*, which once offered 'Pragger Wagger', the Prince of Wales, 'wagger pagger bagger', waste paper basket etc] **1** [late 19C+] (*UK/US campus*) a student in their first term at a university. **2** [1910s] a new arrival among a group of soldiers.

freshie *n.* [colloq. *fresh*, cheeky, forward] [1910s] (*US*) one who is considered sexually or verbally forward.

freshish *adj. see* FRESH *adj.*[1].

fresh meat *n.* [SE *fresh* + MEAT *n.* (1); pun] **1** [19C+] a newly fledged prostitute. **2** [20C+] any form of novice, e.g. a new recruit. **3** [1960s+] a new sexual partner. **4** [1950s+] (*US Und.*) a new, young inmate, esp. a potential victim of predatory prison homosexuals.

fresh out of *phr.* [20C+] (*US/Can.*) absolutely bereft of; usu. used of some form of commodity.

Freshwater *adj.*

SE in slang uses

IN COMPOUNDS

❑ **Freshwater Bay** *n.* [the then adjacent Fleet River; the prison closed in 1842, the market in 1826] [early–mid-19C] (*UK Und.*) **1** the Fleet prison. **2** Fleet Street Market. ❑ **Freshwater mariner** *n.* (*also* **freshwater seaman**) [mid-16C–17C] (*UK Und.*) 'their shippes were drowned in the playne of Salisbury' (Harman), such criminal beggars claimed to have suffered shipwreck or piracy and requested alms to return home. ❑ **Freshwater soldier** *n.* [early 17C] a professional beggar who trades on his spurious reminiscences of battles and campaigns of which, in fact, he has no personal experience. ❑ **Freshwater trout** *n.* [play on FISH *n.*[1] (1)] [1940s] (*US black*) an attractive woman, usu. in a group.

freshwater *n.* **1** [mid–late 19C] an emigrant who works their passage rather than pays a fare. **2** [20C+] (*W.I., Trin.*) a West Indian who visits America and comes back with a US accent.

fress *v.* [Yid. *fress*, to eat; thus play on EAT *v.* (4)] (*orig. US*) **1** [mid-19C+] to eat greedily, to snack. **2** [1960s+] to perform either form of oral intercourse, usu. cunnilingus.

fresser *n.* [FRESS *v.*] (*US*) **1** [late 19C+] a glutton. **2** [1960s+] one who performs cunnilingus or fellatio.

fret one's fat *v.* [late 19C+] to worry; also as phr. *God fret my fat*.

frey *v. see* VRY *v.*

friar tuck *n.* [rhy. sl. = FUCK *n.* (1)] [1950s+] sexual intercourse; thus as a euph.

friar tuck *v.* [FRIAR TUCK *n.*] [1960s+] to have sexual intercourse.

friar tucked *adj.* [FRIAR TUCK *n.*] [1990s+] a euph. for FUCKED *adj.*[1].

frib *n.* [ety. unknown] [mid–late 18C] (*UK Und.*) a stick.

fribble *n.* (*also* **fribler, fribbler**) [echoic + ? SE *frivol*] [mid-17C–mid-19C] a sexually inadequate male; thus adjs. *fribbled, fribbling*; as v., to behave in a sexually inadequate manner; the underlying inference is of effeminacy.

frick *n.* [1930s+] a euph. for FUCK *n.*; also as excl.

frick and frack *n.* [echoic of the sound of their knocking together; ult. *Frick and Frack*, the 1920s–30s Swiss comedy skating team, who performed in the US and Europe. They were famous for a routine where they would put the heels of their skates together, bend their knees and skate in large circles with their bodies leaning outwards] [1980s+] (*US black*) the testicles.

frickinchaten *n.* [? FRIGGING *n.* (3)/FRICKING *adj.* + SE *chatting*] [2000s] (*US black*) talking seductively to a woman.

fricking *adj.* [1930s+] a euph. for FUCKING *adj.* (1).

Friday *n.* [mid-19C] (*US Und.*) hanging day.

SE in slang uses

IN COMPOUNDS

❑ **Friday face** *n.* (*also* **February face**) [Friday's trad. status as a day of abstinence either from all food or from meat] [late 16C–1910s] a miserable or dour face; thus *Friday-faced*, miserable, gloomy.

IN PHRASES

❑ **frighten Friday** *n.* [SE *frighten*, frightened + FRAIDY *adj.*, or *Man Friday*, the black character in Daniel Defoe's *Robinson Crusoe* (1719)] [20C+] (*W.I.*) a timid person. ❑ **that'll be frosty Friday** [1940s+] (*Can./N.Z.*) never, that is very unlikely, 'that'll be the day'.

fridge *n.* **1** [1910s+] (*Aus.*) a prison. **2** [1990s+] a person, usu. a woman who is frigid.

fridge freezer *n.* [rhy. sl. = GEEZER *n.*[1] (1)] [2000s] a man.

fried *adj.* [fig. uses of SE] **1** [1920s+] very drunk; thus *fried to the gills/tonsils*, extremely drunk. **2** [1960s–70s] (*US*) dead. **3** [1960s+] (*drugs*) extremely intoxicated by a drug, usu. cannabis. **4** [1960s+] (*US campus*) (*also* **fried out**) angry. **5** [1970s+] (*US*) very tired, worn out, hungover. **6** [1980s] (*US campus*) defunct. **7** [1980s] (*US campus*) sunburned.

SE in slang uses

IN COMPOUNDS

❑ **fried carpet** *n.* [? resemblance of the fried fish] [late 19C] fish and chips. ❑ **fried fish wrapper** *n. see* FISH-WRAPPER *under* FISH *n.*[1]. ❑ **fried shirt** *n.* [var. on BOILED *adj.*] [19C+] (*US*) a heavily starched shirt, a dress shirt.

frieda *adj.* [initial letter] **1** [2000s] (*S.Afr. gay*) sexually frustrated. **2** [2000s] (*S.Afr. gay*) frigid. **3** [2000s] (*S.Afr. gay*) fickle, unfaithful.

fried bread *adj.* [rhy. sl.] [1990s+] dead.

fried, dyed, laid to the side *adj.* (*also* **fried, dyed, swooped to the side; fried, dyed, swept to the side**) [FRY (ONE'S HAIR) *under* FRY *v.*; the three processes that are undertaken to straighten and arrange black hair] [1970s+] (*US black*) of straightened black hair that is attempting to emulate the texture and even colour of a white person's hair.

fried eggs *n.*[1] [rhy. sl.] [20C+] (*Aus.*) legs.

fried eggs *n.*[2] [supposed resemblance] [1930s+] (*orig. Aus.*) small or undeveloped female breasts.

fried out *adj.* **1** *see* BURNED OUT *adj.*[2] (1). **2** *see* FRIED *adj.*[1] (4).

fried potato *n.* (*also* **baked potato**) [rhy. sl.; note Cockney pron. 'pertater'] [1920s] (*US*) a waiter.

fried rice *n.* [rhy. sl.] [20C+] (*Aus.*) the price.

friend *n.* **1** [early 19C; 1950s–60s] a prostitute's boyfriend or lover, but not necessarily her pimp. **2** [1940s+] (*US black*) menstruation; thus euph. phr. *I have friends to stay*, I am menstruating.

IN PHRASES

❑ **my friend** *n.* (*also* **my little friend, my others**) [20C+] (*Aus./Ulster/US*) menstruation. ❑ **my unconverted friend** *n.* [mid–late 19C] (*US*) a revolver, a pistol.

SE in slang uses

IN PHRASES

❑ **friend of Dorothy('s)** *n. see* DOROTHY'S FRIEND *n.* ❑ **friend of Oscar** *n.* [the gay icon, playwright *Oscar* Wilde (1854–1901)] [1920s+] a male homosexual.

friendly lead *n.* [late 19C] a subscription to help an unfortunate friend, usu. held by a 'whip-round' in a public house.

friendly road, the *n.* [1930s] (*N.Z.*) of workers, the decision to side with one's employer during an industrial dispute.

fries *n.*

IN PHRASES

❑ **do fries go with that shake?** *see under* SHAKE *n.*[1]. ❑ **I don't make the fries** [the image of a worker in a junk-food restaurant] [1990s+] (*US teen*) a phr. used to express the fact that one does not have any influence on the outcome of life.

frig *n.* [FRIG *v.*] **1** [late 18C–19C] an act of masturbation. **2** [late 19C+] sexual intercourse. **3** [1920s–60s] a curse; as in phr. *not give a frig*. **4** [1940s+] a euph. for FUCK *n.* in various uses. **5** [1960s] (*US*) a general derog. term of address. **6** [1990s+] (*US gay*) lesbian sexual intercourse, based on the partners rubbing against each other's body.

IN COMPOUNDS

❑ **frigpot** *n.* [1940s] (*Irish*) a term of abuse.

frig *v.* [Lat. *fricare*, to rub; note 18C SE *frication*, rubbing, in sexual context masturbating a partner] **1** [early 16C+] to have sexual intercourse. **2** [late 16C+] to masturbate. **3** [mid-17C+] to masturbate another person. **4** [mid-18C+] to trifle or fool around (with), to waste time. **5** [1920s–50s] to cheat. **6** [1920s+] a euph. for FUCK *v.* (3); thus excl. *frig it! frig you!* **7** [1950s+] to perform lesbian sex, where the genitals are rubbed together.

DERIVATIVES

❑ **friggish** *adj.* [1960s] sexy.

IN COMPOUNDS

❑ **frig-beard** *n.* [SE *beard*; the image is of the adult, bearded male] [early 18C] a degenerate, a seducer. ❑ **frig-pig** *n.* [late 18C–19C] a fussy, trifling person.

IN PHRASES

❑ **frig about** *v.* (*also* **frig around**) [1920s+] to trifle, to waste time, to fool around. ❑ **frig off** *v.* **1** [20C+] to masturbate, oneself or another. **2** [1940s+] to leave, to go away. ❑ **frig up** *see* separate entries. ❑ **frig-your-buddy week** *n.* (*also* **screw-your-buddy week**) [1960s] (*orig. US milit. use*) a response to any moment or act of betrayal, i.e. *I see, it's frig your buddy week.*

IN EXCLAMATIONS

❑ **frig off!** [1980s+] a euph. for FUCK OFF! *excl.* ❑ **frig you!** [1940s+] a semi-euph. synon. for FUCK YOU! *excl.* ❑ **go frig yourself!** [1930s+] a general excl. of dismissal. ❑ **I'll be frigged!** *see I'LL BE FUCKED! under* FUCKED *adj.*[1].

frigate *n.* (*also* **frigot**) [SE *frigate*, a light, swift vessel; there may also be some punning connection to FRIG *v.* (1)] **1** [mid-17C–19C] a woman. **2** [early 19C] a prostitute.

frigate on fire *n.* [FRIGATE *n.* (2) + FIRE *n.* (1)] [early–mid-19C] a prostitute who has venereal disease.

frigged out *adj.* [FRIG *v.* (2)] [late 19C] exhausted by excessive masturbation and thus incapable of ejaculation.

frigged-up *adj.* [1970s] (*W.I.*) improved, smartened up.

frigger *n.* [FRIG *v.*] **1** [late 17C] the finger or hand with which one masturbates. **2** [late 17C] the penis. **3** [late 19C–1900s] a masturbator; one who masturbates a partner. **4** [1950s] a general derog. term.

frigging *n.* [FRIG *v.*] **1** [late 16C+] masturbation. **2** [late 19C] an act of anal copulation. **3** [late 19C+] the act of copulation. **4** [1920s] a beating, lit. or fig.

frigging *adj.* [FRIG *v.*] **1** [late 18C] insignificant, petty, worthless. **2** [late 19C+] a euph. for FUCKING *adj.* **3** [1940s–50s] pertaining to sex; thus *frigging book*, a pornographic magazine. **4** [1940s+] as infix.

frigging A! *excl. see* FUCKING A! *excl.*

friggish *adj. see under* FRIG *v.*

frigg-up *n. see* FRIG-UP *n.*

frigg up *v. see* FRIG UP *v.*

frightener *n.* (*also* **fright, frighteners**) **1** [1930s+] (*also* **frights**) threats, violence, anything that will terrify a given person into doing what is required. **2** [1960s+] a thug, esp. as used by gangsters, casino-owners etc to commit violence for them.

IN PHRASES

❑ **get the frighteners** *v.* [1960s] fear; thus *get the frighteners*, to become terrified. ❑ **put the frighteners on** *v.* (*also* **put the frighteners in, stick the frighteners on**) [1950s+] (*UK Und.*) **1** to menace, to blackmail, to threaten with violence. **2** to terrify (with no criminal overtones).

frighten Friday *v. see under* FRIDAY *n.*

frighten the (living) daylights out of *v. see under* DAYLIGHTS *n.*

frigot *n. see* FRIGATE *n.*

frigster/frigstress *n.* [FRIG *v.* (2) + -STER *sfx/-stress*] [late 16C–17C] a masturbator.

frig-up *n.* (*also* **frigg-up**) [FRIG UP *v.*; semi-euph. for FUCK-UP *n.* (1)] [1940s+] (*orig. Aus.*) a disaster, a blunder, a mess.

frig up *v.* (*also* **frigg up**) [FRIG *v.* (6); semi-euph. for FUCK UP *v.*] [1930s+] (*orig. Aus.*) to make a blunder, to make a mess of; as adj., *frigged up*.

frijole-eater *n.* (*also* **frijole chomper, ...guzzler**) [Mex. Sp. *frijol*, a bean + SE *eater*] [1940s+] (*US*) a derog. term for a Mexican.

frikkie *n.* (*also* **frikky**) [? FRIG *v.* (1)] [1970s+] (*S.Afr.*) a condom.

frill *n.* [her clothing] [1900s–60s] a woman.

SE in slang uses

IN PHRASES

❑ **get among (a woman's) frills** *v.* (*also* **get up someone's frills**) [late 19C–1910s] to seduce a woman.

frimped *adj.* [? SE *frump*] [1920s–40s] (*US black*) ugly, unattractive; thus *frimpet*, n., a term of abuse.

fringe *v.* [? to hang around the *fringes* of the targeted person] [1940s] (*US black campus*) to sponge.

fringer *n.* [1940s–50s] an outcast; one who exists on the *fringes* of a given group.

fringes *n.* [1940s] (*US black campus*) eyes.

frip *n.* (*also* **friphead**) [? SE *frippery* or FRIPPING *n.*] [1970s+] (*US campus*) a weak, ineffectual person.

frippet *n.* [? *flibbertigibbet*] [20C+] a frivolous or showy young woman.

fripping *n.* [? SE *fripperies* or Lancs. dial. *frip*, something worthless] [1910s–20s] domestic bickering between husband and wife.

'Frisco *n.* [abbr.] **1** [mid-19C+] (*US*) San *Francisco*; thus *Friscoite*, a person from San Francisco. **2** [1920s–30s] as a nickname, e.g. *'Frisco Bill*.

frisco *n.* (*also* **frisko**) [a 'frisky' person] [mid-17C] a term of endearment.

frisco *v.* [? stereotyping of 'FRISCO *n.*] **1** [1930s] (*US gang*) to act in a provocative manner. **2** [1940s] to stutter.

'Frisco speedball *n.* (*also* **'Frisco special, 'Frisco push**) [SPEEDBALL *n.*[1]] [1960s–70s] (*drugs*) a drug cocktail containing LSD, cocaine and heroin.

frisk *n.*[1] (*also* **frisking**) [FRISK *v.*[2]] [late 18C+] (*orig. UK Und.*) a search.

IN PHRASES

❑ **skin frisk** *n.* [1930s+] (*US prison*) a skin search. ❑ **stand frisk** *v.* [19C] to be searched.

frisk *n.*[2] **1** [early 19C+] sexual intercourse. **2** [early–mid-19C] fun, amusement.

frisk *v.*[1] [early 16C–19C] to have sexual intercourse; to be adulterous; also as n., *frisker*, one who engages in sexual intercourse, a prostitute; *frisking*, foreplay.

IN PHRASES

❑ **frisk in a hempen cravat** *v. see under* HEMPEN *adj.*

frisk *v.*[2] [one's hands or schemes 'frisk' over the victim] **1** [early 18C+] (*also* **fisk, friz**) (*orig. Und.*) to search, usu. for weapons, illicit drugs, stolen goods etc; usu. of people, occas. things. **2** [late 18C+] (*orig. US*) to rob or steal, esp. from a sleeping or helpless person. **3** [early 19C] to trick, to hoax. **4** [mid-19C; 1960s] to search in a non-criminal context, e.g. one's own pockets. **5** [1910s] to obtain, to get hold of.

frisk and frolic *n.* [rhy. sl.] [late 19C–1910s] carbolic (soap).

frisker *n.* [FRISK *v.*[1]] **1** [19C+] a pilferer, a petty thief; a pickpocket. **2** [mid-19C] (*UK Und.*) one who conducts a body search.

frisking *n. see* FRISK *n.*[1].

frisking-do *n.* [FRISK *v.*[2] (1)] [mid-19C] (*UK Und.*) a search (of person or premises).

frisko *n. see* FRISCO *n.*

frisky *adj.* [late 19C–1900s] ill-tempered.

SE in slang uses

IN COMPOUNDS

❑ **frisky powder** *n.* [its effects] [1950s+] (*drugs*) cocaine.

frit *n.* [SE colloq. *frit*, frightened; his supposed cowardice] [1940s–60s] (*US*) an effeminate male homosexual.

frito *n.* [advertisements for *Frito Bandito* cornchips, which feature a stereotypical 'Mexican bandit'] [1950s–60s] (*US*) a derog. term for a Mexican or Spanish-American.

fritter *n.*

IN PHRASES

❑ **on the fritter** *adj. see ON THE FRITZ under* FRITZ *n.*[2].

fritters! *excl.* [1900s] (*Aus.*) an excl. of dismissal or contempt.

Fritz *n.* (*also* **Fritzer, Fritzey, Fritzie**) [Ger. dimin. of proper name *Friedrich*, esp. as used of 'Old Fritz', Friedrich II of Prussia; the English-language usage emerged *c.*1880 and came into widespread use during WW1, although it fell from favour afterwards; Brophy & Partridge, *Songs and Slang of the British Soldier* (1930), suggest it was generally replaced by JERRY *n.* (1) after 1915] [late 19C+] a German, esp. a German soldier.

Fritz *adj.* (*also* **Fritzie**) [FRITZ *n.*] [1910s] German.

fritz *n.*[1] (*also* **pork fritz**) [Ger. name *Fritz*, linked to a German sausage] [20C+] (*Aus.*) a large, but not especially spicy, sausage.

fritz *n.*[2]

IN PHRASES

❑ **on the fritz** *adj.* [? German proper name *Fritz* and thus propagandist dislike of all things German, or *fritz* as onomat. for the sparking of a faulty wire or connection] [20C+] **1** drunk. **2** of a person, unhealthy, out of sorts. **3** (*also* **away to the fritz**) of an object, not functioning properly; thus antonym *on the fritz*, working. **4** of a situation, position, job, in jeopardy. **5** (*also* **on the fritter**) of machinery, broken down, not working. **6** impoverished. ❑ **put the fritz on** *v.* (*also* **put on the fritz, put on the fritzerine, put the fritz to**) [20C+] to spoil, to render out of order, to put a stop to.

fritz *v.* [*ON THE FRITZ under* FRITZ *n.*[2]] (*US*) **1** [1910s+] (*also* **fritz out**) to go out of order, to break down. **2** [1940s+] to put out of order.

Fritzer/Fritzey/Fritzie *n. see* FRITZ *n.*

fritzy *n.* [*ON THE FRITZ under* FRITZ *n.*[2]] [1930s] (*US Und.*) an epileptic beggar, or one who poses as such.

friz *v. see* FRISK *v.*[2] (1).

friz out *v.* [ext. FRITZ *v.* (1)] [1990s+] (*US teen*) to lose one's temper, to argue.

frizzle *n.*[1] [abbr. *OLD FRIZZLE under* OLD *adj.*] [18C] the vagina.

frizzle *n.*[2] [? FIZZ *n.*[1] (3)] [mid-19C] champagne.

frizzled in eggs and fresh butter *phr.* [mid-19C] (*UK Und.*) standing in the pillory and pelted with rotten eggs and mud.

frizzler *n. see* SIZZLER *n.* (2).

fro *n.*[1] *see* AFRO *n.*

fro *n.*[2] *see* FROE *n.*[1].

frock *n.*[1] **1** [1900s–10s] a man wearing a frock-coat; a frock-coat. **2** [1920s] (*US Und.*) a suit of clothes. **3** [1980s+] (*US gay*) the man who poses as a lesbian's 'husband' for the sake of 'passing' in an intolerant society [the image of the lesbian as a trouser-wearing woman for whom a frock is automatically unnatural].

SE in slang uses

IN COMPOUNDS

❑ **frock-hitcher** *n.* [late 19C–1900s] a milliner.

frock *n.*[2] [1980s+] (*UK juv.*) a euph. substitute for FUCK *n.* in various contexts.

frocked down *adj.* [SE *frock*] [1940s] (*US black, Harlem*) of a woman, dressed up.

frocker *n.* [1900s–10s] (*Aus.*) a woman dressed up in a (fashionable) frock; thus *frocky*, fashionably dressed.

froe *n.*[1] (*also* **fro, frow**) [Du. *vrouw* or Ger. *Frau*, a woman] **1** [mid-17C–1950s] a woman; thus *fro file*, a female pickpocket. **2** [mid-18C–mid-19C; 1920s] a prostitute.

froe *n.*[2] [ety. unknown] [late 19C–1930s] (*US black*) a trad. plantation slave pocket knife.

Frog *n.* [orig. 14C SE *frog*, a contemptible or offensive person; used in early 17C to refer to Jesuits, then in 1650 to the Dutch, England's national enemy; when they were replaced by the French the definition changed accordingly] **1** [mid-17C–18C] a Dutch person. **2** [mid-17C+] (*also* **Bullfrog**) a French person. **3** [mid-19C] (*US*) a contemptible person. **4** [1910s] (*Aus.*) a French franc. **5** [1920s+] the French language. **6** [1970s+] (*Can.*) a French-Canadian. **7** [1980s] (*US*) a Cajun.

DERIVATIVES

❑ **Frogolia** *n.* [on model of SE *Mongolia*] [1970s+] (*N.Z.*) a derog. term for France; thus *Frogolian*, a French person.

IN COMPOUNDS

❑ **Frogland** *n.* [mid-19C; 1990s+] France. ❑ **Froglander** *n.* [note SE *frogland*, marshy land that is full of frogs, orig. used of the Fens and of Holland] [late 17C–mid-19C] a Dutch person. ❑ **frog's wine** *n.* [brandy is always linked to France; gin to Holland] [mid-19C] **1** brandy. **2** gin.

SE in slang uses

IN COMPOUNDS

❑ **frog-eater** *n. see* separate entry. ❑ **frog-swallower** *n.* [late 19C] a derog. term for a French person.

frog *n.*[1] [his sudden 'leaping' onto criminals] [mid–late 19C] (*US*) a policeman.

SE in slang uses

IN COMPOUNDS

❑ **frogmarch** *v. see* separate entry. ❑ **frog's eggs** *n.* (*also* **frog eggs, frog's eyes, frogspawn**) [1910s+] (*Aus./N.Z./UK juv.*) boiled sago or tapioca pudding. ❑ **frog's eyebrows** *n. see* BEE'S KNEES *n.* ❑ **frog's hair** *n.* [late 19C+] the very smallest degree; in phr. like *within a frog's hair, to a frog's hair.* ❑ **frogskin** *n. see* separate entries. ❑ **frog's march** *v. see* FROGMARCH *v.* ❑ **frogsticker** *n.* [mid-19C+] (*US*) a long-bladed pocket-knife; in milit. use a bayonet. ❑ **frogtown** *n.* [the swampy, frog-ridden pond that is trad. associated with such rural settlements] [19C+] (*US*) a small or out-of-the-way place.

frog *n.*[2] [SE *frog*, an elastic, horny substance growing in the middle of the sole of a horse's hoof] [late 19C–1900s] a foot; thus *on the frog*, walking.

frog *n.*[3] (*also* **frogskin**) [such notes are/were green; Franklyn, *Dict. of Rhyming Slang* (1961), suggests rhy. sl. *frogskin* = SE *sovereign*] **1** [20C+] (*US black/campus/Und.*) (*also* **alligator skin, fish-skin**) a banknote, $1 bill. **2** [1920s] (*US Und.*) a counterfeit dollar bill. **3** [1930s–60s] (*Aus.*) a £1 note. **4** [1960s] (*US Und.*) a bad cheque.

frog *n.*[4] [initial letters] **1** [1940s–70s] (*US campus*) a freshman. **2** [1960s+] (*US campus*) a grade of F.

frog *n.*[5] [abbr. FROGSKIN *n.*[1]] [1960s+] (*orig. Aus.*) a condom.

frog *n.*[6] **1** *see* FROG (AND TOAD) *n.* **2** *see* FROG (SPAWN) *n.*

frog *adj.* [1910s+] French.

frog *v.*[1] [FROG *n.*[3]] **1** [late 19C] to write for money. **2** [1900s] (*US campus*) to cheat.

frog *v.*[2] [1960s] (*US black*) to leap, to jump.

frog (and toad) *n.* [rhy. sl.] [mid-19C+] the road.

frog and toad *v.* [FROG (AND TOAD) *n.* ; note WW1 *frog it*, to march] **1** [late 19C] (*also* **frog it**) to walk. **2** [1980s+] (*Aus. prison*) to leave, esp. to escape.

frog and toe *n.* [ety. unknown] [mid-19C] **1** London [Franklyn suggests that it was a destination towards which one travels on FROG *n.*[2]]. **2** (*US Und.*) New York City.

frog-eater *n.* [late 18C+] a French person; thus adj. *frog-eating.*

froggie *n.* (*also* **froggee, froggy**) [FROG *n.* (2)/FROG *n.* (5)] **1** [mid-19C+] (*orig. US*) a French person. **2** [1930s+] the French language.

froggy *adj.*[1] (*also* **froggie**) [FROGGIE *n.* (1)] [mid-19C+] French.

froggy *adj.*[2] (*also* **froggish**) [1960s+] (*US black*) aggressive, belligerent, keen to fight, keen to start 'jumping'.

IN PHRASES

❑ **feel froggy** *v.* (*also* **feel froggish**) [1970s+] (*US black*) to feel like fighting; thus the challenge *if you feel froggy, then leap*, if you want a fight, then let's get on with it.

frog in the throat *n.* [rhy. sl.] [1950s+] a boat.

frogmarch *v.* (*also* **frog's-march**) [the image of a spreadeagled frog] [mid-19C+] to carry someone face-down, one person holding onto each limb; used on drunks or recalcitrant prisoners.

frogsh *n.* [abbr. *frogshit*] [1910s] (*Aus.*) nonsense, rubbish.

frogskin *n.*[1] [pun on FROG *adj.*, i.e. FRENCH LETTER *n.*; or var. on FROG *n.*[5]] [1940s+] (*orig. Aus./N.Z.*) a condom.

frogskin *n.*[2] *see* FROG *n.*[3].

frog (spawn) *n.* [rhy. sl. = HORN *n.*[2] (1b)] [1990s+] an erection.

frolic pad *n.* (*also* **frolic**) [SE *frolic* + PAD *n.*[2] (2)] [1940s] (*US black*) a nightclub.

from *prep.* [20C+] because of, as a result of; used in a variety of combs., e.g. *from hunger, from grief.*

fromage, the *n.* [play on CHEESE, THE *n.* (2); ult. Fr. synon. *fromage*] [mid-19C–1900s] of people, objects, experiences: the best of a type or style, the superlative.

fromage *adj.* [Fr. *fromage*, cheese, thus CHEESY *adj.*[2] (1)] [1920s+] (*US campus*) objectionable.

from back *phr.* [abbr. SE *from way back*, from a long time ago] [1930s–50s] (*US black*) for a long time.

from go to whoa *phr.* [1970s+] (*Aus.*) from start to finish.

from in front *phr.* [1950s–60s] (*orig. US black/jazz*) from the beginning.

from now on *n.* [1930s–50s] (*US Und.*) a life sentence; indefinite confinement on the punishment block.

frompy *adj.* [pron. of SE *frumpy*] [1930s–40s] (*US black*) of a woman, dowdy, ill-kempt.

froncey *n.* [mispron. of Fr. *Français*, French] [mid–late 19C] a Frenchman, the French language.

frone *n.* [? Ger. *Frau*, woman or SE *frown* + *crone*] [1940s] (*US black*) an unattractive woman.

Front, the *n.* **1** [1940s+] (*UK gay/Und.*) any street that is known as a centre for prostitution, e.g. Piccadilly, Oxford Street. **2** [1950s] (*UK teen*) the main street of a gang's territory.

front *n.*[1] **1** [19C+] (*orig. UK society*) (*also* **frontage**) cheek, audacity. **2** [mid-19C+] self-respect, 'face'. **3** [mid-19C+] a respectable appearance, esp. as a mask for illegal activities; of both people and places. **4** [late 19C–1920s] (*US Und.*) a watch and chain; jewellery. **5** [late 19C–1970s] (*US*) a suit. **6** [late 19C+] (*UK Und.*) anything one needs – smart clothes, a clever line of speech, a personal style, a mental attitude – for the successful promotion of one's schemes. **7** [20C+] one who maintains a respectable appearance for the pursuit of crime. **8** [1910s] (*US Und.*) an assistant, usu. for purposes of diversion, in a criminal act. **9** [1920s] (*US Und.*) a high bail bond. **10** [1940s] in pl., a woman's breasts. **11** [1950s+] (*US black*) in pl., clothes. **12** [1980s] (*US drugs*) a payment for drugs, i.e. not on consignment. **13** [2000s] (*US black*) in pl., the teeth. **14** *see* FRONT MONEY *n.*

IN PHRASES

❏ **get one's front uptight** *v.* [1970s] (*US black*) to assemble the 'props' required to present oneself in a desired manner, usu. expensive material possessions. ❏ **more front than Brighton (beach)** [pun on SE (*sea-*)*front*] [1930s+] a phr. used of one who is very cheeky, daring or outspoken. ❏ **more front than Buckingham Palace** [1980s+] a phr. used of one who is very cheeky, daring or outspoken. ❏ **more front than Harrods** [Harrods, the very large London department store] [1970s+] a phr. used of one who is very cheeky, daring or outspoken. ❏ **more front than Milne's** [Milne's, once a large department store in Auckland] **1** [2000s] (*N.Z.*) extremely cheeky. **2** [2000s] (*N.Z.*) of a woman, large-breasted. ❏ **more front than Myers** (*also* **more front than Foy and Gibson's, ...the National Bank**) [large department stores in respectively Melbourne and Adelaide] [1950s+] (*Aus.*) a phr. used of one who is very cheeky, daring or outspoken.

front *n.*[2] [1950s] (*US black*) a place.

front *n.*[3] [? FRONT, THE *n.*] [1990s+] (*UK Und.*) prostitution.

front *n.*[4] **1** *see* FRONT LINE *n.* **2** *see* FRONT MONEY *n.*

front *adj.* [FRONT *n.*[1] (3)] [1930s+] providing a respectable image for illegal activities.

IN COMPOUNDS

❏ **front gee** *n.* [1930s–40s] (*US Und.*) a member of a pickpocket team who diverts the victim. ❏ **front man** *n.* [1930s+] (*orig. US*) anyone who covers for illegal activities, posing as a 'legitimate' citizen. ❏ **front marriage** *n.* [1950s+] (*US gay*) an unconsummated marriage between a gay man and gay woman to satisfy the norms of non-gay society. ❏ **front money** *n.* *see* separate entry.

SE in slang uses

IN COMPOUNDS

❏ **front attic** *n.* [19C] the vagina. ❏ **front bottom** *n.* [1980s+] the vagina. ❏ **front bum** *n.* [BUM *n.*[1] (1)] [1980s+] the labia majora; the vagina. ❏ **front door** *see* separate entries. ❏ **front entrance** *n.* [late 19C] the vagina. ❏ **front garden** *n.* (*also* **front gate**) [19C] the vagina. ❏ **front gut** *n.* [19C] the vagina. ❏ **front job** *n.* [SE *front*, i.e. of the bank (rather than the hidden strongroom) + JOB *n.*[2] (1)] [1930s] (*US Und.*) a bank robbery in which no money is taken from the safe; only that in the tellers' drawers. ❏ **frontline** *n.* *see* separate entry. ❏ **front load** *v.* *see* separate entry. ❏ **front parlour** *n.* [late 19C] the vagina. ❏ **front porch** *n.* **1** [1910s] (*US*) a protruding stomach. **2** [1970s] the penis. ❏ **front room** *n.* **1** [early 19C] the vagina. **2** [1930s–50s] (*US Und.*) a sedan; a limousine. ❏ **front street** *n.* *see* separate entry. ❏ **front tottie** *n.* [1980s] (*Aus.*) the female genitals. ❏ **front window** *n.* **1** [19C] the vagina. **2** [mid-19C] in pl., the eyes. **3** [1900s–10s] in pl., spectacles.

front *v.*[1] [SE *confront*] **1** [late 16C; mid-19C+] to confront. **2** [mid-19C–1910s] (*UK Und.*) of a pickpocket team, to distract a victim's attention while the actual theft is carried out. **3** [1940s+] (*Aus.*) to appear in front of. **4** [1960s+] (*also* **front up**) to approach. **5** [1960s+] (*US campus/black*) (*also* **front on**) to disrespect, to snub.

IN PHRASES

❏ **front off** *v.* [1980s+] (*US prison*) **1** to betray, to inform on. **2** to confide in. **3** to confront. **4** to put someone else in trouble. ❏ **front on** *v.* *see* sense 5 above. ❏ **front oneself off** *v.* [1960s] (*orig. US black*) to reveal oneself, one's motives, actions etc. ❏ **front someone off** *v.* [1980s+] (*US black*) **1** to reveal information about another person that puts that person in an embarrassing or otherwise difficult position. **2** to confront (someone) with talk about something they either should or should not have done. ❏ **front up** *v.* [i.e. in *front* of the judge] **1** [1960s+] (*Aus./N.Z. Und.*) to appear, esp. in court. **2** *see* sense 4 above.

front *v.*[2] [FRONT *n.*[1]] **1** [1910s] (*US Und.*) to act as a decoy for a fellow criminal. **2** [1920s+] (*orig. US*) to maintain a respectable image for what is in fact a criminal organization, e.g. a restaurant, a nightclub. **3** [1930s] (*US Und.*) to take blame. **4** [1960s+] (*US black*) to deceive. **5** [1970s+] (*US black*) to show off, to pose. **6** [1990s+] (*US campus*) to act foolishly. **7** [1990s+] (*US black*) to back down.

IN PHRASES

❏ **front for** *v.* **1** [20C+] to work as a decoy or a falsely respectable con-man; also used of a place, building or similar. **2** [1920s+] to act as the public face of anyone, criminal or otherwise, who prefers to retain their privacy. **3** [1960s] to represent, e.g. as a lawyer. ❏ **front (off)** *v.* [1970s+] (*orig. US black*) **1** (*also* **front out**) to pose as something one is not. **2** to trick or deceive with glib verbosity for some gain, usu. monetary or sexual. **3** to show off. **4** to talk nonsense, to be 'all talk, no action'.

front *v.*[3] [1960s+] to advance either money or any other commodity (esp. drugs) as a loan or a sample of goods on offer; when buying drugs the seller may ask for the money to be 'fronted' so he in turn, can make a bulk purchase from his superior in the sales chain.

fronta *n.* [it provides a *front* to the marijuana within] [20C+] (*W.I., Rasta*) tobacco leaf used to roll a marijuana cigarette.

frontage *n.* *see* FRONT *n.*[1] (1).

front and rear *n.* [rhy. sl.] [1990s+] a year.

front door *n.* [late 19C+] the female genitals.

IN COMPOUNDS

❏ **front-door man** *n.* [2000s] (*US*) in the context of adultery, the husband, the regular male partner. ❏ **front-door mat** *n.* [1950s+] the female pubic hair.

IN PHRASES

❏ **do a bit of front door work** *v.* [19C] to have sexual intercourse.

front door *adj.* [1980s+] (*Aus. prison*) honest.

fronter *n.* [FRONT *v.*[2]] **1** [1930s] (*US tramp*) one who maintains a respectable appearance as a mask for criminality. **2** [1970s+] (*US black*) a show-off.

frontispiece *n.* **1** [18C–1910s] the face. **2** [mid-19C] the forehead. **3** [1900s] the nose.

front line *n.* (*also* **front, line**) [weakened/fig. use of milit. *front line*, the place where two opposing armies face each other] [1970s+] **1** (*W.I./UK black teen*) the main street or area, the main area of attraction or focus of activities. **2** (*UK black*) that area of a city where the black community is most likely to clash with the forces of white law and order, e.g. All Saints Road, Notting Hill, Railton Road, Brixton etc.

frontload *v.* [SE *frontload*, 'to concentrate a load at the front of (a vehicle)' (*OED*)] [1990s+] (*US campus*) to get drunk before attending an event where no alcohol will be available.

front money *n.* (*also* **front**) [FRONT *adj.*] **1** [1920s+] any form of money paid over in advance. **2** [1930s+] (*US*) money to show and impress others. **3** [1960s+] (*drugs*) money advanced to a dealer for the purchase of drugs.

front street *n.* (*also* **Front Street**) [note the actual Front Street, New York City, once a mercantile centre] [1960s+] (*US black*) **1** the main street of a town, the street on which most of the (illegal) action takes place. **2** in fig. use, the state of being on public display and thus open to attack, whether verbal or physical; a situation in which one must be responsible for one's words and deeds.

IN PHRASES

❑ **play on front street** *v.* [1990s+] to abandon pretence, to act openly. ❑ **put one's business on front street** *v.* (*also* **play on front street, put on front street, put one's business on the street, put one's shit on the street**) **1** [1960s+] (*US black*) to make indiscreet disclosures about oneself or another person. **2** [1960s+] (*US black*) to trick, to deceive. **3** [1990s+] (*US prison*) to confront, to defy.

front-wheel skid *n.* (*also* **backward skid, four-wheel skid, front-wheeler**) [rhy. sl. = YID *n.*[1]] [1920s+] a derog. term for a Jewish person.

frosh *n.* (*also* **froshie**) [*freshman* + ? Ger. dial. *Frosch*, frog, a grammar-school pupil] [1910s+] (*US*) **1** a college freshman. **2** a member of a freshman sports team. **3** (collective) freshmen.

frost *n.* **1** [late 19C+] (*orig. theatre*) a failure. **2** [late 19C+] coolness (between two people). **3** [1950s+] (*US black*) cocaine.

IN COMPOUNDS

❑ **frost-bitten** *adj.* [2000s] (*US drugs*) under the influence of cocaine.

frost *v.* [late 19C+] (*US*) **1** to treat in a distant manner. **2** to anger; to cause coolness in relations. **3** (*US campus*) to shock; esp. in phr. *wouldn't that frost you.*

frost a cake *v.* (*also* **cut a cake**) [1900s; 1960s] (*US*) to make a difference.

frosted *adj.* [FROST *n.* (3)] [1950s–60s] (*drugs*) heavily intoxicated by cocaine.

frosty *n.* (*also* **frostie**) [1950s+] (*Aus./US*) a chilled glass or can of beer.

frosty *adj.* [FROST *v.*] **1** [late 19C] (*US*) very unfriendly. **2** [1900s] unsuitable, inappropriate, 'bad'. **3** [1950s] (*US drugs*) under the influence of cocaine. **4** [1970s+] cool, unemotional. **5** [1980s+] stylish, fashionable.

frosty *adv.* [1900s] (*US*) problematically.

frosty face *n.* **1** [late 18C–19C] one whose face is pitted with smallpox scars. **2** [20C+] (*Ulster*) the joker in a pack of cards. **3** [1920s–70s] (*also* **Miss Frosty Pants**) a severe person.

frot *v.* [Fr. *frottage*, rubbing (in a sexual context); note Urquhart, *The Complete Works of Rabelais* (1653): 'These two did oftentimes do the two-backed beast together, joyfully rubbing and frotting their bacon against one another'] [1970s+] to rub up against (for sexual pleasure and usu. in a clandestine manner).

froth *n.* [early–mid-17C] beer.

froth and bubble *n.* [rhy. sl.] [1960s+] (*Aus.*) **1** a racing double, the daily double. **2** trouble.

frottage *n.* [FROT *v.* + -AGE *sfx*] [2000s] (*US black*) sexual desire.

frotting *n.* [FROT *v.* + sfx *-ing*] [1990s+] the rubbing of bodies together for sexual pleasure.

frow *n.* see FROE *n.*[1].

froze *adj.* [FROST *n.* (3)] [1980s] under the influence of cocaine.

frozen *adj.* [one is rendered immobile, i.e. *frozen* to the spot] **1** [1980s] (*US black*) extremely intoxicated by a drug. **2** [1990s+] (*US black*) condemned to a lengthy prison sentence.

SE in slang uses

IN COMPOUNDS

❑ **frozen fruit** *n.* [pun on SE *frozen* + FRUIT *n.* (2)] [1970s] (*US gay*) a sexually frigid gay man. ❑ **frozen face** *n. see* FROZEN MITT *under* MITT *n.* ❑ **frozen mitt** *n. see under* MITT *n.* ❑ **frozen mitten/word** *n. see* FROZEN MITT *under* MITT *n.*

IN PHRASES

❑ **give someone the frozen eye** *v. see* GIVE SOMEONE THE FISH-EYE *under* FISH-EYE *n.*[1].

fru-fru *n.* [2000s] (*W.I.*) a dirty, unkempt person.

fruit *n.* [the image is of being 'ripe' or 'soft' and 'easy picking'] **1** [late 19C–1930s] (*US*) a dupe, an easy victim, one who is easily influenced. **2** [20C+] (*also* **fruit-eater**) a derog. term for a male homosexual; in general use any homosexual; in gay use esp. one who pays for sex; thus *canned fruit, crushed fruit*, a homosexual who does not reveal his sexual proclivity; *fruitette* a school-age homosexual. **3** [1900s–40s] a promiscuous woman. **4** [1900s–50s] something or someone delightful or pleasant; thus OLD FRUIT below. **5** [1930s; 1980s+] (*US teen*) an unintelligent, dull person. **6** [1940s+] an eccentric person.

IN COMPOUNDS

❑ **fruitball** *n.* (*also* **fruitbar, ...bat, ...basket, ...head, ... merchant**) [-HEAD *sfx* (1)/MERCHANT *n.* (1)] [1970s+] (*US*) an eccentric. ❑ **fruit boots** *n.* [in more restrained eras, such shoes were seen as badges of effeminacy] [1950s–70s] (*orig. US gay*) **1** white tennis shoes, white suede shoes. **2** 'Beatle boots' or any Italian-style shoes with pointed toes. ❑ **fruitcake** see separate entries. ❑ **fruit-eater** *n.* see sense 2 above. ❑ **fruit factory** *n.* [1960s] (*Aus.*) a psychiatric institution. ❑ **fruit-fly** *n.* **1** [1950s+] a homosexual man. **2** [1960s+] (*US gay*) a heterosexual woman who enjoys the company of homosexual rather than heterosexual men. **3** [2000s] (*US Und.*) a heterosexual man who specializes in robbing homosexuals whom he has fooled into believing he is looking for gay sex. ❑ **fruit hustler** *n.* [HUSTLER *n.* (3)] [1950s+] (*US*) one who pursues passive homosexuals for sex. ❑ **fruit jockey** *n.* [JOCKEY *n.*[2] (3b)] [1980s] (*US prison*) a homosexual. ❑ **fruit juice** *n.* [JUICE *n.*[1] (2a)] [1970s+] (*US gay*) semen. ❑ **fruitloop** *n.* see separate entries. ❑ **fruit picker** *n.* **1** [1960s] (*US gay*) an ostensibly heterosexual man who enjoys homosexual encounters. **2** [1970s+] (*US gay*) one who blackmails or robs homosexuals. ❑ **fruit-plate** *n.* [1930s+] (*US*) a male homosexual. ❑ **fruit roller** *n.* [ROLLER *n.* (5)] [1980s+] (*US*) a thug who specializes in mugging or beating up homosexuals; thus v. *fruit-roll*. ❑ **fruit stand** *n.* (*also* **fruit corner**) [1960s] (*US gay*) a place to find male homosexual prostitutes.

IN PHRASES

❑ **fruit for monkeys** *n.* [1930s–70s] (*US*) (derog.) a passive homosexual man. ❑ **fruits in suits** *n.* [2000s] (*N.Z.*) homosexual men who frequent smart urban bars. ❑ **old fruit** *n.* (*also* **old tin of fruit**) [1920s+] a general term of affectionate address. ❑ **over-ripe fruit** *n.* [1950s+] (*gay*) an ageing male homosexual. ❑ **passion fruit** *n.* [1960s] (*US gay*) a masculine homosexual. ❑ **ripe fruit** *n.* [1970s+] (*US gay*) someone who is just discovering their homosexuality.

SE in slang uses

IN COMPOUNDS

❑ **fruit salad** *n.* see separate entries. ❑ **fruitful vine** [it 'bear flowers' (menstruation) every month] [19C] the vagina.

IN PHRASES

❑ **fruit for the sideboard** *n.* [the implication is of 'extras' or luxuries; fruit would normally be placed on the table and soon eaten] [1950s+] (*Aus.*) **1** 'easy money', esp. as won while gambling. **2** (*also* **fruit on the sideboard**) a person who is seen as a source of 'easy money'.

fruit *adj.*[1] (*also* **fruity**) [it is 'soft'] [1900s] (*US campus*) easily achieved.

fruit *adj.*[2] (*also* **fruit-eating**) [FRUIT *n.* (2)] [1920s+] (*US*) homosexual, pertaining to homosexuality.

fruit *v.* [1930s–40s] (*US*) **1** to romance, to seductively persuade. **2** to waste time. **3** to fool or joke.

fruitcake *n.*[1] [they are NUTS *adj.* (2)] [1910s+] an eccentric, a peculiar person; esp. in phr. *nutty as a fruitcake*; thus *fruitcake factory*, a psychiatric institution.

IN PHRASES

❑ **fruitcake around** *v.* [1930s] (*US black*) 'doing something slightly naughty' (*American Speech* XIII).

fruitcake *n.*[2] [FRUIT *n.* (2)] [1930s+] a male homosexual.

fruitcake *n.*[3] [visual resemblance + ? ext. of FRUITCAKE *n.*[2]] [2000s] (*S.Afr. gay*) one who suffers badly from acne or a similar skin problem.

fruitcake *adj.* [FRUITCAKE *n.*[1] (1)] [1940s+] (*US*) crazy, eccentric.

fruitcake *v.* [1930s] (*US black*) to bluff.

fruiter *n.* [FRUIT *n.* (2)] [1910s+] (*US*) a male homosexual.

fruiting *n.* [FRUIT *n.* (3)] [1940s+] (*US black*) promiscuity.

fruit loop *n.*[1] [pun on the US breakfast cereal *Fruit Loops*/FRUIT *n.* (2)] [1980s+] **1** (*US campus*) the small loop (ostensibly for hanging the shirt when no hanger is available) on the upper back of many shirts; such a loop, supposedly, can be used to hold a victim ready for buggery. **2** (*US*) a homosexual man. **3** (*US gay*) a freedom ring, one of a set of six metal rings in the colours of the rainbow worn to indicate that one is homosexual or sympathetic to homosexual causes.

fruit loop *n.*[2] [pun on the US breakfast cereal *Fruit Loops*/LOOPY *adj.* (1)] [1980s+] (*US*) a crazy or stupid person.

fruit salad *n.*[1] [pun on SE, suggested by the assorted colours] **1** [1940s+] badges, medals. **2** [1960s+] (*US drugs/teen*) a random combination of any pills or capsules of drugs available, including psychotropic and medicinal, on which to get intoxicated. **3** [2000s] (*S.Afr. gay*) the male genitals [presumed resemblance to a banana and apples].

IN PHRASES

❑ **do a fruit salad** *v.* [1980s+] (*US campus*) of a man, to expose one's genitals in public.

fruit salad *n.*[2] [pun on FRUIT *n.* (2)] **1** [1960s] (*US*) sexually attractive young women. **2** [1970s+] (*US gay*) a group of gay men.

fruit salad bowl *n.* [pun] [1980s+] (*US drugs*) a pipe or bowl filled with a mix of marijuana and hashish.

fruity *n.* [abbr.] [2000s] a *fruit* machine.

fruity *adj.*[1] [the fig. *fruit* is 'ripe' for enjoyment] **1** [20C+] full of a rich or strong quality, highly interesting, attractive or suggestive. **2** [1910s+] sexually aroused. **3** [1930s] painful. **4** *see* FRUIT *adj.*[1].

fruity *adj.*[2] [FRUITCAKE *n.*[1]] [1910s+] (*US*) crazy.

fruity *adj.*[3] [FRUIT *n.* (2)] [1910s+] (*US*) homosexual; effeminate.

frummagem *v.* (*also* **frammagem**) [mid-17C–mid-19C] (*UK Und.*) to choke, to strangle, to spoil; usu. as *frummagemed*, choked, strangled, spoiled.

frumper *n.* [late 18C–mid-19C] 'a sturdy blade' (Potter, *New Dict. Cant*, 1795).

fruppencies *n.* [Cockney pron. of SE *three-pences*] [1970s] the female breasts.

fry *n.* (*also* **napfry**, **skull fry**) [*FRY (ONE'S HAIR) under* FRY *v.*] **1** [1940s] (*US black*) the act of having one's hair straightened; thus the straightened hair. **2** [1990s+] (*US drugs*) crack cocaine.

IN COMPOUNDS

❑ **fry daddy** *n.* [DADDY *n.* (6)] [1980s+] (*US drugs*) crack cocaine and marijuana; a marijuana cigarette laced with crack cocaine. ❑ **fry sticks** *n.* [2000s] (*US drugs*) marijuana cigarettes either dipped in PCP or formaldehyde.

fry *v.* [fig. uses of SE] **1** [1910s+] (*US*) to punish or be punished. **2** [1920s+] (*US Und.*) to electrocute or be electrocuted in the electric chair. **3** [1960s+] (*US*) to ruin someone, or something, esp. to impair the mind. **4** [1960s+] (*US*) to infuriate. **5** [1970s+] to be electrocuted, to get an electric shock. **6** [1980s+] (*US drugs*) to experience the effects of taking LSD.

IN PHRASES

❑ **fry ass** *v.* [1960s] (*US*) to be executed in the electric chair. ❑ **fry one's brains** *v.* [1970s+] to indulge in an excess of drugs. ❑ **fry (one's hair)** *v.* [the treatment with Congolene, a liquid that burns the scalp, that is part of straightening black hair] [1930s+] (*US black*) to straighten the hair. ❑ **fry someone's ass** *v.* [1960s+] (*US*) to have completely at one's mercy; to punish comprehensively, to infuriate.

SE in slang uses

IN EXCLAMATIONS

❑ **go and fry your face!** (*also* **go and fry your boots!**) [late 19C+] a general excl. of dismissal or contempt.

fryer *n.* [FRY *v.* (2)] [1990s+] the electric chair.

fryers *n.* [SE *fryer*, a small chicken used for frying] [1940s+] (*US black/W.I.*) an insignificant person; a sidekick.

frying pan *n.*[1] [late 18C–early 19C] (*UK Und.*) counterfeit halfpennies.

frying pan *n.*[2] [resemblance] [mid-19C] (*UK Und.*) a large, silver pocket watch.

frying pan *n.*[3] [rhy. sl.] [20C+] **1** an old man. **2** a hand.

frying pan *n.*[4] [1930s] (*US prison*) the electric chair.

frying-pan *adj.* [shearer jargon *frying-pan brand*, a crude brand laid over the legitimate one by a cattle-thief; some rustlers literally used a red-hot frying pan] [mid-19C; 1960s] (*Aus. Und.*) small-time, petty.

f.s. *n.* [abbr. *f*ace *s*itter] [1960s+] a woman who likes to sit on a man's face while he performs cunnilingus.

f sharp *n.* [play on B FLAT *n.*] [mid-19C] a flea.

F-60 *n.* [the pharmaceutical identification stamped on the capsule] [1980s+] (*drugs*) a three-quarter grain capsule of Histadyl.

F-66 *n.* [the pharmaceutical identification stamped on the capsule] [1980s+] (*drugs*) a 1.5 grain capsule of Tuinal.

F. S. man *n.* [*f*ree by *s*ervitude] [late 19C] (*Aus.*) a convict who, after transportation, has worked long enough to gain their freedom.

f.t.b. *phr.* [abbr. *f*ull *t*o *b*ursting] [1910s] a phr. used to denote that one has had more than enough to eat.

f.t.d. *v. see FUCK THE DOG (AND SELL THE PUPS) under* DOG *n.*[2].

FTM *n.* [abbr. *f*emale *t*o *m*ale] [1990s+] (*US gay*) a female to male transsexual.

f.t.w.! *excl.* [abbr.] [1970s+] (*US, mainly bikers/campus*) fuck the world!

f.u.! *excl. see* FUCK YOU! *excl.*

fu *n.* [? Sp. *fumar*, to smoke] [1960s+] (*drugs*) marijuana.

fu *adj. see* FOU *adj.*[1].

f.u.b.a.r. *adj.* [abbr. *f*ucked *u*p *b*eyond *a*ll *r*ecognition] **1** [1940s+] (*orig. US milit.*) extremely unhappy. **2** [1940s+] (*orig. US milit.*) totally beyond repair and/or control. **3** [1970s+] (*US campus*) very unattractive. **4** [1990s+] (*also* **foob**) (*US campus*) very drunk; completely intoxicated by a given drug. **5** [1990s+] (*US*) exhausted. **6** [1990s+] (*US campus*) unfortunate, out of luck.

f.u.b.a.r. *v.* [F.U.B.A.R. *adj.* (2)] [1940s+] (*orig. US milit.*) to blunder, to make a mess, to make a mistake.

f.u.b.b. *phr.* [abbr. *f*ucked *u*p *b*eyond *b*elief] [1950s+] (*US, orig. milit.*) in a very parlous state, whether from physical injury, emotional instability, the effects of drink and/or drugs.

f.u.b.i.s. *phr.* [abbr.] [1940s+] *f*uck *y*ou *b*uddy, *I'm s*hipping out.

fuck *n.* [FUCK *v.* (1)] **1** in direct sexual uses. (**a**) [mid-17C+] an act of copulation. (**b**) [late 17C–early 18C; 1930s+] copulation. (**c**) [late 19C; 1970s+] semen. (**d**) [late 19C+] a person (usu. a woman but of both sexes since 1970s) considered purely as a sex object; thus a *good/bad fuck*, someone who is seen as a sexual adept or incompetent. (**e**) [1900s] the penile thrust. (**f**) [1980s] (*gay*) anal intercourse. **2** in fig. uses. (**a**) [20C+] anything at all, usu. in negative (i.e. nothing), usu. in phr. like GIVE A FUCK *v.*; NOT GIVE A FUCK *v.*; NOT WORTH A FUCK *phr.* (**b**) [1910s+] indicating quantity, usu.

excessive, e.g. AS FUCK below; TO FUCK below. (**c**) [1930s+] used with *as*, *like* or *than* in comparisons, e.g. *as big as fuck, hurts like fuck, bigger than fuck;* LIKE FUCK *adv.* (**d**) [1970s+] the essence, the spirit, 'the daylights', e.g. *kick the fuck out of.* (**e**) [1970s+] indicating difference or importance, usu. in negative, e.g. *that don't make a fuck.* (**f**) [1970s+] a general negation of the previous statement, usu. a v., e.g. *do I fuck, is it fuck.* (**g**) [1970s+] a turn of ill-fortune, a piece of bad luck, e.g. *I lost the gig, ain't that a fuck.* **3** constructed with *the*. (**a**) [1910s+] (*also* **fuck, in the fuck, in the eff**) var. on HELL, THE *phr.*, e.g. *why the fuck did you do that? who the fuck wants to know? the fuck I care.* (**b**) [1950s+] as infix, e.g. *shut the fuck up.* (**c**) *see* WHAT THE FUCK...? *phr.* **4** [1920s+] a person, esp. despicable and usu. with qualifying adj., e.g. *dumb fuck, useless fuck.*

DERIVATIVES

❑ **fuckfest** *n.* [-FEST *sfx*] [1970s] (*US*) an orgy. ❑ **fuckmobile** *n.* [-MOBILE *sfx*] [2000s] a car that improves one's attractiveness to the opposite sex. ❑ **fucko** *n.* [-O *sfx* (1)] (*orig. US*) **1** [1960s+] a general term of address, with no specific overtones whether positive or negative. **2** [2000s] an unpleasant person.

IN COMPOUNDS

❑ **fuck-all** *see* separate entries. ❑ **fuckbag** *n.* (*also* **fuckpot**) [-BAG *sfx*/-POT *sfx*] [1970s+] a general term of contempt for an unpleasant, disgusting person. ❑ **fuckball** *n.* [-BALL *sfx*] [1990s+] a general derog. term. ❑ **fuck-bar** *n.* [1970s] (*US gay*) a bar which provides a back room for sexual activity. ❑ **fuck book** *n.* [1940s+] pornography. ❑ **fuck boy** *n.* [1950s] **1** one who is victimized by their superiors or associates. **2** a passive male homosexual, a catamite. ❑ **fuckbrain** *n.* [1970s+] a fool, a simpleton; thus *fuckbrained*, stupid. ❑ **fuck buddy** *n.* [BUDDY *n.* (1)] [2000s] one with whom one has a sexual, but no deeper, relationship. ❑ **fuck-chops** *n.* [CHOPS *n.*[1] (1)] [1990s+] an imbecile, a stupid person. ❑ **fuckdog** *n.* [DOG *n.*[2] (3c)] [1970s+] a promiscuous woman; one who is eager for sex. ❑ **fuckdust** *n.* [2000s] a general term of abuse. ❑ **fuck-eye, the** *n.* [1980s+] (*US campus*) a flirtatious, sexually encouraging glance. ❑ **fuckface(d)** *see* separate entries. ❑ **fuck-film** *n.* [1970s+] a pornographic film. ❑ **fuck-flaps** *n.* [FLAP *n.*[1] (7)] [1990s+] the labia. ❑ **fuck flick** *n.* [SE *flick*] [1990s+] (*orig. US*) a pornographic film. ❑ **fuck handles** *n. see* LOVE HANDLES *under* LOVE *n.* ❑ **fuckhead(ed)** *see* separate entries. ❑ **fuckhole** *n.* [HOLE *n.*[1] (1b)] **1** [late 19C+] the vagina; the female genitals. **2** [1950s+] an unpleasant, disgusting place. **3** [1980s+] a contemptible, unpleasant person. ❑ **fuck-in** *n.* [on the pattern of SE *love-in*] [1960s–70s] (*orig. US, mainly hippie*) an orgy. ❑ **fuck job** *n.* [JOB *n.*[2] (2)/JOB *n.*[2] (4a)] **1** [1970s+] victimization, an act of victimization. **2** [2000s] (*US*) a term of abuse. ❑ **fuck-knuckle** *n.* [a mix of FUCKWIT below and KNUCKLEHEAD *n.*, the first of which implies plain stupidity, the second adds physical inadequacy] [1980s+] (*Aus./N.Z.*) a fool, an incompetent. ❑ **fuckload** *n.* [1960s+] a great many, a large amount. ❑ **fuck muscle** *n.* [1980s+] (*US gay*) the penis. ❑ **fucknob** *n.* [KNOB *n.* (1a)] [1990s+] a fool, an unpleasant person. ❑ **fuck-nut** *n.* (*also* **fucknuts**) [1980s+] (*UK juv.*) a general term of abuse. ❑ **fuck-nutty** *n.* [NUTTY *adj.*[2] (2)] [1940s] obsessed with thoughts of sex. ❑ **fuck one** *n.* [an emphatic/coarse var. on SE *day one*] [1970s] the very beginning. ❑ **fuck pad** *n.* (*also* **fuck nest**) [PAD *n.*[2] (2)] [1950s+] (*orig. US*) a room or apartment that a man keeps for seductions and sex; thus ext. to any place where a lot of sex happens, whether kept by a man or woman. ❑ **fuckpig** *n.* [1920s+] a general term of derision; the implication is of grubbiness, slovenliness. ❑ **fuck-plug** *n.* [1980s+] **1** a contraceptive diaphragm. **2** a general term of abuse. ❑ **fuckpole** *n.* [SE *pole*/POLE *n.* (1)] [1990s+] **1** the penis. **2** a general term of abuse. ❑ **fuckpot** *n. see* FUCKBAG above. ❑ **fuck-rubber** *n.* [RUBBER *n.*[2] (3)] [1980s] a contraceptive sheath. ❑ **fuck-sauce** *n.* [SE *sauce* but note SAUCE *n.*[1] (7)] [1990s+] semen. ❑ **fuck show** *n.* [1960s+] a live sex show. ❑ **fuck sock** *n.* [1990s+] a sock used as a repository for the ejaculation that climaxes masturbation. ❑ **fuckstick** *n.* [SE *stick*/STICK *n.* (1a)] [1950s+] **1** (*also* **fucking stick**) the penis. **2** a worthless, contemptible or despicable person; also as a term of address. ❑ **fuck-struck** *adj.* [1960s] obsessed with sex. ❑ **fuck truck** *n.* [1970s+] (*Aus.*) any vehicle, usu. a small van (poss. with a mattress in the back), in which a young man hopes to seduce women. ❑ **fuck udders** *n.* [1990s+] the female breasts. ❑ **fuckwad** *n.* [-WAD *sfx*] [1970s+] (*US*) a fool, a stupid or contemptible person; often in direct address. ❑ **fuckwit** *n.* [1980s+] **1** a fool; thus *fuckwitted* stupid. **2** a general term of derision, the implication is of stupidity.

IN PHRASES

❑ **as fuck** *adv.* [1970s+] a general intensifier, the coarse synon. for 'as anything'. ❑ **beat (the) fuck out of** *v.* [1970s+] to beat someone up severely. ❑ **dry fuck** *n. see* separate entry. ❑ **fuck knows** [1970s+] a general phr., underlining one's ignorance or disinterest. ❑ **fuck of a, a** [1920s+] (*orig. US*) **1** a large or notable amount of. **2** a general intensifier. ❑ **fucks to** [2000s] a dismissive phr.; synon. with TO HELL WITH...! *under* HELL *n.* ❑ **get the fuck** *v.* [1990s+] (*Aus.*) to be dismised from one's job. ❑ **get the fuck out** *v.* [1940s+] to leave, to go away; the use of fuck intensifies the urgency. ❑ **go like the hammers of fuck** *v. see* GO LIKE THE HAMMERS OF HELL *under* HELL *n.* ❑ **kick (the) fuck out of** *v.* [1970s+] to beat someone up severely. ❑ **on the fuck** [mid-19C] working as a prostitute. ❑ **scare the fuck out of** *v.* [1990s+] to terrify. ❑ **sure as fuck** *see under* SURE AS... *phr.* ❑ **talk fuck** *v.* **1** [late 19C] to talk about sex. **2** [1960s+] to murmur or shout obscenities during sexual intercourse for the gratification of one or both partners. ❑ **throw a fuck into** *v.* [1940s+] (*US*) to have sexual intercourse with; also homosexual use. ❑ **to fuck** *adv.* [1910s+] a general intensifier: utterly, completely. ❑ **what the blue fuck** *see* WHAT THE FUCK...? *phr.*

IN EXCLAMATIONS

❑ **get the fuck out!** [1950s+] **1** an intensified var. on *go away!* **2** an intensified var. on *get out of here!* and similar phr. of (joc.) disbelief. ❑ **get to fuck!** (*also* **get to Falkirk! get to fuck out of here/it!**) [note synon. Scot. *awa' tae fuck!*] [1920s+] a harsh demand to go away. ❑ **go to fuck!** [1990s+] an excl. of dismissal.

fuck *adj.* [FUCK *v.*] **1** [1940s+] (*orig. US*) describing something obscene or pornographic, e.g. *fuck movie.* **2** [1950s+] as an intensifier.

fuck *v.* [strictly, the ety. of *fuck* remains unknown, although the word has been linked to a supposed, if unsubstantiated, ME v. *fuken*. Neither Ger. *ficken*, nor the Fr. *foutre* (f. Lat. *fotuere*), both of which mean the same, can be linked semantically. *HDAS* notes MDu. *fokken*, to thrust, to copulate with; Norw. dial. *fukka*, to copulate, Swed. dial. *focka*, to strike, to push, to copulate + *fock*, the penis. Given the plethora of euphemisms equating intercourse or penetration with striking or hitting (BANG *v.*[1] (2a), SCREW *v.* (2a), POKE *v.* (1) etc), there may be some substance in Partridge's suggestion of a root in the Lat. *pugnare*, to fight or strike. Considered (with CUNT *n.* (1) and MOTHERFUCKER *n.*) as the ultimate in taboo terms, fuck is in fact SE, but has been listed as taboo, and thus as slang, since *c.*1690. The first print citation is dated 1508, in a line from the poetry of William Dunbar (?1456–?1513); the first dict. listing is in Florio's *Worlde of Wordes* (1598): '*Fottere*, to iape, to sard, to fucke, to swive, to occupy.' By the 18C, if printed at all, the form was usu. *f—k*. The term returned to literary use with James Joyce's much-banned *Ulysses* (1922) but remained taboo in the popular media and in 'polite' speech. This position has been eroded ever since, with the term and its compounds appearing today in films, books and on television, although the press, esp. the tabloids, pretend to a continuing squeamishness. 'Officially', for all that the realities of everyday speech (irrespective of class) disprove the theory, *fuck* remains an outlaw in conversation] **1** [16C+] to have sexual intercourse, usu. of a man, but increasingly of either sex; also of anal intercourse. **2** in fig./ext. uses. (**a**) [mid-19C+] to harm someone irreparably, to cheat, to victimize, to betray, to deceive. (**b**) [1920s+] to stop, to abandon or give up (on). (**c**) [1940s+] to trifle with, to 'mess around', to interfere. (**d**) [1960s+] to blunder, to make a mess (of), to ruin. (**e**) [1960s+] to kick, to stomp on. (**f**) [1970s+] to throw. (**g**) [1980s] to use or exploit for one's benefit. (**h**) [1980s+] to dismiss, to expel. **3** [1920s+] used as a synon. for TO HELL WITH...! *under* HELL *n.*

DERIVATIVES

❑ **fuckability** *n.* [1960s+] sex appeal. ❑ **fuckable** *adj.* **1** [late

19C+] sexually desirable. **2** [1970s+] (*US campus*) sexually available. ❑ **fuckaholic** *n.* [-AHOLIC *sfx*] [1980s+] one who is obsessed with having sexual relations. ❑ **fuck-a-rama** *n. see* separate entries. ❑ **fuckathon** *n.* [sfx *-athon* on model of SE *marathon*] [1960s+] (*orig. US*) a long sexual encounter or orgy. ❑ **fuckation** *n.* [mid–late 17C] sexual intercourse. ❑ **fuckish** *adj.* [late 19C+] sexually forward. ❑ **fucksome** *adj.* [SE sfx *-some*] [late 19C+] of a woman, sexually desirable. ❑ **fuckster** *n.* [-STER *sfx*, implying agency or 'doing'] [late 17C; late 19C] a promiscuous man; occas. woman. ❑ **fuckstress** *n.* [sfx *-stress*, a female agent or 'doer'] [19C+] **1** a prostitute. **2** a female sexual sophisticate. **3** a nymphomaniac.

(IN COMPOUNDS)

❑ **fuckarse** *see* separate entries. ❑ **fuck-beggar** *n.* [18C] 'An impotent or almost impotent man whom none but a beggar-woman will allow to "kiss" her' (Grose, 1785). ❑ **fuck-eyes** *adj. see* FUCK-ME EYES *under* FUCK-ME *adj.* ❑ **fuck-fist** *n.* (*also* **fuck-finger**) [late 19C–1900s] a male or female masturbator. ❑ **fuck-me** *adj. see* separate entry.

(IN PHRASES)

❑ **fuck-a-bush** *adj.* [lit. one who 'fucks in the bushes'] [1950s+] (*W.I., Jam.*) promiscuous. ❑ **fuck about** *see* separate entries. ❑ **fuck a duck** *v. see* separate entry. ❑ **fuck along** *v.* [1960s+] (*US black*) to walk. ❑ **fuck around** *v. see* separate entries. ❑ **fuck away** *v.* [1970s+] to waste, to squander. ❑ **fuck into a cocked hat** *v. see* KNOCK INTO A COCKED HAT *under* KNOCK INTO *v.* ❑ **fuck like a bunny (rabbit)** *v.* [20C+] to copulate enthusiastically. ❑ **fuck like a mink** *v.* [1910s+] (*Aus./US*) of a woman, to copulate enthusiastically. ❑ **fuck like a rattlesnake** *v.* (*also* **root like a rattlesnake, shag...**) [20C+] to copulate enthusiastically; often used of a woman who is presumed to be a sexual enthusiast, usu. in phr. *I bet she...* ❑ **fuck like a stoat** *v.* [late 19C+] to copulate enthusiastically. ❑ **fuck Mrs Palmer** *v.* [1990s+] to masturbate. ❑ **fuck off** *see* separate entries. ❑ **fuck one's ass off** *v.* (*also* **fuck one's head off**) [despite the presence of ASS *n.* (2), and the usu. male subjects of the phr., there is no implication of anal intercourse/homosexuality; the ref. is merely to the movement of the male buttocks and/or a general intensity] [1930s+] to copulate enthusiastically, usu. from the male point of view. ❑ **fuck one's fist** *v.* (*also* **fist-fuck**) [late 19C; 1960s+] to masturbate. ❑ **fuck out** *v.* **1** [1970s+] to break down; thus *fucked out*, usu. of a man, exhausted by an excess of intercourse [on pattern of SE *wear out*]. **2** [1980s] to be sexually unfaithful [to have sex 'out' of the house, 'out' of one's relationship]. **3** *see* FUCK OFF *v.* ❑ **fuck out of** *v.* **1** [mid-19C+] to cheat someone. **2** [2000s] (*Irish*) to eject, to throw out. ❑ **fuck over** *v. see* separate entries. ❑ **fuck someone's brains out** *v. see under* BRAIN *n.*[1]. ❑ **fuck someone's head** *v. see* FUCK (WITH) SOMEONE'S MIND *under* FUCK WITH *v.* ❑ **fuck the arse off someone** *v.* (*also* **fuck someone's arse/socks off, fuck the ass off, ride the arse off, shag...**) [RIDE *v.* (1a)/SHAG *v.*[1] (1) + ARSE *n.* (1)/ASS *n.* (2)] [1940s+] (*orig. US*) usu. of a man, to have energetic sexual intercourse, to make someone the object of one's enthusiastic or aggressive love-making; often in wishful phr. voiced by a man of a passing woman, *I could/I'd like to fuck the arse off that.* ❑ **fuck the crap out of someone** *v.* (*also* **fuck the shit out of someone, fuck the cum...**) [CRAP *n.*[1] (8)/SHIT *n.* (5)/CUM *n.* (1)] [1970s+] of a man, to have sexual intercourse; usu. very energetically and repeatedly. ❑ **fuck the dog (and sell the pups)** *v. see under* DOG *n.*[2]. ❑ **fuck the duck** *v.* (*also* **stroke the duck**) [1960s+] **1** to waste time; to relax. **2** to make a mistake. ❑ **fuck up** *see* separate entries. ❑ **fuck with** *v. see* separate entries. ❑ **fuck you** *see* separate entries. ❑ **fuck-your-buddy week** *n.* [BUDDY *n.* (1)] [1950s+] (*orig. US milit.*) a response to any moment or act of betrayal; usu. as *So it's fuck-your-buddy week then...* ❑ **I wouldn't fuck her with a borrowed prick** (*also* **I wouldn't fuck her with your prick**) [PRICK *n.* (1)] [20C+] a general term of masculine distaste, spoken on seeing what is considered an unattractive or unpleasant woman. ❑ **you can fuck me but you can't make me like the baby** [1980s+] (*Aus. prison*) a phr. meaning that a prisoner may endure his punishment but need not necessarily enjoy it.

(IN EXCLAMATIONS)

❑ **fuck a duck!** *see* separate entry. ❑ **fuck-a-rama!** *see* separate entry. ❑ **fuck around!** *see* separate entry. ❑ **fuck 'em all!** (*also* **fuck 'em!**) [the orig. words for the bowdlerized soldiers' song 'Bless 'Em All'] [1940s+] a general excl. of dismissal, bravado, 'to hell with them'. ❑ **fuck me!** *see* separate entry. ❑ **fuck my days!** (*also* **frig my days! fuck me days!**) [1970s–80s] (*UK black*) an excl. of surprise, annoyance etc. ❑ **fuck my luck!** [1990s+] I don't believe it! ❑ **fuck my old boots!** [1970s+] an excl. denoting one's astonishment; orig. milit. use, sometimes euph. as *seduce my ancient footwear!* ❑ **fuck that!** [20C+] a dismissive excl., often ext., e.g. *fuck that for a bowl of cherries! fuck that for a comic song! fuck that for a top hat!* and see below. ❑ **fuck that/this for a game of soldiers!** (*also* **bugger...! feck...! sod...! stick...! ...game of cowboys! ...game of darts!**) [1950s+] an excl. of derision, indicating that something is not working or that one is giving up. ❑ **fuck that/this for a lark!** (*also* **fuck this for a geg! fuck this lark! shag that for a lark!**) [1970s+] **1** an excl. of derision, indicating something is not working or that one is giving up. **2** don't expect me to get mixed up in that! that's a stupid idea! ❑ **fuck that/this for a laugh!** [1940s+] an excl. of derision, indicating something is not satisfactory or rejecting an idea that is unfeasible. ❑ **fuck that noise!** *see under* NOISE *n.*[1]. ❑ **fuck the begrudgers!** [1980s+] (*Irish*) a general excl. of defiance or scorn. ❑ **fuck them all but six/eight!** [1910s+] (*US, orig. milit.*) a general oath of annoyance and hostility; often ext. with *...and save them for pallbearers!* ❑ **fuck you!** *see* separate entry. ❑ **go fuck a duck!** (*also* **go fuck a dog! go fuck a fishnet! go kiss a duck!**) [1950s+] an excl. of dismissal, or disbelief. ❑ **go fuck your mother!** (*also* **go fuck your sister!**) [1930s+] an all-purpose dismissive excl., generally seen as a supremely offensive remark. ❑ **go fuck yourself!** (*also* **go and fuck yourself! go diddle yourself! go fiddle yourself! go flog yourself! go fug yourself! go jerk yourself! go shoot yourself!**) [1920s+] a general excl. of dismissal.

fuck! *excl.* **1** [1910s+] an excl. of anger, surprise, dismay, disbelief, resignation, esp. in combs. **2** [1970s+] a verbal punctuation, with no real meaning.

(IN EXCLAMATIONS)

❑ **do I fuck!** (*also* **will I fuck! will I shite!**) [1920s+] an excl. of absolute rebuttal, i.e. the hell I will! no I certainly won't/don't!; also used with 'you', 'we', etc. ❑ **fuckshit!** [1970s] (*US*) an excl. of rage. ❑ **fuck's sake!** *see* FOR FUCK'S SAKE! *excl.*

-fuck *sfx* [1960s+] (*orig. US*) a sfx implying the destruction of the appended n.; usu. of something subversive or something that overturns the familiar order of things, e.g. GENDER-FUCK *n.*, HEAD-FUCK *n.*, MINDFUCK *n.* (2).

fuck-about *n.* (*also* **fuck-around, fuckarow**) [FUCK ABOUT *v.*] [1960s+] (*US*) bad treatment, messing about, time-wasting; also of a person; thus *play fuckaround*, to treat someone badly or contemptuously.

fuck about *v.* (*also* **fuck around, fuck round**) [fig. use of FUCK *v.* (1) + SE *about/around*] **1** [1910s+] to mess about, to waste time, to fool around. **2** [1920s+] to annoy, to inconvenience, to waste someone's time. **3** [1960s+] to wander about aimlessly. **4** [1960s+] to have sex outside one's primary relationship. **5** [1970s+] to astonish.

fuck a duck *v.* [FUCK *v.* (1) + assonance] [1930s+] to live a sexually promiscuous life.

fuck a duck! *excl.* [cited occas. as rhy. sl., but only by redup., and not a genuine version] [1930s+] an excl. of surprise, disbelief, dismissal or rejection.

fuck all *n.* (*also* **fok-all, stuff-all**) **1** [1910s+] none, nothing, often extended to *SWEET FUCK ALL under* SWEET *adj.*[1]. **2** [2000s] a second-rate or worthless person.

fuck-all *adj.* [FUCK ALL *n.*] [1930s+] no, none, very little; as an intensifier.

(IN PHRASES)

❑ **fuck (all) else** *n.* [1950s+] absolutely nothing, e.g. *there's fuck else to do around here.*

fuck-all! *excl.* [1910s+] an ext. version of FUCK! *excl.*

fuck-a-rama *n.*[1] [FUCK *v.* (1) + -ORAMA *sfx*] [1960s+] (*orig. US*) a long sexual orgy.

fuck-a-rama *n.*[2] [FUCK-UP *n.* (1) + -ORAMA *sfx*] [1990s+] an absolute disaster, utter chaos.

fuck-a-rama! *excl.* [ext. of FUCK! *excl.*] [1990s+] an excl. of frustration, annoyance.

fuck around *v.*[1] [FUCK *v.* (1) + SE *around*] [1930s+] to have a promiscuous sex life.

fuck around *v.*[2] *see* FUCK ABOUT *v.*

fuck around! *excl.* [1990s+] (*US*) an excl. of mild annoyance.

fuckarow *n. see* FUCK-ABOUT *n.*

fuckarse *n.* (*also* **fuckass**) [FUCK *v.* (1) + ARSE *n.* (1)] [1960s+] a general term of contempt.

fuckarse *v.* (*also* **fuckass**) [FUCKARSE *n.*] [2000s] to play the fool, to act stupidly.

fucked *adj.*[1] [fig. uses of FUCK *v.* (1)] **1** [1920s+] of people, exhausted, unhappy, wretched. **2** [1920s+] cheated, tricked, defeated, deceived. **3** [1940s+] of things, broken, out of order, ruined, spoilt. **4** [1950s+] in serious trouble. **5** [1960s+] intoxicated by a drug or drink. **6** [1960s+] lacking in good sense, crazy. **7** [1960s+] very bad, offensive, rotten, unfair. **8** [1970s+] psychologically maladjusted. **9** [1980s+] bothered, usu. in negative, e.g. *I'm not fucked, you have it.*

IN COMPOUNDS

❑ **fucked duck** *n.* [1930s–60s] (*US*) one who is about to die or doomed to die.

IN PHRASES

❑ **fucked by the fickle finger of fate** [1940s+] (*orig. US*) a phr. describing a victim of adverse circumstances, bad luck. ❑ **fucked off** *adj.* [1940s+] annoyed, furious. ❑ **fucked out** *adj.* **1** [mid-19C+] exhausted by an excess of sex. **2** [1940s+] (*orig. US*) exhausted. ❑ **fucked over** *adj.* [1970s+] **1** suffering (not always painfully) from the use of drugs or alcohol to excess. **2** unpleasant, rotten, sick, dazed. ❑ **fucked to a fair-thee-well** [1980s+] (*US*) ruined beyond repair. ❑ **fucked up** *adj. see* separate entry. ❑ **fucked with no Vaseline** [the use of Vaseline to facilitate sexual (usu. anal) intercourse] [1990s+] suffering extreme physical or emotional pain. ❑ **get fucked** *v. see* separate entries.

IN EXCLAMATIONS

❑ **I'll be fucked!** (*also* **I'll be frigged!**) [1950s+] a general excl. of surprise, frustration, anger etc.

fucked *adj.*[2] (*also* **fugged**) [1940s+] used as an intensified version of damned; often as *fucked if…*

fucked up *adj.* [fig. use of FUCK *v.* + SE *up*] **1** [1930s+] of objects, intentions or plans, broken, wrecked, ruined. **2** [1940s+] (*also* **f'd up**) of people, distressed, unhappy, mentally unstable. **3** [1940s+] (*also* **fuck-up**) suffering (not always painfully) from the use of drugs or alcohol to excess; completely intoxicated. **4** [1940s+] (*orig. US milit.*) of people, badly hurt, wounded or killed. **5** [1940s+] worthless, contemptible, miserable. **6** [1940s+] an intensified var. on DAMNED *adj.* **7** [1950s] (*US*) confused, in a muddle. **8** [1960s+] (*also* **fuck-up**) of places, unpleasant. **9** [1970s] in trouble. **10** [1970s+] unappealling, unpleasant. **11** [1980s+] exhausted, worn out. **12** [1990s+] weird, strange, unusual.

fuckee *n.* [FUCK *v.*] **1** [late 19C] the 'passive' or recipient person during copulation. **2** [1970s] one who is treated badly; one who suffers harm or punishment.

fuckee-fuckee/-suckee *n. see* FUCKY-FUCKY *n.*

fucker *n.* (*also* **fugger**) [FUCK *v.* (1)] **1** [late 16C+] one who has sexual intercourse. **2** [19C] a pimp. **3** [early 19C; 1920s+] (*also* **facker, fecker, fugger, fugher**) a general term of abuse, e.g. *You stupid fucker!* **4** [1910s] (*Aus.*) an English private soldier [either tongue-in-cheek or the result of deliberate misinformation]. **5** [1920s–40s] a vagina. **6** [1920s+] (*also* **fugger, fugher**) a man, a fellow, with no particular abuse intended and even some degree of affection. **7** [1940s+] (*also* **fecker, fogger, fugger, fugher**) an unspecified object, irrespective of its qualities; an animal. **8** [1940s+] a difficult or irritating thing or task. **9** [1960s+] an extreme example, whether positive or negative. **10** [1970s+] one who harms others.

fuckermother *n.* [2000s] var. on MOTHERFUCKER *n.* (1).

Fuckerware party *n.* [a play on a *Tupperware* party] [1980s+] (*US*) a party organized for the sale of erotic toys and clothing.

fuckery *n.*[1] [FUCK *v.* (1) + sfx *-ery*; 'a place where an indicated article or service may be purchased or procured' (*OED*)] [19C] a brothel.

fuckery *n.*[2] [FUCK UP *v.* (1)] **1** [1970s+] unfairness, ill treatment; treachery. **2** [1970s+] (*UK black*) (*also* **fuckry**) nonsense. **3** [2000s] the personification of senses 1 + 2 above, i.e. a stupid mean person.

fuckery *adj.* [FUCKERY *n.*[2]] [1970s+] (*W.I., Rasta*) **1** wrong, unfair. **2** stupid, nonsensical.

fuckface *n.* [FUCK *n.* (1) + SE *face*] [1960s+] (*orig. US*) a fool, an idiot, a generally contemptible person.

fuckfaced *adj.* [1940s+] **1** having an ugly, miserable face. **2** drunk. **3** bleary-eyed, half-awake.

fuck-fuck *n. see* FUCKY-FUCKY *n.*

fuckhead *n.* [FUCK *n.* (1) + -HEAD *sfx* (1)] [1960s+] a fool, a complete idiot; the use of fuck merely intensifies the disdain by its own taboo status; esp. as a term of address.

fuckheaded *adj.* (*also* **fuckhead**) [FUCKHEAD *n.*] [1970s+] stupid, moronic, incompetent, contemptible.

fucking *n.* [FUCK *v.* (1)] **1** [mid-16C+] the act of copulation. **2** [mid-19C+] (*also* **fuggin**) harsh and/or unfair treatment.

IN COMPOUNDS

❑ **fucking stick** *n. see* FUCKSTICK *under* FUCK *n.*

IN PHRASES

❑ **fucking is a town in China** *see* INNOCENT *adj.*

fucking *adj.* (*also* **facking, facquing, farking, focking, fucken, funking**) **1** [mid-19C+] a general intensifier, e.g. *fucking idiot.* **2** [mid-19C+] pertaining to sexual intercourse. **3** [20C+] implying a variety of negatives, e.g. vile, despicable, unpleasant, corrupt, dirty. **4** [1910s+] as infix *-fucking-* e.g. ABSOFUCKINGLUTELY *adv.*; FANFUCKINGTASTIC *adj.*; GUARANFUCKINGTEE *v.*

IN PHRASES

❑ **double-fucking** *adj.* [note one-time use in 1910s, used by Robert Graves in *Goodbye to All That* (1929) in recounting a soldier's comments during WW1] [1910s; 1990s+] an intensified form of FUCKING *adj.* (1). ❑ **fucking-A** *see* separate entries.

IN EXCLAMATIONS

❑ **fucking Ada!** (*also* **bloody Ada!**) [the *Ada* is either a nonsense word or a euph. for the stronger alternative *fucking arseholes!*; as with *fucking hell!*, the *fu* may be deliberately abandoned; thus *'kin' Ada!* etc] [20C+] a general excl. ❑ **fucking Nora!** (*also* **bleeding Nora! bloody Nora!**) [var. on prev.] [1990s+] an excl. used to denote astonishment, dismay, acceptance, praise, recognition.

fucking *adv.* **1** [mid-19C+] a general intensifier, totally, completely, e.g. *fucking stupid.* **2** [1970s+] used, usu. in the negative, to imply definitely (not), certainly (not), e.g. *fucking thanks.*

IN PHRASES

❑ **fucking well** *adv.* (*also* **shagging well**) [1910s+] generally used for emphasis, absolutely, very well, very much, extremely.

fucking A *n.* [1960s] (*orig. US*) very little, as good as nothing, e.g. *I don't know fucking-A about it.*

fucking-A *adj.* (*also* **fuggin ay**) [FUCKING *adv.* (1) + A-OK *adj.*] **1** [1940s+] excellent, superb, best. **2** [1950s+] goddamned, damned. **3** [1950s+] right, correct.

fucking-A *adv.* (*also* **bricking-A, mucking-aye**) [1950s+] completely, totally, absolutely, very well, very much, extremely; e.g. *You're fucking-A right…* or *fucking-A well.*

fucking A! *excl.* (*also* **frigging A!**) **1** [1950s+] (*also* **fucking-aye!**) an excl. generally used for emphasis, absolutely! definitely! **2** [1970s+] an excl. used to denote astonishment, dismay, acceptance, praise, recognition.

fucking hell! *excl.* (*also* **funking hell! shagging hell!**) [FUCKING *adj.* (1)] [1910s+] an excl. of surprise, annoyance, wonder etc.

fuckingly *adv.* [FUCKING *adj.* (1)] [1920s+] extremely, very much, damned.

fuck it! *excl.* (*also* **fuck it all!**) [1920s+] a general dismissive excl.

fuck-it-all *adj.* (*also* **fuck-it**) [FUCK IT! *excl.*] [1940s+] laissez-faire, nonchalant, carefree.

fuck-me *adj.* (*also* **do-it-to-me**) [1980s+] outrageous, esp. when extremely sexy.

IN COMPOUNDS

❑ **fuck-me boots** *n.* (*also* **FM boots, fuck-me booties**) [1980s+] (*US*) sexually alluring footwear, usu. as worn by a woman, and thus featuring high heels. ❑ **fuck-me eyes** *n.* (*also* **fuck eyes**) [1980s+] (*US*) flirtatious, sexually encouraging stares or glances. ❑ **fuck-me shoes** *n.* (*also* **follow-me-home-and-fuck-me shoes, fuck-me pumps, fuck-me's, hump-me pumps**) [allegedly first worn, at least for mass delectation, by film star Joan Crawford (1906–77)] [1970s+] ankle-strapped, wedge-heeled shoes.

fuck me! *excl.* [1910s+] **1** an excl. of surprise, astonishment, resignation; often in combs., e.g. *fuck me rigid! fuck me insensible! fuck me dead!* **2** (*US campus*) an excl. of annoyance, of contempt; shut up! go away! you make me sick!

IN EXCLAMATIONS

❑ **fuck me backwards!** [1940s+] a general excl. ❑ **fuck me dead!** [1970s+] (*N.Z.*) used in a variety of exuberant excls. ❑ **fuck me gently!** [1910s+] a general excl. of surprise, alarm etc. ❑ **fuck me gently with a chainsaw!** [1980s+] a general expression of surprise or annoyance. ❑ **fuck me hard!** (*also* **fuck me harder!**) [1980s+] (*US*) an expression used in response to an unwanted and undesirable action done to the speaker. ❑ **fuck me ragged!** [1980s] a general excl. ❑ **fuck me sideways!** [1940s+] a general excl.

fuck-off *n.* [FUCK OFF *v.*] **1** [1940s+] (*also* **fug-off**) a lazy or inefficient person, who prefers to *fuck off* rather than work. **2** [1980s+] a gesture of contempt. **3** [1980s+] a statement of prohibition. **4** [1980s+] an irritating or frustrating situation.

fuck-off *adj.* [FUCK OFF *v.*] **1** [1950s+] arrogant, ostentatious. **2** [1960s+] lazy, idle. **3** [1990s+] annoying. **4** [1990s+] large, showy.

fuck off *v.* (*also* **fack off, fuck out**) **1** [1910s+] to leave, to go away. **2** [1940s+] (*orig. US*) (*also* **f.o.**) to waste time, to idle, to avoid one's duties; thus *fucking off*, wasting time, acting lazily. **3** [1940s+] a synon. for GO TO HELL! *under* HELL *n.* **4** [1960s+] (*US black*) to waste, to squander. **5** [1960s+] to disregard, to brush aside, to put off. **6** [1970s] to miss out on something through one's own or another's ineptitude. **7** [1980s] to expel, to reject. **8** [1990s+] to stop. **9** [2000s] to annoy.

IN COMPOUNDS

❑ **fuck-off money** *n.* [2000s] a sum of money or an income large enough to give one the power of freedom from everyday constraints, i.e. one could tell one's employer to *fuck off*.

fuck off! *excl.* **1** [1930s+] in aggressive use, 'go away!'; often compounded to *fuck off out of it!* **2** [1980s+] in joc. use, 'don't be silly!'

fuck over *v.* [1960s+] **1** of people, to harm, to beat up, to hurt emotionally, to act cruelly, to interfere, to mess around with. **2** of ideas or objects, to adulterate.

fuckstrated *adj.* [FUCK *n.* (1) + SE *frustrated*] [1980s+] (*US campus*) sexually frustrated.

fuck-up *n.* [FUCK UP *v.*] (*orig. US*) **1** [1930s+] an error, a mistake, bungling, incompetence. **2** [1940s+] a bungler, an incompetent, a hopeless failure. **3** [1990s+] (*US*) a negative attitude.

fuck-up *adj.* (*also* **fucky**) [FUCK-UP *n.* (2)] **1** [1950s+] (*orig. US*) incompetent, inadequate. **2** *see* FUCKED UP *adj.* (3).

fuck up *v.* [ext. use of FUCK *v.* (2)] **1** [1910s+] to ruin, to destroy; to make a mess of; thus *fucker-up*, that which ruins or destroys. **2** [1940s+] to confuse, to confound. **3** [1950s+] to blunder, to make a mistake. **4** [1960s+] (*US black*) to fool around. **5** [1960s] (*US black*) to waste. **6** [1960s+] (*orig. US black*) to hurt, to injure. **7** [1960s+] to cause problems for someone. **8** [1960s+] (*orig. milit.*) to kill, to thwart. **9** [1970s+] to make drunk or drugged. **10** [1990s+] to infect with a venereal disease. **11** [1990s+] to go wrong, to malfunction, to break down.

IN PHRASES

❑ **fuck up someone's pussy** *v. see under* PUSSY *n.*

fuck up! *excl.* [1980s+] (*Irish*) shut up! stop it!

fuck with *v.* [lit. and fig. uses of FUCK *v.* (1)] **1** [1940s+] to mess about with, to become involved with. **2** [1940s+] to interfere, often by physical or mental intimidation. **3** [1960s+] to copulate with (a partner is usu. cited). **4** [1960s+] (*US black*) to impress, to overwhelm, to manipulate. **5** [1960s+] to play around with. **6** [1980s] to associate with.

IN PHRASES

❑ **fuck with someone's head** *v.* [1970s+] to disturb and harm someone emotionally. ❑ **fuck (with) someone's mind** *v.* (*also* **fuck someone's head**) [1960s+] to intimidate, astonish or confuse another or oneself.

fucky *adj.* [FUCK *v.* (1) + sfx *-y*] **1** [20C+] nubile, ostensibly sexually enthusiastic; usu. of a woman. **2** *see* FUCK-UP *adj.*

fucky-fucky *n.* (*also* **fuckee-fuckee, fuckee-suckee, fuck-fuck, fucky-sucky**) [FUCK *v.* (1) + redup.] [20C+] sexual intercourse; esp. as used in Asia, often by prostitutes.

fuck-you *n.* [FUCK YOU! *excl.*] [1970s] (*US*) a statement of dismissal or contempt; general aggressiveness.

fuck-you *adj.* [FUCK YOU! *excl.*] **1** [1930s+] dismissive, contemptuous. **2** [1980s+] hostile, aggressive; also as an infix.

fuck you! *excl.* (*also* **f.u.! fuck yourself!**) [1930s+] a general excl. of dismissal, contempt, I don't believe you! go to hell! nonsense! don't make me laugh!

IN COMPOUNDS

❑ **fuck-you money** *n.* [1950s+] a store of money that gives one the power of freedom from everyday constraints; i.e. one can say to one's employer *fuck you!*

IN EXCLAMATIONS

❑ **fuck you, Charley!** [1930s+] a general excl. of dismissal; often reversed as *Chuck you, Farley!*, but fooling no one. ❑ **fuck you, Jack, I'm all right!** [orig. naut. catchphrase, denoting utter selfishness and disinterest in the plight of anyone else; general milit. use by WW1 and thence to civilians; the best known use is bowdlerized in the film title *I'm Alright, Jack* (1959), which burlesqued bloody-minded industrial relations] [late 19C+] a general dismissive excl., don't bother me! I don't care!

fud *n.* [dial. *fud*, a rabbit's tail] [late 18C–19C] the pubic hair.

fuddle *n.* [FUDDLE *v.*] [late 17C–1940s] **1** drink, alcohol; thus *on the fuddle*, on a drunken spree. **2** intoxication, an intoxicated or generally muddled state; thus *fuddle-headed*, generally confused.

fuddle *v.* [ety. unknown; *OED* suggests poss. links to Du. *vod*, soft, slack, loose, or Ger. dial. *fuddeln*, to swindle] **1** [mid-17C–1910s] to become drunk, to make oneself drunk; thus *fuddling school*, an ale house. **2** [18C–mid-19C] to render drunk.

fuddlecap *n.* [FUDDLE *n.* (1)] [mid-17C–mid-19C] a drunkard; thus *fuddle-caps' hall*, a tavern.

fuddled *adj.* (*also* **fuddle-headed, fuddling**) [FUDDLE *v.* (1)] [17C+] drunk.

fuddy-duddy *n.* (*also* **fuddy, fuddy-dud**) [? Cumberland dial. *duddy fuddiel*, a ragged fellow] [20C+] a fussy, pernickety, narrow-minded person, often with the assumption of their being old.

fuddy-duddy *adj.* [FUDDY-DUDDY *n.*] [20C+] fussy, pernickety, narrow-minded.

fudge *n.* [SE *fudge*, a sweetmeat] **1** [1960s+] (*US*) excrement, usu. in association with homosexual practices. **2** [1990s+] (*US black*) a dark-skinned black person.

IN COMPOUNDS

❑ **fudge baby** *n.* [1990s+] a piece of excrement. ❑ **fudge-nudger** *n.* [1990s+] a derog. term for a male homosexual, a sodomite. ❑ **fudge-packer** *n.* (*also* **packer**) [1980s+] (*US*) a derog. term for a homosexual man; thus n., *fudge-packing*. ▫ **fudgepot** *n.* [1990s+] (*US gay*) the anus. ▫ **fudge tunnel** *n.* [1990s+] the anus.

IN PHRASES

▫ **drop fudge** *v.* [1990s+] to defecate. ▫ **pack fudge** *v.* [1970s+] to perform anal intercourse. ▫ **park one's fudge** *v.* [1990s+] to defecate. ▫ **stir fudge** *v.* [1970s+] to perform anal intercourse.

fudge *v.* [FUDGE *n.* (1)] [1980s+] (*US*) to foul with excrement.

fudgsicle *n.* [proprietary name of the *Fudgsicle* ice-cream-bar, although the bar is, in fact, all-chocolate; the usual image in such terms, e.g. APPLE *n.*[1] (1), OREO (COOKIE) *n.*, is of something that, while coloured outside, is white within] [1940s–60s] (*US*) a black person who is criticized by other blacks for behaving in a 'white' manner.

fuel *n.* [1980s+] **1** (*drugs*) marijuana mixed with insecticides. **2** (*drugs*) phencyclidine. **3** (*US campus/Aus. prison*) food or drink.

fuete *n.* [Cuban Sp. *fuete*, a whip] [1980s+] (*drugs*) a hypodermic needle.

fug *n.*[1] [FUG *v.*] [1940s+] a euph. for FUCK *n.* in all senses.

fug *n.*[2] [SE *fug*, a dense, smoky atmosphere] [2000s] (*US prison*) a cigarette.

fug *v.* (*also* **fog, fugg**) [coined by Norman Mailer (b.1923) as an all-purpose replacement for the taboo word in his book *The Naked and The Dead* (1948)] [1940s+] a euph. for FUCK *v.* (1) in a variety of senses (cf. FUGH *v.*).

IN PHRASES

▫ **fug the dog** *v. see* FUCK THE DOG (AND SELL THE PUPS) *under* DOG *n.*[2].

IN EXCLAMATIONS

▫ **go fug yourself!** *see* GO FUCK YOURSELF! *under* FUCK *v.*

fugazi *adj.* [acronym *F*ucked *U*p, *G*ot *A*mbushed, *Z*ipped *I*n] (*US*) **1** [1980s+] a euph. for FUCKED UP *adj.* **2** [1990s+] fake, artificial, false; also as n.

fugel *v.* (*also* **fugle**) [? Yorks. dial. to trick, to deceive] [early 18C–19C] to seduce; to have sexual intercourse.

fugg *v. see* FUG *v.*

fugged *adj. see* FUCKED *adj.*[2].

fugger *n. see* FUCKER *n.*

fuggin *n. see* FUCKING *n.* (2).

fuggin ay *adj. see* FUCKING-A *adj.*

fugging *adj.* (*also* **fuggen, fuggin, fughing**) [FUG *v.*] [1940s+] a euph. for FUCKING *adj.*

fugh *n.* [FUGH *v.*] [1950s+] a euph. for FUCK *n.* in a variety of senses.

fugh *v.* [used mainly by its popularizer Brendan Behan (1923–64) in his autobiographies *Borstal Boy* (1958) and *Confessions of an Irish Rebel* (1965)] [1940s+] a euph. for FUCK *v.* (1) in a variety of senses.

fugh! *excl. see* FAUGH! *excl.*

fugher *n. see* FUCKER *n.*

fughing *adj. see* FUGGING *adj.*

fugle *v. see* FUGEL *v.*

fugly *n.* [FUGLY *adj.*] [2000s] a very unattractive woman.

fugly *adj.* [elision of FUCKING *adj.* (1) + *ugly*] [1980s+] (*orig. US black*) very unattractive.

fugo *n.* [Cornish dial. *fogo/fougo*, a cave or underground storage chamber] [17C–18C] the rectum or anus.

fug-off *n. see* FUCK-OFF *n.* (1).

f.u.j.i.a.m.a. *phr.* [abbr.; note US milit. *f.u.j.i.g.m.o.*, *f*uck you *J*ack, *I* *g*ot *m*y *o*rders] [1930s] written across an envelope back, *f*uck *y*ou *J*ack, *I* *a*m all right.

fulhams *n.* (*also* **fullams, fullums**) [*Fulham*, southwest London, presumably a centre of their manufacture, although Walker, *A Manifest Detection of Dice-play* (1552), recommends the King's Bench, the Marshalsea and, above all, 'Bird, in Holborn, is the finest workman.'; Nares dismisses such criminality in 'so quiet a village', and suggests that the dice were 'full, or loaded, with some heavy metal on one side, so as to produce a bias', i.e. SE *full*] **1** [mid-16C–mid-19C] (*UK Und.*) crooked dice that appear to be perfectly honest but have in fact been weighted with lead to ensure that they roll as the user wishes. **2** [mid-17C] in ext. use, a trick.

Fulham tractor *n.* [the popularity of SUVs among the rich inhabitants of Fulham, London SW10] [2000s] a sports utility vehicle.

Fulham virgin *n.* [? the louche reputation of the Cremorne Gardens, in neighbouring Chelsea] [19C] a prostitute.

fulke *v.* [coined by Lord Byron in *Don Juan* (1819–24)] [early 19C] to have sexual intercourse.

fulker *n.* [Ger. *fucker, fugger*, a usurer, a great merchant] [mid–late 16C] a pawnbroker or moneylender.

full *adj.* **1** [mid-19C+] (*later use mainly Aus.*) (*also* **full of it**) drunk. **2** [1960s+] absolute, complete, total. **3** [1980s] drugged. **4** [1990s+] good, amazing.

IN PHRASES

▫ **full as...** *see* separate entry. ▫ **full to the bow-tie** *adj.* [1950s] very drunk, or having drunk a large quantity. ▫ **full to the bung** *adj.* (*also* **full to the brim**) [mid–late 19C] very drunk. ▫ **full to the gills** *adj.* [GILLS *n.* (1)] [1910s+] (*orig. US*) very drunk. ▫ **full to the knocker** *adj. see under* KNOCKER *n.*[1].

SE in slang uses

DERIVATIVES

▫ **fullness** *adv.* (*also* **to the fullness**) [1950s+] (*W.I., Rasta*) completely, absolutely, totally.

IN COMPOUNDS

▫ **full bottom** *n.* [his 'full-bottomed' wig] [mid-19C] (*UK Und.*) a judge. ▫ **full bucket, the** *n.* [1990s+] (*Aus.*) a knowledgeable person. ▫ **full buf** *adv.* [BUF *adj.*] [1980s] (*US teen*) dressed up in one's finery, 'dressed to kill'. ▫ **full enchilada** *n. see* WHOLE ENCHILADA *under* WHOLE... *n.* ▫ **full French** *n. see* FRENCH *n.* (4). ▫ **full hand** *n. see* separate entry. ▫ **full house** *n.* [theatrical use] **1** [mid-19C+] a very busy time. **2** *see* FULL HAND *n.* (3). ▫ **full jerry** *see* separate entries. ▫ **full monty** *n. see* MONTY *n.* ▫ **full moon** *n. see under* MOON *n.* ▫ **fullmouth** *adj.* [image of 'talking with one's mouth full'] [20C+] (*W.I.*) bad-mannered, unrestrained. ▫ **full quid, the** *n.* (*also* **full deener, ...pound**) [QUID *n.* (3)/SE *pound*; lit. the 'whole pound'] [1940s+] (*Aus./N.Z.*) sensible, intelligent, aware, trustworthy, 'all there'; esp. in negative phr. *not (quite) the full quid* etc, not very intelligent, slightly eccentric, odd. ▫ **full stop** *n.* [mid-19C] in boxing, a hard blow. ▫ **full team** *n. see* WHOLE TEAM (AND THE DOG UNDER THE WAGON) *under* TEAM *n.*

IN PHRASES

▫ **at full belt** *adv. see under* BELT *v.* ▫ **at full scream** *adv. see under* SCREAM *n.* ▫ **full about** *see* FULL OF *adj.* ▫ **full of...** *see* separate entries. ▫ **full on** *see* separate entries. ▫ **full suit of mourning** *n. see under* MOURNING *n.* ▫ **full two bob** [lit. worth the two shillings that is charged] [1960s+] (*Aus.*) worthwhile, as good as advertised. ▫ **full up** *adj. see* separate entries.

full! *excl.* [1990s+] an affirmative excl.

fullams *n. see* FULHAMS *n.*

full as... *adj.* [16C+] used in various phrs. to mean very drunk.

IN PHRASES

▫ **...a boiled owl** *see* DRUNK AS A BOILED OWL *adj.* ▫ **...a boot** [1940s+] ▫ **...a bull** (*also* **...a bull's bum**) [1940s+] (*Aus./N.Z.*) ▫ **...a goat** [late 19C+] ▫ **...a goose** (*also* **...a goog (egg)**) [1920s+] ▫ **...a lord** [1900s] ▫ **...an egg** [early 18C+] ▫ **...a pommie complaint box** [1960s+] ▫ **...a state school** (*also* **...a Catholic school**) [1960s+] ▫ **...a tick** [19C+] ▫ **...a tun** [early 16C–mid-17C] ▫ **...the family po** [i.e. the family chamber*pot*] [1940s+]

full-blown stallone *n.* [rhy. sl. = BONE *n.*[1] (2c); ult. US film star Sylvester *Stallone* (b.1946), known for his macho 'hard' roles] [1990s+] an erection.

fuller's *n.* [the *Fuller Bros.*, contemporary impresarios and owners of many theatres and cinemas + ? SE *earthy*] [1910s+] (*N.Z.*) New Zealand.

fuller's earth *n.* [SE *Fuller's earth*, 'a hydrous silicate of alumina, used in cleansing cloth' (*OED*); thus gin is a scourer and 'cleaner out'] [early–mid-19C] gin.

full hand *n.* [1940s+] (*Aus.*) **1** the equivalent of the US/UK 'full house' (one pair plus three of a kind) in poker. **2** a life sentence. **3** (*also* **full house**) a simultaneous dose of both syphilis and gonorrhoea. **4** an infestation of both head lice and body lice. **5** (*US milit.*) a combination of any varieties of disease.

IN PHRASES

❑ **play a full hand** *v. see under* PLAY *V.*

fullie *n.* (*also* **fully**) [SE *fully automatic*] [1990s+] (*US gang*) an automatic weapon, e.g. an Uzi, Glock or Tech Nine, as used in gang wars.

fullied *adj.* [FULLY *v.*] [mid-19C–1930s] committed for trial.

fullies *n. see* FOLLIES *n.*

full jerry *n.* [FULL JERRY *adj.*] [20C+] (*Aus./N.Z.*) the whole truth, all the information, 'the facts'.

full jerry *adj.* [SE *full* + JERRY *adj.* (1)] [late 19C+] knowledgeable, informed.

full of *adj.* (*also* **full about**) [mid-19C–1910s] (*Aus.*) thoroughly displeased by, 'fed up with'.

full of... *phr.*

SE in slang uses

IN PHRASES

❑ **full of beans** *see under* BEANS *n.*[3]. ❑ **full of crap** (*also* **full of bean soup, full of feces, full of prunes**) [1930s+] (*orig. US*) contemptible, stupid, nonsensical. ❑ **full of glue** *see under* GLUE *n.* ❑ **full of hop** *see under* HOP *n.*[3]. ❑ **full of it** **1** [late 19C] pregnant. **2** [1940s+] of a person, lying, spinning a line, telling tales [euph. for FULL OF SHIT *phr.*]. **3** *see* FULL *adj.* (1). ❑ **full of oats** *see FULL OF BEANS under* BEANS *n.*[3]. ❑ **full of puha** [Maori *puha, puwha*, a (prickly) sowthistle] [2000s] (*N.Z.*) talking nonsense.

full of shit *phr.* (*also* **full of doo doo, ...sand, ...shite, ... shitshat, ...stuff**) [SHIT *n.* (1a)] [1930s+] **1** of a person, lying, spinning a line, telling untrue tales of an experience. **2** unpleasant, distasteful.

full on *adj.* **1** [1970s+] (*US*) intense, strong. **2** [1980s+] (*US*) total, absolute, complete, utter.

full on *adv.* [FULL ON *adj.*] [1980s+] (*Aus.*) completely, wholeheartedly.

fullums *n. see* FULHAMS *n.*

full up *adj.*[1] [var. on FED UP *adj.*] [late 19C+] (*Aus.*) disgusted with, surfeited with.

full up *adj.*[2] [20C+] (*W.I.*) of an unmarried woman, pregnant.

fully *n. see* FULLIE *n.*

fully *v.* [phr. *the prisoner was fully committed for trial*, commonly found in penny-a-line journalism] [mid-19C–1930s] to commit for trial; thus *fulley*, a trial.

fumble *v.* [joc. uses of SE] **1** [16C+] to indulge in sexual foreplay; the inference is usu. of feebleness, as exhibited by an ageing lecher. **2** [mid-17C–19C] to be impotent.

fumbler *n.* [FUMBLE *V.* (1)] **1** [late 17C–18C] an impotent man, esp. a husband; thus *fumbling*, adj., impotent. **2** [early 18C] a young lecher.

IN COMPOUNDS

❑ **fumbler's hall** *n.* **1** [late 17C–early 18C] the vagina. **2** [mid-17C–early 18C] a metaphorical place where impotent men might be confined as punishment for their failings.

fumigate (one's brains) *v.* (*also* **fume**) [late 19C–1960s] (*US campus*) to smoke.

fummy-nobbed *adj.* [mid-19C] (*UK Und.*) soft-headed, eccentric.

f.u.m.t.u. *phr.* [abbr.] [20C+] fucked up more than usual.

fun *n.*[1] [SE *fundament*] [late 17C–early 19C] the buttocks, the backside.

fun *n.*[2] [late 17C–19C] a cheat, a trick.

fun *n.*[3] *see* FOON *n.*

fun *v.* [FUN *n.*[2]] [late 17C–19C; 1960s+] to cheat, to deceive; thus phr. *put the fun upon*, to trick, to cheat.

fun and frolics *n.* (*also* **flowers and frolics**) [rhy. sl. = BALLOCKS *n.* (2)] [1940s+] the testicles.

funbags *n.* (*also* **funsacks**) [SE *fun* + BAGS *n.*[1] (1)] [1960s+] the female breasts, esp. when large.

funch *n.* [FUCK *V.* (1) + SE *lunch*; the trad. genteel term is euph. MATINÉE *n.*] [1970s+] sexual liaisons at lunchtime.

funds *n.* [late 19C+] (*US black/campus*) money.

fungoo! *excl. see* BAH-FUNGOO! *excl.*

fungus *n.* **1** [late 18C+] (*also* **fungus face**) an unpleasant person. **2** [20C+] a moustache; a beard; thus as insult *fungus-face*. **3** [1910s] an old man.

fun joint *n.* [Chi. *fun*, a measure of opium + JOINT *n.* (3a)] [1940s–50s] (*US drugs*) an opium den.

Funk *n. see* PETER FUNK *n.*

funk *n.*[1] **1** [late 17C–18C] tobacco. **2** [late 17C–18C] tobacco smoke. **3** [late 17C–early 19C; 1940s+] a stench. **4** [1930s+] (*orig. US black*) sweat generated during sex, dancing, general body odour. **5** [1930s+] (*orig. US black*) anything basic, elemental, earthy; the essence of being. **6** [1970s] (*US*) anything attractive or beautiful. **7** [2000s] (*US campus*) any sexually transmitted disease. **8** [2000s] (*US drugs*) marijuana.

funk *n.*[2] [orig. Oxford Univ. use; ult. Flemish *fonck*, fear] **1** [18C+] (a state of) cowardice, terror; thus *funk it*, to avoid an issue or an act through fear. **2** [late 18C+] a black mood; a state of depression; thus adj., *funking*, furious. **3** [mid-19C+] a coward. **4** [late 19C] (*US Und.*) a cheat, swindler. **5** [1900s] (*Aus./US Und.*) an informer. **6** [1920s–30s] (*US tramp*) a sneak thief.

IN COMPOUNDS

❑ **funkhole** *n.* [1910s+] (*orig. milit.*) anywhere one can hide. ❑ **funkstick** *n. see* FUNKER *n.* (2).

IN PHRASES

❑ **like funk on a skunk** *adv. see LIKE STINK ON SHIT under* SHIT *n.*

funk *adj. see* FUNKY *adj.*[2].

funk *v.*[1] [FUNK *n.*[1]] [late 17C+] **1** to smoke a pipe. **2** to make a stench. **3** to blow smoke on someone. **4** of an object, to smoke.

IN PHRASES

❑ **funk the cobbler** *v.* [the trick was apparently first performed by blowing the foul fumes into the cracks in a cobbler's stall] [late 17C–early 19C] (*UK juv.*) to 'smoke out' a schoolmate, usu. with asafoetida. ❑ **funk up** *v.* [1960s] (*US black*) fig. or lit. to 'stink out', to make a smell.

funk *v.*[2] **1** [early 18C+] (*also* **funk on**) to act in a cowardly manner, to flinch or shrink through fear; to worry. **2** [19C–1910s] (*also* **funkify**) to frighten or scare someone. **3** [early–mid-19C] (*UK Und.*) to cheat. **4** [early 19C+] to try to back out of anything, to fight shy of, to wish or try to shirk or evade (an undertaking, duty etc). **5** [late 19C–1910s] to fear, to be afraid of someone.

funked out *adj.* [1990s+] **1** in the style of the music and clothes promoted by the funk bands of the 1970s, esp. George Clinton's Parliament/Funkadelic. **2** sophisticated, blasé.

funked-up *adj.*[1] [FUNK *n.*[1] (6)] [1990s+] (*US black*) excellent, splendid, first-rate.

funked-up *adj.*[2] [FUNK *n.*[2] (1)] [2000s] (*US*) hurt, painful.

funken *adj. see* FUCKING *adj.*

funker *n.* [FUNK *v.*[2] (1)] **1** [19C] a petty criminal, rated as the lowest order of thieves. **2** [mid-19C+] (*also* **funkstick**) one who is a coward, a weakling or a shirker. **3** [late 19C] a prostitute who quits the streets when the weather is bad.

funkey *n.* [FUNK *n.*[1] (3)] [1960s] (*US black*) the buttocks.

funkify *v. see* FUNK *v.*[2] (2).

funking *adj. see* FUCKING *adj.*

funking hell! *excl. see* FUCKING HELL! *excl.*

funkum *n.* [FUNK *n.*[1] (3)] [1930s] lavender, as sold in sachets.

funky *adj.*[1] [FUNK *n.*[1] (3) + sfx *-y*] [late 17C; 20C+] lit. or fig. smelling very unpleasant.

funky *adj.*[2] (*also* **funk**) [FUNK *n.*[2] (1) + sfx *-y*] [early 19C+] fearful, timid, nervous, cowardly.

funky *adj.*[3] [fig. use of FUNKY *adj.*[1]] (*orig. US black*) **1** [20C+] soulful, elemental. **2** [1950s+] pertaining to funk music; thus n., *funkateer*, one who likes funk. **3** [1960s+] (*also* **funky-ass**) fashionable, 'with it'. **4** [1980s+] (*US campus*) weird.

IN COMPOUNDS

□ **funky-ass** *adj. see* separate entry. □ **funky butt** *n.* [1980s] (*US black*) an attractive woman. □ **funky-butt** *adj. see* FUNKY-ASS *adj.* (2). □ **funky-fresh** *adj.* (*also* **fonky fresh**) [FRESH *adj.*[2] (2)] [1980s+] (*US black*) a general adj. of high praise, the most sophisticated, the smartest, the most attractive.

funky *adj.*[4] [FUNK *n.*[2] (1) + sfx *-y*] **1** [20C+] a general term of disparagement: unpleasant, unappealing etc. **2** [1990s+] (*US teen*) wrong, unsatisfactory.

IN COMPOUNDS

□ **funky-ass** *see* separate entries.

funky *adv.* [FUNKY *adj.*[4] (1)] [1960s] (*US*) unkindly.

funky ass *n.* [FUNKY-ASS *adj.* (1)] [1960s+] (*US black*) a general term of abuse, implying bad odours.

funky-ass *adj.* [FUNKY *adj.*[4] + -ASS *sfx*] [1960s+] (*US black*) **1** a general term of derision, with overtones of bad odours. **2** (*also* **funky-butt**) thus, on bad = good model, excellent, exciting [FUNKY *adj.*[3] (3) + BUTT *n.*[1] (1a)].

funna *v. see* FINNA *v.*

funnel *n.* **1** [early 18C; 1900s] the throat. **2** [20C+] (*orig. US black*) a drunkard.

funnies *n.* **1** *see* FUNNY BUSINESS *n.* **2** *see* FUNNY PAGES *n.*

funny *n. see* FUNNY MONEY *n.* (1).

funny *adj.*[1] [SE *feeling funny*] **1** [mid-18C–mid-19C] tipsy, slightly drunk. **2** [1990s+] (*US campus*) intoxicated by marijuana. **3** in terms below, insane, crazy.

IN COMPOUNDS

□ **funny cigarette** *n. see* HAPPY CIGARETTE *under* HAPPY *adj.* □ **funny farm** *n.* [1950s+] a psychiatric institution. □ **funny house** *n.* (*also* **funny bin, ...factory, ...place**) [20C+] (*US*) a psychiatric institution. □ **funny stuff** *n.* [? a revival of sense 1 above] [1980s+] (*Aus. prison*) alcohol.

funny *adj.*[2] **1** [late 19C+] difficult, problematic; out of the ordinary. **2** [20C+] corrupt, fraudulent; of playing cards, tampered with. **3** [20C+] weak, out of control. **4** [20C+] (*US*) sexually aroused.

IN COMPOUNDS

□ **funny business** *n. see* separate entry. □ **funny bunny** *see* separate entries. □ **funny money** *n. see* separate entry. □ **funny paper** *n. see* FUNNY MONEY *n.* (1). □ **funny stuff** *n. see* FUNNY BUSINESS *n.* □ **funny-time** *adj.* [1950s–70s] (*US black*) strange, bizarre. □ **funny work** *n. see* FUNNY BUSINESS *n.*

IN PHRASES

□ **get funny with** *v.* (*also* **turn funny**) **1** [late 19C+] to provoke, to act in an offensive manner; thus the threat *don't get funny with me!* **2** [20C+] to reveal that one has been offended. **3** [20C+] to make sexual advances towards.

SE in slang uses

IN COMPOUNDS

□ **funny-face** *n.* **1** [late 19C+] a term of derision. **2** [1920s+] a term of affectionate address.

IN PHRASES

□ **funny as a bit of string** (*also* **funny as a piece of string**) [1930s+] (*N.Z.*) highly amusing. □ **funny as a box of worms** [1900s] (*N.Z.*) very funny; often used ironically.

funny *adj.*[3] [abbr. fig. use of SE *funny one, funny fellow*] [1930s+] of a man, homosexual, effeminate; of a woman, lesbian.

funny bunny *n.* [FUNNY *adj.*[2] (2) + redup.] [1960s] (*US*) a victim.

funny-bunny *adj.* [1960s+] (*US*) weird, odd, eccentric.

funny business *n.* (*also* **funnies, funny stuff, ...work**) [late 19C+] deceitful or underhand practices.

funny money *n.* [FUNNY *adj.*[2] (2) + SE *money*] (*UK/US Und.*) **1** [1910s+] (*also* **funny, funny paper**) counterfeit money. **2** [1960s–70s] substitute money, i.e. coupons, certificates etc. **3** [1960s+] tricks, deceits. **4** [1960s+] foreign money. **5** [1980s] (*US black*) a small amount of money. **6** [1980s+] any money that has been gained illegally, usu. through some form of fraud.

funny pages *n.* (*also* **funnies, funny papers**) [1910s+] those pages which newspapers reserve for comic strips; thus the comics themselves.

funsacks *n. see* FUNBAGS *n.*

funt *n.* (*also* **foont, phunt**) [Ger. *pfund*, thence Yid.] [mid-19C+] £1.

fur *n.* **1** [late 16C+] (*also* **fur-bush, pussy fur**) the female pubic hair. **2** [18C+] the vagina. **3** [1950s–60s] (*US black*) a woman's wig. **4** [1960s] (*US black*) a woman.

IN COMPOUNDS

□ **furburger** *n. see* separate entry. □ **fur pie** *n.* [1930s+] the female pubic hair and genitals.

SE in slang uses

IN COMPOUNDS

□ **furman** *n.* [the fur trimmings that adorn his official robes] [late 17C–mid-19C] (*UK Und.*) an alderman. □ **fur trade** *n.* [the fur trimmings on judicial robes] [mid-19C] (*UK Und.*) the legal profession.

furbelow *n.* [SE *furbelow*, an adornment to a dress or other garment, ult. f. *falbala*, trimming for women's petticoats, scarves etc + pun on FUR *n.* + SE *below*; the term begins as a ref. to a petticoat typically worn by a whore, then by metonymy to the woman herself, thence the pubic hair and/or vagina] [18C–mid-19C] the female pubic hair; the vagina.

furburger *n.* [FUR *n.* (1) + play on SE *hamburger*] **1** [1960s+] the vagina, esp. during the act of cunnilingus when it is 'eaten'. **2** [1980s] a hairpiece, a wig.

IN PHRASES

□ **eat a furburger** *v.* [1980s+] (*US*) to perform cunnilingus.

furgle *v.* (*also* **fergle, flurgle**) [euph. for FUCK *v.* (1)] [1920s–70s] to have sexual intercourse; thus n., *furgler, fergler*.

furilla *adv. see* ON THE FURILLA *under* FOR REAL *adv.*

furk *n.* [1920s+] a euph. for FUCK *n.* in a variety of senses.

furking *adj.* [1920s+] a euph. for FUCKING *adj.*

furniture *n.* [early 19C] in pugilism, the face.

IN PHRASES

□ **dust the furniture with** *v. see* DUST THE FLOOR/FURNITURE WITH *under* DUST *v.*[1].

furniture polish *n. see* SHOE-POLISH *under* POLISH *n.*

furphy *n.* (*also* **furph**) [proper name John *Furphy*, the proprietor of sanitary carts used by the Australian forces in WW1; the gossip and chat around these carts developed into the general word. Furphy, a former ironfounder, made his carts of iron, and on them was inscribed 'Good, better, best, / never let it rest, / till your good is better / and your better best.' The same slogan was also inscribed in Pitman's shorthand. Note UK services, *Elsan gen*, a rumour, lit. news from the chemical toilet] [1910s+] (*Aus.*) a groundless rumour; thus *furphy-king, furphy-monger*, a gossip.

furrow *n.* [17C–19C; 1980s+] the vagina.

IN PHRASES

□ **die in the furrow** *v.* (*also* **fail in the furrow**) [19C] of a man, to lose one's erection during intercourse. □ **fall in the furrow** *v.* [20C+] to ejaculate.

furry *adj.* [? ext. of such woman = animal terms as MINK *n.* (1), PUSSY *n.* (6)] [1990s+] (*US campus*) of a woman, attractive.

furry hoop *n.* [SE *fur*/FUR *n.* (1) + SE *hoop*/HOOP *n.* (2a)] [1960s+] the vagina.

furschlugginer *adj. see* FERSCHLUGGINER *adj.*

FURTB *phr.* [abbr.] [2000s] (*N.Z.*) full up and ready to burst.

further behind than Walla Walla *phr.* [proper name of the racehorse *Walla Walla*, celebrated for his ability to come from far behind and still win] [1950s+] (*Aus.*) delayed, at a disadvantage.

furthermucker *n. see* FATHER-FUCKER *n.*

furze-bush *n.* [SE *furze*, a spiny evergreen shrub with yellow flowers + BUSH *n.*[1] (2a)/SE *bush*] [mid-19C] the female, occas. male, pubic hair.

fusby *n.* [?FUSSOCK *n.*] [early 18C–mid-19C] a woman (in any negative context).

fuse *n.* [the image of the cigarette as a lit fuse attached to the 'bomb', i.e. the head] [1970s] (*S.Afr.*) a cigarette.

fusebox *n.* [1940s–60s] (*orig. US black*) the head.

fushme *n.* [ety. unknown] [mid–late 19C] 5 shillings (25p).

fusilier *n.* [1900s] beer.

fusil oil *n.* (*also* **fusel oil**) [SE *fusel oil*, 'a term for a mixture of several homologous alcohols, chiefly amylic alcohol, and especially applied to this when in its crude form' (Syd. Soc. Lex. 1885).] [late 19C–1900s] (*US*) whisky.

fusled *adj. see* FOOZLED *adj.* (1).

fuss *n.* [abbr. FUSSOCK *n.*] [mid-17C–early 18C] a lazy, fat woman.

fuss *v.* [SE *make a fuss (of)*] (*US*) **1** [late 19C+] to quarrel, to pick a fight. **2** [1900s–20s] to court, to date. **3** [1920s–30s] (*US*) to engage in sexual activity short of intercourse.

fusser *n.* [FUSS *v.* (2)] [1900s] (*US*) a womanizer.

fussock *n.* (*also* **fussocks, fuzzock**) [Yorks. dial. *fussock*, a stupid person, a coarse, fat woman] [late 17C–19C] a lazy, fat woman; thus *fat fussock*, a fat, strapping woman; *old fussock*, an ill-kempt old woman.

fussock *v.* [SE *fuss*] [1910s–20s] to make a fuss, to cause a commotion, to be noisy.

fusspot *n.* [SE *fuss* + *pot*; one who has certain characteristics] [1920s+] a notably fussy person.

fustian *n.* [SE *fustian*, a kind of coarse cloth made of cotton and flax; cognate with SATIN *n.* (1a)] [late 18C–mid-19C] alcohol, usu. wine or port.

fustilugs *n.* (*also* **fusty luggs**) [lit. 'dirty ears'] [17C–mid-19C] 'a Fulsom, Beastly, Nasty Woman' (B.E.).

futhermucker *n.* [1960s+] (*US*) a joc. reverse of MOTHERFUCKER *n.*

futt about *v.* [1930s] a euph. for FUCK ABOUT *v.* (1).

futter *n.* [FUTTER *v.* (1)] [late 19C] sexual intercourse.

futter *v.* [Fr. *foutre*, to fuck] **1** [17C; late 19C+] to have sex with. **2** [1990s+] to waste time, i.e. semi-euph. for FUCK ABOUT *v.* (1).

future *n.* [ety. unknown; ? link to LATER FOR *phr.* (1)] **1** [1970s+] (*US campus*) an unattractive man. **2** [1980s] the male genitals.

futy *n.* [FUTZ *n.* (3)] **1** [1960s+] the vagina. **2** [1970s+] (*US gay*) the passive partner in homosexual intercourse.

futz *n.* [FUTZ *v.*] (*US*) **1** [1930s–50s] (*also* **phutz**) a fool, an unpleasant person. **2** [1940s+] a euph. for FUCK *n.* **3** [1940s+] the vagina [? link to PFOTZ *n.*].

futz *v.* (*also* **futz around, phutz around**) [Ger. *furzen*, to fart or Yid. *arumfartzen zikh*, to fart around; the term is also a euph. for FUCK AROUND *v.*[2]] (*US*) **1** [1910s+] to waste time, to mess around, to trifle with. **2** [1940s+] to fiddle with. **3** [1940s+] to treat with contempt.

IN PHRASES

□ **futz off** *v.* [var. on/euph. for FUCK OFF *v.* (1)] [1920s+] to leave, to go away. □ **futz out** *v.* [1960s] (*US*) to spoil, to confound. □ **futz up** *v.* (*also* **fotz up**) [1940s–60s] (*US*) to spoil, to confound, to mess up.

futzer *n.* [FUTZ *v.*] [1930s] a foolish or unpleasant person.

futzing *adj.* [FUTZ *n.* (2)] [1930s–60s] (*US*) a euph. for FUCKING *adj.*

fuz-chats *n.* [SE *furze* + CHEAT *n.* (1)] [late 19C] (*UK tramp*) those who sleep in the open air.

fuzz *n.*[1] (*also* **fuz**) [? SE *fuss*, which a police officer makes; or ? MAN WITH THE FUZZY BALLS *under* BALLS *n.*; note without detailed context senses 1 and 2 can be indistinguishable] **1** [1920s+] (*orig. US*) a police officer; the police in general. **2** [1930s–40s] (*US*) a detective.

DERIVATIVES

□ **fuzzmobile** *n.* [-MOBILE *sfx*] [1970s–80s] (*US*) a police car.

fuzz *n.*[2] **1** [1930s+] pubic hair. **2** [1960s+] (*US black*) a goatee beard.

IN COMPOUNDS

□ **fuzz bumper** *n.* (*also* **fuzz bumping pebble-licker**) [SE *bumper*/BUMPER *n.*[7]] [1980s+] (*US campus*) a lesbian. □ **fuzzburger** *n.* [play on SE *hamburger*, var. on FURBURGER *n.* (1)] [1960s+] the vagina, esp. during the act of cunnilingus.

IN PHRASES

□ **bump fuzz** *v.* [1980s+] (*US campus*) to have sexual intercourse.

SE in slang uses

IN COMPOUNDS

□ **fuzzface** *n.* (*also* **fuzzbeard**) [20C+] (*US tramp*) a young tramp or boy (whose beard has not properly grown). □ **fuzzhead** *n.* [1980s] (*US black*) a woman with tightly curled or 'nappy' hair. □ **fuzz-nutted** *adj.* [? the image of immaturity, i.e. one's pubic hair is as yet no more than *fuzz*] [1970s–80s] stupid; thus *fuzz-nuts*, a general term of abuse. □ **fuzztail** *n. see* FUZZY TAIL *under* FUZZY *adj.*

fuzz *v.*[1] [? SE *fuzz*, light, insubstantial particles; the obvious link, FUZZY *adj.*, drunk, is a later coinage] [late 17C–early 18C] to make drunk; esp. as *fuzzed*, tipsy, drunk.

fuzz *v.*[2] [? onomat. sound of riffling cards, or SE *fuss*] **1** [mid-18C] to deal twice together with the same pack of cards, for luck's sake, at whist. **2** [mid-18C–19C] to shuffle cards very carefully; to change the pack.

fuzz-brain *n.* [SE *fuzz(y)*, blurred + sfx *-brain*] [1960s+] a stupid person.

fuzz-brained *adj.* (*also* **fuzzy-assed**) [FUZZ-BRAIN *n.*] [1960s+] (*US*) stupid.

fuzzle *n. see* FOOZLE *n.*

fuzzled *adj. see* FOOZLED *adj.* (2).

fuzzock *n. see* FUSSOCK *n.*

fuzzy *n.* [FUZZ *n.*[1] (1) + sfx *-y*] [1940s+] a police officer.

fuzzy *adj.* [late 18C+] drunk; thus *fuzziness*, drunkenness.

SE in slang uses

IN COMPOUNDS

□ **fuzzy-assed** *adj. see* FUZZ-BRAINED *adj.* □ **fuzzy-face** *n.* [his light facial hair] [1920s–60s] (*US*) a young man. □ **fuzzy tail** *n.* (*also* **fuzz tail**) [? the way the fur of an angry or frightened animal bristles] **1** [1910s–30s] (*US tramp*) the lowest category of vagrant or tramp. **2** [1920s–30s] an ill-natured person. **3** [1930s] a conceited person.

IN PHRASES

□ **fuzzy end of the lollipop** *n.* [coined by Billy Wilder for Marilyn Monroe in the film *Some Like It Hot* (1958)] [1950s; 1990s+] (*US*) hostile or unfair treatment.

fuzzy-wuzzy *n.*[1] (*also* **fuzzy**) [orig. the Sudanese method of dressing the hair; latterly used of anyone with tightly curled 'fuzzy' hair (and black skin)] **1** [late 19C+] a soldier's derog. nickname for a Sudanese warrior. **2** [20C+] 'a coloured native of other countries, such as Fiji and New Guinea' (*OED*).

fuzzy-wuzzy *n.*[2] [? their obscurantism, i.e. they render things 'fuzzy'] [1900s] (*Aus.*) a derog. term for an intellectual.

fye-buck *n. see* SYEBUCK *n.*

f.y.f.i. *phr.* [abbr.] [1960s+] *f*or *y*our *f*ucking *i*nformation, acronym often appended to memos in business.

f.y.o. *n.* [abbr. *fill your own*; i.e. a beer flagon] [1980s+] (*N.Z.*) an invitation to a party at which the guests are asked to supply the drink.

fyst *see under* FOIST.

G *n.* **1** [1920s+] (*orig. US*) (*also* **gee**) 1000 (usu. dollars or pounds) [abbr. GRAND *n.*[1] (1)]. **2** [1930s+] (*US Und.*) constr. with *the*, the US government. **3** [1970s] (*US gang*) the multiple rape of a woman; usu. as *pull a G*, to engage in this [GANGBANG *n.* (1)]. **4** [1970s–80s] (*UK black*) a Giro cheque. **5** [1980s] (*US campus*) a smart and attractive male. **6** [1980s+] (*US black*) a gangster. **7** [1980s+] (*US black*) a friend, a partner; also as a term of address. **8** [1990s+] (*US black*) money. **9** [2000s] a G-string. **10** *see* G-MAN *under* G *adj.*[1]. **11** *see* GEE *n.*[7].

IN COMPOUNDS

❑ **G-man** *n.* **1** [1940s+] a garbage man. **2** [1990s+] (*drugs*) a cocaine dealer. ❑ **G-note** *n.* [1930s+] (*US*) a $1000 note. ❑ **G-pack** *n.* [abbr. PACKAGE *n.* (4)] [1990s+] (*US drugs*) a wholesale purchase of 100 vials of crack cocaine, which can be merchandised for $1000. ❑ **G-smack** *n.* [SMACK *v.* (2)] [2000s] (*US black*) the police.

IN PHRASES

❑ **do the G** *v. see under* GEORGIA *v.* ❑ **G off** *v.* [1990s+] (*US drugs*) to make $1000 in a day's drug dealing. ❑ **half-a-G** *n.* (*also* **half-a-grand, half-G**) [1930s+] (*US Und.*) $500.

G *adj.*[1] [i.e. *g*overnment] [1930s+] (*US*) Federal.

IN COMPOUNDS

❑ **G-girl** *n.* [1930s] (*US*) a female Government employee. ❑ **G-guy** *n.* [1930s] (*US*) an agent of the FBI. ❑ **G-heat** *n.* [HEAT *n.* (3a)] [1930s–60s] (*US*) trouble from, or agents of, federal law enforcement agencies. ❑ **G-man** *n.* [note pre-US use as a political detective in pre-Independence Ireland] **1** [1920s+] (*US*) (*also* **G**) an FBI agent, lit. 'Government-man'. **2** [1980s] (*S.Afr.*) the vice and liquor squad.

G *adj.*[2] [1990s+] (*US black/gang*) gangster.

IN COMPOUNDS

❑ **G-check** *v.* [2000s] (*US black*) to rob. ❑ **G-money** *n.* [MONEY *n.* (6)] [1990s+] (*US black/teen*) a term of affectionate address. ❑ **G-ride** *n.* (*also* **g-ride**) [RIDE *n.* (2a)] [1990s+] (*US black*) any type of automobile favoured by teen gangs, usu. stolen (cf. GANGSTER RIDE *under* GANGSTER *adj.*).

g *n.*[1] (*also* **gee**) [abbr.] **1** [1920s] (*US tramp*) a gallon of liquor. **2** [1950s+] (*drugs*) one grain, usu. of morphine. **3** [1990s+] (*drugs*) one gram, orig. of heroin or cocaine, and latterly also of cannabis. **4** [2000s] a girlfriend. **5** [2000s] grime music. **6** [2000s] (*drugs*) gamma hydroxybutyrate (GHB).

IN PHRASES

❑ **get the g** *v.* [ety. unknown; ? the initial 'g' of SE *get*, to understand] [20C+] (*W.I.*) to understand, to 'get the hang of'. ❑ **half-g** *n.* [1980s+] (*N.Z.*) a flagon of draught beer.

g *n.*[2] [abbr. GAFF *n.*[3] (1)] [1940s–60s] (*US*) a cheating device.

g *n.*[3] [abbr. GOODIES *n.* (7)] [1970s+] (*US black*) the female genitals, the vagina.

IN PHRASES

❑ **get one's G on** *v.* [2000s] (*US teen*) to have sexual intercourse.

g *n.*[4] [abbr. SE *generic*, no-brand] [1990s+] (*US prison*) prison-made cigarettes.

gaan kak! *excl.* [KAK *v.* (2); lit. 'go shit!'] [1970s+] (*S.Afr.*) var. on GO TO HELL! *under* HELL *n.*

gaan to bed *phr.* [1950s+] (*W.I. Rasta*) following a verb of liking or loving, it has a superlative meaning; can be used in any context, such as *I love hafu yam gaan to bed!*

gaats! *excl. see* GATS! *excl.*

gab *n.*[1] [Scot. *gab*, the mouth] [18C+] the mouth.

IN COMPOUNDS

❑ **gab-box** *n.* **1** [20C+] (*US*) the mouth. **2** [2000s] a chatterer. ❑ **gab string** *n.* (*also* **gob string**) [GOB *n.*[1] (1)] [late 18C–early 19C] a bridle.

IN PHRASES

❑ **blow one's gab off** *v. see* BLOW ONE'S GOB OFF *under* GOB *n.*[1]. ❑ **blow the gab** *v.* [mid-18C–1910s] to inform, to betray. ❑ **flash one's gab** *v.* [early 19C] to talk, esp. to brag, to boast. ❑ **flash the gab** *v.* [early 19C] to show off, to act ostentatiously. ❑ **give the gab** *v.* [late 18C–early 19C] to betray a secret, to inform against. ❑ **hold one's gab** *v. see* HOLD ONE'S GOB *under* GOB *n.*[1]. ❑ **shoot one's gab** *v.* [1910s–30s] to talk excitedly. ❑ **shut one's gab** *v. see* SHUT ONE'S GOB *under* GOB *n.*[1]. ❑ **sling a gab** *v.* [1910s–20s] to talk a language.

IN EXCLAMATIONS

❑ **stop your gab!** (*also* **stow your gab!**) [late 18C–1950s] be quiet!

gab *n.*[2] [Scot. *gab*, talk volubly] **1** [19C+] (*also* **gabs**) idle chatter. **2** [mid-19C+] (*also* **gabbie**) talk, conversation, esp. charming and persuasive. **3** [late 19C] a (foreign) language. **4** [1920s] (*US*) one who talks freely, cannot keep a secret. **5** [1990s+] as *the gabs*, a propensity to talk too much.

IN PHRASES

❑ **stow one's gab** *v.* (*also* **cheese one's gab, cut…, hold…**) [early 19C+] to stop talking, esp. as imper.

gab *v.* (*also* **gabber**) [GAB *n.*[1] (1); considered SE by the *OED*, but used in so many sl. combs. below] [late 18C+] to talk.

DERIVATIVES

❑ **gabfest** *n.* (*also* **gab session, jabfest**) [-FEST *sfx*; *jab* is mis-sp. of *gab*] [late 19C+] (*orig. US*) **1** a gathering for talk; a spell of talking; a prolonged conference or conversation. **2** garrulous, unrestrained talk. ❑ **gabster** *n.* [-STER *sfx*] [19C] a chatterer, an idle talker.

IN COMPOUNDS

❑ **gab-artist** *n.* [-ARTIST *sfx*] [1940s+] (*US*) a talker, esp. a convincing talker. ❑ **gab-bag** *n.* [SE *bag*/-BAG *sfx*] [1940s] (*Aus.*) a gossip. ❑ **gabslick** *n.* [SLICK *n.*[1] (2)] [20C+] (*Ulster*) a talkative person.

IN PHRASES

❑ **gab one's head off** *v. see* TALK ONE'S HEAD OFF *under* TALK *v.*

g.a.b.a. *n.* [abbr. the *g*reat *A*ustralian *b*ugger *a*ll] [1980s] (*Aus.*) the outback.

gabba *n.* [Heb. *chaver*/Yid. *khaver*, a comrade] [1960s+] (*S.Afr.*) a friend.

gabber *n.*[1] [GABBER *v.*] [mid-19C] talk, loquacity.

gabber *n.*[2] [colloq. *gab*] **1** [1930s+] a chatterer; an indiscreet talkative person; a gossip. **2** [1940s] a lawyer. **3** [1940s–60s] (*US*) a radio commentator. **4** [1980s] a police officer.

gabber *v.* [var. on SE *jabber*] **1** [mid-17C–mid-19C] to talk, to chatter; thus *gabbering*, verbose; *gabbery*, foolish chatter. **2** *see* GAB *v.*

gabberlooney *n.* (*also* **gobaloon, gobberloony**) [Scot. *gaberlunzie*, a strolling beggar; ? colloq. *gab*, to chatter + LOONY *n.* (1)] [20C+] (*Ulster*) one who talks too much and acts the fool.

gabbie *n.*[1] *see* GAB *n.*[2] (2).

gabbie *n.*[2] *see* GABBY *n.*[1].

gabbleblooter *n.* [SE *gabble* + BLOOTER *n.*] [20C+] (*Ulster*) a loudmouth, a prattler.

gabbletrap *n.* [SE *gabble*] [mid-19C] (*Aus.*) a silly chatterer.

gabbo *n.* (*also* **gabo**) [colloq. *gab*, to chatter + -O *sfx* (7)] [1930s–50s] (*US*) a chatterer.

gabby *n.*[1] (*also* **gabbie**) [? Abor.] [mid-19C+] (*Aus.*) water.

gabby *n.*[2] *see* GABY *n.* (1).

gabby *adj.* [? GAMMY *adj.*[1]] [1940s–50s] (*Irish*) bad, ailing, broken.

gabby row *n.* [SE *gabby*, talkative + SE *row*; the closeness of the houses leads to much neighbourly conversation] [20C+] (*US*) the area of town where the poor live.

gabo *n. see* GABBO *n.*

gaboon *n. see* GOBOON *n.*

gabriel *n.* [the archangel *Gabriel* who announces the 'last trump'] **1** [1930s–40s] (*US black*) a trumpet player. **2** [1930s–40s] (*US black*) a puritan, a 'kill-joy', a 'bible-thumper'. **3** [1930s–50s] (*UK prison*) the chapel organist.

gabs *n. see* GAB *n.*[2] (1).

gabshite *n. see* GOBSHITE *n.* (2).

gaby *n.* [Yorks. dial. *gabes*, a fool, one who gapes or stares vacantly] **1** [late 18C–1960s] (*also* **gabby**) a fool. **2** [1920s] an effeminate man, a homosexual.

gack *n.*[1] (*also* **gak**) [? link to dial. *gack*, to chatter, to talk idly, i.e. one of the drug's primary effects] [1990s+] (*UK drugs*) cocaine.

gack *n.*[2] *see* GECK *n.*

gack *adj.* [? echoic of a sound of distaste] [1980s] unappealing, pretentious.

gacked *adj.* [echoic of the vomiting that may accompany this + ? GACK *n.*[1]] [1990s+] overcome by drink and/or drugs.

gacky *adj.* [GACK *n.*[2]] [2000s] stupid.

gad *n.*[1] [late 16C+] a euph. for God, used in a variety of oaths, which have become gradually milder as the decline of religiosity has robbed them of their import.

(IN EXCLAMATIONS)

❑ **gadsbobs!** (*also* **gadsbud!**) [late 17C–1920s] a mild excl., lit. 'God's body!'. ❑ **gadsbodikins!** (*also* **gadsbudlikins!**) [early 17C–mid-18C] a mild excl., lit. 'God's little body!'. ❑ **gadslid!** [late 16C–mid-17C] a mild excl., lit. 'God's eyelid!'. ❑ **gadsniggers!** (*also* **gadsnigs!**) [ety. unknown for *nigs/niggers*; 'not found in other contexts, and probably ... corrupt or fabricated' (*OED*)] [early–mid-17C] a mild excl. ❑ **gadsnouns!** (*also* **gadzoons! gadzounds!**) ['SNOUNS! *excl.*] [late 17C] a euph. for God and used as a mild excl., lit. 'God's wounds!'. ❑ **gadso!** (*also* **gad-so! gads O!**) [note poss. link to GADSO *n.*] [late 17C–mid-19C] a general excl. ❑ **gadsokers!** (*also* **gadsookers! gadswookers!**) [late 17C–mid-18C] a euph. for God and used as a mild excl., lit. 'God's hooks!'. ❑ **gadsprecious!** [late 17C] a mild excl., lit. 'God's precious (heart)!'. ❑ **gadswogs!** [early 19C] a mild excl., lit. 'God's wounds!'. ❑ **gadswoons!** (*also* **gad zoons!**) [late 17C–early 18C] a mild excl., lit. 'God's wounds!'. ❑ **gadzooks!** (*also* **Cadzooks! gadsooks!**) [*hooks* either means the nails used in the crucifixion or the hands, i.e. HOOK *n.*[1] (1a)] [17C+] lit. 'God's hooks!'; a general oath, one of many ways of euphemizing God.

gad *n.*[2] (*also* **gadder**) [SE *gad*, to rush from place to place] [mid-17C; mid-19C] a loose woman, a slattern.

gad! *excl.* (*also* **gads!**) [GAD *n.*[1]] [late 16C+] a semi-euph. excl., i.e. *God!*

'gad! *excl. see* EGAD! *excl.*

gadaha *n.* [Hind. *gadha*, a donkey; used as a general derog. term by East Indians; the female version *gadahee* is more offensive] [20C+] (*W.I.*) a fool, an idiot.

gad-cracked *adj.* [GAD *n.*[1]] [mid-19C] (*UK Und.*) half-crazy.

gadder *n. see* GAD *n.*[2].

gadderman *n.* [Irish *cadramán*, a boor] [20C+] (*Ulster*) a rogue.

Gadfrey *n. see* GODFREY *n.*

gadget *n.* (*also* **gidget**) [1940s+] (*US*) the penis; thus in pl., the male genitals.

gadgy *n.* (*also* **gadge, gadgie, gage**) [Rom. *gorgio*, a non-Gypsy male, and thus fig. in a sexual context a STRAIGHT *n.*[2] (2)] **1** [mid-19C+] any male, incl. a husband. **2** [1960s+] (*gay*) a male prostitute's client.

gads! *excl. see* GAD! *excl.*

gadso *n.* [Ital. *cazzo*, the penis] [17C–early 19C] **1** the penis. **2** a fool.

gad the hoof *v. see under* HOOF *n.*

gaff *n.*[1] [Rom. *gav*, a town, esp. a market town] **1** [mid-18C–early 19C] a fair. **2** [late 18C–1950s] a cheap music hall or theatre. **3** [19C+] a show, an exhibition. **4** [early 19C] a brothel. **5** [late 19C+] a prison. **6** [late 19C+] a place, an area, e.g. a street. **7** [1910s] (*UK Und.*) a warehouse. **8** [1910s–60s] a job, an occupation. **9** [1920s+] a house or shop, a home. **10** [1930s] a dance hall. **11** [1930s] (*UK Und.*) a place chosen for a robbery. **12** [1930s–40s] (*US Und.*) a crooked casino or similar place designed to fleece innocent victims. **13** [1930s+] a hotel. **14** [1930s+] a bar. **15** [1930s+] a restaurant. **16** [1940s+] a club. **17** [1960s] (*UK Und.*) a prostitute's room, where she works, but usu. does not live.

(IN PHRASES)

❑ **blow the gaff** *v.* **1** [early 19C+] to reveal a secret, esp. a hoax or deception. **2** [late 19C+] (*US*) to make a mess of, to bungle. ❑ **frame the gaff** *v.* [1940s] (*US Und.*) of a confidence trickster, to set up the room where a victim is to be fleeced. ❑ **penny gaff** *n.* [mid–late 19C] a cheap theatre or music-hall.

gaff *n.*[2] [? SE *gaff*, the steel spur attached to a fighting cock; ? Fr. *gaffe*, a verbal blunder or Scot. *gaff*, to talk loudly and merrily or dial. *gaff*, loud, coarse talk] **1** [early 19C–1910s] an outcry, a noise [? also link to GAFF *n.*[1] (1), a fair, where 'outcry' would naturally be the order of any day]. **2** [late 19C–1920s] (*US*) constructed with *the*, a dismissal; ridicule. **3** [late 19C–1960s] humbug, nonsense. **4** [late 19C–1960s] (*US*) severe treatment, criticism, punishment or hardship. **5** [1910s] a legitimate job, work. **6** [1920s] talk. **7** [1920s–50s] interrogation. **8** [1940s] (*Ulster*) news, gossip.

(IN PHRASES)

❑ **give the gaff** *v.* [mid-19C–1910s] to deliver severe treatment/criticism. ❑ **stand the gaff** *v.* (*also* **get the gaff, take the gaff**) [late 19C+] (*US*) **1** to receive severe treatment, criticism etc. **2** to suffer interrogation, beatings, or any adverse conditions. **3** to sustain a situation, good or bad.

(IN EXCLAMATIONS)

❑ **stow your gaff!** [late 19C–1910s] be quiet!

gaff *n.*[3] [SE *gaff*, a spur for a fighting cock + GAFF *n.*[1] (1), a fair where such gambling was most likely to be found] **1** [early 19C+] a cheating device in gambling, orig. a small hook set in a ring used by a card-sharp. **2** [1930s+] (*US Und.*) a fraud, a racket. **3** [1940s] (*US Und.*) the place – a fake 'bookmaker's' or 'stockbroker's office' – in which a confidence trick is carried out. **4** [1940s–50s] (*US*) in pl., crooked dice. **5** [1940s–60s] a gimmick, a hidden trick.

gaff *n.*[4] [SE *gaff*, a barbed fishing spear] [1960s+] **1** (*US*) the penis, thus sexual intercourse. **2** (*US*) the vagina, thus a promiscuous woman. **3** (*US gay*) a tight-fitting strip of rubber worn to disguise the male genitals, by female impersonators.

gaff *adj.*[1] [ety. unknown; ? link to dial. *gaff*, to laugh loudly] [19C+] excellent, simple.

gaff *adj.*[2] [GAFF *n.*[3]] [1920s+] (*US gambling*) rigged.

(IN COMPOUNDS)

❑ **gaff joint** *n.* [JOINT *n.* (3b)] [1920s–50s] (*US Und.*) a casino where the games are crooked.

gaff *v.*[1] [dial. + GAFF *n.*[3]] (*gambling*) **1** [19C] to gamble, esp. to toss coins. **2** [20C+] (*US*) to cheat, to rig, to fix. **3** [1930s+] (*US*) to make a game crooked or dishonest, typically to tamper with a fruit machine or roulette wheel.

gaff *v.*[2] [GAFF *n.*[1] (2)] [mid–late 19C] to play or perform in a music-hall.

gaff *v.*[3] [GAFF *n.*[2]] **1** [late 19C] (*US*) to tease. **2** [late 19C+] (*orig. Scot.*) to talk; to talk loudly; to talk nonsense. **3** [1980s+] (*US campus*) to insult, to ignore.

gaff *v.*[4] [GAFF *n.*[2]] **1** [1920s–30s] (*US tramp*) to stay where one is for too long. **2** [1930s] (*US tramp*) to punish. **3** [1940s] to be caught in the act. **4** [1970+] (*US campus*) to endure.

gaffer *n.*[1] [abbr. of *granfer*, i.e. SE *grandfather*] **1** [18C] a husband. **2** [late 19C–1960s] one's father. **3** [1900s–60s] (*Anglo-Irish*) a boy, a young fellow.

gaffer *n.*[2] [GAFF *n.*[1]; note Lincolnshire dial. *gaffman*, the bailiff or superintendent of a farm] **1** [18C+] a boss or master, esp. of a show or circus; also as a term of address. **2** [late 19C+] (*US*) a foreman, esp. an electrician. **3** [1980s+] (*Aus. prison*) a dominant prisoner.

gaffer *n.*[3] [GAFF *v.*[1] + sfx *-er*] **1** [early 19C+] one who tosses up coins in a gambling game based on guessing heads or tails. **2** [1970s] the 'straight' front man for any form of fraud or marginal business.

gaffing *n.* [GAFF *v.*[1] (1) + sfx *-ing*] [mid-19C] **1** tossing three coins in a hat in order to determine who pays for drinks; he who guesses right is exempt from payment. **2** coin-tossing, pitch-and-toss.

gaffle *n.* [GAFFLE *v.*] [1990s+] (*US black*) defeat, failure, betrayal.

gaffle *v.* [dial. *gaffle*, to encumber, to tease, to incommode] **1** [20C+] (*US*) to snatch, to steal, to round up. **2** [1950s+] (*US Und.*) to arrest. **3** [1960s] (*US prison*) to lock up in solitary confinement. **4** [1970s+] (*US*) to hoax, to deceive. **5** [1990s+] (*US teen*) to ruin someone's plans. **6** [1990s+] to have sexual intercourse. **7** [2000s] (*US prison*) to place in handcuffs.

gaffled *adj.* [GAFFLE *v.* (5)] [1990s+] **1** in an unfortunate condition. **2** (*US black*) dead.

gaffler *n.* [GAFFLE *v.* (1)] [1990s+] (*US black*) a business person, a thief.

gaffus *n.* [? SE *gaff*, a hook] [1960s+] (*drugs*) a hypodermic needle.

gafone *n. see* GAVONE *n.*

g.a.f.u. *n. see* S.N.A.F.U. *n.*

gag *n.* (*also* **geg**) [fig. uses of SE *gag*, something thrust into the mouth to procure the victim's silence. Note that Share suggests ON *gaghals*, with one's neck thrown back] **1** [early 19C+] a joke, a tease; thus *gaggist*, a joke-teller. **2** [early 19C+] a deception, a lie; thus *gaggery*, deception. **3** [mid-19C–1910s] (*US*) a fool, a laughing stock. **4** [mid-19C–1930s] the sales talk of a street-seller of broadsides; the 'patter' of a beggar; a piece of publicity. **5** [mid-19C–1950s] an ad-lib remark. **6** [mid-19C+] a plan, a scheme. **7** [late 19C] oratory, speechifying. **8** [late 19C] chatter (as in a restaurant or bar). **9** [late 19C–1920s] (*UK tramp*) an account; a begging tale. **10** [late 19C–1930s] (*US*) any form of behaviour or practice, or thing. **11** [1900s] (*US drugs*) narcotic drug addiction. **12** [1900s–10s] (*US*) a thing or aspect.

IN PHRASES

❑ **lounge the gag** *v.* [early 19C] (*UK Und.*) to beg. ❑ **on the high gag** [late 18C–mid-19C] (*UK Und.*) begging surreptitiously; telling secrets. ❑ **on the low gag** [late 18C–mid-19C] (*UK Und.*) extremely poor, reduced to the lowest level of beggary. ❑ **pull a gag** *v.* [20C+] (*US*) to play a trick. ❑ **stand the gag** *v.* [? earlier use of sense 4 above] [late 18C] to cry out. ❑ **strike the gag** *v.* [SE *strike*, to desist from] [mid-19C] to stop playing around, to stop joking.

gag *adj.* [GAG *n.* (1)] [1990s+] joking.

gag *v.* (*also* **gagg**) [SE *gag*, to choke, to mute; the image is of making someone 'swallow' a lie or imposture] **1** [mid-18C–mid-19C; 1930s] (*UK Und.*) to beg. **2** [late 18C+] (*also* **gagger**) to deceive, take in or impose upon (a person). **3** [early 19C+] to amuse. **4** [mid-19C] to scold, to nag. **5** [mid-19C+] to ad lib. **6** [late 19C] (*also* **gag on**) to inform against, to betray. **7** [late 19C–1920s] to persuade, to boost, to promote. **8** [late 19C+] to make a joke. **9** [1910s] to fix a horserace. **10** [1960s] to fake, to falsify. **11** [1980s] (*US campus*) to find disgusting. **12** [1990s+] (*US prison/drugs*) to cheat; to sell fake drugs; thus n. *gagger*, a seller of fake drugs. **13** [1990s+] (*US black*) to arrest.

IN COMPOUNDS

❑ **gag high** *v.* [mid-19C] (*UK Und.*) to beg in genteel circles.

SE in slang uses

IN COMPOUNDS

❑ **gag-awful** *adj.* [1980s] (*US campus*) terrible.

IN EXCLAMATIONS

❑ **gag me with a spoon!** (*also* **gag me with a blowdryer! ...snow shovel!**) [1980s+] (*US teen*) an expression of disgust.

gag! *excl.* [SE *gag*, to choke] [1980s] (*US campus*) an excl. of disgust.

gaga *n.*[1] (*also* **gagagootz**) [GAGA *adj.* (1)] [1930s+] an eccentric or senile person.

gaga *n.*[2] [? play on the *ga-ga* noises of babytalk or GAGA *adj.* (2)] (*US gay*) **1** [1940s+] an inexperienced, immature homosexual. **2** [1960s] homosexual foreplay.

gaga *adj.* (*also* **gugga**) [Fr. *gaga*, a senile person] **1** [1910s+] eccentric, senile. **2** [1920s+] also ext. as *gaga over*, sentimental (about), infatuated (with). **3** [1930s] sexually aroused. **4** [1930s+] drunk. **5** [1930s+] confused, disorientated.

gaga *v.* [GAGA *adj.* (2); + ? the *ga-ga* noises of babytalk] (*US*) **1** [1930s] to act sentimentally. **2** [1990s+] to persuade, to 'sweet talk'.

gaga *adv.* [GAGA *adj.* (1)] [2000s] madly, both lit. and fig.

gagagootz *n. see* GAGA *n.*[1].

gage *n.*[1] [SE *gage*, a measure or, alternatively, a pledge, and thus, in the drinking context, a toast] **1** [mid-15C–18C] (*UK Und.*) (*also* **gauge**) a mug holding a quart (2pt/1l) of beer; occas. a pint. **2** [17C–mid-19C] (*also* **gagg**) any mug or container. **3** [mid-17C–1940s] (*also* **gagg**) a pipe, a pipeful of tobacco. **4** [mid-19C] a small quantity; thus a *gage of tobacco*, a *gage of gin*. **5** [1930s–50s] (*US Und.*) cheap whisky.

gage *n.*[2] (*also* **gauge**) [1930s+] (*US drugs*) marijuana; thus *gage joint*, *gage pad*, a place to smoke marijuana.

IN COMPOUNDS

❑ **gage butt** *n.* (*also* **gauge butt**) [BUTT *n.*[1] (2b)] [1930s–50s] (*drugs*) a marijuana cigarette.

IN PHRASES

❑ **blow gage** *v.* (*also* **blow gauge**) [1940s+] (*orig. US black*) to smoke marijuana. ❑ **gage up** *v.* [1930s+] (*US black*) to smoke marijuana. ❑ **get a gage up** *v.* (*also* **get one's gauge up**) [1930s+] to excite or stimulate oneself, esp. from smoking marijuana or drinking alcohol.

gage *n.*[3] *see* GADGY *n.*

gage *n.*[4] **1** *see* GAUGE *n.*[1]. **2** *see* GAUGE *n.*[2].

gaged *adj.* (*also* **gauged**) [GAGE *n.*[1] (1)/GAGE *n.*[2]] **1** [1930s–40s] (*US*) drunk. **2** [1950s] (*US drugs*) (*also* **gage**) intoxicated by marijuana.

gager *n. see* OLD GAGER *under* OLD *adj.*

gagers *n.* (*also* **gaggers**) [? they gauge the situation] [mid-19C] (*US*) the eyes.

gagg *n.* **1** *see* GAGE *n.*[1] (2). **2** *see* GAGE *n.*[1] (3).

gagg *v. see* GAG V.

gagged *adj.* [SE *gag*, to choke] [1960s–70s] (*US campus*) disgusted, upset.

gagger *n.*[1] [GAG *v.*] **1** [late 18C–early 19C] a confidence trickster, a cheat, esp. when telling 'sob-stories' or posing as a deaf-mute. **2** [mid-19C–1910s] a joker. **3** [1930s] a tramp, a beggar. **4** [1940s] (*US Und.*) a receiver of stolen goods. **5** [1940s] (*US tramp*) a tramp who makes a living by telling stories.

gagger *n.*[2] [JOCKUM-GAGGER *under* JOCKUM *n.*] [1920s–30s] (*US tramp*) one who pimps his own wife.

gagger *n.*[3] [SE *gag*, to choke + sfx *-er*] [1980s+] (*US campus*) a disgusting person or thing, lit. a 'sickener'.

gagger *n.*[4] [GAGGING FOR IT *under* GAGGING FOR *phr.*] [2000s] (*Aus.*) a promiscuous female.

gagger *v. see* GAG *v.* (2).

gaggers *n. see* GAGERS *n.*

gaggery *n. see* GAG *n.* (2).

gagging *n.* [GAGGER *n.*[1] (1)] [early 19C] (*UK Und.*) a form of confidence trick, based on persuading a stranger that one is an old, if forgotten friend.

gagging for *phr.* (*also* **gagging to**) [SE *gag*, to choke] [1970s+] desperate for/to.

IN PHRASES

❑ **gagging for it** *adj.* [1980s+] desperate for sex; usu. but not invariably of a woman.

gagging lark *n.* [GAG *v.* (1) + LARK *n.*[3] (6)] [1930s] begging.

gaggler's coach *n.* [one *gags*, i.e. chokes, on the gallows] [mid-19C] (*UK Und.*) a hurdle, on which the condemned were dragged to the gallows.

gaggy *adj.* [SE *gag*, to choke, to vomit] [1970s+] (*US gay*) sordid, highly distasteful.

gag on *v. see* GAG *v.* (6).

gah damn *n. see* GOR DAMN *n.*

gahn! *excl. see* GO ON! *excl.*

gail *v.* [initial letter of SE *gabble* or ? SE *gossip*] [2000s] (*S.Afr. gay*) to chatter.

Gainesburger *n.* [proprietory brandname Gainesbury Puppy Chow, i.e. dog food] [1970s+] (*US prison*) Salisbury steak; hamburger.

gaishen *n. see* GATION *n.*

gait *n.* [SE *gait*, manner of walking or stepping, bearing or carriage while moving] **1** [mid-19C–1900s] (*US*) one's trade, occupation. **2** [1930s] one's manner or way of being; thus *get a gait on*, to hurry.

gaiter *n.* [cognate with BLACKLEG *n.*[1] (1)] [mid-19C] (*UK Und.*) a (racecourse) gambler.

gajillion *n. see* ZILLION *n.*

gajoungas *n. see* GAZONGAS *n.*

gak *n.*[1] [1990s+] (*US black*) a gun.

gak *n.*[2] *see* GACK *n.*[1].

gak *n.*[3] *see* GECK *n.*

gakk *n.* [? GECK *n.*]

IN PHRASES

❑ **put the gakk on** *v.* [1960s] (*US campus*) to tell off, to reprimand.

gal *n.* [SE *girl*] **1** [late 18C+] a young woman, a woman. **2** [mid-19C+] a general term of address to a woman. **3** [1970s+] attrib., pertaining to a woman, female.

IN COMPOUNDS

❑ **gal-boy** *n.* **1** [19C+] (*US*) a tomboy. **2** [late 19C+] a feminine young man, thence an effeminate (young) homosexual; a prison catamite. ❑ **gal-pal** *n.* **1** [1940s–50s] (*US black*) a lesbian. **2** [1970s+] (*US gay*) a homosexual's female friend [PAL *n.* (1)].

IN PHRASES

❑ **gal a tek life** *n.* [lit. 'girl (who) takes life' thus play on KILLER *n.* (2a)] [1990s+] (*W.I.*) a very attractive woman.

gal *v.* [GAL *n.* (1)] [mid-19C–1930s] (*US*) to court young women; thus *go a-gallin*, to go courting.

galah *n.* [SE *galah*, the rose-breasted grey-backed Aus. cockatoo 'much given to chatter'] [1930s+] (*Aus.*) **1** a fool; thus adj. *galah-ish*. **2** a chap, a fellow.

IN COMPOUNDS

❑ **galah session** *n.* [1950s+] (*Aus.*) an interval set aside regularly on the Flying Doctor radio network for anyone who wishes to exchange news and gossip rather than make emergency calls.

galan(e)y *n. see* GALENY *n.*

galay *v.* [Fr. *galeux*, itching, suffering from scabies, thus the image is of one who is constantly scratching their head – in this context through perplexity. In 19C Fr. sl. the term, from the same basic meaning, also meant boss or master] [20C+] (*W.I., Trin.*) to hesitate, to speak or act indecisively.

galdarned *adj. see* GOLDARNED *adj.*

gale *n. see* WHALE *n.* (4).

gale *adj.* [for ety. *see* GALAY *v.*] [20C+] (*W.I.*) covered in scabs, itching, suffering from scabies, eczema or some other skin disease.

galeeny *n. see* GALENY *n.*

galeery *adj.* [ety. unknown; ? link to ON *gola*, to howl or GALLEY *adj.*] [20C+] (*Ulster*) foolish.

galena *n.* [*Galena*, Illinois, a centre of the pork rearing and packing industry] [mid-19C] (*US*) salt pork.

galeny *n.* (*also* **galan(e)y, galeeny**) [Sp. *gallina morisca*, a Moorish hen] [late 18C–1900s] **1** a guinea-fowl. **2** any sort of fowl.

Galilee stompers *n.* [*Galilee* as metonymic for Jesus Christ, trad. pictured in sandals + SE *stompers*] [1970s–80s] (*gay*) sandals; thongs.

galimaufry *n. see* GALLIMAUFRY *n.*

galimony *n.* [GAL *n.* (1) + SE *alimony*] [1990s+] (*US gay*) the lesbian version of palimony.

gall *n.* [SE *gall*, bitterness of spirit, asperity, rancour] [mid-19C+] (*orig. US*) impudence, arrogance, self-possession.

galla *v.* [Xhosa *ukurhala*, to be greedy for] [1960s+] (*S.Afr.*) to crave for, to desire very much, esp. of food.

gallagher and sheehan *n.* [pun on *Gallagher and Shean*, Irish/Jewish vaudeville stars, touring America from 1920–25; *Gallagher* was Ed Gallagher (*c.*1872–1929); *Sheehan*, spelled thus, was of course Irish – there weren't many Jews on the force – but the real Al Shean was the Marx Brothers' uncle, Al Schoenberg (1868–1949), and wrote their hit show *Home Again* in 1914] [1910s] (*US*) a policeman.

gallery *n. see* SHOOTING GALLERY *n.*

IN COMPOUNDS

❑ **gallery 13** *n.* [SE *gallery*, a floor of cells + the trad. bad luck associated with the number 13] [1990s+] (*US Und.*) a prison cemetery.

IN PHRASES

❑ **flash the gallery** *v. see* FLASH THE RANGE *under* RANGE *n.*

galley *n.* (*also* **gallery**) [Scot. *galliard*, cheerful, lively] [20C+] (*Irish*) fun, enjoyment.

galley *adj.* (*also* **gallery**) [GALLEY *n.*] [20C+] (*Irish*) cheerful, lively.

galley-west *adv.* (*also* **gally-west**) [Eng. dial. *colleywest(on)*, contrarily, askew; Collyweston is an actual village in Northamptonshire, although sources do not specify its particular skewedness; it is usu. found in relation to Collyweston roofing slates] [19C+] (*US*) askew, crooked, scattered in all directions; usu. as *go galley-west, knock galley-west*.

gallfired *adj.* [1900s] (*US*) a euph. for GOD-DAMN *adj.*

gallied *adj.* [? dial. *gally*, to frighten, to alarm] **1** [early 18C–1940s] hurried. **2** [late 19C–1900s] worried.

gallies *n.* [? SE *galligaskins*, leggings or wide hose] [mid–late 19C] shoes.

galligaskins *n.* (*also* **galligastins, gally-hosen, garragaskins**) [SE *galligaskins*, a form of wide hose popular in the 16C–17C; later use is joc.; Nares suggests 'GALLO-GASCOINS, being a kind of trowsers first warn by the Gallic Gascons, i.e. the inhabitants of Gascony'] [late 16C–1950s] a joc. term for any form of breeches.

gallihoot *v. see* GALLYHOOT *v.*

gallimaufry *n.* (*also* **galimaufry**) [SE *gallimaufry*, a mess or jumble (usu. of food)] **1** [late 16C–17C] a mistress, a sexually appealing woman. **2** [19C] the vagina.

gallion *n.* [17C SE *galion*, the fore-parts of a ship; thus that part in which slaves were transported from Africa and, once landed, the slave quarters of a plantation] [1940s] (*US black*) the slave quarters; thus the black ghetto and fig. the black world.

gallipot *n.* [SE *gallipot*, a small earthen glazed pot, esp. one used by apothecaries for ointments and medicines; *gallipot* itself means lit. a pot that has been carried/imported in a galley] [mid-18C–mid-19C] an apothecary.

gallivant *n.* [SE *gallivant*, to parade around in a showy fashion, esp. with persons of the other sex] [early–mid-19C] 'a nest of whores' (Bee); thus v. *go to gallivant*, to search for a prostitute.

gallon *n.*

SE in slang uses

IN PHRASES

❑ **get one's gallon** *v.* [SE *gallon*, a container used by manual labourers for holding drinks] [1960s+] (*Irish*) to be dismissed from a job.

galloot *n. see* GALOOT *n.* (2).

gallop *n.* **1** [1970s] an act of sexual intercourse. **2** [1950s] (*Aus.*) a fight.

galloper *n.* [they tumble speedily over the table] [1910s–80s] (*US gambling*) in pl., dice.

galloping *adj.* [early 17C+] (*orig. US*) worsening or increasing.

SE in slang uses

IN COMPOUNDS

❑ **galloping bones** *n.* (*also* **galloping cubes, ...horses, ...ivories, animated cubes, ...ivories**) [BONES *n.*[1] (1)/ CUBE *n.*[1] (1)/fig. use of SE *horse*/IVORY *n.* (1)] [1920s+] (*US gambling*) dice. ❑ **galloping dandruff** *n.* (*also* **crawling dandruff, leaping..., mechanized..., mobile..., travelling..., walking...**) [1910s+] (*Aus./US*) head or body lice. ❑ **galloping dominoes** *n.* [DOMINO *n.*[1] (3)] [1920s–70s] (*US*) dice. ❑ **galloping freckles** *n.* [1920s] (*US*) head or body lice. ❑ **galloping horse** *n.* (*also* **gallup**) [play on SE *horse*/HORSE *n.* (7)] [1950s+] (*drugs*) heroin.

gallop one's antelope *v.* (*also* **gallop one's maggot, gallop the antelope, ...maggot**) [1930s+] to masturbate.

gallop the (old) lizard *v. see under* LIZARD *n.*

gallous *see* GALLOWS *adj.*

gallows *n. see* GALLOWS-BIRD *n.*

SE in slang uses

IN COMPOUNDS

❑ **gallows-apple** *n.* [the victim hangs from the TRIPLE TREE *n.*] [late 17C–early 19C] a candidate for the gallows. ❑ **gallows-bird** *n. see* separate entry. ❑ **gallows-blade** *n. see* GALLOWS-BIRD *n.* (2). ❑ **gallows-clappers** *n.* see separate entry. ❑ **gallows-trap** *n.* [TRAP *n.*[1] (3)] [early 19C] (*UK Und.*) a policeman.

IN PHRASES

❑ **make gallows-apples of** *v.* [the victim hangs from the TRIPLE TREE *n.*] [early–mid-19C] to hang someone.

gallows *adj.* (*also* **gallous, gallus**) [20C+ use is US; on pattern of BLOODY *adj.* (1), i.e. fig. use of violence as synon. for extremism; Scot. *gallows*, rascally, dissolute] **1** [mid-16C; late 18C+] a general intensive, very great, excellent, fine, absolute etc, often in criminal contexts; also used ironically. **2** [mid-19C+] lively, spirited.

gallows *adv.* (*also* **gallowsly, gallus**) [GALLOWS *adj.*] [late 18C–19C] extremely, very much, e.g. *gallows poor*, very poor.

gallows —! *excl.* [mid-19C] an excl. of annoyance, lit. go/send to the gallows.

gallows-bird *n.* (*also* **gallows, gallus**) [the image is of one destined to 'fly' to the gallows] **1** [late 16C–mid-19C] a thief or pickpocket or one who associates with them. **2** [late 18C–1930s] (*also* **gallows blade**) a general insult, i.e. one who is destined for the gallows. **3** [mid-19C] the corpse of one who has been hanged. **4** [1920s–40s] one who has been sentenced to be hanged.

gallows-clappers *n.* [mid-16C–mid-17C] a general insult, i.e. one who is destined for the gallows.

gallowsly *adv. see* GALLOWS *adv.*

gallup *n. see* GALLOPING HORSE *under* GALLOPING *adj.*

galluptious *adj. see* GOLOPSHUS *adj.*

gallus *see under* GALLOWS.

gallus *n.*[1]

IN PHRASES

❑ **do something at the slack of one's galluses** *v.* [SE *gallus*, braces; coined in the UK or play on SE *gallows*] [20C+] (*Ulster*) to do something with ease.

gallus *n.*[2] *see* GALLOWS-BIRD *n.*

gallus tree *n. see* TRIPLE TREE *n.*

gallyhoot *v.* (*also* **gallihoot**) [SE *gallivant* + US regional *scallyhoot*, to be off, to 'skedaddle'] [1940s+] (*US*) to go gallivanting; thus n. *gallihoot*, a spree.

gally-hosen *n. see* GALLIGASKINS *n.*

gallyslopes *n.* [SE *galligaskins*, wide breeches or hose] [late 19C] leggings, gaiters.

gally-west *adv. see* GALLEY-WEST *adv.*

galoot *n.* [? pfx *ga-* = KER- *pfx-* + Scot. *loot*, lout] **1** [19C–1910s] a soldier or a marine. **2** [19C+] (*orig. US*) (*also* **galloot, galoon, galoosh**) an awkward or uncouth person, often used affectionately.

IN PHRASES

❑ **on the gay galoot** [late 19C] on a spree, very cheerful.

galopshus/galoptious *adj. see* GOLOPSHUS *adj.*

galtee *v.* [ety. unknown] [late 19C] (*UK tramp*) to spend.

galter *n.* [? GALTEE *v.*] [mid-19C] (*UK Und.*) a racecourse swindler; a gambler.

galumptious *adj. see* GOLOPSHUS *adj.*

galvanized *adj.* [joc. mispron.] [late 19C–1910s] (*US*) in disguise.

galvo *n.* [SE *galv(anized)* + -O *sfx* (3)] [1970s+] (*Aus.*) galvanized iron.

Galway *n.* [the birthplace of many such priests] [late 19C–1930s] (*US*) a Catholic priest.

galway *n.* [such whiskers are popular in Co. Galway, Ireland] [1920s] (*US*) a style of facial whisker, grown on the upper part of the cheek only.

gam *n.*[1] (*also* **gamb**) [Fr. *jambe*, a leg or Ling. Fr. *gamba*, a leg] **1** [late 18C+] usu. in pl., a leg; esp. [20C+] (*US*) a female leg. **2** [2000s] (*Aus.*) a tampon, a sanitary towel [the position of the vagina at the top of the legs].

IN COMPOUNDS

❑ **gam case** *n.* [late 18C; 1940s+] (*later use mostly US black*) a stocking.

IN PHRASES

❑ **queer gams** *n.* [late 18C] bandy legs.

gam *n.*[2] [mid-19C] (*US Und.*) theft.

gam *n.*[3] (*also* **gamb**) [abbr.] [late 19C–1900s] (*US*) a gambler.

gam *n.*[4] (*also* **gamb**) [GAM *v.*[2] (1)] [20C+] an act of fellatio.

gam *v.*[1] [GAMMON *v.* (4)] **1** [early 19C–1900s] (*US*) to chat, to pay a social call. **2** [late 19C] (*US*) to steal. **3** [1920s+] (*US black*) to boast, to show off.

IN PHRASES

❑ **tip the gam** *v.* [early 19C] to talk (in a given manner).

gam *v.*[2] (*also* **gam around, gamb**) [abbr. GAMAHUCHE *v.*] **1** [mid-19C+] to fellate. **2** [1980s] (*US campus*) to kiss.

gamahuche *n.* [GAMAHUCHE *v.*] [late 19C] an act of cunnilingus.

gamahuche *v.* (*also* **gama, gamahoosh, gamahouch, gamaroosh, gamaruche**) [? Gk *gamos*, wedding; or ? Northumbrian dial. *rouched*, wrinkled, puckered] [mid-19C+] to perform oral sex; thus *gamhuching*, fellatio or cunnilingus.

gam around *v. see* GAM *v.*[2].

gamb *see also under* GAM.

Gamble and Proctor *n.* [rhy. sl.] [1990s+] a doctor.

gambler *n.* [Johnson, *Dictionary* (1755), cites it as 'a cant word, I suppose, for...gamester' and defines it as 'a knave whose practice it is to invite the unwary to game and cheat them'. The cheating inference had worn off by early 19C; even so, the modern professional gambler is assumed to depend on skill, albeit honest, rather than on luck] **1** [mid-18C] a confidence trickster who drops a supposedly valuable object, e.g. a ring, a wallet, and rather than claim it for himself, persuades a passer-by to buy it from him. **2** [mid-18C–19C] a cheating card- or dice-player.

SE in slang uses

IN COMPOUNDS

□ **gambler's roll** *n. see under* ROLL *n.*

gambolier *n.* [joc. blend of SE *gambol* + *gambler*] [mid-19C–1910s] (*US*) a gambler.

gamdiddle *v.* [GAMMON *v.* (4) + DIDDLE *v.*^{2} (2)] [late 19C] to cheat.

game *n.* **1** (*UK Und.*) in the context of sexuality. (**a**) [late 16C–early 19C] (*also* **daughters of the game**) a group of prostitutes, esp. in a brothel. (**b**) [late 16C–19C] sexual intercourse. (**c**) [mid-17C+] the world of prostitution; esp. in phr. ON THE GAME below. (**d**) [mid-18C] homosexual sexual behaviour. (**e**) [1980s] any variety of un-conventional sexual 'play', e.g. sado-masochism. **2** [mid-17C] (*UK Und.*) the proceeds of a robbery. **3** [mid-17C+] constr. with *the*, an occupation, differing as to the group concerned; thus for lovers [17C+] sexual intercourse; for sportsmen [late 17C–early 18C] cock-fighting; for criminals [early 19C] robbery; for sailors [mid-19C] slave-trading; and for prostitutes [mid-19C+] commercial sex. **4** [late 17C–19C] a fool, a simpleton, esp. a victim [he provides a 'game' for his tormentors]. **5** [18C–mid-19C] (*UK Und.*) the profession of robbery. **6** [18C+] (*later use US black*) any attempt to manipulate humanity for one's own ends, usu. financial ones. **7** [19C+] any form of negative activity, e.g. deception, fooling around. **8** [mid-19C–1910s] an amusing incident, a piece of fun, a 'lark'. **9** [mid-19C–1920s] spirit, 'pluck'. **10** [mid-19C+] (*orig. US*) a calling, business or interest; esp. in phr. *what's your game?* **11** [mid-19C+] (*US*) a situation, a state of affairs. **12** [1950s+] expert ability at a particular skill; knowledge, power or influence in a particular industry or environment. **13** [1960s] (*US*) money, possessions. **14** [1960s+] (*US black*) the sophisticated, streetwise person's lifestyle. **15** [1960s+] (*US black*) in spec. use of sense 14, drug-dealing. **16** [1960s+] (*US black*) in spec. use of sense 14 above, prostitution and/or pimping. **17** [2000s] (*US Und.*) benefits or gains that, while illegally obtained, are seen as worth the poor reputation such actions might engender; thus *have the game without the name*.

IN COMPOUNDS

□ **gameball** *adj. see* separate entry. □ **game face** *n.* [play on sporting *game face*, an agressive look adopted for sporting encounters] [1980s+] (*US black*) one's public face. □ **game room** *n.* [1960s+] in sado-masochistic sex, a torture chamber.

IN PHRASES

□ **against the game** [late 19C–1900s] (*US*) in difficulties. □ **come off one's game** *v.* [1970s] (*US black*) to abandon a pose, to act in a spontaneous, genuine manner. □ **daughters of the game** *n. see* sense 1a above. □ **get in someone's game** *v.* [1970s] (*US black*) to interfere in someone else's business. □ **get one's game together** *v.* [1960s+] (*orig. US black*) **1** to be in full control of a situation. **2** as a pimp, to define one's image by a variety of material/symbolic 'props'. □ **have one's game together** *v.* (*also* **have one's game uptight, have one's program together**) [1960s+] (*orig. US black*) to be in full control of a situation. □ **heavy game** *n.* (*also* **strong game**) [HEAVY *adj.* (5c)/SE *strong*] [1970s] (*US black*) a well conceived and executed plan of action. □ **in the game** *adj.* [1920s] (*Aus.*) wealthy. □ **kick game** *v.* [KICK *v.*^{5}] [1980s+] (*US black*) to use any means whereby one attempts to gain economic, psychological or other advantages over a rival or victim. □ **keep the game up** *v.* [late 19C] to continue enjoying oneself. □ **let one's game slip** *v.* [1960s+] (*US black*) to lose control of a situation or plan. □ **lift one's game** *v.* [1960s+] (*US black*) to improve one's situation financially, emotionally etc. □ **on the game** (*also* **on the business**) **1** [mid-19C–1920s] working as a thief. **2** [late 19C+] involved in prostitution. **3** [1970s+] (*US gay*) walking the streets looking for sex. □ **out of the game** *adj.* [2000s] incoherent, unconscious, collapsed (through drink or drugs). □ **peep game** [PEEP *v.*^{3}] [1990s+] a phr. meaning, listen up, I'm about to tell you a secret. □ **play games** *v.* [20C+] to manipulate, to manoeuvre, to act in a deceptive, dishonest manner; thus adj. *game-playing*. □ **play the whole game** *v.* [? one has to play to one's utmost – the whole extent of one's game – to ensure defeat; presumably the context is of a cheat aiming to ensnare a victim, for whom this will be their only success] [late 18C–early 19C] to play at cards or dice with the intention of losing. □ **put game on someone** *v.* [1970s+] (*US black*) to confuse, to play tricks on, to deceive. □ **put salt in someone's game** *v.* [1990s+] (*US black*) to interfere in another person's planned seduction. □ **put shit in the game** *v.* [SHIT *n.* (3a)] (*US black*) **1** [1960s] to take advantage. **2** [1960s+] to trick, to deceive. □ **put snow in one's game** *v.* [SNOW *n.*^{1} (1e)] [1960s+] (*US black*) to ensnare a white person for financial gain. □ **put the high game on** *v.* [18C] (*UK Und.*) to rob, to pick someone's pocket. □ **rank someone's game** *v. see under* RANK *v.*^{2}. □ **run (a) game on** *v.* [1960s+] (*US black*) to bamboozle, to deceive, to seduce, to confuse, to obtain money by trickery. □ **run down game** *v.* [RUN DOWN *v.* (3)] [1960s+] (*US black*) of a pimp, to explain the principles of the pimping business, both from experienced pimps to novices and from the pimp to his prostitutes, telling them the tricks of their trade. □ **talk game** *v.* (*also* **spit game**) [1970s+] (*orig. US black*) to talk, to chatter, but spec. of a pimp, to chatter about pimping, whoring and those involved; note earlier colloq. phr. *talk a good game*. □ **whip a game on** *v.* [1960s+] (*US black*) to hoax, to trick, to deceive, esp. when selling drugs. □ **whup the game** *v. see under* WHUP *v.*

IN EXCLAMATIONS

□ **game on!** *see* separate entry.

SE in slang uses

IN COMPOUNDS

□ **game-stock** *n.* [SE *game*, an object of ridicule, laughing-stock] [1940s+] (*W.I.*) a risible figure, a laughing-stock.

game *adj.*^{1} **1** [late 17C+] of women, promiscuous; thus adj. *gamey*. **2** [late 18C+] criminal or associated with the underworld; thus *game woman*, a prostitute; *game publican*, a publican who affects not to notice the breaking of the law. **3** [early 19C] of an animal, cantankerous. **4** [early 19C–1920s] of men, cunning, villainous. **5** [1990s+] (*US campus*) attractive, seductive.

IN COMPOUNDS

□ **game pullet** *n.* [SE *pullet*, a young chicken; the 'Game Chicken', however, was the nickname for the early 19C prize-fighter Henry 'Hen' Pearce] [18C] a young prostitute; a promiscuous young woman.

game *adj.*^{2} *see* GAMMY *adj.*^{2}.

game *v.* **1** [late 17C+] to jeer, to mock, to delude. **2** [early 19C] (*UK Und.*) to encourage or turn a blind eye to theft. **3** [1960s+] (*US black*) to manipulate humanity for one's own ends, usu. financial ones; to trick, to deceive.

IN PHRASES

□ **game on** *v. see* separate entry. □ **reverse game** *v.* [1970s] (*US black*) of a pimp, to manipulate the relationships of his whores to his best advantage.

game as... *adj.* [SE *game*, enthusiastic, keen, 'up for']

IN PHRASES

□ **...a badger** [1910s] (*US*) very enthusiastic, 'raring to go'. □ **...a meat-ant** (*also* **...an ant, ...bulldog ant, ...goats, ...hornets**) [*meat ant*, a large ant with a painful bite] [late 19C+] (*Aus.*) very brave. □ **...a pebble** (*also* **game as pebbles**) [mid-19C+] extremely courageous, 'raring to go'. □ **...a pissant** [*piss ant*, a large ant with a painful bite] [late 19C+] (*Aus.*) brave, courageous. □ **...Ned Kelly** [proper name *Ned Kelly* (1855–80), Australia's most celebrated bushranger, who ended his days on the gallows, remarking 'Such is life'] [1930s+] (*Aus.*) plucky, courageous, willing to go up against overwhelming odds.

gameball *adj.* [SE *gameball*, the final round in a game of handball] [1910s+] (*Irish*) excellent, first-rate; thus as an affirmative excl.

game of nap *n.* [rhy. sl.] [1960s+] **1** a cap. **2** excrement [= CRAP *n.*[1] (2)].

game on *v.* (*also* **game off**) [GAME *v.* (3)] [19C+] (*orig. US black*) to act deceitfully, to manipulate, to get an advantage over someone by underhand means.

game on! *excl.* [darts jargon *game on!* the game is about to start] [1980s+] **1** an excl. of excitement or anticipation, usu. about a possible sexual conquest, or when a night out or drinking session is arranged. **2** an excl. of triumph at having sorted out initial arrangements.

gamer *n.* [GAME *n.* (6)] **1** [1970s] a pimp, a confidence trickster, one who lives by their wits. **2** [1990s+] (*US campus*) one who is willing to take a challenge.

gamester *n.* [GAME *n.* + -STER *sfx*] **1** [17C–early 18C] a womanizer, a promiscuous male. **2** [17C–mid-19C] a prostitute; a promiscuous woman. **3** [late 17C] a mistress. **4** [early 18C] a pimp.

gamfral/gamfril/gamful *n. see* GAMPH *n.*

gaming *n.* [GAME *v.* (3)] [late 19C+] (*US black*) playing a confidence trick or otherwise manipulating another.

gammat *n.* [proper name *Muhammad*] [1950s+] (*S.Afr.*) **1** the stereotypical Cape Malay, esp. as the subject of jokes. **2** a Muslim boy.

IN COMPOUNDS

❑ **gammat-taal** *n.* (*also* **gamtaal**) [1950s+] (*S.Afr.*) a street-gang argot, a mix of English, Afrikaans and Xhosa.

gammocks *n.* [dial. *gammocking*, rough horseplay] [19C] unrestrained, noisy activities.

gammon *n.*[1] [early–late 18C] (*UK Und.*) **1** a pickpocket's accomplice who jostles the victim while the pickpocket actually performs the theft; a shoplifter's accomplice. **2** the cover provided by the accomplice.

IN PHRASES

❑ **give gammon** *v.* (*also* **keep in gammon**) [early 18C] (*UK Und.*) to stand next to a person while an accomplice picks their pocket.

gammon *n.*[2] [GAMMON *v.*] **1** [mid-18C–early 19C] the language or jargon of thieves, i.e. cant. **2** [late 18C+] nonsense, lies, humbug; thus *gammoner, gammoning*. **3** [19C] chatter. **4** [early–mid-19C] persuasive talk.

IN COMPOUNDS

❑ **gammon and patter** *n.* [PATTER *n.*] [late 18C–19C] **1** criminal cant. **2** any form of jargon or 'professional slang'. **3** verbose chatter. ❑ **gammon and pickles** *n.* (*also* **gammon and jalap, ...spinach**) [pun on SE; for *jalap see* ety. at JOLLOP *n.*] [early 19C+] nonsense, rubbish, humbug.

IN PHRASES

❑ **come the gammon** *v.* [19C] to wheedle. ❑ **pay out the slack of one's gammon** *v.* [late 19C] to recount too many anecdotes. ❑ **pitch gammon** *v.* [early 19C] to concoct a story, to 'tell the tale'. ❑ **tip the gammon** *v.* [mid-19C] to 'shoot a line', to attempt seduction. ❑ **up to gammon** *adj.* [early 19C] (*UK Und.*) aware, knowing, capable.

gammon *n.*[3] [SE *gammon*, ham, i.e. the haunch of a pig; note Urquhart, *The Complete Works of Rabelais* (1653): 'And therefore, that we lose no time, put on, thrust out your gammons'] [1990s+] the vagina.

gammon *v.* [? GAME *v.* (1) or SE (*back*)*gammon* or fig. tying up of a *gammon* or ham] **1** [late 17C–early 18C] to cheat (at a game). **2** [mid-18C] (*UK Und.*) to help. **3** [late 18C] to talk criminal slang. **4** [late 18C+] to deceive, to fool, to talk humbug, to pretend. **5** [19C] to persuade. **6** [mid-19C] to tease amicably.

IN PHRASES

❑ **gammon a maim** *v.* [early 19C] (*UK Und.*) of a beggar, to pose as ill. ❑ **gammon lushy** *v.* (*also* **gammon queer**) [LUSHY *adj.*[1] (1)/QUEER *adj.* (1)] [early 19C] to pretend to be drunk. ❑ **gammon the draper** *v.* [early 19C] 'When a man is without a shirt, and is buttoned up close to his neck, with merely a handkerchief round it, to make an appearance of cleanliness, it is termed, '*gammoning the draper*' (Egan, *Life in London*, 1821). ❑ **gammon the twelve (in prime twig)** *v.* [SE *twelve*, generic for the jury + IN FINE TWIG *under* TWIG *n.*[1]] [late 18C–early 19C] (*UK Und.*) to gain an acquittal in court; the implication is that the defendant has managed to fool the jurymen.

gammon! *excl.* [GAMMON *v.* (4)] [19C] nonsense! humbug! rubbish!

gammoner *n.* [GAMMON *v.* (4)] **1** [early 19C] one who covers for an accomplice. **2** [19C–1950s] one who 'spins a yarn' or tells deceitful tales; thus a *prime gammoner*, an expert at such tale-spinning.

gammy *n.*[1] [? GAMMON AND PATTER *under* GAMMON *n.*[2]] [late 18C] (*UK Und.*) cant or criminal language; thus *stoll the gammy*, to understand thieves' jargon.

gammy *n.*[2] [GAMMY *adj.*[2]] **1** [mid-19C+] a lame person. **2** [late 19C–1900s] (*Aus.*) a fool.

gammy *n.*[3] (*also* **gummer**) [SE *gammer*, i.e. grandmother] [20C+] (*US*) grandmother.

gammy *adj.*[1] [according to Mayhew, *London Labour and the London Poor* (1862), Welsh *gam*, crooked, queer] [mid–late 19C] (*UK Und.*) bad; usu. in combs. below.

IN COMPOUNDS

❑ **gammy lour** *n.* [mid–late 19C] (*UK Und.*) counterfeit coins. ❑ **gammy monicker** *n.* [mid–late 19C] (*UK Und.*) a forged signature. ❑ **gammy stuff** *n.* [mid–late 19C] (*UK Und.*) spurious soap or medicine.

gammy *adj.*[2] (*also* **game, gamy**) [GAM *n.*[1] (1) + sfx *-y* but ? ext. of GAMMY *adj.*[1]; note Share suggests Shelta *geamhchaoch*, bad; note dial. *gammy*, left-handed] **1** [mid-19C+] lame, crippled; usu. as *gammy leg*, a lame leg. **2** [late 19C] idle, lazy. **3** [1970s+] in fig. use, spoilt, useless, second-rate.

gam on *v.* [GAMMON *v.* (4)] [1940s+] (*Irish*) to pretend, to make out that.

gamot *n.* [ety. unknown] [1970s+] (*drugs*) morphine; heroin.

gamp *n.* [the fictional Sarah *Gamp*, created by Charles Dickens in *Martin Chuzzlewit* (1843–4)] **1** [mid–late 19C] an interfering busybody. **2** [mid-19C–1920s] a monthly nurse, a midwife. **3** [mid-19C–1920s] an umbrella.

gamph *n.* (*also* **gamfral, gamfril, gamful**) [Scot. *gamf*, a fool, an idiot] [20C+] a fool, a buffoon.

gamtaal *n. see* GAMMAT-TAAL *under* GAMMAT *n.*

gamy *adj. see* GAMMY *adj.*[2].

gan *n.* (*also* **ganns, gans**) [? Welsh *geneu*, Cornish *ganau*, mouth; Scot. *gane* or *ganne*, mouth, orig. of a fish; itself linked to Norw. *gan*, a fish-gill] [mid-16C–mid-19C] (*UK Und.*) the mouth; in pl., the lips; occas. the throat.

ganaglii *n.* [SE *gang*] [1940s+] (*W.I.*) a bully.

ganch *n.* (*also* **gaunch**) [Irish *gaimse*, a fool] [20C+] (*Ulster*) a fool, a boor.

gandanga *n.* [*gandanga*, a style of tuning, also known as *mvembe*, used in Zimbabwe's *mbira* music] [1990s+] (*S.Afr.*) a terrorist.

gander *n.*[1] [reverse anthropomorphism] **1** [late 18C–19C] a husband. **2** [mid–late 19C] (*US*) a man or husband who is away from home, a 'grass-widower'.

gander *n.*[2] [Fr. *gandin*, a fop] [early–mid-19C] a dandy, a fop.

gander *n.*[3] [GANDER *v.*[2]] [1910s+] a look, a survey.

IN PHRASES

❑ **take a gander at** *v.* (*also* **cop a gander at**) [1910s+] (*orig. US*) to look at, to glance at.

gander *v.*[1] [early 19C SE *ganderheel*, to wander aimlessly] [mid-19C–1950s] (*orig. Aus.*) to walk.

gander *v.*[2] [the bird's long neck] [20C+] to have a look at.

Gandhi's revenge *n.* [1980s] an upset stomach.

g. and t. *n.* [abbr.] [1970s+] a gin *and* tonic.

gandy dancer *n.* [railroad jargon *gandy dancer*, one who works in a railroad maintenance crew; ult. the *Gandy Mfg. Co.*, maker of railroad repair equipment. Such workers might spend their unemployed time tramping the country] (*US*) **1** [20C+] an Italian. **2** [1910s+] a petty crook, a tramp. **3** [1940s–60s] a jitterbug.

gandy stiff *n.* [GANDY DANCER *n.* (2) + STIFF *n.*[1] (4a)] [1910s] (*US tramp*) **1** a street beggar. **2** a tramp who occas. takes a short-term job.

ganef *n. see* GONNOF *n.*

ganeys *n.*

IN EXCLAMATIONS

❑ **by ganeys!** (*also* **by gannies!**) [JANEY MACK! *excl.*] [1940s–50s] a general excl.

gang *n.*[1] (*also* **ging**) **1** [late 16C+] (*orig. US*) any social group (with no criminal overtones). **2** [19C+] (*US*) a large amount of anything.

SE in slang uses

IN COMPOUNDS

❑ **gangbang/banger/banging** see separate entries. ❑ **gangbash** *see* GANG-SPLASH below. ❑ **gangbuster(s)** *see* separate entries. ❑ **gangfuck/fucker** *see* separate entries. ❑ **gang roll** *n.* [ROLL *v.* (1)] [late 19C] (*US*) a sexual orgy or gang rape. ❑ **gang-shack** *n. see* GANG-SHAG *n.* (1). ❑ **gang-shag** *see* separate entries. ❑ **gang-splash** *n.* (*also* **gang-bash**) [SE *splash*, i.e. of bodily fluids] **1** [1960s+] (*Aus./N.Z.*) a heterosexual orgy or multiple rape. **2** [1970s+] (*US gay/prison*) a homosexual rape or orgy.

gang *n.*[2] [GANG *v.* (3)] [1980s] (*US*) an act of usu. non-consensual intercourse, involving a number of men and a single woman.

gang *v.* (*US*) **1** [1910s+] to act or move as a group. **2** [1920s+] to attack or kill as part of a gang, to gang up on. **3** [1930s+] to engage in multiple, usu. non-consensual sexual intercourse with one woman as part of a gang.

ganga *n. see* GANJA *n.*

gangbang *n.* [SE *gang* + BANG *n.*[1] (2b)] **1** [1940s+] the multiple rape of (usu.) a woman, or in gay use, a man. **2** [1950s] (*US drugs*) a number of individuals taking drugs together, esp. a group marijuana smoking session. **3** [1950s+] (*US black*) a (gang) fight. **4** [1950s+] an orgy, irrespective of sexuality, in which there is no compulsion. **5** [1960s] (*Aus.*) a woman willing to take on multiple sexual partners in a single session. **6** [1970s+] (*US*) a confusing or chaotic situation.

gangbang *adj.*[1] (*also* **gangbanger**) [GANGBANG *v.* (1)] [1960s+] willing to indulge in multiple sex.

gangbang *adj.*[2] [GANGBANGER *n.*] [1990s+] (*orig. US black*) pertaining to the lifestyle of a teen gang member.

gangbang *v.* [GANGBANG *n.*] **1** [1940s+] to engage in (usu. coerced) multiple sexual intercourse with one woman (or gay man) as part of a gang. **2** [1970s+] of a woman, to offer sex to a group of men. **3** [1970s+] (*US*) to belong to a gang or to engage in a gang fight; to engage in general gang activities. **4** [1970s+] (*US*) to victimize or destroy. **5** [1990s+] to target as a group, in order to influence or persuade someone.

gangbanger *n.* [GANGBANG *v.* (3)] **1** [1970s+] (*US black*) a member of a teenage gang. **2** [1980s] (*US prison*) a member of an aggressive prison gang.

gangbanger *adj. see* GANGBANG *adj.*[1].

gang-banging *n.*[1] [GANGBANG *v.* (1)] [1960s+] (*orig. US*) gang rape.

gang-banging *n.*[2] [GANGBANG *v.* (3)] (*US black*) **1** [1970s] fighting, esp. in a group. **2** [1980s+] being and living the life of a member of a US youth gang, usu. in Los Angeles.

gangbang, thank you ma'am *phr. see* WHAM-BAM-THANK-YOU-MA'AM *phr.*

gangbuster *n.* [fig. use of SE *gangbuster*, one (usu. a police officer) who pursues and breaks up criminal gangs] [1930s+] (*US*) **1** an exciting and successful person, thing or event. **2** a thug, a hoodlum.

gangbusters *adj.* (*also* **gangbuster**) [GANGBUSTER *n.* (1)] [1990s+] (*US*) **1** rousing, inspiring, successful, impressive. **2** over-zealous.

gangbusters *adv.* [GANGBUSTER *n.* (1)] [1980s+] (*US*) in a successful manner, impressively; usu. as *do/go gangbusters*, to be very successful.

gange *n. see* GANJA *n.*

gangfuck *n.* [GANGFUCK *v.*] **1** [1940s+] the multiple rape of (usu.) a woman. **2** [1970s+] (*US gay*) a male homosexual orgy.

gangfuck *v.* [SE *gang* + FUCK *v.* (1)] [1910s+] to engage in the multiple rape of (usu.) a woman.

gang fucker *n.* [GANGFUCK *v.*] [1960s] one who joins in the multiple rape of a woman.

gangie *n.* (*also* **gangy**) [abbr. GANGBANG *n.*] [1980s+] (*Aus./N.Z.*) **1** a woman who participates in sex with multiple men. **2** the act of gang rape.

gangie *v.* [GANGIE *n.* (1)] [1980s] (*Aus.*) of a woman, to make oneself available for sex with a number of males in sequence.

gang-shag *n.* [GANG SHAG *v.*] [1920s+] **1** (*orig. US*) (*also* **gang shack**) sexual intercourse between a single woman and a group of men (either voluntary or as mass rape); also in gay use. **2** (*US black*) a riotous, noisy party.

gang shag *v.* [SE *gang* + SHAG *v.*[1] (1)] [1920s+] (*orig. US*) of a group of men, to have sexual intercourse (voluntary or otherwise) with a single woman.

gangsta *n.* (*also* **G-ster**) [SE *gangster*; the spelling is deliberately geared to emphasize the anti-establishment pose. The gangsta image, as propounded through rap music, offers an alluring mix of sex (often coerced), violence, drugs and illicitly gained money, but those same characteristics have made it a threatening force for conformists, whether black or white] [1980s+] (*US black*) **1** a rebellious, non-conformist individual, who refuses to accept establishment (white) authority. **2** a gangster, a criminal, esp. a member of organized crime or an urban gang.

IN COMPOUNDS

❑ **gangsta-ass** *n.* [-ASS *sfx*] [1990s+] (*US black*) pertaining to the street culture of a black urban *gangsta*. ❑ **gangsta bitch** *n.* [BITCH *n.*[1] (1)] [1990s+] (*US*) a woman who associates with a male gang and may participate in its activities. ❑ **gangsta class** *n.* [1980s+] (*US black*) the style affected by a young street thug and/or drug dealer. ❑ **gangsta juice** *n.* [JUICE *n.*[1] (3a)] [1980s+] (*US black gang*) Old English malt liquor; Night Train wine. ❑ **gangsta lean** *n. see* GANGSTER LEAN *n.* ❑ **gangsta limp** *n.* [1990s+] (*US black*) a style of walking, characterized by a slight dip in the stride, adopted by young urban black men. ❑ **gangsta roll** *n.* [ROLL *n.* (2)] [1980s+] (*US black*) a large wad of paper money.

gangsta *adj.* [GANGSTA *n.* (1)] [1980s+] (*US black*) used to describe the hedonist, violent lifestyle as epitomized in the lyrics of 'gangsta' rappers.

gangster *n.* [? its rebel image, but note GANJA *n.* (1)] **1** [1960s+] (*US black*) marijuana. **2** [1970s] (*US black*) a cigarette. **3** [1980s+] (*US black*) a troublemaker; an aggressive, abusive person. **4** [1980s+] (*US black*) a rebellious, non-conformist individual. **5** [2000s] (*US prison*) HIV/AIDS.

gangster *adj.* [GANGSTER *n.* (4)] **1** [1980s+] (*US black*) pertaining to a rebellious, non-conformist lifestyle. **2** [1990s+] (*orig. US*) in pl., the female breasts [? link to *GANGSTER FRONT* below, which, with its wide lapels, emphasized the chest area].

IN COMPOUNDS

❑ **gangster doors** *n.* [the style of car preferred by prominent ghetto criminals] [1970s+] (*US black*) a four-door saloon. ❑ **gangster front** *n.* [FRONT *n.*[1] (5); the style of suit worn by the (movie) gangsters of the 1920s–30s and adopted by latter-day ghetto criminals] [1980s+] (*US black*) a double-breasted suit. ❑ **gangster lean** *see* separate entries. ❑ **gangster pills** *n.* [? they slow down the gangster's natural energy] [1960s] (*US black*) barbiturates. ❑ **gangster ride** *n.* [RIDE *n.* (2a)] [1970s+] (*US black*) an old-fashioned, large, poss. black car (cf. *G-RIDE under* G *adj.*[2]). ❑ **gangster stick** *n.* [STICK *n.* (6d)] [1950s+] (*US black*) a marijuana cigarette. ❑ **gangster walls** *n.* [SE (*white*)-*walls*; i.e. the style of wheel preferred by successful ghetto villains] [1970s+] (*US black*) white-walled tyres.

gangster *v.* [GANGSTER *n.* (3)] [1970s+] (*US Und.*) to take by force.

gangster lean *n.* (*also* **gangsta lean**) [GANGSTER *adj.* (1) + SE *lean*] [1970s+] (*US black*) the supposedly sophisticated style of driving a car, with one's elbow out of the window and the body leaning in the same direction; thus, fig., an attitude to life and a lifestyle.

gangster lean *v.* [GANGSTER LEAN *n.*] [1970s+] (*US black*) to adopt the driving posture known as the GANGSTER LEAN *n.*

gangy *n.* [GANGIE *v.*] [1990s+] (*Aus.*) **1** a friend. **2** a fellow gang member. **3** *see* GANGIE *n.*

ganja *n.* (*also* **ganga, gange, ganj, ghanja, gunga, gunja**) [Hind. *ganja*, the hemp plant] [1920s+] marijuana, spec. that grown in Jamaica; thus *ganja man*, a marijuana dealer.

IN COMPOUNDS

❑ **ganja stick** *n.* [SE *stick*] [1950s] (*W.I.*) a device for smoking marijuana.

IN PHRASES

❑ **black ganja** *n.* [1970s+] (*drugs*) dark-coloured marijuana.

gank *n.* (*also* **ganker**) [GANK *v.*] [1980s+] (*drugs*) fake crack cocaine.

gank *v.* (*also* **jank**) [? SKANK *v.*] **1** [1980s+] to trick, to tease. **2** [1990s+] (*also* **gee**) to rob, to steal. **3** [1990s+] (*US black teen*) to shoot someone. **4** [2000s] in weak form of sense 2 above, to obtain, to get.

IN PHRASES

❑ **on the gank** [1990s+] (*US black*) looking for a violent confrontation.

ganky *n.* [ety. unknown] [2000s] (*Irish*) an unattractive woman.

gannet *n.* [SE *gannet*] [1920s+] (*orig. naut.*) a glutton, a heavy eater; a greedy person (for items other than food).

ganns *n. see* GAN *n.*

ganov *n. see* GONNOF *n.*

gans *n. see* GAN *n.*

ganting *n.* [SE *gant*, yawn or gape, thus a mouth hanging open] [20C+] (*Scot.*) begging (for).

gaol *see also under* JAIL and its combs.

gaolbird *n.* (*also* **gaol rat, jailbird, prison-bird**) [SE f. 1800; SE *gaol/jail* + BIRD *n.*[1] (1)] [17C–18C] a prisoner, a former prison inmate; also attrib.

gaoler's coach *n.* [SE *hurdle* was a kind of frame or sledge on which traitors used to be drawn through the streets to execution; this remained part of the legal punishment for high treason until 1870] [late 17C–19C] a hurdle.

g.a.p. *n.* [abbr.] [1960s+] (*US*) the Great American Public.

gap *n.*[1] **1** [17C+] the vagina. **2** [20C+] the mouth.

IN COMPOUNDS

❑ **gap-stopper** *n.* **1** [18C] a pimp or whoremaster. **2** [19C] the penis.

IN EXCLAMATIONS

❑ **stop your gap!** [late 19C+] shut up! be quiet!

gap *n.*[2] [GAP *v.* (1)] [1900s–40s] (*US*) a look, a glance.

gap *v.* [SE *gape*] **1** [late 19C–1950s] (*US*) to stand and stare, esp. at a crime and not take part. **2** [1930s] (*US drugs*) to exhibit the yawning that is a symptom of the onset of withdrawal from narcotics.

gape for gudgeons *v. see under* GUDGEON *n.*

gaper *n.* [SE *gaper*, one that gapes; one that stares or gazes in wonder or curiosity] **1** [1930s+] (*US gambling*) a small mirror or similar used for cheating in card games. **2** [1940s] (*US black*) a mirror, a looking-glass.

Gaperies, the *n.* [elision of the cliché *gay Paris* + sfx *-eries*; plus an image of the gaping British visitor] [1900s] Paris.

gapeseed *n.* [SE *gape* + *seed*. The term is usu. derog.; such 'excitements' are presumed to appeal to the gullible or unsophisticated] **1** [late 16C–mid-19C] anything considered worthy of pause, an exciting event; esp. in phr. *seek, buy* or *sow gapeseed*, to gaze in wonder when one should be getting on with work, business etc. **2** [mid-18C–mid-19C] one who stares (with open mouth).

IN PHRASES

❑ **look for gapseed** *v.* [19C] to be inattentive, to let one's mind wander.

gapia-mouth *n.* [SE *gape* + *mouth*, but note Du. *gapen*, one who yawns from hunger] [20C+] (*W.I., US V.I.*) one whose mouth hangs open or gapes.

gaping *n.* [GAP *v.* (2); the yawning that is typical of an addict suffering from withdrawal] [1950s–60s] (*drugs*) a desire for narcotics.

gapper *n.*[1] [SE *gape*/GAP *v.* (1)] **1** [1910s–50s] (*US Und.*) a foolish bystander; esp. one who witnesses a crime but is not taking part. **2** [1930s+] (*US prison*) a mirror used as a periscope to watch a prison guard; thus the lookout who uses one.

gapper *n.*[2] [GAP *v.* (2); the immediate effect of such a drug is to make one sleepy, thus one's mouth 'gapes' open; yawning is also a symptom of withdrawal] **1** [1930s–50s] a narcotics user in the first stages of withdrawal. **2** [1950s–70s] (*US black*) a narcotic drug, usu. heroin.

gapper *n.*[3] [GAP *n.*[1]] **1** [1960s+] (*US*) a view of a fully exposed vulva. **2** [1980s+] (*US*) the mouth.

gappings *n.* [? phr. 'fill the gap'] [1930s–40s] (*US black*) pay, wages, salary.

gar *n.*[1] [late 16C–1900s] a euph. for *God*.

gar *n.*[2] [ety. unknown] [early 18C] (*UK Und.*) a lip.

gar *n.*[3] [abbr. 'neegar', i.e. NIGGER *n.*[1] (1)] [1960s+] (*US*) a derog. term for a black person.

garage *n.* **1** [1910s] (*US*) a restaurant. **2** [1960s] the vagina.

IN PHRASES

❑ **garage door is open** [1970s+] (*US*) a phr. used to warn a man that his fly is open.

garb *n.* (*also* **garby**) [GOB *n.*[2] (4b)] [1910s] (*US*) a sailor.

garbage *n.* [fig. uses of SE; note orig. 15C–19C SE *garbage*, 'the offal of an animal used for food; esp. the entrails. Rarely, the entrails of a man' (*OED*)] **1** [late 16C–early 17C] (*UK Und.*) stolen goods, esp. parcels or packages. **2** [late 19C+] nonsense, often as used in criticism, e.g. of a record. **3** [20C+] bad food. **4** [1940s–50s] cabbage. **5** [1960s+] (*drugs*) poor-quality or heavily adulterated drugs; orig. heroin, but since ext. to cover all drugs. **6** [1970s+] trivia, anything unimportant. **7** [1980s] (*drugs*) drugs that have the potential for adverse effects.

IN COMPOUNDS

❑ **garbage head** *n.* [-HEAD *sfx* (4)] (*drugs*) **1** [1960s+] (*also* **garbage freak**) a user who will consume anything on offer, irrespective of quality, purity etc. **2** [1980s+] users who buy crack cocaine from street dealers instead of cooking it themselves.

SE in slang uses

IN COMPOUNDS

❑ **garbage can** *n.* [1920s–70s] (*US*) a disgusting person, esp. an old prostitute. ❑ **garbage guts** *n.* [1970s+] (*N.Z.*) a greedy eater. ❑ **garbage hound** *n.* [-HOUND *sfx* (1)] [1960s] (*US prison*) a voracious eater who enjoys even prison food. ❑ **garbage mouth** *n.* [1970s+] a regular, even obsessive user of obscenity or profanity; thus v., to abuse; also attrib. ❑ **garbage wagon** *n.* [1950s+] a motorcycle that still retains its basic style and specifications, before being adapted for use by an outlaw motorcycle gang. ❑ **garbage worker** *n.* [1960s] (*US carnival*) one who sells vegetable cutters.

garbar *n.* [Hind. *garbar*, disorder, chaos] [20C+] (*W.I./ Guyn./ Trin.*) nonsense, confusion; thus *make garbar*, to make trouble; *play garbar*, to play the fool.

garbo *n.* [SE *garbage* + -O *sfx* (3)] [1950s+] (*Aus.*) a garbage man, a dustbin man.

garbonzas *n.* [var. on GAZONGAS *n.*] [1980s+] (*US*) the breasts.

garbonzo *n.* [? GONZO *n.*] [1980s+] (*US*) a crazy idiot.

garboon *n.* [ety. unknown; ? made-up Viz word] [1990s+] one who sniffs bicycle seats for sexual excitement.

garbroth *n.* [lit. broth made from the *garfish*, generally seen as the food of the very poorest and as such not properly fit for human consumption] [mid-19C+] (*US*) any poor or worthless person; often in phrs. *mean as garbroth, poor as garbroth*.

garby *n. see* GARB *n.*

Garden, the *n.* [abbr.] **1** [mid-17C–1930s] Covent *Garden* market, London; initially as an area frequented by prostitutes. **2** [mid-18C–19C] Covent *Garden* Theatre, London. **3** [late 19C–1950s] Hatton *Garden*, London. **4** [1930s+] Madison Square *Garden*, New York City.

IN COMPOUNDS

❑ **Garden goddess** *n.* (*also* **Garden whore**) [early 19C] a Covent *Garden* prostitute. ❑ **Garden gout** *n.* [+ ? link to GARDEN *n.* (1)] [early 19C] venereal disease, whether syphilis or gonorrhoea.

garden *n.* **1** [mid-18C+] the vagina. **2** [19C+] pubic hair.

IN COMPOUNDS

❑ **garden engine** *n.* [ENGINE *n.* (1) / play on SE *garden engine*, 'a portable force-pump used for watering gardens' (*OED*)] [19C] the penis. ❑ **garden gate** *n. see* separate entry. ❑ **garden house** *n. see* separate entries.

IN PHRASES

❑ **drag it through the garden** *v. see under* DRAG *v.*[1]. ❑ **garden of Eden** *n.* (*also* **garden of Venus**) [play on SE] [16C–17C; 20C+] the vagina. ❑ **garden of pleasure** *n.* (*also* **garden of delight**) [play on SE] [mid-17C] the vagina.

SE in slang uses

IN COMPOUNDS

❑ **garden rake** *n.* [late 19C] a comb. ❑ **garden stuff** *n.* [late 19C] (*UK Und.*) information, i.e. against one's confederates. ❑ **garden tool** *n.* [pun on HO *n.* (1)/SE *hoe*] [1990s+] (*US campus*) a sexually promiscuous woman, a 'whore'. ❑ **garden violet** *n. see* VIOLET *n.*

gardener *n.*[1] [which 'works' in the GARDEN *n.* (1)] [mid-19C] the penis.

gardener *n.*[2] [the relative status of their employment, the implication being that this coachman would make a better gardener] [mid-19C] an insult hurled at a second-rate, incompetent coachman.

garden gate *n.* [rhy. sl.] **1** [mid-19C+] a magistrate. **2** [1940s+] (*bingo*) the number eight. **3** [1960s+] £8. **4** [1960s+] a friend [= MATE *n.* (1)].

garden gates *n.* [rhy. sl.] [20C+] rates, taxes.

garden gnome *n.* [rhy. sl.] [1990s+] a comb.

garden hop *v.* [rhy. sl. = SHOP *v.*[1] (2)] [1930s+] (*UK Und.*) to inform against, to betray.

garden hose *n.* (*also* **fireman's hose**) [rhy. sl.] [2000s] the nose.

garden house *n.*[1] [? GARDEN *n.* (1) or abbr. SE *Covent Garden* + HOUSE *n.*[1] (1)] **1** [17C–19C] the house where one's mistress was kept, or which either sex kept for secret assignations. **2** [19C] a brothel.

garden house *n.*[2] [20C+] (*US*) an outside lavatory, a privy.

gardenia *n.* [1960s] (*US short order*) an onion.

garden plant *n.* [rhy. sl.] [20C+] an aunt.

gargle *n.* [orig. medical student use] **1** [mid-19C+] a drink, a measure of alcohol. **2** [late 19C+] alcoholic drink in general.

IN COMPOUNDS

❑ **gargle factory** *n.* (*also* **gargle house**) [late 19C+] a public house or bar. ❑ **gargle trap** *n.* [1940s] the throat.

IN PHRASES

❑ **on the gargle** *adj.* [1940s+] drinking.

gargle *v.* [GARGLE *n.* (1)] [late 19C+] to have a drink.

gargled *adj.* [GARGLE v.] [20C+] drunk; thus *sob-gargled*, maudlin drunk.

gargler *n.* [SE *gargle*] [late 19C] the throat.

gargoyle *n.*

IN PHRASES

❑ **up the gargoyle** *see* UP THE SPOUT *under* SPOUT *n.*[2].

Garibaldi biscuit *v.* [rhy. sl.] [20C+] to risk it.

gark *n.* [? the word equates to the roughness of a scratch] [2000s] (*N.Z.*) a nick or scratch, e.g. in wood.

garlic-eater *n.* (*also* **garlic, garlic destroyer, ...mouth**) [mid-19C–1940s] (*US*) a derog. term for a French, Spanish, Portuguese or Italian person; thus *garlic-eating*, foreign (in a derog. context).

garlic-snapper *n.* [1940s] (*US*) an Italian.

garm *n.* [abbr. SE *garment*] [1990s+] (*UK black*) usu. in pl., clothes, clothing.

IN PHRASES

❑ **garm up** *v.* [1990s+] (*UK W.I.*) to dress oneself up.

garment-peg *n. see* CLOTHES-PEG *n.*[1].

garmouth *v.* [SE *gar*, a fish that is generally considered not worth eating other than in the direst extremity] [20C+] (*US*) to boast, to brag, to make empty threats.

garn! *excl. see* GO ON! *excl.*

garnish *n.* [SE *garnish*, to embellish, to add on] [late 16C–mid-19C] **1** money extorted from a new prisoner, either as a gaoler's fee or as drink-money for the other prisoners [the practice was abolished in 1824, after which time the term was restricted to SE]. **2** fetters [although both Johnson, *Dictionary* (1755) and F&H both cite this meaning, it may have stemmed from a mis-reading of sense 1 above].

garnish *v.* [GARNISH *n.* (2)] [mid-18C–19C] to fit a prisoner with fetters.

garp *n.* [1960s–70s] (*US campus*) nonsense.

garret *n.* **1** [late 18C–1930s] the head (cf. *UPPER STOREY under* UPPER *adj.*). **2** [early 19C–1930s] (*UK Und.*) the fob pocket. **3** [late 19C] the mouth. **4** [late 19C+] a woman's handbag.

IN PHRASES

❑ **abroad in the garret** *adj.* [early 19C] dazed. ❑ **have a rat in the garret** *v.* [2000s] (*N.Z.*) to act eccentrically. ❑ **shut up one's garret** *v.* [late 19C] to be quiet, to stop talking.

garreter *n.* (*also* **garreteer**) [SE *garret* + sfx *-er*, doer, agent] [mid–late 19C] (*UK Und.*) a thief who crawls over house-tops and breaks in through garret windows.

garreting *n.* [SE *garret*/GARRET *n.* (1)] **1** [early 19C] in card games, securing the good cards behind the head or in one's hat. **2** [mid-19C] (*UK Und.*) robbing a house by entering through an upper or garret window.

garrison hack *n.* [ironic use of SE *garrison hack*, a regular attender at military balls. Such a woman, like the horse, can be 'ridden' by anyone] [late 19C] a prostitute.

garrot *n.* [ety. unknown] [1960s+] (*W.I., UKVI*) one who is not a native of the Virgin islands, an outsider.

garrotty *adj.* [? SE *garrotte*] [1980s+] crazy, insane.

garter *n.* [SE *garter*, which stretches] [1930s+] (*US prison*) an indeterminate prison sentence.

Gary Glitter *n.* [rhy. sl.; ult. pop singer *Gary Glitter*, real name Paul Gadd (b.1940)] **1** [1980s+] (a pint of) bitter. **2** [1990s+] the anus [= SHITTER *n.*[1] (1)].

gas *n.*[1] [fig. uses of SE *gas*] **1** pertaining to verbosity. (**a**) [late 18C+] (*also* **gas works**) idle or boastful talk, bombast, humbug. (**b**) [1970s] one who is verbose, affectedly talkative. **2** [1910s+] (*US*) energy; thus *out of gas*, tired out. **3** [1910s+] (*orig. Irish*) as a positive descriptor. (**a**) a very enjoyable, pleasant situation or experience. (**b**) someone who is very pleasing, exciting, impressive. **4** [1920s–60s] (*US tramp*) any form of very strong, if poss. poisonous, drink.

IN COMPOUNDS

❑ **gasbag** *see* separate entries. ❑ **gas-hound** *n.* [-HOUND *sfx*] [1920s–40s] (*US tramp*) a drinker of wood alcohol, ether, and similar intoxicating, if poss. poisonous, stimulants. ❑ **gasman** *n. see* GASBAG *n.* ❑ **gaspipe** *n. see* separate entry. ❑ **gas works** *n. see* sense 1a above.

IN PHRASES

❑ **all (is) gas and gaiters** [image of a pompous, sermonizing (and be-gaitered) bishop] **1** [mid-19C+] satisfactory, as desired. **2** [1920s+] nonsense, rubbish, pomposity, bombast. ❑ **it's a gas** [1960s+] (*US/UK teen*) a phr. indicating that everything is fine, 'it's all wonderful'. ❑ **out of gas** *adj.* [1940s] (*US*) unsuccessful, past one's prime.

SE in slang uses

pertaining to SAmE *gas*, gasoline, i.e. petrol

IN COMPOUNDS

❑ **gas buggy** *n. see* BUGGY *n.*[2] (1). ❑ **gas-guzzler** *n.* (*also* **guzzler**) [colloq. *guzzler*, a heavy drinker/eater] [1970s+] the trad. enormous US automobile, profligate of petrol and dwarfing its European rivals; symbolic of the 1950s, out of favour in the energy-conscious 1970s, it staged a renaissance in the 1990s; 2000s saw the term applied to the controversial SUVs. ❑ **gas jockey** *n.* [JOCKEY *n.*[2] (3b)] [1950s+] (*US*) a gas/petrol station attendant. ❑ **gas queen** *n.* [-QUEEN *sfx* (3)] [1980s] (*US gay*) a man who picks up male prostitutes from his car. ❑ **gas wagon** *n.* **1** [1900s–30s] (*US*) a car. **2** [1930s] in fig. use, a band-wagon, i.e. the prevailing trend.

IN PHRASES

❑ **give (it) the gas** *v.* (*also* **give her the gass**) [1920s+] (*US*) to move fast, to accelerate. ❑ **punch the gas** *v.* [1970s+] (*US*) to accelerate an automobile; to drive fast. ❑ **take the gas pipe** *v.* (*also* **have a gas supper**) [1940s+] (*US*) to commit suicide by inhaling gas.

general uses

IN COMPOUNDS

❑ **gasface** *n.* [? the image is of a user of laughing gas; coined by the hip-hop group *3rd Bass*] [1980s+] (*US teen*) a contorted face, either with pleasure or disgust. ❑ **gas-house mick** *n. see* separate entry. ❑ **gaslighter** *n.* [early 19C] (*UK Und.*) a stunning blow. ❑ **gas-meter bandit** *n.* [the biggest 'job' he attempts is robbing the gas-meter] [1970s] a petty thief. ❑ **gaspipe** *n. see* separate entry.

IN PHRASES

❑ **give gas** *v.* **1** [mid–late 19C] to beat. **2** [mid-19C+] (*US*) to scold, to verbally abuse or ridicule. ❑ **put the gas on** *v.* [1900s] (*Aus.*) **1** to test out a person or a statement. **2** to put a stop to. **3** to exert pressure on a person for a loan, a favour, sexual compliance etc. ❑ **take gas** *v.* **1** [1950s+] (*US*) to be scolded and abused. **2** [1960s] (*US campus*) to do badly. **3** [1960s+] to kill oneself, by any method. ❑ **take the gas** *v.* [the *gas* that knocks one out at the dentist's] [20C+] to endure punishment, esp. in a boxing ring.

gas *n.*[2] [GAS *v.*[2]] [1940s+] (*US black*) hair that has been artificially straightened or 'processed'.

IN COMPOUNDS

❑ **gashead** *n.* [1960s+] (*US black*) **1** one who has had their hair straightened with a 'process' haircut. **2** in fig. use, a black person who rejects their racial origins.

gas *adj.* [GAS *n.*[1] (3)] **1** [1930s+] of objects or people, enjoyable, exciting, funny. **2** [1960s+] impressive, extraordinary. **3** *see* GASSY *adj.*[1] (2).

gas *v.*[1] [GAS *n.*[1] (1)] **1** [mid-19C+] (*also* **gas off**) to chatter, to talk inconsequentially and continually, to offer only 'hot air'. **2** [mid–late 19C; 2000s] (*US campus*) to deceive. **3** [late 19C–1910s] to boast. **4** [1940s] (*US black*) to tell, to inform.

IN PHRASES

❑ **gas it** *v.* [1960s] (*US campus*) to do badly on an examination. ❑ **gas one's head off** *v. see* TALK ONE'S HEAD OFF *under* TALK *v.* ❑ **gas off** *v. see* sense 1 above. ❑ **gas round** *v.* [late 19C–1910s] to ferret out information in a clandestine manner.

gas *v.*[2] [one's hair is 'cooked'] [1940s+] (*US black*) to straighten one's hair.

gas *v.*[3] [GAS *n.*[1] (3)] [1940s+] **1** to enjoy, to have a good time. **2** to impress or please enormously. **3** to excite or thrill.

gas *v.*[4] [1970s+] (*US drugs*) **1** to sniff gasoline fumes. **2** to commit suicide by inhaling car exhaust fumes.

SE in slang uses

IN PHRASES

❑ **gas up someone's head** *v.* (*also* **gas someone's head up**) [fig. use of SAmE *gas up*, to fill up with petrol] [1990s+] **1** (*US*) to destroy someone, usu. emotionally but occas. physically. **2** to pressurize.

gas! *excl.* [GAS *n.*[1] (1)] [mid-19C] rubbish! nonsense!

gasbag *n.* (*also* **gasman**) [GAS *n.*[1] (1)] [mid-19C+] a talkative person.

gasbag *v.* [GASBAG *n.*] [1950s+] to talk excessively.

gaseous *adj.* **1** *see* GASSY *adj.*[1] (1). **2** *see* GASSY *adj.*[2].

gash *n.*[1] [as simple anatomy in the 18C, e.g. Burns c.1786: 'The lasses they hae wimble-bores [i.e. small holes] / The widows they hae gashes'; but 20C+ use is derog. thus poss. augmented by GASH *adj.*] **1** [late 18C+] the vagina. **2** [mid-19C–1960s] (*US*) the mouth. **3** [1910s+] any girl or woman, incl. a prostitute. **4** [1930s+] sexual gratification. **5** [1950s+] (*US*) an effeminate, passive homosexual. **6** [1970s+] (*US gay*) the anus, in the context of sodomy.

IN COMPOUNDS

❑ **gash-eater** *n.* [SE *eater* but note EAT *v.* (4)] [1940s+] one who performs cunnilingus. ❑ **gash-grinder** *n.* [GRIND *v.* (1a)] [1990s+] (*US*) a promiscuous woman; thus a general derog. term for a woman. ❑ **gash-hound** *n.* (*also* **gashman**) [-HOUND *sfx*] **1** [1910s–60s] (*US*) a womanizer. **2** [1950s+] (*US prison*) an older homosexual man with a taste for young men or boys. ❑ **gash-mag** *n.* [1990s+] a pornographic magazine.

IN PHRASES

❑ **flash one's gash** *v.* [1990s+] (*Aus.*) of a woman, to expose her vagina as an incitement/invitation to intercourse. ❑ **grease the gash** *v.* [20C+] of a woman, to masturbate. ❑ **peddle the gash** *v. see* PEDDLE ONE'S ASS *under* PEDDLE *v.* ❑ **rubber gash** *n.* [1980s+] **1** a fake 'vagina' sold as a masturbation aid. **2** (*also* **rubber cunt**) a term of abuse.

gash *n.*[2] [? var. on SE *cut a dash*]

IN PHRASES

❑ **cut (some) gash** *v.* [1910s] to show off.

gash *n.*[3] [printers' jargon *gash*, waste matter] [1940s–50s] (*Aus.*) a second helping.

gash *n.*[4] [ety. unknown] [1980s+] (*drugs*) marijuana.

gash *adj.* [? dial. *gaishen*, a skeleton, something or someone ridiculous, an obstacle] [1940s+] extra, superfluous, spare.

gash *v.* [GASH *n.*[1]] **1** [1940s+] (*US*) to have sexual intercourse. **2** [1990s+] to suffer from any form of sexually transmitted disease.

gas-house mick *n.* [they live near the original gas-houses that lined New York's East River between 14th Street and 22nd Street. The first gas-house appeared in 1842 and its peers followed over the next 50 years; the orig. Gas-house district covered 3rd Avenue to the river and 14th Street to 27th Street. The smell of leaking gas and the poor neighbourhood housing meant that few lived there by choice, but among those who did were the feared thugs of the Gas-house gangs] [1920s–30s] (*US*) a poor or lower-class Irish person.

gasket *n.* **1** [1940s] (*US*) a doughnut or flapjack [resemblance]. **2** [1960s–70s] (*US drugs*) anything used to seal a hypodermic needle to a syringe.

SE in slang uses

IN PHRASES

❑ **blow a gasket** *v.* (*also* **bust a gasket, ...one's gasket, blow one's gauge**) **1** [1940s+] to explode with rage, to go crazy; to collapse. **2** [2000s] to lose, to fail.

gasolene bronc *n. see* BENZINE BUGGY *n.*

gasoline *n.* [1900s–20s] alcohol, esp. Jack Daniel's whisky.

IN COMPOUNDS

❑ **gasoline buggy/cart/go-cart** *n. see* BENZINE BUGGY *n.*

gasp *n.* [? the effect on one's throat] [late 19C] a drink, a shot of liquor.

gasp *v.* [GASP *n.*] [late 19C] to drink a dram of spirits.

gasper *n.* (*also* **gasp**) **1** [1910s+] a cigarette, esp. a cheap brand (orig. Virginia rather than the more exotic Turkish tobacco); also a cigar. **2** [1980s+] (*drugs*) a marijuana cigarette.

gas pipe *n.*[1] [GAS *n.*[1] (1) + SE *pipe*] [mid-19C–1910s] (*US*) a talkative person.

gas pipe *n.*[2] [visual resemblance to SE] **1** [late 19C] a shotgun. **2** [late 19C] in pl., tight trousers. **3** [1930s–40s] (*US*) a slide-trombone.

gassed *adj.*[1] (*also* **gassed up**) [fig. use of SAmE *gas*, petrol] [1910s+] drunk or drugged; thus *half-gassed*, tipsy.

gassed *adj.*[2] [GAS *v.*[2]] [1940s+] (*US black*) used of hair that has been chemically straightened.

gassed *adj.*[3] [GAS *v.*[3]] [1950s–60s] (*US*) delighted.

gassed-out *adj.* [one has run out of GAS *n.*[1] (2)] [1960s] (*US*) worn out.

gassed up *adj.* **1** [1990s+] (*US black*) enraged. **2** see GASSED *adj.*[1].

gasser *n.*[1] [GAS *v.*[1] (1)] [mid-19C–1950s] a loudmouth, a chatterer.

gasser *n.*[2] [GAS *n.*[1] (3)] **1** [1940s+] anything considered very enjoyable, superlative, first-rate. **2** [1950s–60s] a man or woman highly admired, considered to be the best. **3** [1960s] a friend.

gassing *n.* [the image of throwing petrol, US *gas*, over a victim] [2000s] (*US prison*) throwing a liquid substance on an officer from a cell.

gassy *n.* [GASSY *adj.*[1] (2)] [1930s–50s] (*US prison*) a chatterer.

gassy *adj.*[1] [fig. uses of SE + GAS *v.*[1] (1)] **1** [mid–late 19C] (*also* **gaseous**) irascible, likely to 'flare up' without warning. **2** [mid-19C+] (*also* **gas**) talkative, verbose, boastful; also as a nickname.

gassy *adj.*[2] (*also* **gaseous**) [GAS *n.*[1] (3) + sfx *-y*] [1960s–70s] (*US*) superlative, fantastic.

gasumph *v.* see GAZUMP *v.*

gat *n.*[1] (*also* **gatt**) [*Gatling* gun; note British Army use *gatt*, a rifle during 2003 Iraq War] **1** [late 19C+] (*orig. US*) a pistol or revolver. **2** [1920s] (*US*) a gunman. **3** [2000s] (*US prison*) a prison-made knife.

IN PHRASES

❑ **gat up** *v.* [1920s–30s] (*US Und.*) **1** to hold someone up with a gun. **2** to arm oneself.

gat *n.*[2] [Afk. *gat*, hole, vent] [1940s+] (*S.Afr.*) the buttocks, the anus; esp. as an excl.

IN COMPOUNDS

❑ **gat-creeper** *n.* [1980s+] (*S.Afr.*) a sycophant, a toady.

gat *v.* [GAT *n.*[1]] [1930s] to shoot; thus *gatting*, shooting, a shoot-out.

gata *n.* [Sotho sl. *legata*, a member of the police force, lit. 'catch a thief' or GAT *n.*[1], f. their guns] [1970s+] (*S.Afr.*) **1** the police. **2** a prison warder.

Gate, the *n.* [abbr.] **1** [early 18C–19C] Newgate prison. **2** [mid-19C–1940s] Billingsgate. **3** [1950s+] Notting Hill Gate, London W11.

gate *n.* [note Shakespearian use of *gate*, the vulva] **1** [1910s+] (*orig. Aus./N.Z. milit.*) the mouth. **2** [1930s+] (*US black*) (*also* **gates**) a person, a man, esp. as a term of address [jazz jargon *gate*, a swing musician, ult. the 'swinging' of a gate + abbr. GATEMOUTH *n.*; the term, at its peak 1935–43, was popularized by the comedian Jerry Colonna, who used it widely on Bob Hope's radio show]. **3** [1950s–70s] (*US drugs*) the vein into which one injects a narcotic. **4** [1990s+] one's appearance, looks.

SE in slang uses

DERIVATIVES

❑ **gatey** *adj.* [the opening of the prison *gate*] [1950s] (*UK prison*) suffering from the nervousness that precedes the end of one's sentence.

IN COMPOUNDS

❑ **gate fever** *n.* [1920s+] (*UK prison*) the nervous feeling that overtakes many prisoners as their sentence draws to its close. ❑ **gate money** *n.* [1930s–60s] (*US prison*) money given to a prisoner on release. ❑ **gatemouth** *n.* see separate entry. ❑ **gate swinger** *n.* [1970s+] (*US gay*) a bisexual.

IN PHRASES

❑ **from the gate** *adv.* [racecourse jargon] [1940s+] from the outset, from the beginning. ❑ **gate is open** see THE BARN DOOR IS OPEN *under* BARN *n.*[2]. ❑ **get the gate** *v.* [1910s+] (*US*) to be ejected, to be dismissed. ❑ **give someone the gate** *v.* [20C+] (*US*) to dismiss, to reject, to get rid of; to terminate a relationship. ❑ **out of the gate** *adv.* [horseracing imagery] **1** [1990s+] from the very beginning. **2** [2000s] (*Irish*) completely, comprehensively. ❑ **swing the gate** *v.* see *under* SWING *v.*

gatemouth *n.* [allegedly coined by jazz maestro Louis Armstrong (1901–71); Columbia records ad. 1926: 'Gate Mouth...is the kind of mouth that strecthes from ear to ear and buttons in back'] [1920s–40s; 1990s+] (*US black*) **1** a person, a man. **2** a gossip, a loudmouth.

gater *n.* see GATTER *n.*[1].

gates *n.*[1] [i.e. one's front *gate*] [1950s+] (*W.I. Rasta/UK black*) one's home.

gates *n.*[2] **1** [1970s] (*N.Z.*) the lips. **2** [1970s+] (*US gay*) the buttocks.

gates *n.*[3] see GATE *n.* (2).

gates of heaven *n.* [rhy. sl.] [1940s] the number seven.

gates of Rome *n.* [rhy. sl.] [20C+] home.

gather *n.* [GATHER *v.*] [2000s] (*UK Und.*) a detective.

gather *v.* [1970s] (*Aus. Und.*) to arrest.

SE in slang uses

IN PHRASES

❑ **gather straws** *v.* see *DRAW STRAWS under* STRAW *n.*

gather-em-up *n.* (*also* **gather-up**) [Irish/Ulster *gather-up*, a rag-and-bone man] [1970s+] (*Irish*) a useless person.

gation *n.* (*also* **gaishen, gashun**) [Scot. Gael. *gaisean*, a stalk; thus a young boy] [20C+] (*Ulster*) a very thin person.

gatkas *n.* [synon. Yid.] [20C+] trousers.

gatling *n.* [abbr. *Gatling gun*, a form of machine gun, invented by Dr R.J. *Gatling* (1818–1903), and first used in the American Civil War (1861–5)] [late 19C–1960s] (*US*) a gun.

gato *n.* [Sp.] [1980s+] (*drugs*) heroin.

gator *n.*[1] [abbr. ALLIGATOR *n.* (10)] [1930s–50s] (*orig. US black*) **1** a jazz fan. **2** any person considered to be in the swing of things. **3** a term of address used between two men.

gator *n.*[2] [colloq. *gator*, an alligator, in ext. uses] (*orig. US*) **1** [1950s+] an alligator skin shoe; thus in pl., a pair of such shoes. **2** [1980s] (*US campus*) a typical fraternity boy [the alligator emblem that is the trademark of Izod shirts, popular among fraternity wearers].

SE colloq. in slang uses

IN COMPOUNDS

❑ **gator-bait** *n.* [1970s+] (*US*) a black person. ❑ **gator-faced** *adj.* (*also* **gator-mouthed**) [1940s–50s] (*US black*) someone who has a long face and a large mouth. ❑ **gator-mouth** *n.* [1990s+] (*US campus*) **1** a person who talks too much. **2** a fellatrix.

gator *n.*[3] [abbr. ALLIGATOR *n.* (6)] [1960s+] (*US*) an inhabitant of Florida.

gats! *excl.* (*also* **gaats!**) [euph. for Afk. *Gots*, God] [1910s+] (*S.Afr.*) a general excl. of dismay, annoyance, surprise etc; synon. with *God!*

gatt *n.* see GAT *n.*[1].

gatter *n.*[1] (*also* **gater, gatta**) [ety. unknown; Partridge in *DSUE* suggests poss. Ling. Fr. or mix of *agua* + *water*] **1** [19C–1900s] beer; esp. in phr. *shant of gatter*, a pot of beer. **2** [mid-19C] gin.

gatter *n.*[2] [2000s] (*S.Afr. prison*) a police officer or prison warder.

gatter *v.* [GATTER *n.*[1] (1)] [late 19C] to drink beer.

gattering *n.* [GATTER *n.*[1]] [mid–late 19C] a public house; a drinking spree.

gattes *n.* [? Sotho *gata*, to trample or Yid. *khates*, a bad person] [1960s+] **1** (*S.Afr. black*) the police. **2** (*S.Afr. Jewish*) an Afrikaaner.

gatvol *adj.* [GAT *n.*[2] + Afk. *vol*, full] [1980s+] (*S.Afr.*) bored of, disgusted by, 'having a bellyful' of.

gaubey *n.* [Irish *gabhgaire*, an onlooker (at a card-game)] [early 19C+] (*Irish*) a gawper, one who looks on while others are doing something.

gaubshite *n. see* GOBSHITE *n.* (3).

gauch *v. see* GOUCH (OUT) *v.*

gauge *see also under* GAGE and combs.

gauge *n.*^{1} (*also* **gage**) [1930s–50s] temper.

IN PHRASES

❑ **blow one's gauge** *v. see* BLOW A GASKET *under* GASKET *n.* ❑ **get one's gauge up** *v.* (*also* **get one's gage up**) [1930s–50s] **1** to become angry. **2** to become intoxicated.

gauge *n.*^{2} (*also* **gage**) [abbr. *12-gauge*, a 12 bore] [1970s+] (*US black*) a shotgun.

gauger *n. see* GOUGER *n.*

gauldarned *adj. see* GOLDARNED *adj.*

gaulder *see under* GULDER.

gauldurned *adj. see* GOLDARNED *adj.*

gaully! *excl. see* GOLLY! *excl.*

gaum *n. see* GOM *n.*^{2}.

gaunch *n. see* GANCH *n.*

gauzer *n.* (*also* **gawzer**) [? SE *gorgeous* or *gaze*, to stare at] [20C+] (*Irish*) a very pretty girl or young woman.

gavacho *n.* [Sp. *gabacho*, a derog. term for a French person or foreigner] [1960s+] (*US Hisp.*) a white person.

gavone *n.* (*also* **cafone, gafone**) [? JIBONE *n.*] [1960s+] a derog. term for an Italian; by ext., a fool.

gaw *n.* (*also* **gawd, gor**) [mid-19C+] mispron. of, or euph. for, *God*.

gawd blimey! *excl. see* GORBLIMEY! *excl.*

gawdelpus *n.* (*also* **God-help-us, gordelpus**) [SE excl. *God help us!*] **1** [late 19C–1900s] an impoverished labourer ['from his ordinary excl. "Gordelpus – what's a cove to do?"' (Ware)]. **2** [20C+] an irritating or helpless person; often used of a child, e.g. *You 'orrible little gawdelpus!* [unstated is 'what shall we do about you?']. **3** [1900s] a generally miserable looking person.

gawd love-a-duck! *excl.* (*also* **cor love-a-duck!**) [*gawd* is Aus. use, *cor* is general] [20C+] a general expletive.

gawf *n.* [? 'go for more'; note 'Gawfs are sweet and sour at once ... and fit only for mixing' (Mayhew)] [mid-19C] a red-skinned apple, considered inferior produce but capable, with judicious polishing, to be sold as something better.

gawie *n.* [Afk. *gawie*, lout] [1960s+] (*S.Afr.*) a country bumpkin, an unsophisticated peasant.

gawks, the *n.* [echoic of vomiting] [1990s+] (*Irish*) feelings of nausea; thus phr. *have the gawks*, to feel sick.

gawm *n. see* GOM *n.*^{2}.

Gawney Mac! *excl.* (*also* **Gawney Jack! Gawny!**) [1980s+] (*Irish*) a euph. for *Jesus!* (pron. 'Jaysus!').

Gawsave *n. see* GOD SAVE *under* GOD *n.*^{1}.

gawzer *n. see* GAUZER *n.*

gay *n.*^{1} [GAY *adj.* (6)] **1** [1920s+] a male homosexual; thus *gayety*, a state of homosexuality. **2** [1990s+] (*mainly UK juv.*) a term of abuse for an unpopular individual.

IN COMPOUNDS

❑ **gay-basher** *n.* [BASH *v.* (1)] [1980s+] a person who specializes in beating and terrorizing homosexual men. ❑ **gay-bashing** *n.* [BASH *v.* (1)] [1970s+] (*orig. US*) the homophobic beating up of homosexual men; thus *gay-bash*, to beat up homosexuals.

gay *n.*^{2} [GALAH *n.* or JAY *n.*^{1} (4)] [1930s–60s] (*Aus.*) a dupe, a sucker, a gullible person.

gay *n.*^{3} **1** *see* GAY AND FRISKY *n.* **2** *see* GAY AND HEARTY *n.*

gay *adj.* [the use of *gay* as a self-description by homosexuals originated shortly after WW1, prob. an abbr. of US tramp sl. GAYCAT *n.*, the young homosexual companion of an older tramp; (but note Rodgers, *The Queen's Vernacular* (1972): 'fr. 16th cent Fr. *gaie* = homosexual man'; the wider use in the heterosexual world did not begin until c.1970, with the emergence of the Gay Liberation Front, first in the US and subseq. in the UK. With the decline of derog. terms, such as QUEER *adj.* (4), *gay* is now effectively SE; thus note Melly, *Owning Up* (1965): 'I'd never heard the word "gay" at that time [i.e. 1945]. "Queer" was in more general use even among homosexuals'] **1** [late 14C; mid-19C–1920s] of a woman, leading an immoral life, working as a prostitute. **2** [17C–1930s] promiscuous, dissipated. **3** [mid-18C–1920s] slightly drunk, tipsy. **4** [mid-19C–1920s] (*orig. US*) (*also* **gey**) fine, first-rate. **5** [late 19C–1910s] (*US*) forward, impertinent, over-familiar; esp. in phr. *get gay (with)*, to be cheeky, impertinent (towards). **6** [1920s+] (*orig. US*) of sexual orientation, homosexual; thus adv. *gayly*. **7** [1920s+] of a place, catering for or frequented by homosexuals. **8** [1920s+] of behaviour, mannerisms, feelings, events, social circles etc, homosexual. **9** [1980s+] (*orig. US campus*) a general pej.; stupid, ugly, eccentric, weak; of a man, lacking in masculinity but not actually homosexual.

pertaining to female promiscuity or prostitution

IN COMPOUNDS

❑ **gay bit** *n. see under* BIT *n.*^{1}. ❑ **gay girl** *n.* (*also* **gay woman**) [mid-19C] a promiscuous girl or woman. ❑ **gay house** *n.* [HOUSE *n.*^{1} (1)] [18C–1900s] a brothel. ❑ **gay lady** *n.* [mid–late 19C] a prostitute.

IN PHRASES

❑ **gay in the arse** *adj.* (*also* **gay in the groin**) [ARSE *n.* (2a)] [19C] of a woman, promiscuous. ❑ **go gay** *v.* **1** [16C] to commit adultery. **2** [late 19C] to pursue a career as a prostitute. **3** [1930s] to become homosexual. **4** [1940s–60s] (*Aus.*) to have sexual intercourse.

pertaining to homosexuality

DERIVATIVES

❑ **gayola** *n.* [-OLA *sfx*; on pattern of SE *payola*] **1** [1960s+] (*US Und.*) pay-offs and bribes made to police or organized crime to permit the running of gay clubs. **2** [1980s+] (*US*) a homosexual man.

IN COMPOUNDS

❑ **gaybo** *n.* [abbr. of next] [1980s] a male homosexual. ❑ **gay boy** *n.* [1950s+] (*US*) a male homosexual. ❑ **gaycat** *see* separate entries. ❑ **gaychick** *n.* [CHICK *n.*^{1} (2)] [1980s+] (*US gay*) a lesbian. ❑ **gaydar** *n.* [play on SE *radar*] [1980s+] (*gay*) the (alleged) sensory perception that lesbians and gays have of detecting other gay people in their midst. ❑ **gay girl** *n.* [1970s+] (*US gay*) a stereotypically effeminate homosexual man. ❑ **gay goddess** *n.* [1990s+] (*US gay*) a heterosexual woman who prefers the company of gay men. ❑ **gaylord** *n.* [2000s] a homosexual. ❑ **gay trade** *n.* [TRADE *n.* (3)] [1940s+] a homosexual man who is happy to fellate or to perform anal intercourse but will not reciprocate in return (although he may kiss and otherwise fondle his partner).

SE in slang uses

IN COMPOUNDS

❑ **gay deceivers** *n.* [pun on original use, a deceitful rake] **1** [1940s+] a padded brassiere that accentuates the shape and dimensions of otherwise diminutive female breasts. **2** [1960s] (*US gay*) a large artificial penis worn beneath the trousers to accentuate one's apparent sexual allure.

IN PHRASES

❑ **do the gay** *v.* [late 19C] to have a good time. ❑ **gay tyke boy** *n.* [SE *tyke*, a dog] [mid-19C] a dog-fancier. ❑ **Gay White Way** *n. see* separate entry. ❑ **get gay (with)** *v.* **1** [late 19C–1910s] to be aggressive; to behave unpleasantly. **2** [late 19C–1960s] (*mainly US*) to tease, to provoke, to be flippant. **3** [1900s–50s] to go into action, to get on with things. **4** [1940s] (*US drugs*) to take drugs, to get intoxicated.

gay and frisky *n.* (*also* **gay, gay and frisk**) [rhy. sl.] [1910s+] whisky.

gay and hearty *n.* (*also* **gay**) [rhy. sl.] [1930s+] (*Aus.*) a party.

gaycat *n.* [ety. unknown; the best possibility is that sense 1 and 2 were often homosexual, and thus sense 4 which in turn may suggest a transitional point between SE *gay*, cheerful, and GAY *adj.* (6); note 'The Kid' who appears in the eponymous *The Gay-cat* (1921) is not openly homosexual, although this too may be contemporary self-censorship by the author] **1** [late 19C–1950s]

(*US tramp*) a young or inexperienced tramp. **2** [late 19C–1950s] (*US tramp*) (*also* **cat**) a hobo who accepts occasional or seasonal work. **3** [1900s–40s] (*US Und.*) the junior member of a criminal gang, employed to run errands or spy out possible crimes. **4** [1910s–20s] (*US tramp*) (*also* **geycat**) a tramp's younger, homosexual companion. **5** [1920s] (*US Und.*) a thief who only works when he needs money.

gaycat *v.*[1] (*also* **geycat**) [GAYCAT *n.*] [late 19C–1950s] **1** (*US tramp*) to act as a tramp's (homosexual) companion. **2** (*US Und.*) to act as a spy for a criminal gang.

gaycat *v.*[2] (*also* **geycat**) [SE *gay* adj. + CAT *n.*[5] (1)] [1920s–40s] (*US black*) **1** to have a good time. **2** to loiter and chat in the street.

gay gordon *n.* [rhy. sl.] [1990s+] (*US*) a traffic warden.

gaying instrument *n.* [GAY *adj.* (1)/GAY *adj.* (2) + SE *instrument*] [18C] the penis.

gaying it *n.* [GAY *adj.* (1)/GAY *adj.* (2)] [19C] having sexual intercourse.

gayoungas *n. see* GAZONGAS *n.*

gayumbas *n. see* GAZONGAS *n.*

Gay White Way *n.* [the term, in which *gay* is used in the conventional SE manner, i.e. cheerful, jolly, was a short-lived alternative to the longer-lasting GREAT WHITE WAY *n.*] [1910s–30s] Broadway, New York City; thus used generically for similar entertainment centres in other cities.

gazabo *n.* (*also* **gazab, gazabe, gazaboo, gazaybe, gazebo, gazebu, gazee, gazooney, gezeybo**) [? Sp. *gazapo*, a sly fellow + SE *gaze*, i.e. their vacant stares] [late 19C+] (*Irish/US*) an awkward, strange or stupid person; thus fem. *gazaboine*; also any fellow.

IN PHRASES

❑ **high gazabo** *n.* [1930s] an important person.

gaze at the melody *v.* [play on SE *face the music*] [late 19C] to deal stoically with a problem or difficult situation; to take one's punishment.

gazebo *n.*[1] [SE *gazebo*, a form of garden hut, or a turret on the roof of a house] [1900s] (*US*) the mouth.

gazebo *n.*[2] *see* GAZABO *n.*

gazebos *n.* [? nonce-word] [1980s] (*US*) the testicles.

gazebu/gazee *n. see* GAZABO *n.*

gazelle *n.* [late 19C–1940s] (*US*) a young woman.

gazer *n.*[1] [SE *gaze*, to stare at] **1** [1930s–40s] (*US black*) a flirtatious woman looking for a new partner [the assumption being that she is *gazing* at other men in the hope of finding a new husband]. **2** [1930s–50s] (*US Und.*) a federal narcotics agent.

gazer *n.*[2] [1940s] (*US black*) **1** a mirror. **2** a window.

gazlon *n.* [Yid. *gozlin*, a swindler, an unethical person] [20C+] (*UK Und.*) a small-time, poss. timid, thief.

gazob *n.* [var. on GAZABO *n.*] [1900s–40s] (*Aus.*) a fool, simpleton.

gazock *n. see* GAZOOK *n.* (3).

gazongas *n.* **1** [1960s+] (*also* **gajoungas, gayumbas, gazonkas, gazungas**) the female breasts, usu. large. **2** [2000s] the male breasts.

gazoo *n.* [var. on KAZOO *n.*] **1** [1960s+] (*also* **gazool**) the anus. **2** [1970s] (*also* **gazookus**) the vagina.

IN PHRASES

❑ **up the gazoo** (*also* **up the gazops**) [1950s+] (*orig. US*) full up, as much as one can handle, to excess.

gazook *n.* (*also* **gazoo, gazoop, gazoopus**) [GAZABO *n.*] **1** [1900s–60s] (*US*) a lout, a boor, a fool. **2** [1900s–30s] (*also* **gazooka**) a person, a fellow. **3** [1930s–40s] (*US tramp*) (*also* **gazock**) a tramp's young (homosexual) companion.

gazookus *n.*[1] [ety. unknown] (*US*) **1** [1920s–40s] a lout, a boor, a fool. **2** [1920s–60s] (*also* **gazukus**) a thing; thus *the real gazookus*, the genuine article.

gazookus *n.*[2] *see* GAZOO *n.* (2).

gazool *n. see* GAZOO *n.* (1).

gazooma *n.* [1950s] (*US Und.*) a thug, a stupid man.

gazoomph *v. see* GAZUMP *v.*

gazooney *n.*[1] [Anglo-Irish *gossoon*; ult. Irish *garsuin*, a boy, a lad] [1910s+] (*US tramp*) a young, homosexual sidekick who accompanies a tramp.

gazooney *n.*[2] **1** [1990s+] (*US*) an amusing person. **2** *see* GAZABO *n.*

gazoop *n. see* GAZOOK *n.*

gazoopie *n.* (*also* **gazoopy, gazupie**) [? GAZOO *n.* (2)] [1930s–70s] (*US*) a sex show.

gazoopus *n. see* GAZOOK *n.*

gazops *n.*

IN PHRASES

❑ **up the gazops** *see UP THE GAZOO under* GAZOO *n.*

gazukus *n. see* GAZOOKUS *n.*[1] (2).

gazump *n.* [var. on GAZABO *n.*] [1920s] (*US*) a general pej.

gazump *v.* (*also* **gasumph, gazoomph, gazumph, gezump, gezumph, gezzump**) [? Yid. *gezumph*, to cheat or to overcharge] **1** [1920s+] to swindle. **2** [1970s+] (*orig. estate agent*) to accept a stated price for one's property and then to raise that price, using as a threat a supposed, but usu. non-existent, 'offer' from elsewhere; alternatively, the seller accepts one price and then, tempted by a genuinely greater offer, dumps the first buyer without sorrow or ceremony; thus *gazumper*, a swindler. **3** [2000s] in ext. use of sense 2 above, to take over, to usurp (in non-housing contexts).

gazungas *n. see* GAZONGAS *n.*

gazupie *n. see* GAZOOPIE *n.*

g.b. *n.*[1] [abbr. SE *grand* + BOUNCE *n.*[1] (5)] [late 19C–1920s] (*US*) grand bounce, a forceful ejection or dismissal.

IN PHRASES

❑ **get the g.b.** *v.* [*get the go by* or *grand bounce*] [late 19C–1910s] (*US*) to be snubbed, to be ignored.

g.b. *n.*[2] [ety. unknown] [1950s] (*W.I.*) gym shoes or boots that lace at the front with buckles at the side.

g.b. *n.*[3] [GOOFBALL *n.*[1] (2)] [1960s+] (*drugs*) a barbiturate, a depressant.

g.b. *n.*[4] *see* GREENBACK *n.* (1).

g.b. *phr.* [abbr.] [1970s+] (*US campus*) goodbye.

G-clip *n.* [ety. unknown; ? link to G *n.* (8) or ? G *n.* (6)] [2000s] (*US black*) a sign that indicates to a woman that one wishes to have sex.

G.D. *adj.* (*also* **G.d., g.d.**) [abbr.] [mid-19C+] (*US*) God-damned; thus *g.d.f.*, God-damned fool.

g.d.i. *n.* [abbr. *God-damned independent*] [1960s+] (*US campus*) a student who is not a fraternity or sorority member.

G-down *adj.* [G *n.* (6)] [1970s+] (*US black gang*) dressed in gang clothes.

G'd up *adj.* [G *n.* (6)] [1990s+] (*US black/campus*) dressed in the style currently favoured by black urban GANGSTA *n.* (1) youth.

g'd up *adj. see* GEED-UP *adj.*[2].

ge *n.* [Afk. *gê*, trash, rubbish] [1980s+] (*S.Afr.*) **1** a friend, a pal. **2** a tough, a thug.

geach *n.* [? Scot. *geck*, an act of deception; ult. Ger. *Gecken*, tricks] [early 19C] a thief.

geach *v.* [GEACH *n.*] [early 19C] to steal.

gear *n.* [14C+ SE *gear*, accoutrements] **1** [mid-16C–early 18C; late 19C] the female genitals. **2** [mid-16C–mid-18C; 1970s+] (*also* **geer**) the male genitals; thus [17C] *gear-itch*, lecherousness. **3** [mid-16C+] an object or objects; things, varying as to context. **4** [late 17C–early 18C] trash, rubbish. **5** [1930s–70s] (*US prison*) a homosexual. **6** [1950s+] stolen property. **7** [1950s+] (*US*) an important or influential person [SE 16C–18C]. **8** [1960s] in the sex industry, photographs, magazines, films etc. **9** [1960s+] (*W.I.*) in pl., one's best clothing. **10** [1960s+] (*drugs*) drugs, esp. cannabis, heroin. **11** [1970s+] the equipment used in sado-masochistic sex. **12** [2000s] (*US black*) one's personal space.

IN COMPOUNDS

❑ **gear job** *n.* [JOB *n.*[2] (2)] [1970s] (*US prison*) a homosexual.

IN PHRASES

❑ **ace gear** *n.* [ACE *adj.* (1)] [1960s+] (*US gay*) a sexually talented homosexual, capable of both active and passive roles. ❑ **drop one's gear** *v.* (*also* **drop the gear**) [1950s+] (*Aus./N.Z.*) to undress. ❑ **gear up** *v.* [1990s+] (*US black gang*) to get dressed in one's gang clothes. ❑ **in one's gears** *adj.* [late 17C–early 18C] **1** dressed, ready. **2** ready to get to work. ❑ **out of one's gears** *adj.* [late 17C–early 18C] unsettled, out of sorts. ❑ **pack the gear** *v.* [1970s] (*US*) to achieve a given standard; lit. to 'carry the equipment'. ❑ **that's the gear** [1920s+] (*orig. milit.*) a general term of approval, 'that's the stuff'.

SE in slang uses

IN COMPOUNDS

❑ **gearhead** *n.* [mechanical sense of SE *gear* + -HEAD *sfx* (3)] **1** [1970s+] (*orig. US campus*) an engineering student, someone mechanically minded; thus ext. to one who is obsessed with automobiles. **2** [1990s+] (*US*) a car factory worker. ❑ **gear-lever** *n.* [2000s] (*S.Afr. gay*) the penis. ❑ **gear stick** *n. see* JOYSTICK *under* JOY *n.*

IN PHRASES

❑ **get into gear** *v.* (*also* **put it into gear**) [1980s+] (*US*) to get going, to get busy. ❑ **get one's ass in(to) gear** *v.* (*also* **get one's arse in gear, ...balls in gear, ...rear in gear**) [fig. uses of ASS *n.* (2)/ARSE *n.* (1)/BALLS *n.* (1)/REAR *n.* (1)] [1950s+] to stop wasting time, to put some effort and commitment into one's activities, to start doing something useful and positive. ❑ **throw in one's gears** *v.* [1930s] (*US black*) to leave quickly.

gear *adj.*[1] (*also* **geer**) [GEAR *n.* (3); at peak popularity one of the Beatles' supposed favourite words; post-1960s use is ironic] [1910s+] excellent, wonderful, just right; often as *the gear*.

gear *adj.*[2] [GEAR *n.* (5) + rhy. sl. = QUEER *adj.* (4)] [1930s+] homosexual.

geared *adj.* [GEAR *adj.*[2]] [1930s+] (*US Und.*) sexually aberrant.

geared up *adj.* [GEAR *n.*] **1** [1930s+] (*US*) intoxicated. **2** [1960s+] (*Scot./US black*) dressed up. **3** [1970s+] (*US*) very (sexually) excited. **4** [1990s+] prepared, ready.

geck *n.* (*also* **gack, gak, gheck**) [dial. *geck*, a fool; ? modern US use abbr. *gecko*] **1** [early 19C; 1990s+] an odd, eccentric-looking person. **2** [20C+] (*Ulster*) a person who tells tales behind another's back, a gossip. **3** [1990s+] a person who uses LSD.

geck *v.* [? GECK *n.* (3)] [1990s+] to lose one's self-confidence.

gecko *n.*

IN PHRASES

❑ **have a gecko at** *v.* [play on DEKKO *v.* + ? GANDER *n.*[3]] [1970s+] (*US*) to take a look at, to glance at.

geddit? *phr. see* GET IT? *phr.*

gedoente *n.* [Afk. *gedoente*, bustle] [1970s+] (*S.Afr.*) a fuss, a carry-on, a to-do.

gee *n.*[1] [abbr. SE *gee-gee*, a horse] [late 19C–1930s] a horse.

gee *n.*[2] [GEE (UP) *v.* (1)] **1** [late 19C+] (*Aus.*) (*also* **gee-er, gee man**) one who 'gees up' the potential customers into a sideshow, strip-club, confidence trick etc. **2** [1920s+] idle chatter, empty talk, 'blarney'.

IN PHRASES

❑ **put in the gee** *v.* [1920s+] to deceive, to 'tell the tale'. ❑ **put on the gee** *v.* [1920s+] to boast, to brag, to 'swank about'.

gee *n.*[3] [GUY *n.*[2] (1)] [20C+] (*US*) **1** a male, esp. a male friend. **2** as *the gee, the whole gee*, the most important person in a given environment; the leader.

gee *n.*[4] [? Irish sl. *gowl*, the vagina; ult. Irish *gabhal*, the fork (of the body)] **1** [1910s+] a woman considered solely as a sex object. **2** [1930s; 1990s+] (*also* **gee box**) the vagina.

gee *n.*[5] [abbr.] [1930s] (*US tramp*) a glass of alcohol.

gee *n.*[6] [? initial letter *g* of various opium-related words, e.g. GONG *n.*[2] (2); GOW *n.*[1] (2); GUM *n.*[3] (1) or of SE *guy*, which is synon. with BOY *n.*[2] (4a), i.e. heroin; ? even more far-fetched is poss. pun on SE *gee-up!*, used of horses, thus linked to HORSE *n.* (7), heroin; Maurer, *Language of the Underworld Narcotic Addict* Pt.2 (1938), suggests Hindi *ghee*, refined butter; also note Chinese *yí-yín*/GEE YEN *n.*, seconds, i.e. opium residue] [1930s–60s] (*US drugs*) **1** opium. **2** narcotics other than opium.

IN COMPOUNDS

❑ **gee-fat** *n. see* separate entry. ❑ **gee stick** *n.* [SE *stick*/STICK *n.* (6b)] [1930s–50s] (*US drugs*) an opium pipe.

gee *n.*[7] (*also* **boo-gee, G, gee rag, g-rag**) [? ext. of GEE *n.*[6] (1) but, despite dates, poss. abbr. GASKET *n.* (2). Note that, unlike in the UK, where registered addicts (and via them other users) were allowed to use proper medical syringes, US users were often forced to make their own WORKS *n.* (4a), a do-it-yourself assemblage of a hollow needle and an eye-dropper] [1930s+] (*US*) a paper 'collar' used by a drug user to secure the needle to the eye-dropper prior to injecting the heroin/water solution; earlier use in opium smoking.

gee *n.*[8] **1** *see* G *n.* (1). **2** *see* G *n.*[1].

gee *n.*[9] *see* GANK *v.* (2).

gee *n.*[10] *see* GUEE *n.*

gee *v.*[1] (*also* **jee**) [? pron. of initial letter of SE *go*] [late 17C–1920s] to fit, to suit, to behave as required or expected; usu. in phr. *it won't gee*, it doesn't suit, it doesn't work.

gee *v.*[2] [? fig. use of SE *gee up*, to urge a horse forward, thus play on RIDE *v.* (1a)] [1970s+] (*US black*) to have sexual intercourse.

gee *v.*[3] *see* GANK *v.* (2).

gee *v.*[4] *see* GEE (UP) *v.*

gee! *excl.* (*also* **by jee! by the hully gee! hully chee! ...gee! ...Jee! jee! my gee!**) [mid-19C+] (*US*) a mild oath, a euph. for *Jesus!*

geeba *n.* [CHEEB *n.*] [2000s] (*US campus*) marijuana.

gee bag *n.* [? GEE *n.*[4]] [2000s] (*Irish*) a term of abuse.

gee box *n. see* GEE *n.*[4] (2).

geebung *n.* [SE *geebung*, a shrub or tree of the genus *Persoonia*] [mid-19C–1910s] (*Aus.*) **1** an unsophisticated, uncultured, philistine native-born Australian, who values material gain above everything else; personified as *Tommy Geebung*. **2** a place-name for any out-of-the-way place. **3** a gadget.

geech *n.* [? GEETUS *n.*] [1960s] (*US*) money.

geechee *n.* [proper name *Geechee*, an inhabitant (usu. black) of the coastal areas of Georgia, North Carolina or north Florida; the language such people speak is itself *Geechee*] [20C+] (*US black*) a derog. term for anyone (typically a rural southerner, newly migrated to the urban north) whose speech is made incomprehensible by a heavy accent.

geechie *adj.* (*also* **geechy**) [GEECHEE *n.*] (*US black*) **1** [20C+] unintelligible; thus unsophisticated, provincial. **2** [1980s] of a black person, light-skinned, or having Native American forbears.

geed-up *adj.*[1] [ety. unknown] **1** [1900s–60s] (*US*) crippled, in disrepair. **2** [1930s] (*US drugs*) impoverished.

geed-up *adj.*[2] (*also* **g'd up**) [? GEE (UP) *v.*] (*US*) **1** [1920s–70s] (*US*) drunk [? link to GEE *n.*[5]]. **2** [1920s+] excited. **3** [1930s–70s] intoxicated by drugs [? link to GEE *n.*[6]]. **4** [1990s+] modified and thus increased in value.

geedus *n. see* GEETUS *n.*

gee-er *n. see* GEE *n.*[2] (1).

gee-eyed *adj.* [2000s] (*Irish*) drunk.

gee-fat *n.* [? Chi. *gee-yen*, the residue left in an opium pipe] [1930s–50s] (*US drugs*) narcotics, usu. the residue of opium.

gee fuzz! *excl. see* GEE WHIZ! *excl.*

gee-gee *n.*[1] [GEEZER *n.*[1] (1)/GEE *n.*[3] (1) + redup.] [1920s] a man, a fellow.

gee-gee *n.*[2] [? play on SE *gee-gee* a horse, i.e. it is 'ridden' during intercourse + note GEE *n.*[4]] [1960s–70s] (*US*) the anus or vagina.

gee-gee *n.*[3] [redup. of G *n.* (1)] [1980s] (*UK Und.*) one thousand pounds.

geegeeree *adj.* [? pron. SE *jittery*] [2000s] (*W.I., Trin.*) nervous, scared.

gee-hair *n. see* GNAT'S EYEBROW *under* GNAT *n.*

gee hee *n.* [? initials of *go* to *hell*] [late 19C] (*US tramp*) a problem, an instance of bad luck.

geehosaphat! *excl. see* JEHOSHAPHAT! *excl.*

geek *n.*[1] [dial. *geck*, a fool; 20C+ use was popularized by the notoriety of one Wagner, of Charleston, West Virginia, who had a celebrated touring snake-eating act; known as a geek, his ballyhoo ran in part, 'Come and see Esau / Sitting on a see-saw / Eatin' 'em raw!'; thus note *Variety* 8 Sep. 1922: 'The old and reliable snake charmer retired to make room for the snake eater, and weird creatures appeared in dens filled with small reptiles, outside of which huge banners proclaimed the fact that "Bosco" or "Esau" "eats 'em alive"'] **1** [late 19C+] (*US*) (*also* **geke, geekoid**) a clumsy, eccentric or offensive person. **2** [20C+] a carnival freak who specialized in biting the heads off live chickens or snakes; also as v. **3** [1940s] a generally unpleasant person, irrelevant of class. **4** [1950s+] (*US black/teen*) one who is considered intellectual and thus alien to the peer group, esp. an obsessive; thus *geekware*, clothing that appeals to such individuals. **5** [1980s+] (*US teen*) a vulgar, lower-class youth. **6** [1980s+] (*US campus*) one who is considered to devote too much time to their books; thus *geek out*, to work (too) hard. **7** [1980s+] (*orig. US campus*) a devotee of and expert in computers and computer-related culture; thus *geekware*, technology that appeals to such individuals; *geekize*, to render something thus appealing [specific ext. of sense 4 above].

(DERIVATIVES)

❑ **geekiness** *n.* [1980s+] social ineptitude. ❑ **geekish** *adj.* (*also* **geekified, geeking**) [1990s+] eccentric, freakish.

(IN PHRASES)

❑ **geeked up** *adj.* [1990s+] (*US*) naively excited or thrilled by something. ❑ **geek it** *v.* (*also* **geek out**) [1930s–50s] (*US*) to quit or back down. ❑ **geek up** *v.* [i.e. to render someone a *geek*] **1** [1980s+] (*US*) to frighten, to make nervous. **2** [1990s+] (*US black*) to teach, to introduce.

geek *n.*[2] [Cornish dial. *geek*, to peer, to look intently] [1910s+] (*Aus.*) a glance, a look.

geek *n.*[3] [1980s+] (*drugs*) a mix of crack cocaine and marijuana; thus *geek joint*, a cigarette filled with such a mix.

(IN COMPOUNDS)

❑ **geek monster** *n.* [-MONSTER *sfx*] [1990s+] (*US campus*) a CRACK *n.*[7] whore.

geek *adj.*[1] [GEEK *n.*[1]] **1** [1960s+] clumsy, uncoordinated. **2** [1980s+] with reference to the world of obsessives, esp. in the context of computing, the Internet etc.

geek *adj.*[2] [2000s] (*N.Z. teen*) excellent.

geek *v.*[1] [GEEK *n.*[2]] [1910s+] (*Aus./N.Z.*) to stare at, to look at.

geek *v.*[2] [GEEK *n.*[1]] **1** [1950s+] (*US black/drugs*) (*also* **geek out**) to experience severe symptoms of heroin withdrawal; also to deal obsessively with surrounding inanimate objects after a binge on strong amphetamine drugs. **2** [1980s+] (*orig. computing/US campus*) (*also* **geek out**) to devote oneself to one's own (computing, obsessive) pursuits in an environment where such pursuits are disdained. **3** [1980s+] (*US campus*) to act stupidly, or in a way that counters the cultural norm. **4** [2000s] (*US*) to fool someone, to render stupid.

geek *v.*[3] [? GEEK *n.*[1] (5)] [1990s+] (*US*) to sell items in the street.

geekoid *n. see* GEEK *n.*[1] (1).

geek out *v.* **1** *see* GEEK *v.*[2] (1). **2** *see* GEEK *v.*[2] (2).

geeky *adj.* [GEEK *n.*[1] + sfx *-y*] **1** [1970s+] (*US gay*) unethical, villainous. **2** [1980s+] (*US black*) of a man, unattractive. **3** [1990s+] (*orig. US campus*) socially inept, overly studious.

gee man *n. see* GEE *n.*[2] (1).

geemany crimany!/geeminy criminy! *excl. see* JIMINY CRICKET! *excl.*

gee-miny! *excl. see* GEMINI! *excl.*

geep *n.* (*also* **geepo**) [? GEEK *n.*[1] (1)] [1940s–50s] (*US*) an obnoxious, inept or suspicious-looking person.

geer *n. see* GEAR *n.* (2).

geer *adj. see* GEAR *adj.*[1].

gee rag *n. see* GEE *n.*[7].

gees! *excl. see* JEEZ! *excl.*

geese *n.*[1] [ety. unknown] [1950s] (*US street gang*) a theft.

geese *n.*[2] *see* GOOSE *n.*[2].

geese *v.*[1] [? SE *disguise*] [1990s+] (*US black*) to trick, to deceive.

geese *v.*[2] *see* GEEZE *v.*

geeser *n.* **1** *see* GEEZER *n.*[1] (1). **2** *see* GEEZER *n.*[3] (1).

geetus *n.* (*also* **geedus, geetas, geeters, geetis, geets, ghedis, gietus**) [ety. unknown; ? SE *get us*] [1920s+] (*US*) **1** money. **2** power.

gee up *n.* [GEE (UP) *v.*] **1** [1920s+] (*Aus.*) a spree, any form of merry-making. **2** [1940s] (*also* **jee up**) encouragement, stimulus.

gee (up) *v.* [SE *gee up*, to urge a horse forward] **1** [mid-19C+] to encourage, to persuade, to incite, esp. when working as a showman's or market-trader's assistant. **2** [1930s] to act as an *agent provocateur*, esp. when using entrapment for sexual crimes. **3** [1930s+] to provoke trouble deliberately, to tease maliciously, to deceive; thus *geed up*, furious, very angry. **4** [1940s+] (*orig. UK prison*) to inform (against a fellow prisoner); thus *gee-er*, an informer. **5** [1990s+] to give up, to surrender [may be SE *give up*, to hand over].

gee vet! *excl.* [Afk. *gee vet*, lit. 'to give grease'] [20C+] (*S.Afr.*) hurry up! get a move on! 'step on it!'.

gee whillikins! *excl.* (*also* **geewhilligins! gee whillikers! gee whiskers! geewhittaker(s)! gee whizzserkins! gee wittikins! jeewillikens! jewhilliken! jewhitiker! whillikins!**) [mid-19C+] (*mainly US juv.*) a mild, euph. excl.

gee-whiz *adj.* (*also* **geewhizzly**) [GEE WHIZ! *excl.*] [1950s+] exciting; as an intensifier.

gee whiz *phr.* [GEE WHIZ! *excl.*] [1930s] a phr. epitomizing popular speech-forms.

gee whiz! *excl.* (*also* **gee fuzz! gee wizard! geeziz!**) [late 19C+] a euph. for *Jesus!* or *Jesus Christ!* and as such a mild excl.

geewhizzly *adj. see* GEE-WHIZ *adj.*

gee whizzserkins!/gee wittikens! *excl. see* GEE WHILLIKINS! *excl.*

gee yen *n.* (*also* **yi-yen**) [Chinese *yí-yín*] [late 19C–1930s] (*US drugs*) the residue that collects inside the stem of an opium pipe; it may be collected and then resold.

geez *n.*[1] (*also* **geeze**) [GEEZE *v.* (1)] [1960s–70s] (*drugs*) an injection of narcotics.

geez *n.*[2] [abbr. GEEZER *n.*[1] (1)] [1960s–70s] a man, a fellow, a 'bloke'.

geeze *v.* (*also* **geese, geez, geeze up**) [GEEZER *n.*[3] (1); given the date of the root n., Spears, *Slang and Jargon of Drugs and Drink* (1986), is surely right to suggest 'this may be much older than the attestations suggest'] (*drugs*) **1** [1950s+] to inject narcotics. **2** [2000s] to inhale cocaine.

geez(e)! *excl. see* JEEZ! *excl.*

geezed *adj.* [sense 2 GEEZE *v.* which suggests sense 1] **1** [1920s–30s] (*US*) drunk. **2** [1950s+] (*US drugs*) (*also* **geezed up**) intoxicated by drugs.

geezer *n.*[1] [dial. pron. of 15C *guiser*, a mummer (*OED*); Partridge wonders if Wellington's troops might not have picked it up from the Basque *giza*, a man, during the Peninsular War (1808–14)] **1** [late 19C+] (*also* **geeser, geyser, gheeser**) a man, a 'bloke'; occas. a woman. **2** [late 19C+] (*US*) an old man, occas. a woman; often as *old geezer* (*see also* below). **3** [1910s+] a term of address. **4** [1940s–50s] in fig. use of sense 2 above, staleness, tiredness. **5** [1950s] a well-dressed, stylish man. **6** [1970s] a confidence trickster's victim; a whore's client. **7** [1970s] (*UK gay*) a young male prostitute's older client. **8** [1970s+] an authority figure. **9** [2000s] (*UK black*) one who fails to achieve the standards of the 'street' lifestyle, the opposite of a 'brother'.

(IN PHRASES)

❑ **old geezer** *n.* [joc. use of sense 1 above] [1910s+] one's wife; often as *the old geezer*.

geezer *n.*[2] [Lincolnshire dial. *geezer*, a state of drunkenness] [1910s–40s] (*US*) a drink of whisky or strong alcohol.

geezer *n.*[3] [? ext. of GEE *n.*[6] (1)] (*drugs*) **1** [1920s+] (*also* **geeser**) an injection of a narcotic drug. **2** [1920s+] the equipment with which one injects. **3** [1960s+] (*US*) a heroin addict.

geeze up *v. see* GEEZE *v.*

geeziz! *excl. see* GEE WHIZ! *excl.*

geezo *n.* [GEEZER *n.*[1] (1) + -O *sfx* (3)] [1930s] (*US prison*) a convict.

Gee-zus Christ! *excl. see* JESUS! *excl.*

gefoetered *adj. see* BEFOKTE *adj.*

geg *n. see* GAG *n.*

geggy *n.* [GEGS *n.*] [2000s] spectacle-wearing.

gegor *n.* [? GAGGER *n.*[1] (3)] [mid–late 19C] a beggar.

gegs *n.* [GIG-LAMPS *n.* (1)] [2000s] spectacles.

gehuncled *adj.* [? Ger. *gehunkelt*, hobbled] [1920s–60s] (*US*) crippled.

gek *adj.* [Du. *gek*, mad] [mid-19C+] (*S.Afr.*) foolish, obsessed, insane.

geke *n. see* GEEK *n.*[1] (1).

gekko *n.* [var. on DEKKO *n.*] [2000s] (*N.Z.*) a look, a glance.

gel *v. see* JELL *v.*

geld(t) *n. see* GELT *n.*

geli'/gellie *n. see* JELLY *n.*[2].

gelly *n.* **1** *see* JELLY *n.*[2]. **2** *see* JELLY *n.*[3].

gellyhead *n.* (*also* **jellyhead**) [JELLY *n.*[2] (1) + -HEAD *sfx* (1)] [1990s+] (*N.Z.*) a fool.

gel on *v.* [ext. of JELL *v.*] [1980s+] (*US campus*) to break an appointment.

gelt *n.* (*also* **geld, geldt, gelter, ghelt**) [Yid. *gelt*, money or Ger. *gelt*, gold; note S.Afr. colloq. *geld*, money f. Du.] [late 17C+] money.

gemini! *excl.* (*also* **gee-miny! geminy! gemunee!**) [mid-17C] a euph. for *Jesus!* and used as such in oaths (cf. JIMINY! *excl.*).

gemmie *n.* [GAME *adj.*[1] (4)] [1960s] (*Scot.*) a tough, ruthless young man.

gemors *n.* [synon. Afk.] [1970s+] (*S.Afr.*) **1** a mess, a confusion. **2** an insulting form of address.

gemunee! *excl. see* GEMINI! *excl.*

gen *n.*[1] [? abbr. *argent*, silver, or abbr. GENERALIZE *n.*, a supposed backsl. formation of *shilling*] [mid-19C–1950s] a shilling (12 old pence/5p).

gen *n.*[2] (*also* **jen**) [? RAF *gen*(*eral information*) for all ranks] [1940s+] information, facts.

IN PHRASES

❑ **gen out** *v.* [1940s] (*US*) to figure out, to plan. ❑ **gen up** *v.* [1940s+] (*US*) to provide someone with information, to learn a lot of information in a short space of time (usu. on a specific subject); thus *genned up*, well informed.

gendarme *n.* [Fr. *gendarme*, police officer] **1** [20C+] a police officer; also as v., to police. **2** [1950s] (*Aus.*) a large, tough man employed to keep order in a club.

gender-bender *n.* [SE + ? a pun on FENDER-BENDER *n.*; the term was popularized during the rise to fame of the pop star Boy George, whose outrageous clothes and ostentatious make-up managed to disturb many observers] [1980s+] **1** a synon. for a transvestite or a transsexual, bending or eroding the line between the two sexes; thus v. *gender-bend*. **2** an act or example of something that bends the line between the two sexes; thus adj. *gender-bending*.

gender-fuck *n.* [SE *gender* + -FUCK *sfx*; extreme ext. of GENDER-BENDER *n.*] [1970s+] **1** a man who shocks the heterosexual world by openly adopting women's clothes, thus destroying the assumptions about male/female separatism; similarly a woman doing the opposite. **2** an act of destroying such assumptions.

genderfuck *adj.* [GENDER FUCK *v.*] [2000s] describing something that is completely blurring/destroying the boundaries between male and female.

gender fuck *v.* [SE *gender* + FUCK *v.* (2a)] [1960s+] (*gay*) of a man, to shock the heterosexual world by openly adopting women's clothes, blurring (or destroying) the assumptions about male/female separatism.

general *n.*[1] [SE] **1** [1950s] a non-specific term of address to a man whose name one does not know. **2** [1950s+] (*W.I. Rasta*) a smart man, a 'cool operator'. **3** [1970s+] (*S.Afr. Und.*) a high rank in a prison gang.

general *n.*[2] [1960s+] (*US*) the penis.

General Booth *n.* [rhy. sl.; ult. the founder of the Salvation Army, *'General' William Booth* (1829–1912)] [20C+] a tooth.

generalize *n.* [backsl.] [mid-19C–1950s] a shilling.

generalize *v.* [GENERALIZE *n.*] [mid–late 19C] (*middle-class*) to give or lend a shilling; usu. in phr. *can you generalize?*

generating tool *n.* (*also* **generation tool, ...tube, tool of generation**) [SE *generate*, to procreate + TOOL *n.*[1] (1a)] [mid-17C–19C] the penis.

generic *n.* [SE *generic*, not marked with the producer's brandname, and available at a lower price because of plain, cheap packaging] [1990s+] (*US*) a black person.

Gene Tunney *n.* [rhy. sl.; ult. US boxer *Gene Tunney* (1898–1978)] [1960s+] (*Aus./N.Z.*) **1** money. **2** a lavatory [DUNNY *n.*[2]].

Gene Tunney *adj.* [rhy.sl.; ult. *see* prev.] [1980s] (*Aus.*) sunny.

Geneva print *n.* [pun on *Geneva*, the kind of type used in a Geneva Bible, the English translation of the Bible first printed at Geneva in 1560 + *Genever*, Dutch gin] [17C–mid-18C] gin; thus *read Geneva print*, to drink gin; thus phr. *been at Geneva*, drunk.

gen net *n.* (*also* **net-gen**) [backsl.; GEN *n.*[1] + NET *n.*[1]] [mid-19C] ten shillings (50p).

gennitraf *n.* (*also* **genitrave**) [backsl.] [late 19C] a farthing.

genny *n.* [abbr.] [1960s] (*Aus.*) a generator.

genol *adj.* [backsl.] [mid–late 19C] long.

gent *n.*[1] [abbr.; note SE *gent*, genteel, noble, of good rank] **1** [late 18C+] (*orig. US*) a *gent*leman, a man, a fellow. **2** [mid-19C+] a *gent*leman, but only when 'applied derisively to men of the vulgar and pretentious class who are supposed to use the word, and as used in tradesmen's notices' (*OED*); thus adj. *gentish*.

IN COMPOUNDS

❑ **gent's gent** *n. see* GENTLEMAN'S GENT *under* GENTLEMAN'S *n.*

gent *n.*[2] [abbr. Fr. (*une femme*) *gentille*, a gentlewoman] [mid–late 19C] a mistress; usu. as *my gent*.

gent *n.*[3] [abbr. Ital. *argento*, silver] [mid-19C+] (*Ling. Fr./Polari*) money, usu. silver.

gentleman *n.* [on pattern of CITIZEN *n.* (1); ALDERMAN *n.* (5); LORD MAYOR *n.*[1]: smaller and larger versions of the tool] [late 18C–19C] (*US Und.*) a crowbar.

SE in slang uses

IN COMPOUNDS

❑ **gentleman commoner** *n.* [the Oxford version of Cambridge's FELLOW COMMONER *n.*; commoners, as opposed to scholars, were seen as empty-headed] [late 18C–early 19C] (*orig. Oxford Univ.*) an empty bottle. ❑ **gentleman-outer** *n.* [early 18C] a highwayman. ❑ **gentleman-usher** *n.* [? pun on SE *gentleman usher of the Black Rod*; note Williams: 'gentleman usher [...] a male attendant on a lady, sometimes providing a sexual or pimping service'] **1** [late 16C–early 18C] the penis. **2** [17C] a woman's male companion.

IN PHRASES

❑ **do the gentleman** *v.* [1920s] to urinate. ❑ **gentleman in blue (and white)** *n.* [the uniform] [mid–late 19C] a policeman. ❑ **gentleman in brown** *n.* [late 19C] a bedbug. ❑ **gentleman in red** *n.* [late 18C] a soldier. ❑ **gentleman of...** *n. see* separate entry. ❑ **gentleman who pays the rent** *n.* [late 19C] (*Irish*) a pig.

gentleman of... *n.*

IN PHRASES

❑ **gentleman of the back door** *n.* (*also* **usher of the back door**) [BACK-DOOR *n.* (1)] [late 18C–19C] a sodomite. ❑ **gentleman of the brush** *n.* [early 19C] an artist, a painter. ❑ **gentleman of the drop** *n.* [late 18C] (*UK Und.*) a confidence trickster who preys on naïve countrymen, persuading them that they can win money by playing cards with a supposedly drunk person – who of course is a confederate. ❑ **gentleman of the matt and feather** *n.* [late 18C] (*US*) an aficionado of cock-fighting. ❑ **gentleman of the**

pad *n.* [PAD *n.*[1] (1)] **1** [18C] a highwayman. **2** [early–mid-19C] a street-robber. ❑ **gentleman of the road** *n.* **1** [19C] a highwayman. **2** [1920s–50s] (*N.Z./US*) (*also* **man of the road**) a tramp. ❑ **gentleman of the round** *n.* [play on SE *gentleman of the round*, 'a gentleman soldier, but of low rank [...] whose office it was to visit and inspect the sentinels, watches, and advanced guard. It was, therefore, an office of some trust, though little dignity' (Nares) + pun on one who 'does the rounds'] [late 16C–early 17C] a discharged or invalided soldier who makes his living by begging. ❑ **gentleman of the short staff** *n.* [his truncheon] [mid-19C] a constable. ❑ **gentleman of the swag** *n. see under* SWAG *n.*[1]. ❑ **gentleman of the three ins** *n.* [late 18C] 'In debt, in gaol, and in danger of remaining there for life; or, in gaol, indicted and in danger of being hanged in chains' (Grose, 1796). ❑ **gentleman of the three outs** *n.* (*also* **gentleman of four outs**) [variations include 'out of pocket, out of elbows, and out of credit' (Bulwer-Lytton, *Paul Clifford*, 1830); *...of the four outs*, 'without wit, without money, without credit and without manners' (Hotten, 1864)] [late 18C–19C] 'Without money, without wit, and without manners; some add another out, i.e. without credit' (Grose, 1785).

gentleman's *n.* [abbr. GENTLEMAN'S COMPLAINT below] [1920s+] (*W.I.*) a euph. for any form of venereal disease.

IN COMPOUNDS

❑ **gentleman's companion** *n.* [late 18C–19C] a louse. ❑ **gentleman's complaint** *n.* [1920s+] (*W.I.*) a euph. for gonorrhoea. ❑ **gentleman's disease** *n.* [late 16C–17C] venereal disease. ❑ **gentleman's gent** *n.* (*also* **gent's gent**) [1920s–30s] a valet. ❑ **gentleman's master** *n.* [his temporary ascendancy over his social betters] [18C] a highwayman. ❑ **gentleman's pleasure-garden** *n.* [late 19C–1900s] the vagina.

gently Bentley! *excl.* [BBC radio's weekly comedy *Take It From Here* (1940–60), used as catchphrase by Jimmy Edwards (1920–88), addressed to Dick *Bentley*] [1940s–60s] a general excl. of restraint, hang on! take it easy! not too fast! etc.

gentoo *n.* (*also* **jentoe, jintoe**) ['named for the *Gentoo*, a ship which arrived at Cape Town in the mid-19th century with a group of women passengers who became prostitutes; the countries of origin of the women and the ship, and the circumstances of their arrival at the Cape are obscure and in dispute' (*DSAE*). The main theories point to the UK, whose authorities sent out 46 women spec. recruited for the task, or the French] [late 19C+] (*S.Afr.*) a prostitute; thus *gentoo house*, a brothel, usu. entertained by a Malay band.

gentry *n.*

SE in slang uses

IN COMPOUNDS

❑ **gentry-cove** *n.* (*also* **gentry cofe, ...cuffin**) [COVE *n.* (1)/ CUFFIN *n.* (1)] [mid-16C–1900s] (*UK Und.*) a nobleman, a gentleman. ❑ **gentry-cove's ken** *n.* (*also* **gentry cove ken, gentry ken**) [KEN *n.*[1] (1)] [mid-16C] (*UK Und.*) a nobleman's or gentleman's house. ❑ **gentry crib** *n.* [CRIB *n.*[1] (1)] [mid-19C] (*UK Und.*) a gentleman's house. ❑ **gentry mort** *n.* [MORT *n.* (1)] [mid-16C–mid-19C] (*UK Und.*) a noblewoman, a gentlewoman.

gents *n.* [abbr.] [1930s+] the *gentleman's* lavatory.

genuffel *v.* [? backsl. 'loving'] [1930s+] (*S.Afr.*) to flirt.

gen up? *phr.* [SE *genuine*] [1990s+] do you mean it? are you telling the truth?; also as a statement, truly, honestly.

Geoff Hurst *n.* [rhy. sl.; ult. England footballer *Geoff Hurst* (b.1941), famous for his hat-trick in the 1966 World Cup Final] [1990s+] a first-class degree.

Geoffrey Chaucer *n.* [rhy. sl.; ult. *Geoffrey Chaucer* (c.1343–1400), author of *The Canterbury Tales*] [20C+] a saucer.

geography *n.*[1] [one 'explores' it] [1920s+] the vagina.

geography *n.*[2] [euph.] [1920s+] the lavatory.

Geordie *n.* [proper name] **1** [mid-19C+] a Tynesider; thus *Geordie-land*, Tyneside. **2** [1910s+] (*Aus./N.Z.*) a Scot. **3** [1940s+] the Tyneside dialect and accent.

George *n.*[1] [the image of St *George* engraved on the coin] **1** [late 16C–17C] a noble (worth 6s 8d or one-third of a pound). **2** [mid-17C–mid-19C] a half crown, 2s 6d (12½p). **3** [early 18C] a guinea; a pound. **4** [1990s+] money in general.

George *n.*[2]

IN EXCLAMATIONS

❑ **by George!** (*also* **before George! George!**) [synon. for *by Jesus!*] [late 17C+] a general excl.

George *n.*[3] [note RAF jargon *George*, a familiar form of address to any stranger; (1920s+) air crew jargon *George*, the automatic pilot in milit. and civil aircraft; N.Z. WW2 milit. *George*, an Egyptian; note Rowse, *Doughboy Dope from A to Z* (1918) p.25: 'The mysterious George, who did the things you didn't do yourself on the outside, doesn't seem to have enlisted in this man's army'] **1** [early–mid-19C] (*N.Z.*) a generic term for a Maori. **2** [1900s–40s] (*US*) a generic term for a black male. **3** [1920s–50s] (*Can./US*) a generic name for an otherwise nameless black Pullman porter. **4** [2000s] (*US black*) a boyfriend.

IN PHRASES

❑ **let George do it** [1910s–40s] (*US*) let someone else do the work or take the responsibility.

George *n.*[4] [the portrait of *George* Washington on the note] [1940s+] (*US*) a $1 bill or as *big George*, a quarter.

George *n.*[5] *see* GRANDMA (GEORGE) *n.*

George *adj.* [? var. on JERRY *adj.* (1)] **1** [1900s–10s] (*US Und.*) wise, in the know; thus *be George*, to understand. **2** [1930s–70s] (*US*) acceptable, satisfactory.

IN PHRASES

❑ **real George, the** *n.* [1940s–50s] (*US teen*) the best, the ideal.

George! *excl. see* BY GEORGE! *under* GEORGE *n.*[2].

george *n.*[1] [ety. unknown; but note the habit of giving pet names to parts of one's body, usu. the genitals] [1940s+] (*W.I.*) a sore or swollen leg or foot; elephantiasis.

george *n.*[2] [ety. unknown] [1970s] (*US prison*) a one-year prison sentence; thus one of anything.

george *v. see* GEORGIA *v.*

George and Ringo *n.* [rhy. sl.; ult. the Beatles members *George* Harrison (1943–2001) and *Ringo* Starr (b.1940)] [1990s+] bingo.

George Bernard Shaw *n.* [rhy. sl.; ult. the Irish-born playwright *George Bernard Shaw* (1856–1950)] [1940s–50s] a door.

George Blake *n.* [rhy. sl.; ult. Soviet spy *George Blake* (b.1922)] [1960s] a snake.

George Bohee *n.* (*also* **bohee**) [rhy. sl.; ult. the name of a once well-known banjo player, but note *bohea*, the best variety of black tea, from the Wu-i hills in north Fukien, China] [1900s–40s] tea.

george called *phr.* [20C+] (*Aus./US*) a phr. indicating that a woman is menstruating.

George Gerrard *n.* [the proper name of *George Gerrard*, a well-known (and presumably big-talking) character] [20C+] (*Aus.*) a gross exaggeration.

George Plateroon *n.* [mid-17C–early 18C] (*UK Und.*) 'silver' plate that is in fact mainly copper with a thin silver coating.

George Raft *n.* [rhy. sl.; ult. US film star *George Raft* (1895–1980)] [1930s+] **1** a draught. **2** a banker's draft. **3** hard work, i.e. GRAFT *n.*[2] (1).

George Robey *n.* [rhy. sl. = TOBY *n.*[2] (2); ult. UK comedian Sir *George Robey* (1869–1954)] [1910s–30s] (*UK tramp*) the road.

george (smack) *n.* [GEORGE *adj.* (2) + SMACK *n.*[2] (1)] [1960s–70s] (*US drugs*) high-quality heroin.

George Street backblocker *n.* [George Street, a major artery in Sydney, thus generic for urban life and concerns + SAusE *backblocks*, the remote interior] [1910s] (*Aus.*) a business man who owns land in the outback but rarely if ever visits.

George the Third *n.* [1980s+] **1** a *third*-class degree [abbr.]. **2** a piece of excrement, a TURD *n.*[1] (1) [rhy. sl.].

Georgette *n.* [1980s] (*US camp gay*) a term of address to a fellow homosexual male.

George Washington *n.* [*George Washington* (1732–99), 1st President of the US] **1** [1900s] (*Aus./US*) a 'tall tale' [Washington's legendary assurance that 'I cannot tell a lie'].

2 [1930s+] (*US*) a $1 bill [the portrait of Washington printed on the notes]. **3** [1990s+] (*US*) in pl., money, in unspecified sums [ext. of sense 2 above].

Georgia *adj.* [the stereotyping of the state and its natives as poor and backward] [20C+] (*US*) a general derog. term, usu. found in a variety of combs., *see* below.

IN COMPOUNDS

❑ **Georgia buggy** *n.* **1** [1910s+] (*orig. US black*) a wheelbarrow. **2** [1930s] a wheeled rail used to transport racks of clothes. ❑ **Georgia ham** *n.* [its popularity in Georgia + the pinkness of both foodstuffs] [1940s–70s] (*US*) watermelon. ❑ **Georgia ice-cream** *n.* [1970s+] (*US*) grits. ❑ **Georgia overdrive** *n.* [1950s+] (*US*) coasting or freewheeling in order to save petrol. ❑ **Georgia peach** *n.* [the trad. *Georgia peach* is white and female] [1970s+] (*US gay*) a black man. ❑ **Georgia skin** *n.* [abbr. *Georgia skin game*, a card-game] [1930s+] (*US black*) (*also* **skin**) a kind of card-game.

georgia *n.* [abbr. carnival use *Georgia scuffle*, a form of confidence trick] [1960s+] (*US black*) a swindle, esp. that worked by a prostitute on a customer.

IN PHRASES

❑ **send to Georgia** *v. see* GEORGIA *v.* (3).

georgia *v.* (*also* **george, georgy**) [GEORGIA *n.*] [1960s+] (*US black*) **1** to play a confidence trick on a person who has newly arrived from the south and is thus naïve as regards the northern, urban world. **2** to be seduced into a sexual liaison by a woman. **3** (*also* **do the G, send to Georgia**) of a prostitute's client, to accept her services but to renege on payment; thus to rape.

georgie *n.* (*also* **georgy**) [early 19C] **1** (*orig. Und.*) a quartern loaf [*BROWN GEORGE under* BROWN *adj.*[2]]. **2** a penny [the picture of George IV on the coin].

Georgie Best *n.* [rhy. sl.; ult. UK footballer and fabled drinker *George Best* (1946–2005)] [1960s+] **1** a guest. **2** a (drunken) pest. **3** a female breast.

georgie bundle *n.* [ety. unknown; ? anecdotal] [20C+] (*W.I.*) **1** a small bundle that nonetheless can hold all one's few possessions. **2** a collection of odds and ends.

Georgie Moore *n. see* RORY (O'MOORE) *n.* (1).

georgy *n. see* GEORGIE *n.*

georgy *v. see* GEORGIA *v.*

Geraldine *n.* [initial letter of SE *g*eriatric] [2000s] (*S.Afr. gay*) an older, i.e. over 40, homosexual man.

geranium *n.* **1** [late 19C] a red nose. **2** [late 19C] the head. **3** [1900s] (*US Western*) a person, a fellow. **4** [1920s] (*US*) in pl., cabbage.

gerbil *n.* [1980s+] (*US*) a stupid, insignificant or unpleasant person.

gercha! *excl.* (*also* **gertch! gertcha! gertcher!**) [lit. or fig. *get away with you!*/GET ALONG WITH YOU! *excl.*] [1920s+] a mocking response, either aggressive or affectionate.

gerdoing!/gerdoying! *excl. see KERDOINC! under* KER- *pfx.*

gere *n. see* JERE *n.*

geri *n.* (*also* **gerri, gerry**) [abbr. SE *geriatric*] [1970s+] a term for the old (and middle-aged).

germ *n.* (*also* **jerm**) **1** [1940s+] (*US*) a contemptible person. **2** [1990s+] (*US black*) constr. with *the*, AIDS. **3** [2000s] (*US prison*) a cigarette.

Germaine Greer *n.* [rhy. sl.; ult. Aus. writer *Germaine Greer* (b.1939)] [1990s+] (*Aus.*) a beer.

German *n.* **1** [late 19C] a German sausage, a wurst. **2** [1990s+] (*US drugs*) a Dominican cocaine dealer.

IN COMPOUNDS

❑ **German comb** *n.* [the supposed lack of sophistication in German immigrants, who prefer their fingers to a comb] [late 19C+] (*US*) the hand. ❑ **German delight** *n.* [1900s] (*US Und.*) beer. ❑ **German duck** *n. see* separate entries. ❑ **German goitre** *n.* [the stereotyped German capacity for beer] [20C+] (*US*) a beer belly, a noticeable paunch. ❑ **German gospel** *n.* [a speech delivered in November 1897 by Prince Henry of Prussia to his brother Kaiser Wilhelm II (1859–1941), which was full of such fulsome phrases as: 'The gospel that emanates from your Majesty's sacred person...'] [late 19C] vain boasting, megalomania, self-aggrandizement. ❑ **German helmet** *n.* [1950s+] (*orig. gay*) the glans penis. ❑ **German marching pills** *n.* [used by Ger. soldiers, among others, in WWII and later conflicts] [1950s+] (*gay*) amphetamines, esp. Methedrine, a German invention.

IN PHRASES

❑ **polish the old German helmet** *v.* (*also* **burnish the German helmet**) [1990s+] (*US*) to perform oral sex.

German bands *n.* (*also* **German**) [rhy. sl.] [1910s+] the hands.

German duck *n.*[1] [the popularity of the dish among the German sugar-bakers of London's East End] [late 18C–mid-19C] half a sheep's head boiled with onions.

German duck *n.*[2] [orig. Yorks. dial.; ? racial stereotyping] [mid-19C] a bedbug.

German flutes *n.* [rhy. sl.] [mid-19C–1960s] a pair of boots.

Geronimo *n.* [it leads one to excesses, supposedly similar to those of an Apache warrior] [1980s+] (*drugs*) a mixture of alcohol and barbiturates.

Geronimo! *excl.* [proper name *Geronimo*, nickname of Apache leader, Goyathlay ('One Who Yawns') (1829–1909); note NYHT 19/5/1941: ' The use of "Geronimo" dates back to the early days of the 501st Parachute Battalion, 'way back in last October. Two sergeants got into an argument about being afraid, when the first left the plane. One said that to prove he was not scared stiff he would yell something as he jumped. When he left the plane the only thing that came to mind was the name of the famous Indian chief. So he hollered out "Geronimo!"'] [1940s+] (*US, orig. army*) a cry made when leaping or about to start a fight.

gerook *adj.* [Afk. *gerook*, smoked] [1970s+] (*S.Afr.*) intoxicated by drink or a drug, usu. cannabis.

IN PHRASES

❑ **spookgerook** *adj.* [2000s] (*S.Afr.*) paranoid through smoking.

gerri *n. see* GERI *n.*

Gerry *n. see* JERRY *n.*

gerry *n.*[1] [ety. unknown; *DSUE* suggests Lat. *gero*, I carry. Note Devon dial. *gerred*, bedaubed, filthy] [16C] excrement; thus imper. *gerry gan*, be quiet.

gerry *n.*[2] *see* GERI *n.*

gerry *v. see* JERRY *v.* (2).

gerry riddle *n.* [rhy. sl. = PIDDLE *n.* (2)] [1930s+] (*Aus.*) urination.

gert and daisy *adj.* [rhy. sl.; ult. characters created on BBC radio in the 1930s by comediennes Elsie (d.1990) and Doris Waters (d.1978)] [1950s+] lazy.

gertch!/gertcha!/gertcher! *excl. see* GERCHA! *excl.*

Gertie *n.* **1** [1910s+] a prostitute, a promiscuous woman. **2** [1930s+] (*camp gay*) (*also* **Gertrude**) a general term of address to a fellow homosexual man. **3** [1970s+] (*S.Afr. gay*) a heterosexual woman.

gertie *n.* [initial letter] [2000s] (*S.Afr. gay*) gonorrhoea.

Gertie Gitana *n.* [rhy. sl.; ult. music-hall star *Gertie Gitana* (1888–1957)] [20C+] banana.

gertoss *n.* [? SE *girl* + TOSSER *n.*[1] (3)] [2000s] (*N.Z. teen*) a young woman.

Gertrude *n.* [? generic use of female name as derog.] **1** [1940s] (*US milit.*) a clerk. **2** *see* GERTIE *n.* (2).

Gertrude *adj.* [? generic use of name as derog.] [2000s] (*S.Afr. gay*) unattractive.

Gerty Lee *n.* [rhy. sl.; ult. late 19C actress *Gertie Lee*] [1910s+] (*bingo*) the number 33.

gerund-grinder *n.* [early 18C–19C; 1940s] a schoolteacher, esp. a pedant; thus *gerund-grinding*, instruction in Latin grammar, pedantic instruction generally; *gerund-grindery*, a classical school; *gerund-stone*, the imaginary grindstone of a *gerund-grinder*.

gerver *n.* [var./mispron. of GOPHER *n.*[2] (3)] [1910s–20s] (*US Und.*) a safe breaker.

gessein *v.* (*also* **gesseiner**) [? Yid., but note Scot. *gess*, to leave clandestinely] [1940s–50s] (*S.Afr./UK prison*) to trick, to hoax, to dupe; thus *gesseiner*, valuables, belongings.

gessump *v.* [GAZUMP *v.*] [1940s–50s] (*UK prison*) to acquire anything by fraud or a confidence trick.

gestapo *n.* (*also* **gestaps**) [fig. use of Ger. *Geheime Staatspolizei*, the *Gestapo*, the internal police force used by the German Nazi regime 1933–45; note WW2 UK milit. use *gestapo*, military police] **1** [1950s+] (*US black/Aus. Und.*) the police. **2** [1980s+] (*Aus. prison*) the security section.

gesuip *adj.* [Afk. *suip*, to drink, used of an animal] [1980s] (*S.Afr.*) drunk.

get *n.*^{1} (*also* **gett, ghett**) [orig. 16C SE *get*, bastard, brat; the term lapsed into sl. by 18C] **1** [18C+] a bastard child. **2** [1920s+] any creature or object. **3** [1930s+] an idiot, a fool; an unpleasant person; a general term of abuse.

IN PHRASES

❑ **whore's get** *n.* [1920s+] (*Irish*) a bastard child, a general term of abuse.

get *n.*^{2} [GET *v.* (2a)] [late 19C] a swindle, a trick, a means of defrauding a victim.

get *n.*^{3} [GET *v.* (1b)] [late 19C–1950s] (*Aus./N.Z.*) an escape; usu. *do a get*, to leave quickly, to run off.

get *n.*^{4} [i.e. what the robbers *get*; 14C–17C SE] [1940s–60s] (*US*) the profit, the take, the booty of a robbery.

get *v.* **1** in senses of movement. (**a**) [mid-18C+] to start, to commence, with an implication of urgency, e.g. 'get moving', 'get walking' etc. (**b**) [mid-19C+] (*orig. US*) (*also* **git**) to go away; esp. as GET! *excl.* **2** in senses meaning to attack, lit. or fig., physically or verbally. (**a**) [mid-19C+] to trick, to cheat, to victimize. (**b**) [late 19C] to surpass. (**c**) [late 19C+] to succeed in killing for retribution, to 'do for'. (**d**) [late 19C+] to get even with, to take vengeance on, e.g. *I'll get you, just you wait and see*. (**e**) [late 19C+] to have sexual intercourse. (**f**) [20C+] (*also* **get a body**) to kill, to wound. (**g**) [20C+] to corner someone, to get hold of, to track down. (**h**) [1920s+] to attack, to hit. (**i**) [1990s+] to tease, to make someone look foolish. **3** [late 19C] to eat a meal. **4** [1910s–30s] to be punished, to get one's deserts [abbr. SE *get one's deserts*]. **5** [1910s+] to notice, to look at; usu. as derog. imper., e.g. *get him!* look at him (isn't he stupid). **6** [1950s] (*US*) to perceive. **7** [1990s+] (*US black*) to meet, to make contact with.

IN EXCLAMATIONS

❑ **get her!** (*also* **get him!**) [orig. camp gay, 'her' being someone acting exceptionally affectedly, but now general use] [1950s+] an excl. of derision, mockery (both affectionate and otherwise). ❑ **get this!** (*also* **get that!**) [20C+] now listen! take note! this is amazing! ❑ **get you!** [1940s+] a teasing, mocking phr., used to deflate someone who is seen as showing off, overdressing etc; thus *get me!*, teasing oneself; the tone is usu. stereotypically effeminate/homosexual.

SE in slang uses

IN COMPOUNDS

❑ **getabit** *n.* [1900s–20s] a thief. ❑ **get-'em-up** *adj.* (*also* **git-'em-up**) [i.e. his demand *get your hands up!*] [1930s] describing armed robbers, pertaining to hold-up with a gun. ❑ **get-go** *n.* see GIT-GO *n.* ❑ **get-high** *n.* [*see under* HIGH *adj.*^{1}] **1** [1980s+] (*US black*) any form of drug. **2** (*US drug*) a drug user's equipment. ❑ **get-out** *n.* [worn when one 'gets out' of the house] [1940s–50s] (*US black/N.Z.*) an outfit, a suit of clothes.

IN PHRASES

❑ **get...** *v.* **1** *see also* separate entries. **2** *see also under* relevant n. or adj. ❑ **get a body** *v. see* GET *v.* (2f). ❑ **get across** *v.* [1910s+] **1** to irritate, to annoy. **2** (*US black*) to succeed. **3** to seduce. **4** to acquire status. ❑ **get among it** *v.* [1910s+] (*Aus.*) **1** to make a large amount of money. **2** to seduce a woman. ❑ **get around** *v.* **1** see GET UP *v.*^{1} (2). **2** *see* WRAP ONESELF AROUND *under* WRAP *v.* ❑ **get 'em** *v.* (*also* **get them**) [*them* are the SHAKES, THE *n.* (1)] [20C+] **1** to suffer delirium tremens. **2** to be mad. **3** to be frightened. ❑ **get 'em off** *v. see* GET IT OFF *under* GET IT *v.* ❑ **get it in** *v. see under* IT *n.*^{1}. ❑ **get ketch** *v. see* GET CATCH *under* CATCH *v.*^{2}. ❑ **get laid** *v. see under* LAY *v.*^{1}. ❑ **getme?** [SE colloq. *get*, to understand] [2000s] (*orig. black*) a phr. meaning you understand? often used as an all-purpose phr. to punctuate sentences. ❑ **get me, Steve?** (*also* **got me Steve?**) [1910s] (*Aus.*) are you with me? do you understand? ❑ **get money at the best** *v. see under* BEST *v.* ❑ **get much?** *see* GETTING ANY (LATELY)? below. ❑ **get one** *v.* ['one' is a fit] [1910s] to lose emotional control. ❑ **get one at it** *v. see under* IT *n.*^{1}. ❑ **get one going** *v. see under* ONE *n.*^{1}. ❑ **get one off** *v. see* GET IT OFF *under* GET IT *v.* ❑ **get one on** *v. see under* ONE *n.*^{1}. ❑ **get one over (on)** *v. see under* ONE *n.*^{1}. ❑ **get one in** *v. see under* ONE *n.*^{1}. ❑ **get one's** *v.* (*also* **have one's**) **1** [late 19C+] (*orig. US*) to suffer in some way. **2** [20C+] (*orig. US*) to be killed, to die, usu. by accident or through violence. **3** [20C+] (*orig. US black*) to get one's share, usu. of material pleasures, to get what one deserves; usu. as *get mine*. **4** [1960s] (*US*) to get sexual satisfaction. ❑ **get one's a into g** *v.* [abbr. of GET ONE'S ASS IN(TO) GEAR *under* GEAR *n.*, with added element of trying to calculate something] [1970s+] (*N.Z.*) to get on with things, to hurry up. ❑ **get one's — on** *v.* [1990s+] (*US*) used with a n. to describe an activity. ❑ **get one up** *v. see* GET IT UP *v.*^{2} (1). ❑ **get out at...** *v. see* GET OFF AT... *v.* ❑ **get out on** *v.* [1930s] to get away with. ❑ **get someone at it** *v. see under* IT *n.*^{1}. ❑ **get them** *v. see* GET 'EM above. ❑ **get them in** *v. see* GET ONE IN *under* ONE *n.*^{1}. ❑ **get the name out** *v. see under* GET UP *v.*^{1} (2). ❑ **get through** *v.* [1970s+] (*drugs*) to obtain drugs. ❑ **getting any (lately)?** (*also* **get much?**) [ANY *n.* (1)] [1940s+] (*orig. Aus.*) a popular greeting between men. ❑ **getting much?** [the 'much' is sex] [1920s+] (*US*) a male-to-male greeting.

IN EXCLAMATIONS

❑ **get out of here!** [1910s+] (*orig. US black*) a general excl. of disbelief, dismissal, I don't believe you! you must be joking! don't be silly! who do you think you're fooling?

get! *excl.* [GET *v.*] [mid-19C+] get moving! start walking! go away!

get-a-life *adj.* [GET A LIFE! *excl.*] [2000s] describing someone whose preoccupations are considered pitiful.

get a life! *excl.* [1980s+] a dismissive excl. used in any context where the speaker wishes to show disdain for the previous speaker and their ideas, suggestions or opinions.

get along with you! *excl.* (*also* **go along with you!**) [mid-19C+] a general excl. of dismissal and ridicule, esp. as a response to what is seen as excessive or insincere flattery, don't be so silly! you can't fool me!

get at *v.* **1** [late 19C–1920s] (*US*) to begin; to start work on, to turn one's attention to. **2** [late 19C+] to attack, usu. verbally. **3** [late 19C+] to tease, to banter. **4** [late 19C+] to corrupt, to bribe, to tamper with; thus *got at*, bribed, corrupted, subverted. **5** [late 19C+] to hint, to imply; usu. in phr. *what are you getting at?* **6** [1990s+] (*US campus*) to get in touch. **7** [2000s] (*US black*) to invite to fight.

getaway *n.* **1** [mid-19C–1920s] a sudden dash, esp. from the starting point in a game or sport. **2** [mid-19C+] (*orig. UK Und.*) an escape. **3** [mid-19C+] the mode of escape, i.e. a road or alley. **4** [mid-19C+] (*US Und.*) a train or vehicle used for escape. **5** [late 19C–1900s] (*US*) the very start. **6** [20C+] an excuse. **7** [1900s] (*US Und.*) a successful act of robbery.

getaway car *n.* [GETAWAY *n.* (2)] [1930s+] (*US*) a car used by criminals escaping from a crime.

get away (with) *v.* [late 19C+] to get the better of, to beat.

get-back *n.* [SE colloq. *get back (at)*, to retaliate] [20C+] (*US*) revenge.

get back *v.* [1980s] (*US black*) to think again.

SE in slang uses

IN EXCLAMATIONS

❑ **get back in your box!** [late 19C+] (*orig. US*) a general excl. of rebuke, be quiet! I don't want to know! that's quite enough of that!

get back! *excl.* [the image of holding back people crowding to view something special] [mid-19C; 1980s+] (*UK Und./US campus*) an expression of admiration.

get-by *n.* [SE colloq. *get by*, to survive] [1950s] (*US*) a way of life, usu. a difficult one.

get-down *n. see* GIT-DOWN *n.*

get-down *adj.* [GET DOWN *v.*[2] (2)] [1970s] (*US*) committed to enjoying oneself.

get down *v.*[1] [the 'putting down' of one's wager] [late 19C+] (*US*) to place a bet.

get down *v.*[2] [abbr. SE phr. *get down to business*] **1** [1910s+] (*orig. US*) to commit oneself, to make a serious effort. **2** [1950s+] (*orig. US*) to dance, to have a good time. **3** [1950s+] (*orig. US*) to have sexual intercourse. **4** [1960s+] (*orig. US*) to concentrate. **5** [1960s+] (*US black*) to establish oneself, to work. **6** [1960s+] (*orig. US*) (*also* **get down with one's bad self**) to do something especially well. **7** [1970s] (*US Und.*) of a prostitute, to start work for the night. **8** [1970s+] to make something happen, to reach a successful conclusion. **9** [1970s+] to join in with, to take part in. **10** [1970s+] (*US black*) to fight. **11** [1980s] (*US black*) to attempt seduction.

IN PHRASES

▫ **get down dirty** *v.* (*also* **get down fonky, ...shitty**) [SE *dirty*/ FONKY *adj.*[2]/SHITTY *adj.*[1] (3)] [1980s+] (*US black*) to become abusive, to cause trouble. ▫ **get down from the Y** *v.* [? the Y represents the torso and the arms] [1970s+] (*US black*) to fight. ▫ **get down heavy** *v.* [HEAVY *adv.* (3)] [1930s–70s] (*US black*) to enjoy oneself, to enter wholeheartedly into the spirit of an occasion. ▫ **get down with one's bad self** *v. see* sense 6 above.

SE in slang uses

IN PHRASES

▫ **get down to the ground (and move it round and round)** *v.* [1980s] (*US black*) to have sexual intercourse. ▫ **get down to the nitty-gritty** *v. see under* NITTY-GRITTY *n.* ▫ **get down to tin tacks** *v. see under* TIN TACKS *n.*

get down *v.*[3] (*also* **get down on**) [1930s] (*US*) to perform fellatio or cunnilingus.

get down *v.*[4] [DOWN *adj.*[1]] [1950s+] (*US*) to take a narcotic or other recreational drug, usu. heroin.

get down! *excl.* [GET DOWN *v.*[2] (2)] [1960s+] an excl. of encouragement, usu. in the context of a musical performance, whether live or created by a DJ playing records/tapes.

get down on *v.*[1] [DOWN ON *under* DOWN *adj.*[1]] [late 19C+] (*US*) to develop a dislike for or grudge against, to be hostile or oppressive to.

get down on *v.*[2] [SE *get down*, i.e. to bend down to pick something up] [20C+] (*Aus./N.Z.*) to steal; to get hold of.

get down on *v.*[3] *see* GET DOWN *v.*[3] (1).

get 'em off *v. see GET IT OFF under* GET IT *v.*

get fucked *v.* [FUCK *v.* (1)] [1960s+] to have sexual intercourse, used of both men and women.

get fucked! *excl.* [FUCKED *adj.*[1] although this predates slightly] [1910s+] a general excl. of dismissal or contempt; thus euph. *get intercoursed!*

get going *v.* (*also* **have going, set going**) [late 19C+] **1** to drive someone into a temper, to make someone lose control through teasing. **2** to excite someone sexually. **3** to excite someone (other than sexually). **4** to worry or unnerve someone. **5** of a rumour or piece of gossip, to persuade someone of its veracity. **6** to start someone talking, usu. in an angry or neurotic manner.

get in *v.*

IN PHRASES

▫ **get in tow with** *v.* [2000s] (*N.Z.*) to conduct a relationship with, usu. amatory.

IN EXCLAMATIONS

▫ **get in there!** (*also* **in there!**) [1920s+] a general exhortation; in post-1980s UK, typically of a man's friends who are watching his approaches to an unknown woman; often ext. as *get in there, my son!*

get into *v.* (*also* **get in**) **1** [late 18C; 1960s+] to become aware of, to understand. **2** [late 19C+] to penetrate either the vagina or anus; in weak use, to seduce. **3** [1910s+] (*orig. N.Z.*) to attack, whether lit. in a fight, or fig. food, a task etc. **4** [1920s+] (*US*) to defraud, to become indebted to. **5** [1920s+] to enjoy, to become involved in. **6** [1940s+] to develop, to happen; usu. in phr. *what's got into you/him/her?* **7** [1950s+] to argue about. **8** [1960s+] to grow close to.

IN PHRASES

▫ **get into it** *v.* **1** [1960s+] (*US*) to fight with, to argue with. **2** [2000s] to have sexual intercourse.

get it *v.* **1** [early 19C] to be assaulted or beaten up. **2** [mid-19C+] (*US*) to be shot, wounded or killed. **3** [mid-19C+] to be punished or reprimanded. **4** [late 19C+] to be subjected to abuse or nagging. **5** [1930s+] of a man, to have sexual intercourse; of a woman, to be subjected to intercourse. **6** [1940s] to catch a venereal disease. **7** [1940s+] (*US*) to go at great speed. **8** [1960s+] (*US*) to be pleasing, attractive, used in negative contexts, e.g. *Sorry, but he just doesn't get it.*

IN PHRASES

▫ **get it all** *v.* [1900s] (*US Und.*) to get life imprisonment. ▫ **get it down** *v.* [1990s+] (*US*) to master, e.g. a job of work. ▫ **get it hot** *v. see under* HOT *adv.* ▫ **get it in** *v. see under* IT *n.*[1]. ▫ **get it in one** *v.* (*also* **get there in one**) [1930s+] to succeed in doing, in understanding etc at the first try, esp. in a sexual context. ▫ **get it in the back/collar button/guts** *v. see* GET IT IN THE NECK *v.* ▫ **get it in the neck** *v. see* separate entry. ▫ **get it in the throat** *v. see* GET IT IN THE NECK *v.* ▫ **get it off** *v.* (*also* **get 'em off, get one off**) [GET OFF *v.*[2]] [1930s+] (*US*) to reach orgasm, to copulate, to derive pleasure. ▫ **get it off with** *v.* [var. on HAVE IT OFF *v.*] [1970s+] of a man, to have sexual intercourse. ▫ **get it on** *see* separate entries. ▫ **get it up** *v. see* separate entries. ▫ **get it where Maggie wore the beads** *v.* [i.e. GET IT IN THE NECK *v.* (1)] [1900s–20s] to be hit or hurt, to suffer in the worst place, or fig. in the worst poss. way given the context. ▫ **get it where the chicken got the axe** *v.* [i.e. GET IT IN THE NECK *v.* (1)] [late 19C–1910s] to suffer in the worst possible way, according to context.

get it? *phr.* (*also* **geddit?**) [SE colloq. *get*, to understand] [20C+] do you understand? esp. referring to the point of a joke.

get it! *excl.* (*also* **get it, girl!**) [1980s+] (*US campus*) an excl. of encouragement.

get it in the neck *v.* (*also* **cop it in the neck, get it in the back, ...collar button, ...guts**) [late 19C+] **1** (*also* **get it in the throat**) to be punished severely, to suffer badly, to be harshly criticized. **2** (*orig. US*) to be killed or badly wounded.

get-it-on *adj.* [GET IT ON *v.* (2)] [1970s] active, motivated, energetic.

get it on *v.* **1** [20C+] (*US*) to start a fight; to fight; lit. and fig. **2** [1950s+] (*orig. US black*) to start, to take positive action. **3** [1970s] to get an erection. **4** [1970s] to enjoy oneself. **5** [1970s+] (*also* **get it on with, g.i.o.**) to seduce, to have sexual intercourse.

get it on! *excl.* [1970s+] (*orig. US*) a shout of encouragement, enthusiasm, e.g. directed at a musician.

get it up *v.*[1] [late 19C+] to harass, to target for unkindness, to tease.

IN PHRASES

▫ **get it up for** *v.* [1920s+] **1** to concoct evidence against, to frame. **2** to provoke.

get it up *v.*[2] (*also* **get one up, get up**) (*orig. US*) **1** [1930s+] to achieve an erection; occas. in fig. use of a woman. **2** [1960s] to find a required sum of money. **3** [1970s+] in fig. use, to maintain enthusiasm for an idea, situation etc.

get it up *v.*[3] [1950s] (*US Und.*) to amass and produce a sum of money, e.g. in payment of an outstanding debt.

get lost *v.* [20C+] to vanish, to disappear; the implication is of stopping causing trouble.

get lost! *excl.* [Yid. *ver farvalgert*, disappear, move on, go away] [1940s+] a general excl. of dismissal, go away! be off!

get-off *n.* [SE colloq. *get off*, to get away with] [early 19C] (*US*) an excuse.

get off *v.*[1] [late 19C] (*US*) to steal.

get off *v.*[2] **1** [20C+] to gain satisfaction. **2** [1920s+] (*US black*) to achieve one's object. **3** [1930s+] (*US*) to improvise or play music skilfully. **4** [1930s+] (*orig. US black*) to enjoy, to be stimulated by. **5** [1940s+] (*orig. US*) to achieve orgasm. **6** [1970s+] to bring one's partner to orgasm. **7** [1970s+] to masturbate. **8** [1990s+] to please or stimulate someone else. **9** [2000s] of a prostitute, to find a client.

IN PHRASES

❑ **get off with** *v.* **1** [1910s+] to strike up a relationship with a potential sexual partner (short of actual seduction). **2** [1930s+] to seduce, and poss. have sexual intercourse with. **3** [1990s+] (*teen*) to indulge in a session of French kissing.

get off *v.*^{3} **1** [1950s+] (*drugs*) to quit a drug (or alcohol) addiction. **2** [1950s+] (*drugs*) (*also* **get off on**) to get intoxicated with a drug, to experience the effects of a drug. **3** [1950s+] (*drugs*) to inject oneself with a drug. **4** [1960s] to attack. **5** [1970s] to get drunk.

SE in slang uses

IN PHRASES

❑ **get off at...** *v. see* separate entry. ❑ **get off on** *v. see* separate entries. ❑ **get off steam** *v. see* BLOW OFF STEAM *under* STEAM *n.* ❑ **get off the bra-strap** *v.* (*also* **get off the jock strap**) [1980s] (*US black*) to have sexual intercourse. ❑ **get off the dime** *v.* (*also* **get off the nickel**) [the image of a person being stuck on a small spot, i.e. one the size of a *dime* or *nickel* coin] [1920s+] (*US*) to move from a stationary position, esp. of a dancer; to stop idling, to start; also in fig. use, to stop acting/talking in a given manner. ❑ **tell someone where to get off** *v.* (*also* **tell someone where they get off, ...where to go, ...where to head in, show someone where to get off**) ['where they get off' or 'go' is hell] [20C+] (*orig. US*) to scold someone for interfering. ❑ **where does someone get off** [20C+] a phr. implying criticism of another's action.

IN EXCLAMATIONS

❑ **get off!/get off it!** *see* separate entries. ❑ **get off the earth!** [late 19C] (*US*) an excl. of dismissal. ❑ **get off the grass!** [1980s+] (*N.Z.*) an excl. of dimissal, contempt.

get off! *excl.* **1** [early 19C+] a general excl. of disbelief; don't talk nonsense! **2** [1950s+] stop it! **3** [1970s+] (*US campus*) an expression of admiration.

get off at... *v.* (*also* **get out at...**) [1970s+] used in terms meaning to perform coitus interruptus, to withdraw well before ejaculation; specific usages are usu. regional but can be found further afield.

IN PHRASES

❑ **...Broadgreen** (*also* **get out at Broadgreen**) [*Broadgreen* is the station before Edge Hill which is the station before Liverpool Lime Street] [1980s+] ❑ **...Edge Hill** (*also* **get out at Edge Hill**) [*Edge Hill* is the station before Liverpool Lime Street] [1980s+] ❑ **...Gateshead** (*also* **get out at Gateshead**) [*Gateshead* is the railway station before Newcastle-upon-Tyne; note RN use *get off at Fratton* in which Fratton is the stop immediately before Bristol dockyard] [1980s+] ❑ **...Green Island** (*also* **get out at Green Island, get off at Papakura**) [*Green Island*, the station before the terminal at Dunedin; *Papakura* is a couple of stops prior to the terminal at Auckland] [2000s] (*N.Z.*) ❑ **...Haymarket** (*also* **get out at Haymarket**) [used by the natives of Edinburgh, where *Haymarket* is the railway station immediately preceding their own] [1980s+] ❑ **...Hillgate** (*also* **get out at Hillgate**) [a notional place, poss. playing on *hill* = the *mons veneris*, and *gate*, i.e. the entry to the vagina] [1970s] ❑ **...Paisley** (*also* **get out at Paisley**) [used by Glaswegians, where *Paisley* is the railway station immediately before Glasgow] [1980s+] ❑ **...Redfern** (*also* **get out at Redfern**) [*Redfern* is the railway station immediately before Sydney Central] [1980s+] (*Aus.*)

get off it! *excl.* [1910s+] stop teasing! stop exaggerating!

get off on *v.*^{1} [GET OFF *v.*^{2} (4)] **1** [1940s+] to enjoy, to be stimulated by, esp. sexually. **2** *see* GET OFF *v.*^{3} (2).

get off on *v.*^{2} [1970s+] **1** to defeat in a fight. **2** to insult, to get angry with.

get-on *n.* [1900s–50s] (*US Und.*) the entrance to a streetcar.

get on *v.*^{1} **1** [late 19C+] to have sexual intercourse, orig. of a man; to behave in a sexually provocative way [his 'mounting' of his partner]. **2** [1970s] to physically attack.

IN PHRASES

❑ **get on (at)** *v.* [1910s+] to abuse, to scold, to nag. ❑ **get on that** *v.* [late 19C–1940s] (*Aus./US*) to understand, to look at.

IN EXCLAMATIONS

❑ **get on!** *see* GO ON! *excl.*

get on *v.*^{2} (*orig. US black*) **1** [1940s] to take drugs, to become intoxicated. **2** [1960s] to become addicted. **3** [1960s] to get drunk. **4** [1980s+] (*Aus. prison*) to buy drugs.

get on *v.*^{3} [1970s+] (*orig. US black*) to pursue a goal or aim.

get onto *v.* **1** [late 19C+] to suspect. **2** [late 19C+] (*US*) to understand, to work out. **3** [late 19C+] to look (at), to observe. **4** [20C+] to interrogate, to pressurize. **5** [1910s] to attack verbally, to criticize. **6** [1910s+] (*Aus.*) to join in, to participate.

get-over *n.* [GET OVER *v.*^{1} (5)] [1980s] (*US campus*) a lucky benefit.

get over *v.*^{1} **1** [mid-19C+] to take advantage of, to get around. **2** [late 19C–1910s] to astonish, to impress. **3** [1910s+] (*US*) to achieve a goal, to do well, to prosper. **4** [1940s+] (*Aus.*) to intimidate. **5** [1970s+] (*US black/prison*) (*also* **get over on**) to improve one's own image/reputation by putting someone else at a disadvantage. **6** [1980s] (*US black*) to make oneself understood. **7** [1990s+] (*US drugs*) to help someone in need of drugs. **8** [1990s+] (*US drugs*) to take the regular dose of drugs that sustains an addiction. **9** [2000s] (*US*) to get something for nothing. **10** *see* GET UP *v.*^{1} (2).

SE in slang uses

IN PHRASES

❑ **get over it** [1980s] (*US campus*) as imper., calm down, forget it.

get over *v.*^{2} [the physical act of 'mounting' a woman] [late 19C; 1970s+] (*US black*) to seduce, to have sexual intercourse.

SE in slang uses

IN PHRASES

❑ **get over her garter** *v.* (*also* **get over the garter**) [note D'Urfey, *Pills to Purge Melancholy* (1719–20): 'The Barn's a brave place to steal garters'; 'The Maid she held her Legs so wide, / The Young man slipt between, / Such tying of a Garter, / You have but seldom seen'] [mid-17C–late 18C; 1940s] to caress a woman sexually.

get round *v.* [i.e. SE *get around* someone] **1** [mid-19C+] (*orig. US*) to trick, to fool. **2** [mid-19C+] to persuade, to 'con'. **3** [late 19C+] to escape from an obligation or activity; to arrange events as one prefers them. **4** [1900s] (*Aus.*) to get equal, to achieve equality in a business deal.

gets *n.* [abbr. GETAWAY *n.* (2)] [1950s] (*US Und.*) an escape from prison.

gett *n. see* GET *n.*^{1}.

getter *n.* **1** [early 16C; late 19C–1920s] (*US Und.*) a thief; thus *stone-getter*, a diamond thief. **2** [1940s] (*UK Und.*) a criminal who steals letters for forgery gangs.

get-there *n.* [GET THERE *v.* (2)] [late 19C] (*US*) ambition, energy.

get there *v.* [fig. uses of SE] **1** [mid-19C+] of a man, to have sexual intercourse, esp. to deflower. **2** [late 19C+] (*US campus*) to achieve an aim. **3** [1980s+] to achieve orgasm. **4** [1990s+] to become intoxicated by drink or drugs.

IN PHRASES

❑ **get there in one** *v. see* GET IT IN ONE *under* GET IT *v.*

get to *v.* **1** [late 19C] to start doing something. **2** [late 19C+] to effect, to influence emotionally, to worry. **3** [20C+] to corrupt, to bribe, to influence. **4** [1910s+] (*N.Z.*) to attack physically; to kill. **5** [1920s] (*US Und.*) to gain or possess information about. **6** [1960s+] to listen; thus *get to this*, listen to this. **7** [1960s+] to watch.

get-up *n.*^{1} (*also* **git-up**) [mid-19C+] (*US*) energy, spirit.

get-up *n.*^{2} [something 'got up' to allay suspicions or enquiries] [1900s–50s] lies, a ruse, a subterfuge, a false charge.

get-up *n.*^{3} [SE *get up*, i.e. in the morning] **1** [1910s+] (*US prison*) the date of one's release as given by a parole board. **2** [1930s+] an amount of heroin, used in the morning to prevent withdrawal symptons.

get up *v.*[1] **1** [mid-17C; 19C+] to penetrate sexually (whether the vagina or anus). **2** [1980s+] (*also* **get around, ...over, ...the name out**) of a graffiti artist, to inscribe one's name or signature. **3** [1990s+] (*Aus.*) to beat, to get the better of. **4** *see* GET IT UP *v.*[2] (1).

IN PHRASES

❑ **get oneself up** *v.* **1** [mid–late 19C] to dress up. **2** [1970s] to prepare oneself emotionally. ❑ **get up with** *v.* [1970s+] (*US black/campus*) **1** to meet someone; to get in touch with. **2** to have a romantic encounter; to have sexual intercourse. **3** to fight. ❑ **get up off** *v.* [1930s–50s] (*US black*) **1** to experience the effects of a drug. **2** to resist a way of doing things. **3** to give up something important or valuable. **4** to make oneself sexually available. **5** to refrain from gossiping about a third party. ❑ **get up (on)** *v.* [1960s+] (*US black*) to get excited by, to become interested in; as a command to become aware, 'get wise,' or with n., to act.

SE in slang uses

IN PHRASES

❑ **get up and get** *see* separate entries. ❑ **get up in** *v.* [1990s+] (*US black/prison*) to intefere in, to force oneself upon, to fig. enter where one is unwelcome/forbidden.

get up *v.*[2] [GET-UP *n.*[3] (1)] [1930s] (*US prison*) to reach the end of one's sentence.

get up *v.*[3] *see* GET IT UP *v.*[2].

get up! *excl.* [1980s+] (*US campus*) an expression of admiration.

get-up-and-get *n.* (*also* **git-up-and-git**) [GET UP AND GET *v.*] [late 19C–1950s] (*US*) energy.

get up and get *v.* (*also* **git up and git**) [mid-19C+] (*US*) to leave in a hurry, to move rapidly; to act energetically.

get with *v.* **1** [1930s+] (*orig. US black*) to understand, to join in, to accept the party line. **2** [1940s–50s] (*US black/campus*) as *get with it*, to enjoy oneself. **3** [1950s+] (*US teen/campus*) to have sexual intercourse. **4** [1990s+] to associate with, to join forces with.

IN EXCLAMATIONS

❑ **get with it!** [1950s+] (*orig. US teen/campus*) stop acting stupidly!

gevrek *adj.* [Afk. *vrek*, used of animals and contemptuously of humans, to die; ult. Ger. sl. *verrecken*, to die] [2000s] (*S.Afr.*) stupid and lazy.

gey *adj. see* GAY *adj.* (4).

geycat *see under* GAYCAT.

geyser *n.*[1] [play on SPOUT *v.*[1] (1)] [1900s] (*Aus.*) a talker of nonsense, of empty words.

geyser *n.*[2] *see* GEEZER *n.*[1] (1).

geyser *adj.* [GEEZER *n.*[1] (2)] [1900s] (*US*) old, old-fashioned.

gezeybo *n. see* GAZABO *n.*

gezump(h)/gezzump *v. see* GAZUMP *v.*

g.f. *n.* [abbr.] [1920s–50s] (*US*) a girlfriend; used by either gender.

g.h. *n.* [orig. printers' jargon: *George Horne*: stale news; supposedly the name of a compositor given to recounting such irrelevances] [1900s] stale or irrelevant news.

g'hal *n.* ['Irish' pron. of GAL *n.* (1); for background *see* B'HOY *n.*] [mid-19C] (*orig. US*) the female companion of a 'lad', a young rowdy.

'Ghan *n.* [abbr.] (*Aus.*) **1** [20C+] an *Afghan*. A term that is extended to cover Turks and Arabs; thus *Ghan Town*, an area primarily populated by 'Ghans'; also as adj. **2** [1930s+] as the *Ghan*, a train running between Port Augusta and Oodnadatta on the Central Australian Railway, its main passengers being Afghan camel teamsters, heading for their jobs; suspended in 1984, it was relaunched on an extended track in 2004, joining the cities of Darwin and Adelaide.

ghanja *n. see* GANJA *n.*

gheck *n. see* GECK *n.*

ghedis *n. see* GEETUS *n.*

ghee *n.*[1] [SE *guy*] [20C+] (*US*) a man, a fellow.

ghee *n.*[2] *see* GUEE *n.*

gheeser *n. see* GEEZER *n.*[1] (1).

ghelt *n. see* GELT *n.*

gherkin *n.* [1930s+] (*Aus. prison*) the penis.

IN PHRASES

❑ **jerk one's gherkin** *v.* [1930s+] to masturbate.

ghett *n. see* GET *n.*[1].

ghetto *adj.* [SE *ghetto*] [1990s+] (*US*) **1** second-rate, old-fashioned, inferior, badly made [negative connotations]. **2** superior, first-rate [bad = good model]. **3** tough, aggressive, confrontational [perceived positive connotations].

SE in slang uses

IN COMPOUNDS

❑ **ghetto bird** *n.* [BIRD *n.*[1] (6); the use of police surveillance helicopters above ghetto areas] [1990s+] (*US black*) a police helicopter. ❑ **ghetto blaster** *n.* (*also* **ghetto box, ...guitar, ...buster**) [its orig. link to black ghetto youths; thus derog. stereotyping; note BOX *n.*[1] (4b)] [1980s+] a large stereo tape recorder-cum-radio carried by youths. ❑ **ghetto booty** *n.* (*also* **ghetto bootie**) [BOOTY *n.*[2] (2)] [1990s+] (*US black*) attractive female buttocks. ❑ **ghetto champagne** *n.* [2000s] (*US black*) cheap, potent liquor. ❑ **ghettofabulous** *adj.* [1990s+] (*US black*) referring to anything flashy and impressive in black culture, spec. fashion. ❑ **ghetto onion** *n.* [2000s] (*US black*) a large, well-rounded pair of buttocks. ❑ **ghetto sled** *n.* [SLED *n.* (1)] [1990s+] (*US black*) a large, 70s-model automobile. ❑ **ghetto star** *n.* [SE *star*/STAR *n.*[1] (5)] [1990s+] (*US black gang*) a leading gangster.

ghinny *see under* GUINEA.

ghinzo *n. see* GINZO *n.*

ghoef *see under* GOEF.

ghomey *n. see* GOM *n.*[2].

ghost *n.* **1** [late 19C+] an individual who does the work on behalf of the person who is publicly credited. **2** [1900s–30s] (*US*) a paymaster or cashier. **3** [1920s–50s] (*US drugs*) an opium smoker. **4** [1930s] (*US Und.*) a beggar who simulates the symptoms of tuberculosis in order to excite sympathy. **5** [1950s+] (*US*) (*also* **phantom**) a fictitious name created for fraudulent purposes. **6** [1960s] (*Aus.*) a creditor, i.e. one who gives the debtor an unpleasant shock. **7** [1960s+] (*drugs*) LSD. **8** [1970s+] (*US black*) a white person. **9** [1970s+] (*US campus*) an absentee, someone who has opted out of normal social life. **10** [2000s] a crack cocaine addict.

IN PHRASES

❑ **do a ghost** *v.* [1990s+] (*US black*) to leave. ❑ **get ghost** *v.* [1990s+] (*US black*) **1** to act quietly, to 'keep a low profile'. **2** to leave. ❑ **I'm ghost** [1990s+] (*US black*) I've left, I'm leaving.

SE in slang uses

IN COMPOUNDS

❑ **ghost-story** *n.* [late 19C–1960s] (*US tramp*) a fanciful or lying story; esp. a romantic story of tramp life.

IN PHRASES

❑ **the ghost walks** [the *ghost* is a joc. ref. to that of Hamlet's father] [early 19C+] (*orig. theatre*) a phr. indicating that weekly salaries are about to be given out.

IN EXCLAMATIONS

❑ **by ghost!** [1910s–60s] (*Aus.*) a general excl.

ghost *v.* **1** [late 19C+] (*orig. US*) to shadow, to follow surreptitiously. **2** [1920s+] (*US*) to write a book or article for someone else who takes the credit; also of singing. **3** [1960s] (*US prison*) to escape from jail. **4** [1970s+] (*US/UK prison*) to move a prisoner from one prison to another during the night, both departure and arrival taking place when the other prisoners are locked in their cells; thus *ghosting*, the late-night/early-hours transfer of prisoners from one prison to another with the intention of avoiding riots, frustrating external investigations etc [such prisoners are 'spirited away']. **5** [1980s+] (*US black*) (*also* **ghost out**) to leave, to go somewhere; as phr. *pull a ghost*. **6** [1980s+] to share lodgings or a hotel room with someone unbeknown to the proprietor.

IN PHRASES

□ **ghost-train** *n.* [1970s+] (*UK/US prison*) the transfer of prisoners, under cover of night, from one gaol to another.

ghostbusting *n.* [play on 1984 film title *Ghostbusters*] [1980s+] (*drugs*) when taking a drug, usu. heroin, cocaine or crack cocaine, searching for every particle of it.

ghoul *n.* (*US*) **1** [mid-19C–1920s] (*US Und./police*) a man who attempts to blackmail a woman who is deceiving her husband. **2** [late 19C] a grave robber. **3** [1900s] an undertaker. **4** [1900s–10s] a morgue attendant. **5** [1940s–70s] an unattractive-looking woman.

ghoul *v. see* GOAL *v.*

ghow *n. see* GOW *n.*[1].

GI *adj.*

SAmE in slang uses

IN COMPOUNDS

□ **GI bug/craps** *n. see* GIs *n.* □ **GI gin** *n.* [1960s+] (*orig. US milit.*) cough syrup with a high alcohol content popular with addicts when heroin supplies are short. □ **GI haircut** *n.* [1940s+] (*US*) a very short haircut, imported into civilian life by former soldiers. □ **GI Jane** *n.* [1940s+] (*US*) a female member of the armed forces. □ **GI Joe** *n.* (*also* **Joe**) [1930s+] (*US*) a male American soldier. □ **GI trots** *n. see* GIs *n.*

g.i. *v.* [the practice of US soldiers or GIs] [1940s+] to extinguish a cigarette before it is fully smoked, so that it can be re-lit later.

giant powder *n.* [the original tradename] [late 19C–1940s] (*US*) a brand of dynamite.

gib *n.* [abbr. *Gibraltar*, orig. a convict settlement to which prisoners were transported up until 1875] [late 19C] a prison.

gibber *n.*[1] [? SE *jib*, of a horse, to back away, to refuse to go forward] [mid-18C] a horse dealer.

gibber *n.*[2] [late 19C] (*Aus.*) a stone thrown by a young criminal.

gibber *v. see* JIBBER *n.*

gibbs *n. see* JIB *n.*[1] (5).

gibby *n.* [Los Angeles use; ? dial. *gib*, a tom-cat] [1960s] (*US black*) a reckless, foolhardy person.

gibface *n.* [Hotten (1860) states 'properly the lower lip of a horse' but this is not in *OED* or *EDD*; poss. mistake for dial. *gib*, the upper lip of a fish; note also dial. *gib*, a hook, thus *gib-nosed*, hook-nosed] [mid–late 19C] an ugly person, esp. one with a heavy lower jaw.

giblets *n.* **1** [mid-16C] the male genitals. **2** [mid–late 19C] (*also* **jiblets**) the intestines; thus an obese man. **3** [1990s+] the vagina, esp. with pronounced labia.

IN PHRASES

□ **join giblets** *v.* (*also* **mix giblets**) [the *OED* offers a 1681 and 1769 citation for *join giblets*, to marry, but the 1681 seems fig. and the 1769 might poss. have been a mistakenly delicate translation of a piece of 18C coarseness] **1** [late 17C–19C] to have sexual intercourse. **2** [late 18C–early 19C] to cohabit without being married.

gibroney *n.* [? JIBONE *n.*] [1960s] (*US*) an Italian.

gibs *n.* [SE *giblets*] **1** [1980s] (*US prison*) the buttocks, the anus. **2** *see* JIB *n.*[1] (5).

gibstopper *n.* [SNZE *gib*, a gibraltar board, 'an interior cladding that requires the services of a gibstopper to smooth over the cracks' (McGill, *Reed Dict. N.Z. Slang*, 2003)] [2000s] (*N.Z.*) a male homosexual, the active sexual partner in a relationship.

gib teenuck *n.* [backsl.] [mid-19C+] a large vagina, lit. 'big cunt'.

gib teesurbs *n.* [backsl.] [mid-19C+] big breasts, usu. said of a passing woman.

gick *n.* [var. on GUCK *n.*] **1** [1950s] (*US*) viscous matter. **2** [1990s+] (*Irish*) anything disgusting, esp. excrement; thus *give someone the gick*, to disgust.

gicker *n.* [GICK *n.* (2)] [2000s] (*Irish*) the buttocks or anus.

gicky *adj.* [GICK *n.* (2)] [1990s+] (*Irish*) disgusting.

giddie *n.* [1990s+] (*US campus*) **1** sexual activity. **2** something pleasing, attractive.

giddy *adj.*

IN PHRASES

□ **get giddy with** *v.* [late 19C–1900s] (*US*) to treat in a bizarre manner.

giddyack *n.* [2000s] (*US black*) one's own area.

giddyap *n.* (*also* **giddyup**) [SE *giddyap!* a sound made to urge a horse forward] **1** [1920s–30s] (*US*) a racehorse. **2** [1970s+] (*orig. US*) (*also* **gitty-up**) the beginning; usu. in phr. *(right) from the giddyap, straight from…*

giddy goat *n.* [rhy. sl. = TOTE *n.*] [1920s+] (*Aus.*) the Totalizator.

giddy gout *n.* [rhy. sl.; note popular juv. rhyme 'Giddy, giddy gout, your shirt is hanging out!'] [20C+] (*Aus.*) a boy scout.

giddyup *n. see* GIDDYAP *n.*

gidget *n. see* GADGET *n.*

gidgy *n.* ['baby talk' *gidgy, gidgy, gidgy*] [1950s–60s] (*US*) an affectionate tickling under the chin or caressing, usu. directed at an infant; thus sexual caressing.

gietus *n. see* GEETUS *n.*

gieve *n.* [JIVE *n.*[1] (2)] [1930s] (*US black/prison*) talk, esp. when misleading.

gieve *v.* [JIVE *v.*[1] (2)] [1930s] (*US black/prison*) to deceive; to confide in.

giff *n. see* JIFFY *n.*

giffed *adj.* [abbr. *t.g.i.f.*, thank God it's Friday, i.e. time to stop work and go out for pleasure] [1970s+] tipsy, drunk.

giffle gaffle *n.* [? dial. *jiffle*, shuffling, confusion] [mid-19C] nonsense.

giffy *n. see* JIFFY *n.*

gift *n.* **1** [mid-19C] (*UK Und.*) anything that has been stolen and then is sold off cheaply. **2** [mid-19C–1920s] in ext. use of sense 3 below, a person who is seen in a positive light, presenting a good opportunity. **3** [mid-19C+] anything seen as especially easy, requiring no effort to perform or obtain.

gift that keeps on giving, the *phr.* [joc. use of an advertising slogan] [1980s+] (*US campus*) venereal disease; AIDS.

gig *n.*[1] (*also* **gigg**) [ME *gig*, a foolish, coquettish, or lewd young woman / UK dial. *gig*, a flighty fellow, a trifler / ? SE *gig*, a whirling top, thus a trifle] **1** [mid-17C–early 19C] the female genitals. **2** [late 18C–mid-19C] a term of disparagement. **3** [1940s+] (*also* **gig ape, gighead**) (*Aus.*) a fool, an idiot; thus adj., *gig-headed*.

IN COMPOUNDS

□ **gig shop** *n.* [late 18C] a brothel.

gig *n.*[2] (*also* **gigg**) [ety. unknown] **1** [mid-17C–early 19C] the nose. **2** [mid–late 19C] the mouth.

gig *n.*[3] (*also* **gige, gigg**) [GIGGER *n.*[1] (1)] [late 17C–mid-19C] a door.

IN PHRASES

□ **dub the gig** *v. see under* DUB *v.*[1]. □ **strike the gig** *v.* [early 18C–mid-19C] (*UK Und.*) to open a door.

gig *n.*[4] [ety. unknown] [late 18C–early 19C] a suit of clothes.

gig *n.*[5] [ety. unknown] **1** [late 18C+] (*Irish*) a joke, fun [*HDAS* sees this, and thus subseq. uses, as development of gambling use at GIG *n.*[7] but chronology would appear to mitigate against this; ? poss. imagery of SE *gig*, a spinning top, i.e. a plaything]. **2** [20C+] (*orig. US*) business, a state of affairs. **3** [20C+] (*orig. US*) a musical performance or act at a particular venue. **4** [1940s+] a job, an occupation. **5** [1950s+] (*US teen*) an event, a party. **6** [1950s+] (*US black*) a jazz party or jam session. **7** [1950s+] (*US*) a trick or swindle. **8** [1950s+] (*US Und.*) a criminal job; a criminal charge. **9** [1960s] (*Aus.*) a successful coup. **10** [1960s+] (*US*) one's special interest, practice or plan. **11** [1980s] any form of event. **12** [1980s+] (*US campus*) a brief sexual entanglement.

IN PHRASES

□ **blow the gig** *v.* [1960s] **1** to lose a job. **2** to resign from a job.

gig *n.*[6] [? GRIG *n.*[1]] [mid–late 19C] a farthing.

gig *n.*[7] [mid-19C–1960s] (*US*) **1** a set of three numbers forming a bet in 'policy' or 'numbers' gambling. **2** by ext., any set of three.

gig *n.*[8] [abbr. GIG-LAMPS *n.*] **1** [late 19C] one who wears spectacles. **2** [1920s] (*US*) an eye. **3** [1920s+] (*Aus.*) a look, a glance. **4** [1970s+] (*Aus.*) an inquisitive person, a 'busybody'.

gig *n.*[9] **1** [1900s–40s] (*US*) a goading or gibing. **2** [1970s] (*US campus*) a disciplinary report.

gig *n.*[10] [abbr. SE *gigolo*] **1** [1920s+] (*US*) a gigolo; a dedicated womanizer. **2** [1950s] (*Aus.*) one who watches others working.

gig *n.*[11] [abbr. FIZGIG *n.*[2] (1)] **1** [1930s+] (*Aus.*) an informer. **2** [1930s+] (*Aus.*) a detective, or any intrusive person; an eavesdropper. **3** [1950s+] (*Aus. prison*) a visitor, esp. a busybody. **4** [1970s] (*Aus.*) a visitor, a stranger.

gig *n.*[12] [SE *gig*, a whipping top] [1950s] (*W.I.*) a dumpling that resembles a top.

gig *n.*[13] *see* GIGGY *n.*

gig *v.*[1] [GIG *n.*[8] (3)] **1** [18C; 1950s+] (*later use Aus.*) to look at, to stare. **2** [1920s+] (*Aus.*) (*also* **gig about**) to look on when one ought to be working.

gig *v.*[2] [? GIG *n.*[13]] [mid-18C] to have a form of sexual intercourse considered as 'deviant', poss. anal intercourse.

gig *v.*[3] [ety. unknown] [late 18C–early 19C] to hamstring (an animal).

gig *v.*[4] [? SE *gig*, to spear with a *gig*, a form of fish-spear] **1** [late 19C+] (*Aus./US*) to mock, to tease; to irritate, to annoy. **2** [1910s–60s] (*US*) to cheat or swindle, to fool. **3** [1990s+] (*US campus*) to make an obscene gesture.

gig *v.*[5] (*also* **gig around**) [GIG *n.*[5] (3) and subseq. senses] **1** [1930s+] orig. music business, to play at a particular venue, to perform. **2** [1970s] (*US campus*) to give a party. **3** [1970s] (*US*) to work, esp. at a number of short-lived jobs. **4** [1980s+] (*US campus*) to have a single night's sex with someone [GIG *n.*[5] (12) + GIG *n.*[10] (1)]. **5** [1990s+] to go to a musical performance. **6** [2000s] to socialize.

gig-a-boo *n. see* JIGABOO *n.*

gig about *v. see* GIG *v.*[1] (2).

gig ape *n. see* GIG *n.*[1] (3).

gig around *v. see* GIG *v.*[5].

gige *n. see* GIG *n.*[3].

gigg *n.*[1] see JIG *n.*[2] (1).

gigg *n.*[2] *see also under* GIG.

gigger *n.*[1] (*also* **gyger**) [JIGGER *n.*[1] (1)] [mid-16C–19C] a door.

IN COMPOUNDS

❑ **gigger-dubber** *n. see JIGGER-DUBBER under* JIGGER *n.*[1].

IN PHRASES

❑ **dub the gigger** *v. see under* DUB *v.*[1].

gigger *n.*[2] [GIG-LAMPS *n.* (1); the *locus classicus* was its use as a schoolboy nickname for the bespectacled Rudyard Kipling and, as such, used for his fictional alter ego, 'Beetle', in *Stalky & Co* (1899)] [late 19C] one who wears spectacles.

gigger (me)! *excl. see* JIGGER! *excl.*

gigger out! *excl.* [? SE *look out*, based on GIG-LAMPS *n.*] [2000s] (*US prison*) a shout of warning.

giggle *adj.*

SE in slang uses

IN COMPOUNDS

❑ **giggle academy** *n.* (*also* **giggling academy**) [1940s+] (*US*) a psychiatric institution. ❑ **giggle bin** *n.* [1980s] (*Aus.*) a psychiatric institution. ❑ **giggle dust** *n.* [1990s+] (*US drugs*) cocaine. ❑ **giggle factory** *n.* [1910s+] (*Aus./N.Z.*) a psychiatric institution. ❑ **giggle house** *n.* [1910s+] (*Aus./ N.Z.*) a psychiatric institution. ❑ **giggle juice** *n.* **1** [1930s+] (*Aus./ US*) alcohol. **2** [1970s] (*US*) gasoline. ❑ **giggle soup** *n.* [1930s–40s] (*US*) strong alcohol. ❑ **gigglestick** *n. see* separate entries. ❑ **giggle-water** *n.* [1920s+] (*orig. US*) **1** alcohol, esp. whisky or gin. **2** champagne. ❑ **giggleweed** *n.* (*also* **giggle-grass, giggle-smoke**) [one of the drug's effects is to make one giggle] [1930s+] (*drugs*) cannabis.

giggle and titter *n.* (*also* **chirrup..., laugh..., smile...**) [rhy. sl.] [20C+] bitter beer.

giggler *n.* [SE *giggle* or ? ME *gig*, a foolish, coquettish or lewd young woman] [early 18C–19C] (*UK Und.*) a young woman, esp. a prostitute.

gigglestick *n.*[1] [rhy. sl. (although not the rhy. sl. format of full phr.) = PRICK *n.* (1); the word may be equally placed among the various terms that equate penis with 'weapon' or laughter] [20C+] (*orig. US*) the penis.

gigglestick *n.*[2] **1** [1920s+] (*Aus.*) a swizzlestick, used for stirring cocktails. **2** [1930s+] cannabis; a cannabis cigarette [STICK *n.* (6d); note one of the drug's effects is to make one giggle].

giggling *adj.*

SE in slang uses

IN COMPOUNDS

❑ **giggling academy** *n. see* GIGGLE ACADEMY *under* GIGGLE *adj.* ❑ **giggling gas** *n.* [1940s–50s] (*US black/teen*) nitrous oxide. ❑ **giggling gear** *n.* [1960s] the mouth. ❑ **giggling-pin** *n.* [PIN *n.* (1a)] [20C+] (*US*) the penis.

giggy *n.* (*also* **gig**) [ety. unknown; ? link to GIG *n.*[1] (1) + note late 17C *gig*, a hole in the ground for drying flax or gig] [mid-18C+] the anus.

IN EXCLAMATIONS

❑ **up your giggy!** (*also* **up your gig!**) [1950s+] (*US*) a general excl. of contempt, dismissal.

gighead *n. see* GIG *n.*[1] (3).

gig-lamps *n.* (*also* **gigs, jig-lamps, lamps**) [SE *gig-lamps*, the two lights placed to either side of a gig or light carriage] **1** [mid-19C+] spectacles; thus a nickname for one who wears spectacles. **2** [late 19C–1900s] (*US*) jewellery; thus *gig-lamped*, wearing jewellery. **3** [20C+] a person wearing spectacles. **4** [1900s–30s] eyes.

gigolo *v.* [SE *gigolo*, a professional male dancing-partner or escort; a 'kept' man. Formed *c.*1920 as a masculine version of the French *gigole*, a tall, thin woman and hence a woman of the streets or public dance-halls. One 'who lives off women's money [...] one of those incredible and pathetic male creatures, who, for ten francs would dance with any woman wishing to dance in the cafés, hotels, and restaurants of France' (*Woman's Home Companion*, 1922)] [1980s+] (*US black*) **1** to steal a friend's lover, to cheat on one's lover or partner. **2** to fool, to hoax, to deceive.

gigs *n.*[1]

IN EXCLAMATIONS

❑ **by gigs!** [mid-16C–17C] a mild euph. for *by Jesus!*

gigs *n.*[2] *see* GIG-LAMPS *n.*

gigster *n.* [GIG *v.*[5] + -STER *sfx*] [1990s+] **1** (*Aus. teen*) one who attends a rock concert or similar event. **2** one who performs at concerts.

gigunda *adj.* (*also* **gigundo, gigundus**) [pig Lat.] [1970s] (*US campus*) gigantic.

gil *n.*[1] [? JOL *n.*] [2000s] (*S.Afr. gay*) fun; thus as v., to enjoy oneself, esp. loudly.

gil *n.*[2] *see* GILL *n.*[1].

gilda *adj.* [initial letter] [2000s] (*S.Afr. gay*) guilty.

gilded moonshine *n.* [MOONSHINE *n.* (1)] [early 19C] sham IOUs or other bills of credit that have no actual financial backing.

gilder *n.* [1900s] (*UK Und.*) a sixpence gilded so as to counterfeit a half-sovereign.

Giles's breed *n. see* ST GILES'S BREED *under* ST GILES *n.*

gilgadget *n. see* GILLGADGET *n.*

gilhickie *n.* [naut. use *gilguy*, a gadget + DOHICKEY *n.*[1]] [1920s+] anything for which one has forgotten the name.

gilks *n.* (*also* **gilkes, gilk(e)s for the jigger**) [? GILT *n.*[2] (1) + JIGGER *n.*[1] (1)] [17C] skeleton keys or picklock tools.

gill *n.*[1] (*also* **gil**) [ety. unknown] **1** [late 16C–1950s] a gullible person. **2** [19C–1910s] a general term for a man. **3** [early 19C] an interfering person. **4** [late 19C] (*UK Und.*) oneself.

IN PHRASES

❑ **his gills** *n.* (*also* **her gills, his jills**) [late 19C–1910s] (*Aus.*) a self-important person, an authority, 'his nibs'.

gill *n.*[2] [? SE *gill*, a quarter-pint, i.e. a measure of liquid] [early 19C] (*UK Und.*) a household of people.

gill *n.*[3] [ext. use of SE *gill*, a small measure of liquid (one quarter of a pint)] **1** [late 19C–1940s] (*W.I.*) one (old) penny; then three farthings. **2** [1950s] (*US*) a coin.

gill *n.*[4] *see* JILL *n.*

gill *v.* [GILL-FLIRT *n.* (2)] [early 18C] to flirt, to tease.

Gillette *v.* [play on the *Gillette* safety razor which *cuts*/CUT *v.*[6] (4a)] [1930s] (*US*) to adulterate whisky.

gill-flirt *n.* (*also* **gill-flurt, jill-flirt**) [SE *gill*, a lass, a wench + *flirt*] **1** [late 16C–mid-19C] a proud, vain woman. **2** [17C–19C] a flirt, a tease; a prostitute (cf. *FLIRT-GILL under* FLIRT *n.*).

gillgadget *n.* (*also* **gilgadget**) [? naut. jargon *gilguy*, a gadget] [1930s+] (*US*) any object that one has forgotten the name for.

Gillian *n. see* JILL *n.*

gillie *n. see* GILLY *n.*

gillie potters *n.* [rhy. sl.; ult. comedian *Gillie Potter* (1887–1975)] [1950s+] **1** pig's trotters. **2** the human feet.

gilligan (hitch) *n.* (*also* **gilligan guzzler**) [US naut. jargon *gilligan hitch*, an out-of-the-ordinary or speedily tied knot/GUZZLE *n.* (1); Ersine, *Underworld and Prison Slang* (1933), suggests 'Mr. *Gilligan*, an old-time strong-arm actor'] [1930s–50s] (*US Und.*) a stranglehold.

gills *n.* [SE *gill*, a fish's breathing apparatus, situated on each side of the neck] **1** [17C+] the cheeks; often in phr. *red in the gills* or *pink in the gills*, embarrassed. **2** [19C] the corners of a stand-up shirt-collar.

IN PHRASES

❑ **for one's gills** *adv.* [mid-19C] (*UK Und.*) to one's gain, to one's advantage. ❑ **grease one's gills** *v.* (*also* **grease the gills**) [late 19C–1900s] to eat heartily and substantially. ❑ **green about the gills** *adj.* (*also* **green around the gills, blue..., pale..., queer..., white..., yellow...**) [mid-19C+] feeling and looking sick, esp. from an excess of alcohol. ❑ **pink around the gills** *adj.* [1960s] (*US campus*) drunk. ❑ **to the gills** *adv.* [1920s+] absolutely, completely.

gilly *n.* (*also* **gillie, gilly gawkie**) [? GILL *n.*[1] (1)] [late 19C–1930s] (*US*) **1** a yokel or simpleton. **2** an outsider, an amateur, e.g. as regards confidence trickery, carnival work.

gilly *v.* [ety. unknown] [1930s] (*US*) to dispose of, to abandon.

gilpin *n. see* JOHN GILPIN *n.*

gilt *n.*[1] [SE *gilt*, silver plate, ult. Ger. *gelt*, although this means gold] [late 16C–19C] gold, money.

gilt *n.*[2] [ety. unknown] (*UK Und.*) **1** [early 17C–early 19C] a burglar. **2** [late 17C–mid-19C] a skeleton key. **3** [mid-19C] (*UK Und.*) a crowbar.

IN COMPOUNDS

❑ **gilt-dubber** *n.* [DUBBER *n.*[1]] **1** [late 17C–early 19C] (*UK Und.*) an expert pick-lock. **2** [late 19C] (*US Und.*) a hotel thief.

gilt *n.*[3] [? SE *gilt*, a young sow or female pig] [late 17C–early 18C] 'a slut or light housewife' (B.E.).

gilt *n.*[4] *see* JILT *n.*[1].

gilter *n.* [GILT *n.*[2] (2)] [late 17C–mid-19C] a housebreaker who employs a skeleton key.

gim *n.* (*also* **gimmer**) [? misprint GLIM *n.* (2); or *see* GIM *v.*] [1940s] (*US black*) in pl., the eyes.

gim *v.* [? *give me the eye*] [1940s] (*US black*) to stare at.

gimblet-eyed *adj.* [late 18C–early 19C] squinting.

gimcrack *n.* [SE *gimcrack*, a showy, but insubstantial trifle] **1** [early 17C–early 19C] a fop, an affectedly showy person. **2** [late 17C–mid-19C] a pert young woman. **3** [19C] the female genitals.

gimix *n.* [SE *gimmicks*] [1920s–40s] (*US*) a gadget.

gimme *n.* [SE *give me*] **1** [1930s–60s] (*Aus.*) an acquisitive, greedy woman. **2** [1960s+] (*also* **gimmee, gimmie**) something given away for free, or a bargain. **3** [2000s] (*UK Und.*) a bribe.

IN COMPOUNDS

❑ **gimme cap** *n.* [the practice of emblazoning objects with a logo and offering them free in order to spread the brandname began with cigarette papers, which were given away free with the purchase of loose tobacco. Buyers would demand *Give me...* a pack of papers, a cap or whatever was on offer] [1970s+] (*US*) a baseball cap carrying the logo of a sports team, manufacturer or other commercial institution. ❑ **gimme girl** *n.* [1990s+] (*US*) a greedy, materialistic young woman.

gimmer *n. see* GIM *n.*

gimmes *n. see* GIMMIES, THE *n.*

gimmick *n.* [ety. unknown, but note US journal *Words* (Nov. 1936): 'The word gimac means "a gadget". It is an anagram of the word magic, and is used by magicians the same way as others use the word "thing-a-ma-bob".'] **1** [1910s+] a tricky or ingenious device, gadget, idea, esp. one adopted for the purpose of attracting attention or publicity. **2** [1920s–30s] (*US*) a foolish person. **3** [1920s+] (*orig. US*) a gadget; spec. a contrivance for dishonestly regulating a gambling game or an article used in a conjuring trick. **4** [1920s+] (*US Und.*) that which helps implement a criminal scheme. **5** [1930s] (*US tramp*) a lame person. **6** [1940s] (*US*) affairs, business. **7** [1960s] (*US*) the penis. **8** [1960s+] (*drugs*) in pl., the equipment used for injecting a narcotic drug.

gimmick *v.* [GIMMICK *n.* (3)] [1950s–60s] (*US*) to adapt, to alter the function, typically of an electronic component.

gimmie *n. see* GIMME *n.* (2).

gimmies, the *n.* (*also* **gimmes**) [SE *give me/gimme*] **1** [1910s–60s] greediness. **2** [1930s–60s] (*US black*) an irritable mood.

gimming *n.* [GIM *v.*] [1940s] (*US black*) staring at, gazing at.

gimp *n.*[1] [Scot. *gimp*, slender, neat] [late 19C+] **1** (*US*) courage, bravery, spirit. **2** (*Irish/US*) swagger, elegance.

gimp *n.*[2] [? GAMMY *n.*[2]; note letter passed on by Terence Blacker 13/6/2000: "When I lived in Adelaide Australia in 1986 the word 'Gimp' was slang for a mentally retarded person or with the advent of political correctness now known as someone with learning difficulties. It derived from the acronym for The Glenelg Institute for Mental Patients and had expanded to encompass all those South Australians perceived to have some form of mental aberration"] **1** [1910s+] a cripple, esp. a crippled beggar. **2** [1920s+] a limp. **3** [1920s+] a fool. **4** [1970s+] (*orig. US campus*) a weakling, an inadequate; also as adj. **5** [1990s+] in sado-masochism, a person dressed all in leather or rubber, incl. the face. **6** [1990s+] (*UK juv.*) (*also* **gimp-ass**) a fool; a toady.

IN COMPOUNDS

❑ **gimp pram** *n.* [1990s+] a wheelchair. ❑ **gimp-legged** *adj.* [1960s] (*US*) limping. ❑ **gimp stick** *n. see* separate entry.

gimp *adj. see* GIMPY *adj.*[2].

gimp *v.* [GIMP *n.*[2] (1)] **1** [1920s+] to limp. **2** [1960s] to cripple. **3** [1970s+] (*US campus*) (*also* **gimp up**) to ruin, to spoil.

gimped out *adj.* [GIMP *v.* (3)] [1990s+] messed-up.

gimped up *adj.* [GIMP *v.*] **1** [1940s+] (*US*) crippled, disabled; lit. and fig. **2** [1970s+] (*US campus*) confused, at a loss, mixed up.

gimper *n.* (*also* **gimpster**) [GIMP *n.*[2] (1); note newspaper jargon *gimper*, a human interest 'sob' story featuring illness, invalidity etc] [1970s+] (*US*) a disabled person.

gimp stick *n.* [GIMP *n.*[2] (1) + SE *stick*] [1930s] (*US*) a crutch or walking-stick.

gimp up *v. see* GIMP *v.* (3).

gimpy *n.* [GIMP *n.*[2] (1)] [20C+] **1** a cripple, often as a nickname, or term of contempt. **2** the police; thus a term of contempt. **3** someone who is inadequate in some manner.

gimpy *adj.*[1] (*also* **gimpty**) [GIMP *n.*[1] (1)] [mid-19C+] (*US*) spritely, brave, energetic.

gimpy *adj.*[2] (*also* **gimp**) [GIMP *n.*[2] (1)] **1** [1920s+] (*also* **gimpty**) crippled. **2** [1970s] botched, second-rate. **3** [1980s+] in ext. use, a general insult.

gin *n.*[1] [Dharuk *diyin*, woman; also (quite coincidentally) the abbr. for *Aborigine*] **1** [19C+] (*Aus.*) (*also* **black gin, ginny**) a black Aborigine woman. **2** [1970s] (*Aus.*) any woman.

IN COMPOUNDS

□ **gin-banger** *n.* [BANG *v.*[1] (2a)] [1910s] (*Aus.*) a white man who enjoys sexual relations with Aborigine women. □ **gin-burglar** *n.* [1940s+] (*Aus.*) a white man who enjoys sexual relations with Aborigine women; thus *gin-burglary*, having sex with a 'gin'. □ **gin-cuddler** *n.* (*also* **gin-dozzler**) [*dozzler*, ety. unknown; ? SE dazzle; or ? DO *v.*[1] (1a)] [1950s–70s] (*Aus.*) a white man who enjoys sexual relations with Aborigine women. □ **gin-jockey** *n.* [SE *jockey*, i.e. play on RIDE *v.* (1a)] [1950s+] (*Aus.*) a white man who enjoys sexual relations with Aborigine women. □ **gin-man** *n.* [1960s] (*Aus.*) a white man who enjoys sexual relations with Aborigine women. □ **gin-masher** *n.* (*also* **gin-hunter**) [MASHER *n.* (3)] [1900s] (*Aus.*) a white man who enjoys sexual relations with Aborigine women. □ **gin-shepherd** *n.* [20C+] (*Aus.*) **1** a white man who enjoys sexual relations with Aborigine women; thus *gin-shepherding*, searching for Aborigine women for sexual purposes. **2** a white person who attempts to prevent miscegenation between his peers and Aborigine women. □ **gin-stealer** *n.* [1900s–20s] (*Aus.*) a white man who enjoys sexual relations with Aborigine women.

IN PHRASES

□ **gin around** *v.* [1970s+] (*Aus.*) to waste time. □ **hopping around like a gin at a christening** [1960s+] (*Aus.*) on one's best behaviour, esp. when slightly nervous, socially uncomfortable.

gin *n.*[2] [GIN *v.*[2] (2)] [1960s+] (*US black*) a street fight; thus *gin time*, time to fight.

gin *n.*[3] [? play on SE *gin*, an engine; cocaine makes one 'work' faster] [1970s+] (*drugs*) cocaine.

gin *n.*[4]

SE in slang uses

IN COMPOUNDS

□ **gin blossom** *n. see under* BLOSSOM *n.*[2]. □ **gin bottle** *n.* [late 19C] a 'dirty, abandoned, flabby, debased woman, generally over thirty; the victim of alcoholic abuse, within an ace of inevitable death' (Ware). □ **gin bud** *n.* [early 19C] a facial spot or ulcer resulting from excessive gin-drinking. □ **gin crawl** *n.* [CRAWL *n.* (2)] [late 19C] a tour of public houses for the purpose of drinking a series of gins. □ **ginhead** *n.* [-HEAD *sfx* (4)] [1920s+] (*orig. US*) a gin drinker. □ **gin ken** *n.* [KEN *n.*[1] (1)] [mid-18C–mid-19C] a gin shop. □ **gin lane** *n.* [presumably acknowledging William Hogarth's celebrated engraving of 1751] [mid–late 19C] the mouth; the throat. □ **gin-mill** *n. see* separate entry. □ **gin-slinger** *n.* [late 19C] (*US*) a bartender. □ **gin-soak** *n.* [SOAK *n.*[1] (1)] [1930s+] (*US*) an alcoholic, a gin-drinker. □ **gin-spinner** *n.* **1** [late 18C–19C] a distiller. **2** [19C] a dealer in spirits. **3** [early 19C] a wine-vault. □ **gin-trap** *n.* [SE *trap*/TRAP *n.*[1] (4)] [early 19C; 1950s] the mouth. □ **gin-tub** *n.* [mid-19C] a drunkard.

IN PHRASES

□ **dry gin** *n. see under* DRY *adj.*[1]. □ **Gin and Gospel Gazette** *n.* [its preoccupations] [mid–late 19C] the *Morning Advertiser* newspaper. □ **gin and jag** *see* separate entries.

gin *n.*[5] *see* GUINEA *n.*[1].

gin *v.*[1] **1** [early 19C] to ply someone with gin. **2** [mid-19C+] to drink gin.

IN PHRASES

□ **gin up** *v.* [late 19C–1920s] (*US*) to drink alcohol.

gin *v.*[2] [the threshing action of a cotton *gin*] **1** [1910s–60s] (*US black*) to thrash, to beat. **2** [1930s+] to fight, to scuffle. **3** [1940s–60s] to engage in sexual intercourse.

gina *n.* [? initial letter of synon. GANJA *n.* (1)] [2000s] (*S.Afr. gay*) marijuana.

ginal *n.* (*also* **ginnal, jinal, jinnal**) [an ironic play on SE *general*] [1920s+] (*W.I., Jam.*) a trickster, a confidence man.

ginal *adj.* (*also* **ginnal, jinal, jinnal**) [? GINAL *n.* or abbr. SE *original*] [1920s+] (*W.I., Jam.*) sharp, able to find a quick efficient solution to a problem; thus *ginalism*, a philosophy that basically says that the end justifies any means, fair or foul.

gina la salsa *n.* [ext. of camp gay nickname *gina* + Sp. *salsa*, sauce] [1950s+] (*camp gay*) an Italian male effeminate homosexual.

gin and Jag *adj.* (*also* **gin and Jaguar**) [the preoccupations of the inhabitants; JAG *n.*] [1960s+] pertaining to any wealthy area near a metropolitan city, e.g., the wealthy Home Counties around London.

IN COMPOUNDS

□ **gin and Jag belt** *n.* [1960s+] a wealthy area near a metropolitan city; usu. Home Counties surrounding London, and, as such, considered ripe for robbery. □ **gin and Jag bird** *n.* [1970s] a louche, raffish woman from this area, presumed, while prob. married, not to be averse to something 'on the side'.

gin and jag *n.* [GIN AND JAG *adj.*] [1950s+] (*UK Und.*) a crime committed in an upmarket area; presumably burglary.

gin and lime *n.* [rhy.sl.] [1940s] the number nine.

ginch *n.* [ety. unknown, but note dial. *ginch*, a small piece] **1** [1930s+] an attractive woman, esp. when seen as a sex object. **2** [1950s+] the vagina; thus the act of sexual intercourse. **3** [1970s] (*gay*) an attractive young man.

ginchy *adj.* [GINCH *n.* (1) + sfx *-y*] [1950s+] attractive, sexy.

giner *n.* [abbr. SE va*gina*] [2000s] (*US campus*) the vagina.

ging *n.*[1] [it 'gingers up' its targets] [20C+] (*Aus.*) a catapult.

ging *n.*[2] *see* GANG *n.*[1].

gingambobs *n.* [SE *jiggumbob*] [late 18C–19C] **1** toys, baubles. **2** the testicles.

ginger *n.*[1] [SE *ginger*, f. the colour or spiciness] **1** [early–mid-19C] a showy, fast horse. **2** [early 19C+] a red-haired or sandy-haired person. **3** [mid-19C+] high spirits, verve, vigour.

IN PHRASES

□ **give someone ginger** *v.* [1920s] to treat brusquely, to 'make someone jump'. □ **like ginger** *adv.* [late 19C] to a great extent.

ginger *n.*[2] (*also* **ginger-cake, gingerer, ginger girl**) [? on model of orig. meaning of TART *n.* (1), one who is 'sweet', she also offers the 'spiciness' of ginger] **1** [mid-19C–1900s] (*UK Und.*) a young woman; poss. as sense 2 below. **2** [1940s+] (*Aus.*) a prostitute who robs her customer of his wallet. **3** [1940s+] (*Aus.*) the act of robbing a prostitute's client; thus *gingering joint*, a brothel where such practices are common.

IN PHRASES

□ **work a ginger** *v.* [1940s+] (*Aus.*) of a prostitute and her accomplice, to rob her customer.

ginger *n.*[3] a euph. for *Jesus* in combs. below.

IN EXCLAMATIONS

□ **by ginger!** [mid-19C–1930s] (*US*) a mild expletive; euph. for *by Jesus!* □ **ginger blue!** [late 19C–1920s] (*US*) an excl. used to mock someone who is seen as behaving in a socially unacceptable way.

ginger *n.*[4] **1** *see* ON SOMEONE'S GINGER *under* GINGER ALE *n.* **2** *see* GINGER (BEER) *n.*

ginger *adj.*

SE in slang uses

IN COMPOUNDS

□ **ginger-cake** *n.* (*also* **gingerbread**) **1** [19C+] (*US*) a mulatto [the ginger-toned shade of the person's skin]. **2** [1980s] (*S.Afr.*) a policeman [the brown uniform]. **3** *see* GINGER *n.*[2]. □ **gingerbread** *n. see* separate entry. □ **ginger-girl** *n. see* GINGER *n.*[2]. □ **ginger-hackled** *adj.* [cock-fighting jargon *ginger*, a red cock] [late 18C] red-haired. □ **ginger-nob** *n.* [NOB *n.*[1] (1)] [20C+] a red-headed person. □ **ginger peachy** *adj.* [1940s+] (*US*) usu. ironic use, splendid. □ **gingersnap** *n.* [1940s–50s] (*US black*) a black person.

ginger *v.* [GINGER *n.*[2] (2)] [1950s] (*Aus.*) of a prostitute, to rob a client.

ginger ale *n.* [rhy. sl.] [20C+] **1** (*Aus./US*) a gaol. **2** (*Aus./N.Z.*) (*also* **steak and ale**) bail. **3** (*Aus.*) a tail. **4** (*Aus.*) the mail.

IN PHRASES

❑ **on someone's ginger** [rhy. sl. = ON SOMEONE'S TAIL *under* TAIL *n.*] [1960s+] (*Aus.*) following, in pursuit of.

ginger (beer) *n.* [rhy. sl. = QUEER *n.* (4)] [1940s+] a male homosexual; also as adj.

ginger beer *n.* [rhy. sl.] (*Aus.*) **1** [1940s+] an engineer, in both civilian and milit. contexts. **2** [2000s] an ear.

gingerbread *n.*[1] [the gold colour] **1** [late 17C–mid-19C] money; thus *have the gingerbread*, to be rich; as adj., showy, ostentatious. **2** *see* GINGER-CAKE *under* GINGER *adj.*

gingerbread *n.*[2] [rhy. sl.] [1930s] the head.

gingerer *n. see* GINGER *n.*[2].

ginger-pop *n.* [rhy. sl. = COP *n.*[1] (1)] [late 19C] a policeman.

gingery *adj.* [GINGER (BEER) *n.*] [1940s+] pertaining to homosexuals or homosexual culture.

gingleboy *n.* (*also* **jingleboy**) [the noise it makes in one's pocket] [17C] **1** a sovereign (£1 sterling); thus any gold coin. **2** [mid-17C–mid-18C] (*also* **gingle-cash**) one who possesses gold coins.

gingler *n. see* JINGLER *n.*

gingumbob *n.* [late 17C–mid-19C] a trifle.

ginicomtwig *v.* [like THINGUMABOB *n.* it could also mean a 'nameless item' and is thus also a euph.] [late 16C–early 17C] to have sexual intercourse.

ginigog *n. see* GUINEA BIRD *n.*[2] (2).

ginj *v.* [dial. *ginj*, to strangle, using a piece of wire; ult. fishing use *ginj*, to protect the line near the hook by twisting a piece of wire around it; thus, in turn, SE synon. *gange*] [1940s] (*W.I.*) to fill with lies.

gink *n.*[1] [? link to Scot. *gink*, trick] **1** [20C+] (*orig. US*) (*also* **ginkerino**) a stupid, useless person. **2** [1910s] (*orig. US*) a peasant. **3** [1910s–20s] (*US tramp*) a tramp who worked seasonally or occasionally. **4** [1910s–60s] (*US*) a fellow, a person (not pej.); also as jovial/affectionate term of address. **5** [1920s] an animal, esp. a stubborn one. **6** [1920s] (*US Und.*) a traitor. **7** [1940s+] (*US*) an East Asian.

gink *n.*[2] [? GIG *n.*[8] (3)] [1950s+] (*Aus.*) a look, a glance.

ginky *adj.* [GINK *n.*[1] (1)] [1960s–70s] (*US*) unfashionable or stupid-looking.

gin-mill *n.* (*also* **whiskey-mill**) [SE *gin* + *mill* + pun on *gin*, a type of mill] (*US*) **1** [mid-19C+] a bar or nightclub, orig. a speakeasy specializing in cheap, and prob. adulterated, liquor; thus *gin-millist*, a bartender; *gin-mill row*, a street of bars. **2** [1960s] a liquor store.

ginnal *see under* GINAL.

ginned up *adj.*[1] (*also* **ginned**) [SE *gin*] [20C+] (*US*) drunk, tipsy.

ginned up *adj.*[2] [ety. unknown; ? the image of one who frequents 'gin palaces'] [1920s] (*US*) dressed up.

ginner *n.* [var. on GINGER *n.*[1] (3)] [2000s] a person with ginger hair.

ginnery *n.* [mid-19C] a public house dedicated to the sale of gin.

ginney *see under* GUINEA.

ginny *n.*[1] [JEMMY *n.*[3] (1), but note SE *gin*, engine, machine + dial. *ginny*, a simple form of crane] [late 17C–early 19C] (*UK Und.*) 'an instrument to lift up a Grate, the better to Steal what is in the window' (B.E.).

ginny *n.*[2] [abbr.] [1980s] (*US black*) the vagina.

ginny *n.*[3] *see* GIN *n.*[1] (1).

ginny *n.*[4] *see* GUINEA *n.*[1].

ginny *adj.* [SE *gin*] **1** [late 19C] of the liver or kidneys, adversely affected by excessive gin drinking. **2** [20C+] very keen on gin. **3** [1920s+] (*US*) tipsy; also in fig. use.

ginny gall *n.* (*also* **guinea gall, jimmy gall**) [proper name *Guinea*, a region in West Africa] [1900s–50s] (*US black*) anywhere considered as far away, unpleasant and culturally alien.

ginzo *n.* (*also* **ghinzo, ginso**) [GUINEA *n.*[1] (1)] [1930s+] (*US*) **1** a derog. term for an Italian person or their language; also adj. use. **2** a thug working for the US Mafia. **3** any worthless or unpleasant person.

g.i.o. *v. see* GET IT ON *v.* (5).

Giorgio Armani *n.* [rhy. sl. = SARNIE *n.*; ult. fashion designer *Giorgio Armani* (b.1935)] [1990s+] a sandwich.

gip *see under* GYP.

gipe *n.* (*also* **gype**) [Scot. *gipe*, an awkward person, a fool] [20C+] (*Ulster*) **1** a fool. **2** a clumsy, awkward person. **3** a person with long legs. **4** a foolish young woman.

gippo *see under* GYPO.

gippy *n.* [abbr.] **1** [1900s] an Egyptian cigarette. **2** [1910s+] an Egyptian, esp. an Egyptian soldier. **3** [1910s+] a gypsy.

gippy *adj. see* GYPO *adj.*

IN COMPOUNDS

❑ **gippy tummy** *n. see* GYPPY TUMMY *n.*

gipsy *see under* GYPSY.

giraffe *n.* [US milit. *giraffe*, a form of game] [mid-19C–1910s] the swindle, the deception.

IN PHRASES

❑ **come the giraffe** *v.* [mid-19C–1910s] to hoodwink, to swindle.

giraffe *v.* [GIRAFFE *n.*] [mid-19C] (*US*) to hoodwink.

girl *n.*[1] **1** [mid-17C–19C] a (street-walking) prostitute. **2** [19C+] (*US*) any black woman, irrespective of age. **3** [late 19C+] (*US*) used in direct address to a man, without homosexual implication. **4** [1920s+] (*also* **girlie**) a male homosexual, esp. a prostitute; also used in direct address as an insult or term of endearment. **5** [1940s+] (*gay*) used as an affectionate term of address between two homosexual men. **6** [1950s–60s] (*US*) a queen of any suit in cards. **7** [1980s+] (*US black*) a general form of address between two women, irrespective of age. **8** [1990s+] (*US*) an insult aimed at a heterosexual male.

IN COMPOUNDS

❑ **girl-scout** *n. see under* SCOUT *n.* ❑ **girl-shop** *n.* [late 19C] a brothel.

IN PHRASES

❑ **girl about town** *n.* (*also* **girl of the town**) [18C–1900s] a streetwalking prostitute. ❑ **girl of the pave** *n. see* NYMPH OF THE PAVE *n.* ❑ **girl out** *v.* [2000s] (*US*) of a man, to make another man behave as a passive rather than an active homosexual, to subject another man to anal intercourse or fellatio.

SE in slang uses

IN COMPOUNDS

❑ **girl-boy** *n.* **1** [late 16C; late 19C+] (*orig. US*) a feminine young man, an effeminate homosexual boy; also as a general insult. **2** [1960s+] (*US prison*) a heterosexual prisoner engaging in homosexual acts. ❑ **girl-catcher** *n.* [19C] the penis. ❑ **girl-deb** *n. see* DEB *n.*[2]. ❑ **girlfriend** *n. see* separate entry. ❑ **girl-getter** *n.* [? *girl-begetter*, an effeminate man would be unable to produce 'macho' boys] [late 19C–1900s] an effeminate male. ❑ **girl-hopping** *n.* [1990s+] (*US black*) seducing young women. ❑ **girl's blouse** *n. see* BIG GIRL'S BLOUSE *under* BIG *adj.*

IN PHRASES

❑ **girls are bandy at Urandangie, the** *see* separate entry. ❑ **go girling** *v.* [late 18C–1930s] to go out looking for female companionship and possible seduction. ❑ **sweet girl** *n. see* SWEET KID *under* SWEET *adj.*[1].

girl *n.*[2] [the image of cocaine as a 'feminine' drug, the injecting of which gives a sexual thrill (although heroin, too, has that effect on some users), as opposed to heroin or BOY *n.*[2] (4a), a 'masculine' drug, i.e. one that 'knocks you down'] [1950s+] (*drugs*) **1** cocaine. **2** heroin [may be a mis-reading].

IN COMPOUNDS

❑ **girlfriend** *n. see* separate entry.

girl abductor *n.* [rhy. sl.] [1900s–10s] (*Aus.*) a tram conductor.

girl and boy *n.* [rhy. sl.] **1** [mid-19C–1930s] a saveloy. **2** [20C+] a toy.

girled up *adj.* [mid-19C] (*US campus*) of a heterosexual man, obsessively in love.

girlery *n.* [SE *girl* + sfx *-ery*, the place where an occupation is carried on] [19C] a brothel.

girlesk *n.* (*also* **girlesque**) [SE *girl* + *burlesque*] [1930s–50s] (*US*) a show featuring striptease women.

girlfriend *n.*[1] **1** [1950s+] (*S.Afr. Und.*) the male lover of another prisoner. **2** [1970s+] (*US black*) a form of address from a man to a woman, not necessarily known. **3** [1980s+] a form of address between lesbians, not necessarily in a relationship. **4** [1980s+] a form of address between gay men. **5** [1990s+] (*US black*) a form of address between women. **6** [1990s+] (*US gay*) any friend, irrespective of gender/sexuality; a lesbian. **7** [1990s+] (*US black*) a woman.

girlfriend *n.*[2] [ext. GIRL *n.*[2] (1)] [1970s+] (*US black*) cocaine.

girlie *n.* **1** [late 19C+] a woman, irrespective of age although orig. young, usu. as a term of endearment. **2** [1920s+] a nickname for an effeminate boy. **3** *see* GIRL *n.*[1] (5).

girlie *adj.* (*also* **girl-girl, girlie-girlie, girly**) **1** [1910s+] (*orig. US*) used of a young woman employed in some form of the sex or glamour industry. **2** [1960s+] of a woman, sexually alluring. **3** [1990s+] of a man, effeminate.

IN COMPOUNDS

❑ **girlie bar** *n.* [1990s+] (*orig. US*) a bar or 'nightclub' at which the hostesses may double as prostitutes. ❑ **girlie book** *n.* (*also* **girlie mag, ...magazine, ...rag**) [1920s+] (*orig. US*) a pin-up magazine. ❑ **girlie show** *n.* [1940s+] (*orig. US*) a strip show.

girls and boys *n.* [rhy. sl.] [20C+] noise.

girls are bandy at Urandangie, the *phr.* [assonance] [1960s+] (*Aus.*) a phr. used to denote an unsatisfactory situation.

girly *adj. see* GIRLIE *adj.*

girlyboy *n.* [var. on *GIRL-BOY under* GIRL *n.*[1]] [2000s] a male homosexual.

GIs *n.* (*also* **GI bug, ...craps, ...trots**) [i.e. the food poisoning to which soldiers posted abroad might be susceptible; BUG *n.*[5] (3)/ CRAPS, THE *n.*/TROTS *n.*] [1940+] (*US*) diarrhoea; thus the *GI pill*, a pill designed to combat the malady.

Gis *n.*

IN EXCLAMATIONS

❑ **by Gis!** *see BY JIS! under* JIS *n.*

gism *n. see* JISM *n.*

gismo *n. see* GIZMO *n.*

gissum *n. see* JISM *n.*

git *n.*[1] [var. on GET *n.*[1] (3)] [1940s+] a fool, a worthless person.

git *n.*[2] *see* GITBOX *n.*

git *v. see* GET *v.* (1b).

IN COMPOUNDS

❑ **git-'em-up** *adj. see GET-'EM-UP under* GET *v.* ❑ **git-up** *n. see* GET-UP *n.*[1].

IN PHRASES

❑ **git up and get** *see under* GET UP AND GET.

git! *excl.* [SE *get away*/GET *v.* (1b)] [mid-19C+] (*US*) go away!

gitbox *n.* (*also* **git, git flip, gitter (box)**) [orig. jazz jargon] **1** [1930s+] (*US*) a guitar. **2** [1950s] (*US black*) a juke box.

gitch *n.* [ety. unknown; ? link to SE *breech(es)*] [1990s+] (*Can.*) male underpants.

git-down *n.* [1990s+] (*US*) the start, the beginning; the crux of a matter.

IN COMPOUNDS

❑ **git-down time** *n.* [1950s+] (*US*) the start of a prostitute's working 'day', when she *gets down to business*.

gitfiddle *n.* [*git* (*get*) *your fiddle and play*] [1930s+] (*US*) a guitar.

git flip *n. see* GITBOX *n.*

git-go *n.* (*also* **get-go**) [SE *get going*] [1960s+] (*orig. US black*) the beginning, esp. in phrs. below.

IN PHRASES

❑ **from the git-go** *adv.* (*also* **from the get, from the get-go, from the git**) [1960s+] (*orig. US black*) from the very start.

gitney *n. see* JITNEY *n.*

gitter *n. see* JITTER *n.*

gitter (box) *n. see* GITBOX *n.*

gitty-up *n. see* GIDDYAP *n.* (2).

give *v.*[1] [late 19C] (*US*) to renege on one's debts or bills.

give *v.*[2] **1** [late 19C+] to impart information; esp. in dismissive, sceptical phrs. *what are you giving me?* or *don't give me that*. **2** [late 19C+] to act in a specific manner; usu. as *giving it*, e.g. 'giving it the old emotion'. **3** [1930s+] (*orig. US*) of a young woman, to be willing to engage in sexual intercourse; thus GIVE OUT *v.* (3). **4** [1930s+] (*US*) to give up, to surrender. **5** [1950s+] (*US Und.*) to be an active 'masculine' homosexual [i.e. to 'give' rather than to receive].

SE in slang uses

IN PHRASES

❑ **give...** *v.* **1** *see also* separate entries. **2** *see also under* relevant n. or adj. ❑ **give a rusty fuck** *v. see* GIVE A FUCK *v.* ❑ **give birth to a copper** *v.* (*also* **give birth (to it)**) [fig. use of COPPER *n.* (3)] [1990s+] (*Aus.*) to defecate. ❑ **give cuts** *v. see under* CUT *n.* ❑ **give good** *v.* [20C+] (*W.I.*) to berate, to scold severely, to tell off. ❑ **give good...** *v.* (*also* **give great...**) [usu. as *give good head*, i.e. *GIVE HEAD under* HEAD *n.*] [1970s+] (*US*) used in phrs. where a singular n. is used as a generic, e.g. *give good/ great spiel*, to be notable for talking. ❑ **give her one** *v. see under* ONE *n.*[1]. ❑ **give it** *v.* [2000s] to state. ❑ **give off** *v.* [20C+] (*Irish*) to make a fuss. ❑ **give to fucks** *v. see* GIVE A FUCK *v.* ❑ **not give a...** *v.* **1** *see* separate entries. **2** *see also under* relevant n. or adj.

give *v.*[3] [Yid. *vi geht's?* what gives?] [1930s+] (*orig. US*) to happen; usu. in phrs. below.

IN PHRASES

❑ **what gives?** (*also* **what goes? what makes? what's giving?**) [1940s+] **1** a general greeting. **2** as a query, what is going on? what is happening? thus *what gives with —?* how is —? what is going on with —?

give! *excl.* **1** [late 19C+] (*orig. US*) explain! confess! **2** [1920s] an expression of contempt.

give a damn *v.* (*also* **give a dam, ...dang**) [backform. f. NOT GIVE A DAMN *v.*] [1930s+] to care, usu. in a negative sense, e.g. *who gives a damn?* or *like I give a damn*.

IN PHRASES

❑ **don't-give-a-damn** *adj.* (*also* **don't give a shit**) [1960s+] (*US*) careless, carefree.

give-a-fuck *n.* (*also* **give-a-shit**) [GIVE A FUCK *v.*] [1970s+] (*US*) the desire to do something, the state of being motivated towards, enthusiastic for.

give a fuck *v.* (*also* **give a rusty fuck, ...two fucks**) [backform. f. NOT GIVE A FUCK *v.*] [1930s+] (*orig. US*) to care about, to be concerned; usu. in negative sense, e.g. *who gives a fuck?*

give and get *n.* [rhy. sl.] [1990s+] a bet.

give and take *n.* [rhy. sl.] [1960s+] **1** a cake. **2** a bundle of notes [fig. use of sense 1 above but note CAKE *n.*[2] (2)].

give a rusty fuck *v. see* GIVE A FUCK *v.*

give-a-shit *n. see* GIVE-A-FUCK *n.*

give a shit *v.* [backform. f. NOT GIVE A SHIT *v.*] [1960s+] (*orig. US*) to care, usu. in negative sense, e.g. *who gives a shit?* or *I could give a shit*.

give-away *n.* [GIVE AWAY *v.* (1)] [late 19C+] a betrayal of something, usu. a secret; usu. as *dead give-away*.

give away *v.* **1** [mid-19C+] to betray. **2** [late 19C+] (*Aus.*) to give up, to abandon, to forsake.

give it away *v.* [1940s+] **1** (*Aus.*) to stop, to give up, to abandon. **2** (*US*) of a woman or male or female prostitute, to permit sexual intercourse for free.

give it to *v.* **1** [late 18C–mid-19C; 1930s+] to shoot, poss. to kill. **2** [19C] (*UK Und.*) to rob. **3** [19C] to deceive, to take advantage of credulity. **4** [19C+] to hit, to beat, to stab.

5 [mid-19C+] to admonish severely. **6** [late 19C+] to punish severely. **7** [20C+] of a man, to have sexual intercourse. **8** [1920s+] of a woman, to permit intercourse. **9** [1920s+] (*US Und.*) to murder, to execute. **10** [1970s] to tease, to provoke.

give it up *v.* **1** [1940s+] to explain, to impart information. **2** [1960s+] (*orig. US*) to accede to seduction or forced intercourse. **3** [1960s+] to surrender oneself to pleasure (non-sexual). **4** [1970s+] to hand over, usu. money, but also drugs etc. **5** [1990s+] to applaud; usu. in phr. *let's give it up for...* **6** [1990s+] (*US black*) to show gang hand signals.

(IN EXCLAMATIONS)

❑ **give it up!** [1970s+] **1** an aggressive demand from one male that another accept his sexual advances, esp. in prison. **2** the same demand for sex, made from a man to a woman.

given! *excl.* [SE *given*, something that is automatically accepted, 'taken as read'] [1990s+] (*US campus*) an expression of agreement.

give out *v.* [fig. uses of SE] **1** [19C+] (*Irish*) to make a fuss, to complain. **2** [1930s+] (*US black*) to talk emotionally, to talk with great feeling; thus phr. *give out yards.* **3** [1930s+] of a young woman, to make herself available for sexual intercourse. **4** [1940s] as *give out with*, to speak in a given manner. **5** [1940s+] to play music or sing. **6** [1950s] to scream. **7** [1950s] to offer, to present. **8** [1950s+] to make out, to imply, to pretend. **9** [1980s+] to reprimand, to criticize, to attack.

give over! *excl.* [late 18C+] (*usu. northern*) stop it! shut up!

giver *n.* [GIVE *v.*² (5)] [1970s+] (*US gay/prison*) an active prison homosexual.

give sky-high *v.* see BLOW SKY HIGH *v.* (1).

give two fucks *v.* see GIVE A FUCK *v.*

give-up *n.* [GIVE UP *v.*] [1970s+] **1** (*US Und.*) a payment made under duress. **2** (*US*) submission, surrender. **3** (*US Und.*) a robbery or hijacking in which the driver is in league with the hijackers. **4** (*Aus. prison*) an informer.

give up *v.* **1** [mid-19C+] (*Aus./US Und.*) to betray, to inform against. **2** [late 19C+] (*US Und.*) to pay money, esp. under duress. **3** [late 19C+] (*US Und.*) to reveal, to explain.

(IN PHRASES)

❑ **give up the work to someone** *v.* [1960s] (*US*) of a lesbian, to take the active role in sexual intercourse.

giz *n.* [abbr. of GIZMO *n.*] **1** [1940s] (*US*) any small thing for which one has temporarily forgotten the correct name. **2** [1940s] (*US*) ammunition, explosives. **3** [1970s+] (*US*) the vagina. **4** [1990s+] an annoying thing, which is impossible to get rid of.

gizm *n.* see JISM *n.*

gizmo *n.* (*also* **gismo**) [ety. unknown] [1940s+] **1** (*orig. US*) any (small) thing for which one has temporarily forgotten the correct name, a gadget. **2** (*US drugs*) the paraphernalia used for injecting narcotics. **3** (*US*) the vulva or vagina. **4** (*US*) the penis. **5** (*US*) a foolish man.

gizz *n.* (*also* **gizzard**) [Mezzrow & Wolfe, *Really the Blues* (1946): 'Gizzard has a subtle overtone here: a gizzard is stuffed, and stuff means jive or kidding in hip talk, so the implication is: don't come up with no stuff, in other words, don't kid me, make sure that you pay me'] [1940s] (*US black*) a general term of address to a fellow man.

gizzard *n.* [10C SE *gizzard*, animal or insect stomachs; ult. Lat. *gicerium*, the cooked entrails of a fowl] **1** [mid-17C+] the stomach, the solar plexus. **2** [mid-19C+] the heart. **3** [20C+] (*US*) courage, guts. **4** [1920s+] the throat or mouth.

(IN PHRASES)

❑ **hate someone's gizzard** *v.* see *HATE SOMEONE'S GUTS* under GUT *n.*

(IN EXCLAMATIONS)

❑ **bust my gizzard!** [mid-19C] (*US*) a mild oath.

gizzard *v.* [GIZZARD *n.* (1)] [1950s] to cut out someone's guts.

gizzem/gizzum *n.* see JISM *n.*

glabb-huffles *n.* [ety. unknown; ? SE *snuffles*] [mid-19C] (*UK Und.*) a bad cold.

glad *adj.* **1** [mid-18C+] tipsy, drunk. **2** [late 19C–1900s] foolish; cheeky.

(IN COMPOUNDS)

❑ **glad bag** *n.* [play on tradename *Glad Bags*] [1980s+] (*US*) a body bag. ❑ **glad lad** *n.* [1940s] (*US teen*) an attractive boy. ❑ **glad money** *n.* [1930s] (*US Und.*) money distributed by a gangster to ensure popular support in his local community. ❑ **glad pad** *n.* [PAD *n.*² (2)] [1920s–40s] (*US black*) a nightclub, a dancehall or similar establishment. ❑ **glad rag** *n.* [the use of a proprietary *Glad* Bag for holding the liquid inhalant] [1960s+] (*US drugs*) **1** a rag soaked with an intoxicating chemical, the fumes of which one inhales. **2** one who sniffs such inhalants. ❑ **glad stuff** *n.* [the effects] [1950s+] (*drugs*) any form of hard or narcotic drug.

(IN PHRASES)

❑ **glad-time girl** *n.* [var. on SE *good-time*, of a woman, promiscuous] [1980s+] (*W.I.*) a promiscuous woman.

gladiator school *n.* (*also* **gladiator camp, kindergarten**) [1960s+] (*US prison*) **1** a maximum-security prison; thus *gladiator*, a violent prisoner; *gladiator fight*, a fight put on to entertain other prisoners. **2** a prison with a notably harsh regime and a violent atmosphere.

Gladstone *n.* [Prime Minister William *Gladstone*'s reduction, in 1860, of the duty on French wine] [mid–late 19C] cheap claret.

glahm *v.* see GLOM *v.*

glaise *n.* see GLAZE *n.*

glam *v.* see GLOM *v.*

glamity *n.* [W.I. dial. *glami*, sticky and elastic; ult. SE *clammy*, wet, moist, sticky] [1980s+] (*W.I./UK black teen*) **1** the vagina. **2** sexual intercourse. **3** the 'ability' of a vagina, i.e. a woman's sexual prowess.

glamour *adj.*

SE in slang uses

(IN COMPOUNDS)

❑ **glamour boy** *n.* (*also* **glamour girl, glamour queen**) [orig. used of RAF, esp. flying crews] [1930s+] a glamorous young man or woman. ❑ **glamour pants** *n.* [1930s–70s] an attractive young woman, occas. a man. ❑ **glamour puss** *n.* (*also* **glamour pussy**) [PUSS *n.*¹ (2a)] [1940s+] an ostentatiously well-dressed, lavishly made-up etc (young) person, usu. a woman.

glamour fart *n.* [? rhy. sl. = TART *n.* (1)] [1980s+] (*Aus. prison*) a woman, esp. when attractive.

glands *n.* (*US*) **1** [1910s–20s] the testicles. **2** [1970s+] the breasts.

glanthem *n.* [ety. unknown] [late 18C] money.

glarum goggles *n.* [SE *glare* + GOGGLES *n.* (2)] [mid-19C] (*UK Und.*) large, prominent eyes.

Glasgow *adj.*

proper name in slang uses

(IN COMPOUNDS)

❑ **Glasgow kiss** *n.* [20C+] a head butt. ❑ **Glasgow magistrate** *n.* (*also* **Glasgow baillie**) ['When George IV visited Scotland, a wag placed some salt herrings on the iron guard of the carriage belonging to a well-known Glasgow magistrate, who made one of a deputation to receive his Majesty' (Hotten, 1867). The *Scots Magazine* (December 1950) attributes the term to Walter Gibson, 'a merchant of Glasgow and Provost of that city in 1688'] [mid-19C–1930s] a salt herring.

Glasgow Rangers *n.* (*also* **Glasgows**) [rhy. sl.; ult. the football team] [1920s+] strangers, esp. as used by lookout men working with unlicensed street pitchmen.

glasheen *n.* (*also* **glawsheen**) [SE *glass* + dimin. sfx *-een*] [20C+] (*Irish*) a small glass of strong drink.

glasier *n.* see GLAZIER *n.*

glass *n.*¹ [the length of time it takes for sand to run through an *hour-glass*] [mid-19C] an hour.

glass *n.*² (*also* **glassware**) **1** [20C+] (*US Und.*) a diamond; thus *genuine glass*, a high-quality diamond; *fake glass*, a worthless diamond. **2** [1940s+] (*UK Und.*) any form of jewellery.

3 [1940s+] (*drugs*) a hypodermic needle, early versions of which were made of glass. **4** [1940s+] the penis [one 'blows' glass to make it larger]. **5** in drug uses [the shininess of the powders]. (**a**) [1970s+] methamphetamine. (**b**) [1980s+] heroin.

IN PHRASES

❑ **blow someone's glass** *v.* [1970s+] to perform fellatio on a man.

SE in slang uses

IN PHRASES

❑ **glass of lunch** *n.* (*also* **glass of steak**) [1960s] (*Aus.*) a drink, a 'liquid lunch'. ❑ **glass of water** *n.* [such a person, like water, is seen to lack strength] [1950s] (*US*) a tall, thin person. ❑ **use the glass** *v.* [1900s–30s] to use a broken glass or bottle as a weapon in a fight, typically in a public house. ❑ **under glass** *adj.* [the image of a show case] [1920s+] (*orig. US*) imprisoned, arrested.

glass *adj.* [1910s+] (*US, orig. boxing*) used of any weak or vulnerable part of the body, e.g. *a glass chin* or GLASS JAW *n.*

SE in slang uses

IN COMPOUNDS

❑ **glass dick** *n.* [fig. use of DICK *n.*[1] (5)] [1990s+] (*drugs*) a pipe for smoking crack cocaine. ❑ **glass gun** *n.* [early syringes were made of *glass*; they gave one a SHOT *n.*[1] (6b)] [1940s+] (*drugs*) a hypodermic needle. ❑ **glass eyes** *n. see* separate entries. ❑ **Glass House** *n. see* separate entry. ❑ **glasshouse** *n. see* separate entry. ❑ **glass jaw** *n. see* separate entry. ❑ **glass legs** *n. see* HOLLOW LEG *n.* (1).

glass *v.* [abbr. *USE THE GLASS under* GLASS *n.*[2]] [1930s+] to hit in the face with a (broken) glass.

glass case *n.* [rhy. sl.] [mid-19C] a face.

glasses *n.*

SE in slang uses

IN PHRASES

❑ **have one's glasses on** *v.* [stereotyped association of spectacles with intelligence] [1930s–40s] (*US black*) to pose as an intellectual, to lay down the law.

glass eyes *n.*[1] (*also* **glasseye**) [late 18C–1950s] one who wears spectacles.

IN PHRASES

❑ **have glass eyes** *v.* [18C] to be drunk.

glass eyes *n.*[2] (*also* **glassy eye**) [the effect on one's eyes] [1940s–50s] (*drugs*) a drug user.

Glass House, the *n.* [the design] [1960s+] (*US*) the Los Angeles County Jail.

glasshouse *n.* [the glass-roofed North Camp military prison at Aldershot] **1** [1910s+] a military prison or guardroom. **2** [1960s+] a police station.

glass jaw *n.* [GLASS *adj.*] **1** [1910s+] (*orig. boxing*) a conspicuously weak jaw, which breaks or fractures when hit and loses its possessor his fights. **2** [1920s+] (*US campus*) a coward.

glass of beer *n.* [rhy. sl.] [20C+] an ear.

glass of plonk *n.* [rhy. sl. = CONK *n.*[1] (1); ult. PLONK *n.*[1] (1)] [20C+] the nose.

glassware *n. see* GLASS *n.*[2].

glassy (alley), the *n.* (*also* **agate, glassy agate**) [marbles use *glass alley*, a specially prized type of marble + SE *glassy*, of a surface, smooth, unruffled, absolutely flat] [20C+] (*Aus.*) the best, the favourite, the most admired.

IN PHRASES

❑ **just the glassy (marble)** *adj.* [1900s–50s] (*Aus.*) wholly satisfactory, just as required.

glassy (eye) *n.* [dead fish lying on the slab have 'glassy' eyes] [1910s+] (*Aus.*) a cold, disdainful stare.

glassy eye *n. see* GLASS EYES *n.*[2].

glasyer *n. see* GLAZIER *n.*

glaum *see under* GLOM.

glaver *v.* [orig. dial.] [late 17C] to fawn, to flatter.

glawsheen *n. see* GLASHEEN *n.*

glaze *n.* (*also* **glaise**) [SE *glaze*, a vitreous composition used for glazing pottery etc] **1** [late 17C–19C] a window; thus *on the glaze*, robbing jewellers' shops after smashing the windows; *mill a glaze*, to smash a window. **2** [late 18C] (*US Und.*) a bottle. **3** [late 18C–early 19C] a mirror. **4** [early 19C] a lantern.

IN PHRASES

❑ **snap the glaze** *v.* [late 18C–early 19C] (*UK Und.*) to smash shop windows. ❑ **spank the glaze** *v.* (*also* **spank a glaze**) [SPANK *v.*[1] (2)] [early–mid-19C] (*UK Und.*) to break a shop window, reach in and grab whatever one can reach, having previously tied up the shop door so the shopkeeper cannot pursue. ❑ **star the glaze** *v.* [SE *star*, to make a star-shaped crack or hole] **1** [late 18C–mid-19C] (*also* **star it**) to break shop windows for the purpose of theft. **2** [early 19C] to hit in the eye. **3** [mid-19C] to break any window. **4** [mid-19C] (*US*) to vandalize plate glass by scratching it with a glazier's diamond.

glazier *n.* (*also* **glasier, glasyer**) [SE *glasier*] **1** [mid-16C–mid-19C] in pl., the eyes. **2** [mid-17C–mid-19C] (*UK Und.*) a thief who breaks into houses after removing an accessible window, or into shops by smashing the shop window. **3** [mid-18C] (*UK Und.*) a window.

SE in slang uses

IN PHRASES

❑ **is your father a glazier?** [mid-18C–1950s] a rude phr. used to embarrass one who is obstructing one's view.

gleaming *adj.* [1990s+] (*US campus*) first-rate, excellent.

glean *v.* [SE *glean*, to gather, to harvest] [mid–late 19C] to steal.

gleaner *n.* [GLEAN *v.*] **1** [mid–late 19C] a thief. **2** [1920s] in weak use, a sponger.

gleat *n.* (*also* **gleet**) [OF *glette*, slime, filth, purulent matter] **1** [late 17C+] urethritis. **2** [1940s+] (*Aus.*) venereal infection in the rectum.

glee *v.* [dial. *glee*, to squint, to glance sideways] [mid–late 18C] (*UK Und.*) to see, to look at.

gleep *n.* [ety. unknown; *HDAS* suggests 'perhaps intended to represent a Chinese speaker's pron. of CREEP *n.* (3)'; but note *Time* 25 Aug. 1947, 74: 'Britain's first pile...began operation last week. Officially it is a gleep (*g*raphite *l*ow *e*nergy *e*xperimental *p*ile)'] [1940s+] (*US campus*) an odd or stupid person.

gleep *v.* [ety. unknown; ? link to CLIP *v.*[1] (4)] [1950s+] (*US Und., motorcycle gang*) to steal; often *gleep a cage*, to steal a car.

gleet *n. see* GLEAT *n.*

Glenn Hoddle *n.* [rhy. sl. = DODDLE *n.*; ult. soccer star and later England team manager *Glenn Hoddle* (b.1957)] [1970s+] something very easy.

glib *n.* (*also* **glibb**) **1** [mid–late 18C] a ribbon. **2** [early 19C–1900s] loquacity, verbosity. **3** [mid-19C–1930s] the tongue; thus *slacken your glib*, loosen your tongue [resemblance to sense 1 above; but note SE *glib*, voluble but essentially trivial].

IN PHRASES

❑ **slacken your glib!** [late 19C] shut up! be quiet!

glibe *n. see* GYBE *n.*

glick *adj.* (*also* **glic**) [Irish *glic*, cunning, crafty] [1980s+] (*Irish*) cunning, clever.

glide *n.* [1990s+] (*US*) an expensive car.

glide *v.* **1** [late 19C] (*Aus.*) to die. **2** [late 19C+] (*later US black*) to walk, to move, to arrive.

glim *n.* (*also* **glym**) [SE *gleam*] **1** [early 17C; late 19C–1960s] a look, a glimpse. **2** [late 17C–1940s] a lantern, esp. a dark lantern used by thieves (later a flashlight or torch). **3** [18C+] a candle; any form of light, e.g. a star. **4** [mid-18C] a 'fiery' drink. **5** [mid–late 18C] (*UK Und.*) fire. **6** [late 18C–1950s] (*also* **glimm**) often in pl., the eye. **7** [19C] a fake account of a dramatic fire, as sold in the streets. **8** [mid–late 19C] a venereal disease. **9** [mid-19C–1900s] (*also* **shade-glim**) a window. **10** [mid-19C–1940s] (*mainly US*) in pl., spectacles, eye-glasses; thus (*Aus.*) *glim-faking*, selling spectacles at inflated prices. **11** [late 19C–1940s] a match. **12** [1930s] (*US tramp*) in pl., dawn. **13** [1930s] (*US tramp*) an eyeglass. **14** [1940s] a lighter.

IN COMPOUNDS

□ **glim-dropper** *n.* [GOLD-DROPPER *n.*] [1940s–50s] (*US Und.*) a confidence trick whereby a trickster allegedly drops an artificial eye in a shop. He offers a reward if it is found. The merchant cannot do so, but a second conman arrives, only to find the eye. He then says he will claim the reward, until the merchant, who also wants it, buys it off him. There is no reward. □ **glim-fenders** *n.* (*UK Und.*) **1** [late 17C–mid-19C] andirons. **2** [19C] handcuffs [puns on sense 1 above as 'hand irons']. □ **glim-flashy** *adj.* (*also* **glimflashly, grimflushly**) [one fig. *flashes* a *glim*] [late 17C–mid-19C] angry, impassioned. □ **glim-gibber** *n.* (*also* **glim-glibber**) [? fig. use of sense 2 above as generic for underworld + SE *gibber*, to mutter, to talk incomprehensibly] [mid-19C] a particular jargon or professional slang. □ **glim-jack** *n.* [generic proper name *Jack*] [late 17C–mid-19C] **1** (*also* **glym jack**) a link boy, hired to guide people to a destination through dark streets. **2** (*UK Und.*) a thief who works only at night. □ **glim-lurk** *n.* [LURK *n.* (1)] [19C] (*UK Und.*) the pleading for alms after suffering a supposed fire. □ **glim star** *n.* [like a SE *star* it gives off light] [mid-18C] (*UK Und.*) a ring, usu. a diamond ring. □ **glim-stick** *n.* (*also* **glym stick**) [late 17C–mid-19C] (*UK Und.*) a candlestick; thus *rum glimstick*, a silver candlestick; *queer glimstick*, a brass or pewter candlestick.

IN PHRASES

□ **dark glim** *n. see under* DARK *adj.* □ **douse the glim** *v.* **1** [mid-18C–1940s] (*also* **douse the glimmer, shoot the glim, top the glim**) to turn off the light; usu. as imper. **2** [mid-19C–1920s] (*US.Und.*) to give someone a black eye. **3** [late 19C–1900s] to kill someone.

glim *v.* [GLIM *n.*] **1** [late 17C–early 19C] (*UK Und.*) to burn on the hand, to brand. **2** [mid-18C] (*UK Und.*) burned (by a housefire). **3** [late 19C–1960s] (*also* **glimb**) to see, to catch sight of. **4** [20C+] (*UK Und.*) to beg. **5** [1910s–20s] (*US Und.*) to illuminate, to light. **6** [1950s] (*US*) to know, to realize.

glimmer *n.* (*also* **glim, glimmar, glymmer**) [SE *glimmer*, to shine; ult. Du./Ger. *glimmer*, to shine] **1** [mid-16C–early 19C; 1940s] (*UK Und.*) fire; thus a lantern etc. **2** [late 17C–mid-18C] venereal disease. **3** [19C–1960s] the eye; often in pl. **4** [late 19C] (*US*) a match, a locomotive headlight, a kerosene lamp. **5** [1910s] (*US*) a cut gem. **6** [1930s] a person who watches vacant motorcars. **7** [1930s] (*US*) a black eye. **8** [1930s–70s] an electric light, a torch. **9** [1940s–70s] a beggar, esp. one who claims to have lost all his possessions in a fire. **10** [1960s] (*US*) a sight, a view.

IN PHRASES

□ **douse the glimmer** *v. see* DOUSE THE GLIM *under* GLIM *n.*

glimmerer *n.* (*also* **glimmering mort, glymmerer**) [GLIMMER *n.* (1) + MORT *n.*)] **1** [late 16C–early 19C] a beggar who claims to have lost all their possessions as the result of a fire. **2** [mid-17C] a person, usu. a woman, who gains entry to a house on the pretext of getting a light for the fire and, while inside, steals whatever she can. **3** [mid-17C–mid-18C] one who deliberately sets fire to a house, hoping to take advantage of the confusion in order to steal. **4** [early 18C] (*UK Und.*) a link-boy, hired to guide one along the unlit streets.

glimmers *n.* [GLIMMER *n.* (3)] [1930s–60s] (*US Und.*) spectacles.

glimming *n.* [GLIM *v.* (3); note London cab-driver jargon, *glim*, to look for a cab] [late 19C–1940s] **1** (*US black*) watching, observing. **2** (*UK Und.*) watching out for cabs etc for wealthy people, in return for a tip.

glimpse *n.* **1** [1910s] in pl., the eyes. **2** [1950s+] (*W.I.*) an albino [they tend to have poor eyesight].

glint *n.* [20C+] a look, a glimpse; thus *have/take a glint at*, to observe, to glance at.

glisten *n.* [mid-19C] (*US*) a collective term for diamonds.

glistener *n.* [the coin's shine] [early 19C–1920s] a gold coin.

glister *n.* [SE *glister*, a bright light, brilliance, lustre] [late 19C] a glass, a tumbler; thus *glister of fish-hooks*, a glass of Irish whisky.

glister-pipe *n. see* CLYSTER-PIPE *n.* (2).

glitch *n.* [Ger. *glitschen*, to slip, via Yid. *glitshen*, to slide or skid; orig. mainframe computer jargon *glitch*, 'a sudden interruption in electric service, sanity, continuity, or program function' (*New Hacker's Dict.*, 1992). This was adopted c.1960 by astronauts, who gave it the more general definition, and it moved into mainstream sl. with the spread of the personal computer culture] [1960s+] a hitch, a snag, a malfunction.

glitter *n.* [they all sparkle or shine] **1** [1900s–10s] (*Aus.*) money. **2** [1940s] (*US Und.*) in pl., cheap or imitation jewellery. **3** [1950s+] (*US prison*) salt. **4** [1960s–70s] (*US gay*) powdered methamphetamine.

glitterati *n.* [SE *glitter* + *literati*] [1940s+] (*orig. US*) those fashionable writers, academics and sundry critics etc, who have transcended their usual obscurity into the dubious limelight of the New York and London gossip columns.

glitter gulch *n.* [the lurid neon signs, hotel architecture etc] **1** [1950s] the South Side of Chicago [ironic use of sense 2 below]. **2** [1950s+] (*US*) the Las Vegas downtown casino area.

glittery *n.* [1970s] (*US*) gold.

glitz *n.* [backform. f. GLITZY *adj.*] [1950s+] (*orig. US*) an extravagant but superficial display; thus *glitz up*, to make glitzy.

glitzy *adj.* [Ger. *glitzern*, glittering; or comb. of SE *glitter* + RITZY *adj.* (1)] **1** [1950s+] fashionable, sophisticated, glamorous. **2** [1970s] (*US campus*) very capable.

gloak *n.* (*also* **gloach, gloke, gloque**) [Shelta *gloch*, ? cognate with Irish *loach*, hero] [mid-18C–mid-19C] a man, a fellow.

gloak *v.* [ety. unknown] [1920s–30s] (*UK tramp*) to induce pity by one's tale.

glob *n.* (*also* **globber**) [? *blob* + GOB *n.*[2]] **1** [20C+] a mass or lump of some liquid or semi-liquid substance. **2** [1930s] (*US*) a plain sundae. **3** [1960s] (*US campus*) in pl., a great deal, a large quantity.

globe *n.* **1** [late 17C] in pl., the testicles. **2** [18C–early 19C] a round, pewter pot. **3** [mid-19C+] in pl., the female breasts. **4** [late 19C] a bowler hat. **5** [1970s+] in pl., the buttocks.

globular *adj.* [? the sufferer is 'going round in circles'] [18C] drunk.

glock *n.* [Irish *gloichd*, a fool] [mid–late 19C] a fool.

gloik *n.* [GLOCK *n.*] [1910s+] (*Aus.*) a fool, a simpleton.

gloke *n. see* GLOAK *n.*

glom *n.*[1] [? echoic of the solidity/dullness of the individual] [1930s+] (*US*) a fool.

glom *n.*[2] (*also* **glaum**) [GLOM *v.*] (*US*) **1** [1930s+] a hand. **2** [1940s] a look. **3** [1950s+] (*US*) a grab, a snatch, an act of stealing.

glom *v.* (*also* **glahm, glam, glaum, glomm, glom onto, glom up, gloom, glum**) [Scot. *glaum*, to snatch, to grab, to seize with the jaws, to eat greedily] **1** [late 19C+] (*US*) to steal. **2** [1910s+] (*US*) to arrest. **3** [1910s+] (*US*) to get (hold of), to obtain, to seize upon. **4** [1910s+] (*US*) to look, to see, to realize. **5** [1920s–40s] (*US Und.*) to pick fruit or crops. **6** [1930s+] (*US*) to eat, usu. to eat greedily. **7** [1970s+] (*US*) to stick, to entangle.

glomp *v.* [? GLOM *v.*] [1980s] to grab, to suck up.

gloom *n.* (*also* **gloom shedder**) [1910s–30s] (*US*) a depressed and/or depressing individual.

IN COMPOUNDS

□ **gloom bug** *n.* [1920s] a depressed individual.

IN PHRASES

□ **gloomed up** *adj.* [1910s] (*US*) depressed or depressing.

gloom *v. see* GLOM *v.*

gloomer *n.* [1960s] (*S.Afr.*) an undertaker.

gloom shedder *n. see* GLOOM *n.*

gloomy-drawers *n. see* GRUMPY-DRAWERS *n.*

gloomy gus *n.* [created c.1904 as a comic-strip character in *Happy Hooligan* by Frederick Burr Opper (1857–1937)] [20C+] (*US*) a very unhappy, pessimistic person.

gloop *n. see* GOOP *n.*[2].

gloops *n.* [? play on SE *gloom/grump*] [1930s] (*Aus.*) misery, a bad mood.

gloopy *adj.* [GOOP *n.*[2] (1)] [1960s+] **1** viscous, sticky. **2** stupid.

glop *n.* [onomat. of such a substance falling onto a hard surface; coined by cartoonist Elzie Segar (1894–1938) as a sound made by the baby Swee'pea in the cartoon 'Popeye the Sailor'] **1** [1940s+] a liquid or viscous substance or mixture. **2** [1940s+] unappetizing food. **3** [1950s+] (*US*) silly nonsense.

gloque *n. see* GLOAK *n.*

Gloria Gaynors *n.* [rhy. sl.; ult. US pop singer *Gloria Gaynor* (b.1947)] [1990s+] trainers.

glorioski! *excl.* (*also* **gloriosky!**) [SE *glory be...!* + -SKI *sfx*] [1950s+] (*US*) an excl. used to express surprise.

glorious *adj.* [late 18C–1900s] very drunk.

glorious *adv.* [mid-19C] (*UK Und.*) very.

glorious sinner *n.* [rhy. sl.] [mid-19C; 1930s–40s] dinner.

glory *n.*

SE in slang uses

IN COMPOUNDS

❑ **glory-grinding** *n.* [late 19C] (*Aus.*) preaching. ❑ **glory hole** *n. see* separate entries. ❑ **glory-outfit** *n.* [1910s] (*US cowboy*) a funeral procession. ❑ **glory pole** *n.* [POLE *n.*] [1950s] (*US*) the penis. ❑ **glory roll** *n.* [ROLL *n.* (2)] [1930s–40s] (*US black*) a large bankroll, produced as often as possible in order to impress one's acquaintances.

IN PHRASES

❑ **get the glory** *v.* [Tempest, *Lag's Lexicon* (1950), suggests that far from actual faith, such prisoners 'imagine that by crawling round the chaplain or priest they will get preferential treatment'] [1940s–50s] (*UK prison*) to become suddenly and fervently religious while serving a prison sentence.

IN EXCLAMATIONS

❑ **glory be to Pete!** *see under* PETE *n.*[1].

glory be *n.* [rhy. sl.] [1990s+] tea.

glory hole *n.*[1] [SE *glory hole*, anywhere in which things are heaped together without any attempt at order; ult. *glaur*, to make muddy] **1** [mid-19C] a small, holding cell in the court buildings, in which prisoners are kept during their trial. **2** [late 19C–1900s] a meeting place used by the Salvation Army. **3** [20C+] (*Irish*) the space under the stairs, or similar confined place (a place of punishment for badly behaved children). **4** [1960s+] (*US*) a bar frequented by homosexuals [also plays on GLORY HOLE *n.*[2] (2)].

glory hole *n.*[2] [SE *glory*, splendour, magnificence, esp. as pun on *go to glory*, to ascend to heavenly bliss + *hole*] **1** [1920s+] (*orig. US*) the vagina. **2** [1940s+] (*gay*) a hole cut in the side of a public toilet cubicle; one man pushes his penis through while another, anonymous, man fellates him.

glossy *adj.* [1900s] (*US*) very pleasant, enjoyable.

glouter *n.* [? Scot. *cloiter*, a vile wet mess] [20C+] **1** a sticky mess. **2** tapioca pudding.

glove *n.*[1] [the term is used in Thomas Dekker's book of 'manners', *The Guls Hornebooke* (1609), in a list of similar containers: 'hoopes, cans, half-cans, Gloues, Frolicks, and flap-dragons'] [17C] some form of unspecified drinking-vessel.

glove *n.*[2] [note Williams for 17C use of *glove* as metaphor for vagina] [1950s+] (*Aus./US*) a condom.

glow *n.* [the reddening of some drinkers' faces] [1950s+] the euphoric state of being intoxicated by drink or drugs.

IN PHRASES

❑ **get a glow on** *v.* (*also* **have a glow on**) [1950s–70s] (*orig. US*) to become intoxicated by drink or drugs.

gluck *n. see* GUCK *n.*

glucose-slinger *n.* [? nonce-word] [late 19C] (*Aus.*) a publican.

glue *n.* [appearance] **1** [mid-19C] gonorrhoea; thus a *glueing*, a case of gonorrhoea. **2** [late 19C] semen. **3** [late 19C–1940s] (*US*) money. **4** [1920s–40s] (*US*) beer. **5** [1940s] (*US*) alcohol. **6** [1960s] (*US*) blood. **7** [1980s+] (*Aus. prison*) porridge.

IN COMPOUNDS

❑ **gluehead** *n. see* GLUEY *n.* ❑ **glueneck** *n.* (*also* **gluepot**) [1920s–70s] (*US*) a dirty prostitute; thus adj. *gluenecked*. ❑ **gluepot** *n. see* separate entry.

IN PHRASES

❑ **full of glue** *adj.* [1920s] (*US*) worthless, contemptible. ❑ **have one's glue** *v.* [1960s+] (*Irish*) a dismissive retort. ❑ **in the glue** [1960s+] (*US*) in trouble, in difficulties.

glue *v.* [1920s–70s] (*orig. US*) **1** to steal. **2** to arrest.

glued *adj.*[1] [late 19C] (*US campus*) enthusiastic about.

glued *adj.*[2] [GLUE *n.* (5) + the lassitude of a drunkard's speech and movements] [1940s–60s] (*US*) drunk.

glued *adj.*[3] [SE *have one's head glued on*] [1980s+] (*orig. US campus*) stable, sane.

glued *adj.*[4] [2000s] under the influence of glue or similar substances.

gluepot *n.*[1] **1** [late 18C–early 19C] a parson [he 'joins together' married couples]. **2** [late 19C–1930s] a part of the road so muddy that vehicles stick in it. **3** [late 19C–1930s] (*Irish/S.Afr.*) a particularly pleasant public house [one wishes to be or finds oneself 'stuck' there]. **4** [1920s–40s] (*US Und.*) a post office. **5** [1920s–60s] (*US*) an old horse, suggested by use of horse carcasses in glue manufacture. **6** *see* GLUENECK *under* GLUE *n.*

gluepot *n.*[2] [rhy. sl. = TWAT *n.* (1); but note GLUE *n.* (2)] [20C+] the vagina.

gluey *n.* (*also* **gluehead**) [SE *glue* + -*y*/-HEAD *sfx* (4)] [1960s+] (*drugs*) a person who sniffs glue.

gluggar *n.* [Irish *ubh ghlugair*, a rotten egg] [20C+] (*Irish*) a general term of abuse.

glum *v. see* GLOM *v.*

glutes *n.* [medical Lat. *gluteus maximus*, one of the large muscles that form the buttock; ult. Gk *glutos*, the rump] [1980s+] (*US*) the buttocks.

glutton *n.* [SE glutton, but ? link to Suffolk dial. *glutton*, a glut (of commodities) or Scot. *gluther*, to swallow voraciously] **1** [early–mid-19C] an enthusiast; in boxing, one who is a 'glutton for punishment'. **2** [mid-19C] enthusiasm, ardour, greediness. **3** [1940s+] (*gay*) (*also* **glut**) a man obsessed with sex to the exclusion of other considerations.

IN COMPOUNDS

❑ **glutton for punishment** *n.* [1940s+] (*gay*) a fellator who continues sucking the penis even when orgasm has been reached.

glybe *n. see* GYBE *n.*

glym *n. see* GLIM *n.*

glym jack *n. see* GLIM-JACK *under* GLIM *n.*

glymmer *n. see* GLIMMER *n.*

glymmerer *n. see* GLIMMERER *n.*

glym stick *n. see* GLIM-STICK *under* GLIM *n.*

g.m. *n.* [abbr. *g*ood *m*orning] [late 19C–1950s] (*Aus./US*) the morning.

g.m.b.u. *n.* (*also* **g.m.f.u.**) [abbr. *g*rand *m*ilitary *b*alls-*u*p/*g*rand *m*ilitary *f*uck-*u*p] [1940s+] a disaster, utter chaos.

'gnac *n.* (*also* **yak**) [abbr.] [1990s+] (*US black*) cognac.

gnarlacious *adj. see* GNARLY *adj.* (3).

gnarler *n.* (*also* **gnawler**) [GNARL (UPON) *v.*] [early 19C–1920s] **1** a small watchdog. **2** an informer.

gnarl (upon) *v.* [SE *gnar, gnarl*, to snarl] [late 18C–early 19C] (*UK Und.*) to spy on, to inform against; thus *gnarling*, likely to act as an informer.

gnarly *adj.* [SE *gnarly*; popularized in the film *Fast Times at Ridgemont High* (1982)] [1970s+] **1** (*US campus*) bizarre, frightening, amazing. **2** (*US*) a general term of disapproval, disappointment, disgust. **3** (*US campus*) (*also* **gnarlatious, gnarley, knarly, narly**) wonderful, first-rate [on bad = good model].

gnashers *n.* [1960s+] the teeth.

gnasp *v.* [16C SE *gnasp*, to snap at] [early–mid-18C] to annoy.

gnat *n.* [characteristic of the insect] [1940s+] (*US campus*) an unattractive man, esp. one who pesters women.

IN COMPOUNDS

❑ **gnatbrain** *n. see* BEETLE-BRAIN *under* BEETLE *n.*[1]. ❑ **gnat's eyebrow** *n.* (*also* **gnat's balls, ...bristle, ...ear, ...eye, ...elbow, ...hair, ...heel, ...nip, ...nut, ...prick, ...toe-nail, gee hair**) [mid-19C+] (*US*) something very small; esp. in phrs., e.g. *down to a gnat's eyebrow*, to the finest detail; *sharp enough to split the* *hair on a gnat's ass*, extremely fine. ❑ **gnat's liver** *n.* [1930s] (*US black*) an unattractive woman. ❑ **gnat's piss** *n.* (*also* **gnat's pee, ...widdle, tiger's piss**) [1920s+] a derog. description of any liquid, esp. alcohol, that is weak, thin, tasteless etc.

gnaw *v.* [1980s+] (*N.Z.*) to kiss.

SE in slang uses

IN PHRASES

❑ **gnaw the bone** *v. see under* BONE *n.*[1]. ❑ **gnaw the 'nana** *v. see under* NANA *n.*

gnawler *n. see* GNARLER *n.*

gnerts! *excl. see* NERTS! *excl.*

gnof *n. see* GONNOF *n.*

gnome *n.* [1950s+] (*US*) an insignificant person, esp. a low-level employee.

gnostic *n.* [SE *gnostic*, an intellectual, one who possesses esoteric spiritual knowledge] [early–mid-19C] a 'knowing one', thus a cheat or sharper; thus *gnostically*, knowingly, artfully.

Go, the *n. see* GO-SHOP, THE *n.*

go *n.*[1] (*also* **goe**) **1** as a measure or portion. (**a**) [late 18C–1970s] a measure (of alcohol), e.g. a *go of gin*; esp. a three-halfpenny bowl of gin and water, available at a *go shop*; also used of portions of food. (**b**) [early 19C+] a portion, 'a time'. (**c**) [late 19C–1900s] (*Aus.*) a helping of food. (**d**) [1930s–50s] (*US drugs*) a measure of drugs; an injection of a given drug. (**e**) [1940s] (*US drugs*) a very small quantity of drugs wrapped in paper. **2** in the context of fashion, sophistication [SE *go*, spirit, energy, dash]. (**a**) [late 18C+] the height of fashion. (**b**) [early 19C] a dandy, a fashionable man. (**c**) [mid-19C] a wonderful person, esp. an attractive woman. **3** [late 18C+] an event, circumstances, a state of affairs; esp. as *rum go*, an odd situation. **4** [late 18C+] a success. **5** [early 19C+] an enjoyable time, a spree. **6** as a single instance. (**a**) [mid-19C+] an attempt, a try, e.g. *have a go (at)*, to make an attempt. (**b**) [mid-19C+] a turn in a game, an opportunity to do something; thus *at/in one go*, at/in one attempt; *have a go*, take a turn. (**c**) [late 19C–1930s] a bout of, a spell of. **7** [late 19C–1930s] a bargain, an agreement, a 'deal'; usu. in phr. *it's a go*, that's settled. **8** as a physical or verbal set-to. (**a**) [late 19C+] a contest, a fight, esp. a boxing-match or a street fight. (**b**) [1950s+] an argument, a verbal attack; usu. in phr. *have a go at (someone)*. **9** [1920s–30s] a bet. **10** [1940s+] (*Aus.*) a chance; an opportunity. **11** [1960s+] (*Aus.*) news, information. **12** [1960s+] (*Aus./US*) the important, relevant thing. **13** [1980s+] (*Aus. prison*) a plan. **14** in drug uses. (**a**) [1980s+] (*drugs*) cocaine. (**b**) [2000s] (*drugs*) amphetamine.

IN COMPOUNDS

❑ **go pill** *n.* [amphetamines give one energy and 'go'] [1950s–60s] (*US*) a pill or capsule of amphetamine.

IN PHRASES

❑ **all the go** *adj.* [late 18C+] fashionable. ❑ **give something a go** *v.* (*also* **give it a go, give someone a go**) [20C+] (*orig. Aus.*) to try something or someone out, to take a chance on, to make an attempt. ❑ **half-go** *n.* [late 19C–1900s] three pennyworth of spirits, usu. mixed with water. ❑ **have a go** *v.* [late 19C+] **1** to fight; usu. with *at*. **2** to attack verbally. **3** to pick a fight. ❑ **make a go of** *v.* **1** [1920s+] to succeed (despite the odds). **2** [1930s] to put up with, to tolerate. ❑ **square go** *n.* [SQUARE *adj.* (1)] [20C+] a fair fight, a fight without weapons. ❑ **sweet go** *n.* [SWEET *adj.*[1] (3)] [1990s+] (*Aus. Und.*) an easy crime.

go *n.*[2] [abbr.] [20C+] (*Aus.*) a goanna.

go *n.*[3]

IN PHRASES

❑ **give someone the go** *v. see under* GO-BY *n.*

go *v.* **1** in the context of sexuality. (**a**) [17C–18C] to have an orgasm. (**b**) [mid-17C+] usu. of a woman, to perform sexual intercourse; usu. in interrog. phr. used between two men, *Does she go?* **2** [late 17C; mid-19C+] to be acceptable, to be permitted. **3** [late 17C+] to succeed, to win approval or applause; thus adj. *goingest*, best. **4** in the context of monetary investment. (**a**) [mid-18C+] to bet, to wager; thus *gone*, having lost a bet. (**b**) [mid-19C] to bet on; also in fig. use, to trust. (**c**) [mid-19C+] to pay for. **5** [mid-19C+] to tolerate, to bear, to put up with. **6** in the context of physical collapse. (**a**) [mid-19C+] (*US*) to be killed; to die. (**b**) [1950s] (*US prison*) to be executed. (**c**) [1960s+] (*US*) to go to prison. (**d**) [2000s] to collapse, to fall down. **7** [late 19C+] to deal with, to find appealing or acceptable, to like or prefer. **8** [late 19C+] (*orig. US*) to be accepted or carried into effect, to have authority or effectiveness, to be obeyed without question; esp. in phr. *what I say goes*. **9** [late 19C+] to eat or drink, e.g. *I could go a couple of beers*. **10** [late 19C+] to match, to get along. **11** [late 19C+] for something to work out in a specific way, esp. of a political contest, e.g. *go Labour, go Republican*. **12** [20C+] (*Aus./US*) to attack, verbally or physically. **13** [1920s+] (*US*) to choose, esp. to become a member of; thus *go something*. **14** [1920s+] to say, to talk, e.g. *I go 'How are you?', and he goes 'Lousy'*. **15** [1940s] (*US black*) to make an effort. **16** [1950s] to characterize, to explain, to make sense of.

IN COMPOUNDS

❑ **go-about** *n.* [1910s–30s] (*US*) a tramp. ❑ **go-along** *n.* (*also* **go-alonger**) **1** [early–mid-19C] (*UK Und.*) a fool [he 'goes along' when someone orders him]. **2** [mid-19C] a thief. ❑ **go-boy** *n.* (*Can./Irish*) **1** [1940s+] a young hoodlum, a juvenile delinquent. **2** [1970s] an escapee, successful or otherwise. **3** *see* GOFER *n.* ❑ **go-'long** *n.* [one has no choice but to fig. or lit. *go along*] **1** [20C+] (*US black*) consequences, inevitable developments, circumstances; thus *be caught in the go-'long*, to be a victim of circumstances. **2** [1920s–40s] (*US black*) the police truck in which arrested people are taken to the local cells. ❑ **go-slow** *n. see under* SLOW *adj.*

IN PHRASES

❑ **go...** *v.* **1** *see also* separate entries. **2** *see also under* relevant n. or adj. ❑ **go alone** *v.* [early 19C–1900s] to be wary or cautious, to be experienced. ❑ **go from the fists** *v.* (*also* **go from the shoulders, ...the Y, get down from the Y**) [*Y*, i.e. the shape of the two arms and the trunk] [1970s+] (*US black*) to fight. ❑ **go in on** *v.* [mid-19C] (*US*) to attack physically. ❑ **go into** *v.* [1950s] to take advantage of, to obtain money from. ❑ **go like...** *v. see* separate entry. ❑ **go one's death** *v.* [mid-19C] (*US*) to do one's utmost for, to risk one's all on, to bet to the limit. ❑ **go the whole...** *v. see* separate entry. ❑ **go to...** *v. see also under* relevant n. or adj. ❑ **go to it** *v. see under* IT *n.*[1] (2). ❑ **have someone going** *v.* [1910s–20s] to excite sexually, to render infatuated.

SE in slang uses

IN PHRASES

❑ **don't (even) go there** (*also* **you don't want to go there**) [1990s+] (*orig. US black*) a phr. advising someone to avoid a course of action or a particular argument etc; emphasis is on an abstract 'there', rather than an actual place. ❑ **go backwards** *v.* [the position of the anus + the usu. siting of the privy at the back of the house] [18C] to visit an outdoor privy. ❑ **go beyond** *v.* ['beyond' the world one knows] [mid-19C] (*Anglo-Irish*) to suffer judicial transportation. ❑ **go by hand** *v.* [1920s–50s] (*US tramp*) to travel on foot (as opposed to train). ❑ **go-by-the-ground** *n.* [late 18C–early 19C] a short person. ❑ **go by the wall** *n.* [late 16C] a strong ale. ❑ **go in the tank** *v. see* TANK *v.*[1] (1). ❑ **go into one** *v. see under* ONE *n.*[1]. ❑ **go to Denmark** *v. see* GO TO COPENHAGEN *under* COPENHAGEN *n.* ❑ **go to rack and manger** *v. see* LIE AT RACK AND MANGER *under* LIE *v.*[1].

IN EXCLAMATIONS

❑ **go along with you!** *see* GET ALONG WITH YOU! *excl.* ❑ **go girl!** (*also* **you go! you go girl!**) [1990s+] (*orig. US black/campus*) an excl. of encouragement among young women. ❑ **go there!** [1980s] (*UK black*) an excl. of approval.

go... *v.* to have sexual intercourse; in phrs. below.

IN PHRASES

❑ **go...** *see also under* relevant n. or adj. ❑ **go all the way to Cockfosters** *v.* [1990s+] ❑ **go facemaking** *v.* [the *face* is that of a newly conceived child] [late 18C–19C] ❑ **go fleshing it** *v.* [mid–late 19C] ❑ **go goosing** *v.* [mid–late 19C] ❑ **go jock-**

hunting *v. see under* JOCK *n.*[1]. ▫ **go jumming** *v. see under* JUMM *v.* ▫ **go motting** *v. see under* MOT *n.* ▫ **go rumping** *v.* [19C+] of a man, to have sexual intercourse. ▫ **go rump splitting** *v.* [19C] of a man, to have sexual intercourse. ▫ **go slops** *v. see under* SLOPPY SECONDS *n.* ▫ **go star-gazing (on one's back)** *v. see under* STAR *n.*[1]. ▫ **go strumming** *v. see under* STRUM *v.* ▫ **go the distance** *v.* [boxing/horseracing imagery] [1950s+] ▫ **go the limit** *v.* [1920s+] to have or permit sexual intercourse. ▫ **go tromboning** *v.* [the physical action] [late 19C+] ▫ **go tummy-tickling** *v.* [mid–late 19C] ▫ **go vaulting** *v.* [late 16C–late 17C] ▫ **go working the double oracle** *v.* (*also* **go working the dumb oracle, ...hairy oracle**) [SE *work* + ORACLE *n.* (2)] [late 18C–mid-19C]

goad *n.* [SE *goad*, a spur] [16C–early 18C] (*UK Und.*) a decoy at a horse-fair.

goadie *n. see* GODY *n.*

goak *n.* [SE *joke* + dial. *gowk*, a fool] [mid-19C–1930s] (*Aus.*) a prank, a practical joke.

goal *v.* (*also* **ghoul, gool**) [SE *goal*; *ghoul/gool* are dial. prons.] [1910s–30s] (*US*) to knock down, to stun, to defeat; thus *knock someone for a goal*, to astonish.

goanna *n.*[1] [fig. uses of SAusE *goanna*, a variety of lizard (ult. SE *iguana*)] **1** [late 19C] (*Aus.*) a virile man. **2** [1960s] (*Aus.*) any old person.

IN COMPOUNDS

▫ **goanna oil** *n.* [1950s] (*Aus.*) any supposedly remarkable medicinal cure.

goanna *n.*[2] [rhy. sl.; var. on JOANNA *n.*] [1910s+] (*Aus.*) a piano.

go-around *n.*

IN PHRASES

▫ **give someone the go-around** *v.* (*also* **give something the go-around**) [var. on *GIVE SOMEONE THE GO-BY under* GO-BY *n.*] [late 19C+] of a person or thing, to reject, to avoid, to jilt.

go around *v.* [1940s] (*US*) to argue, to fight, to be obsessed with something bad.

SE in slang uses

IN PHRASES

▫ **go around with** *v. see GO ROUND WITH under* GO ROUND *v.*

goat *n.*[1] [the trad. characteristics of the animal, i.e. lechery, stubbornness etc] **1** [late 16C+] a womanizer, a lecher; usu. as *old goat*. **2** [17C; late 19C+] a dupe, a fool. **3** [mid-19C; 1910s+] (*US*) an offensive (old) man, occas. woman. **4** [mid-19C; 1940s] the buttocks. **5** [late 19C] (*US Und.*) a Catholic priest. **6** [1900s–60s] (*US*) a racehorse. **7** [1910s] (*US*) temper [backform. f. *GET SOMEONE'S GOAT* below]. **8** [1910s] (*US*) a slow or worthless horse. **9** [1960s] (*US campus*) a student being initiated into a fraternity, a fraternity pledge; thus *goat room*, the room used for initiation. **10** [1960s+] (*US*) a Pontiac GTO automobile [pron./reversal of GTO; note hotrod jargon *goat*, an old racing car, generally used when speaking of a driver 'herding his goat']. **11** [1970s] (*US teen*) an attractive boy. **12** [1980s] a caddy.

DERIVATIVES

▫ **goatish** *adj.* [17C] lecherous.

SE in slang uses

IN COMPOUNDS

▫ **goat-and-galah** *adj.* [the main inhabitants are *goats* and *galahs*] [1920s–50s] (*Aus.*) used of a small hotel, town or other place to indicate the lack of amenities. ▫ **goat breath** *n.* [1980s] (*US campus*) a derog. term of contempt. ▫ **goat-fuck/-fucking** see separate entries. ▫ **goat-hair** *n.* [1900s–60s] (*US black*) homemade or bootleg liquor. ▫ **goat hill** *n.* (*also* **goat's gulch, goat town, ...woods**) [note one such *goat's gulch* in Kansas was gentrified and re-nicknamed *Angora Heights*] [20C+] (*US*) an area of town where a certain class of people live, usu. the poor, but sometimes the better-off. ▫ **goatmilker** *n.* [note SE *goatmilker, goatsucker*, a name given to the bird *Caprimulgus europæus*, f. a belief that it sucks the udders of goats] [mid-19C] **1** the vagina. **2** a prostitute. ▫ **goat-mouth** *n.* [20C+] (*W.I.*) the ability that certain individuals supposedly possess to cause problems or frustrate the efforts of others; thus *put goat-mouth on*, to cause such problems; *goat-mouth bite you?* a question asked of one who seems unhappy or worried. ▫ **goat-rope** *n. see* GOAT-FUCK *n.* ▫ **goat roper** *n.* [their stereotypical occupation] [20C+] (*US*) a peasant, a rural person, an unsophisticated person. ▫ **goat-screw** *n. see* GOAT-FUCK *n.* ▫ **goat's genolickers** *n.* [var. on DOG'S BALLOCKS *n.*] [1940s–50s] (*Irish*) the real thing, the ultimate example. ▫ **goat's gulch** *n. see GOAT HILL* above. ▫ **goat's jig** *n.* [the perceived sexuality of the goat] [late 17C–19C] sexual intercourse; thus *dance the goat's jig*. ▫ **goat skin** *n.* [1970s] (*US gay*) a long foreskin. ▫ **goat town/woods** *n. see GOAT HILL* above.

IN PHRASES

▫ **dance the goat's jig** *v. see under* DANCE *v.* ▫ **get someone's goat** *v.* (*also* **burn one's goat, get on one's goat, get someone's nannygoat**) [SE *get*, to irritate, to annoy + SE *goat*; ? the goat's propensity to butt when in a bad temper] [20C+] **1** to annoy someone; thus *goat-getting*, deliberate provocation to gain a psychological advantage; *goat-getter*, a malicious teaser. **2** to impress, to move emotionally. **3** to render nervous. ▫ **look goats and monkeys at** *v.* [the trad. propensities of these two animals] [mid-18C–19C] to gaze lecherously at, to leer. ▫ **lose one's goat** *v.* [1910s] to lose one's courage, one's ability to fight. ▫ **no goat's toe** [20C+] (*Ulster*) used of one who is sensible, 'nobody's fool'. ▫ **play the goat** *v.* **1** [18C] to copulate energetically. **2** [late 19C–1920s] to lead a degenerate, dissipated life. **3** [1910s] to mess around, to act ineffectually. ▫ **take the goat's tail** *v.* [1940s] (*Aus.*) to surpass, to win.

goat *n.*[2] [abbr.] (*US*) **1** [late 19C+] a *goat*ee beard. **2** [1910s+] a scape*goat*.

goat *v.* [? to butt like a goat] [mid-19C–1900s] to beat, to thrash.

goatees *n.* [? SE *gonads* + ref. to goatish lechery] [1970s] (*US gay*) the testicles.

goater *n.* [mid-19C] (*US Und.*) a dress.

goat-fuck *n.* (*also* **goat-rope, goat-screw**) [such a coupling is seen as an epitome of chaos] [1970s+] (*orig. US milit.*) a fiasco, a mess, chaos, confusion.

goat-fucking *adj.* (*also* **goatfucker**) [1960s] a euph. for MOTHERFUCKING *adj.*

go-away *n.* **1** [mid-19C] (*Aus./US Und.*) a railroad train; a tram, a bus. **2** [late 19C] (*UK society*) the dress in which a bride departs from her reception to begin her honeymoon.

go away *v. see under* AWAY *adj.*

gob *n.*[1] [orig. northern dial.] **1** [mid-16C+] (*orig. UK Und.*) (*also* **gub**) the mouth. **2** [mid-19C+] verbosity. **3** [late 19C] the face. **4** [1960s] a blow to the mouth.

IN COMPOUNDS

▫ **gob-box** *n.* [late 18C–early 19C] the mouth. ▫ **gob-crockery** *n.* [1980s] (*Aus.*) false teeth. ▫ **gob-iron** *n.* [1950s+] a mouth organ. ▫ **gob-job** *n.* [JOB *n.*[2] (2)] [1980s+] **1** fellatio. **2** (*US gay*) fellatio performed on a sailor [adds pun on GOB *n.*[2] (4b)]. ▫ **gob-lock** *n.* [SE *lock*; their inarticulacy] [1990s+] a fool. ▫ **gob off** *v.* [2000s] to talk (loudly). ▫ **gob out** *v.* [early 19C] to talk. ▫ **gob-organ** *n.* [1930s] (*Aus.*) a mouth-organ. ▫ **gobshite** *n. see* separate entry. ▫ **gobsmacked** *adj. see* separate entry. ▫ **gob-stick** *n.* **1** [late 18C–19C] (*US*) usu. pl., (silver) forks or spoons. **2** [1920s–50s] (*orig. US*) (*also* **gobblestick**) a clarinet or fife. ▫ **gob-string** *n. see GAB STRING under* GAB *n.*[1]. ▫ **gobstruck** *adj. see* GOBSMACKED *adj.*

IN PHRASES

▫ **blow one's gob off** *v.* (*also* **blow one's gab off**) [GAB *n.*[1] (1)] [1910s] to lose one's temper. ▫ **hold one's gob** *v.* (*also* **hold one's gab, ...mug**) [GAB *n.*[1] (1)/MUG *n.*[1] (1d)] [19C+] to be quiet; often as imp. ▫ **shut one's gob** *v.* (*also* **shut one's gab**) [GAB *n.*[1] (1)] [20C+] to be quiet; esp. in imper. *shut your gob!*

gob *n.*[2] [the term appears mid-16C as SE; it gradually declined in status over the next 300 years] **1** [mid-16C+] a lump or clot of some slimy substance. **2** [early 17C; 19C+] a lump, a mouthful. **3** [late 19C+] (*UK Und.*) a theft carried out by a thief who spits on man's coat, alerts him to the problem then robs him while pretending to 'help' him clean up. **4** [late 19C+]

one who is typified by their spitting. (**a**) a coastguard or a quarterdeck man ['When a meeting takes place the men indulge in a protracted yarn and a draw of the pipe. The session involves a considerable amount of expectoration all round, whereby our friends come to be known as gobbies' (F&H)]. (**b**) (*US*) (*also* **gobshite**) any sailor. (**c**) a sailor's hat. **5** [1910s] (*UK public school*) someone who makes one feel sick. **6** [1930s+] a lump; thus adj. *gobby*, lumpy. **7** [1970s] spit. **8** *see* GOBSHITE *n.* (3).

(IN COMPOUNDS)

❑ **gob-gobbler** *n.* [GOBBLER *n.*[2]] [1980s+] (*US gay*) a gay man who prefers sailors as partners. ❑ **gobhawk** *n. see* separate entry.

gob *n.*[3] [16C SE *gob*, a large amount of money] [19C+] a large amount; esp. as *gobs* (*of*).

gob *v.* [GOB *n.*[1] (1)/GOB *n.*[2]] **1** [18C–19C] to swallow in large mouthfuls, to 'choke down'. **2** [early 19C] to hit in or on the mouth. **3** [late 19C+] to spit; to dribble.

(IN PHRASES)

❑ **gob the knob** *v. see under* KNOB *n.*

gob! *excl.* [20C+] God!

go-back *n.* [20C+] **1** (*Aus.*) a reply, a retort. **2** (*US Und.*) a second (or subsequent) attempt at the same crime.

go back *v.* [SAmE *go back*, to retreat to a wild state] [20C+] (*US black*) of processed hair, to return to its normal state.

gobaloon/gobberloony *n. see* GABBERLOONEY *n.*

gobble *n.* [GOBBLE *v.*[1] (2)] [1930s+] an act of fellatio; both hetero- and homosexual.

SE in slang uses

(IN EXCLAMATIONS)

❑ **shut your gobble!** [late 19C] shut up! be quiet!

gobble *v.*[1] [SE *gobble*, to eat food greedily] **1** [mid-19C–1900s] (*US*) to grab, to steal, to apprehend. **2** [1920s+] (*also* **gobble off**) to fellate; thus n. *gobbling*, fellatio [play on EAT *v.* (4)].

(IN COMPOUNDS)

❑ **gobble-gut** *n.* [early–mid-17C] a glutton. ❑ **gobblepipe** *n.* [1930s] (*US*) a saxophone. ❑ **gobble-prick** *n.* [sl. use is too late, hence SE *gobble* + PRICK *n.* (1)] [late 17C–18C] a sexually active woman. ❑ **gobblestick** *n. see GOB-STICK under* GOB *n.*[1].

(IN PHRASES)

❑ **gobble the goo** *v.* (*also* **gobble the gook, ...goop, ...goose, ...gravy**) [GOO *n.*[1] (1)/GOOK *n.*[4] (1)/GOOP *n.*[2] (1)/SE *goose*/GRAVY *n.* (1b)] [1910s+] (*orig. US*) to fellate.

gobble *v.*[2] [SE *gabble* + ? the turkey's *gobbling*] [1930s–40s] (*US*) **1** to chatter. **2** to talk incoherently.

gobbledygoo *n.* (*also* **gobblegoo**) [*GOBBLE THE GOO under* GOBBLE *v.*[1]] [1930s–40s] (*US*) **1** a prostitute who performs fellatio. **2** fellatio.

gobble-gobble *n.* [GOBBLE *v.*[2] (1) + redup.] [1920s–40s] (*US black*) talk, chatter.

gobble off *v. see* GOBBLE *v.*[1] (2).

gobbler *n.*[1] [despite its appearance in Grose (1785), and in Bailey, *Universal Etymological English Dict.* (1721 et seq.), as 'cant', *gobbler*, a turkey-cock, is SE] **1** [mid-16C–late 18C] a duck, a goose. **2** [1910s] (*Aus.*) a Turkish soldier [play on SE *gobbler*, turkey].

gobbler *n.*[2] (*also* **bone gobbler**) [SE *gobble*/GOBBLE *v.*[1] (2)] [1920s+] (*US*) an individual who performs oral sex.

gobbler's knob *n.* (*also* **gobbler hill**) [1930s–60s] (*US*) a generic nickname for anywhere considered far away.

gobby *n.*[1] [GOB *n.*[2] (4)] [late 19C–1920s] **1** a sailor. **2** a coastguardsman.

gobby *n.*[2] [GOBBY *adj.*] [1920s] (*US*) a socially unacceptable person.

gobby *adj.* [GOB *n.*[1] (1) + sfx *-y*] **1** [late 19C+] talkative, esp. in a domineering manner. **2** [1940s] showy. **3** [1950s] greedy.

gobdaw *n.* (*also* **daw**) [Irish *gabhdán*, a gullible person] [1940s+] (*Irish*) a gullible simpleton.

gobhawk *n.* [GOB *n.*[2] (1) + SE *hawk*, to spit] [late 19C–1900s] (*Irish*) an uncouth person.

goblet of jam *n.* [transl. of Arabic, *m'jun-i akbar*] [1960s] (*US drugs*) marijuana.

goblin *n.* [abbr. JEMMY O'GOBLIN *n.*] [late 19C–1920s] a sovereign.

gob off! *excl.* [euph.] [1990s+] go away!

goboon *n.* (*also* **gaboon, goopon**) [GOB *v.* (3) + sfx *-oon*] [1920s–40s] (*US*) a spittoon.

gobshite *n.* [lit. and fig. uses of GOB *n.*[1] (1) + SHITE *n.*] **1** [late 19C–1910s] (*US*) an expectorated wad of tobacco. **2** [20C+] (*also* **gabshite**) a fool, a dupe. **3** [1960s+] (*also* **gaubshite, gob**) a general term of abuse. **4** [1990s+] nonsense, rubbish; thus as adj., stupid. **5** [1990s+] one who talks nonsense. **6** *see* GOB *n.*[2] (4b).

gobsmacked *adj.* (*also* **gobstruck**) [orig. northern dial.; lit. SE *smacked* in the GOB *n.*[1] (1)] [1950s+] flabbergasted, amazed, speechless.

go-buggy *n. see* BENZINE BUGGY *n.*

go-by *n.*

(IN PHRASES)

❑ **give someone the go** *v.* [1900s; 1980s+] (*Aus./N.Z.*) **1** to reject a suitor. **2** to give up a job, leave a country etc. ❑ **give someone the go-by** *v.* (*also* **give someone the go-long**) [SE *go-by*, the action of going] **1** [late 17C+] to reject, to avoid, to jilt, of a person or thing. **2** [19C–1920s] to overtake, to pass. **3** [early 19C] to surpass.

goby *n.* [abbr. SE *go-between*] [1970s] a middleman in criminal dealings, an underworld fixer.

go-cart *n.* [1910s–70s] (*US*) a car.

gock *n.* [var. on GOOK *n.*[4] (1)] [1970s] (*US*) any form of sticky substance, ointment, cream.

God *n.*[1] (*also* **God's**) [late 17C+] used in a number of oaths that, when coined, had a good deal more resonance, given their blasphemous context, e.g. *GOD'S TEETH!* below.

SE in slang uses

(IN COMPOUNDS)

❑ **God-awful** *see* separate entries. ❑ **God-bird** *n.* [dial. *god-bird*, the youngest bird in a nestful] [1950s] (*W.I.*) the much-loved and petted 'baby' of the family. ❑ **God-blasted** *adj.* [20C+] a general oath. ❑ **God-blessed** *adj.* [1960s+] (*US*) a euph. for GOD-DAMN *adj.* ❑ **God-botherer/-bothering** *see* separate entries. ❑ **God-box** *n.* **1** [1910s+] a church. **2** [1930s+] an organ. ❑ **God-dam(n)/-dammit/-damned** *see* separate entries. ❑ **God-hopper** *n.* [1940s–50s] (*US*) an evangelist or very religious person. ❑ **God permit** *n.* [such coaches were advertised as starting 'if God permit'] [late 18C–mid-19C] a stage-coach. ❑ **God save** *n.* (*also* **Gawsave, God saves**) [it starts 'God save our gracious king/queen'] [1900s–30s] the British national anthem. ❑ **Godsown** *n. see* separate entry. ❑ **God's (own) medicine** *n.* [1930s+] (*drugs*) opium, morphine, heroin. ❑ **God squad** *n.* (*also* **god squatter**) **1** [1960s+] any form of proselytizing religious group (often evangelical), esp. as found within a university or similar institution. **2** [1980s+] (*Aus. prison*) prison officers responsible for security. **3** [1990s+] (*US*) the Endangered Species Committee [they are accused of 'playing God' with nature]. ❑ **God-thumper** *n. see BIBLE-THUMPER under* BIBLE *n.*

(IN PHRASES)

❑ **God bless the Duke of Argyle** [ult. a row of iron posts that were erected in Glasgow by the contemporary duke. The story goes that grateful lice-ridden citizens were able to use them as scratching-posts. Another version suggests that the posts were erected around the duke's various estates; primarily for the benefit of sheep, they were adopted by verminous shepherds] [mid-19C] a remark made on observing one's companion shrug their shoulders; the insinuation is that they have lice. ❑ **God-blind-me** *n.* [the ironic excl. by one who sees them] [1950s] (*W.I.*) flashy footwear. ❑ **God-dam-me** *n. see DAMME-BOY under* DAMME! *excl.* ❑ **God-help-us** *n. see* GAWDELPUS *n.* ❑ **God's green apple** *n.* (*also* **God's green gooseberry patch**) [20C+] (*US*) the Earth.

IN EXCLAMATIONS

❑ **God blind old Reilly!** *see under* O'REILLY *n.* ❑ **God-damn!/god-damn it!** see separate entries. ❑ **God's hat!** [mid-16C] an excl. of surprise. ❑ **God's lid!** [late 16C–early 17C] a general semi-blasphemous excl.; lit. 'God's eyelid!'. ❑ **God's teeth!** (*also* **God's bones! ...bread! ...fast! ...fishhooks! ...foot! ...grease! ...guts! ...knockers! ...precious! ...sides! ...wounds!**) [16C+] an excl. used to express astonishment or annoyance. ❑ **God stiffen us!** (*also* **God stiffen you!**) [lit. 'let us grow dead and stiff'] [late 19C–1940s] a general excl. ❑ **God's trousers!** [1900s–50s] (*Aus.*) a mild oath.

God *n.*[2] [1990s+] (*US black*) a term of address to a male friend.

God almighty *n.* [rhy. sl.] [1990s+] a nightie, a nightdress.

God-awful *adj.* [late 19C+] (*orig. US*) especially appalling; also *God-awfullest*.

God-awful *adv.* [GOD-AWFUL *adj.*] [1930s+] appallingly.

God-botherer *n.* **1** [1920s+] (*orig. milit.*) an evangelist. **2** [1960s+] a sanctimoniously pious person.

God-bothering *n.* [GOD-BOTHERER *n.*] [2000s] religious ceremonies, esp. when excessively and sanctimoniously pious.

God-bothering *adj.* [GOD-BOTHERER *n.* (2)] [1960s+] unctuously pious.

Goddam *n.* [the stereotyped English propensity for the oath GOD-DAMN! *excl.*; note more recent French *les fuckoffs*, the English, coined for similar reasons] [late 18C–19C] as used by a foreigner, an English person.

goddam *n.* (*also* **God-dam, God-damn**) [1910s+] a damn; thus NOT GIVE A (GOOD) GODDAM V.

IN PHRASES

❑ **like god-dam** *adv. see* LIKE HELL *under* HELL *n.*

goddamit *adj.* (*also* **goddammit**) [GOD-DAMN IT! *excl.*] [1960s+] (*US*) a general intensifier.

God damn *n.*[1] [rhy. sl.] [1990s+] jam.

God-damn *n.*[2] *see* GODDAM *n.*

God-damn *adj.* (*also* **god-damned, god-damnedest**) **1** [17C+] a general intensifier, lit. 'most damnable'. **2** [mid-19C+] (*US*) exasperating, most strange. **3** [1940s+] as infix. **4** [1980s] a term of affection, admiration.

IN EXCLAMATIONS

❑ **I'll be goddamned!** [1940s+] a general excl. of emphasis, implying one's refusal to accept a given situation; lit. 'cursed'.

god-damn *v.* **1** [17C+] to curse. **2** [1910s–30s] to swear.

God-damn! *excl.* (*also* **God-dam! goddam! goddamn!**) [note WW1 Aus. milit. *goddam-guy*, an American] [17C+] a generally pej. excl. expressing anger, astonishment etc.

god-damned/-damnedest *adj. see* GOD-DAMN *adj.*

god-damn it! *excl.* [mid-19C+] a general excl. of exasperation.

God-dang *adj.* (*also* **God-darn**) [1910s–60s] a euph. for GOD-DAMN *adj.* (1).

goddess *n.* [1980s+] (*US campus*) an ambitious, successful woman.

goddess Diana *n.* [rhy. sl. = TANNER *n.*] [mid-19C] a sixpence (2½p).

godfather *n.* **1** [late 16C–early 19C] (*also* **godfather-in-law**) a juryman. **2** [late 18C–early 19C] one who pays the bill after a meal or a session of drinking; thus *will you stand godfather and we will take care of the brat*, you pay now and we will repay you later.

God forbid *n.* [rhy. sl.] **1** [late 19C+] (*also* **lord-forbids**) a child [= KID *n.*[1] (1)]. **2** [1930s–70s] a hat [= LID *n.* (1)]. **3** a Jew [= YID *n.*[1] (1)].

Godfrey *n.* (*also* **Gadfrey**) [mid-19C+] (*orig. US*) a euph. for *God* and used as such in various mild oaths, e.g. *by Godfrey! Godfrey mighty!*

God in heaven *n.* [rhy. sl.] [20C+] the number seven.

God love her *n.* [rhy. sl.] [1970s] one's mother.

go-down *n.* **1** [mid-17C–early 18C] a drink [it 'goes down']. **2** [1940s+] (*US black*) a basement flat or apartment (cf. GO-UP *n.*).

go-down *adj.* [GO DOWN *v.* (6)] [1960s] describing a person who enjoys giving oral sex.

go down *v.* **1** [mid-19C–1910s] (*UK/US Und.*) to rob, to steal from [*go down* into the pockets]. **2** [late 19C–1930s] to lose one's money, e.g. in a wager; to become bankrupt. **3** [late 19C; 1960s+] (*S.Afr./US*) to die. **4** [20C+] (*also* **go down below**) to be sent to prison; to be punished while in prison. **5** [20C+] (*W.I.*) to be admitted to a psychiatric hospital. **6** [1910s+] (*orig. US*) (*also* **go down on**) to perform fellatio or cunnilingus. **7** [1940s+] (*orig. US black*) to happen, to take place, often of a fight or other dramatic encounter. **8** [1950s] (*US street gang*) (*also* **come down, go down on, go down with**) to attack a rival gang. **9** [1950s+] (*US*) to copulate readily. **10** [1980s] (*US black*) (*also* **go down with**) to help a friend.

IN PHRASES

❑ **what's going down?** [1970s+] (*US black/campus*) a greeting.

SE in slang uses

IN PHRASES

❑ **go down in food** *v.* [20C+] (*W.I., Bdos*) to eat ravenously. ❑ **go down like a dinner** *v.* [colloq. *go down*, to be acceptable] [1940s+] to be extremely popular, also used ironically. ❑ **go down like a pork chop at a Jewish wedding** *v. see under* PORK CHOP AT A JEWISH WEDDING *phr.* ❑ **go down the bay** *v.* [late 19C–1900s] (*US*) to spend heavily. ❑ **go down the chutes** *v.* (*also* **go down the garbage can, ...mine, chute the chutes**) [late 19C+] (*US*) to be ruined, to meet with disaster. ❑ **go down the weather** *v.* [one suffers an 'ill wind'] [17C] to become bankrupt. ❑ **go down to** *v.* [1900s] (*Aus.*) to fall asleep. ❑ **go down to the ground** *v.* [17C] to defecate.

God's *n. see* GOD *n.*[1].

God save the queens *n.* [rhy. sl. = SE *greens*] [20C+] vegetables.

gods for clods *n.* [1970s+] (*US campus*) a course in basic comparative religion.

God's in heaven *n.* [rhy. sl.] [1940s+] (*bingo*) the number seven.

Godsown *n.* (*also* **Godzone**) [abbr. SE *God's own country*] **1** [1910s+] (*N.Z.*) New Zealand. **2** [1970s+] (*mainly Aus.*) Australia; occas. also of other natives about their own country.

gody *n.* (*also* **goadie**) [? SE *gourd*, a water carrier] [20C+] (*W.I.*) a hugely swollen testicle, due to a rupture; known in medical jargon as *hydrocele*, a water tumour.

goe *n. see* GO *n.*[1].

goef *n.* (*also* **ghoef, goof**) [synon. Afk.] [1960s+] (*S.Afr.*) a swim.

goef *v.* (*also* **ghoef, goof**) [GOEF *n.*] [1960s+] (*S.Afr.*) to swim.

goer *n.* [GO *v.* (1b)] **1** [20C+] an enthusiastic if not always competent amateur. **2** [1910s] a flirt. **3** [1920s+] a promiscuous, sexually available woman.

IN PHRASES

❑ **straight goer** *n.* [STRAIGHT *adj.*[1] (3)] [20C+] (*orig. Aus.*) an honest, dependable person.

goers *n.* [they make one *go*] [19C] the feet.

goeters *n.* [Afk. *goeters*, good things] [2000s] (*S.Afr. Und.*) (stolen) goods.

goey *n.* (*Aus./drugs*) **1** [1990s+] cocaine. **2** [2000s] amphetamine.

go-fast *n.* (*also* **go-faster**) [its effects] [1960s+] (*drugs*) methcathinone.

gofer *n.* (*also* **go-boy, gopher**) **1** [1930s+] (*orig. US*) an assistant, an errand boy or girl, a runner, anyone who is told to *go fer*... some requirement. **2** [1960s] (*US drugs*) a person who offers to buy drugs for a naive addict, and keeps them for himself instead.

gofer *v.* (*also* **gopher**) [GOFER *n.*] [1960s+] (*orig. US*) to run errands, to go out for something.

G off *v. see under* G *n.*

goffel *n.* [1970s] (*S.Afr. coloured*) an ageing prostitute. [1990s+] a mixed-race person.

goffer *n.* [? fig. use of RN *goffer*, mineral water or lemonade, orig. that manufactured by *Goffe* & Sons Ltd. The image is of an angry person who is excited in the way that the bubbles in aerated water are. The mineral water use is extant in Aus.] [late 19C–1910s] a blow, a punch.

goffer *v.* [GOFFER *n.*] [late 19C–1900s] to pull or crush a person's hat over their eyes, thus temporarily blinding them.

goffo *n.* [ety. unknown; ? SE *go for (a ride)*] [1950s+] (*Irish*) a free ride on the back bumper of a car, van or lorry, unknown to the driver.

go for *v.*[1] **1** [late 19C+] to find sexually or otherwise attractive or appealing. **2** [1930s+] to accept, to believe, to be deceived.

SE in slang uses

IN PHRASES

❑ **go for an oatie** *v.* [? the arctic explorer Captain Lawrence Oates (1880–1912), whose last words were allegedly his announcement that he was leaving the communal tent to relieve himself] [2000s] (*N.Z.*) to go to the lavatory. ❑ **go for it** *see* separate entries.

go for *v.*[2] **1** [1920s+] to resemble, to 'pass' as. **2** [1970s] (*US black*) 'a pseudo-relationship in which two persons agree to present themselves and act toward each other in this relationship' (Roberts, *Third Ear*, 1971), e.g. *going for cousins*, of an intimate heterosexual couple, to claim they do not have a sexual interest in each other.

go for *v.*[3] [1950s+] to be in one's favour, to be favourable or advantageous to; esp. in phr. *have something going for one*.

go-for-broke *adj.* [GO FOR BROKE *v.*] [1970s+] absolute, committed, unreserved.

go for broke *v.* [GO *v.* (4a) + BROKE *adj.*[1]] [1950s+] (*orig. US*) to commit oneself unreservedly, esp. in a gambling or betting context; also adj. use.

go for it *v.* [GO FOR *v.*[1]] **1** [late 19C+] to commit oneself wholeheartedly. **2** [1920s+] of a woman, to be sexually enthusiastic. **3** [1970s+] to make an effort, to overcome one's fears, to get on energetically. **4** [1970s+] (*US campus*) to seduce.

go for it! *excl.* [1970s+] (*orig. US campus*) **1** an exhortation to make an effort, to overcome one's fears, to get on energetically. **2** a general exhortation to those present, urging them to act crazily, the intention being thus to have fun.

go-forwards *n.* [20C+] (*W.I.*) a thong sandal that, if one does not keep walking forwards, is liable to fall off the foot.

gog *n.* [16C+] a euph. form of *God*, and used as such in oaths.

go-getter *n.* [SE *go-getter*, an active, enterprising individual] [1910s] (*US*) an attractive person or thing.

gog-eye *n.* [? SHANGHAI *n.*[1]] [20C+] (*Aus. juv.*) a catapult.

gogga *n.* [Nama *xo xo*, an insect] (*S.Afr.*) **1** [20C+] an insect, a 'creepy-crawly'. **2** [20C+] a term of affection aimed at a child or a small adult. **3** [1930s+] something menacing or frightening, a dangerous person or thing.

goggle box *n.* (*also* **goggle**) [SE *goggle (at)*, to stare at + *box*/BOX *n.*[1] (4f)] [1950s+] the television.

goggle-eyed *adj.* **1** [16C–17C] having prominent, staring eyes [SE after 17C]. **2** [early 18C; mid-19C+] (*US*) wearing spectacles. **3** [late 19C–1930s] (*US*) (*also* **goggly, google-eyed, googly-eyed**) drunk. **4** [20C+] (*Aus.*) (*also* **google-eyed**) dazed.

goggles *n.* [SE *goggle (at)*, to stare at] **1** [mid-17C] one who stares. **2** [mid-17C–1910s] the eyes; in sing., the white of the eye. **3** [early 19C+] spectacles, esp. when round. **4** [mid-19C] a monocle. **5** [20C+] the nickname of someone who wears spectacles.

goggy *n.* [? GOGGLES *n.* (3)] [1980s+] a school child who has been rejected by its fellows.

go-go *n.*

SE in slang uses

IN PHRASES

❑ **have go-go in one's eyes** *v.* [i.e. one wishes to 'go'] [1990s+] (*US prison*) to wish to escape.

gohuddy *v.* [ety. unknown] [2000s] (*US black*) to go fast, to accelerate.

go-in *n.* **1** [mid-19C] a share in. **2** [mid-19C] a good time. **3** [mid-19C–1900s] an attack or onslaught upon; also, a spell of work upon. **4** [late 19C] (*Aus.*) an attempt; a try at. **5** [late 19C+] (*Aus. Und.*) a criminal attack or onslaught upon, e.g. an act of bush-ranging; also in fig. (non-criminal) use. **6** [1930s] (*UK Und.*) an escape (attempt).

going on *phr.*

IN PHRASES

❑ **have it going on** [1990s+] (*US black*) living in the swing of things, being chic or fashionable.

going-over *n.* [SE *go over*, to inspect, in lit. or fig. uses] (*orig. US*) **1** [late 19C+] a scolding, a telling-off. **2** [1910s+] an inspection. **3** [1930s–40s] petting, sexual caressing. **4** [1930s+] treatment, doctoring. **5** [1930s+] a thrashing, a beating. **6** [1940s+] a police interrogation, also other interrogation.

go it *v.* **1** [late 17C; mid-19C+] to move at great speed. **2** [late 18C+] (*also* **go it hot**) to commit oneself fully, usu. to a course of self-indulgent pleasure or as in a fight. **3** [early 19C] to work as a prostitute. **4** [late 19C+] (*Aus.*) to accept, to believe in.

IN PHRASES

❑ **go it blind** *v.* [mid-19C–1900s] (*US*) to enter on an undertaking without proper preparation or planning. ❑ **go it hot** *v. see* sense 2 above. ❑ **go it strong** *v. see* COME IT STRONG *under* COME IT *v.*[1].

go it! *excl.* [GO IT *v.*] [mid-19C+] a general excl. of encouragement; in full *go it you cripples, crutches are cheap!*

IN EXCLAMATIONS

❑ **go it, boots!** (*also* **go it, lemons!**) [mid-19C–1910s] (*US*) a general cry of encouragement.

golblamed *adj.* [1920s] (*US*) a euph. for GOD-DAMN *adj.*

gold *n.* **1** [late 18C–early 19C] human excrement [the colour of faeces]. **2** [late 19C+] money. **3** in the context of drugs [? the colour or the value]. (**a**) [1940s–50s] a hypodermic syringe. (**b**) [1960s+] marijuana. (**c**) [2000s] crack cocaine. (**d**) [2000s] heroin.

IN COMPOUNDS

❑ **gold-finder** *n.* **1** [early 17C–19C] (*also* **gold-digger**) a latrine cleaner. **2** [mid-18C] a confidence trickster. ❑ **gold nuggets** *n. see* NUGGET *n.* (4).

SE in slang uses

IN COMPOUNDS

❑ **gold-dig/-digger/-digging** *see* separate entries. ❑ **gold-dropper** *n. see* separate entry. ❑ **gold dust/duster** *see* separate entries. ❑ **gold hunter** *n.* [the Gold Rush of 1849] [mid–late 19C] (*US*) a Californian.

IN PHRASES

❑ **dig for gold** *v. see under* DIG *v.*[1]. ❑ **give up the gold** *v.* [2000s] (*US teen*) of a woman, to lose one's virginity prior to marriage.

gold *adj.*

SE in slang uses

IN COMPOUNDS

❑ **goldback** *n.* [US currency notes are all green, so ref. is to the high value rather than the colour] [1920s] (*US*) a $100 bill. ❑ **goldbrick/bricking** *see* separate entries. ❑ **gold drop** *n.* [late 18C] a gold coin. ❑ **goldfinch** *n.* [play on the bird species] **1** [17C–mid-19C] one who always has money in his pocket or purse, thus a target of thieves. **2** [late 17C–early 19C] a golden guinea or sovereign. ❑ **goldfish** *n. see* separate entries. ❑ **goldskin** *n.* **1** [late 19C–1930s] (*US gay*) a young male light-skinned black prostitute. **2** *see* BRASS GUTS *under* BRASS *adj.*[1]. ❑ **gold star** *n.* (*also* **gold shield, ...tin**) [1960s+] (*US*) a gold-shield police detective. ❑ **gold tooth** *n.* [1950s] (*US*) a derog. term for a Puerto Rican. ❑ **gold watch** *n. see* separate entry.

IN PHRASES

❑ **gold and silver** *adj.* [the two metals seen as opposites]

[1980s] bisexual. ▫ **gold-backed ones** *n.* (*also* **gold-backed 'uns**) [mid–late 19C] body lice. ▫ **gold-badge man** *n.* [1950s] (*US*) a city detective. ▫ **gold-end man** *n.* [17C] an itinerant jeweller, a buyer of gold and silver. ▫ **gold-star lesbian** *n.* [1990s+] (*US gay*) a lesbian who never has had and never will have sex with a man or a bisexual woman.

Golda *n.* [common Jewish female name, underpinned by former Israeli prime minister *Golda* Meir (1898–1978)] [2000s] (*S.Afr. gay*) a Jewish homosexual.

goldang! *excl.* [mid-19C+] a euph. for GOD-DAMN! *excl.*

goldanged *adj. see* GOLDARNED *adj.*

goldarn *adj.* (*also* **goldang, goldurn**) [mid-19C+] (*US*) a euph. version of GOD-DAMN *adj.* (1).

goldarn! *excl.* (*also* **goldarn it! goldurn!**) [early 19C+] a euph. for GOD-DAMN! *excl.*

goldarned *adj.* (*also* **galdarned, gauldurned, goldanged, goldarndest, goll darned, gol-walloped**) [GOLDARN *adj.*] [mid-19C+] damned, cursed.

Goldberg *n.* (*also* **Goldstein**) [the stereotyped 'Jewish' surname and as such usu. derog.] [1950s+] (*US black*) any Jew, esp. the shop-owners of Harlem and other ghettos.

goldbrick *n.* [the trick of selling a supposed 'gold' (in fact, painted lead or brass) brick to the gullible. The scheme was originated by one Reed Waddell who, in 1880, sold his first brick for $4000 and thereafter never dropped his price below $3,500 – making an alleged $250,000 in five years] **1** [late 19C+] (*also* **bat**) a confidence game in which the victim buys a 'gold' (actual gold-painted lead) brick. **2** [1900s] (*US campus*) an unattractive, dull girl or woman. **3** [1900s–40s] (*US Und.*) a swindle; anything bogus. **4** [1900s–50s] (*also* **goldbricker**) a swindler. **5** [1910s+] (*US*) (*also* **goldbricker**) a shirker, a loafer, a lazy person. **6** [1970s] one who obtains money without working for it.

goldbrick *v.* [GOLDBRICK *n.*] (*US*) **1** [1900s–30s] to swindle. **2** [1910s+] to shirk, to loaf, to act lazily.

goldbricking *n.* [GOLDBRICK *v.* (2)] [1930s–50s] (*US*) wasting time, loafing, avoiding work.

goldbricking *adj.* [GOLDBRICK *v.* (2)] [1910s–50s] lazy, shirking.

gold dig *v.* [backform. f. GOLD-DIGGER *n.*[1] (2)] [1920s+] usu. of a woman, to obtain money and other gifts in exchange for sexual favours.

gold-digger *n.*[1] **1** [1910s–20s] (*US*) a prostitute. **2** [1910s+] (*orig. US*) a young woman, orig. typically from the chorus line, who swaps sexual favours for the monetary and material gifts of a (usu.) older lover [faltered after WW2 but has been revived in US black use]. **3** [1920s+] anyone, of either gender, who seeks money through advantageous relationships.

gold-digger *n.*[2] *see* GOLD-FINDER *under* GOLD *n.*

gold-digging *n.* [GOLD-DIGGER *n.*[1] (2)] [1920s+] of a (young) woman, swapping sexual favours for material comforts.

gold-digging *adj.* [1920s+] seeking monetary and other material benefits from an advantageous, if not esp. enjoyable, relationship.

gold-dropper *n.* (*also* **dropper, money-dropper**) [late 17C–19C] (*UK Und.*) a rogue who specializes in dropping something supposedly valuable where it will be found by a potential victim, who is either lured into a game or persuaded to buy the 'valuable', while the conman claims that although they should, by rights, share the profits, he will sell his share and let the victim have the whole benefit; alternatively the victim is introduced to some of the sharp's friends, who propose a game of cards or dice, in which they rob him.

gold dust *n.* [the high price of narcotics] (*US drugs*) **1** [1930s+] cocaine. **2** [1970s] heroin [+ ref. to the colour of, presumably, the Chinese (brown) variety of heroin].

SE in slang uses

IN PHRASES

▫ **gold dust twins** *n.* [the twin black boys who featured in adverts for *Gold Dust* washing powder, c.1900; the slogan declared: 'Let the Gold Dust twins do your work'] [20C+] (*US*) close friends.

gold duster *n.* [GOLD DUST *n.* (1)] [1960s] a cocaine user.

golden *adj.* **1** [late 19C; 1950s+] (*orig. US campus*) fine, successful, secure. **2** [1980s+] (*US*) lucrative.

SE in slang uses

IN COMPOUNDS

pertaining to human waste

▫ **golden screw** *n.* [SE *golden*, yellow-coloured + SCREW *n.*[1] (1b)] [1970s+] (*US gay*) anal intercourse culminating in urination rather than ejaculation. ▫ **golden shower** *n. see* separate entry.

general uses

▫ **golden chub** *n.* [a pun on the fish name + CHUB *n.*[1] (1)] [early 18C] a dupe, a fool. ▫ **golden cream** *n.* [its colour] [late 19C] (*UK Und.*) rum. ▫ **golden doughnut** *n.* [1970s] the vagina. ▫ **golden girl** *n.* **1** [1960s+] (*US black*) a very attractive woman, esp. when white. **2** [1970s+] (*drugs*) heroin [GIRL *n.*[2] (2) but note heroin is more usu. BOY *n.*[2] (4a); presumably the golden, i.e. brown, colour is more pertinent to the image here]. ▫ **golden googie** *n.* [GOOG *n.*[1] (1); ? ref. to 'the goose that laid the golden eggs'] [1900s] (*Aus./N.Z.*) a golden coin, a sovereign. ▫ **golden leaf** *n.* [SE *golden*, resembling gold in value + *leaf*] [1920s+] (*drugs*) top-quality marijuana. ▫ **golden rivet** *n.* **1** [1940s–50s] the anus. **2** [1960s] (*US gay*) the penis.

golden gate *n.* [rhy. sl.] [1980s] £800.

golden hind *adj.* [rhy. sl.; ult. *Golden Hind*, the ship in which Francis Drake circumnavigated the globe in 1577–80)] [20C+] blind.

golden shower *n.* (*also* **golden rain**) [SE *golden*, yellow-coloured + *shower* n.; note 17C use of *golden shower* as a euph. for copulation, the image coming f. the Greek myth of Danäe, who was seduced by Zeus in the form of a shower of gold] **1** [1940s+] urolagnia, i.e. the act of urinating on one's partner as part of sexual experimentation. **2** [1970s] (*US gay*) one who displays contempt for other people, i.e. he 'pisses on' them.

IN COMPOUNDS

▫ **golden shower queen** *n.* (*also* **golden stream queen, GSQ**) [-QUEEN *sfx* (3)] [1960s+] a homosexual who enjoys being urinated on.

goldfish *n.*[1] [? its role as a pet] [1900s] (*Aus.*) a man suitable to be made into one's husband.

goldfish *n.*[2] [orig. milit. use *goldfish*, herrings] **1** [1900s–40s] (*Aus./US*) any form of canned fish. **2** [1940s–70s] (*US black*) sliced, canned peaches.

goldfish *n.*[3] [fig. uses of SE, i.e. the image of being trapped or isolated from the outside world in a goldfish bowl] **1** [1920s–40s] (*US*) a beating of a prisoner to extract a confession; also the rubber hose used in such beatings; thus *see the goldfish*, to suffer a beating; *show the goldfish*, to beat up [the prisoner is the isolated goldfish, the interrogators gather round]. **2** [1930s] (*US Und.*) a prisoner standing in an identification line-up. **3** [1950s–60s] (*US black*) a married woman, esp. one who is ripe for seduction; thus *fish for goldfish*, to seduce married women.

IN COMPOUNDS

▫ **goldfish bowl** *n.* (*also* **goldfish room**) [GOLDFISH *n.*[3] (1)] **1** [1930s–60s] (*US*) an interrogation room in a police station. **2** [1970s] any small room, where a discussion takes place.

goldie *n.* [2000s] (*N.Z.*) any impressive object.

Goldie Hawn *n.* [rhy. sl.; ult. US film star *Goldie Hawn* (b. 1945)] [1990s+] a prawn.

goldies *n.* [1910s] (*Aus.*) the teeth.

goldilocks *n.* [rhy. sl. = POX *n.*[1] (3)] [1990s+] venereal disease.

gold ring *n.* [rhy. sl.] [20C+] a king.

Goldstein *n. see* GOLDBERG *n.*

goldurn *adj. see* GOLDARN *adj.*

goldurn! *excl. see* GOLDARN! *excl.*

gold watch *n.*[1] [rhy. sl. = SE *Scotch*; the orig. ref. was to WATERBURY WATCH *n.*] [1950s+] Scotch whisky.

gold watch *n.*[2] [2000s] a general positive term, something or someone excellent.

gole/goles *n.*

IN PHRASES

❑ **by gole/goles!** *see* BY GOLL! *under* GOLL *n.*[2].

goley *n.*

IN EXCLAMATIONS

❑ **by goley!** *see* BY GOLLY! *under* GOLLY! *excl.*

golfed *adj.* [? GOOF *n.*[2] (1)] [1990s+] (*US campus*) drunk.

golgotha *n.* [a pun on Gk *golgotha*, the place of skulls] [mid-19C] a hat.

Goli *n.* [Zulu *egoli*, place of gold] [1940s–60s] (*S.Afr.*) Johannesburg.

go like... *v.*

IN PHRASES

❑ **go like a cut cat** *v.* (*also* **go like a scalded cat**) [SE *cut*, castrated] [1960s+] (*N.Z.*) to act quickly or leave speedily. ❑ **go like a cut snake** *v.* [2000s] (*N.Z.*) to run fast. ❑ **go like a dingbat** *v. see under* DINGBAT *n.*[2]. ❑ **go like a strangled fart** *v. see under* FART *n.* ❑ **go like frozen Daiquiris in hell** *v.* [1940s] (*US*) of a product or commodity, to sell out quickly. ❑ **go like hot cakes** *v.* (*also* **go like hot cross buns, ...hot pies**) [late 19C+] (*orig. US*) **1** of a product or commodity, to sell out quickly. **2** of anything, to occur quickly, plentifully. ❑ **go like the clappers** *v. see under* CLAPPERS *n.*[3].

goll *n.*[1] [ety. unknown; ? link to Irish *gabhlach*, a forked instrument used in fishing, used in modern Irish sl. as *golly-fishing*] [17C; early 19C] the hand.

goll *n.*[2] [mid-18C–1900s] a synon. for God in a variety of oaths (cf. GOLLY! *excl.*).

IN EXCLAMATIONS

❑ **by goll!** (*also* **by gole! by goles! by golls!**) [mid-18C–19C] a euph. for *by God!*

goll darned *adj. see* GOLDARNED *adj.*

IN EXCLAMATIONS

❑ **I'll be goll darned!** *see I'LL BE DARNED! under* DARNED *adj.*

gollier *n.* (*also* **gollyer**) [GOLLY *v.*] [1930s+] (*Irish*) a lump of phlegm.

gollies! *excl. see* GOLLY! *excl.*

gollion *n.* [GOLLY *v.*] [1940s] (*Aus.*) **1** a lump of phlegm. **2** a term of abuse.

golliwog *n.*[1] [rhy. sl.] **1** [1910s–70s] in pl., constr. with *the*, greyhound racing [= DOGS, THE *n.*]. **2** [1990s+] fog.

golliwog *n.*[2] [it supposedly resembles the child's toy] [1920s+] (*Aus.*) a large, hairy caterpillar.

golliwog *n.*[3] *see* GOLLY *n.*[2].

golls *n.*

IN PHRASES

❑ **by golls!** *see* BY GOLL! *under* GOLL *n.*[2].

gollsocker *n. see* GOLLYWHOPPER *n.*

gollumpus *n.* [? Scot. *golamus*, ungaily, large, unshapely] [late 18C–early 19C] a large, loutish, uncoordinated person.

golluptious *adj. see* GOLOPSHUS *adj.*

golly *n.*[1] [backform. f. GOLLY! *excl.*] [20C+] a euph. for *God*; in phr. such as *golly for you* or *golly help you*.

golly *n.*[2] (*also* **golliwog**) [SE *golliwog*; for the problems of the Robertson's jam/marmalade *golly*, *see* my *Words Apart* (1996)] [1950s+] a derog. term for a black person.

golly *n.*[3] [GOLLY *v.*] [1960s–70s] (*Aus.*) a lump of phlegm.

golly *v.* [? Scot. *golly*, to shout hoarsely; ult. Scot. *gollar*, to utter loud but thick and scarcely articulate sounds, to shout] [1930s+] (*Aus.*) to spit; thus *golly-gum*, chewing gum; *golly-pot*, a spittoon.

golly! *excl.* (*also* **gaully! gollies! golly dog! golly Moses! great golly! my golly!**) [*DSUE* suggests a black origin, but the *OED* citation (G. White, *Journals*, 1775) talks of: 'Golly, a sort of jolly kind of oath, or asseveration much in use among our carters, & lowest people'] [mid-18C+] (*mainly US/UK juv.*) an extra-mild euph. for *God!*

IN EXCLAMATIONS

❑ **by golly!** (*also* **by goley! by gollies! by jolly! for golly sakes!**) [mid-19C+] a mild euph. for *by God!*

gollyer *n. see* GOLLIER *n.*

gollywhopper *n.* (*also* **gollybuster, gollysocker**) [GOLLY! *excl.* + WHOPPER *n.*/BUSTER *n.*[1] (1d)/SOCK *v.*[1] (1)] [20C+] (*US*) an outstanding example of its kind.

gollywobbles *n.* [var. on COLLYWOBBLES *n.*] [1940s+] (*US*) feelings of tension, fear or sickness, usu. seen as stemming from the stomach.

go-long *n.*

IN PHRASES

❑ **give someone the go-long** *v. see* GIVE SOMEONE THE GO-BY *under* GO-BY *n.*

golopshus *adj.* (*also* **galluptious, galopshus, galoptious, galumptious, golluptious, goloptious, goluptious**) [echoic of the smacking of one's lips] [mid-19C–1930s] delicious, flavoursome, luscious.

golpe *n.* [Sp. *golpe*, a jolt, a blow] [1970s+] (*drugs*) heroin.

golumptiously *adv.* [GOLOPSHUS *adj.*] [late 19C] wonderfully, delightfully.

goluptious *adj. see* GOLOPSHUS *adj.*

gol-walloped *adj. see* GOLDARNED *adj.*

g.o.m. *n.* [abbr. *GOD'S (OWN) MEDICINE under* GOD *n.*[1]] [1940s+] (*drugs*) opium, morphine.

gom *n.*[1] (*also* **goom**) [Lancashire dial.] [early–mid-19C] a euph. for *God*, and as such used in mild oaths.

gom *n.*[2] (*also* **gaum, gawm, ghomey, gomey, gommouge, gorm**) [Irish *gamal*, a simpleton] [mid-19C+] (*orig. Irish*) a painfully stupid or gullible person, a fool.

gom *n.*[3] (*also* **gommie**) [GOMTOR *n.*] [1960s+] (*S.Afr.*) a fool, an idiot.

goma *n.* [Sp. *goma*, gum/GUM *n.*[3]] [1960s] (*drugs*) opium; black tar heroin.

goma de moto *n.* [Sp. *goma de moto*, gum of dust] [1980s+] (*drugs*) hashish.

gombay *n.* [dial. *gombay*, drum or drummer; ult. Kongo *nboma*, a goatskin drum] [1940s+] (*W.I.*) a very dark-complexioned black person.

gome *n.* [GOMER *n.*[2]] [1980s+] (*US campus*) a devotedly hard worker.

gomer *n.*[1] [poss. 'a large pewter dish' (*DSUE*)] [1900s] (*Irish*) a measure of drink.

gomer *n.*[2] [the proper name *Gomer Pyle*, a fictional T.V. comic yokel character; apparent link to GOM *n.*[2] may be coincidental] [1960s+] (*US*) a fool, a rustic simpleton.

gomer *n.*[3] [? abbr. *g*et *o*ut of *m*y *e*mergency *r*oom; note Doug Wilson posting to American Dialect Society List 21/7/01: 'The acronym-etymology is spurious, I think; another bogus candidate is "Grand Old Man of the Emergency Room". I think the origin is related to the other "gomer" – like in "Gomer Pyle" [...] maybe the original form was "old gome" or so, and maybe "gome" = "man" (from OE "guma" or so; cf. "gome" [and "gomerel"] in OED) [...] Probably reinforced [...] by "gummer" = "one who gums (i.e., chews without having any teeth)" and maybe by "gnome".'] [1960s+] an old, dirty, difficult or chronically ill hospital patient, usu. male; thus *gomere*, the female equivalent.

gomeral *n.* (*also* **gomeril**) [Irish *gomaral*, *gamal*, a lout, a boor; *gomeril* is also found throughout dial.] [19C–1910s] (*Irish*) a lout.

gomer pyle *n.* [for ety. *see* GOMER *n.*[2]] [1980s+] (*US*) a fool, a yokel.

gomey *n. see* GOM *n.*[2].

gommie *n. see* GOM *n.*[3].

gommouge *n. see* GOM *n.*[2].

gomtor *n.* [synon. Afk.] [1960s+] (*S.Afr.*) an uncouth or common loutish person.

gomus *n.* [GOM *n.*[2]] [mid-19C–1910s] (*Anglo-Irish*) a fool.

gon *n.*[1] (*also* **gonnie, gonny**) [abbr.] [1930s–70s] (*US*) gonorrhoea.

gon *n.*^{2} see GONNOF *n.*

gonaff *n.* see GONNOF *n.*

gonce *n.* (*also* **gons**) [? Yid. *gunz*, the lot] [late 19C–1930s] (*Aus.*) money.

gonda *n.* [? SE *gondola*] [2000s] (*S.Afr. gay*) the vagina.

gondola *n.* **1** [1920s–70s] (*US*) a large clumsy shoe. **2** [1930s–50s] (*US Und.*) a large stolen automobile.

gone *adj.*^{1} [fig. uses of *gone*, lost] **1** [mid-16C+] (*US*) describing someone or something considered to be a lost cause, a hopeless case. **2** [17C; mid-19C+] of a person or animal, dead or doomed; usu. in combs., *see* below. **3** [mid-17C+] drunk, intoxicated by a drug; also in fig. use; thus HALF-GONE *adj.* **4** [mid-19C+] insane, crazy, bizarre. **5** [late 19C+] worn out, exhausted; old. **6** [1940s+] (*orig. US black*) a general positive intensifier, excellent, extraordinary, weird and wonderful, lost in music, drugs etc; esp. *gone cat, gone chick*. **7** [2000s] (*US campus*) asleep. **8** *see* GONE ON below.

DERIVATIVES

❑ **gonesville** *adj. see* separate entry.

IN COMPOUNDS

❑ **gone chicken/chuck** *n. see under* CHICKEN *n.* ❑ **gone coon** *n.* (*also* **gone ginny, ...sucker**) [COON *n.* (4)/GUINEA *n.*^{1} (4)/SUCKER *n.*^{1} (3a)] [mid-19C+] (*orig. US*) one who is utterly doomed, without hope of escape. ❑ **gone goose** *n.* (*also* **gone gander, ...goon, ...gosling**) [note 19C naut. jargon *gone-goose*, a ship deserted or given up in despair] [mid-19C+] (*orig. US*) a person or thing that is beyond all hope. ❑ **gone in** *adj.* [mid–late 19C] (*US*) exhausted. ❑ **gone up** *adj.* [as in *gone up* to heaven] [mid–late 19C] **1** discovered. **2** dead. **3** finished, defeated. **4** unfashionable.

SE in slang uses, with link to senses above

IN COMPOUNDS

❑ **gone on** *adj.* (*also* **gone, well gone**) **1** [late 19C–1900s] impressed by. **2** [late 19C+] obsessed by, esp. when in love.

IN PHRASES

❑ **gone to buggery** *adj. see under* BUGGERY *n.* ❑ **gone to Gowings** *adj.* [the mail-order male apparel firm and self-styled 'blokatorium' *Gowings* of Sydney; the phr. was popularized in late 1940s when the well-known criminal Darcy Dugane escaped from jail and left a note on his cell wall reading 'Gone to Gowings!'] [1940s+] (*Aus.*) useless, wrecked. ❑ **gone to Moscow** *adj.* [pun on MOSK *v.*] [1910s+] (*Aus.*) in pawn. ❑ **gone to Ratisbon** *adj.* (*also* **gone to Rot-His-Bone**) [pun on the religious colloquy or Diet of Ratisbon + lit. *rot his bone*] [late 18C–early 19C] dead. ❑ **well gone** *adj. see* GONE ON above.

gone *adj.*^{2} [abbr. *gone with child*] [late 16C; 19C+] pregnant.

gone *adv.* [1920s+] (*US*) a general intensifier, very, completely, thoroughly.

gone *phr.* [1990s+] (*US campus*) goodbye.

gone and forgotten *adj.* [rhy. sl.] [20C+] (*Aus.*) rotten.

gonee *n.* (*also* **gonie, gonnie**) [ety. unknown; poss. linked to a *tsotsi* stereotype of members of the Angoni tribe of Nyasaland] [1980s+] (*S.Afr.*) a knife.

gonef *n.* see GONNOF *n.*

goner *n.*^{1} (*also* **gonner**) [GONE *adj.*^{1}] **1** [mid-19C] a failure, an impossibility. **2** [mid-19C+] one who is dead, or something that is ruined. **3** [mid-19C+] a doomed person, anyone who cannot avoid an unpleasant fate, one on the verge of death; also fig. **4** [mid-19C+] an obsessed person, i.e. one who is 'gone' on something or someone. **5** [late 19C] in weak use, one who is very ill. **6** [1900s] (*Aus./US*) one who has departed. **7** [1940s] a sucker, a pushover.

goner *n.*^{2} [GONE *adj.*^{1} (6)] [1940s] (*US*) a general positive, something or someone impressive.

gonesville *adj.* [SE *gone*/GONE *adj.*^{1} + -VILLE *sfx*^{1}] **1** [1950s+] knocked out, lit. and fig. **2** [1990s+] vanished, escaped, gone. **3** [2000s] dead. **4** [2000s] eccentric, insane. **5** [2000s] in weak use of sense 4, emotionally carried away.

goney *n.* see GOONEY *n.*

gong *n.*^{1} [OE *gang*, the act of walking or going; thus it is, however remotely, an ancestor of the child's plaint, 'I've got to go'] [11C–16C] the privy.

IN COMPOUNDS

❑ **gong farmer** *n.* [mid-15C–16C] a cleaner-out of privies, a nightsoil man. ❑ **gong house** *n.* [11C] a privy.

gong *n.*^{2} [? transliteration of a Chinese word] (*US drugs*) **1** [1910s–50s] an opium pipe. **2** [1930s–50s] opium. **3** [1970s+] marijuana.

IN COMPOUNDS

❑ **gong-kicker** *n.* (*also* **gong-beater**) **1** [1930s–70s] (*US*) an opium smoker. **2** [1950s] a marijuana smoker.

IN PHRASES

❑ **bang the gong** *v.* [late 19C–1940s] (*US drugs*) to smoke opium. ❑ **beat the gong** *v.* [1930s–60s] (*drugs*) to smoke opium. ❑ **hit the gong** *v.* (*also* **hit the gonger**) [1930s+] (*drugs*) to smoke opium. ❑ **kick the gong around** *v.* (*also* **boot the gong around, kick it around, ...the pipe around, ...the rag around, ...the toy around**) **1** [late 19C–1950s] (*drugs*) to use drugs, esp. opium, heroin or morphine. **2** [1940s+] (*US black*) in fig. use, to behave, to do something, to fool around. **3** [1940s+] to gossip, to chat. **4** [1950s] (*drugs*) to smoke marijuana. **5** [1970s+] (*US*) to masturbate.

gong *n.*^{3} [Anglo-Ind. *gong*, a metal disc, not musical, used for striking the hour, thus imported by Indian Army veterans] [1910s+] (*orig. milit.*) a medal; thus any form of award, e.g. a knighthood, an OBE.

gong *n.*^{4} [1920s–40s] the bell (later replaced by a siren) on a police car.

gong *n.*^{5} [supposed resemblance] **1** [1960s–70s] (*US campus*) the penis. **2** [1970s] (*US black*) a gun.

gonga *n.*^{1} [GANJA *n.* (1)] [1930s–50s] (*US prison*) marijuana.

gonga *n.*^{2} see GUNGA *n.*^{1}.

gonga *adj.* [GONG *n.*^{2} (2)] [1930s] (*US Und.*) intoxicated by opium.

gonger *n.*^{1} [GONG *n.*^{2}] [1910s+] (*US drugs*) **1** an opium pipe; thus the dimin. *gongerine*, a small pipe; *up against the gonger*, addicted to opium. **2** an opium addict. **3** opium. **4** any form of opium derivative.

IN PHRASES

❑ **hit the gonger** *v. see* HIT THE GONG *under* GONG *n.*^{2}.

gonger *n.*^{2} [GONG *n.*^{4}] [1930s–40s] in pl., police patrolling in cars.

gongola *n.* [ext. GONG *n.*^{2} (1)] [1930s–60s] (*drugs*) an opium pipe.

gongs *n.* [they 'clang' together + ? SE *gonads*; note GONG *n.*^{5} (1)] [1950s] (*US gay*) the testicles.

gonicles *n.* [SE *gonads*] [1950s] (*US*) testicles.

gonie *n.* [Angoni (Nyasaland) *goni*, to stab] [1960s+] (*S.Afr.*) a knife.

gonies *n.* [abbr. SE *gonads*] [1990s+] the male genitals.

gonif *see under* GONNOF.

gonk *n.* [the large cuddly homunculoid dolls briefly popular in 1960s; but note milit. use *gonk*, to sleep] **1** [1960s+] (*UK juv.*) a fool. **2** [1960s+] a contemptuous description of a prostitute's client. **3** [2000s] an obsessive, an eccentric.

gonkulator *n.* [onomat. noise *gonk* + *calculator*] [1990s+] a word used in place of the actual technical term for a mechanical device.

gonner *n.* see GONER *n.*^{1}.

gonnie *n.* see GON *n.*^{1}.

gonnof *n.* (*also* **ganef, ganov, gnof, gon, gonaff, gonef, gonif, gonnif, gonnofer, gonnoph, gonof, gonoph, gonov, gonovim, gunnif**) [Heb. *gannabh*, thief; Hotten (1860) suggests that the word is 'as old as Chaucer's time', but his ref. is to *gnoff*, a peasant, a lout, which comes from East Frisian *knufe*, lump and *gnuffig*, thick, rough, coarse, ill-mannered; note S.Afr. *goniva*, a stolen diamond] **1** [mid-19C+] a thief; an 'amateur pickpocket' (Hotten, 1859). **2** [mid-19C+] a scoundrel, fool.

IN PHRASES

❑ **arch-gonnof** *n.* [mid–late 19C] (*UK Und.*) the leader of a gang of thieves.

gonnof *v.* (*also* **gonif, gonoph, gunove**) [GONNOF *n.* (1)] [mid-19C–1910s; 2000s] to steal, to rob, to deceive; thus *gonnofing* or *gonophin*, stealing, deception.

gonny *n. see* GON *n.*[1].

gonof *n. see* GONNOF *n.*

gonoph *see under* GONNOF.

gonov/gonovim *n. see* GONNOF *n.*

gons *n. see* GONCE *n.*

gonsel *n.* (*also* **gonsil, gonzel, guncel, gunsel, gunshel**) [Ger. *gänslein*, a little goose, thence Yid. *genzel*, a man's young male lover, a catamite; the *locus classicus* is as the description of Elmer, the young, inadequate hoodlum of Dashiell Hammett's *The Maltese Falcon* (1930, film 1941); given that he is also a criminal's sidekick, the term is often mistranslated as 'gunman'. However, while Raymond Chandler is convinced of this, *HDAS* still quotes *The Maltese Falcon* as a source for *gunsel*, 'a gunman; thug', suggesting a root in GUN *n.*[1] (9) or GUN-SLINGER *n.* (1)] **1** [late 19C+] (*US tramp*) a youth, a naïve boy. **2** [1910s–40s] (*US tramp/prison*) a young, homosexual boy who accompanies a tramp or acts as lover to a masculine prisoner. **3** [1930s–70s] (*US*) a stupid or contemptible man. **4** [1940s+] an informer, a criminal, a gunman. **5** [1950s+] (*US prison*) a (young) troublemaker.

gonski *adj.* [GONE *adj.*[1] + -SKI *sfx*] [2000s] gone, in the sense of not working properly.

gonus *n.* [GOONEY *n.* (2)] [mid-19C+] (*US campus*) a fool, a stupid person.

gonzel *n. see* GONSEL *n.*

gonzo *n.* [GONZO *adj.*[1] (1)] [1970s+] (*orig. US*) an anarchic eccentric.

gonzo *adj.*[1] [GONE *adj.*[1] (2) + CRAZO *n.* or cod Ital. sfx *-zo* + pun on GUNG-HO *adj.*; coined and pioneered as a journalistic form by US writer Hunter S. Thompson (b.1939) in *Rolling Stone* magazine 1970] [1970s+] **1** eccentric, bizarre, extraordinary, groundbreaking; esp. in comb. *gonzo journalism*, a form of extreme 'New Journalism', in which reporters, rather than taking the typical distanced, neutral position, interpolate their thoughts, emotions and actions into the story. **2** out of control. **3** crazy about. **4** psychotic, crazy. **5** in the sex industry, unrestrained, extreme.

gonzo *adj.*[2] [GONE *adj.*[1]] [1970s+] **1** gone, absent. **2** finished, defeated, useless. **3** (*US*) drunk.

gonzoed *adj.* [GONZO *adj.*[2] (3)] [1980s] (*US*) very drunk or intoxicated.

Gonzo (the Great) *n.* [rhy. sl.; ult. the Muppet Show character] [1990s+] a state (usu. of drunken excess).

goo *n.*[1] [? abbr. BURGOO *n.*] **1** [20C+] (*orig. US*) anything sticky or viscid, e.g. blood, semen, glue. **2** [1920s] patter, e.g. of a carnival tout. **3** [1920s+] sickly sentimentality, esp. in speech or writing.

goo *n.*[2] [1990s+] (*Irish*) a glimpse, a look.

goo *v.* [GOO *n.*[1] (1)] **1** [1910s] (*US*) to render sticky. **2** [20C+] (*Aus.*) (*also* **goob**) to spit out a lump of phlegm. **3** [2000s] (*US black*) to feel stupid, angry, stuck.

goober *n.*[1] [SAmE *goober*, a peanut, the state's main crop] **1** [mid-19C+] (*US*) an inhabitant of North Carolina, Alabama, Arkansas or Georgia. **2** [1920s+] (*US*) the penis. **3** [1940s] the testicles. **4** [1970s+] (*US campus*) a small child. **5** [1970s+] (*US campus*) a small mole, spot or similar skin blemish. **6** [2000s] a generic term for any rural person.

IN COMPOUNDS

❑ **goober-brain** *n.* [1960s+] (*US*) a silly person. ❑ **goober-head** *n.* [-HEAD *sfx* (1)] [1980s+] (*US*) a general derog. term, typically describing an eccentric, a fussy person, one who drives badly.

goober *n.*[2] (*also* **goob, goobette**) [fig. uses of SAmE *goober*, a peanut, thus an insignificant object; ult. f. African langs.] **1** [mid-19C+] an idiot, a fool, an incompetent; a country bumpkin; also affectionate use; thus *goob*, to act irritatingly. **2** [1960s+] (*Aus./N.Z./US*) (*also* **goobie**) a gob of phlegm; thus as v., to drool. **3** [1980s+] (*US campus*) someone not attuned to the peer group norms. **4** [1990s+] (*US campus*) nasal mucus.

IN PHRASES

❑ **goob out** *v.* [1980s+] (*US campus*) to disgust, to repel.

goober-grabber *n.*[1] (*also* **gauber-grubber, goober-grabbler/-grubber, gruber-grubber**) [SAmE *goober*, the peanut, grown widely in all these states; the term means lit. 'one who grabs or digs peanuts'] [mid-19C+] (*US*) an inhabitant of North Carolina, Arkansas or Georgia.

goober-grabber *n.*[2] [GOOBER *n.*[2] (1) + SE *grabber*] **1** [1950s] (*US Southern*) a sexually voracious woman. **2** [1990s+] (*US*) a male homosexual.

goobette *n. see* GOOBER *n.*[2].

goobie *n. see* GOOBER *n.*[2] (2).

gooby *n.*[1] [GABY *n.*] [late 19C] a fool, a dullard.

gooby *n.*[2] [GOO *n.*[1] (1)] [1940s–50s] (*US prison*) food.

gooch *v.* [GOO *n.*[1] (1) + SMOOCH *v.*[1] (1)] [1970s] (*US campus*) to kiss.

good *n.* **1** [mid–late 19C] (*orig. US*) alcohol; thus *get good*, to get drunk. **2** [1970s+] (*drugs*) phencyclidine. **3** [2000s] heroin. **4** [2000s] marijuana.

good *adj.*[1] **1** [late 16C; late 19C+] solvent, able to pay for or lend; usu. as *good for*. **2** [early 19C] (*UK Und.*) of a place or person, able to be robbed easily; thus *good upon the crack*, easily broken into. **3** [late 19C+] able to sustain a given situation.

IN PHRASES

❑ **do good** *v.* [1970s] (*US Und.*) to make substantial amounts of money through crime.

SE in slang uses

IN COMPOUNDS

❑ **good buddy** *n.* [BUDDY *n.* (1)] **1** [1950s+] the popular form of address among users of Citizen's Band radios; also in general use. **2** [1950s+] a CB radio user. **3** [1980s+] (*US*) a homosexual. ❑ **good-cut** *n.* [1950s] (*US*) high-quality marijuana. ❑ **good-doer** *n.* [a play on *do-gooder*] [1910s+] a smart person, who 'knows a thing or two'; thus *good-doing*, smart, knowledgeable. ❑ **good eating** *n.* [the image is of food; the sexual use of *eat* is coincidental] [1920s+] (*Aus.*) an attractive young woman. ❑ **good egg** *n. see* separate entry. ❑ **goodfellas** *n.* [ety. unknown; ? link to the film *Goodfellas* (1990)] [1980s+] (*drugs*) fentanyl. ❑ **good gal** *n.* [1930s] (*US*) a girlfriend. ❑ **good gas** *n. see* GREAT GAS *under* GREAT *adj.*[3]. ❑ **good giggles** *n.* [its effect] [1970s] (*drugs*) marijuana. ❑ **good girl** *n.* (*also* **good one**) [ironic + she is *good for* sex] [17C–18C] a prostitute, a wanton. ❑ **good go** *n.* [GO *n.*[1] (1)] **1** [1930s] (*US prison*) anything seen as admirable, useful, easy etc. **2** [1950s–70s] (*drugs*) the proper amount of drugs for the money paid. ❑ **good guts** *n.* [GUT *n.* (2e)] [1910s+] (*Aus.*) the facts, the essential information. ❑ **good guy** *n.* [1920s+] a friendly individual, male or female, esp. if on one's side; often in pl. as *one of the good guys*. ❑ **good hair** *n.* [*good* because such white-styled hair was considered superior or more acceptable] [1950s+] (*US black*) soft, wavy hair, as opposed to tighter black-style curls; ext. to an attractive body. ❑ **good head** *n.* **1** [19C+] an expert. **2** [1920s–70s] (*orig. US Und.*) a trustworthy, admirable person. ❑ **good ink** *n.* [? journalistic imagery] [1910s+] (*Aus./N.Z.*) something agreeable, pleasant; usu. in phr. *that's good ink*. ❑ **good leave** *n.* [? cricketing imagery] [2000s] (*N.Z.*) a judicious action. ❑ **good-looker** *n.* [late 19C+] (*orig. US*) an attractive person, usu. a woman. ❑ **good luck** *n. see* LUCK *n.* ❑ **good man** *n.* **1** [early 17C–early 19C] a boon companion, a roisterer; an admirable person, defined according to context. **2** [18C] a gaoler. ❑ **good news** *n.* [1970s+] a general term of approval, whether of people, things or events. ❑ **good oil** *n.* [OIL *n.* (2c)] [1910s+] (*Aus.*) the honest truth, true facts. ❑ **good one** *n. see* separate entry. ❑ **good people** *n. see under* PEOPLE *n.* ❑ **good shake** *n. see* EVEN SHAKE *under* SHAKE *n.*[1]. ❑ **good shit** *n. see* separate entries. ❑ **good sick** *n. see under* SICK *n.* ❑ **good stuff** *n.* [STUFF *n.* (5b)]

1 [early 19C; 1960s] hard liquor. **2** [1960s+] (*US drugs*) (*also* **bad stuff**) effective, high-quality, pleasant drugs. **3** [1970s–80s] (*US black*) sexual sophistication. **4** [1980s] success in a confidence trick, in deception. ❑ **good thing** *n. see* separate entry. ❑ **good time** *n. see* separate entries. ❑ **good-time Charlie/Jane** *see* separate entries. ❑ **good 'un** *n. see* separate entry. ❑ **good woman** *n.* (*also* **quiet woman, silent...**) [the implication is that her 'goodness' stems from the fact that bereft of a head she cannot scold. A similar sign depicts an *honest lawyer*, the absence of his head deprives him of the ability to lie] [late 18C–mid-19C] a common public house sign representing a woman without a head. ❑ **good-woolled** *adj.* [Lincolnshire dial. *good-wooled*, said of a sheep that has a good fleece] [mid-19C] used of a plucky, spirited person. ❑ **goodyear** *n. see* separate entries.

IN PHRASES

❑ **all good** *adj.* [ext. of SE use] [1990s+] (*US black teen*) fine, great. ❑ **as good as caz** *adj. see under* CASSAN *n.* ❑ **as good as you would desire to piss (up)on** *adj.* [late 17C–early 19C] excellent, first-rate. ❑ **get good to someone** *v.* [1990s+] (*US black*) to be carried away by one's enthusiasms while performing a task. ❑ **get in good (with)** *v.* [1920s+] (*US*) to find favour with. ❑ **good a piece as ever strode a pot** *n.* [a woman 'bestrides' a chamberpot to urinate] [19C] a phr. used of an admirable woman, as good as one might find. ❑ **good at the game** *n.* (*also* **good at it**) [GAME *n.* (1b)/IT *n.*[1] (1)] [19C] an enthusiastic, skilful lover. ❑ **good-looking pictures** *n.* [late 18C] (*UK Und.*) coins bearing the monarch's head. ❑ **goodman turd** *n.* (*also* **goodman fool**) [*GOOD MAN* above + TURD *n.*[1]] [late 16C–early 17C] a derog. description of another person. ❑ **goodnight...** *see* separate entry. ❑ **good on the fang** *adj.* (*also* **good on the tooth**) [1940s+] (*Aus.*) a phr. used of one known as an enthusiastic eater. ❑ **good on the star** *adj.* (*also* **good on the crack**) [the 'starring' of the window when one breaks the glass] [early–mid-19C] (*UK Und.*) easy to break into, usu. of a window. ❑ **good to go** *adj.* [GO *v.* (1b)] [1990s+] (*US black teen*) sexually available; usu. said by men when referring to a woman they presume they would be able to have sex with, e.g. *babe's good to go*; also by a man, as a positive reply to 'how are you?'. ❑ **good voice to beg bacon** *n.* (*also* **bien squawl to maund bacon**) [BENE *adj.* + SQUALL *n.*[2] + MAUND *v.*] [late 17C–early 19C] a very unmelodious singing voice and therefore good only for begging.

IN EXCLAMATIONS

❑ **good biz!** *see under* BIZ *n.*[1]. ❑ **good cess to you!** *see* BAD CESS TO YOU! *under* BAD *adj.* ❑ **good deal!** [1940s+] (*US*) an expression of approval or congratulation, well done! that's wonderful! ❑ **good egg!** *see* separate entry. ❑ **good future!** [1980s+] (*US campus*) a sarcastic response to the speaker's announcement of some form of menial employment, i.e. what a good job! aren't you lucky! ❑ **good gravy!** [mid-19C+] (*Aus.*) a mild expeletive. ❑ **good grief!** (*also* **great grief! spare my grief!**) [dial.] [20C+] a general excl. of surprise and/or dismay. ❑ **good iron!** [quoits jargon *good iron*, a good throw] (*Aus.*) **1** [mid-19C–1900s] a general excl. of approval, congratulations. **2** [1900s] an expression of incredulity. ❑ **good-o!** *see* separate entry. ❑ **good on you!** [invariably linked to Aus., the term is equally common in Ireland. Share suggests that the origin lies in Irish *rinne sé mhaith orm*, lit. 'he made/did his good on me'] [20C+] (*Aus./Irish*) a general expression of approbation, thanks etc; also abbr. to *good*.

good *adj.*[2] [orig. used on frontier as *good Indian*, a dead Indian] [late 19C+] worthless or dead, esp. of an enemy or a criminal.

good and bad *n.* [rhy. sl.] [20C+] one's father, i.e. 'dad'.

goodbye Charlie *phr.* (*also* **goodbye McGinnis**) [1930s–40s] (*US*) a phr. meaning 'it is all over', the end, the finish; usu. in phr. *and it's goodbye Charlie*.

goodbye, John *phr.* [late 19C–1900s] (*US*) a phr. meaning 'it is all over', the end, the finish.

good egg *n.* (*also* **nice egg**) [EGG *n.*[2] (1)] **1** [late 19C–1920s] a good thing. **2** [20C+] an admirable person; thus *good-eggishness*, the quality of being such a person.

good egg! *excl.* [GOOD EGG *n.* (1)] [20C+] that's good! that's lucky!

gooden *n.* [ety. unknown] [2000s] (*US black*) a very fat woman.

goodie *n.* [SE *goodie*, a sweet] (*US*) **1** [1950s+] the vagina. **2** [1970s] the female breast and/or nipple.

goodie and baddie *n.* [rhy. sl. = PADDY *n.* (1)] [20C+] an Irish person.

goodie-book thumper *n. see BIBLE-THUMPER under* BIBLE *n.*

goodies *n.* **1** [mid-19C+] objects, things, presumably beneficial. **2** [1950s+] drugs; in sing., a marijuana cigarette. **3** [1950s+] possessions. **4** [1960s] (*US*) sexual intercourse. **5** [1960s] (*US campus*) alcohol. **6** [1960s] (*US*) information, facts. **7** [1960s+] (*US*) the genitals, the female breasts.

goodle *n.* [SE *good deal*] [1950s+] (*Ulster*) a lot.

goodnight... *phr.* [fig. uses of SE, though for Vienna note *Goodnight, Vienna*, a romantic operetta by Eric Maschwitz and George Posford (1929)] [late 19C+] used to indicate incipient trouble or one's resignation in the face of a problem or disaster; thus elaborated on in phrs. below.

IN PHRASES

❑ **goodnight Irene** [1910s+] ❑ **goodnight Joe Doyle** [1910s+] (*Irish*) ❑ **goodnight McGuinness** [1910s–30s] (*N.Z.*) ❑ **goodnight nurse** [20C+] ❑ **goodnight Vienna** [1930s+]

goodnight kiss *n.* [rhy. sl. = PISS *n.* (2)] [20C+] an act of urination.

good-o *adj.* (*also* **good-oh, goody-oh**) [20C+] (*orig. Aus./N.Z.*) excellent, wonderful, as it should be.

goodo *adv.* (*also* **good-oh**) [20C+] (*Aus.*) very well, excellently.

good-o! *excl.* (*also* **good-oh!**) [usu. associated with somewhat dated schoolboy use] [1910s+] (*orig. Aus./N.Z.*) an excl. of approbation or assent.

good one *n.* **1** [late 18C+] (*also* **good 'un, merry one**) a joke; usu. as *that's a good one*. **2** [19C+] an implausible statement, thus a lie. **3** [mid-19C+] a hard blow. **4** [late 19C] a gullible fool, a SUCKER *n.*[1] (3a). **5** [1950s] (*US*) a long drink. **6** *see GOOD GIRL under* GOOD *adj.*[1]. **7** *see* GOOD 'UN *n.*

Goodrich game *n.* [? a contemporary confidence man; note Asbury, *Sucker's Progress*, (1938): 'According to [anti-gambling writer Jonathan] Green, the [*Secret Band of*] *Brothers* were a great organization of gamblers, robbers and counterfeiters, formed in 1798 at Hanging Rock, in the western part of Virginia, with one Goodrich at the head of the band'] [mid-19C] (*US Und.*) pretending to have been robbed to avoid paying one's bill.

goods *n.* **1** [18C; 1910s+] the female body, usu. in the context of prostitution. **2** [late 19C+] constr. with *the*, the real thing, the ideal thing or person. **3** [20C+] (*US Und.*) constr. with *the*, stolen goods, contraband; usu. *catch someone with the goods*, to catch someone in the act. **4** [20C+] constr. with *the*, accurate information, the truth, esp. when used in an unfriendly manner towards its subject. **5** [1900s] (*US*) alcohol. **6** [1900s] (*US Und.*) money. **7** [1910s] (*US*) an attractive woman. **8** [1920s+] the male genitals. **9** [1930s+] drugs. **10** [1980s] constr. with *the*, sexual intercourse.

IN PHRASES

❑ **deliver the goods** *v.* (*also* **deliver, show the goods**) **1** [late 19C+] to meet expectations, to fulfil one's promises. **2** [1920s+] to perform sexual intercourse. ❑ **have the goods on someone** *v.* (*also* **get the goods on someone**) [20C+] **1** to place someone else at a disadvantage, in any confrontation, physical, mental, financial etc; thus to arrest. **2** to have or obtain incriminating evidence, negative facts etc about something or someone, esp. to the subject's disadvantage, orig. used for racehorses and athletes.

good ship Venus *n.* [rhy. sl.; ref. to the eponymous 'rugby song'] [20C+] the penis.

good shit *n.*[1] [SHIT *n.* (3f)/SHIT *n.* (6a)] [1960s+] (*orig. US*) anything of high quality, esp. drugs.

good shit *n.*[2] [1970s] (*US*) an admirable person.

good thing *n.* [orig. horseracing use, a certain winner] **1** [early 19C+] an advantageous opportunity, usu. in business or in horserace gambling. **2** [20C+] (*Aus./US*) one who can easily be duped, a 'sucker'.

good time *n.*[1] [TIME *n.* (1)] **1** [late 19C+] time off for good behaviour. **2** [1970s+] a jail sentence that is suffered without any particular problems.

good time *n.*[2] [1920s+] (*US black*) an especially acceptable, likeable person.

good time *n.*[3] [its role in sex] [1960s+] the penis.

good-time Charlie *n.* [SE *good time* + CHARLIE *n.*[2] (1)] [1920s+] a playboy, a dissolute man; occas. of a woman; thus *good-time Charlene*.

good-time-Charlie *v.* [GOOD-TIME CHARLIE *n.*] [1920s–50s] (*US*) to act in a jovial, (over-)friendly manner.

good-time Jane *n.* (*also* **good-time Madge**) [SE *good time* + JANE *n.*[2] (1)] [1920s–60s] (*US*) a sexually promiscuous woman.

good 'un *n.* (*also* **good one**) **1** [19C+] a dependable, trustworthy, admirable person or creature. **2** [1920s+] used similarly of an object or situation. **3** *see* GOOD ONE *n.* (1).

(IN PHRASES)

❑ **like a good 'un** *adv.* [mid-19C+] enthusiastically, keenly.

goody-bar *n. see* SISSY-BAR *under* SISSY *n.*

goodyear *n.*[1] [? *gouge*, a slattern, a soldier's companion; ult. Fr. argot *gouge*, a slut; the link between Fr. *goujère*, a hypothetical derivative of 'the French word gouje, which signifies a common Camp-Trull' is considered 'curiously plausible,' by the *OED*, but, it adds, 'there is no evidence that the definite meaning of 'pox' was really intended by any of the writers who used the word; and the alleged etymology is [thus] utterly inadmissible'] [late 16C–early 17C] venereal disease, esp. gonorrhoea.

goodyear *n.*[2] [the *Goodyear* Rubber Company; thus pun on SPARE TYRE *under* SPARE *adj.*] [1960s+] the ring of excess flesh around a portly stomach that may be seen in a kinder light by those who appreciate the Rubenesque figure.

goody-oh *adj. see* GOOD-O *adj.*

gooey *n.* [GOOEY *adj.*] **1** [20C+] (*Aus.*) a lump of phlegm. **2** [20C+] a man of weak character; a fool. **3** [1980s+] a pretty girlfriend.

gooey *adj.* [fig. uses of GOO *n.*[1] (1) + sfx *-y*] **1** [1900s] (*US campus*) bizarre, strange. **2** [1910s+] sentimental, mawkish. **3** [1910s+] sticky, viscid. **4** [1930s] distasteful and distressing.

goof *n.*[1] [dial. *goof*, a fool, a clown, an oaf] **1** [20C+] (*also* **goofhead**) a fool, a blunderer. **2** [1910s] a form of derog. address. **3** [1910s+] an eccentric, crazy person. **4** [1950s] (*US*) something very unpleasant. **5** [1950s] (*US*) an unsophisticated rustic. **6** [1960s+] (*US*) a mistake. **7** [1960s+] (*US*) a joke, a surprise; thus *goofs*, fun. **8** [1970s] an average person, no foolishness implied.

(IN COMPOUNDS)

❑ **goofball** *see* separate entries. ❑ **goofhead** *n. see* sense 1 above.

goof *n.*[2] [GOOF *v.*[1] (2)] (*US*) **1** [1940s] alcohol, a drinker. **2** [1940s–70s] (*also* **goof burner**) a marijuana smoker. **3** [1950s–60s] (*drugs*) psychotropic drugs, esp. marijuana or barbiturates. **4** [1950s–60s] the relaxed state that follows the taking of a drug, usu. marijuana or a barbiturate; thus *on the goof*, drowsy from the effects of a drug.

(IN COMPOUNDS)

❑ **goof burner** *n. see* sense 2 above. ❑ **goof butt** *n.* (*also* **goofy-butt**) [1940s+] (*drugs*) a marijuana cigarette.

goof *n.*[3] *see* GOEF *n.*

goof *v.*[1] **1** to lack focus or concentration. (**a**) [1910s+] (*also* **goof around, goof on, goof out**) to fool (with); to play around. (**b**) [1910s+] (*also* **goof around**) to dawdle, to waste time, to avoid work; thus *goof time*, a period of relaxation. (**c**) [1940s+] (*Aus./US*) to gawk, to stare mindlessly, esp. at the television; thus *goof box*, a TV set. (**d**) [1940s+] (*also* **goof it**) to blunder, to make a mistake; thus *goof oneself*, to get into trouble. **2** [1940s+] (*US*) in the context of intoxication. (**a**) to take drugs; thus *goofing, goofed up, on the goof*, under the influence of drugs; occas. drink. (**b**) thus fig. use, to be addicted to/obsessed with, usu. a person. (**c**) to render someone into a state that approximates that which follows drug use. (**d**) (*drugs*) to relax, to go to sleep under the influence of drugs, usu. heroin. (**e**) to become drunk. **3** [1950s] to wander. **4** [1950s+] (*US*) to mistreat, to victimize. **5** [1950s+] to make a mess of. **6** [1970s] of an object, a machine, to malfunction. **7** [1980s+] to give oneself up.

(IN COMPOUNDS)

❑ **goofball** *n. see* separate entry. ❑ **goofbang** *n. see* separate entry. ❑ **goof pill** *n. see* separate entry.

(IN PHRASES)

❑ **goof it** *v. see* sense 1d above. ❑ **goof off** *see* separate entries. ❑ **goof on** *v.* (*also* **goof over**) **1** [1940s+] (*US*) to laugh at, to find amusing. **2** [1950s+] to get excited by. **3** *see* sense 1a above. ❑ **goof out** *v. see* sense 1a above. ❑ **goof up** *see* separate entries.

goof *v.*[2] *see* GOEF *v.*

goofball *n.*[1] [GOOF *v.*[1] (2)] **1** [1930s–50s] marijuana. **2** [1940s+] (*drugs*) a barbiturate, a tranquillizer; thus *goofballed*, under the influence of barbiturates. **3** [1950s] a sleeping pill. **4** [1950s+] (*Aus./US*) a knockout drop. **5** [1950s+] (*drugs*) cocaine and heroin.

goofball *n.*[2] [GOOF *n.*[1] (3)] [1940s+] (*US*) a silly, amusing, eccentric or insane person.

goofball *adj.* [GOOFBALL *n.*[2]] [1940s+] crazy, eccentric.

goofbang *n.* [GOOF *v.*[1] (1), but note later GOOF *n.*[1] (7) + BANG *n.*[1] (2b)] [1950s] casual sex.

goofed *adv.* [GOOFED (UP) *adj.* (1)] [1960s] (*US*) foolishly.

goofed (up) *adj.* [GOOF *v.*[1]] **1** [1930s] (*US*) made a fool of. **2** [1940s+] (*US*) drunk. **3** [1940s+] (*S.Afr./US*) intoxicated by a drug, esp. cannabis or barbiturates. **4** [1950s] nervous. **5** [1950s] second-rate. **6** [1950s–60s] crazy, infatuated or bewildered. **7** [1960s] messed up, ruined.

goofer *n.*[1] (*also* **goopher**) [GOOF *n.*[1]] **1** [1910s+] (*US*) a lout, an oaf, a clumsy fool. **2** [1940s+] a homosexual prostitute who will take active roles in fellatio or anal intercourse.

goofer *n.*[2] [GOOF *v.*[1] + GOOFBALL *n.*[1] (2)] **1** [1940s–70s] one who 'plays around' with drugs, esp. amphetamines or barbiturates. **2** [1960s–70s] often in pl., a barbiturate.

go-off *n.* (*also* **off-go**) **1** [mid-19C+] the starting time; at the start; usu. in phr. the *first go-off*. **2** [2000s] one who runs away, abandons the group.

go off *v.* **1** [late 17C–19C] to die. **2** [mid-18C; 1920s+] to have an orgasm. **3** [mid-18C–19C] of a woman, to get married. **4** [early 19C+] to happen, to take place, esp. of a fight, a riot. **5** [mid-19C] to be disposed of, whether of people or objects. **6** [mid-19C+] (*also* **go off it, go off pop**) to lose emotional control. **7** [late 19C–1910s] (*society*) to not take place, to fail to happen. **8** [20C+] to pass out, to go to sleep. **9** [1910s+] (*Aus.*) to be sent to prison. **10** [1920s+] (*Aus.*) to suffer a police raid, usu. because a hotel or public house is breaking local drinking laws. **11** [1940s+] (*Aus.*) to be fined. **12** [1970s+] (*US black*) to do something exceptionally well. **13** [1970s+] (*US*) to talk about. **14** [1980s+] (*US campus*) to become foolish or silly. **15** [1980s+] (*US campus*) to act intensely. **16** [1980s+] (*US campus*) to move from topic to topic while talking.

(IN PHRASES)

❑ **go off at the fall of the leaf** *v. see* GO OFF WITH THE FALL OF THE LEAF *under* LEAF *n.* ❑ **go off it** *v. see* sense 6 above. ❑ **go off like a two-bob watch** *v.* (*also* **go off like a tin of bad fish**) [pun on SE *go off*/sense 1 above] [1960s+] (*Aus.*) of a woman, to be highly sexed. ❑ **go off on** *v.* [1960s+] (*US black*) **1** to lose one's temper, to attack verbally, usu. at length. **2** to attack physically. ❑ **go off one's ass** *v.* [1970s] (*US*) to lose control, to lose one's temper. ❑ **go off pop** *v. see* sense 6 above. ❑ **go off with the fall of the leaf** *v. see under* LEAF *n.*

goofie *n. see* GOOFY *n.*

goofily *adv.* [GOOF *n.*[1] (1)] [1930s+] foolishly.

goofiness *n.* [GOOF *n.*[1] (1)] [1920s+] stupidity, foolishness.

goof-off *n.* [GOOF OFF *v.* (1)] **1** [1940s+] (*US*) a loafer, idler. **2** [1960s+] (*US*) an error or blunder. **3** [1980s] a joker.

goof off *v.* [ext. GOOF *v.*[1]] **1** [1930s+] (*orig. milit.*) to act lazily, to mess around instead of working. **2** [1930s+] to blunder; to wreck. **3** [1940s] to go mad. **4** [1940s–60s] (*US drugs*) to go to sleep, esp. under the influence of drugs. **5** [1950s] (*US*) to leave. **6** [1950s–70s] to chat, to socialize. **7** [1960s] (*US*) to gain pleasure from, to be enthralled by. **8** [1980s] to turn down an invitation; to avoid a meeting.

goo food *n.* [GOOK *n.*[3] (1) or, as ref. to consistency of some dishes, GOO *n.*[1] (1)] [1990s+] (*US campus*) East Asian food.

goof pill *n.* (*also* **goofy**) [var. GOOFBALL *n.*[1] (2)] [1950s–70s] (*drugs*) a barbiturate.

goof up *n.* [GOOF UP *v.*] [1950s+] (*US*) **1** a blunder. **2** a person who blunders or messes up, causing trouble for themselves.

goof up *v.* [ext. GOOF *v.*[1] (1d)] [1940s+] (*US*) to blunder, to spoil, to injure.

goofus *n.* (*also* **goovus**) [GOOF *n.*[1]] [1910s+] (*US*) an idiot.

goofy *n.* (*also* **goofie**) [GOOFY *adj.*] **1** [1920s–40s] (*US campus*) a fool. **2** *see* GOOF PILL *n.*

goofy *adj.* [GOOF *n.*[1] (1) + sfx *-y*; the personification of the term (albeit anthropomorphic) is the eponymous Disney character] [1910s+] **1** uncoordinated, inept. **2** drunk. **3** (*also* **goofy-ass**) silly, foolish; thus *goofiness*, foolishness. **4** of a place, bizarre. **5** mad. **6** (*US*) obsessed, keen on. **7** incomprehensible. **8** disorientated, confused. **9** (*US drugs*) suffering from narcotics withdrawal.

goofy *adv.* [GOOFY *adj.* (3)] [1920s] (*US*) oddly.

goofy-butt *n. see* GOOF BUTT *under* GOOF *n.*[2].

goog *n.*[1] (*also* **googie, googy**) [Scot. *goggie*/Irish *gogaí*, nursery term for an egg] **1** [20C+] (*Aus.*) an egg. **2** [1910s+] a fool [link to GOO-GOO *n.*[4]].

goog *n.*[2] [GOOGS *n.*] [1920s–30s] (*US*) a black eye.

goog *v.* [SE *goggle (at)*] [1950s] to stand around; to watch others.

googeen *adj.* [synon. Irish *guaigin*] [20C+] (*Irish*) usu. of a woman, fidgety.

googie *n. see* GOOG *n.*[1].

google-eyed *adj.* **1** *see* GOGGLE-EYED *adj.* (3). **2** *see* GOGGLE-EYED *adj.* (4).

googlum *n. see* GOOZLUM *n.*

googly-eyed *adj. see* GOGGLE-EYED *adj.* (3).

goo-gobs *n.* [ety. unknown; note SE *googol*, 10 to the 100th power] [1970s+] (*US black*) a very large or infinite amount.

googons *n. see* GOOGS *n.*

goo-goo *n.*[1] [? echoic of a supposedly unintelligible language] (*US*) **1** [late 19C–1950s] (*also* **gu-gu**) a derog. term for an Asian or dark-skinned foreigner; esp. a Filipino. **2** [1970s] an unintelligible foreign language.

goo-goo *n.*[2] [SE *good government* + *goodie*] [late 19C+] (*US*) a supporter of political reform.

goo-goo *n.*[3] [backform. f. GOO-GOO EYES *n.*] [1910s] an eye.

goo-goo *n.*[4] [? *goo-goo* noises of stupidity] **1** [1910s+] (*US*) a silly fool; thus as adj., foolish; mawkish, sentimental. **2** *see* GOO-GOO EYES *n.*

goo-goo *adj.* **1** [1900s] sweet, sickly. **2** [1960s] (*US*) effeminate.

goo-goo *v.* [GOO-GOO EYES *n.*] [1900s–40s] (*US*) to make eyes at someone.

goo-goo eyes *n.* (*also* **goo-goo, goo-goo lamp, goo-goos, oogle eyes**) [? SE *goggle (at)* + the double 'o' is reminiscent of two rounded eyes; *goo-goo* is also a classic piece of 'baby-talk' and as such reflects the infantility of such glances] [late 19C+] an amorous glance directed at a loved, or hopefully soon to be loved, one.

goo-goo watch *n.* [ety. unknown; ? SE *cuckoo*] [1930s–40s] (*US black*) dawn and the period just preceding it.

googs *n.* (*also* **googons**) [? GOGGLES *n.* (3) or play on GOO-GOO EYES *n.*] [1920s–50s] (*US Und.*) spectacles.

googy *n. see* GOOG *n.*[1].

googy eyes *n.* [GOO-GOO EYES *n.*] [1910s] (*US*) amorous glances.

googy-googy *adj.* [GOOG *n.*[1] (2)] [1960s] given to playing pranks, fooling around.

gooh *n.* [ety. unknown] [mid-19C] (*US Und.*) a prostitute.

gooi *n.* [GOOI *v.* (1)] [1940s+] (*S.Afr.*) a fling, a spree, a party.

gooi *v.* [Afk. *gooi*, to throw, to fling] [1940s+] (*S.Afr.*) an all-purpose v. used to signify movement and/or action, e.g. to throw, to fling, to give someone something, to use something.

IN PHRASES

❑ **gooi a canary** *v.* [the canary as a stereotypical songbird] [1940s+] to whistle a warning. ❑ **gooi ankers** *v.* [Afk. sl. *ankers*, the brakes] [1980s+] to brake suddenly. ❑ **gooi a spasm** *v.* [SE *spasm*] [1980s+] to react with joy or enthusiasm. ❑ **gooi a Uie** *v.* [U-IE *n.*] [1980s+] to make a U-turn. ❑ **gooi grief** *v.* [i.e. GIVE SOMEONE GRIEF *under* GRIEF *n.*[1]] [1990s+] to annoy somebody. ❑ **gooi pomp** *v.* [POMP *v.*] [1980s] to have sexual intercourse. ❑ **gooi tackie** *v.* [SAfrE *tackie*, a tyre] [1980s+] to accelerate.

gook *n.*[1] [? GOWK *n.*] [mid-19C–1910s] a street-walker.

gook *n.*[2] [? GOWK *n.*] **1** [1910s+] (*orig. US*) (*also* **gouk**) a dull, stupid, foolish person. **2** [1900s] a tramp.

IN PHRASES

❑ **gook-eyed** *adv.* [1950s] (*US*) stupidly, foolishly, vacantly.

gook *n.*[3] [ety. unknown; ? GOO-GOO *n.*[1] (1) + *goo-goo*, baby-talk, a ref. to the incomprehensibility of East Asian languages in Western ears; or nursery excl. of disgust, *gucchh!* denoting Western distaste for the omnivorousness of some East Asian cuisines; neither seems very likely] [1910s+] (*orig. US milit.*) **1** a derog. term for a foreigner, esp. East Asian, e.g. (in chronological order of use) Filipino, Japanese, Korean, Vietnamese; thus *Gookland*, Vietnam. **2** any other foreigner. **3** any foreign language.

IN COMPOUNDS

❑ **gook wagon** *n.* (*also* **gook car**) [sense 2 above, as synon. for a taste for gaudiness and excess] [1950s–60s] (*US*) an inferior car over-decorated with chrome and accessories.

gook *n.*[4] [ext. of GOO *n.*[1] (1)] **1** [1940s+] (*US*) slimy, sticky, dirty viscid matter, also distasteful food. **2** [1980s+] (*US*) anything unpleasant; nonsense.

IN PHRASES

❑ **gook up** *v.* [1950s] to smear such a substance on someone.

gook *adj.* [GOOK *n.*[3]] [1920s+] (*US*) foreign, spec. Italian or East Asian; by late 20C+ usu. Korean or Vietnamese.

gooky *adj.* [GOOK *n.*[4] (1) + sfx *-y*] [1960s+] (*US*) **1** unpleasantly sticky. **2** in fig. use, awkward.

gool *v. see* GOAL *v.*

goola *n.*[1] [Ital. *culo*, the anus] [1940s] (*US*) the anus.

goola *n.*[2] [ety. unknown] [1940s–50s] (*US black*) a piano.

goola box *n.* [GOOLA *n.*[2] + SE *box*] [1930s–50s] (*US black*) a jukebox or 'nickarola'.

goolie *n.* (*also* **gooley**) [? Hind. *golí*, a bullet, ball or pill or dial. *gullies*, marbles; given the common equation of the male genitals with weaponry, one might also note dial. *gully*, a large knife, although that would more properly represent the penis; also note New South Wales Aborigine *goolie*, a stone] **1** [late 18C+] (*also* **goon**) usu. in pl., a testicle. **2** [1940s+] (*US/Aus./N.Z.*) (*also* **goonie**) a small stone or pebble.

IN PHRASES

❑ **have someone by the goolies** *v.* [1980s] to have the upper hand.

goom *n.* [? Jagara *goom*, water] [1960s+] (*Aus.*) **1** methylated spirits, as an alcoholic's drink. **2** (*also* **goomy**) a drinker of methylated spirits.

goombah *n.* (*also* **gumbah**) [Italian *compare*, godfather, one of the names (*see* Mario Puzo, *The Godfather*, 1969) used for a leader of the Italian-American Mafia] **1** [1950s+] (*US, orig. US Ital.*) a close male friend. **2** [1950s+] (*US*) a stupid person. **3** [1950s+] an Italian-American. **4** [1960s+] (*US*) (*also* **gumba**) a thug, a gangster; spec. a member of an organized crime syndicate, usu. the US Mafia. **5** [1960s+] (*US Und.*) in the US Mafia, a patron, lit. a 'godfather'. **6** [1990s+] (*US campus*) an outsider, social outcast.

goom-bye *phr.* (*also* **goomba, goom bi, goon-bye**) [1900s–70s] (*US*) goodbye.

goomer *n.* [GOMER *n.*[2]] [1960s+] (*US*) a fool, a failure.

goomp *n. see* GUMP *n.*[1].

goomy *n. see* GOOM *n.* (2).

goon *n.*[1] [? cartoon character, Alice the *Goon* from the comic *Thimble Theatre* (1919) by E.C. Segar (1894–1938). Given the implication of stupidity, note GOONEY *n.* (2), a fool; note *Indep. Review* 25/10/99 suggests link to a 'family saying' by F. L. Allen in *Harper's Mag.* Dec. 121/1 (title) 'The Goon and his Style'. Ibid. 121/2: 'A goon is a person with a heavy touch as distinguished from a jigger, who has a light touch. While jiggers look on life with a genial eye, goons take a more stolid and literal view'] (*orig. US*) **1** [20C+] (*also* **goony**) a stolid, stupid person. **2** [1930s+] a thug; thus adj. *goonish*, thuggish. **3** [1930s+] non-union labour used for strike breaking, intimidation etc. **4** [1930s+] a police officer. **5** [1940s] a derog. term for a black person.

IN COMPOUNDS

❑ **goonhead** *n.* [-HEAD *sfx* (1)] [1980s+] (*US*) a fool. ❑ **goon squad** *n.* **1** [1930s+] a group of thugs, usu. organized for a specific purpose – strike-breaking, extortion etc. **2** [1940s] (*US black*) the police. **3** [1960s+] (*US prison*) a squad of prison guards used to quell riots or any other form of trouble. ❑ **goon suit** *n.* [1990s+] (*US*) army surplus clothing.

goon *n.*[2] (*also* **goon crystal, goon dust**) [its effects may turn the user into a GOON *n.*[1] (1)] [1970s+] (*drugs*) phencyclidine.

goon *n.*[3] (*also* **bag of goon, goonbag, gooner, goonsack**) [? mispron./abbr. SE *flagon*; or ? GOOM *n.*] [1980s] (*Aus.*) a flagon of cheap wine.

goon *n.*[4] *see* GOOLIE *n.* (1).

go on! *excl.* (*also* **gahn! garn! ger on! get on (with you)! go on out of that! go on with you! g'wan!**) [*garn!* etc is Cockney pron.] **1** [mid-19C+] an excl. used to imply incredulity. **2** [1970s+] (*US campus*) an excl. of admiration.

goonbag *n. see* GOON *n.*[3].

goon-bye *phr. see* GOOM-BYE *phr.*

go on circuit *v.* [1900s] (*Aus.*) of a prostitute, to tour diggings and camps selling her services.

goon crystal/dust *n. see* GOON *n.*[2].

gooned (out) *adj.* [GOON *n.*[1] (1)] [1960s+] (*US*) intoxicated on drugs or by alcohol.

gooner *n.*[1] [SE *gone* or GONER *n.*[1] (3)]

IN PHRASES

❑ **get the gooner** *v.* [1920s–30s] to be dismissed from a job. ❑ **give someone the gooner** *v.* [1920s–30s] **1** to dismiss someone from a job. **2** to jilt, to terminate a relationship.

gooner *n.*[2] **1** [1990s+] (*US prison*) a member of the GOON SQUAD *under* GOON *n.*[1]. **2** see GOON *n.*[3].

gooney *n.* (*also* **goney, goonie**) [OE *ganian*, to gape] **1** [mid-19C] (*UK Und.*) a newly arrived prisoner, esp. one who is not of the criminal underworld. **2** [mid-19C+] (*US*) a fool, an idiot. **3** [1920s+] (*US*) (*also* **gooner**) a foreigner, an enemy, esp. a Chinese communist soldier. **4** [2000s] (*Aus.*) cheap, cask wine.

goonie *n. see* GOOLIE *n.* (2).

go on out of that! *excl. see* GO ON! *excl.*

goonsack *n. see* GOON *n.*[3].

go on with you! *excl. see* GO ON! *excl.*

goony *n. see* GOON *n.*[1] (1).

goony *adj.* [GOON *n.*[1] (1) + sfx *-y*] [1930s+] (*US*) silly, crazy.

goony-bird *n.* [1950s+] (*US teen*) a fool, an eccentric.

goop *n.*[1] (*also* **gooper**) [? var. on GOOF *n.*[1] (1); coined by Gelett Burgess (1866–1951) in 1900 for a 'race' of fantasy childlike creatures] [20C+] (*orig. US*) a fool, an idiot, a boor.

goop *n.*[2] (*also* **gloop**) [var. on GOO *n.*[1] (1)] **1** [1910s+] (*US*) any slimy, sticky viscous matter, esp. hair oil, sticky sweets, cosmetics. **2** [1930s–40s] (*Aus.*) a fool. **3** [1960s] (*US*) gelignite, nitroglycerine.

IN COMPOUNDS

❑ **goop-gobbler** *n.* [GOBBLER *n.*[2]] [1960s–70s] (*US gay*) a fellator or fellatrix.

goop *v.* [SE *gawp* + ? link to GOOP *n.*[1]] [1950s] (*N.Z.*) to stare.

gooper *n. see* GOOP *n.*[1].

goopher *n.* **1** *see* GOOFER *n.*[2]. **2** *see* GOPHER *n.*[2] (2).

goopher feathers *n.* [1920s–40s] (*US*) nonsense.

goopon *n. see* GOBOON *n.*

goopy *adj.* [GOOP *n.*[2] (1)/GOOP *n.*[1] + sfx *-y*] (*US*) **1** [20C+] sticky. **2** [20C+] lacking in energy, exhausted. **3** [1950s+] silly.

goorie *n.* (*also* **goory, kuri**) [Maori *goorie*, a mongrel dog] [1930s+] (*N.Z.*) a general term of abuse.

goose *n.*[1] [theatrical use, *get the goose*, to be hissed] **1** [mid-19C–1920s] a scolding, a reprimand. **2** [1940s–50s] an instruction, a warning to act in the required manner. **3** *see* WINCHESTER GOOSE *n.*

goose *n.*[2] [? pron. of *goose* as *joose*, i.e. Jews; *HDAS* suggests SE *goose*, a tailor's iron, and the link of Jews to tailoring] [late 19C–1940s] a Jew.

goose *n.*[3] [GOOSE *v.*[3]] **1** [1930s+] a poke into the genital area with a finger or some form of implement. **2** [1940s] anal intercourse.

IN COMPOUNDS

❑ **goose hole** *n.* [1970s+] (*US gay/prison*) the anus.

goose *n.*[4] **1** [1960s] (*US campus*) an effeminate man. **2** [1960s–70s] (*US campus*) a socially unacceptable person. **3** [1970s] (*Aus. Und.*) a shopkeeper; a shop assistant.

SE in slang uses

IN COMPOUNDS

❑ **goose-cap** *n.* [coined in the UK, it had lapsed by the 18C but was picked up in the US during the 19C] [late 16C–mid-19C] a fool, an idiot, a numbskull. ❑ **goose egg** *n. see* separate entry. ❑ **goosefoot** *n.* **1** [late 19C] (*US*) a man who stands firmly for one political party, come what may. **2** [1910s] (*US*) a detective. ❑ **goose grease** *n.* [late 19C] vaginal secretions. ❑ **goose-head/-headed** *see* separate entries. ❑ **goose shearer** *n.* [such a villain 'shears' a foolish SE *goose*] [18C–19C] (*UK Und.*) a beggar; thus a confidence trickster. ❑ **goose's neck** *n. see* separate entry. ❑ **goose tracks** *n.* [mid-19C+] (*US*) illegible handwriting.

IN PHRASES

❑ **do someone's goose** *v. see* COOK SOMEONE'S GOOSE *v.* (2).

goose *n.*[5] *see* GOOSE (AND DUCK) *n.*

goose *v.*[1] [SE *goose*, a fool] **1** [mid-19C] to ruin, to spoil. **2** [1930s+] to make a fool of, to deceive.

goose *v.*[2] [theatrical use, *get the goose*, to be hissed] [mid-19C–1920s] to hiss disparagingly, orig. at a play.

goose *v.*[3] **1** [late 19C+] to pursue women, to womanize. **2** [20C+] to poke or tickle a person in the genital or anal area, usu. by a man to a woman. **3** [20C+] (*US*) of emotions, to press, to push, to provoke, to enliven. **4** [1910s+] of a person, to push, to poke. **5** [1920s+] to have sexual intercourse. **6** [1930s+] (*US*) to accelerate a car; thus *goose up*, to move forward a short distance. **7** [1940s] to perform anal intercourse. **8** [1960s] (*US*) to grab. **9** [1960s+] to increase the volume on a radio, sound system or TV. **10** [1970s] (*US campus*) to grasp someone's testicles from behind, as a prank. **11** [1970s+] to improve, to cajole into progress. **12** [1980s] (*US black*) to stab. **13** [2000s] to excite sexually. **14** [2000s] to augment, to increase.

goose (and duck) *n.* [rhy. sl. = FUCK *n.* (1a)] [late 19C+] sexual intercourse.

gooseberries *n.* [supposed resemblance] [20C+] a small boy's testicles.

gooseberry *n.* **1** [19C] a fool [punning on the popular dessert, a *gooseberry fool*, which is also SOFT *adj.* (1)]. **2** [mid-19C–1940s] (*US tramp*) (*also* **gooseberry bush**) laundry hanging on a washing-line, and therefore vulnerable to theft [from the era when clothes were draped over bushes to dry]. **3** [1940s] (*US*) a small piece of excrement around the anus [var. on DINGLEBERRY *n.* (3)].

IN COMPOUNDS

❑ **gooseberry bush** *n.* **1** *see* sense 2 above. **2** *see also* SE uses below. ❑ **gooseberry lay** *n.* (*also* **gooseberry picking**) [LAY *n.*[3] (1)] [mid-19C–1940s] (*UK/US Und.*) the stealing of linen drying in the open air by tramps and thieves. ❑ **gooseberry picker** *n.* [1940s] (*US tramp*) one who steals from clotheslines.

SE in slang uses

IN COMPOUNDS

❑ **gooseberry bush** *n.* [ext. of BUSH *n.*[1] (2a); it is this bush, of course, rather than the fruiting variety, beneath which a child is allegedly born] **1** [19C] the pubic hair. **2** *see also* compounds above. ❑ **gooseberry grinder** *n.* [ety. unknown; ? ref. to the effect on the digestion and thus defecation of unripe gooseberries] [late 18C–19C] the buttocks; esp. in phr. *ask Bogey the gooseberry grinder*, euph. for 'ask my arse'. ❑ **gooseberry-eyed** *adj.* [late 18C–19C] having eyes that look like boiled gooseberries, grey and lifeless.

gooseberry *v.* [GOOSEBERRY *n.* (2)] [1910s–40s] (*US Und.*) to steal clothes from a clothes-line.

gooseberry pudding *n.* (*also* **gooseberry pudden**) [rhy. sl.; *pudding* pron. 'pudden'] **1** [mid-19C–1950s] a woman; esp. as the *old gooseberry*, one's wife. **2** [1920s–40s] a promiscuous woman.

gooseberry ranch *n. see* GOOSING RANCH *n.*

gooseberry tart *n. see* RASPBERRY TART *n.*

goosed *adj.* [GOOSE *v.*[1] (1)] **1** [mid-19C+] ruined, finished. **2** [20C+] (*Aus./US*) drunk. **3** [1920s] (*Aus.*) fooled.

goose egg *n.* (*also* **egg, gooser**) [visual resemblance] **1** [mid-19C+] zero, nothing [shape of the egg/zero; note cricket jargon a *duck's egg*, a score of nothing]. **2** [1940s+] (*US*) a large bruise or swelling that comes up on the head after striking it or being struck a blow.

goose-head *n.* [SE *goose*, a fool + -HEAD *sfx* (1)] [mid-19C–1910s] (*US*) an idiot.

goose-headed *adj.* [GOOSE-HEAD *n.*] [1900s] (*US*) foolish.

gooser *n.*[1] [? such a blow would COOK SOMEONE'S GOOSE *v.*] [mid–late 19C] **1** a knockout blow. **2** in fig. use, a waste, a failure. **3** the end, a goner.

gooser *n.*[2] [GOOSE *v.*[3] (2)] **1** [late 19C] the penis. **2** [20C+] (*Can.*) a pederast.

gooser *n.*[3] *see* GOOSE EGG *n.*

goose's neck *n.*[1] [supposed resemblance] [late 19C] the penis; thus *have a bit of goose's neck*, to have sexual intercourse.

goose's neck *n.*[2] [rhy. sl.] [20C+] a cheque.

goosey *adj.* (*also* **goosy**) [GOOSE *v.*[3] (2) but note GOOSE *n.*[4] (1)] **1** [20C+] nervous, jittery, on edge. **2** [1920s+] effeminate or homosexual. **3** [1930s+] foolishly excited. **4** [1960s] ticklish in the anal area.

goosie *n.* [GOOSE *n.*[4] (1)] [1950s+] **1** (*S.Afr. prison*) the passive, 'female' partner of a homosexual couple. **2** (*S.Afr.*) (*also* **ousie**) a young woman, a girlfriend. **3** (*S.Afr.*) a prostitute.

goosing crib *n.* [ety. unknown; chronology defeats link to otherwise logical senses at GOOSE *v.*[3] although this may represent an early use; + CRIB *n.*[1] (1)] [mid-19C] (*UK Und.*) a brothel.

goosing ranch *n.* (*also* **gooseberry ranch**) [GOOSE *v.*[3] (5) + SE *ranch*] [1920s–40s] (*US*) a brothel.

goosing slum *n.* [var. on GOOSING CRIB *n.* + SLUM *n.*[1] (1)] [mid-late 19C; 1950s] (*orig. UK Und.*) a brothel-cum-low saloon.

goosy *adj. see* GOOSEY *adj.*

goot *n.* [? Ger. *gut*, good] [2000s] (*US black*) something pleasant.

gooter *n.* [ety. unknown] [1980s+] (*Irish*) the penis.

go-out *n.* [GO OUT *v.* (2)] [1930s] (*US Und.*) a death, a murder.

go out *v.* [fig. uses of SE] **1** [early 19C] (*UK Und.*) to work as a thief. **2** [early 19C+] (*Aus./US/US prison*) to die. **3** [1920s+] to escape from prison. **4** [1930s+] (*orig. US*) to faint, to lose consciousness; esp. in phr. *go out like a light*. **5** [1980s+] (*US black*) to act, to behave. **6** [1990s+] (*US black*) to sell out, to abandon one's principles.

IN PHRASES

❑ **go out by Had'em, and come round by Clapham home** *v. see* HADDUMS *n.* ❑ **go out of the country** *v.* [early 19C] (*UK Und.*) to be transported. ❑ **go out the back door** *v.* [1950s+] (*US prison*) to back down under pressure. ❑ **go out with the blades** *v.* [shearing jargon *blades*, hand-held shears, discarded by most shearers in the early 20C+] [1950s–60s] (*Aus.*) to become obsolete.

go over *v.* **1** [late 19C–1900s] to rob, after running one's hands over and through the victim's clothes. **2** [late 19C–1920s] (*US Und.*) to be sent to prison. **3** [20C+] (*orig. US*) to succeed. **4** [1910s] (*UK Und.*) to commit a robbery. **5** [1910s+] to inspect. **6** [1940s+] (*Aus.*) of a man, to become a homosexual [fig. to *go over to the other side* in one's sexuality; note mid-19C clerical use *go over*, to convert to Roman Catholicism]. **7** [2000s] (*drugs*) to overdose [i.e. go over the limit].

IN PHRASES

❑ **go over big** *v.* [1910s+] (*orig. US*) **1** to be notably successful. **2** to make a good impression. ❑ **go over like a lead balloon** *v. see under* LEAD *n.*

SE in slang uses

IN PHRASES

❑ **go over the fence** *v.* [1950s] (*Aus.*) to be unreasonable. ❑ **go over the highside** *v.* [HIGHSIDE *v.*] [1960s+] (*US*) **1** to lose control, to lose one's composure. **2** to show off. **3** to fall off one's motorbike when turning a corner. ❑ **go over the hill** *v. see under* HILL *n.* ❑ **go over the hump** *v.* **1** *see* BLOW ONE'S HUMP *v.* (1). **2** *see under* HUMP *n.*[1]. ❑ **go over the Styx** *v. see* GO ACROSS THE RIVER *under* RIVER *n.* ❑ **go over the tops of trees** *v.* [late 18C] to be very drunk.

goovus *n. see* GOOFUS *n.*

goozer *n.*[1] [? GUZZLE *v.*[2] (3)] [1980s+] (*Irish*) a kiss.

goozer *n.*[2] [? SE *gooseberry*, an unwanted third party] [1990s+] (*UK juv.*) one who attempts to join a group among whom they are not numbered and/or welcome.

goozle *n.* (*also* **goozlem, goozle pipe, goozler, gozzle**) [GUZZLE *n.* (1)] [late 19C+] (*US*) usu. of an animal, the windpipe; of a human, the throat, the Adam's apple.

goozlum *n.* (*also* **googlum**) [GOO *n.*[1] (1)] [20C+] (*US*) any viscous, treacly substance, often a foodstuff.

gopher *see under* GOFER.

gopher *n.*[1] [SE *gopher*, a burrowing rodent of the genera *Geomys* and *Thomomys*, native to these states; the image is of the animal's burrowing or its role as vermin] (*US*) **1** [mid-19C] a Floridian. **2** [mid–late 19C] an Arkansan. **3** [mid-19C–1940s] a Minnesotan. **4** [mid-19C–1940s] (*US*) an offensive or stupid person. **5** [mid-19C–1950s] (*US*) a primitive form of plough. **6** [1920s] (*Can.*) a mounted police officer.

gopher *n.*[2] [their use of underground hideouts: like the SE *gopher*, they 'burrow' beneath the ground] (*US Und.*) **1** [late 19C–1960s] a member of a notorious New York City street gang; thus generic for any thug or gangster [the Gophers, whose 'turf' encompassed New York's 'Hell's Kitchen' (the West side between 42nd Street and 14th Street), used the area's cellars and basements as their preferred hideouts]. **2** [late 19C–1950s] (*also* **goopher**) a safe; thus *kick in the gopher*, to blow open a safe. **3** [late 19C–1960s] a robber who specializes in safes, strongboxes or bank vaults; thus *gopher racket*, safe-cracking; *gopher man/worker*, a safe-breaker; *pull a gopher*, to tunnel into a bank vault. **4** [1920s–40s] a robber who tunnels to his target; thus *gopher gang, gopher mob*, gangs who work in this way.

gopp *n.* [mid-19C] (*UK Und.*) a criminal gang.

goppy *adj.* [1970s] (*US*) sentimental, tearful.

gops *n.* (*also* **gopse**) [ety. unknown] [1960s+] (*S.Afr.*) **1** the backwoods, a backward, rural area. **2** an uncouth or common loutish person.

go queueing *v.*

IN PHRASES

❑ **go queueing** *v. see under* Q *adj.*

gor *n. see* GAW *n.*

gor! *excl.* (*also* **by gor! Goramity! gor-a-war!**) [17C+] a euph. for *God!*

gorb *n.* (*also* **gorby-guts**) [dial. *gorb*, a gluttonous person or animal; ? ult. Scot. *gorb*, an unfledged bird; note also SE *gorbelly*, a (person with) a fat stomach] [20C+] (*Irish*) a glutton.

Gorbals kiss *n.* [ironic use of SE] [1930s+] a head butt.

gor bli!/gor blime! *excl. see* GORBLIMEY! *excl.*

gorblimeries *n.* [its Cockney/villainous population, for whom GORBLIMEY! *excl.* is a stereotyped excl. Note a parallel use as an adj.: 'the Gorblimey aspect of history, the feelings of the ordinary man on the spot at the time' (*Oxford Magazine*, 27 February 1958)] [late 19C] Seven Dials, London.

gorblimey *adj.* [20C+] **1** uncouth. **2** indicative of a working-class background.

gorblimey! *excl.* (*also* **cor blimey! gawd blimey! gor bli! gorblime! gorblimey O'Reilly! gor glomey!**) [late 19C+] a mild, euphemistic oath, lit. 'God blind me!'.

gorby-guts *n. see* GORB *n.*

gor damn *n.* (*also* **gah damn**) [rhy. sl.] [late 19C–1910s] jam.

gordelpus *n. see* GAWDELPUS *n.*

Gordon & Gotch *n.* [rhy. sl.; ult. the firm of book and periodical importers] [20C+] a watch.

Gordon Bennett! *excl.* (*also* **Bennett!**) [either f. James *Gordon Bennett* (1795–1872), the founding editor of the New York *Herald*, or his similarly named son (1841–1918); or Gordon Bennett, promoter of motor- and air-races before 1914] [20C+] a euph. for GORBLIMEY! *excl.*

Gordon Hutter *n.* [rhy. sl.; ult. the contemporary racing and wrestling commentator *Gordon Hutter*] [1930s–40s] (*N.Z.*) butter.

gore *v.* [SE *gore*, to stab with a sharp weapon] [1980s] (*UK black*) to stab, to slash with a knife.

goree *n.* (*also* **gory**) [proper name of *Fort Goree*, on the Gold Coast, a centre for slave trading and gold] [late 17C–early 19C] money.

gore-stained *adj.* [1900s] (*Aus.*) a euph. for BLOODY *adj.* (1).

gorge *n.* [SE *gorge*, that which has been swallowed + *gorge*, to eat to excess] **1** [late 19C–1900s] a heavy meal; a feast. **2** [1920s] a glutton.

gorge out *v.* [SE *gorge*, a ravine with rocky walls] [1960s+] (*US campus*) to commit suicide by jumping from a high cliff.

gorger *n.*[1] [Rom. *gorgio*, a non-Romany] **1** [early 19C] any man, irrespective of appearance. **2** [early–mid-19C] a dandy, an exceptionally well-dressed man [? + SE *gorgeous*].

gorger *n.*[2] [? SE *gouge*, to cheat, to impose upon] [mid-19C] an employer.

gor-glomey! *excl. see* GORBLIMEY! *excl.*

gorgon *n.* [the mythical Gorgon, whose hair was made of writhing snakes] [1950s+] **1** (*W.I. Rasta*) outstanding dreadlocks. **2** (*W.I.*) a thug, a ruffian.

gorgonzola *adj.* [play on CHEESE, THE *n.* (2)] [1940s+] (*Aus.*) very good.

goric *n.* [SE *paregoric elixir*, a camphorated tincture of opium flavoured with aniseed and benzoic acid; opium and heroin addicts use paregoric when stronger drugs are unavailable] [1950s–70s] (*drugs*) opium.

goril *v. see* GORILLA *v.*

gorill *n.* [abbr.] (*US*) **1** [mid-19C] a guerilla. **2** [1930s–40s] a thug [GORILLA *n.*[1] (1)].

gorilla *n.*[1] [the image of the animal as a brutal monster; note the conundrum: Where does a 500-pound gorilla sleep? Anywhere it wants to] **1** [mid-19C+] (*US*) a thug, a ruffian, a violent person. **2** [1950s] a large person, not necessarily a thug. **3** [1960s–70s] a person. **4** [1970s] (*US*) a prostitute's customer who likes to beat up the woman. **5** [1970s] (*US campus*) an unattractive, often overweight, young woman. **6** [1980s+] (*US*) something or someone irresistible or posing difficulty; often modified as *600-pound gorilla, 800-pound gorilla* etc. **7** [1990s+] a monster success, a smash hit. **8** *see* GORILLA PIMP *under* GORILLA *adj.*

IN COMPOUNDS

❑ **gorilla biscuits** *n.* (*also* **gorilla tabs**) [1970s+] (*drugs*) phencyclidine. ❑ **gorilla game** *n.* [1960s] (*US Und.*) the forcing of a woman into prostitution. ❑ **gorilla pills** *n.* [1960s+] (*drugs*) barbiturates.

IN PHRASES

❑ **go gorilla (on)** *v.* [1980s] to attack physically, to beat up.

SE in slang uses

IN COMPOUNDS

❑ **gorilla milk** *n.* [2000s] (*US black*) a black man's semen. ❑ **gorilla salad** *n.* [1970s+] (*US gay*) the pubic hair, esp. if luxuriant.

IN PHRASES

❑ **feed one's gorilla** *v. see* FEED ONE'S HABIT *under* HABIT *n.*

gorilla *n.*[2] [SE *gorilla*, i.e. the size of the primate, a huge MONKEY *n.* (11a)] [1950s+] (*US drugs*) a severe heroin addiction.

gorilla *n.*[3] [i.e. twice the size of a MONKEY *n.* (7)] [1970s] £1000, A$1000.

gorilla *adj.* [GORILLA *n.*[1] (1)] **1** [1920s+] (*US*) aggressive, menacing, thuggish. **2** [1970s+] large, substantial.

IN COMPOUNDS

❑ **gorilla dick** *n.* [DICK *n.*[1] (5)] [2000s] (*US*) a large handgun. ❑ **gorilla pimp** *n.* (*also* **gorilla**) [1960s+] (*US black*) a pimp who controls his prostitutes by threats and actual violence.

gorilla *v.* (*also* **goril, gueril, guerrilla**) [GORILLA *n.*[1] (1)] [1950s+] (*US black/Und.*) to use violence, to intimidate; to rape.

IN PHRASES

❑ **gorilla in the washing-machine** *v.* [1970s] (*US black*) to perform cunnilingus.

gork *n.* [GEEK *n.*[1] (1) + DORK *n.* (2); note hospital jargon *gork*, an imbecile or comatose patient, f. acro. *G*od *o*nly *r*eally *k*nows] [1960s+] (*US campus*) an inadequate, an incompetent.

gorked *adj.* (*also* **gorked-out**) [GORK *n.*] [1970s+] (*US*) mindless, dumb.

gorm *n.*[1] [? GORM *v.*/SE *gourmandize*] [1920s–30s] (*UK tramp*) chewing tobacco.

gorm *n.*[2] *see* GOM *n.*[2].

gorm *v.* [SE *gourmandize*] [late 19C–1920s] (*orig. US*) to eat heartily.

gormagon *n.* [? SE *gorgon* + *dragon*, the nonsense word was supposedly 'Chinese'. 'A monster with six eyes, three mouths, four arms, eight legs, five on one side and three on the other, three arses, two tarses, and a **** [cunt] upon its back' (Grose, 1785). Note mid-18C secret society, the Gormogons, a short-lived imitation of the Freemasons] [18C] a man on horseback with a woman riding side-saddle behind him.

gormed *adj.* [coined by Charles Dickens for Mr Peggotty in *David Copperfield* (1850)] [mid–late 19C] a euph. for GOD-DAMN *adj.*

gormy-ruddles *n.* [SE *gormy ruttles*, 'the strangles', i.e. horses' quinsies or tonsillitis] [19C] the stomach, the intestines.

gornet *n.* [fig. use of SE *gurnard*] [20C+] (*Ulster*) a fool.

go-round *n.* [late 19C+] a fight.

go round *v.* [late 19C] to go out on the town.

IN PHRASES

❑ **go round with** *v.* (*also* **go around with**) **1** [1950s+] to have a relationship with. **2** [1970s] to fight with, physically or verbally.

gorrel *n.* [Afk. *gorrel-(pyp)*, the throat] [1980s+] (*S.Afr.*) the throat.

gorry! *excl.* (*also* **gorree! garra! by kori!**) [mid-19C+] (*orig. US*) a euph. for God and used as such in various mild excls., e.g. *gorry mighty!*

IN EXCLAMATIONS

❑ **by gorry!** (*also* **by gorram!**) [mid-19C+] (*orig. US*) a euph. for *by God!*

Gor Save *n.* [1900s] (*Aus.*) the British National Anthem: 'God save the King/Queen'.

gorse-eater *n.* (*also* **goss-eater**) [2000s] (*N.Z.*) a general derog. term; usu. of a woman.

gorsepocket *n.* [2000s] (*N.Z.*) a miser.

gory *n.*[1] [ety. unknown] [early 19C] a person, a fellow.

gory *n.*[2] *see* GOREE *n.*

gory *adj.* [late 19C–1900s] (*Aus.*) a euph. for BLOODY *adj.*

gos *n. see* GOSS *n.*[1].

gosh *n.* [mid-18C+] a euph. for God; usu. in combs., e.g. *gosh-awful, gosh-darned,* or excls., e.g. *by gosh!my gosh!*

IN COMPOUNDS

❑ **gosh-awful** *adj. see* separate entry. ❑ **gosh-damned** *adj.* (*also* **goshblamed, gosh-damn, gosh-dinged**) [20C+] (*US*) a euph. used in excls. and mild oaths, lit. GOD-DAMNED/-DAMNEDEST *adj.* ❑ **gosh-darned** *adj. see* separate entry.

IN EXCLAMATIONS

❑ **gosh all!** [mid-19C+] (*US*) a euph. for *God almighty!*; usu. in combs, e.g. *gosh all fish-hooks! gosh all hemlock(s)! gosh all Potomac! gosh all Tarnation!* ❑ **gosh-almighty!** [19C+] a euph. excl., lit. *God almighty!* ❑ **gosh-ding!** [20C+] (*US*) a mild oath, euph. for GOD-DAMN! *excl.* ❑ **gosh-darn!** *see* separate entry. ❑ **my gosh!** [1920s+] a general excl., euph. for *my God!*

gosh! *excl.* (*also* **good gosh! great gosh!**) [early 18C+] (*UK/US juv. 20C+*) an extra-mild euph. for *God!*; also as *oh my gosh!*

IN EXCLAMATIONS

❑ **by gosh!** (*also* **begosh!**) [mid-18C+] a mild euph. for *by God!* ❑ **I'll be goshed!** [late 19C] a euph. for *I'll be damned!*

gosh-awful *adj.* [20C+] (*orig. US*) especially appalling; a euph. for GOD-AWFUL *adj.*

DERIVATIVES

❑ **gosh-awfulness** *n.* [1920s+] appallingness.

gosh-darn! *excl.* (*also* **goshdang! gosh-darnit! gosh-dash! gosh-dern! gosh drat! gosh durn!**) [late 19C+] (*US*) a euph. used in excls. and mild oaths, lit. GOD-DAMN! *excl.*; also as v.

gosh-darned *adj.* (*also* **gosh-danged, gosh-darn, gosh-dashed, gosh-derned, gosh-drat**) [mid-19C+] (*US*) a euph. for GOD-DAMN *adj.*

gosher *n.* [? it makes the recipient say GOSH! *excl.*] [late 19C–1910s] a heavy punch.

Go-Shop, the *n.* (*also* **Go, the**) [GO *n.*[1] (1a) + SE *shop*] [late 18C–early 19C] the Queen's Head tavern, Duke's Court, Bow Street, London WC2.

gospel *n.*

SE in slang uses

IN COMPOUNDS

❑ **gospel bird** *n.* (*also* **gospel fowl**) [the practice of rewarding itinerant preachers with a chicken dinner] [1930s–60s] (*US black/tramp*) a chicken. ❑ **gospel-cove** *n.* [COVE *n.* (1)] [1900s–10s] (*Aus.*) a clergyman. ❑ **gospel gab** *n.* [GAB *n.*[2] (1)] [late 19C] supposedly pious, but actually empty, hypocritical talk about religion. ❑ **gospel-grinder** *n.* (*also* **gospel-dealer, -hawk, -huckster, -gent, -peddler, -plugger, -postillion, -shark, -shooter, -slinger, -whanger**) **1** [late 18C+] (*US*) a preacher. **2** [mid-19C–1910s] an evangelistic missionary or tract-distributor, a Sunday School teacher. **3** [20C+] an unctuous, self-satisfied, smug person. **4** [1910s] (*US*) a well-behaved, law abiding person. ❑ **gospel-gun** *n.* [late 19C] (*Aus.*) a preacher. ❑ **gospel mill** *n.* (*also* **gospel shop**) [SE *mill*, a place where a given industry is performed] [late 18C–1910s] (*US*) a chapel, a church. ❑ **gospel-pipe** *n.* [it 'preaches' to the vagina] [1910s–20s] (*US*) the penis.

Gospel Oak *n.* [rhy. sl.] [1990s+] a joke.

goss *n.*[1] (*also* **gos**) [? Virginia dial. *give gorse*, to thrash] [mid-19C–1910s] (*orig. US*) punishment; thus in phrs. below.

IN PHRASES

❑ **get goss** *v.* (*also* **catch goss**) [mid-19C] to receive a beating, punishment. ❑ **give goss** *v.* [mid–late 19C] to beat, to dole out punishment.

goss *n.*[2] (*also* **gozz**) [abbr.] [1980s+] news, information, *gossip*.

goss *v.* (*also* **gozzy**) [? Devon dial. *goss*, to guzzle or drink] [1990s+] (*UK juv.*) to spit.

gossamer *n.* (*also* **goss**) [SE *gossamer hat*, fashionable c.1830 and costing 4s 9p (23½p); such hats were made of *gossamer* silk] [mid-19C–1910s] a hat.

goss-eater *n. see* GORSE-EATER *n.*

gossip *n.*

SE in slang uses

IN PHRASES

❑ **up to the gossip** *adj.* [late 18C–mid-19C] aware of what is going on, shrewd, experienced.

gossled *adj. see* GUZZLED *adj.*

goster *n.* [Irish *gastaire*, a chatterer; note UK-wide dial. *gauster, goster*, to gossip, to talk, to waste time chatting] [20C+] (*Irish*) chat, conversation; also as v., to chat.

gotcha *n.* [SE *got you!*] [1950s+] (*orig. US*) **1** a sudden humiliation, esp. the inadvertent exposure of the buttocks or genitals. **2** in fig. use, something that surprises, esp. with the potential for humiliation.

gotcha! *excl.* (*also* **gotcher!**) [SE *got you!*] **1** [1920s+] I understand! OK! **2** [1930s+] I have got you! [the *locus classicus* was the 1981 *Sun* newspaper headline *Gotcha!* on the drowning of the crew of the Argentine warship *Belgrano*].

IN EXCLAMATIONS

❑ **gotcha back!** [lit. 'I've got your back'] [1990s+] (*US campus*) an expression of support. ❑ **gotcha covered!** [lit. 'I've got you covered'] [1950s+] (*US campus*) an expression of support.

gotch-gutted *adj.* [dial. *gotch*, a pot-bellied jug] [18C–early 19C] pot-bellied.

goth *n.* [SE *Goth*, one who behaves like a barbarian; a rude, uncivilized or ignorant person] [mid-19C] a fool.

go the whole... *v.*

IN PHRASES

❑ **go the whole animal** *v.* (*also* **go the entire animal, ...extreme animal, ...whole quadruped**) [var. on GO THE WHOLE HOG *under* WHOLE HOG *n.*] [mid–late 19C] (*US*) to go on to the end, to do completely and exhaustively. ❑ **go the whole coon** *v.* [SE *racoon*] [late 19C] (*US*) to go on to the end, to do completely and exhaustively. ❑ **go the whole critter** *v.* [var. on GO THE WHOLE HOG *under* WHOLE HOG *n.*] [mid-19C] (*US*) to do thoroughly, to go all the way, to commit oneself unreservedly. ❑ **go the whole figure** *v.* [mid-19C–1910s] (*US*) to risk or do everything possible. ❑ **go the whole hog** *v. see under* WHOLE HOG *n.* ❑ **go the whole way** *v. see* GO ALL THE WAY *under* ALL THE WAY *adv.*

go through *v.* **1** [mid-19C–1900s] (*orig. US*) to search. **2** [mid-19C+] (*US*) to thrash, to beat up; to attack or defeat, both lit. and fig. **3** [mid-19C+] (*US*) to suffer, to be defeated. **4** [mid-19C+] (*US/Aus.*) to rifle through someone's clothes, to rob, after searching the victim's clothes. **5** [late 19C+] (*Aus.*) to rob; lit. and fig. **6** [late 19C+] of a man, to have sexual intercourse; sometimes extended to *go through like a dose/packet of salts*. **7** [1900s] (*US Und.*) to fool, to trick. **8** [1900s] (*US*) to work out, to succeed. **9** [1920s+] (*Aus.*) to give up, to desist. **10** [1940s+] (*orig. milit.*) to desert one's responsibilities, to shirk one's work.

SE in slang uses

IN PHRASES

❑ **go through one for a short cut** *v.* [1980s+] (*Irish*) to criticize severely. ❑ **go through the card** *v.* [orig. betting use, to bet on every horse in a race] [1960s+] to cover comprehensively and completely, e.g. to order extensively from a menu. ❑ **go through the hackles** *v.* [SE *hackle*, a flax-comb, an instrument set with parallel steel pins for splitting and combing out the fibres of flax or hemp] [20C+] (*US*) to suffer, to endure an excess of bad luck. ❑ **go through the ox-house to bed** *v.* [phr. used of an old man with a young wife, *ox* refers to the cuckold's HORNS *n.*] [late 17C–early 19C] of an old man, to marry a young woman (and thus to risk cuckoldry). ❑ **go through the ring** *v.* [one fig. jumps through a *ring* or hoop] [mid-19C] to become bankrupt.

go through on *v.* [1930s+] (*Aus.*) **1** to leave, esp. without giving prior warning. **2** to go absent without leave. **3** to escape from prison or abscond while on bail.

go to grass *v.* [fig. uses of SE *go to grass*, of an animal, to be put to pasture] **1** [19C+] (*US*) (*also* **come to grass**) to be knocked down; to collapse [lit. idea of falling to the grass during open-air prizefights]. **2** [mid-19C] to vanish suddenly, to disappear, to be dismissed. **3** [mid-19C–1900s] of a limb, to waste away. **4** [mid-19C+] (*US*) to die, to be ruined, to retire. **5** [late 19C] to lose (a competition).

go to grass! *excl.* [? a comparison of the subject with a farm animal or with King Nebuchadnezzar, whose madness was denoted by his appetite for grass; Hotten (1859) suggests 'a corruption of "go to GRACE," *grace* being written *gras* in olden times'] [19C+] (*US*) a dismissive excl. either demanding that the subject leaves or suggesting that their statement is nonsense; also as *go to grass and eat hay!*

got out of pawn *adj.* [rhy. sl.] [20C+] born.

gotrocks *n.* (*also* **gotrox**) [SE *got* + ROCKS *n.* (1) + link to the millionaire Rockefeller family] [1930s+] (*US*) a rich person, used as a surname, e.g. *Mr Gotrocks*; thus wealth.

gotta love that *phr.* (*also* **gotta like that**) [1980s+] (*US campus*) an expression of approval of another's good fortune.

gotto *n.* [? SE *got to*, i.e. poverty dictates that one has no choice but to buy such cheap footwear] [1940s] (*W.I.*) a rope-soled shoe.

got your eye full? [1950s+] addressed to someone who is staring, with the undoubted suggestion that they should stop at once; it can be followed with 'Want a picture?'.

gouch (out) *v.* (*also* **gauch, gouge**) [ety. unknown; ? next or link to GOW *n.*[1] (2) or joc. ref. to the clichéd image of a sleeping *gaucho*] [1980s+] to fall asleep or collapse, whether through exhaustion or an excess of drink or drugs; thus n. *gouch/gouch-out*, the state that follows heroin use.

gouchy *adj.* [? Scot. *gowk*, to stare vacantly] [20C+] (*Scot.*) depressed.

gouda, gouda, gouda *n.* [SE *gouda*, a popular Dutch cheese; thus one who is CHEESY *adj.*[2] (1)] [1990s+] (*US campus*) an unappealing, unpopular person.

gouge *n.* [SE *gouge*, to cheat] **1** [mid–late 19C] (*US*) a swindle, a cheat. **2** [1920s] swindling, cheating. **3** *see* GOUGER *n.* (2).

gouge *v.*[1] [backform. f. GOUGER *n.* (2)] [mid-19C+] (*orig. US*) to take something from another person, to cheat someone out of, to insult; thus excl. *gouge!* uttered after a successful insult or theft.

gouge *v.*[2] *see* GOUCH (OUT) *v.*

gouger *n.* (*also* **gauger**) [SE; note SE *gouger*, one who gouges out another's eye in a fight] [19C+] **1** (*Irish*) a thug, a lout. **2** (*also* **gouge**) a swindler, a cheat.

Goughed *adj.* ['J. B. Gough, "the temperance spouter", had recently gone missing; it was found that he had been on a bender' (G. A. Thompson, personal correspondence)] [mid-19C] (*US*) drunk.

gouk *n. see* GOOK *n.*[2] (1).

goul *n.* [Ital. *culo*, the anus] [1960s–70s] (*US*) the anus.

goulash *n.* [? bridge use *goulash*, a re-deal of unshuffled cards after the hands have been thrown in without bidding; thus fig., a mess] **1** [1920s] a fool. **2** [1920s–50s] (*US*) nonsense. **3** [1920s+] (*UK Und.*) prison stew (which is not goulash), also as in any institution.

goulash *adj.* [the 'national dish'] [1910s] (*US*) Hungarian.

go under *v.* (*orig. US*) **1** [19C+] to die. **2** [mid-19C+] to go bankrupt. **3** [late 19C–1900s] in fig. use, to fail or decrease in some way. **4** [1980s+] (*Aus. Und.*) to be imprisoned.

SE in slang uses

IN PHRASES

▫ **go under the house** *v.* [1940s–70s] (*US black/gay*) to perform cunnilingus. ▫ **go under the South Pole** *v.* [the belief that those who went on long sea voyages suffered from fevers + ? the image of the genitals being in the 'southern' part of the body] [late 16C] to suffer from syphilis or venereal disease.

go-up *n.* [1940s–50s] (*US black*) an upstairs flat or apartment (cf. GO-DOWN *n.* (2)).

go up *v.*[1] **1** [early–mid-19C] to be killed or hanged, to die, to be done for; esp. in phr. *to be gone up*. **2** [mid-19C] to be unavailable (through lack of funds). **3** [mid–late 19C] (*US*) to be ruined, to be destroyed, to become bankrupt. **4** [late 19C–1920s] to become explosively angry. **5** [1920s] (*US*) to surrender one's money in a hold-up.

go up *v.*[2] [abbr. GO UP THE RIVER *under* RIVER *n.*] **1** [mid-19C+] (*orig. US*) to go to prison. **2** [1900s–50s] (*Aus.*) to be punished (in a non-custodial manner).

go up *v.*[3] [one gets HIGH *adj.*[1] (2)] [1960s+] (*US drugs*) to become intoxicated by psychotropic drugs.

gourd *n.* [the hollow centre of the plant; note OF *gourd*, a swindle] **1** [mid-16C–18C] (*UK Und.*) a crooked die, which has been hollowed out to affect the throw. **2** [mid-19C; 1960s+] (*esp. drugs*) the head. **3** [1970s] (*US campus*) a stupid, empty-headed person.

IN COMPOUNDS

▫ **gourd-head** *n.* [-HEAD *sfx* (1)] [mid-19C–1970s] (*US*) a blockhead, a fool; as phr. *make gourds*, make a fool of.

IN PHRASES

▫ **blow one's gourd** *v.* (*also* **flip one's gourd, lose...**) [BLOW *v.*[2] (3c)/FLIP *v.*[3] (2)] [1970s+] (*orig. US*) to lose emotional control. ▫ **out of one's gourd** *adj.* (*also* **off one's gourd**) [1960s+] **1** extremely affected by a given drug, usu. cannabis or a hallucinogen. **2** extremely drunk. **3** crazy, insane.

SE in slang uses

IN PHRASES

▫ **gourd of hog's lard** *n. see* TUB OF LARD *under* TUB *n.*[1].

Gourock ham *n.* [*Gourock*, on the Clyde 40km (25 miles) from Glasgow, was once a fishing port] [mid-19C] a salt herring.

gouster *n. see* GOWSTER *n.*[2].

gov *n.* [abbr. SE/GOVERNOR *n.*] **1** [mid-19C+] (*US*) a state governor. **2** [late 19C–1910s] one's father. **3** [1930s+] one's boss. **4** [1940s+] a prison officer. **5** [1990s+] (*US*) the government. **6** *see* GUV *n.* (1).

governess *n.* **1** [late 19C] a prostitute. **2** [1960s+] a dominatrix.

government *n.*

SE in slang uses

IN COMPOUNDS

▫ **government cheese** *n.* [2000s] (*US black*) welfare payments and similar handouts. ▫ **government grapes** *n.* [their being issued on a National Health Service prescription and the similarity of the pills to grapes] [1990s+] temazepam. ▫ **government-inspected meat** *n.* [MEAT *n.* (1)] [1960s+] (*US gay*) a gay man serving in the US armed forces. ▫ **government man** *n.* [19C] a prisoner. ▫ **government name** *n.* [1990s+] (*US black*) one's given name, as used on official papers, as opposed to one's street name. ▫ **government rag** *n.* [mid-19C] (*N.Z.*) a paper currency worth five shillings, issued in 1844 by Governor Fitzroy. ▫ **government securities** *n.* [pun] [mid–late 19C] handcuffs or fetters. ▫ **government signpost** *n.* [it points the way to the next world] [mid-19C] the gallows. ▫ **government stroke** *n.* [the deliberately minimal rate of work put out by convict labourers] [mid-19C+] (*Aus.*) **1** lazy working. **2** relief work, subsidized by the state.

governor *n.* **1** [19C+] an employer, a superior. **2** [early 19C+] a father. **3** [early 19C+] a general term of address to any strange man. **4** [mid-19C; 1950s] (*UK Und.*) a crime boss, usu. of a local area. **5** [1950s+] a publican. **6** [1970s+] an acknowledged expert.

IN COMPOUNDS

▫ **governor's stiff** *n. see under* STIFF *n.*[1].

Governor Green *n.* [1920s] (*US prison*) freedom, the state of having escaped.

govnor *n. see* GUVNOR *n.*

govo *n.* (*also* **gubbo**) [SE *government*, i.e. the adminstrator of the home + -O *sfx* (3)] [1980s] (*Aus.*) a member of a home for disadvantaged or delinquent children.

govy *n.* (*also* **govey**) [abbr.] [1900s] a governess.

gow *n.*[1] (*also* **ghow**) [Chinese *yao-kao*, opium; ult. *yao*, drug + *kao*, an oily, fatty substance, esp. an unguent] (*US drugs*) **1** [1900s] alcohol. **2** [1920s+] opium, heroin or morphine. **3** [1930s–

50s] an opium pipe. **4** [1940s] a pleasurable drug experience.

IN COMPOUNDS

❑ **gowhead** *n.* [-HEAD *sfx* (4)] [1930s–50s] (*US*) a drug addict, usu. of opium. ❑ **gow job** *n.* [? SE *go* or fig. use of sense 2 above + JOB *n.*[2] (2)] [1940s] **1** (*US*) a 'hot rod' car modified for high performance. **2** (*US campus*) a flashily dressed girl or woman. ❑ **gow joint** *n.* [JOINT *n.* (3a)] [1930s] (*US prison*) an opium den; a place where narcotics are sold.

IN PHRASES

❑ **hit the gow** *v.* [1930s+] (*drugs*) to smoke opium.

gow *n.*[2] [abbr. HOOSEGOW *n.*] [1900s–40s] (*US*) a prison.

gow *n.*[3] [? GOO *n.*[1] (1)] [1960s] (*US prison*) sauce.

gow *n.*[4] [backsl. = WOG *n.*[1] (1)] [1970s] (*Aus. teen*) a derog. term for a black or East Asian person.

gow *v.*[1] [GOW *n.*[1] (2)] [1930s] (*US drugs*) to remove opium residue from the pipe.

gow *v.*[2] [GOW *n.*[2] (1)] [1930s] (*US Und.*) to arrest, to imprison.

gowed (up) *adj.* [GOW *n.*[1] (2); note 1910s USN *gowed*, intoxicated by liquor] [1930s+] (*US*) very intoxicated by narcotics.

go with *v.* **1** [mid-19C+] to have an affair or relationship with someone, to have sexual intercourse with. **2** [late 19C+] to go around with, to be friends with. **3** [1960s+] to accept and act upon a plan or suggestion.

IN PHRASES

❑ **go with the flow** *v.* [a mass popularization of the more complex dictum of US psychologist Carl Rogers (1902–87), who saw life as 'floating with a complex streaming of experience'] [1960s+] to accept a situation and make no attempt to alter it, to act passively.

gowk *n.* [GOOK *n.*[2] (2)] [19C–1930s] a tramp.

gowl *n.* [Irish *gabhal*, a fork, a junction] [1990s+] (*Irish*) **1** the vagina. **2** a fool.

gowster *n.*[1] [GOW *n.*[1] (2) + -STER *sfx*] [1930s–60s] (*US drugs*) an opium addict or habitual user of marijuana, heroin etc.

gowster *n.*[2] (*also* **gouster**) [ety. unknown] [1970s] (*US black*) a young man dressed in bell-bottom trousers and a wide-lapelled jacket.

goy *n.* (*also* **goyisher, goyus**) [Heb. *goy*, a nation, thence Yid.; pl. *goyim*] [late 19C+] a gentile, a non-Jew; thus pl. *goyim*.

goy *adj.* (*also* **goyish, goyisher**) [GOY *n.*] [late 19C+] gentile.

goynk *n.* [? JUNK *n.*[1] (7a)] [1940s–50s] (*US drugs*) narcotics, esp. opium.

goyno *n. see* GUINO *n.*

goyus *n. see* GOY *n.*

gozz *n. see* GOSS *n.*[2].

gozzle *n. see* GOOZLE *n.*

gozzle *v.* [GUZZLE *n.* (1)] [1940s–50s] (*US*) to throttle; thus n. *gozzling*.

gozzy *n.* [GOSS *v.*] [1990s+] (*UK juv.*) saliva or phlegm, in the context of spitting.

gozzy *v. see* GOSS *v.*

G.P. *n.* [the sentence is determined at the Governor's Pleasure] [1980s+] (*Aus. prison*) a person serving an indeterminate sentence by reason of insanity, usu. for murder.

g.p. *n.* [abbr.] **1** [1940s+] (*US black*) general principles. **2** [1950s] (*juv.*) grand passion. **3** [1980s] (*US campus*) good plan.

g.q. *adj.* [ref. to *GQ* or *Gentleman's Quarterly* magazine] [1980s+] (*US campus*) fashionably dressed.

graal *n.* (*also* **grawl**) [fig. use of Scot. *grawl*, a young salmon] [19C+] (*Ulster*) a growing boy, a large young lad.

grab *n.*[1] **1** [mid-18C+] an arrest, a theft; thus *put the grab on*, to steal or kidnap. **2** [19C+] a robbery, an act of theft. **3** [early 19C] a thief; a body stealer. **4** [early 19C] (*UK Und.*) booty, the spoils of a robbery. **5** [mid–late 19C; 1950s] a police officer. **6** [1900s] (*US*) a 'go', a 'time'. **7** [1900s–30s] (*US*) a hand, a handful. **8** [1920s] (*US*) profit. **9** [1940s–50s] (*UK prison*) one's pay.

grab *n.*[2]

IN EXCLAMATIONS

❑ **by grab!** (*also* **by grabs!**) [late 19C+] (*US*) a euph. for *by God!*

grab *v.* [fig. uses of SE] **1** [18C+] to steal, to take or obtain for oneself. **2** [mid-18C+] (*also* **grab off**) to arrest. **3** [1900s–60s] (*US*) to grasp, to comprehend. **4** [1910s+] to appeal to; esp. as *HOW DOES THAT GRAB YOU?* below. **5** [1920s+] (*US*) to capture, to kidnap, to abduct (other than in a judicial context). **6** [1920s+] (*US*) to catch some form of transport, usu. a train or taxi. **7** [1960s] (*US*) to irritate. **8** [1970s+] (*US*) to make a turn in a vehicle. **9** [1980s] to have sexual relations.

DERIVATIVES

❑ **grabalicious** *adj.* (*also* **grabilicious**) [1970s–80s] (*UK black*) greedy, grabby.

IN COMPOUNDS

❑ **grab-all** *n.* **1** [late 19C] (*Aus./US*) a greedy person. **2** [late 19C–1930s] a bag to carry odds and ends. ❑ **grab-ass** *n. see* separate entry. ❑ **grabhooks** *n.* [HOOK *n.*[1] (1)] [1910s–40s] (*US*) the hands or fingers. ❑ **grab joint** *n.* [JOINT *n.* (3b)] [1940s+] (*US*) a snack bar, cafeteria.

IN PHRASES

❑ **grab ass** *v. see* separate entry. ❑ **grab a cloud** *v.* [1970s] to raise one's hands. ❑ **grab a handful of** *v.* (*also* **grab an armful, grab an armload of airplane**) [1910s+] **1** (*US tramp*) to steal a ride. **2** (*US*) to take, to steal, to secure for oneself. ❑ **grab a hat** *v. see GET ONE'S HAT under* HAT *n.* ❑ **grab air** *v. see GRAB SKY* below. ❑ **grab a root** *v.* [mid-19C+] (*US*) to hold tight, to get busy, to go ahead. ❑ **grab a stump to rest your rump** *v. see under* STUMP *n.* ❑ **grab-it-and-growl** *n.* (*also* **grab-it-and-gallop**) [the speed of one's eating] [1930s+] (*US*) a diner, a lunch counter. ❑ **grab off** *v. see* sense 2 above. ❑ **grab on** *v.* **1** [mid-19C] to survive, to get along. **2** [1960s] (*US campus*) to make sexual advances towards, to neck. ❑ **grab one's dick** *v. see under* DICK *n.*[1]. ❑ **grab sky** *v.* (*also* **claw sky, grab air, reach for the moon, ...roof, ...sky, ...stars, ...stratosphere**) [20C+] (*US*) to put one's hands in the air. ❑ **how does that grab you?** (*also* **how does that grab your ass?**) [a slightly aggressive implication, a challenge is assumed] [1910s+] what do you think of that?

grab-ass *n.* [SE *grab* + ASS *n.* (2)] [1940s+] (*US*) fighting, fooling around.

IN PHRASES

❑ **play grab-ass** *v.* [1950s+] (*US*) to make physical advances towards someone.

grab-ass *v.* [GRAB-ASS *n.*] [1950s+] to play around, to mess about, esp. in a sexual context; thus *grab-assing*, fooling around.

DERIVATIVES

❑ **grabasstic** *adj.* [2000s] (*US black*) used of one who persistently harasses others, esp. in a sexual manner.

grabber *n.* **1** [mid-19C] in pl., boots. **2** [mid–late 19C] (*UK Und.*) a garrotter. **3** [mid-19C–1940s] (*US Und.*) a thief; thus (*Irish*) a cattle thief. **4** [mid-19C+] a hand, often in pl. **5** [1910s–20s] a pickpocket. **6** [1940s+] (*US*) a selfish or greedy person. **7** [1960s+] (*US*) something that captures people's attention. **8** [1980s] (*Aus.*) in pl., the teeth.

grabble *v.* [*OED* lists it as SE (ult. synon. Du. *grabbelen*), although it cites Grose (1796)] [late 18C–19C] to snatch, to grab, to seize; thus *grabble the bit*, to snatch someone's money.

grabbling irons *n. see* GRAPPLING IRON *n.* (2).

grabby *n.* [? SE *grubby*, or their propensity to *grab*, i.e. loot] [mid-19C–1910s] (*orig. RN*) an infantryman.

grace-card *n.* ['A Kilkenny gentleman, named GRACE, being solicited, with promises of royal favour, to espouse the cause of William III, gave the following answer, written on the back of the six of hearts, to an emissary of Marshal Schomberg's, who had been commissioned to make the proposal to him: — "Tell your master I despise his offer; and that honour and conscience are dearer to a gentleman than all the wealth and titles a prince can bestow."' Hotten 1864, but adds in 1873: 'This would have been a much better story had James II been a better King, and had he not earned for himself, even among Catholic Irishmen, a disgraceful name, through his craven conduct at the Battle of the Boyne'] [mid-19C] **1** (*Irish*) in cards, the six of hearts. **2** the ace of hearts.

Gracemans *n.* [abbr. *Gracechurch* + -MANS *sfx*] [17C] (*UK Und.*) 'Gracious' (Gracechurch) Street market, the corn and hay market of medieval London.

gracie *n.* [GRASS *n.*[4]] [2000s] (*S.Afr. gay*) marijuana.

gracing *n.* (*also* **greycing**) [contraction of SE] [1920s+] greyhound racing.

grad *n.* [abbr.] [late 19C+] (*orig. US*) **1** a *graduate*, lit. or fig.; thus *undergrad*. **2** in non-academic contexts, a person who has 'graduated', e.g. an ex-convict.

grade A *n.* (*also* **grade V**) [the US division of milk into three classes: Grade A for infants and children; Grade B for adults only; Grade C for cooking purposes only] [1930s–50s] (*US*) an order of milk in a snack bar.

grade A *adj.* (*also* **A-grade**) [1920s+] (*orig. US*) excellent, best.

gradoo! *excl.* [according to Eble, *Campus Slang*, 2 Nov. 1973: 'literally bird faeces', although in what language is not stated] [1970s] (*US campus*) an excl. of frustration or disgust.

graduate *n.* **1** [late 19C] an up-market prostitute. **2** [late 19C] a clever, cunning man. **3** [1930s–40s] (*US Und.*) one who has served a sentence.

graduate *v.* **1** [1920s–40s] (*US prison*) to complete one's sentence. **2** [1930s+] to increase, through knowledge and sophistication, one's status within the ranks of one's peers in the streets and the criminal milieu. **3** [1970s+] (*drugs*) to stop using drugs altogether or to progress to stronger drugs.

graf *n.* [abbr.] [1990s+] *graffitti*.

IN COMPOUNDS

❑ **graf-head** *n.* (*also* **graffer**) [-HEAD *sfx* (3)] [1980s+] (*orig. US black*) a graffiti-artist.

graft *n.*[1] [? link to GRAFT *n.*[2] (1) or fig. use of SE *graft*, to insert or fix in or upon something] **1** [mid-19C+] any form of illicit, underhand – but not necessarily criminal – money-making. **2** [mid-19C+] (*UK Und.*) one's criminal speciality. **3** [late 19C–1940s] (*US*) an easy job or sinecure. **4** [late 19C+] corruption. **5** [late 19C+] (*US Und.*) an act of theft. **6** [late 19C+] work, esp. in the context of working to take up or waste time. **7** [20C+] the proceeds of corruption, political bribery etc. **8** [1910s–20s] influence.

graft *n.*[2] [? poss. prev. or ? fig. use of SE *graft*, the depth of earth that may be thrown up at once with a spade (see *OED*, which separates this from prev.)] [mid-19C+] efforts, hard, usu. physical, labouring work.

IN COMPOUNDS

❑ **graft china** *n.* [CHINA (PLATE) *n.* (1)] [1940s–50s] (*UK prison*) a companion with whom one works regularly, as opposed to a SNOUT CHINA *under* SNOUT *n.*[2].

graft *v.*[1] [SE *graft*, to fix onto, in this case the cuckold's HORNS *n.*] [late 16C–18C] **1** to cuckold. **2** to have vaginal or anal intercourse.

graft *v.*[2] [GRAFT *n.*[2] (1)] [mid-19C+] to work hard, to make an effort, to struggle.

graft *v.*[3] [GRAFT *n.*[1]] **1** [mid-19C+] to acquire (money) through trickery, fraud. **2** [mid-19C+] to steal; thus *grafting pal*, one with whom one forms a team of thieves. **3** [20C+] to live as a professional criminal. **4** [20C+] to acquire political gain though bribery or extortion. **5** [20C+] to fool, to hoax. **6** [1910s] to take bribes. **7** [1910s] to live as a parasite. **8** [1930s–50s] (*US*) to bribe. **9** [1950s] in a non-criminal context, to pretend, to fake. **10** [2000s] (*UK drugs*) to sell drugs.

grafted *adj.* [GRAFT *v.*[1] (1) + sfx *-ed*] [late 17C–early 19C] cuckolded.

grafter *n.*[1] [GRAFT *v.*[3]] **1** [mid-19C+] a pickpocket, a thief. **2** [late 19C–1920s] a parasite. **3** [late 19C+] a swindler, esp. one who works at a fair, carnival, mock-auction etc. **4** [20C+] one who is involved in corruption. **5** [1930s+] a street salesman, a hawker. **6** [2000s] (*UK drugs*) a drug dealer's assistant.

grafter *n.*[2] [GRAFT *v.*[2] (1)] [20C+] a hard worker, one who perseveres.

g-rag *n. see* GEE *n.*[7].

graham cracker *n.* [the tan-coloured sweet cracker (biscuit) invented by Sylvester Graham (1795–1851), a promoter of temperance, vegetarianism and whole-wheat flour] [2000s] (*US black*) one who is mixed-race, black and white.

grain *n.* [var. on CORN *n.*[1] (1)] [2000s] (*US teen*) money.

grammel *v.* [? SE *grope* + *fumble*] [20C+] (*Irish*) to grope for, to fumble at.

granary *n.* [mid-19C] the stomach.

grand *n.*[1] (*also* **gran, grands**) [1910s+] (*orig. US*) 1000, usu. dollars or pounds, thus half-(a-)grand, $500.

grand *n.*[2] *see* GRANDSTAND PLAY *under* GRANDSTAND *v.*

grand *adj.*

IN COMPOUNDS

❑ **grand bag** *n.* [BAG *n.*[1] (1a)] [1940s–70s] (*gay*) a large scrotum. ❑ **grand charge** *see* separate entries. ❑ **grand-daddy** *n. see* separate entry. ❑ **grand duchess** *n.* [on the model of QUEEN *n.* (2a)] [1950s+] (*gay*) **1** a heterosexual woman who occupies pride of place in a homosexual male coterie. **2** an experienced, older, sophisticated homosexual man. ❑ **grandfather/grandmother** *n. see* separate entry. ❑ **grand quay** *n.* [? SE *dock*] [mid-19C–1910s] (*US Und.*) a state prison. ❑ **grand slam** *n.* [ironic use of colloq. *grand slam*, an absolute and overwhelming success + SE *slam*, i.e. the violence of the act] [2000s] simultaneous vomiting and defecation. ❑ **grandstand** *v. see* separate entry. ❑ **grand strut** *n.* [mid-19C] used of various fashionable promenading areas of London, e.g. Rotten Row or the Broad Walk in Hyde Park, or Bond Street, W1. ❑ **grand theft** *v.* [US legal jargon *grand theft*, synon. for *grand larceny*, the theft of sums exceeding a figure established by local penal codes] [1960s] (*US black*) a large amount of (stolen) money. ❑ **grand tobyman** *v.* [*TOBY-GLOAK under* TOBY *n.*[2]] [mid-19C] a highwayman.

grand *v. see* GRANDSTAND *v.*

Grand Canyon *n.* (*also* **Lincoln Tunnel**) [1970s+] (*US gay*) a loose anus; thus *Grand Canyon Suite*, noisy, sloppy-sounding anal intercourse.

Grand Central Station *n.* [pun on the numerous SE *tracks*/ TRACKS *n.* (1)] [1960s+] (*US gay*) the scarred arm of a long-term heroin user.

grand charge *n.* [Fr. *grand*, great, big + *charge*, exaggeration] [20C+] (*W.I.*) an empty bluff, loud but hollow boasting.

grand charge *v.* (*also* **make grand charge**) [GRAND CHARGE *n.*] [20C+] (*W.I./UK black*) to present a false but self-aggrandizing image.

grand-daddy *n.* [superior to the DADDY *n.* (6)] [20C+] the extreme example, the most outstanding (of a kind).

grandfather *n.* [rhy. sl.; *grandfather clock* = COCK *n.*[3] (1)] [1950s+] the penis.

grandfather/grandmother *n.* [late 19C+] a general intensifier, added to a n.; thus a *grandmother of a...*

grandma *n.* [the image of a slow-driving grandmother] **1** [1940s+] (*US*) the lowest gear of a vehicle. **2** [1970s+] (*US gay*) an old(er) homosexual; thus *grandpa*, an ageing lesbian.

IN COMPOUNDS

❑ **grandma change** *n.* [1930s–40s] (*US black*) a very rich person.

grandma (George) *n.* (*also* **George**) [euph.] [1950s+] (*US*) menstruation; thus *grandma's coming*.

grandmother *n.* **1** [1960s] the vagina. **2** *see* GRANDFATHER/ GRANDMOTHER *n.*

SE in slang uses

IN PHRASES

❑ **do I know my grandmother?** *see* DOES A BEAR SHIT IN THE WOODS? IS THE POPE A CATHOLIC? *phr.*

IN EXCLAMATIONS

□ **my grandmother!** *see* MY GRANNY! *under* GRANNY *n.*[1]. □ **your grandmother!** *see* YOUR GRANNY! *under* GRANNY *n.*[1].

grands *n. see* GRAND *n.*[1].

grandstand *v.* (*also* **grand**) [sporting imagery, the performance is in front of the grandstand] [20C+] to make oneself conspicuous, to show off.

IN PHRASES

□ **grandstand artist** *n.* (*also* **grandstander, grandstand-jockey, -player**) [-ARTIST *sfx*/JOCKEY *n.*[2] (3b)/SE *player*] [1920s+] (*US*) an exhibitionist, a show-off. □ **grandstand play** *n.* (*also* **grand, grandstand, grandstand eye**) [late 19C+] (*US*) a conspicuous, often ostentatious, action.

granger *n.* [SAmE *Granger*, a member of the Patrons of Husbandry (a farmers' organization)] [late 19C–1930s] (*US*) a farmer or countryman.

graniers *n. see* GRAVIERS *n.*

granite boulder *n.* [rhy. sl.] [late 19C+] a shoulder.

granite-boy *n.* [mid-19C+] a native of New Hampshire, known for its granite quarries.

granite jug *n.* [SE *granite* + JUG *n.*[1] (2a)] [1930s–50s] Dartmoor Prison, west Devon.

granite-rocked *adj.* [pun on STONE BROKE *adj.*] [late 19C] totally penniless.

grannam *n.*[1] (*also* **granmer**) [SE *grain/grannary*] [mid-16C–early 19C] corn.

grannam *n.*[2] (*also* **grannum**) [SE *grand-dam*] [17C–mid-19C] grandmother; thus a term of address to an old woman.

IN COMPOUNDS

□ **grannam-gold** *n.* (*also* **grannam's gold**) [late 17C–mid-19C] old, hoarded coin.

Granny *n.* [? its style and attitudes] [late 19C+] (*Aus.*) the *Sydney Morning Herald*.

granny *n.*[1] (*also* **grannie**) [stereotypes of SE *granny/grandmother*] **1** [late 18C–mid-19C; 1950s+] an old woman. **2** [mid-19C–1900s] (*Aus.*) nonsense, rubbish, 'old wives' tales'; usu. in *MY GRANNY!* below. **3** [mid-19C+] (*orig. naut.*) a badly tied knot which will not hold. **4** [20C+] a fussy person, not necessarily old or female. **5** [1940s–50s] (*UK Und.*) a legitimate business that serves only as a front for criminal activities. **6** [1960s+] (*US*) menstruation; thus (*Aus./US*) *granny's coming*, a woman is menstruating. **7** [1970s+] (*US*) the lowest (thus slowest) gear of a vehicle.

IN COMPOUNDS

□ **granny rag** *n.* [20C+] (*US*) homemade sanitary towels, made of pieces of cloth.

IN PHRASES

□ **in your granny's** [20C+] (*Irish*) a state of absolute comfort, both physical and psychological. □ **she'll be grannies** [*Granny Smith*, a brand of apple; originated in Aus. and named for Maria Ann 'Granny' Smith (d.1870); thus synon. *she'll be* APPLES *adj.* (1)] [1960s] (*Aus.*) everything will be all right.

SE in slang uses

IN COMPOUNDS

□ **granny chills** *n. see* GRANNY GRUNT *n.*[2]. □ **granny-dodger/-dodging** *see* separate entries. □ **granny grunt** *n. see* separate entries. □ **granny-jazzer/-jazzing** *see* separate entries. □ **granny lane** *n.* [the stereotyped cautious driving of old women] [1970s+] (*US*) the right-hand lane of a highway, the slow lane.

IN EXCLAMATIONS

□ **granny farts!** [2000s] (*W.I.*) an excl. of annoyance. □ **my granny!** (*also* **be grannied! my grandmother! my granny and me! my granny's knickers! (on) your granny!**) **1** [late 18C+] rubbish! nonsense! **2** [mid-19C] (*also* **by granny!**) an excl. of astonishment. □ **your granny!** (*also* **your grandmother!**) [early 19C+] (*US*) a general response of incredulity, disbelief, 'you must be joking!'.

granny *n.*[2] (*also* **grannie**) [ety. unknown] [mid-19C] (*US*) a dollar.

granny *n.*[3] [? the supposed experience of a grandmother, or phr. *teach your grandmother to suck eggs*] **1** [mid-19C] knowledge, importance, pride; thus *take the granny off*, to humiliate, to 'bring down a peg', thus to make dirty. **2** [late 19C] a knowledgeable person.

granny *n.*[4] [2000s] (*UK Und.*) the essence, the 'guts'; as in phr. *bash the granny out of*.

granny *v.*[1] [the wolf's disguise in the story of 'Little Red Riding Hood'] **1** [mid-19C] to swindle, to cheat. **2** [20C+] to defeat comprehensively, to allow one's opponent no score at all. **3** [1910s–20s] to disguise oneself.

granny *v.*[2] [mid-19C] **1** to recognize; to understand. **2** (*UK Und.*) to survey, to look over (prior to a robbery).

granny-dodger *n.* [on pattern of MAMMY-DODGER *n.*] [1970s] **1** (*US black*) a contemptible person [euph. for FUCKER *n.* (3)]. **2** (*US prison*) a rapist of elderly women [euph. for FUCKER *n.* (1)].

granny-dodging *adj.* [GRANNY-DODGER *n.* (1)] [1960s–70s] contemptible.

granny grunt *n.*[1] [rhy. sl. = CUNT *n.* (4)] [20C+] a fussy, irritating person, although not necessarily female or old.

granny grunt *n.*[2] (*also* **granny chills**) [20C+] (*US*) a stomach ache, menstruation.

granny grunt *n.*[3] [1930s–40s] (*US black*) a mythical figure to whom otherwise unanswerable questions are referred.

granny-jazzer *n.* [JAZZ v. (1)] [1970s–80s] (*US*) a euph. synon. for MOTHERFUCKER *n.*

granny-jazzing *adj.* [GRANNY-JAZZER *n.*] [1960s] (*US*) a synon. for MOTHERFUCKING *adj.*

granny's wrinkle *n.* [rhy. sl.] [20C+] a winkle (a form of crustacea).

granola(-groid) *n.* [the supposedly healthy US cereal *Crunchy Granola*] [1980s+] (*US campus*) (*also* **granola-breath, -head**) a natural-looking person who pursues a healthy lifestyle; an environmentalist; used derog. to indicate one who pursues a 'Sixties' lifestyle.

IN COMPOUNDS

□ **granola dyke** *n.* (*also* **earthy-crunchy dyke**) [DYKE *n.*] [1990s+] (*US gay*) a lesbian who pursues a 'Sixties' lifestyle.

grape *n.*[1] **1** [late 16C+] (*also* **grapes, the grape**) wine. **2** [late 19C+] any form of liquor. **3** [1950s–70s] (*Aus./US black*) in pl., haemorrhoids. **4** [1970s+] (*US prison*) an alcoholic. **5** [1980s] in pl., the female breasts. **6** [1990s+] in pl., the testicles. **7** see GRAPEVINE *n.*[1].

IN COMPOUNDS

□ **grape-cat** *n.* [CAT *n.*[5] (2b)/CHICK *n.*[1] (2)] [1940s] (*US black*) an alcoholic who prefers wine to other drinks; thus the female version, *grape-chick*. □ **grapeshot** *adj.* [play on SE and sense 1 above + pattern of *CUPSHOT under* CUP *n.*] [19C] drunk.

IN PHRASES

□ **grapes of wrath** *n.* [sense 1 above + pun on the biblical use + the then-recent publication of John Steinbeck's novel *The Grapes of Wrath* (1939)] [1940s] (*US black*) wine.

SE in slang uses

IN COMPOUNDS

□ **grape-juice** *n.* (*also* **juice of the grape**) [early 18C+] wine. □ **grape-nut** *n.* [the healthiness of the breakfast cereal, *Grape-Nuts*] [1980s+] (*US campus*) one who identifies with the styles and concerns of the Sixties. □ **grape parfait** *n.* [when packaged in purple pills] [1970s+] (*drugs*) LSD. □ **grape-stomper** *n.* (*also* **grape-squasher**) [the viticulture practised in these countries] [1940s+] any person of Mediterranean origin, e.g. Italian, French, Spanish, Portuguese, Greek. □ **grapevine** *n. see* separate entry.

IN PHRASES

□ **grape on the business** *n.* [? SE phr. *sour grapes*] [1940s+] (*Aus.*) **1** a puritan. **2** a bore, one who depresses or irritates the company by their presence. □ **grape up** *v.* [1960s] (*US*) to be sycophantic. □ **have a grape on** *v.* (*also* **be a grape on**) [? SE *sour grapes*] [1920s+] (*Aus.*) to feel hostile towards someone or something.

(IN EXCLAMATIONS)

❑ **go peel a grape!** *see* GO PEDDLE YOUR FISH! *under* PEDDLE *v.*

grape *n.*[2] [abbr.] [2000s] (*N.Z.*) gang *rape*.

grape *n.*[3] *see* GRAPEVINE *n.*[1].

grape, the *n. see* GRAPE *n.*[1] (1).

grapefruit *n.* [resemblance] [1960s–80s] usu. in pl., the female breasts.

grapes *n.*[1] [the 'richness' of wine] [1960s–70s] (*US black*) money.

grapes *n.*[2] [they grow on the GRAPEVINE *n.*[1]] [2000s] (*US prison*) gossip.

grapes *n.*[3] *see* GRAPE *n.*[1] (1).

grapes *adj.* [1930s] (*US*) fine, good.

grapevine *n.*[1] (*also* **grape**) [mid-19C+] a network of unofficial sources, rumours, half-truths etc, which seems to spread the news around a circle or group faster than any sanctioned announcement; coined during US Civil War, and abbr. 'a despatch by grape-vine telegraph'.

(IN COMPOUNDS)

❑ **grapevine cinch** *n.* [CINCH *n.*[1] (2)] [late 19C] (*US*) a certainty. ❑ **grapevine telegraph** *n.* [var. on BUSH TELEGRAPH *n.*] [mid-19C–1970s] (*US*) a network of unofficial but often highly efficient communications. ❑ **grapevine wireless** *n.* [1930s] (*US*) a network of unofficial but often highly efficient communications.

grapevine *n.*[2] [rhy. sl.] [20C+] a washing-line.

grapey *adj.* [? through an excess of the GRAPE *n.*[1] (1)] [mid-19C] (*US*) grumpy.

grapp *n.* [? GRAB *n.*[1] (7)] [mid-19C] (*UK Und.*) a full pocket; a full purse.

grapple *n.* [SE *grapple*] [mid–late 19C] the hand; often in pl.

grappler *n.* (*also* **mug-grappler**) [SE *grapple*] **1** [mid-19C] a hand; thus *grapplers*, fingers. **2** [1960s] a wrestler.

grapple the rails *n.* [the effects of the alcohol mean one has to hang on to keep upright] [18C–early 19C] (*Irish*) a glass of rough whisky.

grappling hook *n.* [late 19C+] (*US*) usu. in pl., fingers or hands.

grappling iron *n.* [note WW1 Aus. milit. *grappling irons*, spurs] **1** [early–mid-19C] in pl., handcuffs. **2** [mid-19C–1910s] (*also* **grabbling irons**) in pl., the fingers. **3** [late 19C] (*US*) in pl., spurs.

grap up *v.* [pron. of GRAF *n.*] [2000s] to spray graffitti.

grass *n.*[1] **1** [early 18C; mid-19C+] pubic hair. **2** [1910s–50s] hair; thus *cut the grass*, to cut the hair.

SE in slang uses

(DERIVATIVES)

❑ **grassville** *n. see* separate entry.

(IN COMPOUNDS)

❑ **grass-eater** *n.* [1970s+] (*US*) a police officer who accepts small bribes; thus *grass-eating*. ❑ **grass-fighter** *n.* [fighting on the grass rather than on canvas; note John Healy book title *The Grass Arena* (1988)] [1950s+] (*Aus.*) **1** a bare-knuckle boxer; thus *grass-fighting*, bare-knuckle boxing. **2** one who fights in public rather than in the prize-ring. **3** anyone known for losing their temper and brawling in public. ❑ **grasshopper** *n. see* separate entry. ❑ **grass sandwich** *n.* [1910s–50s] (*US*) an alfresco act of sexual intercourse. ❑ **grass seed** *n. see* HAYSEED *n.*

(IN PHRASES)

❑ **grass before breakfast** *n.* [? *grace before breakfast* or GO TO GRASS *v.* (1)] [mid-18C–mid-19C] (*Irish*) a duel. ❑ **go to grass** *v. see* separate entries. ❑ **go to the grass** *v.* [i.e. the countryside] [1900s] (*N.Z.*) to run off, to abscond. ❑ **in the grass** [1940s+] lying low, esp. of someone one hasn't seen for some time; thus *wait for someone in the long grass*, to lie low, to maintain a 'low profile'. ❑ **on the grass** [late 19C–1950s] (*Aus. Und.*) free (of prison). ❑ **put out to grass** *v.* [animal imagery] **1** [late 16C–early 17C] to send out to work as a prostitute. **2** [1940s+] (*also* **put out to pasture**) to send into retirement. ❑ **send to grass** *v. see* GRASS *v.*[1] (1).

grass *n.*[2] [asparagus use SE in 18C] [mid-19C+] green vegetables, esp. asparagus.

grass *n.*[3] [rhy. sl.; *grasshopper* = SHOPPER *n.*] [1920s+] an informer.

(IN PHRASES)

❑ **come grass** *v.* [1930s+] to turn informer.

grass *n.*[4] [note WW1 Aus. milit. *grass*, Army issue tobacco] [1930s+] marijuana.

(IN COMPOUNDS)

❑ **grass-head** *n.* [-HEAD *sfx* (4)] [1960s+] (*drugs*) a regular smoker of marijuana. ❑ **grasshopper** *n. see* separate entry.

grass *v.*[1] [i.e. to knock onto the *grass*] **1** [19C] (*also* **send to grass**) to knock down [outdoor prize-fights were held on the grass]. **2** [mid-19C–1900s] to kill, to defeat. **3** [1940s+] (*US black*) to have sexual intercourse outdoors, esp. lit. on the grass.

grass *v.*[2] (*also* **grass someone off, grass someone up**) [GRASS *n.*[3]] [1930s+] to inform, to tell tales, to betray.

grasser *n.* [GRASS *v.*[2]] [1940s+] an informer.

grasshopper *n.*[1] **1** [mid-19C–1910s] a waiter at a tea-garden [he 'hops across the grass']. **2** [late 19C] a thief [? he 'hops' from theft to theft]. **3** [20C+] (*Aus.*) a waiter at a picnic [he 'hops across the grass']. **4** [1950s+] (*Aus.*) a tourist, esp. one who is visiting Canberra [they descend on a town or tourist site like a plague of hungry insects].

SE in slang uses

(IN COMPOUNDS)

❑ **grasshopper-crusher** *n. see* BEETLE-CRUSHER *under* BEETLE *n.*[1].

grasshopper *n.*[2] [rhy. sl.] **1** [1920s+] a police officer [= COPPER *n.* (3); note WW1 milit. *grasshopper*, a military policeman]. **2** [1940s+] an informer [= SHOPPER *n.*].

grasshopper *n.*[3] [GRASS *n.*[4] + pun] [1930s+] a marijuana user.

grasshopping *adj.* [GRASSHOPPER *n.*[2] (2)] [1940s–50s] tale-telling, informing; thus v. *grasshopper*, to inform on.

grass in the park *n.* [ext. of GRASS *n.*[3] + rhy. sl. = NARK *n.* (1)] [1990s+] an informer.

grass someone off/up *v. see* GRASS *v.*[2].

grassville *n.* [var. on DAISYVILLE *n.*] [early 19C] the countryside.

grassy *adj.* [GRASS *n.*[3]] [1950s] (*US Und.*) likely to become an informer.

gratters *n.* [abbr. SE + -ER *sfx*] [1900s–60s] (*UK school/ university*) congratulations.

gravalicious *adj.* [SE *greedy* + *avaricious*] [1930s+] (*W.I.*) covetous.

grave-bait *n.* [pun on JAILBAIT *n.* (2) although this woman is likely to get one killed, rather than sent to jail] [1940s] a young woman, flirtatious and sexy, but linked to a powerful and dangerous man.

grave-digger *n.*[1] [alcohol often proved fatal to white men in India] [late 19C] (*Anglo-Ind.*) strong drink.

grave-digger *n.*[2] [rhy. sl. = NIGGER *n.*[1] (1) + ref. to SPADE *n.*] [20C+] a black person.

gravel *n.* [consistency] **1** [1900s–30s] (*US*) granulated sugar. **2** [1980s+] (*drugs*) crack cocaine [play on ROCK *n.* (4d)]. **3** [1990s+] (*S.Afr.*) marijuana.

SE in slang uses

(IN COMPOUNDS)

❑ **gravel-agitator** *n.* [his marching and drilling] [late 19C+] (*US*) an infantryman. ❑ **gravel-crusher** *n.* **1** [mid-19C+] (*also* **gravel-cruncher, mud-crusher**) an infantryman; thus *gravel-crushing*, marching. **2** [late 19C+] (*Anglo-Irish*) a tramp. **3** [20C+] (*Anglo-Irish*) a heavy boot, typically worn by a farmer or agricultural worker. ❑ **gravel-digger** *n.* [mid-19C] an agile dancer. ❑ **gravel-grinder** *n.* **1** [mid-19C] a drunkard, esp. one who has a drunken fall and scratches their face. **2** [late 19C+] (*US*) an infantryman. ❑ **gravel path** *n.* [the SE *gravel path* is raked, the hair is combed; both for neatness] [1900s] (*Aus.*) the human hair. ▫ **gravel rash** *n.* [mid-19C–1940s] abrasions caused by a fall on a gravelly or uneven surface, esp. in the context of drunkenness. ▫ **gravel tax** *n.* [mid-19C] (*UK Und.*) the proceeds of street robbery. ▫ **gravel-train** *n.* **1** [1910s–30s] (*US Und.*) a go-between of lobbyists who buy up legislators. **2** [1910s–30s] (*US*) a sugar bowl [sense 1 above]. ▫ **gravel-walloper** *n.* [1900s] (*US*) an infantryman.

IN PHRASES

▫ **get gravel for one's goose** *v.* [1930s+] (*US*) to have sexual intercourse. ▫ **hit the gravel** *v. see* HIT THE GRIT *under* GRIT *n.*[2].

gravelled *adj.* [lit. falling on the *gravel*] [20C+] drunk.

Gravesend sweetmeat *n.* [*Gravesend*, a town on the Thames estuary] [mid–late 19C] a shrimp.

Gravesend twins *n.* [the sewerage outfall at *Gravesend*] [mid-19C] solid pieces of excrement.

grave-sheet *n. see under* SHEET *n.*

graveyard *n.* [the supposed resemblance of the teeth to tombstones] **1** [19C–1930s] the mouth. **2** [20C+] (*US*) prominent front teeth. **3** [20C+] (*US*) false teeth. **4** *see* GRAVEYARD SHIFT *n.*

SE in slang uses

IN COMPOUNDS

▫ **graveyard juice** *n.* [the fatal effects of excessive drinking] [1940s–50s] (*US*) whisky. ▫ **graveyard shift** *n. see* separate entry. ▫ **graveyard stew** *n.* (*also* **graveyard poultice, ...soup**) [such toast is generally given to the ill; thus the idea that once his or her appetite has been reduced to such a meal the sufferer has nowhere to go but the graveyard] [late 19C–1940s] (*US*) milk toast.

graveyarder *n. see* CHURCHYARD COUGH *under* CHURCHYARD *n.*

graveyard shift *n.* (*also* **graveyard, graveyard trick, ...watch**) [usu. in the context of paid employment, but also used of gamblers, prostitutes and any other late-night 'workers'] [20C+] the overnight shift, the late shift; the personnel who work that shift.

graviers *n.* (*also* **graniers**) [perhaps f. Fr. *grave*, heavy, given that the weight of crooked dice was generally affected in one way or another; however, the *OED* suggests poss. alternative sp., notably *graniers* (cited in Thomas Dekker, *The Bellman of London*, 1608), which offers no obvious origin] [mid-16C–early 17C] (*UK Und.*) crooked dice.

gravney *n.* [ety. unknown] [mid–late 19C] a ring.

gravy *n.* **1** as a bodily fluid. (**a**) [late 17C–early 18C; 1920s+] vaginal secretions; thus *gravy bowl*, the vagina. (**b**) [18C+] semen; thus *gravy-receiver*, the vagina. (**c**) [mid-19C+] blood. (**d**) [1960s+] (*drugs*) the mix of blood and heroin solution that is created in a hypodermic syringe before it is reinjected into the vein; it can coagulate while in the syringe and, when this happens, must be heated before the injection. (**e**) [1970s] sweat. **2** in fig. use, i.e. as a bonus, something extra. (**a**) [late 19C+] money, esp. profit when easily acquired, a tip or bonus, something that comes 'on top of' something that is already very good. (**b**) [1910s+] (*orig. US*) extras, perquisites, the best; money paid as bribes. (**c**) [1910s+] good fortune. (**d**) [1930s+] (*US*) emotional stimulation. **3** [1940s+] (*Aus.*) any form of tinned food.

IN COMPOUNDS

▫ **gravy boat** *n.* [var. on GRAVY TRAIN *n.*] **1** [1940s+] (*US*) a sinecure, a simple, substantially profitable situation from which one can benefit easily. **2** [1960s] a wealthy person. ▫ **gravy case** *n.* [var. on GRAVY TRAIN *n.*] [1940s+] (*US*) a sinecure, a simple, substantially profitable situation from which one can benefit easily. ▫ **gravy-giver** *n.* (*also* **gravy-maker**) [19C] **1** the vagina. **2** the penis. ▫ **gravy rider** *n.* [1920s–50s] (*US*) a person with an easy job. ▫ **gravy street** *n.* [1970s] (*US*) an easy, profitable or successful situation. ▫ **gravy strokes** *n. see* VINEGAR STROKES *under* VINEGAR *n.* ▫ **gravy train** *n. see* separate entry.

IN PHRASES

▫ **bring home the gravy** *v. see* BRING HOME THE BACON *under* BACON *n.*[1]. ▫ **dish out the gravy** *v. see under* DISH OUT *v.* ▫ **go down for the gravy** *v.* [1950s+] to perform oral sex. ▫ **give one's gravy** *v.* [19C] **1** of a man, to reach orgasm. **2** of a man, to bring a partner to orgasm (presumably simultaneous with his own ejaculation). **3** to hit, to beat. ▫ **in the gravy** *adj.* [1940s+] rich, prospering. ▫ **ride the gravy boat** *v. see* RIDE THE GRAVY TRAIN *under* GRAVY TRAIN *n.* ▫ **shoot gravy** *v.* [1960s+] (*drugs*) of a narcotics addict, to reinject the blood that has been drawn into the syringe and there mixed with the heroin solution. ▫ **swap gravy** *v. see under* SWAP *v.*

SE in slang uses

IN COMPOUNDS

▫ **gravy-eyed** *adj.* [late 18C–19C] bleary-eyed, having mucus-filled eyes. ▫ **gravy noodles** *adj. see* GRAVY *adj.* ▫ **gravy ring** *n.* [resemblance to a ring of gravy staining a cloth] [20C+] (*Ulster*) a doughnut.

IN PHRASES

▫ **good as gravy** *adj.* [1950s] very good. ▫ **have gravy on one's grits** *v.* [the image of a brimming plate] [1930s+] (*US black*) to be enjoying a materially successful life.

IN EXCLAMATIONS

▫ **by gravy!** (*also* **good gravy!**) [euph. for 'by God!'] [mid-19C+] (*US*) a mild oath.

gravy *adj.* (*also* **gravy noodles**) [1930s+] a general term of approbation, easy, privileged, wonderful, perfect.

gravy train *n.* [GRAVY *n.* (1) + SE *train*; Dillard, *Lexicon of Black English* (1977), suggests the image of a gambler who is in the 'gravy' and thus pursued by a 'train' of those who wish to benefit] [late 19C+] (*orig. US*) a sinecure, a simple, substantially profitable situation from which one can benefit easily; thus phr. below.

IN PHRASES

▫ **ride the gravy train** *v.* (*also* **ride the gravy boat**) [20C+] (*US*) to enjoy a comfortable life.

grawl *n. see* GRAAL *n.*

grawler *n.* [early 19C] a beggar.

IN PHRASES

▫ **sweeten a grawler** *v. see under* SWEETEN *v.*

gray/grey *see also under* GREY; the spelling of gray/grey remains debatable; according to the *OED* there have been various choices over the years, but there seems to have been little real consistency. For the purposes of this dict., and based as far as possible on the pre-eminent style of the respective countries, 'gray' will be used for US terms and 'grey' for UK/Aus. and other 'Commonwealth' uses.

gray *n.* (*also* **grey**) **1** [1940s+] (*US black*) a white person. **2** [1980s] (*US campus*) a black person who behaves like and associates with white people. **3** *see* GREY *n.* (1).

gray *adj.* (*also* **graymeat, grey**) [skin colour, but also f. what blacks perceive as the 'colourless' behaviour and character of whites, esp. the middle-classes] [1940s+] (*orig. US black*) used of a white person, esp. when racist; usu. in combs., e.g. *gray cat*, a white man; *gray broad*, a white woman; also extended to a Latino or Chicano by 1980s.

IN COMPOUNDS

▫ **gray boy** *n.* (*also* **grey boy**) [SE *boy* + conscious counter to the racists' 'black boy'] [1950s+] (*US black*) a derog. term for a white person. ▫ **gray dog** *n.* [DOG *n.*[2] (6a)] [1970s+] (*US black*) the police. ▫ **gray gal** *n.* (*also* **grey gal, gray chick, grey chick**) [GAL *n.* (1)/CHICK *n.*[1] (2)] [1950s+] (*US black*) a white woman. ▫ **gray-suit** *n. see* SUIT *n.*[1] (3). ▫ **grey nayga** *n.* [NAYGAH *n.*/SE *owl*] [1960s] (*W.I.*) an albino. ▫ **grey puss** *n.* [PUSS *n.*[3]] [1950s+] (*W.I.*) an albino. ▫ **grey-white nigger** *n.* [NIGGER *n.*[1] (1)] [1950s] (*W.I.*) a mulatto.

SE in slang uses

IN COMPOUNDS

▫ **grayback** *n. see* separate entry. ▫ **graybar hotel** *n.* (*also* **greybar hotel**) [its *grey* walls and steel *bars*] [1940s+] (*US*) prison. ▫ **gray coat** *n. see* GRAYBACK *n.* ▫ **Gray Goose** *n. see* separate entry. ▫ **grayhair** *n.* [1980s+] (*US campus*) an old person. ❑ **gray mule** *n. see under* MULE *n.* ❑ **gray one** *n.* see GRAYBACK *n.* ❑ **graystone college** *n.* (*also* **gray house, graystone hotel, gray-rock hotel, greystone college**) [1930s–60s] (*US Und.*) prison.

grayback *n.* (*also* **graycoat, gray one**) [colour of the uniform or, for lice, the body] (*US*) **1** [early 19C] a professed Christian. **2** [mid-19C] an unreliable or worthless person (fig. use of *grayback*, a treasury note issued by the Confederate government). **3** [mid–late 19C] a Confederate soldier in the US Civil War. **4** [mid-19C+] (*also* **greyback**) a head or body louse.

Gray Goose *n.* [1970s+] (*US Und.*) a converted Greyhound bus, painted grey, that is used for transporting prisoners securely between jails, courts etc.

graymeat *n. see* GRAY *adj.*

graze *n.* [1960s+] (*S.Afr.*) food.

graze *v.* **1** [mid-18C; 1950s] (*US prison*) to eat prison food. **2** [1960s+] to eat.

grazer *n.* [GRAZE *v.* (2)] [1990s+] **1** a person who snacks. **2** (*UK Und.*) a tramp who rifles through rubbish bins for food.

greapha *n. see* GREEFO *n.*

grease *n.*[1] **1** in fig. uses. (**a**) [19C+] money, esp. when given as a bribe or paid as protection money [GREASE *v.*[1] (1)]. (**b**) [mid-19C+] flattery, persuasion. (**c**) [1940s+] (*US*) political influence. **2** in lit. uses. (**a**) [mid-19C+] (*orig. US campus*) (*also* **grease pot**) butter or margarine. (**b**) [1910s–50s] (*US drugs*) opium [the viscosity of the drug]. (**c**) [1920s+] (*US black*) vaginal secretions. (**d**) [1920s+] (*US Und.*) nitroglycerine. (**e**) [1950s+] (*US black/campus*) a meal, food. (**f**) [1960s+] (*gay*) any form of lubricant – KY Jelly etc – that facilitates anal intercourse.

IN COMPOUNDS

❑ **grease-hand** *n.* (*also* **grease-palm**) [1970s] (*W.I.*) a bribe. ❑ **grease job** *n.* [JOB *n.*[2] (2)] **1** [1940s] (*US*) a bribe. **2** [1940s–50s] (*US*) insincere flattery. **3** [1950s+] anal intercourse using Vaseline, KY Jelly or a similar lubricant. ❑ **grease-man** *n.* [1970s] (*US Und.*) a safe-blower, who uses nitroglycerine. ❑ **grease pit** *n.* **1** [1950s–70s] (*US drugs*) anywhere a drug seller sets up their business. **2** *see also* SE compounds below. ❑ **greasepot** *n.* **1** see sense 2a above. **2** *see also* SE compounds below.

IN PHRASES

❑ **hit the grease** *v.* [1950s] to smoke opium. ❑ **in the grease** (*also* **in the dripping**) [1910s–60s] (*US*) in serious trouble. ❑ **in the grease pit** [1950s] smoking opium. ❑ **swim in golden grease** *v. see under* SWIM *v.*

SE in slang uses

IN COMPOUNDS

❑ **greaseball** *n. see* separate entry. ❑ **greaseburger** *n.* (*also* **greasebomb**) [1960s+] (*US*) a very greasy or unappetizing hamburger. ❑ **grease-burner** *n.* (*also* **burner**) [1920s–60s] (*US*) a cook. ❑ **grease-gun** *n.* [it goes as fast as 'greased lightning'] [1940s+] an automatic weapon. ❑ **grease-gut** *n.* [1960s] (*US*) a derog. term for a Mexican or Mexican-American. ❑ **greasehound** *n.* [1910s–40s] (*US*) a mechanic. ❑ **grease joint** *n.* [JOINT *n.* (3b)] [1910s+] (*US*) **1** (*also* **grease-garage**) a cheap or inferior restaurant. **2** a hamburger or hot dog stand. ❑ **grease monkey** *n.* (*also* **grease-monk**) [MONKEY *n.* (2c)] [1910s+] a mechanic. ❑ **greasepaint** *n.* [1920s] a generic term for actors. ❑ **grease parlor** *n.* [1940s] (*US black*) a hairdresser's, a beauty parlour. ❑ **grease patty** *n.* [1990s+] (*US prison*) prison-cooked, chicken-fried steak. ❑ **grease pit** *n.* **1** [1960s] an unpleasant place. **2** [1960s+] a cheap restaurant. **3** *see also* slang compounds above. ❑ **grease pot** *n.* **1** [1910s–60s] (*US*) a cook, orig. and usu. in a prison or camp. **2** [1990s+] a term of abuse. **3** *see also* slang compounds above. ❑ **grease pusher** *n.* [1950s] (*US*) a mechanic. ❑ **grease spot** *n.* [mid-19C+] (*US*) **1** an infinitesimally tiny quantity. **2** the fig. state to which one is reduced either after losing a violent fight or suffering extremely hot weather.

IN PHRASES

❑ **melt one's grease** *v.* [mid-19C] to work very hard.

grease *n.*[2] [1920s–70s] (*US black*) a black man.

grease *n.*[3] [abbr. GREASER *n.*[1] (5)] [1960s+] **1** motorcycle riders (Rockers, as opposed to Mods); also collectively as *the grease*. **2** (*US*) a white working-class youth, a member of a hot-rod, motorcycle or juvenile gang.

grease *n.*[4] [GREASE *v.*[5]] [1960s+] (*US*) death.

grease *v.*[1] **1** [early 16C+] to corrupt, to bribe. **2** [17C] to cheat, to deceive. **3** [20C+] to smooth over problems, esp. from authorities. **4** [20C+] to curry favour with, to toady to. **5** [20C+] to embellish, to add to.

IN PHRASES

❑ **grease a fat sow in the arse** *v.* (*also* **grease a fat pig in the arse, ...tail, stuff a fat sow in the arse, ...fat pig in the tail**) [late 17C–early 19C] to give money to a rich man or woman. ❑ **grease a man in the fist** *v.* [late 16C–early 19C] to bribe someone. ❑ **grease one's mitts** *v. see under* MITT *n.* (3).

SE in slang uses

IN PHRASES

❑ **grease down** *v. see* separate entry. ❑ **grease (off)** *v.* [mid-19C–1920s] **1** (*also* **do a grease**) to slip away. **2** (*also* **grease out**) to go away. ❑ **grease one's chops** *v. see under* CHOPS *n.*[1]. ❑ **grease one's/the gills** *v. see under* GILLS *n.* ❑ **grease one's throat** *v.* (*also* **grease one's tonsils**) [1900s–10s] (*US*) to drink alcohol. ❑ **grease someone's duke** *v. see under* DUKE *n.*[3]. ❑ **grease the gash** *v. see under* GASH *n.*[1]. ❑ **grease the rails** *v.* (*also* **grease the track**) [ironic use of SE] [1910s–40s] (*US*) to be run over by a train; to commit suicide by throwing oneself on the tracks. ❑ **grease the weasel** *v. see under* WEASEL *n.* ❑ **grease the wheel** *v.* [mid-19C–1900s] to have sexual intercourse. ❑ **grease up** *v.* [1970s+] (*Aus. prison/US gay*) to prepare with a lubricant for anal sex.

IN EXCLAMATIONS

❑ **grease me!** [1940s] (*US black campus*) a non-specific expression of approval.

grease *v.*[2] [GREASE *n.*[1] (2b)] [1920s–50s] (*US drugs*) to smoke opium.

grease *v.*[3] [GREASE *n.*[1] (2d)] [1930s–50s] (*US Und.*) to open a safe using nitroglycerine.

grease *v.*[4] (*also* **grease down**) [SE *grease*/GREASE *n.*[1] (2e)] [1930s+] (*US*) **1** to eat. **2** in fig. use, to fellate.

grease *v.*[5] [1960s+] (*orig. US milit.*) to kill.

greaseball *n.* **1** [1910s+] (*orig. US milit.*) (*also* **greaseball grunt**) a short-order cook; a kitchen worker. **2** [1910s+] (*US*) any filthy or offensive person; thus the lowest category of tramp. **3** [1920s+] (*orig. US*) a derog. term for a person of any Latin race, e.g. Italian, Greek, Puerto Rican, various South Americans etc. **4** [1930s] (*US*) an automobile factory worker; a garage mechanic. **5** [1950s+] a derog. term of address to a Latin person.

greased *adj.* **1** [1920s–50s] (*US*) drunk. **2** [1960s+] killed [GREASE *v.*[5]].

greased mitt *n. see under* MITT *n.*

grease down *v.* [GREASE *n.*[1] (2c)] **1** [1980s+] (*US campus*) to have sexual intercourse. **2** *see* GREASE *v.*[4].

greaser *n.*[1] [SE *grease*; note Asbury, *The Barbary Coast* (1933): 'According to Hubert Howe Bancrott in his *California Pastoral* [1888], this term was first applied by the Spaniards to the American and English traders who bought hides and tallow. The traders promptly transferred the appellation to the Spaniards who sold these products, and it soon became a term of contempt applied to all Spanish-Americans, and particularly to Mexicans'] **1** as a racial insult. (**a**) [mid-19C+] (*orig. US*) a derog. term for a Mexican, orig. as an inhabitant of Spanish California and thus a member of another Latin race. (**b**) [late 19C+] a Spaniard, or an object pertaining to Spain, e.g. a vessel. (**c**) [1900s] the Spanish language. (**d**) [1970s+] a native of the Middle East or the Indian subcontinent. **2** [1950s+] a 1950s Teddy Boy, his hair larded with Brylcreem or a similar unguent. **3** [1950s+] (*N.Z.*) a fall, a setback; esp. in phr. *come a greaser*, to fall (lit. or fig.). **4** [1960s] a finger. **5** [1960s+] (*orig. US*) a member of a motorcycle gang or (California) a hotrodder. **6** [1970s+] (*US campus*) an old-fashioned person, whose style harks back to 1950s youth cults.

IN COMPOUNDS

❑ **greaser yacht** *n.* [1980s] (*orig. US*) a large flashy car, as driven by Mexicans.

greaser *n.*[2] [GREASE *v.*[1] (4) + sfx *-er*] **1** [late 19C+] (*US*) an objectionable person. **2** [20C+] a sycophant. **3** [1900s–60s] (*US campus*) a person who studies a great deal.

greaser *n.*[3] [GREASE *v.*[4] (1)] [1920s–70s] (*US black*) an enthusiastic eater, esp. of soul food.

greaser *adj.* [GREASER *n.*[1] (1)] [mid-19C+] (*US*) a derog. ref. to a Mexican/Latin person or culture.

greasies *n.* [1940s+] (*Aus./N.Z.*) food, esp. fish and chips or some form of take-away fast food.

greasy *n.*[1] (*Aus./N.Z./US*) **1** [mid-19C–1940s] a butcher. **2** [late 19C+] a cook, esp. in an institution. **3** [1920s] (*US*) a garage mechanic. **4** [1960s+] a seller of fast or takeaway food.

greasy *n.*[2] [SE *greasy*, wool that has not yet been cleaned] [1930s+] a shearer.

greasy *n.*[3] *see* GREASY (MOP) *n.* (1).

greasy *adj.*[1] [fatty food is both tasty and bad for one's health] [1960s–70s] (*US black*) used of something that is simultaneously appalling and appealing.

IN PHRASES

❑ **do greasy** *v.* [2000s] (*US prison*) to treat someone badly. ❑ **keep it greasy** [1990s+] (*US*) a phr. of farewell; 'it' being a metaphorical vehicle. ❑ **talk greasy** *v.* [2000s] (*US black*) to rap smoothly and stylishly.

SE in slang uses

IN COMPOUNDS

❑ **greasy chin** *n.* [the effects of the treat or dinner] **1** [mid-18C–early 19C] a treat given to parish officers in recompense for registering the birth of a bastard. **2** [mid-19C] a dinner. ❑ **greasy fingers** *n.* [objects 'stick' to such fingers] [1930s–40s] (*US black*) a pickpocket. ❑ **greasy grind** *n. see* GRIND *n.* (3d). ❑ **greasy guts** *n.* [-GUTS *sfx*] [1940s] (*US*) a fat person. ❑ **greasy Mac** *n.* [proper name *McDonalds*, purveyors of fast-food; development of GREASY SPOON *n.*[1]] [1980s] (*US*) any fast-food restaurant. ❑ **greasy spoon** *n. see* separate entry.

greasy *adj.*[2] [GREASE *n.*[1] (2b)] [1970s] (*US drugs*) anything concerning drugs and their sale.

IN COMPOUNDS

❑ **greasy bag** *n.* [BAG *n.*[1] (7)] [1970s] (*US drugs*) a bag in which heroin is transported and/or sold. ❑ **greasy junkie** *n.* [JUNKIE *n.* (1)] [1960s] (*US drugs*) a heroin addict who maintains their own supplies by running errands for dealers or by prostitution.

greasy (mop) *n.* [rhy. sl. = COP *n.*[1] (1)] [20C+] (*Aus.*) a police officer.

greasy spoon *n.*[1] (*also* **dirty spoon**) [the state of its cutlery and the texture of its product] [late 19C+] a cheap café or restaurant.

greasy spoon *n.*[2] [rhy. sl. = HOON *n.* (3)] [1980s+] (*Aus. prison*) a lout or hooligan.

great *adj.*[1] [late 17C+] (*Irish*) close, very friendly; thus *great with*, close to, esp. of lovers.

IN PHRASES

❑ **great as shirt and shitten arse** *adj.* [late 18C–early 19C] very intimate, as close as possible.

great *adj.*[2] [abbr. *POOR-GREAT under* POOR *adj.*] [20C+] (*W.I.*) proud but impoverished, unwilling to take charity no matter how much it might be needed.

great *adj.*[3]

SE in slang uses

IN COMPOUNDS

❑ **great divide, the** *n.* [pun on the *Great Divide*, in the Blue Mountains, or the US equivalent in the Rocky Mountains, cited in the celebrated poem 'Eskimo Nell'] **1** [20C+] the vagina. **2** [1930s+] (*Aus.*) the cleavage between a woman's breasts. ❑ **great gas** *n.* (*also* **good gas**) [GAS *n.*[1] (3)] [1910s+] (*Irish*) something, or someone, extremely enjoyable. ❑ **great house** *n.* [the size of the building in comparison with the original homes of its inmates] [mid-19C] the workhouse. ❑ **great joseph** *n.* [ext. JOSEPH *n.* (1); the biblical *Joseph*'s 'coat of many colours'] [18C–early 19C] (*UK Und.*) an overcoat. ❑ **great mucky-muck** *n. see* HIGH MUCK-A-MUCK *n.* ❑ **great pot** *n. see* BIG POT *n.* ❑ **great shakes** *n. see under* SHAKE *n.*[1]. ❑ **great shucks** *n. see* GREAT SHAKES *under* SHAKE *n.*[1]. ❑ **Great Stoush** *n. see* BIG SNARL *n.* ❑ **great tobacco** *n.* [20C+] (*drugs*) opium.

IN PHRASES

❑ **Great White Way** *n. see* separate entry.

great! *excl.* [late 19C+] an excl. of approval, often in ironic use.

great...! *excl.*

IN EXCLAMATIONS

❑ **by the great horn spoon!** [mid-19C+] (*usu. US*) (*also* **by the great anchor**) a mild excl; a euph. for *by God!* ❑ **great balls!** (*also* **great flaming blue-headed balls of Jesus! great thundering cannonballs!**) [20C+] (*orig. US*) an excl. of surprise, amazement. ❑ **great Caesar!** (*also* **great Caesar's ghost! great Christo! great Christopher! great esau! great Jehos(h)aphat! great Jonah! great Nathan!**) [mid-19C+] a mild oath, a euph. for *great God!* ❑ **great grief!** *see GOOD GRIEF! under* GOOD *adj.*[1]. ❑ **great guns!** (*also* **great gooseberries! great sky-rockets! great snuffboxes! great thundering snakes!**) [19C+] (*US*) a general excl. of surprise or annoyance; also as *great guns and little fishes! great guns and little pistols!* ❑ **great pip!** [1900s–60s] an excl. of surprise or irritation. ❑ **great Scott!** (*also* **scott! great scots!**) [? euph. for *great satan!* or *good God!*; but note *Out West*, Oct. 1911 241: 'The expression 'Great Scott' dates back to the Mexican war in which General Winfield Scott distinguished himself and is an example of the tenacity with which a phrase clings to our vocabulary long after the sense has departed from it'] [19C+] a mild oath.

greatest, the *adj.* [1940s+] (*US*) excellent, fantastic, a general term of approval.

great jumping...! *excl.* [late 19C+] (*US*) a mild oath; in a variety of combs.

Great White Way *n.* [SE *great* + *white way*, a street lit with electric lights. The first *white way* was a stretch of Broadway between 14th Street and 23rd Street, on which electric lights were introduced on 20 December 1880. As used with its qualifying adj., the term was coined by Oscar Gude, a New York advertising man who pioneered the use of electrical advertising, starting with a sign erected over Madison Square in 1892, and began erecting signs in Times Square (then Longacre Square) in 1900. His first use of the term came in 1901. Alternatively, and as claimed by Barry Popik orig., it derives f. the title of Albert Bigelow Paine's novel, *The Great White Way* (1901), although this story, set in the Antarctic, referred not to light but to snow. The link supposedly came when a reporter, Shep Friedman, viewed mid-town Broadway under a blanket of snow] [20C+] (*US*) Broadway, New York City, esp. its theatrical district around Times Square.

grebo *n.* (*also* **greb, greebo**) [? *greb*, a general term of abuse used in north of England schools since 1930s] [1980s+] a British youth cult featuring a cultivatedly sordid appearance, a boorish manner and devotion to heavy metal music.

Grecian *n.* [GREEK *n.* (3)] [mid-17C; 19C+] an Irish immigrant; thus *Grecian accent*, the brogue.

Grecian *v.* [? SE *Grecian bend*, 'an affected carriage of the body, in which it is bent forward from the hips' (*OED*)] [1940s] (*W.I.*) of a woman, to walk in a self-consciously 'stylish' manner, either arrogantly or proudly.

Grecian bend *n.*[1] (*also* **Grecian bender**) [ety. unknown] [late 19C] a revolver.

Grecian bend *n.*[2] [play on SE *Grecian bend*, 'an affected carriage of the body, in which it is bent forward from the hips' (*OED*)] [late 19C] 'the bends' or caisson disease.

Greco *n.* [1940s] (*Aus.*) a Greek.

greebo *n. see* GREBO *n.*

greeby *adj.* [? var. on SE *grubby*; note GREBO *n.*] [1940s–60s] (*US teen*) ugly, unattractive.

greed *n.* [mid–late 19C] money.

greedhead *n.* [SE *greed* + -HEAD *sfx* (1)] [1970s+] (*US*) an avaricious person.

greedies, the *n.* [1960s] (*US*) avariciousness.

greedy *adj.* [i.e. one who is 'not satisfied' with attraction to one sex] [1990s+] bisexual.

greedy-gut *n.* (*also* **greedy-guts, greedy gutz**) [US use is 19C+] [mid-16C+] a glutton, a selfish person.

greefo *n.* (*also* **greapha, greefa, grefa, griefo, grifa, griffa, griffo, grifo**) [Mex. Sp. sl. *grifo*, under the influence of marijuana; the original use of *grifo* is tangled or frizzy hair; thus the image of mental fuzziness/frizziness] [1930s+] marijuana.

Greek *n.* [the 'foreignness' of Greek whether as a language or person] **1** [16C+] a cunning, sly individual, esp. a gambler or swindler [20C+ use is derog.]. **2** [late 16C+] unintelligible language, esp. cant or sl.; esp. in phr. *it's all Greek to me*, suggesting that something is incomprehensible; occas. of actions or ideas. **3** [mid-17C; 19C+] a derog. term for an Irish immigrant to the US or UK. **4** [mid-19C] a newcomer. **5** [1930s+] (*US campus*) (*also* **Greek freak**) a member of a college fraternity or sorority; thus as adj. [the use of *Greek* letters as the names of such societies]. **6** [1930s+] a person who engages in anal intercourse, not necessarily but usu. a homosexual [the stereotyped identification of Greeks with homosexuality]. **7** [1930s+] anal intercourse; often used on a prostitute's 'bill of sale'.

(IN COMPOUNDS)

❑ **Greek freak** *n. see* sense 5 above.

(IN PHRASES)

❑ **excuse my Greek** [var. on EXCUSE MY FRENCH *under* FRENCH *n.*] [1990s+] a phr. meaning 'forgive my coarse language'. ❑ **go Greek** *v.* [1970s+] (*US campus*) to join a college fraternity or sorority.

Greek *adj.* [GREEK *n.*] **1** [mid-19C] Irish. **2** [late 19C+] (*also* **Persian**) a generic term for homosexual. **3** [late 19C+] pertaining to anal intercourse; esp. in combs. below.

(IN COMPOUNDS)

❑ **Greek culture** *n.* [1960s+] anal intercourse, usu. in homosexual advertisement use. ❑ **Greek love** *n.* **1** [1930s+] (*gay*) pederasty. **2** [1970s] anal intercourse, irrespective of age. ❑ **Greek side** *n.* [1930s+] (*gay*) the buttocks. ❑ **Greek way** *n.* (*also* **Greek fashion, Greek style, greeking**) [GREEK *adj.* (3)] [1960s+] **1** (*gay*) pederasty. **2** anal intercourse.

SE in slang uses

(IN COMPOUNDS)

❑ **Greek back** *n. see* MEDITERRANEAN BACK *n.* ❑ **Greek fire** *n.* [the burning sensation; SE *Greek fire*, a highly combustible composition used in warfare] [late 19C] (*UK Und.*) bad whisky. ❑ **Greek lightning** *n. see* JEWISH LIGHTNING *under* JEWISH *adj.* ❑ **Greek sauna** *n. see* DUTCH OVEN *under* DUTCH *adj.*[1].

Greek *v.* [GREEK *n.*] **1** [early 19C] to cheat at cards; thus n. *Greeking*. **2** [1970s+] (*gay*) to engage in anal sex; thus n. *Greeking*.

Greek's, the *n.* [Greek immigrants, who specialize in such establishments] [1930s+] (*orig. Aus.*) a generic term for any small café.

green *n.*[1] [SE *green*, naïve] [19C] an unsophisticated, naïve person.

SE in slang uses

(IN PHRASES)

❑ **green in one's eye** *n.* [early 19C+] stupidity, naivety; always in phrs. meaning do you think I'm a fool? do I look stupid?; usu. as *do you see any green in my eye?*

green *n.*[2] [the colour; whether of currency, marijuana or glass bottles] **1** [late 19C+] (*US*) (*also* **welcome green**) money, dollar bills. **2** [20C+] a $1 bill; thus often in pl. **3** [1950s+] (*US drugs*) (*also* **Miss Green**) marijuana, esp. of inferior quality. **4** [1970s+] phencyclidine. **5** [1980s+] ketamine. **6** [1990s+] (*US black*) a bottle of beer. **7** [1990s+] (*Aus.*) Victoria bitter beer. **8** *see* GREEN MONEY *under* GREEN *adj.*[1].

green *adj.*[1] [early use SE *green*, ripe; latterly GREEN *n.*[2] (1)] [mid-19C+] of money, liquid or in funds.

SE in slang uses

(DERIVATIVES)

❑ **greenmans** *n.* [-MANS *sfx*] [early 17C] fields, countryside.

(IN COMPOUNDS)

❑ **green and blacks** *n.* [the colour of the capsules] [1960s–80s] (*UK prison/drugs*) librium capsules. ❑ **green and greasy** *n.* [the colour and texture of well-used dollar bills] [1920s] (*US Und.*) banknotes. ❑ **green and yellow fellow** *n.* [SE *greenery-yallery*, of, pertaining to, or affecting the colours green and yellow, in accordance with the style or fashion of the Aesthetic Movement and thus, in short, affected] [late 19C] a male homosexual. ❑ **green-apple quickstep** *n.* (*also* **green-apple nasties, ...trots, ...two-step**) [the result of eating sour fruit + pun on SE*trot*/TROTS *n.* (1)] [1950s+] (*US*) diarrhoea. ❑ **green ashes** *n.* (*also* **green mud**) [1930s–50s] (*US drugs*) opium residue. ❑ **green-ass** *adj.* [-ASS *sfx*] [1940s+] (*US*) naïve, inexperienced. ❑ **greenback** *see* separate entries. ❑ **green bag** *n.* [the green cloth that was trad. used to make lawyers' bags, used to carry briefs and other documents. 'These gentlemen carry their clients' deeds in a green bag; and, it is said, when they have no deeds to carry, frequently fill them with an old pair of breeches...to give themselves the appearance of business' (Grose, 1785). *Green bags* were replaced by *blue bags* (barristers) and *red bags* (King's or Queen's Counsel)] **1** [late 17C–19C] a lawyer. **2** [19C] in phr. *what's in the green bag?*, 'what is the charge to be preferred against me?' ❑ **green banana** *n. see* BANANA *n.* (2a). ❑ **green bean** *n.* **1** [1950s+] (*US*) a naïve person [SE *green*, naïve]. **2** [1980s+] (*S.Afr.*) (*also* **greenfly**) a township municipal police officer [colour of the uniform]. **3** *see* BEAN *n.*[1] (1c). ❑ **green belly** *n.* [SE *green*, naïve] [1950s] (*US*) a novice, an unsophisticated person, esp. a new arrival in the city from the country. ❑ **green boys** *n.* (*also* **green fellows**) [the colour of dollar bills/GREEN *n.*[2] (1)] [mid-19C] paper money, notes. ❑ **green bud** *n.* [colour/GREEN *n.*[2] (3) + BUD *n.*[2] (3b)] [1980s+] (*US drugs*) marijuana that is green, usu. of a superior quality. ❑ **green cart** *n.* [1930s+] (*Aus.*) a vehicle, actual or metaphorical, in which people are taken to a psychiatric hospital. ❑ **green certificates** *n. see* GREEN MONEY below. ❑ **green death** *n.* [play on SE *Black Death*] [1960s–70s] (*US campus*) sickness and diarrhoea, supposedly caused by student canteen food. ❑ **green dragons** *n.* (*drugs*) **1** [1930s+] heroin [a stamp on the box]. **2** [1970s+] barbiturates [the colour of the pills]. **3** [1970s+] amphetamines [the colour of the pills]. **4** [1980s+] LSD [a type of LSD distributed on squares of blotter stamped with a *green dragon*]. ❑ **green fellows** *n. see* GREEN BOYS above. ❑ **greenfly** *n. see* GREEN BEAN above. ❑ **green goddess** *n.* [the colour of the marijuana leaves and the pleasure of the drug] [1930s–50s] (*US drugs*) marijuana. ❑ **green gold** *n.* [? SE *green gold*, an alloy of gold and silver; high-quality cocaine sparkles] [1980s+] (*drugs*) cocaine. ❑ **green goods** *n. see* separate entry. ❑ **green goose** *n.* [SE *green goose*, a gosling, a young goose; a simpleton or SE *green* + *goose*, a fool] [late 16C–mid-17C] a young, innocent girl, soon to be made into a prostitute. ❑ **green gown** *n. see* separate entry. ❑ **greengrocer(y)** *see* separate entries. ❑ **green grove** *n.* [GREENS *n.*[1]] [19C] the pubic hair. ❑ **green ham** *n. see* GREENHORN *n.* (1). ❑ **green handshake** *n.* [GREEN *n.*[2] (1)] [1970s] (*US*) a bribe, a tip, a bonus. ❑ **greenhead** *n.* [late 17C–early 19C; 1910s] an inexperienced young man. ❑ **greenhorn** *see* separate entries. ❑ **green hornet** *n.* [the colour of the pill or uniform + ref. to the NBC radio series *The Green Hornet*] **1** [1960s] (*US*) a New York City police patrol car, suggested by the colour scheme of the time. **2** [1960s] (*Can. Und.*) a Toronto motorcycle police officer. ❑ **green horse** *n. see* GREENHORN *n.* (1). ❑ **greenhouse** *n. see* separate entries. ❑ **green lamp house** *n.* [1900s] (*US*) a police station. ❑ **Greenland** *n. see* separate entry. ❑ **green leaves** *n.* [the parsley with which PCP was often smoked] [1980s+] (*drugs*) phencyclidine. ❑ **green-light hotel** *n.* (*also* **green light, green lights**) [the green light that marks the building] [1910s–40s] (*US*) a prison or police station. ❑ **green meadow** *n.* [GREENS *n.*[1]] [mid-19C] the vagina. ❑ **green money** *n.* (*also* **green, green certificates, ...materials**) [1900s–10s; 1970s+] (*US*) US currency, esp. as forbidden in prison and used for illegal transactions. ❑ **Green Mountain Boy** *n.* *see* separate entry. ❑ **green mud** *n.* *see* GREEN ASHES above. ❑ **green nigger** *n.* [similar inferior status to a black NIGGER *n.*[1] (1) but *green*, i.e. Irish from the national colours] [20C+] (*US*) an Irish person. ❑ **green one** *n.* [the colour] **1** [1910s] (*US*) $1 bill. **2** [1930s+] £1. **3** [1990s+] a piece of phlegm, in the context of spitting. ❑ **green pea** *n.* **1** [1910s–70s] (*US*) a naïve person [SE *green*, naïve]. **2** [1950s–70s] a key [rhy. sl.]. ❑ **green pill** *n.* *see* BLACK PILL *under* PILL *n.* ❑ **Green Pop** *n.* *see* separate entry. ❑ **Green River** *n.* *see* separate entry. ❑ **green room** *n.* [its green-painted walls] [1950s+] (*US prison*) the gas chamber. ❑ **Green Sod** *n.* *see* OLD SOD *n.* ❑ **green stamp** *n.* [play on *Green Shield* trading stamps, first issued (as S&H Green Stamps) in the US in 1930s and in the UK in 1960s] (*US*) **1** [1950s+] $1 bill; thus *green stamps*, money. **2** [1970s] a traffic offence summons. ❑ **green stuff** *n.* [the colour] **1** [mid-19C+] paper currency, notes. **2** [late 19C–1900s] (*US*) absinthe. **3** [1940s+] (*US black*) marijuana. ❑ **green tea** *n.* **1** [1950s] (*US drugs*) marijuana, esp. of inferior quality [TEA *n.* (4a)]. **2** [1980s+] (*drugs*) phencyclidine [rhy. sl. or the common mixing of the drug with parsley, which may resemble sense 1 above]. ❑ **green thumb** *n.* **1** [1960s] (*US gay*) the penis [? its fecundity]. **2** [1970s+] (*US black*) one who has the knack of making money [GREEN *n.*[2] (1) + play on the more usual gardeners' 'green fingers']. ❑ **green tiger** *n.* *see* GREENIE *n.*[2] (5). ❑ **green tobacco** *n.* [2000s] (*N.Z. drugs*) marijuana. ❑ **green verbs** *n.* [SE *green*, unripe, immature, thus unsophisticated] [20C+] (*W.I.*) poorly spoken, ungrammatical English, esp. when used by one who would be expected to speak correctly. ❑ **green weenie** *n.* [SE *green*, of food, decaying, 'off' + WEENIE *n.*[1] (5)] **1** [1940s+] (*US, orig. milit.*) anything bad; thus *eat/get/have had the green weenie*, to be killed. **2** [1960s–70s] (*US campus*) to break a date; to end a relationship. **3** [1980s] (*US campus*) a Heineken beer. ❑ **green wellies** *n.* *see* WELLIES *n.*

IN PHRASES

❑ **green about/around the gills** *adj.* *see under* GILLS *n.*

green *adj.*[2] [1950s+] (*US*) out of order, in a mess.

green *v.* [SE *green*, naïve] [late 19C] to deceive, to hoax, to swindle, to render gullible.

greenback *n.* [colour] **1** [mid-19C+] (*US*) (*also* **g.b.**) a $1 bill; usu. in pl. **2** [1950s+] (*Aus./UK/Irish*) a £1 note.

greenback *v.* [GREENBACK *n.* (1)] [1970s] (*US*) to pay, esp. a bribe.

greenback *adv.* [GREENBACK *n.* (1)] [1970s] (*US*) in cash.

greener *n.*[1] [SE *green*, naïve] **1** [late 19C] an inexperienced workman used as a strike-breaker. **2** [late 19C+] (*orig. US*) a novice, an innocent, one who has newly arrived. **3** [1940s] (*UK prison*) (*also* **greeney**) a young or new prison inmate.

greener *n.*[2] [the colour of dollar bills] [1940s+] (*US*) a $1 bill.

greener *n.*[3] *see* GREENIE *n.*[2] (5).

greenery *n.* [GREEN *n.*[2]] **1** [1970s] (*US black*) money. **2** [1990s+] (*UK black*) marijuana.

greeney *n.* *see* GREENER *n.*[1] (3).

greengages *n.* (*also* **greens**) [rhy. sl.] [1930s+] wages.

green goods *n.* [the colour of the bills] **1** [late 19C–1950s] (*US Und.*) counterfeit banknotes; thus *green goods business/game/racket*, selling counterfeit money as 'real' money allegedly made from a plate stolen from the government; *green goods man*, a counterfeiter. **2** [1910s+] paper currency.

green gown *n.*

IN PHRASES

❑ **get a green gown** *v.* (*also* **take a green gown**) [pun on SE *green*, with its general meanings of both countryside and innocence + the green stains that come from rolling on the grass] [late 16C–19C] to lose one's virginity, usu. out of doors. ❑ **give someone a green gown** *v.* (*also* **green-gown, give a green mantle**) [late 16C–19C] to have sex outdoors, poss. involving the loss of the woman's virginity.

greengrocer *n.* [play on legit. *bumboating*, selling provisions to ships and BUM *n.*[1] (2)] [late 18C] a prostitute.

greengrocery *n.* [euph.] [early 19C] an illicit bar or 'speakeasy'.

greenhorn *n.* [15C SE *greenhorn*, a young animal, spec. an ox with 'green' or young horns. The term is first used in a milit. sense, describing a new recruit. Grose (1785) defines it as 'an undebauched young fellow, just initiated into the society of bucks and bloods'. Its post-19C use has been mainly US; note that 1815 1st edn of *Guy Mannering* has Scot. *callant*, a youth, a stripling] **1** [late 17C+] (*also* **green ham, ...horse**) a novice, an unsophisticated person, esp. a new immigrant or a new arrival in the city from the country. **2** [late 19C] a virgin; a sexual novice.

greenhorn *adj.* [GREENHORN *n.* (2)] [1980s] (*US*) virginal.

greenhouse *n.*[1] [1900s–70s] (*Irish*) a public lavatory.

greenhouse *n.*[2] [GREEN *n.*[2] (3) + pun on SE] [1980s+] (*drugs*) a place known for selling drugs, esp. marijuana.

greenie *n.*[1] (*also* **greeny**) [abbr. GREENHORN *n.*] [mid-19C+] a novice, an unsophisticated person, esp. a new arrival from the country.

greenie *n.*[2] [the colour] **1** [1930s–70s] (*Aus./US/N.Z.*) $1 or £1. **2** [1960s+] (*US teen*) (*also* **greeny, gremlin, grolly**) a lump of phlegm. **3** [1960s+] (*drugs*) an amphetamine. **4** [1970s] (*US*) in pl., green vegetables. **5** [1970s+] (*S.Afr.*) (*also* **greener, green tiger**) a ten-rand note. **6** [1980s+] (*US campus*) beer, spec. Heineken lager, which comes in predominantly green-labelled bottles or cans. **7** [1990s+] MDMA.

greenie *n.*[3] (*also* **greeny**) [the *Green* party] [1970s+] (*Aus./N.Z.*) an environmentalist, a conservationist.

Greenland *n.* [SE *green*, naïve + SE *land*] **1** [mid-19C] the fig. world of innocence; thus *greenlander*, a gullible, innocent person. **2** [mid–late 19C] (*US*) Ireland; thus *Greenlander*, an Irish person; *from Greenland*, used of an unsophisticated, ignorant person [also play on SE *green*, Ireland's national colour].

Green Mountain boy *n.* [lit. meaning of Vermont, France *verts monts*, green mountains] [late 18C+] (*US*) a native of Vermont.

Green Pop *n.* [SE *green* + POP *n.*[1] (2a); the predominantly green glass bottle] [1940s] (*US*) Rolling Rock beer.

Green River *n.*

SE in slang uses

IN PHRASES

❑ **go up Green River** *v.* [the *Green River* brand of knife, made in Texas] [mid-19C–1940s] (*US*) to die; thus *send someone up Green River*, to kill.

greens *n.*[1] [GREEN GOWN *n.*] [mid-19C+] sexual intercourse; thus *get one's greens, have one's greens*; also *give one's greens*, to consent to sexual intercourse.

IN PHRASES

❑ **have a bit of curly greens** *v.* [late 19C+] to have sexual intercourse. ❑ **hawk one's greens** *v.* [1930s] to work as a prostitute.

greens *n.*[2] [the colour] [1980s+] (*Aus. prison*) prison uniform; thus used as a generic for prisoner activities.

greens *n.*[3] [1980s+] (*drugs*) marijuana.

greens *n.*[4] *see* GREENGAGES *n.*

greens and brussels *n.* [rhy. sl.] [20C+] muscles.

Greenwich barber *n.* [such retailers 'shaved' the sand for their product] [late 18C–early 19C] a seller of sand from the Greenwich sandpits.

Greenwich goose *n.* [proper name *Greenwich* + SE *goose*] [late 18C–19C] a pensioner of Greenwich Royal Naval Hospital, founded in 1692 by Queen Mary.

greeny *n.*[1] [the colour] [1990s+] (*US drugs*) the best grade of marijuana.

greeny *n.*[2] *see also under* GREENIE.

greeper *n.* [? SE *gripper*] [1990s+] (*US drugs*) withdrawal symptoms.

greet *n.* [abbr.] [20C+] (*US*) a greeting; thus *greets*, greetings.

greeter *n.* (*also* **greta**) [? misreading of GREEFO *n.*] [1940s–60s] (*drugs*) marijuana.

grefa *n. see* GREEFO *n.*

greg *v.* (*also* **grig**) [Irish *griog*, to tease] [mid-19C+] (*Irish*) to tease, to fool.

grego *n.* [SE *grego*, a coarse jacket with a hood, worn in the Levant, ult. Lat. *Graecus*, Greek] [mid-19C] a rough greatcoat, with a hood.

Gregorian tree *n.* [pun on proper name *Gregory* Brandon; for details *see* GREGORY *n.*] [mid-17C–early 19C] the gallows.

gregory *n.* [*Gregory* Brandon, who worked as executioner under James I (1601–25), to be succeeded by his son Richard, better known as 'Young Gregory'] [early 17C] a hangman.

Gregory Peck *n.* [rhy. sl.; proper name of US actor *Gregory Peck* (1916–2003)] [1950s+] **1** the neck. **2** a cheque. **3** (*Aus.*) in pl., spectacles, glasses [= SPECS *n.* (1)].

gregory peg *n.* [rhy. sl.; pun on GREGORY PECK *n.* + SE *peg-leg*] [20C+] (*Aus.*) the leg.

gremlin *n.*[1] [? SE *goblin*; orig. use in 1929 refers to troublesome or unimportant officers. Popularized through WW2 RAF use, where the meaning was as above, although one citation claims the term was invented in WW1 by the Royal Flying Corps] [1910s+] an unidentified source of trouble or malfunctioning.

gremlin *n.*[2] *see* GREENIE *n.*[2] (2).

greng-greng *n.* [Twi *greng*, rough, rugged, coarse] [20C+] (*W.I., Trin.*) coarse, short hair.

gret *see under* GRETTE.

greta *n.*[1] [movie star *Greta* Garbo (1905–90) and her alleged declaration, 'I want to be alone'] [2000s] (*S.Afr. gay*) one who prefers solitude.

greta *n.*[2] *see* GREETER *n.*

grette *n.* (*also* **gret**) [abbr.] [1960s–70s] (*US campus*) a cigarette.

grette *v.* (*also* **gret**) [GRETTE *n.*] [1960s] (*US campus*) to smoke, possess or obtain a cigarette.

Greville Starkey *n.* [rhy. sl. = DARKIE *n.*; ult. UK horseracing trainer *Greville Starkey* (b.1939)] [1990s+] a derog. term for a black person.

grey/gray *see also under* GRAY; the spelling of gray/grey remains debatable; according to the *OED* there have been various choices over the years, but there seems to have been little real consistency. For the purposes of this dict., and based as far as possible on the pre-eminent style of the respective countries, 'gray' will be used for US terms and 'grey' for UK/Aus. and other 'Commonwealth' uses.

grey *n.* [Rom. *gry*, a horse, thus linked to PONY *n.* (1)] **1** [early 19C+] (*20C+ mainly Aus.*) (*also* **gray**) a halfpenny or other coin, having two heads or two tails, esp. as used in cheating games. **2** [mid-19C] money in general [the colour of 'silver' coins once they have been some time in circulation].

grey *adj.*

SE in slang uses

(IN COMPOUNDS)

❑ **greyback** *n.* **1** [1970s–80s] (*UK black*) an old person. **2** *see* GRAYBACK *n.* (4). ❑ **greybeard** *n.* [such jugs had the figure of a man with a large beard stamped on them. The name was also given to Dutch earthenware jugs, used for smuggling gin along the east coast] [late 18C–19C] an earthenware jug used in public houses. ❑ **grey biscuit** *n.* [the colour of the tablet] [1990s+] (*drugs*) MDMA. ❑ **greycoat** *n.* [the prison uniform] [1900s] (*Aus. Und.*) a prisoner. ❑ **grey death** *n.* [1950s+] (*Aus. prison*) weak prison stew; similarly porridge. ❑ **grey ghost** *n.* (*also* **grey bomber**) [the colour of the uniform] [1970s+] (*Aus.*) a NSW parking police officer; the same officer in Victoria is a *grey meanie*. ❑ **greyhound** *see* separate entries. ❑ **grey parson** *n.* (*also* **grey-coat(ed) parson**) [*grey* as 'light black' in an adj. use of 'black', referring to matters clerical. The use of *grey* to mean amateur or partial is similar to 20C+ *grey import*, an unofficial, but not actually illegal, import, typically of computer hardware manufactured elsewhere that has yet to become available in the country in which it is sold] [late 18C–19C] a farmer who rents out the tithes normally due to a vicar or rector.

greycing *n. see* GRACING *n.*

greyers *n. see* GREYS *n.*

greyhound *n.*[1] [1920s] (*US Und.*) a professional gambler who travels and works on ocean liners.

greyhound *n.*[2] [SE *greyhounds* are very thin dogs] [1970s+] (*N.Z.*) a very thin hand-rolled cigarette.

greyhound *n.*[3] [it is only an inch from the 'hare'] [1990s+] a very short skirt.

greyhound *v.* [GRAY *adj.* (1)+ SE *hound* v.] (*US black*) **1** [1940s–50s] to run fast. **2** [1970s] to pursue white sexual partners.

grey mare *n.* [rhy. sl.] [1930s–50s] the fare.

grey nurse *n.* [rhy. sl.] [1960s+] (*Aus.*) a purse, a wallet.

greys *n.* (*also* **greyers**) [SE *grey* (-ER *sfx*)] [1900s–40s] grey flannel trousers, once a staple of the 'off-duty' uniform of the British middle-class male.

greys, the *n.* [late 18C–1920s] a fit of yawning, a feeling of laziness, lassitude.

gribber *n.* [? UK dial. *gribble*, to remove matted wool and dung from the tails of sheep; ult. dial. *gribble*, a small pellet or grain] [1970s] small pieces of excrement adhering to the anal hairs.

grick *n.* [var. on GRIG *n.*[1]] [early 19C] a farthing.

grid *n.*[1] [abbr. SE *gridiron*/GRIDIRON *n.* (4)] **1** [1920s+] (*1940s+ mainly Aus.*) a bicycle. **2** [1950s] a car. **3** [1950s] a piano.

grid *n.*[2] [SE *grid*] [2000s] **1** the human face [? the teeth form a grid or grating]. **2** (*US*) the rows of dialling buttons on a modern telephone.

griddle *n.* (*also* **grid**) [? rhy. sl. = SE *fiddle*] [late 19C–1900s] a violin.

griddle *v.* [ety. unknown] [mid–late 19C; 1930s] (*later use US*) to beg, to peddle, to scrounge, esp. as a street-singer.

griddler *n.* [GRIDDLE *v.* (1)] **1** [mid–late 19C; 1950s] a street singer who performs without benefit of a lyric sheet. **2** [1930s] a wandering tinker, a gypsy tramp.

gridiron *n.* [resembance to a SE *gridiron*] **1** [early 19C] (*Anglo-Irish*) a public house sweetheart [? she is 'hot stuff']. **2** [mid-19C] in London, a county court summons [the arms of the City of Westminster, which resemble a *gridiron*]. **3** [late 19C] the bars on a prison-cell window. **4** [late 19C–1940s] (*US*) a football field [post-WW2 use is SE]. **5** [1920s+] a bicycle.

grief *n.*[1] **1** [late 19C+] misery, problems, troubles. **2** [1970s+] (*US gay*) a homophobic thug.

(IN PHRASES)

❑ **give someone grief** *v.* [1960s+] to make miserable, to harm in any way.

grief *n.*[2] [abbr. GREEFO *n.*] [1970s+] (*Aus. drugs*) marijuana.

grief *v.* [GRIEF *n.*[1] (1)] [1970s+] (*US campus*) to trouble, to bother, to annoy.

griefer *n.* [GREEFO *n.*] [1930s–50s] (*US drugs*) a habitual marijuana user.

griefo *n. see* GREEFO *n.*

grievous *n.* [abbr.] [1940s–50s] (*Aus.*) *grievous* bodily harm.

grifa *n. see* GREEFO *n.*

griff *n. see* GRIFFIN *n.*[3].

griff *v.* [? pickpocket jargon *griff*, to jostle one's way through a crowd, picking pockets] [2000s] (*US black*) to fight.

griffa *n. see* GREEFO *n.*

griffin *n.*[1] [SE *griffin*, a mythical animal, with the head and wings of an eagle and the body of a lion] **1** [18C–19C] a fool; thus adj. *griffinish*, foolish. **2** [early 19C–1920s] a menacing woman, a 'gorgon'. **3** [late 19C] (*US*) a young thief.

griffin *n.*[2] [SE *griffin* (*see* prev.) but link unknown; ? it resembles wings; or ? as used by 'fast' young men in London] [mid-19C] an umbrella.

griffin *n.*[3] (*also* **griff**) [? pun on Indian Army jargon *griffin*, a cadet newly arrived from the UK to join the Indian Army or Civil Service; in modern use mainly as Liverpool dial.] [late 19C+] news, reliable information, a tip (in betting), a hint; esp. as *straight griffin*.

griffmetoll *n.* [ety. unknown] [mid–late 18C] (*UK Und.*) a sixpence.

griffo/grifo *n. see* GREEFO *n.*

grift *n.* [GRAFT *n.*[1]] **1** [1910s–40s] one's criminal occupation. **2** [1910s+] (*US Und.*) any crime that depends not upon violence/coercion but on 'lightness of touch and quickness of wit' (Maurer, *The Big Con* 1940), e.g. professional confidence trickery, pickpocketing, professional gambling, circus/carnival work. **3** [1910s+] as *the grift*, the world of crime. **4** [1920s] in ext. use of sense 1 above, a non-criminal occupation. **5** [1920s–50s] corruption; the proceeds of corruption, political bribery etc. **6** [1930s] (*US Und.*) the proceeds of a theft. **7** [1930s–40s] a plan, a scheme, an intention. **8** [1950s] an opinion. **9** *see* GRIFTER *n.* (1).

(IN PHRASES)

❑ **on the grift** [1990s+] working as a confidence trickster, gambler etc.

grift *v.* [GRIFT *n.*] **1** [1910s+] to work as a confidence trickster or petty thief; thus *grifting*, confidence trickery, swindling. **2** [1930s–50s] to trick, to hoax. **3** [1950s+] to steal. **4** [1990s+] (*US campus*) to scrounge off other people.

grifter *n.* [GRIFT *v.*] **1** [1910s+] (*US Und*) (*also* **grift**) a confidence trickster; any form of non-violent criminal living primarily on his or her wits. **2** [1910s+] (*US Und.*) a small-change swindler, thus any small-time gambler. **3** [1910s+] (*US Und.*) a thief. **4** [1930s–50s] a worker, a struggler. **5** [1990s+] (*US campus*) a scrounger, someone living off other people.

grig *n.*[1] [ety. unknown, but all meanings of SE *grig* (a dwarf, a short-legged hen etc) imply dimin. size. Johnson suggests that its original meaning was 'anything below the natural size'] [mid-17C–mid-19C] a farthing; in pl., money, cash.

grig *n.*[2] [ety. unknown] [1990s+] (*US*) anything or anyone that the speaker dislikes or does not require.

grig *v. see* GREG *v.*

gril *n.* [play on SE *girl*] [1990s+] (*US campus*) an affectionate term of address between women.

grill *n.*[1] **1** [1940s] (*US black*) the stomach. **2** [1980s+] (*US black/teen*) the face or mouth; thus one's personal space. **3** [1990s+] (*also* **grille**) the teeth. **4** [1990s+] (*US black*) an intense stare.

(IN PHRASES)

❑ **all up in someone's grill** [1990s+] (*US campus*) aggressively confronting someone, whether verbally or physically. ❑ **bust someone's grill** *v.* [2000s] (*US teen*) to beat up; to hit in the mouth.

grill *n.*[2] [the near-monopoly of Greeks on the running of small cafés] [1950s+] (*Aus.*) a southern European immigrant, esp. a Greek.

griller *n.* [1970s] (*Aus. Und.*) deliberately negative testimony by the police against a criminal with the aim of ensuring a lengthy sentence.

grim and gory *n.* [rhy. sl.] [20C+] (*Aus.*) a story.

grimbo *n.* [SE *grim* + BIMBO *n.* (2)/DUMBO *n.* (1)] [1980s+] (*US campus*) a contemptible or unattractive person.

grimflushly *adj. see* GLIM-FLASHY *under* GLIM *n.*

Grimsby Docks *n.* [rhy. sl.] [1990s+] socks.

grin *n.*[1] [note Egan, *Life in London* (1821): 'A low *slang* term made use of in opposition to the stylish phrase of QUIZ. It is considered rather an unpleasant circumstance to persons entering a splendid ball-room who are not accustomed to it. At all times it should be executed in a graceful manner'] [early 19C] an inquisitive, challenging stare.

(IN PHRASES)

❑ **stand the grin** *v.* [early 19C] to suffer ridicule.

grin *n.*[2] [the trad. 'grinning' skull] [mid-19C] (*US*) a skeleton.

grin *n.*[3] [1960s+] (*US*) amusement; thus *for (shits and) grins*, for fun.

(IN PHRASES)

❑ **ain't life a grin** [1970s] (*US campus*) a cynical expression of misfortune. ❑ **on the grin** *adj.* [1910s] smiling, cheerful.

grin, the *n.* [SE *grin*, a snare] [early 19C] an interrogation.

grin *v.*

SE in slang uses

(IN PHRASES)

❑ **grin in a glass case** *v.* [many criminals were dissected after their execution and their skeletal remains preserved under glass in hospitals] [late 18C–19C] to be anatomized. ❑ **grin in the canyon (of love)** *v. see* YODEL IN THE CANYON (OF LOVE) *v.* ❑ **grin like a basket of chips** *v.* (*also* **smile like a basket of chips**) [SE *basket* + *chips*, small pieces of wood sawn or chiselled off by a carpenter; f. an older Salop. saying, *smile like a basket of chips*] [late 18C–1900s] to grin broadly. ❑ **grin like a cheese-gash** *v.* [late 19C] (*Aus.*) to grin broadly. ❑ **grin like a street-knocker** *v.* [? one's teeth shine like a well-polished knocker] [mid-19C+] to grin broadly. ❑ **not to be grinned at** *see* NOT TO BE SNEEZED AT *under* SNEEZE *v.*[1].

grinagog (the cat's uncle) *n.* [SE *grin* + *agog*] [mid-16C–18C] a simpleton who has a fixed grin on his face.

grincam/grincom(e)/grincum *n. see* CRINKUM *n.*

grind *n.* [GRIND *v.*] **1** as mocking, persuasive or deceptive speech. (**a**) [mid-19C–1920s] (*US*) a swindle. (**b**) [late 19C] (*US campus*) a satirist. (**c**) [late 19C–1930s] (*US campus*) a joke, usu. personal. (**d**) [1930s] (*US tramp*) patter used to lure customers into a sideshow or similar attraction. (**e**) [1930s–50s] (*US Und.*) the 'salestalk' that is used to persuade a confidence man's victim. **2** as a sexual action or performance. (**a**) [mid-19C+] an act of sexual intercourse. (**b**) [late 19C] a person (female or gay male) regarded as a sex object, further qualified as a *good grind*, *bad grind*; thus a promiscuous young woman. (**c**) [1940s–50s] (*orig. US black*) a striptease performance. (**d**) [1940s+] the rubbing of one's body, esp. the genital area, against one's partner while dancing; thus similar movements by a solo dancer or singer; esp. in phr. *bump(s) and grind(s)*. (**e**) [1970s] masturbation. **3** as tiring mental or physical labour. (**a**) [mid-19C+] hard, continuous, wearing work, esp. academic work. (**b**) [late 19C–1900s] (*US campus*) a demanding instructor. (**c**) [late 19C–1900s] (*US campus*) a demanding course. (**d**) [late 19C+] (*US campus*) (*also* **greasy grind**) a student who studies constantly. (**e**) [late 19C+] anything wearing, monotonous, exhausting, debilitating. (**f**) [1900s] (*US campus*) a tiring or boring person or task. (**g**) [1910s–50s] a hard worker, a daily worker. (**h**) [2000s] (*Irish*) in pl., extra tuition. **4** [1980s] (*US campus*) in pl., food.

(IN COMPOUNDS)

❑ **grind house** *n. see* separate entry. ❑ **grind joint** *n. see* separate entries. ❑ **grind show** *n.* [1920s–50s] (*US*) an entertainment show that runs continuously. ❑ **grindsman** *n.* [20C+] (*W.I. Rasta*) one who displays great prowess in bed. ❑ **grindstone** *n.* [mid-19C+] the vagina.

(IN PHRASES)

❑ **get one's grind on** *v.* [2000s] to have sexual intercourse. ❑ **on the grind** **1** [late 19C] nagging, complaining. **2** [late 19C+] involved in hard, demanding work. **3** [late 19C+] having sexual intercourse.

grind *v.* **1** in the context of sex. (**a**) [mid-16C+] to have sexual intercourse; also *do/have a grind*; of a man, *grind one's tool*. (**b**) [1920s+] (*US*) to rotate the hips in a sensuous manner while dancing. (**c**) [1940s+] to rub one's body, esp. the genital area, against one's partner while dancing. (**d**) [1970s] (*also* **grind off**) to masturbate. **2** to work laboriously; to exhaust oneself. (**a**) [mid-19C+] to work hard, esp. at an unrewarding but necessary task; thus adj. *grinding*, hard-working, dedicated. (**b**) [mid-19C+] to devote an unreasonable amount of time and effort to one's studies. (**c**) [late 19C–1900s] to tire, to exhaust; to annoy. (**d**) [late 19C–1900s] to cause someone to work hard. (**e**) [1930s] (*US Und.*) of a confidence man, to devote a great deal of time to persuading a potential victim. **3** to speak mockingly or persuasively. (**a**) [late 19C–1900s] to ridicule, to satirize. (**b**) [1920s–30s] (*US*) to tout a carnival sideshow. **4** [1980s+] (*US campus*) to eat, to have some food; thus as n., an event where a large amount of food is consumed.

(DERIVATIVES)

❑ **grindage** *n.* [-AGE *sfx*] [1990s+] (*US teen*) food.

IN PHRASES

❑ **grind coffee** *v.* [1920s–60s] (*US*) **1** to rotate one's hips during intercourse. **2** to rotate one's hips in a manner suggestive of copulation. ❑ **grind off** *v. see* sense 1d above. ❑ **grind one's coffee** *v.* [1920s] (*orig. US black*) to have sexual intercourse. ❑ **grind someone's jaw** *v. see* TIGHTEN SOMEONE'S JAW *under* JAW *n.*

grinder *n.*[1] [GRIND *v.*/SE *grind*] **1** [late 16C+] a tooth; usu. in pl., the teeth [their function and f. 14C SE *grinder*, a molar; the term moved into sl.]. **2** [19C] a private tutor. **3** [mid-19C] a highly diligent student. **4** [mid–late 19C] a coarse gesture, which involves placing the tip of one's thumb on one's nose and using the other hand to work an imaginary coffee-grinder; the gesture is used to refute what the subject feels is an unjustified attack on their credulity. **5** [1920s–30s] (*US tramp*) a sideshow tout. **6** in sexual contexts. (**a**) [1940s] (*US*) the penis. (**b**) [1940s–60s] the vagina. (**c**) [1950s+] (*US*) a striptease artist. (**d**) [1960s] a striptease dancer. (**e**) [1960s+] a sexually promiscuous or powerful male. **7** [1950s+] (*US*) a large sandwich made of two slabs of bread cut lengthwise from the loaf and containing a variety of ingredients.

IN PHRASES

❑ **take a grinder** *v.* [mid-19C] to make a coarse gesture similar to thumbing one's nose and using the other hand to work an imaginary coffee-grinder.

grinder *n.*[2] [ety. unknown; ? idea of working someone hard for very little pay] [20C+] (*Aus.*) a small coin.

grind house *n.* [SE *grind*/GRIND *v.* (1b)] **1** [1920s+] (*also* **grind joint**) a cinema that shows continuous performances; these were second-rate theatres, rarely showing any first-run feature films, often screening pornography; also the movie exhibited [the physical turning of the early projectors, similar to the rotation of the arm of a coffee grinder + the second-rate films, which a studio simply 'grinds out']. **2** [1930s+] (*orig. US black*) a strip club. **3** *see* GRIND JOINT *n.*[2].

grinding *n.* [SE *grind (it) out*] [1990s+] (*US black teen*) selling drugs of any kind on the street.

grinding-house *n.*[1] [SE *grind*; a ref. to the work one does as part of one's punishment] [17C–18C] a house of correction.

grinding-house *n.*[2] [GRIND *v.* (1a) + HOUSE *n.*[1] (1)/SE *shop*, a place of business or work] [19C] a brothel.

grinding mill *n.* [GRIND *v.* (1a) + MILL *n.*[1] (1)] [1930s] (*US black*) the vagina.

grinding tool *n.* [GRIND *v.* (1a) + TOOL *n.*[1] (1a)] [19C] the penis; thus *grind one's tool*, to copulate.

grind joint *n.*[1] [SE phr. *grind it out* + JOINT *n.* (3b)] [1920s+] (*US*) **1** an entertainment establishment that uses a front-man to solicit customers and runs continuous performances. **2** a third-rate casino.

grind joint *n.*[2] (*also* **grind house**) [GRIND *v.* (1a) + JOINT *n.* (3b)/HOUSE *n.*[1] (1)] **1** [1960s+] (*US*) a brothel. **2** *see* GRIND HOUSE *n.* (1).

gringo gallop *n.* [1960s] (*US*) diarrhoea suffered by tourists.

gringy *adj. see* GRUNGY *adj.*

grinkcome/grinkham/grinkum *n. see* CRINKUM *n.*

grinning bear *n.* [ext. BEAR *n.* (5b)] [1950s–60s] (*US*) the vulva.

grip *n.* [one either grips onto it, or it has one in its grip] **1** [mid-19C] (*US Und.*) something that is easy to achieve or obtain. **2** [1900s–50s] (*Aus.*) a steady job, regular employment. **3** [1970s] (*S.Afr.*) sexual intercourse. **4** [1970s+] (*US black*) an expense, a problem. **5** [1980s+] (*US black*) money; a sum of money. **6** [1990s+] (*US campus*) (*also* **gripa**) a substantial amount, a lot of. **7** [1990s+] (*US campus*) a long time. **8** [1990s+] (*US black*) the male genitals. **9** [2000s] (*US black*) a weapon. **10** [2000s] (*US black*) talent.

IN PHRASES

❑ **clock a grip** *v.* [1990s+] (*US black*) to make a sudden windfall of money, esp. through drug sales or some other illegal scheme.

SE in slang uses

IN PHRASES

❑ **get a grip on things** *v.* [pun] [1990s+] to masturbate.

grip *v.*[1] [? GRIPE *v.* (2)] [1960s] (*US black*) to boast and then to retreat from one's claims.

grip *v.*[2] **1** [1960s+] (*US prison*) to curry favour with a more powerful inmate or with the authorities. **2** [1970s] (*S.Afr.*) to take, to steal. **3** [1980s] (*S.Afr.*) to fondle. **4** [2000s] to apprehend and arrest.

SE in slang uses

IN PHRASES

❑ **grip the pencil** *v.* (*also* **grip it**) [PENCIL *n.* (2)] [1970s] to masturbate.

gripa *n. see* GRIP *n.* (6).

gripe *n.*[1] (*also* **griper**) [SE *gripe*, the act of grasping] **1** [mid-16C–early 17C] (*UK Und.*) any cheating gamester, spec. the member of a team who makes bets with the victim. **2** [mid-17C–19C] (*UK Und.*) a miser. **3** [late 18C] (*Irish*) a hand.

IN COMPOUNDS

❑ **gripe-fist** *n.* (*also* **gripe-penny, gripe-well**) [17C; 19C] a money-lender, a miser.

gripe *n.*[2] [GRIPE *v.*] [1920s+] (*US*) a complaint or tedious person or thing; thus *gripe session*, an airing of complaints.

gripe *v.* [SE *gripes*, the pains of colic, of which one complains] **1** [1900s–30s] (*US*) to disgust. **2** [1920s+] (*orig. US*) to complain, to make a fuss. **3** [1940s+] (*US*) to anger, to annoy.

IN PHRASES

❑ **gripe someone's soul** *v.* [1930s+] (*US campus*) to anger or disgust greatly.

griped *adj.* [GRIPE *v.* (3)] [1920s–60s] (*US*) angry.

griper *n.*[1] [SE *griper*, one who grasps] **1** [early 19C+] (*Irish*) (*also* **gripper**) a bailiff. **2** [mid-19C] (*UK Und.*) a fingernail.

griper *n.*[2] (*also* **gripes, gripper, gripster**) [GRIPE *v.*] [1930s] (*US*) a moaner, a complainer.

griper *n.*[3] *see* GRIPE *n.*[1].

gripes *n.* [SE *gripe*, to grasp; ? underpinned by SE *gripe*, a vulture] [late 17C–18C] a miser, a banker, a usurer.

gripper *n.*[1] [SE *grip*] [late 19C] a miser.

gripper *n.*[2] **1** *see* GRIPER *n.*[1] (1). **2** *see* GRIPER *n.*[2].

grippers *n.* **1** [1940s] (*US black*) shoes, esp. new ones. **2** [1980s] (*US campus*) men's briefs.

gripples *n.* [SE *gripple*, a small ditch or trench, ult. synon. 11C *grip*] [1980s] (*US black*) the anus.

grips *n.*[1] [1990s+] (*US black*) a pair of trainers.

grips *n.*[2] [abbr. *BUGGER'S GRIPS under* BUGGER *n.*[1]] [2000s] sideburns; thus *gripper*, one who has sideburns.

gripster *n. see* GRIPER *n.*[2].

gristle *n.* (*also* **gris, grist**) [SE *gristle-bone*, any part of the body consisting of gristle] [early 17C+] the penis.

IN COMPOUNDS

❑ **gristle-gripper** *n.* **1** [1980s] (*Aus.*) a masturbator. **2** [1990s+] the vagina. ❑ **gristle-hammer** *n.* [2000s] the penis.

IN PHRASES

❑ **give someone the gristle** *v.* [2000s] (*US black*) of a man, to have sexual intercourse.

grit *n.*[1] [19C+] (*US*) solidity or strength of character, spirit, pluck, stamina; thus *be the grit*, to be the 'right sort', the 'genuine article'.

IN COMPOUNDS

❑ **real grit** *n.* [? strengthened by NITTY-GRITTY *n.* (1)] **1** [mid-19C] (*also* **pure grit**) the genuine item, the 'real thing'. **2** [mid–late 19C] (*US*) (*also* **true grit**) an admirable person. **3** [1970s] (*US black*) the absolute truth, the essential facts.

IN PHRASES

❑ **grit out** *v.* [1980s+] (*US*) to endure hardship.

grit *n.*[2] [SE *grit*, the ground; SE in 20C+] [mid-19C] (*US*) land or property.

IN PHRASES

❑ **hit the grit** *v.* **1** [mid-19C+] (*US*) (*also* **cut grit, hit the gravel, ...turf, wallop the flint**) to leave, to get moving, to travel fast. **2** [mid-19C+] (*US*) to die. **3** [1900s–30s] (*US tramp*) (*also* **hit the gravel**) to jump or be forced to jump off a moving train.

grit *n.*[3] [orig. RAF, but likely SE *hominy grits*, a staple of black and white food in the US South] **1** [1940s–70s] (*orig. RAF*) food. **2** *see* GRITS *n.*[1] (1).

IN PHRASES

□ **grit (it)** *v.* [1960s–70s] (*US black/campus*) to eat; thus *gritting place*, a restaurant.

grit *n.*[4] (*also* **gritty**) [for ety. *see* prev.] **1** [1960s+] (*orig. US black*) a white person, esp. a southerner or redneck. **2** [1980s] (*US campus*) a working-class white student.

grit *n.*[5] [abbr./pron.] [1980s+] (*US campus*) a cigarette.

grit *n.*[6] [its consistency] [2000s] (*US drugs*) crack cocaine.

grit *v.*[1] [SE *grit one's teeth*] [1970s] (*US prison*) to stop talking to another inmate.

grit *v.*[2] [SAmE *grits*, coarse oatmeal widely eaten in Southern US] [1990s+] (*US black*) to eat.

gritch *v.* [GRIPE *v.* (2) + BITCH *v.* (3)] [1960s+] (*US campus*) to nag, to complain.

gritchy *adj.* [GRITCH *v.* + sfx *-y*] [1970s+] (*US campus*) irritable, grouchy.

grits *n.*[1] (*also* **grit**) [lit. + fig. uses of SE *grits*, coarse oatmeal, a trad. Southern or black food] [1950s+] (*US black*) any form of food.

IN PHRASES

□ **get one's grits** *v.* [1960s] (*US black*) to enjoy something. □ **up in someone's grits** [2000s] (*US black*) of a man, having sexual intercourse.

grits *n.*[2] [NITTY-GRITTY *n.*] [1970s+] **1** anything seen as a necessity, e.g. money or sex. **2** one's business.

gritter *n.* [GRIT *n.*[4] (2)] [1990s+] (*US campus*) a white working-class teenager.

gritty *n.*[1] *see* GRIT *n.*[4].

gritty *n.*[2] *see* NITTY-GRITTY *n.*

gritty *adj.*[1] [GRIT *n.*[1] (1) + sfx *-y*; subseq. use is SE] [mid-19C–1950s] (*US*) determined, firm, plucky.

gritty *adj.*[2] [one is 'down in the grit', i.e. dirt] **1** [late 19C] impoverished, penniless. **2** [1950s+] in 'straitened circumstances'.

grizzie *n.* [? it looks like 'grizzled' hair or Fr. *gris*, grey] [late 18C] a wig.

grizzle *n.* [GRIZZLE (ONE'S GUTS) *v.*] **1** [late 17C–early 19C] a grumbler, a whinger. **2** [20C+] a fit of whingeing, grumbling or sulking, a peevish mood.

grizzle (one's guts) *v.* [despite the lack of citations (the first is in a ballad recorded in 1842), the v. is prob. contemporary with GRIZZLE *n.* (1)] [mid-19C+] to whine, to cry slightly but continually, usu. of a child.

IN COMPOUNDS

□ **grizzle-guts** *n.* [GUT *n.* (1a)] [1940s+] (*Aus.*) a grumbler, a whinger.

IN PHRASES

□ **street grizzling** *n.* [1930s] (*UK tramp*) the practice of singing pitiful songs to beg money; thus *grizzler*, a singing tramp.

grizzler *n.* [GRIZZLE (ONE'S GUTS) *v.*] [1900s–30s] a beggar who pretends blindness or physical disability.

grizzly *n.* [SE *grizzly bear*] **1** [mid–late 19C; 1990s+] (*US*) a brute. **2** [late 19C] a Russian; the Russian people [BEAR *n.* (2)]. **3** [1970s] (*US black*) an unattractive woman [BEAR *n.* (1d)].

groady *n. see* GRODY *adj.*

groak *n.* (*also* **growk**) [synon. Scot. *groak*] [20C+] (*Ulster*) a child who sits watching others eating, in the hope of being asked to join them.

groan and grunt *n. see* GRUMBLE (AND GRUNT) *n.*

groan-box *n.* [1920s–50s] (*orig. US black*) a musical instrument, esp. an accordion, radio or juke box.

groaner *n.* (*also* **sigher**) [his exaggeratedly enthusiastic, albeit completely spurious, devotions, which draw the congregants' attention away from his actual purpose] [late 18C–mid-19C] (*UK Und.*) a pickpocket who specializes in robbing members of a church congregation.

groatable *adj.* [? SE *groats*, hulled and/or crushed grain of various kinds; poss. used in brewing; or SE *groat*, fourpence, the price of a drink] [early 18C] (*US*) drunk.

groaty *adj. see* GRODY *adj.*

grob *adj.* [Ger./Yid. *grob*, loutish, vulgar, coarse] [1940s+] (*S.Afr.*) unpleasant, coarse.

groceries *n.*[1] (*also* **grocery**) [mid-19C–1910s] sugar, esp. when added to a hot alcoholic drink.

groceries *n.*[2] [? link to GREENS *n.*[1]] **1** [1960s+] (*US gay*) the male genitals. **2** [1980s] the vagina. **3** [1980s] the breasts.

grocer's cart *n.* [rhy. sl.] [20C+] (*Aus.*) the heart.

grocer's shop *n.* [rhy. sl. = WOP *n.*[1] (1)] [1970s] an Italian.

grocery *n.*[1] [? its suitability for buying groceries] [mid-18C–early 19C] small change.

grocery *n.*[2] [mid-19C–1940s] a liquor store or small bar; a speakeasy.

SE in slang uses

IN COMPOUNDS

□ **grocery-boy** *n.* [he is a constant visitor to his local grocery] [1930s–50s] (*US drugs*) an addict, in the throes of withdrawal, whose appetite has returned.

IN PHRASES

□ **charter the grocery** *v. see* CHARTER THE BAR *under* BAR *n.*[2].

grocery *n.*[3] [? SE *gross*] [2000s] (*US black*) a large amount.

grocery *n.*[4] *see* GROCERIES *n.*[1].

grockle *n.* [the term originated in the West Country, spec. in Torbay, where a local remarked that the stream of visitors to the town resembled little Grocks (the celebrated clown *Grock*, real name Charles Adrien Wettach, 1880–1959), but spread throughout Britain's holiday resorts where the local people thus derided the flocks of annual visitors to their area; however, note Quinion WWW (14/7/00): 'GROCKLE An interesting note has arrived from Dr Jeremy Marshall, an associate editor of the *Oxford English Dictionary*. The *OED* has worked on the word, preparatory to writing the entry for it (which will not, however, appear for some years). "The word was popularized because of its use in the film *The System* in 1962, the script-writer having picked the word up from the locals during filming in Torquay. According to research by a local journalist in the mid-1990s, the word in fact originated from a strip cartoon in the comic *Dandy* entitled 'Danny and his Grockle'. (The grockle was a magical dragon-like creature.) A local man, who had had a summer job at a swimming pool as a youngster, said that he had used the term as a nickname for a small elderly lady who was a regular customer one season. During banter in the pub among the summer workers, the term then became generalized as a term for summer visitors. I have the impression that this had occurred in, or only shortly before, the summer in which *The System* was filmed: we know of no instances of the word from the 1950s, or indeed from before the release of *The System*"'. As usual, we are left with loose ends, in particular where the writer of the cartoon got the name from, but this seems pretty definitive] [1960s+] **1** a tourist. **2** (*UK society*) an outsider, with overtones of unpleasantness and boorishness.

grody *adj.* (*also* **groady, groaty, grodie, grotey**) [GROTTY *adj.*; ult. SE *grotesque*] [1960s+] **1** (*US teen*) disgusting, unpleasant; often ext. as *grody to the max* [TO THE MAX *under* MAX *n.*]. **2** (*US campus*) noisy, vulgar, e.g. of a party.

groe *n.* [abbr. SE *Negro*; esp. New England use] [1990s+] (*US*) a derog. term for a black person.

grog *n.*[1] [abbr. SE *grogram*, 'a coarse fabric of silk, of mohair and wool, or of these mixed with silk' (*OED*). Orig. applied as a nickname for Admiral Vernon, known as 'Old Grog', because he wore a grogram cloak. The name was transferred to the mixture of rum and water, which in August 1740 he ordered should be served instead of the RN's usual issue of neat rum; however, the 19C *Roxburghe Ballads* collection includes one such ballad, dated 1672–85, which contains the word 'grog' and would thus seem to overturn this otherwise accepted ety. Further note M. Quinion (letter 14/03/08): 'Ebsworth, [...] was a scrupulous editor, and his dating ought to be on the mark. But it's a one-off example. I'm also bothered by finding the same line in a ballad about a sailor named Jack Robinson, which was published in a collection of comic songs by Thomas Hudson in 1818. The three lines read "In a public-house then they both sot down / And talk'd of admirals of high renown / And drunk'd as much grog as come to half-a-crown." The unknown author may just have borrowed a couple of good lines, of course (such plagiarism was common) but the reference to admirals, and the general tone of the piece, hints that it (and presumably therefore the supposed Roxburghe Ballad) might have been written after 1740 in knowledge of the Vernon story.'] **1** [late 17C+] (*also* **Mr Grog**) alcohol, orig. rum but soon generic for any intoxicating liquor, whether beer or spirits. **2** [late 19C] a party at which grog is drunk. **3** [1950s] (*Aus.*) a drink of beer. **4** [1950s] (*mainly juv.*) tea.

IN COMPOUNDS

❑ **grog artist** *n.* [-ARTIST *sfx*] [1990s+] (*Aus./N.Z.*) a heavy drinker, a drunkard. ❑ **grog blossom** *n. see under* BLOSSOM *n.*[2]. ❑ **grog-den** *n. see* GROG SHOP below. ❑ **grog fight** *n.* [mid-late 19C] (*orig. milit.*) a drinking party. ❑ **groghead** *n.* [-HEAD *sfx* (4)] [1960s] (*US*) a drunkard. ❑ **grog hole** *n.* [mid-19C] (*US*) a public house. ❑ **grog mill** *n.* [on pattern of GIN-MILL *n.*] [1940s] (*US*) a rough or illicit drinking place. ❑ **grog shanty** *n.* [mid-19C–1930s] (*US/Aus./N.Z.*) a public house. ❑ **grog shop** *n.* (*also* **grog-den**) **1** [late 18C+] a public house. **2** [mid-19C] the mouth.

IN PHRASES

❑ **dry grog** *n. see under* DRY *adj.*[1]. ❑ **grog talking** *see* IT'S THE BEER TALKING *under* TALK *v.* ❑ **hit the grog** *v.* [1980s] to get drunk. ❑ **on the grog** *adj.* [1950s+] (*Aus.*) very drunk.

grog *n.*[2] [? Shetland Isles *grog*, sediment, grounds] [1990s+] (*Scot. juv.*) spittle.

grog *v.*[1] [GROG *n.*[1] (1)] [early 19C+] (*Aus.*) to drink; thus *grogging*, drinking.

IN PHRASES

❑ **grog-on** *n.* (*also* **grog-up**) [1950s+] (*Aus./N.Z.*) a drinking session, a party. ❑ **grog up** *v.* (*also* **grog on**) [1950s+] to drink heavily, to drink to excess.

grog *v.*[2] [GROG *n.*[2]] [1990s+] (*Scot. juv.*) to spit.

grogan *n.* [ety. unknown] [1990s+] (*orig. Aus.*) a large piece of excrement.

grogans *n.* [generic Irish family name *Grogan*; such whiskers were popular among Irish-Americans] [1900s–20s] (*US*) muttonchop sidewhiskers.

grogged *adj.* [GROG *v.*[1]] [mid–late 19C] tipsy.

groggery *n.* [GROG *n.*[1] (1)] [early 19C+] (*US/N.Z.*) a saloon, a public house.

groggery *adj.* [GROG *n.*[1] (1)] [early 19C] (*US*) tipsy.

groggified *adj. see* GROGGY *adj.* (1).

groggist *n.* [GROG *n.*[1] (1) + sfx *-ist*] [late 19C] (*Aus.*) the landlord of a public house.

groggy *n.* [GROG *n.*[1] (1) + sfx *-y*] [late 19C] (*US*) **1** a seller of alcohol. **2** an opponent of prohibition.

groggy *adj.* [GROG *n.*[1] (1) + sfx *-y*] **1** [mid-18C+] (*also* **groggified**) drunken, tipsy; under the influence of a drug. **2** [19C+] weak, unsteady, semi-conscious; thus *grog out*, to become comatose, unstable.

grogham *n.* [ety. unknown] [late 18C–19C] (*UK Und.*) a horse.

groid *n.* [abbr. *Negroid*] [1970s+] (*US Southern campus*) a derog. term for a black student; by ext., an unpopular person.

groin *n.* (*also* **growne, groyne**) [ety. unknown; *OED* links it to the body's physical *groin*, but the link seems unlikely] [1910s+] (*UK Und.*) any ring containing a gemstone, esp. a diamond.

grok *v.* [coined by SF author Robert Heinlein (1907–88) in *Strangers in a Strange Land* (1961), it was 'Martian' for 'to drink'] [1960s+] in popular HIPPIE *n.*[2] (3) and mystic use, to appreciate, to understand and experience completely; usu. in phr. *grok the fullness*.

grollies *n.* [? var. on GOOLIE *n.* (1)] [2000s] testicles.

grolly *n. see* GREENIE *n.*[2] (2).

grommet *n.*[1] [SE *grommet*, a ring of rope, a washer] [late 19C–1940s] (*US*) **1** the vagina; thus generic for an attractive woman. **2** (*Aus.*) the anus. **3** sexual intercourse.

grommet *n.*[2] [surfing use *grommet*, a novice] [1990s+] (*Aus.*) a surfer.

IN COMPOUNDS

❑ **grommet dude** *n.* [2000s] (*N.Z. teen*) a boy.

gronk *n.* **1** [1960s] (*US campus*) dirt between the toes. **2** [1980s+] (*Aus. prison*) (*also* **gronkster**) a thug, a bully. **3** [1990s+] an act of defecation. **4** [1990s+] a contemptible person.

gronk *adj.* [GRONK *n.*] [1990s+] disgusting, contemptible.

gronked *adj.* [? echoic of snoring] [1960s+] (*US*) drunk, passed out, tired out, fast asleep.

gronkster *n. see* GRONK *n.* (2).

groody *n.* [coined by A. Burgess, *A Clockwork Orange* (1962)] [1990s+] (*US teen*) in pl., the female breasts.

grooh *adj. see* GRUESOME *adj.*

grool *n.* [GROOLY *adj.*] [1950s] a sinister person; fig., an ugly person.

grooly *adj.* [SE *gru*(*esome*) + (*gris*)*ly*] [1920s–70s] sinister.

groom *v.* [1930s] (*US tramp*) to beat (with a weapon).

grooner *n.* [? SE *gurn*, to pull faces] [2000s] a drunken tramp.

grootbek *n.* [Afk. *groot*, big + *bek*, mouth] [1940s+] (*S.Afr.*) a braggart, a boaster.

grootpraat *n.* [Afk. *groot*, big + *praat*, talk] [1940s+] (*S.Afr.*) boasting, bragging.

groove *n.*[1] [physiognomy + latterly play on IN THE GROOVE *under* GROOVE *n.*[2]] [late 19C–1960s] the vagina.

groove *n.*[2] [widely popularized and generally ascribed to US jazz] **1** [1900s; 1930s+] a way of life, a way of thinking and dealing with people, events etc. **2** [1940s+] a delight, a pleasure, anything enjoyable. **3** [1950s–60s] an amusing or attractive person. **4** [1960s+] a party. **5** [1960s+] (*US*) a record or cassette recording.

IN PHRASES

❑ **bust one's groove** *v.* [2000s] (*US campus*) to annoy someone. ❑ **get one's groove on** *v.* [1990s+] **1** to get going, to dance. **2** (*US black*) to have sexual intercourse. ❑ **in the groove** *adj.* [1930s+] (*orig. US*) **1** carried away by music. **2** perfect, ideal. **3** aware, up to date. ❑ **on the groove** *adj.* [1960s] satisfactory, working properly.

groove *v.* [GROOVE *n.*[2]] **1** [1930s+] (*US*) to play jazz or (latterly) rock music. **2** [1950s+] to enjoy oneself, e.g. at a party; thus *grooved*, happy; *grooviness*, pleasure, enjoyment. **3** [1950s] to praise. **4** [1950s+] to give pleasure, to amuse someone. **5** [1950s+] (*also* **groove with**) to accomodate oneself to, to get along with. **6** [1960s+] to travel along, to move. **7** [1960s+] to have sexual intercourse. **8** [1960s+] to dance; to enjoy music.

IN PHRASES

❑ **groove on** *v.* (*also* **groove behind**) [1950s+] to enjoy or appreciate a situation or other stimulus. ❑ **groove with** *v. see* sense 5 above.

groover *n.* [GROOVE *v.*] [1960s+] a person, neutral when coined in the 1960s but by 1980s+ usu. slightly derisory, since the term, and by ext. the person described, is *de facto* old-fashioned; but still some positive use.

grooving *n.* [GROOVE *v.* (2)] [1960s+] **1** (*orig. US*) enjoying oneself. **2** (*drugs*) the state of having an enjoyable time while using a drug.

grooving *adj. see* GROOVY *adj.*[1] (2).

groovy *n.* [SE *groove*] [1960s–70s] (*Scot.*) a scar.

groovy *adj.*[1] [SE *groove*, a routine life] **1** [late 19C–1910s] staid, conservative. **2** [1960s+] (*US campus*) (*also* **grooving**) not using drugs; not fashionable.

groovy *adj.*[2] [Mezzrow & Wolfe, *Really the Blues* (1946): 'He's groovy, the way musicians are groovy when they pool their talents instead of competing with each other, work together and slip into the same groove'] **1** [1930s+] delightful, wonderful, pleasant, enjoyable etc. **2** [1940s–70s] intoxicated by a drug, usu. marijuana. **3** [1940s+] fashionable. **4** [1960s+] attractive. **5** [1980s+] (*US teen*) passé, out-of-date, esp. when referring to the tastes and styles of the 1960s, during which time sense 1 above was the only accepted meaning.

groovy *adv.* [1960s+] a positive intensifier, e.g. *groovy cool.*

groovy! *excl.* (*also* **groovy cool!**) [GROOVY *adj.*[2] (1)] [1960s+] a general excl. of approval, pleasure.

grope *n.* [GROPE v. (1)] [late 18C+] (*US*) a welcome or unwelcome fondling or handling of the breasts, buttocks or genitals.

IN PHRASES

❑ **come the grope** *v.* (*also* **go the grope**) [1960s+] (*Aus.*) to fondle someone sexually.

grope *v.* **1** [14C+] (*also* **grople**) to fondle or touch the breasts, buttocks or genitals of someone, esp. a potential partner in order to assess their response to one's advances. **2** [20C+] to kiss passionately. **3** [1980s] (*US campus*) to act in a clumsy manner.

IN COMPOUNDS

❑ **gropehole** *n.* [early 18C] the anus. ❑ **grope-in** *n. see* LOVE-IN *n.* (2).

IN PHRASES

❑ **grope for trout in a peculiar river** *v.* [coined by Shakespeare in *Measure for Measure* (1603)] [early 17C–19C] to have sexual intercourse.

groper *n.*[1] [SE *grope*] **1** [late 17C–mid-19C] a blind man, both actually and in the game of Blind Man's Buff. **2** [18C–19C] a midwife. **3** [late 18C–mid-19C] a pocket [one gropes in it for money]. **4** [early 19C] in pl., the hands. **5** [late 19C] (*US*) a blind beggar. **6** [1980s+] (*US drugs*) a deep inhalation of cannabis from a pipe [it tends to be followed by a coughing fit as one's lungs *grope* for air].

groper *n.*[2] [abbr. SAND-GROPER *n.*] [late 19C+] (*Aus.*) a Western Australian.

IN COMPOUNDS

❑ **groperland** *n.* (*also* **Groperdom**) [20C+] (*Aus.*) West Australia; thus *Groperlander*, an inhabitant of West Australia.

groperess *n.* [GROPER *n.*[1] (1) + fem. sfx *-ess*] [mid-19C] a blind woman.

grople *v. see* GROPE v. (1).

gropus *n.* [var. GROPER *n.*[1] (3); one has to grope into its depths to find small items] [mid-19C] a coat pocket.

gross *adj.* (*also* **grossy**) [1920s; 1950s+] (*orig. US teen campus*) disgusting.

gross! *excl.* [GROSS *adj.*] [1950s+] (*mainly US teen/campus*) disgusting!

grossed-out *adj.* [GROSS OUT v.] [1960s+] (*US campus*) disgusted, repelled, appalled.

grosser *n.* [GROSS *adj.*] [1970s+] (*US*) a disgusting or ugly person.

gross-out *n.* [GROSS OUT v.] [1960s+] **1** (*orig. US*) something or someone disgusting. **2** (*US campus*) a contest between students to see who can be most disgusting.

gross-out *adj.* [GROSS OUT v.] [1970s+] disgusting, repellent, shocking.

gross out *v.* [GROSS *adj.*] (*orig. US campus*) **1** [1960s+] to disgust someone, to shock someone; thus excl. *gross me out!* that really disgusts me! **2** [1980s] to be overwhelmed by disgust.

grossy *adj. see* GROSS *adj.*

grosvenor squares *n.* [rhy. sl.] [1970s] flares (flared trousers).

grot *n.* [GROTTY *adj.*; note N.Z. school/institutional use *grot*, lavatory] **1** [1960s+] (*Aus./US*) a dirty, untidy person. **2** [1980s+] dirt, detritus.

grot *adj. see* GROTTY *adj.*

grote *n.* [ety. unknown] [late 19C–1910s] an informer.

grotey *adj. see* GRODY *adj.*

groth *n.* [? echoic] [1990s+] (*UK juv.*) spittle.

grotty *adj.* (*also* **grot**) [SE *grotesque*; esp. popular during the Beatlemania era of the early 1960s as it was used in the film *Hard Day's Night* (1964) and allegedly coined by them (or more likely the writer of the screenplay Alun Owen although he has claimed that it was existing Liverpool sl.)] [1960s+] disgusting, unattractive.

grouce *adj. see* GROUSE *adj.*

grouch *n.* [? backform. f. GROUCHY *adj.* but *see* ety. there] [late 19C+] (*orig. US*) **1** a bad temper. **2** a grumpy, complaining person, or creature. **3** a complaint.

IN COMPOUNDS

❑ **grouch-bag** *n.* [the image, among the actors who coined the term, of one who saved their money being a grumpy person] **1** [20C+] a hidden pocket or purse, in which money can be secured. **2** [1910s] the money hidden in it; thus *grouch money*, savings.

grouch *v.* [GROUCH *n.*; note OF *groucier*, to murmur, to grumble] [1910s+] (*orig. US*) to mope, to grumble, to complain; thus *grouched*, angry, petulant.

groucho *n.* [rhy. sl.; *Groucho Marx* = SPARKS *n.*[2] (2); ult. US comedian *Groucho Marx* (1890–1977)] [20C+] an electrician.

grouchy *adj.* (*also* **grouched**) [? *OED* suggests a root in GROUCH *n.* (1), but *HDAS* prefers the reverse and roots *grouchy* in SE *grudge*, synon. dial. *grutch* or Yorks./US dial. *grouty*, grumpy] [late 19C+] ill-tempered, sour.

grounation *n.* [? ety. unknown; ? Fr. *grosnation*, a great nation or fig. use of SE *groan*, i.e. shout out + sfx *-ation*] [1950s+] (*W.I. Rasta*) a large, island-wide meeting-cum-celebration for Rastafarians.

ground *n.* [1950s+] (*W.I. Rasta*) one's home, one's plot of land.

IN PHRASES

❑ **on the ground** [20C+] (*US prison*) on the streets, free.

SE in slang uses

IN COMPOUNDS

❑ **ground angel** *n.* [1940s] (*US black*) a pretty young woman. ❑ **ground biscuit** *n.* [1920s+] (*US*) a brick or stone when used as a missile. ❑ **ground control** *n.* (*also* **ground man**) [SE *ground control*, a ground-based individual who communicates with an astronaut] [1960s+] (*drugs*) a guide or caretaker during a hallucinogenic experience; such a person is either not taking the drug or a veteran user. ❑ **ground grabbers** *n.* (*also* **ground grippers**) [1910s–60s] (*US black*) shoes, esp. new ones. ❑ **ground-hog** *n. see* separate entries. ❑ **groundpad** *n. see* separate entry. ❑ **ground parrot** *n.* [play on COCKATOO *n.*[2] (3)] [late 19C] (*Aus.*) a small farmer. ❑ **ground pounder** *n.* [1940s+] (*US*) an infantry soldier; also attrib. ❑ **ground rations** *n.* [pun] [1930s+] (*US black*) sexual intercourse (cf. UNDER RATIONS *n.*). ❑ **ground smasher** *n.* [1950s] (*US black*) in pl., feet; also shoes. ❑ **ground sweat** *n.* [late 17C–mid-19C] a grave; thus as v. or *take a ground-sweat*, to be buried.

IN PHRASES

❑ **from the ground up** [late 19C+] **1** (*US*) of a person, sturdy. **2** (*orig. US*) from the very beginning, from first principles, in essence.

ground *v.* [SE *ground*, to prevent an aircraft from flying] **1** [1930s+] (*US*) to suspend from work; usu. as *grounded*. **2** [1950s+] (*orig. US*) (*also* **house**) to restrict someone, usu. an errant teenager, from enjoying their regular social life as a punishment for some real or perceived misdemeanour; usu. as *grounded*.

grounded *adj.* [SE *grounded*, used of an aircraft that cannot fly] **1** [1930s] dead. **2** *see* GROUND v.

grounder *n.* [something that is either *on the ground* or knocks one *to the ground*] **1** [late 19C] a knock-down blow. **2** [1930s; 1990s+] (*US*) a cigarette that is picked up from the ground to be smoked. **3** [1970s+] (*US drugs*) a barbiturate.

ground-hog *n.*[1] [1910s–50s] (*US*) a sausage, a frankfurter, a hot dog.

ground-hog *n.*[2] **1** [1920s+] (*US*) a caisson worker, working under compressed air, digging and laying the foundations of bridges etc. **2** [1960s+] (*Can.*) a meteorologist.

SE in slang uses

IN COMPOUNDS

❑ **groundhog case** *n.* [image of the trapped animal] [late 19C–1950s] (*US, Western*) a tight corner, an inescapable situation.

groundpad *n.* [1930s–40s] (*US black*) **1** in pl., feet. **2** a shoe; usu. in pl.

IN COMPOUNDS

❑ **groundpad bag** *n.* [1940s] (*US black*) in pl., socks. ❑ **groundpad spade** *n.* [1940s] (*US black*) a shoehorn.

grounds *n.* [1960s] (*drugs*) the residue left after an injection of heroin.

group grope *n.* [SE *group* + GROPE *n.*] **1** [1960s+] an orgy. **2** [1970s+] (*US campus*) in fig. use, an encounter group, esp. one that stresses physical contact.

groupie *n.*[1] (*also* **grouper**) [SE *group*, a collection of people] [1960s+] a devotee of group sex.

groupie *n.*[2] (*also* **grouper, groupy**) [SE *group*, a pop/rock band] **1** [1960s+] a girl or young woman who associates herself with rock bands, offering her body in return for a share of their celebrity. **2** [1970s+] anyone, male or female, who is an obsessive fan; the adoration need not run to sex, nor are the subjects necessarily rock stars.

grouse *n.*[1] [SE *grouse*, the small game bird] [mid-19C+] a young woman; thus sexual intercourse.

IN PHRASES

❑ **do a grouse** *v.* [Lancashire dial. *grouse*, to have sexual intercourse] [mid–late 19C] to search for sexually complaisant women.

grouse *n.*[2] [GROUSE *v.*[1]] [1910s+] a complaint; thus *grouser*, a complainer.

grouse *n.*[3] [GROUSE *adj.*] [1960s–70s] (*Aus. Und.*) a tailor-made, rather than a prison-issue cigarette.

grouse, the *n.* [GROUSE *adj.*] [1920s+] (*Aus./N.Z.*) the best, the ultimate, the ideal.

grouse *adj.* (*also* **grouce**) [ety. unknown; ? UK dial. *crouse*, happy, lively, pleased] [1920s+] (*Aus./N.Z.*) wonderful, attractive, excellent, an all-purpose term of approval; also ironic use.

IN COMPOUNDS

❑ **grouse gear** *n.* [GEAR *n.* (3)] [1950s+] (*Aus. teen*) a particularly attractive woman.

IN PHRASES

❑ **go for the grouse** *v.* [1970s+] (*Aus.*) to look for whatever is seen as worthwhile.

grouse *v.*[1] [? OF *groucier*, to murmur, to grumble] [late 19C+] (*orig. milit.*) to grumble, to complain; thus n. *grouser*, one who grumbles; adj. *grousy*, ill-tempered, complaining.

grouse *v.*[2] [GROUSE *n.*[1]] [late 19C+] to engage in sexual activity.

grouter *n.* [ety. unknown; ? Yorks. dial. *grout*, to rummage or root about] [20C+] (*Aus.*) **1** a piece of good luck, an unfair advantage; esp. in phrs. *come in on the grouter, run the grouter*. **2** as excl.

IN PHRASES

❑ **go the grouter** *v.* [1980s+] (*Aus. prison*) to grope a woman.

grouter *v.* [GROUTER *n.*] [20C+] (*Aus.*) to get hold of something through luck rather than judgement, to take unfair advantage of a situation.

grouthead *n.* [SE *grout*, lit. coarse meal, taken as something large and rough and/or SAmE *grout*, to grumble + -HEAD *sfx* (1)] [16C–mid-17C; mid-19C–1900s] (*later use US*) a fool, a simpleton.

groutnoll *n.* (*also* **grout-nold, grutnol**) [SE *grout*, lit. coarse meal, taken as something large and rough + *noll*, head] [early–mid-17C] a fool.

Grove, the *n.* [abbr.] [1950s+] (*orig. UK black*) Ladbroke *Grove*, London W11/W10.

grovel *v.* [1980s+] (*US campus*) to neck, to enjoy sexual relations, esp. with someone who is not one's regular partner.

grove of the evangelist *n.* (*also* **shady grove of the evangelist**) [pun; the area was well-known for its up-market courtesans and 'kept women'] [mid-19C–1910s] St John's Wood, London NW8.

grover *n.* [the head of US President *Grover* Cleveland (1837–1908), which is printed on the bill] [1980s] (*US*) a $1000 note.

grow horns *v.* [the horns are those of a bull] **1** [1970s+] (*US campus*) to become angry. **2** *see under* HORNS *n.*

growk *n.* *see* GROAK *n.*

growl *n.*[1] [1930s] (*US*) food, a snack.

growl *n.*[2] [abbr. GROWL AND GRUNT *n.*] [1940s+] **1** the vagina. **2** women, viewed as sex-objects. **3** sexual intercourse.

growl and grunt *n.* *see* GRUMBLE (AND GRUNT) *n.*

growl at the badger *v.* *see under* BADGER *n.*[1].

growl-biter *n.* [GROWL *n.*[2] (1) + SE *bite*] [1940s+] one who performs cunnilingus.

growl-biting *n.* [GROWL-BITER *n.*] [1940s+] cunnilingus.

growler *n.*[1] [they all 'growl'] **1** [early 19C+] a dog. **2** [early 19C+] a cannon. **3** [1910s] a horse. **4** [1930s] an iceberg. **5** [1960s] (*US*) a police car siren; the car itself. **6** [1970s] a lion. **7** [1990s+] (*UK juv.*) a nagging woman. **8** [2000s] (*UK prison*) a menacing prison inmate who resists using physical violence.

growler *n.*[2] [either a pun on SE *sulky* (although this was a one-horse, two-wheeled vehicle), or the creaks and rattles of the cab, or the stereotypically poor temper of the driver] [mid-19C–1910s] a four-wheeled cab.

IN COMPOUNDS

❑ **growler-shover** *n.* [late 19C–1910s] a cab driver.

IN PHRASES

❑ **work the growler** *v.* [late 19C–1910s] to hire a cab to accompany one on a 'pub-crawl'.

growler *n.*[3] [ety. unknown; ? the growling, grating noise of the can as it slid, full of beer, across the bar, or the 'growling' or grumbling of the children who were sent on the errand, or the drunken arguing that ensued among recipients of the liquor; for full discussion *see* Cohen, *Studies in Slang* VI (1999) pp.1–20] **1** [late 19C–1930s] (*US*) a whisky-flask. **2** [late 19C–1940s] (*US*) a container, usu. a covered pail with a carrying handle, in which beer is purchased at a tavern, then brought home for consumption; thus *growler money, growler boy, growler bag*. **3** [1920s–50s] (*US prison*) any form of container, used for coffee, conveying illicit homebrewed alcohol etc.

IN PHRASES

❑ **rush the growler** *v.* (*also* **chase the growler, work...**) [late 19C+] (*US*) to buy beer from a tavern and bring it home for drinking there; thus n., adj. *growler-rushing*.

growler *n.*[4] [the noise, either of someone straining to defecate or of incarcerated prisoners] (*US*) **1** [1940s–70s] a lavatory, usu. in a prison cell. **2** [1980s] a prison.

growler *n.*[5] [GROWL AND GRUNT *n.*] [1990s+] **1** the vagina. **2** in ext. use, an unattractive woman.

growler *n.*[6] [? one's stomach is growling with hunger] [2000s] food.

growl in her busby *v.* *see under* BUSBY *n.*

grown-ass *adj.* (*also* **grown, grown-assed**) [SE *grown* + -ASS *sfx*] [1930s] (*US black*) adult, mature, grown-up.

growne/groyne *n.* *see* GROIN *n.*

grrl *n.* [1990s+] (*US gay*) a young lesbian, reasonably but not wholly masculine in style.

grub *n.*[1] [SE *grub*, the larva of an insect] **1** [mid-17C–18C; 1940s+] 'a person of slovenly attire and unpleasant manners' (*OED*). **2** [mid-18C+] a dirty, unkempt person, esp. a child. **3** [1950s] (*Aus.*) tuberculosis. **4** [1960s] (*US campus*) a student kitchen worker.

grub *n.*[2] [SE *grub*, to dig] **1** [mid-17C+] food [one has 'grubbed it up']. **2** [mid-19C+] (*US campus*) a hard worker, one who works to the exclusion of other interests [he 'grubs up' facts]. **3** [1940s+] a meal; thus *grub palace*, a restaurant [ext. of sense 1 above].

IN COMPOUNDS

❑ **grub and bub** *n.* (*also* **bub and grub**) [BUB *n.*[1] (1)] [late 18C–19C] food and drink. ❑ **grub-crib** *n.* [CRIB *n.*[1] (1)] [mid-19C] an eating house. ▫ **grub hooks** *n.* [HOOK *n.*[1] (1); ult. SE *grub-hook*, an implement used to 'grub up' roots etc] [1920s+] (*US*) fingers or hands. ▫ **grub-liner** *n.* (*also* **grub-rider**) [fig. use of cowboy jargon *line*, the boundary of a ranch] [1900s–60s] (*US*) an itinerant, out-of-work cowboy who subsists on hand-outs; thus *RIDE THE GRUB LINE under* RIDE *v.* ▫ **grub-mill** *n.* [late 19C] (*US*) the mouth. ▫ **grub-pile** *n.* [late 19C–1940s] (*US, Western*) a meal. ▫ **grub-shop** *n.* [mid-19C] **1** an eating house. **2** the mouth. ▫ **grub-slinger** *n.* [1910s] (*US*) **1** a cook. **2** a waiter or waitress. ▫ **grub-spoiler** *n.* [late 19C–1950s] (*US*) a cook. ▫ **grubstake** see separate entries. ▫ **grub station** *n.* [1900s] (*US*) a restaurant. ▫ **grub thirst** *n.* [late 19C] (*US*) hunger; appetite. ▫ **grub-trap** *n.* [SE *trap*/TRAP *n.*[1] (4)] [mid–late 19C] the mouth. ▫ **grub warehouse** *n.* [mid-19C] the stomach.

IN PHRASES

▫ **get one's grub on** *v.* [1990s+] (*US black*) to eat, esp. voraciously. ▫ **in grub** [early 19C] employed. ▫ **like grub** *adv.* [SE *grub*, to dig, to root up] [late 19C] keenly, enthusiastically.

grub *adj.* [GRUB *n.*[2] (1)] [1990s+] of food, tasty.

grub *v.*[1] [GRUB *n.*[2] (1) + SE *grub up*, to uproot, i.e. whatever can be found/begged] **1** [18C+] (*also* **grub out, grub up**) to eat. **2** [19C–1920s] to provide with food. **3** [late 19C] to scavenge. **4** [late 19C+] to beg, to scrounge; thus phr. *on the grub*.

grub *v.*[2] [dial. *grub*, to potter about] [mid-19C] (*UK Und.*) to walk (unsteadily).

IN PHRASES

▫ **grub along** *v.* [late 19C+] to subsist, to struggle along.

grub *v.*[3] [SE *grub*, to dig up, to root around] **1** [mid-19C+] (*US campus*) to study hard. **2** [1960s+] to kiss passionately. **3** [1960s+] to have sexual intercourse.

grub! *excl.* [1900s] (*Aus.*) a mild excl.

grubber *n.*[1] [SE *grub* v./GRUB *n.*[1] (2); note Yid. *grobber*, a coarse or rude person] **1** [late 18C–1940s] (*US*) a beggar [GRUB *v.*[1] (4)]. **2** [19C] a promiscuous woman. **3** [20C+] a vagrants' casual night shelter or workhouse. **4** [1920s+] (*US*) a disgusting person. **5** [1930s] (*US*) a working man [note also *GRUB ALONG under* GRUB *v.*[2]]. **6** *see NAIL GROPER under* NAIL *n.*[1].

grubber *n.*[2] [GRUB *v.*[1] (1)] [mid-19C–1900s] an eater; thus *heavy grubber*, an enthusiastic, if unmannered, eater.

grubber *n.*[3] [GRUB *v.*[3] (1)] [late 19C] (*US campus*) a diligent student.

grubbery *n.* [GRUB *n.*[2] (1)] [19C] **1** food. **2** a public meal. **3** a cookshop; an eating house. **4** a dining room. **5** the stomach. **6** (*UK Und.*) a workhouse.

grubbies *n.* see GRUBS *n.*

grubbiken *n.* (*also* **grubbing-ken**) [GRUB *n.*[2] (1) + KEN *n.*[1] (1)] [mid-19C] a workhouse where one is fed without performing the usual mandatory labour.

grubbing *n.* [GRUB *v.*[1] (1)] [19C] eating.

IN COMPOUNDS

▫ **grubbing-crib** *n.* [CRIB *n.*[1] (1)] [mid-19C] a cookshop; thus *grubbing-crib fencer*, the proprietor of an eating house. ▫ **grubbing place** *n.* [late 19C] a restaurant, a café.

grubbins *n.*[1] [GRUB *n.*[2] (1)] [mid-19C] (*US*) food.

grubbins *n.*[2] (*also* **grubbing**) [GRUB *v.*[1] (4)] [1910s] (*UK/US Und.*) money.

grubby *n.* [GRUB *n.*[2] (2)] [1940s] (*US campus*) an ostracized student.

grub out/up *v. see* GRUB *v.*[1] (1).

grubs *n.* (*also* **grubbies**) [SE *grubby*] (*US campus*) **1** [1960s+] old or comfortable, informal clothes or shoes. **2** [2000s] smelly or dirty feet.

grubshite *v.* [SE *grubby* + SHITE *v.* (1)] [late 18C–early 19C] to foul, to make dirty.

grubstake *n.* [GRUB *n.*[2] (1) + SE *stake*, the sum of money one places on a bet; immediate root is US mining jargon *grub stake*, 'the outfit, provisions etc furnished to a prospector on condition of participating in the profits of any find he may make; a lay-out' (*Century Dict.*)] **1** [mid-19C+] (*orig. US*) enough money to buy one a meal; ext. to any form of deposit or any form of advance that allows one to work. **2** [1900s–40s] (*also* **grubstakes, grubsteaks**) food, rations.

grubstake *v.* [GRUBSTAKE *n.* (1)] [late 19C+] (*orig. US*) to provide one with sufficient money with which to eat, live etc.

Grub Street news *n.* [proper name *Grub Street*, the notional home of hack journalism. There actually was a Grub Street, poss. named for a Mr Grubbe, near Moorfields in the City of London; it was renamed Milton Street in 1830; Andrew Marvell coined the phr. to epitomize the world of hackery. Grub Street, according to Johnson (1755), was 'much inhabited by writers of small histories, dictionaries, and temporary poems'] [late 17C–early 19C] rumours, lies; thus *Grub Street philosopher*, one who spreads such rumours; *Grub Street crew*, the gossips.

grudge fuck *n.* [GRUDGE-FUCK *v.* (2)] [2000s] (*US*) an act of intercourse undertaken simply as a result of a grudge, e.g. against an absent partner.

grudge-fuck *v.* **1** [1970s+] usu. of a woman, to make intercourse unsatisfying or even impossible. **2** [1990s+] usu. of a woman, to have intercourse with a third party as an act of revenge or anger towards a partner.

grue *adj. see* GRUESOME *adj.*

gruel *n.* [the thin, unpalatable gruel one receives in prison] **1** [late 18C–1900s] punishment. **2** [late 19C] (*US*) sentimental, 'thin' poetry.

IN PHRASES

▫ **get one's gruel** *v.* (*also* **have one's gruel**) [19C] to be punished. ▫ **give someone gruel** *v.* [mid-19C] to kill or defeat. ▫ **take one's gruel** *v.* [late 19C–1900s] to receive and accept punishment.

gruel *v.* [*see* prev.] [late 19C] to ejaculate (into).

grueller *n.* [SE *gruel*, to punish, to exhaust] **1** [mid-19C] a problem, esp. a particularly difficult one. **2** [late 19C] a knock-down blow.

gruesome *adj.* (*also* **grooh, grue**) [1930s+] (*US*) awful, unattractive.

IN COMPOUNDS

▫ **gruesome twosome** *n.* [1940s+] (*orig. US*) **1** a couple in a steady relationship. **2** a pair of individuals, esp, when unpopular, e.g. two teenage girls sharing a very close friendship, a lesbian couple.

gruesome and gory *n.* [rhy. sl. = CORIE *n.*] [20C+] the penis.

grulch *n.* [synon. Scot. *grulsh*] [20C+] (*Irish*) a small stocky person, usu. somewhat uncouth and less than amicable.

grumble *v.* [1920s] (*US tramp*) to pray.

SE in slang uses

IN COMPOUNDS

▫ **grumble-guts** *n.* (*also* **grumble-gizzard**) [Yorks. dial.; note synon. Lancashire dial. *grumble-belly*] [late 18C+] a habitual complainer.

IN PHRASES

▫ **grumble in the gizzard** *v.* [late 17C–early 19C] to be annoyed, but to keep one's feelings to oneself.

grumble (and grunt) *n.* (*also* **groan and grunt, growl and grunt**) [rhy. sl. = CUNT *n.* (1)] [1930s+] **1** the vagina. **2** a generic term for women. **3** sexual intercourse.

grumble and mutter *n.* [rhy. sl. = FLUTTER *n.*[1] (4)] [1960s+] a bet.

grumbler *n.* [the landlord *grumbles* at the customer's economy; the drink makes one's stomach *grumble*] [early 19C] fourpennyworth of grog.

grumbletonian *n.* [a pun on two late 17C religious sects, the Muggletonians (founded 1651 by Lodowicke Muggleton) and Grindletonians (? the Yorks. village of Grindleton); the term was used first as specific political jargon *c.*1690 when the 'Court Party' apostrophized as *grumbletonians* their 'Country Party' rivals, whom, they claimed, resented their personal ambitions being thwarted] [late 17C–mid-19C] a constant grumbler, esp. as regards the 'state of the country'.

grummet *n.* [SE *grummet*, a ring of rope, a washer] **1** [mid–late 19C] (*also* **grummit**) the vagina. **2** [late 19C] sexual intercourse. **3** [1960s+] (*orig. N.Z. surfing*) a woman, esp. as a sex object. **4** [1980s+] (*N.Z. juv.*) someone or something disliked.

grummy *adj.* [ety. unknown] [1920s] (*US*) unhappy, depressed.

grumper *n.* [? SE *rump*] [1970s] (*US*) the buttocks.

grumpus *n.* [SE *grumpy*] [1960s] (*US*) a bad-tempered person.

grumpy-drawers *n.* (*also* **gloomy-drawers**) [1980s+] (*mainly UK juv.*) an ill-tempered, depressive person.

grundies *n.* [rhy. sl. = UNDIES *n.*; ult. Aus. media executive *Reg Grundy* (b.1923)] [1980s+] (*UK juv.*) underwear.

grundy *n.* [GRUNDIES *n.*] [1990s+] (*UK juv.*) a school 'game' whereby the waistband of the victim's underwear is grasped and pulled up hard, thus causing them pain.

grunge *n.* (*orig. US*) **1** [1960s+] sticky, dirty, unpleasant substances. **2** [1960s+] a general term of abuse, a repugnant, odious, dirty or boring person or thing. **3** [1970s+] a form of rock music, epitomized by the work of the Seattle band Nirvana, but first used in relation to the New York Dolls, *c.*1973 (also known, among many rivals, as the 'godfathers of punk'). **4** [1980s+] the fashion style that developed out of the rock music, favouring a dishevelled appearance.

IN COMPOUNDS

□ **grungehole** *n.* [HOLE *n.*[1] (2b)] [1980s] (*US*) a dirty room or place.

grunge *v.* [? GRIPE *v.* (2) + SE *whinge*] [1960s+] **1** to whine, to complain. **2** to assault, to attack, to terrify.

grunged-out *adj.* [GRUNGY *adj.*] [1980s+] (*US*) dirty, messy, unappetizing, unappealing.

grungie *n.* [GRUNGE *n.* (3)] [1980s] (*US*) a person who is interested in the GRUNGE *n.* fashion and music scene.

grungy *adj.* (*also* **gringy, grungey**) [SE *grubby* + SE *dingy*] **1** [1960s+] dirty, messy, unappetizing, unappealing. **2** [1990s+] dressed in the style of GRUNGE *n.* (4).

grunt *n.* [SE *grunt*, i.e. the sounds involved in eating, working hard, defecating etc] **1** [1920s–40s] (*US*) the bill, usu. for food or drink. **2** [1920s+] (*US*) a slice of ham or pork; bacon [GRUNTER *n.* (1)]. **3** [1920s+] (*US*) any person doing menial work; an assistant. **4** [1940s+] (*US*) (*also* **grunties**) excrement; thus fig., 'the daylights', the essence. **5** [1960s] (*US black*) a bowel movement. **6** [1960s] (*US*) an ill-tempered, constantly complaining person. **7** [1960s+] (*US*) a combat soldier, a Marine soldier or a non-flying Airforce officer [the soldier's endless complaining]. **8** [1970s+] (*also* **grunts**) food, esp. snack food. **9** [1970s+] (*US*) a stupid or unpleasant person. **10** [1980s+] (*N.Z.*) of a vehicle, horsepower. **11** [1990s+] an extremely unattractive woman [play on PIG *n.* (1c)]. **12** *see* GRUNTER *n.* (1).

IN COMPOUNDS

□ **grunt work** *n.* [1970s+] (*US*) menial work, drudgery.

SE in slang uses

IN COMPOUNDS

□ **grunt horn** *n.* (*also* **grunt iron**) [1920s–30s] (*US*) a tuba.

grunt *v.* [SE *grunt*/GRUNT *n.*] **1** [late 18C+] to complain. **2** [1930s–40s] (*US*) to do menial work. **3** [1960s] (*US*) to defecate. **4** [2000s] (*UK juv.*) to break wind.

grunter *n.* **1** [early 17C–1950s] (*also* **grunt, gruntler**) a (sucking) pig. **2** [late 18C–early 19C] a shilling (5p) [play on HOG *n.* (1a)]. **3** [early 19C; 1990s+] a police officer, a country constable [play on PIG *n.* (2a)]. **4** [mid–late 19C] (*also* **half a grunter**) sixpence (5p). **5** [1900s] (*Aus.*) a Boer soldier. **6** [1900s–20s] an automobile, a steam engine. **7** [1940s+] (*Aus.*) a prostitute; a promiscuous girl or woman [? the (simulated) grunts of passion with which she embellishes her services]. **8** [1980s+] an old person out of sympathy with current youth enthusiasms [their grunts of complaint].

IN COMPOUNDS

□ **grunter's gig** *n.* [GIG *n.*[2] (1)] [late 18C–19C] the flesh of a smoked pig's face.

grunties *n. see* GRUNT *n.* (4).

grunting-cheat *n.* (*also* **grunting-chete, gruntling-cheat, -chete**) [SE *grunt* + CHEAT *n.* (1)] [mid-16C–mid-19C] (*UK Und.*) a pig, pork.

grunting peck *n.* [SE *grunting* + PECK *n.*[1] (1)] [mid-17C–mid-19C] pork, bacon or any pigmeat.

gruntler *n. see* GRUNTER *n.* (1).

grunts *n. see* GRUNT *n.* (8).

grush *v.* (*also* **grushie**) [synon. Scot. *grush*] [1900s–30s] of children, to scramble for a handful of small change tossed to them, typically after a wedding.

grutnol *n. see* GROUTNOLL *n.*

gruts *n.*[1] [ety. unknown] [early 19C] tea.

gruts *n.*[2] [? GRUNDIES *n.*] [2000s] (*N.Z.*) underpants.

G-shot *n.* [it SE *gees* one up + SHOT *n.*[1] (6b)] [1960s+] (*drugs*) a small dose of drugs used to hold off withdrawal symptoms until a full dose can be taken.

GSQ *n. see* GOLDEN SHOWER QUEEN *under* GOLDEN SHOWER *n.*

G-ster *n. see* GANGSTA *n.*

G-string *n.* [SE *G-string*, the minimal 'loin-cloth' worn by striptease artists etc] [1970s+] **1** (*US black*) any device – a tampon, towel etc – used to staunch the flow of menstrual blood. **2** (*US gay*) an athletic supporter, a jockstrap.

g.t.a. *phr. see* G.T.T. *phr.*

g.t.f.o.! *excl.* (*also* **g.t.f.o.o.m.w.**) [abbr. of *GET THE FUCK OUT! under* FUCK *n.*; often ext. to *get the fuck out of my way*] [1990s+] a general dismissive excl.

g.t.h.! *excl.* [abbr. *GO TO HELL! under* HELL *n.*] [1910s] (*US*) an excl. of dismissal.

g-thang *n.* (*also* **g-thing**) [1990s+] (*US black*) **1** anything that is seen as a male preserve, a 'guy thing'. **2** anything that concerns a street thug, a 'gangster thing' [G *n.* (6)]. **3** anything that is seen as a female preserve, a 'girl-thing'.

G-town *n.* [abbr.] [1980s] (*US*) *Georgetown*, Washington D.C.

g.t.t. *phr.* (*also* **g.t.a.**) [abbr.] [mid-19C–1900s] (*US*) *gone to Texas/Arkansas*; the sign affixed to the door of an absconding businessman.

Guam *n.* [orig. naut. use] [late 19C+] a generic term for any very distant place.

guaranfuckingtee *v.* (*also* **guarandamntee**) [SE + FUCKING *adj.* (4)/DAMN *adj.* (3)] [1940s+] an intensified form of SE *guarantee*.

guardhouse lawyer *n. see* BARRACK-ROOM LAWYER *n.*

Guat *n.* [abbr.] [1990s+] a *Guat*emalan.

guava *n.*[1] [Afk. *koejawel*, backside] [1970s+] (*S.Afr.*) the buttocks, the posterior; thus *come on one's guava*, to make a fool of oneself.

guava *n.*[2] [abbr. *grown/growing up and very ambitious*] [1980s] (*S.Afr.*) South African version of the YUPPIE *n.*

gub *n.*[1] (*also* **gubbah, gubber, Mr Gub**) [? SE *garbage* or SE *government*; note Seal, *The Lingo* (1999): 'The origins of the word [...] may derive from GOVERNMENT BLANKET, widely pronounced [...] as GUBMENT BLANKET, sometimes GUBBY BLANKET. Such blankets were often identified with a red stripe or other device sewn along them. It is said that Aboriginal people would spend many hours unpicking these stitches and over the years this hated symbol of dependence on white handouts has been honed to its present usage'; note 1887 *Bulletin* (Sydney) 15 Oct. 12/3: 'At La Perouse, Sydney, there lives a black who goes by the exalted and sacred name of "The Gubnor."'] [1970s+] (*Aus. Aborigine*) a usu. derog. term for a white man.

gub *n.*[2] *see* GOB *n.*[1] (1).

guban *n.* [Irish *gobán*, an old-fashioned incompetent tradesman] [20C+] (*Irish*) a general term of abuse, esp. an unpleasantly negative critic whose attacks are not based on actual expertise or knowledge.

gubbah/gubber *n. see* GUB *n.*[1].

gubberigine *n.* [GUB *n.*[1] + SE *Aborigine*] [1980s+] (*Aus. prison*) an Aborigine who is considered by his peers to have sold out to white society.

gubbins *n.* [SE *gubbins*, fragments, esp. of fish; fish-parings] **1** [1900s–50s] a fool, a simpleton. **2** [1910s+] an indefinite n. for any nameless object.

gubbo *n. see* GOVO *n.*

gubby *adj.* [? southwest UK dial. *gubby*, a pile, a heap] [mid-19C] (*UK Und.*) pot-bellied.

Gucci queen *n.* [brandname *Gucci* + -QUEEN *sfx*] [1970s] (*US gay*) an affected, fashion-conscious older homosexual.

guccis *n.* [pun] [2000s] (*S.Afr. gay*) bags under the eyes.

guck *n.* (*also* **gluck**) [echoic] [1950s+] (*orig. US*) any form of sticky substance, ointment, cream.

gucky *adj.* [GUCK *n.* + sfx *-y*] [1960s+] (*UK society*) of an event or person, as much as of food or drink, sickening, likely to make one vomit.

gudgeon *n.* [SE *gudgeon*, a small freshwater fish, often used as bait] [late 16C–1920s] a gullible person, one who will 'swallow' anything.

IN PHRASES

❑ **gape for gudgeons** *v.* (*also* **give a gudgeon**) [late 16C–19C] to be duped, fooled.

gudgeon *v.* [GUDGEON *n.*] [late 18C–early 19C] to render oneself gullible, to become a victim.

guee *n.* (*also* **gee, ghee**) [abbr.] [mid-19C–1940s] (*US*) a derog. term for a Portuguese person.

gueril *v. see* GORILLA *v.*

Guernsey highball *n.* [famed Guernsey dairy cows] [1940s] (*US*) milk.

guerrilla *n.* [mid–late 19C] (*US*) a swindler, a crooked gambler.

guerrilla *v. see* GORILLA *v.*

guess *n.*

SE in slang uses

IN PHRASES

❑ **by guess and by God** [1930s+] by sheer luck. ❑ **by guess and by godfrey** [naut. use; to steer 'at hazard without a set course or without the guidance of landmarks' (*OED*)] [1900s] taking a course of action or movement without any real plan. ❑ **by guess and by golly** (*also* **by guess and by gosh**) [late 19C+] (*US*) haphazardly, without a planned direction, at random.

guesser *n.* [1900s] (*N.Z.*) a dishonest racing tipster, hired by bookmakers to persuade punters to bet on useless horses.

guessing-gear *n.* [1900s] (*Aus.*) the head, the brain.

guff *n.*[1] [SE *guff*, a puff, a whiff] **1** [mid-19C+] (*also* **guffery**) lies, nonsense, twaddle. **2** [late 19C+] insolence. **3** [20C+] talk. **4** [1990s+] (*US campus*) trouble, problems.

guff *n.*[2] [dial. *guff*, an offensive smell] [1980s+] a fart.

guff *v.*[1] [GUFF *n.*[1] (3)] **1** [late 19C] (*US*) to chat. **2** [1920s] (*Aus.*) to fool, to deceive.

IN PHRASES

❑ **guff off** *v.* [? dial. *guff*, to talk nonsense, to babble] [20C+] (*Aus.*) to shirk, to act lazily.

guff *v.*[2] [GUFF *n.*[2]] [1980s+] to break wind.

guffery *n. see* GUFF *n.*[1] (1).

guffin *n.* [northern dial.] [mid-19C–1960s] a clumsy fool.

gugag *n. see* HEWGAG *n.*

gugga *n. see* GAGA *adj.*

guggle *n.* [SE *guggle*, to make a gurgling sound, like that of water pouring from a narrow-necked bottle] [late 17C] the windpipe, the throat.

guggy *n.* [Irish *gogaí*, nursery term for an egg] [20C+] (*Irish*) an egg.

gu-gu *n. see* GOO-GOO *n.*[1] (1).

Guguland *n.* [GOO-GOO *n.*[1] (1) + SE *-land*] [1900s] (*US*) the Philippines.

guided missile *n. see under* MISSILE *n.*

guide-post *n.* [he is supposed to guide the congregation to heaven] [late 18C–1900s] a clergyman.

guido *n.* (*also* **guidette**) [Ital. proper name *Guido*; the initial ref. was to the young working-class Italians who lived outside Manhattan and came into the city for their entertainment] **1** [1970s] (*US*) an Italian. **2** [1980s+] (*US campus*) someone acting in an ostentatiously masculine (or feminine) manner. **3** [1990s+] a hairstyle, a MULLET *n.*[2].

guilderhead *n.* [Scot. *guldie*, 'a tall, black-faced, gloomy-looking man' (*EDD*) + -HEAD *sfx* (1)] [1970s+] (*Ulster*) a stupid, clumsy person.

guin *n. see* GUINEA *n.*[1].

Guinea *n.*[1] [the far distance of African Guinea] [late 19C+] (*US*) a euph. for hell, e.g. in phr. *go to Guinea*.

SE in slang uses

IN COMPOUNDS

❑ **guinea bird** *n. see* separate entry. ❑ **guinea gall** *n. see* GINNY GALL *n.* ❑ **Guinea ship** *n.* [SE *Guinea ship*, a ship bringing slaves – in terribly crowded conditions – from West Africa] [1920s+] (*W.I.*) a crowd, a large number of people.

Guinea *n.*[2] [the common use of words with the initial G in this way, e.g. GOSH *n.*, GOLLY *n.*[1]] [1930s–60s] (*US*) a euph. for *God*, e.g. *swear to Guinea*.

guinea *n.*[1] (*also* **ghinny, gin, ginney, ginny, guin, guiney, guinny, guinzo**) [18C *guinea*, a black. The original guineas were black slaves from the Guinea Coast of Africa, and the term gradually evolved to mean anyone with a notably dark complexion, although it is rarely if ever used to describe a black person in 20C+ other than in the SE *Guinea Negro*, a mixed-race group native to Maryland, Virginia and West Virginia, who call themselves *Our People* or *Melungeons*] (*US*) **1** [late 19C+] an Italian person, usu. an immigrant to the US. **2** [1910s+] a derog. term for various other non-Anglo nationalities, usu. Mediterranean, e.g. a Greek, a Portuguese, a Jew. **3** [1900s] (*US Und.*) a woman. **4** [1910s+] a foolish, gullible or insignificant man. **5** [1940s] a Japanese person, a Pacific native. **6** [1950s] a groom in a horseracing stable [US grooms were often of Italian immigrant origins]. **7** [1950s–60s] the Italian language.

IN PHRASES

❑ **get one's guinea up** *v.* [1930s] to become angry, to make one angry.

guinea *n.*[2]

SE in slang uses

IN COMPOUNDS

❑ **guinea bird** *n. see* separate entry. ❑ **guinea-dropper** *n.* [late 17C–early 18C] a confidence trickster who drops counterfeit guineas to ensnare the gullible. ❑ **guinea hen** *n.* [pun on SE *guinea hen*/SE *guinea* + HEN *n.* (2), i.e. a girl who costs a guinea] [17C–early 18C] a courtesan, a prostitute. ❑ **guinea pig** *n. see* separate entry.

IN PHRASES

❑ **guinea to a gooseberry** *n.* (*also* **guinea to a goose, … goosegog**) [var. on LOMBARD STREET TO A CHINA ORANGE *phr.*] [late 19C–1920s] the longest possible odds, thus an absolute certainty.

guinea *adj.* (*also* **ginney, ghinny**) [GUINEA *n.*[1] (1)] [20C+] (*US*) used to describe an Italian person or culture.

IN COMPOUNDS

❑ **guinea football** *n.* [i.e. the popularity of fireworks in the Italian community] [20C+] (*US*) a large firecracker; a home-made bomb. ❑ **guinea red** *n.* [SE *red* (*wine*); the making of wine by Italian immigrants (and their descendants)] [1930s+] (*US*) cheap red wine, poss. homemade. ❑ **guinea stinker** *n.* [STINKER *n.*[1] (3)] [late 19C+] a cheap, malodorous cigar supposedly preferred by Italian-Americans. ❑ **guinea town** *n.* [1960s] (*US*) the Italian area of a city.

guinea bird *n.*[1] [? her price] [17C; mid-19C] a prostitute.

guinea bird *n.*[2] [the state of Guinea + SE *bird*/BIRD *n.*[1] (3a)] (*W.I.*) **1** [early 19C] an African-born black person; so called by the Creoles, who were born in the West Indies. **2** [1980s] (*also* **ginigog**) a person who is superior in some way, either positively or negatively.

guinea pig *n.*[1] [all puns on SE with ref. to their availability for money] **1** [mid-18C–19C] a general term of opprobrium.

2 [early 19C] anyone whose fee comes to one guinea, e.g. a doctor. **3** [mid-19C] (*UK Und.*) a man who receives a guinea for talking up a second-rate horse. **4** [late 19C–1930s] anyone working only part-time, e.g. a company director who only attends board-meetings, a clergyman serving as a deputy. **5** [1980s] (*US Und.*) an informer, a stool pigeon.

guinea pig *n.*[2] [rhy. sl.] [1990s+] a wig.

guiney/guinny *n. see* GUINEA *n.*[1].

guino *n.* (*also* **goyno**) [? SE *guinea*] [1920s–50s] (*Irish*) money.

guinzo *n. see* GUINEA *n.*[1].

Guitar Town *n.* [the 'home of country music'] [1970s] (*US*) Nashville, Tennessee.

guiver *n.*[1] (*also* **guyver, gyver**) [ety. unknown] (*mainly Aus./N.Z.*) **1** [mid-19C+] insincerity, pretension; flattery. **2** [1900s–10s] a lie.

IN PHRASES

❑ **poke guiver (at)** *v.* [1910s] to tease.

guiver *n.*[2] [GUIVER *adj.*; note WW1 milit. *guyvo*, a dandy] [late 19C] a hairstyle, in which the hair is brushed forward over the forehead, affected by Cockney dandies; thus *guiver-lad*, a working-class dandy.

IN PHRASES

❑ **put on the guiver** *v.* (*also* **put on the gyver**) [late 19C+] (*UK Und.*) to affect an upper-class accent.

guiver *adj.* [ety. unknown; ? Romany] [mid-19C] fashionable, smart.

guiver *v.* [GUIVER *n.*[1]] **1** [late 19C] to cheat, to trick. **2** [late 19C] (*Aus.*) to abuse. **3** [20C+] (*Aus./N.Z.*) to pretend, to put on airs.

gulder *n.* (*also* **gaulder**) [Scot. *gulder*, a noisy, energetic shout] [20C+] (*Ulster*) a shout.

gulder *v.* (*also* **gaulder**) [GULDER *n.*] [20C+] (*Ulster*) to shout.

gulf *n.* [mid-16C–mid-18C] the vagina.

gull *n.* [SE *gull*, to dupe, to deceive; note *gull*, simpleton, dupe, despite inclusion in Grose (1785) is SE] [late 16C–17C; early 19C] a trickster, a cheat.

gulley (hole) *n. see* GULLY (HOLE) *under* GULLY *n.*[2].

gulley-raker *n.* (*also* **gully-raker**) [? GULLY (HOLE) *under* GULLY *n.*[2] + SE *raker*; or ? SAusE *gully-raker*, a cattle whip, a cattle thief] [19C] **1** the penis. **2** a womanizer.

gull-finch *n.* [SE *gull*, a simpleton, a dupe + *finch*] [17C] a simpleton, a fool.

gull-groper *n.* [SE *gull* + *grope*; 19C nautical jargon has *gull-sharper*] [17C–early 19C] (*UK Und.*) a money-lender who specializes in loaning money – often to gamblers – and then defrauding them by avoiding repayment when due, but rather entrapping them in a legal suit, the only resolution of which is the handing over not of the original loan, but of land or valuables that are worth much more.

gull-groping *n.* [GULL-GROPER *n.*] [16C–18C] the swindling of a fool or innocent.

gullion *n.*[1] [Irish *góilin*, a creek] [20C+] (*Ulster*) a muddy hole, an open sewer.

gullion *n.*[2] [play on SLUM *n.*[3] (4)/SLUMGUDGEON *n.*] [1950s] (*US Und.*) jewellery, esp. stolen jewellery; thus *gullion-joint*, a jewellery store; *gullion-poke*, a jewellery salesman's gem wallet.

gullivers *n.* [the sufferer 'travels' to the lavatory for relief] [1980s] (*Aus.*) diarrhoea.

gully *n.*[1] [pron. of SE *girlie* but note GULLY (HOLE) *under* GULLY *n.*[2]] [1990s+] (*UK/US black*) a woman.

gully *n.*[2]

SE in slang uses

IN COMPOUNDS

❑ **gully-gut** *n.* [one can pour food and drink down someone as you can down a *gully*] [mid-16C–17C; 1930s+] (*later use US black*) a glutton. ❑ **gully (hole)** *n.* (*also* **gulley (hole)**) [19C] **1** the throat. **2** the vagina. ❑ **gully-jumper** *n.* [20C+] (*US*) a farmer, a peasant. ❑ **gully-washer** *n.* [20C+] (*US*) a heavy downpour of rain.

gully *adj.* [fig. use of SE *gully*, a gutter, which has the same credibility as STREET *adj.*] [1950s+] (*orig. US*) basic, fundamental.

gully *v.* [SE *gull*, to deceive] [mid-19C–1900s] to trick, to fool, to lie.

gully-raker *n. see* GULLEY-RAKER *n.*

gully-raking *n.* [SAusE *gully-raker*, a cattle whip, a cattle thief] [mid-19C–1950s] (*Aus.*) cattle-rustling.

gulp *v. see* SWALLOW *v.*

gulpin *n.* (*also* **gulp**) [he will 'gulp down' anything; orig. naut. jargon for a Royal Marine; note Irish *guilpin*, a lout, Scot. *gulpin*, a simpleton, a gullible fool] [early 19C+] a fool.

gulpy *adj.* [GULPIN *n.* (1)/SE *gull* + *gulp*] [late 19C–1900s] gullible.

gum *n.*[1] [SE *gum*] **1** [mid-18C–mid-19C] impertinent, abusive talk, chatter; thus one who talks impertinently. **2** [mid–late 19C] (*US*) a trick or deception.

IN COMPOUNDS

❑ **gum-raggem** *n.* [RAG *v.* (1a)] [mid-19C] (*UK Und.*) abusive talk.

SE in slang uses

IN COMPOUNDS

❑ **gum action** *n.* [-ACTION *sfx*] [1940s] (*US black*) conversation, talk. ❑ **gum beat/-beater/-beating** *see* separate entries. ❑ **gum-bumping** *n.* [BEAT ONE'S GUMS *v.*] [2000s] (*US*) arguing. ❑ **gum-digger** *n.* [1910s+] (*Aus./N.Z.*) a dentist; thus *gum-digging*, dentistry. ❑ **gum-flapping** *n.* [BEAT ONE'S GUMS *v.*] [1990s+] empty, boastful chatter. ❑ **gum-job** *n.* [var. on BLOW JOB *n.*] [1980s+] (*US*) fellatio. ❑ **gum-knocking** *n. see* GUM-BEATING *n.* ❑ **gum-puncher** *n.* [1950s+] (*Aus.*) a dentist. ❑ **gum-smasher** *n.* [late 19C–1920s] a dentist. ❑ **gumsuck/-sucker/-sucking** *see* separate entries. ❑ **gum-tickler** *n.* **1** [early–mid-19C] (*US*) an alcoholic drink. **2** [late 19C] (*orig. US*) a dentist.

IN PHRASES

❑ **beat one's gums** *v. see* separate entry.

gum *n.*[2] [*God*, or abbr. *God almighty*] [19C+] a euph. for *God (almighty)* and used in various phrs., esp. below.

IN EXCLAMATIONS

❑ **by gum!** (*also* **by gom! by gums! gum! my gum!**) [19C+] a euph. excl. for *by God!*

gum *n.*[3] (*also* **guma**) [the stickiness of the drug] [late 19C+] (*drugs*) opium.

IN PHRASES

❑ **chewing the gum** [1950s] (*drugs*) using and/or addicted to opium.

SE, meaning rubber, in slang uses

IN COMPOUNDS

❑ **gumball** *n.* (*also* **gumball light, ...machine**) [joc. equation of the shape] [1960s+] (*US*) **1** the flashing light on a police car. **2** a police car. ❑ **gumboot** *n.* [the SE *gumboots* that epitomize the speakers] **1** [1990s+] (*N.Z.*) rough, forthright, mainly rural language, i.e. that of fishermen, roustabouts etc. **2** *see* GUMSHOE *n.* ❑ **gumboot tea** *n.* [2000s] (*N.Z.*) trad. Indian tea, rather than herbal or other 'exotic' varieties. ❑ **gumdrop** *see* separate entries. ❑ **gumfoot** *see under* GUMSHOE. ❑ **gum game** *n. see* separate entry. ❑ **gumheel** *n.* [1930s+] (*US prison*) a police officer. ❑ **gumshoe** *see* separate entries. ❑ **gumshoer** *n. see* GUMSHOE *n.* ❑ **gum-sucker** *n. see* separate entry.

gum *n.*[4] [Scot. *gum*, the palate] [1980s+] (*Irish*) a taste for, a desire.

gum *v.*[1] [GUM *n.*[1] (2)] [mid–late 19C] **1** (*US*) to cheat, to delude, to humbug. **2** (*US campus*) to cheat (in an examination).

gum *v.*[2] (*also* **gum up**) **1** [20C+] (*US*) to mess up, to spoil. **2** [1930s+] to talk nonsense.

IN COMPOUNDS

❑ **gumbrain** *n.* (*also* **gumbook, gumhead**) [1950s+] (*US*) an idiot.

IN PHRASES

❑ **gum the game** *v.* (*also* **gum the play, ...show**) [1910s–60s] to spoil. ❑ **gum (up) the works** *v.* (*also* **gum up the job**) [1910s+] to make a mess, to cause an obstruction.

gum *v.*[3] [1980s+] (*US gay*) for a person using dentures to remove them before performing fellatio.

gum! *excl. see* BY GUM! *under* GUM *n.*[2].

guma *n. see* GUM *n.*[3].

gumba(h) *n. see* GOOMBAH *n.*

gum beat *v.* [BEAT ONE'S GUMS *v.*] (*US black*) **1** [1940s] to tell, to recount. **2** [1940s+] to chatter.

gum-beater *n.* [GUM BEAT *v.*] [1940s–70s] (*US*) a chatterer or complainer; a braggart.

gum-beating *n.* (*also* **gum-knocking**) [GUM BEAT *v.*] [1930s+] (*orig. US*) incessant, frivolous, tedious chatter.

gumbler *n. see* KNULLER *n.*

gumby *n.*[1] [ety. unknown] [1980s] (*US campus*) a large quantity.

gumby *n.*[2] [the green character, *Gumby*, a toy, portrayed by Eddie Murphy on U.S. TV's *Saturday Night Live* and/or the character in BBC TV's *Monty Python's Flying Circus* (1969–74); echoic of his monosyllabic incoherence] [1980s+] a fool, an idiot.

IN COMPOUNDS

❑ **gumbyhead** *n.* [-HEAD *sfx* (1)] [1980s+] (*US campus*) someone who does something stupid.

gumdigger's dog *n.* [1960s+] (*N.Z.*) used in various phrs. of comparison, e.g. *mad as a…, skinny as a…*

gumdrop *n.*[1] [late 19C] **1** (*US campus*) a boy- or girlfriend. **2** (*US Und.*) a person, esp. one to be duped.

gumdrop *n.*[2] [1970s+] (*drugs*) **1** barbiturate, esp. seconal. **2** any kind of drug available in pill or capsule form.

gumdrop *adj.* [play on SE] [late 19C] (*US*) sweet and silly.

gum game *n.* [the activity of the opossum, which, in its efforts to elude the hunter, climbs to the very top of a gum tree, thus taking itself beyond the hunter's reach and, since it was hunted at night, beyond his eyesight] [mid–late 19C] (*US*) a trick or dodge.

IN PHRASES

❑ **come the gum (game) over** *v.* [19C] (*US*) to hoodwink, to trick.

gummed up *adj.* [1910s+] (*US*) in trouble; out of favour.

gummer *n.* **1** [mid–late 19C] an old, toothless pit-bull or other fighting dog. **2** [1900s–30s] a toothless person. **3** [1990s+] (*US*) an act of fellatio from an old, toothless person.

gummers *n. see* GUMS *n.*[2] (1).

gummey *n.* [? its stickiness] [late 19C] (*US*) medicine.

gummy *n.*[1] **1** [19C–1940s] a fool, a tedious person. **2** [late 19C–1910s] a toothless person or animal.

gummy *n.*[2] [Fr. *gommeux*, dandy] [late 19C] a dandy, a swell.

gummy *adj.*[1] [orig. dial.; ult. ety. unknown; ? the rubberiness of their movements] **1** [mid-18C–mid-19C] puffy, swollen, esp. of the ankles of a horse or human. **2** [mid-19C] clumsy, drunken. **3** [1950s+] (*US drugs*) used of one who has become lethargic after smoking cannabis.

gummy *adj.*[2] [1920s–40s] (*US*) dubious, untrustworthy.

gummy! *excl.*[1] [var. on BY GUM! *under* GUM *n.*[2]] [mid-19C–1920s] a mild oath.

gummy! *excl.*[2] [1980s] (*W.I., Jam.*) a general excl. of praise: excellent! wonderful!

gump *n.*[1] (*also* **goomp, gumph, gump-head**) [Yorks. dial. *gump*, homely, parochial, awkward, well-meaning; the role of a pathetic *gump* was adopted as a trademark by the 20C+ UK comedian Norman Wisdom (b.1915)] **1** [early 19C+] a fool; thus *gump-headed*, foolish. **2** [1910s+] (*US*) nonsensical or cheeky talk. **3** [1980s+] (*US prison*) a passive homosexual, the target of predatory prison homosexuals.

gump *n.*[2] [? its innate stupidity; ? link to Scot. *gump*, an overgrown child] [late 19C+] (*US*) a chicken, a fowl; esp. a sick or dying chicken given by a dealer to a begging tramp.

gump *n.*[3] [abbr. SE *gumption*, natural intelligence] [1920s–60s] intelligence, native wit.

gumph/gump-head *n. see* GUMP *n.*[1].

gumption *n.* [ext. of SE *gumption*, intelligence] [1990s+] (*W.I.*) a woman's ability to intensify the pleasures of intercourse.

gums *n.*[1] **1** [17C; 19C; 1930s–40s] the eyes. **2** [1940s] (*US black*) the lips, the mouth.

gums *n.*[2] [*elastic gum*, India rubber] **1** [mid-19C–1900s] (*US*) (*also* **gummers**) rubber-soled shoes. **2** [1900s] (*US*) braces (US suspenders).

gums *n.*[3]

IN EXCLAMATIONS

❑ **by gums!** *see* BY GUM! *under* GUM *n.*[2].

gumshoe *n.* (*also* **gumboot, gumfoot, gumshoer**) [lit. or fig. rubber-soled shoes used for creeping around, whether as investigator or thief] **1** [20C+] a private detective or police officer. **2** [1900s–40s] (*US*) a sneak thief or prowler. **3** [1950s] (*US*) a hanger-on.

IN COMPOUNDS

❑ **gumshoe artist** *n.* [ARTIST *n.* (1)] **1** [late 19C–1900s] a sneak thief, a street robber. **2** [1930s+] (*US*) a plain-clothes detective. ❑ **gumshoe worker** *n.* [WORKER *n.*[1]] [1900s–50s] (*US Und.*) **1** a private detective. **2** a sneak thief. **3** an informer.

gumshoe *adj.* [GUMSHOE *n.* (1) + SE *man*/GUY *n.*[2] (1)] [20C+] (*US*) **1** describing a private detective, e.g. *gumshoe man, gumshoe guy*. **2** of an action, surreptitious, undercover; pertaining to being a private detective.

gumshoe *v.* [GUMSHOE *n.* (1)] [20C+] **1** (*also* **gumfoot**) to investigate, esp. used of policemen or private detectives. **2** to walk softly, to creep around. **3** to walk, to stroll. **4** (*US teen*) to search out amorous couples in parked cars in order to surprise them by shining a light on them.

gumsuck *v.* [SE *gum* + *suck*] [late 19C–1920s] (*US*) to humbug or deceive.

gum-sucker *n.*[1] [the proliferation of gum trees] (*Aus.*) [mid-19C–1940s] a European native Australian (esp. a Victorian) or a Tasmanian.

gum-sucker *n.*[2] [SE *gum*] [1900s–50s] a fool or simpleton.

gum-sucking *n.* (*also* **jowl-sucking**) [late 19C] (*orig. US campus*) kissing (esp. in public and thus seen as excessive).

gum up *v. see* GUM *v.*[2].

gun *n.*[1] **1** [mid-17C; 1930s] the vagina. **2** [mid-17C+] the penis; thus *shoot one's gun, get one's gun*, to ejaculate, to masturbate. **3** [18C–early 19C; 1960s] a tobacco pipe. **4** [late 19C+] (*Aus./N.Z.*) the fastest shearer in a shed (usu. 200+ sheep a day); also as adj. **5** [20C+] (*US drugs*) a hypodermic syringe; thus *gun-toter*, one who uses such a syringe. **6** [20C+] a first-rate or important person. **7** [1910s–20s] a general pej. term, e.g. a 'rascal', a 'terror'; thus *great gun*, a cheery scamp. **8** [1910s+] (*US*) throttle power; thus *give her the (full) gun*, to accelerate; *cut the gun*, to turn off the motor. **9** [1910s+] (*US*) by metonymy, a gunman, a gangster; esp. in phr. *hired gun*, a professional gunman who kills, wounds or merely intimidates as required by his employer. **10** [1980s+] (*US prison*) in pl., the fists. **11** [1980s+] (*US campus*) in pl., the biceps. **12** [1980s+] (*US black*) in pl., the female breasts. **13** [2000s] (*US prison*) any form of edged weapon.

IN COMPOUNDS

❑ **gunstick** *n.* [mid-17C] a penis.

IN PHRASES

❑ **big gun** *n.* **1** [mid-19C+] (*orig. US*) an important person. **2** [1900s] (*US Und.*) a leading thief. **3** [1920s+] (*Aus./N.Z.*) the fastest sheep shearer. ❑ **get one's gun (off)** *v.* (*US*) **1** [1910s+] of a man, to ejaculate, to reach orgasm. **2** [1940s+] in fig. use, to excite, to invigorate, to stimulate, to satisfy. ❑ **get someone in the gun** *v.* [1950s–60s] to get someone into trouble. ❑ **get someone's gun off** *v.* **1** [1940s+] to delight someone. **2** [1960s] (*US black*) to give someone an orgasm. ❑ **get the gun** *v.* [1950s] (*Aus.*) to be dismissed from one's job. ❑ **give it the gun** *v.* [1910s+] (*orig. US*) to accelerate, to drive a car or other vehicle fast. ❑ **gun (it)** *v.* [1990s+] (*Aus./US drugs*) to inject a large amount of a drug; to maintain a heroin addiction. ❑ **polish someone's gun** *v.* [1990s+] (*Aus.*) to fellate.

SE in slang uses

IN COMPOUNDS

❑ **gun artist** *n.* [ARTIST *n.* (1)] (*US*) **1** [1920s] a Western gun-fighter. **2** [1940s] a gun expert. ❑ **gun baggage** *n.* [1990s+] underage gangsters who carry weapons for adults. ❑ **gunboat** *n. see* separate entries. ❑ **gun boss** *n.* [1940s] (*US*) the leader of a gang of Western gunmen. ❑ **gun bull** *n.* [BULL *n.*[5] (3)] [1920s–60s] (*US prison*) an armed guard who surveys the prison yard from a guntower. ❑ **gun dog** *n.* [1940s–50s] (*US*) a Western gun-fighter. ❑ **gun-fighter** *n.* (*US*) **1** [1950s+] a wild, undisciplined fighter. **2** [1960s+] an aggressively forceful political candidate or campaigner. ❑ **gun-flint** *n.* [trad. nickname] [late 19C] (*US*) a native of Rhode Island. ❑ **gun-foot** *n.* [the narrow, tubular trousers are reminiscent of a shotgun barrel] [1940s] (*W.I.*) long trousers, esp. narrow ones. ❑ **gun gang** *n.* [they work 'under the gun'] [1970s+] (*US Und.*) the chain gang or any gang of workers who are taken outside the prison and are thus supervised by armed guards. ❑ **gun hand** *n.* [on model of SE *farm hand*] [1950s+] (*US*) a gun-fighter. ❑ **gunhawk** *n.* [1940s+] (*US*) an expert gun-fighter. ❑ **gun moll** *n. see* separate entry. ❑ **gun-mouth (pants)** *n.* [20C+] (*W.I.*) a (young) man's trousers that are too short and narrow. ❑ **gun opera** *n. see* HORSE OPERA *under* HORSE *n.* ❑ **gunpoke** *n.* (*also* **gunpoker**) [on model of SE *cowpoke*] [1900s–30s] (*US*) a gun-fighter. ❑ **gunpowder** *n. see* separate entry. ❑ **gun-sharp** *n.* (*also* **gun-shark**) [on model of SE *cardsharp*/SHARK *n.*] **1** [1900s] an artillery expert. **2** [1920s+] (*US*) an expert gun-fighter. ❑ **gunshot** *n.* **1** [1920s] (*Irish*) a strong rough whisky. **2** [1980s+] reversing a cannabis cigarette, placing the lit end between one's lips, then exhaling the smoke into another person's mouth. ❑ **gun-slammer** *n. see* GUN-SLINGER *n.* ❑ **gunslick** *n.* [SLICK *adj.* (1)] [1930s–50s] (*US*) an expert gun-fighter. ❑ **gun-slinger** *n. see* separate entry. ❑ **gun-thrower** *n.* [1910s–50s] (*US*) a gun-fighter as found in the real/fictional 'Wild West'. ❑ **gun-tosser** *n.* [mid-19C] (*US*) a gun-fighter as found in the real/fictional 'Wild West'. ❑ **gun-toter** *n.* [1920s–40s] (*US*) a gun-fighter as found in the real/fictional 'Wild West'. ❑ **gun-wadding** *n.* [1910s–50s] (*US*) soft white bread.

IN PHRASES

❑ **gun in her baggy** *n.* [BAGGY *n.*] [1990s+] (*W.I.*) a woman with venereal disease. ❑ **gun up** *v.* **1** [1980s+] (*US prison*) to get oneself ready for a fight (irrespective of the weapon used). **2** [2000s] in fig. use, to prepare oneself, to 'buck up'. ❑ **in the gun** [one is 'under fire'] **1** [1910s–20s] (*Aus.*) facing dismissal from one's job. **2** [1910s+] (*Aus.*) unpopular, of ill repute, in trouble, likely to attract criticism or punishment. ❑ **under the gun** [chaingangs who work supervised by gun-carrying guards] [1940s+] (*orig. US*) under great pressure, stress.

gun *n.*[2] ['perhaps from an allusion to a vessel called a gun, used for ale in the universities' (Grose, 1785)] [mid-17C–18C] a flagon of ale.

IN PHRASES

❑ **in the gun** *adj.* [late 17C–early 19C] drunk, tipsy.

gun *n.*[3] [Partridge prefers to define this 'a lie'] [late 17C–18C] a strange and unaccountable story.

gun *n.*[4] [early 19C; 1910s–30s] (*UK/US Und.*) a view, a look, an observation; taking notice.

gun *n.*[5] [abbr. GONNOF *n.*; note Sutherland, *The Professional Thief* (1936): 'The term "cannon" is used to designate the pickpocket and also the racket of picking pockets. The theory of the origin of this term is that the pickpocket some centuries ago was called a *gonnif*, which is the Jewish word for thief. This term was then abbreviated to "gun"; later someone in a moment of smartness referred to a pickpocket as a "cannon" to designate a big gun, and the term "cannon" then became general. The term "gun" is still used to refer to pickpockets, and the female pickpocket who operates upon men is called a "gun-moll".'] **1** [mid-19C] a fool, a bungler. **2** [mid-19C–1960s] a thief. **3** [mid-19C–1960s] a pickpocket. **4** [1900s–20s] (*Aus.*) a confidence trickster.

IN COMPOUNDS

❑ **gun hat** *n.* [late 19C] (*Aus. Und.*) a soft felt hat. ❑ **gun-maker** *n.* [1900s–30s] (*US Und.*) an older thief who instructs young criminals, esp. pickpockets. ❑ **gun mob** *n.* [1910s–50s] (*US Und.*) an expert pickpocketing team. ❑ **gun moll** *n. see* separate entry. ❑ **gunsmith** *n.* **1** [mid-19C] a thief. **2** [1930s] (*US*) an older thief who trains young criminals.

IN PHRASES

❑ **beef gun** *v.* [1940s] (*US Und.*) to shout out that one's pocket has been picked. ❑ **on the gun** [1920s–40s] (*US Und.*) working as a pickpocket. ❑ **punch (the) gun** *v.* [1910s] (*US Und.*) to use criminal slang.

gun *n.*[6] [abbr./pron.] [late 19C+] *gonorrhoea.*

gun *n.*[7] [1980s] (*US*) the arm.

gun *v.*[1] [the aggression of the stare equates with a pointed gun] **1** [early 19C+] (*UK/US Und.*) to stare at, to look over, to examine; to look out for; thus *on the gun*, on the lookout. **2** [1940s+] (*orig. US black*) to stare aggressively or pointedly. **3** [1950s] to stare with sexual interest/intent. **4** [2000s] (*UK teen*) to insult.

gun *v.*[2] [lit. or fig. use of a weapon] **1** [mid-19C–1930s] (*UK Und.*) to steal. **2** [late 19C+] (*US*) (*also* **gun out, pistol**) to shoot, whether human targets or game. **3** [1920s] (*US Und.*) to work as a swindler, a confidence trickster. **4** [1930s+] (*US black*) to attack, physically or verbally. **5** [1980s] (*US campus*) to have sexual intercourse. **6** [1980s] (*US black*) to look for trouble, to start a fight. **7** [1990s+] (*drugs*) to inject a drug.

SE in slang uses

IN PHRASES

❑ **gun down** *v.* [1960s+] (*US*) to reject a suitor or to refute facts.

gun *v.*[3] [GUN *n.*[1] (8)] [1920s+] to rev an engine hard; thus to accelerate.

gunboat *n.*[1] [SE *gunboat*, considered oversized and awkward by sailors] **1** [mid-19C+] (*US*) a large shoe, usu. in pl. **2** [late 19C] (*US*) an armed stage-coach. **3** [1920s–70s] (*US tramp*) a water bucket made from a gallon can [its unwieldiness]. **4** [1930s–40s] (*US tramp*) a steel coal wagon.

gunboat *n.*[2] [GUN *n.*[1] (2) + SE *boat* + pun] [1940s] (*US*) a river-boat being used as a brothel.

gunch *n.* [GUNCH *v.*] [1960s] (*US gay*) a male homosexual.

gunch *v.* [? SE *gay* + MUNCH *v.*[1] (2)] [1960s–70s] (*US gay*) to fellate.

Gundaroo bullock *n.* [*Gundaroo*, a town in southeast New South Wales] [late 19C] (*Aus.*) cooked koala meat.

gundiguts *n.* [Scot. *gundie*, greedy + -GUTS *sfx*] [late 17C–early 19C] a fat person.

guness *n.* [GUN *n.*[5] (2)] [mid-19C] (*UK Und.*) a female thief or pickpocket.

Gunga *n.* [the Rudyard Kipling poem 'Gunga Din' (1892)] [1910s] (*Aus.*) a generic term for an Indian.

gunga *n.*[1] (*also* **gonga, gunger**) [? GONG *n.*[1]; but note Rudyard Kipling poem 'Gunga Din' (1892): 'though I've belted you and flayed you...', i.e. on the backside] **1** [1940s+] (*Aus./N.Z.*) the anus. **2** [1960s] (*US campus*) an unattractive woman. **3** [1980s] (*Aus./N.Z.*) the vagina.

IN PHRASES

❑ **in one's gunga** *adv.* [1950s] (*Aus.*) directly, openly.

IN EXCLAMATIONS

❑ **up your gunga!** [20C+] a euph. synon. for UP YOUR ARSE! *excl.*

gunga *n.*[2] *see* GANJA *n.*

Gunga Din *n.* [rhy. sl.; ult. *Gunga Din*, water carrier in poem by Rudyard Kipling (1865–1936)] **1** [20C+] the chin. **2** [1970s+] (*Aus.*) gin (and water).

gunge *n.*[1] **1** [20C+] (*Ulster*) sweets, cakes, desserts. **2** [1960s+] a sticky mess, poss. when in the form of gravy or sauce, but equally often merely resembling such foods. **3** [1960s+] (*US*) a skin irritation of the male genitals, a mythical disease believed to make a man rot from his genitals outwards, prevalent among soldiers in Vietnam.

gunge *n.*[2] [abbr. GUNGEON *n.*] [1970s+] (*US drugs*) **1** potent marijuana. **2** heroin.

gunge *v.* [GUNGE *n.*^{1} (2)] [1960s+] to clog up with a sticky or messy substance, to become clogged up.

gungeon *n.* (*also* **gungion, gungun, gunion**) [? GANJA *n.*] [1940s+] (*drugs*) potent marijuana, usu. from Mexico or Africa.

(IN PHRASES)

❑ **black gungeon** *n.* (*also* **black gunion**) [1960s+] (*drugs*) an especially potent form of marijuana.

gunger *n. see* GUNGA *n.*^{1}.

gung-ho *n.* [GUNG-HO *adj.*] [1980s+] (*Aus. prison*) enthusiastic prison guards.

gung-ho *adj.* (*also* **gungy**) [Chinese *keng ho*, awe-inspiring (lit. 'more fiery'). The term was initially popularized as the motto of the US Marine Corps Second Raider Battalion, introduced there in 1942 by Lieutenant Colonel Evans F. Carlson] [1940s+] (*orig. US*) often of soldiers or sportspeople, enthusiastic, usu. aggressively so; thus as v., to do something in an aggressive manner.

gung-ho *adv.* [GUNG-HO *adj.*] [1940s+] enthusiastically, vigorously.

gungion/gungun *n. see* GUNGEON *n.*

gungy *adj.*^{1} [GUNGE *n.*^{1} (2)] [1960s+] **1** second-rate, inferior; of food, spoilt. **2** sticky, messy, slimy. **3** revolting.

gungy *adj.*^{2} *see* GUNG-HO *adj.*

gunion *n. see* GUNGEON *n.*

gunja *n. see* GANJA *n.*

gunjie *n.* [ety. unknown] [1990s+] (*Aus. Aboriginal*) a white person; by ext., a police officer.

gunk *n.*^{1} [? Irish *gonc*, to snub, to rebuff] **1** [20C+] (*Ulster*) an unpleasant shock, a major disappointment; thus *gunked*, disappointed. **2** [1940s+] (*US*) nonsense. **3** [1960s+] (*US*) a fool, a dullard. **4** [1990s+] a school child who has been rejected by its fellows.

gunk *n.*^{2} [orig. a proprietary name patented in 1932 by A.F. Curran Co. for 'liquid soaps and liquid cleaners for hard surfaced materials or articles'] [1930s+] (*orig. US*) a viscous or liquid substance.

(IN PHRASES)

❑ **gunk up** *v.* [1960s+] (*orig. US*) to mess up with viscous or liquid substances.

gunky *adj.* [GUNK *n.*^{2} + sfx *-y*] [1970s+] (*US*) sticky, viscous; messed up with or looking like gunk.

gun moll *n.* [SE *gun*/GUN *n.*^{5} (2) + MOLL *n.*] (*US Und.*) **1** [20C+] a female, gun-carrying gangster or female accomplice of a gunman. **2** [1900s–40s] a female pickpocket.

gunned *adj.* [1980s–90s] (*US campus*) drunk.

gunner *n.*^{1} (*also* **gunster**) [GUN *n.*^{3}] [early 18C] one who spreads malicious rumours.

gunner *n.*^{2} [because someone taking aim with a gun uses one eye only] [late 19C] a one-eyed person.

gunner *n.*^{3} [GUN *n.*^{5} (2)] [late 19C] (*UK Und.*) a thief.

gunner *n.*^{4} [SE *gun for*, to go wholeheartedly after someone or something] (*US campus*) **1** [1920s–60s] a zealous woman-chaser; a sexual athlete; also of a sexually enthusiastic woman. **2** [1970s+] an ambitiously competitive student.

gunner *n.*^{5} [play on SHOOT *v.* (3b)] [1930s–50s] the person who is throwing the dice in a game of dice craps.

gunner *n.*^{6} [GUN *n.*^{1}] **1** [1930s–70s] (*US Und.*) a gunman. **2** [1990s+] (*US drugs*) a heroin addict. **3** [1990s+] a term of abuse.

gunner *n.*^{7} [GUN *v.*^{1} (3)] [2000s] (*US prison*) a prisoner who masturbates while looking at a female warder.

gunnif *n. see* GONNOF *n.*

gunny *n.*^{1} [SE *gun*/GUN *n.*^{1} (9)] [1930s+] (*US*) a gunman, a gangster.

gunny *n.*^{2} [abbr. GUNGEON *n.*] [1960s+] (*drugs*) marijuana.

gunny *adj.* [GUN *n.*^{1} (6)] [1970s–80s] (*N.Z.*) first-class, superior.

gun out *v. see* GUN *v.*^{2} (2).

gunove *v. see* GONNOF *v.*

gunpowder *n.* [all plays on 'going off with a bang'] **1** [late 17C–early 19C] (*UK Und.*) an old woman [presumably a cantankerous one who 'goes off with a bang'. In *Henry IV Pt 1* Shakespeare uses the term in such a manner to describe the irascible 'gunpowder Percy']. **2** [mid-18C] a fiery drink; prob. gin [the short-lived 18C UK use was revived in US black use, see next]. **3** [1900s–30s] (*US black*) gin. **4** [1970s] (*US drugs*) opium. **5** [1990s+] (*US drugs*) cocaine.

gunpowder tea *n.* [note British Army sl. *gunfire*, an early morning cup of tea served out to troops before going on first parade] [mid-19C] (*US*) gunfire.

gunsel *n. see* GONSEL *n.*

gun-slinger *n.* (*also* **gun-slammer**) [all 'shoot down' their target] **1** [1920s+] (*US*) a gunman, esp. in the (fictional) 'Wild West'. **2** [1960s] (*US black*) a sexually powerful man. **3** [1990s+] (*US campus*) a woman who rejects a man's attentions rudely. **4** [1990s+] an employee dedicated to troubleshooting. **5** [1990s+] an aggressive male; a troublemaker.

gunster *n. see* GUNNER *n.*^{1}.

gunston *n.* [var. on GUNGEON *n.*] [1970s] (*S.Afr. drugs*) marijuana.

gunterpake *n.* [ety. unknown; ? link to Scot. *gant*, to gape] [20C+] (*Ulster*) a fool.

gunty *adj.* [ety. unknown] [2000s] (*N.Z. teen*) excellent, first-rate.

guntz *n.*^{1} [synon. Ger. *ganz*] [1950s+] the whole lot.

guntz *n.*^{2} [abbr. GONSEL *n.*] [1980s] (*US*) a worthless person.

gunyah *n.* [SAusE *gunyah*, an Aboriginal hut or other dwelling; as sl. the term is thus derisively racist] [late 19C+] (*Aus.*) a white person's hut or house.

gunzel *v.* (*also* **gunzle**) [? misreading of GONSEL *n.*] [1980s] (*US black*) to fight.

gup *n.*^{1} (*also* **gup-gup**) [Hind. *gap*, prattle, which borrowed in turn from the Turkish *gep* or *geb*, word, saying or talk and the Persian *guftan* or *guptan*, to say. The word made its way to the UK *c.*1868, the year in which a highly critical account of South Indian society was published, under the pseudonym of 'Gup'] [mid-19C–1950s] gossip.

gup *n.*^{2} [? GUP *n.*^{1} or SE *gulp*] [1930s–40s] (*Aus.*) a fool, a simpleton.

gup *v.* [GUP *n.*^{1}] [19C–1930s] (*orig. Anglo-Ind.*) to chat, to gossip.

gup-gup *n. see* GUP *n.*^{1}.

guppie *n.* [abbr.] [1980s+] **1** (*US gay*) gay urban professionals, i.e. the gay equivalent of YUPPIE *n.* **2** (*US*) grown-up urban professional, i.e. one who has transcended the yuppie phase.

guppy *adj.* [GUP *n.*^{2}] [1930s+] (*orig. Aus.*) silly, foolish.

guppy-gobbler *n.* [the former Catholic 'fish-day' of Friday] [1960s] (*US*) a Catholic.

gur *n.*

(IN PHRASES)

❑ **on the gur** [? GURRIER *n.*; or ? the *gur-cake*, a fruit pastry slice popular with poor Dublin children, consumed when truanting] [1920s–40s] (*Irish*) truanting.

gurgle *n.* [SE *gurgle*, to swallow] [1940s+] (*Aus./US*) liquor, a drink.

gurk *v.* [echoic] **1** [1920s] to belch. **2** [1940s] (*Aus.*) to break wind.

gurly *adj.* [synon. Scot.] [20C+] (*Ulster*) boisterous, ill-tempered.

gurrell *n.* [? link to dial. *gorrell*; *gurrel*, a glutton, a fat-stomached person] [mid-19C] a fob, a small pocket either in the waistband of the breeches or, latterly, in the waistcoat.

gurrier *n.* [? Fr. *guerrier*, a fighter; ? link to Fr. argot *guéri*, free; ? *gur-cake*, a fruit pastry slice popular with poor Dublin children] [1950s+] (*Irish*) a street urchin.

guru *n.* [Hind. *guru*, a holy man] **1** [1960s] (*drugs*) a guide or caretaker during a hallucinogenic experience. Such a person is either not taking the drug or a veteran user. **2** [1980s] (*US campus*) an expert.

gush *n.*^{1} [both 'gush out'] **1** [mid-19C] a whiff, a smell. **2** [mid–late 19C] (*US*) a good deal of a commodity.

gush *n.*^{2} [GUSH *v.*] [mid-19C+] an objectionably effusive or sentimental display of feeling, esp. as spoken.

DERIVATIVES

❑ **gushy** *adj.* [mid-19C+] sentimental, emotional.

IN PHRASES

❑ **penny gush** *n.* [late 19C] the effusive journalese found in penny newspapers, the late 19C tabloids.

gush *v.* [mid-19C+] to speak in a cloying sentimental manner; thus *gushing*, an extravagant display of feeling or sentiment.

gusher *n.* [GUSH *v.*] **1** [mid-19C–1940s] (*also* **gusheress**) one who talks to excess, uttering usu. insincere and sentimental remarks. **2** [1990s+] a crying fit [SE *gusher*, a well from which the oil flows without pumping].

gusset typing *n.* [1990s+] female masturbation; thus *gusset typist*, a woman who masturbates.

gussie *n.* [proper name *Augustus*, seen as stereotypically effeminate] [late 19C+] (*Aus./US*) a weak, effeminate man; thus a male homosexual.

gussy up *v.* (*also* **gussy**) [GUSSIE *n.*; the implication is usu. of excessive smartness and, in men, effeminacy] [1910s+] to smarten up, to dress up; esp. as *gussied up*, of people, dressed up, esp. for a night out; of objects, ornamented, disguised.

gusto *n.*[1] [SE *gusto* as used in the 1966 advertising slogan for Schlitz beer, 'Schlitz. Grab for the gusto!', an abbr. of the orig. line 'You only go around once in life, so grab for all the gusto you can.'] [1960s+] (*orig. US black*) beer.

gusto *n.*[2] [1980s+] (*US black*) money.

gut *n.* **1** in physical senses. (**a**) [early 16C+] in pl., the stomach. (**b**) [mid-16C+] in pl., the insides, the contents. (**c**) [late 16C+] in pl., a notably fat person; thus *tub of guts*, a grossly obese person. (**d**) [mid-19C+] in pl., a glutton. (**e**) [1910s–30s] (*US Und.*) (*also* **redgut**) a sausage. (**f**) [1960s+] constr. with *a*, a fat stomach. **2** in fig. senses. (**a**) [mid-17C+] (*also* **bowels**) in pl., courage, bravery, staying power. (**b**) [mid-18C+] in pl., energy, vigour, power in performance. (**c**) [20C+] in pl., the essence of a matter, the underlying meaning. (**d**) [1910s–50s] in pl., cheek, audacity, 'nerve'. (**e**) [1910s+] (*orig. Aus.*) in pl., the facts, the information; esp. as GOOD GUTS *under* GOOD *adj.*[1]. **3** pertaining to instinct. (**a**) [late 19C; 1960s+] the source of true feelings; thus *at gut level*, instinctively. (**b**) [20C+] (*US campus*) an easy course; thus *gut gunner*, one who succeeds in such a course. (**c**) [1920s] (*US*) a certainty. (**d**) [1970s+] (*US*) an easy task. (**e**) [2000s] (*US*) a *gut* feeling, an instinct. **4** [1910s–30s] (*US Und.*) in pl., the undercarriage of railroad trains on which tramps hitched a ride. **5** [1920s+] (*US*) the main street; thus *shoot the gut*, to drive along or cruise the main street. **6** [1940s+] constr. with *the*, Strait Street, Valetta, the centre of Malta's red-light district. **7** [1950s] (*Aus. gambling*) in pl., in two-up, the centre of the betting circle into which betted money is tossed.

DERIVATIVES

❑ **gutful/gutfull** *n. see* GUTSFUL *n.* ❑ **gutless** *see* separate entries.

IN COMPOUNDS

❑ **gut-ache** *n.* (*also* **guts-ache**) **1** [late 18C+] a stomach-ache. **2** [1950s] (*UK juv.*) a greedy person. **3** [1950s+] (*N.Z.*) an irritating person; also used as a term of address. ❑ **gut-bomb** *n.* [its deleterious effects] [1960s+] (*US*) a very greasy hamburger or similar food. ❑ **gut-bracer** *n. see* GUT-WARMER below. ❑ **gutbucket** *see* separate entries. ❑ **gut-burner** *n. see* GUT-WARMER below. ❑ **gut-buster** *n.* [it 'busts one's guts'] **1** [1930s] a funny person. **2** [1930s+] something powerful and dramatic; thus *gutbusting*, powerful, energetic, overwhelming. **3** [1950s+] (*N.Z.*) a very steep hill. **4** [1980s+] (*US*) something very funny, e.g. a joke or performance. ❑ **gut burglar** *n. see* BELLY BURGLAR *under* BELLY *n.* ❑ **gut-butcher** *n. see* GUT-REAMER below. ❑ **gut-check** *n.* [orig. sporting use] [1970s+] (*US*) a quick reassessment of strategy and stiffening of morale. ❑ **gutfatty** *n. see* FATGUTS *under* FAT *adj.* ❑ **gut-foot** *n.* [ety. unknown] [1930s–40s] (*US black*) fallen arches, i.e. flat feet. ❑ **gut-foundered** *adj.* [mid-17C–18C] extremely hungry. ❑ **gut-fucker** *n.* (*also* **gut-monger, -sticker**) [FUCKER *n.* (1)/sfx *-monger*/SE *sticker*] [late 19C–1900s] a sodomite. ❑ **gut-head** *n.* [-HEAD *sfx* (1)] [early 17C] one who is stupefied by an excess of food. ❑ **gut-heater** *n. see* GUT-WARMER below. ❑ **gut-hooks** *n.* [1930s+] (*US*) spurs. ❑ **gut-piece** *n.* [1960s] (*US*) the abdomen. ❑ **gut pudding** *n.* [sausages were orig. encased in animal gut] [late 16C–19C] a sausage. ❑ **gut-puller** *n.* [mid–late 19C] a poulterer. ❑ **gut-reamer** *n.* (*also* **gut-butcher, -stretcher, -stuffer**) [1920s–70s] (*US*) a pederast. ❑ **gut-ripper** *n.* [1940s] (*US*) any kind of knife used as a weapon. ❑ **gut-robber** *n.* [orig. logging jargon] [20C+] (*US*) a cook, esp. a bad one. ❑ **gut-rot** *n.* [its presumed effect on one's innards] **1** [1910s+] cheap wine or spirits (cf. ROTGUT *n.*). **2** [1930s+] unpalatable drink or food; also fig. use. ❑ **guts-ache** *n. see* GUT-ACHE above. ❑ **guts and garbage** *n.* [late 18C–early 19C] a very fat person. ❑ **gutsball** *see* separate entries. ❑ **gut-scraper** *n.* [the violin's catgut strings] [early 18C+] a fiddle player, a violinist. ❑ **guts-high** *adj. see* GUTS UP *adj.* ❑ **gut-shoot** *v.* [1930s+] (*US*) to shoot in the stomach. ❑ **gut-shot** *v.* (*US*) **1** [1970s+] wounded in the stomach. **2** [1980s+] in fig. use, deeply hurt. ❑ **gutstick** *n. see* separate entry. ❑ **gut-sticker** *n. see* GUT-FUCKER above. ❑ **gut-stretcher/-stuffer** *n. see* GUT-REAMER above. ❑ **guts-up** *see* separate entries. ❑ **gut-wagon** *n.* [1920s+] (*US*) a truck that carries cattle carcasses. ❑ **gut-warmer** *n.* (*also* **gut-bracer, -burner, -heater**) [1940s+] (*US*) a strong alcoholic drink. ❑ **gut-wrench** *n.* [1940s+] (*US*) the penis.

IN PHRASES

❑ **break someone's guts** *v.* [1930s] (*US prison*) to beat a prisoner in order to break their will and spirit. ❑ **bust a gut** *v.* (*also* **bust one's gut, break a gut, rupture..., split...**) **1** [late 17C+] to work very hard. **2** [1910s+] (*US*) to be overcome with emotion, e.g. rage, delight etc. **3** [1920s+] (*also* **blow a gut**) to strain oneself (esp. by laughing). **4** [1940s] to beat someone up. ❑ **carry guts to a bear** *v.* (*also* **pack guts to a bear, tote..., carry guts to a barrel, pack...**) [late 17C+] to perform an extremely distasteful or absolutely basic task, usu. implying inadequacy or stupidity; thus *he's not fit to..., he hasn't enough/the brains to...* ❑ **come one's guts** *v.* (*also* **give one's guts**) [1930s–70s] to give information. ❑ **double-guts** *n.* **1** [early 19C+] a very fat person. **2** [20C+] (*US*) a large stomach, a pot belly. ❑ **drag the gut** *v. see under* DRAG *v.*[1]. ❑ **drop one's guts** *v.* **1** [1970s–80s] (*N.Z. prison*) to act in a cowardly manner; to back down. **2** [1990s+] to break wind. ❑ **eat one's guts out** *v.* [1960s] to agonize. ❑ **flog one's guts out** *v.* [1970s+] to work very hard, to make an extreme effort. ❑ **get one's guts in a knot** *v.* [1910s+] (*Aus.*) to become angry, esp. for no good reason. ❑ **get one's guts up** *v.* [1970s] (*Aus.*) to have sexual intercourse. ❑ **give one's guts** *v. see* COME ONE'S GUTS above. ❑ **gut it** *v.* **1** [1910s+] (*US campus*) to stay up all night working without any amphetamines for stimulation but purely through strength of will and character. **2** [1960s+] (*US*) (*also* **gut (it) out**) to be strong, tough, in the face of adversity. ❑ **gut plunge on butch** *n.* [1920s–30s] (*US*) scrounging for meat from a butcher's shop by a tramp. ❑ **gut through** *n.* [GUT IT above] [1970s+] (*US*) to endure courageously. ❑ **hate someone's guts** *v.* (*also* **hate someone's gizzard, ...hide, loathe someone's guts**) [1920s+] to loathe, to detest. ❑ **have guts in one's brains** *v.* [mid-17C–early 19C] to be sensible, to show some intelligence. ❑ **have someone's guts for garters** *v.* (*also* **have someone's guts for (a) garter(s), make garters of someone's guts, wear someone's guts for earmuffs**) [late 16C; late 18C; 1930s+] to punish comprehensively, to hurt. ❑ **hold one's guts** *v.* (*also* **keep one's guts**) [late 19C+] to remain silent under questioning. ❑ **kick someone's guts in** *v.* [1930s] to beat, to assault. ❑ **lose one's guts** *v.* [1950s] to vomit. ❑ **more guts than a Bedford truck** [1990s+] (*Aus.*) used of a brave and admirable individual. ❑ **more guts than brains** [late 18C–early 19C] a phr. said of someone who is foolish but determined in their stupidity. ❑ **my great guts are ready to eat my little ones** [late 18C–early 19C] I am very hungry. ❑ **my guts are potato chips** [1970s] (*Aus.*) I am absolutely terrified. ❑ **my guts chime twelve** (*also* **my guts cry cupboard, ...curse my teeth**) [late 18C–19C] I am very hungry. ❑ **pack guts to a barrel/bear** *v. see* CARRY GUTS TO A BEAR above. ❑ **plenty of guts but no bowels** [SE *bowels*, 'pity, compassion, feeling, 'heart'' (*OED*)] [late 18C–early 19C] a phr. used of one who is tough and ruthless but lacks compassion. ❑ **pop a gut** *v.* **1** [late 17C+] to work very hard. **2** [late 19C+] to laugh uproariously. **3** [1940s+] to be furious. ❑ **puff guts** *n.* [mid-17C–early 19C] a fat man. ❑ **pull-guts** *n.* [his 'evisceration' of the fish] [late 17C–early 18C] a fishmonger. ❑ **rupture a gut** *v. see* BUST A GUT above. ❑ **scare the guts out of** *v.* [1950s] to terrify. ❑ **she has to cross her legs to keep her guts from falling out** [1960s] (*US*) used of a promiscuous or supposedly promiscuous woman. ❑ **shut one's guts** *v.* [1950s+] (*Aus.*) to stop talking. ❑ **split a gut** *v. see* BUST A GUT above. ❑ **sweat one's guts out** *v.* (*also* **slave one's guts out, slog..., slug..., tear...**) [late 19C+] to work to one's utmost. ❑ **suck one's guts** *v. see* SUCK ONE'S FACE *under* SUCK *v.*[1]. ❑ **throw one's guts** *v.* **1** [1920s–60s] (*US tramp*) to inform. **2** [1930s+] (*US*) to vomit. ❑ **tote guts to a bear** *v. see* CARRY GUTS TO A BEAR above. ❑ **wear someone's guts for ear-muffs** *v. see* HAVE SOMEONE'S GUTS FOR GARTERS above. ❑ **up in someone's guts** [2000s] (*US black*) of a man, having sexual intercourse.

SE meaning entrails, in slang uses

IN COMPOUNDS

❑ **gut-eater/-eating** *see* separate entries.

gut *adj.* [one knows 'in one's guts'; GUT *n.* (3)] **1** [1910s+] (*US campus*) easy. **2** [1950s+] (*orig. US*) based on instinct, feeling. **3** [1960s+] of fundamental importance.

gut *v.*[1] [GUT *n.* (1a)] **1** [17C–1900s] to eat like a glutton. **2** [late 17C–1900s] to empty; esp. in phr. *gut a quart pot*, to drink the pot to the dregs; *gut a house*, to empty a house of its furnishings.

gut *v.*[2] [GUT *n.* (2a)] **1** [1940s] (*US*) to display one's courage. **2** [1960s+] (*US black*) to punch in the stomach; lit. and fig. use.

gutbucket *n.*[1] [lit. + fig. derivations of saloon use *gutbucket*, the small bucket to catch drippings or 'gutterings' from the barrels that is found in cheap bars and saloons. Such jazz was played in these 'low' saloons] **1** [1920s+] (*orig. US black*) a very basic, raw, unsophisticated style of jazz; thus ext. to rock music. **2** [1930s–60s] (*US black*) a bucket used to carry food or drink, thus inferior liquor. **3** [1940s–50s] (*US black*) a low place or dive. **4** [1960s+] (*US*) a washtub bass. **5** [1970s] a jazz musician.

gutbucket *n.*[2] [GUT *n.* (1a)] **1** [1930s+] (*US*) a (pompous) fat person. **2** [1940s] (*US*) a toilet. **3** [1950s+] (*US*) the belly.

gutbucket *adj.* [GUTBUCKET *n.*[2] (1)] [1930s+] (*US black*) contemptible.

gut-eater *n.* [their taste for offal, despised by whites] [1920s–60s] (*US Western*) a Native American.

gut-eating *adj.* [GUT-EATER *n.*] [1940s–60s] (*US Western*) used derog. of a Native American.

gutless *adj.* [20C+] cowardly.

IN COMPOUNDS

❑ **gutless wonder** *n.* **1** [1930s+] a coward. **2** [1960s] in fig. use, a useless object.

gutless *adv.* [1980s+] as intensifer: to a very great extent, in a very intense manner etc.

guts *v.* [GUT *n.* (1)] [late 19C+] (*Aus.*) to overeat.

-guts *sfx* [metonymy; GUT *n.* (1a)] [late 16C+] a person, e.g. GREEDY-GUT *n.*; LUSTY-GUTS *n.*; WORRYGUTS *n.*

gutsa *n. see* GUTSER *n.*[2].

guts ball *n.* [GUT *n.*] [1960s+] (*US*) **1** any kind of fiercely aggressive and competitive ball game. **2** any action requiring aggression, courage and determination.

gutsball *adj.* [GUTS BALL *n.* (2)] [1960s+] (*US*) plucky, courageous.

gutser *n.*[1] (*also* **gutzer**) [GUT *n.* (1d)] [1910s+] a greedy person.

gutser *n.*[2] (*also* **gutsa, gutzer**) [note WW1 milit. use 'to get into serious trouble'; orig. Scot. for suffering a 'bellyflop'] [1910s+] (*Aus.*) **1** in lit. or fig. use, a heavy fall, a collision; thus *come a gutser*, to trip over and fall; *bring someone a gutser*, to engineer someone's downfall. **2** a disappointment, a let-down; a misfortune.

gutser *v.* [GUTSER *n.*[2] (1)] [1950s] to be beaten or overcome, to lose.

gutsful *n.* (*also* **gutful, gutfull**) [GUT *n.* (1) + SE *full*] [1920s+] (*orig. Aus./N.Z.*) a sufficiency, quite as much of anything as one wants or cares to take; often as *have a gutful*.

IN PHRASES

❑ **gutsful of grunts** *n.* [1910s+] (*Aus.*) an unpleasant person.

gutsing *n.* [the stolen goods are hidden in the GUT *n.* (1a) area] [2000s] (*N.Z.*) shoplifting.

gutso *n.* [GUT *n.* (1) + -O *sfx* (1)] [1950s+] a fat person.

gutstick *n.* [late 19C; 1970s+] the penis.

IN PHRASES

❑ **have a bit of gutstick** *v.* [late 19C; 1970s+] of a woman, to have sexual intercourse.

guts up *adj.* (*also* **guts high**) [GUT *n.* (2a)] [1950s–60s] (*US*) fearless.

guts up *v.* [GUTS *v.*] [mid-19C+] (*Aus.*) to eat.

gutsy *adj.* [GUT *n.* + sfx -*y*] **1** [late 19C+] tough, spirited, brave; thus *gutsiness*, courage, spirit. **2** [1950s+] greedy, very hungry.

gutta-percha *n.*[1] [? the prevalence of the gutta-percha tree (*Isonaudra Gutta*) in the state] [late 19C–1910s] (*Aus.*) an inhabitant of the state of Victoria.

gutta-percha *n.*[2] [the use of *gutta-percha* leaf as a covering] [1920s] (*US*) the foreskin.

gutted *adj.*[1] [GUT *n.* (1b)] [early 19C–1900s] impoverished, without money.

gutted *adj.*[2] [abbr. of phr. *sick to one's guts*, the term originated in prison use, but has become widespread since mid-1970s] [1960s+] deeply disappointed, sick and tired, fed up, utterly depressed, very upset.

gutter *n.* **1** [late 19C] the vagina. **2** [1930s+] (*drugs*) a vein into which a drug is injected. **3** *see* GUTTER-ALLEY below.

SE in slang uses

IN COMPOUNDS

❑ **gutter-alley** *n.* (*also* **gutter**) [17C–19C] the throat. ❑ **gutter blood** *n.* [SE *gutter*, suggesting low class + BLOOD *n.*[1] (1)] [early–mid-19C] **1** a lout, a hoodlum. **2** a parvenu, a vulgar man who puts on airs. ❑ **gutter chaunter** *n.* [CHANTER *n.* (1)] [mid–late 19C] a street-singer. ❑ **gutter gripper** *n.* [1950s+] (*Aus.*) a motorist who drives with one hand stuck through the open window, gripping the gutter that runs around the car's roof. ❑ **gutter hype** *n.* (*also* **gutter hyp, ...junkie**) [SE *gutter*, suggesting low class + HYPE *n.*[2] (1)/JUNKIE *n.*] [1920s–50s] (*drugs*) a very low-level narcotics user. ❑ **gutter lane** *n.* [? proper name *Gutter Lane*, a small street in 17C London and the source of phr. *go down Gutter Lane*, to be a drunkard or glutton. Partridge, however, suggests links to Lat. *guttur*, the throat and to Devon dial. *gutter*, to eat greedily, as well as to colloq. *guttle*, to eat heartily and GUZZLE *v.*[1] (1)] [late 17C–19C] the throat. ❑ **gutter snipe** *n.* **1** [late 19C] (*UK tramp*) a derog. term for a male servant. **2** [1960s] (*US prison*) in a woman's prison, an inmate who turns temporarily to homosexuality.

guttered *adj.* [the image of falling into a *gutter*] [1950s+] very drunk.

guttie *n.* (*also* **gutty**) [GUT *n.* (1d)] **1** [19C] a glutton. **2** [19C+] a very fat person. **3** [1910s+] (*Irish*) one who has no redeeming features, a street urchin; also as adj., thus *guttiest*.

gutties *n.* [SE *gutta-percha*, a tree (*Isonaudra Gutta*) the juice of which is used in their manufacture] [20C+] (*Irish*) plimsolls, trainers.

IN PHRASES

❑ **sink the gutties** *v.* [1980s+] (*Irish*) to drive very fast, i.e. to push one's plimsoll-clad foot down on the accelerator.

gutty *adj.*[1] [GUTSY *adj.* (1)] **1** [1940s+] tough, spirited, brave. **2** [1960s–70s] unpleasant, hard to bear.

gutty *adj.*[2] [SE *gutter*, thus the lifestyle of those who lived 'in the gutter'] [1950s–60s] (*US black*) raw, unsophisticated.

gutzer *n. see under* GUTSER.

Guv *n.* (*also* **old guv**) [var. on GOV *n.*] **1** [late 19C+] (*also* **gov**) a general term of address, usu. to someone seen as or actually higher in the social order. **2** [1900s] one's father. **3** [1950s+] a senior figure, the 'boss'.

guvnor *n.* (*also* **govnor, guvner**) [pron. GOVERNOR *n.*] [mid-19C+] **1** a boss, an important, influential person. **2** a general term of address. **3** (*also* **my old guvnor**) one's father.

guvnor *adj.* [GUVNOR *n.* (1)] [1970s] the most important.

guy *n.*[1] [fig. uses of the negative image of *Guy* Fawkes (1570–1606), leader of the Gunpowder Plot of 1605] **1** [19C+] a fool. **2** [early–mid-19C] a dark lantern; thus *stow the guy*, cover or douse the lantern. **3** [mid-19C] an ugly or badly dressed person. **4** [mid-19C] a crimp, one who tricks men into joining the navy. **5** [mid-19C–1910s] (*US*) a comical fellow, a SMART ALECK *n.* **6** [mid-19C–1910s] (*US*) a trick or hoax, a joke. **7** [late 19C–1950s] an act of running off, of leaving surreptitiously; usu. in phrs. below.

IN PHRASES

▫ **do a guy** *v.* **1** [mid-19C+] to leave, esp. when stealthily or secretly. **2** [late 19C] to escape. **3** [late 19C] to take a false name. **4** [late 19C–1900s] to absent oneself from work without asking permission. ▫ **give someone the guy** *v.* **1** [late 19C] to run away from, to 'give the slip'. **2** [late 19C+] (*US*) to make a fool of someone, to tease.

guy *n.*[2] **1** [late 19C+] (*US*) a man or boy; thus *MAIN GUY under* MAIN *adj.* **2** [1910s+] a general term of address, repopularized in 1970s+ among young UK blacks, and now in general teen use. **3** [1910s+] (*US*) a woman. **4** [1960s] a boyfriend, a lover. **5** [1970s+] a person, irrespective of gender. **6** [1980s+] (*US campus*) in ironic reversal, an incompetent, an inadequate. **7** [1980s+] (*US*) an object, a thing.

guy *n.*[3] [rhy. sl.; *Guy Fawkes* = walk] [late 19C+] a walk, thus an expedition or journey.

guy *n.*[4] [1940s+] (*US*) a euph. for *God*.

guy *adj.* [GUY *n.*[2] (1)] [1990s+] (*US*) particularly or only of interest to men; thus *it's a guy thing*.

guy *v.*[1] [GUY *n.*[1] (1)] [mid-19C+] to tease, to fool, to mock.

guy *v.*[2] *see* GUY-A-WHACK *v.*

guy-a-whack *n.* (*also* **guy-away**) [GUY-A-WHACK *v.*] [20C+] (*Aus.*) a defaulting bookmaker.

guy-a-whack *adj.* [GUY-A-WHACK *v.*] [20C+] (*Aus.*) useless, incompetent.

guy-a-whack *v.* (*also* **guy**) [ety. unknown; *AND* suggests ext. of GUY *n.*[1] (7)/GUY (OFF) *v.* + *a-whack* as var. on SE *away*] [late 19C–1910s] (*Aus.*) to run off, to leave quickly.

guyess *n.* [GUY *n.*[2] (1)] [2000s] a woman or girl.

guy (off) *v.* [*DO A GUY under* GUY *n.*[1]] [late 19C–1930s] (*UK Und.*) to run away, to escape.

guyver *n. see* GUIVER *n.*[2].

guzinter *n.* [SE *goes into*] **1** [1910s+] (*Aus.*) in pl., an animal's innards. **2** [1940s–50s] (*Aus.*) a schoolteacher [basic maths, e.g. 'how many times does two *go into* four?].

guzunder *n.* [it *goes under* the bed] [20C+] a chamberpot.

guzzle *n.* [? OF *gosiller*, to vomit or to chatter + OF *gosier*, throat] **1** [mid-17C+] the throat. **2** [mid-17C+] liquor, a drink; thus *guzzling*, drinking heavily. **3** [late 17C] beer. **4** [mid-19C] the eating of a meal, a mouthful of food. **5** [1920s+] a swig, a gulp.

DERIVATIVES

▫ **guzzlery** *n.* [late 19C+] (*US*) a cheap saloon or bar.

IN COMPOUNDS

▫ **guzzle shop** *n.* (*also* **guzzle crib**) [CRIB *n.*[1] (3)] [late 19C+] (*US*) a cheap saloon or bar.

guzzle *v.*[1] [17C+] to drink (greedily); to eat voraciously.

IN COMPOUNDS

▫ **guzzle-guts** *n.* [-GUTS *sfx*] **1** [late 18C+] a drunkard. **2** [1950s] (*UK juv.*) a greedy person.

IN PHRASES

▫ **guzzle the grass** *v.* [1980s] (*Aus.*) to vomit.

guzzle *v.*[2] [lit. + fig. uses of GUZZLE *n.* (1)] **1** [late 18C] to lie. **2** [mid–late 19C] to swindle. **3** [late 19C+] to strangle, to throttle, to murder; thus *guzzler*, one who employs this method. **4** [1930s] to understand, to 'swallow'. **5** [1930s+] (*UK Und.*) to arrest; to interrogate. **6** [1930s+] to indulge in sexual foreplay, to 'neck'.

guzzled *adj.* (*also* **gossled**) [GUZZLE *v.*[1]/GUZZLE *v.*[2] (3)] (*US*) **1** [late 19C–1930s] drunk. **2** [1920s–30s] assaulted, subjected to intimidation, killed.

guzzling *n.* [GUZZLE *v.*[2] (6)] [1930s] kissing and cuddling.

g.v. *n.* [abbr.] [1900s–10s] a governor.

gwaai *n.* [Zulu *ugwayi*, tobacco, snuff] [1980s+] (*S.Afr.*) **1** tobacco. **2** a cigarette, a 'smoke'.

gwaan! *excl.* [lit. *go on!*] [20C+] (*W.I./UK black teen*) a term of encouragement or appreciation, i.e. go ahead! get going!

g'wan! *excl. see* GO ON! *excl.*

gweeb *n.* (*also* **gweebo, gweep**) [var. on DWEEB *n.*] [1980s+] (*US campus*) a person entirely lacking in social skills and style.

gweva *n.* [Xhosa *igweva*, an illicit diamond buyer] [1960s+] (*S.Afr. township*) a bootlegger.

gybe *n.* (*also* **glibe, glybe, jibe, jybe**) [ety. unknown; Partridge suggests Ger. *schreiben*, a writing; if so then also ? SE *scribe*] **1** [mid-16C–mid-19C] (*UK Und.*) a written paper, esp. a counterfeit pass or licence, carried by many of the mendicant villains. **2** [mid-19C] (*UK Und.*) a coiner.

gybe *v.* [SE *gybe*, of a sail, to swing from one side to the other] [late 17C–18C] to whip, to beat; thus *gybed*, whipped.

gyger *n. see* GIGGER *n.*[1].

gylrig *n.* [Polari; ? backslang of SE *girl* or *girly*] [1950s] (*UK gay*) **1** a desirable person. **2** sexual activity.

gym *v.* [? dial. *gan*, to walk] [1930s] (*UK Und.*) to travel to or gain admission to, without paying the full charge; often of a racecourse.

gym hat *n. see JIMMY CAP under* JIMMY *n.*[4].

gym rat *n.* (*also* **gym bunny**) [SE *gym* + RAT *n.*[1] (1h)] **1** [1970s+] (*US*) a sports enthusiast; usu. one who frequents gyms and training grounds; often used of young gay men obsessed with body building. **2** [1990s+] (*US*) in fig. use, anyone fanatically pursuing a course of activity, a career etc.

gynae *n.* (*also* **gynie**) [abbr.] [1940s+] **1** *gynae*cology. **2** a *gynae*cologist.

gyno *n.* [1960s+] a gynaecologist.

gyp *n.*[1] [abbr. SE *gypsy* and as such an ethnic slur] (*orig. US*) **1** [mid-19C+] (*also* **gip**) a thief. **2** [1910s+] (*also* **jip**) an act of deception, a fraud or hoax. **3** [1920s+] a cheat, a swindler; one who fails to pay his due debts. **4** *see* GYP JOINT below. **5** *see* GYPO *n.*

IN COMPOUNDS

▫ **gyp artist** *n.* [ARTIST *n.* (1)] [20C+] a swindler. ▫ **gyp joint** *n.* (*also* **gyp, gyp flat**) [JOINT *n.* (3b)] [1920s+] (*US*) anywhere, esp. a club, bar etc, where the unwary will be swindled. ▫ **gyp moll** *n.* [MOLL *n.* (1)] [20C+] (*US*) a female swindler. ▫ **gyp racket** *n.* [RACKET *n.*[1] (1)] [20C+] (*US*) swindling, fraud.

IN PHRASES

▫ **get the gyp** *v.* [1910s–30s] to be swindled, cheated.

gyp *n.*[2]

IN PHRASES

▫ **give gyp** *v.* (*also* **give gip, give jip**) [? *OED* implies contraction of GEE UP *n.* in dial. but note Yorks. dial. *jip*, a sound thrashing, heavy punishment] [20C+] to cause pain or trouble; usu. as *give one gyp* or *give someone gyp*; thus *get gip/gyp*, to receive such pain. ▫ **give someone gyp** *v.* (*also* **give someone gip, ...jip**) [late 19C+] (*UK tramp/ Scot.*) to admonish, to punish.

gyp *adj.* (*also* **gypping**) [GYP *v.* (1)] [1920s+] cheating, deceitful.

gyp *v.* (*also* **gip, jip, gypsy**) [GYP *n.*[1]] (*orig. US*) **1** [late 19C+] to cheat, to deceive, to renege on one's debts. **2** [1910s–40s] to steal; to rob from. **3** [1920s–30s] to disappoint. **4** [1970s] to play truant from school.

gyp *adv.* [1950s] (*US*) in a second-rate manner.

gype *n. see* GIPE *n.*

gypo *n.* (*also* **gippo, gyp, gyppo, gyppy, jippo**) [abbr.; note UK services sl. *gyppo*, gravy, grease, stew; S.Afr. milit. *gyppo*, to shirk duty] **1** [late 19C+] *gypsy*, usu. derog. **2** [late 19C+] an

Egyptian. **3** [1920s–70s] (*US*) contract work, a sub-contractor, a piece-worker [the implication is that the worker fulfils the contract then moves on, like a gypsy]. **4** [1990s+] (*UK juv.*) an impoverished, badly dressed schoolchild.

gypo *adj.* (*also* **gippo, gippy, gyppo**) [GYPO *n.*] **1** [1910s+] Egyptian. **2** [1930s+] pertaining to a gypsy or gypsy culture.

gypper *n.* [GYP v. (1)] [1920s+] (*US*) a swindler.

gypping *adj. see* GYP *adj.*

gyppo *see under* GYPO.

gyppy *n. see* GYPO *n.*

gyppy tummy *n.* (*also* **gippy tummy, gyppo gut**) [GYPO *n.* (2)] [1930s+] stomach troubles, diarrhoea; orig. that contracted in Egypt, but now ext. to any such problems that UK tourists experience abroad or in ethnic restaurants at home.

Gypsie Lee *n.* [rhy. sl.] [1930s+] (*Aus.*) tea.

gypsies *n.* [they wander about] [2000s] (*S.Afr. gay*) a pair of shoes.

gypsy *n.* (*also* **gipsy**) [1950s+] (*US*) **1** an independent trucker or the truck they own. **2** an independent cab-driver or taxicab. **3** a prostitute who travels around for trade or lives in a trailer park. **4** used in a variety of combs. (*see* below), usu. stereotyping Romanies as untrustworthy.

IN COMPOUNDS

❑ **gypsy joint** *n.* [JOINT *n.* (3b)] [1960s] (*US*) a palm-reader's. ❑ **gypsy queen** *n.* [QUEEN *n.* (2)/play on SE] [2000s] a homosexual. ❑ **gypsy's deal** *n.* (*also* **gipsy's deal**) [1990s+] (*US*) a business deal that never actually materializes. ❑ **gypsy's leave** *n.* (*also* **gipsy's leave**) [20C+] departure without warning and without settling one's debts. ❑ **gypsy's warning** *n. see* separate entry. ❑ **gypsy switch** *n.* [1950s] (*US Und.*) a form of criminal sleight of hand in which a high-denomination note is palmed and swapped for a low-denomination one.

gypsy *adj.* (*also* **gipsy**) [the negative image of the Romanies] **1** [20C+] (*W.I.*) interfering, irritatingly inquisitive. **2** [1980s+] independent of any organization, legal or otherwise.

gypsy *v. see* GYP *v.*

gypsy's (kiss) *n.* (*also* **gipsy's**) [rhy. sl. = PISS *n.* (2)] [1970s+] an act of urination.

gypsy's warning *n.*[1] (*also* **gipsy's warning**) [rhy. sl.] [20C+] morning; also as 'good morning'.

gypsy's warning *n.*[2] (*also* **gipsy's warning**) [negative stereotyping] [20C+] no warning at all.

gyrene *n.* [ety. unknown; *HDAS* rejects popular ety. *GI* + *marine*; suggests Gk *gyrinos*, tadpole, pollywog, as ref. to the Marine's 'amphibious' role] [late 19C+] (*US*) a US Marine.

gytch *v.* [ety. unknown] [1950s] (*US*) to steal.

gyve *n.* [JIVE *n.*[1] (5a)] [1930s–50s] (*drugs*) a marijuana cigarette.

gyvel *n.* [SE *gyve*, a shackle, a fetter] [late 18C–19C] (*Scot.*) the vagina.

gyver *n.*[1] *see* GUIVER *n.*[1].

gyver *n.*[2]

IN PHRASES

❑ **put on the gyver** *v. see* PUT ON THE GUIVER *under* GUIVER *n.*[2].

gyvo *n.* [GUIVER *n.*[1] (1)] [1930s+] (*Aus.*) flattery, insincerity, pretence.

gyzm *n. see* JISM *n.*

H *n.* [abbr.] **1** [mid-19C+] (*orig. US*) *h*ell. **2** [1920s+] (*drugs*) (*also* **aitch, Big H, the H**) *h*eroin. **3** [1950s] a *h*ypodermic syringe. **4** [1980s+] (*US drugs*) *h*ashish.

ha *n. see* HA-HA *n.*^{2}.

hab *n.* [Fr. *habitant*, an inhabitant. The name was adopted deliberately by the Montréal Canadiens, to display their pride as French, rather than British, Canadians] [20C+] (*Can.*) a derog. term for a share-cropper, a tenant farmer.

habdabs *n. see* ABDABS *n.*

habe *n.* [abbr. legal jargon] [1970s+] *hab*eas corpus, an order compelling its subject to attend court.

haberdasher of (nouns and) pronouns *n.* [the expanded version is late 17C–18C only] [late 17C–early 19C] a schoolmaster; a tutor.

habit *n.* [note that earliest citations are more SE than sl., e.g. in 1887, 'May he continue to wage war against Chinese opium dens until the habit has been swept entirely out of existence'; and the term was adopted by drug users in the 1910s. Note 'William Lee', *Junkie* (1953): 'A junk habit. It takes at least a month of daily use to get a needle habit, two months for a smoking habit, four months for an eating habit.'] **1** [late 19C+] (*drugs*) a drug addiction, usu. to an opiate; thus the sense of needing more drugs to sustain physical comfort. **2** [20C+] ext. to other addictions. **3** [1920s–30s] withdrawal symptoms.

IN PHRASES

❑ **bend the habit** *v.* [1950s] (*drugs*) to decrease one's narcotics intake in an attempt to withdraw from addiction. ❑ **chippie habit** *n.* (*also* **chippy habit**) [CHIPPIE *v.*^{1} (1)] [1930s+] (*drugs*) the occasional use of a narcotic, rather than the regular use necessitated by addiction. ❑ **feed one's habit** *n.* (*also* **feed one's gorilla**) [1950s+] (*drugs*) **1** to inject oneself with a narcotic, usu. heroin. **2** to habitually consume any drug or alcohol. ❑ **get one's habit on** *v.* [1920s–30s] to be using narcotics; to be drunk. ❑ **get the habit off** *n.* [1930s] (*drugs*) to take enough of a narcotic to stop the pain of withdrawal. ❑ **have a habit** *v.* [1930s] (*drugs*) to be suffering from withdrawal symptoms. ❑ **kick the habit** *v.* (*also* **boot the habit, break..., bust..., kick out one's habit**) **1** [1920s+] (*drugs*) to stop taking an addictive drug, usu. heroin (cf. KICK *v.*^{4} (1)). **2** [1950s+] in fig. use, to stop doing something. ❑ **lamp habit** *n.* [the SE *lamp* at which the opium pipe is lit] (*drugs*) **1** [1930s–40s] the passive inhalation of opium, which over a period can lead to addiction. **2** [1930s–50s] an opium addiction. ❑ **mouth habit** *n.* [1930s–50s] (*US drugs*) the consumption of narcotics orally and the subsequent addiction. ❑ **smoke the habit off** *v.* **1** [1930s] to smoke enough to prevent withdrawal symptoms. **2** [1930s–50s] (*US drugs*) of an opium user, to smoke heavily after a period of abstinence. ❑ **stomach habit** *n.* [1950s–70s] (*drugs*) heroin addiction (through inhalation rather than injection).

habitch *n.* [abbr./pron.] [1950s] a *habit*ual criminal.

habra, dabra and the crew *phr.* [? SE *abracadabra*] [20C+] (*W.I., Bdos*) everybody one can think of, a large, undifferentiated crowd.

hache *n.* [Sp. *hache*, the letter H] [1950s+] (*drugs*) heroin.

hachi *n.* (*also* **hotchee, hotchie**) [Jap. *shakuhachi*, 50cm (20in); imported by US veterans of the Korean War (1950–53); but note HATCHI *n.*] [1950s+] (*orig. US milit.*) the penis; thus *eat/suck a hachi!* go to hell!

hack *n.*^{1} [abbr. SE *hackney* carriage/cab-driver; non-vehicular refs. reflect the idea of being available 'for hire'; note Ward, *The London Spy* (1699): 'His beard [...] was as well-grown as a *Hackney-Writers* in the middle of a *Long Vacation*'; note *Gradus ad Cantabrigiam* (1803): 'HACK, a hack preacher "the common exhibitioners of St. Mary's, employed in the service of defaulters and absentees"'] **1** [late 17C–1910s] (*also* **hackman**) the driver of a hackney carriage. **2** [late 18C–19C] a prostitute; one who is sexually experienced [abbr. HACKNEY *n.* (1)]. **3** [19C+] a reporter, a journalist, formerly derog. but recently popular, if tongue-in-cheek. **4** [mid-19C+] (*US*) a taxicab. **5** [late 19C–1960s] (*US*) a hearse. **6** [1920s–50s] (*US*) a car. **7** [1920s+] (*Aus./US*) a taxi-driver. **8** [1930s+] an automobile (other than a taxi). **9** [1950s–70s] anyone who acts as a 'yes-man', esp. in politics. **10** [1950s+] an incompetent, an inadequate. **11** [1960s] (*N.Z.*) a customer, as in a pub. **12** [1990s+] a worker of any type, the image is of monotonous 'grind'. **13** [2000s] (*US Und.*) a rented gun.

IN COMPOUNDS

❑ **hack-pusher** *n.* (*also* **hack pilot**) [1930s–60s] (*Aus./US*) a taxi-driver. ❑ **hack-rack** *n.* [1970s] (*US*) a taxicab stand.

IN PHRASES

❑ **away on a hack** *adj.* (*also* **away in a hack**) [1930s+] (*Irish*) lucky, successful. ❑ **make a hack of** *v.* [fig. use of SE *hack*, a horse for ordinary riding, as distinguished from cross-country, milit., or other special riding] [late 19C] to wear the same dress every day. ❑ **make hack** *v.* [1970s] (*US black*) to move fast.

hack *n.*^{2} [SE *hackneyed*, banal, lacking novelty] [19C+] **1** an embarrassment, an embarrassing situation. **2** an annoying characteristic.

hack *n.*^{3} [? HAWK *n.*^{1}] **1** [1910s–50s] (*US/Can. Und.*) a night watchman. **2** [1920s+] (*US*) a police officer. **3** [1930s] (*US black*) a generic term for any white person. **4** [1930s+] (*US/Can. Und.*) a prison guard; a warder. **5** [1950s–60s] a bodyguard.

hack *v.*^{1} **1** [late 19C+] (*US campus*) to socialize, to waste time, to idle. **2** [1940s–60s] (*US*) to neck, to kiss, to engage in sexual activity.

IN PHRASES

❑ **hack around** *v.* (*also* **hack about, hack off**) **1** [1920s+] (*US campus*) to socialize, to fool about. **2** [1950s–70s] (*US*) to joke, to tease. **3** [1960s+] (*US*) to waste time.

hack *v.*^{2} [SE *hack*, to chop] **1** [late 19C+] (*also* **hack off, hell-hack**) to irritate, to annoy. **2** [20C+] (*US campus*) to tease gently. **3** [1970s+] (*orig. computing*) to tinker with a computer system for pleasure and as a proof of one's expertise. **4** [1980s+] (*orig. computing*) to gain unauthorized access to a computer system (and poss. use that access for illegal activities).

hack *v.*^{3} [HACK *n.*^{1}] [late 19C+] (*US*) to ride in or drive a hackney coach or taxicab.

hack *v.*^{4} [HACK *n.*^{3}] [1910s] (*US Und.*) to work as a night watchman.

hack *v.*^{5} [SE *hack*, to cut through] (*US*) **1** [1950s+] to accomplish. **2** [1970s] to understand.

IN PHRASES

❑ **hack it** *v.* [1950s+] **1** to manage, to tolerate, to bear a difficulty, to solve a problem, to succeed; thus *hack it out, hack* *it over*, to work out, to make a plan. **2** [1960s+] (*also* **hack up**) to achieve, to succeed in a task.

hack *v.*[6] [SE *hack*, to cough] [1970s] (*US campus*) to vomit.

hack *v.*[7] *see* HAWK *v.* (3).

hacked (off) *adj.* [HACK *v.*[2]] (*orig. US*) **1** [late 19C–1910s] exhausted. **2** [1930s+] very angry. **3** [1950s+] grumpy, bored.

hacker *n.*[1] [HACK *n.*[1] (7)] [1930s–60s] (*US*) a taxi-driver.

hacker *n.*[2] [HACK *v.*[1] (1)] [1960s] (*US campus*) an idler, a time-waster.

hacker *n.*[3] [HACK IT *under* HACK *v.*[5]] [1970s] (*US*) one who perseveres in the face of challenges; a survivor.

hacker *n.*[4] [HACK *n.*[1] (10); the implication is of a 'jack-of-all-trades'] [1970s+] a run-of-the-mill, average person.

hacker *n.*[5] [HACK *n.*[3] (4)] [1990s+] (*US prison*) a prison guard.

hackette *n.* [HACK *n.*[1] (3) + dimin. fem. sfx *-ette*] [1970s+] a female journalist.

hackie *n.* (*also* **hacky**) [HACK *n.*[1] (1)/HACK *n.*[1] (7)] **1** [late 19C–1910s] (*US*) the driver of a hackney carriage. **2** [1920s+] (*US*) a taxi-driver.

hackle *n.* [SE *hackles*, the long, shining feathers on the necks of certain birds, typically the domestic cockerel] [mid-19C] courage, pluck; thus *show hackle*, to be willing to fight.

hackle *v.* [? HASSLE WITH *under* HASSLE *v.*[1] + ? SE *get one's hackles up*] [1930s+] (*W.I. Rasta*) to bother, to worry, to trouble.

hackle up *adj.* [HACKLE UP *v.*] [1950s+] (*W.I.*) **1** of people, physically deformed. **2** of things, torn, damaged, untidy.

hackle up *v.* [? SE *hack*, to chop up; but note HACKLE *v.*] [1950s+] (*W.I., Baha.*) to beat up.

hackling *n.* [HACKLE *v.*] [1950s+] (*W.I. Rasta*) bothering, worrying, troubling.

hackney *n.* [14C SE *hackney horse*, a run-of-the-mill horse, i.e. not a warhorse or hunter, which was used for everyday riding and subseq. typified as the sort of horse available for hire] **1** [mid-15C–18C] (*also* **lady hackster, hackney jade, hackster**) a prostitute. **2** [early 16C] a pimp. **3** [mid-19C] (*UK Und.*) a penny; thus *half a hackney*, a halfpenny.

hackneyed *adj.* [HACKNEY *n.* (1)] [early 17C–mid-18C] pertaining to prostitution; as v., to work as a prostitute.

Hackney marsh *n.* [rhy. sl. = glass; *Hackney marshes* = glasses] [1960s+] **1** a glass (of alcohol). **2** in pl., spectacles, glasses.

Hackney wick *n.* [rhy. sl. = PRICK *n.* (1)] [1940s+] the penis.

hackslaver *v.* [SE *hack*, to stammer + *slaver*, to salivate] [19C] to stutter.

hackster *n. see* HACKNEY *n.* (1).

hack the hog *v. see under* HOG *n.*

hackum *n.* [SE *hack*, i.e. he fig. *hacks about* him] **1** [late 17C–early 18C] a braggart. **2** [late 19C] (*US*) one who uses a knife.

hacky *n. see* HACKIE *n.*

had *adj.* [HAVE *v.*] **1** [late 17C; early 19C+] seduced. **2** [late 18C+] tricked, hoaxed, deceived.

haddit *adj. see* HAD IT *adj.*

haddock *n.* [the once popular belief that assigned the dark marks on the shoulders of a haddock to the impression left by St Peter's finger and thumb, when he took the tribute-money out of the fish's mouth at Capernaum. Note 16C proverbial phr. *bring haddock to paddock*, to spend or lose everything] **1** [early–mid-19C] a purse; thus *haddock stuff'd with beans*, a purse full of guineas. **2** [mid-19C] (*US*) money.

haddock and bloater *n.* [rhy. sl.] [1950s+] a *motor*-car.

haddock and cod *n.* [rhy. sl. = SOD *n.*[1] (1)] [20C+] an irritating person, also as an affectionate name for a child.

haddums *n.* (*also* **had 'em**) [the punning phr. 'been at had 'em and come home by Clapham' (cf. CLAP *n.*)] [mid-17C–18C] venereal disease.

Hades *n.* [late 19C+] a euph. for hell, in all senses.

IN PHRASES

❑ **not a hope in Hades** *see* NOT A HOPE IN HELL *under* HELL *n.*
❑ **raise Hades** *v. see* RAISE HELL *under* HELL *n.*

had it *adj.* (*also* **haddit**) [HAVE HAD IT *v.*] [1960s+] (*N.Z.*) useless, second-rate.

haemorrhage *n.* [SE *haemorrhage*, a flow of blood] [1940s] (*US*) tomato ketchup.

haemorrhoid *n.* (*also* **hemo**) [pun on a PAIN IN THE ARSE *n.*] **1** [1970s+] (*US campus*) an annoying person. **2** [1980s+] (*Aus. prison*) a prison officer.

haffie *n.* [SE *half*] [1970s] (*S.Afr.*) a 375ml half-bottle of spirits or wine.

haffies *n. see* HALVIES *n.*

hag *n.* [SE *hag*, an ugly old woman] **1** [1920s–60s] (*US campus*) an unattractive or sexually promiscuous young woman; thus derog. *hag party*, a party for women. **2** [1980s] an unattractive (older) homosexual man.

hagarian *adj.* [SE *hog*] [1940s+] (*W.I.*) oafish, uncouth, rough.

haggard *n.* [SE *haggard*, an intractable person (esp. a woman) who refuses to abandon their own desires. Orig. applied to a wild falcon that would not be tamed] [late 16C] (*UK Und.*) a potential dupe who refuses to fall into the trap that has been prepared.

haggerawator *n. see* AGGERAWATOR *n.*

Haggisland *n.* [SE *haggis*, the 'national' dish, which was once equally popular in England] [mid-19C+] Scotland.

hagsmash *n.* [SE *hog* + *smash*] [20C+] (*Ulster*) a botched, inadequate piece of work.

ha-ha *n.*[1] (*also* **hah-hah**) **1** [late 19C–1960s] (*US*) a laugh of ridicule or derision. **2** [1960s] of a person, an object of derision.

IN PHRASES

❑ **give someone the ha-ha** *v.* [late 19C+] (*US*) to laugh at, to ridicule and take advantage of.

ha-ha *n.*[2] (*also* **ha, haha**) [abbr. BREWHA *n.*] [1970s+] (*US campus*) beer.

ha-ha *n.*[3] [abbr./pron. mari*juana*] [1970s+] (*drugs*) marijuana.

hail *n.* **1** [1930s–50s] (*US*) ice cubes, as in a drink. **2** [1980s+] (*drugs*) crack cocaine.

hail and rain *n.* [rhy. sl.] [1920s] a train.

hail Columbia *n.* (*also* **hail Columbus**) [*Hail Columbia*, a patriotic song publ. in 1798 by Joseph Hopkinson (1770–1842)] (*US*) **1** [mid-19C] America. **2** [mid-19C–1960s] a euph. for *hell*. **3** [mid-19C+] a punishment, a telling-off, a scolding.

hailer *n.* [1920s+] (*Irish*) the prayer 'Hail Mary'.

hail Mary *adj.* [a Catholic prayer for spiritual help. Note 1980s+ football/basketball jargon *hail Mary*, of a pass or throw, very long, often the last of the game, only likely to succeed through divine intervention] [1990s+] (*US*) desperate, last-ditch.

hailstorm *n.* [mid-19C] (*US*) any cocktail made with crushed ice.

haim *n.* (*also* **hame, haym**) [ety. unknown; orig. jazz use *hame*, a job other than in the music business; ? ref. to COLLAR AND HAMES *under* COLLAR *n.*] [1940s+] (*US black*) a job, usu. tedious or unpleasant.

IN PHRASES

❑ **cop a haim** *v.* [1960s] (*US black*) to get a job.

haincty *see under* HINCTY.

Haines! *excl.* (*also* **Hanes!**) [MY NAME IS HAINES *phr.*] [mid-19C–1900s] (*orig. US*) a warning shout.

hair *n.* **1** [mid-19C–1920s] pubic hair. **2** [mid-19C–1950s] a generic term for the female sex; thus *hair-monger*, a womanizer; *plenty of hair*, large numbers of women; *put down some hair*, of a man, to have sexual intercourse. **3** [mid-19C–1970s] (*US*) the scalp, as a trophy; usu. in phr. *lift or raise hair*. **4** [mid-19C+] (*US*) a curative drink for a hangover [abbr. HAIR OF THE DOG (THAT BIT ONE) *n.*]. **5** [20C+] (*Ulster*) a hair-pulling fight between women. **6** in fig. uses. (**a**) [1910s+] composure. (**b**) [1950s+] (*US campus*) courage, masculine prowess [the image of the hairy-chested macho man; note 1960s US sports use *show hair*, for a sportsman to play aggressively and well]. **7** *see* HAIR OF THE DOG (THAT BIT ONE) *n.*

IN COMPOUNDS

❑ **hairburger** *n.* [1970s–80s] (*US*) the female genitals. ❑ **hair**

court *n.* [19C] the female pubic hair. ❑ **hair-divider** *n.* (*also* **hair-splitter**) [mid-19C+] the penis. ❑ **hair-monger** *n.* [late 19C] a womanizer. ❑ **hair pie** *n.* (*also* **hairy pie**) [SE *pie* (which one can EAT *v.* (4)), plus pun on SE *hare pie*; one of many sl. examples of equating sex with food] **1** [1930s+] (*orig. US*) cunnilingus. **2** [1950s+] (*orig. US*) the vagina. **3** [1970s] (*US*) the penis in the context of fellatio.

(IN PHRASES)

❑ **after hair** [late 19C] in pursuit of a woman for sexual purposes. ❑ **bit of hair** *n.* [late 19C+] sexual intercourse; thus *get/have a bit of hair.* ❑ **get one's hair cut** *v.* [euph., with overtones of an adulterer's excuse] [late 19C] of a man, to visit a woman for the purpose of sexual intercourse. ❑ **get one's hair off** *v.* (*also* **get one's wool off**) [1930s] (*Aus.*) to become angry. ❑ **hair out** *v.* [1990s+] to be fearful. ❑ **hair to sell** [late 19C] a phr. used of a woman who is willing to prostitute herself. ❑ **lose one's hair** *v.* [1900s–30s] to lose one's temper. ❑ **shall I put a bit of hair on it?** [the hair in question would be female and pubic] [20C+] directed at a workman who is failing to put something into something else. ❑ **up in one's hair** [2000s] pestering, irritating. ❑ **keep one's hair on** *v. see* separate entry. ❑ **take a turn on hair court** *v.* [19C] to have sexual intercourse.

SE in slang uses

(DERIVATIVES)

❑ **hairless** *adj. see* separate entry.

(IN COMPOUNDS)

❑ **hairbag** *n.* (*US*) **1** [1950s+] a veteran police officer. **2** [1970s+] an unpleasant, disgusting person. ❑ **hairball** *n.* [SE *hairball*, a mass of hair found in the stomachs of various animals, e.g. a cat] [1980s+] a general term of derision for a situation or person. ❑ **hairbrain** *n.* [late 16C–18C; 1950s+] a fool. ❑ **hairburner** *n.* (*also* **hair bender**) [1960s–80s] (*US gay*) a gay male hairdresser. ❑ **hair fairy** *n.* [FAIRY *n.*[1] (3)] [1960s–70s] (*US*) an effeminate male homosexual, with long or styled hair. ❑ **hairpin** *n. see* separate entry. ❑ **hair-shifter** *n.* [1900s] (*Aus.*) a barber. ❑ **hair shirt** *n.* [1940s] (*US teen*) a prude.

(IN PHRASES)

❑ **hair about the heels** (*also* **hair about the fetlocks, hairy about the fetlocks, ...heels, touch of the hairy heel**) [bloodstock use: the image is of a carthorse as compared to a racehorse] [late 19C–1930s] (*UK society*) betraying one's lower-class origins; of poor breeding, socially inferior. ❑ **hair of the dog (that bit one)** *n. see* separate entry. ❑ **hair of the same wolf** *n.* [var. on HAIR OF THE DOG (THAT BIT ONE) *n.*] [17C] a hangover cure that consists of drinking more of the alcohol that created the hangover. ❑ **have a hair across one's ass** *v.* (*also* **have a hair in one's ass, have a hair up one's ass/prat**) [fig. use of ASS *n.* (2)] [1960s+] (*US*) to be irritable, to complain. ❑ **have hair on it** *v.* [the way mould appears on ancient, rotting fruit or vegetables, but note SE *hoary*, white with age, musty and mouldy] [20C+] of a joke or anecdote, to be old, to be out of date, no longer to be amusing or pertinent. ❑ **put hair on** *v. see* *PUT BALLS ON under* BALLS *n.* ❑ **swallow a hair** *v. see under* SWALLOW *v.*

haircut *n.*[1] **1** [late 19C] (*US*) a blow over the head. **2** [1940s] (*US black*) a week [the notional cutting of one's hair on a weekly basis]. **3** [1940s+] (*UK prison*) a short term of imprisonment, in a local prison from a few weeks to two or three months or in a convict prison for three to five years [the relatively short period and the cutting of one's hair on arrival in prison]. **4** [1960s] (*US Und.*) a verbal telling-off. **5** [2000s] (*N.Z.*) winding back a car's odometer.

SE in slang uses

(IN PHRASES)

❑ **from haircut to breakfast time** *see* *FROM ARSEHOLE TO BREAKFAST TIME under* ARSEHOLE *n.*

haircut *n.*[2] [? euph.] [1960s+] (*US drugs*) marijuana.

haired up *adj.* (*also* **haired off**) [HAIR *n.* (6a)] [20C+] (*US*) annoyed, furious, upset.

hairless *adj.*

(IN PHRASES)

❑ **go hairless** *v.* [? one tears one's hair out with rage; note HAIR *n.* (6a)] [1980s] to get mad, go crazy.

hair of the dog (that bit one) *n.* (*also* **blood of the dog, hair**) [the alcoholic 'wolf' that has 'bitten' the sufferer] [mid-16C+] a hangover cure that consists of drinking more alcohol, usu. the same alcohol that created the hangover; occas. ext. to drugs.

hair on one's chest *n.* an emblem of masculinity; in phrs. below.

(IN PHRASES)

❑ **have hair on one's chest** *v.* (*also* **have hair on one's ass, have wild hair**) [20C+] to be brave, to be plucky (cf. *HAVE A WILD HAIR UP ONE'S ASS under* ASS *n.*). ❑ **put hair(s) on one's chest** *v.* (*also* **grow hairs on one's chest**) **1** [1920s+] to embolden, to make stronger, usu. used of sex, food, drink. **2** [1940s] to cheer up, to strengthen; esp. in context of offering a drink, e.g. *that'll put hair on your chest.*

(IN EXCLAMATIONS)

❑ **more hair on your chest!** [20C+] (*Aus.*) a general excl. of approval, acclamation, 'good for you!', 'well done!' etc.

hairpin *n.* **1** [late 19C+] (*US*) a fool, a simpleton. **2** [1920s–60s] (*US*) a woman. **3** [1950s] (*US*) a thin person. **4** [1950s] (*Aus.*) a despised person. **5** [1950s–70s] (*US gay*) a homosexual.

(IN PHRASES)

❑ **drop hairpins** *v. see* separate entry.

hairy *n.*[1] **1** [1910s] a horse. **2** [1920s+] (*Scot.*) a woman, esp. (*Glasgow*) a poor woman [the premise is that a wealthier woman would wear a hat and hide her hair].

hairy *n.*[2] [pron. 'hair-o-in'] [1950s+] (*drugs*) heroin.

hairy *n.*[3] (*also* **hairyback**) [a hairy back is seen as an image of animality] [1960s+] (*S.Afr.*) an Afrikaner.

hairy *adj.*[1] [HAIR *n.* (2)] [mid-19C–1960s] desirable, sexy; thus *feel hairy*, to feel sexually inclined.

hairy *adj.*[2] [ety. unknown] **1** [mid-19C+] difficult. **2** [late 19C] excellent, first-rate. **3** [1910s+] wary, sharp. **4** [1910s+] dangerous, exciting. **5** [1920s–50s] (*orig. Irish*) impressive, sometimes used as an intensive. **6** [1940s+] (*US*) bad or unsatisfactory. **7** [1960s–70s] (*US*) stylish, excellent. **8** [1960s+] weird, complicated.

(IN PHRASES)

❑ **hairy eyeball** *n.* [EYEBALL *n.*[2] (1)] [1960s+] (*US*) a hostile look.

hairy *adj.*[3] [*see HAIR ABOUT THE HEELS under* HAIR *n.*] [1900s–40s] ill-bred, bad-mannered.

(IN COMPOUNDS)

❑ **hairy-heeled** *adj.* **1** [1900s] used of racehorses, fast [bloodstock use]. **2** [1930s+] (*also* **hairy-tailed**) of people, of poor breeding, socially inferior, naïve.

(IN PHRASES)

❑ **hairy about the heels/fetlocks** *see HAIR ABOUT THE HEELS under* HAIR *n.*

SE in slang uses

sexual uses

(IN COMPOUNDS)

❑ **hairy-bank** *n.* [1990s+] (*W.I.*) the vagina; thus *make deposits at the hairy-bank*, of a man, to be generous with material gifts to a girlfriend. ❑ **hairy clam** *n.* [CLAM *n.*[1] (2)] [2000s] the vagina. ❑ **hairy cup** *n.* (*also* **hairy goblet**) [1990s+] the vagina. ❑ **hairy Cyclops** *n. see ONE-EYED CYCLOPS under* ONE-EYED *adj.* ❑ **hairy oracle** *n.* [late 18C–mid-19C] the female pubic hair; the vagina. ❑ **hairy ring** *n.* [RING *n.* (1a)] [late 19C] the female genital area.

(IN PHRASES)

❑ **work the hairy oracle** *v.* [late 19C] to have sexual intercourse.

general uses

(IN COMPOUNDS)

❑ **hairyback** *n. see* HAIRY *n.*[3]. ❑ **hairy belly** *n.* (*also* **hairy-guts**)

[1910s] (*Aus.*) a sycophant. ❑ **hairy crunchy** *n. see* CRUNCHY (GRANOLA) *n.* ❑ **hairy legs** *n.* [2000s] (*N.Z.*) in cards, the joker. ❑ **hairy maclary** *n.* [joc. redup.; ? link to LEERY *adj.* (2)] [2000s] (*N.Z.*) a woman who stops short of sexual intercourse.

hairy *adj.*[4] [HAIR *n.* (6a)] [1910s–70s] annoyed, furious, upset.

hairy ape *n.* [rhy. sl.] [1970s–80s] (*N.Z. prison*) rape.

hairy-arsed *adj.* (*also* **hairy-ass, hairy-assed**) [SE *hairy* + -ARSED *sfx* (2)/-ASS *sfx*/-ASSED *sfx* (2)] **1** [1940s+] (*also* **hairy**) overtly, aggressively masculine. **2** [1960s+] veteran, mature.

hairy-assed *adv.* [1970s] (*US*) completely, unreservedly.

hairyfordshire *n.* [pun on English county *Herefordshire* and the pubic HAIR *n.* (1)] [mid-19C+] the vagina.

IN PHRASES

❑ **go to Hairyfordshire** *v.* [mid–late 19C] to have sexual intercourse.

hairy Mary *n.*[1] [SE *hairy* + MARY *n.* (2a)] [1960s+] (*US gay*) a masculine homosexual.

hairy Mary *n.*[2] (*also* **hairy Molly**) [1960s+] (*Irish*) the female genitals.

ha-ja *n. see* HALF-JACK *n.*

haka *n.* [1960s+] (*N.Z.*) a fuss.

IN PHRASES

❑ **dance a haka** *v. see under* DANCE *v.*

halal *n.* [Arabic *halal*, lawful; in this context ritually slaughtered meat, eaten by Muslims] [1990s+] a derog. term for a Muslim, esp. a Pakistani immigrant.

halal *adj.* [*see* prev.] [2000s] acceptable, correct.

hale and hearty *n.* [rhy. sl.] [1970s+] a party.

half *n.* [abbr.] **1** [mid-19C] (*US*) half a dollar. **2** [late 19C] half a gill (70ml) of spirits. **3** [20C+] half a pint (280ml) of beer; esp. in phr. *a swift half*. **4** [1920s+] £50 or $50. **5** [1930s–70s] ten shillings (50p). **6** [1940s+] (*drugs*) a half-ounce.

IN COMPOUNDS

❑ **half-piece** *n.* [PIECE *n.* (7a)] [1930s+] (*drugs*) a half- ounce (14g) of heroin or cocaine (cf. *QUARTER PIECE under* QUARTER *n.*).

SE in slang uses

IN PHRASES

❑ **— and a half** [mid-19C+] a general intensifier, e.g. *a cunt and a half*, a very unpleasant person indeed; *a party and a half*, a really good party.

half *adv.* [mid-19C+] nearly, almost.

half-... *adj. see also under* relevant adj.

half-(a-)... *n. see also under* relevant n.

half-a-cock *n.* [rhy. sl.; SE *half* + COCK AND HEN *n.*] [1950s+] £5.

half-a-crown *n.* [SE *half-a-crown*, in pre-decimal coinage 2s 6d (12½p)] [1940s+] (*bingo*) the number 26.

half-a-crowner *n.* (*also* **half-crowner**) [SE *half-a-crown*, in pre-decimal coinage 2s 6d (12½p)] **1** [late 19C] any publication costing 2s 6d. **2** [late 19C–1950s] one who pays half-a-crown for a seat at a show.

half-a-dollar *n.*[1] [rhy. sl.] [late 19C+] a collar.

half-a-dollar *n.*[2] *see* HALF-DOLLAR *n.*[1].

half-a-foot *n.* [1920s+] (*W.I.*) a person with a wooden leg.

half a joint *n.* [ety. unknown] [1900s–10s] (*Aus.*) half a pint.

half-alligator *adj.* [HALF-HORSE, HALF-ALLIGATOR *adj.*] [mid–late 19C] aggressive, tough, rambunctious.

half a man *n.* [1970s+] (*US black*) a passive homosexual.

half-a-man *n.* **1** *see* HALF-MAN *n.* **2** *see under* MAN *n.*[1].

half a mo *n.*[1] [MO *n.*[1] (3)] [late 19C+] a very short time, lit. 'half a moment'.

half a mo *n.*[2] [? the delaying excuse, 'Half a mo, I'm just having a fag'] [1910s–30s] a cigarette.

half a mo *phr.* [HALF A MO *n.*[1]] [late 19C+] wait a moment, hang on.

half a mongrel *n.* [? DOG *n.*[2] (3a)] [1990s+] (*Aus.*) a semi-erect penis.

half and between *adj.* [20C+] (*Ulster*) **1** of a person, slightly mad, eccentric. **2** neither one thing nor another.

half-and-half *n.* **1** [19C+] (*US*) a 'half-breed', a person of mixed race; a person whose parents are of different religions. **2** [mid-19C] second rate. **3** [1930s–60s] (*US black*) a hermaphrodite. **4** [1930s+] as offered by a prostitute, fellatio plus full intercourse. **5** [1960s] (*Irish*) a homosexual. **6** [1970s+] (*US gay*) fellatio plus anal intercourse.

half-and-half *adj.* **1** [early 19C–1900s] (*US Und.*) (*also* **half-and-half-and-half, half-half-and-half**) drunk, tipsy. **2** [1900s] married. **3** [1970s+] (*US campus*) bisexual.

SE in slang uses

IN COMPOUNDS

❑ **half-and-half cove** *n.* (*also* **half-and-half boy, ...man**) [SE *half-and-half* + COVE *n.* (1)] [early–mid-19C] a would-be dandy, who fails to make the grade.

half-an-hour *n.* [rhy. sl.] [20C+] (*Aus.*) flour.

half-a-nicker *n.* (*also* **half-nicker**) [rhy. sl.; ult. *HALF-A-NICKER under* NICKER *n.*[2]] [20C+] a vicar.

half a note *n.* (*also* **half-note**) [abbr. SE *half a pound note*; the ten shillings itself was also a note] [late 19C–1970s] (*Aus./Irish*) ten shillings, a ten-shilling note.

half-an-ounce *n.* [the contemporary measurement of silver at five shillings an ounce] [early 18C–early 19C] half-a-crown, 2s 6d (12½p).

half-a-pint *n. see* HALF-PINT *n.*

half-arsed *adj. see* HALF-ASSED *adj.*

half a sheet *n.* [based on HALF A NOTE *n.*] [1930–50s] (*UK prison*) a punishment for wardens, usu. a fine.

half-ass *n.* [SE *half* + ASS *n.* (2)] [1920s+] (*US*) a stupid, incompetent person.

half-assed *adj.* (*also* **half-arse, half-arsed, half-ass**) [SE *half* + ASS *n.* (2)/ARSE *n.* (1)] (*orig. US*) [mid-19C+] careless, inadequate, incompetent, second-rate.

half-assed *adv.* (*also* **half-arsed, half-ass**) [HALF-ASSED *adj.*] **1** [1920s+] (*orig. US*) carelessly, incompetently. **2** [1960s+] not seriously. **3** [1970s+] reasonably.

IN PHRASES

❑ **half-assed backwards** [1960s+] (*US*) back-to-front.

half-a-surprise *n.* [Charles Coborn's song lyric (*c.*1886), 'Two lovely black eyes/Oh what a surprise'] [late 19C–1900s] a single black eye.

half-a-thick *n. see HALF-THICK ('UN) under* THICK 'UN *n.*

half-away *adj.* [i.e. NOT ALL THERE *adj.*] [20C+] (*Ulster*) insane.

half-bake *n.* [SE *half-baked*] [1940s–60s] a fool, an inadequate.

half-chat *n.* [ety. unknown] [2000s] a mixed-race person.

half-cocked *adj.* [late 18C+] drunk.

half-crowner *n. see* HALF-A-CROWNER *n.*

half-cut *adj.*[1] [SE *half-cut quality*, those who look down on everyone other than those who look down on them] [19C] (*US*) crude, uncultivated.

half-cut *adj.*[2] [SE *half* + CUT *adj.*[1]] **1** [19C+] more than mildly drunk but not yet incapable. **2** [late 19C+] (*Aus./N.Z.*) foolish, silly.

half-dollar *n.*[1] (*also* **half-a-dollar**) [a period when £1 sterling was worth around $4, i.e. five shillings (25p) to a dollar] [late 18C+] half-a-crown, 2s 6d (12½ p.).

half-dollar *n.*[2] [SE *half* + fig. use of SE *dollar* to mean 100] [1970s] (*US prison*) one who is serving 50 years in jail.

halfer *n.* [1930s–40s] (*US*) a half-dollar coin.

half-foolish *adj.* [mid-19C] ridiculous.

half-gone *adj.* [SE *half* + GONE *adj.*[1]] **1** [19C] simple, stupid. **2** [late 19C+] drunk. **3** [1940s] (*US milit.*) hungry.

half-half-and-half *adj. see* HALF-AND-HALF *adj.* (1).

half-hitch *v.* [rhy. sl. = SNITCH *v.* (2)] [1970s+] (*N.Z.*) to steal.

half-horse, half-alligator *adj.* [characteristics of the animals] [19C+] (*US*) of a man, notably tough, esp. of a river-boatman; also used of a woman.

half-hundred *n.* [1970s+] (*N.Z.*) a £50 note.

halfie *n.* [abbr.] **1** [1910s–60s] (*Aus.*) a *half*-caste. **2** [1990s+] a *half*-brick.

halfies *n. see* HALVIES *n.*

half-inch *n.* [HALF-INCH *adj.*] [1950s+] (*W.I.*) an inferior workman.

half-inch *adj.* [? ref. to the size of one's penis] [1950s+] (*W.I.*) inadequately equipped for a job.

half-inch *v.* [rhy. sl. = PINCH *v.*] **1** [20C+] to steal; thus *half-inching*, theft. **2** [1990s+] to arrest.

half-iron *n.* [SE *half* + IRON (HOOF) *n.*] **1** [1940s+] a man who enjoys the company but not the specific predilections of homosexuals. **2** [1980s+] a bisexual.

half-jack *n.* (*also* **ha-ja**) [SE *half* + *jack*, a gill, i.e. a quarter-pint] [1960s+] (*S.Afr.*) **1** a 375ml half-bottle of spirits or wine. **2** brandy.

half-lo *n. see under* LOAD *n.*

half-man *n.* (*also* **half-a-man**) [Scot. *halfman*, half a bottle of spirits; note MAN *n.*[1] (5)] [1930s–40s] (*US black*) a half-bottle of spirits, esp. whisky.

half-mile *n.*

(IN PHRASES)

❑ **the dirty half-mile** *n. see under* DIRTY *adj.*

half-moon *n.* [resemblance] **1** [early 17C–19C] the female genital area. **2** [18C–19C] a wig; also as alternative to head. **3** [1970s] a patch of sweat under the arm. **4** [1970s+] in drug uses. (**a**) a piece of hashish moulded in a half-moon shape. (**b**) a piece of peyote cactus.

half-mourning *n. see under* MOURNING *n.*

half-nicker *n. see* HALF-A-NICKER *n.*

half-note *n. see* HALF A NOTE *n.*

half-off *adj.* (*also* **half-on**) [late 19C] tipsy, semi-drunk.

half of marge *n.* [rhy. sl. = SARGE *n.*; ult. SE *marge*, margarine] [1980s+] (*UK Und.*) a police *sergeant*.

half-one *n.* [20C+] (*Irish*) a small glass of whisky.

half-ounce *v.* [rhy. sl. = BOUNCE *v.*[1] (5)/BOUNCE *v.*[1] (17)] [1960s+] **1** to cheat, to short change. **2** to beat up.

half-ounce of baccy *n.* [rhy. sl. = PAKI *n.* (1)] [1970s+] a derog. term for a person of Indian, Pakistani, Bangladeshi or Ugandan Asian blood.

half-ouncer *n.* [rhy. sl. = BOUNCER *n.*[1] (9)] [20C+] a security person at a nightclub, dancehall or similar place.

half past a colored man *phr.* [i.e. midnight is pitch black] [1940s–50s] half past midnight; usu. in answer to one who asks what time it is.

half past a monkey's ass *phr.* [i.e. midnight is pitch black] [1970s] (*US black*) half past midnight.

half past eight *adj.* [ety. unknown] [1980s] (*US*) sneaky, shady.

half past kissing time (and time to kiss again) *phr.* (*also* **half an hour past hanging time**) [late 19C–1920s] a catchphrase used in answer to the query, 'What time is it?'.

half past two *n.* [rhy. sl.] [20C+] a Jew.

half-pay *n.* [SE *half-pay*, an officer, currently unemployed and thus receiving only half-pay] [1940s] (*Irish*) a general term of derision.

halfpenny dip *n.* [rhy. sl.] [mid-19C+] a ship.

halfpenny howling swell *n.* [HOWLER *n.* (3)] [late 19C] an imitation dandy, a pretentious man.

halfpenny stamp *n.* [rhy. sl.] [20C+] a tramp.

half-pie *adj.* [? Maori *pai*, good] [1910s+] (*Aus./Canada/N.Z.*) imperfect, mediocre.

half-pie *adv.* [HALF-PIE *adj.*] [1910s+] (*Aus./N.Z.*) partially, vaguely.

half-pint *n.* (*also* **half-a-pint, half-pinter**) [late 19C+] (*orig. US*) a short person or child.

half-pint *adj.* **1** [20C+] small, undersized. **2** [1930s+] (*US*) of a child, short; thus *quarter-pint*, even smaller.

half-portion *n.* [1900s–60s] a diminutive person.

half-portion *adj.* [HALF-PORTION *n.*] [1900s] tiny; usu. of a person.

half-quarter *n. see under* QUARTER *n.*

half-rats *adj.* [DRUNK AS A RAT *adj.*] [late 19C] tipsy, mildly drunk.

half-rinsed *adj.* [RINCE *v.*] [1910s+] (*Aus./N.Z.*) tipsy, semi-drunk.

half-rocked *adj.* [? one who has not been fully rocked in the cradle and is thus still infantile] [mid-19C–1910s] incompetent, inadequate, foolish.

half seas over *adj.* [either naval imagery, an unstable boat is more likely to ship water, or Du. *op-zee zober*, overseas strong beer (cf. UPSEE *adj.*)] [late 17C+] **1** drunk. **2** thus intensely emotional, whether with joy, love etc.

half-section *n.* [orig. UK Services] [1950s+] (*S.Afr.*) a friend.

half set *n.* [presumably from SET *n.*[1] (2), with SE *half* indicating the dissatisfaction] [1950s–60s] (*mainly drugs*) an unacceptable offer, usu. in the context of a drug deal.

half-shot *adj.* [SE *half* + SHOT *adj.* (1); note CUPSHOT *under* CUP *n.*] [mid-19C+] (*orig. US*) tipsy, mildly drunk.

half-slewed *adj.* [SE *half* + SLEWED *adj.* (1)] [early 19C+] tipsy, half-drunk.

half-stamp *n.* [rhy. sl.] [20C+] a tramp.

half step *v.* [milit. *half-step*, a form of slow marching] **1** [1940s+] to loaf, to idle, to go slowly. **2** [1980s+] (*US black/Und.*) to make a feeble effort, to act in an inappropriate or ineffectual manner. **3** [1980s+] (*US black*) to make promises, e.g. of sexual favours, that are not carried through. **4** [1990s+] (*US black*) to sneak up on.

half-stepper *n.* [HALF STEP *v.* (3)] [1980s+] (*orig. US prison*) one who promises things, but never properly achieves them, thus one who cannot be depended upon.

half-stepping *adj.* [HALF STEP *v.* (3)] [1980s+] (*US black/Und.*) unreliable, untrustworthy.

half-strainer *n.* (*also* **half-way strainer**) [dial. *half-strain*, a mongrel; *half-strained gentry*, shabby-genteel individuals] [late 19C–1910s] (*US, Southern*) a social climber.

half the bay over *adj.* [var. on HALF SEAS OVER *adj.* (1)] [late 19C] drunk.

half-there *adj.* [var. on NOT ALL THERE *adj.*] **1** [20C+] simple, stupid. **2** [1950s] (*Aus.*) tipsy, semi-drunk.

half-tiz *n.* [SE *half* + TIZZY *n.*[1]] [late 19C–1900s] (*N.Z.*) threepence.

half-tore *adj.* [SE *half* + TORE UP *adj.* (3)] [20C+] (*Ulster*) tipsy, half-drunk.

Half-Way House *n.* [the volume of mentally disturbed inmates, making it a 'half-way house to Broadmoor' (the UK's main prison for the criminally insane)] [1930s] (*UK Und.*) Parkhurst prison, Isle of Wight.

halfway house *n.* (*also* **halfway**) [there are 99 numbers available to the caller] [1940s+] (*bingo*) the number 45 or 50.

half-way strainer *n. see* HALF-STRAINER *n.*

halfy *n.* [he has only 'half' his body] [1910s–60s] (*US/S.Afr.*) a legless person, usu. a beggar.

half your luck! *excl. see under* LUCK *n.*

Halifax *n.* [17C+] a euph. for SE *hell.*

(IN PHRASES)

❑ **go to Halifax** *v.* [1900s] to go the long way round.

(IN EXCLAMATIONS)

❑ **go to Halifax!** [mid-17C–19C] a euph. for *GO TO HELL! under* HELL *n.*

Halifax *v.* [HALIFAX *n.*] [17C–19C] **1** to kill, thus send to hell. **2** to beat.

Halifax mutton *n.* [its being imported from *Halifax*, Nova Scotia] [late 19C+] (*W.I.*) salt codfish.

Hall, the *n.* [orig. used as the market for 'foreigners', i.e. out-of-Londoners, the Hall burnt down in 1666 and was rebuilt as a meat, poultry, fish and vegetable market. The current buildings date f. 1881] [mid-19C] Leadenhall Market.

hall *n.* [abbr. DR HALL *n.*] [1920s–30s] (*US Und.*) alcohol.

hallan shaker *n.* (*also* **halland shaker**) [Scot. *hallan*, the partition of a cottage wall, esp. when it cuts off the front door from the fire + SE *shaker*] [16C–18C] a 'sturdy' or able-bodied and poss. violent beggar.

hallelujah *n.* **1** [20C+] (*US*) a euph. for SE *hell*. **2** [1930s] (*UK tramp*) a Salvation Army hostel for the homeless.

hallelujah *adj.* [late 19C–1960s] pertaining to the Salvation Army; or any religious group.

IN COMPOUNDS

❑ **hallelujah garment** *n.* [late 19C] (*Aus.*) a swallow-tailed morning coat (as typically worn by a preacher). ❑ **hallelujah-hawking** *n.* [SE *hawk*, to peddle] [1910s–50s] (*Aus.*) working as a door-to-door evangelist. ❑ **hallelujah lass** *n.* (*also* **hallelujah maid, lulyah lass**) [late 19C–1950s] a young female Salvationist. ❑ **hallelujah-peddlar** *n.* [1920s–30s] (*US*) a Salvation Army or any other affiliation of preacher. ❑ **hallelujah stew** *n.* [20C+] the stew served out at Salvation Army hostels.

Halley's comet *n.* [rhy. sl.] [1990s+] (*Aus.*) vomit.

halloo-wach *n.* [*Halloo-Wach*, brandname of a German drug sold over the counter as a stimulant, like Pro Plus] [1980s+] (*drugs*) amphetamine.

halter *n.* [16C+] (*US 20C+*) the noose used in a judicial hanging.

halter *v.* [HALTER *n.*] [16C+] to hang someone.

halter-sack *n.* [the noose is the *halter*, their body the *sack*] [late 16C–early 17C] a villain whose destination will be the gallows; thus as a term of abuse.

halvers *n.* [SE *half*] [19C+] equal shares; usu. as *halvers!* I demand half!

halvies *n.* (*also* **haffies, halfies, halvsies**) [SE *half*] [20C+] equal shares.

ham *n.*[1] **1** [late 16C–mid-19C; 1940s+] (*later use US black*) in pl., the legs. **2** [mid-17C–mid-19C] in pl., breeches, trousers.

IN COMPOUNDS

❑ **ham cases** *n.* [? Rom. *hamyas*, knee breeches or SE *ham*, the back of the thigh and buttock + *cases* or sense 1 above] [late 18C–19C] breeches, trousers.

IN PHRASES

❑ **press ham** *v.* [1960s+] (*US campus*) to press a bare buttock against a window in order to shock passers-by; also to press the genitals against glass where they can be seen. ❑ **slap ham** *v.* [1980s] (*US campus*) to have sexual intercourse. ❑ **slip some ham** *v.* [1950s] to press one's bare buttocks against a car window.

SE in slang uses

IN COMPOUNDS

❑ **ham and** *n.* [late 19C–1940s] (*US*) an order of ham and eggs. ❑ **ham and beef** *n. see* separate entries. ❑ **ham-and-egg** *adj.* [20C+] **1** (*US*) unskilled. **2** (*orig. US*) second-rate. ❑ **ham-and-egger** *n.* [SE *ham and eggs*, the image is of its commonness] [20C+] (*US, orig. boxing*) an ordinary, run-of-the-mill person or an incompetent individual. ❑ **ham and factory** *n.* [HAM AND above] [1900s] a restaurant. ❑ **hambone** *see* separate entries. ❑ **hamfat** *see* separate entries. ❑ **hamhead** *n. see* separate entry. ❑ **ham-heaver** *n.* [1930s] (*US black*) a waiter. ❑ **ham-hock** *n.* [stereotypical black food] **1** [20C+] in pl., the legs. **2** [1930s–80s] (*US black*) the female legs or ankles. **3** [1980s+] (*US*) a black person. ❑ **ham-match** *n.* [fig. use of SE *match*, a contest] [late 19C–1900s] a stand-up luncheon. ❑ **ham sandwich** *n. see* separate entries. ❑ **ham snatcher** *n.* [lit. one who steals hams] [1960s+] (*US black*) a looter, breaking into stores during urban riots. ❑ **ham stealer** *n.* [note Wepman et. al., *The Life* (1976): 'Ham stealing: stealing just to eat, rather than for profit. A ham stealer is thus the lowest-status player in the Life'] [1950s–70s] (*US black*) one who robs for no more than subsistence.

ham *n.*[2] [abbr. *hamfatter*, a second-rate and thus impoverished actor who was forced to rub hamfat over their face, as a base for the powder that was then applied, rather than being able to afford sweeter smelling oils; the *Century Dict.* (1889) suggests an origin in a black song 'The Ham-Fat Man'; hamfat was also used by old-time jazzmen to grease the slides of their trombones – thus the 1930s band The Harlem Hamfats; note U. of Missouri (in 1931) *ham*, 'one of unpolished manners' and Baker et al., *College Undergraduate Slang Study* (1967–8), 'a person who always fools around'; note also 1939 ref. to a *lard actor*, 'an early professional version of "ham actor",' in a Federal Writers' Project essay on Vaudeville, suggesting that lard, rather than 'hamfat' was a substitute for cold cream as a basis for make-up] **1** [mid-19C+] an incompetent, esp. one who poses as more expert than his performance – often in sport – shows him to be. **2** [late 19C–1920s] (*US*) an incompetent boxer, a poor fighter. **3** [late 19C+] an over-theatrical or incompetent performer. **4** [1930s+] (*US*) an inexpert or over-theatrical performance.

ham *n.*[3] [backform. f. *hamfisted*, plus shape and mis-pron] [1910s–40s] (*US*) the hand.

ham *n.*[4] (*also* **radio ham**) [? SE *amateur* + *ham-fisted*] [1910s+] a student or amateur telegraphist, subseq. an amateur radio operator, i.e. one who makes a hobby of picking up and transmitting radio messages.

ham *n.*[5] [HAMBONE *n.*[3] (2)] [1940s+] the penis.

ham *n.*[6] [rhy. sl.] [1980s] home.

ham *adj.* [HAM *n.*[2]] **1** [1920s–60s] clumsy, ineffective, incompetent. **2** [1920s+] theatrical, melodramatic.

IN COMPOUNDS

❑ **ham scram** *n.* (*also* **ham scam**) [SCAM *n.*[1]/SE *scram*; note dial. *hamstram*, a difficulty] [1920s–40s] (*US black*) a tough time, a difficult period in one's life.

ham *v.*[1] [HAM *n.*[1] (1)] [1910s–60s] (*US Und.*) to walk.

ham *v.*[2] (*also* **ham it up**) [HAM *n.*[2] (3)] [1930s+] (*orig. US*) to act in an exaggerated manner, to ruin a situation by foolishly excessive behaviour.

ham and beef *n.*[1] [1940s–50s] (*Aus.*) a corner shop.

ham and beef *n.*[2] [rhy. sl.] [1940s+] (*UK prison*) the *chief* officer.

ham and cheesy *adj.* [rhy. sl.] [2000s] easy; in fig. sense, willing.

ham and eggs *n.* [rhy. sl.] [1920s+] legs.

hambo *n.* [HAM *n.*[2] + HAMBONE *n.*[1]] [1920s–50s] (*US*) a posing incompetent, esp. on stage.

hambone *n.*[1] [var. on HAMFATTER *n.*] **1** [late 19C–1910s] (*US*) a bad 'nigger minstrel'. **2** [late 19C+] a second-rate actor. **3** [late 19C+] a second-rate performance; thus adj. *hambony*. **4** [1950s+] (*US*) a show-off.

hambone *n.*[2] [rhy. sl.] **1** [20C+] a telephone. **2** [1930s] (*US*) a trombone.

hambone *n.*[3] **1** [1900s–60s] (*US*) in pl., the knees. **2** [1920s–70s] (*US black*) the penis. **3** [1920s–70s] (*US black*) the vagina.

hambone *n.*[4] [the stereotyped black diet is pig-based] [1960s+] (*orig. US black*) **1** shorthand for the black cultural experience. **2** a black person.

hambone *adj.* [HAMBONE *n.*[4]] [1960s+] referring to blacks.

hambone *v.*[1] [HAMBONE *n.*[1]] (*US*) **1** [1920s+] to live as a travelling performer. **2** [1940s+] to live frugally. **3** [1960s+] to show off.

hambone *v.*[2] [? SE *hams*, the buttocks and back of the thighs] [1960s+] (*Aus.*) of a man, to strip off his clothes in public, usu. at a drunken party.

hambone *v.*[3] [HAMBONE *n.*[1]] [1960s+] (*US*) to trick, to cheat.

hamburger *n.* **1** [1930s+] (*US*) (*also* **hamburgerhead**) a stupid or worthless individual or creature, i.e. one who has no more brains than a hamburger. **2** [1980s+] (*drugs*) MDMA [? the circular shape of the tablet].

SE in slang uses

IN COMPOUNDS

❑ **hamburger helper** *n.* [the resemblance to SE *hamburger helper*, i.e. MSG (monosodium glutamate), which looks like white crystals] [1990s+] (*drugs*) **1** heroin. **2** crack cocaine.

hame *n. see* HAIM *n.*

hamfat *n.*[1] [the stereotypical black diet is pig-based] [late 19C–1940s] (*US*) a derog. term for a black person.

hamfat *n.*^{2} [ext. of HAM *n.*^{2}] [1900s–50s] (*US black*) a mediocrity, whether a person or thing.

hamfat *n.*^{3} [1950s] (*US black*) a euph. for SE *hell*.

hamfat *adj.* [HAMFAT *n.*^{2}] [1900s–70s] mediocre, second-rate.

hamfatter *n.* [see full ety. at HAM *n.*^{2}] **1** [late 19C] (*US*) a vociferous, but non-participating critic. **2** [late 19C–1950s] (*US*) an ineffective actor or performer, a mediocre jazz musician. **3** [1900s] (*US Und.*) a second-rate confidence trickster. **4** [1930s] (*US*) a loudly dressed and loudly decorated dandy.

hamhead *n.* [SE *ham/hamburger* + -HEAD *sfx* (1)] **1** [1910s–50s] (*US*) a fool; thus *ham-headed*, stupid. **2** [1950s] (*US Und./prison*) a police officer.

hamilton *n.* (*also* **Mr Hamilton**) [the portrait of US politician Alexander Hamilton (1755–1804) on the note] [1940s+] (*US*) a $10 note.

haming *n.* [HAIM *n.*] [1960s] (*US black*) working, having a non-criminal job.

hamlet *n.* [note Yorks. dial. *play Hamlet with*, to 'play the devil' with] **1** [late 17C–mid-19C] (*UK Und.*) a high constable. **2** [mid-19C] (*US Und.*) a police captain.

hamma *n.* (*also* **hammer**) [? they 'knock one on the head'; but note HAMMER *n.*^{1} (5)] [1960s+] (*US black*) a very attractive black woman, occas. extended to men.

hammer *n.*^{1} **1** [late 16C–mid-19C; 1930s+] (*later use US black*) the penis. **2** [late 18C] the testicles. **3** [19C] (*also* **hammer man**) a strong puncher. **4** [late 19C+] a bodyguard, a thug. **5** [1960s+] (*US black*) a woman's thigh. **6** [1970s+] (*US*) the accelerator; thus *put the hammer down* or *drop the hammer*, to accelerate. **7** [2000s] (*Irish*) a turn, e.g. *take a right-hand hammer*.

SE in slang uses

IN COMPOUNDS

❑ **hammer-handle** *n.* (*also* **hoe-handle**) [supposed resemblance] [1920s–50s] (*US*) the penis. ❑ **hammerhead/headed** see separate entries. ❑ **hammer-man** *n.* **1** [1920s–70s] (*US black*) an authoritarian figure. **2** *see* sense 3 above. ❑ **hammer-school** *n.* [early 19C] a boxing school.

IN PHRASES

❑ **down as a hammer** *see under* DOWN *adj.*^{1}. ❑ **drop the hammer (on)** *v.* **1** [1970s+] (*orig. US*) to take decisive action (against). **2** [1980s] to shoot. **3** [2000s] to humiliate. ❑ **how's your hammer hanging?** [1930s+] (*US*) a phr. used to inquire about someone's state of well being; the typically facetious answer being: 'A little to the left and in the dirt.'. ❑ **just the hammer** (*also* **that's the hammer, just the gears**) [Stock Exchange/auction-house imagery] [1910s+] ideal, perfect, exactly what is wanted. ❑ **put the hammer on** *v.* (*US*) **1** [1940s+] to take decisive action. **2** [1960s+] to demand money. **3** [1980s+] to attack verbally, to slander. ❑ **put the hammers to** *v.* [1940s] (*US*) to beat up. ❑ **swing the hammer** *v. see* SWING THE LEAD *under* SWING *v.* ❑ **under the hammer** [1950s+] in trouble, at a disadvantage.

IN EXCLAMATIONS

❑ **by the hammers of hell!** [1950s] an excl. of surprise or disappointment.

hammer *n.*^{2} [play on KNOCK *v.* (3a)] **1** [mid–late 19C] an unashamed lie. **2** [late 19C+] an unjust or carping criticism.

IN COMPOUNDS

❑ **hammer duet** *n.* [1900s] (*US*) a fig. 'duet' formed of any group devoted to negative criticism.

IN PHRASES

❑ **throw the hammer** *v.* **1** [late 19C–1900s] to obtain money under false pretences. **2** [1900s] (*US*) to criticize negatively, to disparage.

hammer *n.*^{3} *see* HAMMA *n.*

hammer *n.*^{4} *see* HAMMER AND TACK *n.*

hammer *v.*^{1} **1** [late 16C; mid-19C+] to copulate (vigorously) with. **2** [early 19C+] to beat up, to hurt physically, to defeat comprehensively; thus *hammerer*, an aggressive fighter; *hammering*, a comprehensive beating; also used fig. **3** [late 19C+] (*Aus./US*) to drive at maximum speed. **4** [20C+] to assail, to pressurize. **5** [1980s+] (*US campus*) to drink fast, usu. of beer. **6** [1990s+] (*US campus*) to excel. **7** [2000s] to take a large amount of a drug, usu. cocaine. **8** [2000s] to masturbate.

IN PHRASES

❑ **hammer a job** *v.* [JOB *v.*^{1} (1)] [1940s+] (*Irish*) to have sexual intercourse. ❑ **hammer ass** *v.* [ASS *n.*] [1950s+] (*US*) to work very hard. ❑ **on the hammer** [1940s+] (*Aus.*) in pursuit, 'on someone's back'.

hammer *v.*^{2} [SE *hammer* (*away*), to persist; compare PUT THE HAMMER ON *under* HAMMER *n.*^{1}] [1960s–70s] (*US Und.*) to solicit money for drinking.

hammer *v.*^{3} *see* HAMMER (AND NAIL) *v.*

hammer and discus *n.* [rhy. sl.] [1990s+] whiskers.

hammer and jack *n. see* HAMMER AND TACK *n.* (5).

hammer (and nail) *v.* [rhy. sl. = TAIL *v.* (2)] [20C+] to follow.

hammer and saw *n.* [rhy. sl. = *officer of the law*] [1920s] (*US*) a police officer.

hammer and tack *n.* (*also* **hammer**) [rhy. sl.] **1** [late 19C+] (*Aus./N.Z.*) a sixpence [= ZAC *n.*]. **2** [1920s+] (*Aus.*) a road [= SE *track*]. **3** [1930s+] (*Aus./US*) the human back. **4** [1980s] (*Aus.*) dismissal from a job [= SACK *n.* (2a)]. **5** [1980s+] (*also* **hammer and jack**) (*Aus./N.Z.drugs*) heroin [= SMACK *n.*^{2} (1)].

IN PHRASES

❑ **on someone's hammer** [rhy. sl. = ON SOMEONE'S BACK *under* BACK *n.*^{1}] (*Aus.*) **1** [1920s+] very close behind. **2** [1940s+] hounding, pestering.

hammer and tack *adv.* [rhy. sl.] [1990s+] back (in time).

hammered *adj.* [fig. uses of SE *hammer*] **1** [1950s+] very drunk. **2** [1980s+] (*US drugs*) extremely intoxicated by a drug. **3** [1990s+] (*US campus*) of a car, loaded up with accessories.

hammerhead *n.*^{1} [SE *hammer* + -HEAD *sfx* (1); but note HAMMER *n.*^{1} (1) thus synon. with DICKHEAD *n.*] **1** [16C–17C; 20C+] (*US*) anyone stupid and obstinate, often used of a horse. **2** [1970s] a black person.

hammerhead *n.*^{2} [joc. use of SE or HAMMER *n.*^{1} (1) + SE *head*] [1990s+] the penis.

hammerheaded *adj.* [HAMMERHEAD *n.*^{1}] [late 16C–early 17C; 20C+] stupid, stubborn.

hammerish *adj.* [fig. use of SE *hammer*] **1** (*US*) [mid-18C] drunk. **2** [early–mid-19C] very well aware.

hammock *n.* [resemblance; but note the hammock is for a 'lazy cunt', punning on CUNT *n.* (4)/CUNT *n.* (1), which is 'lazy' because it is not available for intercourse] [1990s+] (*UK juv.*) a sanitary towel.

hammy *adj.* [HAM *n.*^{2}] [late 19C+] **1** incompetent, second-rate. **2** typical of bad acting. **3** sentimental, false, bogus.

hamps *n.*^{1} [abbr.] [1990s+] (*US black/drugs*) a Hav-a-Tampa cigar, as used for rolling marijuana cigarettes.

hamps *n.*^{2} *see* HAMPSTEAD(S) *n.*

Hampstead donkeys *n.* [ety. unknown] [mid–late 19C] lice.

Hampstead Heath sailor *n.* [apart from the Round Pond and a number of bathing ponds, the Heath is dry land] [late 19C] a very poor sailor, no sailor at all.

Hampstead(s) *n.* (*also* **Edward Heath, hamps, Hampstead Heath(s)**) [rhy. sl.; ult. *Hampstead Heath* in North London] [late 19C+] a tooth, the teeth.

Hampton Court *n.* [rhy. sl.; Cockney pron.] [20C+] salt.

Hampton rock *n.* [rhy. sl. = COCK *n.*^{3} (1)] [late 19C+] the penis.

Hampton (Wick) *n.* [rhy. sl. = PRICK *n.* (1)] **1** [20C+] the penis. **2** [1960s+] a fool.

ham sandwich *n.*^{1} [the absolute insignificance thereof] [1970s] (*US*) nothing.

ham sandwich *n.*^{2} [pun on part of name] [2000s] (*US black*) a Cadillac Brougham.

ham shank *n.*^{1} [rhy. sl.] **1** [1940s+] an American [= YANK *n.* (1)]. **2** [1990s+] an act of masturbation [= WANK *n.* (1)].

ham shank *n.*[2] [HAM SHANKER *n.*] [2000s] a third-rate, insignificant person.

ham shank *v.* [rhy. sl. = WANK *v.*] [1990s+] to masturbate.

ham shanker *n.* [rhy. sl. = WANKER *n.*] [1990s+] **1** a masturbator. **2** an unpleasant, stupid, despised person.

hanced *adj.* [abbr. SE *enhanced*] [17C] tipsy.

Hancock *v.* [abbr. JOHN HANCOCK *n.*] [1920s] (*US*) to sign, to affix one's signature.

hand *n.*[1] [metonymy] [early 19C+] a person; often as *cool hand, loose hand*.

SE in slang uses

IN COMPOUNDS

❑ **hand-and-pocket shop** *n.* [one must put one's *hand in one's pocket*] [late 18C–mid-19C] an eating house where one must pay cash and credit is not available. ❑ **hand artillery** *n.* (*also* **hand cannon**) [1920s+] (*US*) a pistol. ❑ **handbag** *n.* **1** [1960s+] (*Aus.*) a woman's male escort. **2** [2000s] (*UK black*) of a man, one's wife or girlfriend. **3** *see* ABO'S HANDBAG *under* ABO *n.* ❑ **handball** *n. see* separate entries. ❑ **hand-basket portion** *n.* [note 16C SE *handbasket sloy*, an unpleasant term for a woman] [late 18C–mid-19C] a woman whose family continually gives money to her husband. ❑ **hand book** *n.* [BOOK *n.* (2b)] [late 19C–1970s] (*US*) a small bookmaker or illegal betting establishment. ❑ **handbrake** *n.* [1980s] (*S.Afr. campus*) a regular girlfriend. ❑ **hand crank** *n. see* CRANK *n.*[3] (2). ❑ **handcuff** *n.* [a negative view of marriage] **1** [1920s–40s] (*US*) an engagement (ring), a wedding (ring). **2** [1960s] (*US teen*) a parent. ❑ **hand gallop** *see* separate entries. ❑ **hand gig** *n.* [1940s+] (*gay*) **1** a homosexual prostitute who specializes in masturbating his clients or joining in mutual masturbation with them. **2** mutual masturbation. ❑ **hand grenade** *n.* **1** [1970s] (*US black*) an amorous letter or note. **2** [1980s] (*Aus.*) a hamburger. ❑ **hand jig** *see* separate entries. ❑ **hand jive** *see* separate entries. ❑ **hand job** *see* separate entries. ❑ **handmade** *adj.* (*also* **hand-raised, hand-reared**) [the idea that masturbation has changed its shape] [1960s–70s] (*US*) of the penis, bent noticeably in one direction or another or particularly large. ❑ **hand queen** *n.* [-QUEEN *sfx* (3)] [1960s+] (*US gay*) someone who prefers masturbating a partner or being masturbated to other forms of sex. ❑ **hand-saw** *n. see under* SAW *n.*[2]. ❑ **handshake/shaker** *see* separate entries. ❑ **hand shandy** *see* separate entries. ❑ **hand solo** *n.* (*also* **han solo**) [pun on the character Han Solo in the *Star Wars* films of the 1970s–80s] [1990s+] masturbation. ❑ **hands up** *n.* [the bottle has the Red Hand of Ulster on its label] [1920s] (*Irish*) a bottle of Allsop ale. ❑ **handsupper** *n.* [those Boers who surrendered, i.e. *put their hands up*, at the end of the Anglo-Boer Wars (1880–1, 1899–1902)] [1940s+] (*S.Afr.*) a traitor.

IN PHRASES

❑ **down hand on someone** *v. see under* DOWN *v.*[2]. ❑ **drop hand** *v. see under* DROP *v.*[1]. ❑ **hands off (your) cocks, feet in (your) socks** (*also* **drop one's cock and grab one's socks**) [1910s+] a joc. wake-up cry, orig. RAF, but general in the services, institutions and similar sites of dormitory accommodation. ❑ **hand-to-fist** *adv.* [mid-17C–early 19C] intimately, right up close to each other. ❑ **have one's hand out** *v.* **1** [late 19C+] to beg, to scrounge. **2** [20C+] to be amenable to a bribe. ❑ **make a hand of** *v.* (*also* **take a hand of**) [20C+] (*Irish*) to tease, to mock, to make fun of. ❑ **on one's own hands** [mid-19C] looking after oneself, taking responsibility for one's own life. ❑ **put one's hand down** *v.* [i.e. down into one's trouser pocket] [20C+] to pay, to stand one's turn. ❑ **put one's hand up** *v.* [classroom practice] [1970s+] to confess. ❑ **put one's hand out** *v.* [1950s+] to go through a drunk person's pockets looking for cash and/or valuables. ❑ **throw hands** *v.* (*also* **throw 'em**) [1970s+] (*orig. US black*) to punch, to hit; to fight.

hand *n.*[2] [SE *handful*] **1** [1960s] (*Aus.*) a five-year prison sentence [the five fingers on a hand]. **2** [1960s+] (*S.Afr. drugs*) a small measure of marijuana.

hand *adj.* [1990s+] (*US campus*) the very best.

hand *v.* [ext. of SE] (*US*) **1** [late 19C–1950s] to inflict a blow, to impress upon, to conquer. **2** [late 19C+] to tell with intent to deceive, e.g. *hand someone a line of nonsense*, to talk nonsense.

SE in slang uses

IN COMPOUNDS

❑ **hand-me-down shop** *n.* [SE *hand-me-down shop*, a second-hand clothes shop] [mid-19C–1910s] an illicit pawnbroker's.

IN PHRASES

❑ **hand in one's checks** *v. see under* CHECK *n.*[1]. ❑ **hand in one's chips** *v. see under* CHIP *n.*[2]. ❑ **hand in one's dinner-pail** *v.* (*also* **pass in one's dinner pail, turn in...**) **1** [1920s+] to die. **2** [1930s+] to resign from one's job; to stop what one is doing. ❑ **hand it out** *v.* [1920s–40s] (*US*) to harm, to kill. ❑ **hand it to** *v.* (*also* **give it to**) **1** [1900s–40s] to tell off, to reprimand, to tease. **2** [1910s–50s] (*orig. US black*) to shoot at someone; to attack. ❑ **hand out** *see* separate entries. ❑ **hand over** *v. see* separate entries. ❑ **hand someone one** *v. see* GIVE SOMEONE ONE *under* ONE *n.*[1]. ❑ **hand someone the hat** *v.* [1910s+] to reject, to dismiss. ❑ **hand someone the ice-bowl** *v.* [i.e. to treat coldly] [1900s] to offer a rejection, to fail to pay a debt. ❑ **hand someone the kick-along** *v.* [1930s] (*UK tramp*) to refuse someone something.

hand! *excl.* [abbr.] [1990s+] (*US campus*) an excl. used to wish that someone will *have a nice day*.

handball *n.*[1] [*SE hand* + BALL *v.*[3] + pun on SE *handball* and BALLS *n.* (1)] **1** [1970s+] (*US gay*) fondling one's own balls from the comfort of one's pocket. **2** [1980s+] (*US gay*) the insertion of one's hand and forearm into one's partner's anus or vagina.

handball *n.*[2] [ety. unknown] [1980s+] (*drugs*) crack cocaine.

-handed *adj.* **1** [mid-19C+] (*UK Und.*) describing the size of a gang of criminals, which can be *two-, three-, four-handed* etc; thus MOB-HANDED *under* MOB *n.*[2]; TEAM-HANDED *under* TEAM *n.*; also used of any group, e.g. police. **2** [2000s] equipped.

hander *n.* [one who gives a *hand*] [1960s+] (*Scot./Aus. prison*) a helper, an assistant.

handful *n.* **1** [17C] (*UK Und.*) a long penis, the unit of measurement of a penis. **2** in senses of the hand's five fingers. (**a**) [1930s+] (*UK Und.*) a five-year prison sentence. (**b**) [1940s+] a £5 note or cheque for £5; thus *two-handful*, £10. (**c**) [1950s] (*US teen*) $500.

IN PHRASES

❑ **get a handful of sprats** *v.* (*also* **have a handful**) [play on FISH *n.*[1] (1a) and similar terms meaning the vagina] [late 19C+] to grope a woman's genital area.

hand-gallop *n.* [SE *hand-gallop*, an easy gallop] [1970s+] an act of masturbation.

hand gallop *v.* [HAND-GALLOP *n.*] [1970s+] to masturbate.

handicap *n.* [rhy. sl. = CLAP *n.*] [20C+] venereal disease.

handicap chase *n.* [rhy. sl.] [1990s+] the face.

handicapped *adj. see* PARALYSED *adj.*

handies *n.*

IN PHRASES

❑ **play at handies** *v.* [1910s+] (*Aus.*) of a pair of lovers, to hold hands.

hand jig *n.* (*also* **three-fingered hand jig**) [SE *hand* + *jig*, a fidgety movement] [1930s–70s] (*US prison*) masturbation, usu. of one prisoner by another.

hand jig *v.* [HAND JIG *n.*] [1930s–70s] to masturbate.

hand jive *n.* [HAND JIVE *v.* (3)] [1970s+] an act of masturbation.

hand jive *v.* [JIVE *v.*[1] (3)] **1** [1950s+] (*US*) to move and slap the hands in time to the rhythm of music. **2** [1970s] to feign a hand-slap for the purpose of passing money and drugs between a customer and a dealer. **3** [1970s+] (*US*) to masturbate, usu. someone else.

hand job *n.* [SE *hand* + JOB *v.*[1]] **1** [1930s+] an act of masturbation, performed by a partner; often offered as such in a prostitute's price list. **2** [1970s+] (*US*) an act of insincere flattery. **3** [1970s+] any form of deceit, misinformation. **4** [1980s+] (*US*) an obnoxious person.

IN PHRASES

❑ **do a hand job** *v.* [1960s+] to masturbate.

hand job *v.* (*also* **hand gig**) [HAND JOB *n.* (1)] [1960s+] to masturbate.

handkerchief *n.*

(IN PHRASES)

❑ **give someone the handkerchief** *v.* [1980s] to give someone a signal.

handkerchief-head *n.*[1] [the covering of one's expensively straightened hair with a handkerchief; black militants of the 1960s, who advocated the AFRO *n.* (1) as a symbol of emancipation, saw such hairstyles as selling out to white standards] (*US black*) **1** [1940s+] a subservient, role-playing, white-stereotyped black person. **2** [1940s+] a middle-class black person, irrespective of gender. **3** [1970s+] one who has straightened or 'processed' hair, worn under a headscarf.

handkerchief-head *n.*[2] [SE *handkerchief* + -HEAD *sfx* (2); along the lines of *TOWEL-HEAD under* TOWEL *n.*; ult. the *keffiyeh* head-dress worn by Arabs] [1970s+] (*US*) a derog. term for an Arab or a man who wears a turban.

handle *n.* **1** [16C–early 18C; 1960s+] (*later use US*) the penis. **2** [late 18C–1940s] the nose. **3** [early 19C+] a name, a nickname, a title (esp. as spoken rather than written); thus a *handle to one's name*, a title, an honorific. **4** [mid-19C] a fool. **5** [late 19C; 1960s+] (*US*) an influence on; a role in. **6** [1910s] (*US Und.*) in pl., side-whiskers. **7** [1940s+] (*Aus./N.Z.*) a glass of beer with a handle (as oppposed to a 'straight' glass). **8** [1980s+] (*US campus*) a ring of excess fat around one's stomach, a 'spare tyre'. **9** [1980s+] (*US*) in pl., the female breasts. **10** [1980s+] (*US*) a reference to, a clue; an understanding of.

(IN PHRASES)

❑ **get a handle** *v.* [? abbr. phr. *get a handle and turn yourself off* or synon. colloq. *get a grip*] [1960s+] (*US*) to calm down, to control oneself.

handle *v.* [euph.] **1** [19C] to masturbate. **2** [19C; 1970s] to have sexual intercourse. **3** [1910s–40s] (*US*) to manhandle. **4** [1980s+] (*S.Afr.*) to believe, to find credible.

handlebars *n. see* LONG HANDLEBARS *under* LONG *adj.*

handle cranker *n.* [rhy. sl. = WANKER *n.*] [1980s+] (*Aus. prison*) a masturbator.

handle it! *excl.* [1970s] (*US black*) a general exhortation, differing as to context.

handle up (on) one's business *v.* [2000s] (*US prison*) to fight.

hand-out *n.* **1** [late 19C+] (*orig. US*) food or money given to a beggar. **2** [1920s+] in ext. use, any food or a meal. **3** [1950s+] (*US Und.*) a bribe.

hand out *v.* [late 19C–1930s] (*US*) to impart information that is insincere or aiming to impress.

(IN PHRASES)

❑ **hand out the b.a.** *v. see* B.A. *v.*

hand over *v.* [late 18C–mid-19C] (*UK Und.*) to pay a bribe so as to have a case dropped; to drop an argument, to abandon a court case.

hands *n.*[1] [rhy. sl. on *hands and feet*] [20C+] (a piece of) meat.

hands *n.*[2] [euph.] [1980s+] (*US campus*) the female breasts.

handsell *v.* [SE *handsell*, to give a present] [mid-19C] to hawk goods in the street; thus *handseller*, a street or open-air seller.

handshake *v.* [1910s–60s] (*US*) to curry favour.

handshaker *n.* [SE *handshake*/HANDSHAKE *v.*] **1** [late 19C] (*US*) a swindler. **2** [late 19C–1930s] (*US*) an insincere person. **3** [1930s–50s] a toady, a sycophant.

hand shandy *n.* [SE *shandy*, a fizzy drink combining beer and lemonade] [1980s+] the act of masturbation.

hand shandy *v.* [HAND SHANDY *n.*] [1980s+] to masturbate.

handsome *adv.* [mid-19C+] satisfactorily, as required or desired.

handsome! *excl.* [16C SE *handsome*, becoming, courteous, gracious] [1970s+] a general term of approval, excellent! wonderful!

handsome harry *n.* (*also* **handsome hank**) [1930s+] a womanizer, esp. one whose seductive 'line' cannot be trusted.

hand-to-hand *adj.* [1950s+] (*drugs*) of drugs, delivered immediately.

(IN COMPOUNDS)

❑ **hand-to-hand man** *n.* [1980s+] (*drugs*) transient dealers who carry small amounts of crack cocaine.

handy wagon *n.* [its SE *handiness* for making arrests] [1920s–30s] (*US*) a police patrol car.

Hanes! *excl. see* HAINES! *excl.*

hang *n.*[1] [HANG! *excl.*] [mid-19C+] a euph. for DAMN *n.*

hang *n.*[2] [abbr.] [1950s] (*US*) a *hang*over.

hang *n.*[3] [SE *hang*, to hold on to] [1950s+] (*US black*) a job, esp. one that may not be ideal but supports one's living.

hang *n.*[4] [HANG *v.*[3]] (*orig. US campus*) **1** [1980s+] a loiterer, someone who spends a lot of time at a place. **2** [1980s+] (*also* **hang spot**) a place where one 'hangs out'. **3** [1990s+] a social occasion, a rock or other concert, a party. **4** [1990s+] time spent relaxing, loitering.

hang *v.*[1] [late 16C+] a euph. for *TO HELL WITH…! under* HELL *n.*

(IN EXCLAMATIONS)

❑ **go hang…!** **1** [late 16C+] a dismissive excl. euph.; thus *tell someone to go hang!, go hang crepe on oneself!* **2** [early 17C] of a plan, to collapse, to go wrong, to fail. **3** [1900s] to allow to fail or die. ❑ **hang it all!** [late 16C+] a general excl. of frustration, annoyance.

hang *v.*[2] **1** [mid–late 19C] to be in difficulties; thus *hanging*, in great difficulties [sporting jargon *hanging man*, one who is facing great problems, usu. in the form of debts]. **2** [20C+] (*US*) to impose upon, to blame, to make a criminal charge against [SE *hang*, to kill with a noose/*hang*, to put on a hook].

(IN PHRASES)

❑ **hang on someone's door** *v.* [sense 2 above] [1950s] (*UK prison*) to place blame on someone. ❑ **hang something on** *v.* **1** [1920s+] (*US*) to bring a charge against a criminal, whether justified or not, to allot blame; often as *hang one on*. **2** [1970s] to name.

SE in slang uses

(IN COMPOUNDS)

❑ **hangaround** *n.* [SE *hang around*, to loiter] [20C+] an aimless person, a loiterer. ❑ **hang dog** *adj.* [? US phr. *till the last dog is hung*, till everything is used up] [1940s+] (*W.I.*) plentiful. ❑ **hang-down** *n.* [its flaccid posture] [1970s+] the penis (cf. HANG-LOW *n.*). ❑ **hang-house** *n.* [1940s] (*UK prison*) the room or building that holds the gallows. ❑ **hang-in-chains** *n.* [the corpses of villains were trad. hung in chains as an 'awful warning' to passers-by] [late 18C–early 19C] a villain, a desperate looking person. ❑ **hang-low** *n. see* separate entry. ❑ **hangman** *n. see* separate entry. ❑ **hang-on** *n.* [SE *hang on*, to wait] [1960s] (*US*) an idler.

(IN PHRASES)

❑ **hang a hat on someone** *v. see PUT A HAT ON SOMEONE under* HAT *n.* ❑ **hang a pin** *v. see under* PIN *n.* ❑ **hang a pinch on** *v. see under* PINCH *n.* ❑ **hang a shanty on** *v. see under* SHANTY *n.*[1]. ❑ **hang in** *see* separate entries. ❑ **hang in the bellropes** *v.* [mid-18C] to postpone marriage even after the banns have been read in church. ❑ **hang in the hedge** *v.* [late 17C–early 18C] to be undecided, usu. of a lawsuit. ❑ **hang it on** *v. see* separate entries. ❑ **hang it out** *v. see* separate entries. ❑ **hang it up** *v. see* separate entries. ❑ **hang one's ass/fanny out** *v. see under* ASS *n.* ❑ **hang oneself out** *v.* [the image of hanging out over a long drop] [1990s+] (*US black*) to take a risk. ❑ **hang one's face up** *v.* [mid-19C] to drink on credit. ❑ **hang one's hat** *v.* (*also* **hang one's socks**) **1** [late 19C+] to make a commitment towards, to rely on. **2** [20C+] (*also* **hang up one's hat**) to live, to stay. ❑ **hang one's hat up** *v.* [mid-19C–1950s] to become engaged; thus *hang one's hat up to*, to propose to a woman; *hanging one's hat up*, engaged. ❑ **hang one's jib** *v. see* JIB *n.*[1] (5). ❑ **hang one's latchpan** *v.* [SE *latchpan*, a pan to catch the drippings from roasting meat. In this context the 'drippings' are presumably tears] [late 19C–1900s] to look miserable; to pout. ❑ **hang on someone's bra strap** *v.* [1990s+] (*US black*) of a woman, to impose upon or bother another woman. ❑ **hang out** *see* separate entries. ❑ **hang paper** *v. see under* PAPER *n.* ❑ **hang someone out to dry** *v.* (*also* **hang someone up to dry, leave someone out to dry, ...up to dry**) [1920s+] (*orig. US*) to treat someone particularly harshly; to make an example of someone. ❑ **hang the moon** *v.* [only someone very important, e.g. God, could have *hung the moon* in the sky] [1950s+] (*US*) to be very important; thus *think one hung the moon*, to think very highly of oneself. ❑ **hang up** *see* separate entries.

IN EXCLAMATIONS

❑ **hang a bootie!** [1980s+] (*US campus*) **1** good luck! **2** wait! [joc. pron. of HANG ABOUT! *excl.*]. ❑ **hang about!** *see* separate entry. ❑ **hang five!** [1990s+] (*Aus.*) wait a moment! ❑ **hang it in your ass!** [1950s+] (*US*) an excl. of contempt, often accompanied by a gesture, the right forefinger is hooked over the left thumb, which is making a circle with the left forefinger. ❑ **hang it in your ear!** [1960s+] (*US campus*) don't bother! forget it!

hang *v.*[3] **1** [1920s+] to loiter, to stand around aimlessly, to relax. **2** [1990s+] to inhabit, to live.

IN COMPOUNDS

❑ **hang spot** *n. see* HANG *n.*[4] (2).

IN PHRASES

❑ **hangin', bangin' and slangin'** [BANG *v.*[1] (1) + SLANG *v.*[3] (1)] [1990s+] (*US black gang*) a phr. used to describe the GANGSTA *n.* lifestyle: associating with one's friends and fellow gangsters, fighting with other gangs and selling drugs. ❑ **let's go hangin'** [1990s+] (*US teen*) let's go somewhere and do nothing in particular.

hang *v.*[4] **1** [1930s+] (*US*) to behave, usu. in combs., e.g. HANG LOOSE *v.*; HANG TOUGH *v.* **2** [1980s+] to endure, to suffer, to handle pressure. **3** [1980s+] to leave someone waiting.

IN PHRASES

❑ **hang black** *v.* [20C+] (*US black*) to associate primarily, if not wholly, with one's black peers. ❑ **hang loose** *see* separate entries. ❑ **hang tight** *v.* [1940s+] (*US*) to sit, to wait, esp. under pressure. ❑ **hang tough** *see* separate entries. ❑ **hang with** *v.* **1** [1930s+] (*US*) to associate with, to spend time with. **2** [1970s+] (*US*) to handle a situation, to endure. ❑ **how does that hang?** [1980s+] (*US black*) what do you think?

IN EXCLAMATIONS

❑ **hang (it) easy!** [1950s–60s] (*US*) take it easy!

hang *v.*[5] [1950s–70s] (*Aus./US drugs*) **1** to be under the influence of drugs. **2** to be in need of some drugs.

hang *v.*[6] [1950s+] (*US*) **1** to murder. **2** to beat up.

IN PHRASES

❑ **hang one on** *v. see under* ONE *n.*[1]. ❑ **hang someone's ass** *v. see under* ASS *n.*

hang *v.*[7] [1960s+] (*orig. US*) to turn a corner in a motorcar; as in *hang a left, hang a right.*

IN PHRASES

❑ **hang a lilly** *v.* [initial letters] [1960s+] to turn left. ❑ **hang a louie** *v. see under* LOUIE *n.*[2]. ❑ **hang a ralph** *v.* (*also* **hang a ralphie, ...roscoe**) [initial letters] [1960s+] to turn right. ❑ **hang a Sam** *v.* [initial letters] [1960s] (*US*) to go straight on. ❑ **hang a U-ie** *v. see under* U-IE *n.*

hang! *excl.* (*also* **by hang! stretch!**) [SE *hang*] [late 16C+] a general excl.; *see also* HANG IT! *excl.*; HANG ME! *excl.*

hang about! *excl.* [1960s+] wait a minute! don't go!

hangara *adj. see* HANG OF A *phr.*

Hangar Lane *n.* [rhy. sl.; ult. *Hangar Lane gyratory*, a large roundabout in West London] [1990s+] pain.

hangashun *adj.* [phonetic sp. of nonce-form *hangation* on model of SE *damnation*] [1920s+] (*Aus./N.Z.*) a general intensive, describing something extreme or large.

hangava *adj. see* HANG OF A *phr.*

hang bluff *n.* [rhy. sl.] [mid-19C] snuff.

hang-doodle *adj.* [1950s] a large amount; a general intensifier.

hanged *adj.* [SE *hang*] [late 16C+] a euph. for DAMNED *adj.*

IN EXCLAMATIONS

❑ **I'll be hanged!** (*also* **hanged! I'll be scragged! I'll be hung, swung and clubbed! I'm hanged!**) [SCRAGGED *adj.* (1)] [late 16C+] a general excl. of surprise, annoyance or impatience; often abbr. to *hanged!*

hanger *n.* **1** [early 17C] in pl., the testicles. **2** [mid-18C] (*UK Und.*) a sword [SE *hanger*, the strap that suspends a sword]. **3** [late 19C–1910s] in pl., gloves, esp. when unworn but held in the hand for ornamental purposes. **4** [1930s+] (*Aus./US*) in pl., the female breasts. **5** [1930s+] (*US Und.*) a wallet protruding from a pocket or purse, thus ripe for pickpocketing.

hang in *n.* [1930s+] (*US*) influence.

hang in *v.* (*also* **hang in there, hang on in (there)**) **1** [1930s+] to stay, to maintain a position, usu. with implication of pressures to surrender. **2** [1970s+] to exist, to survive, to be living.

IN PHRASES

❑ **hang in there** [1980s+] used as a farewell.

hanging *n.* [such extras fig. 'hang' off the primary task, occupation etc] [mid–late 19C] (*Aus.*) a perquisite, a bonus, an 'extra'.

hanging *adj.*[1] **1** [late 19C+] (*Irish*) drunk. **2** [1960s+] (*US campus*) feeling ill, esp. hungover.

hanging *adj.*[2] [the image of hanging game until it has become 'high'] [2000s] **1** of a woman, very unattractive. **2** of food, disgusting.

hanging bee *n.* [early 19C–1940s] (*US*) a public hanging.

hanging cheat *n.* [SE *hanging* + CHEAT *n.* (1); lit. 'hanging thing'] [16C–19C] the gallows.

hanging johnny *n.* [JOHNNY *n.*[1] (8)] [late 19C+] the flaccid penis.

hanging out *adj.* [HANG OUT *v.*[2] (2)] [1980s+] (*N.Z. drugs*) suffering from withdrawal symptoms.

hangin' on the leg *phr.* [LEG *n.*] [1990s+] (*US prison*) of a prisoner, to fraternize with the prison authorities; thus *leg-hanger*, one who pursues such acquaintances.

hangi pants *n.* [Maori *hangi*, an earth oven, thus cognate with HOT PANTS *n.* (2)] [2000s] (*N.Z.*) a sexually voracious female.

hang it! *excl.* [HANG! *excl.*] [late 16C+] a general excl.

hang it on *v.*[1] [the image is of hanging something on a peg and forgetting it] [early 19C] **1** to protract, to put into abeyance. **2** to cohabit with a woman, to form a temporary sexual relationship.

SE in slang uses

IN PHRASES

❑ **hang it on the limb** *v.* (*also* **hang it on a bush**) [ety. unknown; ? image of a member of a work gang removing his prison uniform and hanging it from a tree or bush before running] [1920s–50s] (*US prison*) to escape from prison or from a chain gang.

hang it on *v.*[2] [var. on *HANG ONE ON under* ONE *n.*[1]] [1910s] (*US*) to hit hard.

hang it out *v.* **1** [late 19C–1940s] (*Aus.*) to endure [HANG OUT *v.*[1] (3)]. **2** [1960s+] (*US*) to run a risk, risk one's life, to go to extremes [*HANG ONE'S ASS OUT under* ASS *n.*].

hang (it) up *v.* [the placing of records of debt on a piece of paper nailed to a tavern or shop wall] [early 18C–19C] to offer credit, to defer payment, to record as a debt.

hang it up *v.* [the image of hanging up something that is no longer in use] **1** [mid-19C+] to stop doing something. **2** [1950s] (*US Und.*) to escape from prison. **3** [1950s+] to give up trying, to accept defeat, to acknowledge that a target will never be achieved.

hang-loose *adj.* [HANG LOOSE *v.*] [1950s+] (*orig. US*) very informal.

hang loose *v.* [HANG *v.*[4] (1) + SE *loose*/LOOSE *adj.* (5); note personal corresp. from Paul Kunino Lynch (Sydney, Aus.): 'Boswell remarks that he had never heard of an occasional contributor to literary journals of the time named F Lewis. Then he overheard Johnson describe him to an acquaintance: "He lived in London and hung loose on society."'] [1950s+] (*orig. US*) to relax, to take things as they come.

hang loose! *excl.* [HANG LOOSE v.] [1950s+] (*orig. US*) an imper. excl., relax! enjoy yourself! don't worry!

hang-low *n.* [1990s+] (*US black*) the penis (cf. HANG-DOWN *under* HANG v.[2]).

IN PHRASES

❑ **get some stanky on the hang-low** *v.* (*also* **get some stank for my hang-low**) [2000s] to have sexual intercourse.

hangman *n.* [i.e. one who ought to be hanged] [mid-19C+] (*N.Z./W.I.*) a reprobate, a ruffian.

SE in slang uses

IN COMPOUNDS

❑ **hangman's day** *n.* [mid-19C] Friday. ❑ **hangman's wages** *n.* [the equivalent of a Scot. mark, the sum instituted as the executioner's fee by James VI and I (1566–1625). It was divided into one shilling for the execution and three halfpence for the rope] [late 17C–19C] 13½p, 1s 1½d (approx. 6p).

hang me! *excl.* [HANG! *excl.*] [late 16C+] a general excl.

hangnail *n.* [rhy. sl. = SE *snail*] [1990s+] a slow, shambling person.

hang of a *phr.* (*also* **hangara, hangava, hanguva**) [euph. for HELL OF A, A *under* HELL *n.*] [1940s+] (*orig. N.Z./S.Afr.*) a general intensifier, describing something extreme or large of its kind, e.g. *a hang of a headache*.

hang-out *n.*[1] [HANG OUT v.[1]] **1** [mid-19C] (*US campus*) a party, a celebration. **2** [mid-19C+] a lodging, a place of residence. **3** [late 19C+] a place where a group tends to meet.

hang-out *n.*[2] **1** [1960s+] the penis. **2** [1960s+] (*also* **hing-oot**) a general term of abuse, applied equally to either sex.

hangout *adj.* [HANG OUT v.[1] (4)] [1960s+] pertaining to those with whom one associates regularly.

hang out *v.*[1] (*also* **hang up**) **1** [early 19C+] to live, to make one's home. **2** [mid-19C] (*UK/US campus*) to treat. **3** [late 19C–1940s] (*Aus.*) to endure, to survive. **4** [late 19C+] to meet, to collect together at a regular venue, to frequent. **5** [late 19C+] to idle away time with friends. **6** [20C+] to exist, to be situated, to be available, to happen. **7** [1980s+] to lie in wait.

IN PHRASES

❑ **go the hang-out road** *v.* [1970s+] to tell the complete truth. ❑ **hang (out) cool** *v.* [COOL *adj.* (2)] [1970s+] (*US*) to remain calm, to relax.

SE in slang uses

IN PHRASES

❑ **hang out the bloody flag** *v. see* BLOODY FLAG IS OUT *under* BLOODY *adj.* ❑ **hang out the flag of distress** *v. see under* FLAG OF DISTRESS *n.*

hang out *v.*[2] [i.e. have one's tongue hanging out for] **1** [1960s+] to be desperate for something. **2** [1980s+] (*Aus./N.Z. drugs*) of an addict, to be desperate for drugs.

hang tough *n.* [HANG TOUGH v.] [1960s+] a tough character.

hang tough *adj.* [HANG TOUGH v.] [1960s+] stubborn.

hang tough *v.* [HANG v.[4] + TOUGH *adj.*] [1930s+] (*orig. US*) **1** to behave in an aggressive, tough manner, to persist in a course of action whatever the problems; thus *hang tough tit*, to stick to a decision. **2** as imper.: wait a minute, bear with me.

hang-up *n.*[1] **1** [mid-16C–mid-17C] one who is to be hanged. **2** [late 19C] one who is in serious trouble, whether criminal or financial. **3** [1970s] (*US prison*) a suicide who kills themselves by hanging.

hang-up *n.*[2] (*also* **hangup**) [one's mind gets fig. 'hung up' on the problem or emotion] **1** [1940s+] (*orig. US*) a problem, a delay. **2** [1950s+] neurosis, obsession. **3** [1960s] (*US drugs*) an addiction. **4** [1960s] (*US*) a boring, irritating person.

hang-up *adj.* [HUNG UP *adj.* (7)] [1960s] (*UK drugs*) addictive.

hang up *v.*[1] [the placing of records of debt on a piece of paper nailed to a tavern or shop wall] **1** [early 18C+] (*also* **hang it up**) to leave a bill unpaid at a public house; to buy on credit (with the intention of defrauding the creditor. **2** [late 19C] (*US*) to pawn. **3** [late 19C–1950s] (*US*) to charge exorbitantly.

hang up *v.*[2] **1** [mid-19C–1910s] to rob in the street, to garrotte, to 'mug'. **2** [1950s+] (*US prison*) to commit suicide by hanging.

hang up *v.*[3] [SE/*HANG UP ONE'S HAT under* HANG UP ONE'S… v.] **1** [mid-19C+] (*US*) to stop work, to retire, to quit. **2** [late 19C] (*US*) to be quiet, to stop talking. **3** [1950s] to reject, to refuse.

hang up *v.*[4] **1** [late 19C+] to delay, to hold up. **2** [1940s–50s] (*US*) to place under arrest.

hang up *v.*[5] **1** [1950s+] to distress, to annoy. **2** [1980s] (*US black*) to insult.

IN PHRASES

❑ **hang someone up** *v.* [1950s+] (*orig. US*) **1** to put at a disadvantage. **2** to depress. **3** to desert.

hang up *v.*[6] *see* HANG OUT v.[1].

hang up one's… *v.* [image of hanging up on a peg the item required for the job] [mid-19C+] used in a variety of phrs., usu. linked to the occupation in question, meaning to retire; thus fig. to die.

IN PHRASES

❑ **hang up one's fiddle** *v.* [mid-19C–1930s] (*US*) **1** to stop what one is doing. **2** to retire. **3** to die. ❑ **hang up one's gloves** *v.* (*also* **hang up the gloves**) [orig. prize-fighting jargon] [1920s+] (*US*) **1** to retire from one's profession. **2** to give up. **3** to die. ❑ **hang up one's harness** *v.* (*also* **hang up one's iron, …tackle**) [late 19C–1910s] **1** (*also* **drop one's harness**) to retire. **2** to die. ❑ **hang up one's hat** *v.* [mid-19C+] **1** to die. **2** to retire. ❑ **hang up one's hat to** *v.* [1900s–10s] (*Aus.*) to make advances to.

hanguva *adj. see* HANG OF A *phr.*

hank *n.*[1]

IN PHRASES

❑ **have a hank on** *v.* [SE *hank*, a restraining or curbing hold] [late 17C–early 19C] to have the advantage over, the implication is of potential blackmail.

hank *n.*[2] [? SE *hank*, a restraint, a power of check or dial. *hank*, a cluster, a gang] [late 18C–mid-19C] the baiting of an animal; thus *Smithfield hank*, an ox 'rendered furious by over-driving and barbarous treatment' (Grose, 1785); *hank*, to bait; *hanker*, one who takes part in a baiting.

hank *n.*[3] [dial. *hank*, a hook, a loop; i.e. one is fig. 'hung on a hook', rather than moving back to work] [19C] a break from work, gained by pretending to be feeling unwell or some other small lie.

hank *n.*[4] (*also* **ank**) [ety. unknown; ? dial. *be in a hank*, to be confused, mixed up] [late 19C–1950s] nonsense.

hank *n.*[5] (*also* **hank of hair**) [SE *hank* of hair] **1** [1940s+] (*US Und./campus*) a slut, a promiscuous woman. **2** [1960s+] (*US campus*) an unpopular person. **3** [1960s+] (*US gay*) the penis.

IN PHRASES

❑ **take one's hank** *v.* [1960s–70s] (*US prison*) to masturbate.

hank *v.* [HANK *n.*[2]/SE *hank*, a restraint] **1** [early 19C–1910s] to tease, to bait, to persecute. **2** [late 19C–1940s] to hesitate, to draw back.

hank freak *n.* [? the masturbator ejaculates into a *hand*kerchief; or ? HANK *n.*[5] (3)] [1960s] (*US prison*) a compulsive masturbator.

hankie-head *n.* [SE *hankie* + -HEAD *sfx* (2); ult. the *keffiyeh* head-dress] [1970s+] a derog. term for an Arab.

hankins *n.* [? dial. *hank*, a skein or measure of material + dimin. sfx *-ins*] [early 18C] breeches, trousers.

Hank Marvin *adj.* [rhy. sl.; ult. the guitarist *Hank B. Marvin* (b. 1941), best-known as a member of Cliff Richard's band The Shadows] [2000s] starving.

Hank Snow *n.*

IN PHRASES

❑ **pull a Hank Snow** *v.* (*also* **do a Hank Snow**) [song 'I'm Moving On' by Country and Western star *Hank Snow* (b.1914)] [1960s+] (*US*) to leave, to move on.

hanktelo *n.* [ety. unknown] [late 16C–mid-19C] a fool, a simpleton.

hankty *adj. see* HINCTY *adj.*

hankypanky *n.* (*also* **hanky pank**) [? Rom. *hakk'ni panki*, or redup. of the *hanky* (handkerchief) used by a conjuror in some tricks; thus note theatrical jargon *hank-panky bloke*, a conjuror] **1** [mid-19C+] trickery, deceit, esp. of a sexual nature. **2** [late 19C+] (*US*) a carnival game. **3** [20C+] (*US*) silly talk. **4** [20C+] sexual intercourse. **5** [20C+] kissing and cuddling.

IN PHRASES

❑ **play hanky-panky** *v.* [1980s+] to have sexual intercourse.

hankypanky *adj.* [HANKYPANKY *n.*] **1** [20C+] (*Aus.*) cranky, silly. **2** [1940s–50s] (*US*) (*also* **hanky-pank**) counterfeit or obtained through trickery or deceit.

hanky-spanky *adj.* [HANKYPANKY *n.* + SPANKING *adj.* (1)] [mid-19C–1910s] stylish, fashionable, well cut.

Hannah *n.* [note Texas prison use, *Hannah*, the sun] (*US*) **1** [late 19C–1910s] a proper name used as the subject of various general phrs., e.g. *that's what's the matter with Hannah*, a phr. of agreement or certainty; *since Hannah died, since Hannah was a rag doll*, for a very long time; *dead as Hannah Emerson*, totally dead; *he/she doesn't amount to Hannah*, referring to a worthless individual. **2** [20C+] a euph. for *God* and used in various mild oaths, such as *so help me Hannah!* **3** [1930s] an opinion, information.

Hannibal Lecter *n.* [rhy. sl.] [1990s+] a ticket inspector.

Hanover jack *n.* [? counterfeit sovereigns produced in Germany and bearing the head of James II or *Jac(obus)*; they were infiltrated into England and circulated during the reign of William III (r.1689–1702)] [late 19C–1910s] an imitation sovereign.

Hans *n.* [the common name] **1** [late 16C–17C] a Dutchman. **2** [late 19C+] a German.

Hans Carvel's ring *n.* ['Hans Carvel, a jealous old doctor, being in bed with his wife, dreamed that the Devil gave him a ring, which, so long as he had it on his finger, would prevent his being made a cuckold, waking, he found he had got his finger the Lord knows where' (Grose)/RING *n.* (1a)] [mid-18C–19C] the vagina.

hansel and gretel *n.* [rhy. sl.; ult. the fairy-tale characters] [20C+] a kettle.

hanseller *n.* [SE *handseller*, which Hotten cites as sl.] [mid–late 19C] a street salesman, a 'cheap jack'.

Hans-en-Kelder *n.* (*also* **Hans in kelder**) [joc. use of Du. *Hans-en-Kelder*, Jack in the cellar] [early 17C–early 19C] an unborn child, often used as a toast.

han solo *n. see* HAND SOLO *under* HAND *n.*[1].

hansom cab *n.* [rhy. sl.] **1** [20C+] (*Aus.*) a scab, a non-unionist [= SCAB *n.*[1] (4)]. **2** [20C+] (*also* **hanson cab**) a body louse [= SE *crab*, a louse].

hans wurst *n.* [Ger. proper name *Hans* + *wurst*, a sausage or salami] **1** [mid-19C+] (*US*) a fool, an idiot. **2** [1920s+] nonsense; also attrib.

hanus *adj. see* HEINOUS *adj.*

hap *n.*[1] (*also* **haps**) [abbr.] [1960s+] (*US black*) happening; thus *what's the haps (on the craps)?* used as a greeting; *no haps*, no indeed; *the haps*, something good.

hap *n.*[2] [synon. Afk.] [1970s+] (*S.Afr.*) a bite, a mouthful, a morsel.

hapas capas *n. see* HAPUS CAPUS *n.*

ha'penny *n.* [usu. middle-class euph.] [20C+] the female genital area.

IN PHRASES

❑ **keep your hand on your ha'penny (till the right man turns up)** [20C+] advice to young women to retain their virginity until the advent of 'Mr Right'.

ha'penny *adj.*

SE in slang uses

IN COMPOUNDS

❑ **ha'penny boy** *n.* [1960s+] (*Irish*) a worthless, unimportant person. ❑ **ha'penny place** *n.* [1960s+] (*Irish*) a worthless, unimportant place, position or status.

hap'orth o' coppers *n.* [rhy. sl.] [late 19C] (*Aus.*) habeas corpus.

happa *n.* [Jap. *hampa*, half] [1980s+] (*US campus*) a person who is half-Asian.

happen *v.* **1** [1940s+] (*orig. US music industry*) to attract publicity and be successful. **2** [1960s+] (*US*) to appear, to function or work. **3** [1950s+] (*drugs*) used euph. in a variety of questions, e.g. *anything happening?*, i.e. do you have any drugs?; *nothing happening*, I have no drugs, there are no drugs around.

IN PHRASES

❑ **it's all happening** [1930s+] there is much activity or success, everything is working out as desired. ❑ **nothing happening** [1940s–50s] (*US*) used as a response to the greeting *WHAT'S HAPPENING?* below and meaning things are normal. ❑ **what happen?** (*also* **wha'appen, what happening?**) [1950s+] (*W.I./UK black*) a general form of greeting, 'Hello, how are you?'. ❑ **what's happening?** (*also* **happening? wha'ppen? what's been happening?**) [1950s+] a greeting, hello and how are you? what are you/have you been doing?

happening *adj.* [rarely used 1980s + other than ironically/historically] [1960s+] fashionable, chic, up-to-the-minute.

IN PHRASES

❑ **what's happening** (*also* **that's what's happening, what's going down**) [1960s+] (*orig. US black*) the fashionable, chic, smart event, place, show etc; thus *not what's happening*, the opposite.

happenings *n.* [1950s+] **1** (*US*) goings-on, esp. those of an intimate nature. **2** (*US drugs*) any illicit narcotics. **3** (*US black*) in fig. use, women.

happy *n.* [coined in late 1990s US TV show *Buffy the Vampire Slayer*] [1990s+] a pleasurable feeling.

happy *adj.* [euph.] **1** [late 18C+] drunk. **2** [1950s] (*US drugs*) intoxicated.

IN COMPOUNDS

❑ **happy shack** *n.* [1970s+] (*US black*) a liquor store. ❑ **happy shop** *n.* [1960s–70s] (*US black*) a liquor store.

pertaining to intoxication

❑ **happy box** *n.* [1980s+] (*S.Afr.*) wine sold in 2½- or 5-litre (4½–8¾-pint) containers, placed in a cardboard box. ❑ **happy cigarette** *n.* (*also* **funny cigarette**) [1970s+] (*drugs*) a marijuana cigarette. ❑ **happy drugs** *n.* [1960s] anti-depressants. ❑ **happy dust** *n.* [DUST *n.* (6)] **1** [1910s+] (*orig. US drugs*) cocaine; thus *happy duster*, a cocaine user or seller. **2** [1920s+] morphine. **3** [1930s+] heroin. ❑ **happy gas** *n.* **1** [1930s] marijuana. **2** [1940s] (*US*) heroin. **3** [2000s] (*US*) laughing gas or nitrous oxide. ❑ **happy grass** *n.* [GRASS *n.*[4]; among its effects is the promotion of laughter] [1960s+] (*US drugs*) marijuana. ❑ **happy herb** *n.* [HERB *n.*[1] (1); among its effects is the promotion of laughter] [1980s+] (*Aus. drugs*) cannabis. ❑ **happy juice** *n.* [1920s–50s] (*US*) good humour, usu. resulting from alcohol or drug intoxication. ❑ **happy pill** *n.* (*also* **happiness pill**) [1950s+] a tranquillizer or stimulant. ❑ **happy powder** *n.* [1940s+] (*drugs*) **1** cocaine. **2** heroin; morphine. ❑ **happy sticks** *n.* (*US drugs*) **1** [1950s+] marijuana. **2** [1980s+] marijuana laced with phencyclidine. ❑ **happy stuff** *n.* [1920s+] (*US*) cocaine.

general uses

❑ **happy bag** *n.* **1** [1970s+] (*UK Und.*) the bag in which a shotgun is carried on an armed robbery; the gun makes the victim 'happy' to pass over his money. **2** [2000s] (*US*) the scrotum [BAG *n.*[1] (1a)]. ❑ **happy camper** *n.* [1980s+] (*US campus*) one who is perfectly satisfied with their life and the circumstances in which they find themselves; also as negative, *not a happy camper*, a dissatisfied, unhappy person; the deliberate levity of the phrase often hides a genuinely deep unhappiness or dissatisfaction. ❑ **happy Eliza** *n.* [the relentless good humour of such individuals; *Eliza* is generic for a Salvation Army girl] [late 19C–1900s] a female Salvationist. ❑ **happy endings** *n.* [2000s] (*US*) a massage that concludes with masturbation of the male client. ❑ **happy farm** *n.* [var. on *FUNNY FARM under* FUNNY *adj.*[1]] [1960s+] (*US*) a psychiatric institution.

❑ **happy house** *n.* (*also* **happy home**) [1960s+] a psychiatric institution. ❑ **happy hunting grounds** *n.* [Native American imagery] (*orig. US*) **1** [mid-19C+] death. **2** [late 19C] the vagina. ❑ **happy returns** *n.* [pun] [late 19C–1950s] (*Aus.*) the act of vomiting. ❑ **happy shopper** *n.* [brandname *Happy Shopper*, a cheap grocery store, with the idea of being indiscriminate] [1990s+] a bisexual. ❑ **happy trail** *n.* (*also* **the divine line, snail trail, treasure...**) [1990s+] (*US*) a line of chest hair down the middle of a man's torso leading to the penis. ❑ **happy valley** *n.* [note milit. use *happy valley*, first an area of the Somme battlefield and, later, anywhere that is suffering heavy bombing] **1** [1930s+] (*Aus.*) an area of shantytowns. **2** [1960s+] the female genitals. **3** [1960s+] (*US gay*) the cleft of the buttocks. ❑ **happy wagon** *n.* [ironic] [1950s–60s] (*US*) a prison or police van.

-happy *sfx* [1930s+] (*orig. milit.*) **1** slightly insane as a result of a circumstance, e.g. *demob-happy, bomb-happy*. **2** obsessed with.

happy as... *adj.* [mid-19C+] in phrs. meaning either very happy or very unhappy.

(IN PHRASES)

❑ **...a bastard on father's day** [1950s+] (*Aus.*) very unhappy. ❑ **...a black in a barrel of treacle** [1900s] extremely happy. ❑ **...a boxing kangaroo in fog time** [20C+] (*Aus.*) very discontented, very unhappy. ❑ **...(a box of) birds** [the chirping of birds] [late 19C+] (*Aus./UK/US*) in very high spirits. ❑ **...a bug in a rug** (*also* **happy as a bug on a hot stove, happy as a bedbug/June bug, lively as bugs in a rug**) [1910s+] (*US*) very happy. ❑ **...a clam** (*also* **happy as a clam at high tide/water, happy as a cricket, happy as a sand-bag, happy as a horned toad**) [mid-19C+] (*US*) very happy, totally satisfied. ❑ **...a dog with two tails** (*also* **happy as a dog with a tin tail, happy as a dog with two dicks, happy as a dog with a bellyful of soup and a streetful of lamp-posts**) [1950s+] very happy. ❑ **...a flea at a dog-show** (*also* **happy as moths in a best blanket**) [20C+] (*N.Z.*) very happy. ❑ **...a hophead** [1940s] (*US*) very happy. ❑ **...a nun weeding the asparagus** [1910s+] (*Can.*) very cheerful (with obvious sexual overtones given the 'phallic' asparagus). ❑ **...a pig in shit** (*also* **happy as pigs in shit, ...a pig in clover, ...muck, ...mud, ...shite, ...hogs in shit, ...pigs in mud**) [19C+] extremely happy. ❑ **...a sick eel on a sandpit** (*also* **happy as a hooked fish, ...horned toad**) [1940s] (*N.Z.*) very unhappy. ❑ **...Larry** (*also* **happy as Harry**) [ety. unknown; 'possibly but not certainly commemorating the noted Australian pugilist Larry Foley (1847–1917)' (Baker, 1966)] [20C+] (*orig. Aus.*) perfectly happy, quite content.

happy-clappies *n.* [a derog. term that emphasizes the differences between the lower- and lower-middle-class evangelicals and the middle- and upper-class Church of England] [1980s+] (*orig. S.Afr.*) members of an evangelical church, whose services involve a good deal of 'audience participation', e.g. singing, responding, clapping of hands.

happy-clappy *adj.* [HAPPY-CLAPPIES *n.*] [1980s+] naïve, gullible, i.e. typical of the evangelical church and its devotees.

happy hour *n.* [rhy. sl.] **1** [20C+] (*also* **early hour, happy half-hour**) in pl., flowers [orig. use by Covent Garden Market porters]. **2** [1950s+] (*Aus.*) a shower.

haps *n. see* HAP *n.*[1].

hapus capus *n.* (*also* **hapas capas**) [a speedy, lazy pron. of Lat. *habeas corpus*, thou (shalt) have the body (in court). The prerogative writ *habeas corpus ad subjiciendum*, requiring the body of a person restrained of liberty to be brought before the judge or into court so that the lawfulness of the restraint may be investigated and determined. This writ is seen as the basis of all open, honest and democratic legal systems] [1940s–50s] (*US prison*) a prison inmate who has made himself into a self-taught lawyer, to pursue his own case, combat prison corruption or help his fellow inmates.

harbour light *phr.* [rhy. sl.] [late 19C+] all right; usu. as phr. *all harbour*.

harbour (of hope) *n.* [idea of the penis sheltering] [late 17C–1900s] the vagina.

harbour shark *n. see under* SHARK *n.*

harch off *v.* [orig. milit. use; ? parade-ground pron. of 'march' as 'harch'] [1940s+] (*Aus.*) to abandon, to leave.

hard *n.* **1** of alcohol or drugs. (**a**) [late 17C–early 19C] sour or stale beer. (**b**) [mid-19C+] plug tobacco. (**c**) [mid-19C+] (*US 20C+*) (*also* **the hard**) hard cider or whisky. (**d**) [late 19C–1950s] hard labour in prison. (**e**) [1960s+] (*US/N.Z. drugs*) hard drugs, i.e. cocaine and heroin. **2** [mid-19C+] (*UK Und.*) coins (as opposed to notes). **3** [late 19C+] an erection [underpinned by HARD-ON *n.* (1)]. **4** [1960s+] a thug, a hoodlum [HARD CASE *n.* (2)].

(IN PHRASES)

❑ **give hard for soft** *v.* (*also* **give a bit of hard for a bit of soft**) [late 19C] of a man, to have sexual intercourse. ❑ **give soft for hard** *v.* [19C] of a woman, to have sexual intercourse. ❑ **on the hard** [1960s] of a penis, being erect.

hard *adj.* **1** [18C+] pertaining to cash, coins, change (as opposed to notes). **2** [19C+] tough, aggressive, violent. **3** [1900s] (*US*) of alcohol, strong. **4** [1930s+] (*orig. US black/teen*) on bad = good model, excellent, fashionable, admirable. **5** [1950s+] (*drugs*) of narcotics, usu. heroin. **6** [1980s+] (*US*) of clothing, in a tough style, rugged.

(IN COMPOUNDS)

❑ **hard-ass** *see* separate entries. ❑ **hard baby** *n.* [late 19C] (*US*) a thug, a rough, tough man. ❑ **hardback** *n.* [2000s] (*UK black*) a villain, a thug, a 'tough guy'. ❑ **hardball** *see* separate entries. ❑ **hard boy** *n.* [2000s] a thug. ❑ **hard case** *see* separate entries. ❑ **hard chaw** *n.* (*also* **hardjaw**) [SE *chaw*, chew] [20C+] (*Irish*) a tough person. ❑ **hard daddy** *n.* [DADDY *n.* (12)] [1960s+] (*orig. US prison*) a masculine, 'butch' lesbian. ❑ **hard dick** *n.* [DICK *n.*[1]] [1970s+] (*US*) a 'tough guy'. ❑ **hard guy** *n. see* separate entry. ❑ **hard horse** *n.* [early 19C–1920s] (*US*) a brutal, tyrannical person. ❑ **hardjaw** *n. see* HARD CHAW above. ❑ **hard knock** *n.* [SCHOOL OF HARD KNOCKS *n.*] [1980s] a tough, aggressive individual. ❑ **hard leg** *see* separate entries. ❑ **hard lot** *n.* [mid-19C–1900s] (*US*) a rough, aggressive individual. ❑ **hard mack** *n.* [MACK *n.*[2] (1)] [1970s+] a tough, aggressive, brutal pimp. ❑ **hard man** *n. see* separate entry. ❑ **hard morris** *n.* [? anecdotal; i.e. proper name *Morris* or SE *morris* (dancing), i.e. the 'dancing' around of a fighter] [1940s+] (*W.I.*) a tough fighter. ❑ **hard nut** *n. see* separate entry. ❑ **hardrocker** *n.* [HARD ROCK *n.*] [1970s+] (*US*) a thug, a tough person. ❑ **hard root** *n.* [1920s+] (*Irish*) a tough, devil-may-care individual. ❑ **hard stuff** *n. see* separate entry. ❑ **hard thomas** *n.* [? biblical doubting *Thomas*] [1950s] (*W.I.*) a stubborn man. ❑ **hard ticket** *n.* **1** [late 19C+] (*US*) a ruthless, uncompromising, tough person. **2** [20C+] (*US*) a difficult situation. **3** [1960s+] (*Irish*) a humorist, an eccentric.

SE in slang uses

(IN COMPOUNDS)

❑ **hard-back** *adj.* [the onset of back problems with advancing age] [20C+] (*W.I.*) **1** approaching middle-age or older. **2** used of one who ought to know better. ❑ **hard-baked** *adj.* **1** [mid-19C] (*orig. US*) stern, unrelenting. **2** [mid–late 19C] constipated. ❑ **hard bit** *n. see* separate entries. ❑ **hard body** *n.* [1980s+] (*US*) a physically trim, sexually attractive person. ❑ **hard-boiled** *adj. see* separate entry. ❑ **hard cheese** *n.* (*also* **hard Cheddar, hard fodder**) [late 19C+] bad luck; usu. as *hard cheese on… , hard cheese for…*; the phr. may well imply minimal or non-existent sympathy. ❑ **hardcore** *see* separate entries. ❑ **hard-cutting** *adj.* [var. on HARD-HITTING *adj.*] [1940s] (*US black*) extremely good, fashionable. ❑ **hard doer** *n.* [ext. of DOER *n.*[2] (2)] [20C+] (*Aus.*) **1** a character, an eccentric, one who never gives up despite any circumstances. **2** an amusing fellow, a 'good sport'. ❑ **hard drink** *n.* [late 16C–early 18C] stale, sour drink. ❑ **hard dumpling** *n.* [mid-19C] in boxing, a fist. ❑ **hard-ears** *see* separate entries. ❑ **hard-eye/eyes** *see* separate entries. ❑ **hard hair** *n.* [1950s+] (*US black/W.I.*) a black person's naturally kinky hair. ❑ **hard hat** *n.* **1** [1930s–40s] (*US*) a bowler hat. **2** [1940s+] (*US*) a construction worker. ❑ **hardhead** *n. see* separate entries. ❑ **hard-hitter/-hitting** *see* separate entries. ❑ **hard hustle** *n. see under* HUSTLE *n.* ❑ **hard john** *n.* [JOHN *n.*[1]] [1930s–40s] (*US black*) an FBI agent. ❑ **hard knocker** *n. see* HARD-HITTER *n.* ❑ **hard lines** *n. see* separate entry. ▫ **hard money** *n.* [pun on sense 2 above and SE *hard*, difficult] [1940s] (*US Und.*) counterfeit money. ▫ **hardmouth** *see* separate entries. ▫ **hard neck** *n.* [i.e. to be able to *STICK ONE'S NECK OUT under* NECK *n.* because it is so hard] [late 19C+] (*Irish*) **1** cheek, impudence. **2** an impudent person. ▫ **hard-nose/-nosed** *see* separate entries. ▫ **hard nut** *n. see* separate entry. ▫ **hard oil** *n.* [*hard oil*, any form of grease, used for lubrication, that will not flow; orig. used in WW1 for butter] [1910s–40s] (*US*) butter, margarine, lard. ▫ **hard-on** *see* separate entries. ▫ **hard one** *n. see* separate entries. ▫ **hard-pay man** *n.* [1950s] (*W.I.*) a bad debtor, through either his inability or his unwillingness to pay. ▫ **hard puncher** *n.* [such a cap identifies the wearer as a thug] [mid–late 19C] a fur cap typically worn by a London tough. ▫ **hard-pushed** *adj.* [mid-19C–1920s] in poor economic circumstances, in difficulties. ▫ **hard rock** *see* separate entries. ▫ **hard-shell** *see* separate entries. ▫ **hard shit** *n. see* HARD STUFF *n.* (3). ▫ **hard shot** *see* separate entries. ▫ **hard skull-fry** *n.* [the hot lye that is placed on the head to straighten one's hair] [1940s–50s] (*US black*) a straightened or 'processed' hairdo that is covered in hair-oil or cream. ▫ **hard sledding** *n. see* SLEDDING *n.* ▫ **hard spiel** *n. see under* SPIEL *n.* ▫ **hard tack** *n.* [TACK *n.*[1]] **1** [early 19C–1940s] inadequate rations [naval use *hard tack*, ship's biscuits, coarse food; SE *hard*, difficult/intoxicating]. **2** [1910s] (*Aus.*) hard work. **3** [1960s+] (*Irish*) spirits, as opposed to beer. ▫ **hard tail** *n.* **1** [1910s–80s] (*US*) a mule, thus adj. *hard-tailed*. **2** [1930s–70s] (*US*) an experienced man. ▫ **hard thing** *n. see* HARD SHOT *n.* ▫ **hard time/-timer** *see* separate entries. ▫ **hard times** *n.* [SE *hard times*, a period of poverty] [mid-19C–1950s] (*US*) a cheap, poor quality fabric, which resembles heavy wool but is not much better than cotton shoddy and used for the cheapest of clothes; thus *hard times party*, someone who wears worn-out or seedy clothes. ▫ **hard titty** *n. see TOUGH TITTY under* TITTY *n.* ▫ **hard-up** *see* separate entries. ▫ **hard washer** *n.* [1930s] (*US*) a strong alcoholic drink. ▫ **hard way** *n.* **1** [20C+] (*gambling*) the making of an even point in a dice game by throwing a pair rather than two separate numbers; thus in pool, the making of a pot through a difficult rather than easy shot; also in fig. use. **2** [1980s] (*UK prison*) a sentence served without remission. ▫ **hard word** *n. see* separate entry.

IN PHRASES

▫ **hard as lard** *adj.* [assonance] [1940s–60s] (*US black*) excellent, wonderful, as good as one could desire.

IN EXCLAMATIONS

▫ **hard scran!** *see under* SCRAN *n.*

hard *adv.* [note George Parker, *Life's Painter* (1789): 'He went off at the *fall* of the *leaf*, at *tuck 'em fair* — he died d—d hard, and was as *bad* as *brass*'] **1** [19C+] to a great extent, in a zealous manner. **2** [mid-19C–1920s] very, extremely. **3** [late 19C–1950s] in a painful, problematic manner, e.g. of a prison sentence. **4** [1980s+] (*US black*) in an aggressive, hostile manner; intensely [ext. of sense 2].

IN PHRASES

▫ **take it hard** *v.* [1930s+] (*US*) to react emotionally, usu. when distressed or angry.

hard-ass *n.* (*also* **hard-arse**) [HARD-ASS *v.*] **1** [1960s+] (*orig. US*) a tough person, a thug. **2** [1990s+] (*US*) an insensitive nature; a 'thick skin'.

IN PHRASES

▫ **give someone the hard ass** *v.* [1970s+] (*US*) to give someone a hard time.

hard-ass *adj.* (*also* **hard-arse, hard-arsed, hard-assed**) [HARD *adj.* (2) + -ASS *sfx*] **1** [late 19C; 1960s+] tough, no-nonsense, uncompromising. **2** [1960s+] mean, miserly.

hard-ass *v.* [one has, fig., a *hard* ASS *n.* (2)] [1940s+] (*US*) **1** to bully, to treat severely. **2** to endure, to tough it out.

hardball *n.*[1] [the hard balls used in professional baseball, as opposed to softball] [1970s+] (*US*) aggressive tactics.

IN PHRASES

▫ **play hardball** *v.* [1970s+] (*orig. US*) to act ruthlessly and single-mindedly in pursuit of a goal; thus *hardballer*, one who is ruthless and aggressive.

hardball *n.*[2] [HARD *adj.* (5) + SPEEDBALL *n.*[1]] [1980s+] (*US drugs*) **1** a mixture of heroin and cocaine. **2** crack cocaine.

hardball *adj.* [HARDBALL *n.*[1]] [1970s+] (*US*) aggressive, intimidatory.

hardball *v.* (*also* **hardball it**) [HARDBALL *n.*[1]] [1970s+] (*orig. US*) to act aggressively towards, to coerce or intimidate.

hard bit *n.*[1] [late 19C+] an erect penis.

hard bit *n.*[2] [SE *hard* + BIT *n.*[1] (3b)] [1960s+] (*US prison*) an unpleasant time in prison because of one's personality, or crime (which may alienate other prisoners), or inability to adapt etc.

hard-boiled *adj.* [HARD-BOILED EGG *n.*] [20C+] tough, mean, unpleasant.

SE in slang uses

IN COMPOUNDS

▫ **hard-boiled collar** *n.* [1920s–50s] a stiff, starched, detachable collar. ▫ **hard-boiled hat** *n.* (*also* **hard-boiled lid**) [1900s–60s] (*US*) a stiff hat. ▫ **hard-boiled shirt** *n.* [ext. of *BOILED SHIRT under* BOILED *adj.*] [1910s–30s] (*US*) a stiff, starched detachable shirt front.

hard-boiled egg *n.* [they 'can't be beat'; note P. Tamony on its origin in *American Speech* XII:4 Dec. (1937) 258–61] [late 19C–1960s] (*US*) a tough man, esp. a boxer.

hard case *n.* [HARD *adj.* (2) + CASE *n.*[1] (2b)] **1** [mid–late 19C] (*US*) a native of Oregon. **2** [mid-19C+] (*orig. US*) a tough, ruthless person. **3** [late 19C+] (*Aus./N.Z.*) a cheeky or amusing person. **4** [late 19C+] (*Aus./N.Z.*) a sexually available woman. **5** [20C+] (*Aus.*) an indefatigable person, who struggles on irrespective of any obstacle. **6** [1920s] an incorrigible hedonist.

hard-case *adj.* [HARD CASE *n.*] [1940s+] tough, ruthless.

hardcore *n.* **1** [1950s+] one who is considered the most serious, the most dedicated. **2** [1960s+] the strongest varieties of pornography, usu. featuring uncensored still or moving pictures of intercourse, plus such personal preferences as paedophile shots, bestiality, extreme sado-masochism etc.

hardcore *adj.* [HARDCORE *n.*] **1** [1960s+] (*orig. US*) a general term of approval, serious, experienced, committed, full-time; the implication is that the word, act or person thus qualified is the ultimate of the type. **2** [1970s+] pertaining to the more extreme forms of pornography. **3** [1980s+] substantial in quantity. **4** [1990s+] aggressive, criminal. **5** [1990s+] (*US teen*) true to what you believe. **6** [2000s] (*US campus*) of a test or examination, difficult.

hardcore *adv.* [2000s] (*US campus*) to a great extent, intensely.

hard-ears *n.* [HARD-EARS *adj.*] [late 19C+] (*W.I.*) disobedience.

hard-ears *adj.* [late 19C+] (*W.I.*) obstinate, stubborn.

hardegat *n.* [HARDEGAT *adj.*] [1950s+] (*S.Afr.*) an obstinate person.

hardegat *adj.* [Afk. *harde*, hard + GAT *n.*[2]] [1950s+] (*S.Afr.*) stubborn.

hard-eye *v.* [HARD EYES *n.*] [1980s] (*US*) to stare aggressively.

hard eyes *n.* [1950s+] (*US*) an unpleasant look, a disapproving stare.

hard guy *n.* (*also* **hard one**) [HARD *adj.* (2) + SE *guy*] **1** [1910s+] (*US*) a criminal character, a 'tough guy'. **2** [1980s+] (*US campus*) a difficult person.

hardhead *n.* [SE *hard-headed*; such a name does reinforce the white cliché that one can never knock out or hurt a black man by hitting him on his head because it is too solid to damage] **1** [mid-19C–1960s] (*US*) a white native of rural Tennessee or Kentucky. **2** [1930s+] (*US black*) a rebellious, non-conformist black person, a hot-tempered person. **3** [1940s+] (*US*) an extremely zealous person. **4** [1950s+] (*Aus.*) a villain, a criminal. **5** [1960s] (*US*) an instransigent, uncompromising person. **6** [1980s+] (*US*) a fool.

hard hit *n.* [rhy. sl. = SHIT *n.* (1b)] [1970s+] an act of defecation.

hard-hitter *n.* (*also* **hard-knocker**) [late 19C+] (*Aus./N.Z.*) a bowler hat.

hard-hitting *adj.* [ext. of HARD *adj.* (4)] [1940s] (*US black*) smart, fashionable.

hard labour *n.* [rhy. sl.] [20C+] a neighbour.

hard leg *n.* (*also* **hard legs**) [HARD *adj.* (2) + SE *leg*] (*US black*) **1** [1940s+] a tough man or boy. **2** [1940s+] a man who devotes all his time and energies to pursuing the street life and the world of strictly male endeavour – pimping, hustling etc. **3** [1960s+] an ugly woman, esp. an old, worn-out prostitute.

hard-leg *adj.* [HARD LEG *n.*] (*US black*) **1** [1940s+] of a male, tough, aggressive. **2** [1940s+] devoted to pursuing the street life and the world of strictly male endeavour – pimping, hustling etc. **3** [1960s+] of a woman, ugly, esp. of an old, worn-out prostitute.

hard lines *n.* (*also* **tough lines**) [? biblical use of *lines* as one's 'lot in life', i.e. Ps. 16:6: 'The lines are fallen unto me in pleasant places; yea, I have a goodly heritage'] [early 19C+] bad luck, misfortune; thus *easy lines*, good fortune.

hard man *n.* [HARD *adj.* (2) + SE *man*] **1** [20C+] one who has a high opinion of his own powers, usu. physical. **2** [1930s+] a thug, a professionally violent person. **3** [1960s+] (*Irish*) a term of affection.

hardmouth *n.* [20C+] (*W.I.*) one who argues and resists when it is time to repay a loan or to pay a bill.

hardmouth *v.* [1960s+] to attack verbally, to slander.

hard-nose *n.* [HARD-NOSED *adj.*] **1** [1930s+] (*orig. US*) a mean, unpleasant person; thus *get the hard-nose*, to become angry or irritated. **2** [1960s+] (*Aus.*) an indefatigable person, who will struggle on no matter what the odds. **3** [1970s] a cautious gambler who neither wins nor loses large amounts.

hard-nose *v.* [HARD-NOSED *adj.*] [1950s+] to become angry with someone, to get nasty.

hard-nosed *adj.* (*also* **hard-nose**) (*orig. US*) **1** [1920s+] stubborn, tough, uncompromising. **2** [1970s+] common-sense, sensible, e.g. *hard-nosed practicalities*.

hard nut *n.* [abbr. phr. *hard nut to crack*] [late 19C+] **1** (*also* **hard knut, hard log**) a tough person, a dangerous enemy, anything difficult to achieve; thus *hardnutted*, tough, ruthless. **2** an incorrigible person.

hardo *n.* [HARD *adj.* (2) + -O *sfx* (2)] [2000s] a 'tough guy'.

hard-on *n.* **1** [late 19C+] an erection. **2** [1940s+] passionate, lustful feelings. **3** [1940s+] an obsession, usu. hostile, aggressive feelings towards. **4** [1940s+] (*US*) a bad temper, irrespective of gender. **5** [1950s+] (*US*) used as a term of address, usu. sarcastic and referring to someone's high self-esteem. **6** [1960s+] (*US*) a despicable individual, a tough, aggressive person. **7** [1960s+] in fig. use, positive feelings. **8** [1980s+] (*US*) a difficult task.

IN PHRASES

❑ **die with a hard-on** *v. see under* DIE *v.* ❑ **get a hard-on** *v.* **1** [late 19C+] to have an erection. **2** [1940s] (*US Und.*) to draw a pistol. **3** [1960s] to desire someone. ❑ **have a hard-on for** *v.* [1980s+] to dislike (intensely).

hard-on *adj.* [HARD-ON *n.*] **1** [late 19C+] sexually aroused. **2** [1950s+] tough, aggressive.

hard one *n.*[1] [1920s] (*US tramp*) a dollar.

hard one *n.*[2] [SE *hard*, intoxicating liquor] [1930s] a strong drink.

hard-pan *n.* [SE *hardpan*, hard compacted soil or subsoil] [mid-19C–1950s] the most basic part of something; thus *get down to hard-pan*, to get down to basics, to come down to fundamentals.

hard-pan *adj.* [HARD-PAN *n.*] [late 19C–1900s] (*US*) fundamental, conservative.

hard rock *n.* [1910s+] (*US black*) a tough person, both emotionally and physically.

hardrock *adj.* [HARD ROCK *n.*] (*US*) **1** [1910s+] (*also* **hardrocks**) craggy, physically tough. **2** [1960s+] a general term of approval.

hard-rock hotel *n.* (*also* **hard-rock city**) [the stones from which it is built + ? the rocks that prisoners are made to break] [1930s–70s] (*US*) a prison.

hard-shell *n.* [SE *hard* + *shell*, having a hard shell, e.g. a clam, a crab] **1** [mid-19C–1930s] (*US*) a member of the primitive Baptist Church; thus *softshell*, Baptists who are less severely fundamentalist. **2** [mid-19C–1970s] (*US*) an uncompromising conservative person.

hard-shell *adj.* [HARD-SHELL *n.*] [mid-19C+] **1** (*US*) pertaining to Baptists, of the primitive Baptist Church. **2** (*orig. US*) uncompromising, fundamentalist, unswervingly conservative.

hard shot *n.* (*also* **hard thing**) [HARD CASE *n.*] [late 19C+] (*Aus./N.Z.*) **1** a tough but still witty and amusing daredevil. **2** a sexually available woman.

hard shot *adj.* [HARD SHOT *n.*] [late 19C+] (*Aus./N.Z.*) **1** tough, uncompromising, incorrigible. **2** of a woman, sexually available.

hard stuff *n.* [HARD *adj.* (1) + STUFF *n.*] **1** [late 18C–1940s] money in the form of coins, as opposed to notes. **2** [mid-19C+] spirits, as opposed to beer. **3** [1950s+] (*drugs*) (*also* **hard shit**) drugs like narcotics, rather than tranquillizers, cannabis etc.

IN PHRASES

❑ **hit the hard stuff** *v.* [1950s+] to drink (spirits rather than beer or wine).

hard time *n.* [SE *hard* + TIME *n.* (1)] [20C+] (*orig. UK Und.*) **1** a long or severe prison sentence. **2** having trouble serving a sentence, suffering while in jail (whether from the regime or from self-inflicted problems). **3** on the railways, third class.

IN PHRASES

❑ **give someone a hard time** *v.* [1950s+] (*US*) to harass.

hard-time *adj.* [1990s+] (*US prison*) aggressive, menacing.

hard time *v.* [1960s–70s] to give someone a hard time, to irritate them or scold them.

hard-timer *n.* [HARD TIME *n.*] [20C+] **1** a prisoner. **2** a prisoner who suffers in prison (whether from the regime or from self-inflicted problems).

hard-up *n.*[1] [the collectors/smokers are HARD-UP *adj.*] [mid-19C–1930s] **1** tobacco that is made of broken up cigar stumps or cigarette ends. **2** a collector of cigar or cigarette ends which are dried and sold as tobacco to the very poor. **3** a cigarette or cigar end.

hard-up *n.*[2] [HARD-UP *adj.* (1)] [mid-19C–1960s] an impoverished person.

hard-up *n.*[3] [var. of HARD-ON *n.* (1)] [late 19C+] an erection.

hard-up *adj.* **1** [19C+] impoverished; thus *hardupness*, *hardup(p)ishness*, poverty. **2** [late 19C] drunk. **3** [late 19C+] in fig. use, at a loss, desperate, in need of something. **4** [20C+] (*W.I.*) unable to attract a steady partner. **5** [1930s+] (*US*) in need of sexual gratification, sexually frustrated [note HARD-UP *n.*[3]].

hardware *n.* **1** [early 19C–1960s] strong liquor, whisky. **2** [mid-19C] (*US Und.*) counterfeit coins. **3** [mid-19C–1960s] (*US*) coins, cash. **4** [mid-19C+] (*orig. UK Und.*) guns, ammunition, safe-cracking equipment and other 'tools of the trade'. **5** [1930s–50s] jewellery. **6** [1990s+] (*drugs*) isobutyl nitrite.

SE in slang uses

IN COMPOUNDS

❑ **hardware shop** *n.* (*also* **hardware store**) [pun on HARD *n.* (3) + SE *shop*/SHOP *n.*[1] (1)] [1950s+] a male homosexual brothel.

hard word *n.* **1** [mid-19C–1910s] (*Anglo-Irish*) a tip-off, a warning; thus *give someone the hard word*, to warn. **2** [1910s] (*Aus.*) an outrageous request.

IN PHRASES

❑ **put the hard word on** *v.* [1910s+] (*orig. Aus./N.Z.*) **1** to make demands (esp. financial or sexual) of someone. **2** to interrogate, to question.

hare *n.* [a poss. link to the dial. *puss*, a hare, and CAT *n.*[1] (1a) + play on SE (*pubic*) *hair*] [mid-16C–mid-19C] a prostitute; a promiscuous woman.

IN COMPOUNDS

❑ **hare-finder** *n.* [play on SE *hare-finder*, a man whose job it is to find hares] [late 16C–mid-18C] a womanizer, a lecher.

IN PHRASES

❑ **swallow a hare** *v. see under* SWALLOW *v.*

hare and hound *n.* [rhy. sl.] [20C+] a round or order of drinks.

haricot *n.*[1] [SE *haricot bean*, i.e. ext. of BEAN *n.*[1] (2a)] [late 19C+] the penis.

haricot *n.*^{2} [rhy. sl.; *haricot bean* = QUEEN *n.* (2)] [1960s+] (*Aus.*) a male homosexual.

harker *n.* [SE *hark*, to listen] [mid–late 19C] (*US*) an ear.

hark-ye *v.* (*also* **harking**) [the image is of drawing one's target to one side and whispering a request for a loan] [late 17C–early 19C] to borrow money.

Harlem *adj.* [proper name *Harlem*, the centre of New York City's black community] [late 19C+] (*US*) used in derog. senses to emphasize the negative stereotypes of African-Americans as lazy, larcenous, stupid, vulgar etc; in combs. below.

(IN COMPOUNDS)

❑ **Harlem credit-card** *n.* [1950s+] (*US*) a piece of hose used to siphon petrol from another car into the tank of one's own. ❑ **Harlem sunset** *n.* [the stereotyped use of razors in black-on-black fights] [1940s; 2000s] (*US*) blood pouring from razor slashes. ❑ **Harlem taxi** *n.* [1960s] (*US police*) a large, fin-tailed, brightly coloured car. ❑ **Harlem toothpick** *n.* [1930s–40s] (*US black*) a knife.

harlequin *n.* [SE *Harlequin*, a character in English pantomime who wears parti-coloured, bespangled tights; the shininess, and thus the colours reflected in it] [late 19C] (*orig. theatre*) a sovereign.

harlot *n.*

(IN PHRASES)

❑ **demure as a harlot at a christening** *see* DEMURE AS A WHORE AT A CHRISTENING *under* WHORE *n.*

harman *n.* (*also* **beck-harman, harman-beck, harminbeck**) [ety. unknown; ? *OED* suggests elision of SE *hard-man*; *DSUE* prefers *ha-man*, i.e. one who shouts *ha!*, stop; ult. dial. *har*, stop! + SE *beck*, beak] **1** [mid-16C–19C] (*UK Und.*) a constable. **2** [late 17C–19C] a beadle. **3** [mid-19C] a sheriff.

harmans *n.* (*also* **harmin, hartmans**) [fig. use of HARMAN *n.* or ? SE *hard* + -MANS *sfx*, thus lit. a 'hard state of being'] [mid-16C–mid-19C] (*UK Und.*) the stocks.

Harmony hair spray *n.* [the brandname of the popular hair spray] [1970s+] the act of ejaculating into a woman's hair.

Harmy *n.* [rhy. sl.] [late 19C–1900s] (*Aus.*) the Salvation Army.

harness *n.* **1** [early 17C+] (*US*) clothes, esp. a uniform; thus *Sunday harness*, one's best clothes. **2** [mid-19C] (*UK Und.*) a watchman, a constable, a policeman. **3** [1920s–40s] the settings that hold jewels, e.g. a gold ring surrounding a diamond.

(IN COMPOUNDS)

❑ **harness bull** *n.* (*also* **harness boy, ...cop, ...gent, ...guy, ...man**) [SE *harness*, i.e. the Sam Browne belt some forces in the US favour + BULL *n.*^{5} (1)] [20C+] (*US Und.*) a uniformed police officer.

(IN PHRASES)

❑ **harness up** *v.* [1900s–20s] (*US*) to get dressed. ❑ **in harness** [working horse imagery] [mid-19C+] employed, in work; incl. working for a pimp.

Harold *n. see* LLOYD *n.*

Harold Holt *n.* [rhy. sl.; ult. Aus. Prime Minister *Harold Holt* (1908–67), who died in mysterious circumstances, apparently drowned in the Bass Strait] [1970s+] (*Aus.*) **1** salt. **2** a bolt, an act of absconding; thus *do a Harold Holt*, to abscond.

Harold Lloyd *n. see* LLOYD *n.*

Harold Macmillan *n.* [rhy. sl.; ult. UK Prime Minister *Harold Macmillan* (1894–1986)] [1960s+] a villain.

Harold Pinter *n.* [rhy. sl.; ult. UK dramatist *Harold Pinter* (b.1930)] [1980s+] a splinter.

harolds *n.* [rhy. sl.; *Harry Taggs* = BAGS *n.*^{2}] [20C+] (*Aus.*) **1** trousers. **2** knickers.

harp *n.*^{1} [the reverse of an Irish coin once pictured Hibernia and her harp, the 'national instrument' of Ireland] **1** [late 18C–mid-19C] a woman. **2** [late 18C+] (*Irish*) the 'tail' (reverse side) of coin; thus a halfpenny. **3** [late 19C+] (*US*) an Irish person.

SE in slang uses

(IN PHRASES)

❑ **play the harp** *v.* (*also* **play a harp**) [the harp-playing angels of heaven] [late 19C+] to die.

harp *n.*^{2} [abbr. SE *Jew's harp*] **1** [late 19C+] (*orig. US*) a harmonica, a mouth organ. **2** [1930s–40s] (*US*) a vibraharp or vibraphone.

harp *adj.* [HARP *n.*^{1}] [1970s] (*US*) Irish.

harp and fiddle *n.* [rhy. sl. = PIDDLE *n.* (2)] [1950s] (*Aus.*) an act of urination.

harper *n.* [the Irish coin has a harp on it] [late 16C–17C] a penny.

harpic *adj.* [the eponymous lavatory cleaner, which uses the advertising slogan 'clean around the bend'; thus pun on *ROUND THE BEND under* ROUND THE... *phr.*] [1930s+] crazy, insane.

harpoon *n.* **1** [late 19C–1950s] (*US*) ridicule or victimization. **2** [20C+] the penis. **3** [1930s–60s] a hypodermic syringe, as used by drug addicts.

(IN PHRASES)

❑ **get the harpoon** *v. see GET THE SPEAR under* SPEAR *n.* ❑ **throw the harpoon in(to)** *v.* (*US*) **1** [late 19C–1900s] to persuade, to trick, to attack. **2** [1960s+] to have sexual intercourse (with). **3** [1960s+] to flirt with.

harpoon *v.* [HARPOON *n.*] [mid-19C+] (*US*) to ridicule, to criticize, to victimize.

harp six *adv.* [the *harp* engraved on the reverse of Irish coins] [20C+] (*Ulster*) head-over-heels; esp. as *go down harp six*, to fall head-over-heels.

harpy *n.* [SE *harpy*, 'A fabulous monster, rapacious and filthy, having a woman's face and body and a bird's wings and claws, and supposed to act as a minister of divine vengeance' (*OED*); in Homer the Harpies personified hurricanes and whirlwinds] [1940s+] (*US black*) an old woman.

Harriet Lane *n.* [proper name *Harriet Lane*, the victim and wife of the murderer Henry Wainwright, executed 1875; coincidentally the US Harriet Lane, launched 1857, was commanded by one Jonathan Wainwright, who was killed on board her during the US Civil War; the ship, however, was named for the niece of President James Buchanan] [late 19C–1920s] Australian chopped meat.

Harrington *n.* [Sir John *Harrington* (1561–1612) obtained a patent from James I to mint farthings] [early–mid-17C] a farthing.

Harris *adj.* (*also* **Harriet**) [initial letter] [2000s] (*S.Afr. gay*) of a man, hirsute, hairy.

Harris Tweed *n.* [rhy. sl. = WEED *n.*^{3} (2)] [1950s] a weakling.

harry *n.*^{1} [proper name, used as a generic] [early 18C–1950s] a countryman, a peasant.

harry *n.*^{2} (*also* **Harry Jones**) [initial letters; also note heroin is a 'masculine' drug, see BOY *n.*^{2} (4a)] [1930s+] (*drugs*) heroin.

harry *n.*^{3} [ety. unknown] [1970s] (*S.Afr.*) a glass or bottle.

harry *v.* [echoic] [1960s] (*US campus*) to vomit.

harry bluff *n.* [rhy. sl.] [mid–late 19C] snuff.

Harry Common *n.* [generic use of proper name *Harry* + SE *common*] [late 17C–18C] a womanizer.

Harry Dash *n.* [rhy. sl. = FLASH *n.*^{1} (5c)] [2000s] a glimpse.

Harry Dash *adj.* [rhy. sl. = FLASH *adj.* (1a)] [1990s+] showy, ostentatious.

Harry —-ers *phr.* [? HARRY FREEMAN'S *n.* + 'Oxford' -ER *sfx*; note 19C Cantab. *harry sophs*, students who kept all terms required to become Bachelor of Law, f. *harisophs*, a corruption of Gk *herisophos*, erudite] [1940s+] a verbal style, orig. in services, affected in 1950s by society and formerly widespread although now mainly obs., in which various words are prefixed by *Harry* and suffixed by *-ers*, e.g. *Harry flakers*, tired out; *Harry crashers*, asleep etc.

Harry Fat *n. see* FAT *n.* (2).

harry freeman's *n. see* FREEMAN'S *n.*

harry-harry *n.* [ety. unknown] [1940s+] (*W.I.*) rum.

Harry High Pants *n.* [2000s] (*Aus.*) an unsophisticated man, usu. identifiable due to the high waist of his trousers.

Harry Holt *n.* [rhy. sl = BOLT *n.*^{1} (1)] [1980s+] (*Aus. prison*) an escape.

harry huggins *n.* [rhy. sl. = MUGGINS *n.*^{1} (1)] [20C+] a fool, an idiot.

Harry James *n.* [puns on the trumpet played by US bandleader *Harry James* (1916–83)] **1** [1950s] the nose. **2** [1970s] (*US prison*) the brand of *Bugler* smoking tobacco.

Harry Jones *n.* see HARRY *n.*[2].

Harry Lauder *n.* [rhy. sl.; ult. the Scot. music-hall star *Harry Lauder* (1870–1950)] [20C+] a prison warder.

Harry Lime *n.* [rhy. sl.; ult. *Harry Lime*, the anti-hero of the film *The Third Man* (1949)] [1950s+] time (of day).

harry monk *n.* [rhy. sl. = SPUNK *n.* (5)] [2000s] semen.

harry nash *n.* [rhy. sl.] [20C+] cash.

Harry Randall *n.* [rhy. sl.; ult. the music-hall comedian *Harry Randall* (1860–1932)] [20C+] **1** handle. **2** candle.

Harry Ronce *n.* see CHARLIE RONCE *n.*

Harry's hideaway *n.* [1980s+] (*Aus. prison*) isolation cell.

Harry Tate *n.* [rhy. sl.; ult. *Harry Tate* (1872–1940); note also WW1 milit. use *Harry Tate's Cavalry*, the Yeomanry (cf. FRED KARNO'S ARMY *n.*), *Harry Tate's Navy*, the Royal Naval Volunteer Reserve, the Fleet Auxiliary and the Motor Boat Reserve] **1** [1910s+] (*bingo*) the number eight. **2** [1910s+] a plate. **3** [1920s+] a state of nerves. **4** [1950s+] in pl., Player's Weights cigarettes.

Harry Tate *adj.* [rhy. sl.; ult. *see* HARRY TATE *n.*] [20C+] **1** late. **2** incompetent, disorderly, amateur [= SE *in a state*].

harry, tom and dick *adj.* [rhy. sl.] [20C+] sick.

Harry Wragg *n.* [rhy. sl. = FAG *n.*[4] (2); ult. *Harry Wragg*, the jockey and trainer whose career peaked in the 1930s] [1930s–70s] a cigarette.

harsh *adj.* **1** [1970s+] (*US campus/teen*) very unpleasant, exceptionally rude, ill-mannered, extremely bad. **2** [1980s+] (*US drugs*) used of marijuana that, whether through strength or dryness, makes one cough.

harsh *v.* [HARSH *adj.*] **1** [1970s+] (*US campus*) to mistreat, to be very unfair towards; thus *harsh me out!* that's very unfair! **2** [1990s+] (*US*) to ruin, to damage.

IN PHRASES

❑ **harsh on** *v.* [1980s+] (*US campus*) to criticize, to belittle.

hartmans *n.* see HARMANS *n.*

harvest *v.* **1** [late 19C–1900s] to guard, to watch over. **2** [1920s–30s] (*US Und.*) to arrest a group of criminals.

harvest buzzard *n.* see *under* BUZZARD *n.*

harvest moon *n.* [rhy. sl. = COON *n.* (5)] [20C+] a derog. term for a black person.

Harvey Drew *n.* [rhy. sl. = SE *spew*] [1990s+] (*Aus.*) vomit.

Harvey Nichol *n.* (*also* **harvey**) [rhy. sl. = colloq. *pickle*; ult. the store in Knightsbridge, London SW3] [1930s–70s] a problem, a difficult situation; thus personified as a man or woman who acts in a stupid or naïve fashion; sometimes abbr. as *Harve*.

Harvey Nichols *n.* [rhy. sl.; ult. *see* prev.] [20C+] pickles, condiments.

harvy *n.* [abbr.] [mid-19C] (*US campus*) a Harvard student.

has-beens *n.* [rhy. sl.] [20C+] (*mainly UK prison*) greens, vegetables.

hasbian *n.* [SE *has been* + *lesbian*] [2000s] (*US gay*) a woman who used to be a lesbian but is now heterosexual.

hash *n.*[1] [SE *hash*, a mess or jumble] [mid-19C+] food or a meal, often of reheated left-overs.

IN COMPOUNDS

❑ **hash-burner** *n.* [1940s] (*US*) a cook. ❑ **hash factory** *n.* (*also* **hash bazaar, ...emporium, ...foundry**) [late 19C–1940s] (*Aus./N.Z./US*) a cheap café or restaurant, a 'greasy spoon'; a boarding house. ❑ **hash hook** *n.* [1910s–20s] (*US*) a fork. ❑ **hash hotel** *n.* see HASH-HOUSE *n.* ❑ **hash-hound** *n.* [-HOUND *sfx*] [1910s–40s] (*US*) anyone notably keen on their food, a glutton. ❑ **hash-house** *n.* *see* separate entry. ❑ **hash job** *n.* [i.e. chopped up for *hash*] [1950s] (*US*) a knifing, a razoring. ❑ **hash joint** *n.* *see* HASH-HOUSE *n.* ❑ **hash-juggling** *n.* [1900s–10s] (*Aus.*) working as a waiter/waitress. ❑ **hash-man** *n.* [late 19C] (*US*) a restaurant owner. ❑ **hash-slinger** *n.* *see* separate entry. ❑ **hash-trap** *n.* [SE *trap*/TRAP *n.*[1] (4)] [1940s+] (*US*) the mouth.

IN PHRASES

❑ **chop no hash** [1900s] (*US*) a phr. meaning something makes no impression or is of no importance. ❑ **settle the hash** *v.* **1** [19C+] (*also* **cook the hash, fix the/someone's..., settle someone's gruel, ...hash**) to deal with someone who has wronged you, to take revenge. **2** [early–mid-19C] to deal with a situation. **3** [mid-19C+] (*also* **settle one's hash**) to resolve one's difficulties. ❑ **wrestle one's hash** *v.* [mid–late 19C] (*US*) to dine.

hash *n.*[2] [abbr.] [1940s+] (*drugs*) *hash*ish.

IN COMPOUNDS

❑ **hash-bash** *n.* [BASH *n.*[1] (4)] [1990s+] (*drugs*) an evening spent sitting around smoking hashish. ❑ **hash-cake** *n.* [20C+] a cake of any sort into the ingredients of which hashish has been mixed; such cakes, thanks to the cooking process, render the hashish a good deal more potent than simply smoking it. ❑ **hash-head** *n.* [-HEAD *sfx* (4)] [1950s+] (*US*) a habitual user of hashish. ❑ **hash-monster** *n.* [-MONSTER *sfx*] [1980s+] (*US drugs*) a crumb of hashish burned on the point of a pin; the smoke is trapped in a container and then inhaled through a straw. ❑ **hashover** *n.* [play on the drinkers' *hangover*] [1960s+] the after-effects of an evening's heavy indulgence in smoking hashish. ❑ **hash-rat** *n.* [2000s] a smoker of hashish.

IN PHRASES

❑ **black hash** *n.* [opium is black; thus darkening the usu. khaki-coloured hashish] [1980s+] (*drugs*) dark hashish, often the result of its being mixed with opium during its manufacture.

hash *n.*[3] *see* HESH *n.*

hash *v.*[1] [HASH *n.*[1]] [late 19C+] **1** to work as a waiter/waitress in a café. **2** to provide, to serve up.

hash *v.*[2] *see* FLASH THE HASH *under* FLASH *v.*[1].

Hashbury *n.* [HASH *n.*[2] + *Haight-Ashbury*] [1960s–70s] (*US*) the Haight-Ashbury area of San Francisco.

hashed out *adj.* [HASH *n.*[2]] [1970s] heavily intoxicated by smoking hashish.

hasher *n.* (*also* **hashee**) [HASH *n.*[1]] [late 19C+] (*Aus./US*) a waiter or waitress.

hash girl *n.* (*also* **hesh girl**) [? Zulu *héshe*, swooping onto, or *heshe*, a hawk] [1970s+] (*S.Afr.*) a woman who frequents shebeens (drinking clubs) to rob the male patrons.

hash-house *n.* (*also* **hashery, hash joint, ...hotel**) [HASH *n.*[1] + SE *house*] (*US/Aus.*) **1** [mid-19C+] a cheap café or restaurant. **2** [late 19C–1930s] a boarding house, a cheap hotel.

IN COMPOUNDS

❑ **hash-house Greek** *n.* [GREEK *n.*; such jargon included *slaughter in the pan*, beefsteak; *red mike with a bunch o' violets*, corned beef and cabbage; *two of a kind*, fishballs; and *sheeny funeral with two on horseback*, roast pork and boiled potatoes] [20C+] (*US*) the jargon of US fast-food restaurants and cafés.

hashmagandy *n.* [? SE *salmagundi*, a dish composed of chopped meat, anchovies, eggs, onions with oil and condiments; ? HASH *n.*[1]] [late 19C–1940s] (*Aus./N.Z.*) a basic stew, served on sheep stations and in the army.

hash-slinger *n.* [HASH *n.*[1] + SLINGER *n.* (1)] [mid-19C+] (*US*) **1** (*also* **hash-hoister**) a short-order cook or waiter/waitress; thus adj., *hash-slinging*. **2** a college student waiter in a mountain resort hotel.

hashy *n.* [HASH *n.*[2] + *-y*] [1940s] (*UK drugs*) hashish.

IN COMPOUNDS

❑ **hashy fag** *n.* [FAG *n.*[4] (2)] [1940s] (*UK drugs*) a cigarette blending tobacco and hashish.

hasie *n.* [Afk. *haas*, hare] [1960s+] (*S.Afr.*) a male homosexual.

hasikara *n.* [? Hind. *hasiikar*, ludicrous, ridiculous] [20C+] (*W.I.*) a noise, a commotion; thus *make hasikara*, to cause an argument, to make trouble, to make a noise.

hassle *n.* (*also* **hass, hassel**) [? Cumbrian dial. *hassle*, to hack or cut at with a blunt edge, using a sawing motion] [1940s+] (*orig. US*) a dispute, a quarrel, a problem, a nuisance, anything requiring irritating effort.

hassle *v.*[1] [HASSLE *n.*] **1** [1950s+] (*orig. US*) to annoy, to nag, to pressurize; thus n. *hassling*, nagging. **2** [1950s+] (*US*) to quarrel.

IN PHRASES

❑ **hassle with** *v.* (*also* **hassle out**) [1960s+] (*US*) **1** to sort something out through discussion, to argue. **2** to worry about, to be bothered with.

hassle *v.*[2] [HASSLE *v.*[1] (1)] **1** [1960s] to sell. **2** *see* HUSTLE *v.* (3).

hasta *phr.* [Sp. *hasta la vista*, see you later; ? popularized by the use of 'Hasta la vista' (usu. after an act of extreme violence) by film star Arnold Schwarzenegger in *Terminator 2* (1991)] [1980s+] (*US campus*) goodbye, see you later.

hasta la bye-bye *phr.* [Sp. *hasta la vista* + SE *bye-bye*] [1980s+] (*US*) see you later.

hasta la pasta *phr.* [play on Sp. *hasta la vista*] [1980s+] (*US campus*) see you later, goodbye.

haste! *excl.* [1950s+] (*Aus.*) stop it! look out!

haste it up! *excl.* [1940s] (*Aus.*) shut up! hurry up and finish – what you're saying is boring!

hasty banana *phr.* [a play on Sp. *hasta mañana*] [1940s+] (*US*) goodbye.

hasty pudding *n.*[1] [pun; the couple have been 'hasty', the child is the 'pudding'] [mid–late 17C] a bastard, an illegitimate child.

hasty pudding *n.*[2] [SE *hasty pudding*, a pudding made of flour stirred into boiling milk or water to the consistency of a thick batter] [late 18C–19C] a muddy road.

hat *n.* [all things that are 'put on'] **1** [mid-18C–mid-19C] the vagina [also abbr. OLD HAT *n.*; it too is 'frequently felt' (Grose, 1796)]. **2** [early 19C–1900s] a prostitute. **3** [late 19C+] (*US*) a general term for sexual intercourse. **4** [1940s–50s] (*US prison*) a male homosexual. **5** [1940s–60s] (*US black*) a woman, esp. a wife or sweetheart; thus *wear a hat*, to be married or have a girlfriend. **6** [1980s+] (*US*) a contraceptive sheath [note Yid. *Schmeckeldecke*, a condom, lit. 'cock ceiling']. **7** [1970s] (*US*) the head. **8** [1990s+] (*US*) hair. **9** [1990s+] (*US campus*) a fraternity member [the fashion of wearing baseball caps].

SE in slang uses

IN COMPOUNDS

❑ **hat job** *n. see* HEADJOB *under* HEAD *n.* ❑ **hat-making** *n.* [mid-19C] (*UK Und.*) stealing hats. ❑ **hat-peg** *n.* (*also* **hat holder**) [that which one 'hangs' one's hat on] [mid-19C; 1940s–60s] (*later use US black*) the head. ❑ **hat-rack** *n.* **1** [20C+] (*Aus./US*) a scraggy animal, usu. a horse. **2** [1920s–60s] the head. ❑ **hat time** *n.* [note prison farm jargon *hat time*, the moment when the captain takes off his hat and waves it to signal the end of the chain gang's working day] [1970s] (*US black*) the end of a day's work, thus used as synon. for *goodbye*. ❑ **hat-tree** *n.* [1980s] (*S.Afr. gang*) one who is wearing any form of headgear.

IN PHRASES

❑ **dress a hat** *v. see under* DRESS *v.* ❑ **get one's hat** *v.* (*also* **check one's hat, grab a hat, make one's hat**) **1** [1940s+] (*US black*) to leave, esp. to leave quickly. **2** [1950s] (*US prison*) to be released. ❑ **hat up** *v.* [one puts on one's hat] [1970s+] (*US black*) to leave, to exit. ❑ **have one's hat nailed to the ceiling** *v.* [the excitement so produced] [1910s–30s] (*US*) to be fellated. ❑ **have one's little hat on** *v.* [18C] to be drunk. ❑ **in the hat** [2000s] (*US prison*) targeted for death. ❑ **knock someone's hat off** *v.* [1940s+] to astonish, to amaze. ❑ **make one's hat** *v. see* GET ONE'S HAT above. ❑ **put a hat on someone** *v.* (*also* **hang a hat on someone**) **1** [mid-19C–1900s] (*UK Und.*) to beat someone, to put them in their place. **2** [1970s+] (*US black*) to dislike someone intensely. **3** [1970s+] (*US black*) to single someone out for revenge. **4** [1990s+] to inform against, to betray. ❑ **ring someone's hat** *v. see* RING SOMEONE'S BELL *under* BELL *n.*[1]. ❑ **talk through one's hat** *v. see under* TALK *v.* ❑ **under one's hat** *adj.* (*also* **under one's bonnet, ...the hat**) [late 19C+] (*US*) secret. ❑ **up in one's hat** *adj.* **1** [late 19C] drunk. **2** [1920s] (*Irish*) elated. ❑ **up to the hat** *adj.* [1900s] (*US*) full, of food and/or alcohol. ❑ **where did you get that hat?** [late 19C–1910s] (*orig. US*) a general jeer or shout of derision.

IN EXCLAMATIONS

❑ **get hat!** [1970s] (*US black*) go away! ❑ **hat up!** [1970s] (*US black*) go away! ❑ **in your hat!** [1930s–50s] a dismissive retort. ❑ **my sainted hat!** *see* MY AUNT! *under* AUNT *n.*

hat *v.* [HATTER *n.*[1]] [mid-19C+] (*Aus.*) to live by oneself in a remote area.

hat and coat *n.* [rhy. sl.] [20C+] a boat, esp. a refrigerated cargo ship.

hat and feather *n.* [rhy. sl.] [20C+] weather.

hat and scarf *n.* [rhy. sl.] [20C+] a bath.

hatch *n.*[1] (*US*) **1** [20C+] a psychiatric institution; thus HATCH UP *v.* **2** [1900s–30s] (*also* **hatch house**) a prison.

hatch *n.*[2] [1920s+] (*US, orig. naut.*) the throat or mouth.

IN PHRASES

❑ **down the hatch!** (*also* **d.h.**) [1920s+] (*orig. naut.*) a popular toast before taking a drink.

hatchet *n.* **1** [mid-19C+] (*US*) the female genitals. **2** [late 19C–1930s] an ugly or debauched woman. **3** *see* HATCHET MAN below.

SE in slang uses

IN COMPOUNDS

❑ **hatchet job** *n.* **1** [1940s+] (*orig. US*) a particularly vicious piece of criticism, slanderous gossip etc. **2** [1970s] (*US campus*) a broken date. ❑ **hatchet man** *n.* (*also* **hatchet**) [SE *hatchet man*, a Chinese assassin, who uses a hatchet] [1940s+] (*orig. US Und.*) **1** a man who is used to punish, or even murder, selected victims on the orders of his boss; also in fig. use. **2** anyone who takes on, or is told to take on, unpleasant tasks, such as, in a company, firing members of staff, broaching distasteful but necessary topics etc. **3** a person who is willing to perform a HATCHET JOB above in support of a cause or political party. ❑ **hatchet thrower** *n.* [Hispanic 'Indians' were equated with Native Americans] [1930s–40s] (*US black*) a derog. term for a Spanish-speaking man living in Harlem.

IN PHRASES

❑ **throw the hatchet** *v.* (*also* **fling the hatchet, sling...**) [mid-19C] to tell lies, to exaggerate.

hatchi *n.* [? SE *hatch*] [1960s+] (*lesbian*) the vagina.

hatch up *v.* [HATCH *n.*[1] (1)] [1970s] to commit to a psychiatric institution.

hatchway *n.* (*orig. naut.*) **1** [early–mid-19C] the mouth. **2** [mid–late 19C] the vagina.

hate, the *n.* [1990s+] (*US campus*) something unpleasant.

SE in slang uses

IN PHRASES

❑ **get a hate on** *v.* [1960s] (*US*) to become extremely angry. ❑ **have a hate on** *v.* [1940s+] (*Aus./US*) to dislike intensely.

hate on *v.* [1990s+] to do something bad to somebody else.

hater *n.* **1** [1990s+] (*US gang*) an informer. **2** *see* PLAYER-HATER *under* PLAYER *n.*

hate someone's guts *v. see under* GUT *n.*

hatstand *n.* [1930s] (*US*) the head.

hatter *n.*[1] [? mining jargon *hatter*, a miner who works independently rather than in a partnership, but note ...A HATTER *under* MAD AS... *adj.*] [mid-19C+] (*Aus.*) an eccentric individual, esp. one who lives and works alone; occas. of an animal.

hatter *n.*[2] *see* BROWN-HATTER *n.*

haul *n.* **1** [late 18C+] (*orig. US*) a large amount of loot or profit. **2** [mid-19C+] (*US*) a robbery. **3** [late 19C–1930s] (*also* **haul-in**) a round-up of suspects, criminals.

haul *v.* [fig. use of SE *haul*, to pull with violence; note colloq. phr. *haul over the coals*] **1** [late 17C–mid-18C] to pester, to irritate. **2** [late 19C–1910s] to call to account, to bring up for a reprimand. **3** [1970s] to beat.

SE in slang uses

IN COMPOUNDS

❑ **haul-cly** *n.* [CLY *n.* (2)] [18C] a pickpocket; pickpocketing; thus *haul a cly*, to pick a pocket. ❑ **haul-devil** *n.* [mid-19C–1900s] a clergyman.

IN PHRASES

❑ **get one's ashes hauled** *v.* (*also* **get one's rocks hauled**) [? mispron. of ARSE *n.*/ASS *n.*] [late 19C+] to have sexual intercourse. ❑ **haul ankles/arse** *v. see* HAUL ASS *v.* ❑ **haul ashes** *v.* [euph. for HAUL ASS *v.* (1)] [1930s] to leave, to run off. ❑ **haul ass** *v. see* separate entry. ❑ **haul bottom** *v. see* HAUL ASS *v.* ❑ **haul buggy** *v.* [euph. for HAUL ASS *v.*] **1** [1970s+] to leave, to escape, to run off. **2** [1990s+] to increase one's efforts, to work harder. ❑ **haul buns/butt** *v. see* HAUL ASS *v.* ❑ **haul feet** *v. see* HAUL ASS *v.* ❑ **haul freight** *v.* [late 19C+] a euph. for HAUL ASS *v.* ❑ **haul hindparts/hiney/hips** *v. see* HAUL ASS *v.* ❑ **haul in** *v.* (*also* **haul**) [1910s+] (*US*) to arrest; thus n. *haul-in*, a raid. ❑ **haul leg** *v. see* HAUL ASS *v.* ❑ **haul one's ashes** *v.* (*also* **shake ones ashes**) [*GET ONE'S ASHES HAULED* above] [1920s+] (*US*) to have sexual intercourse; to give sexual pleasure; thus *ash-haul job*, an act of intercourse. ❑ **haul oneself** *v.* (*also* **haul one's ass, ...cookies, ...tail, ...skin**) [SE *haul* + ASS *n.* (2)/TAIL *n.* (2)/SE *skin*] **1** [20C+] (*W.I.*) to leave, esp. as imper., *haul yourself!* get the hell out! **2** [1940s+] (*also* **haul it**) to move. ❑ **haul plug** *v. see* HAUL ASS *v.* ❑ **haul the mail** *v.* (*also* **tote the mail**) [the image of the indomitable US mailman] [20C+] (*US*) to go or run fast. ❑ **haul up** *see* separate entries.

haul! *excl.* (*also* **haul it!**) [20C+] (*US/W.I.; orig. naut.*) go away! get out!

haul and pull *adj.* [HAUL AND PULL *v.*] [20C+] (*W.I.*) messy, confused, upset.

haul and pull *v.* [20C+] (*W.I.*) to upset, to make a mess of, to confuse.

haul ass *v.* (*also* **haul, haul ankles, ...arse, ...bottom, ...buns, ...butt, ...feet, ...hindparts, ...hiney, ...hips, ...leg, ...plug**) [SE *haul* + ASS *n.* (2)/ARSE *n.* (1)/BUNS *n.* (1)/BUTT *n.*[1] (1a)/HEINIE *n.* (1)] **1** [1910s+] (*orig. US*) to leave, to escape, to run off; as excl. *haul ass!* let's go! hurry up! get out of here! **2** [1960s+] (*orig. US*) to move fast, to rush. **3** [1970s+] (*US*) to increase one's efforts, to work harder. **4** [1990s+] (*US*) to be extremely successful.

haul-up *adj.* [the position of one's arms and shoulders, huddled against the pain or cold] [20C+] (*W.I.*) unhealthy-looking, sick-looking.

haul up *v.*[1] [early 19C+] to round-up wrong-doers, usu. suspects or criminals.

haul up *v.*[2] [1940s–50s] to run off.

havage *n.* [southwest dial. *havage*, a lineage, a family tree] [early–mid-19C] a family or group of criminals.

hava-hava! *excl. see* HUBBA HUBBA! *excl.*

have *n.* [HAVE *v.* (3)] (*Aus.*) **1** [late 19C–1900s] a swindle, a hoax. **2** [20C+] a disappointment.

have *v.* **1** [16C+] to seduce, usu. a woman; to have sexual intercourse, both heterosexual and homosexual. **2** [late 16C+] (*also* **have it**) to have received punishment. **3** [19C+] (*also* **have on**) to deceive, to trick, to cheat. **4** [early 19C+] to capture; to arrest. **5** [early 19C+] to place in a situation from which there is no escape. **6** [mid-19C+] (*UK Und.*) to recognize. **7** [mid-19C+] to understand, to see through a deception. **8** [late 19C+] to harm, to beat, to punish. **9** [20C+] to be killed, to be injured. **10** [20C+] to rob. **11** [1990s+] (*orig. US black*) to protect [abbr. *HAVE SOMEONE'S BACK under* BACK *n.*[1]]. **12** [1990s+] to have something covered.

IN PHRASES

❑ **have...** *v. see also under* relevant n. or adj. ❑ **have a beat** *v. see under* BEAT OFF *v.* ❑ **have a berry** *v. see* BROWN BERRY *n.* ❑ **have across** *v.* [2000s] of a man, to have sexual intercourse. ❑ **have off** *v.* [1930s+] (*orig. US black*) **1** to berate, to attack verbally. **2** to attack, to beat up. **3** in fig. use, to defeat. **4** *see* HAVE (IT) OFF *v.* ❑ **have on** *v. see* HAVE *v.* (3). ❑ **have someone in** *v.* [1940s+] (*orig. US*) to swindle, to cheat, to deceive. ❑ **let someone have it** *v.* [mid-19C+] (*orig. US*) **1** to hit, to kill, esp. with gunfire. **2** to challenge, to pose a difficult question, to reprimand severely, to criticize. **3** in fig. use, to do something energetically.

SE in slang uses

IN COMPOUNDS

❑ **have-to** *n.* [1950s+] (*US*) anything inescapable, esp. something that is forced upon one by social convention; thus *have-to wedding*, a wedding that is arranged after the putative bride is found to be pregnant.

IN PHRASES

❑ **have...** *v. see also under* relevant n. or adj. ❑ **have again** *v.* [20C+] (*W.I., Gren.*) to have as much as one desires. ❑ **have been around** *v. see* separate entry. ❑ **have going** *v. see* GET GOING *v.* ❑ **have had enough** *v.* [mid-18C+] drunk, e.g. *you've had enough*. ❑ **have had it** *v. see* separate entry. ❑ **have hot balls** *v. see* EYEBALL *n.*[2]. ❑ **have it...** *v. see* separate entries. ❑ **have one's** *v. see GET ONE'S under* GET *v.* ❑ **have oneself** *v.* **1** [1920s+] to indulge oneself, to provide for oneself; usu. in phrs., e.g. *have oneself a good time*, *have oneself some fun*; often as *HAVE ONESELF A TIME under* TIME *n.* **2** [1970s+] (*US gay*) to be excited. **3** [1980s+] (*US black*) to masturbate. ❑ **have only fifty cards in one's deck** *v. see* NOT PLAYING WITH A FULL DECK *phr.* ❑ **have someone on** *v. see* separate entries.

have a cook *v.* [rhy. sl., but note ety. of COOK *n.*[2]] [20C+] to have a look.

have been around *v.* **1** [1920s+] to be experienced in life. **2** [1950s+] to be experienced sexually; if used of a woman, usu. derog.

have had it *v.* **1** [19C+] to have been seduced. **2** [1930s+] to have failed, to have broken down, collapsed, died; often ext. with *in a big way*. **3** [1930s+] to be in trouble; esp. in the minatory phr. *you've had it*, you're in serious trouble. **4** [1940s+] (*orig. N.Z.*) (*also* **have had**) constr. with *with*, to have finished with, to have had a surfeit of, to be tired of or bored with, to have lost one's patience.

IN PHRASES

❑ **have had it up to here** *v.* [1940s+] to be exasperated, to have lost all one's patience; usu. accompanied by a gesture indicating how far up the body one has 'had it'.

have it *v.* [IT *n.*[1]; note music-hall song 'A Little of What You Fancy ...': 'I always hold with having it if you fancy it,/If you fancy it, that's understood .../'Coz a little of what you fancy does you good'] **1** [late 17C+] (*also* **have one**) to have sexual intercourse. **2** [mid-19C+] to have a fight. **3** [1960s+] to be brave. **4** *see* HAVE *v.* (2).

have it all on *v.* [1900s] to achieve fully.

have it away *v.* (*also* **have it, have it away on one's toes, take it on one's toes**) [1950s+] **1** to escape, usu. from prison or impending arrest. **2** to walk, to leave, to exit. **3** to go to, to visit.

have it away (with) *v.*[1] [1920s+] to steal an object.

have it away (with) *v.*[2] [1960s+] to have sexual intercourse; sometimes ext. as *have it away together*.

have it for *v.* [1930s–60s] (*US*) to be in love with.

have it in *v.* [late 19C+] to have sexual intercourse.

have (it) off *v.* (*also* **get it off**) **1** [mid-19C+] (*UK Und.*) to carry out a successful crime. **2** [1930s+] to be successful in any area, but in a specific task. **3** [1950s+] (*UK Und.*) of police, to make a successful raid and arrest.

have it off *v.* [HAVE *v.* (1)] [1930s+] to copulate.

have it on someone *v.* (*also* **have it all over someone**) [20C+] (*Aus./US*) to have someone at a disadvantage; to feel superior towards.

have it up *v.* [late 19C+] to have sexual intercourse.

haverel *n.* (*also* **haveril**) [synon. dial. *haverel*; ult. SE *haver*] [20C+] (*Irish*) an ignorant man, a slatternly woman.

have someone on *v.*[1] [mid-19C+] to tease, to hoax, to engage someone's attention with the longer term intention of deceiving them; thus to swindle, to cheat.

have someone on *v.*[2] [dial.] (*Aus./N.Z.*) **1** [1940s–60s] to accept sexually. **2** [1940s+] to prepare oneself to fight, to accept a challenge. **3** [1950s+] to attack physically.

havey cavey *adj.* (*also* **havy cavy**) [dial.] [late 18C–early 19C] **1** higgledy-piggledy, confused, doubtful; thus *on the havey-cavey*, questioning, doubting. **2** drunken.

havidge *n.* [? dial. *havage*, parentage, lineage, ext. to give image of a collection of criminals] [early 19C] a criminal slum; a gathering of criminals.

havil *n.* [ety. unknown; dial. *havil*, a small crab] [early 18C–mid-19C] (*UK Und.*) a sheep.

Hawaii *n.* (*also* **Hawaiian**) [TV series *Hawaii Five-O*] [1990s+] £50.

Hawaiian *n.* [1970s+] (*drugs*) marijuana grown in and exported from Hawaii.

Hawaiian *adj.*

proper name in slang uses

IN COMPOUNDS

❑ **Hawaiian disease** *n.* [1980s+] **1** the lack of female company. **2** (*gay*) being homosexual, i.e. the lack of women [from sense 1 above, but also Hawaii's large homosexual population]. ❑ **Hawaiian eye** *n.* [play on the eponymous 1960s television programme but note -EYE *sfx*] [1970s+] (*gay*) the anus. ❑ **Hawaiian sunshine** *n.* [1970s+] (*drugs*) LSD.

Hawaii 5-0 *n. see* FIVE-OH *n.*

hawbuck *n.* [? SE *haw*, hedge + *buck*, a man] [19C] a country bumpkin, a lout.

Hawcubite *n.* (*also* **Hawkubite**) [? SE *hack about*; but note Brewer, *Dict. of Phrase and Fable* (1894): 'The succession of these London pests after the Restoration was...The Muns, the Tityre-Tus, the Hectors, the Scourers, the Nickers, then the Hawkubites (1711–14), and then the Mohocks – most dreaded of all. (Hawkubite is the name of an Indian tribe of savages)'] [early 18C] one of a band of dissolute young men infesting the streets of London at this period; a street-bully, a ruffian.

haw-haw toff *n.* (*also* **haw-haw, haw-haw fellow**) [his 'haw-haw' laugh + TOFF *n.* (2)] [mid-19C–1920s] a dandy, an aristocrat.

IN PHRASES

❑ **bit of haw-haw** *n.* [late 19C–1900s] a fop, a dandy.

hawk *n.*[1] **1** [late 17C–19C] a cardsharp, a confidence trickster ['pouncing upon [their victims] mercilessly' (Bee)]. **2** [late 18C+] a bailiff, a constable, a police officer; thus excl. *ware hawk*, a cry of warning. **3** [late 19C+] (*Irish*) any person; often as *QUEER HAWK under* QUEER *adj.* **4** [20C+] (*US black*) a prison officer. **5** [1930s+] (*US black*) chilly winter winds, esp. as experienced in northern cities; usu. as *the hawk*. **6** [1940s+] (*US prison*) one who looks out for the arrival of authorities, e.g. a prison inmate, a carnival worker. **7** [1960s] (*US campus*) an unattractive woman. **8** [1960s] (*US campus*) a very hard worker. **9** [1960s+] (*US*) a person, esp. in public office, government or business, who advocates an aggressive policy. **10** [1960s+] (*S.Afr.*) a 'masculine' male homosexual. **11** [1970s] (*US gay*) a lesbian who picks women up in the street. **12** [1970s+] (*S.Afr./US*) an older male homosexual with a preference for young boys. **13** [1970s+] (*US*) a robber or mugger.

hawk *n.*[2] [1960s–70s] (*drugs*) **1** LSD. **2** an LSD user. **3** an LSD seller.

hawk *adj.* [HAWK *n.*[1]] [1960s+] politically aggressive; also fig.

hawk *v.* **1** [mid-19C–1900s] to act as a decoy, esp. for a card-sharper or a cheapjack. **2** [late 19C–1900s] to pounce upon, to capture, esp. of a criminal seizing upon a victim. **3** [late 19C+] (*US black*) (*also* **hack**) to keep a suspicious and close watch on. **4** [late 19C+] (*US*) to pilfer, to steal. **5** [1960s] (*US campus*) to work hard. **6** [1960s–70s] to walk quickly. **7** [1960s+] (*orig. US black*) to participate in an athletic activity for fun. **8** [1970s+] (*UK black*) to greet, to speak to. **9** [1990s+] to stare someone down. **10** [1990s+] to beg a favour.

IN PHRASES

❑ **hawk off** *v.* [16C–18C SE *hawk after* (*for*): to hunt after, to endeavour to catch] [late 19C] to carry away, to arrest.

SE, meaning to sell, in slang uses

IN PHRASES

❑ **hawk it** *v.* [late 19C+] to work as a street prostitute. ❑ **hawk one's brawn** *v.* [SE *brawn*, a form of potted pork] [1970s+] **1** (*Aus.*) to work as a prostitute. **2** (*UK Und.*) to work as a male prostitute. ❑ **hawk one's brown** *v. see under* BROWN *n.* ❑ **hawk one's brownie** *v. see under* BROWNIE *n.*[1]. ❑ **hawk one's fork** *v. see under* FORK *n.*[1]. ❑ **hawk one's greens** *v. see under* GREENS *n.*[1]. ❑ **hawk one's meat** *v. see under* MEAT *n.* ❑ **hawk one's mutton** *v. see under* MUTTON *n.* ❑ **hawk one's pearly** *v.* [rhy. sl.; *pearly king* = RING *n.* (1a)] [1970s+] to act in a promiscuous manner, to offer one's body for sexual enjoyment.

hawker *n.* [SE *hawk*, to spit, to cough up] [1970s+] (*US*) a gob of expectorated phlegm.

hawker *v.* [HAWKER *n.*] [1970s+] (*US*) to cough up phlegm.

Hawkesbury duck *n.* [SE *Hawkesbury duck*, an ear of maize or a corncob with the kernels intact, which road gang convicts used to steal from fields when hungry] [1980s] (*Aus.*) little or nothing to eat.

Hawkesbury rivers *n.* (*also* **Hawkesburies**) [rhy. sl.] [1940s+] (*Aus.*) the cold shivers.

hawkeye *n.*[1] [mid-19C+] (*US*) a native or inhabitant of Iowa, popularly called the *Hawk-eye State*.

hawkeye *n.*[2] [1980s+] (*Aus. prison*) a prison officer.

hawkeye *v.* [1970s] (*US black*) to keep watch.

Hawkins *n.*[1] [the 'hanging judge' Sir Frederic *Hawkins*] [late 19C–1900s] a severe disciplinarian.

Hawkins *n.*[2] (*also* **'Awkins**) [the line by music-hall star Albert Chevalier (1862–1923): 'And 'Enery 'Awkins is a first-class name'] [late 19C–1900s] a superior costermonger.

Hawkins *n.*[3] (*also* **Mister Hawkins**) [HAWK *n.*[1] (5)] [1930s+] (*US black*) very cold weather.

hawks *n.* [mid-19C] an advantage.

hawkshaw *n.* [*Hawkshaw the Detective* created by Henry Cecil Bullivant in such books as *The Ticket-of-Leave Man* (1935), itself taken f. *The Ticket-of-Leave Man* (1863), a play by the English dramatist Tom Taylor (1817–1880); also in the comic strip *Hawkshaw the Detective* by the American cartoonist Gus Mager (d.1956)] [20C+] (*US/W.I.*) a detective.

hawkshaw *v.* [HAWKSHAW *n.*] [1940s] to investigate, as a police officer.

Hawkubite *n. see* HAWCUBITE *n.*

haw maws *n.* [rhy. sl. = *baws*, i.e. BALLS *n.* (1)] [1960s–70s] (*Scot.*) the testicles.

hay *n.* **1** [20C+] a bed; also in the context of a place for sexual intercourse; thus *great in the hay*, an above-average sexual performer [the use of hay for stuffing mattresses]. **2** [1920s+] as a metaphor for insignificance. (**a**) a small sum of money; usu. in phr. *that ain't hay*, remarking on a substantial sum. (**b**) in fig. use, something worthy of notice. **3** [1930s+] as something smokeable [note Kipling 'The Taking of Lungtungpen' (1880): ''Tis no good [...] fillin' my pouch wid your chooped hay. Canteen baccy's like the Army. It shpoils a man's taste for moilder things']. (**a**) (*US*) tobacco; cigarettes. (**b**) (*US drugs*) marijuana.

IN COMPOUNDS

❑ **hay butt** *n.* [BUTT *n.*[1] (2b)] [1940s+] (*drugs*) a marijuana cigarette. ❑ **hayhead** *n.* [-HEAD *sfx* (4)] [1940s–70s] (*US*) a smoker of marijuana.

IN PHRASES

❑ **bale of hay** *n.* [1960s] a stock of money. ❑ **hit the hay** *v.* (*also* **go to the hay, hit the haystack, ...slats, hunt the hay**) **1** [20C+] to go to bed; thus *in the hay*, asleep. **2** [1900s–20s] (*also* **beat the hay**) to sleep. **3** [1940s+] to have sexual intercourse, to 'go to bed with'. **4** [1950s+] (*drugs*) to smoke marijuana. ❑ **that ain't hay** (*also* **that isn't hay, that ain't/isn't peanuts, ...chopped liver, there ain't no persimmons**) [the perceived insignificance of the various items] [1930s+] (*US*) a phr. used to mean that something is a large and/or significant amount.

SE in slang uses

IN COMPOUNDS

❑ **hayband** *n.* [SE *hay*, the supposed content + the cigar-band] [mid-19C] a second-rate cigar. ❑ **hay burner** *n. see* separate entries. ❑ **hay eater** *n.* [? derog. ref. to white farmers] [late 19C–1930s] (*US black*) a white person. ❑ **hayfoot** *n.* (*also* **strawfoot**) [the placing of a piece of hay and one of straw in the right and left boots so that otherwise ignorant farmboys could learn the difference] [late 19C–1950s] (*US*) a farmer; also as a term of derision, a peasant, a rustic. ▫ **hay-footed** *adj.* [late 19C–1950s] (*US*) rustic, unsophisticated. ▫ **hay-kicker** *n.* see HAYMAKER *n.*[1] (2). ▫ **haymaker** *n.* see separate entries. ▫ **hay motor** *n.* see HAY BURNER *n.*[1]. ▫ **hayneck** *n.* see HAYSEED *n.* ▫ **haypile** *n.* [1900s–30s] (*US*) a bed or mattress. ▫ **hay-pitcher** *n.* [late 19C–1940s] (*US*) a farmer, a peasant. ▫ **hay-pounder** *n.* (*also* **hay-shagger, hay-shaker**) [20C+] (*Aus./N.Z./US*) a farmer, a simple peasant. ▫ **hay rube** *n.* see RUBE *n.*[1]. ▫ **hayseed** see separate entries. ▫ **hay-tosser** *n.* [early 17C; 1900s–10s] (*US*) a farmer.

Hay (and) Hell and Booligal *n.* [*Booligal*, a town in western New South Wales] [late 19C+] (*Aus.*) a mythical place that is beyond all the bounds of civilization and devoid of any proper comforts.

haybag *n.* [US milit. jargon *haybag*, a camp-follower] [mid-19C+] (*US*) a fat old woman, often a slovenly drunkard; thus ext. as *old haybag*; also as v.

hay burner *n.*[1] (*also* **hay motor**) [the animal's food] **1** [20C+] (*Aus./US*) a horse. **2** [1900s–20s] a cheap automobile. **3** [1940s] (*US*) a Western film.

hay burner *n.*[2] [HAY *n.* (3)] **1** [1920s–40s] (*US*) a tobacco pipe. **2** [1930s+] (*US*) a smoker of marijuana.

haym *n.* see HAIM *n.*

haymaker *n.*[1] **1** [mid-19C–1920s] (*US*) (*also* **old haymaker**) the sun. **2** [mid-19C–1950s] (*US*) (*also* **hay-kicker**) a farmer, a rustic; thus a term of abuse.

haymaker *n.*[2] [the image of a man swinging a scythe to cut hay] **1** [20C+] a swinging, roundhouse punch, which counts more on energy and ire than on skill and direction; thus adj., *haymaking*. **2** [1950s+] in fig. use, a 'knockout blow'.

Haymarket hector *n.* [proper name *Haymarket*, a centre of London prostitution + HECTOR *n.*] [19C] a pimp.

Haymarket ware *n.* [London's Haymarket, a centre of 19C prostitution] [late 19C] prostitutes in general.

Hays *n.* [*Hays*, the name of a High Constable at the time] [mid-19C] used as a warning among thieves, meaning that they should run away.

hayseed *n.* (*also* **grass-seed, hayneck, hayseeder**) [naut. phr. *he hasn't got the hayseed out of his hair*] [mid-19C+] a farmer, a simple peasant, a novice.

hayseed *adj.* (*also* **hayseedy**) [HAYSEED *n.*] [mid-19C+] (*Aus./US*) rustic, unsophisticated.

haystack *n.*[1] [rhy. sl.] [20C+] the *back* of a building etc.

haystack *n.*[2]

SE in slang uses

IN PHRASES

▫ **hit the haystack** *v.* see *HIT THE HAY under* HAY *n.*

haystack game *n.* [1900s] (*US Und.*) a card game played on an unsophisticated level.

hazard-drum *n.* [SE *hazard*, a gambling game + DRUM *n.*[3] (3)] [mid-19C] a casino, a gambling house.

haze *n.* [abbr. *PURPLE HAZE under* PURPLE *adj.* + its effect] **1** [1970s+] (*drugs*) LSD. **2** [1990s+] (*drugs*) a kind of marijuana.

hazel *n.*[1] [its colour; note WITCH-HAZEL *n.*] [1940s+] (*drugs*) heroin.

hazel *n.*[2] [2000s] (*S.Afr. gay*) male homosexual sex.

hazel-gild *v.* (*also* **hazel-geld**) [B.E. has sp. *hazel-geld*, but this may be a printer's error] [late 17C–early 19C] to beat with a hazel rod.

hazel-nuts *n.* [mid-19C] (*UK Und.*) copper coins.

hazel oil *n.* see *OIL OF HAZEL under* OIL OF... *n.*

hazer *n.* [1920s] (*UK Und.*) one who distracts the police and passers-by in the aftermath of a smash-and-grab raid; thus v. *haze*, to distract.

hazy *adj.* **1** [early 19C–1910s] tipsy, drunk. **2** [1950s] under the influence of a drug.

h.b. *n.* see HIGHBALL *n.*[1].

h.b.i. *n.* [abbr.] [mid-19C+] (*UK Und.*) *h*ouse *b*reaking *i*mplements.

H caps *n.* [H *n.* (2) + CAP *n.*[4] (1)] [1960s+] (*drugs*) heroin.

h.d. *n.* [abbr. *h*usband *d*ependent] [1980s+] (*US campus*) a man who lives off a woman.

he *n.* (*also* **him**) [the dating is almost random, as Partridge says, this personification is 'prob. almost immemorial'] **1** [late 16C; 20C+] the penis. **2** [1960s] (*US gay*) (*also* **he-bitch**) used by lesbians in the same way as male homosexuals refer to each other as 'she'.

Heab *n.* see HEBE *n.*

head *n.* **1** [19C+] a lavatory, a privy [naut. jargon *head* or *heads*, the ship's lavatory, which was orig. sited at the 'head' of a ship, near the bowsprit]. **2** in the context of the mouth and/or face. (**a**) [mid-19C–1920s] a postage stamp [the monarch's head appears on all UK stamps]. (**b**) [mid-19C+] (*US*) the mouth; in phrs. below. (**c**) [1930s+] (*also* **head play**) oral intercourse, usu. fellatio, but also cunnilingus. (**d**) [1960s+] (*US*) facial appearance, usu. constr. with 'bad', e.g. *she's got great tits, but that's a bad head.* **3** with ref. to drugs. (**a**) [mid-19C; 1950s+] (*orig. US drugs*) the regular user of any kind of drug; orig. of alcohol. (**b**) [1950s+] a drug-induced state. (**c**) [1960s+] a state of mind, other than drug-influenced. (**d**) [1980s+] (*Aus. prison*) high-grade marijuana. (**e**) [2000s] (*UK black*) a cannabis cigarette. **4** in senses of a painful head. (**a**) [late 19C+] a hangover, e.g. *I've got an awful head this morning.* (**b**) [1940s] a sickness resulting from contaminated homemade alcohol. **5** in senses of a tough or aggressive individual [HARDHEAD *n.*]. (**a**) [late 19C+] a professional gambler. (**b**) [20C+] a long-term prisoner. (**c**) [1910s–20s] (*Aus.*) a person in authority. (**d**) [1980s] (*US black*) a belligerent, aggressive person. **6** with ref. to the penis. (**a**) [late 19C+] the end of the penis. (**b**) [1950s+] (*US*) the erect penis. **7** [1900s–30s] (*UK Und.*) a thief. **8** [1920s–30s] (*US Und.*) an illegal immigrant [? such immigrants were counted as 'heads']. **9** with ref. to a young woman. (*US*) (**a**) [1930s+] a young woman. (**b**) [1970s+] a sexually appealing young woman. **10** [1930s+] a user, a performer. **11** [1930s+] (*US*) a person. **12** [1970s+] (*US campus*) beer. **13** [1980s+] (*US black*) a white person, seen as a potential victim of street crime. **14** [1990s+] (*Irish*) as a form of address as in *Howaya head?*

IN COMPOUNDS

▫ **head artist** *n.* [1970s] (*US*) a fellator or fellatrix. ▫ **head cheese** *n.* [its odour and its appearance near the *head* of the penis] [1940s+] smegma. ▫ **head drugs** *n.* [they affect the head (though so do all drugs)] [1960s+] (*drugs*) amphetamines. ▫ **head gasket** *n.* [1960s+] (*US*) a condom. ▫ **head-hunter** *n.* [1970s+] (*US*) one who performs oral sex, esp. in exchange for drugs. ▫ **head job** *n.* [nominalization of -HEAD *sfx* (4)] [2000s] (*N.Z.*) a fool. ▫ **headjob** *n.* (*also* **hat job**) [JOB *n.*[2] (2); SE *hat* plays on the idea of the mouth 'putting a hat' on the penis] [1960s+] (*orig. US*) an act of oral intercourse, usu. fellatio. ▫ **head jockey** *n.* [1950s+] a man who performs cunnilingus. ▫ **head play** *n.* see sense 2c above. ▫ **head queen** *n.* [-QUEEN *sfx* (3)] [1940s–70s] (*US gay*) a male homosexual who frequents public toilets in search of sex. ▫ **head-set** *n.* [var. on SE *mind-set*] [1970s+] (*US*) a state of mind, a mood. ▫ **head shop** *n.* **1** [1960s+] (*orig. US*) a shop specializing in drug paraphernalia [the first such emporium was San Francisco's Psychedelic Shop, opened in Jan. 1966]. **2** [1980s] (*US*) a pornographic bookshop. ▫ **head-worker** *n.* [1910s+] (*US gay*) a fellator.

IN PHRASES

▫ **get head** *v.* [1990s+] to receive oral sex, thus to be fellated. ▫ **give head** *v.* (*orig. US*) **1** [1950s+] to perform oral sex, usu. to fellate. **2** [1960s+] to give flattering comments, usu. with sexual innuendo. ▫ **have a head on** *v.* [late 19C–1950s] to have a hangover. ▫ **keep one's head shut** *v.* [1900s–50s] to be quiet. ▫ **open one's head** *v.* [late 19C–1910s] (*US*) to open one's mouth, to speak (indiscreetly or excessively). ▫ **run one's head** *v.* [var. on *RUN ONE'S MOUTH under* MOUTH *n.*] [1970s+] (*US*) to talk at length or out of turn; thus *head-running*, talking to excess. ▫ **shoot one's head** *v.* [1910s–30s] **1** to complain, to make a fuss, to argue. **2** to talk, esp. boastfully. ▫ **shut one's head** *v.* (*also* **shut one's neck, shut up one's head**) [mid-19C+] (*US*) to be quiet; usu. as imper. *shut your head!/ shut your neck!*

SE in slang uses

based on SE *head*, the chief or senior figure

IN COMPOUNDS

❑ **head-beetler** *n.* [SE *beetle*, any implement used in a variety of industrial processes for crushing, bruising, beating, flattening or smoothing] [mid–late 19C] **1** 'the bully of the workshop, who lords it over his fellow-workmen by reason of superior strength, skill in fighting &c' (Hotten, 1864). **2** a foreman. ❑ **head buck-cat** *n.* [Irish *buc*, he-goat] [1960s–70s] (*Irish*) a person in authority. ❑ **head bummaroo** *n.* (*also* **head bummer**) [? BUMPER *n.*[2] (3)] [mid-19C–1940s] the chief, the person in charge. ❑ **head cheese** *n. see* BIG CHEESE *n.* ❑ **head chick** *n.* [CHICK *n.*[1] (2)] **1** [1930s–40s] (*US black*) a female lover, a favourite girlfriend; one's wife; esp. an expert fellatrix. **2** [1950s–60s] the top prostitute in a pimp's 'stable'. ❑ **head cock** *n.* [1970s] (*US*) the person in charge. ❑ **head hen** *n.* [1930s–50s] (*US black*) a landlady. ❑ **head knock** *n.* [the image of the deity 'knocking' and summoning one to heaven/hell] [1940s–50s] (*US black*) **1** God, Jesus. **2** an important, outstanding person.

IN PHRASES

❑ **head bully of the pass** *n.* (*also* **head bully of the passage bank, head cully of the pass, head cully of the passage bank**) [BULLY *n.*[1] (2) + PASS-BANK *n.*] [late 17C–early 19C] a gang boss or top criminal who levies a tax on all games of chance in the area of which he is in control. ❑ **head cook and bottle-washer** *n. see* CHIEF COOK AND BOTTLE-WASHER *n.* ❑ **head nigger in charge** *n.* (*also* **big nigger in charge, black..., boss..., head negro (in charge)**) [the implication being that, given institutional racism, the authority lies in the title not in the actual job; according to Darryl Pinckney (*New York Review of Books*, Dec. 1995), coined to describe the authoritarian black rights campaigner Booker T. Washington (1856–1915)] [20C+] (*US black*) a sarcastic ref. to any black authority figure.

general uses

IN COMPOUNDS

❑ **headache/-acher** *see* separate entries. ❑ **headbang/banger/banging** *see* separate entries. ❑ **headbeater/beating** *see* separate entries. ❑ **headbin** *n.* [var. on HEADCASE *n.* (1)] [20C+] (*Ulster*) an unstable person, an eccentric. ❑ **headbone** *n.* [1930s+] (*US black*) the skull. ❑ **headbreaker/buster** *n. see* HEADBEATER *n.* ❑ **headbusting** *adj. see* HEADBEATING *adj.* ❑ **headcase** *n. see* separate entry. ❑ **head doctor** *n.* **1** [1950s+] (*US*) (*also* **head doc**) a psychiatrist, a psychotherapist. **2** [2000s] (*drugs*) a drug dealer. ❑ **head-feeler** *n.* [1940s] (*US*) a psychotherapist. ❑ **headfuck/fucker** *see* separate entries. ❑ **head game** *n.* [1970s+] (*orig. US*) psychological trickery and manipulation, usu. hostile or negative in intent; usu. in pl. ❑ **head hunt/hunter** *see* separate entries. ❑ **headkicker** *n.* [1990s+] (*Aus.*) a person in authority who is aggressive. ❑ **head knocker** *n.* (*US*) **1** [late 19C+] a boss. **2** [1960s+] a thug, a violent person. **3** [1960s+] a brutal police officer. ❑ **head-knocking** *adj.* [1960s+] (*US*) violent. ❑ **headlamps** *n.* (*also* **searchlights**) **1** [mid–late 19C] the eyes. **2** [1950s+] (*US*) spectacles. **3** [1960s+] the female breasts. ❑ **headlight** *see* separate entries. ❑ **headpiece** *n. see* separate entries. ❑ **head rails** *n.* (*also* **muzzle rails, nob rails**) [Grose cites it as a 'sea phrase'] [mid-18C–1930s] the teeth. ❑ **head robber** *n.* **1** [mid-19C] a butler [SE *head*, chief + *robber*, used by those with a low opinion of servants]. **2** [late 19C] a boxer, a prize-fighter [he 'takes your head away']. ❑ **headshot** *n.* [1990s+] (*US black teen*) **1** a shot to the head from any firearm. **2** in rap music, freestyle rapping. ❑ **head-shrinker** *n. see under* SHRINK *n.*[1]. ❑ **head smack** *see* separate entries. ❑ **headsman's daughter** *n.* [early 19C] the guillotine. ❑ **headstaggers** *n.* [SE *staggers*, a disease of horses and sheep] [20C+] (*Irish*) mental illness or instability. ❑ **head-top** *n.* [1970s–80s] (*UK black*) the hair. ❑ **head-topper** *n.* [mid–late 19C] a wig. ❑ **headtrip/-tripper** *see* separate entries. ❑ **headwhipper** *n.* [WHIP *v.*[3] (2)] [1950s+] (*US black*) a police officer. ❑ **headwrecker** *n.* (*also* **headwreck**) [1990s+] something, or someone, which causes a great deal of anxiety or unhappiness.

IN PHRASES

❑ **do someone's head in** *v. see under* DO IN *v.* ❑ **get one's head down** *v.* [1940s+] **1** to have some sleep. **2** (*Aus.*) to plead guilty in court [one nods an assent to the charge]. ❑ **get one's head out of one's ass** *v.* [1940s+] (*US*) to stop being stupid, to stop acting stupidly. ❑ **get one's head together** *v.* [1960s+] to sort oneself out, to calm down. ❑ **get one's head up** *v.* **1** [1960s+] (*US drugs*) (*also* **get one's head uptight**) to take a drug, usu. cannabis. **2** [1970s+] (*US*) to cheer up. ❑ **give a man's head the bastinado** *v.* [SE *bastinado*, to beat, to cudgel; 'the lover's penis is the cudgel and the bumps that it "raises" on the unsuspecting husband's head are the cuckold's horns' (Henke, *Gutter Life and Language*, 1988)] [early 17C] of a man, to cuckold a husband. ❑ **give someone the head** *v.* [1960s] to head-butt. ❑ **go head on** *v.* [1930s] (*US black*) to stop trying to fool someone, usu. as imper. ❑ **go head up** *v.* [1980s] (*US black*) to take part in some form of activity with another person. ❑ **go upside someone's head** *v.* [1950s+] (*US black*) to hit in the face, to beat up. ❑ **have a head full of proclamations** *v.* [late 17C–18C] to have one's head full of nonsense. ❑ **have a head like a beaten favourite** *v.* (*also* **have a head like a half-sucked mango, ...like a robber's dog, ...like a twist**) [1960s+] (*Aus.*) to be ugly or unattractive. ❑ **have a head like a drover's dog** *v.* (*also* **have a head like a robber's dog**) [1940s+] (*Aus.*) to be suffering a very bad hangover. ❑ **have a head on** *v.* [SE *have a head/smart head on one's shoulders*] [late 19C–1950s] to be aware, to be alert. ❑ **have a swelled head** *v.* **1** *see under* SWELLHEAD *n.*[1]. **2** *see under* SWELLHEAD *n.*[2]. ❑ **have heads on them like boils** *v.* (*also* **have heads on them like mice**) [1940s+] (*Aus.*) used to describe any strong or powerful combination, whether of a hand of cards, a succession of good throws of the dice or a group of people. ❑ **have one's head in a sling** *v. see under* SLING *n.*[2]. ❑ **have one's head screwed on** *v. see under* SCREW *v.* ❑ **have one's head up one's arse** *v.* (*also* **have one's head (stuck) up one's ass**) [1940s+] (*orig. US*) **1** to be completely and deliberately stupid. **2** to be obsessed with oneself and one's own interests. **3** to ignore what is happening. ❑ **have one's head wedged** *v.* [it is wedged 'up one's ASS *n.* (2)'] [1960s+] (*US*) to be very stupid. ❑ **head-and-heels** *n.* [one has to lift the boy by his *head and heels* to position him for sex] [1970s] (*US gay*) a young, inexperienced homosexual. ❑ **head down, arse up** [2000s] (*N.Z.*) a phr. used of a hard worker. ❑ **head over teakettle** *adv.* (*also* **...tinkettle, ...tincup**) [1940s+] head-over-heels. ❑ **head over turkey** *adv. see under* TURKEY *n.*[1]. ❑ **head-the-ball** *n.* [i.e. one who has headed the ball so often that their brains are scrambled] [1990s+] (*Irish/Scot./Welsh*) **1** a fool. **2** a usu. derog. term of address. **3** a violent psychotic. ❑ **head-to-head** *see* separate entries. ❑ **hit one's head on the ceiling** *v.* [1970s] (*US campus*) to make a mistake. ❑ **hold one's head** *v.* [? the holding of a horse's head] [20C+] (*US black*) to be patient, to restrain oneself. ❑ **keep one's head cool** *v.* (*also* **keep one's head right**) [1980s+] (*US black*) to keep control of oneself, both emotionally and physically. ❑ **keep one's head down** *v.* [1950s+] **1** to be careful. **2** to maintain a 'low profile'. ❑ **knock the head off** *v. see* KNOCK THE TOP OFF *under* TOP *n.* ❑ **loose in the head** *adj. see* LOOSE IN THE BEAN *under* BEAN *n.*[1]. ❑ **make one's head** *v.* [late 18C–mid-19C] (*Irish*) to acquire a tolerance or 'head' for drink. ❑ **off one's head** *adj. see* separate entry. ❑ **on one's head** *adj.* [1900s–30s] (*US*) emotional, in a state. ❑ **on the head** *adv.* [1940s+] exactly. ❑ **out of one's head** *adj.* **1** [mid-19C+] eccentric, insane, obsessive, delirious; occas. as an adv. **2** [1930s+] desperate, highly emotional. **3** [1940s+] (*orig. US*) experiencing the effects of a drug. **4** [1960s+] very drunk. **5** [1990s+] an intensifier, usu. with meaning utterly bored or miserable. ❑ **pull someone's head** *v.* [1990s+] (*Aus.*) to gain or divert someone's attention. ❑ **put a head on** *v. see* GIVE SOMEONE THE NUT *under* NUT *n.*[1]. ❑ **put a (new) head on someone** *v.* **1** [mid-19C–1920s] (*US*) to punch or assault another, to disfigure in a fight. **2** [late 19C] to defeat, to overcome. **3** [late 19C] to silence, to make someone be quiet. ❑ **put one's head out** *v.* [2000s] (*US black gang*) to murder.

❑ **run upside one's head** *v.* [1950s+] (*US black*) to beat up. ❑ **suck heads** *v. see* SUCK FACE *under* SUCK *v.*[1]. ❑ **talk one's head off** *v.* (*also* **talk one's ass off, ...leg off, gab one's head off, gas...**) [SE *talk*/GAB *v.*/GAS *v.*[1] (1)] [1910s+] (*orig. US*) to talk incessantly. ❑ **want one's head read** *v.* (*also* **need one's head read, ...examined, ought to have one's head read, want one's head looked at**) [1920s+] to be very stupid or eccentric; also as excl. *GET YOUR HEAD READ!* below. ❑ **wear one's head large** *v.* [late 19C] to be suffering from a hangover.

IN EXCLAMATIONS

❑ **get your head read!** [20C+] (*Aus.*) a general derisive excl. ❑ **go soak your head!** *see under* SOAK *v.*[1]. ❑ **pull your head in!** (*also* **pull your head in your hole! pull your horns in! ...lid in! ...skull in!**) [the action of the tortoise] [1940s+] (*US/Aus.*) an excl. of annoyance, mind your own business! don't interfere! ❑ **pull your head out!** [i.e. of one's ASS *n.* (2)] [1960s+] (*US*) stop being so stupid!

head *v.*[1] [the betting on 'heads or tails'] [late 19C+] (*Aus.*) **1** to play 'two-up'. **2** to throw 'heads' in a game of two-up.

head *v.*[2] [HEAD *n.* (2c)] [1980s+] to fellate.

-head *sfx* **1** [16C+] used in a variety of combs. in which *-head* is linked to a n. to create a term meaning fool or idiot; the implication is that the head in question is shaped like or otherwise resembles the n.; also less frequently used with adj., e.g. AIRHEAD *n.* (1); BLOCKHEAD *n.*[1]; BONEHEAD *n.*[1] (1); CABBAGE-HEAD *n.* (1); DICKHEAD *n.*; EGGHEAD *n.*[1]; MEATHEAD *n.*; PINHEAD *n.* (2); POINTY-HEAD *n.* (1); SHITHEAD *n.* (1). **2** [mid-19C+] (*US derog.*) a person of a specific (and alien) ethnic origin, e.g. HANDKERCHIEF-HEAD *n.*[2]; *POPE-HEAD under* POPE *n.*; RAG-HEAD *n.* **3** [1910s+] a fan or devotee of a particular thing, e.g. a certain type of music, e.g. CHIPHEAD *n.*; *HOG-HEAD under* HOG *n.*; METALHEAD *n.*; PETROL-HEAD *n.* **4** [1920s+] a habitual user of a drug or a particular drink, e.g. A-HEAD *n.*; HOPHEAD *n.*[1]; JICKHEAD *n.*; POTHEAD *n.*[2].

headache *n.* **1** [1920s+] (*orig. US*) a problem, a cause of anxiety, a worry. **2** [1930s] (*US*) one's husband or wife, boyfriend or girlfriend.

IN COMPOUNDS

❑ **headache-man** *n.* [1940s–50s] (*US drugs*) a Federal narcotics agent. ❑ **headache-stick** *n.* [1910s–70s] (*US black*) a stick used as a club, a police baton or truncheon.

head-acher *n.* [mid-19C] in boxing, a blow to the head.

headbang *v.* [1970s+] to shake one's head violently when watching or listening to heavy-metal music; thus *headbanging music*.

headbanger *n.*[1] **1** [1960s+] a psychotic, a randomly, obsessively violent person, someone who cannot control their temper. **2** [1980s] (*US black*) something crazy and/or astonishing. **3** [2000s] in weak or affectionate use of sense 1.

headbanger *n.*[2] [HEADBANG *v.*] [1970s+] in the music business, a fan of loud, monotonous, 'heavy metal music', usu. a youth who plays a make-believe (or even cardboard) guitar and shakes his head violently as he watches or listens to his heroes.

headbanging *adj.* [HEADBANGER *n.*[1] (1)] [1990s+] psychotic, emotionally unstable.

headbeater *n.* (*also* **headbreaker, headbuster**) **1** [1950s+] (*US black*) a brutal police officer. **2** [1950s+] (*US*) a thug, incl. one who works for a ruthless criminal.

headbeating *adj.* (*also* **headbusting**) [1950s–70s] of police officers, brutal, in full strength.

headcase *n.* [SE *head* + CASE *n.*[1] (2d)] [1950s+] **1** an eccentric, bizarre person. **2** someone undergoing, or in need of, psychiatric treatment. **3** a violent person, a psychotic. **4** a state of psychosis. **5** a clever person, or one who believes themselves to be so.

header *n.* **1** [early 19C] a blow to the head. **2** going lit. or fig. 'head-first'. (**a**) [mid–late 19C] in fig. use of sense 2b, a bet, usu. spontaneous and unthought-out. (**b**) [mid-19C+] a head-first dive, usu. into water. (**c**) [1920s] a social decline. (**d**) [1990s+] one who jumps, usu. for the purposes of suicide, off a high building, bridge etc. **3** [1950s+] (*US*) an act of oral copulation [HEAD *n.* (2c)]. **4** [1960s+] (*Irish*) a psychotic, an unstable or bizarre person.

head-fuck *n.* [HEADFUCK *v.*] [1990s+] **1** a severe depression or that which causes it. **2** the extreme effects of a drug, usu. strong cannabis. **3** something that causes problems, a worry.

headfuck *adj.* [HEAD-FUCK *n.*] [2000s] pertaining to a depression.

headfuck *v.* [SE *head* + FUCK *v.* (2a)] [1970s+] (*orig. US*) to confuse, to mislead, to disorientate.

headfucker *n.* [HEADFUCK *v.*] [1970s+] (*drugs*) an especially powerful drug, esp. a hallucinogen.

head hunt *v.* [1920s+] (*US black*) to look for trouble, to start a fight.

head hunter *n.* **1** [1920s] (*US*) a person who tracks down wanted criminals. **2** [1960s+] (*US*) a police officer who reports on another officer. **3** [1980s+] (*Aus. Und.*) a criminal who specializes in preying on other, successful and thus wealthy, criminals. **4** [1980s+] (*US*) an aggressively selfish and single-minded individual.

headie *n.* [1940s+] (*Aus.*) in the game of two-up, a better who favours 'heads'.

heading *n.* [1940s–50s] using the top of the head to butt someone in a fight.

heading 'em *phr.* [1900s–10s] (*Aus.*) **1** playing 'two-up'. **2** making and saving money.

headlight *n.* [the supposed resemblance] **1** [late 19C–1950s] a large and ostentatious tie pin, usu. a diamond one. **2** [late 19C+] (*US*) in pl., the eyes. **3** [late 19C+] (*orig. US*) a precious stone, usu. a diamond. **4** [20C+] in pl., the female breasts, esp. when prominent and well shaped. **5** [20C+] (*Aus./US*) spectacles, glasses, esp. tinted or dark glasses. **6** [1920s–40s] (*US short order*) in pl., eggs. **7** [1920s+] (*US*) (*also* **headlight to a snowstorm**) a black person, esp. one who is light-skinned [the golden skin colour].

headlight *v.* [HEADLIGHT *n.* (2)] [late 19C+] (*US*) to focus one's eyes on.

head-piece *n.* **1** [late 16C+] the head, the mind. **2** [early 18C] a cuckold's horns. **3** [late 19C–1900s] (*US tramp*) a hat. **4** [20C+] (*Irish*) an intelligent person; a responsible person; thus *have the head-piece on one*, to be intelligent.

heads *n.* **1** [1990s+] (*US black*) one's children. **2** [1990s+] (*Aus. drugs*) marijuana [the *heads* of the marijuana plants].

heads and tails *n.* **1** [late 18C–1950s] (*Aus.*) the act of SIXTY-NINE *n.* (1). **2** [late 19C+] for two people to sleep in the same single bed lying in the opposite direction from each other.

head smack *n.* [SE *head* + SMACK *n.*[2], playing on SMACK *n.*[1] (5)] [1960s+] (*US*) a dose of morphine or heroin inhaled through the nose.

head smack *v.* [HEAD SMACK *n.*] [1960s+] (*US*) to inhale heroin through the nose.

headstaggers *n.* [SE *head* + *staggers*, a disease of horses and sheep] [20C+] (*Irish*) mental illness or instability.

heads up *n.* [1990s+] **1** information, facts. **2** (*US black*) a greeting, an act of recognition. **3** a warning.

heads-up *adj.* [1930s+] (*US*) **1** alert and skilful, esp. in sport. **2** of a fight, one-on-one, thus open, honest.

heads up *phr.* [HEADS UP *n.* (1)] **1** [1930s] (*US*) honestly. **2** [1960s+] a phr. used to indicate affirmation.

heads up! *excl.* [lit. 'get your heads up (and look)'] [1910s+] **1** a shout by lookouts for illegal street traders or street gamblers to warn of an approaching police officer. **2** a general warning.

head-to-head *n.* [1980s+] (*US*) a private conversation.

head-to-head *adj.* [1970s+] at close-quarters.

head trip *n.* (*also* **h.t.**) [SE *head* + TRIP *n.*[4]] **1** [1960s+] (*orig. US drugs*) a drug-induced fantasy, reverie. **2** [1970s+] (*US*) something requiring challenging thought. **3** [1980s+] (*US*) deception or flattery.

head trip *v.* [HEAD TRIP *n.*] [1960s+] (*orig. US*) **1** to daydream, usu. under the influence of drugs. **2** to confuse, to deceive.

head-tripper *n.* [HEAD TRIP *v.*] **1** [1970s+] (*US*) a psychotherapist. **2** [1990s+] a day-dreamer.

head up *v.* [HEAD UP *adv.*] [1980s+] (*US black gang*) to start a fight; as n., a fist fight.

head up *adv.* [1980s+] in direct confrontation.

heady *adj.*[1] [SE *heady*, intoxicating, stupefying] [mid-19C–1910s] drunk, intoxicating.

heady *adj.*[2] [the contents of one's head] [20C+] **1** (*mainly Aus./N.Z.*) ingenious, shrewd. **2** (*US*) arrogant, opinionated.

Healtheries, the *n.* [late 19C] the Health Exhibition, held in London in 1884.

heap *n.*[1] [SE *heap*, a pile; note also the earlier SE *heap*, a great company of people] [17C+] a large amount, often of money.

heap *n.*[2] **1** [early 19C+] a woman, usu. with some derog. adj., e.g. *lazy heap, fat heap*. **2** [1920s+] a man [note HEAP OF COKE *n.*]. **3** [1920s+] (*orig. US*) an automobile [abbr. *heap of scrap, heap of junk*]. **4** [1940s+] (*US*) an (old) aeroplane. **5** [1950s–60s] (*Aus./US Und.*) a large prison.

IN COMPOUNDS

❑ **heap-clouting** *n.* [CLOUT *v.*[2] (1)] [1950s+] (*US Und.*) stealing automobiles.

heap *adv.* [supposedly a representation of the speech of Native Americans] [mid-19C+] (*orig. US*) very, much; usu. as *a heap*.

heap of coke *n.* (*also* **heapy**) [rhy. sl. = BLOKE *n.* (3)] [mid-19C+] a man.

hear *v.* (*also* **hear that**) [SE *hear*, in this context with an implication, the product of drugs/New Age philosophizing, of a deeper understanding than the pure SE implies; note jazz use of *hear*, to become emotionally involved with the music, to concentrate absolutely on what one is hearing] [1930s+] (*US*) to understand, to agree with someone completely; often as *I HEAR YOU* below.

IN PHRASES

❑ **hear something knock** *v.* [mid-19C] to take a hint. ❑ **I hear you** [1930s+] an emphatic way of saying 'I understand', 'yes'.

IN EXCLAMATIONS

❑ **I heard that!** [1980s+] (*US campus*) an excl. of agreement.

hearing cheats *n.* [SE *hearing* + CHEAT *n.* (1)] [mid-16C–mid-19C] (*UK Und.*) the ears.

hearse *n.* (*US*) **1** [late 19C] (*also* **hearse-driver**) a pessimistic person. **2** [late 19C] a police patrol wagon. **3** [20C+] an ambulance. **4** [20C+] a large automobile.

IN COMPOUNDS

❑ **hearse-chaser** *n.* [1930s–50s] (*US Und.*) one who preys on the relatives of newly deceased people, esp. by claiming there are outstanding bills to be paid.

hearseman *n.* [1930s] (*US prison*) a convicted murderer.

heart *n.* [metonymy] **1** [1930s+] (*orig. US Und.*) courage, bravery, spirit. **2** [1960s–70s] (*drugs*) an amphetamine; a dexedrine [abbr. *PURPLE HEARTS* ***under*** PURPLE *adj.*].

IN COMPOUNDS

❑ **heart check** *n.* [2000s] (*US prison*) testing the resilience of an inmate, spec. giving a member of a prison gang a mission, such as a murder, to test his loyalty.

SE in slang uses

IN COMPOUNDS

❑ **heart-starter** *n.* [1960s+] (*Aus.*) the first alcoholic drink of the day.

IN PHRASES

❑ **heart of the raul** *n.* (*also* **heart of the rowl**) [? Scot. *rail, raul*, a line; or ? corruption of SE *royal*; or ? f. *Irish Roll* tobacco (manufactured by Messrs. T.P. & R. Goodbody, Co. Offaly, in 1843), the centre being the freshest] [1940s+] (*Irish*) the best person.

heart and dart *n.* [rhy. sl.] [mid-19C–1920s] a fart.

heart and lung *n.* (*also* **liver and lung**) [rhy. sl.] [1920s–30s] (*US*) the tongue.

heartbreaker *n.* [its supposed effect on the opposite sex] [mid-17C–19C] a curled love-lock.

heartbreak hotel *n.* [1956 song 'Heartbreak Hotel' by Axton, Durden & Presley] (*US*) **1** [1970s] anything designed to elicit pity. **2** [1980s+] a prison.

heartburn *n.* [its effects] [late 19C–1920s] a bad cigar.

hearth-rug *n.* [rhy. sl.] [1910s+] **1** a fool, a simpleton [= MUG *n.*[1] (2a)]. **2** a drinking mug. **3** a bedbug.

heart of oak *adj.* (*also* **hearts of oak**) [rhy. sl. = BROKE *adj.*[1]; ult. *Hearts of Oak* Benefit Society] [20C+] out of funds, impoverished.

heart-on *n.* [play on HARD-ON *n.* (1) + the stimulating effect on the heart] [1980s+] (*drugs*) an inhalant.

heartsease *n.* [both 'ease the heart' in their separate ways] [mid-17C–early 19C] **1** a 20-shilling piece. **2** a measure of gin.

hearts of oak *adj.* *see* HEART OF OAK *adj.*

hearty *n.* [mid-19C–1910s] strong drink.

hearty *adj.* [HEARTY *n.*] [mid-19C–1910s] drunk.

heat *n.* (*US*) **1** in the context of emotion [HOT *adj.* (1); note Shakespearian heat, sexual or amatory enthusiasm]. (**a**) [mid-16C–18C; 1920s–60s] sex appeal, pornography; thus *give the heat*, to make sexual advances. (**b**) [1960s] sexual excitement [? f. sense 1a]. (**c**) [1980s+] popularity [HOT *adj.* (2b)]. (**d**) [1980s+] (*US campus*) constr. with *the*, the best, the most attractive. (**e**) [1980s+] anger, excitement [HOT *adj.* (4a)]. (**f**) [1990s+] excessive emotion, e.g. enthusiasm, terror. **2** in the context of drink or drugs. (**a**) [1900s–60s] (*US*) drunkenness. (**b**) [1900s–60s] (*US*) a drink. (**c**) [1920s–70s] (*US tramp*) the crude alcohol that is drunk in solution as a substitute for alcohol. (**d**) [1950s] an intoxication from drugs; usu. as *have a heat on*. (**e**) [1970s+] (*drugs*) the heating of powdered heroin before smoking it. **3** in fig. use as pressure [HOT *adj.* (5)]. (**a**) [1920s+] (*orig. Und.*) intensive police activity of any kind; pressure, esp. on criminals from the police. (**b**) [1920s+] pressure, irrespective of its source. (**c**) [1930s] physical violence. (**d**) [1930s] (*US Und.*) a police record. (**e**) [1930s+] as *the heat*, a police officer, or the police in general. (**f**) [1930s+] (*US*) problems, difficulties, trouble, bad feeling. **4** [1920s+] (*US*) weapons, arms. **5** [1930s+] gunfire. **6** [1940s] (*US Und.*) constr. with *the*, the electric chair. **7** [1990s+] electricity.

IN COMPOUNDS

❑ **heathead** *n.* [-HEAD *sfx* (4)] [1920s+] (*US*) a consumer of crude alcohol. ❑ **heat-packer** *n.* [PACK *v.*[1] (3)] [1940s+] (*US Und.*) a gunman, an armed gangster.

IN PHRASES

❑ **catch heat** *v.* [1970s+] (*US*) to get into trouble. ❑ **dead heat** *n. see under* DEAD *adj.* ❑ **give heat** *v.* [1930s+] to murder, to kill. ❑ **give someone (the) heat** *v.* [1970s+] (*US*) to place under (verbal) pressure. ❑ **heat on** *v.* [1990s+] (*US black*) to tease. ❑ **heat's on** [1950s+] a phr. meaning the police are exerting exceptional pressure on the community. ❑ **pack heat** *v.* [PACK *v.*[1] (3)] [1920s+] (*US*) to carry a gun. ❑ **put the heat on** *v.* [1920s+] to pressurize, to threaten. ❑ **take heat** *v.* [1920s+] (*US*) **1** to suffer or endure punishment or criticism. **2** to lose money. ❑ **take the heat** *v.* [1950s+] (*orig. US*) to accept responsibility. ❑ **take the heat off** *v.* [1950s+] to relieve pressure on (a person). ❑ **turn on the heat** *v.* (*also* **turn up the heat (on)**) [1930s+] **1** (*orig. US*) to pressurize, to put pressure on. **2** (*US*) to cover or shoot with a gun.

heat *adj.* **1** [1960s] (*US*) pertaining to sex. **2** [1980s] (*US campus*) very attractive.

heated *adj.* [HEAT *n.*] **1** [1980s+] (*US campus*) drunk. **2** [1990s+] (*US black*) angry.

heated up *adj. see* HET UP *adj.*

heater *n.* **1** [late 18C] a foot. **2** [1910s–30s] (*US*) an overcoat. **3** [1910s+] (*US*) a cigar. **4** [1920s+] (*also* **heatrola**) a pistol, revolver. **5** [1930s–60s] (*US*) the female genitals. **6** [1990s+] (*US campus*) an exceptionally attractive man.

IN PHRASES

❑ **pack a heater** *v.* [PACK *v.*[1] (3)] [1920s+] (*US*) to carry a gun.

heathen philosopher *n.* [image of Greek philosophers who trad. scorned the niceties of dress] [late 17C–early 19C] a ragged vagrant, whose flesh can be seen through his garments.

heather *n.* [film *Heathers* (1988)] [1980s+] (*US campus*) a superficial young woman, pretty but lacking in intelligence.

heather c *n.* [? film *Heathers* (1988)] [1990s+] a fat, ugly person who stutters.

heatrola *n. see* HEATER *n.* (4).

heat-seeking (moisture) missile *n. see under* MISSILE *n.*

heat up *v.* [HEAT *n.*] **1** [1930s+] (*US Und.*) to bring pressure upon someone. **2** [1930s+] (*US Und.*) of the victim of a confidence trick, to make a fuss or call in the authorities. **3** [1930s+] (*US Und.*) for pressure of discovery or suspicions to intensify. **4** [1930s+] (*orig. US Und.*) to infuriate, to annoy. **5** [1970s] to arouse sexually. **6** [2000s] (*US*) of a restaurant, to become busy.

heave *n.* [19C] a flagrant attempt to deceive, to swindle, to persuade.

heave *v.* [SE *heave*, to lift and carry away] **1** [mid-16C–mid-19C] to rob. **2** [mid-19C+] to vomit [the sensation in one's stomach].

IN PHRASES

❑ **heave a bough** *v.* (*also* **heave a booth**) [SE *bough*, booth] [mid-16C–early 19C] (*UK Und.*) to rob or rifle a booth; thus *booth-heaver*, one who performs such a robbery. ❑ **heave a case** *v.* [CASE *n.*[3] (1)] [18C–early 19C] to rob a house. ❑ **heave it into** *v.* [late 19C–1900s] (*US*) to persuade, to impose a story upon.

heave-ho *n.* (*also* **heave, heavus**) [naut. jargon *heave-ho!*, a sailor's cry when hauling on the anchor cable, pulling in sails and performing similar strenuous tasks. In this case the task was that of the BOUNCER *n.*[1] (9), who grasped his victim by the scruff of the neck and the seat of the trousers and tossed him through the saloon door] **1** [1930s+] rejection, ejection; often as *the old heave-ho*. **2** [1940s+] an act of vomiting.

heaven *n.* [19C–1900s] the vagina.

SE in slang uses

IN COMPOUNDS

❑ **heaven dust** *n.* [DUST *n.* (6)] (*drugs*) **1** [1930s+] cocaine. **2** [1940s+] heroin; morphine. ❑ **heaven-eleven** *n.* [SE *heaven*, since if the shooter throws eleven on the first throw the bet is won] [1960s+] (*US gambling*) the point of eleven in craps dice.

IN PHRASES

❑ **go to heaven in a string** *v.* [orig. applied in 16C to the Jesuits whose faith could bring them judicial death] [late 16C–mid-18C] to be hanged; thus *feel like going to heaven in a string*, to be so deliriously happy as not to mind even the possibility of imminent death. ❑ **to heaven** *adv.* [17C; late 19C+] (*US*) strongly, very much.

heavenly bliss *n.* [rhy. sl.] [1930s–40s] (*US*) a kiss.

heavenly days! *excl.* [1950s] (*US*) intensifying excl.

heavenly plan *n.* [rhy. sl.] [late 19C+] (*Aus.*) a man.

heaven reacher *n.* [1920s] (*US tramp*) a preacher.

heaver *n.*[1] [the cliché, the breast *heaves* with emotion] **1** [late 17C–early 19C] (*UK Und.*) the female breast. **2** [18C–19C] a person in love. **3** [mid-19C] the male chest. **4** [1980s+] (*US black*) a self-styled great lover, esp. of the more earthy, animalistic type.

heaver *n.*[2] [HEAVE *v.*] [mid-18C–early 19C] (*UK Und.*) a thief who specializes in stealing tradesmen's shop books.

heaver *n.*[3] *see* COAL (HEAVER) *n.*

heavies *n.*[1] [HEAVY *v.*] **1** [1970s+] emotional intensity, usu. depressing. **2** [1980s+] (*N.Z.*) threats.

heavies *n.*[2] *see* HEAVY MOB *n.* (2).

heaving *adj.* [? euph. for FUCKING *adj.*] [1960s] a general intensifier.

heavy *n.* **1** [late 19C–1940s] (*US*) (*also* **heavy merchant**) an actor playing a serious or tragic part in a melodrama; occas. of an actress. **2** in the context of violence. (**a**) [late 19C+] a heavyweight boxer. (**b**) [1910s+] a thug, a villain, esp. a violent criminal (also as portrayed in cinema and theatre); also in fig. use, e.g. a moralizer [note B.E.: 'A heavy Fellow, a dull Blockish Slug']. **3** in fig. use, an important, meaningful person. (**a**) [1910s–20s] (*US campus*) a girlfriend, a boyfriend, an important date. (**b**) [1920s+] (*US*) an important or powerful person. **4** [1920s–40s] (*US*) a large, fat person. **5** [1930s–50s] (*US Und.*) (*also* **heavyman**) a bankrobber. **6** [1940s+] (*US/Aus.*) hard work, heavy labour. **7** [1950s+] (*drugs*) a hard drug (heroin, cocaine) rather than a soft one (cannabis etc). **8** [1960s] (*Aus.*) a detective. **9** in the context of emotion. (**a**) [1970s+] emotional intensity, usu. depressing. (**b**) [1980s+] (*N.Z.*) threats. **10** *see* HEAVY WET *n.*

IN PHRASES

❑ **come the heavy** *v.* [1970s] to act in an aggressive or moralistic manner. ❑ **do the heavy** *v.* [late 19C+] to swagger, to show off. ❑ **lay heavy on** *v.* (*also* **lay on the heavy**) [1970s] (*US/Aus.*) to lecture, to sermonize, to reprimand. ❑ **on the heavy** (*also* **at the heavy**) **1** [1920s+] doing violent crime, armed robbery. **2** [1930s–50s] (*US Und.*) working as a bank robber.

heavy *adj.* **1** [mid-19C] respectable. **2** in lit. uses [the weight of one's purse or wallet, or the gun]. (**a**) [mid-19C+] (*US*) in possession of a great deal of a commodity, usu. money; flush. (**b**) [20C+] of money, substantial. (**c**) [1990s+] armed. **3** [mid-19C+] (*US*) of an object or idea, remarkable in a positive or negative way. **4** fig. uses in negative senses. (**a**) [mid-19C+] ponderously dignified; stern, repressive, unbending, esp. as *heavy father, heavy uncle*. (**b**) [mid-19C+] thuggish, violent, unpleasant. (**c**) [1920s+] intense, urgent, busy. (**d**) [1920s+] of words or of atmosphere, shocking, frightening, threatening. (**e**) [1970s+] physically menacing. **5** fig. uses in positive senses. (**a**) [mid-19C+] (*US*) of a person, powerful, wealthy, influential, popular. (**b**) [1920s] (*US/W.I.*) enthusiastic. (**c**) [1920s+] meaningful, important, emotionally strong; a general intensifier, esp. loved by late 1960s hippies and radicals, varying as to context. (**d**) [1930s+] (*US/W.I.*) physically attractive, sexy. (**e**) [1930s+] intellectual, highbrow. (**f**) [1940s+] (*US black*) wonderful, amazing, admirable. (**g**) [1940s+] very passionate; either physically or emotionally. (**h**) [1960s+] (*US black*) highly intelligent. **6** [1950s+] of a jail sentence, substantial, lengthy. **7** [1950s+] (*US*) in drug uses [the fig. 'weight' of the drugs]. (**a**) in possession of drugs. (**b**) referring to a narcotic drug rather than a soft drug such as cannabis. **8** [1970s+] of a crime, important, large-scale. **9** [1970s+] in sex, pertaining to sado-masochism.

IN COMPOUNDS

❑ **heavy cruising** *n.* [1970s] (*US gay*) sexual encounters between studiously masculine rather than effeminate male homosexuals. ❑ **heavy game** *n. see under* GAME *n.* ❑ **heavy gee** *n.* [1930s–40s] (*US Und.*) a safe-blower. ❑ **heavy gun** *n. see* HEAVY MAN *n.* (2). ❑ **heavy guy** *n. see* HEAVY MAN *n.* ❑ **heavy hen** *n.* [1940s] (*US black/Harlem*) a mature woman (as opposed to a young girl). ❑ **heavy hitter** *n.* [baseball imagery] **1** [1970s+] an important, influential person, esp. in the world of business, politics or crime. **2** [1970s+] (*US*) a violent criminal, a hired thug. **3** [1980s+] (*US*) an alcoholic [HIT *v.* (3b)]. ❑ **heavy job** *n.* [1900s–30s] (*US Und.*) a violent crime. ❑ **heavy lard** *n.* [1940s] (*US black*) **1** any impressively, convincingly told story. **2** a 'tall story', a dramatic but unfeasible story. ❑ **heavy lump** *n.* [pun on SUGAR HILL *n.* (1)] [1940s] the fashionable area of contemporary Harlem, New York City, otherwise known as Coogan's Bluff, between Amsterdam and Edgecombe Avenues, between 138th and 155th Streets. ❑ **heavy man** *n. see* separate entry. ❑ **heavy manners** *see* separate entries. ❑ **heavy merchant** *n. see* HEAVY *n.* (1). ❑ **heavy mob** *n. see* separate entry. ❑ **heavy number** *n. see under* NUMBER *n.* ❑ **heavy rackets** *n.* [1900s–40s] (*US Und.*) those forms of crime that depend on violence or coercion for their success. ❑ **heavy sledding** *n. see* TOUGH SLEDDING *under* TOUGH *adj.* ❑ **heavy stuff** *n.* [STUFF *n.* (5b)] [1960s] (*drugs*) drugs like narcotics, rather than tranquillizers, cannabis etc. ❑ **heavy sugar** *n. see under* SUGAR *n.*[1]. ❑ **heavy swell** *n. see* separate entry.

SE in slang uses

IN COMPOUNDS

❑ **heavy baggage** *n.* [they weigh down the man who is in

pursuit of pleasure or focused on work; note milt. use *heavy baggage*, equipment that is not easily carried] [late 18C–19C] women and children. ❑ **heavy brown** *n.* (*also* **brown gater droppings**) [mid-19C] (*UK Und.*) brown ale. ❑ **heavy cavalry** *n.* (*also* **heavy dragons, ...dragoons, ...horsemen**) [mid-19C–1930s] bedbugs, lice etc. ❑ **heavy (cheer)** *n.* [SE *cheer*, happiness, contentment, esp. as a result of drinking alcohol] [early–mid-19C] a mixture of porter and beer. ❑ **heavy-duty** *adj. see* separate entry. ❑ **heavy-foot** *n.* [identified as such by his shoes] [1930s–40s] (*US Und.*) a plain-clothes detective. ❑ **heavy horsemen** *n.* **1** [mid-19C] Thames thieves who pose as dock-hands to enter ships and steal the cargoes. **2** *see* HEAVY CAVALRY above. ❑ **heavy plodder** *n.* (*also* **heavy toddler**) [mid-19C] (*UK Und.*) a stockbroker. ❑ **heavy roller** *n. see* HIGH ROLLER *n.* (1). ❑ **heavy soul** *n.* [its long-term effects] [1950s] (*drugs*) heroin. ❑ **heavyweight** *see* separate entries. ❑ **heavy wet** *n. see* separate entry.

heavy *v.* [HEAVY *adj.*] **1** [1950s+] to threaten, to menace. **2** [1990s+] to render depressing, to 'bring down'.

heavy *adv.* **1** [20C+] to a large extent. **2** [1920s+] of money, possessing, or spending, a large amount. **3** [1930s+] enthusiastically, keenly. **4** [2000s] in possession of a gun.

IN PHRASES

❑ **run heavy** *v.* [2000s] to carry a gun.

heavy-duty *adj.* [SE *heavy-duty*, hard-wearing] **1** [1930s+] (*orig. US*) intense, serious, committed. **2** [1970s+] (*US*) tough, unpleasant. **3** [1970s+] (*US*) terrific, first-rate. **4** [1980s+] (*US*) deeply committed, heavily involved. **5** [1980s+] (*US drugs*) strongly addictive.

heavy man *n.* (*also* **heavy guy, heavy worker**) [HEAVY *n.* (2b)/HEAVY *n.* (3b)] **1** [1910s+] a safebreaker. **2** [1920s] (*US Und.*) (*also* **heavy gun**) a gang leader, a senior racketeer. **3** [1930s+] a thug, a criminal who is prone to use violence. **4** [1990s+] (*W.I.*) an influential man.

heavy manners *n.* [HEAVY *adj.* (4a) + SE *manners*; also used by the authorities to denote their own firm measures in the fight against crime] [1970s+] (*orig. W.I. then UK black*) any form of oppression or repression experienced by blacks (esp. at the hands of the police); thus *under heavy manners*, under strict discipline.

heavy manners *v.* (*also* **manners**) [HEAVY MANNERS *n.*] [1980s] (*UK black*) to dictate, to bully.

heavy mob *n.* (*also* **heavies, heavy squad**) [HEAVY *adj.* (4b)] [1950s+] (*UK Und.*) **1** a gang of thugs. **2** physically tough police or prison officers used in violent situations. **3** officers from the Flying Squad and, formerly, the Special Patrol Group.

heavy swell *n.* (*also* **howling swell**) [HEAVY *adj.* (5a)/HOWLING *adj.* + SWELL *n.*[1]] [mid-19C–1910s] a dandy, an aristocrat or one who tries to pose as such; thus *heavy swelldom*, the world of such individuals.

heavyweight *n.* **1** [late 19C+] an important person with power and influence. **2** [1910s] (*US Und.*) a thief. **3** [1910s+] (*US Und.*) a violent criminal. **4** [1970s] (*US*) a fat person, esp. a fat woman. **5** [1970s+] (*US gay*) the possessor of a larger-than-average penis. **6** [1970s+] (*US campus*) a heavy drinker.

heavyweight *adj.* [HEAVYWEIGHT *n.* (1)] [20C+] important, influential.

heavy wet *n.* (*also* **heavy, heavy whet**) ['Heavy wet, malt liquor, because the more a man drinks of it, the heavier and more stupid he becomes' (Hotten, 1867)] **1** [early 19C] a heavy drinking bout. **2** [early 19C+] malt liquor; also a mixture of porter and beer. **3** [1930s–40s] (*US black*) a downpour, a rainstorm.

Hebe *n.* (*also* **Heab, Hebie, Heeb**) [abbr. SE *Hebrew*, a Jew] [1920s+] (*orig. US*) a derog. term for a Jew.

hebe *adj.* [HEBE *n.*] [1920s+] Jewish.

he-biddy *n. see under* BIDDY *n.*[1].

Hebie *n. see* HEBE *n.*

Hebrew *n.* [18C–19C] unintelligible language.

Hebrew hoppers *n. see* AIR HEBREWS *n.*

heck *n.* (*also* **hicks**) [late 19C+] a euph. for *hell*.

IN PHRASES

❑ **all to heck** [1950s] (*US*) a general intensifier. ❑ **beat the heck out of** *v. see* BEAT (THE) HELL OUT OF *under* HELL *n.* ❑ **holy heck to pay** *see* HELL TO PAY *under* HELL *n.* ❑ **raise heck** *v. see* RAISE HELL *under* HELL *n.*

IN EXCLAMATIONS

❑ **what the heck!** *see* WHAT THE HELL! *under* HELL *n.*

heck! *excl.* (*also* **by heck! by heckelum! heckers! hick!**) [early 19C+] a euph. for HELL! *excl.*

hecka *adv.* [HECK *n.*] [1980s+] (*US campus*) very.

heckashin *adj. see* HELLACIOUS *adj.*

heckuva *adj. see* HELLUVA *adj.*

he-concubine *n. see* HE-WHORE *n.*

he-coon *n.* [SE *he* + COON *n.* (3)] [late 19C–1970s] (*US*) an important, powerful man.

hector *n.* (*also* **bully-hector**) [an ironic use of the Trojan hero *Hector*, son of Priam and Hecuba, husband of Andromache, 'the prop or stay of Troy'; thus note Shadwell, *The Squire of Alsatia* (1688): 'They are all of them as stout as Hector'] [mid-17C–mid-19C] a blustering, swaggering bully, a thug, a bouncer, esp. of a brothel.

IN PHRASES

❑ **...as/than Hector** [? euph. for SE *hell*] [20C+] (*US*) used in a variety of phrs., e.g. *dead as Hector, mad as Hector, meaner than Hector*.

hector *v.* [mid-17C+] to bluster, to swagger.

hedge *n.*[1] [play on FENCE *n.*[1] (1)] [early 19C] (*UK Und.*) a criminal receiver.

hedge *n.*[2] **1** [1900s] (*US*) a moustache. **2** [1940s+] (*UK Und.*) the crowd that gathers round illicit street traders or gamblers. **3** [1980s+] the pubic hair.

SE in slang uses

IN PHRASES

❑ **hedge off** *v.* [mid-19C] to run off, to escape. ❑ **hedge on the dyke** *n.* [*dyke* is SE; there is no ref. to lesbianism] [19C] the female pubic hair. ❑ **on the wrong side of the hedge** (*also* **fall on the wrong side of the hedge**) [one lands off the road and in a field] [late 19C] to be thrown from a coach, thus in any unfortunate situation.

hedge *adj.* [SE *hedge*, implying dirty, inferior, lit. plying one's trade beneath a hedge] [late 16C–1950s] a general pej., used in a number of combs. below.

IN COMPOUNDS

❑ **hedge-alehouse** *n. see* HEDGE-TAVERN below. ❑ **hedge-bird** *n.* (*also* **hedge-mumper**) [SE *bird*/BIRD *n.*[1] (3a)/MUMPER *n.* (2)] [17C–mid-19C] a general derog. term esp. for a tramp or vagrant, i.e. one who lives or might as well live in a hedge. ❑ **hedge-bird trull** *n.* [mid-17C] a prostitute who plies her trade in the open air, under bushes. ❑ **hedge-bit** *n.* (*also* **hedge and ditch, hedge-bird**) [BIT *n.*[1]] [late 17C–mid-19C] a low-grade prostitute who carries on operations in the open air. ❑ **hedge-creeper** *n.* (*UK Und.*) **1** [mid-16C–mid-17C] a sneak thief, a general rogue. **2** [late 17C–mid-19C] a thief who steals laundry from the hedges on which it is laid to dry. **3** [mid-19C] (*also* **hedge-prowler, hedge ranger**) a prostitute, presumably working in the countryside. ❑ **hedge-priest** *n.* (*also* **hedge-parson**) [late 16C–early 19C] (*UK Und.*) a priest, or a beggar who poses as such, who works in rural areas, ministering to other beggars and the local peasantry; the implication is that such clergy were not true priests. ❑ **hedge-tavern** *n.* (*also* **hedge alehouse**) [late 17C–mid-19C] a low tavern, often the home of criminals, card-sharps and similar underworld figures. ❑ **hedge-whore** *n.* (*also* **hedge-wench**) [late 16C+] a prostitute who plies her trade in the open air.

hedge! *excl.* [1900s–10s] (*Aus. Und.*) usu. on a racecourse, a cry of warning at the approach of police.

hedge and ditch *n.* [rhy. sl.] **1** [late 19C] a market pitch. **2** [1910s+] a cricket or football pitch.

hedgehog *n.*[1] **1** [mid-19C] veal [the two meats are supposedly not dissimilar when cooked]. **2** [1970s] an unattractive woman.

hedgehog *n.*[2] [rhy. sl. = WOG *n.*[1] (1)] [20C+] a derog. term for a foreigner, esp. a black or Asian person.

hedgie *n.* [abbr.] [1990s+] (*Aus./N.Z.*) a hedgehog.

hedging and ditching *n.* [1980s] (*Irish*) sexual intercourse.

Heeb *n. see* HEBE *n.*

heebie-jeebies *n.* (*also* **hebe-jebes, heebs, heebies**) [? ety. unknown, although the *heebie-jeebie*, a dance popular c.1926, was alleged to have taken its name f. the incantations of an Indian witch-doctor before making a human sacrifice; more likely a nonce coinage by the US cartoonist Billy Derbeck and first noted in his strip *Barney Google* in the *New York American* on 26 Oct. 1923] **1** [1920s+] (*orig. US*) unpleasant fantasies, nameless terrors, anything the mind can conjure up to produce nerves and fear. **2** [1920s+] a hangover, delirium tremens. **3** [1980s+] the physical and mental symptoms that accompany heroin or cocaine withdrawal.

hee-haw *n.* [the trad. transliteration of the donkey's bray] **1** [mid-19C+] a donkey. **2** [20C+] (*US*) loud, offensive laughter, esp. if scornful. **3** [20C+] derision, nonsense.

hee-haw *v.* (*also* **haw-haw**) [HEE-HAW *n.* (2)] [20C+] (*US*) to laugh scornfully; to smile.

hee-haw shoes *n.* [1960s] large, clod-hopping shoes, the sort a donkey-riding rustic would choose.

heel *n.* [? SE *down-at-heel* or the image of an unwanted person, continually at one's heels] **1** [1900s–30s] (*US Und.*) constr. with *the*, 'The racket of stealing by sneaking' (Sutherland, *The Professional Thief*, 1937). **2** [1910s+] (*orig. US*) a petty criminal. **3** [1910s+] (*orig. US*) a general derog., esp. a dishonest, untrustworthy person, esp. one who treats women badly. **4** [1920s+] (*US Und.*) an informer.

IN PHRASES

❑ **drag one's heels** *v. see under* DRAG *v.*[1]. ❑ **on the heel** [1910s–40s] (*US Und.*) **1** working as a criminal. **2** till-tapping. ❑ **play the heel** *v.* [1910s+] (*US*) to act unpleasantly, to be mean or cruel.

heel *v.*[1] [SE *heel*] **1** [mid-19C+] (*US*) (*also* **heel it, heel out**) to run away, to escape, to walk quickly. **2** [1910s–30s] (*US Und.*) to walk stealthily, to stalk, to follow. **3** [1940s–60s] (*US Und.*) to leave without paying one's bill.

IN PHRASES

❑ **cop a heel** *v.* (*also* **cop and heel**) **1** [1920s+] (*US Und.*) to run off, to escape. **2** [1930s–50s] (*US prison*) to attack from behind.

heel *v.*[2] [cock-fighting jargon *heel*, to arm a game-cock with a gaff or spur] **1** [late 19C+] (*also* **heel up**) to arm oneself with a firearm. **2** [1900s–40s] (*US*) to lend money.

heel *v.*[3] [HEEL *n.*] **1** [late 19C+] (*US*) to court, to flatter for personal advantage. **2** [1920s+] (*US Und.*) to rob a store using an accomplice to distract the clerk or cashier. **3** [1930s+] (*US*) to cheat a hotel or similar establishment by sneaking in another person without registering.

heel-and-toe *n.* [HEEL-AND-TOE *v.*] [1930s+] (*US*) the act of running or walking quickly; thus *take it on the heel-and-toe*, to escape.

IN COMPOUNDS

❑ **heel-and-toe boy** *n.* (*also* **heel-and-toe man, ...walker**) [20C+] one who walks speedily, runs away or escapes.

heel-and-toe *v.* **1** [early 19C+] (*US*) (*also* **heel-toe**) to run or walk quickly. **2** [mid-19C] to dance. **3** [late 19C] to have sexual intercourse where the man's strokes are very long, deep into the vagina and then almost all the way out.

heel-ball *n.* [SE *heel-ball*, a shoemaker's tool] [1990s+] (*Irish*) **1** a busy, energetic person. **2** a term of abuse.

heeled *adj.* [SE *heeled*, used of a fighting cock, which had sharpened spurs tied to its heels] **1** [mid-19C+] (*orig. US*) (*also* **well-heeled**) armed. **2** [late 19C+] (*orig. US*) prepared, well provided for, wealthy, rich. **3** [1900s] in possession of (other than money or guns). **4** [1910s] busy. **5** [1950s+] intoxicated by or in possession of drugs.

heeler *n.* [SE *heel*, of a dog, to follow at the heels] **1** [mid-19C–1950s] (*US Und.*) a criminal's unskilled accomplice; any type of hired thug. **2** [late 19C–1920s] a lurch to one side. **3** [late 19C–1960s] (*US*) a hanger-on who performs tasks for a politician or political party in the hope of personal aggrandizement. **4** [1910s+] (*US Und.*) a sneak thief.

heel-grifter *n.* [HEEL *n.* (2) + GRIFTER *n.* (1)] [1940s] (*US Und.*) a small-time or second-rate con-man.

heel on *v.* [1910s+] (*US black*) to leave, to depart.

heeltap *n.* [SE *heel-tap*, a layer of leather used in making a shoe heel] **1** [late 18C–1930s] (*also* **bootheel**) the liquor left at the bottom of a glass; thus *no heeltaps!* (occas. *no bootheels!*) or *take off your heeltap!* drain your glasses! **2** [1930s] knockout drops.

IN PHRASES

❑ **and no heeltaps** [late 19C] without any doubt.

heel-thief *n.* (*also* **shoe thief**) [1930s–70s] (*US*) a petty criminal.

heel-toe *v. see* HEEL-AND-TOE *v.* (1).

heesh *n.* [abbr.] [1940s+] (*US drugs*) hashish.

heezie *n.*[1] [dimin./pron. of SE *house* + -IZ- *infix*] [2000s] (*US teen*) a house, a home.

heezie *n.*[2]

IN PHRASES

❑ **off the heezie** *see* OFF THE HOOK *under* HOOK *n.*[1].

heffa *n. see* HEIFER *n.* (3).

heffer *n. see* HEIFER *n.*

he-fluesy *n. see* FLOOZY *n.*

he-he boy *n.* [*he-he*, representation of giggling] [1930s] a homosexual man.

heifer *n.* (*also* **heffer**) **1** [late 16C–early 17C; 1920s+] a promiscuous woman; a prostitute. **2** [mid-19C+] (*also* **heffa**) a woman, a girl. **3** [late 19C+] (*later US black*) an unattractive, obese woman. **4** [1960s+] (*US black*) an immoral woman, esp. one who chooses to defy the current moral codes.

IN COMPOUNDS

❑ **heifer-den** *n.* [1930s] (*US tramp*) a brothel. ❑ **heifer-dust** *n.* [SE *heifer + dust*, rubbish, garbage; i.e. euph. for BULLSHIT *n.* (1)] **1** [1920s–40s] (*US*) Bull Durham brand tobacco. **2** [1920s+] (*US*) nonsense, rubbish. **3** [1920s+] (*Aus.*) a girl or woman. ❑ **heifer-dust act** *n.* [1920s] (*US*) an arrest and interrogation by the police. ❑ **heifer paddock** *n.* [late 19C+] (*Aus.*) a girls' school.

heigh-ho *n.* [the SE excl. *heigh-ho* was used to indicate to a potential buyer that such yarn was on offer] [mid-19C] (*UK Und.*) stolen yarn.

heighty-toity *n. see* HIGHTY-TIGHTY *n.*

Heinie *n.* **1** [20C+] (*also* **Heiney, Hiney**) a derog. term for a German; also attrib. [Ger. proper name, *Heinz*]. **2** [1970s+] (*US*) (*also* **Heiny**) a bottle or can of *Hein*eken lager beer [abbr.].

heinie *n.* (*also* **heiney, heiny, hiney, hinie**) [euph. dimin. of SE *hind end* or *hinder parts*] **1** [1920s+] (*orig. US black*) the buttocks; ext. as fig. ref. to oneself. **2** [1970s+] (*US campus*) a woman, considered sexually. **3** [1970s+] (*US campus*) a handsome man.

IN COMPOUNDS

❑ **heinie highway** *n.* (*also* **heinie hideout**) [20C+] (*US*) the anus.

IN PHRASES

❑ **from head to heinie** [1990s+] from top to bottom.

IN EXCLAMATIONS

❑ **my hiney!** [late 17C+] a general excl. of disdain, dismissal, arrogant contempt.

heino *n.* [abbr.] [2000s] (*Irish*) Heineken beer.

heinous *adj.* (*also* **hanus**) [intensified use of SE] **1** [1970s+] (*US campus*) terrible. **2** [1990s+] (*US teen*) fantastic. **3** [1990s+] very drunk.

Heiny *n. see* HEINIE *n.* (3).

heiny *n. see* HEINIE *n.*

Heinz *n.* (*also* **Heinz dog, Heinz 57**) [the *57 varieties* offered by H.J. Heinz] **1** [1920s+] (*orig. US*) a mongrel. **2** [1940s+] (*bingo*) the number 57. **3** [1940s+] (*gambling*) any combination bet.

4 [1940s+] anything, e.g. a concert, that combines a variety of disparate items.

heirhead *n.* [play on SE *heir* + AIRHEAD *n.*] [1980s+] a rich, hedonistic, stupid young woman, due to inherit a large fortune; occas. of a man.

heist *n.* [HEIST *v.* (1)] [1930s+] (*US Und.*) **1** a robbery. **2** the site of a robbery or break-in.

IN COMPOUNDS

▫ **heist artist** *n.* (*also* **heist guy**) [-ARTIST *sfx*/GUY *n.*²] [1930s+] (*US*) a robber, a 'stick-up man'. ▫ **heist job** *n.* (*also* **hist job**) [1920s+] a robbery. ▫ **heist man** *n. see* HEISTER *n.*

IN PHRASES

▫ **pull a heist** *v.* [1950s+] (*US Und.*) to commit a robbery. ▫ **put the heist on** *v.* [1960s] (*US Und.*) to steal.

heist *v.* (*also* **hist, hyst**) [var. on HOIST *v.* (1)] **1** [1920s+] (*US Und.*) to steal, to hold up; thus *heisting*, burglary. **2** [1940s] to increase, e.g. of a sum of money.

heister *n.* (*also* **heist man, hister**) [HEIST *v.* (1)] **1** [1920s+] a robber, a hold-up man. **2** [1970s] a car thief.

he-landlady *n.* [1900s] a pimp.

hel-bat *n.* [backsl.] [mid-19C] a table.

Helen! *excl.* (*also* **Helena! Helen Blazes! Helen Maria! Helena Montana!**) [20C+] (*US*) a euph. for HELL! *excl.* and used in various mild oaths.

helen *n.* [the initial letter] [1970s+] (*drugs*) heroin.

helitywhoop *adv. see* LICKETY-SPLIT *adv.*

helium-brain *n.* (*also* **helium-head**) [SE *helium* + sfx *-brain/-HEAD sfx* (1)] [1930s+] (*US campus*) a silly person.

hell *n.* **1** [late 16C+] the vagina [misogyny + *PUT THE DEVIL INTO HELL under* PUT THE… *v.*]. **2** used to describe a variety of unpleasant or 'sinful' places [note J. Taylor *News from Hell, with a short description of the Hell at Westminster* (1639), which describes a 17C tavern: 'Within this Hell is good content and quiet, / Good entertainment, various sorts of diet' etc]. (**a**) [mid-17C] Bridewell prison. (**b**) [late 17C–early 18C] a debtor's prison near Southwark, for the King's debtors who were never freed. (**c**) [mid-18C+] a casino, a gambling house; a billiard-hall. (**d**) [1910s] (*Aus.*) an opium den. **3** [1920s] (*US black*) anger. **4** [1920s+] (*US black*) an expert, an admirable or impressive person [HELL *adj.*].

DERIVATIVES

▫ **hellite** *n.* [mid-19C] a professional gambler.

SE in slang uses

DERIVATIVES

▫ **heller** *n.* **1** [late 19C+] one who lives an unfettered, undisciplined and adventuresome life. **2** [late 19C+] (*US*) a very difficult, formidable or exciting thing or person. **3** [1960s+] (*US campus*) an exciting, dramatic party.

IN COMPOUNDS

▫ **hell-all** *n.* (*also* **hell-in-all**) [var. on DAMN-ALL *n.*] [1930s+] (*US*) absolutely none, nothing whatsoever. ▫ **hell and tommy** *n.* [mid-19C–1940s] chaos, disorder (cf. *PLAY HELL AND TOMMY* below). ▫ **hell-bender** *n.* (*also* **hell-bending fool**) **1** [19C+] (*US*) a formidable, outrageous thing or individual [fig. use of US dial. *hellbender*, the American salamander or alligator (cryptobranchus)]. **2** [late 19C] a drinking bout [ext. of BENDER *n.*²]. ▫ **hell-bending** *adj.* [late 19C+] (*US*) hellish, arduous. ▫ **hellbent** *adj. see* separate entry. ▫ **hell-box** *n.* **1** [late 19C] (*US*) a pulpit. **2** *see* BOX *n.*¹ (4d). ▫ **hell-broth** *n.* [SE *hell-broth*, 'a decoction of infernal character or prepared for an infernal purpose' (*OED*)] [mid-19C–1910s] liquor, whether actually 'off' or seen as morally evil by teetotallers. ▫ **hell buster** *n.* **1** [1910s–30s] (*orig. US*) (*also* **hell blazer**) an amazing, riotous or violent thing or person. **2** [1930s] a preacher. ▫ **hell-cart** *n.* [? its lack of comfort] [mid–late 17C] a hackney carriage. ▫ **hell-cat** *n.* (*also* **hellicat, hell-kite**) [as termagant, of a woman and dating to early 17C, is SE, despite its inclusion by Grose] [late 17C+] a lewd bawdy person; also a mischievous young boy, a lively animal, a spiteful person. ▫ **hell-clinking** *adj. see* CLINKING *adj.* ▫ **hell-driver** *n.* **1** [late 17C] a coachman, presumably one who drives recklessly. **2** [1940s] a similarly inclined car-driver. ▫ **hell dust** *n.* [DUST *n.* (6a)] [1930s+] (*drugs*) heroin. ▫ **hellfire club** *n.* [presumably inspired by the original 18C *Hellfire Club*, a coterie of aristocratic debauchees, though not known for S&M] [1980s] (*US gay*) a club for devotees of hardcore sado-masochism. ▫ **hell-fired** *adj.* (*also* **hell-fire**) **1** [mid-18C+] (*orig. US*) a general intensifier. **2** [1950s] as an infix. ▫ **hell-hack** *v. see* HACK *v.*² (1). ▫ **hellicat** *n. see HELL-CAT* above. ▫ **hell-in** *see* separate entries. ▫ **hell-in-all** *n. see HELL-ALL* above. ▫ **hell night** *n.* [the initiatory rituals, known as *hazing*, that accompany such an event] [1940s+] (*US campus*) the night of initiation into a fraternity or sorority. ▫ **hellpig** *n.* [PIG *n.* (1c)] [1980s+] (*US campus*) a fat unattractive woman. ▫ **hell-raiser** *n.* [1910s+] one who deliberately causes trouble. ▫ **hell-raising** *n.* [1910s+] causing trouble. ▫ **hell-raising** *adj.* (*also* **hell-ripping**) [1920s+] trouble-making. ▫ **hell-raker** *n.* [19C+] a violent, forceful or exuberant person or thing. ▫ **hell-raking** *adj.* [backform. f. SE *rake-hell*] [17C+] dramatically violent, chaotic. ▫ **hell-roarer** *n.* [late 19C+] (*US*) a wild, uncontrolled individual or situation. ▫ **hell-roaring** *adj.* (*also* **hell-tearing**) [late 19C+] (*US*) wild, out of control. ▫ **hell's bottom** *n.* (*also* **hell's hollow, hell's point**) [20C+] (*US*) any disreputable or out-of-the-way area. ▫ **hell's delight** *n.* [early 19C+] pandemonium, chaos; often in phr. *play hell's delight* (*with*), to cause chaos (cf. *KICK HELL'S DELIGHT* below). ▫ **hell's front porch** *n.* (*also* **devil's front porch**) [1990s+] (*US prison*) prison. ▫ **hell's half acre** *n.* [mid-19C+] (*orig. US*) any disreputable area or place, esp. the slum area of a town or a low-class dancehall or bar; thus *all around/over hell's half-acre*, all over the place, everywhere. ▫ **hell's kitchen** *n.* [proper name *Hell's Kitchen*, the Irish-black slum area that covered part of the West Side of New York City from *c.*1850 to 1910, bounded by the Hudson River and Eighth Avenue, it ran from 39th Street to 59th Street. The name may have applied initially only to a single tenement or it may have been picked up from the name of a saloon in the red-light area of Corlear's Hook. The toughest part of Hell's Kitchen was known, at least to the writer O. Henry, as the *stovepipe*, a narrow enclave running along Eleventh and Twelfth Avenues] (*orig. US*) **1** [mid-19C+] any very unpleasant or dangerous place. **2** [late 19C+] a generic term for any urban slum area, esp. one that serves also as a lower class entertainment centre, or any dangerous or seedy place. ▫ **hell's mint** *n.* [late 19C–1910s] (*US*) a large quantity. ▫ **hellsnorting** *adj. see* SNORTING *adj.* ▫ **hell's own** *adj.* [late 19C+] (*orig. US*) used as a general intensifier. ▫ **hell-stick** *n.* [20C+] (*US*) a sulphur match. ▫ **hell week** *n.* **1** [1930s+] (*US campus*) the period of initiation for pledges to a college fraternity. **2** [1990s+] (*US campus*) examination week.

IN PHRASES

as an intensifier

▫ **as all hell** *adv.* (*also* **as sin, as hell's kitchen**) [20C+] a general intensifier: very, extremely. ▫ **like fucking hell** *adv.* [late 19C+] in no way whatsoever, absolutely not. ▫ **like hell** *adv.* (*also* **hell-ass-like, like hell for Texas, like god-dam, like merry hell, like sin**) **1** [mid-19C+] a general intensifier: recklessly, intensely, very much, very quickly. **2** [20C+] an ironic excl. of negation and denial, usu. as *like hell I will.* ▫ **shot to hell** *adj.* [1910s+] lit. or fig., destroyed. ▫ **sure as hell** *see under* SURE AS… *phr.* ▫ **to beat hell** *adv.* [late 19C+] to the utmost, very much. ▫ **to hell** *adv.* [late 19C+] a general intensifier, esp. as *hope to hell, wish to hell* to desire intensely.

pertaining to hopelessness

▫ **hoot in hell** *n.* [ext. of HOOT *n.*² (1)] [late 19C+] (*US*) a very small amount, the least bit. ▫ **no more chance than a cat in hell without claws** [late 18C–mid-19C; 1930s] absolutely no chance at all. ▫ **no more chance than a snowball in hell** (*also* **…a baldy, …a fart in a windstorm, …an ice-cream cornet in hell, last as long as a snowball in hell**) [late 19C+] absolutely no chance at all (cf. *NOT HAVE A SNOWBALL'S CHANCE IN HELL* below). ▫ **not a hope in hell** (*also* **not a hope in the hot place, …in Hades**) [1910s+] no chance whatsoever. ▫ **not have a cat in hell's chance** [1930s+] to have no chance at all. ▫ **not have a snowball's chance in hell** (*also* **not have a supply sergeant's chance in hell, snowflake in hell**) [20C+] to have no chance at all (cf. *NO MORE CHANCE THAN A SNOWBALL IN*

HELL above). ❑ **useless as an egg in hell** [1910s] (*Aus.*) utterly useless.

pertaining to time

❑ **until hell freezes (over)** (*also* **until hell wouldn't**) [mid-19C+] for a very long or indefinite time, for ever; thus (*W.I.*) *from hell freeze.*

pertaining to an unpleasant or distant place

❑ **hell and gone** (*US*) **1** [mid-19C+] far away, godforsaken; usu. as *TO HELL AND GONE* below. **2** [1920s] a long time ago. ❑ **hell and half Georgia** [1950s+] (*US*) an extremely large area; the second half of the phr. varies according to the speaker's locality, e.g. *hell and part of Groton, hell and half of New York state.* ❑ **hell west and crooked** (*also* **hell west and winding**) [late 19C+] (*orig. US*) in all directions, disarray, confusion. ❑ **to hell and go** [1930s+] (*W.I., Guyn.*) a general intensifier. ❑ **to hell and gone** (*also* **from here to hell and gone, to hellangone**) (*US*) **1** [mid-19C+] very far away, a very long time. **2** [1920s+] (*also* **to hell and back**) irretrievably, thoroughly, enormously.

pertaining to speed or diversity

❑ **from hell to breakfast** (*also* **from boots to breakfast, from here to Christmas**) [late 19C+] (*US*) **1** in all directions, everywhere. **2** decisively, violently. **3** for a long time, for a long distance. **4** to a very great extent. ❑ **from hell to Hackney** [early 19C] extensively, to a great degree. ❑ **hell for breakfast** *adv.* [20C+] rushed, hurriedly, at top speed. ❑ **hell for leather** *adv.* (*also* **hellbent for leather**) [the leather is due to the phr.'s origin in riding and refers to the harness] **1** [late 19C+] very fast, at top speed, rip-roaringly. **2** [20C+] vehemently. **3** [20C+] rip-roaringly.

pertaining to movement

❑ **get the hell out (of)** *v.* (*also* **get the hell off**) [20C+] (*orig. US campus*) to leave, to depart, e.g. *if you don't want to stay here, then get the hell…*, usu. with a place-name. ❑ **get the hell out of Dodge** *v. see under* DODGE *n.* ❑ **go like a bat out of hell** *v.* (*also* **go like a bat through hell**) [1910s+] (*orig. US*) to move exceptionally fast. ❑ **go like hell** *v.* (*also* **go like the devil**) [18C+] to go very fast, to be very busy. ❑ **go like the hammers of hell** *v.* (*also* **go like the hammers of fuck**) [1920s+] to go very fast.

pertaining to activity or disturbance

❑ **kick hell's delight** *v.* [20C+] (*Can.*) to cause a great deal of trouble or disturbance. ❑ **kick up merry hell** *v.* (*also* **kick up holy hell, curse all holy hell**) [1920s+] to cause a great deal of fuss. ❑ **play hell and tommy** *v.* (*also* **raise hell and tommy, raise thunder and tommy**) [? proper names Henry VIII ('Hal') (r.1509–47) and Thomas Cromwell ('Tommy') (c.1485–1540), the chief engineers of the English Reformation, or SE *hell and torment*] [mid-19C+] to cause absolute chaos (cf. *HELL AND TOMMY* above; *HELL AND TOMMY!* below). ❑ **play (merry) hell with** *v.* (*also* **play hell on, play holy hell**) **1** [1910s+] to give someone a hard time. **2** [1930s] to act aggressively. **3** [1940s+] to damage (an object, a plan etc). ❑ **raise hell** *v.* (*also* **raise blazes, …blue hell, …Hades, …heck, …holy hell, …merry hell, raise the deuce, …the dickens**) [ext. of SE; earlier citations invalidate the popular ety. crediting the phr. to a slogan, *Kansas should raise less corn and more hell*, attributed *c.*1896 to Mrs Mary Ellen Lease (1853–1933)] **1** [mid-19C+] (*orig. US*) to cause a good deal of trouble deliberately; to make a fuss. **2** [1920s+] to celebrate rowdily. **3** [1920s+] to castigate; sometimes intensified as *raise merry hell and put a shingle under it; raise hell and stick a prop under it*.

pertaining to the essence or 'stuffing', thus to beat lit. or fig.

❑ **beat hell** *v.* (*also* **beat to all hell, beat the hell out of**) [mid-19C+] to surpass, to exceed in expectation, to surprise; often as *if this don't beat hell, don't that beat hell.* ❑ **beat (the) hell out of** *v.* **1** [1920s+] (*orig. US*) (*also* **bat…, beat the living Jesus, …the heck, …the holy hell, …the living hell, …the shining hell, bite…, blast…, kick…, knock…, paste…, pound…, punch…, slap…, shake…, thump…, whop…, wipe…, zap…**) to beat severely. **2** [1970s] to do something to excess. **3** [1970s+] (*orig. US*) to amaze, to confound. ❑ **billy hell** *n.* **1** [19C] (*US*) a fantasy place that epitomizes the ultimate in bleakness and desolation, usu. in comparative phrs. for intensification, e.g. *meaner than…, hot as…* **2** [late 19C+] (*US*) used in phrs. as a synon. for STUFFING *n.*[1] etc, e.g. *knock the billy hell out of.* ❑ **knock hell out of** *v.* [20C+] (*orig. US*) to destroy comprehensively. ❑ **knock (the) hell of out** *v.* (*also* **knock blazes, knock hell's blazes out of, knock the heck out**) [mid-19C+] (*orig. US*) to beat severely, to destroy comprehensively. ❑ **rip hell out of** *v.* [1910s+] (*orig. Aus.*) **1** to defeat comprehensively. **2** to tell off, to reprimand. **3** to tease unmercifully.

pertaining to suffering

❑ **catch hell** *v.* [mid-19C+] **1** (*orig. US*) to get into trouble, to suffer a telling-off. **2** to suffer. **3** (*W.I./US*) to find it hard to make enough money to live, to subsist, to suffer great hardship. ❑ **get hell** *v.* (*also* **cop hell**) [1920s+] **1** to suffer. **2** to be severely told off or scolded. ❑ **give someone hell** *v.* **1** [mid-19C+] (*orig. US*) (*also* **give someone fuck, …heck, …holy hell, play hell**) to give someone a 'hard time', to scold severely. **2** [20C+] (*orig. US*) (*also* **give someone fuck, …heck, …holy hell, play hell**) to hurt, to inflict punishment on. **3** [1960s+] to cause pain. **4** [1960s+] of an inanimate object, to prove difficult. ❑ **scare (the) hell out of** *v.* [1930s+] to terrify. ❑ **see hell** *v.* [1950s] (*UK/W.I.*) to suffer, to have a hard time, to find it hard to make enough money to live. ❑ **smell hell** *v.* [mid-19C+] (*US*) to face danger, punishment.

general uses

❑ **all to hell** (*also* **gone to hell**) [19C+] **1** financially ruined. **2** wasted. **3** in chaos. **4** worn out. **5** utterly destroyed. **6** completely. **7** (*N.Z.*) mistaken, in error. ❑ **for the (sheer) hell of it** (*also* **just for…**) [1920s+] (*orig. US*) with no other justification than a (momentary) whim or self-indulgence. ❑ **from hell** (*also* **out of hell**) [1960s+] (*orig. US*) appalling, very unpleasant, usu. with a n., e.g. *the professor from hell, a game from hell.* ❑ **hell-a-mile** *adj.* **1** [late 19C–1930s] (*US*) terrible, hellish. **2** [1930s] (*US*) as general excl., the meaning varies according to context. ❑ **hell-a-tootin'** *adv. see HELL TO SPLIT* below. ❑ **hell beating tanbark** (*also* **devil beating tanbark**) [mid-19C–1900s] (*US*) a general intensive, usu. meaning very fast, in phrs. such as *quicker than hell beating tanbark.* ❑ **hell for** (*US*) **1** [mid-19C+] intent on, insistent upon. **2** [1940s+] as a general intensifier, exceedingly. ❑ **hell of a, a** (*also* **one hell of a, the hell of a**) **1** [late 18C+] hellish, awful; often abbr. to HELLUVA *adj.* **2** [mid-19C+] (*orig. US*) extraordinary, surprising (as often positive as negative). **3** [mid-19C+] to a very great extent. ❑ **hell of a note** *n.* [late 19C+] (*US*) very bad news. ❑ **hell on** **1** [mid-19C–1960s] (*US*) very fond of. **2** [1920s+] difficult or problematic for. **3** [1940s+] (*US*) very hard on, opposed to. ❑ **hell on wheels** *n.* (*also* **hell on roller-skates**) [mid-19C+] (*orig. US*) anyone or anything regarded as the equivalent of hell, usu. referring to character, speed or enthusiasm. ❑ **hell or high water** *see* separate entry. ❑ **hell's a popping** (*also* **hell a-popping, hell is popping, hell pops (loose), hellzapoppin'**) [late 19C+] (*orig. US*) a general phr. of intensification, implying aggression, chaos, forcefulness. ❑ **hell to pay** (*also* **holy heck to pay**) [the myth of the 'Faustian bargain'] [19C+] serious consequences will follow; usu. as *there'll be hell to pay.* ❑ **hell to split** *adv.* (*also* **hell-a-tootin', hell to toot**) [19C+] (*US*) at breakneck speed. ❑ **hell with the lid off** *n.* [late 19C+] (*US*) something extremely difficult or hard to bear. ❑ **I'll go hopping to hell** (*also* **I'll go to hell, I'll go hopping, I'll go hopping to hell backwards**) [20C+] a phr. implying the speaker's amazement, approval or admiration. ❑ **look like hell** *v.* [1930s+] of a person, to appear extremely unwell, whether through actual illness or through the effects of drink or drugs. ❑ **out of hell** *see FROM HELL* above. ❑ **seven kinds of hell** (*also* **seven kinds of shit, seven shades**) [20C+] intense unpleasantness; usu. with *knock/kick/beat/thump…*, to beat severely. ❑ **what the hell** [1920s+] whatever.

IN EXCLAMATIONS

❑ **get to hell (out of)!** [1920s+] a harsh demand that one go away. ❑ **go to hell!** [mid-18C+] a general excl. of dismissal. ❑ **go to hell across lots!** **1** [mid-19C–1940s] (*US*) a general intensified excl. of dismissal; the implication is that they should go with speed. ❑ **go to hell and pump thunder!**

[late 19C] an excl. of derision and dismissal. ❑ **go to hell, Hull and Halifax!** [the 16C prayer 'from hell, Hull and Halifax Good Lord deliver us', which refers to the Halifax Gibbet Law under which a prisoner was executed first and his guilt or innocence ascertained afterwards; for an eyewitness account *see* Taylor, *News from Hell, Hull and Halifax* (1639) pp. 26–9] [16C+] a general excl. of dismissal. ❑ **go to hell or Connaught!** [a law, passed in 1654, forcing Irish landowners out of Ulster, Munster and Leinster] [mid-17C–19C] an excl. of aggressive dismissal, go where you want but don't expect me to be bothered! ❑ **hell and tarnation!** *see* TARNATION! *excl.* ❑ **hell and tommy!** (*also* **hell and maria!**) [mid-19C+] a general excl. ❑ **hell's bells!** (*also* **hell's boots! ...britches! ...fire! ...flames! ...fury! ...smokes! ...teeth!**) [mid-19C+] a general mild. excl., usu. implying irritation or disappointment. ❑ **I'll be go to hell!** [1920s+] (*US*) a mild excl.; euph. for *I'LL BE DAMNED!* *under* DAMNED *adj.* ❑ **the hell with it!** (*also* **the hell with...!**) [20C+] a mild oath of annoyance or dismissal. ❑ **to hell with...!** [early 19C+] a dismissive excl., go away! be done with! ❑ **to hell with it!** [mid-19C+] a mild dismissive excl., I'm done with it! ❑ **what in hell?** (*also* **how in (holy) hell? what in blazes? what in hell and all? why in hell?**) [mid-19C+] a general intensifier of a query. ❑ **what the hell!** (*also* **what the heck! what the sweet hell!**) [mid-19C+] **1** a statement of resignation, of acceptance. **2** a general excl. indicative of annoyance or surprise. ❑ **who in hell?** (*also* **who in red hell? where in hell?**) [1930s+] a general, emphatic question.

hell *adj.* [on the bad = good model] [late 19C+] very good.

hell *v.* **1** [mid-17C] to place in hell or in a situation similar to hell, to cause someone to experience their personal hell. **2** [mid-17C] to make into a hell. **3** [mid-17C–1930s] to scold, to reprimand, to *GIVE SOMEONE HELL under* HELL *n.* **4** [late 19C+] to hurry, to 'fly' around (esp. in some activity disapproved of by the speaker), to go *HELL FOR LEATHER under* HELL *n.* **5** [late 19C+] to cause a commotion, to 'raise hell'; often as HELL AROUND *v.*

hell, the *phr.* **1** [mid-19C+] (*orig. US*) used to intensify a variety of prepositions, such as *what, why, where, how, who, when*; also as *who the hell's gates.* **2** [mid-19C+] a general intensifier to express anger, annoyance, impatience, also (ironically) disbelief or contempt, used to dismiss another speaker's assertion. **3** [late 19C+] (*also* **hell**) a general intensifer implying quantity, intensity.

hell! *excl.* (*also* **by hell! hell and...! hellfire! hell up! 'sdeath and hell!**) [late 16C+] a general expletive.

IN EXCLAMATIONS

❑ **— hell!** *see* separate entry. ❑ **hell and tarnation!** *see* TARNATION! *excl.* ❑ **hell no!** [1930s+] an excl. of denial, absolutely not! ❑ **hell yes!** (*also* **hell yeah!**) [1960s+] an affirmative excl.

— hell! *excl.* as a rhetorical question, implying the answer no, in a variety of excls., including those listed below; also used with different personal pronouns.

IN EXCLAMATIONS

❑ **could I hell!** an excl. implying resignation, acceptance. ❑ **did I hell!** implying negation, e.g. *Did I steal that car, did I hell!*; similarly *will I hell!* = no, I certainly won't! ❑ **do I hell!** [20C+] an excl. of absolute rebuttal, i.e. the hell I will! no I certainly won't/don't! ❑ **is he/she/it hell!** (*also* **are we/you/they hell!**) [20C+] a general phr. of aggressive dismissal, countering or negating the previous statement.

hella *adv.* [abbr. HELLUVA *adj.*] [1980s+] (*US campus*) **1** very, extremely, really. **2** a lot (of), many.

hellabad *adj.* (*also* **helluvbad**) [1990s+] amazing, excellent.

hellacious *adj.* (*also* **heckashin, hellashin, hellashus, hellation**) [HELL *adj.*/SE *hell* + BODACIOUS *adj.*; on model of SE *damnation*] [1920s+] (*US*) **1** wonderful, amazing, extraordinary. **2** difficult, demanding; also as excl.

hellafied *adj. see* HELLIFIED *adj.*

hell-around *adj.* [HELL AROUND *v.*] [1960s] (*US*) trouble-making.

hell around *v.* [HELL *v.* (5)] [late 19C+] (*US*) to cause trouble or a disturbance.

hellashin/hellashus/hellation *adj. see* HELLACIOUS *adj.* (2).

hellbent *adj.* [lit. 'determined on hell'] **1** [mid-19C+] (*orig. US*) determined, stubborn. **2** [1910s] in fig. use, a general intensifer.

IN PHRASES

❑ **hellbent for breakfast** *adv.* [20C+] rushed, hurriedly, at top speed. ❑ **hellbent for election** *adv.* (*also* **...Sunday, ... Georgia**) [fig. uses of *election/Sunday*; the enthusiasm of politicians for the fruits of power/workers for their day of rest; the link to *Georgia* is unclear] [late 19C+] (*US*) hurriedly, recklessly. ❑ **hellbent for leather** *adv. see HELL FOR LEATHER under* HELL *n.*

hellicking *adj.* [1960s] (*Aus.*) large and noisy.

hellie! *excl. see* HELLY! *excl.*

hellified *adj.* (*also* **hellafied**) [1960s+] (*US black*) extreme, excessive.

hellifying *adj.* [1970s] (*US*) wonderful or very bad.

hell-in *n.* [1960s+] (*S.Afr.*) a fury, a temper.

hell-in *adj.* [1960s+] (*S.Afr.*) furious, angry.

hell in, the *adv.* [1960s+] (*S.Afr.*) furiously, angrily, e.g. *he's going the hell in on everyone today.*

helling *n.* [1930–40s] carousing, causing a disturbance, living a hedonistic lifestyle.

hellishing *adj.* (*also* **hellishun, hellishly**) [1930s+] (*usu. Aus./N.Z.*) a general intensifier.

hellity-split *adv. see* LICKETY-SPLIT *adv.*

hello! *excl.*[1] (*also* **hello Mary!**) [20C+] (*US*) a euph. for HELL! *excl.* or hail Mary!

hello! *excl.*[2] **1** [20C+] (*also* **hullo!**) a general response to someone making a comment; there is no inference of greeting. **2** [20C+] (*also* **halloa! halloo! hillo! hollo! holloa! hullo!**) a general excl. of surprise and disbelief, I don't believe this! what's happening? **3** [1950s] (*also* **hello Mary!**) a cry of surprise to no one in particular when a beautiful woman is seen. **4** [1980s+] (*US teen*) a dismissive excl., implying that the individual at whom it is aimed should stop talking foolishly, or saying things in which they patently do not believe. **5** [1990s+] (*US campus*) an expression of agreement, sympathy. **6** [2000s] (*Aus.*) used by a young woman to announce the sight of an attractive man.

IN PHRASES

❑ **hello, nurse!** [1990s+] (*US teen*) a comment made on seeing an attractive member of the opposite sex.

hello-girl *n.* [she answers all calls with *Hello*] [late 19C+] (*US*) a female telephone operator.

hello Mary! *excl. see* HELLO! *excl.*[1].

hello, nurse! *excl. see* HELLO! *excl.*[2].

hell or high water *n.* [20C+] an intensely unpleasant experience; in different phrs. such as *go through hell and high water, between hell and high water.*

IN PHRASES

❑ **come hell or high water** [1940s+] no matter what the circumstance. ❑ **through hell or high water** [1940s+] to any extent, irrespective of any possible problems.

hellova *adj. see* HELLUVA *adj.*

helluva *adj.* (*also* **heckuva, hellova**) [representation of *HELL OF A, A under* HELL *n.*] [1920s+] a general intensifier.

helluvbad *adj. see* HELLABAD *adj.*

helly! *excl.* (*also* **hellie!**) [1960s] a synon. for HELL! *excl.*

hellza *adj.* [var. on HELLUVA *adj.*] [1990s+] a lot of.

helmet *n.* **1** [1950s+] (*also* **copper's helmet**) the glans penis. **2** [1970s+] a haircut. **3** [1980s+] (*US black teen*) a condom. **4** [1980s+] thus, a woman. **5** [1990s+] (*US campus*) a man.

IN PHRASES

❑ **buff one's helmet** *v. see BUFF THE BANANA under* BANANA *n.*

helo *n.* [abbr.] [1960s+] (*US*) a *heli*copter.

helpa *n.* [backsl.] [mid-19C] an apple.

helpers *n.* [? the Rolling Stones' song 'Mother's Little Helper' (1966)] [1960s] (*US drugs*) amphetamine pills.

helter-skelter *n.* [rhy. sl.] **1** [1940s] an air-raid shelter. **2** [1950s+] a bus shelter.

he-male *n.* [late 19C–1900s] a manly man.

hemo *n. see* HAEMORRHOID *n.*

hemp *n.* [the literal name of *cannabis sativa*, generally used in the context of textiles rather than intoxication] [late 19C+] (*drugs*) marijuana.

IN PHRASES

❑ **pull hemp** *v. see STRETCH (THE) HEMP under* STRETCH *v.*

hemp *v.* [19C use is US] **1** [mid-17C–19C] to hang, to choke to death; thus n., *hemp office*, the condemned cell; *hemp take someone*, an oath. **2** [mid-19C] to garrotte in order to rob.

hempen *adj.* (*also* **hemp**) [SE *hempen*, made of hemp, i.e. like the hangman's noose] in phrs. below, pertaining to judicial execution by hanging.

IN COMPOUNDS

❑ **hempen ballast** *n.* [mid-19C] (*UK Und.*) money paid to thief takers and others involved in the conviction of felons. ❑ **hempen casement** *n.* [lit. 'hempen window'] [late 18C–mid-19C] (*UK Und.*) the hangman's noose. ❑ **hempen collar** *n.* [late 16C–1940s] a hangman's noose. ❑ **hempen consummation** *n.* [early 19C] death by judicial hanging. ❑ **hempen cravat** *n.* (*also* **hempen circle, ...garment, ... garter, ...halter, ...hood, ...hornpipe, ...knot, ...necktie, ... quinsy, ...ring, ...tackle, ...wings, hemp necktie, ...neck-cloth**) [SE *quinsy*, a form of tonsillitis] [late 16C–1940s] the hangman's noose; also one who is to be hanged, gallows bait. ❑ **hempen fever** *n.* (*also* **hemp fever**) [18C–early 19C] a judicial hanging. ❑ **hempen fortune** *n.* (*also* **hempen furniture**) [late 18C–mid-19C] (*UK Und.*) money paid to thief takers and others involved in the conviction of felons. ❑ **hempen habeas** *n.* [pun on *habeas corpus*, lit. 'thou shalt have the body'; a writ whereby an accused and imprisoned person must be brought before the court and the reason for his imprisonment justified] [early 19C] a hangman's noose. ❑ **hempen tippet** *n.* [SE *tippet*, a loose scarf] [late 16C–early 17C] a hangman's noose. ❑ **hempen widow** *n.* [late 17C–1940s] a woman whose husband is hanged. ❑ **hemp fever** *n. see HEMPEN FEVER* above. ❑ **hemp necktie/neck-cloth** *n. see HEMPEN CRAVAT* above. ❑ **hemp party** *n.* (*also* **hemp stretching**) [late 19C] (*US*) a hanging, esp. a lynching. ❑ **hempseed** *n.* [late 16C–18C; 1940s] one who is destined to hang. ❑ **hemp-string** *n.* (*also* **hemp-strings**) [mid-17C] a term of abuse, a thief.

IN PHRASES

❑ **frisk in a hempen cravat** *v.* [19C] to be hanged. ❑ **hemp's grown for you, the** (*also* **there's hemp-seed sown for you**) [17C–mid-19C] a warning phr. implying that the person in question is bound to end on the gallows if they pursue their current lifestyle. ❑ **look through a hempen window** *v.* [17C] to be hanged.

hemp roller *n.* [1950s] (*US drugs*) one who smokes marijuana cigarettes.

hems *n.* [abbr.] [1980s] *haemorrhoids*.

hen *n.* **1** [late 16C+] a woman, usu. over 30. **2** [17C–early 19C] a prostitute. **3** [early 17C–19C] a mistress, a girlfriend, a wife. **4** [late 19C] a quart pot. **5** [late 19C+] (*Scot.*) (*also* **hinny**) a term of address to a woman. **6** [20C+] (*US campus*) a female student. **7** [20C+] (*S.Afr./W.I., Tob.*) a male homosexual. **8** [1920s–30s] (*Aus.*) wine. **9** [1920s+] (*US black*) an unkempt, unattractive woman, esp. with messy hair.

DERIVATIVES

❑ **hen-fest** *n.* [-FEST *sfx*] [1940s+] (*US*) a women-only party or gathering.

IN COMPOUNDS

❑ **hen and chickens** *n.* (*also* **hens and chickens**) **1** [mid-19C] large and small pewter pots. **2** [1930s] (*US gambling*) large or small stakes. ❑ **hen-cock** *n.* [mid-19C] (*UK Und.*) an effeminate or homosexual man. ❑ **hen college** *n.* [1920s+] (*US*) a women's college. ❑ **hen-coop** *n.* (*also* **hen-roost**) **1** [early 19C] a brothel. **2** [1900s] (*US campus*) (*also* **hennery**) a women's dormitory. **3** [1920s] (*US*) a beauty parlour. ❑ **hen fight** *n.* [1960s] a fight between two (occas. more) women. ❑ **hen frigate** *n. see* HEN HOUSE *n.* (1). ❑ **hen fright** *n.* [mid-19C] a man who is dominated by his wife. ❑ **hen house** *n. see* separate entry. ❑ **hen hussy** *n.* [dial. *hen hussy*, a woman who looks after the poultry] [late 19C–1940s] (*US*) a man who is seen to be over involved in household affairs and similar 'women's concerns'; thus an effeminate man. ❑ **hen mill** *n.* [1960s] (*US Und.*) a women's prison. ❑ **hen party** *n.* (*also* **hen night, hen picnic**) [late 19C+] a women-only get-together. ❑ **hen pen** *n.* **1** [20C+] (*US Und.*) a women's prison [PEN *n.*[2] (1)]. **2** [1960s] (*Aus.*) a women-only room in a local hotel (i.e. public house). ❑ **hen-roost** *n. see HEN-COOP* above. ❑ **hen skin** *n.* [1900s–50s] (*US*) a cowboy's blanket or underwear, usu. filled with feathers. ❑ **hen-whipped** *adj. see PUSSY-WHIPPED under* PUSSY *n.*

IN PHRASES

❑ **hen of the game** *n. see* separate entry. ❑ **hen of the walk** *n. see* HEN OF THE GAME *n.* (1). ❑ **spin a hen** *v.* [1940s] (*US black*) to dance with an older woman.

SE in slang uses

IN COMPOUNDS

❑ **hen fruit** *n.* (*also* **hen's fruit**) [mid-19C+] (*US*) chicken's eggs. ❑ **hen-headed** *adj.* (*also* **hen-witted**) [characteristics of the barnyard fowl] [20C+] (*US*) stupid, foolish, scatter-brained. ❑ **hen track(s)** *n. see* separate entries.

hen *adj.* [HEN *n.*] [late 18C+] pertaining only to women or gay men.

hen *v.* [the timidity of the fowl] [19C] to act cautiously; to back down.

hencackle *n.* [mountaineering jargon *hencackle*, an easy climb] [1940s+] (*N.Z.*) a trifle, anything unimportant.

hench *n.* (*also* **blench**) [2000s] (*UK teen*) **1** a large, muscular person; thus as adj., muscular. **2** a friend.

henfire *n.* [1920s] (*US black*) used in a variety of phrs. as a euph. for hell/damnation; including *how the henfire, I'll be henfired!, hen-fired*.

heng-pan-nail *n.* [W.I. pron. of SE *hang upon a nail*, whether in one's house or in the shop] [20C+] (*W.I.*) **1** unpressed and bedraggled clothes; thus a term of abuse. **2** ready-made clothes, rather than individually tailored garments.

hen house *n.* [HEN *n.* (1)] **1** [late 18C–early 19C] (*also* **hen frigate**) any house where the wife rather than the husband rules [note naut. jargon *hen frigate*, a ship where the captain's wife travelled with her husband]. **2** [late 19C–1900s] a women's hostel or lodging house [note US Army *hen house*, the Officers' Club, 'where all the chicken hangs out']. **3** [1900s] a prison in general. **4** [1900s–40s] (*US prison*) a women's prison; the women's section of a prison.

hen is on, a *phr.* [ety. unknown] [late 19C–1940s] (*US*) something important is about to happen.

Henley Regatta *n.* [rhy. sl. = SE *natter*] [1990s+] a chat, a gossip.

hennery *n. see HEN-COOP under* HEN *n.*

Henny *n.* [abbr.] [1990s+] (*US black*) *Hennessey* brandy.

hen of the game *n.* [HEN *n.* (1) + GAME *n.* (1b)/SE *walk*] **1** [early 17C–19C] (*also* **hen of the walk**) a prostitute. **2** [late 19C] a stalwart working-class woman.

Henrietta *n.* [rhy. sl.] [1990s+] a letter.

Hen-Rock *n.* [abbr. + ROCKS *n.* (7)] [1990s+] *Hennessey* brandy over ice.

henry *n.* **1** [20C+] (*US*) a Ford automobile [*Henry* Ford I (1863–1947), the patriarch of the automobile assembly line]. **2** [1950s+] (*drugs*) heroin [initial letter; also note heroin is seen as a 'masculine' drug, *see* BOY *n.*[2] (4a)]. **3** see HENRY VIII *n.* **4** *see* HOORAY (HENRY) *n.*

henry berry *n.* [rhy. sl.] [1990s+] (*Aus.*) sherry.

Henry Fonda *n.* [rhy. sl.; ult. US film star *Henry Fonda* (1905–82)] [1990s+] a Honda 90 motorcycle, esp. as used by trainee taxi-drivers or 'knowledge boys'.

Henry Halls *n.* [rhy. sl. = BALLS *n.* (1); ult. popular UK bandleader *Henry Hall* (1898–1989)] [1950s+] the testicles.

Henry Hase *n.* [the signature of the banking official] [early 19C] a banknote, usu. defined as to its amount, e.g. a *£10 Henry Hase.*

henry nash *n.* [rhy. sl.] [20C+] cash.

Henry Neville *n.* (*also* **Henry Nevil**) [rhy. sl.; ult. the G.R. Sims ballad 'Tottie' (1887): 'What the Henry Neville/Do you think you're doing there?'; ? elision of *henry neville* = *hell*] [late 19C] the devil.

Henry VIII *n.* (*also* **henry**) [abbr.] [2000s] (*drugs*) an eighth of an ounce of a drug, e.g. cannabis or cocaine.

Henry III *n.* (*also* **Henry the Third**) [rhy. sl.] **1** [1950s+] a piece of human excrement; thus as a contemptible person [= TURD *n.*[1]]. **2** [1980s+] a word.

hen track *v.* [1940s] (*US black/Harlem*) to sign one's name.

hen tracks *n.* **1** [late 19C–1970s] (*US*) illegible handwriting. **2** [1940S] (*US black*) a signature.

IN PHRASES

❑ **knock off hen tracks on a rolling piano** *v.* [? typewriters were usu. reserved for business use] [1940s] (*US black*) to use a typewriter to compose a personal letter.

hep *n.*[1] [HEP *adj.* (1)] **1** [1910s] understanding. **2** [1930s+] (*US*) someone who is aware of the situation, esp. within non-establishment circles. **3** *see* JOE HEP *n.*

hep *n.*[2] [abbr.] [1960s+] *hep*atitis.

hep *adj.* [rooted in the 19C SE *hep*, shrewd, which comes in turn from *Hep!*, the exhortation of the ploughman or driver urging his horses to 'Get up!' and get lively; the suggestion, as in Gold, *A Jazz Lexicon* (1964), that the term was first used by jazz fans in the 1940s (but not the musicians, who only used it 'derisively') and that those fans simply heard a black inflexion of HIP *adj.* (1) is erroneous due to the earlier dating; the suggested link to a real-life Chicago barman, one Joe Hep, is presumably a popular ety. only] **1** [20C+] aware, sophisticated, in the know. **2** [1950s+] fashionable.

IN PHRASES

❑ **get hep** *v.* [20C+] (*orig. US*) **1** to find out (about). **2** to see one's own interest, to learn what is going on, to become aware. ❑ **hep to the jive** *adj.* (*also* **hep to the groove, hep with**) [1940s+] aware, informed, sophisticated, in the know. ❑ **put (someone) hep** *v.* [20C+] to render (someone) knowledgeable.

hep *v. see* HIP *v.*[2].

hep-cat *n.* (*also* **hip-cat, hepped cat**) [HEP *adj.* (1) + CAT *n.*[5]; note Gold, *A Jazz Lexicon* (1964), 143–4: 'though frequently represented as jazz slang...jazzmen have never used this term in speech except derisively. Its etymology...is based on a Northern white hearing a Southern negro speak *hip* with a diphthongized vowel sound'] **1** [1920s+] (*also* **hep bird**) an aware, sophisticated person. **2** [1930s+] (*US black*) a jazz or swing fan. **3** [1950s+] a general term for a black person.

hepkitten *n.* [joc. dimin. of HEP-CAT *n.* (2)] [1970s] (*US*) a young woman who is a fan of swing music.

hepped *adj.* [HEP *adj.* (1)] [1930s+] (*US*) enthusiastic about, keen on; also constr. with *on*.

IN PHRASES

❑ **hepped up** *adj.* **1** [1930s+] (*US*) agitated, excited. **2** [1940s+] (*US*) intoxicated by drugs or alcohol.

hepster *n.* [HEP *adj.* (1) + -STER *sfx*] [1930s–50s] a jazz or swing fan; also attrib.

her *n.* **1** [1950s+] (*also* **herself**) one's wife. **2** [1960s+] (*drugs*) cocaine [GIRL *n.*[2] (1)].

her and him *n.* [partial rhy. sl.] [20C+] (*Aus.*) a hymn; often in pl. as *hers and hims*.

Herb *n. see* HERBERT *n.*

herb *n.*[1] (*also* **herbs, herba**) **1** [1940s+] (*drugs*) marijuana [orig. used in Jamaica, the religious role of marijuana for Rastafarians is emphasized in the 'natural' image of *herb*, also known as the 'herb of meditation' + a poss. ref. to Ps. 104:14, 'He causeth the grass to grow for the cattle, and herb for the service of man']. **2** [1960s] (*US campus*) a cigarette. **3** [1960s–70s] a marijuana cigarette.

IN COMPOUNDS

❑ **herb and al** *n.* [abbr. SE *alcohol*] [1980s+] (*drugs*) marijuana and alcohol.

herb *n.*[2] [? abbr. *Herb*ert, a common cockney name] [1950s] a character, also used of children.

herb *n.*[3] [HERBERT *n.*] **1** [1990s+] (*US black*) an unsophisticated person, one who has no knowledge of street life; thus *herbette*, the female equivalent [attrib. to an early 1990s Burger King commercial featuring a pathetic character named *Herb*; but note HERB *n.* as abbr. of HERBERT *n.*]. **2** [2000s] (*US campus*) homosexual.

herba *n. see* HERB *n.*[1].

herbal *n.* [1990s+] (*US drugs*) a pure marijuana cigarette, as opposed to one that has been laced with cocaine or another drug.

herbalist *n.* [HERB *n.*[1] (1)] [1970s–80s] (*UK black*) a drug seller.

herbalz *n.* [1990s+] (*US black*) **1** marijuana [HERB *n.*[1] (1)]. **2** semen [ety. unknown].

Herbert *n.* (*also* **Herb**) [1930s+] a simple person; thus *Herbert music*, music-hall jokes mixed with rock music.

Herbie Hides *n.* [rhy. sl. = STRIDES *n.* (1); ult. heavyweight boxer and former WBO champion *Herbie Hide* (b.1973)] [1990s+] trousers.

herbland *n.* [mid-19C] (*UK Und.*) the convict settlement of Botany Bay, New South Wales.

herbs *n.*[1] [ety. unknown; ? fig. use SE *herbs*, which 'spice up' a dish or are ? given to horses, i.e. 'horse power'] [1930s+] (*Aus./N.Z.*) **1** a car's speed, power, responsive to the accelerator. **2** enthusiasm, praise, flattery. **3** beer.

IN PHRASES

❑ **give it the herbs** *v.* (*also* **give it the berries**) [1950s+] (*Aus.*) to accelerate a car or fig. to give someone power.

herbs *n.*[2] *see* HERB *n.*[1].

herder *n.* [ext. of SE *herd*, to drive and control animals] [20C+] (*US prison*) a prison guard who works in the prison yard, controlling the prisoners.

herd (of camels) *n.* [pun] [1930s–40s] (*US black*) a pack of Camel cigarettes.

here and now *n.* [rhy. sl. = CHOW *n.*] [1990s+] (*Aus.*) a derog. term for an East Asian person.

here and there *n.* [rhy. sl.; the phr. is never truncated] **1** [1930s] (*Aus.*) hair. **2** [1930s+] (*orig. US*) a chair.

here-and-thereian *n.* [he wanders *here and there*] [late 18C–early 19C] a wanderer, a nomad.

Here Before Christ *n.* [initials] [1950s] (*US*) the Hudson Bay Company.

here goes! *excl.* (*also* **here's a go! here's fun! here's luck!**) [mid-19C+] a popular toast.

here's how! *excl.* [mid-19C+] a popular toast when drinking.

here's looking at you! *excl.* (*also* **here's into your face!**) [immortalized (and clichéd) after Humphrey Bogart's rendition in the film *Casablanca* (1941)] [late 19C+] a toast before drinking.

here's looking up your kilt(s)! *excl.* [1940s] (*Aus.*) a facetious toast.

here's luck! *excl. see* HERE GOES! *excl.*

here's mud in your eye! *excl.* (*also* **here's spit in your eye! mud! mud in your eye(s)! with mud in your eye!**) [orig. milit. use; thus ? ref. to the muddy trenches of WW1] [1920s+] a toast when drinking.

here's off *phr.* [1900s] (*Aus.*) goodbye.

her indoors *n.* [coined by Leon Griffiths in the *Minder* series on Thames TV, 1979; note Jap. *uichinomono*, wife, lit. 'the one inside'] [1970s+] one's wife.

herky-jerky *adj.* (*also* **herky-jerk**) [1940s+] (*US*) awkward, uneven, foolish.

her ladyship *n. see* LADY *n.* (3).

Her Majesty's bad/hard bargain *n. see* HIS MAJESTY'S BAD BARGAIN *n.*

Her Majesty's carriage *n.* (*also* **Her Majesty's omnibus, His Majesty's carriage**) [late 19C] a prison van.

Her Majesty's naval police *n.* (*also* **His Majesty's...**) [they swim near warm-water ports and thus prevent sailors from attempting to desert ship by swimming ashore] [late 19C–1900s] sharks.

Her Majesty's pictures *n.* [late 17C] money.

Herman *n.* [quasi-rhy. sl. + Germanic name] [1910s–40s] (*Aus.*) a German.

Herman (the one-eyed German) *n.* **1** [1970s] (*US*) a large breast. **2** [1990s+] (*US campus*) the penis.

herms *n.* [ety. unknown] [1980s+] (*drugs*) phencyclidine.

hernandies *n.* [play on song title 'Hernando's Hideaway' (1954), with lyrics: 'I know a dark, secluded place...'] [1970s+] (*US gay*) the buttocks.

heroin-head *n.* [SE *heroin* + -HEAD *sfx* (4)] [1940s] (*US Und.*) a heroin addict.

herone *n.* [? Sp.] [1970s+] (*drugs*) heroin.

hero (of the underworld) *n.* (*also* **heroina**) [1950s+] (*drugs*) heroin.

herp *n.* [abbr.] [1970s+] (*US*) genital *herpes*.

herped *adj.* [HERP *n.*] [1970s+] (*US*) carrying the virus for herpes.

herring *n.* **1** [late 16C+] a foolish, offensive or inconsequential person [? the commonness of the fish]. **2** [1930s–40s] (*US*) $1; a dollar [play on FISH *n.*[1] (2b)].

(IN COMPOUNDS)

❑ **herring-faced** *adj.* [early 17C+] worthless.

SE in slang uses

(IN COMPOUNDS)

❑ **herring-choker** *n.* [their consumption of herrings] [late 19C+] **1** (*Can.*) a nickname for a native or inhabitant of the Maritime Provinces. **2** (*US*) a Scandinavian-born immigrant. ❑ **herring-destroyer** *n.* [late 19C+] (*US*) a Scandinavian-born immigrant. ❑ **herring-gut/-gutted** *see* separate entries. ❑ **herring-Jew** *n.* [1960s] (*W.I.*) a derog. term for a Jewish or Syrian immigrant, who founded their fortunes on peddling salt-fish. ❑ **herring pond** *n.* (*also* **herring-brook**) **1** [late 17C+] the sea, esp. the Atlantic; thus *be sent across the herring pond* or *cross the herring pond at the King's expense*, to be transported (albeit to Botany Bay, Australia, rather than America). **2** [mid-19C–1940s] the English Channel. ❑ **herring-snapper** *n.* [late 19C+] (*US*) a Scandinavian-born immigrant.

herring-gut *n.* [backform. f. HERRING-GUTTED *adj.* (1)] [1910s] (*Aus.*) a thin man.

herring-gutted *adj.* **1** [early 18C–1940s] of a person, thin. **2** [late 19C+] cowardly, 'gutless'.

hers and hims *n. see* HER AND HIM *n.*

herself *n. see* HER *n.* (1).

Hershey *adj.* [brandname of *Hershey Bars*, a popular US chocolate bar; thus CHOCOLATE *adj.* (2)] [1970s+] (*US*) used in ref. to the anus and thus male homosexuality; usu. in combs. below.

(IN COMPOUNDS)

❑ **Hershey highway** *n.* (*also* **Hershey bar highway, Hershey Road**) [1970s+] (*US*) the anus. ❑ **Hershey squirt** *n.* **1** [1970s+] (*US*) (*also* **Hershey squirts**) diarrhoea. **2** [1980s+] (*US campus*) (*also* **Hershey stains**) faecal stains on one's underwear due to liquid emitted when breaking wind or through a badly cleaned anus. ❑ **hitchhiker on the Hershey highway** *n.* [1990s+] (*US*) a male homosexual.

(IN PHRASES)

❑ **take the Hershey highway** *v.* (*also* **ride the Hershey highway**) [1980s+] (*US*) to perform (homosexual) anal intercourse.

Hertfordshire kindness *n.* [stereotyped as a Hertfordshire custom] [late 17C–early 19C] a favour that is granted in return for one favour received, repaying one positive gesture with another; the phr. particularly refers to an exchange of congratulatory toasts.

he-say-she-say *n. see under* SAY *v.*

hesh *n.* (*also* **hash**) [SE *he* + *she*] [1930s+] a male homosexual.

he-she *n.* **1** [late 19C; 1960s+] a transvestite, transsexual or homosexual person. **2** [1960s+] a 'masculine' lesbian.

hesher *n.* [? *heavy metal* + *thrash*] [1980s+] (*US campus*) a fan of heavy metal music.

hesh girl *n. see* HASH GIRL *n.*

he/she sings in our choir *phr.* [1990s+] (*US gay*) a phr. used of a fellow male/female homosexual.

hesitation marks *n.* **1** [1960s+] scars on one's wrist denoting a failed or insufficiently committed suicide attempt. **2** [1970s] (*US gay*) excessive weight [the idea that extra weight is enough to make gay men suicidal].

hessian *n.* [SE *Hessian*, a Hessian mercenary employed by the British during the War of Independence (1775–83); thus a general term of derision. Note also the *hessian fly*, supposedly imported by the Hessian troops, the larvae of which devastate wheat crops] [20C+] **1** (*US*) a troublesome, mischievous person, esp. a fussy woman. **2** (*US*) a mischievous, ill-behaved child. **3** (*US prison*) a Secret Service agent.

hessle *n.* [? HASSLE *n.*, i.e. the problems involved in buying it, the addiction etc] [20C+] (*drugs*) heroin.

he-strumpet *n. see* HE-WHORE *n.*

het *n.* [abbr.] [1970s+] a *het*erosexual.

hetero *n.* (*also* **heter**) [HETERO *adj.*] [1950s+] *hetero*sexual.

hetero *adj.* [abbr.] [1930s+] *hetero*sexual.

heterosex *adj.* [1950s] *hetero*sexual.

het up *adj.* (*also* **heated up**) [SE *heat*, thus lit. 'heated up'; in general use 14C–16C but subseq. in dial. or sl. only] **1** [late 19C+] (*orig. US*) tense, nervous, angry, excited. **2** [1920s+] sexually aroused.

hewgag *n.* (*also* **gugag, hugag**) [SE *hewgag*, a toy musical instrument; ult. orig. unknown; ? *gewgaw*, a jew's harp'] (*US*) **1** [mid-19C+] a bugle or trumpet. **2** [late 19C] (*US campus*) something for which one has no specific name. **3** [1970s+] a battle cry [f. sense 1].

he-whore *n.* (*also* **he-concubine, he-strumpet**) **1** [mid-17C–early 18C; 1970s+] a male homosexual, usu. a prostitute. **2** [2000s] a promiscuous man.

hey *n.* [euph. + SE *hey!*] [1960s+] (*US*) a synon. for *hell*; thus *what the hey*, what the hell.

hey! *excl.* [SE *hey!*, a greeting] [mid–late 19C; 1970s+] a piece of verbal punctuation, used as a form of intimacy, suggesting a complicity between addressee and addressed.

(IN PHRASES)

❑ **make hey-hey** *v.* [1930s] (*US*) to act in a boisterous, celebratory manner.

heyderdan *n.* [? facet. use of popular ballad chorus 'hey derry down!'] [mid-18C] (*UK Und.*) an old brothel-keeper who has been whipped 'at the cart's tail'.

hey-diddle-diddle *n.* [rhy. sl.] [20C+] **1** a fiddle. **2** an act of urination [= PIDDLE *n.* (2)]. **3** the middle.

hey-hey *n.* **1** [1930s] (*US*) a 'good-time girl'. **2** [1930s] (*US*) problems, controversy, action. **3** [1940s–60s] (*orig. US black*) sexual intercourse.

hey-hey *adj.* [HEY-HEY *n.*] [1930s] of a woman, promiscuous.

hey-nonny-no *n.* [used in SE as a chorus in songs/ballads + SE *nonny-no*, a trifle, a 'nothing'] [late 16C–mid-18C] the vagina.

hey rube *n.* [HEY RUBE! *excl.*] [late 19C+] a fight, orig. between circus or carnival people and local townspeople.

hey Rube! *excl.* [SE *hey!* + RUBE *n.*[1] (1); *Hey Rube!* was the trad. rallying cry of circus or carnival employees when faced with any trouble from locals] [late 19C+] a call for help.

hey-wow *n.* [mockery of the hippie's cries of 'Hey, wow, man, can you dig that...' etc] [1980s+] (*US campus*) someone who clings to the styles of the 1960s.

H/H *n.* [1960s+] used in sex contact advertisements, *h*igh *h*eels.

hi-ball *n. see* HIGHBALL *n.*[1].

hic *n. see* HICK *n.*[1] (2).

hiccius (doccius) *adj.* [SE *hiccius doccius*, a juggler; ? ult. real Lat. *hicce est doctus*, this or here is the learned man, or ? pig Lat. formula used, like the conjuror's *abracadabra*, to accompany a juggling trick. Note SE *hiccup*] [18C] drunk.

hice yourself! *excl.* [Scot. *hoise*, to lift up, to raise] [20C+] (*W.I.*) get up and get out!

hick *n.*[1] [popular corruption of the personal name *Dick*, seen as generic] **1** [late 17C+] any inhabitant of the countryside, a peasant, a farmer. **2** [late 17C+] (*also* **hic**) a potential victim, a gullible simpleton. **3** [1920s] anyone parochial and limited, irrespective of origin. **4** [1960s+] (*US*) a Puerto Rican. **5** [1960s+] (*US campus*) one who lacks social and/or academic abilities.

(DERIVATIVES)

▫ **Hickster** *n.* [-STER *sfx*] [1990s+] a gullible, unsophisticated person. ▫ **Hicksville** *see* separate entries.

(IN COMPOUNDS)

▫ **hick town** *n.* [20C+] (*US*) a small town.

hick *n.*[2] [1920s] (*US Und.*) a dollar.

hick *adj.* [HICK *n.*[1] (1)] **1** [20C+] rural, countrified. **2** [1920s+] (*US*) unsophisticated, naïve.

hick! *excl. see* HECK! *excl.*

hickey *n.*[1] [abbr. DOHICKEY *n.*[1] (1)] [20C+] (*N.Z./US*) any small, otherwise nameless object; occas. an unknown person.

hickey *n.*[2] (*also* **hicky**) [ety. unknown; ? abbr. DOHICKEY *n.*[2]] **1** [1910s+] (*US*) a pimple, a boil. **2** [1940s+] (*orig. US*) a love bite, usu. on the neck. **3** [1940s+] (*US*) the penis. **4** [1950s+] (*US*) a bruise, a bump.

hickey *n.*[3] [HICK *n.*[1] (1)] [1940s+] (*Aus.*) any inhabitant of the countryside, a peasant, a farmer; with derog. implications.

hickey *adj.*[1] [SE *hiccup*] [late 18C–19C] drunk, tipsy.

hickey *adj.*[2] *see* HICKY *adj.*

hickey hockey *n.* [rhy. sl.] [1920s+] (*Aus.*) a jockey.

hickory *v.* [SE *hickory*, a walking-stick of hickory wood] [mid-19C] (*US*) to whip, to thrash.

hickory-dock *n.* (*also* **hickory-dickory**) [rhy. sl.] [1930s+] (*Aus./US*) a clock.

hickory oil *n.* (*also* **hickory tea**) [SE *hickory* (*stick*) + joc. use of *oil*/*tea*] [early 19C–1950s] (*US*) a whipping.

hickory towel *n.* [mid-19C] (*US*) a hickory switch.

hicks *n. see* HECK *n.*

hicksius doxius *adj.* (*also* **hictius-doctius**) [var. on HICCIUS (DOCCIUS) *adj.*] [late 18C–early 19C] drunk.

Hicksville *n.* [HICK *n.*[1] (1) + SE *ville*] [1920s+] (*US*) a generic term for any small, rural town.

Hicksville *adj.* [HICKSVILLE *n.*] [1920s+] (*US*) rustic, rural.

hicky *n. see* HICKEY *n.*[2].

hicky *adj.* (*also* **hickey**) [HICK *n.*[1] (1)] [1940s+] (*US*) countrified, rural, unsophisticated.

hictius-doctius *adj. see* HICKSIUS DOXIUS *adj.*

hid *adj.* [abbr. SE *hid*eous] [1980s+] (*US campus*) very ugly.

hidden forest *n.* [2000s] (*US black*) the vagina of a fat woman.

hidden magic *n. see under* MAGIC *n.*

hiddy *adj.* [SE *hideously*] [1980s+] (*US campus*) drunk.

hiddybugger *n.* [2000s] (*N.Z. teen*) an unattractive person.

hide *n.* [SE 11C–16C] **1** skin or its products, whether human or otherwise. (**a**) [17C+] the human skin, thus one's life; esp. in phrs. like *save one's hide* etc. (**b**) [20C+] a person. (**c**) [1930s–60s] (*US*) a horse. (**d**) [1930s–70s] (*jazz*) drums. (**e**) [1930s+] (*US*) a wallet. **2** by metonymy, as a woman or her body. (**a**) [18C] the female genitals. (**b**) [20C+] (*US*) a woman, usu. considered as a sex object. (**c**) [20C+] (*US*) an old crone, a hag, an ugly old woman. (**d**) [1940s–50s] (*US*) an effeminate male homosexual. **3** [late 19C+] (*usu. Aus./N.Z.*) in fig. use, impudence, effrontery, cheek.

(IN COMPOUNDS)

▫ **hide-beater** *n.* [HIDE *n.* (1d) + SE *beater*] [1930s–40s] (*US*) a drummer.

(IN PHRASES)

▫ **hate someone's hide** *v. see* HATE SOMEONE'S GUTS *under* GUT *n.* ▫ **let the hide go with the tallow** *v. see* LET THE TAIL GO WITH THE HIDE *under* TAIL *n.* ▫ **loosen someone's hide** *v.* [1900s] to thrash, to flog. ▫ **more hide than Jessie** (*also* **more arse than Jessie**) [a favourite elephant *Jessie* (1872–1939), which could be visited at the Taronga Park Zoo] [1950s+] (*Aus.*) a phr. used of one who is very cheeky. ▫ **tan someone's hide** *v.* [17C+] to beat someone severely, to spank someone severely.

hide *v.*[1] [a practice carried out on 18C plantations to discipline rebellious slaves] [late 18C] (*W.I.*) to murder, dismember and bury secretly.

SE in slang uses

(IN COMPOUNDS)

▫ **hideaways** *n.* [one *hides* one's money etc] [1930s–40s] (*US black*) pockets. ▫ **hide-up** *n.* [1920s+] (*Aus.*) a hideout.

(IN PHRASES)

▫ **hide one's/the baloney** *v. see under* BALONEY *n.* ▫ **hide the salami** *v. see under* SALAMI *n.* ▫ **hide the sausage** *v. see under* SAUSAGE *n.* ▫ **hide the weenie** *v. see under* WEENIE *n.*[1].

hide *v.*[2] [SE *hide*/HIDE *n.* (1a), the human skin] [early 19C–1900s] to thrash, to flog.

hide and seek *n.* [rhy. sl.; never truncated] [20C+] cheek, insolence.

hided *adj.* [HIDE *v.*[2]] [19C; 1990s+] beaten up.

hi-de-hi *n.* [1930s] (*US*) the exemplar; the very best.

hi-de-hi...ho-de-ho *phr.* [orig. used by US bandleader Cab Calloway in 'The Hi-De-Ho Man' but popularized in BBC TV's situation comedy, *Hi De Hi!* (1970s–80s), which was set in a 1950s holiday camp] [1930s+] a popular style of greeting and the requisite response.

hidey *phr.* (*also* **hidey herb, i.d. herb**) [SE *hi* + HOWDY DOODY *phr.*] [1920s+] (*Aus.*) a general greeting, how are you? how do you do?

hi-diddle-diddle *n.* [rhy. sl.] [1950s+] **1** the middle. **2** an act of urination [= PIDDLE *n.* (2)]. **3** a fiddle.

hi-diddle-diddle *v.* [rhy. sl.; PIDDLE *v.* (1)] [20C+] (*Aus.*) to urinate.

hiding *n.* [HIDE *v.*[2]] [early 19C+] a thrashing; thus fig. a severe sporting defeat.

hieser *n.* [1920s] (*US tramp*) a tramp.

hiez-haad *adj.* [pron. of *ears-hard*] [20C+] (*W.I. Rasta*) thick-skulled, stubborn, unwilling or unable to hear.

hifalutin *adj. see under* HIGHFALUTIN.

hig *adj.* [HID *adj.* + SE *ugly*] [1980s+] (*US campus*) disgusting, ugly.

higgledy-piggledy *adv.* (*also* **higgle-piggle, higgle-te-piggle-te, higglety-pigglety**) [the way in which pigs huddle together in the sty; Johnson saw *higgledy* as based in *higgle*, a confused mass, but *OED* prefers the development via *pig*: *pigly, higly-pigly*] [late 16C+] thrown together, out of order, jumbled up.

high *n.* (*also* **highness**) [HIGH *adj.*[1]] **1** [1940s+] (*drugs*) the euphoric, pleasurable state induced by taking drugs; the emotional, undrugged equivalent. **2** [1960s+] (*US*) a drink, a drug or anything that induces an intoxicated state. **3** [1970s] on the lines of *a drunk*, a person when intoxicated by drugs. **4** [1970s+] a general feeling of well-being; esp. in phr. *on a high*, feeling very happy and positive. **5** [1970s+] (*US*) in pl., high-topped sneakers or trainers. **6** *see* HIGHBALL *n.*[1].

(IN COMPOUNDS)

▫ **high-stick** *n.* [1950s] (*US teen*) a marijuana cigarette.

(IN PHRASES)

▫ **going high** *n.* [1960s] a state of 'full' intoxication. ▫ **hold one's high** *v.* [1980s+] (*US black/drugs*) to maintain control while intoxicated by alcohol or a drug.

high *adj.*[1] **1** [17C+] intoxicated with drink or poss. religious/spiritual enthusiasm. **2** [1930s+] intoxicated with drugs. **3** [1930s+] very enthusiastic about or taken with something;

often as HIGH ON below. **4** [1930s+] exhilarated; experiencing the sensation of drugs but without having taken any. **5** [2000s] in fig. use, successful [on the pattern of DOPE *adj.*[1]].

IN PHRASES

❑ **get high** *v.* **1** [mid-19C+] to drink, to be drunk. **2** [1930s+] (*drugs*) to experience a drug. ❑ **get high behind** *v.* [1950s+] (*drugs*) to experience a drug. ❑ **half-high** *adj.* [1960s–70s] (*US*) tipsy, mildly drunk. ❑ **high as a Georgia pine** *adj.* (*also* **higher than a Georgia pine**) [1920s+] (*US black*) very drunk. ❑ **high as a kite** *adj.* **1** [20C+] in fig. use, very happy, or excited. **2** [1910s+] a general intensifier. **3** [1930s+] very drunk [+ addition of rhy. sl. *high as a kite* = TIGHT *adj.* (7)]. **4** [1930s+] intoxicated by a drug. ❑ **high as ninety** *adj.* [mid-19C] (*US*) drunk [the use of *ninety* may be ext. of trad. image of *nine* as a lucky number]. ❑ **high on** [1930s+] (*orig. US*) **1** enthusiastic about. **2** in ample possession of.

SE in slang uses

IN COMPOUNDS

pertaining to the UK Und., implying superior

❑ **high beak** *n.* (*also* **high bloke**) [BEAK *n.*[1] (1)/BLOKE *n.* (2)] [mid-19C] (*US Und.*) a judge. ❑ **high cape** *n.* [mid-19C] (*UK Und.*) a dashing swindler. ❑ **high gammon** *n.* [GAMMON *n.*[2] (2)] [mid-19C] (*UK Und.*) adopting an aristocratic persona for the purposes of swindling. ❑ **high-gloak** *n.* [mid-19C] (*UK Und.*) a well-dressed highwayman. ❑ **high-go** *n.* [GO *n.*[1] (3)] [early 19C] a frolic, a spree. ❑ **high mob** *n.* (*also* **high mobsmen**) [late 19C] (*UK Und.*) leading criminals. ❑ **high pad** *n.* [PAD *n.*[1] (3)] (*UK Und.*) **1** [mid-16C–early 17C] the highway. **2** [mid-17C–mid-19C] (*also* **high-padsman**) a highwayman; also as n., *high-padding*, highway robbery. ❑ **high spicer** *n.* [late 18C–mid-19C] (*UK Und.*) a highwayman. ❑ **high tober** *n.* [note Partridge suggests a mis-reading of HIGH-TOBY *n.* and thus mis-definition] [late 18C–mid-19C] (*UK Und.*) an elite highwayman; (*US Und.*) a superior thief.

general uses

❑ **high-ass** *adj.* (*also* **high-assed**) [-ASS *sfx*/-ASSED *sfx*] [1930s+] (*US*) haughty. ❑ **highball/baller** *see* separate entries. ❑ **highbeams** *n.* [SE *highbeams*, automobile headlights when they are not dipped] [1980s+] **1** (*drugs*) the wide eyes of a person on crack cocaine. **2** (*US campus*) prominent nipples. ❑ **highbinder** *n. see* separate entry. ❑ **high blower** *n.* [its heavy breathing] [late 18C–mid-19C] a broken-down horse. ❑ **high boy** *n.* **1** [18C] a High Churchman, and thus usu. a supporter of Jacobitism. **2** *see* HIGHBALL *n.*[1]. ❑ **highbrow** *see* separate entries. ❑ **high brown** *see* separate entries. ❑ **high-cap** *v.* [1990s+] (*US black*) to show off. ❑ **high class** *n.* [2000s] (*US prison*) hepatitis C. ❑ **high cockalorum** *see* separate entries. ❑ **high colour** *n. see* HIGH BROWN *n.* ❑ **high cotton** *n. see* separate entry. ❑ **high-daddy** *adj.* [DADDY *n.* (6)] [late 19C+] (*US*) slick, deceptive, excellent, pleasing. ❑ **high dive** *v.* [DIVE *v.*] **1** [1930s+] (*US*) to pickpocket. **2** *see* TAKE A DIVE *under* DIVE *n.*[1]. ❑ **high diver** *n.* [DIVE *v.*] **1** [1930s+] (*US*) a pickpocket. **2** [1930s+] one who performs cunnilingus. ❑ **high drag** *n.* [DRAG *n.*[1] (8b)] [1960s] (*US gay*) formal clothing of the opposite sex. ❑ **high Dutch** *n.* [presumably fig. use not of 'Dutch' but *Hochdeutsch*, High German, the German spoken in the southern part of the country] [17C–mid-19C] nonsense, unintelligible gibberish. ❑ **high-end** *adj.* [orig. commercial use] [1960s+] (*US*) expensive or first-class. ❑ **highfalutin** *see* separate entries. ❑ **high femme** *n.* [FEMME *n.* (3); compare LOW FEMME *under* LOW *adj.*] [1990s+] (*US gay*) a very feminine lesbian. ❑ **high five** *see* separate entries. ❑ **high fly/-flyer/-flying/** *see* separate entries. ❑ **high guy** *n.* [GUY *n.*[2] (1)] [late 19C+] (*US*) an important person. ❑ **high-gyve** *v. see* JIVE *v.*[1] (7). ❑ **high hard yard** *n.* [1940s] (*US black*) a high stuff collar. ❑ **high hat/hatted/hatter/hatty** *see* separate entries. ❑ **high-headed** *adj.* [orig. used of horses, referring to the way a horse carries its head high] [20C+] (*US*) arrogant, haughty, self-important. ❑ **high-heeled/-heeler** *see* separate entries. ❑ **high iron** *n.* [1930s–60s] (*US tramp*) the railroad, esp. as regards the main rather than branch lines. ❑ **highjacker** *n.* [HIJACK *v.* (1)] [1930s] (*US Und.*) a criminal or tramp who robs other criminals or tramps. ❑ **high jinks** *n.* [SE *high jinks*, any form of game, usu. involving some form of forfeit, that is played by drinkers] [late 17C–mid-19C] a gambler who drinks with his victim in order to render the latter more malleable. ❑ **high-jive** *v. see under* JIVE *v.*[1]. ❑ **high jump** *n. see* separate entry. ❑ **high-kicker** *n.* **1** [late 19C+] (*US*) a dissolute person [image of a troublesome horse that kicks out]. **2** [1900s] (*Aus.*) a chorus girl [the focal point of her performance]. ❑ **high law/lawyer** *see* separate entries. ❑ **high living** *n.* [pun] [late 18C–early 19C] esp. of a thief, living in a garret or cockloft, i.e. a very small room immediately above the garret; thus *high-liver*, one who occupies a garret. ❑ **highlow** *n.* [1990s+] (*US black*) a variety of hairstyle, similar to the FADE *n.*[1] (4). ❑ **highlows** *n.* [such footwear stands between *low* shoes and *high* boots] [19C] laced boots that reach the ankles. ❑ **high maintenance** *adj.* [1980s+] (*US*) emotionally (or otherwise) demanding; thus *low maintenance*, easy-going. ❑ **high men** *n.* [mid-16C–early 18C] crooked dice that will always produce a high number. ❑ **high muck-a-muck** *n. see* separate entry. ❑ **high nation** *n.* [-NATION *sfx*] [20C+] (*W.I.*) a high-caste East Indian. ❑ **high nellie** *n.* (*also* **high maggie**) [20C+] (*Irish*) an old-fashioned ladies' bicycle. ❑ **high nose/nosed** *see* separate entries. ❑ **high octane** *see* separate entries. ❑ **high one** *n. see under* ONE *n.*[1]. ❑ **high pike** *n.* [SE *pike*, the toll paid at a turnpike] [mid-19C] an exorbitantly high price. ❑ **high-play** *v.* [1960s] (*US Und.*) to act in an ostentatious manner. ❑ **highpockets** *n.* (*also* **high pocket**) [1910s+] (*orig. US*) a tall man; thus a nickname. ❑ **high power** *n.* **1** [1940s+] (*US prison*) the maximum security section. **2** [1970s] a TRUSTY *n.*[2]. ❑ **high pressure** *see* separate entries. ❑ **high-prime** *v. see under* PRIME *v.* ❑ **high queen** *n.* [2000s] (*S.Afr. gay*) an active homosexual man, as opposed to a passive one, a TOP MAN *under* TOP *adj.* ❑ **high-rent/-rented** *see* separate entries. ❑ **high roll/roller/rolling** *see* separate entries. ❑ **high-season brown** *n.* [1900s–60s] (*US black*) a beautiful, brown-skinned woman. ❑ **high-shoe/-shoed** *see* separate entries. ❑ **high shoon** *n. see* HIGH-SHOE *n.* ❑ **high shot** *adj.* [var. on BIG SHOT *n.* (1)] [1920s+] (*orig. US*) a superior person or one who claims to be superior. ❑ **highside/sider/-siding** *see* separate entries. ❑ **high sign** *see* separate entries. ❑ **high-steam** *adj.* [? SE *high esteem*] [1940s] (*W.I.*) very good, superior. ❑ **high-step/-stepper/-stepping** *see* separate entries. ❑ **hightail** *v. see* separate entry. ❑ **high tec** *n.* [play on SE *high tec*(*hnology*)] [2000s] (*drugs*) alkyl nitrites. ❑ **high thrower** *n. see* HIGH ROLLER *n.* (1). ❑ **high tide** *n.* [late 17C–mid-19C] a state of financial security. ❑ **high-toby** *n. see* separate entry. ❑ **high-tone** *see* separate entries. ❑ **high-top fade** *n.* [FADE *n.*[1] (4)] [1980s+] a style of haircut favoured by young blacks. ❑ **high-up** *see* separate entries. ❑ **highwater/waters** *see* separate entries. ❑ **high yellow** *see* separate entries.

IN PHRASES

❑ **as high as Gilderoy** *adj. see* HIGHER THAN GILDEROY'S KITE *adj.* ❑ **high and dry** *see* separate entries. ❑ **high as (the hair on) a cat's back** *adj. see* HIGHER THAN A CAT'S BACK *adj.* ❑ **high collar and short shirt** *n.* [late 19C] an imitation dandy. ❑ **higher than...** *see* separate entries. ❑ **high on the hog** (*also* **high off the hog**) [that area of the animal from which come the choicest cuts of pork and its by-products] [mid-19C+] living a comfortable, secure and well-off life; esp. in phr. *eat high off the hog, live high on/off the hog*. ❑ **high-school harry** *n.* (*also* **harry high school**) [1950s+] (*US campus*) an immature male student. ❑ **to high heaven** *adv.* [ext. of TO HEAVEN *under* HEAVEN *n.*] [1940s+] (*US*) strongly, very much; usu. as STINK TO HIGH HEAVEN *under* STINK *v.*

high *adj.*[2] **1** [mid-18C–1940s] (*US*) impressive, attractive, splendid. **2** [late 19C; 2000s] (*orig. US*) expensive. **3** [1940s] (*US*) exaggerated. **4** [1950s] (*W.I.*) fashionable, stylish. **5** [1950s–60s] (*drugs*) pure [a sample of such a drug has a *high* percentage of the stated drug, rather than of the CUT *n.* (11c)].

IN PHRASES

❑ **how's that for high?** (*also* **how is that for high?**) [mid-19C–1940s] (*US*) what do you think of that?

high *adj.*[3] [SE *high*, of meat, slightly tainted but still desirable] [late 19C] often of a prostitute, suffering from venereal disease.

high and dry *n.* [abbr. *High Church*] [mid-19C–1900s] belonging to the Church of England, Anglican.

high and dry *adj.* [1910s] (*Aus.*) imprisoned.

high and goodbye *n.* [SE *hi!* + *goodbye*, i.e. their inability to stay lit. or fig. in one place] [1950s+] (*US black*) an unreliable person.

highball *n.*[1] (*also* **hi-ball, high, highboy, h.b.**) [? the tall or *high* glass in which it is served] [late 19C+] (*US*) whisky and soda; also attrib.

highball *n.*[2] [the small hanging ball used as a signal] [late 19C+] (*US*) a signal, orig. used by roailroads, meaning 'proceed'.

IN PHRASES

□ **give someone the highball** *v.* [? railroad jargon *highball*, a fast train; thus the individual who ends the affair is fig. 'taking a fast train' out] [1960s+] (*US*) to reject, to brush off, esp. to end a relationship or love affair.

highball *v.* [HIGHBALL *n.*[2]] [1910s+] (*US*) **1** pertaining to speed. (**a**) [1910s+] to leave at high speed. (**b**) [1920s–30s] to call (urgently). (**c**) [1920s+] to drive fast. **2** [1930s–50s] to make a gesture with one's hand. **3** [1960s] to witness.

highballer *n.* [HIGHBALL *v.*] [1910s+] (*US*) one who moves fast, works hard etc.

highbinder *n.* [SE *high*, haughty, pretentious, arrogant + BENDER *n.*[2], a hard drinker or drinking spree. Note, however, *high-binder*, an early 19C New York City gang, composed orig. of butchers' boys and simultaneously known as the *Hide-binders*; ult. f. the similarly named mid-19C Chinese secret society, supposedly terrorizing fellow-Chinese throughout the US] **1** [early 19C+] (*US*) a rowdy person, a vandal; a gangster, a thug. **2** [early 19C+] (*UK/US prison/Und.*) a criminal; a prison inmate. **3** [late 19C–1950s] (*US*) a member of a secret society supposedly existing among the Chinese in the US for the purpose of blackmailing, extortion and murder. **4** [late 19C–1950s] (*US*) a criminal or fraudulent politician. **5** [20C+] a snobbish person.

highbrow *n.* (*also* **brow**) [HIGHBROW *adj.*] [20C+] (*orig. US*) a clever person, an intellectual; depending on context there is often a nuance of jealous attack; thus n. *highbrowism*.

highbrow *adj.* (*also* **high-browed**) [a large forehead supposedly indicates great intelligence] [20C+] intellectual; often with pej. overtones.

high brown *n.* (*also* **high colour, Vaseline brown**) **1** [1910s+] (*US*) a mulatto, usu. a woman or girl. **2** [1930s] (*US black*) a sophisticated individual or object.

high-brown *adj.* [HIGH BROWN *n.* (1)] [1910s+] (*US*) mulatto.

high cockalorum *n.* [*see* next] [late 19C+] (*orig. US*) an important person; also attrib.

high cockalorum! *excl.* ['an ejaculation or exclamation; also a boy's game in which one set of players jump astride the others (who present a chain of 'backs'), calling out *Hey cockalorum, jig, jig, jig!* (*Hey cockalorum jig!* is given as refrain of a popular song c 1800)' (*OED*)] [early 19C–1960s] a general excl.

high cotton *n.* (*also* **tall cotton**) [the wealth that comes from a high cotton crop] [1940s+] (*orig. US black*) the good life, the materially successful life.

IN PHRASES

□ **shit in high cotton** *v.* (*also* **shit in tall cotton**) [1930s+] (*US*) to live prosperously, to feel happy, to be important; euph. alternatives include *fly in high cotton, live in high cotton, travel in high cotton*.

higher than a cat's back *adj.* (*also* **high as (the hair on) a cat's back**) (*US*) **1** [mid-19C+] very tall, very high. **2** [late 19C+] in fig. use, of money or a limit in gambling. **3** [20C+] very expensive. **4** [1960s] drunk [pun on SE *high*/HIGH *adj.*[1] (1)].

higher than a Georgia pine *phr. see* HIGH AS A GEORGIA PINE *under* HIGH *adj.*[1].

higher than Gilderoy's kite *adj.* (*also* **as high as Gilderoy**) [phr. *to be hung higher than Gilderoy's kite*, to be punished more savagely than one's fellow-criminals. The 17C Scot. robber *Gilderoy* of whom a ballad notes: 'Of Gilderoy sae fraid they ware/They bound him mickle strong,/Tull Edenburrow they led him thair,/And on a gallows hong;/They hong him high above the rest, ...' so high that he resembled 'a kite in the air'] [mid-19C–1900s] (*US*) extremely high.

higher-up *n.* [20C+] a person in authority; one who holds a superior rank (to oneself).

highfalutin *n.* (*also* **hifalutin**) [HIGHFALUTIN *adj.*] [mid-19C–1950s] (*US*) snobbery, pomposity.

highfalutin *adj.* (*also* **hifalutin, high-fallootin', highfaluten, highfaluting, hiki-fallootin'**) [SE *high* + unknown *falutin*; ? f. *floating, flighting* or *flown*; Hotten (1860) suggests Du. *verlooten*, to go and cast lots; other poss. etys. include Yid. *hifelufelem*, extravagant, boastful talk; Cohen (ed.), *Studies in Slang* II (1989), suggests US milit. jargon *high saluting*, saluting in accordance with military training (crisply, with a sharp snap of the wrist) rather than the somewhat lackadaisical salute of everyday milit. practice] [mid-19C+] (*orig. US*) snobbish, pompous; thus *highfaluter*, a snob.

highfalutin *adv.* [1900s] (*US*) snobbily, pompously; in a boastful manner.

high five *n.*[1] [the number of fingers on a hand and the height of the gesture; cf. LOW FIVE *n.*] [1980s+] a greeting or celebratory gesture that takes the form of raising the arm and ritualistically slapping palms with someone.

high five *n.*[2] [the letters of HIV = abbr. of SE *high* + *V*, roman numeral for five] [2000s] (*US teen*) HIV, AIDS.

high five *v.* [orig. used in sports as a greeting or sign of congratulations] **1** [1980s+] to greet someone by raising the arm and ritualistically slapping each other's palm. **2** [1990s+] to slap hands as a form of celebration, affirmation, congratulation etc.

high fly, the *n.* [late 19C–1910s] showing off, acting in a superior, arrogant manner.

high-flyer *n.* (*also* **flier, high flier**) **1** [late 17C–early 19C] a High Churchman, a Tory, a Jacobite. **2** [late 17C–late 19C] a daring adventurer. **3** [late 17C+] a pretentious or fashionable strumpet, a promiscuous woman. **4** [18C] a patron of the gallery at a theatre. **5** [18C–19C] a piece of hurried revision. **6** [late 18C–1910s] a pretentious or exaggerated statement. **7** [19C] a genteel beggar or swindler. **8** [19C] a 'swell' beggar, who poses as a fashionable gentleman; thus HIGH FLYING *n.* **9** [mid-19C+] (*US*) an important person or one who poses as such. **10** [late 19C] a begging-letter writer. **11** [late 19C–1900s] a gentleman who has fallen on hard times. **12** [20C+] (*US black*) one who lives well, one who enjoys material success.

IN PHRASES

□ **on the high-fly** [mid–late 19C] working as a beggar, a cadger or a begging-letter writer pretending to be a gentleman fallen on hard times.

high flying *n.* [HIGH-FLYER *n.*] **1** [19C] (*also* **go the highfly, on the highfly**) the practice of posing as a fashionable gentleman to swindle the gentry. **2** [20C+] (*US*) immorality, hedonism, extravagance.

high-flying *adj.* [HIGH-FLYER *n.*] **1** [late 17C; late 18C–1950s] of a statement, pretentious. **2** [mid-19C+] (*US*) arrogant, pretentious.

high hat *n.* [the *high hat* or top hat, whether as joc. resemblance or a sign of expensive lifestyle or tastes] **1** [late 19C–1950s] (*US drugs*) a large opium pill. **2** [1900s–50s] a glass of whisky and soda. **3** [1920s+] (*orig. US*) (*also* **high hatter**) a member of the social élite. **4** [1920s+] an arrogant, superior person, a snob. **5** [1930s+] a slight, a snub; usu. as *give someone the high hat*, or *put on the high hat*, to put on airs.

high-hat *adj.* [note Philip 'Vaudeville' (in Federal Writers' Project 1939): '"High hat," another term used in the same sense, is quite obvious. For example: John Juggler, who has been performing in white flannels, or other cheap costume, appears in new wardrobe presenting his act in a full dress suit and top hat, i.e. – a "high hat." This new ensemble indicates greater prestige, apparent prosperity, and a professional advance. Other vaudevillians, upon commenting upon it might remark: "I see John has gone high hat."'] [1920s+] of items and individuals, snobbish, pertaining to the upper-class.

high hat *v.* (*also* **give someone the high hat, hi-hat**) [1920s+] (*orig. US*) to act in a superior manner towards others, to snub.

high-hat *adv.* [HIGH-HAT *adj.*] [1960s] arrogantly.

high hatter *n.* see HIGH HAT *n.* (3).

high-hatty *adj.* (*also* **high-hatted**) [1920s+] (*orig. US*) snobbish, stuck up.

high-heeled *adj.* (*also* **high-heeling**) [wearing high-heeled shoes is a sign of superiority] [mid-19C–1910s] (*US/Aus.*) arrogant.

IN PHRASES

❑ **have on one's high-heeled shoes** *v.* (*also* **...high-heeled boots**) [mid-19C–1910s] (*US*) to be arrogant, self-important, snobbish.

high-heeled time *n.* [wearing high heels denotes a special evening out] [20C+] (*US*) an exciting or enjoyable time.

high-heeler *n.* [? SE *high* + HEELER *n.*] [1900s–20s] (*US Und.*) a female beggar, posing as a cripple with a built-up shoe.

IN COMPOUNDS

❑ **high-heel game** *n.* [1900s–20s] (*US Und.*) of a female beggar, posing as a cripple with a built-up shoe.

high jump *n.* [? steeplechasing; or of trouble so bad that one will metaphorically have to 'jump very high' to get over it; but ? image of death by judicial hanging] **1** [late 19C–1940s] the gallows, thus death. **2** [20C+] serious problems. **3** [1960s+] (*Aus.*) the criminal court.

IN PHRASES

❑ **in for the high jump** (*also* **in for the jumps, on the high jump**) [1920s+] in serious trouble.

highland *n.* **1** [1960s+] (*US*) in pl., the prosperous parts of a town, where the wealthy élite live [the way in which the wealthy gravitated to the higher ground in an era when the lowlands, usu. near the river, had a higher incidence of disease]. **2** [1970s] (*US black*) the northern, often black, area of a city.

highland fling *n.*[1] [rhy. sl.] **1** [20C+] (*Aus.*) string. **2** [20C+] a (wedding) ring. **3** [1960s+] in cards, the king.

highland fling *n.*[2] [1980s+] (*Aus. prison*) masturbation.

highland fling *v.* [rhy. sl.] [1950s+] to sing; thus *highland flinger*, a singer.

highland flute *n.* see FLUTE *n.*[2].

Highland frisky *n.* [rhy. sl. + its effects on the drinker] [late 19C] whisky.

high law *n.* [SE *highway* + LAW *n.* (1)] [mid-16C–early 17C] (*UK Und.*) highway robbery.

high lawyer *n.* [HIGH LAW *n.*] [late 16C–early 17C] a highwayman.

high lonesome *n.* [late 19C+] (*US*) a solo drinking spree.

IN PHRASES

❑ **hit the high lonesome** *v.* [1930s] to go out alone.

highly *n.* [HIGH *adj.*[1] (2) + ? SE *leaf*] [1970s] (*W.I.*) marijuana.

highmadandy *n.* [SE *high* + *dandy*] [20C+] (*Ulster*) someone who has more money than brains.

high muck-a-muck *n.* (*also* **big mucky-muck, great mucky-muck, high mickey-doodle, ...monkey-muck, ...muckety-muck, ...muckty-muck, ...mucky-muck**) [Chinook jargon *hiu*, plenty + MUCK-A-MUCK *n.*] [mid-19C+] (*US*) a superior or important person, whether in fact or through pretension; hence sometimes God.

highness *n.* see HIGH *n.*

high noon *n.* [rhy. sl.; ult. the film *High Noon* (1952)] [1950s+] a spoon.

high nose *n.* [HIGH-NOSED *adj.*] [20C+] (*US*) arrogance, snobbery.

high-nosed *adj.* (*also* **high-nosey**) [the subject's sticking their nose in the air] [late 18C–1940s] arrogant, supercilious; intellectual, pretentious.

high octane *n.* [HIGH-OCTANE *adj.*] [1990s+] (*US*) **1** very strong alcohol. **2** strong caffeinated coffee.

high-octane *adj.* [SE *high octane*, of gasoline; cf. LOW-OCTANE *under* LOW *adj.*] **1** [1980s+] dynamic, high-powered. **2** [1990s+] of alcohol and drugs, highly intoxicating. **3** [1990s+] of coffee, strong, highly caffeinated.

high pressure *n.* [HIGH-PRESSURE *v.*] [1920s] (*US*) a boss, a powerful man.

high-pressure *v.* [1920s+] to pressurize, to intimidate.

high-rent *adj.* [opposite of LOW-RENT *adj.*] [1970s] **1** (*US campus*) moral. **2** sophisticated, superior.

high-rented *adj.* [pun on colloq. *high-rented*, hot, thus HOT *adj.* (5c)] [late 19C] (*UK Und.*) of a villain, extremely well known to the police.

high roll *v.* [HIGH ROLLER *n.*] (*orig. US*) **1** [20C+] to spend money freely; to live hedonistically. **2** [1900s] to act boldly or aggressively.

high roller *n.* [SE *high* + *roller*, a dice-player] **1** [late 19C+] (*orig. US*) (*also* **big roller, heavy..., high thrower**) one who spends extravagantly, one who gambles for high stakes. **2** [20C+] (*US*) an expensive prostitute. **3** [1920s] (*US*) God. **4** [1920s] (*US*) one who behaves outrageously. **5** [1930s] (*US black*) a type of hat worn by gamblers. **6** [1980s+] (*W.I./UK/US black teen*) a materially successful person, usu. a rich ghetto drug dealer, as used by the Los Angeles gang, the Crips. **7** [1990s+] (*US*) a senior manager.

high-rolling *adj.* [HIGH ROLLER *n.*] [late 19C+] (*orig. US*) **1** extravagant, betting or spending heavily. **2** in ext. use, important, influential.

high seas *n.* [rhy. sl.] [1920s] (*US*) the knees.

high-shoe *n.* (*also* **high shoon**) [? the heavy footwear favoured by country-dwellers] [mid-17C–early 19C] a rustic, a peasant.

high-shoed *adj.* [HIGH-SHOE *n.*] [late 17C–early 19C] countrified, gullible.

highside *v.* [1960s+] (*US black*) to behave in an arrogant, boastful manner, to show off.

highsider *n.* [HIGHSIDE *v.*] [1990s+] an arrogant person, a person who shows off their material wealth.

high-siding *n.* [HIGHSIDE *v.*] [1960s+] (*US black*) showing off, bragging, often in the ostentatious display of jewellery, expensive clothes, cars etc.

high sign *n.* **1** [late 19C+] (*orig. US*) a warning, a recognition signal, a secret sign, esp. when denoting one's membership of a group; a signal that the 'coast is clear'. **2** [1920s–30s] a sign to leave, a rejection; as *give someone the high sign*.

high sign *v.* [HIGH SIGN *n.*] **1** [1920s+] (*US*) to warn, to give a sign of recognition, to signal that there is no danger. **2** [1970s+] (*US black*) to show off, to upstage someone.

high-step *v.* [1910s–20s] (*Aus.*) to feel pleased with oneself.

high-stepper *n.*[1] (*also* **stepper**) [orig. of a horse that lifts its feet high when walking or trotting] **1** [late 19C–1930s] a fashionably dressed or smoothly mannered person; a hedonist [20C use is SE]. **2** [1920s–60s] (*US black*) a tough, resilient person. **3** [1950s] (*Aus.*) a self-satisfied person.

high-stepper *n.*[2] [rhy. sl.] [1910s–60s] pepper.

high-stepping *adj.* [HIGH-STEPPER *n.*[1] (1)] [1910s+] (*Aus./US black*) aristocratic, smart, thus boastful, arrogant, showing off.

highstrikes *n.* [mispron.] [mid-19C–1930s] hysterics.

hightail *v.* (*also* **hightail it, hi-tail**) [reverse anthropomorphism] [1910s+] (*orig. US*) to leave quickly, to run off, to escape.

high-toby *n.* **1** [late 18C–19C] (*also* **main toby**) the highway, the main road. **2** [late 18C–1940s] highway robbery. **3** [early–mid-19C] a highwayman.

IN COMPOUNDS

❑ **high-toby gloak** *n.* (*also* **high-tober-gloak, high-toby gloque**) [GLOAK *n.*; Andrewes, *Dict. Slang & Cant* (1809), like *Sinks of London* (1848), erroneously omits 'toby'] [19C] a mounted highwayman. ❑ **high-toby man** *n.* [19C] a highwayman. ❑ **high-toby spice** *n.* (*also* **high-spice toby, high-toby splice, high-toby spree**) [late 18C–19C] the highway; highway robbery.

IN PHRASES

❑ **on the high-toby** [early 19C] living the 'high' life, usu. of a gambler.

high-tone *n.* (*also* **high-toner**) [HIGH-TONE *adj.*] [late 19C+] (*US*) an important person, a pretentious person.

high-tone *adj.* (*also* **high-toned, high-toney**) **1** [late 18C+] superior, high quality. **2** [late 19C+] stand-offish, snobbish; upper-class.

high tone *v.* [HIGH-TONE *adj.*] [1910s–20s] (*US*) to snub, to ignore.

highty-tighty *n.* (*also* **heighty-toity, hity-tity**) [first cited in B.E. – who spells it 'hightetity'; although HOITY-TOITY *n.* is earlier, *OED* notes the contemporary pron. of 'oi' as 'igh', as in oil = ile, boil = bile, and thus sees it as no more than 'a variant'] **1** [late 17C–18C] a promiscuous young woman. **2** [early 19C–1920s] an aloof, snobbish person. **3** [late 19C] snobbery.

highty-tighty *adj.* [HIGHTY-TIGHTY *n.*] [early 19C–1920s] aloof, snobbish, supercilious.

highty-tighty *adv.* [HIGHTY-TIGHTY *adj.*] [early 19C–1920s] aloofly, superciliously.

highty-tighty! *excl.* [HIGHTY-TIGHTY *adj.*] [early 19C–1920s] an excl. of disdain, annoyed surprise, infuriation.

high-up *n.* [HIGH-UP *adj.*] [1930s+] (*orig. US*) the boss, the leader, anyone senior to or more powerful than the speaker.

high-up *adj.* [1910s+] (*orig. US*) influential, important.

high water *n.* [like the real high water, such an economic 'tide' will ebb in time, so the image is of impermanence] [late 18C–mid-19C] financial security.

highwater *adj.* [mid-19C+] (*US*) too short, usu. of trousers, occas. of other clothing or hair; thus n. *highwaters*, trousers that are too short.

high waters *n.* [1980s+] (*US black*) an erection.

high yellow *n.* (*also* **high yalla, ...yaller, yalla**) [HIGH-YELLOW *adj.*] [1910s+] a mulatto woman or girl; occas. a man.

high-yellow *adj.* (*also* **high-yaller**) [SE *high* + YELLOW *adj.* (2b)] (*US*) **1** [1920s+] mulatto. **2** [1970s+] arrogant, superior [ext. of sense 1, i.e. considered better than black]. **3** [2000s] in colour, light brown.

higrade *v.* [1920s] (*US tramp*) to obtain something illegally.

hi-hat *v. see* HIGH HAT *V.*

hijack *n.* [according to Cohen, *Studies in Slang* II (1989), based on *high jack*, zinc ore, a term used *c.*1899 in the mines of Webb City, Missouri, then the world's greatest lead/zinc mine. This zinc ore was more valuable than the basic lead among which it was found, and miners would steal it to further enrich themselves. The term was virtually SE by 1900, as are the later meanings referring to the holding up of vehicles, including aircraft, and the killing or ransoming of their occupants] **1** [late 19C–1920s] (*US*) the robbery of tramps as they sleep in the 'hobo jungles'; the individual who does this. **2** [late 19C+] (*orig. US*) a hold-up followed by the theft of goods (often exercised by one criminal upon another). **3** [1920s] a robber who uses violence.

hijack *v.* [HIJACK *n.*] **1** [1900s–20s] (*US tramp*) to rob another tramp as they sleep in the 'hobo jungles'; later to rob a fellow criminal. **2** [1920s+] (*US*) to subject to extortion. **3** [1920s+] (*US gay/prison*) to rape another man. **4** [1920s+] (*US*) to remove or move a person against their will. **5** [1930s] (*US prison*) to violently rob a fellow prisoner.

hi jimmy knacker *n.* [rhy. sl.; ult. the name of an old street game] [20C+] tobacco.

hike *n.*[1] [SE *hike*, to walk] [mid-19C+] a vigorous or laborious walk; a tramp or march, a long journey by car.

IN PHRASES

▫ **take a hike** *v.* (*also* **make a hike**) [20C+] (*orig. US*) to leave; esp. as imper. *take a hike!*

hike *n.*[2] [? comb. of KIKE *n.* (1) + HUNKY *n.* (1)] [late 19C] (*US*) a derog. term for an Italian immigrant.

hike *v.* [dial.] **1** [1940s] to store up, to put away, esp. a valuable object. **2** [1950s] to send away. **3** [1950s–60s] to take someone for a walk, with the implication being that they will be assaulted or killed.

hike (off) *v.* [dial. *hike*, to run off with, to snatch] **1** [early 18C+] (*UK Und.*) (*also* **hike, hike out**) to leave, to go home. **2** [mid–late 19C] (*UK Und.*) to arrest. **3** [1950s] (*US*) to trick or cheat.

hiker *n.*[1] (*US*) **1** [1900s] a countryman. **2** [1930s–40s] a small-town marshal.

hiker *n.*[2] [SE *hike*] [1910s–20s] (*US*) a leg.

hiki-fallotin' *adj. see* HIGHFALUTIN *adj.*

hikori *n.* (*also* **hikuli**) [? Amerindian] [20C+] (*drugs*) peyote.

Hilda Handcuffs *n.* [1980s+] (*camp gay*) a police officer, usu. male.

Hill, the *n.* [1950s+] (*N.Z. Und.*) Mt Eden Prison in Auckland (which is in fact sited in a valley behind the hill).

hill *n.*

SE in slang uses

IN PHRASES

▫ **go over the hill** *v.* [orig. escaping outdoors work gangs, using hills as cover from one's pursuers] **1** [late 19C+] (*US prison*) to escape. **2** [late 19C+] (*US milit.*) to abscond, to desert. **3** [1960s] (*US*) to go mad. ▫ **hill of Venus** *n. see* VENUS'S HIGHWAY *n.* ▫ **on the hill** **1** [1950s+] (*US*) pregnant [the shape of one's stomach]. **2** [1980s+] (*Aus. prison*) in prison. ▫ **over the hill** **1** [1910s+] free, escaped, esp. of an escaped prisoner or a soldier who has deserted etc. **2** [1930s+] worn out, useless, too old, dead, crazy.

hill and dale *n.* [rhy. sl. = TALE *n.*[1]] [1940s+] confidence trickery.

hillbilly heroin *n.* [SAmE *hillbilly*, used as a general derog. adj., equivalent to 'poor man's'] [2000s] (*US drugs*) oxycontin.

hillman hunter *n.* [rhy. sl. = PUNTER *n.* (5); ult. the motorcar *Hillman Hunter*] [20C+] a customer.

hillocks *n.* [1970s+] (*US gay*) the buttocks.

hill of beans, a *phr.* (*also* **row of beans, ...pins, hill of shit**) [mid-19C+] an insignificant or useless thing, nothing; often in phr. *not amount to a hill of beans*.

IN PHRASES

▫ **not worth a hill of beans** [mid-19C+] worthless, useless.

him *n.* **1** [1960s+] (*drugs*) heroin [the perceived 'masculinity' of the drug; cf. BOY *n.*[2] (4a)]. **2** *see* HE *n.*

himbette *n.* [HIMBO *n.* + sfx *-ette*] [2000s] a younger, and perhaps more attractive HIMBO *n.*; the male equivalent of a BIMBETTE *n.*

himbo *n.* [SE *him* + BIMBO *n.*; allegedly coined in *Tatler* magazine] [1980s+] a gigolo.

himmer *n.* [SE *him*; Rodgers, *Queens' Vernacular* (1972), suggests an old joke, the punchline of which puns on SE *hymn/him*] [1950s–70s] a male homosexual.

hinaki *n.* (*also* **hinake**) [Maori slang *hinake*, eel trap] [1940s+] (*Aus./N.Z.*) prison.

hinchinarfer *n.* [SE *inch and a half*, the supposed length of her husband's penis – her grumpiness is due to sexual frustration] [late 19C] a grumpy, gruff-voiced woman.

hincty *n.* (*also* **hinckty, haincty**) [HINCTY *adj.*] (*US black*) **1** [1920s+] a snob, an arrogant, self-opinionated person. **2** [1960s+] a white person.

hincty *adj.* (*also* **haincty, hinckty, hinkty**) [ety. unknown; a suggestion that the word is an elision of HANDKERCHIEF-HEAD *n.* has no linguistic backing and the term is anyway later; ? note Lincolnshire dial. *hinch*, meanness, miserliness] (*US black*) **1** [1920s+] snobbish, pretentious, putting on airs. **2** [1960s+] a derog. epithet for any black abandoning racial pride in an attempt to ape white manners or styles. **3** *see* HINKY *adj.*

hind *n.* (*also* **hind-end**) [abbr. BEHIND *n.*] [1930s+] (*US black*) the buttocks, the posterior.

hind coach-wheel *n.* [the 'hind' or rear coach-wheels are larger than the front ones] [late 17C–early 19C] a five-shilling piece (25p), a crown.

hind fist *n.* [1900s] (*Aus.*) a leg, a foot.

Hindoo *n.* (*also* **Hindu**) [facet. uses of SE *Hindoo/Hindu*, a follower of Hinduism and thus, broadly, an Indian] **1** [1900s–10s] (*US*) a person with special ability, a wizard. **2** [1950s] a spell.

hind paw *n.* [18C–19C] a foot, a leg.

hindside *n.* (*also* **hindparts, hind-quarter, hind sights**) [HIND *n.*/SE *hind*; var. on BACKSIDE *n.*] [mid-19C+] the buttocks, the posterior.

Hindu *n.* [play on the 'untouchable' caste (properly *harijan* or *dalit*) and TOUCH *v.*[1]] **1** [1930s] (*US Und.*) one who cannot be bribed. **2** *see* HINDOO *n.*

Hindustani jig *n.* [? a supposed predilection of Hindus for sodomy] [1960s+] (*gay*) anal intercourse.

Hiney *n. see* HEINIE *n.* (1).

hiney *n. see* HEINIE *n.*

hinge *n.* [the turning of one's head] [1930s+] (*US*) a look; usu. in phr. *get/take a hinge*, to look at.

IN PHRASES

❑ **take a hinge at** *v.* [the turning of one's head] [1930s–50s] (*US*) to look at.

hinged dub *n.* [mid–late 18C] (*UK Und.*) a buttoned pocket.

hinges *n.* [20C+] (*US*) the joints of the human body; thus *one's hinges are creaking*, one is getting old.

hinie *n. see* HEINIE *n.*

hink *n.* [HINKY *adj.* (1); this and all derivatives may be nonce-words found in Ellroy only, and used historically by him] [1950s] suspicious information or rumour, suspicious activity.

hinked *adj.* [HINKY *adj.* (2); note comment at HINK *n.*] [1950s] frightened of, nervous about.

hink (out) *v.* [HINKY *adj.* (2); note comment at HINK *n.*] [1950s–60s] (*US*) to become or appear nervous, frightened.

hinky *n.* [HINKY *adj.* (3)] [1920s] (*US*) something or somewhere cheap and unsophisticated.

hinky *adj.* (*also* **hankty, hincty, hinkie, hinkty**) [Scot. *hink*, a hesitation, a misgiving] **1** [1920s+] (*US police*) suspicious. **2** [1950s+] (*US*) scared, jumpy, nervous. **3** [1960s] (*US*) very cheap, petty.

hinky-dinky *adj.* [the nickname of Michael 'Hinky Dink' Kenna (1858–1946), alderman and politician of Chicago] (*US*) **1** [1900s–30s] excellent. **2** [1900s–40s] little, short in stature.

hinny *n. see* HEN *n.* (5).

Hip, the *n.* [abbr.] [1920s] the *Hippodrome*, New York.

hip *n.*[1] [SE, but note also HIP, THE *n.*] [1910s] (*US Und.*) a burden, a problem.

IN PHRASES

❑ **on one's hip** [1910s] **1** of a person, acting as a burden, a dependant. **2** having someone following one.

hip *n.*[2] (*also* **hipness**) [HIP *adj.* (1)] [1940s+] (*orig. US black*) sophistication, the prevailing fashion.

hip *n.*[3] [one lies on one's hip when partaking of opium] [1950s] (*drugs*) a narcotics user.

SE in slang uses

IN COMPOUNDS

❑ **hip-chick** *n.* [1950s] (*US*) a prostitute who works in hotels. ❑ **hip-hitter** *n.* [1970s] (*gay*) a male homosexual [the physical movements of anal intercourse]. ❑ **hip inside/outside** *n.* [mid-19C] (*UK Und.*) inside and outside coat pockets. ❑ **hip layer** *n.* [1930s–50s] (*US drugs*) an opium smoker. ❑ **hip peddler** *n.* [1900s–40s] (*US*) a prostitute. ❑ **hipper nipper** *n.* [1970s] (*Aus.*) in pl., girls' bikini panties. ❑ **hip-tosser** *n.* [1950s] a male homosexual.

IN PHRASES

❑ **get one's hips up (on one's shoulders)** *v.* (*also* **get one's hips in a sling**) [1920s–40s] (*US black*) to get upset, annoyed or hurt. ❑ **have hip disease** *n.* [1920s+] (*Aus.*) to carry a hip-flask. ❑ **it's your little hip pocket** [? the position of the hip pocket over the buttock; thus one is about to receive a KICK IN THE PANTS *under* KICK *n.*[5]] [1950s+] (*US black*) you're in great trouble. ❑ **lay it on someone's hip** *v.* [the pre-mobile phone pager was often clipped to the belt at *hip* level] [2000s] (*US black*) to call someone on their pager. ❑ **on the hip** **1** [late 16C+] in a position of control, near absolute superiority [wrestling imagery, and used as such in the sport: the victim's hip would be on the ground when knocked down; however, note Nares: 'This phrase seems to have originated from hunting, because, when the animal was seized upon the hip, it is finally disabled from flight'; Dr. Johnson (in *Notes on Shakespeare*, 1765) suggests a link to the cross-buttock throw in wrestling but opted for the hunting link in later editions of his *Dictionary*]. **2** [1900s–30s] carrying alcohol in a *hip*-flask; usu. in phr. *got anything on your hip?*; thus drunk. **3** [1900s–60s] (*drugs*) (*also* **take it on the hip, laying on your ear**) using narcotics, whether opium, heroin or, latterly, crack cocaine [opium smokers rested on one *hip* as they smoked]. ❑ **peddle one's hips** *v. see* PEDDLE ONE'S ASS *under* PEDDLE *v.* ❑ **put a dent in one's hip** *v.* [one's wallet is carried on one's hip] [1970s+] (*US black*) to cost an appreciable amount of cash.

hip, the *n.* (*also* **hipp, hipps, hips, hyps**) [SE *hypochondria*] **1** [18C–19C] neuroses, misery, esp. when brought on by excessive drinking (cf. HYPO *n.*[1]). **2** [1920s] as *hips*, bad luck, a misfortune.

hip *adj.* [HEP *adj.* (1) or ? the posture of the opium smoker, reclining on their *hip* and the idea that the term, e.g. 'are you hip?', was used as a form of recognition between smokers; a link to Wolof *hepi*, to see or *hipi*, to open one's eyes has been posited. As relating to HIPSTER *n.* the word had a more specific meaning to jazz buffs/beatniks of 1950s, but now the general use is predominant] **1** [20C+] sophisticated, aware, in tune with events, ideas and situations; often as *hip to*. **2** [1920s+] (*US*) infatuated, excited. **3** [1940s–50s] (*US*) insolent, cheeky. **4** [1940s+] (*US black*) splendid, enjoyable. **5** [1960s+] (*US black*) in possession of or able to supply drugs.

IN COMPOUNDS

❑ **hip-cat** *n. see* HEP-CAT *n.*

IN PHRASES

❑ **get hip (to)** *v.* [20C+] to understand, to recognize, to work out. ❑ **have one's hip boots on** *v.* [pun on sense 1 above/SE *hip + boots*] [1930s–60s] to be sophisticated, aware. ❑ **hip to the tip** [1950s] (*US black*) to the greatest extent, e.g. dressed up in one's best clothes. ❑ **hip up** *v.* [1970s] (*US*) to understand, to appreciate. ❑ **too hip to slip** [var. on *TOO COOL FOR SCHOOL under* COOL *adj.*] [1990s+] very fashionable, well-dressed.

hip *v.*[1] [HIP, THE *n.*] [mid–late 19C] to depress.

hip *v.*[2] (*also* **hep, hip on, hip to, hyp**) **1** [1910s+] (*orig. US black*) to explain, to initiate into; thus *hepped*, *hept*, initiated, aware. **2** [1930s+] to inform, to tell about. **3** [1950s] as interog., to understand.

IN PHRASES

❑ **hip someone's ship** *v.* [1950s] (*US black*) to make clear, to explain.

hip *adv.* [HIP *adj.* (1)] [1950s+] smartly, fashionably.

hip-and-drop *v.* (*also* **hop-and-drop**) [20C+] (*W.I.*) to limp, either because of a temporary injury or a permanent deformity.

Hip City *n.* [? HIP *adj.*] [20C+] (*US black*) Cleveland, Ohio.

hipe *n. see* HYPE *n.*[1] (1).

hipidity *n.* [HIPPIE *n.*[2] (3)] [1970s] (*US campus*) a usu. young person, preaching a philosophy of 'love and peace', backed by a wide spectrum of drug use, esp. cannabis and hallucinogens.

Hip McCoke *n.* [rhy. sl. = BLOKE *n.* (3)] [1960s] (*S.Afr.*) a man, esp. a gambler.

hip Michael, your head's on fire! *excl.* (*also* **hyp Michael, your head's on fire!**) [mid-18C–early 19C] an excl. aimed at any passing red-headed man.

hipp *n. see* HIP, THE *n.*

hipped *adj.*[1] [HIP, THE *n.*] **1** [early 18C+] (*also* **hippish, hypped**) miserable, unhappy, in low spirits. **2** [mid-19C+] angry, irritated. **3** [late 19C–1940s] (*US campus*) impoverished. **4** [1900s–30s] (*US*) defeated, done for.

hipped *adj.*[2] **1** [late 19C+] obsessed with, convinced of; usu. as *hipped on* [fig. use of the opium smoker's lying on their *hip*, thus the image is of addiction, in this case to an idea or person rather than a drug]. **2** [1920s–70s] (*US black*) (*also* **hip on**) aware, well-informed; often ext. as *hipped to the play, hipped to the jive* [HIP *adj.*].

IN PHRASES

❑ **half-hipped** *adj.* [1940s] (*orig. US black*) ill-informed, unsophisticated.

hipped *adj.*[3] [SE *hip*] [1920s–40s] (*US Und.*) **1** carrying a weapon. **2** carrying a hip-flask.

hipper *n.* [? they carry a gun on their *hip*] [1900s] (*US Und.*) a police officer or sheriff.

hippie *n.*[1] [a bottle small enough to be kept in one's hip pocket] [20C+] (*W.I., Guyn.*) a half-bottle.

hippie *n.*[2] (*also* **hippy**) [like many terms, *hippie* crossed from the black to white worlds; unlike most, however, it altered its meaning, in this case from negative to, in peer-group eyes at least, positive. Since the 1960s/early 1970s the negative image has returned, although not as a failed *hipster* but as a 1960s throwback] **1** [1950s–60s] (*US black*) one who poses (with little or no success) as a HIPSTER *n.* **2** [1950s–70s] (*orig. US*) a sophisticated, cool, 'hip' person. **3** [1960s+] (*orig. US*) (*also* **hippiehead**) a (usu.) young person, preaching a philosophy of 'love and peace', backed by a wide spectrum of drug usage, esp. of cannabis and hallucinogens; also attrib.

IN COMPOUNDS

❑ **hippie crack** *n.* [CRACK *n.*[7]] [1980s+] (*drugs*) nitrous oxide.

hippie *adj.* (*also* **hippy**) [HIPPIE *n.*[2] (3)] [1960s+] pertaining to the style or fashion of the sixties.

hippins *n.* [SE *hips*] [1930s] (*US tramp*) a mattress.

hippish *adj. see* HIPPED *adj.*[1] (1).

hippo *n.* **1** [1970s+] (*S.Afr.*) an armoured police vehicle [abbr. SE *hippopotamus*]. **2** *see* HYPO *n.*[1] (1).

hippodrome *n.* [SE *hippodrome*, a course or circus for horseraces and chariot-races] [late 19C–1900s] (*US sporting*) any race or sporting contest in which the result has been fixed in advance.

hippodrome *v.* [HIPPODROME *n.*] [late 19C–1940s] (*US sporting*) to fix a sporting competition.

hipps *n. see* HIP, THE *n.*

hippy *see also under* HIPPIE.

hippy-dippy *adj.* (*also* **hippy-dip**) [HIPPIE *adj.* + DIPPY *adj.* (1); note Cooper, *The Scene* (1960): 'Hippy-dippy, sometimes kiddy, cry for your bottle when you want your titty' used to berate one who is acting childishly] **1** [1960s] (*US black*) immature, juvenile. **2** [1960s+] eccentric with added overtones of hippiedom.

hippy-trippy *adj.* (*also* **trippy-hippie**) [HIPPIE *adj.* + TRIPPY *adj.*] [1970s+] eccentric with added overtones of hippiedom.

hips *n. see* HIP, THE *n.*

hipsidoodle *n.* [1990s+] (*US*) a HIPPIE *n.*[2] (3), or someone who resembles one.

hipster *n.* [HIP *adj.* + -STER *sfx*; black use dropped by 1940s] [1930s+] (*orig. US black*) one who espouses the fashionable Bohemian stance of the period; the essence was a conscious downplaying of emotional display, a stance poss. facilitated by heroin addiction.

hipsy hoy *n.* [rhy. sl.] [20C+] a boy.

hiram *n.* **1** [1910s] (*US Und.*) an initiate into criminality; a thief [a metaphor taken from freemasonry]. **2** [1930s+] (*US*) a rustic, a peasant [the proper name, used in the Old Testament and thus popular among Puritan immigrants].

hiray *n.* (*also* **hiray**) [? SE *hire*] [20C+] money.

hi-res *adj.* [abbr. SE *high resolution*, used to define image quality on a video monitor] [1930s+] (*US*) fine, satisfactory, admirable.

hirey *n. see* HIRAY *n.*

his highness *n. see* HIS (ROYAL) HIGHNESS *n.*

His Majesty's bad bargain *n.* (*also* **Her Majesty's bad bargain, ...hard bargain, king's bad bargain, ...hard bargain, queen's bad bargain, ...bad shilling, ...hard bargain, Q.H.B.**) [the quality of his service does not justify his pay] [late 18C–1900s] a worthless soldier; a malingerer; a soldier jailed in a civilian prison.

His Majesty's carriage *n. see* HER MAJESTY'S CARRIAGE *n.*

His Majesty's naval police *n. see* HER MAJESTY'S NAVAL POLICE *n.*

his (royal) highness *n.* [late 19C+] used by a woman as a sarcastically 'respectful' description of her husband; the implication is of laziness, or someone considered to be pompous, overbearing.

hisser *n.* [ext. of N.Z. cross-country walking *hiss*, echoic of high-speed movement, thus one who moves fast and is, as such, admirable] [2000s] (*N.Z.*) something welcome or admired.

hissy *n.* (*also* **hissy fit**) [? SE *hysterical* or *hiss*] [1970s+] (*US*) a tantrum, an outburst of bad temper.

hist *adj.* [*BE HISTORY under* HISTORY *n.*] [1980s+] (*US campus*) finished, over, completed.

hist *v. see* HEIST *v.*

hist *phr.* [*BE HISTORY under* HISTORY *n.*] [1980s+] (*US campus*) goodbye.

hister *n. see* HEISTER *n.*

history *n.*

IN PHRASES

❑ **be history** [1920s+] (*orig. US*) to be out-of-date, no longer relevant, dead. ❑ **I'm history** [1980s+] goodbye; thus *make history*! go away!

history of the four kings, the *n.* (*also* **book of the four kings, the**) [mid-17C–19C] a pack of cards; thus *study the history of the four kings*, to play cards.

hit *n.* **1** in fig. use, a success. (**a**) [18C+] a successful coup of any sort, usu. based on crime. (**b**) [18C+] a success, usu. in show business. (**c**) [early 19C+] (*US gambling*) a winning series of numbers in gambling. (**d**) [20C+] a good impression. **2** in the context of crime or violence. (**a**) [19C+] an attempted crime, esp. a robbery. (**b**) [1950s+] (*UK Und.*) a murder, esp. a 'contracted' gangster killing. (**c**) [1950s+] (*US Und.*) the target/victim of an assassination. (**d**) [1960s+] (*US Und.*) an attack against a rival gang or gang member. **3** a portion of alcohol or drugs. (**a**) [20C+] a single drink of alcohol. (**b**) [20C+] a swig of liquid, a measure of anything. (**c**) [1910s+] the effect that follows the taking of any drug or drink. (**d**) [1930s+] (*drugs*) a purchase of a drug. (**e**) [1950s+] (*drugs*) a puff on a cigarette, marijuana cigarette or pipe. (**f**) [1950s+] (*drugs*) a portion of any drug, a tablet of amphetamine or barbiturate; an injection or a line of heroin or cocaine, a 'trip' of LSD etc. (**g**) [1960s+] (*drugs*) the act of injecting a narcotic drug; the injection itself. (**h**) [1980s+] (*drugs*) a puff on a crack cocaine pipe. (**i**) [1990s+] in fig. use, a stimulus. **4** an example of suffering or loss. (**a**) [1940s–60s] (*US Und.*) a prison sentence or denial of parole. (**b**) [1960s+] (*US Und.*) an arrest. (**c**) [2000s] a loss. **5** a single example. (**a**) [1970s+] (*US*) an instance, an attempt or time. (**b**) [1980s+] in gambling, a single card.

DERIVATIVES

❑ **hitsville** *n.* [-VILLE *sfx*[1]] [1960s+] the fig. world of success.

IN COMPOUNDS

❑ **hit-head** *n.* [-HEAD *sfx*] [1980s+] a user of crack cocaine. ❑ **hit house** *n.* **1** [1930s] (*US black*) an illegal bar that sells contraband liquor. **2** [1950s+] (*drugs*) a house where users go to inject narcotics and leave the owner drugs as payment. ❑ **hit list** *n.* [1970s+] **1** a list of those scheduled for assassination. **2** any list that details tasks that are to be carried out. ❑ **hit man** *n.* **1** [1930s+] (*US Und.*) a hold-up man. **2** [1950s+] (*orig. US*) a hired or 'contract' killer. **3** [1970s] in fig., non-violent use. **4** [1990s+] one who performs non-lethal violence for money. ❑ **hit woman** *n.* (*also* **hit lady**) [1970s+] (*US*) a female hired killer.

IN PHRASES

❑ **make a hit** *v.* [mid-19C+] (*orig. US*) to make a favourable impression. ❑ **one-hitter** *n.* (*also* **one-hit bowl**) [BOWL *n.* (2)] [1970s+] (*drugs*) a marijuana pipe that contains just enough for a single inhalation. ❑ **on hit** *adj.* [1990s+] (*US campus*) fashionable, chic. ❑ **take a hit** *v.* [2000s] to suffer.

hit *adj.* **1** [1910s] (*US*) in love. **2** [1990s+] (*US campus*) in trouble.

SE in slang uses

IN PHRASES

❑ **hit under the wing** *adj.* [mid-19C] drunk.

hit *v.* [sporting imagery] **1** [early 16C+] to arrive at something in one's mind, to discover, to guess correctly; often as *hit it*. **2** as lit. or fig. violence. (**a**) [late 16C–17C; 1920s+] (*orig. US*) (*also* **hit pussy**) to have sexual intercourse with a woman (**b**) [1920s+] to rob, to hold up; lit. and fig. uses. (**c**) [1950s+] to kill, to assassinate. (**d**) [1960s; 2000s] to seduce. (**e**) [1960s+] to attack, to criticize. (**f**) [2000s] (*US*) to sodomize. **3** in the context of consumption. (**a**) [mid-17C] of an aphrodisiac, to take effect. (**b**) [mid-19C+] (*drugs*) to use or consume drugs or alcohol. (**c**) [late 19C+] (*US campus*) to use. (**d**) [1920s+] to inject narcotics. (**e**) [1920s+] of a (narcotic) drug, to take effect; occas. of alcohol. (**f**) [1940s+] to give someone an injection of narcotics. (**g**) [1940s+] (*drugs*) (*also* **hit on**) to take a puff of a cigarette or marijuana cigarette. (**h**) [1960s+] (*drugs*) to adulterate drugs before selling them. **4** to request. (**a**) [mid-18C; mid-19C+] (*US*) to beg, to ask for a loan, to accost. (**b**) [1950s+] to charge money, e.g. as rent. (**c**) [1990s+] (*US black/drugs*) to call someone on a pager. **5** in criminal contexts. (**a**) [19C+] (*US*) to send to prison. (**b**) [1950s+] to raid an establishment; usu. of police. (**c**) [1990s+] to stop and search, usu. of a vehicle. **6** to attain an aim. (**a**) [early 19C] to succeed, to work out. (**b**) [late 19C–1920s] to defeat, to overcome. (**c**) [late 19C+] (*US campus*) to pass an exam with a high grade. (**d**) [20C+] to succeed, to do well. (**e**) [1910s+] to make a successful bet. (**f**) [1930s+] (*US black*) to work hard. (**g**) [1940s+] of a bet, to prove successful. **7** in the context of motion. (**a**) [late 19C+] to go to, to visit; to arrive at; of people but also objects. (**b**) [1910s] to meet. (**c**) [1920s+] to do something, usu. involving motion. **8** (*orig. US*) to give. (**a**) [late 19C+] to pay, to hand over money, to bet. (**b**) [1920s+] to deal out a card, esp. in imper. *see* HIT ME! below. (**c**) [1930s+] to give someone a drink. (**d**) [2000s] to present, of a gesture or a grimace. **9** to obtain, legally or otherwise. (**a**) [20C+] to take. (**b**) [1960s] to make money. **10** [1940s+] to switch on or off, to apply, e.g. the lights or the brakes of a vehicle.

IN PHRASES

□ **hit...** *v. see also under* relevant n. or adj. □ **hit a 180** *v.* [180°] [1990s+] to make an abrupt reversal; to change one's mind. □ **hit a tap** *v. see* HIT A LICK (AT A SNAKE) *under* LICK *n.*[2]. □ **hit for** *v. see* separate entry. □ **hit it** *v. see* separate entry. □ **hit on** *v. see* separate entry. □ **hit on all (four) cylinders** *v.* (*also* **hit on all six**) [automobile imagery] [1910s+] to work properly. □ **hit one's hobbles** *v.* [racing use *hit the hobbles*, for a horse to keep galloping despite a hobble chain] [1950s+] (*Aus.*) to make a comeback. □ **hit on the head by the tavern bitch** *adj. see* BIT BY THE TAVERN BITCH *under* BIT BY... *phr.* □ **hit pussy** *v. see* HIT *v.* (2a). □ **hit red** *v.* [1960s+] (*US drugs*) to draw blood into the syringe, where it mixes with the water/narcotic solution prior to injection. □ **hit someone off** *v.* [1990s+] (*US black*) to give someone (something). □ **hit someone on the hip** *v.* [1990s+] (*US black*) to page someone. □ **hit someone up** *v.* [1980s+] (*US black*) **1** to attack physically. **2** to challenge verbally. **3** (*also* **hit someone back**) to approach, to get in touch with someone. □ **hit someone with** *v.* **1** [1950s] to approach someone with a plan. **2** [1950s+] to give someone something. □ **hit the ball** *v. see* separate entry. □ **hit the books** *v. see* separate entry. □ **hit the bottle** *v.* (*also* **hit the flask, ...jug**) [late 19C+] (*orig. US*) to drink heavily. □ **hit the ceiling** *v. see* separate entry. □ **hit the fan** *v. see* SHIT HITS THE FAN, THE *under* SHIT *n.* □ **hit the gas** *v.* [1920s+] (*US*) to accelerate in a motorcar. □ **hit the gate** *v.* [1990s+] (*US Und./prison*) to leave prison, to be released. □ **hit the hike** *v. see* HIT THE ROAD *v.* □ **hit the pit** *v.* **1** [20C+] (*US Und.*) to be imprisoned. **2** *see under* PIT *n.* □ **hit the road** *v. see* separate entry. □ **hit the roof** *v. see* HIT THE CEILING *v.* (4). □ **hit the ties** *v.* [SE *tie*, a railway sleeper] [1900s–30s] (*US*) **1** to walk along railway tracks, esp. after quitting one's job in a work camp. **2** in fig. use, to be out of a job. □ **hit the trail** *v.* (*also* **hit the track**) [late 19C+] (*orig. US*) to leave; as *hit the smoky trail*, leave by a railway. □ **hit up** *v. see* separate entries.

IN EXCLAMATIONS

□ **hit me!** **1** [1930s+] (*orig. US gambling*) an invitation to the dealer to give one another card. **2** [1940s+] (*orig. US*) an invitation to a bartender to pour one another drink.

hi-tail *v. see* HIGHTAIL *v.*

hit (and miss) *n.* (*also* **hit or miss**) [rhy. sl.] [1930s+] **1** a kiss. **2** urine [= PISS *n.* (1)]. **3** urination [= PISS *n.* (2)].

hit and miss *v.* [rhy. sl. = PISS *v.* (2)] [1980s] (*Aus.*) to urinate.

hit and missed *adj.* [rhy. sl. = PISSED *adj.*[1]; unlike most rhy. sl. this phr. is never truncated] [1960s+] drunk.

hit and run *n.* [rhy. sl.] [1990s+] the sun.

hit and run *adj.* [rhy. sl. = DONE *adj.* (4)] [20C+] cheated, deceived.

hitch *n.*[1] [SE *hitch*, a temporary fastening, as with a loop or knot] **1** [mid-19C+] (*US*) a period of time, esp. of employment of any sort. **2** [20C+] (*US milit.*) a term of enlistment in one of the US armed forces. **3** [1920s+] (*US*) a prison sentence.

hitch *n.*[2] [HITCH *v.*[2]] [1920s+] an act of hitchhiking, e.g. *I got a hitch up to London*.

hitch *n.*[3] [1950s] (*US drugs*) in pl., punctures and scar tissue from injections that accumulate along the veins of a regular heroin addict.

hitch *v.*[1] [? abbr. *hitch up one's sleeves*] [late 19C–1920s] (*US*) to start fighting.

hitch *v.*[2] [abbr.] [1920s+] to *hitch*hike.

hitch *v.*[3] *see* HITCH (UP) *v.*

hitched *adj.* (*also* **hitched up**) [HITCH (UP) *v.*] [mid-19C+] (*orig. US*) married; thus *unhitched*, divorced; *hitching-on*, a marriage ceremony.

hitchhike *v. see* DRIVE THE CAR *under* CAR *n.*

hitch it *v.* [var. on HITCH (UP) *v.*] [1910s] (*Aus.*) to get married.

hitch-up *n.* [HITCH (UP) *v.* (1)] [19C] (*US*) **1** a marriage. **2** a married couple.

hitch (up) *v.* (*also* **hitch on**) [SE *hitch*, to fasten, esp. in a temporary way] **1** [mid-19C+] to establish a relationship with, to marry; thus *rehitch*, to remarry; *hitcher up*, one who is getting married. **2** [20C+] to join two people in marriage.

IN PHRASES

□ **hitch horses together** *v.* [hitching two horses to the same post] [19C] (*US*) **1** to agree upon, to get along well. **2** to marry. □ **hitch teams** *v.* (*also* **hitch one's wagon, hitch tackle**) [mid-19C–1900s] to get married, to marry.

hitch up *v.* [the *hitching up* of one's team to a wagon or coach before setting off on a journey] [late 19C–1900s] (*US*) to start, to set off.

hitch up the reindeers *v.* [play on the relationship of reindeer to SNOW *n.*[1] (2a)] (*drugs*) **1** [1930s–50s] to prepare the needle etc for an injection of cocaine. **2** [1930s+] to inhale cocaine.

hitey-titey *adj.* [HIGHTY-TIGHTY *adj.*] [1950s+] (*W.I. Rasta*) aloof, snobbish, supercilious.

hit for *v.* [ext. of HIT *v.*] **1** [late 19C+] (*US*) to beg, to ask for a loan, to accost. **2** [1900s–50s] (*US*) to travel towards, to leave for. **3** [1950s+] to purchase, esp. drugs. **4** [2000s] to cost.

hit it *v.* **1** [early 19C+] to have a given experience, usu. with a combining adj. that implies some form of success. **2** as *hit it up* or *hit things up*. (**a**) [late 19C+] to act positively, to succeed, to do something. (**b**) [20C+] to get drunk. (**c**) [20C+] to behave in an aggressive, noisy manner. **3** [1900s–40s] (*Aus./US*) to get on with, to establish good relations; also constr. with *with*. **4** [1920s–40s] (*US*) constr. with *off*, to leave, to depart. **5** to consume drink or drugs. (**a**) [1920s+] (*US/N.Z.*) to drink (heavily). (**b**) [1970s+] to smoke cannabis. (**c**) [1980s+] to smoke crack cocaine or heroin. **6** [1970s+] (*US gay*) to perform to the best of one's ability. **7** [1980s+] (*US black*) to have sexual intercourse. **8** [2000s] (*US prison*) to masturbate; to have anal sex. **9** *see* HIT THE BOOKS *v.* **10** *see* HIT THE ROAD *v.* (1).

hit it! *excl.* **1** [1940s+] (*US*) get moving! **2** [1960s] (*US prison*) be quiet!

hit on *v.* **1** [20C+] to approach, e.g. for help, to ask. **2** [1950s] (*US*) to criticize. **3** [1950s+] (*orig. US black*) (*also* **hit**) to make advances to, to make attempts to seduce. **4** [1950s+] (*US black*) to ask, to approach, usu. against the subject's wishes. **5** [1960s+] (*US*) to attempt to swindle or victimize. **6** [1960s+] in pimp use, to attract a woman to one's team of prostitutes. **7** [1970s+] (*US*) to rob. **8** [1990s+] (*US*) to enjoy, to indulge in. **9** *see* HIT *v.* (3g).

hit or miss *n. see* HIT (AND MISS) *n.*

hitter *n.* [HIT *n.*/HIT *v.*] **1** [1950s+] a thug, esp. a hired killer. **2** [1960s+] a success, a star, an influential individual; usu. with overtones of violence or criminality; also attrib. **3** [1960s+] (*drugs*). (**a**) a narcotics user. (**b**) a user of crack cocaine. (**c**) a small crack pipe, designed for only one puff. **4** [1980s+] one who derives sexual satisfaction from beating a partner. **5** [1990s+] (*US teen*) a pager, a beeper.

(IN COMPOUNDS)

▫ **period hitter** *n.* [1960s] (*drugs*) an occasional drug user.

hit the ball *v.* **1** [20C+] (*US*) to leave quickly [railway jargon *highball*, a signal directing the train to go at full speed]. **2** [1910s+] (*US*) to work hard, to be diligent at a job [sporting imagery].

hit the books *v.* (*also* **hit it**) [1920s+] (*US campus*) to study hard.

hit the ceiling *v.* **1** [20C+] (*orig. US*) to increase to a new level; usu. of prices. **2** [20C+] (*orig. US*) to become shocked, from surprise or pain. **3** [1900s] (*US campus*) to fail an examination. **4** [1910s+] (*orig. US*) (*also* **hit the roof**) to explode with temper, to become extremely annoyed. **5** [1950s] (*US drugs*) to smoke opium or marijuana.

hit the road *v.* [late 19C+] (*orig. US*) **1** (*also* **hit it, hit the hike**) to leave, to set out on a journey; thus imper. *hit the road/hit the road, Jack*, get out, go away. **2** to leave prison. **3** to take up a life of crime.

hitting *adj.* [1990s+] (*US black*) excellent.

Hittite *n.* [pun on SE *hit/Hittite*] [early 19C] those who fought in and patronized the Prize Ring.

hit up *v.* **1** in senses of consumption. (**a**) [late 19C–1950s] (*US*) to drink. (**b**) [1900s] to buy (a round of drinks). (**c**) [1950s+] (*orig. US*) (*also* **hit up the hypo**) to inject a drug; thus n. *hitting up*, injecting. (**d**) [1980s+] to inject someone else with a drug. **2** in lit. or fig. senses of movement towards. (**a**) [late 19C+] (*US*) (*also* **hit up for**) to visit. (**b**) [1910s] (*US*) to attend to, concentrate on. (**c**) [1970s+] (*US*) to make affectionate and/or sexual advances towards. **3** in senses of action or performance. (**a**) [1900s–30s] to perform, to do, to make. (**b**) [1920s–30s] (*US*) to accelerate a vehicle. (**c**) [1990s+] (*US Und.*) to rob, to mug. (**d**) [2000s] (*US campus*) to contact by mobile phone. **4** [1990s+] (*US*) to win a bet.

hit up (for) *v.* [late 19C+] (*orig. Aus./N.Z.*) to ask someone for something, usu. money.

hity-tity *n. see* HIGHTY-TIGHTY *n.*

hive *n.* [as a receptacle for HONEY *n.*[1] (2b); see Williams for 17C metaphorical uses] [mid–late 19C; 1970s] the vagina.

hive off *v.* [SE *hive off*, to break away from a group] [1910s+] (*Aus.*) to leave.

hiver *n.*[1] [SE *hive* (*off*) of bees, to swarm; the image is of whores 'swarming like bees' to the newly settled Western towns] [late 19C] (*US, Western*) a travelling bawd; usu. in pl.

hiver *n.*[2] [SE *HIV* (human immuno-deficiency virus)] [1980s+] a derog. term for a person with AIDS.

hizzo *n.* [HO *n.* (4) + -IZ- *infix*] [2000s] (*US black*) an extremely promiscuous woman.

hizzy *n.*

(IN PHRASES)

▫ **off the hizzy** *see* OFF THE HOOK *under* HOOK *n.*[1].

H.M.I.C. *n.* [*h*ead *m*otherfucker *i*n *c*harge] [1970s+] (*US*) the dominant figure in a given situation or institution.

HMP *n.* [the legal phr. 'detained at *H*er *M*ajesty's *P*leasure'] [1990s+] prison, time in prison.

h.n. *n. see* HOUSE NIGGER *n.*

h.n.i.c. *n.* [abbr. HEAD NIGGER IN CHARGE *under* HEAD *n.*] [1960s+] (*US black*) a sarcastic ref. to any black authority-figure.

ho *n.* (*also* **hoe, who, whoe**) [black pron. of SE *whore*] **1** [1950s+] (*orig. US black*) a prostitute. **2** [1960s+] a generic term describing any woman [ostensibly neutral, but the undertones of its ety. still make it controversial]. **3** [1970s+] (*US gay*) a passive sexual partner. **4** [1980s+] (*US black/campus*) a promiscuous or seductively dressed young woman. **5** [1980s+] a girlfriend. **6** [1980s+] a person indiscreet in sexual matters. **7** [1980s+] (*US black*) a sexually promiscuous man. **8** [1990s+] an unfriendly person, either male or female. **9** [1990s+] (*US black*) a coward, i.e. a man who acts like a woman; also attrib. **10** [2000s] (*US campus*) a form of friendly address. **11** [2000s] (*drugs*) cannabis; also attrib [? it is available to anyone with the money; it is a soft, thus 'feminine' drug compared to harder, 'male' narcotics].

(IN COMPOUNDS)

▫ **ho-ass** *adj.* [-ASS *sfx*] [1990s+] (*US black*) a general term of address, used of a man. ▫ **ho-bag** *n.* [1990s+] (*US*) a derog. term for a woman. ▫ **ho-bitch** *n.* [BITCH *n.*[1] (1a)] [1990s+] (*US campus*) a general negative when applied to any woman. ▫ **ho boots** *n.* [1970s+] (*US black*) ostentatiously sexy, high, tight, high-heeled woman's boots. ▫ **ho cake** *n.* [1990s+] (*US black*) the vagina. ▫ **ho-catcher** *n.* [1970s] (*US black*) a smart suit. ▫ **ho jockey** *n.* [JOCKEY *n.*[2] (3b)] [2000s] (*US black*) a successful pimp or womanizer. ▫ **ho layer** *n.* [LAY *v.*[1] (1)] [1980s+] (*US black*) **1** one who conducts most (or all) of his sex life with prostitutes. **2** a womanizer, a ladies' man. ▫ **ho stroll** *n.* [STROLL *n.* (3)] [1960s+] (*orig. US black pimp*) the street or streets in a town or city where prostitutes work regularly. ▫ **ho train** *n.* [2000s] (*US black*) a group of prostitutes that accompany their pimp on the street.

ho *v.* [HO *n.* (1)] **1** [1950s+] (*US black*) to work as a prostitute. **2** [1980s+] (*US black teen*) to sell out, to prostitute oneself.

hob *n.* (*also* **hoblob**) [earlier use is SE; corruption of proper name *Robin* or *Robert*] [mid-16C–19C] a rustic, a simpleton; often found as a generic proper name.

hobbinol *n.* (*also* **hobbinal**) [HOB *n.* + NOLL *n.*; orig. a characte in Spenser's *Shepherd's Calendar* (1579)] [17C–early 19C] a rustic, a simpleton.

hobbit *n.* [the peacable, country-dwelling creatures created by J.R.R. Tolkien in his books *The Hobbit* and *Lord of the Rings*] **1** [1980s+] (*US campus*) a socially unappealing, studious student. **2** [2000s] (*UK prison*) a compliant prisoner.

hobble *n.* [Scot. *habble*, a difficulty, a perplexity] **1** [late 18C–1940s] a difficult situation, from which it is hard to extricate oneself. **2** [1950s] (*Irish*) a troublesome person, a term o abuse.

(IN PHRASES)

▫ **in a hobble** [18C–19C] in trouble, perplexed, committed fo trial.

hobble *v.* [SE *hobble*, orig. of an animal, to restrain] **1** [18C–early 19C] (*UK Und.*) to steal. **2** [18C–early 19C] (*UK Und.*) to arrest. **3** [late 19C–1900s] (*US*) to restrain. **4** [1980s+] (*US campus*) to have sexual intercourse.

hobbled *adj.* [HOBBLE *v.* (2)] [late 18C–mid-19C] arrested committed to trial; thus *hobbled upon the legs*, transported sent to the hulks.

hobby *n.* [play on PONY *n.* (3a)] [mid-19C] (*US*) an English translation of a text in a foreign language.

hobby bobby *n.* [SE *hobby* + BOBBY *n.* (1)] [1980s] a specia constable.

hobby horse *n.* **1** [late 16C–early 17C] a fool, a jester [SE *hobby horse*, the performer, in a morris dance, who manipulates with much capering, the wicker horse that is part of the trad 'cast']. **2** [late 16C–18C] (*also* **she-hobby**) a prostitute, a promiscuous woman; a mistress [SE *hobby horse*, a small horse she can be 'ridden' by all and sundry].

hobby horse man *n.* [HOBBY HORSE *n.* (2)] [early 17C] a womanizer, an adulterer.

hob-job *n.* [HOB *n.* + SE *job*] [mid–late 19C] an unskilled job, an odd job, e.g. holding horses, carrying parcels; also as v.

hob-jobber *n.* [HOB-JOB *n.*] [mid–late 19C] a man or boy walking the streets on the lookout for small jobs.

hobnail *n.* (*also* **hopnail**) [the heavy footwear, studded with hobnails, used by country-dwellers] [late 16C–19C] a rustic, a simpleton.

hobnailed *adj.* [HOBNAIL *n.*] [late 16C–19C] rustic, boorish.

hobnail express *v.* [1910s+] (*N.Z./US*) to walk, to travel b foot.

hob nob *v.* [according to Grose (1785), the custom dates to the late 16C: 'When great chimnies were in fashion, there was at each corner of the hearth...a small elevated projection, called the *hob*, and behind it a seat. In winter time the beer was placed on the hob to warm; and cold beer was set on a small table, said to have been called the *nob*, so that the question, Will you have hob or nob, seems only to have meant Will you have warm or cold beer?' Skeat, *Etymological Dict.* (1909), opts for AS *hab*, have, and *nabban*, not have, thus 'take it or leave it', i.e. the choice is yours] [mid-18C–mid-19C] to invite to drink and then to clink glasses; thus *hob nob/hob a nob*, a toast.

hobnobs *n.* [NOB *n.*^{2} (1)] [1960s+] (*Scot./Irish*) members of the upper classes.

hobo *n.* [ety. unknown; claims have been made for *hoe-boy*, a migrant farm-worker and the cry *Ho, boy!* used regularly by northwestern railway mail handlers *c.*1880–90; note Mencken, *The American Language* (3rd edn, 1936): 'Tramps and hoboes are commonly lumped together, but in their own sight they are sharply differentiated. A *hobo* or *bo* is simply a migratory laborer; he may take some longish holidays, but soon or late he returns to work. A *tramp* never works if it can be avoided; he simply travels. Lower than either is the *bum*, who neither works nor travels, save when impelled to motion by the police'; note WW1 milit. *hobo*, a cadger, a useless person] (*US*) **1** [late 19C–1960s] the penis [fig. use of sense 2, i.e. it 'wanders around']. **2** [late 19C+] a tramp, a vagrant, an itinerant worker, often using the US rail system as a means of free transport. **3** [1900s–20s] the vagrant cell. **4** [1910s+] (*N.Z.*) a rough, lowly person, not necessarily a tramp. **5** [1970s+] someone whose poverty renders them effectively a tramp.

(IN COMPOUNDS)

❑ **hobo cage** *n.* [1900s–20s] (*US*) the iron cage in a prison for locking up minor offenders. ❑ **hobo cocktail** *n.* [1940s] (*US*) a glass of water, esp. when requested (rather than alcohol) in a restaurant. ❑ **hobo coffee** *n.* [1960s] coffee made without the use of a filter, which one has to allow to settle before drinking. ❑ **hobo soup** *n.* [1990s+] (*US*) ketchup mixed with hot water.

(IN PHRASES)

❑ **hobo's delight (on a rainy night)** *n.* [2000s] (*US*) a throw of twelve in craps dice.

hobo *adj.* [HOBO *n.* (2)] [late 19C+] (*US*) pertaining to tramps or their culture; used lit. and fig.

hobo *v.* [HOBO *n.* (2)] [late 19C+] (*US*) **1** to live or travel as a tramp. **2** in fig. use, i.e. to travel or catch a free train ride.

Hoboken *n.* [proper name of *Hoboken*, New Jersey; poss. f. an imagined identification with HOBO *n.* (2) although the name is, in fact, Indian] [20C+] (*US*) **1** an insignificant, out-of-the-way place. **2** hell.

hobosex *n.* [HOBO *n.* (2) + SE *(hetero)sexual*] **1** [1970s+] (*US gay*) a sexual partner who performs badly or whose anus is not as tight as it once was. **2** [1990s+] sex with a number of strangers in a short period of time; thus *hobosexual*, one who enjoys such random adventuring.

ho-boy *n.* (*also* **hobey-man**) [SE *hautboy*, *hoboy*, an oboe, humorously applied to a clyster-pipe or enema] [19C] (*US*) a nightsoil carrier.

Hobson's (choice) *n.* [rhy. sl.; f. SE *Hobson's choice*, no choice at all. Named for Tobias Hobson or Jobson (d.c.1630), the Cambridge carrier (commemorated by John Milton (1608–74) in two epitaphs), who let out horses and is said to have compelled customers to take the horse that happened to be next to the stable-door or to go without; orig. *Hodgson's choice* and cited as such by Ernest Weekley as occurring in 1617, 13 years before Hobson's death] [20C+] the human voice.

hoch *n.* [Ger. excl. *hoch!*] [1910s] (*Aus.*) a German.

hochmagandy *n.* *see* HOUGHMAGANDY *n.*

hock *n.*^{1} [SE *hock*, a joint in the back leg of a quadruped, between the knee and the fetlock, which points backwards; *curby* f. *curb*, a disease of horses manifested in a swelling on the hock] [late 18C+] the foot, or the foot and ankle; usu. in pl., thus *curby hocks*, round or clumsy feet.

(IN PHRASES)

❑ **rattle one's hocks** *v.* [1900s] (*US*) to go fast.

hock *n.*^{2} [Du. *hok*, hutch, hovel, prison; but note gambling jargon, *see* Asbury, *Sucker's Progress* (1938) 15–16: '*In hock*—The last card in the box was said to be *in hock*. Originally it was known as the *hockelty card*, and in the early days of Faro, when it counted for the bank, a player who had bet on it was said to have been caught *in hock*. Also, a gambler who had been trimmed by another sharper was said to be *in hock* to his conqueror; and as late as the middle 1880's, in the underworld, a man was *in hock* when he was in jail. The phrase is now principally used in reference to pawnshop pledges, but it seems to have acquired that meaning in recent years.'] [late 19C+] the state of being pawned; usu. in phr. *IN HOCK* below.

(IN COMPOUNDS)

❑ **hock sheet** *n.* [1990s+] (*US police*) a list of stolen goods that may have been pawned. ❑ **hock shop** *n.* **1** [late 19C+] a pawnbroker's shop. **2** [1950s] a prison.

(IN PHRASES)

❑ **caught in hock** [mid-19C] caught in the act. ❑ **hock off** *v.* [2000s] (*N.Z.*) to get rid of, to dump. ❑ **in hock** **1** [mid-19C–1950s] in prison; thus the reverse, *out of hock*. **2** [late 19C+] indebted to, owing both money and metaphorical debts; thus the reverse, *out of hock*. **3** [late 19C+] in pawn; thus the reverse, *out of hock*. **4** [1920s] in trouble. ❑ **on hock** [2000s] on credit. ❑ **on the hocks** [1930s] (*US tramp*) impoverished.

hock *n.*^{3} [rhy. sl. = COCK *n.*^{3} (1)] [1950s+] a male homosexual.

hock *n.*^{4} **1** *see* HOCKER *n.* **2** *see* HOCKIE *n.*

hock *v.*^{1} [HOCK *n.*^{2}] **1** [late 19C+] (*orig. US*) to pawn; thus adj. *hockable*. **2** [1930s–70s] (*US*) to steal. **3** [1950s+] to sell. **4** [1960s] (*N.Z.*) to get hold of, to obtain.

hock *v.*^{2} [HOCKIE *n.* (2)] [1960s] (*US*) to talk nonsense, to joke.

hock *v.*^{3} [? HOCK *n.*^{1}] [1970s] (*US*) to kick.

hock-dockies *n.* [HOCK *n.*^{1} + redup.] [mid-19C] shoes.

hocker *n.* (*also* **hock**) [SE *hawk*, to clear one's throat of phlegm] [1960s+] (*US teen*) a gob of phlegm or spit.

hockey *n.* *see* HOCKIE *n.*

hockey *adj.* (*also* **hocky**) [orig. Cumb. dial; ety. unknown; such beer, sold cheap to the farmer, was trad. served at harvest-homes or harvest-suppers, celebrating the successful completion of the annual harvest] [late 18C–mid-19C] drunk, spec. with strong, stale beer known as *old hock*.

hockey *v.* *see* HOCKIE *v.*

hockey stick *n.* [1940s+] (*N.Z.*) a mutton chop.

hockie *n.* (*also* **hock, hockey, hocky**) [? CACKY *n.*] **1** [late 19C+] excrement, both human and animal. **2** [1930s+] (*US*) in fig. use, nonsense, lies. **3** [1980s+] semen.

hockie *adj.* (*also* **hocky**) [HOCKIE *n.*] [1970s] (*US campus*) unpleasant, nasty.

hockie *v.* (*also* **hockey, hocky**) [HOCKIE *n.*] [20C+] to excrete.

hock-pintled *adj.* (*also* **hock-pointed**) [SE *hock* + PINTLE *n.* (1)] [18C–19C] suffering from penile strabismus, lit. 'a squint of the penis', i.e. a painful condition in which the penis is painfully bent out of shape.

hocks *n.* *see* HOCK *n.*^{1}.

hocky *see also under* HOCKIE.

hocky *adj.* *see* HOCKEY *adj.*

hocus *n.* [HOCUS *v.*; fig. use of SE *hocus*, imposture, trickery] **1** [early 19C–1900s] drugged liquor. **2** [1930s+] (*US drugs*) heroin, morphine or cocaine in solution, prepared for injection. **3** [1930s+] (*drugs*) (*also* **hokus**) opium, morphine, heroin or cocaine. **4** [2000s] (*drugs*) marijuana.

hocus *adj.* [abbr. HOCUS-POCUS *adj.*] [early 18C–19C] drunk.

hocus *v.* [SE *hocus*, to confuse] **1** [early 19C+] (*UK Und.*) to drug a person with a mixture of a narcotic (e.g. laudanum, opium) or snuff and beer before robbing them; also of animals, e.g. race-horses. **2** [mid-19C] in general use, to adulterate.

hocus-pocus *n.*^{1} (*also* **hocus**) [joc. play on POKE *n.*^{2} (2)] [mid-17C; 1930s–50s] (*US Und.*) a purse or wallet.

hocus-pocus *n.*[2] [SE *hocus-pocus*, confusion; note HOCUS-POCUS *adj.*] **1** [19C] drugged alcohol. **2** [1980s+] marijuana.

hocus-pocus *adj.* [SE *hocus-pocus*, deceitful, confused] [18C] drunk.

hod *n.* (*also* **brother hod**) [SE *hod*, by metonymy] [late 18C–early 19C] a bricklayer's mate or labourer.

hodad *n.* (*also* **ho-daddy, hodag**) [surfing jargon *hodad*, a non-surfer, thus a fool; ult. ety. unknown; poss. greeting *Ho! Dad*] [1960s+] (*US*) a stupid, obnoxious person.

hoddie *n.* [the hod he carries] [1950s+] (*Aus.*) a bricklayer's mate, a hod-carrier.

hoddy-doddy *n.* [dial. *hoddy-doddy*, a snail] **1** [mid-16C–early 19C] a short, squat person; thus rhy. phr. *hoddy doddy, all arse and no body*. **2** [late 16C–18C; 20C+] (*later use US*) a fool, a simpleton.

hoddy peak *n.* [dial. *hoddy-doddy*, a snail + SE *peak*, head] **1** [16C] a fool, a simpleton. **2** [late 16C–17C] (*also* **hoddy-peel**) a cuckold [the snail's horns become those of the cuckold].

hodedor *n.* [phonetic pron. of Sp. *jodedor*, one who makes a mess, who fouls up] [1970s] (*US/P.R.*) a thug, a hoodlum, a gangster.

hodge *n.* [corruption of proper name Roger, supposedly 'rustic'] [late 16C–1940s] a rustic, a simpleton.

hodmandod *n.* (*also* **hodmedod, hodmendod**) [SE *hodmandod*, any form of shelled snail] [mid-17C–18C] a crippled or deformed person; thus *hodmandod*, short and clumsy.

hod of mortar *n.* [rhy. sl.] [mid-19C] a pot of porter.

hoe *n.* see HO *n.*

hoe check *n.* [HO *n.* (9) + SE *check*] [2000s] (*US prison*) a beating given to a prison inmate to see how he will react.

hoe-handle *n.* see HAMMER-HANDLE *under* HAMMER *n.*[1].

hoe into *v.* [agricultural imagery] (*mainly Aus.*) **1** [late 19C+] to begin a task with energy and enthusiasm. **2** [1950s+] to use enthusiastically.

hoffing *n.* [? HUFF *v.*] [1970s] (*US black*) a fight.

hog *n.* **1** as money [picture of a pig engraved on the early shilling]. (**a**) [mid-17C–1930s] one shilling (5p); thus *hog and a kye*, one shilling and sixpence (1s 6d/7½p). (**b**) [18C–early 19C] sixpence (2½p). (**c**) [mid-18C–1900s] half-a-crown, 2s 6d (12½p). (**d**) [mid-19C–1940s] (*US*) a ten-cent piece. (**e**) [1940s–50s] (*US*) (*also* **hoggie**) $1. **2** in the context of greediness, 'hoggishness'. (**a**) [late 17C+] a miser, a mean person; a generally foolish person. (**b**) [1950s+] (*drugs*) anyone who uses more drugs (orig. narcotics, but later extended to cover cannabis) than the speaker does. **3** a (large and powerful) vehicle [fig. ref. to the size and power of a SE *hog*]. (**a**) [late 19C+] (*US*) an engine used for hauling freight cars. (**b**) [20C+] (*later use US black*) any large automobile, esp. a Cadillac [note *Hy Lit's Unbelievable Dict. of Hip Words* (1968): 'the reasons it's called a HOG is because it eats up all your bread through monthly payments to the finance company']. (**c**) [1960s+] (*orig. Hell's Angels*) a motorcycle (usu. a Harley-Davidson) modified and cut down for outlaw gang use. (**d**) [1970s+] (*US*) any large vehicle or aircraft that uses quantities of fuel. **4** of those possessing 'masculine' characteristics [the toughness of the animal]. (**a**) [1920s+] (*US*) a stoic, a tough individual. (**b**) [1960s+] (*US prison*) a tough prisoner who survives hardship stoically. (**c**) [1980s] (*US campus*) a man who epitomizes good looks, intelligence and sexual prowess. **5** as a term of abuse. (**a**) [1940s+] (*US*) a derog. term for a police officer; usu. as *the hogs*, the police [devel. of PIG *n.* (2a); note 'Sayers' and Heenan's Great Fight' in Hindley, *Curiosities of Street Literature* (1871): 'So those heroes were surrounded / By a lot of Hampshire hogs', ref. to the police breaking up a prizefight in 1860]. (**b**) [1960s+] (*US campus*) (*also* **boo-hog**) a male term for an unattractive woman, occas. a woman's term for a man. **6** [1960s+] (*US*) the penis. **7** [1970s+] (*drugs*) phencyclidine [the original use of phencyclidine (PCP) as an animal tranquillizer, often of pigs].

IN COMPOUNDS

❑ **hog-head** *n.* (*also* **hogshead**) [-HEAD *sfx* (3)] [1910s–40s] (*US tramp*) a railroad engineer.

IN PHRASES

❑ **half-a-hog** *n.* (*also* **half-hog**) **1** [late 17C–late 19C] sixpence. **2** [mid-19C] (*US Und.*) a five-cent piece, a nickel. ❑ **hog in armour** *n.* **1** [mid-17C–19C] a well-dressed lout, of either sex. **2** [mid-19C] (*US*) a blustering official. ❑ **hog in togs** *n.* [TOGS *n.* (1); such a man lived by his wits, often off foolish women, and worked, if at all, as a ROPER *n.*[2] (2) or SHILL *n.*[2] (1) for a gambling house or similar establishment] [mid-19C] (*US*) a man-about-town, a loafer with no visible means of support but an endless appetite for good clothes, parties and places of entertainment. ❑ **make a hog of oneself** *v.* see MAKE A PIG OF ONESELF *under* PIG *n.* ❑ **mint hog** *n.* [MINT *n.*[1] + image of the hog as a source of income (cf. GENTLEMAN WHO PAYS THE RENT *under* GENTLEMAN *n.*)] [early 19C] an Irish shilling.

SE in slang uses

IN COMPOUNDS

❑ **hog-age** *n.* [mid-19C–1900s] (*US*) male adolescence. ❑ **hog and hominy** *n.* [late 18C+] (*US*) pork with hominy grits or cornbread; thus fig. as the basics of existence. ❑ **hog-bosom** *n.* see SOW-BELLY *n.* ❑ **hog-caller** *n.* (*US*) **1** [1940s–60s] a loudspeaker. **2** [1940s–60s] one who makes themselves heard, with complaints, arguments, orders etc. **3** [1940s+] a loud and piercing scream, akin to those used by farmers calling their pigs. ❑ **hog-cutter** *n.* [1930s] (*US black*) an unintelligent person. ❑ **hog-drunk** *adj.* [1950s–60s] (*US*) very drunk. ❑ **hog-eye** *n.* see separate entry. ❑ **hog-fat** *n.* [1920s+] (*Aus.*) a useless person, a parasite, a 'good-for-nothing'; lit. very fat. ❑ **hog-grubber** *n.* (*also* **hog-grunter**) [GRUBBER *n.*[1]] [late 17C–mid-19C] a mean, miserly, sneaking person. ❑ **hog heaven** *n.* [the perceived stupidity of the animal] [1940s+] (*US*) a state of bliss or blissful ignorance. ❑ **hog island** *n.* (*also* **hog town, hog waller**) [i.e. a 'pig sty'] [late 19C+] (*US*) a generic term for any small, impoverished, out-of-the-way settlement; thus adj. *hog-wallowing*, to refer to an inhabitant of such a place. ❑ **hog-killing** *n.* [the hog, born on the farm, costs nothing; killing it provides food etc] [late 19C–1910s] (*US*) an unexpected or large financial profit. ❑ **hog-killing (time)** *n.* (*also* **hog wallow**) [trad. throwing of a party to coincide with the annual killing of a farm's hogs] [mid-19C–1950s] (*US*) a boisterous party, a celebration. ❑ **hog-leg** *n.* see separate entry. ❑ **hog-mouth** *adj.* [1930s] (*W.I.*) uncouth. ❑ **hog pen** *n.* [1920s–60s] (*US black*) a disgusting or filthy place. ❑ **hog ranch** *n.* [derog. use of SE; ? an actual brothel thus named] [late 19C+] (*US*) a brothel. ❑ **hog-rich** *adj.* [i.e. one has had one's 'snout in the trough'] [1980s] (*US*) very wealthy. ❑ **hog rubber** *n.* [lit. 'one who rubs hogs'] [17C] a rustic, an ignorant peasant, a disgusting, filthy person. ❑ **hog's eye** *n.* see HOG-EYE *n.* ❑ **hogshead** *n.* see HOG-HEAD above. ❑ **hog-stomp** *n.* see HOG-WRESTLE below. ❑ **hog-thomas** *n.* [THOMAS *n.*[1]] [20C+] (*W.I.*) a crude, loud person. ❑ **hog town** *n.* see HOG ISLAND above. ❑ **hog train** *n.* [late 19C] (*US tramp*) the world of tramping. ❑ **hog waller** *n.* see HOG ISLAND above. ❑ **hog wallow** *n.* see HOG-KILLING (TIME) above. ❑ **hogwash** see separate entries. ❑ **hog-whimpering** *adj.* [20C+] (*orig. US*) extremely drunk. ❑ **hog-wild** *adj.* **1** [20C+] (*US*) (*also* **hoggy-wild**) out of control; also adv. **2** [1910s] absolutely determined; also adv. ❑ **hog-wrestle** *n.* (*also* **hog-stomp, hog-wrastle**) **1** [20C+] (*US*) a noisy, inelegant, low-class dance. **2** [1940s] a rowdy argument.

IN PHRASES

❑ **bar-hog** *n.* [1960s+] (*US*) a part-time prostitute, who frequents bars and uses them as a base for soliciting. ❑ **drive one's hogs (to market)** *v.* see *under* DRIVE *v.*[1]. ❑ **like a hog on ice** *adv.* [late 19C] (*US*) unsteadily, clumsily. ❑ **on the hog (train)** [negative image of hogs in a sty] [late 19C+] **1** (*US*) living as a tramp. **2** (*US*) out of order, chaotic, of objects, in bad condition. **3** (*US campus*) at a disadvantage. **4** (*also* **on the pork**) (*US*) of people, in bad condition, penniless. **5** (*US*) depressed. **6** (*US campus*) honest. ❑ **sell a hog** *v.* see HOG *v.* (1b). ❑ **sure as hogs are made of bacon** see *under* SURE AS… *phr.* ❑ **whole hog** *n.* see separate entry.

verbs meaning to masturbate

❑ **beat one's hog** [1970s] ❑ **belt one's hog** [1940s+] ❑ **flog the hog** [1990s+] ❑ **hack the hog** [1990s+] ❑ **hug the hog** [1990s+]

IN EXCLAMATIONS

❑ **I'll be hog-wallered!** *see* I'LL BE JIGGERED! *under* JIGGERED *adj.*[1].

hog *v.* **1** to attack, lit. or fig. (**a**) [19C] to have sexual intercourse [the puritan image of 'swinishness' allied to sex]. (**b**) [1960s–70s] (*US prison*) (*also* **sell a hog**) to subject to assault, esp. homosexual rape. **2** [mid–late 19C] (*US*) to defraud, to cheat. **3** [mid-19C+] (*US*) to steal. **4** [late 19C+] (*orig. US*) to grab for oneself, to act greedily or selfishly.

IN PHRASES

❑ **hog at** *v.* (*also* **hog up**) [20C+] (*W.I.*) **1** to speak roughly to, to humiliate verbally. **2** to eat ravenously. ❑ **hog for** *v.* [1910s] (*Aus.*) to desire intensely. ❑ **hog it** *v.* [1910s–40s] to sleep deeply, esp. when accompanied by snores.

hogan *n.* [? fig. use of SE *hog*, to eat greedily; Dr Walter Bergdorf suggests: 'don't you think this comes from the name for a Navaho stone and dirt house, now used mainly for ceremonial purposes. They are dome-shaped and easily visualized as breasts'] [1960s+] (*US*) **1** in pl., the female breasts. **2** a mouthful, used as a unit of measurement when describing the size of a woman's breasts, therefore often in pl. **3** in pl., a young woman.

hogan-magan *n.* (*also* **hogan, hogen-mogen**) [Du. *Hoogmogendheiden*, lit. 'High Mightinesses', the title of the States-General] **1** [mid-17C–mid-18C] an important person or one who presumes himself to be one. **2** [late 17C–early 18C] a Dutchman.

hogan-magan *adj.* (*also* **hogen-mogen**) [HOGAN-MAGAN *n.*] **1** [mid-17C–mid-18C] pretentious, high and mighty. **2** [mid-17C–mid-18C] of drink, strong. **3** [late 17C–early 18C] Dutch.

IN COMPOUNDS

❑ **hogan-mogan rug** *n.* [17C SE *rug*, a strong drink] [mid-17C] a strong drink.

Hogan's ghost *n.* [rhy. sl.] [1960s] (*Aus.*) toast.

hogan's ghost! *excl.* [? an unknown anecdote] [20C+] (*Aus.*) a general expression of amazement.

hogan's goat *n.* [a fanciful animal owned by a fictitious Irishman] [1950s+] **1** (*US*) an obnoxious thing; thus phr. *stinks like hogan's goat*, to be bad, objectionable, a failure etc. **2** (*Irish*) a kept woman.

hogen-mogen *see under* HOGAN-MOGAN.

hog-eye *n.* (*also* **hog's eye**) [supposed resemblance] **1** [1900s] (*US*) a hamlet or small village. **2** [1910s+] (*US*) the female genitals; thus *hog's-eye man*, a womanizer. **3** [1930s] (*US prison*) a skeleton key. **4** [1930s+] (*US Und.*) a lock. **5** [1990s+] the anus [-EYE *sfx*]. **6** [1990s+] the urethral hole in the head of the penis [poss. a misdef. of sense 5].

hog-eye man *n.* [mid–late 19C] (*US*) a sailor, often black, who manned the 'hog-eye boats', running between Cape Horn and San Francisco at the time of the Calif. Gold Rush.

hoggenheimer *n.* [a 1902 stage character, amplified into a cartoon character created *c.*1913 by D.C. Boonzaaier of *Die Burger*] [1910s] (*S.Afr.*) a generic name for the stereotypical Jewish capitalist (esp. as based in Johannesburg); thus *Hoggie*.

hogger *n.*[1] [negative stereotyping of the animal] **1** [late 19C+] (*Irish*) a street-corner idler. **2** [1960s+] (*US campus*) a fat, homely young woman. **3** [1960s+] (*US campus*) a sexual athlete. **4** [1980s+] (*US*) the penis.

hogger *n.*[2] [HOG *n.* (3a)] [1910s–50s] (*US tramp/railroad*) a locomotive engineer.

hoggers *n.* [SE *Hogmanay* + -ER *sfx*] [1990s+] (*Scot.*) Hogmanay.

hoggins *n.* [SE *hoggings*, i.e. a pig's portion] [20C+] a due share in pleasure, usu. sexual pleasure.

hoggish *adj.* (*also* **hoggy**) [the negative image of the animal; *hoggish*, rude or filthy, is SE despite inclusion by Harman and Grose] [20C+] (*US*) greedy, avaricious.

Hoggishland *n.* [? SE *Hogmanay*] [mid-18C] Scotland.

hogleg *n.* (*also* **hog's leg**) [resemblance; the nickname of the Colt Single-Action Army, also known as the *Peacemeaker* and launched in 1870] **1** [1910s+] (*US*) a large handgun; occas. a shotgun. **2** [1940s] (*US*) the penis. **3** [1990s+] (*US campus/drugs*) a large marijuana cigarette.

hogmagundy *n. see* HOUGHMAGANDY *n.*

hogmarket somebody *n.* [they have porcine manners] [late 19C] (*W.I.*) an ill-mannered person.

hogo *n.* [HOGO *adj.*] [mid-17C+] a stench.

hogo *adj.* [20C+ use Ulster only; Fr. *haut goût*, a 'high' flavour, thus also SE *high*] [late 18C–mid-19C] stinking, esp. of rotting meat.

Hogopolis *n. see* PORKOPOLIS *n.*

hogwash *n.* [fig. uses of 15C *hogwash*, the swill of a brewery, which was given to the pigs] **1** [late 17C–1960s] thick and bad beer; occas. inferior wine, or tea. **2** [late 19C+] (*also* **hogswaddle**) nonsense, rubbish.

hogwash! *excl.* [HOGWASH *n.* (2)] [late 19C+] rubbish!

h.o.h.a. *phr.* [abbr. *h*it *o*ne, *h*it *a*ll; pron. 'haitch-oh-haitch-ay'] [20C+] (*Irish*) a street challenge, esp. from a weaker to a stronger person or group.

hoha *n.* [HOHA *adj.*] [1970s] (*N.Z.*) an annoying person.

hoha *adj.* [synon. Maori] [1970s+] (*N.Z.*) irritated, tetchy, 'fed up'.

ho-hum *adj.* [SE *ho-hum!*, an excl. of boredom] [1960s+] non-committal, inconclusive, dull.

hoick *v.*[1] [? SE *hike*, drag] [late 19C+] **1** to lift or hoist, with a jerk or snatch. **2** to drag (out of). **3** to spit out.

hoick *v.*[2] [SE *hawk*] [20C+] (*Aus.*) to spit; also as n., a glob of phlegm.

hoist *n.* [SE *hoist*, to lift] **1** [early 18C+] (*UK Und.*) (*also* **hoys**) constr. with *the*, the act of shoplifting or breaking into houses. **2** [late 18C+] (*UK Und.*) a shoplifter or burglar. **3** [late 18C+] a pickpocket. **4** [1930s] the profits from a robbery. **5** [1930s+] (*US*) a hold-up or hijacking. **6** [1930s+] (*also* **hyste**) any form of robbery.

IN COMPOUNDS

❑ **hoist-lay** *n.* [LAY *n.*[3] (1)] [19C] (*UK Und.*) **1** shoplifting. **2** robbing a man by holding him upside down and shaking the money out of his pockets. ❑ **hoist-merchant** *n.* [MERCHANT *n.*] [19C] a shoplifter.

IN PHRASES

❑ **go upon the hoist** *v.* [late 18C–early 19C] to shoplift. ❑ **on the hoist** (*also* **on the hoys**) [early 19C+] working as a shoplifter.

hoist *v.* **1** in criminal use. (**a**) [late 18C–19C] (*UK Und.*) to turn a man upside down and shake him until the money falls out of his pockets. (**b**) [19C+] (*UK/US Und.*) to shoplift; in weak use, to steal [HOIST *n.* (1)]. (**c**) [mid-19C+] to break into, to rob. (**d**) [late 19C–1910s] (*US*) to kick or thrash someone. (**e**) [1920s+] (*US Und.*) to commit an armed robbery or a hold-up. (**f**) [2000s] (*UK Und.*) to be arrested. **2** [mid-19C+] to drink; thus *hoist/hoist a few*, to have a drink/drinks; *on the hoist*, out drinking [one *hoists* one's elbow]. **3** [1970s] (*US gambling*) to defeat soundly.

IN COMPOUNDS

❑ **hoist-in** *n.* [mid-19C–1910s] a drink.

IN PHRASES

❑ **hoist one** *v.* [mid-19C+] to have a drink.

SE in slang uses

IN PHRASES

❑ **hoist tail** *v. see under* TAIL *n.* ❑ **hoist the blue flag** *v.* [the blue apron trad. worn by the publican] [late 18C–early 19C] to take on the running of a public house.

hoister *n.* **1** in criminal use [HOIST *n.*]. (**a**) [18C+] (*UK Und./US tramp*) (*also* **hoisterman, hoyster, hyster**) a shoplifter. (**b**) [19C+] (*orig. UK Und.*) a pickpocket. (**c**) [1980s+] (*Aus. prison*) one who steals from warehouses. **2** [late 19C–1900s] a drunkard [HOIST *v.* (2)].

IN COMPOUNDS

❑ **hoister-mort** *n.* [early–mid-19C] (*UK Und.*) a female shoplifter.

hoisting *n.* [SE *hoist*/HOIST *v.*] **1** [late 18C–mid-19C] street robbery, 'mugging'. **2** [19C+] shoplifting.

hoisting engineer *n.* [HOIST *v.* (2) + pun] [1910s–30s] (*US*) a drunkard.

hoitch *n.* [HO *n.* (1) + BITCH *n.*[1] (1a)] [1980s+] (*US campus*) an unpopular, unpleasant woman.

hoity-toity *n.* [SE *hoity-toity*, giddy behaviour, flightiness; *see also* ety. of HIGHTY-TIGHTY *n.*] **1** [mid-17C–early 19C] an immodest, lively woman, a 'romping girl'. **2** [18C] sexual play or joking.

hoity-toity *adj.* [SE *haughty* + redup., though Weekley, *Etymological Dict. of Modern English* (1921), notes that the synon. mid-17C phr. *upon the hoyty-toyty* has poss. link to walking on a high wire] **1** [mid-17C+] (*also* **haytie twaity, highty-tighty, hoighty-toighty**) aloof, snobbish. **2** [1910s] (*US*) irritable. **3** [1950s] dull, formal, staid.

hoity-toity! *excl.* [HOITY-TOITY *adj.*] [late 17C–1900s] an excl. of surprise or disdain.

Ho-Jo *n.* [abbr.] [1960s+] (*US*) a Howard Johnson's motel.

hoke *n.* [HOKUM *n.*] **1** [1920s] (*US*) a fool. **2** [1920s–50s] sentimental melodrama; thus nonsense.

hoke *v.* [abbr. HOKUM *n.* (1)] [1920s+] (*US*) to flatter, to string along, to hoax.

(IN PHRASES)

❑ **hoke up** *v.* [1920s+] (*US*) to embellish, to render fraudulent.

hokey *n.*[1]

(IN EXCLAMATIONS)

❑ **by hokey!** (*also* **by hoky-poky! by hookity! by hooky!**) [? euph. for *hell!* or f. SE *hocus-pocus*] [19C+] (*US*) a mild excl.

hokey *n.*[2] [HOKUM *n.*] **1** [1950s–60s] (*US*) a fool. **2** [1960s+] nonsense.

hokey *adj.* [HOKUM *n.*] [1920s+] (*US*) fake, false, banal.

hokey cokey *n.* [rhy. sl.; note also the trad. Cockney dance 'The Hokey-Cokey'] [1990s+] karaoke.

hokey-dokey *see under* OKEY-DOKE.

hokey-pokey *n.*[1] [SE *hocus-pocus*] **1** [mid-19C+] swindling and other illicit activities. **2** [late 19C+] nonsense. **3** [1940s] an unspecified object.

hokey-pokey *n.*[2] [rhy. sl. = CHOKEY *n.* (1)] [late 19C] solitary confinement.

hokey-pokey *n.*[3] [ety. unknown; street cry 'hokey-poky, a penny a lump!' The ices were sold by Italians, sometimes doubling as organ-grinders, at one penny or a halfpenny each, but despite the popular ety., it does not come f. Ital. *o che poco!* 'o how little!'; more likely is a link to HOKEY-POKEY *n.*[1], i.e. the passing off of cheap versions of superior products] [late 19C+] **1** a cheap variety of ice-cream, sold by street vendors. **2** (*N.Z.*) a toffee-like sweet.

hokey-pokey *adj.* [HOKEY-POKEY *n.*[1] (1)] [mid–late 19C] duplicitous, untrustworthy, swindling.

Hokitika swindle *n.* [proper name *Hokitika*, a town on the west coast of New Zealand + SE *swindle*] [1930s+] (*N.Z.*) a bar game, based on betting on a sequence of numbers, e.g., on a £1 note, to determine who will buy the round of drinks.

hokonui *n.* [*Hokonui* Hills, where an illegal whisky comes from] [2000s] (*N.Z.*) illegally distilled alcohol.

hokum *n.* [? SE *hocus-pocus* + BUNKUM *n.*. Orig. theatrical jargon *hokum*, to use comedy or sentimentality to appeal to an unsophisticated audience] **1** [20C+] nonsense, flattery, lying. **2** [1910s+] (*orig. theatrical*) sentimental or melodramatic speechifying or 'business'.

hokum *adj.* (*also* **hokumy**) [HOKUM *n.* (2)] [1920s+] sentimental, melodramatic, nonsensical.

hokum-snivvy *n.* [fig. use of HOOK AND SNIVEY, WITH NIX THE BUFFER *n.*] [20C+] (*US*) a stew or boiled dinner made of unspecified ingredients.

hoky-poky *n.*

(IN EXCLAMATIONS)

❑ **by hoky-poky!** *see* BY HOKEY! *under* HOKEY *n.*[1].

hol *n. see* HOLE *n.*[1] (1a).

Holborn Hill *n.*

(IN PHRASES)

❑ **walk backwards up Holborn Hill** *v.* (*also* **ride backwards up Holborn Hill, push the cart up Holborn Hill, ride in a cart up Holborn Hill, sail up Holborn Hill**) [the road to Tyburn led from Newgate jail along Holborn. Criminals trad. stood in the cart facing backwards, poss. to increase their ignominy, but more likely to avoid seeing the approaching gallows until the last possible moment] [mid-17C–18C] to go to the gallows.

hold *v.*[1] (*US drugs*) **1** [late 19C+] to be in possession of money, usu. large sums; often as *holding*. **2** [1930s–60s] for a supply of drugs to suffice an addict for a given period of time. **3** [1930s+] to be in possession of drugs, esp. for selling. **4** [1960s–70s] (*US black*) to borrow. **5** [1970s–80s] (*UK black*) to take, to steal. **6** [1970s+] (*US Und.*) to be armed. **7** [1970s+] to be in possession of anything.

(IN PHRASES)

❑ **do you hold?** [late 19C] (*Aus.*) a phr. indicating that it is someone's turn to buy the drinks. ❑ **hold heavy** *v.* [HEAVY *adv.* (2)] [20C+] to have a good deal of money. ❑ **hold light** *v.* [20C+] to have only a little money, to be out of pocket.

SE in slang uses

(IN COMPOUNDS)

❑ **hold-door trade** *n.* [whores standing around brothel doorways in the hope of attracting passing trade] [late 16C–early 17C] the world of prostitution.

(IN PHRASES)

❑ **hold...** *v. see also under* relevant n. ❑ **hold a fresh** *v.* [1990s+] (*W.I.*) to take a shower. ❑ **hold a tangi** *v.* [Maori *tangi*, a formal lamentation, a dirge] [1940s] (*N.Z.*) to analyse, to hold a 'post mortem', to have a feast or party. ❑ **hold court in the street** *v. see under* STREET, THE *n.* ❑ **hold foot** *v.* [20C+] (*Ulster*) to sustain, fig. to keep up with. ❑ **hold onto the slack** *v. see under* SLACK *n.*[1]. ❑ **hold out** *see* separate entries. ❑ **hold over someone** *v.* [mid–late 19C] (*US*) to have an advantage over someone. ❑ **hold still for** *v. see* STAND STILL FOR *under* STAND *v.*[2]. ❑ **hold the bag** *v. see* separate entry. ❑ **hold up** *see* separate entries.

(IN EXCLAMATIONS)

❑ **hold it!** *see* separate entry. ❑ **hold tight!** [orig. a bus- or tram-driver's shout] **1** [1910s+] stop! don't move! **2** [1960s+] (*W.I.*) calm down! ❑ **hold your kitties!** [20C+] be patient! remain calm! ❑ **hold your mouth!** *see under* MOUTH *n.* ❑ **hold your whiz!** *see under* WHIZ *n.*[1].

hold *v.*[2] [1900s] (*Aus.Und.*) to rob on the street. to 'mug'.

hold down *v.* **1** [late 19C–1910s] (*US tramp*) to ride atop a freight car, despite it being known by the crew. **2** [late 19C+] to keep a job for some time, to occupy. **3** [20C+] (*W.I.*) of a woman, to control one's partner, esp. to stop him from having other sexual relationships. **4** [20C+] (*W.I.*) of a man, to assault a woman sexually. **5** [1980s+] (*US campus*) to wait; esp. as imper. *hold down!*

(IN PHRASES)

❑ **hold-me-down** *n.* [late 19C] (*US tramp*) a regular job.

holder *n.* [HOLD *v.*[1] (3)] [1990s+] (*US prison*) an inmate entrusted with keeping a gang's supply of drugs.

holding *adj.* [fig. use of SE *hold*/HOLD *v.*[1]] **1** [1930s+] (*drugs*) in possession of drugs, esp. for dealing, selling; or money to obtain drink or drugs. **2** [1980s] (*US campus*) of dress, attractive. **3** *see* HOLD *v.*[1] (1).

hold it! *excl.* (*also* **hold everything! hold it right there!**) [the subject is supposed to freeze in position. Partridge suggests orig. painters' jargon] [20C+] stop what you're doing! be quiet! etc.

(IN EXCLAMATIONS)

❑ **hold it down!** [1940s+] be quiet! calm down!

hold-out *n.* [HOLD OUT (ON) *v.*] [20C+] (*US*) an act of evasion; something that has been held back, e.g. money; thus an individual who 'holds out'.

(IN COMPOUNDS)

❑ **hold-out artist** *n.* [ARTIST *n.*] [1950s+] a gambler or cheat who will never admit how much money they have made out of a game.

hold out *v.* [mid-19C+] (*US*) to live, to reside.

hold out (on) *v.* [20C+] (*orig. US*) to withhold something from someone; to resist.

hold the bag *v.* (*also* **hold the sack**) [SE *bag*] **1** [mid-18C+] to take responsibility. **2** [20C+] to be in a disadvantageous position. **3** [20C+] (*UK Und.*) of a villain, to be left with full responsibility for a crime in which one's associates have not been legally involved. **4** [1960s+] (*drugs*) to be in possession of a quantity of drugs, to deal drugs [note BAG *n.*[1] (7a)].

hold-up *n.* [HOLD UP *v.*[1]] **1** [late 19C+] (*orig. US*) an armed robbery. **2** [late 19C+] (*orig. US*) (*also* **hold-up man**) an armed robber. **3** [1900s–50s] (*US*) an instance of extortion; lit. or fig.

hold up *v.*[1] [the demand that victims should hold up their hands] **1** [mid-19C+] to commit an armed robbery. **2** [late 19C–1950s] to cheat, to blackmail. **3** [late 19C–1960s] (*US*) to demand, esp. to charge an exorbitant price.

SE in slang uses

IN PHRASES

❑ **hold up one's clothes/dress at** *v.* [20C+] (*W.I.*) of a woman, to raise her skirts and expose her buttocks as a gesture of derision.

hold up *v.*[2] [the pretence of 'holding up' the structure against which one leans] [mid-19C+] (*joc.*) to lean against, to support.

hold up! *excl.* (*also* **hole up!**) [20C+] a general excl. requesting a pause in either activity or speech.

hole *n.*[1] [SE *hole*] **1** as a part of the body. (**a**) [late 14C+] (*also* **hol**) the anus. (**b**) [late 16C+] the vagina. (**c**) [mid-19C+] the mouth; usu. as SHUT ONE'S HOLE below. (**d**) [20C+] the buttocks. (**e**) [20C+] sexual intercourse; usu. in phr. GET ONE'S HOLE below. (**f**) [1940s+] (*US*) a (promiscuous) woman, a prostitute. (**g**) [1970s+] (*US*) a passive homosexual man, esp. when promiscuous. (**h**) [2000s] an underage girl used for paedophile exploitation. **2** as an unpleasant place. (**a**) [mid-16C+] (*orig. UK prison*) the punishment cells [the orig. *Hole* was found in the Counter or Compter debtors' prison in Wood Street, London, where it was the nickname for that cell, a notably squalid one, in which the poorest prisoners were confined. The rich enjoyed the 'masters' side', while the middle classes went to the 'knights' side'; all were entered in the prison's Black Book. William Fennor's *Counter's Commonwealth* (1617) gives an extensive survey of life within the prison. A similar form of dungeon, not apparently sl., was the *hell*, cited by the OED and Nares, who suggests it was 'something worse than the *hole*']. (**b**) [18C+] a derog. description of any small, dirty, clandestine place, often one where illegal occupations were planned or carried out; thus (*US*) *rum hole*, a squalid drinking place. (**c**) [1920s+] (*US campus*) a student's room. (**d**) [1930s–50s] (*US Und.*) a hideout. (**e**) [1930s+] (*US*) the subway or one of its stations. (**f**) [1940s+] (*US*) a space or slot, a position, e.g. in a race. (**g**) [1990s+] (*US Und*) a railroad side track. (**h**) [1990s+] (*Aus./US*) a prison. **3** [late 18C+] in fig. use: a difficult situation, a fix, a scrape, a mess.

IN COMPOUNDS

❑ **hole and corner work** *n.* [mid–late 19C] sexual intercourse. ❑ **hole-monger** *n.* see HOLER *n.* ❑ **hole nervous** *adj.* [1970s] (*US Und.*) suffering from the nervousness that arises from a lengthy period spent in hiding or keeping a low profile. ❑ **holes and poles** *n.* [POLE *n.*] [1960s+] (*US campus*) sex education classes. ❑ **hole time** *n.* [TIME *n.*] [20C+] (*US prison*) time spent in the punishment cells.

IN PHRASES

❑ **break someone's hole** *v.* [1970s] (*US*) to beat up. ❑ **dark hole** *n.* see *under* DARK *adj.* ❑ **get one's hole** *v.* (*also* **get one's hole away**) [1960s+] (*Scot./Irish*) of a man, to have sexual intercourse. ❑ **give him a hole to hide it in** *v.* (*also* **lend him a hole to hide it in**) [IT *n.*[1] (2)] [late 19C+] of a woman, to permit sexual intercourse. ❑ **in the hole** (*also* **in a hole**) [mid-19C+] (*orig. US*) **1** in debt, owing, usu. connected with gambling. **2** in difficulties. ❑ **keep a tight hole** *v.* see KEEP A TIGHT ASSHOLE *under* ASSHOLE *n.* ❑ **make the hole** *v.* see WORK THE HOLE *under* WORK *v.* ❑ **put someone in the hole** *v.* [mid-19C] to make someone feel inferior, to 'put down'. ❑ **shut one's hole** *v.* [1940s+] to be quiet, esp. in imper. *shut your hole!* ❑ **up someone's hole** [1970s+] (*US*) immediately behind and therefore irritating, bothering.

IN EXCLAMATIONS

❑ **in your hole!** (*also* **in your pants! ...shite!**) [1970s+] a dismissive rejoinder. ❑ **my hole!** [late 17C+] a general excl. of disdain, dismissal, arrogant contempt.

SE in slang uses

IN PHRASES

❑ **can you see any holes in my head?** [1930s] (*US*) a retort, do you think I am stupid? ❑ **hole in** *v.* see HOLE UP *v.* ❑ **hole in one's head** *n.* see separate entry. ❑ **hole in the road** *n.* see HOLE IN THE WALL *n.* (4). ❑ **hole in the wall** see separate entries. ❑ **hole up** see separate entries. ❑ **hunt one's hole** *v.* [mid-19C–1960s] (*US*) to run away, to seek refuge. ❑ **make a hole in** *v.* [20C+ use is SE] **1** [early 17C–19C] to use up a great deal of, esp. money or a dish of food. **2** [1930s] (*US Und.*) to escape from prison. ❑ **make a hole in one's manners** *v.* (*also* **put a hole in one's manners**) [mid–late 19C; 1970s+] (*later use Aus.*) to behave rudely. ❑ **make a hole in the water** *v.* [mid-19C–1910s] to commit suicide by diving or jumping into water and drowning.

IN EXCLAMATIONS

❑ **hole in one!** [golf imagery] [1970s+] absolutely correct!

hole *n.*[2] [ety. unknown] [1930s] (*UK tramp*) a shilling (5p).

hole *v.* [HOLE *n.*[1] (1b)] **1** [late 19C] 'to effect intromission' (F&H); thus *holing*, womanizing, whoring. **2** see HOLE UP *v.*

hole card *n.* [poker jargon *hole card*; the card that, in five-card stud, is dealt face down] [1920s+] (*orig. US*) a secret, which can be either a weakness that, once discovered, can be exploited, or a hidden strength.

IN PHRASES

❑ **peep someone's/one's hole card** *v.* [PEEP *v.*[3] (2)] [1950s+] (*US prison/black*) to work out a person's (or consider one's own) hidden attitudes and emotions.

holed *adj.* [HOLE *n.*[1] (1)] [late 19C+] of a man, enjoying sexual intercourse.

hole in my shoe *n.* [rhy. sl.] [1960s+] (*bingo*) the number 82.

hole in one's head *n.* **1** [1940s+] (*US*) a lack of common sense. **2** [1950s] nonsense, lies.

SE in slang uses

IN PHRASES

❑ **need like a hole in the head** *v.* (*also* **need like a third nut**) [joc. use of SE but note Yid. *ich darf es vi a loch in kop*, 'I need that like a hole in the head'] [1940s+] to not need at all.

hole in the ground *n.* [rhy. sl.] [20C+] £1.

hole in the wall *n.* [either f. the holes in the walls of English debtor's prisons, through which the inmates could obtain supplies and money to alleviate their situation, or f. the small shops and similar establishments found in the broad stone walls of fortified medieval cities. *Hole in the wall* became a generic term, although the US West had its *Hole in the Wall*, an outlaw hideaway in the gorges and cliffs that straddle the Wyoming, Colorado and Utah state lines (a sometime refuge for Butch Cassidy and the Sundance Kid and the real-life Wild Bunch), while 1860s New York City boasted the *Hole in the Wall* on Water Street, where its proprietor, Gallus Meg (a monstrous Englishwoman), bit the ears off ill-behaved customers and preserved her trophies in a pickle jar displayed behind the bar] **1** [mid-17C] a brothel. **2** [mid-19C–1930s] (*US*) an illicit liquor store or bar; *see also* sense 6 below. **3** [mid-19C–1950s] a small shop. **4** [mid-19C+] (*US*) (*also* **hole in the road**) a small, insignificant, remote place. **5** [late 19C+] a tiny, cramped apartment. **6** [1910s+] (*US*) a bar; *see also* sense 2 above. **7** [1920s–40s] a restaurant. **8** [1980s+] an automatic teller machine (ATM), installed in the external wall of a bank or building society branch.

hole in the wall *adj.* [HOLE IN THE WALL *n.* (4)] [mid-19C+] (*orig. US*) second-class, inferior.

hole (out in one) *v.* [golfing imagery] [1910s+] (*Aus.*) to become pregnant after one's first act of sexual intercourse, esp. on one's marriage night.

holer *n.* (*also* **hole-monger**) [HOLE *n.*[1] (1b) + SE sfx *-monger*; note 13C–15C SE *holour*, a fornicator or whoremonger and, as such, applied to men only] **1** [16C+] a womanizer, a successful seducer. **2** [19C] a male prostitute. **3** [19C] a pimp. **4** [late 19C] a prostitute.

-holer *sfx* [1940s+] (*US*) applied to an outside lavatory or privy and denoting the number of seats available, e.g. *one-holer*, *two-holer* etc.

hole up *n.* [HOLE UP *v.*] [late 19C+] a hideout.

hole up *v.* (*also* **hole, hole in**) [SE *hole up*, (of an animal) to retire to a hole for hibernation or security] [late 19C+] to take up residence, with a possible but not invariable implication of hiding away or taking refuge.

hole up! *excl. see* HOLD UP! *excl.*

holey dollar *n. see* HOLY DOLLAR *under* HOLY *adj.*

holhanger *n.* [HOL *n.* + SE *hang around*, to loiter] [1990s+] (*S.Afr.*) a lounger, a lazy person.

holiday *n.* [i.e. a *holiday* from normal life] [late 19C] a prison sentence.

IN PHRASES

▫ **take a holiday** *v.* [1940s] (*UK Und.*) to serve a prison sentence.

holing *n. see* HOLE *v.*

holla boys, holla *n. see* HOLLER BOYS, HOLLER *n.*

H.O.L.L.A.N.D. *phr.* [abbr. *here our love lives and never dies*] [1940s+] an affectionate message, written on envelopes of love letters.

holland *n.* [play on HOLE *n.*[1] (1a) + NETHERLANDS *n.* (2)] [late 16C] the anus.

Holland tape *n.* (*also* **hollands**) [SE *Holland* + TAPE *n.*] [mid-18C–19C] gin.

holler *n.* [HOLLER *v.*] [late 19C+] (*US*) a complaint, a fuss, esp. to the police.

IN PHRASES

▫ **get one's holler on** *v.* [2000s] (*US black*) to talk to a woman with the intent of seduction. ▫ **put up a holler** *v.* [1950s] to make a fuss.

holler *v.* **1** [early 18C+] (*also* **hollow**) to shout, to scream, to complain. **2** [mid-19C–1920s] (*US*) to surrender, to admit defeat. **3** [1940s+] to confess, to betray one's criminal associates. **4** [1960s] to sing. **5** [1980s+] (*US black*) to ridicule, to abuse. **6** [1990s+] (*US campus*) to visit. **7** [2000s] (*US black*) to demand, to ask for. **8** [2000s] (*US teen*) to greet. **9** [2000s] (*US campus*) to phone or talk to someone.

IN PHRASES

▫ **holler (bloody) murder** *v. see under* MURDER *n.* ▫ **holler calf-rope** *v.* (*also* **say calf-rope, yell calf-rope**) [19C+] (*US, orig. Western/Southern*) to give in, to surrender, to admit defeat, esp. in children's games. ▫ **holler copper** *v. see* separate entry. ▫ **holler New York** *v.* [echoic] [1960s+] (*US*) to vomit. ▫ **holler uncle** *v. see* CRY UNCLE *under* UNCLE *n.*

holler boys, holler *n.* (*also* **holla boys, holla; 'oller boys, 'oller**) [rhy. sl.; ult. HOLLER *v.* (1)] [20C+] a (stiff) collar.

holler copper *v.* (*also* **holler cop, ...police, squeal copper, yell...**) [HOLLER *v.* (1)/SE *yell*/SQUEAL (ON) *v.* + COPPER *n.* (3)] [1920s+] to inform.

holliers *n.* [1940s+] (*Irish*) holidays.

hollow *n.* **1** [early 19C] poultry, when served for a meal [the hollow cavity within a cooked bird]. **2** [late 19C+] (*US*) in a variety of combs., describing an area of a town or an out-of-the-way area; usu. combined with a ref. to poor or foreign groups, e.g. *dead man's hollow*, *frog hollow*, *Irish hollow*, *piggy hollow*, *punkin hollow*, *skunk hollow*, *sleepy hollow*, *smoky hollow*, *snuff hollow*.

hollow *v. see* HOLLER *v.* (1).

hollow *adv.* (*also* **holler**) [ety. unknown] [mid-17C+] completely, utterly; esp. in phr. *beat* or *knock hollow*, to trounce completely.

Holloway *n.* [pun on 'hollow way'] **1** [mid-19C–1920s] the vagina. **2** [1930s] the throat.

Holloway castle *n.* (*also* **the Castle, royal place of Holloway**) [before its mid-20C+ remodelling the gateway of the original Holloway prison (now England's main women's prison) had 'castellated' architecture, copied in part from Caesar's Tower, Warwick Castle; the pub across the road is still called the Holloway Castle] [late 19C–1930s] Holloway prison.

Holloway, Middlesex *n.* [Holloway, London N7/N19; puns on both words] [mid-19C–1900s] the stomach.

hollowhead *n.* (*also* **hollow brain**) [SE *hollow* + -HEAD *sfx* (1)] [mid-19C+] (*US*) an idiot.

hollow leg *n.* **1** [20C+] (*orig. US*) (*also* **glass legs**) a capacity for heavy drinking, a heavy drinker; occas. of over-eating. **2** [1920s+] a person who can indulge to a great extent.

hollow-legged *adj.* [HOLLOW LEG *n.*] [late 19C+] used of a serious drinker.

hollow log *n.* [rhy. sl.] **1** [1960s+] (*Aus.*) a derog. term for any non-white person [= WOG *n.*[1] (1)]. **2** [1970s+] (*Aus.*) a (racing) dog. **3** [1980s+] (*Aus. prison*) an informer [= DOG *n.*[2] (6b)].

Hollyweird *n.* [the negative image of the film capital] [1950s+] (*US*) Hollywood, California.

Hollywood *n.* [2000s] (*S.Afr. gay*) jail, prison.

proper name in slang uses

IN PHRASES

▫ **do a Hollywood** *v.* [2000s] (*N.Z.*) to fake or act in some way. ▫ **go Hollywood** *v.* [stereotypes of Hollywood as sexually licentious and the home of excessive, if faked, emotion] **1** [1940s+] (*US*) to sodomize. **2** [1960s+] (*US campus*) to lose emotional control, to act hysterically; to act egotistically.

Hollywood *adj.* [1930s+] (*US*) used generically to imply luxury, self-indulgence, etc; occas. disparagingly so.

IN COMPOUNDS

▫ **Hollywood eyes** *n.* [1950s] (*US black*) an attractive woman. ▫ **Hollywood hustler** *n.* [HUSTLER *n.* (7)] [1970s+] (*US*) a male homosexual prostitute. ▫ **Hollywood stew** *n.* [the apparent 'luxury' of the dish] [20C+] (*US prison*) creamed cod fish. ▫ **Hollywood stop** *n. see* CALIFORNIA STOP *under* CALIFORNIA *adj.* ▫ **Hollywood swoop** *n.* [such manoeuvres are reminiscent of, or learned from, film or TV police chase sequences] [1970s+] (*US black/west coast*) an automobile manoeuvre whereby one cuts in front of another vehicle, stopping one's own car and thus forcing the other vehicle to halt.

holmes *n.* (*also* **holm slice**) [pun on HOMES *n.*; *Larry Holmes*, heavyweight champion; also note NO SHIT, SHERLOCK! *excl.*] [1970s+] (*US campus*) an affectionate dimin. of HOMEBOY *n.* (3).

holnaai *n.* [Afk. 'hole fuck'] [2000s] (*S.Afr.*) anal intercourse.

holus-bolus *adv.* [pig Lat. or a ponderous pun on Gk *holos bolos*, the whole lump] [early 19C–1900s] in a mess, jumbled up.

holy *n.*

IN EXCLAMATIONS

▫ **by the holy!** [19C–1900s] a general excl. of surprise, excitement, alarm etc.

holy *adj.* **1** [mid-19C+] a general intensifier. **2** [1990s+] (*UK juv.*) excellent, the best.

IN COMPOUNDS

▫ **holy horror** *n. see* HOLY TERROR *n.* ▫ **holy terror** *n. see* separate entry.

SE in slang uses

IN COMPOUNDS

▫ **holy alls** *n.* [20C+] (*Irish*) the end result. ▫ **Holy City** *n.* [the city's many churches; thus the alternative nickname the *city of churches*] [late 19C–1910s] (*Aus.*) Adelaide, South Australia; thus *Holy State*, South Australia. ▫ **Holy Cod** *n.* [a mockery of religious fish-eating; note Fr. equivalent *La Sainte Morue*] [late 19C–1920s] Good Friday. ▫ **holy dollar** *n.* (*also* **holey dollar**) [mid–late 19C] (*Aus.*) a silver dollar out of which a circle has been punched. ▫ **holy father** *n.* [SE *holy father*, the Pope, used as an excl. by such boys] [late 18C–19C] 'A butcher's boy of St Patrick's Market, Dublin or any other Irish blackguard' (Grose, 1785). ▫ **holy ghost shop** *n.* [late 19C–1900s] a church.

❑ **holy ground, the** *n.* *see* HOLY LAND *n.* (2). ❑ **holy herb** *n.* (*also* **holy weed**) [the use of marijuana as sacramental by Rastafarians; WEED *n.*[1] (4); HERB *n.*[1] (1)] [1960s+] marijuana. ❑ **holy Joe** *n.* *see* separate entry. ❑ **holy lamb** *n.* *see under* LAMB *n.*[1]. ❑ **holy land** *n.* *see* separate entry. ❑ **holy Mary** *n.* [1950s+] (*Irish*) of a man or woman, a religious hypocrite, one who pretends to great and showy religiosity. ❑ **holy Moses** *n.* **1** [early 17C] a cuckold [paintings of Moses displayed him with a part-halo, the curves of which resemble horns protruding from his head]. **2** [1960s] (*US*) a (street) preacher or religious fanatic. ❑ **holy unction** *n.* [mid-19C] (*UK Und.*) pea soup. ❑ **holy weed** *n.* *see* HOLY HERB above. ❑ **holy week** *n.* **1** [1960s] (*US*) the time of menstruation. **2** [1970s] (*gay*) any time one abstains from sex, e.g. when one has VD. ❑ **holy Willie** *n.* [the subject of Robert Burns's poem 'Holy Willie's Prayer' (1785)] [late 19C+] a sanctimonious, hypocritically pious person.

holy...! *excl.* used in various oaths, usu. in conjunction with a euph. for *God* or *Jesus*; popularized in non-religious uses by the 1960s *Batman* TV series, when Robin, the superhero's sidekick, created a wide variety of excls. on the model of 'holy..., Batman!'.

IN EXCLAMATIONS

❑ **holy balls!** *see under* BALLS! *excl.* ❑ **holy biddy!** *see* HOLY HELL! below. ❑ **holy bones!** [1900s] a mild. excl. ❑ **holy cats!** [20C+] a mild excl. of surprise, dismay, alarm. ❑ **Holy Christ!** *see* CHRIST! *excl.* ❑ **Holy Christmas!** *see* CHRISTMAS! *excl.* ❑ **Holy Christopher!** *see* CHRISTOPHER! *excl.* ❑ **holy cow!** [1910s+] (*orig. US*) an excl. of surprise or disappointment. ❑ **holy crap!** [CRAP *n.*[1] (2)] [1930s+] (*US*) a general excl. of amazement, surprise, annoyance etc. ❑ **holy cripes!** [CRIPES! *excl.*] [20C+] a general excl. of surprise, alarm etc. ❑ **holy crow!** (*also* **jeezum-crow!**) [1960s+] (*US*) a phr. of amazement, surprise. ❑ **holy dooley!** [? link to LARRY DOOLEY *n.*] [1940s+] (*Aus.*) a general expression of surprise. ❑ **holy Egypt!** *see* HOLY HELL! below. ❑ **holy fly!** (*also* **holy flyback! by the...!**) [20C+] (*Aus./Irish*) a mild oath. ❑ **holy frost!** [19C] (*Aus.*) a general oath. ❑ **holy fuck!** [FUCK! *excl.*] [1940s+] (*orig. US*) a general excl. used to express surprise, astonishment. ❑ **holy gee!** (*also* **holy ginger! ...jeez! hully chee! ...gee!**) [mid-19C+] a mild excl. of surprise, dismay, alarm. ❑ **holy hailstones!** [1960s] (*US*) an excl. of astonishment. ❑ **holy hell!** (*also* **holy biddy! ... Egypt! ...hokey! ...horror! ...Jack the Ripper! ...snakes!**) [mid-19C+] a mild excl. of surprise, dismay, alarm. ❑ **holy James Street!** *see* JAMES STREET! *excl.* ❑ **holy Joe!** *see* separate entry. ❑ **holy jumped-up Jesus!** (*also* **holy Creeping Jesus! holy jumped-up be-jeebers! holy jumped-up Jehosophat! holy sneaking Jesus!**) [1910s–50s] a general excl. ❑ **holy jumping...!** *see* separate entry. ❑ **holy mackerel!** *see* separate entry. ❑ **holy mackinaw!** (*also* **old mackinaw!**) [1900s–70s] (*US*) a mild excl. ❑ **holy moly!** (*also* **holy moley!**) [var. on *HOLY MOSES under* HOLY *adj.* The catchphrase favoured by the comic-book character Captain Marvel] [1920s+] (*orig. US juv.*) a general excl. of amazement or shock. ❑ **holy monkey!** [1950s] an excl. of surprise, disbelief. ❑ **holy Moses!** (*also* **Holy Mike! Holy Moe!**) [mid-19C+] a general excl. of amazement or shock. ❑ **holy Peoria!** [*Peoria*, Illinois] [1960s] an excl. of surprise. ❑ **holy pretzel!** [1960s] (*US campus*) an excl. of surprise. ❑ **holy shit!** (*also* **holy piss! holy shit on a shamrock!**) [SHIT *n.* (1a)] [1960s+] a general excl. of surprise or astonishment. ❑ **holy smoke!** *see* separate entry. ❑ **holy snakes!** *see* HOLY HELL! above. ❑ **holy wars!** [1900s–10s] a general excl.

holy friar *n.* [rhy. sl.; never truncated] [late 19C+] a liar.

holy ghost *n.* [rhy. sl.] **1** [20C+] (*Aus.*) the post, the mail. **2** [1940s] the post, i.e. the start-line for a horserace. **3** [1950s+] toast.

holy ghosts *n.* [rhy. sl.] [20C+] (*Aus.*) fence posts.

holy Joe *n.* [orig. naut. jargon] **1** [mid-19C+] a clergyman, esp. in the services or in a prison. **2** [late 19C+] anyone of a religious bent. **3** [late 19C+] (*also* **holy Josie**) a prudish, sanctimonious, narrow-minded puritan; thus *holy joeism*.

holy Joe! *excl.* [20C+] an excl. of surprise.

holy jumping...! *excl.* [late 19C+] a general excl.; a euph. for JESUS! *excl.* or JUMPING JESUS! *excl.*; usu. with *jimminy, jemima,* etc and other words beginning with *j*, but also can be used with any other n. Common ones include *mother of god*, *beans*, *cats*.

holy land *n.* [SE *holy ground/land*, an area within church jurisdiction in which villains or persecuted people could gain sanctuary. The slums and criminal ghettos were often impervious to the law; St Giles is the patron saint of beggars; Ribton-Turner, *A History of Vagrants* (1887), notes: 'An old *fancy* chaunt [that] ends every verse thus: "For we are the boys of the holy ground / And we'll dance upon nothing and turn us around."'] **1** [19C] (*orig. US*) a red-light district or slum. **2** [mid-19C] (*also* **holy ground**) the area around St Giles, London, including Seven Dials. **3** [late 19C+] any area of a city populated by or frequented by Jews. **4** [late 19C+] (*Aus.*) Tasmania.

holy mackerel! *excl.* (*also* **holy mac!**) [late 19C+] an excl. of surprise, shock, wonder or amazement.

holy nail *n.* [rhy. sl.] [late 19C+] legal bail.

holy poker *n.*[1]

IN EXCLAMATIONS

❑ **by the holy poker!** (*also* **by poker! by the hoky-poky! by the holy iron! by the holy poker of hell! holy poker!**) [the instrument of punishment used in Purgatory] [early 19C+] (*Irish*) a mild oath.

holy poker *n.*[2] [mid-19C+] the penis.

Holy Roller *n.* [their physical twitchings and 'rollings' at the height of their apparent religious ecstasy] (*US*) **1** [mid-19C+] (*also* **Roller**) a member of a Pentecostal church. **2** [1940s+] a sanctimonious person or a religious fundamentalist.

holy-rolling *n.* [HOLY ROLLER *n.*] [1920s] (*US*) religious fervour.

holy-rolling *adj.* [HOLY ROLLER *n.* (2)] [1940s+] (*US*) sanctimonious.

holy show *n.* (*also* **holy spectacle, show**) [mid-19C+] (*Aus./Irish*) the cause of a scandal or embarrassment, esp. in phr. *make a holy show of oneself*, to make an exhibition of oneself.

holy smoke *n.* [rhy. sl.] [20C+] **1** coke, the fuel. **2** Coke, the drink Coca-Cola.

holy smoke! *excl.* (*also* **by the holy smokes! holy smokes! smoke! smoly hoke!**) [late 19C+] an excl. of surprise, shock, wonder or amazement.

holy terror *n.* (*also* **holy horror**) [HOLY *adj.*] [late 19C+] **1** a person of exasperating habits or manners. **2** a terrible place or event.

holy water *n.* [rhy. sl.] [20C+] a daughter.

hom *n.*[1] [abbr. SE *homosexual*] [1990s+] a general term of abuse.

hom *n.*[2] *see* HOMEBOY *n.* (3).

homa *n.* *see* OMEE *n.*

hombre *n.* (*also* **ombrey**) [Sp. *hombre*, man, but widely popularized through 20C+ spread of the Hollywood Western film] **1** [mid-19C+] a man. **2** [late 19C+] a term of address; thus *hombresse*, a woman. **3** [1990s+] (*orig. US campus*) a male friend.

hombrecitos *n.* [Sp. *hombrecitos*, little men; ? those that one sees after taking the hallucinogen] [1970s+] (*drugs*) psilocybin.

hombug *n.* *see* HUMBUG *n.*

Home *n.* [apparently criminals were welcome to use this as a base as long as they did not operate locally] [late 19C–1940s] (*US Und.*) St Paul, Minnesota.

home *n.* [abbr. HOMEBOY *n.*] **1** [1940s+] (*orig. US black*) a friend, often used in direct address. **2** [1970s+] (*US campus*) a person from the same home town, a friend.

SE in slang uses

IN COMPOUNDS

❑ **homebake** *see* separate entries. ❑ **home biscuit** *n.* [1980s+] (*US campus*) a friend. ❑ **homeboy** *n.* *see* separate entry. ❑ **homebrew** *n.* *see* BREW *n.*[1] (7). ❑ **home-buddy** *n.* *see* HOMEBOY *n.* (1). ❑ **home chicken** *n.* [1980s] (*US campus*) a male or female homosexual. ❑ **home chop** *n.* [? affectionate use of SE *lambchop*] [1980s+] (*US campus*) a friend, usu. of the opposite sex. ❑ **home cooking** *n.* *see* separate entry. ❑ **home folks** *n.* [19C+] (*US*) **1** one's immediate or extended family. **2** people from the area in which one grew up, from one's home community. ▫ **homegrown** *n. see* separate entry. ▫ **home guard** *n. see* separate entry. ▫ **homegirl** *n. see* separate entry. ▫ **homelady** *n. see* HOMEGIRL *n.* (1). ▫ **homeland** *n.* [1960s–70s] (*US black*) the black area of a city. ▫ **home-made** *n.* [1940s–60s] (*US*) a home-made pistol, a 'zip gun'. ▫ **homemade shit** *n.* [SE *homemade* + SHIT *n.* (3b)] [1970s] (*US campus*) unpleasant, depressing feelings. ▫ **home rule/ruler** *see* separate entries. ▫ **home run** *n. see* separate entry. ▫ **home skillet** *n.* [SKILLET *n.* (2); var. on HOMEBOY *n.*] [1980s+] (*orig. US black*) a fellow black person. ▫ **home slice** *n.* [var. on HOMEBOY *n.* (2)] **1** [1980s+] (*also* **home dirt**) (*US campus/prison*) someone from one's town, area, state; ext. to any friend. **2** [1990s+] (*US campus*) a dull person who rarely goes out. **3** [1990s+] (*US black teen*) a fellow black person. ▫ **home squeeze** *n. see under* SQUEEZE *n.*[1]. ▫ **homestone** *n.* [STONED *adj.* (2)] [1980s+] (*US drugs*) marijuana grown on private premises. ▫ **homework** *n.* [1930s+] (*orig. US*) **1** petting, necking, sexual intercourse. **2** a girlfriend.

(IN PHRASES)

▫ **get home on** *v.* **1** [1900s–10s] (*Aus.*) to take advantage of; to steal from. **2** [1900s] to hit, lit. or fig. ▫ **get home to** *v.* [orig. boxing use, but latterly an emotional impression too] [early 19C+] to make an impression on. ▫ **go home** *v.* [note SE phr. *go to one's last home*, to die] **1** [early 19C–1910s] to die. **2** [20C+] (*W.I., Gren.*) to defame a member of one's own or someone else's family. **3** [1920s+] of an article of clothing, to wear out. ▫ **go home by beggar's bush** *v.* [to be reduced, like a beggar, to sleeping under a bush] [late 16C–18C] to be ruined. ▫ **go home by Woodcock's cross** *v.* [ety. unknown; ? anecdotal] [17C] to regret one's actions, to fail badly; thus *go crossless home by Woodcock's cross*, to repent and then to be hanged. ▫ **home and fried** *adj.* [play on colloq. *home and dried*] [1910s] (*Aus.*) safe and sound. ▫ **home and hosed** *adj.* (*also* **home with a rug on**) [1940s+] (*Aus./N.Z.*) **1** safe and sound. **2** accomplished without having to make any real effort. ▫ **home of rest** *n.* [1910s] a prison. ▫ **what's that when it's at home?** (*also* **who's he/she when he/she's at home?**) [late 19C+] a deliberate misunderstanding of a word or statement, which the speaker is implying to be too 'clever' for them to understand.

(IN EXCLAMATIONS)

▫ **go (home) and eat coke!** [? punning on Marie Antoinette's supposed (but fictional) dismissal of the starving Paris mob, *Let them eat cake*] [late 19C+] a general excl. of contempt or dismissal.

homebake *n.* (*also* **bake**) [HOMEBAKE *v.*] **1** [1980s+] (*Aus./N.Z. drugs*) the manufacture of homemade heroin or morphine from codeine phosphate. **2** [1990s+] (*US drugs*) baking soda when mixed with crack cocaine.

homebake *v.* (*also* **bake**) [the use of heat in the manufacturing process] [1980s+] (*Aus./N.Z. drugs*) to manufacture homemade heroin or morphine from codeine phosphate; thus *homebaker*, one who does this; *homebaking*, the process.

homeboy *n.* **1** [late 19C+] (*also* **home-buddy**) someone who stays mainly at home. **2** [late 19C+] a neighbourhood person [*homeboy* originated in the South and was used by all races before it migrated, with the black population, to the urban ghettos; its modern use in rap music has rendered it once again trans-cultural]. **3** [late 19C+] (*also* **hom**) a good friend; thus as a term of address. **4** [late 19C+] a naïve person, newly arrived in the city from the countryside. **5** [1910s+] (*S.Afr./US*) someone who has come to the city from the same rural or provincial area as oneself; *see also* HOMEGIRL *n.* **6** [1950s–60s] (*Irish*) an ex-inmate of a religious institution. **7** [1970s+] (*US black*) a young black or Hispanic member of a street gang. **8** [1980s+] (*US black*) a fellow black person.

home cooking *n.* **1** [1930s–40s] (*US black*) anything outstanding, wonderful or first-rate [the presumed excellence of home cookery]. **2** [1960s] (*US*) sexual intercourse, usu. from a man's point of view with his wife.

homee *n. see* OMEE *n.*

homegirl *n.* [var. on HOMEBOY *n.*] (*orig. US black*) **1** [1910s+] (*also* **homelady**) a woman from one's home town or neighbourhood. **2** [1980s+] a woman. **3** [1980s+] a close female friend. **4** [1980s+] a female gang member.

homegrown *n.* **1** [1970s+] (*drugs*) marijuana that has been grown at home [such marijuana was usu. seen as inferior before the introduction of new techniques, e.g. hydroponics, that have revolutionized the former cottage industry over the last 20 years]. **2** [1990s+] (*US prison*) a 'masculine' lesbian.

home guard *n.* [20C+] **1** (*US*) a regular worker, one who stays on one job in one locality rather than a transient. **2** (*US*) a beggar or tramp who stays in one place. **3** (*US Und.*) a con-man's victim who lives in the same city/town as that in which he is fleeced. **4** (*US Und.*) a local, as opposed to an itinerant, confidence man.

home on the range *n.* [rhy. sl.] [20C+] (*Aus.*) small change.

home on the range *adj.* [rhy. sl.] [1990s+] strange.

homer *n.*[1] (*US*) **1** [late 19C+] in sports, a referee who favours the home team. **2** [1980s+] a friend.

homer *n.*[2] **1** [1980s+] (*US campus*) a penis [? it goes for a HOME RUN *n.*]. **2** *see* HOME RUN *n.*

homer *n.*[3] *see* OMEE *n.*

home rule *n.* [play on FENIAN *n.*] [late 19C–1900s] Irish whisky.

home ruler *n.* [? the stereotypical Irish diet of potatoes. The period saw a major agitation by the Fenians in favour of Irish Home Rule] [late 19C] **1** a baked potato, cooked and sold in the street. **2** (*Irish*) a pint bottle of stout.

home run *n.* [baseball imagery] **1** [1900s] an escape from prison. **2** [1940s+] (*Aus.*) (*also* **homer**) a soldier who is badly injured or dead and will be sent home from the battlefield. **3** [1960s+] (*US*) (*also* **homer**) sexual intercourse; both heterosexual and homosexual (cf. FIRST BASE *n.* (1); *SECOND BASE under* SECOND *adj.*; *THIRD BASE under* THIRD *adj.*).

(IN PHRASES)

▫ **hit a home run** *v.* (*also* **score a home run, get run**) [1980s+] (*US campus*) to have sexual intercourse.

homes *n.* [*see also* HOLMES *n.*] [1970s+] (*orig. US black*) an affectionate dimin. of HOMEBOY *n.* (3), usu. as a term of address, e.g. *Hey, homes...*

home sweet home *n.*[1] [late 19C–1920s] the vagina.

home sweet home *n.*[2] [rhy. sl.] [1980s] (*Aus.*) a comb.

homey *n.*[1] (*also* **homie**) **1** [1920s+] (*Aus./N.Z.*) an Englishman; a British immigrant, esp. one newly arrived or still nostalgic for the 'home country'. **2** [1940s] (*US black*) a stay-at-home person. **3** [1940s+] (*orig. US black*) an affectionate dimin. of HOMEBOY *n.* (3), used as n. or form of address. **4** [1990s+] (*US campus*) a partner in a casual sexual relationship. **5** [1990s+] a relative.

(IN PHRASES)

▫ **homey don't play dat** [the catchphrase of the character Homey the Clown in the TV show *In Living Color*] [1990s+] (*US campus*) a phr. indicating one's refusal to cooperate with, consent to or accept something.

homey *n.*[2] *see* HOMIE *n.*[1].

homey *n.*[3] *see* OMEE *n.*

homey *adj. see* HOMY *adj.*

homicide *n.* [MURDER *n.* (2)/SE *murder*] **1** [1950s] (*US*) someone or something formidable. **2** [1990s+] (*US drugs*) a cocktail of heroin and/or cocaine plus various prescription drugs, incl. scopolamine, a sea-sickness remedy, used to increase the heart-rate, and dextromethorphan, usu. used as a cough medicine. The effects are generally negative, including paranoia, hallucinations and memory loss, and can lead to death, usu. by heart attack.

homie *n.*[1] (*also* **homey**) [abbr.] [1940s+] (*US*) a *homo*sexual.

homie *n.*[2] [HOMEY *n.*[1] (3)] [1990s+] (*Aus.*) a person who wears expensive brands of sportswear.

homie *n.*[3] *see* HOMEY *n.*[1].

homie *n.*[4] *see* OMEE *n.*

homie *adj.* [HOMIE *n.*[1]] [1960s] homosexual.

hominy *n.* [the main constituent of prison meals]

IN COMPOUNDS

❑ **hominy bus** *n.* [1950s] (*Aus. prison*) the bus that runs between Darlinghurst Prison and Long Bay Prison. ❑ **hominy gazette** *n.* [1910s+] (*Aus. prison*) internal prison rumours. ❑ **hominy pimples** *n.* [1950s] (*Aus. prison*) an itchy rash, prevalent in summer, which prisoners ascribe to the monotonous diet. ❑ **hominy prick** *n.* (*also* **hominy cock**) [1950s] (*Aus. prison*) a substitute 'penis' made by stuffing a sock with hominy and used by women prisoners for masturbation.

homi-polone *n. see* OMEE-POLONE *n.*

homo *n.*[1] [Ling. Fr.; ult. Lat. *homo*, a man] [early 19C–1920s] a man.

homo *n.*[2] [abbr. of SE] **1** [1920s+] a male *homo*sexual. **2** [1960s+] gay pornography. **3** [1970s+] (*US campus*) a weakling, an inadequate [no specific sexuality is implied].

IN COMPOUNDS

❑ **homogrips** *n.* [2000s] (*N.Z.*) sideboards/sideburns. ❑ **homo heaven** *n.* [1960s] (*US gay*) any public area where homosexuals meet, pick each other up etc.

IN PHRASES

❑ **do a homo and blow** *v.* [pun on BLOW *v.*[1] (4d)/BLOW *v.*[2] (1c)] [1990s+] (*US black*) to leave, usu. as imper.

homo *adj.* [HOMO *n.*[2] (1)] [1920s+] homosexual.

homoney *n.* [Lat. *homo*, a man] [mid–late 18C] a woman; a wife.

ho-monga *n.* [US black pron. of archaic SE *whoremonger*, a lecher, a fornicator] [2000s] (*US teen*) a man who has a number of girlfriends at the same time.

homy *adj.* (*also* **homey**) **1** [mid-19C] feeling like home, thus comfortable, secure. **2** [1920s+] homely, conventional, dominated by 'family values'.

honch *n.* [? initial letters] [1970s] (*US drugs*) heroin.

honcho *n.* [Jap. *han'cho*, group leader; imported to the West by US forces in Korea] **1** [1940s+] (*orig. US*) a leader, employer, boss, the head person of any job or other situation. **2** [1960s+] (*US*) a fellow man. **3** [1990s+] a well-built, attractive man.

honcho *v.* [HONCHO *n.*] [1950s+] (*orig. US*) to lead, to direct others in a task or plan.

hondoo *n.* [Sp. *honda*, 'the eye or eyelet on the loop of a rope through which the main line is passed to form a loop for roping' (Logsden, *Whorehouse Bells Were Ringing*, 1989)] [1910s–60s] (*US*) the vagina.

hone *n.* [SE *hone*, a whetstone used to grind knives] [18C] the vagina.

hone *v.* [OF *hogner, hoigner*, to grumble, mutter or murmur, to whine like a child, or dog] [20C+] (*US*) **1** to pine for, to yearn after. **2** to look for, to search out.

hone out *v.* [? one has *honed* the edge of one's appetite] [1980s+] (*US campus*) to eat voraciously.

honest Injun *adj.* [HONEST INJUN *phr.*] [20C+] honourable.

honest Injun *phr.* (*also* **honest Indian**) [the term was orig. sarcastic (Indians being seen as essentially dishonest) but became used at face value, esp. by children] **1** [mid-19C+] (*orig. US*) on my honour; also as interrog. meaning 'really?'. **2** [20C+] an affirmative phr. meaning really, definitely.

honest john *n.* (*also* **honest Jack**) [SE *honest* + JOHN *n.* (1)/JACK *n.*[2] (1)] **1** [early 17C; late 19C+] (*US*) (*also* **honest Joe**) an honest citizen, a hard-working person. **2** [1930s] (*US prison*) a naïve person who does not know how to 'work the system'.

honest lawyer *n.* [mid-19C] a public house sign showing a headless man dressed in lawyer's robes, the implication being that his honesty is only possible since, headless, he is bereft of the chance to speak.

honest-to-Hannah *adj.* [euph. var. on SE *honest-to God*] [1950s–60s] genuine, pure.

honest-to-John *adj.* [euph. var. on SE *honest-to-God*] [1940s+] (*US*) genuine, sincere, proper; also as excl. of affirmation.

honest to Pete *adv. see under* PETE *n.*[1].

honey *n.*[1] **1** senses based on the sweetness. (**a**) [mid-14C+] (*also* **honey-chops**) a term of endearment, whether male to female or vice versa; occas. to a child of either sex. (**b**) [late 14C+] a sweetheart, a lover. (**c**) [early 19C+] (*orig. US*) anyone or anything good of its kind. (**d**) [1920s+] an attractive young woman. (**e**) [1920s+] (*US*) a female term for an endearing, attractive man. (**f**) [1930s+] (*orig. US*) in ironic use of sense 1c, something problematical. **2** senses based on the texture. (**a**) [late 17C+] semen. (**b**) [18C+] vaginal secretions. **3** [19C+] (*US*) one whose personality makes them hard to associate with but who has no appreciation of the fact [abbr. *she's a honey but the bees don't know it*]. **4** senses based on the colour. (**a**) [1900s] (*US Und.*) a black person. (**b**) [1920s+] (*US*) (*also* **honeydew**) human excrement; thus *honey-pit, honey-vat*, a cesspit; *honey gatherer, honeyman*, a cesspit cleaner.

as terms of endearment

IN COMPOUNDS

❑ **honey-baby** *n.* (*also* **honey-babe, honey-boy**) [1920s–50s] a general term of affection. ❑ **honey-bun** *n.* (*also* **honey-bunch, honey-bunny, honeybugs, honeypie**) **1** [20C+] a general term of affection. **2** [1950s] a girlfriend. ❑ **honeychile** *n.* (*also* **honey child**) [1920s+] (*US*) a general term of affection, usu. in Southern and/or black use. ❑ **honey-chops** *n. see* sense 1a above. ❑ **honey-dip** *n.* [1990s+] (*US black*) a pretty young woman with a golden-brown complexion, the image is of her being dipped in honey; also as adj. ❑ **honeyfuck** *see* separate entries. ❑ **honey-thighs** *n.* [1940s+] (*orig. US*) a general term of affection from a man to a woman; occas. vice versa.

IN PHRASES

❑ **strobe-light honey** *n.* [1990s+] (*US black teen*) a woman who is attractive at a distance or in poor light, e.g. in a club, but less so in close-up.

pertaining to excrement or defecation

IN COMPOUNDS

❑ **honey-bucket** *n.* (*also* **honeypot**) [1930s+] a bucket used for night-soil. ❑ **honey-cart** *n.* [the term has been adopted by airlines, railway companies and other owners of public transport that provide mobile lavatory facilities] **1** [1920s+] (*US*) a vehicle for collecting human excrement. **2** [1950s+] (*US*) a portable outdoor toilet. ❑ **honey dew** *n.* **1** *see* HONEY *n.*[1] (4b). **2** *see also* SE compounds below. ❑ **honey-dipper** *n.* (*also* **honey-digger, honey dripper**) [1920s+] a latrine cleaner; thus *honey-dipping*, the removal of excrement or sewage; thus a term of abuse. ❑ **honey house** *n.* [20C+] (*US*) a privy or outside lavatory. ❑ **honey-wagon** *n.* (*US*) **1** [1920s+] a vehicle for collecting human (occas. animal) excrement. **2** [1930s] a manure cart used for cleaning out barns. **3** [1940s] a garbage wagon. **4** [1940s+] a portable toilet. **5** [1970s] a vehicle used to spread manure on a field.

other uses

IN COMPOUNDS

❑ **honeydripper** *n.* (*also* **honey-drips**) [1960s+] (*US black*) a sexual partner.

SE in slang uses

IN COMPOUNDS

❑ **honey bum** *n.* [BUM *n.*[1] (1)] [1940s–50s] (*Aus.*) a passive homosexual. ❑ **honey cooler** *n.* [mid-19C–1900s] (*US*) an extraordinary person or thing. ❑ **honey dew** *n.* (*also* **honey dip**) **1** [20C+] (*US*) whisky. **2** *see also* sl. compounds above. ❑ **honey fall** *n.* [mid-19C] a piece of good luck. ❑ **honey pot** *n. see* separate entry.

honey *n.*[2] [rhy. sl. on *pot o' honey*] [mid-19C+] (*US*) money.

honey *adj.* [HONEY UP *v.*] [1940s] (*US*) affectionate.

honey (around) *v. see* HONEY UP *v.*

honeyfuck *n.* [HONEYFUCK *v.*] [1970s+] **1** a very sexy woman. **2** a prepubescent girl, viewed as a sex object.

honeyfuck *v.* [HONEY *n.*[1] (1d) + FUCK *v.*] [1960s+] (*US*) **1** to have sexual intercourse in innocent or idyllic circumstances. **2** to have sex with a prepubescent girl.

honeyfuggle *n.* [HONEYFUGGLE *v.*] [1980s+] lies, deceit.

honeyfuggle *v.* (*also* **honeyfackle, honeyfogle, honeyfugle**) [dial. *connyfogle*, to entice by flattery, to hoodwink; or dial. *gallyfuggle*, to deceive or trick] (*US*) **1** [early 19C–1940s] to swindle, to trick, to fool. **2** [mid-19C–1940s] to 'sweet talk', to flatter, to entice. **3** [mid-19C+] to cuddle up to. **4** [mid-19C+] to have sex, esp. with a prepubescent girl.

honeyfuggler *n.* (*also* **honeyfoogler, honeyfugler**) [HONEYFUGGLE *v.* (2)] [mid-19C–1940s] (*US*) a flatterer; one who makes alluring but empty promises.

honeymoon (stage) *n.* [1930s+] (*drugs*) the early use of heroin, before actual addiction, during which period the user can stop without any real physical or mental pain.

honeypot *n.* [Puxley, *Cockney Rabbit: A Dick 'n' Arry of Rhyming Slang* (1992), suggests rhy. sl. = TWAT *n.* (1), but the chronology militates against this; D'Urfey, *Pills to Purge Melancholy* (1719), credits the lines to the poem 'To chuse a Friend, but never Marry' by the Earl of Rochester, but offers no date] **1** [late 17C+] the vagina. **2** [1930s+] (*also* **nectar pot**) an attractive woman; also as a term of address.

honey up *v.* (*also* **honey, honey around, honey it up**) [var. on HONEYFUGGLE *v.* (2)] [mid-19C+] to cajole, to flatter, to sweet talk.

Hongers *n. see* HONKERS *n.*

Hong Kong *n.* [rhy. sl. = PONG *n.*[1]] [1990s+] a smell.

Hong Kong *adj.* [rhy. sl.] [1990s+] wrong.

Hong Kong dog *n.* [1990s+] diarrhoea or any form of stomach problem picked up by visitors to Hong Kong.

honk *n.*[1] [? Maori *haunga*, ill-smelling] [1920s+] (*orig. Aus.*) an unpleasant smell.

honk *n.*[2] [abbr. HONKYTONK *n.*[1]] **1** [1940s–60s] a wild, uproarious party. **2** [1970s+] (*US*) country and western or honky-tonk music.

honk *n.*[3] [? its similarity to a HONKER *n.*[1] (2)] [1960s–70s] (*US*) the penis.

honk *n.*[4] [HONK *v.*[4]] [1980s+] (*US drugs*) an inhalation of a narcotic.

honk *n.*[5] [Du. *honk*, one's aim or target, that which has to be done] [2000s] (*S.Afr. prison*) prison work detail.

honk *n.*[6] *see* HONKIE *n.*

honk *v.*[1] [SE *honk*, to make a honking noise] **1** [20C+] (*US*) (*also* **honk on**) to talk loudly in a boastful manner. **2** [1960s+] to vomit. **3** [2000s] to snore.

honk *v.*[2] [HONK *n.*[1]] **1** [1920s+] (*orig. Aus.*) to smell unpleasant, to stink; often intensified as *honk like a gaggle of geese*. **2** [1970s+] (*US campus*) to be very offensive or unattractive.

honk *v.*[3] [representative sound of the actions] **1** [1940s+] to have sexual intercourse, to seduce. **2** [1970s+] (*US campus*) to be sexually aroused. **3** [1970s+] (*US Und.*) to kill someone.

honk *v.*[4] [HONKER *n.*[1] (2)] [1960s–70s] (*US*) to inhale or snort a narcotic.

honk *v.*[5] [the image of squeezing or 'honking' an old-fashioned horn or hooter] [1970s+] (*US*) to squeeze the penis or breast.

honkatonk *n. see* HONKYTONK *n.*[1].

honked (off) *adj.* [HONK OFF *v.*] [1950s+] (*US campus*) angry.

honked up *adj.* [HONK *v.*[1] (1)] [1960s+] (*US campus*) excited.

honker *n.*[1] **1** [mid-19C+] (*US*) a goose. **2** [1940s+] the nose [SE *honk*, a nose]. **3** [1960s+] (*US*) a player of a brass instrument.

honker *n.*[2] [HONK (IT ON) *v.*] [1960s+] (*US*) a very fast vehicle.

honker *n.*[3] [HONK *v.*[5]] **1** [1970s+] a large penis. **2** [1970s+] (*US*) in pl., the female breasts, esp. if large.

honker *n.*[4] [HONK *v.*[2]] **1** [1970s+] (*US campus*) an offensive or unattractive person. **2** [1980s+] (*US teen*) anyone considered odd or eccentric.

honker *n.*[5] [HONK *v.*[1] (2)] [1980s+] (*US*) a gob of phlegm.

Honkers *n.* (*also* **Hongers**) [*Hong Kong* + -ER *sfx*] [1920s+] Hong Kong, usu. among UK ex-patriates stationed or working in East Asia.

honkers *n.* [SE *haunches*] [1940s] (*US black*) in pl., the buttocks.

honk, honk! *excl.* [1930s] a toast when drinking.

honkie *n.* (*also* **honk, honkey, honky**) [abbr. BOHUNK *n.* (1); the black use is a development of the white HUNKY *n.* (1), the orig. name for Poles who worked in Chicago stockyards. The change of the white 'u' to the black 'o' supposedly accentuates the black desire, embodied in the black militants of the 1960s, to distance themselves as far as possible from the object of their distaste] **1** [1940s+] (*US black*) a white person, occas. a light-skinned Latino. **2** [1940s+] an ice-cream bar. **3** [1970s] a phoney person. **4** [1980s+] a man, usu. derog. and used by any race.

DERIVATIVES

❑ **honkymobile** *n.* [-MOBILE *sfx*] [1970s] (*US black*) any car seen as unfashionable and thus driven only by whites.

IN COMPOUNDS

❑ **honkietown** *n.* [1970s] (*US black*) the predominantly white area of a town.

honkie *adj.* (*also* **honkie-ass, honky**) [HONKIE *n.*] [1940s+] (*orig. US black*) **1** a derog. term for white or pertaining to white lifestyle/culture. **2** fake, pseudo, second-rate.

honking *adj.*[1] [SE *honk*] [1940s+] very drunk.

honking *adj.*[2] [? var. on SE *hulking*] [1980s+] (*US campus*) enormous, huge.

honking brown *n.* [HONK *v.*[1] (1)] [1940s] (*US black*) an ostentatious tan-coloured suit of clothes.

honk (it on) *v.* [? the *honking* of the horn that accompanies such a progress] [1960s+] (*US*) to drive or go at top speed.

honkoe *n.* [? HONKIE *n.*, but with no racial overtones or HONK *v.*[2]] [1930s–60s] (*Aus.*) a general term of abuse.

honk off *v.* [HONK *v.*[2]] [1950s+] (*US campus*) to anger, to annoy.

honk on *v.* (*also* **honk off**) [? HONK (IT ON) *v.*] [1970s] (*US campus*) to go away, to leave one alone.

honky *see under* HONKIE.

honky *n. see* HUNKY *n.* (2).

honky-dooley *adj. see* HUNKY-DORY *adj.* (1).

honkytonk *n.*[1] (*also* **honkatonk**) [the *honky-tonk* piano that was often a feature of such establishments. The UK comedian Dick Emery (1918–83) used 'hello honky-tonk/tonks' as a catchphrase, but it has not survived his death, other than historically] **1** [late 19C+] (*orig. US*) a seedy bar which may also offer music, gambling, prostitutes; thus *honky-tonker*, a promiscuous woman who haunts such bars. **2** [1980s+] (*US*) a small town.

honkytonk *n.*[2] [rhy. sl. = PLONK *n.*[1] (1)] [20C+] (*Aus.*) cheap wine.

honkytonk *adj.* (*also* **honky-tonky**) [HONKYTONK *n.*[1] (1)] [1920s+] (*orig. US*) seedy, sordid, run down, mediocre.

honky-tonk *v.* [HONKYTONK *n.*[1] (1)] [1950s+] (*US*) to go out on the town.

honyock(er) *n. see* HUNYAK *n.*

hoo *n. see* HOOHA *n.*

hooa *n. see* HOOER *n.*

hooch *n.*[1] (*also* **hootch**) [*hoochinoo*, an alcoholic liquor made by Alaskan Indians, esp. the Hoochinoo people] **1** [late 19C+] (*orig. US*) alcohol, liquor. **2** [late 19C+] any inferior alcoholic drink (esp. whisky) in Alaska and the Can. northwest. **3** [late 19C+] (*orig. US, esp. prison*) illicitly distilled liquor, often made from surprisingly unorthodox ingredients. **4** [1970s+] (*US drugs*) (*also* **hoochie**) cannabis.

IN COMPOUNDS

❑ **hooch dog** *n.* [1980s+] (*US campus*) a marijuana cigarette. ❑ **hooch-hive** *n.* [1960s] (*S.Afr.*) an illicit drinking club. ❑ **hooch hound** *n.* [-HOUND *sfx*] **1** [1930s] a Prohibition agent. **2** [1940s–60s] (*orig. US black*) a drunkard.

hooch *n.*[2] *see* HOOCHIE *n.*[1].

hooch *n.*[3] *see* HOOTCH *n.*[1].

hooch *n.*[4] *see* HOOTCHY-KOOTCHY *n.*

hooch *v.* [HOOCH *n.*[1]] [1900s] to drink alcohol.

hooched (up) *adj.* [HOOCH *n.*[1]] [1920s+] (*US/S.Afr.*) tipsy.

hoochie *n.*[1] (*also* **hooch, hootchie, hoochie mama, hootchie..., hootchy...**) [HOOTCHY-KOOTCHY *n.* (1)] **1** [1920s+] (*US black*) a promiscuous girl or woman; *hoochie* *mama* is the intensified form; thus v. *hoochie-mama*, to act outspokenly, shamelessly. **2** [1990s+] (*US black*) an affectionate term of address.

hoochie *n.*[2] *see* HOOCH *n.*[1] (4).

hoochie *n.*[3] *see* HOOTCHY-KOOTCHY *n.*

hoochie-coocher *n.* [HOOTCHY-KOOTCHY *n.* (1)] [1930s–40s] (*orig. US black*) a striptease artist.

hoochie-coochie *n. see* HOOTCHY-KOOTCHY *n.*

hoochie-coochie man/woman *n.* (*also* **hootchie-cootchie..., hootchy-cootchy...**) [HOOTCHY-KOOTCHY *adj.* + SE *man/woman*] [late 19C+] (*US black*) a practitioner of voodoo.

hoochie mama *n. see* HOOCHIE *n.*[1].

hoochie-pap *n.* [? the exaggerated movement of the buttocks when dancing the *hoochie-coochie*] [1920s] (*US black*) **1** the buttocks, the posterior. **2** copulation.

hoochie papa *n.* (*also* **hoochie-pap**) [1990s+] (*US black*) a womanizer.

hoochy *n. see* HOOTCHY-KOOTCHY *n.*

hoochy-coochy *n. see* HOOTCHY-KOOTCHY *n.*

hood *n.*[1] [abbr. HOODLUM *n.*] **1** [late 19C+] (*US*) a gangster, a thug. **2** [20C+] (*Aus.*) the police. **3** [20C+] a street ruffian.

hood *n.*[2] [? its foreskin] [1950s+] (*W.I. Rasta*) the penis.

SE in slang uses

IN EXCLAMATIONS

❑ **by my hood!** [late 14C–16C] a mild oath or excl.

hood *n.*[3] [abbr. SE *neighbourhood*] **1** [1960s+] (*US black*) the area in which one lives, one's home ground. **2** [1980s+] (*US prison*) a friend who has come from one's own neighbourhood.

IN COMPOUNDS

❑ **hood rat** *n.* [1990s+] (*US black teen*) **1** an unattractive and/or promiscuous woman. **2** a young person living in the (black) neighbourhood or part of a gang, usu. female. **3** (*US campus*) a gangster, a thug.

IN PHRASES

❑ **from the hood** [1990s+] (*US black gang*) being a member of a neighbourhood gang. ❑ **put someone on the hood** *v.* [1990s+] (*US black gang*) to enrol in a gang.

hoodickie *n.* (*also* **hoodackie**) [DOHICKEY *n.*[1] (1)] [1940s+] (*N.Z.*) an otherwise nameless object, often a gadget.

hoodie *n.* (*also* **hoody**) [abbr.] **1** [1980s+] (*orig. US*) a *hood*ed sweatshirt, as worn by many young people, esp. those involved in rap music, as a semi-uniform. **2** [2000s] (*orig. US*) by metonymy, the wearer, esp. when perceived as a threat.

hoodle-do *n. see* HOODOO *n.* (2).

hoodle-hoodle wagon *n. see* HOODLUM WAGON *n.*

hoodlelacky *n.* [1940s+] (*N.Z.*) an otherwise nameless object, often a gadget.

hoodlum *n.* [ety. unknown. The term was coined in San Francisco c.1870–2 and spread across the US by the end of the decade, generating a number of popular etymologies. Among them, according to H.L. Mencken (1880–1956), is the idea of a local newspaperman who, keen to coin a term to describe the street gangs that were plaguing the city's streets, decided simply to reverse the name of a leading gangster, one Muldoon. This created *noodlum*, and a printer's error, substituting 'h' for 'n', did the rest. Other theories include a reference to a gang rallying-cry, 'Huddle 'em!', and to roots in the Bavarian dialect term *Hodalump*, which carries exactly the same meaning, in various terms in Spanish and among US Indian languages. B&L's suggestion of an origin in the pidgin English *hood lahnt*, lazy, is not feasible. It is tempting to bring in the near-synon. SE *hooligan*, but that word was British and was noted only when it began appearing in London police reports c.1898; *see* Asbury, *The Barbary Coast* (1933), pp.150–3 for possible etys., and his persuasive opting for the 'huddle 'em' theory] [late 19C+] (*orig. US*) **1** an unpleasant person or a street ruffian. **2** a thug or gangster.

hoodlum *adj.* [HOODLUM *n.*] **1** [late 19C+] lowlife, criminal, frequented by unpleasant characters. **2** [1970s] in fig. use, working badly, acting up.

hoodlum wagon *n.* (*also* **hoodle-hoodle wagon**) [note cowboy jargon *hoodlum wagon*, the bed wagon] [late 19C–1960s] (*US*) a police patrol wagon.

hoodoo *n.* [SE *hoodoo*, the practice of witchcraft] (*US*) **1** [late 19C] a party or celebration. **2** [late 19C+] (*also* **hoodledoo**) a curse, a jinx, a run of bad luck.

hoodoo *adj.* (*also* **hoodooed**) [HOODOO *n.* (2)] [late 19C–1940s] jinxed, cursed.

hoodoo *v.* (*also* **hoodoodle**) [HOODOO *n.*] [late 19C+] (*US*) to cheat, to deceive, to take advantage of; to suffer or give bad luck.

hoods *n.* [hoods for one's eyes] [1970s+] (*US gay*) dark glasses.

hoody *n. see* HOODIE *n.*

hoody *adj.* [HOOD *n.*[1]] [1960s+] (*US*) acting in a thuggish manner; resembling a thug.

hooer *n.* (*also* **hooa, hoor, hua, huer**) [SE *whore*] **1** [1950s+] (*Aus.*) a term of general disapproval, applied to either sex. **2** [1960s] (*Aus.*) any creature.

IN PHRASES

❑ **like a hooer at a christening** [1960s+] (*N.Z.*) in a state of confusion.

hooey *n.* [? Rus. (translit.) *hooey*, sl. for penis, i.e. cock, thus 'load of old cock', or COCK *n.*[5] (2)] [1910s+] rubbish, nonsense.

hooey! *excl.* [HOOEY *n.*] [1920s+] nonsense!

hoof *n.* **1** [late 16C+] the human foot. **2** [1960s+] a shoe.

IN PHRASES

❑ **beat the hoof** *v.* (*also* **bang the hoof**) [early 17C–early 19C] to walk. ❑ **gad the hoof** *v.* [mid-19C] to walk without shoes. ❑ **get the hoof** *v.* [late 19C+] to be thrown out, either of a place or of one's employment. ❑ **on the hoof** [1930s+] **1** in existence. **2** passing by, casual. ❑ **shake a hoof** *v. see under* SHAKE *v.* ❑ **take it on the hoof** *v.* [1900s] (*US*) to run off, to leave quickly.

hoof *v.* (*also* **hoof it**) [HOOF *n.*] **1** [mid-17C+] (*also* **huff it**) to walk, to go on foot. **2** [late 19C+] to run. **3** [20C+] to kick, also in fig. use. **4** [1920s+] (*also* **hoofer**) to dance. **5** [1950s] (*US*) to work hard. **6** [1980s+] (*US campus*) to hurry. **7** [1990s+] to engage enthusiastically in something.

IN COMPOUNDS

❑ **hoofball** *n.* [1910s] (*Aus.*) Australian Rules Football.

IN PHRASES

❑ **hoof out** *v.* [late 19C+] to throw out, to expel. ❑ **hoof the pad** *v. see under* PAD *n.*[1].

hoofer *n.* [HOOF *n.*] [1910s+] (*US*) a dancer of either sex; a chorus-girl or chorus-boy.

hoofer *v. see* HOOF *v.* (4).

hoofery *n.* [HOOF *v.* (4)] [1940s–60s] (*orig. US black*) a dancehall.

hoofing *n.* [HOOF *v.*] **1** [late 17C+] travelling on foot. **2** [20C+] (*orig. US*) dancing.

hoof it *v.* [? fig. use of HOOF *v.* (3), with the idea of 'kicking someone up the arse'] **1** [2000s] (*US prison*) to hide contraband in one's rectum. **2** *see* HOOF *v.*

hoofler *n.* [HUFFLE *v.*] [20C+] (*Irish*) a general term of abuse.

hoogie *n.* (*also* **hoogy, hoojer**) [? HOOJAH *n.*/HOOSIER *n.*] [1970s+] (*US black*) a derog. term for a white person, esp. a racist.

hooha *n.* (*also* **hoo, hoohah**) [Yid. *hu-ha*, a hullabaloo] **1** [1930s+] an uproar, commotion. **2** [1970s+] (*orig. milit.*) nonsense, rubbish, twaddle.

hoojah *n.* [1920s] (*US black*) a derog. term for a white person.

hoo-jahs, the *n.* (*also* **the hoo-has, the hoo-hoos**) [1930s+] (*Aus./US*) delirium tremens.

hoojer *n. see* HOOGIE *n.*

hook *n.*[1] **1** in senses of the shape of a hook. (**a**) [late 18C+] a finger; usu. in pl., thus a hand. (**b**) [late 19C+] (*orig. Aus.*) a spur, usu. in pl. (**c**) [1910s–60s] (*US prison*) a straight razor used as a weapon. (**d**) [1940s+] (*US*) a jack or seven in poker [i.e. the shape of 'J' or '7']. (**e**) [1960s+] (*US campus*) the grade C; thus *hook and a half*, the grade C+. (**f**) [1960s+] (*US black*) a derog.

term for a Jew [the popular stereotype of hook-nosed Semites]. (**g**) [1970s] (*US Und.*) a key. (**h**) [1970s+] (*US gang*) a weakling, a conformist, esp. a non-gang member [? the stereotypically studious Jew is seen as unlikely to join a gang; note WW1 milit. *hook*, a shirker]. **2** in senses of lit. 'hooking' or grasping. (**a**) [mid-19C+] (*also* **breech hook**) the pickpocket who actually steals the wallet, money etc rather than his various accomplices; thus *lady hook*, a female pickpocket. (**b**) [late 19C+] (*Aus.*) any expert thief. (**c**) [1940s–50s] an arrest. (**d**) [1940s+] (*Irish*) a confidence trickster, a cheat. (**e**) [1980s] (*US black/Und.*) a piece of cheap jewellery. (**f**) [1980s] (*Aus.*) a prison. (**g**) [2000s] (*US black/Und.*) the police. **3** in fig. senses, that which 'hooks'. (**a**) [late 19C] in fig. use, one's skill, one's ability. (**b**) [late 19C+] a catch, a drawback. (**c**) [late 19C+] a gimmick or angle. (**d**) [late 19C+] an imposture. (**e**) [1930s+] (*US*) an influential patron or contact; political influence. (**f**) [1930s+] (*US*) any form of influence, e.g. blackmail. **4** [1940s+] (*US campus*) the telephone [telephonic imagery: one 'hangs it up'; early models had a hook on which the receiver was hung].

IN PHRASES

▫ **do the hook** *v.* [1930s] (*US Und.*) to serve a life sentence. ▫ **get one's hooks on** *v.* (*also* **get one's hooks into, have one's hooks into**) [20C+] to grasp, to grab, to obtain, esp. when the object is most desired or currently held by a rival. ▫ **off the hook** (*also* **off the heezie, ...hizzy**) [1990s+] **1** (*US black/teen*) used of something so good as to transcend description. **2** (*US*) completely unacceptable, crazy, out of control. ▫ **on one's own hook 1** [early 19C+] (*also* **on one's own pock-nook**) looking after oneself, taking responsibility for one's own life, on one's own initiative or volition; the var. is Scot. **2** [1910s+] (*US*) of an achievement or action, done with no help from anyone else, on one's own. ▫ **pay with a hook** *v.* [late 19C] (*Aus.*) to steal. ▫ **put the hooks in** *v.* **1** [1940s] (*US*) to take advantage of. **2** [2000s] to entrap, lit. or fig. ▫ **sling one's hook** *v.* [SE *sling* + sense 1 above] **1** [mid–late 19C] to pick pockets. **2** *see also* separate entry. ▫ **toss the hooks** *v.* [1900s] (*US*) to box.

SE in slang uses

IN PHRASES

▫ **drag one's hook** *v. see under* DRAG *v.*[1]. ▫ **drop off the hook(s)** *v. see under* DROP OFF *v.*[1]. ▫ **drop the hook on** *v. see under* DROP *v.*[1]. ▫ **get the hook** *v.* [the long pole or *hook* used to drag unpopular performers off stage; introduced in 1903 at Harry Minor's Bowery Theatre, New York City] [late 19C–1920s] (*US*) **1** to be ejected. **2** in fig. use, to take second place; to suffer a rejection. ▫ **give someone the hook** *v.* [1900s] (*US*) **1** to imprison. **2** to betray, to double-cross. **3** to punish, to treat unkindly. ▫ **let someone off the hook** *v.* [*OFF THE HOOK* below] [1960s+] to excuse (someone) from punishment. ▫ **off the hook** [1950s+] out of trouble, freed of a difficult situation ▫ **off the hook(s) 1** [mid-17C–19C] ill-tempered, peevish; 'in a state'. **2** [mid-17C–1900s] crazy, eccentric. ▫ **off the hooks** [the ancient practice of exposing the head and limbs of executed traitors in public places around a city] [mid-19C+] dead; thus *drop/go off the hooks*, to die; *knock off the hooks*, to kill, to murder. ▫ **on the hook** [as opposed to *OFF THE HOOK* above] [1940s+] (*US*) responsible (for) something that went wrong. ▫ **take a/one's/the hook** *v. see* SLING ONE'S HOOK *v.* ▫ **throw the hooks into** *v.* (*US*) **1** [late 19C–1940s] to criticize viciously. **2** [late 19C+] to cheat or swindle, to lure a victim. **3** [1910s] to trick, to fool. **4** [1910s] to attack with a weapon.

hook *n.*[2] [HOOK *v.*[1] (2f)] [1930s+] (*drugs*) an addiction.

IN PHRASES

▫ **off the hook** [1930s–60s] (*US drugs*) ceasing to take narcotic drugs. ▫ **on the hook** [1940s+] (*drugs*) addicted to a drug.

hook *n.*[3] [*HOOK DOWN under* HOOK *v.*[1]] [1970s] (*US drugs*) a puff on a pipe.

hook *n.*[4] and its combs., *see* HOOKER *n.*[3].

hook *adj.* **1** [1940s] (*S.Afr. prison*) difficult, problematic. **2** [1980s+] (*US black*) physically attractive [the attraction is a 'hook'].

hook *v.*[1] **1** UK Und. uses, in senses of using a lit. or fig. hook. (**a**) [early 17C–19C] to steal, to pilfer, esp. by cutting a hole in a shop window and 'fishing' for its contents with a hook on a string. (**b**) [late 18C+] to steal, to rob; to pick a pocket. **2** in senses of SE *hook*, to ensnare. (**a**) [18C+] to fool, to practise a confidence trick upon, to swindle. (**b**) [early 18C+] (*US*) to arrest, to catch in a crime. (**c**) [early 19C+] to attract, esp. into marriage. (**d**) [late 19C+] to attract, to catch the eye of. (**e**) [20C+] to (over)charge. (**f**) [1920s+] (*drugs*) to make someone addicted to drugs. (**g**) [1990s+] (*US black*) to cost. **3** (*also* **hook it**) in senses of SE *hook*, move with a sudden twist or turn. (**a**) [mid-18C+] to run off, to escape. (**b**) [mid-19C+] to go about one's own business. (**c**) [20C+] (*US*) to play truant. **4** in senses of grabbing or grasping. (**a**) [1930s+] (*US, orig. tramp*) to steal a ride on a train or other vehicle, to hitchhike. (**b**) [1980s+] to catch a train, a bus etc. (**c**) [1980s+] (*US campus*) to engage in love making. (**d**) [1980s+] (*US black*) to search for. (**e**) [1990s+] (*US campus*) to help. (**f**) [1990s+] (*US drugs*) to find or obtain something. **5** [1950s] (*drugs*) to inject narcotics.

IN PHRASES

▫ **hook in** *v.* **1** [19C+] (*US*) to get introduced to or put in touch with, to entice. **2** [late 19C+] to associate oneself with. **3** [20C+] (*Aus./US*) to get involved in. ▫ **hook jack** *v.* [late 19C–1910s] (*US*) to play truant. ▫ **hook one's bait** *v.* (*also* **hook one's mutton**) **1** [1920s+] (*Aus./N.Z.*) to escape, to run off. **2** [2000s] (*N.Z.*) to dance with someone. ▫ **hook up** *v.* [1900s] (*US*) to enter into a relationship, e.g. marriage. ▫ **on the hook 1** [mid-19C–1940s] engaging in theft. **2** [1900s–40s] (*US*) playing truant. **3** *see* HOOKED *adj.*[2]. ▫ **on the hook(s) 1** [late 19C] under control. **2** [1950s–70s] in debt to, whether actual or fig.; under the influence of.

SE in slang uses

IN PHRASES

▫ **hook down** *v.* [1960s] to swallow, usu. in the context of drugs. ▫ **hook it up** *v.* [1990s+] (*US*) to finish, to bring to a conclusion. ▫ **hook onto** *v.* **1** [late 19C+] to attach oneself to someone, to follow about. **2** [20C+] to discover.

hook *v.*[2] **1** [1910s+] (*Aus./US*) to punch, to fight. **2** [1970s] (*US black*) to kill, to murder.

hook *v.*[3] [HOOKER *n.*[3] (1); while there appears to be no evidence of this use before 1940s, it seems unlikely that the word was not in unrecorded use as much as a century earlier] [1940s+] to engage in prostitution.

IN PHRASES

▫ **hook it up** *v.* [2000s] (*US black*) to be a prostitute or to act like one.

hook *v.*[4] [HOOK *n.*[1] (1e)] [1970s+] (*US campus*) to get a grade C.

hook *v.*[5] [echoic + SE *hawk*, to spit] [1990s+] (*UK juv.*) to vomit.

hook *v.*[6] *see* HOOK UP (WITH) *v.* (8).

hook-and-eye *n.* [? rhy. sl, although rhyme is uncharacteristically on the first element] [1920s] a crook.

hook and snivey/snivvy *see under* HOOKEM-SNIVEY.

hook and snivey, with nix the buffer *n.* [late 18C–early 19C] (*UK Und.*) a criminal trick designed to feed a dog and an additional man for nothing, when food has to be purchased per head.

hooked *adj.*[1] [HOOK *v.*[1] (2a)] [late 17C+] tricked, fooled, deceived, ensnared; usu. in the context of a confidence trick or blackmail.

hooked *adj.*[2] (*also* **hooked on, on the hook**) [HOOK *v.*[1] (2b)] **1** [mid-19C+] obsessed with, infatuated with, in love, 'caught'. **2** [1910s+] married.

hooked *adj.*[3] [HOOK *v.*[1] (2f)] [1920s+] addicted (usu. to a narcotic drug).

hooked *adj.*[4] **1** [1980s] (*US campus*) sorted out, taken care of. **2** [1990s+] (*US black/campus*) physically attractive.

hooked into *adj.* [1970s] (*US*) involved with.

hooked on *adj.* [20C+] (*Aus.*) of a woman, 'picked up' in the street or in some other informal situation.

hooked up *adj.*[1] [SE *hook up*, to join with] [1910s+] (*US*) dating, 'going steady'.

hooked up *adj.*[2] [one has been *hooked up* to heaven] [1920s] dead.

hooked up *adj.*[3] [*hooked up* with what is fashionable, interesting] [1970s+] (*US*) **1** well-dressed. **2** intelligent, culturally aware.

hookem-snivey *n.* (*also* **hook and snivey/snivvy, hook 'em snivey, hookem-snivvy, hookum-snivey/-snivvy**) [abbr. of HOOK AND SNIVEY, WITH NIX THE BUFFER *n.*] **1** [late 18C] (*Irish*) a blow. **2** [late 18C–19C] a trick or deceit, spec. a contrivance for undoing the bolt of a door from the outside; a device to help with putting on boots. **3** [late 19C] nobody.

hookem-snivey *adj.* (*also* **hook and snivey/snivvy, hook 'em snivey, hookem-snivvy, hookum-snivey**) [HOOKEM-SNIVEY *n.*] [mid-19C–1930s] deceitful, tricky.

hookem-snivey *v.* (*also* **hook and snivey/snivvy, hook 'em snivey, hookem-snivvy, hookum-snivey**) [HOOKEM-SNIVEY *n.*] [mid–late 19C] to deceive, esp. by faking an illness.

hooker *n.*[1] (*also* **hook**) [HOOK *v.*[1]] **1** [mid-16C–18C] a thief, orig. one who uses a pole with a hook at one end to 'fish' items from open windows, unguarded market stalls, passing carts etc; thus *bene hooker boy*, an expert thief. **2** [late 19C–1950s] a pickpocket, esp. of watches.

hooker *n.*[2] [HOOK *v.*[1] (2a)] [17C] a confidence trickster.

hooker *n.*[3] (*also* **hook**) [SE *hook*, to catch, to lure, to entice. Popular ety. suggests the denizens of *Corlear's Hook*, known as *The Hook*, a red-light area on the New York City waterfront. The view is sanctified by Bartlett's *Dict. of Americanisms* (1859), which defines *hooker* as 'a resident of The Hook, i.e. a strumpet, a sailor's trull'. Also stated by Nell Kimball (1854–1934), 'Her Life as an American Madam': 'The moniker hooker came about in the Civil War...General Joe Hooker, a handsome figure of a man, was a real quif-hunter, and he spent a lot of time in the houses of the redlight district, so that people began to call the district Hooker's Division.' However, the term is attested as early as 1835. Thus the ety. is prob. the SE, but with strong reinforcement f. the geographical ref.; ? link to 19C SE *hooker*, a sailor's affectionate term for a vessel and thus synon. with various terms equating a whore with a ship, e.g. *LAND CARRACK under* LAND *n.*[2]; PINNACE *n.*] **1** [mid-19C+] (*orig. US*) a prostitute. **2** [1990s+] (*US campus*) an idiot, a stupid person, a general term of abuse.

(IN COMPOUNDS)

❑ **hook house** *n.* [HOUSE *n.*[1] (1)/SE *house*] [late 19C+] (*US*) a brothel. ❑ **hook joint** *n.* [JOINT *n.* (3b)] [1950s] (*US Und.*) a brothel; anywhere that swindles its patrons. ❑ **hook shop** *n.* (*also* **hooker shop**) [mid-19C+] a brothel.

hooker *n.*[4] [HOOK *v.*[1] (2b)] [1930s–40s] (*US Und.*) a warrant for an arrest.

hooker *n.*[5] [HOOK *n.*[1] (3b)] [1960s+] (*US*) a trick or concealed drawback.

hooketty/hookety *adj. see* HOOKITY *adj.*

hookey *n.* [the popular stereotype of hook-nosed Semites] [late 19C] the nickname of a hook-nosed man, thus a Jew.

hookey *adj. see* HOOKY *adj.*

hookey (walker) *n.* [HOOKEY WALKER! *excl.* (1)] [mid–late 19C] bad luck, trouble.

hookey walker! *excl.* (*also* **hooky walker! with a hook!**) [according to Bee, the proper name of *John Walker*, 'an outdoor clerk' at Longman, Clementi and Co.'s in Cheapside; Walker had a hooked or crooked nose and was used by the 'nobs of the firm' to spy on his fellow employees. Those upon whom he spied naturally declared that his reports were nonsense and since there were more of him than them, they tended to prevail. Hotten (1867) offers an alternative view, basing the phr. on 'a person named Walker, an aquiline-nosed Jew' who exhibited an orrery 'the Eidoranion' along which he would 'take a sight', which action, using an extended arm and a finger raised to the eye, was the equivalent of a dismissive gesture; Hotten also suggests another hook-nosed Walker, a magistrate] [early 19C–1900s] **1** an expression of incredulity, nonsense! rubbish! **2** go away! be off! thus *play Hookey Walker*, to run off.

hookface *n. see* HOOKNOSE *n.*

hook house *n. see under* HOOKER *n.*[3].

hookie bookie *n.* [HOOKY *n.*[3] (1) + assonance] [2000s] (*US black*) time-wasting, acting as a parasite.

hook it up *v. see* HOOK UP (WITH) *v.* (13).

hookity *n.*

(IN EXCLAMATIONS)

❑ **by hookity!** *see BY HOKEY! under* HOKEY *n.*[1].

hookity *adj.* (*also* **hooketty, hookety**) [1900s] (*Aus.*) dubious, unacceptable, underhand, unfair.

hook joint *n. see under* HOOKER *n.*[3].

hooknose *n.* (*also* **hookface**) [physiological stereotyping; also note Folb, *Runnin' Down Some Lines* (1980): 'Whites who display characteristics associated with what is seen as Jewish behavior or looks are often labeled as such. I heard a variety of non-Jewish people, such as Italians, Armenians, and Greeks, being called by these terms because they showed stereotypic Jewish features or they behaved in some manner associated with Jews'] [mid-19C+] a derog. term for a Jew; also a derog. term of address.

hook off *v.*[1] [HOOK *v.*[1]] [late 19C] to steal.

hook off *v.*[2] [HOOK *v.*[1] (3a)] [1930s+] (*N.Z.*) to escape, to run off.

hook shop *n. see under* HOOKER *n.*[3].

hookum-snivey/-snivvy *see under* HOOKEM-SNIVEY.

hook-up *n.* **1** [1900s] a fight. **2** [1900s–50s] a connection between one person and another. **3** [1910s+] a connection between one thing and another. **4** [1980s+] (*US campus*) an ability to get proper connections with certain people or things, e.g. drugs. **5** [1980s+] (*US drugs*) a place where drugs are sold. **6** [1980s+] (*US*) a brief sexual or romantic relationship or the person with whom one has a relationship. **7** [2000s] (*US prison*) a story made up by a prison officer to cause trouble for a prisoner. **8** [2000s] (*US prison*) various items purchased from the commissary. **9** [2000s] (*US black*) a suit of clothes, an outfit.

(IN PHRASES)

❑ **get the hook up** *v.* [lit./fig. uses of sense 6 above] [2000s] (*US teen*) for a situation to surpass one's expectations; to enjoy a satisfactory sexual relationship.

hook up (with) *v.* **1** [20C+] to meet. **2** [20C+] to form a relationship with; sexual or otherwise. **3** [20C+] to get married. **4** [1910s] (*US*) to corrupt, to suborn. **5** [1940s+] to introduce, to bring two parties together in a commercial transaction, to connect. **6** [1950s+] (*US Und.*) to involve a fellow criminal in or to advise of a potentially lucrative scheme. **7** [1970s] (*US Und.*) to work as a prostitute. **8** [1970s+] (*also* **hook**) to be sexually active with someone, whether kissing or having sex. **9** [1980s+] (*US campus*) to give, to hand over, to provide. **10** [1980s+] to obtain drugs for someone. **11** [1990s+] (*US black*) to create something according to one's own taste, e.g. clothing, house decoration, holiday plans. **12** [1990s+] (*US*) to take an academic course. **13** [1990s+] (*US teen*) (*also* **hook it up**) to get more than one is entitled to, to get something for free. **14** [2000s] (*US prison*) to get an address and phone number.

hooky *n.*[1]

(IN PHRASES)

❑ **do hooky** *v.* [? a *hook* nose / HOOKEY WALKER! *excl.* (1)] [mid–late 19C] to make the coarse gesture of applying the thumb and fingers to one's nose.

hooky *n.*[2] [HOOK *n.*[1] (1)] [1930s] (*US Und.*) a thief.

hooky *n.*[3] [abbr. PLAY HOOKY *v.*] [1940s+] (*US*) truanting.

(IN COMPOUNDS)

❑ **hooky house** *n.* [1990s+] (*US teen*) anywhere that tenagers gather outside the supervision/control of their parents. ❑ **hooky party** *n.* [1990s+] (*US black*) a group of teenagers who skip school to drink malt liquor or liquid crack cocaine.

hooky *n.*[4] [popular stereotype of hook-nosed Semites] **1** [1950s] a Jew. **2** [1970s] (*US black*) a white person [generic or euph. var. on sense 1].

hooky *n.*^{5}

IN EXCLAMATIONS

▫ **by hooky!** *see* BY HOKEY! *under* HOKEY *n.*^{1}.

hooky *adj.* (*also* **hookey**) [HOOK *v.*^{1} + pun on BENT *adj.* (2)] [1940s+] illegal.

hooky *v.* [HOOKY *n.*^{3}] [1960s+] to play truant.

hooky walker! *excl. see* HOOKEY WALKER! *excl.*

hool *v.* [SE *hooligan*] [2000s] (*N.Z.*) to drive fast (and potentially dangerously).

hooley *n.* (*also* **hoolie**) [? Irish *ceilidh*, a gathering for the playing of music, telling of tales and general conversation (pron. 'kayley'). Share (1997), however, opts for Anglo-Ind. *hooly*, ult. Hind. *holi*, the Hindu spring festival in honour of Krishna; note also HOOLIHAN *n.*] [late 19C+] (*orig. Irish*) a rip-roaring party.

hooley-dooley! *excl.* (*also* **hooly-dooly!**) [1960s+] (*Aus.*) an excl. of astonishment.

hoolie *n.*^{1} (*also* **hooley**) [abbr.] [2000s] a *hooligan*.

hoolie *n.*^{2} *see* HOOLEY *n.*

hoolihan *n.* [*Hoolihan*, an Irish surname, thus the stereotyped image of the riotous Irish + ? SE *hooligan*; however, note cowboy jargon *hoolihan*, to throw down a steer with a quasi-wrestling hold, poss. orig. anecdotal] [1930s+] (*US*) a riotous event, a boisterous party.

IN PHRASES

▫ **throw the hoolihan** *v.* [1930s–40s] to celebrate riotously.

hoolihan *v.* [HOOLIHAN *n.*] [1940s+] (*US*) to have a very good time, esp. of a cowboy going out on the town.

hooly-dooly! *excl. see* HOOLEY-DOOLEY! *excl.*

hoon *n.* [ety. unknown. Baker suggests, esp. for sense 2, a contraction of Jonathan Swift's *houyhnhnm* (the anthropomorphic horses of *Gulliver's Travels*, 1726), but they are seen as intelligent beings. It is their human slaves, the *yahoos*, who are the fools – and noted as such in dictionaries; note also N.Z. WW2 use by religiously motivated conscientious objectors to describe those with political or humanitarian (rather than religious) agendas] **1** [1930s+] (*Aus./N.Z.*) a show-off with limited intelligence; a flashy lout or hooligan. **2** [1930s+] (*Aus./N.Z.*) a pimp, a procurer of prostitutes. **3** [1930s+] (*Aus./N.Z.*) one who drives in a dangerous, showing-off manner. **4** [1980s+] (*N.Z.*) an exploit that involves 'hoonish', i.e. exhibitionist, loutish behaviour.

DERIVATIVES

▫ **hoondom** *n.* [1980s+] (*N.Z.*) the world of loutish exhibitionists. ▫ **hoonery** *n.* [1980s+] (*N.Z.*) loutish behaviour. ▫ **hoonish** *adj.* [1980s+] (*N.Z.*) of a person or their behaviour, exhibitionist, loutish.

IN COMPOUNDS

▫ **hoon bin** *n.* [SIN BIN *under* SIN *n.*] [1980s+] (*N.Z.*) an enclosure where drunken sports supporters are detained during a match. ▫ **hoonchaser** *n.* [1980s+] (*N.Z.*) a police officer.

hoon *v.* [HOON *n.*] **1** [1970s] to exploit, to take advantage of. **2** [1980s+] to behave in a loutish manner.

IN PHRASES

▫ **hoon it up** *v.* [1980s] (*N.Z.*) to have a noisy, boisterous party.

hoop *n.* **1** [mid-19C–1960s] a ring, e.g. a wedding ring [SE 16C–early 19C]. **2** [1930s+] in sexual contexts. (**a**) the vagina. (**b**) the anus. (**c**) (*US prison*) sodomy. **3** [1930s+] (*Aus.*) a jockey [by metonymy, based on the hooped 'colours' worn by some jockeys]. **4** [1970s+] (*US*) (*also* **hoops**) the game of basketball [the basketball *hoop*, thus the basketball film *Hoop Dreams* (1994)]. **5** [1990s+] (*Aus. drugs*) the tourniquet that isolates a vein prior to injecting a narcotic drug.

IN COMPOUNDS

▫ **hoop action** *n.* (*also* **hoopage, hooping**) [1970s+] (*US*) the game of basketball. ▫ **hoop-stretcher** *n.* [1990s+] a male homosexual.

hoop *v.*^{1} [fig. SE *put through the hoop*] [mid-18C–1900s] to beat.

IN PHRASES

▫ **hoop someone's barrel** *v.* [18C] to beat.

hoop *v.*^{2} [echoic] [mid-19C; 1980s] (*US*) to vomit.

hoop *v.*^{3} (*also* **hoop down, hoop it, hoop out**) [HOOP *n.* (4)] [1970s+] (*US*) to play basketball.

hoop *v.*^{4} [SE *hoop*, to bind or fasten with hoops, to surround with a hoop] [2000s] (*US black*) to steal.

hoop along *v.* [2000s] (*N.Z.*) to move fast.

hoopdee/hoopdie *n. see* HOOPTIE *n.*

hoopdie swoop *v.* [1970s+] (*US black*) to move in on and pick up a man or woman with great speed and efficiency.

hooped *adj.* (*also* **hoopsy coopsy**) [? ref. to a barrel *hoop*] [mid-18C; 1940s+] (*N.Z.*) drunk.

hoopee! *excl. see* WHOOPEE! *excl.*

hoop it *v.* **1** [mid–late 19C] (*Aus./UK Und./US*) to run away, to escape. **2** *see* HOOP *v.*^{3}.

hoopla *n.* (*also* **hooplah**) [SE *hoop-la!* an expression accompanying a sudden movement, esp. of some trick on stage or in a circus ring; ult. Fr. *houp-là!*] [late 19C+] a fuss, a commotion.

hoopla *adj.* [HOOPLA *n.*] [1910s–30s] crazy, wild, confused.

hoople *n.*^{1} [Du. *hoepel*, a hoop, orig. used in New York City] [1920s–30s] (*US Und.*) a ring.

hoople *n.*^{2} [? *Major Hoople*, a US cartoon strip character, created by Gene Ahern, in 'Our Boarding House', in 1923] **1** [1920s+] (*US*) (*also* **hooplehead**) a fool, an idiot. **2** [1970s] (*US black*) a white person.

hoopsy coopsy *adj. see* HOOPED *adj.*

hoop-te-doodle *n.* [1920s] (*US*) anything for which one has no specific name.

hooptie *n.* (*also* **hoop, hoopdee, hoopdie, hoopty, whoop de**) [? the noise the car makes] **1** [1960s+] (*US orig. California*) a car, esp. the latest model. **2** [1990s+] (*US black*) a worn-out, falling-to-pieces automobile.

hoop up *v. see* WHOOP IT UP *v.*

hoopy *adj.* [? SE *hoop*, i.e. var. on LOOPY *adj.*] [1980s] crazy.

hoor *n. see* HOOER *n.*

hoorah *see under* HURRAH.

hoorah (Henry) *n. see* HOORAY (HENRY) *n.*

hooraw *v. see* HURRAH *v.*

hooray *adj.* (*also* **hurray**) [HOORAY (HENRY) *n.*] [1960s+] noisily and affectedly upper-class.

hooray fuck! *excl.* [SE *hooray* + FUCK! *excl.*] [1940s+] (*N.Z.*) used as a farewell excl., esp. to someone one dislikes or has just been insulting.

hooray (Henry) *n.* (*also* **hoorah (Henry), henry, whooray**) [despite the term's virtually invariable appearance in a UK context, note its US coinage] [1930s+] (*orig. US*) a rich young man given to much public exhibitionism, drunkenness and similar anti-social activities, all based on an excess of snobbish self-esteem; thus fem. *hooray Henrietta*.

hooride *n.* (*also* **who-ride**) [HOOPTIE *n.* (2) + RIDE *n.* (2a)] [1980s+] (*US black*) a run-down automobile.

hooride *v.* [SE excl. *hoorah!*] [1980s+] (*US black*) **1** to act in a rowdy manner. **2** to shoot, to assassinate.

hooroo! *excl.* (*also* **ooroo!**) [SE excl. *hoorah!*] **1** [1900s–50s] hoorah! hooray! **2** [1910s+] (*Aus.*) (*also* **aroo! hurroo!**) goodbye.

hooroosh *n.* (*also* **hurroosh, hurroo**) [SE *hurrish, hurroosh.* 'To drive with the cry "hurrish!" or "hurroosh!"' (*OED*). ? ult. *hooray!*] [20C+] (*orig. US*) an uproar, a great fuss.

hoosegow *n.* (*also* **hoozegow, house-gow**) [Sp. *juzgado*, a tribunal or court of justice] [20C+] (*US*) **1** a prison. **2** any form of institution to which inmates are sent rather than volunteer for entrance. **3** an outhouse, a privy.

hoosegow *v.* [HOOSEGOW *n.* (1)] [20C+] to imprison.

hoosey *adj. see* HOOSIER *adj.*

hoosh *v.* [*hoosh!*, excl. used when driving animals] **1** [mid-19C+] to shove up, to lift, to give a leg up. **2** [late 19C+] to deride. **3** [1900s–40s] of animals and people, to herd, to drive. **4** [1950s] to rush around.

hoosheroon *n. see* HOOSIEROON *n.*

hooshier *n. see* HOOSIER *n.* (1).

hooshierina *n. see* HOOSIERINA *n.*

hooshta *n.* (*also* **hooshter**) [cry of *hooshta!*, used to urge the camel forward] [1910s] (*Aus.*) a camel.

hoosier *n.* [ety. unknown; the suggestion of Cumbrian dial. *hoozer*, something large of its kind is not backed up by US use (a substantial discussion of possible ety. can be found at http://www.indiana.edu/~librcsd/internet/extra/hoosier.html)] **1** [19C+] (*US*) (*also* **hooshier, hosier, hoozier**) a peasant, a rustic simpleton. **2** [19C+] (*US*) a native of Indiana. **3** [mid-19C+] (*US Und.*) a gullible person. **4** [late 19C+] (*US tramp*) a 'farmer'. **5** [late 19C+] (*US*) an amateur, novice or incompetent. **6** [20C+] (*US black*) a white person, esp. a racist. **7** [1910s] (*US Und.*) a local small-town police officer. **8** [1930s–40s] (*US prison*) a prison visitor.

(IN COMPOUNDS)

❑ **hoosier fiend** *n. see* FIEND *n.* (2).

(IN PHRASES)

❑ **hoosier up** *v.* [1920s] (*US tramp*) to act like a simpleton.

hoosier *adj.* (*also* **hoosiery, hoosey**) [HOOSIER *n.* (1)] [late 19C–1960s] peasant, rustic, simple.

hoosier *v.* [HOOSIER *n.* (3)] [20C+] (*US*) to cheat, to make someone a victim of trickery.

hoosierina *n.* (*also* **hooshierina**) [HOOSIEROON *n.*] [mid–late 19C] (*US*) a female native of Indiana.

hoosieroon *n.* (*also* **hoosheroon**) [HOOSIER *n.*] [mid–late 19C] (*US*) a native of Indiana.

hoosiery *adj. see* HOOSIER *adj.*

hoot *n.*[1] (*also* **hootoo, hout, hutu**) [Maori *utu*, money paid as recompense] [mid-19C+] (*Aus./N.Z.*) money; esp. money as paid in return for something, e.g. work.

hoot *n.*[2] [? fig. use of SE *hoot*, an abrupt, sharp cry] [late 19C+] **1** (*orig. US*) (*also* **two hoots**) a very small amount. **2** (*orig. US*) anything or anyone considered unimportant, insignificant. **3** (*US*) a tot of liquor, a drink. **4** (*US*) a euph. for hell.

(IN PHRASES)

❑ **give a hoot** *v.* (*also* **...two hoots, ...a hoot in hell, care two hoots**) [1910s+] to care, usu. in negative use, e.g. *who gives a hoot?* ❑ **hoot in hell** *n.* [late 19C+] (*US*) the least bit.

hoot *n.*[3] [abbr. HOOTENANNY *n.* (5)] [late 19C; 1940s+] (*US*) a party.

hoot *v.*[1] [20C+] (*orig. Aus.*) to smell badly, to stink.

hoot *v.*[2] [HOOT *n.*[3]] [1960s+] to have a good time, to carouse.

hootch *n.*[1] (*also* **hooch**) [SE *hutch*] [1960s+] (*orig. US milit. in Vietnam*) any form of shelter from a peasant hut, to a bunker, to an office building; now general word.

hootch *n.*[2] *see* HOOCH *n.*[1].

hootchie *n. see* HOOCHIE *n.*[1].

hootchie-cootchie man/woman *n. see* HOOCHIE-COOCHIE MAN/WOMAN *n.*

hootchie-kootchie *n. see* HOOTCHY-KOOTCHY *n.*

hootchie mama *n. see* HOOCHIE *n.*[1].

hootchy-cootchy man/woman *n. see* HOOCHIE-COOCHIE MAN/WOMAN *n.*

hootchy-kootchy *n.* (*also* **hooch, hoochie, hoochie-coochie, hoochy, hoochy-coochy, hootchie-kootchie, hootchy, kutch**) [ety. unknown; perhaps no more than a showman's idea of an 'exotic' or 'Oriental' name, the vowels of which suggest the sinuous gyrations of the dancer] **1** [late 19C+] (*orig. US*) a form of highly suggestive belly-dance, usu. performed at carnivals; also attrib. **2** [1980s+] (*US*) sexual activity.

hootchy-kootchy *adj.* [HOOTCHY-KOOTCHY *n.*] [20C+] (*orig. US*) erotic, suggestive, sexy.

hootchy mama *n. see* HOOCHIE *n.*[1].

hooted (up) *adj.* [HOOT *n.*[2] (3)] [late 19C–1930s] (*US*) drunk.

hootenanny *n.* [ety. unknown] **1** [1910s] (*US*) a bedbug, a body louse. **2** [1920s+] (*US*) an imaginary object; something for which one cannot remember the name. **3** [1920s+] a general term of abuse. **4** [1920s+] nonsense, rubbish, anything insignificant; a euph. for *a damn*, and used similarly, e.g. *I don't give a hootenanny*. **5** [1940s+] (*US*) a party. **6** [1950s+] (*US*) a performance of folk music.

hooter *n.*[1] [HOOT *n.*[2]] [mid-19C–1900s] (*US*) an insignificant amount.

hooter *n.*[2] [late 19C] (*US*) a drink.

hooter *n.*[3] [the supposed resemblance to an old-fashioned automobile *hooter*] **1** [1950s+] the nose. **2** [1970s–80s] (*US*) a telephone. **3** [1970s+] a female breast; usu. in pl. **4** [1980s+] (*US*) a woman with large breasts.

(IN PHRASES)

❑ **get some hooter** *v.* [? sense 2 above] [1980s] (*US campus*) to have sexual intercourse.

hooter *n.*[4] [? the sound of defecation] [1960s] (*N.Z.*) the lavatory.

hooter *n.*[5] **1** [1980s+] (*drugs*) a marijuana cigarette. **2** [1980s+] (*N.Z. drugs*) a tube (generally of rolled cardboard) used to inhale smoke from heated drops of cannabis oil.

hooter *n.*[6] [1990s+] (*Ulster*) a person who boasts.

hooter *n.*[7] [2000s] (*US black*) a police officer.

hooting-tooter *see* HOOTY *n.*

hootoo *n. see* HOOT *n.*[1].

hoots and toots *n.* [rhy. sl.] [1960s] (*S.Afr.*) a suit; a pair of boots.

hooty *n.* (*also* **hooting-tooter**) [? the stereotypically ostentatious display associated with gay men] [1980s] (*US black*) a homosexual.

hooty *adj.*[1] [ety. unknown] [1930s–40s] (*US*) angry.

hooty *adj.*[2] [SE *hoot*, something funny] [1970s+] (*US campus*) crazy.

hoover *adj.* [US President Herbert *Hoover* (1874–1964), during whose administration (1929–33) the US suffered the worst privations of the Depression] [1930s–70s] (*US*) a generic adj. used in a variety of combs., all referring to events or objects engendered by the poverty that accompanied the Great Depression, e.g. *Hooverville*, a shanty town; *Hoover blankets*, newspapers used to wrap up in for warmth; *Hoover flush*, an unfinished flush in poker.

(IN COMPOUNDS)

❑ **hoover buggy** *n.* (*also* **hoover cart, ...wagon**) [1930s–70s] (*US*) any makeshift vehicle horsedrawn and dedicated to hauling hay. ❑ **hoover dust** *n.* [1930s] (*US*) cheap tobacco. ❑ **hoover flags** *n.* [1930s] (*US*) empty pockets turned inside out. ❑ **hoover gravy** *n.* [1930s–70s] (*US*) particularly thick gravy, often virtually all a family had to eat. ❑ **hoover hog** *n.* [1930s+] (*US*) **1** a wild rabbit. **2** an armadillo, a cheap form of meat for poor farmers during the Depression. ❑ **hoover pork** *n.* [1930s–50s] (*US*) **1** sow belly. **2** rabbit meat. ❑ **hoover's ham** *n.* [1930s–40s] (*US*) salt pork. ❑ **hoover wagon** *n. see* *HOOVER BUGGY* above.

hoover (up) *v.* [suggested by the brandname of *Hoover* vacuum cleaners, used generically meaning to vacuum, thus to 'suck up'] **1** [1970s–80s] (*UK black*) to smoke a (cannabis) cigarette. **2** [1980s+] (*orig. US*) to inhale drugs. **3** [1980s+] (*orig. US*) to eat or drink, esp. greedily. **4** [1980s+] (*orig. US*) to snatch, esp. greedily. **5** [1980s+] (*orig. US*) to fellate vigorously; thus n. the act of vigorous fellatio. **6** [2000s] (*US black*) to follow someone around, to be clingy. **7** [2000s] (*US teen*) to obtain an abortion.

hoozegow *n. see* HOOSEGOW *n.*

hoozier *n. see* HOOSIER *n.* (1).

hoozy *adj. see* WOOZY *adj.*

hop *n.*[1] **1** [late 17C+] (*also* **hopser**) a dance [note *Sinks of London* (1848) defines such dances as 'a sixpenny, a dancing room where sixpence is the price of admission']. **2** [19C] a dancing academy. **3** [1900s] (*US*) an organized dance, held in a dancehall and frequented by lower class young people.

(IN COMPOUNDS)

❑ **hop merchant** *n.* [MERCHANT *n.*] **1** [late 17C–mid-19C] a dancing master. **2** [19C] a fiddler.

(IN PHRASES)

❑ **house hop** *n.* [20C+] (*orig. US black*) a party at which the guests buy their refreshments to help pay the rent.

SE in slang uses

(IN PHRASES)

❑ **from the hop** [1960s] (*N.Z.*) from the start.

hop *n.*[2] [SE *hops*, the main constituent of beer] **1** [mid-19C+] beer [later use is Aus/N.Z./US black]. **2** [1900s] (*US prison*) tea.

(IN COMPOUNDS)

❑ **hophead** *n. see* separate entry. ❑ **hop joint** *n.* [JOINT *n.* (3b)] [late 19C+] (*US*) a saloon bar. ❑ **hop juice** *n.* [JUICE *n.*[1] (3a)] [late 19C] (*US*) beer. ❑ **hop shop** *n.* [late 18C] a tavern.

(IN PHRASES)

❑ **go the hops** *v.* [1940s–50s] (*Aus.*) to enjoy drinking beer. ❑ **on the hops** [1920s–60s] drinking.

hop *n.*[3] (*also* **hops**) [ety. unknown; ? pidgin Chinese term from Mandarin *ho ping*/Cantonese *nga pin* = tranquillity, bliss, peace] **1** [late 19C+] opium. **2** [20C+] heroin. **3** [1910s–50s] a regular drug user. **4** [1920s–40s] morphine. **5** [1920s+] any type of illicit drug. **6** [1940s] in fig. use, a 'drug', e.g. religion.

(IN COMPOUNDS)

❑ **hop-crazy** *adj.* [1930s] under the influence of opium. ❑ **hop fiend** *n.* [late 19C–1940s] a drug user. ❑ **hop fighter** *n.* [1910s] (*US drugs*) an opium smoker. ❑ **hop gun** *n.* [GUN *n.*[1] (5)] [1930s–50s] (*US drugs*) a hypodermic syringe. ❑ **hophead** *see* separate entries. ❑ **hop joint** *n.* [JOINT *n.* (3a)] [late 19C+] a room or apartment where patrons gather to smoke opium or, more recently, to take heroin. ❑ **hop layout** *n. see* LAYOUT *n.* (6). ❑ **hop merchant** *n.* [MERCHANT *n.*] [1910s] (*US Und.*) a drug peddler. ❑ **hop pad** *n.* [PAD *n.*[2] (2)] [1920s–40s] (*drugs*) a room or apartment where patrons gather to smoke opium or to take heroin. ❑ **hop party** *n.* [1920s+] (*US drugs*) a party where drugs of some sort are consumed. ❑ **hop stick** *n.* [SE *stick*/STICK *n.* (6)] [1930s] (*US drugs*) **1** an opium pipe. **2** a cannabis cigarette. ❑ **hop talk** *n.* [the implication is that such talk is promoted by opium smoking] [late 19C+] (*US*) foolish or exaggerated talk. ❑ **hop toy** *n.* (*also* **hen toy**) [late 19C–1950s] **1** (*drugs*) a container for opium, and part of the opium LAYOUT *n.* (6b). **2** in fig. use, a fantasy (although not actually based on opium).

(IN PHRASES)

❑ **full of hop** (*also* **full of hops**) [1900s–20s] (*US*) behaving as if one were drugged, acting without sense. ❑ **hit the hop** *v.* [1940s–60s] (*US drugs*) to use a narcotic drug, usu. heroin. ❑ **hop (someone) up** *v.* [2000s] (*US*) to give an injection (of legal or illegal drugs). ❑ **on the hop** [1930s–50s] using narcotics.

hop *n.*[4]

(IN PHRASES)

❑ **play the hop** *v.* (*also* **go on the hop**) [*HOP THE WAG under* HOP *v.*[1]] [1930s–60s] to play truant from school.

hop *n.*[5] (*also* **hopper**) [abbr. *BELLHOP under* BELL *n.*[1]] **1** [1930s+] (*US*) a hotel porter. **2** [1960s] a delivery man.

hop *n.*[6] *see* JOHN HOP *n.*

hop *v.*[1] **1** [late 19C] a general greeting in phr. *how hops it?* **2** [late 19C+] (*US*) to jump onto (occas. off) a moving vehicle, esp. a train; to get a lift or ride; to catch a train or aeroplane. **3** [late 19C+] to depart. **4** [late 19C+] (*US*) to assault. **5** [1910s–40s] to make someone jump, to admonish and thus frighten someone. **6** [1920s–60s] (*US black*) to dance, to cavort, to play. **7** [1920s+] to move from place to place. **8** [1920s+] (*US*) usu. of a man, to engage in sexual intercourse. **9** [1950s+] (*orig. US black*) of a place, e.g. a party or club, to pulsate with excitement.

(IN PHRASES)

❑ **hop bail** *v.* [1900s–50s] (*US*) to forfeit one's bail by fleeing. ❑ **hop bells** *v. see under* BELL *n.*[1]. ❑ **hop one's frame** *v. see under* FRAME *n.*[1]. ❑ **hop over a broom** *v. see* JUMP (OVER) THE BROOMSTICK *v.* ❑ **hop the ball** *v.* [Gaelic football *hop the ball*, to set the game in motion] [20C+] (*Irish*) to make a provocative remark. ❑ **hop the charley** *v.* [var. on *HOP THE WAG* below/ CHARLEY-WAG *v.*] [late 19C] to run off, to decamp. ❑ **hop the coop** *v. see under* COOP *n.*[1]. ❑ **hop the twig** *v. see* separate entry. ❑ **hop the wag** *v.* [dial. *wag*, to move, to go] [mid-19C+] to play truant from school. ❑ **on the hop** **1** [late 19C+] running away, escaping, on the run. **2** [1990s+] (*Irish*) to play truant. ❑ **take it on the hop** *v.* (*also* **take it on the arches**) [1960s+] (*US*) to run away; to escape.

SE in slang uses

(IN COMPOUNDS)

❑ **hop harry** *n.* [play on SE *hop*, to move/*bowl*, to move] [1920s–40s] (*Aus.*) a bowler hat. ❑ **hop-over** *n.* [WW1 Aus. milit. *hop-over*, a battle, an assault] [1910s] (*Aus.*) a celebration, a party, esp. if rowdy.

(IN PHRASES)

❑ **hop-and-drop** *v. see* HIP-AND-DROP *v.* ❑ **hop it** *v. see* separate entry. ❑ **hop off** *v. see* separate entries. ❑ **hop on** *v. see* separate entry. ❑ **hop someone's bones** *v.* [1950s] to have sexual intercourse. ❑ **hop the twig** *v. see* separate entry.

(IN EXCLAMATIONS)

❑ **go hop in the bowl!** [1920s] (*US, mainly juv.*) a general excl. of dismissal/abuse. ❑ **hop along!/hop for it!** *see* HOP IT! *excl.* ❑ **hop it!** *see* separate entry. ❑ **hop to it!** *see* HOP IT! *excl.*

hop *v.*[2] [HOP *n.*[3]] [1910s] (*US*) to give a horse some form of drug to alter its natural performance.

hope *v.*

SE in slang uses

(IN PHRASES)

❑ **hope-to-die** *adj.* [abbr. *hope to die if...*] (*orig. US black*) **1** [1960s+] absolute, total. **2** [1980s+] closest, most trusted, best. ❑ **hope to hell** *v. see* WISH TO HELL *v.*

(IN EXCLAMATIONS)

❑ **hope to my die!** [*hope to die + I hope I may die*] [1920s–30s] (*US*) a strong excl. used to underline the veracity or sincerity of the speaker's statement. ❑ **hope to tell you!** (*also* **hope to shout!**) [20C+] (*US*) a strong excl. used to underline the speaker's statement.

hopeful *n.* [early 18C+] an optimist; thus *young hopeful*, a neophyte, a beginner, often used ironically.

hophead *n.*[1] [HOP *n.*[3] + -HEAD *sfx* (4)] [20C+] (*drugs*) **1** an opium, morphine or heroin addict; thus *hophead house*, a place where addicts buy and take narcotics. **2** a cocaine addict. **3** the user of any drug. **4** a marijuana smoker. **5** an unstable person.

hophead *n.*[2] [HOP *n.*[2]/SE *hops* + -HEAD *sfx*] **1** [1940s+] (*US/N.Z.*) a drunkard or a beer-drinker; an alcoholic. **2** [1940s+] (*N.Z.*) a wild, eccentric person. **3** [1970s+] (*US*) a German-American.

hophead *adj.* (*also* **hopheads, hopheaded**) [HOPHEAD *n.*[1] (1)] [20C+] **1** (*drugs*) addicted to a narcotic drug, usu. opium or heroin; pertaining to that addiction. **2** as a general insult, implying mental deficiency.

hop in(to) *v.* (*Aus.*) **1** [1930s+] to start, to begin, e.g. *hop into the grub*, to start eating, often used as an invitation or imper. **2** [1940s–50s] to fight, to attack.

SE in slang uses

(IN PHRASES)

❑ **hop in for one's chop** *v. see under* CHOP *n.*[1].

hop it *v.* [HOP IT! *excl.*] **1** [20C+] to leave, to run off. **2** [1950s+] to die.

hop it! *excl.* (*also* **hop along! hop for it! hop to it!**) [20C+] go away! run along! etc.

hop it and scram *n.* [rhy. sl.] [20C+] ham.

Hopkins *n. see* MR HOPKINS *under* MR *n.*

hopnail *n. see* HOBNAIL *n.*

hop off *v.*[1] **1** [late 18C–1920s] to die or kill. **2** [20C+] to leave.

hop off *v.*[2] [20C+] **1** (*Ulster*) to beat, to thump violently. **2** (*Irish*) (*also* **have a hop of**) to tease, to make fun of.

hop off *v.*[3] [1970s] to happen, to transpire.

hopola *n.* [HOP ON *v.* (1) + -OLA *sfx*] [1990s+] (*US black*) a woman.

hop on *v.* [20C+] **1** to have sexual intercourse. **2** to put pressure on. **3** to attack, to beat up. **4** (*US teen*) to take an admiring look.

IN PHRASES

❑ **hop on a babe** *v.* [BABE *n.* (3)] [1990s+] (*US campus*) to have sexual intercourse; the implication is that the man, lacking greater finesse, has made a pounce (prob. when drunk) to initiate the activity.

hop-out *n.* [HOP OUT *v.*] [1910s] (*Aus.*) argument; controversy.

hop out *v.* [20C+] (*Aus.*) to challenge someone to fight; thus excl. *hop out!* are you ready to fight?

hopped out *adj.* [HOP *n.*[2]] [1980s+] (*N.Z.*) drunk.

hopped (up) *adj.* [lit. + fig. uses of HOP *n.*[3]] **1** [1910s+] (*US drugs*) under the influence of drugs; thus v. *hop oneself up*, to take drugs. **2** [1920s+] (*US*) in fig. use, excited, impatient, obsessed with. **3** [1930s+] (*US*) crazy. **4** [1940s–50s] (*US*) embellished, 'jazzed up.'. **5** [1940s+] (*US*) of a car, improved beyond its basic specifications.

IN PHRASES

❑ **hopped to the gills** *adj.* [*TO THE GILLS under* GILLS *n.*] [1920s+] totally intoxicated by a drug, esp. opium or heroin.

hopper *n.*[1] [SE *hopper*, a chute] **1** [mid-19C–1910s] the mouth. **2** [1950s+] (*US*) a toilet.

hopper *n.*[2] **1** [late 19C] (*US*) a locust. **2** [late 19C+] (*Irish*) a flea.

hopper *n.*[3] [SE *hip-hopper*] [1990s+] (*US black*) a young (black) man.

hopper *n.*[4] *see* HOP *n.*[5].

hopper arse *n.* (*also* **hopper breech, ...hips**) [HOPPER-ARSED *adj.*] **1** [16C–1950s] large buttocks. **2** [early 17C] as a term of abuse.

hopper-arsed *adj.* (*also* **hopper-hipped, -rumped, -tailed**) [SE *hopper* + -ARSED *sfx*] [16C–1950s] large-buttocked.

hopper-dockers *n.* [ety. unknown; ? var. on HOCK-DOCKIES *n.*] [early 19C] shoes.

hopping *n.* [HOP *n.*[1] (1)] [late 19C] dancing.

hopping *adj.* [abbr. SE *hopping mad*] **1** [late 19C–1920s] (*US*) furious. **2** [1950s+] (*US teen*) tense, exciting, lively. **3** [1970s+] (*Irish*) crazy.

hopping around like a gin at a christening *phr. see under* GIN *n.*[1].

hopping Giles *n.* [proper name *St Giles*, the patron saint of cripples] [late 18C–19C] a lame, limping person.

hopping pot *n.* [rhy. sl.] [late 19C+] the lot.

hop-pole *n.* [mid-19C] a tall, thin person.

hoppy *n.*[1] [HOP *n.*[1] (1)] **1** [mid–late 19C] a dancing master. **2** [late 19C] a fiddler.

hoppy *n.*[2] **1** [mid-19C+] (*US*) a lame person. **2** [1960s+] a flea; usu. in pl.

hoppy *n.*[3] (*also* **hoppie**) [HOP *n.*[3]] [1900s–50s] (*drugs*) orig. an opium addict, a drug addict.

hoppy *adj.*[1] **1** [mid-19C+] lame, limping. **2** [1930s+] lively, full of movement.

hoppy *adj.*[2] [HOP *n.*[3]] [1940s] (*US drugs*) characteristic of, or relevant to, drugs or drug-taking.

hoppy *adj.*[3] [HOP *n.*[3]] [1940s–50s] (*US drugs*) **1** well-supplied with narcotics, esp. opium. **2** smelling of opium.

hops *n.*[1] [1990s+] (*US black*) the ability to jump high during a game of basketball.

hops *n.*[2] [? you 'hop around' together] [1990s+] (*US black*) a close friend.

hops *n.*[3] *see* HOP *n.*[3].

hopscotch *n.* [rhy. sl.] [1990s+] a watch.

hopscotch *v.* **1** [1900s] (*US Und.*) to take a chance. **2** [1910s–40s] (*US Und.*) to move frequently from place to place. **3** [1940s] (*US Und.*) to travel the country with a confidence game. **4** [1960s] (*US*) to have many sexual partners.

hopser *n. see* HOP *n.*[1] (1).

hopster *n.* [HOP *n.*[3]] [1940s–50s] (*US drugs*) an opium addict.

hop the twig *v.* **1** [late 18C–1900s] (*UK Und.*) (*also* **jump the twig**) to run away. **2** [late 18C+] (*also* **leap the twig**) to die.

IN PHRASES

❑ **hopped the twig** [mid-19C] (*US Und.*) hanged.

hori *n.* [lit. Maori transcription of 'George'] [1940s+] (*N.Z.*) a semi-derog. term for a Maori.

horie *n. see* HORRIE *n.*

horizontal *n.* [Fr. *grande horizontale*; she is, of course, 'horizontal' on a bed or *chaise longue*] **1** [late 19C–1950s] (*also* **horizontalist**) an up-market prostitute, a kept woman. **2** [late 19C+] (*US*) (*also* **the horizontals**) sexual intercourse; usu. as *do a horizontal*.

horizontal *adj.*

SE in slang uses, pertaining to sexual intercourse

IN COMPOUNDS

❑ **horizontal dancing** *n.* (*also* **horizontal barn-dancing, ...bop, ...exercise, ...folk-dancing, ...handshake, ...hula, ...mambo, ...polka, ...polo, ...rhumba, ...rumb, ...tango, ...twist and shout, ...two-step**) [1940s+] sexual intercourse. ❑ **horizontal jogging** *n.* (*also* **horizontal exercise**) [note US milit. *horizontal fatigue*, a nap] [1950s+] sexual intercourse. ❑ **horizontal refreshment** *n.* [mid-19C–1930s] sexual intercourse. ❑ **horizontal relaxation** *n.* [1940s+] (*Aus./N.Z.*) sexual intercourse. ❑ **horizontal worker** *n.* [late 19C+] (*US*) a prostitute.

IN PHRASES

❑ **get horizontal** *v.* (*orig. US*) **1** [late 19C; 1990s+] to drink or drug oneself into a stupor. **2** [1980s+] to have sexual intercourse. **3** [1990s+] to lie down, to go to sleep.

horizontalize *v.* [HORIZONTAL *n.* (2)] [1980s+] (*US*) to have sexual intercourse.

hork *v.* [? HOICK *v.*[1] (1)] [1980s+] (*US campus*) to steal, to take without permission, to borrow without asking.

hormone *n.* [1980s+] (*US campus*) a sexually aggressive person, whether verbally or physically.

SE in slang uses

IN COMPOUNDS

❑ **hormone fix** *n.* [FIX *n.*[3] (5)] [1980s+] (*US campus*) any form of sexual encounter, from the most marginal to full intercourse. ❑ **hormone queen** *n.* [-QUEEN *sfx* (3)] [1960s–70s] (*US*) a male transvestite who takes oestrogen.

Horn, the *n.* [ety. unknown] [late 17C] the Compter prison, in London.

horn *n.*[1] [the obvious link is to HORN *n.*[2] (1a), the penis, but the term apparently comes from an old German farming practice of grafting the spurs of a castrated cock on the root of the severed comb. These transplants would grow into horns, sometimes several inches long. The German word *hahnreh* or *hahnrei*, meaning cuckold, orig. meant capon, a castrated cock; an older theory took the posture of 'missionary position' intercourse, in which the man represented a head and the woman's legs, spread and raised, were his horns; thus note Ward, 'The Dancing School' (1700): 'I should hate a Husband with horns, were they even of my own grafting'] [mid-15C+] an all-purpose term for cuckoldry, a symbol of cuckoldry; usu. in pl.

IN COMPOUNDS

❑ **horn-child** *n.* [20C+] (*W.I.*) the offspring of an adulterous relationship. ❑ **horn fair** *n. see* separate entry. ❑ **horn-grower** *n.* (*also* **horn-merchant**) [18C–19C] a married man. ❑ **horn-headed** *adj.* [18C] cuckolded. ❑ **horn-maker** *n.* [late 16C–17C] one who cuckolds. ❑ **horn work** *n.* [early 17C–mid-19C] cuckoldry.

IN PHRASES

❑ **blow one's horn** *v.* [early 18C] to be a cuckold, to be cuckolded. ❑ **give horns** *v.* [19C+] to cuckold. ❑ **grow horns** *v.* [17C–18C] to become the victim of cuckoldry. ❑ **horns-to-**

sell *n.* [18C–19C] **1** a promiscuous wife. **2** a cuckold. ▫ **plant horns** *v.* [mid-18C] to make someone into a cuckold. ▫ **put horns on** *v.* [1950s] to make someone into a cuckold. ▫ **put the horns on** *v.* [fig. use] [1940s+] (*US*) **1** to jinx. **2** to cuckold. ▫ **take a horn** *v.* [20C+] (*W.I.*) to accept that one's partner is having/has had an affair without making an issue out of it. ▫ **wear the horns** *v.* [17C+] to be cuckolded.

horn *n.*[2] [resemblance to an SE *horn*] **1** in sexual contexts. (**a**) [late 16C+] the penis. (**b**) [late 17C+] sexual excitement or lust. (**c**) [late 18C+] an erection. (**d**) [1960s] (*US campus*) a male sexual athlete. **2** [19C+] (*US*) a drink [SE *horn*, a form of drinking vessel]. **3** [mid-19C+] the nose. **4** [1930s+] an ear; in phr. *between the horns*, in the centre of the forehead. **5** [1930s+] (*orig. jazz*) as a wind instrument. (**a**) a trumpet. (**b**) a trombone. (**c**) any kind of wind instrument. **6** [1940s+] (*US*) a telephone; esp. in phr. *on the horn*.

IN COMPOUNDS

▫ **hornbag** *n.* [HORN *n.*[2] (1b) + -BAG *sfx*/BAG *n.*[1] (3); or SE *bag*, a receptacle for HORN *n.*[2] (1a)] [1980s+] an attractive woman. ▫ **horn-colic** *n.* [late 18C–1950s] **1** an involuntary erection. **2** male sexual frustration. ▫ **horndog** *see* separate entries. ▫ **horn movie** *n.* [1950s+] a pornographic film. ▫ **horn-pill** *n.* [20C+] an aphrodisiac. ▫ **horn smoker** *n.* [2000s] a fellator or fellatrix. ▫ **hornsmoking** *n.* [2000s] fellatio.

IN PHRASES

▫ **blow someone's horn** *v. see* RING SOMEONE'S BELL *under* BELL *n.*[1]. ▫ **blow your horn if you don't sell fish** [1900s] (*US*) a phr. used after someone has blown their nose noisily. ▫ **on the horn** in a state of sexual excitement. ▫ **scrape one's horns** *v.* (*also* **cut one's horns**) [1960s+] (*US*) **1** of a man, to engage in sexual activity, esp. after a period of abstinence. **2** to masturbate. ▫ **smoke a horn** *v.* [SMOKE *v.*[3]] [2000s] to fellate.

SE in slang uses

IN COMPOUNDS

▫ **horn-thumb** *n.* [the sheath of horn worn by a cutpurse to protect his thumb from the knife-blade] [mid-16C–early 17C] a cutpurse.

IN PHRASES

▫ **blow one's horn** *v. see* separate entry. ▫ **diamond a horn** *v. see under* DIAMOND *n.* ▫ **get the horn to** *v.* [1970s] (*US*) to pressurize. ▫ **toot one's horn** *v. see* BLOW ONE'S HORN *v.* (2).

IN EXCLAMATIONS

▫ **pull your horns in!** *see* PULL YOUR HEAD IN! *under* HEAD *n.*

horn *v.*[1] [HORN *n.*[1]] [mid-16C+] to cuckold.

IN PHRASES

▫ **horn (with)** *v.* [20C+] (*W.I.*) to be unfaithful to one's husband, wife or lover by having sex with or dating another person.

horn *v.*[2] [HORN *n.*[2] (3)] [1950s+] (*US drugs*) to inhale a narcotic.

horn *v.*[3]

SE in slang uses

IN PHRASES

▫ **horn in** *v.* (*also* **horn in on**) [20C+] (*orig. US*) to intrude, to interfere. ▫ **horn off** *v.* (*also* **horn out**) [fig. to use one's horns] [mid-19C–1910s] (*US*) to impose upon, to force someone. ▫ **horn out** *v.* [1910s] (*US*) to escape.

horndog *n.* [HORN *n.*[2] (1b) + DOG *n.*[2] (1a)] **1** [1980s+] (*US campus*) a sexually aggressive person. **2** [1990s+] a sexually frustrated person.

horndog *v.* [HORNDOG *n.*] [1980s+] (*US campus*) to pursue sexually.

horned-up *adj.* [HORN *n.*[2] (1b)] [1940s+] (*orig. US*) sexually excited.

horner *n.* [HORN *n.*[1]] [16C+] an adulterer; thus [20C+] (*W.I.*) *horner-man*.

hornet *n.* [mid-18C] (*UK Und.*) a watchman.

horney *n.*[1] [OLD HORNIE *under* OLD *adj.*] [mid-18C+] (*UK Und.*) a member of the watch, an officer of the law.

horney *n.*[2] [its shape] [early 19C] the nose.

horney *n.*[3] *see* HORNY *n.*[2].

horn fair *n.* [Horn Fair was a real occasion, held annually from the 12C until 1768 at Charlton, Kent on St Luke's day, 18 Oct; St Luke bearing the evangelistic sign of the Ox, and thus wearing HORNS *n.*; processions of revellers, all wearing horns and sometimes masks, walked from Cuckold's Point near Deptford, to Charlton. For an extensive discussion of the actual *Horn Fair* see Ward, 'A Frolic to Horn-Fair' in *Writings* (1704), pp.194–222 (esp. 211–13 in which he attributes the custom to a dalliance of King John); Grose (1785, et seq.) and Ebsworth *Roxburghe Ballads* (VII pt. 1, pp.195–6)] [mid-17C–early 19C] the state of being cuckolded; a fig. gathering of cuckolds.

hornies, the *n.* [HORNY *adj.*] [1920s+] (*US*) sexual desire.

hornified *adj.* [HORNIFY *v.*] [late 18C–19C] cuckolded.

hornify *v.* [HORN *n.*[1]] [17C–19C] to cuckold.

horniness *n.* [HORNY *adj.*] [1960s+] sexual excitement, lust.

horn-mad *adj.* [SE *horn-mad*, enraged, the image is of a horned beast that is ready to gore anyone in its way, but note, HORN *n.*[2] (1b)/HORN *n.*[1]] **1** [late 16C–19C] extremely jealous, esp. as a victim of cuckoldry. **2** [late 16C–1950s] lecherous, maddened by lust; thus *horn-madness*, the condition of lustfulness; *horn-madded*, lustful.

horn of plenty *n.* [rhy. sl.] [1990s+] (*bingo*) the number 20.

hornpipe *n.* [HORN *n.*[2]] [late 16C–18C] **1** sexual intercourse, often adultery; usu. as *dance the hornpipe*. **2** a penis.

horns *n. see* HORN *n.*[1].

hornswoggle *n.* [HORNSWOGGLE *v.*] [19C+] (*US*) nonsense, humbug; thus *hornswoggler*, a fraud, a cheat.

hornswoggle *v.* [ety. unknown] (*US*) **1** [19C+] to embarrass, to confuse, to disconcert. **2** [late 19C+] (*also* **horn-swaggle**) to cheat, to swindle.

hornswoggled *adj.* (*also* **cornswoggled, onswoggled**) [HORNSWOGGLE *v.*] [19C+] (*US*) a euph. for DAMNED *adj.*

hornswoggling *n.* [HORNSWOGGLE *v.*] [mid-19C+] (*US*) cheating, deceiving.

horny *n.*[1] [HORN *n.*[1]] [18C] a cuckold.

horny *n.*[2] (*also* **horney**) [orig. Scot.] [20C+] (*Aus.*) a cow, a bullock; thus *horney-steerer*, a bullock-driver; thus used generically for the beef interest.

horny *n.*[3] [HORNY *adj.*] [1970s] (*US*) one who is sexually excited, desirous of sex.

horny *adj.* [HORN *n.*[2] (1b)] **1** [early 19C+] sexually eager, aroused. **2** [1930s+] sexually arousing, erotic, pornographic, e.g. a *horny picture*.

horrible *n.* **1** [1920s–50s] (*Aus.*) a rascal, a villain; a Bohemian, one who acts without regard for social convention. **2** [1960s] (*US campus*) an unattractive woman.

horribly *adv.* [1910s] a positive intensifier.

horrid horn *n.* [Erse *omadhun*, a fool] [mid–late 19C] (*Anglo-Irish*) a fool.

horrie *n.* (*also* **horie**) [HORI *n.*] [1980s] (*Aus.*) a derog. term for an Asian.

horrie *adj.* [abbr. SE *horrible*] [1990s+] (*Aus.*) overwhelming.

horries *n.* [Afk. *horries*, DTs, but note HORRORS, THE *n.*] (*S.Afr.*) **1** [1950s+] delirium tremens. **2** [1970s+] a phobia, a visceral fear.

horrorbag *n.* [SE *horror* + BAG *n.*[1] (3) but note WHOREBAG *under* WHORE *n.*] [1980s] (*Aus.*) a, usu. unattractive, girl or woman.

horrors, the *n.* **1** [mid-18C+] a fit of depression, unpleasant worries. **2** [mid-19C+] delirium tremens; often as *in the horrors*; ext. as *blue horrors*; *cast-iron/stonewall horrors*. **3** [mid-19C+] a hangover. **4** [1920s+] unpleasant reactions suffered during the withdrawal from narcotic drugs. **5** [1960s+] unpleasant experiences (usu. paranoid fantasies) brought about occas. by the effects of smoking cannabis, opium or from taking a hallucinogen.

IN PHRASES

▫ **dig the horrors** *v. see* separate entries. ▫ **dry horrors** *n. see under* DRY *adj.*[1]. ▫ **get the horrors** *v. see* DIG HORRORS *v.*[1].

horrorshow *n.* [1950s+] (*US*) a disgusting or embarrassing person, thing or situation.

horrorshow *adj.* [HORRORSHOW *n.* on bad = good model, but note use in Anthony Burgess, *A Clockwork Orange* (1962), where it means excellent and is based on Rus. *horosho*] [1990s+] (*US teen*) extremely good.

hors d'oeuvre *n.* [rhy. sl. = PERV *n.* (1)] [1960s] (*Aus.*) a paedophile.

hors d'oeuvres *n.*[1] [SE *hors d'oeuvres*, the first dish of a meal, usu. of mixed items and intended to whet the appetite; a prelude to stronger, more exotic pleasures] [1970s+] (*drugs*) barbiturates or amphetamines.

hors d'oeuvres *n.*[2] [rhy. sl.] [1990s+] nerves.

Horse, the *n.* (*also* **Old Horse, the**) **1** [mid-19C] Horsemonger Lane prison, Southwark, London [erected 1799 as a model prison, it lasted until the 1880s; it was outside this prison on 13 November 1847 that Charles Dickens witnessed the public hanging of the murderers Frederick and Maria Manning]. **2** [mid-19C] Bridge Street prison, Blackfriars.

horse *n.* **1** in gambling. (**a**) [mid–late 18C] a lottery ticket that is hired out by the day. (**b**) [late 19C] (*US*) a queen in cards. (**c**) [late 19C–1930s] (*US gambling*) a selection of four numbers to be played simultaneously. (**d**) [1950s] (*US*) gambling in general. **2** as money. (**a**) [19C] a £5 note [? play on PONY *n.* (1b)]. (**b**) [1960s] (*Irish*) a half-crown. **3** (*also* **hoss**) as a human being, usu. in congratulatory senses. (**a**) [19C+] (*US*) a strong, athletic man or an admirable, good fellow. (**b**) [mid-19C] (*US*) one's husband. (**c**) [mid-19C+] (*US*) (*also* **cholly, cholly hoss**) a form of address by one man to another. (**d**) [mid-19C+] a fine specimen; usu. constr. with *of*. (**e**) [late 19C–1910s] (*US campus*) an exceptionally able student. (**f**) [20C+] (*Aus.*) one's wife. (**g**) [1980s+] (*US*) a large, ungainly woman. **4** [mid-19C] (*also* **embalmed horse**) corned beef. **5** [late 19C–1910s] (*US campus*) as plays on PONY *n.* (3a). (**a**) a literal translation used in preparing a lesson. (**b**) help in an examination. **6** as language [? SE *horse laugh*]. (**a**) [late 19C+] (*US*) (*also* **hoss**) a joke, esp. a joke at someone else's expense; thus *horseplay*, teasing. (**b**) [1900s–40s] (*US*) nonsense, rubbish. **7** [1930s+] (*drugs*) (*also* **hoss**) heroin. **8** [1940s–60s] (*US*) a motorcycle. **9** [1950s+] (*US*) a prostitute, one of a group of women working for a pimp [she is part of his STABLE *n.*; but also similar pron. to SE *whore*]. **10** [1950s+] (*US prison*) a visitor or prison warder who is willing to smuggle contraband in and out of prison [var. on MULE *n.* (4c)]. **11** [1960s+] venereal disease, spec. gonorrhoea [rhy. sl. *horse and trap* = CLAP *n.*]. **12** *see* CHARLEY HORSE *n.* **13** *see* *HORSEFLESH* below.

IN COMPOUNDS

❑ **horse-head** *n.* [-HEAD *sfx* (4)] [1950s+] (*US*) a heroin addict.

IN PHRASES

❑ **horsed out** *adj.* [1980s+] (*drugs*) intoxicated on heroin.
❑ **red horse** *n.* [mid-19C+] (*US*) corned beef.

SE in slang uses

IN COMPOUNDS

❑ **horse apple** *n.* (*also* **apple, horseball, ...bean, ...biscuit, ... doughnut, ...dumpling, ...plum**) [supposed resemblance] [mid-17C; early 18C+] a piece of horse manure found lying in the road. ❑ **horse-ass** *n. see* HORSE'S ASS *n.* ❑ **horse-ass** *adj.* [-ASS *sfx*] [1950s] (*US*) stupid, incompetent. ❑ **horse blanket** *n.* **1** [late 19C+] (*US black, orig. milit.*) an overcoat. **2** [20C+] (*US*) (*also* **monkey blanket, saddle...**) a griddle cake. ❑ **horsebreaker** *n. see* PRETTY HORSE BREAKER *n.* ❑ **horseburger** *n. see* HORSESHIT *n.* (2). ❑ **horse buss** *n.* [SE *buss*, a kiss; ult. earlier *bass*] [late 18C–early 19C] **1** a loud smacking kiss. **2** a bite. ❑ **horse-capper** *n.* [SE *horse-coper*, a horse dealer] [mid-19C] (*US Und.*) a dishonest horse-dealer. ❑ **horse-chaunter** *n.* [CHANTER *n.* (2)] [mid-19C] a crooked horse dealer; thus *horse chaunting*, crooked horse dealing. ❑ **horsecock/cocked** *see* separate entries. ❑ **horse-collar** *see* separate entries. ❑ **horse cop** *n. see under* COP *n.*[1]. ❑ **horsecrap** *n.* [CRAP *n.*[1] (6)] [1930s+] (*US*) nonsense; also as adj., second-rate. ❑ **horse dookie** *n.* [DUKIE *n.*[2] (1)] [1970s+] (*US*) nonsense. ❑ **horse doughnut/dumpling** *n. see* *HORSE APPLE* above. ❑ **horse-faker** *n.* [FAKER *n.* (1)] [late 19C] a horse dealer. ❑ **horsefeathers** *n. see* separate entry. ❑ **horseflesh** *n.* (*also* **horse**) [ult. SE phr. *dead horse*, anything that is beyond saving or use and cannot be revived. The work, which will bring in no further money, is no more use than a 'dead horse'] [late 17C] work that is charged for before it is actually done. ❑ **horse-fly** *n.* (*also* **hoss-fly**) [mid-19C–1930s] (*US*) a fellow. ❑ **horsefuck/fucking** *see* separate entries. ❑ **horse godmother** *n.* [late 18C–mid-19C] a large masculine woman, 'a gentlemanlike kind of lady' (Grose, 1785). ❑ **horse heads** *n.* [1970s+] (*drugs*) amphetamines. ❑ **horse heavy** *n.* [1940s] (*US black*) a fat person. ❑ **horse hockey** *n.* (*also* **horse frocky**) [HOCKIE *n.* (2)] [1950s+] (*US*) nonsense. ❑ **horse joint** *n.* [JOINT *n.* (3b)] [1950s] (*US Und.*) a bookmaker's 'office'. ❑ **horse kiss** *n.* [the image is of a horse's mouth, with large teeth and lips] [late 17C–18C] a rough, heavy kiss. ❑ **horse leech** *n.* [ult. ref. to SE *horse-leech*, a sucking worm] **1** [late 16C–mid-18C] (*also* **leach**) a quack doctor [SE *horse-leech*, a veterinary surgeon]. **2** [17C; 1900s] a general term of abuse. **3** [mid-17C] a prostitute. ❑ **horseman** *n. see* separate entry. ❑ **horse manure** *n.* [euph.] [1910s+] (*US*) nonsense, rubbish; also as excl. ❑ **horse marine** *n.* [trad. sailors' disdain for the poor seamanship of the Royal Marines; a 'horse marine' is an impossibility] [mid-19C–1900s] an awkward person. ❑ **horsemeat** *n.* [play on SE meat/MEAT *n.* (2)] [1980s+] (*US gay*) a large penis. ❑ **horse-nails** *n.* [SE *horse-nail*, a nail used to secure a horseshoe] [mid-19C] money. ❑ **horse opera** *n.* **1** [mid-19C–1940s] (*US*) a show featuring trained horses. **2** [1920s+] (*orig. US*) (*also* **gun opera, hoss opry**) a Western, whether on film or television [on model of SOAP OPERA *n.*]. ❑ **horse-pad** *n.* [early 18C] (*UK Und.*) a highwayman. ❑ **horse piss** *n.* [PISS *n.* (4a)] [20C+] (*US*) weak coffee or weak beer; any unpleasant tasting food. ❑ **horse player** *n.* [1930s+] (*US*) a person who bets on horseracing. ❑ **horse-plum** *n. see* *HORSE APPLE* above. ❑ **horse-pox** *n.* [mid-17C–18C] an especially severe strain of venereal disease, esp. as used in excl. ❑ **horse pucky** *n.* [PUCKEY *n.*] [1970s+] (*US*) nonsense; also as excl. ❑ **horse radish** *n.* [euph.] [1910s+] (*US*) nonsense; also as excl. ❑ **horse room** *n.* (*also* **horse parlour**) [1940s–50s] (*US*) a bookmaking establishment. ❑ **horse's arse** *n. see* HORSE'S ASS *n.* ❑ **horse's ass** *n. see* separate entry. ❑ **horse's can/cock/foot** *n. see* HORSE'S ASS *n.* ❑ **horse's hangdown** *n.* [SE *hangdown*, i.e. the animal's penis, on the model of PRICK *n.* (3)] [20C+] a fool, an idiot. ❑ **horseshit** *see* separate entries. ❑ **horseshite** *n. see* HORSESHIT *n.* (2). ❑ **horseshoe** *see* separate entries. ❑ **horse's meal** *n.* [cf. synon. Scot. and Yorks. dial. *horse-feast*] [late 18C–mid-19C] a meal that has no accompanying drink, alcoholic or otherwise. ❑ **horse's neck** *n.* **1** [20C+] (*orig. US*) ginger ale flavoured with lemon peel, with or without whisky, brandy or gin [ety. unknown]. **2** [1920s–70s] (*US*) a fool, an idiot, a general term of abuse [partial euph. for HORSE'S ASS *n.*]. ❑ **horse's necklace** *n.* [late 19C–1930s] (*Aus. prison*) the hangman's noose. ❑ **horse's nightcap** *n.* [late 16C–1930s] the cap pulled over the condemned man's head before his death; thus the noose itself. ❑ **horse's patoot** *n.* (*also* **horse's patootie**) [partial euph. for HORSE'S ASS *n.*] [1940s+] (*US*) a fool, an idiot, a general term of abuse. ❑ **horse's rear** *n. see* HORSE'S ASS *n.* ❑ **horse thief** *n.* [1910s+] (*US*) a dishonest person. ❑ **horse tranquilizer** *n.* (*also* **pig tranquilizer**) [the legitimate use of the drug as an animal tranquillizer] [1970s+] (*drugs*) phencyclidine. ❑ **horse-turd** *n. see* HORSESHIT *n.* (1). ❑ **horsewoman** *n.* [they 'ride' their partner] [1940s+] a masculine lesbian.

IN PHRASES

❑ **...and the horse you rode in on** [Wild West imagery] [1970s+] (*US*) a dismissive, antagonistic phr., the pfx FUCK YOU! *excl.* is used or unspoken. ❑ **bet on the horses** *v.* [1950s] to be addicted to morphine [*sic*]. ❑ **die in a horse's nightcap** *v. see under* DIE *v.* ❑ **go to rest in a horse's nightcap** *v. see* *DIE IN A HORSE'S NIGHTCAP* *under* DIE *v.* ❑ **horse and dog show** *n. see* *DOG AND PONY SHOW* *under* DOG *n.*[2]. ❑ **horse of another colour** *n.* [SE by 20C+] [late 18C–1920s] a very different topic. ❑ **play horse with** *v.* **1** [late 19C–1910s] (*US*) to indulge in horseplay. **2** [late 19C–1950s] (*US campus*) to ridicule, to tease. **3** [1900s] (*US campus*) to overcome easily; to confuse. ❑ **play the horse(s)** *v. see* *PLAY THE PONIES* *under* PONY *n.* ❑ **talk horse** *v.* [late 19C–1900s] to boast, to 'talk big'. ❑ **wouldn't that tie your horse** [1900s] (*US*) a phr. of mild exasperation or surprise, isn't that amazing/infuriating.

(IN EXCLAMATIONS)

▫ **damn me for a horse if I do!** *see under* DAMN! *excl.*

horse *v.* **1** [late 16C–17C; 1930s+] to have sexual intercourse. **2** [late 17C–19C] to flog, to whip; thus *horsed*, held on another person's back before receiving a flogging [the victim is placed across a wooden frame or 'horse']. **3** [19C+] (*US*) to yearn for, to want eagerly, to lust after [? a horse straining at the bit or dial. *horse*, for a mare to be in heat]. **4** in the context of using horse-like strength. (**a**) [mid-19C] to work very hard, to work harder than another person. (**b**) [20C+] (*US*) to haul or drag with great effort. (**c**) [1920s] to move energetically. **5** to deceive, to cheat. (**a**) [mid–late 19C] to swindle, to cheat. (**b**) [late 19C–1960s] (*US*) to trick, to deceive, to tease. **6** [late 19C–1900s] (*US campus*) to amaze. **7** [late 19C–1910s] (*US campus*) to study with the help of a translation [HORSE *n.* (5a)]. **8** *see* HORSE AROUND below.

(IN PHRASES)

▫ **horse around** *v.* **1** [20C+] (*also* **horse**) to joke, to mess about. **2** [1920s+] (*US*) to make sexual advances to, to indulge in sexual horseplay. **3** [1950s+] (*US*) to be keen on becoming married. **4** [1950s+] (*US*) to sleep around, to philander. ▫ **horse (it)** *v.* (*also* **hoss it**) [the strength and stamina of the animal] [late 19C–1960s] (*US*) to walk fast.

horse! *excl. see* HORSESHIT! *excl.*

horse and carriage *n.* [rhy. sl.] [20C+] a garage.

horse and cart *n.* [rhy. sl.] **1** [late 19C–1900s] the heart. **2** [20C+] (*Aus.*) the start. **3** [1960s+] a tart. **4** [1970s+] a breaking of wind [= FART *n.* (1)].

horse and cart *v.* [rhy. sl. = FART *v.* (1)] [1970s+] to break wind.

horse and donk *n.* [rhy. sl. = PLONK *n.*[1] (1)] [1960s+] (*Aus.*) cheap wine.

horse and foal *n.* [rhy. sl.] [20C+] (*Aus.*) the dole.

horse and trap *n.* [rhy. sl.] **1** [20C+] venereal disease, spec. gonorrhoea [= CLAP *n.*]. **2** [1950s+] excrement [= CRAP *n.*[1] (2)].

horse and trough *n.* [rhy. sl.] [20C+] a cough.

horsecock *n.* **1** [1920s–50s] (*US*) on basis of COCK *n.*[5] (2) (**a**) an idiot, a fool. (**b**) nonsense. **2** on basis of COCK *n.*[3] (1). (**a**) [1940s+] (*US*) a sausage, salami. (**b**) [1970s] a gun. (**c**) [1990s+] (*US*) a large penis.

horsecocked *adj.* [HORSECOCK *n.* (2c)] [2000s] having a large penis.

horse-collar *n.* [supposed resemblances] **1** [late 19C+] the vagina, esp. when considered larger than average. **2** [1900s–10s] (*US*) a zero, esp. in sport. **3** [1920s–50s] (*Can./US*) a clerical or man's high collar.

horsecollar! *excl.* [1920s+] (*US*) nonsense!

horsed *adj.* **1** [1990s+] (*US campus*) drunk. **2** *see* HORSE *v.* (2).

horsed out *adj. see under* HORSE *n.*

horsed up *adj.* [ASTOR'S PET HORSE *n.*] [1950s+] (*US*) of a woman, showy, overdressed, overly made-up.

horsefeathers *n.* (*also* **feathers**) [euph. for HORSESHIT *n.*; supposedly coined by the comic strip artist William de Beck] [1920s+] (*orig. US*) nonsense, rubbish.

horsefuck *v.* [SE *horse* + FUCK *v.* (1)] [1970s+] to have sexual intercourse with the man using rear entry.

horse-fucking *adj.* [1960s] (*US*) very large.

horseman *n.* **1** in sexual contexts, playing on RIDE *v.* (1a). (**a**) [18C+] a promiscuous man, a philanderer. (**b**) [late 19C] the penis. **2** [1920s] (*US Und.*) one who collects protection money and passes it on to gangsters, corrupt police etc. **3** [1940s] (*US Und.*) a corrupt police officer. **4** [1960s] (*US campus*) a habitual cheat, one who 'rides' on the efforts of their fellow students. **5** [1970s] (*Can. Und.*) a member of the Royal Canadian Mounted Police (RCMP).

horses *n.* [abbr.] [20C+] *horse*power.

horses! *excl.* [abbr. HORSESHIT *n.*] [1920s] (*US*) an excl. used to express anger or disappointment.

horses and asses *n.* [rhy. sl.] [2000s] (*Irish*) drinking glasses.

horses and carts *n.* [rhy. sl.] [20C+] darts.

horse's ass *n.* (*also* **horse-ass, horse's arse, ...behind, ...can, ...cock, ...foot, ...rear**) [SE *horse* + ASS *n.* (2)/ARSE *n.* (1)/BEHIND *n.* (1)/CAN *n.*[1] (1b)/COCK *n.*[3] (1)] [mid-19C+] **1** a fool, an idiot. **2** a general term of abuse.

horseshit *n.* [SE *horse* + SHIT *n.* (1a)] **1** [1920s+] (*also* **horse-turd**) horse dung. **2** [1920s+] (*also* **horseburger, horseshite**) rubbish, nonsense. **3** [1940s] (*US*) a damn, e.g. *that isn't worth horseshit*.

horseshit *adj.* [HORSESHIT *n.*] [1930s+] (*US*) contemptible, offensive, worthless.

horseshit *v.* [var. on BULLSHIT *v.*] [1950s+] (*US*) to lie, to flatter.

horseshit! *excl.* (*also* **horse!**) [HORSESHIT *n.*] [1920s+] (*US*) an excl. of disgust, disappointment, disbelief.

horseshoe *n.* [the trad. association of horseshoes and luck] [1910s–20s] (*US*) **1** a propensity for good luck. **2** as *horsehoes*, a nickname for a very lucky person.

horseshoe *v.* [1900s] (*Aus.*) to disparage, to criticize harshly.

horse's hoof *n.* [rhy. sl. = POOF *n.* (1)] [1950s+] a male homosexual.

horse's rug *n.* [rhy. sl. = MUG *n.*[1] (2a)] [1980s] (*Aus.*) a fool.

horsewoman *n.* [they 'ride' their partner] [1940s+] a masculine lesbian.

hortical *adj.* [? SE *exhort*] [1950s+] (*W.I./UK black teen*) genuine, sincere, respected.

(IN COMPOUNDS)

▫ **hortical don** *n.* [DON *n.* (3)] [1970s+] (*W.I. Rasta*) a respected, acclaimed person.

hose *n.*[1] [joc. uses of SE] **1** [1920s+] (*US*) the penis, usu. large. **2** [1940s+] (*UK Und.*) sexual intercourse. **3** [1980s] (*US campus*) a boyfriend.

(IN COMPOUNDS)

▫ **hosebeast** *n.* [BEAST *n.*] [1990s+] (*US*) a sexually promiscuous person. ▫ **hose job** *n.* [JOB *n.*[2] (2)] [1970s+] (*US*) fellatio. ▫ **hoseman** *n.* [1970s] (*US*) an exceptionally virile man. ▫ **hose monster** *n.* (*also* **hose monger**) [-MONSTER *sfx*/-MONGER *sfx*] [1980s+] (*US*) a sexually promiscuous person, usu. a woman. ▫ **hose queen** *n.* [-QUEEN *sfx* (2)] [1980s+] (*US campus*) a sexually promiscuous woman.

(IN PHRASES)

▫ **psycho hosebeast** *n.* [PSYCHO *adj.* (2)] [1980s] (*US campus/teen*) a very attractive, sexy, hopefully promiscuous young woman.

SE in slang uses

(IN COMPOUNDS)

▫ **hose-head** *n.* [-HEAD *sfx* (1)] [1980s+] (*US campus*) a stupid person.

hose *n.*[2] [HOSE *v.*[2] (3a)] [1980s] (*US campus*) a difficult test or examination.

hose *n.*[3] [? HO *n.* (4) or HOSE *v.*[2] (2a)] [1980s+] (*US campus*) a promiscuous woman.

(IN COMPOUNDS)

▫ **hosebag** *n.* (*also* **hose wagon**) [+ ? pun, she is a 'bag' for the male HOSE *n.*[1] (1)] **1** [1970s+] (*orig. US campus*) a derog. term for a promiscuous woman. **2** [1980s+] (*US campus*) an unattractive person, often female.

hose *v.*[1] [SE *hose (down)*] **1** [1910s+] to fire at, orig. with a machine gun. **2** [1920s+] (*US orig. police/Und.*) to beat with a rubber hose, to punish. **3** [1940s+] (*US*) to cheat, to victimize. **4** [1970s+] (*US campus*) to defeat. **5** [1980s+] (*S.Afr.*) to urinate in one's underwear. **6** [1990s+] to lie.

(IN PHRASES)

▫ **hose in** *v.* [1980s+] (*N.Z.*) to win easily. ▫ **hose off** *v.* [1950s+] (*N.Z.*) to annoy, to infuriate. ▫ **hose out** *v.* [1970s+] (*N.Z.*) to beat comprehensively. ▫ **take a hosing** *v.* [1940s+] (*US*) to be cheated or badly treated.

hose *v.*[2] [HOSE *n.*[1]] **1** [1920s] (*US campus*) to curry favour with. **2** in sexual contexts. (**a**) [1930s+] (*also* **hose down**) to copulate with (always from a man's point of view). (**b**) [1960s+] (*gay*) to sodomize. (**c**) [1980s+] (*US campus*) of a woman, to search for a sexual partner. **3** based on image of

PISS ON *v.* (1). (**a**) [1980s+] (*US campus*) to fail, to do badly, to be rejected. (**b**) [1990s+] (*US campus*) to be treated badly. (**c**) [1990s+] (*US campus*) to have too much work to do. **4** [1990s+] to urinate on.

hosed *adj.* [HOSE *v.*[1] (3)] **1** [1980s] (*US campus*) drunk. **2** [1990s+] (*US black*) in trouble, in difficulties.

hosed out *adj.* [SE *hose*] [1960s] (*US*) exhausted.

hoser *n.* [HOSE *n.*[1] (1)] (*Can./US campus*) **1** [1960s+] a promiscuous man or woman. **2** [1980s+] a fool, an idiot, an uncultured, boorish person.

hosier *n.* see HOOSIER *n.* (1).

hosing *n.* [HOSE *v.*[2] (2a)] **1** [1930s+] sexual intercourse. **2** [1960s+] (*gay*) sodomy.

hospital *n.*

SE in slang uses

IN COMPOUNDS

❑ **hospital heroin** *n.* [a synthetic opiate used in hospitals as a substitute for heroin] [1980s+] (*drugs*) Dilaudid.

IN PHRASES

❑ **do you like hospital food?** [the potential assailant asks this of a victim, who prob. replies 'No' and is told 'Well you'd better get used to it'] [1980s+] a threatening phr. used immediately before administering a beating. ❑ **in hospital** [euph.] [1900s–20s] (*US*) in prison.

hoss *n.*[1] (*US campus*) **1** [1980s] a successful womanizer. **2** [1990s+] any large thing or person.

hoss *n.*[2] *see* HORSE *n.*

hoss-fly *n. see* HORSE-FLY *under* HORSE *n.*

hossie *n.* [abbr.] [1960s–70s] (*Aus.*) a hospital.

hoss it *v. see* HORSE (IT) *under* HORSE *V.*

hoss opry *n. see* HORSE OPERA *under* HORSE *n.*

hostie *n.* [abbr.] [1960s+] (*Aus.*) an air *host*ess.

hostile *adj.*

IN PHRASES

❑ **go hostile at** *v.* (*also* **go hostile on**) [orig. Aus./N.Z. milit. use] [1930s+] (*Aus.*) to become angry with.

hot *n.* [George Parker, *Life's Painter* (1789): 'a mixed kind of liquor, of beer and gin, with egg, sugar and nutmeg, drank mostly in night-houses, but when drank in a morning, it is called flannel'] **1** [late 18C–19C] beer mixed with gin, plus egg and spices. **2** [20C+] (*US*) a hot meal; thus *hot up*, to heat up (usu. leftovers); thus phr. *collar a hot*, to eat a meal. **3** [1910s–20s] (*US*) sexual intercourse [HOT *adj.* (1a)]. **4** *see* HOT PROPERTY *under* HOT *adj.*

IN COMPOUNDS

❑ **hot with** *n.* [mid-19C] hot spirits and water with sugar.

IN PHRASES

❑ **three hots and a cot** *n.* [1960s+] (*US*) three meals a day plus a bed for the night, often used as a rate of payment.

hot *adj.* **1** in sexual senses. (**a**) [14C+] sexually aroused, sexually available. (**b**) [late 19C+] of books, films etc, erotic, sexually arousing; thus of language, obscene. (**c**) [late 19C+] orig. applied by men to women, sexy, sexually attractive. **2** in senses of immediacy, action. (**a**) [mid-16C+] urgent, pressing, poss. dangerous. (**b**) [late 19C+] in constant use; busy, hectic. (**c**) [late 19C+] current, of the moment, up-to-date. (**d**) [late 19C+] (*US*) fast or powerful. **3** [late 16C+] unpleasant; usu. in phr. *make it hot (for)*. **4** with ref. to the emotions. (**a**) [late 16C+] furious, extremely angry. (**b**) [late 16C+] zealous, eager, enthusiastic. (**c**) [mid-17C+] of people, reckless, boisterous. (**d**) [18C+] lively, energetic. (**e**) [mid-19C+] severe. (**f**) [1910s] annoying/unacceptable. (**g**) [1920s+] tense. **5** in Und. and related uses. (**a**) [late 16C+] dangerous, thus unsafe for criminal activity. (**b**) [17C+] in weak use of sense 1, in difficulties (other than criminal). (**c**) [mid-19C+] of people or objects, known to or wanted by the police, suspect. (**d**) [20C+] of goods, stolen. (**e**) [1920s–60s] (*US Und.*) of a house or place, occupied while being robbed. (**f**) [1920s+] of money or documents, forged or counterfeit. (**g**) [1930s] (*US Und.*) marked for death. (**h**) [1930s+] (*US prison*) smuggled. (**i**) [1940s–50s] of dice or other form of gambling equipment, crooked. **6** with ref. to the human body. (**a**) [17C–19C] suffering from venereal disease or pubic lice. (**b**) [17C+] (*US*) drunk; usu. in combs., e.g. *hot as a red wagon, hotter than love in haying-time, hotter than a skunk*. (**c**) [1930s+] (*US drugs*) of an injection or drug, likely to cause death. (**d**) [1940s+] healthy; usu. as a negative, e.g. 'not feeling too hot'. (**e**) [1950s+] (*US*) of a part of a body, an organ, seriously physically infected. **7** in senses of excellence or skill. (**a**) [early 17C; mid-19C+] (*US*) first-rate. (**b**) [mid-19C+] very adept, skilful. (**c**) [20C+] of a sportsman, playing well, on top form; also used fig. of any contestant or performer, or in business etc. **8** indicative of something positive. (**a**) [mid-19C+] (*orig. US*) highly amusing, esp. if ironic, ludicrous; thus a *hot one*. (**b**) [mid-19C+] attractive, pleasurable, a general term of approval. (**c**) [20C+] very promising, potentially useful, thus commercially successful. (**d**) [1970s+] (*US*) lucky. **9** used of inanimate objects. (**a**) [20C+] in the context of gunfire etc, dangerous. (**b**) [1930s+] (*US*) electrified. (**c**) [1940s+] (*US*) radioactive. (**d**) [1950s+] of a bullet, loaded into the weapon's chamber; of a gun, loaded.

IN COMPOUNDS

❑ **hot...** *see also* separate entries. ❑ **hot armchair** *n. see* HOT CHAIR below. ❑ **hot baby** *n. see under* BABY *n.* ❑ **hot-backed** *adj.* [17C] of a woman, promiscuous, sexually voracious. ❑ **hot biscuit** *n.* [1980s+] (*US*) something exciting. ❑ **hot book** *n.* [1940s+] (*US*) a pornographic magazine, book. ❑ **hot-bot** *n.* (*also* **Lady Hot-bot**) [abbr. SE *bottom*] [20C+] a promiscuous, sexually voracious woman. ❑ **hot boy** *n.* [late 19C+] (*orig. US black*) a fashionable young man, a 'young blood'. ❑ **hot-bummed** *adj. see* HOT-ARSED *adj.* ❑ **hot buns** *n. see under* BUNS *n.* ❑ **hot burglary** *n.* [1970s] (*US Und.*) aggravated burglary. ❑ **hot cack** *adj.* [CACK *n.*[2] (1); ? euph. for SHIT-HOT *adj.*] [1940s+] (*Aus.*) very good. ❑ **hot card** *n. see under* CARD *n.*[2]. ❑ **hot chair** *n.* (*also* **hot armchair, ...stool**) [1920s+] (*US*) the electric chair. ❑ **hot chance** *n. see* FAT CHANCE *n.* ❑ **hot chocolate** *n. see under* CHOCOLATE *n.*[1]. ❑ **hot corner** *n.* **1** [mid-19C–1900s] a difficult situation in which one finds oneself threatened, bullied or otherwise under attack. **2** [2000s] a corner that is a site for drug-selling. ❑ **hot crate** *n. see under* CRATE *n.* ❑ **hot-cunted** *adj. see* HOT-ARSED *adj.* ❑ **hot-dish** *adj.* (*also* **hot-slop**) [late 19C] (*US campus*) attractive, fashionable. ❑ **hot drawers** *n. see* HOT PANTS *n.* ❑ **hot-duke** *v. see under* DUKE *n.*[3]. ❑ **hot enchilada** *n. see* HOT TAMALE *n.* (3). ❑ **hot end** *n.* [SE *end*, with the idea of a lollipop] [late 19C] (*US*) problems. ❑ **hot fat injection** *n.* [INJECTION *n.* (2)] [1930s–50s] (*Aus./US*) sexual intercourse. ❑ **hot fling** *n.* [SE *fling*, a fit of self-indulgence. Note 16C *fling*, to wriggle the buttocks during sex] [20C+] a particularly active bout of sex, esp. with a new partner. ❑ **hot hay** *n.* [HAY *n.* (3b)] [1930s] (*US drugs*) marijuana. ❑ **hot head** *n.* [1970s] (*US prison*) a prison homosexual. ❑ **hot-headed** *adj.* **1** [late 17C] hungover. **2** [late 17C–18C] drunk. ❑ **hot iron** *n. see* HOT-ROD *n.* (2). ❑ **hot item** *n. see under* ITEM *n.* ❑ **hot-lips** *n.* [1920s+] (*US*) a nickname applied to someone with a reputation for passionate kissing. ❑ **hot load** *n.* [1970s+] (*US*) a powerful firearm cartridge. ❑ **hot lot** *n. see* HOT MEMBER *n.* ❑ **hot meat** *n.* **1** *see* HOT BEEF *n.* **2** *see under* MEAT *n.* ❑ **hot meat injection** *n.* [MEAT *n.* (2) + INJECTION *n.* (2)] [1930s+] sexual intercourse. ❑ **hot meds** *n. see* MED *n.* (3). ❑ **hot minute** *n.* (*also* **hot second**) [1930s+] (*US*) a moment. ❑ **hot number** *n. see under* NUMBER *n.* ❑ **hot nuts** *n.* [NUTS *n.*[2] (1)] [1930s+] (*US*) usu. of a man, strong sexual desire. ❑ **hot oil** *n.* [1980s] (*US black*) a self-opinionated person, an important person. ❑ **hot papa** *n. see under* PAPA *n.* ❑ **hot paper** *n. see under* PAPER *n.* ❑ **hot patootie** *n. see under* PATOOTIE *n.* ❑ **hot plate** *n.* [pun on SE *hot plate*] [1940s] (*US Und.*) the electric chair. ❑ **hot pockaroo** *n.* (*also* **potcharooney**) [1960s+] (*US gay*) the buttocks. ❑ **hotpoint** *v.* [the trickster *points out* something that is supposedly *hot*] [1970s+] (*Aus.*) to fool, to take advantage by trickery; thus *hotpointer*, one who does this. ❑ **hot-pot** *n.* **1** [20C+] (*Aus.*) in horseracing, the favourite. **2** [1920s–30s] (*US black*) a sexually promiscuous woman. ❑ **hot property** *n.* (*also* **hot**) [1950s+] a success, a sensation. ❑ **hot rail** *n.* [2000s] (*US prison*) an instance where a group of inmates stand around a particular prisoner during visiting time so that he can have sex with his partner. ❑ **hot school** *n. see under* SCHOOL *n.* ❑ **hot second** *n. see* HOT MINUTE above. ❑ **hot session** *n.* [1920s+] (*US*) a good time (orig. sexual intercourse). ❑ **hot settee** *n. see* HOT SEAT *n.* (1). ❑ **hot-slop** *adj. see* HOT-DISH above. ❑ **hot slough** *see under* SLOUGH *n.*[1]. ❑ **hot squat** *n. see* HOT SEAT *n.* (1). ❑ **hot stick** *n. see under* STICK *n.* ❑ **hot stool** *n. see* HOT CHAIR above. ❑ **hot-tailed** *adj.* (*also* **hot-tail**) [TAIL *n.* (4)] **1** [late 17C–18C] infected with venereal disease. **2** [1960s+] of a woman, lecherous, lascivious. ❑ **hot tomato** *n. see under* TOMATO *n.* ❑ **hot tongue** *n.* [1920s–30s] (*US tramp*) a sexually passionate woman. ❑ **hot topic** *n.* [1990s+] one who has a far-reaching reputation. ❑ **hot trap** *n. see under* TRAP *n.*[2]. ❑ **hot 'un** *n.* **1** [mid-19C] a gulp of liquor. **2** [mid-19C+] a painful, punishing blow or fight. **3** [late 19C–1900s] a debauchee, a degenerate. ❑ **hot-up** *n. see* HOT-ROD *n.* (2). ❑ **hot willie dog** *adj.* [late 19C] (*US campus*) smart, fashionable, showy.

IN PHRASES

❑ **come hot** *v.* [1930s–40s] (*US Und.*) for a confidence man to go ahead with his plan, even when the victim knows that he is being swindled. ❑ **get hot on** *v.* [1920s] (*US*) to get busy, to put in extra effort. ❑ **get the hot end of** *v.* [20C+] (*US*) to be victimized, to be given a hard time. ❑ **have a hot back** *v.* [late 16C] to be sexually aroused or available. ❑ **have a hot mouth** *v.* [20C+] (*W.I., Guyn.*) to answer cheekily, to talk back. ❑ **have a hot stomach** *v.* [one is warm enough without the pawned garments and one's stomach is *hot* (sense 4b above) for drink] [late 18C–early 19C] to pawn one's clothes to get money for buying liquor; also ext. as *have so hot a stomach as to burn the clothes off his back.* ❑ **hot as...** *see* separate entry. ❑ **hot enough to fuck** *adj.* [FUCK *v.* (1)] [1960s+] (*US*) very angry, furious. ❑ **hot for** *adj.* (*also* **hot about, ...on, ...over, ...to, ... upon**) [18C+] (*orig. US*) enthusiastic, keen on, esp. sexually. ❑ **hot in the biscuit** *adj. see under* BISCUIT *n.*[1]. ❑ **hot in the socks** *adj.* [1920s] (*US*) very energetic and lively. ❑ **hot-lot it** *v.* [1970s] (*US*) to go at great speed. ❑ **hotter than...** *see* HOT AS... *adj.* ❑ **hot (up)** *v.* **1** [late 19C+] to heat, to warm up. **2** [20C+] of events, to become more exciting, more dramatic. **3** [1960s] (*S.Afr.*) to go out on a spree. ❑ **make it hot for** *v.* (*also* **make it warm for**) [mid-19C+] to punish, to make life difficult for someone. ❑ **not so hot** [1920s+] (*orig. US*) a general negative phr., not very good, unattractive, displeasing etc. ❑ **run hot** *v.* **1** [1980s+] (*Aus. prison*) to do something illegally with a strong chance of being found out. **2** [1980s+] (*Aus. prison*) to have a run of good luck, e.g. in gambling. **3** [1990s+] (*W.I.*) to be wanted, whether by fans or the police. **4** [1990s+] (*W.I.*) to have prolonged sexual intercourse.

SE in slang uses

IN COMPOUNDS

❑ **hot...** *see also* separate entries. ❑ **hot and nice** *n.* [1940s] (*W.I.*) a meat patty. ❑ **hotbed** *n.* [the beds are continually occupied] [1930s+] (*US*) **1** a bed in a cheap rooming-house that could be hired for 25 cents for eight hours. **2** a cheap rooming-house. **3** (*also* **hot-bed hotel**) a cheap brothel or hotel that rents out beds to prostitutes and their short-time clients. ❑ **hot belly** *n.* [racial stereotyping: Mexicans like hot, peppery food; var. on PEPPER BELLY *under* PEPPER *n.*] [20C+] (*US*) a Mexican. ❑ **hot flannel** *n.* (*also* **warm flannel**) ['a play on the old name "lambswool."' (Hotten, 1874)] [18C–19C] heated gin and beer with nutmeg, sugar and spices. ❑ **hot-knife** *v.* [1980s+] (*drugs*) to smoke cannabis from a heated knife; the fumes are sucked up through a broken-off milk-bottle neck. ❑ **hot milk** *n.* [late 19C; 1970s] semen. ❑ **hot pepper belly** *n. see* PEPPER BELLY *under* PEPPER *n.* ❑ **hotpot** *n.* [late 17C–early 19C] a hot drink made of ale and brandy. ❑ **hot pup** *n. see* HOT DOG *n.*[1] (1). ❑ **hotsmoke** *n.* [1980s+] (*drugs*) the smoking of crack cocaine. ❑ **hot stepper** *n.* [he runs off 'as if his feet were on fire'] [20C+] (*W.I./UK black teen*) a prison-breaker, a fugitive from prison or a penal institution. ❑ **hot stopping** *n.* [mid-19C] hot spirits and water. ❑ **hot tiger** *n.* [mid-19C] a mixture of hot-spiced ale and sherry, originated at Oxford University.

IN PHRASES

❑ **like a hen on a hot griddle** (*also* **like a hen on a hot plate, ...hot brick, like a chicken on a hot griddle, like a duck..., like a flea..., like a bear over/on hot iron, like a bug on a hot frying pan, like a goose on a hot plate**) [mid-19C+] (*US/Irish*) in an agitated or nervous manner.

IN EXCLAMATIONS

❑ **hot baby!** [1920s] (*US*) an excl. of surprise. ❑ **hot diggety (dog)!** *see* separate entry. ❑ **hot dog!** *see* separate entry. ❑ **hot puppy!** (*also* **hot pup! hot puppies!**) [var. on HOT DOG! *excl.*] [1920s+] (*US*) an excl. of pleasure. ❑ **hot spit!** [1930s+] (*US*) an excl. in response to anything good, exciting, sexually attractive. ❑ **hot ziggety!** (*also* **hotzickity! hot ziddity! hot-ziggedy!**) [var. on HOT DIGGETY (DOG)! *excl.*] [1900s–50s] (*US*) used to express excitement, enjoyment; also as adj., very enthusiastic.

hot *v.*[1] [to cause HEAT *n.* (3)] **1** [1920s] to tell off, to reprimand. **2** [1930s] (*Irish*) to beat. **3** [1990s+] to unmask, to cause trouble for.

hot *v.*[2] *see* HOTTING *n.*

hot *adv.* (*also* **hot-hot**) [HOT *adj.*] **1** [mid-19C+] ardently, eagerly, violently, severely, angrily. **2** [1930s+] well, much. **3** [1970s] of gambling, successfully.

IN PHRASES

❑ **cop it hot** *v. see under* COP IT *v.* ❑ **get it hot** *v.* **1** [mid-19C–1920s] to be punished (lit. or fig.) severely. **2** [late 19C–1900s] to be scolded with great venom. ❑ **give it hot (and strong)** *v.* **1** [late 17C+] to castigate severely. **2** [mid-19C+] to attack and/or punish severely. ❑ **hot off the bat** *adv. see* RIGHT OFF THE BAT *under* BAT *n.*[2].

hot air *n.* (*also* **air hot, hot water**) [late 19C+] (*orig. US*) nonsense, rubbish, empty chatter.

IN COMPOUNDS

❑ **hot-air artist** *n.* (*also* **hot-air merchant**) [-ARTIST *sfx*/MERCHANT *n.*] [20C+] a loquacious person, a person who talks nonsense.

IN PHRASES

❑ **chew hot air** *v.* [1910s] to talk nonsense.

hot and cold *n.*[1] [initial letters, plus fig. ref. to the effects of the drugs] [1970s–80s] (*US drugs*) a combination of heroin and cocaine.

hot and cold *n.*[2] [rhy. sl.] [1990s+] gold.

hot and heavy *phr.* [mid-19C+] intense(ly).

hot and heavy like a tailor's goose *phr.* [SE *goose*, a tailor's iron, the neck of which supposedly resembles that of the bird; + ? the hissing noise it makes when the heated iron meets the dampened cloth] [late 17C–18C] a phr. applied to a passionate lover.

hot-arsed *adj.* (*also* **hot-ass, hot-assed, hot-bummed, hot-cunted**) [HOT *adj.* (1a) + -ARSED *sfx* (2)/-ASSED *sfx* (2)/BUM *n.*[1] (1)/CUNT *n.* (1)] **1** [late 17C+] of a woman, lecherous, lascivious. **2** [1970s] in fig. use, exciting, stimulating.

hot as... *adj.* (*also* **hotter than...**) [play on SE *hot*/HOT *adj.*] used in combs. below meaning extremely hot, whether in a SE use, i.e. temperature or various sl. uses, usu. sexuality.

IN PHRASES

❑ **...a fire-cracker** [1910s+] **1** (*Can.*) sexually promiscuous. **2** (*US*) sexually aroused. **3** (*US*) under suspicion, liable to arrest. ❑ **...a fresh-fucked fox in a forest fire** (*also* **hot as a hen laying a goose egg, hot as a forty-balled tomcat, hotter than...**) [1930s+] (*US*) extremely hot, whether as to temperature or sexuality. ❑ **...a (three-dollar) pistol** (*also* **hot as a two-dollar pistol, ...ten-cent-pistol, hotter than...**) **1** [1930s+] (*US*) (*also* **hot as a bad girl's dream, ...July jam, ... mustard**) very angry. **2** [1930s+] (*US*) (*also* **hot as a 45**) suspicious, wanted by the police. **3** [1940s+] (*US*) very popular or successful. **4** [1950s] (*US*) very hot. **5** [1970s] (*US black*) sexually aroused. ❑ **...a witch's tit** [1940s] (*US*) very hot. ❑ **hotter than a little red wagon** (*also* **hotter than a bitch-wolf**) [1970s] (*US*) of a woman, sexually voracious.

hot-ass *adj.* [SE *hot* + -ASS *sfx*] **1** [1960s+] a general superlative. **2** *see* HOT-ARSED *adj.*

hot ass *v.* [1970s] (*US*) to go out drinking and enjoying oneself.

hot-assed *adj. see* HOT-ARSED *adj.*

hot beef *n.* (*also* **hot meat, ...mutton**) [HOT *adj.* (1a) + BEEF *n.*[1]/ MEAT *n.* (1)/MUTTON *n.*] [19C] a promiscuous woman.

hot beef! *excl.* (*also* **beef!**) [early 19C–1930s] a cry of alarm, synon. with and rhyming on SE 'stop thief!'.

IN PHRASES

❑ **cry (hot) beef** *v.* (*also* **give (hot) beef, squeak beef**) [late 18C–19C] to give the alarm, to call a hue and cry. ❑ **sing out beef** *v.* [early 19C] to cry 'stop thief!'. ❑ **whiddle beef** *v.* [HOT BEEF! *excl.*] [late 18C] to raise the alarm.

hot beef injection *n.* *see* BEEF INJECTION *under* BEEF *n.*[1].

hot box *n.*[1] [HOT *adj.* (5b) + SE *box*] [late 19C–1900s] (*US*) **1** a difficult situation. **2** a tantrum.

hot box *n.*[2] [HOT *adj.* (9) + SE *box*] **1** [1900s] a crematorium, the actual cremator. **2** [1940s] (*US*) a steak. **3** [1960s] a battery used for applying torture by electricity.

hot box *n.*[3] *see under* BOX *n.*[1].

hot box *v.* **1** [1940s+] (*drugs*) to hold onto a marijuana cigarette for too long before passing it. **2** [1980s+] (*US drugs*) to fill a small sealed room with the smoke of cannabis or crack cocaine. **3** [1980s+] to take a deep draw on a cigarette.

hotch *v.* [Scot. *hotch*] [20C+] to swarm with, to burst with.

hotcha *n.* [HOTCHA! *excl.*] **1** [1930s+] (*orig. US*) hot jazz music, any flashy, exciting entertainment. **2** [1940s+] (*US*) an exciting, attractive young woman.

hotcha *adj.* [HOTCHA *n.*] [1930s+] (*US*) sexy, exciting.

hotcha! *excl.* [echoic] [1920s+] (*orig. US*) an excl. of enthusiasm and approval; esp. in phr. *with a hey nonny-nonny and a hotcha-cha.*

hotchee/hotchie *n.* *see* HACHI *n.*

hot cock *n.* *see under* COCK *n.*[5].

hot cock *adj.* [HOT *adj.* (1a) + COCK *n.*[3] (1)] [1970s] (*US*) of a woman, sexually voracious.

hot-cocked *adj.* [SE *hot* + COCK *n.*[4] (1)] [1950s] (*US*) sexually voracious.

hot coffee *n.* [SE *hot coffee*/HOT *adj.* (5b)] [late 19C–1900s] (*Aus.*) something problematic.

hot coffee *adj.* [HOT COFFEE *n.*] [1900s] (*Aus.*) in a temper.

hot coppers *n.* [SE *hot* + *copper*, a large saucepan used for boiling either food or laundry] [mid-19C–1900s] a mouth and throat parched through excessive drinking; thus, a hangover.

IN PHRASES

❑ **clear one's coppers** *v.* [mid-19C] to clear one's throat.

hot cross bun *n.* [rhy. sl.] [20C+] (*Aus.*) the sun.

hot cross bun *phr.* [rhy. sl.] [1950s+] on the run.

hot damn! *excl.* (*also* **hot dammit! hot dang!**) [var. on GOD-DAMN! *excl.*] [1920s+] (*US*) a general excl., usu. implying pleasure rather than fury.

hot diggety (dog)! *excl.* (*also* **diggity dank! hot diggerty damn! hotdiggery! hot jiggety!**) [20C+] (*US*) a general excl. of pleasure or surprise.

hot dinner *n.* [rhy. sl.] [20C+] a winner.

hot dog *n.*[1] [SE since *c.*1939, when it was served under that name by the Coney Island Chamber of Commerce to President Franklin D. Roosevelt and his guests, King George VI and Queen Elizabeth of Great Britain and Northern Ireland, the hot dog started life as sl. It prob. comes from heavy-handed mid-19C humour focusing on the supposed use of horse- and dog-meat as sausage filling, a concept that was accentuated by the 1843 scandal concerning the use of dog-meat for human consumption. The image was intensified by the use (*c.*1860) by German immigrants of *Hundewurst*, dog sausage, to mean smoked frankfurter sausages (larger sausages were *Pferdwurst*, horse baloney). The dachshund, of course, is a 'sausage dog'. The term originated *c.*1895 at the Yale Club (as well as at Harvard, Cornell and other US 'Ivy League' colleges) where lunch wagons were known as 'dog wagons' and frankfurters known as 'hot dogs'] **1** [late 19C+] (*orig. US*) (*also* **hot pup**) a spiced, heated sausage or frankfurter, served on a split roll and trad. garnished with sauerkraut and mustard. **2** [1920s+] (*orig. US*) (*also* **pup**) the penis. **3** [1970s+] (*US*) a homosexual. **4** [1990s+] (*orig. US*) a piece of canine excrement.

hot dog *n.*[2] [HOT *adj.* (7)/HOT *adj.* (8) + DOG *n.*[2] (2b)] (*orig. US campus*) **1** [late 19C+] one who is particularly proficient at an occupation or activity, esp. a successful gambler. **2** [late 19C+] a show-off. **3** [1960s+] in ironic use, an unpleasant or incompetent person. **4** [1960s+] something exciting, amusing.

hot dog *adj.*[1] [HOT DOG *n.*[2]] **1** [late 19C+] (*orig. US campus*) good, excellent. **2** [1920s+] (*US*) showy, flamboyant.

hot dog *adj.*[2] [HOT DOG *n.*[1] (2), punning on HOT *adj.* (1b)] **1** [1960s–70s] (*US prison*) pornographic. **2** [1970s] (*US*) homosexual.

hot dog *v.*[1] **1** [1950s] to prioritize, to find important. **2** [2000s] to grab for oneself.

hot dog *v.*[2] [HOT DOG *n.*[2]] **1** [1960s+] to show off. **2** [1960s+] to chase, to harass, to pursue. **3** [1990s+] (*US*) to perform very well.

hot dog! *excl.* (*also* **hot doggies!**) [20C+] (*orig. US campus*) an expression of delight or strong approval.

hot-dogger *n.* [HOT DOG *n.*[2]] [20C+] (*US teen/campus*) **1** a show-off, a braggart. **2** a successful, talented individual.

hote *n.* [abbr. of SE *hotel*] [1900s] (*US*) a cheap lodging house.

hotel *n.* **1** [19C] the vagina. **2** [early 19C+] (*orig. US*) a prison. **3** [1930s] (*US*) a brothel. **4** [1980s] (*S.Afr.*) the police cells.

hotel beat *n.* [SE *hotel* + BEAT *v.* (1)] [late 19C–1900s] one who stays in hotels and then leaves without paying the bill.

Hotel de Garvie *n.* (*also* **Hotel de Garvey**) [its governor, one *Garvey*] [1900s] (*N.Z.*) the Wellington prison.

hotel de gink *n.* [SE *hotel* + GINK *n.*[1]; the orig. *Hotel de Gink* was founded in Seattle in 1913 and flourished until 1915, a chain of similarly named hotels were then founded across the US; used in WW2 by US Air Transport Command for its hotels] [1910s+] (*US, orig. tramps*) a lodging house; subseq. used for transient officers' quarters in US forces.

Hotel de Hash *n.* [the regular appearance of hash (meat stew) on the prison menu] [late 19C] (*US Und.*) a prison.

hot foot *n.* **1** [mid-19C+] (*orig. US*) speedy action, a quick movement or journey; as phr. *on the hot foot* [HOT FOOT *v.*]. **2** [late 19C+] (*US*) the act of beating the soles of someone's feet or shoes, e.g. of a rough sleeper by a police officer. **3** [1930s–50s] (*US*) a malicious trick played on an unsuspecting sleeper. Matches are thrust end-first into the gap between the upper and sole of the shoe (or between naked toes if vulnerable); the matches are lit, and the shoe 'catches fire' or the flesh is painfully singed. **4** [1940s–50s] (*US*) in fig. use, an unpleasant surprise.

IN PHRASES

❑ **do the hot-foot act** *v.* [1910s] to run off.

hot foot *v.* (*also* **hot foot it, hot heel**) **1** [mid-19C+] (*orig. US*) to rush around, to hurry, to run. **2** [20C+] to escape from. **3** [1910s–20s] to chase away.

hot-hot *adv.* *see* HOT *adv.*

Hotlanta *n.* (*also* **Hot Town**) [the city's actual and fig. temperature] [1970s+] (*US*) Atlanta, GA.

hot mama *n.* (*also* **hot mamma, hot momma, red hot, red-hot mama**) [HOT *adj.* (1c) + MAMA *n.* (1); note the entertainer Sophie Tucker (1884–1966), who billed herself as 'the last of the red hot mamas'] [1920s+] **1** (*US*) a flighty young woman. **2** (*orig. US black*) a large, hedonistic woman, often a habituée of saloons, bars and nightclubs; occas. used of men (cf. *HOT PAPA under* PAPA *n.*). **3** (*US*) a sexy woman, irrespective of her figure.

hot mama *v.* [HOT MAMA *n.*] [1920s] (*US*) to flirt.

hot member *n.* (*also* **hot lot**) **1** [late 19C] a debauchee, a degenerate; in weak use, one who lives for pleasure. **2** [late 19C–1900s] one who flouts convention. **3** [late 19C–1900s] a troublesome, bad-tempered, quarrelsome person. **4** [late 19C–1910s] (*US*) the penis [MEMBER *n.*[1] (1)]. **5** [late 19C–1940s] (*US*) a sexually attractive woman, also a prostitute.

hotnot *n.* [SE *Hottentot*] [1940s+] (*S.Afr.*) a derog. term for a black person.

hot-on *n.* [HOT *adj.* (1a)] [1960s] **1** (*US black*) lust; lustful feelings. **2** (*US campus*) an unpleasant person.

hot on *adj.*[1] [HOT *adj.* (1)] [late 19C+] very severe towards, intent on.

hot on *adj.*[2] [HOT *adj.* (7b)] [1930s+] very skilful at.

hot on *adj.*[3] *see HOT FOR under* HOT *adj.*

hot one *n.* [HOT *adj.* + SE *one*/ONE *n.*[1]] **1** [mid-19C–1900s] a violent blow. **2** [late 19C] a promiscuous woman. **3** [late 19C+] an admirable individual, a good example, usu. with sexual overtones. **4** [late 19C+] a 'difficult' person. **5** [late 19C+] (*gambling*) a winning tip. **6** [20C+] something shocking, surprising or exciting, or funny. **7** [1940s+] something or someone appealing. **8** [1970s] a good idea or plan. **9** [1980s+] (*UK black gang*) a murder.

hot pants *n.* (*also* **hot drawers, warm britches**) [HOT *adj.* (1a) + SE *pants*] **1** [1920s+] (*US*) strong sexual desire; often as *have hot pants for*. **2** [1930s+] a sexually eager woman. **3** [1960s–70s] (*US*) extreme keenness. **4** [1960s+] a term of address to a sexually eager woman (or one who is seen as such).

hot pants *adj.* [HOT PANTS *n.*] **1** [1920s+] sexually eager. **2** [1960s+] sexy, provocative.

hot pillow *n.* [1950s+] (*US*) a casual, short-time sexual encounter; usu. attrib., in combs., e.g. *hot-pillow motel* (cf. HOT-SHEET *adj.*).

(IN COMPOUNDS)

❑ **hot-pillow trade** *n.* the sex industry, spec. casual prostitution.

hot potato *n.*[1] (*also* **hot potato jacket, hot spud**) **1** [mid-19C+] (*orig. US*) a problem, a difficult person, a trying situation, anything those concerned would prefer not to handle. **2** [late 19C+] (*US*) an admirable, clever or energetic person [HOT *adj.* (2b) + POTATO *n.* (2)].

(IN EXCLAMATIONS)

❑ **take a red-hot potato!** (*also* **hold your hot-potato!**) [the effect of a *red-hot potato* in the mouth] [mid-19C–1920s] be quiet! shut up!

hot potato *n.*[2] [rhy. sl.; Cockney pron. 'pertater'] [late 19C–1900s] a waiter (cf. COLD POTATO *n.*[2]).

hot potato *adv.* [rhy. sl.; Aus. pron. 'pertater'] [2000s] (*Aus.*) later.

hot prowl *n.* [HOT *adj.* (5e) + SE *prowl*] [1930s+] (*US police/Und.*) a burglary while the occupants of the building are present; thus *hot prowler*, the burglar.

hot-prowl *v.* [HOT PROWL *n.*] [1930s+] (*US police/Und.*) to burgle a property while the residents are there.

hot rock *v.* [HOT ROCKS *n.*[2]] [1980s+] (*drugs*) to drop burning lumps of cannabis from a cigarette onto one's clothes.

hotrock *adv.* [1940s–50s] absolutely, intensely.

hot rocks *n.*[1] [HOT *adj.* + SE *rocks*/ROCKS *n.* (8)] **1** [1920s] (*US campus*) someone or something splendid. **2** [1930s] (*US*) biscuits. **3** [1940s+] (*US*) esp. of a man, strong sexual desire. **4** [1950s] (*US*) as a form of address, usu. ironically.

hot rocks *n.*[2] [1980s+] (*Irish/Aus. drugs*) hot ash, dropped from a joint, which makes small burn holes; also, when sucked through a pipe and it burns one's throat.

hot-rod *n.* [HOT *adj.* (2d) + SE piston *rod*] **1** [1930s+] (*US*) an aggressive, unruly young man. **2** [1940s+] (*also* **hot iron, hot-up, rod**) a car modified for speed and flashiness. **3** *see* ROD *n.* (1).

hot-rod *adj.* [HOT-ROD *n.*] [1950s+] (*US*) energetic, aggressive.

hot-rod *v.* [1940s+] (*US*) to drive fast and aggressively; also in fig./ext. use.

hot-rodder *n.* (*also* **rod**) [HOT-ROD *n.* (2)] [1940s+] a person who drives or races a car that has been modified for speed and style.

hots, the *n.* [HOT *adj.* (1a)] [1940s+] (*orig. US*) **1** sexual desire; usu. in phr. *have the hots for*, to desire sexually. **2** in fig. use, any form of excitement or enthusiasm.

hot scone *n.* [rhy. sl. = JOHN *n.*[1]] [1920s+] (*Aus.*) a police officer, a detective.

hot seat *n.* **1** [1920s+] (*US*) (*also* **hot settee, ...spot, ...squat, seat**) the electric chair; thus, as v., to be subjected to the electric chair [HOT *adj.* (3b)]. **2** [1930s–40s] any situation in which the subject, consciously or not, is exposed, esp. for the purposes of a confidence trick [note Davis, *Phenomena in Crime* (1941): 'So called because the hooked "mug" is on tenterhooks re the materialization of the investments he has handed over to the crooks']. **3** [1950s+] an unpleasant situation, esp. in a courtroom or public enquiry; esp. as *in the hot seat*. **4** [1950s+] the seat in an interrogation room on which the prisoner sits. **5** [1960s+] any form of interrogation, in a non-official context.

(IN PHRASES)

❑ **take the hot squat** *v.* [1920s+] (*US*) to be executed in the electric chair.

hot sheet *n.* [the items that are HOT *adj.* (5c)] **1** [1920s+] (*US police*) a list of stolen property and of crimes under investigation. **2** [2000s] (*US black*) the list of members of opposite gangs that are considered serious enemies.

hot-sheet *adj.* [such beds are in near-continuous occupation and thus stay warm] [1930s+] (*US*) used in combs. below of any lodging place where the customers take rooms for short-term sexual encounters (cf. HOT PILLOW *n.*).

(IN COMPOUNDS)

❑ **hot-sheet hotel** *n.* (*also* **hot-sheet flop, ...house, ...motel**) a hotel that rents out some or all of its rooms to prostitutes, adulterous couples and others who wish to use the beds for short periods rather than for overnight accommodation.

hot shit *n.* (*also* **that hot shit**) [HOT *adj.* (7) + SHIT *n.* (2b)] [1950s+] (*orig. US*) **1** something important, vibrant, exciting, fashionable etc. **2** an important person or someone who thinks they are.

(IN PHRASES)

❑ **hot-shit around** *v.* [1970s] (*US*) to act in an arrogant manner.

hot-shit *adj.* [HOT SHIT *n.*] [1960s+] (*orig. US*) **1** splendid. **2** offensively self-conceited.

(IN PHRASES)

❑ **hot-shit for** *adj.* [1970s+] (*US*) keen or enthusiastic.

hot-shit! *excl.* [1940s+] (*US*) an expression of excitement, enthusiasm.

hot-shot *n.* [HOT *adj.*] **1** [17C] a sexual athlete, used of either sex [note 17C *hot-shot*, one who discharged his firearm too enthusiastically]. **2** [early 19C+] (*orig. US*) (*also* **hot**) an important, influential person or one who believes that they are. **3** [late 19C–1920s] (*US*) a cutting or sarcastic remark [SHOT *n.*[1] (3a)]. **4** [1920s–30s] (*US tramp*) a stolen car. **5** [1920s–50s] (*US tramp*) a fast freight train. **6** [1930s+] (*drugs*) the substitution of cyanide, strychnine or battery acid for white powdered heroin; when injected by the addict, it causes instant death and leaves no trace; also as v., to sell or take such a preparation [SHOT *n.*[1] (6b)]. **7** [1940s+] ironic use of sense 2, usu. as a term of address.

hot-shot *adj.* [HOT-SHOT *n.*] [1920s+] (*orig. US*) **1** conceited, self-opinionated, ostentatious. **2** first-rate [? backed up by *hot-shot*, a truck-freighting term from *c.* 1920: rapid; offering through or non-stop service].

(IN COMPOUNDS)

❑ **hotshot Charlie** *n.* [CHARLIE *n.*[2]; coined in Milton Caniff's comic strip 'Terry and the Pirates' (1940s)] [1940s–70s] (*US*) a nickname for a brash, egotistical young man.

hot spot *n.* [HOT *adj.* + SPOT *n.*[5]] **1** [20C+] a dangerous or difficult situation. **2** [1900s–20s] (*US Und.*) an area where there is likely to be a good deal of police presence or similar security. **3** [1920s+] (*US*) a popular, fashionable nightclub, bar. **4** *see* HOT SEAT *n.* (1).

hot stuff *n.*[1] (*US*) **1** [mid-19C+] spiced rum, strong alcohol. **2** [1920s–30s] coffee.

hot stuff *n.*[2] [HOT *adj.* + SE *stuff*] (*orig. US*) **1** [late 19C+] something or someone considered first-rate, excellent, especially intelligent or capable. **2** [late 19C+] an attractive woman. **3** [late 19C+] something or someone pornographic or sexy. **4** [1920s+] (*US*) stolen goods. **5** [1930s] (*UK Und.*)

fraudulent literature used in financial swindling. **6** [1950s] extremely well-dressed.

hot stuff! *excl.* [HOT STUFF *n.*[2]] [late 19C+] (*orig. US*) a form of address, often implying that the person in question has a higher opinion of themselves than does the audience.

hotsy-totsy *n.* (*also* **hotsy**) [1910s–40s] (*US*) **1** a pretty young woman. **2** a magazine devoted to pin-ups.

hotsy-totsy *adj.* (*also* **hotsy**) [ext. of HOT *adj.* (2b); coined by cartoonist William 'Billie' de Beck, c.1925] [1920s+] (*orig. US*) **1** excellent, satisfactory, just right. **2** of a place, sophisticated.

IN PHRASES

❑ **play hotsy-totsy** *v.* [1960s] to play games with, lit. or fig.

hot tamale *n.* (*also* **tamale, tomale**) [HOT *adj.* (2b)/HOT *adj.* (1c) + Sp. *tamale*, a Mexican dish consisting of corn husks wrapped around a variety of fillings] **1** [late 19C–1930s] (*US*) a clever person, often used ironically. **2** [late 19C+] (*US*) an attractive, sexy, young woman. **3** [1920s+] (*US gay*) (*also* **hot enchilada**) a Hispanic homosexual man.

hot tamale! *excl.* [HOT TAMALE *n.*] [1940s+] (*US*) an excl. of excitement, pleasure.

hotted-up *adj.* [HOT-ROD *n.* (2)] [1950s+] (*US*) of a car engine, customized.

Hottentot *n.* [proper name Hottentot, poss. meaning 'stutterer' or 'stammerer'. 'One of the two sub-races of the Khoisanid race (the other being the Sanids or Bushmen), characterized by short stature, yellow-brown skin colour, and tightly curled hair. They are of mixed Bushman-Hamite descent with some Bantu admixture, and are now found principally in South-West Africa' (*OED*). Since 18C the term has been used abusively, to describe someone 'uncivilized' and of inferior intelligence and culture] **1** [18C–1910s] a fool, a simpleton. **2** [18C+] (*S.Afr.*) a derog. term for a black person. **3** [late 19C–1910s] used in the East End of London to denote a stranger; thus cry *Hottentots!* strangers coming! **4** [20C+] in pl., the buttocks [the nakedness of African tribespeople].

IN COMPOUNDS

❑ **Hottentot apron** *n.* [the physical characteristics of 'Hottentot' women] [20C+] elongated labia.

hotten up one's copper *v.* [1940s+] (*N.Z.*) to have something warm to eat and drink.

hot ticket *n.* [orig. theatre use, a successful show or performer] [1960s+] (*US campus*) a person, event or object that is currently fashionable or stylish.

hot ticket! *excl.* [HOT TICKET *n.*] [1990s+] (*US campus*) an excl. of affirmation.

hottie *n.*[1] [abbr.] **1** [20C+] (*orig. Aus.*) a *hot*-water bottle. **2** [2000s] (*drugs*) hashish or marijuana smoked off a hot knife.

hottie *n.*[2] (*also* **hotty**) [HOT STUFF *n.*[2]] **1** [1910s] an outstanding person. **2** [1910s; 1980s+] (*US black/campus*) a good-looking or promiscuous member of the opposite sex.

hottie *adj.* (*also* **hotty**) [HOTTIE *n.*[2]] [1990s+] (*US*) very attractive.

hotting *n.* [? UK descendant of US *hotrod*] [1990s+] joy-riding, or, in legal parlance, *taking and driving away*; the 'hotter' steals a high-performance car and, often to an appreciative crowd, puts it and his own driving skills through their paces, emphasizing skids, spins and hand-brake turns.

hot toddy *n.* [rhy. sl.] [20C+] a body.

Hot Town *n. see* HOTLANTA *n.*

hotty *see under* HOTTIE.

hot water *n.* (*also* **warm water**) **1** [mid-16C+] difficulties, problems; usu. as *in hot water*. **2** [late 19C] (*US*) in a restaurant, a cup of tea. **3** see HOT AIR *n.* (1).

hot water! *excl.* [HOT WATER *n.*] [2000s] (*US prison*) a warning that an officer is coming.

hot-water house *n.* [f. the pot of hot water kept constantly heated for lodgers to make tea or coffee on payment of a half-penny] [mid-19C] (*UK Und.*) the lowest, most basic type of lodging house for tramps and beggars.

hot wire *n. see under* WIRE *n.*[1].

hot-wire *v.* [the 'hot' electric spark produced by touching two wires] **1** [1950s+] (*orig. US*) (*also* **wire**) to start a car without an ignition key by making the required connection between two wires. **2** [1980s+] to illegally connect to the electricity supply.

Houdini *n.* [joc. ref. to Harry *Houdini* (1874–1926), US conjuror and escape artist] **1** [1920s+] (*US*) someone who avoids something, usu. work. **2** [1980s+] (*US drugs*) marijuana [the smoker 'escapes' reality].

IN PHRASES

❑ **pull a Houdini** *v.* (*also* **do a Houdini**) [1920s+] (*US*) to escape, to vanish suddenly, to leave stealthily.

Houdini *v.* [HOUDINI *n.*] [1920s+] (*US Und.*) to escape, to disappear.

hough! *excl. see* FAUGH! *excl.*

houghmagandy *n.* (*also* **hochmagandy**) [? *hough*, the hollow part of the human knee joint, the adjacent section of the thigh + *canty*, cheerful, lively, brisk or *gundy*, a push; or ? fig. use of HASHMAGANDY *n.* or SE *hogmanay*; Ebsworth, *Bagford Ballads* (1880), prefers an interpretation of *gandy* as a var. pron. of 'go over gaudy', extramarital intercourse 'over the broomstick'] [18C+] (*Ulster/Scot.*) (adulterous) sexual intercourse.

hou jou bek! *excl.* [Afk. *bek*, an animal's mouth, when used of a human it is sl.; note Fr. *ferme ta gueule*, shut your gob, in which *gueule*, usu. of an animal is sl. when used of a human] [1910s+] (*S.Afr.*) shut your trap!

hoult *n.* [pron. of SE *hold* n.] [20C+] (*Irish*) **1** a sexually attractive woman, often qualified as a *fine/great/goodhoult*. **2** sexual intercourse.

hound *n.* **1** based on the negative characteristics of the dog, synon. with DOG *n.*[2] (1). (**a**) [mid-18C+] an unpleasant person. (**b**) [mid-19C+] a gangster, a hoodlum. (**c**) [1920s+] (*US black*) an indiscriminatingly promiscuous man. (**d**) [1930s+] (*Aus.*) a lazy, good-for-nothing person. (**e**) [1960s] (*US*) a coward. (**f**) [1980s+] (*Aus. prison*) an informer. (**g**) [1980s+] an unattractive woman. **2** [1910s+] (*US*) an enthusiast, a devotee [-HOUND *sfx*]. **3** [1950s+] (*US black*) a Grey*hound* Corporation bus. **4** [1960s] (*US*) 'the daylights', 'the stuffing'; thus *kick/knock the hound out of*.

IN PHRASES

❑ **come the hound** *v.* [1970s] (*Irish*) to deceive, to trick.

hound *adj.* [HOUND *n.* (1e)] [1960s] (*US prison*) cowardly.

hound *v.* [HOUND *n.* (1c)] [1980s+] (*US black/campus*) **1** to have sex with. **2** to go out looking for sex.

-hound *sfx* [1910s+] an enthusiast, usu. for 'pleasures of the flesh', e.g. PUSSY-HOUND *under* PUSSY *n.*, SAUCEHOUND *under* SAUCE *n.*[1].

hound-dog *v.* [HOUND *v.* (2)] [1990s+] to go out looking for a (sexual) companion or criminal.

houndish *adj.* [SE *hound*, a glutton, but the n. form is rarely found] [20C+] (*W.I., Guyn.*) shamelessly gluttonous.

hound pudding *n.* [1950s] (*mainly juv.*) mince.

Hounslow Heath *n.* [rhy. sl.] [mid–late19C] the teeth.

hour-grunter *n.* [watchmen patrolled the streets, calling out the time] [late 17C–early 18C] a watchman.

hours *phr.* [1980s] (*UK black*) an expression of farewell.

house *n.*[1] **1** [16C+] a whore-house, a house of ill-repute, a brothel. **2** [mid-17C–1920s] a public house, a hotel, an illegal drinking house. **3** [mid-19C–1900s] a poor-house, a workhouse; a tramps' lodging house. **4** [late 19C–1930s] (*UK society*) a group of guests at a ball or dance who sit, eat and dance within their own circle only. **5** [20C+] (*US Und.*) a police station. **6** [1920s+] (*US Und.*) a single prison cell; thus *house time*, a sentence in jail. **7** [1940s–70s] (*US black/teen*) a prison.

IN COMPOUNDS

❑ **house girl** *n.* [1950s] (*US Und.*) a prostitute who works in a brothel. ❑ **house-keeper** *n.* [euph.] **1** [late 18C–1940s] (*US Und.*) a madame. **2** [1930s–70s] a kept mistress. ❑ **house mother** *n.* [1950s+] in the sex industry, a madame.

IN PHRASES

❑ **at the top of the house** (*also* **in the top of the house, up the…, at the housetop, in the…, up the…**) [late 17C–mid-18C] very angry. ❑ **dead house** *n. see under* DEAD *adj.* ❑ **hit a**

house *v.* [20C+] (*US prison*) to search a cell. ▫ **house of call** *n. see* CALL HOUSE *n.* (1). ▫ **house of civil reception** *n.* (*also* **house of civil entertainment**) [mid-18C–early 19C] a brothel. ▫ **house of conveniency** *n.* [18C] a brothel. ▫ **house of delight** *n.* (*also* **house of entertainment, ...pleasure**) [18C] a brothel. ▫ **house of profession** *n.* [17C] a brothel. ▫ **house of resort** *n.* [late 16C–early 17C] a brothel. ▫ **house of sale** *n.* [late 16C–early 17C] a brothel. ▫ **house of state** *n.* [17C] a brothel. ▫ **house of waste** *n.* [the moral standpoint] [late 18C–early 19C] a tavern. ▫ **in the house** **1** [1970s] (*US black*) at home. **2** [1980s+] lit., present and fig., aware, 'on the ball' etc. **3** [1980s+] (*orig. US black/teen*) excellent. ▫ **play house** *v.* **1** [20C+] (*US*) to cohabit. **2** [1930s+] (*US campus*) to have sexual intercourse. **3** [1950s] to insult one's peers with ref. to their mother. **4** [1960s] of two homosexuals, to play around in a sexual manner.

SE in slang uses

pertaining to a lavatory

IN PHRASES

▫ **House of Commons** *n.* [pun on SE/COMMONS *n.*] [late 18C–mid-19C] a privy, a lavatory. ▫ **house of easement** *n.* (*also* **chapel of ease, house of..., office of..., place of convenience, ...resort**) [euph.] [17C–19C] a privy. ▫ **house of office** *n.* [17C–mid-19C] a privy. ▫ **house of parliament** *n.* (*also* **houses of parliament, parliament house**) ['where all the big pricks hang out'] [1960s+] (*UK/N.Z.*) a lavatory, esp. a public lavatory.

general uses

IN COMPOUNDS

▫ **house-a-blazes** *adv.* [1940s] (*W.I.*) utterly, completely. ▫ **house ape** *n.* [1960s+] (*US*) a small child. ▫ **house-bit** *n.* *see under* BIT *n.*[1]. ▫ **house connect** *n. see under* CONNECTION *n.* ▫ **house dog** *n.* [1930s] (*US tramp*) one who takes jobs in private houses. ▫ **house-fed lamb** *n.* [mid-19C] (*UK Und.*) a kept mistress. ▫ **house fee** *n.* [1980s+] (*drugs*) a fee charged for entry into a room or apartment where one can smoke crack cocaine. ▫ **house furniture** *n. see* PIECE OF FURNITURE *under* PIECE *n.* ▫ **house hop** *n. see under* HOP *n.*[1]. ▫ **house-knacker** *n.* (*also* **house-farmer**) [SE *house-knacker*, one who buys old houses to strip out their materials or to convert them for profitable use] [late 19C] a landlord who rents third-rate accommodation to the poor. ▫ **houseman** *n.* [his specializing in house-breaking rather than safe-cracking etc] [1900s–40s] (*US*) a burglar. ▫ **house-piece** *n. see under* PIECE *n.* ▫ **house-plant** *n.* [1910s+] (*US*) an indolent person who does nothing but sit around. ▫ **house rat** *n.* [1960s] (*US*) a child. ▫ **housework** *n.* [1900s–20s] (*US Und.*) burglary; thus *house-worker*, a burglar.

IN PHRASES

▫ **dark house** *n. see under* DARK *adj.* ▫ **house for rent** *n.* [a widow becomes 'vacant' for a new (male) 'tenant'] [18C–19C; 1930s] **1** a widow's weeds. **2** the widow herself. ▫ **house of countless drops** *n.* (*US black*) **1** [1930s–40s] a bar that sells grilled food as well as the usual liquor. **2** [1990s+] the House of Detention. ▫ **house of D** *n.* [abbr.] [1960s+] (*US prison*) a *house of detention*; spec. the Women's House of Detention in NYC. ▫ **house of knowledge** *n. see* KNOWLEDGE BOX *n.* (2). ▫ **house of many slammers** *n.* [1940s+] (*US*) a prison. ▫ **house of noodles** *n. see under* NOODLE *n.*[1]. ▫ **house of pain** *n.* (*US black*) **1** [1940s] the dentist's. **2** [1990s+] a prison. ▫ **house that Jack built** *n.* (*also* **Jack's house**) **1** [late 19C–1930s] a prison [the generic hangman *Jack Ketch*]. **2** [1920s+] (*Aus.*) the Government Savings Bank in Sydney, opened 1928. ▫ **house under the hill** *n.* [the image of the vagina as being 'down there' and beneath the fig. *hill*, or pubic mound; note Aubrey Beardsley's title for his sole and unfinished erotic novel *Under the Hill* (1898)] [late 19C+] the vagina. ▫ **house with green shutters** *n.* [1930s] (*US prison*) the gas chamber. ▫ **house without chairs** *n.* [1920s–40s] (*US black*) a temporarily unfurnished apartment or house; usu. as used for parties.

house *n.*[2] *see* BRICKHOUSE *n.*[2] (2).

house *v.*[1] [abbr. of ROUGHHOUSE *v.*] **1** [1980s+] (*US*) to outdo, to defeat. **2** [1990s+] (*US*) to attack someone violently. **3** [1990s+] (*US black*) to take over, to exert one's authority.

house *v.*[2] [SE *house*, to take into a house] **1** [1980s+] (*US black/rap music*) to take for oneself, to steal. **2** [1990s+] (*US black*) to go, to come or move towards. **3** [1990s+] (*US teen*) to give, to take or bring. **4** *see* GROUND *v.*

house *v.*[3] [? SE *bring down the house*] [1980s+] (*US black/rap music*) to excite and impress an audience.

housed *adj.* [1990s+] (*US campus*) drunk.

house-gow *n. see* HOOSEGOW *n.*

house in a state *n.* [rhy. sl.] [1960s] (*bingo*) the number 78.

housemaid's knee *n.* [rhy. sl.] [1970s] the sea.

house nigger *n.* (*also* **h.n.**) [the slavery-era division between 'house' and 'field niggers', i.e. those who worked as indoor servants and those who worked in the fields; the former were seen as 'softer' than the latter] [1970s+] (*US black*) **1** a black person employed, often as the 'token nigger', i.e. token black worker, in a mainly white organization. **2** a black person who is seen as preferring white friends and opinions to those of their own community. **3** a subservient person, a 'yes-man', irrespective of race.

IN PHRASES

▫ **big house nigger** *n.* [1950s] (*US black*) any proud, arrogant person.

house of fraser *n.* [rhy. sl.; usu. as 'howser'; ult. *House of Fraser*, a department store] [20C+] a razor, either as a weapon or for shaving.

House of Lords *n.* [rhy. sl.] [20C+] cords, i.e. corduroy trousers.

house of wax *n.* [rhy. sl. = JACKS *n.*[2]] [2000s] (*Irish*) the lavatory.

house to let *n.*[1] [rhy. sl.] [1930s] (*UK Und.*) a bet.

house to let *n.*[2] *see* APARTMENT TO LET *n.*

housewife *n.* [metonymy, but note poss. play on 18C *housewife*, a small (pocket-sized) case for needles, thread, scissors etc] [late 19C] the female genitals.

SE in slang uses

IN COMPOUNDS

▫ **housewife's hour** *n.* [play on radio scheduling jargon] [1960s+] (*US gay*) the afternoon, esp. as used for masturbation since nothing else is happening.

housewives' choice *n.* [rhy. sl.; ult. the BBC radio programme] [1950s+] a voice.

housey-housey *adj.* [rhy. sl.; ult. UK synon. for *bingo*] [20C+] lousy, i.e. unwell.

hout *n. see* HOOT *n.*[1].

houtkop *n.* (*also* **hout, houtie**) [Afk. *hout*, wood + *kop*, head] [1950s+] (*S.Afr.*) a blockhead, a fool; thus a general term of abuse for a black person; often abbr. to *hout*, *houtie*.

hover *n.* [it gets the user HIGH *adj.*[1] (2)] [1990s+] (*US drugs*) $10 worth of crack cocaine.

how about that (then)? *phr.* (*also* **how's about that?**) [1930s+] an interrog. phr. calling for agreement that something is worthy of praise or approval.

how are they coming? *phr. see* HOW'S IT HANGING? *phr.*

how (are) they hanging? *phr. see* HOW'S IT HANGING? *phr.*

how (are) they hitting? *phr. see* HOW (ARE) YOU HITTING THEM? *phr.*

how are they stacking up? *phr.* (*also* **how are they running?**) [1900s–30s] (*US*) a greeting.

how are you! *excl.* [1910s+] (*Irish*) an expression of disbelief, a dismissive retort.

how are you diddling? *phr. see under* DIDDLE *v.*[1].

how are you going? *phr.* (*also* **how are you coming up?**) [1910s+] (*orig./mainly Aus.*) a general phr. of greeting.

how (are) you hanging? *phr. see* HOW'S IT HANGING? *phr.*

how (are) you hitting them? *phr.* (*also* **how (are) they hitting?**) [sporting imagery] [late 19C+] (*US*) a phr. of greeting, how are you?

how are you making? *phr.* [MAKE OUT *v.* (2)] [1950s] (*US*) a greeting.

how are you off for soap? *phr. see under* SOAP *n.*[1].

how are your poor feet? *phr. see under* FOOT *n.*

how came you so *phr.* (*also* **how come you so, how fare ye, Lord how came you so**) [? a blasphemous ref. to a biblical quotation] **1** [late 18C–19C] drunk. **2** [19C–1910s] (*US*) pregnant.

how does that grab you? *phr. see under* GRAB *v.*

how does that hang? *phr. see under* HANG *v.*[4].

how-do-you-do *n.* (*also* **how-de-do, howdy-do, how-d'ye-do**) [rhy. sl.] **1** [19C] (*US*) a thrashing. **2** [mid-19C+] a problem, a difficulty, a fuss; usu. as a *fine/pretty how-do-you do* [= STEW *n.*[1]]. **3** [1930s] a shoe; often in pl. **4** [1930s] in pl., trousers. **5** [1930s] (*US*) in pl., ladies underwear, pyjamas.

how do you like them apples? *phr.* (*also* **how do you like that for apples? how do you like them berries? ...onions? ... your eggs done?**) [1910s+] (*US*) an ironic, rhetorical demand, 'What do you think of that then and what are you going to do about it?' The implication is that whatever one thinks, one can do nothing.

howdy doody *phr.* (*also* **howdy-do-dee!**) [SE *how do you do?* + the NBC-TV puppet Howdy Doody, launched 27 December 1947] [late 19C+] (*US*) a general greeting; also as v.

how-d'ye-do *n. see* HOW-DO-YOU-DO *n.*

how fare ye *phr. see* HOW CAME YOU SO *phr.*

how is it (there)? *phr.* [IT *n.*[1]] [1910s–50s] a phr. of greeting.

how is that for high? *phr. see* HOW'S THAT FOR HIGH? *under* HIGH *adj.*[2].

howitzer *n.* [SE *howitzer*, a light cannon] (*US*) **1** [late 19C–1960s] a large pistol or revolver. **2** [1970s] the penis. **3** [2000s] a large female breast.

howl *n.* **1** [late 19C+] (*US*) a noisy objection, a complaint. **2** [1910s] a miserable person. **3** [1930s+] a highly amusing story, situation, experience or person.

IN PHRASES

❑ **put up a howl** *v.* [1900s] to make a fuss.

howl *v.* [fig. use of SE] **1** [20C+] (*US*) to celebrate wildly. **2** [20C+] (*US*) to complain. **3** [1980s] (*US preppie*) to mock, to tease [the howls of derision that accompany such teasing].

IN PHRASES

❑ **howl on** *v.* [1990s+] (*Aus. Und.*) to complain about. ❑ **on the howl** [late 19C–1910s] (*Aus./US*) on a drunken spree.

howler *n.* **1** [late 19C] a boisterous lout. **2** [late 19C] a heavy fall, a bad accident; thus *come/go a howler* [one *howls* with pain]. **3** [late 19C–1910s] a dandy, a fop, a fashionable dresser [his clothes and personality 'howl' for attention]. **4** [late 19C–1930s] an expert. **5** [late 19C+] a notable blunder (esp. in an examination), a gross error, a social solecism [such errors 'howl out' for notice]. **6** [1930s–60s] a great success.

howlet *n. see* MADGE HOWLET *n.*

howleybags *n.* [*HOWLING BAGS under* BAGS *n.*[2]] [2000s] (*N.Z.*) nappies or knickerbockers.

howling *adj.* [mid-19C+] great, extreme, pronounced.

IN COMPOUNDS

❑ **howling bags** *n. see under* BAGS *n.*[2]. ❑ **howling rags** *adj.* [? one's clothes are awry] [1910s] (*Aus.*) very drunk. ❑ **howling swell** *n. see* HEAVY SWELL *n.* ❑ **howling thing** *n.* [late 19C–1900s] (*US*) a particularly exciting individual.

SE in slang uses

IN COMPOUNDS

❑ **howling stick** *n.* [mid–late 19C] a flute.

how much? *excl.* [mid-19C+] an excl. of incredulity, a demand for further detail or information, esp. when what has been offered seems unbelievable; it need have no ref. to price, but is delivered in response to what the listener considers to be a far-fetched statement.

how's a...? *phr.* [1910s] (*Aus.*) a general interrog.

how's about that? *phr. see* HOW ABOUT THAT (THEN)? *phr.*

how's by you? *phr.* [1960s] (*US*) a greeting.

how's high? *phr.* [late 19C] (*US*) how are you?

how's it bouncing? *phr. see under* BOUNCE *v.*[1].

how's it going? *phr.* (*also* **how's it? how's it happening? how's she going?**) [20C+] a general phr. of greeting.

how's it hanging? *phr.* (*also* **how (are) they hanging? how (are) you hanging? what's hanging?**) [IT *n.*[1] (2); 'they' being the testicles, the popular answer to the pl. form is 'One in front, for speed'] [1970s+] a man-to-man greeting, what are you up to? how are you?

how's it shaking? *phr. see* WHAT'S SHAKING? *under* SHAKE *v.*

how's she cutting? *phr. see under* CUT *v.*[2].

how's that for high? *phr. see under* HIGH *adj.*[2].

how's the boy? *phr.* (*also* **how's the girl?**) [1910s–30s] a phr. of greeting: how are you?

how's the way? *phr.* [20C+] (*N.Z.*) a phr. of greeting.

how's-yer-father *n.*[1] (*also* **how's-your-father**) [coined in a music-hall sketch performed by the comedian Harry Tate (1872–1940) and popularized by services during WW1] **1** [20C+] sexual intercourse; often as a *bit of how's-yer-father.* **2** [20C+] used of anything for which one either does not know or prefers not to mention the name. **3** [20C+] nonsense, rubbish. **4** [20C+] occas. use as a general euph., *swear like how's yer father*, i.e. swear 'like fuck'. **5** [1990s+] petty criminality. **6** [1990s+] a condom.

how's-yer-father *n.*[2] [rhy. sl. = SE *lather*] **1** [20C+] a state of excitement or fear. **2** [2000s] (*N.Z.*) a fight.

how's your ass? *phr. see under* ASS *n.*

how's your bod? *phr. see under* BOD *n.*

how's-your-father *n. see* HOW'S-YER-FATHER *n.*[1].

how's your hammer hanging? *phr. see under* HAMMER *n.*[1].

how the devil! *excl. see* WHAT THE DEVIL! *excl.*

how to go! *excl. see* WAY TO GO! *excl.*

howzit? *phr.* (*also* **howza wawda?**) [1930s+] hello, how are you?

hoxter *n.* [SE *oxter*, the armpit] [19C] an inside pocket.

hoy *n.* [HOOEY *n.*] [1910s] (*US*) rubbish, nonsense.

hoy *v.* [dial. *hoy*, to throw, to heave/SE *haul*] (*Aus.*) **1** [1920s+] to drag, to take. **2** [1930s+] to get rid of, to discard. **3** [1960s] to throw.

hoys *n. see* HOIST *n.* (1).

hoyster *n. see* HOISTER *n.* (1).

hozzy *n.* [abbr.] [1990s+] a hospital.

h.p. *n.* [abbr.] [1990s+] (*US black teen*) the Hunter's Point area of San Francisco.

h.q. *n.* [abbr. *half-quarter*] [1980s+] (*US drugs*) an eighth of an ounce (5g) of cannabis.

h.r.n. *n.* [abbr.] [1950s+] (*drugs*) heroin.

h.t. *n.*[1] [abbr.] [1940s] (*US black campus*) a heart throb.

h.t. *n.*[2] *see* HEAD TRIP *n.*

H town *n.* **1** [1970s+] (*US*) Houston, Texas. **2** [2000s] (*US black*) Harlem, New York City.

hua *n. see* HOOER *n.*

Hub, the *n.* [self-styled as the 'hub of the solar system/universe'] [mid-19C+] Boston; thus *Hubite*, a Bostonian.

hub *n. see* HUBBY *n.*

hubba *n.* [HUBBA HUBBA! *excl.*] [1980s+] **1** (*US campus*) an attractive man. **2** (*drugs*) crack cocaine [fig. use denoting its energizing effect].

hubba-hubba *n.* [HUBBA HUBBA! *excl.*] **1** [1940s] (*US*) nonsense. **2** [1940s+] a lively, energetic spirit.

hubba hubba! *excl.* (*also* **hava hava!**) [SE *hubba! hubba!*, a college cheer; according to posting on American Dialect Society List: 'At one of the WWII training bases in the U.S. there was a sergeant who was known for shouting "A HUB A HUB A HUB" and who was thereby nicknamed Sergeant Hubba Hubba. One day two soldiers were in the town near the base (the author of the account and a friend). They became temporarily separated, when the author of the account spotted two beautiful, charming women walking in his direction. The author wanted to call his friend immediately to take a look at the two women, but he did not want to do so in an obvious and socially gauche manner. So he shouted out something that his friend would understand but would mean nothing to the civilians: HUBBA HUBBA. Later they told the story of this incident about the beautiful women to their buddies back at the base. And HUBBA HUBBA became a local expression on the base in reference to seeing a beautiful woman. A few months later Bob Hope was scheduled to perform at the base, and his advance men (as they always did) visited the base beforehand to pick up anything of local interest that could be used by Bob Hope in his act. They picked up the story about HUBBA HUBBA and gave it to Hope, who did use the expression in his act. That was the seal of approval'] [1940s+] (*orig. US teen/campus*) a term of approval, esp. when directed at a passing girl or woman.

hubberlush *n.* [HUBBA HUBBA! *excl.* + LUSH *n.*[3] (3)] [2000s] (*N.Z.*) an attractive woman.

hubbie *n. see* HUBBY *n.*

hubble *n.* [? abbr. HUBBLE-BUBBLE *n.*] [20C+] (*Ulster*) fuss and bother.

hubble-bubble *n.* [SE *hubble-bubble*, the confused noise emanating from a person talking so fast as to be incomprehensible; rhy. sl. = trouble] [mid-18C–1900s] confusion, chaos; thus *hubble-bubble fellow*, a fool.

hubble de shuff *adv.* [milit. jargon *fire hubble de shuff*, fire quickly and irregularly; ? the orig. root of both is 16C northern dial. *hubbleshow*, a hubbub, a disturbance] [late 18C–19C] confusedly, chaotically.

hubbub *n.* [mid-19C] (*US*) a stomach-ache.

hubby *n.* (*also* **hub, hubbie**) [abbr./corruption of SE] **1** [late 17C+] a husband. **2** [1980s] (*US campus*) (*also* **husband**) a steady boyfriend.

hubcap biter *n.* [1980s] (*Aus.*) a woman who choses the men she goes after on the basis of their cars.

huck *n.* [? proper name *Huckleberry Finn*, hero of Mark Twain's novel *The Adventures of Huckleberry Finn* (1884)] **1** [late 19C–1910s] (*US*) a person. **2** [1920s+] a black person.

huckery *adj.* [? Maori *pakaru*, ruined] [2000s] (*N.Z.*) a general negative, unattractive, unpleasant.

huckle *n.* [? dial. *huckle*, to bend the body; he 'bends over' for penetration] [20C+] (*US*) an effeminate male homosexual.

huckle *v.* [? dial. *huckle*, to stoop, to bend the body] [1950s+] to be seized or arrested.

huckleberry *n.* [SE *huckleberry*, the fruit; influenced by the proper name in Mark Twain's *Adventures of Huckleberry Finn* (1884)] **1** [mid-19C+] (*US*) a small amount, degree or extent. **2** [mid-19C+] (*US*) a fellow, a boy. **3** [late 19C+] (*US*) the person who suits one's wishes [SE *huckleberry*, a sweetheart]. **4** [late 19C+] (*US*) a person of little importance. **5** [late 19C+] (*US*) constr. with *the*, bad treatment. **6** [1920s+] (*US*) a nickname for a black person. **7** [2000s] (*US drugs*) a very compact marijuana bud 5cm (2in) or less in length [resemblance to the fruit].

IN PHRASES

❑ **huckleberry above (one's) persimmon** (*also* **...over one's persimmon, huckleberry below a persimmon**) [proverbial phr.; the disparate 'status' of the fruits] [mid-19C+] (*US*) **1** beyond one's capabilities, esp. when the task cited is, in fact, simple. **2** (*also* **...to one's persimmon**) superior, to a single degree, to what it is compared with.

huckleberry finn *n.* [rhy. sl.; ult. novel *The Adventures of Huckleberry Finn* (1884) by Mark Twain] [20C+] (*Aus.*) gin.

huckleberry hound *n.* [rhy. sl. = SE *pound*] [1960s+] (*Aus. prison*) a punishment cell; solitary confinement.

huckle-my-buff *n.* (*also* **huckle and buff, huckle-my-butt, huckle-my-muff**) [dial. *huckle*, to jog along, thus lit. 'jog my skin/my buttocks'] **1** [mid-18C–early 19C] a mixture of gin and ale. **2** [late 18C–early 19C] a drink made by heating beer, eggs and brandy together. **3** [20C+] (*US*) bourbon and milk poured over crushed ice, recommended as a hangover cure.

hue *v.* [SE *hue*, colour (of the flesh after a beating), or SE *hue*, to assail, to drive, or *hew*, to cut with blows] (*UK Und.*) **1** [late 17C–mid-19C] to beat, to whip. **2** [19C] to hit with a cudgel.

huer *n. see* HOOER *n.*

huevos *n.* [Sp. eggs] [2000s] (*W.I.*) the testicles.

Huey *n. see* HUGHIE *n.*

huey *n.*[1] (*also* **hughey**) [ety. unknown; ? SE *hue*, to chase with shouts, or a *hue and cry*; such fates might befall a hapless tramp] [mid–late 19C] (*tramp*) a town or village.

huey *n.*[2] [SE *hue and cry*] [mid-19C–1920s] (*UK/US Und.*) a newspaper that lists stolen articles; spec. the National Police Gazette (NY).

huff *n.* [SE *huff*, to puff, to blow up] **1** [mid-16C–mid-19C] a blusterer, a bully. **2** [late 16C+] a bad temper. **3** [mid-19C] a dodge or trick. **4** *see* HUFFCAP *n.*

IN PHRASES

❑ **take the huff** *v.* [1920s+] to lose one's temper, to take offence.

huff *v.* **1** to act arrogantly, aggressively [SE *huff*, to bully, to hector; note 1910s–20s milit. jargon *huff*, to kill]. (**a**) [late 16C–early 19C] to swagger. (**b**) [late 17C–early 19C] to scold, to reprove, to bully. (**c**) [18C+] to annoy, to offend. (**d**) [early 19C] to throw one's arms over a victim's shoulders and then take the money from his pockets; the assault requires two partners, one to grab and one to rifle the clothes. **2** [1960s+] (*drugs*) to sniff solvents or similar volatile substances; thus *huffing*, inhaling [SE *huff*, to blow].

IN PHRASES

❑ **stand the huff** *v.* [STAND *v.*[2] (2) + SE *huff*/sense 1a above; the image is of the boastfulness that can underpin the gesture] [late 18C–early 19C] to take responsibility for the bill in a public house.

huff! *excl.* (*also* **huffa!**) [imitative of a blast of air through some form of orifice] [late 15C–16C] 'an exclamation attributed to a swaggerer or bully, esp. when introduced on the stage' (*OED*).

huff and ding *v.* [HUFF *v.* (1a) + DING *v.*[1] (2)] [late 17C–early 18C] to swagger and boast.

huffcap *n.* (*also* **huff**) [HUFF *v.* (1) + SE *cap*, i.e. that which raises the cap] **1** [late 16C–early 18C] a swaggerer, a blusterer [the bully sets his cap at a swaggering angle]. **2** [late 16C–19C] a form of strong ale.

huffer *n.*[1] [HUFF *v.* (1)] [mid-17C–18C] a bully, a braggart, a boaster.

huffer *n.*[2] [HUFF *v.* (2)] [1960s+] (*drugs*) an inhalant abuser.

huffish *adj. see* HUFFY *adj.*

huff it *v. see* HOOF *v.* (1).

huffle *v.* [SE *huff*, to blow; 'a piece of bestiality too filthy for explanation' (Grose, 1785)] [late 17C–18C] to fellate; to perform frottage with the armpit.

huff-snuff *n.* [his swaggering, threatening presence; Urquhart translates French *Lifrelofres*, synon. used for Germans or Swiss; the editor adds 'Here it is a buffooning term for an impertinent philosopher'] [late 16C–mid-18C] a bully, a braggart.

huffy *adj.* (*also* **huffish**) [HUFF *n.* (2)] [late 17C+] angry, bad-tempered; thus adv. *huffily*.

hufty-tufty *n.* (*also* **hufty, huftie-tuftie**) [HUFTY-TUFTY *adj.*] [17C] a swaggering, boastful individual.

hufty-tufty *adj.* [HUFF *v.* (1) + redup.] [late 16C–17C] swaggering, boastful.

hug, the *n.* [SE *hug*, to grasp tightly] [mid-19C] (*UK Und.*) the act of garrotting, i.e. sneaking up on a victim, choking them from behind with a forearm across the throat and rifling their pockets with the free hand.

IN PHRASES

❑ **put the hug on** *v.* (*also* **put on the hug**) [mid-19C+] to choke, to throttle.

hug *v.* [HUG, THE *n.*] [mid-19C] (*US*) to choke.

SE in slang uses

IN COMPOUNDS

❑ **hug-booby** *n.* [BOOBY *n.*[1] (1)] [late 17C–18C] a pej. term for a married man. ❑ **hug-drug** *n.* [its effects; the drug makes users want to touch everyone around them] [1980s+] (*drugs*) MDMA.

IN PHRASES

❑ **hug brown bess** *v. see under* BROWN BESS *n.* ❑ **hug the hog** *v. see under* HOG *n.* ❑ **hug the porcelain god/goddess** *v. see* KISS THE PORCELAIN GOD *under* PORCELAIN GOD *n.*

hugag *n. see* HEWGAG *n.*

huge *adj.* (*also* **hugeacious, hugeous**) [mid-19C; 1950s+] (*US*) wonderful, great, impressive.

huggar *adj.* (*also* **hugar**) [SE *hugger-mugger*, confused, disorderly] [mid-19C] (*UK Und.*) drunk.

hugger *n. see* TREE-HUGGER *under* TREE *n.*

hugger-mugger *n.*

IN PHRASES

❑ **in hugger-mugger** *adv.* [SE *hugger-mugger*, concealment, secrecy] [early 16C–early 19C] secretly, clandestinely.

huggle-my-buff *n.* [mid-18C] a form of mixed, hot drink.

huggy-bear *v.* [1960s+] (*US*) to cuddle.

hughey *n. see* HUEY *n.*[1].

Hughie *n.* (*also* **Huey**) [echoic of the noise of vomiting] [1950s+] (*US/Aus.*) used in phrs. pertaining to vomiting.

IN PHRASES

❑ **call (for) Hughie** *v.* (*also* **call (for) Bill**) [1960s+] (*UK society*) to vomit. ❑ **cry Hughie** *v.* (*also* **talk to Huey**) [1960s+] to vomit.

hugh prowler *n.* [generic use of proper name *Hugh* + SE *prowler*] [16C] a generic nickname for a small-time thief.

hugmatee *n.* [? SE *hug me t'ye*, hug me to you] [late 17C–early 18C] a type of ale.

hugs and kisses *n.* [rhy. sl. = MISSUS *n.*] [20C+] one's wife.

hulahaka *n.* [2000s] (*N.Z.*) a person of mixed Maori and Pacific Island descent.

hula raider *n.* [play on SE *hula-hoop*/HOOP *n.* (2b)] [1990s+] a male homosexual.

hulk *n.* [SE *hulk*, a big, unwieldy person; popularized by the 1962 comic-book character, the *Incredible Hulk*, created by Stan Lee and Jack Kirby] **1** [early 19C–1920s] (*US*) the body, the torso. **2** [1940s+] (*US*) a large, muscular man.

IN PHRASES

❑ **hulk out** *v.* [1980s] to increase one's musculature through exercise.

hulk *v.* [mid-19C] to hang about in the hope of an invitation.

hulked *adj.* [HULK *n.*; the *Incredible Hulk* would turn into his superhero form only when emotionally aroused] [1980s+] (*US campus*) angry.

hull-cheese *n.* [orig. Yorks. dial. *hull-cheese*, 'the strong ale of Hull' (*EDD*)] [17C] malt liquor and water; thus *eat hull-cheese*, to become drunk.

hully *n.* [1970s+] (*US black*) an especially fat person.

hully chee! *excl. see* GEE! *excl.*

hully gee! *excl. see* GEE! *excl.*

hully-gully *n.* [SE *hully-gully*, a form of dance, based on the *frug*; thus a fan of the dance] [1960s+] (*W.I.*) **1** a young ruffian. **2** a playboy.

hulverhead *n.* [Norfolk dial. *hulver*, holly; the wood of a holly bush is notably hard] [17C–early 19C] a fool.

hulver-headed *adj.* [HULVERHEAD *n.*] [17C–early 19C] stupid.

hum *n.*[1] [abbr. HUMMING ALE *n.*] [17C–18C] strong beer.

hum *n.*[2] [abbr. SE *humbug*] **1** [mid-18C–19C] nonsense, a trick, a hoax; a whispered lie. **2** [mid-19C] (*UK Und.*) a liar, equated in all recorded citations with a Methodist [also HUM-BOX *n.*]. **3** [late 19C] something unpleasant. **4** [1910s–30s] (*Aus.*) a cadger, a scrounger; thus *on the hum*, begging, cadging.

hum *n.*[3] [? their mumbling or 'humming' of prayers, hymns or responses; ? abbr. SE *humble*] [late 18C–mid-19C] a member of a church congregation.

hum *n.*[4] [HUM *v.*[2]] [late 19C+] an unpleasant smell.

hum *n.*[5] [var. on BUZZ *n.* (3c)] [1970s+] (*US drugs*) a mild intoxication from drug use.

hum *v.*[1] [SE *humbug*] **1** [late 17C–mid-19C] to trick, to hoax, to humbug; thus *humming*, teasing, hoaxing, fooling. **2** [late 19C+] (*Aus.*) (*also* **humm**) to scrounge, to borrow with no intention of giving back.

IN COMPOUNDS

❑ **hum job** *n.* [JOB *n.*[2] (2)] [1980s+] a deception.

hum *v.*[2] ['the humming of fermentation in an active manure heap' (Ware)] [late 19C+] to smell disgusting; lit. and fig.

hum *v.*[3] [HUMMER *n.*[6]] [1960s] (*US Und.*) to arrest on false charges.

hum *v.*[4] [abbr. HUMMER *n.*[8]] [1960s+] to give fellatio.

IN COMPOUNDS

❑ **hum job** *n.* [JOB *n.*[2] (2)] [1960s+] (*US*) fellatio, which is intensified by the fellator humming as he/she sucks.

humangous *adj. see* HUMONGOUS *adj.*

humble *n.* **1** [1940s+] (*US Und.*) an arrest on false or petty charges [var. on HUMMER *n.*[6]]. **2** [1950s+] (*US black*) (*also* **humbolt, hummel**) a self-defeating act; any situation that puts one at a disadvantage.

SE in slang uses

IN PHRASES

❑ **one's humble** [SE *your humble servant*] [late 19C–1900s] a person, as *your humble, his humble* etc.

hum-box *n.* [the preacher's droning tones] **1** [early 18C–mid-19C] a pulpit. **2** [mid-19C] (*US*) an auctioneer's rostrum.

IN COMPOUNDS

❑ **hum-box patterer** *n.* [ironic use of PATTERER *n.* (2)] [mid-19C] a preacher.

humbug *n.* (*also* **hombug**) [ety. unknown; 'facts as to its origin appear to have been lost, even before the word became common enough to excite attention' (*OED*). Hotten (1859) traces the first use back to c.1735, finding it in Ferdinando Killigrew's *The Universal Jester* (the *OED* dates this edn to 1754), where it is cited in a list of 'merry conceits, facetious drolleries, &c., clenchers, closers, closures, bon-mots and humbugs'. He also notes that the mid-18C radical Orator Henley was sometimes nicknamed 'Orator Humbug'. As to ety., he suggests either *hum* or the German town of Hamburg, 'from which town so many false bulletins and reports came during the war in the last century'. After 1800 its use spread 'in periodical literature, and in novels not written by squeamish or over-precise authors'. However, note HUMMER *n.*[1] (1), an obvious lie, is earlier] **1** [mid-18C+] a trick, a hoax, an imposture. **2** [early 19C+] nonsense, esp. moralizing hypocrisy. **3** [early 19C+] one who employs such ploys, a hypocrite. **4** [mid-19C+] (*US; later use US black*) anything worrying, complicated, unpleasant, offensive, troublesome or a misunderstanding, esp. if trivial. **5** [1960s+] (*US black*) a fight. **6** [1970s] (*US black*) a gang. **7** [1970s+] (*US Und.*) a false arrest on trumped-up charges [var. on HUMMER *n.*[6]].

humbug *v.* [HUMBUG *n.*] **1** [mid-18C+] to cheat, to delude, to deceive; thus *humbuggery*, cheating, deception. **2** [mid-19C] to waste time talking. **3** [1960s+] (*US black*) to fight, to act tough; thus *humbugger*, a thug, a fighter; *humbugging*, fighting, brawling.

IN PHRASES

❑ **humbug about** *v.* [19C] to play the fool; to waste (someone's) time. ❑ **humbug into** *v.* [19C+] to persuade into doing something.

humbug! *excl.* [HUMBUG *n.* (2)] [early 19C+] nonsense! rubbish!

humbugger *n.* [HUMBUG *v.*] [mid-18C–19C] **1** a cheat. **2** a hoaxer. **3** one who 'plays about' all the time.

humbugging *adj.* [HUMBUG *v.* + sfx *-ing*] **1** [mid-18C+] hoaxing, swindling, deceiving. **2** [late 19C] hypocritical.

hum cap *n.* [late 17C–19C] very old, very strong beer.

humdinger *n.* [? HUMMER *n.*[1] (4) + DING *v.*[1] (1); note, the earliest (print) uses are either two words or include a hyphen] [20C+] (*orig. US*) a remarkable and excellent object, event or person.

humdinging *adj.* [HUMDINGER *n.*] [20C+] extraordinary, first-rate.

humdrum *n.* [SE *humdrum*, a dull, monotonous person; ult. SE *hum*, to murmur on] **1** [17C–early 19C] a wife, a husband. **2** [18C–19C] a parson.

humdudgeon *n.* (*also* **humdurgeon**) [? HUMBUG *n.* (1) + SE *dudgeon*, ill humour] [late 18C–mid-19C] any imaginary illness, low spirits; thus *humdurgeoned*, annoyed.

humgumptious *adj.* [fanciful formation] **1** [early–mid-19C] artful, cunning, knowing; thus *humgumption*, a pretence of knowledge. **2** [1910s] (*US*) fine, grand, pretentious.

humm *v. see* HUM *v.*[1] (2).

hummal-hack *n.* [SE *humble* + *hack*, implying availability for hire] [mid-19C] (*UK Und.*) a curate.

hummel *n. see* HUMBLE *n.* (2).

Hummer *n.* [1990s+] (*US*) a Humvee military vehicle, also produced for civilian use.

hummer *n.*[1] [HUMMING *adj.* (2)] **1** [late 17C–early 19C] an obvious lie. **2** [late 17C+] a very energetic or lively person, a powerful lively thing. **3** [late 18C] a liar. **4** [late 19C+] something or someone exceptional of their type. **5** [2000s] an erection.

hummer *n.*[2] [HUMBUG *n.* (1)] **1** [mid-18C–early 19C] a cheat, an imposter. **2** [1950s–70s] (*US black*) something deceptive, a minor or insignificant mistake.

hummer *n.*[3]

IN PHRASES

❑ **on the hummer** [ety. unknown; ? the sound of malfunctioning machinery, ext. to the human context] [20C+] **1** (*US*) of machinery, out of order. **2** (*US*) of a person, feeling unwell, unhappy, annoyed. **3** (*US*) at a disadvantage. **4** (*US tramp*) living comfortably as a tramp [? SE *humming along*].

hummer *n.*[4] [HUM *v.*[2]] [1900s] one who smells.

hummer *n.*[5] [HUM *v.*[1]] **1** [1910s–40s] (*Aus.*) a scrounger. **2** [1960s–70s] (*US campus*) a stupid or inconsequential person.

hummer *n.*[6] [HUMMER *n.*[1]] [1930s+] (*Und.*) an arrest on false or petty charges.

hummer *n.*[7] [? link to HUM *n.*[1] or HUMDINGER *n.*] [1960s+] (*US*) a heavy drinking session.

hummer *n.*[8] [1970s+] (*US*) fellatio, esp. when the testicles are held in the mouth and the woman hums; thus in fig. use.

humming *n. see* HUM *v.*[1] (1).

humming *adj.* [? SE *hum*, i.e. sense 1 causes a humming in the drinker's head, while sense 2 is so big it virtually hums] **1** [mid-17C–mid-19C] of liquor, strong, frothing, esp. in HUMMING ALE *n.* **2** [mid-17C+] notably large or active, energetic, intense.

IN COMPOUNDS

❑ **humming ale** *n. see* separate entry. ❑ **humming bub** *n. see* BUB *n.*[1]. ❑ **humming gee** *n.* [1930s] (*US drugs*) an opium pipe. ❑ **humming October** *n.* [early 18C–19C] very strong ale, made from the new season's hops.

humming ale *n.* (*also* **humming beer, ...bub, ...liquor, ...punch, ...stuff, ...tipple**) [HUMMING *adj.* (1) + BUB *n.*[1] (1)/ STUFF *n.* (5a)/TIPPLE *n.* (1)] [mid-17C–mid-19C] strong beer.

humming bird *n.* [electricity hums] [late 19C–1930s] (*US prison*) **1** a type of torture using electricity. **2** the electric chair.

hummum *n.* [Arabic *hammam*, a hot or Turkish bath. The original *Hummum* was set up in Covent Garden in 1631; it later became a hotel] [late 17C–early 19C] a brothel.

humongous *adj.* (*also* **humangous, humongeous, humongoid, humungo, humungous**) [sugg. by SE *huge/ monstrous/tremendous*] [1960s+] (*orig. US*) enormous, outsized, huge.

Hump, the *n.* [1920s–30s] (*US tramp*) the Rockies; thus *go over the Hump*, to cross the Rockies on one's trek from east coast to west.

hump *n.*[1] **1** [late 19C+] constr. with *the*, a fit of bad-humour, a sulk; usu. as *GET THE HUMP* below [abbr. SE phr. *hump the back*, to sulk]. **2** [1910s+] (*US Und.*) the midpoint of one's prison sentence [image of the hump as a midpoint]. **3** (*orig. US*) in sexual contexts [HUMP *v.*[1] (1); the physical movement of 'missionary position' intercourse]. (**a**) [1910s+] an act of sexual intercourse. (**b**) [1910s+] (*US*) playing on sense 3a, a semi-euph. for FUCK *n.* (2a), e.g. *I don't give a hump.* (**c**) [1920s+] a person, usu. a woman, considered purely as a sexual object. (**d**) [1940s–50s] (*US prison*) a (passive) male homosexual. **4** with ref. to the defining physical aspect of the zoological camel. (**a**) [1910s+] (*Aus.*) a camel. (**b**) [1920s+] (*US*) a Camel (brandname) cigarette. **5** [1950s+] as a person. (**a**) a contemptible person, esp. a man. (**b**) a general term for a person, basically a peasant or manual worker. **6** *see HUMP DAY* below.

IN COMPOUNDS

❑ **hump house** *n.* [HOUSE *n.*[1] (1)] [1920s] (*US*) a brothel. ❑ **hump-nutty** *adj.* [NUTTY *adj.*[2]] [1920s] (*US*) obsessed with sex.

IN PHRASES

❑ **blow one's hump** *v.* [1950s+] to reach orgasm. ❑ **dry hump** *see* separate entries. ❑ **get the hump** *v.* (*also* **capture the hump, get the humps, take the hump**) [mid-19C+] **1** to be depressed, miserable. **2** to be over-sensitive or 'touchy', thus angry. ❑ **give someone the hump** *v.* [mid-19C+] to annoy, to irritate. ❑ **have a hump in one's back** *v.* [1990s+] (*US black*) of a man, to be in the middle of sexual intercourse. ❑ **have one's hump up** *v.* [mid-19C] to be in a bad mood. ❑ **make a hump in one's back** *v.* [the missionary position] [1960s] of a man, to have sexual intercourse. ❑ **on the hump** [1980s+] having sexual intercourse. ❑ **peddle one's hump** *v. see PEDDLE ONE'S ASS under* PEDDLE *v.* ❑ **throw someone a hump** *v.* [1950s+] to have sexual intercourse with someone.

IN EXCLAMATIONS

❑ **my hump!** [late 17C+] a general excl. of disdain, dismissal, arrogant contempt.

SE in slang uses

IN COMPOUNDS

❑ **hump day** *n.* (*also* **hump, hump night**) [SE *hump*, the critical point of an undertaking. Once Wednesday has passed one is coasting 'downhill' towards the weekend] [1950s+] (*US*) Wednesday, the middle of the week.

IN PHRASES

❑ **bust one's hump** *v.* [1950s+] (*US*) to work very hard. ❑ **bust someone's hump** *v.* [1970s+] (*US*) to harass, to annoy, to persecute. ❑ **crawl someone's hump** *v.* [CRAWL *v.*[2] (3)] [19C+] (*US*) to attack, to assault. ❑ **get a hump on** *v.* [one *humps* one's back with effort] [late 19C+] (*US*) to hurry, to exert oneself. ❑ **get one's hump up** *v.* [the way a cat arches its back when angry or threatened] [mid-19C; 1950s] to get in a temper, to become irritated. ❑ **go over the hump** *v.* **1** [1940s] to finish a job. **2** [1940s+] (*US*) to pass one's prime, to decline in ability. **3** *see* BLOW ONE'S HUMP *v.* ❑ **hit the hump** *v.* [1910s] (*US prison*) to make an escape attempt. ❑ **over the hump** **1** [1910s+] (*orig. US*) over the worst, past the midpoint of a job or experience, usu. an unpleasant one. **2** [1940s–60s] gone beyond return or reversal. **3** [1950s] (*US drugs*) enjoying the peak of a drug experience.

hump *n.*[2] [HUMP *v.*[1] (2b)] [1970s+] (*US*) an arduous journey; hard walking.

hump *v.*[1] **1** [mid-17C+] to have sexual intercourse [the *hump* in the man's back, when in the 'missionary position'; orig. UK until early 19C, then to the US early 20C; revived in UK mid-20C+]. **2** lit. + fig. uses of SE *hump*, to make a hump in one's back f. effort etc. (**a**) [mid-19C–1920s] (*US*) to take pride in oneself, to fancy oneself. (**b**) [mid-19C+] (*US*) to exert oneself, to work hard; as imp. *hump yourself!*, get on with it! (**c**) [mid-19C+] (*US*) to travel fast, of people or objects. (**d**) [mid-19C+] (*US/ Aus.*) to carry heavy objects; esp. in milit. use, patrolling with a heavy pack, weapon, supplies etc. (**e**) [late 19C+] (*orig. Aus.*) often constr. with *it*, to tramp, to trudge, to go on foot; also in fig. use. **3** fig. uses of sense 1 on model of FUCK *v.* (2). (**a**) [mid–late 19C] to botch, to spoil. (**b**) [late 19C] (*US*) to beat up. (**c**) [20C+] (*US*) to act lazily, to loaf around, to be idle. (**d**) [1940s+] as a dismissive v. or excl. (**e**) [1950s+] to make someone else suffer, to exploit, to harm. (**f**) [1960s+] to suffer.

IN COMPOUNDS

❑ **humphead** *n.* [-HEAD *sfx* (1)] [1990s+] (*US*) a general term of abuse; synon. with FUCKHEAD *n.* ❑ **hump-me pumps** *n. see FUCK-ME SHOES under* FUCK-ME *adj.*

IN PHRASES

❑ **hump 'em and dump 'em** [DUMP *v.* (6)] [1980s+] a popular male catchphrase suggesting that seduction and then abandonment are the best ways of relating to women. ❑ **hump it** *v.* (*also* **hump off**) **1** [20C+] to leave. **2** [1920s] to die. ❑ **hump one's bluey/drum/Matilda/swag** *v. see under* relevant n.

hump *v.*[2] [HUMP *n.*[1] (1)] [20C+] to take offence.

humper *n.* [HUMP *v.*[1]] **1** [early 19C; 1970s+] a seducer. **2** [1900s] (*Aus.*) a vagrant. **3** [1960s+] a carrier of heavy objects, esp. in rock music use describing those who lift a band's equipment. **4** [1970s+] (*US*) a thing, poss. annoying. **5** [1970s+] (*US*) a hard-working person.

Humphrey *n.* [ety. unknown] [mid-19C] (*US Und.*) a coat with no pockets, just holes through which the thief passes his booty into concealed inner pockets or suspended bags.

humpie *n. see* HUMPY *n.*[1].

humping *n.* [HUMP *v.*[1]] [1950s+] sexual intercourse.

humping *adj.* [HUMP *v.*[1]; thus a euph. for FUCKING *adj.*] **1** [1940s+] (*US*) a general intensifier, positive or negative according to context. **2** [1980s+] (*US black*) very attractive.

humpsome *adj. see* HUMPY *adj.*[2] (2).

humpty *n.* (*also* **humpty-bump, humpty-hump, humpty-dumpty**) [HUMP *v.*[1]] [1980s+] sexual intercourse.

IN PHRASES

❑ **do the humpty-bump/hump** *v.* [1990s+] (*US campus*) to have sexual intercourse.

humpty *adj.*[1] [HUMP *n.*[1] (1)] [1990s+] irritated, tetchy.

humpty *adj.*[2] *see* HUMPTY-DUMPTY *adj.*

humpty *adj.*[3] *see* HUMPY *adj.*[1].

humpty-bump *n. see* HUMPTY *n.*

humpty-doo *adj. see* UMPTY-DOO *adj.*

humpty-dumpty *n.*[1] (*also* **humty dumty**) [redup.; the two liquors are 'humped together'] [late 17C–mid-19C] a hot drink made of ale and brandy boiled together.

humpty-dumpty *n.*[2] [abbr. *Humpty-Dumpty*, the nursery-rhyme character who, despite his posturing, 'fell off a wall'] **1** [late 18C–19C] a short, squat person. **2** [mid-19C] a hunchback. **3** [1920s+] (*US*) (*also* **humpty**) an outright failure, an incompetent person, esp. in sport.

humpty-dumpty *n.*[3] *see* HUMPTY *n.*

humpty-dumpty *adj.* (*also* **humpty**) [HUMPTY-DUMPTY *n.*[2]] **1** [mid-19C] of a person, short and thick. **2** [late 19C+] (*US*) generally down on one's luck, tiresome, incompetent, foolish, ridiculous, ill.

humpty-hump *n. see* HUMPTY *n.*

humpy *n.*[1] (*also* **humpie**) [their defining physical characteristic] **1** [mid-18C+] a hunchback; also used as a derog. name. **2** [1930s–40s] (*Aus.*) a camel. **3** [2000s] (*N.Z.*) a hump-backed whale.

humpy *n.*[2] [HUMP *v.*[1]] **1** [1920s] a sexually attractive woman. **2** [1970s+] (*US gay*) a good-looking man.

humpy *adj.*[1] (*also* **humpty**) [HUMPY *n.*[1] (1)] [late 19C+] (*US*) hunchbacked.

humpy *adj.*[2] [HUMP *n.*[1] (1)] **1** [late 19C+] depressing. **2** [1900s–10s] (*also* **humpsome**) depressed, miserable.

humpy *adj.*[3] [HUMP *v.*[1]] [1970s+] (*US gay*) good-looking; sexually attractive, often comb. with *number*.

humpy-pumpy *n. see* RUMPY-PUMPY *n.*

humty-dumty *n. see* HUMPTY-DUMPTY *n.*[1].

humungo/humungous *adj. see* HUMONGOUS *adj.*

Hun *n.* [Ger. *Hunnen*, one of an Asiatic race of warlike nomads, who invaded Europe *c.*375, and under their leader Attila (*c.*406–453), overran much of Europe *c.*450. The original Huns were the Chinese *Hiong-nu* or *Han*. The modern use originated during WW1 and stemmed directly from the speech made by Kaiser Wilhelm II to German troops setting sail for China on 27 July 1900: 'No quarter will be given, no prisoners will be taken. Let all who fall into your hands be at your mercy. Just as the Huns a thousand years ago...gained a reputation in virtue of which they still live in historical tradition, so may the name of Germany become known in...China that no Chinaman will ever again even dare to look askance at a German'] **1** [19C+] a derog. term for a German, the German army. **2** [1990s+] (*Scot.*) a Protestant, thus Glasgow Rangers FC (trad. a Protesant team).

Hun *adj.* (*also* **Hunnish, Hunny**) [1910s+] German; thus *Hunland*, Germany.

hun *n.* [abbr.] **1** [late 19C] an attractive, wonderful thing or person [HONEY *n.*[1] (1c)]. **2** [late 19C+] a *hundred*, $100.

hunch *v.* [? SE *hunch*, either one's hand or ? one's back in sense 2] **1** [1920s] (*US black*) to grab and squeeze a woman's breast. **2** [1940s–50s] (*US*) to betray, to doublecross.

hunchy *n.* [its hump] [1910s–30s] (*Aus.*) a camel.

hundred *n.* [1990s+] (*Aus. drugs*) A$100 worth of heroin.

hundred to eight *n.* [rhy. sl.] [1990s+] a plate.

hung *adj.* **1** in the context of the body. (**a**) [mid-17C; 1930s+] having a large penis; often in phr. *hung like a* — (see below); thus *underhung*, having a small penis. (**b**) [1950s+] having large breasts. **2** physically run down. (**a**) [1940s+] (*US*) suffering from a minor illness, e.g. a hangover [SE *hungover*]. (**b**) [1950s] drunk. **3** in emotional contexts [HUNG UP *adj.*]. (**a**) [1940s+] (*orig. US*) depressed or upset. (**b**) [1950s+] obsessed with or infatuated by. (**c**) [1960s+] in trouble, facing problems.

IN PHRASES

❑ **hung for** [1950s+] (*US teen*) in need of, lacking; thus *hung for bread*, in need of cash. ❑ **hung like a donkey** (*also* **hung like a bull, ...hoover hose, ...mule**) [1960s+] possessing a large penis. ❑ **hung like a doughnut** [1960s+] (*US gay*) describing a woman, i.e. one who has a vagina (a hole). ❑ **hung like a hamster** [2000s] possessing a very small penis. ❑ **hung like a horse** (*also* **hung like a showdog, ...stallion, ...stud (horse)**) **1** [1960s+] possessing a large penis; thus adj. *horse-hung*. **2** [1990s+] (*US*) having influence with the police. ❑ **hung like a humming bird** [1970s+] possessing a very small penis. ❑ **hung like a jack donkey** (*also* **hung like a jackass**) [1960s+] possessing a large penis. ❑ **hung like a mouse** (*also* **hung like a field mouse**) [1960s+] possessing an extremely small penis. ❑ **hung like a mule** *see* HUNG LIKE A DONKEY above. ❑ **hung like an ass** [17C] possessing a large penis. ❑ **hung like a (stud) mosquito** [1960s+] (*US*) possessing a very small penis. ❑ **hung low** [1990s+] (*US black*) equipped with a notably large penis. ❑ **hung out** **1** [1960s+] (*US campus*) obsessed with, fascinated by. **2** [1980s+] (*US drugs*) addicted. ❑ **hung to** [1950s–60s] (*US black*) obsessed with.

hungarian *n.* [pun on SE *hungry* + racial slur] [17C] a hungry person, a glutton.

hungarian *adj.* [for ety. *see* HUNGARIAN *n.*] **1** [late 17C–early 18C] thievish, marauding, needy, beggarly. **2** [1990s+] (*US campus*) hungry.

IN COMPOUNDS

❑ **Hungarian champagne** *n.* [racial slur] [1990s+] (*Aus.*) soda water.

hung beef *n.* [early 19C] a dried bull's penis, esp. when used as a whip.

hunger street *n.* (*also* **hungry-go-naked place, hungry gulch, ...hill, ...hollow, ...lane, ...ridge, ...street**) [20C+] (*US*) the poor area of a town.

hungries *n.* [SE *hungry*] [1970s+] (*US*) an appetite, esp. one developed after smoking marijuana.

hungry *adj.* [intensified version of SE *hungry*, 'having or characterized by a strong desire or craving' (*OED*)] **1** [mid-19C+] ambitious, enthusiastic, driven. **2** [20C+] (*Aus.*) mean, grasping, stingy, obsessed with money; often used as a nickname, e.g. Hungry Scott. **3** [20C+] (*US campus*) sexually excited. **4** [1950s] (*US drugs*) in need of narcotics.

IN COMPOUNDS

❑ **hungry croaker** *n.* [CROAKER *n.*[5] (1)] [1950s+] (*drugs*) a doctor who, for one reason or another, is willing to prescribe drugs for any user who asks for them.

SE in slang uses

IN COMPOUNDS

❑ **hungry-belly** *adj.* [20C+] (*W.I.*) esp. of children, starving, malnourished. ❑ **hungry hill/gulch/hollow/lane** *n. see* HUNGER STREET *n.* ❑ **hungry mile** *n.* [1930s–70s] (*Aus.*) a stretch of Sussex Street, Sydney, frequented by dockers in search of work. ❑ **hungry ridge/street** *n. see* HUNGER STREET *n.* ❑ **hungry track** *n.* [late 19C+] (*Aus.*) a section of the road on which a vagrant finds it hard to find either food or work.

IN PHRASES

❑ **hungry enough to eat the ass out of a dead skunk** [1950s+] (*Can.*) very hungry; also in vars. ❑ **hungry-go-naked place** *n. see* HUNGER STREET *n.*

-hungry *sfx* [HUNGRY *adj.* (1)] [20C+] keen, desperate for.

hung up *n.* [SE *hang* but poss. inference of HUNG UP *adj.*] [2000s] (*US prison*) a prisoner who tries to hang himself.

hung up *adj.* **1** [late 19C+] (*orig. society*) self-obsessed, snobbish. **2** [late 19C+] delayed or hindered. **3** [20C+] desperate, poor, in trouble. **4** [1940s+] (*orig. US*) unhappy, depressed, neurotic, anxious. **5** [1940s+] (*orig. US*) (*also* **hung on**) obsessed or infatuated. **6** [1940s+] (*US drugs*) intoxicated. **7** [1940s+] (*US drugs*) addicted.

IN PHRASES

❑ **hung up on** [1940s+] **1** obsessed with, esp. in love with someone. **2** (*US drugs*) addicted to.

hunk *n.*[1] [19C US dial. *hunk*, bulk; a large body] **1** [19C+] (*US*) a country bumpkin, a peasant, a farmer. **2** [late 19C+] a dull, slow, stupid person. **3** [1930s+] (*US*) sexual intercourse, thus a sexual partner, usu. a woman. **4** [1940s+] (*also* **hunker**) a large man or woman. **5** [1940s+] (*US*) a sexually attractive woman. **6** [1940s+] (*US*) an attractive, rugged, well-built man, poss. somewhat unintelligent [appears to have been coined as a description of the film star Victor Mature, first described as a 'beautiful hunk of a man' and a 'wonderful hunk of a man' by Sheilah Graham in a syndicated column on 3/4/1941].

hunk *n.*[2] [abbr. SE *Hungarian* as generic for all Central European immigrants] **1** [late 19C+] (*US*) an immigrant from Central Europe, e.g. a Hungarian, Lithuanian, Slav, Pole; thus *hunky town*, the area of a town in which such immigrants congregate. **2** *see* HUNKY *n.* (2).

hunk *adj.* [SAmE *hunk*, in a safe or good position or condition, all right; ult. E.Fris. *hunk*, corner, nook, retreat, home in a game; thus SE adv. *hunk*, in a safe position, all right] [mid-19C–1930s] (*US*) satisfactory, fine.

IN PHRASES

❑ **get hunk (with)** *v.* [mid-19C–1950s] (*US*) to get even with. ❑ **go the hunks** *v.* [late 19C+] (*US*) to take equal shares.

hunk *v.* [1990s+] (*US*) to vomit.

hunker *n. see* HUNK *n.*[1] (4).

hunker *v.* [one fig. *hunkers* down awaiting orders] [20C+] (*Ulster*) to act as a parasite, to curry favour with.

hunker-slider *n.* [HUNKER-SLIDING *n.*] [20C+] (*US/Irish*) one who acts deceitfully.

hunker-sliding *n.* [Scot. *hunkersliding*, dishonourable or shifty conduct] [20C+] (*US/Irish*) acting unfairly, deceitfully.

hunkey *adj. see* HUNKY *adj.*[1] (1).

hunkey-dorey/hunkidori *adj. see* HUNKY-DORY *adj.* (1).

hunkie *see under* HUNKY.

hunking *adj.* [HUNK *n.*[1]] [1980s+] **1** (*US campus*) large. **2** attractively well-built.

hunko *adj.* [HUNKY *adj.*[4]] [1960s+] (*US*) of someone's physique, short, stocky.

hunk of ass/arse/butt *n. see* PIECE OF ASS *under* PIECE *n.*

hunk of meat *n. see* PIECE OF MEAT *under* PIECE *n.*

hunks *n.* [ety. unknown; ? *Hunks*, the name of a well-known bear, kept in 17C London for baiting: bearlike, the miser 'hugs' his money and a *bear* (cf. *bear with a sore head*) is a grumpy person] **1** [17C–1920s] a miser, also a surly person. **2** [19C–1920s] (*US*) a worthless, good-for-nothing person.

hunkum-bunkum *adj.* [? HUNKY *adj.*[1] (1)] [mid-19C–1910s] (*US*) excellent.

hunky *n.* (*also* **hunkie**) [abbr. BOHUNK *n.*] **1** [late 19C+] (*US*) an immigrant from Central Europe, e.g. a Hungarian, Austrian, Lithuanian, Slav, Pole; thus *Hunky Town*, the area of a town in which such immigrants congregate. **2** [1920s+] (*US*) (*also* **honky, hunk**) a derog. term for a black person. **3** [1950s+] (*US black*) a derog. term for a white person.

hunky *adj.*[1] [abbr. HUNKY-DORY *adj.*] **1** [mid-19C+] (*US*) (*also* **hunkey**) excellent, satisfactory, lucky, pleasurable, in good condition, 'safe and sound'. **2** [late 19C–1910s] (*US*) friendly, ingratiating.

hunky *adj.*[2] (*also* **hunkie**) [HUNKY *n.* (1)] [20C+] pertaining to an immigrant from Central Europe, e.g. a Hungarian, Lithuanian, Slav, Pole.

hunky *adj.*[3] [1930s] (*US*) aggressive.

hunky *adj.*[4] [HUNK *n.*[1] (6)] [1970s+] of a man, good-looking, well-built.

hunky chunk *v.* [ety. unknown; link to SE *hunk/chunk*] [mid-19C] (*US Und.*) to steal food.

hunky-doke *adj.* [HUNKY-DORY *adj.* (1) + OKEY-DOKE! *excl.*] [1940s] in good/proper order; functioning as required.

hunky-doodle *adj.* [var. on HUNKY-DORY *adj.*] [1900s] (*US*) fine, satisfactory.

hunky-dory *adj.* [Du. *hunk*, home (in a game; the word was first used by youngsters in New Amsterdam and thence New York); thus adv. *hunk*, in a safe position, all right; *dory*, ety. unknown; ? redup. Note Quinion *World Wide Words* 27/11/99: HUNKY-DORY [...] The suggestion is that the term was introduced in America about 1865 by a popular variety performer named Japanese Tommy. [...] it is said to have been sailors' slang for a street in Yokohama named Honki-Dori, whose inhabitants "catered for the pleasures of sailors", as he puts it. The word was a play on the existing word 'hunky' for something that was fine, splendid or satisfactory, which itself probably derives from the adjective 'hunk' with much the same sense. That can be traced back to the 1840s and has links to another reduplicated term, 'hunkum-bunkum'.] (*orig. US*) **1** [mid-19C+] (*also* **honky-dooley, hunkey-dorey, hunkidori**) wonderful, excellent, first-rate. **2** [1980s+] close, cosy, intimate; thus in ironic use, unsophisticated.

hunky-dory *adv.* [HUNKY-DORY *adj.*] [20C+] in an excellent manner.

hunky-dunky *adj.* [var. on HUNKY-DORY *adj.*] [1950s+] (*US*) fine, excellent.

hunky-peroodlum *adj.* [1900s] very attractive and sexually inviting.

Hunnish/Hunny *adj. see* HUN *adj.*

hunt *v.* **1** [20C+] (*Aus.*) to drive away, to chase off. **2** [1970s+] (*US campus/gay*) to search for a partner for romance or sex.

SE in slang uses

IN COMPOUNDS

❑ **hunt-about** *n.* [mid-19C–1920s] **1** a prostitute. **2** an interfering, meddlesome gossip. ❑ **hunt-buggy** *n.* [BUGGY *n.*[2] (1)] [1960s] (*US gang*) a police car.

IN PHRASES

❑ **hunt a placebo** *v. see under* PLACEBO *n.* ❑ **hunt a tavern fox** *v.* [pun on SE *fox*/FOXED *adj.*] [mid–late 17C] to get drunk. ❑ **hunt grass** *v.* [var. on GO TO GRASS *v.* (1)] [mid–late 19C] (*US*) **1** to be knocked down. **2** to be extremely confused. ❑ **hunt one's hole** *v. see under* HOLE *n.*[1]. ❑ **hunt the dummy** *v. see under* DUMMY *n.*[2]. ❑ **hunt the elephant** *v. see SEE THE ELEPHANT under* ELEPHANT *n.* ❑ **hunt the hay** *v. see under* HAY *n.* ❑ **hunt the squirrel** *v.* [the coaches veer from side to side as does a frightened squirrel] [late 18C–19C] of two coachmen, to attempt to upset each other's vehicles as they race along a public road, typically one being a hackney coach, the other a stage. ❑ **hunt up a cow** *v. see CHASE (UP) A COW under* COW *n.*[1].

hunter *n.* [19C] the penis.

hunting *n.* (*also* **squirrel hunting**) [late 17C–mid-19C] (*UK Und.*) searching for a victim whether for a theft, a confidence trick etc.

SE in slang uses

IN COMPOUNDS

❑ **hunting license** *n.* [20C+] (*US prison*) a commitment to kill an inmate, often ordered by a gang leader.

hunyak *n.* (*also* **honyock, honyocker, hunyok**) [? *Hun(garian)* + (Pol)*ack*] **1** [20C+] (*US*) an immigrant from central or eastern Europe, e.g. a Hungarian or Pole. **2** [1920s+] (*US*) an ignorant, inexperienced or unsophisticated person, esp. a rustic, a peasant.

hura *n.* [Sp.] [1960s+] (*US*) the police.

hurdy-gurdy *n.* (*also* **hurdy, hurdy-gurdy house**) [SE *hurdy-gurdy*, i.e. the sound of the instrument] **1** [mid-19C+] (*US*) a dancehall, a dancer in a dancehall; thus *hurdy-gurdy house, hurdy-gurdy girl*. **2** [1940s] (*US Und.*) Cedar Rapids, Iowa.

hurdy-gurdy *adj.* [HURDY-GURDY *n.* (1)] [1970s] noisy, brash, bright, i.e. mimicking the image of a thronging dancehall.

hurkle *v.* [dial. *hurkle*, to crouch, to squat, to shrink from the cold] [20C+] (*Ulster*) to look on rather than offer help when others are working.

hurl *v.* [1950s+] (*Aus./S.Afr.*) **1** to vomit. **2** in fig. use, to enrage, to make sick.

hurler *n.* [? SE *hurl*, to toss, i.e. what is tossed into the glass] [20C+] (*Irish*) a measure of whisky.

hurley foot *n.* [? Irish game of *hurley/hurling*, in which the ball is hit with a stick or club] [20C+] (*Irish*) a club-foot.

hurrah *n.* (*also* **hoorah**) [SE *hurrah!*] **1** [mid-19C+] (*US*) a boisterous party, a ruckus, uproariousness. **2** [1970s] insincere, effusive talk.

IN COMPOUNDS

❑ **hurrah boys** *n.* [mid-19C–1920s] (*US*) **1** a supporter, a fan. **2** college students [the ritualized college cheers popular among students]. ❑ **hurrah clothes** *n.* [i.e. the wearing of such clothes to events at which one may applaud] [20C+] (*orig. US*) one's best clothes, one's 'Sunday suit'. ❑ **hurrah joint** *n.* [1930s] (*US*) a noisy, uproarious place, e.g. a nightclub.

IN PHRASES

❑ **on a (great) hurrah** **1** [late 19C] (*US*) on a spree. **2** [1900s–10s] (*Aus.*) in a rush, at speed, chivvying.

hurrah *adj.* (*also* **hoorah**) [HURRAH *n.*] [late 19C+] (*US*) **1** wild and disorderly. **2** boisterous, noisy.

hurrah *v.* (*also* **hoorah, hooraw**) [HURRAH *n.*] [20C+] (*US*) **1** to tease, to harass. **2** to cause a commotion, to raise a ruckus.

hurrah's nest *n.* [*hurrah*, an imaginary bird] [early 19C+] (*US*) a confused, tangled or disorderly mess, a state of confusion or disorder.

hurray *adj.* see HOORAY *adj.*

hurricane deck *n.* [SE *hurricane-deck*, a light upper deck on a steamer] [mid-19C+] (*US*) the back of a horse or mule.

hurricane lamp *n.* [rhy. sl.] [20C+] a tramp.

hurroo *n.* see HOOROOSH *n.*

hurroo! *excl.* see HOOROO! *excl.* (2).

hurroosh *n.* see HOOROOSH *n.*

hurry-buggy *n.* [it 'hurries' one to prison] [1920s–40s] a police van.

hurry-come-up *n.* [1930s–60s] (*W.I.*) a parvenu, esp. with overtones of a bad reputation.

hurry-up *n.* **1** [20C+] anything or anyone that goes fast. **2** [20C+] an emergency, anything urgent. **3** [20C+] (*US*) a request for money; thus *on the hurry-up*, begging. **4** [1940s] (*US*) a romantic proposition. **5** [1970s–80s] (*N.Z. prison*) a reprimand, a telling-off.

IN COMPOUNDS

❑ **hurry-up wagon** *n.* (*also* **hurry-up van**) [the speed with which it is driven] [19C+] (*US*) a police van or car.

IN PHRASES

❑ **bit of a hurry-up** *n.* [1950s] (*Aus.*) a rushed piece of work. ❑ **give someone a bit of hurry-up** *v.* [20C+] (*Aus.*) to stimulate, to encourage to act more energetically. ❑ **on the hurry-up** [1950s+] at great speed, in a hurry.

hurry-up *adj.* [20C+] (*US*) urgent, in emergency.

hurry up the cakes *v.* see *under* CAKE *n.*[1].

hurry-whore *n.* [the speed with which she deals with a customer] [early–mid-17C] a street-walker.

hurt *n.*

IN PHRASES

❑ **put the hurt on** *v.* (*also* **put a hurting on, put a hurt on, put on a hurt, put the hurt to**) [1960s+] (*orig. US black*) to hurt deliberately, to assault physically and/or emotionally.

hurt *adj.* **1** [1960s+] (*US black/campus*) unattractive. **2** [1980s] (*US black/drugs*) extremely intoxicated by a given drug or hungover from alcohol excess.

hurt *v.* **1** [1900s] to be anxious or impatient. **2** [1910s+] (*US*) of an inanimate object, to cause problems for, to injure. **3** [1950s] (*UK Und.*) to wound severely, to kill. **4** [1950s+] (*drugs*) of a drug addict, to suffer the lack of their drug of choice. **5** [1960s+] of a person, to suffer; also ironic use.

IN PHRASES

❑ **hurt for** *v.* [1940s+] to want something desperately, usu. to alleviate current unhappiness.

hurting *n.*

IN PHRASES

❑ **put a hurting on** *v.* see PUT THE HURT ON *under* HURT *n.*

hurting *adj.* (*also* **hurting for**) [HURT *v.*] (*US*) **1** [1940s+] short of money. **2** [1950s+] generally miserable or in trouble. **3** [1950s+] (*drugs*) urgently needing narcotics to sustain one's regular dosage. **4** [1980s+] (*US campus*) (*also* **hurtin' cowboy**) drunk. **5** [1980s+] (*US campus*) bad, out of condition.

IN COMPOUNDS

❑ **hurting dance** *n.* (*also* **hurt dance**) [1950s+] (*orig. US*) sadness, frustration, jealousy, usu. in a relationship in which one person has another *doing a hurting dance*.

IN PHRASES

❑ **hurtin' for certain** [1950s+] (*US black*) **1** distressed, in trouble. **2** ugly, very unattractive. **3** in great need, esp. of drugs or sex.

hus *n.* [? HUSTLE *v.* (4)] **1** [1960s–70s] (*US*) a favour. **2** *see* HUSS *n.*

husband *n.* **1** [1930s+] the supposedly 'aggressive' partner of a homosexual couple. **2** *see* HUBBY *n.* (2).

SE in slang uses

IN COMPOUNDS

❑ **husband game** *n.* [mid-19C] (*US Und.*) a confidence trick where a prostitute has her 'husband' knock on the door after she has been paid but before she has performed. ❑ **husband's tea** *n.* [? a husband's inadequacy as opposed to that of a lover] [mid-19C] very weak tea.

husband and wife *n.* [rhy. sl.] [20C+] (*US*) a knife.

hush *n.* [early 18C; 1930s–40s] a bribe.

SE in slang uses

IN COMPOUNDS

❑ **hush-house** *n.* [coined by columnist Walter Winchell (1897–1972) but note *HUSH-SHOP* below] [1920s–40s] (*US*) a speakeasy. ❑ **hush money** *n.* see separate entry. ❑ **hush mouth** *see* separate entries. ❑ **hush-shop** *n.* (*also* **hush-crib**) [the sales are made 'on the hush'] [mid–late 19C] an unlicensed beer or liquor shop. ❑ **hush-up** *n.* [1920s] (*US*) a 'cover-up' of crime.

hush *v.* [SE *hush*, to silence] [early 18C–19C] (*UK Und.*) to murder.

hush-hush *n.* [SE *hush*, silence/*hush-hush*, most secret, undercover + ref. to HUSH *v.*] [1930s–60s] **1** (*US Und.*) a pistol with a silencer. **2** (*US*) secrecy. **3** (*US*) a secret.

hush money *n.* (*also* **hush dough**) [SE *hush*, silence] [18C+] a bribe paid to ensure that embarrassing facts are suppressed.

hush mouth *n.* [it shuts the drinker up] [1940s] (*US black*) a sip of whisky.

hush-mouth *adj.* [1920s] (*US black*) secret, silenced.

hush puppy *n.* [rhy. sl.] [1980s+] a YUPPIE *n.*

husk *n.* [1910s] (*US*) a well-built man.

husk *v.* [SE *husk*, to remove a shell] [1940s] (*US black*) to undress, to strip.

huskings *n.* [HUSK *v.*] [1940s] (*US black*) a pile of clothes, esp. those discarded immediately after undressing.

Husky *n.* (*also* **husky**) [SE *husky*, an Eskimo/Inuit dog; ult. 18C sp. *Ehuskemay*] [mid-19C–1940s] (*US*) **1** a derog. term for an Inuit. **2** a derog. term for the Inuit language.

huskylour *n.* [SE *husky*, dry (as a corn husk) + LOUR *n.*; thus lit. 'dry money', i.e. hard cash] [late 17C–19C] (*UK Und.*) a guinea.

huss *n.* (*also* **hus**) [abbr. HUSTLER *n.*] (*US black*) **1** [1950s] a fellow, a man, used in direct address. **2** [1960s] a smart, stylish man's suit.

huss *adj.* (*also* **hus**) [HUSS *n.* (2)] [1960s] (*US black*) smart, fashionable stylish.

hustle *n.* [HUSTLE *v.*] **1** [1940s+] (*orig. US Und.*) a swindle, a hoax, a get-rich-quick scheme. **2** [1940s+] (*US*) any means of survival, often providing little more than subsistence. **3** [1940s+] (*US black*) a job, a means of earning a living. **4** [1940s+] (*US black*) working as a pimp, prostitute or tramp. **5** [1970s+] (*US*) flattery, deception. **6** [1970s+] (*US*) a means of seduction, a pass. **7** [1970s+] (*US*) a criminal scheme or activity. **8** [2000s] toughness, aggression.

IN PHRASES

❑ **get a hustle on** *v.* **1** [late 19C–1930s] (*US*) to get moving, to get going, to get on with the job etc. **2** to sustain one's existence by whatever means available. ❑ **hard hustle** *n.* [1950s+] (*US*) any form of complex and thus potentially highly lucrative confidence trick. ❑ **on the hustle** [1940s+] (*US*) **1** living as a confidence trickster, a swindler. **2** working as a prostitute. **3** working hard.

SE in slang uses

IN COMPOUNDS

❑ **hustle-buggy** *n.* [1920s–30s] (*US*) a police car.

hustle *v.* (*also* **hussle**) [SE *hustle*, to push around or against, to jostle; ult. Du. *husselen*, *hutselen*, to shake, to toss] **1** [19C] to have sexual intercourse. **2** [mid-19C+] to practise swindling or petty theft. **3** [mid-19C+] (*orig. US*) (*also* **hassle**) to use one's initiative to obtain or secure; to live by one's wits. **4** [late 19C+] (*US*) to work hard, to make an effort. **5** [late 19C+] (*US*) to sell goods, esp. in an aggressive manner, to promote; thus in phrs. *hustle hash*, to work as a waiter or waitress; *hustle shoes*, to work as a shoe-shine; *hustle sheets*, to sell newspapers. **6** [late 19C+] (*US*) to work as a prostitute. **7** [20C+] to urge someone to work harder. **8** [20C+] to obtain money or some other commodity through begging. **9** [1910s] (*US prison*) to steal. **10** [1930s+] (*orig. US*) to deceive or to con. **11** [1940s+] (*US*) to make sexual advances. **12** [1960s+] to work as a male prostitute. **13** [1970s] to pimp. **14** [1970s+] (*drugs*) to attempt to obtain drug customers, to sell drugs.

IN PHRASES

❑ **hustle one's bustle** *v.* **1** [1930s+] to work as a prostitute. **2** [1970s+] to hurry.

hustler *n.* [HUSTLE *v.*] **1** [19C] (*US Und.*) one of a pickpocket gang. **2** [late 19C–1930s] (*US*) a racetrack tout. **3** [late 19C+] (*US*) a hard-working, ambitious person, also an energizer, one who exhorts his fellows to harder work, greater commitment. **4** [late 19C+] anyone who makes a living through their wits and ingenuity, rather than accepting the restraints of a conventional job; their occupations are often, but not invariably, criminal or virtually so. **5** [20C+] (*W.I.*) a confidence man, a well-dressed beggar. **6** [1910s+] (*Und.*) a pimp. **7** [1920s+] (*US*) a prostitute of either sex. **8** [1930s+] a gambler or player of pool, bowling etc, who uses skill and poss. cheating to make a living against lesser opponents. **9** [1960s+] (*US campus*) a man who succeeds in seducing women, a womanizer. **10** [1960s+] a tout.

IN PHRASES

❑ **hustlers don't call showdowns** [1960s+] (*US black*) a phr. meaning one who is on the receiving end of a hand-out does not cause trouble because that might terminate the flow of free gifts.

hustling *n.* [HUSTLE *v.*] **1** [early 19C+] street robbery; bag-snatching. **2** [late 19C+] selling objects, ideas, one's services etc, esp. in an aggressive manner. **3** [late 19C+] living by one's wits; also as adj. **4** [1920s+] working as a prostitute. **5** [1960s] (*US black*) making a nervous sign at someone. **6** [1960s+] cadging, begging.

IN COMPOUNDS

❑ **hustling-ass** *adj.* [-ASS *sfx*] [1980s+] (*US black*) aggressively self-aggrandizing, hard-working, self-promoting etc. ❑ **hustling broad** *n.* (*also* **hustling dame, ...girl, ...woman**) [BROAD *n.*[2] (2)/SE *dame*, *girl/woman*] [1930s+] (*US Und.*) a female prostitute.

hut *n.* **1** [1900s] (*US*) an apartment, a dwelling place; one's home. **2** [1920s+] (*US prison*) a cell.

hutch *n.* **1** [1900s–10s] (*Aus.*) a home, a house. **2** [1930s+] (*US*) an office, usu. small. **3** [1950s] (*US*) a nightclub.

hutu *n. see* HOOT *n.*[1].

huxter *n.* [? ext. of SE *huckster*, a small trader] [mid-19C] (*UK Und.*) money.

Hyde Park *n.* [rhy. sl. = NARK *n.* (1)] [20C+] an informer.

Hyde Park railings *n.* [the row of bones that make up such a breast resemble the fencing of the London park] [late 19C–1900s] a breast of mutton.

hydraulic *n.* [pun on SE *hydraulic jack*] [1960s+] (*Aus.*) a light-fingered person, who'll 'lift anything that isn't nailed down'.

hydraulics *n.* [rhy. sl. = BALLOCKS *n.* (3)] [1990s+] nonsense, rubbish.

hydro *n.* [abbr.; senses 2 and 3 ? the chemical process used in the manufacture] [1980s+] (*US drugs*) **1** hydroponically grown marijuana. **2** crack cocaine. **3** amphetamine.

hydroplug *n.* [HYDRO *n.* (1)] [1980s+] (*US drugs*) a pipe for smoking marijuana.

hyena *n.* [mid-19C–1950s] (*US*) a lazy or stupid person.

hygelo *n.* [ety. unknown; ? link to HIGH *adj.*[1] (2)] [1930s–50s] (*US drugs*) a narcotics addict.

hyke *v.* [CHI-IKE *v.* (2)] [late 19C–1900s] to attract someone's attention, to shout after someone.

hykey *n.* [? fig. use of HIKE *v.* (1)] [mid–late 19C] pride.

Hymie *n.* [the stereotypical Jewish name *Hyman*/Ger. name *Herman*] [20C+] (*orig. US*) **1** a derog. term for a Jew. **2** a derog. nickname for a German.

Hymie *adj.* [1970s+] (*orig. US*) used derog. of a Jew.

hymie *n.* **1** [1930s] (*US gay*) the anus. **2** [1930s–40s] (*US gay*) an adolescent lover/cook. **3** [1950s] (*US tramp*) sexual intercourse.

hymied *adj.* [HYMIE *n.* (1)] [2000s] (*US*) cheated.

Hymietown *n.* [HYMIE *n.* (1) + SE *town*] [1980s+] (*US*) a derog. nickname for New York City.

hymnslinger *n.* [late 19C] (*Aus.*) a preacher, a clergyman.

hyp *n.* **1** *see* HYPE *n.*[2]. **2** *see* HYPO *n.*[1] (1).

hyp *v. see* HIP *v.*[2].

hype *n.*[1] [SE *hyperbole*] **1** [1910s+] (*US Und.*) (*also* **hipe**) a short-change swindle in which the criminal persuades a shopkeeper that he has paid with a larger denomination note than he actually has, thus gaining extra change. **2** [1920s+] (*US*) a swindle, a confidence trick, fraud, lies or exaggeration. **3** [1920s+] (*US Und.*) a confidence trickster; a 'short-change artist'. **4** [1920s+] (*US*) an exorbitant increase in prices. **5** [1930s+] any contrived situation or scheme designed to fleece a victim. **6** [1950s+] publicity, promotion, esp. wild statements guessing about something's nature (whether positive or negative).

IN PHRASES

❑ **drop a hype** *v.* [1940s] (*US black*) to air one's opinions, to tell one's story. ❑ **throw hype** *v.* [1990s+] (*US black*) to talk in a self-aggrandizing manner.

hype *n.*[2] [abbr.] **1** [1910s+] (*US drugs*) (*also* **hyp**) a hypodermic syringe or injection; thus *hype kit*, the equipment used for narcotic injections. **2** [1920s+] (*US drugs/Und.*) (*also* **hyp, hyp man**) a heroin or morphine addict, any narcotics addict. **3** [1970s] (*US pimp*) a prostitute who works simply to support her narcotic addiction. **4** [1990s+] (*US drugs*) narcotic drugs.

5 [1990s+] (*US campus*) a regular user of marijuana.

IN COMPOUNDS

❑ **hype joint** *n.* [1960s] a place frequented by narcotics users. ❑ **hype talk** *n.* [1950s] the slang of narcotics users. ❑ **hype tank** *n.* [1960s–70s] (*US drugs/prison*) a cell reserved for narcotics users.

hype *adj.* [HYPE *n.*[1]] **1** [1970s] (*US*) fraudulent. **2** [1980s+] (*US campus*) uptight, upset, jittery, nervous, worried. **3** [1980s+] (*US black*) splendid, exciting, cool or attractive. **4** [1990s+] (*US campus*) excited in a positive sense. **5** [1990s+] dramatic.

hype *v.*[1] [HYPE *n.*[1]] **1** [1910s+] (*US Und.*) to operate a short-change racket, to swindle, to cheat. **2** [1910s+] to work up one's emotions, to become stimulated, to make more exciting. **3** [1920s] (*US*) to overcharge. **4** [1930s+] (*US black*) to fool or cajole, to outsmart. **5** [1940s+] (*orig. US*) to promote a person or commodity through an excess of overzealous, grandiose publicity, esp. in rock or show business use. **6** [1940s+] to excite. **7** [1960s+] (*US campus*) to annoy.

hype *v.*[2] (*also* **hype up**) [HYPE *n.*[2] (1)] [1930s+] (*drugs*) to inject a drug.

hyped *adj.* (*also* **hyped-up, hyphy**) [HYPE *v.*[1]] **1** [1910s+] intense, excited. **2** [1930s+] intoxicated by narcotic drugs, or a stimulant. **3** [1960s] artificial, fake, all HYPE *n.*[1] (6) and no substance. **4** [1970s+] tense, nervous.

hyper *n.* [HYPE *n.*[1]] **1** [1910s–50s] (*US Und.*) one who works the short-change racket. **2** [1940s] (*US black*) a persuasive talker. **3** [1960s] a publicist.

hyper *adj.* [abbr. SE *hyperactive*] **1** [late 19C; 1940s+] tense, over-emotional, 'wired'. **2** [1940s+] betraying one's feelings, esp. towards an attractive person.

hyper *v.* [abbr. SE *hyperactive*] [mid-19C–1950s] (*US*) to hurry, to run.

IN PHRASES

❑ **hyper down** *v.* [1980s+] (*US*) to calm down.

hyperjacks *n.* [HYPE *v.*[2] + JACK (AND JILL) *n.* (4)] [1980s+] (*drugs*) ampoules of heroin.

hype stick *n.* [HYPE *n.*[2] (1) + STICK *v.* (4c)] [1910s] (*US drugs*) a hypodermic needle.

hyp Michael, your head's on fire! *excl. see* HIP MICHAEL, YOUR HEAD'S ON FIRE! *excl.*

hypnotist *n.* [HYPE *v.*[1] (2) + pun] [1980s+] (*US campus*) an eccentric.

hypo *n.*[1] [abbr. SE *hypochondriac*] **1** [18C+] (*also* **hippo, hyp**) a feeling of mild depression, of being out of sorts. **2** [mid-18C+] (*also* **hippo, hypps**) a hypochondriac. **3** [1900s] (*US campus*) a notably hard worker.

hypo *n.*[2] [HYPE *n.*[2]] (*drugs*) **1** [late 19C+] (*also* **hypo-smecker**) a drug addict. **2** [20C+] a hypodermic syringe. **3** [20C+] a hypodermic injection.

IN PHRASES

❑ **pull a hypo** *v.* [1940s] (*drugs*) to sell poor quality drugs.

hypo *n.*[3] [HYPE *n.*[1]] [1950s] encouragement, excitement.

hypo *v.*[1] [HYPO *n.*[2] (2)] [1920s+] to administer a hypodermic injection.

hypo *v.*[2] [ext. of use of HYPO *v.*[1], i.e. to 'inject' the dice with something that helps the cheat] [1930s] (*US Und.*) to 'load' a pair of dice.

hypo *v.*[3] [HYPE *v.*[1]] [1930s+] (*US*) to promote or enhance, to stimulate enthusiasm.

hypped *adj. see* HIPPED *adj.*[1] (1).

hyps *n. see* HIP, THE *n.*

hyst *v. see* HEIST *v.*

hyste *n. see* HOIST *n.* (6).

hyster *n. see* HOISTER *n.* (1).

I

I *n.* [mid-19C+] (*US, mainly Southern/Midwest*) used in place of SE *by* in a variety of combs. euph. referring to *God* or *Jesus*, e.g. *I golly! I Godfrey!*

i *n.* [abbr.] [1910s–20s] (*US*) an *i*dea.

iah *n.* [proper name *Jah*, i.e. Jehovah, Rastafarian use for God + Rastafarian pfx *i-* to imply the spirituality that encompasses all humans, thus obviating the need for individual personal pronouns] [1990s+] (*W.I.*) a term of address to a friend.

I and I *n.* (*also* **Iyah Nyah**) [I AND I *pron.*] [1960s+] (*W.I. Rasta/UK black teen*) a Rastafarian.

I and I *pron.* [1960s+] (*W.I. Rasta/UK black teen*) us, we; you and I.

Ian Rush *n.* [rhy. sl.; ult. UK footballer *Ian Rush* (b.1961)] [1980s] a brush.

I bet you say that to all the boys/girls *phr.* see under SAY *v.*

i.b.m. *n.* [abbr. *i*tty *b*itty *m*eat (i.e. MEAT *n.* (2)] [1960s+] (*US*) a small penis.

Ice, the *n.* [2000s] (*N.Z.*) Antarctica.

ice *n.*[1] [fig. uses of visual and physical properties of SE *ice*] **1** (*US*) as that which keeps things 'cool' or satisfactory. (**a**) [late 19C+] money in general. (**b**) [late 19C+] profit from the illegal sale of tickets for the theatre, cinema etc. (**c**) [20C+] protection money, bribes. **2** indicative of emotional chilliness. (**a**) [late 19C+] (*US*) a cool reception, a brush-off. (**b**) [1990s+] (*US black*) an emotionless person, one who has no qualms about saying and doing what they feel. (**c**) [1990s+] courage; ruthlessness. (**d**) [2000s] failure to pay a debt. **3** [late 19C+] (*orig. US*) jewellery, esp. diamonds. **4** [1960s+] (*US black*) something or someone excellent [COOL *adj.* (6)]. **5** [1970s+] in US drugs uses. (**a**) cocaine. (**b**) methamphetamine.

IN COMPOUNDS

❑ **ice-cube** *n.* [1930s+] a diamond. ❑ **ice-house** *n.* [1930s+] (*US Und.*) a jewellery store. ❑ **ice palace** *n.* **1** [1920s–30s] (*US Und.*) an upmarket saloon or brothel. **2** [1940s+] (*US black*) a jewellery store.

IN PHRASES

❑ **give someone the ice** *v.* [20C+] (*US*) to give someone a cool reception. ❑ **on ice** *adj.* **1** [mid-19C+] (*orig.US*) in reserve. **2** [late 19C–1940s] certain, definite, a foregone conclusion, esp. of a sporting contest. **3** [late 19C+] (*orig. US*) out of the way; in storage. **4** [20C+] (*orig. US*) dead. **5** [1930s] (*US Und.*) of stolen goods, waiting to be sold. **6** [1930s+] (*US Und.*) in prison, under arrest. **7** [1930s+] (*orig. US*) in hiding, esp. from the police. **8** [1940s–50s] (*orig. US*) in secret, on the quiet. **9** [1950s] (*US Und.*) suffering confinement in a punishment cell. **10** [1990s+] in protective custody. ❑ **on ice** *adv.* [1920s+] (*US*) to the greatest extent, to the limit. ❑ **play ice for** *v.* [1930s] to criticize, to look down on. ❑ **put on ice** *v.* **1** [late 19C+] (*orig. US*) of a person, to hide away, to keep out of the limelight until required, e.g. a witness, the 'star' of a newspaper exclusive etc. **2** [1910s+] of a project, idea etc, to put aside for later development or use. **3** [1930s] (*US campus*) to forget deliberately. **4** [1930s+] (*orig. US*) to maintain a distant, minimally emotional relationship. **5** [1930s+] (*also* **pack on ice**) to kill, to murder; to knock out. **6** [1930s+] (*US*) to imprison.

SE in slang uses

DERIVATIVES

❑ **ice-o** *n.* [-O *sfx* (3)] [1920s+] (*Aus.*) an iceman.

IN COMPOUNDS

❑ **ice jack** *n.* [1910s–20s] an ice-cream salesman. ❑ **ice job** *n.* [JOB *n.*[2] (2)] [1960s+] (*US gay*) an act of fellatio in which the fellator has ice cubes in his/her mouth. ❑ **ice-wagon** *n.* **1** [late 19C–1950s] (*US*) a slow-moving person or vehicle. **2** *see* WATER WAGON *under* WATER *n.*[1].

ice *n.*[2] [abbr. SE *isolation*] [1970s] (*US prison*) solitary confinement.

ice *adj.* **1** [1970s+] (*US black*) a synon. for COOL *adj.* (2). **2** [1970s+] (*US black*) a synon. for COOL *adj.* (3). **3** (*N.Z.*) [2000s] perfectly clean.

ice *v.* **1** to conclude [SE *to put the icing on the cake*]. (**a**) [20C+] to ensure victory, orig. in a sporting contest. (**b**) [1980s+] to complete, to round off. **2** [1930s+] (*US*) to pay bribes or protection money [ICE *n.*[1] (1)]. **3** to reject, to ignore. (**a**) [1930s+] (*US*) (*also* **ice out**) to snub, to treat coldly. (**b**) [1960s+] (*US black*) to reject, to turn down, to cease. (**c**) [1980s+] to break an appointment with, to abandon or cancel a plan or scheme. **4** to isolate. (**a**) [1930s+] (*US Und.*) (*also* **ice down**) to imprison. (**b**) [1930s+] (*US prison*) to place in solitary confinement. (**c**) [1990s+] to hide. **5** to attack physically. (**a**) [1940s+] to murder, to kill. (**b**) [1940s+] to hit, to knock out. (**c**) [1970s+] in fig. use, to harm, to cause trouble for.

IN EXCLAMATIONS

❑ **ice that!** [1970s] (*US black*) stop that! calm down!

iceberg slim *n.* [SE *iceberg*, an unemotional person; more immediately the street name of Robert *Iceberg Slim* Beck (1918–92), one-time pimp and author of a series of autobiographical books; such gangsta rappers as Ice T (real name Tracy Marrow) took their names from his] [1960s] (*US black*) a pimp.

icebox *n.* **1** [20C+] (*US*) an unemotional person, esp. a sexually unresponsive woman. **2** [1920s+] (*Can./US prison*) a solitary confinement cell [note SE *isolation* and ICE *n.*[2]]. **3** [1920s+] (*US prison*) the morgue. **4** [1930s–40s] (*US prison*) a life sentence. **5** [1930s+] (*US*) the vagina. **6** [1930s+] (*US*) a prison. **7** [1940s] (*US Und.*) a safe. **8** [1970s+] a coffin.

ice-cream *n.* **1** [1920s+] (*US drugs*) cocaine, morphine, heroin, crack cocaine [the whiteness of the drugs and the pleasure they give]. **2** [1960s+] semen. **3** [1980s] (*US campus*) alcoholic drink.

IN COMPOUNDS

❑ **ice-cream man** *n.* **1** [1950s] a dealer in narcotics. **2** [1990s+] (*US black/drugs*) a seller of crack cocaine.

SE in slang uses

IN COMPOUNDS

❑ **ice-cream habit** *n.* [HABIT *n.* (1); on the premise that one likes ice-cream but doesn't want it all the time] [1930s+] (*drugs*) the irregular use of an otherwise addictive drug. ❑ **ice-dream pants** *n.* [the colour] [20C+] (*US*) lightweight, light-coloured summer trousers. ❑ **ice-cream suit** *n.* [late 19C+] (*orig. Aus./US*) a white linen suit.

ice-cream *adj.* [var. on APPLE PIE *adj.*] [2000s] (*US*) perfect, as desired.

ice-creamer *n.* (*also* **ice-creamo**) [the stereotyped occupation of Italian immigrants] [1930s+] an Italian.

ice-cream (freezer) *n.* [rhy. sl. = GEEZER *n.*[1] (1)] **1** [1950s+] a man. **2** [1980s] a person who can be easily duped. **3** [1980s] (*US campus*) a form of address to a good friend.

iced *adj.*[1] [ICE *v.* (4)] **1** [1930s+] (*US prison*) placed in the punishment block, in solitary confinement. **2** [1970s+] (*US black*) isolated; ignored.

iced *adj.*[2] (*also* **iced down, iced out**) [ICE *n.*[1] (3)] [1950s+] (*US*) wearing (diamond) jewellery.

iced *adj.*[3] [ICE *n.*[1] (5)] [1970s+] (*drugs*) intoxicated by (crack) cocaine.

IN PHRASES

❑ **iced to the eyebrows** *adj.* [1950s] extremely drunk.

iceman *n.* [ICE *n.*[1]] **1** [1920s+] (*US Und.*) a diamond thief. **2** [1940s+] an emotionless person. **3** [1940s+] a paid killer, a 'hit man'. **4** [1960s+] one, e.g. a corrupt police officer, who is given bribes by gangsters etc. **5** [1960s+] the frontman who pays or receives protection money on behalf of illegal gamblers or the authorities.

icer *n.* [early 19C] a bottle of soda-water.

ice-tong doctor *n.* [*ice tongs*, i.e. a nickname for the tools used by an illegal abortionist, who often compounded one crime with another] [1930s–50s] (*US drugs*) a doctor who is happy to supply illegal drugs.

ichiban *n.* [Jap. *ichiban*, number one, picked up by US troops serving in the Korean War (1951–3)] [20C+] (*US*) the best.

icing expert *n.* (*also* **icing queen**) [resemblance of semen to SE *icing*] [1940s+] (*gay*) a fellator.

ick *n.*[1] (*also* **ickaroo**) [ICKY *n.* (1)] [1930s+] (*US black*) a fool, a sucker.

ick *n.*[2] [backform. f. ICKY *adj.* (3)] **1** [1940s+] (*also* **ickem**) anything disgusting, e.g. greasy dirt. **2** [1990s+] in fig. use, something unpleasant.

ick *adj.* [abbr. ICKY *adj.* (1)] [1960s+] (*US*) sickly, over-sentimental, distasteful.

ickaroo *n.* see ICK *n.*[1].

ickem *n.* see ICK *n.*[2] (1).

icky *n.* [ICKY *adj.* (1); thus lit. one who likes only bad, 'sweet' jazz] [1930s–50s] (*US black*) **1** a stupid person, a person who is conventional. **2** a member of the upper classes.

icky *adj.* (*also* **icky-boo, icky-poo**) [echoic of SE *sticky/sicky* + 'baby-talk' sfx *-boo/-poo*] **1** [1920s+] (*orig. US*) of a person or an object (typically a film or play), sickly, over-sentimental. **2** [1920s+] (*mainly US teen*) usu. of food, sticky, sweet, unpleasant. **3** [1920s+] (*mainly teen*) (*also* **yicky**) distasteful, nauseating, unpleasant. **4** [1960s] (*US drugs*) feeling sick as part of heroin withdrawal.

icky-boo *adj.* [cod-'nursery' version of SE *sick*] [1920s] sick, nauseous.

ickyness *n.* [ICKY *adj.* (3)] [1960s+] (*US teen*) disgust.

icky-poo *adj.* see ICKY *adj.*

i'cod! *excl.* see ECOD! *excl.*

I could eat... *phr.* see under EAT *v.*

icy-blues *n.* see BABY-BLUES under BABY *n.*

icy eye *n.* see COLD-EYE *n.*

icy mitt *n.* see FROZEN MITT under MITT *n.*

icy pop *n.* [SE *icy* + POP *n.*[1] (2)] [1990s+] (*US campus*) beer.

i.d. *n.*[1] [abbr.] [1940s+] **1** an *id*entification. **2** an *id*entification photograph or card.

i.d. *n.*[2] [I.D. *n.*[1]; pun on the phr. *Let's see your I.D.*] [1950s+] (*US*) the penis.

i.d. *v.* [abbr.] [1940s+] (*orig. US*) to *id*entify.

Ida *n.* (*also* **Indiana, Ira, Irene, Ivy**) [initial letter] (*S.Afr. gay*) an Indian homosexual.

Idaho rainstorm *n.* (*also* **Idaho brainstorm, ...rain, ...shower**) [1930s+] (*US*) a dust storm.

i.d.b. *phr.* [abbr. *in daddy's business*] [1980s+] used by privileged young men to describe their occupation.

idea box *n.* (*also* **idea pot**) [1930s+ use is US black] [late 18C–19C; 1930s+] the brain, the head, knowledge.

ideal home *n.* [rhy. sl.] [1950s+] a comb.

I'd eat my chips out of her knickers *phr.* see under KNICKERS *n.*

I declare *n.* see I DON'T CARE *n.*

identity *n.* see OLD IDENTITY under OLD *adj.*

I desire *n.* [rhy. sl.] [mid-19C–1940s] a fire.

i.d. herb! *excl.* see HIDEY *phr.*

I didn't come down in the last shower (of rain) *phr.* [20C+] (*Aus.*) a phr. used when claiming a greater degree of experience or knowledge than that with which one is being credited.

I didn't fall off a Christmas tree *phr.* [1940s+] I'm not stupid, don't take me for a fool.

idiot *n.*

SE in slang uses

IN COMPOUNDS

❑ **idiot box** *n.* (*also* **idiot, idiot's lantern**) [SE *box*/BOX *n.*[1] (4f); note TV jargon *idiot girl*, the woman who holds up cue cards for an announcer or other performer; *idiot card*, a cue card] **1** [1950s+] (*orig. US*) the television, implying that TV watchers are less than normally intelligent. **2** [1990s+] a computer. ❑ **idiot fringe** *n.* [late 19C–1920s] a popular hairstyle for girls and young women. ❑ **idiot juice** *n.* [the substances' effects] **1** [1970s+] (*US drugs*) a mixture of nutmeg and water, used mainly in prisons. **2** [2000s] any form of spirits. ❑ **idiot oil** *n.* [alcohol's effects] [1980s+] **1** alcohol. **2** a metaphorical 'liquid', immersion in which renders one stupid. ❑ **idiot pills** *n.* [the effects] [1960s+] (*drugs*) barbiturates, any strong sedatives. ❑ **idiot spoon** *n.* [the supposed level of intelligence of those that wield them] [1940s–60s] (*US*) a shovel. ❑ **idiot stick** *n.* [the supposed level of intelligence of those who wield them; note also US Army use in Vietnam to mean (1) a rifle, (2) a wooden yoke used by the Vietnamese to carry two baskets, water buckets etc] [1930s+] (*US*) **1** a shovel. **2** a hoe. **3** a metaphorical 'stick' which, when wielded, confers stupidity upon the victim. ❑ **idiot tube** *n.* [TUBE *n.*[1] (7)] [1960s+] (*US*) the television.

IN PHRASES

❑ **half-idiot** *n.* (*also* **half-a-idiot**) [20C+] (*W.I., Bdos*) a complete fool.

idjeet/idjet/idjit/idjut *n.* see EEJIT *n.*

Idle Hall *n.* [20C+] (*W.I.*) a notional place used fig. to mean a state of unemployment.

IN PHRASES

❑ **work at Idle Hall** *v.* [20C+] (*W.I.*) to be unemployed.

idle jubbie *n.* [SE *idle* + JUBBIE *n.*] [1990s+] (*W.I.*) a young unemployed person.

idleset *n.* [20C+] **1** (*Ulster*) a fat stomach [it is evidence of one's idleness]. **2** (*Scot.*) unemployment.

I don't care *n.* (*also* **I declare**) [rhy. sl.] [1930s–40s] (*US*) a chair.

I don't make the fries *phr.* see under FRIES *n.*

I don't think *phr.* [mid-19C+] an ironic phr. used at the end of a declaratory statement as a means of negating whatever has just been said, e.g. *She's a real sweetie. I don't think!*

idrin *n.* [W.I. pron. of SE *brethren*] [1950s+] (*orig. W.I. Rasta*) one's fig. 'brothers'.

iez-haad *adj.* [W.I. pron. 'ears-hard'] [1950s+] (*W.I. Rasta*) thick-skulled, stubborn, unwilling or unable to hear.

i'fecks! *excl.* (*also* **by my feckins! i'fac! i'fackins! i'facks! i'fags! i'feaks! i'fegs! ifeekins! fegs! yfeck!**) [17C–1920s] a mild excl., lit. 'in faith'.

iffy *adj.* (*also* **iffey**) [SE *if*] [1930s+] (*orig. US*) **1** marginal, not wholly acceptable, unpalatable. **2** involved with criminality. **3** difficult. **4** ambiguous.

if you can't be good, be careful! *excl.* see BE GOOD! *excl.*

ig *n.* (*also* **igg**) [IG *v.*] [1960s–70s] (*US black*) a snub, a rejection.

IN COMPOUNDS

❑ **ig man** *n.* [20C+] (*US black*) an *ig*norant *man*, a fool.

ig *v.* (*also* **igg**) [abbr. SE *ignore*] [1930s+] (*orig. US black*) **1** to ignore a person deliberately, to snub. **2** to overlook something, to ignore the facts.

IN PHRASES

❑ **give the ig** *v.* [1960s] to ignore, to snub. ❑ **put the ig on** *v.* [1960s] to ignore, to snub.

i'gad! *excl. see* EGAD! *excl.*

igaree *v.* (*also* **igri, iggery, iggry**) [IGAREE! *excl.*] [1910s] to hurry up, to go quickly.

igaree! *excl.* (*also* **igri, iggery, iggry**) [Arabic *igaree*, quick] [1910s] hurry up! quickly! thus ext. *get an igri on!*, hurry up.

igg *see under* IG.

ight *phr. see* A-IGHT *phr.*

ignant *n.* [abbr./pron. of SE *ignorant*] [1940s+] (*US black*) an *ignorant*, stupid person.

ig'nant oil *n. see under* IGNORANT *adj.*

ignite (oil) *n.* [it sets the drinker 'on fire'] [1980s+] (*US black*) whisky.

ignorance *n.* [IGNORANT *adj.*] [1940s+] (*W.I.*) extreme anger that threatens the other person.

ignorant *adj.* [dial. *ignorant*, uncouth, ill-mannered] (*W.I./UK black*) [1940s+] **1** angry, irascible, short-tempered. **2** unpleasant. **3** arrogant, ill-natured, bullying.

IN COMPOUNDS

❑ **ignorant oil** *n.* (*also* **ig'nant oil**) [1960s+] (*US black*) alcohol. ❑ **ignorant stick** *n.* [var. on *IDIOT STICK under* IDIOT *n.*] [1950s+] (*US*) a shovel; a long-handled hoe.

IN PHRASES

❑ **get ignorant** *v.* [20C+] (*W.I.*) to lose one's temper, to be rude; thus *get someone ignorant*, to enrage, to infuriate. ❑ **ignorant as Paddy's pig** *adj. see under* PADDY *n.* ❑ **make ignorant** *v.* [1940s+] (*UK Und.*) to irritate, to annoy.

I got it like that *phr.* [1980s+] (*US black teen*) a phr. indicating that one is doing well.

igri *see under* IGAREE.

I guess yes! *excl.* [late 19C+] (*US*) yes indeed! absolutely!

igxagxa *n.* [Xhosa *ukugxagxa*, one who has become poor and squalid] [1950s+] (*S.Afr. black*) **1** a poor white. **2** one who falls between two ethnic cultures.

I hate it/that *phr.* [1980s+] (*US campus*) a sarcastic expression of pleasure.

i jacks! *excl. see under* JACKS *n.*[1].

ijet/ijit/ijjit/ijut *n. see* EEJIT *n.*

ijuwishi *n.* [JEWISH *n.*] [1960s+] (*S.Afr. black*) expensive clothing.

Ike *n.* [abbr. the 'rural' or Jewish name *Isaac*] (*US*) **1** [late 19C+] (*also* **country ike**) an ignorant rustic male. **2** [20C+] a self-important, pretentious person. **3** [20C+] a derog. term for a Jew.

IN PHRASES

❑ **big Ike** *n.* [1900s–10s] (*US*) an important person. ❑ **wise Ike** *n.* [20C+] (*US*) a self-important, pretentious person.

ikey *n.* [abbr. IKEY-MO *n.*; lit. or fig. refs. to stereotyped Jewish characteristics] **1** [early 19C+] the 'inevitable' nickname for a Jew or one who has 'Jewish' features. **2** [mid-19C] (*UK Und.*) a Jewish receiver and seller of stolen goods. **3** [mid-19C+] a derog. term for a Jew. **4** [late 19C+] one who plays a duplicitous 'sharp' trick. **5** [20C+] a pawnbroker (irrespective of racial origin). **6** [20C+] a moneylender. **7** [1910s+] (*S.Afr.*) a student of the University of Cape Town; thus *Ikeys*, the university itself [despite the obvious racial implication, the term is regularly used in sports reports without further comment]. **8** *see* IKEY-MO *n.* (5).

DERIVATIVES

❑ **ikeyness** *n.* [late 19C+] the derog. stereotypes attributed to Jewishness, *i.e.* artfulness, craftiness, greed, financial chicanery etc (the subject need not be a Jew).

ikey *adj.* [IKEY *n.* (1)] **1** [late 19C+] Jewish. **2** [late 19C+] extraordinary, showy. **3** [late 19C+] smart, cunning. **4** [late 19C+] (*US*) (*also* **iky**) impertinent, cheeky. **5** [late 19C+] melodramatic, done for effect (the image of the over-emotional Jew). **6** [1900s] (*Aus.*) a large amount.

ikey *v.* (*also* **iky**) [IKEY *n.*] [1930s–60s] (*US*) to cheat financially.

ikey-mo *n.* [SE *Isaac* + *Moses*, two typical Jewish given names; note Kentish dial. *ikey*, proud; 'probably popularized by the *Ikey Mo* who was partner in the nefarious doings of the original Ally Sloper, the first British strip-cartoon 'character', in the series which started in *Judy* magazine, 1867, and ran for many years' (*DSUE*)] **1** [early 19C+] a derog. term for a Jew; thus the various stereotypes. **2** [early 19C+] a Jewish receiver, moneylender, pawnbroker, peddler. **3** [mid-19C+] a loafer, a layabout. **4** [mid-19C+] a tip, information. **5** [mid-19C+] (*Aus.*) (*also* **ikey, Mo, Moses**) a bookmaker. **6** [20C+] (*Aus.*) a mean person.

ikey-mo *adj.* [IKEY-MO *n.*] **1** [late 19C+] Jewish. **2** [late 19C+] artful, crafty, knowing. **3** [late 19C+] having a good opinion of oneself, stuck-up. **4** [1960s] dandified.

iky *adj. see* IKEY *adj.* (4).

iky *v. see* IKEY *v.*

ilie *adj.* [lit. use of SE *highly*] [1950s] (*W.I. Rasta*) describes something valuable, exalted, sacred.

Ilie Nastase *n.* [rhy. sl. = CARSEY *n.* (4); ult. Romanian tennis player *Ilie Nastase* (b.1946)] [1990s+] the lavatory.

ilk *n.* [ILL *adj.* (2)] [2000s] (*US black*) something unpleasant, bizarre, distasteful.

ill *adj.* [fig. uses of SE *ill*, unwell] (*US black/teen*) **1** [1900s; 1980s+] angry, frustrated, of an animal, vicious. **2** [1970s+] aggressive, offensive, bad. **3** [1980s+] on the bad = good model, wonderful, first-rate. **4** [1990s+] bizarre, surprising. **5** [1990s+] unattractive.

IN EXCLAMATIONS

❑ **that's so ill!** [1980s+] (*US teen*) an all-purpose denunciation of an object or activity.

SE in slang uses

IN COMPOUNDS

❑ **ill fortune** *n.* [unfortunate in that it is not a whole shilling] [late 17C–early 19C] ninepence (a coin). ❑ **ill music** *n. see* separate entry. ❑ **ill piece** *n. see under* PIECE *n.* ❑ **ill willie** *adj.* [SE *ill will*] [20C+] (*Ulster*) uncooperative.

ill *v.* [ILL *adj.*] (*orig. US black teen*) **1** [1980s+] to act crazily, aggressively, wildly. **2** [1990s+] to do something very well.

Illadelphia *n.* [ILL *adj.* (3)] [2000s] (*US black*) Philadelphia, PA.

I'll be... for all combs. *see* the relevant n., adj. or v.

I'll be! *excl.* [1920s+] abbr. of *I'll be damned!*

I'll be one up on your taw presently *phr.* (*also* **I'll be a marble (upon your taw), I'll be one marble...**) [marbles imagery; SE *taw*, the large marble with which a player shoots] [late 18C–19C] a threatening phr. meaning 'I'll deal with you in due course', 'I'll get even'.

I'll be there *n.* [rhy. sl.] [20C+] a chair.

illegim *n.* [abbr.] [1900s] (*Aus.*) an *illegi*timate child.

illegit *n.* [1980s] (*N.Z.*) an *illegit*imate child.

illegit *adj.* [abbr.] [1910s+] *illegit*imate; criminal.

illegitimate *n.* [paradoxically, a *legitimate* settler was a criminal who had been sentenced to transportation] **1** [19C] (*Aus.*) a free, i.e. non-convict, Australian settler. **2** [early 19C] counterfeit sovereigns; thus *young illegitimate*, a counterfeit half-sovereign. **3** [mid-19C] a poor class of costermonger looked down on by the mainstream costers, selling pea soup, sweetmeats, spice-cakes etc.

I'll go he! *excl.* [1950s+] (*N.Z.*) an excl. of surprise or of confidence.

I'll go hopping to hell *phr. see under* HELL *n.*

illing *n.* (*also* **illin'**) [ILL *v.* (1)] [1980s+] (*orig. US black/teen*) acting or thinking wildly, aggressively, crazily.

illing *adj.* (*also* **illin'**) [ILL *v.* (1)] [1980s+] **1** (*US campus*) annoyed, unhappy. **2** (*US campus*) in a difficult or unpleasant situation, under severe stress. **3** (*US campus*) drunk. **4** (*US campus*) unattractive, old-fashioned. **5** (*US black*) performing superbly.

I'll knock out your eight eyes *phr. see under* EYE *n.*

I'll make you sing o-be-joyful on the other side of your mouth *phr. see under* O-BE-JOYFUL *n.*

ill music *n.*

IN PHRASES

❑ **make ill music** *v.* [SE *ill*, bad + fig. use of *music*] [late 17C–early 18C] a phr. used of unwelcome news, e.g. *that makes ill music here.*

illuminated *adj.* [play on LIT (UP) *adj.* (1)] [20C+] drunk.

illustrated shirt *n.* [mid-19C] a coloured shirt, as favoured by costermongers.

illy *n.*[1] [? ILL *adj.* (3)] [1980s] (*drugs*) marijuana.

illy *n.*[2] [ILL *adj.* (1)] [1990s+] (*US black/teen*) an angry or frustrated person.

illy-gump *n.* [ety. unknown] [1970s] (*US black*) information.

illywhacker *n.* [AND offers no ety; Baker (1945) offers: 'the following terms for sharpers and those who live by their wits: *spieler, eeler-spee, eeler-whack* and *illywhacker* (the last three are formed by transposition and mutilation of the first.'] [1940s+] (*Aus.*) a professional confidence man, esp. an itinerant following fairs and country shows.

I'm a Dutchman *phr.* (*also* **I'll be a Dutchman, I'm a bishop, ...Chinaman, ...Chink, ...nun, ...tailor, ...tinker, ...Trojan, ... Turk, I'm Dutch**) [late 16C; late 18C+] a phr. used to refute a suggestion or hypothesis, usu. preceded by *If that's... then I'm a...*

I'm afloat *n.* [rhy. sl] **1** [mid-19C–1940s] (*UK/US*) a boat. **2** [late 19C+] (*also* **armour float**) a coat.

i-man *pron.* [1950s+] (*W.I. Rasta*) I, me, mine.

I'm a nigger *phr.* (*also* **I'm a coon, ...coyote, ...horned sinner, ...monkey, ...monkey's uncle, ...ring-tailed baboon**) [NIGGER *n.*[1]] [mid-19C+] a phr. used to refute a suggestion or hypothesis, and as an excl. of astonishment.

I'm a wreck *n. see* NERVOUS WRECK *n.*

imbo *n.* [SE *imbecile* + -O *sfx* (3)] [1950s–70s] (*Aus.*) a fool, a simpleton.

imbuggerance *n.* [phr. *I don't give a bugger*] [1960s+] (*Aus.*) irrelevance.

I'm Dutch *phr.* see I'M A DUTCHMAN *phr.*

imey-wimey *n.* [? SE *whine* or elision of *I ... me ... why me?* + onomat.] [1920–70s] (*US black*) a meek-sounding, whining voice.

I'm from Missouri *phr.* (*also* **I'm from Texas**) [orig. *I come from Missouri. You have got to show me*; the image is of the cautious countryman refusing to fall for the wiles of the city slicker. The phr. was popularized, though not actually coined, by Missouri Congressman Willard D. Vandiver (1854–1932) — see Cohen (1998) 105-28 for a detailed discussion] [late 19C+] (*US*) a phr. used to denote one's scepticism and suspicions; usu. ext. with some form of *so you'll have to show me!*

immense *adj.* [mid-18C+] extremely good, first-rate, splendid.

immense *adv.* [mid-18C–mid-19C] splendidly, well.

immensikoff *n.* [coined by the music-hall star Arthur Lloyd (1840–1904), who called himself *Immensikoff* and appeared on stage in such a coat to sing, c.1868, his hit 'The Shoreditch Toff'] [late 19C–1900s] a bulky, fur-lined overcoat.

immensikoff *adj.* [IMMENSIKOFF *n.* (1)] [late 19C–1900s] splendid, esp. as regards one's dress.

immies *n.* [SE *immy*, a highly rated marble, made to resemble a semi-precious stone, e.g. cornelian, agate] [1940s+] (*US*) the eyes.

immigrant chic *n. see* PORTAGEE COLONIAL *under* PORTAGEE *n.*

I'm missing *phr.* [1990s+] a phr. meaning 'I'm leaving'.

imo *adj.* (*also* **immo**) [abbr. SE *imitation*] [1940s+] (*US black/campus*) imitation, counterfeit.

imoogie *adj. see* MOEGIE *adj.*

imperence *n.* [SE *impudence*] [mid-18C–19C] impudence, impertinence.

DERIVATIVES

❑ **imperent** *adj.* [mid-19C] impudent.

impimpi *n.* [SE *pimp* or Zulu *umbimbi*, a conspiracy or *iphimpi*, a species of cobra] [1960s+] (*S.Afr.*) a police informer.

implement *n.* [late 17C–18C] a fool who is persuaded to take part in a dangerous or foolhardy enterprise.

importance *n. see* COMFORTABLE IMPORTANCE *under* COMFORTABLE *adj.*

impos *adj.* [abbr.] [1900s–20s] *impossible.*

impost-taker *n.* [SE *impost*, a tax or customs levy + *taker*] [late 17C–early 19C] one who lends money to losing gamblers, taking advantage of their desperate need for new funds to extort the highest possible interest.

impot *n.* [abbr. SE *imposition*] [late 19C–1920s] (*UK juv.*) a (public) school punishment, usu. writing 'lines'.

impudence *n.* [mid-18C–late 19C] the penis.

impudent stealing *n.* **1** [18C–19C] 'Cutting out the backs of coaches and robbing the seats' (Grose 1788). **2** [mid-19C] (*US*) cutting off the tails of a man's coat.

impure *n.* [late 18C–19C] a prostitute.

imshee *v.* (*also* **imshi, imshy**) [IMSHEE! *excl.*] [1910s+] (*orig. milit.*) **1** to go away, to vanish. **2** to hurry someone along.

imshee! *excl.* (*also* **imshi! imshy!**) [Arab. *imshi*, go away, adopted by WWI troops serving in the Middle East] [1910s+] (*orig. milit.*) be off! go away!

I'm so (frisky) *n.* [rhy. sl.] [late 19C+] whisky.

I'm there *phr.* [1970s+] (*US campus*) an expression of support.

I'm willing *n.* [rhy. sl.] [20C+] a shilling (5p).

in *n.* **1** [1920s+] (*orig. US*) a means of infiltrating otherwise closed groups, usu. those holding power and influence. **2** [1940s] (*US*) a means of infiltrating a building.

IN PHRASES

❑ **have an in** *v.* [1930s+] to have a means of infiltrating an otherwise closed group. ❑ **on the in** [1920s+] (*orig. US*) being an insider, having inside information.

in *adj.* **1** [19C+] (*UK Und.*) being part of a closed or influential group, often through the payment of bribes, wielding of influence etc. **2** [mid-19C] in season. **3** [mid-19C+] fashionable. **4** [late 19C+] (*US Und.*) a member of a confidence trick team, or, as a 'civilian', aware and tolerant of their activity. **5** [20C+] guaranteed of success in a given project, e.g. sexual seduction. **6** [20C+] socially acceptable. **7** [20C+] partaking in a game, e.g. of cards or pool. **8** [1950s+] (*US*) being a member of one of the armed services. **9** [1960s+] (*drugs*) connected with drug suppliers. **10** [1960s+] limited to a small circle, e.g. a shared sense of humour. **11** [1980s+] a member of the police force.

in *adv.* **1** [late 18C–19C] in pawn. **2** [19C+] in prison. **3** [20C+] (*US*) facing trouble, under scrutiny. **4** [1920s] (*US*) in love. **5** [1970s] in debt.

IN PHRASES

❑ **get someone in** *v.* [1920s+] (*Aus.*) to fool, to trick.

in a horn *phr.* [? dial. *in a horn*, expression of incredulity] [mid-19C+] (*US*) a general phr. of dismissal.

in a man's beef, be *v. see under* BEEF *n.*[1].

in-and-in *n.* see IN-AND-OUT *n.*[1] (2).

in and in *adv.* [1920s] (*US*) participating positively.

in-and-out *n.*[1] **1** [mid-17C–mid-19C] (*also* **in and to**) the penis. **2** [mid-17C+] (*also* **in-and-in, in-out, outs and ins**) sexual intercourse. **3** [late 19C] a pauper who alternates between living in a workhouse and street begging [i.e. *in* and *out* of the workhouse]. **4** [1960s] in attrib., use, relating to the penis and/or sexual intercourse.

IN PHRASES

❑ **play at in and out** *v.* (*also* **play in and out**) [17C] to have sexual intercourse. ❑ **want to know the ins and outs of a**

cat's arsehole (*also* **...duck's bum, ...nag's arse**) [20C+] to be very inquisitive.

in-and-out *n.*[2] [rhy. sl.] [20C+] **1** the nose [= SE *snout*]. **2** a cigarette [= SNOUT *n.*[2]]. **3** a bottle of stout. **4** a tout, a racecourse tipster. **5** gout. **6** (*Aus.*) the throat [= SE *spout*].

in-and-out boy *n. see* IN-AND-OUT MAN *n.* (1).

in-and-outer *n.*[1] [in and out of success/prison/police station] **1** [late 19C–1950s] (*US*) an incompetent, esp. in sport. **2** [1950s] (*US Und.*) a second-rate, petty criminal. **3** [1970s] (*US Und.*) a criminal who is arrested, but never actually charged and jailed.

in-and-outer *n.*[2] [1940s] (*US black*) a door.

in and out like a fiddler's elbow *phr.* [20C+] **1** rapid and enthusiastic copulation. **2** (*Aus.*) all over the place, in terms of useless over-activity.

in-and-out man *n.* **1** [1920s–50s] (*also* **in-and-out boy**) a second-rate criminal, i.e. one whose life alternates between being in and out of prison. **2** [1950s+] (*UK Und.*) an opportunist thief [one who goes quickly in and out of the house he is robbing].

in-and-out-of *n.* [1940s] (*US black*) a door.

in and to *n. see* IN-AND-OUT *n.*[1] (1).

in-between *n.*[1] [rhy. sl. = QUEEN *n.* (2)] [1950s+] (*Aus.*) a male homosexual.

in-between *n.*[2] [i.e. *in between* the legs] [1990s+] (*US black*) the vagina.

in-betweens *n.* [1970s+] (*drugs*) a mixture of amphetamines and barbiturates.

in cahoots *phr.* (*also* **cahoots, in cahoot, in cahoots with**) [? Fr. *cahute*, cabin, or *cohorte*, company; other suggestions include US *cahot*, a pothole, or the *pfx* KER – + *hoot*, albeit the latter remains inexplicable] [early 19C+] (*orig. US*) in partnership (with), usu. implying a slightly disreputable or surreptitious alliance.

Inca message *n.* [because of the relation of cocaine to South America] [1980s+] (*drugs*) cocaine.

incandescent *adj.* [1900s] (*US campus*) tipsy, mildly drunk.

inch *n.* [17C+] used, by metonymy, to describe the penis; a specific size is usu. appended.

inch *v.* [abbr. HALF-INCH *v.*] [1990s+] (*US campus*) to steal.

in chancery *adv.* ['the tenacity and absolute control with which the Court of Chancery holds anything, and the certainty of cost and loss to property "in chancery"' *OED*] [19C–1900s] in an awkward situation.

inch and pinch *v.* [20C+] (*Ulster*) to live frugally.

in co *phr.* [abbr. *in* company with] [early 19C–1910s] (*orig. US*) along with.

incog *adj.* [Scot. dial. *cogue*, a drinking vessel or dram] [19C] drunk.

incognita *n.* [Lat. *incognita*, an unknown woman] [mid–late 19C] a courtesan, a high-class prostitute.

incubator *n.* [1900s] (*Aus., Sydney*) a wife.

inde *adj.* [abbr.] [1960s] *ind*ependent.

indescribables *n.* [late 18C–19C] trousers.

index *n.* **1** [early 19C] the nose. **2** [early–mid-19C; 1930s–40s] (*also* **indexer**) the face [20C+ use is US black].

india *n.* [Sp. *india*, a peasant woman] [1950s–70s] (*camp gay*) a plain man, with homely, peasant features.

India man *n. see* INDIA WIPE *n.*

Indian *n.* (*US*) **1** [mid-19C+] an uncouth, rowdy person, irrespective of actual race. **2** [mid-19C+] a person. **3** [late 19C] a cent [a picture of a Native American was engraved on the reverse]. **4** [late 19C+] a quick temper.

IN PHRASES

❑ **big Indian** *n.* [mid-19C+] (*US*) an influential, important person. ❑ **dead Indian** *n. see under* DEAD *adj.* ❑ **get one's Indian up** *v.* [note B&L differentiate: 'to say that one has his "Indian up", implies a great degree of vindictiveness, while Dutch wrath is stubborn but yielding to reason'] [late 19C+] (*US*) to lose one's temper. ❑ **Indian (up)** *v.* (*also* **Indian around**) [19C+] (*US*) to sneak up without alerting one's targets. ❑ **play Indian** *v.* [1920s] (*US*) to ambush. ❑ **play the sober Indian** *v.* [mid-19C] (*US*) to resist joining in a drinking session.

Indian *adj.* used in the following combs. as a negative stereotype.

IN COMPOUNDS

❑ **Indian coffee** *n.* [the assumption being that 'Red Indians' deserved nothing better than such coffee] [mid-19C+] (*US*) coffee made from reheated grounds. ❑ **Indian giver** *n.* [the racist stereotype of the untrustworthy 'Red Indian'] (*orig. US*) **1** [mid-18C+] one who when giving, expects a gift in return; thus *Indian gift* and *Indian giving*. **2** [20C+] one who first gives, then takes back a gift. ❑ **Indian haircut** *n.* [the stereotype of the warlike 'Red Indian', tomahawk in hand] [20C+] (*US*) scalping. ❑ **Indian hay** *n.* [HAY *n.* (1)] [1930s+] (*drugs*) marijuana. ❑ **Indian hunting** *n.* [19C] (*US*) a fight between two men. ❑ **Indian liquor** *n.* (*also* **...rum, ... whisky**) [based on the assumption that anything could be palmed off on 'Red Indians'] [late 18C–19C] (*US*) the lowest quality spirits. ❑ **Indian pow-wow** *n.* [early 19C+] (*US*) a noisy discussion or gathering. ❑ **Indian rug** *n.* [RUG *n.*[1] (1)] [1960s+] (*gay*) a cheap wig done in braids. ❑ **Indian side** *n.* [the Indian practice of mounting a horse from the right, as opposed to whites who mounted from the left] [1920s+] (*US, mainly Western*) the right-hand side, esp. of a horse; in fig. use as correct. ❑ **Indian time** *n.* [1960s+] (*US, mainly West*) unpunctuality, a relaxed attitude to time-keeping.

IN PHRASES

❑ **burn Indian hay** *v.* (*also* **burn an Indian**) [1950s+] to smoke marijuana. ❑ **put the Indian sign on** *v.* (*also* **get..., hang..., have ...**) [note SE *Indian sign*, a smoke-signal] [20C+] (*US*) to put a curse on someone, based on the belief that Native Americans have the power of cursing.

Indiana *n.* see IDA *n.*

Indian charm *n.* [rhy. sl.] [1990s+] the arm.

Indian joe *n.* [rhy. sl.] [2000s] (*Irish*) a toe.

India wipe *n.* [late 18C–early 19C] (*also* **India man**) a handkerchief made of Indian (Asian) cotton.

indie *n.* [1920s+] an independent (record label, film company etc).

indigo *adj. see* BLUE *adj.*[3].

indispensables *n.* [mid-19C] trousers.

indispensible *n.* [early 19C] a small satchel or bag worn by a woman.

Indo *n.* [abbr. *Indonesia*] **1** [1960s–70s] (*orig. Aus.*) Indonesia; an Indonesian. **2** [1980s+] (*drugs*) marijuana.

Indonesia *n.* [SE *Indonesia*, the origin] [1980s+] (*US drugs*) (*also* **Indonesian bud**) marijuana.

indoor *adj.*

SE in slang uses

IN COMPOUNDS

❑ **indoor golf** *n.* [1920s–50s] (*US*) craps dice. ❑ **indoor money** *n.* [1960s+] (*UK Und.*) a reserve of cash for use in day-to-day life rather than the proceeds of a robbery. ❑ **indoor sledging** *n.* [20C+] sexual intercourse.

indorse *v.* [SE *in* + *dorse*, the back] [18C–19C] to sodomize.

indorser *n.* [INDORSE *v.*] [early 18C–19C] a male homosexual.

indorse with a cudgel *v.* [SE *indorse*, stamping the flesh of one's victim] [late 18C–19C] to thrash, to beat with a stick.

industrial *adj.* [the image of an industrial worker as a 'real man'] [1980s+] (*US campus*) extremely masculine.

industrial debutante *n.* [1980s+] (*US*) a prostitute who specializes in attending US business conventions.

ineffable *n.* **1** [19C] constr. with *the*, the vagina [lit. the 'unspeakable' [thing]]. **2** [mid-19C] a supreme dandy.

ineffables *n.* [19C] trousers.

in effect mode *phr.* [1980s+] (*US black teen*) to be in a relaxed, stress-free state of mind.

inexpressibles *n.* (*also* **innominables, insuppressibles**) [euph.; note 20C+ Romanian *indispensabili*, underpants] [late 18C–1900s] trousers.

i-ney! *excl.* [ety. unknown] [1950s+] (*W.I. Rasta*) a greeting.

inferior half *n.* see BETTER HALF *n.*

in flaggers *phr.* [abbrev. Lat. *in flagrante delicto*, lit. 'in flagrant lust'] [1920s–60s] (*Aus.*) (caught) in the act, usu. of sexual intercourse.

info *n.* [abbr.] [20C+] *information.*

in for (it) *phr.* **1** [18C] drunk. **2** [mid-19C+] willing, committed to, eager. **3** [1910s–20s] pregnant.

in front see *under* UP FRONT.

in full effect *phr.* [1990s+] (*orig. US black*) present, going on, happening.

ing-bing *n.* [? var. on WING-DING *n.*] [1920s–40s] (*US*) a fit, an emotional outburst.

ingler *n.* [? dial. *ingle*, to fondle; thus he 'fondles' the horse to persuade it to go with him. Note SE *ingle*, a catamite] [late 18C–mid-19C] a horse thief who toured country fairs looking for victims.

in goat heaven and kiddie kingdom, be *v.* [20C+] (*W.I., Bdos*) to be in a state of absolute bliss.

ingogo *n.* [Zulu *ingogo*, a half-crown or 25 cents] [1970s+] (*S.Afr.*) a cheap prostitute.

in guts gully *phr.* [20C+] (*W.I.*) in serious difficulties.

inhale *v.* [late 19C+] **1** to eat very fast, to gobble up. **2** to drink.

in heat *adj.* see ON HEAT *adj.*

in high feather *phr.* see *under* FEATHER *n.*

in hog heaven and john crow paradise *v.* [20C+] (*W.I., Bdos*) to be in a state of absolute bliss.

Iniskillen men *n.* [the original *Iniskillen* regiment distinguished itself in Ireland; the militia was less impressive, 'soon raised, as soon set down' (B.E.)] [late 17C–18C] a derog. term for the militia.

in'it *n.* [the ubiquitous INNIT! *excl.*] [1990s+] (*UK Asian*) a teenage gang.

in it *adj.* **1** [early 19C+] (*mainly Aus.*) agreeing to participate, taking a share. **2** [late 19C] at the heart of society. **3** [late 19C+] conforming to one's ideas and attitudes, worthy of notice, often as NOT IN IT *phr.* **4** [late 19C+] in trouble. **5** [late 19C+] (*US*) aware, alive. **6** [1960s+] (*Aus.*) having sexual intercourse.

IN PHRASES

❑ **I wouldn't be in it** [1940s+] (*Aus.*) I wouldn't join in, take part.

iniversal *adj.* [the substitution by Rastafarians of 'i' for 'you' or the sound 'u'] [1960s+] (*W.I./UK black teen*) universal.

in jail at Innisfail *phr.* [1960s+] (*Aus.*) an assonant/rhyming phr. used to denote an unsatisfactory situation.

injection *n.* [see Williams (1994) for metaphorical use in 17C] **1** [mid-18C] semen, at the point of ejaculation. **2** [late 19C] sexual intercourse; the intromission of the penis.

Injiny *adj.* [1900s] (*US*) Native American.

Injun *n.* (*also* **Injen, Injin, Injunn**) [early 19C+] (*US*) a Native American; a Native American language.

Injun *v.* [derog. association of INJUN *n.*] [late 19C] to creep up on, to ambush.

ink *n.* [colour] **1** [20C+] (*Aus./N.Z./US*) a cheap red wine [*DNZE* also suggests rhy. sl. = *drink*]. **2** [1910s–40s] (*US*) (*also* **ink face**) a derog. term for a black person, esp. with a very dark complexion. **3** [1920s–40s] strong, bitter coffee. **4** [1930s+] publicity; a mention in the newspapers. **5** [1980s+] a tattoo. **6** [1990s+] (*US*) a police or prison record.

IN PHRASES

❑ **get some ink** *v.* [1910s+] to receive coverage in the printed media for one's actions, speech etc. ❑ **make black ink** *v.* [SE *black ink*, as opposed to red ink, denotes the profit side of a ledger] [1930s] (*US*) to make money. ❑ **shed ink** *v.* [late 19C] to write, usu. more general than the professional *SLING INK* below. ❑ **sling ink** *v.* **1** [mid-19C+] (*orig. US*) (*also* **spill ink**) to write, esp. professionally, to work as a journalist. **2** [1930s] (*US*) to compose or arrange music. **3** [1990s+] (*US prison*) to apply a tattoo.

SE in slang uses

IN COMPOUNDS

❑ **ink-bottle** *n.* [note Royal Navy jargon *ink-slinger*, the purser's clerk] [late 19C–1900s] a clerk. ❑ **ink-flinging** *n.* [late 19C] journalism, writing. ❑ **ink-jerker** *n.* [Farmer (1889) has the lesser known synon. *adjective-jerker*] [mid-19C–1910s] (*US*) a writer, esp. a journalist. ❑ **ink-pot** *n.* **1** a sly, dishonest lawyer. **2** [1910s–50s] (*US Und.*) a place where criminals gather. ❑ **ink-slinger** *n.* (*also* **ink-walloper**) **1** [mid-19C+] (*orig. US*) a writer, esp. a journalist. **2** [1910s–60s] a clerk. **3** [1930s] a musician who arranges music. ❑ **ink-slinging** *n.* **7** [late 19C+] the profession of writing or journalism. ❑ **ink-spiller** *n.* (*also* **ink-shedder, -splasher, -waster**) [mid-19C–1910s] a writer, usu. a journalist or clerk. ❑ **inkspot** *n.* [1910s–60s] (*US*) a black person, usu. derog. ❑ **inkwell** *n.* (*also* **inkhorn**) [1940s+] (*US*) the vagina.

ink *v.* **1** [1940s+] (*orig. US*) to sign a contract. **2** [1970s+] to take fingerprints. **3** [1980s+] (*US*) to tattoo [INK *n.* (5)].

inked *adj.* [INK *n.* (1)] [late 19C+] (*Aus./N.Z.*) drunk.

ink face *n.* see INK *n.* (2).

inkos *n.* [Xhosa/Zulu *inkosi*, chief] [late 19C] (*S.Afr.*) a white man.

inky *adj.* (*also* **inky-poo**) [INKED *adj.*] [1900s–60s] (*orig. Aus.*) drunk.

inky blue *n.* [rhy. sl. = flu] [1970s+] influenza.

inky-dink *n.* [note the popular fictional schoolboy Billy Bunter's Indian rajah friend, Hurree Jamset Ram Singh, nicknamed *Inky*] [1900s–40s] (*US black*) a particularly dark-skinned person.

inky-poo *adj.* see INKY *adj.*

inky smudge *n.* [rhy. sl.] [late 19C–1970s] (*UK Und.*) a judge.

inlaid *adj.* (*also* **inlayed, well-inlaid, well-inlayed**) [SE *inlaid*, ornamented, usu. with precious metals] [late 17C–early 19C] rich, well-off.

in-law *n.* see *WIFE-IN-LAW under* WIFE *n.*

in like Flynn *phr.* [the alleged sexual prowess of the actor Errol *Flynn* (1909–59); however, note Michael Quinion's website *World Wide Words* 11/9/99: 'Reference books almost universally assert that this set phrase, an American expression meaning to be successful emphatically or quickly, especially in regard to sexual seduction, refers to the Australian-born actor Errol Flynn [...] the phrase is said to have been coined following his acquittal in February 1943 for the statutory rape of a teenage girl. This seems to be supported by the date of the first example recorded, in *AS* in December 1946, which cited a 1945 use in the sense of something being done easily. The trouble with this explanation is that examples of obviously related expressions have now turned up from dates before Flynn's trial. Barry Popik of the American Dialect Society found an example from 1940, as well as this from the sports section of the *San Francisco Examiner* of 8 February 1942: "Answer these questions correctly and your name is Flynn, meaning you're in, provided you have two left feet and the written consent of your parents". To judge from a newspaper reference he turned up from early 1943, the phrase could by then also be shortened to 'I'm Flynn', meaning "I'm in". It's suggested by some writers that the phrase really originated with another Flynn, Edward J Flynn – "Boss" Flynn – a campaign manager for the Democratic party during FDR's presidency. Flynn's machine in Chicago was so successful at winning elections that his candidates seemed to get into office automatically. The existence of the examples found by Mr Popik certainly suggest the expression was at first unconnected with Errol Flynn, but that it shifted its association when he became such a notorious figure'] **1** [1940s+] (*orig. US*) a dead certainty, esp. in areas of sexual conquest. **2** [1990s+] intimate with.

in my bollocks *phr.* (*also* **in my arse, ...belt, ...bollix, ...boot, ...brown, ...hole, ...ring, ...wick, in your tail-board, on my pratt**) [1920s+] a general intensifier, usu. negating the previous statement.

inna *adj.* [20C+] (*W.I./UK black teen*) inside, in the, in.

inner tube *n.* see RUBBER CHEQUE *n.*

innie *n.* (*also* **insy**) [1970s+] an indented navel.

innit! *excl.* (*also* **ennit!**) [SE *isn't it*] [1940s+] all-purpose, otherwise meaningless term, used at the end of sentences.

innocent *n.* **1** [mid-19C] (*US*) a corpse. **2** [mid-19C–1930s] (*US Und.*) a prisoner [since the prisoner is locked up they cannot be accused of any subsequent crimes until release; Irwin suggests the near universal claim by criminals that they are innocent]. **3** [late 19C+] (*UK Und.*) a sentence passed on an innocent man. **4** [1960s] (*US black*) ironic ref. to white liberals wishing to become involved in the black struggle [from stock liberal disavowals of racism, prejudice, the responsibility for slavery etc].

innocent *adj.*
SE in slang uses

IN PHRASES

▫ **she is/was so innocent she thinks fucking is a town in China** [pun on *Fukien*, an area in southeast China] [1940s+] a phr. used of an especially naïve young woman.

innominables *n. see* INEXPRESSIBLES *n.*

in on *adv.* [late 19C+] involved with, esp. a plan or scheme, legal or otherwise.

in one's *phr.* [phr. *in one's life*] [mid-19C–1940s] (*US*) part of one's circumstances, e.g. *none of that in mine*, no thank you.

in one's ackee/salt *phr.* [these positive emotions arise from being well-fed on *ackee*, a popular W.I. fruit of the *Blighia sapida* tree, usu. accompanied by saltfish] [1940s+] (*W.I.*) energetic, cheerful.

in-out *n. see* IN-AND-OUT *n.*[1] (2).

ins *n.* [abbr.] (*US*) **1** [1930s+] *in*formations. **2** [1950s] *in*terests. **3** [1970s] *in*fluence(s). **4** [1990s+] (*US campus*) money [money is an IN *n.*].

insane *adj.* [on bad = good model] [1940s+] (*orig. US black*) wonderful, admirable, excellent.

insangu *n.* [synon. Xhosa *intsangu*/Zulu *insangu*] [2000s] (*S.Afr. drugs*) marijuana.

insects (and ants) *n.* [rhy. sl. = SE/SAmE *pants*] [20C+] **1** trousers. **2** knickers, i.e. underwear.

Inside, the *n.* [late 19C+] (*Aus.*) central Australia.

DERIVATIVES

▫ **insider** *n.* [late 19C+] (*Aus.*) person who lives in central Australia.

inside *n.* (*also* **insides**) [late 19C+] (*US*) information, esp. when privileged.

IN PHRASES

▫ **dark as the inside of a cow** *adj. see under* DARK *adj.*

inside *adj.* **1** [mid-19C+] (*also* **on the inside**) in prison. **2** [late 19C+] of information, privileged, intimate. **3** [1940s] in a psychiatric hospital.

IN COMPOUNDS

▫ **inside dope** *n.* [early 20C+] privileged or intimate information. ▫ **inside job** *n.* (*also* **inside work**) [JOB *n.*[2] (1)] [late 19C+] a crime that has been committed with the aid or cognizance of an employee of the company or servant of the house in question. ▫ **inside kid** *n.* [KID *n.*[1] (5)] [1920s–30s] one who has privileged information or knowledge. ▫ **inside man** *n.* **1** [late 19C] (*UK Und.*) a police spy. **2** [20C+] (*orig. UK Und.*) (*also* **inside**) anyone involved in a crime, usu. a large-scale robbery of a firm or private house, who is employed on site and helps the robbers with information etc. **3** [1930s+] (*orig. UK Und.*) a tipster who locates prospects for robbers or safe-blowers. **4** [1930s+] (*orig. UK Und.*) in a three-card monte team, an accomplice who poses as a normal bettor but acts only to encourage the real victims of the game. **5** [1930s+] (*US Und.*) in any confidence trick, that member of the team who takes the lead role in tricking the victim; the *roper* or *outside man* brings the victim to the *inside man*. ▫ **inside track** *n.* [late 20C use is SE; note racing jargon *inside track*, the truth] [mid-19C–1950s] exclusive information; an advantageous position. ▫ **inside wire** *n.* [1960s] privileged, 'inside' information, esp. in the context of a crime [WIRE *n.*[1] (3)].

IN PHRASES

▫ **on the inside** [20C+] privy to restricted information.

inside and outside! *excl.* [abbr. *inside of a cunt and outside of a jail!*] [early–mid-19C] a popular toast.

inside right *adj.* [rhy. sl. = SE *tight* mean] [1990s+] mean, grasping.

insides *n. see* INSIDE *n.*

inspector *n.* [he moves from job to job, 'to see what they are like'] [1930s–40s] (*US*) an itinerant worker.

IN PHRASES

▫ **inspector of city buildings** *n.* [1920s+] (*Aus.*) one who is unemployed and not especially keen on finding work. ▫ **inspector of manholes** *n.* (*also* **manhole inspector**) [pun on SE *manhole/man hole*, i.e. the male anus] [1930s+] a male homosexual; usu. the active partner. ▫ **inspector of public buildings** *n.* [late 19C–1910s] an unemployed person. ▫ **inspector of (the) pavements** *n. see under* PAVEMENT *n.*

inspired *adj.* [euph.] [late 19C+] drunk.

instant boot camp *n.* [BOOT *v.*[7] (1)+ pun on milit. *boot camp*, a notably vile environment] [1970s+] (*US campus*) the act of vomiting.

instant zen *n.* [the contemplative world of *Zen* Buddhism] [1960s+] (*drugs*) LSD.

instrument *n.* **1** in sexual contexts. (**a**) [16C+] (*also* **generation tool**) the penis. ext. as *instrument of copulation/generation/propagation*. (**b**) [late 16C–17C] the vagina. (**c**) [mid-17C] in pl., the testicles. **2** [1900s–50s] (*US Und.*) the pickpocket who actually takes the object from the victim.

insuppressibles *n. see* INEXPRESSIBLES *n.*

insurance policy *n.* [1970s] (*US teen*) a condom.

insy *n. see* INNIE *n.*

intellex *n.* [? tradename or ? SE *intelligent*] [2000s] (*US drugs*) the drug 4-methylaminorex.

intense *adj.* (*US campus*) **1** [1970s+] very good, excellent. **2** [1980s+] very difficult.

intense! *excl.* [INTENSE *adj.* (1)] [1980s+] (*US campus*) a general excl. of approval.

interior decorating *n.* [euph.] [1980s+] (*UK society*) sexual intercourse during the day.

interlazzer *n.* [mid-19C] (*UK Und.*) a parasite.

international bitch *n.* [1960s] a female INTERNATIONAL NIGGER *n.*

international milk thief *n.* [1970s+] (*UK police*) an ironic term for any petty villain.

international nigger *n.* [NIGGER *n.*[1] (11)] [1950s–70s] (*US black*) a person who dresses in expensive, imported clothes.

interplanetary mission *n.* [the 'mission' is to get HIGH *adj.*[1] (2), term from *Star Trek*] [1990s+] (*drugs*) of a user, going around from one *CRACK HOUSE under* CRACK *n.*[7] to another in the hope of getting some drugs.

in the jigs *phr. see* JIGGERED *adj.*[1] (3).

in the lurch *n. see* LEFT IN THE LURCH *n.*

in the mood *n.* [rhy. sl.] [20C+] food.

in the nooer *phr.* [SE *manure*] [1970s] (*Aus.*) in difficulties.

in the nude *n.* [rhy. sl.] [1970s+] food.

in the park *n. see* BUSHY PARK *n.*[2].

in there *adj.* **1** [1930s–60s] (*orig. US black*) involved, aware, informed; doing well, prospering. **2** [1940s+] (*US black*) looking attractive. **3** [1950s+] sexually successful. **4** [1950s+] (*US campus*) pleased and excited.

IN PHRASES

▫ **you're in there** [1950s+] you'll find no problems with seduction.

in there! *excl. see GET IN THERE! under* GET IN *v.*

intimate *n.* [the shirt's proximity to one's body] [19C] (*US Und.*) a shirt.

into *prep.*[1] [abbr. *pitch into* etc] [mid-19C+] fighting.

into *prep.*[2] [late 19C+] (*orig. US*) **1** owing money to. **2** having taken a payment for a job.

into *prep.*[3] **1** [late 19C+] (*Aus.*) sexually involved with. **2** [1930s+] involved in a money-making scheme of some form, esp, criminal. **3** [1960s+] aware of, interested in, involved with, attracted by; thus *be into* [abbr. *deeply into* or similar; a HIPPIE *n.*[2] (3) phrase that emerged during the late 1960s and thence proceeded to general speech as well as use in a variety of New Age therapies; ult. from 19C SE *into*, meaning involved with]. **4** [1980s+] of the police, pursuing, investigating.

in tow *phr.* [1980s+] (*Aus. prison*) susceptible to bribery.

intro *n.* [abbr.] [1910s+] an *intro*duction, whether to a person or to a piece of writing, music etc.

IN PHRASES

❑ **intro up** *v.* [2000s] to *intro*duce.

introduce charley *v. see under* CHARLIE *n.*[11].

introduce her to Fagan *v. see under* FAGAN *n.*

-invasion *sfx* [1980s+] (*US campus*) in comb. with a relevant n., denoting a quantity, a large number, e.g. *hunk invasion*, a lot of handsome boys.

Inventories *n.* [late 19C] the Inventions Exhibition, London 1885.

invertebrated *adj.* [SE *invertebrate*, without a backbone, i.e. one has collapsed] [1980s+] (*US campus*) drunk.

invigorator *n.* [mid-19C] **1** a drink. **2** an oyster.

in with *phr.* **1** [late 17C–19C] intimate with [SE post-1800]. **2** [mid-19C–1900s] suspicious of a person, getting even with. **3** [mid-19C+] fashionable, socially aware. **4** [late 19C] in comparison with, compared with.

in you go says bob munro *phr.* [ety. unknown; ? anecdotal or simply assonant] [1950s+] (*N.Z.*) a general phr. of encouragement at the outset of a project, competition etc.

in your dipper! *excl.* [? ref. to sheep dip] [1920s+] (*N.Z.*) a general excl. of rejection, dismissal.

in your tailboard *phr. see* IN MY BOLLOCKS *phr.*

ipsal dixal *n.* [Lat. *ipse dixit*, an unproved statement, a dictum, lit. 'he himself said it'] [mid-19C–1900s] an unsupported statement.

ipse *n.* [Lat. *ipse*, itself; thus 'the very thing'. Note the Umbrian wine *Est! Est! Est!*, lit. 'It is, it is, it is!', i.e. it is the best/the thing] [early 18C] a variety of ale.

ipsydinxy *n.* (*also* **ipse dixit**) [? echoic of the slurred tones of a drinker; ? positive challenge to a drunkard to say the Lat. phr. *ipse dixit*] [late 18C–mid-19C] whisky.

I.R.A. *adj.* [rhy. sl. = GAY *adj.* (6)] [1980s] (*Aus.*) homosexual.

Ira *n. see* IDA *n.*

ira *n.* [Partridge suggests 'centre slang', but ? mis-sp. of RIAH *n.*] [1970s] (*gay*) hair.

Irene *n. see* IDA *n.*

irey *adj.* (*also* **irie**) [HIGH *adj.*[1]] [1950s+] (*W.I. Rasta*) pleasing, powerful, euphoric; orig. in the context of the sensations that followed smoking cannabis; thus used as an affirmative greeting.

Irish *n.* **1** [mid-19C+] (*orig. US*) temper. **2** *see* IRISH ARMS *under* IRISH *adj.*

Irish *adj.* [the stereotypical Irishman or woman is stupid, short-tempered, violent (whether on the street or in the home), addicted to potatoes, keen on brawling and usu. employed in a menial, labouring task, often rural; all these traits are reflected in the combs. that follow, and all combs. with *Irish* should be assumed to be derog. (if seen as joc. by the coiner/speaker) unless otherwise stated] [18C+] a general negative racial epithet; usu. in combs. below.

IN COMPOUNDS

I. pertaining to work

a. the wheelbarrow

❑ **Irish ambulance** *n.* [1910s–30s] (*US*) a wheelbarrow. ❑ **Irish baby buggy** *n.* [1910s+] (*US*) a wheelbarrow. ❑ **Irish buggy** *n.* (*also* **Irish pluggy**) [1920s+] (*US*) a wheelbarrow. ❑ **Irish chariot** *n.* [1940s] (*US*) a wheelbarrow. ❑ **Irish local** *n.* [1930s+] (*US*) a wheelbarrow [SAmE *local*, a local train line].

b. tools for physical labour

❑ **Irish banjo** *n.* (*also* **Irish spoon**) [mid-19C+] a spade, a shovel. ❑ **Irish fan** *n.* [1920s+] (*US*) a spade, a shovel. ❑ **Irish local** *n.* [1900s] a hand-car, propelled by pushing a handle backwards and forwards. ❑ **Irish screwdriver** *n.* [20C+] a hammer. ❑ **Irish toothpick** *n.* [1920s] (*US*) a pickaxe. ❑ **Irish tumble-dryer** *n.* [1980s] a cement mixer.

II. pertaining to food

a. the potato

❑ **Irish apple** *n.* [late 18C+] a potato. ❑ **Irish apricot** *n.* (*also* **Irish wall-fruit**) [late 18C+] a potato. ❑ **Irish football** *n.* [1970s] (*US*) a potato. ❑ **Irish grape** *n.* [1940s–70s] (*US*) a potato. ❑ **Irish lemon** *n.* [late 19C+] (*US*) a potato. ❑ **Irish root** *n.* [mid-19C] a potato.

b. other foodstuffs

❑ **Irish cherry** *n.* [1930s+] (*US*) a carrot. ❑ **Irish cocktail** *n.* [play on MICKEY FINN *n.*] [1980s] (*US*) a drink containing a substance that causes unconsciousness. ❑ **Irish goose** *n.* [mid-19C] (*US*) cooked codfish. ❑ **Irish horse** *n.* [mid-18C+] tough, undercooked salt beef. ❑ **Irish nachos** *n.* [1990s+] (*US*) fried potato wedges and (refried) beans. ❑ **Irish turkey** *n.* [popularized by its use in the *Jiggs and Maggie* comic strip] [mid-19C+] (*US*) corned (UK: salt) beef and cabbage.

III. pertaining to sex

❑ **Irish clubhouse** *n.* [1960s+] (*US gay*) a sophisticated, expensive brothel. ❑ **Irish confetti** *n.* [1980s+] semen spilled outside the vagina (through coitus interruptus practised by pious Catholics). ❑ **Irish dip** *n.* [1960s+] (*gay*) sexual intercourse. ❑ **Irish disease** *n.* [1990s+] the state of having a small penis. ❑ **Irish fortune** *n.* [19C] the vagina. ❑ **Irish horse** *n.* [1950s+] (*gay*) an impotent penis. ❑ **Irish inch** *n.* [a slur on Irish penis size] [1970s–80s] (*US*) the erect penis. ❑ **Irish jig** *n. see* separate entry. ❑ **Irish marathon** *n.* [20C+] a lengthy session of sexual intercourse. ❑ **Irish potato** *n.* [? play on SPUD *n.*[3]/STUD *n.*] [1990s+] (*W.I.*) a young man who is 'kept' by an older woman. ❑ **Irish promotion** *n.* [20C+] (*gay*) masturbation. ❑ **Irish rise** *n.* [late 19C+] sexual detumescence. ❑ **Irish root** *n.* [19C+] the penis. ❑ **Irish toothache** *n.* (*also* **i.t.a., Paddy's toothache, Dutch salute**) **1** [19C+] an erection. **2** [20C+] pregnancy. ❑ **Irish toothpick** *n.* [1980s+] (*US gay*) the erect penis. ❑ **Irish virgin** *n.* [? pious Irish virgins who become nuns] [20C+] (*US*) one who is a virgin and is likely to remain one. ❑ **Irish way** *n.* [the belief that pious Catholics used anal intercourse as their sole means of contraception] [1970s+] heterosexual anal intercourse. ❑ **Irish wedding** *n.* [20C+] (*gay*) masturbation. ❑ **Irish whist** *n.* [19C] sexual intercourse.

IN PHRASES

❑ **dance the Irish jig** *v. see under* DANCE *v.* ❑ **give a hot poultice for the Irish toothache** *v.* [late 19C] of a woman, to have sexual intercourse. ❑ **Irish by birth but Greek by injection** [GREEK *adj.* (2) + INJECTION *n.*] [1960s+] of a man, homosexual. ❑ **play at Irish whist (where the jack takes the ace)** *v.* [late 19C] to have sexual intercourse.

IV. pertaining to lack of sophistication

❑ **Irish comics** *n.* (*also* **Irish funnies, Irish sports pages**) [because of supposed Irish illiteracy] [1970s+] the obituary columns in a newspaper. ❑ **Irish compliment** *n.* [mid-19C+] a back-handed compliment. ❑ **Irish dividend** *n.* [mid-19C+] (*US*) a non-existent or fictitious profit, a deficit, a stock assessment. ❑ **Irish hint** *n.* [mid-18C+] (*US*) a very broad hint. ❑ **Irish promotion** *n.* [late 19C+] a cut in one's pay. ❑ **Irish rise** *n.* (*also* **Irish raise**) [mid-19C+] a cut in one's pay. ❑ **Irish shave** *n.* [1920s+] the act of defecation. ❑ **Irish sidewalk** *n. see* IRISHMAN'S SIDEWALK *under* IRISHMAN'S *adj.* ❑ **Irish sports pages** *n. see* IRISH COMICS above. ❑ **Irish wash** *n.* [1960s+] (*US*) the turning or reversing of a garment or other object to hide rather than actually remove the dirt.

V. pertaining to physique

❑ **Irish arms** *n.* (*also* **Irish**) [mid-18C–mid-19C] thick legs. ❑ **Irish channel** *n.* [down which alcohol flows] [1900s] the throat. ❑ **Irish draperies** *n.* [1980s+] drooping female breasts. ❑ **Irish evidence** *n.* [1960s] (*gay*) pendulous breasts. ❑ **Irish legs** *n.* [late 18C+] heavy female legs. ❑ **Irish stamps** *n.* [mid-19C] (*UK Und.*) thick, clumsy legs.

VI. pertaining to violence

❑ **Irish beauty** *n.* [late 18C+] a woman with a pair of black eyes. ❑ **Irish bouquet** *n.* [1960s–70s] (*US*) any form of projectile, usu. a stone or brick. ❑ **Irish coat of arms** *n. see* *IRISHMAN'S COAT OF ARMS under* IRISHMAN'S *adj.* ❑ **Irish confetti** *n.* [from *c.*1832 until the adoption of asphalt, NY streets were paved with bricks] [20C+] (*also* **confetti**) bricks, esp. as thrown during riots. ❑ **Irish dividend** *n.* [1920s] (*US Und.*) a shake-down by the police. ❑ **Irish hoist** *n.* [the stereotypically boorish, brawling Irishman] [mid-19C+] a kick in the behind. ❑ **Irish invitation** *n.* [late 18C] a challenge to a duel. ❑ **Irish karate** *n.* [1990s+] (*Aus.*) the use of a shotgun. ❑ **Irish parliament** *n.* [1940s] a heated argument. ❑ **Irish rose** *n.* [1930s] (*US*) a stone, for throwing. ❑ **Irish wake** *n.* [mid-19C+] any boisterous occasion and not necessarily a wake. ❑ **Irish wedding** *n.* (*also* **wedding**) [late 18C–19C] a brawl, 'where black eyes are given instead of favours' (Grose 1796).

VII. general uses

❑ **Irish assurance** *n.* [like the Greek myth, which proclaims that being dipped in the River Styx gives a child invulnerability, 'so it is said, that a dipping in the River Shannon totally annihilates bashfulness' (Grose 1785)] [late 18C–19C] boldness, shamelessness. ❑ **Irish clubhouse** *n.* [20C+] (*US*) a police station [plays on SE *club*, association/*club* to hit, i.e. police violence]. ❑ **Irish confetti** *n.* [1980s+] (*N.Z.*) gravel, stones. ❑ **Irish curtains** *n.* [1960s+] (*Aus./US*) cobwebs. ❑ **Irish draperies** *n.* [late 19C+] cobwebs. ❑ **Irish evidence** *n.* [late 18C–19C] a perjuring witness; perjury. ❑ **Irish flag** *n.* [1960s] (*US*) a diaper, a nappy. ❑ **Irish lace** *n.* [1950s+] a spider's web. ❑ **Irish merino** *n.* [2000s] (*N.Z.*) a wild pig. ❑ **Irish necktie** *n.* [late 19C] (*US*) a rope. ❑ **Irish nightingale** *n.* [mid-19C–1940s] (*US*) a bullfrog. ❑ **Irish pasture** *n.* [20C+] (*US*) a fainting fit, esp. a pretended one. ❑ **Irish rifle** *n.* [19C] a small toothcomb. ❑ **Irish shift** *n.* (*also* **Irish switch**) [the supposed propensity of Irish politicians to blow with the prevailing wind; given the year of first use – 1960 – the Irish in question may have been the Kennedys, whose scion John was elected president that year] [1960s+] (*US*) political hypocrisy. ❑ **Irish twins** *n.* [the stereotypical fecundity – and lack of contraceptive practice – of trad. Irish families] [1960s+] (*US*) two siblings born within a 12-month period. ❑ **Irish wedding** *n.* [19C] the emptying of a cesspool.

SE in general slang uses

IN PHRASES

❑ **as Irish as Paddy Murphy's pig** (*also* **as Irish as paddy's pig, as Irish as Patrick Murphy's pig**) [late 19C+] quintessentially Irish.

Irish jig *n.* [rhy. sl.] [20C+] **1** wig. **2** (*Aus.*) a term of abuse for an Irish person, a pig. **3** a cigarette [CIG *n.*].

Irish lasses *n.* [rhy. sl.] [20C+] glasses.

Irishman's *adj.* possessive of the same stereotypical qualities as IRISH *adj.*

IN COMPOUNDS

❑ **Irishman's buggy** *n.* [1920s] (*US*) a wheelbarrow. ❑ **Irishman's coat of arms** *n.* (*also* **Irish coat of arms**) [mid-18C+] a black eye and a bloody nose. ❑ **Irishman's dinner** *n.* ['a smoke and a visit to the urinal' (Hotten 1874) + ref. to Irish Famine 1845–6] [19C+] a fast. ❑ **Irishman's harvest** *n.* [used by London costermongers; indigent Irishmen presumably picked up rotten oranges] [19C] the orange season. ❑ **Irishman's pocket** *n.* [20C+] (*US*) a pocket that is both large and empty. ❑ **Irishman's rest** *n.* [late 19C–1900s] mounting a ladder carrying a hod of bricks. ❑ **Irishman's sidewalk** *n.* (*also* **Irish sidewalk**) [racial stereotyping; either the despised Irish ought to walk in the street, rather than on the pavement where more civilized people walked, or they were too stupid to know the difference] [mid-19C–1930s] (*US*) the street. ❑ **Irishman's turkey** *n.* [1910s+] (*US*) corned beef and cabbage.

Irish mike *n. see* PAT AND MIKE *n.*[1].

Irish rose *n.* [rhy. sl.] [20C+] the nose.

Irish stew *adj.* [rhy. sl.] [20C+] **1** true, esp. in the phr. below. **2** blue.

IN PHRASES

❑ **too Irish (stew)** *adj.* (*also* **too bloody Irish (stew)**) [20C+] too true.

Irishy *n.* [late 19C] (*Aus.*) an Irish immigrant to Australia.

iron *n.* [later use is US] **1** [16C–early 18C; 1930s+] the penis. **2** as a metal coin. (**a**) [late 18C–1920s] money. (**b**) [1900s–10s] (*US*) $1 in cash. **3** as a metallic object. (**a**) [early 19C–1910s] (*US*) bullets or shells. (**b**) [mid-19C+] (*US*) (*also* **ironware, piece of iron**) a gun. (**c**) [1920s] (*US Und.*) a drill bit. (**d**) [1920s+] (*US prison*) handcuffs. (**e**) [1930s+] (*US*) a discontinued model of motor car, a run-down, dilapidated car. (**f**) [1940s] a housebreaker's implement, a crowbar. (**g**) [1960s–70s] (*US*) a motorcycle. (**h**) [1960s+] (*US*) weights, as used in bodybuilding exercises. (**i**) [1970s+] a knife. **4** [mid-19C; 1990s+] in fig. use, courage. **5** [1980s+] (*W.I., Jam.*) a thug, a gangster.

IN COMPOUNDS

❑ **iron boy** *n.* [1910s–20s] (*US*) $1. ❑ **iron dollar** *n.* [1900s–20s] (*US*) $1 in cash. ❑ **iron freak** *n.* [-FREAK *sfx*] [1960s] (*US*) a weight-lifting enthusiast. ❑ **ironhead** *n.* [1990s+] (*US prison*) one who works out with body-building weights. ❑ **iron louie** *n.* [late 19C] (*US*) $1. ❑ **iron man** *n.* **1** [20C+] (*US*) $1; usu. in pl. **2** [1940s–60s] (*US*) $1000. **3** [1940s–70s] (*orig. Aus.*) £1 note. **4** [1960s] (*US*) $100. ❑ **ironware** *n. see* sense 3b above. ❑ **iron-whip** *v.* [1970s] (*US Und.*) to pistol-whip.

IN PHRASES

❑ **carry iron** *v.* [1930s] (*US Und.*) to go armed, esp. as a gangster's bodyguard. ❑ **draw iron** *v. see under* DRAW *v.*[4]. ❑ **iron out** *v.* [2000s] of money, to spend freely. ❑ **piece of iron** *n. see* sense 3b above. ❑ **pump iron** *v.* (*also* **bump iron, drive..., throw...**) [1960s+] (*orig. US*) to work out with weights, to practise bodybuilding. ❑ **push iron** *v.* [1960s–80s] (*US*) to exercise with weights. ❑ **put an iron on one's shoulder** *v.* [1980s+] (*N.Z.*) to become indebted, lit. or fig.

iron, the *n. see* IRON HORSE *n.*[2].

iron *adj.* [mid-19C] courageous, feerless.

SE in slang uses

IN COMPOUNDS

❑ **iron bar** *v.* (*also* **bar**) [1980s+] (*Aus. prison*) to make a surprise attack (irrespective of the weapon used). ❑ **iron ben** *n.* [1940s] (*US Und.*) a bullet-proof vest. ❑ **iron boots** *n. see IRON GAITERS* below. ❑ **iron-bound** *n.* [late 18C–early 19C] a silver-laced hat. ❑ **iron butterfly** *n.* (*also* **butterfly**) [shape; the curved finger-holes are the 'wings' of the butterfly] [1950s+] an old-fashioned hypodermic syringe made of metal and glass. ❑ **iron cross** *n.* [SE *cross*, a burden] [1960s+] (*US black*) extremely unfavourable circumstances from which it is hard to extract oneself. ❑ **iron cunny** *n.* [pron. SE *candy*] [1950s] (*W.I.*) a tough sugar candy, extremely hard to chew. ❑ **iron cure** *n.* (*also* **steel and concrete cure**) [the *iron* bars of the cell] [1930s–50s] (*US drugs*) a 'cure' for addiction given in prison: the prisoner is deprived of drugs and forced to withdraw in his cell. ❑ **iron doublet** *n.* [Carew (1785–1882), Kent (1835), 'Sinks' (1848) and F Diunscombe (c.1850) all offer erroneously *iron-doublet*, a parson] **1** [17C–early 19C] a prison. **2** [late 19C] (*US*) innocence. ❑ **iron eye** *n.* [1940s] (*US*) a hard and hostile stare. ❑ **iron feed** *n.* [such a starchy dish is very 'hard'] [1940s] (*W.I.*) corn meal cooked with rice. ❑ **iron gaiters** *n.* (*also* **iron boots, ...garters**) [mid-18C–mid-19C] leg-irons. ❑ **iron hat** *n.* [note WW1 US milit. *iron derby*, a steel helmet] [1910s–30s] (*US*) a derby hat. ❑ **iron house** *n.* **1** [1910s+] (*US Und.*) (*also* **iron hotel**) a prison. **2** [1990s+] a punishment cell. ❑ **iron jaws** *n.* [1970s+] (*US gay*) an exceptionally competent fellator. ❑ **iron lung** *n.* **1** [1940s] a deep air-raid shelter in the London underground. **2** [1950s] the Central Line, in its extension from Shoreditch to Essex. **3** [1960s+] (*Irish*) an aluminium keg of beer, usu. Guinness. **4** [1970s+] an open-air urinal. ❑ **iron parenthesis** *n.* [it provides a *parenthesis* in one's on-going life] [early 19C] a prison. ❑ **iron pile** *n.* [SE/IRON *n.* (3h)] [20C+] (*US Und.*) **1** a prison. **2** (*also* **weight pile**) the weight-lifting and body-building facilities in a prison. ❑ **iron rivets** *n. see* RIVETS *n.* ❑ **iron theatre** *n.* [1920s–30s] (*US Und.*) a prison.

iron *v.* **1** [late 19C+] to kill. **2** [1950s+] (*Aus.*) to defeat in a fight. **3** [1970s+] (*Aus.*) to get drunk.

IN PHRASES

❑ **iron out** *v.* [fig. uses of SE] [20C+] **1** to correct a situation, to put things right. **2** to overwhelm in a fight. **3** to kill, to murder. **4** to reform, to impose morality [? IRON *n.* (3b)].

iron duke *n.* [rhy. sl. = FLUKE *n.*[2] (1); the orig. *Iron Duke* was the Duke of Wellington (1769–1852)] [late 19C+] a lucky chance.

ironed *adj.* [mid-18C] (*US*) handcuffed.

iron girder *n.* [rhy. sl.] [1990s+] murder; usu. in fig. uses, e.g. 'get away with iron girder'; 'there'll be iron girder if..

Ironhead *n.* [the German soldier's helmet] [1940s] (*Aus.*) a German soldier.

ironhead *n.* [the hardness of iron] [1910s+] (*US*) a fool.

ironheaded *adj.* [IRONHEAD *n.*] [1940s] stupid.

iron (hoof) *n.* [rhy. sl. = POOF *n.* (1)] [1930s+] a male homosexual.

iron hoop *n.* [rhy. sl.] [late 19C–1910s] soup.

iron horse *n.*[1] [1920s] (*US Und.*) prison.

iron horse *n.*[2] [rhy. sl.] **1** [1930s+] (*also* **the iron, the ironing**) a toss (note Cockney pron. *torss*). **2** [1950s+] a racecourse.

iron horse *n.*[3] [the original *iron horse* was the mid-19C railroad] [1970s+] (*US black*) the subway.

iron horse *v.* [IRON HORSE *n.*[2] (1)] [1930s+] to toss (as in coins).

ironing, the *n. see* IRON HORSE *n.*[2].

iron Mike *n.*[1] [play on SE *iron* + 'anthropomorphic' nickname] [1940s] (*US Und.*) brass knuckles.

iron Mike *n.*[2] [rhy. sl. = SE *bike*] [1940s+] a bicycle.

ironmongery *n.* [20C+] firearms, weapons.

irons *n.* **1** [late 17C+] (*US*) handcuffs. **2** [1920s+] utensils, knife and fork [abbr. EATING IRONS *n.*]. **3** [1980s+] knuckledusters.

iron tank *n.* [rhy. sl.] [1910s+] a bank.

irrigate *v.* [mid-19C–1900s] (*Aus./US*) **1** to drink. **2** to give a drink to someone else.

irrigation *n.* [IRRIGATE *v.*] [mid–late 19C] alcoholic refreshment.

irrits *n.*

(IN PHRASES)

❑ **give someone the irrits** *v.* [abbr. SE *irritate*] [20C+] (*Aus.*) to annoy, to irritate.

irvine *n.* (*also* **irv**) [? joc. use of proper name] [1970s+] (*US black*) the police.

isaac *n.* [? generic use of Isaac as a rural, thus 'foolish' name] [late 17C] a fool.

isabella *n.* (*also* **isabeller**) [rhy. sl.] [mid-19C+] an umbrella.

is all *phr.* [1940s+] (*orig. US*) abbr. of *that is all*.

isda *n.* [? Sp.] [1970s+] (*drugs*) heroin.

ish, the *n.* [SHIT *n.* (2b)] [1990s+] (*US black*) **1** something bad. **2** the very best, the ultimate.

ish *adj.* [? abbr. CUNTISH (*see under* CUNT *n.*) but poss. backsl. SHIT *n.*] [1980s+] (*UK juv.*) a general negative, use varying as to context.

i-shence *n.* (*also* **ishen**) [SE *essence*] [1950s+] (*W.I. Rasta*) marijuana, often particularly potent strains.

ish kabibble *phr.* (*also* **ish kabbible**) [for etym. *see* ABIE KABIBBLE *n.*] [1910s+] (*US*) it is of no importance to me, 'I should worry'.

I shot him lightly and he died politely *phr. see under* SHOOT *v.*

I should be so lucky *phr. see under* LUCKY *adj.*

I should blush to murmur *phr.* [late 19C] (*US*) a phr. of affirmation.

I should cocoa! *excl. see under* COFFEE AND COCOA *v.*

I should snicker to smile *phr. see under* SMILE *v.*

I should worry *phr.* [Yid.] [20C+] I don't care.

is it? *phr.* **1** [1910s] used as a challenging phr. **2** [1960s+] (*S.Afr.*) a non-committal expression used to convey polite disbelief, astonishment, 'Really?' 'You don't mean to say?'.

Island, the *n.* **1** [mid-19C+] Riker's Island prison, near New York. **2** [late 19C–1930s] (*US Und.*) Blackwell's Island Asylum, NYC. **3** [late 19C] (*S.Afr.*) Robben Island prison. **4** [20C+] the Isle of Wight and, thus the prisons of Parkhurst, Portland or Camp Hill, both of which are situated on the island.

island *n.*

(IN PHRASES)

❑ **drink out of the island** *v. see under* DRINK *v.*

island nigger *n.* [SE *island* + NIGGER *n.*[1] (1); the premise being that, as foreigners and non-whites, Puerto Ricans are *de facto* niggers] [1980s+] (*US*) a derog. term for a Puerto Rican.

isle of France *n.* [rhy. sl.] [mid-19C–1900s] a dance.

Isle of Man *n.* [rhy. sl.; never shortened] [20C+] a pan.

Isle of Wight *n.* [rhy. sl.] [1950s+] **1** the right side. **2** right, permission.

Isle of Wight *adj.* [rhy. sl.] [20C+] **1** light. **2** tipsy [= TIGHT *adj.* (7)]. **3** all right. **4** mean, grasping [= TIGHT *adj.* (6a)].

ism *n.* (*also* **izm**) [ety. unknown] [1980s+] (*US drugs*) marijuana.

ism and skism *n.* (*also* **isms and skisms, ism and schism**) [? coined by Bob Marley] [1970s+] (*W.I./UK black teen*) a phr. that denotes society's ways, class consciousness, sub-systems and/or classifications.

isn't that special *phr.* [1980s+] (*US campus*) a dismissive phr. implying that *that* is not special at all.

iso *n.* [abbr.] [1930s] (*US prison*) the *iso*lation cells.

Isro *n.* (*also* **Izro, Jewfro**) [SE *Israel* + AFRO *n.*] [1970s+] (*US*) a bushy hairstyle worn by white people, often curly-headed Jews.

Issey *n. see* IZZY *n.*

issue *n.* [1910s+] (*Aus.*) everything, the lot, all there is.

(IN PHRASES)

❑ **the whole issue** *n.* [1910s+] (*Aus.*) everything, the lot, all there is.

issue *v.* [1990s+] (*US drugs*) to cheat; to sell fake drugs.

I.S.T. *n.* [abbr. *I*ndian *S*tretchable *T*ime; cultural/national stereotyping] [1990s+] (*US*) a lack of punctuality.

I suppose *n.* [rhy. sl.] [mid-19C+] a nose.

I swan *phr.* (*also* **I swanny**) [abbr./pron. of SE oath *I shall warrant*] [early–mid-19C] (*US*) a phr. of asseveration, 'I declare'.

it *n.*[1] [euph.] **1** [17C+] sexual intercourse. **2** [mid-17C+] the male genitals. **3** [19C] a chamberpot. **4** [late 19C+] the female genitals. **5** [late 19C+] (*US*) a fool or an unpleasant person, a term of contempt. **6** [late 19C+] (*orig. US*) the acme of fashion, the ultimate, usu. when applied to a person, e.g. *he really thinks he's it*. **7** [20C+] (*US*) money. **8** [20C+] a cover-all for such special qualities that are required for social or professional success. **9** [20C+] sex appeal [note that although the term was popularized in Elinor Glyn's *It* (1927), see R. Kipling 'Mrs Bathurst' (1904) for earlier use. Cited as such in the OED and by Andrew Lycett in *Rudyard Kipling* (1999) who adds 'Possibly he gleaned this idea from Lord Milner, who had courted Glyn']. **10** [1910s+] a person. **11** [1920s] ejaculation. **12** [1930s] (*US*) excrement. **13** [1930s] (*US Und.*) death; also fig. use. **14** [1930s+] a ref. to a casual, picked-up partner as opposed to a lover. **15** [1930s+] sexually available females. **16** [1940s+] virginity. **17** [1950s] (*US*) a dose of an addictive drug. **18** [1950s+] (*US black*) the quintessence of black spirit, sensitivity etc. **19** [1970s] masturbation.

(IN PHRASES)

❑ **at it** **1** [late 16C+] fighting, lit. or fig. **2** [17C+] indulging in sexual intercourse. **3** [18C+] involved in something illegal, or bad. **4** [19C–1900s] kissing and cuddling. **5** [mid-19C] drinking heavily. **6** [late 19C+] involved in an argument, emotionally moved. **7** [1920s+] teasing, provoking. ❑ **get it in** *v.* [1920s+] **1** of a man, to enter a woman before sexual intercourse. **2** to seduce. ❑ **get someone at it** *v.* [*at it* sense 7 above] [1940s+] to tease, to drive into a fury. ❑ **go to it** *v.* **1** [early 17C–early 18C; 1960s] to have sexual intercourse, to pet. **2** [1950s+] to fight. ❑ **have it** *v. see* separate entry. ❑ **have it all on** *v. see* separate entry. ❑ **have it away** *v. see* separate entries. ❑ **have it for** *v. see* separate entry. ❑ **have (it) off** *v. see* separate entry. ❑ **have it in** *v. see* separate entry. ❑ **have it on someone** *v.* (*also* **have it all over someone**) *see* separate entry. ❑ **have it up** *v. see* separate entry. ❑ **put it**

about *v.* [1960s+] to indulge in a wide-ranging sex life; to work as a prostitute. ❑ **put it down** *v.* [1950s+] (*US*) to sit down. ❑ **put it in and break it** *v.* [the erect penis 'breaks' after orgasm] [late 19C+] of a man, to have sexual intercourse. ❑ **put it to** *v.* [note Shakespeare's *Love's Labour's Lost* (*c.*1595): 'If their daughter be capable, I will put it to them'] [1930s+] to have sexual intercourse with. ❑ **put it up** *v.* [mid-19C; 1990s+] of a man, to have sexual intercourse. ❑ **put it up to** *v.* ['it' being a fist or boot] **1** [1910s] (*US*) to attack verbally, to criticize. **2** [1990s+] (*Irish*) to attack physically.

it *n.*[2] [late 19C+] as an indefinite object, used with a v., e.g. *walk it, cab it*.

i.t.a. *n. see* IRISH TOOTHACHE *under* IRISH *adj.*

ital *n.* [ITAL *adj.*] [1980s+] (*W.I.*) marijuana.

ital *adj.* (*also* **i-tal**) [SE *vital* + Rastafarian use of pfx *i-*] **1** [1950s+] (*orig. W.I. Rasta*) essential, basic, *echt* Rastafarian. **2** [1950s+] (*W.I. Rasta*) vital, organic, natural, wholesome, referring both to a way of cooking and of life. **3** [1960s+] (*W.I./UK black teen*) of food, natural, unprocessed (fresh vegetables, fruits etc) or prepared without salt.

Italian *n.* [stereotyping] [1990s+] (*US*) anger, bad temper.

Italian *adj.* [seen as a 'dirty' and 'foreign' practice] **1** [late 16C–17C; 1900s–1930s] (*also* **Italick**) devoted to hetero- or homosexual anal intercourse. **2** [17C] in fig. use, referring to anything 'backward' or reversed. **3** [mid-17C] pertaining to syphilis.

IN COMPOUNDS

❑ **Italian airlines** *n.* [the stereotyped inefficiency of Italian air companies] [1950s+] (*gay*) walking. ❑ **Italian fence climbers** *n.* [1990s+] (*US*) shoes, boots. ❑ **Italian football** *n.* [derog. stereotyping of Italian anarchists] [1940s–80s] (*US Und.*) a bomb. ❑ **Italian hero** *n.* [its 'heroic' size, or ? f. stereotype of Italians as placing sexual – the phallic sandwich – above martial prowess] [20C+] (*US*) a large sandwich made of two slabs of bread cut lengthwise from the loaf and containing a variety of ingredients. ❑ **Italian mean time** *n.* [2000s] unpunctuality. ❑ **Italian (pad)lock** *n. see* SPANISH PADLOCK *under* SPANISH *adj.* ❑ **Italian perfume** *n.* [1940s] (*US*) garlic. ❑ **Italian quarrel** *n.* [stereotyping; the image is of the corrupt Borgia family] [late 19C–1900s] death, murder, poisoning, treachery. ❑ **Italian salute** *n.* [the gesture originated in Italy and was imported by immigrants] [1950s+] (*US*) an obscene gesture of contempt or derision; one arm is bent and the fist and forearm thrust upwards while the other hand grasps the forearm or bicep. ❑ **Italian sin** *n.* (*also* **Italian tricks**) [17C] hetero- or homosexual anal intercourse. ❑ **Italian special** *n.* (*also* **Italian straws**) [20C+] (*US*) pasta, spaghetti. ❑ **Italian tune-up** *n.* [SE *tune-up*, service for a car] [1990s+] (*US*) the act of driving one's car into the desert and speeding at 100 mph to check that everything works.

italist *n.* [ITAL *adj.*] [1990s+] (*W.I.*) one who leads a natural 'organic' lifestyle; often of Rastafarians.

I.T.A.L.Y. *phr.* [abbr.] [1940s+] *I* *t*rust *a*nd *l*ove *y*ou, written on envelopes of love letters.

itch *n.* (*also* **itching**) **1** [17C+] sexual excitement. **2** [17C+] syphilis. **3** [1950s+] (*drugs*) an addiction to narcotics.

itch and scratch *n.* [rhy. sl.] [1910s+] a match.

itcher *n.* [ITCH *n.* (1)] [19C] the vagina.

itchified *adj.* [ITCH *n.* (2)] [mid-18C] syphilitic; as a term of abuse.

itching *n. see* ITCH *n.*

itching jenny *n.* [ITCH *n.* (1); note JENNY *n.*[1] (3) despite dates] [19C] the vagina.

itchland *n.* [derog. stereotyping of Wales and Scotland as lands of overt sexuality or of infestations of body-lice; thus early 18C ballad 'The Curse of Scotland': 'So God keep me from Scotland, and all that mangy race / For it is a nasty, mangy, lousy, itchy, dirty place'] **1** [late 17C–early 18C] Wales. **2** [18C–mid-19C] Scotland. **3** [mid-19C] (*UK Und.*) Ireland.

DERIVATIVES

❑ **Itchlander** *n.* [early 19C] a Scot.

Itchyamtown *n.* [ITCHLAND *n.* (2)] [mid-19C] (*UK Und.*) Edinburgh.

itchy eye *n.* [SE *itchy* + ROUNDEYE *n.* (1); a typical symptom is an itching sensation of the sphincter] [1990s+] (*US*) haemorrhoid.

Ite *n. see* EYETIE *n.*

item *n.* **1** [19C–1900s] (*US*) a hint, an inkling, a piece of information, thus one who hints. **2** [1940s+] (*US*) a person. **3** [1940s+] (*orig. US*) a couple.

IN COMPOUNDS

❑ **hot item** *n.* [the exploits of such fashionable individuals provide items for newspaper gossip columnists] [1980s+] (*US*) a couple having a romantic relationship.

item *v.* [ITEM *n.* (1)] [19C] to pass on information to a confederate.

I-Tie *n. see* EYETIE *n.*

Itie *see under* EYETIE.

-itis *sfx* [SE *-itis*, used with a proper noun to create the name of a disease, often an inflammation of the part in question, e.g. arthritis, nephritis] [20C+] used humorously to create imagined 'diseases', e.g. *Zeppelinitis*, a fear of aerial bombardment during WW1; *danceitis*, an obsession with dancing; *workitis*, a pathological dislike of work.

it's my way or the highway *phr.* [the image of a boy ejecting a girl from his car, some way from home, after she has refused to have sex] [1980s+] (*US*) do as I say or you will suffer.

it's one o'clock (at the button factory) *phr.* (*also* **it's two o'clock..., it's three o'clock..., ...at the waterworks**) [20C+] advice to a man that his fly is open.

itzy house *n.* [? DITZY *adj.*[2] (1)] [1930s] (*US*) a psychiatric institution.

IV *v.* [1990s+] (*US drugs*) to inject a drug *i*ntra*v*enously.

ivads! *excl. see* EGAD! *excl.*

Ivan *n.* [the stereotypical Slavic/Russian name] [1940s+] **1** generic for a Russian; thus a Communist. **2** a generally stupid east European person.

ivory *n.* [lit. or fig. uses of SE *ivory* used in manufacturing all these items] **1** [early 18C+] in pl., dice. **2** [late 18C+] a tooth, usu. in pl. **3** [mid-19C+] a piano; in pl., piano keys. **4** [late 19C–1930s] (*US*) poker chips. **5** [late 19C–1950s] billiard balls.

pertaining to a piano

IN COMPOUNDS

❑ **ivory-bender** *n.* [1920s] (*US*) a piano-player. ❑ **ivory-hammerer** *n.* (*also* **ivory-spanker**) [late 19C+] a pianist. ❑ **ivory-hound** *n.* [1930s] (*US*) a piano player [+ -HOUND *sfx*]. ❑ **ivory-pounder** *n.* [20C+] (*US*) a piano player. ❑ **ivory-thumper** *n.* [1920s+] (*US*) a piano player. ❑ **ivory-tickler** *n.* (*also* **tickler**) [1910s+] (*US*) a piano player.

general uses

IN COMPOUNDS

❑ **ivory-box** *n.* [19C+] the mouth. ❑ **ivory-carpenter** *n.* (*also* **ivory-picker, ...-puller, ...-snatcher**) [1940s–50s] (*US*) a dentist. ❑ **ivory dome** *n.* [DOME *n.* (1)] **1** [20C+] a bald-headed person. **2** [1910s–30s] (*US*) a fool. ❑ **ivory-domed** *adj.* [1910s–1930s] (*US*) stupid. ❑ **ivory-turner** *n.* [early–mid-19C] a skilful dice-player.

IN PHRASES

❑ **flash one's ivory** *v.* (*also* **flash the ivories, ...ivory**) [19C] to smile, to grin. ❑ **rattle the ivories** *v.* [mid-19C+] to throw dice. ❑ **roll in one's ivory/ivories** *v.* [sing. use until mid-19C] [late 18C–late 19C] to kiss. ❑ **sport one's ivory** *v.* [late 18C–early 19C] to grin. ❑ **wash one's ivories** *v.* (*also* **sluice one's ivories**) to drink.

ivory float *n.* [rhy. sl.] [1920s–50s] (*US*) a coat.

ivory pearl *n.* [rhy. sl.] [1930s] a girl.

Ivy *n.*[1] [2000s] (*S.Afr. gang*) a 1970s youth subculture that prioritized smart clothes over inter-gang violence.

Ivy *n.*[2] *see* IDA *n.*

ivy bush *n.* [late 19C] (*US*) a heavily bearded man.

I Won't Work *n.* [1900s–20s] (*US*) derog. term for a member of the Industrial Workers of the World (IWW).

ixnay *prep.* [pig Lat., the reverse of *nix*] [1920s+] (*US*) no.

-iz- *infix* [note the earlier use of an infix *-eas-* found in a number of terms used by US carnival workers, e.g. *ceasarnie* (a CARNIE *n.*[3]), *measark* (a MARK *n.*[1]), *heasar* (here), *neasix* (NIX *n.*) etc] [1940s+] (*US black*) used as a general infix, e.g. in BIZALLS *n.*, BIZNATCH *n.*, HIZZO *n.*, SHIZNIT *n.* etc.

izm *n. see* ISM *n.*

Izro *n. see* ISRO *n.*

izzelly *n.* [ety. unknown] [mid-19C] (*UK Und.*) an associate.

IN COMPOUNDS

▫ **izzellywicket** *n.* [? SE *wicket* in cricket] [mid-19C] (*UK Und.*) one who betrays their associates (to save their own life).

Izzy *n.* (*also* **Issey**) [Jewish name *Isaac*] [20C+] a nickname for a Jew.

J *n.* **1** *see* JAVA *n.* **2** *see* JAY *n.*[1] (3). **3** *see* JAY *n.*[1] (4).

j *n.* (*also* **jay, jaybird, j-bo**) [abbr. JOINT *n.* (5c)] [1960s+] (*drugs*) a cannabis cigarette.

IN COMPOUNDS

❑ **jay smoke** *n.* [abbr. J *n.* + SMOKE *n.* (2a)] [1960s+] (*drugs*) marijuana.

IN PHRASES

❑ **on one's j** *see* ON ONE'S JOB *under* JOB *n.*[2].

Ja *n.* (*also* **JA**) [abbr.; see also JAMDUNG *n.*] [20C+] (*W.I. Rasta*) Jamaica.

j.a. *n.* [abbr.] **1** [1970s] (*W.I.*) a Jamaican. **2** [1990s+] (*US*) a Japanese-American.

j.a. *adj.* [J.A. *n.* (2)] [1990s+] (*US*) Japanese-American.

jaap *n.* (*also* **japie, jarpie**) [Afk. *jaap*, f. proper name *Jacob*, a typical 'country' name. *DSAE* claims that 'no examples of the word in use by non-South Africans have been found', but cf. YARPIE *n.*, common in Aus., albeit transliterated] (*S.Afr.*) **1** [1940s+] an Afrikaner. **2** [1960s+] a peasant, a rustic, an unsophisticated person.

jab *n.* [note earlier JAB *v.* (1)] **1** [20C+] (*US*) in fig. use, an attempt, a try. **2** [1910s+] an injection. (**a**) (*drugs*) an injection of a narcotic drug. (**b**) (*orig. milit.*) an inoculation, any form of injection, esp. against diseases such as TB and polio. **3** [1970s+] (*US/Irish*) an act of copulation. **4** [2000s] (*Irish*) a woman's breast; usu. in pl.

IN PHRASES

❑ **big jab** *n.* (*also* **stainless steel ride**) [2000s] (*US prison*) a lethal injection, used in executions.

jab *v.* **1** [20C+] (*drugs*) to inject drugs. **2** [1960s+] (*US campus*) of a man, to have sexual intercourse.

IN COMPOUNDS

❑ **jab job** *v.* [JOB *n.*[2] (2)] [1950s+] (*drugs*) to inject a drug. ❑ **jaboff** *n.* (*also* **jabpopp, jabpoppo**) [POP *n.*[1] (4a)] [1930s–50s] (*US prison*) an injection of drugs; the sensation that follows it.

jaba *n.* [? SE *jabber*, to talk nonsense] [2000s] (*US teen*) marijuana.

ja-baas *n.* [Afk. *ja baas*, yes, master] [1960s+] (*S.Afr.*) a servile, subservient black person.

jabber *n.* **1** one who SE *jabs*. (**a**) [1900s–40s] (*US prison*) a prize-fighter. (**b**) [1910s+] any person who is prone to fighting. **2** in drug context [JAB *v.* (1)]. (**a**) [1910s] (*US prison*) a hypodermic syringe. (**b**) [1930s–50s] (*US drugs*) a drug addict.

jabber-juice *n.* [SE *jabber*, to talk unrestrainedly + JUICE *n.*[1] (3d)] [1970s] (*US prison*) sodium-pentothal.

Jabe *n.* [*Jabez*, a typical rural name; thus peasant cunning] [1900s] (*US*) a generic for a peasant, an unsophisticated person.

jabez *v.* [*Jabez*, a typical rural name; thus peasant cunning] [1910s–20s] to play an underhand trick.

jabfest *n.* *see* GABFEST *under* GAB *v.*

jabone/jaboney *n.* *see* JIBONE *n.*

jabongoes *n.* [nonce-word, var. on BAZONGAS *n.*] [1960s] (*US*) the female breasts.

jabonie *n.* *see* JIBONE *n.*

jabooby *n.* [? play on JOINT *n.* (5c)] [1950s+] (*drugs*) marijuana.

jabpopp/jabpoppo *n.* *see under* JAB *v.*

jab trotters *v.* *see under* TROTTER *n.*

Jabus! *excl.* *see* BEJABERS! *excl.*

Jack *n.* **1** [1970s+] (*US*) (*also* **Jack D, Jackie D, Jack's**) *Jack Daniel's* brand of whisky [abbr.]. **2** *see* JACK KETCH *n.*

Jack- *pfx* [18C] denoting a nationality; eg *Jack French*.

jack *n.*[1] [abbr. SE *jackass*] [14C–17C; 20C+] a fool.

IN COMPOUNDS

❑ **jack act** *v.* [SE *jackass*] [1920s+] (*Irish*) to play the fool.

IN PHRASES

❑ **lay on the jack** *v.* (*also* **be on the jack**) [16C] to beat or scold severely. ❑ **play the jack** *v.* **1** [17C] to act the villain. [play on *jack* = the 'knave' in cards]. **2** [19C] to play the fool.

jack *n.*[2] [later 20C+ usage is US black] **1** [late 15C+] a man or boy; a commoner as distinct from a gentleman. **2** [late 17C] a general term of abuse. **3** [mid-18C+] as term of address to a man [20C+ usage is primarily US]. **4** [mid-19C+] (*US*) (*also* **country jack**) a rustic, a peasant; a simpleton [underpinned by JAKE *n.*[1] (1)].

IN COMPOUNDS

❑ **jack blunt** *n.* [late 19C–1910s] a blunt person. ❑ **jack boots** *n.* [early 19C] the 'boots' or bootboy at an inn. ❑ **jack bragger** *n.* (*also* **jack brag**) [mid–late 16C] a boaster, a braggart. ❑ **jack cove** *n.* (*also* **jake cove**) [late 18C–mid-19C] (*UK Und.*) a dirty, contemptible man. ❑ **jack fool** *n.* [the term survived in 1940s Kansas dial.] [17C] a foolish person. ❑ **jack gentleman** *n.* [late 17C–18C] a man of low birth or manners who has pretensions to be a gentleman, an insolent fellow, an upstart. ❑ **jack gentlewoman** *n.* [late 18C] a large masculine woman. ❑ **jack mot** *n.* *see* JACK-WHORE below. ❑ **jack mum** *n.* [MUM *adj.*] [20C+] (*Irish*) a discreet person, esp. in the phr. *between you and me and jack mum*. ❑ **jack nasty** *n.* [mid–late 19C] a sneaking, slovenly person. ❑ **jack nasty face** *n.* [punning on the general use, 'a dirty fellow, seldom seen' (J.Bee). Note merchant navy jargon *jack nasty face*, a cook's assistant, or anyone considered ugly] [19C] the vagina. ❑ **jack papish** *n.* (*also* **Jack Priest**) [early 18C–mid-19C] a derog. term for a Roman Catholic. ❑ **jack poke** *n.* [JACK *n.*[2] (1) + POKE ALONG *under* POKE *v.*] [1930s–40s] (*US*) a slow, listless person. ❑ **jack pudding** *n.* [innate humour of a SE *pudding*] [mid-17C–1910s] a jester or clown, travelling with a mountebank or itinerant quack. ❑ **jack-rat** *n.* [mid-19C] (*UK Und.*) a sneak-thief. ❑ **jack sauce** *n.* [mid-16C–early 18C] a saucy or impudent fellow. ❑ **jack stickler** *n.* [mid-16C–mid-17C] a meddlesome or interfering person, a busybody. ❑ **jack straw** *n.* [ref. to *Jack Straw*, leader of the failed Peasants' Revolt, 1381] [late 16C–17C] a nonentity, lit. a 'man of straw'. ❑ **jack weight** *n.* [late 18C–19C] a fat man. ❑ **jack-whore** *n.* (*also* **jack mot**) [MOT *n.* (1)] **1** [mid-18C–mid-19C] a large, tough prostitute. **2** [mid-19C–1920s] a womanizer.

IN PHRASES

❑ **fat jack of the bone-house** *n.* [mid-19C–1900s] a very fat man [obs. SE *bonehouse*, the human body]. ❑ **jack-at-a-pinch** *n.* **1** [late 17C–mid-19C] a temporary clergyman, hired when the regular incumbent is absent. **2** [mid-19C] one who is required only in an emergency or as a gapstop; thus an insignificant person. **3** [late 19C] an odd-job man. ❑ **jack at the stiff** *n.* [mid-19C] (*UK Und.*) a friend in need. ❑ **jack in the pulpit** *n.* [SE *pulpit*, i.e. one who sets themselves up as a preacher, lit. or fig.] [19C] a pretender, an upstart. ❑ **jack in the water** *n.* [mid–late

19C] a waterman's attendant, who helps passengers on and off boats. ▫ **jack of clubs** *n.* [19C] (*US*) a good fellow, man. ▫ **jack of dover** *n.* [late 14C–17C] a Dover sole. ▫ **jack of legs** *n.* [folk legend of *Jack of Legs*, a supposed giant, some 3m (14ft) tall, who is allegedly buried in the churchyard at Weston, Hertfordshire. A large thigh bone, excavated in the graveyard, was given to the naturalist Sir John Tradescant (1608–62)] [late 18C–19C] **1** a tall, long-legged man. **2** an outsize clasp-knife. ▫ **jack of the clockhouse** *n.* [SE *jack of the clockhouse*, which 'goes upon screws, and his office is to do nothing but strike'; the actual *jack* was a figure of a man which strikes the bell on the outside of a clock] [17C] (*UK Und.*) a confidence trickster, specializing in selling supposedly purpose-written pamphlets, poems etc, which flatter the vanity of the purchaser but which are, in fact, mass-produced with a personalized dedication tacked on. ▫ **jack out of doors** *n.* [late 16C–17C] a vagrant, one who has been thrown out of his house. ▫ **jack-the-wrong-man** *n.* [mid-19C] (*UK Und.*) a policeman. ▫ **single-jack** *n.* [1920s–30s] (*US tramp*) a one-legged, one-armed or one-eyed beggar.

jack *n.*[3] [SE *jack*, a device for lifting things] **1** [17C; 19C+] the penis. **2** [late 19C+] an erection; thus phr. *on jack*, erect; thus often as sexual desire. **3** [1950s+] copulation. **4** [1980s+] an act of masturbation. **5** [1990s+] (*US black*) a gun.

IN PHRASES

▫ **get jack in the orchard** *v.* [ORCHARD *n.* (1)] [19C] to penetrate a woman. ▫ **when the jack takes the ace** *n.* [ACE *n.* (1)] [mid-19C] sexual intercourse.

jack *n.*[4] **1** [late 17C–mid-19C] a farthing. **2** [19C+] (*US*) money. **3** [mid-19C] (*also* **half-jack**) a counter, similar in size and shape to a sovereign or half-sovereign, used in gambling houses and casinos [strangely enough, *jack* and *half-jack* are gambling counters worth a whole/half a sovereign, and *half-jack* (below) contemporaneously means a half-sovereign, but *jack* alone never seems to equal a whole sovereign]. **4** [20C+] (*Aus.*) in two-up, a double-headed coin. **5** *see* JACK'S (ALIVE) *n.*

IN PHRASES

▫ **half-jack** *n.* **1** [mid–late 19C] 10 shillings (50p), half a sovereign. **2** *see* sense 3 above. ▫ **make one's jack** *v.* [late 18C–1900s] (*US*) to prosper, to make one's fortune.

jack *n.*[5] (*also* **jackie, jackshite, jacky**) [abbr. JACK TAR *n.*[1] (1)] [late 17C+] a sailor.

IN COMPOUNDS

▫ **jack ashore** *adj.* [his habits when in port] [late 19C–1900s] larky, excited, tipsy.

jack *n.*[6] [JAKES *n.*] [late 18C–19C] a lavatory.

jack *n.*[7] [abbr.] **1** [late 18C+] (*US*) a donkey or *jack*ass. **2** [19C] (*US*) a flap*jack*. **3** [mid-19C+] a black*jack* or cosh. **4** [late 19C] a *jack*al. **5** [20C+] (*US/Can.*) a lumber*jack*. **6** [1900s–10s] (*US*) a *jack*pot. **7** [1930s] (*US*) the card-game black*jack*. **8** [1960s] a *jack*et.

jack *n.*[8] [ety. unknown, but note SE *jack*, used for a variety of machines] [early 19C] a post-chaise, a travelling carriage seating two or four, with the coachman or postilion riding one of the horses.

IN COMPOUNDS

▫ **jack-boy** *n.* [early 19C] a postilion, one who rides one of a carriage's leading horses rather than riding on the box.

jack *n.*[9] [mid-19C] (*UK Und.*) a low-ranking prostitute.

jack *n.*[10] (*also* **jacky**) [SE *laughing jackass*] [late 19C–1950s] (*Aus.*) a kookaburra.

jack *n.*[11] [orig. northern dial., now general] [late 19C+] **1** a detective. **2** a police officer. **3** constr. with *the*, the Military Police.

jack *n.*[12] [abbr. JACKSIE *n.*[1] (1)] [late 19C+] the anus.

jack *n.*[13] **1** [late 19C+] (*US*) illegally distilled liquor, based on various fruits and vegetables and usu. specified as such, e.g. *tater jack* (potatoes), *prune jack*, *raisin jack*. **2** [20C+] (*W.I.*) illegally distilled rum. **3** [1930s+] methylated spirits, used as a drink, thus *jack man*, one who habitually drinks meths.

jack *n.*[14] [? play on SE *jackass*, i.e. the sort of student who requires a crib; or ? SE *jack*, i.e. it 'lifts up' grades] [1900s–40s] (*US campus*) a translation or hidden notes.

jack *n.*[15] [abbr. JACK ROLLER *n.* (1)] [1920s+] (*US*) a mugger, a thief.

IN COMPOUNDS

▫ **jack-boy** *n.* [1980s+] (*US police*) an armed robber. ▫ **jack racket** *n.* [1930s+] the act of mugging.

IN PHRASES

▫ **run a jack** *v.* [1930s+] to grab a man's shirt and pull it over his head, before robbing him.

jack *n.*[16] [1940s] (*US milit.*) a corporal.

jack *n.*[17] [rhy. sl. *Jack McNab* = SCAB *n.*[1] (4)] [1940s+] (*Aus.*) a non-union labourer, a strike-breaker, spec. a member of the Permanent and Casual Waterside Workers' Union.

jack *n.*[18] [1950s+] (*US black*) a (public) telephone.

jack *n.*[19] [SE *hijack*] [2000s] (*UK black*) a street robbery, a mugging.

jack *n.*[20] **1** *see* CHEAP JOHN *n.*[1] (3). **2** *see* CUT UP JACK *v.* **3** *see* JACK NOHI *n.* **4** *see* JACKSHIT *n.*

jack *n.*[21] **1** *see* JACK (AND JILL) *n.* **2** *see* JACK (IN THE BOX) *n.* (1).

jack, the *n.* [abbr. JACK (IN THE BOX) *n.*] [1940s+] (*Aus.*) venereal disease.

jack *adj.*[1] [late 19C+] (*Aus.*) aware (of).

jack *adj.*[2] [abbr. NEW JACK *n.* (1)] [1980s+] (*US black*) flashy, ostentatious.

IN COMPOUNDS

▫ **jack move** *n.* [MOVE *n.* (6)] [1980s+] (*US black*) a wild, foolish, eccentric move or type of behaviour.

jack *adj.*[3] *see* JACK (JONES) *adj.*

jack *v.*[1] [JACK *n.*[14]] [1900s] (*US campus*) to use a translation or hidden notes to pass an examination.

jack *v.*[2] **1** [1910s+] (*US Und.*) to beat with a blackjack. **2** [1940s+] to masturbate or make a masturbatory gesture. **3** [1950s+] (*US prison*) to serve a prison sentence. **4** [1950s+] to break open. **5** [1970s+] (*US prison*) to stun a fellow inmate with a blackjack before raping. **6** [1980s+] to stab or punch, usu. as JACKED *adj.*[1] (5).

IN PHRASES

▫ **jack out** *v.* **1** [mid–late 19C] (*US*) to knock unconscious. **2** [1940s] (*Aus.*) to refuse or avoid a task.

jack *v.*[3] **1** [1930s+] (*orig. US*) to steal (from), to hijack, to take forcibly. **2** [1980s+] to seduce. **3** [1990s+] (*drugs*) to steal someone else's drugs. **4** [1990s+] (*US*) to search.

IN PHRASES

▫ **jack rec** *v.* [sense 1 above + JACK AROUND *v.* (1) + SE *recreation*] [2000s] (*US prison*) to waste time, to mess up recreation by causing a disturbance.

jack *v.*[4] [1980s+] (*N.Z.*) to take charge of; to get ready.

jack *v.*[5] **1** *see* JACK AROUND *v.* **2** *see* JACK (IN) *v.* **3** *see* JACK (UP) *v.* **4** *see* JACK UP *v.*[4] (2).

jack *v.*[6] for masturbation combs., *see under* JACK OFF *v.*[1].

jack act *v.* [SE *jackass*] [1920s+] (*Irish*) to play the fool.

Jack Adams *n.* [? anecdotal] [late 17C–19C] a fool; thus *Jack Adams' parish*, Clerkenwell.

jack (a) dandy *n.* [rhy. sl.] [mid-19C+] brandy.

jack-a-dandy *n.* (*also* **jack of dandy, jacky-dandy**) [SE pfx *jack*, a person, esp. in derog. or contemptuous contexts + *dandy*] [early 17C–19C] an insignificant person, a fop.

jackal *n.* [19C] **1** (*US Und.*) a steamboat thief, spec. the thief who actually removes the booty. **2** a moneylender's tout.

jackaloo *adj. see* JAKELOO *adj.*

jack an' danny *n.* (*also* **jacky danny**) [1990s+] **1** the vagina [rhy. sl. = FANNY *n.*[1] (1)]. **2** nonsense, time-wasting, prevarication [rhy. sl. = FANNY *n.*[2]].

jack (and jill) *n.* [rhy. sl.] **1** [1930s+] a hill. **2** [1930s+] a bill. **3** [1930s+] a till. **4** [1960s+] a pill, esp. of heroin; usu. in pl. **5** [1970s+] (*Aus.*) a fool [= DILL *n.*].

(IN PHRASES)

❑ **on the jack (and jill)** [2000s] taking birth control pills.

jack-and-jill-off *n. see* JACK-OFF *n.* (2).

Jack and Joan *adj.* [rhy. sl.] [1990s+] on own's own.

jack and shit *n. see* JACKSHIT *n.*

jackanory *n.* [rhy. sl.; ult. the UK children's TV programme, *Jackanory*, which involved stories being read aloud] [1970s+] **1** a story. **2** a lie, i.e. a 'tall story'.

jackaroo *n.* (*also* **jackeroo**) [late 19C+] (*Aus.*) **1** a white man living beyond the bounds of 'civilization' [Jagara *dhugai-tu*, a wandering white man]. **2** a man newly arrived from Britain to gain experience in the bush [Baker, *The Australian Language* (1945), suggests Queensland Aborigine *tchaceroo*, the shrike, which 'talks' a great deal, orig. applied to a group of German missionaries settled near Brisbane and thence all whites; a corruption of JACKY RAW *n.*; JACK *n.*^{10} + SE *kangaroo*]. **3** a young hired hand.

jackaroo *v.* (*also* **jackeroo**) [JACKAROO *n.* (2)] [late 19C+] (*Aus.*) to pick up experience.

jack around *v.* (*also* **jack**) [1960s+] **1** to waste time. **2** as sense 1 with sexual, adulterous overtones. **3** (*US campus*) to tease. **4** (*US*) to treat badly, with deceit or contempt.

jackass *n.* [JACK *n.*^{13} (1) + it turns the drinker into a SE *jackass*] [1920s–40s] (*US*) home distilled liquor, e.g. brandy or corn whisky.

jackass *adj.* [? SE *jackass*, used of things that are gross and stupid] [mid-19C+] large, substantial.

jackass rope *n.* [1950s+] (*W.I., Jam.*) home-grown tobacco, twisted into a rope.

Jack Benny *n.* [rhy. sl.; ult. US comedian *Jack Benny* (1894–1974)] [20C+] a penny.

jack boy *n.* **1** *see* JACK *n.*^{8} (1). **2** *see* JACK *n.*^{15} (1).

Jack Bull *n. see* JOHN BULL *n.*

Jack Canuck *n. see* CANUCK *n.*

Jack Catch *n. see* JACK KETCH *n.*

Jack Cornstalk *n. see* CORNSTALK *n.* (2).

Jack D *n. see* JACK *n.* (1).

jack dandy *n. see* JACK (A) DANDY *n.*

jackdaw *n.* [rhy. sl.] [mid-19C+] a jaw.

Jack Dee *n.* [rhy. sl. = PEE *n.*^{1} (2)/WEE *n.*; ult. UK comedian *Jack Dee* (b.1962)] [1990s+] an act of urination.

jack-deuce *adj.* [1930s] (*US*) at an angle or slanted.

Jack Doyle *n. see* CONAN DOYLE *n.*

Jack Drum's entertainment *n.* (*also* **John Drum's entertainment, Tom Drum's...**) [they are 'drummed out' of the house] [late 16C–early 19C] a rough reception, esp. the throwing out of an unwelcome guest.

jacked *adj.*^{1} **1** [late 18C–19C] of a horse, spavined. **2** [late 19C+] (*Aus.*) angry, annoyed, tired of. **3** [1960s+] (*US campus*) physically broken down. **4** [1980s] (*US drugs*) to be under the influence of cocaine. **5** [1980s+] stabbed, attacked [JACK *v.*^{2} (6)].

jacked *adj.*^{2} [1990s+] (*US campus*) **1** muscular. **2** of coffee, caffeinated.

jacked *adj.*^{3} *see* JACKED (UP) *adj.*

jacked off *adj.* [fig. use of JACK OFF *v.*^{1} (1)] [1980s+] (*US*) enthusiastic, very keen.

jacked out *adj.* [JACKED *adj.*^{1} (2)] [1970s+] (*US campus*) annoyed, irritated, angry.

jacked (up) *adj.* (*also* **jack**) [JACK (UP) *v.*] **1** [1930s+] (*US drugs*) suffering (usu. negatively) from the effect of a given drug and/or alcohol. **2** in non-drugs uses. (**a**) [1960s+] (*US teen*) upset, anxious, waiting anxiously for time to pass. (**b**) [1960s+] (*US campus*) unfair. (**c**) [1970s+] (*US*) excited, exhilarated, happy. (**d**) [1970s+] (*US gay*) sexually excited. (**e**) [1980s+] intense, energised. (**f**) [1980s+] focused, alert.

jacked up *adj.*^{1} [? JACK UP *v.*^{1} (3)] **1** [mid–late 19C] ruined, given up, abandoned. **2** [1900s–10s] (*US*) pregnant.

jacked up *adj.*^{2} [JACK (IN THE BOX) *n.* (1)] [20C+] (*Aus.*) infected (usu. with venereal disease).

jacked up *adj.*^{3} [JACK UP *v.*^{4} (4)] [1950s+] (*US Und.*) charged with an offence, esp. while already serving a sentence.

jacked up *adj.*^{4} [JACK UP *v.*^{3} (3)] [1960s+] (*N.Z.*) arranged, sorted out, 'fixed'.

jackeen *n.* (*also* **Dublin jackeen**) [JACK *n.*^{2} (1) + dim. *-een*] [mid-19C+] (*Anglo-Irish*) **1** a Dubliner, as opposed to a country person. **2** a self-assertive but worthless person.

jacker *n.* [JACK *v.*^{3} (1)] **1** [1960s+] (*US*) a hijacker. **2** [2000s] a street robber, a thief.

jacker-off *n. see* JACK-OFF *n.* (1).

jackeroo *see under* JACKAROO.

jackery *n.* [JACKAROO *n.* (3)] [late 19C–1900s] (*Aus.*) a popular station-hand; usu. in pl.

jackery-pokery *n. see* JIGGERY-POKERY *n.*

jacket *n.* **1** [17C–19C] (*US*) the human skin; usu. in phr. below. **2** [20C+] (*W.I.*) refs. to illegitimacy [the jacket 'dresses up' a man and thus confers respectability on the child]. (**a**) a child fathered by a woman's lover rather than by her husband. (**b**) any child who has no 'official' father; thus *wear a jacket for*, for a husband to accept the child as his own. (**c**) a man who accepts the role of father to a child he knows is not his. **3** [1930s+] (*US Und.*) ext./fig. uses. (**a**) the police/prison file on a criminal, recording previous convictions etc; one's criminal record. (**b**) a reputation, usu. bad; thus *fruit jacket*, a reputation as a homosexual. (**c**) a jail sentence. (**d**) a witness to a crime. (**e**) a military service record. **4** [1960s+] (*US*) a condom. **5** *see* *YELLOW JACKET under* YELLOW *adj.*

(IN PHRASES)

❑ **dust someone's jacket** *v. see under* DUST *v.*^{1}. ❑ **fruit jacket** *n. see* sense 3b above. ❑ **give someone a jacket** *v.* [20C+] (*W.I., Jam.*) for a married woman to conceive and bear a child by her lover and pass it off to her husband as his. ❑ **hang a jacket on** *v.* [1950s+] (*US prison*) for one inmate to accuse another of informing. ❑ **lick someone's jacket** *v.* [LICK *v.*^{1} (1)] [18C] to thrash, to beat up. ❑ **line one's jacket** *v.* [17C–early 19C] to fill one's stomach; either with food or drink. ❑ **punk jacket** *n.* [PUNK *n.*^{1} (2)] [1990s+] (*US prison*) a reputation for cowardice. ❑ **put someone on the heavy jacket** *v.* [1980s+] (*N.Z.*) to ostracize. ❑ **rat jacket** *n.* [RAT *n.*^{1} (1)] [1970s+] (*US prison*) a reputation as an informer. ❑ **snitch jacket** *n.* [SNITCH *n.*^{1} (3)] [1960s+] (*US Und.*) a reputation as an informer. ❑ **thrash someone's jacket** *v.* [late 17C–early 19C] to beat, to thrash. ❑ **under one's jacket** [19C] (*US*) in one's stomach. ❑ **wet one's jacket** *v.* [early 19C] (*US*) to get drunk.

jacket *v.*^{1} **1** [19C] to 'remove a man by underhand and vile means from any birth or situation he enjoys, commonly with a view to supplant him' (Vaux). **2** [19C] to betray a confidence. **3** [1960s] (*W.I.*) to seduce someone else's lover.

jacket *v.*^{2} **1** [late 19C–1900s] to threaten someone with confinement in a lunatic asylum [abbr. *strait-jacket*]. **2** in Und. uses [JACKET *n.* (3)]. (**a**) [mid-19C–1930s] (*US Und.*) to be identified or caught in the act. (**b**) [1950s] (*US*) (*also* **fit someone for a jacket**) to threaten someone with an arrest and prison sentence. (**c**) [1970s+] (*US prison*) to be labelled untrustworthy or given any form of bad reputation by fellow prisoners.

jacket and vest *n.* [rhy. sl.] [1930s] the *West* End of London.

jacketing *n.* [Lincs./Sussex dial. *jacket*, to thrash] [mid-19C–1900s] a thrashing, a beating; also verbal.

jacket job *n.* [SE *(strait) jacket* + JOB *n.*^{2} (2)] [1990s+] something, or someone, liable to drive one crazy, thus mad, insane.

jackey *n.*^{1} *see* JACKY *n.*^{1}.

jackey *n.*^{2} *see* JACKY JACKY *n.*

jack flash *n.* [rhy. sl. = HASH *n.*^{2}; + ? ref. to Rolling Stones' song 'Jumping *Jack Flash*' (1968)] [1960s+] (*Aus.*) hashish.

jack-gagger *n. see* *JOCKUM-GAGGER under* JOCKUM *n.*

jackhammer *n.* [play on SE; note HAMMER *n.*^{1} (1)] [1970s+] (*US gay*) the erect penis.

jackhandle *n.* [1960s] (*US*) an erect penis.

jackhouse *n. see* JAKEHOUSE *n.*

jackhunt *v. see* JACKROLL *v.* (1).

jackie *n.* **1** *see* JACK *n.*[5]. **2** *see* JAKE *n.*[3].

Jackie D *n. see* JACK *n.* (1).

Jackie (Dash) *n.* [rhy. sl. = SLASH *n.* (2a); ult. UK dockers' leader *Jack Dash* (1906–1989)] [1990s+] an act of urination.

Jackie Howe *n.* (*also* **Jacky Howe, Jimmie Howe, Jimmy Howe**) [proper name of *Jackie Howe* (1855–1922), an Australian shearer who in 1892 established a world shearing record by shearing 321 merino sheep with hand shears in 8 hours 40 minutes] [1930s+] (*Aus./N.Z.*) a navy blue or black woollen singlet worn by Aus. and N.Z. shearers and bushmen.

Jackie Robinson *n.* [proper name of *Jackie Robinson* (1919–72), who in 1947 became the first black man to play in major league baseball (for the Brooklyn Dodgers)] (*US black*) **1** [1940s+] any black person who is the first to gain entry to a profession. **2** [1950s] the penis [note JACK ROBINSON *n.*].

jackies *n.* [JACK TAR *n.*[1] (1)] [1910s] American sailors.

Jackie Trent *adj.* [rhy. sl. = BENT *adj.* (2); ult. singer/songwriter *Jackie Trent* (b.1940)] [1990s+] corrupt, untrustworthy.

jack (in) *v.* (*also* **jack, jack it, jack it in, jack it up, jag it in**) [? dial. *jack*, to give up suddenly, to relinquish, to abandon or SE *chuck*, to throw] [late 19C+] to stop doing something, to give in, to abandon, to resign; thus *jacked in*, abandoned, given up.

(IN PHRASES)

❑ **jack the contract** *v.* [1910s+] (*Aus.*) to give up or leave a job when it proves too difficult.

jack in a box *n.* [*DSUE* claims prob. from JACK IN THE BOX *n.*[1] (1)] [late 16C–mid-19C] a cheat, spec. a thief who deceives tradesmen by the substitution of identical boxes: his own filled with gold pounds, the one that the tradesman finds himself left with filled with silver shillings.

jacking off *n.* [JACK OFF *v.*[1] (1)] [20C+] (*gambling*) **1** racking up the pool balls. **2** shaking dice with a movement that might be seen as resembling masturbation.

jack (in the box) *n.* [rhy. sl. = POX *n.*[1] (3)] [20C+] venereal disease.

jack in the box *n.*[1] **1** [mid-16C–17C] the consecrated host. **2** [late 17C–early 18C] (*UK Und.*) (*also* **jack in a box**) a street pedlar; usu. one who doubles as a confidence trickster [the box of goods that is carried]. **3** [late 18C–early 19C] an unborn child. **4** [mid-19C] (*UK Und.*) a form of screw used in safe-breaking [BOX *n.*[1] (2d)]. **5** [late 19C+] the penis [it 'pops up']. **6** [20C+] (*US Und.*) breaking and entering a house or apartment [BOX *n.*[1] (3b)].

jack in the box *n.*[2] [rhy. sl.] [20C+] socks.

jack in the box *n.*[3] [JACK *n.*[3] (1) + BOX *n.*[1] (1)] [1960s+] (*US black*) the state of having one's penis inside one's partner's vagina.

jack in the (low) cellar *n.* [trans. of Du. HANS-EN-KELDER *n.*] [mid–late 18C] an unborn child.

jack iron *n.* [20C+] (*W.I.*) a form of unlicensed and very potent rum, distilled secretly in the countryside.

jack it *v.* [fig. use of JACK IT IN/UP *v.*] **1** [late 19C–1900s] to die. **2** *see* JACK (IN) *v.*

jack it in/up *v. see* JACK (IN) *v.*

jack job *n.* [JACKSHIT *n.*] [1970s+] (*US campus*) unfair treatment.

jack (jones) *adj.* [rhy. sl.] [20C+] alone.

(IN PHRASES)

❑ **on one's jack (jones)** (*also* **on one's jacks, on one's jacksy**) [20C+] on one's own, by oneself.

Jack Ketch *n.* (*also* **Jack, Jack Catch, Master Ketch, Mr Ketch**) [proper name of the common executioner *Jack Ketch* (*c.*1663–86). Partly on account of his barbarity at the executions of Lord Russell, the Duke of Monmouth and other political offenders, and partly perhaps from the obvious links with the SE *catch*, his name became widely known. When it was given to the hangman in the puppet-play of *Punchinello*, which arrived from Italy shortly after his death, his immortality was assured] **1** [mid-17C+] (*orig. UK Und.*) the hangman. **2** [late 19C] ext. to anyone chosen to carry out a death sentence. **3** [late 19C+] a jail sentence [STRETCH *n.* (1c)].

(IN COMPOUNDS)

❑ **Jack Ketch's certificate** *n.* [early 19C] a judicial flogging; it is 'given under his hand'. ❑ **Jack Ketch's frame** *n.* [mid-19C] the gallows. ❑ **Jack Ketch's kitchen** *n.* [18C–19C] that room in Newgate prison where the hangman boiled the quarters of those dismembered for high treason. ❑ **Jack Ketch's necklace** *n.* [NECKLACE *n.* (2)] [early 19C] the hangman's noose. ❑ **Jack Ketch's pippin** *n.* [PIPPIN *n.* (2)] [late 17C–19C] a candidate for the gallows. ❑ **Jack Ketch's warren** *n.* [19C] the slum area in and around Turnmill Street, Clerkenwell.

jack-knife *v.* [1980s] (*US*) to have a prolonged session of sexual intercourse.

Jack Lang *n.* (*also* **old Jack Lang**) [rhy. sl.] [1960s–80s] (*Aus.*) slang.

jack lattin *n.* (*also* **jack latten**) [*John Lattin* of Morristown House, Co. Kildare, won a bet after dancing, as wagered, a distance of over 32km (20 miles), changing his dance-step every furlong] [20C+] (*Irish*) a threat of punishment.

jackleg *n.* [JACKLEG *adj.* (1)] (*US*) **1** [mid-19C+] an incompetent, unskilled or unprincipled worker or professional person, esp. a quack doctor, a corrupt lawyer, a hypocritical preacher. **2** [20C+] an itinerant preacher.

jackleg *adj.* (*also* **jack-legged, jakeleg**) [US dial. *jackleg*, unskilled, ult. UK dial. *jack-a-legs*, a large clasp knife, as used by a second-rate carpenter] (*US*) **1** [mid-19C+] untrained, unprofessional, dishonest. **2** [20C+] thrown-together, makeshift. **3** [20C+] (*US black*) bogus; not adhering to black people's cultural standards.

jackleg *v.* [JACKLEG *n.*] [mid-19C+] (*US*) to act in an incompetent, unskilled or unprincipled way.

jackman *n.* [apparently derived f. a misspelling of JARKMAN *n.*, as printed in the 1575 edn of Awdeley, *Fraternitie of Vagabondes*] [mid-16C–mid-19C] (*UK Und.*) a mendicant villain who used his abilities of reading and writing to forge counterfeit begging licences.

jack Mormon *n.* [? JACKLEG *adj.* (1) + *Mormon*] **1** [mid-19C+] a non-Mormon who sympathizes with the Mormons. **2** [20C+] an apostate Mormon.

jack nohi *n.* [Maori pron. of SE *nosey*] **1** [1940s+] (*N.Z.*) an inquisitive person, a 'nosey parker'. **2** [1970s+] (*also* **jack**) a look-round; a glance.

(IN PHRASES)

❑ **have a jack (nohi)** *v.* [1970s+] (*N.Z.*) to take a look.

jacko *n.* [SE *jack*, a laughing jackass or kookaburra] (*Aus.*) **1** [1910s] (*also* **jacky**) a Turkish soldier. **2** [1940s] a kookaburra.

jack of *adj.* [JACK UP *v.*[1]] [late 19C+] (*Aus.*) bored with, tired of.

(IN PHRASES)

❑ **get jack of** *v.* [late 19C+] (*Aus.*) to resent, to be bored with, to be fed up with.

jack of dandy *n. see* JACK-A-DANDY *n.*

jack-off *n.* [JACK OFF *v.*[1] (1)] [1930s+] (*US*) **1** (*also* **jacker-off**) a general insult, lit. a masturbator. **2** (*also* **jack-and-jill-off**) an act of masturbation; thus fig., something worthless or pointless. **3** as a derog. term of address. **4** in fig. use, a hoax, a confidence trick.

jack-off *adj.* [1930s+] **1** pertaining to the act of masturbation. **2** a general term of abuse, disdain; fig. use of sense 1.

jack off *v.*[1] [JACK *n.*[3] + JERK OFF *v.*] **1** [1910s+] (*also* **jack oneself, jack oneself off**) to masturbate. **2** [1920s+] to masturbate someone else. **3** [1940s–60s] in fig. use, to blink, i.e. to move the eyelid up and down fast. **4** [1940s+] (*US*) to fool around, to do nothing. **5** [1950s+] (*drugs*) to pump backwards and forwards with the plunger of the hypodermic without finally injecting the blood and heroin mix into the arm [the up-and-down gesture of masturbation and the figurative 'jacking off' instead of reaching a climax]. **6** [1960s+] (*US*) to take advantage of, to deceive or tease someone. **7** [1990s+] (*US*) to fantasize.

(IN COMPOUNDS)

❑ **jack book** *n.* (*also* **jack flicks, jack pictures**) [1970s+] (*US* *prison*) pornography. ❑ **jack bumps** *n.* [1960s+] (*US*) acne, allegedly caused by masturbation.

IN PHRASES

❑ **jack one's jaw(s)** *v.* (*also* **jack off one's jaw, jerk one's jaw(s)**) [1960s+] (*US*) to chatter at length (and aimlessly). ❑ **jack one's jizz** *v.* [JIZZ *n.*] [1930s+] to masturbate. ❑ **jack the dog** *v.* [SE *dog*] [1940s] (*US*) **1** to waste time, to loaf on the job. **2** to bungle, to blunder.

jack off *v.*[2] [1930s–60s] (*UK tramp*) to leave.

jack one's jaw *v. see under* JACK OFF *v.*[1].

jackpot *n.* [sources claim a link to poker's *jackpot*, a large 'pot' of money, but there seems no real proof] [late 19C+] (*Can./US*) **1** a dilemma, a difficult situation, trouble. **2** an arrest.

IN PHRASES

❑ **in the jackpot** [1980s] in trouble.

jackpot *v.* **1** [20C+] (*US prison*) to fight, usu. with fists [JACKPOT *n.* (1)]. **2** [1970s+] (*US Und.*) to chat, to gossip, to reminisce [abbr. of gambling *cut up jackpots*, to reminisce over card-games].

jack rabbit *n.*[1] **1** [late 19C–1960s] (*US*) a mule. **2** [1970s+] (*US prison*) an escaped convict.

IN COMPOUNDS

❑ **jackrabbit parole** *n.* [1970s+] (*US prison*) an escape from prison.

jack rabbit *n.*[2] [rhy. sl. = HABIT *n.* (1)] [1980s+] (*Aus. prison*) narcotics addiction.

jack rabbit *n.*[3] [1990s+] (*Aus.*) the penis.

jackrabbit *adj.* [1950s] (*US*) insignificant.

jackrabbit *v.* [JACK RABBIT *n.*[1] (2)] [1970s+] (*Can./US*) to run, escape.

jack randall *n.* (*also* **jack randle, jerry randle, johnny randle, ron randell**) [rhy. sl.; ult. Jack Randall (1794–1828), a noted pugilist (Hotten 1873)] [mid-19C+] a candle.

jack-ready *adj.* [1970s] (*US*) absolutely ready, ready and waiting.

jack rees *n.* [rhy. sl.] [20C+] (*Aus.*) fleas.

Jack Robinson *n.*

IN PHRASES

❑ **before one can say Jack Robinson** (*also* **before one could say Jack Robinson, while one could say..., quicker than one can say..., before one can say Jack Robertson**) [there is no specific *Jack Robinson*; perhaps it was a minor tongue-twister; note Grose (1785) suggests a real 'Jack Robinson ... a very volatile gentleman of that appellation, who would call on his neighbours, and be gone before his name could be announced'] [late 18C+] instantly, at once, very quickly.

jackroll *v.* **1** [1910s+] (*also* **jackhunt**) to rob a victim (often one of one's own companions) while they are drunk or sleeping [JACK *n.*[2] (1) + ROLL *v.* (3a)/SE *hunt*]. **2** [1990s+] (*S.Afr.*) to abduct, then rape a woman, usu. a schoolgirl, to gang-rape; thus *jack-rolling*, abducting and raping [despite logical link to sense 1, *DSAE* suggests a song by Womack & Womack, with lyrics 'Love is just a ballgame, sometimes you lose – jackroll'].

jack roller *n.* [JACKROLL *v.*] **1** [1920s+] (*US*) a robber who specializes in stealing from drunk, drugged or otherwise incapacitated victims. **2** [1990s+] (*S.Afr.*) an individual, usu. one of gang, who abducts and rapes women.

Jack's *n.* see JACK *n.* (1).

jacks *n.*[1]

IN EXCLAMATIONS

❑ **by jacks!** (*also* **by Jakers! by Jack! i jacks! Jakers!**) [late 18C+] used in mild oaths as a euph. for *by Jesus!*

jacks *n.*[2] [JAKES *n.*] [1940s+] (*Irish*) the lavatory (cf. JAX *n.*[1]).

jacks *n.*[3]

IN PHRASES

❑ **on one's jacks** *see under* JACK (JONES) *adj.*

jack's (alive) *n.* (*also* **jax**) [rhy. sl.] [1910s+] five, esp. as £5 note.

jack scratches *n.* [rhy. sl.] [20C+] (*Aus./US*) matches.

jacksey *n.* see JACKSIE *n.*[1].

jack shea *n.* (*also* **jack shay**) [? rhy. sl. = tea (in Irish pron. 'tay')] [late 19C+] (*Aus.*) a tin container, holding a quart (2 litre) of liquid, used for brewing tea and, when empty, containing a smaller vessel for drinking the tea.

jackshit *n.* (*also* **jack, jack and shit**) [JACK *n.*[1] + SHIT *n.* (3i)] **1** [1960s+] (*orig. US*) absolutely nothing, always used with a qualifying negative v., e.g. *you don't know jack shit about...* **2** [1970s+] (*US*) nonsense. **3** [1970s+] (*US*) a stupid, contemptible person.

jackshit *adj.* [JACKSHIT *n.*] [1990s+] (*US*) worthless, useless, negligible.

jackshite *n.* see JACK *n.*[5].

Jack's house *n. see* HOUSE THAT JACK BUILT *under* HOUSE *n.*[1].

jacksie *n.*[1] (*also* **jacksey, jaxi**) [ety. unknown; ? link to JACK *n.*[3]] **1** [late 19C+] the anus; thus *up your jacksie*, a derog. response to an unpalatable idea or opinion. **2** [20C+] (*Aus.*) a brothel.

IN EXCLAMATIONS

❑ **stick it up your jacksie!** [1940s+] a general excl. of dismissal or derision. ❑ **up your jacksie!** (*also* **up your jack!**) [JACKSIE *n.*[1] (1)] [late 19C+] an alternative version of UP YOUR ARSE! *excl.*

jacksie *n.*[2] [rhy. sl.] [1940s] a taxi.

jack smithers *n.* [? anecdotal] **1** [1900s–40s] (*Aus.*) a drink taken by one who is drinking alone. **2** [1930s+] a solitary drinker.

Jackson *n.*[1] [mid–late 19C] used in mild oaths as a euph. for *by Jesus!*

Jackson *n.*[2] [the portrait of President Andrew *Jackson* (1767–1845) printed on the bill] [mid-19C+] (*US*) a $20 bill; thus money in general.

Jackson *n.*[3] [ext. JACK *n.*[2] (3)] [1930s+] (*US*) a form of address, usu. between men.

Jackson Pollocks *n.* [rhy. sl. = BALLOCKS *n.*; ult. the US abstract expressionist painter *Jackson Pollock* (1912–56)] [2000s] **1** the testicles. **2** nonsense, rubbish.

jack sprat *n.*[1] [the name survives mainly in the nursery rhyme, which itself post-dated it: its first appearance in print was 1570, while the nursery rhyme was first published in 1639] [late 16C–19C] a small person, a dwarf.

jack sprat *n.*[2] [rhy. sl.] [20C+] **1** fat (on meat). **2** a brat, an irritating small child.

jack squat *n.* [1980s+] (*US*) a partial euph. for JACKSHIT *n.*

jackstraw *n. see under* JACK *n.*[2].

Jack Straw's Castle *n.* [JACKSTRAW *n.*; the common sl. image of the vagina as a trifle, a nothing] [19C] the vagina.

jack surpass *n.* [rhy. sl.] [mid-19C] a glass.

jacksy *n.*

IN PHRASES

❑ **on one's jacksy** *see* ON ONE'S JACK (JONES) *under* JACK (JONES) *adj.*

jack tar *n.*[1] [JACK *n.*[2] (1) + *tar*, i.e. the 17C naut. practice of smearing canvas breeches with tar to provide a primitive form of waterproofing. The term gradually evolved into SE during the 19C] **1** [18C+] a sailor. **2** [19C] a hornpipe.

jack tar *n.*[2] [rhy. sl.; ult. JACK TAR *n.*[1]] **1** [20C+] a bar (in a public house). **2** [1960s] ten shillings [= HALF A BAR *under* BAR *n.*[1]]. **3** [2000s] a bar (in a jail cell).

Jack the Bear *n.* [rhy. sl.; Wolfe & Mezzrow (1946) 'When you're *like Jack the Bear, you ain't nowhere*, because for a good part of the year a bear is just huddled snugly in a hole, oblivious to the world. His brother, *No Fu'er*, is in the same sorry predicament, far from alert'] [1940s–60s] (*US black*) a general derog. term: a failure, a fool; occas. used positively to mean a success; often abbr. to just *the Bear*.

jack the dancer *n.* [rhy. sl.] [20C+] (*Aus.*) cancer.

jack the dog *v. see under* JACK OFF *v.*[1].

Jack the Jew *n.* [racial stereotyping] [19C] a receiver of stolen goods, usu. of the least valuable type.

jack the lad *n.* [JACK *n.*[2] (1) + SE *lad*; note Egan in *Captain Macheath* (1842): 'For sounding, frisking any clie, / Jack was the lad, and never shy'] [1970s+] a show-off, anyone particularly pleased with themselves and keen to ensure that everyone knows it.

jack the lad *adj.* [rhy. sl.] [20C+] bad.

jack the painter *n.* [the stain it leaves on the cup or teapot or its smell, supposedly similar to paint] [mid-19C–1940s] (*Aus.*) a strong, coarse green tea, which stained the drinker's lips.

Jack the Ripper *n.* [rhy. sl.; ult. *Jack the Ripper*, the late 19C mass-killer] **1** [20C+] a kipper [like his victims, kippers are slit open]. **2** [1980s+] a slipper. **3** [2000s] a stripper.

jack the slipper *n.* [late 19C] a prison treadmill.

Jack, Tom and Harry *n. see* TOM, DICK AND HARRY *n.*

jack-up *n.*[1] [SE *jack up*, to raise] **1** [1940s+] (*Aus.*) an argument, a dispute, a refusal to cooperate, esp. at work or in the office. **2** [1980s+] (*Aus./N.Z.*) a 'frame-up', an act of calculated deception.

jack-up *n.*[2] [JACK UP *v.*[4] (1)] [1990s+] a confrontation; violent or otherwise.

jack (up) *v.* (*orig. US drugs*) **1** [1930s+] to inject narcotics; usu. as JACKED (UP) *adj.* **2** [2000s] in non-drug contexts, e.g. drinking coffee.

jack up *v.*[1] [note dial. uses; to give up anything in a bad temper (Sussex); to become bankrupt or insolvent (Leicester); later mainly JACK (IN) *v.*] **1** [late 19C–1910s] to give up, esp. a love affair, to abandon, to leave. **2** [late 19C+] to collapse, either physically or financially, to be completely exhausted. **3** [late 19C+] to ruin, to exhaust completely, to mess up. **4** [late 19C+] (*Aus.*) (*also* **jack up on**) to refuse to carry out an instruction, to refuse to work, to offer resistance; thus *jacked up/up on*, annoyed with, disenchanted. **5** [20C+] (*UK Und./Aus.*) to plead 'not guilty'. **6** [1990s+] (*US campus*) to fail to work, to be injured.

jack up *v.*[2] **1** [late 19C+] (*US*) to criticize, to rebuke, to discipline or call to account. **2** [late 19C+] (*US*) to suspend in disgrace, to take disciplinary action.

jack up *v.*[3] (*also* **jack**) **1** [20C+] (*orig. US*) to raise, to increase, e.g. to raise rents. **2** [1910s–60s] (*US*) to urge, to incite. **3** [1920s+] (*N.Z.*) to arrange, to organize, to put right, to spruce up. **4** [1960s+] (*US*) to excite, to stimulate. **5** [1980s] to accelerate a vehicle.

IN PHRASES

❑ **jack oneself up** *v.* [1920s+] **1** to settle in; thus to make oneself or someone else at home. **2** to pull oneself together.

jack up *v.*[4] [1960s+] (*US black*) **1** to assault, to attack, to beat up, to hold up, to mug; usu. in a group. **2** (*also* **jack**) to have sexual intercourse. **3** of the police, to interrogate; to stop and search. **4** to arrest, to be charged, to be jailed. **5** to take aside for a conversation. **6** to stop.

IN PHRASES

❑ **jack it up someone's ass** *v.* [SE *jack*, to force up + ASS *n.* (2)] [1960s+] (*US*) to punish or victimize someone.

jack up *v.*[5] [1990s+] (*US*) to vomit.

jack with *v.* [var. on JACK AROUND *v.*] [1960s] (*US*) **1** to annoy, to irritate, to 'mess around'. **2** to become involved with.

jacky *n.*[1] (*also* **jackey**) [? a gin distiller] [late 18C–1920s] gin.

jacky *n.*[2] **1** *see* JACK *n.*[5]. **2** *see* JACK *n.*[10]. **3** *see* JACKO *n.* (1). **4** *see* JACKY JACKY *n.*

Jacky Bull *n. see* JOHN BULL *n.*

jacky-dandy *n. see* JACK-A-DANDY *n.*

jacky danny *n. see* JACK AN' DANNY *n.*

jacky howe *n. see* JACKIE HOWE *n.*

jacky jacky *n.* (*also* **jackey, jacky**) [popular nickname *Jacky* + redup.] [mid-19C+] (*Aus./N.Z.*) **1** a white man's derog. name for an Aborigine, the 'typical' Aborigine. **2** a coconut.

IN PHRASES

❑ **sit up like jacky** *v.* [SE *sit up*; or *Jacky*, the trad. name for the organ grinder's monkey] [1940s+] (*Aus./N.Z.*) to sit up straight and confident.

Jacky Lancashire *n.* [rhy. sl.] [1900s] (*Aus.*) a handkerchief (pron. 'hankercher').

jacky raw *n.* (*also* **jimmy raw**) [JACK *n.*[2] (1) + *raw* + ? JACKAROO *n.* (2)] [20C+] (*Aus.*) a new immigrant.

jacky rue *n.* [? JACKY RAW *n.* + JACKAROO *n.*] [20C+] (*Aus.*) a squatter.

jacob *n.*[1] [the biblical story of *Jacob*'s ladder] **1** [mid-18C] (*UK Und.*) a thief who uses a ladder. **2** [mid-18C–1970s] (*UK Und.*) a ladder. **3** [19C+] the penis [it 'climbs up' the vagina].

jacob *n.*[2] [play on JAY *n.*[1]] [late 18C–19C] a fool.

jacobite *n.* [? the 'false' claims of the *Jacobites* to the British throne] [late 17C–mid-19C] a shirt collar, a fake shirt.

Jacob's crackers *adj. see* CREAM CRACKERED *adj.*

jacob's ladder *n.* [one 'climbs' up it] [19C] **1** (*orig. theatre*) a 'ladder' in a pair of tights or stockings. **2** the vagina.

jacobus *n.* [the Lat. name *Jacobus*, (King) James I (r.1603–25) inscribed on it] [early 17C–18C] a guinea.

jacque's *n. see* JAKES *n.*

Jacques Cousteau job *n.* [*Jacques Cousteau* (1910–97) the aquanaut + JOB *n.*[2] (2)] [1980s+] in football, a dive.

jacum-gag *n. see* JOCKUM GAGE *under* JOCKUM *n.*

jade *n.* [? one becomes SE *jaded*] [mid-19C+] (*Aus./US*) a long jail sentence.

jadrool *n.* (*also* **jadroney**) [ety. unknown] [1960s+] (*US, esp. US Ital.*) a stupid or unpleasant person.

jafa *n.* [abbr.; *j*ust *a*nother *f*ucking *A*ucklander] [2000s] (*N.Z.*) a person from Auckland.

jaffa *n.* [the size of a *Jaffa* orange] [1990s+] (*UK juv.*) a male who has notably large testicles.

Jag *n.* [abbr.] [1950s+] a *Jag*uar motorcar.

jag *n.*[1] [dial. *jag*, as much liquor as one can hold, a 'load'. Note *S.F. Alta* 4 Aug. 1889 [title] What a Jag Is: 'An inquirer asks us the meaning of 'Jag' applied to inebriety. It is a new slang. In the rural districts the cargo of a wagon that is hauling wood, when [holding] all that the wagon can carry, is called a 'load.' When it is less than up to the full capacity it is called a 'Jag.' Therefore when a man is less than dead drunk he has not a load on but merely a Jag'] **1** [late 17C+] a drunken spree; thus *have/get a jag on*, to be drunk or *on a jag*, on a spree. **2** [late 19C–1940s] a drunkard. **3** [late 19C+] a drink. **4** [late 19C+] (*drugs*) the consumption of a drug, usu. defined by the drug in question. **5** [20C+] the experience of taking a specific drug. **6** [20C+] in fig. uses. (**a**) (*US*) a period of indulgence, a fit, a spree of any kind. (**b**) (*orig. US*) a breakdown, an emotional collapse; often as *crying jag*, lengthy and profound sobbing. **7** [1930s] a hangover. **8** [1950s] a drugs party. **9** [1950s] a trance.

IN COMPOUNDS

❑ **jag-feeder** *n.* [late 19C–1900s] (*US*) a drink. ❑ **jag line** *n.* [1910s] a police line-up of those arrested as 'drunk and disorderly'. ❑ **jag parlor** *n.* [1900s] a bar, a saloon. ❑ **jag snakes** *n.* [late 19C] (*US*) hallucinations from delirium tremens.

IN PHRASES

❑ **dry jag** *n. see under* DRY *adj.*[1]. ❑ **get a jag on** *v.* (*also* **have a jag on**) [late 19C+] to get drunk, to be drunk. ❑ **get the jags** *v.* [1900s] to get depressed. ❑ **on a jag** **1** [20C+] on a drunken spree. **2** [1950s+] (*orig. US*) elated.

jag *n.*[2] [JACK *n.*[1]? or fig. use of JAG *n.*[1] (2)] [late 19C+] **1** a foolish notion. **2** (*US*) a strange or stupid person.

jag *v.*[1] [dial. *jag*, to cut roughly] **1** [late 19C] to vaccinate. **2** [late 19C–1900s] to assault with a knife. **3** [1960s] (*US*) to copulate with a woman. **4** [1960s–70s] to make pregnant. **5** [1980s+] (*drugs*) to inject oneself or someone else [note JACK (UP) *v.* (1)].

jag *v.*[2] [JACK AROUND *v.*] [20C+] (*Aus./N.Z.*) to depress, to irritate.

jag *v.*[3] [? dial. *jag*, a journey; but note dial. *jag*, to tear roughly, i.e. the gossips 'tear someone to pieces'] [1940s+] (*N.Z.*) to pay a social call.

IN PHRASES

❑ **go jagging** *v.* [1940s+] (*Aus./N.Z.*) to go visiting for the purpose of exchanging gossip.

jag *v.*[4] (*also* **jag up**) [JAG *n.*[1]] [1950s+] (*drugs*) to maintain one's drugged or drunken state.

jagabat *n.* [? Hind. *jaggery*, sugar, sweet + *bat*, language] **1** [20C+] (*W.I.*) a prostitute or notably promiscuous woman. **2** [1990s+] (*W.I.*) (*also* **jagga-bite**) a person of the lowest class and style of behaviour.

jagamaree *n. see* JIGAMAREE *n.*

jagged *adj.*[1] (*also* **jagged up**) [JAG *n.*[1]] **1** [mid-18C+] drunk; also fig. use. **2** [1930s+] intoxicated by drugs.

jagged *adj.*[2] [JAG *v.*[2]] [20C+] (*N.Z.*) tired; depressed; irritating.

jagger *n.*[1] [Ger. *Jäger*, a sportsman] [mid-19C] a gentleman.

jagger *n.*[2] **1** [1940s] (*US carnival*) a tattoo artist. **2** [2000s] a heroin user [JAG *v.*[1] (5)].

jag it in *v. see* JACK (IN) *v.*

jag-off *n.* [JACK-OFF *n.* (1)] [1930s+] (*US*) a masturbator, thus an idiot, dolt.

jag-off *adj.* [JAG-OFF *n.*] [1980s] (*US*) stupid.

jag off *v.* [JACK OFF *v.*[1]/JACK AROUND *v.*] **1** [1950s–60s] (*US drugs*) to inject a narcotic, esp. slowly. **2** [1960s+] (*US*) to masturbate. **3** [1970s+] (*US*) to fool around, to mess about. **4** [1970s+] (*US*) to tease or deceive someone.

jags *adj.* [Afk. *jags*, of an animal, in season, on heat] [20C+] (*S.Afr.*) randy, lecherous.

jague *n.* [? JAKES *n.*, since both are seen as repositories of filth] [mid-17C–mid-19C] (*UK Und.*) a ditch.

jail *see also under* GAOL and its combs.

jail *n.*

SE in slang uses

(IN COMPOUNDS)

❑ **jailbait** *n. see* separate entry. ❑ **jailhouse** *adj. see* separate entry. ❑ **jail-jumper** *n. see* *JUMP JAIL under* JUMP *v.* ❑ **jail lawyer** *n. see* *JAILHOUSE LAWYER under* JAILHOUSE *adj.* ❑ **jail radio** *n. see* *BUSH RADIO under* BUSH *n.*[1]. ❑ **jail tail** *n.* (*also* **jailhouse pussy**) [var. on JAILBAIT *n.* (2)] [1960s] (*US gay*) a young boy who is below the age of sexual consent, with whom sex would mean prison.

jail *v.* [1960s+] (*US*) to spend time in prison, spec. to create the best possible situation for oneself given the overriding circumstances.

jailbait *n.* **1** [1930s+] (*US*) a young person who is (seen as) a troublemaker and thus likely to be sent to prison. **2** [1930s+] (*orig. US*) (*also* **Alcatraz bait, bait, penitentiary bait**) a young person, usu. a girl, who is under the age of sexual consent; having sex with such an individual is to invite a jail sentence. **3** [1950s+] in fig. use, dangerous; of people, attractive but dangerous. **4** [1960s–70s] (*US*) a charge of statutory rape.

jailhouse *adj.*

SE in slang uses pertaining to prison

(IN COMPOUNDS)

❑ **jailhouse bitch** *n.* [BITCH *n.*[1] (1f)] [1990s+] a wife or grilfriend who pays regular visits to her partner while he is in jail. ❑ **jailhouse daddy** *n.* [DADDY *n.* (14)] [1950s–60s] (*US prison*) a dominating male homosexual prisoner who exploits or protects his partner. ❑ **jailhouse lawyer** *n.* (*also* **gaolhouse lawyer, jail lawyer**) [1920s+] (*US Und.*) a prison inmate who has become a self-taught lawyer, either to pursue their own case, combat prison corruption or help fellow inmates. ❑ **jailhouse pussy** *n. see* *JAIL TAIL under* JAIL *n.* ❑ **jailhouse salute** *n.* [1970s] (*US*) an obscene gesture. ❑ **jailhouse turnout** *n.* (*also* **j.t., j.t.o.**) [1960s–70s] (*US*) a prisoner who is forced to engage in homosexual practices or who becomes a homosexual while in prison [TURN OUT *v.*[4] (2)].

jailic *n.* [SE *jail* + *Gaelic*] [1970s+] (*Irish*) Irish as learned while imprisoned in the prison at Long Kesh, Belfast.

jailing *n.* [JAIL *v.*] (*US prison*) **1** [1960s+] accustoming oneself to life in jail and adapting one's lifestyle to make one's time there as tolerable as possible. **2** [1990s+] wearing one's trousers in such a way that a few inches of one's underwear is visible; such a fashion was very popular among black youth and their white imitators in 1990s. **3** [2000s] serving time in the punishment cells. **4** [2000s] of a prisoner's friends or family, visiting regularly.

jaina *n.* [Sp.] [1960s+] (*US*) a girlfriend.

jajazy *n. see* JASEY *n.*

jakalorum *adj.* [JAKE *adj.*[1] (2)] [1900s] (*Aus.*) as required, satisfactory, in order.

jake *n.*[1] (*also* **country jake**) [the 'rural' proper name *Jacob*] **1** [mid-19C+] (*US*) a farmer, a rustic. **2** [1920s–40s] (*orig. US black*) a general term of address. **3** [1980s+] (*US campus*) an unsophisticated person, a misfit, a fool. **4** [1990s+] (*US*) a Jamaican.

(IN COMPOUNDS)

❑ **jake cove** *n. see* *JACK COVE under* JACK *n.*[2]. ❑ **jake flake** *n.* [FLAKE *n.*[2] (1)] [1950s+] (*US black*) anyone interested in themselves above anything or anyone else.

jake *n.*[2] [JAKE *adj.*[1] (2)] [1910s] (*Can./US*) an admirable example.

jake *n.*[3] (*also* **jackie, jakers, jakey**) [abbr. *Jamaica*] **1** [1920s+] (*US*) Jamaica ginger, a drink with intoxicating properties [esp. popular during Prohibition (1919–33)]. **2** [1920s+] (*US*) methylated spirits, or surgical spirits, used as an alcoholic drink; thus *jake-drinker*, a meths drinker; thus JAKELEG *n.* **3** [1930s–70s] (*US prison*) a drunkard.

(IN COMPOUNDS)

❑ **jakehead** *n.* (*also* **jakehound**) [-HEAD *sfx* (4)/-HOUND *sfx*] [1920s–30s] (*US*) an addict of Jamaica ginger.

jake *n.*[4] **1** [1970s] (*US*) coffee [? f. JAKE *n.*[3] (1) or elision of JAMOKE *n.*[1]; note JOE *n.*[4]]. **2** [1980s+] (*US*) a New York City police patrolman [? he drinks so much coffee].

jake *n.*[5] **1** *see* JAKELEG *n.* **2** *see* JAKES *n.*

jake *adj.*[1] [? SE *chic*] **1** [1910s–20s] (*US Und.*) aware, in the know. **2** [1910s+] (*Aus./N.Z./US*) satisfactory, as required, esp. in phr. *she's/she'll be/we're jake*, it's fine, things will be fine, we are fine.

(IN PHRASES)

❑ **all jake** [1910s+] (*US*) right, OK, satisfactory.

jake *adj.*[2] [2000s] (*US black*) unsatisfactory, disappointing.

jake *v.* [? SE *jerk* oneself out of] [1990s+] (*US campus*) to cancel an appointment without prior notice, to drop out of an arrangement.

jake *adv.* [1910s+] satisfactorily.

jakealoo/jake-a-pie *adj. see* JAKELOO *adj.*

jaked *adj.* [JAKE *adj.*[1] (2)] [1980s+] (*US campus*) **1** excited, happy, thrilled. **2** drunk.

jakehouse *n.* (*also* **jackhouse**) [JAKES *n.* + SE *house*] [1900s–10s] a privy, a lavatory.

jakeleg *n.* (*also* **jake**) [1930s–70s] paralysis of the leg or legs caused by an excess of JAKE *n.*[3], thus *jakeleg liquor/whisky*, 'bad' liquor or whisky (which may well cause paralysis); *jake-legged*, paralysed.

jakeleg *adj. see* JACKLEG *adj.*

jake leg *v.* [JAKELEG *n.*] [1990s+] (*US*) to tease, playfully deceive.

jakeloo *adj.* (*also* **jackaloo, jakealoo, jake-a-pie, jakerloo**) [JAKE *adj.*[1]; note A.G. Pretty (ed.), *Glossary Of Slang [...] in the A.I.F. 1921–1924* (1924) (rev. t/s): ' JAKERLOO OR JAKE. "Jake" was in use before the war, in Australia by drivers & others to indicate that the load and harness were secure and everything ready for a start. It was also used to indicate that all was well with the speaker. The addition of the last two syllables appear to have been made in the A.I.F. abroad; perhaps the outcome of the observation by certain members of the "force" of the "Bakerloo" the name of the underground railway that connected Waterloo station with Baker Street, both in London. Some contend that the term was introduced on the Western Front by the Canadians and that it is a relic of the French Revolution when the plotters were known as "Jaques 1", "Jaques 2" etc in order to avoid detection'] [1910s+] (*Aus./N.Z.*) excellent, wonderful, very good.

jakers *n. see* JAKE *n.*[3].

jakes *n.* (*also* **jacque's, jake, jaxe**) [? *jack's* or *jack's place*; using SE *jack* as generic for a man. Note synon. 1930s+ Virginia dial. *jack-house*; note also Nares (1822): 'Its etymology is uncertain, unless we accept the very bad pun of Sir John (Harington), who derives it (in jest indeed) from an old man who, at such a place, cried out *age akes, age akes*, meaning that age causes aches'] [mid-16C+] a lavatory; occas. in sing.

IN COMPOUNDS

❑ **jakes-farmer** *n.* (*also* **jakes barreller**) [SE *farmer*, one who cleanses] [late 16C–mid-17C] a man employed to clean out privies.

jake the rape *v.* [1980s+] (*Aus. prison*) to escape.

jakey *n.*[1] [1960s] (*US gay*) the penis.

jakey *n.*[2] [JAKE *n.*[3] (2)] **1** [1980s+] a beggar; an alcoholic vagrant. **2** *see* JAKE *n.*[3].

jakey *adj.* [JAKE *n.*[1] (1)] [1950s+] (*US*) unsophisticated, gauche, rustic, characteristic of a country person.

jalino *n.* [ety. unknown] [1940s] (*US*) a disadvantage; usu. as *have someone by the jalino.*

jalobies *n.* [ety. unknown] [1960s+] nipples.

jalopy *n.* (*also* **jalop, jaloppy, jilopi, jollopi, joppy, loppy**) [ety. unknown; ? Sp.; echoic of the car's unsteady progress] [1920s+] (*orig. US*) **1** a decrepit car. **2** a worthless or unattractive person or object.

Jam *n.* [abbr.] [1970s+] a *Jam*aican.

jam *n.*[1] [SE *jam*, a crush;19C SE *crush*, a party] **1** [19C–1920s] (*US*) a social gathering or party; a crowd. **2** in fig. uses, i.e. that which crushes. (**a**) [late 19C+] a problem, a difficult situation, usu. *in a jam*. (**b**) [20C+] (*US*) (*also* **jamb**) a disagreement or a fight. (**c**) [1930s–50s] (*US drugs*) an overdose ['it gets you in a jam' (Spears, 1986)]. **3** [1930s+] (*US black*) swing or other popular music. **4** [1950s+] (*US black*) a party with music. **5** [1950s+] music in general, a song, a record, a performance of jazz, rock or rap music (orig. with a dance routine). **6** [1970s+] (*US gay*) a spontaneous party that ends in an orgy or a big fight. **7** [1990s+] (*W.I.*) a crowd in a venue that is at full capacity.

IN COMPOUNDS

❑ **jambox** *n.* [BOX *n.*[1] (4b)/SE *box*] [1980s+] (*US campus*) a portable stereo tape deck.

IN PHRASES

❑ **blind jam** *n.* [fig. use of SE *blind*, i.e one cannot 'see' a charge] [1930s] (*US Und.*) an arrest without a specific charge.

jam *n.*[2] [SE *jam*, the fruit conserve] **1** in context of pleasure, advantage [orig. sporting jargon *real jam*, anything exceptionally good]. (**a**) [mid-19C+] profit, an advantage. (**b**) [mid-19C+] something very enjoyable. (**c**) [mid-19C+] anything easy. **2** [late 19C+] (*Aus.*) images of excessive 'sweetness'. (**a**) affectation, pretentiousness; thus *put on the jam, show jam*, to act in an affected manner. (**b**) toadying. **3** [1920s–40s] (*US Und.*) small stolen articles, i.e. personal jewellery. **4** bodily fluids. (**a**) [1940s+] (*US gay*) faeces; often in the context of homosexual foreplay. (**b**) [1960s+] menstrual blood. (**c**) [1960s+] (*US black*) semen. (**d**) [2000s] vaginal secretions.

IN COMPOUNDS

❑ **jam fag** *n.* [FAG *n.*[5] (1)] [1940s+] a homosexual with no other sexual interests. ❑ **jam rag** *n.* [1960s+] a tampon, a sanitary towel.

IN PHRASES

❑ **eat jam** *v.* [SE *eat*/EAT *v.* (4) + sense 4a above] [1940s+] (*US gay*) to lick the anus. ❑ **give her the jampot** *v.* [sense 4c above] [1980s] (*US black*) to have sexual intercourse. ❑ **jam off** *v.* [2000s] to ejaculate. ❑ **put on jam** *v.* (*also* **lay on jam**) (*Aus.*) **1** [late 19C–1900s] to put on airs. **2** [1900s] to flatter. ❑ **real jam** *n.* (*also* **real Peruvian doughnuts**) [orig. sporting jargon] [mid-19C–1910s] of objects or people, the best, the superlative.

SE in slang uses

IN COMPOUNDS

❑ **jam sandwich** *n.* (*also* **jam butty**) [the fluorescent coloured stripe running round the middle of the car] [1980s+] a police car.

IN PHRASES

❑ **jam on your egg** *n.* [? SE *do you want jam on it?*, a phr. meaning to stop complaining/being so demanding] [2000s] (*Irish*) wishful thinking.

jam *n.*[3] [JAM TART *n.* (2)] [late 19C+] **1** an attractive woman. **2** sexual intercourse with a woman. **3** (*later use US black*) the vagina.

IN PHRASES

❑ **bit of jam** *n.* **1** [late 19C] the vagina; thus *have a bit of jam*, to have sexual intercourse. **2** [late 19C–1900s] an attractive woman. ❑ **elderly jam** *n.* ['Elderly jam is – elderly jam, and heaven preserve it, for man turns from it' (Ware)] [late 19C] an old woman. ❑ **lawful jam** *n.* [late 19C–1900s] one's wife. ❑ **no-beyond jammer** *n.* [late 19C–1900s] an extremely attractive woman.

jam *n.*[4] [acronym] **1** [1960s+] (*gay*) a heterosexual man [? abbr. for *just a man*, but this may be a camp joke and the real ety. is unknown]. **2** [1980s+] (*Ulster*) a second-rate teacher [abbr. *junior assistant mistress*].

jam *n.*[5] [1970s+] **1** (*US black/drugs*) cocaine. **2** (*US drugs*) (*also* **jammie**) amphetamine.

IN COMPOUNDS

❑ **jam cecil** *n.* [? CECIL *n.*[2]] [1970s+] (*drugs*) amphetamine. ❑ **jam house** *n.* [1970s] (*US black*) a place where cocaine can be both purchased and then snorted in convivial surroundings.

jam *n.*[6] **1** *see* JAM JAR *n.* (1). **2** *see* JAM ROLL *n.* (1).

jam *n.*[7] *see* JEM *n.*[1].

jam *adj.* see JAM-UP *adj.*

jam *v.*[1] [one's head is 'jammed' into the noose; ? ref. to the original method of hanging, jamming the neck into a forked piece of wood] [mid-18C–early 19C] to hang; usu. as JAMMED *adj.*[1].

jam *v.*[2] **1** [mid-19C+] to injure, to damage by striking or crushing. **2** [mid-19C+] to strike hard and suddenly. **3** [mid-19C+] to cause trouble for, to put in danger; often as JAM UP *v.* (1). **4** [1920s] (*US*) to persist forcefully. **5** [1940s] (*US*) to impede. **6** [1960s+] (*US black*) to confront, to fight, to overcome or defeat. **7** [1970s+] to threaten, to harass, to arrest. **8** [1980s+] (*US black*) to defeat verbally.

jam *v.*[3] [JAM *n.*[1]] **1** [1930s+] (*W.I./US black*) to play or, of an instrument or of music in general, to be played so as to encourage vigorous dancing; thus *jamming*, dancing in an abandoned manner. **2** [1930s+] (*orig. US*) of musicians, to play together without set scores or arrangement for the pleasure and the spontaneous music thus created. **3** [1950s+] (*US black/campus/drugs*) (*also* **jam down**) to have fun, a good time, also by taking drugs. **4** [1970s+] (*US black*) to talk forcefully, esp. in a group. **5** [1970s+] (*US black/campus*) (*also* **jam back**) to dance. **6** [1980s+] (*US campus*) to do very well.

IN PHRASES

❑ **jam out** *v.* [1980s+] (*US campus*) **1** to listen to music. **2** to play music intensely. ❑ **jam the box** *v.* to play music on a jukebox, portable stereo.

jam *v.*[4] [JAM *n.*[3] (2)] **1** [1940s+] (*orig. US black/W.I.*) to have sexual intercourse. **2** [1990s+] (*US black/gay*) to have anal intercourse. **3** [2000s] in fig. use, i.e. euph. for FUCK *v.* in a variety of senses.

jam *v.*[5] [JAM *n.*[5] (1)] [1960s–70s] (*US black*) to sniff cocaine.

jam *v.*[6] [? SE *jam* one's foot on the accelerator] [1960s+] (*US teen*) to leave, to exit fast.

jam *adv.* [JAM *n.*[2] (1)] [mid-19C] (*US*) comfortably, easily.

Jamaica discipline *n.* [? pun on *do you make her*] [1960s+] (*gay*) a wife's denial of sexual favours to her husband.

Jamaican coat-of-arms *n.* [rice and peas is the Jamaican national dish] [1940s+] (*W.I.*) a dish of rice and peas.

Jamaica rum *n.* [rhy. sl.] [20C+] a thumb.

jamb *n. see* JAM *n.*[1] (2b).

jambas *n.* [Sp.] [1960s+] (*US*) theft, robbery.

jamberoo *n.* [var. on JAMBOREE *n.* (1)] [late 19C–1950s] (*Aus.*) a drunken spree.

jambo *n.* [JAM TARTS *n.*] [1980s+] (*Scot.*) a supporter of the football club Heart of Midlothian.

jambone *adj.* [? var. on JIBONE *n.*] [1980s] (*US*) worthless, contemptible.

jamboree *n.* [best known in 20C+ as a SE description of any large Boy Scout rally, the first of which, the International Rally of Boy

Scouts, was held in 1920] **1** [mid-19C+] (*orig. US*) a spree, a noisy revel. **2** [late 19C–1950s] (*US*) a disturbance or fight.

jamboree *v.* [JAMBOREE *n.*] [1920s] to go on a spree.

jam duff *n.* [rhy. sl. = PUFF *n.* (3a)] [20C+] a male homosexual.

Jamdung *n.* (*also* **Jam Down**) [SE *jam*, press + *dung* (W.I. pron.), down; refers to oppression of the Jamaican proletariat] [1950s+] (*W.I., Jam.*) Jamaica.

james *n.* **1** [19C] a cooked sheep's head [JEMMY *n.*[1] (3)]. **2** [19C–1950s] a housebreaker's implement [play on the nickname *Jemmy*/JEMMY *n.*[3] (1)]. **3** [mid–late 19C] (*also* **jemmy**) a sovereign [orig. use as 16C *James Royal*, a Scot. silver coin of James VI of Scotland (r.1567–1603), the sword dollar]. **4** *see* JOHN *n.*[2] (1a).

(IN PHRASES)

❑ **half-James** *n.* [late 18C–19C] ten shillings (50p).

James Burke *n.* [rhy. sl. = JERK *n.*[1] (1); ult. UK TV producer and historian *James Burke* (b.1936)] [2000s] (*N.Z.*) an act of male masturbation.

James Christe! *excl. see* JESUS! *excl.*

James Crow *adj. see* JIM CROW *adj.*

james crow *n. see* JIM CROW *n.*[2].

james earl dog *n.* [? ref. to *James Earl Ray* (1928–98), the alleged killer of Martin Luther King in 1968] [1980s+] (*US campus*) a marijuana cigarette.

James Hunt *n.* [rhy. sl.; ult. UK motor racing champion *James Hunt* (1947–93)] [20C+] **1** audacity, cheek [= FRONT *n.*[1] (1)]. **2** the vagina [= CUNT *n.* (1)].

James Street! *excl.* (*also* **Holy James Street! Holy James's Street and Jacobs!**) [*James Street*, Dublin, site of the Guinness brewery, and Jacobs Biscuit factory] [20C+] (*Irish*) a general excl.

jamette *n.* [? Fr. sl. *jeanette*, a prostitute, or Fr. *diamètre*, diameter, i.e. the line between two halves of the social world] [20C+] (*W.I.*) **1** a prostitute. **2** a woman widely recognized to be promiscuous. **3** a woman's breast.

jam foutre *n. see* JEAN FOUTRE *n.*

jam it *v.*[1] (*also* **jam for Sam**) [JAM *v.*[3]] [1930s+] to listen to music.

jam it *v.*[2] [JAM *v.*[6]] [1960s+] to drive a car or bike fast.

SE in slang uses

(IN EXCLAMATIONS)

❑ **jam it up your arse!** *see* SHOVE IT UP YOUR ARSE! *excl.*

jam it! *excl.* [var. on SHOVE IT! *excl.*] [1950s+] (*Aus./US*) a threatening excl.

jam jar *n.* [rhy. sl.] **1** [1910s+] (*also* **jam**) initially a tram car, a motor car. **2** [1950s] a farthing [= *far*].

jammed *adj.*[1] [JAM *v.*[1]] [mid-18C–19C] (*UK Und.*) hanged, murdered, killed.

jammed *adj.*[2] [JAM *n.*[1] (2)] **1** [mid-19C; 1920s] (*US*) drunk or intoxicated. **2** [late 19C+] (*US Und.*) in trouble with the law, arrested. **3** [1910s] subject to discipline. **4** [1970s+] (*US*) troubled, upset.

jammed out *adj.* [JAM *adj.*] [early 19C–1940s] (*US*) dressed up.

jammed up *adv.* [JAM *n.*[1] (2)] **1** [1920s+] in a difficult situation, in trouble, e.g. arrested. **2** [1960s] having taken an overdose of drugs.

jammer *n.*[1] [JAM *v.*[3]] [1980s+] (*US*) a player of music.

jammer *n.*[2] [1990s+] (*US prison*) an ice-pick.

jammer *n.*[3] [JAM IT *v.*[2]] [2000s] (*Irish*) a (stolen) car.

jammie *n.* **1** *see* JAM *n.*[5] (2). **2** *see* JAMMY *n.*[1].

jammin' *n.* [JAM *v.*[3] (1)] [1960s+] (*W.I. Rasta*) having a good time, dancing calypso/soca.

jamming *n.* [JAM *v.*[2]] [20C+] (*W.I.*) severe criticism, physical assault.

jamming *adj.* [JAM *n.*[2] (1)] [1980s+] (*orig. US black*) exciting, pleasing, excellent, the best; also as excl. of pleasure.

jammy *n.*[1] (*also* **jam, jammie**) [abbr. JAM JAR *n.* + dimin. sfx *-y*] [1960s+] (*S.Afr.*) a motorcar.

jammy *n.*[2] [? JIMMY *n.*[4] (1)] [1980s+] (*US black*) **1** the penis. **2** a handgun, a pistol.

jammy *n.*[3] [JAM *n.*[2] (4b)] [1980s+] a tampon, thus *n., jamming*, menstruating.

jammy *n.*[4] [ext. of JAM *n.*[1] (5)] [1990s+] (*US black*) a film.

jammy *adj.*[1] **1** [late 19C+] easy, simple, lucky, profitable [JAM *n.*[2] (1a)]. **2** [1900s] (*Aus.*) pretentious [JAM *n.*[2] (2a)]. **3** [1910s] bloodsoaked [? JAM *n.*[2] (4b)].

jammy *adj.*[2] [lit. covered in jam] [1960s+] (*Aus.*) unwashed.

jammy dodger *n.* [rhy. sl. = ROGER *v.*[1]] [1990s+] an act of sexual intercourse.

jamoke *n.*[1] (*also* **jamoch, jamocha, jamok, jamoka, jomoke**) [*Java* + *Mocha* coffee beans] [late 19C+] (*US*) coffee.

jamoke *n.*[2] (*also* **jamouche**) [a WW1 soldier's nickname] [1940s+] (*US*) a stupid or objectionable fellow.

jamoke *n.*[3] [ety. unknown; ? ext. of JAMOKE *n.*[2] on pattern of DORK *n.* etc, where the term means both a fool and a penis] [1960s] (*US*) the penis.

jam pies *n.* [rhy. sl.] [1990s+] the eyes.

jampot *n.* **1** [late 19C–1950s] (*Aus.*) a high collar [resemblance]. **2** [late 19C+] the vagina [JAM *n.*[3] (3)]. **3** [1940s+] (*US black/gay*) the anus [JAM *n.*[2] (4a)].

jam roll *n.* [rhy. sl.] **1** [1970s+] (*UK prison*) (*also* **jam**) parole. **2** [1990s+] the dole. **3** [2000s] the anus, as in 'arsehole'; thus a pej. description.

jams *n.* [abbr. JIM-JAMS *n.* (1)] [late 19C–1910s] delirium tremens, a hangover.

jam session *n.* [jazz use *jam session*, an impromptu concert. The first session, according to Mezzrow & Wolfe (1946), took place in late 1927 at 22 North State Street, Chicago, in the cellar of the Three Deuces speak-easy. Among those involved were Bix Beiderbecke, Bing Crosby and Mezzrow himself. 'I think the term "jam session" originated right in that cellar. Long before that, of course, the colored boys used to get together and play for kicks, but those were mostly private sessions, strictly for professional musicians, and the idea was usually to try and cut each other, each one trying to outdo the others and prove himself best. Those impromptu concerts of theirs were generally known as "cuttin' contests." Our idea [...] was to play together, to make our improvisation really collective [...] to see could we fit together and arrive at a climax all at once. Down in that basement concert hall, somebody was always yelling over to me, "Hey Jelly, what you gonna do?" [...] and almost every time I'd cap them with, "Jelly's gonna jam some now," just as a kind of play on words. We always used the word "session" a lot, and I think the expression "jam session" grew up out of this playful yelling back and forth.'] **1** [1920s+] (*orig. US*) an informal gathering, a get-together, esp. of musicians, a group discussion. **2** [1930s+] (*W.I./UK black*) any occasion which is accompanied by a large, boisterous audience. **3** [1970s+] sexual foreplay or intercourse.

jam tart *n.* [rhy. sl.] **1** [mid–late 19C] a mart. **2** [mid-19C+] a sweetheart, a girlfriend. **3** [20C+] the heart, whether anatomically or as a card suit.

jam tart *v.* [rhy. sl. = FART *v.* (1)] [1980s] (*Aus.*) to break wind.

Jam Tarts *n.* [rhy. sl.] [1990s+] (*Scot.*) Hearts, i.e. Heart of Midlothian F.C.

jam-up *adj.* (*also* **jam**) [image of SE *jam*, e.g. on bread in addition to butter, as conferring extra pleasure] [early 19C+] (*orig. US*) splendid, fine, excellent, first-rate.

(IN PHRASES)

❑ **jam-up and jelly-tight** (*also* **jelly-tight**) [JELLY *n.*[1] (3); the overall implication is sexual] [1960s+] (*US black*) splendid, first-rate.

jam up *v.* [ext. of JAM *v.*[2] (3)/(5)] **1** [mid-19C+] (*US*) to cause trouble, to put someone or oneself in a difficult position. **2** [1920s] (*US prison*) to arrest. **3** [1990s+] (*also* **jam**) to discipline. **4** [1990s+] (*US prison*) to confront, to question.

(IN PHRASES)

❑ **jam someone up** *v.* **1** [1950s] (*US*) to cause trouble for. **2** [1960s+] (*US black*) to rape. **3** [1960s+] (*US black*) to beat, to overpower. **4** [1970s+] (*US black*) to talk forcefully, to challenge, to confront.

jam-up *adv.* [JAM-UP *adj.*] [early 19C–1940s] thoroughly, totally, keenly.

jan *n.* [ety. unknown; ? Rom.] [17C] (*UK Und.*) a purse.

janasmug *n. see* JANUSMUG *n.*

jancro(w) *n. see* JOHN CROW $n.^{1}$.

jancy! *excl. see* JANEY MACK! *excl.*

Jane *adj.* [JANE $n.^{2}$ (1)] [1920s] (*Scot.*) of a woman, smart, sophisticated.

jane $n.^{1}$ [SE *jane*, a small silver coin from Genoa, introduced into England towards the end of the 14C] [mid-19C–1900s] a sovereign.

jane $n.^{2}$ [generic use of the proper name] **1** [late 19C+] a woman, a sweetheart, a girlfriend. **2** [1940s–70s] an effeminate or homosexual man. **3** [1950s+] (*US*) a women's lavatory. **4** [1950s+] (*camp gay*) the embodiment of one's feminine side. **5** *see* JEAN *n.*

jane $n.^{3}$ [abbr. MARY JANE $n.^{2}$] (*US drugs*) **1** [1970s+] marijuana. **2** [1990s+] cocaine [note cocaine is a 'feminine' drug, cf. GIRL $n.^{2}$].

Jane Crow *n.* [after JIM CROW *n.*] [1970s] discrimination against women.

Jane Doe *n.* [1970s+] the female version of JOHN DOE *n.*

Jane Q Public *n.* (*also* **Jane Q Citizen**) [1970s+] (*US*) the average, typical woman.

Jane Russell *n.* [rhy. sl.; ult. US film star *Jane Russell* (b.1921)] [20C+] a mussel.

Jane Russell special *n.* [the voluptuous Hollywood star *Jane Russell* (b.1921)] [1990s+] (*US*) two poached eggs on toast.

Jane Shore *n.* [rhy. sl.; ult. *Jane Shore* (d.1527), mistress of Edward IV] **1** [mid–late 19C] the floor. **2** [1930s] a prostitute [= SE *whore*].

janet *n.* [rhy. sl. on *Janet Street-Porter*; ult. UK TV personality *Janet* Street-Porter (b.1944)] [1980s+] (*drugs*) a quarter ounce of cannabis.

janey mack! *excl.* (*also* **bejaney-mack-tonight! jancy! janey!**) [1920s+] (*Irish*) a general excl., euph. for *Jesus Christ!*

janga-manga *n.* [? *jangga*, a river prawn, eaten by poor peasants + *manga* = Fr. *manger*, to eat] [1940s] (*W.I.*) a person of the lowest class.

jangle *v.* [SE *jangle*, to squabble] [1960s+] **1** to speak ill of someone, to gossip. **2** to unnerve.

janissary *n.* [SE *janissary*, ult. Turk. *yeni-tsheri* (*yeni* new, modern + *tsheri* soldiery), a body of Turkish infantry] [late 17C–mid-19C] **1** a bailiff and/or his assistants. **2** the mob.

jank *adj.* see JANKY *adj.* (1).

jank *v. see* GANK *v.*

jankers *n.* [orig. milit. jankers, punishment for defaulters; ety. unknown; thus Kersh (1941) 'What is jankers, Sergeant?' 'It's a sort of general word meaning punishment.']

IN COMPOUNDS

❑ **jankers-man** *n.* [1920s–40s] an authority figure.

IN PHRASES

❑ **on jankers** [20C+] in prison or undergoing some form of punitive discipline.

jankie *n.* (*also* **janky**) [? SE *Yankee*, i.e. a negative comment on white people] [1990s+] (*US black*) bad luck.

janky *adj.* [JANKIE *n.*] [1990s+] (*US black teen*) **1** (*also* **jank**) second-rate, inferior, unpleasant, bizarre. **2** stupid.

jannie *n.* [? abbr. JANE $n.^{3}$ (1)] [1980s+] (*US drugs*) a meticulously rolled, large cannabis cigarette that burns smoothly.

jannock *adj.* (*also* **jonic, jonnick, jonnuk**) [dial. *jannock*, fair, straightforward] [mid-19C+] sociable, fair-dealing, honest; thus *die jannock*, to die bravely.

janny *n.* [abbr.] [1920s] (*US*) a *jan*itor.

janusmug *n.* (*also* **janasmug**) [*Janus*, the Roman god with two faces i.e. MUG $n.^{1}$ (1)] [mid-19C–1940s] (*Und.*) one who works as the intermediary between a thief and a receiver of stolen goods.

Jap *n.* (*also* **jap**) [abbr. + negative stereotyping f. the lingering dislike of the Japanese as America's 'trad. enemy', esp. in the context of the surprise attack on Pearl Harbor in WW2] **1** [mid-19C+] a derog. term for a *Jap*anese person. **2** [1940s] (*US gang*) a sneak, a spy. **3** [1950s–70s] (*US gang*) a surprise attack by a teenage gang, thus *pull a jap*, to launch a surprise attack. **4** [1960s+] (*US campus*) an unexpected test, a bad surprise.

IN COMPOUNDS

❑ **Japland** *n.* [1940s+] Japan. ❑ **Jap's eye** *n.* [its resemblance to a 'slit eye' and thus racial stereotyping] [1990s+] the urethral opening at the end of the penis. ❑ **Jap-slap** *v.* [racist stereotyping of the Japanese as specialists in surprise attacks, e.g. Pearl Harbour] [1980s+] (*US*) to slap someone suddenly, also used fig. and as n. ❑ **Jap wise** *adj.* [? stereotype of Japanese stealing Western skills and reproducing the form but still lacking the innate knowledge that helped create them] [20C+] (*US*) partially or insufficiently informed.

IN PHRASES

❑ **pull a jap** *v.* [1940s+] (*US*) to take by surprise, to ambush. ❑ **you wouldn't give it to a Jap on ANZAC Day** [*ANZAC day*, the Aus./N.Z. memorial to their joint forces landing at Gallipoli in 1915; then ext. to WW2] [1970s+] (*Aus.*) said of anything that is absolutely unacceptable.

Jap *adj.* [mid-19C+] pertaining to Japan or Japanese lifestyle/culture.

IN COMPOUNDS

❑ **Jap crock** *n.* [abbr. SE *crockery*] [late 19C] (*UK society*) Japanese porcelain. ❑ **Jap hash** *n.* [*chow mein*, itself an ersatz form of Chinese food, invented for Western consumers, has nothing to do with Japanese cuisine] [20C+] (*US*) chow mein. ❑ **Jap moll** *n.* (*also* **Asian moll**) [SE *Asian* + MOLL *n.* (2)] [1970s+] (*N.Z.*) a prostitute who specializes in Asian or Japanese customers. ❑ **Jap safety boots** *n.* [1980s+] (*Aus. prison*) sandals; thongs. ❑ **Jap scrap** *n.* [1980s+] (*US campus*) a motorcycle or appliance made in Japan, slightly derog. ❑ **Japstick** *n.* [STICK *n.* (1)] [1950s+] (*gay*) the penis of an Asian man.

j.a.p. *n.* [abbr. *J*ewish-*A*merican *p*rincess] [1970s+] (*US*) a rich, spoiled Jewish girl, also of a boy, i.e. *prince*.

jap *n.* [late 19C+] (*US*) a derog. term for a black person.

jap *v.* [JAP *n.*] **1** [1940s+] (*US*) to attack, esp. of street gangs. **2** [1960s] (*US campus*) to steal. **3** [1960s+] (*US*) to undermine someone's plans or efforts, to surprise. **4** [1960s+] (*also* **jap out**) to back down, to renege on an appointment. **5** [1960s+] to swindle, to be cheated. **6** [1980s+] to hit, to knock. **7** [1990s+] (*US black*) to punch.

japan *n.* [fig./journ. use of SE *Japan*, varnish, veneer] [mid-19C–1900s] in prize-fighting, the skin.

japan *v.* [SE *japan*, to make black and glossy. The ref. is to the black clerical garb. Note Aus./US prison use *japanned*, said of a convict who has been converted by the chaplain] **1** [mid-18C–19C] to ordain a priest. **2** [late 19C] (*US*) of a prisoner, to take up religion. **3** [1930s] (*US Und.*) to force the truth from someone.

Japanese knife-trick *n.* [the image is of chopsticks] [late 19C–1900s] eating from one's knife, esp. peas.

Japanese roller skate *n.* [1970s] (*US*) a small car of Japanese manufacture.

japanning *n.* [the *japanned* surface of such a box] [1900s] (*Aus.*) stealing cash-boxes.

jape *v.* [in 1599 *jape* appears in Florio alongside the first ever listing of *fuck*. Note its survival in 20C+ in certain US states, esp. NC, WVa and Va, and in the Appalachians] **1** [late 14C–16C] to seduce a woman. **2** [mid-15C–16C] to have sexual intercourse.

japers! *excl.* [1940s+] (*Irish*) a general excl., a euph. for JESUS! *excl.* (cf. BEJABERS! *excl.*).

japie *n. see* JAAP *n.*

jappa-jappa *adj.* [? Yoruba *jaba-jaba*, higgledy-piggledy, Krio *jagbajagba*, worthless stuff] [20C+] (*W.I.*) rough, indifferent, esp. of work or personal appearance.

Jappy *n.* (*also* **Jappo**) [abbr.] [1900s–50s] (*Aus./US*) a derog. term for a *Jap*anese person.

Jappy *adj.* [JAP *n.*] [1900s–10s] (*Aus.*) Japanese; in a Japanese style.

jar *n.*[1] **1** [20C+] (*Anglo-Irish*) a stone hot-water bottle. **2** [1920s+] a glass of beer, thus phr. *with a few jars on*, to be drunk. **3** [1960s+] (*drugs*) a quantity of pills, usu. 500 or 1000 [the amount in the jars supplied to pharmacists].

jar *n.*[2] [? SE *jargoon*, a zircon or fake diamond] [1940s–70s] fake jewellery, usu. so well made that it can pass for real.

IN PHRASES

❑ **do a jar-up** *v.* [1950s] (*UK Und.*) to sell a piece of fake jewellery.

jar *v.* [mid-19C+] to drink.

jarboni *n. see* JIBONE *n.*

jarbox *n.* (*also* **jawbox**) [Scot.] [20C+] (*Ulster*) the kitchen sink.

jarg *adj.* [SE *jargoon*, a zircon, thus a counterfeit precious stone] [2000s] illegal, stolen, counterfeit.

jarhead *n.*[1] [US dial. *jarhead*, a mule; ult. f. pron. of *jawhead*] (*US black*) **1** [1930s–40s] a black man. **2** [1940s+] a fool, a slow, stupid person; thus as adj., *jar-headed*.

jarhead *n.*[2] [SE *jar* (of liquor) + -HEAD *sfx* (4)] [1930s+] **1** an alcoholic, a heavy drinker. **2** (*US*) a US Marine.

jark *n.* [ety. unknown] **1** [mid-16C–19C] (*UK Und.*) (*also* **jarke, jasker, jerke, jurk**) a seal. **2** [19C] any trinket worn on a watch-chain. **3** [19C] (*UK campus*) a safe-conduct pass. **4** [19C] a watch.

jark *v.* [JARK *n.* (1)] [18C] to seal.

jarke *n. see* JARK *n.* (1).

jark it *v.* [? fig. use of SE *jerk*] [mid-19C] to run away.

jarkman *n.* (*also* **jarkeman**) [JARK *n.* (1) + -MANS *sfx*] [mid-16C–mid-19C] (*UK Und.*) a mendicant villain who used his abilities of reading and writing (Latin) to forge counterfeit begging licences.

jar loose *v.* [late 19C+] (*US*) to let go, to leave; thus hand over.

jaro *n.* (*also* **jyro**) [Maori *whauran*, to scold] [late 19C+] a telling off, a scolding.

IN PHRASES

❑ **give jaro** *v.* [? Maori] [20C+] (*N.Z.*) to scold.

jar of jam *n.* [rhy. sl.] **1** [20C+] a pram. **2** [1930s+] a tram.

jarpie *n. see* JAAP *n.*

Jarrahland *n.* [SAusE *jarrah*, a type of eucalyptus found in Western Aus.] [20C+] (*Aus.*) the state of Western Australia; thus *jarrah-jerker*, anyone who works in the bush.

jarred *adj.*[1] [JAR *n.*[1] (2)] [1930s+] **1** drunk. **2** used fig., in a mess.

jarred *adj.*[2] [SE *jar*] [1990s+] (*orig. US teen*) emotionally disturbed, upset.

jar someone's frame *v. see* CLIMB SOMEONE'S FRAME *under* FRAME *n.*[1].

J. Arthur (Rank) *n.* [rhy. sl.; ult. the cinema magnate J. Arthur *Rank* (1888–1972)] **1** [1940s+] a bank. **2** [1970s+] masturbation [= WANK *n.* (1)]. **3** [1970s+] a fool [= WANK *n.* (6)].

jarvel *n.* [early 19C] (*US Und.*) a jacket.

jarvey *n.* (*also* **jarvis, jervis, jervy**) [generic use of proper name *Jarvis*] **1** [late 18C+] a hackney coachman; thus *jervis' upper benjamin*, a coachman's greatcoat. **2** [19C] (*US*) a waistcoat. **3** [19C; 1950s] a hackney coach.

IN PHRASES

❑ **resurrection jarvey** *n.* [mid-19C] a driver of a night hackney carriage.

jarvey *v.* [JARVEY *n.* (1)] [early 19C] to drive a hackney coach.

jasbo *n. see* JAZZBO *n.*

jasey *n.* (*also* **jajazy, jarsey, jazey**) [? proper name *Jersey*, a variety of flax used in the making of a certain type of wig] **1** [late 18C–1930s] a wig, esp. one made of worsted; thus *bloke with the jasey*, a judge. **2** [mid-19C] (*US*) a man with a great deal of facial hair.

IN EXCLAMATIONS

❑ **dash my jasey!** *see* DASH MY WIG(S)! *under* DASH! *excl.*

Jasez! *excl. see* JESUS! *excl.*

jasker *n. see* JARK *n.* (1).

jasm *n.* [var. on JISM *n.* (1)] [mid–late 19C] (*US*) spirit, energy.

jason's fleece *n.* [the Greek myth, where *Jason* stole the Golden Fleece + a pun on SE *fleece*, to strip someone of their money or possessions] (*UK Und.*) **1** [17C] the gold pieces that are used to trap the victim in a money-switching fraud. **2** [late 17C–early 19C] a citizen who has been swindled of their money.

JASP *n.* [SE *J*ewish + WASP *n.*] [1970s] (*US*) a Jew who has assimilated into the Anglo-Saxon elite culture.

jasper *n.* [generic use of male proper name] **1** [late 19C+] (*US*) a man, esp. a rustic, a peasant. **2** [1910s+] (*US*) a black person. **3** [1950s] (*US*) the penis. **4** [1950s+] (*US prison/black*) a lesbian.

jasper *adj.* [1950s–60s] (*US*) lesbian; pertaining to the world of lesbians.

Jasper Carrot *n.* [rhy. sl.; ult. UK comedian *Jasper Carrot* (b. 1945)] [1990s+] a parrot.

jass *v. see* JAZZ *v.*

jassack *n.* (*also* **jass-onkey**) [SE *jackass* + *donkey*] [mid-19C+] (*US*) a mule; thus a term of abuse.

jastick *n.* [ety. unknown] [mid-19C] (*UK Und.*) a watch.

jaul *see under* JOL.

java *n.* (*also* **J, javy, jay**) [*Java* coffee beans] [mid-19C+] (*US/Can.*) coffee.

javin *n.* [late 18C] (*US Und.*) a jacket.

jaw *n.* [SE *jaw*] **1** [mid-18C+] talk, conversation, a speech; thus *hold/stop your jaw*, stop talking. **2** [19C–1910s] a lecture, a speech. **3** [early 19C–1950s] a telling-off, a ridicule. **4** [1940s] braggadocio.

DERIVATIVES

❑ **jawsome** *adj.* [late 19C] talkative, verbose. ❑ **jawfest** *n.* [JAW *n.* (1) + -FEST *sfx*] [1910s+] (*US*) a long chat or talking session.

IN COMPOUNDS

❑ **jawbox** *n. see* JARBOX *n.* ❑ **jaw-flapping** *n.* [1940s+] (*US*) empty chatter; as n., *jawflaps*, a talkative person. ❑ **jaw-mag** *n.* [MAG *n.*[5] (1)] [late 19C–1900s] talk, conversation, a speech. ❑ **jaw music** *n.* [1920s] (*US*) conversation, chatter, esp. when verbose or tedious. ❑ **jaw-work** *n.* [mid-18C–19C] talk, conversation; thus as n., *jaw-worker*, a talker.

IN PHRASES

❑ **all jaw (like a sheep's head)** [late 19C–1910s] overly talkative, a chatterbox. ❑ **crack one's jaw** *v. see under* CRACK *v.*[1]. ❑ **flap one's jaw** *v.* [1940s+] (*US*) to talk idly, to gossip. ❑ **hold one's jaw** *v.* (*also* **haul up one's jaw, keep one's jaw, stop one's jaw**) [mid-18C+] to be quiet, often as imper. *hold your jaw!* ❑ **run one's jaws** *v.* [2000s] to brag, to boast, to fantasize. ❑ **stow one's jaw** *v.* [1920s] (*US*) to stop talking, usu. as imper. ❑ **tie up one's jaw** *v.* [1950s] (*Aus.*) to stop talking.

SE in slang uses

IN COMPOUNDS

❑ **jawbreaker** *n. see* separate entry. ❑ **jaw-breaking** *adj. see* separate entry. ❑ **jawbuster/cracker/puller** *n. see* JAWBREAKER *n.* ❑ **jawsmith** *n.* **1** [late 19C+] (*US*) a talkative person, a demagogue. **2** [1930s–40s] (*US*) a dentist. ❑ **jaw-twister** *n. see* JAWBREAKER *n.*

IN PHRASES

❑ **tighten someone's jaw** *v.* (*also* **grind someone's jaw**) [1960s–70s] (*US black*) to make someone angry.

jaw *v.*[1] [JAW *n.*] **1** [mid-18C+] to talk, to argue. **2** [19C+] to address censoriously or abusively, to scold or lecture. **3** [mid-19C] (*US*) to yell. **4** [late 19C] to tell, e.g., a lie.

IN COMPOUNDS

❑ **jaw-ass** *v.* [-ASS *sfx*] [1960s+] (*US*) to talk at length. ❑ **jaw-cove** *n.* [COVE *n.* (1)] [mid-19C] (*US Und.*) **1** a lawyer. **2** an auctioneer. ❑ **jaw-me-dead** *n.* (*also* **jaw me dad**) [late 18C–1900s] a chatterer. ❑ **jaw-tackle (fall)** *n.* [mid-19C–1910s] (*US*) the mouth, the tongue, as used in talking.

IN PHRASES

❑ **have one's jawing tackle on board** *v.* [19C–1910s] to be impudent, to be cheeky. ❑ **jaw someone's head off** *v. see* TALK SOMEONE'S HEAD OFF *under* TALK *v.*

jaw *v.*[2] [? Rom. *java*, I go or Hind. *jao*, go] [mid–late 19C] to go.

jawbation *n.* [17C–early 19C] a tedious scolding; thus *jawbatious*, tedious, argumentative, ill-humoured; a noisy argument that takes place in the street.

jawblock *v.* [one 'blocks one's jaw' with words] [1940s] (*US black*) to talk.

jawbone *n.*[1] [mid-19C] (*US*) **1** a castanet, usu. in pl. **2** a Jew's harp.

jawbone *n.*[2] [the verbal persuasiveness required to get goods on credit, to make political speeches etc] **1** [mid-19C–1970s] (*orig. Can./US*) credit. **2** [late 19C+] (*US*) empty talk, exaggerated promises that are not kept.

IN PHRASES

❑ **diarrhoea of the jawbone** *n. see* DIARRHOEA OF THE MOUTH *under* DIARRHOEA *n.*

jawbone *adj.* [JAWBONE *n.*[2] (1)] [mid-19C–1970s] (*orig. Can./US*) on credit.

IN COMPOUNDS

❑ **jawbone time** *n.* [1910s+] (*US Und.*) time spent in jail awaiting sentencing [i.e. 'credit' towards one's jail time]. ❑ **jawbone wedding** *n.* [1920s] (*US army*) an informal agreement to live as man and wife.

jawbone *v.* [JAWBONE *n.*[2]] **1** [late 19C–1970s] to persuade someone into extending credit, to sell or buy on credit. **2** [1950s+] to talk, to chatter. **3** [1960s+] (*US*) to persuade, esp. in politics.

jawbone breaker/doctor *n. see* JAWBREAKER *n.* (2).

jawboning *n.* [JAWBONE *v.* (3)] [1960s+] (*US*) a political or industrial tactic whereby a negotiator or leader attempts to talk two warring sides out of making unreasonable demands.

jawbox *n. see* JARBOX *n.*

jawbreaker *n.* (*also* **jawcracker, jaw-twister**) **1** [mid-19C+] a word that the speaker considers so long or complex that its pronunciation threatens to be harmful. **2** [1920s+] (*US*) (*also* **jawbone breaker, jawbone doctor, jawbuster, jaw puller, jaw cracker**) a dentist.

jaw-breaking *adj.* (*also* **jaw-cracking**) [JAWBREAKER *n.*] [mid-19C+] of words and speech, hard to pronounce.

jawelnofine *phr.* [Afk. *ja*, yes + SE *well* + *no* + *fine*; coined by R.J.B. Wilson, broadcaster with South African Broadcasting Association] [1980s+] (*S.Afr.*) a general response (usu. ironical and resigned) to any form of information; fair enough, what can I say? that's life; also attrib.

jawer *n.* [JAW *v.*[1] (2)] [1900s] (*Aus.*) one who nags.

jawing *n.* [JAW *v.*[1]] **1** [late 18C+] talk, a conversation, often when seen as pointless. **2** [19C+] a telling-off, a scolding.

jawing-tackle *n.* [JAW *v.*[1]] [late 18C–19C] the mouth, the tongue, as used in talking.

jawjab *n.* [1990s+] (*N.Z. teen*) conversation.

jaw-jack *v.* [US black pron. of *jaw-jerking/jerking off*, i.e. 'verbal masturbation'] [1960s+] (*US black*) to talk excessively, loudly or inconsequentially.

jaw-jaw *n.* [JAW-JAW *v.*] [1950s+] conversation, chatter.

jaw-jaw *v.* [JAW *v.*[1] (1) + redup.; usu. first attrib. to Winston Churchill in a speech at the White House on 26 June 1954, in the dictum: 'To jaw-jaw is always better than to war-war'] [1950s+] to talk, to converse, to discuss.

jawl *see under* JOL.

jawn *n.* [ety. unknown] [1980s+] (*US campus*) an indiscriminate term, usu. used of something or someone that causes happiness, joy or excitement; also used as adj.

jaws *n.* [the myth of the *vagina dentata*] [1940s+] (*US*) the labia majora.

jaws, the *n.* [? the grinding of one's teeth] [1960s+] (*US*) anger.

jawsing *n.* [JAW *v.*[1] (4)] [2000s] (*US teen*) lying.

Jax *n.* [abbr.] [1920s+] (*US*) Jacksonville, Florida.

jax *n.*[1] (*also* **jaxx**) [JAKES *n.* but later use might be f. JACKS *n.*[2] given prob. difference in pron.; later use Irish] [16C; 1940s+] the lavatory.

jax *n.*[2] *see* JACK'S (ALIVE) *n.*

jaxey/jaxie/jaxi *n. see* JACKSIE *n.*[1].

jaxx *n. see* JAX *n.*[1].

jaxy *n.* (*also* **joxy**) [? JACKSIE *n.*[1] (1)] [20C+] the female genitals.

jay *n.*[1] (*also* **jaybird**) [SE *jay* (*Garrulus glandarius*), a bird noted, *inter alia*, for its noisiness and bright colouring, and its boorishness towards other birds] **1** [early 16C–early 17C] a cheeky chatterer. **2** [late 16C–17C; late 19C+] a showy woman, a prostitute [later use is US, mostly black]. **3** [late 19C–1920s] (*US campus*) (*also* **J**) a person who does something disagreeable or foolish. **4** [late 19C+] (*also* **J**) (*orig. US*) a rustic, a simpleton, a novice, a newcomer.

IN COMPOUNDS

❑ **jay-naked** *adj. see* NAKED AS A JAYBIRD *under* JAYBIRD *n.*[1]. ❑ **jay town** *n.* (*also* **jayville**) [sense 3 above + SE *town*/-VILLE *sfx*[1]] [late 19C–1920s] (*US*) a small town.

jay *n.*[2] **1** *see* J *n.* **2** *see* JAVA *n.*

jay *adj.*[1] [late 19C] (*US campus*) enjoyable.

jay *adj.*[2] [JAY *n.*[1] (4)] **1** [late 19C–1910s] (*US*) naive, worthless, unsophisticated. **2** [1900s–10s] gullible.

jay *v.*[1] [JAYHAWK *v.*] [1990s+] (*US*) to steal.

jay *v.*[2] [1990s+] (*US black*) to have sexual intercourse.

jay! *excl.* [initial letter] [1920s+] Jesus!

jaybee *n. see* J.B. *n.*[2].

jaybird *n.*[1] [JAY *n.*[1] (4)] [late 19C+] (*US*) a rustic, a simpleton, a novice, a newcomer.

SE in slang uses

IN PHRASES

❑ **naked as a jaybird** *adj.* (*also* **jaybird, jaybird-naked, jay-naked, naked as a nuthatch**) [1930s+] (*US*) stark naked.

jaybird *n.*[2] **1** *see* J *n.* **2** *see* JAY *n.*[1].

jaybird *adj.* [JAYBIRD *n.*[1]] [late 19C+] (*US*) inferior, contemptible.

jayhawk *n.* [JAYHAWKER *n.*] **1** [20C+] (*US*) a rustic, a simpleton, a novice, a newcomer. **2** [1910s+] (*US*) a mythical bird used as an emblem of Kansas. **3** [1930s+] (*US*) a native of Kansas [combines senses 1 + 2].

jayhawk *v.* [negative image of the SE *jay*, the bird] [mid-19C+] (*US esp. army, orig. Civil War*) to raid, to plunder, to steal, to operate as a guerrilla soldier.

jayhawker *n.* [the alleged similarity of Kansans – raping and pillaging during the US Civil War (1861–5) – to the SE *jay*, noted for its aggressive, bullying relations with other birds; Schele de Vere (1872) claims the term was imported from Aus. convicts] **1** [mid-19C+] (*US*) a native of Kansas, spec. in the context of murderous activities carried on before and during the Civil War. **2** [late 19C–1950s] (*US*) a rustic, a simpleton.

jayhoo *n. see* JEHU *n.* (3).

jay-o *v. see* J.O. *v.*

Jays *n.* [initial letter] [20C+] (*Irish*) members of the Society of Jesus, the Jesuits.

jay smoke *n. see under* J *n.*

Jaysus! *excl. see* JESUS! *excl.*

Jayzus! *excl. see* JESUS! *excl.*

jazbo *n. see* JAZZBO *n.*

jaze! *excl. see* JEEZ! *excl.*

jazey *n. see* JASEY *n.*

Jazus! *excl. see* JESUS! *excl.*

jazz *n.* [the ety. of jazz remains one of the most fiercely debated and heavily researched; roots in French, in West Africa, in African-American sex slang and elsewhere have been suggested, and abandoned. The current position links the term to mid-19C *jism*, meaning spirit or energy; its first use has been traced to players on the 1913 San Francisco Seals baseball club, as reported by one 'Scoop' Gleason in the San Francisco *Bulletin*. The progress from baseball to music is uncharted, but examples of the latter usage appear almost contemporaneously. For an extensive study of the ety. see Cohen (ed.) *Comments on Etymology* 32:4–5 (Dec.–Jan. 2002–03)] **1** [1910s–60s] (*orig. US black*) sexual intercourse. **2** [1910s+] (*US*) spirit, energy, excitement. **3** in fig. uses. (**a**) [1910s+] (*orig. US*) misleading, untrue, empty or pretentious talk, nonsense. (**b**) [1910s+] (*US*) anything, stuff.

(**c**) [1920s] energetic time-wasting. (**d**) [1950s] fighting, confrontation. (**e**) [1960s+] (*US drugs*) heroin. **4** [1930s+] (*US*) semen. **5** [1960s] (*US*) a social gathering. **6** [1960s+] a thrill, a moment of pleasure. **7** [1980s] (*US*) harassment.

(IN COMPOUNDS)

□ **jazz baby** *n.* [BABY *n.* (3); whether the jazz refers to sex or music, or to something of both, remains debatable. Note Merrill and Jerome's popular US song, 'Jazz Baby' (1919)] [1910s–40s] a flighty girl or young woman, usu. middle-class, in her late teens or very early 20s, who sported short, bobbed hair, lipstick, skimpy dresses and generally led a lifestyle as far as possible removed from that of her parents. □ **jazzbo** *see* separate entries. □ **jazz house** *n.* [HOUSE *n.*[1] (1)] [1920s] (*US*) a brothel. □ **jazz joint** *n.* [JOINT *n.* (3b)] [1920s] (*US black*) a brothel. □ **jazz mag** *n.* [sense 3 above + MAG *n.*[4] (1)] [1990s+] an 'adult' pornographic magazine.

(IN PHRASES)

□ **all that jazz** [sense 3a above] [1950s+] (*orig. US*) that sort of thing, usu. following a list of proper nouns ...*and all that jazz.*

jazz *v.* (*also* **jass**) [JAZZ *n.*; note Pierre Guiraud in his "Dictionnaire érotique" (Paris 1978, 1984, 1993) has 'jaser = coiter' and gives as a quotation 'Tu as les genoux chauds, tu veux jaser' (La Comedie des proverbes XVIe s.) As his source he gives 'Glossaire érotique de la langue francaise depuis son origine jusqu'à nos jours' by Louis de Landes, Bruxelles 1861; this quote is used in Farmer *Vocabula Amatoria* (1896)] **1** [1910s+] (*orig. US black*) to have sexual intercourse. **2** [1910s+] (*US*) to enliven, to inspire, to excite. **3** in fig. uses. (**a**) [1910s+] (*US*) to mess up, to confuse. (**b**) [1920s+] (*US*) to tease. (**c**) [1940s+] to lie, to deceive. (**d**) [1950s] to take liberties, synon. with FUCK WITH *v.* **4** [1920s] to dance someone around. **5** [1920s+] to enjoy oneself, to be inspired or excited. **6** [1980s+] (*Aus. prison*) to sodomize.

(IN COMPOUNDS)

□ **jazzhound** *n. see* separate entries. □ **jazz talc** *n.* [1990s+] (*drugs*) cocaine. □ **jazz water** *n.* [1920s] (*US*) bootleg alcohol.

SE in slang uses

(IN PHRASES)

□ **jazz around** *v.* [1910s+] **1** to fool about, to idle, to lead a fast life, mainly in pursuit of sex. **2** thus, of money, to squander. **3** to rush about. □ **jazz up** *v.* **1** [1910s+] of people, places or objects, to brighten up, to improve, to make more gaudy, to pep up. **2** [1950s] to improve performance. **3** [1970s] to mess up.

jazzbo *n.* (*also* **jasbo, jazbo, jazz-bo**) [? proper name *Jasper* or SE *jazz*/JAZZ *n.* (2) + SE *boy*] **1** [1910s–20s] in vaudeville, slapstick comedy. **2** [1910s–20s] a black vaudeville performer, esp. in a 'black and white minstrel' show. **3** [1910s–20s] syncopated music. **4** [1910s–60s] a black person, esp. a man or soldier. **5** [1910s+] (*US*) a fellow, a man, esp. a fashionable young man. **6** [1920s+] (*US/US campus*) a fool, an idiot; or something eccentric or crazy-looking [? BOZO *n.*[1] (3)].

jazzbo *adj.* [JAZZBO *n.* (5)] [1910s+] stylish, up-to-date.

jazzed (up) *adj.* [JAZZ *v.* (2)/JAZZ UP *under* JAZZ *v.*] **1** [1910s–60s] (*US*) intoxicated by drugs or alcohol. **2** [1910s+] (*US campus*) excited, thrilled, pleased; thus *unjazzed*, depressed. **3** [1930s+] augmented, embellished (esp. in a flashy, vulgar manner). **4** [1940s–50s] of a woman, overtly sexual. **5** [1940s+] ostentatious, showy.

jazzer *n.*[1] (*also* **jazzist**) [SE *jazz*] [1910s+] (*orig. US*) **1** a jazz musician. **2** a jazz fan. **3** a party goer.

jazzer *n.*[2] [JAZZ *v.* (1)] [1920s+] (*Irish*) one who has sexual intercourse.

jazzhound *n.*[1] [JAZZ *n.* (1) + -HOUND *sfx* (1)] **1** [1920s] (*US*) a sexually promiscuous man. **2** [1960s+] (*S.Afr. gay*) a heterosexual male prostitute, one who services women only.

jazzhound *n.*[2] [SE *jazz* + -HOUND *sfx*] [1920s] (*US*) a jazz enthusiast.

jazzing *n.* [JAZZ *v.* (1)] [1920s–50s] (*US*) having sexual intercourse.

jazzist *n. see* JAZZER *n.*[1].

jazzy *adj.*[1] [SE *jazz*; both senses refer to the music and its image rather than to the sl. use] **1** [1910s+] (*US*) bright, lively, exciting. **2** [1920s+] (*US*) ostentatious, brash.

jazzy *adj.*[2] [JAZZ *n.* (1)] [1920s+] (*US black*) sexy.

jazzy-ass *adj.* [JAZZY *adj.*[1] (2) + -ASS *sfx*] [1970s] flashy, ostentatious, vulgar.

J.B. *n. see* JOHN BULL *n.*

j.b. *n.*[1] [abbr.] [1930s–40s] a hat made by the *John B.* Stetson Company.

j.b. *n.*[2] (*also* **jaybee**) [abbr. *j*et *b*lack; also a pun on *j.c.* or *jaycee*, a respectable, middle-class white person] [1940s+] (*US*) a black person.

j-bo *n.* see J *n.*

J. Carroll Naish *n.* [rhy. sl. = SLASH *n.* (2); ult. US actor *J. Carroll Naish* (1900–73)] [1970s+] urination.

j.c.o. *n.* [*j*ust *c*ome *o*ver] [1940s] (*US*) a newly arrived immigrant.

j.d. *n.* [abbr.] **1** [1950s+] *j*uvenile *d*elinquent. **2** [1970s] (*US Und.*) JOHN DOE *n.* **3** [1990s+] (*also* **JD**) *J*ack *D*aniels whisky.

j.d. *v.* [J.D. *n.* (1)] [1960s] to behave as a juvenile delinquent.

jeal *adj. see* JEL *adj.* (1).

jeames *n.* [deliberately tortured pron. of proper name *James* and thus a generic term for a footman or a pej. for a flunkey. This in turn based on Thackeray's servant *Jeames* in the *Diary of C. Jeames de la Pluche, Esq.* (1846). Until it was swallowed up by the *Daily Telegraph* (in 1937), the ultra-conservative *Morning Post* was the paper of choice for the British upper classes] [mid-19C] the *Morning Post* newspaper.

jeames *adj.* [JEAMES *n.*] [1910s] (*Aus.*) of journalism, snobbish.

jean *n.* (*also* **jane**) [the female equivalent of a JOHN *n.*[2] (1c)] [1960s+] (*US*) a female prostitute's female client.

jean *v.* [JEANS *n.*] [1910s] (*US Und.*) to place (a wallet) into a pocket.

Jean Crapeau *n. see JOHNNY CRAPOSE under* JOHNNY- *pfx*.

jean foutre *n.* (*also* **jam foutre**) [stereotypical Fr. excl. *je m'en foutre!*, the fuck with it!] [mid-17C–18C] a Frenchman.

jean potage *n.* [Fr. *Jean potage*, John(ny) soup] [19C] (*US*) a French-born immigrant.

jeans *n.*

(IN PHRASES)

□ **in one's jeans** [late 19C–1960s] in one's trouser pockets.

jeasley/jeasly *adj. see* JEEZLY *adj.*

Jebby *n.* [abbr.] [1940s+] (*US*) a Jesuit.

jeckle *adj. see* JEKYLL (AND HYDE) *adj.*

'jects *n.* (*also* **'jecks**) [abbr.] [1990s+] (*US black*) the projects the lowest class of housing.

'jects *adj.* ['JECTS *n.* considered to be the lowest form of housing] [1990s+] (*US black teen*) cheap, rubbishy.

J. Edgar *n.* [FBI boss *J. Edgar* Hoover] [1970s+] (*US black*) the police.

jee *see under* GEE.

jeebies *n.* (*also* **jeeby**) [abbr. HEEBIE-JEEBIES *n.*] [1930s+] (*US*) unpleasant fantasies, nameless terrors, anything the mind can conjure up to produce nerves and fear.

jeefies! *excl. see* JEEPERS! *excl.*

jee gee *n.* [? DUJI *n.*] [1970s+] (*drugs*) heroin.

jeep *n.*[1] [Eugene the *Jeep*, an animal with amazing powers, created in 1936 by E.C. Segar (1894–1938) and incorporated in his cartoon *Popeye*] **1** [1930s–50s] (*US campus*) a greedy, materialistic young woman. **2** [1930s+] (*US*) a stupid, inept or inexperienced person. **3** [1940s] (*US black*) a drunkard.

jeep *n.*[2] [var. on GEE *n.*[7] (1)] [1960s] (*drugs*) a paper 'collar' used by a drug user to secure the needle to an eye-dropper before injecting the heroin/water solution.

jeep *v.* [2000s] (*US black*) to steal.

jeepers! *excl.* (*also* **jeefies!**) [1920s+] (*orig. US*) a mild oath euph. for JESUS! *excl.*

jeepers creepers! *excl.* (*also* **jeepers deepers! ...peepers!**) [ext. of JEEPERS! *excl.* as a euph. for JESUS! *excl.*] [1920s+] a mild oath.

jeer *n.*[1] [late 17C–early 18C] (*UK Und.*) a sealed document.

jeer *n.*[2] *see* JERE *n.*

jeesunk *n. see* JUNK *n.*[1] (7a).

jeeter *n.* [*Jeeter* Lester, the poor white peasant protagonist of Erskine Caldwell's novel *Tobacco Road* (1932)] [1930s–60s] (*US*) a rustic, a peasant.

jeez! *excl.* (*also* **gees! geez! geeze! jayz! jaze! jees! jeese! jeesy! jeeze! jeezum! jeezuz! je's! jez!**) [1920s+] (*orig. US*) a mild excl., euph. for JESUS! *excl.*

jeezer *n.* [it makes one exclaim JESUS! *excl.*] [1980s] (*US*) something remarkable.

jeezle-peezle! *excl.* (*also* **jeezle! jeezy peezy! jeezy-wheezy!**) [1940s+] (*US*) a mild oath, euph. for JESUS! *excl.*

jeezly *adj.* (*also* **jeasley, jeasly**) [var. on JESUSLY *adj.*] **1** [1930s+] (*US*) darned. **2** [1990s+] (*US*) inferior.

jeezum!/jeezuz! *excl. see* JEEZ! *excl.*

Jeezus! *excl. see* JESUS! *excl.*

Jeezus K. Reist! *excl. see* JESUS H CHRIST! *excl.*

jeezy peezy!/jeezy-wheezy! *excl. see* JEEZLE-PEEZLE! *excl.*

jef *n. see* JIFFY *n.*

jefe *n.* [Sp. *jefe*, boss, chief] [1990s+] (*US drugs*) a senior cocaine dealer.

Jeff *n.* [late 19C–1900s] (*US Und., New York City*) the Jefferson Market Court, New York City, esp. in its role as the night court for the trial of prostitutes.

jeff *n.* [abbr. proper name *Jefferson Davis* (1808–89), president of the Confederate States 1861–5. Note mid-19C circus jargon *tight-jeff*, a tight-rope, *slack-jeff*, a slack rope] **1** [1930s–40s] a dull, stupid person, a pest. **2** [1930s–60s] (*US black*) a derog. term for a white rustic, a peasant, esp. a Southerner. **3** [1950s] an admirable person. **4** [1950s–60s] a white person, esp. if a racist. **5** [1960s+] a black person who is obsequious towards whites.

jeff *v.* [abbr. proper name *Jefferson Davis* (1808–89), president of the Confederate States during the US Civil War 1861–5] [1960s+] **1** (*US Und.*) to lie, to work a confidence trick, to fool a victim; usu. as *jeffing*. **2** (*US prison*) to tease, to joke with. **3** (*US black*) to talk, to chatter, esp. to seduce, to fool or deceive with a 'line'; thus *tight jeff*, well-rehearsed patter; *slack jeff*, spontaneous ad-libbed chatter. **4** (*US black*) to behave obsequiously, esp. towards whites, to humiliate oneself.

IN COMPOUNDS

❑ **jeff artist** *n.* [ARTIST *n.* (1)] [1960s+] **1** (*US*) a liar, a confidence trickster. **2** (*US black*) a black person who behaves subserviently towards whites.

Jeff Davis *n.* [abbr. proper name *Jefferson Davis* (1808–89), president of the Confederate States 1861–5] **1** [1940s] (*US black*) a rustic, a peasant, usu. from the South. **2** [1960s+] (*US black*) a black person who behaves subserviently towards whites.

jeffer *n.* [JEFF *n.*] [1960s+] (*US black*) a rustic, a peasant.

jefferson airplane *n.* [*Jefferson Airplane*, one of the most successful 'psychedelic bands' of the 1960s] [1960s+] (*US drugs*) a split match that is used as an improvised holder for the last fraction of a marijuana cigarette.

jeffey *n.* **1** [mid-19C] (*US Und.*) lightning. **2** *see* JIFFY *n.*

jeffing *n. see* JEFF *v.* (1).

jeffy *n. see* JIFFY *n.*

jehoshaphat! *excl.* (*also* **geehosaphat! jehosiphat! jehosophat!**) [mid-19C+] used in a variety of mild oaths; a euph. for JESUS! *excl.*

jehu *n.* [ext. joc. SE *Jehu*, a coachman, ult. II Kings 9:20: 'The driving is like the driving of Jehu the son of Nimshi: for he driveth furiously'] **1** [mid-19C–1950s] a cab-driver. **2** [mid-19C+] any form of driver. **3** [1900s–40s] (*US*) (*also* **jayhoo**) a rustic, simpleton [JAY *n.*[1] (4)].

jejo *n. see* YEYO *n.*

jekyll (and hyde) *adj.* (*also* **jeckle**) [rhy. sl. = SNIDE *adj.* (1); ult. *Dr Jekyll and Mr Hyde* (1866) by R.L. Stevenson] [1920s+] crooked, fake, spurious, counterfeit.

jekyll and hydes *n.* [rhy. sl. = STRIDES *n.*] [20C+] (*Aus.*) trousers.

jel *n.* (*also* **jell**) [abbr. JELLO-BRAIN *n.*] [1980s+] (*US teen*) an appalling, unacceptable person.

jel *adj.* (*also* **jeal**) [abbr.] [1980s+] (*US*) *jealous*.

jeldi/jeldy *see under* JILDI.

jell *n.*[1] [SE *jelly*] [1950s+] (*Aus.*) a coward.

IN PHRASES

❑ **jell (it)** *v.* [1950s+] (*Aus.*) to act in a cowardly way.

jell *n.*[2] *see* JEL *n.*

jell *v.* (*also* **gel, jell around, jell out, jelly, jelly around**) [SE *gel*/ SAmE *jel*, to solidify into a jelly-like substance; the image is of a jelly slowly melting; to turn into *Jell-O*/*jelly*] [1930s+] (*US campus*) to relax, to waste time, to hang about; esp. at a soda fountain or café.

jellhead *n.* (*also* **jelly**) [JELLY *n.*[1] (7)] [1990s+] (*UK drugs*) a habitual drug-user, whose mental faculties have been, it is implied, thus impaired.

jellied *adj.* [JELLY BEAN *n.* (5a)] [1980s+] under the influence of tranquillizers.

jellied eels *n.* [rhy. sl.] [20C+] wheels, i.e. transport.

jellied out *adj.* [JELLY BEAN *n.* (1)] [1930s] (*US campus*) dressed up.

jellies *n. see* JELLY *n.*[1] (7).

jellies, the *n.* [1950s] a fit of nerves or anxiety.

jello-brain *n.* (*also* **bag of jello, jello**) [someone whose brain is like jelly; *Jell-O* the brandname of a gelatine dessert/+ sfx *-brain*] (*US campus*) **1** [1960s+] a foolish, scatterbrained person. **2** [1960s+] an older person. **3** [1980s+] a drug user [JELLY *n.*[1] (7)/JELLY BEAN *n.* (5)].

jello-brained *adj.* [JELLO-BRAIN *n.* (1)] [1960s+] stupid, foolish.

jello squad *n.* [JELLO-BRAIN *n.* + SE *squad*] [1970s+] (*US campus*) an imaginary gathering or club of all those students considered beyond the social pale of their peers on campus.

jelly *n.*[1] **1** [17C+] semen; vaginal fluid. **2** [late 19C+] a buxom, pretty young woman [she 'wobbles']. **3** [1920s+] (*US black*) the penis or the vagina. **4** [1920s+] (*US black*) sexual intercourse. **5** [1930s–40s] (*US black*) anything given free. **6** [1940s] (*US black*) male sexual prowess; sexuality. **7** [1980s+] (*UK drugs*) temazepam; usu. in pl. as *jellies* [the gel-like content of the capsules]. **8** *see* JELLHEAD *n.*

IN COMPOUNDS

❑ **jelly baby** *n.* **1** [1920s+] secretions from the anus or vagina during or after intercourse. **2** [1970s+] (*drugs*) amphetamine. ❑ **jelly-bag** *n.* [17C–19C] **1** the scrotum [BAG *n.*[1] (1a)]. **2** the vagina. ❑ **jelly-box** *n.* [SE *box*/BOX *n.*[1] (1a)] [1950s+] (*orig. US*) the vagina. ❑ **jelly jewellery** *n.* [1990s+] ejaculated semen, covering the face and throat of one's partner. ❑ **jelly sandwich** *n.* [1970s+] (*US black*) a sanitary towel. ❑ **jelly snatchers** *n.* [1970s] (*US black*) the hands.

IN PHRASES

❑ **it must be jelly, 'cause jam don't shake like that** [1920s+] (*US black*) a phr. used between males to express their appreciation of an especially attractive female. ❑ **sling one's jelly** *v.* [19C] of a woman, to masturbate.

SE in slang uses

IN COMPOUNDS

❑ **jelly-bellied** *adj.* [JELLY BELLY below] **1** [late 19C+] fat. **2** [1930s+] (*Aus./US*) (*also* **jelly-belly**) cowardly. ❑ **jelly belly** *n.* **1** [mid-19C+] a fat person. **2** [1930s+] (*Aus./US*) a coward.

IN PHRASES

❑ **bowl of jelly** *n.* (*also* **can of jelly**) [1930s+] (*US*) a notably fat person.

jelly *n.*[2] (*also* **geli', gellie, gelly**) [abbr./pron.] **1** [1930s+] (*orig. Aus.*) gelignite. **2** [1970s+] napalm.

IN COMPOUNDS

❑ **jelly baby** *n.* [1940s–70s] a robber who specializes in gelignite to open safes.

jelly *n.*[3] (*also* **gelly**) [abbr. of JELLY ROLL *n.* (2)] [1960s+] (*US*) a close friend, esp. a girlfriend or boyfriend.

jelly *v.* **1** [1930s–50s] (*US*) to dance. **2** [1940s] (*US*) to walk provocatively. **3** [1950s–60s] (*US black*) (*also* **jello**) to have sexual intercourse. **4** [1970s–80s] (*US street gang*) to beat someone up.

IN PHRASES

□ **jelly-ass** *v.* [? the shaking of one's ARSE *n.*] [1930s–60s] (*US*) to dance.

jelly (around) *v. see* JELL *v.*

jelly bean *n.* **1** a person who is 'sweet' or 'soft'. (**a**) [1910s–60s] (*US*) a sweetheart. (**b**) [1910s+] (*US*) a foolish, inept, dishonest or effeminate person. (**c**) [1920s–30s] one who is devoted to pleasure rather than work; esp. used of a high-school student. (**d**) [1920s–30s] a fashionably dressed young man, a womanizer. **2** [1930s+] a pimp. **3** [1960s] (*US gay*) a small penis. **4** [1960s+] (*US black*) a term of address. **5** in drug uses [the drugs resemble sweets]. (**a**) [1960s+] (*drugs*) any form of pill, e.g. a barbiturate, an amphetamine. (**b**) [1990s+] (*US campus*) a painkiller. (**c**) [1990s+] (*drugs*) crack cocaine.

jelly bean *adj.* [JELLY BEAN *n.* (1)] [1990s+] (*Aus.*) unpleasant, lying.

jelly-date *n.* (*also* **bean-date, cake-date, coke-date**) [the relevant SE food; JELLY (AROUND) *v.* + DATE *n.*[1]] [1920s–40s] (*US campus*) **1** a date to take a girlfriend to the soda fountain or similar, where one sits and chats. **2** the person who is one's date in that situation.

jellyfish *n.* [the invertebrate SE *jellyfish*] [20C+] a weak, ineffectual, cowardly person.

jellyfish *adj.* [1900s–1910s] (*US*) common, ordinary.

jellyhead *n. see* GELLYHEAD *n.*

jelly roll *n.* [? JELLY *n.*[1]; note earlier chronology here; SAmE *jelly roll*, a doughnut, which has a hole at its centre] **1** [20C+] (*orig. US black*) sexual intercourse. **2** [1910s+] (*orig. US black*) a lover, a spouse; also attrib. **3** [1910s+] (*orig. US black*) the female genitals, thus *jelly roll gum drop*, the clitoris. **4** [1950s] (*US*) a male hair style, popular in the 1950s. **5** [1970s+] (*US black*) a sanitary napkin.

jelly roll *v.* [JELLY ROLL *n.* (1)] [1920s+] (*orig. US black*) to have sexual intercourse.

jelly roller *n.* [JELLY ROLL *v.*] [1920s–60s] (*US black*) a womanizer, a seducer.

jelly-tight *adj. see* JAM-UP AND JELLY-TIGHT *under* JAM-UP *adj.*

jem *n.*[1] (*also* **jam**) [SE *gem*] [18C–1900s] (*UK Und.*) a jewel, a gold ring; thus *rum-jem*, a diamond ring.

jem *n.*[2] (*also* **jembo**) [abbr. JEMMY *n.*[2] (1)] [1940s+] (*Irish*) a generic name for a Dubliner.

jemima *n.*[1] [generic use of proper name] **1** [late 19C] a servant girl. **2** [late 19C–1900s] a chamberpot [its removal is one of the servant's tasks]. **3** [1900s–30s] in pl., elastic-sided boots [ety. unknown; ? a brandname or link to JEMMY *adj.*[1] (3)].

jemima *n.*[2] [AUNT JEMIMA *n.*, the stereotypical black 'mammy'] [1950s+] (*gay*) the black female genitals.

jemima *v.* [AUNT JEMIMA *n.* (1)] [1960s] (*US black*) of a black woman, to act in a seductive but servile manner towards a white man.

jemima! *excl.* [mid-19C+] (*US*) a euph. for JESUS! *excl.*; used in a variety of mild oaths; also in comparatives *like Jemima; nice as Jemima*.

jeminy-o! *excl.* [late 17C–1900s] a general excl., euph. for JESUS! *excl.*

jem mace *n.* (*also* **jim mace**) [rhy. sl.; ult. the UK prize-fighter *Jem Mace* (1831–1910)] [20C+] face.

jemmy *n.*[1] (*also* **jimmy**) [ety. unknown] **1** [early 17C] a fool. **2** [mid-18C] a wig. **3** [mid-18C–1910s] a sheep's head [Bee (1823) suggests an actual butcher *Jemmy* Lincomb, who lived near Scotland Yard]. **4** [mid–late 19C] a large human head.

jemmy *n.*[2] [16C SE *gim*, smart, spruce and thus ? linked to Scot. *jimp*, slender] **1** [mid-17C–early 19C] (*also* **jemmy fellow**) a dandy. **2** [mid–late 18C] a light cane, as carried by a dandy. **3** [mid-19C–1910s] a shooting coat, a great coat.

jemmy *n.*[3] (*also* **jemmy rook, jenny, London jemmy, London jimmy**) **1** [late 17C+] (*UK Und.*) a house-breaker's short crowbar. **2** [mid-18C] a walking stick.

jemmy *n.*[4] **1** [mid-19C] (*UK Und.*) twopence. **2** *see* JAMES *n.* (3).

jemmy *adj.*[1] [JEMMY *n.*[2] (1)] **1** [mid–late 18C] clever, 'sharp'. **2** [mid-18C–mid-19C] dandified, e.g. a *jemmy fellow*, a smart, well-turned out, dandified man; *jemminess*, neatness, smartness; *jemmily*, smartly. **3** [mid-19C] smart, of superior class.

jemmy *adj.*[2] (*also* **jimmy**) [mid-19C–1900s] rubbishy, nonsensical.

IN PHRASES

□ **all jemmy** (*also* **all jimmy**) [late 19C] all nonsense.

jemmy *v.* [JEMMY *n.*[3] (1)] [late 19C+] to break open with a crowbar.

jemmy jessamy *n.* [JEMMY *adj.*[1] (2) + JESSAMY *n.*] [mid-18C–mid-19C] a smart, well-turned-out fellow.

jemmy jessamy *adj.* [JEMMY JESSAMY *n.*] [mid-18C–mid-19C] smart, well-turned-out.

Jemmy O'Goblin *n.* (*also* **Jimmy O'Gob, Jimmy O'Goblin**) [rhy. sl.] [late 19C–1930s] (*orig. theatre*) a sovereign, in pl., money.

jemmy rook *n. see* JEMMY *n.*[3].

jemson *n.* (*also* **jimmison**) [? SE *jimsonweed*, i.e. the penis also grows] [1930s–50s] (*US, Ozarks*) the penis.

jen *n. see* GEN *n.*[2].

jeng-jeng *n.* [Carib.E. *jege*, rags, tatters + ? Ngombe *jengé*, disorder] [20C+] (*W.I., Jam./Bel.*) **1** anything considered worthless, a useless collection of bits and bobs. **2** of things or of personal appearance, a general state of confusion.

jeng-jeng *adj.* [JENG-JENG *n.*] [20C+] (*W.I., Jam./Bel.*) disreputable, unpleasant.

Jennie Howlet *n. see* MADGE HOWLET *n.*

Jennifer Justice *n.* [initial letters] [2000s] (*S.Afr. gay*) a police officer, usu. male.

jenny *n.*[1] **1** [late 18C+] a donkey [play on the songbird SE *jenny-wren*, i.e. a ref. to the donkey's bray; post-18C uses are US]. **2** [mid-19C–1950s] (*Scot./US*) a young woman [dial. *jenny*, a country girl]. **3** [1990s+] the vagina.

jenny *n.*[2] [? abbr. SE, it *generates* warmth; note TV/film jargon *jenny*, a generator] [late 19C–1920s] a hot-water bottle.

jenny *n.*[3] *see* JEMMY *n.*[3].

jenny *adj.* (*also* **jenny-ass, jinny, jinny-ass, jinny-wing**) [the female name] [1930s+] (*Irish/US black*) of a man, effeminate.

jenny *v.*[1] [ety. unknown; ? link to JERRY *v.* (2)] [late 19C–1900s] (*UK Und.*) to understand.

jenny *v.*[2] (*also* **jinny**) [SE *jenny*, used as a pfx denoting the female sex] [20C+] of a woman, to nag, to henpeck.

jenny *v.*[3] (*also* **jenny off**) [feminized version of JACK OFF *v.*[1] (1)] [1990s+] (*S.Afr. gay*) of a woman, thence homosexual man, to masturbate.

jenny-ass *adj. see* JENNY *adj.*

jenny darby *n.* [Fr. *gendarmes* + ref. to DARBIES *n.* (1)] [mid-19C] a policeman.

jenny lee *n.* (*also* **jenny lea**) [rhy. sl.; later uses f. Baroness Lee of Asheridge (1904–88), Scottish Labour politician] **1** [late 19C+] a flea. **2** [1930s–60s] a key. **3** [1930s+] tea.

Jenny Lind *n.* [rhy. sl.; ult. the Swedish soprano *Jenny Lind* (1820–87)] [20C+] wind, either in the context of weather or the human stomach; thus *Jenny Lindy*, windy.

Jenny Linda *n.* (*also* **Jenny Linder**) [rhy. sl.; ult. *see* JENNY LIND *n.*] [mid–late 19C] a window.

jenny off *v. see* JENNY *v.*[3].

jenny riddle *n. see* JIMMY (RIDDLE) *n.*

jenny wine *n.* [? JENNY *adj.*/SE *genuine*] [20C+] (*Irish*) a non-drinker, a teetotaller.

Jenny Wren *n.* [rhy. sl.] [20C+] Ben Truman beer.

jentoe *n. see* GENTOO *n.*

jere *n.* (*also* **gere, jeer**) [Rom. *jeer*, excrement] [mid-16C–17C] (*UK Und.*) a piece of human excrement.

jeremiah *n.* [rhy. sl.] [1930s+] a fire.

Jeremy Beadle *n.* [rhy. sl. = NEEDLE *n.*; ult. UK TV entertainer *Jeremy Beadle* (1948–2008)] [1980s+] irritation, annoyance.

jeremy diddler *n. see* DIDDLER *n.*[2].

Jericho *n.* [anecdote in 2 Sam. 10:5 when David ordered his servants to stay in that city until their beards were grown] **1** [mid-17C–1920s] a place of retirement, banishment or concealment, a far-distant place, esp. in phr. *let someone go to jericho*. **2** [mid-18C–19C] a privy, an outside lavatory. **3** [1910s+] a synon. for SE *hell*.

IN PHRASES

□ **go to Jericho** *v.* [fig. use of sense 1 above] [mid-18C–early 19C] to become drunk.

IN EXCLAMATIONS

□ **go to Jericho!** [late 19C–1920s] an excl. of dismissal.

jerk *n.*[1] **1** [1930s+] (*US*) a male masturbator [JERK OFF *v.*; despite cites, may be orig. sense]. **2** [1930s+] (*orig. US*) a general term of abuse; a fool, an idiot, a failure. **3** [1940s+] (*US*) a soda-fountain clerk [abbr. SAmE *soda jerk*]. **4** [1960s+] (*US*) an ice-cream soda.

DERIVATIVES

□ **jerko** *n.* [-O *sfx*] [1940s+] (*US*) a stupid, contemptible person. □ **jerky** *adj.* [1930s+] (*US*) silly, idiotic.

IN COMPOUNDS

□ **jerk-ass** *n.* [-ASS *sfx*] [1960s+] (*US*) a contemptible idiot. □ **jerkface** *n.* [1970s+] (*US campus*) a foolish, dull person. □ **jerkhead** *n.* [sense 2 above + -HEAD *sfx*] [1950s+] (*US*) a stupid, contemptible person. □ **jerkwad** *n.* [JERK *v.*[2] (7) + -WAD *sfx*/WAD *n.*[4] (1)] [1990s+] (*US*) a masturbator, a general term of abuse. □ **jerkweed** *n.* [sense 2 above + *DICKWEED under* DICK *n.*[1]] [1990s+] (*US*) a stupid, contemptible person.

SE in slang uses

IN PHRASES

□ **get a jerk on** *v.* [1920s–40s] to hurry up. □ **put a jerk in(to) it** *v.* [1910s–30s] to act vigorously, smartly or quickly.

jerk *n.*[2] *see JERKWATER TOWN under* JERKWATER *adj.*

jerk *adj.*[1] [abbr. of JERKWATER *adj.*; as in SAmE *jerk line*, branch railroad] [late 19C–1940s] (*US*) small-time, second-rate, mediocre; of a railroad, secondary.

jerk *adj.*[2] [JERK *n.*[1] (2)] [1930s+] foolish, stupid.

jerk *v.*[1] [17C–18C] (*UK Und.*) to counterfeit.

IN PHRASES

□ **jerk a gybe** *v.* [GYBE *n.*] [mid-17C–mid-18C] (*Und.*) to forge a licence.

jerk *v.*[2] **1** [17C–18C; 1970s] to copulate. **2** [mid-17C–mid-19C] to accost; to beat. **3** [late 18C–19C] to write or utter. **4** [mid-19C] (*US*) to take, to snatch. **5** [mid-19C+] (*US*) to draw a gun or weapon. **6** [late 19C+] (*US*) to draw beer, soda etc from a tap. **7** [late 19C+] to masturbate. **8** [20C+] (*Aus./US*) to dismiss, to disqualify, to withdraw; thus the *sudden jerk*, the ending of an affair. **9** [1980s+] (*US*) to cheat, to mistreat. **10** [1980s+] (*also* **jerk over**) (*US campus*) of a person, to mess around, to annoy deliberately, to harass; of a situation, to make a mess, to interfere with. **11** [1990s+] (*US black*) to spend freely.

IN COMPOUNDS

□ **jerk-silly** *adj.* (*also* **jerk-simple**) [1930s+] (*US*) mentally unbalanced, supposedly from chronic masturbation.

IN PHRASES

□ **jerk a knot** *v.* [SE *knot*, a lump or bruise] [1940s+] (*US*) to hit or punch someone. □ **jerk around** *v.* **1** [1930s+] (*US*) (*also* **jerk off**) to treat badly, to tease someone, to mess someone about, as *jerk someone around*. **2** [1960s+] (*US campus*) to waste time, to fool around. □ **jerk one's bird** *v. see under* BIRD *n.*[3] (1). □ **jerk one's gherkin** *v. see under* GHERKIN *n.* □ **jerk one's jelly** *v.* (*also* **jerk one's juice**) [JELLY *n.*[1] (1)/JUICE *n.*[1] (2a)] [20C+] to masturbate. □ **jerk one's joystick** *v.* (*also* **jerk one's mutton, ...rod, ...rope, ...turk, ...turkey**) [*JOYSTICK under* JOY *n.*/MUTTON *n.* (3)/ROD *n.* (1)/SE *rope*/*TURKEY NECK under* TURKEY *n.*[1]] [20C+] to masturbate. □ **jerk over** *v. see* sense 10 above. □ **jerk someone's joint** *v.* [JOINT *n.* (1)] [1990s+] to masturbate someone else, e.g. of a prostitute and her client.

IN EXCLAMATIONS

□ **go jerk yourself!** *see GO FUCK YOURSELF! under* FUCK *v.*

SE in slang uses

IN PHRASES

□ **jerk across the Jordan** *v.* [SE *jerk* + River Jordan, fig. used as a place that had to be crossed in death] [1910s] (*Aus.*) to be executed by hanging. □ **jerk baldheaded** *v. see SNATCH BALD-HEADED under* BALD-HEADED *adv.* □ **jerk chin music** *v. see under* CHIN MUSIC *n.* □ **jerk one's jaw(s)** *v. see JACK ONE'S JAW(S) under* JACK OFF *v.*[1]. □ **jerk someone's chain** *v.* (*also* **jerk someone's bird**) [SE *jerk*, as an owner drags on a dog's lead to control it + *chain*/BIRD *n.*[3] (1)] [1960s+] to annoy, to distract forcefully, to taunt. □ **jerk the cat** *v.* [var. on WHIP THE CAT *v.* (3)] [early 17C] to vomit. □ **jerk the tinkler** *v.* [TINKLER *n.*[2]] [mid-19C] to ring a bell. □ **jerk to Jesus** *v.* [late 19C–1930s] (*US*) to execute by hanging. □ **jerk up** *v.* **1** [mid-19C–1940s] (*US*) to arrest. **2** [20C+] (*US*) to reprimand. **3** [1990s+] (*US*) to impose upon, to mess someone around.

jerke *n. see* JARK *n.* (1).

jerked *adj.* (*also* **jerked off, ...up**) [JERK *n.*[1] (2)] [1950s+] (*US*) exceedingly stupid.

jerker *n.*[1] [JERK *v.*[2] (6)] (*US*) **1** [late 19C+] (*also* **soda-juggler**) a soda-fountain clerk; usu. as *soda-jerker*. **2** [1930s] a drinker; often as *BEER-JERKER under* BEER *n.* **3** [1950s] a bartender; in comb. such as *whiskey-jerker* or *BEER-JERKER under* BEER *n.*

jerker *n.*[2] [JERK OFF *v.*] **1** [1940s+] a masturbator, esp. one who frequents striptease shows or similar. **2** [1990s+] (*US black*) in fig. use, one who talks nonsense.

jerking *n.* [SE *jerk*] [2000s] (*UK prison*) a thrusting attack with a sharp object by one prisoner at another.

jerk-nod *n. see* YERKNOD *n.*

jerk-off *n.* [JERK OFF *v.*] **1** [1920s+] (*US*) an act of masturbation. **2** [1930s+] (*US*) a useless, despised person, a lazy incompetent. **3** [1970s+] (*US*) a fraud, a pretence.

jerk-off *adj.* [JERK OFF *v.*] [1930s+] (*US*) **1** pertaining to masturbation. **2** stupid, worthless, despicable.

jerk off *v.* **1** [mid-19C+] to masturbate. **2** in fig. uses. (**a**) [late 19C] (*Aus.*) to do quickly and perfunctorily, esp. in the context of writing. (**b**) [1950s+] (*US*) to mess around, to waste time or energy. (**c**) [1960s] (*US*) to get out, to go away, often in imper. (**d**) [1960s] to waste time, to work at a pointless task. (**e**) [1960s+] (*US*) to tease, to cheat, to treat badly, to infuriate someone; as *jerk someone off.* (**f**) [1990s+] to flatter. **3** [1920s+] to masturbate a partner. **4** [1950s+] (*US drugs*) to inject a drug, pumping the blood/heroin/water mixture in and out of the vein. **5** [1960s+] to move one's hand over an object in a way that is either obviously masturbatory or else just a nervous or repetitive fiddling.

jerks *n.*[1] **1** [19C] a hangover. **2** [late 19C–1900s] (*US*) constr. with *the*, the physical writhings that are evinced by one who is supposedly possessed of the Holy Spirit. **3** [late 19C; 1940s] (*US*) constr. with *the*, acute anxiety.

IN PHRASES

□ **give someone the jerks** *v.* [? fig. use of sense 3 above or ? predecessor to *JERK AROUND under* JERK *v.*[2]] [1910s–30s] to tease, to hoax.

jerks *n.*[2] [abbr. *FLY JERKS under* FLY *n.*[3]] [20C+] (*Aus.*) the pieces of cork that are suspended from a hatbrim to distract flies.

jerk town *n.* [abbr. *JERKWATER TOWN under* JERKWATER *adj.*] [late 19C–1950s] (*US*) a small provincial or rural town.

jerkwater *n.* [JERKWATER *adj.* (2)] [1950s+] (*US*) a fool, an idiot.

jerkwater *adj.* [railroad use, as *jerkwater railroad*, a small remote rural location where trains didn't stop except to pick up water. These places had a trackside water tower and a trough from which a train could scoop or *jerk water* from between the tracks without actually stopping. An alternative ety., based on earlier railroad practice, suggests that the crew had actually to leave the train and *jerk* the *water* in buckets from local wells, then run with it to the waiting locomotive. A further suggestion cites buckets that were attached to the locomotive by a leather strap and that were used to *jerk* the *water* from streams running alongside the track] **1** [late 19C+] (*US*) small-time, second-rate, mediocre. **2** [1950s+] (*US*) stupid, foolish.

IN COMPOUNDS

❑ **jerkwater town** *n.* (*also* **jerk, jerkwater**) [20C+] (*US*) a small, insignificant town.

jerm *n. see* GERM *n.*

jerran *adj.* [mid-19C] (*Aus.*) afraid.

jerrawicke *n.* [? dial. *jerry beer*, second-rate beer] [mid-19C] (*Aus.*) Australian-brewed beer.

jerri *n. see* JERRY *n.*[5].

jerried *adj.* [SE *jerry*, a second-rate builder] **1** [late 19C+] in fig. non-building use, botched. **2** [1920s] injured.

Jerry *n.* (*also* **Gerry**) [abbr.; Brophy & Partridge (1930) suggest this was the preferred WW1 term subseq. to 1915] [1910s+] a derog. name for a *German*.

Jerry *adj.* [JERRY *n.*] [1910s+] German.

jerry *n.*[1] [ety. unknown] [19C] (*UK Und.*) a fog, a mist.

jerry *n.*[2] [TOM AND JERRY *n.* (2)] [mid-19C] (*US*) a spree.

IN PHRASES

❑ **jerry-wag** *n.* [early–mid-19C] a tipsy individual, out on a spree; thus a *jerry-wag shop*, a coffee stall, much frequented by such people.

jerry *n.*[3] [SE *Jeremiah*] [mid-19C] a pessimist, a complainer.

jerry *n.*[4] [abbr. SE *jerry hat*] [mid–late 19C] a round felt hat.

jerry *n.*[5] (*also* **jerri**) [abbr. SE *jereboam*, a double magnum of wine] **1** [mid-19C+] a chamberpot. **2** [1980s] a lavatory.

IN PHRASES

❑ **jerry-come-tumble** *n.* [mid–late 19C] a lavatory. ❑ **jerry-go-nimble** *n.* **1** [mid–late 19C] diarrhoea. **2** [late 19C] a crafty, untrustworthy person.

jerry *n.*[6] [late 19C–1930s] (*UK Und.*) a watch; thus *jerry-getting*, *jerry-nicking*, *jerry-stealing*, watch stealing.

jerry *n.*[7] [1920s] the penis.

jerry *n.*[8] *see* JERRY SHOP *n.*

jerry, the *n.* [? stereotyped link of police and a 'typically Irish' given name] [1910s] (*UK Und.*) the police.

jerry *adj.* [JERRY *v.* (2)] **1** [20C+] (*orig. US*) (*also* **jerry to**) aware, knowledgeable, informed. **2** [1900s–30s] (*US*) good, fine. **3** [1980s] (*Aus.*) (*also* **jerry to**) interested in.

IN PHRASES

❑ **full jerry** see separate entries. ❑ **get jerry on** *v.* (*also* **get jerry to**) [1900s–40s] (*US*) to be aware of, to understand.

jerry *v.* [? abbr. JERRYCUMUMBLE *v.*] **1** [mid–late 19C] to tease, to chaff, to sneer at. **2** [late 19C+] (*also* **gerry**) to understand, to work out, to recognize, to discern.

IN PHRASES

❑ **take a jerry** *v.* [1910s+] to change one's behaviour or course of action (for the better). ❑ **take a jerry to** *v.* [1910s+] (*Aus./N.Z.*) to investigate and understand something, to work something out.

jerrycumumble *v.* (*also* **jerrymumble**) [? rhy. sl.] **1** [early 18C–19C] to shake about, to tumble. **2** [20C+] to understand, to work out [TUMBLE *v.*[2]/RUMBLE *v.*[2] (1)].

jerry-diddle *n.* [rhy. sl. = SE *fiddle*] [20C+] **1** a violin. **2** (*Aus.*) a drink 'on the house' [the implication that the publican is 'fiddling' himself out of a profit].

jerry lynch *n.* [? anecdotal] [mid-19C–1900s] a poor quality pickled pig's head.

jerrymumble *v. see* JERRYCUMUMBLE *v.*

Jerry O'Gorman *n.* [rhy. sl.] [20C+] a Mormon.

jerry randle *n. see* JACK RANDALL *n.*

jerry riddle *n. see* JIMMY (RIDDLE) *n.* (1).

jerry rumble *v.* [JERRY *adj.* + RUMBLE *v.*[2] (1); ? rhy. sl. *jerryrumble* = TUMBLE *v.*[2] (1)] [1900s] (*N.Z.*) to discover, to understand.

jerry shop *n.* [abbr. *TOM-AND-JERRY (SHOP) under* TOM AND JERRY *n.*] [early–late 19C] **1** (*also* **jerry, jerry-house**) a cheap tavern. **2** a pawnbroker.

jerry sneak *n.*[1] [*Jerry Sneak*, a character in *The Mayor of Garrat* (1764) by Samuel Foote, who is dominated by his wife] [late 18C–19C] a hen-pecked husband; thus *jerry-sneakery*, henpecking.

jerry sneak *n.*[2] [JERRY *n.*[6] (1)+ SNEAK *n.*[1] (1)] [19C] a thief who specializes in stealing watches.

jerry sneak *adj.* [JERRY SNEAK *n.*[2]] [early 19C] underhand, deceitful.

Jersey *n.* [1940s] (*US*) milk.

Jersey *adj.* pertaining to the state of New Jersey.

IN COMPOUNDS

❑ **Jersey eagle** *n.* (*also* **Jersey bird**) [the abundance of mosquitoes in the state] [1900s–30s] (*US*) a mosquito. ❑ **Jersey lightning** *n.* [mid-19C–1960s] (*US*) a strong kind of apple-jack, peach brandy or illicitly distilled whisky. ❑ **Jersey side** *n.* [the position of New *Jersey*, the 'wrong' side of the Hudson River from Manhattan] [1940s] (*US black*) the wrong side, the inferior type etc.

IN PHRASES

❑ **Jersey side of the snatch play** [*JERSEY SIDE* above + SNATCH *n.* (1d); lit. on the wrong side of one's sexual peak] [1940s] (*US black*) over 38 years old.

jersey *n.* [Cheshire dial. *jersey*, 'a contemptuous term for a head of hair' (*EDD*)] [late 19C–1940s] (*Aus.*) a red-head.

Jersey city *n.* [rhy. sl. = TITTY *n.* (1)] [1930s–70s] (*US*) a female breast; often in pl. *jerseys*.

Jersey highball *n.* [SE *jersey* (cow) + HIGHBALL *n.*[1]] [1940s] (*US black*) cow's milk.

Jerusalem *n.* [according to the Bible, Christ rode into Jerusalem on a donkey, but note (Egan), *Real Life in Ireland* 91: [note] 'Donkeys and their riders are so called in honour to a late entry into Jerusalem by some female crusaders against common decency'] [19C] a donkey.

proper name in slang uses

IN PHRASES

❑ **go to Jerusalem** *v.* [? drunkenness being 'the promised land'] [mid-18C–early 19C] to get drunk. ❑ **Jerusalem the Golden** *n.* (*also* **Jerusalem-by-the-Sea**) [the large number of Jews who retire to Brighton and other towns along Britain's south coast] [late 19C+] Brighton. ❑ **little Jerusalem** *n.* [1910s] (*US*) the Jewish area of a town or city.

Jerusalem *adj.* [mid-19C–1920s] a euph. for DAMNED *adj.*

proper name in slang uses

IN COMPOUNDS

pertaining to Jews or Judaism, usu. stereotyped

❑ **Jerusalem apple** *n.* [1910s] (*US*) a tomato. ❑ **Jerusalem cruisers** *n.* [1990s+] sandals. ❑ **Jerusalem cuckoo** *n.* [1920s] (*Irish*) a Jew.

general uses

❑ **Jerusalem artichoke** *n.* [rhy. sl. = MOKE *n.*[1] (1)] [late 19C–1930s] a donkey. ❑ **Jerusalem cuckoo** *n.* [its 'hee-haw' bray presumably reminiscent of the cuckoo's 'cuc-oo'] [1910s–40s] a donkey. ❑ **Jerusalem Ford** *n.* [1930s] (*US*) a donkey. ❑ **Jerusalem hobby** [late 18C] a donkey. ❑ **Jerusalem overtaker** *n.* [late 19C] (*US West*) a comb. ❑ **Jerusalem parrot** *n.* [20C+] a flea. ❑ **Jerusalem pony** *n.* [19C] a donkey. ❑ **Jerusalem slim** *n.* [1920s–70s] (*US tramp*) Jesus Christ.

Jerusalem! *excl.* [mid-19C+] used in a variety of mild oaths; euph. for JESUS! *excl.*

IN EXCLAMATIONS

❑ **Jerusalem artichokes!** [1940s] euph. for JESUS! *excl.* ❑ **Jerusalem cricket!** (*also* **Jerusalem crickets! ...June bugs!**) [euph. for JESUS! *excl.*] [mid-19C–1900s] (*US*) a mild oath.

jerve *n.* (*also* **jerv**) [abbr. JERVIS *n.*] **1** [mid-19C–1950s] (*US Und.*) a waistcoat or waistcoat watch pocket; thus *jerver*, a pickpocket. **2** [1910s] (*US Und.*) in a pickpocket team, the one who actually does the stealing.

jervis *n. see* JARVEY *n.*

jervy *n. see* JARVEY *n.*

je's! *excl. see* JEEZ! *excl.*

jessamy *n.* (*also* **jessimy**) [SE *jessamine*, jasmine. Lit. a man who scents himself with perfume or who wears a sprig of jessamine in his buttonhole; the implication is of effeminacy as well as dandyism] [late 17C–mid-19C] a fop or dandy.

jesse *n.* (*also* **jessie**) [play on Isa. 11:1 'There shall come forth a rod out of the stem of Jesse'] [1910s–30s] (*US Und.*) a bluff or threat.

IN PHRASES

❑ **give someone jesse** *v.* (*also* **give someone jessie/jessy, catch Moses**) [mid-19C–1940s] to punish, to beat, to scold soundly; sometimes used with other verbs, such as *administer*; also with *catch/get*, to be punished.

Jesse James *n.* [US outlaw *Jesse James* (1847–82)] [1960s] a dangerous, hardened criminal.

Jesse James killer *n.* [? Robert Ford, killer of the outlaw *Jesse James*, was a former member of his gang; thus a traitor and a 'slimy' figure] [1940s] (*US black*) any heavy, sticky hair pomade, usu. with a distinctive smell.

Jessica! *excl.* [2000s] (*S.Afr. gay*) a euph. for JESUS! *excl.*

jessie *n.*[1] (*also* **jessie-boy**) [use of generic female name] **1** [1920s+] a male homosexual. **2** [1930s+] a weakling, an ineffectual person; thus *woman-jessie*, a weak man who physically abuses women. **3** [2000s] (*S.Afr. gay*) a Jewish homosexual man.

jessie *n.*[2] [JERSEY *n.*] [1940s] (*US black*) a red-haired girl or woman.

jessie *n.*[3] *see* JESSE *n.*

jessie-boy *n. see* JESSIE *n.*[1].

jessimy *n. see* JESSAMY *n.*

jester *v.* [1970s] (*W.I.*) to play the fool.

Jesu! *excl. see* JESUS! *excl.*

Jesuit *n.* [the contemporary suspicion of Jesuits, who were thus branded with a suitably repellent image] [mid-17C–early 19C] a male homosexual; thus the *jesuits' fraternity*, the world of homosexuality; thus *Jesuit box*, to masturbate.

Jesus *n.* [1920s+] a synon. for 'hell', used as an intensifier.

IN PHRASES

❑ **beat the living Jesus out of** *v. see* BEAT (THE) HELL OUT OF *under* HELL *n.*

IN EXCLAMATIONS

❑ **sweet...Jesus!** *see* SWEET BLEEDING JESUS! *under* SWEET *adj.*[1]. ❑ **what the Jesus!** [1920s–50s] (*US tramp*) an excl. of irritation.

proper name in slang uses

IN COMPOUNDS

❑ **Jesus boots** *n.* (*also* **Jesus gliders, ...shoes, ...slippers, ... weejuns**) [Christ is trad. portrayed as wearing sandals] [1940s+] (*orig. US*) footwear, orig. boots, now usu. sandals. ❑ **Jesus dust** *n. see* DUST *n.* (6a). ❑ **Jesus freak** *n.* [-FREAK *sfx*] [1960s+] (*orig. US*) a fervent or evangelical Christian; usu. used contemptuously. ❑ **Jesus guy** *n. see* MISSION STIFF *under* MISSION *n.* ❑ **Jesus screamer** *n.* (*also* **Jesus shouter**) [1950s+] (*US*) a street preacher. ❑ **Jesus stiff** *n.* [STIFF *n.*[1] (4a)] [1920s–50s] **1** (*US Und.*) a religious tramp. **2** (*US prison*) a prisoner who adopts religious beliefs while serving a sentence.

IN PHRASES

❑ **(bloody) Jesus** *n. see* BEJAZUS *n.* ❑ **sweet jesus** *n. see under* SWEET *adj.*[1]. ❑ **tell it to Jesus** [1930s] (*US tramp*) a request to be quiet.

Jesus *adj.* (*also* **Jesus Christ**) [1920s+] (*US/W.I.*) a general intensifier, e.g. *not one Jesus shilling*, not one DAMNED *adj./* cursed shilling.

Jesus! *excl.* (*also* **Christ Jesus! do Jesus! Gee-zus Christ! James Christe! Jasez! Jaysus! Jayzus! Jazus! Jeezus! Jesu! Jesus Christ! Jesus Christ alive! Jesus-please-us! Jesus Priest! Weeping Jesus!**) [late 14C+] a general and blasphemous oath.

IN EXCLAMATIONS

❑ **Jesus Christ and the cows got out!** [1930s] (*US tramp*) an excl. of despair. ❑ **Jesus Christ on a raft!** (*also* **Jesus Christ on a pogo stick! ...bicycle! ...crutch!**) [cf. CHRIST ON A BIKE! *under* CHRIST! *excl.*] [1940s+] a mild excl. ❑ **Jesus, Mary and Joseph!** [20C+] a mild oath; an excl. of surprise. ❑ **Jesus shit!** [SHIT! *excl.* (1)] [1960s+] an excl. of exasperation or astonishment. ❑ **Jesus tonight!** [20C+] (*Irish*) a general excl., a euph. for *Jesus Christ!*

Jesus H Christ! *excl.* (*also* **Jeezus K. Reist! Jesus F. Christ! Jesus H. Mahogany Christ! Jesus Johnnycake Christ! Jesus X Christ! Judas H Christ!**) [the H is redundant other than for rhythm, although *DARE* suggests a link to *IHS*, the monogram for Jesus; note Quinion 5/8/00: 'There have been various theories, but the one that seems most plausible is that it comes from the Greek monogram for Jesus, 'IHS' or 'IHC'. This is formed from the first two letters plus the last letter of His name in Greek (the letters iota, eta, and sigma; in the second instance, the C is a Byzantine Greek form of sigma). The H is actually the capital letter form of eta, but churchgoers who were unfamiliar with Greek took it to be a Latin H.'] [late 19C+] a mild oath.

jesusly *adj.* [JESUS *adj.* (1)] [19C] (*US*) a general intensifier; a euph. for DARNED *adj.*, DAMNED *adj.*

Jesus Priest! *excl. see* JESUS! *excl.*

Jesus wept! *excl.* [20C+] a general and blasphemous oath.

Jesus X Christ! *excl. see* JESUS H CHRIST! *excl.*

jet *n.*[1] [the *jet* black gown] [early 18C–19C] a lawyer.

jet *n.*[2] [its 'accelerating' effect on the mental processes] [1980s+] (*drugs*) ketamine.

jet *v.* [SE *jet*, to travel by jet aircraft; note 16C–17C SE *jet*, to move along jauntily, to caper] [1950s+] (*US black/campus/teen*) **1** (*also* **jet out**) to leave in a hurry, to move very fast. **2** to excite someone.

jet one's juice *v. see under* JUICE *n.*[1].

Jew *n.* **1** [17C+] a mean person, a skinflint. **2** [1900s] (*Aus.*) a bookmaker. **3** [1940s–50s] (*US black*) the boss, irrespective of their actual religion. **4** [1950s+] (*W.I.*) any rich person, presumably white but with no religious overtones, other than the worldwide derog. stereotype.

Jew *adj.* (*also* **Jew's**) [17C+] in slang, reflecting centuries of Christian teaching, the Jew is grasping, avaricious, wealthy, untrustworthy, deceitful and mean (as well as circumcised and abstaining from pork). Thus virtually all combs. with *Jew/Jewish* are derog. and play on these stereotypes.

IN COMPOUNDS

❑ **Jew baby** *n.* [1910s–50s] a derog. term for a Jew. ❑ **Jew bagel** *n. see* BAGEL *n.* (1). ❑ **Jew bail** *n.* (*also* **Jew's bail**) [the belief that while Jews will offer bail in any situation, they will not be there to pay it if the criminal absconds] [late 18C–19C] insufficient bail. ❑ **jewbox** *n.* [1930s] (*US*) an electric-powered vehicle. ❑ **Jew butter** *n.* [the popularity among Jews of *schmaltz*, fat as a spread] [late 19C] (*US*) goose or chicken dripping. ❑ **Jew canoe** *n.* (*also* **Jew buggy, Jewish submarine, Jew's canoe**) [CANOE *n.*[2] (1)] **1** [1970s+] (*US*) a Cadillac. **2** [1980s+] (*UK society*) a Jaguar. ❑ **Jew cheque** *n.* [the stereotyping of Jews as devious money-makers] [1980s+] (*US*) any form of cheque that is obtained through fraud, e.g. on Social Security. ❑ **Jew flag** *n. see* JEWISH FLAG *under* JEWISH *adj.* ❑ **Jew food** *n.* [in mockery of the Jewish dietary prohibition on all pork products] [20C+] ham. ❑ **Jew joanna** *n. see* JEWISH JOANNA *under* JEWISH *adj.* ❑ **Jew joint** *n.* [JOINT *n.* (3b)] [20C+] (*US*) a second-hand clothes store. ❑ **Jew's bail** *n. see* JEW BAIL above. ❑ **Jew's Bentley** *n.* (*also* **Jew's Rolls Royce**) [the stereotyped association of Jaguars and *nouveaux riches* Jews] [1930s–60s] a Jaguar motorcar. ❑ **Jew's canoe** *n. see* JEW CANOE above. ❑ **Jew's compliment** *n.* (*also* **Jewish compliment, Judische compliment**) **1** [mid-19C+] of a man, having a large penis but no money or presents [the premise is that the penis is free, but to the stereotypically mean Jew, presents involve losing money]. **2** [1950s+] (*gay*) a circumcised penis. ❑ **Jew shave** *n.* [traces of a beard that still remain on some swarthy Jewish men's faces despite their shaving] [1930s] (*US*) covering one's face with talcum powder instead of shaving. ❑ **Jew sheet** *n.* [1950s+] (*gay*) an account, often imaginary, of money lent to friends. ❑ **Jew's lance** *n.* [1950s+] (*gay*) a Jewish circumcised penis. ❑ **Jew's poker** *n.* [the lighting of fires (and in more recent years, the turning on of electric lights), is among many prohibitions against 'work' on the Sabbath. The Yid. term for the same individual is *shabbas goy*, Sabbath gentile] [late 19C] the gentile who, in religious households, is brought in to light the fires on the Sabbath. ❑ **Jew's Rolls Royce** *n. see* JEW'S BENTLEY above. ❑ **Jew's typewriter** *n.* [racial stereotyping, the Jew as moneygrabber] [20C+] a cash register.

SE in slang uses

IN COMPOUNDS

❑ **Jew-fencer** *n.* [-FENCER *sfx*] [mid-19C] a Jewish street-seller. ❑ **Jew town** *n.* [late 19C+] (*US*) a Jewish community within an urban area.

jew *v.* (*also* **jew down, ...out, ...up**) [racial stereotyping; the cheater need in no way be Jewish] [early 19C+] to cheat financially; also to haggle.

Jew beanie *n. see* BEANIE *n.*[1] (4).

Jew boy *n.* [not initally derog. (although note the US use of *boy* to address blacks)] **1** [late 18C+] a young Jewish man [SE by late 19C, though rarely used in 20C+]. **2** [mid-19C+] a derog. term for a male Jew, irrespective age; thus fem. *Jew-girl*; also attrib.

Jewburg *n.* [the city's large Jewish population + a pun on the usual nickname, *Jo'burg*] [1900s–50s] (*S.Afr.*) Johannesburg; thus *Jewburger/Jewburgher*, a rich Johannesburg merchant.

Jew chum *n.* **1** [1930s–50s] (*Aus.*) a Jewish refugee from Germany or central Europe [pun on NEW CHUM *n.* (2)]. **2** [1940s–50s] (*US*) a tramp [rhy. sl. = BUM *n.*[3] (1)].

jew down *v. see* JEW *v.*

jewel *n.* **1** [late 15C+] (*also* **jewelry**) in pl., the male genitals. **2** [mid-16C+] (*also* **jewel case, jewelery, jewelry, jewels**) the vagina. **3** [late 18C–1950s] (*US/Irish-Amer.*) a fellow, a man, oft. as term of address.

IN COMPOUNDS

❑ **jewel box** *n.* **1** [1960s] the vagina. **2** [1970s] (*US gay*) the scrotum.

jewel *adj.* [2000s] (*US black*) excellent, first-rate.

jewellery *n.* [late 19C–1940s] (*US prison*) handcuffs, shackles, chains.

jewels *n. see* JEWEL *n.*

Jewey *n. see* JEWY *n.*

Jewfro *n. see* ISRO *n.*

Jewhannesburg *n.* [its large Jewish population] [1900s] (*Aus.*) Johannesburg, Sth. Africa.

jewhilliken!/jewhitiker! *excl. see* GEE WHILLIKINS! *excl.*

jewhillikin *adj.* [late 19C] (*US*) exemplary.

Jewie *n. see* JEWY *n.*

Jewie Louie *n. see* JEWY LOUIS *n.*

Jewish *adj.* used in the following combs. as a negative stereotype.

IN COMPOUNDS

❑ **Jewish airlines** *n.* [Jews are too mean to pay airfares] [1960s+] (*gay*) as a mode of transport, on foot. ❑ **Jewish Alps** *n.* **1** [20C+] (*US*) Washington Heights, New York City, home of many successful Jews. **2** [1960s+] (*US*) the Catskill Mountain resort area, patronized by Jewish New Yorkers. ❑ **Jewish-American princess** *n. see* JEWISH PRINCESS below. ❑ **Jewish bonfire** *n. see* JEWISH LIGHTNING below. ❑ **Jewish champagne** *n.* [1930s] (*US*) celery tonic. ❑ **Jewish compliment** *n. see* JEW'S COMPLIMENT *under* JEW *adj.* ❑ **Jewish corned beef** *n.* [BEEF *n.*[1] (3)] [1960s+] a circumcised penis. ❑ **Jewish flag** *n.* (*also* **Jew flag**) [the avaricious Jew has no nation, only money; the same image as of the Communist derog. phr. 'rootless cosmopolitans'] [1910s+] (*US*) a currency note. ❑ **Jewish foreplay** *n.* [the supposed frigidity of the JEWISH PRINCESS below] [1950s+] (*US*) the man pleads for sex, his partner refuses all physical contact. ❑ **Jewish forest** *n.* ['mittel-European' pron.: 't'ree t'rees'] [20C+] in poker, three threes. ❑ **Jewish joanna** *n.* (*also* **Jew joanna**) [*Jewish* + JOANNA *n.* = JEWISH PIANO below] **1** [20C+] a taximeter. **2** [1960s+] a cash register. ❑ **Jewish lightning** *n.* (*also* **Jewish bonfire, ...fire sale, Greek lightning**) [20C+] deliberate arson in order to gain the insurance on an otherwise unprofitable business. ❑ **Jewish muscles** *n.* [1940s] shoulder-padded jackets. ❑ **Jewish national** *n.* [the ref. is to the *Hebrew National* brand of kosher salami] [1950s+] (*US gay*) a circumcised penis. ❑ **Jewish nightcap** *n.* [late 19C–1950s] a foreskin. ❑ **Jewish overdrive** *n.* [20C+] (*US*) freewheeling down hills to save petrol. ❑ **Jewish Oxo** *n.* [*Oxo*, the brandname of a beef extract; like the kitchen stand-by, money makes 'gravy'] [1960s+] money. ❑ **Jewish penicillin** *n.* [despite its essentially humorous content, the term has some medical reality: the effect of hot soup on the mucous membranes is to make them work harder and thus help clear the nose of the blocking that comes with a cold] [1960s+] (*US*) chicken soup. ❑ **Jewish piano** *n.* (*also* **Jewish pianola**) **1** [20C+] a taximeter. **2** [1930s+] a cash register. ❑ **Jewish prince** *n.* [1980s+] (*US*) a (middle-class) Jewish man who is spoiled and/or dominated by his mother. ❑ **Jewish princess** *n.* (*also* **Jewish-American princess**) [1970s+] (*US*) a young, conceited, (middle-class) Jewish woman. ❑ **Jewish renaissance** *n.* [1950s+] (*gay*) over-elaborate furniture in doubtful taste. ❑ **Jewish screwdriver** *n.* (*also* **Yiddish screwdriver**) [the supposed inability of stereotypically cerebral/entrepreneurial Jews to perform manual tasks] [20C+] a hammer. ❑ **Jewish sidewalls** *n.* [1950s–60s] (*US*) white rubber sidewalls, glued onto otherwise black tyres in an attempt to make them look more fashionable. ❑ **Jewish (standard) time** *n.* (*also* **j.s.t.**) [the supposed propensity of Jews to arrive late for any meeting or appointment] [1930s+] (*US*) unpunctuality; derog. only if used by a non-Jew. ❑ **Jewish submarine** *n. see* JEW CANOE *under* JEW *adj.* ❑ **Jewish waltz** *n.* [1980s+] (*US*) deal-making, haggling. ❑ **Jewish windbreaker** *n.* [1960s] (*US*) a mink coat.

IN PHRASES

❑ **Jewish by hospitalization** *adj.* [1950s+] (*gay*) circumcised but not Jewish.

jewish *n.* [racial stereotyping, the 'invariably' rich Jew] [1960s+] (*S.Afr. black*) smart, expensive clothing.

jewish *adj.*[1] [1940s] (*US*) odd, abnormal.

jewish *adj.*[2] [JEWISH *n.*] [1960s+] (*S.Afr. black*) of clothes or other material objects, smart, expensive, chic.

jewish *v.* [JEWISH *n.*] [1960s+] (*S.Afr. black*) to dress someone up in smart clothes.

jewlark *v.* [SE *gill/jill*, a girl or woman + LARK *v.*] [mid-19C+] (*US*) to flirt, to court.

jewlarker *n.* (*also* **jewlarky**) [JEWLARK *v.*] [late 19C+] (*US*) **1** a sweetheart. **2** a dandy.

Jewman *n.* [var. on JEW BOY *n.*] [20C+] (*Irish*) a moneylender.

Jew's *n.* [the three balls that signify a pawnbroker and the fact that most Harlem pawnbrokers were Jews; note 1887 *Bulletin* (Sydney) 5 Nov. 8/3: 'The Red Sea was divided and held back as a wall on either hand for the ancient pawn brokers to pass over'] [1970s] (*US black*) a pawnbroker.

Jew's *adj. see* JEW *adj.*

Jew's eye *n.* [? Ital. *gioie* or Fr. *joaille*, a jewel or, given the prevailing stereotype, the medieval practice of extorting money from the Jewish community on pain of threatened torture, which may or may not have involved blinding] [late 16C–1900s] something valuable or desirable, usu. as *worth a Jew's eye*.

jew up *v. see* JEW *v.*

Jewy *n.* (*also* **Jewey, Jewie**) [late 19C+] an 'inevitable' nickname for a Jew, esp. when surnamed Moss; a derog. name for a Jew; also adjectival use.

Jewy Louis *n.* (*also* **Jewie Louie**) [1970s+] (*UK society*) a flashy, vulgar style of interior decoration, poss. featuring (fake) Louis XV or Louis XVI furniture.

Jew York *n.* [the large Jewish population in that city] [20C+] derog. term for New York city; thus *Jew Yorker*; similarly *Jewnited States, Jewnited Nations*.

jeysey ears *adj.* [1970s] (*W.I.*) of a person, dirty, filthy.

jez! *excl.* see JEEZ! *excl.*

j.g.e. *n.* [*j*ust *g*ay *e*nough] [2000s] (*N.Z. gay*) a heterosexual who is nonetheless acceptable within the homosexual community.

J-hole *n.* [coined on TV show *Saturday Night Live*] [2000s] (*US campus*) a contemptible person.

jib *n.*[1] (*also* **jibb**) [Rom. *chib*, *jib*, the tongue; Hind. *tschib*, language] **1** [mid-19C] (*UK tramp*) the tongue. **2** [mid-19C] the face or expression. **3** [mid-19C] language. **4** [late 19C+] (*orig. US Und.*) speech, impudent talk. **5** [20C+] (*US black*) (*also* **gibbs, gibs, jibbs, jibs**) the mouth [dial. *jib*, the underlip; thus the mouth]. **6** [1950s–60s] (*US black*) a tooth; usu. in pl., *jibs*.

IN PHRASES

❑ **diarrhoea of the jib** *n.* see DIARRHOEA OF THE MOUTH *under* DIARRHOEA *n.* ❑ **flap at the jibs** *v.* [1950s+] (*US black*) to talk wildly, out of control, in a panicky, unrestrained manner. ❑ **flip off at the jibs** *v.* [see sense 5 above] [2000s] (*UK black*) to speak in such a manner as to provoke a fight. ❑ **flying jib** *n.* [1930s–60s] a talkative person. ❑ **hang one's jib** *v.* [naut. imagery] [late 18C–19C] to look miserable, lit. to 'hang one's underlip'. ❑ **run one's jibs** *v.* (*also* **jaw at the jibs, run one's gibs**) [RUN OFF *under* RUN *v.*)/JAW *v.*[1] (1)] [1960s+] to chatter aimlessly. ❑ **slide one's jib** *v.* [1930s–40s] (*US black*) to talk unrestrainedly.

jib *n.*[2] [abbr. proper name Antoine *Gibus*, the Fr. inventor who patented the hat in 1837] [late 19C–1900s] (*UK society*) an opera hat, i.e. 'flat-folding "chimney-pot" hat, closed by springs set in centre of vertical ribs' (Ware).

jib *n.*[3] see JIBBER *n.*

jib *v.*[1] [? JIBBER *n.*] **1** [mid-19C+] to depart quietly, to slip away. **2** [20C+] to leave behind, to abandon.

jib *v.*[2] (*also* **jibb**) [JIB *n.*[1] (4)] [mid-19C+] to talk, to chatter; esp. at length and without meaning.

jib *v.*[3] **1** see JIBBER *n.* **2** see JIBB (IN) *v.*

jibb *n.* **1** [1990s+] (*US drugs*) a gram of hashish [ety. unknown; ? SE *jib*, the 'arm' of a crane; thus pun on getting one HIGH *adj.*[1]]. **2** see JIB *n.*[1].

jibb *v.* see JIB *v.*[2].

jibba-jabba *n.* (*also* **jibber-jabber**) [JIB *v.*[2] + SE *jabber*] [1950s+] (*US black*) excessive conversation.

jibber *n.* (*also* **jib, gibber**) [SE *jib*, of a horse, to back away, to refuse to go forward] **1** [mid-19C–1960s] a worn-out horse, an uncooperative horse. **2** [20C+] (*orig. Irish*) in fig. ext. of sense 1, a coward.

jibber the kibber *v.* [a lantern is tied to a horse's neck and the horse itself has one foot tied. The movement this produces appears, from out on a dark sea, to resemble a moving ship's light. Ety. unknown; Patridge suggests *jibber*, to confuse, but it does not appear until 1824; *jib*, for a horse to move in fits and starts, is also 19C; ?17C dial. *jibby-horse*, a flashy, showy woman is East Anglian, but Grose (1785) links such wrecking to 'our western coasts'; *kibber* may be reduplication, it may relate to Cornish dial. *kib*, to steal] [late 18C–early 19C] to set up a device deliberately to wreck ships for the potential plunder.

jibbery *adj.* [JIBBER *n.* (1)] [late 19C] uncooperative.

jibb (in) *v.* (*also* **jib**) [? JIB *v.*[2], the idea of talking oneself in, or GYP *v.*] [1960s+] to gain admission to an event or service (e.g. a bus ride) without a ticket and without paying, thus *jibber*, one who gets in for free.

jibbs *n.* see JIB *n.*[1] (5).

jibe *n.*[1] see GYBE *n.*

jibe *n.*[2]

IN PHRASES

❑ **no jibe** see NO JIVE *under* JIVE *n.*[1].

jib-jibe *n.* (*also* **ji-jibe**) [JIB *v.*[2]] [1960s+] (*US black*) talk that goes in one ear and out the other, unimportant chatter.

jiblet *n.* [ety. unknown] [1960s+] (*drugs*) barbiturate.

jiblets *n.* see GIBLETS *n.* (2).

jibone *n.* (*also* **jabone, jaboney, jabonie, jarboni, jiboney, jumbloney, shaboney**) [? Milanese *giambone*, ham, cf. JAMBONE *adj.*] **1** [1920s+] (*US*) a novice, an innocent, a newly arrived immigrant, a fool. **2** [1920s+] (*US*) a heavy, a thug, a muscleman, as which a newly arrived immigrant was often used. **3** [1950s] (*US Und.*) an Italian.

jibs *n.*[1] [SE *jib*, a protruding sail at the bow of the ship] **1** [1910s] (*US*) clothes. **2** [1950s+] (*US black*) the buttocks. **3** [1980s+] (*US*) a woman's breasts.

jibs *n.*[2] see JIB *n.*[1].

jick *n.* [JIGGER *n.*[3]] [1920s–40s] (*US black*) alcohol, esp. bootleg alcohol.

jickajog *n.* [echoic of the action] [17C–mid-19C] a shoving, a commotion.

jickhead *n.* [JICK *n.*+ -HEAD *sfx* (4)] [1930s–70s] (*US black*) a drunkard.

jidder *n.* [? JUDY *n.*[1] (1)] [1910s] (*Aus.*) a woman, a girl.

jiffy *n.* (*also* **giff, giffy, jef, jeffey, jeffy, jif, jiff, jiffey, jiffin**) [the vars. *jeffey, jeffy* are 19C only] **1** [late 18C+] a moment, a very short time, almost invariably in phr. *in a jiffy*, occas. *in a jiff*, also intensified as *half a jiffy*. **2** [late 19C] a very small amount.

jig *n.*[1] [SE *jig*, a lively dance] **1** [17C–18C] sexual intercourse, often as *double entendre* with *dance*. **2** [18C–19C] a joking, mocking nickname for a person. **3** [1980s] (*US campus*) a promiscuous man.

SE in slang uses

IN PHRASES

❑ **get a jig on** *v.* [1900s] (*Aus.*) to hurry up.

jig *n.*[2] [late 16C SE *jig*, a comical performance, usu. given in the interval or at the conclusion of a play] **1** [17C+] (*also* **gigg**) a trick, a swindle; thus (late 18C+) *the jig is up*, the game is up. **2** [1910s] (*US Und.*) a problem; a mistake.

jig *n.*[3] [abbr. JIGGER *n.*[1] (1)] [18C–early 19C] a lock or door.

jig *n.*[4] (*also* **jigg**) [abbr. JIGABOO *n.*] (*orig. US*) **1** [1920s+] a derog. term for a black person. **2** [1920s–40s] as used by a black person, thus not derog.; also as term of address.

IN COMPOUNDS

❑ **jig-chaser** *n.* [SE *chaser*] [1920s–40s] (*US*) a white person who pursues the company of blacks. ❑ **jig cut** *n.* [1920s–70s] (*US*) a razor or knife slash. ❑ **jig shop** *n.* [pun] [1920s] (*US Und.*) a blacksmith's. ❑ **jig-town** *n.* [1920s+] (*US*) a black community within an urban area. ❑ **jigwalker** *n.* (*also* **jigwalk, jigwawk**) [JIG *n.*[4] (1) + play on SE *jaywalker*] [1900s–60s] (*US*) a derog. term for a black person, unless used by blacks. ❑ **jig water** *n.* (*also* **jig juice**) [late 19C+] (*US*) alcohol, spirits.

jig *n.*[5] [1990s+] (*US black*) clothing.

jig *adj.* [JIG *n.*[4] (1)] [1920s+] (*US*) referring, in a derog. manner to a black person or the black lifestyle and culture.

jig *v.*[1] [JIG *n.*[1] (1)] [17C–18C] to have sexual intercourse.

jig *v.*[2] [1960s] (*Aus.*) to play truant.

jig *v.*[3] [SE, *jig* someone around] [1960s+] (*US*) to bother, to irritate.

jig *v.*[4] [1980s+] (*US*) to prod with a knife, to stab.

jigaboo *n.* (*also* **gig-a-boo, jigabo, jiggaboo, zigabo, zigaboo, ziggerboo**) [either SE *jig*, a dance, ult. Fr. *giguer*, to leap, to gambol, to frolic (the classic 19C black stereotypes); or modelled on SE *bugaboo*, which, in the 13C, was the name of a demon, and since the 18C, the fear of demons in general; or Bantu *tshikabo*, a meek and servile person, used as derog. by slaves. Paradoxically, the first approximate use of *jigaboo* – in the song 'I've got rings on my fingers' by Weston, Barnes & Scott – appears to have referred to Asians. Certainly the lyrics are set in India, although the ref. to 'Mistress Mumbo Jumbo Ji-ji-boo J O'Shea' would imply that the writer was of the 'they all look alike to me' persuasion] **1** [1920s+] (*orig. US*) a derog. term for a black person. **2** [1920s+] as used by a black person, non-derog. **3** [1940s] (*US black campus*) a crazy person. **4** [1950s] (*US*) an unsophisticated peasant, a farmer.

IN COMPOUNDS

❑ **jigaboo cig** *n.* [1990s+] (*US drugs*) a cannabis cigarette. ❑ **jigaboo joy shop** *n.* [stereotyping of the tastes of black car buyers] [1920s–50s] (*US*) an automobile supply store specializing in cheap but ostentatious chrome accessories.

jig-a-jig *n.* (*also* **jig-a-jog, jig-jig**) [redup. indicative of the movements of copulation; note JIG *n.*[1] (1)] [17C; late 18C+]

sexual intercourse, often found in pidgin slangs; also attrib.

IN COMPOUNDS

❑ **jig-a-jig joint** *n.* [1970s] a brothel.

jig-a-jig *v.* [JIG-A-JIG *n.*] [20C+] to have sexual intercourse.

jigamaree *n.* (*also* **jagamaree, jiggamaree**) [var. on JIGGUMBOB *n.*] **1** [early 19C+] (*US*) a thing, a gadget, a fanciful contrivance. **2** [mid-19C] anything the speaker considers ridiculous or worthless. **3** [mid–late 19C] a cunning trick.

jigg *n. see* JIG *n.*[4].

jigga *n.* [? JIG *v.*[1]] [2000s] (*US teen*) a womanizer.

jiggaboo *n. see* JIGABOO *n.*

jiggalorum *n.* [on pattern of JIGGUMBOB *n.*] [early 17C; 1920s] a trifle, a fanciful thing.

jiggamaree *n. see* JIGAMAREE *n.*

jiggam-bob *n. see* JIGGUMBOB *n.*

jiggambob *v. see* JIGGER *v.*[1] (1).

jigged *adj.* [JIGGERED *adj.*[1]] **1** [1900s–50s] (*US*) a euph. for DAMNED *adj.* **2** [20C+] (*Aus.*) broken, useless.

jigger *n.*[1] [? link to Lancashire dial. *jigger*, a narrow entry between houses, although the cant very likely preceded it; Ribton-Turner, *A History of Vagrants* (1887), suggests Welsh *gwddor*, a gate] **1** [mid-16C–19C] (*UK Und.*) a door. **2** [late 18C–19C] a doorkeeper. **3** [19C] (*UK Und.*) a key. **4** [late 19C+] a prison or cell.

IN COMPOUNDS

❑ **jigger-dubber** *n.* (*also* **gigger-dubber**) [DUB *v.*[1]] [late 18C–19C] a turnkey.

IN PHRASES

❑ **dub the jigger** *v. see DUB THE GIG(GER) under* DUB *v.*[1]. ❑ **strike a jigger** *v.* [STRIKE *v.* (1)] [mid-19C] (*UK Und.*) to pick a lock, to break down a door.

jigger *n.*[2] [the sufferer *jigs* with the pain] [18C–early 19C] (*UK Und.*) a whipping post.

jigger *n.*[3] [SE *jig*, to shake, with idea of JIGGER *n.*[1] too as under lock and key] (*US*) **1** [late 18C–19C] (*also* **chigger**) a clandestine, illicit still. **2** [19C] (*UK Und.*) one who operates an illicit still and sells the liquor. **3** [19C] bootleg liquor. **4** [mid–late 19C] a drink of spirits, a dram [SE in 20C+]. **5** [mid-19C+] a small glass or metal cup, a measure used in mixing cocktails. **6** [mid-19C+] a whisky cocktail. **7** [1920s] (*US*) a young man who frequents soda fountains in the hope of picking up girls.

IN COMPOUNDS

❑ **jigger stuff** *n.* [STUFF *n.* (5a)] [early–mid-19C] liquor made at a secret still. ❑ **jigger worker** *n.* [SE *worker*/WORKER *n.*[1] (1)] **1** [mid-19C–1900s] a seller of illicitly distilled spirits. **2** [late 19C] a drinker of such illegal spirits, esp. whisky.

jigger *n.*[4] [? JIGGER *n.*[1] or JIGGER *n.*[5] (1) or SE *jig*, to move up and down] **1** [mid–late 19C] the penis. **2** [mid-19C–1940s] the vagina.

jigger *n.*[5] (*also* **jiggie, jiggus**) [SE *jig*, a mechanical contrivance] **1** [mid-19C+] (*US*) a thing, a gadget, any small, mechanical contrivance. **2** [late 19C–1940s] (*US tramp*) (*also* **jiggers**) a fake sore, wound or bandage to elicit sympathy. **3** [1900s] (*US*) a tattoo. **4** [1900s–10s] (*US*) a scoop of ice-cream. **5** [1900s–20s] a bicycle. **6** [1910s] a motorcycle. **7** [1910s–20s] a car. **8** [1950s+] (*Aus. Und.*) an improvised radio receiver, used in prison.

jigger *n.*[6] (*also* **jiggers**) [JIGGER! *excl.* (2)] [late 19C–1930s] (*US*) a police officer.

jigger *n.*[7] [euph. for BUGGER *n.*[1]] [20C+] a person; often a foolish person.

jigger *n.*[8] [JIGABOO *n.* (1)] [1920s+] (*orig. US*) a derog. term for a black person.

jigger *n.*[9] (*also* **jigger man**) [JIGGER! *excl.* (2)] [1920s+] (*US prison/Und.*) a lookout man.

jigger *n.*[10] [initial letter on model of NIGGER *n.*[1] (1)] [2000s] (*US black*) a Jew.

jigger *v.*[1] [SE *jig*, to move around] **1** [mid-19C] (*also* **jiggambob**) to shake or jerk rapidly. **2** [mid-19C+] to break, to destroy, to ruin. **3** [late 19C–1930s] (*US*) (*also* **jiggeroo**) to fool, to cheat, esp. in passive.

jigger *v.*[2] [JIGGER *n.*[1]] **1** [late 19C–1920s] to lock up, to imprison. **2** [1970s] to unlock.

jigger *v.*[3] [late 19C–1930s] a euph. for to damn, i.e. to hell with.

jigger *v.*[4] [JIGGER *n.*[5]] **1** [1900s] (*US*) to tattoo. **2** [1910s–30s] (*US Und.*) to deface, to mar (the flesh), thus to create a fake sore.

jigger *v.*[5] [JIGGER *n.*[9]] [1960s] (*US prison/Und.*) to act as a lookout.

jigger! *excl.* (*also* **gigger (me)! jigger me tight! jiggers!**) [? a euph. for JESUS! *excl.*, although usu. used in v. forms; ? semi-euph. for BUGGER *v.*[1]] **1** [early 19C+] used as a vaguely indecent oath, e.g. as *by jiggers! jigger it! I'll be jiggered! be jiggering well careful!* etc. **2** [1910s+] (*US*) (*also* **jiggeroo!**) a warning that someone hostile, e.g. the police, a teacher, one's parents, is coming.

IN PHRASES

❑ **give jiggers** *v.* (*also* **give jiggs**) [1910s–60s] (*US*) to be a lookout, to keep a lookout.

IN EXCLAMATIONS

❑ **by jiggers!** (*also* **by jickers! by jiggurs! by jigs! by ziggity!**) [late 19C–1920s] (*orig. US*) a mild oath, euph. for *by Jesus!*

jiggered *adj.*[1] [JIGGER *v.*[1] (2)] **1** [mid-19C+] (*also* **fiddled**) a euph. for DAMNED *adj.*, with some feeling of confusion; often in phrs. below. **2** [mid-19C+] exhausted, worn out, beaten, often as *jiggered up*. **3** [1920s–40s] (*also* **in the jigs**) drunk. **4** [1990s+] in fig. use, unstable.

IN EXCLAMATIONS

❑ **I'll be jiggered!** (*also* **...hog-wallered! ...jiggerooed! ...jig-swiggered! ...jimjammed! ...jumped up!**) [mid-19C+] a general excl. of surprise, irritation.

jiggered *adj.*[2] [JIGGER *n.*[3] (1)] [late 19C] **1** contraband, smuggled. **2** secret.

jigger-foot market *n.* [Carib.E *jigger-foot*, a foot infested with *jiggers* or larval mites, which lay their eggs beneath the skin. The poor are often prone to such infestation] [1940s+] (*W.I.*) a residential area and market of the very poorest people.

jiggering *adj.* [JIGGER! *excl.*] [late 19C–1930s] a mild pej.

jigger man *n. see* JIGGER *n.*[9].

jiggeroo *v. see* JIGGER *v.*[1] (3).

jiggeroo! *excl. see* JIGGER! *excl.* (2).

jiggerooed *adj.*

IN EXCLAMATIONS

❑ **I'll be jiggerooed!** *see I'LL BE JIGGERED! under* JIGGERED *adj.*[1].

jiggers *n.* **1** *see* JIGGER *n.*[5] (2). **2** *see* JIGGER *n.*[6].

jiggers! *excl. see* JIGGER! *excl.* (1).

jiggery-pokery *n.* (*also* **jackery-pokery, jiggery**) [synon. dial. *jiggery-pokery*, ? ult. Scot. *joukery-pawkery*, a trick] [late 19C+] tricks, lies, underhand activities in general.

jiggie *n. see* JIGGER *n.*[5].

jiggle *adj.* (*also* **jiggly**) [JIGGLE *v.*] [20C+] of a woman, amorously inclined.

jiggle *v.* [mid-19C–1940s] to have sexual intercourse.

jiggle and jog *n.* [rhy. sl. = FROG *n.* (2)] [1970s+] a Frenchman.

jiggler *n.*[1] [SE *jiggle*, i.e. using the sleight of hand required to turn the lock, but note JIGGER *n.*[1]] [1940s+] (*UK Und.*) skeleton keys for use on pin tumbler locks.

jiggler *n.*[2] [1980s] (*US*) a female breast.

jiggling bone *n.* [JIGGLE *v.*+ SE *bone*/BONE *n.*[1] (1)] [19C] the penis.

jiggly *adj. see* JIGGLE *adj.*

jigglywhack *adj.* [2000s] (*US black*) eccentric, extreme.

jiggs *n.*[1] (*also* **Jiggs and Maggie**) [popularized in the *Jiggs and Maggie* comic strip] [1940s] (*US*) corned beef and cabbage.

jiggs *n.*[2] [JIG *n.*[4] (1)] [2000s] (*US black*) a fellow black person.

jiggs *n.*[3]

(IN PHRASES)

❑ **give jiggs** *v. see* GIVE JIGGERS *under* JIGGER! *excl.*

jiggumbob *n.* (*also* **jiggam-bob**) [var. on THINGUMABOB *n.*] **1** [17C; 1920s] (*US*) something strange, peculiar, unknown. **2** [mid-17C] euph. for the vagina.

jiggus *n. see* JIGGER *n.*[5].

jiggy *n.* [JIGGER *n.*[6] (1)] [1990s+] (*US black*) the police.

jiggy *adj.* [SE *jig*, to move around] **1** [1920s+] (*US*) crazy, nervous, fidgety. **2** [1990s+] (*orig. US black*) sexually excited or exciting. **3** [1990s+] (*US black*) acting in a sophisticated, moneyed manner and looking the part.

jiggy-jig *n.* [var. JIG-A-JIG *n.* (1); *DSUE* quotes 'a Hindi-English dictionary', which defines it as an 'exclamation of delight used by Indian women during sexual intercourse'] [19C–1930s] (*Anglo-Ind.*) sexual intercourse.

jig-jagging *n.* [SE *jig* v.] [1900s–20s] (*US black*) dancing with absolute abandonment.

jig-jig *n. see* JIG-A-JIG *n.*

jig-lamps *n. see* GIG-LAMPS *n.*

jiglets *n.* [ety. unknown; ? fig. use of SE, *giblets*, i.e. generic use of one's innards as one's whole being] [late 19C–1910s] (*US*) oneself, as in *his jiglets*.

jigs *n.*

(IN PHRASES)

❑ **in the jigs** *adj.* (*also* **in the blue jigs**) [JIGGERED *adj.*[1]] **1** [1940s+] very drunk. **2** [1950s+] very frightened. ❑ **jigs on the green** *n. see* WIGS ON THE GREEN *under* WIG *n.*[2].

jigs! *excl.* [abbr. JIGGER! *excl.* (2)] [1920s–40s] (*US*) a cry of warning.

jig-swiggered *adj.*

(IN EXCLAMATIONS)

❑ **I'll be jig-swiggered!** *see* *I'LL BE JIGGERED!* *under* JIGGERED *adj.*[1].

ji-jibe *n. see* JIB-JIBE *n.*

jildi *n.* (*also* **jildy, juldee**) [Hind. *jaldi*, quickness] [late 19C+] haste, speed; esp. in phrs. *on the jildi*, in a hurry, quickly; *move a jildi*, hurry up.

jildi *adj.* (*also* **jildy**) [JILDI *n.*] [late 19C+] quick, speedy.

jildi *v.* (*also* **jildy, juldee, juldi**) [JILDI *n.*] [late 19C+] to move fast, to hurry, to smarten up; often as excl. *jildi!* hurry up!

jildi *adv.* (*also* **jeldi, jeldy, jildy**) [JILDI *n.*] [late 19C+] quickly.

jill *n.* (*also* **gill, Gillian**) [late 15C+] (*US*) a young woman.

jillaroo *n.* [play on JACKAROO *n.*] [1940s+] (*Aus.*) **1** a white woman newly arrived in Australia, a white woman living in the bush. **2** a land girl.

jill-flirt *n. see* GILL-FLIRT *n.*

jillion *n.* [on model of SE *million, trillion*] [1940s+] (*orig. US*) an indefinite, extremely large number; thus *jillionaire*, an extremely wealthy person.

jill (off) *v.* ['feminized' version of JACK OFF *v.*[1] (1)] [1980s+] (*orig. US gay*) of a woman, to masturbate; thus *jilling*, female masturbation.

jills *n.* [Shelta] [mid-19C–1900s] the self, used with possessive pron., e.g. *my jills*, I; *his jills*, he.

jilly *adj.* [1960s] (*Aus.*) a euph. for BLOODY *adj.* (1).

jilopi *n. see* JALOPY *n.*

jilt *n.*[1] (*also* **gilt**) [SE *jilt*, 'a woman who gives her lover hopes, and deceives him' (Johnson); ult. *gillet/jillet*, a loose or wanton woman] [early 17C–19C] a prostitute, esp. one who tricks her client.

jilt *n.*[2] [GILT *n.*[2] (1)] **1** [mid-18C] a thief who robs travellers staying in taverns or alehouses. **2** [mid-19C–1900s] a crowbar, housebreaking tools in general.

jilt *v.* [JILT *n.*[2]] [mid-19C–1900s] (*orig. US*) to break into a house or to enter a building under false pretences – both for the purpose of theft.

jilter *n.* [JILT *v.*] [mid-19C+] (*orig. US*) a sneak thief.

jil to woodrus *v.* [? Scot. *woodrum*, a state of confusion] [1930s] to go crazy, to lose control.

Jim *n.* **1** [late 19C+] (*US, esp. black*) a title for a fellow man (usu. black), usu. used as shorthand for making a gesture of friendship. **2** [late 19C+] (*S.Afr.*) a derog. all-purpose generic name for black men. **3** [1910s] (*Aus.*) generic for the average Australian.

jim *n.*[1] [SE *gem* or a play on TOM *n.*[8] (1)] [19C+] jewellery, diamonds.

jim *n.*[2] [play on JOHN *n.*[2] (5)] [1900s] (*US campus*) a urinal, also as *v.*, to urinate.

jim *n.*[3] [? abbr. JIMMY O'GOB(LIN) *n.*] **1** [1900s–20s] (*Aus.*) £1; thus *half jim*, ten shillings. **2** [1930s] money.

jim *n.*[4] [abbr. *Jim Crow* and thus CROW *adj.*] [1910s] (*US Und.*) something second-rate, worthless.

jim *n.*[5] [generic use of proper name; based on JOHN *n.*[2] (1c)] [1970s+] a man who likes to watch prostitutes at work (or just a 'dirty old man' who frequents 'adult' bookshops, stripshows etc) but offers no actual sexual threat.

jim *n.*[6] *see* JIMBROWSKY *n.*

jim *v. see* JIM (UP) *v.*

jim *adv.* [1920s] (*US black/W.I.*) an intensifier; completely.

jim and jack *n.* [rhy. sl.] [1960s] the back.

jim and joe *n.* [ety. unknown; there seems to be no link to the US presidents some of whose heads adorn dollar bills of various denominations; (James Madison appears in PORTRAIT OF MADISON *n.* but the denomination is too large)] [1900s] (*US*) a dollar.

jim britts *n. see* JIMMY BRITTS *n.*

jim brown *n.* [rhy. sl.] [late 19C+] town, the West End of London; or any city.

jimbrowsky *n.* (*also* **jim, jim browski, jimbrowski**) [? JIMMY *n.*[4] (1)] [1980s+] (*US black*) the penis.

jim crack *n.* [euph.] [mid-19C+] (*US*) an act of defecation.

jimcrack *n.* [GIMCRACK *n.* (1)] [1900s–50s] (*US*) **1** a fop, an affectedly showy person. **2** a fool. **3** a lie.

jimcracker *n.* (*also* **jimcrack, jimcracky**) [GIMCRACK *n.* (1)] [mid-19C–1970s] (*US*) a remarkable person or thing.

Jim Crow *n.* (*also* **John Crow**) [early 19C Kentucky plantation song with the chorus 'Jump *Jim Crow*' and the 'black face' entertainer Thomas Dartmouth Rice (1808–60), who first performed it in Louisville in 1828; its popularity in the UK followed Rice's appearance at the Adelphi theatre in 1836, in a 'farcical Burletta' entitled 'A Flight to America, or, Twelve Hours in New York'; for details see Hindley (1878) pp. 267ff.; note also Schele De Vere (1872): 'We have no ballad and no song that can be called American. The nearest approach [...] was the dramatic song *Jim Crow*, brought out about the year 1835 by an enthusiastic Yankee on the boards of a theatre in New York; it created a sensation, for it was new in form and conception, and no doubt rendered still more attractive by the strange guise in which it was presented. It was quickly followed by several other songs of the same kind, such as *Zip Coon*, *Longtailed Blue*, *Ole Virginnynebber tire*, *Settin' on a Rail*, etc [...] For a time this African inroad drove nearly every other song from the publisher's store and the drawing-room'] **1** [early 19C+] a patronizing if not actively derog. generic term for a black person. **2** [mid-19C] (*Irish*) a negro. **3** [mid-19C+] (*also* **Jim Crowism**) white racist discrimination against blacks and the *Jim Crow* laws that embody it; usu. attrib., as JIM CROW *adj.* (4). **4** [late 19C] (*US*) a small touring theatrical company.

(IN PHRASES)

❑ **jump Jim Crow** *v.* **1** [mid-19C] to reverse one's political allegiance. **2** [mid-19C–1930s] to become agitated, to 'hop around', thus as adj.

Jim Crow *adj.* (*also* **James Crow**) [JIM CROW *n.*] **1** [mid-19C] (*US*) a derog. adj. describing a black person. **2** [mid-19C–1960s] small-time, incompetent, fraudulent. **3** [mid-19C+] (*US*) (*also* **jim-crowed**) of or for use by blacks only, segregated, eg *Jim Crow car*. **4** [mid-19C+] (*US*) describing legislation that is racially prejudiced against blacks; thus racist in general.

Jim Crow *v.* [JIM CROW *n.* (3)] [20C+] (*US black*) to treat a black person in a patronizing and authoritative manner, to discriminate against black people.

Jim Crow *adv.* [1940s] (*US*) in a segregated manner.

jim crow *n.*[1] [JIM CROW *n.* (1)] **1** [mid-19C] a soft felt hat with broad brim and low crown. **2** [late 19C–1900s] (*US black*) a small card, resembling a currycomb, used by negroes in rural areas.

jim crow *n.*[2] (*also* **james crow**) [rhy. sl. = *saltimbanco*, a street clown] [mid–late 19C] a street clown (with no racial inference); a black minstrel.

jim-crowed *adj. see* JIM CROW *adj.* (3).

Jim Crowism *n. see* JIM CROW *n.* (3).

jim dandy *n.* [? 1844 song 'Dandy Jim ob Caroline'. The song, apparently written by a black rather than white author, trumpets the admirable qualities of this especially 'dandy nigger'. Alternatively, dial. *gim/jim*, neat, spruce + DANDY *adj.*; *gim* ult. ? Scot. *jimp*, slender, delicate, graceful. Cohen (1989) suggests that the popularization of the term may have come through its use in baseball c.1890s] [late 19C+] (*US*) an excellent person or thing.

jim-dandy *adj.* [JIM DANDY *n.*] [late 19C+] (*US*) of a thing or situation, excellent, satisfactory; of a person, first-rate, admirable.

jim fish *n.* [? the character *Jim Fish*, who was used in miners' training films in the 1940s as an example of what not to do] [1930s+] (*S.Afr.*) a derog. term of address to a black man.

Jim Gerald *n.* [rhy. sl.] [20C+] (*Aus.*) *The Herald* newspaper.

jim-hickey *n.* [? JIM DANDY *n.* + DOHICKEY *n.*[1] (1)] **1** [late 19C–1900s] an excellent or admirable person or thing. **2** [1900s] as the equivalent of *HELL OF A, A under* HELL *n.*

Jim Hill *n.* [? anecdotal] [1930s] (*US tramp*) a freight wagon.

jiminetty! *excl.* [var. on JIMINY! *excl.*] [20C+] (*US*) used in mild oaths as a euph. for JESUS! *excl.*

jiminy! *excl.* (*also* **jeeminee! jiminy! jimmini! jimmy!**) [late 17C+] a euph. for *Jesus!* and used as such in oaths.

(IN EXCLAMATIONS)

❑ **by jiminy!** (*also* **by Jim! by Jimmy!**) [early 19C+] a mild oath, euph. for *by Jesus!*

jiminy cricket *n.* [rhy. sl.] [1980s] (*Aus.*) a ticket.

jiminy cricket! *excl.* (*also* **geemany crimany! geeminy criminy! jiminy crickets! ...crikey! ...criminy! ...cripes! ... whiz! jimmety whiskers! jimminny crimminny! jimminy Christmas! ...froth!**) [? Ger. interj. *jemine*, oh dear!, gracious! = Lat. Jesu domine; *cricket* = euph. for Christ] [mid-19C+] (*orig. US*) a euph. for JESUS! *excl.*

jim-jam *n.* [ety. unknown, but of similar pattern to FLIM-FLAM *n.*; WHIM-WHAM *n.*] **1** [mid-16C–late 19C] a fanciful or trivial article, a knick-knack. **2** [1990s+] (*Aus.*) nonsense, rubbish.

jimjam *adv.* [1960s] (*US black*) jumpily.

jimjammed *adj.*

(IN EXCLAMATIONS)

❑ **I'll be jimjammed!** *see I'LL BE JIGGERED! under* JIGGERED *adj.*[1].

jim-jams *n.* (*also* **jim-jims**) [ety. unknown] **1** [mid-19C–1960s] (*orig. US*) delirium tremens, a hangover. **2** [late 19C–1920s] odd manners, personal peculiarities. **3** [late 19C+] 'nerves', apprehension, a fit of depression.

jimkwim *n. see* DR JIM *n.*

jim mace *n. see* JEM MACE *n.*

jimmety whiskers! *excl. see* JIMINY CRICKET! *excl.*

jimmey *n. see* JIMMY *n.*[2].

jimmied up *adj.* [1900s] (*US*) in a mess, in chaos.

Jimmie Howe *n. see* JACKIE HOWE *n.*

jimmies *n.*[1] [abbr. JIM-JAMS *n.*] **1** [20C+] a sense of fear, apprehension, a fit of depression. **2** [1900s–30s] delirium tremens, a hangover.

jimmies *n.*[2] *see* JIMMY BRITTS *n.*

Jimmie Valentine *n.* [the anti-hero of an O. Henry short story 'Jimmie Valentine' (1910)] [1920s] (*US Und.*) a safe-cracker.

jimminny crimminny!/jimminy Christmas!/jimminy froth! *excl. see* JIMINY CRICKET! *excl.*

jimmison *n. see* JEMSON *n.*

jimmiwoodser *n. see* JIMMY WOODSER *n.*

jimmunt *n. see* DR JIM *n.*

Jimmy *n.* [generic use of the name] [20C+] (*mainly Scot.*) used as a term of address to a person whose actual name one does not know.

jimmy *n.*[1] [abbr. JEMMY O'GOBLIN *n.*; note ety. at JACOBUS *n.*] **1** [mid-19C–1930s] a guinea. **2** [late 19C–1910s] a sovereign (£1.00).

jimmy *n.*[2] (*also* **jimmey**) [var. on JEMMY *n.*[3] (1)] [mid-19C+] (*mainly US Und.*) a short house-breaker's crowbar; also attrib.

jimmy *n.*[3] [1940s+] (*US*) a vehicle manufactured by the General Motors Corporation.

jimmy *n.*[4] [? JIMMY *v.*[1] (4)] **1** [1980s+] the penis. **2** [1990s+] (*US black/campus*) a condom.

(IN COMPOUNDS)

❑ **jimmy cap** *n.* (*also* **gym hat, jimmy hat**) [1980s+] (*US black*) a condom. ❑ **jimmy protector** *n.* [1980s+] (*US black*) a condom. ❑ **jimmy wine** *n.* [1990s+] semen.

(IN PHRASES)

❑ **sooty jimmy** *n.* [SE *sooty* + JIMMY *n.*[4] (1)] [1980s+] (*US black*) a black penis.

jimmy *n.*[5] **1** *see* JEMMY *n.*[1]. **2** *see* JIMMY GRANT *n.* **3** *see* JIMMY HIX *n.* **4** *see* JIMMY (RIDDLE) *n.*

jimmy *adj.* [? JEMMY *adj.*[1] (2); 16C SE *jump*, exact, precise, coinciding; 1750 *OED* 'a jemmy fellow'] **1** [mid-19C–1920s] (*US*) exact, fit, stylish, fashionable. **2** *see* JEMMY *adj.*[2].

jimmy *v.*[1] [JIMMY *n.*[2]] **1** [late 19C+] (*US Und.*) to break into, using a small crowbar. **2** [1900s–50s] to gain access to something whether mental or physical, but without violence, to 'wriggle' into or out of something. **3** [1910s–50s] (*US Und.*) to injure, wound or spoil. **4** [1910s–60s] (*US*) to copulate. **5** [1920s–30s] (*US*) to steal from, to extract from someone, to cajole or cheat. **6** [1970s+] to get in without paying.

jimmy *v.*[2] [JIMMY (RIDDLE) *n.*] [1930s+] to urinate.

Jimmy Boyle *n.* [rhy. sl.; ult. ex-prisoner and writer *Jimmy Boyle* (b.1940)] [2000s] (*drugs*) kitchen foil, as used for smoking heroin or to CHASE THE DRAGON *v.*

Jimmy Britts *n.* (*also* **Jim Britts, jimmies**) [rhy. sl. = SHITS, THE *n.*; ult. proper name of *Jimmy Britt* (1879–1940), a US-born boxer who toured Australia during WW1] [1940s+] (*orig. Aus.*) **1** diarrhoea. **2** fig. nerves, fears.

(IN PHRASES)

❑ **have the Britts (up)** *v.* [1940s] (*Aus.*) to be in a nervous state.

jimmy dancer *n.* [rhy. sl.] [20C+] (*Aus.*) cancer.

jimmy dog *n.* [ety. unknown] **1** [20C+] (*Irish juv.*) the penis. **2** [1980s+] (*US campus*) a marijuana cigarette.

jimmy gall *n. see* GINNY GALL *n.*

jimmy gee! *excl. see* JIMMY JEE! *excl.*

jimmy grant *n.* (*also* **jimmy, jimmy grunt**) [rhy. sl.] [mid-19C–1960s] (*Aus./N.Z./S.Afr.*) an immigrant.

jimmy-heel *n.* [1920s] (*US*) a worthless, despicable person.

jimmy hills *n.* [rhy. sl.; ult. UK TV soccer pundit *Jimmy Hill* (b. 1928)] [20C+] pills.

jimmy hix *n.* (*also* **jimmy, jimmy hicks, sister hicks**) [rhy. sl.] **1** [late 19C+] (*US gambling*) the point of 6 in craps dice; a six in poker. **2** [1950s+] (*UK Und.*) an injection of narcotics [= FIX *n.*[3] (1)].

jimmy hope *n.* [rhy. sl.] [1910s+] (*US prison*) soap.

Jimmy Howe *n. see* JACKIE HOWE *n.*

Jimmy Jee! *excl.* (*also* **Jimmy Gee! Jimmy Jesus!**) [1900s–40s] (*Aus.*) a mild excl.; a euph. for JESUS! *excl.*

jimmy lee *n.* [rhy. sl.] [20C+] (*Aus.*) tea.

Jimmy Logie *n.* [rhy. sl. = BOGEY *n.*[3] (1); ult. soccer star *Jimmy Logie* (1919–1984), who played for Arsenal 1939-55] [1950s+] a piece of nasal mucus.

jimmy low *n.* [? a local New South Wales 'character'] [late 19C] (*Aus.*) a timber-tree, *eucalyptus resinefera*.

jimmy mason *n.* [rhy. sl.; ult. *James Mason*, Hollywood film star (1909–1984)] [20C+] a basin.

Jimmy Nail *adj.* [rhy. sl.; ult. UK actor and singer *Jimmy Nail* (b.1954)] [1990s+] stale.

Jimmy O'Gob(lin) *n. see* JEMMY O'GOBLIN *n.*

Jimmy Prescott *n. see* CHARLIE PRESCOTT *n.* (1).

jimmy raw *n. see* JACKY RAW *n.*

jimmy (riddle) *n.* (*also* **jenny riddle, jerry riddle, J.R.**) [rhy. sl.; *Jimmy Riddle* = PIDDLE *n.*] [1930s+] an act of urination; and as a request to use the lavatory.

jimmy rollocks *n. see* TOMMY ROLLOCKS *n.*

jimmy rounds *n.* [Fr. *je me rends*, the cry supposedly offered by hapless French sailors when faced with the might of the RN; however the *Sporting Mag.* (Oct. 1800) suggests an infantry encounter in Holland] [early 19C–1900s] Frenchmen.

Jimmy Sangster *n.* [rhy. sl.] [1980s] (*Aus.*) a gangster.

jimmy skinner *n.* (*also* **jim skinner, joe skinner, johnny skinner, ned skinner**) [rhy. sl.] [late 19C+] dinner.

jimmy-swing *n.* [note *Captain Swing* 'the Kent rick-burner' who terrorized farmers *c.*1830 in an attempt to put off the spread of farm machinery that was seen as a threat to farm-workers' livelihoods] [1940s+] (*W.I.*) a poor, common young man.

Jimmy Wilde *n.* [rhy. sl.; ult. world flyweight champion *Jimmy Wilde* (1892–1969)] [20C+] *mild* beer.

Jimmy Woodser *n.* (*also* **Jimmiwoodser, Jimmy Woods, Johnny Woods, Johnny Woodser**) [a character in a poem by B.H.T. Boake, publ. in *The Bulletin* (7 May 1892): 'At the thought the hearts beats quicker/Than an old Bohemian's should ... /I'll go and have a liquor/With the genial "Jimmy Wood".' Poss. a genuine person, a loner named Jim Woods] (*Aus./N.Z.*) **1** [late 19C+] anyone who drinks alone, a drink that is taken by oneself; thus *jimmy woodsing*, drinking by oneself; similarly one of a group who pays only for his own drink. **2** [1900s–10s] a drink that one buys for oneself, despite being in company. **3** [1900s–50s] a solitary person, an orphan.

Jimmy Woodser *v.* [JIMMY WOODSER *n.* (1)] [1900s–60s] (*Aus.*) to drink by oneself.

Jimmy Young *n.* [rhy. sl.; ult. the singer turned UK radio personality *Jimmy Young* (b. 1923)] [1990s+] **1** a bribe [= BUNG *n.*[1] (4)]. **2** the tongue.

jimplecute *n. see* JIMSECUTE *n.*

jimpson *n.* [1920s] (*US*) the penis.

jim-rags *n.* [dial. *jamrags*, tatters, rags] [late 19C] (*Aus.*) tiny pieces, shreds, esp. in the phr. *kick someone to/knock someone into jim-rags.*

jims *n.* [abbr. JIM-JAMS *n.*] [late 19C–1930s] (*Aus./US*) **1** delirium tremens. **2** a fit of 'nerves' or depression.

jimscreech *v.* [1980s+] (*UK black*) to con, to gain entry.

jim-screechy *adj.* [JIMSCREECH *v.*] [1990s+] (*W.I.*) underhand, deceitful.

jimsecute *n.* (*also* **jimplecute**) [? dial. *jimpsey*, neat, smart, pretty + SE *cute*] [mid–late 19C] (*US, Southern*) a sweetheart.

jim skinner *n. see* JIMMY SKINNER *n.*

Jimson *n.* [ext. JIM *n.* (1)] [1950s] (*US black*) a term of address to a man.

jimswinger *n.* (*also* **jimswigger**) [? JIM *n.*, a generic black name + the swinging of the coat's tails] [late 19C–1940s] (*US, mainly Southern black*) a tailcoat.

jim town *n.* [? *gimcrack* or JIM *n.*] [late 19C–1960s] (*US*) **1** a shanty town. **2** the poor (thus often black or Hispanic) part of a town.

jim (up) *v.* [? JIM *n.*; if so, a racist slur; cf. *A*FRICAN ENGINEERING *under* AFRICAN *adj.*] [20C+] (*US*) **1** to spoil, ruin or botch, to injure. **2** to fool around.

jim-whizzed *adj.* [fanciful; ? link to JESUS! *excl.*] [late 19C] (*US*) a euph. for DAMNED *adj.*, usu. in the phr. *I'll be jim-whizzed!*

jin *n.* [abbr. INJUN *n.*] [1940s] (*US black*) a Native American.

jinal *see under* GINAL.

jing *n.*[1] [it 'jingles' in one's pocket] [1970s+] (*US campus*) money.

jing *n.*[2]

IN EXCLAMATIONS

❑ **by jing!** *see* JINGS! *excl.*

jing-bang *n.* **1** [mid-19C–1920s] the whole lot, as in the phr. *the whole jing-bang.* **2** [1940s+] (*W.I.*) a noisy, dirty crowd. **3** [1940s+] (*W.I.*) a low-class, rough, noisy person. **4** [1940s+] (*W.I.*) a promiscuous woman.

jing-jang *n.* [echoic of the movements of sex] [1940s+] (*US gay*) **1** the penis. **2** the vagina. **3** sexual intercourse.

jingle *n.* **1** [early 19C] wit. **2** [mid-19C] (*US*) spirit, energy. **3** [late 19C–1920s] (*US*) an alcoholic drink [? the rattle of ice-cubes in one's glass]. **4** [20C+] (*orig. Aus.*) money [its noise in one's pocket]. **5** [1910s] a light, pleasant state of intoxication. **6** [1940s+] (*US*) a telephone call.

jingle *adj. see* JINGLE-BRAINED *adj.* (2).

jingle *v.* [JINGLE *n.*] **1** [1940s] (*US*) to telephone. **2** [1990s+] to sell.

jingleberry *n.* [var. on DINGLEBERRY *n.* (1)] **1** [1930s] (*US*) in pl., a wealthy person. **2** [1930s–50s] (*US*) a testicle.

jingleboy *n. see* GINGLEBOY *n.*

jingle-brained *adj.* [JINGLE-BRAINS *n.*] **1** [1920s] (*US*) foolish. **2** [1930s+] (*also* **jingle**) intoxicated.

jingle-brains *n.* (*also* **jingle-brain**) [late 17C–early 19C] a fool, a dunce.

jingled *adj.* [JINGLE *n.* (3)] [1900s–30s] (*US*) drunk.

jingle-jangle *n.* [late 17C; 1950s] (*later use Irish*) an argument; unpleasantness.

jingler *n.* (*also* **gingler**) [SE *jingle*] **1** [17C–early 19C] a crooked horse-dealer [the noise of the harness, but perhaps more f. a further SE meaning, to play with words, verbal facility being the stock-in-trade of the horse-trader]. **2** [late 19C–1920s] (*US*) usu. pl., money, coins [note also GINGLEBOY *n.*].

jingling johnny *n.* **1** [late 19C] an Indian cart and horse. **2** [late 19C–1940s] (*Aus./N.Z.*) hand shears [the clicking noise of the shears]. **3** [late 19C–1940s] (*Aus./N.Z.*) a hand-shearer. **4** [20C+] the musical instrument known as a Chinese pavilion or Chinese crescent [it 'consists of a pole, with several transverse brass plates of some crescent or fantastic form, and generally terminating at top with a conical pavilion or hat. On all these parts a number of very small bells are hung which the performer causes to jingle' (*Grove's Dict. of Music*). A later Aus. version, which uses bottle tops tacked loosely onto an old broomstick, is the *lagerphone*].

jingo *n.* [play on JOINT *n.* (5c)] [1980s+] (*drugs*) a cannabis cigarette.

jingo! *excl.* (*also* **by Gingo! by jingo! by jingoes!**) [presumably a euph. for JESUS! *excl.*, but ? *St Gingoulph* (Hotten, 1867, Schele de Vere 1872); Ribton-Turner, *A History of Vagrants* (1887), suggests a Romani root via Basque *Jinkoa*, God. (lit. 'He who is on high'), adopted by the gypsies of northern Spain and southern France; it may also have been imported by soldiers from those areas who served in Edward I's conquest of Wales in 1284] [late 17C+] euph. for *by Jesus!* also intensified as *by the living jingo!*

jings! *excl.* (*also* **by jing! by jings!**) [euph. for JESUS! *excl.*] [late 18C+] (*orig. and usu. Scot.*) used as a mild oath (cf. JINKS *n.*; JINGO! *excl.*).

jink *n.*[1] [the noise of one coin hitting another] [mid-19C–1900s] money.

jink *n.*[2] [SE *jink*, to move jerkily; note dial. *jinked*, hurt in the loins or back] [1960s+] (*US black*) a disabled person, anyone seen as bizarre, unpleasant.

jink *v.* [Scot. *jink*, to dodge] [1920s+] (*Aus.*) to swindle.

jinkers *n.*

IN EXCLAMATIONS

❑ **by jinkers!** *see* BY JINKS! *under* JINKS *n.*

jink one's tin *v. see* TIN *n.* (1).

jinks *n.*

IN EXCLAMATIONS

❑ **by jinks!** (*also* **by jinkers!**) [mid-19C+] a general euph. excl. (cf. JINGS! *excl.*).

jinky *adj.* [SE *jinx*] [1950s–80s] (*US black*) difficult, problematical, unpleasant.

jinnal *see under* GINAL.

jinna rumble *n.* [ety. unknown] [1940s] (*W.I.*) makeshift crutches, made of sticks and used to help walking.

jinnit *n.* [Sp. *jinete*, a light horseman] [20C+] (*Irish*) a mule.

IN PHRASES

❑ **act the jinnit** *v.* [20C+] (*Irish*) to play the fool, to act irrationally.

jinny *n.* [the *gin* available there] [1920s–40s] (*US*) a speakeasy or unlicensed drinking place.

jinny *v. see* JENNY *v.*[2].

jinny (-ass/-wing) *adj. see* JENNY *adj.*

jintoe *n. see* GENTOO *n.*

jip *see also under* GYP.

jip *n.*[1] [? US sporting jargon *gyp*, a bitch (dog); ult. abbr. *gypsy*, used as a popular dog's name] [mid-19C–1940s] (*US*) a derog. term for a woman, esp. a black woman.

jip *n.*[2] [? GIVE GYP *under* GYP *n.*[2]] [1940s+] (*Aus.*) energy, 'pep'.

jip *n.*[3] [2000s] (*Irish*) semen.

jip *adj.* (*also* **jip-job**) [dial. *jip*, to trick, to cheat] [20C+] (*Ulster*) badly done, poorly produced, botched.

jip *v. see* GYP *v.*

jippo *n. see* GYPO *n.*

jippogat *n.* [? GYPO *n.* (1) + GAT *n.*[2]] [2000s] (*S.Afr.*) a malingerer.

jirk-nod *n. see* YERKNOD *n.*

Jis *n.*

IN EXCLAMATIONS

❑ **by Jis!** (*also* **by Gis! by Gys!**) [16C–17C] a mild oath, a euph. for 'by Jesus!'.

jis *v. see* JIZ *v.*

jislaaik! *excl.* [? *Jesus*; pron. 'yis-like'] [1950s+] (*S.Afr.*) a general excl., the meaning of which varies as to context and the speaker's mood, usu. surprise, but also annoyance, grievance, dismay.

jism *n.* (*also* **chism, gism, gissum, gizm, gizzem, gizzum, gyzm, jiss, jissom, jiz, jizz, jizzum**) [ety. unknown; note northeast US dial. *jasm*, energy] **1** [mid-19C+] (*orig. US*) energy, spirit, thus *jizzless*, apathetic. **2** [late 19C+] (*orig. US*) semen. **3** [1930s–40s] (*US, mainly Southern*) gravy. **4** [1990s+] (*US*) an ejaculation, lit. and fig. an emission.

IN COMPOUNDS

❑ **jizzbag** *n.* (*also* **jizzbucket**) [1980s+] **1** a contraceptive sheath. **2** a general term of abuse, also as term of address. ❑ **jizzbags** *n.* [SE *bag*/BAG *n.*[1] (1)] [1990s+] the testicles. ❑ **jizzrag** *n.* (*also* **jiz rag**) [1990s+] a handkerchief or similar piece of material into which one masturbates. ❑ **jizz rocket** *n.* [2000s] (*US*) the penis. ❑ **jizzwater** *n.* [2000s] semen.

IN PHRASES

❑ **lick someone's jizz** *v.* [1980s+] (*US*) to be impressed.

jiss *v. see* JIZ *v.*

jit *n.*[1] [1910s] (*Aus.*) a cigarette.

jit *n.*[2] [JITNEY *n.* (1)] **1** [1910s+] (*US*) a nickel, a 5-cent coin. **2** [1930s–40s] (*US*) a black person. **3** [1990s+] (*US black*) a derog. term for a young person, a foolish person.

jit *n.*[3] [? var. on JISM *n.* (2); or the SE *jet* of ejaculated semen] [1970s] (*US campus*) semen.

IN COMPOUNDS

❑ **jitbag** *n.* [SE *bag*/-BAG *sfx*] [1990s+] **1** a condom. **2** a general term of abuse.

jit *n.*[4] *see* JITTERBUG *n.* (3).

jitney *n.* (*also* **gitney**) [the five-cent fare charges on the original *jitney* omnibuses. *DARE* quotes a source claiming *jitney* to be 'Jewish slang', but there is no evidence] **1** [20C+] (*US*) a 5-cent piece, a nickel. **2** [1910s+] (*US*) a small, cheap car or vehicle. **3** [1910s+] (*US*) (*also* **jitney bus**) a bus charging a fixed fare. **4** [1940s–70s] (*US black*) a cab.

IN COMPOUNDS

❑ **jitney bus** *n. see* sense 3 above. ❑ **jitney girl** *n.* [1950s–60s] (*US*) a prostitute who drives around in her own car soliciting customers.

jitney *adj.* [JITNEY *n.*] [1910s+] anything cheap, improvised or ramshackle; thus *jitney dance*, a pay-per-dance or 'taxi-dance' dancehall.

jitney *v.* [JITNEY *n.*] [1910s+] (*US*) to travel by bus or small vehicle.

jits *n.* [abbr. of JITTERS, THE *n.*] [1930s+] (*US*) anxiety, nervousness.

jitter *n.* (*also* **gitter**) [? JITTERBUG *n.* or the movement of dancing to such bands] [1980s+] (*UK teen*) a fan of 'heavy metal' music.

jitter box *n.* [1940s] (*US*) a guitar.

jitterbug *n.* [JITTERS, THE *n.* + BUG *n.*[4] (3d); app. coined 1934 by US band leader Cab Calloway (1907–94); *jitterbug*, the dance and a dancer is SE] **1** [1930s–60s] (*orig. US*) a nervous person. **2** [1930s+] a fan of swing music. **3** [1940s+] (*US*) (*also* **jit**) an adolescent who is naïve or foolish. **4** [1960s+] (*US black*) a voluble, indiscreet person, a chatterer. **5** [1960s+] (*US black*) a youth who lives a street life but is not invariably a criminal.

jitterbug *v.* [JITTERBUG *n.*] **1** [1940s–70s] (*US*) to fool around. **2** [1940s–70s] (*US black*) to saunter, to swagger. **3** [1950s–70s] (*US*) (*also* **jitterhop**) to participate in gang fighting.

jitterbugged *adj.*

IN EXCLAMATIONS

❑ **I'll be jitterbugged!** [1930s] (*US black*) an excl. of surprise.

jitterdoll *n.* (*also* **jitterjane**) [for ety. *see* JITTERBUG *n.*] [1940s] (*US black*) a woman who loves to dance.

jitter joint *n.* [JITTERBUG *n.* (2) + JOINT *n.* (3b)] [1940s–50s] (*US*) a cheap dancehall.

jitters, the *n.* [supposedly f. the Spoonerism 'bin and *jitters*' for 'gin and bitters' and orig. used of one who has drunk too much of that mixture] **1** [1920s+] extreme nervousness, a state of emotional and often physical tension, agitation. **2** [1930s–40s] (*US*) a hangover, delirium tremens.

jittery *n.* [JITTERY *adj.*] [1950s] a nervous, unstable person.

jittery *adj.* [JITTERS, THE *n.*] [1930s+] nervous, tense, 'on edge'.

jive *n.*[1] [SE *jibe*, to scoff, to sneer] **1** [1920s–70s] (*US black*) sexual intercourse, also a sex partner. **2** [1920s+] (*orig. US black*) nonsense, rubbish, insincere, deceitful or pretentious talk [note Burley, *Original Handbook of Harlem Jive* (1944): 'Jive is a distortion of that staid, old, respectable English word "jibe" — jibber — speak fast and inarticulately, chatter [...] Jibberish — unintelligible speech, meaningless sounds, jargon, blundering or ungrammatical talk'; he dates it to Chicago, 1921; Mezzrow & Wolfe, *Really the Blues* (1946): 'The word *jive* probably comes from the old English word *jibe*, out of which came the words *jibberish* and *gibberish*, describing sound without meaning, speech that isn't intelligible'; Mezzrow further suggests, quoting black journalist Earl Conrad, that 'Jive talk may have been originally a kind of "pig Latin" that the slaves talked with each other, a code – when they were in the presence of whites'. Note that *jive*, swing music is SE]. **3** [1930s+] (*US*) Afro-American slang, esp. as coined in Harlem and thence used by jazz musicians. **4** [1930s+] (*US*) any thing, stuff, goings-on, situation. **5** in drug uses. (**a**) [1930s+] marijuana. (**b**) [1950s+] (*drugs*) heroin. (**c**) [1990s+] recreational drugs in general; also attrib. **6** [1960s–70s] a second-rate person. **7** [1960s–70s] one's personality or material possessions. **8** [1970s] a proposition, a suggestion.

IN COMPOUNDS

❑ **jive artist** *n.* [-ARTIST *sfx*] [1930s] (*orig. US black*) a pretentious person. ❑ **jive kit** *n.* [1950s] (*US drugs*) the equipment – needle, spoon, eye-dropper, cotton – used for taking narcotics. ❑ **jive stick** *n.* [STICK *n.* (6d)] [1950s+] (*drugs*) a marijuana cigarette. ❑ **jive talk** *see* separate entries.

IN PHRASES

❑ **collar the jive** *v.* [1930s+] (*US black*) to understand every aspect of a situation. ❑ **knock the jive out of** *v.* [1940s] (*US black*) to play the piano. ❑ **no jive** (*also* **no jibe**) [1930s+] (*US*) honestly, no fooling; also attrib. ❑ **shoot the jive** *v.* [1960s] (*US*) to gossip, talk inconsequentially. ❑ **what's your jive?** *see* WHAT'S YOUR TALE? *under* TALE *n.*[1].

jive *n.*[2] [abbr. JIVE-ASS *n.*[1] but note the earlier *JIVE ARTIST under* JIVE *n.*[1]] [1950s+] (*US black*) **1** a deceitful, arrogant or pretentious person. **2** an unsophisticated person.

jive *adj.* [JIVE *n.*[1] (2)] (*orig. US black*) **1** [1940s+] a generally negative term, applicable to a range of dubious actions, fake, phoney, deceitful, unappealing, hypocritical, insincere etc. **2** [1960s+] unimportant, trivial, foolish.

(DERIVATIVES)

❑ **jivey** *adj.* **1** [1940s+] (*US*) redolent of jive music, lively, aware [SE *jive*, swing music]. **2** [1960s+] (*US*) pretentious, insincere, phoney, hypocritical etc [fig. use of sense 1].

(IN COMPOUNDS)

❑ **jive hand** *n.* [SE *hand*, the cards that one has been dealt] [1970s+] (*US black*) an undesirable situation that puts one person at an unfair disadvantage, one is dealt 'a bad hand'. ❑ **jive nigger** *n. see* JIVE-ASS *n.*[1]. ❑ **jive roller** *n. see* ROLLER *n.* (7). ❑ **jivetime** *adj.* [JIVE *n.*[1] (2) + ? pun on the radio daypart *drivetime*] [1960s+] (*US black*) insincere, dishonest, stupid. ❑ **jive turkey** *n.* [TURKEY *n.*[1] (4a)] [1970s+] (*US black*) an insincere, deceitful, dishonest person.

jive *v.*[1] [JIVE *n.*[1]; Burley, *Original Handbook of Harlem Jive* (1944), suggests that the original use of *jiving* was as a synon. for the DOZENS *n.*] (*orig. US black*) **1** [1920s+] to engage in sexual intercourse. **2** [1920s+] (*also* **jive up**) to talk nonsense, to deceive, trick or flatter by apparently empty chatter; thus *jive about with*, *give some jive*, to play with, to mess around. **3** [1930s+] to play or dance to jive music, to have a good time. **4** [1930s+] to tease, to make fun of. **5** [1940s–70s] to converse, to talk. **6** [1960s–70s] to idle, to loaf about. **7** [1960s+] to saunter, to swagger, to dodge.

(IN PHRASES)

❑ **high-jive** *v.* (*also* **high-gyve**) [1930s+] (*US*) to tease, to provoke. ❑ **jive and juke** *v.* [JUKE *v.*[3]] [1970s+] (*US campus*) to have a very good time. ❑ **jive around** *v.* **1** [1930s+] to tease, to make fun of, to fool around. **2** [1960s+] to tell lies, to deceive. ❑ **jive (someone) out of** *v.* [1960s] to deceive, to trick, to cheat.

SE in slang uses

(IN COMPOUNDS)

❑ **jive bomber** *n.* [play on SE *jive*, to dance/*dive-bomber*] [1940s] (*US teen*) a good dancer.

jive *v.*[2] [SE *jibe*] [1940s+] to fit in, to make sense, to agree, esp. in negative uses, e.g. *that don't jive*, that doesn't make sense.

jive-ass *n.*[1] (*also* **jive nigger**) [JIVE-ASS *adj.* (1)] [1950s+] (*orig. US black*) a deceitful, arrogant or pretentious person.

jive-ass *n.*[2] [JIVE *v.*[1] (3) + -ASS *sfx*] [1960s+] (*US*) one who loves fun or excitement.

jive-ass *adj.* [JIVE *n.*[1] (2) + -ASS *sfx*] (*orig. US black*) **1** [1950s+] (*also* **jive-end**) deceitful, pretentious, arrogant, insincere. **2** [1960s+] (*also* **jiving-assed**) a general derog. epithet.

jive-ass *v.* [JIVE-ASS *adj.* (1)] [1960s+] (*orig. US black*) to talk nonsense, to swagger, to boast.

jiver *n.* [JIVE *v.*[1] (2)] **1** [1920s–60s] (*US black*) a trickster, a deceiver, a flatterer, an insincere person. **2** [1940s–50s] (*also* **jivester**) a jazz fan. **3** [1970s] a rock musician.

jive talk *n.* [JIVE *n.*[1] (3)] [1940s+] (*orig. US black*) slang-talking.

jive-talk *v.* [JIVE TALK *n.*] [1960s+] (*orig. US black*) to talk slang.

jive up *v. see* JIVE *v.*[1] (2).

jiz *n.* and combs. *see under* JISM *n.*

jiz *v.* (*also* **jis, jiss, jizz, jizz up**) [JISM *n.*] [1970s+] (*orig. US*) to ejaculate, thus *jizzed out*, sexually exhausted.

(DERIVATIVES)

❑ **jizzer** *n.* [2000s] an ejaculator.

jizz *n.* and combs. *see under* JISM *n.*

jizzle-gaffers *n.* [mid-19C] (*UK Und.*) a burglar's tools.

jizzum *n. see* JISM *n.*

jizz up *v. see* JIZ *v.*

j.k. *phr.* [abbr.] [1980s+] *just kidding.*

j.o. *n.* [abbr. JERK-OFF *n.*/JACK OFF *v.*[1] (1)] [1970s+] **1** an act of masturbation. **2** a general term of abuse.

j.o. *v.* (*also* **jay-o**) [abbr. JERK OFF *v.* (1)/JACK OFF *v.*[1] (1)] [1950s+] in sex industry, to masturbate.

jo *n. see* JOE MAXI *n.*

jo *v.* [? abbr. SE *joke*] **1** [early 19C] (*US*) to spoil. **2** [1930s] (*US*) to be exhausted. **3** [1980s] (*US gambling*) to rig a game.

joan *n.* [the commonness of the proper name] [16C–1930s] a homely woman.

joanie *n.* [? the character *Joanie* in the US sitcom *Happy Days*, set in late 1950s and early 1960s; note JOAN *n.*] [1980s+] (*US teen*) an out-of-date, unfashionable young woman.

joaning *n.* (*also* **joning**) [ety. unknown, but note dial. *Joan Blunt*, an outspoken woman] [1930s+] (*US black/Southern*) indulging in a ritualized exchange of insults.

joanna *n.* (*also* **joanner, joanno, joano, johanna**) [rhy. sl.; the single 19C citation is for *joano*; *joanna* appears in 1900] [mid-19C+] a piano.

Joan of Arc *n.*[1] [rhy. sl.; ult. *Joan of Arc* (*c*.1412–31)] **1** [20C+] a park. **2** [20C+] a lark, a situation; thus *sod this for a Joan of Arc.* **3** [1940s–50s] (*Aus.*) a shark.

Joan of Arc *n.*[2] [punning ref. to FAGGOT *n.*[1] (3)/the *faggots* with which St Joan was burned] [1950s–80s] (*camp gay*) an ostentatious, camping homosexual.

joan (on) *v. see* JONE *v.*

j.o.b. *n.*

(IN PHRASES)

❑ **get on one's j.o.b.** *see GET ON ONE'S JOB under* JOB *n.*[2]. ❑ **on one's j.o.b.** *see ON ONE'S JOB under* JOB *n.*[2].

job *n.*[1] (*also* **jobey**) [? 15C SE *job*, a small compact portion of some substance; a piece, lump (cf. THICK 'UN *n.*)] [late 17C–mid-19C] a guinea, a pound.

(IN PHRASES)

❑ **half-a-job** *n.* [late 17C–18C] half a guinea.

job *n.*[2] **1** in Und. uses. (**a**) [late 17C+] (*orig. UK Und.*) any form of criminal activity, esp. a robbery, often with a qualifying name, e.g. *the Barclays Bank job*. (**b**) [late 19C–1910s] (*US*) a trick, a hoax. (**c**) [late 19C–1910s] a jab; a blow; a physical assault. **2** [late 18C; late 19C+] a type, a variety or a procedure, e.g. *the desk was a teak-oiled job, his moustache was a bushy brown job, a boob job, a nose job*. **3** [mid-19C+] a bowel movement; thus *do a job*, to defecate [euph.]. **4** of a person. (**a**) [1920s+] (*orig. US*) a person of either sex, a type of person, with adj. e.g. a *cute little job*, a *first-class job*. (**b**) [1930s+] (*Aus.*) a drunkard. (**c**) [1930s+] (*Aus.*) a fool, a poor worker. (**d**) [1940s+] (*N.Z.*) a prostitute. **5** [1920s+] (*orig. US*) an aircraft, a motorcar or any other vehicle; of a vehicle, a brand, a make, a style. **6** [1940s] an effort, a problem. **7** [1960s] (*US*) a way of life. **8** *see* BLOW JOB *n.* (1).

(IN PHRASES)

❑ **big job** *n.* **1** [mid-19C] (*US*) murder, assassination; thus *do the big job*, to kill [euph.]. **2** [1930s] anything notably large of its type, e.g. an automobile. ❑ **do a job** *v.* **1** [early 19C+] (*UK Und.*) to commit a crime, esp. a robbery. **2** [mid-19C+] (*also* **do a jobbie**) to defecate. **3** [20C+] (*Aus.*) to make pregnant. ❑ **do a job for oneself** *v.* [20C+] to defecate. ❑ **do a job on** *v.* **1** [early 19C+] (*also* **do the job on**) to beat up, to murder. **2** [1950s] to make someone the victim of a confidence trick or allied hoax or deception. **3** [1950s+] to cause trouble for, to harass, to persecute. **4** [1950s+] (*US*) of a man, to have sexual intercourse. **5** [1970s] to curse, to place a spell on. ❑ **do one's job over** *v.* [1970s] (*Aus.*) to become obsessed (with). ❑ **do someone's job for them** *v.* (*also* **do someone's business**) [var. on *DO A JOB ON* above] **1** [18C–1920s] to ruin. **2** [late 19C] to beat, to kill. ❑ **do the job** *v.* (*also* **give a job**) [ext. of JOB *v.*[1] (1)] [mid-17C–1970s] to have sexual intercourse. ❑ **get on one's job** *v.* (*also* **get on one's j.o.b.**) [1980s] (*US black*) to concentrate on one's life, involvements, pursuits. ❑ **job of work** *n.* [19C] any form of criminal enterprise. ❑ **job out** *v.* [19C] (*US Und.*) to distribute counterfeit money to criminal associates and dealers. ❑ **just the job** *see JUST THE TICKET under* TICKET *n.* ❑ **make a job** *v.* [20C+] (*Aus.*) to beat up, to defeat severely. ❑ **on one's job** (*also* **on one's j, on one's j.o.b.**) [1950s+] (*US black*) alert, in control; successful at a given task. ❑ **on the job** [SE *job*/JOB *v.*[1] (1)] [late 19C+] **1** a euph. for engaged in sexual activity. **2** working properly. **3** in the process of doing something. **4** aware, au fait. ❑ **pull a job** *v.* [1910s+] (*orig. US*) to carry out a robbery or other criminal act. ❑ **put up a job (on)** *v.* [late 19C+] (*US*) **1** to trick, to deceive (someone). **2** to concoct an injurious story.

SE in slang uses

IN PHRASES

❑ **couldn't get a job on a shit house cart** [1990s+] (*Aus.*) a phr. used of a complete inadequate/incompetent.

IN EXCLAMATIONS

❑ **get a job!** [1950s+] (*US campus*) find something constructive to do with yourself!

job *n.*[3] (*also* **jobe**) [the biblical proper name *Job*, who received a lengthy telling-off from his supposed 'comforters'] [mid-19C–1920s] a hen-pecked husband.

job *v.*[1] [SE *job*, to pierce, to thrust something into] **1** [mid-16C+] to have sexual intercourse; thus *jobbing*, sexual intercourse. **2** [late 19C+] (*Aus.*) to hit, to beat up. **3** [1970s] (*drugs*) to inject a narcotic; thus as n. an injection. **4** [1980s] to harm, to injure.

job *v.*[2] (*also* **jobe**) [JOB *n.*[3]; Grose suggests 'Cambridge term'] [late 17C–1900s] to scold, to tell off.

job *v.*[3] [SE *job*, to do a piece of work] **1** [mid-19C+] to finish. **2** [1970s–80s] (*US*) to fire from a job.

job *v.*[4] [JOB *n.*[2] (1)] **1** [late 19C+] to cheat, to betray, to 'frame up'. **2** [1960s] (*US*) to steal.

jo-bag *n.* [JOHNNY *n.*[1] (12) + SE *bag*/BAG *n.*[1] (1)] [1960s+] a condom.

jobbed *adj.*[1] [JOB *v.*[3]] [mid-19C] concluded, finished, usu. in the phr. *(that) job's jobbed*.

jobbed *adj.*[2] [JOB *v.*[4] (1)] [1900s–40s] (*UK Und.*) accused or 'framed' on false evidence.

jobber *n.*[1] [JOB *v.*[1] (2)] [early 19C] a blow to the head.

jobber *n.*[2] [1900s–70s] (*US*) a job, employment, a difficult chore.

jobber knot *n.* [? mis-reading of colloq. *jobbernowl*, a stupid person, ult. f. SE *noll*, the crown of the head] [mid-19C] a tall man.

jobbie *n.*[1] [JOB *n.*[2]/SE *job* + sfx *-ie*] **1** [1900s–30s] (*US*) a man or woman. **2** [1950s+] (*US*) (*also* **jobby**) a thing. **3** [1990s+] a job.

jobbie *n.*[2] (*also* **jobby**) [JOB *n.*[2] (3) + sfx *-ie*; note W.I. use, for children only] [1980s+] **1** (*orig. Scot.*) a piece of excrement, a turd. **2** a general term of abuse.

IN COMPOUNDS

❑ **jobby jouster** *n.* (*also* **jobby jabber**) [1990s+] a male homosexual.

IN PHRASES

❑ **do a jobbie** *v.* *see* DO A JOB *under* JOB *n.*[2].

jobe *n.* *see* JOB *n.*[3].

jobe *v.* *see* JOB *v.*[2].

jobey *n.* *see* JOB *n.*[1].

Job's ward *n.* (*also* **Job's dock**) [the suffering therein] [late 18C–early 19C] the venereal disease ward at St Bartholomew's Hospital in London.

IN PHRASES

❑ **be laid up in Job's dock** *v.* [late 18C–early 19C] to be treated in hospital for a venereal disease.

Job's wife *n.* (*also* **Job's comforter**) [the biblical story of *Job*] [19C–1930s] a scolding, promiscuous woman.

Joburg *n.* (*also* **Jo'burg, Johburg**) [abbr.] [late 19C+] (*orig. milit.*) Johannes*burg*, South Africa, thus *Joburgher*, a dweller in the city; also attrib.

Jocelyn *n.* (*also* **Jozlin**) [the perceived 'effeminacy' of the name] [1990s+] (*UK juv.*) a male homosexual.

Jock *n.* [the stereotypical Scot. given name *Jock*, f. *John*] **1** [mid-18C–19C] a Northcountry seaman, esp. a crewman of a collier. **2** [mid-18C+] (*also* **Jockey, Jockie, Jocky**) a generic for a Scotsman. **3** [late 19C+] as a term of address to a Scot.

IN COMPOUNDS

❑ **Jockland** *n.* [2000s] Scotland.

Jock *adj.* [JOCK *n.* (2)] [1980s+] Scottish.

jock *n.*[1] (*also* **jocum**) [JOCKUM *n.*] **1** [mid-18C+] the genitals, both male and female; also in fig. use [the word vanished from the mainstream but remains in US black in the late 20C+]. **2** as a garment. (**a**) [1920s+] an athletic support or 'jock strap'. (**b**) [1950s+] (*Aus./US*) (*also* **jokettes**) in pl., men's underwear. **3** [1940s+] (*also* **jocko, jockette, jockstrap**) (*US campus and sports*) a sportsman, esp. an assiduously keen one. **4** [1960s+] (*US campus*) a politically conservative, white, middle-class young man. **5** [1960s+] (*US campus*) as ext. of sense 3, a devoted and diligent student, e.g. *math jock, computer jock*. **6** [1980s+] (*US*) a stupid, unimaginative person, a nerd. **7** *see* JOCKER *n.*[1] (3).

IN COMPOUNDS

❑ **jock major** *n.* [1960s+] (*US campus*) a student who majors in physical education. ❑ **jock-piece** *n.* [1920s+] (*US*) the penis. ❑ **jock-rot** *n.* (*also* **jock itch**) [1960s+] (*US*) a skin infection of the genital area. ❑ **jocksniffer** *n.* [joc. use of sense 1 above + SE *sniffer*, note reported 2003 US Army use, a civilian who is very wrapped up in military affairs] [1960s+] (*US*) a (presumably male) sports groupie who likes to hang around sports stars. ❑ **jockstrap** *n.* **1** [1960s+] (*US*) a stupid, insignificant fellow. **2** *see* sense 3 above.

IN PHRASES

❑ **black jock** *n.* **1** [late 18C] the pubic hair. **2** [late 19C] (*also* **brown jock, grey jock**) the vagina. ❑ **go jock-hunting** *v.* [late 19C–late 1900s] to have sexual intercourse. ❑ **hang up one's jock** *v.* [HANG UP ONE'S... *v.*] [1980s+] (*US*) **1** to retire, to give up. **2** to be killed. ❑ **knock someone's jock off** *v.* (*also* **beat someone's jock off**) [1950s+] (*US*) to overcome completely. ❑ **lose one's jock** *v.* [1960s+] (*US*) to be fooled. ❑ **on someone's jock(strap)** [1980s+] (*US*) pursuing, esp. of a woman sexually harassing a man.

jock *n.*[2] [abbr.] **1** [early 19C+] a *jock*ey. **2** [1940s+] (*orig. US*) a disc *jock*ey. **3** [1960s+] (*US*) a worker, an operator, e.g. *construction jock, elevator jock* [abbr. JOCKEY *n.*[2] (3b)].

jock *adj.* [JOCK *n.*[1] (3)] **1** [1960s] (*US black/campus*) of a woman, having an attractive figure. **2** [1960s+] (*US*) athletic, sporty.

jock *v.*[1] [JOCK *n.*[1]] **1** [late 17C–early 19C; 1960s+] to have sexual intercourse. **2** [1960s+] (*US*) to engage in athletics. **3** [1970s] to be lively and have a good time. **4** [1980s+] (*US black*) to imitate, to irritate (cf. *on someone's jock(strap)* under JOCK *n.*[1]). **5** [1980s+] (*US black teen*) to idolize, to pay someone lots of attention, trying to impress them.

IN PHRASES

❑ **jock someone's style** *v.* [2000s] (*US black*) to imitate.

jock *v.*[2] [? JACK *v.*[3] (1)] [1980s+] (*US black*) **1** to steal, either an object or a person, e.g. a lover. **2** to copy, e.g. song lyrics.

jockam *n.* *see* JOCKUM *n.*

jock and boxer *n.* [the names of two varieties of underwear] [20C+] (*gay*) a young man and his older friend.

jocker *n.*[1] [JOCK *v.*[1]] **1** [late 19C+] (*US*) a tramp who travels with a younger partner, working for him and poss. acting as his catamite. **2** [20C+] (*also* **jocky**) (*US*) a male homosexual, the 'husband' of the couple. **3** [1910s+] (*also* **jock, joko**) (*US*) a predatory homosexual, esp. in the context of prison, who forces his attentions on younger/weaker men or boys. **4** [1960s–70s] (*US*) a lecher.

jocker *n.*[2] [JOCK *n.*[1] (2a)] [2000s] an athletic support, 'jock strap'.

jockette *n.* *see* JOCK *n.*[1] (3).

Jockey *n.* *see* JOCK *n.* (2).

jockey *n.*[1] [JOCKUM *n.*; note *double entendre* on a man's name in D'Urfey, *Pills to Purge Melancholy*, (1719): 'You've been ranting, playing the Wanton, / Keeping of Jockey Company'] [17C; 1920s–30s] the penis.

jockey *n.*[2] **1** [late 18C–mid-19C] a man. **2** [mid–late 19C] (*UK Und.*) the expert, the exemplar. **3** any form of worker. (**a**) [mid-19C–1940s] an accomplice or assistant, usu. of a driver of a cab or utility vehicle. (**b**) [mid-19C+] a worker in a particular job, e.g. *swab jockey*, washer-up, *pump jockey*, petrol pump attendant, *grunt-and-squeal jockey*, a stock hauler, *juice jockey*, a gasoline-truck driver, *suicide jockey*, a nitroglycerine hauler, *disc jockey*. (**c**) [1910s+] any form of driver, esp. of cabs, buses. **4** [1900s–30s] (*US Und.*) a horse thief. **5** [1930s] a pimp. **6** [1930s] (*UK Und.*) a gang member. **7** [1930s+] a whore's client. **8** [1940s+] (*US*) in homosexual uses. (**a**) a homosexual tramp. (**b**) a masculine lesbian. **9** [1950s] (*gypsy*) a general term of address, e.g. *Hello jockey*. **10** [1950s–70s] a user of drugs or one who is habituated, e.g. *hop-jockey*, drug addict, *horse-jockey*, heroin user.

IN COMPOUNDS

❑ **jockey's breakfast** *n.* [1990s+] (*Irish*) sexual intercourse and a slice of bacon.

jockey *v.* **1** [late 18C–19C] (*US Und.*) to trick, to defraud [one 'rides' the victim in a required direction]. **2** [1930s+] to do a job of work. **3** [1940s–60s] (*US black/teen*) to drink. **4** [1940s+] (*US*) to drive a vehicle, to pilot a plane. **5** [1960s+] to work someone hard.

IN PHRASES

❑ **jockey around** *v.* [1900s–70s] (*US*) to move from place to place, job to job.

jockeying *n.* [late 19C] racing carriages along the streets of London.

jockey's (whip) *n.* [rhy. sl.] **1** [1940s–50s] a bed, a sleep [KIP *n.*[1]]. **2** [1960s+] in pl. potato chips.

jock-gagger *n. see* JOCKUM-GAGGER *under* JOCKUM *n.*

Jockie/Jocky *n. see* JOCK *n.* (2).

jockies *n.*

IN EXCLAMATIONS

❑ **by jockies!** (*also* **by Jockey!**) [mid–late19C] (*US*) euph. for *by Jesus!*

jocko *n.* [generic use of name *Jock* but ? dial. *jockey*, a peasant, a countryman] (*US*) **1** [1910s+] a stupid or contemptible man or boy; also a term of address. **2** [1950s+] a friendly form of address. **3** *see* JOCK *n.*[1] (3).

jocks *n.* [euph. for JESUS! *excl.*] [late 19C–1920s] (*US*) used in mild oaths, typically *by jocks!, i jock!*

jockum *n.* (*also* **jockam**) [ety. unknown] [mid-16C–1900s] the penis.

IN COMPOUNDS

❑ **jockum cloy** *v.* (*also* **jockum**) [fig. use of CLOY *v.*] [late 17C–early 19C] of a man, to have sexual intercourse. ❑ **jockum gage** *n.* (*also* **jacum-gag**) [GAGE *n.*[1] (2)] [late 17C–early 19C] (*UK Und.*) a chamberpot; thus *rum jockum gage*, a silver chamberpot. ❑ **jockum-gagger** *n.* (*also* **jack-gagger, jock-gagger**) [JOCK *n.*[1] (1)/ JOCKUM *n.* + GAGGER *n.*[1] (3), lit. 'penis-beggar'] [late 18C–early 19C] a man who lives on his wife's prostitution, a pimp.

jocky *n.*[1] [JOCKUM *n.*] [mid–late 17C] the penis.

jocky *n.*[2] *see* JOCKER *n.*[1] (2).

jocum *n. see* JOCK *n.*[1].

Jodrell (Bank) *n.* [rhy. sl. = WANK *n.*; ult. the *Jodrell Bank* power station] [1950s+] **1** masturbation. **2** a tired-out old prostitute.

Jody *n.* (*also* **Jodie**) [JOE THE GRINDER *n.*] **1** [1940s+] (*US*) used derisively by US troops, prisoners and other isolated men, the lover who takes the 'girl you've left behind'. **2** [1940s+] (*US*) used derog. by soldiers, a male civilian; thus *jody clothes*, men's civilian clothes. **3** [1970s+] (*US gay/prison*) a homosexual prisoner's younger lover.

Joe *n.*[1]

IN EXCLAMATIONS

❑ **by Joe!** [mid-19C–1940s] (*US*) a mild oath; euph. for *by Jesus!*

Joe *n.*[2] *see GI JOE under* GI *adj.*

joe *n.*[1] [proper name *Joe*, abbr. of *Joseph*] **1** generic uses of the proper name. (**a**) [18C–early 19C] (*Scot*) a friend. (**b**) [mid-19C+] a generic name for a person, e.g. *joe average, joe citizen*, the average man in the street; also one who has a job or position, e.g. *joe plainclothes*, a plain-clothes police officer, *working joe* one who is employed etc; see also combs. below. (**c**) [1910s+] (*US*) a (likeable) person, often used in direct address. (**d**) [1960s+] (*Can.*) a French Canadian. **2** (*also* **joey**) in Aus. uses [orig. on the goldfields a trooper enforcing the regulations laid down by Gov. Charles *Jo*seph LaTrobe (1801–75) and the cry *Joe!/Joe-Joe!*, issued by a miner at the approach of police]. (**a**) [mid-19C] a policeman, a trooper. (**b**) [mid–late 19C] by ext. of (a), a term of abuse hurled at anyone who was not a miner. **3** [mid-19C–1940s] (*US campus*) (*also* **joe house**) a privy; thus as v., meaning to use a lavatory; *joe-wad*, toilet paper [supposedly f. the burning of the privies at Hamilton College on one Nov. 5, following the refusal of the President, *Joseph* Penney, to have them cleaned]. **4** [1970s+] (*US campus*) beer [the *Jo*seph Schlitz Brewing Co. of Milwaukee].

as a generic name

IN COMPOUNDS

❑ **Joe Bloggs** *n.* [1940s+] a generic name used for any otherwise unnamed man. ❑ **Joe Blow** *n.* (*also* **Joe Bloe**) [orig. the horn player in a band, who 'blows'] **1** [1920s+] (*Aus./N.Z./US*) any man. **2** [1930s] (*US Und.*) a drugs carrier [BLOW *n.*[3] (4)]. ❑ **Joe Chink** *n.* [CHINK *n.* (1); the link of heroin (or properly opium) to the Orient] **1** [1960s] a generic term for the Chinese. **2** [1970s] (*US drugs*) a heroin addiction. ❑ **Joe Citizen** *n.* [1930s+] (*US*) an average person. ❑ **Joe College** *n.* (*also* **college joe, Kid College**) [SE *college*] [1930s+] (*US*) a college boy, esp. one who is self-satisfied and self-indulgent; also attrib. ❑ **Joe Cool** *n.* (*also* **Johnny Cool, Mr Cool**) [COOL *adj.* (3); note character 'Joe Cool' in Burnett *Asphalt Jungle* (1949)] [1960s+] one who is, or more likely sees themselves, as sophisticated, wordly, etc. ❑ **Joe Crap** *see JOE SHIT (THE RAG MAN)* below. ❑ **joe job** *n.* [SE *job*] [1980s+] (*US campus/teen*) a menial, low-paid task. ❑ **Joe lunchpail** *n.* (*also* **Joe lunchbox, Joe lunchbucket**) [SE *lunchpail/lunchbox/lunchbucket*] [1960s+] (*US*) an ordinary working man. ❑ **Joe Muggins** *n. see* MUGGINS *n.*[1] (1). ❑ **Joe Public** *n.* (*also* **John Public**) [SE *public*] [1930s+] (*orig. US*) the general public, thus fem. *Josephine Public*. ❑ **joe sad** *n.* [SE *sad*/SAD *adj.* (2)] [1920s+] (*US black*) a miserable or unpopular person. ❑ **Joe Schmo** *n.* (*also* **Joe Schmoe, Joe Shmo, Joe Shmoe**) [SCHMO *n.*] [1940s+] (*orig. US*) anyone, 'Mr. Average'. ❑ **Joe Shit (the rag man)** *n.* (*also* **Joe Crap**) [SHIT *n.* (2)/CRAP *n.*[1] (9)] [1940s+] (*US*) an extremely contemptible person, a nobody. ❑ **Joe Six-pack** *n.* [SE *six-pack*] [1970s+] (*US*) an ordinary, beer-drinking man. ❑ **Joe Zilch** *n.* (*also* **joe zilsch**) [ZILCH *n.*[1] (2)] [1920s+] (*US*) the average, otherwise unnamed man.

IN PHRASES

❑ **not for Joe** (*also* **not for Joseph**) [ety. unknown; ? anecdotal; ? sense 1b above] [mid-19C–1920s] by no means, not on any account. ❑ **quality joe** *n.* (*also* **quality folks**) [ironic use of SE the *quality*, the upper classes + *Joe Public* (above)/SE *folks*] [1950s] (*US drugs*) a non-addict. ❑ **random joe** *n. see under* RANDOM *adj.* ❑ **regular joe** *n.* (*also* **right Joe**) [*REGULAR GUY under* REGULAR *adj.*/RIGHT *adj.* (1)] [20C+] a conventional, conservative person; as such seen as honest and dependable.

joe *n.*[2] [abbr.] **1** [late 18C–mid-19C] (*US*) a *Jo*hannes, a Portuguese gold coin properly the *dobra de quatro escudos*, minted by Joannes or João V (1703–50), of the value of appx. 36s. sterling. **2** [1960s] (*US*) a Navajo Indian.

joe *n.*[3] [? JOEY *n.*[1] (1)] **1** [mid-19C+] (*W.I.*) sixpence (post-1969 value 5 cents). **2** [1930s] (*N.Z.*) one penny.

joe *n.*[4] [Java; ? elision of JAMOKE *n.*[1]; or play on Stephen Foster song 'Old Black Joe'] [1910s+] (*US*) coffee.

joe *n.*[5] [? JOE BLAKES *n.* (1)] [1920s] (*US*) a fit, occasioned by drug withdrawal or alcoholic excess.

joe *n.*[6] **1** *see* JOE (BLAKE) *n.* **2** *see* JOE GURR *n.* **3** *see* JOE (HUNT) *n.* **4** *see* JOE MILLER *n.* **5** *see* JOEY *n.*[1] (1). **6** *see LITTLE JOE under* LITTLE *adj.*

joe *adj.*[1] [ety. unknown, but note northern dial. *to be joe*, to the master, presumably a generic use of the name] (*US*) **1** [1900s–20s] aware, in the know. **2** [1950s–60s] used for anything exceptionally strong, large or extraordinary.

joe *adj.*[2] [? JOE *n.*[1] (1b)] [1990s+] (*US*) tedious or inconsequential.

joe *v.* (*also* **joey**) [JOE *n.*[1] (1)] **1** [mid–late 19C] (*Aus./N.Z.*) to abuse. **2** [mid–late 19C] (*Aus./N.Z.*) to warn. **3** [1980s] to steal from handbags.

Joe Baxi *n.* [rhy. sl.; ult. US heavyweight boxer *Joe Baksi* (1922–77)] [1980s+] a taxi.

joe (blake) *n.* [rhy. sl.] **1** [20C+] cake. **2** [20C+] (*Aus.*) a snake. **3** [1930s+] (*Aus./US*) steak. **4** [1980s+] (*Aus.*) a stake, a bet.

joe blakes *n.* [rhy. sl.] (*Aus./N.Z.*) **1** [late 19C+] the shakes. **2** [20C+] delirium tremens [= SNAKES *n.*].

Joe Blake the Bartlemy *v.* [? rhy. sl. *joe blake* = FAKE *v.*[1] (1) + *Bartlemy* = Bartholomew Fair] [mid-19C] to visit a prostitute.

joe bonce *n.* [rhy. sl.; PONCE *n.* (1)] [1930s+] a pimp.

joe brown *n.* [rhy. sl.] [late 19C+] town.

joe buck *n.* [rhy. sl. = FUCK *n.* (1); note the heterosexual male prostitute hero of the novel *Midnight Cowboy* (1965): 'Joe Buck'] [1930s+] (*Aus.*) an act of copulation.

Joe Cotton *n.* [1910s] (*US*) the point of four in craps dice.

Joe Daki *n.* [rhy. sl. = PAKI *n.*] [1990s+] a derog. term for a British Asian.

joe dandy *n.* [var. on JIM DANDY *n.*] [late 19C–1940s] an excellent person or thing.

Joe de Grinder *n. see* JOE THE GRINDER *n.*

joe doakes *n.* (*also* **Joe Dokes**) [circus jargon *Joe Doakes*, the ringmaster; note JOHN DOE *n.*] [1920s+] (*US*) any anonymous man.

Joe Erk *n.* [rhy. sl. = BERK *n.*, note ERK *n.*] [1950s+] a fool, a general term of abuse.

joe gardiners *n.* [proper name of *Joe Gardiner Ltd*, a boot- and shoe-maker of Sydney] [1950s] (*Aus.*) boots.

joe goss *n.* [rhy. sl.; ? ult. late-19C US prize-fighter *Joe Goss*] [20C+] (*Aus./US*) **1** the boss; thus a political boss. **2** a police officer.

joe gurr *n.* (*also* **joe, joe ghirr**) [rhy. sl. = STIR *n.*[1] (1); ult. *Joe Gurr*, Amelia Earhart's radio consultant on her 1937 Round-the-World flight] [1930s+] prison.

joe heath's mare *n.* [ety. unknown; presumably anecdotal] [20C+] (*W.I.*) a workhorse; thus *like joe heath's mare*, exerting oneself, behaving in an excited manner.

joe hep *n.* (*also* **hep, joe hept, joe hip**) [HEP *adj.* (1)/HIP *adj.* (1)] [20C+] (*US*) an aware, wise person.

joe hep *adj.* (*also* **joe hept, joe hip, johnny hep**) [JOE HEP *n.*] [1900s–40s; 1980s] (*US*) smart, aware, knowledgeable.

joe hook *n.* [rhy. sl.] **1** [1930s+] a villain, a crook; as adj., untrustworthy. **2** [1950s+] a book.

joe hope *n.* [rhy. sl.] [20C+] (*Aus.*) soap.

joe (hunt) *n.* (*also* **Joey (Hunt)**) [rhy. sl. = CUNT *n.*] [20C+] a fool, a general derog. term.

IN PHRASES

□ **make a joe of oneself** *v.* [1960s+] (*N.Z.*) to make a fool of oneself.

joe jorgensen *n.* [proper name *Joe Jorgensen*, a well-known goal kicker for Balmain Aus. Rules Football team] [1950s] (*Aus.*) one who kicks while fighting.

Joe Loss *n.* [rhy. sl.; ult. UK bandleader *Joe Loss* (1909–90)] [20C+] a toss, as in a DAMN *n.*

Joe Louis *n.* [proper name of US heavyweight champion *Joe Louis* (1914–81), reflecting either his size or his strength] [1940s–50s] **1** (*W.I.*) a large, solid cake. **2** (*W.I., Jam.*) home-distilled rum. **3** (*US*) 'bad' or homemade liquor.

Joe MacBride *n.* [rhy. sl. = RIDE *n.* (1); ult. US jazz musician *Joe McBride*] [20C+] sexual intercourse.

joe marks *n.* [rhy. sl.] [1930s–40s] (*Aus.*) sharks.

joe maxi *n.* (*also* **jo, jo maxi**) [rhy. sl.] [1990s+] (*Irish*) a taxi.

Joe McGee *n.* [? anecdotal] **1** [1920s–70s] (*US*) a stupid, unreliable person. **2** [1930s] a mean person, spec., a non-tipping hotel guest.

Joe McGee *adj.* [1930s] (*US*) fake.

Joe McNab *v.* [rhy. sl.] [1970s–80s] (*N.Z. prison*) to stab.

Joe Miller *n.* (*also* **joe**) [proper name of *Joe Miller* (1684–1738), a comedian whose name was attached to the bestselling *Joe Miller's jests, or the Wit's Vade-mecum*, written by John Mottley and published in 1739, after Miller's death] **1** [late 18C–1900s] a joke-book. **2** [early 19C+] (*also* **Joe Millerism**) a joke, esp. an old 'chestnut'; thus *I don't see the Joe Miller of it*, I don't see what's funny about it. **3** [mid-19C+] a joke-teller, a humourist.

joe morgan *n.* [rhy. sl.] [1940s] (*Aus.*) an organ.

joe morgans *n.* [? anecdotal; note contemporary references to Joe Morgan, a 'famed' drunk, e.g. Ade, *Knocking the Neighbors* (1921) 157: He was the original Blotter. [...] According to all the Laws of Heredity the only Son was cast for the Part of Joe Morgan; or Ade, *The Old-Time Saloon* (1931), 109: Every one who quaffed at the bar was Joe Morgan, the village sot] [1920s] (*N.Z.*) delirium tremens.

joe poke *n.* [abbr.] [late 19C–1910s] a Justice of the Peace.

Joe Rail *n.* [rhy. sl.= TALE *n.*[1]] [1900s] (*Aus.*) a hard-luck story aimed to obtain money.

joe rocks *n.* (*also* **tommy rocks**) [rhy. sl.] [20C+] (*Aus./UK/US*) socks.

joe roke *n.* [rhy. sl.] [1920s+] (*US*) smoke.

Joe Ronce *n. see* CHARLIE RONCE *n.*

Joe Rook *n.* [rhy. sl.] **1** [1930s+] a book i.e. a bookmaker. **2** [1950s+] a crook.

Joe Rookie *n.* [rhy. sl. = BOOKIE *n.* (1) + play on ROOK *v.*[1] (1)] [1990s+] a bookmaker.

joe rourke *n.* [rhy. sl.] **1** [1930s] (*UK Und.*) a thief [FORK *n.*[1] (2)]. **2** [20C+] a fork.

joes *n.*[1] [abbr. rhy. sl.; *joe blakes* = SHAKES, THE *n.*] [1910s+] (*Aus.*) **1** a fit of depression. **2** an attack of nerves.

joes *n.*[2] [2000s] (*US prison*) cigarettes.

joe savage *n.* [rhy. sl.] [mid-19C] a cabbage.

joe skinner *n. see* JIMMY SKINNER *n.*

joe soap *n.* [rhy. sl. = DOPE *n.*[2] (1)] **1** [1930s+] a self-description, e.g. *joe soap here ...* **2** [1930s+] a fool, a gullible individual. **3** [1980s+] any man.

Joe Strummer *adj.* [rhy. sl. = BUMMER *adj.*; ult. *Joe Strummer* (1952–2002), a member of the early punk band, *The Clash* (1977–86)] [1970s+] unpleasant, disappointing.

Joe the Grinder *n.* (*also* **Joe de Grinder**) [generic use of proper name *Joe* + GRIND *v.* (1)] [1930s+] (*US black*) the mythical seducer, who specializes in married women or those with boyfriends; thus JODY *n.*

joey *n.*[1] [uses of proper names] **1** as a coin. (**a**) [mid-19C] (*US*) four. (**b**) [mid–late 19C] (*also* **joe**) a fourpenny piece, a groat [radical politician *Joseph Hume* MP (1777–1855), who encouraged the introduction of the coin. The term was coined by the London cabbies, who lost money by the coin's invention, when the *joey* replaced the sixpence as the usual payment for shorter journeys]. (**c**) [1900s–50s] a threepenny bit. **2** in Aus. uses [JOE *n.*[1] (2)]. (**a**) [mid–late 19C] in the goldfields, an outsider. (**b**) [mid-19C+] a police officer; in WW1 a military policeman. **3** [late 19C–1940s] a circus clown [abbr. proper name Joseph Grimaldi, the British clown (1779–1837)]. **4** [1980s+] (*also* **deacon**) a general derog. implying physical inadequacy and used on the pattern of SPASTIC *adj.* [proper name Joey Deacon, disabled child who featured on popular children's TV programme *Blue Peter* in the 1980s; but note also JOEY *n.*[6] (2)].

joey *n.*[2] [? HOLY JOE *n.*] **1** [mid-19C–1940s] a hypocrite. **2** [20C+] an excuse, a small 'white' lie.

joey *n.*[3] [SAusE *joey*, a young kangaroo] **1** [late 19C+] (*Aus.*) a child, usu. a white child. **2** [20C+] (*Aus.*) a sodomite, an active male homosexual. **3** [1910s+] (*Aus.*) a worthless cheque; like the animal, it 'bounces'. **4** [1970s] (*Aus. gay*) a young male prostitute or the young lover of an older man.

IN PHRASES

❑ **slip a joey** *v.* [SE *slip*, of animals, to miscarry, to give birth prematurely] [20C+] (*Aus.*) **1** to have a miscarriage. **2** to give birth.

SE in slang uses

IN PHRASES

❑ **have a joey in the pouch** *v.* [1950s–60s] (*Aus.*) to be pregnant.

joey *n.*[4] [ety. unknown] **1** [1940s+] (*UK prison*) any form of contraband, letters, parcels etc, smuggled into a prison. **2** [2000s] (*drugs*) a drug addict who works as a drug mule. **3** [2000s] (*drugs*) £10 worth of heroin.

joey *n.*[5] [1970s+] (*N.Z.*) a condom.

joey *n.*[6] **1** see JOE *n.*[1] (2). **2** see JOE (HUNT) *n.*

joey *v.* see JOE *v.*

Joeys *n.* (*also* **Johies, Jozi**) [abbr.] [1940s+] (*S.Afr.*) Johannesburg.

jo-fired *adv.* [var. on ALL-FIRED *adv.*] [early–mid-19C] (*US*) a general intensifier, complete, absolute, total, utter.

jog *v.* **1** [late 16C–19C] (*UK Und.*) to move, to leave. **2** [17C–mid-19C] of a man, to have sexual intercourse. **3** [1970s] of a homosexual man, to have anal intercourse. **4** see JOOK *v.*

jogar *n.* (*also* **jogah**) [JOGAR V.] [1920s+] a busker.

jogar *v.* (*also* **jogger**) [Ital. *giocare*, to play] [late 19C+] (*Ling. Fr./Polari*) to sing, to play, to entertain.

jogari omee/polone *n.* (*also* **joggering omee/polone**) [JOGAR *v.* + OMEE *n.*/POLONE *n.*] [late 19C+] an entertainer, a busker.

jogue *n.* (*also* **jug**) [the term survives in 20C+ market traders' jargon *joag*] [early 19C–1900s] (*UK Und.*) one shilling; thus *five jogue*, 5 shillings etc.

jogul *v.* [Sp. *jugar*, to play] [mid-19C] to play a game, esp. a card-game.

johanna *n.* see JOANNA *n.*

Johburg *n.* see JOBURG *n.*

Johies *n.* see JOEYS *n.*

John *n.* (*also* **john**) [commonness of the name; note police/legal jargon *John Doe*, any anonymous male suspect, victim etc] **1** [late 16C+] a generic term for a man. **2** [18C–1900s] a male servant. **3** [early 19C–1900s] (*US*) an Englishman [abbr. JOHN BULL *n.*]. **4** [mid-19C–1940s] a derog. term for a Chinese man [abbr. JOHN CHINAMAN *n.*]. **5** [mid-19C+] a general term of address, orig. of white men by immigrants etc, irrespective of actual name, e.g. *Hello, John, got a new motor* etc. **6** [late 19C+] (*S.Afr.*) a generic term for any male black servant. **7** [1900s–50s] (*US*) a jack in poker [punning on the name *Jack*].

IN COMPOUNDS

❑ **john farmer** *n.* [sense 1 above + SE *farmer*] [1900s–70s] (*US*) an ordinary farmer. ❑ **john-hold-my-staff** *n.* [note sense 2 above] [17C] a servile attendant.

john *n.*[1] (*also* **john darme, johndarm**) [abbr./mispron. of Fr. *gendarme*] [mid-19C+] a police officer, usu. male.

IN COMPOUNDS

❑ **john elbow** *n.* [he grabs one by it] [20C+] a police officer. ❑ **john law** *n.* (*also* **johnnie law**) [JOHN *n.* (1) + SE *law*] [20C+] (*orig. Und. US*) a policeman, esp. a senior one. ❑ **john palace** *n.* (*also* **john house**) [SE *palace*] [1900s] (*Aus.*) a police station.

IN PHRASES

❑ **big john** *n.* [1970s+] (*US black*) the police.

john *n.*[2] **1** in Und. uses, a victim, a source of money. (**a**) [1900s–60s] (*US Und.*) (*also* **james**) an easy victim, a sucker; a free spender. (**b**) [1910s+] (*US Und.*) any law-abiding man. (**c**) [1910s+] (*orig. US*) a female or male prostitute's client. (**d**) [1940s–60s] (*US black*) a gullible white man. (**e**) [1980s] (*US black*) a man susceptible to feminine trickery. **2** [1910s] (*Aus.*) a boyfriend. **3** [1910s+] the penis [abbr. JOHN THOMAS *n.* (1)]. **4** [1920s+] a skilled, professional tramp [such a top-class tramp is well dressed and thus resembles a 'normal' citizen]. **5** [1930s+] (*orig. US college*) the lavatory, usu. for men [? abbr. CUZ JOHN *n.*]. **6** [1950s+] (*gay*) an older man who supports a younger one without actually sharing a long-term relationship with him. **7** [1960s+] (*US*) one's signature [abbr. JOHN HANCOCK *n.*]. **8** [1960s+] (*US gay*) among lesbians, a man who associates with female homosexuals. **9** [1960s+] a condom. [note JOHNNY *n.*[1] (12)]. **10** [1970s] (*US*) the menstrual period. **11** [1990s+] (*US drugs*) heroin [fig. use of JOHN *n.* (1), based on BOY *n.*[2] (1) and the idea that heroin is a 'masculine' drug].

IN COMPOUNDS

❑ **john catcher** *n.* [1950s] (*US*) a prostitute. ❑ **john walker** *n.* [JOHN *n.* (1) + SE *walk*, ie to remove] [1970s] (*US Und.*) a security man in a brothel.

IN PHRASES

❑ **john among the maids** *n.* [19C] a whoremonger, a promiscuous man. ❑ **play john** *v.* **1** [mid-19C] of a man, to flirt. **2** [1980s] (*US*) (*also* **play Jim**) to fool about.

john *n.*[3] [rhy. sl.; *John Bull* = PULL *v.* (2b)] [1950s+] an arrest.

john *n.*[4] **1** see JOHN *n.* **2** see JOHN DAVIES, THE.

john *v.* [mid–late 18C] (*UK Und.*) to recognize.

john- *pfx* see JOHNNY- *pfx*.

john-and-joan *n.* [the proper names] [late 18C–mid-19C] a hermaphrodite.

John Audley *phr.* ['Ex. the actor-manager John Richardson (d. 1837), who used to ask 'Is John Audley here?' whenever another 'house' was waiting, though tradition (Hotten, 1864) has it that John Audley or Orderly taught him the wheeze' (*DSUE*)] **1** [mid-18C] (*UK Und.*) quietly. **2** [late 19C] stop doing that. **3** [1920s] quickly, be quick.

John B *n.* [abbr.] [1930s] (*US*) a hat made by the *John B.* Stetson Company.

John Bates *n.* see MR BATES *under* MR *n.*

John Bradbury *n.* see BRADBURY *n.*

john brown *n.* (*also* **john D, ...esquire, ...handle, ...Q, ... rogers, ...smith, ...willy**) [all vars. on JOHN HANCOCK *n.* (1)] [1960s] (*US*) one's signature.

john brown *v.* [the abolitionist *John Brown* (1800–59), who was hanged for his part in the attack on Harper's Ferry, Virginia] [mid–late 19C] (*US*) to execute by hanging; thus *be john-browned*, to be 'hanged'.

IN EXCLAMATIONS

❑ **I'll be John-Browned!** [20C+] (*US*) a joc. euph. for *I'LL BE HANGED!* under HANGED *adj.*

John Bull *n.* (*also* **Bull, Jack Bull, Jacky Bull, J.B., Johnnie Bull, Johnny Bull, Miss Bull**) [first used to name a character in John Arbuthnot's *The History of John Bull* (1712), in which he also coined *Nic Frog* + *Louis Baboon*, for the Dutch- and Frenchman respectively] **1** [early 18C+] an Englishman, the British, Great Britain; an English ship; thus *John Bull-land*, England/Britain. **2** [1900s] an English woman.

IN COMPOUNDS

❑ **John Bull's bastard** *n.* [1940s–50s] (*Irish*) an Englishman.

John Bull *adj.* [JOHN BULL *n.* (1)] [late 18C+] characteristically English, thus *John Bullism*.

john bull *n.* [rhy. sl.] [20C+] **1** a pull, a tug. **2** an arrest [= PULL *n.* (2c)]. **3** a seduction, or the hope of it; thus *go out on the John Bull*, to go out looking for sex [= PULL *v.* (2e)].

john bull *adj.* [rhy. sl. = FULL *adj.* (1)] [1960s+] (*Aus.*) drunk.

John Canoe *v.* see CANOE *v.*[1].

John Chinaman *n.* (*also* **China John, johnnie Chinaman/Chinee, johnny Chinaman/Chinee**) [early 19C–1940s] a derog. term for a Chinese man.

John Cleese *n.* [rhy. sl.; ult. UK writer of and actor in Monty Python, *John Cleese* (b. 1939)] [2000s] cheese.

John Cornstalk *n.* see CORNSTALK *n.* (2).

John Crappo *n.* see *JOHNNY CRAPOSE under* JOHNNY- *pfx*.

John Crow *n.*[1] (*also* **jancro, jancrow**) [*john crow*, the carrion crow] [1940s+] (*W.I.*) a general derog. description of a person.

John Crow *n.*[2] see JIM CROW *n.*

john D *n.* see JOHN BROWN *n.*

johndarm/john darme *n.* see JOHN *n.*[1].

John Davies, the (*also* **john**) [ety. unknown; ? anecdotal] [late 19C] (*US*) money.

John Deal *n. see* DEALER *n.*

john dillon *n.* [rhy. sl.] [1930s+] (*N.Z.*) one shilling (5p).

John Doe *n.* [18C+ police/legal jargon *John Doe*, any anonymous male suspect, victim etc] [20C+] an anonymous person, a pseudonym.

John Dory *n.* [rhy. sl.] **1** [1990s+] (*Aus.*) a story. **2** [2000s] (*N.Z.*) in fig. sense, one's signature.

John Drum's entertainment *n. see* JACK DRUM'S ENTERTAINMENT *n.*

john dunn *n.*[1] [rhy. sl.] [late 19C–1900s] (*Aus.*) £1.

john dunn *n.*[2] [mispron. of Fr. *gendarme*; note JOHN *n.*[1]] [1910s+] (*Aus.*) a police officer, usu. male.

john esquire *n. see* JOHN BROWN *n.*

Johney Croppi *n. see* JOHNNY CRAPOSE *under* JOHNNY- *pfx.*

john family *n. see* JOHNSONS *n.*[1].

john gilpin *n.* (*also* **gilpin**) [? tradename, but note the 'trusty sword' carried by the eponymous hero of William Cowper's poem 'John Gilpin' (1783)] [1950s] (*W.I.*) a large cutlass with a curved back and flared blade.

john hall *n.* [var. on HALL *n.*] [1920s–30s] (*US*) alcohol.

John Hancock *n.* [the particularly large signature of *John Hancock* (1737–93) on the US Declaration of Independence, 1776] [late 19C+] (*US*) one's signature, esp. on some form of legal or otherwise official document.

John Hancock *v.* [JOHN HANCOCK *n.*] [1960s+] (*US*) to sign one's name.

john handle *n. see* JOHN BROWN *n.*

john henry *n.* **1** [late 19C–1940s] (*US black*) a hard-working black man, tough and indomitable in the face of appalling challenges. **2** [late 19C+] the penis [var. on JOHN THOMAS *n.* (1)]. **3** [1910s+] (*US*) one's signature, esp. on some form of legal or otherwise official document [var. on JOHN HANCOCK *n.*].

IN PHRASES

❑ **play john henry** *v.* [1930s] (*US black*) of a man, to make advances towards a woman.

john hop *n.* (*also* **hop, johnny hop, johnny hopper, jon-hop, jonnjonna, jonnop, jonop**) [rhy. sl. = COP *n.*[1] (1)] [20C+] (*Aus.*) a police officer, usu. male.

John Knox *n.* [rhy. sl. = POX *n.*[1] (3)] [1960s–70s] (*Scot.*) venereal disease.

johnnie *see also under* JOHNNY *n.*[1] and its combs.; note that wherever I have source material, I have given alternative spellings; in those cases where there is a single spelling, I have given only the one I found. The alternative may, none the less, exist.

Johnnie Bates *n. see* MR BATES *under* MR *n.*

johnnie-boy *n. see under* JOHNNY *n.*[1] (2c).

johnnie law *n. see* JOHN LAW *under* JOHN *n.*[1].

Johnnie Nab *n.* [JOHNNY *n.*[2] (1)+ NAB *v.*[1] (2)] [1940s] (*US black*) a police officer, usu. male.

Johnnie Rollocks *n.* (*also* **Johnnie Rollox**) [rhy. sl. = BALLOCKS *n.* (3)] [late 19C] nonsense; something fraudulent.

Johnnie Warby *n.* [? WARB *n.*] [1950s] a tell-tale.

Johnny *n.* (*also* **Johnnie**) [1950s+] *Johnny* Walker whisky; differentiated as *Johnny Red, Johnny Black*, denoting labels/strength.

johnny *n.*[1] (*also* **johnnie**) **1** [late 17C–1900s] a sweetheart, a lover. **2** generic uses for a person. (**a**) [18C+] a man. (**b**) [mid-19C+] used in direct address to any man, name unknown. (**c**) [late 19C–1940s] (*also* **johnnie-boy**) an idle, vacuous young aristocrat, a smart young man about town; thus *johnniedom*, the world of such young men. **3** a novice [abbr. JOHNNY RAW *n.*]. (**a**) [19C] (*esp. Aus.*) a new immigrant. (**b**) [late 19C+] an inexperienced youngster, a raw recruit, a new hand. **4** [mid-19C] (*Anglo-Irish./Scots*) a half-glass of whisky. **5** in respect of national or local populations. (**a**) [mid-19C] (*US*) a Confederate soldier [abbr. *Johnny Reb* under JOHNNY- *pfx*; generic (and slightly contemptuous) use of proper name]. (**b**) [mid-19C–1940s] a soldier in the Indian Army. (**c**) [late 19C–1910s] a Gurkha. (**d**) [1910s] a German soldier. (**e**) [1910s–20s] a Turk. (**f**) [1910s–40s] an Arab. (**g**) [1950s+] an onion-seller from Brittany. (**h**) [1980s] (*S.Afr. black*) a soldier. **6** [mid-19C; 1930s+] (*US*) a lavatory [var. on JAKES *n.* (1)/JOHN *n.*[2] (5)]. **7** [mid-19C–1900s] a rustic simpleton or fool. **8** [mid-19C+] the penis [abbr. JOHN THOMAS *n.* (1)]. **9** [20C+] (*Aus.*) a kookaburra. **10** [1900s] (*Aus.*) the government, esp. as a tax-gatherer [JOHNNY- *pfx* + SE *government*]. **11** [1930s] (*US*) a jack in poker [JOHN *n.* (7)]. **12** [1960s+] (*also* **johnny bag**) a condom. **13** [2000s] (*US prison*) a sandwich in a sack. **14** *see* JOHNNY HORNER *n.*

IN COMPOUNDS

❑ **johnny all sorts** *n.* [mid-19C–1910s] (*Aus.*) a general dealer, usu. in second-hand goods. ❑ **johnny-at-the-rat-hole** *n.* [RATHOLE *n.*] [1900s–30s] (*US*) an exceptionally enthusiastic, greedy person; thus *play johnny-at-the-rat-hole*, to eavesdrop, to interfere in other people's affairs. ❑ **johnny-come-lately** *n.* [mid-19C+] a novice, an unsophisticated person, a recent arrival or recruit; also attrib. ❑ **Johnny Grab** *n.* [? GRAB *v.* (2)] [mid-19C] (*US Und.*) an executioner. ❑ **johnny green** *n.* [mid–late 19C] a naïve person. ❑ **johnny house** *n.* [1930s+] (*US*) a privy, an outside lavatory. ❑ **johnny johnson** *n. see* JOHNSON *n.* (1). ❑ **johnny jumper** *n.* [early 19C] a black slave driver. ❑ **johnny-just-come** *n.* (*also* **just-come**) [20C+] (*W.I.*) a newcomer. ❑ **johnny newcome** *n.* (*also* **johnny newcomer**) **1** [early 19C–1940s] a newcomer or novice. **2** [mid–late 19C] a newborn child. ❑ **johnny no stars** *n.* [from the rating of fast-food restaurant personnel] [2000s] a fool.

johnny *n.*[2] [JOHN *n.*[1]] [mid-19C+] a police officer; a prison guard.

IN COMPOUNDS

❑ **johnny-be-good** *n.* [play on rock song 'Johnny B. Goode' (1958)] [1970s–80s] (*US black*) the police. ❑ **johnny ham** *n.* [play on PIG *n.* (2)] [1930s+] (*US*) a detective. ❑ **johnny law** *n.* [LAW *n.* (3)] [1920s+] (*US*) a police officer, usu. male.

johnny *v.* [late 19C] to realize, to understand.

johnny- *pfx* (*also* **John-**) [modern use tends to be facetious/ironic] [19C+] used as a pfx, as in *johnny-darkie, johnny-gyppo* etc; occas. as sfx.

IN COMPOUNDS

❑ **Johnny Congress** *n.* [SE *Congress*] [early 19C] (*US*) the US Congress. ❑ **Johnny Crapose** *n.* (*also* **Jean Crapeau, John Crappo, Johney Cropp, Johnny Crapaud, ...Crapeau, ...Crapo, ...Crappoi, ...Croppo**) [Fr. *crapaud*, a toad] [19C–1930s] a Frenchman. ❑ **Johnny Reb** *n.* (*also* **Johnny Red**) [SE *rebel*] [mid-19C+] (*US*) a Southerner, esp. a fighter for the Confederacy.

Johnny Armstrong *n. see* CAPTAIN ARMSTRONG *under* CAPTAIN *n.*

Johnny Bliss *n.* (*also* **Arthur Bliss, Micky Bliss, Mike**) [rhy. sl. = PISS *n.*] [20C+] (*Aus./UK*) an act of urination; also as in the phr. 'take the piss'.

Johnny Bull *n. see* JOHN BULL *n.*

johnny bum *n.* [a euph. for *Jack-ass*] [late 18C–early 19C] a donkey.

johnny cake *n.* [a cornmeal bread made by Indians and early settlers] **1** [mid-19C–1930s] (*US*) a countryman, esp. a New Englander. **2** [20C+] (*US/Can.*) a French-born immigrant.

Johnny Cash *n.* [rhy. sl.; ult. US country singer *Johnny Cash* (1932–2003)] **1** [1960s+] urination [= SLASH *n.* (2a)]. **2** [1960s+] (*Aus.*) hashish [= HASH *n.*[2]]. **3** [1980s+] (*Aus. prison*) a hiding place [= STASH *n.*[2] (3)].

johnny Chinaman/johnny Chinee *n. see* JOHN CHINAMAN *n.*

Johnny Cool *n. see* JOE COOL *under* JOE *n.*[1].

Johnny Cotton *adj.* (*also* **Dolly Cotton**) [rhy. sl.] [1930s+] rotten.

johnny darbies *n.* [DARBIES *n.* + JOHNNY DARBY *n.*] [mid-19C+] handcuffs.

johnny darby *n.* [JOHNNY *n.*[2]; added pun on Fr. *gendarme*, a policeman] [mid–late 19C] a policeman.

johnny gee *n.* [? GEE (UP) *v.* (1)] [1930s] (*N.Z.*) methylated spirits, as drunk by alcoholics.

johnny hep *adj.* *see* JOE HEP *adj.*

johnny hop/hopper *n.* *see* JOHN HOP *n.*

Johnny Horner *n.* (*also* **Charlie Horner**) [rhy. sl.] [late 19C+] the corner, esp. a public house on a corner.

johnny-jump-up *n.* [joc. ref. to its effects] [20C+] (*Irish*) a bottle of cider, or mix of beer and cider.

Johnny O'Keefe *n.* [rhy. sl.; ult. the Australian rock and roll singer *Johnny O'Keefe* (1935–78)] [1980s+] (*Aus. prison*) the teeth.

johnny-on-the-spot *n.* (*also* **Johnny-on-the-job**) [JOHNNY *n.*[1] (1) + SE *spot/job*; note NY Sun Apr. 1896: 'A 'Johnny on the spot' is a man or youth who may be relied upon to be at a certain stated place when wanted and on whose assured appearance confident expectation may be based. It is not sufficient that an alert and trustworthy individual, to be thought deserving of the name 'Johnny on the spot,' should restrict his beneficent activity to the matter of being at a certain place when needed. He must, in addition, render such service and attend to such business when there as the occasion may require, and such a 'Johnny' must be on the spot not merely to attend to the business of others, but also to look after his own. Hence an individual who is prompt and farseeing, alive to his own interests and keenly sensible of means for promoting his own advantage is a 'Johnny on the spot'.'] **1** [late 19C+] (*US*) a reliable, punctual or decisive person, or thing; also attrib. **2** [1970s] (*US*) a portable latrine.

johnny-on-the-spot *adv.* [1950s] (*US*) promptly.

Johnny Peasoup *n.* see PEASOUP *n.*[1] (2).

johnny-pump *n.* [1970s] (*US*) a water hydrant.

johnny randle *n.* *see* JACK RANDALL *n.*

johnny rann *n.* [rhy. sl. = SCRAN *n.* (2)] [20C+] food.

johnny raper *n.* [rhy. sl.] [1980s+] **1** (*Aus.*) newspaper. **2** (*Aus. prison*) a cigarette paper. **3** (*Aus. prison*) a caper, a criminal exploit.

Johnny Raw *n.* (*also* **Johnnie Raw, Jonny Raw, raw**) [JOHNNY *n.*[1] (1) + SE *raw*] **1** [19C] a rustic, an unsophisticated country dweller. **2** [19C; 1960s] an inexperienced youngster, a raw recruit, a new hand, a novice. **3** [late 19C+] (*esp. Aus.*) a new immigrant.

Johnny Raw *adj.* [JOHNNY RAW *n.*] [19C] inexperienced, naïve.

Johnny Ray *adj.* [rhy. sl. = *gay*] [1980s] (*Aus.*) homosexual.

Johnny Rocks *n.* [rhy. sl. = POX *n.*[1] (1)] [1920s] (*Irish*) syphilis.

Johnny Ronce *n.* *see* CHARLIE RONCE *n.*

Johnny Rowsers *n.* (*also* **Charlie Rousers, jolly rousers**) [rhy. sl.] [1920s–60s] (*US*) trousers.

Johnny Russell *n.* [rhy. sl.; ult. ? politician Lord *John Russell* (1792–1878)] [1900s–40s] (*Aus.*) bustle, hustle.

IN PHRASES

□ **on the Johnny Russell** [1900s–40s] (*Aus.*) **1** bustling about. **2** struggling for existence.

johnny rutter *n.* [rhy. sl.] [1930s+] butter.

johnny skinner *n.* *see* JIMMY SKINNER *n.*

Johnny Tapp *v.* [rhy. sl. = CRAP *v.*[2] (1)] [1980s+] (*Aus. prison*) to defecate.

Johnny Tinplate *n.* [a mocking allusion to his badge] [1910s–20s] (*US*) a rural sheriff.

Johnny Walker *n.*[1] [rhy. sl. = talker; ult. *Johnnie Walker*, a brand of whisky] [20C+] **1** a talker, a garrulous person. **2** an informer.

Johnny Walker *n.*[2]

IN PHRASES

□ **do a Johnny Walker** *v.* [1900s] to let off, to escape scot free.

johnny warder *n.* [proper name of *John Ward* who kept a public house in Sussex Street, Sydney, in which he allowed such people to drink] (*Aus.*) **1** [late 19C] a drunken layabout. **2** [1910s–30s] anyone who drinks alone, a drink that is taken by oneself.

johnny wet-bread *n.* [anecdote of a Dublin beggar who moistened his bread in the city's fountains] [20C+] (*Irish*) a teasing rather than aggressive term of mockery.

Johnny Whopstraw *n.* *see* WHOPSTRAW *under* STRAW *n.*

johnny woodser/johnny woods *n.* *see* JIMMY WOODSER *n.*

johnny yeg *n.* *see* YEGG *n.*

John O'Brien *n.* [ety. unknown; ? anecdotal] (*US*) **1** [1900s–50s] a freight train or one of its boxcars; a side-door Pullman. **2** [1910s] an empty safe. **3** [1920s] a hand-car.

John O'Groat *n.* [rhy. sl.] [20C+] a coat.

John O'Groats *n.* [rhy. sl. = OATS *n.*[2]] [1920s+] sexual satisfaction.

John Pigtail *n.* *see* PIGTAIL *n.* (4).

John Public *n.* *see* JOE PUBLIC *under* JOE *n.*[1].

John Q *n.* *see* JOHN BROWN *n.*

John Q. Law *n.* [JOHN LAW *under* JOHN *n.*[1] + JOHN Q. PUBLIC *n.*] [1980s+] (*US*) a police officer, usu. male.

John Q. Public *n.* (*also* **John Q. Citizen, John Q. Voter**) [JOHN *n.* (1) + ? ref. to US President *John Q(uincy) Adams* (1767–1848)] [1930s+] the average, law-abiding citizen.

John Roberts *n.* [*John Roberts*, MP, the author of the Sunday Closing Act, which was applied to Wales] [late 19C] enough alcohol to last a drinker from Saturday night to Sunday night.

john rogers *n.* *see* JOHN BROWN *n.*

john roper's window *n.* [pun] [mid-16C] the hangman's rope.

John Roscoe *n.* *see* ROSCOE *n.*

john sap *n.* *see* SAP *n.*[2].

John Selwyn *n.* [rhy. sl.; ult. UK Conservative politician *John Selwyn Gummer* (b.1939)] [1980s] **1** an unpleasant reaction to drugs [= BUMMER *n.*[4] (1)]. **2** any unpleasant experience or person [= BUMMER *n.*[3] (3)].

john smith *n.* *see* JOHN BROWN *n.*

johnson *n.* [analogous with JOCK *n.*[1] (1) or JACK *n.*[3] (1); later use ? link to boxing champion Jack *Johnson* (1878–1946)] **1** [mid–late 19C; 1960s+] (*also* **johnny johnson**) the penis (later usage esp. US black). **2** [1950s+] a pimp; a man living off a prostitute's earnings. **3** [1970s] (*US*) a dildo. **4** [1970s+] (*US*) a thing. **5** in US drugs uses. (**a**) [1970s+] marijuana. (**b**) [1980s+] crack cocaine. **6** [1980s] the buttocks.

IN PHRASES

□ **pull a Johnson** *v.* [the shape of the 'J' in Johnson] [1990s+] (*US teen*) to execute a U-turn in the middle of the street, usu. as a last-minute decision. It is illegal in most states.

johnson bar *n.* [? railroad jargon *johnson bar*, the reverse bar of an early 20C+ locomotive; note JOHNSON *n.*] **1** [1920s+] (*US*) a penis. **2** [1960s–70s] (*US*) a dildo.

johnsons *n.*[1] (*also* **john family, johnson-boys, johnson brothers, johnson-man**) [? the commonness and thus potential anonymity of the name; or railroad jargon *johnson bar*, the reverse bar of an early 20C+ locomotive, used as a weapon or cosh] [1920s+] (*US*) a generic term for the world of professional criminals.

johnsons *n.*[2] [ety. unknown; ext./misreading of JOHNSON *n.* (1)] [1970s] (*US*) a woman's breasts.

john stagger-back *n.* [20C+] (*W.I.*) a variety of codfish fritter, so tough and chewy that one 'staggers back' when one bites it.

john thomas *n.* **1** [late 17C+] (*also* **John Thomson, Sir Thomas**) the penis. **2** [mid–late 19C] a liveried servant [generic name or ? like the former, the latter 'stands' in the presence of a lady].

John Wayne *n.*[1] [suggestive of heroic film characters played by the Hollywood actor *John Wayne* (1907–79)] [1960s+] (*US*) anything or anyone seen as heroic, macho, manly.

John Wayne *n.*[2] [rhy. sl.; ult. *see* prev.] [1990s+] a train.

John Wayne *adj.* [JOHN WAYNE *n.*[1]] [1960s+] (*US*) heroic, macho, manly.

John Wayne *v.* [JOHN WAYNE *n.*[1]] [1960s+] (*US*) to act decisively, daringly, in an aggressive manner; often in ironic use.

john willie *n.* [var. on JOHN THOMAS *n.* (1); note WILLIE *n.*[4]] [1930s+] the penis.

john willy *n. see* JOHN BROWN *n.*

john yegg *n. see* YEGG *n.*

join *n.* [20C+] (*Ulster*) a pool or 'kitty' of money to provide a round of drinks.

join *v.*

SE in slang uses

IN PHRASES

❑ **join giblets** *v. see under* GIBLETS *n.* ❑ **join out** *v.* [late 19C–1920s] **1** (*US tramp*) for two or more tramps to become companions on the road; to be hired. **2** (*US Und.*) to join a criminal gang. ❑ **join paunches** *v.* [18C–19C] to have sexual intercourse. ❑ **join the bird family** *v. see under* BIRD *n.*[1]. ❑ **join the gang** *v.* [late 19C] to become a professional thief.

join-boy *n.* [? Fanakalo *joyin*, a contract + SE *boy*] [1940s+] (*S.Afr.*) a newly recruited miner.

joined *adj.* [note *join giblets* under JOIN *v.*] [late 19C] married.

joint *n.* **1** [17C; mid-19C; 1930s+] (*US*) the penis. **2** a man or woman. (**a**) [late 19C–1900s] a wife. (**b**) [late 19C–1950s] (*Aus.*) a person, a fellow, a 'chap'. (**c**) [1990s+] (*US black/gay*) a feminine male homosexual partner. **3** a place [according to the *OED* the orig. use applied spec. to Chinese-run opium dens and thence to illicit saloons; in both cases the *joint* was seen as a gathering place for criminals, a low-life nuance that remains with the word, even in its more general sl. use]. (**a**) [late 19C–1950s] (*US drugs*) (*also* **pipe joint**) an opium den. (**b**) [late 19C+] (*orig. US*) any place, esp. a bar or club, a brothel, a gambling establishment, a restaurant. (**c**) [20C+] (*orig. US tramp*) a meeting place. (**d**) [1910s] a factory. (**e**) [1910s] (*Aus.*) a public-house bar. (**f**) [1910s+] one's house or home. (**g**) [1910s+] a country, geographical area, a town, a city. (**h**) [1920s–50s] (*Aus./US carnival*) any 'sideshow' devoted to gambling. (**i**) [1920s+] (*US*) prison, also as *the joint*. (**j**) [1960s] (*US*) a police station. (**k**) [1980s] (*US*) a detoxification facility. (**l**) [1990s+] in fig. use; of any kind of object or place; often unspecified. **4** in Und. uses. (**a**) [late 19C+] a swindling set-up or a place to be robbed. (**b**) [1900s] (*Aus. Und.*) a swindle. (**c**) [1940s] (*US Und.*) (*also* **top of the joint**) the total amount taken in a single confidence trick. **5** (*orig. US*) in drug uses. (**a**) [1930s+] an opium pipe or hypodermic syringe and other drug paraphernalia [the 'joining' of the opium and its pipe]. (**b**) [1950s] a cigarette laced with paregoric. (**c**) [1950s+] a marijuana or hashish cigarette [the 'joining' of the drug with tobacco to make the cigarette; by the 1990s the drug reference had become sufficiently common for the word to be used almost without comment or identifying quotation marks]. (**d**) [1990s+] marijuana. **6** [1940s+] (*US*) a gun. **7** [1970s+] (*orig. US black*) something excellent, as in the phr. *the serious joint*, the real thing. **8** [1980s+] (*orig. US black*) an artistic creation, typically a record or film [popularized by film-maker Spike Lee (b.1956) who credits his films 'Another Spike Lee Joint'; subseq. used by many hip-hop/rap artists to describe their music]. **9** [2000s] (*US black/prison*) a prison sentence.

DERIVATIVES

❑ **jointwise** *adj.* [-WISE *sfx*] [1930s–50s] (*US prison*) well-adjusted to prison life, capable of sustaining one's existence in prison.

IN COMPOUNDS

❑ **jointman** *n.* [JOINT *n.* (1) + SE *man*] [1920s+] (*Can./US prison*) any prisoner who toadies to the authorities. ❑ **joint togs** *n.* [TOGS *n.* (1)] [1950s] (*US Und.*) the clothes worn by a whore in a brothel.

IN PHRASES

❑ **all over the joint** [1950s] (*US*) everywhere. ❑ **black joint** *n.* [1920s] (*US black/Harlem*) any black nightclub catering spec. to white 'tourists'. ❑ **blast a joint** *v.* [1950s+] (*drugs*) to smoke marijuana. ❑ **book the joint** *v.* [1970s+] (*US teen*) to look over a place, to check its amenities. ❑ **bust a joint** *v.* [1950s–70s] (*drugs*) to smoke a cannabis cigarette. ❑ **crack a joint** *v.* [late 19C] to smoke an opium pipe. ❑ **daffy joint** *n. see* DAFFY HOUSE *under* DAFFY *adj.* ❑ **do a joint** *v.* [1960s+] (*drugs*) to smoke marijuana. ❑ **get to the joint** *v.* (*also* **go to the joint**) [late 19C–1930s] (*US*) to come to the point, to achieve one's aim, esp. in a criminal context. ❑ **have someone by the joint** *v.* [1970s] of a woman, to have a man sexually enslaved. ❑ **hot joint** *n.* [HOT *adj.* (5)] [1920s–60s] (*US tramp*) somewhere that is robbed while the owners are in occupation. ❑ **jump the joint** *v.* [ext. use of SAusE *jump*, to take possession of a parcel of land, esp. in a deceitful or illegal manner] [1910s–50s] (*Aus.*) to take command. ❑ **pipe joint** *n. see* sense 3a above. ❑ **pull one's joint** *v.* (*also* **pull one's meat**) **1** [1930s+] to masturbate. **2** [1970s] to whine, to complain. ❑ **real joint** *n.* [1950s] (*US Und.*) any nightspot frequented by criminals, spec. pimps and prostitutes. ❑ **spread the joint** *v.* [1930s–50s] (*US drugs*) to prepare the equipment for smoking opium. ❑ **stand on one's joint** *v.* [1940s] (*US*) to have an erect penis. ❑ **top of the joint** *n. see* sense 4c above.

joint of beef *n.* [rhy. sl.] [20C+] the chief, i.e. the boss.

jojee *n.* [var. on DUJI *n.*] [1960s+] (*drugs*) heroin.

jo-jo *n.*[1] [proper name *Jo-Jo*] **1** [late 19C–1900s] (*Aus.*) a man with a very heavy beard and side-whiskers [a Russian 'dog-man' who was exhibited as a sideshow freak in Melbourne, c.1880]. **2** [20C+] (*US*) a funny character [a dog-faced boy exhibited by P.T. Barnum (1810–91)].

jo-jo *n.*[2] [ety. unknown] [1960s+] (*Can. prison*) a bulky coat without pockets.

jojo *n.* [? JOHN *n.*[2] (3)/JOHNSON *n.* (1)] [1960s+] (*US black*) the penis.

IN COMPOUNDS

❑ **jojo book** *n.* [1990s+] (*US*) a pornographic book.

joker *n.*[1] [they make a joke of the situation] **1** [early 19C+] (*orig. Aus.*) a man, a person, sometimes with implications of incompetence. **2** [mid-19C+] (*US*) any thing or situation that poses a problem, a hidden catch, a surprise [card imagery]. **3** [20C+] (*W.I.*) anyone who is given authority but performs their work with irritating incompetence, thus 'a disgrace to one's profession'. **4** [1920s] a negro. **5** [1950s] (*US gay*) a masculine homosexual.

IN PHRASES

❑ **my joker** [late 19C] a term of affectionate address.

joker *n.*[2] [1920s–50s] (*US drugs*) **1** a hypodermic syringe. **2** an injection of morphine.

jokes *adj.* [2000s] (*UK black*) amusing, funny.

jokettes *n. see* JOCK *n.*[1] (2b).

joko *n. see* JOCKER *n.*[1] (3).

jol *n.* (*also* **jaul, jawl**) [Afk. *jol*, a dance, a party] (*S.Afr.*) **1** [1950s+] a good time, merry-making, enjoyment, entertainment. **2** [1960s+] a party, a festival or other social occasion. **3** [1980s+] a joke, a stunt, a game. **4** [1980s+] a holiday, a trip taken for pure enjoyment. **5** [1980s+] an act of sexual intercourse; a person characterized by their sexuality. **6** [2000s] (*S.Afr. prison*) a prison sex-worker's client. **7** [2000s] a fuss. **8** *see* JOLLY *n.*[1] (8).

jol *adj. see* JOLLY *adj.*

jol *v.* (*also* **jaul, jawl**) [JOL *n.*] (*S.Afr.*) **1** [1940s+] to go out, to stroll, to run, to depart, to look for some fun or entertainment. **2** [1960s+] to have an affair with, to flirt, to 'carry on'. **3** [1970s+] to tease, to joke. **4** [1970s+] to play, to frolic, to have fun, to 'party'. **5** [1980s] to hang around, to loiter.

jola *n.* [Carib.E *jola*, a large jute sack] [1950s+] (*W.I.*) an over-sized handbag.

joller *n.* [JOL *v.* + sfx *-er*] (*S.Afr.*) **1** [1960s+] a hedonist. 'The term 'joller' is believed to have originated from the Afrikaans word 'jol', meaning a festive party. People who attended such parties were accordingly referred to as 'jollers', but the word has degenerated in meaning and now signifies any person who 'celebrates' any and every occasion by fighting, swearing, drinking, and smoking dagga' (Freed [1963]). **2** [1960s+] one who frequents 'unsavoury' bars, dance-halls and similar places of low-life entertainment. **3** [1980s+] one who attends a party, concert or social gathering. **4** [1980s+] a player of a game.

jollier *n.* **1** [late 19C–1930s] (*UK Und.*) (*also* **jolly**) a card sharp's accomplice, who pretends to be a member of the public. **2** [1900s] a flatterer.

jollies *n. see* JOLLY *n.*[1] (9).

jolling *n.* [JOL *v.* + sfx *-ing*] (*S.Afr.*) **1** [1960s+] flirting. **2** [1980s+] merry-making, 'partying'.

jollo *n.* [SE *jollification* + -O *sfx* (3)] [20C+] (*Aus.*) **1** a party, a celebration, usu. involving drinking. **2** intense activity, not necessarily pleasurable.

jollocks *n.* (*also* **jollock, jollux**) [SE *jolly*, but note dial. *jollus*, fat, fleshy, *jollock*, jolly, hearty] **1** [mid-18C–early 19C] a fat person. **2** [late 18C–19C] a parson.

jollop *n.* [SE *jalap*, a purgative drug obtained from the tuberous roots of *Exogonium* (*Ipomoea*) *purga*] **1** [late 19C+] a purgative, a medicine. **2** [1920s+] strong liquor or a measure of liquor.

jollopi *n. see* JALOPY *n.*

jolly *n.*[1] **1** [late 18C–mid-19C] the head [abbr. *JOLLY NOB under* JOLLY *adj.*]. **2** [early–mid-19C] an accomplice [? they 'jolly one along']. **3** [early 19C–1940s] a marine; thus *tame jolly*, a militiaman, *royal jolly*, a royal marine [OED suggests n. use of SE *jolly*, cheerful, gallant, brave etc, but Bowen (*Sea Slang*, 1929) and Fraser & Gibbons (1925) say it was adapted from the nickname of the City Trained Bands, a 'Tame Jolly' (which may also have come from SE)]. **4** pertaining to speech. (**a**) [mid-19C] praise, esp. when spoken for an ulterior and/or criminal purpose. (**b**) [mid-19C] (*UK Und.*) a rude or aggressive comment. (**c**) [mid-19C] (*UK Und.*) a warning. (**d**) [mid–late 19C] a cheer. (**e**) [mid–late 19C] a sham purchaser, who praises up inferior goods in order to facilitate their sale to an innocent buyer; similarly used for a fairground stallholder's or crooked gambler's accomplice. (**f**) [mid-19C+] (*US*) light-hearted teasing, bantering, often as *the jolly*. **5** [mid–late 19C] a ruckus, a fracas. **6** [mid–late 19C] the person who encourages or initiates a ruckus. **7** [mid-19C–1910s] a deception or hoax. **8** [late 19C+] (*also* **jol**) a party, a merry-making [abbr. SE *jollification*]. **9** [late 19C+] (*also* **jollies**) a thrill of pleasure or excitement. **10** [1960s+] (*US*) an orgasm. **11** [1990s+] sexual play, whether or not including intercourse.

(IN COMPOUNDS)

❑ **jolly-bag** *n.* [SE *bag*/BAG *n.*[1] (1a)] [1980s+] (*US*) a condom. ❑ **jolly beans** *n.* (*also* **jolly pills**) [sense 9 above] [1960s+] (*drugs*) amphetamine.

(IN PHRASES)

❑ **get one's jollies** *v.* [1950s+] **1** to enjoy oneself. **2** to have sex. ❑ **give (someone) a jolly** *v.* **1** [mid–late 19C] to deceive, to tell a tale in order to trick someone. **2** [late 19C] to applaud. ❑ **start a jolly** *v.* [late 19C] to start the applause, for a performer or turn, at a music-hall or theatre.

jolly *n.*[2]

(IN EXCLAMATIONS)

❑ **by jolly!** *see BY GOLLY! under* GOLLY! *excl.*

jolly *adj.* (*also* **jol**) [mid-17C+] tipsy, drunk.

SE in slang uses

(IN COMPOUNDS)

❑ **jolly nob** *n.* [NOB *n.*[1] (1)] [late 18C–mid-19C] the head. ❑ **jolly stick** *n.* [STICK *n.* (1a)] [1970s] the penis.

(IN PHRASES)

❑ **jolly for polly** [20C+] sexually available.

(IN EXCLAMATIONS)

❑ **jolly d!** [? abbr. SE *jolly delightful/decent*; note D *adj.*] [1940s+] (*juv.*) wonderful! excellent! fantastic!

jolly *v.* **1** [mid-19C] to make a sham bid at an auction. **2** [mid-19C–1920s] (*orig. US?*) to tease roughly, to chaff, to abuse, to trick. **3** [mid-19C+] (*also* **jolly along, ...for, ...up**) to treat someone in an agreeable manner, with the intention of keeping them happy and/or obtaining a favour from them; esp. in the phr. *jolly up, jolly along*. **4** [late 19C] to cheer. **5** [late 19C] (*US campus*) to have a good time.

jolly dog *n.* [SE *jolly* + DOG *n.*[2] (1); later use is SE] [18C–19C] a boon companion; thus *jolly-doggy-ness*.

jolly joker *n.* [rhy. sl.] [20C+] a poker.

jolly member *n. see under* MEMBER *n.*[1].

jollyo *n.* [JOLLY *n.*[1] (8) + -O *sfx* (1)] [1970s] a celebration.

jolly roger *n.* [rhy. sl.] [20C+] a lodger.

jolly rousers *n. see* JOHNNY ROWSERS *n.*

jolly-up *n.* [JOLLY *n.*[1] (8)] **1** [1900s–20s] a drinking bout, a spree. **2** [1920s–50s] a good time. **3** [1920s+] an informal dance, a party.

Jolson story *n.* [rhy. sl. = CORIE *n.*; ult. *The Jolson Story*, a biopic of the singer Al *Jolson* (1886–1950), released in 1946] [1970s–80s] the penis.

jolt *n.* **1** in context of drink or drugs. (**a**) [20C+] (*US drugs*) a measure of a drug as taken by a user, esp. an injection of a narcotic; occas. of a non-recreational drug; thus *OVERJOLT* below. (**b**) [20C+] a stiff drink of spirits, esp. brandy, whisky or bourbon. (**c**) [1920s+] (*US*) the effects of a drug or alcohol, a 'kick'. (**d**) [1950s] as non-drug ext. of (c) a thrill. **2** [1910s+] (*US Und.*) a prison sentence, usu. with the number of years specified, e.g. a *seven-year jolt*. **3** [1940s] (*US*) a job. **4** [1950s] execution in the electric chair. **5** [1960s] (*US*) a train.

(IN PHRASES)

❑ **overjolt** *n.* [SE *over* + sense 1 above] [1950s+] (*US drugs*) a drug overdose. ❑ **pass someone a jolt** *v. see* JOLT *v.* (2). ❑ **shake one's jolt** *v.* [1950s] (*US prison*) to interfere with the way another person is dealing with their sentence.

SE in slang uses

(IN PHRASES)

❑ **give someone the jolts** *v.* [SE *jolts*, electric shocks] [1970s] (*US*) to execute in the electric chair.

jolt *v.* **1** [17C–18C] to have sexual intercourse. **2** [mid-19C+] (*orig. US*) (*also* **pass someone a jolt**) to hit or kill someone. **3** [1910s+] (*US*) (*also* **jolt up**) to drink. **4** [1920s–30s] (*US Und./prison*) to sentence to prison. **5** [1950s+] (*US drugs*) to inject a drug. **6** [1960s–70s] (*Scot.*) to abscond.

jolter *n.* [JOLT *n.* (1)] [1910s] (*drugs*) a drug user.

jolterhead *n.* (*also* **jolter-pate, jolthead**) [dial; ult. ? SE *jowl*, a bump on the head] [late 16C–19C] a fool, a stupid person.

jolter-headed *adj.* (*also* **jolt-headed**) [JOLTERHEAD *n.*] [late 16C–19C; 1980s+] stupid, foolish.

jo maxi *n. see* JOE MAXI *n.*

jombie *n. see* JUMBIE *n.*

jomer *n.* [? Rom./Polari] [mid–late 19C] a girlfriend, the antonym of BLOWER *n.*[1].

jomoke *n. see* JAMOKE *n.*[1].

jonah *n.* [naut. sl. *Jonah*, a person who personifies bad luck; such individuals were sometimes tossed overboard, esp. in a storm, to placate the elements. The term in itself goes back to the biblical prophet *Jonah*, who, while supposedly 'fleeing the Lord', was similarly tossed overboard and swallowed by 'a great fish', presumably a whale] **1** [mid-19C+] one who brings bad luck; thus *Jonahness*; also of objects. **2** [late 19C+] one who suffers severe misfortune. **3** [1950s] a heckler. **4** [1960s] (*US prison*) a misfortune; also attrib.

(IN PHRASES)

❑ **bring one's Jonah on** *v.* [20C+] (*W.I.*) to attack verbally, to vilify.

jonah *v.* [JONAH *n.*] **1** [late 19C+] to bring bad luck. **2** [1960s] (*US black*) to trick, to swindle.

jonah's whale *n.* [rhy. sl.] [late 19C–1910s] a tail.

Jonathan *n.* [abbr. SAmE *Brother Jonathan*, a generic for the US and for its people; note Bartlett, 1848: 'When General Washington [...] came to Massachusetts to organize it and make preparations for the defence of the country, he found a great want of ammunition and other means necessary to meet the powerful foe he had to contend with [...] On one occasion at that anxious period, a consultation of the officers and others was had, when it seemed no way could be devised to make such preparation as was necessary. His Excellency, Jonathan Trumbull the elder, was then

Governor of the State of Connecticut, on whose judgment and aid the General placed the greatest reliance, and remarked, "We must consult 'Brother Jonathan' on the subject." The General did so, and the Governor was successful in supplying many of the wants of the army. When difficulties afterwards arose, and the army was spread over the country, it became a by-word [...] The term Yankee is still applied to a portion, but "Brother Jonathan" has now become a designation of the whole country, as John Bull has for England'; there is no evidence for this popular story, however, in Washington's papers] **1** [late 18C–mid-19C] (*US*) a New Englander. **2** [late 18C–1900s] (*orig. US*) an American; thus fem. *Jonatheena*.

Jonathan Aitken *adj.* [rhy. sl.; ult. *Jonathan Aitken* (b. 1942), former Conservative MP and convicted perjurer] [2000s] eggs and bacon.

Jonathan Ross *n.* [rhy. sl.; ult. UK TV personality *Jonathan Ross* (b. 1960)] [1980s+] **1** a drink, spec. beer [SAUCE *n.*[1] (5)]. **2** a TOSS *n.*[1] (1).

Jonathan Simonizer *n.* [var. on APPLE-POLISHER *n.*; *Jonathan*, a kind of apple + *Simonizer*, a brand of wax] [1930s–40s] (*US campus*) a toady, a sycophant.

jone *v.* (*also* **joan (on)**) [JOANING *n.*] **1** [1970s+] (*US black*) to indulge in a session of ritualized mutual insults; usu. as JONING *n.* **2** [1980s+] (*US campus*) to be idle while pretending to be busy. **3** [1990s+] (*US teen*) to gossip (maliciously).

jones *n.*[1] [the common family name; its link to craving remains unexplained; note *HHC* Dec. 1999: 'According to our colleagues at the Online Rap Dictionary, it comes from Jones Alley in Manhattan where junkies, with their ever-present longing, used to live'] **1** [1960s+] (*US drugs*) (*also* **Mr. Jones**) drug addiction, esp. to heroin. **2** [1960s+] (*US drugs*) a heroin addict. **3** [1960s+] (*US drugs*) heroin. **4** [1960s+] the symptoms of heroin withdrawal. **5** [1970s+] (*US*) a strong craving or habit, whether for cigarettes, food, a person or anything, e.g. a *love jones*, a *chocolate jones*. **6** [1980s] (*US drugs*) a marijuana cigarette.

IN COMPOUNDS

▫ **jones man** *n.* (*also* **jones boy**) [1970s+] (*US black/drugs*) a heroin dealer.

jones *n.*[2] [? JOHNSON *n.* (1)] [1960s+] (*US black*) **1** the penis. **2** sexual intercourse.

IN PHRASES

▫ **get one's jones off** *v.* [1960s+] (*orig. US black*) to reach orgasm; also fig. to enjoy. ▫ **get one's jones on** *v.* [1980s] (*US black*) to have a sexual partner on hand.

jones *n.*[3] [generic use of surname] [1970s+] (*US black*) a black person.

jones *v.* [JONES *n.*[1]] **1** [1970s+] (*drugs*) to suffer from narcotics addiction or the withdrawal symptoms that accompany it. **2** [1980s+] in fig. use, to be obsessed by, to be dependent on. **3** [1980s+] to want very much. **4** [1980s+] (*US campus*) to intrude and try to prevent someone who is attempting to seduce another. **5** [1990s+] (*US campus*) to do wrong, to cause someone to be unhappy.

joneser *n.* [JONES *n.*[1] (1)] [1980s+] (*US*) an addict, esp. of cocaine.

jonesing *adj.* [fig. use of JONES *v.* (1)] [1980s+] (*US campus*) boring.

Jones's locker *n. see* DAVY JONES'S LOCKER *n.*

jong *n.*[1] [Cape Du. *jongen*, a young lad] (*S.Afr.*) **1** [early 17C–late 19C] a black servant. **2** [early 19C] an informal mode of address, irrespective of sex. **3** [20C+] a derog. term for a black man. **4** [1970s] a boyfriend.

jong *n.*[2] [? JOHN *n.*[2] (3) + SCHLONG *n.* (1)] [1920s–50s] (*US*) the penis.

jong! *excl.* [? JONG *n.*[1]/JONG *n.*[2]] [1950s+] (*S.Afr.*) an excl. of surprise, delight, exasperation, approval etc.

jon-hop *n. see* JOHN HOP *n.*

jonic *adj. see* JANNOCK *adj.*

joning *n. see* JOANING *n.*

jonn(a) *n. see* JONNOP *n.*

jonnick/jonnuk *adj. see* JANNOCK *adj.*

jonnop *n. see* JOHN HOP *n.*

Jonny Raw *n. see* JOHNNY RAW *n.*

jont *n.* [var. on JOINT *n.* (8)] [2000s] (*US prison*) a thing, an object.

joog *v.* **1** [1980s] (*US black*) to have sexual intercourse. **2** *see* JUKE *v.*[1]. **3** *see* JUKE *v.*[2]. **4** *see* JUKE *v.*[3].

joogie *n.* [? JUKE *n.*[1] (1) + BOOGIE *n.*[2] (1)] [1970s–80s] (*US black*) a black person, occas. derog. use.

jook *see also under* JUKE and combs.

jook *n.*[1] [1990s+] (*US black*) a burglary.

jook *n.*[2] *see* JUK *n.*

jook *v.* (*also* **jog, joog, jug**) [JUKE *v.*[2] (3)] [1970s+] (*US gay*) to sodomize.

jookass *n.* [pron.] [1920s] (*US black*) a jackass.

jookery *n. see* JUKE *n.*[1].

jook-halter *n.* [Scot. *jouk*, to trick + SE *halter*] [19C+] (*Ulster*) one who has only just escaped hanging.

jook out someone's eye *v.* [fig. use of JUKE *v.*[2] (1)] [1950s+] (*W.I.*) to cheat in a business deal.

jooks *n.* [JUKE *v.*[1] (1)] [1990s+] (*black*) a fool.

jook-the-beetle *n.* [fig. use of Scot. *jouk*, to trick + *beetle*, a hammer, in this case a masher for the vegetables] [20C+] (*Ulster*) **1** a bad cook. **2** a lump in mashed potatoes or porridge.

jook-the-bottle *n.* [fig. use of Scot. *jouk*, to trick + SE *bottle*] [20C+] (*Ulster*) a teetotaller.

joop *v. see* JUKE *v.*[2] (3).

joppy *n. see* JALOPY *n.*

jordan *n.*[1] (*also* **jordain, jouden, jurden**) [origin unknown, one theory suggested that the term is an abbr. of *Jordan-bottle* – a bottle of water brought from the River Jordan by crusaders or pilgrims – but this ignores the orig. form of the word, as found in *Prompt. Parv.* (1440) *inter alia*, *jurdanus*, which has no links to *Jordanes*, the contemporary Lat. for the Jordan. An earlier SE use was a kind of pot or vessel formerly used by physicians and alchemists; such pots might often have held urine for analysis; thus leading to the sl. term] [late 14C–1970s] a chamberpot.

jordan *n.*[2] (*also* **jordain**) [ety. unknown; ? f. use of 'go over the Jordan' as euph. for die; such a blow might kill the recipient] [late 17C–mid-19C] (*UK Und.*) a blow with a staff.

jordan *adj.* [mid-19C] (*US*) disagreeable, difficult.

jork *n.* [JERK *n.*[1] (2) + DORK *n.* (2)] [1990s+] (*US campus*) an idiot, a fool.

j.o. scene *n.* [J.O. *n.* (1) + SCENE *n.* (5)] [1960s+] **1** masturbation. **2** mutual masturbation.

Joseph *n.* [all are biblical] **1** [mid-17C–mid-19C] a (usu. woman's) overcoat or cloak; thus *rum Joseph*, a first-rate overcoat, *queer joseph*, a tattered, worn-out cloak [Joseph's 'coat of many colours']. **2** [mid-17C–late 19C] a bashful young man [Joseph fled from Potiphar's wife]. **3** [1950s] (*juv.*) a dreamer [Joseph's dream].

joseph *adj.* [ext. of JOE *adj.*[1] (1)] [1900s–20s] (*US*) aware, in the know; thus as n., one who is aware.

Josephus rex *n.*

IN PHRASES

▫ **you are Josephus rex** [pun on SE abbr. *jo* + Lat. *rex*, king] [late 18C–early 19C] you are joking.

Josh *n.* [JOSKIN *n.*] [mid-19C–1900s] (*US*) a rustic, simpleton.

josh *n.* [JOSH *v.*] [late 19C+] (*US*) a good-natured joke or piece of banter; thus adj. *joshy*; also attrib.

josh *v.* [proper name *Josh* Billings (Henry Wheeler Shaw, 1818–85), an American humorist] (*US*) **1** [mid-19C+] to ridicule or tease someone. **2** [late 19C+] to indulge in teasing or banter; thus n. *joshing*, as phr. *put the josh on someone*.

josh! *excl.* [JOSH *n.*] [mid-19C] (*US*) a cry of encouragement.

josher *n.*[1] [JOSH *v.*] [late 19C–1920s] (*US*) a teaser.

josher *n.*[2] [? JOSH *v.* or play on Suffolk dial. *josh*, an old cow] [late 19C–1940s] (*Aus.*) an immoral old woman.

josies *n.* [1970s+] (*Irish*) women's breasts.

joskin *n.* [dial. *joss*, bump + SE *bumpkin*; 20C+ use is US] **1** [early 19C+] a country bumpkin. **2** [late 19C] a foreigner, esp. one from the British Colonies.

joss *n.* [pidgin *joss*, a Chinese god; ult. Port. *deos* and Javanese *dejos*] **1** [late 19C–1950s] (*Aus./US*) a derog. term for a Chinese person. **2** [late 19C+] luck; thus *good joss, bad joss*.

josser *n.*[1] [JOSS *n.*] **1** [late 19C] an ageing roué. **2** [late 19C–1900s] a swell, a grandee. **3** [late 19C–1940s] (*Aus.*) a clergyman, a minister.

josser *n.*[2] [var. on PROSSER *n.*] [late 19C–1910s] one who begs for loans, a 'sponge'.

josser *n.*[3] [? Polari *josser*, an outsider] [late 19C–1920s] a simpleton, a fool.

josser *n.*[4] [? a 'beggar' ie JOSSER *n.*[2]] **1** [late 19C+] a man, a fellow, usu. with *old*. **2** [1900s] as a term of address.

jossop *n.* [ety. unknown; ? link to JOLLOP *n.*; ? ult. ME *jussell*, a broth] [mid-19C+] gravy.

joss-pidgin-man *n.* (*also* **joss-house-man**) [SE *joss-man*, a priest of a Chinese religion, ult. *joss*, a Chinese idol or image; thus luck (f. Pidgin version of Port. *deos*, god). Note RN use *jossman*, Plymouth gin, which carried a picture of a monk on the bottle] [late 19C–1920s] a clergyman, esp. a missionary.

joss temple *n.* [pidgin *joss*, a Chinese god] [late 19C] (*US*) an opium den.

jostle *v.* **1** [late 18C–1960s] (*UK Und.*) to cheat; thus n. *jostle*. a trick. **2** [1960s+] (*US Und./police*) to pickpocket; thus *jostle operation*, pickpocketing. **3** [1990s+] to masturbate.

jostler *n.* [JOSTLE v.] [1920s–60s] (*US Und./police*) a pickpocket or petty thief.

joto *n.* [Mex. Sp.] [1970s+] (*US gay/prison*) a male homosexual, esp. the passive/effeminate member of a couple.

jottle *n.*

IN PHRASES

❑ **do a jottle** *v.* (*also* **go jottling**) [Lincolnshire dial. *jot*, to shake roughly, to jerk about + *jottle*, to busy oneself with trifles] [late 19C–1900s] to have sexual intercourse.

jouden *n. see* JORDAN *n.*[1].

jouk *n. see* JUKE *n.*[1].

joukoutoo *pron.* [Fr. *jusqu'à tu*, as far down (socially) as you] [20C+] (*W.I.*) a derog. pron., even you, unimportant you; thus, as adj., insignificant, unimportant.

jounce *v.* [SE *jounce*, to shake] **1** [19C] of a man, to have sexual intercourse. **2** [2000s] (*US campus*) to punch.

jour *n.* [abbr.] [19C] a *jour*neyman worker, e.g. a printer, a cabinet-maker.

journey *n.* [late 19C–1930s] a spell of work, a time or occasion.

journeyman soul-saver *n.* [mid–late 19C] a scripture-reader.

journo *n.* [abbr. SE + -O *sfx* (3)] [1960s+] (*orig. Aus.*) a journalist.

Jove *n.*

IN EXCLAMATIONS

❑ **by Jove!** (*also* **by Joves!**) [late 16C+] by God!

jow *v.* [Hind.] [mid–late 19C; 1980s] to go away, to leave; usu. as imper. *jow!* go away! be off!

jowl-sucking *n. see* GUM-SUCKING *n.*

joxer *n.* [? northern dial. *jock*, a seaman] [20C+] (*Irish*) **1** an idler. **2** one who is out of work.

joxy *n. see* JAXY *n.*

Joy, the *n.* [abbr.] [late 19C+] (*Anglo-Irish*) Mount*joy* Prison, Dublin.

joy *n.* [the effects] (*drugs*) **1** [1940s+] marijuana. **2** [2000s] heroin.

IN COMPOUNDS

❑ **joy dust** *n.* [DUST *n.* (6)] [1930s+] (*US drugs*) heroin, morphine or cocaine. ❑ **joy flakes** *n.* [FLAKE *n.*[1]] [1940s+] (*US drugs*) heroin, morphine or cocaine. ❑ **joy hemp** *n.* (*also* **joy roots**) [1940s] (*US black*) marijuana. ❑ **joy powder** *n.* [1920s+] (*US drugs*) heroin, morphine or cocaine. ❑ **joy smoke** *n.* [1930s–60s] (*drugs*) marijuana. ❑ **joy weed** *n.* [WEED *n.*[1]] **1** [1910s] (*US*) tobacco. **2** [1930s–40s] (*US drugs*) marijuana.

SE in slang uses

IN COMPOUNDS

❑ **joy bang** *n.* [SE *joy* + BANG *n.*[1] (4); such an injection would usu. be subcutaneous rather than intravenous] [1950s+] (*drugs*) an occasional injection of a narcotic by anyone who is not addicted. ❑ **joy box** *n.* **1** [1910s] the stomach. **2** [1940s–60s] (*US black*) a radio or a piano [ext. BOX *n.*[1] (4)]. **3** [1970s] (*US*) the vagina [BOX *n.*[1] (1)]. ❑ **joy boy** *n.* **1** [1920s+] (*US*) a foolish joker, or (ironically) a bad-tempered person. **2** [1960s+] a male homosexual. **3** [1960s+] a homosexual prostitute. **4** [1990s+] (*US*) a drug addict. ❑ **joy button** *n.* (*also* **joy buzzer**) [note BUTTON *n.*[1] (1c)] [1970s+] (*US*) the clitoris. ❑ **joy germ** *n.* [1960s] (*N.Z.*) a pessimist, a complainer. ❑ **joy girl** *n.* (*also* **joy lady**) [lit. trans. Fr. *fille de joie*] [1910s–70s] (*US*) a prostitute. ❑ **joy hole** *n.* [note HOLE *n.*[1] (1)] [1930s+] (*US*) the vagina. ❑ **joy house** *n.* (*also* **joy club, joy shop**) [note HOUSE *n.*[1]] [1910s–70s] (*US*) a brothel. ❑ **joy jelly** *n.* (*also* **joy jell**) [1970s+] (*US*) fruit-flavoured vaginal lubricant jelly. ❑ **joy joint** *n.* (*also* **joy parlor**) [JOINT *n.* (3)] [late 19C–1960s] (*US*) a saloon bar. ❑ **joy juice** *n.* [note JUICE *n.*[1] (3)] **1** [20C+] (*US*) liquor, alcohol. **2** [1950s] (*US*) rubbing alcohol. **3** [1950s+] (*US black/campus*) beer. **4** [1950s+] (*US drugs*) liquid amyl nitrite. **5** [1960s+] (*US drugs*) chloral hydrate. **6** [1960s+] (*US drugs*) a depressant. **7** [2000s] the drugs used in an execution by lethal injection. ❑ **joy knob** *n.* [note KNOB *n.* (1c)] **1** [1940s–70s] (*US*) a knob screwed to a vehicle's steering wheel, to facilitate steering with one hand. **2** [1950s+] (*US*) the penis. ❑ **joy lady** *n. see* JOY GIRL above. ❑ **joy prong** *n.* [PRONG *n.* (1)] [1910s–70s] the penis. ❑ **joy ride** *n.* [RIDE *n.* (1a)] [1940s–60s] (*US*) sexual intercourse. ❑ **joy rider** *n.* **1** [1920s–30s] (*US*) a legless beggar who transports themselves on a wheeled platform. **2** [1930s–60s] (*US drugs*) an occasional narcotic drug user. ❑ **joy shop** *n. see* JOY HOUSE above. ❑ **joy shot** *n.* [SHOT *n.*[1] (6b); note later JOY POP *n.*] [1920s] (*drugs*) an occasional injection of a narcotic by anyone who is not addicted. ❑ **joystick** *n.* [Puxley (1992) suggests rhy. sl. *joystick* = PRICK *n.* (1), but this is unlikely] **1** [1910s+] (*orig. US*) (*also* **gear stick**) the penis. **2** in drug uses [STICK *n.* (6)]. **(a)** [1930s–50s] (*drugs*) an opium pipe. **(b)** [1960s+] a marijuana cigarette. ❑ **joy trail** *n.* [1970s+] the vagina. ❑ **joy water** *n.* **1** [1900s–30s] (*US*) alcohol. **2** [1910s] (*Aus.*) champagne.

Joyce *n.* [Irish writer *James Joyce* (1882–1941) whose portrait was on the Irish £10 note; the Irish currency is now the euro] [2000s] (*Irish*) £10.

Joynson-Hicks *n.* [rhy. sl.; ult. *William Joynson-Hicks* (1865–1932), Conservative Home Secretary 1924–29] [1920s] (*bingo*) the number six.

joy of my life *n.* [rhy. sl.] [20C+] one's wife.

joy pop *n.* [JOY POP *v.*] **1** [1930s+] (*drugs*) an occasional injection of a narcotic by anyone who is not addicted. **2** [1990s+] in fig. use.

joy pop *v.* [SE *joy* + POP *v.*[1] (4a)] [1930s+] (*drugs*) to inject narcotic drugs irregularly.

joy-popper *n.* [JOY POP *v.*] **1** [1930s+] (*drugs*) an occasional taker of illegal drugs, esp. injectable narcotics. **2** [1960s] a delight.

joy-popping *n.* [JOY POP *v.*] [1920s–70s] (*drugs*) the occasional use of drugs.

Jozi *n. see* JOEYS *n.*

Jozlin *n. see* JOCELYN *n.*

J.R. *n. see* JIMMY (RIDDLE) *n.*

j.s.t. *n. see* JEWISH (STANDARD) TIME *under* JEWISH *adj.*

j.t. *n.* [abbr. JOHN THOMAS *n.*] [20C+] the penis.

j.t.(o.) *n. see* JAILHOUSE TURNOUT *under* JAILHOUSE *adj.*

Juan *n.* [1990s+] (*US*) generic for a male Puerto Rican.

juanita *n.* (*also* **juana**) [play on the Sp. name *marijuana*, lit. 'Mary Jane'] [1930s+] (*drugs*) marijuana.

juba *n.* [1960s] (*S.Afr.*) a white man.

jubbie *n.* [? JUBBIES *n.*] [1990s+] (*W.I.*) a friend, a girlfriend.

jubbies *n.* (*also* **jubblies, jumblies**) [? SE *chubby*] [20C+] breasts.

jubes *n. see* JUJUBES *n.*

jubilee *n.* [coined by the *Sporting Times* at the time of Queen Victoria's Golden Jubilee (1887) + a play on the 'arse-end' of the century] [late 19C] the buttocks, the posterior.

judas *n.* [SE *judas-hole*; *judas-slit*, a peep-hole; ult. the biblical *Judas*, the betrayer of Christ] **1** [mid-19C+] (*US Und.*) the spyhole set into a solid cell door. **2** [1960s] (*Irish*) an unexpected blow, delivered from behind.

judas-haired *adj.* [the biblical *Judas* was supposedly red-haired] [mid-19C] **1** red-haired. **2** deceitful.

Judas H Christ! *excl. see* JESUS H CHRIST! *excl.*

Judas Priest! *excl.* (*also* **Judas! Judast! Judas H. Priest!**) [late 19C+] (*orig. US*) a euph. for *Jesus Christ!*

judder bars *n.* [2000s] (*N.Z.*) haemorrhoids.

jude *n.* [JUDY *n.*[1]] **1** [late 19C] a prostitute. **2** [late 19C] (*US*) a good-looking and thus as an insult, effeminate man. **3** [late 19C–1910s] a woman. **4** [1910s] (*Aus.*) a man.

jude *adj.* [JUDE *n.* (2)] [late 19C] (*US*) of a man, good-looking, thus effeminate.

judge *n.* **1** [early–mid-19C] (*UK Und.*) an experienced criminal. **2** [mid–late 19C] (*US*) used in direct address to a man whose real name is unknown. **3** [1950s+] (*S.Afr.*) a senior figure in a prison gang, among whose tasks is to authorize the assassination of a fellow prisoner. **4** [1960s+] (*Aus.*) a manual labourer who shirks on the job [such a person is 'always sitting on a case'].

judge *v.* [ety. unknown; ? the idea of a judge refusing to relinquish their robes] [1950s+] (*W.I. Rasta*) to wear one's everyday or ordinary clothes or shoes in the yard or in the bush.

Judge Dredd *n.* (*also* **Judge Dread**) [rhy. sl.; the comic book hero] [1990s+] the head.

Judge Lynch *n.* [SE *lynch law*, ult. the court held by *Captain William Lynch* (1742–1820) of Pittsylvania in Virginia *c.*1776–80] [mid-19C–1940s] (*US*) lynch law.

judgin' *adj.* [JUDGE *v.*] [20C+] (*W.I. Rasta*) ref. to everyday or ordinary clothes or shoes worn in the yard or in the bush, as in *judgin' boot*.

Judi Dench *n.* [rhy. sl.; ult. UK actor Dame *Judi Dench* (b.1934)] [1990s+] a stench, a stink.

Judische compliment *n. see* JEW'S COMPLIMENT *under* JEW *adj.*

judy *n.*[1] [Punch's wife *Judy* in the puppet-show 'Punch and Judy'; 20C+ use mainly in Liverpool dial. + Aus.] **1** [19C+] (*orig. UK Und.*) a generic term for a woman. **2** [19C+] (*orig. UK Und.*) a promiscuous woman or prostitute. **3** [mid-19C+] (*orig. UK Und.*) a girlfriend, or wife. **4** [20C+] a ludicrous-looking woman. **5** [1960s] (*Aus.*) a feminine lesbian. **6** [1980s+] (*US campus*) a fat woman.

IN COMPOUNDS

❑ **judy-slayer** *n.* [play on SE *lady-killer*] [late 19C–1900s] a successful ladies' man.

IN PHRASES

❑ **crack a judy** *v.* (*also* **crack a judy's tea-cup**) [early 19C+] to deflower a woman. ❑ **flop a judy** *v.* [late 19C] to lay a woman down preparatory to intercourse. ❑ **judy with the big booty** *n.* [BOOTY *n.*[2] (2)] [1970s+] (*US black*) a fat woman. ❑ **stalk a judy** *v.* [late 19C+] to follow a woman in the hope of sex. ❑ **tap a judy** *v.* [TAP *v.*[2] (1a) + sense 1 above, ie pun on to deflower] [mid–late 19C] to cause one's nose to bleed with a blow.

judy *n.*[2] [early 19C–1940s] (*orig. US*) a fool.

judy *n.*[3] (*also* **jupe balls**) [ety. unknown] [20C+] (*US prison*) a particularly unappealing item of food served to prisoners in solitary confinement; the meal consists of a ground patty, approx. 10 x 10 x 8cm (4 x 4 x 3in), which is composed of the entire meal's ingredients put together through a blender; it is trad. burned on the outside and raw within.

judy and punch *n.* [rhy. sl.] [20C+] lunch.

jued up *adj. see* JUICED *adj.*

juff *n.* [? Fr. *joues*, cheeks] [late 19C+] the buttocks, the posterior.

Jug *n. see* YUG *n.* (1).

jug *n.*[1] **1** [18C–early 19C] the buttocks, the posterior [abbr. DOUBLE JUGG(S) *under* DOUBLE *adj.*]. **2** as a lit. or fig. container, often as a place. (**a**) [early 19C+] prison; thus as *the jug*, solitary confinement, *jugged*, in prison. (**b**) [mid-19C] the mouth, esp. as a receptacle for alcoholic drink. (**c**) [mid-19C–1960s] (*US*) a safe. (**d**) [mid-19C+] (*orig. UK Und.*) a bank. (**e**) [1930s] (*US*) a post office. **3** in the context of liquor. (**a**) [1920s+] (*US*) a bottle of whisky or wine. (**b**) [1960s+] a drink, esp. a pint of beer. **4** [1930s] (*UK Und.*) a forged cheque. **5** [1930s] (*US*) a dilapidated old vehicle. **6** [1940s+] (*US*) a carburettor. **7** [1950s+] (*orig. US*) (*also* **juggs**) in pl., the female breasts, esp. when large. **8** [1960s+] (*drugs*) vials of amphetamine and later of crack cocaine.

IN COMPOUNDS

nouns

❑ **jug-heavy** [1920s–40s] (*US Und.*) a safecracker. ❑ **jug-heel** [HEEL *n.* (2)] [1900s–30s] (*US Und.*) a bank robber. ❑ **jug-heistman** (*also* **jug heister**) [HEISTER *n.* (1)] [1940s–50s] (*US Und.*) a bank robber. ❑ **jug-house** [1930s–60s] (*US*) a prison. ❑ **jug man** (*also* **jugman**) [1920s–50s] (*US Und.*) a bank robber. ❑ **jugrooter** [ROOTER *n.*[4]] [1930s] (*US Und.*) a bank robber. ❑ **jug touch** [TOUCH *n.*[1] (3)] [1900s–30s] (*US Und.*) the robbery of people as they come out of banks.

adjectives

❑ **jug-bitten** (*also* **bitten**) [early 17C] drunk. ❑ **jug-broke** [mid-17C] drunk. ❑ **jug-steamed** [mid-19C] (*US*) drunk.

IN PHRASES

❑ **knock a jug** *v.* **1** [1920s–30s] (*US black*) to get drunk. **2** [1940s] (*US black*) to buy a drink. ❑ **on the jug** [1940s–50s] (*US Und.*) working as a bank robber. ❑ **shoot the jug** *v.* [1930s–40s] (*US Und.*) to blow open a safe.

SE in slang uses

IN PHRASES

❑ **by a jugful** [early 19C+] (*US*) by a great deal, 'by a long chalk', usu. in negative.

jug *n.*[2] [17C uses SE *jug*, pet name for Joan, generic for the quintessential country girl; late 19C use is abbr. JUGGINS *n.*] [late 19C–1950s] a fool, a gullible person.

jug *n.*[3] *see* JOGUE *n.*

jug *v.*[1] [JUG *n.*[1] (2)] **1** [mid-19C+] to imprison, to incarcerate. **2** [1930s] (*UK Und.*) to rob someone as they leave a bank.

jug *v.*[2] [JUKE *v.*[1]] **1** [late 19C–1960s] to deceive, either jokingly or through some form of illegality. **2** [2000s] (*US prison*) to provoke; to harass.

jug *v.*[3] (*also* **juge, jugg**) [JUKE *v.*[2] (3)] [1960s] (*US black*) to have sexual intercourse.

jug *v.*[4] [SNZE *jug*, a litre bottle of beer] [1970s+] (*N.Z.*) to hit or slash with a beer bottle.

jug *v.*[5] **1** *see* JOOK *v.* **2** *see* JUG UP *v.* (2). **3** *see under* JUKE.

jug and pail *n.* [rhy. sl.] [20C+] jail.

juge *v. see* JUG *v.*[3].

jugelow *n.* [Rom. *guggal*, a dog; note market traders' jargon *juck*, *juckle*, a dog] [early 19C] (*UK Und.*) a dog.

jug-fuck *n.* [such an image, copulation with a jug, is seen as absurd] [1980s+] (*US*) an awful mess or terrible situation.

jugg *v.* **1** *see* JUG *v.*[3]. **2** *see under* JUKE.

jugged *adj.* [JUG *n.*[1] (2a)/JUG *n.*[1] (3a)] **1** [early 19C+] imprisoned. **2** [1920s+] (*US*) (*also* **jugged up**) drunk.

jugger *n.* [JUG *n.*[1] (2d)/JUG *n.*[1] (3a)] **1** [1910s–30s] (*US Und.*) a banker. **2** [1920s–60s] (*US Und.*) a bank robber. **3** [1960s–70s] (*US*) a drunk.

jugging *n.* [JUG UP *v.* (2)] [2000s] (*UK prison*) a form of punishment inflicted on sex offenders by other prisoners, involving scalding with hot water and sugar.

jugging law *n.* [? unknown use of SE *jug* (slang uses are too late) + LAW *n.* (1)] [late 16C] (*UK Und.*) criminality as it pertains to the corrupt practice of certain games, e.g. dicing or skittles.

juggins *n.* [var. on MUGGINS *n.*[1] (1); Note Henry Ernest Schlesinger Benzon, better known to London's sporting fraternity as the *Jubilee Juggins*. Benzon, the son of a Birmingham umbrella frame-maker, went through an inheritance of £250,000 (a massive sum at the time) in less than two years. His last pennies went in 1887, the year of Queen Victoria's Golden Jubilee, thus earning him his nickname. Only the kindness of his fellow patrons of the raffish Romano's Restaurant in the Strand, who established a fund that sustained him on £7 a week for life, saved him from absolute penury] [late 19C–1950s] a fool, a dupe, esp. someone who is so foolish that they can be prevailed upon to buy every round of drinks.

juggle *v.* [SE *juggle*] **1** [mid-16C–early 18C] to have sexual intercourse. **2** [1910s; 1990s+] (*Aus./W.I./UK black*) to do any form of illicit business; to cheat. **3** [1960s+] (*US drugs*) to sell drugs, esp. to support one's own habit.

juggler *n.* **1** [mid-16C–early 18C] a fornicator, a womanizer [JUGGLE *v.* (1)]. **2** [1950s] someone who keeps many relationships going at the same time. **3** in drug uses [JUGGLE *v.* (3)]. (**a**) [1960s+] (*drugs*) an addict who sells drugs to help finance their own addiction. (**b**) [1980s+] a street dealer, orig. of marijuana, latterly of crack cocaine. **4** [1970s] (*US Und.*) an expert at fraudulent manipulation of accounts [14C SE *juggler*, one who deceives by trickery; a trickster].

juggler's box *n.* [mid-17C–early 19C] (*UK Und.*) a machine used to brand criminals on the hand.

juggs *n. see* JUG *n.*[1] (7).

jughead *n.*[1] [orig. use denoted a horse or mule with a large chunky head; such a head supposedly denoted stubbornness and stupidity; ? link to JUGGINS *n.*] (*US*) **1** [late 19C+] a fool, a general term of abuse. **2** [1910s+] a mule or a horse.

jughead *n.*[2] [JUG *n.*[1] (3a) + -HEAD *sfx* (4)] [1940s–70s] a drunkard.

jugheaded *adj.* [JUGHEAD *n.*[1] (1)] [1930s+] (*US*) stupid.

jug-up *n.* [JUG UP *v.* (1)] [1960s+] (*Can. prison*) mealtime.

jug up *v.* [SE *jug*/JUG *n.*[1] (2a)] **1** [1960s+] (*US prison*) to eat prison food. **2** [2000s] (*UK prison*) (*also* **jug**) to attack a fellow inmate with a jug of scalding water.

juice *n.*[1] **1** in financial contexts, often illegal or corrupt. (**a**) [early 16C–early 17C] the profits of a profession or office. (**b**) [late 17C; 1920s+] (*later use US*) money, esp. from bribery, corruption, loan-sharking. (**c**) [1930s–50s] protection money. (**d**) [1930s+] (*US*) political or criminal influence; anything involving corruption, pay-offs, favours. (**e**) [1950s+] (*US gambling*) a bookmaker's percentage. (**f**) [1960s+] recognition, publicity, respect. (**g**) [1970s+] (*US*) interest on a debt or loan. **2** lit. or fig. bodily fluids [despite chronology as determined by available cites seems likely that sense b came first as it does with JISM *n.*]. (**a**) [mid-17C+] (*also* **cock juice, cunt juice**) semen or vaginal fluid. (**b**) [18C+] spirit, vitality, energy, usu. sexual. (**c**) [20C+] (*orig. US*) blood. (**d**) [1940s–60s] (*US black teen*) vomit. (**e**) [1970s] (*US gay*) sweat. (**f**) [1970s+] (*US*) 'the daylights', or a fig. use of urine, i.e. PISS *n.* as in such phr. as *knock/scare the juice out of*. (**g**) [1980s+] (*US black*) sexual intercourse. **3** drink or drugs. (**a**) [mid-17C+] alcohol, wine. (**b**) [20C+] (*US Und.*) any form of alcohol illicitly made inside a prison. (**c**) [20C+] (*US*) whisky or any other strong liquor. (**d**) [20C+] any form of drugs, esp. heroin or methadone in liquid, phencyclidine, crack cocaine; in prison use, the tranquillizer Largactil. (**e**) [1960s] (*US*) beer. (**f**) [1970s+] (*S.Afr.*) methylated spirits, as drunk by alcoholics. (**g**) [1970s+] steroids. **4** fuel. (**a**) [late 19C+] electricity. (**b**) [20C+] petrol. (**c**) [1910s] (*US*) mercury, as in a thermometer. (**d**) [1920s–60s] (*US Und.*) nitroglycerine. (**e**) [1950s] energy. (**f**) [1990s+] gas. (**g**) [1990s+] of a vehicle, power. **5** as a conversational 'lubricant' [both 'lubricate' communication]. (**a**) [1930s–60s] (*US*) flattering talk. (**b**) [1960s+] (*US*) gossip. **6** [1930s+] senses pertaining to guns. (**a**) a gun. (**b**) gunfire; the power of a weapon. **7** [1980s+] enjoyment, satisfaction, stimulation [JUICE *v.* (4d)].

IN COMPOUNDS

❑ **juice box** *n.* (*also* **juice can**) [1940s–60s] (*US*) a battery. ❑ **juice-freak** *n.* [-FREAK *sfx*] [1970s] (*US campus*) a person who drinks, as opposed to taking drugs. ❑ **juice-head** *n.* (*also* **juice-hound**) [-HEAD *sfx* (4)/-HOUND *sfx* (1)] [1950s+] (*US*) a heavy drinker, an alcoholic; thus as derog. term of address. ❑ **juice house** *n.* [1930s] (*US tramp*) an electric railway. ❑ **juice joint** *n.* [JOINT *n.* (3b)] **1** [1920s+] (*US*) a tavern, a bar, any establishment selling liquor. **2** [1940s+] (*US gambling*) a crooked gambling establishment operating electronically controlled games. **3** [1980s+] (*drugs*) a marijuana cigarette sprinkled with crack cocaine. ❑ **juice junkie** *n.* [2000s] an alcoholic. ❑ **juice man** *n.* **1** [1920s–50s] (*US*) an electrician. **2** [1950s+] (*US Und.*) the collector of loans for an illegal money-lender. **3** [1970s] (*US*) an influential person.

IN PHRASES

❑ **big juice** *n.* [1960s–70s] (*US black*) a white gang-boss. ❑ **blow one's juice** *v.* [1990s+] to reach orgasm. ❑ **get the juice** *v.* [1910s–30s] (*US Und.*) to be executed in the electric chair. ❑ **give juice for jelly** *v.* [JELLY *n.*[1]] [19C] of a woman, to have sexual intercourse. ❑ **jet one's juice** *v.* [late 19C–1970s] of a man, to achieve orgasm. ❑ **sling one's juice** *v.* [19C] of a man, to masturbate.

SE in slang uses

IN PHRASES

❑ **juice of the cow** *n. see* COW JUICE *under* COW *n.*[1]. ❑ **juice of the grape** *n. see* GRAPE-JUICE *under* GRAPE *n.*[1].

juice *n.*[2] [pron. of DEUCE *n.*[1] (2)] [1920s–60s] (*Irish*) twopence.

juice *adj.* [JUICY *adj.*] [1990s+] (*US*) privileged, pleasant, convenient.

juice *v.* **1** pertaining to alcohol/drinks [JUICE *n.*[1] (3a)]. (**a**) [late 19C+] (*US*) (*also* **juice back, juice (it) up**) to drink alcohol, to get drunk. (**b**) [1910s–70s] (*US*) to milk a cow, also used facetiously. (**c**) [1950s] to render drunk. **2** pertaining to power/energy [JUICE *n.*[1] (4a)]. (**a**) [1920s+] (*US*) to electrocute, to kill or torture with electricity. (**b**) [1940s+] (*orig. US*) (*also* **juice up**) to increase the power of a machine, usu. an automobile. (**c**) [1960s+] (*US black*) to intensify, to augment, to liven up, to excite. (**d**) [1970s–80s] (*US*) to attack with a weapon, to fire a gun. (**e**) [2000s] to provide with electrical power. **3** in financial contexts [JUICE *n.*[1] (1b)]. (**a**) [1950s] to bribe, esp. in context of organized crime paying off the authorities. (**b**) [1950s+] to add interest to a loan, debt. (**c**) [1990s+] to extort money, through threats or trickery. **4** pertaining to sexual activity [JUICE *n.*[1] (2a)]. (**a**) [1970s+] (*US black/campus*) to have sexual intercourse. (**b**) [1970s+] (*US gay*) of man, to sweat, esp. during sex. (**c**) [1980s+] (*US*) to dampen with vaginal secretions. (**d**) [1980s+] (*US*) in fig. use, to get excited. (**e**) [1990s+] to stimulate one's female partner to sexual arousal. (**f**) [1990s+] (*also* **juice up**) to become damp with sexual arousal.

IN PHRASES

❑ **juice a woody** *v. see under* WOODIE *n.*[2].

juiced *adj.* (*also* **jued up, juiced up**) [JUICE *v.*] **1** [late 19C+] (*orig. US*) drunk or intoxicated by drugs. ext. as *juiced to the skin*. **2** [1970s+] (*US*) excited, nervous; energized, hyperactive. **3** [1980s+] of a woman, sexually aroused. **4** [1990s+] (*US campus*) strong, unadulterated.

juice harp *n.* [pron.] [mid-19C–1920s] a harmonica, a Jew's harp.

juicer *n.* [JUICE *n.*[1]] **1** [1920s+] (*US*) an electrician. **2** [1940s] (*US*) one who chews rather than smokes tobacco [the tobacco/saliva 'juice' created]. **3** [1960s+] (*US*) a heavy drinker, an alcoholic. **4** [1980s+] (*drugs*) a woman who barters sex for drugs, esp. crack cocaine.

juicery *n.* [JUICE *n.*[1] (3a)] [mid–late 19C] a drinking house.

juicily *adv.*[1] [JUICY *adj.* (1b)] [1910s+] vigorously, excellently.

juicily *adv.*[2] [JUICY *adj.* (2b)] [1960s+] suggestively.

juicy *n.* [1970s] (*US*) a kiss.

juicy *adj.* **1** something 'suitable for sucking dry'. (**a**) [early 17C–1950s] wealthy; financially rewarding. (**b**) [late 19C+] excellent, first-rate. (**c**) [20C+] pleasant, enjoyable. **2** sexually or otherwise stimulating. (**a**) [early 17C+] intellectually stimulating. (**b**) [late 17C+] suggestive, racy, sexy. (**c**) [1920s+] dramatic, exciting. **3** [late 17C+] secreting vaginal fluids, ready for sex. **4** [mid–late 19C] of weather, raining, very wet.

juicy about *phr.* [1920s+] (*Aus.*) aware of.

juicy fruit *n.*[1] [JUICY *adj.* (2b) + FRUIT *n.* (2); also a pun on the epon. chewing gum brandname] [1930s+] (*Aus./US black*) a male homosexual.

juicy fruit *n.*[2] [rhy. sl. = ROOT *n.*[1] (1d)] [1950s+] (*Aus.*) sexual intercourse.

juicy-spicy *n.* [JUICY *adj.* (2b) + SPICY *adj.* (3)] [mid-19C] (*US, Texas*) a boyfriend, the object of a young woman's affections.

ju-ju *n.* [SE *ju-ju*, a charm, an amulet, a fetish; the image is of the exoticism of drugs] (*drugs*) **1** [1940s+] a marijuana cigarette; marijuana [abbr. SE *marijuana*]. **2** [1980s+] any drugs in capsule form.

jujubes *n.* (*also* **jubes**) [SE *jujube*, a suckable lozenge, flavoured so as to represent the jujube fruit (*Zizyphus vulgaris*). Jujube is a very much altered form of the orig. Gk *zizuphon*] [1960s+] the female breasts.

juk *n.* (*also* **jook**) [JUKE *v.*[2]] [1940s+] (*W.I.*) **1** a stab. **2** a hypodermic injection.

juk *v.* **1** *see* JUKE *v.*[2]. **2** *see* JUKE *v.*[3] (3).

juke *n.*[1] (*also* **jook, jookery, jook house, jouk, juke house, juke joint**) [? Gullah *jook/joog house*, a disorderly house, a house of ill-repute; ? ult. Bambara (dial. of Mandingo) *jugu*, wicked, violent] **1** [1930s+] (*orig. US black*) any establishment offering drink, food, music or dancing. **2** [1930s+] (*orig. US black*) cheap, raucous music played at similarly inclined roadhouses, cafés and brothels. **3** [1940s+] (*US*) (*also* **juker**) a jukebox.

juke *n.*[2] [JUKE *v.*[1] (1)] [1970s+] a trick, a dodge, whether physical or mental.

juke *n.*[3] *see* DUKE *n.*[3] (1).

juke *v.*[1] (*also* **joog, jook, jug, jugg**) [? Scot. *jouk*, to trick] **1** [mid-19C+] to evade, to dodge, to avoid, to hide. **2** [mid-19C; 1980s+] (*US/Ulster*) to trick, to cheat, to victimize. **3** [20C+] (*Ulster*) to play truant.

juke *v.*[2] (*also* **chook, joog, jook, jug, jugg, juk**) [? Fulani *jukka*, to poke, to knock down, to spur; note South Carolina dial. *joog/jook*, to prick, to poke, to stab] (*orig. W.I./US black*) **1** [late 19C+] to pierce or stick, as with a needle, thorn or a long pointed stick; to stab. **2** [late 19C+] to hit, to beat up. **3** [1930s+] (*also* **joop**) to have sexual intercourse, often quick and casual when the man is keen but the woman is reluctant. **4** [1990s+] to shoot. **5** [2000s] to spoil.

juke *v.*[3] (*also* **joog, jook, jug, jugg**) [? Bantu *juka*, Wolof *dzug*, thence to Gullah *juke, joog*, disorderly, wicked] [1930s+] (*orig. US black/campus*) **1** to dance, to party, to play music, to frequent dance-halls etc. **2** to have a good time. **3** (*also* **juk**) to boost, to improve.

IN PHRASES

❑ **juke up** *v.* [1930s+] to improve, to boost.

jukey *n.* [abbr.] [1990s+] a *juke*box.

juk-maka *n.* [JUKE *v.*[2] (1) + SE *maker*. He is 'sharp enough to prick a thorn' (Cassidy & LePage)] [1940s] (*W.I.*) a cunning person.

jukrum *n.* [JARK *n.*] [late 17C–early 19C] a licence.

juldee/juldie *see under* JILDI.

julip *n.* [SE (*mint*) *julep*, 'a mixture of brandy, whisky, or other spirit, with sugar and ice and some flavouring, usually mint' (*OED*)] [2000s] (*US prison*) home-made alcohol, usu. fermented juice.

Julius Caesar *n.*[1] [mid-19C–1910s] the penis.

Julius Caesar *n.*[2] [rhy. sl.] [20C+] **1** a cheeser, i.e. 'cheesecutter' cap. **2** a freezer.

jum *n.* (*also* **jumb**) [JUMBO *n.* (6)] (*drugs*) **1** [1980s+] an outsize vial or rock of crack cocaine. **2** [2000s] a sealed plastic bag containing crack cocaine.

jumbie *n.* (*also* **jombie, Jumbee, jumby**) [? one of several Bantu languages incorporating *nsmabi*, God or devil] [mid-19C+] (*W.I.*) a ghost or spirit, a duppy.

jumble *n.* [pron. of *John Bull*; used by West African immigrants/students in UK and popularized in the books of Colin MacInnes (1914–76)] [1950s–60s] a white person.

jumble *v.* (*also* **jumble up**) [late 16C–19C] to have sexual intercourse.

jumblefuck *v.* [CLUSTERFUCK *n.* (1)] [1930s] (*US*) to participate in an orgy or group sex.

jumble-giblets *n.* [17C–19C] the penis; thus *do/perform a jumble-giblets*, to have sexual intercourse.

jumble-gut lane *n.* [late 17C–early 19C] a rough, badly-maintained road.

jumbler *n.* [JUMBLE *v.* (1)] [17C–18C] a womanizer, a promiscuous man.

jumblies *n. see* JUBBIES *n.*

jumbloney *n. see* JIBONE *n.*

jumbo *n.* [? *Mumbo-Jumbo*, a West African (Mandingo) deity. Popular ety. links the term to *Jumbo*, the celebrated elephant of the Regent's Park Zoo, sold to Barnum and Bailey's Circus in 1881. However, the Zoo opened in 1828 and Jumbo and a female, Alice, did not arrive until 1863; note also chronology: the term was initially applied to people rather than, as is assumed, vice versa] **1** [early 19C+] a large and clumsy person. **2** [late 19C–1930s] the Elephant and Castle public house in south London. **3** [1910s] (*Aus.*) as an affectionate term of address. **4** [1940s+] (*N.Z.*) the buttocks, the posterior. **5** [1940s+] a fool, simpleton. **6** in drug or drink use. (**a**) [1950s] (*US drugs*) a large capsule of heroin. (**b**) [1980s+] (*US drugs*) an outsize vial of crack cocaine. (**c**) [1980s+] (*US*) a quart (40-oz.) bottle of beer.

jumbo *adj.* [JUMBO *n.* (1)] **1** [late 19C+] very large. **2** [1990s+] in fig. use, very successful.

jumbo! *excl.* [1900s–30s] a euph. for JESUS! *excl.*

jumbo's trunk *adj.* [rhy. sl.] [late 19C] drunk.

jumby *n. see* JUMBIE *n.*

jumm *adj.* [Scot. *jumm*, a clumsily built, awkward-looking house] [1990s+] (*Ulster*) used of something that is large but unwieldy and as such virtually worthless.

jumm *v.* [abbr. JUMBLE *v.*, but note dial. *jum*, a sudden jolt] [17C] to have sexual intercourse.

IN PHRASES

❑ **go jumming** *v.* [17C] to have sexual intercourse.

Jump, the *n.* [early 19C] the Black Jack Tavern, Portugal St, London.

jump *n.* **1** in UK Und. uses. (**a**) [late 16C–early 17C] a robbery carried out around dusk by a number of rogues, who mill about, walking slowly along a street and opening every accessible window they can, grabbing whatever they can reach and moving on. (**b**) [late 18C] a robbery that uses a man posing as a lamp-lighter, who can lean his ladder against a house without suspicion, climb it and enter through any window he can open. (**c**) [19C] a ground-floor window. (**d**) [19C] a robbery that involves breaking in through a ground-floor back window; thus *jump the glaze*, to open the window. (**e**) [late 19C] an escape, while committing a burglary. **2** in sexual contexts. (**a**) [mid-19C+] an act of sexual intercourse. (**b**) [1930s–40s] (*US*) a sexually promiscuous woman. (**c**) [1970s+] (*US gay/prison*) gang-rape. **3** in sense of movement. (**a**) [mid-19C+] (*US*) usu. constr. with *the*, the beginning, the outset; thus *at/from/on jump/the jump*, from the start. (**b**) [late 19C+] (*orig. US*) a journey, esp. from coast to coast or city to city; thus (*US tramp*) a free trip on a train or a boat. (**c**) [1980s] a fig. start, a chance. **4** in sense of physical effort. (**a**) [late 19C–1940s] (*US*) liveliness, energy. (**b**) [20C+] an ambush, an attack, a surprise, an advantage; esp. in phr. *get a/the jump on (someone)*. (**c**) [1930s+] (*orig. US black*) a party where the guests buy their refreshments to help pay the rent. (**d**) [1940s–80s] (*US gang/black*) a dance party. (**e**) [1950s+] (*US*) a gang fight. **5** [1970s] (*US gay*) one's home [JUMP *v.* (10a)]. **6** [1970s+] (*orig. W Aus.*) a public house bar. **7** [1980s+] (*Aus.*) a barmaid. **8** [1990s+] a shop counter. **9** [2000s] (*US prison*) homemade alcohol.

IN COMPOUNDS

❑ **jump city** *n.* [-CITY *sfx* (1)] [1980s+] (*US*) the start, esp. in phr. *from jump city*, from the very beginning. ❑ **jump jobber** *n.* [SE *jobber*, 'one who does jobs or odd pieces of work; one employed to do a job' (*OED*)] [1940s–60s] (*US*) a pimp. ❑ **jump joint** *n.* [1930s+] **1** (*orig. US black*) a party where the guests buy their refreshments to help pay the rent. **2** (*US*) a cheap roadhouse or brothel, esp. an establishment providing food, drink and music for dancing. ❑ **jump street** *n.* [1970s+] (*US*) the start, esp. in phr. *from jump street,* from the very beginning.

IN PHRASES

❑ **at a jump** *see* ON THE JUMP below. ❑ **get a jump on** *v.* (*also* **have a jump on**) [20C+] (*orig. US*) to gain a lead on, get an advantage over (someone); to hurry. ❑ **give someone a jump** *v.* [20C+] of a man, to have sexual intercourse. ❑ **go the jump** *v.* [mid-19C] (*UK Und.*) to enter a house by a window. ❑ **jump in the sack** *n.* [SACK *n.* (4)] [1990s+] an act of casual sexual intercourse. ❑ **off one's jump** [1950s] (*Irish*) crazy, insane. ❑ **on the jump 1** [mid-19C+] restless, unsettled, nervous, busy. **2** [mid-19C+] (*also* **at a jump, on a jump, on the keen jump**) promptly, immediately, very quickly. **3** [1900s–30s] (*US Und.*) on the run. ❑ **put on the jump** *v.* [1900s] (*US*) to alert, to get someone moving, to 'ginger up'.

SE in slang uses

IN EXCLAMATIONS

❑ **go and take a running jump at yourself!** (*also* **go and take a crawling jump at yourself! ...creeping jump at yourself! go take a run and a jump!**) [20C+] a general excl. of dismissal and distaste.

jump *v.* **1** in sexual senses. (**a**) [17C+] to have sexual intercourse. (**b**) [1940s+] to rape; to attack sexually. (**c**) [1960s+] (*US black/campus*) to seduce, to make determined or aggressive sexual advances. **2** in Und. uses. (**a**) [mid–late 18C] (*UK Und.*) to open, i.e a window. (**b**) [late 18C–mid-19C] to break into, for the purpose of robbery. (**c**) [late 18C–late 19C] (*UK Und.*) to cheat, to defraud. **3** to use lit. or fig. force; to oppose. (**a**) [mid-19C+] to ambush, to attack, esp. a surprise attack; also to surprise (without violence). (**b**) [mid-19C+] (*US, orig. West*) to rob, unlawfully to take possession of another's property etc. (**c**) [late 19C] (*S.Afr.*) to seize goods wrongfully. (**d**) [late 19C–1960s] (*US Und.*) of police, to raid. (**e**) [late 19C+] (*US*) to rebuke, to criticize. (**f**) [late 19C+] to stop and question, as of police. (**g**) [1900s] (*US campus*) to punish. (**h**) [1900s] (*US*) to accuse. (**i**) [1920s+] (*Aus./US/UK black*) to arrest. (**j**) [1940s+] to beat up. **4** in sense of movement or evasion. (**a**) [mid-19C+] (*US*) to leave, to abscond, to quit, from duty or to avoid payment. (**b**) [late 19C–1930s] (*US*) to leave without paying one's bill. (**c**) [late 19C+] (*US campus*) to miss a class; to drop a course. (**d**) [1920s+] (*US*) to leave a job. (**e**) [1930s+] (*also* **bust a light**) to fail to stop at a red traffic light or stop signal, usu. in phr. *jump the lights*. **5** [late 19C] (*Aus.*) of a convict, to become a prison warder. **6** [late 19C+] (*Ulster*) to convert from Catholicism to Protestantism for the material advantages such a change would confer. **7** [1910s+] (*Aus.*) to understand, to work out [? play on SE *jump to a conclusion*]. **8** [1920s] to travel on the railway without paying. **9** [1930s] (*US*) to inform. **10** in sense of pleasure. (**a**) [1930s+] (*orig. US black*) of a place of entertainment, e.g. a nightclub, to pulsate with energy, to be full of excitement, usu. as *jumping*, esp. in phr. *joint is jumping*. (**b**) [1940s+] (*US black*) to dance, to have fun. **11** [1930s+] (*US black*) to act, to behave; usu. in combs. such as *JUMP SALTY* below etc. **12** [1940s+] (*US black*) to occur, to happen; see also JUMP OFF *v.* (3).

IN PHRASES

❑ **jump all over** *v.* [note synon. US dial. uses *jump out, jump up*] [20C+] (*orig. US*) to attack verbally, to berate. ❑ **jump bad** *v.* [1940s–70s] (*orig. US black*) to misbehave. ❑ **jump bail** *v.* [mid-19C+] (*orig. US*) to disappear (usu. by leaving the country) and thus avoid a possible prison sentence while remanded on bail before trial. ❑ **jump in someone's shit** *v.* [SHIT *n.* (3k)] [1960s+] (*US*) to scold, to reprimand. ❑ **jump jail** *v.* [late 19C] to escape from prison; thus n., *jail-jumper*. ❑ **jump off the perch** *v.* [1990s+] to commit suicide. ❑ **jump one's bill** *v.* (*also* **jump one's board**) [late 19C–1930s] (*US*) to abscond, esp. from a hotel or lodging, without paying one's bill. ❑ **jump salty** *v.* (*also* **fly salty**) [SALTY *adj.*] [1930s+] (*orig. US black*) to be annoyed or irritated, to take offence. ❑ **jump ship** *v.* [SE *jump ship*, for a sailor to leave the ship (at a port) before the voyage has finished] [1930s+] (*US*) to quit, to renege. ❑ **jump smart** *v.* [1970s] (*US black*) to act in a foolishly 'clever' manner. ❑ **jump someone's hand** *v.* [fig. use of SE *hand* (*of cards*)] [1970s+] (*US black*) to threaten or victimize someone. ❑ **jump steady** *v.* (*also* **jump smooth**) [1930s–50s] (*US black*) to act properly, to be honest, usu. in context of a sexual relationship. ❑ **jump stink** *v.* [1940s+] (*US*) to attack, to turn hostile. ❑ **jump up someone's ass** *v.* (*also* **jump up someone's butt**) [ASS *n.* (2)/ BUTT *n.*[1] (1a)] [1970s+] (*US*) to attack, verbally or physically. ❑ **on the jump 1** [1910s] speedily. **2** [1910s–20s] immediately. ❑ **what's jumping?** [1980s+] (*US campus*) a greeting.

IN EXCLAMATIONS

❑ **go jump yourself!** [20C+] (*orig. US*) a coarse dismissive excl; euph. for *GO FUCK YOURSELF! under* FUCK *v.*

SE in slang uses

IN COMPOUNDS

❑ **jump-and-jive** *n.* [JIVE *v.*[1] (3)] [1940s] (*W.I.*) a shoe made from old automobile tyres and very common during WW2. ❑ **jump-out boy** *n.* [1990s+] (*US*) one who performs an ambush. ❑ **jump-steady** *n.* [1930s+] (*US black*) alcohol, which ensures that one keeps 'jumping'.

IN PHRASES

❑ **jump in** *v. see* separate entries. ❑ **jump (in) the box** *v.* [one 'jumps' into the witness box] [1960s+] (*Aus.*) to give evidence. ❑ **jump it** *v.* [1960s] to desert, to run off. ❑ **jump Jim Crow** *v. see under* JIM CROW *n.* ❑ **jump off** *v. see* separate entries. ❑ **jump on** *v. see* separate entry. ❑ **jump one's horse over the bar** *v.* [late 19C–1900s] (*Aus.*) to barter one's horse for liquor. ❑ **jump (on) someone's bones** *v. see under* BONES *n.*[1]. ❑ **jump out** *v. see* separate entries. ❑ **jump (over) the broomstick** *v. see* separate entry. ❑ **jump the fence** *v.* [1930s+] (*US prison*) to make an escape. ❑ **jump the glaze** *v. see* JUMP *n.* (1d). ❑ **jump the joint** *v. see under* JOINT *n.* ❑ **jump the rattler/train** *v. see under* RATTLER *n.* ❑ **jump the twig** *v. see* HOP THE TWIG *v.* ❑ **jump the rails** *v.* [horseracing imagery] [20C+] to lose control, to disappear. ❑ **jump the wrong tree** *v. see* BARK UP THE WRONG TREE *v.* ❑ **jump through one's ass** *v.* [ASS *n.* (2)] [1960s+] (*US*) to panic, to lose control, to be terrified. ❑ **jump through one's asshole** *v.* [ARSEHOLE *n.*] [1970s] (*US*) to throw a tantrum; to scream and shout. ❑ **jump up** *v. see* separate entries. ❑ **jump upon** *v. see* JUMP ON *v.* ❑ **jump up (and down)** *v.* [1970s+] (*US black*) to have sexual intercourse.

IN EXCLAMATIONS

❑ **jump back!** [1960s+] (*US black/campus*) an expression of astonishment. ❑ **jump up my ass!** *see under* ASS *n.*

jumpabout *n.* [rhy. sl.] [1980s] (*Aus.*) a ticket.

jumped up *adj.*

IN PHRASES

❑ **I'll be jumped up!** *see I'LL BE JIGGERED! under* JIGGERED *adj.*[1].

jumper *n.* **1** UK Und. uses. (**a**) [late 18C–early 19C] (*also* **jump**) a thief who enters a house through a window. (**b**) [1980s+] a thief who steals from offices. **2** [early–mid-19C] a Scot. coin, worth 10 pence [the image of a man on horseback carried on one face of the coin]. **3** in lit. uses, someone or something that jumps. (**a**) [early 19C–1930s] a flea or any small jumping insect. (**b**) [mid-19C–1940s] (*Can./US*) a light buggy, a basic form of sledge. (**c**) [20C+] a travelling bus or rail inspector. (**d**) [1960s–70s] (*US black*) in pl., gym shoes [their use in basketball]. (**e**) [1960s+] (*US*) someone who makes or attempts a suicide jump from a height. (**f**) [1980s+] (*US*) someone who attempts or makes a suicide jump onto the subway tracks. (**g**) [1990s+] (*US black*) an expensive bicycle, esp. when stolen. **4** in fig. uses. (**a**) [mid-19C–1940s] (*Aus.*) one who jumps a mining claim [JUMP *v.* (3b)]. (**b**) [1940s+] one who absconds while on bail [JUMP *v.* (4a)]. **5** [1990s+] (*US drugs*) an injection or portion of a narcotic drug, esp. the first of the day [it gets one 'up and jumping']. **6** [2000s] (*W.I.*) a member of a fundamentalist Christian church.

jump in *v.* [JUMP *v.* (3j); the initiation involves the new member being beaten up by one or more of their putative peers] [1980s+] (*US Und.*) **1** to initiate someone into a street gang. **2** in passive, to be initiated into a street gang.

IN PHRASES

❑ **jumped in port** [1930s–40s] (*US black*) newly arrived.

jumping *adj.*[1] [early 19C+] (*orig. US*) used as the first half of a number of combs. that make up mild, euph. oaths, e.g. *jumping beans! …catfish! …fire! …gee whillikers! … grasshoppers! …hyenas! …jacks! …jeepers! …Jehovah! … Jehu! …jemima jane! …jenny! …Jerusalem! …jews! …jews harps! …Joseph! …Judas!*

jumping *adj.*[2] [JUMP *v.* (10a)] **1** [late 19C] intense. **2** [1940s+] (*orig. US*) (*also* **jumpin**) lively, energetic, exciting.

jumping beans *n.* [1930s] (*US*) dice.

jumping cat *n.* [JUMPING *adj.*[2] + CAT *n.*[5] (1)] [1950s+] (*US black*) **1** a sophisticated, poised older person. **2** anyone successful in their occupation, legitimate or criminal.

jumping cats! *excl.* (*also* **jumping bullfrogs! …butterballs! … caterpillars! …fish-hooks! …nannygoats! …rattlesnakes! … toadstools!**) [1900s–40s] (*US/Aus.*) a mild excl.

jumping china *n.* [JUMP *v.* (4a) + CHINA (PLATE) *n.*] [1980s+] (*UK Und*) someone with whom one is escaping.

jumping jack *n.* [rhy. sl.] [20C+] the *black* ball in snooker.

jumping Jehoshaphat! *excl.* (*also* **jumping Jeremiah! … jewfish! …jewsharps! …joey! …John! …Joshua! …Rodgers!**) [20C+] one of a variety of phr. that euphemize the once blasphemous JESUS! *excl.*

jumping Jesus! *excl.* (*also* **jumping Christ! …jeepers!**) [1920s+] used as a mildly blasphemous oath or intensifier.

jumping Moses! *excl.* (*also* **jumping Mo!**) [mid-19C+] (*US*) a mild oath, great heavens!

jumpo *n.* [JUMP *n.* (2a) + -O *sfx*] [1950s] (*US*) the penis.

jump-off *n.* [1910s+] (*orig. US/Can. milit.*) the outset, the beginning.

jump off *v.* **1** [mid-19C+] to begin, e.g. of a military attack. **2** [late 19C] (*US*) to leave. **3** [1930s+] to happen, to start happening. **4** [1970s] of a person, to start doing something.

jump on *v.* (*also* **jump upon**) **1** [mid-19C+] to attack, verbally or physically, someone who is seen to have exposed themselves to such an assault by their behaviour or their weakness. **2** *see* STEP ON *V.*

jump-out *n.* [var. on JUMP-OFF *n.*] [20C+] (*Aus.*) the beginning.

jump out *v.*[1] [1900s] (*US Und.*) to steal.

jump out *v.*[2] [JUMP *v.* (4a)] **1** [1960s+] (*US Und.*) to throw out (of a place). **2** [1980s+] (*US black*) to be unfaithful. **3** [1990s+] (*US Und.*) to expel from a street gang, a ritual that involves beating up the departing member [opposite of JUMP IN *v.*].

jump (over) the broomstick *v.* (*also* **jump (over) the broom, …hurdle, hop over a broom**) [the uses are all fig. in 20C+ although they were once actual actions] [17C+] to enter into a common-law marriage; no civil or religious ceremony is undertaken, but the couple 'make their vows' by jumping over a broomstick or any of the other obstacles/implements.

jumps, the *n.* [fig. uses of SE] **1** [late 19C–1950s] (*orig. US*) delirium tremens. **2** [20C+] (*US*) nervousness. **3** [1920s] excitement, 'the fidgets'.

jump-up *n.* **1** [mid-19C–1940s] (*Aus.*) a paste made of flour, water and sugar [it jumps in the pan when boiling]. **2** [late 19C] (*Aus.*) the witness box. **3** [1940s+] (*UK Und.*) hi-jacking a lorry and/or stealing its contents [JUMP UP *v.* (2)]. **4** [1950s+] (*W.I.*) a wild dancing party [orig. held as a funeral wake, but now in general use; note US *jump-up/jump-up song*, a lively song with ad hoc lyrics, often extemporized from various proverbial sayings]. **5** [1970s+] (*US black*) sexual intercourse [*jump up (and down)* under JUMP *v.*].

IN COMPOUNDS

❑ **jump-up merchant** *n.* (*also* **jump-up man**) [MERCHANT *n.*] [1940s+] one who steals from lorries, trucks etc.

jump up *v.* (*also* **jump up on**) [JUMP *v.*] **1** [mid-19C–1900s] to criticize harshly. **2** [1940s+] to steal a lorry and/or its contents. **3** [1960s] (*US*) to arrest.

Junction, the *n.* [1960s+] the area of south London near Clapham Junction railway station.

june around *v.* [late 19C–1900s] (*US campus*) to make a great deal of apparent effort, without any concrete accomplishment.

junebug *n.* [SE *junior boy*] [mid-19C–1950s] (*US black*) a boy who is named after his father.

jungle *n.* **1** a geographical area. (**a**) [late 19C–1920s] (*US*) the backwoods, the suburbs. (**b**) [20C+] (*W.I.*) an area in West Kingston, Jamaica. (**c**) [1910s+] (*US*) that area of a town or city, often outside the city limits, where criminals, tramps and vagrants congregate; also as *hobo jungle*; also attrib. (**d**) [1960s+] (*US*) the black area of a town or city. **2** an unpleasant place. (**a**) [20C+] (*US*) a prison. (**b**) [1930s] (*UK tramp*) a very cheap London lodging house for tramps. **3** [1930s+] (*US*) a derog. term for a black person. **4** [1980s] (*S.Afr.*) a knife.

IN COMPOUNDS

❑ **junglebird** *n.* [BIRD *n.*[1] (3a)] [1920s–30s] (*US*) a tramp. ❑ **jungle bunny** *n.* [their alleged origins in the *jungle*] [1950s+] (*US*) a derog. term for a black person; also attrib. ❑ **jungle buzzard** *n.* (*also* **jungle bum, jungle buzzer**) [BUZZARD *n.*] [1910s+] (*US tramp*) a parasite on other tramps; a tramp who robs his fellows. ❑ **jungle hound** *n.* [1930s] a frequenter of tramp encampments. ❑ **jungle meat** *n.* [MEAT *n.*] [1960s+] (*gay*) a black man or his penis. ❑ **jungle stiff** *n.* (*also* **jungle-wallah**) [STIFF *n.*[1] (4a)] [1920s–40s] (*US tramp*) one who frequents that area of a town or city where criminals, tramps and vagrants congregate.

IN PHRASES

❑ **jungle up** *v.* **1** [1910s+] (*US tramp*) to share a campsite with other hoboes; to live in a hoboes' encampment; to cook up a meal. **2** [1960s] to gather together, in non-tramp context. **3** [1960s] to be allies, to work together. **4** [1960s] (*US gay*) to share a bed with many people, to cuddle up. **5** [1970s+] (*US gay/tramp*) to have homosexual anal intercourse.

SE in slang uses

IN COMPOUNDS

❑ **jungle juice** *n.* *see* separate entry. ❑ **jungle sex** *n.* [the image of 'black natives' and their lusts; thus racial stereotyping] [1990s+] an intense, rough and speedy bout of sexual intercourse. ❑ **jungle telegraph** *n.* [1940s+] a network of gossip and rumour that brings news (often inaccurate) before the official sources.

jungle *adj.* [JUNGLE *n.* (1e)] [1930s+] (*US*) **1** pertaining to the black area of a town or city. **2** used, orig. derog., in reference to black people or culture.

IN COMPOUNDS

❑ **jungle fever** *n.* (*also* **black fever**) [the term, generally outlawed as racist in white use, changed its emphasis with the release of Spike Lee's film *Jungle Fever* in 1991] **1** [1960s+] (*US*) the desire of whites (usu. men) to have sex with black partners. **2** [1990s+] (*US black*) the desire of blacks to have white partners.

jungle juice *n.* [SE *jungle* + JUICE *n.*[1]] **1** [1940s+] (*orig. Aus.*) any form of strong, home-distilled liquor, often made of jungle-grown fruits and plants, herbs etc by soldiers with no 'regular' drinks. **2** [1950s] (*mainly juv.*) tea. **3** [1970s] (*US*) men's aftershave that supposedly enhances virility and sexual appeal. **4** [1990s+] (*US campus/UK juv.*) semen or vaginal secretions. **5** [2000s] (*US*) sweat.

jungler *n.* [JUNGLE *n.* (1c)] [1910s] (*US tramp*) a frequenter of a tramp encampment.

junglist *n.* [20C+] (*W.I., Jam.*) someone who comes from the area in West Kingston, Jamaica known as JUNGLE *n.* (1b).

jungly *adj.* [racist stereotyping] [1980s+] (*UK society*) disorganized, chaotic, less than smart.

junior *n.* [1950s–80s] (*US black*) a socially and/or sexually inept male.

junior jumper *n.* [SE *junior* + JUMP *v.* (1a)] [1990s+] (*US black*) a juvenile (under 16) who commits rape and robbery.

Junior Walker and the All Stars *n.* [R&B star *Junior Walker* (Autry DeWalt II), b. 1942] [1970s+] (*US black*) the police.

juniper *n.* [late 19C–1940s] (*US*) a rustic.

juniper (juice) *n.* (*also* **juniper ale, juniper water**) [SE *juniper*, its primary constituent] [18C+] gin.

juniper lecture *n.* (*also* **juniper letter**) [the sharpness of the juniper-berry] [late 19C–early 19C] a severe reprimand, a 'telling-off'.

junjo *n.* [1990s+] (*W.I.*) a term of abuse.

junk *n.*[1] **1** food [naut. jargon *junk*, old or second-rate cable or rope; ? + overtones of SE *junk*, a lump, a chunk]. (**a**) [mid-18C–1930s] (*also* **salt junk**) salt beef. (**b**) [mid-19C+] poor or indigestible food. **2** [mid–late 19C] (*UK prison*) oakum (loose fibre, obtained by untwisting and picking old rope), the 'picking' of which provided the main cell task for 19th century prisoners. **3** inanimate objects. (**a**) [mid-19C+] (*orig. US*) usu. negative description of possessions or other unspecified objects; used dismissively of objects that are in fact sound but that the speaker no longer likes; as adj., *junky*, of an object, old, dilapidated. (**b**) [20C+] (*Aus.*) the dregs of a bottle or glass of alcohol. (**c**) [20C+] (*US Und.*) jewellery. (**d**) [1920s+] a run-down vehicle. (**e**) [1930s+] something unpleasant. (**f**) [1990s+] (*US*) cheap or inferior liquor. **4** [20C+] (*US*) rubbish, nonsense. **5** [1900s] (*US*) money. **6** [1910s–20s] (*US*) a mean, despicable man. **7** in drugs use. (**a**) [1910s+] (*also* **jeesunk**) opiates, orig. opium, later usu. heroin. (**b**) [1910s+] non-recreational drugs in general, often medicinal. (**c**) [1950s–60s] cannabis. (**d**) [1960s] amphetamine, benzedrine. (**e**) [1960s] an injectable medicine. **8** [1990s+] (*US campus*) offensive or abusive speech. **9** [1990s+] (*US campus*) the male genitals. **10** [1990s+] (*US campus*) constr. with *the*, the very best.

IN COMPOUNDS

❑ **junkball** *n.* [1990s+] (*US campus*) annoying, disappointing. ❑ **junk box** *n. see* JUNKER *n.* (3). ❑ **junk guy** *n. see JUNKMAN* below. ❑ **junk hawk** *n.* [1970s+] (*US drugs*) a heroin user whose entire existence centres on the drug. ❑ **junkhead** *n.* [-HEAD *sfx*] [1950s+] (*US drugs*) a drug addict or drug dealer. ❑ **junkheap** *n.* (*also* **junkpile**) [SE *heap*] **1** [1910s] a railroad train. **2** [1920s+] a disgusting, filthy place. **3** [1940s+] an old, battered automobile; also attrib. ❑ **junk hog** *n.* [1930s–50s] (*US drugs*) a drug addict who is seen as excessive in their consumption. ❑ **junk hound** *n.* [-HOUND *sfx*] [1930s] (*US drugs*) a narcotics addict. ❑ **junkhouse** *n.* [2000s] (*US drugs*) a place – an apartment, a house – used for the consumption of narcotics, crack cocaine, etc. ❑ **junkman** *n.* (*also* **junk guy**) [1940s+] (*US drugs*) **1** a heroin dealer. **2** a cocaine dealer. ❑ **junk pile** *n. see* JUNKER *n.* (3). ❑ **junk tank** *n.* [TANK *n.*[2] (1), with pun on *DRUNK TANK under* TANK *n.*[1]] [1960s+] (*US police*) a cell reserved for drug abusers and alcoholics.

IN PHRASES

❑ **junk in the trunk** *n.* (*also* **junk in one's trunk**) [SAmE *trunk*, the 'boot' of a car] [1990s+] (*US black*) large buttocks. ❑ **on the junk** [1950s+] (*US Und.*) using narcotics. ❑ **pop junk** *v.* [1940s+] (*US*) to gossip.

junk *n.*[2] [abbr. JUNKIE *n.*] [1950s+] (*Aus.*) a heroin addict.

junk *adj.* (*also* **junky**) [JUNK *n.*[1]] **1** [1960s] (*drugs*) pertaining to heroin or the hard drug culture. **2** [1960s+] rubbishy, second-rate, inferior.

junked *adj.* (*also* **junked up**) [JUNK *n.*[1] (7a)] [1930s+] (*drugs*) intoxicated by drugs.

junker *n.* (*US drugs*) **1** [1920s+] a drug addict [var. on JUNKIE *n.*]. **2** [1920s+] a drug seller. **3** [1940s+] (*US*) (*also* **junk box, junkolo, junk pile**) a near-derelict but just drivable second-hand car, or motor-bike, one step from the junkyard [JUNK *n.*[1] (3a)].

junket-brain *n.* (*also* **junket-head**) [SE *junket*, whey, + SE *brain/head*, thus 'soft brain'] [1950s] (*Aus.*) a general term of abuse.

junkette *n.* [JUNKIE *n.* (1) + fem. sfx *-ette*] [1960s+] (*drugs*) a young female drug taker or heroin addict.

junket trumpet *n. see SPUNK-TRUMPET under* SPUNK *n.*

junkie *n.* (*also* **junkey, junkster, junky**) [JUNK *n.*[1] (7a)] **1** [1920s+] (*drugs*) a heroin addict. **2** [1950s–70s] (rare) a heroin seller. **3** [1960s+] a (regular) user of any drug. **4** [1970s+] fig. an addict of any sort, e.g. *vinyl junkie*, a collector of vinyl (rather than cassette or CD) recordings.

IN COMPOUNDS

❑ **junkie fold** *n.* [1950s] (*drugs*) a method of folding a square of paper, one end tucking into the other and top folding into the resulting 'slot', in which a measure of narcotics can be held.

junkie *adj.* [JUNKIE *n.*] (*orig. drugs*) **1** [1950s+] (*also* **junkey, junky**) used of one who is addicted to narcotics; pertaining to the world of narcotics. **2** [1970s+] addicted to anything. **3** [1970s+] addictive.

junko *n.* [JUNK *n.*[1] (7a)] [1970s+] (*US*) a drug addict.

junkolo *n. see* JUNKER *n.* (3).

junkster *n. see* JUNKIE *n.*

junky *n.* **1** [1930s–70s] (*US*) a collector of rubbish, a 'rag-and-bone' man. **2** *see* JUNKIE *n.*

junky *adj.* **1** [1960s] (*US*) nonsensical, absurd. **2** *see* JUNK *adj.* **3** *see* JUNKIE *adj.* (1).

junz *n.* [2000s] (*UK black*) a (promiscuous) young woman.

jupe *n.* [1970s] (*S.Afr.*) alcohol, wine.

jupe balls *n. see* JUDY *n.*[3].

jurden *n. see* JORDAN *n.*[1].

jurk *n. see* JARK *n.* (1).

jury leg *n.* [ety. unknown; ? on pattern of naut. jargon *jury-rigged* or *jury-mast*, temporary rigging or a temporary mast, a short-term arrangement that replaces equipment swept away in a gale or after a battle] [mid-18C–early 19C] a wooden leg.

jury nobbling *n. see under* NOBBLE *v.*[2].

just *adv.*

IN PHRASES

❑ **just as cheap** [1950s+] (*W.I. Rasta*) just as well. ❑ **just fallen off the cabbage truck** (*also* **just fallen off the turnip truck**) [play on SE *green*, naïve] [1980s] (*US*) very naïve, unsophisticated. ❑ **just quietly** [1910s+] (*Aus./N.Z.*) just between you and me, confidentially. ❑ **just the shiner** (*also* **just the shining**) [var. on *just the shiny shilling* (*see JUST THE SHINY BOB under* BOB *n.*[3])] [1920s+] (*Aus.*) exactly what one requires.

just as I feared *n.* [rhy. sl. from the Edward Lear limerick (1846): 'There was an old man with a beard / Who said "It is just as I feared! Two owls and a hen / Four larks and a wren / Have all built their nests in my beard."'] [20C+] a beard.

just-come *n. see JOHNNY-JUST-COME under* JOHNNY *n.*[1].

justice *n.*

IN PHRASES

❑ **do justice** *v.* [late 17C–early 18C] to toast a person, to drink to a person.

Justice Child *n.*

IN PHRASES

❑ **do Justice Child** *v.* [Sir Francis *Child* (1642–1715), banker and lord mayor of London] [late 17C–mid-18C] (*UK Und.*) to act as an informer.

justin *n.* [2000s] (*N.Z.*) a half-gallon container of beer: *just in* case you run out.

jute *n.*

IN PHRASES

❑ **give jute to** [? link to Scot. *jute*, a derog. term for a woman] [1980s+] (*N.Z.*) to tease.

juve *n.* (*also* **juvey, juvie**) [abbr.] **1** [1930s–50s] (*US*) a *juvenile*, e.g. on stage. **2** [1930s+] (*US*) (*also* **juve delinq**) a *juvenile delinquent*. **3** [1960s+] (*US*) a *juvenile* court or detention establishment. **4** [1960s+] (*also* **Juvi**) (*US*) *Juvenile* Hall, reform school. **5** [1960s+] pornography featuring supposed '*juveniles*'. **6** [1990s+] (*US black*) *juvenile* court.

juvie *adj.* [JUVE *n.* (2)] [1970s+] (*US Und/Police*) pertaining to juvenile crime.

juxies *n.* [mid-19C] (*UK Und.*) burglar's tools.

jybe *n. see* GYBE *n.*

jyro *n. see* JARO *n.*

K *n.* [abbr.; since 1980s *K* has replaced the equivalent G *n.* (1) in popularity] **1** [1940s+] a kilometer. **2** [1960s+] 1000, esp. as $1000 or £1000 [SE *kilogram*, 1000 grams]. **3** in drug uses. (**a**) [1970s+] a kilogram of any illicit drug. (**b**) [1980s+] ketamine hydrochloride, a mildly hallucinogenic drug, developed as a battlefield anaesthetic, associated chemically with phencyclidine (PCP) and often used as a legal substitute for MDMA. (**c**) [1980s+] phencyclidine [? mis-reading of sense 3b above]. **4** [1990s+] (*US campus*) money [from sense 2 above].

K! *excl. see* KAY! *excl.*

ka…! *excl. see also under* KER…!

kaalgat *adj.* [Afk. *kaal*, bare + GAT *n.*[2]] [1960s+] (*S.Afr.*) naked.

kaalvoet *adj.* [synon. Afk.] [late 19C+] (*S.Afr.*) barefoot.

kaartjie *n.* [Afk. *kaartjie*, a ticket, a card, in turn f. UK *card*, a small measure of opium or Mex. Sp. *cachuca*, a capsule of drugs, which is f. Chilean sl. *cachuca*, a small comet] [1950s+] (*S.Afr. drugs*) a very small measure of cannabis.

kaaskop *n.* [Afk. *kaas*, cheese + *kop*, head] [1970s+] (*S.Afr.*) a Dutchman.

kabac genals *n. see* KABGNALS *n.*

kaba-kaba *n.* [KABA-KABA *adj.*] [20C+] (*W.I.*) a low-class, worthless, rough person.

kaba-kaba *adj.* [Yoruba *kaba-kaba*, orig. used of speech to mean haltingly, then second-rate, of inferior quality] [20C+] (*W.I.*) **1** of people, slovenly, ill-kempt, boorish-looking. **2** of animals and things, cheap, worthless.

kabayo *n. see* CABALLO *n.*

kabeezer *n.* [CABEZA *n.*] [1960s+] (*US*) **1** the head. **2** the face.

kabgnals *n.* (*also* **kabac genals**) [the word itself is *backslang* spelt backwards and its use – spoken very quickly – is a coded way of asking, 'Do you understand backslang, and shall we use it for this conversation?'] [late 19C] backslang.

kabillion *n.* (*also* **kajillion, kazillion**) [KER- *pfx* + play on SE (*m*)*illion*] [1980s+] (*US*) an uncountable large number.

kabitz *n. see* KIBITZ *n.*

kabitzer *n. see* KIBITZER *n.*

kablooey! *excl.* [KER- *pfx* + BLOOEY! *excl.*] [1970s+] an onomat. term indicating an explosion.

kabloom! *excl.* (*also* **kablamo!**) [KER- *pfx* + SE *boom/bloom*] [1970s+] an onomat. term indicating a large explosion.

kaboodle *n. see* CABOODLE *n.*

kaboolies *n.* [var. on CAJOOBLIES *n.*] [2000s] (*US*) the female breasts.

kaboom *n.* [KABOOM! *excl.*] [1940s+] a loud bang or noise.

kaboom! *excl.* [KER- *pfx* + SE *boom*] [1940s+] an onomat. term indicating a loud noise or explosion.

kaboona *n.* [? var. on KADOOVA *n.*] [1970s] (*Aus.*) the head.

kabosh *n. see* KIBOSH *n.*

kabuki *n.* [ety. unknown] [1980s+] (*drugs*) a crack cocaine pipe made from a plastic rum bottle and a rubber sparkplug cover.

kabump! *excl.* [KER- *pfx* + SE *bump*; note *belly-cabump*, (US) to throw oneself face-down onto a sled preparatory to sliding down a hill] [1970s+] an onomat. term indicating the noisy landing of one object or person on another.

kachew! *excl.* (*also* **kerchew!**) [KER- *pfx* + SE (*ti*)*shoo*] [20C+] an onomat. term indicating the sound of a sneeze.

kaching! *excl.* (*also* **kachang! k-chung!**) [KER- *pfx* + SE *ching*] [1960s+] an onomat. term indicating the noise of a metal object striking another and giving a sharp, bell-like note.

kack *n.*[1] [CACK *n.*[3] (1)] **1** [1900s–50s] (*US black*) an important person. **2** [1920s] (*US black*) a negro. **3** [1920s–40s] (*US black*) a snobbish person.

kack *n.*[2] [? CACK *n.*[2]] **1** [1960s] an old horse. **2** [1960s] (*Aus.*) luck [? i.e. link to LUCK *n.* (1)].

kack it *v. see* CACK *v.*[1] (2).

kacks *n. see* KECKS *n.*

kacky-hander *n.* [CACK-HANDED *adj.*] [1980s] (*Aus.*) a clumsy person.

kadi *n.* (*also* **kadie, kady, katie, katy**) [? Rom. *stadi*, a hat; note also CADY *n.*] [late 19C+] a hat.

kadoodle *v.* [KER- *pfx* + TODDLE *v.*] [late 19C] (*US*) to hang around, to frequent, to wander about.

kadooment *n.* [dial. *'k*, look + *do*(*o*)*ment*, 'doings', disturbance, entertainment; thus lit. 'look, excitement!'] [20C+] (*W.I.*) **1** noise, confusion. **2** usu. as *Kadooment*, open-air fun and excitement.

kadoova *n.* [? KADI *n.*, thus fig. *head*] [late 19C] (*Aus.*) the head.

IN PHRASES

❑ **off one's kadoova** *adj.* [late 19C+] (*Aus.*) crazy, eccentric, mentally unstable.

kady *n. see* KADI *n.*

kafferboetie *n. see* KAFFIRBOETIE *n.*

kafferpak *n.* [Afk. *kaffer*, KAFFIR *n.*[1] + *pak*, a hiding] [1930s+] (*S.Afr.*) a thorough beating, a thrashing, a comprehensive defeat.

kaffir *n.*[1] [Arab *kefir*, an infidel; orig. a Xhosa-speaking African and by extension, any African; orig. (18C) seen as a simple description of a given ethnic group, the term became insulting and abusive and its use is now actionable] (*orig. S.Afr.*) **1** [mid-19C+] a derog. term for a black person. **2** [mid-19C–1900s] a pimp, an unpleasant person.

IN COMPOUNDS

❑ **Kaffirland** *n.* [mid-19C] the Cape provinces; latterly South Africa. ❑ **kaffir's tightener** *n.* [TIGHTENER *n.*; such a meal supposedly satisfies even an African] [mid-19C] (*S.Afr.*) a large, heavy meal.

IN PHRASES

❑ **go to the kaffirs** *v.* [derog. var. on SE colloq. phr. *go to the dogs*] [1950s+] to deteriorate, to decline socially. ❑ **Jack Kaffir** *n.* [late 19C] a generic term for black people. ❑ **kitchen kaffir** *n.* [1980s+] pidgin Zulu language. ❑ **white kaffir** *n.* **1** [mid-19C+] a derog. term for a white perceived as behaving badly by their peers. **2** [mid-19C+] a white who has become overly close to or assimilated into the black community. **3** [1930s+] an albino.

kaffir *n.*[2] *see* CAFFER *n.*

kaffir *adj.* [for ety. see KAFFIR *n.*[1]] **1** [late 18C+] (*S.Afr.*) in combs. meaning of or pertaining to black people. Like *nigger*, *Jewish*, *Chinese*, *Mexican* etc, the term is used in a wide variety of combs., all of which are *de facto* insulting. **2** [1930s–60s] (*S.Afr.*) bad, unreliable.

IN COMPOUNDS

❑ **kaffir appointment** *n.* [1950s+] (*S.Afr.*) an appointment for which one fails to arrive on time. ❑ **kaffir beer** *n.* [late 19C+] (*S.Afr.*) a drink made from fermented prickly pears and honey. ❑ **kaffir bread** *n.* [early 19C+] (*S.Afr.*) the Encephalartos (a form of mollusc). ❑ **kaffir corn** *n.* [late 18C+] (*S.Afr.*) a form of sorghum. ❑ **kaffir dog** *n.* [mid-19C+] (*S.Afr.*) a species of long-tailed, sharp-muzzled, lean dog, popular among indigenous Africans. ❑ **kaffirmeid** *n.* [1960s+] (*S.Afr.*) an insulting form of address or reference to a black woman. ❑ **kaffir piano** *n.* [late 19C+] (*S.Afr.*) any of a number of multi-stringed wooden percussion instruments. ❑ **kaffir sheeting** *n.* [mid-19C+] (*S.Afr.*) a coarsely woven, thick cotton fabric used for clothes or cheap curtains. ❑ **kaffir taxi** *n.* [1980s+] (*S.Afr.*) **1** a run-down car. **2** brandy plus Coca-Cola or some other sweet fizzy drink [? it 'gets you going']. ❑ **kaffir tobacco** *n.* [1960s+] (*S.Afr. drugs*) marijuana.

kaffirboetie *n.* (*also* **kafferboetie**) [KAFFIR *n.*[1] (1) + BOET *n.*] [1930s+] (*S.Afr.*) a white sympathizer with black causes.

kafoom! *excl.* [KER- *pfx* + *foom*, echoic of an explosion; var. on KABLOOM! *excl.*, KABOOM! *excl.*] [1960s+] an onomat. term indicating the sound of an explosion.

kafooster *n.* [KER- *pfx* + ? PHOOEY! *excl.*] [1970s+] (*US*) useless talk, idle chatter.

kagg *n. see* CAG *n.*

kagou *adj.* [Fr. *cagot*, sanctimonious] [20C+] (*W.I., Trin.*) looking miserable, unenthusiastic, 'sorry for oneself'.

kahoonas *n.* (*also* **cahoonas, kazooms**) [joc. use of KAHUNA *n.*] [1970s+] large female breasts.

kahuna *n.* [Hawaiian *kahuna*, priest or wise man, orig. used for an expert surfer] [1980s+] (*US*) a large or important person or thing; often in the phr. *the big kahuna*.

kaifa *n. see* KYFER *n.*

kai-kai *see under* KI-KI.

Kaintuck *n. see* KENTUCK *n.*

kaiser baby *n.* [SE *kaiser*, a metaphor for power] [1920s–30s] (*US black*) a woman who leaves home and returns married to a successful, wealthy (and usu. white) husband.

kajees *n.* [ety. unknown] [1980s+] (*drugs*) cannabis.

kajillion *n. see* KABILLION *n.*

kak *n.* [S.Afr. Du. *kak*, excrement; but note CACK *n.*[2]] **1** [1970s+] (*chiefly S.Afr.*) excrement, also used fig. **2** [1970s+] (*S.Afr.*) rubbish, nonsense. **3** [1990s+] (*S.Afr.*) trouble, chaos.

IN PHRASES

❑ **give someone kak** *v.* [1980s+] to nag. ❑ **in kak** [1980s+] in trouble. ❑ **up to kak** *adj.* [1970s+] useless.

IN EXCLAMATIONS

❑ **kak!** [1980s+] an excl. of annoyance, resignation, SHIT! *excl.*

kak *adj.* [KAK *n.*] [1970s+] (*S.Afr.*) unpleasant, nasty.

kak *v.* [KAK *n.*] **1** [1960s+] (*US*) to vomit. **2** [1970s+] (*S.Afr.*) to defecate. **3** [1980s] in fig. use, to be frightened, worried.

kaka/ka-ka *see under* CACA and its combs.

kaker *n.* [Yid. *kaker*, excrement] **1** [1930s+] anything, or anyone, unpleasant or distasteful. **2** [1960s+] cannabis [i.e. SHIT *n.* (6b)].

kakked-out *adj.* [KAK *v.* (2), i.e. var. on POOPED (OUT) *adj.* (1)] [2000s] (*S.Afr.*) worn out.

kakker-boosah *n.* [CACA *n.*/KAK *n.* + *boosah*, ety. unknown] [19C] prematurely voided excrement; vomiting.

kakpot *n.* [KAK *n.* + SE *pot*] [1970s+] (*S.Afr. Und.*) a latrine.

kaks *n.* [ety. unknown; ? link to KAK *n.* or KECKS *n.*] [20C+] (*Irish*) the testicles.

Kalahari wishing well *n.* [the *Kalahari* desert, with the idea of digging a hole] [1970s+] (*S.Afr.*) an outdoor privy.

kale *n.* (*also* **kale seed, kile**) [its greenness connotes the vegetable, but ? note COLE *n.*] [20C+] (*US*) money.

kali *n.* (*also* **cooly, kally**) [ety. unknown; ? link to COOL *adj.* (8a) or Carib.E *coolieweed*, a variety of fern and thus a play on WEED *n.*[1] (4)] [1950s+] (*W.I. Rasta*) marijuana.

kalumpus! *excl.* [KER- *pfx* + SE *lump*] [mid-19C] an onomat. term indicating the noise made when an object falls onto a hard surface.

ka me, ka thee *phr. see* CLAW ME AND I'LL CLAW YOU *under* CLAW *v.*

kamie *n.* [abbr.] [1940s] (*US*) an attack by Japanese kami-kazi pilots.

kamma *adj.* [Nama *khamo*, like, similar] [20C+] (*S.Afr.*) esp. of emotions or illness, fake, trumped up, spurious.

Kanacka *n. see* CANUCK *n.*

Kanaka *n.* (*also* **Canaka, Kanacka**) [Hawaiian *kanaka*, man] [mid-19C+] (*orig. Aus.*) **1** a Pacific Islander, esp. one brought to Australia as an indentured labourer on the Queensland cotton or sugar plantations. **2** (*also* **Kanock**) a Hawaiian, sometimes derog. **3** *see* CANUCK *n.*

IN COMPOUNDS

❑ **Kanakaland** *n.* (*Aus.*) **1** [late 19C–1940s] Queensland. **2** [1920s] Hawaii. ❑ **Kanakalander** *n.* [late 19C–1940s] (*Aus.*) a Queenslander.

IN PHRASES

❑ **white Kanaka** *n.* [1910s] (*Aus.*) a white person seen as having 'gone native' and as such disdained.

kanga *n.*[1] [rhy. sl.; abbr. SE *kangaroo*] **1** [1950s] (*UK prison*) (*also* **kangar**) chewing tobacco [CHEW *n.* (1)]. **2** [1950s+] (*Aus.*) money [SCREW *n.*[1] (5)].

kanga *n.*[2] [abbr. SE *kangaroo*] **1** [1970s] (*orig. Aus.*) a pneumatic drill [like the SE *kangaroo*, it 'jumps up and down']. **2** [1980s] (*Aus.*) a white child [the TV series *Skippy, the Bush Kangaroo*].

kangaroo *n.*[1] **1** [mid-19C+] (*US*) an Australian; an Australian soldier; an Aborigine. **2** [late 19C–1900s] a thin, slope-shouldered person [the supposed resemblance to the animal].

IN COMPOUNDS

❑ **kangaroo feathers** *n.* [kangaroos do not have feathers] [1910s] (*Aus.*) an impossible thing, often an unlikely story. ❑ **kangaroo hop** *n.* [late 19C] (*Aus.*) a short-lived feminine affectation in which the hands were held palm-down at the breast, a pose reminiscent of the kangaroo. ❑ **Kangarooland** *n.* [1900s–50s] (*Aus.*) Australia. ❑ **kangaroo shit** *n.* [1940s+] (*Aus.*) defecation in a squatting position. ❑ **kangaroo straight** *n.* [suggested by the gaps or 'jumps'] [1950s+] (*US*) a poker hand which resembles a straight but has a card or cards missing, thus a worthless hand. ❑ **Kangaroo Valley** *n.* [1960s+] Earls Court, London, base for many expatriate Australians.

IN PHRASES

❑ **have kangaroos in one's top paddock** *v.* (*also* **have possums...**) [SE *top paddock*, used fig. for the head] [20C+] (*Aus./N.Z.*) to be eccentric, to be mentally unstable. ❑ **there's a kangaroo loose in the top paddock** [1990s+] (*Aus.*) a phr. describing a fool.

kangaroo *n.*[2] (*also* **kanga**) [rhy. sl.] **1** [20C+] (*Aus./US*) a shoe. **2** [1920s+] a Jew. **3** [1920s+] a prison warder [SCREW *n.*[1] (2c)].

kangaroo *v.* [SAusE *kangaroo*, to hop in the manner of the animal] **1** [20C+] (*US*) to convict unjustly, orig. as in a 'kangaroo court'. **2** [1910s] (*US*) to beat up. **3** [1950s–60s] (*US black*) to make one hyperactive, often used of a drug. **4** [1950s+] (*Aus.*) usu. constr. with *it*, to defecate in a squatting position, usu. with one's feet on the seat. **5** [1970s+] of a car, to jerk along rather than run smoothly; thus *kangaroo start*, a jerky, shuddering start, typically that of a learner driver.

kangarooster *n.* [SE *kangaroo* + sfx *-ster*] [1920s+] (*Aus.*) an amusing or eccentric person.

kango *n.* [abbr. SE *kangaroo*] [1940s+] an Australian.

kangse *n.* (*also* **koks, konks**) [? dial. *conk*, a blow on the nose] [20C+] (*W.I.*) a light blow, usu. given to a child and usu. on the head.

kangse *v.* [KANGSE *n.*] [20C+] (*W.I.*) to hit lightly.

kani *n.* [SE *consumption*, pre-20C name for tuberculosis] [1940s+] (*W.I.*) **1** a bad cough, usu. with a temperature. **2** a person who is suffering from this.

kanits *n.* [backsl.] [mid-19C] a stink.

kanitseno *n.* [backsl.; KANITS *n.*] [mid-19C] a stinker, lit. 'stinking one'.

Kansas *n.*

IN COMPOUNDS

❑ **Kansas City roll** *n.* [1940s+] (*US black/gambling*) a show bankroll in which one large-denomination note is exhibited on the outside, concealing a quantity of small bills. ❑ **Kansas City workout** *n.* [1970s+] (*US gay*) watching men go by. ❑ **Kansas neck-blister** *n.* [late 19C–1900s] (*US*) a Bowie knife. ❑ **Kansas yummy** *n.* [YUMMY *n.* (1)] [1960s+] (*US*) a young woman who proves hard to seduce; she need not necessarily come from Kansas, but the implication is of small-town/rural innocence and morality.

kant *n. see* CANT $n.^{2}$.

Kanuck/Kanuk *n. see* CANUCK *n.*

kanurd *adj.* (*also* **kenird, kennurd**) [backsl.] [mid-19C–1930s] drunk.

kap *v. see* CAP $v.^{2}$.

kapeesh! *excl. see* CAPEESH! *excl.*

kapello *n.* [Ital. *capello*, a coat] [mid-19C+] (*Ling. Fr./Polari*) a coat.

kaplunk! *excl.* (*also* **kerplunk!**) [KER- *pfx* + SE *plunk*] [late 19C+] an onomat. term indicating one object hitting another with a dull thump, or a solid object falling into liquid; occas. as v. *kerplunk*.

kapow! *excl.* (*also* **kapowie! kerpow!**) [KER- *pfx* + SE *pow!*, echoic of a blow or sudden noise] [1930s+] an onomat. term indicating a sudden noise or shock, typically an imitation of a handgun firing.

kappa *n.* [abbr. SE *handicapped*] [1990s+] (*UK juv.*) a disabled person; thus, as a general insult.

kaps *n.* [? SE *capsules*] [1970s+] (*drugs*) phencyclidine.

kaput *adj.* [Ger. *kaputt* and Fr. (*être*) *capot*, (to be) without tricks in the card-game of piquet] [1910s+] **1** out of order, utterly ruined or exhausted; thus *get the kaput*, to be rejected, dismisssed. **2** dead, finished.

kark *v. see* CARK *v.*

karzee/karzi/karzie/karzy *n. see* CARSEY *n.*

kaschnickered *adj.* [KER- *pfx* + ? SHICKERED *adj.* (1)] [1970s+] (*US black*) drunk, intoxicated.

kashoom! *excl.* [KER- *pfx* + SE *shoot/zoom*] [1970s+] an onomat. term indicating speedy movement.

kasj *adj. see* CAS *adj.*

kass kass *n.* (*also* **kas-kas**) [SE *curse/cuss* + redup. or Twi *kasakasa*, to dispute verbally] **1** [1940s+] (*W.I. Rasta*) a quarrel or contention. **2** [1960s] (*WI/Jam.*) malicious rumour-mongering. **3** [1970s+] an argumentative person.

kat *n.* **1** *see* CAT $n.^{1}$ (1a). **2** *see* CAT $n.^{5}$ (1).

Kate, the *n.* [abbr. KATE CARNEY *n.*] [late 19C+] the British army.

kate *n.* **1** [16C–1930s] (*Scot.*) (*also* **cate, katy**) a prostitute [generic use of proper name; Irwin also suggests Du. *kat*, 'a wanton']. **2** [mid-17C–mid-19C] in UK Und. uses [the dimin. of the SE name *Katherine*, and on the model of other burglars' tools, e.g. BETTY *n.*, JEMMY $n.^{3}$]. (**a**) a skeleton key. (**b**) a pick-lock.

kate and sidney *n.* (*also* **kate and sydney**) [rhy. sl.] [20C+] steak and kidney.

Kate Carney *n.* (*also* **Kate Karney, Kate Kearney**) [rhy. sl.; ult. music-hall singing star *Kate Carney* (1869–1950)] [20C+] the British army.

kath *n. see* KATHLEEN MAVOURNEEN *n.*

Katharine Docks *n.* [rhy. sl.= ult. *St Katharine's Docks* in London] [20C+] socks.

kathleen maroon *n.* [KATHLEEN MAVOURNEEN *n.* (2)] [1910s+] (*Aus.*) a three-year prison sentence.

kathleen mavourneen *n.* (*also* **kath**) [the song 'Kathleen Mavourneen', the chorus of which runs 'It may be for years, it may be forever'] **1** [mid-19C+] an indeterminate period of time. **2** [1910s+] (*Aus.*) a prison sentence of indeterminate time. **3** [1910s+] (*Aus.*) a habitual criminal. **4** [1910s+] (*US*) a promise; usu. in the context of paying back a loan. **5** [1920s] (*Aus.*) a pack [presumably refers to the time a vagrant carries his pack].

IN COMPOUNDS

❑ **kathleen mavourneen system** *n.* (*also* **Cathleen Mavoureen system**) [business jargon, *Kathleen Mavourneen*, a defaulting debtor] [1920s–80s] (*Aus.*) hire purchase.

katie *n. see* KADI *n.*

Katie-bar-the-door *phr. see* KATY BAR THE DOOR *phr.*

Katie catch wagon *n.* [SE + fem. name as with BLACK MARIA *n.* (1)] [2000s] (*S.Afr. gay*) a police van.

katonk *n.* (*also* **kotonk**) [the theory, propounded by Hawaii-born Japanese, that tapping their heads would give the sound *katonk* like that of a coconut] [1940s+] (*US, Hawaiian*) a Japanese-American from the USA rather than from Hawaii.

katoo *v.* [SE *kowtow*] [late 19C] (*Aus.*) to act as a sycophant.

katookus *n.*

IN PHRASES

❑ **bet one's katookus** *v. see* BET ONE'S (SWEET) ASS *v.*

katootin'! *excl.* [KER- *pfx* + TOOTING *adj.* (1)] [1920s+] (*US*) a general intensifier, as in *durn katootin' right*.

katsing *n. see* CATSING *n.*

Katy *n.* [initial letters] [late 19C–1960s] (*US tramp*) the Missouri, Kansas and Texas Railroad.

katy *n. see* KADI *n.*

Katy bar the door *phr.* (*also* **Katie-bar-the-door, Katy bar the gate**) [adoption of a popular US fiddle tune, thus entitled] [20C+] (*US*) used as a warning, to indicate impending danger.

katzenjammer *n.* [Ger. *katzen*, cats + *jammer*, distress, wailing] (*US*) **1** [mid-19C+] a hangover or its symptoms. **2** [20C+] anxiety or jitters. **3** [1940s] a catsuit.

katzenjammer *adj.* [KATZENJAMMER *n.*] [1930s] stupid.

kawhallop *v. see* KERWHALLOP *v.*

kay *n.* [K *n.* (1)] [1980s+] (*S.Afr.*) one kilometre.

kay! *excl.* (*also* **K! kay-okay!**) [abbr. OK! *excl.*] [1950s+] all right! everything is in order!

kaya $n.^{1}$ [var. on *amakhaya*, lit. people from home, thus = HOMEBOY *n.* (7)] [1960s+] (*S.Afr. gang*) a gang girl.

kaya $n.^{2}$ [orig. Jam. use; ety. unknown; ? link to Carib.E. *kayakiit*, a form of medicinal herb, thus note HERB $n.^{1}$ (1)] [1980s+] (*drugs*) marijuana.

KayCee *n. see* K.C. *n.* (1).

kaycuff foe! *excl.* [backsl. FUCK OFF! *excl.*] [20C+] go away!

Kaye *n.* [the proper name most like the brandname] [2000s] (*S.Afr. gay*) KY jelly or similar lubricant.

kayf *n. see* CAF *n.*

kaykirp *n. see* CURP *n.*

kayo *see under* K.O.

kayoe *adj. see* K.O. *adj.*

kay-okay! *excl. see* KAY! *excl.*

Kay See *n. see* K.C. *n.*

kaze *n. see* CASE $n.^{2}$.

kazi *n. see* CARSEY *n.*

kazillion *n. see* KABILLION *n.*

ka-zip *n.* (*also* **kerzip**) [ety. unknown] [1900s–30s] the human head.

IN PHRASES

❑ **off one's kazip** *adj.* (*also* **off one's kerzip**) [1900s–30s] (*US*) insane, eccentric.

kazoo *n.* [? KEISTER *n.* (6) or play on SE *kazoo*, a rudimentary *wind instrument*] [1960s+] the anus, the buttocks, the vagina or penis; thus *up the kazoo*, either lit. 'up the arse' or implying completeness or excess, e.g. *I've got customers up the kazoo*.

kazooms *n. see* KAHOONAS *n.*

kazoonie *n.* [GAZOONEY $n.^{1}$ (1)] [1950s] (*US prison*) a child.

k.b. $n.^{1}$ [abbr. KNOCKBACK *n.*] [20C+] **1** (*UK prison*) a rejection, esp. of parole. **2** any form of rejection.

k.b. $n.^{2}$ [abbr.; the initials are preferred to the offensive term KAFFIR BEER *under* KAFFIR *adj.*] [1960s+] (*S.Afr.*) kaffir beer (a form of beer brewed with malted sorghum millet).

k.b. *n.*[3] [KIND *n.* (2) + BUD *n.*[2] (3)] [1990s+] (*US black/drugs*) top-quality marijuana.

k.b. *v.* [abbr. KNOCK BACK *v.* (4)] [20C+] to reject.

k.b.o. *phr.* [abbr.] [1940s] *k*eep *b*uggering *o*n, i.e. persevere, stick to the job.

K-boy *n.* [SE *k(ing)* + *boy*] [1940s+] (*US*) a king in cards.

K.C. *n.* (*also* **casey, KayCee, Kay See**) [late 19C+] (*US*) Kansas City, Missouri.

K.C. Brown *n. see* CASEY BROWN *n.*

k-chung! *excl. see* KACHING! *excl.*

k'daar *n. see* KY'DAAR *n.*

keaster *n. see* KEISTER *n.*

keck *n.* (*also* **keek**) [KICK *n.*[4]] [late 19C–1910s] (*US*) a pocket.

keck-handed *adj.* (*also* **keck-fisted**) [dial.; note SE *cack-handed*, maladroit] [late 19C+] left-handed.

kecks *n.* (*also* **kacks, kaks, keks, kex**) [orig. Liverpool var. of KICKS *n.*[1]] **1** [late 19C+] trousers. **2** [1960s+] knickers, underpants.

kedger *n.* [Cockney pron. of SE *cadger*] [19C] a beggar who gains money for performing small jobs; thus *kedger's coffee-house/hotel*, a centre for beggars.

kee *n. see* KEY *n.*[2].

keebler *n.* [ety. unknown] [1990s+] (*US black*) a white person.

keech *n.* (*also* **keegh, keek**) [Scot. *keech*, excrement] [1970s+] **1** excrement. **2** something distasteful, disgusting. **3** nonsense, rubbish.

keechter *n.* [KEECH *n.* (1)] [1990s+] the posterior, the buttocks.

keed *n.* [pron. of KID *n.*[1] (4)] [1920s+] (*US*) a person, used in direct address.

keef *n. see* KIF *n.*

keegh/keek *n. see* KEECH *n.*

keek-cloy *n.* [? KECKS *n.*/KICKS *n.*[1] + CLY *n.* (2)] [early 19C] (*UK Und.*) a trouser pocket.

keel *n.* [naut. imagery; SE *keel*, the bottom of a boat] [late 19C+] the buttocks.

keel-haul *v.* [naut. jargon *keel-haul*, 'To haul (a person) under the keel of a ship, either by lowering him on one side and hauling him across to the other side, or, in the case of smaller vessels, lowering him at the bows and drawing him along under the keel to the stern' (*OED*)] [late 18C+] to treat badly, to punish, to beat, to ruin.

keel-hauling *n.* [20C+ use is W.I.; KEEL-HAUL *v.* + joc. use of KEEL *n.*] [mid-19C; 1940s+] a flogging.

keelie *n.* (*also* **keeler**) [Scot. *keelie*, a kestrel] [mid-19C+] (*Scot.*) a thief; latterly a street thug, esp. from Glasgow.

keel off *v.* (*also* **keel out**) [var. on SE *keel over*, to collapse, to fall over] [20C+] (*W.I.*) **1** to collapse. **2** to die.

keen *adj.* [SE *keen*, eager or shrewd] [late 19C+] (*US*) splendid, competent, sharply dressed etc; thus *keen society*, high society.

keener *n.* (*also* **keenie**) [SE *keen* + sfx *-er*] **1** [mid-19C+] (*US*) a hard bargainer, a cheat, a card-sharp. **2** [2000s] (*Can. juv.*) a toady, a sycophant.

keeno *adj.* [ext. of KEEN *adj.*] [1910s+] excellent, wonderful, first-rate etc.

keep *n.* [abbr.] **1** [1940s] (*US black/Harlem*) a house*keep*er. **2** [1960s] (*US*) a barman [SAmE *barkeep*].

keep *v.* [early 19C] to remain a virgin.

SE in slang uses

IN COMPOUNDS

❑ **keep-miss** *n.* (*also* **keep-woman**) [20C+] (*W.I.*) a kept woman. ❑ **keep-up** *n.* [SE *keep up appearances*] [1970s+] (*US black*) anyone who looks after the home, spec. a maid.

IN PHRASES

❑ **can you keep one down?** [1910s] (*Aus.*) an invitation to drink. ❑ **keep a fuss** *v.* [20C+] (*W.I.*) **1** to make a noise or a disturbance. **2** to quarrel loudly. ❑ **keep a nestling** *v.* [imagery of a worried mother bird] [late 17C–early 18C] to be restless, uneasy. ❑ **keep an ironmonger's shop (by the side of the common)** *v.* (*also* **keep an ironmonger's shop where the sheriff sets up**) [late 18C–early 19C] to be hanged in chains. ❑ **keep a swannery** *v.* [the mocking phr. 'all his geese are swans'] [late 18C–early 19C] to boast, to boost one's own achievements. ❑ **keep cave** *v.* (*also* **keep cavvy**) [Lat. *cave*, beware; but Ware suggests *K.V.* as in *on the qui vive*, on the lookout] [mid-19C+] (*juv.*) to keep a lookout. ❑ **keep doggo** *v. see* LIE DOGGO *under* LIE *v.*[1]. ❑ **keep down** *v.* [SE *hold down*] [20C+] (*Aus.*) to maintain one's job despite the problems entailed. ❑ **keep in tow** *v.* (*also* **keep in a tow-line, keep on a string**) [early 19C–1900s] (*UK Und.*) to keep someone in suspense. ❑ **keep it between the ditches** *v. see under* DITCH *n.* ❑ **keep it up** *v.* [pun on SE *keep it up*, to maintain an erection] [late 18C–1900s] to live a fashionable life; to prolong a debauch. ❑ **keep nikko** *v. see under* NICK *v.*[3]. ❑ **keep one's foot in someone's ass** *v. see under* ASS *n.* ❑ **keep one's game tight** *v. see* TIGHTEN UP ONE'S GAME *under* TIGHTEN (UP) *v.* ❑ **keep one's hair on** *v. see* separate entry. ❑ **keep one's hand in** *v.* [20C+ use is SE] [early 18C–19C] to maintain one's skills (in a job). ❑ **keep one's hips on one's shoulders** *v.* [1940s] (*US black*) to stop, to calm down. ❑ **keep on keeping on** *v.* [1910s+] (*orig. US black*) to persist in one's efforts. ❑ **keep out of the rain** *v.* [late 19C+] (*orig. Aus.*) to avoid trouble. ❑ **keep shoatie** *v.* [presumably SHUT-EYE *n.*[1], but rather than closing the eyes, one is keeping them wide open; also Scot. *shut-eye*, a trick or swindle; or link to *shotgun*, i.e. one who backs up, lit. or fig. a protangonist] [20C+] (*Scot.*) to keep a lookout. ❑ **keep six** *v. see* GIVE SIX *under* SIX! *excl.* ❑ **keep the faith** [best known in the slogan *keep the faith, baby*, popularized by the controversial US Congressman Adam Clayton Powell Jr (1908–72)] [1960s+] (*orig. US black*) stay loyal, don't desert us. ❑ **keep your hand on your ha'penny (till the right man turns up)** *v. see* HA'PENNY *n.* ❑ **keep yow** *v.* [*yow*, onomat. for a cry of alarm] [1940s+] (*Aus.*) to keep a lookout, esp. in a criminal context.

IN EXCLAMATIONS

❑ **keep your hair on!** *see under* KEEP ONE'S HAIR ON *v.*

keeper *n.* [20C+] **1** any form of weapon [i.e. it keeps one safe]. **2** (*US*) a person of worth.

keeping *n.*

SE in slang uses

IN PHRASES

❑ **in keeping** [18C–early 19C] (*UK Und.*) of a prostitute, kept by a given client; also of the man who lives off a whore. ❑ **on one's keeping** [late 19C+] (*Irish*) in hiding, i.e. 'keeping oneself out of sight'.

keeping cully *n.* [SE *keep* + CULLY *n.*[1] (2)] [late 17C–early 19C] **1** 'one that maintains a Mistress and parts with his money very generously to her' (B.E.). **2** 'one who keeps a mistress, as he supposes, for his own use, but really for that of the public' (Grose, 1785); thus *keeping lady*, a mistress/prostitute.

keeping the passover *phr.* [orig. known as *hold a Rag Fair* or *hold a Monmouth Street*. The association of Jewish old-clothes sellers with Monmouth Street led to the introduction of *Passover*, the Jewish spring festival commemorating the Exodus from Egypt; presumably + added ref. to the 'passing over' of the fresh air] [late 19C] (*W.I.*) spreading out one's clothes for an airing.

keep one's hair on *v.* (*also* **keep one's skin on**) [? the image of tearing out one's hair when in a rage; or ? (though prob. a folk ety. at best) the need of members of US pioneering wagon trains to keep calm in the face of an Indian attack (were they to panic, they might well be scalped, thus losing their hair)] [late 19C+] to keep calm, to keep one's temper; thus *get one's hair off*, to lose one's temper.

IN EXCLAMATIONS

❑ **keep your hair on!** (*also* **keep your head on! ...hairs on! ... tits on!**) [late 19C+] calm down! don't lose (emotional) control!

keeshkas *n. see* KISHKES *n.*

keester *see under* KEISTER.

keeva *adj.* [ety. unknown] [1990s+] (*US campus*) excellent, worthy of admiration.

kef *n. see* KIF *n.*

keffal *n.* (*also* **keffel**) [Welsh *ceffyl*, a horse; its use often implied that the horse was second-rate] [late 17C–mid-19C] (*UK Und.*) a horse.

keg *n.* (*also* **beer keg**) **1** [late 19C+] (*US*) the stomach. **2** [1940s+] (*Aus./N.Z.*) beer, a barrel of beer[abbr. SE *beer keg*]. **3** [1970s] (*US drugs*) 5 lbs of marijuana [? the amount of marijuana that would fill a beer keg].

(IN COMPOUNDS)

❑ **keg-fly** *n.* [on pattern of BAR-FLY *n.*] [1980s+] (*US campus*) someone who hovers around the beer keg at parties. ❑ **keg-legs** *n.* [1990s+] (*UK juv.*) an insult aimed at a girl with fat thighs or esp. calves.

(IN PHRASES)

❑ **carry the keg** *v.* [pun on SE *keg*/CAG *n.*] [early 19C] to be easily annoyed, to be unable to take a joke. ❑ **come off the keg** [1910s+] (*Aus.*) don't talk nonsense. ❑ **have a keg on board** *v.* [late 19C] (*US*) to be drunk. ❑ **keg it up** *v.* [1990s+] (*N.Z.*) to drink, usu. in a party or public house. ❑ **open a keg of nails** *v.* [20C+] to have a drink, to get drunk.

keg *v.*[1] [KEG *n.*; the image is of leaving the beer in the keg] [late 18C–mid-19C] (*US*) to abstain from drinking alcohol.

keg *v.*[2] *see* CAG *v.*

kegger *n.* (*also* **X kegger**) [SE *keg*/KEG *n.*] **1** [1910s+] a person who buys alcohol legally, and then takes it to a teetotal or 'dry' area of the country for consumption. **2** [1960s+] (*US campus*) a party featuring a large supply of beer.

kegging *n.*[1] [SE *beer keg*] (*N.Z.*) **1** [1910s+] buying alcohol legally, and then taking it to a teetotal or 'dry' area of the country for consumption. **2** [1970s+] indulging in a keg-party, i.e. a party where kegs of beer are consumed.

kegging *n.*[2] [1990s+] stripping as part of sexual bullying by boys.

kegging *adj.* [? the positive qualities of a SE *keg* of beer] [1990s+] (*US campus*) excellent, worthy of admiration.

kegmeg *n.* [SE *kegmeg*, rotten meat or a tough old goose] **1** [mid-19C] tripe; thus *kegmeg shop*, a tripe shop. **2** [late 19C] an intimate conversation [? pun on TRIPE *n.*[1]; or TRIPE *n.*[2] (1), as a moral disapproval of the 'rotten-ness' of gossip].

keifer *n. see* KYFER *n.*

keister *n.* (*also* **keaster, keester, keyster, kiester, kister**) [Ger. *kiste*, a box, a case + Ger. sl. the rump] **1** [late 19C+] (*US*) a suitcase, a satchel, a handbag, a salesman's sample case. **2** [late 19C+] (*US Und.*) a burglar's bag of safe- or house-breaking tools. **3** [1910s+] (*US Und.*) a safe, a strongbox (often within a safe). **4** [1930s–40s] (*US*) the female genitals. **5** [1930s–60s] (*US, esp. prison*) anal copulation. **6** [1930s+] (*orig. US*) the anus, the buttocks. **7** [1940s–60s] (*US*) a prison. **8** [1960s+] (*US*) one's self.

(IN COMPOUNDS)

❑ **keister bandit** *n.* [-BANDIT *sfx* (2)] [1930s+] (*US prison*) a 'masculine' male homosexual; by ext., a womanizer, a rapist. ❑ **keister bunny** *n.* [1990s+] (*US prison*) an inmate who places contraband items – tobacco, drugs – in his rectum. ❑ **keisterman** *n.* [1930s–50s] (*US Und.*) a thief who specializes in stealing suitcases on railway stations. ❑ **keister plant** *n.* [PLANT *n.* (17)] [1930s–70s] (*US drugs*) a cache of drugs hidden, usu. in some form of hollow metal container, in the rectum. ❑ **keister shafting** *n.* [SHAFT *v.* (1)] [1980s+] (*US gay*) anal intercourse. ❑ **keister stash** *n.* [STASH *n.*[2]] [1960s] (*US Und.*) any slim, hollow item, e.g. a biro tube, that can be placed in the anus and used to transport money, drugs etc. ❑ **keister stab** *v.* [STAB *v.*] [1980s+] (*US gay*) to have anal intercourse. ❑ **keister-stashed** *adj.* [1960s] (*US prison*) hidden in the anus.

(IN PHRASES)

❑ **grease someone's keister** *v.* [2000s] (*US*) to sodomize.

keister *v.* (*also* **keester**) [KEISTER *n.* (6)] (*US, esp. prison*) **1** [1930s+] (*also* **ass-keister**) to hide something in the rectum. **2** [1930s+] to sodomize. **3** [1960s+] to betray, to harm [fig. use of sense 2].

Keith Moon *n.* [rhy. sl.; ult. rock drummer *Keith Moon* (1947–78)] [1960s+] an eccentric, a loon.

keks *n. see* KECKS *n.*

kelch *n. see* KELT *n.*

kelder *n. see* HANS-EN-KELDER *n.*

kell *n.* [northern dial. *kell*, the equivalent of SE *caul*] [20C+] (*Ulster*) a ring of dirt that reveals an unwashed neck.

kelly *n.*[1] [fig. uses of proper name *Kelly*] **1** [20C+] (*Aus.*) an axe; thus *swing kelly*, to swing an axe [brandname of *Kelly* Axe Manufacturing Co., Charleston, West Virginia]. **2** [1940s–50s] (*Aus.*) a bus or tram inspector [the bushranger Ned *Kelly* (1855–80); like him the inspectors pounce suddenly on their victims]. **3** [2000s] money [play on colour *Kelly green*].

kelly *n.*[2] [Cumbrian dial. *kelp*, a young crow] [20C+] a crow.

kelly *n.*[3] [pun on a *Derbyhat*; ? rhy. sl. DERBY KELLY *n.*] [1900s–70s] (*US*) a man's hat.

Kelly gang *n. see under* NED KELLY *n.*[1].

kelly ned *n.* [rhy. sl.; ult. the bushranger *Ned Kelly* (1855–80)] [20C+] (*Aus./US*) the head.

kelly's eye *n.* [? a lost anecdote] [20C+] (*bingo*) the number one.

kelp *n.*[1] (*also* **calp**) [Turkish *calpac*, a Turkish and Tartar felt cap] [mid-18C–mid-19C] a hat.

kelp *n.*[2] [? Scot. *gilpp*, a growing girl] [20C+] a self-conscious, awkward teenager, usu. a girl.

kelp *v.* [KELP *n.*[1]] [early–mid-19C] to raise one's hat to an acquaintance.

kelsey *n.* [presumably a punning ref. to *TIGHT AS KELSEY'S NUTS under* KELSEY'S NUTS *n.*] [1930s–70s] (*US black*) **1** a prostitute. **2** straight hair: a popular hairstyle, favoured by many prostitutes [orig. carnival use].

Kelsey's nuts *n.* [punning ref. to the US *Kelsey* Wheel Company, founded in 1910 to produce automobile wheels. The need for nuts and bolts to be exceptionally tight fitting to preclude wobbly wheels gave rise to the saying] [1930s+] (*US Und.*) used alone to imply the best, the absolute; used in phr. below as a superlative to mean 'extremely', 'the most'.

(IN PHRASES)

❑ **cold as Kelsey's nuts** *adj.* (*also* **colder than Kelsey's ass**) [1960s+] extremely cold. ❑ **dead as Kelsey's nuts** *adj.* (*also* **deader than Kelsey's nuts**) [1930s+] (*US*) very, definitely dead, out of favour; lit. or fig. ❑ **safe as Kelsey** *adj.* [1910s+] extremely conservative. ❑ **tight as Kelsey's nuts** *adj.* [1980s+] (*US Und.*) extremely mean, stingy.

kelt *n.* (*also* **kelch, kelsey, keltch, keltz**) [? Scot. *kelt*, a homespun cloth, usu. of black and white wool mixed, once used for outer garments by country people] [1910s+] (*US black*) **1** a white person. **2** used to mean a light-skinned black person, in phr. such as *three-quarter kelt*.

kelter *n.* [northern dial.] [late 18C–mid-19C] money, cash.

kembla (grange) *n.* [rhy. sl.; ult. *Kembla Grange*, an area of Wollongong, New South Wales] [1950s+] (*Aus.*) small change.

kemels *n.* [? brandname] [1940s] (*US black*) shoes.

kemesa *n. see* CAMESA *n.*

kemo sabe *n.* [according to scriptwriter Frank Striker, the 'Native American' term 'trusty scout' applied to the loyal Indian companion, Tonto, in the *Lone Ranger* radio and television series created by George Trendle in 1933; for some of the alternative theories of the phr. see http://www.write101.com/kemosabe.htm] [1930s+] (*US*) a friend, used in direct address.

kemp *n.* (*also* **kimp**) [ety. unknown] [1950s] (*US*) a car.

Ken *n.* [the popular male companion for *Barbie*] [1980s+] (*US campus*) a painstakingly fashionably dressed and groomed man.

ken *n.*[1] [poss. abbr. SE *kennel* (in a non-canine mode) or f. Hind. *khan(n)a*, a house or room, which is also found in combs., e.g. *buggy-khanna* (coach house) or *bottle-khanna* (drinking house); Hotten (1867) attributes it to 'Gypsey and Oriental' and notes that 'all slang and cant words which end in *-ken* are partly of Gypsey origin' on which basis Partridge (1984) opts for a root in Rom. *tan*, a place; the term vanished from sl. *c.*1860, but has survived in costermonger jargon] **1** [16C+] (*UK Und.*) (*also* **kennel**) a house; a home, a room. **2** [17C–1920s] (*UK Und.*) a disreputable drinking room. **3** [19C] (*UK tramp*) a bed. **4** *see* PATTEN-KEN *n.*

IN COMPOUNDS

❑ **ken-burster** *n.* [early–mid-19C] a house-breaker. ❑ **ken-cadger** *n.* [early 19C] (*UK Und.*) the lowest rank of beggar. ❑ **ken-cracker** *n.* [late 18C–19C] a house-breaker. ❑ **ken-miller** *n.* [MILL *v.*[1] (1)] [mid-17C–mid-19C] a house-breaker.

IN PHRASES

❑ **burn the ken** *v.* [early 18C–early 19C] to stay at an inn, then leave without paying one's bill.

ken *n.*[2] [SE colloq. *barbie*, a barbecue; punning on *Ken* and Barbie, the fashion dolls] [1990s+] (*Aus.*) a cleaning implement for a barbecue.

ken *n.*[3] [2000s] (*Irish*) a can or bottle or draft of Heineken beer.

kenchlin *n.* [mid-19C] (*UK Und.*) a firm promise.

IN COMPOUNDS

❑ **kenchlinnigger** *n.* [mid-19C] (*UK Und.*) an untrustworthy villain.

ken cove *n. see* COVE OF THE KEN *under* COVE *n.*

Ken Dodd *n.* [rhy. sl. = WAD *n.*[1] (1); ult. UK comedian *Ken Dodd* (b.1927)] [1960s+] a large roll of banknotes.

Ken Dodds *n.* [rhy. sl.; *see* prev.] [1960s+] in pl. the testicles [CODS *n.*[1] (1)].

kenird *adj. see* KANURD *adj.*

kennedy *n.* [anecdotal: one *Kennedy* who was apparently killed with a poker] **1** [early 19C–1900s] a poker. **2** [early 19C–1900s] a blow inflicted with a poker [f. a man who allegedly suffered thus in London's St Giles slums]. **3** [1980s+] the penis [fig. use of sense 1].

IN PHRASES

❑ **give someone kennedy** *v.* [early 19C–1900s] to strike someone with a poker.

kennedy *v.* [KENNEDY *n.*] [mid-19C] to strike or beat to death with a poker.

kennedy rot *n.* **1** [20C+] (*Aus./US*) a sot [rhy. sl.]. **2** *see* BARCOO ROT *under* BARCOO *n.*

kennedy swoop *n.* [1970s+] (*US black*) a hairstyle in which black hair is straightened, then brushed to one side in a manner loosely resembling the hairstyles of John F. *Kennedy* (1917–63) and Robert *Kennedy* (1925–68).

kennel *n.*[1] [SE *kennel*, a gutter] [late 17C–19C] the vagina.

IN COMPOUNDS

❑ **kennel-raker** *n.* [SE *raker*; SE *kennel-raker* 'a raker of the gutter; a scavenger; also used as a term of abuse' (*OED*)] [19C] the penis.

kennel *n.*[2] [1900s–20s] **1** (*tramp*) a house. **2** (*US*) a booth, any small structure reminiscent of a dog-kennel.

SE in slang uses

IN COMPOUNDS

❑ **kennel show** *n.* [play on DOGS *n.*[1] (1)] [1940s] (*US milit.*) foot inspection.

IN PHRASES

❑ **dog kennels** *n.* [play on SE *dogs*/DOGS *n.*[1] (2)] [1920s] (*US*) shoes. ❑ **roll me in the kennel** *n.* [SE *kennel*, the gutter; the drunken toper will sleep anywhere] [early–mid-18C] gin. ❑ **snoring kennel** *n.* [late 17C–early 18C] a bedroom.

IN EXCLAMATIONS

❑ **go to the kennel!** [1900s] (*Aus.*) go away! be quiet! ❑ **kennel up!** [1910s] (*Aus.*) stop talking!

kennetseeno *adj.* [backsl.] [mid-19C] putrid, stinking, 'off'.

kennick *n.* [KEN *n.*[1] (1) + ? model of *Celtic*] [mid–late 19C] a mixture of criminal cant and the slang talked in a lodging house.

Kennington Lane *n.* [rhy. sl.; ult. *Kennington Lane*, a south London thoroughfare] [20C+] pain.

kennuck *n.* (*also* **kenuck**) [? KILKENNY *n.*[2]] [mid–late 19C] a penny.

kennurd *adj. see* KANURD *adj.*

keno! *excl.* [used in game of *keno* to describe a winning set of numbers] [late 19C–1930s] (*US*) an excl. used to express excitement or success.

kenobe *n.* [mid-19C] (*UK Und.*) a thief.

Kenso *n.* [*Kens(ington)* + -O *sfx* (3)] [1940s+] (*Aus.*) **1** Kensington, a suburb of Sydney. **2** the University of New South Wales at Kensington.

Kent *n.* [ety. unknown; ? as favoured in *Kent*, the UK county] [19C] any variety of coloured handkerchief; thus also *Kent clout*, *Kent rag*.

Kentish Town *n.* [rhy. sl. = BROWN *n.* (1); ult. area of northwest London] [20C+] a penny.

kentry *n.* [late 19C] (*US Und.*) a gang's territory.

Kent Street ejectment *n.* (*also* **Kent Street distress**) [Kent Street, Southwark, a very poor area in 16C London, where the landlords originated the practice] [late 18C–19C] the removal of the front door when tenants are more than two weeks in rent arrears.

Kentuck *n.* (*also* **Kaintuck**) [abbr.] [early 19C+] (*US*) a Kentuckian, Kentucky; also as adj.

Kentucky *adj.* [geographical stereotyping] [early 19C] (*US*) pertaining to violence.

based on negative connotations of the state

IN COMPOUNDS

❑ **Kentucky argument** *n.* [late 19C] (*US*) a dispute which escalates to the drawing of firearms. ❑ **Kentucky bite** *n.* [mid-19C] (*US*) a cutting bite to the ear or nose during a fight. ❑ **Kentucky blue** *n.* [joc. ref. to *Kentucky blue grass*] [1960s+] (*US drugs*) a variety of marijuana grown in Kentucky. ❑ **Kentucky breakfast** *n.* [the supposed favourite breakfasts of the classic 'Southern gentleman'] [late 19C+] (*US*) **1** popularly defined as 'three cocktails and a chew of terbacker'. **2** a bottle of bourbon, a three-pound steak and a setter dog; the dog is there to eat the steak. ❑ **Kentucky oysters** *n.* [late 19C+] (*US, mainly black*) chitterlings, pig intestines. ❑ **Kentucky treat** *n.* (*also* **Kentucky**) [1910s–50s] (*Aus./US*) a supposed 'treat' for which everyone present has to contribute.

Kentucky *v.* [2000s] (*S.Afr. gay*) to have anal intercourse.

kenuck *n. see* KENNUCK *n.*

kenwood *n.* [rhy. sl.; *Kenwood mixer* = SHIKSA *n.* (1)] [2000s] a Gentile woman.

kenz *adj.* [Scot. *kensy*, a general term of abuse for a rough, rude person] [20C+] (*W.I., USVI*) gullible, simple-minded, easily fooled.

keo *n.* (*also* **keo-boy**) [Scot. *kiow-ow*, a trifle in speech or conduct] [20C+] (*Ulster*) **1** an entertaining, if less than respectable, individual. **2** a term of abuse, a contemptible person. **3** a womanizer. **4** a trickster.

keptie *n.* (*also* **keptee**) [SE *kept* + fem. sfx *-ie*] [1930s–60s] (*US*) a mistress, a kept woman.

ker- *pfx* [most dictionaries (*OED*, Webster, F&H) link the pfx to onomatopoeia, but beyond that the precise meaning of *ker-* becomes more problematical. A range of possibilities is listed by George Cohen, whose detailed analysis is recommended for further study (Cohen 1985, pp.1–28): (i) f. simple onomatopoeia. (ii) f. Ger. past participle pfx *ge-*. (iii) f. dial. *cur-*/*car-* and Gaelic *car-*, wrongly, confusedly; ult. f. Gaelic *car*, a twist, a turn. (iv) the initial *crrr-* pron. of words such as *crash* and *crunch* (Cohen's own belief)] [mid-19C+] (*orig. US*) a pfx used in a wide variety of combs. to indicate the sound of falling, of collision or of movement; other synon. pfxs include *ca-, che-, co-, com-, con-cor-, cul-, cur-, ga-, k'-, ka-, ke-, ko-, ku-*.

IN COMPOUNDS

❑ **ker...** *see also under* KA... ❑ **kerbolluxed** *adj.* [BALLOCKS (UP) *v.*] [20C+] messed up, confused, with overtones of attendant noise. ❑ **kerflooey** *adj.* (*also* **caflooey, gaflooey, kerfluey**) [*KERFLOOEY!* below] [1910s+] crazy, chaotic, disorganised; usu. in phr. *go kerflooey*, to go to pieces, to break down. ❑ **kerflummox** *adv.* (*also* **kerflumix**) [*KERFLUMMOX* below] [mid-19C–1900s] (*US*) of falling, heavily or noisily, with a thump. ❑ **kerflummox** *v.* (*also* **curflummux, kerflumix, kerflummox,**

kuflummux) [FLUMMOX *v.* (4)] **1** [mid-19C–1900s] (*US*) to confound, to flabbergast. **2** [late 19C] to ponder. **3** [late 19C–1900s] (*US*) to fall heavily or noisily. ❑ **kerlaraping** *n.* [? *larrup*, to thrash] [late 19C] (*US*) cavorting, jumping around excitedly. ❑ **kershlunk** *adv.* [*slunk/slink*] [1940s+] an onomat. term indicating the clandestine, slinking movement of an animal or human, e.g. *The cat went kershlunk into the bushes.* ❑ **kerwhallop** *see* separate entries.

(IN EXCLAMATIONS)

❑ **ker...!** *see also under* KA...! ❑ **kerbam!** [SE *bam*] [20C+] an onomat. term indicating a sudden noise or sharp shock. ❑ **kerbang!** [SE *bang*] [late 19C+] an onomat. term indicating a sudden sharp noise or explosion. ❑ **kerbiff!** [BIFF *n.*[1] (1)] [late 19C+] an onomat. term indicating a sudden blow. ❑ **kerbim!** [echoic *bim*] [mid-19C] an onomat. term indicating a sudden blow. ❑ **kerblam!** [SE *blam*] [late 19C+] an onomat. term indicating a sudden shock or explosion. ❑ **kerblinketyblank!** (*also* **kerblinketyblink! kerblinketyblunk!**) [BLANKETY-BLANK *phr.*] [late 19C] an onomat. term indicating annoyance, irritation. ❑ **kerblip!** [echoic *blip*] [20C+] an onomat. term indicating the noise of something hitting the (soft) ground. ❑ **kerblump!** [SE *bump/blump*; var. on *KERPLUMP!* below] [1940s+] an onomat. term indicating the noise of a solid object hitting the (soft) ground. ❑ **kerbonk!** [BONK *n.* (1)] [1980s+] an onomat. term indicating the noise of a solid object hitting (or being hit by) another one. ❑ **kerchug!** [SE *chug*] [20C+] an onomat. term indicating the sound of an ailing motor engine turning over. ❑ **kerchunk!** (*also* **cachunk! cajunk! cashunk!**) [SE *chunk*] [mid-19C+] an onomat. term indicating the sound of a solid object hitting the ground or two solid objects colliding. ❑ **kerdap!** [echoic *dap*] [1930s] (*US*) an onomat. term echoic of something liquid hitting a solid surface. ❑ **kerdash!** [? SE *splash*] [mid-19C] (*US*) an onomat. term indicating the sound of an object hitting a liquid. ❑ **kerdiff!** [*diff*, echoic of a sudden noise] [mid-19C] (*US*) an onomat. term indicating a sudden shock or noise. ❑ **kerdoing!** (*also* **gerdoing! gerdoying! kerdoink! kerdoying!**) [*doing*, echoic of a sudden noise] [1950s+] an onomat. term indicating a sudden noise. ❑ **kerflap!** [SE *flap*] [20C+] an onomat. term indicating a sudden shock or gesture. ❑ **kerflip!** [SE *flip*] [1930s+] an onomat. term indicating the sound of a solid body hitting a soft one or hitting liquid. ❑ **kerflooey!** (*also* **gaflooey! kaflooey!**) [FLOOEY! *excl.*] [1910s+] an onomat. term indicating a sudden explosion. ❑ **kerflop!** [SE *flop*] [late 19C+] an onomat. term indicating the sound of a solid body hitting a soft one or hitting liquid. ❑ **kerflunk!** (*also* **kaflunk!**) [echoic *flunk*] [1980s+] an onomat. term indicating something solid falling to the ground. ❑ **kerplooey!** (*also* **kaplooey!**) [echoic *plooey*; var. on *KERFLOOEY* above] [1930s+] an onomat. term indicating the noise made by the explosion of something soft and messy, e.g. a large fruit or a living body. ❑ **kerplop!** [SE *plop*] [late 19C+] an onomat. term indicating the sound of a solid body falling, usu. into liquid, or of a bubble bursting in liquid. ❑ **kerplump!** [echoic *plump*] [1930s+] an onomat. term indicating the sound of a solid body hitting a soft surface. ❑ **kerplumpus!** (*also* **kerlumpus**) [ext. of *KERPLUMP!* above] [mid-19C] an onomat. term indicating the sound of a solid body hitting a soft surface. ❑ **kerpoomph!** [echoic *poomph*] [1950s] an onomat. term indicating the sound of a solid body hitting a soft surface. ❑ **kershewey!** [? *Jesus*] [1940s+] (*US*) a euph. interj., the equivalent of *by Christ* or *by Jesus*. ❑ **kerslam!** [SE *slam*] [late 19C–1910s] an onomat. term indicating a sudden noise or action. ❑ **kerslap!** [SE *slap*] [mid-19C+] an onomat. term indicating a sudden noise or, usu., action. ❑ **kerslash!** [SE *slip/crash*] [mid-19C] (*US*) an onomat. term indicating a sudden crash, as caused by tripping over an object. ❑ **kerslesh!** [SE *slash*] [mid-19C] (*US*) an onomat. term indicating movement at speed. ❑ **kerslosh!** (*also* **kerslush! kerswosh! kerwash! kerwosh!**) [SE *slosh/slush/wash*] [mid-19C+] an onomat. term indicating movement through a wet or soft substance, or the falling of a solid object into such a substance, e.g. viscous mud. ❑ **kerslung!** (*also* **kersling!**) [echoic] [mid-19C] an onomat. term indicating a sudden movement. ❑ **kersmack!** [SMACK *v.* (2)] [1930s+] an onomat. term indicating a sudden movement or a sharp blow. ❑ **kersmash!** (*also* **co-smash!**) [SE *smash*] [mid-19C+] an onomat. term indicating a sudden crash or collision. ❑ **kersouse!** (*also* **kasouse! kesouse!**) [SE *souse*] [mid-19C] an onomat. term indicating a fall into liquid. ❑ **kersplash!** (*also* **kersplosh!**) [SE *splash*] [late 19C+] an onomat. term indicating a fall into liquid. ❑ **kersplat!** (*also* **kasplat!**) [SPLAT! *excl.*] [1980s+] an onomat. term indicating a fall onto a soft surface, esp. with concomitant mess, e.g. a stuntman's dive into a stall of soft fruit and vegetables. ❑ **kerswallop!** (*also* **kerswollop!**) [echoic] [mid-19C] (*US*) an onomat. term indicating a fall or flop. ❑ **kerswash!** (*also* **caswash!**) [echoic] [mid-19C–1960s] an onomat. term indicating a collision or crash, esp. of one object falling on top of another. ❑ **kerswop!** [echoic] [mid-19C] an onomat. term indicating a fall into liquid. ❑ **kerthud!** [SE *thud*] [1940s+] an onomat. term indicating the dull noise of a solid object landing on a solid surface. ❑ **kerthump!** [SE *thump*] [late 19C+] an onomat. term indicating a sudden dull noise. ❑ **kerumph!** (*also* **kerump!**) [echoic] [20C+] an onomat. term indicating an exclamation or sudden shock. ❑ **kerwallux!** (*also* **cawallux! cawhalux!**) [SE *wallop*] [mid-19C] (*US*) an onomat. term indicating the sound of a slap or a box on the ear. ❑ **kerwash!/kerwosh!** *see* *KERWOOSH!* below. ❑ **kerwhackety!** [SE *whack/racket*] [1940s+] an onomat. term indicating noisy, stumbling, erratic progress. ❑ **kerwhammy!** [WHAM! *excl.*] [1940s+] an onomat. term indicating the sound of a sudden collision. ❑ **kerwhop!** (*also* **cawhop!**) [echoic] [mid-19C+] an onomat. term indicating the noise of a solid body falling onto a solid surface. ❑ **kerwoosh!** (*also* **kerwash! kerwosh!**) [SE *whoosh*] [20C+] an onomat. term indicating speedy movement.

kerb *see under* CURB and combs.

kerb and gutter *n.* [rhy. sl.] [20C+] (*Aus.*) butter.

kerboodle *n. see* CABOODLE *n.*

kerbstone *see under* CURBSTONE and combs.

kêrel *n.* (*also* **carol**) [OE *ceorl*, a countryman, a common man] (*S.Afr.*) **1** [early 19C+] a chap, a fellow. **2** [early 19C+] a boyfriend. **3** [early 19C+] a tricky, cunning person. **4** [late 19C+] a term of address to a man. **5** [1970s+] the police.

Kermit the Frog *n.* [rhy. sl.; ult. *Kermit the Frog*, a character in *The Muppet Show* (1976–81)] [1970s+] **1** a lavatory [BOG *n.*[1] (1)]. **2** sexual caressing, stopping short of intercourse [SNOG *n.*].

kero *n.* [abbr. SE *kerosene*] [1930s+] (*Aus.*) **1** *kerosene*; thus *kero-tin*, old tins used for other purposes. **2** beer [implies a form of 'fuel'].

kerosene tin push *n.* [the joc. story that goats are fed on kerosone tins; thus *Bulletin* 11/1/1906 15/1: 'What a multiplicity of uses the kerosene tin is put to in the bush [...] Houses are made of it in some parts and I have heard they feed the goats on kerosene tins about Byrock, but I cannot vouch for that.'] [1900s] (*Aus.*) a flock of goats.

kerp *n. see* CURP *n.*

Kerry Packered *adj.* (*also* **kerried**) [rhy. sl. = KNACKERED *adj.* (1); ult. Aus. media magnate *Kerry Packer* (1937–2005)] [1970s+] exhausted, tired out.

Kerry security *n.* [? negative stereotyping of Kerrymen as corrupt] [late 18C–early 19C] any form of bond or oath that has been sworn in return for money.

Kerry witness *n.* [? negative stereotyping of Kerrymen as corrupt] [late 18C] a witness who is happy to swear to anything (for a price).

kerteever/kerterver *see under* CATEVER.

kertever cartzo *n.* [Ling. Franca *cattivo cazzo*, lit. 'bad cock'] [mid-19C] venereal disease.

kertish *n.* [late 19C–1900s] (*US*) dollars, money.

kerwhallop *v.* (*also* **cowhallop, cowollap, kawhallop, keswollup**) [KER- *pfx* + SE *wallop*] [mid-19C+] to hit hard and suddenly, to smack.

kerwhallop *adv.* (*also* **co-wallop, kawhallop**) [KERWHALLOP *v.*] **1** [mid-19C] (*US*) precisely, exactly. **2** [20C+] indicating suddeness, or a fall.

kerzillion *n. see* ZILLION *n.*

keskydee *n. see* KISKEEDEE *n.*

kesouse! *excl. see* KERSOUSE! *under* KER- *pfx.*

keswollup *v. see* KERWHALLOP *v.*

ket *n.* [abbr.] [2000s] **1** (*drugs*) ketamine. **2** (*N.Z.*) an electric *kettle.*

ketch *v.* [mid-19C] (*UK Und.*) to hang.

ketchup *n.* **1** [20C+] (*Aus.*) beer [the colour of 'brown sauce']. **2** [1940s–70s] (*US*) blood [the colour of tomato ketchup].

kettle *n.*[1] **1** [17C–19C] the vagina [the image of a vagina as a receptacle]. **2** [early 19C–1930s] (*US*) a steam engine [the steam]. **3** a variety of watch [the original large circular pocket watches allegedly resembled kettles]. (**a**) [mid-19C+] a pocket watch; thus *red kettle*, a gold watch; *white kettle*, a silver watch; *dummy kettle*, a toy watch. (**b**) [1920s+] a wrist watch.

IN PHRASES

❑ **get one's kettle mended** *v.* [note the repertoire of bawdy songs in which wandering tinkers 'mend' ladies' *kettles*] [late 19C–1900s] of a woman, to have sexual intercourse.

SE in slang uses

IN COMPOUNDS

❑ **kettle brandy** *n.* [late 19C–1900s] tea, esp. as drunk at tea parties.

kettle *n.*[2] *see* KETTLE (ON A HOB) *n.*

kettle *v.* [? dial. *kittle*, to arouse, to stimulate, to prick] [1920s–30s] (*US*) esp. of a horse, to frighten or become frightened.

kettlebelly *n.* [late 19C–1920s] (*US*) a fat person.

kettled *adj.* [SE *kettle*, as a container (for liquor)] [1990s+] drunk.

kettledrum *n.* [a play on the omnipresent tea kettle + *drum*, 'an assembly of fashionable people at a private house, held in the evening, much in vogue during the latter half of the 18th and beginning of the 19th century ... later, an afternoon tea party, formerly sometimes followed by the larger assembly' (*OED*)] [mid–late 19C] an afternoon tea party on a large scale.

kettledrums *n. see* CUPID'S KETTLEDRUMS *under* CUPID *n.*

kettle (on a hob) *n.* [rhy. sl.] **1** [late 19C+] one shilling (5p) [BOB *n.*[3] (2)]. **2** [20C+] a pet name for someone called Bob.

kev *n.* [2000s] a hooligan, a working-class youth devoted to petty criminality.

Kevin *n.* [the 'commonness' of the name] [1980s+] (*UK upper and middle classes*) a derog. name for lower-middle- or working-class youths, whom they regard as overly flashy and socially unacceptable; a male SHARON *n.*

kevork *v.* [*Jack Kevorkian* (b. 1928), US doctor who assisted patients to commit suicide and was imprisoned from 1999 to 2007] [1990s+] to kill.

kew *n.* [backsl.] [mid-19C–1900s] a week; thus *skew*, weeks.

kewl *adj.* [COOL *adj.*] [1990s+] (*US teen*) a general term of approval.

kewpie *n.* [abbr. *kewpie doll*] **1** [1920s] (*US*) a fool, an unsophisticated person. **2** [1920s–40s] (*US Und.*) a child. **3** [1990s+] (*Aus.*) a prostitute [rhy. sl. = MOLL *n.* (2)].

kex *n. see* KECKS *n.*

key *n.*[1] [lit. and fig. uses of SE *key*] **1** [17C+] the penis [the complement to KEYHOLE *n.*; *see double entendres* in D'Urfey, *Pills to Purge Melancholy* (1719), e.g. 'Ne'er hope to keep a find Cabinet lock'd, / When every Furr'd Gown has a Key, Sir' and 'To have her stock, / So close kept Lock'd, / And put a Key to her Till']. **2** [1910s+] (*Aus./N.Z.*) constr. with *the*, a declaration that one is a habitual criminal, thus the indefinite detention that, following the Habitual Criminals Act (1905) was mandatory for such individuals, who would first serve a specified sentence, then, subject to behaviour etc would begin the indefinite 'key' [SE *throw away the key*]. **3** [20C+] (*US prison*) (*also* **keys**) a prison warder [metonymy SE *key*, which they carry]. **4** [2000s] (*US prison*) a pack of cigarettes [? its role as a means of exchange, thus it 'opens doors'].

IN COMPOUNDS

❑ **key man** *n.* **1** [1960s+] (*Aus.*) a habitual criminal. **2** [1970s+] (*UK Und.*) the member of a criminal gang who clinches the deal.

SE in slang uses

IN COMPOUNDS

❑ **key winder** *n.* [SE *key winder*, a watch that is wound up with a key (ref. to sense 1 above); *stem winder*, a watch that requires no key] [1910s] (*US*) a girl; thus *stem winder*, a boy.

IN PHRASES

❑ **key of the door** *n.* [the trad. year of 'coming of age' (prior to its change to 18) and getting one's own front-door key] [1950s+] (*bingo*) the number 21.

key *n.*[2] (*also* **kee, keye, ki**) [abbr. *k*ilogram] **1** [1960s+] (*drugs*) one *k*ilo of marijuana, hashish or any other drug. **2** [2000s] £1000.

key *n.*[3] [1990s+] (*W.I.*) a friend.

key *adj.* [SE *key*, central, vital] [1970s+] (*US campus*) excellent, admirable.

key *v.* [1980s+] (*orig. US campus*) to scratch an automobile with a key or other pointed object.

keye *n. see* KEY *n.*[2].

keyed *adj.* [? SE *keyed up*, tense or nervous] **1** [1910s–30s] (*US*) drunk. **2** [1990s+] (*US black*) intoxicated by a drug.

keyhole *n.* [SE/KEY *n.*[1] + HOLE *n.*[1] (1)] [17C; 1920s] the vagina.

SE in slang uses

IN COMPOUNDS

❑ **keyhole-whistler** *n.* (*also* **keyhole-whisperer**) [those inside the adjacent house hear whispering/whistling through the keyhole] **1** [mid-19C–1920s] one who sleeps in barns or outhouses, thus a tramp or vagrant. **2** [1930s] (*US Und.*) a criminal in hiding.

keyhole a round-tripper *v.* [ety. unknown] [1930s–40s] (*US black*) to witness a remarkable event; to gaze at an exceptional individual.

keynod *n. see* YERKNOD *n.*

key on *v.* [1980s+] (*US*) to instruct, to teach.

keys *n. see* KEY *n.*[1] (3).

keyster *n. see* KEISTER *n.*

Keystone *n.* [Hollywood's *Keystone Cops*, a group of comical, incompetent policemen created by director Mack Sennett (1884–1960) in 1912; they featured in a number of films made by his Keystone Studios] [1910s+] a police officer.

Keystone cop *n.* [rhy. sl.; for ety. *see* prev.] [1990s+] a chop (pork, beef etc).

K.G. *n. see* COUSIN JACK *n.*

khaki *n.* [all from the colour, usu. of a uniform] **1** [late 19C] pease pudding; thus *cannon and khaki*, a globular steak pudding and a lump of pease pudding on the side. **2** [1940s+] (*S.Afr.*) a non-Nationalist white South African, usu. of English background [Boer War sl. *khaki*, an English soldier]. **3** [1960s] (*N.Z.*) a Maori. **4** [1970s+] (*US*) a county police officer. **5** [1970s+] (*Irish*) a lifeguard.

SE in slang uses

IN COMPOUNDS

❑ **khaki pussy** *n.* [PUSSY *n.* (11)] [1970s+] (*US gay*) a soldier.

❑ **khaki-wacky** *n.* [WHACKY *adj.*] [1940s+] (*US*) used of a woman, one who is enamoured of men in military uniform.

khakis *n.* [abbr.] [1990s+] *khaki* shorts or clothes.

kharzi/khazi *n. see* CARSEY *n.*

khazi *v.* [KHARZI/KHAZI *n.*; play on SHIT ONESELF *v.*] [2000s] to be infuriated.

K-hole *n.* [K *n.* (1); the 'hole' in one's life] [1980s+] (*drugs*) a period of confusion that follows the use of ketamine.

Khyber (Pass) *n.* (*also* **kiber, kyber**) [rhy. sl. = ARSE *n.*] **1** [late 19C] a glass. **2** [20C+] the buttocks. **3** [1960s+] the anus. **4** [1970s+] the rear, e.g. of a car. **5** [1990s+] (*Aus.*) dismissal, rejection.

khyfer *n. see* KYFER *n.*

khyfer *v. see* KYPHER *v.*

ki *n.*[1] [orig. naut. use; supposedly dial. *kyish*, muddy-looking, brown, but *EDD* has no listing] [1940s–70s] (*UK prison*) cocoa.

ki *n.*[2] *see* KEY *n.*[2].

kiaora *n.* [Kiaora: a brand of drink that claimed to contain 50% fruit (i.e. FRUIT *n.* (2)) juice] [1980s+] (*Aus. prison*) a male homosexual who plays both active and passive roles in anal intercourse.

kibbel *n.* [mid-19C] (*UK Und.*) clothes.

kibbitz *v.* see KIBITZ *v.*

kibbitzer *n.* see KIBITZER *n.*

kibbled *adj.* [KIBBLES & BITS *n.* (2)] [1990s+] (*US*) crushed, in bits and pieces.

kibbles & bits *n.* [the brandname of a US petfood] [1980s+] **1** (*US black*) cheap food. **2** (*drugs*) small crumbs of crack cocaine. **3** used of a man who has small genitals.

kiber *n.* see KHYBER (PASS) *n.*

kibitz *n.* (*also* **kabitz**) [KIBITZ *v.* (1)] **1** [1930s+] (*US*) tedious chatter, unwanted advice. **2** [2000s] a conversation.

kibitz *v.* (*also* **kibbitz**) [Ger. *Kiebitz*, a lapwing or peewit, a noisy and inquisitive bird; thus *kiebitzen*, to look over a card-player's shoulder; popularized by Yid. speakers] [1920s+] **1** to watch (a gambling game) and to comment/advise but not to participate. **2** (*also* **kibetz**) to chat, to gossip, to pester, to cajole.

kibitzer *n.* (*also* **kabitzer, kibbitzer**) [KIBITZ *v.* (1)] [1920s+] **1** one who looks over a card-player's shoulder, advising and interfering with the game. **2** anyone who butts in or meddles, offering usu. unwanted advice.

kibo *n.*[1] [? *BEAT AKEYBO under* BEAT *v.*] [1900s] (*US*) an overwhelming success.

kibo *n.*[2] see KYBO *n.*

kibosh *n.* (*also* **kabosh, kiboshery, kybosh**) [? Heb. or Yid. *kabas, kabasten*, to suppress (B&L, but rejected by Rosten, *The Joys of Yiddish* 1968); but note intensifying pfx KER- *pfx* + BOSH *n.*[1]; KYE *n.* + BOSH *n.*[1], i.e. 18 pence, and thus synon. with a *FOURPENNY (ONE) under* FOURPENNY *adj.* (see *DSUE* 8th edn Appendix for further theories); however, note Irish Gaelic *ceip bàis*, death cap, i.e. the black cap used in court and Dolan (1998): 'Irish *caidhp (an) bháis* or *caidhpin (an) bháis*, "cap of death", the black cap or judgment cap worn by judges when pronouncing sentence of death'] **1** [mid-19C+] a bad accident, a defeat. **2** [mid-19C+] rubbish, nonsense, humbug; thus *kiboshery*. **3** [mid-19C; 1930s–70s] (*also* **kye**) eighteen pence i.e. 1/6d predecimalization. **4** [late 19C] the height of fashion. **5** [1940s–50s] an 18-month prison sentence.

IN PHRASES

❑ **give someone the kibosh** *v.* [1900s] to destroy or defeat someone. ❑ **on the kibosh** [1920s+] ruined. ❑ **put the kibosh on** *v.* [mid-19C+] to spoil, to ruin.

kibosh *v.* (*also* **kybosh**) [KIBOSH *n.*] [mid-19C+] to finish off, to destroy.

kick *n.*[1] (*also* **kicky**) [ety. unknown; ? fig. use of SE *kick*, with the image of the sharp impact thereof] **1** [late 17C–19C] the current fashion; thus *all the kick*, the present vogue; *high kick*, the height of fashion. **2** [mid-19C] a fashionable garment. **3** [1940s+] a fashion, a fad, with comb. adj./noun; thus *on a/the … kick*, e.g. *on a writing kick, on the religion kick* etc. **4** [1950s+] one's attitude or opinion.

DERIVATIVES

❑ **kickish** *adj.* [late 18C] fashionable.

kick *n.*[2] [rhy. *six* = *kick*, but not rhy. sl. as such] **1** [18C+] sixpence; thus *two-and-a-kick*, half-a-crown (25p). **2** [20C+] money in general.

IN PHRASES

❑ **get some kick** *v.* [1940s] (*US black*) to obtain some money.

kick *n.*[3] **1** [19C–1900s] a chance, a 'go'. **2** [1910s+] (*US*) something ironic or elusive, a twist. **3** [1940s+] a trick, a 'line'.

kick *n.*[4] (*also* **kicker**) [Ware suggests Und. use only] [mid-19C+] a pocket, esp. in trousers.

IN PHRASES

❑ **hit the kick** *v.* [1970s] (*Aus.*) to spend one's money, e.g. when buying a round of drinks. ❑ **sky kick** *n.* [fig. use of SE *sky*, i.e. an upper garment] [1940s] (*US Und.*) the inside pocket of a jacket or coat.

kick *n.*[5] **1** [mid-19C+] a stimulating or intoxicating effect, usu. from alcohol or drugs. **2** [20C+] (*Aus./US*) a spree; a party. **3** [1910s–50s] energy, vitality. **4** [1910s+] (*orig. US*) a thrill, amusement or excitement. **5** [1930s] an amusing, surprising or stimulating person. **6** [1950s–60s] the sensation any place, situation or thing produces. **7** in context of intoxicants. (**a**) [1940s] (*US drugs*) addiction; thus using drugs. (**b**) [1940s–50s] an injection of or shot of heroin. (**c**) [1950s] (*W.I.*) gin or whisky. (**d**) [1950s+] (*US drugs*) any kind of psychotropic drug. (**e**) [1970s] (*US drugs*) a portion of a drug. **8** [1990s+] (*Aus.*) publicity, promotion.

IN COMPOUNDS

❑ **kick stick** *n.* [STICK *n.* (6d)] [1960s+] (*drugs*) a marijuana cigarette.

IN PHRASES

❑ **bust one's kicks off** *v.* [1960s] (*US*) to reach orgasm. ❑ **for kicks** [1940s+] for pleasure, for amusement. ❑ **get a kick out of** *v.* [1920s+] to enjoy, to appreciate. ❑ **on a kick** [1940s+] (*orig. US*) **1** having a good time. **2** enthusiastic about.

SE in slang uses

IN PHRASES

❑ **kick in one's gallop** *n.* [riding imagery] [late 18C+] (*Ulster*) a weakness of character; thus *put a kick in someone's gallop*, to ruin someone's plans, to 'put a spoke in their wheel'; *odd kick in one's gallop*, an eccentricity. ❑ **kick in the arse** *n.* **1** [1920s+] a setback, a grave disappointment. **2** [1920s+] a salutory punishment. **3** [1940s+] (*Irish*) a very small distance or space of time, lit. or fig. **4** [1950s+] anything that urges one on to greater effort, commitment. ❑ **kick in the bollocks** *n.* [1920s+] a setback, a grave disappointment. ❑ **kick in the guts** *n.* **1** [mid-18C–early 19C] a dram of gin or any other spirit. **2** [1920s+] a setback or disappointment. ❑ **kick in the nuts** *n.* [1920s+] a setback, a grave disappointment. ❑ **kick in the pants** *n.* [note 1751 Smollett, *Peregrine Pickle* xlvi. (1779) II. 88 Our hero...dismissed him with a kick on the breech] **1** [1920s+] a setback, a grave disappointment. **2** [1920s+] a salutory punishment. **3** [1920s+] a joke, a laugh (often used ironically). **4** [1950s+] anything that urges one on to greater effort, commitment; also attrib. ❑ **within a kick** [1910s] (*Aus.*) very nearly. ❑ **within a kick of a brown cow** [1900s] (*Aus.*) very close to.

kick *n.*[6] [i.e. a 'kick against the pricks'] (*orig. US*) **1** [mid-19C+] a complaint. **2** [late 19C+] trouble. **3** [1930s+] a worry or concern.

IN PHRASES

❑ **make a kick** *v.* [mid-19C+] to raise an objection, to complain.

kick *n.*[7] **1** [mid-19C+] a moment. **2** [1950s+] (*US black*) generally any little thing or situation.

IN PHRASES

❑ **in a kick** [mid-19C] in a moment, very soon.

kick *n.*[8] [one 'kicks up one's legs'] [1950s–60s] (*US*) a fit, as in a *laughing kick*.

kick *n.*[9] [1950s+] (*orig. US black*) the beat or rhythm in music.

kick *n.*[10] [KICK *v.*[1] (9)] [1990s+] (*US black*) death, a murder.

kick *n.*[11] [1990s+] (*drugs*) withdrawal from drug addiction.

IN COMPOUNDS

❑ **kick-sweat** *n.* [1990s+] (*drugs*) the sweating that is one of the symptoms of withdrawal from narcotic drugs use.

kick *n.*[12] see KICKBACK *n.*[1] (2a).

kick, the *n.* **1** [late 19C–1900s] a dismissal, 'the sack' [SE *kick*; one is lit./fig. 'kicked out'; var. on BOOT, THE *n.*]. **2** [1920s] (*US Und.*) a beating, during interrogation, by the police.

IN PHRASES

❑ **get the kick** *v.* (*also* **give the kick**) [late 19C–1910s] to be dismissed/to dismiss from a job.

kick *adj.* **1** [1950s+] (*US drugs*) describing anything relating to coming off an addiction, e.g. *kick pad* or *kick ward*, a hospital ward reserved for recovering addicts [KICK *v.*[4] (1)]. **2** [1990s+] (*US teen*) unfashionable [? should be kicked out].

kick *v.*[1] **1** [18C+] to leave, to walk, to wander aimlessly [the image is of kicking stones etc; the combs. are more usu. from the early 19C+]. **2** [late 18C–mid-19C] to ask for money, work etc. **3** [19C–1940s] to rid oneself of something, to reject a lover [abbr. SE *kick out*]. **4** in senses of SE *kick*, to resist, to rebel. (**a**) [mid-19C+] (*US*) (*also* **kick at**) to complain or protest. (**b**) [1980s+] (*US campus*) to be difficult, to prevail over something or someone. **5** [mid-19C+] to die [? abbr. *KICK THE CLOUDS* below or sense 1 above]. **6** [1930s] (*US Und.*) to rob a safe or cash box. **7** [1950s] (*US prison*) of a sentence, to deal with, to manage. **8** [1980s+] (*US black/rap*) to raise, increase or produce, as of a recording, sound or volume [one fig. *kicks* the volume, price etc upwards]. **9** [1990s+] (*US black/Und.*) to kill, to murder. **10** [2000s] (*US black*) to have sexual intercourse (with).

IN PHRASES

❑ **kick flavor** *v.* [1990s+] (*orig. US*) to perform rap music. ❑ **kick raps** *v.* [1990s+] (*US campus*) to play or listen to music. ❑ **kick someone for** *v.* [late 18C–mid-19C] to ask someone for money, to borrow money. ❑ **kick (the) ballistics** *v.* [KICK IT TO *v.* (2)] [1990s+] (*US black*) to explain a situation, to inform. ❑ **kick through (with)** *v.* [1910s+] (*US*) to pay up, to come across with.

SE in slang uses

IN COMPOUNDS

❑ **kick and buck** *n.* [1920s] (*W.I.*) a water tank or cistern made of clay that has been *kicked* and *bucked* (pounded) until it is absolutely water-tight. ❑ **kick-shoe** *n.* [19C] a dancer; a buffoon.

IN PHRASES

❑ **could kick a bullock up the arse and walk away with the hide** [2000s] (*N.Z.*) a phr. said of someone who has large feet. ❑ **could kick the eye out of a mosquito** [late 19C–1920s] (*orig. US*) a phr. said of someone who possesses supreme competence. ❑ **couldn't kick a hen off its nest** [2000s] (*N.Z.*) used of a situation where everything one tries fails. ❑ **kick A** *v. see* KICK ASS *v.* ❑ **kick about** *v. see* KICK AROUND *v.* ❑ **kick a brown dog** *v.* (*also* **kick a yellow dog**) [1900s] (*Aus./US*) to let off steam, to get rid of tension. ❑ **kick a goal** *v.* [1980s+] (*Aus. prison*) to succeed, to win an advantage. ❑ **kick along** *v.* [1970s+] (*Aus.*) to survive reasonably easily, to get along well. ❑ **kick arse** *v. see* KICK ASS *v.* ❑ **kick ass** *see* separate entries. ❑ **kick away the prop** *v.* [the removal of the ladder, cart, stool etc on which the victim stands] [18C] to suffer execution by hanging. ❑ **kick back** *see* separate entries. ❑ **kick behind** *v. see* KICK ASS *v.* ❑ **kick brass** *v.* (*also* **kick dust, kick hell, kick sands**) [? var. on KICK ASS *v.*] [20C+] (*W.I.*) to make a fuss, to cause a commotion. ❑ **kick butt** *v. see* KICK ASS *v.* ❑ **kick down (to)** *v. see* separate entry. ❑ **kick for touch** *v.* [rugby imagery] [2000s] (*N.Z.*) to back down, to avoid confrontation. ❑ **kick him where his mum never kissed** *v.* (*also* **...missed**) [2000s] (*N.Z.*) to kick in the testicles, occas. buttocks. ❑ **kick in** *v. see* separate entries. ❑ **kick-in-the-ass** *adj. see* KICK-ASS *adj.* ❑ **kick in the pants** *v.* **1** [1920s+] to treat harshly. **2** [1980s+] to propel someone into action. ❑ **kick in the tail** *v.* [TAIL *n.* (2)] [1910s+] to kick hard, lit. or fig. ❑ **kick loose** *v.* [var. on KICK BACK *v.*[2] + LOOSE *adj.* (5)] [1930s+] to release, to make available, to let go. ❑ **kick mud** *v.* [backform. f. MUD-KICKER *n.*] [1950s–70s] (*US black*) **1** to perform hard, dirty work. **2** to work as a street prostitute. ❑ **kick on** *v. see* separate entry. ❑ **kick over** *v.* **1** [1920s–30s] (*US Und./police*) to raid an establishment or place. **2** [1930s] to rob. ❑ **kick rocks** *v.* [2000s] (*US prison*) to go away. ❑ **kick sands** *v. see KICK BRASS* above. ❑ **kick someone into touch** *v.* [rugby imagery] [1970s+] to reject, to dismiss, to throw away. ❑ **kick someone's lung out** *v.* [late 19C–1900s] to criticize someone harshly, to attack someone verbally. ❑ **kick stones** *v.* [KICKSTONE & CO *n.*] [20C+] (*W.I.*) to be unemployed. ❑ **kick the beam** *v.* [Gifford (1988): '"Kick the beam" means literally that one arm of a scale is so lightly weighted that it strikes the beam or frame of the scales; hence, figuratively, to be light in weight, and in slang, to experience sudden emotion or orgasm'] [1920s] to experience an intense emotion; to reach orgasm. ❑ **kick the cat** *v.* [the cat being the 'lowest' member of the household and thus most likely to suffer such abuse] [late 19C–1950s] to vent one's frustrations. ❑ **kick the clouds** *v.* (*also* **kick the air, kick the wind**) [SE + HOTEL *n.* (2); public hangings were performed outside the prison where the malefactor had been held] [late 16C–1940s] to be hanged; often ext. as *...before the hotel door.* ❑ **kick the daylights out of** *v. see BEAT THE (LIVING) DAYLIGHTS OUT OF under* DAYLIGHTS *n.* ❑ **kick the dust out of** *v.* [1910s] (*Aus.*) to beat up. ❑ **kick the gong** *v. see* BOOT THE GONG *v.*[1]. ❑ **kick the street** *v.* [1960s+] (*US Und.*) to work as a street prostitute. ❑ **kick to the curb** *v.* [1990s+] **1** (*US black*) to reject someone, esp. to bring a relationship to an end. **2** to reject an idea or object, to stop doing something. ❑ **kick with** *v.* [1990s+] (*US black*) to associate with; to be part of a gang.

kick *v.*[2] [KICK *n.*[4]] **1** [mid-19C] (*UK Und.*) to put in one's pocket. **2** [mid-19C–1960s] by ext. to make money.

kick *v.*[3] [KICK *n.*[5]] (*US*) **1** [late 19C–1900s] to amuse or entertain one's audience. **2** [1930s+] to perform well or with energy, usu. of music. **3** [1950s] to feel the effects of a drug. **4** [1950s+] to delight, to please. **5** *see* KICK IT *v.*[2] (2). **6** *see* BOOT *v.*[6] (1).

kick *v.*[4] [abbr. *KICK THE HABIT under* HABIT *n.*] (*orig. US drugs*) **1** [1920s+] (*also* **kick the monkey**) to stop taking an addictive drug. **2** [1960s+] to stop any form of addiction.

IN PHRASES

❑ **kick off** *v.* [1950s] **1** (*US drugs*) to sleep off the effects of drugs. **2** to withdraw from narcotic addiction.

kick *v.*[5] [1990s+] (*US black*) to empty, to finish, e.g. a bottle of beer.

kick *v.*[6] *see* BOOT *v.*[6].

kickapalaz *n.* [var. on LALLAPALOOSA *n.*] [1900s] (*US*) something excellent, superlative.

kickapoo (juice) *n.* (*also* **kickapoo joy juice, kikipoo**) [coined in 1941 by cartoonist Al Capp in his strip *L'il Abner*, in ref. to patent medicines of 1900s named after the *Kickapoo*, the Algonquian Indians; the ingredients, according to the strip, included 'a barr'l o' kerosene, two dozen chicken haids, a bucket o' somethin' sloppy we swiped off a passin' truck, a motorman's glove, three pairs o' old socks, a dash o' axlegrease, turpentine'] [1940s+] (*US*) strong alcohol, esp. home brewed.

kick around *v.* (*also* **kick about**) [ext. KICK *v.*[1]] **1** [mid-19C+] (*orig. US*) to make a fuss, to complain. **2** [mid-19C+] (*orig. US*) to hang about, to wander aimlessly. **3** [late 19C+] to exist. **4** [1940s+] (*orig. US*) to discuss or consider a topic or idea. **5** [1960s] to put into circulation, to distribute.

kick-ass *adj.* (*also* **kick-arse, kick-butt, kick-in-the-ass**) [KICK ASS *v.*] (*orig. US*) **1** [1970s+] powerful, aggressive, stimulating, thuggish or violent. **2** [1980s+] terrific, exciting.

kick ass *v.* (*also* **kick A, kiss arse, kick behind, kick butt**) [lit. + fig. uses of *KICK SOMEONE'S ASS under* ASS *n.*; + ARSE *n.* (1)/BUTT *n.*[1] (1)] **1** [1950s+] (*orig. US*) to beat someone up, to fight, also fig. use. **2** [1970s+] (*US campus*) to have a good, if boisterous, time. **3** [1980s+] (*orig. US campus*) to do well, to make a successful effort; thus n. *ass-kicking*.

kickback *n.*[1] [KICK BACK *v.*[1]] **1** [1910s+] (*US*) a repercussion, usu. negative. **2** in financial or commercial contexts. (**a**) [1920s+] (*orig. US Und.*) (*also* **kick**) a payment (prob. illegal) made to a person who has facilitated a deal, a transaction, someone's appointment to a job etc. (**b**) [1930s+] a portion of one's profits that is handed over as 'protection money'. (**c**) [1940s+] a commission on a payment made by the payee to the customer, usu. a genteel euph. for a bribe. **3** [1930s–60s] (*US drugs*) a return to addiction despite efforts to abandon drug use. **4** [2000s] (*US*) a response; also attrib.

kickback *n.*[2] [KICK BACK *v.*[2]] [1990s+] (*orig. US black*) a period of relaxation, relaxing.

kickback *adj.* [KICK BACK *v.*[2]] [1980s+] (*US*) relaxing, calm, low-key.

kick back *v.*[1] **1** [1910s+] (*US*) to return something, such as money or stolen goods, to the original owner. **2** [1930s+] to pay a bribe or a commission.

kick back *v.*[2] [KICK *v.*[1] + LAID-BACK *adj.*] [1970s+] (*orig. US black*) to laze around, to relax.

IN COMPOUNDS

▫ **kickback place** *n.* [1990s+] (*US black gang*) anywhere one can relax, away from the stresses and threats of the streets.

kick back *v.*^{3} [1980s+] (*US*) to drink.

kick-cloy *n.* [KICK *n.*^{4} (1) + CLY *n.* (2)] [mid-19C] (*UK Und.*) a pair of trousers.

kick down *v.* [late 18C] to win money at gambling.

kick down (to) *v.* (*also* **kick down with, kick out with**) [? KICK *v.*^{1}] **1** [20C+] to go to, to arrive, visit, wander. **2** [1980s+] (*also* **kick**) (*US*) to give something to, to hand over. **3** [1980s+] (*US black*) to set a person up in the drug business.

kicked *adj.* [KICK *v.*^{4} (1)] [1940s+] (*drugs*) having withdrawn from narcotic addiction.

kicked back *adj.* [KICK BACK *v.*^{2}] [1990s+] (*US*) relaxing, lazing around.

kicked up *adj.* [? KICK *v.*^{6} (1)] [1930s] intoxicated on a drug.

kicker *n.*^{1} **1** [mid-19C] a dancing-master. **2** [mid-19C+] in pl., the feet. **3** [late 19C+] (*US*) in poker, a high card, such as an ace, retained in the hope of matching the pair or as a bluff [? fig. use of SE *kick*, i.e. defeat, surpass]. **4** [1940s+] in pl., shoes. **5** [1940s+] (*US*) in pl., boots with pointed toes, made from rare or exotic reptile skins (e.g. armadillo, alligator, snake); such boots are used spec. for dancing.

kicker *n.*^{2} [KICK *v.*^{1} (4a)] [late 19C+] (*US*) one who complains or grumbles.

kicker *n.*^{3} [KICK *n.*^{5}] **1** [1940s+] (*US*) a thrill. **2** [1990s+] (*US*) a chaser, usu. pertaining to drugs rather than drinks.

kicker *n.*^{4} [KICK *n.*^{3} (2)] [1940s+] (*US*) a consequence or hidden twist.

kicker *n.*^{5} [1950s] (*US*) a cache of money, a find [KICK *n.*^{4}].

kicker *n.*^{6} [it *kicks* the rest along] **1** [1950s+] a culminatory action. **2** [1970s+] (*orig. US*) the last, most problematical piece of information.

IN PHRASES

▫ **for kickers** (*also* **for a kicker, for the kickers**) [1960s+] (*US*) for good measure.

kicker *n.*^{7} *see* SHITKICKER *n.* (3).

kicker *adj. see* SHITKICKER *adj.*

kickeraboo *v.* [pron. of KICK THE BUCKET *v.*] [late 18C–mid-19C] (*W.I.*) to die.

kick-in *n.*^{1} [SE *kick in*] [1900s] (*US Und.*) a form of robbery whereby one member of a gang kicks in the front of a shop and steals the contents while the remainder of the gang stand outside and keep any interference at bay.

kick-in *n.*^{2} [KICK IN *v.*^{2} (1)] **1** [1930s–50s] (*US*) a commission on a payment made by the payee to the customer, usu. a genteel euph. for a bribe. **2** [1960s+] a bribe. **3** [1990s+] a contribution.

kick in *v.*^{1} [ext. of KICK *v.*^{1} (5)] (*US*) **1** [20C+] to die. **2** [1910s+] to give up, to abandon.

kick in *v.*^{2} (*also* **kick, kick in with**) [var. of KICK BACK *v.*^{1}] [20C+] (*US*) to hand over, usu. money.

kick in *v.*^{3} (*also* **kick**) [? KICK *v.*^{3}] **1** [20C+] to do what is required, to join in. **2** [20C+] to begin, to start to happen. **3** [1970s+] to (make something) start working, to accelerate an action, usu. of mechanical objects. **4** [1980s+] of drugs, to take effect, to start to work; also of alcohol. **5** [1990s+] of a musical instrument.

kick in *v.*^{4} **1** [1910s+] (*US Und.*) to smash one's way through a door, to break in and burglarize. **2** [1990s+] (*US black*) to start a fight.

kick in *v.*^{5} **1** [1910s+] (*US*) to speak up, to tell the truth. **2** [1990s+] (*US black*) to express oneself.

kicking *adj.*^{1} [KICK *v.*^{1} (4a)] [late 19C] (*US*) complaining.

kicking *adj.*^{2} (*also* **kickin', kickin' hard**) [KICK *n.*^{5}] **1** [1960s+] excellent, wonderful, first-rate. **2** [1980s+] (*US campus*) difficult, unpleasant.

kicking it *n.* (*also* **kickin' (it)**) [KICK IT *v.*^{2}] [1980s+] (*orig. US black/teen*) lying around, wasting time, relaxing, socializing.

kick in with *v. see* KICK IN *v.*^{2}.

kickish *adj. see under* KICK *n.*^{1}.

kick it *v.*^{1} [abbr. KICK THE BUCKET *v.*] [late 19C+] to die.

kick it *v.*^{2} [KICK IT AROUND *v.*^{1}] **1** [1930s+] (*also* **kick**) to play music. **2** [1980s+] (*orig. US black*) (*also* **kick**) to chatter, to gossip, to relax. **3** [1980s+] (*US black*) to act, to do something well.

IN PHRASES

▫ **kick it live** *v.* [1980s+] (*US black*) to have a good time, to talk, to chatter, to gossip.

kick it *v.*^{3} [KICK *v.*^{1}] [1950s+] (*US*) to leave, to go fast.

kick it *v.*^{4} [put one's foot on the gas pedal] [1970s+] (*US*) to accelerate a vehicle.

kick it *v.*^{5} [KICK *v.*^{3}] [1990s+] **1** (*US*) to get on well with someone. **2** (*US*) to associate with. **3** (*US*) to have an affair over and above one's primary, monogamous relationship. **4** (*US black/prison*) to have sexual intercourse. **5** (*US*) of a man to a woman, to make suggestive comments.

kick it! *excl.* [1990s+] (*US campus*) pay attention!

kick it around *v.*^{1} [KICK AROUND *v.* (2)] [1930s–40s] (*US*) to carouse, to have a good time.

kick it around *v.*^{2} *see* KICK THE GONG AROUND *under* GONG *n.*^{2}.

kick it in the guts *phr.* (*also* **kick her in the guts**) [2000s] (*N.Z.*) **1** a phr. expressing doubt or disbelief in the previous statement. **2** a phr. advising someone to be tougher.

kick it to *v.* [var. of SOCK IT TO *v.*] [1990s+] (*US black*) **1** to give something to someone, 'to let someone have it'. **2** to inform, to explain the facts. **3** to do something in a committed manner.

kick-off *n.* [soccer imagery; Gold (1964) notes the 'signal for the musicians to play by the leader's stamping his foot several times in the desired tempo'] [late 19C+] the beginning, the start.

kick-off *adj.* [KICK-OFF *n.*] [1930s] (*US*) first.

kick off *v.*^{1} **1** [20C+] to die. **2** [1910s–20s] (*US*) to kill. **3** [1910s+] to leave. **4** [1970s+] to attack, to fight; often as *kick it off*. **5** [1990s+] to argue, to shout, to be aggressive.

kick off *v.*^{2} [KICK-OFF *n.*] **1** [1910s+] (*orig. US*) (*also* **kick things off**) to begin, to start, to set in motion. **2** [1970s] of a club or bar, to open.

kick off *v.*^{3} [KICK *n.*^{5} (1)] [1940s–60s] (*US*) to delight, to excite.

kick on *v.* **1** [1940s+] (*Aus.*) to struggle on despite the negative odds. **2** [1980s] (*Aus.*) to continue drinking once somebody has found some money to buy another round with. **3** [2000s] to enjoy onself.

kickout *n.* [KICK OUT *v.*^{1} (1)] **1** [late 19C+] a dismissal, a discharge. **2** [1960s+] one who has been ejected from a job or from their education.

IN PHRASES

▫ **give someone the kickout** *v. see* GIVE SOMEONE THE BAG *under* BAG *n.*^{1}.

kick out *v.*^{1} **1** [late 17C+] to eject, to force to leave. **2** [late 19C+] to die [late 20C+ use only W.I.]. **3** [20C+] to run away. **4** [1910s] (*US Und.*) to appear suddenly. **5** [1910s+] to get out of bed.

IN PHRASES

▫ **I wouldn't kick her out of bed** [1920s+] referring to an attractive woman; a comment usu. made by one of a group of young men observing a passing woman.

SE in slang uses

IN PHRASES

▫ **kick out a hind leg** *v.* [late 18C–early 19C] to bow in an unsophisticated 'rustic' manner.

kick out *v.*^{2} (*US*) **1** [1920s+] to pay up. **2** [1930s] to work something out. **3** [1930s+] to play music. **4** [1980s+] to fail. **5** [1990s+] to produce, to create.

kicks *n.*^{1} [ety. unknown; ? link to UK dial. *kecks*, the (dried) hollowed-out stem of an umbelliferous plant, e.g. a teazle; such stalks were used as candlesticks, water-pipes etc, and the link to trousers, themselves 'hollow stalks', seems feasible] [late 17C–1930s] breeches, thus trousers.

kicks *n.*^{2} [late 19C+] (*US black/campus*) shoes; in later usage, athletic shoes.

kicks *n.*^{3} [KICK *n.*^{5} (4)] [1920s+] (*orig. US*) thrills, pleasure.

(IN PHRASES)

▫ **get one's kicks** *v.* [1930s+] (*orig. US black*) to enjoy oneself. ▫ **get one's kicks off** *v.* [1920s+] (*US*) to come to orgasm.

kick sand *v. see under* SAND *n.*^{1}.

kicksees *n.* **1** *see* KICKS *n.*^{2}. **2** *see* KICKSIES *n.*

kick-sick *n. see* SICK *n.* (2).

kicksies *n.* (*also* **kicksees**) **1** [18C–1910s] (*also* **kickseys, kicksters, kixes**) trousers; thus *kicksies-builder*, a tailor [for ety. *see* KICKS *n.*^{1}]. **2** [late 18C–19C] (*UK Und.*) shoes.

kicksing *n.* [KICKS *n.*^{3}] [1920s+] (*W.I.*) making fun of, not taking seriously.

kickster *n.* [KICKS *n.*^{3}] [20C+] (*W.I.*) a jester, a joker, an irresponsible person.

kicksters *n. see* KICKSIES *n.* (1).

Kickstone & Co *n.* [one is idly 'kicking stones' around] [20C+] (*W.I.*) a notional firm or business, used fig. to mean a state of unemployment.

kicksy *adj.* [Ger. *keck*, bold or SE *kick*] [mid-17C; mid-19C] troublesome, disagreeable.

kick the bucket *v.* (*also* **kick the can, ...pig, ...tin, boot the bucket, clunk the...**) [the contemporary method of slaughtering a pig, in which the animal is suspended from a beam by the insertion of a piece of bent wood (a 'bucket') behind the tendons of its hind legs; the dying animal naturally kicks out at the bucket. Alternatively, and rather less likely, the story of an ostler working at an inn on the Great North Road who killed himself by hanging; to gain the necessary drop he stood on a bucket, kicking it away as required] [late 18C+] to die.

kickumbob *n.* [mid-17C] anything for which one has no proper name.

kick-up *n.* [KICK UP *v.*] **1** [late 18C–1910s] (*orig. US*) a dance, a party. **2** [late 18C–1950s] an argument, a disturbance; esp. a prison riot.

kick up *v.* **1** [mid-18C+] to cause trouble, to react unfavourably, usu. in combs., see below and at individual nouns. **2** [mid-19C+] to create, to make something happen. **3** [1970s+] to raise the volume, e.g. on a stereo. **4** [1990s+] (*US*) to start.

(IN PHRASES)

▫ **kick up a fuss** *v.* [mid-18C+] to cause trouble, to create a disturbance. ▫ **kick up (a) murder** *v.* [BLUE MURDER *n.*] [1920s–60s] to make a great fuss. ▫ **kick up a riot** *v.* [mid-18C+] to cause trouble, to create a disturbance. ▫ **kick up a row** *v. see under* ROW *n.*^{1}. ▫ **kick up a shindy** *v. see under* SHINDY *n.* ▫ **kick up bobsy-die** *v.* [dial. *bobs-a-dying*, a great fuss, pandemonium] [19C+] (*N.Z.*) to make a fuss, a commotion. ▫ **kick up (high) jack** *v. see* CUT UP JACK *V.*

SE in slang uses

(IN PHRASES)

▫ **kick up daisies** *v. see* PUSH UP (THE) DAISIES *V.*

kicky *see* KICK *n.*^{1}.

kicky *adj.*^{1} [KICK *v.*^{1} (4a)] [mid-19C+] (*orig. US*) notable for complaints, filled with complaints.

kicky *adj.*^{2} [lit. providing or creating a KICK *n.*^{5} (4)] [1940s+] (*US*) exciting, lively.

kicky-wicky *n.* [? Fr. *quelquechose*, something] [early 17C] the penis.

kid *n.*^{1} [SE *kid*, a young goat] **1** [late 16C–18C] (*also* **kidd**) a child [SE f. 19C]. **2** [mid-18C–19C] (*UK Und.*) a child of either sex, esp. a juvenile thief, known as 'the kid —' (their surname). **3** [late 18C] (*UK Und.*) a member of a confidence team. **4** [late 18C+] (*also* **kyd**) a person, usu. young (but not a child). **5** [mid-19C+] a friend or fellow, often used in direct address. **6** [late 19C–1930s] a tramp's young companion, poss. a catamite. **7** [late 19C+] (*US*) a young person, usu. a woman, used affectionately, esp. in direct address. **8** [late 19C+] (*orig. US*) as *one's kid*, one's younger sibling. **9** [1910s+] used self-referentially, i.e. 'the kid — '. **10** [1910s+] (*US prison*) a catamite, an underage or young homosexual boy; thus *kid fruit*, *KF*, an older man who prefers sex with such boys. **11** [1970s] (*US black*) a sophisticated person.

(DERIVATIVES)

▫ **kiddish** *adj.* (*also* **kid-like**) [late 19C+] childish. ▫ **kidlet** *n.* [dimin. sfx *-let*] [late 19C+] a small child or an affectionate term for a young woman; often in pl. ▫ **kidling** *n.* [dimin. sfx *-ling*] **1** [early 19C] a young thief, esp. if the father is already 'in the trade'. **2** [late 19C] a baby, an infant.

(IN COMPOUNDS)

▫ **kid bouncing** *n.* [late 19C] (*UK Und.*) frightening simpletons by telling frightening stories. ▫ **kid catcher** *n.* [late 19C] a truant officer, employed by the London School Board to track down those refusing to attend school. ▫ **Kid College** *n. see* JOE COLLEGE *under* JOE *n.*^{1}. ▫ **kid flick** *n.* [play on SKIN FLICK *under* SKIN *adj.*^{2}] [1970s+] (*orig. US*) a film or video recording aimed at the child audience. ▫ **kid glove** *n.* [pun on SE] [late 19C–1920s] (*US Und.*) an elite tramp or criminal. ▫ **kidken** *n.* (*also* **kiddken**) [KEN *n.*^{1} (1)] [mid-19C] a lodging house frequented by young criminals. ▫ **kid lamb** *n. see* LAMB *n.*^{1} (3). ▫ **kid lay** *n.* [LAY *n.*^{3} (1)] [late 17C–mid-19C] (*UK Und.*) robbery that involves waylaying messenger boys and similar youngsters, and defrauding them of the goods they are carrying by offering them money to run a quick errand and promising, during their absence, to look after the goods; thus phr. *work the kid*. ▫ **kid leather** *n.* [pun on SE/LEATHER *n.* (2a)] [mid–late 19C] a very young prostitute; generic for the world of very young female prostitution. ▫ **kid-rig** *n.* [RIG *n.*^{2} (1)] [late 18C–mid-19C] (*UK Und.*) the robbery of children (occas. adults) sent out on errands (their parcel or the money with which they have been entrusted is taken either by guile or by force). ▫ **kid-simple** *adj.* [1920s+] (*gay*) of an older homosexual male, obsessed with young boys; less common for a heterosexual paedophile whose obsession is for young girls. ▫ **kidsman** *n.* [mid–late 19C] (*UK Und.*) one who trains boys to steal and pick pockets. ▫ **kid stretcher** *n.* [19C] a paedophile. ▫ **kid stuffer** *n.* [STUFF *v.*^{1} (1)] [1980s+] (*Aus. prison*) a child molester. ▫ **kidvid** *n.* [1950s+] (*orig. US*) (*also* **kideo**) children's TV or videos. ▫ **kid-walloper** *n.* (*also* **brat-whacker, kid-whacker**) [SE *walloper/whacker*, Yorks. dial.; 20C+ use mainly Aus.] [late 19C–1950s] a schoolmaster; thus v. *kid-whack*. ▫ **kidwy** *n.* [SE *wee*] [early–mid-19C] (*UK Und.*) a thief's child.

(IN PHRASES)

▫ **drop the kids off (at the pool)** *v.* [1990s+] to defecate. ▫ **go upon the kid** *v.* [late 18C] (*UK Und.*) to steal parcels from errand boys by promising to hold them while they make another delivery. ▫ **sweet kid** *n.* under SWEET *adj.*^{1}.

(IN EXCLAMATIONS)

▫ **kid's shit!** [1970s] (*US*) an excl. of disappointment.

kid *n.*^{2} [KID *v.*] **1** [mid-19C–1900s] (*UK Und.*) persuasive talk, aimed at effecting a confidence trick, interrogating a prisoner, etc. **2** [mid-19C+] teasing, mockery, chaff. **3** [1900s–1910s] (*Aus.*) excessive praise. **4** [20C+] nonsense, rubbish; usu. as *no kid*, I am not telling a lie.

(IN PHRASES)

▫ **for kid** [1950s] as a joke. ▫ **have more kid in them than goat** *v.* [pun on sense 2 above + SE *kid*, a baby goat] [1930s+] (*Aus.*) to be an incurable joker or 'kidder'. ▫ **on the kid** [1860s] bantering, teasing. ▫ **play kid** *v.* [1900s] to tease, to joke.

kid *n.*^{3} [abbr.] [mid–late 19C] in pl., kid gloves.

kid *adj.* [KID *n.*^{1} (1)] **1** [late 19C+] (*orig. US*) younger, as in *kid brother*. **2** [20C+] (*orig. US*) pertaining to, or fit for children, as in KID STUFF *n.* **3** [20C+] (*US*) childish.

kid *v.* (*also* **kid around**) [? to treat as a KID *n.*^{1} (1) or to COD *v.*] **1** [19C–1900s] to persuade. **2** [19C+] to tease, to pretend, to fool; used in phr. *I'm not kidding*, I'm absolutely serious; *I kid you not*, I'm telling (you) the truth; *who are/who do you think you're kidding*, who do you think you're fooling (because it certainly isn't me)?

(DERIVATIVES)

▫ **kidment** *n.* [sfx *-ment*] [mid–late 19C] **1** a handkerchief which is attached to the pocket from which it is protruding, so that a pickpocket, however careful, alerts the handkerchief's owner when an attempt is made to remove it. **2** any inducement to dishonesty or crime. **3** a fictitious story or any form of statement written with the intent of deception. **4** a begging letter. **5** 'coarse chaff or jocularity' (Hotten, 1873). ❑ **kidology** *n.* [sfx *-ology*; thus note the nonce-word coined by the author Terry Pratchett (b.1948), *headology*, using one's head rather than force to get what one wants] [1970s+] the art of teasing or fooling a victim, esp. with the intent of obtaining something from them.

(IN PHRASES)

❑ **are you kidding?** (*also* **you have to be kidding**) [1940s+] you can't be serious, surely you're joking. ❑ **I kid you not** [1950s+] (*orig. US*) a phr. implying that the speaker is being absolutely serious. ❑ **kid along** *v.* [1910s+] **1** to tease, esp. with a long and apparently feasible story. **2** (*also* **kid up**) to deceive, to hoax. ❑ **kid on** *v.* [mid-19C+] **1** to encourage someone else to do something. **2** to tease, to deceive. ❑ **kid oneself (up)** *v.* [mid-19C+] to delude oneself. ❑ **kid the pants off** *v.* [1930s+] to tease mercilessly. ❑ **no kidding** (*also* **no kid!**) [late 19C+] (*US*) used interrog. or emphatically, i.e. 'Are you serious?' or 'I'm absolutely serious'. ❑ **you have to be kidding** *see* ARE YOU KIDDING? above.

kidalidaloo *n.* [1980s] (*Aus.*) a small child, old enough to walk.

kid blister *n.* [KID *adj.* (1) + rhy. sl.] [20C+] (*Aus.*) a sister.

Kid Creole *n.* [rhy. sl.; from the rock band *Kid Creole* and Coconuts] [2000s] the dole.

kidd *n. see* KID *n.*[1] (1).

kidded *adj.* [KID *n.*[1] (1)] [late 19C–1900s] pregnant.

kiddeliwink *n.* ['Originally KIDDLE-A-WINK, from the offer made, with a wink, to give you something out of the kettle or kiddle' Hotten 1873.] [mid-19C] **1** a village store or small shop, or ale-shop. **2** a promiscuous woman.

kidden *n.* [KID *n.*[1]] [mid-19C] a low lodging house for boys.

kidder *n.* [SWELL COVE *under* SWELL *adj.*] **1** [late 17C–early 19C] a tradesman's tout. **2** [late 19C+] a teaser, a joker, a hoaxer; thus ext. as (*Aus.*) *kidder from Kiddervile*. **3** [2000s] a general term of address.

kiddey *n. see* KIDDY *n.*

kiddie *see under* KIDDY.

kiddier *n.* [? SE *kidney*] [mid-19C] a pork butcher.

kiddiess *n.* [early–mid-19C] (*UK Und.*) a well-dressed young woman.

kiddiewink *n. see* KIDDIWINK *n.*

kiddily *adv.* [KIDDY *n.* (1)] [early–mid-19C] fashionably or showily; thus *kiddily togged*, smartly dressed.

kidding *n.* [KID *v.* (2)] [mid-19C+] teasing, joking.

(IN PHRASES)

❑ **kidding on the square** (*also* **kidding on the level**) [20C+] (*US*) teasing with underlying serious intent.

kiddiwink *n.* (*also* **kiddiewink**) [ext. of KID *n.*[1] (1)] [20C+] a young child; also used affectionately or sarcastically, of an adult.

kiddken *n. see* KIDKEN *under* KID *n.*[1].

kiddleywink/kiddliwink *n. see* KIDLYWINK *n.*

kiddo *n.* [KID *n.*[1] (1) + -O *sfx* (1)/-O *sfx* (3)] **1** [late 19C+] (*also* **kiddoo**) a general term of address to an adult, sometimes derog. **2** [20C+] a person. **3** [1910s] a girlfriend. **4** [1920s+] (*orig. Aus./N.Z.*) a young person or a child, esp. as a greeting, *Hey, kiddo*.

kiddy *n.* (*also* **kiddey, kiddie**) [fig./joc. uses of KID *n.*[1]] **1** [late 18C–mid-19C] a fashionable, flashy young man, a rake, a pimp or a thief; thus *rolling kiddy*, a dandy-cum-thief, or a dandy who dresses like a smart thief. **2** [19C+] a child. **3** [19C+] a man. **4** [mid-19C] stage-coach driver. **5** [mid-19C] a hat fashionable among small-time but dandified thieves. It featured a broad ribbon passing through a large buckle at its front. **6** [mid-19C–1900s] a pimp. **7** [mid-19C+] (*later US black*) a friend or fellow, a person. **8** [1920s+] as *the kiddy/kiddie*, the most important person. **9** [1970s] (*US black*) one who is seen as less important than the speaker.

(DERIVATIVES)

❑ **kiddyish** *adj.* **1** [early 19C–1910s] stylish, showily dressed. **2** [mid-19C] frolicsome, jovial.

(IN COMPOUNDS)

❑ **kiddy-fiddler** *n.* (*also* **kiddie-fiddler**) [FIDDLE *v.*[1] (2)] [2000s] a paedophile. ❑ **kiddy porn** *n.* (*also* **kiddie porn**) [1970s+] pornography that features the sexual exploitation of young (sometimes very young) children. The practice has been going on for very many years; the term emerged into wider use during the mid-1980s.

kiddy *adj.* [KIDDY *n.*] **1** [late 18C–mid-19C] well-dressed, fashionable, flashy. **2** [late 18C–mid-19C] skilful, esp. in a criminal context. **3** [1920s+] (*also* **kiddie**) pertaining to, or fi[t] for children.

kiddy *v.* [KID *v.* or KIDDY *n.* (1)] [mid-19C] to hoax, to humbug, to subject to confidence trickery.

kideo *n.* KIDVID *under* KID *n.*[1].

kidge *adj.* [mid-19C] (*UK Und.*) healthy, fit.

kidger *n.* [KID *n.*[1] (5) + var. on SE colloq. *codger*] [late 19C+] (*Irish*) a term of endearment to a young boy, occas. to an animal.

kidlywink *n.* (*also* **kiddleywink, kiddliwink**) **1** [mid-19C] 'a woman of unsteady habits' (Hotten, 1864) [? link to W. Country dial. *kiddleywink*, an ale-house]. **2** [1980s] a small child [KID *n.*[1] (1)].

kidman's blood mixture *n.* (*also* **kidman's joy**) [proper name of Sir Sidney *Kidman* (1857–1935) a large-scale grazier] [1930s–40s] (*Aus.*) treacle.

kidnap *v.* [KID *n.*[1] (1) + NAP *v.*[1] (1); SE by mid-19C] [late 17C–mid-19C] to steal children, esp. for use as servants or labourers on the plantations; thus *kidnapper*, one who kidnaps.

kidney *n.* [1980s] (*US black*) the womb.

SE in slang uses

(IN COMPOUNDS)

❑ **kidney-bruiser** *n.* (*also* **kidney-buster/-crusher/-rider/-rotter**) [1940s+] (*Aus./N.Z.*) a frameless pack that, without any support, bangs on one's back and kidneys. ❑ **kidney-buster** *n.* (*US*) **1** [1920s+] (*also* **kidney-cracker, kidney-disturber**) a large penis. **2** [1930s–40s] a vehicle that gives a bumpy ride. ❑ **kidney-foot** *n.* [resemblance] [mid-19C–1930s] (*US*) a flat-footed person; thus *kidney-footed*. ❑ **kidney pie** *n.* [pun on SE *kidney*/KID *v.*] [1930s+] (*Aus./N.Z.*) flattery, humbug, deceit. ❑ **kidney-prodder** *n.* [1930s+] (*US*) a large penis; thus *v. prod someone's kidneys*, of a man, to have sexual intercourse. ❑ **kidney-scraper** *n.* [2000s] a man with an extra-large penis. ❑ **kidney-wiper** *n.* (*also* **kidney-wash**) [late 19C+] (*US*) a large penis.

(IN PHRASES)

❑ **have kidney trouble** *v.* [one's excuse for making so many visits to the lavatory] [1940s+] (*gay*) to frequent public lavatories for sex. ❑ **have one's kidneys afloat** *v. see* HAVE ONE'S BACK TEETH AFLOAT *under* TEETH *n.* ❑ **line one's kidneys** [1950s] (*Aus.*) to have a drink.

kidney punch *n.* [rhy. sl.] [20C+] lunch; usu. as *bit of kidney*.

kid's eye *n.* [orig. Scot.] [early–mid-19C] fivepence.

kidstakes *n.* [rhy. sl. *kidstake* = fake; or KID *n.*[2] (2) + SE *stake*, wager] [1910s+] (*Aus./N.Z.*) flattery, insincerity, deceit, nonsense; in sing. a fake; also as v.

kid stuff *n.* (*also* **kid's stuff**) [KID *adj.* (2) + SE *stuff*; senses 2 and 3 euph. use of sense 1 but note KID STUFFER *under* KID *n.*] **1** [20C+] (*orig. US*) anything considered childish and/or insignificant. **2** [1980s+] pornography that features the sexual exploitation of young children. **3** [1980s+] the children who are exploited in such pornography.

kidult *n.* [KID *n.*[1] (1) + SE *adult*] [1980s+] **1** (*orig. US*) any form of entertainment, usu. film, videotape or television, geared to attract both child and adult audiences. **2** an adult person who indulges in this cross-over entertainment.

kidult *adj.* [KIDULT *n.*] [1980s+] appealing to children and adults simultaneously.

kief *see under* KIF.

kielbasa *n.* [Polish *kielbasa*, a highly seasoned garlicky sausage, usu. poached before it is eaten] [1970s+] (*US*) a penis.

kiester *n. see* KEISTER *n.*

kif *n.* (*also* **kef, keef, kief**) [Arabic *kaif*, the state of bliss reached after smoking hashish] [1950s+] (*drugs*) a variety of hashish produced in Morocco.

kif *adj.* (*also* **kief, kiff**) [fig. use of KIF *n.*; note Afk. *gif*, poison; the similarity in pron. has led to POISON *adj.*, and the nickname for marijuana, DURBAN POISON *n.*; note WW1 milit. *all kiff*, all right] [1950s+] (*S.Afr.*) a general term of approval meaning wonderful, first-rate, excellent; as adv. *kiff-kiff* enthusiastically.

kife *n.*[1] [? var. on KIP *n.*[1] (2)] [late 19C+] a bed.

kife *n.*[2] *see* KYFER *n.*

kife *v.* [KYFER *n.*] **1** [late 19C+] to have sexual intercourse. **2** [1930s+] (*US*) to cheat or to steal.

kifer *n. see* KYFER *n.*

kiff *adj. see* KIF *adj.*

kiffed *adj.* [KIF *n.*] [1960s] (*drugs*) intoxicated on hashish.

kiffle *v.* [? Scot. *kiffle*, a slight cough] [20C+] (*Ulster*) to procrastinate, to act hesitantly, to potter about.

kiff off *v.* [1960s] (*US*) to fall asleep.

kike *n.* (*also* **kyke**) [poss. rhyming with the common Jewish name *Ike*, i.e. Isaac (cf. IKEY-MO *n.* (1)); or f. Yid. *kikel*, a circle, the mark used by some illiterate Jewish immigrants rather than a cross when signing immigration papers at Ellis Island, New York City, *c.*1900, or f. common sfx *-ki, -ski*, which was found in many European Jewish names. P. Tamony (*Maledicta* I:2, 269ff) rejects these, preferring Ger. *kieken*, to peep. In this case the ref. is to the (predominantly Jewish) US clothes manufacturers who 'peeped' at smarter European fashions and produced mass-market knock-offs for popular, poorer customers] [20C+] (*orig. US*) **1** (*orig. US*) a derog. name for a Jew, esp. an East European late 19C immigrant to US rather than the older, German immigrants of earlier decades. **2** (*US Und*) a Jewish thief. **3** (*orig. US*) a grasping, dishonest if also shrewd person (irrespective of race).

IN COMPOUNDS

❑ **kiketown** *n.* [1920s–60s] (*US*) the Jewish area of a city.

IN PHRASES

❑ **kike it** *v.* [the stereotypically mean Jew prefers not to pay fares] [20C+] (*US*) to walk.

kike *adj.* [KIKE *n.*] [20C+] (*orig. US*) Jewish.

kikey *adj.* [KIKE *n.*] [1920s+] (*orig. US*) Jewish.

kiki *n.* (*also* **ki-ki**) [play on QUEEN *n.* (2) or CHICHI *adj.* (1)] (*US gay*) **1** [1930s+] a homosexual who is equally happy in active or passive sex roles. **2** [1930s+] a bisexual. **3** [1940s+] a lesbian who takes neither an overtly feminine nor masculine role. **4** [1960s] a male homosexual who engages in oral and genital sex simultaneously. **5** [1960s–70s] sexual intercourse between two homosexual men of the same 'type', ie passive and passive or active and active.

kiki *adj.* (*also* **kai-kai**) [KIKI *n.*] [1940s] (*US gay*) one who enjoys anal sex; thus effeminate.

kiki *v.* (*also* **kai-kai**) [KIKI *n.*] [1940s] (*US gay*) to have (anal) sex.

kikipoo *n. see* KICKAPOO (JUICE) *n.*

kilkenny *n.*[1] [proper name *Kilkenny*, a county and city in Leinster in the Republic of Ireland; *frieze* is a variety of coarse woollen cloth usu. made in Ireland] [late 17C–early 19C] a frieze coat.

kilkenny *n.*[2] [rhy. sl.] [1930s–60s] a penny.

kill *n.*[1] (*also* **kilo**) [abbr.] [1910s–20s] a kilometre.

kill *n.*[2] **1** [1930s–50s] (*US*) a murder. **2** [1930s–50s] (*UK Und.*) in fig., use, the actual moment of bringing a confidence trick to a climax. **3** [1940s–50s] (*US back*) an impressive person or thing [abbr. of KILLER *n.* (2)]. **4** [1980s+] a major coup, esp. in criminal terms. **5** *see* KILLING *n.*

IN PHRASES

❑ **have a kill** *v. see* KILL *v.* (5a). ❑ **make a kill** *v. see* MAKE A KILLING *under* KILLING *n.*

kill *n.*[3] [abbr. KILLER *n.* (5a)] [1970s+] (*drugs*) high-grade, strong marijuana; thus *smoke some kill*.

kill *adj.* [abbr. KILLER *adj.*; on bad = good model] [1980s+] (*US*) fashionable, smart, sophisticated.

kill *v.* **1** (*orig. US*) to affect another person in a non-lethal way. (**a**) [mid-19C+] often constr. with *dead*, to amaze or delight, esp. an audience [note earlier SE use in 17–18C, usu. as *kill one with...* or *kill at first sight*]. (**b**) [late 19C+] to cause to convulse with laughter, to delight, to bowl over; esp. as *that kills me*; often ironic. **2** to consume, to terminate, to turn off. (**a**) [mid-19C+] (*orig. US*) to eat (enthusiastically) or to drink. (**b**) [mid-19C+] (*orig. US*) to suppress information, to cancel. (**c**) [late 19C+] (*orig. US*) to cut the engine of a vehicle or the power on a machine. (**d**) [1910s+] to turn off in general, to stop, esp. of noise or talking; often as KILL IT below. (**e**) [1920s+] to turn off lights, esp. in TV or film studios. (**f**) [1920s+] to finish, esp. a drink, hence *killer*, a heavy drinker. (**g**) [1920s+] to use up, to expend, e.g. time. (**h**) [1940s+] to put out a cigarette. (**i**) [1990s+] (*US*) to get rid of or remove an item, usu. of clothing or food. (**j**) to cover a wall or other object in graffiti. **3** (*US campus*) to overcome, to succeed. (**a**) [20C+] to pass an exam, esp. well. (**b**) [20C+] to do well, esp. easily. (**c**) [2000s] to punch; also in fig. use, to succeed. **4** [1970s+] (*US campus*) to fail, to do badly. **5** in sexual contexts. (**a**) [1990s+] (*US*) (*also* **have a kill, kill it, kill off**) to masturbate. (**b**) [2000s] (*US campus*) to have sexual intercourse with.

IN PHRASES

❑ **kill a number** *v. see under* NUMBER *n.* ❑ **kill it** *v.* **1** [1910s+] (*orig. US*) to stop talking; usu. as imper. *kill it!*, shut up! **2** *see* sense 5a above. ❑ **kill off** *v. see* sense 5a above.

SE in slang uses

as nicknames, usu. for alcoholic drinks

IN COMPOUNDS

❑ **kill-cobbler** *n.* [? the propensity of shoemakers for gin-drinking] [early–mid-18C] gin. ❑ **kill-devil** *n.* **1** a drink or drug. (**a**) [mid-17C–19C] (*US*) rum, or newly made rum, also known as *rumbullion*. (**b**) [mid-19C–1960s] (*US*) strong alcohol, esp. whisky. (**c**) [1950s] (*US, Ozarks*) very strong tobacco. **2** [late 17C–19C] a gun [revived in late 19C use is US]. ❑ **kill-dick swig** *n.* [mid-19C] (*UK Und.*) British-distilled brandy. ❑ **kill-grief** *n.* [its emotional anaesthesia] [early–mid-18C] gin or rum. ❑ **kill-priest** *n.* (*also* **kill-preacher**) [the clergy's supposed partiality to the drink] [late 18C–19C] port wine, also whisky.

IN PHRASES

❑ **kill-me-quick** *n.* [the effect of such food or drink] **1** [mid-19C–1900s] (*US*) whisky. **2** [late 19C–1900s] (*Aus.*) a form of fritter. **3** [1940s+] (*S.Afr.*) a form of strong liquor drunk in the townships, made of bread, syrup, brown sugar, yeast and bran. ❑ **kill-the-beggar** *n.* [19C] rough whisky.

general uses

IN COMPOUNDS

❑ **kill-boy lodge** *n.* [mid-19C] (*UK Und.*) Newgate prison. ❑ **kill-calf** *adj.* (*also* **kill-cow**) [SE *kill-calf/-cow*, a butcher] [late 16C–mid-18C] murderous. ❑ **kill-cow** *n.* ['I could kill a cow with one blow'] [late 16C–late 19C] an unrestrained braggart. ❑ **killpig** *n.* [2000s] an appalling situation.

IN PHRASES

❑ **kill a Chinaman** *v. see under* CHINAMAN *n.* ❑ **kill-a-ho** *adj.* [lit. *kill a whore*] [1990s+] (*US black teen*) used of the lyrical style of rap bands who specialize in extreme misogynism. ❑ **kill a snake** *v. see under* SNAKE *n.*[1]. ❑ **kill a worm** *v.* [late 19C–1910s] to take a drink, spec. to drink a glass of absinthe. ❑ **kill one's dog** *v. see under* DOG *n.*[6]. ❑ **kill some babies** *v.* [1990s+] (*US*) to masturbate. ❑ **kill someone's buzz** *v. see under* BUZZ *n.*

killed *adj.* [KILL *v.* (1)] [1980s+] (*US*) intoxicated by drugs or alcohol.

killed off *adj.* [19C] dragged out from one's recumbent position beneath a table after drinking to excess.

killem-shots *n.* [mid-19C] (*UK Und.*) sparkling eyes.

killer *n.* **1** [mid-19C] (*UK prison*) the treadmill. **2** someone or something exceptional (both positive and negative). (**a**) [mid-19C+] (*orig. US*) an outstanding, formidable person, often attractive, occas. menacing. (**b**) [1910s+] of an object, something exceptional of its type. (**c**) [1910s+] (*orig. US*) something very difficult to manage. (**d**) [1930s+] of performers/performances, the very best. **3** [1940s+] (*orig. Aus.*) the 'clincher', the final word in an argument. **4** [1940s+] (*Aus./US*) a womanizer [abbr. SE *lady-killer*]. **5** in drug uses. (**a**) [1940s+] (*also* **killer stick**) marijuana, a marijuana cigarette. (**b**) [2000s] phencyclidine. (**c**) [2000s] OxyContin. **6** [1970s+] as a term of address.

killer *adj.* (*orig. US*) **1** [1970s+] terrific, amazing, effective. **2** [1980s+] ghastly, terrible, demanding. **3** [1980s+] extreme, ultimate.

killer beans! *excl.* (*also* **killer boots!**) [ext. of *cool beans! see* under COOL *adj.*] [1990s+] (*US teen*) a general expression of approval meaning really wonderful, absolutely excellent.

killer-diller *n.*[1] [KILLER *adj.* + redup.] [1930s+] (*US*) something considered the very best; also ironically.

killer-diller *n.*[2] [KILLER *n.* (1) + redup.] [1930s+] (*orig. US*) a ladies' man.

killer-diller *adj.* (*also* **thriller-diller**) [KILLER-DILLER *n.*[1]] [1930s+] (*orig. US*) excellent, wonderful.

killers *n.* [late 18C] the human eyes.

killer stick *n. see* KILLER *n.* (5a).

killer weed *n.* [SE *killer* + WEED *n.*[1] (4); orig. a non-sl. epithet applied to discourage use, now used ironically] [1970s+] (*drugs*) **1** marijuana. **2** phencyclidine.

killing *n.* (*also* **kill**) [now SE] [mid-19C+] (*US*) a great success, usu. financial.

IN PHRASES

❑ **make a killing** *v.* (*also* **make a kill, ...cleaning**) **1** [late 19C+] (*orig. US*) to make a profit by gambling, whether at the races, on the stock market, in a casino etc. **2** [1900s] (*US campus*) to answer all of a teacher's questions correctly.

killing *adj.* [17C SE *killing*, captivating, bewitching] **1** [mid-18C–1940s] fashionable, stylish. **2** [mid-19C+] (*orig. US*) fascinating, very interesting, wonderful. **3** [mid-19C+] extremely funny.

killing floor *n.* [1960s+] (*US black*) **1** (*also* **slaughter floor, slaughtering floor**) anywhere used for the purpose of sexual intercourse. **2** a place where victims are robbed and/or cheated by a confidence trickster.

kill-me-dead *n.* [rhy. sl.] [1930s] (*UK tramp*) bread.

killout *n.* [1930s–40s; 1980s+] (*US black*) an amazing person, an enthralling topic or thing.

kill out *v.* [1930s] (*US black*) to feel good, exhilarated.

kill out oneself *v.* [20C+] (*W.I.*) to exhaust oneself.

Killsome *n.* [1980s+] (*W.I.*) Kingston, Jamaica.

kilo *n. see* KILL *n.*[1].

kilt *adj.* [hyperbolic use of SE *killed*] [19C+] (*Irish*) suffering, whether mentally or physically.

kilter *n.* [? it puts one *out of kilter*] [1960s] (*US drugs*) marijuana.

kim *n.* [abbr.] [1950s] (*Aus.*) a *kimono*.

kimbaw *v.* [SE *akimbo*, crossed or crooked] [late 17C–mid-19C] (*UK Und.*) **1** to cheat, to rob, to deceive. **2** to beat up.

Kimberley *adj.* [*Kimberley*, an area of northwest Australia] [20C+] (*Aus.*) a general derog. name used in various combs., e.g. *Kimberley mutton*, roast goat, *Kimberley oyster*, a meat fritter.

kimblock *n.* [mid-19C] (*UK Und.*) a rich fool, as such a potential target for robbery, thus adj. *kimblocky*, having more money than sense.

kimible *n.* [? SE (*arms*) *akimbo*] [1960s+] (*US black*) an exaggerated, identifiable pimp walk.

kimible *v.* (*also* **kimble**) [KIMIBLE *n.*] [1960s+] (*US black*) to use the exaggerated 'pimp's walk'.

kimino/kimona *n. see* WOODEN KIMONO *under* WOODEN *adj.*

kimono *adj.* [2000s] (*S.Afr. gay*) vulgar, tasteless.

kimp *n. see* KEMP *n.*

kin *n.* [SE *kin*, family] [18C] (*UK Und.*) a thief.

kinarkey *n.* [1990s+] (*W.I.*) a woman wearing garish make-up.

kinat *n.* (*also* **canat, kinnat, kinnatt**) [Irish *cnat*, a gnat] [20C+] (*Irish*) an impertinent, conceited youngster.

kinchin *n.* (*also* **kinch, kinchen, little kinchin**) [Ger. *Kindchen*, MDu. *kindeken*, a little child] (*UK Und.*) **1** [mid-16C–1900s] a (small) child. **2** [mid-18C–mid-19C] a young woman, a little girl.

IN COMPOUNDS

❑ **kinchin co** *n.* (*also* **kitchin co, kynchin-co**) [*co* = COVE *n.* (1)] [mid-16C–early 19C] (*UK Und.*) a child who has been brought up to thieving as a profession. ❑ **kinchin cove** *n.* (*also* **kinchen cove**) [COVE *n.* (1)] (*UK Und.*) **1** [late 17C–mid-19C] a little man. **2** [late 17C–mid-19C] a child brought up as a thief. **3** [late 18C–mid-19C] a man who steals children for gypsies, beggars, etc. ❑ **kinchin lay** *n.* (*also* **kynchin lay**) [LAY *n.*[3] (1)] [mid-19C–1900s] **1** street stealing from children. **2** in fig. use, i.e. devoting oneself to the topic of children. ❑ **kinchin mort** *n.* (*also* **king's mot, kitchin mort**) [MORT *n.* (1)] [mid-16C–mid-19C] (*UK Und.*) **1** a beggar's child, or any child carried by a beggar in order to excite pity. **2** a young, virgin girl, destined to be a prostitute or beggar's companion. ❑ **kinchin prig** *n.* [mid-19C] (*UK Und.*) a young thief.

kind *n.* [Hawaiian surf sl. *da kine*, anything of which one forgets the precise name] constr. with *the* **1** [1960s+] (*US*) anything good such as food, drugs or liquor. **2** [1980s+] (*US drugs*) superior quality cannabis.

kinder *n.* (*also* **kinda, kindie, kindy**) [abbr.] [1950s+] (*Aus.*) the *kinder*garten class in a primary school.

Kinder Eggs *n.* [brandname of a popular sweet] [1990s+] (*drugs*) MDMA.

kindergarten *n.* **1** [1950s] (*US Und.*) a reform school. **2** *see* GLADIATOR SCHOOL *n.*

Kinder Surprise *n.* [*Kinder Surprise*, the popular egg-shaped sweet] [1990s+] (*UK juv.*) a female who has large breasts, waist and thighs but thin legs.

kindheart *n.* [17C] a dentist.

kindie *n. see* KINDER *n.*

kindy *n.* **1** [2000s] (*N.Z.*) a suburb where young people train to be gang members. **2** *see* KINDER *n.*

'kin'ell! *excl.* (*also* **'king hell!**) [abbr. FUCKING HELL!] [20C+] an excl. of surprise, annoyance, wonder etc.

King *n.* [abbr.] **1** [late 19C+] (*S.Afr.*) King William's Town, Eastern Cape; once capital of the provinces of Queen Adelaide and British Kaffraria. **2** [1990s+] (*US black*) Burger King.

king *n.* **1** [mid-19C+] (*US campus*) the best, usu. used with a suitable n. or v., as -KING *sfx*,. **2** [20C+] (*Aus./US*) a respected figure, e.g. in a prison, or the leader of a gang of larrikins. **3** [1960s+] (*gay*) a masculine lesbian. **4** [2000s] (*US black*) a term of address.

IN COMPOUNDS

❑ **king daddy** *n.* [sense 2 above + DADDY *n.* (6)] [1990s+] (*US teen*) the very best of a person, place or thing; thus the female counterpart QUEEN MAMA *n.* ❑ **King Rat** *n.* [1970s+] (*Aus.*) a much admired person.

SE in slang uses

IN COMPOUNDS

❑ **king muck** *n. see* LORD MUCK *under* MUCK *n.*[1]. ❑ **king's bad hard bargain** *n. see* HIS MAJESTY'S BAD BARGAIN *n.* ❑ **king's elevator** *n. see* ROYAL SHAFT *under* ROYAL *adj.* ❑ **king's mot** *n. see* KINCHIN MORT *under* KINCHIN *n.* ❑ **king's peg** *n. see under* PEG *n.*[4]. ❑ **king's pictures** *n.* [the royal features as engraved or printed on money] [mid-17C–mid-19C] money. ❑ **king's plate** *n.* [the ult. royal control of prisons and the police] [early 19C] chains, fetters. ❑ **king's throne** *n. see* THRONE *n.*

IN PHRASES

❑ **draw the king's picture** *v. see under* DRAW *v.*[4].

king *adj.* [20C+] (*Aus.*) excellent, wonderful, perfect.

IN COMPOUNDS

❑ **king-hell** *adj.* [on pattern of terms like KING HIT *n.*; or abbr. FUCKING HELL!] [1960s+] (*orig. US*) formidable, impressive.

king *v. see* KING HIT *v.*

-king *sfx* [KING *n.* (1)] [mid-19C+] (*US campus*) used with a suitable n. or v. to denote the best of something, e.g. *surferking, tokingking* (cf. -QUEEN *sfx*).

King Billy *n.* (*also* **Billy**) [King William IV of England (r.1830–7)] [late 19C+] (*Aus.*) **1** a generic term for any Aboriginal leader. **2** any Aboriginal singled out from the rest.

king billy *adj.* [rhy. sl. = SILLY] [1970s–80s] (*N.Z. prison*) foolish, stupid; mad.

king canutes *n. see* DAISY ROOTS *n.*

King Country spanner *n.* [2000s] (*N.Z.*) a bottle-opener.

king (death) *n.* [rhy. sl.] [20C+] (bad) breath.

king dick *n.*[1] [rhy. sl.] [late 19C+] a brick; thus *king dickie*, a brickie, a bricklayer.

king dick *n.*[2] [generic use of proper name] [20C+] (*Aus.*) the leader, the boss, the 'guv'ner'.

IN PHRASES

❑ **not for king dick** *see* NOT FOR ALL THE TEA IN CHINA *under* TEA *n.*

king dick *adj.* [rhy. sl. = THICK *adj.* (1)] [20C+] stupid, dull.

kingdom come *n.* [rhy. sl.] **1** [20C+] rum. **2** [1970s+] the buttocks [= BUM *n.*[1] (1)].

King Farouk *n.* [rhy. sl.] [1950s] a book.

kingfish *n.* [the original *Kingfish* was the populist Governor and Senator Huey P. Long (1893–1935) of Louisiana; Long, who declared that he 'looked around at the little fishes present and said "I'm the Kingfish", fought his campaigns on the slogan 'Everyman a King but no man wears a crown'. The name was also given to a character in the hit US radio show *Amos 'n' Andy*] [1920s+] (*US*) a political leader or 'boss'.

'king hell! *excl. see* 'KIN'ELL! *excl.*

king hit *n.* [SE *king*, supreme, extreme + *hit*] [1940s+] (*Aus.*) **1** a knockout blow. **2** a thug, a bully. **3** a surprise punch.

king-hit *adj.* [KING HIT v.] (*Aus.*) **1** [1940s+] thuggish, pertaining to thuggery; usu. as *king-hit merchant*, one who specializes in thuggery. **2** [2000s] knocked out, struck down.

king hit *v.* (*also* **king**) [KING HIT *n.*] [1940s+] (*Aus.*) **1** to knock down. **2** to deliver a surprise punch.

King Kong *n.* [the name of the fictitious monster ape, who 'starred' in the film *King Kong* (1933)] **1** [1930s–60s] (*US black*) (*also* **kong**) cheap, potent, homemade whisky. **2** [1970s] (*US drugs*) a strong addiction.

IN PHRASES

❑ **King Kong pills** *n.* [1960s+] (*drugs*) barbiturates.

King Kong *v.* (*also* **Kong**) [1930s] (*US black*) to drink KING KONG *n.* (1) whisky.

King Lear *n.* [rhy. sl.] **1** [1930s+] an ear. **2** [1940s+] a male homosexual [QUEER *n.* (4)].

King Lear *adj.* [KING LEAR *n.* (2)] [1940s+] homosexual.

king of Spain *n.* [rhy. sl.] [20C+] (*Aus.*) **1** rain. **2** a train. **3** an airplane.

king of Spain's trumpeter *n.* [pun on SE *Don Key/donkey*] [late 18C–early 19C] a donkey.

kingpin *n.* [US use is late 19C, then Aus. early 20C+, UK 1950s+; SE *kingpin*, synon. with *kingbolt*, the most important or largest bolt in a mechanical structure, itself linked to *kingpost*, the central post that holds up a roof-truss] [mid-19C+] (*orig. US*) the central figure, the most important figure in an organization or team.

kingpin *adj.* [mid-19C+] of a person, most important, most central or authoritative in an organization.

kings (and queens) *n.* [rhy. sl.] [20C+] baked beans; thus *kings on holy ghost*, baked beans on toast.

King's College *n.* [late 18C–early 19C] the King's Bench prison.

King's Head Inn (in Newgate Street) *n.* (*also* **Chequer Inn in Newgate Street**) [late 17C–mid-19C] Newgate prison.

king shit *n.* (*also* **king spit**) [SE *king*] **1** [1940s+] (*orig. US*) an important person; usu. in negative, an arrogant, self-opinionated person [SHIT *n.* (2a)]. **2** [1990s+] a major drug dealer [SHIT *n.* (6)].

IN PHRASES

❑ **think one is king shit** *v.* [1940s+] (*US*) to be extremely conceited.

kingsize *adj.* [1950s+] (*US*) complete, utter, total.

kingsize *adv.* [1980s+] (*US*) to a very large extent, completely, absolutely.

kingsman *n.* [mid–late 19C] **1** (*also* **kinsman**) a silk handkerchief in a variety of colours, as worn by costermongers of both sexes. **2** a silk handkerchief with a green base and a yellow pattern; thus *kingsman of the rortiest*, a very gaudy variety.

king spit *n. see* KING SHIT *n.*

king's proctor *n.* [rhy. sl.] [20C+] a doctor.

King Street *n.*

IN PHRASES

❑ **up King Street** [*King Street*, Sydney, the site of the Supreme Court, which hears bankruptcy cases; note SE phr. *in carey street*] [1950s] (*Aus.*) in financial difficulties; thus *go up King Street*, to become bankrupt.

Kingswood lion *n.* [the village of Kingswood, known for the keeping of donkeys by the colliers who lived there] [early 19C] a donkey.

kinifee *n.* [exaggeratedly lit. pron. of SE *knife*] [1950s–60s] (*Aus. teen*) a knife.

kink *n.*[1] (*also* **kinkhead**) [typically 'kinky' black hair] [mid-19C–1940s] (*US*) a derog. term for a black person.

IN PHRASES

❑ **come the kink** *v.* [mid-19C] to steal a black slave from the country, and dispose of them in town.

kink *n.*[2] [? fig. uses of SE *kink*, a bend] [1910s–60s] (*US Und.*) **1** a criminal, later esp. a car thief. **2** a non-criminal tramp or a criminal who specializes in a style of theft different from that practised by the speaker.

kink *n.*[3] [SE *kink*, an eccentricity] **1** [1920s+] a perversion, esp. in sexual activity. **2** [1960s+] a sexually abnormal person, an eccentric.

IN PHRASES

❑ **go into kinks** *v.* [20C+] (*Irish*) to double up with hysterical laughter.

kinked *adj.* [SE *kink*, an eccentric] [1950s] (*Aus.*) eccentric.

kinked out *adv.* [KINK *n.*[3] (1)] [1990s+] dressed in a sexually perverse manner.

kinker *n.* [1900–40s] (*US*) a circus performer.

kinkey *adj. see* KINKY *adj.* (3).

kinkhead *n. see* KINK *n.*[1].

kinkless *adj.* [SE *kink*] [1920s] having straight(ened) hair.

kinko *n.* [SE *kink*, an eccentric/KINK *n.*[3] (1) + -O *sfx* (1)] [1960s+] (*US*) **1** an eccentric person. **2** a person with bizarre sexual tastes.

kinky *n.*[1] [abbr. KINKYHEAD *n.*] [1920s–40s] (*US*) one who has kinky hair, thus usu. a black person.

kinky *n.*[2] [KINKY *adj.* (2a)] [1920s–40s] (*US Und.*) anything that has been obtained dishonestly, esp. a stolen car.

kinky *n.*[3] [KINKY *adj.* (3)] **1** [1950s+] a sexual eccentric. **2** [1960s+] a film portraying unconventional sexual acts.

kinky *adj.* [SE *kink*, a bend] **1** of people (or animals). (**a**) [mid-19C+] (*US*) odd, bizarre, eccentric. (**b**) [late 19C+] immoral or unladylike. (**c**) [1900s–50s] (*US*) of livestock, frisky, of people, high-spirited. (**d**) [2000s] cheeky. **2** in (*US Und.*) uses, as vars. on BENT *adj.* (2) or BENT *adj.* (4). (**a**) [1900s–70s] dishonest or criminal. (**b**) [1920s–50s] stolen. **3** (*also* **kinkey**) in sexual contexts, from KINK *n.*[3] (1). (**a**) [1940s+] sexually eccentric, esp. sadomasochistic. (**b**) [1950s+] also in fig. use, i.e. almost perversely interested in.

IN COMPOUNDS

❑ **kinky boots** *n.* [1960s+] boots worn by women, usu. thigh-high and usu. skin-tight, and associated with the trad. 'dominatrix' figure.

IN PHRASES

❑ **get kinky** *v.* [2000s] to have sexual intercourse. ❑ **kinky about/over** *adj.* [1970s+] sexually excited by.

kinkyhead *n.* [SE *kink*] [mid-19C+] (*US black*) one who has kinky hair; hence a black person.

kinky-headed *adj.* [KINKYHEAD *n.*] [mid-19C+] (*US black*) of a person, having kinky hair; thus black

kinnat/kinnatt *n. see* KINAT *n.*

kinney *n.* [? KIND *n.* (2)] [2000s] (*US black/drugs*) very high quality marijuana.

Kinsey 6 *n.* [the categorization by sexologist Alfred Kinsey (1894–1956) in his book *Sexual Behavior in the Human Male* (1947), popularly known as the 'Kinsey Report'] [1950s] (*US gay*) a person who is completely homosexual, as opposed to one with some bisexual inclinations.

kinsler *n. see* KITSLER *n.*

kinsman *n. see* KINGSMAN *n.* (1).

kin teet *adj.* [pron. of *skin teeth*; the skin has drawn back from the teeth through *rigor mortis*] [1950s] (*W.I.*) dead.

'kin teet' *v. see* SKIN (ONE'S) TEETH *under* SKIN *v.*[1].

kioodle *n. see* KIYOODLE *n.*

kip *n.*[1] [Danish *kippe*, hut, a low alehouse, *horekippe*, a brothel] **1** [mid-18C+] a brothel; thus *kip-keeper*, a brothel-keeper, a madame. **2** [mid-19C+] a bed. **3** [late 19C+] the place where one sleeps, one's home. **4** [late 19C+] sleep, a nap; thus *akip*, asleep. **5** [late 19C+] a lodging house, a hotel room, an institutional home for the homeless. **6** [1920s–40s] (*Anglo-Irish*) a job. **7** [1920s–40s] (*US Und.*) a nightwatchman. **8** [1930s+] (*mainly Irish*) any form of place, building.

DERIVATIVES

❑ **kipsville** *n.* [-VILLE *sfx*[1]] [1910s] (*US Und.*) a hotel.

IN COMPOUNDS

❑ **kip dough** *n.* (*also* **kip jack**) [DOUGH *n.* (1)/JACK *n.*[4] (2)] [1930s–60s] (*US tramp*) money to pay for one's lodging. ❑ **kiphouse** *n.* (*also* **kip-house, kipping house**) **1** [late 19C+] a lodging house, night shelter or similar refuge for homeless people. **2** [1990s+] a brothel. ❑ **kip shop** *n.* [SHOP *n.*[1] (3)] **1** [1920s–30s] a lodging house. **2** [1930s+] (*Scot.*) a brothel.

IN PHRASES

❑ **in kip** [1910s] in bed, asleep. ❑ **tatter a kip** *v.* [mid-18C] to wreck a brothel.

kip *n.*[2] [mid-19C] (*UK Und.*) a foolish person.

kip *n.*[3] [late 19C+] (*Aus.*) the spatula-like wooden bat used for tossing pennies in the game of two-up.

IN PHRASES

❑ **pass the kip** *v.* [1900s–10s] in fig. use, to allow someone else to speak. ❑ **rush the kip** *v.* [1900s–10s] (*N.Z.*) to make a precipitate, over-hasty decision.

kip *n.*[4] [Scot. *kip*, a promontory on a hill, a turned-up nose] [1990s+] (*Scot.*) the face.

kip *v.* [KIP *n.*[1]] **1** [early–mid-19C] to play truant. **2** [early 19C+] (*also* **kip down, kipp**) to sleep. **3** [late 19C+] to lodge. **4** [1900s] to sit, to lie. **5** [1950s] to put someone to bed. **6** [1970s+] (*US teen/Und.*) to sleep on the streets.

IN COMPOUNDS

❑ **kip-in** *adj.* [lit. 'sleep-in'] [20C+] easy, undemanding.

IN PHRASES

❑ **kip in** *v.* [1940s+] **1** to be quiet, to stop talking, esp. as imper. **2** to go to bed. ❑ **kip out** *v.* [late 19C–1960s] to sleep in the open air.

kipe *v.* (*also* **kype**) [? dial. *kip*, to take property through fraud or violence] [1930s+] (*US*) to steal.

kipped *adj.* [KIP *v.* (2)] [1920s–30s] (*US Und.*) of a place, guarded by an all-night watchman who sleeps on the premises.

kipper *n.*[1] [an affectionate nickname] **1** [late 19C–1960s] a person, esp. a young or small person, a child. **2** [1940s+] (*Aus.*) an Englishman, an English immigrant, also attrib. [like the *kipper*, he is 'two-faced with no guts']. **3** [2000s] one's face. **4** [2000s] (*Irish*) a red-head.

SE in slang uses

IN PHRASES

❑ **done up like a kipper** *see under* DONE UP *adj.*[1]. ❑ **do (up) like a kipper** *v. see under* DO *v.*[1]. ❑ **you couldn't box kippers** [1920s+] a phr. used to decry a person as a physical weakling.

kipper *n.*[2] [KIP *v.* (2)] [20C+] anywhere one can sleep, a 'dosshouse', a hotel; one's bed.

kipper *v.*[1] [? a herring is 'ruined' by kippering; or var. on SCUPPER *v.*] [1920s+] to ruin someone else's chances.

kipper *v.*[2] [1930s] (*UK tramp*) to get sunburnt.

kipper and bloater *n.* [rhy. sl.] [1970s+] a motor.

kipper and plaice *n.* [rhy. sl.] [20C+] the face.

kippered *adj.* [1900s] (*US*) drunk.

Kipperland *n.* [2000s] (*N.Z.*) the United Kingdom.

kipping *n.*[1] (*also* **kippings**) [1910s–20s] lodging.

IN COMPOUNDS

❑ **kipping house** *n. see* KIPHOUSE *under* KIP *n.*[1].

IN PHRASES

❑ **make one's kippings** *v.* [1910s] (*US*) to live.

kipping *n.*[2] [the 'two-up' KIP *n.*[3] (1), the piece of wood on which the pennies are placed before throwing them into the air; like other similarly shaped objects it can be synon. for the penis] [1950s] (*Aus.*) masturbating.

kipples *n. see under* DANCE *v.*

kippy *adj.* [ety. unknown] [1910s–80s] (*US*) attractive, striking, lively.

kipsie *n.*[1] (*also* **kipsey**) [SE *keep*] **1** [mid-18C–19C] a wicker basket, usu. to hold cherries. **2** [late 19C] (*UK Und.*) a tramp's bag or container for his provisions and personal property. **3** [1930s] (*UK Und.*) a woman's handbag.

kipsie *n.*[2] (*also* **kypsey, kippsie**) [KIP *n.*[1] (3)] **1** [20C+] (*Aus.*) a home, a house, a lodging house. **2** [1910s] (*Aus.*) a dugout, a shelter in WW1. **3** [1910s+] (*Aus.*) a cheap lodging house.

kirb *n.* [backsl.] [mid-19C] a brick.

Kirby *n.* [? anecdotal, poss. late 19C Sydney undertaker P. Kirby] [late 19C] (*Aus.*) an undertaker.

kirk *n.*[1] [ext. use of Scot. *kirk*] [early 19C–1910s] (*UK/US Und.*) a church.

IN COMPOUNDS

❑ **kirk-buzzer** *n.* [BUZZER *n.*[1]] [mid-19C] (*US Und.*) a pickpocket who specializes in the robbery of church congregations.

IN PHRASES

❑ **crack a kirk** *v.* [CRACK *v.*[2] (2c)] [mid-19C] (*UK Und.*) **1** to break into a church. **2** to break into a house while its owners are at church.

kirk *n.*[2] *see* CIRQ *n.*

kirkling *n.* [KIRK *n.*[1]] [late 19C] (*UK Und.*) breaking into houses that are temporarily deserted while the occupants are at church.

kirk pilot *n. see* SKYPILOT *under* SKY *n.*[2].

kisheda *n.* [2000s] (*US black*) a man who goes with lots of women, usu. ugly ones.

kishkes *n.* (*also* **keeshkas, kishka, kishkas**) [Yid. *kishkes*, intestines] [20C+] (*orig. US*) the guts, the stomach; also in fig. use, courage, pluck (or lack thereof).

kiskeedee *n.* (*also* **keskydee**) [Fr. *qu'est-ce qu'il dit?*, what is he saying?] [mid-19C–1950s] (*US*) a French-speaking person.

kisky *adj.* [? rhy. sl. = whisky or ? Rom. *kushto*, feeling good or happy] [mid-19C] drunk, tipsy.

k.i.s.s.! *excl.* [abbr.; orig. milit. usage, later general, also popular in drug rehabilitation circles] [1960s+] (*US*) keep it simple, stupid.

kiss *n.* **1** [1910s–20s] (*US*) a drink from a bottle. **2** [1920s+] (*US teen*) a blow or hit.

kiss *v.* **1** in sexual contexts. (**a**) [16C–mid-19C] to have sexual intercourse [note Fr. *baiser*, lit. to kiss, in sl. to have sexual intercourse]. (**b**) [19C–1960s] (*also* **kiss it**) to fellate or perform cunnilingus. **2** [1910s+] (*US*) to hit or strike hard. **3** [1970s+] (*US teen*) to reject, to do without etc [abbr. KISS OFF *v.*/SE *kiss* *goodbye*]. **4** [1990s+] to approach, to draw near, e.g. of a birthday or date.

(IN PHRASES)

❑ **kiss one's arse/ass goodbye** *v.* (*also* **kiss one's asshole goodbye**) [ARSE *n.* (1)/ASS *n.* (2)/ASSHOLE *n.* (1)] [1970s+] to give up completely, to abandon all hope. ❑ **kiss oneself goodbye** *v.* **1** [1900s] (*US*) to give up hope, to surrender. **2** [1980s+] to commit suicide. ❑ **kiss someone's arse/ass** *v. see* separate entry. ❑ **kiss someone's dick** *v. see SUCK SOMEONE'S DICK under* DICK *n.*[1]. ❑ **kiss someone's ring** *v.* (*also* **kiss someone's toe, ...thumb**) [SE *kiss the ring*, to pay homage, but note RING *n.* (1) thus var. on KISS SOMEONE'S ARSE *v.*] [19C+] to fawn, to act the sycophant, to toady. ❑ **kiss someone's tail** *v. see* KISS SOMEONE'S ARSE *v.* ❑ **kiss the babe** *v.* (*also* **kiss the baby**) [mid-19C–1950s] (*orig. US*) to take a drink. ❑ **kiss the baby** *v.* [the imminent kissing goodbye of one's child] [1990s+] (*US Und.*) to face a certain term of imprisonment. ❑ **kiss the Clink** *v.* (*also* **kiss the Counter, Kiss Newgate**) [CLINK *n.*[1] (1)/SE *counter/Newgate*, a prison attached to a city court] [mid-16C–18C] to be confined in either of these prisons. ❑ **kiss the cross** *v.* [SE *cross*, a blow in boxing + pun on religious use] [1920s+] (*Aus.*) to be knocked out. ❑ **kiss the dog** *v.* [1930s–50s] (*US Und.*) of a pickpocket, to steal from a person while face-to-face. ❑ **kiss the dust** *v.* [orig. mid-18C boxing *kiss the dust*, to be knocked down] [20C+] (*orig. US*) to die. ❑ **kiss the maid** *v.* [SE *maiden*, a form of early guillotine used at Edinburgh in late 16C; occas. applied to the Halifax gibbet] [late 17C–18C] to be executed on a primitive form of the guillotine. ❑ **kiss the parson's wife** *v.* [the belief that those who wish for such luck must 'kiss the parson's wife'] [late 18C–early 19C] to be lucky in the choosing of or betting on horses. ❑ **kiss the worm** *v.* [WORM *n.*] [1940s+] to fellate.

(IN EXCLAMATIONS)

❑ **go kiss a duck!** *see GO FUCK A DUCK! under* FUCK *v.* ❑ **kiss it where the sun don't shine!** (*also* **kiss me where the sun don't shine! kiss a fat lady in the ass!**) [1940s+] (*orig. US*) a general excl. of derision or dismissal. ❑ **kiss me neck!** [1940s+] (*W.I. Rasta*) a common excl. of surprise. ❑ **kiss my arse/ass!** *see* separate entry. ❑ **kiss my foot!** [mid-19C; 1940s+] (*US/Aus.*) a general statement of contempt or dismissal. ❑ **kiss my tail!** [TAIL *n.* (2); var. on KISS MY ARSE!] [late 16C–late 19C] a general statement of contempt or dismissal. ❑ **kiss my tuna!** [TUNA *n.*; var. on KISS MY ARSE!; the implication is that the oral sex that is invited is *de facto* distasteful] [1980s+] (*US teen*) an all-purpose excl. of rejection.

SE in slang uses

(IN COMPOUNDS)

❑ **kissing trap** *n.* [TRAP *n.*[1] (4)] [mid–late 19C] (*orig. boxing*) the mouth. ❑ **kiss wagon** *n. see PASSION WAGON under* PASSION *n.*

(IN PHRASES)

❑ **kiss goodbye** *v.* [20C+] to reject, to do without, 'say goodbye' to. ❑ **kiss mary** *v.* [MARY *n.* (3)] [1960s] to smoke marijuana. ❑ **kiss teeth** *v.* (*also* **kiss teet, suck teeth**) [1920s+] (*orig. W.I. Rasta*) to make a hissing noise of disapproval, dislike, vexation or disappointment; also as n.

(IN EXCLAMATIONS)

❑ **kiss kiss!** [the kisses offered on saying goodbye] [1990s+] (*US campus*) goodbye.

kiss! *excl.* [1970s] (*W.I.*) a euph. for *Christ!*

kiss and cuddle *n.* [rhy. sl.] [20C+] a muddle.

kiss-arse *n.* (*also* **kiss-ass**) [KISS-ARSE *adj.*] [1950s+] (*orig. US*) a toady, a sycophant.

kiss-arse *adj.* (*also* **kiss-ass**) [KISS SOMEONE'S ARSE *v.*] [1910s+] (*orig. US*) sycophantic.

kiss arse *v.* (*also* **kiss ass, kiss butt**) [KISS SOMEONE'S ARSE *v.*] [1910s+] (*orig. US*) to be subservient, to toady, to act as a sycophant.

kisser *n.* (*orig. boxing*) **1** as a physical feature. (**a**) [mid-19C+] the mouth. (**b**) [late 19C+] the face. (**c**) [1970s] the anus. **2** as abbr. lit. *ass-kisser*/ASS-KISSER *n.* (**a**) [20C+] a male homosexual. (**b**) [1950s+] a toady, a sycophant.

kissing cousin *n. see* COUNTRY COUSIN *n.*

kiss me hardy *n.* [rhy. sl.] [20C+] a measure of Bacardi rum.

kiss-me-quick *n.* [rhy. sl. = PRICK *n.*] [1990s+] **1** the penis. **2** a fool.

kiss my arse *adj. see* KISS-MY-ASS *adj.*

kiss my arse! *excl.* (*also* **kiss mine! ...my ass! ...my ass(orted peanuts)! ...my axle! ...my bender! ...my blackass! ...my breech! ...my butt! ...my royal hindparts! ...my Royal Irish!**) [ARSE *n.*/ASS *n.* note Chaucer, *Miller'sTale* (1386): 'But with his mouth he kiste hir naked ers'] **1** [early 16C+] a general statement of contempt or dismissal; often ext. as *kiss my ass in Macey's window!* **2** [1970s] (*US*) an excl. of surprise.

(IN EXCLAMATIONS)

❑ **I'll be a kiss my ass!** [1950s] a general excl. of surprise, amazement, delight, etc.

kiss my arse fellow *n.* (*also* **kiss-my-toe fellow**) [late 18C–early 19C; 1960s] a sycophant; as *kiss-my-arse man* in 1960s.

kiss-my-ass *adj.* (*also* **kiss-my-arse, kiss my back cheeks, kiss-my-tail**) [KISS MY ARSE! *excl.* (1)] **1** [1960s+] a general pej. **2** [1970s+] arrogant, undaunted, proud.

kiss-off *n.* **1** [1920s+] (*US*) a dismissal, a rejection. **2** [1930s+] (*US*) a conclusion, a farewell, a termination (usu. with sense of one party compelling it on the other). **3** [1940s+] death.

kiss off *v.* [? billiards use or the offering of a farewell kiss] **1** [20C+] to sidetrack someone or something, to marginalize, to slight or disregard. **2** [1910s+] (*US*) to murder or to die. **3** [1930s] to defraud, to cheat. **4** [1930s+] to reject, to ignore, to spurn, esp. a lover; thus excl. *kiss off!*, go away, don't talk rubbish! **5** [1930s+] (*also* **kiss out**) to bring to an end. **6** [1950s] to come to an end. **7** [1960s] (*US campus*) to leave; leave alone.

kiss of life *n.* [rhy. sl.] [20C+] one's wife.

kiss someone's arse *v.* (*also* **kiss someone's ass, ...assets, ...behind, ...brown end, ...bum, ...butt, ...tail**) [ARSE *n.*/ASS *n.*/BUM *n.*[1] (1)/BUTT *n.*[1] (1)/TAIL *n.* (2)] [mid-17C+] to fawn, to act the sycophant, to toady.

kiss-up *n.* **1** [1950s] (*US*) sexual enjoyment. **2** [1960s+] a sycophant [KISS UP (TO) *v.*].

kiss up (to) *v.* [1960s+] to toady to.

kissy *adj.* **1** [1940s–70s] (*US gay*) attractive, appealling [SE *kissable*]. **2** [1970s–80s] (*US*) sycophantic [KISS ARSE *v.*].

kissyface *n.* **1** [1950s+] (*orig. US teen/campus*) the act of kissing. **2** [2000s] used fig. to describe any intimate meeting, conversation etc.

(IN PHRASES)

❑ **play kissyface** *v.* (*also* **kissy-kissy, play kissy-ass, ...kissy-poo**) **1** [1950s+] (*US*) to kiss and cuddle. **2** [2000s] in fig. use, to befriend, often insincerely.

kissy-kissy *n.* [KISS ARSE *v.*] [1980s+] (*US*) sycophantic behaviour.

kissy-poo *n.* [deliberate infantilism] [2000s] a kiss.

kister *n. see* KEISTER *n.*

kit *n.*[1] [SE *kit*, a small fiddle, esp. popular among dancing-masters; ult. ? Gk *cithara*] [early 18C–early 19C] a dancing-master.

kit *n.*[2] **1** [late 18C–mid-19C] a number of things or persons viewed as a whole, a set, a lot, a collection. **2** [19C] the penis and testes. **3** [mid-19C+] clothing [SE *kit*, the uniforms used for various sports; phr. widely popularized by the spread of 1990s 'lad culture' and the magazines that pander to it]. **4** [1920s+] (*drugs*) the equipment, such as a syringe or a spoon, required for injection of a narcotic. **5** [1930s] in (*US Und.*) use. (**a**) a safebreaker's equipment. (**b**) fake documents used to back up the credibility of a financial swindler. **6** [2000s] (*drugs*) drugs, in the context of dealing. **7** *see* KITTY *n.*[1] (3).

(IN PHRASES)

❑ **get one's kit off** *v.* [1970s+] to take off one's clothes, to strip.

kit *n.*[3] [Maori *kete*, flax basket, but note SE *kit*, a kind of basket, esp. one made of straw or rushes for holding fish] [1940s+] (*N.Z.*) a shopping basket.

kit and boiling *n.* see WHOLE KIT AND BILING *under* WHOLE KIT *n.*

kit and caboodle *n.* see WHOLE KIT AND CABOODLE *under* WHOLE KIT *n.*

kit and killybang *n.* see WHOLE KIT AND CARGO *under* WHOLE KIT *n.*

Kitch *n.* [Lord *Kitch*ener] [1910s–20s] (*Aus.*) a British soldier.

kitchen *n.*[1] **1** [late 17C–19C] the vagina. **2** [late 19C+] the stomach. **3** [1910s+] (*Irish*) food, a meal.

IN PHRASES

❑ **clean up the kitchen** *v.* (*also* **scrub the kitchen**) [1930s+] (*US*) to perform anilingus or cunnilingus.

SE in slang uses

IN COMPOUNDS

❑ **kitchen-bitch** *n.* see *under* BITCH *n.*[1]. ❑ **kitchen mechanic** *n.* **1** [late 19C+] (*US*) (*also* **kitchen queen**) a cook or washer-up. **2** [1960s] (*US black*) a prostitute.

IN PHRASES

❑ **give someone the rounds of the kitchen** *v.* [late 19C+] (*Aus.*) to tell off, to scold. ❑ **rounds of the kitchen** *n.* [the victim is beaten up and down the room] [20C+] (*Ulster*) a thrashing.

kitchen *n.*[2] [? it is fig. 'round the back of the house'] [1990s+] (*US black*) the hairs at the nape of one's neck.

kitchen range *n.* [rhy. sl.] [20C+] small change.

kitchen sink *n.* [rhy. sl.] **1** [20C+] a stink. **2** [20C+] a derog. term for a Chinese person [= CHINK *n.* (1)]. **3** [1970s+] (*Aus.*) a drink.

kitchen stoves *n.* [rhy. sl.] [20C+] (*Aus.*) cloves.

kitchin co *n.* see KINCHIN CO *under* KINCHIN *n.*

kitchin mort *n.* see KINCHIN MORT *under* KINCHIN *n.*

kite *n.* [SE *kite*, a bird of prey (*Milvusictinus*)] **1** [mid-16C–19C; 1960s] a despicable person, one who preys on others. **2** [mid-16C–mid-19C; 1990s+] the stomach [the stomach as an 'eater']. **3** as something that 'flies away'. (**a**) [19C+] (*also* **kyte**) a cheque. (**b**) [mid-19C] a promissory note. (**c**) [mid-19C] (*UK tramp*) paper; cigarette paper. (**d**) [mid-19C+] (*US/Can. prison*) a contraband letter or note smuggled into or out of prison. (**e**) [mid-19C+] (*US prison*) any form of written document, note, memo etc used within a prison. (**f**) [mid-19C+] a dud cheque, i.e. one that has insufficient funds to back it. (**g**) [1930s–60s] (*US black*) a letter. (**h**) [1970s] (*US Und.*) a complaint to the police about some form of illegal operation, often from a gambler who has been fleeced. (**i**) [1970s+] (*Aus. prison*) a newspaper. (**j**) [1970s+] (*US campus*) an inveterate drug user, who stays *high as a kite*. (**k**) [1980s+] (*UK Und.*) a credit card, usu. stolen. (**l**) [1990s+] a person involved in some kind of criminal dealings. (**m**) (*US black*) a banknote. **4** [late 19C] a shirt-front. **5** [1900s–40s] (*US*) a prostitute or promiscuous woman. **6** [1950s] (*US drugs*) one ounce of a narcotic. **7** [20C+] (*US*) the human face [the position of the 'eating' mouth in the face]. **8** [20C+] (*Irish*) the anus.

IN COMPOUNDS

❑ **kite-fishing** *n.* [1900s–20s] (*UK Und.*) stealing mail containing bank cheques from homes and offices. ❑ **kite-flyer** *n.* [mid-19C+] a passer of dud cheques. ❑ **kite-flying** *n.* **1** [early 19C+] raising money by persons colluding in the exchange of accommodation bills or cheques on different banks, in none of which they possess sufficient funds. **2** [mid-19C] raising money by transferring accounts between banks and creating an illusory balance against which one cashes cheques. **3** [mid-19C+] passing forged, stolen or unbacked cheques. ❑ **kite-man** *n.* (*also* **kite-merchant**) [sfx *-man*/MERCHANT *n.*] [1920s+] a criminal who specializes in cheque fraud. ❑ **kite-mob** *n.* [MOB *n.*[2] (3)] [1930s–40s] (*UK Und.*) a gang specializing in passing fraudulent cheques.

IN PHRASES

❑ **fly a kite** *v.* **1** [19C+] (*also* **fly the kite**) to obtain credit against bills, whether or not the 'paper' is valid or fraudulent. **2** [late 19C–1910s] to raise money. **3** [20C+] to pass a dud cheque, ext. as *fly a dodgy kite*. **4** [1920s+] (*US prison*) to smuggle a letter out of prison; also, to pass letters within prison. **5** [1940s–70s] (*US*) to send a letter. ❑ **flykite** *adj.* [? the sort of person who could FLY A KITE above] [mid-19C] (*UK Und.*) sharp, perspicacious. ❑ **kite with no string** *n.* [1930s+] (*US black*) **1** an airmail letter. **2** any form of communication, incl. latterly email.

SE in slang uses

IN COMPOUNDS

❑ **kite-flying** *n.* [FLY A KITE below] [early 19C] the enjoyment of extramarital pleasures by a husband. ❑ **kite string** *n.* [1970s+] (*N.Z.*) a close attachment, an 'apron-string'.

IN PHRASES

❑ **blow out the kite** *v.* [the food makes one's stomach expand like the 'belly' of a kite in the wind] [mid–late 19C] to have a full stomach. ❑ **fly a kite** *v.* [fig. uses of SE] **1** [mid-19C] constr. with *at*, to court, to pursue a woman. **2** [late 19C] to make public, to publicize. **3** [late 19C] (*UK Und.*) to write a letter to a receiver of stolen goods, prior to a robbery, to ascertain the value of the goods to be stolen. **4** [20C+] (*US*) to show off, to make a big display. **5** [1920s+] to present a false front or a deceitful line of talk in order to persuade one's victim that one's intentions are other than they really are. **6** [1930s+] to sound out public opinion, by taking initial steps in a given project or idea. **7** [1950s] (*Aus.*) to lie. ❑ **fly the kite** *v.* [mid-19C] to toss excrement from a window. ❑ **raise a kite** *v.* [1940s] (*W.I.*) to grumble, to make a fuss. ❑ **up the kite** *adj.* [1990s+] pregnant.

IN EXCLAMATIONS

❑ **go fly a kite!** [1910s+] a suggestion that an unwanted person should go away.

kite *v.* **1** [mid-19C–1900s] to wander around [SE *kite*, i.e. one i. 'gliding' like a kite]. **2** from KITE *n.* (3). (**a**) [mid-19C+] to pass a dud cheque. (**b**) [1920s+] (*UK/US Und.*) to smuggle letters in and out of prison; similarly passing letters within a prison. (**c**) [1990s+] (*US prison*) to write a letter or note.

DERIVATIVES

❑ **kiter** *n.* [1930s+] a criminal who specializes in cheque fraud.

SE in slang uses

IN PHRASES

❑ **kite around** *v.* [mid-19C+] to rush about; to drag about.

kited *adj.* [one is 'flying high'] [1940s] (*US*) drunk.

kiting *n.* [KITE *v.* (2)] [1930s+] (*UK/US Und.*) passing dud cheques.

IN COMPOUNDS

❑ **kiting-book** *n.* [1960s] a cheque-book.

kit-kat *n.* [rhy. sl.; kit-kat = PRAT *n.*[1] (6)] [1960s+] a fool, general term of abuse.

kit-kat shuffle *n.* [a two-fingered version of the FIVE-FINGER SHUFFLE *under* FIVE-FINGER(ED) *adj.*; the chocolate bar *Kit-Kat*, which comes in two or four fingers; but note KITTY *n.*[2] (1)] [1990s+] female masturbation.

kitskonstabel *n.* [Afk. *kits*, instant + *konstabel*, constable] [1980s+] (*S.Afr.*) a special constable, only partially trained, used to keep order in townships during a state of emergency.

kitsler *n.* (*also* **kinsler**) [ety. unknown] [1960s] (*S.Afr. Und.*) swindler.

kitt *n.* [ety. unknown; ? misuse of KIT *n.*[2] (6) or KIF *n.*] [1980s+] (*drugs*) cannabis.

kitted-up *adj.* [KIT *n.*[2] (3)] [1960s+] dressed, clothed.

kitten *n.* **1** [19C] a pint or half-pint pot [i.e. a small CAT *n.*[4] (1)]. **2** [1900s] (*US Und.*) the junior member of a gang, used to check places susceptible to a robbery, etc [dimin. of SE *cat*, but note CAT *n.*[1] (1)]. **3** a young woman [dimin. of SE *cat* but also play on CAT *n.*[1] (1)]. (**a**) [1900s] an attractive young woman. (**b**) [1920s+] (*US black*) a young, inexperienced girl. (**c**) [1930s+] an affectionate term of address to one's girlfriend or child. (**d**) [1940s+] (*US black*) a girlfriend [a jazz era coinage, plays on CAT *n.*[5] (1)]. **4** [1990s+] the vagina [var. on CAT *n.*[1] (1)].

SE in slang uses

IN COMPOUNDS

❑ **kitten's vest** *n.* see CAT'S PYJAMAS *n.*

IN PHRASES

▫ **have kittens** *v.* (*also* **cast a kitten, get kittens, ...zebras, have a kitty, ...kittens in the granary, ...pups**) [the nervousness of a pregnant cat] [20C+] to worry to excess, to throw a fit, to succumb to one's emotions, to lose one's temper, often through worry or fear. ▫ **real kittens** *n.* [1900s] (*US*) something or someone exceptional.

kittie *n.* (*also* **kittok**) [the popular name + ref. to CAT *n.*[1] (1)] [16C] a prostitute.

kitties *n.* (*also* **kittys**) [? SE *kit*] [late 18C–mid-19C] one's furniture or household effects.

kittle pitchering *n.* [Scot. *kittle*, to puzzle with a question, a riddle etc + *pitcher*, to throw in] [late 18C–early 19C] a way of cutting off a boring talker by continually interrupting them with small queries.

kittock *n. see* KITTIE *n.*

kitty *n.*[1] [Northumbrian dial.; ? f. *kidcote*, the name of the prison in various northern towns, incl. York and Lancaster] **1** [19C–1940s] a prison, a lock-up. **2** [late 19C+] the 'pool' in card-games, or any other game of chance [SE in 20C+, the money is fig. 'imprisoned' while the hand is played]. **3** [1920s+] (*also* **kit**) any reserve of money; or any valuable commodity.

kitty *n.*[2] (*also* **kitty-cat**) [SE *Kitty*, the dimin. of the female name *Katherine*] **1** [late 19C+] the vagina. **2** [20C+] (*US*) a young, inexperienced girl. **3** [1910s+] a woman, esp. in a sexual context. **4** [1930s] used as a pejorative. **5** [1930s+] the equivalent of a jazz/beatnik CAT *n.*[5] (1).

SE in slang uses

IN PHRASES

▫ **have a kitty** *v. see* HAVE KITTENS *under* KITTEN *n.*

kitty *n.*[3] (*also* **cat, kitty-cat**) [pron.] [1930s+] (*US black*) a Cadillac.

kitty-hop *n.* [1910s] (*US Und.*) any form of scheme whereby the criminal cannot lose.

kitty litter *n.* [1990s+] (*US gay*) used by trans-sexuals to denote HIV.

kittys *n. see* KITTIES *n.*

kivey *n.* (*also* **kiver**) [presumably a dimin. of COVE *n.*, though poss. linked to Lat. *civis*, a citizen] [19C] a man.

kiwash *n.* [ety. unknown; ? link to SE *wash*] [1980s] (*US*) money, esp. obtained illegally, and requiring laundering.

Kiwi *n.* [the national bird] [20C+] a New Zealander.

Kiwi *adj.* [KIWI *n.*] [20C+] pertaining to New Zealand or New Zealand culture.

IN COMPOUNDS

▫ **Kiwi grace** *n.* [1970s+] a name for the excl. '2, 4, 6, 8, bog in, don't wait!'; i.e. an allusion to the New Zealander's enthusiasm/greediness for food. ▫ **Kiwi green** *n.* [GREEN *n.*[2] (3)] [1970s+] (*N.Z. drugs*) locally grown marijuana. ▫ **Kiwi haircut** *n.* [1950s+] (*N.Z.*) a 'short-back-and-sides' haircut.

kiwi *n.* [a soft FRUIT *n.* (2)] [1970s+] a homosexual.

ki-yi *n.* [echoic] (*US*) **1** [late 19C–1910s] a noisy dog. **2** [late 19C–1940s] a contemptible fellow, a cur.

ki-yi *v.* [echoic] [late 19C–1940s] (*US*) to shout, to yell.

kiyoodle *n.* (*also* **kioodle, kyoodle**) [? echoic or SE *cur*] (*US*) **1** [late 19C+] a small noisy dog. **2** [20C+] a worthless fellow. **3** [1920s] worthless talk.

k.j. *n.* [abbr. (albeit incorrect) CRYSTAL *n.* (3) + JOINT *n.* (5c)] [1970s+] (*drugs*) phencyclidine.

klaat! *excl.* [abbr. BLOOD CLAAT *n.*] [20C+] (*W.I.*) a general excl. of anger.

kleenex *n.* [*Kleenex*, a popular brand of paper handkerchief] [1980s+] (*US*) **1** a juvenile word used for sex, because 'You pick it up, blow, and throw it away'. **2** among paedophiles, a description of those they exploit.

kleinhuisie *n.* [Afk. *klein*, small + *huis*, house, lit. 'little house'] [1960s+] (*S.Afr.*) an outdoor privy.

klem *v.* [mid-19C] (*UK Und.*) to hit.

klep *n.* (*also* **klepper**) [abbr. SE *kleptomaniac*] [late 19C–1970s] a thief.

klep *v.* [KLEP *n.*] [late 19C–1970s] to steal.

klepto *n.* [abbr.] [1950s+] a *klepto*maniac, an obsessive shoplifter.

klick *n.* (*also* **click, klik**) [abbr.] [1960s+] (*orig. US milit.*) a kilometre.

klika *n. see* CLICA *n.*

klingon *n.* [play on *cling on*; the *Klingons* are the 'bad guys' in the TV series *StarTrek* (from 1966)] **1** [1980s+] (*drugs*) a crack cocaine addict [*clings on* to every morsel of crack]. **2** [1990s+] a piece of excrement *clinging on* to the anal hairs. **3** [1990s+] a tedious or unpleasant person.

klink *n. see* CLINK *n.*[1] (1).

klink *v.* [echoic] [1930s] (*US Und.*) to hit with a gun or a cosh.

klinker top *n.* [1950s] (*US black*) a person with tightly curled 'nappy' hair.

klip *v.* [Afk. *klip*, a small rock] [late 19C] (*S.Afr.*) to place a stone under a vehicle's wheel to stop it running away downhill.

klippy *adj.* [1920s] (*US*) nice and neat.

klobber *see under* CLOBBER.

klondike *n.* [the *Klondike*, site of the Alaskan gold rush in the late 19C; miners worked alone and in darkness] [20C+] (*US prison*) the punishment cells.

klondike *adj.* [the 19C Alaskan gold rush on the *Klondike* river, which rendered diggers mad with greed] [late 19C] mad.

klonkie *n.* [Afk. *klein-jong*, servant-boy] [1950s+] (*S.Afr.*) a young black boy.

kloof *n.* [1910s] (*US*) a fool.

klookhead *n. see* KOOK *n.*

kluck *n. see* CLUCK *n.*[1] (1).

klucker *n.* (*also* **kluck, kluxer, ku klucker**) [late 19C+] (*US black*) a member of the racist Ku Klux Klan.

kludge *n.* (*also* **clooge, kluge**) [computer jargon; note Ger. *kluge*, smart, witty. Coined by J.W. Granholm (*Datamation*, n.d.) and defined by him as 'an ill-assorted collection of poorly matching parts, forming a distressing whole'] [1960s+] anything thrown together more by luck than judgement and with little style or sophistication.

klunker *n. see* CLUNKER *n.*[1].

klunk out *v.* [var. on CONK (OUT) *v.*] [1970s+] (*US*) **1** to break down. **2** to faint or fall down.

klutz *n.* (*also* **clutz**) [synon. Yid.; ult. Ger. *klotz*, a log, a lump of wood] [1950s+] (*orig. US*) a stupid, clumsy, socially inept person.

klutz *v.* [KLUTZ *n.*] [1970s+] (*orig. US*) to bungle or botch.

klutzy *adj.* [KLUTZ *n.*] [1960s+] (*orig. US*) clumsy, inept.

kluxer *n. see* KLUCKER *n.*

k.m. *n.* [abbr. *KITCHEN MECHANIC under* KITCHEN *n.*[1]] [late 19C–1940s] (*US*) a chef or washer-up.

k.m.a.! *excl.* [abbr. KISS MY ARSE! *excl.*] [late 19C–1920s] (*US*) a general statement of contempt or dismissal.

knab *v. see* NAB *v.*[1] (2).

knabs *n. see* NABS *n.*

knack *n.* [SE *knack*, a trinket] **1** [17C] the vagina. **2** [19C] the penis.

knack *adj.* [? NAFF *adj.*[1] + WACK *adj.* (1)] [2000s] (*US campus*) horrible, undesirable.

knacked *adj.* [abbr. KNACKERED *adj.*] [1980s+] exhausted, utterly tired-out.

knacker *n.* [SE *knacker*, a horse-slaughterer] **1** [mid–late 19C] a worn-out horse, fit only for slaughter. **2** [late 19C] by ext. a worn-out, useless person. **3** [1960s] (*Aus.*) a A$2 bill. **4** [1990s+] (*UK juv.*) a general insult aimed at a person. **5** [1990s+] (*UK juv.*) a thief.

knacker *v.* [KNACKERS *n.*/KNACKER *n.* (1)] **1** [mid-19C+] (*Aus.*) to castrate. **2** [late 19C+] to kill, to ruin. **3** [late 19C+] to tire.

knacker drinking *n.* [Irish *knacker*, a tinker] [1990s+] (*Irish*) drinking alcohol in the open air.

knackered *adj.* [KNACKER *v.*] **1** [1930s+] worn-out, exhausted; also fig. use. **2** [1940s] of a person, dead. **3** [1950s+] of machinery, objects, broken, irreparable. **4** [1950s+] stopped from doing what one wishes, thwarted. **5** [1990s+] drunk.

knackering *adj.* [KNACKER *v.*] [1950s+] exhausting, debilitating.

knackers *n.* (*also* **knacks**) [dial.] [mid-19C+] the testicles.

IN PHRASES

❑ **off one's knackers** [2000s] insane, stupid.

IN EXCLAMATIONS

❑ **my knackers!** [var. on *MY BALLS! under* BALLS! *excl.*] [1940s] a general term of derision.

knackers! *excl.* [1930s+] a general excl. of derision or dismissal.

knackety/knacky *adj. see* NAUKY *adj.*

knacks *n. see* KNACKERS *n.*

knap *v.* [var. on NAP *v.*[1] (2)] **1** [late 17C–early 18C] (*UK gambling*) to use sleight-of-hand to cheat in dice-play. **2** [mid-18C] (*UK Und.*) to swear, to take an oath. **3** [mid-18C] to arrest. **4** [late 18C–19C] (*UK Und.*) to steal, to take, to receive; thus *knap a clout*, to steal a handkerchief, *knap seven penn'orth*, to receive a 7-year sentence, *knap/nap the glim, glue*, to catch venereal disease, *knap the swag*, to grab the plunder.

IN PHRASES

❑ **knap a jacob from a danna-drag** *v.* [JACOB *n.*[1] (2) + DANNA *n.* + DRAG *n.*[1] (1)] [early 19C] (*UK Und.*) to steal the ladder from a nightsoil cart in order to use it for burglaries. ❑ **knap it** *v. see NAP IT under* NAP *v.*[1]. ❑ **knap the ding** *v.* [DING *n.*[1]] [early–mid-19C] (*UK Und.*) to take or steal what has already been stolen. ❑ **knap the rust** *v.* [SE *rusty*, of horses, refractory] [19C] to lose one's temper. ❑ **knap the stoop** *v.* (*also* **nab the stoop, nap...**) [SE *stoop*, the position into which the prisoner is forced] [late 18C–mid-19C] to be placed in the pillory.

knap of the case, the *n.* [? SE *knap*, the crest or summit of a hill, but *OED*, which includes it as a derivative, notes 'doubtfully placed here' + CASE *n.*[3] (1)] [mid-16C] (*UK Und.*) the head of the house.

knapped *adj.* [fig. use of KNAP *v.*] [early–mid-19C] (*UK Und.*) pregnant.

knapper *n.*[1] (*also* **knepper**) [dial.] [mid-18C–mid-19C] the knee.

knapper *n.*[2] *see* NAPPER *n.*[1] (1).

knapper *n.*[3] *see* NAPPER *n.*[2] (2).

knapper's poll *n.* [NAP *n.*[2] (1)+ SE *poll*, the head] [18C–early 19C] (*UK Und.*) a sheep's head.

knapping-jigger *n.* (*also* **napping jigger**) [KNAP *v.* (4) + JIGGER *n.*[1] (1)] [mid-19C] (*UK Und.*) a turnpike gate; thus *dub at the knapping-jigger*, to pay at the turnpike gate.

knark *n.* [var. on NARK *n.*] **1** [mid-19C] 'a hard-hearted or savage person' (Hotten 1859). **2** [mid-19C+] a police informer.

knave in grain *n.* [SE *knave* + (*shining*) *grain*, cochineal; note Grose (1785): 'a phrase borrowed from the dyehouse, where certain colours are said to be in grain, to denote their superiority, as being dyed with cochineal, called grain'] [late 17C–early 19C] a first-rate rogue.

knave's grease *n.* [late 16C–early 17C] a flogging.

knawky *adj. see* NAUKY *adj.*

knee *n.* [KNEE *v.*] [1950s+] often constr. with *the*, an attack with one's knee, as used to hit an opponent in the testicles.

SE in slang uses

IN COMPOUNDS

❑ **knee-biter** *n. see ANKLE-BITER under* ANKLE *n.* ❑ **knee-creeper** *n.* [1960s] (*Scot.*) a voyeur who taunts amorous couples in the outdoors. ❑ **knee drill** *n.* [esp. the prayers one needed to offer when claiming free food, drink and lodging from the Salvation Army] [late 19C–1920s] insincere praying, presumably on one's knees. ❑ **knee-knockers** *n.* (*also* **kneebangers**) [1960s+] (*US*) knickerbockers or men's knee-length shorts. ❑ **knee pad** *v.* [1950s] (*US black*) to beg. ❑ **knee-slapper** *n.* [such a joke makes the listener slap their knee with delight] [1960s+] (*US*) an uproarious joke, often used ironically. ❑ **knee-trembler** *n.* (*also* **knee-tremble, knee-wobbler**) ['A standing sexual embrace: low coll.: from ca. 1850; in C.20 predominant meaning is 'copulation in a standing position' (*DSUE*)] [20C+] sexual intercourse when both partners are standing up, popular with cheap prostitutes or with couples who have nowhere to lie down; thus *do a knee-trembler*, to have intercourse standing up; also in fig. use. ❑ **knee-walking** *adj.* (*also* **knee-knocking drunk, knee-walking drunk**) [1960s+] (*US*) very drunk, often preceded by *falling-down*; also of drugs.

knee *v.* [1920s+] to hit someone in the testicles with one's knee.

kneecap *v.* **1** [1970s+] to exact an extra-legal 'punishment' esp. beloved of, and poss. introduced by, the IRA, whereby victims are shot through the kneecaps and, while painfully crippled, are not actually killed. **2** [1970s+] to break someone's kneecaps with a stick or similar weapon. **3** [1980s+] in fig. use, to destroy someone's career.

DERIVATIVES

❑ **kneecapping** *n.* [1990s+] the act of shooting through the kneecaps.

kneel at the altar *v.* [1920s+] (*US gay/prison*) **1** to fellate. **2** to sodomize.

kneesies *n.* (*also* **kneesie**) [1950s+] (*US*) amorous knee contact, usu. covertly under a table; also in fig. use.

knepper *n. see* KNAPPER *n.*[1].

knickers *n.* [abbr. SE *knickerbockers*; spec. the *knickbocker* suits once worn by convicts] [1930s+] (*US prison*) a life sentence or penal servitude.

IN COMPOUNDS

❑ **knickers and stockings** *n.* [1930s] a term of imprisonment. ❑ **knickers bandit** *n.* [1960s+] **1** one who steals from washing lines. **2** a general term for a small-time petty criminal.

IN PHRASES

❑ **get the knickers** *v.* [1930s+] **1** (*US prison*) to get a life sentence. **2** (*UK prison*) to get penal servitude.

SE in slang uses

IN PHRASES

❑ **act as if one's knickers were on fire** *v.* [1960s+] to panic to behave hysterically. ❑ **bore the knickers off** *v. see BORE THE PANTS OFF under* PANTS *n.* ❑ **come home with your knickers torn and say you found the money** *v.* [20C+] a phr. used to indicate the speaker's inability to believe an extremely unlikely story. ❑ **get into someone's knickers** *v. see GET INTO SOMEONE'S PANTS under* PANTS *n.* ❑ **get one's knickers in a twist** *v.* (*also* **get one's tits in a twist, get one's panties in a bunch, ...up one's crack, get one's underwear in a twist**) [1960s+] **1** to become excessively agitated over a problem or situation, to worry to extremes; thus *don't get your knickers in a twist*, stop getting so worried; *knicker-twisting*, agonizingly worrying; thus used with other garments. **2** to make a mistake to be under a misapprehension, to 'get the wrong end of the stick'. ❑ **I'd eat my chips out of her knickers** [var. on *I COULD USE HER SHIT FOR TOOTHPASTE under* SHIT *n.*] [1970s+] a statement of absolute (sexual) devotion. ❑ **shut one's knickers** *v.* [1960s] to be quiet, to stop talking, esp. as imper. ❑ **wet one's knickers** *v. see WET ONE'S PANTS under* PANTS *n.*

IN EXCLAMATIONS

❑ **keep your knickers on!** *see KEEP YOUR PANTS ON! under* PANTS *n.*

knickers! *excl.* (*also* **knickers to you!**) [? euph. for KNACKERS *n.* or use of *knickers* as a juv. 'obscenity'] [1970s+] a general excl. meaning rubbish!, you must be joking! etc; general negation of the preceding speaker's opinion, demand etc.

knick-knack *n.* [SE *knick-knack*, a pleasing or curious trifle] **1** [late 17C; late 19C] the penis. **2** [late 19C] the vagina. **3** [1970s] (*gay*) a small penis. **4** *see* NICK-NACK *n.* (5).

knick-knacker *n.* [SE *knick-knack*, one whose mind is limited by their obsession with trivia] [1960s–70s] (*US*) a fussy, officious person.

knicks *n.* [abbr.] **1** [late 19C+] *knick*erbockers. **2** [1910s+] *knickers*. **3** [1990s+] (*Irish*) (*also* **nicks**) sports shorts.

knife *n.*

SE in slang uses

IN COMPOUNDS

❑ **knife-thrower** *n.* [the laying of tables] [1900s] (*US*) a waiter or waitress.

IN PHRASES

❑ **knife up** *v.* [1980s] (*Aus.*) to share. ❑ **like a knife** *adv.* [mid-19C; 1910s] (*US*) very quickly.

IN EXCLAMATIONS

❑ **knife it!** [i.e. cut it short] [early–mid 19C; 1960s] stop!, don't go on!

knife *v.* [late 19C+] (*US*) to attack, either verbally or in print, in an underhand manner; thus n. *knifing*.

knife and fork *n.* [rhy. sl.] [20C+] pork.

knife and pork *v.* [rhy. sl.] [1980s] (*Aus.*) to walk.

knifer *n.* [late 19C–1920s] a fraud and cadger.

kniff-knaff *n.* [? link to Scot. *kniff*, lively, alert] [late 17C] a joke, a jest.

knight *n.* **1** [16C+] an all-purpose appellation, linked to a variety of occupations; see KNIGHT OF THE... *n.* **2** [late 18C–mid-19C] (*UK Und.*) 'a poor silly fellow' (*Sinks of London*, 1848).

knight and barrow pig *n.* [i.e one who poses as a knight, but is more of a barrow-pig, i.e. a (castrated) pig; note phr. *more hog than gentleman*] [late 18C–early 19C] someone with ideas above their station.

knight of Hornsey *n.* [HORNS *n.*] [mid-17C–early 19C] a cuckold.

knight of St Nicholas *n.* [late 16C–early 19C] a wandering criminal beggar; thus a highwayman.

knight of the... *n.* (*also* **burgess of the...**) [16C+] 'Various jocular (formerly often slang) phrases denoting one who is a member of a certain trade or profession, has a certain occupation or character etc. In the majority of these the distinctive word is the name of some tool or article commonly used by or associated with the person designated, and the number of such phrases may be indefinitely increased.' (*OED*) While the earlier (16C–18C) terms definitely have this occupational basis, the later (19C) ones tend to use the occupation in more of an ironic or joking sense.

IN PHRASES

❑ **...the awl** [mid-19C] a cobbler. ❑ **...the blade** *see* separate entry. ❑ **...the brogan** [BROGAN *n.*] [late 19C] (*US*) a tramp. ❑ **...the brush** **1** [late 18C] a chimney sweep. **2** [late 19C] an artist. ❑ **...the brush and moon** [? SE *brush* that was once used as the sign of a tavern; or a real or generic public house name] [mid-19C] a drunkard. ❑ **...the cleaver** [late 18C–19C] a butcher. ❑ **...the collar** [mid-16C–mid-17C] one who has been hanged. ❑ **...the cross** [mid-19C] (*UK Und.*) a professional criminal. ❑ **...the cue** [late 18C–19C] a billiard-player; a billiard marker. ❑ **...the elbow** [late 17C–mid-18C] a card-sharp, a cheating gambler. ❑ **...the forked order** (*also* **knight of the order of the fork**) **1** [late 16C–17C] a cuckold. **2** [mid-17C–mid-18C] one whose job involves digging with a fork. ❑ **...the golden grummet** [naut. jargon *grummet* = rope ring + *gold* = excrement] [1930s+] (*US Und.*) one who enjoys anal intercourse. ❑ **...the grammar** [late 17C–mid-18C] a teacher. ❑ **...the green cloth** [the green baize of card tables] [late 19C–1920s] (*orig. US*) a gambler. ❑ **...the gusset** *see* BROTHER OF THE GUSSET *under* BROTHER (OF THE)... *n.* ❑ **...the halter** [16C] one doomed to be hanged. ❑ **...the hod** [early–mid-19C] a bricklayer; a bricklayer's labourer. ❑ **...(the) industry** [he 'works' his victims] [mid-17th–19C] a cheating gambler. ❑ **...the Iron Chain** [late 19C] a prisoner in irons who is being transported. ❑ **...the jemmy** (*also* **knight of the jimmy**) [late 19C–1920s] (*UK/US Und.*) a burglar. ❑ **...the knife** [17C] a cutpurse. ❑ **...the lapstone** [mid–late 19C] a cobbler. ❑ **...the napkin** [mid-18C–late 19C] a waiter. ❑ **...the needle** [late 18C–1900s] a tailor. ❑ **...the pad** (*also* **knight of the rumpad**) [PAD *n.*[1] (1)] [mid-17C–mid-19C] a highwayman. ❑ **...the pen** [mid–late 19C] **1** a clerk. **2** a writer. ❑ **...the pencil** [late 19C–1920s] a bookmaker. ❑ **...the pestle** [despite current lack of citations, sense 2 prob. came first] **1** [17C] (*also* **knight of the burning pestle**) someone with a venereal disease, a term of abuse. **2** [mid-17C–19C] an apothecary, esp. one who prescribes for venereal diseases. ❑ **...the petticoat** [late 19C–1900s] a man employed as 'muscle' by a brothel. ❑ **...the pigskin** [late 19C] a jockey. ❑ **...the pisspot** [late 19C] a doctor, an apothecary. ❑ **...the pit** [late 19C] a fan of cock-fighting. ❑ **...the post** *see* separate entry. ❑ **...the quill** [late 17C] an author. ❑ **...the rainbow** [the colours of the uniform, which would represent those of the person served] [late 18C–mid-19C] a footman, a waiter. ❑ **...the road** *see* separate entry. ❑ **...the rumpad** *see* ...THE PAD above. ❑ **...the shears** (*also* **knight of the sheers**) [late 18C–late 19C] a tailor. ❑ **...the spigot** [early 19C] a publican, an inn-keeper. ❑ **...the spout** [SPOUT *n.*[2] (1)] [early 19C] a pawnbroker. ❑ **...the standard** [late 19C] a racecourse bookmaker. ❑ **...the thimble** [late 18C–late 19C] a tailor. ❑ **...the trencher** [late 18C–early 19C] a great eater. ❑ **...the vapour** [17C] a smoker; also known, by the coiner John Taylor the Water Poet (*c.*1578–1653), as *gentlemen of the whiffe, esquires of the pipe*. ❑ **...the wheel** [late 19C] a cyclist. ❑ **...the whip** [late 18C–19C] a coachman. ❑ **...the yardstick** [late 19C] (*Aus.*) a draper, a haberdasher.

knight of the blade *n.* **1** [late 17C–early 19C] (*also* **bully of the blade**) a bully, a thug. **2** [late 18C–mid-19C] a wandering villain, posing as a soldier and living on his wits. **3** [late 19C] (*Aus.*) (*also* **knight of the blades, ...bright blade, ...shining sword, ...sword**) a shearer.

knight of the post *n.* (*also* **post-knight**) [prob. meaning a whipping-post or pillory; despite entry in *Sinks of London* etc. Partridge suggests it was SE by 19C; OED has it SE from its 16C coinage] [late 16C–mid-19C] (*UK Und.*) a notorious perjurer, one who earns a living by giving false evidence.

knight of the road *n.* **1** [mid-17C–1900s] a highwayman. **2** [late 19C] (*Aus.*) a bushranger. **3** [late 19C+] a commercial traveller. **4** [late 19C+] (*mainly Aus.*) a tramp. **5** [1930s] someone on a walking or cycling holiday. **6** [1970s] a truck-driver.

K-9 *n.* [pron. of SE *canine*] (*US prison*) **1** [1980s+] a dog. **2** [2000s] a corrections officer.

knish *n.* [Yid. *knish*, 'a dumpling of flaky dough filled with chopped liver, potato, or cheese, and baked or fried' (OED); ult. Rus. *knish*, a type of cake] **1** [1930s+] (*US*) the vagina. **2** [1940s+] (*US gay*) the anus. **3** [1960s] a typical housewife on a gambling spree.

knits *n.* [1960s–70s] (*US black*) knitwear, esp. garments expensively imported from Italy.

knit the knot *v. see* TIE THE KNOT *under* TIE *v.*

knitting *n.* [the 'feminine' occupation] **1** [1930–40s] girls or women considered collectively. **2** [2000s] (*S.Afr. gay*) male homosexual sexual intercourse [plays on NEEDLE *n.*].

knitting needle *n.* [1960s–70s] the penis; thus *knit*, to masturbate.

knitty *adj. see* NITTY *adj.*

knitty-gritty *n. see* NITTY-GRITTY *n.*

knob *n.* **1** representative of body parts. (**a**) [18C+] the head. (**b**) [late 19C+] (*also* **cock-knob**) the head of the penis. (**c**) [1910s+] the penis. (**d**) [1930s+] (*also* **knobbies**) a female breast, usu. in pl. as *knobs*. (**e**) [1930s+] (*US*) spec. a woman's nipple, usu. in pl. as *knobs*. (**f**) [1940s+] (*US black*) the knee, usu. in pl. as *knobs*. (**g**) [1950s+] (*US teen*) in fig. use of sense 1c, a general term of abuse. **2** in gambling use. (**a**) [mid–late 19C] a swindling fairground game, also called 'under and over'. (**b**) [1920s–40s] (*Aus./N.Z.*) a double-headed penny, esp. as used in the game of two-up, produced by filing down standard coins and welding them together. **3** [1930s–60s] (*US black*) in pl., stylish, up-to-date shoes with shined toecaps [? the shape of the toecap]. **4** [1960s] a blow.

IN COMPOUNDS

❑ **knob artist** *n.* (*also* **nob artist**) [-ARTIST *sfx*] [1990s+] a male homosexual. ❑ **knob-cheese** *n. see* COCK CHEESE *under* COCK *n.*[3]. ❑ **knob-end** *n.* [SE *end*; lit. the glans penis] [1990s+] a general derog. term. ❑ **knob-gobbling** *n.* [GOBBLE *v.*[1] (2)] [1960s+] fellatio; thus *knob-gobbler*, a fellatrix or fellator.

❑ **knobhead** *n. see* separate entry. ❑ **knob-job** *n.* [JOB *n.*[2] (2)] [1960s+] (*orig. US*) fellatio. ❑ **knob-jockey** *n.* [JOCKEY *n.*[2] (1)] [1990s+] a general insult, implying that the male subject is a masturbator or a homosexual. ❑ **knobknot** *n. see* KNOBHEAD *n.* ❑ **knob polisher** *n.* [1960s+] a young male prostitute; thus *knob polish*, to masturbate. ❑ **knob shiner** *n.* [1990s+] **1** a masturbator. **2** a general term of abuse. ❑ **knob snot** *n.* [SNOT *n.*[1] (5)] [1990s+] semen. ❑ **knobstick** *n. see* separate entry. ❑ **knob yoghurt** *n. see* COCK CHEESE *under* COCK *n.*[3].

IN PHRASES

❑ **carve someone's knob** *v.* [1950s] (*US black*) to explain, to make understand. ❑ **do the knob** *v.* [1950s] to take notice. ❑ **get a knob** *v.* [1950s–60s] (*orig. milit.*) to catch a venereal disease. ❑ **gob the knob** *v.* [1990s+] (*US*) to perform fellatio. ❑ **go where the big knobs hang out** *v.* [play on KNOB *n.* (1b)/ NOB *n.*[2] (1)] [1960s–70s] (*Aus.*) to urinate. ❑ **lose one's knob** *v.* [1910s] (*Aus.*) to go mad, to break down. ❑ **polish the knob** *v.* [1970s+] (*US gay*) to fellate. ❑ **slob a knob** *v.* [1940s+] (*US*) to perform fellatio. ❑ **with knobs on** (*also* **with nobs on**) [i.e. with 'extras'] [1920s+] embellished, with 'add-ons', decorations; for certain.

IN EXCLAMATIONS

❑ **with knobs on!** [1930s+] (*usu. juv.*) an excl. retort meaning the same to you and more so!

SE in slang uses

IN COMPOUNDS

❑ **knob-knocker** *n.* [1920s] (*US tramp*) a safe cracker. ❑ **knob-twister** *n.* [the knobs on the betting board] [1980s] (*Aus.*) a bookmaker.

IN PHRASES

❑ **on the knob** *see* ON THE KNOCKER *under* KNOCKER *n.*[1].

knob *v.*[1] [KNOB *n.*] **1** [early 19C–1950s] (*also* **do the knob**) to hit in the face or head. **2** [1990s+] usu. of a man, to have sexual intercourse.

IN EXCLAMATIONS

❑ **knob it!** [sense 2 above, as synon. for FUCK IT! *excl.*] [1990s+] a general phr. of dismisssal.

knob *v.*[2] *see* NOB *v.* (2).

knobber *n.* [KNOB *n.*] **1** [1970s+] (*US*) a male homosexual transvestite prostitute. **2** [1980s+] (*US campus*) fellatio. **3** [1990s+] (*US*) a stupid, obnoxious person. **4** [1990s+] (*US*) the penis; usu. in phr. below.

IN PHRASES

❑ **put some slobber on the knobber** *v.* [1990s+] (*US*) to perform oral sex.

knobbies *n. see* KNOB *n.* (1d).

knobbing *n.* [KNOB *v.*[1] (2)] [1990s+] an act of sexual intercourse.

knobbly-knee *n.* [rhy. sl.] [20C+] a key.

knobby *adj. see* NOBBY *adj.*

knobhead *n.* (*also* **knobknot**) [KNOB *n.* (1) + -HEAD *sfx* (1)/SE *knot*] [1930s+] (*orig. US*) a stupid person.

knobkierie *n.* [2000s] (*S.Afr.*) a penis.

knobs *n. see* KNOB *n.*

knobstick *n.* (*also* **nobstick**) [SE *knobstick*, a club with a rounded head, used by strike-breakers as a weapon] [mid-19C–1920s] a strike-breaker.

knob-thatcher *n. see* NOB-THATCHER *under* NOB *n.*[1].

knock *n.*[1] **1** in sexual contexts. (**a**) [mid-16C–18C; 20C+] sexual intercourse. (**b**) [18C+] the penis. (**c**) [20C+] a prostitute or promiscuous woman; *on the knock*, working as a prostitute. (**d**) [1910s] (*Aus.*) a girlfriend. **2** [late 19C+] in fig. uses. (**a**) a negative opinion, a criticism, an insult. (**b**) (*also* **knockout**) a setback. **3** in (*US prison*) use. (**a**) [1910s] a prison sentence. (**b**) [1990s+] the crime with which one has been charged; the crime one has committed.

IN COMPOUNDS

❑ **knock shop** *n. see* KNOCKING-SHOP *n.*

IN PHRASES

❑ **call the knock** *v.* [SE *knock on the door*] [2000s] to track down, apprehend and arrest. ❑ **do a knock with** *v.* (*Aus.* **1** [1920s+] to arrange a meeting with someone of the opposite sex. **2** [1930s+] to have sexual intercourse; to kiss and cuddle ❑ **give the knock to** *v.* [late 19C] to knock down. ❑ **go the knock on** *v.* [1910s+] (*Aus.*) to steal. ❑ **on the knock** *see* ON THE KNOCKER *under* KNOCKER *n.*[1]. ❑ **put in the knock** *v.* [1910s (*US*) to reject, to refuse. ❑ **put the knock on** *v.* (*also* **put the knocks in**) [late 19C+] to disparage, to criticize. ❑ **take the knock** *v.* **1** [late 19C+] (*orig. US*) to accept the blame. **2** [late 19C+] to suffer an unpleasant surprise. **3** [late 19C+] to suffe financial losses, often in gambling. **4** [1900s–1910s] of a bookmaker, to be defrauded. **5** [1920s+] of a bookmaker, to defraud a bettor. **6** [2000s] to be overcome by drink or drugs.

knock *n.*[2] *see* POSTMAN'S KNOCK *n.*

knock *v.* **1** in senses of lit. or fig. aggression. (**a**) [late 16C+] to have sexual intercourse. (**b**) [mid-18C+] (*UK Und.*) to rob, to steal; thus (late 18C) *knock the lobb*, breaking and entering **2** [mid-19C–1900s] to excel, to surpass [subseq. uses of are SE] (**a**) [mid-19C+] (*US/Aus.*) to kill, to shoot dead, later usage in phr. *knock yourself*, to commit suicide. (**b**) [mid-19C+] to destroy, to defeat. (**c**) [1910s+] to cheat, to defraud, esp. to obtain credit which one has no intention of honouring (**d**) [1920s+] to hit. (**e**) [1940s+] (*US*) to arrest. **3** in senses of lit. or fig. communication. (**a**) [early 17C; mid-19C+] (*also* **give the knock**) (*orig. US*) to disparage, to criticize. (**b**) [late 19C+ (*US*) to complain, to inform on, to betray. (**c**) [late 19C+] (*US*) to explain; esp. to explain to a confidence trickster's victim that he is being swindled. (**d**) [1920s+] (*Aus.*) to flirt with a woman. (**e** [1940s] (*US black*) to speak. (**f**) [1940s–70s] (*US black*) to borrow; to ask for. (**g**) [1960s] (*US black*) to write. **4** in fig senses, to arouse the emotions. (**a**) [early 18C+] to strike with astonishment, alarm or confusion, to confound. (**b**) [mid 19C+] to impress highly, to elicit great admiration, to make big impression, esp. of new fashions, entertainments. **5** [lat 19C+] (*US black*) to give, to do, to perform. **6** [1920s–50s] (*U black*) to consume. **7** [1910s–20s] (*Aus.*) to give in; to b exhausted [abbr. SE knock under]. **8** [1940s–70s] (*US*) to earn.

IN PHRASES

meaning to defeat or beat, or to astound

❑ **knock acock** *v.* [note SE *acock*, defiantly] [19C] to amaze, to shock, to 'knock sideways'. ❑ **knock all to rags** *v.* [late 19C (*US*) to knock senseless. ❑ **knock cats out of** *v.* [1900s] (*Aus.*) to berate. ❑ **knock cold** *v.* (*also* **knock cold as a monkey-wrench knock dead**) **1** [mid-19C] (*also* **kill dead**) to astound, to amaze **2** [20C+] to complete or dispose of something easily or quickly ❑ **knock cuckoo** *v. see under* CUCKOO *adj.* ❑ **knock endways** *v.* (*also* **knock sky-wise and crooked**) [mid-19C–1930s] to astound, to astonish, to shock profoundly, to overturn. ❑ **knock flat** *v. see* KNOCK OUT *v.* (2f). ❑ **knock for a Burton** *v.* [1940s+ to destroy. ❑ **knock for a loop** *v.* (*also* **knock for a dingdong, ...goal, ...ghoul, ...home run, ...trip, ...the loop**) [one is fi knocked 'head-over-heels'] [1920s+] to astound, to astonish, to devastate; also *THROW FOR A LOOP under* LOOP *n.*[2]. ❑ **knock for a row of...** *v.* (*also* **...ashcans, ...flat tires, ...latrines ...Mongolian whipped cream containers, ...silos, ...sou apple trees, ...stumps, ...totem poles**) [1910s+] (*US/N.Z* **1** to hit or knock someone senseless. **2** to impress or amaze. ❑ **knock hell out of** *v. see under* HELL *n.* ❑ **knoc rotten** *v.* [1910s+] (*Aus.*) to kill, to stun. ❑ **knock saucepan out of** *v.* (*also* **knock smoke out of**) (*Aus.*) **1** [late 19C–1900s] to attack aggressively. **2** [1950s] to overcome completel ❑ **knock seven bells out of** *v. see under* BELL *n.*[1]. ❑ **knoc shingles in** *v.* (*also* **knock the roof in**) [the similarity of the nois [1960s+] (*US*) to snore. ❑ **knock sky-wise and crooked** *se* KNOCK ENDWAYS above. ❑ **knock slops off** *v.* [1900s] (*Aus.*) to beat thoroughly. ❑ **knock someone bandy** *v.* [late 19C+] to astound, to stun with a blow. ❑ **knock someone's block off** *see under* BLOCK *n.*[1]. ❑ **knock someone's dick in the dirt** *see KEEP SOMEONE'S DICK IN THE DIRT under* DICK *n.*[1]. ❑ **knoc someone's eye out** *v. see under* EYE *n.* ❑ **knock someone's hat off** *v. see under* HAT *n.* ❑ **knock someone sick** *v. see und*

SICK *adj.*[1]. ❑ **knock stiff** *v. see under* STIFF *adj.*[1]. ❑ **knock the corners off** *v.* (*N.Z.*) **1** [20C+] to punish violently. **2** [2000s] to civilize someone. ❑ **knock the crap out of** *v. see under* CRAP *n.*[1]. ❑ **knock the dick off** *v. see under* DICK *n.*[1]. ❑ **knock the ears off** *v. see under* EARS *n.* ❑ **knock the hindsights off** *v.* (*also* **knock the hindsights out of**) [? SE *hindsight*, the backsight of a rifle] [19C] (*US*) to deal a heavy blow to, to beat up, to defeat. ❑ **knock the jive out of** *v. see under* JIVE *n.*[1]. ❑ **knock the (living) daylights out of** *v. see under* DAYLIGHTS *n.* ❑ **knock the piss out of** *v. see under* PISS *n.* ❑ **knock the shit out of** *v. see under* SHIT *n.* ❑ **knock the socks off** *v.* (*orig. US*) **1** [mid-19C+] to defeat comprehensively. **2** [1930s+] to cause serious problems for, to defeat fig.; to have an intense effect upon. **3** [1960s+] (*also* **blow the socks off, steam the socks off**) to astound. ❑ **knock the stuffing out of** *v. see under* STUFFING *n.*[1]. ❑ **knock the tar out of** *v. see under* TAR *n.*[3]. ❑ **knock the wool out of one's head** *v. see under* WOOL *n.*[1].

general uses

❑ **get knocked** *v.* [1930s+] (*Aus.*) **1** to suffer a setback, a disappointment or defeat. **2** to be killed. ❑ **knock a drill** *v.* [1940s] (*US black*) to leave, to walk. ❑ **knock a nod** *v. see under* NOD *n.*[1]. ❑ **knock a piece** *v. see* KNOCK (OFF) A PIECE *under* PIECE *n.* ❑ **knock a scarf** *v. see under* SCARF *n.* ❑ **knock a statue act** *v.* [1940s–60s] (*orig. US black*) to wait. [1940s] (*US black*) to (take a) walk. ❑ **knock a trot** *v.* [1940s] (*US black*) to escape, run away. ❑ **knock fowl soup** *v.* [1950s] (*US black*) to die. ❑ **knock it down on the box** *v.* (*also* **knock it out of the box**) [KNOCK *v.* + BOX *n.*[1]] [2000s] (*US black*) to have sexual intercourse. ❑ **knock like a ten-ton lorry** *v.* [2000s] of a woman, to copulate enthusiastically. ❑ **knock the back out of** *v. see under* BACK *n.*[1]. ❑ **knock the bottom out of** *v.* [1980s] to have sexual intercourse.

SE in slang uses

(IN COMPOUNDS)

❑ **knock-drops** *n. see* KNOCKOUT DROPS *n.* ❑ **knock-round** *n.* [KNOCKABOUT *n.*] [late 19C] a wander, an aimless progress. ❑ **knock-softly** *n.* [late 19C] a foolish weak person.

(IN PHRASES)

❑ **knock about the bub** *v. see under* BUB *n.*[1]. ❑ **knock across** *v.* (*also* **knock against**) [late 19C–1920s] to encounter, to meet. ❑ **knock a drill** *v.* [1940s] (*US black*) to leave, to walk. ❑ **knock a line with** *v. see* DO A LINE (WITH) *under* LINE *n.*[1]. ❑ **knock along** *v.* [late 19C+] **1** (*orig. Aus.*) to idle, to wander. **2** to travel around rather than settle down. **3** to manage, to subsist. ❑ **knock anthony** *v. see* CUFF ANTHONY *under* CUFF *v.*[1]. ❑ **knock a slice off** *v.* see CUT A SLICE (OFF THE JOINT) *under* SLICE *n.* ❑ **knock at the door** *v.* [? to regain admission to sobriety] [1930s–70s] (*US drugs*) to withdraw from narcotics use. ❑ **knock boots with** *v. see under* BOOTY *n.*[2]. ❑ **knock dog** *v.* [the image of lying around like a dog] [20C+] (*W.I.*) to idle, to do nothing. ❑ **knock dust** *v.* [1970s] (*US prison*) to knock down, to beat up. ❑ **knock flat** *v. see* KNOCK OUT *v.* (2f). ❑ **knock fowl soup** *v.* [1950s] (*US black*) to die. ❑ **knock her dead one on the nose each and every double trey** *v.* [1940s] (*US black*) to get a pay cheque every sixth day (or the sixth day of every week?). ❑ **knocking it back with a stick** [1940s+] (*Aus.*) a phr. used by a man who wishes to boast of the success of his sex life; usu. in answer to a question, e.g. GETTING ANY (LATELY)? *under* GET *v.* ❑ **knock it down** *v.* [late 19C–1900s] to signify one's approval by hammering on the table or stamping on the floor. ❑ **knock it on the head** *v.* (*also* **knock it in the head**) [? the final blow of a hammer that drives in a nail; McGill, *Reed Dict. of N.Z. Sl.* (2003): 'from killing a snake'] [early 19C+] to stop doing something, to finish a task; to bring something to an end. ❑ **knock one's can in** *v.* (*also* **knock one's arse in, ...end in**) [1910s+] (*Aus.*) to surprise, to worry, to confound. ❑ **knock one's nuts out** *v. see under* NUTS *n.*[2]. ❑ **knock one's pipes out** *v. see under* PIPES *n.*[1]. ❑ **knock one's wig** *v. see under* WIG *n.*[2]. ❑ **knock on together** *v.* (*also* **knock on with**) [1950s+] to have an affair. ❑ **knock shingles in** *v.* (*also* **knock the roof in**) [the similarity of the noise] [1960s+] (*US*) to snore. ❑ **knock some skin** *v. see under* SKIN *n.*[1]. ❑ **knock the dew off the lily** *v. see* SHAKE THE DEW OFF THE LILY *under* LILY *n.* ❑ **knock the drawing-room out of** *v.* (*also* **knock the sitting-room out of**) [2000s] (*N.Z.*) to toughen someone up, e.g. a new immigrant. ❑ **knock the dust off the old sombrero** *v.* [20C+] (*US*) to perform oral sex. ❑ **knock the end in** *v. see under* END *n.* ❑ **knock the pad** *v.* [? SE *pad*, i.e. a bed] [1940s+] (*US black*) to have sexual intercourse.

knocka *n. see* KNOCKER *n.*[3].

knockabout *n.* (*also* **knock-around**) [KNOCK AROUND *v.*] **1** [mid-19C] a drinking spree. **2** [late 19C+] (*Aus.*) a tramp, a vagrant. **3** [late 19C+] (*Aus.*) a layabout, a low criminal or idler. **4** [20C+] (*W.I.*) the lowest type of prostitute. **5** [1910s+] a social 'jack-of all trades', a 'regular chap'. **6** *see* KNOCKABOUT MAN *n.* (1).

knockabout *adj.* [SE *knock about*] [late 19C+] (*orig. theatrical*) noisy, violent, rambunctious.

knock about *v.*[1] **1** [early 19C+] to travel around rather than settle down. **2** [mid-19C+] to exist, to be. **3** [mid-19C+] to idle, to waste time. **4** [late 19C+] to associate with.

knock about *v.*[2] *see* KNOCK BACK *v.* (3).

knockabout hand *n. see* LUMPER *n.*[1] (1a).

knockabout man *n.* (*also* **knockabout joey**) [KNOCKABOUT *n.*] **1** [late 19C–1950s] (*Aus.*) (*also* **knockabout**) an unskilled labourer or handyman on a sheep station. **2** [1930s+] a layabout, an idler. **3** [1930s+] a thief, esp. a pickpocket.

knock-all *n.* [1970s] no, none.

knock-around *n. see* KNOCKABOUT *n.*

knockaround *adj.* [KNOCK AROUND *v.* (1)] [1940s+] (*US*) having worldly or criminal experience.

knock around *v.* (*orig. US*) **1** [mid-19C+] to wander, to travel aimlessly [20C+ use is SE]. **2** [20C+] to associate with.

knock at the door *n. see* KNOCK ON THE DOOR, A *n.*

knockback *n.* [SE *knock back*] **1** [late 19C+] a rejection, a refusal. **2** [1940s+] (*UK prison*) the rejection of one's application for parole.

knock back *v.* **1** [20C+] to cost, e.g. *that'll knock you back a bit*. **2** [1910s+] to fine someone. **3** [1910s+] (*also* **bang back, knock about**) to eat, to drink, esp. to finish off one's drink. **4** [1930s+] (*orig. Aus./N.Z.*) to reject [KNOCKBACK *n.* (1)].

knock-down *n.* **1** in senses of lit. or fig. violence or aggression. (**a**) [mid-17C] something astounding, remarkable, that 'knocks one down'. (**b**) [late 17C–19C] (*also* **knocker-down**) strong ale or liquor. (**c**) [19C+] (*US*) a fight; also in fig. use, an undeniable argument. **2** [mid-19C+] (*Aus./N.Z./US*) an introduction, esp. a formal introduction of a man to a woman in whom he is interested; thus *give one a knock-down*, to give one an introduction. **3** [1930s–60s] (*US*) information. **4** [1950s] (*Aus.*) in financial/commercial uses [? abbr. *knock-down money*]. (**a**) a loan. (**b**) a profit, usu. illicit. (**c**) a discount.

(IN COMPOUNDS)

❑ **knock-down money** *n.* [mid-19C; 1980s+] (*US*) tips or gratuities.

(IN PHRASES)

❑ **take a knock-down** *v.* [1950s] (*US black*) to take note.

knock-down *adj.* [KNOCK-DOWN *n.* (1)] [19C+] violent, whether lit. or fig.

knock down *v.* **1** [mid-18C–mid-19C] to choose, to nominate someone [the chairman at a dinner knocking with a hammer before announcing a speaker]. **2** [early 19C+] (*orig. US*) to drink. **3** [mid-19C+] (*Aus./N.Z.*) to spend all of one's money on a celebration; thus *knock down a cheque, drink out a cheque*, to spend an entire season's pay cheque on a single drinking bout. **4** [mid-19C+] (*US*) (*also* **knock down on**) to embezzle, to steal from a firm's takings. **5** [late 19C+] (*Aus./N.Z.*) to make an introduction; thus *knock one down to*, to introduce, e.g. *knock me down to that daisy*, introduce me to that woman. **6** in context of monetary gain. (**a**) [1920s+] (*US*) to earn or obtain money, usu. for work, or by requesting a loan or gift. (**b**) [1950s] (*US*) to accumulate money, usu. through crime. **7** [1990s+] (*US prison*) to serve a sentence. **8** [2000s] (*US black*) to have sexual intercourse.

knock-down (and) drag-out *n.* [one or more participants are knocked unconscious and dragged outside] [early 19C+] (*orig.

US) also constr. with *brawl*, *fight* etc, a vicious violent fight; thus fig. an acrimonious but non-violent dispute.

knock-down-(and)-drag-out *adj.* (*also* **knock-down-and-drag-off, knock-down-and-pull-out, stomp-down and drag-out**) [KNOCK-DOWN (AND) DRAG-OUT *n.*] [early 19C+] lit. or fig., intense, violent.

knock down and drag out *v.* [KNOCK-DOWN (AND) DRAG-OUT *n.*] [early 19C+] to fight violently.

knock-down-(and)-drag-out *adv.* [KNOCK-DOWN (AND) DRAG-OUT *n.*] [1910s+] in a violent manner.

knock down on *v. see* KNOCK DOWN *v.* (4).

knocked *adj.* [KNOCK *v.* (1)] **1** [1950s+] under control, at one's mercy, e.g. *I've got it knocked.* **2** *see* KNOCKED OUT *adj.* **3** *see* KNOCKED UP *adj.* (5).

IN PHRASES

❑ **have it knocked** *v.* [late 19C+] to have a problem, and esp. life in general, absolutely under control.

knocked down for (a/the) crap *v.* [ironic use of KNOCK DOWN *v.* (1) + CRAP *n.*[2] (1)] [early–mid-19C] condemned to execution by hanging.

knocked off *adj.*[1] [KNOCK OFF *v.* (3a)] [1910s+] stolen.

knocked off *adj.*[2] [KNOCK OFF *v.* (2a)] **1** [1920s+] killed, murdered. **2** beaten; defeated.

knocked out *adj.* [KNOCK OUT *v.* (2a)] **1** [late 19C+] (*US*) bankrupt. **2** [late 19C+] (*also* **knocked**) exhausted. **3** [late 19C+] (*also* **knocked**) overwhelmed. **4** [1920s+] (*US*) heavily intoxicated. **5** [1950s+] (*US*) stylish, excellent.

knocked over *adj.* [late 19C–1930s] dead, very ill.

knocked up *adj.* [KNOCK UP *v.* (2)] **1** [late 18C+] tired, jaded, used up. **2** [late 18C+] bankrupt, impoverished. **3** [late 18C; 1930s] dead. **4** [19C–1930s] (*Irish*) drunk. **5** [mid-19C+] (*orig. US*) (*also* **knocked**) pregnant. **6** [late 19C] (*Aus.*) of an animal, angry. **7** [1930s] emotional, floored by emotion. **8** [1960s] defeated, in a difficult situation.

knocked with a French faggot *phr. see under* BLOW WITH A FRENCH FAGGOT-STICK *n.*

knock-'em-dead *adj.* [*KNOCK COLD under* KNOCK *v.*] [1930s+] astounding, amazing, overwhelming.

knock-'em-down *n.* [its effects] [early 16C] a fiery drink.

knock-'em-downs *n.* (*also* **knock-me-downs**) **1** [early 19C] skittles, esp. as played in a public house. **2** [early 19C] a coconut shy.

knock-'em-stiff *n. see under* STIFF *adj.*[1].

knocker *n.*[1] [KNOCK *v.*] **1** in sexual contexts. (**a**) [17C] a promiscuous man, a whoremonger. (**b**) [mid-17C+] the penis. **2** in pl., as a part of the body. (**a**) [late 19C+] the testicles [they 'knock together' but note KNACKERS *n.*]. (**b**) [1930s+] (*orig. US*) the female breasts; occas. in sing. **3** a physically or socially superior individual. (**a**) [early 17C–19C] an outstandingly attractive person or thing. (**b**) [late 19C+] (*US*) the top person, the person in authority, often in comb., e.g. *HEAD KNOCKER under* HEAD *n.*, *top knocker* [their 'striking' appearance]. **4** a form of hair dressing seen as resembling a door-knocker. (**a**) [early–mid-19C] a form of pendant to a wig, similar to a pigtail. (**b**) [19C] a small curl worn flat on the temples, a fashionable hairstyle at that time [abbr. DOOR-KNOCKER *n.* (2)]. **5** in context of communication. (**a**) [late 19C+] (*US Und.*) an informer or complainant. (**b**) [late 19C+] (*orig. US*) a critic, esp. one who relishes making negative comments. (**c**) [late 19C+] a disappointment. (**d**) [1900s–50s] a criticism; negative comments; also as *the knockers*. **6** [1920s–30s] (*UK tramp*) an arrest. **7** [1920s+] in (*Und.*) use. (**a**) a gambler or prisoner who refuses to pay their debts (which cannot be enforced legally in the UK). (**b**) one who passes bad cheques or gains goods on credit — and fails to pay the bill. **8** *see* KNOCKO *n.*

SE in slang uses

IN COMPOUNDS

❑ **knocker-down** *n. see* KNOCK-DOWN *n.* (1b). ❑ **knocker-face** *n.* (*also* **knocker-head**) [reminiscent of an old-fashioned door knocker] [late 19C–1920s] an ugly face, or the person who 'owns' it. ❑ **knocker-worker** *n.* [20C+] a door-to-door pedlar.

IN PHRASES

❑ **dressed up to the knocker** [19C] dressed in one's best clothes. ❑ **full to the knocker** *adj.* [2000s] (*N.Z.*) completely drunk. ❑ **live up to the knocker** *v.* (*also* **live up to the door**) [mid-19C–1900s] to live up to one's means. ❑ **on the knocker** **1** [mid-19C+] (*UK Und.*) (*also* **on the knock**) touring houses, ostensibly to buy or sell goods, but spec. to trick or bully people into selling heirlooms, antiques etc for minimal prices. **2** [1930s+] (*Aus.*) (*also* **on the knob, on the knuckle**) at once, on demand, esp. of cash payments, exactly. **3** [1940s] working as a door-to-door salesman. ❑ **up to the knocker** [KNOCKER *n.*[1] (3a) or fig. use of SE (*door*) *knocker*] **1** [mid-19C–1910s] capable, up to a task. **2** [mid-19C+] fashionably dressed or over-dressed. **3** [late 19C] in prime condition, enjoying oneself. **4** [late 19C] completely.

knocker *n.*[2] [ety. unknown; ? link to Yid. *naches*, pleasure] [late 19C–1900s] (*Aus.*) common sense.

IN PHRASES

❑ **off one's knocker** *adj.* [1900s] (*Aus.*) mad, insane uncontrolled. ❑ **put the knocker on** *v.* [2000s] (*Aus.*) to call a halt, to forbid.

knocker *n.*[3] (*also* **knocka**) [? KNUCKLEHEAD *n.*] [1990s+] (*US black*) a fool.

knocker and knob *n.* [rhy. sl.] [20C+] a job.

knock-in *n.* [ety. unknown; ? one 'knocks in' or plays one's cards] [mid–late 19C] the game of loo; thus a hand at any card-game

knock in *v.*[1] [the money is 'knocked in' to the coster's pocket] [mid-19C–1900s] (*coster*) to make money.

knock in *v.*[2] [2000s] to beat up.

knocking *n.* [KNOCK *v.*] **1** [late 16C+] sexual intercourse **2** [20C+] negative criticism.

IN COMPOUNDS

❑ **knocking-jacket** *n.* [early 18C–19C] a nightdress.

knocking dog *adj.* [ety. unknown] [20C+] (*W.I.*) plentiful, in abundance, usu. of cheap items on sale at a market.

knocking-off *n. see* KNOCK-OFF *n.*

knockings *n.* **1** [1950s] the residue of one's funds; also fig use as nearly dying [? *KNOCK-DOWN MONEY under* KNOCK-DOWN *n.*]. **2** [1990s+] information, facts [KNOCK-DOWN *n.* (3)].

knocking-shop *n.* (*also* **knocking-crib, knocking-house, knocking-joint, knock shop**) [KNOCK *v.* (1) + SE *shop*/CRIB *n.* (1)/HOUSE *n.*[1] (1)/JOINT *n.* (1)] **1** [mid-19C+] a brothel **2** [1910s] (*Aus.*) an untidy or dirty place.

knock in the cradle *n.* [mid-17C–18C] a fool.

IN PHRASES

❑ **have a knock in the cradle** *v.* [mid-17C] to be stupid.

knock into *v.* **1** [late 19C+] to run into. **2** [1910s+] (*Aus.*) to fight with.

SE in slang uses

IN PHRASES

❑ **knock into a cocked hat** *v.* (*also* **fuck into a cocked hat, knock into a coked hat, ...fits**) [mid-19C+] (*orig. US*) to overturn, destroy or beat thoroughly or completely. ❑ **knock into a mish** *v.* [SE *mishmash*] [mid-19C] (*N.Z.*) to overcome, to surpass. ❑ **knock into the middle of next week** *v.* (*also* **... next century, ...next month, ...the north end of creation, sling into the middle of...**) [early 19C+] (*orig. US*) to overturn, destroy or beat thoroughly or completely.

knock it off *v.* [KNOCK OFF *v.* (1)] **1** [mid-19C+] to stop doing something. **2** [20C+] to complete or dispose of something easily or quickly. **3** *see* KNOCK OFF *v.* (2c).

knock it off! *excl.* [KNOCK IT OFF *v.*] [mid-19C+] stop it! be quiet! shut up!

knock (it) out *v.* [1960s+] (*US black*) **1** to have sexual intercourse. **2** to do anything quickly, with neither style nor concentration.

knockman *n. see* KNOCKO *n.*

knock-me *n. see* KNOCK-ME-SILLY *n.*

knock-me-down *n.* [var. on KNOCK-'EM-DOWN *n.*] [mid-18C–1900s] strong beer or any fiery drink.

knock-me-down *adj.* **1** [mid-18C–1920s] violent, aggressive or overpowering. **2** [mid-19C] something or someone remarkable.

knock-me-downs *n. see* KNOCK-'EM-DOWNS *n.*

knock-me-out-drops *n. see* KNOCKOUT DROPS *n.*

knock-me-silly *n.* (*also* **knock-me**) [rhy. sl.] [20C+] (*Aus.*) a billy (used to boil water).

knocko *n.* (*also* **knocker, knockman**) [the knocking at one's door or on one's skull] [1950s+] (*US black*) a police officer, esp. a member of the drugs squad.

knock-off *n.* (*also* **knocking-off, knock-off time**) [KNOCK OFF *v.*] **1** [early 19C+] (*orig. US*) time to leave work, the end of the day; the act of ceasing work; also attrib. **2** [early 19C+] (*orig. US*) a period away from work; a holiday. **3** in Und. uses. (**a**) [1920s+] an underworld killing. (**b**) [1930s+] a robbery; thus *on the knock-off*, working as a thief. (**c**) [1930s–60s] (*US drugs*) an arrest. (**d**) [1950s] (*US Und.*) a police raid. (**e**) [1950s+] something that has been stolen or has the potential for theft. **4** [1950s] an act of sexual intercourse. **5** [1960s+] a fake, a copy; used in the fashion trade to describe cheap copies of 'designer' garments, cheap reproductions of antiques etc.

knock-off *adj.* [1960s+] a cheap version of an originally expensive garment.

knock off *v.* **1** to bring to an end. (**a**) [mid-17C+] to stop work, to stop thieving, hence *knocking-off time*, the end of the day's or shift's work. (**b**) [18C+] to die. (**c**) [late 18C+] to consume, esp. a drink. (**d**) [early 19C+] to conclude or complete speedily, to do quickly and perfunctorily, esp. in the context of writing. (**e**) [early 19C+] to abandon, to cease from. (**f**) [early 19C+] (*US*) to free from work, to stop someone working. (**g**) [late 19C+] (*US*) to abstain or give up a habit. (**h**) [late 19C+] (*N.Z.*) *vtr.*, to dismiss from a job. **2** as lit. or fig. aggression. (**a**) [early 19C+] (*orig. US*) to hang; to kill, to murder; thus n., *knock-off man*, a hired killer. (**b**) [1920s+] to defeat, to overcome, to destroy. (**c**) [1930s+] (*orig. US*) (*also* **knock it off**) to seduce, to have sexual intercourse (often commercial, adulterous or purely hedonistic); also attrib. **3** in (*Und.*) uses. (**a**) [1910s+] (*also* **k.o.**) to steal, to burglarize; also as *knock it off*, to break into a premises. (**b**) [1920s+] (*orig. US police*) to arrest. (**c**) [1920s–50s] to raid; to seize stolen goods. **4** in monetary contexts. (**a**) [1920s–40s] (*US*) to acquire money, usu. easily. (**b**) [1950s] to dispose of, e.g. a debt. **5** [1930s+] (*orig. US*) to marry.

IN PHRASES

❑ **knock off a piece** *v.* (*also* **knock off a little**) [PIECE *n.* (1a)] [1930s+] of a man, to seduce, either a woman or man. ❑ **knock off hen tracks on a rolltop piano** *v. see under* HEN TRACKS *n.* ❑ **knock off the hooks** *v. see* OFF THE HOOKS *under* HOOK *n.*[1]. ❑ **knock oneself off** *v.* [1920s+] to kill oneself.

knock on the door, a *n.* (*also* **knock at the door, a**) [rhy. sl.] [20C+] (*bingo*) the number four.

knockout *n.* [KNOCK OUT *v.* (2a)] **1** [late 19C+] a person or thing of outstanding quality, attractiveness or excellence. **2** [20C+] a pleasant, gratifying surprise. **3** [20C+] a complete success. **4** [1910s] (*US Und.*) the 'badger game', where a man is blackmailed after being lured into a compromising situation with a prostitute. **5** [1930s–40s] a 'knockout' drug or potion. **6** *see* KNOCK *n.*[1] (2b).

knockout *adj.* [KNOCKOUT *n.*] (*orig. US*) **1** [late 19C+] stupefying or liable to cause unconsciousness, orig. of a drug. **2** [20C+] excellent, wonderful, the very best. **3** [20C+] very attractive.

knock out *v.* **1** (*also* **bang out**) in intransitive uses. (**a**) [mid-19C+] to do roughly or quickly, esp. of writing, to create, to make etc. (**b**) [late 19C+] (*orig. Aus.*) to earn a sum of money; e.g. *knock out £200 per week*; although orig. of food, in phr. *knock out tucker*. (**c**) [late 19C+] to obtain for oneself, e.g. *knock out some sleep*. (**d**) [20C+] to sell. **2** in transitive uses. (**a**) [late 19C] to make someone bankrupt. (**b**) [late 19C] to fail an examination candidate. (**c**) [late 19C–1960s] (*US*) to deprive someone, esp. of money. (**d**) [late 19C+] to kill someone. (**e**) [late 19C+] (*orig. US*) to surprise, overcome or defeat. (**f**) [late 19C+] (*esp. US black*) (*also* **knock flat**) to impress, to overwhelm, to delight. (**g**) [1930s–40s] (*US Und.*) to arrest. (**h**) [1940s–70s] to steal, esp. to steal everything from the place one is robbing.

IN PHRASES

❑ **knock oneself out** *v.* [1930s+] (*orig. US*) **1** to have a very enjoyable time, to 'let oneself go', to amaze oneself. **2** to work very hard. **3** to worry.

IN EXCLAMATIONS

❑ **knock yourself out!** [1940s+] (*US*) have a good time!

SE in slang uses

IN PHRASES

❑ **knock out of the box** *v.* [baseball jargon] [late 19C+] (*US*) to defeat, to overcome, to kill. ❑ **knock out one's link** *v.* [? SE *link*, 'a torch...formerly much in use for lighting people along the streets' (*OED*)] [mid-18C] to be very drunk.

knockout *adv.* [KNOCKOUT *n.*] [1920s+] completely, utterly.

knockout artist *n.* [-ARTIST *sfx*] [1990s+] a thug.

knockout drops *n.* (*also* **knock-drops, knock-me-out drops, knockout, knockout pills, k.o. drops, k.o.d., the drop**) **1** [late 19C+] chloral hydrate mixed into a drink to render an innocent victim unconscious. **2** [late 19C+] a soothing linctus, usu. based on laudanum or opium, used to soothe fractious young children. **3** [1900s] in fig. use, something powerful, destructive. **4** [1910s+] (*Aus.*) drugged or adulterated liquor.

knock-over *n.* [KNOCK OVER *v.*] **1** [1920s–30s] (*US Und.*) a police raid. **2** [1920s+] (*US police*) an armed robbery. **3** [1920s+] (*Aus.*) a substantial, if surprising, success. **4** [1970s] (*US*) an easy task.

knock over *v.* **1** [early 19C+] (*orig. US*) to murder, to kill, orig. animals/birds. **2** [mid-19C+] (*US*) to drink, to eat. **3** [1920s] (*US Und.*) to ban. **4** [1920s+] (*orig. US*) to rob or steal, usu. with violence. **5** [1920s+] (*US Und./police*) to arrest. **6** [1920s+] (*US Und./police*) to raid. **7** [1920s+] (*US Und./police*) to get someone into trouble, to punish (a prisoner). **8** [1940s–60s] (*US*) to seduce, to have sexual intercourse; to rape. **9** [1940s+] to impress. **10** [1970s+] (*US*) to defeat or abuse through violence; to beat up.

IN PHRASES

❑ **knock over a/the doll** *v.* [1950s] (*Aus.*) to take the consequences for an act.

knock under *v.* [despite Grose and Hotten, *knock under*, to admit defeat, to submit, is SE] **1** [18C–mid-19C] to die. **2** [1900s] (*Aus.*) to surpass.

knock up *v.* **1** [17C+] to waken; thus *knocker up*, n., one who wakes people up [knocking on the front or bedroom door]. **2** [mid-18C+] to injure, to impair, to wear out, to die, to defeat, thus n. *knock-up*, an impediment, a strain. **3** [early 19C+] (*orig. US*) (*also* **knock**) to impregnate. **4** attrib., pertaining to impregnation. **5** [early 19C+] to put together spontaneously, to arrange at short notice. **6** [mid-19C+] to earn a living, usu. with a noun, e.g. *knock up a crust*. **7** [late 19C+] to amass.

IN COMPOUNDS

❑ **knock-up money** *n.* [1900s–50s] (*US Und.*) the profit from a crime.

IN PHRASES

❑ **knock up a cheque** *v.* [late 19C–1940s] (*Aus.*) to earn money for one's labour.

knockwurst *n.* [Ger. *Knockwurst*, a sausage] [1970s+] (*US*) the penis.

knosh *v. see* NOSH *v.*

knot *n.* **1** [mid-19C+] the swelling at the base of the head of the penis. **2** [20C+] (*US*) the head, esp. one that appears impenetrable by sense [SE *knot*, an especially hard mass of wood; later use is US black]. **3** [1910s+] (*Aus.*) a pack; thus *carry/hump/push the knot*, to travel with a pack [the *knots* that secure the pack or SWAG *n.*[1] (9)]. **4** [1970s+] (*US black*) a substantial roll of dollar bills.

IN PHRASES

❑ **push the knot** *v.* [20C+] (*Aus.*) to live as a tramp.

K-note *n.* [K *n.* (2)] [1960s] (*US*) a $1000 bill.

knothead *n.* [SE *knot*, an imperfection in a piece of wood + -HEAD *sfx* (1). Such spots are harder than the surrounding wood] **1** [1910s+] (*US*) a mule or stubborn animal. **2** [1920s+] a fool.

knot-headed *adj.* (*also* **knotty-headed**) [KNOTHEAD *n.*] **1** [1910s+] (*US*) stupid. **2** [1930s] (*US black*) having tightly curled hair.

knothole *n.* **1** [1940s] (*US black*) a doughnut. **2** [1960s] (*Aus.*) the vagina.

knotted *adj.*

IN EXCLAMATIONS

❑ **get knotted!** [euph. for GET FUCKED! *excl.*] [1940s+] go away! stop bothering me!

knotty *n. see* NATTY *n.*[2].

knotty *phr.* [the knotted DREADLOCKS that betoken a Rasta-man] [1970s+] (*W.I. Rasta*) used as a greeting or farewell.

knotty ash *n.* [rhy. sl.; Knotty Ash, suburb of Liverpool, UK, where comedian *Ken Dodd* (b.1931) comes from; the ref. is to his problems with taxes] [1980s+] cash.

knotty-headed *adj. see* KNOT-HEADED *adj.*

know *v.*

SE in slang uses

IN PHRASES

❑ **know...** *v. see also under* relevant n. or adj. ❑ **know what I mean?** (*also* **knowmean? know what I'm saying? na mean?**) [1960s+] an almost transparent interj., used as much for punctuation as for explication. ❑ **know what I mean, Vern?** [ref. to a nationwide advertising campaign] [1980s+] (*US campus*) do you understand? ❑ **know what time of day it is** *v. see under* TIME *n.* ❑ **know where the barley grows** *v. see* FIND OUT WHERE THE BARLEY GROWS *under* BARLEY *n.*[1]. ❑ **not know...** *see* separate entry. ❑ **want to know the ins and outs of a duck's bum** *v. see under* IN-AND-OUT *n.*[1].

know a thing or two *v.* (*also* **know a thing or six, know a trick or two, learn a few, learn a thing or two, see a..., teach someone a..., tell a..., up/down to a thing or two**) [late 18C+] to be aware, to be knowledgeable.

knowing *adj.* [late 18C–1900s] stylish, fashionable, i.e. knowing what is in style; thus *knowing kiddy, knowing one*, a stylish person.

knowledge *n.*

IN PHRASES

❑ **drop knowledge** *v. see under* DROP *v.*[4].

knowledge box *n.* **1** [late 18C+] (*also* **knowledge bag, knowledge bump**) the head or the mind [UK use faded by early 19C but revived in US black use by 20C+]. **2** [20C+] (*US*) (*also* **house of knowledge, knowledge factory, knowledge stash**) a school.

Knuck *n. see* CANUCK *n.*

knuck *n.* [SE *knuckle/knuckles*] **1** [early 19C–1940s] (*also* **nuck**) a pickpocket or thief. **2** [mid-19C–1950s] (*US*) in pl., the knuckles. **3** [late 19C+] (*orig. US*) (*also* **brass knucks, nucks**) usu. in pl., brass knuckles, worn over the fist to ensure victory in a fist fight [abbr. KNUCKLEDUSTER *n.* (1)].

IN COMPOUNDS

❑ **knuck game** *n.* [1960s+] (*US black*) fist-fighting.

knuck *v.* [abbr. KNUCKLE *v.*[2]] **1** [mid-19C–1900s] to pick pockets. **2** *see* KNUCKLE *v.*[2] (2).

knucka *n.* [? someone you rap knuckles with, plus note MUCKER *n.*[3] (1)] [1990s+] (*orig. US black/teen*) a friend.

knucker *n. see* KNUCKLER *n.*

knuckle *n.* [KNUCKLE *v.*[2]] **1** [late 18C–mid-19C] a pickpocket; thus *go on the knuckle*, to work as a pickpocket; *knucklejill*, a female pickpocket [Grose 1796 et seq. suggests 'a superior kind of pickpockets']. **2** [mid-19C+] (*US*) in pl., a KNUCKLEDUSTER *n.* (1), 'brass knuckles'. **3** [1930+] a fight, violence; thus *go the knuckle/knuckles*, to fight; *knuckle-boy, knuckleman*, n., a fighter. **4** [1990s+] (*US drugs*) a wrapper of heroin [th[e] knuckle-like bulge of the wrapped drug].

IN COMPOUNDS

❑ **knuckleburger** *n.* [SE *knuckle* + (*ham*)*burger*; a play o[n] KNUCKLE SANDWICH below] [1970s+] (*US*) a punch in the mouth. ❑ **knuckle-dabs** *n.* (*also* **knuckle-confounders**) [late 18C–early 19C] **1** handcuffs. **2** the fists. ❑ **knuckle-dragger** *n* [1980s+] **1** a fool, a peasant. **2** a thug; as adj., *knuckle dragging*, violent. ❑ **knuckleduster** *n. see* separate entry ❑ **knucklehead/headed** *see* separate entries. ❑ **knuckl[e] junction** *n.* [1970s+] (*US*) a fist-fight; in phr. *take someon[e] dancing down at knuckle junction*, to administer a beating ❑ **knuckle sandwich** *n.* (*also* **fist sandwich, nuckl[e] sandwich**) [1950s+] (*orig. US*) a blow from a fist, esp. to th[e] mouth. ❑ **knuckle shuffle** *n.* [1990s+] masturbation ❑ **knuckle soup** *n.* [mid-19C] (*US*) a punch in the mouth ❑ **knuckletalk** *n.* [1910s] (*US prison*) coded communicatio[n] between prisoners achieved by rapping their knuckles on thei[r] cell walls.

IN PHRASES

❑ **down on the knuckle** (*also* **close to the knuckle, down o[n] the knucklebone((s) of one's arse), down on one's bac[k] seam**) [mid-19C–1930s] virtually penniless. ❑ **go the knuckl[e]** *v.* [1940s+] (*Aus.*) to have a fist-fight. ❑ **on the knuckle** *see* O[N] THE KNOCKER *under* KNOCKER *n.*[1].

knuckle *v.*[1] (*also* **knuckle to**) [var./abbr. on SE *knuckle unde[r]*] [mid-18C–1950s] (*US*) to give in, to confess, to surrender, t[o] accept something one dislikes but is not strong enough to figh[t].

knuckle *v.*[2] **1** [late 18C–mid-19C] to steal, to pick pocke[ts] 'after the approved method' (Hotten 1859); thus *knuckle wipe*, to steal a handkerchief [SE *knuckle*; 'the approved metho[d] according to Vaux, implies the robbery of notes and cash rath[er] than less valuable items]. **2** [mid-19C+] (*also* **knuck, knuck[le] up**) to hit, to fight.

knucklebone *n.*

IN PHRASES

❑ **down on the knucklebone((s) of one's arse)** *see* DOW[N] ON THE KNUCKLE *under* KNUCKLE *n.*

knuckleduster *n.* **1** [mid-19C+] a metal instrument, tra[ditionally] brass, that covers the knuckles, thus strengthening them whe[n] delivering a blow [SE f. 1900]. **2** [late 19C+] a large, gaud[y] flashy ring.

knucklehead *n.* (*also* **nuckel-head**) [knuckles pressed to th[e] forehead imply the intensity of thought for one who is not ove[r] bright] [1930s+] (*orig. US*) a term of abuse, a description f[or] any foolish, stupid, slow person.

knuckleheaded *adj.* (*also* **knucklehead**) [KNUCKLEHEAD *n*] [1930s+] (*orig. US*) stupid.

knuckler *n.* (*also* **knucker, knucksman**) [KNUCKLE *v.*[2] (1)] [la[te] 18C–19C] a pickpocket.

knuckle to *v. see* KNUCKLE *v.*[1].

knuckle-up *n.* [var. on *PUNCH-UP under* PUNCH *v.*] [1940s-] (*N.Z.*) a fist fight.

knuckle up *v.* **1** [1960s+] (*US black teen*) to prepare to figh[t] by closing and raising one's fists. **2** *see* KNUCKLE *v.*[2] (2).

knuckling cove *n.* [KNUCKLE *v.*[2] + COVE *n.* (1)] [early 19C] pickpocket.

knucksman *n. see* KNUCKLER *n.*

knuller *n.* (*also* **gumbler**) [OE *cyllan*, to knell; the old-fashion[ed] sweep rang a bell to announce his progress along a street] **1** [mi[d-] 19C] a chimney sweep who goes from house to house offeri[ng] his services. **2** [mid-19C–1900s] a clergyman.

knut *n.* (*also* **k-nut, nut**) [post-1920s use is historical] **1** [la[te] 19C] (*Aus.*) a provincial dandy. **2** [1910s–20s] a dandy, a ve[ry] well-dressed, fashionable (if not overly intelligent) young ma[n].

k.o. *n.* (*also* **kayo**) (*orig. US*) **1** [1910s+] a knockout; also f[ig.] use. **2** [1910s+] in fig. use, death or termination; also attri[b.]

IN COMPOUNDS

❑ **k.o. drops** *n. see* KNOCKOUT DROPS *n.*

k.o. *adj.* (*also* **kayo, kayoe**) [joc. reversal of OK *adj.*] [1910s[+]] (*US*) all right, in order.

k.o. *v.*[1] (*also* **kayo, kyo**) [abbr. SE] [20C+] to knock out, lit. or fig.

k.o. *v.*[2] **1** [1970s+] (*US campus*) to die, to be killed [KICK OFF *v.*[1] (1)]. **2** *see* KNOCK OFF *v.* (3a).

koala *n.* (*Aus.*) **1** [1940s+] a diplomat, who is immune from Aus. law [the koala is an officially protected creature]. **2** [1970s+] an unappreciative man [a pun on the phr. he 'eats, roots/ROOT *v.* (5a) and leaves'].

koala-shagger *n.* [2000s] (*N.Z.*) a derog. nickname for an Australian.

koboko *n. see* BOKO *n.*

kochee *n. see* KOOTCH *n.*

kochonni *n.* [Fr. *cochon*, a pig; note synon. Yid. *chaserei*, lit. 'pig things'] [20C+] (*W.I., St Lu./Dmnca*) a piece of junk, anything worthless or useless.

kockamamey *n. see* COCKAMAMIE *n.* (1).

k.o.d. *n. see* KNOCKOUT DROPS *n.*

koda *n.* [initial letter, albeit incorrect] [2000s] (*S.Afr. gay*) cocaine.

kodak *v.* [Kodak, popular brand of camera] **1** [late 19C] to take visual note. **2** [20C+] (*US*) to pose, as in a photograph.

k.o.'ed *adj.* [KNOCKED OUT *adj.* (4)] [1960s–70s] (*US*) very drunk or intoxicated by drugs.

koelie *n. see* COOLIE *n.*[1].

koffie-moffie *n.* [Afk. *koffie*, coffee + MOFFIE *n.*] [1980s+] (*S.Afr.*) a male flight attendant.

Kofifi *n.* [? Sotho (*le*)*fifi*, darkness, (*se*)*fifi*, corpse or (*bo*)*fifi*, mourning] [1950s] (*S.Afr. township*) Sophiatown, a black residential area of Johannesburg, razed during the 1950s after the forcible removal of its inhabitants.

Kohen *n. see* COHEN *n.*

kojak *v.* [US TV show *Kojak* (1973–7) whose epon. hero possessed this facility] [1970s+] (*US teen*) to find a parking space in an area where such discoveries are at best rare.

kojak with a Kodak *n.* [the TV show *Kojak* + the make of camera] [1970s+] (*US*) a police officer manning a radar speed trap.

kojo *n.* [Fante *Kodwo*, a male born on a Monday] [20C+] (*W.I.*) a tough and violent person, usu. from a rural area.

koki *n.* (*also* **cokey**) [proprietary name *Koki*] [1990s+] (*S.Afr.*) a fibre-tipped colouring pen.

koko *n. see* COCO *n.*[1] (2).

kokomo *n.* [play on COKE *n.*[1] (1)] **1** [1930s–50s] (*US drugs*) a cocaine user. **2** [1980s+] (*drugs*) crack cocaine.

koks *n. see* KANGSE *n.*

kombo *n. see* COMBO *n.*[1].

kommie *n. see* COMMIE *n.*

komoppo *n.* [ety. unknown] [1940s] (*US*) an unattractive woman.

kone *n.* [KONIACKER *n.*] [mid-19C] (*UK Und.*) counterfeit money.

Kong *v. see* KING KONG *v.*

kong *n. see* KING KONG *n.* (1).

kongkongsa *adj.* [Twi *kongkongsa*, double-dealing, duplicity, betrayal] [20C+] (*W.I.*) deceitful, hypocritical, biased.

kongo *n. see* CONGO *n.*[1].

koniack *n. see* CONEY *n.*[1].

koniacker *n.* (*also* **coneyacker, coniacker**) [? CONEY *n.*[1]; F&H suggest 'obviously, a play upon COIN, money and HACK, to mutilate'.] [early 19C–1930s] (*US*) a counterfeiter.

konk *see under* CONK and its combs.

konks *n. see* KANGSE *n.*

konoblin rig *n.* [RIG *n.*[2] (1)] [early 19C] (*UK Und.*) stealing large lumps of coal from coalsheds.

kooch *n. see* KOOTCH *n.*

kook *n.* (*also* **cook, klookhead, kuke**) [? CUCKOO *n.*[1] (2) but popularized following the late 1950s US TV show *77 Sunset Strip* in which the supposedly (by 1958 standards) 'eccentric' character Gerald Lloyd Kookson III ('Kookie'), played by actor Edd Byrnes (b.1933), became a teenage idol] **1** [1950s+] (*US*) a crazy person, an eccentric, albeit an acceptable one; also attrib. **2** [1960s] (*US*) a spy. **3** [1960s+] (*orig. US campus*) an annoying or mistaken person.

kookaboo *n.* (*also* **cuckaboo**) [KOOK *n.* (1) + ? SE *kookaburra*, the Australian 'laughing' bird/cuckoo] [1950s+] (*US*) an insane person.

kooked-up *adj.* [KOOK UP *v.*] [1950s+] (*US*) crazy, eccentric.

kookie house *n. see* KOOKY HOUSE *n.*

kookoo *adj. see* CUCKOO *adj.*

kook up *v.* [KOOKY *adj.*] [1950s+] to make eccentric, bizarre.

kooky *adj.* [KOOK *n.*] [1950s+] (*orig. US*) **1** odd, eccentric (often with overtones of charm). **2** infatuated with.

kooky house *n.* (*also* **kookie house**) [KOOKY *adj.* + SE *house*] [1950s+] (*US*) a psychiatric institution.

kool *v.* [backsl.] [mid–late 19C] to look (at).

(IN EXCLAMATIONS)

❑ **kool esclop!** [ESCLOP *n.* (1)] [mid–late 19C] (*UK Und.*) a warning cry of 'look police!'. ❑ **kool toul!** [mid-19C+] look out!

kools *n.* [play on cigarette brandname *Kool*] [1980s+] (*drugs*) phencyclidine.

koon *n. see* COON *n.* (4).

koopa *n.* [ety. unknown] [2000s] (*US black*) a close friend.

koosh *n. see* CUSH *n.*[1] (1).

kooshy *adj. see* CUSHY *adj.* (1).

koota *n. see* COOTIE *n.*

kootch *n.* (*also* **kochee, kooch**) [HOOTCHY-KOOTCHY *n.*] **1** [1920s–70s] (*US*) a form of highly suggestive belly-dance, usu. performed at carnivals; thus *kootcher*, a dancer. **2** [1970s+] the vagina; thus a prostitute. **3** [1970s+] (*US gay*) the anus.

kooti *n. see* COOTIE *n.*

kopasetic/kopasette *n. see* COPACETIC *adj.*

kopec *n.* (*also* **kopek, kopex**) [late 19C–1930s] (*US*) a dollar; thus money.

kopgee *n.* (*also* **kopje, kop-jee**) [Du. *kopje*, a mound or low hill] [late 19C–1900s] the head.

kopjie-walloper *n.* [Du. *kopje*, a hill + SE *wallop*, to thrash] [late 19C+] (*S.Afr.*) a diamond-buyer (often Jewish) who traded directly with miners on their claims; this practice was outlawed by the Diamond Trade Act (1882) *hist.*

koreegro *n.* [SE *Korea* + *negro*] [2000s] (*US black*) an Asian person pretending to be a GANGSTA *n.*

kosh *n. see also under* COSH.

kosher *adj.* [fig. uses of Yid. *kosher*, acceptable according to the Jewish dietary laws; ult. Heb. *kāshēr*] **1** [late 19C+] honest, legitimate, above-board. **2** [20C+] (*US*) Jewish. **3** [1930s] (*US prison*) not guilty. **4** [1930s+] clean, pure. **5** [1940s+] satisfactory, good. **6** [1970s+] safe; thus *unkosher*, dangerous, unsafe.

(IN COMPOUNDS)

❑ **kosher delicatessen** *n.* [everyone one might EAT *v.* (4) will be KOSHER *adj.*, i.e. Jewish] [1960s+] (*gay*) Israel. ❑ **kosher dill** *n.* [1960s+] (*gay*) a circumcised penis. ❑ **kosher nosher** *n.* [pun on *Cosa Nostra* + Yid. *kosher*, religiously acceptable to Jews + Yid. *nosher*, an eater] [1970s+] (*US gay*) a coterie of gay Jewish men. ❑ **kosher (style)** *adj.* [the role of ritual circumcision in Judaism] [1960s+] (*US gay*) circumcised.

kosher *v.* [i.e. rendered 'safe'] [1960s] to smuggle.

kotanga *n.* [pun on pron. SE *coathanger*, sometimes used as an ad hoc car aerial] [2000s] (*N.Z.*) a car aerial.

kotch *see under* COTCH.

kote-si-kote-la *n. see* COTE-SI-COTE-LA *n.*

kotonk *n. see* KATONK *n.*

kouchie *n. see* CUTCHIE *n.*

kow-clink *n.* [ety. unknown; ? link to COW *n.*[1] (2)] [mid-16C] (*Scot.*) a prostitute.

kowtow chow *n.* [SE *kowtow*, lit. 'knock the head', 'the Chinese custom of touching the ground with the forehead in the act of prostrating oneself, as an expression of extreme respect, submission, or worship' (*OED*) + CHOW *n.*[1]] [1970s+] (*US gay*) the act of performing fellatio while kneeling in front of one's partner.

k.p. *n.* [abbr. police jargon *k*nown *p*rostitute] [1940s+] (*Aus.*) a prostitute.

kraak *v.* [Afk. phr. *gaan dat dit so kraack*, 'go like the blazes'] [1950s+] (*S.Afr.*) to speed, to go fast, esp. on a motorbike.

krack *v.* see CRACK *v.*[2] (2c).

krag *n.* [Du. *kracht*, power, strength] [1950s+] (*S.Afr.*) energy, strength, 'oomph'.

krappy *adj.* see CRAPPY *adj.* (3).

kratz (up) *v.* [ety. unknown; ? Ger./Yid.] [1960s] (*US Und.*) to make a mess, to blunder.

kraut *n.* [*Sauerkraut*, a form of pickled, shredded cabbage, supposedly loved by the nation] **1** [mid-19C+] (*orig. US*) a derog. name for a German or Austrian. **2** [1940s+] the German language.

IN COMPOUNDS

❑ **kraut-eater** *n.* [mid-19C–1930s] (*US*) a derog. term for a German. ❑ **krauthead** *n.* (*also* **kraut stomper**) [1910s+] (*US*) a derog. term for a German. ❑ **krautland** *n.* [1950s+] (*orig. US*) a derog. name for Germany.

kraut *adj.* [1940s+] pertaining to Germany or things German.

kreskin *v.* [US TV magician *Kreskin*, George Joseph Kresge (b. 1935)] [1970s+] (*US teen*) to prophesy, to work out intuitively, to foresee.

kridel *n.* [ety. unknown] [1990s+] (*W.I.*) an unattractive woman.

krispy kracker *n.* see CRISPY (CRITTER) *n.*

krissy *n.* (*also* **kroes, kroesie**) [Afk. *kroes*, frizzy] [1940s+] (*S.Afr.*) frizzy hair.

kroeskop *n.* [Afk. *kroes*, frizzy + *kop*, head] [1910s+] (*S.Afr.*) one who has frizzy or tightly curled hair, thus a derog. term for Africans in general.

kronk *n.* see CRONK *n.*

kroon *n.* [2000s] (*S.Afr.*) money.

krop *n.* [backsl.] [mid–late 19C] pork.

krud *n.* see CRUD *n.*

krunk *n.* [ety. unknown] [1990s+] (*US*) an all-purpose euph. used in place of an obscenity, usu. SHIT *n.*

krunk *adj.* [KRUNK *n.*] [2000s] (*US teen*) wild, uninhibited.

krunk *v.* [1990s+] **1** euph. for FUCK *v.* **2** to trek, to travel far to somewhere [joc. use of SE *crunch*].

krunked-up *adj.* [KRUNK *v.*] [1990s+] **1** euph. for FUCKED UP *adj.* (1). **2** euph,. for FUCKED UP *adj.* (3).

krunking *adj.* [KRUNK *v.*] [1990s+] euph. for FUCKING *adj.*

kryptonite *n.* [rhy. sl.; the mineral that weakens even Superman's powers] [2000s] a website.

kuds *n.* [late 17C] *God's* in a variety of oaths.

kuf *n.* [ety. unknown] [1990s+] (*UK drugs*) cocaine.

kuff *n.* [SE *cuff*] [1970s–80s] (*UK black*) a blow, lit.or fig.

kuff *v.* [KUFF *n.*] [1970s–80s] (*UK black*) to hit, to smash.

kuffed up *adj.* [KUF *n.*] [1990s+] (*UK drugs*) experiencing the effects of (crack) cocaine.

kugel *n.* [Yid. *kugel*, a sweet or savoury casserole or pudding] [1960s+] (*S.Afr.*) the daughter of wealthy parents, whose main interest is her wardrobe, appearance, boyfriend (as an acquisition not a person) and the expenditure of money. Such girls, as the etymology implies, are Jewish; black and Boer versions are *ebony-kugel* and *boere-kugel* respectively; thus *kugelese*, the jargon spoken between such young women.

kuka *n.* (*also* **kungse**) [var. on CACA *n.* (1)] [20C+] (*W.I.*) a piece of excrement.

kuke *n.* see KOOK *n.*

ku klucker *n.* see KLUCKER *n.*

kung fu fighter *n.* [rhy. sl.] [2000s] a lighter.

kungse *n.* see KUKA *n.*

kunk *n.* see CONK *v.*[2].

kunker *n.* see CUNKER *n.*

kunumunu *n.* [Yoruba *kunun*, bashful, lacking in self-confidence] [20C+] (*W.I.*) a stupid man, esp. one who is controlled by a woman; an imbecile.

kuri *n.* [Maori *kuri*, a dog] [20C+] (*N.Z.*) **1** a mongrel, a badly-behaved dog. **2** a second-rate racehorse. **3** see GOORIE *n.*

kurl-a-mo/-the-mo *adj.* see CURL-THE-MO *adj.*

kurl the mo *v.* see CURL THE MO *v.*

kush *n.*[1] see CUSH *n.*[1] (1).

kush *n.*[2] see CUSH *n.*[2].

kutch *n.* see HOOTCHY-KOOTCHY *n.*

kuter *n.* see CUTER *n.*[2].

kuti *n.* see COOTIE *n.*

kuzak *n.* [ety. unknown] [1970s] (*S.Afr.*) cash.

kuzat *n.* [ety. unknown] [1960s–70s] (*S.Afr. township*) money.

kvell *v.* [Yid.; ult. Ger. *quellen*, to gush, to swell] [1960s+] to boast, to feel proud or happy, to gloat, to enjoy oneself.

kvetch *n.* [KVETCH *v.*] [1950s+] a nag, a whiner, a complainer.

kvetch *v.* [Yid. *kvetsh*; ult. Ger. *quetschen*, to squeeze, to press] [1950s+] (*orig. US*) to complain, to delay, to nag.

kvetchy *adj.* [KVETCH *v.*] [1940s+] irritable, whiny.

kwaai *adj.* [Afk. *kwaad*, bad, evil, hence on bad = good model] [1970s+] (*S.Afr.*) a general term of approval, fantastic, great.

kwaal *n.* [Afk. *kwaal*, a complaint] [1960s+] (*S.Afr.*) an illness, a complaint.

kwan *n.* [ety. unknown] [2000s] (*US black*) respect.

Kwang *n.* [1910s] (*Aus.*) generic for any Chinese person.

kway *n.* [? SE *takeaway*] [1940s+] (*Aus.*) **1** a general thief, with no real speciality. **2** a man who lives on money taken from a procurer.

K.Y. *n.* (*also* **K-Y, KY**) [abbr.] [1960s+] (*US drugs*) the Federal Narcotics Hospital, Lexington, Kentucky.

kyas *adj.* [? Lat. *quies*, quiet] [mid-19C] (*UK Und.*) silent, quiet.

kyber *n.* see KHYBER (PASS) *n.*

kybo *n.* (*also* **kibo**) [KHYBER (PASS) *n.*] [1970s] (*US*) a privy.

kybosh *n.* see KIBOSH *n.*

kyd *n.* see KID *n.*[1] (4).

ky'daar *n.* (*also* **k'daar**) [Afk. *kykdaar*, look there] [1980s+] (*S.Afr.*) a tourist.

kye *n.* (*also* **kibosh, kybosh**) [ety. unknown; Partridge (1984) suggests the Yid. *kye*, 18; but this is not cited in Rosen] [mid-19C+] one shilling and sixpence.

kyfer *n.* (*also* **kaifa, keifer, khyfer, kife, kifer, kyfering, kypher**) [Arabic *kaif*, absolute enjoyment, perfect contentment, thus 'that which pleases one', one's delight + *keyif*, 'the amiable beauty of a fair woman'; the word is the root of KIF *n.*, a type of hashish, and also meant the pleasure engendered by cannabis] **1** [mid-19C+] the vagina. **2** [late 19C+] women regarded as sex objects; thus *kyfer-mashing*, pursuing women; *bit of kyfer*, a woman, a 'bit o' skirt'. **3** [1990s+] (*US*) a crooked lawyer.

IN PHRASES

❑ **have a bit of keifer** *v.* [late 19C+] of a man, to have sexual intercourse.

kyke *n.* see KIKE *n.*

kylie *n.* [Nat. Aus. *kylie*, a boomerang] [1940s+] (*Aus.*) the small piece of wood used for tossing the coins in the game of two-up.

kynchin-co *n.* see *KINCHIN CO under* KINCHIN *n.*

kynchin lay *n.* see *KINCHIN LAY under* KINCHIN *n.*

kyo *v.* see K.O. *v.*[1].

kyoodle *n.* see KIYOODLE *n.*

kype *v.* see KIPE *v.*

kypher *v.* (*also* **khyfer**) [Fr. *coiffeur* or KYFER *n.*] [late 19C–1900s] to dress one's hair.

kypsey *n.* see KIPSIE *n.*[2].

kyuter *n.* see CUTER *n.*[2].

kyvy *n.* [COVE *n.* (1)] [mid-19C] (*UK Und.*) a corrupt watchman in league with thieves and housebreakers.

L *n.* [abbr.] **1** [mid-19C] (*US*) a $50 banknote [Roman numeral *L*, 50]. **2** [late 19C; 2000s] (*US prison*) a *life* sentence. **3** in drug uses. (**a**) [1960s+] (*US*) LSD. (**b**) [1990s+] (*also* **el**) marijuana [abbr. LOC *n.*[1]]. **4** *see* EL *n.*[1].

l. *n.* [abbr.] [1990s+] (*US black*) a *loss*; usu. in phr. *take a l.*

L.A. *n.* [abbr.; post WWII use is SE] [20C+] (*orig. US*) Los Angeles.

l.a. *n.* [abbr.] [1990s+] (*drugs*) *l*ong-acting *a*mphetamine.

la *n.*[1] *see* LAH *n.*

la *n.*[2] *see* LA-LA *n.*[1].

la *adj.* [? abbr. LA-DI-DAH *adj.* (2)] [1960s] (*US gay*) effeminate.

la! *excl. see* LAWKS! *excl.*

laa-dee-laa *adj. see* LA-DI-DAH *adj.*

laad-mi-don *n.* [lit. 'Lord, me done (for)'] [1940s+] (*W.I.*) **1** the poorhouse, the almshouse. **2** a tuberculosis sanatorium.

laaitie *n. see* LIGHTIE *n.*

laama *n.* [lit. 'Lord! Ma'am', the expression uttered on seeing such finery] [1940s+] (*W.I.*) clothing worn for celebrations and other special occasions.

laanie *n.* (*also* **lahnee, lani, lanie, larney**) [ety. unknown, but ? Fr. *l'orne*, the ornate one, or Malay/Hind. *rani*, a queen] [1970s+] (*S.Afr.*) **1** a boss, an employer. **2** a white person, a rich person. **3** an arrogant person.

laanie *adj.* (*also* **lahnee, lani, lanie, larney**) [LAANIE *n.*] [1970s+] (*S.Afr.*) **1** showy, arrogant. **2** rich; expensive. **3** intellectually sophisticated.

laba *n.* (*also* **laba-laba, labba, labba-labba**) [BLAB *v.*; BLABBER *n.*] [1950s+] (*W.I.*) a chatterbox, a gossip, a talkative person.

laba-laba *adj.* (*also* **labba-labba**) [LABA-LABA *v.*] [1980s] (*UK black*) verbose, effusive.

laba-laba *v.* [LABA *n.*] [1960s] (*W.I.*) to chatter, to gossip, to betray secrets.

labba/labba-labba *n. see* LABA *n.*

labber-mouth *n.* [LABA *n.*; note BLABBERMOUTH *n.*] [20C+] (*W.I.*) a chatterer, a talker.

labdick *n.* [abbr. *L*othian *a*nd *B*orders Constabulary + presumably a link to DICK *n.*[5] (2)] [20C+] (*Scot.*) a police officer.

label *n.* [1910s–50s] (*US*) a person's name.

labes *n.* [abbr.] [1980s+] the labia majora; also as sing.

labonza *n.* (*also* **labonz**) [? Ital. *la pancia*, the paunch] (*US*) **1** [1930s+] the pit of the stomach. **2** [1940s+] the buttocks.

labor skate *n.* [SAmE *labor* + SKATE *n.*] [1930s–60s] (*US*) a union official, the inference is of corruption.

labour, the *n.* [abbr.] [1920s+] the labour exchange, the employment exchange, the job centre.

labour gone in Maxwell Pond *phr. see* MONEY GONE IN MAXWELL POND *under* MAXWELL POND *n.*

labour leather *v. see under* LEATHER *n.*

labrick *n.* (*also* **laverick**) [? dial. *laverick*, a lark or a hare] [late 19C–1910s] (*US*) an idiot.

labrish *n.* [BLAB *v.*] [1940s–60s] (*W.I.*) gossip, chatter.

labrish *adj.* [LABRISH *n.*] [1940s–60s] (*W.I.*) talkative, gossipy.

labrish *v.* [LABRISH *n.*] [1940s–60s] (*W.I.*) to tell tales, to gossip.

labrisher *n.* [LABRISH *v.*] [1940s–60s] (*W.I.*) a chatterer, a telltale.

lac *n.* (*also* **llac**) [abbr.] [1980s+] (*US black*) a Cadil*lac*.

lacatan *n.* [SE *lacatan*, a type of small banana] [1950s] (*W.I.*) a short, stoutish person.

lace *n.*[1] [abbr. LACE CURTAIN *n.*[1] (2)] [1960s+] (*US gay*) the foreskin.

IN COMPOUNDS

❑ **lace queen** *n.* [1980s] (*US gay*) a homosexual who prefers uncircumcised partners.

lace *n.*[2] [? the value or thinness of lace] [1980s] (*US teen*) money.

lace *v.* [SE *lace*, to set upon with a whip or lash] **1** [late 17C+] to beat. **2** [1970s] (*US*) to swindle. **3** [1980s+] to shoot.

IN PHRASES

❑ **lace into** *v.* [early 19C+] to attack, to beat, to thrash; also fig. use. ❑ **lace someone's jacket** *v.* [late 18C–19C] to beat up, to thrash.

lace curtain *n.*[1] (*also* **lace curtains**) **1** [1900s–30s] (*US*) (*also* **chin curtains**) in pl., a beard. **2** [1940s+] (*gay*) a (long) foreskin.

lace curtain *n.*[2] [rhy. sl.] [1930s+] beer, orig. spec. Burton's beer.

lace-curtain Irish *n.* [they adorn their windows with such curtains] [1920s+] (*US*) genteel, petit-bourgeois Irish-Americans.

laced *adj.* [SE *laced*, of a plant, entwined] **1** [late 17C–early 18C] of coffee, sugared. **2** [late 17C+] of a drink, mixed or combined with something [SE in 20C+]. **3** [1970s+] of a drug, mixed or combined with something. **4** [1980s+] (*US*) drunk, intoxicated by a drug [one's blood is *laced* with alcohol]. **5** [2000s] of music, mixed.

SE in slang uses

IN COMPOUNDS

❑ **laced mutton** *n.* [MUTTON *n.* (1); the lacing is that of stays or corsets, embellishing a young, or disguising an ageing, figure. Poss. a pun on the culinary term 'lacing' (making incisions into) a duck or chicken's breast, but this meaning is slightly later] **1** [late 16C–mid-19C] a prostitute. **2** [early 19C] a woman dressed to appear younger than her years. ❑ **laced woman** *n.* [late 18C–mid-19C] (*UK Und.*) a virtuous woman.

IN PHRASES

❑ **laced (by the neck)** *adj.* [image of lace-ornamented garments] **1** [1900s] (*US*) dressed up and bejewelled. **2** [1970s+] (*US black*) extremely sophisticated.

lace-work *n.* [boxing imagery: the rubbing of the glove's laces in the opponent's face and eyes or f. the ideas of 'embroidery'] [late 19C] (*US*) the gathering of evidence for a legal process.

lacing *n.* [SE *lace*, to whip; LACE *v.*] **1** [late 17C+] a judicial flogging; a beating. **2** [1940s+] a verbal attack, criticism.

lack *n.* [abbr. SE *lackey*] [1990s+] (*Irish*) a girlfriend.

lack-a-daisy! *excl. see under* LAWKS! *excl.*

lackanooky *n.* (*also* **lakanuki**) [the re-spelling of a Polynesian word + play on SE *lack of* + NOOKIE *n.* (1)] [1940s+] (*US*) ill-health caused by lack of sexual activity.

lackin *n.* (*also* **laken, lakin**) [ety. unknown] [mid–late 19C] a wife.

la cosa *n.* [Sp. *la cosa*, the thing] [1980s+] (*US drugs*) heroin.

lacy *adj.* **1** [1940s] (*US*) effeminate, homosexual. **2** [1950s] sexy.

lad *n.* [20C+] (*Irish*) **1** any inanimate object. **2** a creature. **3** (*also* **large lad**) a penis. **4** a fox. **5** constr. with *the*, cancer.

lad, the *n. see* AMERICAN LAD *under* AMERICAN *adj.*

ladder *n.* [metonymy] **1** [16C] the gallows. **2** [late 19C] the vagina.

IN PHRASES

❑ **go up the ladder to bed** *v.* (*also* **go up a ladder to rest, mount the ladder**) [late 16C–19C] to be hanged.

laddo *n.* [SE *lad*] **1** [late 19C+] an affectionate term of address. **2** [1990s+] a hooligan.

laddy *n.* (*also* **lassie**) [1990s+] (*US gay*) a boy or a girl with gay parents.

la-di-dah *n.*[1] (*also* **la de dah, laudy-daw**) [LA-DI-DAH *adj.* (1)] [late 19C+] **1** a snob. **2** (*also* **ladidaism**) snobbishness; upper-class and/or wealthy hedonism.

la-di-dah *n.*[2] [rhy. sl.] **1** [20C+] a car, a tram car. **2** [1960s] a trolley car. **3** [1970s+] (*also* **lardy**) a cigar.

la-di-dah *adj.* (*also* **laa-dee-laa, la-dee-da, la-di-da, lahdidah, law-de-dah**) [? LARDY-DARDY *adj.*; or the supposed excl. of *La-di-dah!* in the face of information, experience etc] [late 19C+] **1** stuck up, arrogant, snobbish. **2** effeminate, affected.

la-di-dah *v.* (*also* **do the la-di-dah, la-di-da**) [LA-DI-DAH *adj.*] [late 19C+] to use affected manners or speech.

la-di-dah! *excl.* [LA-DI-DAH *adj.* (1)] [1990s+] a derog. excl. implying the recipient is pretentious or snobbish.

la-di-dah-di *n.* [1980s] a fantasy.

ladle *n.* [play on SPOON *n.* (1)] [mid-19C] (*UK Und.*) a fool.

ladle *v.* [the image of carefully doling out soup] [mid-19C–1910s] to talk slowly and solemnly.

lad of wax *n.* [late 18C–19C] **1** a cobbler. **2** a boy; a weak or unimportant man.

lads of the village *n.* [early 19C] thieves.

lady *n.* **1** [late 17C–19C] a crooked or hunchbacked woman. **2** [late 19C–1900s; 1960s+] (*US*) one's girlfriend or wife. **3** [late 19C+] (*also* **her ladyship**) a queen in a pack of playing cards. **4** [1910s+] (*US prison*) one's effeminate homosexual partner. **5** [1930s+] (*US black*) an independent, high-class prostitute. **6** [1960s+] (*gay*) as a term of address to a fellow homosexual male. **7** [1970s+] (*US gay*) an effeminate homosexual. **8** [1970s+] (*US*) a prostitute belonging to a specific pimp. **9** [1970s+] (*drugs*) cocaine [abbr. of *WHITE LADY under* WHITE *adj.*].

SE in slang uses

IN COMPOUNDS

❑ **ladies' college** *n.* [euph.] [18C] a brothel. ❑ **ladies' delight** *n.* (*also* **ladies' plaything, ladies' treasure**) [note ety. of DILDO *n.*] [19C] the penis. ❑ **ladies' lollipop** *n.* [19C] the penis. ❑ **ladies' tailoring** *n.* [the in-and-out 'sewing' motion of intercourse] [19C] sexual intercourse. ❑ **ladies' walk** *n.* [mid–late 19C] a ladies' lavatory. ❑ **lady abbess** *v. see* ABBESS *n.* ❑ **lady hackster** *v. see* HACKNEY *n.* (1). ❑ **lady hot-bot** *v. see* *HOT-BOT under* HOT *adj.* ❑ **lady love** *v.* [backform. f. *LADY LOVER* below] [1930s+] to engage in lesbian behaviour. ❑ **lady lover** *n.* (*also* **woman-lover**) [1930s+] a lesbian. ❑ **lady-maker** *n. see* *BABY-MAKER under* BABY *n.* ❑ **lady's blush** *n. see* *MAIDEN'S BLUSH under* MAIDEN *n.* ❑ **lady's jewels** *n.* [note JEWEL *n.* (1)] [mid-18C] the testicles. ❑ **lady's leg** *n.* [the shape] [2000s] (*N.Z.*) a liqueur bottle. ❑ **lady's low toupee** *n.* [early 18C; 1990s+] the pubic hair. ❑ **lady's waist** *n.* [1930s+] (*Aus.*) **1** (*also* **lady's finger, lady's wish**) a slender beer glass, with an hour-glass shape. **2** the drink served in such a glass. ❑ **lady ware** *n.* [SE *ware*, goods] **1** [late 16C; 19C] the penis (and testes). **2** [17C] the vagina.

IN PHRASES

❑ **hold the lady down** *v.* [1930s] (*US tramp*) to ride on the 'gunnels' or 'rods' beneath the wagons while a fast train is passing over a bumpy stretch of track. ❑ **lady about town** *n. see* *WOMAN ABOUT TOWN under* WOMAN *n.* ❑ **lady and gentleman racket** *n.* [mid-19C] the theft of barnyard fowls. ❑ **lady five fingers** *n.* (*also* **old lady five fingers**) [1960s+] masturbation. ❑ **lady in mourning** *n.* [mid-19C] (*UK Und.*) a black woman. ❑ **lady of pleasure** *n.* (*also* **daughter of pleasure, woman of pleasure**) [mid-17C+] a prostitute (cf. *PLEASURE-LADY under* PLEASURE *n.*). ❑ **lady of the evening** *n. see* *EVENING STAR under* EVENING *adj.* ❑ **lady of the game** *n.* (*also* **female of the game**) [GAME *n.* (1a)] [late 17C–early 18C] a prostitute. ❑ **lady of the town** *n.* [early 18C] a prostitute. ❑ **lady of the lake** *n.* [SE *lake*, to play amorously; ? ult. LARK *v.*] [mid–late 17C] a prostitute. ❑ **sweet lady** *n. see under* SWEET *adj.*[1].

Lady Berkeley *n.* [var. on BERKELEY (HUNT) *n.* (1)] [19C] the vagina.

ladybird *n.* [SE *ladybird*, a sweetheart] [late 16C+] a prostitute.

Lady Blamey *n.* [*Lady Blamey*, widow of Sir Henry Blamey (1884–1951), who taught soldiers how to cut a beer bottle in two by winding a kerosene-soaked string around it, setting the string alight and then plunging the bottle into cold water, where it broke cleanly] [1940s] (*Aus.*) a drinking vessel made of half a beer bottle with the cut edge rounded by sandpaper.

Lady Dacre's wine *n.* [ety. unknown; ? anecdotal] [early 19C] gin.

lady from Bristol *n.* (*also* **lady of Bristol**) [rhy. sl.] [20C+] (*orig. Aus.*) a pistol.

Lady Godiva *n.* [rhy. sl. = FIVER *n.* (1)] [20C+] (*UK/US*) £5/$5.

Lady Green *n.* [his perceived 'womanishness' + SE *green*, naïve (in the ways of the world and of prison)] [mid-19C] (*UK Und.*) a prison chaplain.

Lady Jane *n.* [euph. use of proper name] [mid-19C+] the vagina.

Lady Laycock *n. see* *MISS LAYCOCK under* MISS *n.*

Lady Muck *n.* [fem. var. on *LORD MUCK under* MUCK *n.*[1]] [1930s+] an arrogant, pretentious woman of any class.

lady of Bristol *n. see* LADY FROM BRISTOL *n.*

lady of Spain *n.* [rhy. sl.] [1960s] (*Aus.*) a plane.

lady snow *n.*[1] [SE *lady* + SNOW *n.*[1] (1d)] [1950s–80s] (*US black*) a respected upper-class white woman.

lady snow *n.*[2] [SE *lady* + SNOW *n.*[1] (2a); note cocaine is a 'feminine' drug, see GIRL *n.*[2]] [1960s] (*drugs*) cocaine.

lag *n.*[1] [? OF *l'aigel/l'aigue*, water] **1** [mid-16C–18C] a bundle of clothes for washing; usu. as LAG OF DUDS *n.* **2** [17C–19C] urine. **3** [17C–19C] weak liquor or wine. **4** *see* LAGE *n.*

lag *n.*[2] (*also* **lagg**) [LAG *v.*[2] (1); note Aus. (Victoria) police jargon *lag*, 'one who informs especially, though not exclusively, against his or her fellow-officers' (Seal, *The Lingo*, 1999)] **1** [mid-18C–19C] (*US Und.*) a term of transportation or penal servitude. **2** [early 19C+] a convict who has been transported or sentenced to penal servitude. **3** [mid-19C] a convict who has finished his sentence or has been released on parole. **4** [mid-19C+] any convict; thus *Lagland*, the underworld. **5** [1910s+] (*Aus./N.Z./US prison*) any length of sentence. **6** [1930s+] (*Aus. prison*) a three-month sentence.

IN COMPOUNDS

❑ **lag fever** *n.* [early 19C] a spurious illness feigned in order to avoid transportation. ❑ **lag's farewell** *n. see* *SOLDIER'S FAREWELL under* SOLDIER *n.* ❑ **lag ship** *n.* [early 19C] a ship used for the transportation of convicts to Australia; a prison hulk.

IN PHRASES

❑ **dead lag** *n. see under* DEAD *adj.*

lag *n.*[3] (*also* **lag-a-bag, lag-lost**) [Scot. *lag/lag-a-bag/lag-lost*, a lazy person] [1910s+] a layabout, a ne'er-do-well, a lazy person.

lag *n.*[4] [synon. Afk] [2000s] (*S.Afr.*) a laugh, a joke.

lag *v.*[1] [LAG *n.*[1]] **1** [mid-16C] (*UK Und.*) to wash (down). **2** [mid 18C–19C] to urinate. **3** [mid-19C] (*UK Und.*) to water down **4** [2000s] to drink.

IN COMPOUNDS

❑ **lagging gage** *n.* [GAGE *n.*[1] (2)] [18C–19C] a chamberpot.

lag *v.*[2] (*also* **leg**) [16C SE *lag*, to carry off, to steal] **1** [mid-18C–19C] to sentence to transportation for more than seven years **2** [early 19C+] (*also* **lag off**) to arrest, to apprehend. **3** [mid 19C] (*UK Und.*) to cause trouble for; to lead to an arrest **4** [mid-19C+] to imprison. **5** [late 19C+] (*Aus.*) to inform on

6 [1910s] (*US Und.*) to imprison on trumped up charges and faked evidence.

lag *v.*[3] [? fig. use of LAG *v.*[1] (2), i.e. 'pissing around'/'piss on'] **1** [1950s+] to talk repetitively and tediously. **2** [1950s+] (*Aus. Und.*) to inform. **3** [1990s+] (*also* **lag off**) to shirk one's duties. **4** [2000s] (*S.Afr.*) to laugh.

IN PHRASES

❑ **take lag** *v.* [1950s] (*W.I./UK black*) to criticize, to attack verbally.

lag *v.*[4] *see* LEG *v.*[2].

lag-a-bag *n. see* LAG *n.*[3].

lage *n.* (*also* **lag, lagge**) [? OF *l'aige/l'aigue*, water] [mid-16C–19C] (*UK Und.*) water.

IN COMPOUNDS

❑ **lag-cull** *n.* [CULL *n.*[1] (3)] [mid-18C] (*UK Und*) a sailor.

lage *v.* [LAGE *n.*] [mid-16C–19C] to wash down or off with water.

lager beer *n.* [rhy. sl.] [1960s+] (*Aus.*) an ear.

lager-head *n.* [mid-19C] (*US*) a German.

lagg *v.* [? misreading of LAG *v.*[2] (1)] [mid-19C] (*US*) to execute by hanging.

lagga lagga *adj.* [SE *lag*, to dawdle, to walk slowly] [1980s] (*W.I.*) slow, time-wasting.

lagge *n. see* LAGE *n.*

lagged *adj.*[1] [LAG *v.*[2]] **1** [late 18C+] imprisoned, transported. **2** [1930s] (*US prison*) to be imprisoned with no hope of release.

lagged *adj.*[2] [LAGG v.] [mid-19C] (*US*) hanged.

lagger *n.*[1] [? LAG *n.*[2] (2)] [late 18C–mid-19C] a sailor; a waterman.

lagger *n.*[2] [LAG *v.*[2]] **1** [early 19C+] a convict; thus *long-lagger*, a convict serving a long sentence. **2** [mid-19C+] (*Aus. 20C+*) a police informer. **3** [1930s+] an ex-convict.

lagger *n.*[3] [poss. link also to Scot. *lagger*, to overload] [mid-19C] ? a full glass or other container.

lagger *n.*[4] [LAG *n.*[3]] [1990s+] a layabout, a 'corner boy'.

lagging *n.* [LAG *v.*[2]] **1** [early–mid-19C] (*UK Und.*) a sentence of transportation; thus *lagging matter*, any crime punishable by transportation. **2** [mid-19C+] (*UK Und.*) any prison sentence. **3** [mid-19C+] a sentence of more than three years' imprisonment.

IN COMPOUNDS

❑ **lagging dues** *n.* (*also* **lagging matter**) **1** [early–mid-19C] transportation; e.g. *lagging dues will be concerned*, this person is liable to be transported. **2** [late 19C] a sentence of penal servitude. ❑ **lagging station** *n.* [20C+] (*UK prison*) a prison for long-term prisoners.

lagging boat *n.* [LAG *n.*[1] (3)] [2000s] a drunkard, an alcoholic.

lag-lost *n. see* LAG *n.*[3].

lag of duds *n.* [LAG *n.*[1] + DUDS *n.*[1] (1); Harman's orig. definition is 'a buck of clothes', f. SE *buck*, a washtub, and thus a 'washtub's measure of clothes', *buck* contemporaneously meant lye, which would be used in the washing process] [mid-16C–19C] a bundle of clothes for washing.

lah *n.* (*also* **la**) [ety. unknown] [1990s+] very strong marijuana.

lahdee *adj.* (*also* **lahdi**) [abbr. LA-DI-DAH *adj.*] [1930s+] smart, fashionable.

lahdidah *adj. see* LA-DI-DAH *adj.*

lahnee *see under* LAANIE.

lahteeache! *excl.* [backsl.] [mid-19C+] all right.

laid *adj.*[1] [LAID OUT *adj.*[1]] [1960s+] (*US black*) intoxicated by alcohol or drugs.

IN PHRASES

❑ **laid to the bone** *adj.* [1960s–70s] (*US black*) drunk.

laid *adj.*[2] [abbr. LAID OUT *adj.*[2]] [1970s+] (*US black*) **1** fashionably dressed. **2** fashionably decorated. **3** worked out.

IN COMPOUNDS

❑ **laid crib** *n.* [CRIB *n.*[1] (1)] [1970s+] (*US black*) an attractive, well-furnished home.

IN PHRASES

❑ **laid to the bone** *adj.* [1970s+] (*US black*) **1** well-dressed. **2** of clothes, cut so well they seem a second skin. ❑ **laid to the natural bone** *adj.* [1970s+] (*US black*) naked.

laid *adj.*[3] *see* LAY *v.*[1] (1).

laid-back *adj.* **1** [1960s+] passive, relaxed, casual. **2** [1960s+] of music, soothing, peaceful. **3** [1970s+] intoxicated by drugs or alcohol.

laid out *adj.*[1] [SE *laid out*, awaiting burial, i.e. one is 'dead' drunk] [1920s+] (*US*) drunk.

laid out *adj.*[2] [1960s+] (*US black*) **1** of a person, well-dressed; good-looking. **2** of a place, smart, neat.

laid, relaid and parlayed *phr. see under* LAY *v.*[1] (1).

laid up in Job's dock, be *v. see* JOB'S WARD *n.*

laigz *n.* [? fig. use of SE *legs*; or *lag*, used in games as 'a chance, an opportunity'] [1940s+] (*W.I.*) **1** a trick. **2** influence.

laimeter *n.* (*also* **lamester, lameter, lamitor**) [Scot. *lamiter*, a lame person, a cripple] [20C+] (*Ulster*) one who is feeling unwell.

lain/laine *n. see* LANE *n.*[2].

lair *n.* (*also* **lare**) [backform. f. LAIRY *adj.* (2)] (*Aus.*) **1** [1920s+] a show-off, one who dresses flashily. **2** [1960s] behaviour considered to be showing off.

DERIVATIVES

❑ **lairish** *adj.* [2000s] ostentatious.

lair *v.* (*also* **lair up**) [LAIR *n.*] [1920s+] (*Aus.*) **1** to dress flashily, to dress up. **2** to act in a showy manner.

IN PHRASES

❑ **lair up** *v.* (*also* **lare up**) [1920s+] (*Aus.*) to brag, to boast, to show off.

laired up *phr.* (*also* **all laired up**) [LAIR *n.*] [1920s+] (*Aus.*) flashily dressed.

lairily *adv.* [LEERY *adj.* (2)] [1990s+] cautiously.

lairize *v.* [ext. of LAIR v.] [1920s+] (*Aus.*) to brag, to boast, to show off; thus as n. *lairizer*, a cheeky show-off.

lairy *adj.* (*also* **lary**) [LEERY *adj.*] **1** [mid-19C+] knowing, conceited, cheeky. **2** [20C+] (*Aus.*) (*also* **leary**) flashy, ostentatious, showy.

lairy *adv.* (*also* **leary**) [LAIRY *adj.* (2)] [20C+] (*Aus.*) showily, ostentatiously.

laka *n.* [ety. unknown] [1960s] (*US gay*) the penis.

lakanuki *n. see* LACKANOOKY *n.*

Lake, the *n.* [1920s] (*US Und.*) Salt Lake City, Utah.

laken *n. see* LACKIN *n.*

laker lady *n.* [for ety. *see* LADY OF THE LAKE *under* LADY *n.*] [18C–19C] a prostitute.

lakes (of Killarney) *adj.* [rhy. sl.] [1910s+] **1** (*also* **lakesy**) mad, eccentric; as *n.*, a mad person [BARMY *adj.*]. **2** two-faced, untrustworthy [CARNEY *adj.* (1)].

lakin *n.*[1]

IN EXCLAMATIONS

❑ **by our lakin!** (*also* **byr'lakin!**) [lit. *by our little lady*] [late 15C–mid-17C] a mild oath, euph. for *by our lady!*

lakin *n.*[2] *see* LACKIN *n.*

La-La *n.* [abbr. of LA-LA LAND *n.*] [2000s] (*US black*) Los Angeles, California.

la-la *n.*[1] (*also* **la**) [abbr./redup.] [1960s+] (*Aus.*) a lavatory.

la-la *n.*[2] [? LOLLA *n.*] [1970s] the vagina.

lala/la-la *n. see* LOLLA *n.*

La-La Land *n.* **1** [1920s] (*US*) Paris [Fr. cliché *ooh-la-la*]. **2** [1970s+] (*orig. US*) Los Angeles [L.A. *n.* but note LA-LA LAND *n.*].

la-la land *n.* [1970s+] (*US*) a fantasy world; thus *in la-la land*, out of touch with reality, drugged or drunk.

lalapalooza/lalapazaza *n. see* LALLAPALOOSA *n.*

lal brough *n.* (*also* **lally**) [rhy. sl.; *Lal* = dimin. of *Alice*, the image is of an old lady, 'Lal Brough', taking snuff] [20C+] snuff.

lal-lah/lallah *n. see* LOLLA *n.*

lallapaloosa *n.* (*also* **lalapalooza, lalapazaza, lallapalooza, lallapaluza, lallypaloozer, lolapaloosa, lollapalo, lollapaloosa, lollapalooza, lollypalooza, lollypaloozer, wollapalooza**) **1** [late 19C+] (*orig. US*) something or someone outstandingly good, stylish or pleasing of its kind. **2** [1920s] a devastating punch. **3** [1940s] an extreme example.

lallie *n.* (*also* **lallette, lally, lyle**) [? shared initial letters] [1960s+] (*Ling. Fr./Polari*) a leg; usu. in pl.

lalligag *v. see* LALLYGAG *v.*

lally *n.* **1** *see* LAL BROUGH *n.* **2** *see* LULLY *n.*[1].

lallycooler *n. see* LOLLYCOOLER *n.*

lallygag *n.* (*also* **lollygag**) [LALLYGAG *v.*] **1** [mid-19C+] foolishness, nonsense, empty chatter. **2** [20C+] (*also* **lollygog**) flirting, love-making; thus lollygagger, one who enjoys flirting. **3** [1940s] a wastrel, an irresponsible person.

lallygag *v.* (*also* **lalligag, lolligag, lollygag**) [ety. unknown, ? link to dial. *lolly*, the tongue or SE *loll* around] **1** [mid-19C+] (*US*) to fool around, to kiss and cuddle; also as n. *lollygagger*. **2** [late 19C] (*US campus*) to surpass, to take advantage of. **3** [late 19C+] (*US*) to dawdle, to dally, to fool about.

lallypaloozer *n. see* LALLAPALOOSA *n.*

lam *n.*[1] [LAM *v.*[2] (1)] **1** [late 19C+] (*US*) (*also* **lamas**) an escape, e.g. from prison. **2** [1990s+] an escape from work or duty.

IN PHRASES

❑ **do a lam** *v.* [mid-19C] to run away, to escape eg. from prison. ❑ **on the lam** **1** [1910s+] quickly, at a run, at top speed. **2** [1920s+] (*US Und.*) on the run from prison or the police, thus fig. on the loose. ❑ **take it on the lam** *v.* [20C+] (*US Und.*) to run away, to escape (esp. from prison).

lam *n.*[2] [LAM *v.*[1]] [1900s–30s] (*US*) a punch or blow.

IN PHRASES

❑ **have a lam on** *v.* [? the temper occasions the blows] [1990s+] to be in a bad temper.

lam *v.*[1] (*also* **lamb, lambo, lamm, lamme**) [linked to ON *lemja*, to lame, as a result of a beating] **1** [late 16C+] to beat or strike; thus *lamming*, a beating, *lam out*, to lash out. **2** [mid–late 19C] (*US*) to defeat in a fight. **3** [late 19C] (*Aus.*) to swindle. **4** [1910s–40s] to throw, to toss, to smash against. **5** [1920s] in fig. use, to do perfunctorily, fast.

IN PHRASES

❑ **give lamb and salad** *v.* [pun] [mid-19C–1900s] to beat, to thrash. ❑ **lam into** *v.* [the term began life as UK sl. but crossed the Atlantic to reappear in criminal milieux] **1** [late 19C+] to beat up. **2** [late 19C+] to do something aggressively, wholeheartedly. **3** [1970s+] to attack verbally.

lam *v.*[2] (*also* **lamb, lam out**) [? early 19C Und. *lammas*, to depart, to leave, or as abbr. of *slam* or from LAM *v.*[1] thus pun on BEAT IT *v.*. Major, *Juba to Jive: A Dict. of Afro-American Slang* (1994), suggests link to Igbo *lam*, to leave, which would be interchangeable in the eyes of US black slave owners] **1** [late 19C+] (*US Und.*) to run away, to escape from prison. **2** [late 19C+] to leave, to go away (without the assumed pressure of sense 1). **3** [1910s–50s] (*US*) to chase, to run after.

IN PHRASES

❑ **lam into** *v.* [1920s] (*US*) to encounter, to run into. ❑ **lam out on** *v.* [1920s+] to run away (from someone).

lam *v.*[3] *see* LAMP *v.*[2] (1).

lamaster *n. see* LAMSTER *n.*

lamb *n.*[1] [note Williams for 17C use of *lamb* as a novice whore] **1** [mid-17C–1960s] a simpleton, a fool, esp. one easily cheated of their money. **2** [late 19C] a rough, a thug. **3** [1920s–70s] (*mainly US prison*) (*also* **kid lamb**) a young homosexual boy, esp. one who accompanies a tramp. **4** [1940s+] (*US black*) an innocent.

IN COMPOUNDS

❑ **lamb-brained** *adj.* [2000s] (*N.Z.*) weak, stupid.

SE in slang uses

IN COMPOUNDS

❑ **lamb and spinach** *n.* [mid-19C] (*UK Und.*) women and gin. ❑ **lamb cannon** *n.* [1990s+] the penis. ❑ **lamb chop** *n.* [1970s+] a term of affection; usu. of a woman, occas. a man. ❑ **lamb-pie** *n.* [a pun on the SE *lamb*/LAM *v.*[1] (1)] [late 17C–early 19C] a beating, a flogging. ❑ **lamb pit** *n.* [1950s–70s] the vagina. ❑ **lamb sauce** *n.* [mid-19C] (*UK Und.*) fine clothes. ❑ **lambskin man** *n.* [the ermine-bordered robes] [late 17C–mid-19C] a judge. ❑ **lamb's tongue** *n.* [1930s–40s] (*US prison*) **1** $1. **2** a $5 bill.

IN PHRASES

❑ **fresh lamb** *n.* [mid-19C] (*UK Und.*) a new prostitite. ❑ **holy lamb** *n.* [a pun on Lat. *agnus dei*, the lamb of God, used as the first words of the Catholic mass. The term lamb was given to the particularly violent troops led by the soldier of fortune Colonel Percy Kirke in 1684–6. Their flag carried an image of the paschal lamb, known in heraldry as the *holy lamb*, and the troops were known as 'Kirke's lambs'. Lambs also referred to gangs of thugs used to intimidate voters at 19C elections, e.g. the 'Nottingham lambs', which flourished 1860–70] [late 18C–19C] (*Irish*) a complete and utter villain.

lamb *n.*[2] [? abbr. FULHAMS *n.* (1)] [late 18C] (*UK Und.*) a dice.

IN COMPOUNDS

❑ **lambsman** *n.* [late 18C] (*UK Und.*) a professional dice cheat.

lamb *v.* **1** *see* LAM *v.*[1]. **2** *see* LAM *v.*[2].

lamb and salad *n.*

IN PHRASES

❑ **give lamb and salad** *v. see under* LAM *v.*[1].

lambasted *adj.* [colloq. *lambaste*, to thrash] [1990s+] drunk.

lamb down *v.* [shearing jargon *lamb down*, to tend ewes at lambing time, usu. used by shearers and other rural workers; but also note the stereotypical innocence/vulnerability of a lamb] [late 19C–1910s] (*Aus./N.Z.*) **1** to persuade someone to spend al[l] their money on alcohol. **2** to calm someone down. **3** to spen[d] all one's money.

IN COMPOUNDS

❑ **lambing-down shanty** *n.* [late 19C–1910s] (*Aus.*) a rura[l] tavern. ❑ **lambing-down shop** *n.* [late 19C–1910s] (*Aus.*) a public house.

lamber-down *n.* [LAMB DOWN *v.* (1)] [late 19C–1910s] (*Aus./N.Z.*) a shanty-keeper or landlord who persuades men to spen[d] all their money on drink.

Lambeth *v.* [the well-known public bath-house in Lambeth] [lat[e] 19C–1900s] to wash.

Lambeth Walk *n.* [rhy. sl.] [1930s+] the chalk used in billiard[s] or snooker.

lamb fry *n. see* LAMB'S FRY *n.*

lambing-down shanty *n. see under* LAMB DOWN *v.*

lambing-down shop *n. see under* LAMB DOWN *v.*

lam black *n. see* LAMPBLACK *n.*

Lambo *n.* [2000s] (*UK black*) a Lamborghini.

lambo *v. see* LAM *v.*[1].

lamborghini *n.* [a make of luxury sports car] [1990s+] (*drugs*) crack pipe made from a plastic rum bottle and a rubbe[r] sparkplug cover (cf. MASERATI *n.*).

lambsbread *n.* (*also* **lamb's breath**) [? a form of plant, cf. S[E] *lamb's lettuce*, corn salad] [1950s+] (*W.I./Rasta*) a form of high quality marijuana.

lamb's fry *n.* (*also* **lamb fry**) [rhy. sl.] [20C+] (*Aus./US*) **1** [a] necktie. **2** an eye, usu. used in the pl.

lamb skin-it *n. see* SKIN-THE-LAMB *n.*

lame *n.* [LAME *adj.*] **1** [1940s+] (*US prison*) a weakling. **2** [1950s+] (*orig. US black*) an unsophisticated person or a foo[l]. **3** [1960s] (*US drugs*) a tobacco cigarette. **4** [1960s+] (*US Und*[.]) a non-criminal and so a possible victim. **5** [1970s+] (*US drug*[s]) one who does not take drugs.

DERIVATIVES

❑ **lamer** *n.* [1950s+] (*US teen*) a general term of contemp[t] disparagement.

lame *adj.* **1** [mid-19C+] (*US*) bankrupted by gambling o[r] speculation. **2** [late 19C+] (*also* **lame-ass**) naïve, clums[y] socially inept, incompetent; thus n. *lameness*, weakness, social ineptitude. **3** [20C+] drunk. **4** [1950s+] (*US black*) contemptible. **5** [1970s+] of drugs, weak.

DERIVATIVES

❑ **lameness** *n.* [1990s+] inadequacy, weakness.

IN COMPOUNDS

❑ **lamehead** *n.* [-HEAD *sfx*] [1970s+] (*US*) a fool.

IN PHRASES

❑ **lame as a mule** *adj.* [1990s+] (*Aus.*) utterly useless.

lamebrain *n.* [SE *lame* + sfx *-brain*] [1910s+] (*orig. US*) a fool, a simpleton; thus *lamebrained*, stupid, foolish.

lamebrain *adj.* (*also* **lamebrained**) [LAMEBRAIN *n.*] [1920s+] stupid, foolish.

lame duck *n.*[1] **1** [mid-18C+] a defaulter on the Stock Exchange; thus anybody who is unable to pay his debts. **2** [early 19C+] any weak, disabled or useless person, and thus falling behind their peers. **3** [mid-19C+] (*US orig. political*) a defeated politician who is working out a period of office, esp. a president who has been defeated in the presidential election in November but does not leave office – in which all decisions are now *de facto* irrelevant – until January; this usage can extend to any similarly placed officials. **4** [1940s] (*Aus.*) a rascal.

lame duck *n.*[2] [rhy. sl. = FUCK *n.*] [1940s+] an act of sexual intercourse.

lame-duck *adj.* [LAME DUCK *n.*[1] (2)] [1920s+] weak, useless, inferior.

lame-o *n.* (*also* **lamo**) [LAME *n.* + -O *sfx* (1)] [1970s+] (*US campus*) a general term of contempt or disparagement, a weakling, an inadequate, one not attuned to the prevailing styles and priorities.

lame-o *adj.* [LAME-O *n.*] [1990s+] second-rate, weak, inadequate.

lameroo *n. see* LAMSTER *n.*

lames *n.* [LAME *n.*; on pattern of HOMES *n.*] [1950s+] (*US black*) a general term of contempt, disparagement; as a term of address.

lamester/lameter *n. see* LAIMETER *n.*

l.a.m.f. *phr.* [abbr.] [1960s+] (*US gang*) *l*ike *a* *m*other *f*ucker; when added to a gang name it implies the toughness and aggressiveness of the person so defined.

laminate *n.* [pun on PLASTIC *adj.*] [1980s+] (*US campus*) something or someone phoney, false.

Lamington *n.* ['a soft felt hat with a curled brim and a dented crown, first worn at Homburg, once a fashionable health-resort' (*OED*). Aus. use plays on SAusE *lamington*, a square of sponge cake coated in chocolate icing and desiccated coconut, ult. Baron Lamington (1860–1940), governor of Queensland] [late 19C–1940s] (*Aus.*) a Homburg hat.

lamister *n. see* LAMSTER *n.*

lamitor *n. see* LAIMETER *n.*

lamm *v. see* LAM *v.*[1].

lammas *v.* [? var. on LAM *v.*[2]; ult. SE *Lammas*, harvest festival] [mid-19C] (*UK Und.*) to run off.

lam-master *n. see* LAMSTER *n.*

lamme *v. see* LAM *v.*[1].

lammie/lammister *n. see* LAMSTER *n.*

lammy *n.* [SE *lambskin*. Note naut. jargon *lammy*, a duffel coat] [mid-19C] a blanket.

lamo *n. see* LAME-O *n.*

lamous *adj.* [? the name of a Chicago company that made fake jewellery] [1910s] (*US tramp*) **1** cheap, inferior, esp. of jewellery. **2** of a person, harmless.

lamp *n.* [joc. abbr. SE *headlamps*] **1** [19C+] an eye, usu. in pl.; thus *queer lamp*, a blind, sore or squinting eye. **2** [late 19C–1900s] in pl., spectacles. **3** [1920s+] (*US*) a look or glance. **4** [1950s] in pl., the female breasts.

IN PHRASES

❑ **smoke (one of) someone's lamps** *v.* [1910s–20s] (*US*) to give someone a black eye.

SE in slang uses

IN PHRASES

❑ **lamp of light** *n.* (*also* **lamp of life**) [19C] the penis. ❑ **lamp of love** *n.* [19C] the vagina.

lamp *v.*[1] [? LAM *v.*[1]] **1** [early 19C+] to beat, to strike, to thrash. **2** [1950s] (*W.I.*) to trick, to deceive.

lamp *v.*[2] [LAMP *n.*] **1** [20C+] (*also* **lam**) (*orig. US*) to look at, to assess visually. **2** [1950s+] to consider, to think about. [the image is of watching other people] **3** [1980s+] (*US black/campus*) to loiter, to 'hang out', to relax while others panic.

lamp along *v.* [a *lamplighter* works quickly] [mid-19C+] (*Irish*) to go along at a great pace.

lampblack *n.* (*also* **lam black**) [? LAM *v.*[1] (1); thus the bruises make one's skin even darker, or SE *lampblack*, carbon residue, often used for blacking up] [1930s–40s] (*US black*) a very dark-skinned black person.

lamp chop *n.* [? lamb chop] [1930s] (*US*) a violin.

lamper *n.* [LAMP *v.*[1] (2)] [1950s] (*W.I.*) a confidence trickster.

lamp habit *n. see under* HABIT *n.* (1).

lampish *adj. see under* PARAFFIN LAMP *n.*

lamp-post *n.* **1** [late 19C+] a teasing name for a tall, thin person. **2** [1920s] (*US*) any large and noticeable piece of jewellery.

lamps *n. see* GIG-LAMPS *n.*

lamster *n.* (*also* **lamaster, lameroo, lamester, lamister, lam-master, lammie, lammister**) [LAM *v.*[2]] **1** [20C+] (*US Und./prison*) an escapee, a fugitive. **2** [1920s] (*US Und.*) a member of a pickpocket team who leaves with the loot.

lam up *v.* [US dial. *lam*, to pick up a small object] [1920s] (*US*) to pick up.

lana *n.* [2000s] (*S.Afr. gay*) the penis.

Lancashire lass *n.* [rhy. sl.] [1930s] a drinking glass.

Lancashire lasses *n.* [rhy. sl.] [1930s+] glasses (spectacles).

lance *n.* (*also* **lancet**) **1** [late 15C–mid-19C; 1960s+] the penis. **2** [1940s–50s] (*US drugs*) a hypodermic needle.

IN PHRASES

❑ **get one's lance waxed** *v.* [1980s] of a man, to have sexual intercourse. ❑ **lance of love** *n.* [19C] the penis.

lance *v.* (*US*) **1** [1900s] to charge, to extract money; the inference is of cheating. **2** [1960s+] of a man, to have sexual intercourse; often ext. in phr. eg *lance with one's pork sword*.

lance-jack *n.* [JACK *n.*[2] (1)] [1910s+] (*orig. UK milit.*) a lance-corporal.

lance-knight *n.* (*also* **lanceman, lance-prigger**) [? Ger. *Landsknechte*, a mercenary soldier who, when not actually fighting, terrorized civilians] [late 16C–mid-17C] **1** a highwayman. **2** a horse-thief who owns his own horse.

lancepresado *n.* (*also* **lanspresado, lansprisado**) [Fr. *lancepessade*, 'the meanest officer in a foot-company' (Cotgrave, *Dict. French and English Tongues*, 1611), used in English as a synon. for *lance-corporal*, the lowest rank of NCO] [17C–mid-19C] one who comes into company, esp. in a tavern or public house, with only a few pence in their pocket; an informer.

lance-prigger *n. see* LANCE-KNIGHT *n.*

land *n.*[1] [SE *land(ed) a blow*] [20C+] (*Irish*) a surprise, usu. a disappointment, a letdown.

land *n.*[2] [2000s] (*US black*) a closed-off area, such as a car that is a place to smoke marijuana in.

SE in slang uses

IN COMPOUNDS

❑ **landbroker** *n.* [mid-19C] (*UK Und.*) an undertaker. ❑ **land carrack** *n.* [SE *carrack*, a large ship; she 'sails' the streets] [17C] a prostitute. ❑ **land-leaper** *n.* (*also* **land-loper**) [SE *leap*/Du. *loopen*, to run] [mid-14C–mid-19C] a criminal vagabond, subsisting on pilfering and often disguised with fake sores and similar blandishments. ❑ **land-lubber** *n.* [LUBBER *n.*] [early 17C–mid-19C] a wandering tramp, a vagrant. ❑ **land-pirate** *n.* **1** [17C–19C] a highwayman, a wandering thief, a gypsy.

2 [early 19C] a thieving prostitute. ❑ **land-rat** *n.* [late 16C–mid-19C] a term of abuse. ❑ **land shark** *n. see under* SHARK *n.* ❑ **land-yard** *n.* [mid-19C] (*UK Und.*) a graveyard.

IN PHRASES

❑ **land o' cakes** [18C–1900s] Scotland. ❑ **land o' darkness** [1930s–40s] (*US black*) Harlem, New York City; thus the black district of any city. ❑ **land of milk and honey** *n.* [MILK *n.* (1a) + HONEY *n.*[1] (4b)] [2000s] (*S.Afr. gay*) the anus. ❑ **land of the wooden hams** *n.* (*also* **land of the wooden nutmegs**) [the concept of such wooden items as symbols of deceit (cf. ety. for NUTMEG (MAKER) *n.*)] [19C–1900s] (*Aus.*) America. ❑ **land of twang** *n.* [the accent] [1900s] (*Aus.*) the United States. ❑ **who has any lands in Appleby?** [late 17C–early 19C] a phr. addressed to 'the man at whose door the glass stands long, or who does not circulate it in due time' (Grose 1785).

IN EXCLAMATIONS

❑ **my land!** (*also* **my lands!**) [euph. for SE *my lord*] [mid-19C+] (*Can./US*) a mild oath.

land *v.* **1** [mid-19C–1900s] to win a bet, to win something by betting. **2** [mid-19C+] to help someone, to aid, to 'set on one's feet'. **3** [late 19C+] (*also* **land out**) to hit someone, i.e. to land a blow on; thus *land one on*; as n., *lander*. **4** [late 19C+] in fig. use, to defeat someone, to 'dish out' to someone. **5** [1910s–30s] to arrest, to capture.

IN PHRASES

❑ **land on** *v.* [1910s+] (*US*) to reprimand severely. ❑ **land someone in the shit** *v. see under* SHIT *n.*

land! *excl. see* LANDSAKES! *excl.*

landed estate *n.* [late 19C–1910s] **1** a grave; thus (WW1 milit.) *become a landowner*, to die. **2** dirt beneath the fingernails.

landlady *n.* [euph.] [late 19C+] (*US*) a madam, a proprietress of a brothel.

land of hope *n.* [rhy. sl.] [20C+] soap.

landprop *n.* [? SE *land*lord + *prop*rietor] [1930s–70s] (*US black*) a landlord or landlady.

landsakes! *excl.* (*also* **for landsakes! land! lands! land's-a-livin'! lands-sake!**) ['Lord's sake!'] [mid-19C+] (*mainly US*) a mild oath.

land's end! *excl.* [var. on LANDSAKES! *excl.*] [1980s] (*US campus*) an all-purpose excl.

Lane, the *n.* **1** [mid–late 19C] Horsemonger Lane jail. **2** [mid-19C–1900s] Drury Lane Theatre, London. **3** [mid-19C–1910s] Leather Lane, a large street market (London EC1). **4** [mid-19C–1930s] Petticoat Lane Market (Middlesex St, London E1). **5** [1910s] (*US*) The Bowery, NYC.

lane *n.*[1] [mid-16C+] the throat.

IN PHRASES

❑ **red lane** *n.* (*also* **red lane alley**) [18C+] the throat.

lane *n.*[2] (*also* **lain, laine**) [? one who lives in a country lane or var. pron. of LAME *n.*] [1930s–60s] (*US black*) **1** a peasant, a rustic. **2** an unsophisticated person. **3** a male. **4** a new inmate in a prison [their lack of knowledge of prison life].

IN PHRASES

❑ **ace lane** *n.* [ACE *adj.* (1)] [1940s] (*US black*) a husband.

Lane Cove *n.* [rhy. sl.] [20C+] (*Aus.*) a stove.

langel *n.* [dial. *langel*, a tether or rope for restraining an animal] [20C+] (*Ulster*) a tall, thin person.

langer *n.* [? joc. var. of SE *long one* or link to LANGOLEE *n.*] [1980s+] (*Irish*) **1** the penis. **2** a contemptible person.

langered *adj.* (*also* **langers**) [Scot. *langer*, weariness] [20C+] (*Irish*) drunk.

langolee *n.* [Welsh *trangluni*, tools] [mid–late 19C] the penis.

langret *n.* [15C Eng. and 15C–19C Scot. var. sp. of *lang*, long] [mid-16C–early 19C] a type of false die, in which one side is fractionally longer than the rest.

language *n.* [early 19C+] 'bad' language, obscenity; rudeness, argument.

language *v.* [LANGUAGE *n.*] [1900s] (*Aus.*) to use obscene language towards.

language! *excl.* [abbr. *Mind your bad language!* or some similar restraint] [mid-19C+] be quiet! shut up!

langulala *n.* [Hausa *langalanga*, a tall, thin person] [1940s+] (*W.I.*) a very tall, thin person.

lani/lanie *see under* LAANIE.

lank *adj.* [Afk. phr. *lank nie sleg nie*, not bad at all] [1970s+] (*S.Afr.*) a general term of approval, usu. from children or young people.

lanky *n.*[1] (*also* **lank**) [SE *lanky*, adj., tall, thin] [mid-19C+] a nickname for a tall, thin person.

IN PHRASES

❑ **lanky drink of cactus juice** *n. see* LONG DRINK OF WATER *under* LONG *adj.*

lanky *n.*[2] [abbr.] [late 19C] (*Aus.*) a person from *Lanc*ashire, England.

lanky fathom of misery *n. see* LONG STREAK OF MISERY *under* STREAK *n.*

Lanna Macree's dog *n.* (*also* **Lanty McHale's dog, Lanty MacHale's goat, Larry McHale's dog**) [? anecdotal] [20C+] (*Irish*) a time-server, one who befriends whoever they happen to be with.

lanny *n.* [abbr.] [2000s] (*N.Z.*) a *Land* Rover.

lanspresado/lansprisado *n. see* LANCEPRESADO *n.*

lantern *n.* [it helps one on one's way (i.e. with one's plans, requests etc)] [mid-19C] a bribe.

IN PHRASES

❑ **dark lantern** *n. see under* DARK *adj.*

Lanty McHale's dog/Lanty MacHale's goat *n. see* LANNA MACREE'S DOG *n.*

lap *n.*[1] [euph.; but note SE *lap*, a fold of flesh] [late 15C–17C] the vagina.

DERIVATIVES

❑ **lapful** *n.* [19C–1920s] **1** a husband; a lover. **2** an unborn child.

IN COMPOUNDS

❑ **lap-clap** *n.* [SE *clap*, a blow] [17C–mid-18C] **1** sexual intercourse. **2** conception; thus *get a lap-clap*, to become pregnant. ❑ **lapland** *n.* **1** [late 17C–19C] the vagina; thus *Lapland witch*, a prostitute. **2** [1920s+] the world of women. ❑ **lap-lover** *n.* [1970s+] one who enjoys cunnilingus.

SE in slang uses

IN PHRASES

❑ **under the lap** *adv.* (*Aus.*) **1** [1930s+] confidentially. **2** [1940s+] clandestinely.

lap *n.*[2] [SE *lap*, to drink] (*UK Und.*) **1** [mid-16C–mid-19C] buttermilk or whey or any thin, non-alcoholic drink. **2** [early 17C–1930s] liquor in general. **3** [mid-17C–mid-19C] soup. **4** [early 18C–1900s] tea.

IN COMPOUNDS

❑ **lap-feeder** *n.* [late 18C–1900s] a silver tablespoon.

IN PHRASES

❑ **go on the lap** *v.* [late 19C–1900s] to go out drinking.

lap *v.* (*also* **lap up**) [fig. use of SE *lap* v./LAP *n.*[2] (2)] **1** [19C+] to drink alcohol, esp. greedily. **2** [mid-19C] (*UK Und.*) to take, to steal. **3** [late 19C+] to enjoy greatly; usu. as *lap it up*. **4** [1930s+] to perform cunnilingus [note LAP *n.*[1]/CUNT-LAPPER *n.*]. **5** [1990s+] to be very fond of.

SE in slang uses

IN PHRASES

❑ **lap the gutter** *v.* [? either *GUTTER-ALLEY under* GUTTER *n.* or GATTER *n.*[1]] [mid–late 19C] to drink; to get drunk.

lap-ears *n.* [SE *lop-ears*, a donkey] [mid-19C] (*US campus*) a notably religious student.

lapper *n.* **1** [19C–1900s] (*UK Und.*) alcohol; thus *rare-lapper*, a hard drinker [LAP *n.*[2] (2)]. **2** [mid-19C] (*US*) the tongue; thus as phr. *cool one's lapper*, have a drink [SE *lap*]. **3** [1930s+] one who performs oral sex [*see* LAP *v.* (4)].

lappie *n.* [Afk. *lappie*, a rag, i.e. that into which the solvent is poured prior to being sniffed] [2000s] (*S.Afr. drugs*) the sniffing of solvents; also as v.

lappy *adj.* [LAP *n.*^{2} (2)] [18C] (*UK Und.*) drunk.

larakin *n. see* LARRIKIN *n.*

larceny *n.* **1** [1920s+] (*US Und.*) an inclination towards theft, a liking for theft; thus *larceny in his heart*. **2** [1940s–60s] (*US black*) in fig. use, thoughts or feelings, usu. unpleasant or antagonistic.

IN PHRASES

❑ **lay one's larceny** *v.* [1940s] to talk to, to 'chat up'.

SE in slang uses

IN PHRASES

❑ **larceny shoes** *n.* [as a status symbol of (orig.) black teens, such shoes are allegedly the badge of criminality; thus a racist slur] [1980s+] (*US*) elaborate, high-priced trainers (cf. FELONY SHOES *n.*).

larceny *v.* [LARCENY *n.* (2)] [1940s–60s] (*US black*) to think badly of, to suspect, to view someone negatively.

lard *n.* [SE *lard*, the fat of an animal] **1** [mid-19C; 1910s+] (*US*) human fat, often in combs. **2** [1920s–50s] (*US*) butter or margarine. **3** [1970s+] (*Irish*) (*also* **beat the meal out of**) the essence, the 'daylights'; usu. in phr. *beat the lard out of*.

DERIVATIVES

❑ **lardo** *n.* [-O *sfx* (1)] [1980s+] (*US*) a fat person, usu. used in direct address.

IN COMPOUNDS

❑ **lard-ass(ed)** *see* separate entries. ❑ **lard ball** *n.* [-BALL *sfx*] [1940s+] an obese person. ❑ **lard batty** *n.* [BATTY *n.*^{2} (1)] [2000s] (*UK black*) a fat person. ❑ **lard-belly** *n.* [1930s+] (*US*) an obese person. ❑ **lard-bladder** *n.* [late 19C–1920s] an obese person. ❑ **lardbrain** *n. see* LARDHEAD *n.* ❑ **lard-bucket** *n.* [1950s+] a fat person. ❑ **lard-butt** *n.* [BUTT *n.*^{1} (1a)] [1960s+] (*US*) an obese person. ❑ **lard-can** *n.* [1920s] (*US*) a fat person. ❑ **lardhead** *n. see* separate entries.

IN PHRASES

❑ **lard up** *v.* [1990s+] to put on weight. ❑ **swim in golden lard** *v. see* SWIM IN GOLDEN GREASE *under* SWIM *v.*

lard and pail *n. see* BUCKET AND PAIL *n.*

lard-ass *n.* (*also* **lard**) [LARD *n.* (1) + ASS *n.* (2); i.e. someone who sits on their posterior and does nothing but cultivate lard] [1920s+] (*orig. US*) **1** an overweight person; often used as a nickname for such a person; thus a lazy, good-for-nothing person. **2** a fat posterior.

lard-assed *adj.* (*also* **lard-ass**) [LARD-ASS *n.*] [1940s+] (*US*) having large buttocks, fat; thus lazy, useless.

larder *n.* [SE *larder*, a cold store] [2000s] (*S.Afr. gay*) the male genital area.

lardhead *n.* (*also* **lardbrain**) [SE *lard* + -HEAD *sfx* (1)] [1930s+] (*US/Aus.*) a stupid person.

lardy *n. see* LA-DI-DAH *n.*^{2} (3).

lardy *adj.* [LARD *n.* (1)] [1920s+] fat, obese.

IN COMPOUNDS

❑ **lardyface** *adj.* [1920s] a derog. description of one with a fat face.

lardy-dardy *adj.* (*also* **lardy**) [var. on LA-DI-DAH *adj.* but actually earlier, so ? simply the sound of the speech] [mid-19C+] affected, supercilious, foppish; thus n. snobbishness, arrogance.

IN PHRASES

❑ **come the lardy-dardy** *v.* [mid–late 19C] to dress in a showy manner. ❑ **do the lardy** *v.* [late 19C] to put on airs.

lardy-dardy *v.* [LARDY-DARDY *adj.*] [late 19C] to act in a supercilious manner.

lare *n. see* LAIR *n.*

lareover *n.* (*also* **layer-over, layover**) [it is 'laid over' the taboo term] [late 17C–18C] a word that is substituted for one that is considered indecent.

lare up *v. see under* LAIR *v.*

large *n.* (*also* **large one**) [1970s+] **1** (*US*) $1,000; usu. in multiples, e.g. *200 large* etc. **2** £1,000; usu. in multiples. **3** (*Aus.*) of a jail sentence, one year.

large *adj.* **1** [late 19C–1910s] (*US campus*) enjoyable, fine. **2** [1910s+] (*W.I./Rasta*) respected. **3** [1920s+] (*US black*) successful, exciting. **4** [1990s+] (*US teen*) impressive.

IN COMPOUNDS

❑ **large-head** *n.* [-HEAD *sfx*] [late 19C–1900s] (*US*) a drunkard. ❑ **large house** *n. see* BIG HOUSE *n.* (1). ❑ **large lad** *n. see* LAD *n.* (3). ❑ **large order** *n. see* TALL ORDER *under* ORDER *n.* ❑ **large one** *n. see* LARGE *n.*

IN PHRASES

❑ **large for** *adj.* [1960s+] (*US*) enthusiastic.

large *adv.* [mid-19C+] unrestrainedly, excessively, in a self-indulgent manner; thus *dress large*, to dress in an ostentatious manner; *play large*, to gamble heavily; *talk large*, to boast.

IN PHRASES

❑ **live large** *v.* (*also* **live big**) [coined as the motto of 'The Executioner', hero of the action adventure series by Don Pendleton, first publ. 1969] [1950s+] (*US*) to live extravagantly and ostentatiously. ❑ **up large** [1980s+] (*N.Z.*) drinking heavily.

large (it) *v.* [1990s+] **1** to live extravagantly, in a showy manner. **2** to show off, to act aggressively.

largie *n.* **1** [1970s+] (*W.I., Bdos*) a 750ml (26fl oz) bottle of rum. **2** [2000s] (*Aus.*) a 750ml (26fl oz) bottle of beer.

larikin *n. see* LARRIKIN *n.*

lark *n.*^{1} [ety. unknown] [early 18C] (*UK Und.*) a boat.

lark *n.*^{2} (*also* **larky**) [play on BIRD *n.*^{1} (3a)] [19C] (*US*) a fellow, a man.

SE in slang uses

IN PHRASES

❑ **have larks for breakfast/supper** *v.* [larks are trad. good singers] [1910s] (*Ulster*) to be especially eloquent.

lark *n.*^{3} [? northern dial. *lake*, to play (its Yorks. pron. might well have sounded more like 'lark') or SE *skylark*, to play tricks, to indulge in rough horseplay] **1** [19C+] a frolic, a game; thus *larkiness*, a propensity for such pleasures; also used ironically/negatively. **2** [early 19C] a propensity for fun and games. **3** [mid-19C] the butt of a joke or 'game'. **4** [mid-19C; 1970s] (*also* **larkey**) an amusing person. **5** [mid-19C+] any form of activity, occupation. **6** [1920s+] (*also* **larks**) a criminal scheme.

IN COMPOUNDS

❑ **lark rig** *n.* [RIG *n.*^{2} (1)] [late 18C] (*UK Und.*) a confidence trick.

IN PHRASES

❑ **and no larks** [1910s] and no fooling around. ❑ **come half-larks with** *v.* [1910s–20s] to deceive, to fool. ❑ **kick up a lark** *v.* [KICK UP *v.*] [early–mid-19C] to cause a commotion. ❑ **on a lark** [mid-19C–1920s] on a spree. ❑ **on the lark** [early–mid-19C] having fun.

lark *v.* (*also* **lark about, lark around, lark it**) [LARK *n.*^{3}] **1** [19C] to masturbate. **2** [19C+] to play tricks, to play around, to enjoy oneself. **3** [mid-19C] to tease. **4** [mid-19C+] to flirt.

IN PHRASES

❑ **and no larking about** [1910s+] and no mistake.

larker *n.* [LARK *v.* (2)] [mid-19C] one who is given to enjoying themselves at others' expense.

larkery *n.* [LARK *v.* (2)] [19C] playfulness (whether rough or gentle).

larkey *n. see* LARK *n.*^{3} (4).

larking *n.* [LARK *v.*] **1** [mid-18C–19C] fellatio, cunnilingus [Grose included the term in his first edn. (1785) as 'a lascivious practice that will not bear explanation'; he omitted it from subsequent edns. It reappears in F&H, who label it 'venery' and define it as 'irrumation'. Partridge, in his edition of Grose's 3rd edn (1796), notes its absence and glosses it as 'irrumation, cunnilingism']. **2** [19C] fun, enjoyment; thus *down to larking*, the excuse offered by one who claims that they were convicted unfairly. **3** [1970s+] (*UK gay*) experimenting with homosexuality.

larks *n. see* LARK *n.*^{3} (6).

larky *n. see* LARK *n.*^{2}.

larky *adj.* (*also* **larkish**) [LARK *n.*^{3} (1)] [early 19C+] frolicsome.

larky-boy *n.* [LARKY *adj.*] [20C+] (*Irish*) a mischief-maker.

larney *see under* LAANIE.

larrikin *n.* [? Warwickshire/Worcestershire/Cornish dial. *larrikin*, a mischievous or frolicsome youth. Other theories include elision of LEERY *adj.* (1) + KINCHIN *n.* (1) or dial. *larack*, to lark/lark about] [late 19C+] (*orig. Aus.*) **1** (*also* **larakin, larikin, larrakin, larry**) a rascal, a villain, a Bohemian, one who acts without regard for conventions; thus *larrikin push*, a street gang; *larrikiness/larrikina*, a female larrikin. **2** [1950s] in fig. use, any object that is rowdy, violent or unpleasant.

DERIVATIVES

❑ **larrikinism** *n.* [20C+] hooliganism.

larruping *adj.* (*also* **tad-larruping**) [fig. use of colloq. *larrup*] [1900s] (*US*) very good, excellent, esp. of food.

larry *n.*^{1} [? LAIRY *adj.*; LEERY *adj.*; note carnival jargon *larry*, a cheap or worthless trinket given as a prize at a gambling game] (*US*) **1** [mid-19C–1900s] deception. **2** [1980s+] a failure.

larry *n.*^{2} [Irish *learaire*, a lounger, an idler] **1** [late 19C] (*Aus.*) idleness. **2** [20C+] (*Irish*) a fool.

larry *n.*^{3} [? the supposed 'effeminacy' of the name] [1990s+] (*UK juv.*) an effeminate or homosexual man.

Larry Dooley *n.*

IN PHRASES

❑ **give someone Larry Dooley** *v.* (*also* **play Larry Dooley**) [ult. *Larry Foley*, late 19C Aus. boxer; the phr. began with the proper name, but *Dooley* soon replaced *Foley*] [1940s+] (*Aus.*) to beat someone, to punish; thus *larry-doo*, a thrashing, a disturbance.

Larry Dugan's eye water *n.* [*Larry Dugan*, a well-known Dublin shoe-black] [late 18C–19C] blacking.

Larry McHale's dog *n. see* LANNA MACREE'S DOG *n.*

larstins *n.* (*also* **larstings**) [? abbr. SE *elastics*] [late 19C–1900s] (*Aus.*) elastic-sided boots.

lary *adj. see* LAIRY *adj.*

las *n.* [colloq. Afk. *las*, to increase] [1970s+] (*S.Afr.*) money, esp. as a loan or a contribution.

lash *n.*^{1} [SE *lash*, a whip] **1** [late 18C] (*US*) a sword. **2** [1910s+] (*Aus.*) violence. **3** [1920s+] (*Aus.*) a trick, a swindle. **4** [1950s+] (*Aus./Irish*) a try, an attempt; thus *give it a lash*, to have a try. **5** [2000s] the penis. **6** [2000s] (*UK black teen*) sexual intercourse.

IN PHRASES

❑ **have a lash (at)** *v.* (*Aus./N.Z.*) **1** [late 19C+] to attack, to fight (with). **2** [1940s+] to take part in, to make a try at.

SE in slang uses

IN PHRASES

❑ **drop the lashes on** *v.* [20C+] (*W.I.*) **1** to beat severely. **2** to make a surprising, shock decision.

lash *n.*^{2} [mid-19C] (*US*) money.

lash *n.*^{3} [var. on LUSH *n.*^{1} (1)] [1980s+] alcohol; a state of inebriation.

IN PHRASES

❑ **on the lash** [2000s] out on a spree.

lash *n.*^{4} (*also* **lasher**) [LASH *v.*^{2}] [1980s+] (*Aus./N.Z Und.*) a general term of abuse; spec. one who does not pay their debts.

lash *v.*^{1} **1** [1930s+] (*Irish*) to rain heavily [as if it is whipping you]. **2** [1950s+] (*W.I.*) to have sexual intercourse, esp. in a vigorous manner. **3** [1960s+] (*US*) to urinate [fig. use of sense 1]. **4** [1980s+] (*UK black*) to mug, to steal from; thus n., *lashing*, a street robbery. **5** [2000s] to discard, to get rid of.

IN PHRASES

❑ **lash in** *v.* [SE *lash out*] [20C+] (*Irish*) to spend money, or provide, or act without restraint.

lash *v.*^{2} [SE *lashes*, neglect in the performance of a legal duty] [1960s+] (*Aus./N.Z. Und*) to fail to honour a debt or obligation.

lashed *adj.* [LASH *n.*^{3}] [1990s+] drunk.

lasher *n.*^{1} [LASH *v.*^{1} (2)] [1950s] (*W.I.*) a womanizer, a sexual athlete.

lasher *n.*^{2} [? SE *luscious*] [1990s+] (*Irish*) an attractive woman, a beauty.

lasher *n.*^{3} *see* LASH *n.*^{4}.

lash larue *n.* [LASH *v.*^{1} (2), but also as pun on proper name of US entertainer *Lash LaRue* 'King of the Bullwhip'] [1950s] (*W.I.*) a womanizer, a sexual athlete.

las mujercitas *n.* [fig. use of Sp. 'little wives'; ? the shape of the mushrooms resembles small breasts] [1970s+] (*drugs*) psilocybin.

lassie *n. see* LADDY *n.*

last *adj.*

SE in slang uses

IN COMPOUNDS

❑ **last heartbeat** *n.* [? an exaggerated phr. of love; 'I will love you until my last heartbeat'] [1940s] (*US black*) a lover, a sweetheart. ❑ **last mile** *n.* [1930s+] (*US prison*) the final walk of a condemned man from death row to the execution chamber. ❑ **last out** *n.* [1940s] (*US black*) death. ❑ **last waltz** *n.* [1930s+] (*US prison*) a condemned man's final walk to the execution chamber.

IN PHRASES

❑ **last part over the fence** *n. see* PART THAT GOES OVER THE FENCE LAST *n.*

last card of the pack *n.* [rhy. sl.] **1** [mid-19C] the human back. **2** [20C+] dismissal from employment [= SACK *n.* (2a)].

lat *n. see* LATS *n.*^{1}.

latch *n.*^{1} [i.e. it secures one's clothes] [late 18C–mid-19C] (*US*) a buckle or breast-pin.

SE in slang uses

IN PHRASES

❑ **latch for the gate to your front yard** *n.* [1930s–40s] (*US black*) fly buttons or a collar pin.

latch *n.*^{2} [SE *latch on to* + *leech*] [1960s–70s] (*US black*) a parasite, a beggar.

IN PHRASES

❑ **put the latch on** *v.* [1950s] to beg from.

latch *v.* **1** [early 18C–19C] (*UK Und.*) to let in. **2** [1930s+] (*US*) to get married. **3** [1950s] (*US campus*) to embrace. **4** [1950s] to take someone's arm.

latchico *n.* [Scot. *latch*, indolent, idle] [1970s–80s] (*Irish*) a wastrel, a rogue.

latchpan *n.* [SE *latchpan*, a dripping pan, lit. a 'catching pan'] [mid-19C–1930s] the lower lip; thus *hang one's latchpan*, to sulk, to pout.

late *adj.*

SE in slang uses

IN COMPOUNDS

❑ **late black** *n. see under* BLACK *n.* ❑ **late bright** *n. see under* BRIGHT *n.* ❑ **late night** *n.* (*also* **late watch**) [1980s+] (*US campus*) a party, usu. at a fraternity house, that does not start until after the bars and clubs close.

late! *excl.* **1** [1960s] (*US black*) an exclamation of amazement, usu. ironic. **2** [1990s+] (*US teen*) see you later!

later *v.* [LATER *phr.*/LATER FOR *phr.*] [1980s+] (*US campus*) to abandon a relationship.

later *phr.* (*also* **later on, laters, later'z, lates, latex**) [1940s+] (*orig. US black*) see you later, goodbye.

IN PHRASES

❑ **later, tater** [1970s+] (*US campus*) a farewell.

later for *phr.* (*also* **later on for**) [1940s+] (*orig. US*) a general phr. of dismissal, synon. with *to hell with*; usu. *later for that*.

IN PHRASES

❑ **later for you** [1980s+] (*US campus*) goodbye.

IN EXCLAMATIONS

❑ **later for you!** [1940s+] (*orig. US black*) shut up! go away! to hell with it!

lath and plaster *n.* [rhy. sl.] [mid-19C] a master, an employer.

lather *n.*[1] [19C–1900s] semen.

IN COMPOUNDS

❑ **lather-maker** *n.* [19C] **1** the vagina. **2** the penis.

lather *n.*[2] (*also* **lathering**) [mid-19C–1950s] a scolding, a beating.

lather *v.* [SE in 20C+] [late 18C+] **1** to thrash. **2** to defeat.

IN PHRASES

❑ **lather up** *v.* [1930s–40s] (*US*) to show affection, to encourage, to excite; esp. of a woman prior to seduction.

lathered *adj.* [SE *lather*, the froth on a liquid, or a state of agitation] **1** [1910s–40s] (*orig. Aus.*) drunk. **2** [1950s] (*US drugs*) intoxicated by a drug. **3** [1970s] (*US*) sexually excited.

lat-house *n. see* LATS *n.*[1].

Latin *n.* [SE *Latin*, one of the communities in Europe, in this case Spain, the manufacturer of *alicante*] [mid-17C] alicante wine.

latitat *n.* [Lat. *latitare*, to lie concealed; thus legal jargon *latitat*, 'a writ which supposed the defendant to lie concealed and which summoned him to answer in the King's Bench' (*OED*)] [mid-16C–mid-19C] an attorney, a lawyer.

latro *phr.* ['Italianized' version of LATER *phr.*] [1990s+] (*US campus*) a farewell, goodbye.

lats *n.*[1] (*also* **lat, lat-house**) [abbr.] [1940s+] (*orig. milit.*) a *lat*rine.

lats *n.*[2] [abbr.] [1960s+] the *lat*issimus dorsi muscles.

lattie/latty *n. see* LETTY *n.*[1].

L.A. turnabouts *n.* [1980s] (*US drugs*) amphetamines.

laudy-daw *n. see* LA-DI-DAH *n.*[1].

laugh *v.*

SE in slang uses

IN PHRASES

❑ **don't make me laugh** [20C+] don't be stupid, ridiculous; thus [1920s–40s] ext. as *don't make me laugh I've got a split lip*. ❑ **give laugh for peas-soup** *v.* [20C+] (*W.I.*) **1** of a visitor, to act in a sufficiently entertaining manner to win an invitation to a meal. **2** to chat or gossip instead of getting on with one's work, thus using one's wit and charm to hide one's actual laziness. ❑ **laugh and scratch** *v.* [what one does when the injection takes effect] [1930s+] (*drugs*) to inject a drug, usu. heroin. ❑ **laugh at the ground** *v.* (*also* **laugh at the carpet, ...grass**) [1960s+] (*Aus.*) to vomit. ❑ **laugh one's ass off** *v.* (*also* **laugh one's balls off, ...box off**) [1970s+] to laugh uproariously.

laugh and joke *n.* [rhy. sl.] [late 19C+] a smoke.

laugh and titter *n. see* GIGGLE AND TITTER *n.*

laughing *adj.* (*also* **away laughing**) [1910s+] (*orig. milit.*) safe, secure; usu. in such phr. as *you're laughing* or *I'm laughing*.

SE in slang uses

IN COMPOUNDS

❑ **laughing academy** *n.* (*also* **laughing farm, ...house, ...school**) [1940s+] (*US*) a psychiatric institution. ❑ **laughing boy** *n.* [? Gilbert & Sullivan song 'A Laughing Boy But Yesterday' in *The Yeoman of the Guard* (1888), about a miserable person] [20C+] **1** an ironic nickname given to someone who seems consistently, or even temporarily, miserable and in low spirits. **2** one who laughs complacently prior to encountered problems. ❑ **laughing gear** *n.* (*also* **laughing tackle**) [GEAR *n.* (3)/SE *tackle*] [1970s+] the mouth. ❑ **laughing-sided boot** *n.* [adopted from Aborigine mispron. of SE] [1930s+] (*Aus.*) an elastic-sided boot. ❑ **laughing soup** *n.* (*also* **laughing-juice, ...water**) [its effects] [20C+] (*US*) an alcoholic drink, esp. champagne. ❑ **laughing weed** *n.* (*also* **laughing tobacco**) [WEED *n.*[1] (4); i.e. its effects] [1920s+] (*US drugs*) marijuana.

laughs and smiles *n.* [rhy. sl. = SE *piles*] [20C+] (*Aus.*) haemorrhoids.

lauk!/lauks! *excl. see* LAWKS! *excl.*

launch *n.* [SE but with ? implication of dial. *launch*, to groan] [late 18C–19C] childbirth, esp. the actual labour.

launching pad *n.* [SE *launch* + PAD *n.*[2] (2); pun on TAKE OFF *v.*[2] (4a)] [1950s–70s] (*US drugs*) a room, flat or house where drug addicts can go to inject.

launder *v.* [the 'dirty' money is invested or deposited and is withdrawn 'clean' of any association with crime; note Jonson *The Alchemist* (1610): 'I'll bring [...] thy neck within a noose, for laund'ring gold, and barbing it' – the reference is to 'sweating' gold plate and to clipping money] [1970s+] to decriminalize money that has been gained through criminal activities by 'washing' it through a legitimate business such as a casino or bank; thus n., *laundry, launderer*.

laundress *n.* [euph.] [17C; late 19C] a prostitute.

laundromat *n.* [SE *Laundromat*, a 'do-it-yourself' laundry shop; LAUNDER *v.*] [1980s+] a business, such as a casino, in which money that has been gained through criminal activities can be decriminalized.

laundry *n.* (*US*) **1** [1940s+] clothes that are being worn, underwear; thus *drop one's laundry*, to undress. **2** [1960s+] (*gay*) the bulge of the genitals under trousers. **3** [1970s] women.

launey day! *excl. see* LAWDY! *excl.*

Laurel and Hardy *n.* [rhy. sl.; ult. comedians Stan *Laurel* (1890–1965) and Oliver *Hardy* (1892–1957)] [1990s+] a Bacardi (rum).

lav *n.* [abbr.] [1910s+] *lav*atory; thus *lav paper*, lavatory roll.

IN PHRASES

❑ **make love to the lav** *v.* (*also* **make love to the loo**) [1960s+] (*Aus.*) to vomit.

lavender *n.* [mid-19C–1920s] **1** something good, desirable. **2** flattery.

SE in slang uses

IN PHRASES

❑ **lay up in lavender** *v. see* separate entry.

lavender *adj.* [1920s+] (*orig. US*) a euph. for homosexual and anything referring to homosexuality.

IN COMPOUNDS

❑ **lavender boy** *n.* (*also* **lavender lad, ...lips**) [1920s+] a male homosexual. ❑ **lavender cowboy** *n.* [1920s+] an effeminate man; thus a male homosexual. ❑ **lavender law** *n.* [1920s+] legal issues, practice and study pertaining to the gay and lesbian community.

IN PHRASES

❑ **streak of lavender** *n.* [1930s] an effeminate man. ❑ **have a dash of lavender** *v.* [1940s+] to be marginally homosexual.

lavender cove *n.* [LAY UP IN LAVENDER *v.* (1) + COVE *n.* (3)] [19C] a pawnbroker.

laverick *n. see* LABRICK *n.*

la vida loca *n.* [Sp. *la vida loca*, the crazy life; coined by the Mexican immigrant gangs, starting with the *pachucos* of the 1930s–40s and the *cholos* of 1950s–60s, who initiated the gang style, subseq. picked up by black teens and their elders] [1960s+] (*US gang*) the gangster lifestyle of the Mexican barrios of the US, esp. Los Angeles.

lavo *n.* (*also* **lavvo**) [abbr. + -O *sfx* (3)] [1920s+] (*Aus./Irish*) the *lav*atory.

la vogue *n.* [? *Vogue* magazine; i.e. the use of the restroom for making up etc] [1980s+] (*US campus*) a restroom or public lavatory for women.

lavvy *n.* [abbr.] [20C+] (*mainly Scot.*) a *lav*atory.

law *n.* **1** [mid–late 16C] (*UK Und.*) a type of criminal activity [OF *lei*; ult. Lat. *legem*, law; synon. with LAY *n.*[3] (1)]. **2** [18C+] (*orig. US*) constr. with *the*, the police. **3** [1910s+] with the article deliberately omitted, a police officer; occas. a private detective. **4** [1940s+] (*US prison*) a prison warder.

IN COMPOUNDS

❑ **law-car** *n.* [1970s] a police car. ❑ **law-dog** *n.* (*also* **law hound**) [SE *dog*/-HOUND *sfx*; note DOG *n.*[2] (6a)] [late 19C+] (*US*) a police officer. ❑ **lawman** *n.* (*also* **lawboy**) [1960s+] a law-enforcement officer. ❑ **law sharp** *n.* [SHARP *n.*[1] (2)] [late 19C–

1940s] (*US*) a lawyer. ❑ **law shop** *n.* [SHOP *n.*[1] (1)] [1970s+] a police station. ❑ **law station** *n.* [1950s] a police station.

IN PHRASES

❑ **down by law** *see under* DOWN *adj.*[1]. ❑ **give law** v. [sporting jargon *give law*, to give a hunted animal a chance of escape] [late 18C–mid-19C] to give someone a chance.

law v. [abbr. SE *outlaw*] **1** [1900s–50s] (*US*) to set the law on, to arrest. **2** [1940s–50s] (*UK Und.*) to impersonate a police officer.

law! *excl.* [euph. for SE *Lord!*] [late 16C+] a mild excl. of surprise or amazement.

law-de-dah *adj. see* LA-DI-DAH *adj.*

lawdy! *excl.* (*also* **launey day! lawny! lawsy! lordy!**) [SE *Lord*] [mid-19C+] a mild excl.

lawful *adj.*

SE in slang uses

IN COMPOUNDS

❑ **lawful blanket** *n. see under* BLANKET *n.* ❑ **lawful jam** *n. see under* JAM *n.*[3]. ❑ **lawful picture** *n. see under* PICTURE *n.* ❑ **lawful tool** *n. see under* TOOL *n.*[1].

IN EXCLAMATIONS

❑ **lawful sakes!** *see* LAW SAKES! *under* LAWS! *excl.*

lawks! *excl.* (*also* **la! lauk! lauks! lawk! oh lawks!**) [mid-18C+] used as a euph. for SE *Lord* in a variety of mild oaths.

IN EXCLAMATIONS

❑ **lawks-a-mussy!** (*also* **lack-a-daisy! lawk-a-daisy! lawks-a-day! Lawks a-mercy! Laws-a-mercy! lor-a-massy! lor-a-mussy!**) [late 18C+] a mild oath, lit. 'Lord have mercy!'.

lawless *adj.* [20C+] (*W.I.*) **1** irresponsible, troublesome. **2** of a woman, promiscuous, unrestrainedly vulgar. **3** of speech, smutty, dirty. **4** sitting with the legs sprawled apart.

lawless as a town bull *adj. see under* TOWN *n.*[2].

lawn *n.*[1] [SE *lawn*, a form of fine linen, resembling cambric] [early 19C] (*UK Und.*) a white cambric handkerchief.

lawn *n.*[2] **1** [1940s+] a crew cut hairstyle; thus *lawnhead*, a person with a crewcut. **2** [1950s+] (*gay*) pubic hair, and if it is shaved it is a *mowed lawn*.

IN COMPOUNDS

❑ **lawn-mower** *n.* [1970s+] (*US*) a cunnilinctor.

IN PHRASES

❑ **mow the lawn** v. **1** [1930s–40s] (*US black*) to cut one's hair. **2** [1930s–40s] (*US black*) to comb one's hair. **3** [1950s+] (*US black*) to shave with an electric razor. **4** [1970s+] to perform cunnilingus. **5** [1980s+] (*Aus./UK*) of a woman, to shave or trim the pubic hair.

lawn mower *n.* [1930s–40s] (*US Und.*) a machine gun.

lawny! *excl. see* LAWDY! *excl.*

laws! *excl.* (*also* **lawsie! lawsy!**) [mid-19C+] (*US*) Lord!

IN EXCLAMATIONS

❑ **law sakes!** (*also* **lawful sakes! lawsy's sakes!**) [mid-19C–1900s] (*US*) a mild oath, lit. 'for the Lord's sake!'. ❑ **law's-a-me!** (*also* **laws me!**) [late 19C] (*US*) a mild oath, lit. 'Lord save me!'.

Laws-a-mercy! *excl. see under* LAWKS! *excl.*

lawsy! *excl. see* LAWDY! *excl.*

lawt *adj.* [backsl.] [mid-19C] tall.

lax (up) v. [abbr.] [2000s] to relax.

lay *n.*[1] [SE *lay*, to wager] [17C–18C] a chance.

lay *n.*[2] [LAY v.[1] (1)] **1** [mid-17C; late 18C; 1920s+] a person with whom one has sexual intercourse, or a promiscuous woman, usu. qualified as *a good lay, a bad lay, an easy lay* etc. **2** [1920s+] (*orig. US*) an act of sexual intercourse.

lay *n.*[3] [OF *lei*, law, which itself is the root of the synon. LAW *n.*] **1** [mid-17C+] (*UK Und.*) any kind of criminal activity, usu. modified by a participle that denotes the speciality, e.g. CHIVING-LAY *under* CHIV *n.*[1]; CLOUTING LAY *n.*; CRACK LAY *under* CRACK *n.*[4]; KID LAY *under* KID *n.*[1]; MAUNDERING LAY *under* MAUNDER v. **2** [18C–1960s] any form of enterprise, business or occupation; often the terms or conditions of such a contract or job. **3** [mid-18C–19C] the life and practice of crime as in *the lay*. **4** [early 19C] stolen goods. **5** [mid-19C–1940s] (*US*) one's (hidden) intention or aim. **6** [mid-19C–1950s] (*UK Und.*) a place considered for robbing. **7** [mid-19C–1950s] (*US*) a state of affairs. **8** [1910s] (*Aus.*) a trick, a deception. **9** [1920s] an obsession, a subject.

IN PHRASES

❑ **on the lay** [mid-18C–1910s] involved in some form of illegal activity. ❑ **pull one's lay** v. [1950s] (*US black*) to do something, e.g. perform music.

lay *n.*[4] [? SE *lay*, to place; i.e. that which is laid on the table, counter etc] [mid-19C] **1** a piece, a portion, e.g. a *lay of pannum*, a piece of bread. **2** goods.

lay *n.*[5] **1** [1910s–30s] (*US*) a place to sleep, a bed. **2** [1920s–50s] (*US drugs*) the act of lying down and smoking opium. **3** [1930s] (*US drugs*) a session in an opium den. **4** [1930s] (*US drugs*) a portion of any type of drug.

lay v.[1] **1** [mid-16C+] (*also* **lay off**) to have sexual intercourse with. **2** [late 17C; 1950s+] to make oneself available for sexual relations; also constr. with *for*.

IN PHRASES

❑ **get laid** v. [1920s+] (*orig. US*) to have sexual intercourse; thus *unlaid*, used of those who have not had intercourse. ❑ **laid, relaid and parlayed** [1950s+] (*US*) **1** having had frequent or protracted sexual intercourse. **2** absolutely deceived, cheated. ❑ **lay bricks** v. [1930s] (*US*) to have sexual intercourse. ❑ **lay it on the line** v. [1940s–50s] (*US*) to have sexual intercourse. ❑ **lay off with** v. [1940s–50s] (*Aus.*) to have sex with. ❑ **lay the leg** v. **1** [17C; 1910s+] to have sexual intercourse. **2** [1940s+] (*US prison*) to sodomize. ❑ **lay the lip** v. [1930s–60s] (*US*) to fellate. ❑ **lay the track** v. [pun on SE] [2000s] (*US prison*) to have (presumably homosexual) sexual intercourse. ❑ **lay up with** v. [1920s+] (*US*) to have sexual intercourse with.

SE in slang uses

IN PHRASES

❑ **lay...** *see also under* relevant n. or adj. ❑ **lay about** v. *see* LAY INTO v. ❑ **lay an egg** v. [RAF sl. *lay an egg*, drop a bomb. The link with US BOMB *n.* (9) may be coincidental. Note *Variety* headline the morning after the 1929 Crash, 'Wall Street Lays an Egg'] [1920s+] **1** to fail completely, esp. in show business. **2** (*Aus./N.Z.*) to worry, to be agitated. **3** (*N.Z.*) to defecate. ❑ **lay a patch** v. (*also* **lay a batch**) [the tyres leave a patch on the road] [1960s+] (*US*) to make tyre marks by accelerating fast in a car. ❑ **lay back** v. see separate entry. ❑ **lay back and front shops into one** v. *see under* SHOP *n.*[1]. ❑ **lay cane upon abel** v. [pun on the biblical brothers *Cain* and *Abel*] [late 17C–early 19C] to beat, to thrash. ❑ **lay dead** v. **1** [late 19C+] (*US black*) to wait. **2** [1940s+] to do nothing, to stop everything. ❑ **lay down** see separate entries. ❑ **lay for** v. *see* LAY INTO v. ❑ **lay giggy** v. [? GIG *n.*[8] (2)] [1930s] (*US juv.*) to keep a lookout. ❑ **lay in(to)** *see* separate entries. ❑ **lay it on** v. *see* separate entry. ❑ **lay low** v. *see* separate entry. ❑ **lay-off** *n. see* separate entry. ❑ **lay on** v. *see* separate entry. ❑ **lay one on someone** v. *see under* ONE *n.*[1]. ❑ **lay one's ass on the table** v. [1970s] (*US*) to be frank. ❑ **lay one's knowledge** v. [1940s] (*US black*) to take advantage of a situation. ❑ **lay (on) the hip** v. [the usu. posture for smoking opium is to lie on one's side] [1930s–50s] (*US*) to smoke opium. ❑ **lay on to** v. *see* LAY INTO v. ❑ **lay out** *see* separate entry. ❑ **lay paper** v. *see under* PAPER *n.* ❑ **lay pit and boxes into one** v. [orig. theatrical jargon. 'A simile borrowed from the playhouse, when for the benefit of some favourite player, the pit and boxes are laid together' (Grose)] [late 18C–early 19C] to remove the physical division between the vagina and the anus. ❑ **lay rubber** v. (*also* **get rubber, lay tread, lay wheels**) [the rubber leaves a mark on the road] [1950s+] (*US*) to drive off at speed, spinning the wheels as one accelerates away. ❑ **lay (some) cable** v. (*also* **lay a cable**) [1970s+] to defecate. ❑ **lay (some) iron** v. (*also* **lay some hot iron**) [the metal cleats on a tap-dancer's shoes] [1930s–60s] (*US black*) to tap-dance, esp. as a professional. ❑ **lay someone trigging** v. [? SE *trig*, the starting line of a race or that from which bowlers deliver the bowl; or SE *trig*, in good physical condition, strong, sound] [late 18C–mid-19C] to knock someone down. ▫ **lay them down** *v.* [mid–late 19C] to play cards. ▫ **lay to** *v. see* LAY DOWN *v.* (1a). ▫ **lay up** *see* separate entries.

lay *v.*[2] (*also* **lie**) [abbr. SE *lay in wait*] [17C+] to watch for, to survey.

lay *v.*[3] **1** [mid-19C–1950s] (*US*) to knock someone unconscious. **2** [1960s+] (*US black*) to idle, to relax, to spend time with. **3** [1980s+] (*US black*) to over-indulge in drugs or drink to such an extent that one is laid on one's back.

lay *v.*[4] [1940s+] (*US black*) an all-purpose v. of action.

IN PHRASES

▫ **lay it** *v.* [note Lincoln University (Oxford, Pennsylvania) use c.1934: 'LAY IT. To do something extremely well'] [1930s–70s] (*US*) to do something in a noteworthy manner, e.g. to play jazz music well. ▫ **lay two ways** *v.* [1960s–70s] (*US black*) to short-change or otherwise rob someone in an ostensibly honest exchange of money.

IN EXCLAMATIONS

▫ **lay some on me!** [1950s+] (*US black*) an invitation to swap ritual hand slaps as a form of greeting.

lay *v.*[5] *see* LAY DOWN *v.* (2).

layaway *n.* [1990s+] (*US campus*) one who interferes with a seduction.

lay back *v.* (*also* **lay low, lay up**) **1** [1940s+] to have sexual intercourse. **2** [1960s+] (*US black*) to relax. **3** [1960s+] to do nothing specific, to pass time (e.g. in prison).

IN PHRASES

▫ **lay back in the cut** *v.* [CUT *n.* (13a)] [1960s+] (*US black*) **1** to relax. **2** to lie in ambush, whether actually or fig.

lay-down *n.* **1** [mid-19C–1950s] a sleep. **2** [late 19C–1900s] (*US*) a refusal or collapse [note LAY DOWN *v.* (1)]. **3** [1900s–30s] a place to sleep. **4** [1920s–30s] (*US drugs*) the price of admission to enter and smoke in an opium den; thus an opium den [LAY DOWN *v.* (2)]. **5** [1930s+] (*UK Und.*) a period of remand in prison. **6** [1930s+] (*US*) a certainty [one can *lay down* money on it]. **7** [1950s] a burial.

lay down *v.* **1** in senses of giving up [boxing imagery]. (**a**) [late 19C+] (*US*) (*also* **lay to**) to volunteer for defeat; thus *lay-down artist*, a defeatist. (**b**) [1910s+] to collapse. (**c**) [1930s+] to accept, to acquiesce. **2** [1930s–60s] (*drugs*) (*also* **lay**) to smoke opium [the smoker's recumbent position]. **3** [1930s+] (*US prison*) to place an inmate in the punishment cells [punishment cells were so cramped there was barely enough room to stand upright]. **4** [1940s+] (*US*) to explain, outline, to present a theory.

IN COMPOUNDS

▫ **lay-down joint** *n.* [JOINT *n.* (3a)] [1930s+] (*US drugs*) a place to smoke opium.

IN PHRASES

▫ **lay down on** *v.* [late 19C+] (*US*) to abandon someone, to fail in a duty.

SE in slang uses

IN PHRASES

▫ **lay down one's knife and fork** *v.* (*also* **chuck in one's knife and fork**) [mid-19C–1930s] to die. ▫ **lay down on the job** *v.* (*also* **lie down (on the job)**) [1910s+] (*orig. Aus.*) **1** to act lazily. **2** to do a job badly. ▫ **lay down some cow** *v. see under* COW *n.*[1]. ▫ **lay 'em down** *v.* **1** [1930s–40s] (*US*) to die [one 'lays down' one's body]. **2** [1940s+] (*US*) to drive very fast [the pressing down of the accelerator].

lay down! *excl.* [1920s–50s] (*US*) be quiet! shut up!

lay-down merchant *n.* [LAY PAPER *under* PAPER *n.* + MERCHANT *n.*] [1950s+] a criminal who specializes in the distribution (*laying-down*) of counterfeit banknotes.

lay-easy *n. see* EASY LAY *under* EASY *adj.*

layer *n.* [in all defs the image is of 'laying down' banknotes or cash] **1** [1900s–10s] a bookmaker. **2** [1910s] (*US Und.*) one who passes bad cheques. **3** [1920s] (*US Und.*) a short- change artist. **4** [1930s–50s] (*US*) a currency note.

layer down *n.* [LAY PAPER *under* PAPER *n.*] [late 19C–1950s] (*US Und.*) one who passes counterfeit currency.

layer-over *n. see* LAREOVER *n.*

lay-in *n.* [1970s+] (*US prison*) a pass allowing a sick prisoner not to work.

lay in *v.* **1** [late 19C] (*US Und.*) to get acquainted. **2** [1900s] (*US*) to act as confederates. **3** [1900s] (*US*) to obtain, to 'look out for'. **4** [1920s] (*US*) to stay, esp. in the context of hiding from pursuit. **5** [1930s+] (*US prison*) to stay in one's cell when one might usu. be out of it.

layin' and playin' *phr.* [1970s+] (*US black*) of a man, idling around the house, usu. with one's female partner.

lay into *v.* (*also* **lay about, lay for, lay in, lay on to**) **1** [mid-19C+] to attack physically. **2** [mid-19C+] to start eating in a voracious manner. **3** [1920s+] to attack verbally.

lay it on *v.* **1** in senses of communication. (**a**) [mid-19C+] to exaggerate; to make an excessive fuss. (**b**) [1910s+] (*orig. US*) to criticize, to berate. (**c**) [1930s–70s] (*US black*) to seek a verbal or physical confrontation, to hit. (**d**) [1950s+] to inform, to pass on information. **2** [1930s+] (*US*) to act or work efficiently or energetically. **3** [1970s] (*US black*) to slap someone's hand in greeting.

lay low *v.* (*also* **lie low, lie under**) **1** [mid-19C+] to hide oneself away, to keep a low profile. **2** *see* LAY BACK *v.*

lay me in the gutter *n.* [rhy. sl.] [1920s+] butter.

lay-off *n.* [var. on LAY-DOWN *n.*] [1920s] (*US drugs*) a smoke of opium.

lay on *v.* **1** [late 19C+] (*also* **lay**) to give, esp. drugs. **2** [late 19C+] to tell, to impose facts upon. **3** [1900s] (*Aus.*) to assail.

IN PHRASES

▫ **lay on a burn** *v.* [BURN *v.* (1)] [2000s] (*US black*) to infect someone with a sexually transmitted disease intentionally.

layout *n.* **1** [mid-19C] an achievement, an activity. **2** in senses of a set, a display. (**a**) [mid–late 19C] a set of equipment or clothes. (**b**) [mid-19C+] the table, dice, cards etc required for setting up a gambling club, whether legitimate or as a prop for a confidence trick. (**c**) [mid-19C+] any form of display, e.g. a showman's stall. **3** [mid-19C–1950s] (*US*) a plan, a scheme. **4** [mid-19C–1960s] (*US*) an association of persons, such as a gang or team. **5** [mid-19C+] (*US*) an apartment, a house, or any place. **6** (*also* **hop layout**) in drug uses [the relevant 'kit' is 'laid out' in front of the user before use]. (**a**) [late 19C–1960s] an opium den. (**b**) [late 19C–1980s] (*drugs*) the various accoutrements – pipe, box, needle etc – required for smoking opium. (**c**) [1920s+] the syringe, cotton etc required for injecting a narcotic. **7** [late 19C+] a situation, the facts. **8** [1900s] a meal, a 'spread'.

IN PHRASES

▫ **layout across the drink** *n.* [sense 5 above + DRINK *n.*[1] (2)] [1940s] (*US black*) Europe.

lay out *v.* **1** (**a**) [early 19C–1950s] (*US*) to defeat or overcome; often as *LAY OUT COLD* below. (**b**) [mid-19C–1960s] (*US*) to kill. (**c**) [mid-19C+] (*orig. US*) to knock someone out in a fight. (**d**) [late 19C–1900s] (*Aus.*) to indulge oneself to excess, e.g. in drinking. (**e**) [late 19C–1960s] (*US*) to amaze or astound. (**f**) [1900s–60s] (*US*) to scold or reprimand; thus n. *laying out*, a scolding. (**g**) [1920s–30s] (*US black*) to stop what one is doing, esp. suddenly. (**h**) [1920s–30s] (*US black*) to avoid someone, to step aside. **2** [1930s+] (*also* **lay it out**) to inform, to pass on information, to make something clear. **3** [1960s+] (*US campus*) to sunbathe. **4** [1970s] (*Irish*) to deceive sexually.

IN PHRASES

▫ **lay it out** *v.* **1** [1960s+] of a homosexual of either sex, to admit and poss. flaunt one's sexual preference. **2** [1990s+] to offer oneself for intercourse. **3** *see* sense 2 above. ▫ **lay it out straight** *v.* [1950s+] to tell all the facts. ▫ **lay out cold** *v.* [early 19C+] (*orig. US*) **1** to knock out, to defeat. **2** to astound, to amaze. ▫ **lay out in lavender** *v.* [1940s+] (*US*) to scold severely, to indulge in a verbal battle. ▫ **lay out like a carpet** *v.* (*also* **lay (out) like a rug**) [1920s–50s] (*US*) to knock unconscious.

layover *n. see* LAREOVER *n.*

lay-up *n.* [LAY UP *v.*] **1** [late 19C] a drink of alcohol. **2** [1930s] a term in jail. **3** [1940s] (*UK Und.*) a hideout. **4** [1990s+] (*US campus*) something easy.

lay up *v.* **1** [mid-19C+] to rest, to relax. **2** [late 19C] (*US*) to die. **3** [1920s] to live, to be in a place. **4** [1920s+] (*US*) to hide, to take refuge. **5** *see* LAY BACK *v.*

IN PHRASES

▫ **lay up in** *v.* [2000s] (*US black*) of a man, to penetrate a woman.

lay up in lavender *v.* [ironic use of SE *lay up in lavender*, to put aside carefully for future use. Lavender was then, as now, kept with stored linen and other fabrics] **1** [late 16C–19C] to pawn. **2** [17C–19C] to put out of harm's way; to hide from the police. **3** [17C–19C] to imprison. **4** [late 17C–19C] to die.

IN PHRASES

▫ **in lavender** **1** [mid-17C; mid-19C–1930s] hidden from the police. **2** [late 18C] in a charity hospital. **3** [mid-19C–1940s] (*US Und.*) in prison. **4** [1930s] (*US Und.*) dead.

laziosis *n.* [SE *lazy* + a play on sfx *-osis* used in words that name illnesses, e.g. tuberculosis] [20C+] (*W.I., Guyn./Belz.*) laziness.

lazy *n.* [mid-19C] time off, sloth.

lazy *adj.*

SE in slang uses

IN COMPOUNDS

▫ **lazy bed** *n.* [late 18C] (*Aus.*) cooked opossum. ▫ **lazy body** *n.* [1980s+] (*W.I./UK black teen*) a devoted idler, someone who is averse to physical exercise and exertion. ▫ **lazyboots** *n.* [on the pattern of SLYBOOTS *under* SLY *adj.*] [19C] a lazy person. ▫ **lazybum** *n.* [1990s+] (*Aus.*) a loafer. ▫ **lazy lob** *n.* *see* LOB *n.*[3].

l.b. *n.* (*also* **el-bee**) [*1lb*; pron. 'el-bee'] [1960s+] (*drugs*) one pound in weight, occas. of flesh.

l.b.j. *n.* [? joc. ref. to US President *L*yndon *B*aines *J*ohnson (1908–73) or from the nickname for the military prison in Vietnam, *L*ong *B*inh *J*ail] [1960s+] **1** (*US drugs*) LSD. **2** (*US drugs*) phencyclidine. **3** (*US drugs*) heroin. **4** (*US*) a large penis.

l.b.w. *n.* *see* LEG BEFORE WICKET *n.*

L.C.N. *n.* [abbr. *L*a *C*ostra *N*ostra] [1980s] (*US*) the Mafia.

l.d. *n.* [abbr.; pron. 'el-dee'] [1970s+] (*US black*) a Cadillac *Eld*orado.

leach *n.* *see* HORSE LEECH *under* HORSE *n.*

lead *n.* (*US*) **1** [19C+] a bullet. **2** [mid–late 19C] a collection of money, e.g. by a street performer. **3** [1900s] a gun.

IN COMPOUNDS

▫ **lead pill** *n.* (*also* **leaden capsule**) [mid-19C–1950s] (*US*) a bullet. ▫ **lead pipe** *n.* **1** [1900s–50s] (*US prison*) prison-cooked spaghetti. **2** *see* LEAD-PIPE CINCH below. ▫ **lead plum** *n.* [1920s–30s] (*US*) a bullet. ▫ **lead poisoning** *n.* (*also* **lead cocktail, ...medicine**) [late 19C+] (*orig. US*) shotgun shells, revolver bullets, esp. when lodged in a victim's body. ▫ **lead-pusher** *n.* (*also* **lead-chucker, -spitter, -sprayer**) [20C+] (*US*) a gun. ▫ **lead sandwich** *n.* [1970s] (*US*) a bullet. ▫ **lead towel** *n.* **1** [mid-18C–early 19C] a pistol. **2** [early 19C] a bullet.

IN PHRASES

▫ **cold lead** *n.* [early 19C–1920s] a bullet. ▫ **eat lead** *v.* [note 16C SE *eat iron*, to be stabbed] [1920s+] (*orig. US*) to be shot, usu. fatally. ▫ **feed (hot) lead** *v.* [1940s–50s] (*US*) to shoot, usu. to shoot dead. ▫ **get the lead** *v.* (*also* **take the lead**) [late 19C–1920s] to be shot. ▫ **get the lead out** *v.* (*also* **get the lead out of one's ass, ...pants, ...tail**) [SE *lead* weighs one down] [1910s+] to hurry up, to stop dawdling; usu. as imper. ▫ **lead in one's pencil** *n.* *see under* PENCIL *n.* ▫ **lead up** *v.* [1990s+] (*US black*) to shoot. ▫ **pump lead** *v.* [late 19C+] (*US*) to fire a gun. ▫ **shake the lead out (of one's arse/ass)** *v.* (*also* **get the lead out of one's arse/ass, shake the lead out of one's pants/shorts**) [1910s+] (*orig. US*) to make an effort, to 'get a move on', to stop being lazy. ▫ **sling lead** *v.* (*also* **squeeze lead**) [1920s+] (*US*) to fire a gun; to shoot. ▫ **swap lead** *v.* *see under* SWAP *v.* ▫ **swing the lead** *v.* *see under* SWING *v.* ▫ **throw lead** *v.* (*also* **spill lead**) [late 19C+] (*US*) to shoot a gun.

SE in slang uses

IN COMPOUNDS

▫ **lead balloon** *n.* [1950s+] (*US*) a failure; usu. in phr. *go over like a lead balloon*. ▫ **leadhead** *n.* [-HEAD *sfx*] [1940s+] (*US*) an idiot. ▫ **lead-pipe cinch** *n.* [the solidity of a SE *lead pipe* + CINCH *n.*[1] (2)] (*US*) **1** [late 19C] a firm grip. **2** [late 19C+] (*also* **lead pipe, pipe cinch**) an absolute certainty, an easy task. ▫ **lead sled** *n.* *see under* SLED *n.*

lead *v.* [LEAD *n.*] [late 19C] to be shot.

leaded *adj.* [gasoline usage] [1990s+] (*US campus*) of coffee, caffeinated.

leaden pill *n.* (*also* **leaden favour**) [19C–1900s] a bullet.

leadfoot *n.* (*US*) **1** [1930s+] a fast driver [the heaviness of a foot on the accelerator]. **2** [1950s] a clumsy person [the heaviness that slows one down].

lead foot *v.* [LEADFOOT *n.*] (*US*) **1** [1930s+] to drive a vehicle very fast. **2** [1950s] to move slowly and clumsily.

lead-footed *adj.* [LEAD FOOT *v.*] (*US*) **1** [1930s+] speeding. **2** [1950s] slow, clumsy.

leading article *n.* **1** [mid–late 19C] the nose. **2** [mid-19C–1900s] the vagina.

leading card *n.* [card-playing jargon; the card that is led sets the initial betting standard for a round of play] [late 17C+] an example or precedent.

lead in one's pencil *n.* *see under* PENCIL *n.*

lead off *v.* [1910s+] (*orig. milit.*) to lose one's temper.

lead sheet *n.* [musical jargon *lead sheet*, a sheet of music containing the melodic line and lyric only; Mezzrow & Wolfe (1946) 'As for *lead sheet*, it's only one sheet of music out of a whole orchestration, with only the melody line on it, and hence thin enough to mean topcoat; whereas the *full orchestration* is, by contrast, thick and bulky, and could only mean a heavy overcoat'] [1930s–40s] (*US black*) an overcoat or other outer garment.

lead-swinger *n.* [SWING THE LEAD *under* SWING *v.*] [1910s+] one who shirks their duties, a malingerer.

lead-swinging *n.* [SWING THE LEAD *under* SWING *v.*] [1910s+] the act of shirking one's duties, malingering.

leaf *n.* **1** [mid-19C] (*US Und.*) autumn. **2** (*US*) in drug uses [the plants from which they are taken]. (**a**) [1910s–30s] (*also* **leaf-gum**) crude opium. (**b**) [1930s+] drugs in general. (**c**) [1940s+] cocaine. (**d**) [1960s+] marijuana. **3** (*US*) as a currency note. (**a**) [1920s–30s] a $100 bill. (**b**) [1920s+] a $1 bill.

SE in slang uses

IN PHRASES

▫ **drop one's leaf** *v.* [autumnal imagery, but note GO OFF WITH THE FALL OF THE LEAF below] [19C] to die. ▫ **fall of the leaf** *n.* [autumnal imagery, but note next] [early 18C] death. ▫ **go off with the fall of the leaf** *n.* (*also* **go off at the fall of the leaf**) [a pun on the leaves or hinged panels of the drop and the dead leaves that fall from a natural, rather than judicial 'tree'. Grose (1796) notes that 'criminals in Dublin being turned off from the outside of the prison by the falling of a board, propped up, and moving on a hinge, like the leaf of a table'; Griffiths, *Chronicles of Newgate* (1884), notes that the adoption of the gallows in England followed the invention of the Dublin 'engine of death'; George Parker *Life's Painter* (1789): '*Fall of the leaf*. The new mode of hanging. The culprit is brought out upon a stage, and placed upon a leaf, when the rope is fixed about his neck he leaf falls, and the body immediately becomes pendant'] [late 18C–19C] to be hanged.

leafless tree *n.* [early–mid-19C] the gallows.

IN PHRASES

▫ **climb the leafless tree** *v.* to be hanged.

leaf of the old author *n.* (*also* **drop of the old author**) [? the *old author* being God] [19C] a drink, esp. of brandy.

leak *n.* **1** [early 18C–19C] the female genitals. **2** [1910s+] (*orig. US*) the act of urination. **3** [1910s+] (*orig. US*) a piece of hitherto secret information that has been revealed. **4** [1920s+] (*Aus.*) an informer. **5** [1930s+] (*Aus.*) a trick, a dodge.

IN PHRASES

❑ **put the leak into** *v.* [mid-19C] (*US*) to trick, to deceive. ❑ **take a leak** *v.* (*also* **spring a leak**) **1** [early 17C] to have a venereal disease. **2** [1910s+] to urinate. ❑ **turn on the leaks** *v.* **1** [1930s] (*US Und.*) to inform, to betray. **2** [1930s] to start crying.

leak *v.* **1** [late 16C+] to urinate. **2** [mid-19C+] to reveal a secret unintentionally, or intentionally [now SE]. **3** [late 19C] (*US*) to lie. **4** [late 19C+] (*US*) to weep. **5** [1900s] (*US*) to rain. **6** [1980s+] (*US*) to bleed.

leake *n. see* LEEK *n.*

leak one's lizard *v. see under* LIZARD *n.*

leaky *adj.* [SE *leak*/LEAK *v.*] **1** [late 17C+] unable to keep a secret. **2** [early 18C] in need of urination. **3** [early 19C–1900s] drunk and thus talkative. **4** [20C+] (*US*) tearful, weepy. **5** [1990s+] (*Irish*) of weather, wet.

leaky bladder *n.* [rhy. sl.] [20C+] a stepladder.

lean *n.* [2000s] (*US drugs*) prescription cough syrup, containing codeine.

lean *adj.* (*also* **leaned**) [2000s] (*UK drugs*) intoxicated by cannabis.

IN PHRASES

❑ **sit on lean** *v.* [1990s+] to be intoxicated by drugs.

lean *v.*[1] [the image is supposedly that of a pimp cruising the streets with his whores] [1970s+] (*US black/west coast*) to drive a car while leaning out of the window.

SE in slang uses

IN PHRASES

❑ **lean against the engine** *v.* [the recumbent posture of opium smokers, and the concomitant smoke] [1940s–50s] (*US drugs*) to smoke opium. ❑ **lean-away** *n.* [late 19C–1950s] (*Aus.*) a drunkard. ❑ **lean over backwards** *v. see* BEND OVER BACKWARDS *under* BEND *v.*[1]. ❑ **lean-to** *n.* [1940s] a lodging house, night shelter or similar refuge for homeless people. ❑ **on a lean** *adj.* [1910s] (*Aus.*) waiting, lit. leaning (e.g. on a wall).

lean *v.*[2] [1990s+] (*drugs*) to be intoxicated by a given drug or combination thereof.

lean *v.*[3] *see* LEAN ON *v.* (1).

lean *adv.* [1980s+] (*US black*) obviously, strongly.

lean and fat *n.* (*also* **leaning fat**) [rhy. sl.] [mid-19C+] a hat.

lean and linger *n.* (*also* **long(ers) and linger(s)**) [rhy. sl.] [1920s+] a finger.

lean and lurch *n.* [rhy. sl.] [mid-19C+] a church.

leaned *adj. see* LEAN *adj.*

lean green *n.* [GREEN *n.*[2] (1)] [1970s+] (*US teen*) money.

leaning fat *n. see* LEAN AND FAT *n.*

leaning house *n.* [SE *lean*, i.e. relax + HOUSE *n.*[1] (1)] [1970s+] (*US black*) a brothel or a place where illicit meetings, drug sales etc take place.

lean on *v.* **1** [1910s+] (*also* **lean**) (*orig. US*) to beat up, to strike. **2** [1920s+] (*orig. US*) to pressurize, to persuade, poss. with violence or threats of violence. **3** [1920s+] to depend on. **4** [1960s+] (*US black*) to disparage or ridicule.

leap *v.* [SE *leap*, of an animal, to copulate] [early 16C–18C] to have sexual intercourse with.

IN COMPOUNDS

❑ **leaping house** *n.* [SE *house*/HOUSE *n.*[1] (1)] [late 16C–18C] a brothel.

IN PHRASES

❑ **leap in the dark** *v.* (*also* **leap up a ladder**) [18C–late 19C] to have sexual intercourse.

SE in slang uses

DERIVATIVES

❑ **leaping** *adj.* [1920s–50s] (*US drugs*) under the influence of drugs or alcohol.

IN COMPOUNDS

❑ **leaping dandruff** *n. see* GALLOPING DANDRUFF *under* GALLOPING *adj.* ❑ **leaping lena** *n.* [its bumpy motion] [1910s–50s] (*US*) a small car.

IN PHRASES

❑ **leap and you will receive** [1970s+] (*US black*) a ritual challenge to a fight. ❑ **leap at a crust** *v.* [mid-17C–mid-18C] to be starving. ❑ **leap at a daisy** *v.* [mid-16C–early 17C] to be hanged [the grass surrounding the gallows]. ❑ **leap at Tyburn** *v.* [TYBURN *n.*] [late 17C–early 19C] to be hanged. ❑ **leap the twig** *v. see* HOP THE TWIG *v.* (2).

IN EXCLAMATIONS

❑ **leaping lizards!** [coined in the comic strip *L'il Orphan Annie* by Harold Gray (1894–1968)] [1920s–70s] (*US*) an excl. expressing surprise.

leaper *n.* (*also* **leapy**) [SE *leap*] **1** [1930s–70s] (*US drugs*) a cocaine addict. **2** [1960s+] (*drugs*) any form of stimulant, amphetamine etc, usu. in pl. **3** [1960s+] a dud cheque, drawn against inadequate funds [note BOUNCE *v.*[2] (4)].

leaps *n.* [the fits that may be part of withdrawal] **1** [1920s–60s] (*US drugs*) withdrawal symptoms from cocaine addiction. **2** [1940s–50s] (*US Und.*) nerves, tension.

lea-rigs *n.* [SE *lea-rig*, a ridge left in grass at the end of a ploughed field] [late 19C] the vagina.

learn a few/learn a thing or two *v. see* KNOW A THING OR TWO *v.*

learn a new way *v.* [1960s+] of a heterosexual man, to turn to homosexuality.

learn French *v. see under* FRENCH *n.*

learn manners in Seville *v.* [pun on *Seville/civil*] [1910s–20s] to learn acceptable, if rather juvenile, manners.

leary *adj.* **1** *see* LAIRY *adj.* (2). **2** *see* LEERY *adj.*

least *n.* [the opposite of MOST, THE *n.*] [1950s] (*US black*) a mediocre or dull person or event.

leather *n.* **1** [14C–19C] the skin; thus *lose leather*, to rub off skin while riding [SE until 18C]. **2** in physiological or sexual contexts. (**a**) [mid-16C+] the vagina. (**b**) [mid-16C+] a promiscuous woman. (**c**) [mid-16C+] sexual intercourse; hence *nothing like leather*, there is nothing as good as sex. (**d**) [1930s+] (*US*) the anus. **3** an item made of leather. (**a**) [mid-18C+] a wallet or purse, or bag. (**b**) [mid-19C+] a leather ball, usu. a cricket ball or football; in the US a baseball. (**c**) [late 19C+] (*US*) a shoe; thus *lay leather*, to walk. (**d**) [1910s–30s] (*US*) a whip. (**e**) [1920s+] (*US*) a holster. (**f**) [1920s+] (*US*) a boxing glove. (**g**) [1920s+] (*US*) a saddle; thus *fork leather*, to ride a horse; *hit leather*, to ride off; *pull/hunt leather*, to grasp the saddle while riding a bucking horse. (**h**) [1930s] (*US Und.*) a pickpocket. (**i**) [1930s–40s] (*US*) by metonymy, a brutal kicking with a boot or shoe. (**j**) [1960s+] a leather coat or jacket. **4** [late 19C] (*US*) liver. **5** [1910s–30s] (*US*) meat.

IN COMPOUNDS

❑ **leather-dresser** *n.* [19C] the penis. ❑ **leather glommer** *n.* [the pickpocket 'lifts' the LEATHER *n.* (3a), while the assistant GLOM *v.* (1) or grabs it and takes it away] [1930s] (*US*) a pickpocket's assistant. ❑ **leather lane** *n.* [pun on the *Leather Lane* market, off Holborn, London] [19C] the vagina. ❑ **leather lay** *n.* [LAY *n.*[3] (1)] [late 18C] (*UK Und.*) the theft of bags. ❑ **leather lifter** *n.* [LIFTER *n.* (1)] [1920s–40s] (*US Und.*) a pickpocket. ❑ **leather-pusher** *n.* [1920s] a boxer; thus *leather pushing*, the sport of boxing. ❑ **leather stretcher** *n.* [19C] the penis. ❑ **leather worker** *n.* [WORKER *n.*[1] (2)] [1900s] (*US Und.*) a pickpocket.

IN PHRASES

❑ **burn leather** *v.* [1930s–40s] (*orig. US black*) to dance; to move fast. ❑ **give someone the leather** *v.* [1930s] **1** to kick a person. **2** to beat with the fist, to punch. ❑ **go leather-stretching** *v.* [late 18C–late 19C] of a man, to have sexual intercourse. ❑ **labour leather** *v.* [late 19C–1900s] to have sexual intercourse. ❑ **lay some leather on** *v.* [1930s] (*US*) to spank, to beat. ❑ **lose leather** *v.* [late 18C–19C] to become saddle-sore from excessive riding. ❑ **pattin' leather** [1930s+] (*US black*) **1** walking the streets. **2** thus fig. being out of work. ❑ **put in the leather** *v.* (*also* **put the leather in, put the leather to, stick the leather in**) [1910s+] to kick someone, esp. during a fight. ❑ **stretch leather** *v.* [17C–19C] to have sexual intercourse; thus *get one's leather stretched*. ❑ **throw leather** *v.* [1930s+] to box.

leather *adj.* [1960s+] (*orig. US gay*) pertaining to leather fetishism in attire and behaviour.

IN COMPOUNDS

❑ **leather bar** *n.* (*also* **leather lounge**) [1960s+] (*orig. US gay*) a bar frequented by leather fetishists and sadomasochistic male homosexuals. ❑ **leather boy** *n.* (*also* **leather man, leather job**) [1960s+] (*gay*) a male leather fetishist homosexual. ❑ **leather dyke** *n.* [DYKE *n.*] [1990s+] (*gay*) a lesbian leather fetishist. ❑ **leather freak** *n.* [-FREAK *sfx*] [1960s+] (*US*) a leather fetishist. ❑ **leather queen** *n.* (*also* **leather Mary**) [-QUEEN *sfx* (3)/MARY *n.* (2a)] [1960s+] (*orig. US gay*) a male homosexual who likes dressing in leather and may also enjoy sadomasochism.

SE in slang uses

IN COMPOUNDS

❑ **leather bottom** *n.* (*also* **leatherbum**) [20C+] a civil servant who is totally dedicated to work and thus never leaves their desk. ❑ **leather-face** *n.* [mid–late 19C] (*US*) an emotionless face or the individual with such a face. ❑ **leatherhead** *n. see* separate entry. ❑ **leather medal** *n.* [a 'real' medal is metal] [early 19C–1940s] (*US*) a fig. medal for failure, laziness, the booby prize. ❑ **leatherneck** *n. see* separate entry. ❑ **leather piece** *n.* [1960s+] (*US black*) any garment, esp. a coat, made of leather. ❑ **leatherskin** *n.* [mid–late 19C] (*US*) a derog. name for a Native American; thus adj., *leather-skinned*.

IN PHRASES

❑ **all leather** *adj.* [the toughness and durability of leather] **1** [19C+] of an object, excellent, first-rate. **2** [1920s] of a person, dependable, trustworthy.

leather *v.* **1** [mid-18C+] to beat, to kick. **2** [late 19C] to criticize severely. **3** [1930s] in fig. use, to consume voraciously, to 'shovel in'. **4** [1930s+] (*gay*) to perform anal intercourse [LEATHER *n.* (2d)].

leathered *adj.* [fig. use of LEATHER *v.* (1)] [1990s+] having consumed a large volume of alcohol in a very short time.

leatherhead *n.* [SE *leather* + -HEAD *sfx* (1)] **1** [early 17C+] a fool, a stupid person. **2** [mid-19C–1900s] (*US*) an inhabitant of Pennsylvania. **3** [mid-19C–1940s] (*US*) (*also* **leatherneck**) a policeman or watchman [the protective leather helmets worn by the police, or the leather badges that New York's first policemen wore]. **4** [1920s] (*US*) a louse [their seeming indestructibility].

IN COMPOUNDS

❑ **leather-headed** *adj.* [late 18C–1910s] foolish, stupid.

leather-lane *adj.* [the *Leather Lane* market off Holborn, London] [early 19C] second-rate, poorly made.

leathern conveniency *n.* (*also* **leathern convenience, leathern sanctuary**) [orig. 17C Quaker jargon] **1** [late 17C–mid-19C] a stage-coach. **2** [19C] a purse.

leatherneck *n.* **1** [late 19C–1960s] (*orig. Aus.*) a roustabout [the effects of the sun on skin]. **2** [20C+] (*UK/US*) a marine [early US marine uniforms had a leather neckband]. **3** [20C+] (*US*) a thug, a lout. **4** see LEATHERHEAD *n.* (3).

leathers *n.* **1** [mid–late 19C] anyone wearing leather leggings or breeches, e.g. a coachman. **2** [1960s+] leather garments, esp. as worn by motorcyclists. **3** [1970s–80s] (*UK black*) shoes.

leave *v.*

SE in slang uses

IN PHRASES

❑ **leave before the gospel** *v.* [i.e. before the church service is fully over] [20C+] to practise coitus interruptus. ❑ **leave it wet for (someone)** *v. see under* WET *adj.*[1]. ❑ **leave one's face** *v.* [1980s+] (*US campus*) to act in an embarrassing way. ❑ **leave shaping** *v.* [the image is of cricket: a batsman is still *shaping* up to play the ball when it passes the bat and bowls him] [20C+] (*W.I.*) to outsmart, to fool. ❑ **leave someone hanging** *v.* [1970s+] (*US black*) to reject or ignore a proffered handshake or to refuse to indulge in the ritualizing hand-slapping used as a greeting. ❑ **leave someone out/up to dry** *v. see* HANG SOMEONE OUT TO DRY *under* HANG *v.*[2]. ❑ **leave someone the bucket** *v.* [the bucket used as a chamberpot that prisoners must empty each morning] [1940s–50s] (*US prison*) to leave jail. ❑ **leave the dead at someone** *v.* [the image of abandoning a corpse] [20C+] (*W.I.*) to abandon when in difficulties, to 'leave holding the baby'. ❑ **leave the world with cotton in one's ears** *v.* [proper name *Cotton*, a 19C Newgate chaplain who would preach a last sermon to the condemned man] [early 19C] to be hanged. ❑ **leave town** *v.* [1900s–60s] (*US black*) to die.

IN EXCLAMATIONS

❑ **leave it out!** [1970s+] a general excl. of admonition: stop doing that!, don't be so stupid! etc. ❑ **leave off!** *see* separate entry.

leave off! *excl.* [mid-19C+] stop it! (esp. in sense of stop telling lies).

leaving shop *n.* [both places where something is left, deposited] **1** [mid–late 19C] an unlicensed pawnshop, specializing in lending very small sums on items that mainstream pawnbrokers reject; the usual rate of income was two (old) pence on the shilling, i.e appx. 16.66%. **2** [late 19C] the vagina.

Leb *n.* (*also* **Lebo**) [abbr.] [1980s+] **1** (*US*) a Lebanese person. **2** (*Aus.*) (*also* **lebbo**) an immigrant from the Lebanon. **3** *Lebanon*.

leb *n.* (*also* **Lebanese**) [abbr.] [1960s+] (*drugs*) Lebanese hashish, usu. qualified as *Red Leb, Lebanese Gold*.

leccy *n. see* LECKY *n.*

lech *see under* LETCH.

lech about *v. see under* LETCH *v.*

lechery-layer *n.* [SE *lechery* + LAY *v.*[1] (1)] [late 17C–18C] a prostitute.

lecky *n.* (*also* **leccy, lekkie, lekky**) [abbr.] [1960s+] **1** electricity, esp. as a utility; thus *fiddle the lecky*, to cheat on one's electricity bill. **2** an electrician.

lecky *adj.* [abbr.] [1960s+] electric; thus *lecky blanket, lecky kettle*.

led by (the head of) one's dick *phr. see under* DICK *n.*[1].

led captain *n.* (*also* **led-friend**) [SE *led horse*, a riderless horse that is often seen in the retinues of the rich and powerful, underlining the extent of their possessions, and the fact that they have them, even if they are of no real use; Grose (1785) adds that 'the small provision made for officers of the army and navy, in time of peace, obliges many ... to occupy this wretched station] [late 17C–mid-19C] **1** a toady or sycophant, 'an humble dependent in a great family, who, for a precarious subsistence, and distant hopes of preferment, suffers every kind of indignity' (Grose 1785). **2** a pimp.

ledge, the *n.* [abbr. of SE *knowledge*] [2000s] (*US black*) the situation, all the facts.

leech out *v.* [1950s] (*US teen*) to leave.

leeg *adj.* [SE *legitimate*] [1990s+] (*UK juv.*) a general negative.

lee-gate *v.* [Sp. sl. *ligando*] [1970s] (*US/P.R.*) to spy on, to act as a peeping Tom.

leek *n.* (*also* **leake**) [a national emblem] [early 18C] a Welsh person.

Leekshire *n.* [the leek is a national emblem] [18C–19C] Wales.

Lee Marvin *adj.* [rhy. sl.; US film star *Lee Marvin* (1924–87)] [1960s+] starving.

leen *n.* [abbr.] [1990s+] (*US black/drugs*) mescaline.

leer *n.* [? LURE *n.* or Sp. *leer*, to read] [late 18C–late 19C] a newspaper.

leerer *n.* [? SE *leer*, looking askance, sly] [mid-19C] (*UK Und.*) an eye.

leery *adj.* (*also* **leary**) [? SE *leer*, looking askance, sly] **1** [early 18C+] bright, alert, aware. **2** [early 18C+] guarded, suspicious of or uneasy about someone or something. **3** [late 19C–1930s] (*US*) hungover, drunk. **4** [20C+] cunning, underhand. **5** [20C+] bad-tempered, disagreeable, cheeky. **6** [20C+] frightened, hesitant. **7** [1930s] (*US Und.*) of goods, damaged.

DERIVATIVES

❑ **leariness** *n.* (*also* **leeriness**) **1** [late 19C+] awareness, sophistication. **2** [1960s+] caution.

IN COMPOUNDS

□ **leary bloke** *n.* [BLOKE *n.* (3)] **1** [mid-19C] a showy dresser. **2** [late 19C] (*Aus.*) a cunning person. □ **leary cove** *n.* (*also* **leary one**) [COVE *n.* (1)] [early–mid-19C] (*UK Und.*) one who is knowing, aware, esp. in criminal contexts.

Lee Van (Cleef) *n.* [rhy. sl.; ult. *Lee Van Cleef* (1925–89), actor most famous for playing the villains in spaghetti westerns] [1990s+] beef.

left *adv.* **1** [late 19C–1910s] (*US*) at a disadvantage, defeated; esp. in *get left*, to be placed at a disadvantage. **2** [1990s+] (*US black*) dead.

left and right *n.* [rhy. sl.] [20C+] a fight.

left-field *adj.* [baseball imagery] [1950s+] (*US*) unorthodox.

leftfielder *n.* [baseball imagery] [1940s–60s] (*US black/teen*) a criminal.

left-footer *n.* **1** [1930s+] (*also* **left-hander**) a Roman Catholic, but used in reverse by Catholics who define themselves as *right-handers*; thus *dig with the left foot*, to be a Catholic [? turf-cutting spades, as used by Catholics, having the lugs – that piece upon which the foot presses down – on the left of the haft. Note Pennsylvania use *left-winger*, a Roman Catholic]. **2** [1980s+] a male homosexual.

IN COMPOUNDS

□ **left-footing** *n.* [1980s] conducting a homosexual lifestyle.

IN PHRASES

□ **kick with the left foot** *v.* [rugby imagery] [1950s+] (*N.Z.*) to be a Roman Catholic.

left-handed *adj.* [lit. trans. of Lat. *sinister*] **1** [early–mid-18C] of sexual relations, extra-marital. **2** [late 19C] sly, surreptitious. **3** [late 19C–1910s] (*UK Und*) second-hand. **4** [late 19C+] undesirable, illicit, evil. **5** [1920s–70s] (*US*) homosexual. **6** [1930s–40s] reverse, back-to-front, also fig. use.

IN COMPOUNDS

□ **left-handed batsman** *n.* [1990s+] a male homosexual. □ **left-handed compliment** *n.* [late 19C+] an insincere or 'back-handed' compliment, a remark that 'damns with faint praise'. □ **left-handed monkey wrench** *n.* (*also* **left-handed spanner**) [1920s+] (*US*) an imaginary tool that an inexperienced worker is sent to find as a prank. □ **left-handed website** *n.* [1990s+] a website specializing in pornography [it causes visitors to use the mouse with their left hand]. □ **left-handed wife** *n.* [mid-17C–1930s] a mistress; thus the masc. form, *left-handed bridegroom*, a male lover.

leftie *see under* LEFTY.

left in the lurch *n.* (*also* **in the lurch**) [rhy. sl.] [late 19C+] a church.

lefto *n. see* LEFTY *n.* (3).

left off! *excl.* [1960s–70s] (*US campus*) a joc. reversal of RIGHT ON! *excl.*

left over *n.* [1930s] (*US*) mashed potatoes.

left raise *n.* (*US black*) **1** [1930s–40s] the left-hand side of one's body plus the relevant limbs. **2** [1930s–40s] the left side. **3** [1940s–50s] a pocket, presumably on the left of one's jacket or trousers.

left turn *n.* [the trad. fear of the 'sinister' left side] [1930s] (*US Und.*) a fool.

lefty *n.* (*also* **leftie**) **1** [mid-19C+] (*orig. US*) a left-handed person or a nickname for one who is left-handed; thus adv. *lefty*, with the left hand. **2** [1910s–60s] a person who has lost their limbs on their left side (arm and leg). **3** [1930s+] (*also* **lefto**) a left-wing political radical.

lefty *adj.* (*also* **leftie**) [LEFTY *n.*] **1** [1930s+] left-handed. **2** [1930s+] left-wing, Communistic.

leg *n.* **1** [mid-18C–mid-19C] someone who is to be transported [LEG *v.*[1] (2)]. **2** [19C] a cheating racehorse or cards gambler; thus *leggism*, the characteristics of such a gambler. **3** [19C–1930s] a bookmaker or professional layer of odds, e.g. in faro [abbr. BLACKLEG *n.*[1]]. **4** [mid-19C] the act of running away, escaping. **5** [mid–late 19C] a round or rubber of a card-game; thus *leg-and-leg*, a situation in which each player in the game has won a leg. **6** by metonymy, one who uses their legs. (**a**) [mid–late 19C] a footman. (**b**) [1960s–70s] (*US*) an infantryman. (**c**) [1970s] (*US*) an errand boy. **7** [20C+] (*Irish*) influence; thus *have a good/great leg of someone*, to have influence with, to be 'well in' with them. **8** [1960s+] (*US*) in sexual contexts [metonymic + poss. euph. DIRTY LEG *under* DIRTY *adj.*]. (**a**) a promiscuous woman. (**b**) (*US black/campus*) a woman. (**c**) female sexuality. (**d**) sexual intercourse.

DERIVATIVES

□ **legged** *adj.* [mid–late 19C; 1970s] chained, in irons; thus imprisoned.

IN COMPOUNDS

□ **leg art** *n.* (*also* **leg picture**) [1930s–50s] actual views or pictures of women revealing their legs. □ **leg bags** *n.* **1** [late 18C–19C] stockings or trousers. **2** [late 19C] trousers. □ **leg business** *n.* **1** [late 19C–1930s] sexual intercourse. **2** [mid–late 19C] (*US*) the ballet. **3** [mid–late 19C] (*US*) any form of entertainment where the focus is on the women's legs. □ **leg drama** *n.* [late 19C] any form of show, whether a musical or full-scale striptease, in which the focus is on a woman's legs. □ **leg-licker** *n.* [1990s+] (*US gay*) a lesbian. □ **leg-lifter** *n.* [early 18C–19C] a promiscuous man, a womanizer; thus *leg-lifting*, casual sexual intercourse. □ **leg picture** *n. see* LEG ART above. □ **leg piece** *n.* **1** [mid–late 19C] any form of stage performance featuring the female leg, e.g. a burlesque show. **2** [1910s–20s] the ballet. □ **leg sacks** *n.* [1930s–40s] (*US black*) socks; stockings. □ **leg-shaker** *n.* [late 19C–1920s] a dancer; a dance. □ **leg shop** *n.* [late 19C] (*US*) a theatre devoted to burlesque, i.e. the display of women's legs. □ **leg show** *n.* [late 19C+] (*orig. US*) any form of show, whether a musical or full-scale striptease, in which the focus is on a woman's legs. □ **leg-stretcher** *n.* [mid-19C] (*US*) whisky.

IN PHRASES

□ **clap one's leg over** *v. see* THROW A LEG OVER below. □ **dead leg** *n. see under* DEAD *adj.* □ **get some leg** *v.* (*also* **get off some leg, get some big leg, get some soft leg**) [1960s+] (*US black*) usu. of a man, to have sexual intercourse. □ **legged for groat** [? SE *groat*, fourpence] [late 19C] (*UK tramp*) a jail sentence of ten years. □ **leg into** *v.* [1920s+] (*Aus. Und.*) to become involved in, to take a share. □ **legs (right) up to her ass** (*also* **...arse, ...bum**) [ASS *n.* (2)/ARSE *n.* (1)/BUM *n.*[1] (1)] [1930s+] (*orig. US*) a male description of a woman with exceptionally long and attractive legs. □ **lift a leg over** *v.* (*also* **lay a leg on, lay a/one's leg over, lift a leg on**) [17C–18C] to have sexual intercourse. □ **lift one's leg** *v.* (*also* **get one's leg lifted**) [early 18C–19C] of either sex, to have sexual intercourse. □ **make a leg** *v.* [a pun on SE *make a leg*, to bow] [1900s–20s] of a woman, to show one's legs. □ **make up one's leg** *v.* (*also* **make leg**) ['the time of smalls, stockings and buckled shoes, when making up the leg was a necessary prelude to going into society' (Ware)] [late 19C–1900s] (*coster*) to make money. □ **on the leg** [the image of a dog rubbing against a human leg] [1990s+] (*US prison*) toadying. □ **play at lift-leg** *v.* [early 18C–mid-19C] to have sexual intercourse. □ **pull someone's leg** *v.* **1** [late 19C] (*US campus*) to curry favour with, to act the toady. **2** [late 19C] to default in payment of a bill. **3** [late 19C+] (*US*) to ask for a loan of money. **4** [1920s] (*Aus.*) to subject to a confidence trick. □ **throw a leg over** *v.* (*also* **clap one's leg over, roll one's leg over, throw one's leg over**) [18C; 1960s+] of a man, to seduce, to have sexual intercourse.

IN EXCLAMATIONS

□ **my hind legs!** [late 17C+] a general excl. of disdain, dismissal, arrogant contempt. □ **oh my leg!** [the ref. is to the leg-irons one wears there] [early 19C] a teasing remark, aimed at anyone recently freed from prison.

SE in slang uses

DERIVATIVES

□ **legless** *adj. see* separate entry.

IN COMPOUNDS

□ **legback** *n.* [1970s–80s] (*UK black*) the female thigh, thus generically, a woman. □ **leg bail** *n.* [SE *bail*, security given against the release of a prisoner pending their trial] [mid-18C–1940s] unauthorized absence; thus *give/tip leg-bail* (*and land* *security*), to escape, to run off. ❑ **leg-breaker** *n.* [1970s+] (*US Und.*) a hired thug. ❑ **leg man** *n. see* separate entry. ❑ **leg-opener** *n.* [on model of EYE-OPENER *n.*[1] (1)] [1950s+] (*orig. Aus.*) a drink given to a woman in the hope of getting her drunk enough for seduction. ❑ **legover** *n. see* separate entry. ❑ **leg-roped** *adj.* [SAusE *leg-rope*, 'a noosed rope used to secure an animal by one hind leg' (*AND*)] [1900s] (*Aus.*) married. ❑ **legshake artist** *adj.* [-ARTIST *sfx*] [20C+] (*orig. Aus.*) a pickpocket.

IN PHRASES

❑ **best leg of three** *n.* [late 19C–1900s] the penis. ❑ **cut one's leg** *v.* [SE/CUT *adj.*[1]] [late 17C–late 18C] **1** to become pregnant. **2** to get drunk. ❑ **fight at the leg** *v.* [back-sword or single-stick rules, in which it is considered unfair to hold the opponent by the leg] [late 18C–19C] to take unfair advantage. ❑ **get a leg in** *v.* [1900s–10s] (*Aus.*) **1** to gain someone's confidence, to win over. **2** to win an advantage. ❑ **get one's leg over** *v.* (*also* **get one's leg across**) [1970s+] of a man, to seduce, to have sexual intercourse. ❑ **give someone a (clean) leg up** *v.* (*also* **give someone a bunch up, give someone a leg**) [mid-19C+] to help someone (occas. something) over an obstacle, wall etc, both physical and fig., esp. to advance themselves professionally; thus *get a leg up*, to gain such an advantage. ❑ **give someone a little leg** *v.* [colloq. phr. *pull someone's leg*] [1960s–70s] to confuse, to tell tales. ❑ **have a loose leg** *v.* [20C+] (*Irish*) to be free to live one's life without restraint. ❑ **have legs on one's belly** *v.* [they facilitate one's 'crawling'] [1940s+] (*Aus./N.Z.*) to be a sycophant, a toady. ❑ **have someone/something by the leg** *v. see* HAVE SOMEONE BY THE BALLS *under* BALLS *n.* ❑ **leg of mutton in a silk stocking** *n.* [SE but note MUTTON *n.* (1b)] [late 17C–late 19C] a woman's leg. ❑ **leg of the law** *n.* [var. on *LIMB OF THE LAW under* LIMB *n.*] [19C] a lawyer. ❑ **lose one's legs** *v.* [mid–late 18C] to be drunk. ❑ **make indentures with one's legs** *v.* [the custom of indenting the top edges of legal documents] [17C–mid-18C] to stumble drunkenly.

leg *v.*[1] **1** [17C+] to run. **2** in (*UK Und.*) uses [the irons on a felon's leg]. (**a**) [mid-18C–mid-19C] to be transported; thus n., *leg*, one who is transported. (**b**) [early 19C] to arrest. (**c**) [mid-19C] to be sentenced to prison; thus *n., legging*, a jail sentence. **3** [mid-19C–1900s] to run errands. **4** [late 19C] to trip someone up by seizing their leg. **5** [1960s] (*US Und.*) to shoplift by hiding goods between the legs. **6** [1970s] to set a bomb. **7** [1970s+] (*orig. US black*) (*also* **leg it**) to have sexual intercourse [note *GET ONE'S LEG OVER under* LEG *n.*]. **8** [1990s+] to chase, i.e. to make someone run (away).

IN PHRASES

❑ **leg it** *v.* **1** [mid-19C+] to run away, to walk. **2** [1910s] to wander, to travel.

leg *v.*[2] (*also* **lag**) [BOOTLEG *v.* (2)] [1920s+] (*US*) to make or distribute illicitly distilled whisky.

leg *v.*[3] *see* LAG *v.*[2].

legal *v.*

IN PHRASES

❑ **get legal** *v.* [1990s+] (*US black/drugs*) to be involved in the use and selling of crack cocaine.

legal beagle *n.* [1940s+] (*orig. US*) a lawyer, esp. an assiduous one.

legal eagle *n.* [rhy. sl., albeit internal] [1930s+] (*orig. US*) a lawyer, with the implication of being an astute one.

legal fleagle *n.* [1970s] (*US*) a lawyer.

leg before wicket *n.* (*also* **l.b.w.**) [rhy. sl., usu. abbr.] [20C+] a ticket, both lit. and fig.; thus *not the l.b.w.*, 'not the ticket'.

legem pone *n.* [the first two words of the fifth division of Ps. 119, which begins the psalms at Matins on the 25th day of the month, associated with 25 March, the year's first quarter day and thus the first major payday of the calendar] [16C–17C] the payment of money, cash down.

legend *adj.* [1990s+] (*Aus./US campus/black*) amazing, excellent; also as *n.* an exceptional person.

leger *n.* [Fr. *lèger*, light] [late 16C] (*UK Und.*) **1** a coal merchant who gives short weight. **2** a London coal merchant who buys wholesale in the country and then retails the coal in London, pretending to be from the country himself.

DERIVATIVES

❑ **legering** *n.* [late 16C] (*UK Und.*) the giving of short measure by colliers.

legger *n.*[1] [? he produces such goods from his breeches pockets or his boot-tops] **1** [late 18C–1900s] one who pretends to be selling smuggled goods, but is in fact selling old or shop-worn stock, obtained cheaply. **2** [1920s–60s] (*US*) a smuggler of contraband liquor, a boot*legger* [abbr.; *OED* cites *legger* as abbr. of 1920s+ *bootlegger*, but sense 1 suggests the practice already existed].

legger *n.*[2] [20C+] (*Irish*) a departure on foot; usu. as *do a legger*.

leggings *n.* [Fr. *legume*, a vegetable] [20C+] (*W.I.*) greens and root vegetables used in soup.

leggins *n.* [1930s+] (*US gay/prison*) copulation when the penis is rubbed between the legs of the sexual partner.

leggner *n.* [pun on STRETCH *n.* (1b)/SE *stretch a leg*] [1940s–50s] (*UK prison*) a 12-month sentence.

leggo *adj.* [backform. f. LEGGO BEAST *n.*] [1940s+] (*W.I. Rasta*) wild, disorderly.

leggo! *excl.* [mispron./mis-sp.] **1** [late 19C+] (*orig. US*) let go! **2** [late 19C+] a shout of warning, let's go! run for it!

leggo beast *n.* [SE *let go*, uncontrolled, without an owner + *beast*] [1940s+] (*W.I.*) **1** a tramp. **2** a person, usu. a woman, with loose morals; by ext. a prostitute.

legit *n.* [abbr. SE *legitimate*] **1** [late 19C–1950s] in theatre, 'straight' dramatic productions rather than variety, etc. **2** [late 19C–1950s] an actor who works in sense 1. **3** [20C+] (*UK/US Und.*) a legitimate employment, occupation or person. **4** [1950s] a legitimate place, usu. of entertainment — as opposed to an 'after-hours' establishment or a speakeasy.

IN PHRASES

❑ **on the legit** *adj.* [1920s+] honest, fair-dealing, trustworthy.

legit *adj.* [abbr.] **1** [1920s+] (*orig. US*) (*also* **ligit**) *legit*imate, and as such the description of anything that, in context, might be considered as otherwise; thus *on the legit*, conducting an honest life/business etc. **2** [1920s+] (*orig. US*) of a person, respectable. **3** [1990s+] (*US black*) authentic; talented.

legit *adv.* [abbr.] [1930s+] legitimately.

legit! *excl.* [LEGIT *adj.*] [1990s+] (*US teen*) an excl. of approval, acceptance, 'you're OK!', 'that's acceptable!'.

legitimacy *n.* [one had 'legal reasons' for the trip] [19C] (*Aus.*) the state of emigrating to Australia as a convict.

legitimate *n.* **1** [19C] (*Aus.*) a settler who arrived in Australia as a transported convict [such settlers had 'legal reasons' to make the trip]. **2** [early 19C] a sovereign (money) [? as opposed to a forgery].

legitimate *adj.* [1970s+] (*US gay*) heterosexual.

legless *adj.* (*also* **footless**) **1** [1940s+] drunk to the extent of nearly or actually falling over. **2** [1990s+] exhausted.

leg man *n.* (*orig. US*) **1** as a user of one's legs. (**a**) [1920s+] a journalist who actively finds the news. (**b**) [1930s+] one who acts as a go-between for organized crime and its 'customers'. (**c**) [1940s+] an assistant. (**d**) [1960s] any form of go-between **2** [1950s+] a man who prefers a woman's legs to any other part of her anatomy; as opposed to an *ASS-MAN under* ASS *n.* or a *TIT MAN under* TIT *n.*[2].

leg of beef *n.* [rhy. sl.] [20C+] a thief.

leg of mutton *n.*[1] [mid-19C] a sheep's trotter.

leg of mutton *n.*[2] [rhy. sl.] [20C+] a button.

leg of pork *n.* [rhy. sl.] [1990s+] a piece of chalk.

legover *n.* **1** [20C+] (*Irish*) assistance, help [image of giving someone a *leg over* a stile or gate]. **2** [1970s+] (*orig. milit.*) sexual intercourse; thus *give/have a bit of legover*, to have sexual intercourse [back form. f. *GET ONE'S LEG OVER under* LEG *n.*]

legs *n.* [i.e. all *legs*, no body] [mid-19C+] a tall, thin person.

legs eleven *n.* [resemblance] **1** [20C+] (*bingo*) the number 11. **2** [1910s] (*Aus.*) a tall thin man. **3** [1950s–60s] £11.

legshake artist *n.* [-ARTIST *sfx*] [20C+] (*orig. Aus.*) a pickpocket.

legume *n.* [Fr. *legume*, a vegetable] **1** [1980s+] (*US drugs*) a piece or 'button' of peyote cactus. **2** [1980s+] (*US campus*) a lazy person, one who lies around doing nothing.

leg work *n.* **1** [late 19C+] (*orig. US*) in terms of a job, a great deal of walking; also in fig. use as a huge amount of research. **2** [1940s+] intercourse between the thighs or the buttocks (without penetration of the anus).

leg worker *n.* [LEG WORK *n.* (1) + pun on SE *leg*] [1930s] (*US*) one who works on the street, on foot, as a tout etc.

Leicester (Square) *n.* [rhy. sl.] [1990s+] a chair.

leisure hours *n.* [rhy. sl.] [late 19C–1900s] flowers.

lekker *n.* (*also* **lekkers**) [abbr.] [2000s] (*N.Z.*) electricity.

lekker *adj.* [Du. *lekker*, pleasant, tasty] [mid-19C+] (*S.Afr.*) **1** an all-embracing term of approval, as n. *lekkerkry* pleasure; as adv., to a great extent. **2** tipsy, slightly drunk.

lekkie *n. see* LECKY *n.*

lekking *n.* [1990s+] (*S.Afr. juv.*) playing outside the house.

lekky *n. see* LECKY *n.*

lem *n.*[1] [ety. unknown] [1970s–80s] (*S.Afr.*) a pocket-knife.

lem *n.*[2] (*also* **lemon**) [abbr.] [2000s] (*US black*) marijuana that smells of lemon when smoked.

lem *v.* [? LEMON *n.* (1a), i.e. one who refuses to socialize] [1980s+] (*US drugs*) to fall asleep immediately after smoking marijuana.

lemac *n.* (*also* **little man**) [backsl.] [2000s] (*US prison*) a Camel cigarette.

lemon *n.* **1** of people and things, in the sense of the sourness and/or unpalatability of the fruit. (**a**) [mid-19C] a person of a sour disposition. (**b**) [mid-19C+] (*also* **citron, lime**) anything or anyone undesirable, esp. used of a woman. (**c**) [1910s+] a disappointment, anything worthless or fraudulent, esp. a poor quality drug purchase. (**d**) [1920s+] a defective car or vehicle; thus the *lemon law*, a law that provides redress for buyers of substandard or defective cars. (**e**) [1950s+] (*US drugs*) (*also* **lemonade**) weak or second-rate narcotics, a diluted or poor-quality drug, esp. poor heroin. (**f**) [1980s+] (*Aus./S.Afr.*) a lesbian. **2** [20C+] a victim, a fool [? pun on SUCKER *n.*[1] (3b)]. **3** the shape. (**a**) [1920s–50s] the head. (**b**) [1930s+] (*US*) the female breasts. **4** [1920s–60s] (*US black*) a light-skinned black person. **5** in the sense of something/someone that can be 'squeezed'. (**a**) [1930s] (*US Und.*) an informer [such a person can be 'squeezed' by an interrogator]. (**b**) [1930s+] (*US black*) the female pubic hair. (**c**) [1930s+] (*US black*) the vagina. (**d**) [1930s+] (*US black*) the male genitals. **6** *see* LEMON CURD *n.* (1).

(DERIVATIVES)

❑ **lemoner** *n.* [1970s+] (*Irish*) a disappointment, something depressing.

(IN COMPOUNDS)

❑ **Lemon Avenue** *n.* (*also* **Lemon Land**) [their lips are eternally pursed with disapproval, as if they had just sucked a lemon] [1910s+] (*Aus.*) the fig. name for the 'spiritual home' of censorious or socially repressive people. ❑ **lemon-eater** *n.* (*also* **lemon-pelter, lemon-sucker**) [the English are seen as sour] [1960s+] (*US derog.*) an English person. ❑ **lemon game** *n.* [GAME *n.* (6)] [20C+] (*US Und.*) a way of cheating at pool, whereby a victim is enticed into the game and allowed to win. Once they are sufficiently confident to bet heavily, their opponent has a 'run of luck' and takes all their money. ❑ **lemon hand** *n.* [HAND *n.*[1] (1)] [1960s] (*US*) a deliberately malicious person. ❑ **lemon-lipped** *adj.* [2000s] (*N.Z.*) very angry. ❑ **lemon-squeezer** *n.* **1** [1920s] (*US*) a subway car. **2** [1940s+] (*Aus./N.Z.*) a hat with a peaked crown and broad, flat brim worn by Aus. and N.Z. soldiers. ❑ **lemon-sucker** *n.* [? SE *sucker* or his stereotypically pursed lips] [1920s–60s] (*US*) an effeminate man. ❑ **lemon twist** *n.* [the sweet] [1990s+] (*Aus. Und.*) when one gang employs a known police informer to give information about its rivals to the police.

(IN PHRASES)

❑ **cut lemons** *v.* [CUT *v.*[3]/ SE; ? lemons are 'sharp'] [late 19C] (*US*) to impress, to appear important; usu. in negative, e.g. *that didn't cut any lemons.* ❑ **hand someone the lemon** *v.* [1910s–30s] (*US*) to disdain, to dismiss. ❑ **have lemon lips** *v.* [2000s] (*S.Afr. gay*) to be in a bad mood, very angry. ❑ **sell lemons** *v.* [1950s+] to sell second-rate or fake drugs. ❑ **shoot the lemon** *v.* [1910s] (*US prison*) to chatter, to gossip. ❑ **squeeze one's lemon** *v.* **1** [1930s+] (*orig. US black*) to have sexual intercourse [esp. in blues use, as a sexual euph.: 'Squeeze my lemon, till the juice runs down my leg']. **2** [1940s] in fig. use, to live life to the full. **3** [1950s+] of a man or woman, to urinate.

SE in slang uses

(IN COMPOUNDS)

❑ **lemon drop** *n.* **1** [1970s] (*US teen*) a contraceptive pill. **2** [2000s] (*US drugs*) a methamphetamine tablet. ❑ **lemonfish** *n.* [1980s+] (*N.Z.*) shark, as used in fish and chip shops.

(IN PHRASES)

❑ **suck lemons** *v.* [20C+] (*US*) to act sourly, to complain, to sulk.

lemon *adj.*[1] [LEMON *n.*] **1** [late 19C–1920s] of a black person, light-skinned. **2** [1900s–20s] (*US*) useless, second-rate.

lemon *adj.*[2] [rhy. sl.; *lemon squash* = FLASH *adj.* (1a)] [2000s] ostentatious.

lemonade *n.* **1** [1970s+] (*US*) urine. **2** *see* LEMON *n.* (1e).

lemon and dash *n.* [rhy. sl. = SE *wash*/SLASH *n.* (2)] [1950s+] a public lavatory.

lemon and lime *n.* [rhy. sl.] **1** [20C+] time. **2** [1990s+] crime.

lemon curd *n.* [rhy. sl.] [1960s+] **1** (*also* **lemon**) a piece of excrement [TURD *n.*[1] (1)]. **2** a derog. term for a person [TURD *n.*[1] (2)]. **3** a woman [BIRD *n.*[1] (1b)].

lemon (drop) *n.* [rhy. sl. = COP *n.*[1] (1)] [1980s+] a police officer.

lemon (flavour) *n.* [rhy. sl.] [1990s+] a favour.

lemons *adv.* [the 'sharpness' of the fruit] [mid-19C–1940s] (*Aus./US*) energetically, enthusiastically; usu. as *go in lemons.*

lemon spread *n.* [rhy. sl.] [1980s] (*Aus.*) the head.

lemon (squash) *n.* [rhy. sl.] [20C+] (*Aus.*) a wash; also as v.

lemon-squeezer *n.* [rhy. sl. = GEEZER *n.*[1] (1)] [1970s+] a man.

lemon squeezy *adj.* [rhy. sl.; also the rhyme *easy peasy lemon squeezy*] [1990s+] easy.

lemon tart *n. see* APPLE TART *n.*

lemon tea *n.* [rhy. sl. = PEE *n.*[1] (2)] [1940s+] an act of urination.

lemony *adj.* [the 'sharpness' of the fruit] [1940s–60s] (*Aus./N.Z.*) angry, irritated.

(IN PHRASES)

❑ **go lemony at** *v.* (*also* **go lemony with**) to lose one's temper with.

lend *n.* [16C+ dial.; 20C+ use is Aus.] [19C+] a loan, e.g. *give us a lend of your barrow.*

lend him a hole to hide it in *v. see* GIVE HIM A HOLE TO HIDE IT IN *under* HOLE *n.*[1].

length *n.* **1** [mid-19C] (*UK Und.*) six months' imprisonment [horseracing imagery, a *length* is half a STRETCH *n.* (1b)]. **2** [1940s+] the penis, usu. by metonymy an act of sexual intercourse, usu. with vtr., *give a length, throw a length* etc [i.e. the 'length' of the penis].

(IN PHRASES)

❑ **slip someone a length** *v.* [1950s+] to have sexual intercourse.

SE in slang uses

(IN PHRASES)

❑ **go the length of a...** *v.* [late 19C] to lend, the amount being specified at the end, e.g. *go the length of a quid.*

Len Hutton *n.* [rhy. sl., ult. cricketer *Len Hutton* (1916–90)] [1930s+] a button.

lenny the lion *n.* [rhy. sl. = IRON (HOOF) *n.*] [1930s+] a homosexual.

leno *n.* [Sp. *leño*, a stick of wood] [1950s+] (*US drugs*) marijuana, a marijuana cigarette.

lens *v.* (*US*) **1** [1920s] to see, to get to know about. **2** [1980s+] to film a movie.

lens lizard *n. see under* -LIZARD *sfx.*

lens louse *n. see under* -LOUSE *sfx.*

Leonie *n.* (*also* **Leonora**) [initial letters] [2000s] (*S.Afr. gay*) a liar.

Leo Sayer *n.* [rhy. sl. = *all-dayer*, ult. pop star *Leo Sayer* (b.1948)] [1990s+] an all-day drinking session or any other form of party.

leper *n.* [1990s+] (*Irish/UK juv.*) a general term of abuse.

Leperland *n.* [its population of lepers] [late 19C] (*Aus.*) a nickname for Queensland.

leper line *n.* [the Western Australia Native Australian Welfare Act (1954), which sought to prevent the spread of leprosy by forcing all sufferers to move to a place south of that parallel] [1950s+] (*Aus., Western*) a line running across Western Australia at 20°S.

lepping *adj.* [fig. use of SE *leap*] [20C+] (*Irish*) angry, keen.

lepping *adv.* [LEPPING *adj.*] [20C+] (*Irish*) very, hugely.

leprosy *n.* [ety. unknown] [1930s–40s] (*Aus.*) cabbage.

ler *n.* [abbr.] [2000s] (*US black, Los Angeles*) a hust*ler*.

leracam *n.* (*also* **lur-a-cham**) [backsl.] [mid-19C] a mackerel.

lergy *n. see* LURGI *n.*

lerricompoop *v.* [? link to LERRICOMTWANG *n.* or dial. *lerry*, a whim, a caprice; note also SE *liripoop*, the long tail hanging down from a graduate's hood — potentially seen as phallic, and dial. *lerrick*, to beat, to flog] [17C] to have sexual intercourse.

lerricomtwang *n.* [the chorus of a contemporary popular song] [mid–late 17C] a fool, a simpleton.

les *n.* (*also* **les-wolf, lez, lezz**) [abbr.] [1920s+] (*orig. US*) a *les*bian.

les *adj.* (*also* **lez**) [LES *n.*] [1940s+] lesbian.

les *v.* [abbr.] [1940s] to indulge in *les*bian sexual relations.

lesb *n.* [abbr.] [1950s+] a *lesb*ian.

lesbie *n.* (*also* **lesby**) [abbr.] [1950s+] a *lesb*ian; thus the punning phr. *lesby friends*.

lesbo *n.* (*also* **lezbo**) [abbr.] [1920s+] (*orig. US*) a *lesb*ian.

lesbo *adj.* [LESBO *n.*] [1970s+] lesbian.

lesie *adj. see* LEZZIE *adj.*

Lesley Crowthers *n.* [rhy. sl.] [2000s] trousers.

leslie *n.* (*also* **Leslie Anne**) [abbr. + a name that serves for men and women] [1940s+] (*Aus.*) a lesbian.

leslies *n.* (*also* **lesleys**) [initial letter] [2000s] (*S.Afr. gay*) the legs.

leso *n.* (*also* **lezo, lezzo**) [abbr. + -O *sfx* (3)] [1940s+] (*Aus.*) a *les*bian.

leso *adj. see* LEZZIE *adj.*

lesser *n. see* LEZZER *n.*

lessie *see under* LEZZIE.

less it! *excl.* [1970s+] (*UK juv.*) excl. of prohibition, e.g. stop that!, be quiet!

less than nothing *n.* **1** [20C+] (*US black*) a derog. term for a passive homosexual. **2** [1980s+] (*gay*) a weak gay man, unable to look after himself.

les-wolf *n. see* LES *n.*

let *v.*

SE in slang uses

IN PHRASES

❑ **let a brewer's fart grains and all** *v.* [late 18C–19C] to foul one's trousers. ❑ **let down someone's blind** *v.* [1910s–20s] to make clear that someone is dead. ❑ **let fly** *v.* [SE *let fly*, to fire, a missile, a gun, etc] **1** [18C] to defecate. **2** [18C–early 19C] to break wind. ❑ **let her flicker** [running a reel of movie film] [mid-19C+] (*Aus./US*) a phr. used at the start of some operations, usu. as *OK, let her flicker …* ❑ **let it all hang out** *v.* [a musicians' term, this migrated to white HIPPIE *n.*[2] (3) use and thence, like a number of similar terms, to the jargon of 'new therapies'] [1960s+] (*orig. US black*) to cast aside any restraints, to do what one wants. ❑ **let leap a whiting** *v.* [mid-16C–late 19C] to let an opportunity slip. ❑ **let me hold some change** *see under* CHANGE *n.* ❑ **let off** *v.* [? play on SE *let off steam*] [mid-19C; 1920s+] to break wind. ❑ **let off at** *v.* [1970s] to shout at, to attack verbally. ❑ **let off steam** *v. see* BLOW OFF STEAM *under* STEAM *n.* ❑ **let (one) go** *v. see under* ONE *n.*[1]. ❑ **let one's hair down** *v.* **1** [1930s+] to admit to being homosexual. **2** [1970s] as *vtr.* to 'out' a previously closeted homosexual. ❑ **let one's horse out of the stable** *v.* **1** [1950s–60s] to urinate. **2** [2000s] to reveal a secret. ❑ **let run a milestone** *v.* [late 17C] (*gaming*) to let a die roll some distance. ❑ **let someone down a buttonhole** *v. see* TAKE SOMEONE DOWN (A BUTTONHOLE) *under* TAKE DOWN *v.* ❑ **let someone have it** *v. see under* HAVE *v.* ❑ **let the badger loose** *v.* [the 'sport' of badger-baiting] [1970s+] (*US, Western*) to celebrate wildly, to 'let off steam'. ❑ **let the priest say mass** [20C+] (*Irish*) a phr. used to reprimand someone who keeps interrupting or offering unwanted suggestions.

IN EXCLAMATIONS

❑ **let 'em trundle!** [late 17C–mid-18C] go away! be off! ❑ **let's be having you!** (*also* **let's have you!**) [20C+] time to start work! get out of bed! drink up! etc.

letari *n. see* LETTARY *n.*

letch *n.* (*also* **lech**) [abbr.] **1** [late 18C+] a strong sexual desire; a yearning. **2** [1940s+] (*orig. US*) a *lech*er. **3** [1960s] sexual play.

DERIVATIVES

❑ **letchy** *adj.* [2000s] lecherous.

IN COMPOUNDS

❑ **letchwater** *n.* [19C] **1** semen. **2** vaginal fluid.

letch *v.* (*also* **lech**) [LETCH *n.* (1)] [1910s+] to lust, crave, thus *leching*.

IN COMPOUNDS

❑ **letching-piece** *n.* [PIECE *n.* (1a)] [1910s+] a promiscuous woman.

IN PHRASES

❑ **letch about** *v.* (*also* **lech about**) [1960s] to act in a sexual manner.

let-down *n.* [mid-19C+] a disappointment.

let-go *n.* [LET GO *v.* (1)] [mid-18C] orgasm, ejaculation.

letgo *n.* [1980s] (*W.I., Jam.*) a release, a way out (of one's problems).

let go *v.* **1** [late 19C+] to reach orgasm. **2** [1900s] to spend money. **3** [1910s] (*US*) to be quiet, usu. as imper. 'forget it!'. **4** [1960s] to urinate. **5** [1990s+] (*US campus*) to relax.

let go a razzo *v. see* RASPBERRY TART *n.* (2).

let go with *v.* [late 19C–1930s] to perform an action, esp. in context of violence.

let-her-go-Gallagher *adj.* [LET HER GO (GALLAGHER) *v.* (1)] [1910s] naked.

let her go (Gallagher) *v.* [? assonance of proper name] **1** [mid-19C+] to allow anything, real or fig., to go at full speed, to remove any impediment to progress. **2** [1910s–40s] (*US*) to vomit.

let her go (Gallagher)! *excl.* [LET HER GO (GALLAGHER) *v.*] [late 19C–1930s] (*Aus./US*) go ahead!

let her rip! *excl.*[1] (*also* **let her roll!**) [? f. steamboat engines that exploded or *ripped* when under excessive pressure. The phr., according to Ware, was common among their captains when urging the crew to put on full steam when racing against a rival boat] [mid-19C+] (*orig. US*) an excl. suggesting that someone should go full speed ahead, whether lit. or fig., to remove any impediment to progress.

let her rip! *excl.*[2] (*also* **let him rip!**) [let them *r*est *i*n *p*eace] [mid-19C+] an excl. of dismissal.

let-in *n.* [LET IN *v.*] **1** [19C–1920s] a hoax, an act of cheating. **2** [1910s–20s] a robbery. **3** [1910s–20s] an illegal victimization.

let in *v.* [image of falling through ice] [mid-19C–1900s] to cheat, to defraud, to victimize.

let into *v.* [mid-19C–1900s] to attack physically.

let into the secret *v.* [late 17C–early 19C] to draw a victim into betting on a crooked race or game and then to defraud them.

let-out *n.* **1** [mid-19C–1900s] (*Anglo-Irish*) (*also* **let off**) a spree, an entertainment, a grand occasion. **2** [1920s] (*US Und.*) money from corruption. **3** [1920s+] an excuse, an alibi.

let out at *v.* [late 19C+] **1** (*Aus.*) to aim a blow at. **2** to admonish.

let out her fore room and lie backwards *v.* (*also* **lies backwards and lets out her fore room**) [late 17C–early 19C] of a woman, allegedly to be working as a prostitute.

let rip *v.* [backform. f. LET HER RIP! *excl.*[1]] [late 19C+] to 'let fly', to let go, esp. with great energy and force.

let's rejoice *n.* [rhy. sl.] [20C+] (*Aus.*) the voice.

lettary *n.* (*also* **letari, letty**) [Ital. *letto*, a bed] [1900s–30s] (*tramp*) a lodging.

letter *n.*

SE in slang uses

IN COMPOUNDS

❑ **letterbox** *n.* [1990s+] a passive homosexual. ❑ **letter-fencer** *n.* [SE *letter* + -FENCER *sfx*] [late 19C–1900s] a postman. ❑ **letter-racket** *n.* [SE *letter* + RACKET *n.*[1] (1)] [early 19C] (*UK Und.*) the sending of fake begging letters.

IN PHRASES

❑ **letter from home** *n.* [the stereotypical link of watermelons and life 'down home'] **1** [1930s+] (*US*) anything that provokes nostalgia. **2** [1950s–70s] (*US black*) a watermelon. ❑ **there's a letter in the post office** (*US*) **1** [mid-19C+] a phr. used to warn a man his fly is undone or his shirt is out, also used to a woman when her slip is showing. **2** [late 19C–1910s] said of a woman who is menstruating.

letter A number 1 *adj. see* A-1 *adj.* (1).

lettered *adj.* [18C–early 19C] (*UK Und.*) branded on the hand.

Lettie *n.* (*also* **letticus, lettie bag, lettuce leaf**) [2000s] (*S.Afr. gay*) a lesbian; thus *lettiquette*, behaving in a boorish manner, supposedly stereotypically lesbian.

lettuce *n.*[1] [the colour green] [20C+] money in notes, sometimes ext. as *lettuce leaves*.

lettuce *n.*[2] [? play on SE *let us*] [2000s] (*US prison*) prisoners who perform gang rapes.

lettuce leaf *n.*[1] [rhy. sl.] [1980s] (*Aus.*) a thief.

lettuce leaf *n.*[2] *see* LETTIE *n.*

letty *n.*[1] (*also* **lattie, latty**) [Ital. *letto*, a bed] [mid-19C+] (*Ling. Fr./Polari*) a bed; thus *letties*, lodgings, accommodation.

letty *n.*[2] *see* LETTARY *n.*

let your father in *n.* (*also* **Tommy get out, and let your father in**) [rhy. sl.] [late 19C] (a glass of) gin.

leucoddy *n.* [Polari] [mid-19C+] the human body.

levant *n.* [*Levant*, the Middle East. The image is of running off to foreign parts; + ? f. racial stereotype of 'oily Levantine'; note the eponymous cardsharp Capt. *Levanter* in Whyte Melville *Digby Grand* (1853); ult. Sp. *levantar la casa*, to break up housekeeping, *levantar el campo*, to break up the camp] [18C–19C] a bet that is made without sufficient funds to cover one's losses; usu. as *run a levant, come the levant*.

IN PHRASES

❑ **throw a levant** *v.* [mid-19C–1900s] to leave, to run off.

levant *v.* [LEVANT *n.*] **1** [18C–19C] to bet without sufficient funds to cover one's losses. **2** [19C–1920s] (*UK Und.*) to run off, to escape trouble, esp. to avoid gambling debts.

levanter *n.* [LEVANT *n.*] [18C–19C] an absconder, esp. one who runs off after placing a losing bet.

level *adj.* [late 19C+] (*orig. US*) honest, trustworthy, true.

level *v.*[1] (*also* **level with**) (*orig. US*) **1** [1910s] to contest. **2** [1910s+] to be honest. **3** [1950s+] to admit, to confess.

level *v.*[2] [1950s] (*drugs*) to experience the ending of a drug's effects.

level (best) *n.* [note that *level best* is SE in UK but sl. in US] [mid-19C+] (*orig. US*) one's very best efforts.

leveller *n.* [19C] a knock-down blow.

level vibes *phr.* [SE *level* + VIBE *n.* (1)] [1980s+] (*W.I./UK black teen*) a satisfactory situation, peace and quiet.

level worst *n.* [reverse of LEVEL (BEST) *n.*] [19C] (*US*) one's worst attempt or effort.

leven *n.* [Hotten (1859) credits this to backsl.] [mid–late 19C] the number eleven; elevenpence.

leventy-leven *adj.* [1970s+] (*US black*) a large, unspecified number.

leven yenneps *n.* (*also* **leven, nevele yeneps**) [backsl.; LEVEN *n.*/NEVELE *n.* + YENNEP *n.*] [mid-19C] elevenpence.

levite *n.* [SE *Levite*, a member of the ancient Hebrew tribe of Levi, one of the two tribes authorized to serve as priests in the Temple] [mid-17C–mid-19C] a priest or parson.

levy *n.* [abbr. (*e*)*levencents*, which was the value of the Spanish *real*, formerly accepted as currency in US] **1** [19C] (*US*) twelve cents. **2** [mid-19C] one shilling (five pence).

levy *v.* [see LEVY (AND FRANK) *n.*] [1950s+] to masturbate.

levy (and frank) *n.* [rhy. sl. = WANK *n.* (1), ult. the name of a chain owned by London restaurateurs *Levy and Franks*] [1950s–70s] an act of masturbation.

lewdie *n.* [SE *lewd*] [1960s] a married woman who frequents singles' bars looking for brief encounters.

Lewis and Whitty *n.* [rhy. sl.; ult. *Lewis and Witty*, a well-known Melbourne department store] **1** [1920s] (*US*) a city. **2** [1940s–50s] (*Aus.*) in pl. the female breasts [TITTY *n.* (1)].

lewis cornaro *n.* [the name of a man renowned for his consumption of water] [early 19C] a drinker of water.

lewy *n. see* LOUIE *n.*[2].

Lex *n.* [abbr.] [1950s–60s] (*drugs*) the Federal drug habilitation hospital at Lexington, Kentucky.

lex *n.*[1] [late 19C] (*US gambling*) the point of nine in craps dice.

lex *n.*[2] [abbr.] [1980s+] (*US black*) a Lexus motorcar, one of the high-status cars preferred by the rap/hip-hop community.

lex *n.*[3] [abbr.] [1990s+] (*UK black*) a Rolex watch.

lex-luther *n.* [LEX *n.*[2] + pun on *Lex Luthor*, an enemy of the comic superhero Superman] [1990s+] (*US black teen*) a Lexus automobile, a coveted status symbol.

lez *see under* LES.

lezbo *n. see* LESBO *n.*

lezo *n. see* LESO *n.*

lezz *n. see* LES *n.*

lezzer *n.* (*also* **lesser, lezza**) [abbr.] [1950s+] (*Aus./Irish/US*) a lesbian.

lezzie *n.* (*also* **lessie, lezzy**) [abbr.] **1** [1930s+] a lesbian. **2** [1990s+] a term of abuse for an unpopular individual, esp. juv.; the inference is of homosexuality.

lezzie *adj.* (*also* **lesie, leso, lessie, lezzo, lezzy**) [abbr.] [1960s+] lesbian.

lezzo *n. see* LESO *n.*

lezzo *adj. see* LEZZIE *adj.*

lezzy *see under* LEZZIE.

l.f. *n. see* LONG FIRM *under* LONG *adj.*

l.g.r. *n. see* LITTLE GIRLS' ROOM *under* LITTLE *adj.*

liar *v.* [1950s] (*US*) to lie to someone.

lib *n.*[1] [LIB *v.* (1)] [17C–18C] **1** a sleep. **2** as *long lib*, death.

lib *n.*[2] [abbr.] **1** [20C+] a *lib*erty; often. in pl.; usu. as *take libs*. **2** [1960s] (*US*) a left-wing person. **3** [1970s] a supporter of women's *lib*eration. **4** [1970s+] (*orig. US*) *lib*eration, usu. in gender political contexts and thus abbr. for 'liberation movement', e.g. *Women's Lib, Gay Lib*.

lib *v.* (*also* **lip, lyp**) [ety. unknown; see LIB-BEG *n.*] (*UK Und.*) **1** [mid-16C–18C] to lie down, to sleep. **2** [late 17C–mid-19C] to sleep together, to have sexual intercourse.

lib-beg *n.* (*also* **libbedge, libbege, libbige, libedge, lyb beg, lybbeg, lyb bege**) [LIB *v.* + sfx *-age* ; Ribton-Turner, *A History of Vagrants* (1887), suggests Gaelic/Erse *leabadh*, a bed, Manx *lhiabbee*, a bed] [mid-16C–mid-19C] (*UK Und.*) a bed.

libben *n.* [LIB *v.*] [late 17C–mid-19C] (*UK Und.*) a private house.

libber *n.*[1] [Irish *leadhb*, a strip, a rag, a slovenly person] [20C+] (*Irish*) an untidy, slovenly person.

libber *n.*[2] (*also* **libbie**) [abbr.] [1970s+] (*orig. US*) **1** a feminist, a member of the Women's *Lib*eration Movement. **2** a member of any *lib*eration group.

libbige *n. see* LIB-BEG *n.*

libb-ken *n. see* LIBKEN *n.*

libbo *n.* (*also* **libo**) [abbr.] [1950s+] a *lib*erty, usu. in phr. *taking libbos*.

libe *n.* [abbr.] [1910s+] (*US campus*) a *library*.

libe *v.* [LIBE *n.*] [1910s+] (*US campus*) to study in a library, *libe out*, to go to the library.

libedge *n. see* LIB-BEG *n.*

liberate *v.* **1** [1940s+] to steal [esp. in 1960s radical use, on the Proudhon principle that 'property is theft' but likewise with a degree of irony/self-mockery given the 1960s obsession with 'freedom' and 'the revolution'. With further irony, the 'radical' use stems f. WW2 'liberating forces' who 'freed' commodities as well as people]. **2** [1990s+] to eat or drink.

liberty *n.* [the liberty that supposedly comes with wealth] **1** [1910s–60s] (*US*) money. **2** [1940s] (*US, esp. black*) a quarter, a 25-cent coin.

libken *n.* (*also* **libb-ken, libkin, lipken, lybkin**) [LIB *v.* + KEN *n.*[1] (1)] [mid-16C–1900s] (*UK Und.*) a house, a lodging.

libo *n. see* LIBBO *n.*

library *n.* **1** [mid–late 17C] a drinking club, a friendly gathering. **2** [1930s+] (*US*) (*also* **outdoor library, reading room, Sears Roebuck library**) a privy [the old catalogues, newspapers etc that were often left there as lavatory paper; the common use of old Sears catalogues as lavatory paper]. **3** [1960s+] (*US*) an 'adult', i.e. pornographic bookstore.

licence *n.*

IN PHRASES

❑ **where did you get your licence?** [1970s+] (*Aus.*) a general excl. of annoyance aimed at a poor or allegedly poor driver, often with a suggestion such as 'Woolworths?' 'Off a Weetabix packet?' etc.

license *v.* [1960s] (*UK Und./police*) for the police to to tolerate a given crime, e.g. prostitution or drug-dealing, in return for bribes.

IN COMPOUNDS

❑ **license money** *n.* [1960s] (*UK Und./police*) regular bribes given to the police by major criminals to ensure the smooth running of their operations.

-licious *sfx* [SE *delicious* + pattern of BOOTYLICIOUS *adj.* (2)] [1990s+] (*orig. US*) sfx implying excellence, appeal.

lick *n.*[1] [? East Anglian dial. *lick-up*, a miserably small pittance of any thing] **1** [mid-18C+] a slight and hasty wash, a quick tidy-up. **2** [mid-19C+] a casual amount of work. **3** [mid-19C+] (*orig. US*) a bit, a cursory amount. **4** [mid-19C+] a pace; usu. with comb. adj. **5** [late 19C+] a portion, e.g. of liquor; a drinking bout.

IN PHRASES

❑ **can't hit a lick** [sense 3 above] [1920s–30s] (*US black*) used of an inability to succeed in a given aim, esp. that of making money either legally or otherwise. ❑ **lick of the tarbrush** *n. see* TOUCH OF THE TARBRUSH *under* TOUCH *n.*[1]. ❑ **throw a lick** *v.* [1950s] (*W.I.*) to give someone a drink of liquor, esp. a 'shot' from a bottle.

lick *n.*[2] [SE *lick*, a blow] **1** [mid-18C+] an effort, an attempt at something. **2** [mid-19C+] (*Aus./N.Z./US*) a (short) sprint; intensified as *lick of one's life*. **3** [mid-19C+] (*US*) a rhythm or pace, spec. on the chain gang. **4** constr. with *the*. (**a**) [mid-19C+] (*US/US black/W.I.*) the correct thing, the proper course of action. (**b**) [1940s+] (*orig. W.I.*) the very best, the supremely fashionable. **5** [1910s+] (*later black*) a turn, a 'go', an attempt; thus *one-lick*, once only. **6** [1930s+] (*US Und.*) a theft. **7** [1930s+] (*orig. US*) a particular phrase of music, i.e. a *guitar lick*. **8** [1940s+] (*US black*) a plan, an idea, a scheme. **9** [1960s+] fig. what one does, an action, one's personal preference. **10** [1970s] (*US black*) an opportunity. **11** [1990s+] (*drugs*) a puff on a crack cocaine pipe.

IN PHRASES

❑ **go for a lick of one's quoit** *v. see* GO FOR ONE'S QUOITS *under* QUOIT *n.* ❑ **hit a lick** *v.* [2000s] (*US prison*) **1** to come into money. **2** to masturbate. **3** to commit armed robbery. ❑ **hit a lick (at a snake)** *v.* (*also* **hit a tap**) [1920s+] (*US*) to make an effort; usu. in negative combs. implying laziness on behalf of the subject of the phr. e.g. *He hasn't hit a lick all week.* ❑ **lick that killed Dick, the** *n.* [1950s–60s] (*US black*) the last straw. ❑ **what's your lick?** *see what's your tale?* under TALE *n.*[1].

lick *n.*[3] [1960s] (*N.Z.*) an ice cream.

lick *n.*[4] *see* LICK-ARSE *under* LICK *v.*[2].

lick *v.*[1] [SE *lick*, a blow; esp. in W.I. combs. e.g. *lick up*, stir up; *lick down*, knock or fling to the ground; *lick 'way*, strike or cut off (as in a tree branch)] **1** [mid-16C+] to beat, to thrash; thus *lick out of*, to change someone's character/beliefs/actions by a threat of violence, to 'knock it out of' someone. **2** [19C+] to defeat, to overcome, to be victorious. **3** [mid-19C+] (*US*) to move fast, also as *lick it*. **4** [1990s+] to shoot.

IN COMPOUNDS

❑ **lick-up** *adj.* [2000s] (*UK black*) overcome by drink or drugs.

IN PHRASES

❑ **lick about** *v.* (*also* **lick around**) [20C+] (*W.I.*) to live an unsettled life. ❑ **lick a shot** *v.* [1990s+] (*orig. W.I.*) to shoot at. ❑ **lick-a-shot** *adj.* [2000s] aggressive, menacing. ❑ **lick creation** *v.* [late 19C–1900s] (*US*) to be really amazing, to be beyond the bounds of possibility. ❑ **lick into fits** *v.* [late 19C–1910s] to beat comprehensively. ❑ **lick someone's jacket** *v. see under* JACKET *n.* ❑ **lick shot** *v.* [1980s+] (*W.I./UK black teen*) **1** to fire a shot from a real or imaginary gun to signal appreciation of music or an event. **2** to fire a gun. ❑ **sweet-lick** *v.* [1980s] (*UK black*) to apply deodorant.

IN EXCLAMATIONS

❑ **licks me!** [mid-19C+] a general excl. of incomprehension.

lick *v.*[2] [1970s+] to fellate or perform cunnilingus; usu. with DICK *n.*[1] (5) for a man or CLIT *n.* for a woman.

IN COMPOUNDS

❑ **lick and shine** *n.* [2000s] of a man, the act of smoking crack cocaine while a prostitute performs fellatio on him. ❑ **lick-box** *n.* [BOX *n.*[1] (1c); note BOX *n.*[1]] [1940s+] a male homosexual.

IN PHRASES

❑ **lick a box** *v. see under* BOX *n.*[1]. ❑ **lick the holy ground** *v.* [play on HOLE *n.*[1] (1b)] [1990s+] to perform cunnilingus.

SE in slang uses

IN COMPOUNDS

❑ **lick-arse** *n.* (*also* **lick**) [LICK SOMEONE'S ARSE below] [1970s+] (*Irish*) a toady, a sycophant. ❑ **lick-boots** *n.* [note late-18C synon. *lick the shoe*] [late 19C+] (*Aus.*) a toady. ❑ **lickdish** *n.* (*also* **lick-platter**) [mid-16C–mid-19C] a general term of abuse, the implication is of gluttony. ❑ **lick-finger** *n.* [note Ben Jonson's *Staple News* (1625): 'Lick-finger, a Master Cooke'] [late 16C–early 18C] a cook. ❑ **lickmouth** *n.* [LICK ONE'S MOUTH below] [20C+] (*W.I.*) cheap, unpleasant gossip; hence the person who gossips. ❑ **lickover** *n.* [late 19C; 1960s+] (*US*) a quick, cursory clean. ❑ **lick-spigot** *n.* [SE *spigot*/SPIGOT *n.*] **1** [late 16C–17C] a bar-man. **2** [17C–19C] a fellatrix.

IN PHRASES

❑ **lick an' pran** *v.* [colloq. *a lick and a promise*] [1950s+] (*W.I.*) to tidy up. ❑ **lick of the cat and a run around the table** *n.* [2000s] (*N.Z.*) a very frugal meal. ❑ **lick-me-lug** *n.* [LUG *n.*[1]; var. on *LICK-ARSE* above] [1990s+] (*Irish*) a toady, a sycophant. ❑ **lick on the whip** *v. see DRINK ON THE WHIP under* DRINK *v.* ❑ **lick one's mouth** *v.* [the participants lick their lips in pleasure] [20C+] (*W.I.*) to carry around or to impart negative gossip. ❑ **lick pap together** *v.* [20C+] (*W.I., UKVI*) to come from the same impoverished background. ❑ **lick someone's arse** *v.* [1940s+] to toady, to be a sycophant. ❑ **lick up (to)** *v.* [1960s+] to curry favour, to be obsequious, to grovel shamelessly in return for favours, esteem etc. ❑ **lick-your-arse** *adj.* [1940s] toadying, sycophantic.

IN EXCLAMATIONS

❑ **lick my froth!** [? inference of sexual secretion/fluids] [1980s] (*US teen*) a general term of abuse or dismissal. ❑ **lick my love-pump!** [*LOVE PUMP under* LOVE *n.*; apparently coined for the movie *This Is Spinal Tap* 1982] [1980s+] (*US campus*) a general dismissive, abusive excl., such as 'shut up! you make me sick!'.

licked *adj.* [LICK *v.*[1] (2)] **1** [19C+] utterly defeated. **2** [1970s+] exhausted.

licker *n.*[1] [LICK *v.*[1] (1)] **1** [18C–1930s] anything that is exceptional in size, power etc. **2** [late 19C+] something that proves beyond one's powers.

licker *n.*[2] **1** [1970s+] (*US black*) the tongue. **2** [1970s+] (*US gay*) one who performs oral sex, usu. a lesbian. **3** *see arse-licker under* ARSE-LICK *v.*

licker *n.*[3] *see* LIQUOR *n.*

licker-head *n. see* LIQUORHEAD *n.*

lickerish *adj.* [SE *lick*] [20C+] never satisfied and wanting everything; gluttonous and aggressively greedy, esp. for food.

lickety-split *adv.* (*also* **helitywhoop, hellity-split, lickerty-brindle, lickerty-clip, lickerty cut, licketysplickety, lickety-spit, lickity-split, lick-to-split, linkety-clink**) [most alternative forms faded by late 19C] [mid-19C+] (*orig. US*) fast, with some onomat. overtones.

IN PHRASES

❑ **go lickety-split** *v.* (*also* **come lickety-split**) [pun] [1990s+] to give oral sex to a woman.

licking *n.* [LICK *v.*[1]] **1** [mid-18C+] a beating. **2** [19C+] a defeat.

IN COMPOUNDS

❑ **licking-match** *n.* [1910s] (*W.I.*) a brawl.

lick out *v.*[1] [1960s+] to perform cunnilingus.

lick out *v.*[2] [1990s+] (*W.I.*) to speak out against.

lickpot *n.* [14C–15C SE. Other finger names are *longman* (middle finger), *ring-man* (third or ring-finger), *little man* (little finger) and *big tom* (the thumb)] [20C+] (*W.I.*) the index finger.

licks *n.* [SE *lick*, a blow] **1** [late 18C+] a thrashing [now mainly UK black]. **2** [20C+] orders [now mainly UK black]. **3** [1980s+] verbal abuse. **4** [1990s+] (*US black*) robbery.

IN PHRASES

❑ **drive licks in someone's skin/tail** *v. see under* DRIVE *v.*[1]. ❑ **get one's licks** *v.* [mid-19C+] (*US*) to get one's chance, to get one's way. ❑ **give someone the licks of Lisbon** *v.* [? ref. to Portuguese colonialism] [20C+] (*W.I., Guyn.*) to berate, to scold severely, to tell off. ❑ **licks like fire** *n.* [20C+] (*W.I.*) **1** a savage beating. **2** an overwhelming victory.

lickskillet *n.* [SE *lick* + *skillet*; cf. SE *lickspittle*] [late 19C–1950s] (*US*) a contemptible person.

lick-to-split *adv. see* LICKETY-SPLIT *adv.*

licky-licky *n.* [LICKY-LICKY *adj.*[1]] [1990s+] (*W.I.*) a parasitical toady.

licky-licky *adj.*[1] [abbr. *LICK SOMEONE'S ARSE under* LICK *v.*[2]] [1920s+] (*W.I.*) fawning, flattering, obsequious.

licky-licky *adj.*[2] (*also* **likki-likki, likky-likky**) [taking tentative licks rather than bites] **1** [1920s+] (*W.I.*) pernickety, choosy, esp. as to one's food. **2** [1920s+] (*W.I.*) never satisfied, in the sense of greedy, gluttonous [f. sense 1]. **3** [1970s–80s] (*UK black*) alcoholic; drinking to excess.

licorice *n.* [2000s] (*US*) a black woman.

licorice stick *n. see* LIQUORICE STICK *n.*

lid *n.* **1** [mid-19C+] a hat, a cap. **2** [late 19C+] (*orig. US*) the head. **3** [20C+] (*orig. US*) constr. with *the*, a restraint, protection or confidentiality, or the lack of it, usu. in the phr. *keep the lid on*, to keep it secret; *blow the lid off*, to reveal secrets. **4** [1910s+] (*US gambling*) limit. **5** [1920s–60s] (*US black*) the sky. **6** [1960s] (*US*) fellatio. **7** [1960s+] (*drugs*) a quantity of marijuana, about 22g (3/4oz) or 40 cigarettes'-worth, and often considered the equivalent of 1oz (28g) [the quantity of the drug that fills the *lid* of a tin of Prince Albert, a popular brand of tobacco].

IN PHRASES

❑ **blow one's lid** *v.* (*also* **blow the lid, fly off the lid**) [1920s+] to go mad, to lose emotional control. ❑ **blow the lid off** *v.* **1** [1920s+] (*also* **blast the lid off**) to reveal, to uncover esp. a scandal involving those 'in high places'. **2** [1960s] to unleash a great deal of trouble. ❑ **dip one's lid** *v.* (*also* **tip one's lid**) [20C+] (*orig. Aus.*) to tip one's hat, esp. in fig. use, i.e. to acknowledge, to pay respect. ❑ **flip one's lid** *v.* [1940s+] (*orig. US*) to go crazy, to lose emotional control. ❑ **fly off the lid** *v. see BLOW ONE'S LID* above. ❑ **have the lid off** *v.* [1910s] of a situation, to be out of control. ❑ **off one's lid** *adj.* [1900s] (*US*) mad. ❑ **put the lid on** *v.* (*also* **put a lid on**) **1** [late 19C+] (*orig. US*) to cover up, to hide, esp. news that is offensive or embarrassing to an establishment; thus imper. *put a lid on it!* be quiet! stop talking! **2** [20C+] to clamp down on activities such as corruption, esp. that of an urban administration. **3** [20C+] to be the ultimate, the 'last straw'. **4** [1920s+] to stop something from happening. **5** [1920s+] (*Aus.*) to shut a bar at the legal closing time. ❑ **that's put the lid on it** [1920s+] (*orig. US*) that's finished it, that's all one can do/say.

lidder *n.* [? someone who puts lids on containers in factories, i.e. one of little intelligence; or ? FLID *n.*] [1990s+] (*UK juv.*) a fool.

lido *n.* [ety. unknown; ? Sp.] [1980s+] (*US drugs*) crack cocaine.

lid-proppers *n.* (*also* **lid-poppers**) [they keep one awake, and 'prop up one's eyelids'] [1960s+] (*drugs*) amphetamines.

lie *v.*[1]

SE, meaning to lie down, in slang uses

IN COMPOUNDS

❑ **lie-down** *n.* [1980s+] a prison sentence.

IN PHRASES

❑ **lie at rack and manger** *v.* (*also* **live.., go to...**) [SE *rack and manger*, the frame that holds an animal's food and the stable in which it is kept; thus lit. to live like an animal] [mid-17C–19C] to live hard. ❑ **lie doggo** *v.* (*also* **doggo, keep doggo, lie doggoh, play doggo**) [late 19C+] to remain hidden and quiet, just like a stalking dog. ❑ **lie down (on the job)** *v. see LAY DOWN ON THE JOB under* LAY DOWN *v.* ❑ **lie in state** *v.* [ironic use of SE; the man is 'dead' after his sexual exertions] [18C–early 19C] of a man, to lie in bed with two or three women. ❑ **lie low** *v. see* LAY LOW *v.* ❑ **lie on** *v.* (*also* **lie over, lie upon**) [16C–18C] to have sexual intercourse. ❑ **lie on one's face** *v.* (*also* **lie on one's ear**) [late 19C–1920s] to drink very heavily until one collapses. ❑ **lie out** *v.* [20C+] (*Ulster*) to play truant. ❑ **lie rough** *v.* [late 17C–early 19C] to go to sleep without first removing one's clothes. ❑ **lies backwards and lets out her fore room** *see* LET OUT HER FORE ROOM AND LIE BACKWARDS *v.* (1).

lie *v.*[2]

SE, meaning to tell untruths, in slang uses

IN PHRASES

❑ **if I'm lying I'm dying** (*also* **if I'm lying I'm flying**) [1930s+] (*US black*) a phr. implying the speaker's attestation of absolute honesty and good faith. ❑ **lie-and-story** *n.* [1940s+] (*W.I.*) gossip, slander. ❑ **lie like a flatfish** *v.* [pun] [1960s+] to lie skilfully and continually. ❑ **lie like a pig** *v.* [20C+] (*Aus.*) to tell plausible lies. ❑ **lie like truth** *v.* [mid–late 19C] to lie in a plausible manner, often used of cheapjacks and other street salesmen.

lie *v.*[3] *see* LAY *v.*[2].

lieu *n. see* LOOIE *n.*[1].

lie under *v. see* LAY LOW *v.*

lieuy *n.* **1** *see* LOOEY *n.*[1]. **2** *see* LOOIE *n.*[1].

life *n.* **1** as abbr. of SE *life sentence*. (**a**) [mid-19C+] imprisonment for a life sentence; thus v. *life* (*up*) to imprison for life. (**b**) [1970s+] in fig. use, i.e. something long-term and permanent but not in prison context. **2** constr. with *the*. (**a**) [20C+] (*orig. US*) the world of prostitution. (**b**) [1910s+] (*UK Und.*) the professional criminal underworld. (**c**) [1940s+] (*US black*) the subculture of petty crime, pimping, drug dealing etc that makes up the alternative world of the streets. (**d**) [1950s+] (*US gay*) the world of homosexuality. (**e**) [1960s–70s] (*US drugs*) the world of drug addiction.

IN COMPOUNDS

❑ **lifeboat** *n.* (*also* **life liner, lifesaver**) [1910s+] (*US prison*) a pardon or the commutation of a sentence.

IN PHRASES

❑ **life off** *v.* (*also* **life up**) [2000s] (*UK Und.*) to give someone a life sentence. ❑ **life on the installment plan** *n.* [1910s+] (*US Und.*) a succession of sentences as served, with periods of freedom, by a recidivist.

SE in slang uses

IN COMPOUNDS

❑ **lifejacket** *n.* [1980s+] (*US campus*) a condom. ❑ **life preserver** *n.* **1** [mid-19C–1910s] the penis [pun on SE *life preserver*, a loaded bludgeon]. **2** [1940s] (*US*) a doughnut [resemblance to SE *life preserver*, a life-buoy]. ❑ **lifesaver** *n.* [2000s] (*Irish*) a condom.

IN PHRASES

❑ **ain't life a grin** *see under* GRIN *n.*[3]. ❑ **not on your life** (*also* **not on your life insurance, not on your sweet life**) [late 19C+] no way at all, totally impossible. ❑ **way of life** *n.* [euph.] [early 19C] the profession of prostitution.

IN EXCLAMATIONS

❑ **on my life!** [19C+] an affirmation of absolute truth in the face of an audience's scepticism.

life and death *n.* [rhy. sl.] [20C+] breath.

Lifebuoy soap *n.* [rhy. sl. = DOPE *n.*[1] (6)] [1980s] (*Aus.*) cannabis.

Life in London *adj.* [mid-19C] of a place, e.g. a lodging house, run-down, filthy.

life off *v. see* LIFE *n.*

life of Larry *n.* [? …LARRY *under* HAPPY AS… *adj.*] [1960s+] (*Irish*) the good life, a comfortable existence.

life of Riley *n.* (*also* **life of Reilly, …Riley**) [? one of a number of late 19C songs. However, the first known use is in 'My Name is Kelly' (1919), written by H. Pease. The relevant line runs 'Faith and my name is Kelly Michael Kelly,/But I'm living the life of Reilly just the same'] [1910s+] the good life, a comfortable existence.

lifer *n.* [SE *life sentence*] **1** [mid–late 19C] one who has been transported for life. **2** [mid-19C+] a life sentence. **3** [mid-19C+] a prisoner serving a life sentence. **4** [1960s+] (*US, orig. milit.*) a career soldier. **5** [1970s+] a pej. term for anyone who appears excessively keen on discipline and its administration on their peers. **6** [1970s+] a person unwilling to change their way of life, esp. a drug addict. **7** [1970s+] one who intends to stay in the same job or career until retirement. **8** [1980s+] (*US campus*) an ironic term for someone who has committed a trivial offence.

Liffey water *n.* [rhy. sl.; the orig. ref. was to Guinness, brewed near the River Liffey in Dublin] [late 19C+] porter (the drink).

lift *n.* **1** [late 16C–early 19C] (*UK Und.*) a thief of parcels or packages; 'he that stealeth or prowleth any plate, jewels, bolts of satin, velvet or such parcels from any place …' (Greene, *2nd part of Coney-Catching*, 1591); a shoplifter or pickpocket. **2** [late 16C–1910s] theft, burglary, shop lifting. **3** [late 19C–1900s] a punch. **4** [1910s] a raise in salary. **5** [1950s–60s] (*orig. US*) the effects of intoxication from alcohol or drugs.

IN COMPOUNDS

❑ **lift pill** *n.* [it gives one 'a lift'] [1960s–70s] (*US drugs*) an amphetamine pill.

SE in slang uses

IN PHRASES

❑ **give someone a lift** *v.* [the victim's body is 'lifted' through the air; note Gorse (1785): 'to give one a lift, to assist'] [late 19C–1900s] to give someone a short, swift kick.

lift *v.* [orig. SE, esp. for cattle thieving] **1** in Und. uses. (**a**) [mid-16C+] (*orig. UK Und.*) to steal. (**b**) [late 18C+] to shoplift; also as *do on the lift*. (**c**) [mid-19C+] to pick pockets. (**d**) (*UK Und.*) [late 19C] to remove or recover one's booty from the place where it has been hidden. (**e**) [1910s+] to arrest [1960s+ use of esp. army and police in Ulster]. (**f**) [1980s+] to move a prisoner from one jail to another. (**g**) to kidnap. **2** [mid–late 19C] (*US*) to raise someone's bet in a poker game. **3** [1910s+] to plagiarize. **4** [1910s+] (*US*) to drink. **5** [1930s–50s] to have an erection. **6** [1990s+] to give someone a lift (in a car).

DERIVATIVES

❑ **lifted** *adj.* [1940s+] (*US*) intoxicated by alcohol or drugs.

IN COMPOUNDS

❑ **lifting law** *n.* [LAW *n.* (1)] [16C–17C] (*UK Und.*) the stealing of parcels or packages.

SE in slang uses

IN COMPOUNDS

❑ **lift-leg** *n.* [? its amorous effects (*see* PLAY AT LIFT-LEG *under* LEG *n.*)] [late 16C–mid-19C] strong ale.

IN PHRASES

❑ **lift one's hand to one's head** *v.* (*also* **lift one's hand to one's mouth**) [late 18C–19C] to drink, esp. to excess. ❑ **lift one's heels** *v.* [18C–19C] of a woman, to lie down preparatory to sexual intercourse. ❑ **lift one's elbow** *v.* (*also* **hold up one's dagger hand, lift the hand, lift the little finger, raise one's elbow, …the elbow**) [17C–early 19C; 2000s] to drink, usu. to excess.

lifter *n.* **1** [late 16C+] one who steals packages and parcels; a shoplifter; a pickpocket [LIFT *v.*]. **2** [late 17C–early 19C] (*UK Und.*) (*also* **lift**) a crutch. **3** [early 19C] an act of swindling. **4** [late 19C] (*US*) a heavy blow [lit. *lifting* the victim off their feet].

lift-leg *n.* [? its amorous effects (*see* PLAY AT LIFT-LEG *under* LEG *n.*)] [late 16C–mid-19C] strong ale.

lig *n.*[1] [? dial. *lig*, to lie down or LIB-BEG *n.*] [early 18C–mid-19C] a bed.

IN COMPOUNDS

❑ **lig robber** *n.* [1930s–40s] a thief who hides under a bed waiting to rob or assault somebody.

lig *n.*[2] (*also* **liggety**) [Scot. *lug*, a fool] [1940s+] (*Ulster*) a fool (*lig* is male, *liggety* female).

lig *n.*[3] *see* LIGGER *n.*

lig *v.* [backform. f. LIGGER *n.*] [1990s+] to sponge, to 'freeload', to gatecrash functions or parties, esp. those connected with show business.

ligby *n.* [? LIG *n.*[1]] [17C] a mistress.

liggen *v.* [dial. *liggen*, to lie down] [17C] to sleep.

ligger *n.* (*also* **lig**) [ety. debatable: acronym of *l*east *i*mportant *g*uest or SE *linger*, to hang around, or Banffshire dial. *lig*, to gossip, to talk too much. Most likely it is dial. *lig*, to lie around. The term became widespread in the early 1970s, but dates at least to 1960 when Colin MacInnes (1914–76) used it in his essay on poncing — 'The Other Man'] [1960s+] a hanger on, esp. in show business, a 'freeloader'.

liggety *n. see* LIG *n.*[2].

light *n.* [orig. printers' use; ? to cast a *light* on one's financial 'darkness'.] **1** [early 19C–1930s] credit; thus *strike a light*, to open a line of credit; *get a light*, to obtain credit; *have one's light put out*, to have one's credit stopped. **2** [early 19C+] in pl., the eyes [20C+ usage is usu. US black]. **3** [20C+] a small amount of money. **4** [20C+] (*W.I.*) insanity, craziness; thus *have a light*, to be crazy [? SE *light-headed*]. **5** [1900s] (*US campus*) a bright, clever person.

SE in slang uses

DERIVATIVES

❑ **lightmans** *n.* (*also* **lightman**) [-MANS *sfx*] [mid-16C–mid-19C] (*UK Und.*) the day; thus *bene lightmans* 'good day'.

IN PHRASES

❑ **bring to light** *v.* [early 19C] of a thief, to produce stolen property in order to claim a reward or quash a prosecution. ❑ **lights are on but there's nobody home** [1970s+] insane, mentally deficient, vacant. ❑ **lights out** *n.* [a fig. evocation of the end of the day in a dormitory or barracks] [20C+] **1** death. **2** unconsciousness. **3** in fig. use, the end. ❑ **put someone's lights out** *v.* (*also* **beat…, blow out…, punch…, shoot…, turn out…**) [fig. use of SE *daylights*; the orig. use may have referred to one's eyes and/or one's intestines, i.e. 'liver and lights', but the 'electrical' imagery has long since superseded this] **1** [early 17C; mid-19C+] to kill, to murder; thus rarely, intransitive use, to die. **2** [late 19C+] to knock unconscious. ❑ **put the light on** *v.* [mid-19C] (*UK Und.*) to inform, to betray a comrade to the police. ❑ **strike a light** *v. see under* STRIKE *v.*

light *adj.* [fig. uses of SE *light*, as in 'light upon her heels', 'light in the head', 'light in the pocket'] **1** [mid-16C–early 19C] of women, promiscuous. **2** [mid-18C; 1930s+] (*US*) intoxicated, esp. by drugs. **3** [1930s+] (*orig. US black*) (*also* **light of, light on**) short of money. **4** [1960s+] (*US black*) stupid. **5** [1960s+] weak. **6** [1990s+] (*US*) unable to consume large quantities of drink and/or drugs.

DERIVATIVES

❑ **lightness** *n.* [late 16C–17C] of a woman, wantonness, promiscuity.

IN COMPOUNDS

❑ **light frigate** *n.* [pun on SE *light frigate*, a light, swift vessel + FRIG *v.* (1)] [late 17C–19C] a prostitute. ❑ **light head** *n.* [1950s] (*US drugs*) one who restricts their drug intake to 'light' drugs, e.g. cannabis. ❑ **light housewife** *n.* [mid-16C–18C] a prostitute. ❑ **light stuff** *n.* **1** [1960s+] (*drugs*) any non-addictive drugs, e.g. cannabis. **2** [1970s+] an unimportant person. ❑ **light upstairs** *adj.* [UPSTAIRS *n.* (5)] [1970s] (*US black*) eccentric, insane. ❑ **lightwit** *n.* [1910s] (*US*) a fool. ❑ **light woman** *n.* (*also* **light lady, light wench**) [late 16C–mid-19C] a prostitute.

IN PHRASES

❑ **light in the ass** *adj.* [1990s+] (*US black*) second-rate, insubstantial.

SE in slang uses

IN COMPOUNDS

❑ **light artillery** *n. see under* ARTILLERY *n.* ❑ **light blue** *n.* [19C] gin. ❑ **light feeder** [ety. unknown] [mid-19C–1900s] a silver spoon. ❑ **light-food** *n.* [late 19C–1900s] chewing tobacco. ❑ **lightfoot** *n.* [neither is seen as 'treading heavily' in the world] **1** [20C+] a male homosexual. **2** [1970s–80s] (*US black*) a neophyte to the raffish world of the streets, one who leads a sheltered life and does not properly participate in the tougher ghetto world. ❑ **light horseman** *n.* [mid-19C] a dockside thief. ❑ **light housekeeping** *n.* [1970s] (*US black*) co-habiting. ❑ **light infantry** *n.* [mid–late 19C] fleas. ❑ **light meat** *n. see under* MEAT *n.* ❑ **light piece** *n. see under* PIECE *n.* ❑ **light-timbered** *adj.* [late 17C–mid-19C] of a person, slender, thin; thus physically weak. ❑ **light time** *n. see under* TIME *n.* ❑ **light troops** *n.* [19C] body lice. ❑ **light wet** *n. see under* WET *n.*

IN PHRASES

❑ **light in the loafers** *adj.* (*also* **light on her feet**) [the image is of the stereotyped effeminate male, tripping along] [1950s+] (*US*) homosexual. ❑ **lightly and politely** *adv.* (*also* **lightly, slightly and politely**) [1930s–60s] (*US black*) smoothly, effortlessly.

light *v.*[1]

SE in slang uses

IN PHRASES

❑ **light a rag** *v.* (*also* **light a shuck**) [late 19C–1970s] (*US Und.*) to leave at high speed, to run off fast. ❑ **light into** *v.* (*also* **light down on**) (*Irish/US*) **1** [mid-19C+] (*also* **light on**) to attack physically. **2** [late 19C+] to attack verbally, to criticize. **3** [late 19C+] to tackle, to attack, whether food or a task. ❑ **light off** *v.* [late 19C+] to have an orgasm [SE *light off*, to ignite as an explosive]. ❑ **light out** *v.* (*also* **light for, light off**) [? naut. use *light out*, to move something along, e.g. a sail] [mid-19C+] (*US*) to leave, to escape, to hurry off.

light *v.*[2] [SE *enlighten*] [20C+] (*US black*) to enlighten someone with general or specific knowledge.

light and bitter *n.* [rhy. sl. = SHITTER *n.*[1] (1)] [2000s] the anus.

light and dark *n.* [rhy. sl.] [1930s+] a park.

lighted up *adj.* see LIT (UP) *adj.* (1).

lighten the load *v. see under* LOAD *n.*

lighten up *v.* [orig. SE 15C] **1** [1940s+] (*orig. US black*) to calm down. **2** [1960s+] to cease from an action. **3** [1960s+] to act more cheerfully, to cheer up. **4** [1960s+] to reduce verbal or psychological pressure. **5** [1990s+] to act more enthusiastically. **6** [2000s] to diminish one's input of a given substance or activity.

lighter *n.* [? LIGHT *adj.* (2)] [1950s] (*US drugs*) a narcotics addict.

lighthead *n.* [SE *light* + -HEAD *sfx* (1); the supposedly minscule weight of the fool's brain] [19C–1960s] a fool, a simpleton.

DERIVATIVES

❑ **lightheaded** *adj.* [early 18C–19C] stupid, foolish, mad.

light heels *n.* [her heels being so 'light', they fail to keep her from falling onto her back; underpinned by the 17C fashion for high cork, i.e. lightweight, heels in women's shoes; being fashionable they were seen as encouraging immorality] [17C–19C] a promiscuous woman, a prostitute; thus *light-heeled*, promiscuous.

DERIVATIVES

❑ **light-heeled** *adj.* [17C–18C] promiscuous.

lighthouse *n.* **1** [early 19C] a watch-house. **2** [early 19C] an especially prominent nose, esp. when reddened by years of drinking. **3** [late 19C–1940s] a lookout man. **4** [1900s–10s] (*N.Z.*) an illicit dealer in alcohol who carries supplies around and canvasses potential customers. **5** [1910s] (*US Und.*) those members of a safecracking team who wait outside while the 'parlor man' lights the fuse to the explosive. **6** [1910s–40s] (*US Und.*) a lookout man or a person who procures customers for a brothel.

IN PHRASES

❑ **dressed up like a lighthouse** *see under* DRESSED *adj.*

lightie *n.* (*also* **laaitie, lighty**) [SE *light-weight*] **1** [1940s+] (*S.Afr.*) a child; a young man. **2** [1970s+] (*S.Afr. Und.*) young men used for sexual purposes by older prisoners.

lightning *n.* **1** [late 18C–mid-19C] (*also* **liquid lightning**) gin. **2** [mid-19C+] (*Aus./US*) (*also* **lightning juice, liquid lightning**) whisky or any form of cheap spirits or strong liquor. **3** [late 19C] (*US*) electricity. **4** [late 19C] (*US*) a telegraph. **5** [1970s+] (*US drugs*) amphetamine or crack cocaine.

IN COMPOUNDS

❑ **lightning jerker** *n.* (*also* **...shover, ...slinger, ...squirter, ... wrestler**) [the use of electricity in the telegraph system; JERKER *n.*[1]/ SLINGER *n.*] [late 19C–1940s] (*US*) a telegraph operator. ❑ **lightning water** *n.* [mid-19C+] (*US*) strong whisky.

IN PHRASES

❑ **chain lightning** *n.* (*also* **chained lightning**) [SE *chain lightning*, lightning that moves rapidly in a forked or zigzag course] **1** [mid-19C] (*US*) misery, punishment, hell. **2** [mid-19C–1900s] potato spirit [the image is of immediacy and strength of the spirit's effect]. **3** [mid-19C–1930s] (*orig. US*) strong, if cheap, whisky [the image is of immediacy and strength of the spirit's effect]. **4** [late 19C–1920s] an exceptionally able person. ❑ **flash of lightning** *n.* [SE *flash* + play on SE] [late 18C–mid-19C] a glass of gin. ❑ **streak of lightning** *n.* [mid-19C] gin.

SE in slang uses

IN COMPOUNDS

❑ **lightning rod** *n.* [ROD *n.* (1)] [1970s] (*Irish*) a penis.

IN PHRASES

❑ **blue lightning** *n.* [the flash when a bullet is fired] [mid-19C] (*US West*) a revolver, a six-gun.

lightning *adj.* [mid-19C+] (*US*) extraordinary, formidable.

light of love *n.* [rhy. sl. *light of love* = abbr. *gov*] [1940s+] (*UK prison*) a prison governor.

light o' love *n.* [euph.; note Nares (1822): 'LIGHT O'LOVE. An old tune of a dance, the name of which made it a proverbial expression of levity, especially in love matters'] **1** [late 16C–1930s] a prostitute. **2** [1900s] a female partner.

lights *n.* [SE *lights*, offal, often considered an inedible piece of the animal] [19C] a fool.

light skirts *n.* [LIGHT *adj.* (1)] [late 16C–17C; mid-19C] a prostitute.

DERIVATIVES

❑ **light skirtedness** *n.* [early 17C] sexual licence.

light-up *n.* [LIGHT UP *v.*[1] (1)] [1990s+] a marijuana cigarette.

light up *v.*[1] **1** to take drink or drugs. (**a**) [mid-19C+] to light a pipe, cigar or cigarette. (**b**) [1900s] (*US*) to have a drink; to become drunk. (**c**) [1920s+] (*US drugs*) to take cocaine. (**d**) [1930s+] (*US drugs*) to smoke marijuana. (**e**) [1940s+] (*drugs*) *vtr.* to supply someone with drugs, usu. marijuana. (**f**) [1980s+] to smoke a crack pipe. **2** in fig. uses. (**a**) [1940s–60s] to reach orgasm. (**b**) [1960s] (*US*) to arouse someone sexually. (**c**) [1960s+] (*US*) to shoot, destroy with gunfire. **3** [1970s+] (*US black*) to hit or attack someone. **4** [1980s+] (*US black*) to dominate, esp. in sports.

light up *v.*[2] [1900s] (*US Und.*) to board a train illegally.

lightweight *n.* [LIGHTWEIGHT *adj.*] **1** [late 19C+] (*orig. US*) (*also* **featherweight**) an insignificant person, a weakling. **2** [1910s–60s] an intellectual mediocrity. **3** [1970s–80s] (*US black*) one who leads a sheltered life and does not properly participate in the tougher ghetto world. **4** [1980s+] one who cannot equal their peers in the sphere of drinking or taking drugs.

lightweight *adj.* (*also* **featherweight**) [now SE] [19C+] (*US*) insignificant, unimpressive.

IN PHRASES

❑ **light weight and way late** *adj.* [1930s] (*US black*) fashionable, sophisticated.

lightweight *adv.* [2000s] (*US black*) to a certain extent, as opposed to very.

lighty *n. see* LIGHTIE *n.*

lig-robber *n. see* LIG *n.*[1].

like *v.*

SE in slang uses

IN PHRASES

❑ **I like it, but it doesn't like me** [late 19C+] a phr. that refers to food and/or drink that, while delicious, has a deleterious effect on the consumer. ❑ **like it or lump it** *v. see under* LUMP *v.*[1].

like *adv.* **1** [19C+] used to express 'kind of', 'in a way' or 'so to speak' when used postpositively, as in *he ran down the road like, and …* **2** [1940s+] (*orig. US black/beatnik*) to express 'approximately', 'just about' or poss. to draw attention to the subject matter when used prenominally, as in *it takes like ten minutes; I feel, like, sick.* **3** [1950s+] (*orig. US jazz/beatnik/hippie/teen*) usu. used as an interjection or excl. to introduce or draw attention to what follows, or to indicate uncertainty, or simply as a meaningless filler as in *Like man, it's out of sight; Like he drove so fast…* **4** [1960s+] as if…; the SE used in a derisive sense, denying the validity of the speaker's last statement. **5** [1980s+] referring to one's feelings/speech as recalled when telling an anecdote.

IN PHRASES

❑ **like, hi** [1990s+] (*US campus*) hello. ❑ **like, wow** [1950s+] a phr. of affirmation, delight.

SE in slang uses

IN PHRASES

❑ **like…** *see also under* relevant n. ❑ **like bringer** *adv.* [mid-19C] (*US*) energetically. ❑ **like di-wa-didy** *adv.* [1920s–60s] uncompromisingly, perfectly, completely. ❑ **like Edgware Road** *adj.* [because 'that's got no ballroom either'; pun on SE *ballroom* + BALLS *n.* (1)] [1940s+] a phr. describing tight trousers. ❑ **like Hunt's dog will neither go to church nor stay at home** [a Shropshire labourer by the name of Hunt whose mastiff was neither happy at home – where he howled whenever his master left for church – or at the church – where he refused to enter] [late 18C–19C] a description of 'discontented and whimsical persons' (Grose 1785). ❑ **like sin** *adv.* **1** [late 19C] speedily. **2** *see* LIKE HELL *under* HELL *n.* ❑ **like stupidness** *adv.* [1950s] (*W.I./UK black*) abundantly, in great supply. ❑ **like two cents** *adj.* [1920s–50s] (*US*) worthless. ❑ **like winkey** *adv.* (*also* **like winkey, like winkie**) [abbr. SE *like winking*] [early 19C–1930s] very quickly.

like a… *phr.* [mid-17C+] a variety of similes, all of which are fig./joc. uses of SE or sl.

IN PHRASES

❑ **like a…** *see also under* relevant n. ❑ **like a beer bottle on the Coliseum** [1940s+] (*Aus.*) conspicuous. ❑ **like a cock-maggot in a sinkhole** [late 19C–1920s] very angry, infuriated. ❑ **like a gravedigger** [phr. 'up to the a-se in business, and don't know which way to turn' (Grose, 1796)] [late 18C–early 19C] extremely busy. ❑ **like a hen on a hot griddle** *see under* HOT *adj.* ❑ **like a lily on a dustbin** (*also* **like a lily on a dirt tin**) [1930s+] (*Aus.*) utterly incongruous or inappropriate. ❑ **like a lord's bastard** [1940s] in great luxury, usu. fig. ❑ **like a nigger girl's left tit** [alt. versions, varying as to chronology, substitute the name of a contemporaneously celebrated black woman] [20C+] (*orig. US*) used of something that, punningly, is 'neither right nor fair'. ❑ **like a pakapoo ticket** (*also* **like a pakapu ticket**) [Chinese pidgin *pak-ah-pu ticket*, a form of betting slip used by Chinese gamblers; properly known as *pai-ke-p'iao*, it was a small square of paper marked with 80 Chinese characters; the gambler chose some of these, usu. ten, and, depending on how many matched that day's winning combination, would make a small profit for their sixpenny stake] [1940s+] (*Aus.*) said of anything untidy, complex, incomprehensible. ❑ **like a rope-dancer's pole with lead at both ends** [late 18C–early 19C] a phr. used of a person considered very stupid and slow. ❑ **like a shag on a rock** [SE *shag*, a cormorant] [1930s+] (*Aus.*) conspicuous; also various phr. denoting solitariness, e.g. *lonely/miserable as a shag on a rock.* ❑ **like a wet week** [20C+] (*Aus.*) to look depressed; usu. as *have a face like a wet week, look like a wet week.* ❑ **like a winter's day – short and dirty** [late 18C–early 19C] a pej. description for an unpopular person.

like arse! *excl. see* LIKE FUCK! *excl.*

like crazy *adv.* [1920s+] **1** intensely, excessively, obsessively, esp. as an answer to 'Do you like … ?' '*Sure, like crazy.*'. **2** as fast as possible.

like five hundred *adv.* [on model of LIKE SIXTY *adv.*] [mid-19C–1900s] (*US*) to excess, very much so, intensely.

like forty *adv.* [on model of LIKE SIXTY *adv.* and LIKE TWENTY *adv.*] [mid-19C+] (*US*) with great force, with absolute commitment.

like fuck *adv.* (*also* **like a fuck**) [LIKE FUCK! *excl.*] [1960s+] intensely, very much.

like fuck! *excl.* (*also* **like arse!**) [1960s+] an excl. of denial or negation, usu. as *like fuck I will!*

like fuckery *adv.* [LIKE FUCK *adv.*] [2000s] to a very great extent.

like fun *adv.* [early 19C+] vigorously, energetically, quickly.

like fun! *excl.* [euph. LIKE FUCK! *excl.*] [1910s+] a dismissive excl., implying the absolute unlikeliness of a given event, opinion, etc.

like hang *adv.* [LIKE HANG! *excl.*] [1960s+] (*Aus./N.Z.*) a general intensive, very much.

like hang! *excl.* [1960s+] (*Aus./N.Z.*) a general intensive excl.

like peas *adj.* [20C+] (*W.I.*) plentiful, abundant.

like peas *adv.* [20C+] (*W.I.*) plentifully, abundantly.

liker *n.* [? Sfk dial. *liker*, a try, an attempt] [late 19C–1910s] a glance, a look.

like sixty *adv.* (*also* **sixty**) [? SE *like sixty men*; on model of LIKE TWENTY *adv.* and LIKE FORTY *adv.*] [mid-19C+] (*orig. US*) with great force or vigour, at a great speed.

IN PHRASES

❑ **swing like sixty** *v.* [SWING *v.* (9a)] [1960s+] (*US teen*) to perform at one's peak, to achieve ultimate success or pleasure.

like that *adj.* **1** [1910s+] extremely intimate. **2** [1970s+] (*US, mainly Southern*) a euph. for pregnant. **3** [1970s+] homosexual.

like the bear – nowhere *phr. see* JACK THE BEAR *n.*

like twenty *adv.* [on the model of LIKE FORTY *adv.* and LIKE SIXTY *adv.*] [mid-19C] (*US*) with great force, with absolute commitment.

likker *see* LIQUOR *n.*

likkered *adj. see* LIQUORED (UP) *adj.*

likki-likki/likky-likky *adj. see* LICKY-LICKY *adj.*[2].

lil *n.* (*also* **lill**) [Rom. *lil*, a book, a paper] **1** [early–mid-19C] a book; a pocket-book or wallet. **2** [mid–late 19C] a £5 note. **3** [mid-19C–1920s] (*UK und.*) a forged bank note; thus *lil-faker*, a counterfeiter. **4** [1900s] any banknote. **5** *see* LILY *n.*

l'il abners *n.* [i.e. the shoes worn by the hero of the cartoon strip *L'il Abner* (1934–79), created by Al Capp] [1940s+] (*US*) square-toed shoes, usu. work shoes.

lilac *n.* [the supposed similarity of a bushy sideburn to a lilac flower] [late 19C–1920s] (*US*) in pl., sideburns or sideboards.

lilac *adj.* [SE *lilac*, a colour seen as stereotypically homosexual] [20C+] effeminately homosexual.

lilies-of-the-valley *n.* [supposed resemblance] [1990s+] (*gay*) haemorrhoids.

lill *n. see* LIL *n.*

Lilley and Skinner *n.* [rhy. sl.; ult. *Lilley and Skinner*, a London shoe shop (est. 1835)] [1920s+] **1** dinner. **2** a beginner.

lillian *n.* [camp feminization, i.e. *Lillian Law*] [1970s+] (*gay*) the police.

Lillian Gish *n.* [rhy. sl.; ult. US film star *Lilian Gish* (1899–1993)] [1920s+] **1** (*Aus.*) a dish. **2** a fish.

Lillian Gished *adj.* [rhy. sl. = PISSED *adj.*[1]; for ety. see LILLIAN GISH *n.*] [1950s–60s] drunk.

Lilly *n.* [the manufacturer's name on the pill, branded as *Lilly F-40*] [1970s+] (*drugs*) Seconal.

lilly *n. see* LILY *n.* (4a).

lilly/lilly law *n. see* LILY LAW *n.*

lilt *v.* [Scot. *lilt*, to dance] [20C+] (*Ulster*) to act foolishly or carelessly.

lily *n.* (*also* **lil**) **1** the symbolic purity or innocence of the flower. (**a**) [late 19C–1950s] (*US*) anything or anyone remarkable or particularly outstanding. (**b**) [1900s–60s] (*US Und.*) a gullible person. (**c**) [1920s–30s] (*US*) a virgin. **2** [1910s–20s] a livid bruise. **3** the whiteness of some varieties of the flower. (**a**) [1910s–60s] (*US*) usu. in pl., a white person's hands; thus *lily-presser*, a handshaker. (**b**) [1960s+] (*US black*) a white person [SE *lilywhite*. Note 14C SE *lily*, a person or thing of exceptional whiteness, fairness or purity]. **4** the implicit 'femininity' of flowers. (**a**) [1920s+] (*also* **lilly**) a derog. term for an effeminate man or a homosexual, esp. one who fears to reveal his sex life. (**b**) [1930s] the queen in cards. (**c**) [1950s–80s] (*camp gay*) a proper name used for a variety of camp nicknames. **5** [1940s+] (*US*) a penis, usu. with ref. to urination or masturbation. **6** [1990s+] (*US black*) the vagina, esp. when loose. **7** *see under* LILYWHITE *n.*

(IN COMPOUNDS)

❑ **lily's whiskers** *n. see* CAT'S WHISKERS *n.*

(IN PHRASES)

❑ **drain the lily** *v.* [1940s] to urinate. ❑ **shake the dew off the lily** *v.* (*also* **knock the dew off the lily, shake the dew off one's wienie**) [1940s+] to urinate. ❑ **wave the lily** *v.* [1970s+] (*US*) of an exhibitionist, to expose and wave one's penis.

lily *adj.*

SE in slang uses, pertaining to white or silver colour

(IN COMPOUNDS)

❑ **lily benjamin** *n.* [BENJAMIN *n.*[1]] [mid-19C] a white greatcoat or overcoat. ❑ **lily shallow** *n.* [19C] a low-crowned white hat, esp. as worn by a coachman. ❑ **lily-tick** *n.* [mid-19C] (*UK Und.*) a silver watch.

lily law *n.* (*also* **lilly, lilly law, Miss Lily**) [female proper name *Lily* + LILY *n.*] [1940s+] (*orig. US gay*) the police.

lily of lagoona *n.* (*also* **Lily of Laguna**) [rhy. sl.; ult. 1898 song title 'Lily of Laguna' by Leslie Stuart] [20C+] (*Aus.*) a schooner, which in Aus. is a tall beer glass; thus beer or a glass of beer.

lily the pink *n.* [rhy. sl.] [2000s] a drink.

lilywhite *n.* **1** [late 17C–early 19C] (*also* **lilly white**) a chimney-sweep [a heavy joke at the expense of the soot-blackened sweep]. **2** [early 19C] (*also* **lily**) a black person [a heavy joke at the expense of the black-skinned individual]. **3** [late 19C–1970s] a young male homosexual. **4** [1900s–40s] (*US black*) (*also* **lilywhiter**) a white person who claims superiority on the grounds of their colour. **5** [1930s] (*orig. US*) in pl., a white person's hands. **6** [1930s–70s] (*US black*) (*also* **lily**) usu. in pl., bedsheets. **7** [1950s] (*US*) one who has no connections with any form of crime or corruption. **8** [2000s] (*also* **clean skin**) a drug trafficker who deliberately eschews ostentation to maximize their chances of avoiding arrest.

lilywhite *adj.* [LILYWHITE *n.* (4)] [20C+] (*US*) bigoted against or segregated from black people.

lilywhite groat *n.* [the coin was silver] [mid-19C–1910s] a shilling (five pence).

limb *n.* **1** as euph. (**a**) [17C–19C] the penis. (**b**) [1990s+] an erection. **2** [early 17C–1920s] a mischievous boy, a 'young rascal' [abbr. SE *limb of Satan*].

(IN PHRASES)

❑ **limb of the bar** *n.* [early–mid-19C] a barrister. ❑ **limb of the law** *n.* [SE *limb*, an extension, a branch] **1** [mid-18C–1920s] a lawyer, spec. a second-rate attorney or any legal functionary, incl. the police. **2** [1930s+] (*Aus.*) a police officer.

limb *v.* [late 19C] to fight.

limber dick *n.* [SE *limber* + DICK *n.*[1] (5); his penis is presumed no longer capable of erection] [1980s+] (*Aus. prison*) an old prisoner.

limbie *n.* (*also* **limby**) [SE *limb*] [1910s+] (*N.Z.*) one who has lost a leg, usu. in battle.

limbo *n.* [SE *limbo*, 'a region supposed to exist on the border of Hell as the abode of the just who died before Christ's coming, and of unbaptized infants' (*OED*)] **1** [late 16C–1920s] prison. **2** [late 17C–mid-18C] pawn. **3** [1970s+] (*drugs*) marijuana from Colombia. **4** [2000s] (*US prison*) time in jail before trial.

limbo room *n.* [SE *limbo*] [1960s+] (*Can. prison*) a place where corporal punishment is administered to prisoners.

Limburger *n.* [ult. *Limburger*, actually a Dutch/Belgian cheese, not a German one] **1** [late 19C–1950s] (*US*) a derog. name for a German. **2** [1980s+] (*US campus*) an unpopular or unattractive young woman.

limby *n. see* LIMBIE *n.*

lime *n.*[1]

(IN PHRASES)

❑ **in the lime** *adj.* [SE *limelight*] [1940s] (*Aus.*) conspicuous, popular, heavily advertised.

lime *n.*[2] [LIME *v.*] [1950s+] (*orig. W.I.*) a spontaneous, unorganized social gathering, usu. of young people. Often qualified by its focus, e.g. *beach lime*, a beach get-together; a *roti lime*, a gathering to eat roti; thus punning phr. *this lime has no juice*, this get-together is boring.

(IN PHRASES)

❑ **coast a lime** *v.* [1950s] (*W.I./UK black*) to hang around chatting and socializing. ❑ **pick a lime** *v.* [? LIMEY *n.* (1), i.e. the groups of US sailors who frequented the Trinidad red-light areas during WW2] [1970s+] (*orig. W.I.*) to sit around and relax with friends or family.

lime *n.*[3] *see* LEMON *n.* (1b).

lime *adj. see* LIMEY *adj.*

lime *v.* [? LIMEY *n.* (1), i.e. the groups of US sailors who frequented the Trinidad red-light areas during WW2. Also US teen use in the 1990s; note late 19C Fr. sl. *limer*, 'To take time in the act of kind'] [1950s+] (*orig. W.I.*) to sit around and relax with friends or family; thus *liming*, hanging around, chatting.

limehouse cut *n.* [rhy. sl. = SE *gut*] [20C+] a paunch.

lime juice *n.* [LIME-JUICER *n.*] **1** [mid-19C–1900s] (*Aus.*) an immigrant from England; thus *hasn't got the lime-juice off*, *smelling of lime-juice* etc, used of newly arrived immigrants. **2** [mid-19C–1900s] (*US*) as *Lime juice country*, England. **3** [1950s] (*US*) English, English idiom.

lime-juicer *n.* [the former habit of serving sailors lime juice as a preventative against scurvy on long voyages] **1** [mid–late 19C] (*Aus.*) an immigrant from England. **2** [mid-19C–1950s] (*US*) an English or British person or sailing ship.

lime-juicer *adj.* (*also* **lime-juice**) [LIME-JUICER *n.*] [mid-19C–1950s] (*US*) English, British.

limer *n.* [LIMEY *n.* (2)] [1970s+] (*W.I.*) a layabout, an idler.

lime-skin *n.* [1970s] (*W.I.*) an old felt hat.

lime-twig *n.* [SE *lime-twig*, a twig smeared with birdlime for catching birds; thus a snare] [late 16C–17C] a thief; thus adj., *lime-fingered*.

lime-twigs *n.* [SE *lime-twig*, a twig smeared with birdlime for catching birds; thus a snare] [16C–17C] (*UK Und.*) playing cards, as used by a confidence trickster or card-cheat; thus fig., any snare.

limey *n.* [LIME-JUICER *n.*] **1** [1910s+] (*orig. Aus.*) an English person or sailing ship. **2** [1940s+] (*W.I.*) a derog. term for a disreputable white person of lower class. **3** [1950s] the English language. **4** [1960s+] (*US short order*) an English muffin.

limey *adj.* (*also* **lime**) [LIMEY *n.* (1)] [1910s+] (*orig. Aus.*) English, British.

limey land *n.* [LIMEY *n.* (1) + SE *land*] [1910s–70s] (*US*) England.

limit *n.* [1920s] (*US Und.*) constr. with *the*, the maximum sentence; the death sentence.

(IN PHRASES)

❑ **lurid limit** *n. see* DIZZY LIMIT *under* DIZZY *adj.*

limo *n.* (*also* **limmie, limmo, limou**) [abbr.] [1920s+] (*orig. US*) a *limo*usine.

limo *v.* [LIMO *n.*] [1960s] (*US*) to travel in a limousine.

limp-dick *n.* (*also* **limp-prick**) [SE *limp* + DICK *n.*[1] (5)/PRICK *n.* (1)] [20C+] an inadequate person, a weakling.

limp-dick *adj.* (*also* **limp-prick**) [LIMP-DICK *n.*] [20C+] inadequate, weak.

limpty *n. see* LIMPY *n.*

limp wrist *n.* [his allegedly extravagantly effeminate gestures] (*orig. US*) **1** [1950s+] (*also* **bent wrist, broken wrist, limp wrister**) a male homosexual. **2** [1990s+] a weakling, a social 'liberal'.

limp-wristed *adj.* (*also* **limp-wrist, weak-wristed, wristy**) [LIMP WRIST *n.*] [1950s+] (*orig. US*) weak, effeminate, homosexual.

limpy *n.* (*also* **limpty**) [1930s–60s] (*US tramp*) a crippled beggar; any person.

lina *n.* [Sp. *lina*, a line] [1990s+] (*drugs*) cocaine.

Linc *n.* [abbr.] [1970s] (*US*) a *Linc*oln automobile.

lincoln *n.* [the face of *Abraham Lincoln* (1809–65), 16th president of the US, is printed on $5 bills] **1** [1930s–70s] (*US*) a $5 note. **2** [2000s] (*US black*) a bag of drugs that has a penny in the middle so that it weighs more.

Lincoln's Inn *n.* [rhy. sl.] **1** [mid-19C+] a hand [FIN *n.*[1] (1)]. **2** [late 19C+] a £5 note [FIN *n.*[2] (1)]. **3** [late 19C+] gin.

Lincoln Tunnel *n. see* GRAND CANYON *n.*

line *n.*[1] [fig. use of SE *line* + abbr. *a line of talk*] **1** [mid-17C+] an area of criminal or dubious activity [SE *line*, an occupation]. **2** as a form of communication [underpinned by racing jargon *the line*, the daily details of the horses running and the odds on them]. (**a**) [mid-19C–1930s] a hoax, a trick; thus *get someone in a line*, to mock, to tease. (**b**) [mid-19C+] (*orig. US*) a smooth verbal style aimed at seduction or at persuading someone else to accept an idea or plan, esp. in sexual or business contexts; hence *FEED A LINE* below and *DO A LINE (WITH)* below. (**c**) [late 19C+] (*orig. US*) a useful tip, a piece of information, usu. acquired confidentially. **3** as a geographical/topographical entity [orig. police jargon; lit. a *line* of buildings]. (**a**) [late 19C+] (*US*) a red-light district; thus *lady of the line*, a prostitute. (**b**) [late 19C+] the area of social life, entertainments etc. (**c**) [2000s] (*US Und.*) a street or block used for drug-dealing. **4** [1930s+] in a brothel, the parade of available prostitutes; thus the women employed by a single pimp. **5** in (*drugs*) use. (**a**) [1930s+] the main vein in the arm used to inject heroin. (**b**) [1950s] injected heroin. (**c**) [1950s+] a small marijuana cigarette. (**d**) [1960s+] a portion of heroin or cocaine scraped into a line across a mirror in order for it to be sniffed into the nostril. (**e**) [1970s+] (*US*) a rough unit of measure used by cocaine dealers. (**f**) [1970s+] a portion of any drug which is inhaled. **6** see FRONT LINE *n.* **7** *see* LINE-UP *n.* (1). **8** *see* MAINLINE *n.* (1).

(IN COMPOUNDS)

❑ **line-shooter** *n.* [*SHOOT A LINE* below] [1940s+] one who talks pretentiously or boasts.

(IN PHRASES)

❑ **dead line** *n.* [fig. use of US milit. jargon *dead line*, a line drawn around a military prison, beyond which a prisoner is liable to be shot down] [late 19C–1920s] (*US*) the red light area of a town or city. ❑ **do a line** *v.* (*also* **do lines**) [1970s+] (*drugs*) to inhale cocaine. ❑ **do a line (with)** *v.* (*also* **knock a line (with)**) [1930s+] **1** (*Aus.*) of a man, to talk amorously and seductively; of either sex, to talk persuasively. **2** [1930s+] (*Irish*) to have a sexual relationship, a courtship. ❑ **down the line** *n.* [1930s] visting a red-light district in search of sexual intercourse. ❑ **dusty line** *n.* [SE *dusty* + sense 2b above] [1980s+] (*US black*) a piece of outmoded slang. ❑ **feed a line** *v.* (*also* **feed**) [1950s+] to deceive through a cunning story or excessive charm, to persuade, to talk smoothly. ❑ **get a line on** *v.* [late 19C+] (*orig. US*) to understand, to acquire information about; thus *give a line on*, to impart information or knowledge. ❑ **get someone in a line** *v.* [early–mid-19C] (*UK Und.*) to engage a victim in conversation while an accomplice is robbing them. ❑ **hand (out) a line** *v.* [20C+] to deceive through a cunning story or excessive charm. ❑ **line of shit** *n.* (*also* **line of bull, ...crap**) [SHIT *n.* (4a) / BULL *n.*[6] (1) / CRAP *n.*[1] (4)] [1920s+] purportedly persuasive nonsense. ❑ **on the line** [1930s] (*US Und.*) working as a street prostitute or in a brothel. ❑ **pull a line (on)** *v.* [1920s–60s] to deceive, to get away with a dubious scheme. ❑ **run a line** *v.* [2000s] (*UK drugs*) to smoke heroin from a sheet of tinfoil, the heated heroin liquefies and runs down the foil, leaving a brown line. ❑ **run down some lines** *v.* [RUN DOWN *v.* (3)] [1980s+] (*US black*) **1** to make conversation. **2** to attempt seduction by smooth talking. ❑ **sell a line** *v.* [1900s–30s] to promote a persuasive patter. ❑ **shoot a line** *v.* (*also* **run a line**) [SHOOT *v.* (5)] **1** [late 19C+] to concoct a smooth patter, esp. with the specific aim of seduction. **2** to send a letter. ❑ **sling a line** *v.* [SLING *v.* (2a)] [1900s] to tell a lie, to deceive. ❑ **stretch a line** *v. see* *STRETCH (THE) HEMP under* STRETCH *v.* ❑ **string (out) a line** *v.* [STRING (ALONG) *v.* (1a)] [1950s] (*Aus.*) to deceive, to tell a 'tall story'. ❑ **take it in the line** *v.* [1930s] to inject into a vein.

SE in slang uses

(IN PHRASES)

❑ **first line** *n.* [SE *first*, best + *line* (of merchandise] [1970s] (*drugs*) morphine. ❑ **go down the line** *v.* [1950s] to make an effort, to commit onself. ❑ **have a line on** *v.* [racing jargon *the line*, the daily details of the horses running and the odds on them] [20C+] to understand, to know what is happening; to know about. ❑ **in line** *adj.* [1940s+] not breaking any rules, law-abiding. ❑ **keep the line** *v.* [hunting jargon *keep one's own line*, to ride straight] [early–mid-19C] to behave properly. ❑ **line of the old author** *n.* [late 17C–early 19C] a drink, esp. of brandy. ❑ **on the line** *see* separate entry. ❑ **out of line** *adj.* [SE *line*, a style of activity, a discipline] [1920s+] (*orig. US*) breaking rules, unacceptable, out of the ordinary. ❑ **over the line** *adj.* [1920s] drunk. ❑ **over the line** *adv.* [1910s] to excess. ❑ **sweat on the top line** *v. see under* SWEAT *v.*[2]. ❑ **under the line** [mid-19C] (*UK Und.*) awaiting execution by hanging.

(IN EXCLAMATIONS)

❑ **hold the line!** [telephone imagery] [1920s–30s] wait a minute!

line *n.*[2] [? BOTTOM LINE *n.*; Mezzrow & Wolfe *Really the Blues* (1946) '*Line two* means the price is a dollar; prices, like times of the day, are often doubled so that outsiders won't understand the details'] [1930s+] (*US black*) **1** money. **2** the cost or price of an item.

line *n.*[3] [1930s+] (*Aus.*) a woman; usu. with a defining adj., e.g. *good line, nice line, slashing line*.

line *n.*[4] *see* FRONT LINE *n.*

line *n.*[5] *see* LINE-UP *n.* (1).

line *v.*[1] [14C SE *line*, to copulate] **1** [16C] to seduce. **2** [1900s] (*Aus.*) to hit. **3** [1940s] (*US*) to copulate, used of both humans and animals.

line *v.*[2]
SE, meaning to cover, in slang uses

IN PHRASES

❑ **line one's flue** *v. see under* FLUE *n.*[1]. ❑ **line one's jacket** *v. see under* JACKET *n.* ❑ **line one's kidneys** *v. see under* KIDNEY *n.* ❑ **line one's tubes** *v. see under* TUBE *n.*[1]. ❑ **line someone with licks** *v.* [SE *lick*, a blow] [20C+] (*W.I.*) to administer corporal punishment.

line *v.*[3] *see* LINE UP *v.* (1c).

linebacker *n.* [1970s] (*US campus*) an outsider, one who is unsociable and unpopular.

lined *adj.*[1] [the couple have signed on the dotted *line*] [late 19C–1920s] married.

lined *adj.*[2] [1930s+] rich, having money.

linen *n.* [1900s] a shirt.

IN PHRASES

❑ **dust someone's linen** *v. see* DUST SOMEONE'S JACKET *under* DUST *v.*[1].

linen armourer *n.* [late 18C–early 19C] a tailor.

linen(-draper) *n.* [rhy. sl.] [mid-19C+] a newspaper.

linen-lifter *n.* [1980s] (*Aus.*) a womanizer.

line out *v.* [late 19C–1900s] (*US*) to head for.

liner *n.*[1] [it *lines* one's stomach or pockets] **1** [20C+] (*Irish*) a substantial meal. **2** [2000s] (*US Und.*) money.

liner *n.*[2] [? he lines up criminals] [1980s+] (*UK black*) a police officer.

line-up *n.* **1** [20C+] (*also* **line**) a police identification parade. **2** [1910s+] gang-rape or group sex. **3** [1930s] (*US Und.*) the personnel of a group, e.g. a criminal hierarchy. **4** [2000s] (*US drugs*) the consumption in quick sucession of a glass of beer, a puff on a marijuana cigarette, a line of cocaine, a shot of whisky and a puff on a cigarette.

IN COMPOUNDS

❑ **line-up girl** *n.* [1950s] a young woman who volunteers herself for multiple sex. ❑ **line-up room** *n.* [1930s] (*US*) the room in which identification parades are held.

IN PHRASES

❑ **run a line** *v.* [1970s+] (*US gay*) to service a queue of men wishing to have anal intercourse with one; or wishing to be given oral sex.

line up *v.* **1** lit. or fig., to stand or place oneself in a line. (**a**) [1900s–70s] (*US*) to associate, to join up with. (**b**) [1910s–50s] (*Aus.*) (*also* **line up to**) to accost, to approach. (**c**) [1920s+] (*orig. US*) (*also* **line**) to arrange, to organize, to plan in advance. (**d**) [1920s+] (*US Und.*) to be subjected to a police identification parade [LINE-UP *n.* (1)]. **2** in senses of assault. [1910s+] (*US*) to subject to or (rare) to be subjected to a gang rape [LINE-UP *n.* (2)]. **3** in vtr. senses. (**a**) [1920s–30s] (*US*) to rob. (**b**) [1930s–70s] (*US*) to arrange an illicit and profitable deal. (**c**) [1950s] (*orig. US*) to put someone in a given position or situation. **4** [1940s+] (*gay*) to gang fellate or sodomize.

IN PHRASES

❑ **line up one's ducks** *v.* [1960s+] (*US*) to set one's affairs in order.

ling *n.* [SE *ling*, a type of fish] **1** [17C] a woman, considered as a sexual object. **2** [mid-17C–19C] (*also* **old ling**) the vagina or the female sexual odour. **3** [1920s+] (*Aus.*) a stench.

IN COMPOUNDS

❑ **ling-grappling** *n.* [19C] womanizing.

ling *v.* [? SE *line*] [1990s+] (*UK juv.*) to throw very hard.

linguist *n.* [abbr.] [1950s+] (*Aus.*) a cunni*linguist*.

link *n.*

IN PHRASES

❑ **on the link** [2000s] (*UK black*) having sexual intercourse.

link *v.* [2000s] (*UK black*) to form a relationship with.

linkety-clink *adv. see* LICKETY-SPLIT *adv.*

link (it) *v.* [early–mid-19C] (*UK Und.*) to pick a pocket by turning it inside out.

link it *v.* [1900s–40s] to walk arm-in-arm.

links *n.* [SE *link*] **1** [late 19C] (*US*) sausages. **2** [1940s] (*US*) handcuffs.

linthead *n.* (*also* **lintbrain**) [SE *linthead*, a worker in a cotton mill] (*US*) **1** [1930s–60s] an insignificant or lower-class person. **2** [1960s+] a stupid person.

lint-scraper *n.* (*also* **lint**) [SE *lint*, the cotton that bandages are made of] [mid-18C–19C] a junior surgeon.

lion *v.* [reverse anthropomorphism] [mid-19C; 1920s+] (*Aus./US*) to frighten, to intimidate; to be cheeky.

Lionel Bart *n.* [rhy. sl. = FART *n.* (1); ult. UK composer and lyricist *Lionel Bart* (1930–99)] [1990s+] breaking wind.

Lionel Blair *n.* [rhy. sl., ult. UK entertainer *Lionel Blair* (b.1931)] [1970s+] **1** a chair. **2** in pl., flares, flared trousers. **3** hair.

lioness *n.* [16C] a prostitute.

lionize *v. see* SHOW THE LIONS (AND TOMBS) *under* SHOW *v.*

lion's bathrobe *n. see* CAT'S PYJAMAS *n.*

lion's lair *n.* (*also* **lion's share**) [rhy. sl.] [20C+] a chair.

lion's roar *n.* [rhy. sl.] [20C+] a snore.

lip *n.*[1] **1** as communication. (**a**) [19C+] cheek, impertinence; thus. (**b**) [1920s+] (*US*) a lawyer, esp. in criminal practice [the concept of 'talking back' (as in cheekiness) in defence of a client]. (**c**) [2000s] lies, deception. **2** in musical contexts. (**a**) [late 19C+] (*US*) musical ability, esp. as a player of brass instruments. (**b**) [1980s] a brass player.

DERIVATIVES

❑ **lipish** *adj.* (*also* **lippish**) [mid-19C] impudent, cheeky.

IN COMPOUNDS

❑ **lip action** *n.* (*also* **lip dancing, lip music**) [20C+] (*US*) oral sex. ❑ **lip-burner** *n.* [1910s–50s] (*US*) a very short cigarette butt. ❑ **lip-loyalty** *n.* [SE *lip service*] [late 19C] (*Aus.*) insincerity. ❑ **lip music** *n.* [1990s+] slangy speech. ❑ **lip read** *v.* **1** [1960s] (*US*) of a lesbian, to perform cunnilingus. **2** [1970s] to kiss. ❑ **lip rug** *n.* [RUG *n.*[1] (1)] [1970s+] (*US black*) a moustache. ❑ **lip service** *n.* [1960s] fellatio. ❑ **lip shield** *n.* [1910s] (*US*) a moustache. ❑ **lip squeezer** *n.* [2000s] (*S.Afr. gay*) a lesbian. ❑ **lip wrestle** *v.* (*also* **mouth wrestle**) [1970s+] (*US*) to indulge in passionate kissing.

IN PHRASES

❑ **dance on someone's lips** *v. see under* DANCE *v.* ❑ **give it lip** *v.* [early 19C+] **1** (*also* **give lip, give some lip**) to be cheeky. **2** (*Aus.*) to speak out loud. ❑ **have a lip** *v.* [1900s] to be cheeky. ❑ **keep a stiff lip** *v.* [SE *keep a stiff upper lip*] [1970s+] (*US black*) to keep quiet, to maintain a secret. ❑ **keep one's lips at home** *v.* [mid-19C] (*US*) to be quiet, to stop being impertinent. ❑ **less (of your) lip** (*also* **none of your lip, not so much (of your) lip**) [mid-19C+] don't be so cheeky. ❑ **slip one's lip** *v.* [1950s] (*US black*) to talk rudely, aggressively.

lip *n.*[2] [? LIBKEN *n.*] [mid-19C] (*UK Und.*) a house.

lip *v.*[1] [SE *lip*] **1** [late 18C–19C] to sing; thus *lip us a chant*, sing us a song. **2** [late 18C–1940s] to speak. **3** [late 19C+] to insult, to abuse, to be impudent. **4** [20C+] (*Ulster*) to eat or drink. **5** [1940s+] to suck on. **6** [1940s+] (*US campus*) to kiss [note 17C–19C poetic SE *lip*, to kiss].

IN PHRASES

❑ **lip in** *v.* [late 19C–1950s] (*US*) to butt into a conversation impolitely. ❑ **lip off** *v.* [1950s+] (*US*) to talk rudely, cheekily or provocatively. ❑ **lipping the dipper** *n.* [1930s–40s] (*US drugs*) sucking the air out of a makeshift syringe.

lip *v.*[2] *see* LIB *v.*

lip and lagging *adj.* (*also* **lippin-leggin**) [Scot. *laggen*, the projecting part of the stave at the bottom of a barrel] [20C+] (*Ulster*) full to the brim.

lipey *n.* [mid-19C] a persuasive, talkative shopkeeper.

lip fart *n.* [1920s+] (*US teen*) a farting noise made with the lips.

lip fart *v.* [LIP FART *n.*] [1920s+] (*US teen*) to make a farting noise with the lips.

lipish/lippish *adj. see* LIP *n.*[1] (1).

lipken *n. see* LIBKEN *n.*

lip-lock *n.* [1970s+] (*US*) **1** a fig. tight hold with the mouth. **2** fellatio. **3** (*also* **lock lip**) a passionate kiss, kissing.

lipper *n.* [mid-19C] (*UK Und.*) a drinking glass.

lippie-chaser *n.* [1960s] (*S.Afr.*) a white man who pursues black women.

lipping (the dipper) *n. see under* LIP v.[1].

lippin-leggin *adj. see* LIP AND LAGGING *adj.*

lippy *adj.* [LIP *n.*[1] (1a)] [mid-19C+] cheeky, talkative, loudmouthed.

Lipton's *n.* (*also* **Lipton tea**) [*Lipton's*, a cheap brand of tea, pun on TEA *n.* (4a)] [1960s+] (*US drugs*) inferior quality cannabis.

liq *n.* (*also* **L.I.Q.**) [abbr.] [1970s+] (*US black*) **1** a *liq*uor store. **2** *liq*uor, alcohol.

liquefied *adj.* (*also* **liquified**) [1930s+] drunk.

liquid *n.* **1** [1960s+] LSD dissolved into a liquid form. **2** [1990s+] a dietary supplement containing furanon di-hydro. **3** [1990s+] phencyclidine.

liquid *adj.*

SE in slang uses

IN COMPOUNDS

❑ **liquid bread** *n.* [1990s+] (*US campus*) very cheap beer. ❑ **liquid comfort** *n.* [1900s] succour gained through alcohol. ❑ **liquid cosh** *n.* [1970s+] (*UK prison*) major tranquillizers used to calm rebellious or 'difficult' prisoners. ❑ **liquid courage** *n.* (*also* **loudmouth soup**) [1940s+] (*US*) courage due to the consumption of alcohol. ❑ **liquid crack** *n.* [CRACK *n.*[7]; the ref. is to the strength of the drug and of the beer] [1990s+] (*US black*) malt liquor. ❑ **liquid crime** *n.* (*also* **liquid damnation, liquid death, liquid fire**) [mid–late 19C] strong, potent alcohol, esp. whisky. ❑ **liquid gold** *n.* [1980s+] (*drugs*) alkyl nitrites. ❑ **liquid grass** *n.* [1970s] (*US drugs*) tetrahydrocannabinol (THC). ❑ **liquid laugh** *n.* (*also* **liquid laughter**) [1960s+] (*orig. Aus.*) vomit. ❑ **liquid lightning** *n. see under* LIGHTNING *n.* (1). ❑ **liquid lunch** *n.* [1960s+] (*orig. Aus.*) a meal that consists of alcohol. ❑ **liquid rouge** *n.* [mid-19C] (*boxing*) blood. ❑ **liquid sky** *n.* [1980s] (*US drugs*) heroin. ❑ **liquid stuff** *n. see* STUFF *n.* (5a). ❑ **liquid sunshine** *n.* [1910s] (*Aus.*) alcohol.

liquidated *adj.* [1980s–90s] (*US campus*) drunk.

liquified *adj. see* LIQUEFIED *adj.*

liquor *n.* (*also* **licker, likker**) **1** [mid-19C–1920s] (*US*) a drink; thus *what's your liquor?*, what will you have to drink? **2** [late 19C–1900s] the water used by unscrupulous publicans to adulterate beer.

IN PHRASES

❑ **have in some liquor** *v.* (*also* **have in (some) rum**) [20C+] (*W.I.*) to be drunk.

liquorate *v. see* LIQUOR (UP) *v.*

liquored (up) *adj.* (*also* **in liquor, in licker, likkered, liquorish**) [LIQUOR (UP) v.] [18C+] drunk.

liquorhead *n.* (*also* **licker-head**) [SE *liquor* + -HEAD *sfx* (4)] [1920s+] (*US*) a drunkard.

liquorice stick *n.* (*also* **licorice stick**) [STICK *n.* (1a)/PRICK *n.* (1)] **1** [1930s+] (*US*) a clarinet, thus *lick the licorice stick*, to play the clarinet. **2** [1970s+] (*US*) a black person. **3** [1970s+] (*US gay*) a (black man's) penis. **4** [1980s+] (*Aus. prison*) a baton.

liquorish *adj. see* LIQUORED (UP) *adj.*

liquorize *v. see* LIQUOR (UP) *v.*

liquor one's boots *v.* **1** [18C] to cuckold. **2** [late 18C–19C] to drink before leaving on a journey.

liquor someone's hide *v.* [pun on LICK v.[1] (1)] [late 17C–early 18C] to thrash, to give a beating.

liquor's talking *phr. see* IT'S THE BEER TALKING *under* TALK *v.*

liquor-up *n.* [LIQUOR (UP) v.] [mid–late 19C] **1** a drinking spree; a party. **2** (*US*) a drink.

liquor (up) *v.* (*also* **liquorate, liquorize**) **1** [19C+] to ply with drink, to supply with alcohol [SE mid-16C–18C]. **2** [early 19C–1940s] to drink alcohol, to get drunk; thus *liquorer*, a hard drinker; *liquoring*, drinking.

lis-dil-lis *adv.* [? legal SE *lis*, a lawsuit] [mid-19C] (*UK Und.*) face to face.

lisp and stutter *n.* [rhy. sl.] [20C+] (*Aus.*) butter.

lispers *n.* [18C–mid-19C] (*UK Und.*) the lips.

listen *v.* [1900s–40s] (*US*) to sound; as in *that listens good/well*.

listener *n.* [early 19C+] (*orig. boxing*) the ear.

listening flap *n.* [1900s] (*Aus.*) the ear.

listing to starboard *adj.* (*also* **listing to port**) [naut. imagery] [19C+] tipsy, drunk.

Lit *n.* (*also* **Lith**) [abbr.] [1920s+] (*US*) a *Lit*huanian.

Lit *adj.* [LIT *n.*] [1920s+] (*US*) Lithuanian.

lit *n.* [abbr.; note also LIT *adj.*] [mid-19C+] *lit*erature.

lit *adj.* [abbr.] [late 19C+] *lit*erary, esp. in combs. *lit. crit.*, literary criticism; *lit. ed.*, literary editor; *lit. supp.*, literary supplement.

literature *n.* [late 19C+] any form of printed material.

Lith *n. see* LIT *n.* (1).

little *n.* [1960s+] (*US*) **1** petting. **2** sexual intercourse.

little *adj.*

SE in slang uses

IN COMPOUNDS

❑ **little Ada** *n. see* ADA FROM DECATUR *n.* ❑ **little black book** *n.* **1** [1920s–40s] (*US Und.*) police files, kept secret. **2** [1930s+] the volume in which every bachelor supposedly keeps lists of available and willing women; also fig. as any address book. ❑ **little black father** *n.* [early 19C] a quart jug. ❑ **little boys' room** *n.* [1930s+] (*orig. US*) a coy euph. for a men's lavatory. ❑ **little breeches** *n.* (*also* **little britches**) [UK use ends/US commences in mid-19C] [late 18C+] an affectionate term of address to a small boy; or a term of abuse. ❑ **little britches** *n.* [ety. unknown] [1930s+] (*US gambling*) the point of three in craps dice or a three in cards. ❑ **little brother** *n. see* separate entry. ❑ **little brown eyeball** *n. see* BROWN EYE *n.* (1). ❑ **little casino** *n. see* separate entry. ❑ **little clergyman** *n.* [his blackened clothes] [late 18C–19C] a young chimney-sweep. ❑ **little davy** *n.* [19C+] the penis. ❑ **little deers** *n.* [double pun on *little dear* and *deer* as a fem. version of STAG *n.*[4] (1), i.e. the single men who frequent the theatre] [late 19C–1900s] young women who are involved in some way with the stage. ❑ **little Dick** *n.* [1930s+] (*US gambling*) in craps, the point of four. ❑ **little eight** *n.* [late 19C] (*Aus.*) a regular per diem payment. ❑ **little eva** *n.* **1** [1950s] (*US black*) a loud-mouthed white woman. **2** [1950s] (*US*) used to reinforce a negative statement [f. sense 1]. ❑ **little four** *n.* [20C+] (*US gambling*) the point of four in craps dice. ❑ **little friend** *n.* [the ref. is to the welcome appearance of a period as a sign that, had one been worried, one was not pregnant] [1920s+] (*orig. Can./Aus.*) menstruation; thus *my little friend has come*, I am menstruating. ❑ **little girls' room** *n.* (*also* **l.g.r.**) [1930s+] a coy euph. for the ladies' lavatory. ❑ **little go** *n. see* separate entries. ❑ **little green man** *n.* [2000s] (*Irish*) a small bottle of whisky. ❑ **little grey cells** *n.* [coined by crime writer Agatha Christie in *The Mysterious Affair at Styles* (1920) and always associated with her fictional sleuth Hercule Poirot] [1920s+] the human brain. ❑ **little house** *n. see* separate entry. ❑ **little jimmy** *n.* [20C+] in bingo, the number one. ❑ **little jobs** *n.* [euph.] [20C+] (*juv.*) urination. ❑ **little Joe** *n.* (*also* **joe, little Joe from Baltimore, little Joe from Kokomo**) [late 19C+] (*US gambling*) the point of four in craps dice, esp. as two twos. ❑ **little Joe (in the snow)** *n.* [SNOW *n.*[1] (2a)] [1920s+] (*drugs*) cocaine. ❑ **little john** *n.* [ety. unknown] [1980s+] (*N.Z. drugs*) a cannabis cigarette made from two papers. ❑ **little joker** *n.* [mid-19C] (*US*) the pea or similar object used in the shell game. ❑ **little josie** *n.* (*also* **little josephine**) [var. on *LITTLE JOE* above] [20C+] (*gambling*) the point of four in craps dice. ❑ **little kinchin** *n. see under* KINCHIN *n.* ❑ **little mama** *n.* [19C+] (*US black*) an attractive black woman. ❑ **little man** *n. see* separate entry. ❑ **little miss big** *n.* [var. on *MISS BIG STOCKINGS under* MISS *n.*] [1990s+] (*W.I.*) a precocious young girl. ❑ **little nigger** *n.* [20C+] (*US*) in poker, a game in which the low spade splits the pot. ❑ **little one** *n.* [1950s] (*US*) the penis. ❑ **little pal** *n.* [1920s] (*US*) a pretty young woman. ❑ **little phoebe** *n. see* PHOEBE *n.* ❑ **little ploughman** *n.* [? pun on SE *plough*/PLOUGH *v.* (1)] [19C] the clitoris. ❑ **little (red)**

wagon *n.* **1** [1930s] (*US tramp*) a dump truck. **2** [1930s–70s] (*US black*) (*also* **red wagon**) a problem, a difficulty; usu. in the phr. *that's your little red wagon.* ❑ **little school** *n. see under* SCHOOL *n.* ❑ **little shot** *n.* [reverse of BIG SHOT *n.* (1)] [1930s+] (*US*) an insignificant person. ❑ **little snakesman** *n.* [SE *little* + SNAKESMAN *n.*; the twisting and turning of the boy in his actions] [late 18C–19C] (*UK Und.*) a small boy in a gang of burglars who is put through a narrow opening into a house, then lets the gang in. ❑ **little wack** *n.* (*also* **little whack**) [SE *little* + WHACK *n.*[2] (1)] [late 19C] a small measure of spirits. ❑ **little wheel** *n.* [play on BIG WHEEL *under* BIG *adj.*] [1950s] (*US*) a secondary rank of gang leader; one who has power but remains less important than an actual boss.

IN PHRASES

❑ **little bit of all right** *see* BIT OF ALL RIGHT, A *phr.* ❑ **little bit of eyes right** *n.* [milit. play on BIT OF ALL RIGHT, A *phr.*] [1910s] (*Aus.*) a woman, usu. attractive. ❑ **little boy blue** *n. see* separate entry. ❑ **little boy in the boat** *n. see* LITTLE MAN (IN THE BOAT) *n.* ❑ **little end of nothing** *n.* [early 19C+] (*US*) anything very insignificant, utterly unimportant; also intensified as *little end of nothing sharpened/whittled down to a point.* ❑ **little end of the horn** *n.* [the *Horn of Plenty*, which in mythology was one of the horns of the goat Amalthea by which the infant Zeus was suckled, and hence a symbol of fruitfulness and plenty. Its large end is depicted as pouring forth its bounty] [19C+] (*US*) failure; usu. in the phr. *come out of the little end of the horn*; thus as opposite, the *big end of the horn*.

IN EXCLAMATIONS

❑ **little more!** [1950s+] (*W.I. Rasta*) a general excl. of farewell, 'see you later!'.

little and large *n.* [rhy. sl.] [1920s+] *margarine.*

Little Barbary *n.* [*see* BARBARY COAST *n.*] [late 17C–19C] the borough of Wapping, site of the Ratcliff Highway, once London's tough port area.

Little Bo-Peep *n.* [rhy. sl.; ult. the nursery rhyme] [late 19C+] sleep.

little boy blue *n.*[1] [the colour of their uniforms] [late 19C; 1960s+] (*later US black*) the police.

little boy blue *n.*[2] [rhy. sl. = SCREW *n.*[1] (2c)] [20C+] a prison warder.

little brother *n.* **1** [mid-19C+] the penis. **2** [1970s+] (*US black*) an affectionate or familiar term of address to a younger man or child.

little brown jug *n.* [rhy. sl.] [20C+] **1** an electric plug. **2** a bath plug. **3** a tampon [fig. use of SE *plug*]. **4** (*Aus.*) a fool [MUG *n.*[1] (2a)].

little casino *n.* [SE *casino*, a card game in which the ten of diamonds, called *great casino*, counts two points, and the two of spades, called *little casino*, counts one; note BIG CASINO *n.*] (*US*) **1** [1900s] any insignificant event or object. **2** [1900s] a term of familiarity, aimed at a woman. **3** [1900s–50s] an insignificant person. **4** [1930s+] gonorrhoea [compares gonorrhoea with syphilis, which would be a 'greater' form of VD].

Little Dublin *n.* [late 18C] an area of St. Giles's, London peopled by Irish beggars.

little go *n.*[1] (*also* **little-go**) [late 18C–mid-19C] a private lottery.

little go *n.*[2] [Oxford University jargon *little go*, the first public examination (usu. taken during or at the end of one's first year and now known as *prelims*) as opposed to finals or *great go*] **1** [late 19C–1900s] (*UK Und.*) one's first experience of prison. **2** [1960s] (*US*) an unimportant, unexciting or incomplete attempt at a task or performance.

little grey home in the west *n.* [rhy. sl.; ult. a song *Little Grey Home in the West*, written in 1911 by Hermann Frederic Löhr and D. Eardley-Wilmot] [1910s–50s] a vest.

little house *n.* **1** [18C+] a lavatory or privy [19C+ use is (*Aus./N.Z./US*)]. **2** [1930s+] (*US Und.*) a local prison; a reformatory.

Little India *n.* [c.1940s a largely residential area in which many who had retired from colonial posts in India lived; followed by later immigrants] [1940s+] Bayswater, West London.

little man *n.* **1** [1960s+] the penis. **2** *see* LEMAC *n.*

little man (in the boat) *n.* (*also* **little boy in the boat, little old man in the boat, man in the boat**) [note LITTLE MAN *n.* (1)] **1** [late 19C–1930s] the navel. **2** [late 19C+] the clitoris.

IN PHRASES

❑ **sink the little man (in the boat)** *v.* [1990s+] of a man, to have sexual intercourse.

Little Miss Muffet *v.* [rhy. sl. = STUFF IT! *excl.*] [1930s+] to get rid of, to ignore.

Little Miss Roundheels *n.* [note Robert Greene in *The Blacke Bookes Messenger* (1592): 'the commonest harlot and hackster ... and with the lightnes of hir heeles bring me in the some crownes'] [1930s+] a promiscuous woman.

little nell *n.* [rhy. sl.] [20C+] a bell, usu. a doorbell.

little peter *n.* [rhy. sl.; note PETER *n.*[2]] [20C+] a gas or electricity meter.

little red ridings *n.* [rhy. sl. = *Little Red Riding Hoods*] [1950s–60s] stolen goods.

little titch *n.* [rhy. sl.; ult. music-hall comedian Harry Relph (*Little Tich*) (1867–1928)] [20C+] an itch.

little titchy *adj.* [LITTLE TITCH *n.*] [20C+] itchy.

littlie *n.* [SE *little* + N.Z. sfx *-ie*, equivalent of Aus. -O *sfx* (3)] [1960s+] (*Aus./N.Z.*) a child.

lit (up) *adj.* **1** [late 19C+] (*orig. US*) (*also* **lighted up**) drunk. **2** [1910s] (*Aus.*) suffering from a sexually transmitted disease. **3** [1920s] (*US*) showily dressed up. **4** [1920s+] (*US drugs*) extremely intoxicated by a drug. **5** [1960s+] (*US gang*) shot. **6** [1970s+] excited. **7** [1990s+] (*US*) angry.

IN PHRASES

❑ **all lit up** *adj.* [1930s+] (*drugs*) under the influence of drugs. ❑ **lit to the gills** *adj.* (*also* **lit to the guards**) [*TO THE GILLS under* GILLS *n.*] [20C+] drunk. ❑ **lit up like a Christmas tree** *adj.* (*also* **...like a birthday cake, ...like a church, ...like a new saloon, ...like an ocean liner, ...like a pier, ...like a sky-rocket, ...like a torch, ...like a triumphal arch, ...like a white way, ...like high mass**) [20C+] very drunk; intoxicated from drugs. ❑ **lit up like Broadway** *adj.* (*also* **...like a Luna park, ...like a White Way, ...like Main Street, ...like Times Square**) **1** [20C+] very drunk. **2** very happy.

litvak *n.* (*also* **litvok**) [late 19C+] a Jew whose family come from Lithuania and are therefore considered lower-class by Jews from Poland.

li-un *n. see* LI-YUEN *n.*

live *adj.* [the image of a live performance] **1** [mid-19C+] (*orig. US*) alert, energetic. **2** [late 19C+] excellent, first-rate, thrilling; thus *a live one*, an admirable person or object. **3** [20C+] of a potential victim of a confidence trick, willing to be tricked; often as LIVE ONE *n.* (3). **4** [1930s–50s] of a house, inhabited, occupied, the opposite of DEAD *adj.* (3).

IN COMPOUNDS

❑ **live blanket** *n. see under* BLANKET *n.* ❑ **live horse** *n.* [antonym of DEAD HORSE *n.*[1] (1)] [mid-19C] work done and not charged for. ❑ **live meat wagon** *n.* see *MEAT WAGON under* MEAT *n.* ❑ **live sausage** *n. see under* SAUSAGE *n.*

live *v.*

SE in slang uses

IN PHRASES

❑ **live at Easy Hall** *v.* [20C+] (*W.I.*) to live comfortably. ❑ **live at rack and manger** *v. see LIE AT RACK AND MANGER under* LIE *v.*[1]. ❑ **live at the sign of the cat's foot** *v. see under* CAT *n.*[1]. ❑ **live at the sign of the Queen's Head** *v.* (*also* **live in Queen Street**) [late 18C–mid-19C] of a man, to be dominated by one's wife. ❑ **live at your aunt** *v. see under* AUNT *n.* ❑ **live bache** *v. see under* BACH *n.* ❑ **live big** *v. see LIVE LARGE under* LARGE *adv.* ❑ **live in a good paddock** *v.* [farming imagery] [1950s] (*N.Z.*) to live comfortably. ❑ **live in someone's ear** *v. see under* EAR *n.*[1]. ❑ **live low** *v.* [1980s+] (*US black*) **1** to have a poor standard of living. **2** to feel depressed. ❑ **live off the land** *v.* [late 19C+] (*Aus.*) to live as a tramp. ❑ **live off the smell of an oil rag** *v.* (*also* **...oily rag, ...oiled rag**) [late 19C+] (*Aus./N.Z.*) to subsist on a bare minimum of material wants. ❑ **live on someone's eye-top** *v.* [one's continual glancing around for a potential donor] [1950s+] (*W.I.*) to scrounge off someone. ❑ **live on the skin of a rasher** *v.* [20C+] (*Irish*) to live very frugally. ❑ **live shallow** *v. see under* SHALLOW *adj.* ❑ **live square** *v. see under* SQUARE *adv.* ❑ **live under the cat's foot** *v. see under* LIVE AT THE SIGN OF THE CAT'S FOOT *under* CAT *n.*[1]. ❑ **well to live** *adj.* [one is enjoying life] [late 17C–mid-19C] tipsy. ❑ **where one lives** [mid-19C+] (*orig. US*) at a vital or central point of one's emotions, e.g. *that gets me right where I live.*

live eels *n.* [rhy. sl.] [mid–late 19C] fields.

livener *n.* [SE *enliven*] **1** [late 19C+] a drink used as a 'pick-me-up', usu. the first drink of the day. **2** [2000s] a small portion of a drug, used for a similar purpose, although the time of day is irrelevant.

live-on *n.* [a husband could *live on her earnings*; the image is of her (unrealized) potential as a prostitute] [late 19C–1900s] an attractive young woman.

live one *n.* [LIVE *adj.*] **1** [late 19C+] (*US*) a notable, popular or well-respected individual. **2** [20C+] (*US*) a winning bet. **3** [20C+] (*orig. UK Und.*) the ideal victim for a proposed hoax, fraud or other deceit. **4** [20C+] (*US*) a generous and enthusiastic patron of nightclubs, theatres and other places of entertainment (incl. brothels). **5** [1910s] (*US*) a success, or one who has the potential so to be. **6** [1940s+] (*gay*) a generous rich client for a prostitute. **7** [1950s+] an enthusiastic participant in a proposed scheme. **8** [1970s] an eccentric, with implications of homosexuality. **9** [1970s+] someone destined to cause trouble in any situation, usu. challenging authority.

liver *n.*

SE in slang uses

IN PHRASES

❑ **liver disturber** *n.* (*also* **liver-lifter, liver-turner**) [late 19C] (*US*) a very large penis. ❑ **liver-jerker** *n.* [late 19C–1900s] a tricycle. ❑ **liver-shaker** *n.* [late 19C–1910s] a riding hack. ❑ **liver-spot** *n.* [1940s+] (*W.I.*) a mulatto. ❑ **liver-string** *n.* (*also* **liver-pin**) [20C+] (*W.I., Guyn.*) a notional source of one's energy; thus *work out one's liver-string*, to exhaust oneself through hard labour. ❑ **that ain't chopped liver** *see* THAT AIN'T HAY *under* HAY *n.*

live rabbit *n.* [19C] the penis; thus *have a bit of rabbit pie*, to have sexual intercourse.

IN PHRASES

❑ **skin the live rabbit** *v.* **1** [19C] to have sexual intercourse. **2** [late 19C–1900s] of a man, to peel back one's foreskin.

liver and lights *n.*

IN PHRASES

❑ **scare the liver and lights out of** *v.* [mid-19C+] to terrify.

liver-faced *adj. see* WHITE-LIVERED *adj.* (1).

liver-lips *n.* [1910s+] (*US black*) **1** large, dark lips. **2** a person with thick, dark lips, often used in direct address.

DERIVATIVES

❑ **liver-lipped** *adj.* [1930s–50s] (*US black*) thick-lipped.

Liverpool kiss *n.* [orig. naut.] [1940s+] a blow to the mouth or face.

livestock *n.* **1** [late 18C–1910s] lice, fleas, any bodily infestation. **2** [mid-19C] (*US*) slaves. **3** [1920s–50s] (*US*) women as objects of sexual interest, or prostitutes [play on CATTLE *n.* (1)].

living *n.*

IN PHRASES

❑ **do a living** *v.* [1980s] (*UK black*) to commit a street robbery.

living *adj.* [late 19C+] (*US black/Aus.*) an intensifier.

IN PHRASES

❑ **stomp the living shit out of** *v. see* BEAT THE SHIT OUT OF *v.*

living color yawn *n. see* TECHNICOLOUR YAWN *n.*

living end *n.* [1950s+] the extreme, the absolute limit.

living off the tit *adv. see under* TIT *n.*[2].

livity *n.* [1990s+] (*W.I.*) a healthy attitude to life.

li-yuen *n.* (*also* **li-un**) [late19C–50s] (*drugs*) top grade smoking opium.

Liz/liz *n. see* LIZZIE *n.*[1] (3).

liza *n.* [SE *lie*, i.e. one 'lies with' the woman substitute] [1970s] (*S.Afr. prison*) a makeshift hole lined with cloth, used to aid masturbation.

lizard *n.* **1** [mid-19C+] an inhabitant of Alabama [lizards are common in the state]. **2** [late 19C+] (*Aus./N.Z.*) a shepherd, a musterer, a mender of boundary fences. **3** [1900s–50s] (*US*) an old or useless racehorse, any horse. **4** [1910s+] a smooth and highly plausible fortune-hunter or womanizer who works his charms in the lounges of hotels, an adventurer. **5** [1910s+] (*US*) a contemptible or unlikeable person. **6** [1950s+] (*US black*) in pl., lizard-skin shoes. **7** [1960s+] (*Aus./US*) the penis. **8** [1980s+] (*US black*) a young woman.

IN PHRASES

❑ **bleed the lizard** *v.* [1990s+] to masturbate. ❑ **choke the lizard** *v.* (*also* **lift..., whip..., ...one's...**) [1960s+] to masturbate. ❑ **drain the lizard** *v.* [1960s+] to urinate. ❑ **flog the lizard** *v.* [1960s] (*Aus.*) to urinate. ❑ **gallop the (old) lizard** *v.* [1960s+] to masturbate. ❑ **give the lizard a run** *v.* [1960s+] (*Aus.*) of a man, to have sexual intercourse. ❑ **leak one's lizard** *v.* [1960s+] (*US*) to urinate. ❑ **milk the lizard** *v.* (*also* **milk the anaconda, ...maggot, ...moose**) [late 19C+] to masturbate. ❑ **pet the lizard** *v.* [1970s+] to masturbate. ❑ **squeeze the lizard** *v.* [2000s] (*Irish*) to urinate. ❑ **stroke one's lizard** *v.* [1960s+] to masturbate.

SE in slang uses

DERIVATIVES

❑ **lizarding** *n.* [the way a lizard basks in the sun] [1970s] (*Aus.*) lazing.

IN PHRASES

❑ **flat out like a lizard drinking** [1930s+] (*Aus.*) moving or working at great speed. ❑ **what's on the rail for the lizard?** [predates sense 7 above, but poss. link] [1940s] (*US black*) what have you got to offer? esp. in the context of money, sexual favours and other exciting, if unrespectable, pleasures.

-lizard *sfx* [1920s+] (*US*) used in combs. to describe a person with a particular habit or type of behaviour; thus *chow-lizard*, a person who eats a lot; *couch-lizard*, a person who frequently lies necking with his girlfriends on a couch etc.

IN PHRASES

❑ **day lizard** *n.* [1920s] an unemployed tramp or beggar who practices as a minor con man. ❑ **lens lizard** *n.* [1920s+] (*US*) a photographer, a film-maker. ❑ **lot lizard** *n.* [SE (*parking*) *lot*] [1980s+] (*US*) a prostitute who works at truck stops.

lizard lap *n.* [? centring on oral sex] [1990s+] (*W.I.*) a sexual position.

lize *n.* [*see* MOSE *n.*] [mid-19C] (*US*) a generic name for New York's 'Bowery g'hals', the female accomplice/equivalent of MOSE *n.*

lizzie *n.*[1] **1** [mid-19C+] (*also* **Liz, liz, Lizzie, lizzie boy**) (*orig. US*) an effeminate youth; a homosexual. **2** [1900s–20s] (*Aus./US campus*) (*also* **Liz, liz, Lizzie**) a young woman. **3** (*also* **Liz, liz, Lizzie**) of vehicles, in affectionate use of the female name. (**a**) [1910s–50s] (*US*) as *the Lizzie*, the Cunard liner Queen Elizabeth. (**b**) [1910s+] (*orig. US*) an early Model Ford car, spec. the Model T, known as the TIN LIZZIE *under* TIN *adj.* **4** [1930s] (*also* **Lizzie**) cheap Portuguese wine [abbr. *Lisbon*, the Portuguese capital].

IN COMPOUNDS

❑ **lizzie-louse** *n.* (*also* **lizzie-lousy, lousy liz**) [1930s–50s] a police officer in a police car. ❑ **lizzie-stiff** *n.* [1920s–30s] a tramp who travels by car.

IN PHRASES

❑ **lizzie up** *v.* [1910s–30s] (*US*) to turn gay, to make homosexual; the implication is of raping someone anally.

lizzie *n.*[2] (*also* **lizzy-bean**) [abbr.] [1940s+] a lesbian.

lizzie *v.* [LIZZIE *n.*[1] (3b)] [1910s+] (*US*) to drive an early Model Ford car, spec. the Model T.

lizzie up *v. see under* LIZZIE *n.*[1] (1).

L.K. Clark *n.* (*also* **Elkie Clark**) [rhy. sl.; ult. *Elkie Clark*, a Glaswegian boxer in the 1920s–30s] [20C+] the mark, i.e. beginning.

llac *n. see* LAC *n.*

llello *n.*[1] [mispron.] [1990s+] (*US black*) hello.

llello *n.*[2] (*also* **lleyo**) [pron. 'yeayo'] [1990s+] (*US drugs*) cocaine.

llelo *n.* [1990s+] (*US black/drugs*) crack cocaine.

llesca *n. see* YESCA *n.*

lleyo *n. see* LLELLO *n.*[2].

lloyd *n.* (*also* **Harold Lloyd, Harold**) [rhy. sl. *Harold Lloyd* = LOID *n.*; ult. silent film star *Harold Lloyd* (1893–1971)] [1950s+] a piece of celluloid used for picking Yale locks.

Lloyd George *n.* [the National Assistance Act (1911) introduced by Lloyd George's govt.] [1940s–50s] National Assistance.

Lloyd's (List) *adj.* [rhy. sl. = PISSED *adj.*[1]] [20C+] drunk.

l.m.c. *adj.* [abbr.] [1990s+] *l*ower *m*iddle *c*lass.

L note *n.* [2000s] (*US prison*) a life sentence.

Lo *n.*[1] (*also* **Mr Lo, Mrs Lo**) [pun on the line 'Lo, the poor Indian' in Pope's *Essay on Man* (1733)] [mid-19C+] (*US*) a Native American.

Lo *n.*[2] [abbr.] [2000s] Po*lo*, the Ralph Lauren brand of clothing.

'lo *phr.* [abbr.] [1920s+] hel*lo*.

load *n.* **1** as a quantity of drink or drugs. (**a**) [late 17C+] drink, usu. in a quantity sufficient to render the drinker drunk; hence a state of drunkenness in phr. *carry a load, get a load on/in, have a load on, take a load on* etc. (**b**) [1920s+] an amount of drugs, e.g. the quantity of heroin required to sustain an addiction. (**c**) [1920s+] an injection. (**d**) [1950s+] 25 or 30 packs of heroin held together in a bundle, the equivalent of an ounce weight. **2** [mid-18C–mid-19C] (*UK Und.*) one's personal possessions or money, also the proceeds of a crime. **3** as abbr. of *'load of rubbish,' 'load of nonsense,' 'load of shit,'* etc. (**a**) [mid–late 19C] (*US campus*) a practical joke. (**b**) [1930s+] (*US*) an old, discontinued model or a run-down, dilapidated vehicle or a stolen car. (**c**) [1930s+] (*orig. US*) utter nonsense. (**d**) [1940s+] (*orig. US black*) an automobile. (**e**) [1940s+] (*US*) a stupid, ridiculous or contemptible person. (**f**) [1970s] (*Aus. Und.*) fabricated evidence. **4** in context of the body or bodily fluids [SE *loaded*, to be burdened with, to be weighed down. Note late 19C use of *load*, measles, smallpox]. (**a**) [mid-19C+] (*US*) faeces, a bowel movement. (**b**) [late 19C+] (*orig. Aus.*) a bout of venereal disease. (**c**) [1920s+] (*US*) an ejaculation of semen or an orgasm (of either sex). (**d**) [1960s+] (*US black*) a large amount of semen in the testes. (**e**) [1970s] a large penis. (**f**) [1980s] (*US black*) the intense urge to have sex.

IN COMPOUNDS

❑ **loaded gun** *n.* [GUN *n.*[1] (2)] [1980s+] (*US gay*) the penis before ejaculation of its 'load' of semen.

IN PHRASES

❑ **blow one's load** *v.* [1970s+] usu. of a man, to ejaculate, to come to orgasm. ❑ **bust a/one's load** *v.* [1990s+] to ejaculate. ❑ **carrying a load** *adj.* [20C+] drunk. ❑ **catch a load of** *v.* [1920s+] (*US*) to catch sight of. ❑ **chuck one's load** *v.* [SE *chuck*/CHUCK *v.*[2] (17)] [1990s+] to ejaculate. ❑ **drop one's load** *v.* **1** [late 19C] to give birth. **2** [1930s] to have a miscarriage. **3** [1940s+] (*US black*) to reduce tension by having sexual intercourse. **4** [1960s+] (*also* **drop one**) to defecate. **5** [1970s] to experience a shock. **6** [1990s+] to act in a cowardly manner; synon, with *SHIT ONE'S LOAD under* SHIT *v.* ❑ **dump a/one's load** *v.* **1** [1960s] to defecate. **2** [1960s+] to vomit. **3** [1980s+] (*N.Z.*) to ejaculate. ❑ **get a load of** *v.* (*also* **take a load of**) **1** [1920s+] (*orig. US*) to notice, to look at deliberately. **2** [1920s+] (*orig. US*) a demand that one's audience listen to something or notice an event; usu. in a sexual context, e.g. *get a load of that!* and usu. between males. ❑ **half-load** *n.* (*also* **half-lo**) [1960s+] (*US drugs*) 15 packs of heroin, each weighing about 1g and thus equivalent to ½ ounce, a typical purchase made by a small pusher. ❑ **lighten one's load** *v.* [1980s+] **1** to masturbate. **2** [2000s] to urinate. ❑ **load off one's behind** *n.* [pun on colloq. phr. *load on one's mind*] [1920s+] a defecation. ❑ **load off one's mind** *n.* [pun on colloq. phr. *load on one's mind*] **1** [1920s+] a haircut. **2** [1960s+] a defecation. **3** [1980s+] (*US gay*) the removal of a penis from the anus. ❑ **shit one's load** *v.* [SHIT *v.* (1a); the image is of terror that leads to involuntary defecation] [1990s+] to be absolutely terrified. ❑ **shoot (off) one's load** *v.* [SHOOT *v.* (1a)/SE *shoot*] **1** [1920s+] to ejaculate; usu. of a man. **2** [1950s+] in fig. use: to expend one's best effort. **3** [1960s] in fig. use: to blame, to pass on a responsibility. ❑ **tie a load on** *v.* [1940s+] (*US*) to get drunk.

SE in slang uses

IN PHRASES

❑ **no load** *n.* [they 'carry no weight'] [1920s+] (*US*) a lazy, unenthusiastic or pessimistic person. ❑ **pull one's load** *v.* (*also* **pull one's freight**) [late 19C+] (*Can.*) to make one's best effort.

load *v.* **1** in context of drink or drugs [LOAD *n.* (1)]. (**a**) [late 19C] to ply someone with drink. (**b**) [1960s] (*drugs*) to take drugs. **2** [late 19C–1950s] (*US*) to lie, to deceive. **3** [1900s] (*US campus*) to prepare for an emergency, eg an exam. **4** [1990s+] (*Aus. Und.*) of police, to plant false evidence.

DERIVATIVES

❑ **loaded** *adj.* [it has been *loaded* up with all possible extras] [2000s] of an automobile, customized.

IN PHRASES

❑ **load in** *v.* [late 19C] to drink. ❑ **load up** *v.* **1** [late 19C] to provide with drink. **2** [late 19C] (*US*) to provide with false information. **3** [late 19C+] to get drunk, to use a drug; also as *load up on* a drink or drug. **4** [late 19C+] to eat heartily. **5** [1930s+] (*Aus./N.Z.*) to infect with venereal disease. **6** [1980s+] (*Aus. prison*) to incriminate through perjured evidence.

loaded *adj.* [LOAD *v.*] **1** in senses suggesting a lit. or fig. additive. (**a**) [19C+] of dice, in some way crooked. (**b**) [1920s+] of anything other than dice, similarly crooked. (**c**) [1920s+] (*US*) laced with alcohol, drugs or poison. [note SE *loaded*, of wine, adulterated to appear full-bodied]. (**d**) [1950s] (*US Und.*) prepared to lie on oath. (**e**) [1970s+] of boxers, to have the hands taped with heavy insulating tape, thus rendering his blows more lethal. (**f**) [1980s] (*Aus. Und.*) (*also* **loaded up**) 'planted' with incriminating evidence. **2** [late 19C+] (*orig. US*) (*also* **loaded up**) drunk. **3** [late 19C+] (*orig. US*) (*also* **loaded up**) intoxicated with a drug. **4** [late 19C+] (*orig. US*) (*also* **loaded down**) rich, either in actual cash or simply, esp. in prison use, in possessions such as tobacco; of a place, filled with money or valuables. **5** [1920s+] in possession of a large amount of a given commodity, e.g. drugs. **6** [1950s+] of a female, well-built, big-breasted. **7** [1970s] pregnant.

IN PHRASES

❑ **loaded for bear** *adj.* (*also* **loaded, loaded for rhino**) [hunting use, bear-shooting requires heavy armament] (*US*) **1** [late 19C–1950s] holding a good poker hand. **2** [late 19C+] fully prepared for all problems, esp. the hardest ones, thus also fully armed and equipped for conflict (cf. ARMED FOR BEAR *phr.*). **3** [1940s] drunk. ❑ **loaded to the…** *adj.* **1** [late 19C+] in var. phrs. as synons. for drunk, incl. *loaded to the barrel, …the earlobes, …the gills, …the guards, …the gunnels, …the hat, … the muzzle, …the Plimsoll Mark, …the tailgate.* **2** [1940s+] (*drugs*) in var. phrs. as synons. for intoxicated by a drug. ❑ **loaded up** *adj.* [it has been *loaded up* with all possible extras] [2000s] of an automobile, customized.

loaded gun *n. see under* LOAD *n.*

loadie *n.* [LOAD *v.* (1)] [1970s+] (*US campus*) a habitual drinker or drug user.

load of *n.* **1** [late 19C+] a great deal of, a lot of, usu. in combs. to form dismissive phr.; thus *load of crap, load of old cobblers, load of old cods, load of old wank* etc. **2** *see also under* relevant n.

load of hay *n.* [rhy. sl.] [mid-19C] a day.

loads *n.* [1990s+] (*US drugs*) a mixture of codeine and Doriden.

loads *adv.* [1920s+] to a very great extent, very much.

loadsamoney *n.* [ult. the 1980s TV character *Loadsamoney* created by Harry Enfield (b.1961)] [1990s+] a great deal of money.

loads of *n.* [17C+] many, a great quantity, esp. of a desirable commodity.

IN PHRASES

❑ **give it loads** *v.* [1990s+] to make a fuss.

load-up *n.* [2000s] a shopping spree.

loaf *n.*[1] [SE *loaf*, to pass time idly, but note Sw. *lofdag*, Du. *verlofdag*, a leave-day, a holiday] [mid-19C–1920s] (*orig. US*) **1** the act of loafing, idling; thus (US) *loaf-day*, a day when no regular work is done. **2** one who idles and does not work. **3** any occupation deemed to require minimal if any effort.

loaf *n.*[2] [LOAF *v.*[2]] [1980s+] (*Irish*) a headbutt.

loaf *v.*[1] [mid-19C–1900s] (*US campus*) to steal, to cadge.

loaf *v.*[2] [LOAF (OF BREAD) *n.*] [1980s+] (*Irish*) to headbutt.

Loafers' Hall *n.* [mid-19C] (*US*) a prison.

loaf (of bread) *n.* [rhy. sl.; note TWOPENNY *n.*[1] suggests earlier usage] [1910s+] a head, esp. brains, intelligence; thus *use one's loaf*, to act sensibly, often as imper. *use your loaf!*

IN PHRASES

❑ **give someone the loaf of bread** *v.* [1940s+] to hit with one's head. ❑ **use one's loaf** *v.* [1930s+] to think, to act intelligently, to work things out.

loaf of bread *n.* [1970s] (*US*) a $1 bill.

loaf of bread *adj.* [rhy. sl.] [1910s–30s] dead.

loan *n.*

SE in slang uses

IN PHRASES

❑ **get the loan of** *v.* (*also* **have a lend of, have the loan of, take the loan of, take a lend of**) [dial. *take the lend of*, to take advantage of, to cajole] [20C+] (*Aus.*) to play a trick on; to treat like a fool.

lo and behold *n.* [the neckline is *lo(w)* and one *beholds* the breasts] [20C+] a plunging neckline.

loaner *n.* [SE *loan*] [1920s+] (*US*) a temporary replacement for an item being repaired; anything on loan/hire.

Loan Land *n.* [Australian debts to 'the mother country'] [1910s] (*Aus.*) Britain.

loan shark *n.* [20C+] a supplier of private loans at maximum interest.

loan sharking *n.* [1910s+] the practice of lending money at usurious rates, esp. by organized crime syndicates.

loap *v.* see LOPE *v.*

loaver *n.* [LOUR *n.*] [mid–late 19C] (*UK Und.*) money.

lob *n.*[1] [echoic of something solid, heavy, clumsy (similar sounding words, with similar meanings, are found in various Teutonic languages)] **1** [18C] a snuffbox, any box. **2** [18C–1940s] (*also* **lobb**) a till, a cash register; thus *dip/frisk/pinch/sneak a lob*, to rob a till; *make a good lob*, to take a large amount of money from the till; *lobber*, a till robber. **3** [early 18C] a form of confidence trick, involving confusing a shopkeeper when giving change [16C-17C SE *lob*, a country bumpkin; i.e. a lumpish person]. **4** [mid-19C–1900s] the head. **5** [mid-19C+] a haul, thus a fortune, a large amount, usu. of money. **6** [1910s–50s] (*Aus./UK prison*) pay.

IN COMPOUNDS

❑ **lob-lay** *n.* [LAY *n.*[3] (1)] [mid-19C] (*UK Und.*) robbing shop tills.

IN PHRASES

❑ **go on the lob** *v.* [late 18C–early 19C] to play a confidence trick on shopkeepers by asking for change for a high-value coin but then switching coins to make a profit.

lob *n.*[2] (*also* **lobb**) [16C–19C SE/dial. *lob*, a country bumpkin. Note Yid. *lobbes*, rascal + Du. *lobbes*, a clown] **1** [mid-19C] (*UK Und.*) an informer. **2** [20C+] a dull, stupid person; thus adj., *lobbish*, stupid. **3** [1910s–20s] (*Aus./UK Und.*) a police officer, esp. an officious one. **4** [1930s] (*US Und.*) an initiate into criminality. **5** [1990s+] (*US prison*) a deliberate insult implying that the subject is weak and/or homosexual; a spur to a fight.

lob *n.*[3] (*also* **lobb**) [SE *lob*, something pendulous] [late 19C+] the penis, esp. when half- or fully erect.

IN PHRASES

❑ **lazy lob** *n.* [20C+] a semi-erect penis.

lob *n.*[4] [racing *lob*, a horse that is bound to lose] [1920s–30s] (*US*) a waste of time; something fated to fail.

lob *n.*[5] *see* LOBBY-GOW *n.*

lob *v.* [16C–18C SE] [early 19C] to droop, to allow to hang heavily.

IN PHRASES

❑ **lob in** *v.* [SE *lob*, to move heavily or clumsily] **1** [20C+] (*Aus.*) to arrive, to turn up, (of a race horse) to win; thus *lobber*, one who turns up; *lob around*, wait around. **2** [20C+] to commence having sexual intercourse. ❑ **lob off** *v.* [SE *lob*, to move heavily or clumsily] [1910s] (*Aus.*) to go away. ❑ **lob onto** *v.* [? SE *lob*, to throw, usu. clumsily] [1910s+] (*Aus.*) **1** to get hold of or find out through a stroke of luck. **2** to associate oneself with. ❑ **lob out** *v.* [SE *lob*, to throw, usu. clumsily] [1940s+] to hand out.

lobb *n. see under* LOB.

lobby-gow *n.* (*also* **lob**) [SE *lobby* + GOW *n.*[1] (2); Asbury, *Gangs of New York* (1927), suggests Cantonese *Lo Bot Gow*, 'Old White Dog'] [late 19C–1970s] (*US*) **1** (*also* **lobby gob**) a hanger-on, a messenger, a servant, an errand boy, esp. one who frequents or works in an opium den or brothel, or a tourist guide in Chinatown. **2** a Chinese police informer. **3** in fig. use, an insignificant person. **4** a ruffian, a low-class thief.

lobby louse *n.* (*also* **lobby lizard, lobby tart**) [SE *lobby* + -LOUSE *sfx*/-LIZARD *sfx*/TART *n.*] [1930s–60s] (*US*) a person who loiters in hotel lobbies, usu. harassing guests.

lobby-sneak *n.* (*also* **lobby-thief**) [mid-19C–1920s] (*UK Und.*) a thief who enters a house, takes what is easily available and leaves.

lobcock *n.* [SE *lob*, a country bumpkin + COCK *n.*[3] (1)] **1** [16C–19C] a fool. **2** [late 17C+] (*also* **lobprick**) a large, flaccid penis; thus attrib. *lobcock*, flaccid, limp. **3** [18C–19C] a penis suffering from penile strabismus.

lob-crawler *n.* (*also* **lob-sneak**) [LOB *n.*[1] (2) + SE *crawl*] [mid-19C–1930s] (*US*) a thief who specializes in robbing shop tills.

lob-crawling *n.* (*also* **lob-sneaking**) [LOB *n.*[1] (2)+ SE *crawl*] [mid-19C–1900s] (*UK Und.*) the robbery of shop tills.

lobkin *n.* [LIBKEN *n.*] [late 17C–early 19C] a lodging house.

loblolly *n.* [? echoic but note dial. *lob*, to bubble while boiling, esp. of a thick substance like porridge + Devon dial. *lolly*, broth, soup or other food boiled in a pot] **1** [late 16C–mid-19C] a thick gruel, both a peasant and a naut. dish, and also used as a simple medicine. **2** [17C–19C] a bumpkin, a peasant, a boor. **3** [early 19C] (*W.I.*) a weakling. **4** [mid-19C–1940s] (*US*) a mud hole. **5** [20C+] (*US*) a fat person.

lobo *n.* [SE *lobo*, a grey wolf] [1940s] **1** (*US black*) an unattractive woman [synon. for DOG *n.*[2] (9)]. **2** (*US*) an outsider, a loner.

lobprick *n. see* LOBCOCK *n.* (2).

lobs *n.*[1] [? SE *lob*, a country bumpkin] [mid-19C] an under-gamekeeper.

lobs *n.*[2] [Rom. *lavaw*, words] [mid-19C] (*tramp*) talk, conversation.

lobs *n.*[3] *see* LOBSTER *n.*[1] (1a).

lobs! *excl.* [ety. unknown] (*UK juv.*) **1** [mid-19C; 1990s+] (*later use Aus.*) a warning shout that heralds an approaching master. **2** [1910s–20s] a call for truce during a game.

lob-sneak *n. see* LOB-CRAWLER *n.*

lob-sneaking *n. see* LOB-CRAWLING *n.*

lob's pound *n.* [LOB *n.*[1] (1) + SE *pound*, an enclosure] **1** [late 16C–mid-19C] a prison or enclosed space. **2** [17C] the vagina. [note LOB *n.*[3]] **3** [mid-18C–mid-19C] fig. use of sense 1, i.e. trouble, a difficult situation.

lobster *n.*[1] **1** from the colour [orig. f. the full suits of armour worn by the Roundheads in Cromwell's New Model Army (spec. Hazelrigg's cuirassiers); then f. the red coats worn by British soldiers of the period; in phr. the unboiled lobster is blue-black, thus resembling a clergyman's black or policeman's blue garb; the boiled lobster turns red, recalling the soldier's scarlet uniform]. (**a**) [mid-17C–1910s] (*also* **lobs**) a soldier, a marine (who also wears scarlet). (**b**) [mid-19C] a policeman. **2** the slow movements of the crustacean, but note LOB *n.*[2] (2). (**a**) [mid-19C+] (*US*) a slow-witted, awkward or gullible person; a general term of abuse; esp. of a socially inept or foolish person. (**b**) [late 19C–1900s] an older man who gives a younger woman presents and/or money in return for sexual favours. (**c**) [late 19C–1910s] a second-rate racehorse. **3** [late 19C–1900s] the penis. **4** [1970s–80s] (*US black*) a rich person [the role of lobsters as luxury food].

IN COMPOUNDS

❑ **lobster-back** *n.* [early–late 19C] a British soldier. ❑ **lobster-box** *n.* **1** [early–mid-19C] a transport ship. **2** [mid-19C] a military barracks. **3** [1930s] (*US Und.*) a cell in a police station. ❑ **lobster-pot** *n.* **1** [19C] the vagina. **2** [1970s+] (*US gay*) a sailor who subjects himself to anal intercourse. ❑ **lobster shift** *n.* (*also* **lobster-trick**) [the slow pace of the crustacean; i.e. such a shift, usu. between 2:00a.m. and 9:00a.m. is rarely busy] [1920s+] (*US*) a late-night work shift.

IN PHRASES

❑ **boil one's lobster** *v.* [late 18C–early 19C] for a clergyman to become a soldier. ❑ **blue lobster** *n. see* RAW LOBSTER *under* RAW *adj.* ❑ **red lobster** *n.* [many were ex-soldiers] [mid-19C] the Metropolitan Police.

SE in slang uses

IN COMPOUNDS

❑ **lobster-palace society** *n.* [*lobster-palace*, one of the elegant, expensive new restaurants that emerged in New York City at this time, which specialized in lobsters and attracted the rich and famous] [late 19C–1910s] (*US*) the world of wealth if not of social position. ❑ **lobstertails** *n.* [? resemblance, based on colour or shape] [1940s–60s] (*US black*) **1** (*also* **lobstertoes**) a case of venereal disease. **2** a case of body lice.

lobster *n.*[2] [ety. unknown; ? pun on idea of being 'boiled alive'] [1980s+] (*Aus. prison*) a 20-year jail sentence.

loc *n.*[1] [LOCOWEED *n.*] [1990s+] (*US black*) marijuana.

loc *n.*[2] (*also* **lok**) [LOC *adj.*] [1990s+] (*US black*) **1** a street gang member. **2** a friend. **3** a general term of address.

loc *n.*[3]

IN PHRASES

❑ **go loc** *v. see under* LOCS *n.*[2].

loc *adj.* (*also* **lok**) [LOCO *adj.*] [1980s+] (*US black*) **1** crazy, mad, whether because of taking drugs or one's emotional state. **2** armed [the image is of one who, once armed, will do something 'crazy'].

loc *v.* [LOC *n.*[1]] [1990s+] (*US black*) **1** to smoke marijuana. **2** to become intoxicated (as a result of drug use).

local *n.* [1940s] (*UK Und./police*) a jail sentence of less than three years.

local *adj.* [LOCO *adj.*] [1940s+] (*S.Afr.*) eccentric, crazy.

local talent *n.* [SE *local* + TALENT *n.* (1) + pun] [1910s+] the attractive women in a neighbourhood; also used in homosexual context of young men.

local yokel *n.* [1940s+] (*US/Aus.*) a naïve and foolish small-town or country person.

locating *n.* [1920s] getting prospects.

location joke! *excl.* [1980s+] (*US campus*) said of a joke which can only be appreciated within a subscribed group, i.e. 'you had to be there!'.

loced-assed *adj.* [ext. of LOC OUT *v.*] [1990s+] (*US black*) ultra-aggressive, dangerously unbalanced.

lochinvar *n.* [rhy. sl. = *bra*] [2000s] a brassiere.

lock *n.*[1] **1** in senses of SE *lock*, an enclosure. (**a**) [17C–19C] (*also* **padlock**) the vagina. (**b**) [late 17C–mid-19C] (*UK Und.*) a place for storing stolen goods. (**c**) [late 17C–mid-19C] (*UK Und.*) a receiver of stolen goods. (**d**) [mid-19C] (*UK Und.*) the office of a corrupt magistrate. **2** in fig. uses [SE *lock*, a grip or trick in wrestling]. (**a**) [early 18C–mid-19C] a chance; thus *stand a queer lock*, to have a poor chance. (**b**) [late 18C–early 19C] character, e.g. *stand a queer lock*, to bear an indifferent character. (**c**) [late 18C–mid-19C] an occupation, a way of life; thus *cut a lock*, to conduct a way of life. (**d**) [early 19C] a scheme, a plan. (**e**) [1940s+] (*US*) a certainty. (**f**) [1960s+] (*US*) complete control over something. **3** *see* LOCKUP *n.* (3).

IN COMPOUNDS

❑ **lock-picker** *n.* [1940s] (*US Und.*) an abortionist.

IN PHRASES

❑ **lock-all-fast** *n.* [late 17C–late 18C] a receiver of stolen goods. ❑ **lock of (all) locks** *n.* [19C] the vagina. ❑ **on lock** *adj.* [2000s] worked out, under control.

lock *n.*[2] [orig. dial.] [20C+] (*Ulster*) a small quantity, e.g. of food; thus *brave lock*, *quare lock*, a substantial amount.

lock *v.*[1] **1** [1930s+] (*US prison*) to occupy a cell. **2** [1960s+] of a pimp, to ensure a prostitute's fidelity, emotional and economic. **3** [1970s+] (*US Und.*) to imprison.

IN COMPOUNDS

❑ **lockdown** *n.* **1** [1970s+] (*orig. US prison*) an instance of the entire prison population being confined to the cells and deprived of exercise or association. **2** [1990s+] solitary confinement. ❑ **lock-in** *n.* [1990s+] a session of drinking that begins after the public house or bar has officially closed for the night.

IN PHRASES

❑ **lock assholes** *v.* (*also* **lock, lock asses**) [ASSHOLE *n.* (1)/ASS *n.* (2)] [1950s+] (*US*) to fight. ❑ **lock down** *v.* **1** [1970s+] (*US Und.*) to imprison. **2** [1990s+] to place in solitary confinement. ❑ **lock into** *v.* [1960s+] to become part of a plan, a group etc, to join. ❑ **lock off** *v.* [20C+] (*W.I.*) to put a choke-hold on someone's neck in order to immobilize and then rob them; also known as *choke-and-rob*. ❑ **lock one's barn door** *v. see under* BARN *n.*[2]. ❑ **lock on with** *v.* [20C+] (*Aus. juv.*) to fight. ❑ **lock up** *v. see* separate entry.

lock *v.*[2] [LOCKS *n.*] [2000s] to arrange one's hair in a Rastafarian dreadlock style.

locked *adj.* [SE *locked*, i.e. shut off from coherent thought or action] [1970s+] (*Irish*) drunk.

locker *n.*[1] [mid-18C] (*UK Und.*) one who leaves goods at a house in the country or a small town and borrows money on them, pretending that they have been made in London, i.e. that they are valuable.

locker *n.*[2] **1** [19C] the vagina. **2** [mid-19C+] (*US*) the stomach. **3** [1900s–40s] (*US Und.*) a safe.

locker room *n.* [its association with all-male amusements] [1980s+] (*drugs*) isobutyl nitrite, amyl nitrite.

locket *n. see* LUCY LOCKET *n.*

lock lip *n. see* LIP-LOCK *n.* (3).

locks *n.* [abbr. SE *dreadlocks*] [1950s+] (*orig. W.I.*) the long knotted hair that is the best-known and typical badge of Rastafarianism.

IN COMPOUNDS

❑ **locksman** *n.* [1950s+] (*orig. W.I.*) a Rastafarian.

locksmith's daughter *n.* [late 18C–late 19C] a key.

lockup *n.* **1** [early 19C+] (*US*) (*also* **lock-up house**) a jail [20C+ use is SE]. **2** [mid–late 19C] (*UK Und.*) a prisoners' cell in a magistrates court or next to the gallows. **3** [1930s+] (*US Und.*) (*also* **lock**) the punishment cell or cells. **4** [1940s] (*US prison*) a jailer, a warder. **5** [1990s+] (*US*) an arrest.

lock up *v.* **1** [1910s+] (*US*) to be in complete control and thus assured of victory. **2** [1930s] (*US black*) to marry. **3** [1930s–70s] (*US black*) to have under one's complete control, to possess absolutely. **4** [1980s] (*US black*) of a pimp, to secure the services of a given prostitute.

lock-up chovey *n.* [SE *lock up* + CHOVEY *n.*] [early 19C] a covered cart in which travelling hawkers carried their goods around the country. It could be locked to secure the stock.

loco *n.* [Sp. *loco*, insane, crazy] **1** [mid-19C+] (*US*) a lunatic. **2** [mid-19C+] (*US*) madness. **3** [1920s] (*US*) a car, a *locomotive*. **4** [1960s+] (*US teen gang*) a Mexican-American gang member. **5** [1960s+] (*US drugs*) marijuana.

loco *adj.* [abbr. *locoweed*, a narcotic weed that affects cattle in the Southwest US; ult. Sp. *loco*, insane, crazy] [late 19C+] (*orig. US*) insane, crazy.

DERIVATIVES

❑ **locoed** *adj.* **1** [late 19C–1970s] crazy. **2** [1900s] in fig. use, unsteady.

IN COMPOUNDS

❑ **loco duds** *n.* (*also* **loco suit**) [DUDS *n.*[1] (1)/SE *suit*] [1940s] (*US Und.*) a strait jacket.

loco *v.* [LOCO *adj.*] [late 19C+] (*US*) to drive mad.

loco *adv.* [1910s–1950s] (*US*) in a mad manner.

locomo *v.* [LOCOMOTE *v.*] [1990s+] (*US teen*) to leave the area.

locomote *v.* [backform. SE *locomotion*] [mid-19C–1910s] (*US*) to move around from place to place.

locomotive *n.* [? play on SE, i.e. it 'gets one moving'] **1** [mid–late 19C] in pl., the legs. **2** [late 19C–1900s] a winter drink made of Burgundy, curaçao, egg yolks, honey and cloves all heated together. **3** [1900s–50s] (*orig. US campus*) 'a cheer characterized by a slow beginning and a progressive increase in speed and used esp. at school and college sports events' (Webster 1966) [SE since the 1960s].

loc out *v.* [LOC *adj.* (1)] [1980s+] (*US black*) to drive crazy, to make exciting.

DERIVATIVES

❑ **loced out** *adj.* (*also* **loc'd out, loqued out**) [1980s+] (*US black*) **1** crazy, under stress. **2** adopting gang styles.

locoweed *n.* [Sp. *loco*, crazy, the supposed effects of cannabis + *locoweed*, milkvetch, or any other plant of the genus *Oxytropis*, which causes erratic behaviour, impaired coordination and poss. lethargy in livestock] [1920s+] (*US drugs*) marijuana.

locs *n.*[1] [pron. with a long 'o'] [1990s+] (*US black*) a hairstyle for black hair that involves natural curls, usu. twisted or braided over months to create the effect.

locs *n.*[2] (*also* **locos, lokes**) [LOC *adj.* (1); i.e. the image of the sunglass-wearer as tough, dangerous and ready for any action – no matter how 'crazy'] [1990s+] (*orig. US black*) sunglasses.

IN PHRASES

❑ **go loc** *v.* [2000s] to prepare onself for a drive-by shooting by putting on dark glasses and any other form of disguise.

loc up *v.* [LOC *adj.* (1)] [2000s] (*US black*) to go crazy.

locus *n.* [? Sp. *loco*, crazy, i.e. the effects of the drink] **1** [late 17C] anything stupefying; thus (*W.I.*) *locus-ale*, an intoxicating drink made from the scum of the sugar cane. **2** [mid-19C–1950s] (*also* **locust**) a drink, drugged with either laudanum or snuff.

locus *v.* [? rhy. with SE *hocus*, though not proper rhy. sl., or LOCUS *n.*] **1** [mid–late 19C] to trick, to fool. **2** [mid–late 19C] to render a victim unconscious with chloroform, usu. to rob them or carry them aboard a ship in need of crew.

locust *n.*[1] [SE *locust wood*, from which the clubs were made] (*US*) **1** [mid-19C] a policeman. **2** [mid-19C–1930s] a billy club or stick.

locust *n.*[2] **1** [late 19C–1900s] (*UK society*) an extravagant person who throws away any left-overs, rather than saving them for possible reuse. **2** [1970s] (*Aus.*) a tourist.

loddy *n.* [abbr.] [early 19C] laudanum or tincture of opium.

lodger *n.* **1** [mid–late 19C] the penis. **2** [mid–late 19C] an unimportant, insignificant person. **3** [late 19C–1910s] in pl., head lice, rats and mice, any kind of vermin. **4** [1990s+] a baby in the womb.

lodgings *n.* **1** [19C] the vagina. **2** [1940s–50s] (*Aus.*) prison.

lodging-slum *n.* [SE *lodging* + SLUM *n.*[2] (3)] [early 19C] (*UK Und.*) the hiring of expensive lodgings with the intention of stealing the furniture etc that one finds there.

loft *n.* [1900s] (*US*) the head.

lofter *n.* [ety. unknown; ? link to SE *loft* but why?] [mid-19C] (*US Und.*) the very lowest class of prostitute.

lofty *n.* [20C+] a nickname for either a very tall or a very short man.

log *n.* [visual or fig. uses of SE *log*] **1** [mid-19C+] a stupid person. **2** [1930s–50s] (*US drugs*) an opium pipe. **3** [1930s+] a piece of excrement. **4** [1950s] (*Aus.*) a large person. **5** [1960s] (*US*) a bar counter [the wood from which it is constructed]. **6** [1960s+] (*US*) the penis. **7** [1970s+] (*US drugs*) phencyclidine [? sense 2 above]. **8** [2000s] an erection.

IN PHRASES

❑ **flog the log** *v.* (*also* **slog the log**) [1950s+] to masturbate. ❑ **go up a log** *v.* [the activity of a snake or lizard] [1910s+] (*Aus.*) to hide. ❑ **log of wood** *n.* [mid-19C+] (*Aus.*) a dull, stupid person; thus *log of ebony*, a stupid black person. ❑ **sink the log** *v. see under* SINK *v.*

loge *n.* [Fr. *horloge*, watch] [late 17C–mid-19C] (*UK Und.*) a watch.

IN PHRASES

❑ **vid loge** *n.* [? Lat. *video*, I look at; Partridge suggests Fr. *vide*, empty, hollow] [mid-18C] a repeating watch.

loges *n.* [Gk *logos*, a word] [17C] (*UK Und.*) a faked pass or warrant.

logey *n.* [SE *log*] [20C+] (*Irish*) a heavy, fat person.

loggerhead *n.* [post-18C use is US, f. SE *logger*, something heavy or clumsy + -HEAD *sfx* (1)] [late 16C+] a fool, a dullard.

DERIVATIVES

❑ **logger-headed** *adj.* [late 16C–early 19C] stupid, dull.

IN PHRASES

❑ **go/come to loggerheads** *v.* [20C+ use is SE] [early 17C–19C] to (get into a) fight.

logie *n.* [theatre jargon *logie*, prop jewels, made mainly of zinc, invented by one David *Logie*] [mid-19C] sham jewellery.

logi-logi *n.* (*also* **logo-logo**) [? SE *log*] [1950s] (*W.I.*) a stupid, oafish person.

log-juice *n.* [the use of SE *logwood* (used in dyeing and in medicine as astringent) to adulterate port] [mid-19C] a cheap port wine.

logs, the *n.* [1910s] (*Aus.*) a lock-up, a prison.

logy *adj.* [US regional *logy*, slow, lethargic, stupid, ult. synon. dial. *louggy, loogy*] **1** [1910s–20s] (*US*) tipsy. **2** [1980s+] (*US drugs*) lethargic after smoking cannabis.

loid *n.* [abbr.] [1950s+] cellu*loid* or a piece of plastic, such as a credit card, used to slip open Yale-style locks when housebreaking.

loid *v.* [LOID *n.*] [1950s+] to open a lock by means of a strip of celluloid.

loiter *n.* [1970s] (*Aus. Und.*) a charge of loitering with intent to commit a felony.

lok *see under* LOC.

lokes *n. see* LOCS *n.*[2].

loksh *n. see* LUKSHEN *n.*

lolapaloosa *n. see* LALLAPALOOSA *n.*

lolla *n.* (*also* **lala, la-la, lal-lah, lallah, lu lu**) [ety. unknown; ? abbr. of LALLAPALOOSA *n.*, but note Grose (1785): 'LOLL, a mother's loll, a favourite child'] [late 19C+] (*US*) something or someone outstanding in some way, whether good, stylish or pleasing, or occas. with negative connotations.

lollapalo/lollapaloosa/lollapalooza *n. see* LALLAPALOOSA *n.*

lollie boy *n.* [SAusE *lolly boy*, 'one who sells refreshments from a tray at a cinema, sports ground, etc' (*AND*)] **1** [late 19C] (*Aus.*) someone or something unimportant. **2** [2000s] (*N.Z.*) a politician's 'gofer'.

lollied *adj.* [? LOLLIPOP *v.*[1]] [1960s–70s] informed against, betrayed to the police.

lollies *n.* [abbr. SE *lollipop*] **1** [mid-19C+] (*Aus.*) all sweets, except for ice lollies. **2** [20C+] the female breasts [they can, like a sweet, be sucked].

lolligag *v. see* LALLYGAG *v.*

lollion *n.* [? SE *loll*] [20C+] (*Ulster*) a fat, clumsy person.

lollipop *n.*[1] [all are 'sweet'] **1** in senses of 'sweetness'. (**a**) [mid-19C–1980s] a woman, esp. an attractive one. (**b**) [20C+] (*also* **lolly**) one's special favourite, the prize article in a collection.

(**c**) [1910s] (*Aus.*) anything easy [play on SWEET *adj.*[1] (3)]. (**d**) [1910s+] (*orig. US*) one's sweetheart, usu. used as a term of affection. (**e**) [1920s+] (*US*) an effeminate man or a homosexual. **2** in sense of that which is sucked or a play on SUCKER *n.*[1] (3a). (**a**) [late 19C+] the penis. (**b**) [1910s+] (*orig. Aus., later US black*) a gullible person who has been 'sucked', i.e. taken advantage of. (**c**) [1940s+] (*also* **pop**) the penis or vagina in the context of oral sex. (**d**) [1950s–60s] an older man who is happy to indulge a younger woman, whether or not he receives any favours in return. (**e**) [1970s] the female breast.

IN COMPOUNDS

❑ **lollipop stop** *n.* [1980s+] (*US gay*) a lavatory, esp. one where one can get quick, anonymous sex.

lollipop *n.*[2] (*also* **lolly, lollypop**) [rhy. sl.] [20C+] **1** a police officer [COP *n.*[1] (1)]. **2** a shop. **3** a monetary tip [DROP *n.*[6] (1)].

lollipop *v.*[1] (*also* **lolly-pop**) [rhy. sl. = SHOP *v.*[1] (2)] [20C+] to inform, to betray.

lollipop *v.*[2] [LOLLIPOP *n.*[1] (2b)] [1950s+] (*US black*) to take advantage of someone.

lollop *n.* (*also* **lollophead**) [LOLLOP *v.*] [mid-19C–1910s] an insignificant, lazy person.

lollop *adj.* [mid-19C] (*UK Und.*) lazy.

lollop *v.* [SE *loll*] [mid-18C+] to lounge, to sprawl.

DERIVATIVES

❑ **lollopy** *adj.* [mid-19C+] lazy.

lolloper *n.* [LOLLOP *v.*] **1** [late 19C+] a lazy, idle or slow person. **2** [1910s+] (*US*) anything or anyone exceptional in quality, size, character etc; as adj., *lolloping*.

lollophead *n. see* LOLLOP *n.*

lollpoop *n. see* LOLPOOP *n.*

lolly *n.*[1] [SE *loll*; orig. boxing use] [early 19C+] the head [20C use is Aus.].

IN PHRASES

❑ **do the lolly** *v.* (*also* **do one's lolly, hit the lolly**) [1940s+] (*Aus.*) to lose one's temper, to lose control of one's emotions or senses. ❑ **sweet as a lolly** *adj. see* SWEET AS (A) NUT *under* SWEET *adj.*[1].

lolly *n.*[2] [? SE *lollipop*] [late 19C] (*US Und.*) a child.

lolly *n.*[3] [LOLLIPOP *n.*[1]] (*Aus. Und.*) **1** [1910s–50s] anything very simple to do or understand. **2** [1920s+] a fool, a dupe.

lolly *n.*[4] [? rhy. sl. *lollipop* = cop = copper] [1940s+] money.

IN COMPOUNDS

❑ **lolly night** *n.* [2000s] (*N.Z.*) the evening of pay day, which brings with it the expectation of picking up a sexual partner.

lolly *n.*[5] *see* LOLLIPOP *n.*[1] (1b).

lolly *n.*[6] *see* LOLLIPOP *n.*[2].

lollycooler *n.* (*also* **lallycooler**) [late 19C+] (*US*) someone or something successful, admirable.

lollygag *see under* LALLYGAG.

lollygog *n. see* LALLYGAG *n.* (2).

lollypalooza/lollypaloozer *n. see* LALLAPALOOSA *n.*

lollypop *n. see* LOLLIPOP *n.*[2].

lolly-pop *v. see* LOLLIPOP *v.*[1].

lollypop court *n.* [1950s] (*US juv*) a juvenile court.

lolly scramble *n.* [SNZE *lolly scramble*, the tossing of a handful of *lollies*, i.e. sweets, for children to grab] [1960s+] (*N.Z.*) an undignified struggle, for money, power, influence, fame etc.

lolly (up) *v.* [rhy. sl. *lollipop* = SHOP *v.*[1] (2)] [1930s+] to inform to the police, or prison authorities.

lollywater *n.* [SE *lollipop* + *water*] [20C+] (*Aus./N.Z.*) a non-alcoholic drink.

lo-lo *n.* [? DOWN LOW *n.*] [2000s] (*US teen*) a state of secrecy.

lolo *n.* [? LOWRIDER *n.*[2]] [1990s+] (*US black*) **1** a lowrider automobile. **2** a member of a gang.

lolpoop *n.* (*also* **lollpoop**) [SE *loll*] [late 17C–early 19C] 'a lazy, idle drone' (B.E.).

lolpoop *v.* [LOLPOOP *n.*] [late 17C–18C] to idle, to laze around.

lombard *n.* [an acronymic pun on the 17C Lombards, natives of Lombardy who provided Europe, including London, with its leading bankers. One of a rash of acronyms coined during the mid-1980s, *lombard* described many of the newly rich young men who populated the City of London] [1980s+] *loads/lots of money but a right/real dickhead.*

Lombard fever *n.* [dial. *lomber*, to idle. The *OED* links the term to dial. *fever-lurden, fever-lurgan, fever-lurgy, fever-largie*, all meaning the same] [late 17C–early 19C] idleness, indolence, laziness, 'the idles' (Grose, 1785).

Lombard Street to a china orange *phr.* (*also* **Lombard Street to a Brummagem sixpence, ...to an eggshell, ...to ninepence; one hundred pounds to a China orange**) [Lombard Street, a centre of London banking since the 12C + SE *china orange*. The sweet orange (*Citrus aurantium*) was first sold in London in the mid-17C and by the 19C it was used figuratively to mean anything of minimal value. The bet wagers the wealth that is available in the street's banks against the almost valueless orange] [mid-18C+] the longest possible odds, an absolute certainty.

London *n.*

SE in slang uses

IN COMPOUNDS

❑ **London fog** *n.* **1** [1910s] a dog [rhy. sl.]. **2** [1960s+] (*Aus.*) any manual worker who does not perform their share of the work [such a person 'will not lift']. ❑ **London ivy** *n.* [both tend to obscure what they 'grow on'] [late 19C] **1** dust. **2** fog. ❑ **London jemmy/jimmy** *n. see* JEMMY *n.*[3]. ❑ **London ordinary** *n.* [*London* (i.e. trippers) + SE *ordinary*, 'a public meal regularly provided at a fixed price in an eating-house or tavern; also, formerly, the company frequenting such a meal, the 'table'' *OED*] [mid-19C] Brighton beach, 'where the "eight-hours-at-the-seas-side" excursionists dine in the open air' (Hotten 1864). ❑ **London particular** *n.* **1** [19C] a type of Madeira wine, imported especially for London merchants. **2** [mid–late 19C] a London fog or smog [? the pale yellow colour of sense 1 or the image of such a fog appearing only in London]. ❑ **London taxi** *n.* [rhy. sl. = JACKSIE *n.*[1] (1)] [20C+] the anus.

IN PHRASES

❑ **London to a brick** [BRICK *n.* (3a)] [1960s+] (*Aus.*) a certainty, the longest possible odds.

Londonderry *n.* [rhy. sl.] [20C+] sherry.

Londrix *n.* [? Fr. *Londres*, London] [mid-19C] London.

lone duck *n.* (*also* **lone dove, quiet mouse**) [late 19C–1900s] a former 'kept woman' who is now a common prostitute and works either from her own room or in a house of assignation.

lone hand *n.* [1920s–30s] (*US Und.*) a thief who operates alone.

lonely *adj.*

SE in slang uses

IN COMPOUNDS

❑ **lonely art** *n.* [apart from its obvious connotations, note the pun on 'lonely heart'] [20C+] masturbation. ❑ **lonelyhearts** *n.* [20C+] (*US prison*) **1** prisoners who maintain a correspondence with people outside prison. **2** men who write letters to female inmates.

IN PHRASES

❑ **lonely as a bastard on Father's Day** *adj.* (*also* **solitary as a bastard on Father's Day**) [1960s+] (*Aus.*) extremely lonely. ❑ **lonely in the weather** *n.* [their head is 'in the clouds'] [1950s] (*W.I.*) a tall, thin person. ❑ **on one's lonely** (*also* **by one's lonely**) [late 19C–1930s] by oneself.

lone ranger *n.* [rhy. sl. = DANGER *n.*] [1990s+] a chance, an opportunity.

lonesome pine *n.* [1990s+] (*UK Und.*) a solitary, eccentric prisoner.

lone star *n.* [1910s] (*US Und.*) a criminal who works independently of a gang.

lone wolf *n.* **1** [1900s–70s] (*orig. US police/Und.*) a criminal (or 'civilian') who works alone, not necessarily a recluse, but not permitting anyone to penetrate their façade [thus SE use, a solitary person, usu. male]. **2** [1950s] (*US prison*) one who does not enter a sexual relationship.

lone wolf *v.* [LONE WOLF *n.*] [1930s–60s] (*orig. US*) to live or act alone; often with *it.*

long *n.* **1** [1930s–40s] (*US*) a long-barrelled revolver; thus *long cut short*, a sawn-off revolver [abbr.]. **2** [1980s+] (*US black*) money [abbr. LONG GREEN *n.* (1)]. **3** [1990s+] (*US*) $1000 [LONG GREEN *n.* (1)].

long *adj.* **1** [mid-18C+] of numbers, large; thus *long odds*, high odds; *long price*, a high price; *long purse*, riches; *long shillings*, good wages. **2** [mid-19C+] (*orig. US Stock Exchange*) abundant, esp. of money. **3** [mid-19C+] (*UK Und.*) a general intensifier, implying the extreme of a type. **4** [1910s+] (*Und.*) used to describe a prisoner who still has most of their sentence to serve. **5** [1950s+] (*US drugs*) of a drug addiction, severe; thus a *long jones*, a severe habit. **6** [1990s+] (*US black*) financially successful.

IN COMPOUNDS

❑ **long bread** *n.* (*also* **long cash, ...dough**) [BREAD *n.*[1] (2)] [1940s+] (*orig. US black*) a large amount of money. ❑ **long dollars** *n.* [1990s+] high-denomination bills. ❑ **long green** *n.* *see* separate entry. ❑ **long 'un** *n.* (*also* **long one**) [1960s+] £100 or £1000.

IN PHRASES

❑ **ain't long enough** *adj.* [1970s+] (*US black*) of money, not enough, insufficient.

SE in slang uses

IN COMPOUNDS

❑ **long belly** *see* separate entries. ❑ **long-bench** *n. see* LONG METER below. ❑ **long bit** *n. see under* BIT *n.*[1]. ❑ **long beer** *n.* [mid-19C+] a glass of beer or a soft drink, as opposed to wine or spirits. ❑ **long clay** *n.* [mid-19C] a churchwarden pipe. ❑ **long-cock** *adj. see under* COCK *n.*[4]. ❑ **long con** *n.* [opposite of SHORT CON *n.*] [1930s+] (*orig. US Und.*) any confidence trick or cheat that is carefully planned for perfect execution. ❑ **long cork** *n.* [the length of cork used for such wine] [late 18C–early 19C] claret. ❑ **long dedger** *n.* [Ital. *undici*, eleven] [mid-19C+] (*Ling. Fr./Polari*) the number eleven. ❑ **long dick** *v. see under* DICK *v.*[2]. ❑ **long draw** *n. see* DRAW *n.*[2] (1). ❑ **long drop** *n.* [1970s+] (*N.Z./S.Afr.*) an outdoor privy. ❑ **long ear/eared/ears** *see* separate entries. ❑ **long end** *n. see under* END *n.* ❑ **long-eye** *n.* **1** [mid–late 19C; 1970s] the vagina. **2** [20C+] (*W.I.*) a promiscuous woman. **3** [20C+] (*W.I.*) greed, covetousness; thus *put one's long eye on, throw long eye on*, to covet, to desire for oneself. ❑ **long-faced one** *n.* (*also* **longnosed chum**) [late 19C–1920s] a horse. ❑ **long fifteen** *n.* [ety. unknown] [early 17C] 'some class of lawyers' (*OED*). ❑ **long firm** *n.* (*also* **l.f.**) [mid-19C+] (*UK Und.*) a fraudulent scheme whereby a firm is set up, small orders placed and paid for to establish good credit, then a massive order is made, its contents quickly sold off, often below par, and the firm vanishes, the warehouse is shut down and the debt, this time huge, is never paid. ❑ **long-foot** *adj.* [20C+] (*W.I.*) long-legged. ❑ **long ghost** *adj.* [mid-19C–1900s] a tall, awkward person. ❑ **long-gone** *adj.* [mid-19C] (*UK Und.*) serving a life sentence in prison. ❑ **long goodbye** *adj.* [the title of a Raymond Chandler novel publ. in 1953] [1950s+] death. ❑ **long grain rice** *n.* [similar shape, if different size] [1940s–50s] (*W.I.*) boiled green banana. ❑ **long gut** *n. see* LONG BELLY *n.* ❑ **long guts** *adj. see* LONG-BELLY *adj.* ❑ **longhair/haired** *see* separate entries. ❑ **long handlebars** *n.* (*also* **handlebars, longhandlers**) [var. on LONG JOHNS *n.*] [20C+] (*US*) long underwear. ❑ **long handles** *n.* (*also* **long-handled underwear**) [late 19C *long-handled hose*; var. on LONG JOHNS *n.*] [1920s+] (*Can./US*) long woollen winter underwear, combinations. ❑ **long-head/-headed** *see* separate entries. ❑ **long heel** *n.* [supposed physiological characteristic] [1950s+] (*US, mainly Southern*) a black person. ❑ **long house** *n.* [a typical brothel of the period had a long central corridor with a number of small bedrooms arranged along either side] [1900s–40s] (*US black*) a brothel. ❑ **long-jaw** *n.* [their jaw drops open at all the sights] [1980s] (*Aus.*) a tourist. ❑ **long john(s)** *see* separate entries. ❑ **long jump** *n.* [1920s–60s] a hanging; thus *take the long jump*, to be hanged; *in for the long jump*, destined for/in trouble. ❑ **long lady** *n.* [late 19C] a farthing candle. ❑ **long lane** *n.* [mid-19C] the vagina. ❑ **long lick** *n.* [late 19C–1920s] (*Aus.US*) molasses. ❑ **long meg** *n.* [proper name of a celebrated 17C woman, *Long Meg* of Westminster] [mid-17C–early 19C] an exceptionally tall woman; thus *as long as Meg of Westminster*. ❑ **long meter** *n.* (*also* **long-bench**) [? *long meet her*, i.e. one who won't go away/one who sits next to you on the *bench* and will not leave] [20C+] (*W.I.*) a boring, long-winded speaker. ❑ **long-mouth** *n.* **1** [20C+] (*W.I.*) a glutton, one who is constantly hungry. **2** [1950s+] (*W.I.*) a boring, long-winded speaker. **3** [1980s+] (*W.I.*) a liar. ❑ **long neck** *n.* [late 19C+] (*Aus.*) a camel. ❑ **long nine** *n.* [? nine inches long] [mid–late 19C] (*US*) a cigar; also *long eighteen* (if extra long). ❑ **long-nose** *n.* **1** [1900s–1940s] a Jew, thus *long-nosed*, Jewish. **2** [1910s] (*Aus.*) a general term of abuse to one seen as greedy. **3** [1920s] (*US*) an upper-class person, an aristocrat. ❑ **longnosed chum** *n. see* LONG-FACED ONE above. ❑ **long on** *adj.* [20C+] well supplied with, expert in. ❑ **long one** *n. see* separate entry. ❑ **long out** *v.* [20C+] (*W.I.*) to purse one's lips or stick out one's tongue in a gesture of deliberate rudeness. ❑ **long paddock** *n.* [1920s+] (*Aus./N.Z.*) the road. ❑ **long rod** *n. see under* ROD *n.* ❑ **long shoe(s)** *see* separate entries. ❑ **long shot** *see* separate entries. ❑ **long-sleeved top** *n.* (*also* **long-sleeved hat**) [late 19C–1910s] a silk hat. ❑ **long-sleever** *n.* [note 1902 *Bulletin* (Sydney) 18 Oct. 14/4 'T.A.D.': 'Anyone know the true derivation of the phrase 'long-sleever' as applied to beer. Heard, the other day, that Bishop Barker (consecrated to the Sydney see in 1854) was fond of his long beer. Hence Sydney's barmaids were asked for a 'lawn-sleever, please,' as a compliment to 'His Lordship.' That degenerated into 'long-sleever.' ['Long-sleever' comes from the resemblance between a pint-pot and a 'long-sleeved hat.' A 'long beer' used to be called in Sydney a 'Bishop Barker' – the bishop was a very tall man.'] [late 19C+] (*Aus.*) a drinking glass of the largest size. ❑ **long spit** *n. see* BIG SPIT *n.* ❑ **longstall** *n.* [1940s] (*S.Afr. Und.*) a lookout. ❑ **long-stem** *n.* [1910s] (*US drugs*) an opium pipe. ❑ **long stomach** *n.* [late 18C–early 19C] **1** a voracious appetite. **2** a greedy eater. ❑ **long-stopper** *n.* [1990s+] (*Aus. Und.*) a lookout. ❑ **long strokes** *n.* [as opposed to SHORT STROKES *n.*] [20C+] the initial stage of sexual intercourse. ❑ **long tail/-tailed** *see* separate entries. ❑ **long tea** *n.* [19C] (*UK juv.*) urine. ❑ **long tickey** *n.* *see under* TICKEY *n.* ❑ **longtimer** *n.* [20C+] (*US prison*) a prisoner with a very long sentence. ❑ **long tog** *n. see under* TOG *n.* ❑ **long tom** *n. see* separate entry. ❑ **long-tongue/-tongued** *see* separate entry. ❑ **long town** *n.* [? its geographical dimension] [19C] (*Anglo-Irish*) London. ❑ **long 'un** *n.* **1** [late 19C–1900s] a pheasant [the length of its tail]. **2** [late 19C+] a tall person. ❑ **long underwear** *n. see* separate entry. ❑ **long 'uns** *n. see* LONG JOHNS *n.* ❑ **long white roll** *n.* [1940s] (*US black*) a cigarette. ❑ **long-winded** *adj. see* separate entry. ❑ **long word** *n.* [mid-19C+] any statement that implies a long time, e.g. *never is a long word.*

IN PHRASES

❑ **as long as one's arm** *adj.* (*also* **as long as a rainy Sunday**) [mid-17C+] extensive, substantial. ❑ **long drink of water** *n.* (*also* **lanky drink of cactus juice**) [Scot. *drink*, a lanky overgrown person; ult. ON *drengr*, a young, unmarried man] [1910s+] a very thin person. ❑ **long in the arm** *see under* ARM *n.* ❑ **long out one's eye** *v.* [20C+] (*W.I.*) to be covetous for. ❑ **the long drop** *n. see* DROP, THE *n.*

long *adv.* [1990s+] (*US*) abundantly.

long acre *n.* [rhy. sl.] **1** [mid–late 19C] a baker. **2** [mid–late 19C] a newspaper.

long and linger *n. see* LEAN AND LINGER *n.*

long and short *n.* [rhy. sl.] [20C+] port (wine).

long-and-shorts *n.* [mid-19C] (*UK Und.*) cards used for cheating.

longas *n.* [? SE *long* +ARSE *n.*] [1950s] (*W.I.*) a very tall man.

long belly *n.* (*also* **long gut**) **1** [1920s] (*US*) a hunger for narcotics. **2** [1950s] (*W.I.*) a greedy person.

long-belly *adj.* (*also* **long-guts**) [LONG BELLY *n.*] [1950s] (*W.I.*) gluttonous, greedy, usu. of a man or a child.

long ear *n.* **1** [mid-19C] a clever person. **2** [mid–late 19C] (*US campus*) a sober, religious student. **3** [1930s–50s] (*US*) an eavesdropper.

long-eared *adj.* [a donkey's long ears] **1** [1910s–50s] stupid. **2** [1950s] eavesdropping.

long-eared chum *n.* [1960s] (*US*) a mule.

longears *n.* [late 19C–1960s] (*US*) a mule, a donkey.

longer and linger *n. see* LEAN AND LINGER *n.* (1).

longers *n. see* LONGIES *n.* (1).

long green *n.* [LONG *adj.* (2) + the colour of dollar bills/marijuana] **1** [late 19C+] (*US*) money, paper money, esp. in large amounts. **2** [1960s] (*US drugs*) a kind of marijuana [GREEN *n.*[2] (3)].

longhair *n.* **1** [mid-19C–1900s] (*US West*) a name for early settlers who wore their hair long. **2** backform. f. LONGHAIRED *adj.* (1). (**a**) [1920s+] (*orig. US*) an intellectual or artist or musician. (**b**) [1930s] (*US*) a moral reformer. (**c**) [1930s+] (*US*) a performer or aficionado of classical music. (**d**) [1950s+] (*US*) classical music. **3** [1960s+] (*US*) a HIPPIE *n.*[2] (3) or a politically liberal person.

longhaired *adj.* [stereotyped image of an intellectual as bearded, sandalled and hirsute] **1** [late 19C+] (*orig. US*) (*also* **longhair**) intellectual, aesthetic, always pej.; thus *longhaired music*, classical music, etc. **2** [1910s–70s] (*esp. milit.*) of a man, female-looking; as in *longhaired bunkie*, a longhaired buddy. **3** [1960s+] HIPPIE *adj.*, politically liberal.

IN COMPOUNDS

❑ **long-haired chum** *n.* (*also* **long-haired mate, ... one**) [play on milit. *long-eared chum*, a mule; note Texas prison *long-haired people*, one's family and loved ones] **1** [late 19C] a horse. **2** [late 19C–1960s] a young woman, a girlfriend.

long-head *n.* [backform. LONG-HEADED *adj.* (1)] [late 18C–1900s] (*US*) an astute, shrewd person.

long-headed *adj.* [fig. use of SE] **1** [late 17C+] discerning, shrewd. **2** [late 19C+] obstinate.

longhorn *n.* [the *longhorn* cattle that were found in Texas] [late 19C–1960s] (*US/mainly West*) a tough, Texan old-timer or cowboy.

longies *n.* **1** [1910s+] (*also* **longers, longs**) long trousers. **2** [1940s+] (*orig. US*) long woollen winter underwear, combinations.

long it *v.* [2000s] to take time, to delay.

long john *n.* [the necessity of removing one's LONG JOHNS *n.* (1)] [2000s] (*N.Z.*) an outdoor lavatory.

long johns *n.* (*also* **long-uns**) [1940s+] (*orig. US*) long woollen winter underwear, combinations.

long one *n.* **1** [mid-19C] a pipe, presumably long-stemmed. **2** [late 19C–1900s] (*Aus.*) a tall glass of beer. **3** [late 19C–1900s] (*US*) a horse that is listed at long odds, an outsider [LONG *adj.* (1)]. **4** [1970s+] (*UK Und.*) a long prison sentence. **5** *see* LONG 'UN *under* LONG *adj.*

IN PHRASES

❑ **put the long ones in** *v.* [the long strides of one who is running away] [1980s+] (*Aus. prison*) to escape.

SE in slang uses

IN PHRASES

❑ **long one with many links** *n.* [1940s] (*US black*) a long key chain, worn with a ZOOT SUIT *n.*

long-pop *n. see* LONG SHOT *n.*[1] (1).

longs *n. see* LONGIES *n.* (1).

longs and broads *n.* [their rectangular shape] [early 19C] cards.

longs-and-shorts *n.* [one or more edges of such cards have been shaved for recognition during a shuffle or deal] [mid-19C] cards purpose-made for cheating.

long-shoe *n.* [the style of footwear preferred by US black pimps at the time] [1950s–80s] (*US black*) **1** a sophisticated, urbane pimp or swindler. **2** as *long-shoe game*, the profession and lifestyle of pimping.

long-shoe *adj.* [LONG-SHOE *n.*] [1950s–70s] (*US black*) pertaining to the world of pimping.

long shoes *n.* [1950s–80s] (*US black*) success; thus *wear long shoes*, to be successful.

longshore lawyer *n.* [SE *longshore*, tough, villainous] [early 19C] a corrupt, ruthless lawyer.

long shot *n.*[1] (*also* **long-pop**) [SE *long* + SHOT *n.*[1] (5b); the inaccuracy of shooting at a distant target, thus a bet laid at long odds on an unlikely contender] [mid-19C+] (*gambling*) a wild guess, an adventurous attempt, a slim chance.

long shot *n.*[2] [1950s–60s] (*UK Und.*) a prostitute's client who spends longer than the usual time — around fifteen minutes — with a client.

long-shot *adj.* [20C+] risky, adventurous.

long tail *n.* [ety. unknown; ? the slow progress of treacle off the spoon] [20C+] (*Aus.*) treacle.

long-tail blue *n.* **1** [early–mid-19C] (*also* **old blue**) a swallowtail jacket, worn by black dandies. **2** [mid–late 19C] the black dandy that wore such a coat.

long-tailed *adj.* [early–late 19C] of a coat, having a long tail.

long-tailed beggar *n.* **1** [mid-19C] a cat [the supposed story of a sailor who came home after his first voyage unable to remember the name of a cat and asked his mother 'What's she called, that 'ere long-tailed beggar?']. **2** [1900s–20s] a large denomination sterling note [LONG-TAILED 'UN *n.*].

long-tailed finnup *n.* [LONG-TAILED 'UN *n.* + FINNIP *n.*] [mid–late 19C] a large denomination sterling note.

long-tailed 'un *n.* [mid-19C+] a large denomination sterling note, £10, £20, £50; thus *long-tailed*, of more than £5 face value.

long tails *n.* [1940s] £5 notes.

long tom *n.* [note naut. *long tom*, a long-barrelled, deck-mounted gun] **1** [mid-19C–1910s] (*US/Aus./N.Z.*) a long-handled shovel. **2** [mid-19C–1960s] a wooden colander trough used in gold hunting, into which men shovelled earth. **3** [late 19C–1900s] the penis. **4** [1930s] (*US prison*) a sawn-off shotgun. **5** [1970s] (*S.Afr.*) a large can of beer.

long-tongue *adj.* [LONG-TONGUED *adj.*] [20C+] (*Irish/W.I.*) talkative, indiscreet.

long-tongued *adj.* [late 16C–1900s] of a chatterer, a gossip, one who is unable to keep a secret; thus *as long-tongued as Granny*. ['Granny was an (actual) ideot (*sic*) who could lick her own eye' (Grose)].

long underwear *n.* [? play on LONGHAIR *n.* (2d)] [1930s–60s] (*US*) jazz music popularized for 'easy listening', also classical music.

IN COMPOUNDS

❑ **long-underwear gang** *n.* [1930s] musicians specializing in 'easy listening' jazz.

long-winded *adj.* **1** [late 17C–mid-19C] used of one who takes a long time to do something, e.g. pay a bill or debt. **2** [1940s+] used of a man (or woman) who takes a long time to reach orgasm.

IN COMPOUNDS

❑ **long-winded paymaster** *n.* [late 17C–early 19C] (*UK Und.*) one who extends lengthy credit.

Lonsdale *n.*

IN PHRASES

❑ **give someone the Lonsdale belt** *v. see* GIVE SOMEONE THE BELT *under* BELT *n.*

lont *n. see* LOON *n.*[1].

Loo, the *n.* (*also* **'Loo**) [abbr.] **1** [1900s–50s] (*Aus.*) Wooloomooloo, a tough, working-class suburb of Sydney. **2** [1940s–70s] (*Aus.*) Borroloola, a town in the Northern Territory, where the majority of the population are native Australians.

loo *n.*[1] (*also* **lou**) [? Fr. *l'eau*, water; the *bordalou*, a portable commode, resembling a sauce boat and carried by 18C ladies in their muff; SE *leeward*, the side of a ship turned away from the wind and as such the side over which one would urinate/defecate; an abbr./pun on *Waterloo*, whether the station or the battle it commemorates] [1930s+] the lavatory.

loo *n.*[2] [US pron. of *loo*-tenant] [1960s+] (*US*) a police or fire lieutenant.

loo *v.* [? the card-game *loo*] [early 19C] (*US*) to cheat, to defraud.

loober *v.* [mid-19C] (*UK prison*) to flog, to thrash.

loocha *n.* (*also* **loocher, lootcha**) [synon. Hind. *luchcha*] [19C] (*Anglo-Ind.*) 'a blackguard libertine, a lewd loafer' (Y&B).

looder *n.* [Irish *liúdar*/Scot. *lowder*, a blow] [late 19C+] (*Irish*) a blow.

looey *n.*[1] (*also* **lieuy, looie, louie**) [echoic] [1970s+] (*US*) **1** a lump of expectorated phlegm. **2** a piece of nasal mucus.

looey *n.*[2] *see* LOOIE *n.*[1].

loof-faker *n.* [backsl. *loof* = flue + FAKER *n.* (1)] [mid-19C] a chimney-sweep.

loogan *n.* (*also* **loogin, lugan**) [? ext. LUG *n.*[2] (1) underpinned by negative racial stereotyping of a concocted 'typical Irish' surname] (*US*) **1** [1910s–60s] a fool, a newcomer. **2** [1930s–40s] a petty crook or ruffian. **3** [1980s] a gun man.

loogee *n. see* LUNGER *n.* (2).

loogie *n.* [var. on LOOEY *n.*[1]] **1** [1980s+] (*US*) a gob of phlegm. **2** *see* BOGEY *n.*[3].

Loogin *n. see* LUGEN *n.*

loogin *n. see* LOOGAN *n.*

looie *n.*[1] (*also* **lieu, lieuy, looey, louie**) [US pron.] [1910s+] (*orig. US milit.*) lieutenant.

looie *n.*[2] *see* LOOEY *n.*[1].

look *v.*

SE in slang uses

IN PHRASES

❑ **cannot look at** [late 19C+] bears no comparison, cannot equal, has no chance of competing with. ❑ **look-at-me** *n.* [2000s] an ostentatious automobile; a limousine. ❑ **look at the ceiling** *v.* [late 19C+] of a woman, to have sexual intercourse in the missionary position. ❑ **look at the maker's name** *v.* (*also* **read the maker's name**) [the name is found on the bottom of an upturned glass] [19C] to drink heavily. ❑ **look at the wall** *v.* [late 17C] of a man, to urinate. ❑ **look for what one ain't put down** *v.* [20C+] (*W.I.*) to be a professional thief. ❑ **look(ing) as if one couldn't help it** [late 18C–early 19C] looking like a fool or simpleton. ❑ **look lively** *v.* [late 19C+] to be drunk. ❑ **look (marlin) spikes at** *v.* (*also* **look pitchforks at**) [SE *marlin spike*, an iron tool tapering to a point, used to separate the strands of rope in splicing] [19C] to glare at, to 'look daggers' at. ❑ **look nine ways for Sunday** *v.* (*also* **look nine ways at thrice**) [16C+] to squint. ❑ **look over the spikes** *v. see under* SPIKE *n.*[1]. ❑ **look seven ways for Sunday** *v.* (*also* **look two ways for Sunday**) [var. on *LOOK NINE WAYS FOR SUNDAY* above] [early 19C+] **1** to squint. **2** in fig. use, to be seriously upset or disturbed. **3** to be physically askew. ❑ **look snappy** *v. see under* SNAPPY *adj.*[1]. ❑ **look through a glass** *v.* [19C] to be drunk. ❑ **look towards** *v.* [mid–late 19C] to drink a health. ❑ **look upon a hedge** *v.* [17C; 1930s+] to urinate. ❑ **what does it look like?** [1970s] (*US campus*) hello.

IN EXCLAMATIONS

❑ **look slippery!** [late 19C–1920s] (*orig. RN*) hurry up! get on with it! ❑ **look slippy!** (*also* **look slimy!**) [mid-19C+] hurry up! get on with it! ❑ **look story!** *see under* STORY *n.*

lookable *adj.* [1990s+] (*W.I.*) of a woman, attractive.

look-a-here! *excl.* [1910s+] (*US*) an imper. calling on one's attention, esp. before delivering some reprimand or lecture.

lookee here! *excl.* (*also* **look here! looky here! looky there!**) [mid-19C+] an imper. calling on one's attention, esp. before delivering some reprimand or lecture.

looker *n.* (*orig. US*) **1** [late 19C+] an attractive woman; occas. man. **2** [late 19C+] in combs., that which looks in a certain way. **3** [20C+] (*US*) in pl., the eyes. **4** [1970s] a client who wishes only to look at a prostitute, who is usu. naked, and occas. fondle her breasts. **5** [1970s] a voyeur.

lookie-lou *n.* (*also* **looky-loo**) [1980s+] (*US black/campus*) an inquisitive person, a peeping Tom.

look-in *n.* [mid-19C+] **1** a brief visit. **2** a chance, an opportunity, usu. with the implication of ultimate success.

looking glass *n.*[1] [one's reflection in the urine, as well, poss., as the attention paid by contemporary physicians to the urine itself. Thus the 18C riddle: 'Q. Why is a Chamber-Pot call'd a Looking-Glass? A. Because many rarely see their Faces in any other'] [early 17C–mid-19C] a chamberpot.

looking glass *n.*[2] [rhy. sl. = ASS *n.* (2)] [1960s] (*US*) the buttocks, the posterior.

look like... *v.*

IN PHRASES

❑ **look like a monkey fucking a football** *v.* [1960s+] (*US*) to look utterly absurd. ❑ **look like a pox doctor's clerk** *v.* [1930s] to be overdressed. ❑ **look like a wet week** *v. see* LIKE A WET WEEK *under* LIKE A... *phr.* ❑ **look like Brown's cows** *v.* [1970s] (*Aus.*) to act in a straggling, uncoordinated manner. ❑ **look like bull-beef** *v.* [late 17C–early 19C] to look stern, grim and threatening; thus phr. *bluff as bull beef*, stern, intimidating. ❑ **look like death eating a sandwich** *v.* [1940s+] (*US*) to look very ill, very emotional or very tired. ❑ **look like death warmed up** *v.* (*also* **look like death/shit warmed over**) [1930s+] to look extremely ill, usu. very pale; cf. FEEL LIKE DEATH WARMED UP *under* FEEL *v.* ❑ **look like God's revenge against murder** *v.* [late 18C–early 19C] to look furious; later as abbr. *look like murder*. ❑ **look like Jock Blunt** *v.* [early 18C–early 19C] for one's face to betray one's disappointment. ❑ **look like one lost a pound and found a sixpence/a halfpenny** *v.* [19C+] to look notably downcast. ❑ **look like Sunday** *v.* [1910s] to be dressed up. ❑ **look like ten bob in the quid** *v.* [1960s] (*Aus.*) to look miserable. ❑ **look like ten cents up** *v.* [1920s] (*US*) to compare unfavourably. ❑ **look like the ant's pants** *v. see* ANT'S PANTS *n.* (1). ❑ **look like the kookaburra that has swallowed the kangaroo** *v.* [1930s+] (*Aus.*) to look elated, to look very happy.

look-look *v.* [20C+] (*W.I.*) to gaze about in a furtive manner, to peep.

looko *n.* [SE *look* + -O *sfx* (3)] [1950s] (*Aus.*) a glance.

lookout *n.* [mid-19C+] (*orig. US*) a problem, a responsibility; usu. as *that's their lookout*.

looksee *n.* (*also* **look-see, looksie**) [? Anglo-Chinese pidgin] **1** [mid-19C+] a glimpse, a glance. **2** [1920s–60s] (*US*) a doctor's licence to practise.

IN COMPOUNDS

❑ **look-see man** *n.* [1920s] (*US*) a tourist or sightseer.

looksee *v.* [mid-19C+] (*orig. US*) to make an inspection, to have a look, to glance at.

look-up *n.* [backform. f. LOOK UP *v.*[1]] [mid-19C+] a brief visit.

look up *v.*[1] [late 18C+] to visit.

look up *v.*[2] [early 19C+] (*orig. commercial*) usu. of a situation, to improve, to be getting better.

looky here! *excl. see* LOOKEE HERE! *excl.*

looky-loo *n. see* LOOKIE-LOU *n.*

looky there! *excl. see* LOOKEE HERE! *excl.*

loolah *n.* [1990s+] a crazy person.

looloo/looly *n. see* LULU *n.*[1] (2).

loom *n.* [euph.] [mid-17C–18C] the vagina.

loon *n.*[1] (*also* **lont**) [SE *lunatic*; ult. Lat. *luna*, moon; such people are supposedly 'moonstruck'. Note mid-15C+ SE *loon*, a worthless person, a rogue, an idler] [late 18C+] a fool, an idiot.

loon *n.*[2] [1980s] (*Aus.*) a pimp.

loon (about/off) *v.* [LOON *n.*[1]] [1960s+] to act crazily or irresponsibly; as *n.* a wild time.

IN COMPOUNDS

❑ **loon pants** *n.* (*also* **loons**) [1970s+] trousers with enormous flared bottoms, esp. beloved of early 1970s hippies.

looney *n. see* LOONY *n.*

looney *adj. see* LOONY *adj.*

looney tune *n.* (*also* **looney tunes**) [*Looney Tunes*, the series of film cartoons created for Warner Bros. by the team of Hollywood animators Hanna-Barbera and released 1930–69, then shown on TV from 1950s; the term was popularized by another Hollywood figure, Ronald Reagan, to describe such figures as Libyan leader Colonel Gaddafi] [1950s+] **1** a crazy person, a lunatic. **2** a cartoon.

looney tune *adj.* (*also* **loony-tune, loony-tunes**) [LOONEY TUNE *n.*] [1960s+] insane, irrational.

loonie *n.*[1] [the representation of a *loon* or diver on its reverse] [1980s+] (*Can.*) the Can. $1 coin, introduced in 1987.

loonie *n.*[2] *see* LOONY *n.*

loon pants/loons *n. see under* LOON (ABOUT/OFF) *v.*

loonslate *n.* (*also* **loonslatt**) [? LOON *n.*[1] + SLAT *n.*[2] (1); lit. 'a fool's half-crown'] [late 17C–early 19C] one shilling and one penny-halfpenny, 1s 1½d.

loony *n.* (*also* **looney, loonie, lunie, luny**) [SE *lunatic*; or LOON *n.*[1]] [mid-19C+] (*orig. US*) a fool, an eccentric, a mad person.

IN COMPOUNDS

❑ **loony bin** *n.* (*also* **looney bin**) **1** [1910s+] a psychiatric institution. **2** [1970s+] in ext./fig. use, a chaotic place, a 'madhouse'. ❑ **loony doctor** *n.* [1920s+] a psychoanalyst, a psychiatrist.

IN PHRASES

❑ **do a loony** *v.* [1990s+] (*UK juv.*) to lose one's temper, to become hysterical.

loony *adj.* (*also* **looney, luny**) [LOONY *n.*] **1** [mid-19C+] (*orig. US*) eccentric, insane, foolish, pertaining to psychiatry. **2** [1970s+] (*US campus*) intoxicated.

IN COMPOUNDS

❑ **loony bird** *n.* [BIRD *n.*[1] (3a)] [1960s–70s] (*US*) a crazy person. ❑ **loony farm** *n.* [1970s] (*US*) a psychiatric institution. ❑ **loony house** *n.* [1930s+] (*US*) a psychiatric institution. ❑ **loony pen** *n.* [1980s+] (*US*) a psychiatric institution. ❑ **loony roost** *n.* [1940s] (*US*) a psychiatric institution. ❑ **loony-tune/-tunes** *adj. see* LOONEY TUNE *adj.*

loop *n.*[1] [backform. f. LOOPY *adj.* (1)] [1940s–50s] (*Aus.*) a fool.

loop *n.*[2] **1** [1980s+] a fig. circle of information; usu. in phr. *in the loop/out of the loop*. **2** [1990s+] a pornographic film. **3** [2000s] (*US black*) sex involving several males and a single female.

IN PHRASES

❑ **out of the loop** [1980s+] (*US teen*) not in on a secret, or unaware of what's going on.

SE in slang uses

IN PHRASES

❑ **put the loop on** *v.* [image of a lasso] [1920s] (*US*) to capture. ❑ **throw for a loop** *v.* [var. on *KNOCK FOR A LOOP under* KNOCK *v.*] [1960s+] to disturb one, to worry one considerably, to put one off one's stride.

loop *v.*[1] [SE *loop*, i.e. one's drunken meandering] [1920s+] (*US*) to go on a drinking spree; thus phr. *go on a loop*.

loop *v.*[2] [SE *loop*, to walk around in a circle] **1** [1960s] (*S.Afr.*) to run off. **2** [1980s] to be a caddie.

looped *adj.* (*also* **looped out, looped up**) [one is 'going round in circles'] (*US*) **1** [1930s+] drunk. **2** [1960s+] infatuated with something or someone, or crazy, demented. **3** [1980s] (*US drugs*) intoxicated with a drug.

looper *n.*[1] **1** [late 19C] a bullet. **2** [1910s] a punch, a blow.

looper *n.*[2] [LOOP *v.*[2]] [1980s] a caddie.

looper *n.*[3] [backf. from LOOPY *adj.* (1)] [1980s+] a crazy, disturbed person.

loopie *n.* (*also* **loopy**) [the 'looping' movement used in swatting sand flies + LOOPY *adj.* (1); i.e. the quality of questions they ask local people] [1970s+] (*N.Z.*) a tourist.

loop-legged *adj.* (*also* **looping**) [1940s+] (*US*) drunk.

loop-o *adj. see* LOOPY *adj.*

loop off *v.* [? SE *lope off*] [early–mid-18C] to run away.

loop-the-loop *n.*[1] (*also* **loopy the loop**) [rhy. sl.; *loopy* is Aus. use] **1** [1920s] (*US*) a ring or hoop. **2** [1940s+] soup.

loop-the-loop *n.*[2] [1960s–70s] mutual oral-genital stimulation.

loopy *n. see* LOOPIE *n.*

loopy *adj.* (*also* **loop-o, loopy-loo**) [? Scot. *loopy*, cunning] **1** [1920s+] (*orig. naut.*) eccentric, crazy. **2** [1990s+] obsessed with, mad about. **3** [1990s+] drunk or drugged.

IN PHRASES

❑ **off one's loop** *adj.* [1940s] eccentric, mad. ❑ **up the loop** *adj.* [1910s–50s] insane, eccentric.

loopy the loop *n. see* LOOP-THE-LOOP *n.*[1].

loor *n. see* LOUR *n.*

loose *n.*

SE in slang uses

IN PHRASES

❑ **make a loose** *v.* [early 18C] to make one's escape.

loose *adj.* **1** [late 19C] of an appointed time, not punctual, round about, e.g. *a loose midday*. **2** [1900s; 1990s+] (*US black*) out of control. **3** [1910s–50s] crazy. **4** [1930s+] (*US campus*) drunk. **5** [1950s+] (*US*) unperturbed, casual, relaxed. **6** [1960s] (*US black*) in possession of money.

IN PHRASES

❑ **get loose** *v.* [1970s+] **1** to relax. **2** to throw some punches; also *get loose on*. **3** to dance, to have fun. ❑ **hang loose** *see* separate entries. ❑ **stay loose** *see* separate entries.

SE in slang uses

IN COMPOUNDS

❑ **loose ball** *n. see under* BALL *n.*[1]. ❑ **loose-bodied gown** *n.* (*also* **loose-kirtle**) [metonymy; thus Nares (1822): 'This being a very customary dress of abandoned women, was sometimes ued as a phrase for such ladies'] [late 16C–17C; mid-19C] a prostitute. ❑ **loose box** *n.* [SE *loose box*, a stall in which a horse can move around freely + pun on euph. *loose woman*] [mid-19C] a brougham or similar vehicle owned by a kept woman or a well-off prostitute. ❑ **loose ends** *n. see under* ENDS *n.*[1]. ❑ **loose fish** *n. see under* FISH *n.*[1]. ❑ **loose house** *n. see LOUSE HOUSE under* LOUSE *n.* ❑ **loose-legged** *adj.* **1** [19C] suffering from diarrhoea. **2** [1960s] (*US*) promiscuous. ❑ **loose link** *n.* [1980s+] (*US black*) an informer. ❑ **loose screw** *n. see under* SCREW *n.*[2]. ❑ **loose wig** *n. see under* WIG *n.*[2]. ❑ **loose-wired/-wiring** *see* separate entries.

IN PHRASES

❑ **have a loose leg** *v.* [20C+] (*Irish*) to be free to live one's life without restraint. ❑ **loose in the bean** *adj. see under* BEAN *n.*[1]. ❑ **loose in the hilt** *adj.* **1** [17C+] suffering from diarrhoea. **2** [mid-17C–early 18C] maritally unfaithful. **3** [mid-18C] drunk. ❑ **loose in the rump** *adj.* (*also* **loose in her rump**) [18C–mid-19C] of a woman, wanton, promiscuous. ❑ **loose up top** *adj.* [*HAVE A SCREW LOOSE under* SCREW *n.*[1]] [late 19C+] mad, eccentric.

loose as a goose *adj.* (*also* **loose as a caboose**) [1930s+] (*US*) very loose, in any sense.

DERIVATIVES

❑ **loosey-goosey** *adj.* [1960s+] (*US*) very loose, in any sense.

loose-coat game *n.* [19C] prostitution.

IN PHRASES

❑ **play at the loose-coat game** *v.* [late 19C] to have sexual intercourse.

loose goose *n.* [LOOSE AS A GOOSE *adj.*] [1950s+] (*US*) a person or thing that is loose, in any sense.

loosely wired *n. see* LOOSE-WIRED *adj.*

loosener *n.* **1** [1900s] (*US*) a giver, usu. of money. **2** [1920s–30s] (*US*) in pl., prunes [their trad. role in curing constipation].

loosen someone's hide *v. see under* HIDE *n.*

loosen (up) *v.* [late 19C+] (*orig. US*) **1** to relax, esp. as an imper. **2** as *loosen up on*, to relax one's restraints on another. **3** to start speaking, esp. as an imper. **4** to spend or hand over money [to loosen one's purse-strings].

loose-wired *adj.* (*also* **loosely wired**) [1950s] out of control.

loose wiring *n.* [1910s] (*US*) mental instability.

loosey-goosey *adj. see under* LOOSE AS A GOOSE *adj.*

loosies *n.* [1980s+] cigarettes bought unpackaged.

loot *n.*[1] **1** [late 18C+] plunder, booty [SE by late 19C, f. Hind. *lut*, plunder, ult. Skrt *lotra*, plunder. Note also Anglo-Ind. *lootie-wallah*, a plunderer or bandit]. **2** [1910s+] money.

loot *n.*^{2} (*also* **Loot, lootie, Lute**) [abbr. US pron.] [late 19C+] (*Aus./US*) a lieutenant; also used in UK in WW1 to describe the rank, but not to address its bearer.

lootcha *n. see* LOOCHA *n.*

looted *adj.* [1990s+] (*US black*) drunk or drugged.

loothy *n.* [Irish *liútar*, big, ungainly] [20C+] (*Irish*) a large, ungainly man.

L.O.P. *adj.* [PUSSY *n.* (2)] [1980s] (*US black*) Lack Of Pussy; sexual frustration.

lop *n.*^{1} (*also* **lophead, loppy**) [LOB *n.*^{2} (2)] **1** [20C+] (*US Und.*) a fool. **2** [1970s+] (*US*) a contemptible person. **3** [1990s+] (*US campus*) an uncoordinated person. **4** [2000s] (*US prison*) a second-rate prison officer.

lop *n.*^{2} [ety. unknown, ? link to dial. *lop*, a flea, i.e. the coin's innate worthlessness] [1930s+] (*Anglo-Irish*) a penny.

lop cock *n.* [SE *lop*, to cut off + COCK *n.*^{3} (1)] [1930s–40s] (*US*) a circumcised penis.

lop down *v.* [East Anglian dial. *lop*, to droop] [mid-19C–1900s] (*US*) to sit down, to lie down.

lope *n.* [abbr.] [2000s] (*US prison*) an env*elope*.

lope *v.* (*also* **loap**) [SE *loup*, to leap] **1** [late 17C+] to go, to run, to run away. **2** [19C] to steal.

IN PHRASES

□ **on the lope** [late 19C+] running away, on the run.

lop-ear *n.* (*also* **flop-ear**) [? the prevalence of rabbits in the state] [mid-19C+] (*US*) a nickname for an inhabitant of Oregon.

lop-eared *adj.* (*also* **flop-eared**) [the *lop-ears* of an animal, but ? LOB *n.*^{2} (2)] [mid-19C+] (*US*) exceptionally stupid or gullible; thus n., *lopear*.

lopes *n. see* MELON *n.* (4).

lope (the mule) *v. see under* MULE *n.*

lophead *n. see* LOP *n.*^{1}.

loppy *n.*^{1} [? dial. *lop*, to idle, to hang about or f. SE *loppy*, infested with 'lops' or fleas] [late 19C–1940s] (*Aus./N.Z.*) a handyman on a rural station, a roustabout.

loppy *n.*^{2} *see* JALOPY *n.*

loppy *n.*^{3} *see* LOP *n.*^{1}.

loppy cull *n.* [? LOP *n.*^{1} + CULL *n.*^{1} (2)] [18C] (*UK Und.*) a drunken man.

loppy dust *n.* [LOP *n.*^{1} +SE *dust*] [1980s+] (*drugs*) cocaine.

loppy pop *n.* [rhy. sl.; ? pun on SE *lollipop*] [2000s] a shop.

loqued out *adj. see* LOCED OUT *under* LOC OUT *v.*

lor! *excl.* (*also* **lors!**) [mid-19C+] an abbr. version of *Lord!*, used in a variety of excl. and mild oaths.

IN EXCLAMATIONS

□ **lor lumme!** *see* LUMME! *excl.*

lor-a-massy/mussy! *excl.* [mid-19C–1930s] a mild oath, 'Lord have mercy!'.

lor blime! *excl.* (*also* **lorblimey!**) [1910s–20s] (*Aus.*) a mild excl., lit. 'Lord blind me!'.

DERIVATIVES

□ **lor-blimer** *n.* [1910s] (*Aus.*) a vulgar, vociferous person.

Lord *n.*

SE in slang uses

IN COMPOUNDS

□ **lord-forbids** *n. see* GOD FORBID *n.* (1). □ **lord muck** *n. see under* MUCK *n.*^{1}.

IN PHRASES

□ **Lord how came you so** *see* HOW CAME YOU SO *phr.* □ **Lord knows how** (*also* **Christ knows what/where, Lord knows what (not), ...where, ...who, ...why**) [mid-17C+] a phr. implying amazement, incredulity or plain ignorance; thus as n., an unknown place, person or reason.

IN EXCLAMATIONS

□ **Lord blue me!** [late 19C] (*Aus.*) a mild excl. □ **lord lumme!** *see* LUMME! *excl.*

lord *n.* [Gk *lordos*, bent backwards; thus the medical term *lordosis*, anterior curvature of the spine] [late 17C–19C] a hunch-backed or badly crippled man; thus also addressed as *His Honour*.

IN PHRASES

□ **my lord** [early–mid-19C] a mocking nickname given to a hunchback.

lord and lady *n.* [1970s–80s] (*N.Z. prison*) sexual intercourse.

lord and mastered *adj.* [rhy. sl. = PLASTERED *adj.*^{1}] [1990s+] drunk.

Lord Harry *n. see* OLD HARRY *n.* (1).

IN EXCLAMATIONS

□ **by the Lord Harry!** (*also* **by Lord Harry! by the living Harry!**) [late 17C–1940s] a mild oath.

Lord John Russell *n.* [rhy. sl.; ult. British politician *Lord John Russell* (1792–1878)] [mid–late 19C] a bustle, a frame used to make a woman's skirt stand out from the hips.

Lord Lovat *v.* [rhy. sl. = SHOVE IT! *excl.*] [20C+] to get rid of, to throw away.

lord love...! *excl.* [mid-19C+] a mild oath.

IN EXCLAMATIONS

□ **lord love-a-duck!** (*also* **love a duck! love-a-Peter!**) [20C+] a mild excl. of surprise etc.

Lord Lovell *n.* (*also* **Lord Lovel**) [rhy. sl.; 20C+ use is mainly US] [mid-19C+] a shovel.

Lord Mansfield's teeth *n.* [*Lord Mansfield* (1733–1821), Lord Chief Justice of the Court of Common Pleas] [late 18C–early 19C] the *chevaux de frize* or row of spikes embedded into the top of the wall of the King's Bench prison.

lord mayor *n.*^{1} [on pattern of ALDERMAN *n.* (5); CITIZEN *n.* (1); GENTLEMAN *n.*: smaller and larger versions of the tool] [late 19C–1950s] a large crowbar.

SE in slang uses

IN COMPOUNDS

□ **lord mayor's coal** *n.* [mid-19C] a piece of slate. □ **lord mayor's fool** *n.* [pvb 'like My Lord Mayor's fool, full of business and nothing to do'] [mid-19C] 'a personage who likes everything that is good, and plenty of it' (Hotten 1864).

lord mayor *n.*^{2} [rhy. sl.] **1** [1910s–70s] an oath, a 'swear'. **2** [1940s–60s] a chair.

lord mayor *v.* [rhy. sl.] [1910s–70s] to swear.

Lord Northumberland's arms *n. see* NORTHUMBERLAND ARMS *n.*

lord (of the manor) *n.* [rhy. sl. = TANNER *n.*] [mid-19C–1970s] a sixpence.

lord rex *n.* [rhy. sl. = *sex*] [1970s–80s] (*Aus./N.Z. prison*) sexual intercourse.

lords and peers *n.* [rhy. sl.] [2000s] the ears.

Lord Sutch *n.* [rhy. sl.; ult. popstar/politician *Screaming Lord Sutch* (1940–99), the leader of the maverick UK political party Monster Raving Loony Party] [1960s+] **1** the clutch. **2** the crotch.

Lord Wigg *n.* [rhy. sl.; ult. UK politician *George Wigg* (1900–83)] [1960s+] a pig.

lordy! *excl. see* LAWDY! *excl.*

lordy me! *excl.* [late 19C+] a euph. for *Lord help me!*

Loretta Young *n.* [rhy. sl.; ult. *Loretta Young* (1913–2000), Hollywood film star] [1990s+] the tongue.

lorna doone *n.* [rhy. sl., ult. the novel *Lorna Doone* (1869) by R.D. Blackmore] [20C+] a spoon.

lorry up *v.* (*also* **lurry up**) [Irish *liúradh*, a beating] [1940s+] (*Irish*) to beat, to thrash, also as *lurry into*, to get stuck into, to attack.

lors! *excl. see* LOR! *excl.*

Los *n.* (*also* **Los Angels**) [abbr.] [1910s+] (*US*) *Los* Angeles.

los *adj.* [Afk. *los*, loose] [1950s+] (*S.Afr.*) usu. of a woman, promiscuous.

los *v.* [Afk.] [1980s+] (*S.Afr.*) to let go, often as excl.

los boy *n.* [1960s] (*S.Afr.*) a layabout.

lose *v.* **1** [mid-19C+] (*US*) to vomit; usu. in phrs. below. **2** [mid-19C+] to suffer a miscarriage, to have a still-birth or have one's child die very early in life. **3** [late 19C+] (*US*) to kill.

4 [late 19C+] (*US*) to evade. **5** [1920s+] (*orig. US*) to get rid of, to dispose of. **6** [1990s+] (*US*) of a CD, radio etc, to turn off.

IN PHRASES

❑ **lose a dinner** *v.* [1950s+] (*Aus./US*) to vomit. ❑ **lose a meal** *v.* [1940s+] (*Aus.*) to vomit. ❑ **lose one's doughnuts** [var. on BLOW ONE'S DOUGHNUTS *under* BLOW *v.*[1]] [1940s+] (*US campus*) to vomit. ❑ **lose one's groceries** *v. see* BLOW ONE'S GROCERIES *under* BLOW *v.*[1]. ❑ **lose one's load** *v.* [1960s] (*Aus.*) to vomit. ❑ **lose one's lunch** *v.* (*also* **blow dinner, blow one's lunch, drop one's lunch, lose one's breakfast**) [1920s+] (*Aus./US*) to vomit.

SE in slang uses

IN PHRASES

❑ **lose leather** *v. see under* LEATHER *n.* ❑ **lose move** *n. see* MOVE *n.* ❑ **lose one's...** *see also under* relevant n. ❑ **lose one's britches** *v.* [var. on *LOSE ONE'S SHIRT under* SHIRT *n.*] [20C+] to lose a good deal of money, usu. through betting. ❑ **lose one's gender** *v.* [1940s+] (*gay*) to abandon homosexuality to become a heterosexual. ❑ **lose one's lollies** *v. see* TOSS ONE'S LOLLIES *under* TOSS *v.* ❑ **lose one's rudder** *v.* [18C] to be drunk and thus lose one's sense of direction. ❑ **lose one's stopper** *v.* [18C] to be drunk and thus lose one's sense of direction. ❑ **lose one's Tampax** *v.* (*also* **lose one's douche bag**) [1960s] (*US*) to become hysterical. ❑ **lose the match and pocket the stakes** *v.* [the male is seen as the 'winner'; the stakes are his ejaculated semen] [19C] of a woman, to have sexual intercourse. ❑ **lose the number of one's mess** *v.* [naut. imagery] **1** [early 19C–1930s] (*also* **get put out of mess**) to die. **2** [1910s] to lose one's position; to fall from social or professional grace. ❑ **lose the run of** *v.* [Irish *ná bí ag rith leat féin mar sin*, lit. 'don't be running with yourself like that'] **1** [1900s] (*Aus.*) to lose control of someone else. **2** [1970s+] (*Irish*) to lose one's self-control.

IN EXCLAMATIONS

❑ **go and lose yourself!** [20C+] (*Aus.*) a general excl. of dismissal or disdain.

lose it *v.* **1** [1950s+] to lose control temporarily; in an extreme case to have an actual mental breakdown, to go mad. **2** [1970s] to lose one's virginity. **3** [1980s+] (*US campus*) to be surprised, to be shocked. **4** [1980s+] (*US campus*) to vomit. **5** [1990s+] to lose one's skills, abilities.

lose out (on) *v.* [note Asbury *Sucker's Progress* (1938) 16: An extraordinary number of the terms, technical and otherwise, which were employed by Faro players in the palmy days of the game have passed into the language [...] Here are some of them: [...] *Losing out*—Betting on a card which loses four times in one deal] [mid-19C+] **1** to fail, to miss an opportunity. **2** (*also* **lose out to**) to be fooled, to be swindled.

loser *n.* **1** [20C+] (*orig. US*) a failure, esp. a socially inadequate person. **2** [20C+] (*US*) a convicted prisoner, one who served a jail sentence; often ext. by a number that denotes the number of sentences; usu. as TWO-TIME LOSER *n.* **3** [1920s+] (*orig. US*) a disappointment, a problem, an obstacle, a useless thing or idea.

loser *adj.* [LOSER *n.*] [1970s+] (*US*) of people or things, second-rate, useless.

loskop *n.* [Afk. *los*, loose + *kop*, head] [1950s+] (*S.Afr.*) a forgetful, scatty person.

loskop *adj.* [LOSKOP *n.*] [1950s+] (*S.Afr.*) crazy, forgetful, eccentric.

lossie *n.* [LOS *adj.*] [1950s+] (*S.Afr.*) a promiscuous woman.

lost and found *n.* [rhy. sl.] **1** [20C+] orig. £10; £1. **2** [1970s–80s] (*N.Z. prison*) the punishment block [POUND *n.*[4]].

lost in the suds *phr. see under* SUDS *n.*[1].

lot *n.*[1] **1** [mid-19C–1940s] a person; often as *BAD LOT under* BAD *adj.*; a small company of asssociates. **2** [1920s] (*UK Und.*) a prison sentence. **3** [1960s+] (*Aus./N.Z prison*) constr. with *the*, a life sentence.

lot *n.*[2] [ext. of SE *the lot*, everything] [late 19C–1900s] the male genitals.

loteby *n.* (*also* **ludby**) [SE *lote*, to skulk or hide] [14C–early 18C] a mistress.

lothario *n.* [in the cast list of Sir William D'Avenant's play *The Cruel Brother* (1627) is a 'Lothario, a frantic young gallant'. The name was used again by Nicholas Rowe in *The Fair Penitent* (1703), and the term's popularity stems from the latter, in which he is characterized as 'The Gay Lothario'] [mid-18C+] a libertine, a rake.

lotion *n.* [late 19C+] a drink.

DERIVATIVES

❑ **lotioned** *adj.* [late 19C] drunken.

lot lizard *n. see under* LIZARD *n.*

lot of, a *adj.* [abbr. SE *whole lot of*] [1940s–60s] (*US black*) exceptionally good, skilful, esp. of musical ability.

lotsa *n.* [pron. of SE *lots of*] [1920s+] (*orig. US*) very many, a large number.

Lot's wife *n.* [1920] salt.

lotta *n.* [pron. of SE *a lot of*] [1910s+] (*orig. US*) very many, a large number.

lottie *n.* [2000s] (*S.Afr. gay*) the penis.

lotties and totties *n.* [theatrical jargon *lotties and totties*, out of work young actresses, in turn f. common names] [late 19C] prostitutes as a group.

lou *n.*[1] *see* LOO *n.*[1].

lou *n.*[2] *see* LOUIS *n.* (3).

loud and clear *adj.* [rhy. sl.] [1990s+] dear, expensive.

loudmouth *n.* [LOUDMOUTH *adj.*] [1920s+] (*orig. US*) **1** a braggart, a boaster. **2** a lawyer.

loudmouth *adj.* (*also* **loudmouthed**) **1** [late 19C+] (*orig. US*) boastful, arrogant, vulgar. **2** [1970s] (*US*) ostentatious, showy.

loudmouth *v.* [LOUDMOUTH *adj.*] **1** [1930s+] (*orig. US*) to brag, to boast. **2** [1930s+] (*US black*) to speak abusively.

loudmouth soup *n. see LIQUID COURAGE under* LIQUID *adj.*

loud one *n.* [late 17C–mid-19C] a gross lie.

loudspeaker *n.* [1930s] (*US*) **1** a braggart, a boaster. **2** one's wife.

loudtalk *v.* [1920s+] (*US black*) to talk in a way that confronts or embarrasses one's hearers, that is deliberately antagonistic; thus n. *loud-talk*, *loud-talking*.

Louie *n.* (*also* **louie**) [? Fr. coin, the pre-Revolutionary *louis d'or*, synon. for the *écu* of the 17C–18C] [late 19C+] (*orig. US*) $1, in pl. *louis*, money.

louie *n.*[1] [the Mortein commercials of 1960s+ which featured *Louie the Fly*] [1960s+] (*Aus.*) a fly.

louie *n.*[2] (*also* **lewy**) [the initial letter] [1960s+] in driving, a left turn; usu. in phr. below.

IN PHRASES

❑ **hang a louie** *v.* (*also* **hang a louis**) [HANG *v.*[7]] [1960s+] to turn left.

louie *n.*[3] **1** *see* LOOEY *n.*[1]. **2** *see* LOOIE *n.*[1].

louies *n.* [abbr.] [1980s+] (*US*) the luxury luggage and clothing manufactured by *Louis* Vuitton.

louis *n.* **1** [1920s–30s] (*US*) a pimp [negative stereotyping of the proper name which is Fr., like ALPHONSE *n.*[2]]. **2** [1980s+] (*UK drugs*) one sixteenth of an ounce of cannabis [play on French King *Louis* XVI]. **3** [1990s+] (*also* **lou**) (*US campus*) an unattractive man.

loulou *n. see* LULU *n.*[1] (2).

lounge *n.* [mid-19C; 1940s] (*Aus./US Und.*) the dock in a court of law.

SE in slang uses

IN COMPOUNDS

❑ **lounge lizard** *n.* (*also* **lounge serpent, lounge snake**) [-LIZARD *sfx* but note LIZARD *n.* (4)] **1** [1910s+] a fortune-hunter or womanizer who works his charms in the lounges of hotels. **2** [1920s+] a poor or miserly man who would rather court a woman in her own house than take her out on the town [note University of Missouri use (in 1931), the synon. *sofa lizard*]. ❑ **lounge louse** *n.* [1930s+] (*Aus./US*) a womanizer, an adventurer; usu. in pl. *lounge lice*.

lounge the gag *v. see under* GAG *n.*

lour *n.* (*also* **loor, loure, lower, lowr, lowre, lowrie, lowyer**) [Fr. *louier*, a reward, then 14C SE *lower*, a reward; cf. Rom. *loor*, to plunder, and *luripen*, booty] [mid-16C–late 19C] (*UK Und.*) money; a purse.

Lou Reed *n.* [rhy. sl. = SPEED *n.* (6); ult. rock star Lou Reed (b.1942)] [1960s+] (*drugs*) amphetamine.

louse *n.* **1** [mid-17C+] an extremely contemptible or untrustworthy individual. **2** [1990s+] (*US black/gay*) as *the lice*, police who arrest transvestites working as street prostitutes.

SE in slang uses

IN COMPOUNDS

❑ **louse bag** *n.* **1** [late 18C–early 19C] a wig or a bag worn over the hair. **2** [1960s] (*Scot.*) a term of abuse. ❑ **lousebound** *n.* [1930s–50s] a general term of abuse, lit. one who is infested with lice. ❑ **louse cage** *n.* (*also* **louse trap**) (*US*) **1** [late 19C–1940s] a cheap hotel or lodging house. **2** [late 19C–1960s] (*US*) a hat. **3** [1920s–60s] a bunkhouse. **4** [1940s] a railroad caboose. ❑ **louse house** *n.* (*also* **loose house, louse dump**) **1** [late 18C–1930s] a prison. **2** [1900s–1940s] a seedy hotel or lodging house, or confined space. ❑ **louse ladder** *n.* **1** [late 18C–19C; 1930s] a ladder, i.e. 'a stitch fallen in a stocking' (Grose 1785). **2** [1920s] a bushy sidewhisker, usu. in pl. ❑ **louse trap** *n.* **1** [mid-18C–mid-19C] (*also* **Scotch louse trap**) a toothcomb. **2** [early 19C] the hair; the head. **3** [20C+] a sideburn or sidewhisker; usu. in pl. ❑ **louse walk** *n.* [mid–late 19C] a back-hair parting.

louse *adj.* [LOUSE *n.*] [1940s+] (*US*) second-rate.

louse v. [LOUSE *n.*] **1** [1940s+] (*Aus.*) to pilfer. **2** *see* LOUSE UP v. (4).

DERIVATIVES

❑ **lousing** *n.* [1960s+] (*Irish*) hanging around on street corners.

IN PHRASES

❑ **louse (around)** *v.* **1** [1910s+] (*US*) to idle, to loiter, to waste time [northern UK dial. *lowse*, to stop working]. **2** [1910s+] (*US*) (*also* **louse up**) to mistreat someone. ❑ **louse up** *see* separate entries.

-louse *sfx* [used with qualifying n.] [1930s+] (*US*) used in combs. to refer to a despicable person, a waster, a hanger-on.

IN PHRASES

❑ **lens louse** *n.* [1920s–70s] (*US*) a person who monopolizes the camera; sometimes ext. to someone who monopolizes a conversation. ❑ **road louse** *n.* [1910s] (*US*) a Ford motor car.

loused *adj.* [1950s+] (*drugs*) covered by sores and abscesses from repeated use of unsterile needles.

louseland *n.* [a derog. suggestion that Scotland is infested with vermin] [late 17C–early 19C] Scotland.

louser *n.* [LOUSE *n.*; also Irish use 1960s+] **1** [1930s+] (*orig. US*) a contemptible individual. **2** [1940s–50s] (*Aus.*) a petty thief.

louse-up *n.* [LOUSE UP v. (4)] [1970s+] (*US*) a situation or thing that is a mess or that is troublesome.

louse up *v.* **1** [1910s–60s] to infest with vermin. **2** [1920s] (*US prison*) to wash one's clothes to remove lice. **3** [1930s] to tease. **4** [1930s+] (*orig. US*) (*also* **louse**) to make a mess of, to ruin, usu. deliberately; thus adj. *loused-up*. **5** [1940s+] to blunder, to fail. **6** [1950s+] to cause a person difficulties, to cause trouble for someone. **7** [1950s+] to make a place or situation unpleasant or nasty.

DERIVATIVES

❑ **loused-up** *adj.* [1950s] ruined, inferior.

lousy *n.* [LOUSY *adj.*] [1930s–50s] a despicable person.

lousy *adj.* [fig. use of SE *louse*] **1** [late 14C+] a general intensifier, usu. with derog. implications. **2** [late 18C+] (*US*) small, insignificant. **3** [1930s–70s] (*Aus.*) mean, tight-fisted. **4** [1970s] (*US Und.*) corrupt.

IN COMPOUNDS

❑ **lousy-looked** *adj.* [lit. 'looking lice-ridden'] [17C] a general epithet of abuse. ❑ **lousy with** *adj.* (*also* **crabby with**) [mid-19C+] full of, abundant with (a commodity, type of person etc).

lousy *adv.* [fig. use of SE *louse*] [16C; 1930s+] a general intensifier, usu. with derog. implications.

Lousy Anna *n.* [1920s+] (*US*) a derog. name for Louisiana.

lousy lou *n.* [rhy. sl.] [20C+] the 'flu, influenza.

love *n.* [early 19C+] any person or thing that is pleasant or attractive, e.g. *it's a real love*.

SE in slang uses

pertaining to sex

IN COMPOUNDS

❑ **love bone** *n.* [BONE *n.*[1] (1)] [1960s+] (*US black*) the penis. ❑ **love box** *n.* [BOX *n.*[1] (1a)/SE *box*] [1980s+] (*US*) the female genitals. ❑ **love bug** *n.* [BUG *n.*[5] (1)] **1** [20C+] an imaginary virus, the symptons of which are being in love; thus the disease itself. **2** [1970s+] (*US gay*) a pubic louse. **3** [1980s] a person who is in love with being in love. ❑ **love button** *n.* [1990s+] (*orig. US*) the clitoris. ❑ **love canal** *n.* [play on SE + pun on 1993 ecological abuse of the *Love Canal*, New York] [1980s+] (*US*) the vagina. ❑ **love crack** *n. see* CRACK *n.*[3] (1). ❑ **love custard** *n.* [note CUSTARD *n.*] [1990s+] semen. ❑ **love dart** *n.* [late 19C+] the penis. ❑ **love envelope** *n.* [1970s+] (*US gay*) a condom. ❑ **love flesh** *n.* [19C] the vagina. ❑ **love gap** *n. see* PASSION GAP *under* PASSION *n.* ❑ **love glove** *n.* [1970s+] (*US*) **1** a condom. **2** a vagina. ❑ **love grenades** *n.* [2000s] the testicles. ❑ **love gun** *n.* [ext. of GUN *n.*[1] (2)] [1970s+] (*US*) the penis. ❑ **love handles** *n.* (*also* **fuck handles, love rungs**) [the idea being that one can hold on to them during sex] [1960s+] the excess flesh around a portly stomach that may be seen in a kinder light by those who appreciate the Rubenesque figure (cf. BAR HANDLES *under* BAR *n.*[2]). ❑ **love hole** *n.* [1980s+] (*US*) the vagina. ❑ **love juice** *n.* [ext. JUICE *n.*[1] (2a)] [late 19C+] **1** semen. **2** vaginal secretions. ❑ **lovelips** *n.* [1990s+] (*US*) the labia. ❑ **love machine** *n.* [1960s+] (*US*) a sexually virile man, a womanizer. ❑ **love muffin** *n.* [MUFFIN *n.*[1] (8)] [1980s+] (*US*) a sexually attractive person. ❑ **love muscle** *n.* [1950s+] (*US*) the penis. ❑ **love nuts** *n. see* LOVER'S NUTS *under* LOVER *n.* ❑ **love pump** *n.* [popularized by the film *This is Spinal Tap* (1984)] [1980s+] (*US*) the penis. ❑ **love rod** *n. see* ROD *n.* ❑ **love rug** *n.* [1990s+] the female pubic hair. ❑ **love rungs** *see* LOVE HANDLES above. ❑ **love's cabinet** *n.* [18C] the vagina. ❑ **love seat** *n.* [late 19C] the vagina. ❑ **love shack** *n.* [1960s+] (*orig. US*) **1** a room or apartment that a man keeps for seductions and sex. **2** a lover, an object of sexual desire (and conquest) [fig. use of sense 1 + ? SHACK-UP *n.* (1)]. ❑ **love staff** *n.* [late 19C] the penis. ❑ **lovesteak** *n.* [1980s+] (*US campus*) the penis. ❑ **love stick** *n.* [STICK *n.* (1a)] [1920s+] (*US*) the penis. ❑ **love torpedo** *n.* [1990s+] the penis. ❑ **love truncheon** *n.* [late 19C; 1990s+] the penis. ❑ **love warrior** *n.* [2000s] the penis.

IN PHRASES

❑ **make (some)one's love come down** *v.* [1930s–60s] (*US black*) to stimulate sexually, to come to orgasm.

general uses

IN COMPOUNDS

❑ **love affair** *n.* [pun on BOY *n.*[2] (4a) + GIRL *n.*[2]] [1970s+] (*drugs*) a mixture of heroin and cocaine. ❑ **love apples** *n. see under* APPLES *n.* ❑ **love curls** *n.* [mid–late 19C] a hairstyle in which the hair is cut short and worn low over the forehead. ❑ **love drug** *n.* [among the drug's primary effects is a sense of world-embracing benevolence] [1980s+] (*drugs*) MDMA. ❑ **love letter** *n.* [1940s] (*US black*) **1** a bullet. **2** a stone or rock thrown at someone. ❑ **love-pot** *n.* [19C] a drunkard. ❑ **love spuds** *n. see under* SPUD *n.*[3]. ❑ **love weed** *n.* [WEED *n.*[1] (4)] [1930s+] (*US drugs*) marijuana.

IN PHRASES

❑ **give love** *v.* [1990s+] (*black*) to respect, to praise. ❑ **love off** *v.* [20C+] (*W.I., Jam.*) to make obvious sexual advances towards. ❑ **much love** *n.* [1990s+] (*US black*) popularity, respect. ❑ **pure love** *n.* [LSD's image as a creator of 'love and peace'] [1970s] (*drugs*) LSD.

IN EXCLAMATIONS

❑ **for the love of Mike!** (*also* **for the love of holy Buddha! ...Heaven! ...Jupiter! ...Moses! ...Pete! ...Peter the hermit!**

...Polly Simpkins!) [*Mike*, like *Pete*, is irrelevant, other perhaps than as a euph. for *Moses*] [mid-19C+] (*orig. US*) a euph. excl. of exasperation or surprise, for goodness' sake!

love a duck! *excl. see under* LORD LOVE…! *excl.*

loveage *n.* [SE *lovage*, a cordial based on the herb lovage (*Ligusticum scoticum*)] [mid-19C] a drink consisting of the dregs collected from the overflow from the pouring taps, the ends of spirit bottles and similar leavings, which was sold cheaply in gin-shops, particularly to women.

love and hate *n.* [rhy. sl.] [20C+] weight.

love and kisses *n.* [rhy. sl. = MISSIS *n.*] [20C+] one's wife.

love and marriage *n.* [rhy. sl.] [20C+] a carriage.

love-a-Peter! *excl. see* LORD LOVE-A-DUCK! *under* LORD LOVE…! *excl.*

loved it *phr.* [1980s+] (*US campus*) an expression of elation.

loved-up *adj.* [LOVE (UP) *v.*] [1990s+] **1** intoxicated from love or romance, often used spec. of having had a lot of sex. **2** under the influence of MDMA.

love-in *n.* [1960s+] (*orig. US*) **1** a group gathering to express mutually loving feelings. **2** (*also* **grope-in**) an orgy. **3** positive, optimistic relations.

love lane *n.* (*also* **love-lane**) [mid–late 19C] the vagina.

IN PHRASES

▫ **take a turn in Love Lane on Mount Pleasant** *v.* [19C] to have sexual intercourse.

lovely *n.* [SE *lovely* adj.] **1** [1930s+] a pretty young woman, a word esp. popular with the tabloid press, seaside entertainers etc, also as term of address. **2** [1970s+] (*US drugs*) (*also* **lovelies, lovely high**) marijuana laced with phencyclidine.

lovely *adj.* **1** [early 17C+] delightful, really excellent; often in ironic use. **2** [mid-19C] (*UK Und.*) suitable and ready for criminal action.

lovely *adv.* [20C+] admirably, enjoyably, well.

lovely grub! *excl.* [1950s+] implies approval of whatever is being considered, whether actual food or not.

lovely high *n. see* LOVELY *n.* (2).

lover *n.* **1** [20C+] (*US*) a pimp [euph.]. **2** [1910s+] (*orig. US*) an affectionate general term of address, though no actual love affair need be implied. **3** [1950s] (*US Und.*) a rapist or bigamist [euph.].

SE in slang uses

IN COMPOUNDS

▫ **lover's nuts** *n.* (*also* **love nuts, lover's balls, lover's knots**) [NUTS *n.*[2] (1)/BALLS *n.* (1)/SE *knots*] [1950s+] (*US*) aches in the testicles caused by sexual stimulation without ejaculation. ▫ **lover's speed** *n. see* SPEED FOR LOVERS *under* SPEED *n.*

IN PHRASES

▫ **lover under the lap** *n.* [1940s–70s] (*Aus.*) a lesbian.

lover-boy *n.* (*also* **lover-man**) **1** [1950s+] a womanizer; the term is often used (esp. by women) ironically. **2** [1960s] (*US gay/teen*) a boyfriend; homosexual and heterosexual use.

lover-girl *n.* [1950s] the female equivalent of LOVER-BOY *n.*

love up *n.* (*also* **luv-up**) [LOVE (UP) *v.*] [1950s+] (*US*) a caress, a hug.

love (up) *v.* (*orig. US*) **1** [late 19C+] to caress, to hug, to embrace, also used fig. **2** [1920s+] to have sexual intercourse. **3** [1990s+] (*drugs*) to render someone intoxicated with MDMA [backf. from LOVED-UP *adj.* (2)]. **4** [2000s] to be very fond of.

lovey-dovey *n.* [SE *love* + redup. + image of billing and cooing turtle-doves] **1** [mid-19C+] (*also* **lovey-ducks**) a term of endearment. **2** [20C+] (*also* **lovey, lovey-dove**) one's lover, partner. **3** [1920s+] (*also* **love-dove**) (*US*) lovemaking.

lovey-dovey *adj.* [LOVEY-DOVEY *n.*] **1** [late 19C+] affectionate. **2** [2000s] maudlin and sentimental.

loving *adj.* [1940s+] (*US*) used as a euph. for FUCKING *adj.*

loving it *phr.* ['it' is life] [1980s+] in a positive or pleasing situation.

low *n.*[1] **1** [1950s+] any form of depression; also in pl. *the lows*. **2** [1960s+] (*US drugs*) a bad reaction to a drug; esp. the negative feelings that may follow the 'high' [opposite of HIGH *n.* (1), and slightly contrived].

low *n.*[2] [abbr. of SE *fellow*] [1990s+] (*US black*) a friend.

low *adj.*

SE in slang uses

IN COMPOUNDS

▫ **low-ass** *adj.* [2000s] (*US*) lowly. ▫ **lowball/baller** *see* separate entries. ▫ **low-bite** *n.* [1990s+] (*W.I.*) an upper class person who likes working class pursuits. ▫ **low belly strippers** *n. see* STRIPPERS *n.* ▫ **low-count** *adj.* [1970s] (*US drugs*) of a measure of drugs, under-weight. ▫ **low countries** *n. see* separate entry. ▫ **lowdown/-downer** *see* separate entry. ▫ **low femme** *n.* (*also* **blue-jeans femme**) [FEMME *n.* (3)] [1990s+] (*US gay*) a feminine lesbian but one that is not quite as stereotypically feminine as a *HIGH FEMME under* HIGH *adj.*[1]. ▫ **low five** *see* separate entries. ▫ **low-flung** *adj.* [mid–late 19C] (*US*) of low character or social position. ▫ **low forehead** *n.* [1900s] (*US*) a foolish person. ▫ **low gagger** *n.* [late 18C] (*UK Und.*) a confidence trickster who elicits compassion (and money) by pretending to be hurt in some way. ▫ **low Greek** *n.* [GREEK *n.* (7)] [1960s+] (*gay*) heterosexual intercourse (because the vagina is lower than the anus). ▫ **low-heel/-heeled** *see* separate entry. ▫ **low jump** *n.* [play on HIGH JUMP *n.* (3)] [1960s+] (*Aus.*) a magistrate's court. ▫ **lowland** *n.* [1930s–70s] (*US black*) the area of a city, usu. the south, where the black ghetto is generally sited. ▫ **lowlands** *n.* [late 18C–19C] the female genitals. ▫ **lowlife** *see* separate entries. ▫ **lowmen** *n.* [mid-16C–early 19C] fixed dice that will always show low numbers. ▫ **low nation** *n.* [-NATION *sfx*] [20C+] (*W.I.*) a low-caste East Indian. ▫ **low-octane** *adj.* [the opposite of HIGH-OCTANE *adj.* (3)] [1990s+] of coffee, decaffinated. ▫ **low pad** *n.* [PAD *n.*[1] (3); as opposed to *HIGH PAD under* HIGH *adj.*[1]] [late 17C–early 19C] (*UK Und.*) a footpad; 'a base Sheep-stealing, half-penny Rogue' (Head 1674); thus n., *low-padding*, petty thievery. ▫ **low pro** *n.* [abbr.] [1990s+] (*US black*) a *low profile*. ▫ **low quarters** *n.* [1930s–70s] (*US black*) Oxford shoes, with laces over the instep. ▫ **low-rate** *v.* [20C+] (*US black/Southern*) to attack verbally, to criticize, to denigrate, to ridicule. ▫ **low rent** *see* separate entries. ▫ **lowride/rider/riding** *see* separate entries. ▫ **low-run** *adj.* [1950s+] (*W.I.*) untrustworthy, hypocritical. ▫ **low tide** *n.* (*also* **low water, low water mark**) [the image of one's economic 'vessel' being stranded by low tide] [late 17C–1920s] a state of financial difficulty, thus v. to *be in low tide*. ▫ **low-toby** *n. see* separate entry.

IN PHRASES

▫ **get low** *v.* [a reverse pun on the usu. *GET HIGH under* HIGH *adj.*[1] with other drugs, due to the relaxing effects of marijuana] **1** [1980s+] (*US campus*) to smoke marijuana. **2** [2000s] to inject a narcotic. ▫ **low in the lay** *adj.* [SE *lay low*, to knock down] [mid-19C–1910s] extremely poor. ▫ **low (man) on the totem pole** *n.* (*also* **low man on the ladder**) [an image of Native American hierarchy] [1940s+] inferior, second-rate, in a junior or uninfluential position at work. ▫ **low neck and short sleeves** *n.* [the foreskin is the 'sleeves'] [1940s+] (*gay*) a circumcised penis. ▫ **take low** *v.* [late 19C+] (*W.I./US black*) to adopt a humble attitude in order to forward one's aims.

lowball *adj.* [poker imagery] [1990s+] (*US*) second-rate, inferior.

lowball *v.* [1950s+] (*US*) in negotiating, to make a lower than realistic offer.

lowballer *n.* [LOWBALL *v.*] [1990s+] (*US*) one who bets – when a spread is on offer – on the assumption of a low score.

low countries *n.* [the 'geography' of the body + a pun on *country*/CUNT *n.* (1)] **1** [late 16C–17C] the anus. **2** [late 16C–19C] the female genitals.

SE in slang uses

IN PHRASES

▫ **Low Country soldier** *n.* [the characteristics of those who have soldiered in the Low Countries or of Dutch troops] [mid-17C] a good drinking companion.

lowdown, the *n.* [20C+] (*orig. US*) privileged information, intimate details, 'the inside story'; thus *adj.*

IN PHRASES

❑ **on the low down** *adv.* [1900s] (*US*) in secret, privately.

lowdown *adj.* (*US*) **1** [mid-19C+] mean, contemptible, unpleasant. **2** [late 19C+] depressed, impoverished, out of luck. **3** [1920s] of a place, run-down. **4** [1920s+] (*US black*) excellent.

lowdown *adv.* [LOWDOWN *adj.* (1)] [20C+] meanly, contemptibly, unpleasantly.

low-downer *n.* [LOWDOWN *adj.* (1)] [mid-19C–1930s] (*US black*) a poor white person, esp. a native of North Carolina.

lower *n. see* LOUR *n.*

lower *adj.*

SE in slang uses

IN COMPOUNDS

❑ **lower end** *n. see* END *n.* (1b). ❑ **lower mouth** *n.* [mid-19C] the vagina. ❑ **lower wig** *n. see under* WIG *n.*[2].

IN PHRASES

❑ **lower than a snake's belly** *adj.* (*also* **lower than a snail's belly, lower than a snake's hip**) [1920s+] **1** (*Aus./US*) as low as one can go. **2** (*orig. US black*) (*also* **lower than a midget's ass in hell**) depressed. ❑ **lower than the belly of a cockroach** *adj.* [1940s+] used of a person categorized as the lowest of the low. ❑ **lower than whale shit** *adj.* [1960s+] (*US*) **1** extremely depressed. **2** (*also* **lower than shark shit**) of no moral worth.

lower *v.*

SE in slang uses

IN PHRASES

❑ **lower (a glass)** *v.* [late 19C+] to take a drink, to empty a glass (or bottle) by drinking its contents. ❑ **lower one's belt** *v. see under* BELT *n.* ❑ **lower the bomb** *v. see under* BOMB *n.* ❑ **lower the boom (on)** *v.* (*also* **drop the boom (on)**) [naut. imagery] [1930s+] (*US*) **1** to hit hard. **2** to give up on. **3** to take decisive action against. **4** to reprimand severely, to put an end to someone's misbehaviour. **5** to murder, to kill. **6** (*Aus.*) of a man, to have sexual intercourse.

lowey *n.* [? LOWHEEL *n.*] [1950s–80s] (*Aus.*) a young woman who is dedicated to hedonism, the equivalent and accomplice of a REV-HEAD *n.*

low five *n.* [the opposite of a HIGH FIVE *n.*[1]] [1980s+] (*US black*) a palm-/hand-slapping ritual, with the hands held low rather than the usual HIGH FIVE *n.*[1].

IN PHRASES

❑ **give oneself a low five** *v.* [1980s+] to masturbate.

low five *v.* [opposite of HIGH FIVE *v.*] [1980s+] (*US black*) to greet someone with a palm-/hand-slapping ritual, where the hands are held low.

lowheel *n.* [the state of one's shoes after constantly walking the streets] [1930s–60s] **1** a prostitute or promiscuous woman. **2** a down-and-out, a tramp.

low-heeled *adj.* [the heels of a working-class labourer's boots are likely to be worn down from use] [1910s] (*Aus.*) tough; ill-bred.

lowie *n.*[1] (*also* **lowy**) [? LOWHEEL *n.* (1)] [1950s+] (*Aus.*) a prostitute or promiscuous woman.

lowie *n.*[2] [LOW *n.*[1] (1) + sfx *-ie*] [2000s] a depression.

lowing cheat *n.* (*also* **lowing chete**) [SE *lowing* + CHEAT *n.* (1), lit. 'lowing thing'] [mid-16C–early 17C] (*UK Und.*) a cow, a calf.

lowing rig *n.* [RIG *n.*[2] (1)] [early 19C] (*UK Und.*) the theft of cattle.

lowlife *n.* (*also* **lowlifer, low lived**) [LOWLIFE *adj.*] [1910s+] (*orig. US*) a contemptible person, esp. a criminal.

lowlife *adj.* (*also* **low-lived**) **1** [early 18C+] (*orig. US black*) unpleasant, contemptible, aggressive, vulgar. **2** [1990s+] in criminal terms, second-rate.

lowr/lowre *n. see* LOUR *n.*

low rent *n.* [LOW-RENT *adj.*] **1** [1960s+] (*US campus*) a worthless individual, a promiscuous woman. **2** [1960s] a second-rate place.

low-rent *adj.* [1950s+] (*orig. US*) cheap, distasteful, unfashionable.

lowride *v.* [LOWRIDER *n.*[2] (1)] [1970s+] (*US*) to cruise the streets in a low-slung, customized car.

IN PHRASES

❑ **get low** *v.* [1970s+] (*US*) to ride in a car so that only one's head is visible.

lowrider *n.*[1] [the fig. 'lowriding' in the area of morals + ethics] **1** [1930s+] (*US black*) a pimp. **2** [1970s] (*US prison*) an inmate who intimidates other prisoners into paying protection money.

lowrider *n.*[2] [since the driving of such cars is illegal, they are fitted with hydraulic systems to adjust the height of the car while driving, making it appear to bounce] (*US*) **1** [1960s+] (*also* **lowride**) a customized car, occas. motorcycle, that has been 'chopped and channelled' to lower the suspension and give it a generally sleeker look. **2** [1960s+] the driver of such a car. **3** [1960s+] a Chicano (among whom lowrider cars are popular). **4** [1990s+] (*orig. US black*) in pl., baggy jeans with a low crotch, worn so low as to reveal one's underpants.

lowriding *n.* [LOWRIDE *v.*] [1970s+] (*US*) cruising the streets in a low-slung, customized car.

lowrie *n. see* LOUR *n.*

low-toby *n.* [TOBY *n.*[2] (1)] [early–mid-19C] (*UK Und.*) highway robbery by footpads (rather than mounted highwaymen); thus the *low-toby lay*, street robbery.

IN COMPOUNDS

❑ **low-toby man** *n.* [19C] a footpad.

lowy *n. see* LOWIE *n.*[1].

lowyer *n. see* LOUR *n.*

lox *n.* [? var. on LUMMOCKS *n.* (1)] [1960s+] (*US*) a fool.

lox jock *n.* (*also* **lox jockey**) [Yid. *laks*, thence SE *lox*, smoked salmon, served with cream cheese and bagels, a favourite Jewish dish] [1940s+] (*US*) a Jew.

loz *n.* [? misreading of the numeral 1, pron. as the letter 'l' + *oz*, abbr. for one ounce] [1990s+] (*drugs*) 1oz (28g) of cannabis.

lozenge *n.* (*also* **lozenger**) [? a fellatrix/fellator sucks it] [1990s+] (*UK juv.*) the penis; thus a general insult.

L.P. *n.* [abbr. *l*esbian *p*otential] [1990s+] (*US gay*) said of a passing woman, poss. a lesbian.

l.p. *adj.* [play on SE *long playing* record, i.e. one 'plays both sides'] [2000s] (*S.Afr. gay*) bisexual.

L-7 *n.* (*also* **l-seven**) [the L and the 7 when put together form a SE *square* thus a pun on SQUARE *n.* (1c); the word can be accompanied by using thumb and forefinger extended at right angles, forming an L and a 7, and when the two are combined they form a square] [1950s+] (*US black/teen*) a conventional, tedious person, unsympathetic to teen interests.

L-7 *adj.* (*also* **l-seven**) [L-7 *n.*] [1950s+] (*US black/teen*) unfashionable, unsophisticated.

l.t.r. *n.* [abbr.] [1970s+] a *l*iving *t*ogether *r*elationship, marriage in all but the legalities.

lubber *n.* (*also* **lub, lubberloon**) [? OF. *lobeor*, a swindler or parasite, ult. *lober*, to deceive, to sponge upon or to mock; it is the basis of the 16C nautical *land-lubber*, a landsman or incompetent sailor. The clumsiness implicit in the nautical use implies a further link to SE *lob*, a country bumpkin, ult. from a variety of Teut. forms all meaning heavy or clumsy; note 16C–19C SE *lubberland*, an imaginary land of plenty without labour; a land of laziness] [mid-14C–1940s] a fool; as adj., *lubbering*, foolish.

lubber *v.* [? SE *belabour*] [mid-19C] to hit.

lubberly *adj.* (*also* **looberly, lubber**) [SE *lubber*, a big, clumsy, stupid person] [mid-16C–19C; 1930s] stupid.

lube *n.* [SE *lubrication/lubricant*; note SE *lube*, abbr. of *lubricant*, used on machinery] **1** [1940s+] (*Aus.*) a drink. **2** [1970s+] (*US*) a lubricated condom. **3** [1970s+] any form of lubricant, e.g. KY Jelly, used to facilitate (anal) sex. **4** [1970s+] (*US gay*) natural lubrication in sex, spec. from pre-semen.

IN COMPOUNDS

❑ **lube job** *n.* [the fluids thus generated + pun] [1940s+] (*US*) oral or sexual intercourse. ❑ **lube on** *n.* [the lubrication of vaginal secretions] [1960s] (*US campus*) of a woman, a state of sexually excitement.

lube *v.* [fig. uses of SE *lubricate*] **1** [1930s+] to keep happy, to entertain. **2** [1950s] to bribe, to tip. **3** [1970s+] to apply a lubricant, e.g. KY Jelly, to facilitate (anal) sex.

lubed *adj. see* LUBRICATED *adj.*

lubie *n.* [LUBE *n.* (2) + sfx *-ie*] [1970s+] (*US*) a lubricated condom.

lubricate *v.* **1** [mid-18C–early 19C] to have sexual intercourse. **2** [late 19C+] to ply with drink. **3** [late 19C+] to drink. **4** [1920s] to bribe.

lubricated *adj.* (*also* **lubed**) [LUBRICATE *v.* (3)] [1910s+] (*orig. US*) drunk.

lubricator *n.* [negative stereotype: his perceived 'greasiness'] [mid–late 19C] (*US*) a derog. name for a Mexican.

luchini *n.* (*also* **lucci**) [? play on SAmE *zucchini*, courgettes, which are 'green'; or ? ext. of SE *lucre*, money] [2000s] (*US black*) money.

luck *n.* (*also* **good luck**) [pvb 'Shitten luck is good luck'] [late 18C–early 19C] stepping into a heap of excrement.

SE in slang uses

IN PHRASES

▫ **break luck** *v.* **1** [1930s+] of a prostitute, to encounter the first customer of the day. **2** [1960s] in general use, to have a piece of good fortune. ▫ **change one's luck** *v.* **1** [1910s–70s] (*US*) for a white person to have sex with a black person (esp. for the first time). **2** [1970s+] (*US gay*) to perform homosexual sex for the first time. ▫ **do one's luck** *v.* [DO IN *v.* (5)] [1910s+] (*Aus.*) to use up or run out of luck. ▫ **luck of a Chow** *n. see* CHINAMAN'S LUCK *under* CHINAMAN *n.* ▫ **luck of Eric Connolly** *n.* [proper name of *Eric Connolly* (d.1944), known as an exceptionally lucky gambler] [1940s–60s] (*Aus.*) a description of any lucky person.

IN EXCLAMATIONS

▫ **half your luck!** [1930s+] (*Aus.*) signifying envy, jealousy of the person addressed, i.e. *I wish I had ...*

luck out *n.* [SE *luck out*, to strike lucky] [1970s+] (*orig. US*) a piece of good luck.

lucky *adj.*

SE in slang uses

IN COMPOUNDS

▫ **lucky bag** *n.* [fairground jargon *lucky bag*, a 'lucky dip'] [19C] the vagina. ▫ **lucky boy** *n.* (*also* **luck boy**) [mid-19C+] (*US*) a crooked professional gambler. ▫ **lucky Pierre** *n.* [? the punchline of a joke] **1** [1940s+] the man in a sexual threesome of two women and one man; or the woman between two men. **2** [1960s+] (*gay*) the middle man in a 'sandwich' of three sexually entwined men. ▫ **lucky shop** *n.* **1** [mid-19C] a public house. **2** [1970s+] (*Aus.*) a Totalizator Agency Board (TAB) betting shop in Victoria.

IN PHRASES

▫ **be lucky** [1930s+] (*mainly London*) goodbye. ▫ **get lucky** *v.* [1930s; 1980s+] of (usu.) a man, to seduce, to have sexual intercourse. ▫ **I should be so lucky** [the word-pattern implies a Yid. origin] [20C+] intimating envy on behalf of a speaker who has just been informed of another's luck, also used ironically. ▫ **lucky as a shithouse rat** *adj. see under* SHITHOUSE RAT *n.* ▫ **lucky for some** *n.* [20C+] (*bingo*) the number 13. ▫ **you should be so lucky** [? a Yid. phr.; certainly orig. identified with Jewish use] [1950s+] usu. in ironic use, you should be so lucky – but there's almost no hope that you will be.

lucky charm *n.* [rhy. sl.] [1990s+] the human arm.

lucky dip *n.* [rhy. sl.] **1** [20C+] a whip. **2** [20C+] in pl. chips, french fries. **3** [1980s+] (*Aus. prison*) LSD [TRIP *n.*[4] (1b)].

Lucozade *n.* (*also* **Luco, Luke**) [rhy. sl.; the brandname of the tonic drink *Lucozade* = SPADE *n.*] [1950s+] a black person.

lucy *n.* **1** [1950s–60s] (*S.Afr./US gay*) one who has a 'loose asshole'. **2** in drug uses [they all help one become SE *loose*; i.e. less tense, less stressed]. **(a)** [1950s+] marijuana. **(b)** [1980s+] heroin. **(c)** [1990s+] (*US black*) a cigarette.

IN PHRASES

▫ **sweet Lucy** *n. see under* SWEET *adj.*[1].

lucy in the sky with diamonds *n.* [the title of Beatles song (1967), the initial letters (and the psychedelic lyrics) of which left no one in doubt – for all the band's disclaimers – as to its subject] [1960s+] LSD.

lucy law *n.* [1960s+] (*gay*) the police.

lucy locket *n.* (*also* **locket**) [rhy. sl.] [1940s+] a pocket.

lud! *excl.* [18C–1940s] a form of *Lord!* and similarly used in mild oaths.

ludby *n. see* LOTEBY *n.*

lude *n.* (*also* **ludes, luds**) [brandname *Quaalude*, manufactured until 1983] [1970s+] (*US drugs*) methaqualone, or other depressant drugs; thus *ludehead*, a habitual user of the drug.

IN PHRASES

▫ **luded out** *adj.* [1980s+] (*US campus*) unable to function, usu. because of drugs.

Ludgate bird *n.* [*Ludgate* Prison, which housed mainly debtors] [17C] a bankrupt, one who has been imprisoned for bankruptcy.

Lud's bulwark *n.* [statues of the mythical King *Lud* and his sons used to stand on this old London gate, which the king had supposedly erected in 66BC, but it was more likely a Roman gate. Brewer, *Dict. of Phrase and Fable* (1894), suggests Ludgate comes from OE *ludgeat*, a postern, while Partridge opts for Norse *ludden*, thick, broad] [late 17C–early 19C] Ludgate prison.

Lud's unlucky gate *n.* [*see* LUD'S BULWARK *n.*] [17C] Ludgate Prison, mainly used for debtors.

luego *phr.* [Sp. *hasta luego*] [1980s+] (*US campus*) goodbye.

luer *n.* [proprietory name *Luer* brand syringe] [1930s–50s] (*US drugs*) a hypodermic syringe.

luff *n.* [echoic of a puff of wind; i.e. that expelled while talking] [early–late 19C] speech, talk.

l.u.g. *n.* [abbr. *l*esbian *u*ntil *g*raduation] [1990s+] (*orig. US campus*) a female student who is not necessarily a lesbian, but who experiments with feminism and lesbian politics and culture; thus var. *b.u.g.*, *b*isexual *u*ntil *g*raduation.

lug *n.*[1] [Scot./northern dial.] [late 16C+] an ear.

DERIVATIVES

▫ **lugful** *n.* [1980s] an 'earful', a sufficiency in being talked to, or in overhearing.

IN COMPOUNDS

▫ **lug-bashing** *n.* [1950s] (*Aus.*) talking effusively, preaching. ▫ **lug-bite** *v.* [late 19C–1930s] (*Aus.*) to cadge, to ask for a loan; thus *lug-biter*, a cadger. ▫ **lug-punch** *n.* [2000s] (*N.Z.*) a friendly chat.

IN PHRASES

▫ **bite someone's lug** *v.* [late 19C+] to borrow money. ▫ **blow down someone's lug** *v.* [1950s] (*Aus.*) to nag. ▫ **chew someone's lug** *v.* [late 19C] to beg. ▫ **put the lug on** *v.* [1960s+] (*US black*) to confront someone either as to their character or actions, to criticize, both seriously and in fun. ▫ **throw on the lug** *v.* [1900s] (*US*) to ask for or spend someone's money.

lug *n.*[2] [SE *lug* v., to drag, to haul. Such a heavyweight would need to be dragged along, mentally or physically. Note Scot. *luggie*, awkward, sluggish; mid 16C SE *lug*, something heavy and clumsy may be only coincidental] (*orig. US*) **1** [late 19C+] a large, stupid man. **2** [1930s] a lout, a sponger. **3** [1930s+] a general term of abuse. **4** [1950s] a person, irrespective of character.

IN COMPOUNDS

▫ **lughead** *n.* [-HEAD *sfx* (1)] [1940s+] (*US*) a stupid person.

IN PHRASES

▫ **put the lug on** *v.* (*also* **drop a lug on, drop the lug on**) **1** [1920s+] to beg; to demand money with menaces, to extort, to blackmail. **2** [1930s–40s] (*US*) to beat up, to use violence against.

lug *v.*[1] [SE *lug*, to drag] **1** [mid-19C+] to escort someone, to bring along a companion. **2** [20C+] to arrest or imprison.

3 [1900s–40s] (*US Und.*) to lure a victim into a confidence game.

IN PHRASES

▫ **lug out** *v.* **1** [late 17C–mid-18C] to draw a sword. **2** [late 19C] (*US*) to draw a gun. ▫ **lug someone's ear** *v.* [20C+] (*Aus.*) to borrow money.

lug *v.*[2] [LUG *n.*[1]] **1** [19C] to pawn. **2** [20C+] (*orig. US*) to beg. **3** [1930s] (*US*) to extend credit. **4** [1960s+] (*US black*) to berate, to criticize harshly.

IN COMPOUNDS

▫ **lug chovey** *n.* [CHOVEY *n.*] [mid–late 19C] a pawnshop.

IN PHRASES

▫ **in lug** [mid-19C] in pawn. ▫ **on the lug** [20C+] begging for a loan.

lug *v.*[3] [? LUG *n.*[1], as in *OED*; however *HDAS* suggests that this *lug* could poss. be a separate word] [1950s–70s] (*US Und.*) to beat up.

lug *v.*[4] [*PUT THE LUG ON under* LUG *n.*[1]] [1970s+] (*Can./US prison*) for one male prisoner to sexually assault another.

Lugan *n. see* LUGEN *n.*

lugan *n. see* LOOGAN *n.*

luge *adj.* [1990s+] (*W.I.*) huge, massive.

Lugen *n.* (*also* **Loogin, Lugan, Lugie, Lugun**) [? LOOGAN *n.* or *Lithuanian*] [1940s+] (*US*) a Lithuanian or person of Lithuanian background.

luggage *n.* **1** [late 19C+] the male genitals [pun on BAG *n.*[1] (1a)]. **2** [1950s+] (*US teen*) bags under the eyes [pun on SE *bags*].

lugger *n.*[1] [LUG *n.*[1]] [mid–late 19C] an earring.

lugger *n.*[2] [LUG *v.*[2]] **1** [1920s–40s] (*US Und.*) a beggar. **2** [1940s–50s] (*Aus.*) a nag.

lugger *n.*[3] [LUG *v.*[1] (3)] **1** [1920s+] (*US Und.*) an accomplice who makes contact with an intended victim or punter, also in a shoplifting team. **2** [1920s+] (*US Und.*) the accomplice (there are usu. two) who helps the actual thief remove the stolen goods from the store. **3** [1960s+] (*Can. prison*) a smuggler of contraband in or out of the prison.

lugging session *n. see WOOFING SESSION under* WOOFING *n.*

lughole *n.* [dial./LUG *n.*[1] (1)] [20C+] an ear.

IN PHRASES

▫ **pin back one's lugholes** *v.* [1940s+] to give one's full attention.

Lugie *n. see* LUGEN *n.*

lugs *n.* [late 19C–1930s] (*US*) affected manners, posing, pride.

IN PHRASES

▫ **put on lugs** *v.* (*also* **pile on lugs**) [late 19C–1930s] (*US*) to put on airs, to act affectedly.

Lugun *n. see* LUGEN *n.*

Luke *n. see* LUCOZADE *n.* (1).

luke *n.* [? northern dial.] [early–mid-19C] nothing.

Luke and Matt Goss *n.* [rhy. sl.; =TOSS *n.*[1]; ult. *Luke and Matt Goss*, the brothers that made up 1980s pop duo *Bros*] [1990s+] an infinitesimal amount; nothing whatsoever.

lukshen *n.* (*also* **loksh, luksh**) [Yid. *lokshen*, noodles, in this context pasta] [20C+] (*US Jewish*) an Italian.

lull *n.* [SE *lull*, a soothing drink] [mid-17C] ale.

lullaby *n.* [it 'puts one to sleep'] [mid–late 19C] the penis.

lullaby-cheat *n.* [SE *lullaby* + CHEAT *n.* (1), lit. 'lullaby-thing'] [mid-17C–mid-19C] (*UK Und.*) a child.

lullo-bump *n.* [? elision of SE *lay low* + *bump*, i.e. the position of the clitoris on the body and its shape] [1990s+] (*W.I.*) the clitoris.

lully *n.*[1] (*also* **lally, lulleys**) [? SE *laundry* or *lilywhite*] [mid-17C–19C] (*UK Und.*) **1** wet or drying linen. **2** a shirt, thus *dabble one's lally*, to wash a shirt.

IN COMPOUNDS

▫ **lully-prigger** *n.* [PRIG *v.*[2] (1)] [mid-18C–late 19C] **1** one who steals from washing lines or from wherever washing has been put out to dry. **2** a thief who catches and strips a child of its clothing. ▫ **lully-prigging** *n.* (*also* **lully-snow-prigging**) [PRIG *v.*[2] (1)] [mid-18C–late 19C] (*UK Und.*) the theft of washing.

lully *n.*[2] [SE *little* or *lullaby*] [late 18C] (*UK Und.*) a child.

lully-lily-berry *n.* [ety. unknown; SE *lily*, white + *berry*, i.e. the nipple, but ? *lully*] [mid-19C] (*UK Und.*) a woman's breast.

lulu *n.*[1] **1** (*also* **luluh**) from the proper name, seen as somewhat exotic. (**a**) [mid-19C–1930s] (*orig. US*) a girlfriend, a gangster's girlfriend. (**b**) [1950s] a silly young woman. **2** (*also* **looloo, looly, loulou**) anyone or anything exceptional [ety. unknown]. (**a**) [mid-19C+] (*orig. US*) anything, or anyone, remarkable, exceptional, wonderful. (**b**) [late 19C+] (*orig. US*) a disaster, an abject failure or a foolish person. (**c**) [late 19C+] (*US gambling*) a remarkable poker hand that beats a royal flush [ironic use of sense 2a]. **3** [1930s–50s] a 'clever' remark.

lulu *n.*[2] [redup. LOO *n.*[1]] [1930s+] the lavatory.

lulu *n.*[3] **1** [1950s] (*US Und.*) a venereally diseased penis; a severe case of gonorrhoea. **2** [2000s] the female genital area.

lulu *adj.* [LULU *n.*[1] (2a)] [1970s] (*US*) notable.

luluh *n. see* LULU *n.*[1] (1).

lulyah lass *n. see HALLELUJAH LASS under* HALLELUJAH *adj.*

lumb *n.* [? LUMBERED *adj.*[2] (1)] [18C–early 19C] (*UK Und.*) too much.

lumber *n.*[1] [17C SE *Lombard*, a bank, money-changer's or money-lender's office, a pawnshop. The Lombards, or natives of Lombardy, were celebrated bankers; thus the medieval *Lombard Room*, where pawnbrokers and bankers stored their pledges] **1** [early 17C–mid-19C] a pawnshop. **2** [early 17C–mid-19C] the state of being in pawn. **3** [mid-18C] stolen goods. **4** [mid-18C+] a house or room, esp. one used for storing stolen goods. **5** [late 18C–mid-19C] anywhere frequented by confidence tricksters and similar villains. **6** [1940s–80s] the flat from which a prostitute works, but does not occupy as a home.

IN COMPOUNDS

▫ **lumber cove** *n.* [COVE *n.* (1)] [late 18C–mid-19C] (*UK Und.*) the landlord of a thieves' meeting-place. ▫ **lumber gaff** *n.* (*also* **lumber joint**) [GAFF *n.*[1] (9)] [1930s–80s] the flat from which a prostitute works but which she does not occupy as a home. ▫ **lumber house** *n.* (*also* **lumber ken**) (*UK Und.*) **1** [18C–mid-19C] a drinking tavern frequented by criminals. **2** [early 19C] a house to which thieves bring stolen property after committing a crime. **3** [mid-19C] a pawnbroker's shop.

IN PHRASES

▫ **in lumber** **1** [early 19C+] (*mainly Aus.*) (*also* **in Lombard Street**) jailed, in prison. **2** [mid-19C] (*UK Und.*) in pawn. **3** [1930s+] in trouble, often extended to *in dead lumber*.

lumber *n.*[2] [? dial. *lumber*, mischief] **1** [1950s] a scheme, usu. criminal, an example of criminal activity. **2** [1960s+] sexual play, petting. **3** [1960s+] (*mainly Scot.*) a prospective sexual partner, a casual pick-up. **4** [2000s] violence, a fight.

lumber *n.*[3] **1** [1970s+] (*US*) the penis [pun on WOOD *n.*[1] (5)]. **2** [1970s+] (*US drugs*) unwanted twiggy stems in marijuana.

lumber *v.*[1] [LUMBER *n.*[1]] **1** [19C] to pawn. **2** [early 19C] (*UK Und.*) to hide oneself. **3** [early 19C+] (*orig. Aus.*) to arrest, to imprison. **4** [mid-19C] to be held subject to legal constraints. **5** [mid-19C] (*UK Und.*) to act as a receiver for stolen goods. **6** [1940s] (*S.Afr. prison*) to smuggle goods into a prison.

IN PHRASES

▫ **lumber out** *v.* [20C+] (*Aus.*) to throw out, to eject.

lumber *v.*[2] [LUMBER *n.*[2]] **1** [mid-19C] to saunter. **2** [mid-19C; 1950s] to steal. **3** [mid-19C+] to court, to 'chat up'; esp. with the intention of robbing the victim. **4** [1930s+] (*mainly Scot./Ulster*) to fondle sexually, to have intercourse. **5** [1930s+] to take, to escort. **6** [1980s+] (*S.Afr.*) to beat up.

IN COMPOUNDS

▫ **lumber joint** *n.* [1960s+] (*Aus.*) a hotel used for sexual assignations.

lumber *v.*[3] [late 19C+] to burden with.

lumbered *adj.*[1] [LUMBER *v.*[1]] **1** [early 19C+] pawned. **2** [early 19C+] (*Aus./UK Und.*) arrested. **3** [mid-19C+] imprisoned. **4** [1950s+] short of money, indebted.

lumbered *adj.*[2] [SE *lumber*, to weigh down, to fill up with; ult. *lumber*, useless, space-consuming objects] **1** [mid-19C+] burdened with, trapped. **2** [late 19C+] defeated, in trouble.

lumberer *n.*[1] [SE *lumber*, i.e. they are forced to sleep on piles of timber] **1** [mid-18C] a poor prostitute. **2** [mid-18C–early 19C] a tramp, a vagrant.

lumberer *n.*[2] [LUMBER *v.*[1]] **1** [mid–late 19C] a pawnbroker. **2** [late 19C] a swindling tipster. **3** [late 19C–1910s] any form of swindler. **4** [1900s–60s] a prostitute or pimp who specializes in robbing her/his clients. **5** [1960s] (*Aus.*) a traffic police officer (c.f. WALLOPER *n.*[1] (6)).

lumberjack *n.* [rhy. sl.; pun on SE *lumbar*] [1990s+] the human back.

lumber-Jill *n.* [a woman that looks like a SE *lumberjack*] [1940s+] an unattractive woman, with whom one cannot achieve an erection.

lumber (sauce) *n.* [SE *lumber*, wood] [1930s–60s] (*US*) a toothpick.

Lumbo *n.* [abbr.] [1970s] (*drugs*) Colombian marijuana.

luminous reader *n. see* READER *n.* (3).

lumme! *excl.* (*also* **lord lumme! lor lumme! lummie! lummy!**) ['Lord love me!'] [late 19C+] an excl. of surprise, shock, disbelief.

lummie! *excl. see* LUMME! *excl.*

lummocks *n.* (*also* **lommix, lummix, lummock, lummokin, lummox, lummux**) [dial. *lummock*, to move heavily or clumsily] [mid-19C+] a large, heavy or clumsy person, an ungainly or stupid lout; a fool.

(DERIVATIVES)

❑ **lummoxy** *adj.* [1950s+] awkward, careless, uncoordinated.

lummy *adj.* [Yorks. dial.] [19C] excellent; thus *lummy lick*, a delicious mouthful; *lumminess*, pleasant things.

lummy! *excl. see* LUMME! *excl.*

Lump, the *n.* [? its occupants are 'lumped together'] [late 19C–1930s] the workhouse, the casual ward, esp. the Marylebone workhouse; ext. as *Lump Hotel*.

lump *n.* **1** [early 16C+] (*also* **lumps**) a lot, a large quantity [*lumps* is 16C; *lump* late 17C+]. **2** [early 19C+] (*Irish*) a good size, usu. of a child. **3** [mid-19C] (*US*) a gold coin. **4** [late 19C–1930s] (*US*) semen; usu. as *BLOW ONE'S LUMP* below. **5** [late 19C+] (*US*) a parcel of food given to a tramp or vagrant [dial. *lump*, a luncheon]. **6** [1930s] (*US*) \$100. **7** [1930s+] (*US*) in pl., a beating, punishment, blame or criticism, usu. constructed with a pronoun and *give/take/get*. **8** [1940s+] (*US campus*) a lazy idler, a stupid person [LUMP *v.*[4]]. **9** [1940s+] (*US*) in pl., the female breasts. **10** [1960s] the head.

(IN PHRASES)

❑ **blow one's lump** *v.* [BLOW *v.*[1] (5)] **1** [late 19C–1930s] (*US*) to achieve orgasm; usu. of men, but also of women. **2** [1930s] (*US black*) to act in the desired manner. **3** [1930s–50s] (*US black*) (*also* **blow one's lumps**) to play very energetically; to give full expression to one's feelings. ❑ **take one's lumps** *v.* (*also* **get one's lumps**) [1940s+] (*orig. US*) to accept and deal with one's problems and setbacks, to 'get one's deserts'.

SE in slang uses

(IN COMPOUNDS)

❑ **lumphead** *n.* [-HEAD *sfx* (1)] [1910s–60s] (*orig. US*) an absolute fool, an idiot, an incompetent.

(IN PHRASES)

❑ **give someone lumps** *v.* [1930s–40s] to beat someone up. ❑ **lump of cake/duff** *n.* see *PIECE OF CAKE under* PIECE *n.* ❑ **lump of sin** *n.* see *PIECE OF SIN under* PIECE *n.* ❑ **lump of soap** *n.* see *under* SOAP *n.*[1] ❑ **lump of stone** *n.* [late 19C–1900s] (*UK Und.*) a local prison (i.e. one outside London). ❑ **lumps and bumps** *n.* [1980s+] (*Aus. prison*) a convict who loses a lot of fights.

lump *v.*[1] [SE *lump*, to look sulky or disagreeable] [late 18C+] (*orig. US*) to accept something, however grudgingly, that has to be endured.

(IN PHRASES)

❑ **like it or lump it** *v.* [late 18C+] to accept a situation, willingly or not; usu. as *You'll have to like it or lump it*, or sometimes the euph. phr. *If you don't like it you'll have to do the other thing*.

lump *v.*[2] (*also* **lump up**) [SE *lump*, to beat or thresh] **1** [late 18C+] to beat; to punch, to hit; as *n.* a blow. **2** [1950s] (*US*) to murder. **3** [1950s+] (*US*) to hit someone over the head with a lump of stone or a brick.

(DERIVATIVES)

❑ **lumping** *n.* [1930s] a beating.

lump *v.*[3] [mid-19C+] to haul about, to carry a heavy weight.

(IN PHRASES)

❑ **lump it** *v.* [mid-19C] (*UK Und.*) to drain a glass in a single swallow, to 'knock back'. ❑ **lump the lighter** *v.* [late 18C–late 19C] to be transported [fig. use of SE *lump*, to load + *lighter*, a vessel used for loading/unloading ships].

lump *v.*[4] (*also* **lump up**) [1940s+] (*US campus*) to act lazily, to do nothing.

lump *v.*[5] [1970s+] (*US*) to defecate.

lump and bump *n.* [rhy. sl. = CHUMP *n.*[1] (2)] [late 19C–1930s] a fool, a simpleton.

lumper *n.*[1] [LUMP *v.*[3]] **1** in (*UK Und.*) uses. (**a**) [late 18C–19C] (*also* **knockabout hand**) a riverside thief. (**b**) [late 18C–1940s] the 'lowest order and more contemptible species' of thief who lurk and grab whatever they can, regardless of value. (**c**) [mid-19C] a seller of goods under false pretences, the old made to look new, the weak strong etc. (**d**) [1950s] (*US prison*) a convict who is an orderly. **2** a type of labourer or contractor. (**a**) [late 18C+] a contractor or a worker who loads and unloads heavy cargo, orig. ship's cargo [cited as slang in Grose 1785]. (**b**) [mid–late 19C] a small contractor, a middleman, an exploitative factory owner. **3** [mid-19C] a militiaman [his stolidity and/or the weight of his equipment and pack; note dial. *lumper*, of a horse, to walk heavily; of a man, to stumble]. **4** [1950s–60s] in pl., a lump sum paid as unemployment compensation.

lumper *n.*[2] *see* LUMP OF LEAD *n.* (1).

lumping pennyworth *n.* [late 17C–mid-19C] a good bargain; thus [late 18C–early 19C] *get/have a lumping pennyworth*, to marry a fat woman.

lump of bread *n. see* LUMP OF LEAD *n.* (1).

lump of chalk *v. see* BALL OF CHALK *v.*

lump of coke *n.* [rhy. sl. = BLOKE *n.*] [mid-19C] a man, a person.

lump of ice *n.* [rhy. sl.] [late 19C–1900s] advice.

lump of lead *n.* [rhy. sl.] **1** [mid-19C+] (*also* **lumper, lump of bread**) the head. **2** [1950s–60s] a hangover, i.e. a HEAD *n.* (4a). **3** [2000s] (*Aus.*) bread.

lump of school *n.* [rhy. sl.] [late 19C–1900s] a fool.

lumpy *n.* [1950s] (*US*) a large man.

lumpy *adj.*[1] [dial. *lumpy*, awkward, sluggish] [early 19C–1900s] tipsy, slightly drunk.

lumpy *adj.*[2] [mid-19C] pregnant.

lumpy work *n.* [1910s] (*US*) unacceptable behaviour.

lun *n.* [UK theatrical manager John Rich, who in 1717 as 'John Lun' performed as 'Harlequin' in a new style of entertainment he called 'pantomime'] [late 18C–early 19C] Harlequin, the *commedia del arte* stock character; by. ext. any stage clown.

lunachick *n.* [pun on SE *lunatic*] [1990s+] (*US campus*) a crazy woman.

lunan *n.* [Rom. *loobni*, a prostitute] [mid–late 19C] (*tramp*) a woman.

lunar *n.* [abbr. SE *lunar observation*] [late 19C–1950s] a look, a glance; thus *take a lunar*, to glance at.

lunatic soup *n.* (*also* **lunatic's broth**) [20C+] (*Aus./Irish/N.Z.*) **1** cheap alcohol; spec. cheap red wine. **2** (*also* **electric soup**) methylated spirits as drunk by alcoholics.

lunch *n.* **1** [1900s] (*US*) a certainty, e.g. in betting. **2** in food-related contexts. (**a**) [1900s–10s] (*US*) the stomach. (**b**) [1910s+] (*US*) the contents of the stomach; *see* LOSE ONE'S LUNCH *under* LOSE *v.* (**c**) [1930s] (*US*) a lunch counter. (**d**) [1950s+] something/someone who is about to suffer or be physically hurt, or is already ruined [is only good to serve as food for some large predator]. **3** in sexual contexts. (**a**) [1920s–30s] cunnilingus. (**b**) [1940s+] the penis. (**c**) [1970s+] (*US gay*) the bulge of the genitals under the trousers. (**d**) *see* BASKET LUNCH *under* BASKET *n.*[1]. **4** [1960s+] (*US campus*) (*also* **lunchie, lunchy**) a dull, stupid person, a fool [i.e, one who is OUT TO LUNCH *adj.*]. **5** [2000s] a bonus, a profit [on the pattern of DRINK *n.*[4] (2)].

IN PHRASES

❑ **have lunch downtown** *v.* [DOWNTOWN *n.*] [1920s+] to engage in oral sex.

SE in slang uses

IN COMPOUNDS

❑ **lunch bag** *n.* (*also* **lunchbox, lunchbucket, lunch pail, lunchsack**) [one who is OUT TO LUNCH *adj.*; note *OnLine Dict. of Playground Slang* (2001): 'from people who brought lunch to school in a bag, then went off to sit and eat it alone because no-one liked them'] [1950s+] (*US campus*) a dull, foolish person, an undesirable person. ❑ **lunch-basket** *n.* (*also* **lunch-wagon**) [1910s] the stomach. ❑ **lunchbox** *n. see* separate entry. ❑ **lunch bucket** *adj.* **1** [1950s+] (*US*) working-class, blue-collar [*LUNCHPAIL* below]. **2** [1950s+] (*US*) stupid, dull, uninspiring [*LUNCH BAG* above]. ❑ **lunchcounter** *n.* (*also* **lunchpails**) [their provision of milk] [1960s] (*US*) the female breasts. ❑ **lunch gut** *n.* [1950s+] (*drugs*) the vomiting that may follow an injection of heroin. ❑ **lunch-hooks** *n.* [SE *lunch hook*, a hook used to remove meat from the pot] **1** [late 19C–1900s] (*US campus*) the teeth. **2** [late 19C+] (*orig. US*) the hand or fingers. ❑ **lunchmeat** *n.* **1** [1970s+] (*US campus*) a stupid, contemptible person. **2** [1970s+] (*US gay*) the bulge of the genitals through the trousers. **3** [1980s+] (*US*) nonsense. **4** [1990s+] (*US*) a victim. ❑ **lunchpack** *n. see* LUNCHBOX *n.* (2). ❑ **lunchpail** *n.* (*also* **lunchpailer**) [metonymy] **1** [1950s+] (*orig. US*) a blue-collar worker. **2** *see LUNCH BAG* above. ❑ **lunchpails** *n. see LUNCHCOUNTER* above. ❑ **lunchsack** *n. see LUNCH BAG* above. ❑ **lunch wagon** *n. see LUNCH-BASKET* above.

IN PHRASES

❑ **anti-lunch** *n.* [either the drink is seen as counteracting one's appetite or the sp. should be *ante-*] [19C] an appetizer, a drink taken before lunch. ❑ **eat someone's lunch** *v.* [1950s+] (*US*) to defeat, injure or outdo someone. ❑ **have someone for lunch** *v.* [1950s] to subject to intense pressure. ❑ **out to lunch** *adj. see* separate entry. ❑ **who opened their lunch?** [1960s–70s] (*Aus.*) who broke wind?

lunch *adj.* [OUT TO LUNCH *adj.*] **1** [1960s+] stupid, foolish, crazy. **2** [1990s+] good, excellent, admirable.

lunch *v.*[1] [LUNCH *n.* (2d)] [1950s+] (*US campus*) to spoil, ruin or fail.

lunch *v.*[2] [OUT TO LUNCH *adj.*] **1** [1980s+] (*US campus*) to lack concentration, to be unaware. **2** [1980s+] (*US black/teen*) to act in a silly or irrational manner; to overreact; to procrastinate. **3** [1990s+] (*US black*) to go insane.

DERIVATIVES

❑ **lunching** *adj.* [1950s+] crazy, stupid.

lunch at the lazy Y *v.* [the Y refers both to the spread legs and to the YMCA/YWCA] [1950s+] (*US*) to perform cunnilingus.

lunchbox *n.* **1** [1970s] (*US black*) the stomach. **2** [1980s+] (*also* **lunchpack**) the male genitals, esp. when large and prominent beneath tight shorts or trousers. **3** [2000s] the female genitals. **4** *see LUNCH BAG under* LUNCH *n.*

IN COMPOUNDS

❑ **lunchbox lancer** *n.* [1990s+] a male homosexual.

IN PHRASES

❑ **open one's lunchbox** *v.* [1980s+] to break wind; thus question *who opened their lunchbox?* ❑ **your lunchbox is open** [1970s] your fly is open.

lunched-out *adj.* [OUT TO LUNCH *adj.*] [1970s+] (*US*) dazed, unaware, stupid.

lunchie/lunchy *n. see* LUNCH *n.* (4).

lunchy *adj.* [OUT TO LUNCH *adj.*] [1960s+] (*US campus*) **1** dull, stupid, absent-minded. **2** carefree, light-hearted, jokey. **3** unfashionable, out of style, e.g. *He looks so lunchy wearing that bow tie.*

lung *n.* [note SE *lungs*, the fire-blower for a chemist] **1** [late 17C–mid-18C] in pl., a powerfully-voiced person. **2** [1930s+] (*orig. US*) (*also* **lungers**) in pl., the female breasts; occas. in sing., thus adj. *lungy*, having large breasts. **3** [1950s] (*US*) constr. with *the*, tuberculosis. **4** [1980s+] (*drugs*) a form of pipe used for smoking cannabis.

SE in slang uses

IN COMPOUNDS

❑ **lung biscuit** *n.* [1980s] (*US campus*) a lump of phlegm. ❑ **lung-box** *n.* [mid–late 19C] the mouth. ❑ **lung-buster** *n.* [1980s+] (*Aus./N.Z.*) a cigarette. ❑ **lung-duster** *n.* [1920s–40s] (*US black*) a cigarette. ❑ **lung warts** *n.* [1940s+] (*US*) the female breasts, esp. when small.

lung *v.* [1900s] (*US campus*) to argue.

lunger *n.* (*US*) **1** [late 19C+] one who is suffering from lung disease (i.e. tuberculosis) or has been wounded in the lungs. **2** [1940s+] (*also* **loogee**) a mouthful of spit, a gob of phlegm; thus *hack up a lunger*, to spit. **3** [1980s] a strong cigarette.

lunie *n. see* LOONY *n.*

lunk *n.* [abbr. LUNKHEAD *n.*] (*US*) **1** [mid-19C+] a fool. **2** [1940s+] an oaf, an ungainly person.

DERIVATIVES

❑ **lunky** *adj.* [1940s+] stupid.

lunk *adj.* [Scot. *lunkie*, close, ult. Norwegian *lunke*, a tepid degree of heat] [late 19C+] (*Irish*) **1** of weather, close, sultry. **2** of a person, feeling ill.

lunker *n.* [? CLUNKER *n.*[1] or LUNK *n.* (2)] (*US*) **1** [mid-19C] something large and unruly. **2** [1970s+] a dilapidated motor car.

lunkhead *n.* [? SE *lump* + -HEAD *sfx* (1)] [mid-19C+] (*orig. US*) an absolute fool, an idiot, an incompetent.

lunkheaded *adj.* [LUNKHEAD *n.*] [late 19C+] slow-witted, foolish.

luny *see under* LOONY.

luokal-mediocal *n.* [W.I. pron. of SE *local mediocre*] [1950s] (*W.I.*) an undependable, untrustworthy person.

luppie *n.* [abbr.] [1990s+] **1** (*US gay*) a lesbian urban professional, i.e. a lesbian YUPPIE *n.* **2** (*US*) a Latino/Latina urban professional, i.e. Hispanic YUPPIE *n.*

luptious *adj.* [SE *voluptuous* + *delicious*] [mid-19C–1900s] delicious, luscious, lovely.

lur-a-cham *n. see* LERACAM *n.*

lurch *n.* [LURCH *v.*[1] (1)] [mid-16C+] a cheat or swindle, often ext. as *give the lurch*; thus *in one's lurch*, at a disadvantage; *have/take at/in lurch*, to have at a disadvantage; *leave in the lurch*, to abandon in difficulty without assistance.

SE in slang uses

IN PHRASES

❑ **on the lee lurch** *adj.* [mid-19C] (*US*) drunk.

lurch *v.*[1] [MHGer. *lurz*, left, wrong, thence *lurzen*, to deceive. The Ger. appears to have been adopted into Fr. as *lourche*, the name of a game similar to backgammon, and in its heyday equally popular in Britain. In it, a *lurch* meant a game in which one player defeats an opponent to a score of zero. Those who lose a game of whist without scoring five are *lurched*] **1** [mid-16C+] to deceive, to get the better of; to steal. **2** [mid-19C] (*UK Und.*) to abandon.

lurch *v.*[2] [2000s] (*Irish*) to dance very close together.

lurcher *n.* [SE *lurcher*, a swindler, a rogue] [20C+] **1** (*Aus.*) a rascal, a villain. **2** (*Aus.*) a Bohemian, one who acts without regard for social convention [LARRIKIN *n.* (1)]. **3** (*Ulster*) one who lurks around waiting for an advantage to present itself.

lurcher (of the law) *n.* [dial. *lurch*, lurk or slink about] [18C–early 19C] the lowest rank of bailiff, a 'bum bailiff'.

lure *n.* [SE *lure*, anything that tempts or entices] [late 17C–18C] 'an idle pamphlet' (B.E.), i.e. a prostitute.

lured *adj.* [ety. unknown] [20C+] (*Ulster*) happy, cheerful.

lurgi *n.* (*also* **lergy, lurgy**) [popularly attrib. to the writers of *The Goon Show* (1953–60), but the *EDD* cites *lurgy*, idleness, loafing

+ *lurgy-fever*, the 'disease' of idleness. The *OED* adds the synon. *fever-lurden, fever-lurgan*, ult. SE *fever* + *lurdan*, 'a general term of opprobrium, reproach, or abuse, implying either dullness and incapacity, or idleness and rascality; a sluggard, vagabond, "loafer"'] [1940s+] any unspecified but deleterious disease or ailment; esp. as the minatory phr. *dreaded lurgi*.

lurid limit *n. see* DIZZY LIMIT *under* DIZZY *adj.*

lurk *n.* [SE *lurk*, to hide oneself, to lie in ambush, to remain furtively or unobserved about one spot] **1** [19C] (*UK Und.*) a form of fraud in which one pretends some form of distress in order to raise money from the credulous; thus *go on a lurk*, get money through false pretences. **2** [mid-19C+] a hideaway, a meeting place; thus *servant lurk*, a public house where duplicitous servants meet criminals to plan mutually beneficial robberies. **3** [mid-19C+] (*Aus./N.Z.*) a dodge, racket or scheme; thus *up to all lurks*, wide-awake, cunning. **4** [late 19C+] (*Aus./N.Z.*) a job. **5** [20C+] (*Aus.*) a hanger-on, an eavesdropper. **6** [1950s–60s] (*Aus.*) the best place to meet someone or find some product or whatever. **7** [2000s] (*S.Afr.*) cheap white wine, 'rotgut'.

DERIVATIVES

❑ **lurkola** *n.* [+ -OLA *sfx*] [1950s+] (*Aus.*) the practice (ostensibly illegal and generally denied by its practitioners) of bribing (with cash or kind) those with access to the public to tout a product. ❑ **lurky** *adj.* [1970s+] (*US campus*) seedy, untrustworthy, weird.

IN COMPOUNDS

❑ **lurkman** *n.* [mid-19C+] (*Aus.*) a confidence trickster, a petty criminal.

IN PHRASES

❑ **lurks and purks** *n.* [1970s] tricks and bonuses.

lurk *v.* [SE *lurk*; i.e. one tends to adopt a 'low profile' while driving in this way] [1960s] (*US black*) to go riding in a stolen car.

lurker *n.* [LURK *n.*] **1** [mid–late 19C] a criminal beggar who travels the country showing off various forged certificates referring to losses in fires, shipwrecks or similar disasters and hoping thereby to get financial aid. **2** [20C+] (*Aus.*) a petty criminal.

lurking *n.* [LURK *n.* (1)] [mid-19C] (*UK Und.*) **1** stealing. **2** fraudulent begging, following the occupation of a fraudulent beggar.

lurp *n.* [play on SE *lurch*] [1990s+] (*US teen*) an extremely clumsy or awkward person; thus adj. *lurpy*.

lurries *n.* [LURRY *n.*] (*UK Und.*) **1** [mid-17C–mid-18C] clothes. **2** [mid-17C–early 19C] a quantity of valuables, e.g. watches and rings.

lurry *n.* [LOUR *n.*] [mid-17C–mid-18C] money.

lurry up *v. see* LORRY UP *v.*

lus *n.* [Afk. *lus vir*, desirous of] [1970s+] (*S.Afr.*) a yearning, a longing; thus *be lus for*, to long for.

lush *n.*[1] (*also* **lusho**) [? Ger. *Loschen*, strong beer, Shelta *lush*, to eat and drink] **1** [late 17C+] alcohol, esp. beer. **2** [mid–late 19C] a drink. **3** [mid-19C+] a drunkard. **4** [mid-19C+] a drinking spree. **5** [1940s–60s] (*US*) in fig. use of sense 3 above, a victim or fool. **6** [2000s] in fig. use, an addict. **7** *see* LUSH ROLL below.

DERIVATIVES

❑ **lusher** *n. see* LUSH WORKER below.

IN COMPOUNDS

❑ **lush betty** *n.* [BETTY *n.* (2)] [mid-19C] (*US*) a whisky bottle. ❑ **lush blowen** *n.* [BLOWEN *n.* (1)] [mid-19C] (*UK Und.*) a drunken woman. ❑ **lushbum** *n.* [BUM *n.*[3] (1)] [1940s] (*US*) an alcoholic tramp. ❑ **lush cove** *n.* [COVE *n.* (3)] [mid-19C] a publican. ❑ **lush crib** *n.* (*also* **lushing crib**) [CRIB *n.*[1] (3)] [19C] a saloon or bar. ❑ **lush dip** *n. see* LUSH ROLL, LUSH WORKER below. ❑ **lush diver** *n. see* LUSH WORKER below. ❑ **lush drum** *n.* [DRUM *n.*[3] (3)] [mid–late 19C] (*UK Und./US*) a saloon or bar. ❑ **lush grafter** *n. see* LUSH WORKER below. ❑ **lush-head** *n.* [-HEAD *sfx* (4)] [1930s–60s] (*US*) a drunkard. ❑ **lush hound** *n.* [-HOUND *sfx* (1)] [1930s–50s] a drunkard. ❑ **lush-house** *n.* [late 19C–1920s] a bar or saloon. ❑ **lush joint** *n.* (*also* **lush dive**) [JOINT *n.* (3b)/DIVE *n.*[2] (1)] [1930s–60s] a saloon, a bar. ❑ **lush ken** *n.* (*also* **lushing ken**) [KEN *n.*[1] (1)] [late 18C–1920s] (*UK/US Und.*) an alehouse, saloon or bar. ❑ **lush kick** *n.* [KICK *n.*[5] (1)] [1950s] (*US*) a sense of drunkenness; the positive effect of alcohol. ❑ **lush lover** *n.* [1930s] (*US black*) a heavy drinker. ❑ **lush merchant** *n.* [MERCHANT *n.*] [late 19C+] (*Aus.*) a drunkard. ❑ **lush-out** *n.* [early 19C–1900s] a drinking bout. ❑ **lushpad** *n.* [PAD *n.*[2] (2)] [1940s] (*US black/Harlem*) a bar. ❑ **lush panny** *n.* [PANNEY *n.*[2] (1)] [19C] a bar, a saloon, a tavern. ❑ **lush roll** *v.* (*also* **lush, lush dip, roll a lush**) [ROLL *v.* (3a)] [1910s–80s] (*orig. US*) to rob a drunk; thus n. *lushrolling*. ❑ **lush roller** *n.* [1910s–60s] (*US*) one who specializes in robbing sleeping or passed-out drunks, esp. in subways. ❑ **lush stash** *n.* [STASH *n.*[2] (3)] [1900s–40s] (*US black*) a bar, a tavern. ❑ **lush-toucher** *n.* [1900s–40s] (*US*) a person who robs a drunk. ❑ **lush trotter** *n.* [19C] (*orig. US*) a boy or girl who is sent to the saloon to bring back beer either for their parents or for working men who cannot leave their jobs. ❑ **lush wallower** *n.* [late 19C] (*Aus.*) a heavy drinker. ❑ **lushwell** *n.* [1960s+] (*US*) a heavy drinker. ❑ **lush worker** *n.* (*also* **lush dip, ...diver, ...grafter, lusher**) [+ WORKER *n.*[1] (1)/DIP *n.*[1] (3)/DIVER *n.* (3)/GRAFTER *n.*[1] (1)] **1** [1900s] (*US*) in fig. use, one who drinks heavily and/or associates with drunks. **2** [1910s+] (*US*) one who specializes in robbing sleeping or passed-out drunks, esp. in subways.

lush *n.*[2] [? SE *luscious*] [mid–late 19C] (*US Und.*) money.

lush *n.*[3] [SE *luscious*] **1** [late 19C] something luscious, i.e. sexually titillating. **2** [1940s–50s] (*US gay*) an extremely attractive heterosexual man. **3** [1980s+] (*US campus*) an attractive woman.

lush *adj.*[1] [LUSH *v.*[1] (1)] [early 19C+] drunk.

lush *adj.*[2] [SE *luscious*] **1** [1910s+] of a woman, very sexually attractive, esp. if voluptuous, also of a man. **2** [1950s+] good, excellent.

IN COMPOUNDS

❑ **lush thrush** *n.* [1940s–50s] a very attractive young woman.

lush *adj.*[3] [LUSH *n.*[2]] (*US*) **1** [1930s–40s] wealthy. **2** [1940s+] hedonistic, luxurious.

lush *v.* [LUSH *n.*[1] (1)] **1** [19C–1900s] to ply with drink, to make drunk. **2** [early 19C+] to drink.

IN PHRASES

❑ **lush (it) up** *v.* **1** [late 19C+] (*also* **lush around**) to drink, usu. alcohol; to become drunk. **2** [1920s+] to ply with drink. ❑ **lush at Freeman's Quay** *v. see* DRINK AT FREEMAN'S QUAY *under* DRINK *v.*

lushed *adj.* [LUSH *v.*[1]] [19C+] drunk.

IN COMPOUNDS

❑ **lushed up** *adj.* **1** [1920s+] drunk. **2** [1950s] intoxicated by drugs.

lusher *n.* [LUSH *v.*[1]] **1** [mid-19C–1950s] (*US*) a heavy drinker, a drunk. **2** [1910s–30s] a prostitute who preys on drunken customers.

lushery *n.* [LUSH *n.*[1] (1)] [mid–late 19C] a saloon or bar.

lushey *adj. see* LUSHY *adj.*[1] (1).

lushie *n. see* LUSHY *n.*

lushing *n.* [LUSH *v.*[1]] [mid-19C+] drinking, usu. to excess.

IN COMPOUNDS

❑ **lushing crib** *n. see* LUSH CRIB *under* LUSH *n.*[1]. ❑ **lushing ken** *n. see* LUSH KEN *under* LUSH *n.*[1].

lushing *adj.* [LUSH *v.*[1]] [mid–late 19C] used of a person who enjoys drinking.

Lushington *n.* (*also* **lushington**) [either LUSH *n.*[1] (1), the proper name *Lushington* (a brewer) or f. 'The "City of Lushington" which, according to the *OED*, 'was the name of a convivial society (consisting chiefly of actors) which met at the Harp Tavern, Russell Street, until about 189? It had a "Lord Mayor" and four "aldermen", presiding over "wards" called Juniper, Poverty, Lunacy, and Suicide. On the admission of a new member, the "Lord Mayor" ... harangued him on the evils of excess in drink.' The society was founded c.1750] [19C] a drunkard; thus *dealing with Lushington, Alderman Lushington is concerned, voting for the Alderman, Lushington is his master*, to be drinking too much.

lusho *n. see* LUSH *n.*[1].

lush up *v.* [LUSH *adj.*[3]] [1960s] to provide with a luxurious standard of living.

lushy *n.* (*also* **lushie**) [LUSH *n.*[1] (3)] [1940s] (*US black*) a drunkard.

lushy *adj.*[1] [LUSH *n.*[1] (1)] **1** [early 19C–1950s] (*also* **lushey**) drunk, tipsy. **2** [mid-19C] drunken.

IN COMPOUNDS

❑ **lushy cove** *n.* [COVE *n.* (1)] [early–late 19C] a drunkard.

lushy *adj.*[2] [LUSH *adj.*[2] (1)] [1980s+] (*US campus*) sexy, voluptuous.

lust dog *n.* [DOG *n.*[2] (3c)] [1970s+] (*US campus*) a male term for an allegedly promiscuous woman.

lustre *n.* [mid-19C] (*UK Und.*) a diamond.

lusty *n.* [2000s] (*N.Z. teen*) an attractive person.

lusty cod *n.* (*also* **jolly cod, rum cod**) [SE *lusty*, massive, substantial + COD *n.*[3] (3)] [late 17C] (*UK Und.*) a substantial sum of money.

lusty-guts *n.* [late 16C–early 17C] a promiscuous man, a womanizer.

lusty lawrence *n.* [a ballad entitled 'Lusty Laurence' is entered in the Stationers' Register 1594] [late 16C–17C] a womanizer, a promiscuous man.

Lute *n. see* LOOT *n.*[2].

lute *n.*[1] [both *doubles entendres*: an 'instrument' upon which one 'plays'] [17C–18C] **1** the vagina. **2** the penis; thus *play a lute solo*, to masturbate.

lute *n.*[2] [abbr.] [1950s+] (*US*) a *Lut*heran.

luv, luv *adj.* [2000s] (*US prison*) wealthy, successful.

luv-up *n. see* LOVE UP *n.*

luvvie *n.* (*also* **luvvy**) **1** [1950s+] a general term of affectionate greeting. **2** [1980s+] a slightly derog. synon. for an actor or actress, esp. of the more demonstrative and overtly emotional type [their stereotyped effusive cries of 'Luvvie! Darling!' on meeting].

lux *v.* [abbr. brandname Electro*lux*] [1970s+] (*N.Z.*) to vacuum a carpet etc.

luxcolquarron luxury *n.* [obs. SE *luxate*, to dislocate, to put out of joint + COLQUARRON *n.*] [mid-19C] (*UK Und.*) 'the breakneck pleasure of being hanged' *New & Improved Flash Dict.* (Duncombe, 1850).

luzz *v.* [1990s+] (*UK juv.*) to throw.

L.W.O.P. *n.* [pron. 'el-wop'; abbr. *l*ife *w*ith*o*ut *p*arole] [2000s] (*US prison*) a life sentence with no possibility of parole.

lyb beg/lybbeg/lyb bege *n. see* LIB-BEG *n.*

lybkin *n. see* LIBKEN *n.*

lydia *adj.* [play on US singer, poet, writer and actress *Lydia Lunch* (Lydia Koch, b.1959), although link is unclear] [2000s] (*S.Afr. gay*) small.

lye *n.* [? US Southern *lye*, hominy (corn)] [1990s+] (*US drugs*) marijuana (smoke).

lying in state *phr. see under* STATE *n.*

l.y.k.a.h. *phr.* [abbr.] [20C+] (*Irish*) *l*eave *y*our *k*nickers *a*t *h*ome, written by men on the back of letters to their loved ones.

lyle *n. see* LALLIE *n.*

Lymps, the *n.* [abbr.] [mid-19C] the O*lymp*ic Theatre, London.

lyp *v. see* LIB *v.*

lyrebird *n.* [pun on SE *lyrebird*] [20C+] (*Aus.*) a liar, a mimic.

lyrics *n.* [1980s+] (*UK black*) **1** fantasies, wild talk. **2** talk with no overtones.

lyricsing *n.* [1980s+] (*UK black*) chatting up, sweet-talking.

M *n.* [abbr.] (*drugs*) **1** [1910s+] (*also* **em**) morphine. **2** [1950s+] marijuana. **3** [1980s+] MDMA.

ma *n.* (*also* **mother**) [1930s+] a derog. title put before a man's name to imply his homosexuality.

maaga *adj.* see MAUGER *adj.*

Maalox moment *n.* [the proprietary antacid *Maalox*; the phr. was coined for an advertising campaign] [1990s+] (*orig. US campus*) a time of stress.

maas *n.* [? fig. use of Jam. *maas*, master] [1990s+] (*W.I.*) money.

maat *n.* (*also* **maatie, maatjie**) [Du. *maat*, a friend] [20C+] (*S.Afr.*) a friend, a chum, a pal.

mab *n.*[1] (*also* **mob**) [SE *mab*, a slattern] [late 18C–early 19C] a prostitute.

IN COMPOUNDS

❑ **mabbed up** *adj.* [late 17C–early 18C] (*UK Und.*) carelessly dressed.

mab *n.*[2] [rhy. sl.] [early–mid-19C] a cab.

mabby *adj.* [? female name *Mab*(*el*)] [mid-19C] (*UK Und.*) cowardly, timid.

Mabel *n.* **1** [1950s] (*US*) a woman, a girl. **2** [1950s] (*Aus.*) a girlfriend. **3** [1970s+] (*US gay*) a black man.

Ma Bell *n.* (*also* **Maw Bell**) [SE *ma*, i.e. mother + the earlier firm, the *Bell* Telephone Company] [1920s+] (*US*) the American Telephone & Telegraph Inc., orig. *Maw Bell*.

mab-ridden *adj.* [mid-19C] (*UK Und.*) frightened (of retribution), suffering a guilty conscience.

Mac *n.* (*also* **mac, mack**) [Irish/Gaelic *mac*, son] **1** [17C+] a Celtic Irishman. **2** [18C+] a male Scot. **3** [20C+] (*Can.*) McMaster University, Hamilton, Ontario. **4** [20C+] (*US*) a term of greeting with no specific ref. to Scottish or Irish men implied. **5** [1990s+] (*also* **mack**) a Mac-10 machine pistol.

Mc- *pfx* (*also* **Mac**) [see McJOB *n.*] [1980s+] (*orig. US campus*) used to emphasize the mediocre or mass-market quality of the combined n.

mac *n.*[1] [abbr.] **1** [late 19C+] (*W.I.*) one shilling (post-1969 value 10 cents) [abbr. MACARONI *n.*[1] (3)]. **2** [1970s] a condom [SE *mac*(*intosh*)].

mac *n.*[2] see MACK *n.*[2].

macadam *n.* [SE *macadam*, a type of road made of compacted layers of stone, invented by *John Loudon McAdam* (1756–1836). The fritter is hard and flat like the road] [1950s] (*W.I.*) a codfish fritter.

macadocious *adj.* see MACKADOCIOUS *adj.*

McAlpine fusilier *n.* [*McAlpine*, a leading UK construction company] [1960s+] a building labourer, a navvy.

mac-and-fip *n.* [MAC *n.*[1] + FIP *n.* (2)] [1940s+] (*W.I.*) one shilling and three pence (post-1969 value 15 cents).

macaroni *n.*[1] **1** [18C] a jolly fool, esp. an Italian one. **2** [mid-18C–1930s] a fop, a dandy, thus *macaroni-stake*, a horserace ridden by a 'gentleman jockey' [the *Macaroni Club*, 'which is composed of all the travelled young men who wear long curls and spying-glasses' (Horace Walpole ed., *Letters of Earl Hertford*, 1764). The travelling, suggests the *OED*, prob. gave the members a taste for foreign foods, hence the name]. **3** [early 19C+] (*W.I.*) (*also* **maccarony**) one shilling (post-1969 value 10 cents) [? the tip commonly proffered by a dandy]. **4** [mid-19C+] (*also* **macaroni bender**) an Italian [note synon. US regional use *macaroni-smacker, macaroni-snapper*].

IN COMPOUNDS

❑ **macaroni queen** *n.* [QUEEN *n.* (2)] [1980s+] (*US gay*) a non-Italian gay man who prefers Italian partners.

macaroni *n.*[2] [rhy. sl.] **1** [mid-19C] (*Aus.*) a pony. **2** [mid-19C+] £25; (*Aus.*) $25 [= PONY *n.* (1b)]. **3** [1920s+] (*Aus.*) nonsense, meaningless talk [joc. use of SE, but note PONY (AND TRAP) *n.* (2)]. **4** [1970s+] a piece of human excrement; thus the act of defecation [PONY (AND TRAP) *n.* (1)].

macaroni *n.*[3] [joc. ext. of MACK *n.*[2] (1)] [1970s+] (*US*) the middleman, usu. a pimp, who stands between the client and prostitute.

IN PHRASES

❑ **macaroni with cheese** *n.* [1970s+] (*US black*) someone involved in a wide variety of activities such as pimping, drug-selling and gambling games.

macaroni *adj.* [MACARONI *n.*[1] (4)] [mid-19C+] Italian.

macaroon *n.*[1] [early 17C+] a buffoon, a blockhead, a dolt.

macaroon *n.*[2] [rhy. sl. = COON *n.* (5)] [20C+] a black person.

McAtah *n.* [W.I. pron. of (Douglas) *McArthur* (1880–1964), US general] [1980s] (*W.I.*) mirrored dark glasses.

macca *adj.*[1] [W.I. dial. *macca*, a thorn, thus cognate with SHARP *adj.* (2)] [1990s+] (*W.I.*) exceptionally good.

IN PHRASES

❑ **macca-man** *n.* [but note *mack man* under MACK *n.*[2]] [1970s] (*W.I.*) a tough, strong, efficient man.

macca *adj.*[2] [1990s+] (*UK juv.*) very large.

macco *n.* see MACO *n.*[1].

McCoy *n.* **1** [1900s–40s] first-rate whisky or beer; often as *clear McCoy*. **2** [1930s] (*US*) money. **3** [1930s–50s] (*US drugs*) medicinal drugs; pure narcotics.

McCoy (the) *n.* see REAL McCOY, THE *n.*

McCoy *adj.* [REAL McCOY, THE *n.*] [1920s–60s] (*US*) genuine, correct, excellent.

McDaddy *n.* see MACK DADDY *n.*

macdaddy *adj.* see MACK DADDY *n.*

mcdumpster kid *n.* [the image is of such a person forced to scavenge in the dumpsters or skips that contain refuse food from a McDonald's restaurant] [2000s] (*US black*) a homeless, starving young person.

Mace *n.* [the prize-fighter Jem *Mace* (1831–1910)] [late 19C] (*Aus.*) physical violence.

mace *n.* [ety. unknown; poss. link to MASON *n.*[1]; SE *mace*, a club, but the violence is only fig.] **1** [mid-18C–1930s] a swindle, a fraud, confidence tricks. **2** [late 18C–19C] a confidence trickster, a swindler, 'a rogue assuming the character of a gentleman, or opulent tradesman, who under that appearance defrauds workmen, by borrowing a watch, or other piece of goods till one [that] he bespeaks is done [swindled] ' (Grose, 1785).

IN COMPOUNDS

❑ **mace-cove** *n.* [COVE *n.* (1)] **1** [early–mid-19C] a confidence trickster, a swindler. **2** [late 19C] (*Aus. Und.*) a housebreaker. ❑ **mace-gloak** *n.* [GLOAK *n.*] [early 19C] a confidence trickster, a swindler. ❑ **maceman** *n.* **1** [19C] a confidence trickster. **2** [mid-19C] one who defaults on their debts. **3** [late 19C] an élite criminal.

IN PHRASES

❑ **on the mace** *adj.* **1** [early 18C–mid-19C] (*UK Und.*) living as a swindler. **2** [mid–late 19C] on credit. ❑ **strike the mace** *v.* [early 19C] to persuade a shopkeeper to sell one goods on credit, although one has no intention of ever making that credit good; to borrow from friends without intending repayment. ❑ **work the mace** *v.* [19C] to swindle.

mace *v.* [MACE *n.*] **1** [late 18C+] to sponge, to swindle. **2** [early 19C–1930s] to fail to pay one's debts; thus *give (something to someone) on the mace*, to obtain goods by persuading the shopkeeper to extend credit that one has no intention of paying. **3** [early 19C–1950s] (*US*) to beg or demand money from. **4** [1920s] (*UK Und.*) to avoid paying one's train fare.

IN PHRASES

❑ **mace the rattler** *v.* [RATTLER *n.* (1)] [late 19C–1930s] to travel by train without buying a ticket.

macer *n.* [MACE *v.*] **1** [early–mid-19C; 1970s] a swindler. **2** [late 19C; 1970s] a thief, a villain.

McFly *n.* [the character George *McFly* in the *Back to the Future* films (1985, 1989, 1990)] [1980s+] (*US campus*) a fool, an empty-headed person; thus *McFly!* wake up!

MacGimp *n.* (*also* **M'Gimp, McGimp, MacGimper, magimp, megimp**) [rhy. sl.] [1910s–60s] (*US*) a pimp.

MacGorrey's Hotel *n.* [the name of a contemporary governor] [late 19C–1900s] Chelmsford prison, Essex.

McGuyver *n.*

IN PHRASES

❑ **pull a McGuyver** *v.* [1980s TV detective show *McGuyver*] [1990s+] (*US campus*) to do something mechanically very clever.

mach *n.* **1** *see* MACON *n.* **2** *see* MECH *n.*

macher *n.* (*also* **mocher**) [Yid.] [1910s+] an influential, powerful person.

machine *n.* **1** in sexual contexts. (**a**) [early 18C] a prostitute. (**b**) [mid-18C–late 19C; 1940s+] (*also* **spit-fire machine, electric machine**) the penis. (**c**) [late 18C–early 19C] a condom. (**d**) [late 19C–1940s] the vagina. **2** [late 19C–1940s] (*N.Z.*) a Totalizator. **3** [20C+] (*US*) an automobile. **4** [1970s] (*drugs*) a hypodermic syringe. **5** [1970s+] (*US campus*) a motorcycle.

-machine *sfx* [1930s+] (*US*) combining form that indicates an enthusiast, a devotee, e.g. *sex-machine, rap-machine*.

machinery *n.* **1** [early 19C] the head. **2** [1930s] (*US prison*) a male homosexual [MACHINE *n.* (1)]. **3** [1930s+] (*US drugs*) the equipment used for injecting a narcotic. **4** [1980s+] the male genitals. **5** [1980s+] (*drugs*) marijuana. **6** [1990s+] a revolver, a pistol.

macing *n.*[1] [MACE *v.*] [19C+] cheating, esp. at three-card monte.

macing *n.*[2] [MACE *n.*] [1900s] a severe thrashing.

mac it *v.* [1960s+] (*US prison*) of a lesbian, to wear men's clothing.

McJob *n.* [brandname *McDonald's*+SE *job*, popularized by Douglas Coupland in his book *Generation X* (1991). The use of McDonald's refers both to the type of job, which epitomizes those available in the fast-food chain, and to what critics see as the disposable, tasteless, non-nutritional quality of the food the chain sells] [1980s+] (*orig. US*) a pointless, usu. menial job with no prospects or job satisfaction.

mack *n.*[1]

IN EXCLAMATIONS

❑ **by the mack!** (*also* **by the mackin! by the maskins!**) [? SE *by the Mass!* or *by Mary!*] [mid-16C–mid-17C] a general oath (cf. HOLY MACKEREL! *excl.*).

mack *n.*[2] (*also* **mac, maque**) [early 15C–mid-17C SE *mackerel*, a pimp, pander or procuress, ult. Fr. *maquereau*, a pimp + ? Du. *makelaar*, a broker; note Larchey *Dict. Historique* (1878): 'In the Middles Ages the word *macque* signified *vente*, the profession of a merchant. From this came *maquerel* and *maquignon*. The *maquereau* is nothing more than a merchant of women] **1** [20C+] (*US Und.*) a pimp. **2** [1940s+] (*US black*) (*also* **the mack, mack talk**) seductive, persuasive talk, spec. the 'chat-up' line used by a pimp to recruit a new woman. **3** [1960s+] (*US black*) a clever, influential person, a smooth operator.

DERIVATIVES

❑ **mackdom** *n.* the world of smooth-talking, successful people.

IN COMPOUNDS

❑ **mack daddy** *n. see* separate entry. ❑ **mackman** *n.* (*also* **mac man**) [1950s+] (*US black*) a pimp; thus *hard-mack*, a pimp who rules through threatened or actual violence; *sweet mack*, a gentle pimp who prefers to use charm.

IN PHRASES

❑ **get the mack on** *v.* [2000s] (*US black/campus*) to make a pass at someone. ❑ **make mac with** *v.* (*also* **make mack with**) [1960s+] (*US black/campus*) to flirt, to pick up a woman. ❑ **put the mack down** *v.* [1990s+] (*US black*) to act in a smooth, sophisticated manner, reminiscent of the idealized pimp. ❑ **sweet mack** *n.* **1** [1960s–70s] a pimp who treats his women well. **2** [1990s+] (*US black*) a person who deceives or tries to charm a member of the opposite sex with seductive words; a successful seducer.

mack *n.*[3] [? abbr. SE *smack*] [1970s] (*US black*) a French kiss.

mack *n.*[4] *see* MAC *n.*

mack *adj.* [MACK *n.*[2] (1)] (*US black*) **1** [1960s] masculine in appearance and behaviour. **2** [1960s+] anything pertaining to a pimp, such as attitude, philosophy, automobile or clothes.

mack *v.*[1] [MACK *n.*[2]] **1** [late 19C+] to work as a pimp. **2** [1960s+] (*US black*) to swagger, to walk rhythmically. **3** [1960s–70s] (*US gay*) of lesbians, to act in a masculine manner. **4** [1960s+] (*also* **mack down**) (*US black*) to talk seductively, to flirt; spec. as a pimp to recruit a prostitute. **5** [1970s] to chat idly. **6** [1970s+] (*US black*) to lie or exaggerate in order to deceive, exploit or influence someone. **7** [1990s+] to have sexual intercourse. **8** [1990s+] to steal. **9** [1990s+] (*US black*) to be successful, usu. sexually.

IN PHRASES

❑ **macked out** *adj.* (*also* **macked up**) [1930s+] (*US*) stylishly or flashily dressed. ❑ **mack on** *v.* (*also* **mack to**) [1970s+] (*US black/teen*) to make a verbally forceful attempt to seduce a person, to flirt heavily.

mack *v.*[2] [MACK *n.*[3]] **1** [1970s+] (*US campus/black*) to kiss, to flirt. **2** [1990s+] (*US campus*) to eat.

IN PHRASES

❑ **mack down** *v.* [underpinned by *McDonald's* hamburgers] [1970s+] (*US campus*) to eat. ❑ **mack on** *v.* [1980s+] (*US campus*) to eat.

macka *n.* [ety. unknown] [1980s+] (*drugs*) amphetamine.

mackadelic *n.* [MACK *adj.* (1)] [1990s+] (*US black*) a first-rate person.

mackadocious *adj.* (*also* **macadocious**) [MACK *adj.* (1)] [1980s+] (*US black*) excellent, the very best.

mack daddy *n.* (*also* **MacDaddy, macdaddy**) [MACK *n.*[2] + DADDY *n.* (6); thus 'The Great *MacDaddy*', protagonist of an African-American rhyme of 1950s] **1** [1950s+] (*US black*) a successful pimp or criminal. **2** [1990s+] (*US black*) an important, influential black man, a power in the community, a very successful or skilful man. **3** [1990s+] (*US black*) a handsome, virile man. **4** [1990s+] (*US campus*) anything or anybody that is considered the best.

macked out *adj. see under* MACK *v.*[1].

macker *n.*[1] [abbr. MACARONI *n.*[2] (1)] [1930s–40s] (*Aus.*) a pony, a horse.

macker *n.*[2] [MACK *n.*[2] (1)] [1930s+] (*US Und.*) a pimp.

mackerel *n.* [Fr. *maquereau*, a pimp] **1** [15C–19C] (*UK Und.*) (*also* **macquerella**) a madam, a procuress. **2** [16C–17C; 1930s+] (*later US Und.*) a pimp. **3** [17C–early 19C] a prostitute. **4** [mid-19C–1920s] (*US*) a worthless or stupid man. **5** [2000s] a hanger-on, a parasite.

SE in slang uses

IN PHRASES

❑ **mackerel-backed** *adj.* (*also* **mackrel back**) [mid-17C–19C] long-backed, tall and thin; also as *n., mackerel-back*, a tall, thin person. ❑ **mackerel-snapper** *n.* (*also* **mackerel-eater, mackerel-gobbler, mackerel-smacker, mackerel-snatcher**) [the eating of fish on Fridays by devout Catholics] [mid-19C; 1920s+] (*orig. US*) a Roman Catholic, thus adj. *mackerel-snatching*.

mackery *n.* [MACK *n.*[2] (1)] [1930s+] (*US*) pimping.

macking *n.* [MACK *v.*[1] (1)] [1990s+] (*US black*) in fig. use, working hard.

mackry *n. see* MONKERY *n.*

McMuff *n.* [MUFF *n.*[1] (1) + play on *Egg McMuffin*, a McDonald's hamburger chain product] [1990s+] (*US*) the vagina.

mcnoon *adj.* [ANDY MCNOON *n.*] [1910s] (*Aus.*) mad.

maco *n.*[1] (*also* **mako, macco**) [Fr. *ma commère*, lit. 'my gossip'] [20C+] (*W.I.*) **1** a gossip, a busybody. **2** a peeping Tom.

maco *n.*[2] (*also* **mako**) [? Fr. *maquereau*, a pimp] [20C+] (*W.I.*) **1** an effeminate man. **2** a fool, an idiot.

maco *adj.* (*also* **mako**) [MACO *n.*[1]] [20C+] (*W.I.*) inquisitive, gossipy, meddlesome; thus *maco-man, maco-woman*.

maco *v.* (*also* **mako**) [MACO *n.*[1]] [20C+] (*W.I.*) **1** to interfere in other people's affairs. **2** to act as a voyeur. **3** to gossip scandalously.

macon *n.* (*also* **maconha, mach**) [Brazilian Port. *maconha*, marijuana] [1960s+] (*drugs*) marijuana.

mac on *v. see under* MACK *v.*[1].

maconha *n. see* MACON *n.*

mac out *v.* [the McDonald's hamburger chain/MACK *v.*[2]] [1980s+] (*US teen*) to overeat, to gorge oneself, esp. on junk food.

McPaper *n.* [MC- *pfx* + SE *paper*] [1980s+] (*US campus*) **1** a sloppily written, poorly researched piece of work. **2** *USA Today*, seen as insufficiently rigorous in its news coverage.

macquerella *n. see* MACKEREL *n.* (1).

macumeh *n. see* MAKOMÉ *n.*

mad *adj.* **1** [1940s+] generally intensifying adj. of approval, whether of objects, e.g. *a mad hat* or of persons, e.g. *you mad bastard*. **2** [1940s+] absurd. **3** [1990s+] (*US black*) (*also* **madd**) a lot of, very much, e.g. *mad piles of cash*.

SE in slang uses

IN COMPOUNDS

❑ **mad haddock** *n.* [? play on ODD FISH *under* ODD *adj.*] [20C+] (*Aus.*) an exceptionally eccentric person. ❑ **madhatter** *n.* [...A HATTER *under* MAD AS... *adj.*] [1990s+] (*US teen*) someone who sells drugs. ❑ **madhouse** *n.* [SE *madhouse*, a psychiatric institution] [1920s–30s] (*US prison*) a prison with especially unpleasant conditions. ❑ **madman** *n.* [melodramatic assessment of the effects] [1970s+] (*drugs*) **1** a notably strong variety of a given drug, e.g. heroin. **2** phencyclidine. ❑ **madmen** *adj.* [1960s] crazy, absurd. ❑ **mad money** *n.* **1** [1920s+] (*orig. US*) money carried by a woman for an emergency, such as being abandoned far from home by her boyfriend when she hasn't agreed to sex [the 'madness' is in the anger of the boyfriend]. **2** [1930s+] (*US*) savings set aside for some spontaneous, unscheduled expenditure, usu. on pleasure [the madness is in the spending]. ❑ **mad Tom** *n.* [? a real-life mad beggar or TOM *n.*[1]] [late 17C–mid-19C] a beggar who counterfeits madness, the 18th rank of criminal beggars. ❑ **mad-up** *adj.* [1970s–80s] (*UK black*) crazy.

IN PHRASES

❑ **he went mad and they shot him** [1940s+] (*Aus.*) a general answer to the question, 'Where is X?'. ❑ **mad as...** *adj. see* separate entry. ❑ **madder than...** *adj. see* separate entry.

mad *v.* [obs. SE usage] [late16C+] (*UK/US/W.I.*) to exasperate, to drive mad, e.g. with jealousy or worry.

madam *n.* **1** with ref. to a woman [? ironic use of SE reflecting a prejudice against foreigners; i.e. the adoption of Fr. *madame*]. (**a**) [17C–early 19C] a courtesan, a kept woman, a prostitute. (**b**) [early 18C+] (*also* **madame**) a bawd; the proprietor of a male or female brothel. (**c**) [19C] a general term of contempt for a woman, esp. one whose lifestyle does not reflect her self-appraisal. (**d**) [mid-19C–1910s] a handkerchief [? its ostensible respectability]. (**e**) [1970s+] (*US gay*) an (older) homosexual man. **2** [1910s–30s] (*UK Und.*) praise, flattery [? the fawning shopkeeper who calls every customer *madam*; or abbr. of MADAME DE LUCE *n.*]. **3** [1920s+] nonsense, rubbish, esp. in phr. *a load of old madam*.

madam *v.* [MADAM *n.* (3) or MADAME DE LUCE *n.*] [1930s+] to tell the tale, to 'pitch a line'; also phr., *put on madame*, to be assertive.

Madam Brown *n. see* MISS BROWN *under* MISS *n.*

madame bishop *n.* [? SE *bishop*, mulled and spiced port. The popular ety. based on a link to the proper name of an Aus. hotel-keeper is prob. specious] [mid-19C–1940s] (*Aus.*) a mixed drink consisting of port, sugar and nutmeg.

Madame de Luce *n.* [rhy. sl. = SPRUCE *v.*] [20C+] deceptive talk.

Madame Thomasina *n. see* AUNT THOMASINA *n.*

Madame Tussaud *adj.* [rhy. sl.] [1990s+] bald.

Madam Van *n.* (*also* **Madam Ran**) [? a real-life whore or madam or (given the contemporary role of the Dutch as 'national enemy') f. the common *van* pfx used in Du. surnames; Grose, 1785, 1796, *Madam Ran*, are misprints] [late 17C–early 19C] (*UK Und.*) a prostitute.

mad as... *adj.* [mid-19C+] (*Aus./US*) completely deranged, utterly furious. Other than those listed below, variations include *mad as a beetle, ... a Chinaman, ... a dingbat, ... a goanna, ... a hornet, ... as tucker, ... as hops*.

IN PHRASES

❑ **...a cut snake** (*also* **mad as a snake, mad as snakes**) [1910s+] (*Aus./US*) completely deranged, utterly furious. ❑ **...a gum-tree full of galahs** [1940s+] (*Aus.*) insane, eccentric. ❑ **...a hatter** [the use in 18C of mercurous nitrate in the tanning of felt hats. This was absorbed by the hatters, in whom the effects could produce mental problems] [mid-19C+] very mad, utterly insane; in a rage. ❑ **...a maggot** [1940s+] (*N.Z.*) very crazy. ❑ **...a (March) hare** [the hare's sexual excitement, which peaks in March] **1** [15C+] very crazy. **2** [18C] lustful. ❑ **...a meat axe** *see under* MEAT AXE *n.* ❑ **...a weaver** [proverbial wisdom associates weavers and insanity] [17C] very crazy. ❑ **...a wet hen** [early 19C+] extremely angry.

madball *n.* [1960s+] a fortune teller's crystal ball.

madball *adj.* [1960s+] (*US*) crazy.

Madchester *n.* [the brief but well-publicized period (*c.*1989–92) when Manchester, rather than London, dominated teen fashion, music and choice of drug consumption. *Mad* refers to the use of MDMA (cf. ECSTASY *n.*), the drug of choice in the city's clubs] [1980s+] Manchester.

madd *adj. see* MAD *adj.* (3).

madder than a woodheap *adj.* (*also* **madder than a wet hen/owl, ...nine hundred dollars, ...seven boiled owls, ...thunder**) [1910s+] very angry.

maddie *n.* [abbr. SE *madam*] [1980s+] (*S.Afr.*) the white mistress of a house, the employer of domestic servants.

maddikin *n.* [? MADGE-KEN *under* MADGE *n.*] [late 18C–19C] the vagina.

maddo *n.* [SE *madman* + -O *sfx* (3)] [1910s] (*Aus.*) a lunatic.

mad dog *n.* [the effects] **1** in context of drink or drugs. (**a**) [late 16C–early 17C] strong ale. (**b**) [1970s+] (*US*) cheap wine, esp. the brand Mogen David 20/20. (**c**) [1970s+] (*drugs*) phencyclidine. **2** [late 19C+] (*Aus.*) an unsettled debt that the debtor refuses to pay, esp. at a public house. **3** in context of instability [SE *mad dog*; note MAD DOG *v.*]. (**a**) [1940s+] (*US*) a violent thug. (**b**) [1970s+] (*US black*) a rebel, a non-conformist, one who refuses to accept their role in society. (**c**) [1990s+] (*US*) a deliberately provocative and aggressive stare.

mad-dog *adj.* [SE *mad dog*] [1940s+] (*US black*) violent, thuggish.

mad dog *v.* [such animals fix their targets with an unwavering, aggressive stare] **1** [1980s+] (*N.Z.*) to nag, to pester. **2** [1990s+] (*US black/prison*) to stare at intensely and threateningly. **3** [1990s+] (*US campus*) to attack verbally.

maddy *n.* [SE *mad*] [1970s+] (*Scot./Aus.*) a psychologically unstable person, a lunatic.

maddy *adj.* [SE *mad*] [20C+] (*W.I.*) crazy, insane, unstable.

made *adj.* **1** [late 17C–19C] (*UK Und.*) stolen [MAKE *v.*]. **2** [1930s+] (*US*) recognized, identified [MAKE *v.* (4)]. **3** [1940s+] (*US black*) usu. of girls or women, describing someone who has had their hair straightened [MAKE *v.* (8)]. **4** [1950s+] (*orig. US Und.*) initiated as a member of the US Mafia [MAKE *v.* (9)]. **5** [1950s+] (*US*) cheated, tricked [MAKE *v.* (1e)]. **6** [1950s+] (*US*) completed successfully. **7** [1950s+] (*drugs*) satisfactorily supplied/intoxicated with drugs, usu. heroin.

IN COMPOUNDS

❑ **made man** *n.* (*also* **made guy**) [1950s+] (*US Und.*) a formally initiated member of the US Mafia.

made (up) *adj.* (*orig. Irish*) **1** [1930s+] lucky, secure, well-off. **2** [1980s+] delighted, pleased.

mad for it *adj.* [orig. Scots local use] [1940s+] extremely enthusiastic, ready to go mad, keen on, willing to do something.

Madge *n.* [joc. use of female proper name] [1950s–70s] (*camp gay*) a tasteless person.

madge *n.* **1** [16C] a woman. **2** [late 18C] (*UK Und.*) a homosexual man. **3** *see* MADGE HOWLET *n.* (1).

IN COMPOUNDS

❑ **madge-cove** *n.* [COVE *n.* (1)] [late 18C–mid-19C] a homosexual man. ❑ **madge-cull** *n.* [CULL *n.*[1] (3)] [late 18C–mid-19C] (*UK Und.*) a homosexual man. ❑ **madge-ken** *n.* [KEN *n.*[1] (1), lit. 'woman-place'] [late 18C–mid-19C] the vagina.

Madge Howlet *n.* (*also* **howlet, Jennie Howlet, madge, Madge Howlett, Madge-owlet, Margerie Howlet**) [dial. *madge howlet*, a barn owl] [17C–19C] the vagina; a prostitute.

IN COMPOUNDS

❑ **madgyland** *n.* (*also* **maggyland**) the world of prostitution.

mad mick *n.* [rhy. sl.] [20C+] **1** (*Aus.*) the penis [PRICK *n.* (1)]. **2** (*Aus./US*) a pick.

madolo *n.* [ety. unknown] [1970s] (*S.Afr. township*) wine.

Mad Town *n.* [abbr.] [1980s+] (*US*) Madison, Wisconsin.

madza *n.* (*also* **medza, medzer, midzer**) [Ital. *mezzo*, a half] [mid–late 19C] (*Ling. Fr./Polari*) a half; thus *madza beargured*, half-drunk, *madza round the bull*, half a pound of steak.

IN COMPOUNDS

❑ **madza caroon** *n.* [CAROON *n.*] [mid–late 19C] half a crown, 2s 6d (12½p). ❑ **madza poona** *n.* [POONA *n.*] [mid–late 19C] a half-sovereign. ❑ **madza saltee** *n.* [SALTEE *n.* (1)] [mid–late 19C] one halfpenny.

Mae West *n.*[1] [rhy. sl.; ult. Hollywood star *Mae West* (1892–1980)] **1** [1930s+] a female breast. **2** [2000s] the best (thing).

Mae West *n.*[2] [the shape; ult. *see* prev.] [1960s] (*US*) a long cruller.

Maf *n.* [1960s+] (*orig. US*) the (usu. US) Mafia.

m.a.f. *adj.* (*also* **mad as fuck**) [abbr. *mad as fuck*] [1990s+] extremely annoyed.

mafa *n.* [2000s] (*US black*) abbr. of 'motherfucker'.

mafeesh! *excl.* (*also* **mafish!**) [colloq. eastern Arab. *mafis*, there is nothing] [late 19C–1960s] (*orig. milit.*) used in a variety of negative senses to mean done with! nothing doing! go to hell!

mafias *n.* [stereotyping] [2000s] (*US prison*) dark sunglasses.

mag *n.*[1] [MADGE *n.* (2)] [early 18C] (*UK Und.*) a sodomite.

mag *n.*[2] [? var. on MUG *n.*[1] (1)] **1** [mid-18C–1910s] a mouth. **2** [late 19C] (*UK Und.*) constr. with *the*, confidence trickery, swindling. **3** [late 19C–1910s] the face.

IN EXCLAMATIONS

❑ **hold your mag!** [19C–1900s] (*Aus.*) be quiet, 'shut up!'.

mag *n.*[3] (*also* **magg, meag, meg**) **1** [mid-18C–1950s] a halfpenny. **2** [early 19C–1950s] a penny, a cent.

IN COMPOUNDS

❑ **mag-flying** *n.* [mid–late 19C] playing pitch and toss.

IN PHRASES

❑ **fly the mags** *v.* [early–mid-19C] (*orig. UK Und.*) to gamble by tossing halfpence, to play pitch and toss.

mag *n.*[4] [abbr.] **1** [mid-18C+] a *magazine*. **2** [1940s+] a *magazine* of bullets. **3** [1950s+] *magnesium*. **4** [1970s+] (*US*) a *magnum* pistol. **5** *see* MAGAZINE *n.* (1). **6** *see* MAGSMAN *n.* (1).

mag *n.*[5] [SE *magpie*, post-19C use mainly Aus.] **1** [late 18C+] talk, chatter. **2** [1910s] nagging. **3** [1910s] (*Aus.*) a lie. **4** [1940s+] a chatterer.

DERIVATIVES

❑ **maggery** *n.* [mid-19C] (*UK Und.*) chatter.

IN COMPOUNDS

❑ **mag-pie** *n.* [late 19C] speech, conversation. ❑ **mag-stake** *n.* [mid–late 19C] money obtained by verbal trickery or fraud.

IN PHRASES

❑ **chuck a mag** *v.* [mid–late 19C] (*UK Und.*) to work as a confidence trickster. ❑ **tip the mag** *v.* [late 19C] to talk, to orate. ❑ **stow one's mag** *v.* [STOW *v.* (1)] [mid-19C] to be quiet, to stop talking, esp. in imper. *stow your mag!*, shut up!

mag *v.* [MAG *n.*[5]] **1** [early 19C] (*Scot.*) to steal. **2** [early 19C+] to chatter, to talk, to scold; thus n. *magging*. **3** [mid–late 19C] (*UK Und.*) to cheat; esp. through insincere talk. **4** [20C+] (*Aus.*) to talk at, to nag; thus n. *magging*.

IN PHRASES

❑ **on the mag** *adj.* [late 19C] working as a confidence trickster.

maga *adj.* [SE *meagre* or Fr. *maigre*, thin] **1** [1950s+] (*W.I., Rasta*) thin. **2** [2000s] (*UK black*) in fig. use, in poverty.

IN PHRASES

❑ **maga dog** *n.* [1950s+] (*W.I., Rasta*) a mongrel; thus as a term of abuse.

magageba *n.* [? Zulu *amakhekheba*, flat, rigid objects] [1970s+] (*S.Afr. black*) money.

magazine *n.* (*also* **mag**) [? the time it takes to read one] [1920s+] (*US Und.*) a six-month jail sentence.

mageegle *v.* [Scot. *maggle*, mangle] [20C+] (*Ulster*) to confuse, to bewilder.

magg *n. see* MAG *n.*[3] (1).

maggery *n. see* MAG *n.*[5] (1).

maggie *n.*[1] [proper name *Maggie*, abbr. Margaret] **1** [17C–early 18C; 1930s] (*also* **Margaretta, meg**) a prostitute. **2** [19C] a generic term for a woman. **3** [20C+] (*Ulster*) in cards, the ace or queen of hearts.

maggie *n.*[2] **1** [20C+] (*Aus.*) abbr. *magpie*. **2** [1910s] (*US Und.*) an automatic pistol [its *magazine* of bullets].

maggie *n.*[3] [1940s+] (*W.I.*) a handcuff, a manacle, usu. in pl.

maggie and jiggs *n.* [the 'lead characters' in a long-running US strip cartoon] [1930s–60s] (*US*) an outdoor privy.

maggie ann *n.* (*also* **maggie anne, maggie ryan, maggy ann(e)**) [pron.] [1910s+] (*orig. milit.*) margarine.

Maggie Mahone *n. see* MIKE MALONE *n.*

maggieman *n.* [Irish *margadh*, a fair] [20C+] (*Irish*) a fairground showman.

Maggie Moores *n.* (*also* **maggies**) [rhy. sl. = drawers] [20C+] (*Aus.*) women's underpants.

maggie rab *n.*[1] (*also* **maggie rob, maggie robb**) [MAG *v.* (2) + SE *rob*; play on proper names] [19C] (*Scot.*) a nagging, unpleasant wife.

maggie rab *n.*[2] (*also* **maggie rob, maggie robb**) [MAG *n.*[3] (1) + SE *rob*; play on proper names] [19C] (*Scot.*) a bad halfpenny.

maggie ryan *n. see* MAGGIE ANN *n.*

maggies *n. see* MAGGIE MOORES *n.* (1).

maggie's pie *n.* [var. on MAGPIE'S NEST *n.*] [20C+] (*US black*) the female genitals.

magging *n.*[1] (*also* **megging**) [MAGSMAN *n.* (1)] [mid–late 19C] confidence trickery, swindling.

magging *n.*[2] *see* MAG *v.* (2).

maggot *n.* [general loathing of the SE *maggot*] **1** as a pejorative. (**a**) [late 17C+] a contemptible person. (**b**) [mid-19C] constr. with *the*, a bad situation. (**c**) [1980s+] (*Aus/N.Z./US black*) a white person. (**d**) [1980s+] (*Aus.*) a general term of abuse, esp. aimed at girls or women [plays on the image of the *maggot* that 'eats your flesh']. (**e**) [1980s+] (*US police*) a criminal, esp. a drug dealer. (**f**) [1980s+] (*US campus*) a very lazy person, esp. one who stays in bed all day [they 'burrow' beneath the sheets]. **2** [1920s] (*Irish*) a state of drunkenness. **3** [2000s] the penis [a *maggot* burrows into flesh].

SE in slang uses

IN COMPOUNDS

❑ **maggot-boiler** *n.* [the maggots that were found in the tallow or animal fat that was used as the basis for candle-making] [late 18C–early 19C] a tallow chandler. ❑ **maggot-brained** *adj.* (*also* **maggot-faced, maggot-headed, maggot-pated, maggot-plated**) [late 17C; 20C+] a general epithet of abuse. ❑ **maggot magnet** *n.* (*also* **maggot taxi**) [2000s] (*N.Z.*) a sheep. ❑ **maggot meat** *n.* [1970s] (*US*) a corpse, a dead person. ❑ **maggot pack** *n.* [1920s] (*N.Z.*) a meat pie.

IN PHRASES

❑ **act the maggot** *v.* [1950s+] (*Irish*) to play the fool, to clown. ❑ **enough to gag a maggot** *n.* [1960s] (*US*) **1** something utterly repulsive. **2** something in great or overwhelming quantity. ❑ **have a maggot in one's tail** *v.* [late 17C–early 18C] of a woman, to be venereally diseased. ❑ **milk the maggot** *v. see* MILK THE LIZARD *under* LIZARD *n.* ❑ **road maggot** *n. see under* ROAD *n.*

maggots! *excl.* [late 19C] excl. of dismissal.

maggoty *adj.* (*also* **maggotish, maggotty**) [the image of a rotting brain] **1** [late 17C–19C] eccentric, whimsical. **2** [20C+] (*Aus.*) ill-tempered, irritable. **3** [20C+] (*Irish/US*) dirty, disgusting. **4** [1920s+] (*US/Irish*) extremely drunk. **5** [1990s+] (*US*) crazy, insane.

maggy ann(e) *n. see* MAGGIE ANN *n.*

magic *n.*

SE in slang uses

IN COMPOUNDS

❑ **magic (dust)** *n.* [DUST *n.* (6e)] [1970s+] (*drugs*) phencyclidine. ❑ **magic mushroom** *n.* (*drugs*) **1** [1960s+] (*also* **magic**) a psilocybe mushroom, a hallucinogen somewhat milder than LSD. **2** [1970s] peyote. ❑ **magic wand** *n.* [either a tribute to masculine power or the myth that sexual intercourse somehow puts an end to quarrels] [1950s–60s] the penis.

IN PHRASES

❑ **hidden magic** *n.* [1960s+] (*US gay*) a penis that is substantially larger than expected when erect. ❑ **tragic magic** *n.* [the potentially unpleasant, if exciting, effects] **1** [1970s+] (*US drugs*) heroin. **2** [1980s+] (*US drugs*) crack cocaine dipped in phencyclidine.

magiffer *n. see* MAGOOFER *n.*

magimp *n. see* MACGIMP *n.*

magistrate *n. see* GLASGOW MAGISTRATE *under* GLASGOW *adj.*

magistrate's court *n.* [rhy. sl. = SE colloq. a *short*, a drink of spirits] [20C+] a measure of spirits, as bought in a public house.

magnet *n.* [its allure] [18C–19C] the vagina.

-magnet *sfx* [1960s+] used to imply allure, usu. sexual, but occas. not, e.g. *COP MAGNET* below.

IN PHRASES

❑ **babe magnet** *n.* (*also* **bitch magnet, poontang…, shag…**) [BABE *n.* (3)] [1980s+] a man who is (or an object which makes a man) irresistibly alluring to a woman. ❑ **chick magnet** *n.* [1990s+] a man who is irresistibly alluring to women. ❑ **cop magnet** *n.* (*also* **copper magnet**) [COP *n.*^{1} (1)] [1990s+] anything or anyone that attracts the unwelcome interest of the police. ❑ **fanny magnet** *n.* [FANNY *n.*^{1}] [1980s+] anything that catches the female eye, e.g. a very attractive (young) man, an attractive motorcar. ❑ **pussy magnet** *n.* [2000s] (*US*) a sporty automobile, supposedly appealing to girls.

magnolia curtain *n.* [SE *magnolia*, generic synon. for the South + play on *Iron Curtain*] [1940s+] (*US black*) the Mason-Dixon (40°N) line that divides the American north and south.

magnolious *adj.* [elaboration of SE *magnificent*] [mid-19C+] (*US*) magnificent, splendid, large; thus *magnoliousness*, the fact or quality of being *magnolious*.

magnoon *adj.* (*also* **magnune**) [Arab. *magnoon*, eccentric] [1910s–40s] (*Aus./N.Z.*) crazy, eccentric.

magnum bonum *n.* [Lat. 'a great good thing'] [early 19C] a bottle holding two quarts of wine.

magoo *n.* [usage infl. by 1932 Broadway comedy *The Great Magoo* by Hecht and Fowler and the character *Mr Magoo* in UPA Studios cartoon series shown on children's television in the 1970s] **1** [1930s–60s] (*US*) a lie, a trick, a hoax, thus *give the magoo*, to deceive someone. **2** [1930s+] (*US*) constr. with *the*, sex appeal. **3** [1930s+] (*US*) an important person. **4** [1930s+] (*US*) a foolish person. **5** [1980s+] (*US campus*) a driver, usu. old and male, who drives very slowly and thus impedes the faster car behind.

magoofer *n.* (*also* **magiffer**) [var. on MACGIMP *n.*, but note MAGOO *n.*] [1950s–60s] (*US*) a pimp.

magoozlum *n.* [? Hollywood jargon *magoo*, the gooey ingredient of 'custard pies'] [1920s+] (*US*) rubbish, trash.

mag-pie *n. see under* MAG *n.*^{5}.

magpie *n.*^{1} **1** [mid-17C–19C] an Anglican bishop [the black chimere and white rochet forming his ordinary ceremonial attire]. **2** [mid–late 19C] (*Aus./UK prison*) convict clothing (coloured yellow and black); thus the convict who wears it. **3** [1910s+] (*Aus.*) a nickname for a South Australian [the black and white colouring of the bird, the ref. is to the convict clothes worn by early settlers]. **4** [1980s] (*Aus.*) a half-caste. **5** [2000s] (*N.Z.*) a thief [the larcenous propensities of the bird].

magpie *n.*^{2} [ext. of MAG *n.*^{3}] [mid-19C] a halfpenny.

magpie's nest *n.* [18C–19C; 1980s] (*US black*) the female genitals.

magsman *n.* [MAG *n.*^{5} (1), i.e. he uses words rather than violence to commit his crimes; Michael Davitt, *Leaves from a Prison Diary* (1885): 'The order of magsmen will comprise card-sharpers, "confidence trick" workers, begging-letter writers, bogus ministers of religion, professional noblemen, "helpless victims of the cruel world", medical quacks and various other clever rogues'] **1** in (*UK Und.*) use. (**a**) [mid-19C] an assistant for a street swindler or pickpocket. (**b**) [mid-19C–1900s] the king of the 19C swindlers, a fashionable swell who appeared as sophisticated a figure as those on whom he preyed. (**c**) [mid-19C+] (*also* **mag**) a street swindler, or thief, esp. one who preys on gullible countrymen. (**d**) [mid-19C+] a card-sharp or other cheating gamester. **2** [20C+] (*Aus.*) a chatterbox, a talker.

mag-stake *n. see under* MAG *n.*^{5} (1).

magtig! *excl.* (*also* **magtie!**) [Afk. *allemagtig*, almighty] [mid-19C+] (*S.Afr.*) a general excl., the equivalent of Lawdy! or Lawks!

maguffy *n.* [? a real name, but note the film jargon *MacGuffin*, a gimmick or plot pretext] [20C+] (*W.I.*) **1** one who thinks that they are more important than they really are. **2** anything large and pretentious.

mahaha *n. see* MAHULA *n.*

maharishee *n.* [proper name *Maharishi Mahesh Yogi* (1917–2008), a popular 1960s guru, espoused by the Beatles and others in search of raised consciousness] [1970s+] (*drugs*) marijuana.

Mahatma Gandhi *n.* [rhy. sl., ult. Ind. freedom fighter *Mahatma Gandhi* (1869–1948)] [20C+] **1** brandy. **2** shandy.

Mahatma Gandhi *adj.* [rhy. sl.; see MAHATMA GANDHI *n.*] [2000s] **1** dandy. **2** randy.

mah jong *n.* (*also* **mahjoun, mahuang**) [the Chinese game] [1970s] (*drugs*) marijuana.

mahog *n.* (*also* **mahoga**) [abbr. SE *mahogany*, thus the colour of the wood and the drink] [1960s+] (*S.Afr. black*) brandy.

mahogany *n.* **1** from the the colour. (**a**) [late 18C–mid-19C] a Cornish drink made of gin and treacle. (**b**) [mid-19C] a strong mixture of brandy and water. (**c**) [mid-19C] a strong dark ale. **2** by metonomy. (**a**) [mid-19C+] a table, esp. a dining table. (**b**) [late 19C+] (*US*) a bar counter. **3** [1900s] pickled beef.

IN COMPOUNDS

❑ **mahogany flat** *n.* [SE *mahogany*, as a symbol of luxury + *flat*] [1970s–80s] (*US black*) an expensive, well-furnished and situated apartment or home. ❑ **mahogany polisher** *n.* [20C+] a barman. ❑ **mahogany slosh** *n.* [play on SE *mahogany* + SLOSH *n.*[1]; its colour and taste] [late 19C–1910s] tea from a cook-shop or coffee-stall. ❑ **mahogany top** *n.* [the colour of the wood/hair] [mid–late 19C] a red-head.

IN PHRASES

❑ **below the mahogany** *adj.* [mid-19C; 20C+] drunk. ❑ **decorate the mahogany** *v.* (*also* **decorate**) **1** [1900s–50s] (*US*) to lay down money, whether for gambling or in payment of a bill. **2** [1930s+] of a man, to hand over one's housekeeping money to one's wife. ❑ **pint of mahogany** *n.* [late 19C] a mug of coffee.

SE in slang uses

IN COMPOUNDS

❑ **mahogany flat** *n.* (*also* **mahogany baxter**) [late 19C+ use is US] [mid-19C–1930s] a bedbug.

mahogany gaspipe *n.* [a joc. rendering of its sound] [20C+] the intonations of the Irish language, also as one who speaks the language.

mahomet *n. see* TURK *n.*[1] (1).

Mahometan gruel *n.* [its origins and popularity in the Middle East] [late 17C–early 19C] coffee.

mahoska, the *n.* [? Irish *mo thosca*, my business; thus cf. *cosa nostra*, 'these things of ours', a synon. for the Sicilian/US mafia] [1930s+] (*US Und.*) anything illicit, esp. drugs, money, a weapon, stolen goods etc.

mahula *n.* (*also* **mahaha, mahoula**) [MAHULA *adj.*] [1900s–40s] (*US*) nonsense.

mahula *adj.* [Yid. *mekhule*, Heb. *mechula*, spoiled, bankrupt] [1920s+] (*US*) bankrupt or ruined.

maiden *n.* [ety. unknown; ? a local plant name] [mid-19C–1910s] (*Aus.*) cloves; peppermint.

SE in slang uses

IN COMPOUNDS

❑ **maiden lane** *n.* [late 19C] (*US*) the 'red-light' area of a town. ❑ **maiden's blush** *n.* (*also* **lady's blush**) [the colour; BARMAID'S BLUSH *n.*[2]] **1** [late 19C–1910s] (*also* **maiden's prayers**) port and lemonade. **2** [1940s+] (*Aus.*) ginger beer and raspberry cordial. ❑ **maiden sessions** *n.* [fig. use of SE *maiden*, a virgin] [late 17C–early 19C] legal sessions where no prisoners are sentenced to death.

Maid Marian *n.* [the morris dancing tradition of having that character played by a local prostitute] [16C] a prostitute.

maids adorning *n.* [rhy. sl.] [mid-19C] the morning.

Maidstone jailer *n.* [rhy. sl.] [mid-19C] a tailor.

maid's water *n.* [late 19C+] (*Aus.*) any weak drink, esp. tea.

mail *n.* **1** [1940s+] (*S.Afr.*) a carrier for an illicit grog-shop. **2** [1960s+] (*Aus.*) a rumour, a report, racing tip; information on crime. **3** [1990s+] (*US black teen*) money [? like the US mail it 'gets through anywhere'].

mail *v.* [MAIL *n.*] [1970s+] (*S.Afr.*) **1** to send someone to buy liquor illicitly. **2** to act as a go-between in such a purchase.

mailer *n.* [MAIL *v.*] [1950s] (*S.Afr. Und.*) a middleman in the illicit liquor trade.

'mailer *n.* [abbr. ? *Bulletin* nonce-word] [1900s] (*Aus.*) a blackmailer.

mail-order cowboy *n.* [1920s–40s] (*US*) a would-be cowboy who has the clothes but is otherwise spurious.

main *n. see* MAINLINE *n.* (2).

main, the *n.*

IN PHRASES

❑ **turn on the main** *v. see* TURN ON THE WATERWORKS *under* WATERWORKS *n.*

main *adj.* [late 19C+] (*US*) used to describe a person or thing with power or importance, usu. in combs., as in *the main cheese, the main cop* etc.

IN COMPOUNDS

❑ **main bitch** *n. see* separate entry. ❑ **main brain** *n.* [1970s] (*US teen*) an important person. ❑ **main burg** *n. see* BIG BURG *under* BURG *n.*[1]. ❑ **main cat** *n.* (*also* **main dog**) [CAT *n.*[5]] [1960s] the leader, the most important person. ❑ **main cheese** *n. see* BIG CHEESE *n.* ❑ **main chick** *n. see* MAIN BITCH *n.* ❑ **main drag** *n. see* separate entry. ❑ **main finger** *n.* [FINGER *n.* (2)] [late 19C–1920s] (*US*) the boss. ❑ **main girl** *n. see* MAIN BITCH *n.* ❑ **main guy** *n.* [GUY *n.*[2]] [late 19C+] (*US*) the boss. ❑ **main ho** *n. see* MAIN BITCH *n.* ❑ **main kazoo** *n.* (*also* **main kazaam**) [play on the self-aggrandizing names of various US societies, esp. the *kleagles* etc of the Ku Klux Klan] [20C+] (*US*) a person of importance. ❑ **main kick** *n.* [KICK *n.*[5] (4)] [1930s–40s] (*US black*) **1** one's favourite activity. **2** the stage or theatre. **3** an addiction to drugs. **4** alcohol. ❑ **main lady** *n. see* MAIN BITCH *n.* ❑ **mainland** *n. see* separate entry. ❑ **mainline(r)** *see* separate entries. ❑ **main man** *n. see* separate entry. ❑ **main mellow/piece** *n. see* MAIN SQUEEZE *under* SQUEEZE *n.*[1]. ❑ **main momma** *n.* [1970s+] (*US black*) one's girlfriend or wife. ❑ **main monkey** *n.* [2000s] (*drugs*) addiction to narcotics; the need for narcotics. ❑ **main mug** *n.* [1940s] (*US*) an important person. ❑ **main ou** *n.* [OU *n.* (2)] [1970s+] (*S.Afr.*) a local hero, esp. in a school or college. ❑ **main queen** *n.* [QUEEN *n.*] **1** [1940s+] (*US black*) one's girlfriend or wife. **2** [1960s] (*US*) an attractive and sexually desired male homosexual. ❑ **main squash** *n.* [1900s] (*US*) the most important person. ❑ **main sqeeeze** *n. see under* SQUEEZE *n.*[1]. ❑ **main stash** *n.* [Mezzrow & Wolfe, *Really the Blues* (1946), '*Main stash* is home, where you and your wife or steady girlfriend live, as distinguished from other secondary "homes" you might have, where other women friends of yours live'] [1940s–60s] (*US black*) one's home. ❑ **main stem** *n. see* separate entry. ❑ **main stroll** *n.* [STROLL *n.* (1)] [1940s] (*US black*) Seventh Avenue in Harlem. ❑ **main stuff** *n. see* MAIN BITCH *n.* ❑ **main thrill** *n.* [1930s–40s] (*US black*) **1** the main street; spec. 7th Avenue in Harlem. **2** one's drug of choice. ❑ **main trill** *n.* [? pron. of prev.] [1940s] (*US black, Harlem*) a main street; an avenue. ❑ **main who'/whore** *n. see* MAIN BITCH *n.* ❑ **main wire** *n.* [1910s] (*US*) the most important person, the manager, the boss. ❑ **main woman** *n.* **1** [1990s+] (*W.I./UK black*) a man's primary partner, poss. the mother of his children, etc. **2** *see* MAIN BITCH *n.*

IN PHRASES

❑ **main on the hitch** *n.* [MAIN MAN *n.* + HITCHED *adj.*] [1930s–40s] (*US black*) a woman's favourite man, esp. her husband. ❑ **main saw on the hitch** *n.* [Mezzrow & Wolfe, *Really the Blues* (1946), 'Your wife is the *main saw on the hitch*; you may have other *saws* to cut your wood, and you might say that you were hitched to them too, but not in such a basic way'; note *MAIN ON THE HITCH* above] [1940s] (*US black*) one's wife. ❑ **take it main** *v.* [1930s] to inject narcotics into a vein.

SE in slang uses

IN COMPOUNDS

❑ **main alley** *n.* [20C+] (*orig. US tramp*) the main street. ❑ **main avenue** *n.* [19C] the vagina. ❑ **main spot** *n.* [mid-18C] the vagina. ❑ **main toby** *n.* [toby] [mid-19C] the main road, the highway.

main *v. see* MAINLINE *v.*

main bitch *n.* (*also* **main chick, ...girl, ...ho, ...lady, ...stuff, ...who', ...whore, ...woman**) [MAIN *adj.* + BITCH *n.*[1] (1)/CHICK *n.*[1] (2)/SE *girl*/HO *n.* (1)/SE *lady*/STUFF *n.* (10)/abbr. SE *whore*/SE *woman*] [1950s+] (*US black*) **1** the favourite prostitute among those a pimp controls. **2** (*also* **main chick**) a man's favourite girlfriend.

main drag *n.* [MAIN *adj.* + DRAG *n.*[1] (1), also note *drag* (*oneself along*), to make one's way wearily, tiredly. The term referred orig. to a town or city's centre of tramp or vagrant life but was extended and then transferred to the main street, whether or not frequented by vagrants. Despite its almost invariably US use today, the term started in the UK and is cited as such by Mayhew, *London Labour & London Poor* (1861–2)] **1** [mid-19C+] the main street of a town or city. **2** [1930s–40s] (*US black*) 7th Avenue in Harlem, New York. **3** [1960s–70s] the main road.

IN PHRASES

❑ **buzz the main drag** *v.* (*also* **mooch the main drag, work the main drag**) [1920s] to beg along a town's main street. ❑ **main drag of many tears** *n.* [the bars and theatres on 125th St (Harlem's main street) where otherwise depressed and frustrated people can attempt to drown their sorrows] [1940s] (*US black*) 125th Street Harlem, New York.

mainer *n.* [1990s+] (*US teen*) driving up and down the main street of a small town.

Mainiac *n.* [pun on SE *maniac*] [mid-19C+] (*US*) a native of Maine.

mainland *n.* [1940s+] (*N.Z.*) the South Island.

DERIVATIVES

❑ **mainlander** *n.* [1940s+] (*Aus.*) one who lives on the mainland of Australia (rather than Tasmania).

mainline *n.* **1** [1930s+] (*US prison*) (*also* **line**) the prison convict population, excluding those who are detained in punishment cells. **2** (*orig. US*) in drug uses. (**a**) [1930s+] (*also* **main, mainliner**) the vein into which an addict injects narcotics. (**b**) [1940s+] (*also* **mainline bang**) an injection into the vein. (**c**) [1950s] narcotics, usu. addiction. **3** *see* MAINLINER *n.*

IN PHRASES

❑ **bust the mainline** *v.* (*also* **burn the mainline**) [1950s+] to take an intravenous injection. ❑ **hit the mainline** *v.* (*also* **bust the mainline, hit the main vein**) [1930s+] (*drugs*) to inject a drug. ❑ **ride the mainline** *v.* (*also* **rock the mainline**) [1950s] (*drugs*) to inject narcotics; to be a narcotics addict.

mainline *adj.* [MAINLINE *n.*] **1** [1930s+] (*US prison*) pertaining to the main prison population (and the rules to which it is subjected). **2** [1950s–60s] (*orig. US drugs*) pertaining to narcotics use and addiction.

mainline *v.* (*also* **main**) [MAINLINE *n.*] (*orig. US drugs*) **1** [1930s+] to inject narcotics directly into a vein. **2** [1960s+] to inject a third party. **3** [1960s+] to inject intravenously in non-drug use; also fig.

mainliner *n.* (*also* **mainline, mainline shooter**) [MAINLINE *v.*] **1** [1930s+] (*orig. US drugs*) a drug addict who injects narcotics into the vein. **2** [1940s–50s] (*US prison*) a convict who is part of the main prison population, rather than those held in punishment cells.

main man *n.* [MAIN *adj.* + SE *man*] (*orig. US black*) **1** [1920s+] a pimp. **2** [1940s+] a lover, a sweetheart, a woman's only boyfriend. **3** [1950s+] (*also* **main boy**) one's best friend; an intimate. **4** [1960s+] (*S.Afr.*) a local hero, esp. in a school or college. **5** [1960s+] any important person, e.g. a chief prison warder or a managing director. **6** [1970s] a hero. **7** [1970s] an accomplice, an informer. **8** [1970s+] a leading drug supplier.

main stem *n.* [SE *main stem*, the central trunk] **1** [late 19C–1930s] (*US*) a person of importance, the boss. **2** [late 19C+] (*also* **big stem**) the main street of a town. **3** [20C+] (*US black*) the elite, the upper class. **4** [1920s–30s] (*US tramp*) the most important street of a town in the context of tramp society and standards. **5** [1920s–50s] Broadway, New York City.

IN PHRASES

❑ **buzz the main stem** *v.* (*also* **mooch the main stem, work the main stem**) [1920s] to beg along a town's main street. ❑ **on the stem** [20C+] (*US tramp*) walking the main street of a town, begging for subsistence.

Main Streeter *n.* [*Main Street*, small-town America, f. the novel of that name by Sinclair Lewis (1920)] [1920s+] a provincial, small-town person.

maj *adj. see* MAJOR *adj.*

majat *n.* [? Malay *madat*, opium] [1950s+] (*S.Afr. drugs*) the third and lowest grade of marijuana on sale in S.Afr.

majesty *n.* [1900s] the penis.

majita *n.* (*also* **majika**) [the film *The Magic Garden* (1951), which depicts, *inter alia*, the life of such a youth] [1950s+] (*S.Afr. black*) a streetwise young man, also as a term of address.

majonda *n.* [? Filipino *majonda*, old, obsolete, although this image seems unlikely] [1950s+] (*US drugs*) heroin.

major *n.* [1970s+] (*US gay*) a lesbian.

major *adj.* (*also* **maj**) [1960s+] (*orig. W.I./US teen*) **1** all-purpose term of great approval. **2** large, extreme, a lot of.

major *adv.* (*also* **majorally**) [1980s+] to a very great extent, extremely.

major-league *adj.* [baseball imagery] [1940s+] (*orig. US*) very important, the most powerful, highly impressive.

major-league *adv.* [1990s+] (*US*) extremely.

majorly *adv.* (*also* **majorally**) [MAJOR *adv.*] [1980s+] (*orig. US campus*) extremely, very much, primarily.

major nasty *adj.* [MAJOR *adv.* + NASTY *adj.* (4)] [1980s+] (*US black/teen*) very unpleasant, very difficult.

major solde *n.* [SOLDI *n.*] [mid-19C] a halfpenny.

make *n.*[1] (*also* **mec**) [Midlands/northern dial.; 20C+ use mainly Dublin] [mid-16C+] (*UK Und.*) a halfpenny.

make *n.*[2] [MAKE *v.*] **1** [mid-19C–1950s] a successful robbery or swindle. **2** [1910s–60s] (*US Und.*) the proceeds of a theft or robbery. **3** [1930s+] a seduction. **4** [1950s+] (*US*) a description or an identification of a suspect, esp. through fingerprinting, photofit or other forms of police records. **5** [1960s+] (*US*) kissing, necking. **6** *see* EASY MAKE *under* EASY *adj.*

IN PHRASES

❑ **lay the make on** *v.* [1960s+] (*US*) to become sexually aggressive. ❑ **on the make** (*orig. US*) **1** [mid-19C+] looking to benefit oneself, ambitious, keen to do whatever will be most useful for one's own advancement or profit. **2** [mid-19C+] engaged in theft or swindling. **3** [late 19C+] seeking sexual activity. **4** [1900s] (*US Und.*) of a police officer, willing to be bribed. ❑ **on the make-game** [GAME *n.* (4)] [mid-19C] (*UK Und.*) working as a criminal; indulging in some form of criminality. ❑ **run a make (on)** *v.* [1970s+] (*US police*) to identify a suspect. ❑ **put the make on** *v.* **1** [1920s] (*US*) to assess. **2** [1950s+] (*US*) to make sexual advances. ❑ **put the make to** *v.* [1960s] to describe.

make *v.* **1** to obtain, to attain a goal. (**a**) [late 17C+] to steal (from). (**b**) [mid-19C+] to promote, to make successful, usu. as *made*. (**c**) [20C+] (*US*) to seduce, to have sexual intercourse with. (**d**) [1910s+] (*US*) to succeed in getting something, constructed with *for*, e.g. *to make a croaker for a reader*, to persuade a doctor to write a prescription for narcotics; *make for a stash*, to steal the drugs another addict has hidden so as to use them oneself. (**e**) [1920s] (*US Und.*) in weaker form of sense 1d, to entice the potential victim of a confidence trick. (**f**) [1920s+] to attain a goal, e.g. *make the team*, *make a club*. (**g**) [1950s–60s] (*US*) to consume drugs or drink. (**h**) [1960s+] (*US*) to make a drug purchase. **2** [mid-19C+] (*US*) to consider, to regard, to estimate as, e.g. *I make it about 10 o'clock*. **3** in senses of movement. (**a**) [mid-19C+] (*US*) to go to, to arrive at, to attend, to pay a visit. (**b**) [1900s] (*Aus.*) to leave. (**c**) [1910s+] spec. use of sense 3a, to catch, e.g. *make a plane*, *make a train*. **4** (*orig. US police/Und.*) in sense of SE *make out*, to discern, abbr. *make an identification*. (**a**) [20C+] to witness or observe, to recognize, to identify a suspect, also as *make one for*, to recognize someone as. (**b**) [1960s+] to stop and search people on the street. (**c**) [1990s+] (*US Und.*) to prove someone guilty in court. **5** [1910s–60s] (*US*) to understand or to empathize with. **6** [1940s+] to appear in the newspaper. **7** [1940s+] (*US, mainly Southern*) to distill liquor illegally. **8** [1940s+] (*US black*) to straighten one's hair. **9** [1950s+] (*US*) to enlist someone as an official member of the US Mafia; usu. as MADE *adj.* (4). **10** [1950s+] (*US*) to bear or endure. **11** [1960s] (*US*) to enjoy, to appreciate.

IN COMPOUNDS

❑ **make-up** *n.* [1950s] (*drugs*) **1** an injection of heroin. **2** the need to find more drugs.

IN PHRASES

❑ **make for** *v.* [1940s+] to identify, to connect to. ❑ **make off** *v.* [1940s] (*US*) to pretend. ❑ **make out** *v.* [SE *make out*, 'to establish by evidence, argument' (*OED*); *see also* separate entry] [late 19C+] to arrive at a conclusion; thus *how do you make that out?* how do you reach that conclusion? ❑ **make over** *v.* [20C+] (*US black*) to flatter. ❑ **make up to** *v.* **1** [late 18C+] to 'make love to', to 'chat up'. **2** [19C+] to curry favour with. ❑ **make with** *v.* (*also* **give with**) [Yid. *macht mit*, make with] [20C+] (*orig. US*) to use, to affect, to perform, to pose as.

SE in slang uses

IN COMPOUNDS

❑ **make-bait** *n.* (*also* **makebate**) [16C–19C] a troublemaker; one who stirs up arguments. ❑ **makeweight** *n.* [late 18C–early 19C] **1** a small candle. **2** a small, slender person.

IN PHRASES

❑ **make...** *v. see also under* relevant n. or adj. ❑ **make a chevy** *v.* [mid-19C] (*Irish*) to escape, to run away. ❑ **make a cow's of** *v.* [abbr. *cow's arse*] [1970s+] to make a mess of. ❑ **make a crush** *v.* [1920s] (*US*) to make a good impression on. ❑ **make a die** *v.* [? pun on *make a day of* ('day' = 'die' in Cockney pron.)] [early 17C–19C] to die. ❑ **make a Federal case out of** *v.* (*also* **make a Federal production out of**) [in the US legal system the Federal, rather than state, legislature often implies greater severity] [1950s+] (*US*) to take very seriously, esp. when the speaker feels that the problem is really minor, 'to make a mountain out of a molehill'; thus *not make a Federal case (out) of*, to not make a minor problem into a major one. ❑ **make a hames** *v.* (*also* **make a haimes**) [SE *hames*, the two pieces of metal placed on each side of a horse's collar; although the link to a 'mess' is unclear] [1930s+] (*Irish*) to bungle, to make a mess. ❑ **make a hare** *v.* [the image of a *hare* as a foolish creature] [mid-19C+] (*Anglo-Irish*) to make someone look foolish; to expose someone's ignorance. ❑ **make a Judy (Fitzsimmons) of oneself** *v.* [ety. unknown; ? anecdotal] [mid-19C] to be a fool, to make an idiot of oneself. ❑ **make a May-game of** *v.* [the trad. Mayday pastimes] [late 17C–18C] to play games with, to trick or deceive. ❑ **make a monster of** *v.* [late 16C–early 17C] to cuckold. ❑ **make a napkin out of one's dishclout** *v.* [the cook wields the *dishcloth*, the wife the *napkin*] [mid-18C–early 19C] **1** to marry one's cook or other servant. **2** to make a foolish, unsuitable marriage. ❑ **make an example** *v.* [late 17C] to get drunk. ❑ **make a one-eighty** *v. see* ONE-EIGHTY *v.* ❑ **make a set** *v.* [sporting imagery] [mid-17C] to have sexual intercourse. ❑ **make a straight coat-tail** *v.* [one's tails are blown out by the wind of one's progress] [mid-19C–1920s] (*US*) to run, to hurry. ❑ **make a strike** *v.* [orig. skittles/bowling, later baseball imagery] [mid-19C+] to be lucky, to be successful. ❑ **make ducks and drakes of** *v. see* PLAY DUCKS AND DRAKES WITH *under* PLAY *v.* ❑ **make free with both ends of the busk** *v. see under* BUSK *n.* ❑ **make indentures with your legs** *v. see under* LEG *n.* ❑ **make one's lucky** *v. see* CUT ONE'S LUCKY *under* CUT *v.*[2]. ❑ **make points** *v.* [basketball imagery] [1960s+] (*US*) to give a good impression, to 'score' with someone. ❑ **make the big door** *v.* [1950s] (*US prison*) to be released. ❑ **make the legal move** *v.* [1950s+] (*US teen*) to get married. ❑ **make time with** *v.* (*US*) **1** [1930s+] to make advances, to court, to flirt. **2** [1950s] to associate with. ❑ **make tortillas** *v.* [1970s] (*US prison*) to sodomize.

make it *v.* **1** in senses of existence, achievement. (**a**) [mid-19C+] to subsist, to survive, often as phr. *just barely making it*, also used in greeting, as in *How you making it?* (**b**) [late 19C+] to achieve (something). (**c**) [20C+] to be successful; thus *make it big, make it good*. (**d**) [1910s+] to manage, usu. in context of movement. (**e**) [1930s–60s] (*US prison*) to be granted parole. (**f**) [1940s+] to survive, to stay alive. (**g**) [1950s+] to get on, to relate. (**h**) [1960s+] to achieve a climax, to orgasm. **2** in senses of action. (**a**) [1930s+] to do something, to visit or be at a place, to arrive. (**b**) [1950s+] to move, to get on, to run off; also as imper. **3** [1950s–70s] (*US drugs*) to take drugs, esp. opiates. **4** [1980s+] to stop doing something, to abandon.

IN PHRASES

❑ **make it (with)** *v.* **1** [1930s+] to have sexual intercourse; either hetero- or homosexual. **2** [1950s+] (*US*) to have an orgasm.

make like (a)... *v.* **1** [late 19C+] (*orig. US*) to imitate, to pretend to be, to behave like or as if; thus *make like a chicken, ... duck*. **2** [1950s+] (*US*) (*also* **do a...**) as part of a number of phrs. all of which mean 'go away', 'get lost', e.g. *make like a fart and blow away, ... dragster and lay rubber, ... drum and beat it, ... banana and split, ... cow pat and hit the trail, ... paper doll and cut out, ... tree and leave, ... rubber and roll on* [an extensive selection can be found in *Maledicta* IV, 1, pp.40–42].

IN PHRASES

❑ **make like a baby and head out** *v.* (*also* **make like a foetus and head out**) [1980s+] (*US campus*) to leave. ❑ **make like an alligator and drag ass** *v.* [pun on DRAG ASS *v.*] [1950s+] (*US*) to leave.

make-out *n.* [MAKE OUT *v.* (3)] **1** [1960s+] (*US campus*) one who is good at seducing others. **2** [1970s+] (*US*) usu. attrib., romantic and sexual behaviour.

make out *v.* [SE *make out*, to manage to do something] **1** [19C+] to get on with, to socialize with; usu. with adv. meaning well or badly. **2** [mid-19C+] (*orig. US*) (*also* **make**) to get along, to make the grade, to succeed. **3** [1930s+] (*US*) to seduce a woman or man. **4** [1940s–50s] to stay, to make one's place. **5** [1940s+] (*US*) to indulge in hetero- or homosexual foreplay or petting but not necessarily intercourse.

IN COMPOUNDS

❑ **make-out artist** *n.* [ARTIST *n.* (1)] [1940s+] (*US*) a ladies' man, a successful seducer. ❑ **make-out line** *n.* [1950s] speech that is designed to facilitate seduction.

make out (like) *v.* [ext. of MAKE LIKE (A)... *v.* (1)] [late 19C+] to pretend, to pose as (if).

maker *n.* [19C] a forger, a counterfeiter.

-making *sfx* [mainly 1930s and general middle-/upper middle-class use, but disinterred regularly by readers of the novels of Evelyn Waugh, esp. *Vile Bodies* (1930)] [1920s+] used with a variety of nouns, e.g. *blush-making, hot-making* [sc. embarrassing], *shy-making, sick-making*, sometimes prefixed by 'too'.

mako *n. see* MACO *n.*[1].

makomé *n.* (*also* **macumeh, makoumé**) [Carib.E *makomé*, one's child's godmother, usu. an elderly female friend; ult. Fr. *macommère*] [20C+] (*W.I.*) an effeminate man.

maku *n.* [? Fr. *maquereau*, a pimp] [20C+] (*W.I.*) **1** an effeminate man. **2** a peeping tom. **3** a fool, an idiot.

mal *adj.* [1980s+] (*S.Afr.*) crazy, weird.

Malabar Hilton *n.* (*also* **Malabar flats**) [1960s+] (*Aus. Und.*) Long Bay prison, New South Wales.

malady of France *n. see* FRENCH DISEASE *under* FRENCH *adj.*

malaky *n. see* MALARKEY *n.*

malalapipe *n.* [Zulu *umalalepayipini*, 'one who sleeps in a pipe'] [1970s+] (*S.Afr.*) a homeless child beggar.

malarkey *n.* (*also* **malaky, malarky, mallarkey, mullarkey**) [? Irish *mullachán*, a strongly built boy, thus a ruffian] (*orig. US*) **1** [1920s+] nonsense, foolishness, 'messing about'; as v., to fool someone. **2** [1940s+] a fool.

malavogue *v.* (*also* **malivogue**) [ety. unknown; a nonce-word] [20C+] (*Irish*) to beat, to manhandle.

Malawi grass *n.* [SE *Malawi* + GRASS *n.*[4]/COB *n.*[2] (2)] [1980s+] (*drugs*) marijuana from Malawi; thus *Malawi cob*, marijuana from Malawi bundled in a shape reminiscent of a cigar.

malazanas *n.* [ety. unknown; ? an African language] [1960s–70s] (*S.Afr. township*) money.

malco *n.* [abbr. SE *malcoordinated*] [1980s+] a general term of abuse; also as v. *malco*, to act in an uncoordinated manner.

maleesh *phr.* [Egyptian Arabic *ma'lesh*, no matter, never mind] [1910s+] (*Aus./N.Z.*) a phr. used to indicate one's lack of interest/dismissal of an idea or thing.

male-hustler *n.* [HUSTLER *n.* (7)] [1960s] (*US gay*) a male prostitute, posing as masculine rather than effeminate.

male-mules *n.* [play on SE; poss. used only in Urquhart's trans. of Rabelais (1653)] [17C] the testicles.

malflor *n.* [Sp. lit. 'an evil flower'] [1960s+] (*US*) a lesbian.

malformy *n.* [? euph. for MOTHERFUCKER *n.*; SE *malformed*] [1970s] (*US black*) a general insult.

malfunction junction *n.* [1970s+] (*US*) a major congestion, usu. a traffic jam.

malhavelins *n. see* MANAVILINS *n.*

malicious *adj.* [20C+] (*W.I.*) **1** tiresomely inquisitive. **2** offensively meddlesome with the aim of causing harm.

ma-liner *n.* [1980s] (*S.Afr. Und.*) a pickpocket.

malivogue *v. see* MALAVOGUE *v.*

malkin *n.* (*also* **malyne, mawkin**) [Scot. *malkin*, a cat. *Grimalkin* is often the name of a witch's feline familiar, while *malkin* itself also means hare, suggesting a link to the rabbit, a trad. 'sexy' animal, that may or may not be coincidental] **1** [late 14C; early 16C–17C] a promiscuous woman. **2** [mid-16C–19C] the vagina.

IN COMPOUNDS

▫ **malkin-trash** *n.* [late 17C–early 19C] an ill-dressed person.

mallacky *n.* [Irish *meallach*, lumpy, globular] [20C+] (*Irish*) cat excrement.

mallarkey *n. see* MALARKEY *n.*

mallee root *n.* [rhy. sl., ult. Abor. *mallee*, eucalyptus] [1940s+] (*Aus.*) a prostitute.

mallet *n.*[1] [their image as a repressive agency] [1970s–80s] (*US black*) the police.

SE in slang uses

IN PHRASES

▫ **on the mallet** [they are *knocked down/out*] [mid-19C] of goods, taken on trust.

mallet *n.*[2] [1990s+] (*UK juv.*) a boy who lacks pubic hair.

mallet *v.* [SE *mallet*] [late 16C–19C; 1980s+] to hit, to beat, lit. and fig.; latterly spec. to defeat.

mallethead *n.* [SE *mallet* + -HEAD *sfx* (1); note earlier MALLETHEADED *adj.*] [1950s+] (*US*) a stupid person.

malletheaded *adj.* [SE *mallet*] [19C] stupid, foolish.

malleting bout *n.* [early–mid-19C] a fist-fight.

Malley's cow *n.* [the story of one *Malley* who was supposed to look after a cow. When his boss returned to find Malley but no cow and asked what had happened, he received the reply 'she's a goner'] [1950s–70s] (*Aus.*) one who has left, gone away.

mallie *n. see* MALL RAT *n.*

mallit *n.* [2000s] (*S.Afr.*) a crazy person.

mallowpuff Maori *n.* [*mallowpuff*, a biscuit brown on the outside and white inside] [1980s+] (*N.Z.*) a Maori who is not committed to Maori culture.

mall rat *n.* (*also* **mallie, mall punk**) [SE (*shopping*) *mall* + -RAT *sfx*] [1980s+] (*US*) a young person who spends the day hanging around shopping malls; a young person who dresses and behaves in a punk fashion.

malmsey nose *n.* [the assumption being that the acned nose is the result of drinking too much *malmsey* wine] [late 17C–early 19C] a heavily acned nose.

Malt *n.* [abbr.] [late 19C–1960s] a *Maltese*.

malt *n.* **1** [19C] as a constituent of beer, used in phr. indicating drunkenness. **2** [early 19C] (*UK Und.*) tea.

DERIVATIVES

▫ **malted** *adj.* [19C] drunk, tipsy. ▫ **malty** *adj.* [early–mid-19C] drunk.

IN COMPOUNDS

▫ **malt cove** *n.* (*also* **malty cove**) [COVE *n.* (1)] [19C] a beer drinker. ▫ **maltpie** *n.* [early 17C] alcohol. ▫ **malt sandwich** *n.* [2000s] (*N.Z.*) a glass of beer. ▫ **maltworm** *n.* [play on SE *maltworm*, a malt-infesting weevil] [mid-16C–early 17C; mid-late 19C] a heavy drinker.

IN PHRASES

▫ **have malt above the meal** *v.* [early 18C–mid-19C] (*Scot.*) to be drunk. ▫ **have malt above the water** *v.* [late 17C–19C] to be drunk. ▫ **have malt above the wheat** *v.* [mid-16C–mid-17C] to be drunk.

malt *v.* (*also* **malt it**) [SE *malt*, a component of beer] [19C] to drink.

maltooling *n.* [MOLL *n.* (1) + *tool* to pick pockets] [mid–late 19C] of a female pickpocket, stealing from people travelling on buses.

maltoot *n.* (*also* **maltout**) [? Fr. *matelot*, a sailor] [late 18C–late 19C] a marine.

mam *n.* [abbr. SE *mammary (gland)*] [1970s+] in pl., the female breasts.

mama *n.* (*also* **mamma**) **1** [1910s+] (*orig. US black*) a woman, esp. when sexy and attractive. **2** [1910s+] (*orig. US black*) a girlfriend or wife, esp. in direct address. **3** [1940s+] a feminine lesbian. **4** [1940s+] anything considered very powerful, large or admirable. **5** [1950s+] (*US*) an effeminate male homosexual; also as camp self-description. **6** [1960s+] (*orig. Hell's Angel*) a woman who rides with the Hell's Angels and is available for sex and allied indignities but is distinguished from the *old ladies* (the actual girlfriends of the riders); the term is an abbr. of *Let's go make someone a mama*. **7** [1970s] (*US prison*) an inmate who poses as a woman. **8** [1980s] a masculine lesbian.

SE in slang uses

IN COMPOUNDS

▫ **mama bear** *n.* [BEAR *n.* (6)] [1970s+] (*US*) a policewoman, esp. in the Highway Patrol. ▫ **mama bitch** *n. see under* BITCH *n.*[1]. ▫ **mama coca** *n.* [lit. 'mother coca'] [1980s+] (*drugs*) cocaine. ▫ **mama man** *n.* [1940s+] (*W.I.*) **1** a man who does women's work. **2** an unmanly man. ▫ **mama's boots** *n.* [1930s] (*US gambling*) a pair of threes in craps dice. ▫ **mama's boss** *n.* [1930s–40s] (*US black*) usu. female usage, a husband or favourite boyfriend.

IN PHRASES

▫ **sweet mama** *n. see under* SWEET *adj.*[1]. ▫ **did your mama have any sons that lived?** [1970s] (*US black*) a phr. used by a woman to rebuff sexual cat-calling by men as she passes them.

mama and papa of… *phr. see* FATHER (AND MOTHER) OF… *phr.*

mamacita *n.* [Sp., lit. 'little mother'] [1970s+] (*US*) an attractive young woman.

mama-huncher *n.* (*also* **mother-huncher**) [1960s+] euph. for MOTHERFUCKER *n.*

mama-jabber *n. see* MAMMY-JAMMER *n.*

mamí *n.* [2000s] (*US black/P.R.*) a woman, usu. black or Puerto Rican.

mamma *n. see* MAMA *n.*

mammapoule *n. see* MAMPALA *n.*

mammock *v.* [dial. *mammock*, to tear into pieces] [mid–late 19C] (*US, mainly west and south*) **1** to beat, to thrash; thus *mommicking*, a thrashing. **2** to mess up, to confuse.

mammy *n.*[1] (*also* **mauma, momma**) [SE *mammy*, mother; note Hurston, *Story in Harlem Slang* (1942), defines it simply as 'a term of insult'] **1** [19C+] (*US*) the ideal black woman as stereotyped by whites; such women would typically be employed as nannies or cooks in white households. **2** [early 19C] (*UK Und.*) the madam of a brothel.

IN COMPOUNDS

▫ **mammy-freak** *n.* [FREAK *n.*[1] (7)] [1950s] (*US*) a prostitute's (white) customer whose sexual tastes demand women who resemble motherly black women.

mammy *n.*[2] [the image of maternal, i.e. *mammy's* abundance, of love, food etc] [1930s+] (*US Und.*) an abundance, a lot, esp. in phr. *money's mammy*, a great deal of money.

mammy-dodger *n.* (*also* **mammy-dugger**) [1920s–30s] (*US black*) euph. for MOTHERFUCKER *n.*

DERIVATIVES

▫ **mammy-dodging** *adj.* [1920s–30s] euph. for MOTHERFUCKING *adj.*

mammyfucking *adj.* [1970s] synon. for MOTHERFUCKING *adj.*

mammy-jammer *n.* (*also* **mama-/mamma-/mammie-jammer, mama-/mamma-/mammie-jabber, mammy-jammy**) [1950s+] euph. for MOTHERFUCKER *n.*

DERIVATIVES

▫ **mammy-jamming** *adj.* (*also* **mama-jabbing**) [1940s+] euph. for MOTHERFUCKING *adj.*

mammy-loving *adj.* [1960s+] a semi-euph. for MOTHERFUCKING *adj.*

mammy-rammer *n.* [1960s–70s] euph. for MOTHERFUCKER *n.*

DERIVATIVES

▫ **mammy-ramming** *adj.* (*also* **mammy-rammy**) [1960s–70s] euph. for MOTHERFUCKING *adj.*

mammy-screwing *adj.* [SCREW *v.* (1)] [1960s] semi-euph. for MOTHERFUCKING *adj.*

mammy-tapper *n.* [1960s] (*US black*) euph. for MOTHERFUCKER *n.*

DERIVATIVES

▫ **mammy-tapping** *adj.* [1960s] euph. for MOTHERFUCKING *adj.*

mampala *n.* (*also* **mammapoule, mampala-man, maparla, maparla-man**) [Sp. *mampolón*, a cock, but not a fighting cock, thus a weakling] [20C+] (*W.I.*) an effeminate man, a homosexual man who plays the 'female' role in sex.

mampy *n.* (*also* **mampi**) [1990s+] (*W.I.*) a fat woman.

mamzer *n.* (*also* **momser, momza, momzer, momzir**) [Heb. *mamzer*, a bastard, adapted in Lat. and thus used throughout the Middle Ages. The modern use, however, is related to Yid., and imported by Jewish immigrants to US and UK] [20C+] a catch-all term implying everything from great affection to deep dislike.

Man *n.* [abbr.] [mid-19C] (*UK Und.*) *Man*chester, UK.

man *n.*[1] **1** as a term of address. (**a**) [late 16C+] used emphatically in direct address [Gold, *A Jazz Lexicon* (1964), and Major, *Juba to Jive: A Dict. of Afro-American Slang* (1994), suggest that the term was adopted by US blacks to counter the common white use of 'boy' when addressing blacks: note McCall, *Makes Me Wanna Holler* (1994): 'More fights started over one person calling another 'boy' than over anything else. To counter that indignity, we addressed each other respectfully as 'man', even though we were not adults']. (**b**) [20C+] used in direct address, without emphasis, usu. to acknowledge a shared social or cultural identity (later usage sometimes includes women, children and animals). **2** as a piece of money [the picture, usu. of a male monarch, that was engraved on most coins + *iron man*, a term for various units of currency]. (**a**) [early 19C] the head of a coin. (**b**) [1910s–60s] (*US*) $1. **3** [mid-19C–1960s] (*US*) (*also* **old man, son**) the penis. **4** (*orig. US*) constr. with *the*. (**a**) [1910s+] the holder of institutional authority, whether an individual, e.g. a prison warden, a senior military officer, or in sing. or pl., a group, e.g. policemen, prison officers. (**b**) [1920s+] the holder of power, in a non-institutional context; anyone deemed exceptional in ability; thus (*US black*) *you the man*, a phr. implying one's acceptance of another person's superiority. (**c**) [1930s+] (*US*) (*also* **the Man above, the big man**) God. (**d**) [1940s+] (*orig. US*) a (major) drug dealer. (**e**) [1940s+] (*US black*) the white ruling class. (**f**) [1950s+] a crime boss, esp. when he masquerades as a respectable businessman. (**g**) [1950s+] (*US black*) the US Government. (**h**) [1990s+] an exemplary person. **5** [1930s–40s] (*US black*) a pint bottle of liquor [Scot. *halfman*, half a bottle of spirits; thus HALF-MAN *n.*]. **6** [1950s+] as a quasi-suffix, a fan, an enthusiast; e.g. LEG MAN *n.* (2).

IN PHRASES

▫ **half-a-man** *n.* [1960s] half a dollar. ▫ **meet the man** *v.* [1970s] (*US black*) to go to work.

SE in slang uses

IN COMPOUNDS

▫ **man-box** *n.* [mid-19C] a coffin. ▫ **man-catcher** *n.* (*also* **man-getter, -grabber, -hunter, -shark**) [1920s–50s] (*US*) a labour recruiter, an employment agency. ▫ **man dumpling** *n.* [the implication is either of being as big as a man, or a man-sized portion] [1950s] (*W.I.*) a very large dumpling. ▫ **man muscle** *n.* [note *love muscle* under LOVE *n.*] [1970s+] (*US black*) the penis. ▫ **man pains** *n.* [1990s+] (*US black teen*) **1** injuries suffered while doing 'manly' things, i.e. lifting a trunk, playing football etc. **2** sexual frustration. ▫ **man-paste** *n.* *see* PASTE *n.*[1]. ▫ **man planter** *n.* [PLANT *v.*[1] (2)] [1920s] (*US tramp*) a grave digger. ▫ **man root** *n.* [19C] the penis. ▫ **man Thomas** *n.* [early 18C–mid-19C] the penis. ▫ **man-trap** *n.* *see* separate entry.

IN PHRASES

▫ **give on a man** *v.* (*also* **give upon a man**) [20C+] (*W.I.*) of a woman, to surrender oneself to male advances. ▫ **man-a-hanging** *n.* [late 19C; 1970s–80s] (*US black*) a person in trouble. ▫ **man and man** *n.* [on pattern of I AND I *pron.*] [1970s–80s] (*UK black*) a person. ▫ **man-better-man** [20C+] (*W.I.*) a phr. used to issue a definite challenge to fight, with the implication of finding out who is the 'better man'. ▫ **man for breakfast** *n.* [1930s] (*US, Western*) a killing. ▫ **man in a grey flannel suit** *n.* [1990s+] (*Aus.*) a shark. ▫ **man in blue** *n.* *see* BOYS IN BLUE *n.* ▫ **man in gray** *n.* [1930s–50s] (*US black*) a postman. ▫ **man in the boat** *n.* *see* LITTLE MAN (IN THE BOAT) *n.* ▫ **man in the moon** *n.* *see* separate entry. ▫ **man of business** *n.* [Carib.E. *man of business*, a handyman] [20C+] (*W.I.*) a woman's lover on whom she relies for various favours. ▫ **man of the road** *n.* *see* *GENTLEMAN OF THE ROAD under* GENTLEMAN OF… *n.* ▫ **man of the town** *n.* [late 17C–early 19C] a debauchee, a libertine. ▫ **man of the world** *n.* [late 19C] a professional thief, usu. a pickpocket. ▫ **man of war** *n.* [its site, on the east bank of the Fleet River; the image is of an anchored warship] [18C–19C] the Fleet prison, London. ▫ **man-o'-man** *n.* [1970s] (*US black*) Manischewitz Wine. ▫ **man outside Hoyt's** *n.* [the commissionaire *outside Hoyt's* Theatre, Melbourne, a gorgeously uniformed individual] [1940s+] **1** (*Aus.*) the source of all rumours; also as phr. *don't know — from the man outside Hoyt's*. **2** (*Aus. Und.*) the source of any stolen property that the police might find with a receiver. ▫ **man upstairs, the** *n.* [1940s+] God. ▫ **man walking** *n.* [2000s] (*US prison*) a signal that a prison officer is approaching. ▫ **man who rides the screaming gasser** *n.* [1930s–40s] (*US black*) a policeman in a patrol car. ▫ **man with a headache stick** *n.* [i.e. his nightstick/truncheon] [1930s–60s] (*US black*) a policeman. ▫ **man with a paper ass(hole)** *n.* [ASS *n.* (2)/ASSHOLE *n.*] [1950s+] (*US black*) a talkative fool – all talk and little or no action. ▫ **man with no hands** *n.* [1940s+] (*Aus.*) a miser. ▫ **man with the book of many years** *n.* [1940s] (*US black*) a judge. ▫ **man with the fuzzy balls** *n.* *see under* BALLS *n.* ▫ **sure as I'm a man fit to wear britches** *adv.* *see under* SURE AS… *phr.*

man *n.*[2] [SE *man*, something powerful, strong] [1950s+] (*W.I.*) a very expensive thing, usu. in phr. *something is a man*.

man *v.* **1** [17C] to work as a pimp. **2** [17C–early 19C] to have sexual intercourse.

manablins *n.* *see* MANAVILINS *n.*

man alive *n.* (*also* **dead alive**) [rhy. sl.] [20C+] (*bingo*) the number five.

man and wife *n.* [rhy. sl.] [1910s+] a knife.

manarolins *n.* *see* MANAVILINS *n.*

manatee *n.* [1960s–70s] (*US gay*) a 'masculine' lesbian.

manavilins *n.* (*also* **malhavelins, manablins, manarolins, manavalins, manavelings**) [ety. unknown, but note contemp. naut. jargon *manarvel*, to pilfer small stores] [mid–late 19C] odds and ends, bits and pieces, typically of food or small change.

Manc *n.* [SE *Manc*unian] [1990s+] a native of Manchester, UK.

Manc *adj.* [MANC *n.*] [1990s+] pertaining to Manchester or Mancunians.

Manch *n.* [abbr.] [2000s] *Manch*ester, UK.

Manchester *n.* [the days when *Manchester* was 'Cottonopolis', the textile capital of the globe] [20C+] (*Aus./N.Z.*) household linen; thus the *Manchester department* in shops.

manchester *n.* [? Scot. *mang*, talk and/or f. Rom. *mag*, to beg] [early 19C] (*UK Und.*) the tongue.

Manchester Cities *n.* (*also* **Manchesters**) [rhy. sl. *Manchester City* = TITTY *n.* (1)] [1950s+] (*Aus./UK*) the female breasts.

mancunt *n.* [SE *man* + CUNT *n.* (1)] [1990s+] (*gay*) **1** anus. **2** a passive homosexual.

manda *v.* (*also* **mandy**) [2000s] (*S.Afr. gay*) to masturbate.

M and C *n.* [M *n.* and C *n.*[3]; see also C AND M *n.*] [1920s–60s] (*US drugs*) a mixture of morphine and cocaine, the equivalent of the heroin and cocaine SPEEDBALL *n.*[1].

mander *n.* [SE *remand*] [mid–late 19C] (*UK prison/Und.*) a remand to prison, pending trial.

manderer *n.* *see* MAUNDER *n.*

mandingo *n.* [proper name *Mandingo*, a member of the peoples of the upper Niger in West Africa, whose ranks supplied many slaves; more immediately a ref. to the book title *Mandingo*, concerning the stereotypical 'black buck' slave and his effect on women, both black and white] [1960s+] (*US black*) a tough, physically strong, virile African-American man.

M&M *adj.* [2000s] (*US teen*) of a person, just about acceptable.

M & Ms *n.* [the US-originated sweet, equiv. of UK *Smarties*/ SMARTIES *n.* (1)] [1960s+] (*drugs*) barbiturates, amphetamines, drugs available as pills.

mandozy *n.* [the Anglo-Jewish prize-fighter *Daniel Mendoza* (1764–1836)] [19C] **1** a powerful blow. **2** a term of endearment among London Jews.

mandrake *n.* [SE *mandrake*, 'Any plant of the genus *Mandragora*...characterized by very short stems, thick, fleshy, often forked, roots, and fetid lance-shaped leaves. The mandrake is poisonous, having emetic and narcotic properties, and was formerly used medicinally. The forked root is thought to resemble the human form, and was fabled to utter a deadly shriek when plucked up from the ground' (*OED*)] **1** [mid-17C] a dildo. **2** [19C+] a sodomite, a male homosexual.

M and S *n.* (*also* **Marks, Marks and Sparks**) [abbr.; note the firm's house magazine is called *Sparks*] [1930s+] nickname for the Marks & Spencer group of department stores.

mandy *n.* (*also* **manny**) [the spelling 'manny' seems to appear only in Fabian & Byrne, *Groupie* (1969) and was coined by them as a deliberate euph.] [1960s+] a Mandrax or methaqualone tablet.

man-eater *n.* [orig. naut. use, a particularly disciplinarian officer, ult. SE, a man-eating tiger] **1** [late 17C–early 18C] a watchman, a constable. **2** [mid–late 19C] (*Anglo-Ind.*) a horse that tends to bite people. **3** [20C+] a sexually predatory woman. **4** [1920s] a swindler. **5** [1920s+] a tough overseer, employer, etc. **6** [1970s+] a homosexual man; a fellator.

(DERIVATIVES)

❑ **man-eating** *adj.* [1970s+] devoted to fellatio.

maneen *n.* [SE *man* + dimin. sfx *-een*] [1910s+] (*Irish*) a little man, a gauche young man.

maneuvra *v.* [SE *manoeuvre*] [2000s] (*US black*) to pick up a woman.

mang *n.*[1] [1970s] (*Aus. teen*) a general insult.

mang *n.*[2] [2000s] (*S.Afr. Und.*) prison.

mang *v.* [Scot. or Rom. *mag*, to beg] [early–mid-19C] to talk or boast.

manga *n. see* MUNGER *n.*

mangarly *n.* (*also* **mangary, mangery, manjary**) [Ital. *mangiare*, to eat] [late 16C; 1930s] (*Ling. Fr./Polari*) food.

mange *n.* [Ital. *mangiare*, to eat] [late 19C–1900s] food.

mange *adj.* [SE *mangy*] [1990s+] (*W.I.*) unpleasant, impolite.

mange *v.* [Ital. *mangiare*/Fr. *manger*, to eat] [1960s+] (*US campus*) to eat.

mangina *n.* [SE *man* + *vagina*; cf. MANHOLE *n.*, MANCUNT *n.*] [2000s] **1** (*gay*) anus. **2** (*US campus*) a reticent, reserved man.

mangle *n.*[1] [19C] the vagina.

mangle *n.*[2] [supposed resemblance] [1940s+] (*Aus.*) a bicycle.

mangle and wringer *n.* [rhy. sl.] [20C+] a singer.

mangled *adj.* [as if wrung through a mangle] **1** [1920s] worn out. **2** [1930s] (*US*) hurt, injured. **3** [1980s+] (*US campus*) dishevelled, unkempt. **4** [2000s] (*Irish*) drunk.

mango *n.* [resemblances] **1** [1980s+] (*N.Z.*) a N.Z. $50 note. **2** [1980s+] (*US*) in pl., the female breasts. **3** [2000s] (*S.Afr. gay*) a hairy anus.

mangsman *n.* [MANG *v.* (1)] [mid-19C] (*UK Und.*) a lawyer.

mangy *adj.* [SE *mangy*, squalid, shabby, lit. 'scabby'] **1** [mid-19C+] contemptible. **2** [20C+] (*Irish*) mean, grasping, avaricious.

manhole *n.* **1** in sexual contexts both based on HOLE *n.*[1] (1). (**a**) [late 19C+] the vagina. (**b**) [1970s+] (*US gay*) the anus. (**c**) [1970s+] (*US gay*) a passive partner in anal intercourse. **2** [1970s+] (*US black*) a bar, a saloon, a club etc, esp. for men only [HOLE *n.*[1] (2b)].

(IN COMPOUNDS)

❑ **manhole cover** *n.* [1950s+] (*Aus./US*) a sanitary towel; thus pl. *manhole covers*, menstruation.

manhole cover *n.*[1] [rhy. sl.] [20C+] a brother.

manhole cover *n.*[2] **1** as food [joc. 'resemblance']. (**a**) [1940s+] bread pudding. (**b**) [1950s] (*US short order*) hot-cakes. **2** *see under* MANHOLE *n.*

manhole inspector *n. see under* INSPECTOR *n.*

manicou-man *n.* [? Carib.E. *manicou*, a 'nocturnal, foul-smelling marsupial rodent the size of a cat' (Allsopp, *Dict. Caribbean English Usage*, 1996); the young of this creature hang onto their mother for transportation] [20C+] (*W.I.*) an effeminate man.

manifest *n.* [the *manifest* of the goods it carries] [1920s–30s] (*US*) a fast freight train.

man in the moon *n.*[1] **1** [mid-17C] a watchman, a constable. **2** [mid-19C] a nickname for the person, necessarily anonymous and quick to disappear, who pays out bribes at elections.

man in the moon *n.*[2] [rhy. sl. *man in the moon* = LOON *n.*[1]] [20C+] a fool, an eccentric.

manjarie *n. see* MANGARLY *n.*

Mank *n.* [abbr.; see also MANC *n.*] [2000s] **1** a Mancunian. **2** Manchester.

manly-warringahs *n.* [rhy. sl.; ult. Aus. Rules football club *Manley Warringah*; *warringah*, a term from the Guringai language means 'sign of rain', 'across the waves' or 'sea'] [1990s+] (*Aus.*) fingers.

manmanpoul *n.* [Fr. *maman poule*, mother hen] [20C+] (*W.I.*) **1** a person who fusses excessively. **2** a gullible fool.

manna from heaven *n.* [2000s] (*US*) the throw of eleven in craps dice.

manne die *n.* [Afk. *man*(*ne*), man + *die*, the; i.e. *the man*] [1960s+] (*S.Afr.*) a local hero, esp. in a school or college.

manners *n.*

(IN PHRASES)

❑ **put manners on** *v.* [1930s+] (*Irish*) to discipline, to force into line. ❑ **under manners** [1990s+] (*W.I./UK black*) behaving as required, submitting to another person's orders.

manners *v.* **1** [1970s–80s] (*UK black*) to seduce. **2** *see* HEAVY MANNERS *v.*

mannish *adj.* [i.e. a child acting beyond its years] [20C+] (*US/W.I.*) usu. of young people, forward, impertinent.

mannish water *n.* [the association of the soup with virility] [20C+] (*W.I., Jam.*) goat-head soup, a highly seasoned, peppery soup made from the head and offal of a goat, eaten on festive occasions. The soup is linked to virility in Jamaica and with placating the spirits of the dead in Tobago.

Manny *adj.* [2000s] Mancunian.

manny *n.*[1] [1970s+] (*US gay*) a lesbian.

manny *n.*[2] *see* MANDY *n.*

mano *n.* [1960s+] (*US Hispanic*) used in direct address, man.

manoeuvre the apostles *v.* [pun on popular phr. *to rob Peter to pay Paul*] [late 18C+] to manipulate one's accounts to pay off one debt while incurring another.

man on the moon *n.* [rhy. sl.] [1960s+] a spoon.

manor *n.* [note 'Walter', *My Secret Life* (1888–94): 'You leave the girl alone, it's my manor'] **1** [1920s+] (*US/UK Und./police*) an area of operations, one's home base. **2** [1930s+] (*UK Und.*) one's local area. **3** [1960s+] an indeterminate place, used generically.

man o' war *n.* [rhy. sl.] [20C+] a bore.

-mans *sfx* (*also* **-man**) [the *OED* cites it as 'unexplained' but Partridge (*DSUE* 8th edn, 1984, *Origins*, 4th edn, 1966) suggests links with Lat. *mens*, mind, Fr. sfx *-ment*, SE *man*, a human being or Skrt *-moni*, mood or mind] [16C–19C] a state of being or a thing; *see* various combs. e.g. CRACKMANS *n.*, RUFFMANS *n.* etc.

manteca *n.* [2000s] (*US drugs*) heroin.

mantee *n.* [ety. unknown] [1930s–60s] a masculine lesbian; thus *manteewalk*, to swagger, *mantee voice*, a deep voice.

mantelpiece *n.*

(IN PHRASES)

❑ **you don't look at the mantelpiece when you're poking the fire** *see under* POKE *v.*

mantovani *n.* (*also* **manto**) [rhy. sl. = FANNY *n.*[1]] [1990s+] women, girls.

man-trap *n.*[1] **1** [late 18C] a widow. **2** [late 18C] (*UK Und.*) the gallows. **3** [late 18C–19C] the vagina. **4** [late 19C] (*Aus.*) a public house. **5** [1910s+] an attractive and available woman.

man-trap *n.*[2] [rhy. sl. = CRAP *n.*[1] (2)] [late 19C–1900s] a piece of excrement.

manual *n.*

IN EXCLAMATIONS

❑ **get a manual!** [computer imagery] [1990s+] (*US campus*) an admonition to find out what is going on.

manual labour *n.* [1990s+] masturbation.

manufacture *n. see* *ENGLISH MANUFACTURE under* ENGLISH *adj.*

manure *n.* [euph. for BULLSHIT *n.* (1)] [1920s–70s] (*Can./US*) nonsense.

Maori *adj.* [20C+] (*N.Z.*) not a sl. term as such, *Maori* has been stereotyped as an all-purpose shorthand for stupid, lazy, or primitive. It is used as such in the combs. that follow.

IN COMPOUNDS

❑ **Maori cannon** *n.* [1930s–40s] (*N.Z.*) a badly played shot in billiards or snooker. ❑ **Maori car** *n.* [1980s] (*N.Z.*) an old or broken-down vehicle. ❑ **Maori day off** *n.* (*also* **MDO**) [1980s] (*N.Z.*) unauthorized absence from the workplace. ❑ **Maori foreplay** *n.* [2000s] (*N.Z.*) a lack of sexual foreplay. ❑ **Maori half-crown** *n.* [the half-crown (12.5p) was worth 30 pennies] [late 19C; 1950s] (*N.Z.*) a penny. ❑ **Maori holiday** *n.* [1970s+] (*N.Z.*) the day after payday. ❑ **Maori mustang** *n.* [the *Mustang* is a much sought-after sports car; the *Ford* is definitely not] [1970s+] (*N.Z.*) the Mark II Ford Zephyr. ❑ **Maori overdrive** *n.* [1970s+] (*N.Z.*) sliding one's car downhill with the engine off and the gears in neutral. ❑ **Maori P.T.** *n.* [SE *P.T.*, physical training] [mid-19C+] (*N.Z.*) taking it easy and doing nothing. ❑ **Maori pyjamas** *n.* [joc. mispron.] [2000s] (*N.Z.*) marijuana. ❑ **Maori roast** *n.* [1970s+] (*N.Z.*) fish and chips or some form of fast food. ❑ **Maori screwdriver** *n.* [2000s] (*N.Z.*) a hammer used to drive in a screw. ❑ **Maori sidestep** *n.* [2000s] (*N.Z.*) barging directly into someone, i.e. no sidestep at all. ❑ **Maori time** *n.* [1980s+] (*N.Z.*) a flexible attitude to time-keeping. ❑ **Maori weed** *n.* [20C+] (*N.Z.*) a wild horse.

map *n.* [? predating in J. Taylor, 'The Water Poet', *Works* (1630): 'Being willing to take slender acquaintance of any map whatsoever, viewing, and circumviewing every man's face I met'] **1** [20C+] the human face. **2** [1920s] the mouth. **3** [1920s+] (*US Und.*) a bank cheque, usu. a fraudulent one.

SE in slang uses

IN PHRASES

❑ **throw a map** *v.* [the supposed similarity of a pool of vomit to a map of Australia] [1940s+] (*Aus.*) to vomit.

map *v.* [MAP *n.* (1)] [1980s+] (*US black*) to hit, esp. to hit in the face.

SE in slang uses

IN PHRASES

❑ **have someone mapped** *v.* [20C+] to have someone completely and accurately assessed, to work out another's movements and attitudes.

maparla *n.* (*also* **maparla-man**) *see* MAMPALA *n.*

maphepha *n.* (*also* **mephepha**) [Xhosa *amaphepha*, papers] (*S.Afr.*) **1** [1970s+] a rand. **2** [1970s+] money in general. **3** [1980s+] an official document, 'papers'.

map of... *phr.* [1900s–60s] (*US*) a phr. used with the name of a country to refer to typical facial features, e.g. a Jew will have a *map of Jerusalem all over his face.*

IN PHRASES

❑ **map of England** *n.* (*also* **map of Africa, map of Ireland**) [note synon. Fr. *carte de France*; [19C] *cartes de géographie*] [1910s+] a semen stain on a sheet, or occas. a garment. ❑ **map of Tassie** *n.* (*also* **mapatasi, map of Tasmania, map o' Tassie**) [the supposed similarity of this shape to the outline of a map of Tasmania] [1980s+] (*Aus.*) the female genitals and pubic hair.

mapusa *n.* (*also* **mapuza**) [? Afr. pron. of SE *police*] [1970s+] (*S.Afr. Und.*) the police.

maque *n. see* MACK *n.*[2].

mara *adj.* [2000s] (*S.Afr. gay*) depressed.

maracas *n.* [? the musical instrument; i.e. one 'plays' on them] **1** [1930s+] (*US*) the female breasts. **2** [1990s+] the testicles [appearance and rhy. sl.; = KNACKERS *n.*].

marahoochie *n. see* MARIHOOCHIE *n.*

marathons *n.* [their effect on one's stamina] [1970s+] (*drugs*) amphetamines.

marble *n.* [1950s+] the clitoris.

IN PHRASES

❑ **roll one's marble** *v.* [1950s] (*US*) of a woman, to masturbate.

SE in slang uses

IN PHRASES

❑ **have a good marble** *v.* [horseracing, to be in a good position at the starting gate; ult. next] [1920s–60s] (*Aus.*) to be in an advantageous position. ❑ **make one's marble good** *v. see* *MAKE ONE'S ALLEY GOOD under* ALLEY *n.*[3].

marble *adj.*

SE in slang uses

IN COMPOUNDS

❑ **marblehead** *n.* **1** [19C] a Greek [the many marble statues of Greece + -HEAD *sfx*]. **2** [1910s–60s] (*US*) (*also* **marble dome**) an idiot [SE *marble* + -HEAD *sfx*]. ❑ **marble heart** *n.* [play on *cold shoulder*] [late 19C–1930s] (*US*) a rejection. ❑ **marble orchard** *n.* (*also* **marble city, marble town**) [note film title *Gardens of Stone* (1987), referring to the US Arlington National Cemetery] [1920s+] (*US*) a cemetery.

marble *v.* [SE *marble*, that rolls along] [mid–late 19C] (*US*) to leave, to go.

marble arch *n.* [rhy. sl.] [1990s+] starch.

marble halls *n.* [rhy. sl. = BALLS *n.* (1)] [20C+] the testicles.

marbles *n.*[1] [? Fr. *morbilles*, small blisters] [late 16C–19C] venereal buboes or pocks.

marbles *n.*[2] [Fr. *meubles*, furniture] [mid–late 19C] furniture.

marbles *n.*[3] [resemblance, but note MARBLE HALLS *n.*] [mid-19C+] the testicles.

IN PHRASES

❑ **crack one's marbles** *v.* [1930s] (*US*) **1** of a man, to achieve orgasm or to induce it in a woman. **2** to delight, to please.

marbles *n.*[4] (*US*) **1** [mid-19C+] personal possessions, esp. money used as gambling stakes. **2** [1930s] pearls. **3** [1930s–50s] dollars; money in general; thus *big marbles*, a large sum of money.

SE in slang uses

IN PHRASES

❑ **have marbles in one's head** *v.* [paradoxically synon. with colloq. phr. *lose one's marbles*] [1950s] (*US*) to be insane, eccentric, foolish. ❑ **pass in one's marbles** *v.* (*also* **roll in one's marble(s), throw in one's marble**) [1900s–50s] (*Aus.*) to die.

marbles! *excl.* [MARBLES *n.*[3]; pun on BALLOCKS! *excl.*] [late 19C] a general excl. of disgust, contempt and negation.

marbles and conkers *adj.* [rhy. sl. = BONKERS *adj.* (2)] [20C+] eccentric, crazy.

marchers *n.* [2000s] (*S.Afr.*) money.

marching money *n.* [19C milit. jargon, money used to pay for a soldier's meals during a march] [1910s+] (*Aus.*) daily travel allowance.

marching powder *n.* (*also* **marching dust**) [1980s+] (*US drugs*) cocaine, as in BOLIVIAN MARCHING POWDER *n.* or *Peruvian marching powder*.

march in the rear of a whereas *v. see* *FOLLOW A WHEREAS under* FOLLOW *v.*

marchioness *n.* [a character in Charles Dickens's *Old Curiosity Shop* (1841)] [mid–late 19C] a maid-of-all-work.

Marco Polo *n.* [Ital. explorer *Marco Polo* (1254–1324)] [1980s+] (*US gay*) an Italian gay man.

marcus clark *n.* [rhy. sl.; ult. *Sir Marcus Clark* (1883–1953), Australian retailer (*Marcus Clark's*) and businessman] [20C+] (*Aus.*) a shark.

mard-arse *n.* [dial. *mardy*, sulky, in turn f. dial. *mar*, to spoil or over-indulge a child + *arse*, used as general pej. rather than actual physical description] [20C+] a sulky person.

mare *n.*[1] [SE *mare*, a female horse; the original sexual connotation being used of a man's partner in copulation, upon whom he 'rides'] **1** [14C–19C] a mistress, a sexually pleasing woman, any woman with sexual overtones. **2** [1920s+] an ill-tempered, unpleasant or spirited woman. **3** [1930s+] an ugly woman. **4** [1940s+] a woman, without pej. overtones.

mare *n.*[2] [abbr. SE *nightmare*] [1980s+] a horrendous situation, person or place.

mare and foal *n.* [rhy. sl.] [2000s] (*N.Z.*) a bankroll.

mare's nest *n.* [SE *mare's nest*, a folly, an impossibility] [1950s–70s] (*N.Z.*) a bar set aside for women and their escorts.

mare with two legs *n.* (*also* **mare with three legs**) [17C–mid-19C] a gallows.

marg *n.* [abbr.] [2000s] (*US*) a *margarita* cocktail.

Margaret (Rose) *n.* (*also* **Mary Rose**) [rhy. sl.; ult. *Margaret Rose* or Princess Margaret (1930–2002), the Queen's sister; the ship *Mary Rose*, a sunken Tudor warship brought to the surface in 1974] [1970s+] the nose.

Margaretta *n. see* MAGGIE *n.*[1].

Margaret Thatcher *n.* [rhy. sl. = SCRATCHER *n.* (6); ult. UK Conservative Prime Minister *Margaret Thatcher* (b.1925)] [2000s] (*Irish*) a bed.

margarine legs *n.* [they are 'easily spread'] [1980s] used to describe a promiscuous woman, e.g. *find a woman with margarine legs*.

margarine mess *n.* [late 19C–1900s] a yellow cab, running in London in the 1890s.

Margate sands *n.* [rhy. sl.] [20C+] the hands.

marge *n.*[1] [the proper name] [1950s+] (*US gay*) a feminine or passive lesbian.

marge *n.*[2] [pun on abbr. for margarine/the woman's name and the fact that it/she 'spreads' easily; note MARGARINE LEGS *n.*] **1** [1990s+] a promiscuous woman. **2** [2000s] (*S.Afr. gay*) a promiscuous gay man.

Margerie Howlet *n. see* MADGE HOWLET *n.*

margery *n.* [the proper name] [mid-18C+] a homosexual man.

margery-prater *n.* ['Here's Grunter and Bleater, / with Tib of the Buttry, / And Margery Prater, / all drest without sluttry' (Richard Brome, *The Joviall Crew*, 1641). *Prater* comes from her constant clucking or 'prating', while *margery* echoes dial. *margery daw*, jackdaw and *margery howlet*, an owl] [mid-16C–early 19C] a hen.

margie *n.* [the initial letter] **1** [1930s] (*US Und.*) morphine. **2** [1980s+] (*Aus. prison*) marijuana.

mari *n.* [abbr.] [1930s–50s] (*drugs*) *marijuana*, a *marijuana* cigarette.

Maria *n. see* BLACK MARIA *n.*

maria (monk) *n.* [rhy. sl. = SPUNK *n.*; ult. *The Awful Disclosures of Maria Monk*, (1836)] [late 19C+] **1** courage. **2** semen.

mariar *n. see* BLACK MARIA *n.*

maribones *n. see* MARROWBONES *n.*

maribou stork *n.* [1990s+] the penis.

Marie *n. see* MARY *n.*

marie *adj.* [2000s] (*S.Afr. gay*) crazy, stupid.

Marie Corelli *n.* [rhy. sl.; ult. *Marie Corelli*, pseudonym of romantic novelist Marie Mackay (1855–1924)] **1** [1910s] the stomach, belly. **2** [1960s+] television [= TELLY *n.*].

marigold *n.*[1] (*also* **marygold**) **1** [mid–late 17C] a gold coin. **2** [mid-19C] £1 million.

marigold *n.*[2] [SE *marijuana* + ACAPULCO (GOLD) *n.*] [1970s] (*drugs*) marijuana.

mari-ha-ha *n.* [joc. pron.] [1960s] (*US drugs*) marijuana.

marihoochie *n.* (*also* **marahoochie, marihooch, marihootee, marihootie, marijooani**) [joc. mispron.] [1970s+] (*drugs*) marijuana.

marinate *v.*[1] [pun on SE *marine*] [late 17C–mid-19C] (*UK Und.*) to transport overseas as a punishment; thus *marinated*, transported to a foreign penal colony.

marinate *v.*[2] [pun on SE *marinate*, to pickle or tenderize in wine and vinegar, herbs and spices] [1990s+] (*US teen*) to idle, to loaf; thus *marinating*, idling, 'hanging out'.

marine *n.* **1** [1940s] (*N.Z.*) a pint bottle of beer [backform. f. DEAD MARINE *under* DEAD *adj.*]. **2** *see* DEAD MARINE *under* DEAD *adj.*

mariner's grave *n.* [rhy. sl.] [1940s–70s] a shave.

Marine Tiger *n.* [1950s] (*US*) a newly-arrived Puerto Rican immigrant.

marish and parish *phr.* [SE *marish*, a marsh + *parish*, a local governmental sub-division. Allsopp, *Dict. Caribbean English Usage* (1996), presumes some lost UK dial. phr. transported to W.I.] [20C+] (*W.I., Bdos/Guyn./Trin.*) everyone.

mariweegee *n.* [joc. mispron.] [1970s+] (*drugs*) marijuana.

marjie *n.* [abbr.] [1940s+] (*Aus.*) *margarine*.

marjoram *n.* [mispron., also punning on HERB *n.*[1] (1)] [1970s] (*drugs*) marijuana.

Marjorie *n. see* MARY *n.* (2).

mark *n.*[1] [SE *mark*, to note down, i.e. one who is noted down as a possible victim] **1** [mid-18C+] (*orig. UK Und.*) the potential and actual victim of a con-man, a gullible person; thus *make a mark*, to ensnare a victim. **2** [mid-18C+] (*UK Und.*) an item to be stolen, a place to be robbed. **3** [mid-19C+] (*UK Und.*) a pickpocket's target. **4** [mid-19C+] (*Aus./US*) a person, usu. in the context of their financial probity, specified as a *good mark* or *bad mark*. **5** [late 19C–1930s] (*UK tramp*) a good place to beg. **6** [late 19C–1930s] (*UK tramp*) a generous giver. **7** [1920s] a newcomer to the world of prostitution. **8** [1930s+] (*drugs*) in pl., the signs of narcotic injections. **9** [1940s–60s] (*US black/teen*) (*also* **marko**) as a term of address. **10** [1950s–60s] a drug dealer's customer. **11** [1950s+] (*US black*) the target of a gang assassination, mugging, robbery etc. **12** [1960s+] (*US Und.*) a prostitute's customer.

IN PHRASES

❑ **easy mark** *n.* **1** [late 19C+] someone or something overcome, mastered or persuaded without difficulty, anything achieved with ease. **2** [1930s] an obvious suspect. ❑ **put the mark up** *v.* [PUT UP *v.*] [1940s] (*US Und.*) of a confidence man, to locate and investigate a well-to-do victim. ❑ **raise a mark** *v.* [1940s] (*US Und.*) to use bluffing to extract more money from a victim. ❑ **soft mark** *n.* [SOFT *adj.* (3)] [late 19C+] a gullible victim. ❑ **string a mark** *v.* [late 19C+] (*US Und.*) for a confidence trickster to entrap a victim.

SE in slang uses

IN PHRASES

❑ **come to the mark** *v.* [thus SE *come up to the mark*] [early 19C] (*UK Und.*) to fulfil a contract, to keep a promise. ❑ **no-mark** *n.* [he/she makes no mark in life] [1980s+] a nobody, a nonentity. ❑ **over the mark** *adj.* [a notional 'mark' that denotes a limit to 'safe' drinking] [19C+] (*Can.*) tipsy.

mark *n.*[2]

IN PHRASES

❑ **when the mark buss** (*also* **when the mark bust, ...burst**) [Carib.E. *mark*, one of the 36 symbols – a centipede, a hog, an old lady – used in the gambling game of *Whe-Whe*. Each is identified by a number and players bet on which number will be found to reveal the winning symbol in a round] [20C+] (*W.I.*) when the truth comes out, when the facts are revealed.

mark *v.* [MARK *n.*[1]] **1** [mid–late 19C] (*UK Und.*) to subject to surveillance, e.g. of criminals by the police. **2** [1910s+] (*US Und.*) to select a prospective victim. **3** [1950s–70s] (*US black*) to tease, to mock.

IN PHRASES

❑ **mark someone's card** *v.* [racecourse use, tipsters *mark race-cards* with their selections] **1** [1930s+] to watch someone, to place someone under surveillance, to pick someone out as a potential victim. **2** [1940s+] to explain, to point out, to warn. **3** [1960s+] to categorize, usu. either as a good or trustworthy or bad or untrustworthy person; to put someone in a specific position. **4** [1960s+] to realize, to see and understand. ▫ **mark up** *v.* **1** [1910s+] to bruise, to leave with scars after a fight. **2** [1980s+] (*Aus. prison*) to tattoo.

marked with a T *phr.* [the ancient habit of branding convicted thieves with a *T*] [late 19C] known as a thief.

marker *n.*[1] [MARK *v.*] **1** [late 16C–early 17C] (*UK Und.*) that member of a pickpocketing or shoplifting team who takes the stolen item from the person who actually picks the pocket. **2** [1950s–70s] (*US black*) a person engaged in ritual teasing or mocking. **3** [1960s+] (*US black*) the bait that lures a victim into some form of swindle or other fraud.

marker *n.*[2] [it has been 'marked down'; see Asbury, *Sucker's Progress* (1938) 17: 'An extraordinary number of the terms, technical and otherwise, which were employed by Faro players in the palmy days of the game have passed into the language [...] *Marker* – An article, sometimes a small piece of ivory provided by the bank, used by a player whose credit was good. He announced the value of the *marker* as he made his bet, and was supposed to settle after each deal'] **1** [1930s+] (*orig. US*) an IOU for a gambling debt; also used fig. for any form of debt. **2** [2000s] (*US Und.*) money.

IN PHRASES

▫ **call in one's marker** *v.* (*also* **call in a marker, ...someone's marker**) [1970s+] to demand repayment of a favour.

market *n.*

IN PHRASES

▫ **go to market** *v.* [late 19C+] (*Aus.*) to lose one's temper, to behave irritably; to make a fuss, to let off steam. ▫ **in the market 1** [1930s] (*US black*) in prison. **2** [1940s] rich, well-off, usu. as the result of gambling or crime.

market dame *n.* [euph., the market being that of Covent Garden] [early 18C] a prostitute.

marketeer *n.* [mid-19C] (*UK Und.*) a professional gambler.

marketplace *n.* [1960s] (*US*) that area of a city or town where street prostitutes work.

mark foy *n.* [rhy. sl.; the name of late 19C London firm of carters or f. a well-known Sydney department store] [1940s+] (*Aus.*) **1** a boy. **2** a young sexual partner.

marko *n. see* MARK *n.*[1] (9).

mark of the beast *n. see under* BEAST *n.*

Marks *n. see* M AND S *n.*

marks *n. see* TRACKS *n.*

Marks and Sparks *n. see* M AND S *n.*

Marlboro country *n.* [suggested by the landscapes featured in advertisements for *Marlboro* cigarettes] [1960s+] (*US*) the remote countryside.

marley *n.* [abbr.] [mid-19C–1950s] a *mar*ble; usu. in pl. *marlies.*

marley stopper *n.* (*also* **marley-slopper**) [MARLEY *n.* + SE *stopper*] [mid–late 19C] one who is splayfooted.

marmalade *n.* [late 19C] (*Aus.*) popular adulation.

marmalade madam *n.* (*also* **marmulet madam**) [? her gaudy clothes or ironic ref. to the 'sweetness' of the preserve or SE *marmalade-eater*, one who has been well brought up + MADAM *n.*] [late 17C–early 18C] a promiscuous woman; a whore.

Marmite *n.* [pun on BROWN *n.* and SE *brown*, the colour of *Marmite*, a popular yeast extract spread in the UK] referring to the anus, stereotypically in male homosexual contexts.

IN COMPOUNDS

▫ **Marmite driller** *n.* (*also* **Marmite miner**) [1990s+] a male homosexual. ▫ **Marmite motorway** *n.* [1990s+] the anal passage.

IN PHRASES

▫ **drill for Marmite** *v.* [1990s+] to sodomize.

marm poosey *n.* (*also* **marm-puss**) [SE *ma'am* + PUSSY *n.*, orig. tailors' use *marm-pussy*, one's wife] [late 19C] a flashily dressed public house landlady.

marmulet madam *n. see* MARMALADE MADAM *n.*

maroon *n.* [SE *maroon*, a former slave] [1940s+] (*US*) a stupid person.

Marquis of Lorne *n.* (*also* **marquis**) [rhy. sl. = HORN *n.*[2]] **1** [mid-19C] the penis. **2** [1960s+] an erection.

marquis of marrowbones *n. see under* MARROWBONES *n.* (1).

marriage music *n.* [late 17C–early 19C] the sound of wailing children.

marriage prospects *n.* [1940s] the penis and testes.

marribones *n. see* MARROWBONES *n.*

married *adj.* **1** [late 18C–early 19C] used to describe convicts who have been chained together for the purposes of moving them from one place to another, or on board a ship that transports them abroad; thus [20C+] handcuffed together. **2** [1930s–70s] (*US gay*) in a homosexual relationship. **3** [1980s+] (*US campus*) in a long-term relationship.

marrobaan *v.* [2000s] (*S.Afr. Und.*) to steal.

marrobaaner *n.* [2000s] (*S.Afr.*) a thief.

marrow *n.* [note Shakespearian use of (*manly*) *marrow*, semen or fig. 'spunk'] **1** [late 16C–mid-19C] semen. **2** [1990s+] (*US black*) the penis.

IN COMPOUNDS

▫ **marrow-pudding** *n.* **1** [late 16C–mid-19C] the penis. **2** [mid–late 19C] a foetus, usu. in phr. *bellyful of marrow-pudding*, pregnant.

marrowbone and cleaver *n.* [note Grose, 1785: 'marrow bones and cleavers, principal instruments in the band of rough musick; these are generally performed on by butchers, on marriages, elections, riding skimmington, and other public, or joyous occasions'] [mid–late 19C] the penis.

marrowbones *n.* (*also* **maribones, marribones, marybones, merrybones**) **1** [mid-16C–1930s] the knees; thus *bring someone down on their marrowbones*, make someone beg forgiveness. **2** [early 17C–mid-19C] the fists when used as weapons.

IN PHRASES

▫ **marquis of marrowbones** *n.* [late 16C–17C] a lackey, a servant.

marrowbone stage, the *n.*

IN PHRASES

▫ **go in/by the marrowbone stage** *v. see* RIDE BY THE MARROWBONE STAGE *under* RIDE *v.*

marrowsky *n.* (*also* **medical Greek, mowrowsky**) [? proper name of a Polish count, poss. Count Joseph Boruwlaski. Popularized by medical students at University College in Gower Street, London] [mid-19C–1960s] a form of slang whereby the user transposes the initial letters of adjacent words; thus *marrowskying*, using this language.

marry *v.*

SE in slang uses

IN PHRASES

▫ **marry brown bess** *v. see under* BROWN BESS *n.* ▫ **marry Mistress Roper** *v.* [the flogging at the 'rope's end' that a recruit would have to endure and because such recruits handle the ships' ropes 'like girls'] [mid-19C] to enlist in the Royal Marines. ▫ **marry the devil's daughter (and live with the old folks)** *v.* [late 18C–early 19C] to marry a termagant. ▫ **marry the widow** *v.* [trans. of Fr. sl. *épouser la veuve*, to be guillotined, lit. 'to marry the widow'] **1** [early 19C] to be hanged. **2** [late 19C–1900s] to make a mess of things.

marry! *excl.* (*also* **mary!**) [SE *the Virgin Mary*] [mid-14C–1920s] **1** a mild oath. **2** in answering a question, implying surprise that it should be asked, 'why, to be sure!'.

marry come up! *excl.* [synon. with HOITY-TOITY! *excl.* or the modern *get you!* under GET *v.*] [late 16C–18C] an excl. used to express indignant or amused surprise or contempt; ext. [late 17C–18C] as *marry come up, my dirty cousin!*, used to tease one who is putting on airs.

Mars and Venus *n.* [rhy. sl.] [20C+] the penis.

Mars bar *n.* [rhy. sl.] [1960s+] a scar.

marsha *n.* [1960s] (*S.Afr.*) money.

marshall *n.* [proper name *Marshall*, chief cashier of the Bank of England, whose name appeared on the notes, *c.*1870] [mid–late 19C] a £5 note.

marshmallow *n.* **1** [1930s+] (*US*) a soft, weak person, or thing. **2** [1940s–60s] (*US black*) a white person. **3** [1970s+] (*drugs*) (*also* **marshmallow reds**) depressants, barbiturates [they soften one's emotions].

marshmallow *adj.* [MARSHMALLOW *n.* (1)] [1960s+] (*US*) sentimental.

marshy *adj.* [1960s] (*US campus*) seedy, unpleasant.

marter *n.* (*also* **martar**) [SE *mart*, to bargain, to do business] [late 16C] **1** a bargainer. **2** a receiver of stolen goods. **3** a dishonest horse-trader who buys stolen horses and disposes of them at fairs.

martext *n. see* PUZZLE-TEXT *under* PUZZLE *n.*[2].

Martha *n.* [2000s] (*S.Afr. gay*) a 'masculine' homosexual male.

martin *n.* [? SE *martin*, a species of bird. It is supposedly lucky for a martin to nest in the eaves of one's house; poss. in this case it is the robbers who see the appearance of such a *martin* as lucky for themselves] [late 16C–mid-17C] the victim of theft, either by a team of confidence tricksters or a highwayman.

(IN COMPOUNDS)

▫ **Martin chain** *n.* [ST MARTIN'S LACE *n.*] [early 17C] an imitation gold chain.

martin drunk *adj.* [SE *St Martin's evil*, drunkenness] [16C] drunk.

martingale *v.* [SE *martingale*, a restraining strap that prevents the horse from rearing or throwing back its head; thus fig. to 'ride one's luck'] [19C] (*gambling*) to double the stakes every time one loses.

Martin-le-Grand *n. see* ST MARTIN'S (LE GRAND) *n.*

Martin Place *n.* [rhy. sl., ult. proper name *Martin Place*, Sydney] [1930s+] (*Aus.*) the face.

Martin Place *adj.* [proper name *Martin Place*, Sydney; the image of the 'big city' as *de facto* wicked] [1930s+] (*Aus.*) in the context of the city, decadence or corruption, or what is seen as such by country people.

Martin's *n. see* ST MARTIN'S (LE GRAND) *n.*

martooni *n.* [a 'drunken' pron. of SE] [1950s+] (*US*) a martini cocktail.

Marty Wilde *n.* [rhy. sl.; ult. pop singer *Marty Wilde* (b.1939)] [1960s+] mild (beer).

marv *n.* [MARV *adj.*] [1990s+] (*US campus/teen*) a highly intelligent person, a scholar.

marv *adj.* (*also* **marvie, marvy, marvy-groovy**) [abbr. SE *marvellous*] [1950s+] (*orig. US*) wonderful, the best, outstanding; also used ironically/negatively.

marvel *v.* [ety. unknown] [mid–late 19C] (*US*) to leave, esp. quickly.

marvin *n. see* MELVIN *n.*

Marvin (the Arvin) *n.* [assonance from Army Republic VietNam; later use is historical] [1960s+] (*US, orig. milit.*) generic name for any member of the South Vietnam military.

marvy *adj. see* MARV *adj.*

marvy-groovy *adj. see* MARV *adj.* (1).

Mary *n.* (*also* **Marie**) [generic use of one of the most common of female proper names, but also offering a touch of Mariolatry] **1** uses based on being female. (**a**) [early 19C+] (*Aus./N.Z.*) (*also* **meri**) an Aboriginal native woman; thus pidgin *White Mary*, a white woman. (**b**) [1900s–10s] (*Irish/Aus.*) (*also* **mary ann, mary jane**) a female servant. (**c**) [1920s–70s] (*S.Afr.*) (*also* **coolie Mary**) an Indian woman, usu. a fruit or vegetable hawker. (**d**) [1940s+] (*S.Afr.*) any black woman, esp. a domestic servant. **2** (*also* **Marjorie**) gay uses. (**a**) [1920s+] the most popular camp proper name; typically in phr. *get you Mary!* (**b**) [1950s+] thus, a gay man's (younger) lover. (**c**) [2000s] (*S.Afr. gay*) a magistrate. **3** drug uses. (**a**) [1940s–50s] (*US drugs*) morphine [the shared initial letter *M*]. (**b**) *see* MARY JANE *n.*[2].

(IN PHRASES)

▫ **go to Mary's room** *v.* (*also* **go to visit aunty, go to visit Mary**) [euph.] [1980s] (*Aus.*) to use the lavatory.

Mary, the *n.* [2000s] (*S.Afr. prison*) a beating.

Mary *adj.* [1960s–70s] (*US gay*) effeminate, homosexual.

Mary! *excl.* [MARY *n.*] [1920s+] a clichéd, camp homosexual excl.

mary! *excl. see* MARRY! *excl.*

mary and johnny *n.* [play on Sp. which translates as 'mary' and 'jane'] [1930s+] (*drugs*) marijuana.

mary ann *n.*[1] [joc. uses of proper name] **1** [late 19C–1900s] (*Aus.*) a girlfriend. **2** [late 19C–1910s] a dressmaker's dummy. **3** [mid-19C+] (*also* **Mary Jane**) an effeminate male homosexual; a young boy used as a catamite in prison. **4** [1970s+] (*US gay*) a US Marine. **5** *see* MARY *n.* (1).

mary ann *n.*[2] [rhy. sl.] [20C+] **1** a fan. **2** a hand; a fist.

mary ann *n.*[3] (*also* **mary anna, maryanne**) [1910s+] (*drugs*) marijuana; a marijuana cigarette.

mary ann *n.*[4] [? MARY JANE *n.*[1] (1)] [1990s+] female pubic hair.

Mary at the cottage gate *n.* [rhy. sl.] [1980s] (*Aus.*) the number eight.

mary banger *n.* [20C+] an extremely plain, dowdy woman.

Mary Blane *n.* (*also* **mary blaine**) [rhy. sl.] [late 19C] a railway train; as v. to meet a train.

marybones *n. see* MARROWBONES *n.*

Mary Decker *n.* [proper name of US athlete *Mary Decker* Slaney (b.1958)] [1980s] (*S.Afr. black*) **1** a black taxi. **2** a fast armoured police vehicle.

Mary Ellen *n.* [1930s] (*US Und.*) a style of robbery whereby the victim is rendered drunk and then robbed.

mary ellens *n.* [rhy. sl. = *melons*, see under MELON *n.*] [20C+] the female breasts.

Mary Fist *n.* (*also* **Mary Ellen, Mary Five-Fingers, Mary Palm**) [1940s+] (*US*) the hand, as used in male masturbation; thus *married to mary fist*, addicted to masturbation.

mary frances *n.* [euph. using the initial letters] [1960s+] euph. for MOTHERFUCKER *n.*

marygold *n. see* MARIGOLD *n.*[1].

mary green *n.* [rhy. sl.] [20C+] in cards, the queen.

mary hick *n.* [20C+] a plain, dowdy woman.

mary jane *n.*[1] [generic use of female name] **1** [mid-19C–1930s] the vagina. **2** [1960s] (*US black*) a skirt with a slit up one side. **3** [1960s+] (*US*) (*also* **mary**) a lesbian.

mary jane *n.*[2] (*also* **mary, mary j., maryjane, mary jonas, merry**) [lit. trans. of Sp.] **1** [1920s+] (*orig. US drugs*) marijuana, cannabis. **2** [2000s] cocaine.

mary jane *n.*[3] *see* MARY *n.* (1).

maryjanes *n.* [the schoolgirl sound of the proper name] [1920s+] (*orig. US*) round-toed shoes with a strap across the foot.

Mary Jo *n.* [1950s] (*US black*) a notably beautiful female.

mary jonas *n. see* MARY JANE *n.*[2].

Marylebone kick *n.* [? a speciality of the area's thugs] [mid-19C] a kick to the stomach.

Marylebone stage, the *n.*

(IN PHRASES)

▫ **go in/by the Marylebone stage** *v. see* RIDE BY THE MARROWBONE STAGE *under* RIDE *v.*

marylou *n.* [rhy. sl.] [20C+] glue.

Mary Palm *n. see* MARY FIST *n.*

mary poppins *n.* [joc. use of film title *Mary Poppins* (1964)] [1960s+] (*US*) the female breasts.

Mary Rose *n. see* MARGARET (ROSE) *n.*

mary walkers *n.* [Dr *Mary Walker* (1832–1919), US campaigner for rational dress for women who would lecture on her subject wearing men's evening dress] [late 19C] (*US*) trousers.

mary warner *n.* (*also* **mary wanner, mary werner, merry wonder**) [pron.] [1920s–70s] (*orig. US drugs*) marijuana.

mary weaver *n.* [pron.] [1930s–70s] (*drugs*) marijuana.

mary werner *n. see* MARY WARNER *n.*

mary worthless *n.* [pun on the camp term MARY *n.* (2) + popular US cartoon *Mary Worth*, launched 1938] [1940s+] (*US gay*) an ageing, unattractive male homosexual.

mascot *adj.* [the diminutive size of a trad. mascot, e.g. the small boy who parades with a soccer team] [1950s+] (*W.I., Rasta*) used of one who is of inferior status.

maserati *n.* [fig. use of the automobile name] [1980s+] (*drugs*) an improvised crack cocaine pipe, using a spark-plug cover and a plastic bottle (cf. LAMBORGHINI *n.*).

masers *n.* [abbr.] [1960s+] a *Maserati* car.

mash *n.*[1] **1** [late 19C–1910s] a person with whom one is infatuated; thus *on the mash*, looking for an opportunity of seduction, *have a mash on*, to make advances towards, *make a mash on*, to be the object of someone's infatuation [MASH v. (2)]. **2** [late 19C–1910s] a dandy [abbr. MASHER *n.* (2)]. **3** [late 19C–1920s] (*orig. US*) an infatuation, a crush on someone [MASH v. (2)]. **4** [late 19C–1930s] an admirer [MASH v. (2)]. **5** [1910s+] (*US/Aus.*) sentimental nonsense [but note MUSH *n.*[1] (2)]. **6** [1920s–30s] (*US*) a blow, a hit [MASH v. (1)]. **7** pertaining to (illicitly distilled) alcohol [abbr]. (**a**) [1930s+] (*US prison*) illicitly distilled whisky, esp. prison-distilled whisky. (**b**) [1990s+] (*US prison*) the ingredients of prison-made alcohol. **8** [1980s] (*US campus*) sexual activity that stops short of intercourse, kissing and foreplay [MASH v. (2)].

IN COMPOUNDS

❑ **mash note** *n.* (*also* **mash letter**) **1** [late 19C+] (*US*) a love letter. **2** [2000s] in fig. use, a begging letter. ❑ **mash-tub** *n.* [note the defunct newspaper the *Morning Advertiser* was known as the 'Morning Mash-tub' because of its brewery interests] [19C] a brewer.

IN PHRASES

❑ **make a mash** v. **1** [late 19C–1920s] (*US*) to 'make a pass', to seduce someone. **2** [1900s] (*US campus*) to please a teacher. ❑ **on the mash** [late 19C] looking for a sexual conquest.

SE in slang uses

IN COMPOUNDS

❑ **mashman** *n.* [onomat. for the noise it makes in one's pocket] [1940s–50s] (*W.I.*) small change. ❑ **mash-mash** *adj.* [lit. mashed, i.e. broken mouth] [1990s+] (*W.I.*) toothless.

mash *n.*[2] [rhy. sl.; *mash and peas* = motor neurone disease] [2000s] motor neurone disease.

mash v. [SE *mash*, to crush, to pulp, hence sexually to render 'soft'; note Rom. *mash*, to allure, to entice] **1** [mid-19C+] (*US*) to beat someone up; to crush. **2** [late 19C+] (*orig. US theatrical*) to make oneself attractive to a member of the opposite sex, to flirt with, to succeed in seduction; thus *MASHING* below. **3** [1940s+] (*US black*) to give one what is due; thus *mash it on me*, give it to me, *mash me a fin*, loan me $5. **4** [1950s] (*W.I.*) to seduce, to rape. **5** [1970s] (*US*) to masturbate. **6** [1980s] (*US black*) to pass over stolen or contraband goods. **7** [1980s+] (*US campus*) to kiss, to neck. **8** [1990s+] (*US black*) to work hard, to commit oneself to a task. **9** [1990s+] to fondle the breasts in an aggressive manner. **10** [2000s] (*US black*) to have sexual intercourse.

DERIVATIVES

❑ **mashing** *n.* [late 19C–1930s] the act of flirting, seducing, making advances.

IN COMPOUNDS

❑ **mashman** *n.* [2000s] (*UK black*) a thug.

IN PHRASES

❑ **mash down** v. [20C+] **1** to apply pressure, to press down on. **2** (*W.I., Rasta*) to destroy, also in fig. sense. ❑ **mash it up** v. (*also* **mosh it up**) **1** [1950s+] (*W.I., Rasta/UK black*) to achieve a huge success; to do something well. **2** [1990s+] (*W.I.*) an expression of encouragement. ❑ **mash the fat** v. [1970s+] (*US black*) to have sexual intercourse. ❑ **mash up** v. (*also* **mash in**) [1920s+] **1** (*orig. US/W.I.*) to destroy, to break, to beat up, of a relationship, to break up. **2** (*W.I.*) to get oneself into trouble. **3** (*W.I.*) to cause trouble. ❑ **mash with** v. [1980s+] (*US campus*) to kiss, to neck.

SE in slang uses

IN PHRASES

❑ **mash flat** v. [*mashing* the accelerator pedal] [1940s] (*W.I.*) to move along, make room, as in a crowded bus; also to accelerate a car.

mash dog! *excl.* [Carib.E. *mash*, a call to a dog, meaning go or walk] [20C+] (*W.I.*) a general phr. of irritation and dismissal, get out! get out of my way!

mashed *adj.* [SE *mashed*, crushed; but Spears, *Slang and Jargon of Drugs and Drink* (1986), suggests link of sense 1 to SE *mash*, the basis of whisky] **1** [late 19C+] (*US*) drunk. **2** [1970s] drugged. **3** [1980s] (*drugs*) under the influence of a recreational drug.

mashed (on) *adj.* [MASH v. (2)] [late 19C–1950s] **1** infatuated, sexually or romantically obsessed (by). **2** in a non-sexual context.

mashed-potato circuit *n. see* RUBBER-CHICKEN CIRCUIT *under* RUBBER *adj.*

masher *n.* [MASH v. (2); senses 2 and 3 are often elided] **1** [late 19C] an individual, of either gender, who uses charm and beauty to succeed. **2** [late 19C–1910s] a dandy; thus *masher blue*, a shade of blue favoured by such men for their waistcoats. **3** [late 19C+] (*orig. US*) a man who forces his unwanted attentions on women, a 'lady-killer'. **4** [1990s+] (*US black*) a hard, committed worker.

DERIVATIVES

❑ **masherdom** *n.* [late 19C] the world of mashers.

IN COMPOUNDS

❑ **mashers corners** *n.* [one could best ogle the chorus-girls from the front stalls] [late 19C–1900s] (*UK society*) the opposite prompt (O.P.) and prompt side (P.S.) entrances to the stalls at the Gaiety Theatre, London.

masher *adj.* [MASHER *n.* (2)] [late 19C–1910s] flashy, dandified, fashionable.

mashers *n.* [SE *mash*] **1** [1930s+] (*W.I.*) cheap shoes, sold initially with rope soles, then with pieces of car tyre. **2** [2000s] the female breasts.

mashing *n.*[1] [1930s] (*UK tramp*) a portion of tea leaves and sugar, enough for one cup of tea.

mashing *n.*[2] *see* MASH v. (2).

mashkin-shop *n.* (*also* **motshkin-shop**) [MOSKENEER v. (1) + SE *shop*] [late 19C] a pawnbroker's.

mashonisa *n.* [? Zulu *mashonisa*, a cause of one's losing heavily] [1970s+] (*S.Afr. township*) a money-lender.

mashugga *adj. see* MESHUGA *adj.*

mash-up *n.* [2000s] a song that is a mix of two completely different songs spliced into one.

mash-up *adj.* (*also* **mosh-up**) [MASH v.] [1980s+] (*orig. US/W.I.*) **1** badly broken or bent, damaged beyond repair. **2** thus in fig. use, e.g. used of someone exhausted or suffering from a hangover.

mash-up *adv.* [2000s] of drug use, to a very great extent.

Mas John *n.* (*also* **Messjohn, Miss John**) [*Mas*, master; the hostility is underlined by the abbr.] [mid-17C–early 19C] a derog. term for a Scot. Presbyterian minister, as opposed to an Anglican or Roman Catholic.

maso *n.* [abbr.] [1960s] (*US*) a *maso*chist.

mason *n.*[1] [the stereotyping of Freemasons as dishonest] [mid-18C] one who acquires goods fraudulently by giving a bill that they do not intend to honour, thus n. *masoning*.

DERIVATIVES

❑ **masoner** *n.* [mid–late 18C] (*UK Und.*) one who gives a promissory note in exchange for a purchase, with no intention of honouring it.

SE in slang uses

IN PHRASES

❑ **mason's maund** *n.* (*also* **mason's mawnd**) [MAUND *n.*] [late 17C–early 19C] a fake sore, placed above the elbow and counterfeiting a broken arm caused by a fall from a scaffold.

mason *n.*[2] (*also* **mason line**) [proper name *Mason-Dixon line*, dividing the US north and south along the 40th parallel] [19C+] (*US black*) a town's main street, esp. when it delineates the line between the black and white communities.

mason *n.*[3] [1940s–50s] (*US gay*) **1** a 'masculine' male homosexual. **2** a lesbian.

ma's plaster *n.* [one who needs a fig. *plaster* from their *ma*, i.e. mother] [20C+] (*Irish*) a whiner, a whinger.

mass *n.* [ety. unknown] [1990s+] (*W.I./UK black teen*) money, currency.

mass *adj.* see MASSIVE *adj.* (3).

Massa Charlie/Charley *n.* see MR CHARLIE *n.*

massage *v.* [1920s+] (*orig. US*) **1** to beat, to injure, to kill. **2** of the police, to beat up a suspect during an interrogation.

mass-ass *adj.* [1980s+] (*US black*) mass.

Massey-Harris *n.* [pun on the *Massey-Harris* self-binder (an early combine harvester); the ref. is to the 'binding' effects of cheese on the digestion] [20C+] (*Aus./Can.*) cheese.

massive *n.* (*also* **masses**) [1980s+] (*W.I./UK black teen*) a group of people who stick together and have shared social interests, such as a dancehall crowd; often specified by a geographical name, e.g. the *Peckham massive*, the *Tottenham massive*.

massive *adj.* **1** [20C+] a general term of great approval; also as excl. **2** [1950s+] (*orig. W.I., Rasta*) respected; ext. as *massive large* for emphasis. **3** [1980s+] (*US campus*) (*also* **mass**) large, a lot of.

mass tom *n.* [lit. 'master tom'; thus joc. use of proper name] [1940s] (*W.I.*) a shark.

mast *n.* [1980s+] (*Aus. prison*) the (erect) penis.

IN PHRASES

❑ **at half-mast** *adv.* **1** [1940s+] in a partially lowered position, used esp. of trousers or a partial erection of the penis. **2** [1970s] thus, *quarter-mast*: a modified version of sense 1.

Ma State *n.* [*ma*, mother; thus the 'mother state'. New South Wales is the oldest Aus. colony] [1900s–50s] (*Aus.*) New South Wales; thus *ma stater*, a native of New South Wales.

master *n.* [20C+] (*US black*) the absolute best.

IN COMPOUNDS

❑ **master blaster** *n.* [BLAST *v.*[1] (5)] [1980s+] (*drugs*) a large amount of freebase cocaine. ❑ **master dog** *n.* [20C+] (*US black*) the supreme authoritarian figure (usu. a white man) within an institutional hierarchy.

SE in slang uses

IN COMPOUNDS

❑ **master-can** *n.* [CAN *n.*[1] (4b)] [18C–19C] a chamberpot. ❑ **master member** *n.* [MEMBER *n.*[1] (1)] [19C] the penis. ❑ **master-piece** *n.* [1900s] (*Aus. Und.*) a tool used by a thief.

Master John Goodfellow *n.* (*also* **Master John Thursday**) [generic use of *John* + SE *goodfellow*, a jovial companion; *John Thursday* was a 17C musician and dancing master, the supposed inventor of a dance known as the 'Hussarde'] [17C–19C; 1940s] the penis.

Master Ketch *n.* see JACK KETCH *n.*

master of… *n.*

IN PHRASES

❑ **master of ceremonies** *n.* **1** [mid-17C] as a tavern term, 'he that stands upon his strength, and begins new healths'; i.e. gets up and proposes a succession of toasts (*The English Liberal Science*, 1650). **2** [19C] the penis. ❑ **master of misrule** *n.* [mid-17C] an uproarious drunkard, i.e. 'He that flings Cushions, Napkins, and Trenchers about the room' (*The English Liberal Science*, 1650). ❑ **master of the black art** *n.* [in *DSUE*, Partridge, who dates it 16C–17C, notes 'the term is suspect'] [16C] any beggar, irrespective of their 'speciality'. ❑ **master of the mint** *n.* [a pun on the SE *herb*] [late 18C–mid-19C] a gardener. ❑ **master of the novelties** *n.* [mid-17C] a playful drunkard, i.e. 'he that is first to begin new frolicks' (*The English Liberal Science*, 1650). ❑ **master of the rolls** *n.* [pun] [mid-17C–mid-19C] a baker. ❑ **master of the wardrobe** *n.* [pun] [18C–early 19C] one who pawns their clothes to get money for drink.

masterpiece *n.* [joc. use of SE + pun on SE *master* + *piece*/PIECE *n.* (1)] [18C–19C] the vagina.

master vein *n.* [SE *master-vein*, a major vein, usu. the carotid artery or jugular vein]

IN PHRASES

❑ **hit on the master vein** *v.* [late 16C] to become pregnant. ❑ **prick the master vein** *v.* [late 17C] of a man, to have sexual intercourse (cf. HIT ON THE MASTER VEIN above).

mat *n.* [abbr. SE *mattress*] [1930s–40s] **1** (*US*) a prostitute or sexually promiscuous woman. **2** (*US black*) one's regular sweetheart, one's wife. **3** see DOORMAT *n.*

SE in slang uses

IN PHRASES

❑ **go back to the mat** *v.* [1970s] (*N.Z.*) to return to nature, to be reduced in rank, circumstances. ❑ **on the mat** [the small *mat* on which an accused soldier stood in the orderly room or the boxing mat; var. of ON THE CARPET *under* CARPET *n.*[1]] **1** [late 19C+] on trial. **2** [late 19C+] facing a reprimand and/or punishment, also in fig. use. **3** [1900s] ready to fight; also in fig. use. **4** [1920s–40s] (*US*) under interrogation. **5** [1930s] in serious trouble, beaten.

mat *v.* see CARPET *v.*

match *n.* [abbr. MATCHBOX *n.* (1)] **1** [1900s] (*US*) a prison. **2** see MATCHBOX *n.*

match *v.* [1950s+] to light a cigarette (for someone).

matchbox *n.* **1** denoting size/flimsiness. (**a**) [1920s+] a very small house, or room. (**b**) [1960s] a small car. **2** [1940s+] (*US drugs*) denoting quantity. (**a**) $10 worth of marijuana, orig. an actual matchbox full, by 1990s more like a thimbleful. (**b**) approx. 10g (½oz) of marijuana. **3** [1980s+] (*UK Und.*) an easily robbed target.

matchstick *n.* [1950s+] a nickname for a very thin person; thus *matchstick with the wood shaved off*, an exceptionally thin person.

mate *n.* [orig. used as sailor's jargon] **1** [late 14C+] (*also* **comate**) a friend; thus (Aus.) *mate up*, to befriend. **2** [19C+] (*orig. Aus.*) a general term of address to a man, usu. by a man.

DERIVATIVES

❑ **mateship** *n.* [1970s] (*Aus.*) the state of friendship.

IN COMPOUNDS

❑ **mate's rates** *n.* **1** [1980s+] (*orig. Aus.*) discounted rates made available to friends of the business/enterprise. **2** [1980s+] (*N.Z.*) payment in cash; no actual friendship need be involved.

mateloe/matelot *n.* see MATLOW *n.*

matey *n.* (*also* **maty**) [MATE *n.*] **1** [early 19C+] a pal, a chum, a companion; usu. as a term of address [Francis-Jackson, *Official Dancehall Dict.* (1995), defines W.I. use as 'a female friend' only]. **2** [1990s+] (*W.I.*) a rival.

matey *adj.* (*also* **maty**) [MATE *n.*] [1910s+] friendly.

matic *n.* [abbr.] [1990s+] (*W.I./UK black teen*) an auto*matic* weapon.

matie *n.* [MAAT *n.*] **1** [20C+] (*S.Afr.*) a student at Stellenbosch University in the Western Cape. **2** [20C+] as *Matieland*, Stellenbosch University; the town of Stellenbosch.

matilda *n.* (*also* **tilly**) [late 19C+] (*Aus.*) a tramp's pack; thus *matilda up*, carrying a pack; *matilda-bearer*, *matilda-carrier*, *matilda-hawker*, *matilda-lumper*, *matilda-man*, *matilda-waltzer*, a vagrant.

IN PHRASES

❑ **carry Matilda** *v.* (*also* **hump Matilda, walking Matilda**) [late 19C+] (*Aus.*) to go on the tramp, carrying one's pack.

matinée *n.* [SE *matinée*, an afternoon theatrical performance] **1** [1940s+] sexual intercourse (usu. adulterous or with a prostitute) in the afternoon. **2** [1950s] a prostitute's client who makes his appointments for the afternoon.

matlow *n.* (*also* **mateloe, matelot, matelow**) [Fr. *matelot*, a sailor] [mid-19C+] (*orig. RN*) a sailor.

mat-man *n.* [the SE *mat* on which he fights] [1920s+] (*orig. US*) a wrestler.

matriculate *v.* [1970s+] (*US campus*) to start on a trip, to go somewhere.

matrimonial *n.* [seen as the usual practice of married couples] [19C] sexual intercourse in the 'missionary position'.

matrimonial peacemaker *n.* (*also* **peacemake**) [mid-17C–19C] the penis, based on sexual intercourse as an agency of peace between married couples.

matrimony *n.* [lit. a 'marriage'] [19C] a mixture of two sorts of food or drink.

matsakaw *n.* (*also* **matsakow**) [ety. unknown] [1970s] (*drugs*) heroin.

mattress *n.* **1** [1920s–30s] (*US*) a beard. **2** [1930s] (*US*) pubic hair. **3** [1940s] (*US*) the face. **4** [1960s+] (*Aus./US*) a woman as a sexual partner; a girlfriend [the man 'lies' on her].

SE in slang uses

IN COMPOUNDS

❑ **mattressback** *n.* **1** [1960s+] (*Aus./US*) a sexually promiscuous woman. **2** [1990s+] (*Aus. prison*) a prisoner who spends a lot of time in their cell. ❑ **mattress jig** *n.* [19C–1920s] (*US*) sexual intercourse. ❑ **mattress job** *n.* [JOB *n.*[2] (2)] [20C+] a beating by police to persuade a person to make a confession. The victim is placed under a mattress and then jumped and stamped upon, so no visible marks are left on the victim's body. ❑ **mattress-muncher** *n.* [his response to anal intercourse] [1960s+] (*orig. Aus.*) a passive homosexual man. ❑ **mattress polo** *n.* [1930s–60s] (*US*) sexual intercourse.

IN PHRASES

❑ **go to the mattress** *v.* (*also* **hit the mattress, ...mattresses**) [the practice of sleeping on mattresses in one's hideout, rather than in one's bed at home. Orig. a US Mafia usage, the phr. was widely popularized by the success of Mario Puzo's book *The Godfather* (1969) and the films that followed] [1930s+] (*orig. US Und.*) to hide, to take refuge, esp. when under siege from another gang.

maty *see under* MATEY.

matzo *n.* [1910s] (*US*) a Jew.

maud *n.* (*also* **maude**) [play on the female proper name] **1** [late 19C–1930s] (*US black*) a woman. **2** [1940s+] a male prostitute. **3** [1960s+] a dowdy or overweight male homosexual.

maud and ruth *n.* [rhy. sl.] [1970s+] the truth.

mauger *adj.* (*also* **maaga, mauga, maugre, mawgah, mawgar, mawgre, meagre**) [Du. *mager*, lean or Fr. *maigre*, thin] [20C+] (*W.I.*) thin, scrawny.

Mauie Wowie *n.* (*also* **Maui wauie, Maui wowee**) [*Maui*, a Hawaiian island + SE *wow!*, an excl. of pleasure or astonishment] [1970s+] (*US drugs*) a potent variety of marijuana, grown in Maui, Hawaii.

mauk *n. see* MAWKES *n.*

maul *v.* **1** [late 19C+] (*US campus*) to have a very passionate petting session. **2** [1960s] to treat something in a sensuous manner.

mauldy *adj.* [? MAULEY *n.* (1)] [1910s–50s] (*Aus.*) left-handed.

mauled *adj.* [late 17C–mid-19C] very drunk.

mauler *n.* (*also* **mawler**) [SE *maul*, to handle roughly] **1** [early 19C+] the hand, the fist. **2** [20C+] (*US*) a boxer. **3** [1920s] a punch. **4** [1950s] brass knuckles.

mauley *n.* (*also* **maulie, mawley, morley, myliers**) [SE *maul*, to handle roughly or Shelta *malya*, ult. transposition of Gaelic *lamh*, hand] **1** [late 18C–1950s] the hand, a fist. **2** [mid-19C] a finger, usu. in pl. **3** [mid-19C+] a signature; handwriting.

IN PHRASES

❑ **fam the mauley** *v.* [early 19C] to shake hands. ❑ **slang the mauleys** *v.* **1** [late 18C–late 19C] to shake hands. **2** [early 19C] to fight with one's hands or fists. ❑ **sling one's mauley** *v.* [late 18C–19C] to shake hands.

mauma *n. see* MAMMY *n.*[1].

mau-mau *n.* [1950s] (*US*) a burglar.

mau-mau *v.* [proper name *Mau-Mau*, Kenyan guerrillas of 1950s who spearheaded the drive to free their nation from British rule. The term is best-known in the title of Tom Wolfe's essay *Mau-Mauing the Flak-Catchers* (1970)] [1960s–70s] (*US*) of black or minority activists, to harass the white establishment for their community's gain, esp. by taking advantage of liberal guilt.

mauming and glauming *n.* [? SE *maul* + Scot. *glaum*, to snatch at] [mid-18C] pawing in an amorous or sexual manner.

maun *n.* [mid-19C] (*UK Und.*) a hand, thus *tip us your mauns*, give me your hands, shake hands.

maund *n.* [MAUND *v.*] (*UK Und.*) **1** [17C] begging; thus a specific begging ruse, e.g. a fake sore. **2** [early 18C] a beggar.

IN PHRASES

❑ **soldier's maund** *n.* (*also* **soldier's mawnd**) [late 17C–18C] (*UK Und.*) a fake wound, assumed by beggars who wish to pose as soldiers returned from the wars; thus the beggar who uses this ruse.

maund *v.* (*also* **maund it, mawnd**) [? Fr. *mendier/quémendier*, to beg, ult. Lat. *mendicus*, a beggar, the root of the SE *mendicant*. Note Rom. *mang*, to beg] [mid-16C–mid-19C] (*UK Und.*) to ask or require; thus to beg.

IN PHRASES

❑ **maund abram** *v.* [ABRAM *n.*] [17C] to beg while posing as a madman. ❑ **maunding cove** *n.* [COVE *n.*] [early 17C–late 18C] a beggar. (*also* **maunding mort**) ❑ **maund on the pad** *v.* [PAD *n.*[1]] [17C] to beg on the street or highway.

maunder *n.* (*also* **manderer, maunderer, mawnder**) [MAUND *v.*] [17C–mid-19C] (*UK Und.*) a beggar.

maunder *v.* [MAUND *v.* (1)] [early 17C–late 18C] to beg; thus *maunder on the fly*, to beg in the streets, *maundering*, begging, prone to begging; *maundering tools*, items used to enhance one's begging image and thus gain more sympathy and alms.

IN PHRASES

❑ **maundering lay** *n.* [LAY *n.*[3]] [mid-19C] (*UK Und.*) begging (under false pretences).

maunderer *n. see* MAUNDER *n.*

maundering broth *n.* [dial. *maunder*, to grumble, to threaten] [late 17C–early 19C] a scolding.

maureen *v.* [2000s] (*S.Afr. gay*) to murder.

mause *n.* [18C] (*UK Und.*) a bundle.

maut *n. see* MORT *n.*

maux *n. see* MAWKES *n.*

maven *n.* (*also* **mavin, mayvin**) [Heb. *mavin*, understanding] [1950s+] (*US*) an expert, a connoisseur.

Mavis *n.* [2000s] (*S.Afr. gay*) an effeminate homosexual man.

maw *n.* [SE *maw*, a (usu. animal's) stomach] **1** [late 14C; early 16C+] the mouth. **2** [1940s+] (*US black*) the vagina.

IN COMPOUNDS

❑ **maw-wallop** *n.* [SE *wallop*, a churning and bubbling, a blow] [late 18C–early 19C] a disgusting dish of food, enough to make the eater vomit.

Maw Bell *n. see* MA BELL *n.*

maw-dicker *n.* [dial. *maw*, mother + DICK *v.*[2] (1)] [1960s+] (*US mainly southwest*) euph. for MOTHERFUCKER *n.*

mawgabraw! *excl.* [Irish *magh go brách*, the field for ever] [20C+] (*Irish*) a general excl. of abuse, usu. delivered as a parting shot, i.e. go to hell!

mawgah/mawgar/mawgre *adj. see* MAUGER *adj.*

mawkes *n.* (*also* **mauk, maux**) [MALKIN *n.*] **1** [late 16C–early 18C] a prostitute. **2** [late 18C–1960s] a slatternly woman.

DERIVATIVES

❑ **mawkish** [early 18C] slatternly.

mawkin *n.* [Scot. *mawkin*, a half-grown girl] **1** [17C+] simpleton. **2** a promiscuous woman.

mawkish *adj. see* MAWKES *n.* (2).

mawler *n. see* MAULER *n.*

mawley *n. see* MAULEY *n.*

mawmouth *n.* [mid-19C] (*UK Und.*) one who splutters when they speak.

mawnd *v. see* MAUND *v.*

mawnder *n. see* MAUNDER *n.*

maw-worm *n.* [proper name *Mawworm*, a character who epitomized hypocrisy, in Bickerstaffe's play *The Hypocrite* (1769); also Lieutenant *Mawworm* in Middleton's play *A Mad World, My Masters* (c.1606), ult. *maw-worm*, a parasitic stomach worm] [mid-19C+] a hypocrite.

(DERIVATIVES)

❑ **maw-wormy** *adj.* [mid–late 19C] **1** hypocritical. **2** pessimistic, fault-finding, nagging.

max *n.* (*also* **maximus, old max**) [all abbr. of SE *maximum*] **1** [early 18C–19C] gin, esp. high-quality gin. **2** [mid-19C] (*UK Und.*) any form of alcohol. **3** [mid-19C+] (*US campus*) the maximum score or achievement in an examination, the student who achieves this. **4** [1950s+] (*US Und.*) the maximum sentence for an offence. **5** [1960s+] (*Can./US*) a maximum security jail. **6** [1970s+] (*US campus*) the highest level or degree. **7** [2000s] (*drugs*) gamma hydroxy butyrate, GBH, dissolved in water and mixed with amphetamines.

(DERIVATIVES)

❑ **maxy** *adj.* [mid-19C] drunk.

(IN COMPOUNDS)

❑ **max-ken** *n.* [KEN *n.*[1] (2)] [mid-18C] (*UK Und.*) a tavern specializing in gin.

(IN PHRASES)

❑ **to the max** *adv.* (*also* **to the maxi**) [SE *maximum*, orig. in the California youth cultures] [1970s+] the best, the most extreme. [1980s+] (*orig. US black*) to do something as well or as enthusiastically as possible.

max *adj.* (*also* **maximum**) [1960s+] (*US*) superlative, outstanding.

max *v.* [MAX *n.*] **1** [mid-19C] to drink. **2** [mid-19C] to treat to a drink. **3** [late 19C+] (*US campus*) to achieve a maximum score or grade in an examination. **4** [1970s+] (*US Und.*) to serve the full length of a jail sentence. **5** [1970s+] (*US*) to give one's maximum effort. **6** [1970s+] (*US*) to exceed the limit. **7** [1980s+] (*US black/campus*) to have a very good time, to relax. **8** [1990s+] (*US Und.*) (*also* **max out**) to give the highest possible sentence for a cited crime.

(DERIVATIVES)

❑ **maxed** *adj.* **1** [mid-19C; 1980s+] drunk or highly intoxicated. **2** [1970s+] (*US*) full to maximum capacity. **3** [1980s+] (*US*) utterly exhausted, drained of energy.

(IN COMPOUNDS)

❑ **maxed out** *adj.* [1980s+] **1** very drunk or highly intoxicated. **2** at one's limits, e.g. of strength or weight or credit.

(IN PHRASES)

❑ **max and relax** *v.* [1980s+] (*US black/campus*) to take life easy, to enjoy oneself; esp. in phr. *maxin' and relaxin'*. ❑ **max out** *v.* **1** [1970s+] (*US prison*) to complete one's sentence without gaining any remission for good behaviour. **2** [1970s+] to indulge to extremes. **3** [1970s+] of an object or person, to reach its limit, esp. of a credit card. **4** [1980s+] (*US*) to succeed. **5** [1980s+] to relax.

max *adv.* (*also* **maximum**) [1950s+] (*US*) extremely, at the maximum, at most.

Max Factor *n.* [rhy. sl.; brandname *Max Factor*, a leading producer of cosmetics and make-up] [20C+] (esp. fig.) an actor, i.e. one who fakes illness or injury, a footballer who 'dives' etc.

max fuckter *n.* [f. brandname *Max Factor*, a leading producer of cosmetics] [1950s–70s] (*gay*) make-up.

maxi *n.* (*also* **maxy**) [abbr. SE *maximum*; ? an obsolete maximum fare on a form of public transport] [1940s+] (*W.I.*) one shilling (5p).

maxie *n.* [Lat. *maximus*, the greatest] [mid-19C] (*Scot.*) a major mistake, a serious blunder.

maximum *adv. see* MAX *adv.*

maximus *n. see* MAX *n.*

Max Miller *n.* [rhy. sl. Cockney pron. 'piller'; ult. comedian *Max Miller* (1895–1963)] [1920s+] a pillow.

maxslummed *adj.* [MAX *n.* (1)] [mid-19C] (*UK Und.*) drunk (on gin).

max walls *n.* [rhy. sl. = BALLS *n.* (1); ult. comedian *Max Wall* (1908–90)] [1930s+] the testicles.

Maxwell House *n.* [rhy. sl., the popular brand of instant coffee] [1960s+] a mouse.

Maxwell Pond *n.*

(IN PHRASES)

❑ **money gone in Maxwell Pond** *n.* (*also* **labour gone in Maxwell Pond**) [proper name of the *Maxwell* (Sugar) Estate in Barbados. No actual pond, however, has ever been traced] [20C+] (*W.I.*) used to describe money or effort that has been wasted or 'thrown away'.

maxy *n. see* MAXI *n.*

maxy *adj. see under* MAX *n.*

mayate *n.* [Mex. Sp.] [1960s+] (*US*) a black person; also as adj.

Maybelline waste *n.* [*Maybelline*, a brandname of cosmetics; i.e. it was not worth getting made-up] [1990s+] (*US campus*) a disappointing social event.

maymay-lippy *adj.* [? SE *mama* + LIPPY *adj.*] [20C+] (*W.I., Antg.*) talkative, gossipy.

ma-yo *n.* [? Chinese] [1970s] (*drugs*) cannabis.

mayo *n.* [? misreading of MA-YO *n.*] [1940s+] (*drugs*) **1** cocaine. **2** heroin; morphine.

mayonnaise midget *n.* [2000s] (*US black*) a white man's penis, stereotyped as small.

mayonnaise monkey *n.* [2000s] (*US black*) a white person.

maypole *n.* [the shape] [17C–18C] the penis.

(IN PHRASES)

❑ **play at maypole** *v.* [1960s] (*gay*) to indulge in sexual activity.

maypop *n.* [pun. on SE *may pop*/US dial. *maypop*, the passion flower] [1980s+] (*US black*) a very worn tyre.

maytag *n.* [the *Maytag* brand of home appliances] [1970s+] (*US prison*) a weak male prisoner who is abused by other inmates, forced to do their menial chores and poss. raped.

maytag *v.* [MAYTAG *n.*] [1970s+] (*US prison*) to perform anal rape.

mayvin *n. see* MAVEN *n.*

may your chooks turn into emus and kick your shithouse down *phr. see under* CHOOK *n.*

may your prick and purse never fail you *phr. see under* PRICK *n.*

mazard *n.* (*also* **mazer, mazzard**) [SE *mazer*, a hard wood (usu. but not invariably maple) used as a material for drinking cups] **1** [17C–1920s] the head. **2** [mid-18C–1940s] the face. **3** [early 19C] (*Anglo-Irish*) the 'head' of a coin.

mazard *v.* (*also* **mazzard**) [MAZARD *n.* (1)] [early 17C] to hit on the head.

mazawattee *n.* [rhy. sl.; ult. Mazawattee, a brand of tea] [20C+] a potty.

mazda crown *n.* [*Mazda*, a popular brand of lightbulb; coined by columnist Walter Winchell (1897–1972)] [1930s] (*US*) a bald-headed man.

Mazda Lane *n.* (*also* **mazda thoroughfare**) [see prev.] [1920s–50s] (*US*) Broadway, New York.

mazeh *n.* (*also* **mazehette**) [Heb. *mah ze?*, what is this?] [1980s+] (*US campus*) a very attractive man or woman.

mazer *n. see* MAZARD *n.*

Mazola party *n.* [*Mazola*, a brand of vegetable oil + SE *party*] [1960s+] (*US*) a party of two or more people who cover their bodies in vegetable oil to engage in sexual activity and intercourse.

mazoo *n.* (*also* **mazoola**) [abbr./var. MAZUMA *n.*] [1950s–80s] (*US*) money.

mazoom *n.* (*also* **mazume**) [abbr. MAZUMA *n.*] [1900s–20s] (*US*) money.

mazuma *n.* (*also* **mazooboe, mazooma, mazume**) [Yid., ult. Heb. *mazuma*, prepared, ready] **1** [20C+] money. **2** [1960s] a dollar bill.

mazuzu *n.* [? an African word or var. on MAZUMA *n.*] [1960s–70s] (*S.Afr. township*) money.

mazzard *n. see* MAZARD *n.*

mazzy *n. see* TEMAZZY *n.*

m.b. *n.* [abbr. brandname] [1930s+] (*Aus.*) Melbourne *B*itter; thus *suffer from m.b.*, to be drunk.

m.b. coat *n.* [abbr. *m*ark of the *b*east; the 'beast' in this context was Popery] [mid–late 19C] a long coat worn by clergymen.

mbongo *n.* [Nguni *imbongi*, a praise-singer] [1910s+] (*S.Afr.*) a political stooge or apologist, a 'yes-man'.

m.b. waistcoat *n.* [orig. worn by tractarians only, *c.*1840, but later adopted by other clergymen] [mid–late 19C] a kind of waistcoat with no opening in front, worn by Anglican clergymen.

M.C. *n.* (*also* **emcee**) [lit. *m*aster of *c*eremonies, as such orig. 1930s] **1** [1950s+] one who is in charge, a leader, a boss. **2** [1980s+] (*orig. US black*) the lead singer of a rap band; e.g. *M.C. Noise.*

Mc/Mac *see under* MAC.

m.c. *v.* [M.C. *n.*] **1** [1930s+] to present a (rock) concert. **2** [1980s+] to perform as a rapper.

M'Coy, the *n. see* REAL MCCOY, THE *n.*

mc² *adj.* [the shorthand for Einstein's theory of relativity + pun on SQUARE *adj.* (10)] [1980s+] (*US campus*) overly studious, over-devoted to books and uninterested in parties, drink, drugs and other forms of pleasure.

m.d.g. *phr.* [abbr. *m*utual *d*esire to *g*rope] [1980s+] (*US campus*) strong physical attraction.

m.d.l. *n.* [abbr. *MUTTON DRESSED AS LAMB under* MUTTON *n.*] [1990s+] a person, usu. a woman, who dresses younger than her years.

me *pron.* [1950s+] used at the end of a sentence to indicate preference or for emphasis, e.g. *I like lard, me.*

— me *phr.* [the *locus classicus* comes in the film *The Sweet Smell of Success* (1957) where the venal columnist J.J. Hunsecker confirms his absolute power over the venal, scrabbling press agent Sidney Falco with the command, *Match me, Sidney*, i.e. Light my cigarette] [1920s+] (*orig. US*) used with a relevant n. to denote an imper., e.g. *pen me*, hand me a pen.

meadow mayonnaise *n.* (*also* **meadow dressing**) [euph. pun on BULLSHIT *n.*] [1910s+] (*Aus./US*) nonsense, rubbish.

meadow muffin *n.* (*also* **meadow cake, trail muffin**) [1970s+] (*US*) a lump of manure.

meag *n. see* MAG *n.*³.

meagre *adj. see* MAUGER *adj.*

meal *n.* [1970s+] (*S.Afr. gang*) an act of sexual intercourse.

SE in slang uses

IN PHRASES

▫ **dive for a meal** *v. see under* DIVE *v.*

mealie-muncher *n.* (*also* **mealie**) [S.Afr.E. *mealie*, maize + SE *muncher*] [1970s] (*S.Afr.*) an Afrikaner.

meal-mouth *n.* [SE *mealy-mouth*, one who fears to speak their mind] [late 17C–18C] one who demands money, but in a sly, sheepish manner.

meals on wheels *n.* **1** [1960s+] (*US gay*) teenagers cruising the streets in their cars. **2** [2000s] jellied eels [rhy. sl.]. **3** [2000s] (*S.Afr. gay*) men on motorcycles.

meal ticket *n.* **1** [late 19C+] (*orig. US*) anyone good for the price of a meal. **2** [late 19C+] (*orig. US*) anyone who provides money or a livelihood for someone else, who thus needs to make less effort; also the object which earns one's income. **3** [late 19C+] (*orig. US*) employment, wages, whatever provides the price of a (fig.) meal. **4** [1950s] (*US*) a personal preference. **5** [1960s+] (*US gay*) as senses 1–3 in homosexual contexts. **6** [1970s] an opportunity.

mealy bustle *n.* [late 19C] (*US short order*) mealy potato.

mealy potato *n.* [1900s] (*Aus.*) the right thing.

mean *n.* [1980s+] aggressiveness.

mean *adj.* **1** [late 19C+] (*orig. US*) very good, very clever, adroit, with implications of 'so good it's unfair', on the 'outlaw' bad = good model. **2** [1920s+] (*US black*) exceptionally attractive or stylish.

IN COMPOUNDS

▫ **mean machine** *n.* **1** [1980s+] (*orig. US*) a fast or stylish car. **2** [1990s+] fig. a powerful team or person.

SE in slang uses

IN COMPOUNDS

▫ **mean-eye** *v.* [1930s] (*US*) to stare at aggressively, in a hostile manner. ▫ **mean-hair** *adj.* [1960s+] (*gay*) unpleasant, cruel. ▫ **mean mug** *v.* [MUG *n.*¹ (1b)] [2000s] (*US black*) to look at someone in a disrespectful and hostile manner. ▫ **mean potatoes** *n. see* SMALL POTATOES *n.* ▫ **mean reds** *n.* [coined by Truman Capote in *Breakast at Tiffany's* (1958)] [1960s+] (*US campus*) a fit of depression. ▫ **mean soup** *n.* [1990s+] (*Aus.*) alcohol. ▫ **mean white** *n.* [SE *mean*, impoverished] [mid-19C–1900s] (*US black*) an extremely poor white person.

IN PHRASES

▫ **too mean to part with one's shit** *adj.* [late 19C+] very mean indeed.

mean-ass *n.* [SE *mean* +-ASS *sfx*] [1950s+] an unpleasant person.

mean-ass *adj.* [MEAN-ASS *n.*] [1950s+] very unpleasant.

me and you *n.* [rhy. sl.] [20C+] **1** (*bingo*) the number two. **2** sexual intercourse [= SCREW *n.*¹ (1)].

me and you *phr.* [1940s–60s] (*US black*) an invitation to start fighting; esp. in phr. *it's gonna be me and you.*

me-and-you *n.* [a play on words rather than rhy. sl.] [1930s+] a menu.

me arse and Katty Barry! *excl. see under* ARSE *n.*

measure *n.*

SE in slang uses

IN PHRASES

▫ **one's measure** *n.* [mid–late 19C] the right person for the circumstances.

measured for a new overcoat, be *v.* (*also* **measured for a new suit of clothes**) [i.e. a *WOODEN OVERCOAT under* WOODEN *adj.*] **1** [late 19C] to receive a beating. **2** [1930s–40s] (*US*) to be buried.

measure (out) *v.* [? SE *measure* out blows; *measure one's length*, to fall prostrate] [1900s–50s] (*US Und.*) to strike hard.

measure over the counter *v.* [mid-19C] to die.

measures *n. see* MEDZERS *n.*

meat *n.* **1** [16C+] a body, usu. a woman's, as an object of sexual pleasure; thus *fond of meat*, amorously inclined. **2** [late 16C+] (*also* **lump of meat, piece of meat**) the penis. **3** [17C+] the vagina. **4** [mid-19C+] (*orig. US*) one's body or flesh. **5** [mid-19C+] prey, as in *he's my meat* referring to a potential victim. **6** [late 19C+] a prostitute; thus *fresh meat*, a novice prostitute, *raw meat*, a woman *in flagrante delicto*, the *price of meat*, the cost of a prostitute. **7** [late 19C+] (*orig. US*) a person of another race as an object of sexual gratification, constructed with a colour; thus *dark meat, white meat.* **8** [late 19C+] (*orig. US*) a person (or thing) that fits the bill, meets one's needs. **9** [20C+] (*US*) a corpse, a wounded person. **10** [1960s+] (*US*) an inferior person, poss. physically robust but mindless or gullible, thus often used to describe sportsmen; also affectionate use. **11** [1980s] (*US*) in pl., a set of car tyres. **12** [1990s+] (*N.Z.*) a sporty, macho man, who places physical development above intelligence.

DERIVATIVES

▫ **meaty** *adj.* [early 19C+] sexually attractive, sexually exciting.

IN COMPOUNDS

▫ **meat axe** *n.* [1970s] (*US*) the penis. ▫ **meatbag** *n.* **1** [mid–late 19C] the stomach. **2** [1990s+] a heavily muscled man. ▫ **meatbeater** *n.* [1980s+] a masturbator, esp. one who masturbates excessively; thus a general term of abuse. ▫ **meat cart** *n.* (*also* **meat crate**) [1930s–40s] (*US*) a hearse.

❑ **meat-cleaver** *n.* [20C+] the penis. ❑ **meat curtains** *n.* [1990s+] the female vaginal lips or labia majora. ❑ **meat fancier's** *n.* [19C] a brothel. ❑ **meat-flasher** *n.* [late 19C–1910s] an exhibitionist, one who exposes themselves indecently; thus *meat-flashing*, exhibitionism. ❑ **meat horn** *n.* [1950s] the penis. ❑ **meathound** *n.* [-HOUND *sfx*] [1930s–60s] **1** (*US*) a lecher. **2** (*US black*) one who indulges in oral sex [they EAT *v.* (4) their partner]. ❑ **meat house** *n.* [HOUSE *n.*[1] (1)/SE *house*] **1** [late 19C] (*US*) one's body. **2** [late 19C–1960s] (*also* **meat shop**) a brothel. **3** [1930s] (*US police*) a morgue. ❑ **meat injection** *n.* [1980s+] (*orig. US*) an act of penetration by the penis. ❑ **meat lance** *n.* (*also* **meat spear, meat stick**) [1970s+] (*US*) the penis. ❑ **meat mag** *n.* [MAG *n.*[4] (1)] [1970s] (*US*) a magazine of homosexual pornography. ❑ **meat-merchant** *n.* [late 19C] a prostitute. ❑ **meat-monger** *n.* [late 18C–19C] a womanizer, a philanderer. ❑ **meat packer** *n.* [play on SAmE *meatpacker*] [1940s] (*US*) an undertaker. ❑ **meat puppet** *n.* [SE *puppet*, both 'jump up and down'] (*US*) **1** [1980s+] a gullible person. **2** [1990s+] the penis. ❑ **meat-roll** *n.* [1990s+] a penis. ❑ **meat salesman** *n.* [1970s] a pimp. ❑ **meat shot** *n.* [1990s+] (*US*) a flesh wound. ❑ **meat skewer** *n.* [late 19C] the penis. ❑ **meat tool** *n.* [TOOL *n.*[1] (1)] [1960s+] (*US*) the penis. ❑ **meat wagon** *n.* [lit. and fig. uses of sense 9 above + SE *wagon*] **1** [1910s+] (*US*) (*also* **live meat wagon**) an ambulance. **2** [1940s+] a vehicle used for conveying prisoners to and from court, police stations, prisons etc, a general police van. **3** [1940s+] (*US*) a hearse. **4** [1980s] a large, expensive automobile. ❑ **meat whistle** *n.* [1930s+] (*US*) the penis, esp. as an object of fellatio. ❑ **meat-works** *n.* [1940s] (*Aus.*) a brothel.

(IN PHRASES)

❑ **beat one's meat** *v.* [1940s+] (*orig. US*) **1** (*also* **flog one's meat**) to masturbate; also fig. and in dismissive phr. *go beat your meat!* **2** to brag, to boast. ❑ **bit of meat** *n.* [early 18C+] **1** the vagina. **2** sexual intercourse. **3** a woman considered as nothing more than a sex object. ❑ **black meat** *n.* **1** [20C+] a black woman's genitals. **2** a black woman. ❑ **bust one's meat** *v.* [2000s] (*UK black*) of a man, to ejaculate. ❑ **don't let your meat loaf** [pun on SE *loaf*, the food/*loaf*, to loiter] [1960s+] (*US*) a general phr. of encouragement, the implication being 'don't procrastinate'. ❑ **fond of meat** *adj.* [19C+] used to describe a man who is fond of sex, esp. with prostitutes. ❑ **give someone some meat** *v.* (*also* **give someone some**) [1970s+] of a man, to have sexual intercourse. ❑ **hang one's meat** *v.* [1900s–10s] (*US*) of a man, to urinate. ❑ **have a bit of meat** *v.* [late 19C+] to have sexual intercourse. ❑ **hawk one's meat** *v.* [19C] to display one's body. ❑ **hot meat** *n.* [HOT *adj.* (1a)] [1940s] (*US*) exposed female flesh. ❑ **light meat** *n.* [1960s] (*US*) white people, usu. women, considered as sex objects. ❑ **make cold meat of** *v.* [var. on SE phr. *make mincemeat of*] [mid-19C+] (*orig. US*) to kill. ❑ **meat and two veg** *n.* (*also* **meat and two bits**) [1960s+] the penis and testicles. ❑ **meat for your master** *n.* [mid-18C] that which is considered out of reach of the speaker, and due only to their superiors. ❑ **pound one's meat** *v.* [1950s+] (*US*) **1** to masturbate. **2** to have sexual intercourse. ❑ **pump one's meat** *v.* [1970s–80s] to masturbate. ❑ **put the meat to** *v.* (*also* **throw the meat to**) [1960s–70s] of a man, to have sexual intercourse. ❑ **sink one's meat** *v.* [1930s] (*US*) to have sexual intercourse. ❑ **stretch some meat** *v.* [1980s+] (*US*) to have sexual intercourse. ❑ **swinging the meat** *adj.* see SWINGING ON THE MEAT *under* SWING *v.* ❑ **take one's meat out of the basket** *v.* [1940s+] (*gay*) to reveal one's genitals to another man.

SE in slang uses

(IN COMPOUNDS)

❑ **meatbrain** *n.* [1960s+] (*orig. US*) a fool. ❑ **meat-eater** *n.* [antonym of GRASS-EATER *under* GRASS *n.*[1]] [1970s+] (*US Und.*) a police officer who, not content with the payoffs, bribes and perks that are freely offered, actively compels people to offer him such monies. ❑ **meat fosh** *n.* [var. on *fish-fosh*, kedgeree] [late 19C] hash, stew. ❑ **meat-grinder** *n.* (*US*) **1** [1940s–50s] a car with a loud engine. **2** [1950s+] any tough situation or place in which an elimination process is being carried out, such as training. **3** [1990s+] someone who controls one and renders one's life unpleasant. ❑ **meathook** *n.* **1** [mid–late 19C] a curl on the temple, then fashionable among London cockneys; thus *meathooks*, curls in general. **2** [1910s+] (*Aus./US*) the arm. **3** [1910s+] (*US*) a hand; often in pl. *meathooks*. **4** [1970s] (*US*) the penis. ❑ **meat man** *n.* [20C+] (*US black*) an ordinary person. ❑ **meat-mincer** *n.* [mid-19C] in boxing, the mouth. ❑ **meat ticket** *n.* [var. on MEAL TICKET *n.*] [1930s+] **1** anyone good for the price of a meal. **2** anyone who provides money or a livelihood for someone else, who thus needs to make less effort. **3** see DEAD-MEAT TICKET *under* DEAD MEAT *n.* ❑ **meat trap** *n.* [SE *trap*/TRAP *n.*[1] (4)] [mid-19C+] (*Aus./US*) the mouth. ❑ **meat water** *n.* [1940s+] (*W.I.*) stock, soup. ❑ **meat wrapper** *n.* see FISH-WRAPPER *under* FISH *n.*[1].

(IN PHRASES)

❑ **meat and drink** *n.* **1** [19C] drunken love-making. **2** [late 19C] (*W.I.*) strong drink in general, but spec. liquor thickened with egg yolks. ❑ **meat and two veg** *adj.* [the stereotypically basic dish, roast meat, potatoes and cabbage] [20C+] plain, unadorned, 'no-frills'. ❑ **meat-drink-washing-and-lodging** *n.* [its image as a universal panacea] [early–mid-18C] gin. ❑ **meat-in-the-pot** *n.* [its use in obtaining food] [mid-19C–1940s] (*US, mainly West*) a rifle, a shotgun, a revolver. ❑ **not for all the meat in China** see NOT FOR ALL THE TEA IN CHINA *under* TEA *n.*

meat and potatoes *n.* [the stereotyped plain meal] [1950s+] (*US*) the essence, the basics, the 'brass tacks'.

meat-and-potatoes *adj.* [MEAT AND POTATOES *n.* (1)] [1950s+] (*US*) average, run-of-the-mill, unexciting, basic.

meat axe *n.* **1** [mid-19C] (*US*) used in similes, *see below*. **2** [1990s+] (*Aus./N.Z.*) an eccentric, a mad person.

(IN PHRASES)

❑ **mad as a meat axe** *adj.* [1920s+] (*Aus./N.Z.*) **1** (*also* **savage as a meat axe, wild as a meat axe**) very angry. **2** completely insane.

meatball *n.* **1** [1930s+] (*US*) a stupid person; thus a potential victim [fig. ext. + ref. to MEATHEAD *n.*]. **2** [1940s+] (*US*) an Italian [the stereotyped partiality of Italians for the dish]. **3** [1950s] an African-American. **4** [1950s+] (*US*) as ext. of sense 1, a prostitute's customer. **5** [1970s+] (*US Und.*) a minor or false criminal charge [backform. f. MEATBALL *adj.*].

meatball *adj.* **1** [1940s+] (*US Und.*) used of a criminal charge for a petty crime, e.g., *meatball beef, meatball rap* [the smallness or commonness, thus unimportance, of the food]. **2** [1960s+] (*US*) stupid [MEATBALL *n.* (1)].

meater *n.* ['said of a dog who only bites meat, that is to say, one who will not fight' (Ware)] [late 19C–1900s] a coward.

Meat-Freezer *n.* [the export of deep-frozen N.Z. lamb] [1900s] (*Aus.*) a New Zealander.

meathead *n.* [SE *meat* + -HEAD *sfx* (1), implying that solid flesh, rather than brains, occupies one's skull] **1** [1920s+] (*US*) a stupid person; thus as term of address. **2** [1940s+] a general term of abuse.

(DERIVATIVES)

❑ **meatheaded** *adj.* [1940s+] stupid, foolish.

meat market *n.* [MEAT *n.* (1); in sense 1c note synon. 1910s US *meet market*] **1** as a place, usu. for sexual encounters. (**a**) [late 19C+] (*also* **market**) a rendezvous for prostitutes of either sex. (**b**) [1940s+] (*US*) any situation or place where people are regarded as commodities, such as a recruiting agency or a modelling agency. (**c**) [1950s+] anywhere that people gather for the primary purpose of finding sexual partners, often used in universities to describe first-year parties. (**d**) [1960s] in fig. use, the world of commercial sexuality. **2** [late 19C+] as a part of the body. (**a**) the female breasts. (**b**) the vagina.

meat pie *n.* [rhy. sl.] [20C+] **1** a fly. **2** a trouser fly. **3** eye, usu. in pl. **4** a necktie. **5** a lie.

meat pie *adj.* [the cheapness of *meat pies*] [1910s+] (*Aus.*) small-time, esp. in *meat pie bookie*, a small-time bookmaker.

meat rack *n.* [pun on SE *meat*/MEAT *n.* (1)/MEAT *n.* (9)] **1** [1960s+] (*orig. gay*) a place, such as a bar or a particular street, where homosexuals display their charms to potential customers. After the 'singles bar' explosion of the 1970s, the term was extended to heterosexuality. **2** [1970s] an ambulance, usu. from a morgue.

IN PHRASES

❑ **off the meat rack** *adj.* [2000s] (*US black*) superlative, first-rate, astonishing.

meaty *n.* [1970s+] (*UK juv.*) a lump of spittle containing a proportion of phlegm.

mebs *n.* (*also* **mebbs**) [1990s+] (*Irish*) the testicles.

mec *n. see* MAKE *n.*[1].

meccano set *n.* [*Meccano*, a popular construction kit used by children] [1950s] (*N.Z. prison*) the portable, silver-painted, steel gallows, moved and erected as and when required.

mech *n.* (*also* **mach**) [abbr.] [1910s+] (orig. RAF) a *mech*anic.

mechanic *n.* **1** [17C–mid-19C] (*also* **mechanick**) a general term of abuse. **2** [late 19C] (*US gambling*) one who invents methods of cheating. **3** [20C+] (*orig. US*) a professional cheat at cards or dice; thus *mechanic's grip*, a way of holding a deck of cards. **4** [20C+] any notably successful player. **5** [20C+] (*W.I.*) a trick, a contrivance, usu. involving some form of physical activity. **6** [1930s–70s] (*US Und.*) a pickpocket or safe-breaker. **7** [1950s] a trainer who uses drugs to stimulate his horses. **8** [1970s+] a hired killer.

SE in slang uses

IN COMPOUNDS

❑ **mechanics' avenue** *n.* (*also* **...alley, ...street, Mechanicsburg**) [SE *mechanic*, a manual labourer + SE *avenue/alley/street*] [mid-19C–1960s] (*US*) a poor or run-down part of a town or city.

mechanic *adj.* [SE *mechanic*, 'pertaining to or involving manual labour' (*OED*)] [late 16C–early 19C] vulgar, contemptible.

mechanical digger *n.* [rhy. sl. = NIGGER *n.*[1] (1)] [20C+] a derog. term for a black person.

mechanized dandruff *n. see* GALLOPING DANDRUFF *under* GALLOPING *adj.*

meckem-peckam *adj.* [? SE *make* + *pernickety*] [1940s+] (*W.I.*) fault-finding, very hard to satisfy.

mecks *n.* [ety. unknown] [mid–late 19C] wines and spirits.

med *n.* [abbr.] **1** [mid-19C+] a *med*ical student; thus (1940s+) *med college*, medical school, *med business*, medical business. **2** [20C+] a doctor. **3** [1930s+] *med*icine; *med*ication; usu. in pl. **4** [1940s+] *med*ical school.

IN COMPOUNDS

❑ **med-man** *n.* [abbr.] **1** [1930s–40s] (*US*) a quack or a patent *med*icine seller. **2** [1940s+] a doctor [SE *medicine man*].

IN PHRASES

❑ **hot meds** *n.* [2000s] (*US prison*) controlled medication.

meddle (with) *v.* [14C–17C SE *meddle*, to have sexual intercourse] **1** [1940s+] (*US*) to have sexual intercourse. **2** [1970s] (*US black*) to be intimate, but not spec. on a sexual level.

Meddy, the *n.* [abbr.] [1940s] the Mediterranean.

medical Greek *n. see* MARROWSKY *n.*

medicine *n.* **1** [mid–late 19C; 1930s+] (*orig. US*) an intoxicating drink. **2** [mid-19C+] punishment, usu. deserved. **3** [mid-19C+] sexual intercourse. **4** [1910s–1930s] (*US*) information, knowledge. **5** [1930s] (*US black*) semen. **6** [1930s+] drugs.

IN COMPOUNDS

❑ **medicine sharp** *n.* [SHARP *n.*[1] (2)] [late 19C–1910s] (*US*) a physician.

IN PHRASES

❑ **make medicine** *v.* [1900s] (*US, Western*) to converse. ❑ **take one's medicine** *v.* **1** [mid–late 19C] to have sexual intercourse. **2** [mid-19C–1930s] to drink. **3** [late 19C+] to accept a (deserved) punishment or reprimand.

medicine *adj.* [the soothing effects of SE *medicine*] [late 19C–1930s] (*US*) persuasive.

medico *n.* [SE late 17C–mid-19C] **1** [mid-19C+] a doctor; thus *she-medico*, a female doctor. **2** [1940s] a medical student.

medieval *adj.* [the stereotype of the Middle Ages as symptomatic of such excesses; the phr. was coined in the Quentin Tarantino film *Pulp Fiction* (1993)] [late 19C+] barbaric, illiberal, cruel.

IN PHRASES

❑ **get medieval on someone's ass** *v.* [1990s+] to treat with extreme savagery.

medina *n.* [? as opposed to Mecca, presumably Manhattan, but note Arab. *medina*, the Arab section of a town; note 1885 Bulletin (Sydney) 17 Jan. 12/1: And it is just to hand, the new crack prima donna [...] at a minute's notice, 'guyed a whack to her own Medina' – which means London] [1990s+] (*US black/rap music*) a nickname for Brooklyn.

meditation *n.* [the loneliness of the punishment] [1960s+] (*US prison*) solitary or segregated confinement.

Mediterranean back *n.* (*also* **Greek back**) [1970s+] (*Aus.*) a supposedly fake illness or incapacity, used to justify malingering, apparently by Italians, Greeks, Yugoslavs and others seen as lazier than 'white' Australians.

medium *n.* **1** [1930s+] (*Irish*) an indeterminate measure, approx 0.3 litres (a half-pint) of beer. **2** [1940s+] (*Irish*) the Irish language [SE *medium of communication*].

medlar (tree) *n.* **1** [late 16C–19C] the vagina. **2** [17C] a promiscuous woman. **3** [mid-19C] (*UK Und.*) a man who smells.

meds *n. see* MED *n.* (3).

medza/medzer *n. see* MADZA *n.*

medzers *n.* (*also* **measures**) [abbr. MADZA CAROON *under* MADZA *n.*; *measures* is mispron.] [1960s–70s] (*Ling. Fr./Polari*) money.

meemies *n.* (*also* **meemees, mimis, miyams**) [? var. on HEEBIE-JEEBIES *n.*; note WW2 US milit. sl. *screaming meemie*, the German *nebelwerfer*, a multi-barrelled mortar] [1940s+] (*orig. US*) hysteria; usu. as *SCREAMING MEEMIES* below.

IN PHRASES

❑ **screaming meemies** *n.* (*also* **screaming meamies, screaming mimis, screemies**) [1940s+] (*US*) **1** nerves, paranoia. **2** delirium tremens.

meerschaum *n.* [SE *meerschaum*, a type of mineral often made into a tobacco pipe] [1930s] (*US*) a saxophone.

meet *n.* **1** [mid-19C] (*UK Und.*) a meeting place. **2** [mid-19C+] (*orig. US*) a meeting, appointment, in [20C+] esp. for illicit purposes such as drug selling [now SE]. **3** [20C+] (*US*) a gathering for the purpose of an activity, usu. sport, e.g. *a swim meet*, also a conference or convention.

meet *v.*

SE in slang uses

IN PHRASES

❑ **meet hell** *v.* [20C+] (*W.I.*) to find it hard to make enough money to live, to subsist, to suffer great hardship. ❑ **meet mary palm and her five sisters** *v.* [1950s+] to masturbate. ❑ **meet rosie hancock** *v.* [pun on name/SE *hand* + COCK *n.*[3]] [1950s+] to masturbate. ❑ **meet with mother thumb and her four daughters** *v.* [1960s+] to masturbate.

meff *n.* [? pron. of SE *meth*ylated spirits, often drunk by alcoholic tramps] [1990s+] a dirty, smelly person; a vagrant.

me for *phr.* [20C+] (*orig. US*) I want.

meg *n.*[1] (*also* **megg**) [generic uses of MAG *n.*[3]] **1** [late 17C–mid-19C] a guinea. **2** [1910s] (*US*) a dollar. **3** see MAG *n.*[3] (1).

meg *n.*[2] (*also* **megg, meggie, meggs**) [var. on MAGGIE ANN *n.*] [1940s+] (*drugs*) marijuana.

meg *v.* [MEG *n.*[1] (1)] [19C] to swindle; thus *megging*, swindling.

mega *adj.* [adopted Greek pfx *mega-*, great] [1960s+] (*orig. US teen*) **1** of an object or person, superlative, excellent, extra-special; usu. as pfx. **2** of an object, huge, enormous, substantial. **3** of a person, very well known or very successful, also later used predicatively e.g. *the movie was mega*. **4** of a person, extreme in type.

mega *adv.* [1960s+] extremely, to a great extent.

megablast *n.* [MEGA *adj.* (1) + BLAST *n.*[1] (3)] [1980s+] (*drugs*) **1** a very deep inhalation of a cannabis cigarette. **2** an act of inhalation from a crack pipe. **3** an extremely exciting, satisfying experience.

megg *n. see under* MEG.

meggie *n. see* MEG *n.*[2].

megging *n. see* MAGGING *n.*[1].

meggs *n. see* MEG *n.*[2].

megilla *n.* (*also* **megillah**) [Yid. *gantse Megillah*, a whole (tedious) story, ult. Heb. *megillah*, roll, scroll. In standard use the term refers to five Old Testament books – the Song of Solomon, Ruth, Lamentations, Ecclesiastes and Esther – that are trad. associated with certain festivals, esp. the Book of Esther, read at Purim] [1940s+] a long, tedious or complicated story, a complicated state of affairs, a long explanation; esp. in phr. *the whole megillah*, everything, the lot.

megimp *n. see* MACGIMP *n.*

Meg Ryan *n.* [rhy. sl. = IRON (HOOF) *n.*; ult. US film actress *Meg Ryan* (b.1961)] [1990s+] a male homosexual.

megsman *n.* [MEG *v.*; var. on MAGSMAN *n.*] **1** [mid–late 19C] the king of the 19C swindlers. **2** [mid-19C+] a petty criminal, a cheat.

mehawn! *excl.* [Irish *mo thón*! my arse!] [1930s+] (*Ulster*) nonsense! rubbish!

meidnaaier *n.* [Afk. lit. 'maid-fucker'] [2000s] (*S.Afr.*) one who has intercourse with black women.

meig *n.* [var. on MEG *n.*[1]] [20C+] (*US*) a nickel, a five-cent coin.

-meister *sfx* [Ger. *meister*, master, Yid. *meyster*, master] [1980s+] (*orig. US campus*) **1** master, i.e. expert; used in comb. with a relevant n. to denote the leader of a profession, although the praise may often be tinged with irony. **2** used in comb. with a personal name or first syllable of a name.

mejoge *n.* (*also* **midjic, midget**) [Shelta] [mid-18C–1950s] one shilling (5p).

mek-mek *n.* [SE *make* (*a fuss*) + redup.] [1940s+] (*W.I.*) **1** a pernickety person, a fault-finder. **2** a quarrel, quarrelling.

mek-mek *adj.* [MEK-MEK *n.* (2)] [1940s+] (*W.I.*) quarrelsome.

mek-mek *v.* [MEK-MEK *n.* (1)] [1940s+] (*W.I.*) to hesitate, to be indecisive, to make a half-hearted attempt.

melancholy hat *n.* [late 16C–early 17C] **1** a mourning hat. **2** a smart, fashionable hat.

Melba *n.*

(IN PHRASES)

❑ **do a Melba** *v.* [1970s+] (*Aus.*) to announce, with great fanfare, one's imminent retirement, only to return, time and time again, for another 'farewell', a practice of Dame Nellie *Melba* (1861–1931) and many other 'showbiz greats'.

Melbourne cup *n.* [1980s+] (*N.Z.*) a chamberpot.

Melbourne Pier *n. see* PORT MELBOURNE PIER *n.* (1).

melching *n.* [MINGE *n.* (2) + FELCH *v.* (1)] [1990s+] sucking the newly ejaculated semen from the vagina (poss. with the aid of a straw).

melia murder! *excl.* (*also* **millia murder!**) [Irish *míle murdar*, lit. 'a thousand murders', thus 'horror of horrors!'] [mid-19C+] (*Irish*) a general excl. of surprise, horror, regret.

melkpens *n.* [Afk. *melk*, milk + *pens*, stomach] [1970s] (*S.Afr.*) a young, naïve and inexperienced person.

mellish *n.* [? Lat. *mel*, honey, thus the image of money as a 'sweetener' and/or the golden colour] [early 19C] a sovereign.

mellow *n.*[1] [late 17C] a smooth drink.

mellow *n.*[2] [MELLOW *adj.*] **1** [1950s–60s] (*US black*) a homosexual. **2** [1960s+] (*US black*) a favourite boy- or girlfriend, a good friend of either sex. **3** [1970s+] (*US*) a state of calm relaxation.

mellow *adj.* **1** [17C+] pleasantly drunk, tipsy. **2** [late 19C+] (*orig. US black*) (*also* **mellowed**) perfect, fine, esp. in phr. *mellow as a cello*. **3** [1930s+] (*US black*) relaxed and comfortable. **4** [1930s+] (*US black*) attractive, stylish. **5** [1940s+] (*US black*) of a friend, close, intimate. **6** [1940s+] calm, peaceful, unconcerned with the material or painful, a state often induced by smoking cannabis. **7** [1970s+] of drugs, relaxing.

(IN COMPOUNDS)

❑ **mellow-back** *adj.* [BACK *adv.*] [1930s–60s] (*US black*) fashionable, chic, well-dressed. ❑ **mellow black** *n.* [1930s–40s] (*US black*) an attractive young black woman. ❑ **mellow dude** *n.* (*also* **mellow fellow**) [DUDE *n.*[1]] [1960s–70s] (*US drugs*) a drug user. ❑ **mellow man** *n.* [1940s] (*US teen*) an attractive boy. ❑ **mellow roof** *n.* [ROOF *n.* (2)] [1930s–40s] (*US black*) the human head.

(IN PHRASES)

❑ **mellow drag with the sag** *n.* (*also* **mellow drag that has that sag**) [1930s–40s] (*US black*) the exaggeratedly long jacket of a ZOOT SUIT *n.* ❑ **mellow drug of America** *n.* [1960s+] MDA (3,4-methylenedioxyamphetamine), a hallucinogenic that resembles LSD in its effects; it has the same chemical formula as MDMA, but is not identical. ❑ **mellow out** *v.* (*also* **mellow off**) [1960s+] (*orig. US*) to calm oneself down, to calm someone down, to relax, esp. under the influence of drugs.

mellow yellow *n.* **1** [1950s–60s] (*US black*) a light-skinned girl or woman; usu. attractive [MELLOW *adj.* (4) + YELLOW *n.* (1) + assonance]. **2** (*also* **yellow**) in drug uses ['*Mellow Yellow*' (1967) a song by HIPPIE *n.*[2] (3) folk-singer Donovan + MELLOW *adj.* (6)]. (**a**) [1960s–70s] dried banana skins, which, according to contemporary rumour, could be smoked. (**b**) [1960s+] (*drugs*) (*also* **yellow**) a variety of LSD. **3** [1980s+] (*S.Afr. township*) (*also* **yellow mellow**) a CASSPIR armoured truck, used to maintain order in the townships [the colour of the vehicles, thence the proprietary name of a yellow-coloured soft drink, ult. f. the song, *see* sense 2].

mellum *n.* [pron. of *melon*, head?] [1930s] (*US*) common sense.

melodies *n.* [rhy. sl. abbr. *melody lingers*] [1970s+] the fingers.

melon *n.* **1** [mid-19C+] (*Aus./ Can./N.Z./US black*) the human head; thus *do one's melon*, *go off one's melon*, to lose one's temper, to become over-excited. **2** [1910s+] (*US*) a windfall or unexpected profit [financial jargon *cut a melon*, to announce an extra dividend]. **3** [1920s+] (*Aus./ Can./N.Z./US black*) a fool. **4** [1940s+] (*also* **cantaloupes, honeydews, lopes**) in pl., the female breasts, esp. when large.

(IN PHRASES)

❑ **cut a melon** *v.* [20C+] (*US*) to divide up, esp. the spoils of a large coup or a crime.

melon-farmer *n.* **1** [1960s] (*US*) an unsophisticated person; a peasant. **2** [1980s+] a euph. for MOTHERFUCKER *n.* often used as the 'equivalent' when dubbing [coined by Alex Cox, director of *Repo Man* (1984) when re-dubbing the film for television].

melonhead *n.* [MELON *n.* (3) + -HEAD *sfx* (1)] [1910s+] (*Aus./US*) a fool; thus *melon-headed*, stupid.

melt *n.*[1] [metonymy of SE *melt*, the spleen] [mid-19C] (*US*) one's self.

melt *n.*[2] [OE *milt*, spleen; the tongue is spleen-shaped] [20C+] (*Ulster*) the tongue, usu. in phrs. *break one's melt*, to infuriate one beyond reason; *keep in your melt*, hold your tongue; *knock in one's melt*, to drive one mad.

melt *v.* **1** [late 17C+] to spend money, esp. on drink. **2** [19C] to come to orgasm. **3** [early 19C] to beat up. **4** [mid-19C–1920s] to cash a cheque or break a note. **5** [late 19C–1930s] (*Aus./N.Z.*) to spend one season's pay on one extended binge. **6** [1930s+] (*US black*) (*also* **melt out**) to run out of money, to have no money. **7** [1930s+] (*US campus*) to drink oneself into unconsciousness. **8** [1940s–60s] (*US campus*) to delight, thrill or attract someone. **9** [1950s–60s] to leave.

(IN COMPOUNDS)

❑ **melted out** *adj.* [1930–40s] (*US black*) without money and thus desperate.

melt! *excl.* [MELT *v.* (9)] [1960s] (*US*) as imper., leave! get lost!

melted *adj.* [SE *melt*] [2000s] (*Irish*) tired.

melted butter *n.* **1** [18C–19C] semen. **2** [1950s–70s] (*US black*) an attractive woman, esp. a mulatto [her 'yellow' skin tone].

melted out *adj. see under* MELT *v.* (6).

melting moments *n.* **1** [19C] two fat people having sexual intercourse. **2** [late 19C] ardent, intense passion.

melting pot *n.* (*also* **baking pot**) [it 'softens' the penis after ejaculation] [19C] the vagina.

melting pot receiver *n.* [late 18C] (*UK Und.*) a receiver of stolen silver plate who melts down the stolen goods, thus rendering them untraceable.

melt one's grease *v. see under* GREASE *n.*[1].

melvin *n.* (*also* **Marvin, Merv, Mervin, Uncle Melvin**) [image of *Melvin* as a 'nerdy' proper name] **1** [1950s+] (*Aus./US*) a dull, tedious, socially inept and otherwise distasteful person. **2** [1980s+] a condition in which clothing gets stuck between the buttocks; thus *give someone a melvin*, to tug someone's underwear up suddenly and roughly; *have a melvin/have melvins/have a murphy*, to receive this [seen as a typical problem for sense 1].

melvin *adj.* [MELVIN *n.* (1)] [1980s+] old-fashioned, socially inept, dull, foolish.

melvin *v.* [MELVIN *n.* (2)] [1980s+] (*US campus*) to tug someone's underwear up suddenly and roughly with the aim of lifting them off the ground.

Melvyn Bragg *n.* [rhy. sl.; ult. UK broadcaster and author *Melvyn Bragg* (b.1939)] **1** [1990s+] sexual intercourse [= SHAG *n.*[1]]. **2** a promiscuous woman [= SLAG *n.*[1] (4)]. **3** a cigarette [= FAG *n.*[4] (2)].

Melvyn Bragg *v.* [MELVYN BRAGG *n.*] [2000s] to have sexual intercourse.

mem *v.* [abbr.] [2000s] to *mem*orize.

member *n.*[1] [prior use is SE, Lat. *membrum virile*, 'the virile member', i.e. the penis] [18C+] the penis.

IN COMPOUNDS

❑ **member mug** *n.* [late 17C–early 19C] a chamberpot.

IN PHRASES

❑ **dropping member** *n.* [19C] the flaccid penis, esp. when afflicted with (temporary) impotence or with venereal disease. ❑ **hot member** *n. see* separate entry. ❑ **jolly member** *n.* [19C] the penis. ❑ **member for cockshire** *n.* [puns on SE *member* and *Cock*(shire)/COCK *n.*[3] (1)] [mid-19C] the penis. ❑ **member for horncastle** *n.* [punning on SE *member* + HORN *n.*[1]; thus *double entendre* in D'Urfey, *Pills to Purge Melancholy* (1719): 'I am a cunning Constable, / And a Bag of Warrants I have here, / To Press sufficient Men and able, / At *Horn-castle* to appear / [...] / *Where I miss the Man I'll press the Wife*'] [late 18C–early 19C] a cuckold. ❑ **unruly member** *n.* [play on usu. sense of tongue, from General Epistle of James, 3:5–8: 'Even so the tongue is a little member [...] But the tongue can no man tame; it is an unruly evil, full of deadly poison'] [19C] the penis.

SE in slang uses

IN PHRASES

❑ **member of the catch club** *n.* [they *catch* villains] [late 18C–early 19C] a bailiff or bailiff's assistant.

member *n.*[2] [SE *member* as abbr. of *member of the community* is SE 16C–17C] **1** [mid-19C–1920s] a fellow, a chap; usu. with adj. e.g. *hot member*. **2** [1960s+] (*US black*) (*also* **club member**) a fellow black person. **3** [1960s+] (*US gay*) a fellow homosexual.

IN PHRASES

❑ **member for Barkshire** *n.* [pun on SE *bark/Berkshire*] [late 18C–early 19C] one who is suffering from a harsh, persistent cough. ❑ **member of the union** *n.* [1990s+] (*US gay*) a member of the homosexual community.

memory box *n.* [1990s+] (*Aus.*) the mind.

Memphis dominoes *n.* [1940s–70s] (*US*) dice.

men *n.* [the pl. of SE *man* implying the homosexuality] [1990s+] (*W.I.*) a homosexual.

menavelings *n.* [? link to naut. jargon *manarvel*, to pilfer from the ship's stores] [mid–late 19C] odd money remaining after the daily accounts are made up at railway offices.

mench *n. see* MENSH *n.*

mendic *adj.* (*also* **mindic**) [Nyungar *mindaik*, sick] [1920s+] (*Aus.*) sick, ill.

men in blue *n. see* BOYS IN BLUE *n.*

meno *n.* [abbr.] [1920s+] the *meno*pause.

meno *adj.* [abbr.] [1920s+] *meno*pausal.

mensch *n.* (*also* **mensh**) [Yid. *mensch*, Ger. *Mensch*, a person] [1910s+] a 'real man', the implication being of character and integrity rather than sexual or physical prowess.

mensh *n.* (*also* **mench**) [abbr.] [1980s+] a *men*tion.

mensh *v.* (*also* **mench**) [abbr.] [1910s+] to *men*tion; usu. in phr. *don't mensh*, don't mention it.

mental *n.* [abbr. SE *mental case/ability/home*] **1** [1910s+] an insane, deranged person, a mental patient. **2** [1970s+] intelligence. **3** [1970s+] (*Aus.*) an emotional outburst, a display of ill temper. **4** [1980s+] (*Irish*) a psychiatric institution.

IN PHRASES

❑ **chuck a mental** *v.* (*also* **crack a mental, do a mental**) **1** [1980s+] (*Aus./N.Z.*) to lose one's temper; to have a fit. **2** [1990s+] to have an emotional breakdown.

mental *adj.* **1** [late 19C+] insane, crazy, out of one's mind. **2** [1990s+] a general intensifier meaning wonderful, bizarre, terrifying, according to context. **3** [1990s+] angry.

IN PHRASES

❑ **go mental** *v.* **1** [1960s+] to become insane, to have a mental breakdown or outburst. **2** [2000s] to have an uproarious time.

SE in slang uses

IN COMPOUNDS

❑ **mental giant** *n.* [1980s+] (*US campus*) a fool, an idiot. ❑ **mental hernia** *n.* [1970s] (*US*) **1** a fool, an idiot. **2** a mental breakdown. ❑ **mental job** *n.* [JOB *n.*[2] (4)] [1920s+] one who is or potentially might be insane. ❑ **mental midget** *n.* [1960s+] (*US*) a stupid person.

mentalist *n.* (*also* **mentaller, mentler**) [1990s+] (*UK juv.*) an eccentric.

mentler *n.* [pron. of MENTAL *adj.*] [1990s+] a crazy person.

IN PHRASES

❑ **do a mentler** *v.* [2000s] to act outrageously.

mentler *adj.* [MENTLER *n.*] [1990s+] insane, crazy.

mephepha *n. see* MAPHEPHA *n.*

Merc *n.* (*also* **Merk**) [abbr.] [1930s+] a *Merc*edes Benz.

merc *n.* [abbr.] [1960s+] a professional *merc*enary soldier.

Mercedes *n.* [the car of the same name and status] [1970s–80s] (*US black*) an elegant woman with good looks and an attractive figure.

mercer's book *n.* [SE *mercer*, a dealer in luxury textiles + SE *book*. Any Elizabethan gallant worth his name was in debt to his clothier] [late 16C–late 17C] debt; thus *in the mercer's book*, the state of being in debt.

IN PHRASES

❑ **drowned in the mercer's book** *adj. see* separate entry.

merch *n.* [abbr.] [1950s] the *merch*ant navy.

merchandise *n.* [euph.] **1** [late 17C; 1950s+] women as sex objects. **2** [1900s] (*US*) constr. with *the*, the real thing, the ideal thing, the ideal person. **3** [1920s+] contraband liquor. **4** [1930s+] (*drugs*) drugs. **5** [1970s+] a man, often a male prostitute, as a sex object.

merchant *n.* [mid-16C–18C; 20C+] a man, a fellow, esp. as an adept of a particular interest, [20C+] use is usu. in a variety of qualifying combs., e.g. *BLAG-MERCHANT under* BLAG *n.*; *BULL MERCHANT under* BULL *n.*[6]; *CAPER MERCHANT under* CAPER *n.*[2]; *FANNY MERCHANT under* FANNY *n.*[2]; *FEATHER MERCHANT under* FEATHER *n.*; *HOIST-MERCHANT under* HOIST *n.*; *HOP MERCHANT under* HOP *n.*[1]; *JUMP-UP MERCHANT under* JUMP-UP *n.*; LAY-DOWN MERCHANT *n.*; *LUSH MERCHANT under* LUSH *n.*[1]; *MUTTON MERCHANT under* MUTTON *n.*; *READER MERCHANT under* READER *n.*; *TIMBER-MERCHANT under* TIMBER *n.*; *TOOTLE-MERCHANT under* TOOTLE *n.*; *WOOD MERCHANT under* WOOD *n.*[1].

merchant banker *n.* (*also* **Swiss banker**) [rhy. sl. = WANKER *n.*] [1980s+] a masturbator; thus a general term of abuse.

merchant of eel-skins *n.* [? his slipperiness, the unlikeliness of their supposed commodity] [mid-16C–late 17C] one who only poses as a merchant.

merck *n.* (*also* **merk**) [the *Merck* pharmaceutical company] [1920s+] (*drugs*) cocaine.

mercy! *excl.* (*also* **for mercy's sake! mercy me! mercy sakes!**) [14C+] a general oath (esp. popular in the 1950s–60s camp gay world, with its overtones of a classic 'Southern belle').

mercy blow through *phr.* [for ety. *see* MERCY BUCKETS *phr.*] [1910s] (*Aus.*) thank you.

mercy buckets *phr.* (*also* **messy buckets**) [intentional malapropism of Fr. *merci beaucoup*, thank you very much] [1930s+] (*Aus./US*) thank you.

mercy buttercups *phr.* [for ety. *see* MERCY BUCKETS *phr.*] [1980s+] (*US campus*) thank you.

mercy fuck *n.* (*also* **mercy pussy**) [SE *mercy* + FUCK *n.* (1)/PUSSY *n.* (1)] [1960s+] (*US*) an act of sexual intercourse engaged in out of pity; thus also v.

mercy mary! *excl.* [MERCY! *excl.* + MARY *n.*] [1950s+] (*gay*) an excl. of surprise.

mercy percy *n.* [1930s] (*US*) an exciting performance.

mercy pussy *n. see* MERCY FUCK *n.*

meri *n. see* MARY *n.* (1a).

Merk *n. see* MERC *n.*

merk *n. see* MERCK *n.*

merk *v.* [2000s] **1** (*US black*) (*also* **mirk**) to leave. **2** (*UK black*) to surpass, in fig. use, to kill.

merkin *n.* [Early Mod. E *malkin*, a mop, thus the false pubic hair as worn by actors and prostitutes, now SE] **1** [mid-17C–18C] the female genitals. **2** [1990s+] a man who poses as the husband or lover of a lesbian who wishes to hide her real sexual preference [pun on BEARD *n.* (3c)].

mermaid *n.* [the mythical fish-women (based on the Greek sirens) reputed to lure sailors to their doom] **1** [16C–17C] a prostitute. **2** [2000s] (*N.Z.*) a police officer at a weigh station [because they are 'cunts with scales'].

mero chingon, el *n.* [Sp. sl., lit. the 'biggest fucker'] **1** [1950s–60s] (*US teen gang*) the leader. **2** [1990s+] (*US*) an exemplary or admirable person.

mero mero *n.* [Sp. lit. 'the biggest biggest'] [2000s] (*US black/teen*) **1** God. **2** a gang leader; thus ext. to any important/admirable person.

merry *n. see* MARY JANE *n.*[2] (1).

merry *adj.* [early 19C+] used in many expressions, e.g. *merry hell*, as an elaboration.

SE in slang uses

IN COMPOUNDS

▫ **merry-arsed Christian** *n.* [*merry-arsed*, cheerful + joc. reversal of CHRISTIAN *n.*[1]] [19C] a prostitute. ▫ **merry-begotten** *n.* [i.e. conceived when the parents were *merry*] [late 18C–19C] a bastard. ▫ **merry bit** *n. see under* BIT *n.*[1]. ▫ **merry bout** *n.* (*also* **bout**) [late 17C–1900s] sexual intercourse. ▫ **merry-go-down** *n.* [16C–17C] a variety of strong ale. ▫ **merry-go-up** *n.* [? its effects after 'going up' the nose] [early–mid-19C] snuff. ▫ **merry grig** *n.* [mid-16C–early 19C] a close companion. ▫ **merry legs** *n. see* MERRY BIT *under* BIT *n.*[1]. ▫ **merry-maker** *n.* (*also* **merry-man**) [19C] the penis. ▫ **merry-merry** *n.* [the cheeriness of the girls or the song] **1** [1900s–20s] (*US*) a chorus line. **2** [1910s] a song. ▫ **merry-thought** *n.* [18C] a turkey.

merry and bright *n.* [rhy. sl.] [20C+] a light, usu. in pl.

merrybones *n. see* MARROWBONES *n.*

merry-go-round *n.*[1] [rhy. sl.] [late 19C+] £1 sterling.

merry-go-round *n.*[2] [US racetracks are oval] (*US*) **1** [1900s–30s] a racetrack. **2** [1940s] a roulette wheel.

merry-go-round *n.*[3] [var. on RUNAROUND *n.* (3)] **1** [1920s+] (*orig. US*) an evasion. **2** [1970s+] (*US black*) one who is attempting to deceive or swindle another person.

merry-go-round *v.* [20C+] (*US Und.*) of a prisoner, to clear all administrative and bureaucratic procedures before being discharged from prison at the end of a sentence.

merryheart *n.* [rhy. sl.] [20C+] a sweetheart.

Merry Mac *n.* [rhy. sl.; ult. *Merry Mac's Fun Parade*, title of the comic section in the *Sunday Post* (publ. in Dundee) in 1960s–70s] [1990s+] (*Scot. drugs*) crack cocaine.

Merry-macka *n.* [lit. 'merry but thorny'; also mispron.] [1990s+] (*W.I.*) America.

merry old soul *n.* [rhy. sl.] [20C+] **1** coal. **2** a hole. **3** the anus [= HOLE *n.*[1] (1)].

merry widow *n.*[1] [Fr. *veuve*, widow + pun on *The Merry Widow* (1906), light opera by Franz Lehár] [20C+] Veuve Cliquot champagne.

merry widow *n.*[2] [a popular brand of condoms] [1920s–30s] (*US*) a condom.

merry wonder *n. see* MARY WARNER *n.*

mersh *n.* [clipping] [2000s] (*UK drugs*) unexceptional, average cannabis, lit. 'commercial'.

Mervin *n. see* MELVIN *n.*

Meryl Streep *n.* [rhy. sl.; ult. US film actress *Meryl Streep* (b.1949)] [1990s+] sleep.

merzer *n.* [abbr. *immerser*] [1980s+] (*Aus. prison*) a homemade piece of equipment for boiling water.

merzky *adj.* [? echoic of a 'myeugh' snort of disgust or Fr. *merde* + 'Slavic' sfx *-ski*] [1990s+] (*US teen*) dirty or nasty.

mesc *n.* (*also* **mezc**) [abbr.] [1960s+] (*orig. US drugs*) mescaline.

mescal *n.* [abbr., note Mex. *mescal*, a drink made from the fermented juice of the agave plant] [1950s+] (*drugs*) *mescal*ine.

meserole *n. see* MEZZROLL *n.*

mesh *adj.* [1990s+] (*W.I.*) well-dressed.

meshuga *n.* (*also* **meshuggina, mishuga, mishugenah, mishugeneh**) [MESHUGA *adj.*] [20C+] a crazy person, an obsessive, an eccentric.

meshuga *adj.* (*also* **mashugga, meshugenah, meshugeneh, meshugga(h), meshuggenah, meshuggeneh, mishugge**) [Yid. *mushuge*, crazy, ult. f. Heb. *shagag*, to wander, to go astray] [late 19C+] crazy, insane, eccentric.

Mesopotamia *n.* [SE *Mesopotamia*, the land between the rivers Tigris and Euphrates, lit. 'between the rivers'; although, much earlier, the Westbourne River once meandered through Belgravia, thus rendering the area 'between' that and the Thames, the implication is less geographical than racist; the Belgravia area was seen as the home of newly rich Jews. Oxford University jargon use is geographical, referring to that area of Oxford between the rivers Cherwell and Isis] [mid-19C] Belgravia.

mess *n.*[1] [SE *mess*, a sufficient quantity to make a dish] [early 19C+] (*US*) a large quantity.

mess *n.*[2] **1** [20C+] excrement, usu. canine or feline; thus *make a mess*, to excrete on a carpet, floor or similar unsuitable place. **2** [1910s–20s] (*US milit./prison*) food. **3** [1920s+] (*US black*) nonsense, rubbish. **4** [1920s+] (*orig. US*) an objectionable, ineffectual or stupid person. **5** [1930s–70s] (*US black*) something good or praiseworthy, if slightly confusing or disturbing [SE *mess*, a state of confusion or muddle]. **6** [1940s+] (*US black*) unspecified 'stuff' in general. **7** [1960s+] semen. **8** [1980s+] (*US campus*) male or female genitalia. **9** [1990s+] (*Irish*) foolish behaviour, fun.

mess *n.*[3] [abbr.] [1970s] (*US black/drugs*) mescaline.

mess *v.* **1** [late 19C+] to interfere, disturb [backform. f. MESS WITH *v.*]. **2** [20C+] to have sexual intercourse, esp. adulterously; thus n. *messing*. **3** [1910s+] (*US*) to fight. **4** [1930s+] (*US*) to defecate. **5** [1980s] (*US*) to gossip maliciously. **6** [1980s+] to tease, to joke. **7** [1990s+] to masturbate.

IN PHRASES

▫ **mess over** *v.* [1960s+] (*US black*) to harm, to mistreat, to annoy.

mess! *excl.* [MESS *n.*[2] (1)] [1910s–20s] a euph. excl. for SHIT! *excl.*

mess about *v.* (*also* **mess around**) **1** [late 19C+] to handle roughly, to mistreat, to swindle, to deceive. **2** [late 19C+] to indulge in varying degrees of sexual intimacy; usu. adulterously. **3** [late 19C+] to waste time, to fool around, to wander off the subject, to distract someone's attention [epitomized in Kenneth Williams's (1926–88) catchphrase *Stop messing about!* used in various Kenneth Horne BBC radio comedy shows and in the UK *Carry On...* films (1950s–80s)]. **4** [1920s–30s] (*US black*) to dance. **5** [1940s] to be involved with. **6** [1960s] to spend time with, to socialize. **7** [1970s] to assault sexually.

IN PHRASES

❑ **no messing (about)** [1930s+] a general intensifier, without a doubt, absolutely, certainly; often as *and no messing about*.

message *n.* [1950s–60s] (*UK Und.*) instructions passed on among criminals.

SE in slang uses

IN PHRASES

❑ **get the message** *v.* [orig. jazz use, but now general] [1950s+] to appreciate, to understand.

mess-around *n.* [1940s+] (*W.I.*) a cake made of flour that must be stirred for a long time.

messed (up) *adj.* **1** [1910s+] ruined in any sense, physically, emotionally or mentally. **2** [1950s+] (*orig. US*) extremely intoxicated by a drug or drink; one of a number of terms that equate extreme drunkenness with suffering violence. Many of such terms can also apply to the effects of drugs. **3** [1970s] injured. **4** [1980s+] (*US black*) troubled, suffering bad luck, wrong, unfair. **5** [1990s+] (*US black*) irrational.

messen *n.* [Scot. *messen*, a small dog; thus synon. with SE *cur*] [20C+] (*Ulster*) a contemptible person.

messenger *n.* [it passes the cheat a 'message'] [late 19C] (*N.Z.*) a false die, used by a cheat.

messer *n.* [MESS ABOUT *v.*] **1** [20C+] one who 'makes a mess', a bungler. **2** [1910s+] an 'amateur prostitute', one who while not actively swapping sex for cash, will take 'presents' from her admirers. **3** [1930s] (*US Und.*) a professional thug. **4** [1930s+] (*Irish*) an extremely incapable or irresponsible person.

Messjohn *n. see* MAS JOHN *n.* (1).

messorole *n. see* MEZZROLL *n.*

mess-up *n.* [MESS UP *v.*] **1** [20C+] a blunder, a botch. **2** [1910s] (*Aus.*) a fight. **3** [1920s+] an inadequate or incompetent person, a person with problems.

mess up *v.* **1** [20C+] (*US*) to ruin, to botch. **2** [1910s+] (*US*) to make a mistake, to get into trouble, to fail. **3** [1910s+] (*orig. US*) to beat up, to assault. **4** [1930s+] to ridicule. **5** [1930s+] to involve in. **6** [1950s+] to confuse, to make an emotional mess of. **7** [1960s+] (*US*) to play around, usu. in a sexual manner.

IN PHRASES

❑ **mess up someone's game** *v.* (*also* **mess up someone's action, ...play, ...style**) [GAME *n.* (2)/ACTION *n.* (4)/PLAY *n.* (2)/STYLE *n.*] [1970s–80s] (*US black*) to interfere in someone else's attempt at seduction.

mess with *v.* (*US*) **1** [19C+] to become involved with, to use, to fool around with. **2** [late 19C+] to harass, to annoy, to interfere with. **3** [1980s+] to laugh at, to ridicule, to tease.

IN PHRASES

❑ **mess with nature** *v.* [NATURE *n.* (2)] [1970s–80s] (*US black*) **1** to lose one's potency, esp. through excess use of narcotics or alcohol. **2** to interfere with a couple who are poised to have sexual intercourse. ❑ **mess (with) someone's mind** *v.* [1950s+] (*orig. US black*) to disturb or harm someone emotionally.

messy *adj.*[1] [1910s+] immoral, unethical.

SE in slang uses

IN COMPOUNDS

❑ **messy attic** *n. see under* ATTIC *n.*

IN PHRASES

❑ **get messy** *v.* [euph.] [1950s] (*US*) to have sexual intercourse.

messy *adj.*[2] [MESS *n.*[2] (5)] [1930s–60s] (*US black*) good, first-rate.

messy buckets *phr. see* MERCY BUCKETS *phr.*

mestee *n. see* MUSTEE *n.*

Met *n.* [abbr.] **1** [late 19C–1910s] the *Met*ropolitan Music Hall, London. **2** [late 19C+] the *Met*ropolitan Railway, part of the London Underground system. **3** [late 19C+] (*also* **Mett**) (*US*) the *Met*ropolitan Opera House, New York. **4** [1940s+] (*also* **Mets**) the *Met*ropolitan Police, serving London. **5** [1940s+] the *Met*eorological Office, responsible for weather forecasting, usu. as the *Met Office*; thus *Met man*, a weather forecaster.

metal *n.* [abbr. *precious metal*] **1** [late 18C+] money. **2** [2000s] a pistol, a revolver, a gun. **3** [2000s] a bullet, ammunition.

metalhead *n.* [SE (*heavy*) *metal* + -HEAD *sfx* (3)] [1980s+] (*orig. US teen*) a fan of heavy metal music.

metal mouth *n.* [1970s+] (*US campus/UK juv.*) a person with orthodontic braces.

mete *adj.* [Sp. *meterse*, to interfere in, to meddle] [20C+] (*W.I.*) meddlesome, interfering.

meter *n.* [the coin then required to operate a gas *meter*] [1930s–40s] (*US black*) a quarter, 25 cents.

SE in slang uses

IN COMPOUNDS

❑ **meter thief** *n.* [their targets never rise above gas meters, parking meters etc] [1960s+] (*UK Und.*) a term of contempt for a petty villain.

meth *n.* [abbr.] (*drugs*) **1** [1960s+] (*also* **meths**) the drug Methedrine, a *meth*amphetamine; thus *methed up*, under the influence of methamphetamine; *meth trip*, the experience of the drug. **2** [1980s+] *meth*adone. **3** [1990s+] marijuana. **4** *see* METHS *n.*

IN COMPOUNDS

❑ **meth fiend** *n.* [2000s] a regular user of amphetamine. ❑ **meth freak** *n.* [-FREAK *sfx*] [1960s+] (*US drugs*) a regular user of Methedrine or methamphetamine. ❑ **meth-head** *n.* [-HEAD *sfx* (4)] [1960s+] (*drugs*) a regular user of Methedrine or methamphetamine. ❑ **meth lab** *n.* [2000s] a laboratory used for the illicit production of methamphetamine. ❑ **meth monster** *n.* [-MONSTER *sfx*] [1960s+] (*US drugs*) **1** a person who has a violent reaction to methamphetamine. **2** a methamphetamine addict.

Metho *n.* [abbr. + -O *sfx* (3)] [1940s+] (*Aus./N.Z.*) a *Metho*dist.

metho *n.* (*also* **methy**) [abbr.] [1930s+] (*Aus.*) **1** *methy*lated spirits, beloved by extreme alcoholics. **2** a drinker of *methy*lated spirits; ext. as *metho fiend, metho king*.

Methody *n.* [mid-19C+] (*Aus./Irish*) a Methodist.

meths *n.* (*also* **meth, metha**) [1920s+] methylated spirits, usu. as drunk by alcoholic tramps or *meth(s)-drinkers*.

methy *n. see* METHO *n.*

met-pot *n.* [dial. *met*, a gathering, a dance, a fair] [20C+] (*W.I.*) a large pot used for cooking for parties, celebrations or any occasions requiring many servings.

metrop *n.* [abbr.] [late 19C+] a *metrop*olis; usu. London.

metros *n.* [1980s] (*US black*) metropolitan police.

mettle *n.* ['the mettle of generation', SE *mettle*, spirit, pluck] [17C–early 19C] semen.

metzel *n.* [Ger. *Metzelsuppe*, metzel soup, made with sausage] [19C] (*US*) a German-born immigrant.

Mex *n.* [abbr.; note late 19C–1940s US forces use *Mex*, any form of foreign currency, esp. that of the Philippine Islands] **1** [mid-19C+] (*US*) (*also* **Mexi**) a Mexican; a nickname for a Mexican. **2** [mid-19C+] (*US*) the Mexican/Spanish language. **3** [late 19C–1950s] (*US*) Mexico or Mexico City. **4** [1900s–10s] (*US*) Mexican money. **5** [1970s+] (*US drugs*) Mexican drugs.

Mex *adj.* [abbr.] **1** [mid-19C+] Mexican. **2** [late 19C–1900s] (*US*) second-rate, inferior; in measurement, half the length/weight/value, etc.

IN COMPOUNDS

❑ **Mex town** *n.* [1950s] (*US*) the area of a town populated by Mexican immigrants.

Mexicali revenge *n.* [the Mexican town of *Mexicali*] [1970s] (*US*) diarrhoea, as contracted by travellers in foreign countries.

Mexican *n.* [such people come from 'south of the border/Down Mexico way'] [1980s+] (*Aus.*) a Victorian as seen from New

South Wales, or a native of New South Wales or Victoria viewed from Queensland.

Mexican *adj.* [20C+] used in a variety of combs. to imply cheapness, inadequacy, stupidity, mediocrity and a dependence on donkeys. The stereotype of Mexicans in the US is uniformly negative.

(IN COMPOUNDS)

general uses

❑ **Mexican athlete** *n.* **1** [1910s+] (*US*) a person who exaggerates [he 'shoots the bull']. **2** [1930s+] (*US*) an unsuccessful candidate for a college or school sports team. ❑ **Mexican bankroll** *n.* [1940s–70s] (*US Und.*) a banknote of high denomination rolled around a large number of notes of small denomination. ❑ **Mexican Bogner's** *n.* [*Bogner's*, a fashionable brand of choice in ski-wear] [1950s+] (*US*) jeans worn as ski pants. ❑ **Mexican boxing glove** *n.* [1990s+] (*Aus.*) a knife. ❑ **Mexican breakfast** *n.* [1930s+] (*US, Texas*) a cigarette and a glass of water (alt. urination), i.e. nothing nourishing at all. ❑ **Mexican Buick** *n.* [the antithetical status of the cars] [1950s+] (*US*) a Chevrolet. ❑ **Mexican bush** *n.* [BUSH *n.*[1] (1)] [1940s] (*US drugs*) an inferior variety of marijuana. ❑ **Mexican Cadillac** *n.* [1960s] (*US*) an old but showily decorated Chevrolet. ❑ **Mexican carriage** *n.* [1950s+] (*US*) a donkey. ❑ **Mexican carwash** *n.* [1950s+] (*US*) washing the car by leaving it out in the rain. ❑ **Mexican cashmere** *n.* [1950s+] (*US*) a sweatshirt. ❑ **Mexican chrome** *n.* [1950s+] (*US*) **1** aluminium paint used to simulate real (and more expensive) chrome on a car. **2** any form of silver paint. ❑ **Mexican cigarette** *n.* (*also* **Mexican cigar**) [1910s+] (*US*) a (poorly made) marijuana cigarette. ❑ **Mexican commercial** *n.* [1940s+] (*US drugs*) average strength Mexican marijuana. ❑ **Mexican crack** *n.* [CRACK *n.*[7]] [2000s] (*US drugs*) methamphetamine. ❑ **Mexican credit card** *n.* [1950s+] (*US*) a piece of hose used to siphon petrol from another car into the tank of one's own. ❑ **Mexican dragline** *n.* [1960s+] (*US*) a shovel or spade. ❑ **Mexican filling station** *n.* [1950s+] (*US*) a hose used to siphon petrol from another car into one's own. ❑ **Mexican foxtrot** *n.* [1950s+] (*US*) diarrhoea, dysentery. ❑ **Mexican hairless** *n.* [pun on SE *Mexican hairless*, a breed of dog] [1950s+] an old, hairless tennis ball. ❑ **Mexican happening** *n.* [racial stereotyping, Mexicans supposedly put everything off until *mañana*] [1960s+] (*US*) something that never happens. ❑ **Mexican hayride** *n.* [1960s] (*US*) an overcrowded automobile. ❑ **Mexican jeep** *n.* [1940s+] (*US*) a donkey. ❑ **Mexican jelly bean** *n.* [the car bounces up and down on its special suspension] [1950s+] (*US*) a Chevrolet that has been lowered in the rear and fitted with a Venetian blind in the rear window. ❑ **Mexican lawnmower** *n.* [1960s+] (*US*) a hand-held tool used to trim hedges and grass. ❑ **Mexican lightning** *n.* [LIGHTNING *n.* (2)] [1970s] (*US*) tequila. ❑ **Mexican lipstick** *n.* (*also* **pasata grin**) [1990s+] smears of blood around the mouth of one who has been having cunnilingus with a menstruating woman. ❑ **Mexican look** *n.* [1910s] (*US*) a hostile stare. ❑ **Mexican Maserati** *n.* [1950s+] (*US*) a Mercury. ❑ **Mexican milk** *n.* [1970s+] (*US*) tequila. ❑ **Mexican motor mount** *n.* [1950s+] inner tubing used as a shock absorber, rather than the purpose-built material. ❑ **Mexican muffler** *n.* (*also* **cherry-bomb muffler**) [SAmE *muffler*, a silencer] [1950s+] (*US*) a homemade silencer made from a tin can stuffed with steel wool that is then attached to the car's exhaust pipe. ❑ **Mexican nightmare** *n.* [1960s+] (*gay*) gaudy ceramic crockery, typical of that sold to tourists in Mexico. ❑ **Mexican nose guard** *n.* [1950s+] (*US*) an athletic support or jockstrap. ❑ **Mexican oats** *n.* [euph. for BULLSHIT *n.* (1)] [1950s+] (*US*) nonsense, rubbish. ❑ **Mexican overdrive** *n.* (*also* **Georgia overdrive**) [1950s+] (*US*) coasting or freewheeling in order to save petrol. ❑ **Mexican promotion** *n.* (*also* **Mexican raise**) [1950s+] (*US*) a better job but one that brings no increase in salary. ❑ **Mexican quarter-horse** *n.* [1960s+] (*US*) a mule. ❑ **Mexican rig** *n.* [1960s+] (*US*) anything that has been poorly constructed. ❑ **Mexican schlock** *n.* [SCHLOCK *n.* (1)] [1960s+] (*US gay*) any art in poor taste, typically that sold to tourists in Mexico. ❑ **Mexican seabag** *n.* [1930s+] (*US*) a newspaper or paper bag in which poor sailors carry their belongings. ❑ **Mexican shower** *n.* [2000s] (*US*) a rudimentary wash, cleaning only the face and armpits. ❑ **Mexican sidewalls** *n.* [1950s+] (*US*) black tyres painted white to imitate expensive white sidewalls. ❑ **Mexican standoff** *n.* **1** [late 19C+] (*orig. US*) a situation in which two parties are at a deadlock, with neither party willing to back down from a stated position and neither party having a superior edge; the result is that both parties give in and walk off. **2** [20C+] (*US*) a partial victory or defeat, but one that still fails to provide a decisive outcome. **3** [20C+] a round in poker when no one is willing to open the betting or no one wins the pot. **4** [20C+] a head-on collision between two trains. **5** [1920s–30s] (*US*) execution by firing squad. ❑ **Mexican straight** *n.* [1950s+] any five cards and a knife in poker. ❑ **Mexican threads** *n.* [1950s–60s] (*US*) a stripped bolt that has been forced into a hole to cut new threads. ❑ **Mexican time** *n.* [1960s+] (*US*) poor timekeeping, unpunctuality. ❑ **Mexican toothache** *n.* [1960s+] diarrhoea, often contracted on a foreign holiday. ❑ **Mexican two-step** *n.* [1950s+] diarrhoea. ❑ **Mexican valium** *n.* [SE *valium*] [2000s] (*US drugs*) Rohypnol. ❑ **Mexican valve-job** *n.* [1950s–60s] (*US*) flushing the carburettor of a running engine with kerosene. ❑ **Mexican window-shade** *n.* [1950s–60s] Venetian blinds in the back window of a car.

pertaining to drugs

❑ **Mexican brown** *n.* (*also* **Mexican tar**) (*US drugs*) **1** [1960s+] high-strength marijuana. **2** [1970s+] heroin, usu. weak, inferior. ❑ **Mexican green** *n.* [GREEN *n.*[2] (3)] [1960s+] (*drugs*) a weak grade and type of marijuana. ❑ **Mexican horse** *n.* [HORSE *n.* (7)] [1970s+] (*drugs*) heroin, presumably from Mexico. ❑ **Mexican jumping beans** *n.* [1970s+] **1** (*drugs, gay*) amphetamines. **2** (*drugs*) barbiturates, esp. Seconal, made in Mexico. ❑ **Mexican mud** *n.* [MUD *n.* (3e)] [1980s+] (*US drugs*) heroin. ❑ **Mexican mushroom** *n.* [the psilocybe *mushroom* grows in Mexico] [1960s+] (*drugs*) psilocybin, psilocin. ❑ **Mexican red** *n.* (*drugs*) **1** [1960s+] a barbiturate. **2** [1970s+] a potent variety of Mexican marijuana.

Mexico *n.*

(IN PHRASES)

❑ **in Mexico** [1910s–50s] (*US Und.*) in prison.

mexicoon *n.* [SE *Mexican* + COON *n.* (5)] [2000s] (*US black*) a black man who pursues Hispanic women.

mexx up *v.* [? SE *mix up*] [2000s] to join, to form a partnership with.

mezc *n. see* MESC *n.*

mezonny *n.* [SE *money* + -IZ- *infix*] [1930s–50s] (*US drugs*) the act of arranging for and taking the delivery of drugs from one's dealer.

mezz *n.* (*also* **mighty mezz**) [the jazz musician and marijuana-dealer *Milton 'Mezz' Mezzrow* (1899–1972)] [1930s+] marijuana, orig. spec. that sold by *Milton 'Mezz' Mezzrow*.

mezz *adj.* [the positive reputation of *'Mezz' Mezzrow* (*see* MEZZ *n.*)] [1930s–70s] (*US black*) honest, dependable.

mezzroll *n.* (*also* **meserole, messorole, mezz's roll**) [MEZZ *n.* + SE *roll*] [1940s+] (*drugs*) a large, generously filled marijuana cigarette.

m.f. *n.* [abbr.] [1950s+] (*orig. US*) euph. for MOTHERFUCKER *n.*

m.f. *adj.* [abbr.] [1950s+] (*orig. US*) euph. for MOTHERFUCKING *adj.*

m'fucka *n. see* MOTHERFUCKER *n.*

m-fugging *adj. see* MOTHERFUCKING *adj.*

m.f.u.t.u. *phr.* [abbr., orig. WW2 milit., inscribed on B-17 bombers with a cartoon of General Hideki Tojo (1885–1948) getting 'the finger'] [1940s] (*US*) a term of abuse, *motherfuck you too.*

m.f.w.i.c. *phr.* [abbr.] [1970s+] (*orig. US milit.*) a term of abuse, *motherfucker who's/what's in charge.*

m.g.a. *phr.* [abbr.] [1970s+] (*Aus.*) Mediterranean gut-ache, an 'illness' supposedly contracted by Greek, Yugoslav and similar 'Mediterranean' immigrants to Aus., seen as innately lazier than their Anglo-Saxon counterparts.

m.h. *n.* [*mental health*] [1990s+] (*US*) a mentally unstable, insane person.

m.h.c. *n. see* MILE HIGH CLUB *n.*

miaow! (miaow!) *excl.* [such a conversation is SE *catty*] [1920s+] used by a third party when overhearing a pair of speakers engaged in malicious gossip.

mic *n.*[1] [abbr.; cf. SE colloq. *mike*, a microphone] [1960s+] a *mic*rophone.

IN PHRASES

▫ **rock someone's mic** *v.* [2000s] (*US black*) of a woman, to fellate.

mic *n.*[2] (*also* **mike**) [abbr.] [1960s+] (*drugs*) one *mic*rogram (one millionth of a gram), the basic measurement of LSD. An average dose of LSD is approx. 250 mics.

mich *v. see* MITCH *v.*

michael *n.* **1** [1910s–30s] (*US*) a hip flask [? the 'Irish' name *Michael* and thus stereotype of Irish drinkers]. **2** [1930s+] (*Aus.*) the vagina [play on *Michael Hunt*, i.e. CUNT *n.* (1); esp. used in joc. phr. 1930s+ 'Has anyone seen Mike Hunt?']. **3** [1940s–50s] (*US*) a 'knockout drop', as placed in a drink [abbr. MICKEY FINN *n.*].

Michael Caine *n.* [rhy. sl.; ult. the English actor *Michael Caine* (b.1933)] [1960s+] (lit. + fig.) a pain.

Michael Miles *n.* [rhy. sl.; ult. British television game show host *Michael Miles* (1919–71)] [1990s+] piles.

Michael Schumacher *n.* [rhy. sl.; Cockney pron. 'terbaccer'; ult. *Michael Schumacher* (b.1969), F1 racing driver] [1990s+] tobacco.

Michael Winner *n.* [rhy. sl.; ult. *Michael Winner* (b.1935), film director and latterly restaurant critic] [1990s+] dinner.

miche *v. see* MITCH *v.*

Michelin (tyre) *n.* [the tyre makers and their 'Michelin man' logo] [1950s+] (*W.I.*) **1** a bulla cake. **2** a dumpling. **3** a fat person.

Michigan *n.* [? anecdotal] [1910s] (*US Und.*) a confidence trick.

Michigan roll *n.* (*also* **Michigan, Michigan bankroll, Michigan stake**) [ROLL *n.* (2)] [1910s+] (*US*) a fake bankroll, a note of a high denomination around a large number of notes of smaller denomination.

mick *n.*[1] **1** with ref. to the given name, esp. as used in Ireland, and thus bearing the 'Irish' stereotypes of Catholicism, manual labouring and potato-eating; note milit. *the Micks*, the Irish Guards; any Irish unit. (**a**) [mid-19C+] (*orig. US*) (*also* **mickie**) an Irish person; usu. but not invariably derog. (**b**) [1920s+] (*Aus./US*) a Roman Catholic. (**c**) [1930s] a labourer on the roads. (**d**) [1930s+] (*US*) a potato. (**e**) [1940s] (*US*) as a generic, an Englishman. **2** [1910s+] (*Aus.*) in female senses [abbr. MICHAEL *n.*]. (**a**) the vagina. (**b**) the queen in a pack of cards [? from sense 2a]. **3** [1960s+] (*US campus*) anything easy, esp. an academic class or test [MICKEY MOUSE *adj.*[1] (4)].

IN PHRASES

▫ **at the micks** *adj.* (*also* **at the mix**) [pun on micks/MIX *v.* + ? ref. to sense (1a) above, a (rowdy) Irishman] [1960s+] causing trouble.

mick *n.*[2] [20C+] (*Aus.*) in two-up, the 'tail' of a coin; thus *mick*, to spin the coins so that they come up tails.

mick *adj.* [MICK *n.*[1]] **1** [late 19C+] (*orig. US*) Irish. **2** [1920s+] (*Aus./US*) Roman Catholic. **3** [1980s+] (*US campus*) easy.

mick doolan/dooley/doolin/doo/do *n. see* MICKEY DOOLAN *n.*

Mickey *n. see* MICKEY MOUSER *n.*

mickey *n.*[1] (*also* **mickie, micky**) **1** ext. or fig. uses of MICK *n.*[1], pertaining to Irishness and its stereotypes. (**a**) [mid-19C+] (*US*) (*also* **mikey**) an Irish person. (**b**) [1920s+] (*Aus./US*) a Roman Catholic. (**c**) [1930s+] (*US*) a potato, esp. a roasted sweet potato. **2** [late 19C+] (*Aus.*) (*also* **micky**) a wild bullock [? the stereotyped 'wild Irishman']. **3** [20C+] (*Irish*) (*also* **mick**) the penis. **4** [1910s+] (*mainly Can./US black*) a small bottle of wine or spirits [MICHAEL *n.* (1)]. **5** [1930s+] (*Irish/Aus./N.Z.*) the vagina. **6** [1930s+] (*US*) (*also* **mickey's**) a knockout drug, usu. administered via an alcoholic drink [abbr. MICKEY FINN *n.*]. **7** [1940s–60s] (*US prison*) a fellow inmate. **8** [1950s–60s] (*US*) a fellow, a person. **9** [1970s] (*US*) aggressiveness, macho.

IN COMPOUNDS

▫ **mickey-muncher** *n.* [1980s+] (*Aus.*) a man who performs cunnilingus.

IN PHRASES

▫ **act the mickey** *v.* [2000s] (*Irish*) to play the fool. ▫ **chuck a mickey** *v.* (*also* **throw a mickey**) [1950s+] (*Aus.*) to lose one's temper, to have a tantrum. ▫ **take the mickey** *v. see* separate entry.

mickey *n.*[2] [rhy. sl. *mickey* = *mike* = SPIKE *n.*[2] (1)] [late 19C+] (*UK tramp*) a casual ward.

mickey *adj.*[1] (*also* **micky**) [rhy. sl.] [late 19C–1900s] sick.

mickey *adj.*[2] [abbr. MICKEY MOUSE *adj.*[1] (1)] [1950s+] (*US*) something second-rate, corny.

mickeydazzler *n.* **1** [1990s+] (*Irish*) a ladykiller. **2** *see* BOBBY-DAZZLER *n.*

Mickey Doolan *n.* (*also* **Micky..., Mick..., ...Do, ...Doo, ... Doolin, ...Dooley, Doolan, Doolie**) [generic Irish name] [20C+] (*N.Z.*) an Irish immigrant; a Roman Catholic.

Mickey D's (rainbow steakhouse) *n.* (*also* **Mickey Dee's (rainbow steakhouse)**) [initial letters of *McDonald/Mickey D*] [1970s+] (*US black/campus*) a McDonald's hamburger restaurant.

Mickey Duff *adj.* [rhy. sl.; = SE *rough*] [1990s+] unwell, 'under the weather'.

mickey-fickey *n.* (*also* **micky-ficky**) [1990s+] (*US black*) euph. for MOTHERFUCKER *n.* (1).

mickey finn *n.* (*also* **mickey, mickey flynn, micky, micky-fine, mike finn**) [the saloon-keeper *Mickey Finn*, who ran Chicago's Lone Star and Palm Saloons *c.*1896–190? He, in turn, had supposedly picked up the recipe from voodoo operators in New Orleans; for a detailed history of Finn and his drug, see Asbury, *The Gangs of Chicago*, (1940) pp.171–6] **1** [late 19C+] (*orig. US*) a knockout drug, poss. chloral hydrate, mixed into an unsuspecting victim's drink. **2** [1940s] (*Aus.*) in carnival use, the person who goes out and touts for business. **3** [1970s–80s] (*N.Z. prison*) a sleeping pill. **4** [1990s+] (*US drugs*) any form of depressant.

IN PHRASES

▫ **slip someone a mickey** *v.* [late 19C+] (*US*) to render a victim unconscious through adding a sedative, esp. chloral hydrate, to their drink.

Mickey Mouse *n.* **1** in derog. senses [MICKEY MOUSE *adj.*[1]]. (**a**) [1930s–70s] (*US black*) a white person. (**b**) [1940s–70s] (*US*) a small, silly or inconsequential person. (**c**) [1940s+] (*US black*) commercialized music, esp. uninspired jazz music. (**d**) [1950s+] (*US*) a trivial, petty or unnecessary activity. (**e**) [1980s+] (*US*) foolish or nonsensical talk. **2** in rhy. sl. (**a**) [1930s+] (*orig. theatre*) a house. (**b**) [1940s+] a Liverpudlian [= SCOUSE *n.* (1)]. **3** [1940s+] (*US*) ref. to the orig. black and white Disney cartoons. (**a**) a black and white police patrol car. (**b**) a police officer. **4** [1950s+] (*US*) a watch [a line of watches manufactured in 1930s with a picture of *Mickey Mouse* on the face].

IN PHRASES

▫ **Mickey Mouse in the house, and Donald Duck don't give a fuck** [1950s+] (*US black*) a phr. used to encourage party guests to move to a new and more abandoned level of self-indulgence.

Mickey Mouse *adj.*[1] [*Mickey Mouse*, Walt Disney's anodyne, albeit hugely successful, cartoon creation, created in 1928; sense 2 very quickly becomes used primarily as sense 3] **1** [1930s+] (*orig. US*) second-rate, badly made, artificial; thus (*US black*) *Mickey Mouse music*, commercialized jazz or pop music. **2** [1940s+] small, miniature. **3** [1950s+] (*orig. US*) silly, puerile, contemptible. **4** [1950s+] (*US campus*) easy, facile.

IN COMPOUNDS

▫ **Mickey Mouse ears** *n.* [1970s] (*US campus*) siren lights on a police car. ▫ **Mickey Mouse habit** *n.* [HABIT *n.* (1)] [1970s+] (*drugs*) a limited addiction to or occasional use of heroin. ▫ **Mickey Mouse money** *n.* [1970s+] **1** any unfamiliar currency, incl. the UK's decimal coins in the immediate aftermath of their introduction. **2** counterfeit money. ❑ **Mickey Mouse ticket** *n.* [2000s] (*US prison*) a disciplinary report.

Mickey Mouse *adj.*^{2} [rhy. sl. = GROUSE *adj.*; ult. *see* MICKEY MOUSE *adj.*^{1}] [1960s+] (*Aus.*) excellent, wonderful, the best.

Mickey Mouse *v.* [MICKEY MOUSE *adj.*^{1}] [1960s+] (*US*) to fool around, to botch; often as *Mickey Mouse around*, *Mickey Mouse it*.

Mickey Mouser *n.* (*also* **Mickey**) [rhy. sl. = SCOUSER *n.* (1)] [2000s] a Liverpudlian.

Mickey Rooney *n.* [rhy. sl.; ult. US film star *Mickey Rooney* (b.1920)] **1** [1930s+] macaroni. **2** [1950s+] an eccentric, a mad person [LOONY *n.*].

Mickey Rourke *n.* [rhy. sl. = FORK *n.*^{1} (5); ult. *Mickey Rourke* (b.1956), Hollywood film star] [2000s] the penis.

Mickey Spillane *n.* [rhy. sl.; ult. popular novelist *Mickey Spillane* (1918–2006)] [1950s+] (*Aus.*) a game.

mickey T *n.* [ety. unknown; ? anecdotal] [1990s+] (*US black*) a woman who pursues powerful and/or wealthy men only.

Mickey the Mouse *n.* [MICKEY *n.*^{1} (1) + play on *Mickey Mouse* (see adj.)] [1930s] (*Aus.*) a Roman Catholic priest.

mickie *n. see* MICKEY *n.*^{1}.

mickser *n.* [MICK *n.*^{1} (1)] [1950s+] an Irishman who has emigrated to the UK.

micky *see also under* MICKEY.

micky bliss *n. see* JOHNNY BLISS *n.*

micro *v.* [abbr.] [2000s] *micro*wave.

micro-chip *n.* [rhy. sl. = NIP *n.* (1) + ref. to Japanese technological expertise] [1970s+] a Japanese person.

microdot *n.* [1970s+] (*drugs*) a small dose of LSD, usu. as placed on squares of blotting-paper.

mid *n. see* MIDDY *n.*

midden *n.* [SE *midden*, a dunghill, manure-heap, refuse-heap] [19C+] (*Scot.*) a filthy, slatternly person.

middle *n.*

SE in slang uses

(IN PHRASES)

❑ **in the middle** *adj.* [1920s+] (*orig. US*) in trouble, in a dangerous or difficult situation.

middle *adj.*

SE in slang uses

(IN COMPOUNDS)

❑ **middle cut** *n.* [1970s+] (*US black*) the vagina. ❑ **middle finger** *n.* **1** [1960s+] a prostitute's trick, involving the middle finger and the man's anus, to ensure that each client arrives at a speedy orgasm so that she can maximize her nightly earning potential. **2** *see* MIDDLE LEG below. ❑ **middle kingdom** *n.* [a pun on SE *Middle Kingdom*, in ancient Egypt, the 11th and 12th dynasties (22–18C BC), doubtless a back-handed tribute to the Victorian fascination with things Egyptian] [19C] the vagina. ❑ **middle leg** *n.* (*also* **middle, middle finger, middle stump**) [late 19C+] the penis. ❑ **middle name** *n.* [20C+] (*orig. US*) something one likes or identifies with strongly; esp. in phr. *… is my middle name*. ❑ **middle piece** *n.* (*also* **middle-pie**) [mid-19C–1900s] the stomach. ❑ **middle storey** *n.* [late 17C–late 18C] the stomach. ❑ **middleweight** *n.* [boxing imagery] [1970s] (*US*) a person, usu. criminal, of medium power and influence.

middle *v.* [SE *middle*, to put in the middle, in this context, of an illicit scheme] [mid-19C] to make a fool of, to cheat.

Middlesex clown *n.* [mid-17C–early 19C] an inhabitant or native of the county of Middlesex.

middlo *n.* [1990s+] a middle-class person.

middy *n.* **1** [19C–1930s] (*also* **mid**) a midshipman. **2** [1940s+] (*Aus.*) (*also* **midi**) a measure of beer, approx. 285ml (10fl oz), or the glass that holds it [the measure is 'middle sized'; however, note Hornadge, *Aus. Slanguage* (1986): 'In New South Wales a middy of beer is a small glass (10oz) while in Western Australia it shrinks [...] down to a 7 oz measure'].

(IN COMPOUNDS)

❑ **middy screamer** *n. see* ONE-POT SCREAMER *n.*

midge-net *n.* [SE *midge*, a gnat] [mid-19C–1900s] a woman's veil.

midge's knee-buckle *n.* (*also* **midge's dick**) [SE *midge*, a gnat] [20C+] (*Ulster*) something infinitesimally small.

midget *n. see* MEJOGE *n.*

midget from Harlem *n.* [1930s] (*US/NY short order*) a small chocolate soda.

midi *n. see* MIDDY *n.* (2).

midjic *n. see* MEJOGE *n.*

Midland Bank *n. see* BARCLAY'S (BANK) *n.*

midlands *n.* [19C] the vagina.

midnight *n.* [1910s–50s] (*US*) the point twelve in craps.

midnight *adj.* [MIDNIGHT (THE CAT) *n.*] [mid-19C+] (*US*) of people, black.

(IN COMPOUNDS)

❑ **midnight lace** *n.* [LACE *n.*^{1}] [1970s+] (*US gay*) a black man's penis. ❑ **midnight queen** *n.* [QUEEN *n.* (2)] [1960s+] (*US gay*) a white homosexual man who prefers black partners.

SE in slang uses

(IN COMPOUNDS)

❑ **midnight cowboy** *n.* [film title *Midnight Cowboy* (1969)] **1** [1960s–70s] (*US*) a male prostitute, esp. when posing as a 'cowboy'. **2** [1980s] (*Aus.*) a man who goes to a male prostitute. ❑ **midnight express** *n.* (*also* **midnight mystery tour**) [1980s+] (*Aus. prison*) the sudden night-time transfer of a convict. ❑ **midnight oil** *n.* [play on phr. *burning the midnight oil*] [1940–50s] (*drugs*) opium. ❑ **Midnight Revue** *n.* [1940s–50s] (*US gang*) a prostitute hired by a group of young boys. ❑ **midnight talk** *n.* [1980s+] (*Aus. prison*) the beating of a prisoner by officers.

midnight (the cat) *n.* **1** [mid-19C+] (*US*) a black person. **2** [1950s–80s] (*US black*) a particularly dark-complexioned black person.

mid-ocean *n.* [late 19C] (*US*) boiled eggs.

midshipman's watch and chain *n.* [late 18C–early 19C] a sheep's heart and pluck (the liver and lungs).

midway *n.* [carnival/fairground jargon *the Midway*, the central avenue along which the major shows and amusements are situated. The term originated in 1893, when the Chicago Exposition featured the *Midway* Plaisance] **1** [late 19C+] (*US*) the main street or streets of a town or city. **2** [1930s+] (*US black*) a hallway or corridor.

midzer *n. see* MADZA *n.*

mierda *n.* [Sp. *mierda*, SHIT *n.*] [1990s+] excrement.

miering *n.* [ety. unknown; ? Afk.] [1960s–70s] (*S.Afr. township*) money.

miff *n.* [an expression of disgust, i.e. 'Mmmpphh!'] **1** [early 17C+] a tantrum, a petty quarrel, a tiff; thus MIFFED *adj.*; *miffiness*, the propensity to take offence at the slightest justification. **2** [1900s] (*US*) a general term of abuse.

(DERIVATIVES)

❑ **miffy** *adj.* [early–mid-19C] tetchy, cantankerous, likely to take offence.

miff *v.*^{1} [MIFF *n.*] **1** [1950s] to become irritated. **2** [1980s] (*US*) to irritate.

miff *v.*^{2} *see* NIFF *v.* (1).

miffed *adj.* [MIFF *n.*] [early 19C+] annoyed.

miffy *n.* [? Fr. *maufé*, the Devil] [18C–19C] the Devil.

miffy *adj. see under* MIFF *n.*

mifky-pifky *n.* (*also* **moofky-poofky, moofty-poofty, mufki pufki**) [ety. unknown] [1970s+] (*US*) silly behaviour, esp. romantic or sexual.

mifty *adj.* [MIFF *n.*] [late 17C–mid-18C] apt to take offence for minimal reason.

mig *n.* [pron. of the SE abbr. *mg*] [2000s] a milligram.

miggle *n.* (*also* **miggies, miggles**) [var. MEG *n.*^{2}] [1940s–70s] (*US drugs*) marijuana.

mighty *n.* [early 19C] a pint of ale.

mighty *adj.*

SE in slang uses

IN COMPOUNDS

❑ **mighty dome** *n.* [1930s–40s] (*US black*) the US Congress building or any similar large, institutional edifice. ❑ **mighty mezz** *n.* see MEZZ *n.* ❑ **mighty mouth** *n.* (*camp gay*) **1** [1950s–70s] a fellator. **2** [1950s+] a gossip or one who boasts. ❑ **mighty quinn** *n.* [the Bob Dylan song 'The Mighty Quinn' (1966), esp. the line 'You ain't seen nothin' like the Mighty Quinn'] [1970s] (*drugs*) LSD.

IN PHRASES

❑ **mighty-come-a-tooting** (*also* **mighty come-a-right, mighty-come-a-shouting, mighty-come-a-whistling, mighty shouting, mighty whistling**) [20C+] (*US*) quite right, usu. preceded by *you're...* ❑ **mighty Joe Young** *n.* [the film *Mighty Joe Young* (1949)] [1960s+] (*drugs*) **1** an extremely heavy narcotics addiction. **2** a depressant.

Mike *n.*[1] [late 19C+] (*US*) **1** a familiar term of address to an unknown male. **2** a generic term for an Irishman.

Mike *n.*[2] see JOHNNY BLISS *n.*

mike *n.*[1] [abbr. *Michael*, the stereotypical Irish forename] **1** [mid-19C–1900s] a labourer, a hod-carrier, esp. when Irish. **2** [1940s–50s] (*Aus.*) a cup of tea.

mike *n.*[2] [joc. use of SE colloq. *mike*, a microphone] **1** [1940s] (*US black*) in pl., ears. **2** see MIC *n.*[2].

mike *v.* [MOOCH *v.*[1], but Hotten (1860) notes racial stereotyping: *Mike* is a generic term for an Irishman and Irish labourers were seen as congenitally idle] **1** [early 19C–1950s] to loiter, to 'hang about'; thus *do/have a mike*, to loiter, to waste time. **2** [1900s–30s] to steal, to make off with.

IN PHRASES

❑ **do a mike** *v.* (*also* **do a mick, do a mickey**) [1910s–60s] to escape, to run away.

mike bliss *n.* see MICKY BLISS *n.*

mike finn *n.* see MICKEY FINN *n.*

Mike Malone *n.* (*also* **Maggie Mahone**) [rhy. sl.] [1930s–80s] a telephone.

mike malone *adv.* see PAT MALONE *n.* (1).

miker *n.* [MIKE *v.* or Gloucestershire dial.] **1** [late 19C+] a loafer, a scrounger. **2** [1920s–30s] a truant.

mikey *n.*[1] [MIC *n.*[2]] [2000s] (*US drugs*) someone who volunteers to personally test illicit drugs.

mikey *n.*[2] see MICKEY *n.*[1] (1).

mil *n.* [abbr.] **1** [1960s+] a *mil*lion, usu. of money. **2** [1990s+] a *mil*ligram, usu. of a drug.

milch-cow *n.* [SE *milch-cow*, a cow 'in milk' + used fig. as an easy source of money] [late 17C–early 19C] (*UK prison*) a prisoner who is generous in bribing warders; one who is easily tricked out of money or property.

mild and meek *n.* [rhy. sl.] [20C+] (*Aus.*) the cheek.

mild bloater *n.* [mid-19C–1900s] a second-rate dandy, 'weak young men who keep bull-dogs, and dress in a "loud" stable style, from a belief that it is very becoming... .' (Hotten, 1864).

mildewed *adj.* [SE *mildewed*, tainted with mildew] **1** [late 19C–1950s] miserable, miserable-looking. **2** [1910s–20s] pitted with smallpox.

mileage *n.* [1960s+] (*orig. US*) **1** experience of life. **2** a criminal record.

mile end *n.* [rhy. sl.] [20C+] a friend.

mile high club *n.* (*also* **m.h.c.**) [1960s+] (*orig. US*) a notional 'club' of those who have enjoyed sex in an aeroplane. This has now been joined by the *mile-deep club*, those who have had sex while travelling through the Channel Tunnel between UK and France.

miler *n.* (*also* **myla**) [Rom. *meila*, a mule, ? ult. Lat. *mulus*] [19C–1900s] a donkey, an ass.

miles's boy *n.* [Bee (1823) cites a tax-collector called Miles, who employed a boy to check on people who might be attempting to default on their dues by moving away] [early–late 19C] 'a very knowing lad in receipt of much information' (*B&L*).

milestone *n.* [they stand at the side of the road] [early 19C] a country bumpkin.

SE in slang uses

IN COMPOUNDS

❑ **milestone inspector** *n.* [1920s–50s] (*tramp*) a professional tramp. ❑ **milestone-monger** *n.* [mid-19C–1910s] (*tramp*) a professional tramp.

milf *n.* [acronym for *m*om *I* would *l*ike to *f*uck; coined in movie *American Pie* (1999)] [2000s] (*US campus*) an attractive (older) woman.

milherm *n.* see MILLIHELEN *n.*

milihelen *n.* see MILLIHELEN *n.*

milish *n.* [abbr.] [mid-19C–1910s] (*US*) the militia.

militant *adj.* [weak use of SE] [1970s+] (*black*) aggressive, energetic, purposive.

military ceremony *n.* (*also* **military wedding**) [play on SHOTGUN WEDDING *n.*] [1910s+] (*US*) a wedding that is forced on the groom through his girlfriend's (soon to be bride's) pregnancy.

milk *n.* **1** bodily fluids. (**a**) [early 17C+] semen; thus *milk-pail, milk-pan*, the vagina. (**b**) [mid–late 17C] vaginal secretions. **2** as a drink. (**a**) [mid-19C+] (*US*) bourbon or beer. (**b**) [1990s+] methylated spirits mixed with water and drunk by down-and-out alcoholics [the resulting white 'milky' colour]. **3** [late 19C–1920s] a weakling [abbr. SE *milksop*].

IN COMPOUNDS

❑ **milk jug** *n.* (*also* **milk pan**) [late 18C–1900s] the vagina. ❑ **milkman** *n.* [late 19C+] **1** the penis. **2** a person who masturbates frequently.

IN PHRASES

❑ **make a milk run** *v.* [1970s+] (*US gay*) to frequent a men's lavatory looking for sex. ❑ **put milk in the coffee** *v.* [1940s+] (*W.I.*) to have sexual intercourse.

SE in slang uses

IN COMPOUNDS

❑ **milk bottle bottoms** *n.* see COKE BOTTLE GLASSES *n.* ❑ **milk can** *n.* (*also* **milk bottle**) **1** [late 19C–1900s] a baby. **2** [1940s+] usu. in pl., the female breasts. ❑ **milk factory** *n.* [1940s–70s] (*US*) in pl., the female breasts. ❑ **milk route** *n.* [1930s] (*US*) a female breast. ❑ **milk shake** *n.* [1910s–70s] (*US*) in pl., the female breasts. ❑ **milk shop** *n.* (*also* **milk walk**) [19C] the female breasts. ❑ **milk wagon** *n.* [1960s+] (*US gay*) in pl. the female breasts. ❑ **milk walk** *n.* [late 19C] (*US Und.*) a beggar's 'beat'. ❑ **milk-woman** *n.* **1** [19C+] (*Scot.*) a wet nurse; thus *green milk-woman*, one who has only recently given birth. **2** [late 19C–1900s] a female masturbator.

IN PHRASES

❑ **bring someone to their milk** *v.* [? image of a baby quietening when given its milk; ? a stubborn calf that refuses to drink but gives in when overwhelmed by hunger] [mid-19C] (*US*) to subdue someone, to bring someone to their senses, to make them accept authority; also *come to one's milk*, to come to one's senses. ❑ **do the milk route** *v.* [the image of a milk roundsman] [1970s+] of one who is searching for or selling sex to tour bus stations or other such places very late at night or very early in the morning looking for trade. ❑ **let the milk down** *v.* [breastfeeding imagery] [1970s+] (*US, South*) to reveal the facts after withholding them for some time. ❑ **milk and honey route** *n.* [1910s–30s] (*US tramp*) a rail route that is renowned for good hand-outs, esp. one passing through Mormon parts of Utah. ❑ **milk in the coconut** *n.* [mid-19C+] (*orig. US*) a puzzling fact or circumstance, a crux, esp. in phr. *that accounts for the milk in the coconut*; a phr. used to respond to someone's explanation of an event or action.

IN EXCLAMATIONS

❑ **milk and water!** *excl.* (*also* **both ends of the busk!**) [the ref. is to the female breasts and the vagina, which give respective milk and urine or vaginal juices; a SE *busk* is a corset, or the wood, stee or whalebone that stiffens it] [late 18C–early 19C] a toast, further defined as 'Both ends of the busk!'.

milk *v.* **1** in senses of taking illegally. (**a**) [16C+] to defraud, to extract money from. (**b**) [mid-19C–1900s] to intercept telegrams addressed to others. (**c**) [1930s+] (*Aus.*) to siphon petrol from a car (whether legally or not). **2** [17C+] to masturbate oneself or someone else, to cause to ejaculate [note in D'Urfey, *Pills to Purge Melancholy* (1719): 'But stupid Honesty; / May teach her how to Sleep all Night / And take a great deal more Delight, / To Milk the Cows than thee'; note MILK *n.*]. **3** [late 19C+] to add milk to tea or coffee. **4** [1900s; 1990s+] to laze around, to be idle.

IN PHRASES

❑ **milk a duck** *v.* [1930s+] (*US*) to attempt the impossible. ❑ **milk the chicken** *v. see* CHOKE THE CHICKEN *under* CHOKE *v.* ❑ **milk the lizard** *v. see under* LIZARD *n.* ❑ **milk the pigeon** *v.* [late 18C–19C] to attempt an impossible task.

milk bar cowboy *n.* [1950s] **1** a person, esp. a motorcyclist, who frequents milk bars. **2** a general term of abuse, usu. aimed at the young.

milken *n. see* MILL-KEN *under* MILL *v.*[1].

milker *n.* [MILK *v.* (2)] **1** [late 19C] one who intercepts telegrams addressed to others. **2** [late 19C–1900s] the vagina [it 'milks' the penis of semen]. **3** [late 19C+] a masturbator. **4** [1900s] an idler. **5** [1930s+] usu. in pl., the female breast.

milker's calf *n.* [SE *milker's calf*, a calf that is still with its mother] [late 19C] (*Aus.*) a petted, favourite child, a 'mother's boy'.

milkie *n.* (*also* **milky**) [late 19C+] **1** a milkman. **2** milk.

milking pail *n.* [note *double entendre* in D'Urfey, *Pills to Purge Melancholy* (1719): 'What Joys are found, / In Russet Gown, / Young, plump and round, / And sweet and sound, / *That carry the Milking Pail*'] [early 18C–19C] the vagina.

milk jug *n.* (*also* **milkie**) [rhy. sl. = MUG *n.*[1] (2a)] **1** [1920s+] (*Aus.*) a fool, a simpleton. **2** *see* MILK *n.* (1).

milkman's horse *adj.* [rhy. sl. = Cockney pron. 'crorss'] [late 19C+] cross, annoyed, irritated.

milko *n.* (*also* **milk-oh**) [SE *milk* + -O *sfx* (3)] **1** [20C+] (*orig. Aus.*) a milkman. **2** [1910s] (*Aus.*) dawn; the very early morning (i.e. milk delivery time). **3** [1940s] (*Aus.*) a cow-hand. **4** [1940s] (*UK drugs*) a mix of heroin and lactose.

milkshake *n.* [resemblance] **1** [1990s+] (*N.Z.*) a mix of bicarbonate of soda, used illegally in the hope of enhancing a racehorse's performance; thus *milkshake*, to administer such a mixture. **2** [2000s] (*N.Z. teen*) fellatio.

milktoast *n. see* CASPAR MILQUETOAST *n.*

milky *n. see* MILKIE *n.*

milky *adj.*[1] [mid–late 19C] (*UK Und.*) white; thus *milky duds*, white clothes; *milky tats*, white rags.

IN COMPOUNDS

❑ **milky duds** *n.* [mid-19C] white linen rags. ❑ **milky way (to bliss)** *n.* [mid-17C–mid-19C] (*UK Und.*) the female breasts.

milky *adj.*[2] [SE *milksop*] [mid-19C+] cowardly.

IN COMPOUNDS

❑ **milky beak** *n.* [BEAK *n.*[1] (1)] [mid-19C] (*UK Und.*) a drunken magistrate.

milky bar kid *n.* [the child advertising the Milky Bar, a sweet, was known as the *Milky Bar Kid*] [1980s+] (*Aus. prison*) a petty criminal.

milky way *adj.* [rhy. sl. = GAY *adj.* (6)] [1990s+] homosexual.

mill *n.*[1] **1** [mid-16C–mid-19C] the vagina [a play on SE *grind*/GRIND *v.* (1)]. **2** in (*UK Und.*) use [SE *mill*, covering a variety of engines and tools]. (**a**) [17C] a housebreaker. (**b**) [17C–early 18C] housebreaking. (**c**) [17C–mid-19C] a chisel. **3** [early 19C–1930s] a fist-fight [MILL *v.*[1] (3)]. (**a**) a prize-fight. (**b**) a fight, a brawl. sometimes a battle. **4** in sense of *going* or *passing* or *putting through the mill*. (**a**) [mid-19C] (*UK Und.*) the Insolvent Debtors' Court. (**b**) [late 19C+] any institution that acts to process its affairs by rote, rather than deal with them on their individual merits. (**c**) [1950s+] (*US drugs*) anywhere that pure heroin, purchased in bulk, is diluted and packaged for street sales. **5** in context of imprisonment. (**a**) [mid–late 19C] a tread*mill*. (**b**) [mid-19C–1940s] a prison. (**c**) [late 19C–1940s] a military prison or guardhouse. **6** [1900s] (*US*) a bar. **7** as a machine. (**a**) [1910s+] (*US*) a typewriter [it 'grinds out' the words]. (**b**) [1910s+] (*US*) an engine of an aircraft or 'souped up' car; thus *turn the mill*, start the engine [note WW1 Fr. sl. *moulin à café*, 'coffee-grinder', i.e. a machine gun, operated by a crank handle]. **8** [1930s] (*US*) by metonymy from sense 1, a woman.

IN COMPOUNDS

❑ **mill-dose** *n.* [mid-19C] (*UK Und.*) a spell of hard labour in prison. ❑ **mill-ken** *n.* [mid-18C] a lodging house. ❑ **mill-lay** *n.* [LAY *n.*[3] (1)] [late 17C–early 19C] breaking and entering for the purpose of robbery; thus *mill-layer*, a housebreaker.

IN PHRASES

❑ **dance the mill** *v.* [mid-19C] (*W.I.*) to walk on the prison treadmill. ❑ **mill on the green** *n. see* WIGS ON THE GREEN *under* WIG *n.*[2].

SE in slang uses

IN COMPOUNDS

❑ **mill-clapper** *n.* [SE *mill-clapper*, an instrument which by striking the hopper causes the corn to be shaken into the mill-stones] [late 17C–19C] a (woman's) tongue.

IN PHRASES

❑ **soak the mill** *v. see under* SOAK *v.*[1].

mill *n.*[2] [abbr.] (*US*) **1** [mid-19C; 1940s+] a *mill*imetre, esp. in the diameter of a tube or gun barrel [Latin, *mille*, thousand]. **2** [1930s+] a *mill*ion, usu. dollars. **3** [1960s] (*drugs*) $1000 worth of heroin [Lat., *mille*, thousand].

mill *v.*[1] [SE *mill*, to grind down, to break into small parts] **1** [mid-16C–19C] (*UK Und.*) to steal, to rob, to break open; thus MILL A KEN below; [late 18C] *mill a go*, to succeed in a robbery or theft; [mid-18C–19C] *mill a quod*, to break out of prison; thus n., *milling*, goods worth stealing. **2** [17C–19C] to smash, to break open, to spoil. **3** [17C+] to thrash, to fight, to overcome; to hit. **4** [late 17C–1900s] to kill, to murder. **5** [mid-18C] to consume.

IN COMPOUNDS

❑ **mill-ken** *n.* (*also* **milken**) [mid-17C–19C] a housebreaker.

IN PHRASES

❑ **mill a cly** *v.* [CLY *n.* (2)] [early 19C] (*UK Und.*) to pick a pocket. ❑ **mill a ken** *v.* [KEN *n.*[1]] [mid-16C–mid-19C] (*UK Und.*) to rob a house. ❑ **mill someone's glaze** *v.* [fig. use of GLAZE *n.* (1)] [late 18C–early 19C] to knock out someone's eye. ❑ **mill the glaze** *v.* [GLAZE *n.*] [late 17C–mid-19C] (*UK Und.*) to break a window, esp. as a means of entering a house.

mill *v.*[2] [MILL *n.*[1] (1)] [mid-19C] to sentence to the treadmill, to imprison.

mill doll *n.* (*also* **mill-dolly**) [MILL DOLL *v.*] [mid-18C–mid-19C] a prison, orig. the Bridewell in Bridge Street, Blackfriars, London.

mill doll *v.* (*also* **mill dolly**) [MILL *n.*[1] (5b) + ? SE *Doll*, a woman's name, a woman's job; ? although chronology mitigates against this, from MILL DOLL *n.*, where doll = woman = play on *bride*] [18C–mid-19C] to beat hemp in prison.

millennium dome *n.* [rhy. sl.] [1990s+] a comb.

miller *n.*[1] [MILL *v.*[1]] **1** [mid-17C–mid-19C] a housebreaker, a thief. **2** [late 17C–early 19C] (*UK Und.*) a killer, a murderer. **3** [early 19C] a vicious, intractable horse. **4** [early–mid-19C] a boxer, esp. one who relies on aggression rather than skill. **5** [1940s+] (*Aus.*) a cicada [the grinding of its legs].

SE in slang uses

IN COMPOUNDS

❑ **miller's reel** *n. see under* DANCE *v.*

IN PHRASES

❑ **give someone the miller** *v.* [mid–late 19C] to pelt someone with flour, grease or other rubbish.

miller *n.*[2] [JOE MILLER *n.*] [early 19C–1920s] **1** a joke, esp. an old 'chestnut'. **2** a joke-book.

miller's daughter *n.* [rhy. sl.] [1910s–20s] water.

Miller's point *n.* [rhy. sl. = JOINT *n.* (1)] [1970s–80s] (*N.Z. prison*) a cannabis cigarette.

milli *n.* [abbr.] [1990s+] (*US black*) a nine *milli*metre pistol.

millia murder! *excl. see* MELIA MURDER! *excl.*

millihelen *n.* (*also* **milherm, milihelen**) [pun on *Helen* of Troy whose face 'launched a thousand ships', in *Doctor Faustus* (1604) by Christopher Marlowe, or, for men, on the Greek god *Hermes*] [1960s+] (*US campus*) an imaginary unit of measurement to calculate female/male beauty; *milherm* is for men.

milliner's shop *n.* [19C] the vagina.

milling *n.* [MILL *v.*[1]] **1** [mid-16C–early 19C] robbing, stealing. **2** [early 19C] of a horse, kicking. **3** [early–mid-19C] a beating, a thrashing. **4** [early–mid-19C] (*also* **milling-bout, milling match**) boxing for money, prize-fighting. **5** [early 19C–1900s] fighting, usu. with the fists.

IN COMPOUNDS

❑ **milling-cove** *n.* (*also* **milling kiddy cove**) [COVE *n.* (1)] [early–mid-19C] a prize-fighter. ❑ **milling-panney** *n.* [PANNEY *n.*[2] (1)] [early 19C] a place where prize-fights are held.

million *n.* [abbr. of SE phr. *million to one*] [1950s+] a sure bet.

SE in slang uses

IN COMPOUNDS

❑ **million-dollar wound** *n.* [equivalent to UK *blighty one* (*see* BLIGHTY *n.*) in WW1] [1940s+] (*US milit.*) any wound that guarantees the victim a passage out of a war zone and back to the USA.

IN PHRASES

❑ **feel like a million dollars** *v.* (*also* **feel like a million big ones, feel like a million bucks, feel like a million seeds**) [1920s+] (*orig. US*) to feel excellent, very cheerful, extremely well, in the best of spirits, thus *taste like a million*, to taste very good. ❑ **go a million** *v.* **1** [1910s] to love very much. **2** [1910s+] to be utterly lost, in a totally hopeless position, at a total disadvantage. ❑ **gone a million** *adj.* [? coined by the profligate John Scadden, Prime Minister of Western Australia, (1911–16)] [20C+] (*Aus./N.Z.*) in a hopeless state. ❑ **go over like a million bucks** *v.* [20C+] to succeed absolutely, to do very well. ❑ **look like a million dollars** *v.* (*also* **dress like a million dollars, feel like a million dollars, look like a million, look like a million bucks, look like a million on a hoof**) [1910s+] (*US*) to be extremely attractive; extremely smartly/ fashionably dressed. ❑ **million to a bit of dirt** [mid–late 19C] a phr. used of a very sure bet.

milltag *n.* (*also* **milltog, milltug, milltuig, mill twig**) [Shelta *melthog*, a shirt] [early–late 19C] a shirt.

Millwall Reserves *n.* [rhy. sl.; ult. Millwall football club, based in Isle of Dogs, London] [1990s+] nerves.

milly *n.*[1] [abbr. MILLTAG *n.*] [20C+] a shirt.

milly *n.*[2] *see* NINE *n.* (2).

milly *adj.* [abbr. MILITANT *adj.*] **1** [1990s+] (*UK black*) aggressive, pugnacious; thus *get milly*, to become aggressive. **2** [2000s] (*S.Afr. gay*) mad, 'dizzy'.

miln up *v.* [proprietary name *Milne*, a firm of locksmiths] [1940s–50s] (*UK prison*) to lock into a cell.

milquetoast *n. see* CASPAR MILQUETOAST *n.*

milt *n.* [SE *milt*, the roe of the male fish] [19C] semen.

IN COMPOUNDS

❑ **milt market** *n.* (*also* **milt shop**) [19C] the vagina.

IN PHRASES

❑ **double one's milt** *v.* [19C] to ejaculate twice without withdrawing.

miltog *n. see* MILLTAG *n.*

milton *n.* [? pun on Gray's *Elegy written in a Country Churchyard* (1751) 'mute inglorious Miltons'] [mid-19C] an oyster.

miltonian *n.* [ety. unknown] [mid–late 19C] a policeman.

Milton Keynes *n.* [rhy. sl.; ult. *Milton Keynes*, town in Buckinghamshire, UK] [1990s+] **1** beans, usu. baked beans. **2** a homosexual [= QUEEN *n.* (2)].

milvad *n.* [Scot.] [mid-19C] a blow.

milvader *v.* [MILVAD *n.*] [early–mid-19C] to beat, to assault; to box, thus *milvadering*, a set-to, fight, boxing-match.

Milwaukee *adj.* used in combs. with ref. to the city's breweries.

IN COMPOUNDS

❑ **Milwaukee cider** *n.* (*also* **Milwaukee special, Milwaukee water**) [1950s–60s] (*US*) beer. ❑ **Milwaukee goitre** *n.* [1930s+] (*US*) a beer belly.

mim *adj.*

IN PHRASES

❑ **as mim as old Betty Martin at a funeral** [dial. *mim*, affectedly modest, demure, primly silent or quiet; the term is imitative of pursed lips. Whether this is the same *Betty Martin* as ALL MY EYE AND BETTY MARTIN *phr.* is unknown] [early 19C] walking in a prim, orderly manner.

mimi hill *n.* [Maori *mimi*, to urinate] [1980s+] (*N.Z.*) on a journey, an opportunity to stop and use a lavatory.

mimis *n.* **1** [1990s+] (*US campus*) sleep. **2** *see* MEEMIES *n.*

mince *n.* **1** [2000s] an act of wandering. **2** *see* MINCE (PIE) *n.*

mince *v.* [1980s+] (*N.Z.*) to work as a prostitute on several different boats in a single night; used by a *SHIP-MOLL under* SHIP *n.*[1].

IN PHRASES

❑ **mince about** *v.* [1980s+] (*N.Z.*) to loiter, to 'hang about'.

mince (pie) *n.* (*also* **mincers**) [rhy. sl.] [mid-19C+] an eye; usu. in pl.

mind *n.*

SE in slang uses

IN COMPOUNDS

❑ **mind detergent** *n.* [1960s+] **1** a psychedelic or psychotropic drug. **2** anything that, through the difficulty of its solution or comprehension, fig. 'bends the mind'. ❑ **mind-expander/-explorer** *n. see* MIND-BENDER *n.* ❑ **mind-bender/ -bending** *see* separate entries. ❑ **mind-blow/-blower/ -blowing** *see* separate entries. ❑ **mindfuck/fucker/fucking** *see* separate entries. ❑ **mind-opener/-spacer** *n. see* MIND-BENDER *n.* ❑ **mind-tripper** *n.* [TRIPPER *n.*] **1** [1960s+] (*US campus/teen*) someone seen as eccentric, odd, abnormal. **2** *see* MIND-BENDER *n.*

IN PHRASES

❑ **get one's mind right** *v.* [1950s–60s] to think clearly, to agree with. ❑ **have five minds to** *v.* [var. on SE *be in two minds*] [20C+] (*W.I.*) to be strongly inclined to do something (usu. rash). ❑ **have mind** *v.* [20C+] (*W.I.*) to possess courage, to be brave. ❑ **take someone's mind** *v.* [1940s–60s] (*US black*) to manipulate someone's mind, usu. for negative purposes.

mind *v.* [MINDER *n.* (1)] (*UK Und.*) **1** [20C+] to protect, to act as a bodyguard. **2** [1950s+] to bribe regularly.

SE in slang uses

IN PHRASES

❑ **mind one's own pigeon** *v.* [corruption of SE *pidgin*, concern, affair] [20C+] (*Aus./N.Z.*) to mind one's own business. ❑ **mind one's own tune** *v.* [1960s] to guard one's behaviour or speech. ❑ **mind the store** *v.* (*also* **watch the store**) [1920s+] (*US*) to take care of someone or something. ❑ **mind your own fish** *v. see under* FISH *n.*[1].

IN EXCLAMATIONS

❑ **mind your eye!** *excl. see under* EYE *n.*

min dae *phr.* [Afk. *min dae*, few days] [1960s+] (*S.Afr.*) used as a greeting in the S.Afr. army by national servicemen who have 40 or fewer days to serve; also the period of service itself.

mind-bender *n.* (*also* **mind-expander, ...-explorer, ...-opener, ...-spacer, ...-tripper**) [SE *mind* + *bend/expand/explore/open/* SPACE (OUT) *v.*[1]/TRIP *v.*[1]] [1960s+] **1** a psychedelic or psychotropic drug. **2** (*also* **mind-bend**) anything that, through the difficulty of its solution or comprehension, fig. 'bends the mind'. **3** a user of hallucinogens.

mind-bending *adj.* (*also* **mind-cracking, mind-crunching, mind-guzzling**) [MIND-BENDER *n.*] **1** [1960s+] amazing, fantastic, remarkable, orig. in the context of hallucinogenic drug use. **2** also in non-drug use.

mind-blow *v.* [BLOW ONE'S MIND *v.*] [1970s–80s] to shock, amaze, surprise.

mind-blower *n.* (*also* **mind-blow**) [MIND-BLOWING *adj.*] **1** [1960s+] something that is astonishing, remarkable. **2** a psychedelic drug. **3** a hallucinogenic drug-user.

mind-blowing *adj.* [BLOW ONE'S MIND *v.*] [1960s+] astounding, amazing, remarkable, orig. in the context of hallucinogenic drug use; thus adv. *mind-blowingly*.

minder *n.* **1** [late 19C+] (*orig. UK Und.*) a criminal's bodyguard, a 'strong-arm man', someone who guards stolen property. **2** [1940s+] (*UK Und.*) a pimp. **3** [1970s] (*UK Und.*) a young criminal's patron, who sets up crimes for his protégé to carry out. **4** [1980s+] extended to a variety of non-criminal milieux, e.g. *governmental minders, journalistic minders*.

mindfuck *n.* [SE *mind* + FUCK *n.* (1)] **1** [1960s+] a fantasy copulation. **2** [1960s+] (*orig. US*) an emotionally overwhelming experience, usu. through drugs. **3** [1970s+] (*US campus*) one who delights in manipulating others. **4** [1970s+] a psychotic individual. **5** [1970s+] deception, bafflement, confusion.

mindfuck *v.* [MINDFUCK *n.* (2)] **1** [1960s+] (*orig. US*) to manipulate emotionally; deceive, to tease, esp. while the victim is under the influence of drugs and thus less emotionally stable. **2** to subject to a fantasy act of intercourse.

(DERIVATIVES)

❑ **mind-fucked** *adj.* [1980s+] (*orig. US/US campus*) **1** drunk, under the influence of drugs. **2** emotionally overcome. **3** unintelligent.

mindfucker *n.* [MINDFUCK *v.*] [1960s+] (*orig. US*) a person or event that is totally confusing or amazing.

mindfucking *adj.* [MINDFUCK *v.*] [1960s+] (*orig. US*) baffling, confusing, amazing.

mindic *n.* see MENDIC *adj.*

mine *n.* (*also* **mines**) [1900s–10s; 1950s+] (*US Und.; latterly US black*) myself, me, usu. as *for mine*.

(IN PHRASES)

❑ **go for mines** *v.* (*also* **got to get mines**) [black var. on SE *mine*] [1990s+] (*US black teen*) to look after oneself, to indulge one's own interests.

mine! *excl.* [1980s+] (*US campus*) my fault!

mine of pleasure *n.* [mid–late 19C] the vagina.

minette *n.* [Fr. *minette*, 'pussycat'] [late 19C] fellatio.

minette *v.* [MINETTE *n.* (1)] [late 19C] to fellate.

ming *n.*[1] [MING *v.* (1) or, given the unpleasant taste, ? ref. to SF character *Ming the Merciless* in the series *Flash Gordon* (from 1936)] [1980s] a marijuana cigarette made of discarded butts.

ming *n.*[2] [MING *v.*] [1980s+] (*Scot.*) a smell, a stench.

ming *v.* [Scot.] [1970s+] (*orig. Scot.*) to stink; in fig. use to be very unattractive.

minga *n.* see MINGER *n.*

minge *n.* [Suffolk dial., ult. synon. Rom. *mingra*, note East Anglian *minge*, to drizzle] **1** [1910s+] (*also* **min**) women in general. **2** [20C+] the vagina; the female pubic hair.

(IN COMPOUNDS)

❑ **minge bag** *n.* **1** [1970s+] an unpleasant or disliked woman. **2** [1990s+] a miser, a general term of abuse. ❑ **minge mouse** *n.* [1940s–50s] a pubic louse. ❑ **minge-muncher** *n.* [1980s+] (*N.Z.*) a cunnilinguist. ❑ **minge wagon** *n.* [1980s] a flashy car seen as an adjunct to the seduction of foolishly impressionable young women.

(IN PHRASES)

❑ **ginge minge** *n.* [abbr. SE *ginger*] [1990s+] ginger female pubic hair.

mingelicious *adj.* see BOOTYLICIOUS *adj.* (2).

minger *n.* (*also* **minga**) [MING *v.*] **1** [1970s+] one who lit. or fig. smells, a 'stinker'. **2** [1990s+] an unattractive and/or stupid person.

minging *adj.* [MINGE *n.* or MING *v.*] [1980s+] **1** a general derog. term: disgusting, ugly, smelly, etc. **2** of a person, unattractive. **3** very drunk.

mingo *n.* [? MING *v.*; Lat. *mingo*, I make water] [late 18C–mid-19C] (*US campus*) a chamberpot.

mingo *v.*[1] [obs. SE *meng*, to have sexual intercourse] [mid-17C] to have sexual intercourse.

mingo *v.*[2] [MINGO *n.*] [mid-18C–mid-19C] (*US campus*) to urinate.

mingy *n.* [MINGY *adj.*] [20C+] a mean, ungenerous person.

mingy *adj.* [? SE *mean/mangy* + *stingy*] [20C+] mean, tight-fisted, miserly.

mini *n.* [abbr.; orig. created as *the* fashion statement of the 'swinging Sixties', more recently resurgent in the 1980s and 2000s] [1960s+] a *mini*skirt.

minibennie *n.* [1970s] (*US drugs*) **1** benzedrine. **2** amphetamine.

Minié rifle *n.* [the power of its effect; ult. SE *Minié rifle*, named after inventor Claude Étienne *Minié* (1804–79), which fired a 'Minié' (or 'minnie') ball] [mid-19C] (*US*) cheap strong bourbon.

mini-mini *n.* (*also* **minny-minny**) [Lat. *minimus*, smallest, but note Twi *mini-mĩnã*, a small, stinging fly + Hausa *míni*, smallness] [1950s+] (*W.I.*) small spots that one sees in front of one's eyes, either as a result of a blow to the head, or from the mild hallucinations that may accompany the smoking of 'ganja'.

Mini Moke *n.* [rhy. sl.; ult. the once-popular *Mini Moke*, a Mini Minor with a 'jeep'-style body] [1990s+] smoke.

minister's face *n.* (*also* **minister's head, minister's snout, parson's face**) [anti-clericalism] [mid-19C–1950s] (*US*) a boiled or roasted hog's head with the eyes and jowls removed.

mink *n.* **1** [mid–late 19C; 1960s+] (*US black*) a pretty, sexy young woman. **2** [20C+] (*US*) the vagina. **3** [1900s–70s] (*US*) a lecher or scoundrel. **4** [1940s] a sexual obsessive. **5** [2000s] (*Irish*) a traveller.

SE in slang uses

(IN PHRASES)

❑ **not for mink** see NOT FOR ALL THE TEA IN CHINA *under* TEA *n.*

mink and manure belt *n.* [1980s+] (*S.Afr.*) **1** the affluent rural areas that lie between Pretoria and Johannesburg. **2** affluent suburbs, typified by wealth and a love of horses, when found outside any city. Their inhabitants can be black or white.

Minnesota *adj.*

(IN COMPOUNDS)

❑ **Minnesota bankroll** *n.* [1960s+] (*US Und.*) an ostensibly substantial bankroll, of which only the visible outer note is high-denomination or, in some versions, even cash. ❑ **Minnesota thirteen** *n.* [the brand of corn used] [1920s+] (*US*) an illegal brand of bourbon.

Minnie *n.* (*also* **Minnie Apples**) [abbr.] [1910s+] (*US*) *Minne*apolis, Minnesota.

minnie five fingers *n.* [1920s] (*US*) the hand, as used in male masturbation.

Minnie Mouse *n.* [rhy. sl.; ult. the Disney character *Minnie Mouse* (created 1928)] [1940s+] (*Aus.*) the house.

minnow *n.* [SE *minnow*, the fish; i.e. small bottle/can] [1970s+] (*US campus*) a 340ml (12fl oz) bottle or can of beer.

minny-minny *n.* see MINI-MINI *n.*

minor *n.* [1990s+] (*UK black*) an unimportant matter.

minor clergy *n.* [? the blackness of their clothes] [late 18C–late 19C] young chimney-sweeps.

minor-league *adj.* [baseball imagery] [20C+] (*orig. US*) small-scale, modest.

minstrel *n.* (*also* **black and white minstrel, nigger minstrel**) [the drug's black and white capsules; thus a pun on the popular *Black and White Minstrel Show* (from 1960)] [1960s–80s] (*drugs*) Durophet.

mint *n.*[1] [8C SE *mint*, money. The term was wholly sl. by 16C, although *the Mint*, as a place, remained SE] **1** [16C–mid-19C]

(*UK Und.*) a piece of money. **2** [mid-16C–early 19C] (*also* **mynt**) gold. **3** [late 18C+] a great deal of money. **4** [1900s] a great deal.

(DERIVATIVES)

❑ **minted** *adj.* [1990s+] wealthy. ❑ **mintful** *n.* [1940s+] a large sum of money.

mint *n.*^{2} [numerous advertisements promoting products with 'a hint of mint'; note earlier MINTY *n.*] [1950s+] (*US gay*) effeminacy; usu. in phr. a *hint of mint*, a trace of homosexual tendencies.

mint *adj.* (*also* **mintox, mont, real mint**) [SE *mint*, unblemished] [1980s+] (*Can./US/UK teen*) a general term of thorough approval.

mint drop *n. see* BENTON'S MINT DROPS *n.*

minted *adj. see under* MINT *n.*^{1}.

mintee *n. see* MINTY *n.*

minter *n. see* AFTER DINNER MINT *n.*

mint hog *n. see* HOG *n.* (1a).

mintie *n.*^{1} [the advertising slogan 'It's moments like these you need Minties', launched by James Stedman-Henderson in 1922, for *Minties*, a peppermint-flavoured lollipop sweet] [1930s+] (*Aus.*) comfort, solace.

(IN PHRASES)

❑ **man with the minties** *n.* [1980s] (*Aus.*) a racing tipster.

mintie *n.*^{2} *see* MINTY *n.*

mint leaf *n.*^{1} (*also* **mint ticket**) [the colour of dollar bills] [1920s+] (*US*) a banknote, money.

mint leaf *n.*^{2} (*also* **mint weed**) [1970s+] (*drugs*) mint or poss. parsley leaves impregnated with phencyclidine (PCP) for smoking.

mintox *adj. see* MINT *adj.*

mint sauce *n.* [laboured pun on SE *mint* + *source*] [early–mid-19C] money.

mint ticket *n. see* MINT LEAF *n.*^{1}.

mint weed *n. see* MINT LEAF *n.*^{2}.

minty *n.* (*also* **mintee, mintie**) [? link to Fr. *minet*, an effeminate young man] [1940s–70s] (*US gay*) **1** an effeminate male homosexual. **2** a masculine lesbian.

minty *adj.*^{1} [MINTY *n.*] **1** [1950s–60s] (*camp gay*) fading, losing one's attractiveness, said of an ageing effeminate male homosexual. **2** [1960s] frequented by homosexuals. **3** [1960s+] effeminate in mannerism, if not actually homosexual.

minty *adj.*^{2} [MINT *adj.* (1)] [1990s+] (*US campus*) excellent, first-rate.

minus *adj.* **1** [19C] lacking, bereft of. **2** [mid-19C] absent. **3** [2000s] (*US campus*) as a negative retort.

minute *n.* [1990s+] (*US black*) a long time.

(IN PHRASES)

❑ **in a minute** [1970s+] (*US black*) a phr. of farewell, goodbye.

miraculous *adj.* [20C+] (*Scot.*) very drunk.

miraculous pitcher (that holds water with the mouth down) *n.* [late 18C–mid-19C] the vagina.

mirk *v. see* MERK *v.*

mirror man *n.* [he is always going to 'look into it'.] [1980s+] (*Aus. prison*) an officer who promises help, advice, information etc, but never manages to provide it.

mis *n.* (*also* **miss**) [abbr.] [late 19C+] **1** a *mis*carriage. **2** (*also* **mizz**) a *mis*ery, a state of unhappiness.

misbehave *n.* [rhy. sl.] [20C+] (*Aus./US*) a shave.

miscarriage *n.* [1970s] (*US*) a term of abuse for an incompetent person.

misdeal *n.* [card imagery] [late 19C–1900s] (*US*) a mistake.

miserable *adj.* [pun on SE *miserable/miser*] [mid-19C+] tight-fisted, grasping, mean.

miserables, the *n.* [late 19C–1920s] a hangover.

misery *n.* [its effects] **1** [early 19C–1930s] gin. **2** [1930s–50s] (*US*) (bad) coffee.

SE in slang uses

(IN PHRASES)

❑ **get the miseries** *v.* [1990s+] **1** (*US*) to be tetchy, to be irritated. **2** (*US black*) to be in pain, to be ill.

miseryguts *n.* [1950s+] a depressing, censorious person.

misfortunate *n.* [early 19C] euph. for a prostitute.

mish *n.*^{1} [Ital. *camisa*, a shirt] [mid-17C–1910s] (*UK Und.*) a shirt, a smock; a sheet.

mish *n.*^{2} [abbr.] **1** [late 19C–1940s] a missionary. **2** [1990s+] in sexual intercourse, missionary position. **3** [2000s] (*N.Z.*) hard work, in the sense of a 'mission'.

mish *v.* [MISH *n.*^{2}] [late 19C–1940s] to work as a missionary.

mishegaas *n.* (*also* **mishegoss, mishigoss**) [Yid.] [late 19C+] nonsense, obsession, tomfoolery.

mish-topper *n.* [MISH *n.*^{1} + SE *topper*, lit. 'shirt topper'] [late 17C–mid-19C] (*UK Und.*) **1** an overcoat. **2** a petticoat.

mishuga/mishugenah/mishugeneh *n. see* MESHUGA *n.*

mishugge *adj. see* MESHUGA *adj.*

mislain/misle/misli *v. see* MIZZLE *v.*

misper *v.* [SE *mis*sing *per*son] [2000s] to go missing.

Miss *n.* (*also* **Mrs, Ms, Princess**) **1** [late 16C+] a title used in comb. with a n. to express the subject's primary characteristic, e.g. *Miss Grind*, a very hard worker; thus 'Frenchified' as *Mademoiselle*. **2** [1920s+] (*gay*) (*also* **Mrs**) a title prefixed to a name to imply that the subject's homosexuality is known or obvious. The pfx was a staple of pre-Gay Liberation Front camp usage, e.g. *Miss Ugly*.

used with specific or metonymic proper names

(IN COMPOUNDS)

❑ **Miss Adams** *n. see* SWEET FANNY ADAMS *n.* ❑ **Miss Alice** *n. see* SWEET FANNY ADAMS *n.* ❑ **Miss Amy** *n.* [Folb, *Runnin' Down Some Lines* (1980), suggests source in Amy Carter, daughter of US President Jimmy Carter] [1960s+] (*US black*) a young white woman. ❑ **Miss Ann** *n.* (*also* **Miss Anne, Miss Annie**) [1920s+] (*US black*) a white woman; esp. when considered to be hostile or patronizing to blacks. ❑ **Miss Astor** *n.* (*also* **Mrs Astor**) [the wealthy *Astor* family, once social arbiters of New York] [1960s+] (*US*) **1** a woman who overdresses. **2** usu. mocking, an elite 'social leader' of a community. ❑ **Miss Big Stockings** *n.* [1950s] (*US black*) an attractive, well-built, conspicuous young woman. ❑ **Miss Brown** *n.* (*also* **Madam Brown**) [joc./euph. use of proper name] [late 18C–19C] the vagina. ❑ **Miss Bull** *n. see* JOHN BULL *n.* ❑ **Miss Carrie** *n.* [pun on *carry/Carrie*] [1960s] (*drugs*) a quantity of drugs carried on one's person. ❑ **Miss Cubba** *n. see* CUBBA *n.* ❑ **Miss Emma** *n.* [the letter *M*] [1930s+] (*drugs*) morphine. ❑ **Miss Emma Jones** *n.* [prev. + JONES *n.*^{1}] [1950s+] an addiction to morphine. ❑ **Miss Fine** *n.* [FINE *adj.* (3)] [1950s–70s] (*US*) form of address aimed at one who is considered to be overly self-opinionated. ❑ **Miss Fist** *n.* [1950s+] the hand, in the context of masturbation. ❑ **Miss Fitch** *n.* [rhy. sl. = BITCH *n.*^{1}] **1** [20C+] an unpleasant woman. **2** [1970s] (*US gay*) a 'feminine' male homosexual. ❑ **Miss Flash** *n.* (*also* **flash queen**) [FLASH *n.*^{1} (8)] [1950s–70s] (*camp gay*) a user of amphetamines or Benzedrine. ❑ **Miss Frosty Pants** *n. see* FROSTY FACE *n.* (3). ❑ **Miss Green** *n. see* GREEN *n.*^{2} (3). ❑ **Miss It** *n.* [1950s+] (*orig. US gay*) a greeting to a fellow homosexual man. ❑ **Miss Jane** *n.* [1950s] (*W.I.*) an effeminate man. ❑ **Miss Lashey** *n.* [? LASHER *n.*^{1}, but while this man also chases women, it is for gossip rather than seduction, thus the effeminate *Miss*] [1950s] (*W.I.*) a male gossip. ❑ **Miss Laycock** *n.* (*also* **Lady Laycock**) [pun on LAY *v.*^{1} + COCK *n.*^{3} (1)] [18C–late 19C] the vagina; thus anthropomorphized in 18C as a prostitute. ❑ **Miss Lillian** *n.* [Folb, *Runnin' Down Some Lines* (1980), suggests link to Lillian Carter, mother of President Jimmy Carter] [1960s–80s] (*US black*) a white girl or woman of any age, but usu. an older woman. ❑ **Miss Lily** *n. see* LILY LAW *n.* ❑ **Miss Lizzie Tish** *n.* (*also* **Miss Tizzie Lish**) [? anecdotal or a joc. use of a generic proper name] [1960s+] (*US*) **1** a woman who overdresses. **2** usu. mocking, an élite 'social leader' of a community. ❑ **Miss Lucy** *n.* [1970s] (*US black*) generic for a white girl or woman of any age, but usu. an older woman. ❑ **Miss Man** *n.* [MAN *n.*[1] (4)] [1970s+] (*US black gay*) the police. ❑ **Miss Molly** *n. see under* MOLLY *n.*[1]. ❑ **Miss Morales** *n.* [1970s+] (*US gay*) a Mexican homosexual. ❑ **Miss Morph** *n.* [MORPH *n.*] [1960s+] (*drugs*) morphine. ❑ **Miss Nancy** *n. see* separate entry. ❑ **Miss One** *n. see* MISS THING *n.* ❑ **Miss Peach** *n.* [PEACH *v.*] [1950s–70s] (*camp gay*) an informer. ❑ **Miss Piggy** *n.* [rhy. sl. = CIGGIE *n.*; ult. the character in the TV puppet series *The Muppets* (1976–80)] [1990s+] a cigarette. ❑ **Miss Placed Confidence** *n.* [19C] (*US, Asian*) venereal disease. ❑ **Miss Prissy-pants** *n. see* PRISSY-PANTS *n.* ❑ **Miss Right** *n. see* MR RIGHT *n.* ❑ **Miss Thing** *n. see* separate entry. ❑ **Miss van Neck** *n.* (*also* **Mrs van Neck**) [joc. use of supposed proper name] [late 18C–early 19C] a woman with large breasts. ❑ **Miss Xylophone** *n.* [the equation of protruding ribs and the metal bars of the instrument)] [1950s–70s] (*camp gay*) a notably thin person.

miss *n.*[1] (*also* **miss of the town, town miss**) [a heavily ironic use of SE] [early 16C–19C] a prostitute, 'a Whore of Quality' (B.E.); a kept woman.

SE in slang uses

DERIVATIVES

❑ **missing** *n.* [mid-19C] courtship.

miss *n.*[2]

IN PHRASES

❑ **give someone/something a miss** *v.* [20C+] to avoid seeing someone or doing something.

miss *n.*[3] *see* MIS *n.*

miss *v.*

SE in slang uses

IN PHRASES

❑ **miss one's figure** *v. see under* FIGURE *n.*[1]. ❑ **miss one's tip** *v. see under* TIP *n.*[5]. ❑ **miss the bus** *v.* (*also* **miss the A-train**) [20C+] to lose an opportunity, to forfeit a chance.

missee *n. see* MISSY *n.*

misses *n. see* MISSIS *n.*

missie *n. see* MISSY *n.*

missile *n.* [its 'explosive' effects] [1980s+] (*drugs*) phencyclidine.

IN COMPOUNDS

❑ **missile basing** *n.* [BASING *n.*] [1980s+] (*drugs*) a mixture of liquid crack cocaine and phencyclidine.

SE in slang uses

IN PHRASES

❑ **guided missile** *n.* [1970s+] (*US black*) the erect penis. ❑ **heat-seeking (moisture) missile** *n.* [1980s+] (*US campus*) the penis.

missing *n. see under* MISS *n.*[1].

mission *n.* [ext. of SE *mission*, 'the commission, business, or function with which a messenger, envoy, or agent is charged' (*OED*); the specific allusion is to the introduction to episodes of the TV series *Star Trek* (from 1966); the overall inference is of the seriousness of such an activity] [1980s+] (*drugs*) **1** a search for drugs, esp. for crack cocaine or cocaine. **2** a binge on crack cocaine.

IN PHRASES

❑ **on a mission** [1980s+] **1** (*US black gang*) searching for, in pursuit of, performing any gang-related activity, esp. killing members of a rival gang or simply penetrating their territory. **2** (*drugs*) looking for and/or bingeing on drugs. **3** (*US campus*) in search of.

SE *mission* house, in slang uses

IN COMPOUNDS

❑ **mission squawker** *n.* [1920s–40s] (*US tramp*) a mission evangelist. ❑ **mission stiff** *n.* [STIFF *n.*[1] (4a)] [20C+] (*US*) **1** a missionary worker. **2** a convert. **3** (*also* **jesus guy, mission bum, mission kid**) a tramp or vagrant who frequents charitable missions, looking for hand-outs, food and shelter, esp. one who pretends conversion.

missionary man *n.* [SE *missionary position*, considered the least adventurous of all the positions of love-making] [1980s+] (*US campus*) an uninspired lover.

missis *n.* (*also* **misses, missus**) [SE *Mrs*] [mid-19C+] one's wife; the mistress of the household.

Mississippi *adj.*

IN COMPOUNDS

❑ **Mississippi marbles** *n.* [1920s+] (*US*) dice, or the game of craps. ❑ **Mississippi mule** *n.* [its 'kick'] [1960s] (*US*) illicitly distilled, 'bootleg' bourbon.

Miss John *n. see* MAS JOHN *n.*

Miss Nancy *n.* [generic use of female name; NANCY *n.* (2a) is a later concept] [early 19C–1940s] an effeminate man, presumably a homosexual; thus *Miss-Nancyfied, Miss Nancyish*, effeminate, *Miss-Nancyism*, effeminacy.

DERIVATIVES

❑ **Miss-Nancyfied** *adj.* effeminate; prim.

IN PHRASES

❑ **talk Miss Nancy** *v.* [19C] to speak in an effeminate manner.

Missouri *adj.*

IN COMPOUNDS

❑ **Missouri-bake** *n.* (*US*) bread that is burnt on the outside but under-cooked inside. ❑ **Missouri bankroll** *n.* [coined by the Industrial Workers of the World (IWW or 'Wobblies'), who designed this form of 'bankroll' to foil the thieves who preyed on newly paid-off workers] [1930s+] (*US*) **1** a roll or wad of blank paper, cut to the same size as dollar bills, surrounded by a few real notes of high denomination. **2** also in fig. use. ❑ **Missouri featherbed** *n.* [late 19C–1960s] (*US, mainly Western*) a straw mattress. ❑ **Missouri hummingbird** *n.* (*also* **Missouri nightingale**) [1910s–20s] (*US*) a mule. ❑ **Missouri mule** *n.* [1990s+] (*US*) a blow to the testicles. ❑ **Missouri toothpick** *n. see* ARKANSAS TOOTHPICK *under* ARKANSAS *adj.*

Miss Thing *n.* (*also* **Miss One, Miss Thang**) **1** [1960s+] (*orig. US gay*) a homosexual man. also as greeting between such men. **2** [1970s+] (*US gay*) one's innate femininity. **3** [1980s+] (*UK black/campus*) any unnamed woman. **4** [1990s+] (*US black*) (*also* **Miss Thang**) a woman who is seen as arrogant and unpleasant.

Missus *n.* [mid-19C+] (*Aus.*) the trad. title of the wife of the owner or manager of a sheep station.

missus *n. see* MISSIS *n.*

missy *n.* **1** [late 17C+] (*also* **missee, missie**) a young girl, esp. as characterized by servants and sometimes derog. **2** [1960s–70s] (*US gay*) an underage boy. **3** [1990s+] (*US drugs*) cocaine [note cocaine is a 'feminine' drug, see GIRL *n.*[2]].

mist *n.* (*drugs*) **1** [1970s+] phencyclidine. **2** [1980s+] smoke created by a crack cocaine pipe. **3** [2000s] (*UK Und.*) a state of high excitement, drug-induced or otherwise.

Mistah Big *n. see* MR BIG *under* MR *n.*

mistake *n.* [euph.] [1950s+] an unplanned pregnancy and the child that follows.

SE in slang uses

IN PHRASES

❑ **and no mistake** (*also* **and no mistake about it, make no mistake**) [early 19C+] a general intensifier, certainly, without any doubt.

Mister/Mr for all combs. of Mister, the abbr. Mr has been used, unless no citations have been found with the abbreviation.

Mr *n.* (*also* **Don, Dr, Earl, Lord, Major, Master, Monsieur, Sir**) [mid-16C+] a title used in comb. with a n. to express the subject's primary characteristic, e.g. *Mr Grind*, a very hard worker.

used with specific or metonymic proper names

IN COMPOUNDS

❑ **Mr Anybody** *n.* [1940s] a generic name for an anonymous member of the public. ❑ **Mr Arnold** *n. see* ARNOLD *n.* ❑ **Mr Astorbilt** *n. see* ASTORBILT *n.* ❑ **Mr Average** *n.* (*also* **Mr Averageman**) [1910s+] the average member of the public.

❑ **Mr Bates** *n.* (*also* **Bates, John Bates, Johnnie Bates**) [? pun on *Mr. Bates*/SE *masturbates*, thus the individual is a JERK *n.*[1]] [1920s–40s] (*US Und.*) a potential victim, a confidence man's dupe. ❑ **Mr Big** *n.* (*also* **Mistah Big, Mister Big**) [1930s+] (*orig. US*) an important, influential person, esp. a 'criminal mastermind'. ❑ **Mr Block** *n.* [1930s] (*US tramp*) a gullible person. ❑ **Mr Blue** *n.* [? a blue elixir of morphine sulphate] [1970s] (*drugs*) hydromorphone, the basis of the synthetic opiate Dilaudid. ❑ **Mr Bobo** *n. see* PO-PO *n.* ❑ **Mr Boozington** *n. see* BOOZINGTON *n.* ❑ **Mr Boss Hoss** *n.* [1980s] (*US*) a slightly mocking ref. to a leader. ❑ **Mr Brown** *n.* [BROWN *n.* (3)] [1950s] a homosexual. ❑ **Mr Chad** *n. see* CHAD *n.* ❑ **Mr Charles** *n. see* CHARLIE *n.* ❑ **Mr Charlie** *n. see* separate entry. ❑ **Mr Chuck** *n. see* CHUCK *n.* ❑ **Mr Clean** *n.* [the character '*Mr Clean*' in advertisements for a brand of household cleaner of the same name, first marketed in late 1950s] **1** [1960s+] (*US*) an obsessively neat and prudish man. **2** [1970s+] (*orig. US*) someone who makes a point of portraying themselves (sincerely or otherwise) as free of corruption; esp. in politics, business, sport or other forms of public life in which a proclaimed moral stance is useful; ext. as *Miss Clean, Mrs Clean*. ❑ **Mr Cool** *n.* [rhy. sl. = TOOL *n.*[1]] **1** [2000s] the penis. **2** *see* JOE COOL *under* JOE *n.*[1]. ❑ **Mr Cracker** *n.* [CRACKER *n.*[3]] [1950s+] (*US black*) a white person. ❑ **Mr Cunningham** *n. see under* CUNNINGHAM *n.* ❑ **Mr Double Tripes** *n. see* DOUBLE TRIPE *n.*[1]. ❑ **Mr Do-you-wrong** *n.* [1970s–80s] (*US black*) a man who mistreats women. ❑ **Mr Eddie** *n.* [generic use] [1920s–50s] (*US black*) a white man. ❑ **Mr Fat** *n. see* FAT *n.* (2). ❑ **Mr Ferguson** *n.* [mid-19C] (*UK Und.*) a phr. used to announce that a policeman is present. ❑ **Mr Fish** *n.* [1930s–50s] (*US drugs*) an addict who volunteers to undergo a Federal cure in prison. ❑ **Mr Five-by-Five** *n.* [title of a 1942 pop song by Don Raye and Gene de Paul] [1940s] (*US*) a very short, fat man. ❑ **Mr Fixit** *n.* [a series of short religious films in 1950s featured '*Mr Fixit*', a carpenter who combined the mending of furniture with delivering pious homilies to the attendant children] **1** [1950s+] a general facilitator. **2** [1980s+] a DIY expert. ❑ **Mister Franklin** *n.* **1** [1950s+] a euph. for MOTHERFUCKER *n.* [initial letters]. **2** *see* BEN FRANKLIN *n.* ❑ **Mr Gotrocks** *n. see* GOTROCKS *n.* ❑ **Mr Green** *n.* [early 19C] a gullible man, a 'sucker'. ❑ **Mr Grim** *n. see* OLD MR GRIM *under* OLD *adj.* ❑ **Mr Grog** *n. see* GROG *n.*[1] (1). ❑ **Mr Gub** *n. see* GUB *n.*[1]. ❑ **Mr Happy** *n.* (*also* **Mister Happy**) [1980s+] (*orig. US*) the penis. ❑ **Mr Happy Helmet** *n.* [1990s+] the penis. ❑ **Mr Harding** *n.* (*also* **Mister Harding**) [SE *hard*] [20C+] (*W.I.*) a hard task-master, a strict superior. ❑ **Mister Hawkins** *n. see* HAWKINS *n.*[3]. ❑ **Mr Hickenbothom** *n.* [late 18C–19C] any nameless object. ❑ **Mr Hombug** *n.* [1980s] (*US black*) a security policeman, e.g. at a school. ❑ **Mr Hopkins** *n.* (*also* **Hopkins**) [pun on SE *hop*; note *Notes and Queries*, March 13, 1858: 'It originated from the ease of one Hopkins, who, having given one of his creditors a promissory note in regular form, added to it this extraordinary memorandum: It is expressly agreed, that the said Hopkins is not to be hurried in paying the above note'] [late 18C–19C] a lame or limping person; thus *don't hurry, Mr Hopkins*, meaning in US 'hurry up', and in UK 'don't bother to go too fast'. ❑ **Mr Horner** *n.* [HORN *n.*[1]] **1** [18C] a promiscuous man, esp. one who cuckolds others. **2** [late 19C] the penis [the object that does the cuckolding but note also HORN *n.*[2] (1a)]. ❑ **Mr Jones** *n. see* JONES *n.*[1] (1). ❑ **Mr Ketch** *n. see* JACK KETCH *n.* ❑ **Mr Lo** *n. see* LO *n.*[1]. ❑ **Mr Lushington** *n.* [19C] a state of drunkenness. ❑ **Mr Maiden** *n.* [early 18C] an effeminate man, who wears female clothing. ❑ **Mr Mason** *n. see* BENNY MASON *n.* ❑ **Mr Mention** *n.* [1980s+] (*W.I./UK black teen*) a person known as a popular figure or as a successful womanizer. ❑ **Mr Milquetoast** *n. see* CASPAR MILQUETOAST *n.* ❑ **Mr Money** *n.* **1** [1950s] a rich person. **2** [1960s+] (*US black*) a derog. name for a Jew. ❑ **Mr Moto** *n.* (*also* **Moto**) [the fictional Jap. detective created by novelist J.P. Marquand (1893–1960)] [1940s–70s] (*US*) a Japanese or Asian man. ❑ **Mr Much** *n.* [rhy. sl. = SE *crutch* = *crotch*] [20C+] (*Aus.*) the groin. ❑ **Mr Muscles** *n.* [1950s] (*US*) a well-built man. ❑ **Mr Nawpost** *n.* [one who, if hungry enough, would 'gnaw a post'] [late 17C–late 18C] a fool, a simpleton. ❑ **Mr Nice Guy** *n.* (*also* **Mr Nice**) [1960s+] a pleasant, amenable person, although that status carries a certain conditionality; thus *no more Mr Nice Guy*, also used ironically. ❑ **Mr Patel** *n.* (*also* **Mr Patel's**) [generic use of *Patel*, the most common Ind. surname in the UK and one borne by many of the Ugandan Asians who arrived in the early 1970s and began running such shops] [1980s+] the local corner newspaper/sweet shop or small grocery. ❑ **Mr Peanut** *n.* ['Mr Peanut' the dandified logo of Planter's Peanuts (created 1916)] [1960s–80s] (*US black*) a white man. ❑ **Mr Peeler** *n. see* PEELER *n.*[2]. ❑ **Mr Peter** *n.* [late 19C] a negro. ❑ **Mr Plod** *n. see* PLOD *n.*[2]. ❑ **Mr Prunella** *n.* [SE *prunella*, a strong textile, orig. silk, commonly used for gowns worn by clergymen, barristers and graduates] [late 18C–early 19C] a parson. ❑ **Mr Richard** *n. see* RICHARD *n.* (2). ❑ **Mr Right** *n. see* separate entry. ❑ **Mr Roper** *n.* [his primary tool] [mid-17C–mid-18C] the hangman. ❑ **Mr Sin** *n.* [1970s–80s] (*US black, Los Angeles*) a member of the vice squad. ❑ **Mr Six-by-six** *n.* [1950s] (*US*) a very large man. ❑ **Mr Smoke-a-Bowl** *n.* [2000s] (*US drugs/teen*) a regular smoker of marijuana. ❑ **Mr Speaker** *n.* (*also* **Mister Speaker**) [its noise + the political office of the *Speaker*, who 'lays down the law' in the US House of Representatives or the British Parliament; 1940s+ use is US black] [mid–late 19C; 1940s] (*US*) a revolver, a pistol. ❑ **Mr Stitch** *n.* [early 18C] a tailor. ❑ **Mr Switch** *n.* [SE *switch*, a whip] [early 18C] a coachman. ❑ **Mr T** *n.* [ety. unknown; ? anecdotal] [1950s+] (*W.I., Rasta*) the boss. ❑ **Mr Ten Per Cent** *n.* [1920s+] (*orig. US*) **1** an agent, usu. in show business, who takes 10% (at least) of their client's earnings. **2** a middleman, esp. between interest groups and politicians, who arranges 'favours' and directs influence for some cut of the subsequent profits. ❑ **Mr Thingstable** *n.* [late 18C–early 19C] 'Mr Constable, a ludicrous affectation of delicacy in the avoiding the pronunciation of the first syllable in the title of that officer, which in sound has some similarity to an indecent monosyllable' (Grose, 1785). ❑ **Mr Thomas** *n. see* UNCLE TOM *n.* ❑ **Mr Three Balls** *n. see* THREE BALLS *n.* ❑ **Mr Tom** *n.* **1** [1970s] (*US black*) the penis. **2** *see* UNCLE TOM *n.* ❑ **Mr Twenty-six** *n.* [1960s–70s] (*drugs*) a 26-gauge hypodermic syringe. ❑ **Mr Two-to-one** *n.* [early 19C] (*UK Und.*) a pawnbroker. ❑ **Mr Warner** *n.* [var. on MARY WARNER *n.*] [1950s–70s] (*drugs*) a marijuana smoker. ❑ **Mr Whipple** *n.* [1990s+] (*US black/drugs*) phencyclidine mixed with formaldehyde. ❑ **Mr Whiskers** *n.* [the trad. portrait of a be-whiskered *Uncle Sam*] [1930s–60s] (*US*) the American government or its law enforcement agencies. ❑ **Mr Wiggins** *n.* [early 19C] a fool, a simpleton. ❑ **Mr Wigsby** *n.* (*also* **wigsby, wigster**) [late 18C–early 19C] a man wearing a wig. ❑ **Mr Wind** *n.* [1930s+] (*US black*) chilly winter winds, esp. as experienced in northern cities. ❑ **Mr Wobbly** *n. see* COMRADE WOBBLY *n.* ❑ **Mr Wong** *n. see* WONG *n.*[1]. ❑ **Mr Wood** *n.* (*also* **Charlie Wood**) [1930s+] a police truncheon. ❑ **Mr Zip-Zip** *n.* [title of a 1917 pop song] [1910s–40s] (*US*) a barber.

IN PHRASES

❑ **Mr Knap is concerned** **1** [19C] (*also* **Mr Knap has been there**) of a woman, pregnant [KNAPPED *adj.*]. **2** [early 19C] (*UK Und.*) this is a matter involving theft [KNAP *v.* (4)]. ❑ **Mr Nash is concerned** *see under* NASH *v.*[1] ❑ **Mr Palmer and his five sons** *n.* [1950s+] (*orig. gay*) the hand, used for masturbation. ❑ **Mr Palmer is concerned** *see under* PALM *v.* ❑ **Mr Pullen is concerned** *see under* PULL *v.*

mister *n.* **1** [20C+] (*US*) a form of address to a man whose proper name one does not know. **2** [1980s] used of a homosexual man considered neither pleasant nor attractive. **3** [1990s+] (*US drugs*) heroin [heroin is a 'masculine' drug; see BOY *n.*[2] (1)].

Mr Charlie *n.* (*also* **Massa Charley, Massa Charlie, Mister Charley, Mister Charlie, Mr. Charley**) [SE *Mr* + generic 'white' name *Charlie*] **1** [1920s+] (*US black*) any white man. **2** [1970s] thus the man in power.

IN PHRASES

❑ **fast-talking charlie** *n.* [1950s+] (*US black*) a Jew, esp. a Jewish storekeeper.

Mr Foot's horse *n.*

IN PHRASES

❑ **take Mr Foot's horse** *v.* (*also* **travel by Mr. Foot's horse**) [early 19C] to go on foot.

mister-man *n.* [1990s+] (*W.I.*) a term of respect.

mister-me-friend *n.* (*also* **mister-me-man**) [1940s–50s] (*Irish*) a person, an acquaintance.

Mr Right *n.* (*also* **Miss Right**) [mid-19C+] the ideal lover, husband, wife, boy- or girlfriend for anyone so searching; also used ironically.

Mistress Princum Prancum *n.* (*also* **Mrs Princum Prancum**) [PRINK *v.* (1)] [late 18C–mid-19C] a woman who is preoccupied by turning herself out neatly, and maintaining a concomitantly 'precise' character.

mit *n. see* MITT *n.*

mitch *n.* [1990s+] (*US Und.*) a fake wad of money used in a confidence trick.

mitch *v.* (*also* **mich, miche, mitche**) [synon. UK dial.] [late 19C+] (*Irish*) to run off, to abandon one's duties, to play truant.

mitcher *n.* [16C] a petty thief.

mite *n.* [SE *mite*, a tiny insect found in cheese] **1** [late 18C–19C] (*also* **mitey**) a cheesemonger. **2** [mid-19C+] a whit or jot, a bit [SE 14C–mid-17C]. **3** [mid-19C+] a particle, a tiny piece [SE 17C]. **4** [1950s] a farthing.

mitigated afflictions *n. see* AFFLICTIONS *n.*

mitre *n.* [SE *mitre*, a bishop's ceremonial headgear] [early 19C] (*US Und.*) a hat.

mitred *adj.* [mid-19C] (*UK Und.*) standing on the gallows wearing a hood, thus awaiting execution by hanging.

mitt *n.* (*also* **mit**) [abbr. SE *mitten*] **1** [early 19C+] (*Aus./US*) usu. in pl., a glove; often a boxing glove. **2** [late 19C–1960s] (*US*) a hand of cards. **3** [late 19C+] (*US*) usu. in pl., the hand. **4** [1910s] (*US prison*) in pl., handcuffs. **5** [1910s–30s] (*US tramp*) usu. in pl, a tramp who has lost one or both hands. **6** [1980s] (*US Und.*) a roll of money.

DERIVATIVES

❑ **mitted** *adj.* [1910s–40s] (*US Und.*) armed.

IN COMPOUNDS

❑ **mitt artist** *n.* [1900s] (*US*) a prizefighter. ❑ **mitt broad** *n.* (*also* **mit artist**) [BROAD *n.*[2] (3)] [1920s–30s] (*US Und.*) a fortune teller, a palm-reader. ❑ **mitt camp** *n.* [1920s–80s] a palmist's or fortune-teller's establishment, tent etc. ❑ **mitt joint** *n.* [JOINT *n.* (3)] **1** [1910s–30s] (*US*) a crooked gambling establishment. **2** [1920s–80s] a palmist's or fortune-teller's establishment, tent etc. ❑ **mitt-juggler** *n.* [1900s] a prize-fighter, a boxer. ❑ **mitt man** *n.* **1** [late 19C–1950s] (*US black*) a religious charlatan who uses his flock's credulity to make himself a sumptuous income. **2** [1960s] (*US Und.*) a confidence man. ❑ **mitt pounding** *n.* [1930s–40s] (*US black*) applause, clapping. ❑ **mitt-pusher** *n.* [1900s–20s] (*US*) a boxer. ❑ **mitt-reader** *n.* [1920s+] (*US*) a fortune-teller, a palmist. ❑ **mitt store** *n.* [1940s] (*US Und.*) a form of confidence trick in which a supposedly legitimate business masquerades as a front for crooked poker games (ostensibly being played 'just to pass the time'). The victim is 'mitted', i.e. dealt into such a game and fleeced of his money.

IN PHRASES

❑ **big mitt** *n.* [1900s–40s] (*US Und.*) **1** a form of swindling involving the use of a stacked hand while playing poker. **2** as *big mitt man*, a confidence trickster. ❑ **chance one's mitt** *v.* [var. on CHANCE ONE'S ARM *under* ARM *n.*] [1900s–30s] to take risks. ❑ **chilly mitt** *n.* [1900s] (*US*) constr. with *the*, a rejection, a snub, usu. in phr. *get/give the chilly mitt*. ❑ **cold mitt** *n.* [1920s] (*US*) a snub, a rejection. ❑ **frozen mitt** *n.* (*also* **frozen face, frozen mitt, frozen mitten, frozen word, icy mitt**) [late 19C+] (*US*) a rejection, an unfriendly reception. ❑ **give someone the mitt** *v.* (*also* **give someone the frosty hand, ...the hand, ...the icy mit**) **1** [late 19C] to say goodbye. **2** [late 19C–1940s] (*US*) to reject, esp. in the context of a proposal of marriage. ❑ **greased mitt** *n.* [GREASE *v.*[1]] [1920s–40s] (*US*) anyone who has been bribed. ❑ **grease one's mitts** *v.* [20C+] (*US*) to accept/solicit bribes; thus *grease someone's mitts*, to bribe. ❑ **hand someone the mitt** *v.* (*also* **hand someone the mitten**) [1900s–20s] (*US*) to reject, to turn down, to dismiss. ❑ **throw the mitt(s)** *v.* [1900s–40s] (*US Und.*) to pick pockets.

mitt *v.* [MITT *n.*] **1** [1900s–20s] (*US*) to punch. **2** [1900s–60s] (*also* **mit**) to shake hands, or to press something into someone's hand, e.g., a bribe. **3** [1910s–50s] (*US Und.*) to handcuff, to arrest. **4** [1930s–40s] to wave to.

IN PHRASES

❑ **mitt in** *v.* [1900s–50s] (*US Und.*) to inveigle someone into a cheating card game.

IN EXCLAMATIONS

❑ **mitt me!** [1930s–40s] (*US*) shake hands, esp. in context of congratulations.

mitten *n.* **1** [19C+] usu. in pl., the hand, esp. the fist. **2** [mid-19C+] (*US*) a rejection or dismissal; usu. in phrs. below. **3** [mid-19C+] a boxing glove; usu. in pl., thus *mitten-mill*, a prize-fight. **4** [late 19C–1930s] a handcuff; usu. in pl. **5** [1920s] (*US Und.*) a knuckle duster.

IN COMPOUNDS

❑ **mitten queen** *n.* [-QUEEN *sfx* (3)] [1990s+] (*US gay*) a man who masturbates other men.

IN PHRASES

❑ **get the mitten** *v.* **1** [mid-19C] (*US campus*) to be expelled from a college. **2** [mid–late 19C] (*US*) to be turned down as a suitor, to be rejected. **3** [late 19C] to be dismissed from employment. ❑ **give someone the mitten** *v.* [mid-19C–1900s] (*US*) to reject a proposal of marriage, to end a relationship. ❑ **tip someone the mitten** *v.* [late 19C] to dismiss from a job.

mitten *v.* [MITTEN *n.*] **1** [mid–late 19C] (*US*) to seize or grab; usu. as *mitten onto*. **2** [late 19C] to reject (someone) as a lover.

mittflop *v.* [MITT *n.* (3) + SE *flop*] [1930s–40s] (*orig. US milit.*) to ingratiate oneself by doing favours; thus *mittflopper*.

mittglom *v.* [MITT *n.* (3) + GLOM *v.* (1)] [1910s–50s] (*US, orig. milit.*) to ingratiate oneself by doing favours; thus *mitt-glommer*, a sycophant.

mittimus *n.* [Lat. *mittimus*, we send. The word is used in legal Lat. as the first word of an arrest warrant and thus of the writ itself] [late 16C–mid-19C] a dismissal from an office or job; thus (mid-19C) *get one's mittimus*, to be dismissed, to be killed, to be sent to prison.

mitting *n.* [ety. unknown] [mid–late 19C] a shirt.

mitts *n. see* MITT *n.*

Mitzi *adj.* [2000s] (*S.Afr. gay*) small, usu. of the genitals.

mivey *n.* see MIVVY *n.*[2] (1c).

mivvy *n.*[1] [? pron.] [late 19C–1910s] a marble.

mivvy *n.*[2] [? ironic abbr. SE *marvel* or Cockney pron. of 'mother' as *muvva*] **1** [late 19C–1920s] in 'female' senses. (**a**) a contemptuous term for a woman. (**b**) in fig. use, a complainer, a whiner, an 'old woman'. (**c**) (*also* **mivey, mivy**) the landlady of a lodging-house. **2** [1900s–50s] an expert, an adept.

mix *n.* **1** [mid-19C+] a fight, a brawl. **2** [late 19C–1910s] a muddle, a mess. **3** [1970s+] (*Aus. drugs*) a combination of cannabis and other herbs, usu. tobacco. **4** [1970s+] (*S.Afr.*) methylated spirits, as drunk by alcoholics. **5** [1970s+] (*US drugs*) a powder used to cut cocaine. **6** [1990s+] (*US black*) one's private life. **7** [1980s] (*US black*) the record turntable or turntables as used by hip-hop and rap DJs, and the music played. **8** [1980s+] (*US black*) in abstract senses. (**a**) a difficult situation. (**b**) the memory. **9** [2000s] an environment in which drugs are involved.

IN PHRASES

❑ **at the mix** *see* AT THE MICKS *under* MICK *n.*[1]. ❑ **in the mix** [orig. record industry jargon] [1980s+] **1** (*US black*) involved, esp. in gang activities. **2** (*US prison*) in prison. ❑ **put the mix in** *v.* [SE *mix things up*] [1950s–60s] to cause trouble deliberately, to interfere in a malicious manner.

mix *v.* [MIX *n.* (1)] **1** [late 19C+] (*US*) to fight. **2** [1970s] to inject a drug, usu. heroin [the *mix* of blood and heroin in solution that forms the injection].

IN PHRASES

❑ **mix in** *v.* [late 19C+] to initiate or join a fight. ❑ **mix it (up)** *v.*

[late 19C+] (*Aus./US*) **1** (*also* **mix matters**) to fight, to foster trouble. **2** to cause trouble for someone else. **3** to enjoy oneself. ❑ **mix it up** *v.* **1** [19C] 'to agree secretly how the parties shall make up a tale, or colour a transaction in order to cheat or deceive another party, as in case of a justice-hearing, of a law-suit, or a cross in a boxing-match for money' (Bee). **2** [2000s] (*US black*) to change a song around or play multiple songs at the same time.

SE in slang uses

IN PHRASES

❑ **mix giblets** *v. see* JOIN GIBLETS *under* GIBLETS *n.*

mix and muddle *n.* [rhy. sl.] [20C+] a cuddle.

mixed *adj.* **1** [late 19C–1910s] confused, at a loss. **2** [late 19C–1930s] slightly drunk. **3** [2000s] (*S.Afr. gay*) a male prostitute who operates as either active or passive partner.

mixed-ale oration *n.* [the assumption is that the speaker is drunk or may as well be so] [late 19C–1900s] a poor political oration, typified by its illiterate use of the language; thus *mixed-aler, mixed-ale philosopher*, a drunken know-it-all.

mix'em *n. see* MIXUM *n.*

mixer *n.* [MIX *v.*] **1** [1910s+] a trouble-maker, a gossip, usu. deliberately malicious, one who 'stirs things up'. **2** [1960s] a fighter, a brawler.

mix-metal *n.* [a silversmith's function] [late 18C–early 19C] a silversmith.

mixologist *n.* [SE *mix* + sfx *-ologist*] [mid-19C+] (*orig. US*) a bartender, esp. as a mixer of cocktails; thus *mixology*, mixing cocktails.

mixum *n.* (*also* **mix'em**) [the mixing of medicines] **1** [early 17C–early 18C] an apothecary. **2** [18C] a vintner.

mix-up *n.* [now SE] [late 19C–1930s] a fist-fight.

IN COMPOUNDS

❑ **mix-up artist** *n.* [-ARTIST *sfx*] [1990s+] (*W.I.*) a troublemaker.

miyams *n. see* MEEMIES *n.*

mizake the mizan *v.* [MAKE *v.* (1) + MAN *n.*[1] (1)] [1930s–50s] (*US drugs*) to buy narcotics.

mizz *n. see* MIS *n.* (2).

mizzard *n.* [MAZARD *n.* (2)] [late 19C] the face, the mouth.

mizzle *v.* (*also* **mislain, misle, misli**) [? Shelta *misli*, to go, note naut. jargon *mizzle one's dick*, to miss one's passage] **1** [late 18C+] to leave, to go quickly, to escape; also as *do a mizzle*; thus excl. *mizzle!* go away! be off! **2** [mid-19C] to die.

IN PHRASES

❑ **do a mizzle** *v.* [1900s] to leave, to run off. ❑ **on the mizzle** [late 19C] leaving, en route.

mizzled *adj.* [? SE *mizmaze*, a state of confusion] [late 16C; mid-19C–1940s] drunk.

mizzler *n.*[1] [SE *mizzle*, to complain, to whimper] [1940s] a whinger, a complainer.

mizzler *n.*[2] *see* RUM MIZZLER *under* RUM *adj.*

Mizzoo *n.* [abbr.] [late 19C–1950s] (*US*) the Missouri River, Missouri.

m.j. *n.* [MARY JANE *n.*[2]] [1960s+] (*orig. US drugs*) marijuana.

mjieta *n.* [Zulu *umjita*, an urbanized man] **1** [1960s+] (*S.Afr.*) a township playboy. **2** [1970s+] as a term of address to a black man or youth.

m.l.a. *n.* [abbr. *massive lip action*] [1980s+] (*US campus*) passionate kissing.

mlungu *n.* [Nguni *umlungu*, a white man. The term was coined in early 19C, ? f. Xhosa/Zulu *lunga*, to be correct or good, to be in good order. The ironic/mocking use developed much more recently] [1980s+] (*S.Afr. black*) used mockingly, a white person.

m.m.'s *n.* [abbr.; SE *marijuana* + MUNCHIE *n.*[1] (2)] [1970s] (*drugs*) the hunger that follows smoking marijuana; i.e. *marijuana munchies*.

Mo *n.*[1] [abbr.; the *Mogul*, near Drury Lane was established in 1850, according to Ware on the site of 'a public garden there...kept by some wonderful Indian'] [mid-19C–1920s] the *Mogul* Music Hall, later the Middlesex.

Mo *n.*[2] [abbr. black pron. of *Fillmo'*] [1990s+] (*US black teen*) the Fillmore area of San Francisco.

Mo *n.*[3] *see* IKEY-MO *n.* (5).

m.o. *n.* [abbr. Lat. *modus operandi*, the way of working] **1** [1950s+] (*UK Und.*) the distinguishing working style of a criminal or gang. **2** [1950s+] way of thinking. **3** [1990s+] as sense 1 in non-criminal contexts, a regular way of life. **4** see MOTA *n.*

mo *n.*[1] [abbr.] **1** [late 19C+] (*Aus./N.Z.*) a moustache. **2** [late 19C+] a *moment*, a second; often as HALF A MO *n.*[1]. **3** [1910s–50s] (*US*) a *month*. **4** [1960s+] (*US campus/UK teen*) a homosexual [abbr. HOMO *n.*[2]].

mo *n.*[2] *see* MOTA *n.*

mo *adj.* [2000s] (*US black*) stupid.

mo *v.*[1] (*also* **mo-out**) [MO *adj.* (1)] [1980s] (*US teen*) to embarrass someone, especially in front of their peers.

mo *v.*[2] [MO *n.*[1] (5)] [1980s+] (*US/UK teen*) to act towards someone in a manner that is perceived as being homosexual.

moab *n.* [joc. ref. to Ps.60:8, 'Moab is my washpot'] [mid–late 19C] a turban-shaped hat, worn by women.

Moabite *n.* [SE *Moabite*, an enemy of the biblical Israelites and occas. used in 16C–17C as a pej. nickname for Roman Catholics] [late 17C–mid-19C] a bailiff.

moa-fugg *n. see* MOFUCK *n.*

moan *n.* [SE to *moan*] [1910s+] (*orig. milit.*) a grievance, a complaint.

IN PHRASES

❑ **put on the moan** *v.* [1930s] (*US*) to complain.

moan and wail *n.* [rhy. sl.] [1930s–40s] a gaol.

moaner's bench *n.* [black English pron. of SE *mourner's bench*] [late 19C+] (*US black*) a special pew reserved during a black church revival for those who wish to be 'saved'. Under the direct eye of the preacher and other church dignitaries, they moan and groan, confess their sins and hope to be 'visited by the Spirit'; thus *moaner*, one who makes a public repentance.

moat *n.* [mid-19C] (*US Und.*) a river; thus *moat palace*, a steamboat.

mob *n.*[1] [var. on MAB *n.*[1] (1)] [mid-17C–early 19C] a prostitute.

mob *n.*[2] (*also* **mobb, mobocracy**) [abbr. *mobile vulgus*, the fickle crowd, *mob* was a term cited by Swift in 1712 as one of those that should be purged from the language. Surprisingly Johnson, whose *Dict.* (1755) eschewed (*inter alia*) *dumfound*, *ignoramus* and *touchy* allowed it] **1** [late 17C+] the rabble, the city proletariat [SE f. 1800]. **2** [early 19C+] a company or group of associates; occas. of non-human groups. **3** [mid-19C+] (*orig. US*) a criminal gang. **4** [mid-19C+] a gang of ruffians or thugs. **5** [1920s+] (*US*) constr. with *the*, the US Mafia. **6** [1990s+] by ext., e.g. in UK, any form of organized crime.

IN COMPOUNDS

❑ **mob-handed** *adv.* [-HANDED *adj.*] [1930s+] accompanied by a large gang.

mob *adj.* [MOB *n.*[2] (3)] [1930s+] (*US*) related to a criminal gang, esp. the US Mafia, or its culture and lifestyle.

IN COMPOUNDS

❑ **mob guy** *n.* (*also* **mob boy, mob gee**) (*US Und.*) **1** [1930s–40s] a member of a criminal gang. **2** [1930s+] a member of the US Mafia; thus. ext. to counterparts in other countries. ❑ **Mob Town** *n.* (*also* **Mob City**) [19C] (*US*) Baltimore, Maryland.

mob *v.*[1] (*also* **mob it**) [MOB *n.*[2]] **1** [late 17C+] to move around with or act in a crowd. **2** [mid-18C+] to attack in a large group. **3** [1930s] (*US Und.*) to be murdered on the instructions of a criminal gang. **4** [1990s+] (*US black*) to associate.

IN PHRASES

❑ **mobbed up** *adj.* (*US Und.*) **1** [1920s+] connected with, usu. in a criminal context, but other than organized crime. **2** [1960s+] connected with or run by organized crime. ❑ **mob up** *v.* [1920s+] (*US Und.*) **1** to join a gang. **2** to collect in a gang. **3** to ally oneself with.

mob *v.*[2] [f. *mobilize*, to drive a car] [1990s+] (*US black*) to go, to travel.

mobb *n. see* MOB *n.*[2].

mobber *n. see* MOBSTER *n.* (1).

mobe *n.* [abbr.] **1** [1900s] auto*mob*ile. **2** [1990s+] a *mob*ile phone.

mobey *n. see* MOBY *n.*

mobi *n. see* MOBY *n.*

mo-bike *n.* [abbr.] [1920s+] a *motorbike*.

mobile *n.* [1980s] (*US drugs*) a large rock of cocaine.

-mobile *sfx* [1960s+] (*US campus*) a vehicle, usu. a car, with a pfx.

mobile dandruff *n. see* GALLOPING DANDRUFF *under* GALLOPING *adj.*

mobility *n.* [backform. from MOB *n.*[2] on model of NOB *n.*[2] (1) and SE *nobility*; Swift allowed *mobility*, while Johnson condemned it as 'cant'] [late 17C–mid-19C] the populace, the masses.

mobilize *v.* (*also* **mopelize, mopolize**) [SE *mob* but note *mopel*, to abort] [1920s–70s] (*US, esp. New York City*) of street gangs, to beat up, to vanquish.

mobocracy *n. see* MOB *n.*[2].

moboton *n.* [? SE *mob* + *marathon*] [20C+] (*W.I.*) a great many, a large amount.

mobsman *n.* [a member of the elite ranks of pickpockets, the SWELL MOB *n.*] **1** [mid-19C–1960s] (*UK Und.*) anyone who uses manual dexterity for theft, a category that includes both pickpockets and shoplifters. **2** [1930s] (*US Und.*) a gangster.

mobster *n.* (*also* **mob, mobber**) [MOB *n.*[2] (3)+ -STER *sfx*] **1** [1910s+] (*orig. US*) a gangster. **2** [1960s+] a member of the US Mafia.

moby *n.* (*also* **mobey, mobi**) [abbr.] [1990s+] a *mobile* telephone.

moby *adj.* [the fictional whale *Moby-Dick*, created by US novelist Herman Melville (1819–91)] [1960s+] (*US campus*) enormous.

moby (dick) *n.* [rhy. sl.; ult. the US novel *Moby-Dick* (1850) by Herman Melville] [late 19C+] **1** prison [= NICK *n.*[3] (1)]. **2** the penis [= PRICK *n.* (1)].

moby (dick) *adj.* [rhy. sl.] [1990s+] ill, sick.

moccasined *adj.* [abbr. phr. *bitten by the moccasin* (*snake*)] [mid–late 19C] (*US*) drunk.

moccasins *n.* [late 19C+] (*US*) any kind of footwear; also used fig. as (*walk a mile*) *in my moccasins*, to experience my life.

moch *n. see* MOCK *n.*[2].

mocha *n. see* MOCKER *n.*

mocha *adj.* [SE *mocha*, a variety of coffee] [mid-19C+] (*US*) of people, black, African-American.

mocha and java *v.* [the brandnames of coffee, thus the image of chatting over a cup of coffee] [late 19C–1900s] to get on, to be friendly.

mocher *n. see* MACHER *n.*

mochie *n.* [2000s] (*S.Afr. prison*) a woman.

mochy *n. see* MOUCHEY *n.*

mock *n.*[1] [? MAG *n.*[3] (1)] [20C+] (*Aus.*) a halfpenny.

mock *n.*[2] (*also* **moch**) [abbr. MOCKIE *n.*] (*US*) **1** [1910s–30s] a newly arrived Jewish immigrant. **2** [1920s+] a Jew.

mocka *n. see* MOCKER *n.*

mocker *n.* (*also* **mocha, mocka, mokker**) [link to Yid. *macha*, a big man, a 'big shot'] [1910s+] (*Aus./N.Z.*) clothing, esp. a woman's dress, occas. a suit or suit pattern.

mockered *adj.* [Rom. *mockodo*, *mookeedo*, dirty, filthy] [mid-19C] of a face, pitted, full of holes (the result of smallpox).

mockered up *phr.* (*also* **all mockered up**) [MOCKER *n.*] [1910s+] (*Aus.*) dressed up in one's best, poss. flashy garments.

IN PHRASES

❑ **mockered up like a pox-doctor's clerk** *adj. see* DONE UP LIKE A POX DOCTOR'S CLERK *under* DONE UP *adj.*[2].

mockers *n.*

IN PHRASES

❑ **put the mockers on** *v.* (*also* **put a mock on, put the mocker on, put the mocks on**) [? Yid. *makkes*, ult. Heb. *makot*, plagues, blows, (evil) visitations. The phr. was poss. orig. used in Aus., but given the ety., there may be a link to 19C London market traders] [1910s+] to jinx, to put a curse on, to frustrate someone's plans. ❑ **put the moz on** *v.* (*also* **put the mozz on**) [1920s+] (*Aus.*) to inconvenience, to jinx.

mockey *n. see* MOCKIE *n.*

mockie *n.* (*also* **mockey, mocky, moxie**) [proper name *Moses*, but cf. SMOUS *n.* and MOUCHEY *n.* *DARE* suggests Yid. *makeh*, a boil or sore] [late 19C+] (*US*) a derog. term for a Jew.

mockie *adj.* (*also* **mocky**) [MOCKIE *n.*] [1930s+] (*US*) Jewish.

mockingbird *n.* [rhy. sl.] **1** [1960s+] (*orig. theatre, UK; Aus.*) a word. **2** [1980s+] (*Aus.*) a piece of excrement [= TURD *n.*[1] (1)].

mock litany men *n.* [such beggars are reminiscent of the origins of the CANTING CREW *n.*] [late 19C–1900s] (*Irish*) beggars who make their demands in a sing-song or versifying manner.

mock out *v.* [SE *mock*] [1960s+] (*US campus*) to tease.

mocktail *n.* [SE *mock* + (*cock*)*tail*] [1980s+] (*US*) a non-alcoholic drink.

mocky *see under* MOCKIE.

mocs *n.* [abbr. SE *moccasins*] [1950s+] (*US*) slip-on shoes.

mod *n.*[1] [abbr.] [1940s+] often in pl., *mod*ification(s).

mod *n.*[2] [abbr. SE *modernist*] [1960s+] **1** a member of a teenage cult orig. *c*.1961, who wore smart clothes, rode motor scooters and fought their main rivals, the motorcycle-riding, leather-clad 'rockers'. **2** (*Aus.*) one who discards the conventional past and looks to the future. **3** (*US campus*) a well-dressed, fashionable person.

DERIVATIVES

❑ **moddy** *adj.* [1970s] in a 'mod' style.

mod *adj.* [abbr. SE *modern*] [1960s+] fashionable, up-to-date.

IN COMPOUNDS

❑ **mod squad** *n.* [1970s–80s] plainclothes police, usu. young and dressed in the prevailing teenage and early 20s fashions, who look for crime in colleges and local youth centres.

IN PHRASES

❑ **(in a) mod bag** *adj.* [1980s] fashionable. ❑ **mod to the bone** *adj.* [TO THE BONE *under* BONE *n.*[1]] [1960s+] (*US black*) very fashionably dressed.

modams *n.* [ety. unknown] [1970s+] (*drugs*) marijuana.

mode *v. see* MOULD *v.*

Model, the *n.* [Pentonville was opened in 1842 and designed as a *model* prison on the 'separate system', i.e. continuous solitary confinement irrespective of one's crime (pioneered in the Haviland Eastern Penitentiary in Philadelphia)] [mid-19C–1900s] Pentonville prison, Caledonian Road, London.

model *v.* [1990s+] (*UK black*) to pose, e.g. at a party or club.

modelling *n.* [1990s+] (*S.Afr.*) the parading of an offender naked through a township as a form of punishment.

Model T *adj.* [the inexpensive Ford *Model T* motorcar, last manufactured in 1927] [1930s–60s] (*US*) out-of-date, cheap.

mo dicker *n.* [*mo*, abbr. SE *mother* + DICK *v.*[2] (1)] [1960s+] (*US*) synon. for MOTHERFUCKER *n.* and as adj. *mo-dickin'*.

modicum *n.* [as well as the comestibles, the vagina is something one can EAT *v.* (4); note Williams (1994) 'This derives, by synecdoche, from the 'woman' sense found in Dekker *Roaring Girle* I i, where a girl visiting a man is termed "a daintier bit or modicum than any lay upon his trencher at dinner."'] [mid-17C–19C] the vagina.

modie *n.* [2000s] (*US black*) a motel.

modigger *n. see* DOJIGGER *n.* (2).

modock *n.* ['a flashy chap who goes around wearing helmet and goggles, and more than likely, leather boots and riding breeches, too, and talking about the big things he is going to do for aviation' (Allen & Lyman, *Wonder Book of the Air*, 1936); ety. unknown. Supposedly a mythical bird, which 'flies backwards to keep the sun out of its eyes', but other than an aviators' joke, this has no validity as an ety.] [1930s–40s] (*US*) one who becomes an aviator for the social prestige or publicity.

modock *v.* [see MODOCK *n.* (1)] [1940s–70s] (*US*) to rush off.

mods and rockers *n.* [rhy. sl. *mods and rockers* = KNOCKER *n.*[1] (1)] [1960s+] the female breasts.

moe *n.* [2000s] (*US prison*) a 'married' prison homosexual.

moegie *adj.* [MOEGOE *n.*] [1960s] tired.

moegoe *n.* (*also* **imoogie, moggo, mogoe, moogie, mugu**) [Afk.] [1940s+] (*S.Afr.*) a lazy lout, a country bumpkin, a gullible person.

moer *n.* **1** [20C+] (*S.Afr.*) the buttocks. **2** [1940s+] a term of obscene abuse, usu. as phr. *jou moer! se moer! your moer!* [Afk. mother/womb]. **3** [1970s+] (*also* **moer se, moersa**) hell; as phr., to hell and gone; the hell in; as adj., hell of a.

moer *v.* [? MOER! *excl.* or Afk. *moor*, murder] **1** [1950s+] (*S.Afr.*) to thrash, to beat up. **2** [1980s] to kill someone.

moer! *excl.* [Du. *moder*, mother, thus fig. 'your mother's womb'] [1940s+] (*S.Afr.*) an abusive term of address or an obscene excl. of fury or disgust; esp. in excls. *jou moer! your moer!* your mother!

DERIVATIVES

❑ **moersa** *adj.* [1980s] enormous, 'motherfucking'.

moer (of) *n.* (*also* **moere, moersa, moerse**) [1980s+] something large, a 'mother of'.

moey *n.* (*also* **mooe, mooey, mouee**) [Rom. *mooï*, the mouth] **1** [mid-19C] (*US Und.*) a petition. **2** [mid-19C+] the mouth. **3** [mid–late 19C; 1990s+] the vagina. **4** [late 19C+] (*Aus.*) a moustache.

moff *n.* (*also* **moph**) [abbr.; note farming jargon *moff*, a dual-purpose farm wagon] [20C+] a hermaphrodite.

moffie *n.* [? Du. sl. *mofrodiet*, a hermaphrodite; note UK naut. jargon *mophy*, 'a delicate well-groomed youth' (*DSUE* 8)] [1950s+] (*S.Afr.*) **1** a homosexual; thus *koffie-moffie*, an airline steward (lit. 'coffee-queen'). **2** a transvestite.

moffry *n.* [abbr.] [20C+] (*W.I.*) **1** a hermaphrodite. **2** a weak, effeminate man.

mofo *n.* (*also* **mo-fo, mo-foe**) [abbr.] **1** [1960s+] synon. for MOTHERFUCKER *n.* (1). **2** [1980s+] synon. for MOTHERFUCKER *n.* (3).

mofo *adj.* (*also* **mo-fo**) [abbr.] [1980s+] synon. for MOTHERFUCKING *adj.*

mofuck *n.* (*also* **moa-fugg, mo-fucker**) [abbr.] [1960s+] synon. for MOTHERFUCKER *n.*

mog *n.*[1] (*also* **mogue**) [? Fr. *se moquer de*, to jeer, to deride] [mid-19C] a lie; thus *no mogue*, no lie.

mog *n.*[2] [abbr. MOGGIE *n.*[1] (2)] **1** [1920s–50s] a fur, a tippet, a fur coat. **2** [1920s+] a cat. **3** [1940s] a monkey.

mog *v.* [ety. unknown] [late 18C–1950s] to amble, to trudge along slowly.

mogadored *adj.* [rhy. sl. = colloq. *floored*, ? ult. Irish *magadh*, to mock, to jeer, to laugh at, ? Rom. *mokardi/mokodo*, tainted] [1930s+] beaten, defeated, confused.

mogambo *n.* [? film *Mogambo* (1953), starring Clark Gable and Ava Gardner big-game hunting in Kenya] [1980s] (*US black*) sexual intercourse.

mogg *v. see* MOG *v.*

moggie *n.*[1] (*also* **moggy**) [? proper name *Maggie* or dial. *moggie*, a calf] **1** [late 17C–19C] an untidily dressed woman, a slattern. **2** [20C+] a cat. **3** [1970s] an unpleasant woman.

moggie *n.*[2] [1980s+] (*drugs*) Mogadon, a mild sleeping pill; thus adj. *moggified*.

moggie *adj.* [2000s] (*S.Afr.*) crazy.

moggo *adj. see* MOEGIE *adj.*

moggy *n. see* MOGGIE *n.*[1].

mogoe *n. see* MOEGOE *n.*

mogue *v.* [MOG *n.*[1]] [mid–late 19C] to trick or deceive.

mogul *n.* [1940s] (*US short order*) ham.

Mohack *n. see* MOHOCK *n.*

mohair *n.* **1** [late 18C–early 19C] a derog. name for a civilian, as named by a soldier [a civilian's mohair-covered buttons; a soldier had the unadorned brass]. **2** [mid-19C] (*US Und.*) an upholsterer.

mohair knickers *n.* (*also* **mohair stockings**) [1980s+] an extremely hairy vagina.

mohasky *n.* (*also* **mohasty, mohoska, mosky**) [ety. unknown; ? play on SE, thus cf. MARIHOOCHIE *n.*] [1930s+] (*drugs*) marijuana.

mohasky *adj.* (*also* **mohasty, mohoska, mosky**) [MOHASKY *n.*] [1930s+] (*drugs*) intoxicated by marijuana.

Mohock *n.* (*also* **Mohack, Mohawk**) [SE *Mohawk*] [early 18C–19C; 1960s] a dissolute and violent young man, usu. an aristocratic rowdy, who caroused through the streets of London beating up passers-by, attacking watchmen, smashing windows etc; occas. of a woman, a prostitute.

IN PHRASES

❑ **act the mohawk** *v.* [1960s] (*Irish*) to misbehave.

mohoska *n. see* MOHASKY *n.*

moisher *v.* [play on the Jewish name *Moishe/Moses*, i.e. the 'wandering Jew'] [1960s] to wander.

moist *n.* [play on DAMP *n.* (1)] [1900s–30s] (*US*) an alcoholic drink.

IN COMPOUNDS

❑ **moistmill** *n.* [1900s–30s] (*US*) a bar. ❑ **moist 'un** *n.* [1900s–30s] (*US*) a drunkard.

moist *adj.* [1990s+] (*US campus*) second-rate, inferior.

moisten *v.*

SE in slang uses

IN PHRASES

❑ **moisten one's wick** *v. see under* WICK *n.*[1]. ❑ **moisten the chaffer** *v. see* MOISTEN ONE'S CHAFFER *under* CHAFFER *n.*[2]. ❑ **moisten the clay** *v. see under* CLAY *n.*

moistie *n.* [2000s] (*N.Z.*) a desirable female.

moist the clay *v. see under* CLAY *n.*

mojo *n.* [? Gullah *moco*, witchcraft, magic, Fula *moco'o*, medicine man.] **1** [1920s+] (*orig. US black*) spirituality, magic, thus power and influence. **2** [1930s+] (*US drugs*) any narcotic drug, esp. morphine. **3** [1970s] (*US black*) a kind of dance.

IN PHRASES

❑ **like a mojo** *adv.* [1980s+] (*US black/campus*) a great deal. ❑ **the mojo and the say-so** *n.* [1920s+] (*orig. US black*) qualities giving one power and influence over others.

mojo *v.* [MOJO *n.* (1)] (*orig. US*) **1** [1930s] to fool, to deceive. **2** [1960s+] to jinx, to charm.

moke *n.*[1] [? Devon/Hampshire dial. *mokus*, a donkey. In *DSUE*, Partridge suggests Rom. *moxio*, a donkey, or *Moke*, the dimin. of the proper name *Margaret*, on the pattern of MOG *n.*[2] (2), MOGGIE *n.*[1] (2); also f. *Margaret*, a cat] **1** [mid-19C–1940s] a donkey, an ass. **2** [mid-19C+] a fool. **3** [late 19C+] (*Aus.*) a horse, often an second-rate one.

IN PHRASES

❑ **cop a moke** *v.* [20C+] (*US prison*) to escape, lit. 'grab a donkey'.

moke *n.*[2] [? Sp. *mocha*, dark-skinned; ult. Sp. *café de Moca* (an Arabian port on the Red Sea), but note SMOKE *n.* (3a)] (*US*) **1** [mid-19C–1950s] a black person, any dark-skinned foreigner. **2** [mid–late 19C] a white person wearing 'blackface' and performing in a 'minstrel show'. **3** [late 19C–1910s] a foolish, tedious person. **4** [1960s] a Hawaiian, esp. a young, thuggish man.

mokker *n. see* MOCKER *n.*

mokuiner *n. see* MOSKENEER *n.*

mokus *n.* [? MOCKERS *n.*] (*US*) **1** [1920s–50s] a depressed state, 'the blues'. **2** [1950s–70s] a very intoxicated state.

mokus *adj.* [MOKUS *n.* (2)] [1950s–70s] (*US*) drunk but wanting another drink.

mola *n. see* MOOLA *n.*

molared *adj. see* MOLO *adj.* (1).

mold *v.* (*also* **mode**) [1980s] (*US campus*) to humiliate; to catch someone out in a contradiction or other error.

moldy *adj.* [1920s+] (*US*) foolishly sentimental.

moldy fig *n.* [i.e. that which is 'stale and shrivelled'] [1940s+] (*orig. US*) a very boring or old-fashioned person, esp. as applied by modern jazz fans to their antitheses, the fans of trad. New Orleans jazz.

mole *n.*[1] **1** [late 19C–1910s] the penis [the animal and the penis 'burrow in']. **2** [late 19C–1910s] a male homosexual [from sense 1]. **3** [1930s] (*US prison*) someone who tunnels into a bank to rob it. **4** [1990s+] (*US prison*) someone who escapes by digging their way out of prison.

IN COMPOUNDS

❑ **mole-catcher** *n.* [late 19C–1910s] the vagina.

mole *n.*[2] [? MOLLY *n.*[1] (2) or MOLL *n.* (1)] [1960s+] (*Aus./N.Z.*) a woman, esp. a promiscuous one.

molehill *n.* [? MOLE *n.*[1] (1)/visual resemblance to SE *molehill*] [early 18C] a pregnant stomach.

moles *n.* [SE *moleskin*, a strong, soft, fine-piled cotton fustian, the surface of which is 'shaved' before dyeing] [late 19C+] (*Aus.*) moleskin trousers.

moleskin *n.* [1990s+] (*US*) derog. term for a black person.

moleskin squatter *n.* [such men wore *moleskin* trousers] [late 19C–1940s] (*Aus./N.Z.*) 'a working man who has come to own a small sheep run.' (*OED*).

moley *n.* [it 'burrows into' the victim's flesh] [1950s] a potato, its surface jagged with the edges of safety razor blades.

moll *n.* [dimin. of proper name *Mary*, reinforced by the early 17C criminal *Moll Cut-purse*, immortalized in Middleton & Dekker's play *The Roaring Girl* (1611)] **1** [17C+] a woman, usu. a promiscuous one. **2** [17C+] a prostitute [now survives only in Aus. use]. **3** [early 19C+] a girlfriend; esp. in *gangster's moll*, a gangster's female companion. **4** [mid-19C] (*UK Und.*) a landlady, a proprietress, the 'lady of the house'; usu. ext. as *moll of the crib*, *moll of the drum*. **5** [1920s–70s] (*US*) an effeminate male homosexual. **6** [1960s] (*S.Afr.*) a female Teddy Boy.

DERIVATIVES

❑ **molled (up)** *adj.* **1** [mid-19C] followed or accompanied by a woman. **2** [mid-19C] sleeping with a woman other than one's wife. ❑ **molling** *adj.* [mid-19C] (*UK Und.*) pertaining to women.

IN COMPOUNDS

❑ **moll buzzer** *n.* [BUZZER *n.*[1]/WORKER *n.*[1]; note Goldin et al., *Dict. of American Und. Lingo* (1950): 'The theft is accomplished in the following manner: An accomplice, known as the buzzer, accosts a victim and asks to be directed to a given place in the neighborhood. The destination is so chosen that the victim must turn her back to the carriage to point. The purse-snatcher now advances from the direction which the victim is facing and deftly seizes the purse. The victim seldom discovers her loss until the thieves have disappeared. Premature discovery requires the buzzer, feigning solicitude, to block pursuit and delay any outcry until the snatcher has escaped.'] **1** [mid-19C+] (*UK/US Und./police*) (*also* **dame buzzer, moll buzzard, moll worker**) a pickpocket or a beggar who specializes in women as victims; thus *moll-buzzing*, purse- or bag-snatching; by ext., any minor thief; v. *buzz a moll*. **2** [late 19C–1930s] (*US Und.*) a female thief, pickpocket or beggar. ❑ **moll crib** *n.* [CRIB *n.*[1] (3)] [mid-19C] a brothel. ❑ **moll hook** *n.* [HOOK *n.*[1] (1)] [late 19C–1910s] a female pickpocket. ❑ **moll house** *n.* [SE *house*/HOUSE *n.*[1] (1)] [18C] a brothel. ❑ **moll-hunter** *n.* [late 19C–1900s] a womanizer. ❑ **moll-knuck** *n.* [KNUCK *n.* (1)] [mid-19C] (*UK Und.*) a female pickpocket. ❑ **moll sack** *n.* [SE *sack*, lit. 'woman sack'] [mid-19C] a handbag; a market basket. ❑ **moll shop** *n.* (*also* **molly shop**) [SHOP *n.*[1] (3)] [20C+] a brothel. ❑ **moll slavey** *n.* see SLAVEY *n.* ❑ **moll-tooler** *n.* (*also* **molley, moll-tool**) [TOOLER *n.*] [mid–late 19C] a female pickpocket. ❑ **mollwhiz** *n.* [WHIZ *n.*[4] (1)] [1930s] (*US Und.*) a female pickpocket. ❑ **moll-wire** *n.* [WIRE *n.*[2]] [mid-19C–1930s] **1** a pickpocket who specializes in robbing female victims. **2** a female pickpocket.

IN PHRASES

❑ **bury a moll** *v.* [mid-19C] to run away from one's mistress. ❑ **like old molls at a christening** *adj.* (*also* **like an old moll...**) [1960s+] (*N.Z.*) **1** noisy, verbose. **2** in a state of confusion. ❑ **moll of the cross** *n.* [CROSS *n.*[1] (4)] [mid-19C] (*UK Und.*) a girl or woman of the Und. ❑ **Moll's three misfortunes** *n.* [the phr., while appearing in the British Library edn, was not transferred into any of the published versions of the *Classical Dict. of the Vulgar Tongue*] [late 18C] 'broke the [chamber-] pot, bes[hi]t the bed and cut her a[r]se' (Grose, 1796). ❑ **posture moll** *n.* [early 18C] a prostitute who specializes in stripping and adopting sexually arousing positions before her customer. ❑ **square moll** *n.* [mid-19C] an honest woman.

moll *v.* [MOLL *n.*] **1** [19C] to go around with women. **2** [late 19C; 1970s] of a man, to act effeminately. **3** [1950s] (*US*) to work as a prostitute.

moll blood *n.* [Scot. nickname] [late 18C–early 19C] the gallows.

Moll Doyle *n.*

IN PHRASES

❑ **give someone Moll Doyle** *v.* [*Moll Doyle's daughters*, a clandestine agrarian society, pitted against rapacious landlords and similar figures] [mid-19C+] (*Irish*) to scold, to reprimand, usu. of a wife to a husband.

IN EXCLAMATIONS

❑ **by the powers of Moll Doyle!** (*also* **by the powers of Moll Kelly!**) [early 19C+] (*Irish*) a mild oath.

molled *adj.* *see* MOLO *adj.*

molley *n.* *see* MOLL-TOOLER *under* MOLL *n.*

mollisher *n.* (*also* **mollesher**) [MOLL *n.* (1); ? link to Rom. *monishi*, a woman] **1** [early–mid-19C] a woman. **2** [mid-19C] a slattern. **3** [mid–late 19C] a thief's mistress.

mollock *v.* [? dial. *marlock*, to frolic, to gambol + *rollick*, coined by Stella Gibbons in *Cold Comfort Farm* (1932)] [1930s+] to cavort, to have a good time, to have sexual intercourse.

Moll Peatley's jig *n.* (*also* **Moll Peatley's gig, Moll Pratley's gig**) [? the name of a well-known contemporary prostitute + GIG *n.*[1] (1)/SE *jig*] [late 18C–early 19C] sexual intercourse, 'a rogering bout' (Grose, 1788).

Moll Thompson's mark *n.* [the sign *M.T.* inscribed on empty packages] [late 18C–mid-19C] used to describe an empty bottle.

molly *n.*[1] [generic use of female name, underlined by Fr. *molle*, soft; note US regional dial. *cut up molly*, to act in an extravagant, frolicsome manner; ballad 'The Maid's Resolution to follow her Love' (*c.*1820) which uses 'Madam Molly' for a woman who poses as a soldier] **1** [late 17C+] (*also* **moll, molly-cull, mollyman, Tom Molly**) a male homosexual, an effeminate man; thus adj. *mollyish*. **2** [early 18C–1940s] (*also* **molley, mollie**) a prostitute. **3** [late 19C+] (*Irish*) a young woman.

DERIVATIVES

❑ **mollying** *adj.* [18C] homosexual. ❑ **mollyish** *adj.* [19C] effeminate.

IN COMPOUNDS

❑ **molly-booby** *n.* [1970s] (*W.I., Bdos*) a fool. ❑ **molly-cull** *n.* [CULL *n.*[1] (3)] [18C] a catamite. ❑ **molly dike** *n.* [1970s–80s] (*US gay*) a lesbian. ❑ **molly-dodger** *n.* [1920s–60s] (*US*) euph. for MOTHERFUCKER *n.* ❑ **molly-dooker** *n.* (*also* **molly-hander**) [? DUKE *n.*[3], with derog. sense that an effeminate man, like a left-handed person, would be clumsy or ? MAULEY *n.*] [1920s+] (*Aus.*) a left-handed person; thus *molly-dook(ed)*, left-handed. ❑ **mollyhead** *n.* (*also* **mollyhawk**) [-HEAD *sfx*] [1900s] a fool, a simpleton. ❑ **molly house** *n.* [SE *house*/HOUSE *n.*[1] (1)] [early 18C–late 19C] a male homosexual brothel. ❑ **molly man** *n.* [1920s+] an effeminate homosexual. ❑ **molly-mop** *n.* [DOLLYMOP *n.*] [early 19C] an effeminate man. ❑ **molly's hole** *n.* [MOLL *n.* + HOLE *n.*[1]] [19C] the vagina. ❑ **molly shop** *n.* see MOLL SHOP *under* MOLL *n.* ❑ **mollyslop** *adj.* [SLOP *n.*[1] (2)] [late 19C] nonsensical, weak, with overtones of effeminacy. ❑ **mollywopper** *n.* [1970s] (*US*) a euph. for MOTHERFUCKER *n.*

IN PHRASES

❑ **Miss Molly** *n.* [18C] an effeminate homosexual. ❑ **Tom Molly** *n.* [early 19C] an effeminate homosexual.

molly *n.*[2] [play on SE *black molly*, a species of tropical fish, which the black pills may be seen as resembling] [1970s+] (*US drugs*) usu. in pl. *mollies*, amphetamines; usu. as *blue mollies*, *black mollies*, or even *yellow mollies*.

IN PHRASES

❑ **black mollies** *n.* [1970s] (*US drugs*) amphetamine.

molly *v.* [MOLLY *n.*[1] (1)] [18C] to sodomize, to bugger; thus *mollying*, very keen on buggery.

Molly Ban/Bawn *n.* [used as (?coined by) the title of a popular ballad by Samuel Lover (1797–1868)] [20C+] (*Irish*) confusion, worry; thus *the times of Molly Bán*, a riotous good time.

mollyfock *n.* [1960s+] euph. for MOTHERFUCK *n.*

mollyfocking *adj.* (*also* **mollyfogging**) [1960s+] euph. for MOTHERFUCKING *adj.*

mollygrubs *n. see* MULLIGRUBS *n.*

molly maguire *n.* [rhy. sl.] [2000s] (*orig. Aus.*) a fire.

Molly Maguired *adj.* [rhy. sl.] [1990s+] tired.

molly (malone) *n.* [rhy. sl.] [20C+] the telephone.

Molly O'Morgan *n.* [rhy. sl.] [20C+] an organ.

mollypuff *n.* (*also* **mullipuff, mullypuff**) [dial. *mullipuff*, the fungus *Lycoperdon Bovista*, a puff-ball, note F&H suggest an alternative meaning, 'a gambler's decoy' but *DSUE* dismisses this as an error] [early 17C–early 18C] a weakling, used as a general term of contempt.

molly (the monk) *adj.* [rhy. sl.] [1960s–70s] (*Aus.*) drunk.

molo *adj.* (*also* **molared, molled, mowlow**) [? SE *molly*, a meeting of ships' captains, poss. for drinking] [20C+] (*Aus.*) drunk.

molocher *n.* (*also* **moloker**) [? SE *lacquered*] [mid–late 19C] a renovated hat, ironed and greased back to something resembling its original condition.

molrower *n.* [MOLROWING *n.*] [mid–late 19C] a womanizer.

molrowing *n.* [MOLL *n.* (1)/MOLL *n.* (2) + SE *row*, a noise (the woman's amatory groans are compared to the screeching of mating cats)] [mid–late 19C] **1** going out on a (whoring) spree. **2** caterwauling, making a noise.

IN PHRASES

❑ **go molrowing** *v.* of a man, to have sexual intercourse.

molvyn *n.* [2000s] (*S.Afr. gay*) a male homosexual.

mom *n.* [1950s–70s] (*US gay*) a passive partner in a lesbian relationship.

mome *n.* [? Fr. *mome*, a little child or an innocent, or *mum*, dumb] [mid-16C–early 18C] a fool, a simpleton.

momick *v.* (*also* **mommuck**) [1920s–30s] (*US*) to beat, to injure, to damage.

momma *n.*[1] [var. on MAMA *n.*] **1** [1930s+] (*US black*) (*also* **mommy**) a woman, any woman, spec. as a term of address. **2** [1960s] a male-to-male term of friendly address. **3** [1960s+] (*US black*) a girlfriend, a lover. **4** [1970s+] synon. for MOTHERFUCKER *n.*

IN COMPOUNDS

❑ **momma's game** *n.* (*also* **momma's dozens**) [1950s+] (*US black*) a name-calling ritual that depends heavily on mutually abusing the participants' mothers.

IN PHRASES

❑ **sweet momma** *n. see* SWEET MAMA *under* SWEET *adj.*[1].

momma *n.*[2] *see* MAMMY *n.*[1].

mommuck *v. see* MOMICK *v.*

mommux *n.* (*also* **momox**) [MOMMUX (UP) *v.*] [mid-19C] a mess, a muddle.

mommux (up) *v.* (*also* **momox**) [? FLUMMOX *v.* (4)] [mid-19C–1950s] (*US*) to confuse, to bewilder, to confound, to botch.

mommy *n.* [2000s] (*S.Afr. gay*) the lesbian equivalent of a DADDY *n.* (8).

mommy up *v.* [SAmE *mommy*, mother] [1980s+] (*US campus*) to love, to hug, to comfort.

momo *n.* (*also* **mo-mo**) [abbr. SE *mo(ron)* + redup.] [1950s+] (*US*) a stupid person.

momox *see under* MOMMUX.

mompara *n.* [Fanakalo *mompara*, a fool, waste matter] (*S.Afr.*) **1** [late 19C+] of black workers, a novice, a greenhorn. **2** [1930s+] a fool, an idiot, also used as a term of affection.

mompie *n.* [Fanakalo (mining slang) *mompara*, a fool, waste material] [1940s+] (*S.Afr.*) a very slow-witted person.

mompyns *n.* (*also* **munpins**) [lit. 'mouth-pins'] [mid-15C] the teeth.

momser *n. see* MAMZER *n.*

momser/momza/momzer *n. see* MAMZER *n.*

momzir *n. see* MAMZER *n.*

mon *n.*[1] (*also* **mun**) [abbr.] [late 19C–1970s] (*US*) *money*.

mon *n.*[2] [imitation of W.I. pron.] [1960s+] (*orig. US campus*) as used in address, man.

monacher/monack/monacker *n. see* MONNIKER *n.*

monaghan *n.* [proper name, presumably of a specific individual] [late 17C–mid-18C] (*Irish*) a fool, a clown.

monaker *n.* **1** *see* MONARCH *n.*[1]. **2** *see* MONNIKER *n.*

Mona Lisa *n.* [rhy. sl.] [1980s+] **1** a freezer. **2** a pizza.

monarch *n.*[1] (*also* **monaker**) [the *monarch*'s head on the coin] [mid-19C–1900s] a sovereign.

monarch *n.*[2] *see* MONNIKER *n.*

Monday *n.*

SE in slang uses

DERIVATIVES

❑ **Mondayish** *adj.* (*also* **Mondayfied**) [mid-19C] disinclined to work, esp. after a festive weekend.

IN COMPOUNDS

❑ **Monday mouse** [MOUSE *n.* (3)] [late 19C–1900s] a black eye, resulting from a Saturday or Sunday night (drunken) fight.

IN PHRASES

❑ **blue Monday** *n. see* separate entry. ❑ **crib-crust Monday** *n.* [? CRIB *v.*[1] + SE *crust*; one has no money for food and must scrounge crusts] [mid-19C] (*UK juv.*) the Monday before Advent. ❑ **Monday and Tuesday** *adj.* [the correct order of the days of the week] [1950s] slow, steady, careful. ❑ **St Monday** *n. see* separate entry.

Monday morning quarterback *n.* (*also* **Saturday morning quarterback, Sunday morning...**) [amateur criticism of the week's pro football matches, played on Sundays] [1930s+] (*US*) a person who criticizes with the benefit of hindsight.

Monday morning quarterback *v.* [see prev.] [1930s+] (*US*) to criticize with the benefit of hindsight.

mondo *adj.* [MONDO- *pfx*] [1980s+] considerable, substantial, huge.

mondo *adv.* [MONDO- *pfx*] [1980s+] (*US teen/campus*) completely, absolutely, very, exceedingly.

mondo- *pfx* [Ital. *mondo*, the world (cf. -CITY *sfx* (1)), first popularized by the Italian cult film *Mondo Cane* (1961) and, like COWABUNGA! *excl.*, DUDE *n.*[1] and other Californian teen/surfer slang, *mondo* gained a new lease of life with the *Teenage Mutant Ninja Turtles* craze of the late 1980s] [1960s+] (*US*) used to describe a bizarre, surprising or anarchic view of the topic under consideration, with the implication of salaciousness or (kitschy) bad taste, usu. combined with a real or cod Italian n., e.g. *mondo trasho, mondo weirdo, mondo bizarro*.

monekeer/moneker/monekur *n. see* MONNIKER *n.*

monet *n.* [a critical view of the work of the Fr. artist Claude *Monet* (1840–1926)] [1990s+] (*US teen*) something that (lit. and fig.) looks good from afar but appears less appealing in close-up.

money *n.* **1** ref. to the commercial potential of the organs. (**a**) [late 18C+] esp. of young girls, the vagina. (**b**) [1970s+] of boys, the anus; thus used as a form of address between homosexual men. **2** [mid-19C] *money's* worth. **3** [late 19C+] (*US*) in general, the critical element or aspect, used fig., e.g. *that's where the money is*. **4** [1980s+] (*US black*) (*also* **money dog, money grip**) one's best friend. **5** a man; a rich man. **6** a general form of address to any man.

IN PHRASES

❑ **put one's money where one's mouth is** *v.* [1940s+] (*orig.*

US) fig., to back one's boasting with suitable action; lit., to back one's opinions with wagered money.

SE in slang uses

IN COMPOUNDS

❑ **money-bag** *adj.* (*also* **money-bags**) [1960s+] wealthy. ❑ **moneybags** *n.* **1** [early 19C+] a lover of money. **2** [late 19C+] (*also* **money-bagger**) a wealthy person; often as *Mr Moneybags*. ❑ **moneybox** *n.* (*also* **moneybag**) [its commercial potential] [19C] the vagina. ❑ **money bug** *n.* [BUG *n.*[1]] [late 19C–1900s] (*US*) a millionaire. ❑ **money-cuffee** *n.* [CUFFEE *n.*] [late 19C] (*W.I.*) a foolish spendthrift. ❑ **money-dropper** *n. see* GOLD-DROPPER *n.* ❑ **money grip** *n. see* MONEY *n.* (4). ❑ **money machine** *n.* [its commercial potential] [1960s–70s] (*US*) the vagina. ❑ **money-maker** *n.* [the commercial potential] **1** [late 19C+] the vagina. **2** [1960s+] (*US*) the female buttocks; also used of gay men. ❑ **money pocket** *n.* [its commercial context] [2000s] (*US black*) the vagina. ❑ **money-puker** *n.* [SE *puke*, to vomit] [1990s+] (*US*) an automatic teller machine. ❑ **money shot** *n.* [SE *money* refers to the commercial potential of such shots + phr. *ON THE MONEY* below; note, however, sense 1a above] **1** [1960s+] in pornographic still or moving pictures, a close-up of the genitalia, male or female at the moment of ejaculation (which for purposes of 'verisimilitude' always takes place outside the body). **2** [1990s+] also fig. use, the big climax. ❑ **money's mammy** *n.* [fig. a 'member of money's family'] [1930s–40s] (*US black*) a very rich person. ❑ **money-spinner** *n.* [its commercial potential] [19C] the vagina.

IN PHRASES

❑ **don't-go money** *n.* [1950s] (*US*) money that one cannot afford to lose. ❑ **money gone in Maxwell Pond** *n. see under* MAXWELL POND *n.* ❑ **money talks – bullshit walks** [1950s+] a dismissive phr. aimed at a person. ❑ **on the money** *adj.* [betting imagery] [1940s+] (*orig. US*) excellent, perfect, just right. ❑ **smart money** *n.* (*also* **right money**) [note milit. jargon *smart money*, compensation for injuries received in service] **1** [1920s+] (*US*) spec. the way in which experienced gamblers bet. **2** [1950s] (*US Und.*) a clever and successful criminal. **3** [2000s] in fig. use, good sense. ❑ **throw money around like a man with no hands** *v.* [1950s] (*Aus.*) to be very mean. ❑ **throw money at** *v.* [1970s+] to spend an extravagant amount of money on something, esp. in the hope of remedying a problem.

money *adj.* (*orig. US*) **1** [1930s+] used prenominally to denote success, proficiency, ability to win or to fulfil high expectations; e.g. *money star*, a famous film star; *money jockey*, a jockey who wins often; *money card*, the card that completes a winning hand in poker; *money shot*, a close up shot of orgasm in a pornographic film; *money quote*, a quote of a sensational exposure in a news story. **2** [1990s+] used without a n. with the same meaning, e.g. *You're money; That's really money!*

mong *n.*[1] [SE *mongrel*] [1940s+] (*Aus.*) a dog, not necessarily of mixed breed.

mong *n.*[2] [abbr. SE *mongol*] [1970s+] a general term of opprobrium. The overriding implication is that of stupidity.

mong *v.* (*also* **do a mong**) [Romany *mong*, to beg] [1910s–50s] (*Aus.*) to cadge.

monged *adj.* (*also* **monged-out**) [MONG *n.*[2]] [1980s+] intoxicated by a drug, usu. MDMA.

mongee *n.* [Fr. *manger*, to eat] [1910s–30s] (*US tramp*) food.

monger *n.* [MONG *v.*] [1900s–10s] (*Aus.*) a cadger.

-monger *sfx* [SE *monger*, a dealer, a trafficker] [late 16C–late 17C; late 19C+] an enthusiast or knowledgeable person.

mongie *adj. see* MONGY *adj.*

mong-mong *n.* [pron. of Carib.E. *Mount St Moritz Bajan*, a poor white one of whose ancestors moved to the Grenadan estate of St Moritz *c.*1870s, working as a market gardener] [20C+] (*W.I., Gren.*) a poor white.

mongo *n.* [MONG *n.*[2], but *Mongo* is a trad. name for a shambling idiot, often the servant of a 'mad professor' in films etc; however, that too may be rooted in SE *mongol*] [1970s+] (*US*) an idiot.

mongo *adj.* [? HUMONGOUS *adj.*] [1980s+] (*US teen/campus*) considerable, substantial, huge.

mongo *adv.* [MONGO *adj.*] [1990s+] extremely.

Mongolian *n.* (*also* **Mongol**) [mid-19C–1910s] (*Aus.*) a Chinese immigrant to Australia, or the United States.

mongolito *n.* [cod Sp. 'little mongol'] [1980s+] (*US campus*) a term of endearment.

mongoloid *n.* [1970s+] a stupid, dumb person; as adj., stupid.

mongoose *n.* [the animal, which has a light-brown coat and reddish eyes] [1900s–50s] (*W.I.*) an albino, esp. as a term of abuse.

mongoose gang *n.* [1950s campaign to eradicate the mongoose in Grenada; those who claimed a bounty for killing the creatures had to produce a tail and became known as the '*mongoose gang*'] [1950s+] (*W.I., orig. Gren.*) a group of thugs working for a politician and acting as a form of private army/secret police.

mongoree *n. see* MUNGAREE *n.*

mong (out) *v.* [MONGED *adj.*] [2000s] to be dully comatose.

mongrel *n.* **1** in UK Und. senses. (**a**) [16C–17C] an accomplice who helps in a confidence trickster's pose as a poor scholar. (**b**) [late 17C–early 19C] a hanger-on among confidence tricksters, a sponger. **2** [late 16C+] (*chiefly Aus./N.Z.*) a general term of abuse; i.e. *you bloody mongrel* [despite the synon. of *mongrel* and *half-breed*, there appears to be no racial implication].

mongrel *adj.* [17C+] an abusive epithet.

mongy *adj.* (*also* **mong, mongie**) [MONG *n.*[2]] [1970s+] stupid, dull.

monica *n.* [1950s+] (*S.Afr. gay*) **1** money. **2** menstruation.

monica/monicher/monick(er)/monika/moniker *n. see* MONNIKER *n.*

monish *n* [imitation of Anglo-Yid. speech] [19C–1920s] (*US*) money.

monk *n.* [abbr. MONKEY *n.*] **1** [mid-19C] (*UK Und.*) a person. **2** [mid-19C; 1940s] a general term of contempt. **3** [mid-19C+] (*orig. US*) a *monkey*. **4** [late 19C–1930s] (*US*) a Chinese person. **5** [1920s] (*US black*) a West Indian. **6** [1930s–40s] (*US Und.*) a Supreme Court judge, often on a State level. **7** [1960s] (*US*) addiction to a drug, usu. heroin [abbr. MONKEY ON ONE'S BACK *n.*].

IN PHRASES

❑ **out the monk** *adj. see* separate entry.

monk *v.* [MONKEY *v.*] (*US*) **1** [late 19C–1950s] to trifle with, to fool around. **2** [1950s–60s] to neck, to engage in sexual activity.

monkery *n.* (*also* **mackry, monkry**) (*UK tramp*) **1** [late 18C–19C] the countryside. **2** [mid-19C] as *the monkery*, the world of tramps and vagrants; thus *on the monkery*, living as a tramp. **3** [mid-19C–1930s] a specific district in which tramps or beggars work.

monkey *n.* **1** [late 16C+] a scamp, a rascal [now SE]. **2** a practitioner or a worker. (**a**) [late 17C] a playhouse girl or prostitute. (**b**) [late 19C–1900s] as used by artisans or manual labourers, a clerk. (**c**) [20C+] (*US*) a person who acts as, works as, or is responsible for something, usu. a workman, used in combs., e.g. *bridge monkey*, a bridge builder. (**d**) [1910s–30s] (*US*) a chorus-girl or a taxi-dancer, a dancehall hostess who charges ten cents a dance to all-comers; thus *MONKEY SHOW* below. (**e**) [1920s–40s] (*US black*) the leader of a band or orchestra [the on-stage cavorting or their MONKEY SUIT *n.*]. (**f**) [1930s–40s] (*US*) one who washes dishes in a restaurant, café etc. (**g**) [1930s–40s] (*US Und.*) a prohibition agent. (**h**) [1940s+] (*US prison*) a correctional officer. **3** an inanimate object. (**a**) [19C] a small bustle [? the image of a baby monkey clinging to its mother's back]. (**b**) [early 19C–1950s] (*UK Und.*) a padlock [ety. unknown; but note SE *monkey*, 'applied to various machines and implements' (*OED*)]. (**c**) [mid-19C] a flask, esp. as used to carry liquor on hunting expeditions [? backform. f. *SUCK THE MONKEY under* SUCK *v.*[1]]. (**d**) [mid-19C–1910s] (*Aus./N.Z.*) a mortgage. **4** in derog. senses. (**a**) [19C+] a general insult, esp. when used derog. since mid-19C by white people of a black or Asian person. (**b**) [20C+] (*Aus./US*) (*also* **monkey**

man) a Chinese person; a Mongolian; any East Asian person. (**c**) [1900s–40s] (*US black*) a West Indian. (**d**) [1910s+] (*Aus./US*) a Japanese person. (**e**) [1910s+] a thug, spec. one with no intelligence. (**f**) [1970s+] (*US black*) a white person. **5** [19C+] a person, with no derog. overtones. **6** [mid-19C–1930s] (*later use US black*) ill temper, tetchiness [? characteristics of the animal]. **7** [mid-19C+] (*also* **monk**) £500, A$500, $500 [ety. unknown]. **8** [late 19C–1950s] (*Aus.*) a sheep. **9** the genitals. (**a**) [late 19C+] (*Aus./US*) the vagina [? punning abbr. MONKEY BUSINESS *n.*]. (**b**) [1980s+] (*US campus*) the penis. **10** a gullible person. (**a**) [1920s] (*US tramp*) a member of the public, a non-tramp. (**b**) [1920s+] (*US Und.*) a victim of a swindler, a dupe. **11** in drug uses [abbr. MONKEY ON ONE'S BACK *n.*]. (**a**) [1930s+] (*drugs*) any form of narcotics addiction, usu. of heroin, morphine; thus the withdrawal symptoms that attend a lack of the drug. (**b**) [1960s–70s] (*drugs*) morphine. (**c**) [1970s] (*US black/drugs*) a drug addict (who is irredeemably 'hooked'). (**d**) [1980s+] (*drugs*) a cigarette made from cocaine paste and tobacco. **12** [1980s+] (*US campus*) 'the other woman', 'the other man', i.e. the individual with whom one's partner is having an affair [such a person 'climbs all over' their partner].

IN COMPOUNDS

❑ **monkey bait** *n.* [1950s+] (*drugs*) free samples of addictive drugs. ❑ **monkey-chaser** *n.* **1** [1910s–30s] (*US*) a man who frequents taxi-dances. **2** [1920s+] (*US black*) a West Indian. **3** [1950s] (*US*) a cocktail composed of gin and ice, with a little sugar and a trace of water. ❑ **monkey clothes** *n.* [MONKEY SUIT *n.*] **1** [1900s–30s] (*US*) men's dress or evening wear. **2** [1920s] (*US Und.*) uniform or plain clothes, as worn by policemen. ❑ **monkey-dodger** *n.* [1900s–40s] a sheep-station hand; thus *monkey-dodging*, mustering sheep. ❑ **monkey drill** *n.* [1950s] (*drugs*) a hypodermic syringe. ❑ **monkey house** *n.* **1** [1900s–60s] (*US*) a psychiatric institution. **2** [1950s] (*US drugs*) an opium den. ❑ **monkey jumps** *n.* [1950s] (*drugs*) the staggering and twitching of one who is addicted to narcotics. ❑ **monkey-juice** *n.* [2000s] semen. ❑ **monkey meat** *n.* **1** [1910s+] (*orig. US milit.*) canned corned beef. **2** [1950s–70s] (*drugs*) a heavily intoxicated drug user. ❑ **monkey medicine** *n.* [1950s] (*drugs*) morphine. ❑ **monkey rum** *n.* [1940s–70s] (*US*) West Indian rum. ❑ **monkey show** *n.* (*also* **monkey hop**) [1910s–30s] (*US*) a taxi-dance or burlesque show. ❑ **monkey spanner** *n.* [2000s] the penis. ❑ **monkey track** *n.* [1960s] the scarred veins that are the product of and indicate heroin addiction. ❑ **monkey wagon** *n.* [1960s] (*US*) an estate car, a 'family' car.

IN PHRASES

❑ **feed the monkey** *v.* **1** [1950s+] (*drugs*) (*also* **scratch the monkey**) to maintain one's addiction to narcotics. **2** [1970s+] (*US gay*) to have sexual intercourse with a woman. ❑ **get one's monkey up** *v.* (*also* **have one's monkey up**) [early–mid-19C+] to lose one's temper, to get into a bad temper; thus *my monkey's up*, I am very annoyed. ❑ **get someone's monkey up** *v.* (*also* **put someone's monkey up**) [mid-19C–1920s] to annoy someone, to infuriate someone. ❑ **give someone the monkeys** *v.* [1930s] to annoy, to distress. ❑ **have the monkeys** *v.* [1910s] to have feelings of irritation. ❑ **kill the monkey** *v.* [1990s+] to end an addiction to narcotics. ❑ **like a monkey on a stick** *adj.* [late 19C+] behaving in an eccentric, bizarre manner. ❑ **like a monkey with a tin tool** *adj.* [mid-19C] impudent, cheeky, self-satisfied. ❑ **monkey on one's back** *n. see* separate entry. ❑ **slap the monkey** *v.* [1990s+] to masturbate. ❑ **suck the monkey** *v. see* under SUCK *v.*[1]. ❑ **touch the monkey's head** *v.* [1990s+] of a woman, to place one's fingers on a man's penis.

SE in slang uses

IN COMPOUNDS

❑ **monkey-assed** *adj.* [ASS *n.* (2)] [1980s+] (*US*) damned. ❑ **monkeyback** *n.* [1920s] (*US black*) a man who dresses in formal dinner wear, a dude. ❑ **monkey bite** *n.* [1940s+] (*US*) a love-bite. ❑ **monkey blanket** *n. see* HORSE BLANKET *under* HORSE *n.* ❑ **monkey board** *n.* [mid–late 19C] the step on a bus on which the conductor stands. ❑ **monkey business** *n. see* separate entry. ❑ **monkey cage** *n.* [20C+] (*Can./US Und.*) a prison cell. ❑ **monkey-catcher** *n.* [the assumed cunningness of monkeys; those who can catch them must be doubly intelligent] [mid-19C–1940s] (*W.I.*) a shrewd, intelligent individual. ❑ **monkey dick** *n.* [DICK *n.*[1] (5)] (*US*) **1** [1960s+] a frankfurter sausage. **2** [1980s+] a contemptible person. ❑ **monkey dust** *n.* [DUST *n.* (6e)] [1970s+] (*drugs*) **1** phencyclidine. **2** morphine. ❑ **monkey-face** *n. see* separate entry. ❑ **monkey fart** *n.* (*also* **monkey shit**) [FART *n.* (1)] [20C+] (*W.I.*) utter rubbish, absolute nonsense. ❑ **monkey farting** *n.* [1960s+] (*orig. Can.*) playing around, 'messing about', wasting time. ❑ **monkey-fuck** *v.* [1990s+] to light one cigarette from the tip of another. ❑ **monkey-hangers** *n. see* APEHANGERS *under* APE *n.* ❑ **monkey hat** *n.* [1950s] (*US*) a hat worn by someone preparing food, as in a sandwich bar. ❑ **monkey iron** *n.* [it is very tough to chew] [1950s] (*W.I.*) a sweetmeat made of coconut boiled with sugar. ❑ **monkey jacket** *n.* **1** [late 18C+] a short, close-fitting jacket, worn by either sex. **2** [1940s+] a dinner jacket. ❑ **monkey Jesus** *n.* [1940s] (*W.I.*) a very ugly person. ❑ **monkey-lip** *n.* (*also* **monkey-shave**) [1900s] (*Aus.*) a form of beard typically worn by puritans and evangelicals. ❑ **monkey lotion** *n.* [1990s+] (*W.I.*) acid that is thrown on someone resulting in burns and disfiguration. ❑ **monkey man** *n.* **1** [1920s–60s] (*US black*) a weak man, usu. one dominated by his wife or girlfriend. **2** [1920s–60s] (*US black*) rarely, a West Indian immigrant. **3** [1950s] (*N.Z.*) one who provides a mortgage [note Ware (1909): 'Monkey on the house (*Soc.*). Expression current in Cambridgeshire. It means that the owner of the house has raised money on it. The natives also say, 'A monkey on the land', the word 'monkey' being exactly equivalent to 'mortgage''']. **4** [1980s+] (*W.I.*) a large, unintelligent man. ❑ **monkey money** *n.* **1** [1910s–30s] (*US*) any foreign currency. **2** [1930s] (*US tramp*) tokens issued instead of cash to be used in a specific shop. **3** [1940s] (*UK Und.*) counterfeit coins. **4** [1990s+] (*W.I.*) a small, insignificant sum of money. ❑ **monkey nut** *n.* (*US drugs*) a given measure of crack cocaine. ❑ **monkey nuts** *n.* **1** [20C+] (*US prison*) prison-cooked meatballs. **2** [2000s] a very small amount. ❑ **monkey parade** *n.* [late 19C–1910s] the evening promenade up and down a main thoroughfare by (Cockney) young people in search of flirtation. ❑ **monkey piss** *n.* [PISS *n.* (1)] [1970s] (*US*) weak beer or bad wine. ❑ **monkey root** *v.* [var. on MONKEY-FUCK above] [1980s+] (*Aus. prison*) to light one cigarette from the tip of another. ❑ **monkey's...** *n. see also* separate entries. ❑ **monkey's allowance** *n.* [late 18C–19C] a minimum of payment and a maximum of harsh treatment, usu. 'translated' as 'more kicks than halfpence'. ❑ **monkey shine** *see* separate entries. ❑ **monkey's tail** *n.* [early–mid-19C] (*orig. naut.*) a short crowbar. ❑ **monkey stick** *n.* [1940s] a malacca cane, as used by a dandy. ❑ **monkey swill** *n.* [1920s–30s] US cheap liquor, strong liquor, manufactured during US Prohibition. ❑ **monkey suit** *n. see* separate entry. ❑ **monkey's wedding** *n.* [1940s+] (*S.Afr.*) a situation of alternating or simultaneous sunshine and rain [fig. use of *monkey's wedding* (*breakfast*), a presumably chaotic occasion (used as such in parts of US), ? ult. synon. Port. *casamento de rapôsa*, a vixen's wedding]. ❑ **monkey tie** *n.* [1940s] (*S.Afr.*) an especially gaudy tie. ❑ **monkey tricks** *n. see* separate entry. ❑ **monkey work** *n.* [late 19C–1960s] (*US*) trickery, mischief.

IN PHRASES

❑ **make a monkey out of** *v.* **1** [late 19C+] (*orig. US*) to make a fool of, to make someone look stupid. **2** to destroy a theory. ❑ **monkey and parrot time** *n.* [late 19C–1900s] (*US*) an unhappy marriage, in which the two partners fight continually. ❑ **monkeys to junkies** *n.* [studying mankind, from its origins as apes to JUNKIE *n.*] [1980s] (*US campus*) a course in anthropology. ❑ **throw a monkey wrench into the machinery** *v.* (*also* **hurl a monkey wrench...**) [20C+] (*orig. US*) to obstruct something deliberately, to go out of one's way to wreck a plan or project; thus *monkey-wrenching*, this form of industrial sabotage, esp. performed by ecologists; *monkey-wrencher*, one who does this. ❑ **too much of the monkey** *n.* [late 19C] (*Aus.*) extreme, 'asking too much'. ❑ **where the monkey puts his nuts** *n.* (*also* **where the monkey shoves his nuts, where the monkey put the pineapple**) [late 19C+] a euph. for the anus, usu. as a phr. of coarse dismissal, *you can shove/put it/them where the monkey...*

monkey *adj.* **1** [1920s+] (*US*) a general derog., esp. in racist contexts. **2** [1950s] difficult, troublesome. **3** [1970s] corrupt, illicit.

monkey *v.* (*also* **monkey about, monkey around, monkey with**) [anthropomorphism] [late 19C+] (*orig. US*) to fool around, to tamper, to fiddle, usu. in a destructive clumsy manner, occas. used as a synon. for the expression 'to busy one's self' with anything, but it cannot be legitimately used of honest, useful work, except when such work is either badly done or is undertaken as a recreation rather than as a legitimate business.

IN PHRASES

❑ **monkey with the band wagon** *v.* [late 19C] (*US campus*) to interfere, to meddle. ❑ **monkey with the buzz saw** *v.* [late 19C–1960s] to interfere foolishly.

monkey business *n.* (*also* **monkey-doodle business, monkey's business**) [late 19C+] (*orig. US*) **1** dubious, underhand or crooked practices. **2** (*also* **monkeydoodle**) foolish activities, 'messing around'. **3** a euph. for sexual intercourse.

monkey-face *n.* **1** [mid–late 19C] a grimace. **2** [late 19C+] a stupid, ugly person, also as term of address.

DERIVATIVES

❑ **monkey-faced** *adj.* [19C+] ugly.

monkey-monk *n.* [HIGH MUCK-A-MUCK *n.* (1)] [late 19C+] (*US*) a superior or important person, whether in fact or through pretension.

monkey on one's back *n.* [ety. unknown; the image is of a monkey, clawing at the sufferer; note Schmidt, *Narcotics Lingo and Lore* (1959): 'in allusion to the once popular carnival and vaudeville monkey-on-the-dog act in which a monkey, riding on a performing dog, held on inseparably to the back of its mount'] **1** [mid–late 19C] anger or a bad temper. **2** [1930s+] (*orig. US drugs*) (*also* **monkey on one's shoulder, gorilla on one's back**) drug addiction, esp. to heroin. **3** [1950s+] in fig. use for any form of addiction or long-term problem.

IN PHRASES

❑ **take the monkey off one's back** *v.* [1960s+] to withdraw from narcotics addiction; also in fig. use.

monkey's *n.* [abbr. *monkey's fuck* (see NOT GIVE A FUCK *v.*)] [1960s+] (*orig. US*) a damn; thus *I don't care a monkey's fuck, I don't give a monkey's ass* etc.

monkey's cousin *n.* [rhy. sl. = a dozen] [1940s+] (*bingo*) the number twelve.

monkey shine *n.* (*also* **monkey shines**) [SE *monkey* + SHINES *n.*] [early 19C+] (*US*) tricks or antics.

monkey-shine *v.* [MONKEY SHINE *n.*] [20C+] (*US*) to misbehave; to play tricks.

monkey spank *n.* [rhy. sl. = WANK *n.*; ult. *SPANK THE MONKEY under* SPANK *v.*[1]] [1990s+] an act of masturbation; lit. and fig.

monkey spanker *n.* [rhy. sl. = WANKER *n.*; ult. *SPANK THE MONKEY under* SPANK *v.*[1]] [1990s+] a masturbator; a general term of abuse.

monkey's tail *n.* [rhy. sl.] [20C+] usu. in pl., a nail.

monkey suit *n.* [late 19C+] (*orig. US*) **1** a uniform or overalls. **2** (*also* **monkey**) a formal dress suit, evening dress; usu. as worn by a man but occas. by a woman. **3** one who is wearing a unform, e.g. a cinema usher. **4** a suit.

monkey's uncle *n.*

IN EXCLAMATIONS

❑ **I'll be a monkey's uncle!** (*also* **I'm a monkey's uncle!**) [1920s+] a general expression of surprise.

monkey tricks *n.* [negative image of the animal + MONKEY *n.* (1)] **1** [18C+] dubious acitivities. **2** [late 18C+] (*also* **monkeys**) (unwanted) sexual advances. **3** [20C+] any action considered irritating.

monkry *n. see* MONKERY *n.*

monniker *n.* (*also* **monacher, monack, monacker, monaker, monarch, monekeer, moneker, monekur, monica, monicher, monick, monicker, monika, moniker, monnicker, monoger**) [? *monogram* or Ling. Fr.; *DSUE* (1984) suggests fig. use of SE *monarch*, a king, who like a name rules a person's life] [mid-19C+] (*orig. tramp*) name, signature; thus *tip someone one's monnicker*, to tell someone one's name; hence an important person.

monniker *adj.* [MONNIKER *n.*] [1970s+] (*US*) pertaining to one's name or nickname; 'trademark'.

monniker *v.* [MONNIKER *n.*] [1920s+] to name.

monocular eyeglass *n.* [mid–late 19C] the anus.

monogen *adj.* (*also* **monogin**) [mid-19C] (*UK Und.*) of jewels, of the highest quality/value.

monoger *n. see* MONNIKER *n.*

monolithic *adj.* [pun on STONED *adj.* (2)] [1960s–70s] highly intoxicated by a drug.

monosyllable *n.* (*also* **divine monosyllable, venerable monosyllable**) [i.e. CUNT *n.* (1)] [18C–19C] the vagina.

monotony *n.* [pun on SE *monogamy*] [1970s+] (*US campus*) one's single, steady girlfriend.

mons *adj.* [? abbr. SE *monster*, ? the WW1 battle of *Mons*] [1980s] a blunder.

mons meg *n.* [a play on *Mons Meg*, a 15C cannon kept at Edinburgh Castle; presumably a coarse ref. to its gaping mouth + poss. play on *mons veneris*] [19C] the vagina.

monster *n.* **1** [1920s–70s] (*US*) a large and formidable car or plane. **2** [1950s+] (*US*) an outstanding person, thing, achievement or success. **3** [1960s] (*US campus*) a difficult course or examination. **4** in drug uses. (**a**) [1970s+] (*drugs*) any exceptionally powerful drug. (**b**) [1990s+] (*US drugs*) methedrine. **5** [1980s+] (*UK prison*) a sexual offender, a child-molester etc. **6** [1990s+] an obsessive, an addict. **7** [2000s] (*US prison*) HIV/AIDS. **8** [2000s] cocaine.

monster *adj.* [MONSTER *n.*] **1** [1930s+] (*US*) great in size, quantity, significance or achievement. **2** [1950s] (*US black*) annoying, irritating. **3** [1970s+] (*US black*) excellent, first-rate, the very best.

monster *v.* [note 1990s journ. use, to subject to intense media scrutiny] [1960s+] (*orig. Aus.*) **1** to harass a woman in the hopes of seduction. **2** to attack (verbally rather than physically), to pressurize.

-monster *sfx* [MONSTER *n.* (2)] [1980s+] (*US*) used with a relevant n. to denote a person's primary characteristic or passion, e.g. *party-monster, munchie-monster*.

monstro *adj.* (*also* **monstrous**) [abbr. SE *monstrous*] [1970s+] (*US*) enormous, outstanding.

mont *adj. see* MINT *adj.*

monte *n.*[1] [abbr. THREE-CARD MONTE *n.*] **1** [mid-19C+] (*Und./gambling*) the three-card trick, 'find the lady'. **2** [late 19C–1900s] (*Aus.*) (*also* **monte-man, monty**) a racecourse tipster. **3** [late 19C+] (*Aus./N.Z.*) (*also* **monty**) an absolute certainty. **4** [1900s] one who plays sense 1. **5** [1930s] (*Aus.*) a lie. **6** [1980s+] (*N.Z.*) an admirable person.

IN COMPOUNDS

❑ **monte-man** *n.* [MONTE *n.*[1] (1) + SE man; however he does not necessarily practise the three-card monte swindle] [1900s] (*Aus.*) a confidence trickster.

monte *n.*[2] [1970s+] good quality marijuana from Mexico [pun on Sp. *monte*, a bush/BUSH *n.*[1] (1)].

monte *n.*[3] [play on the city *Montevideo*] [1990s+] a video.

monte *n.*[4] *see* MONTY *n.*

Monte Cairo *n.* [2000s] a giro cheque.

montezumas *n.* [rhy. sl.] [20C+] bloomers.

Montezuma's revenge *n.* (*also* **Pharaoh's revenge**) [named after the last Aztec emperor, *Montezuma II* (properly Moctezuma c.1470–1520)] [1960s+] (*orig. US*) food poisoning, esp. with diarrhoea, suffered by tourists in Mexico or Egypt.

monthlies *n.* (*also* **monthly**) [late 19C+] the menstrual period.

monthly bill *n.* (*also* **monthly dues, monthly pain**) [20C+] (*US*) menstruation.

Monto *n.* [late 19C–1960s] (*Anglo-Irish*) the run-down, lowlife area surrounding Montgomery Street, Dublin.

montra *n.* [Fr. *montre*, a watch] [early 19C] (*UK Und.*) a watch.

monty *n.* (*also* **full monte, full monty, monte**) [ety. unknown; the success of the 1997 film *The Full Monty* hugely popularized the phr. and the variety of etys for *monty/monte* were proposed, although none has been accepted as authoritative; they range from *monte*, a Sp. and Hisp.Am. game of chance, played with a pack of 45 cards, the tailor's *Montague* Burton, i.e. a full three-piece suit; the 'full English breakfast' purportedly enjoyed by Field Marshall *Montgomery*, during WW2; the gambling town of *Monte* Carlo, in which the *full monte* would equate with 'breaking the bank' and several more] **1** [late 19C+] everything, all that there is, 'the lot'; esp. in phr. *the full monty*. **2** *see* MONTE *n.*[1].

monz *n.* [? SE *monster*] [1990s+] (*UK juv.*) a social reject.

moo *n.*[1] [SE *moo*, strengthened by abbr. MOO-COW *n.*] **1** [late 19C+] a woman, esp. a foolish one; often as *silly old moo*. **2** (*US*) as products of the MOO-COW *n.* (**a**) [1910s–20s] a beefsteak. (**b**) [1940s+] milk or cream.

moo *n.*[2] [abbr. MOOLA *n.*] [1940s–50s] (*US*) money.

mooca *n.* (*also* **moocah**) [? initial letter] [1930s+] (*drugs*) marijuana.

mooch *n.*[1] (*also* **mouch**) [MOOCH *v.*[1] (2); note blurb by Edison Company for the song 'Mootching Along' by Collins & Harlan (1914): 'For a long time, way back in the days before the [first world] war, negroes did a shuffling or lazy man's dance...They called it The Mootch. The shuffle explains the movement of the feet, and the "mootch" defines the lazy movement of the shoulders, and the sway and rhythm of the body'] (*orig. US*) **1** in US Und. uses. (**a**) [mid-19C–1940s] a street robbery. (**b**) [1950s] a street thief who specializes in snatching (drunken) men's jewellery. **2** [late 19C–1900s] a departure or dismissal. **3** [late 19C+] a wander, a saunter. **4** [1910s+] (*also* **moochie**) a sponger, a borrower; a beggar, an idler. **5** [1920s+] (*US gambling*) a gullible or naïve person. **6** [1940s–50s] (*US drugs*) a drug, usu. heroin or opium. **7** [1940s–70s] (*drugs*) a drug addict; thus *KICK THE MOOCH AROUND* below. **8** [1950s+] a general term of abuse.

IN COMPOUNDS

❑ **mooch joint** *n.* [1940s–50s] (*drugs*) a bar where one can buy drugs. ❑ **mooch pusher** *n.* [1940s–50s] (*drugs*) a drug dealer.

IN PHRASES

❑ **do a mook** *v.* [1900s] (*Aus.*) to go to. ❑ **kick the mooch around** *v.* [1950s] (*US drugs*) to smoke opium.

mooch *n.*[2] **1** [20C+] (*US*) a bad mood. **2** [1950s] a problem, a difficult situation.

DERIVATIVES

❑ **moochy** *adj.* [1990s+] tetchy.

mooch *v.*[1] (*also* **mouch**) [? OF *muchier*, to hide or skulk] **1** [early 19C+] (*also* **mootch**) to pilfer, to steal. **2** [mid-19C+] (*also* **moose**) often constr. with *along, off, out* etc, to walk, to go, to amble along. **3** [mid-19C+] to beg, to sponge, to cadge. **4** [late 19C+] to loaf around. **5** [late 19C+] (*tramp*) to live as a tramp. **6** [1910s+] to take. **7** [1910s+] (*US*) to enter surreptitiously. **8** [20C+] (*Ulster*) to play truant, esp. as *ON THE MOOCH* below.

IN PHRASES

❑ **mooch off** *v.* [1920s+] (*US*) to laze around. ❑ **mooch the stem** *v.* [MAIN STEM *n.* (4)] [20C+] (*US*) to beg in a city's main street. ❑ **on the mooch** **1** [mid-19C+] living as a professional beggar. **2** [mid-19C+] in search of a given commodity, e.g. money or drugs. **3** [late 19C] (*also* **on the mouch**) wandering about. **4** [late 19C] on the lookout. **5** [20C+] (*Irish*) playing truant. **6** [1940s–50s] (*drugs*) addicted to drugs.

mooch *v.*[2] [SMOOCH *v.*[1] (1)] [1960s+] (*US*) to kiss.

moocher *n.* (*also* **moucher, moocheress**) [MOOCH *v.*[1]] **1** [mid-19C+] a beggar. **2** [mid-19C+] a loafer, a loiterer. **3** [mid-19C+] (*US*) a petty thief. **4** [1940s–50s] (*drugs*) a drug addict. **5** [1950s] a gangster.

IN COMPOUNDS

❑ **moocher's mile** *n.* [1930s–40s] the stretch of Piccadilly (in London) that runs east across the Circus and on to Leicester Square.

Moocheries *n. see* MUCKERIES, THE *n.*

moochie *n. see* MOOCH *n.*[1] (4).

mooching *adj.* [MOOCH *v.*[1] (4)] [mid-19C+] idling, loafing.

moochy *adj. see under* MOOCH *n.*[2].

moo-cow *n.* (*also* **moo, moo-moo**) **1** [early 19C+] (*UK juv.*) a cow. **2** [1990s+] (*US campus*) an obese person.

moodies *n.* [1960s] depression.

moody *n.* **1** [1930s+] gentle persuasion, 'blarney'. **2** [1950s+] complaints, ill temper, depression. **3** [1950s+] deceit, lies, verbal trickery [rhy. sl.; *Moody & Sankey* = HANKYPANKY *n.* (1); ult. the US evangelists Dwight Lyman *Moody* (1837–99) and Ivo David *Sankey* (1840–1908)]. **4** [1960s+] a fit of 'the sulks'; thus *pull/throw a/the moody*, to sulk.

IN PHRASES

❑ **old moody** *n.* [1930s+] a cunning trick, a fraud; thus *pull the old moody*. ❑ **throw a moody** *v.* [1930s+] to become sulky, truculent, ill-tempered.

moody *adj.* [1940s+] illicit, untrustworthy, false.

IN PHRASES

❑ **go (all) moody (on)** *v.* [1970s] (*UK Und.*) to fail, to go wrong.

moody *v.* [MOODY *n.* (3)] [1950s+] **1** to trick, to defraud, to play a confidence trick. **2** to complain. **3** to lie about, to act lazily. **4** to pretend.

mooe *n. see* MOEY *n.*

mooe/mooey *n. see* MOEY *n.*

mooer *n.* [SE *moo* + sfx *-er*] [19C] a cow.

mooey *n. see* MOEY *n.*

moofky-poofky/moofty-poofty *n. see* MIFKY-PIFKY *n.*

moofty-poofty *n.* [? MUFF *n.*[1] (1) + POOF *n.*] [1990s+] oral intercourse, whether fellatio or cunnilingus.

moogie *adj. see* MOEGIE *adj.*

mooi *adj.* [Du. *mooi*, pretty; note milit. jargon *mooi-moois*, full dress or 'step-out' uniform (lit. 'pretty-pretties')] [early 19C+] (*S.Afr.*) a general term of approval meaning pleasant, pretty good, nice.

moojin *n.* [20C+] (*W.I.*) a fool, a simpleton.

moo juice *n.* (*also* **moo-moo**) [MOO-COW *n.* + SE *juice*] [1930s+] (*orig. US black*) milk.

mook *n.* [? JAMOKE *n.*[2] (1)] [1930s+] (*US*) a general term of abuse, a foolish person.

IN PHRASES

❑ **do a mook** *v. see under* MOOCH *n.*[1].

moola *n.* (*also* **mola, moolah, moolouw, mulla**) [ety. unknown] [1930s+] (*orig. US*) money.

mooley *n.* [abbr.] [2000s] (*US black*) a mulatto.

moolie *n.* [1960s+] (*US*) **1** a country person [? SE *muleskinner*]. **2** a black person [MULENYAM *n.* (1)].

moolouw *n. see* MOOLA *n.*

moo-moo *n.*[1] [? Twi *e-mumu*, a person who is deaf and dumb] [20C+] (*W.I.*) **1** an extremely shy person, too nervous to speak out. **2** a fool, a simpleton.

moo-moo *n.*[2] *see* MOO JUICE *n.*

moon *n.* **1** the moon's circularity. (**a**) [mid-18C; late 19C+] the buttocks, the anus, the rectum; thus *FULL MOON* below. (**b**) [mid–late 19C] (*US*) a large, round biscuit. (**c**) [1910s] (*US*) a silver dollar. (**d**) [1960s+] (*also* **moonie, moony**) the purposeful exposure of the buttocks in a provocative way. **2** in senses of time, as defined by lunar passage. (**a**) [early 19C+] a month's imprisonment, or multiples thereof, e.g. *nine moon*. (**b**) [early 19C+] a month. (**c**) [late 19C–1930s] (*US tramp*) a night; thus phr. *cover with the moon*, sleep in the open air. **3** [1920s+] (*US*) (*also* **moony**) illicitly distilled liquor abbr. MOONSHINE *n.* **4** [1960s+] (*drugs*) (*also* **moon**) a piece of peyote cactus, eaten for the mescaline it contains [? its half-moon shape].

IN COMPOUNDS

❑ **moon pie** *n.* [fig. use of PIE *n.* (1)] [1970s+] (*US*) anal intercourse. ❑ **moon-queerer** *n.* [mid-19C] (*UK Und.*) a link-boy.

IN PHRASES

□ **full moon** *n.* [1970s+] the bared buttocks, deliberately exhibited in public. □ **shoot a moon** *v.* (*also* **shoot moon, shoot the moon**) [1960s+] to bare one's buttocks in public. □ **shoot the moon** *v.* **1** [1940s] to have sexual intercourse; thus of a man, to ejaculate. **2** *see also* SE phrs. below.

IN EXCLAMATIONS

□ **my moon!** [late 17C+] a general excl. of disdain, dismissal, arrogant contempt.

SE in slang uses

IN COMPOUNDS

□ **moon cricket** *n.* [ety. unknown; ? a cricket that emerges at night will appear to be black] [20C+] (*US*) a black person. □ **moon-curser** *n.* [dial. *moon-curser*, a ship-wrecker. Urban *moon-cursers* specialized in working the area near Lincoln's Inn Fields in London] [late 17C–mid-19C] (*UK Und.*) a link-boy who either robs those for whom he provides a light, or who guides his charges towards some villainous confederates who do the job for him. □ **moon-eyed** *adj.* [the drunkard's seeing double, and thus two moons] [18C+] (*US*) drunk. □ **moon-eyed hen** *n.* [SE *moon-eyed*, squinting, orig. used of horses] [late 18C–early 19C] 'a squinting wench' (Grose). □ **moon-face** *n.* [late 19C+] (*US*) an Asian person; thus *moon-faced*, having Japanese or Asian features. □ **moonfeed** *n.* [1980s] (*drugs*) heroin. □ **moon-glow** *n.* [1950s] (*W.I.*) a light-brown complexion. □ **moon juice** *n.* [1970s+] **1** (*US drugs*) cough syrup laced with amphetamine. **2** (*drugs*) heroin. □ **moonman** *n.* *see* separate entry. □ **moon-raker/-raking** *n.* *see* separate entries. □ **moon rock** *n.* [ROCK *n.* (4c)] [1980s+] (*drugs*) a mixture of crack cocaine and heroin. □ **moon-shooter** *n.* *see SHOOT THE MOON* below. □ **moon's man** *n.* *see* MOONMAN *n.* □ **moon stick** *n.* [SE *moon*, i.e. the 'yellow' colour + STICK *n.*] [2000s] (*US black*) a white man's penis.

IN PHRASES

□ **go between the moon and the milkman** *v.* [i.e. to leave the house at or just prior to dawn] [late 19C] to abscond from a house or flat, taking one's furniture and possessions, but avoiding payment of any outstanding rent, utility bills etc. □ **go to the moon** *v.* (*also* **go in the moon**) [1930s] (*Ulster*) to lose one's temper. □ **over the moon** *adj.* [*DSUE* adds a single mid-19C citation, in a private letter; *OED* cites earlier 19C examples of phr. *jump over the moon*] [1930s+] extremely cheerful, delighted, esp. as a clichéd response attributed to sportspeople, particularly professional football players, when interviewed about a successful game or competition. □ **shoot the moon** *v.* [it is done during the night] **1** [early 19C–1950s] (*also* **bolt the moon**) to abscond from a house or flat, taking one's furniture and possessions but avoiding payment of any outstanding rent, utility bills etc; thus *moon-shooter*, one who absconds with their possessions but without paying the rent. **2** [1920s–30s] (*US*) to take a major gamble [ext. of sense 1]. **3** *see also* sl. phrs. above.

moon *v.* [MOON *n.* (1a)] **1** [late 19C–1930s] (*US*) to have anal intercourse with. **2** [1960s+] (*orig. US*) (*also* **shoot a moon**) to drop one's trousers and underpants and present one's bare buttocks to onlookers, often performed through a car window. **3** [1990s+] in weakened form of sense 2, to bare one's buttocks.

mooner *n.* [presumably f. the effect of the moon on the mind, or due to the effects of a full moon, during which time the crime rate supposedly increases] [1950s+] (*US Und.*) a pathological lawbreaker.

mooney *adj.* *see* MOONY *adj.*

Mooney's apron *n.* [20C+] (*Ulster*) in cards, the ten of clubs.

moonie *n.* *see* MOON *n.* (1d).

moonlight *n.* [var. on MOONSHINE *n.*] [19C] smuggled spirits.

SE in slang uses

IN COMPOUNDS

□ **moonlight wanderer** *n.* [early 19C] a tenant who cheats the landlord by leaving lodgings late at night, usu. with their household possessions.

IN PHRASES

□ **let moonlight into** *v.* *see LET THE DAYLIGHT INTO/THROUGH under* DAYLIGHT *n.*[1]. □ **moonlight-pon-tick** *n.* [lit. 'moonlight on a stick'] [1940s+] (*W.I.*) a gas lamp.

moonlight *v.* [to operate by SE *moonlight*] **1** [1940s] (*UK Und.*) to engage in criminal activity at night. **2** [1950s–60s] (*Irish*) to steal cattle. **3** [1950s+] (*orig. US*) to work at two jobs in order to boost one's income. The second job is usu. night work, and the other employer may not know about it.

DERIVATIVES

□ **moonlighting** *n.* [1950s+] taking a second, usu. late-night, job in addition to one's daily employment.

moonlighter *n.* [MOONLIGHT *v.*] **1** [late 19C–1960s] (*UK Und.*) a thief or burglar who operates at night; (*Irish*) usu. a cattle thief. **2** [20C+] one who escapes paying the rent by leaving a house late at night. **3** [1920s–40s] a smuggler of illicitly distilled liquor. **4** [1950s+] one who takes a second job, undeclared for tax purposes. **5** [1960s] (*US teen*) one who betrays their regular partner. **6** [1970s+] (*US black*) a prostitute.

moonlight flit *n.* (*also* **flit, midnight flit, moonlight flitter**) [abbr. 18C MOONLIGHT FLITTING *n.*] [early 19C+] the removal of one's household goods, and with them oneself, late at night in order to escape paying one's rent, usu. in phr. *do a (moonlight) flit*.

moonlight flits *n.* [rhy. sl. = TIT *n.*[2] (1); ult. MOONLIGHT FLIT *n.*] [1990s+] the female breasts.

moonlight flitting *n.* [earlier version of MOONLIGHT FLIT *n.*] [early 18C–mid-19C] leaving a house late at night to avoid paying rent.

moonlighting *n.* *see under* MOONLIGHT *v.*

moonlights *n.* [one wears such clothing at night] [1900s–10s] (*US*) evening dress.

moonman *n.* (*also* **moon's man**) ['A moon-man signifies in English a madman...But these moon-men...are neither absolutely mad, nor yet perfectly in their wits. Their name they borrow from the moon, because, as the moon is never in one shape two nights together, but wanders up and down Heaven like an antic, so these changeable-stuff-companions never tarry one day in a place...' Dekker (1608); this discussion of England's gypsies is the first ever to be printed] [17C–early 19C] a gypsy.

moon-raker *n.* ['It is said that some men of that county, seeing the reflection of the moon in a pond, endeavoured to pull it out with a rake' (Grose, 1796). However, the *OED* notes, 'in Wiltshire a more complimentary turn is given to the story: the men were caught raking a pond for kegs of smuggled brandy, and put off the revenue men by pretending folly'] **1** [late 18C–19C] a native of Wiltshire. **2** [19C] a smuggler.

moon-raking *n.* [MOON-RAKER *n.* (2)] [19C] smuggling.

moonshine *n.* [the content of alcoholic *moonshine* differed as to the county, in Sussex and Kent it referred to white brandy, in Yorks. to gin] **1** [mid-17C+] nonsense, a trifle, nothing at all; flattery, humbug; also as *bag of moonshine*, *moonshine in the mustard pot*. **2** [late 18C+] (*also* **moon**) illicitly distilled or contraband liquor [fig. use of sense 1]. **3** [20C+] adulterated liquor.

IN PHRASES

□ **give someone a mouthful of moonshine** *v.* [late 18C–early 19C] to flatter.

SE in slang uses

IN COMPOUNDS

□ **moonshine darlin'** *n.* [1950s] (*W.I.*) a party to which anyone can come as long as they contribute food or drink. It is held outdoors under the light of the moon.

moonshine *adj.* [MOONSHINE *n.* (2)] [late 18C+] usu. of liquor, illicitly distilled.

moonshine *v.* [MOONSHINE *n.*] [late 19C+] (*US*) to distil illicit liquor, usu. bourbon.

moonshiner *n.* [MOONSHINE *v.*] **1** [mid-19C+] (*orig. US*) a distiller of contraband liquor, usu. whisky. **2** [1960s] (*S.Afr.*) a dealer in illicit goods.

moon's man *n.* *see* MOONMAN *n.*

moontan *v.* [pun on SE *suntan*] [1940s+] (*US*) to indulge in sexual activity at night, out-of-doors.

moony *n.* [MOONY *adj.*] **1** [mid-19C] a fool. **2** *see* MOON *n.* (1d). **3** *see* MOONSHINE *n.*

moony *adj.* (*also* **mooney**) [the supposed effect of the (full) moon on one's brain] **1** [mid-19C] melancholy. **2** [mid-19C–1930s] drunk. **3** [mid-19C+] sentimentally romantic. **4** [1930s] (*Aus.*) idiotic. **5** [1950s] (*US*) drug-crazed.

IN COMPOUNDS

□ **moony cove** *n.* [COVE *n.* (1)] [late 19C–1900s] an eccentric person.

Moor, the *n.* [abbr.] [20C+] (*UK Und.*) Dartmoor prison in west Devon.

Moorgate rattler *n.* [play on dial. *Morgan rattler*, a reckless fighter, anyone or anything exceptional or MORGAN RATTLER *n.* (1). Moorgate is an area in the City of London] [late 19C–1900s] (*East London*) a dandified person.

moose *n.*[1] (*also* **bull-moose, regular moose**) (*orig. Can.*) **1** [20C+] a large, powerful, poss. clumsy man. **2** [1990s+] an unattractive woman. **3** [2000s] (*US campus*) a very close friend.

SE in slang uses

IN COMPOUNDS

□ **moose-face** *n.* [mid-19C–1940s] (*US*) an ugly person who is nonetheless wealthy and thus attractive. □ **moose-fucker** *n.* [SE *moose* + FUCK *v.*] [1990s+] a derog. term for a resident of Canada. □ **moose milk** *n.* (*also* **moose juice**) [1920s+] (*Can.*) some form of home-brewed alcohol concocted on the Yukon, e.g. milk and rum mixed.

IN EXCLAMATIONS

□ **moose shit!** (*also* **moose fuck!**) [1960s+] (*US*) used as an oath.

moose *n.*[2] [Jap. *musume*, daughter, girl] **1** [1940s+] (*US*) a little sister or young girl. **2** [1940s+] (*US*) a girl friend. **3** [1950s+] (*US*) a young Japanese or Korean woman, esp. a prostitute, or the wife or mistress of a serviceman stationed in Japan or Korea.

moose *n.*[3]

IN PHRASES

□ **milk the moose** *v. see MILK THE LIZARD under* LIZARD *n.*

moose *v. see* MOOCH *v.*[1] (2).

moosey *n.* [? dial. *moosie/mosey*, soft, over-ripe; or covered with soft hair] [1920s–50s] (*US*) the vagina.

IN COMPOUNDS

□ **moosey-faced** *adj.* [1990s+] a general term of abuse, lit. 'vagina-faced'.

moosh *n.* **1** *see* MUSH *n.*[2]. **2** *see* MUSH *n.*[5].

mooshay *n.* [Fr. *monsieur*] [20C+] (*W.I.*) a poor white, a descendant of the original Fr. settlers on St Kitts.

mooshe-man *n.* (*also* **mushe-man**) [MUSHE *n.* + SE *man*; the poor image of Middle Eastern immigrants] [1940s+] (*W.I.*) a confidence trickster, a hoaxer.

moota *n.* (*also* **mootah, mooter, mootie, mootos, muta, mutah**) [Sp. *mota*, a clod of turf, a handful of earth, thus the link to GRASS *n.*[4]. Note also weaving jargon *mota*, an imperfection or tangle in wool or cotton, thus the link to a 'tangled' mind] [1930s+] (*drugs*) marijuana.

mootch *v. see* MOOCH *v.*[1].

mo-out *v. see* MO *v.*[1].

Mop *n.* [abbr.] [1920s–30s] (*US tramp*) the Missouri Pacific Railroad.

mop *n.*[1] **1** [early 19C+] the hair of the head. **2** [1940s] (*US*) pubic hair, of either sex. **3** [1940s] (*US black*) a beard. **4** [1950s–70s] (*US black*) hair that has been straightened.

SE in slang uses

IN COMPOUNDS

□ **mop-squeezer** *n.* **1** [late 18C–early 19C] a maidservant. **2** [1940s–60s] (*US*) a queen in poker [joc. use of sense 1]. □ **mopstick** *n.* (*also* **mophead**) [SE *mopstick*, a mop-handle] **1** [late 19C] a fool. **2** [late 19C] (*also* **mop handle**) a thin, scrawny person. **3** [late 19C–1930s] one who loafs around a cheap saloon and cleans up the place in return for drinks.

mop *n.*[2] [SE *mop up* (liquor)] [mid-19C–1910s] **1** a drinking bout, a drunken spree; usu. as *on the mop*. **2** a drunkard.

mop *v.* [SE *mop up*] **1** [late 19C+] usu. in passive, to defeat; thus *mopped out*, ruined. **2** [1950s] (*W.I./UK black*) to beg, to ask for. **3** [1970s+] (*US gay*) to steal, esp. to shoplift.

IN PHRASES

□ **mop ass** *v.* [ASS *n.* (2)] [1990s+] (*US*) to win conclusively. □ **mop down** *v.* [20C+] to empty a glass.

mop! *excl.* [jazz use *mop*, the last beat at the end of a jazz number with a cadence of triplets] [1940s+] (*orig. US*) a word used to indicate a sudden occurrence, e.g. *I'm doing this, then mop! I'm doing that.*

mop and bucket! *excl.* [rhy. sl., euph. for FUCK IT! *excl.*] [20C+] an excl. of annoyance or pain.

mop and pail *n. see* BUCKET AND PAIL *n.*

mope *n.* [MOPE *v.*] [1910s–70s] (*US prison*) a stealthy departure.

IN PHRASES

□ **cop a mope** *v.* (*also* **take a mope**) **1** [1920s–50s] (*US*) to leave. **2** [1930s+] (*US prison*) to escape. **3** [1940s] (*US*) to hold back, to refrain from talking.

mope *v.* **1** [late 19C–1960s] (*orig. US*) to walk or move slowly. **2** [late 19C–1970s] to desert or escape. **3** [1930s–40s] (*US Und.*) to live as a vagrant; thus *on the mope*, to live as a tramp; *mopery*, tramping.

IN COMPOUNDS

□ **moping artist** *n.* [1930s] (*US*) a tramp.

mopelize *v. see* MOBILIZE *v.*

mopery *n.* [SE *mope*] **1** [20C+] (*US Und./police*) stupidity or ineptitude. **2** [20C+] (*US Und./police*) a trivial or minor offence, often used ironically, as in a charge of *mopery and dopery*. **3** [1910s] (*US prison*) contraband. **4** [1970s] a second-rate figure.

mopey as a wet hen *adj.* [20C+] (*Aus./N.Z.*) miserable, gloomy.

moph *n. see* MOFF *n.*

mopoke *n.* (*also* **morepork**) [SE *mope hawk* or *mopoke*, the tawny frogmouth, a species of owl. Its song sounds like 'more pork, more pork'] [mid-19C+] (*Aus.*) a fool.

mopolize *v. see* MOBILIZE *v.*

mopper-up *n.* [they 'mop up' liquor] [1910s–30s] (*Aus.*) a drunkard.

moppery *n.* [MOP *n.*[1] (1)] [early–mid-19C] the head.

moppus *n. see* MOPUS *n.*

moppy *adj.*[1] [SE *mopey*] [early 19C] depressed.

moppy *adj.*[2] (*also* **mopped, moppie**) [MOP (UP) *v.*] [early 19C–1940s] drunk.

mops and brooms *phr.* (*also* **all mops and brooms**) [? the old mop fairs, annual fairs held in the UK West Country, at which servants put themselves up for hire; a young woman would carry a *mop* or *broom* to indicate the job she desired. Such fairs were accompanied by much drinking; Hotten (1874) suggests that the world about them appears to resemble such implements to a very drunken person] [19C–1930s] drunk.

IN PHRASES

□ **mop and broom (it)** *v.* [19C] to drink heavily.

mopsy *n.* (*also* **mopsey**) [SE *mopsy*, a general term of endearment, ult. *mop*, abbr. *moppet*, an affectionate term for a baby] [mid-17C–19C; 1940s] a homely woman, usu. used affectionately.

mopsy *adj.* [MOP (UP) *v.*] [late 19C] drunk.

mop (up) *v.* **1** [early 19C+] to eat greedily, to drink, to empty one's glass; thus *mopped up*, drunk. **2** [mid-19C+] to absorb, to appropriate, to defeat or win. **3** [late 19C+] (*orig. milit.*) to carry out conclusively, esp. of a gangland or military shooting. **4** [1910s–20s] to believe, to acknowledge. **5** [1930s+] to make a good deal of money.

mopus *n.* (*also* **moppus**) [? surname of Sir Giles *Mompesson* (1583–1663), a notoriously corrupt speculator under James I]

1 [late 17C] a farthing. **2** [late 17C–mid-19C] a halfpenny. **3** [late 18C–1900s] usu. in pl., money in general.

IN PHRASES

❑ **touch the mopusses** *v.* [early 19C] (*US*) to win money at gambling.

moragrifa *n.* (*also* **mor a grifa**) [? Sp.; ult. GREEFO *n.*] [1960s+] (*drugs*) marijuana.

moral *n.* [SE *moral certainty*] [mid-19C+] (*mainly Aus.*) a certainty; usu. in phr. *it's a moral*.

IN PHRASES

❑ **to a moral** *adv.* [late 19C–early 20C] perfectly.

moral *adj.* [MORAL *n.*] [1900s] certain, definite.

moral Cremorne *n.* [this otherwise staid exhibition was nonetheless illuminated in the evenings, bringing to mind the original *Cremorne*, the notably immoral Chelsea 'pleasure garden'] [late 19C] (*UK society*) the Fisheries Exhibition of 1883.

more... *phr. see under* relevant n.

moreno *n.* [Sp. *moreno*, dark-skinned] [1960s+] (*US*) a black person.

more or less *n.* [rhy. sl.] [20C+] a dress.

morepork *n. see* MOPOKE *n.*

more power to your elbow! *excl. see under* ELBOW *n.*

more R than F *phr.* (*also* **more F than R**) [abbr.] [mid-19C–1900s] *more rogue than fool*; orig. and usu. of a servant.

Moreton (bay) *n.* (*also* **Morton**) [rhy. sl.; *Moreton Bay fig*; ult. Moreton Bay, from 1824–39 the penal settlement sited at the mouth of the Brisbane River, Queensland] **1** [1950s+] (*Aus. Und.*) an informer [= FIZGIG *n.*[2]]. **2** [1970s+] (*Aus.*) a busybody [= GIG *n.*[8] (4)].

morf *n.* (*also* **morph, morpho**) [abbr.] [20C+] (*drugs*) **1** *morph*ine. **2** a *morph*ine user.

morganize *v.* [one William Morgan, abducted and presumably murdered in 1826] [mid-19C] (*US*) to abduct.

morgan rattler *n.* [the term exists in a popular fiddle tune but ety. unknown and ? anecdotal; unlike the rigid police truncheon, it was made of a flexible material; the *EDD* defines it as 1. 'a hard and reckless fighter', 2. the weighted cane or stick, 3. 'anything good or striking of its kind'] **1** [late 18C] a penis. **2** [1900s] a weighted stick used as a weapon, with a knob of lead at one or both ends, often used by garrotters.

morgue *n.* [the provision of drinks, often adulterated with chemicals to increase their potency, that could damage the brain or even kill the drinker] [late 19C–1900s] (*US*) a very sordid bar or saloon.

moriarty *n.* [rhy. sl.] [20C+] a party.

mork *n.* [Rom. *mooshkeroo*, a constable] [late 19C–1900s] a policeman.

morley *n. see* MAULEY *n.*

Mormon *n.* [the polygamy performed by 19C Mormons] [late 19C–1920s] (*US*) a promiscuous man.

SE in slang uses

IN COMPOUNDS

❑ **Mormon candy** *n.* (*also* **Mormon currency**) [the sect's innate Puritanism eschews sweets] [1930s–40s] (*US*) carrots. ❑ **Mormon dinner** *n.* [1930s–40s] (*US*) a meal that consists mainly of potatoes. ❑ **Mormon poison** *n.* [the Mormon prohibition of any beverages containing caffeine] [1980s] (*US*) coffee. ❑ **Mormon rain** *n.* (*also* **Mormon rainstorm**) [the climate of Utah, the home of Mormonism] [1930s+] (*US*) a dust storm.

morner *n.* [1970s+] (*US gay*) sexual intercourse in the morning.

morning *n.* [abbr.] **1** [early 19C–1930s] a *morning* drink. **2** [late 19C+] a *morning* newspaper.

SE in slang uses

IN COMPOUNDS

❑ **morning drop** *n.* [pun on SE *drop*, a popular form of medicine + *drop*, the fall through the gallows' trapdoor] [19C] the gallows; a hanging. ❑ **morning glory** *n.* [puns on SE *morning glory*, the plant *Ipomoea purpurea*] **1** [1900s–80s] (*US*) something which or someone who fails to maintain an early promise, esp. in sporting contexts. **2** [1950s] (*US drugs*) the first narcotic injection of the day. **3** [1970s+] (*Aus.*) sexual intercourse before one gets up in the morning. **4** [1990s+] an erection on waking. ❑ **morning mick** *n.* [MICK *n.*[1]] [20C+] (*Ulster Protestant*) the *Irish News*, published in Belfast with a definite Catholic/nationalist slant. ❑ **morning pride** *n. see* PRIDE OF THE MORNING *n.* ❑ **morning shot** *n.* [SHOT *n.*[1] (6b)] (*US drugs*) **1** [1960s] a narcotics user's first injection of the day. **2** [2000s] any form of stimulant or amphetamine. ❑ **morning sneak** *n.* [SNEAK *n.*[1] (1b)] [early 18C–mid-19C] (*UK Und.*) one who specializes in thieving early in the morning; thus the act of doing so. ❑ **morning wake-up** *n.* [WAKE-UP *n.* (4)] [1980s+] (*drugs*) the first blast of crack cocaine from the pipe. ❑ **morning wood** *n. see under* WOOD *n.*[1].

IN PHRASES

❑ **morning after the night before** *n.* (*also* **next morning feeling**) [late 19C+] the state of being hungover after an excess of alcohol.

Morningside speed *n.* [the socially select area of Morningside, Edinburgh] [1990s+] (*Scot. drugs*) cocaine.

Morocco *n.*

IN PHRASES

❑ **in Morocco** *adj.* [prob. nonce-word; coined as supposed 'gypsy slang' by H.W. Longfellow (1807–82); ? a pun on *buff*, which can refer, like *morocco*, to leather and can also mean naked in the phr. *in the buff*] [mid-19C] stripped, naked.

morocco man *n.* [late 18C–mid-19C] a tout for lottery insurance.

morotgara *n.* (*also* **murotugora**) [ety. unknown] [1970s+] (*drugs*) heroin.

morph *n. see* MORF *n.*

morphodite *n.* (*also* **morph, morphidite, morphodyke, morphodyte, morphy, murphydyke**) [popular mispron. of SE *hermaphrodite*] **1** [18C+] a hermaphrodite. **2** [1920s+] a male homosexual.

morrice *v. see* MORRIS *v.*

morrie *n.*[1] [ety. unknown; ? a nonce-creation by Cook, in *The Crust on its Uppers* (1962), who defines it as 'reverse of Slag' and slag as 'young third-rate grafters, male or female, unwashed, useless'] [1960s] a sharp young person, eyes on the main chance and willing to take risks to achieve what they want.

morrie *n.*[2] [1970s] (*Aus.*) a male homosexual.

morris *v.* (*also* **morrice**) [the movements of the *Morris* dance] **1** [early 18C–early 19C] to be hanged. **2** [early 18C–mid-19C] to dance. **3** [mid-18C] (*UK Und.*) to sell or lose. **4** [mid-18C–19C] to leave; esp. as *come morris, morris off, do a morris*. **5** [19C] to move quickly.

morris minor *n.* [rhy. sl. = SHINER *n.*[1] (2); ult. the automobile, first launched in 1948 in UK] [1950s+] a black eye.

morry *n.* [abbr.] [1970s] a post mortem.

mort *n.* (*also* **maut**) [ety. unknown; ? SE *mort*, a salmon in its third year, i.e. the popular equation of women with fish; Ribton-Turner, *A History of Vagrants* (1887), suggests Welsh *modryb*, a matron, *morwyn*, a virgin] [mid-16C–1930s] a woman, esp. a prostitute.

IN COMPOUNDS

❑ **mort dell** *n.* [late 16C–19C] an unmarried woman or virgin girl who accompanies a mendicant villain. ❑ **mort wap-apace** *n.* [WAP *v.* and SE *apace* according to B.E.; but Dekker, *O Per Se O* (1612), a primary source for B.E., suggests that the phr. was anecdotal, noting that 'there was an abram, who called his mort Madam Wap-apace'; all subseq. uses are glossarial] [17C–early 19C] (*UK Und.*) an experienced prostitute or sexually active woman.

mortal *n.* [late 19C] (*US*) a certainty.

mortal *adj.*[1] (*also* **mortial**) **1** [early 17C–1900s] a general intensifier, e.g. *all my mortal days*. **2** [late 17C+] extreme, great. **3** [early 19C–1910s] long and tedious.

IN COMPOUNDS

❑ **mortal lock** *n.* [LOCK *n.*[1]] [1950s+] (*US, orig. gambling*) a certainty, a cinch, esp. of a racehorse, a race or a winning hand in cards.

mortal *adj.*^{2} [early 19C+] drunk.

mortal *adv.* (*also* **mortial, mortally**) [15C+] extremely, excessively, e.g. *mortal cold, mortal drunk.*

mortaller *n.* [20C+] (*Irish*) a mortal sin, as set down by Roman Catholicism.

mortallious *adj.* [MORTAL *adj.*^{2} (1)+ sfx *-ious*] [19C] very drunk.

mortally *adv. see* MORTAL *adv.*

mortar *n.* [18C–19C] the vagina.

mortgage alley *n.* (*also* **mortage flat, mortgage heights, mortgagehill, mortgage hollow, mortgage knob, mortgage lane, mortgage manor, mortgage mesa**) [1910s+] (*US*) the prosperous part of a town or city.

mortgage deed *n.* [mid-19C] a pawnbroker's ticket.

mortial *adj. see* MORTAL *adj.*^{1}.

Mortie *n.* [misreading or var. on MATIE *n.* (1)] [1970s+] (*S.Afr.*) a student at the University of Stellenbosch.

Morton *n. see* MORETON (BAY) *n.*

m.o.s. *n.* [abbr.] [1980s+] (*US campus*) member of the opposite sex.

moschineer *n. see* MOSKENEER *n.*

moschkener *n. see* MOSKENEER *n.*

Moscow *n.* [MOSKENEER *v.*] [1910s+] (*Aus.*) a pawnshop; thus *in Moscow, gone to Moscow,* in pawn; *Moscow ticket,* a pawn ticket.

mos def *phr.* [abbr.] [2000s] (*US black*) most definitely.

mose *n.* **1** [mid–late 19C] (*US*) the generic name for a typical 'Bowery b'hoy', a proletarian New Yorker who might work as a fireman but whose main occupation was running with a gang, mixing street thuggery with life as a political mercenary [the name, if not the type, was originated by Edward Judson (1823–86), a political fixer and bullyboy, who wrote a number of blood-and-thunder burlesques featuring *Mose*, Lize and their friend Sykesy; note also B.A. Baker's play, *A Glance at New York* (1848), featuring 'Mose', a character based on the real-life Moses 'Old Mose' Humphreys, a leader of the Bowery B'hoys, a ferocious street brawler and a fireman of Lady Washington Engine Co. No. 40]. **2** [1920s–80s] (*US black*) a black man, esp. one who is subservient to whites [proper name *Moses*, a stereotypically 'black' name].

mosekeno *v. see* MOSKENEER *v.*

Moses *n. see* IKEY-MO *n.* (5).

IN PHRASES

▫ **give Moses** *v. see* BASH THE LIVING MOSES OUT OF *under* BASH *v.*

Moses! *excl.* (*also* **by the mother of Moses! Jesusful Moses! my Moses! Moses wept! Mother of Moses! suffering Moses!**) [mid-19C+] a general excl. of surprise, excitement, alarm etc.

mosey *n.*^{1} [late 18C] a bull.

mosey *n.*^{2} [MOSEY *v.*] **1** [1960s+] a wander or walk around. **2** [2000s] a look.

mosey *v.* (*also* **mosey about, ...along, ...around, ...off, ...on, ...on down, ...over, mousey, mozey, mozy**) [? Sp. *vamos*, let's go, thus US *vamoose*, go away] **1** [early 19C+] (*orig. US*) to leave, to wander off, to wander or hang around. **2** [mid-19C+] to go fast, to make haste. **3** [mid-19C+] to walk along; go to.

mosh *n.* [MOSH *v.*^{2}] [1980s+] violent and aggressive dancing.

mosh *v.*^{1} [MOOCH *v.*^{1}] **1** [late 19C–1900s] to leave a restaurant without paying one's bill; thus *the mosh*, the practice of committing this fraud. **2** [1910s–30s] to pawn.

IN COMPOUNDS

▫ **mosh shop** *n.* [1910s–30s] a pawnbroker's shop.

mosh *v.*^{2} [? SE *mash*; ? MOSH (ABOUT) *v.* (1)] [1980s+] to dance in a violent and aggressive manner, jumping up and down, crashing into other dancers, waving one's arms etc; thus *moshing*, the dance style.

IN COMPOUNDS

▫ **mosh pit** *n.* [1980s+] the area in a club or rock arena where MOSHING *n.* takes place.

mosh (about) *v.* (*also* **mosh around, mosh up**) **1** [1950s+] to hit, to fight; to mess up, to destroy; also as adj. **2** [2000s] to mess about.

mosher *n.* [MOSH *v.*^{2}] [1980s+] a metal fan, more recently a nu metal fan; it has become as much a fashion/lifestyle description as just describing one who moshes.

mosh (game) *n.* [ety. unknown] [1910s–30s] (*Aus.*) any form of illegal gambling.

moshing *n. see* MOSH *v.*^{2}.

moshkeneer *n. see* MOSKENEER *n.*

mosh-up *adj. see* MASH-UP *adj.*

mosk *v.* [abbr. MOSKENEER *v.*] [1900s] to pawn, esp. at a profit.

moskeneer *n.* (*also* **mokuiner, moschineer, moschkener, moshkeneer, moskeener**) [MOSKENEER *v.*] [late 19C] a pawner, esp. one who pawns articles for more than they are worth, for a living.

moskeneer *v.* (*also* **mokuiner, moschkener, mosekeno, moshkeneer, moskeener**) [Heb. *mashkon*, a pledge, whence *mishken*, to pawn] [late 19C–1910s] to pawn, esp. to pawn for more than an article is actually worth.

mosker *n.* [MOSKENEER *v.*] [late 19C–1940s] a swindler who specializes in defrauding pawnbrokers.

mosking *n.* (*also* **mossing**) [MOSKENEER *v.*; ? underpinned by the image of moss growing on the unredeemed article] **1** [late 19C] placing things in pawn. **2** [1940s] (*UK Und.*) put in prison.

moskuiner *n. see* MOSKENEER *n.*

mosky *n. see* MOHASKY *n.*

mosque *n.* [late 18C] (*UK Und.*) a church.

mosquito bites *n.* [1970s+] (*US campus*) small breasts.

mosquitos *n.* [? the marks left by the hypodermic rather than a ref. to the actual drug] [1940–50s] (*drugs*) cocaine; thus *mosquito bit*, addicted to cocaine.

moss *n.* **1** [18C–early 19C] (*UK Und.*) lead ['grows on the top' of buildings]. **2** as forms of hair. (**a**) [mid-18C+] the female pubic hair. (**b**) [1900s–60s] (*US*) hair, esp. of the head. (**c**) [1940s–60s] (*US black*) black hair. (**d**) [1970s+] (*US gay*) chest hair. **3** [mid–late 19C] money [? both are 'green' or pvb 'a rolling stone – ? a tramp – gathers no moss'].

DERIVATIVES

▫ **mossy** *adj.* [20C+] of a person, hirsute.

IN COMPOUNDS

▫ **moss dog** *n.* [his 'grip' on money] [1910s] a miser. ▫ **moss rose** *n.* [19C] the female pubic hair. ▫ **moss snatcher** *n.* [1950s] (*US black*) a barber.

SE in slang uses

IN COMPOUNDS

▫ **moss-grown** *adj.* [late 19C–1900s] of a thing, old-fashioned or conservative.

moss-back *n.* **1** [mid–late 19C] (*US*) (*also* **mossy-back**) someone who hid themselves to avoid conscription during the American Civil War. **2** [late 19C+] (*US*) (*also* **mossy-back, mosshead**) a diehard conservative. **3** [1900s–20s] a recluse.

mossie *n.* (*also* **mozzy**) [1940s+] (*orig. Aus.*) a mosquito.

mossing *n. see* MOSKING *n.*

mossoo *n.* [deliberate mispron. of Fr. *monsieur*, mister, sir] [late 19C–1920s] a Frenchman.

mossy *adj.*^{1} [the image of slow growth or movement] **1** [late 16C–early 17C] stupid, dull. **2** [1900s–40s] (*US*) very conservative or reactionary; old-fashioned, old.

mossy *adj.*^{2} [MOSS *n.* (2)] [20C+] of a person, hirsute.

IN COMPOUNDS

▫ **mossy bank** *n.* (*also* **mossy cave, mossy vale**) [late 18C–19C] the female pubic hair. ▫ **mossy cell** *n.* [19C+] the female genital area. ▫ **mossy doughnut** *n.* [DOUGHNUT *n.*^{1} (3)] [1940s+] (*US*) the vagina. ▫ **mossy face** *n.* [late 18C–19C] the female genitals and pubic hair.

SE in slang uses

IN COMPOUNDS

▫ **mossy-back** *n. see* MOSS-BACK *n.*

most, the *n.* [1950s+] (*orig. US*) the best, the most exciting, the finest, also as phr., *the most on toast.*

mostest *n.* [late 19C+] (*orig. US*) the very best, superlative; thus the popular description of Ella Maxwell (1883–1963), 'the hostess with the mostest'.

most ricky-tick *adv.* [1970s+] (*orig. US milit.*) very quickly.

mot *n.* (*also* **mott, motte**) [prob. Du. *mot*, a woman; less likely is Fr. *amourette*, a girlfriend; note *OED* classifies *mot* as alt. sp. of MORT *n.*] (*orig. UK/US/Irish*) **1** [late 18C–19C] a prostitute. **2** [late 18C+] a woman, a wife. **3** [early 19C] a criminal's accomplice; a female criminal. **4** [mid-19C] a public or lodging-house landlady. **5** [late 19C+] (*also* **motte**) the *mons veneris*; thus the vagina. **6** [late 19C+] pubic hair, whether male or female.

DERIVATIVES

❑ **motting** *n.* [19C] pursuing women, esp. prostitutes.

IN COMPOUNDS

❑ **mot-cart** *n.* **1** [mid-19C] a brougham or similar vehicle owned by a kept woman or well-off prostitute. **2** [late 19C] a mattress. ❑ **mot-case** *n.* [CASA *n.*[1]; note synon. Du. *mot-kasse* CASA *n.*[1] (1)] [mid-19C–1920s] a brothel. ❑ **mot-house** *n.* [SE *house*/HOUSE *n.*[1] (1); note synon. Du. *mot huys*] [mid–late 19C] a brothel. ❑ **mott-carpet** *n.* (*also* **motte-fleece, mott-fleece**) [19C] the female pubic hair.

IN PHRASES

❑ **go motting** *v.* [19C] of a man, to have sexual intercourse.

mot *v.* [MOT *n.* (2)] [19C–1930s] to go out pursuing women, to court.

mota *n.* (*also* **m.o., mo, moto**) [Sp. sl. *mota*, dust; var. on MOOTA *n.*] [1950s+] (*US drugs*) marijuana.

IN PHRASES

❑ **black mote** *n.* (*also* **black mo, ...moat**) [1970s+] (*drugs*) **1** a particularly potent variety of marijuana, with notably dark colouring. **2** marijuana mixed with honey.

mote *v.* [abbr. SE *motor*] **1** [late 19C–1940s] to drive or ride in a car. **2** [1920s+] (*also* **motate**) to move quickly, of a person or a vehicle.

motel hell *n.* [1970+] (*US teen*) any situation or place that is considered appalling or unacceptable – a job, a place to stay, a relationship etc.

moth *n.* **1** [mid-19C–1930s] a prostitute. **2** [1990s+] (*Irish*) a woman, a girl-friend [common Irish English confusion of spoken *t* and *th*].

motha *n.* (*also* **mothah**) see MOTHER *n.* (5).

mothball *n.* [? their mind and speech flits around like a moth] [1940s–50s] (*US black/campus*) an irritating person.

mothbox *n.* [1930s–60s] (*orig. US black*) a piano.

mother *n.* **1** in senses referring to a woman or female occupations. (**a**) [mid-16C–1930s] a madam, a bawd, a procuress; often comb. with a proper name as *Mother —*. (**b**) [late 19C–1920s] a public house landlady or similar. (**c**) [late 19C+] one's wife. (**d**) [1920s+] the self-proclaimed name of a female owner of a pet, esp. a dog; thus *Come to mother, baby*. (**e**) [1970s] (*US black*) a married woman. (**f**) [1970s] (*US black*) the senior member of a pimp's stable of whores. (**g**) [1980s] used as a female self-reference. **2** [late 19C; 1940s+] the ultimate example of something, the extreme version of something, something exceptional [popularized in the 1990s as mockery of the hyperbolic use of the phr. *mother of all battles* by the Iraqi dictator Saddam Hussein (1937–2006) to describe the Gulf War, 1991]. **3** in male homosexual contexts, usu. implying effeminacy. (**a**) [1930s+] (*US black*) an effeminate (or homosexual) man. (**b**) [1940s+] (*US gay*) a homosexual who introduces another into the gay world. (**c**) [1940s+] (*US gay*) a term used by an effeminate gay man to refer to himself, e.g. *Your mother....* **4** [1940s–60s] (*US black*) in pl., constr. with *the*, the ritualistic name-calling based on insulting one's rival's mother. **5** (*also* **motha, mothah, muh, mutha**) as abbr. of var. senses of MOTHERFUCKER *n.* (**a**) [1950s+] a derog. term for a person. (**b**) [1960s] as a comparative. (**c**) [1960s+] an unspecified object or situation. (**d**) [1960s+] something exceptional. (**e**) [1970s+] (*US black*) affectionate term used between men. **6** [1960s+] (*also* **mutha**) in (*drugs*) uses [? MOOTA *n.* or abbr. MOTHERFUCKER *n.* or the role of drug as a comforter, i.e. a *mother*]. (**a**) marijuana. (**b**) a drug seller.

SE in slang uses

as a nickname

IN COMPOUNDS

❑ **Mother Bunch** *n.* [joc. use of the name of a noted late-16C ale-wife] [late 16C–early 17C] water. ❑ **Mother Cunny** *n.* [CUNNY *n.*] [mid-17C] generic for a procuress or bawd. ❑ **Mother Damnable** *n.* [usu. generic but in Caulfield, *Blackguardiana* (1793) is a picture of a bawd entitled 'Mother Damnable of Kentish Town Anno 1676' with an accompanying verse (dated 1676) which notes that 'So fam'd, both far and near, is the reenown, / Of Mother Damnable, of Kentish Town'] [late 17C–18C] a procuress, a madam. ❑ **Mother Fist (and her five daughters)** *n.* (*also* **Mother Five Fingers**) [20C+] the hand, in the context of masturbation. ❑ **Mother Ga-ga** *n.* [GAGA *n.*[1]] [1940s+] (*gay*) a fussy, gossipy, interfering older homosexual. ❑ **Mother Knab-cony** *n.* (*also* **mother nab-cony**) [NAB *v.*[1] (1) + CONY *n.*, lit. 'Mother Snatch-Sucker'] [late 17C–early 18C] a madam, a bawd. ❑ **Mother Midnight** *n.* [late 17C–early 19C] **1** a bawd, a madam. **2** a midwife; esp. one who delivers or aborts illegitimate children. ❑ **Mother Parker** *n.* [1950s–70s] (*US gay*) a tough, older homosexual.

general uses

DERIVATIVES

❑ **motherless** *see* separate entries.

IN COMPOUNDS

❑ **mother abbess** *n.* *see* ABBESS *n.* ❑ **motherfuck/fucker/fucking** *see* separate entries. ❑ **motherfugger** *n.* *see* MOTHERFUCKER *n.* ❑ **motherfugging** *adj.* *see* MOTHERFUCKING *adj.* ❑ **motherlove** *n.* [1940s–60s] (*US gay*) **1** a homosexual man having sex with a heterosexual woman. **2** sexual intercourse between two homosexual men of the same 'type', ie passive and passive or active and active. ❑ **mother nature** *n.* **1** [20C+] (*US*) menstruation. **2** [1960s+] (*drugs*) marijuana [mother nature's own tobacco]. ❑ **mother's blessing** *n.* *see under* BLESS *v.*[1]. ❑ **mother's cramp** *n.* [1900s] a hernia. ❑ **mother's day** *n.* [1960s+] **1** (*US black*) the day when welfare cheques arrive from the government. **2** (*US milit.*) payday. ❑ **mother's friend** *n.* [19C] a quinine pessary, an elementary form of contraceptive, whose inefficiency gave it a parallel name, the *midwife's friend*. ❑ **mother's life** *n.* [1980s] imprisonment for life. ❑ **mother's milk** *n.* **1** [early 19C+] gin. **2** [mid-19C] brandy. **3** [1960s] Guinness stout. ❑ **mother's ruin** *n.* [the drink's supposed effects] [1920s+] gin. ❑ **mother superior** *n.* *see* separate entry.

IN PHRASES

❑ **be mother** *v.* (*also* **be mum**) [1950s+] to serve portions, usu. of food and drink and esp. to pour out cups of tea; thus the invitation *will you be mother?*, will you serve/pour? ❑ **does your mother know you're out?** [mid-19C+] sarcastic comment to a person whom the speaker feels should be elsewhere, due to immaturity, foolishness, inexperience etc. ❑ **has your mother sold her mangle?** (*also* **does your mother keep a mangle?**) [note 1990s TV comedy character 'Arthur Atkins' (the comedian Paul Whitehouse), the cod 1930s music-hall comic with his catchphrase 'Where's my washboard'] [19C] an all-purpose teasing phr., aimed at a passer-by. ❑ **have one mother too many** *v.* [a bastard should not have any mother at all, i.e. should have been left unconceived] [20C+] to be illegitimate. ❑ **mother and father of...** *n.* *see* FATHER (AND MOTHER) OF... *phr.* ❑ **mother-in-law** *n.* *see* separate entry. ❑ **mother of all masons** *n.* [a dig at the Freemasons, for no discernible reason] [19C] the vagina; the phr. is used as a toast. ❑ **mother of all saints** *n.* [a blasphemous joke] [late 18C–19C] the vagina. ❑ **mother of all souls** *n.* [a blasphemous joke] [late 18C+] the vagina. ❑ **mother of St Patrick** *n.* (*also* **mother of St Paul**) [a blasphemous joke] [18C–19C] the vagina. ❑ **mother of that was a whisker** *n.* [? phr. *it has whiskers on it* or WHISKER *n.*[1]] [mid–late 19C] a retort to an utterly implausible story.

❑ **mother of the maids** *n.* [early 17C–mid-19C] a madam, a brothel-keeper. ❑ **mother's little helper** *n.* [Rolling Stones' song 'Mother's Little Helper' (1966)] [1960s+] (*drugs*) the tranquillizer Miltown. ❑ **mother-young-girl** *n.* [1990s+] (*W.I.*) an ageing woman who tries to be younger than her years. ❑ **your mother** *n.* [the 'feminization' underpinning much camp gay sl.] [1940s+] (*camp gay*) oneself; thus *your mother needs a drink* etc.

IN EXCLAMATIONS

❑ **mother of shit!** [1940s] (*US*) an excl. of surprise or exasperation. ❑ **on my mother's dick!** (*US*) an oath, 'on my honour!'.

mother *adj.* (*also* **motherated**) [abbr.] [1940s+] synon. for MOTHERFUCKING *adj.*

mother- *n.*

as a semi-euph. for MOTHERFUCKER *n.*

IN COMPOUNDS

❑ **mother-bugger** [1990s+] (*S.Afr.*) ❑ **mother-feryer** [1930s+] (*US*) ❑ **mother-flicker** [1960s+] (*US*) ❑ **mother-flunker** [1960s+] (*US*) ❑ **mother-fouler** [1940s+] (*US*) ❑ **motherfrigger** [FRIG *v.* (1)] [1930s+] (*US*) ❑ **mother-fuyer** [1930s+] (*US*) ❑ **mother-grabber** (*also* **father-grabber**) [1960s+] (*US*) ❑ **motherhead** [1970s+] (*US*) ❑ **mother-hopper** [1970s+] (*US*) ❑ **mother-hubba** (*also* **mother hubbard, mother hubber, mutha hubbard**) [1950s+] (*orig. US*) ❑ **mother-hugger** [1950s+] (*US*) ❑ **mother-humper** (*also* **mother-hump**) [HUMP *v.*[1]] [1960s+] (*US*) ❑ **mother-jiver** [JIVE *v.*[1] (1)] [1950s+] (*US*) ❑ **mother-jumper** (*also* **mother-jump**) [JUMP *v.* (1)] [1940s+] (*US*) ❑ **mother-lover** [1950s+] (*US*) ❑ **mother-plugger** [PLUG *v.*[1] (1)] [1920s] (*US*) ❑ **mother-raper** [1950s+] (*US black*) ❑ **mother-rubba** (*also* **mother-rubber**) [1970s] (*US*) ❑ **mother-sucker** [SUCK *v.*[1] (1)] [1950s+] (*US*)

as a semi-euph. for MOTHERFUCKING *adj.*

IN COMPOUNDS

❑ **mother-beating** [1930s] (*US*) ❑ **mother-eating** [1940s–60s] (*US*) ❑ **motherfeeling** [1940s–60s] (*US black*) ❑ **mother-flunking** [1960s+] (*US*) ❑ **mother-fouling** [1940s+] (*US*) ❑ **motherfrigging** [1940s+] (*US*) ❑ **motherfreying** [1940s–60s] (*US*) ❑ **mother-grabbing** (*also* **father-grabbing**) [1950s+] (*US*) ❑ **mother-hopping** [1960s+] (*US*) ❑ **mother-humping** [1960s+] (*US*) ❑ **mother-jiving** [1950s+] (*US*) ❑ **mother-loving** (*also* **mammy-loving**) [1950s+] (*US*) ❑ **motherlumping** [1960s] (*US*) ❑ **motherramming** [RAM *v.*[1]] [1960s] (*US black*) ❑ **mother-raping** [1950s+] (*US black*) ❑ **mother-sucking** [1960s] (*US*)

as other euphs.

IN COMPOUNDS

❑ **mother-hugging** *adj.* [1950s+] (*US*) a euph. for a putative lit. n. *motherfucking*, i.e. incestuous intercourse. ❑ **mother-rape** *n.* [1960s] (*US black*) a synon. for MOTHERFUCK *n.* (2). ❑ **mother-rape** *v.* [1960s] (*US black*) a euph. for MOTHERFUCK *v.* (1).

IN EXCLAMATIONS

❑ **mothersomething!** [1960s] (*US*) a euph. for MOTHERFUCKER! *excl.* (1).

mother and daughter *n.* [rhy. sl.] [mid-19C+] water.

Mother Brown *n.* **1** [20C+] town, usu. the West End of London [rhy. sl.]. **2** [2000s] in pl., the knees [popular Cockney song 'Knees up, Mother Brown'].

Mother Carey's chickens *n.* [? play on orig. naut. *Mother Carey's chicken*, the *storm* petrel, as one who enjoys controversy or actively promotes it] [early–mid-19C] two people who are sharing living quarters and the payment for them, or likewise sharing a cab.

Mother Cornelius' tub *n.* [a presumed actual *Mother Cornelius*, whether a nurse or a procuress; but note the masc. 'Cornelius' in Taylor, 'Travels to Bohemia' (1620): 'Or had Cornelius but this tub, to drench / His clients that had practis'd too much French' (i.e., venereal disease); poss. ref. to physician Henry Cornelius Agrippa (1496–1535) a leading advocate of hot baths for medicinal purposes; Henke, in *Gutter Life and Language* (1988), also notes the possible use of a hard dense wood, necessary to withstand the heavy salt brine used in 'pickling' patients, known as *cornel-wood*, 'the wood of *Cornus mascula*, celebrated for its hardness and toughness, whence it was anciently in request for javelins, arrows, etc.' (*OED*); there may be one more pun on *cornel* and the 'cornuted' cuckold] [late 16C–17C] the sweating tub used in the cure of venereal disease.

motheree *n. see* MOTHEREN *n.*

mothereff *n.* [1960s] (*US*) euph. for MOTHERFUCKER *n.*

motheren *n.* (*also* **motheree**) [MOTHEREN *adj.*] [1940s+] (*US*) euph. for MOTHERFUCKER *n.*

motheren *adj.* [pron. of MOTHERING *adj.*; also used adverbially] [1950s+] (*US*) euph. for MOTHERFUCKING *adj.*

motherer *n.* [SE *mother*, to look after] [late 19C+] (*Aus.*) a shepherd.

motherfuck *n.* [abbr. MOTHERFUCKER *n.*] [1960s+] (*orig. US*) **1** a highly derog. term for a person or an object. **2** a damn, as in *I don't give a motherfuck*. **3** the hell, e.g. *get the motherfuck out, what the motherfuck*.

motherfuck *v.* [backform. f. MOTHERFUCKER *n.*] [1940s+] (*orig. US*) a general curse, usu. in imper., e.g., *motherfuck the pigs!*

motherfuck *adv.* [abbr. MOTHERFUCKING *adv.*] [1960s+] (*orig. US*) used as a general intensifier, e.g., *don't you motherfuck forget it!*

motherfuck! *excl.* [MOTHERFUCK *n.*] [1960s+] (*orig. US*) a general excl. of surprise, rage etc.

motherfucker *n.* (*also* **motherfugger, muh-fugger, mutha, muthafucka**) (*orig. US black*) **1** [1920s+] a supreme insult, an expletive based on the incest taboo, prob. the ultimate in obscenities [dating is difficult, the earliest written citation is in 1929 for the euph. *motherplugger*, although R.S. Gold, *Jazz Lexicon* (1964) notes the term was in existence as early as *c.*1900]. **2** [1940s+] (*orig. US*) anything one dislikes, an infuriating or surprising state of affairs. **3** [1950s+] (*orig. US black*) used with a wide variety of meanings, from good to bad, often as a black-to-black term of affection or a compliment, e.g. *Jimi Hendrix was a bad motherfucker on guitar*; also simply meaning 'thing'. Frequently abbr. to *mother* [note Folb, *Runnin' Down Some Lines* (1980) 'You jus' be sayin' dat any way come to your mind. Like you got some o' dem sweet mothafuckas. They righteously together brothers, got they game uptight, they on dey J.O.B.! Right on! Got dem lowlife thugs. They mean mothas. Don't be messin' wid 'em. Blow you away in a minute! Johnny he my ace, now he a bad mothafucka. He together. Strong rap to d' young ladies – and he go down wi'chu right now! We tight. Gots dem little ol' punks. Think they together, be talkin' out d' side dey neck! Jive mothafucka don't hold no air! See like da's one o' dem slangs got all differn' kin'a meaning. Don't be callin' young lady dat. Dude use dat talk 'bout other dude']. **4** [1960s+] a thing, otherwise unnamed. **5** [1960s+] a damn, e.g. *I don't give a motherfucker*. **6** [1960s+] an indefinite standard of comparison, e.g. *crazy as a motherfucker; meaner than a motherfucker*. **7** [1970s+] a large or outstanding example. **8** [1990s+] a place.

IN PHRASES

❑ **for a motherfucker** *adv.* [1960s+] (*orig. US black*) an intensifying expletive; thus *he has guns for a motherfucker*, he has a great many guns, *I'm throwing bricks for a motherfucker*, I'm throwing bricks continually and passionately etc.

IN EXCLAMATIONS

❑ **I'll be a dirty motherfucker!** (*also* **I'm a motherfucker!**) [1960s+] an excl. of commitment, usu. followed by 'if' and some form of negative.

motherfucker! *excl.* [MOTHERFUCKER *n.*] [1960s+] (*orig. US*) a general excl. of surprise, rage etc.

motherfucking *adj.* (*also* **m-fugging, motherfugging, muthafucken, sisterfucking**) [MOTHERFUCKER *n.*] (*orig. US*) **1** [1930s+] a general intensifier. **2** [1960s+] used as an infix, to accentuate or denigrate the word thus altered, e.g. *emanci-motherfucking-pation*.

motherfucking *adv.* [MOTHERFUCKING *adj.*] [1960s+] (*orig. US*) a general intensifier, e.g. *Start motherfucking talking*.

motherfucking A *n.* [ext. of FUCKING A *n.*] [1970s+] (*orig. US*) very little, as good as nothing, e.g. *I don't know motherfucking A about it.*

motherfucking-A *adj.* [ext. of FUCKING-A *adj.*] [1970s+] (*orig. US*) **1** excellent, superb, the best. **2** goddamned, damned.

motherfucking-A *adv.* [ext. of FUCKING-A *adv.*] [1970s+] (*orig. US*) generally used for emphasis, absolutely, very well, very much, utterly, completely.

motherfucking A! *excl.* [ext. of FUCKING A! *excl.*] [1970s+] (*orig. US*) an excl. used to denote astonishment, dismay; acceptance, praise, recognition.

mother hubbard *n.* **1** [late 19C+] a cupboard [rhy. sl.; ult. nursery rhyme *Old Mother Hubbard*]. **2** [1980s+] nonsense, fanciful talk, lies.

mother-huncher *n. see* MAMA-HUNCHER *n.*

mothering *adj.* [abbr.] [1950s+] euph. for MOTHERFUCKING *adj.*

mother-in-law *n.* **1** [late 19C–1950s] a drink composed of equal proportions of old (stout) and bitter. **2** [1980s+] (*S.Afr., Ind.*) (*also* **mother-in-law exterminator, mother-in-law's hell-fire, mother-in-law's masala**) proprietary names for the hottest forms of chilli-based hot sauces or curry powders (masalas).

SE in slang uses

(IN PHRASES)

❑ **mother-in-law's bit** *n.* [the stereotyped meanness of such figures] [late 18C–early 19C] a very small portion.

Mother Kelly *n.* [rhy. sl.] [20C+] **1** jelly. **2** telly, i.e. television.

motherless *adj.* **1** [late 19C+] (*orig. Aus.*) a general expletive adj. **2** [1940s+] (*Irish*) drunk.

motherless *adv.* [late 19C+] (*orig. Aus.*) a general intensifier, esp. as *motherless broke*, completely bereft of funds.

Mother Machree *n.* [rhy. sl.; ult. Irish *mo chroí*, my heart; best known as the title of Rida Johnson Young's 19C ballad] [20C+] (*Aus.*) tea.

(DERIVATIVES)

❑ **Mother Machree-ish** (*also* **Mother McCrea**) [20C+] (*Irish*) mawkish, lachrymose, banal.

mother of pearl *n.* [rhy. sl.] [late 19C+] a girl.

motheroo *n.* [1950s+] euph. for MOTHERFUCKER *n.*

mother's *n. see MOTHER'S RUIN under* MOTHER *n.*

mothers! *excl.* [1980s+] (*S.Afr.*) a general excl.

mother's joy *n.* [rhy. sl.] [20C+] (*Aus.*) a boy.

mother's pride *n.* [rhy. sl.] [20C+] a bride.

mother superior *n.*[1] [1930s–70s] (*camp gay*) **1** an older, experienced and open homosexual. **2** a police sergeant.

mother superior *n.*[2] [1960s] euph. for MOTHERFUCKER *n.*

motion lotion *n.* (*also* **motion potion**) [1970s+] **1** (*US*) alcohol. **2** (*orig. US*) gasoline, petrol.

motivate *v.* [play on SE *motivate* + MOTORVATE v.] **1** [1930s+] (*US black/campus*) to move, to go, to leave. **2** [1950s–60s] (*US black*) to force oneself to do something that one dislikes. **3** [1970s+] (*US campus*) to move around in a group, socializing.

Moto *n. see* MR MOTO *under* MR *n.*

moto *n.*[1] [abbr. *m*aster *o*f *t*he *o*bvious] [1990s+] (*US campus*) a tedious, irritating, boring person.

moto *n.*[2] *see* MOTA *n.*

motor *n.* [SE *motor*, to drive] **1** [late 19C–1900s] a fast, hard-living man-about-town. **2** [late 19C+] a *motorcar*. **3** [1940s+] (*US*) a *motorcycle*. **4** [1970s+] (*US gay*) the buttocks.

SE in slang uses

(IN COMPOUNDS)

❑ **motorcyle** *n.* **1** [1930s+] (*US*) euph. for MOTHERFUCKER *n.*; usu. as *bad motorcycle*. **2** [1950s] (*US black*) a woman (who can supposedly be 'ridden'). ❑ **motorcyle bull** *n. see* BULL *n.*[5]. ❑ **motorhead** *n.* [1970s+] (*US*) **1** a fool. **2** a car or motorcycle enthusiast. ❑ **motorhuckle** *n.* [joc. mispron.] [1980s+] (*US*) a motorcycle. ❑ **motormouth(ed)** *see* separate entries. ❑ **motor scooter** *n.* [1960s+] (*US*) a euph. for MOTHERFUCKER *n.*

motor *v.* **1** [1970s+] to get started, to go well. **2** [1980s+] (*orig. US campus*) to move quickly, to leave.

motor-boat *n.* [rhy. sl.] [1980s] (*Aus.*) the throat.

Motor City *n.* [1930s+] (*US*) Detroit, Michigan.

motorized dandruff *n.* [1940s] (*US milit.*) head lice.

motormouth *n.* [1960s+] (*orig. US*) **1** a chatterer, a gossip; an obsessive talker. **2** the mouth of such a person.

motormouth *v.* [MOTORMOUTH *n.*] [1980s+] (*orig. US*) to talk ceaselessly.

motormouthed *adj.* [MOTORMOUTH *n.*] [1970s+] verbose, chattering.

motorvate *v.* [? nonce-word *motor-vate*, coined for Chuck Berry's song 'Maybelline' (1955)] [1970s+] (*US campus*) to wander about; to leave quickly.

Motown *n.* [the home of *Motown* record company, itself named after the city's original nickname MOTOR CITY *n.*] [1960s+] (*US*) Detroit, Michigan.

motser *n.* (*also* **motsa, motza, motzer**) [Yid. *matze*, the unleavened bread eaten at Passover. In trad. form this resembles an outsize round biscuit, and thus an enormous coin] [1930s+] (*Aus.*) **1** money, esp. as gambling winnings or as a large sum. **2** a 'certainty', which will guarantee such a win.

motshkin-shop *n. see* MASHKIN-SHOP *n.*

mott *n.* plus combs., *see* MOT *n.*

mott *v.* [ety. unknown; ? SE *mott/mete*, to ascertain the dimensions and/or quantity of] [1920s+] (*Aus.*) to stare at fixedly.

mottab *n.* (*also* **mottob**) [backsl.] [mid-19C] the bottom.

motte *n. see* MOT *n.*

motting *n. see under* MOT *n.*

motto *adj.* [Rom.] [late 19C–1950s] (*tramp*) drunk.

mottob *n. see* MOTTAB *n.*

motza *n. see* MOTSER *n.*

motzer *n.* (*also* **matzo, motza, motzey, motzy**) [Heb. *matze*, unleavened bread, trad. eaten at the Jewish festival of Passover] **1** [late 19C–1900s] (*US*) a Jew. **2** *see* MOTSER *n.*

mouch *v. see* MOOCH *v.*[1].

moucher *n. see* MOOCHER *n.*

mouchet *n.* [Fr. *mouche*, a fly] [late 17C–early 19C] a synthetic beauty mark affixed to a woman's face.

mouchey *n.* (*also* **mochy**) [SMOUS *n.* (1)] [mid-19C] a Jew.

mouee *n. see* MOEY *n.*

mould *v.* (*also* **mode**) [SE *mould*, the growth that appears on rotting vegetable matter] [1980s+] (*US campus*) to embarrass, to humiliate.

moulded *adj.* [SE *mould*, a form of fungus that grows on rotting food + SE *old*] [1990s+] (*US black*) old; senile.

mouldies *n.* [late 19C] old clothes; thus *moult one's mouldies*, to change one's clothes.

mouldiworp *n.* [dial. *mouldiwarp*, a mole, lit. 'earth-digger'/ 'earth-thrower'] [19C] the penis.

mouldy *adj.* (*also* **blue-mouldy**) **1** [late 16C+] useless, second-rate, out-of-date. **2** [mid-19C] grey-haired. **3** [late 19C–1970s] boring, gloomy, sick. **4** [1930s+] (*also* **mowldy**) very drunk.

(IN COMPOUNDS)

❑ **mouldy one** *n.* (*also* **mouldy 'un, moulie**) [the colour] [mid-19C–1950s] a copper coin. ❑ **mouldy pate** *n.* [SE *pate*] [mid–late 19C] a servant wearing a grey powdered wig.

mouldy grub *n.* [play on SE *mulligrubs*] [mid-19C] a travelling showman; thus *mouldy grubbing*, performing in the open air.

moulenjam *n. see* MULENYAM *n.*

mouli *v.* [brandname *Moulinex*, ult. Fr. *mouli-légumes*, a food processor] [1980s+] (*Aus. drugs*) to chop cannabis in a parsley grinder.

moulie *n.* [? negative stereotyping of MULENYAM *n.*] [1980s] nonsense.

moulonjam/moulonjohn *n. see* MULENYAM *n.*

moult one's feathers *v. see under* FEATHER *n.* (2).

moult the mouldies *v. see under* MOULDIES *n.*

mounseer *n.* (*also* **mounsear, mounsheer, mounsier, mounsieur**) [Fr. *monsieur*] [16C–1900s] a Frenchman.

Mount, the *n.* **1** [early 18C–late 19C] London Bridge [one approached the Bridge up a short incline]. **2** [20C+] (*Can.*) Montreal.

mount *n.* [MOUNT *v.*[1]/SE *mount*] **1** [mid-19C] a wife, a mistress. **2** [mid-19C–1950s] anything one rides, esp. a dangerous and uncontrollable horse. **3** [1970s+] (*US black*) a promiscuous woman, who is 'ridden'.

SE in slang uses

IN PHRASES

▫ **do a mount** *v.* [one *mounts* the witness box] [20C+] to give evidence.

mount *v.*[1] (*also* **do a mount**) [SE before 19C and when used of animals] [late 16C+] to have sexual intercourse with, spec. to climb on, prior to sexual intercourse.

IN PHRASES

▫ **mount a corporal and a four** *v.* ['the thumb is the corporal, the four fingers the privates' (Grose, 1785)] [late 18C–early 19C] to masturbate.

SE in slang uses

IN PHRASES

▫ **mount the ass** *v.* [old Fr. custom of exhibiting a bankrupt riding backwards on a donkey] [late 18C–19C] to become bankrupt. ▫ **mount the ladder** *v.* [the ladder onto the gallows] [16C–mid-19C] to be hanged. ▫ **mount the red rag** *v. see under* RED RAG *n.*

mount *v.*[2] ['Derived from the borrowed clothes men used to MOUNT, or dress in when going to swear for a consideration' Hotten (1859)] **1** [late 18C–mid-19C] to perjure oneself for money. **2** [1960s+] (*US black*) to brag, to boast, to attack verbally.

mountain *n.* **1** [1970s+] (*US black*) in pl., large, noticeable female breasts. **2** [1990s+] (*US campus*) an erection.

SE in slang uses

IN COMPOUNDS

▫ **mountain canary** *n.* [joc. ref. to its braying] [1920s+] (*US, mainly Western*) a donkey. ▫ **mountain climber** *n.* [play on HIGH *adj.*[1] (2)] [1970s+] (*US campus*) a feeling of intoxication produced by drugs. ▫ **mountain devil** *n.* [the nickname for the thorn-devil (*Moloch horridus*), a Tasmanian lizard] [20C+] (*Aus.*) a native of Tasmania. ▫ **mountain dew** *n. see* separate entry. ▫ **mountain goat** *n.* [1940s–50s] (*US prison*) any form of prison meat. ▫ **mountain guinea** *n.* [GUINEA *n.*[1]] [1960s+] (*US/Ital.*) used by southern Italians, a northern Italian. ▫ **mountain pecker** *n.* **1** [mid–late 19C] a sheep's head. **2** [late 19C] a Welshman. ▫ **mountain wop** *n.* [WOP *n.*[1] (2)] [1960s+] (*US*) a derog. term for an Italian.

mountain dew *n.* (*also* **mountain**) [coined in Scotland and exported to the US, the term is equally popular in W.I. use] **1** [early 19C+] whisky, 'advertised as from the Highlands' (Hotten, 1860). **2** [early 19C+] (*also* **mountain juice**) illicitly distilled alcohol, contraband whisky. **3** [1980s+] (*W.I.*) marijuana.

mountain passes *n.* [rhy. sl. = glasses] [20C+] spectacles.

mountains of Mourne *n.* [rhy. sl. = HORN *n.*[2] (1)] [20C+] an erection.

mounter *n.* [MOUNT *v.*[2] (1)] [late 18C–19C] one who swears false oaths; a perjurer; thus *mounting*, perjury.

mount-faulcon *n.* [lit. 'mount falcon'; coined by lexicographer John Florio (*c.*1553–*c.*1625)] [late 16C–19C] the vagina.

Mount Pleasant *n.* [pun on proper name/MOUNT *v.*[1]] **1** [mid-18C] as *mount pleasant of Rome*, the buttocks of a male homosexual. **2** [mid-18C–19C] the female genital area.

Mount St Moritz Bajan *n.* [20C+] (*W.I., Gren.*) a poor white.

Mount Shasta *n.*

IN PHRASES

▫ **atop Mount Shasta** *adj.* (*also* **from Mount Shasta**) [*Mount Shasta*, an extinct volcano in N. California; ? the image of the addict as one whose strength has vanished] [1930s–50s] (*US drugs*) addicted to narcotics.

mourner's bench *n.* [SAmE *mourner's bench*, a bench set up at revival meetings for those 'in mourning for their sins'] [1900s–30s] **1** (*US*) the court bench on which prisoners sit awaiting trial. **2** (*US prison*) a bench on which new inmates sit, e.g. for indoctrination talks.

mourning *n.*

SE in slang uses

IN COMPOUNDS

▫ **mourning shirt** *n.* [such a shirt needs less regular washing, ref. to the custom of wearing the same clothes through the immediate period of mourning] [mid-17C] a flannel shirt.

IN PHRASES

▫ **butcher's mourning** *n.* [the normal mourning hat was black, but butchers apparently disliked the colour] [mid-19C] a white hat with a black band. ▫ **dress it in mourning** *v.* [1930s] (*US*) of a white male, to have sexual intercourse with a black female. ▫ **full suit of mourning** *n.* [early–mid-19C] a pair of black eyes. ▫ **half-mourning** *n.* [play on IN MOURNING below] [mid-19C–1930s] a single black eye. ▫ **in mourning** (*also* **full mourning**) [the wearing of black as a sign of *mourning*; the SE adj. *mourning*, visibly bruised, is SE from 18C] **1** [early 19C+] having a black eye; thus *have one's eyes in mourning*, to have a pair of black eyes. **2** [late 19C+] (*UK society*) having dirty fingernails, edging the hands like the black border of mourning paper; thus (20C+) *you're in mourning for the cat*, you have dirty fingernails. ▫ **peepers in mourning** *n. see under* PEEPER *n.*

mouse *n.* **1** as a female, or representative of female characteristics [there is no discernible link between senses 1a and 1e]. (**a**) [mid-16C–late 18C] a woman, esp. when applied to a prostitute or a woman arrested for brawling in the street. (**b**) [late 17C] a timid or effeminate man. (**c**) [19C] (*US black*) one's wife; thus *mousetrap*, marriage. (**d**) [late 19C] the vagina. (**e**) [late 19C+] a mistress. (**f**) [1900s–60s] a small, very feminine girl who invites being cuddled. (**g**) [1910s–60s] (*US*) a woman. (**h**) [1930s–80s] (*US Und.*) an effeminate male homosexual; thus a fellator. (**i**) [1940s+] a weakling. (**j**) [1950s] (*Aus.*) in pl., the girls who accompany the Aus. variety of Teddy Boy. **2** [19C] the penis [its penetration of narrow spaces; note dial. *mouldiwarp*]. **3** [mid-19C+] (*also* **mousie**) a black eye [supposed resemblance]. **4** [late 19C–1900s] a barrister, a solicitor. **5** [late 19C+] (*UK Und.*) an informer [play on RAT *n.*[1]]. **6** [1920s+] (*Aus.*) a man who does not consummate his marriage on the wedding night [? f. phr. 'are you a man or a mouse?']. **7** [1940s] (*US black*) a pocket [ety. unknown; ? abbr. SE *mouse-hole*].

IN COMPOUNDS

▫ **mouse-hunt** *n.* (*also* **mouse-hunter**) [late 16C–mid-17C] a womanizer, a wencher.

IN PHRASES

▫ **cop a mouse** *v.* [late 19C] to get a black eye.

SE in slang uses

IN COMPOUNDS

▫ **mousebrain** *n.* [1970s+] (*US*) a fool. ▫ **mousehole** *n.* [19C] the vagina. ▫ **mouse mattress** *n.* [1990s+] (*US*) a tampon. ▫ **mouse potato** *n.* [SE *mouse* + var. on COUCH POTATO *under* COUCH *n.*] [2000s] (*orig. US*) one who spends what is seen as an excessive time using their computer, usu. in the context of the Internet. ▫ **mousetrap** *see* separate entries.

IN PHRASES

▫ **drunk as a mouse** *adj. see* DRUNK AS A RAT *adj.* ▫ **mind mice at the crossroads** *v.* [20C+] (*Irish*) **1** to do anything undemanding and simple. **2** to undertake a task requiring deviousness and patience.

IN EXCLAMATIONS

▫ **by the mouse-foot!** [mid-16C–late 17C] a mild excl.

mouse *v.* **1** [late 17C] to hit in the face [note SE *mouse*, to handle roughly, as a cat does a mouse]. **2** [1920s+] to give a black eye. **3** [1940s–50s] (*US Und.*) to inform on. **4** [1970s] (*US*) to blackmail; thus *the mouse*, extortion [note 19C US *mouse*, to poke about].

(DERIVATIVES)

❑ **moused** *adj.* [1920s+] of an eye, blackened.

mouse! *excl.* [phr. *quiet as a mouse*] [19C] be quiet!

mouser *n.* **1** [19C–1900s] in sexual senses. (**a**) the vagina. (**b**) a fellatrix, esp. one who nibbles rather than sucks the penis. **2** [19C+] a cat o'-nine tails [play on CAT *n.*[3]]. **3** [mid-19C] a detective [SE *mouser*, a cat]. **4** [mid-19C+] a black eye. **5** [1910s–60s] (*US*) a homosexual. **6** [1930s+] (*orig. US*) (*also* **mousie**) a moustache [supposed resemblance].

mousetrap *n.* **1** [late 17C–19C] marriage. **2** [late 17C+] the vagina. **3** [late 19C] a sovereign [the fanciful similarity of the crown and shield (pictured on the reverse) to a set mousetrap]. **4** [late 19C–1900s] the mouth.

mousetrap *v.* [1940s+] (*US*) to fool or mislead by false promises, to entice, to cajole.

mousey *n.* (*also* **mousie**) [SE *mousetrap*] [1910s–30s] (*UK tramp/Aus.*) cheese.

mousey *adj.* [1950s+] (*US*) small, unassuming.

moush-houser *n. see* MUSH *n.*[2].

mousie *n.* **1** *see* MOUSE *n.* (3). **2** *see* MOUSER *n.* (6). **3** *see* MOUSEY *n.*

moustache *n.* (*also* **mustache**) (*US*) **1** [late 19C+] a man with a moustache. **2** [1930s–60s] oral copulation, cunnilingus. **3** [1940s+] the pubic hair.

(IN COMPOUNDS)

❑ **moustache ride** *n.* (*also* **mustache ride**) [SE *moustache* + RIDE *n.* (1)/SE *ride*] [1980s+] (*US*) an act of cunnilingus, from the perspective of a woman. ❑ **moustache Pete** *n.* (*also* **mustache, mustache Pete**) [1930s+] **1** an original Italian immigrant to New York, typified by his heavy moustache; thus extended to describe women. **2** an original member of the US Mafia.

(IN PHRASES)

❑ **have a moustache** *v.* [1940s] to perform cunnilingus.

moutagram *n.* (*also* **moutaphone**) [SE *mouth* + *telegram/telephone*] [1940s] (*W.I.*) a source of gossip and false news.

mout-a-massy *n.* [lit. 'mouth have mercy'] [1940s–50s] (*W.I.*) a gossip, a chatterbox.

moutaphone *n. see* MOUTAGRAM *n.*

mouth *n.* **1** [late 17C–mid-19C] a fool, a dupe, thus *you are a mouth and you will die a lip*, general phr. of abuse/dismissal. **2** [late 17C–mid-19C; 1940s+] (*also* **mouther**) a noisy, talkative, boorish person; thus [early–mid-19C] *rank mouth*, an especially impudent person. **3** [late 19C+] cheek, impudence, verbosity. **4** [late 19C+] the dry, foul-tasting mouth that follows a night's excesses; thus *have a mouth on one*, to be desperate for alcohol. **5** [1940s–60s] (*US*) a lawyer.

SE in slang uses

(DERIVATIVES)

❑ **mouthful** *n. see* SAY A MOUTHFUL *under* SAY *v.*

(IN COMPOUNDS)

❑ **mouth almighty** *n.* [19C+] a noisy, talkative, loud-mouthed person. ❑ **mouth artist** *n.* [-ARTIST *sfx*] **1** [1900s] (*US*) a braggart, an empty boaster. **2** [1940s+] (*US*) a talented fellator/fellatrix. ❑ **mouth bet** *n.* [late 19C] (*US gambling*) a verbal promise of a bet. ❑ **mouth breather** *n. see* separate entry. ❑ **mouth diarrhoea** *n.* [1970s] the act of informing. ❑ **mouth fuck** *see* separate entries. ❑ **mouth habit** *n. see under* HABIT *n.* ❑ **mouth half-cocked** *n.* [fig. use of *half-cocked*, of a pistol that has the cock drawn back] [late 17C–early 19C] a person who gapes stupidly at anything and everything. ❑ **mouth job** *n.* [JOB *n.*[2] (2)] [1970s+] (*US gay*) fellatio. ❑ **mouth music** *n.* [1970s+] the practice of cunnilingus. ❑ **mouth-off** *n.* [1950s+] (*orig. US*) a braggart, a boaster, a chatterer. ❑ **mouth organ** *n.* [puns] [late 19C–1920s] (*US*) **1** a spokesman. **2** the tongue. ❑ **mouth pie** *n.* [late 19C–1900s] feminine scolding, nagging. ❑ **mouthpiece** *n. see* separate entry. ❑ **mouth queen** *n.* see MOUTH-WORKER below. ❑ **mouth-talk** *n.* [1930s] (*US black*) impulsive or thoughtless talk. ❑ **mouth thankless** *n.* [literary euph. coined by Sir Walter Scott (1771–1832)] [19C] the vagina. ❑ **mouthwash** *n. see* separate entries. ❑ **mouthwork** *n.* [1950s] (*US*) bragging, boastfulness, empty words. ❑ **mouth-worker** *n.* **1** [1940s+] (*gay*) (*also* **mouth queen**) a fellator. **2** [1950s+] (*drugs*) one who takes drugs orally. ❑ **mouth wrestle** *v. see* LIP WRESTLE *under* LIP *n.*[1].

(IN PHRASES)

❑ **all mouth and trousers** *adj.* (*also* **all mouth, all mouth and no trousers**) [1960s+] all talk and no action, a braggart, a fake. ❑ **diarrhoea of the mouth** *n. see under* DIARRHOEA *n.* ❑ **dip one's mouth in someone's business** *v. see under* DIP *v.*[2]. ❑ **don't let your (alligator) mouth overload your ass** *v.* [1960s+] (*US*) keep quiet, esp. in a difficult situation where words might complicate matters. ❑ **don't let your mouth buy what your ass can't pay for** *v.* [1970s+] (*US*) keep quiet, esp. when speaking might make matters worse. ❑ **don't let your mouth write a cheque your ass can't cash** *v.* [1960s+] (*orig. US black*) keep quiet, esp. when speaking might make matters worse. ❑ **give (it) mouth** *v.* [late 19C+] to be cheeky. ❑ **have a mouth like a cow's cunt** *v.* [late 19C+] to be very talkative. ❑ **have a mouth like a wrestler's jockstrap** *v.* [1970s+] to be severely hungover, suffering the effects of a heavy night's drinking. ❑ **have a mouth like the bottom of a bird-cage** *v.* (*also* **...like the bottom of a bird cage, ...a parrot-cage**) [the filthiness of the cage] [1920s+] to be suffering the physical results of a night's drinking; also as *one's mouth feels like...* ❑ **have a mouth like the bottom of a cocky's cage** *v.* (*also* **...bottom of a bird's cage, ...parrot cage**) [SE *cockatoo*] [1960s+] (*Aus.*) to have a mouth that is unpleasantly furred, the result of excessive drinking. ❑ **have a mouth like the inside of an Arab's armpit** *v.* [stereotyping of Arabs as dirty] [1940s+] to be suffering such unpleasant physical feelings as are concomitant with a hangover. ❑ **have a mouth like the inside of an Arab's underpants** *v.* (*also* **... like a lorry-driver's crutch, ...like the inside of a Pommie's jockstrap ...like a nun's minge, ...like an Arab's sandal/arse**) [stereotyping] [1960s+] to experience the dry mouth, furred tongue and disgusting taste that can accompany a hangover. ❑ **have a mouth on one** *v.* [late 19C+] to be foul-mouthed or abusive; to be aggressively cheeky. ❑ **have one's mouth full of pap** *v.* [SE *pap*, baby food] [late 18C–early 19C] to act in a childish manner. ❑ **in one's mouth** *adj.* [2000s] (*US prison*) eavesdropping. ❑ **make a wry mouth** *v.* [the rictus of suffocation, ult. SE *make a wry mouth*, to grimace with disapproval] [late 16C–17C] to be hanged. ❑ **mout-hab-nuttin-fe-do** *n.* [lit. 'mouth has nothing (better) to do'] [20C+] (*W.I.*) a chatterbox, a malicious gossip. ❑ **mouth of nature** *n.* [mid-18C] the vagina. ❑ **mouth runs like parch benny** *adj.* (*also* **mouth runs like sick nigger takes salts**) [Carib.E. *parch* = SE *parched* + *benny*, a form of sesame-based cooking oil, used in making sweets] [20C+] (*W.I.*) a phr. used of an incessant irritating chatterer. ❑ **mouth that cannot bite** *n.* [literary euph. coined by Thomas D'Urfey (1653–1723)] [late 17C–early 18C] the vagina. ❑ **mouth that says no words** *n.* [18C–19C] the vagina. ❑ **pass one's mouth on** *v.* [var. on SE *pass an opinion/a remark*] [20C+] (*W.I.*) to slander, to speak rudely about. ❑ **poke one's mouth off** *v.* [1970s+] (*US black*) to lose one's temper. ❑ **put one's mouth in** *v.* [late 19C] to make a comment. ❑ **put one's mouth in one's pocket** *v.* [20C+] (*W.I.*) to be forced to make a heavy payment after losing a libel suit. ❑ **put one's mouth on** *v.* [20C+] (*W.I.*) to denigrate, to slander. ❑ **run one's mouth** *v.* (*also* **fly one's mouth, run one's gab, run one's gums, run one's jaws**) [one's *mouth runs* like an engine] [1930s+] (*orig. US/W.I.*) **1** to gossip, to tell tales. **2** to give advice. **3** to talk without restraint. **4** as *run up one's mouth*, to brag, to boast, to fantasize. ❑ **set mouth on** *v.* [1970s+] (*US black*) to gossip, to malign. ❑ **stand mouth** *v.* [early 19C] to be duped.

(IN EXCLAMATIONS)

❑ **hold your mouth!** [18C+] be quiet!

mouth *v.* **1** [mid-19C] (*US campus*) to bluff a recitation. **2** [1920s+] to insult, to criticize, to speak insolently, also in phr. *give mouth*. **3** [1990s+] (*W.I.*) to make fun of.

IN PHRASES

❑ **mouth off** *v.* [1950s+] (*orig. US*) **1** to speak impudently. **2** (*also* **mouth on**) to boast, to brag.

mouthamassy (Liza) *n.* [? Twi *mmasa-mmasa*, confused words, or f. phr. 'mouth have mercy!'] [20C+] (*W.I.*) a chatterbox.

mouthar *n.* [? SE *mouth*] [20C+] (*W.I.*) a chatterbox, one who cannot be trusted to keep secrets.

mouth-breather *n.* [such individuals are presumed to be breathing heavily] [1910s+] a stupid person, esp. a particularly stupid thug.

DERIVATIVES

❑ **mouth-breathing** *adj.* [1980s+] stupid, often stupid and thuggish.

mouther *n. see* MOUTH *n.* (2).

mouth fuck *n.* [SE *mouth* + FUCK *n.* (1)] [mid-19C] an act of fellatio.

mouth fuck *v.* [MOUTH FUCK *n.*] [1970s+] to fellate.

mouth is sore *n.* [rhy. sl.] [1960s] (*bingo*) the number 44.

mouthpiece *n.* **1** [mid-19C+] a lawyer; in the UK a solicitor or barrister, in the US an attorney [orig. SE]. **2** [1900s–30s] (*US*) an informer. **3** [1990s+] (*US black*) gold caps on one's front teeth.

mouthwash *n.*[1] [rhy. sl. = NOSH *n.* (2) + lit. image] [20C+] food.

mouthwash *n.*[2] **1** [1930s+] a drink of alcohol. **2** [1940s+] (*US prison*) prison coffee.

mouti-mouti *n.* (*also* **mowti-mowti**) [1940s–50s] (*W.I.*) a gossip, a chatterbox; thus as adj.

mouton *n.* [Fr. *mouton*, a sheep. The Fr. sl. means the same] [19C–1900s] 'a spy quartered with an accused person with a view to obtaining incriminating evidence' (*OED*).

move *n.* **1** [early 19C] (*UK Und.*) of a prostitute, a session with a customer. **2** [early 19C+] a trick, a scheme, a stratagem. **3** [1960s] schemes used for seduction; esp. in phr. *put the moves on*. **4** [1960s+] (*orig. US*) a sexual advance. **5** [1960s+] (*orig. US*) in pl., knowledge, ability, 'smarts'; esp. in phrs. *have all the moves, got all the moves*. **6** [1980s+] (*US*) the right thing, the proper way, 'what's happening'. **7** [1990s+] (*drugs*) a shipment of smuggled drugs.

IN PHRASES

❑ **bust a move** *v.* [1980s+] (*orig. US black*) **1** to make a physical move. **2** to make a serious effort, to take action. **3** to snub. ❑ **lose (move)** *n.* [1980s+] (*US campus*) a foolish person or action. ❑ **make a move (on)** *v.* [1980s+] to make sexual advances (towards). ❑ **put a move on** *v.* (*also* **put a move on**) **1** [1960s+] (*orig. US*) usu. of a man, to make advances towards the opposite sex. **2** [1980s] (*US black*) to harass. **3** [2000s] to contact.

move *v.* **1** [mid-18C+] to leave [SE from 15C–mid-18C]. **2** [20C+] (*Irish*) to pick up a member of the opposite sex [SE *move*, to stir, to excite]. **3** [1950s+] (*orig. US*) to dance or play music energetically or with a strong rhythm. **4** [1950s+] (*orig. US*) to move fast, to be exciting or dynamic. **5** [1970s+] (*US drugs*) to sell off or to dispose of merchandise, incl. contraband, drugs and stolen property [ext. of SE *move*, of merchandise, to sell or dispose of].

IN PHRASES

❑ **move in the blind** *v.* [? SE *blind spot* (of the landlord)] [late 19C] to leave one's rented premises without paying the rent, to do a MOONLIGHT FLIT *n.* ❑ **move off** *v.* [mid–late 18C] to die. ❑ **move on** *v.* [1970s+] **1** (*US black/campus*) to hit, to assault, usu. with a weapon. **2** (*US black*) to assault in a group. **3** to approach sexually. ❑ **move one's ass** *v.* (*also* **move one's butt, move one's hump, shift one's ass**) [1970s+] (*orig. US*) to hurry up, to get a move on. ❑ **move out** *v.* [1920s] (*N.Z.*) to expand, to bloom. ❑ **move the crowd** *v.* [1990s+] (*US black*) to leave. ❑ **move the laundry** *v.* [stereotypical image of Chinese running laundries] [1930s–50s] (*US Und.*) to smuggle illegal Chinese immigrants. ❑ **move to** *v.* [mid-19C] to bow to. ❑ **move with** *v.* [1950s+] to associate with, to spend time with. ❑ **move your carcass!** *excl.* (*also* **shift your carcass!**) [20C+] move! get out of the way!

moveables *n.* [17C–early 19C] (*UK Und.*) swords, watches, jewellery and other valuable objects that can be stolen, won at gambling or otherwise taken away from their owner.

mover *n.* [1950s+] **1** an ambitious and successful person, both socially and with the opposite sex; ext. as *movers and shakers, movers and groovers*. **2** someone who moves themselves or others physically and emotionally. **3** an attractive person, usu. female. **4** the person in charge.

IN PHRASES

❑ **big mover** *n.* [1950s+] (*Aus.*) one who is a consistent success, e.g. as a womanizer.

movie *n.* **1** [1960s+] (*US*) a sequence of events that are unpleasant or boring, esp. in phr. *I don't like this movie*, I am not happy or comfortable. **2** [1970s] (*US Und.*) prison [ironic ref. to the austerity of the prison]. **3** *see* PICTURE *n.* (2).

moving dunghill *n. see under* DUNGHILL *n.*[1].

mow *n.* [MOW *v.*] [mid-16C–18C] the act of copulation.

mow *v.* [Scot./northern dial. *mow*, to copulate, and note MOULDIWORP *n.*] [mid-16C–early 19C] to have sexual intercourse.

SE in slang uses

IN PHRASES

❑ **mow on** *v.* [1980s+] (*US campus*) to eat heartily, to gorge oneself. ❑ **mow the brigalo suckers** *v.* [*brigalow*, a form of acacia, found in New South Wales and Queensland. Its rapid growth can render large areas of land unusable] [1990s+] (*Aus.*) to shave one's beard. ❑ **mow the lawn** *v. see under* LAWN *n.*[2].

mower *n.* [its *moo*-ing or its chewing of the grass] **1** [late 17C–mid-19C] (*UK Und.*) a cow. **2** [mid-19C] in fig. use, describing a person.

mow-heater *n.* (*also* **mow beater**) [the drover's habit of sleeping on hay mows + ? drover's 'heating up' of the MOWER *n.*'s behinds as he uses his stick to guide them through gates, down lanes etc] [late 17C–early 19C] (*UK Und.*) a drover.

mowldy *adj. see* MOULDY *adj.* (4).

mowlow *adj. see* MOLO *adj.*

mowly *adj.* [1990s+] (*W.I.*) smelly, malodorous.

IN COMPOUNDS

❑ **mowly-aam** *n.* [1990s+] (*W.I.*) body odour.

mowrowsky *n. see* MARROWSKY *n.* (1).

mowti-mowti *n. see* MOUTI-MOUTI *n.*

moxie *n.*[1] [dial. *mawks*, a slattern, an unkempt woman] [20C+] (*W.I.*) an untidy and thus unattractive young woman.

moxie *n.*[2] (*also* **moxey, moxy**) [from the tradename of a once-popular US soft drink *Moxie*, developed *c.*1880 and patented 1924; it poss. contained *moxie*, or wintergreen; ult. Algonquin root *maski-*, medicine] **1** [1930s+] (*US*) courage, impudence, ability. **2** [1960s–70s] (*US black*) an impudent upstart.

moyo *n.* [Sp.] [1980s+] (*US/P.R.*) a black person.

moz *v.* (*also* **mozz**) [SE *muzzle*] [1940s+] (*Aus.*) to interrupt, to hinder.

moza-motton *n.* [mid-19C] a piece of luck.

Mozart and Liszt *adj. see* BRAHMS (AND LISZT) *adj.*

mozz *v. see* MOZ *v.*

mozzarella *n.* [CHEESE *n.*[1] (1)] [2000s] (*US black*) money.

mozzle *n.* (*also* **moz, muzzle**) [*see* MOZZLE AND BROCHA *n.*] [mid-19C+] luck.

mozzle *v.* [1920s+] (*Aus.*) **1** to hinder, to interrupt. **2** to put a jinx on.

mozzle and brocha *n.* [rhy. sl. = *ON THE KNOCKER under* KNOCKER *n.*[1], ult. Yid. mazel, good luck + *brocha*, a blessing] [20C+] a door-to-door salesman.

mozzy *n. see* MOSSIE *n.* (1).

m.p. *n.* [abbr. *m*ember of the *p*olice] [mid–late 19C; 1960s] (*US/Aus.*) a police officer.

mpata *n.* [Zulu *mpatha*, a greenhorn] [1980s+] (*S.Afr. Und.*) a new inmate, a fool, one who has not yet learned how to cope with prison conditions.

m.r.a. *n.* [REEB *n.*[2] (1); abbr. *m*ajor/*m*assive *r*eeb *a*ction] [1980s+] (*US campus*) unsociable behaviour.

Mrs *n.* [var. of MISSIS *n.*] **1** [1910s+] a wife, esp. as *the Mrs*. The husband's surname is omitted, e.g. *Here is Mr Smith, Mrs is out shopping*; also in homosexual relationships. **2** *see* MISS *n.* (1).

used with proper or metonymic names

(IN COMPOUNDS)

▫ **Mrs Astor** *n. see* MISS ASTOR *under* MISS *n.* ▫ **Mrs Astorbilt** *n. see* ASTORBILT *n.* ▫ **Mrs Astor's pet horse** *n.* (*also* **Mrs Astor's billy goat, ...cow, ...pet cow, ...plush horse**) [var. on ASTOR'S PET HORSE *n.*] [1920s+] (*US*) **1** an over-made-up or overdressed person. **2** an arrogant, haughty person. ▫ **Mrs Evans** *n.* [a witch of that name, who was supposedly wont to turn herself into a cat] [late 18C] a female cat. ▫ **Mrs Fubbs** *n.* [a witch of that name, who was supposedly wont to turn herself into a cat] [late 18C] a female cat. ▫ **Mrs Fubbs' parlour** *n.* [early 19C] the vagina. ▫ **Mrs Goff** *n.* [ety. unknown; ? anecdotal] [early–mid-19C] (*US campus*) a woman. ▫ **Mrs Greenfields** *n.* [imaginary landladies] [20C+] (*UK tramp*) sleeping in the open air; thus *Mrs Ashpits*, sleeping near a lime-kiln. ▫ **Mrs Hand (and her five daughters)** *n.* [1980s+] the hand, as used for masturbation; thus *make a rendezvous with Mrs Hand*, to masturbate. ▫ **Mrs Harris and Mrs Gamp** *n.* [from the two characters, the former 'real' and latter imaginary, in Charles Dickens's *Martin Chuzzlewit* (1843–4)] [mid–late 19C] the *Morning Herald* and the *Standard* newspapers. ▫ **Mrs Jones** *n.* (*also* **Mistress Jones, Mrs Jones's counting house, Mrs Jones's house**) [early–late 19C] the lavatory; thus *visit Mrs Jones*, to use the lavatory; *upset Mrs Jones*, to tip over the water closet. ▫ **Mrs Lo** *n. see* LO *n.*[1] (1). ▫ **Mrs Lukey Props** *n.* [? anecdotal] [19C] a brothel-keeper. ▫ **Mrs Mopp** *n.* [the character *Mrs Mopp* created by Tommy Handley (1892–1949) for the radio comedy series *ITMA* (*It's That Man Again*, from 1939). Her catchphrase was 'Can I do you now, sir?'] **1** [1940s+] a cleaner. **2** [1940s+] a shop [rhy. sl.]. ▫ **Mrs Palm (and her five daughters)** *n.* (*also* **Mrs Palmer and her five daughters**) [1950s+] the hand, as used for masturbation. ▫ **Mrs Philip's purse** *n.* (*also* **Mrs Phillip's purse, Mrs Philip's ware, Mrs Phillip's ware**) ['These machines were long prepared and sold by a matron of the name of *Phillips*, at the Green Canister, in Half-moon Street, in the Strand. That good lady, having acquired a fortune, retired from business, but learning that the town was not well served by her successors, she, out of a patriotic zeal for the public welfare, returned to her occupation; out of which she gave notice by divers hand-bills, in circulation in the year 1776' (Grose, 1796). Whether she was related to Mrs Phillips, that brothel-keeper who, in the mid-19C, ran a house at 11 Upper Belgrave Place, is alas unknown; see Williams (1994) II 1016 for a substantial discussion] [late 18C] a condom. ▫ **Mrs Princum Prancum** *n. see* MISTRESS PRINCUM PRANCUM *n.* ▫ **Mrs Suds** *n.* [mid-18C] a washerwoman. ▫ **Mrs Van Neck** *n.* [late 18C–early 19C] a woman with large breasts. ▫ **Mrs White** *n.* [WHITE *n.* (3)] [1900s–50s] a drug dealer, presumably in white powders, i.e. narcotics.

Mrs Chant *n.* [rhy. sl.; *see* next] [1930s+] an aunt.

Mrs Chant's *n.* [rhy. sl. = *MY AUNT under* AUNT *n.*; ult. Mrs Ormiston *Chant* (1848–1923) a well-known moralist] [1950s+] a lavatory; thus *visit Mrs Chant's*.

M.R.S. (Degree) *n.* (*also* **M.R.S.**) [abbr. and pun on US 'Master of Science'/Mrs; pron. 'missus'] [1970s+] (*US campus*) a husband; i.e. the nickname for the degree that a woman who goes to college mainly to find a husband is said to be studying for.

Mrs Doyle *n.* [rhy. sl; ult. *Mrs Doyle*, character in a 1990s TV sitcom *Father Ted*] [1990s+] a boil.

Mrs Ducket *n.* (*also* **Mrs Duckett**) [rhy. sl.] [1930s+] a bucket.

Mrs Ducket! *excl.* (*also* **Mrs Duckett!**) [1950s+] a euph. for FUCK IT! *excl.*

Mrs More *n.* [rhy. sl.] [1990s+] the floor.

Ms *n. see* MISS *n.*

m.s. *n.* [abbr. *m*orphine *s*ulphate] [1950s+] (*drugs*) morphine.

mshoza *n.* [? SE *shows*, thus showy, well-dressed, good-looking] [1980s+] (*S.Afr.*) the female companion of a township dandy.

M² *n.* [1940s] (*UK gay*) mutual masturbation.

m.t. *n.* [pron./abbr. of *em*p*t*y; similarly used by mid-19C railway porters of an empty carriage] [mid-19C+] an empty bottle.

MTF *n.* [abbr. *m*ale *t*o *f*emale] [1990s+] (*US gay*) a male to female transsexual, transgender or transvestite.

m.t.f. *n.* [abbr. *m*ust *t*ouch *f*lesh] [1980s+] (*UK society*) an overly amorous young man.

MTM *n.* [abbr. *m*ale *t*o *m*ale, var. on FTM *n.*, with the idea being that although the person was biologically a woman to start with they always felt like a man] [1990s+] (*US gay*) a female to male transsexual.

M25 *n.* [the initial letters + the UK's *M25* motorway, an orbital route round London, which played a major part in the siting of the early ecstasy-fuelled raves] [1980s+] (*drugs*) MDMA.

m.u. *n.* [abbr.] [1970s+] (*drugs*) a *m*arijuana *u*ser; but note sometimes for marijuana.

mu *n.* [abbr. MOOCA *n.*] [1930s+] (*drugs*) marijuana.

much *adj.* [1950s+] (*US black*) many, a lot of.

much *v.* [? SE *make much of*] [mid-19C; 1950s] to persuade, to fondle.

much *adv.* [ext. use of SE] [1950s+] (*US black/teen*) very, extremely, to a great extent, defined by a v. or adj. e.g. *unhappy much?*

much! *excl.* [late 16C; mid-19C+] certainly not! not likely!

much clown love *phr.* (*also* **M.C.L.**) [2000s] (*US black*) a phr. implying great affection.

much-fake *v.* [2000s] (*US prison*) to make playing cards out of whatever materials are available.

muchly *adv.* [late 19C+] very much; usu. in TA MUCHLY! *excl.*

mucho *adj.* [synon. Sp.] [1940s+] (*orig. US*) a lot of, many.

mucho *adv.* [MUCHO *adj.*] [1940s+] (*orig. US*) exceedingly.

muck *n.*[1] [SE *muck*, anything filthy, dirty, esp. when part liquid] **1** [14C–mid-19C] in fig. use, money; wealth [the equation of money and dirt]. **2** [mid-19C+] a general term covering anything or anyone seen as disgusting, worthless or abhorrent. **3** [late 19C+] rubbish, nonsense. **4** [late 19C+] semen, esp. in phr. *spill one's muck*. **5** [1910s+] food or drink, not necessarily unpleasant. **6** [1910s+] as euph. for SHIT *n.* **7** [1940s–50s] rudeness, insults.

(IN COMPOUNDS)

▫ **muck-cook** *v.* [? SE *cook*, to concoct + fig. use *muck*, dirt; thus poss. antecedent of *DISH (OUT) THE DIRT under* DIRT *n.*] [late 19C–1900s] to laugh behind someone's back. ▫ **muck-forks** *n.* [mid–late 19C] the fingers. ▫ **muckhill** *n.* [late 17C–early 18C] a pile of money; thus *have a good muckhill at one's doorstep*, to be well-off. ▫ **muckhole** *n.* **1** [1900s–30s] a filthy, unappetizing place or room. **2** [1930s–40s] the anus. **3** [1960s+] (*Aus.*) the vagina. ▫ **muckrag** *n.* [19C] a handkerchief. ▫ **muck savage** *n.* [1990s+] a peasant. ▫ **muck shifter** *n.* [late 19C] a navvy. ▫ **muck-shoveller** *n.* [1940s] (*Aus.*) a tin-miner. ▫ **mucksnipe** *n.* [mid-19C] a gambler (or anyone else) who has lost all their money. ▫ **muckspout** *n.* [early 19C–1910s] one who uses a good deal of obscene language or has a 'smutty' mentality. ▫ **muckstick** *n.* **1** [1910s+] (*US*) a long-handled shovel; thus *muckstick man*, a manual labourer. **2** [1960s] (*N.Z.*) a shotgun.

(IN PHRASES)

▫ **as muck** *adv.* [late 19C+] extremely, utterly; either following a pej. adj., e.g. *as sick as muck* or implying one, e.g. *as rich as muck*. ▫ **blow one's muck** *v.* [1990s+] of a man, to ejaculate, to reach orgasm. ▫ **chuck one's muck** *v.* [1990s+] to ejaculate. ▫ **lord muck** *n.* (*also* **king muck**) [20C+] a hypothetical aristocrat, snobbish and conspicuous in his contempt for lesser mortals, but since he is lord of 'muck' he is, in fact, no better than they are. ▫ **muck and a halfpenny afters** *n.* [late 19C–1900s] (*middle-class*) a pretentious, unpleasant dinner 'spotted at the corners with custard powder preparations, and half dozens of stewed prunes, etc, etc' (Ware).

muck *n.*[2] [abbr. MUCKER *n.*[1]] [late 19C–1930s] a heavy fall.

muck *n.*[3] [abbr. MUCK-A-MUCK *n.* (2)] [1900s–50s] (*US*) an important or self-important person.

muck *n.*[4] [1920s+] euph. for FUCK *n.* in its various forms.

muck *v.*[1] **1** [mid–late 19C] to beat, to surpass, to ruin financially. **2** [late 19C] to dirty. **3** [late 19C] to irritate. **4** [late 19C+] to fail, to make a mess of; esp. as *muck about, muck up*. **5** [1920s] (*US*) to work as a manual labourer, esp. a navvy.

DERIVATIVES

▫ **mucked** *adj.* [late 19C] in trouble.

IN PHRASES

▫ **muck about** *v.* (*also* **muck around**) *see* separate entry. ▫ **muck it** *v.* [1920s+] (*US*) to work at a menial task, lit. 'to get one's hands dirty'. ▫ **muck out** *v.* [mid-19C] (*UK gambling*) to take all one's opponents' money.

muck *v.*[2] [1920s+] euph. for FUCK *v.* in its various forms.

muck about *v.* (*also* **muck around**) **1** [late 19C+] to act half-heartedly, to engage in pointless, time-wasting activity, to mess around. **2** [1910s+] to ruin, to mess up, to annoy; usu. in passive. **3** [1910s+] to fondle intimately, to seduce.

muck-a-muck *n.* [Chinook jargon *muckamuck*, food] (*orig. US*) **1** [mid-19C–1930s] food, drink. **2** [mid-19C+] (*also* **muckety-muck, muck-i-muck, muckti-muck, mucky-muck, mucky-mucky, muckty-muck**) an important or self-important person; esp. as *big muck-a-muck* and HIGH MUCK-A-MUCK *n.*

muck-a-muck *adj.* (*also* **muckety-muck**) [MUCK-A-MUCK *n.* (2)] [1970s] (*US*) arrogant.

mucked *adj. see under* MUCK *v.*[1].

mucked (out) *adj.* [stable imagery] [early 19C–1910s] penniless.

muckender *n.* (*also* **mucketer, muckinder**) [SE *muckender*, a handkerchief or napkin, ult. Fr. *mouchoir*, Sp. *mocador*] [early 18C] a cleaning cloth, a duster.

mucker *n.*[1] [SE *muck*, dirt] **1** [mid-19C+] a heavy fall; thus *come a mucker, go a mucker*, to come to grief, to ruin oneself; also fig. use. **2** in negative descriptions of persons. (**a**) [late 19C–1910s] (*US*) a street urchin or youth who does not go to college. (**b**) [late 19C–1930s] a fanatic, a hypocrite. (**c**) [late 19C+] a rough, coarse person. (**d**) [1900s–20s] (*US campus*) a mean, untrustworthy person; a 'bounder'. **3** [1910s–30s] (*US tramp*) a manual labourer.

DERIVATIVES

▫ **muckerish** *adj.* [late 19C–1900s] (*US campus*) coarse, ill-bred.

IN PHRASES

▫ **go a mucker** *v.* [1930s] to squander, to waste, to 'splash out'.

mucker *n.*[2] [var. on FUCKER *n.* (3)] [late 19C+] an unpleasant person.

mucker *n.*[3] [MUCK IN *v.*] [20C+] (*orig. Aus.*) a companion, a friend; as direct term of address.

mucker *v.* **1** [mid-19C] to come to grief, to fail. **2** [mid-19C–1920s] to cause problems for someone. **3** [mid-19C+] to fall, to 'take a tumble'. **4** [late 19C] to ruin.

Muckeries, the *n.* (*also* **Moocheries**) [MUCK ABOUT *v.*; a pej. ref. to the inventors] [late 19C] the Inventions Exhibition, held in South Kensington in 1885.

mucker-upper *n.* [MUCK UP *v.*] [1940s–50s] a bungler.

mucketer *n. see* MUCKENDER *n.*

muckety-muck *n. see* MUCK-A-MUCK *n.*

muckibus *adj.* [SE *muck* + pig Lat. sfx *-ibus*] [mid-18C–mid-19C] tipsy, slightly drunk.

muck in *n.* [MUCK IN *v.* (1)] [1910s+] a communal activity.

muck in *v.* (*also* **muck into**) **1** [late 19C+] to join in, to lend a hand, esp. in a dirty or unpleasant task. **2** [1930s] to have a sexual relationship with.

muckinder *n. see* MUCKENDER *n.*

mucking *adj.* **1** [late 19C–1900s] repellent, filthy [MUCK *n.*[1]]. **2** [1910s+] euph. for FUCKING *adj.*

mucking-aye *adv. see* FUCKING-A *adv.*

mucking-togs *n.* [joc. mispron., but note MUCKING *adj.* + TOGS *n.*] [mid-19C–1910s] a mackintosh.

mucksuck *v.* [1960s+] (*US*) to act in a disgusting manner.

mucksucker *n.* [MUCKSUCK *v.*] [1960s+] (*US*) one who acts in a disgusting manner.

muckty-muck *n.* [1950s+] (*US black*) **1** nonsense, rubbish, lies. **2** aimless, aggressive talk. **3** *see* MUCK-A-MUCK *n.*

muck-up *n.* [MUCK UP *v.*, post-WW2 uses underlined by FUCK-UP *n.* (1)] [20C+] **1** a blunder, an error, a confusion; also attrib. **2** a mixture. **3** of a person, a mess.

muck up *v.* (*also* **muck up on**) [MUCK *v.*[2]] **1** [late 19C+] make a mess (of), to spoil or ruin. **2** [late 19C+] to fail, to go wrong. **3** [1910s+] (*Aus.*) to play the fool. **4** [1920s] to dirty.

muck-worm *n.* [SE *muck-worm*, a worm that lives in mud] **1** [late 16C–19C] a person of the lowest origin. **2** [late 16C–1910s] a miserly person, a 'money-grubber' [further play on MUCK *n.*[1] (1)]. **3** [mid-17C–mid-18C] one who is mentally or morally degraded. **4** [mid–late 19C] a street urchin.

mucky-muck/mucky-mucky *n. see* MUCK-A-MUCK *n.*

mucosa de rosa *n.* [SE *mucus* + fake Ital. sfx *-a* + assonance of *rosa*; thus an inference of 'pinkness', i.e. effeminate homosexuality] [1950s–70s] (*camp gay*) one who spits.

mud *n.* **1** [18C–19C] a fool. **2** as a thick liquid. (**a**) [late 19C+] (*orig. US*) (*also* **Mississippi mud**) thick, strong coffee. (**b**) [1900s] (*UK Und.*) pea soup. **3** in drug senses [the colour (and consistency); note abbr. *foreign mud*, trans. of Chinese name for opium]. (**a**) [1910s+] unprocessed opium. (**b**) [1920s+] opium, esp. second-rate. (**c**) [1950s+] methadone. (**d**) [1970s+] the residue of heroin or morphine processing. (**e**) [1990s+] heroin. **4** [1970s+] excrement. **5** [2000s] (*US*) problems.

IN COMPOUNDS

▫ **mudbutt** *n.* [BUTT *n.*[1] (1a)] [2000s] (*US campus*) diarrhoea. ▫ **mud check** *n.* [i.e. will one SHIT ONESELF *v.*] [2000s] (*US prison*) a forced confrontation to see how brave a new inmate may be. ▫ **mud dog** *n.* [2000s] (*N.Z.*) an unattractive person. ▫ **mud duck** *n.* [1980s] (*US black*) an attractive woman. ▫ **mud flap** *n.* [20C+] (*US*) a derog. term for a black person. ▫ **mud hen** *n.* **1** [1910s] (*US*) a derog. term for a black woman. **2** [1970s] (*US prison*) a lazy person. ▫ **mud-out** *n.* [2000s] an act of defecation. ▫ **mud-packer** *n.* [20C+] (*US*) a homosexual man. ▫ **mud pads** *n.* [1910s–20s] the feet. ▫ **mud pipes** *n.* [mid-19C–1930s] thick boots, gumboots. ▫ **mud puppy** *n.* [US regional *mud puppy*, a salamander] [1980s+] (*US campus*) an ugly woman. ▫ **mud-pusher** *n.* [late 19C] a street sweeper. ▫ **mud scow** *n.* [SE *scow*, a large flat-bottomed boat] [early 19C–1920s] (*US*) **1** in pl., large, cheap shoes. **2** in pl., feet. ▫ **mud shark** *n.* [2000s] (*US black*) a white woman who prefers black men as partners. ▫ **mud show** *n.* **1** [late 19C–1900s] (*UK society*) an agricultural show or any similar outdoor event. **2** [1920s–30s] (*US*) an old-fashioned circus; thus *mud-showman*, one who runs or works at such a circus. ▫ **mud snake** *n.* [1990s+] (*US*) **1** the penis. **2** a turd. ▫ **mud student** *n.* [mid-19C] an agricultural student. ▫ **mud turtle** *n.* [late 19C–1930s] (*US*) a contemptible person.

IN PHRASES

▫ **hit the mud** *v.* [1950s] to smoke opium. ▫ **hold one's mud** *v.* [a job that one has to do oneself] [1960s+] **1** (*US black*) to keep one's own counsel, to keep quiet. **2** (*US drugs*) to be courageous. ▫ **mud for one's turtle** *n.* [1980s+] (*US*) from a man's point of view, sexual intercourse. ▫ **pack mud** *v.* [1970s+] (*gay*) to have anal intercourse.

SE in slang uses

IN COMPOUNDS

▫ **mud bud** *n.* [BUD *n.*[2] (3)] [1980s+] (*drugs*) homegrown marijuana. ▫ **mudcat** *n.* (*US*) **1** [mid-19C–1940s] a stupid or contemptible person. **2** [late 19C+] a Mississippian [Mississippi is known as the *Mudcat* State]. ▫ **mudcrusher** *n.* **1** [1970s+] (*US black*) an extreme form of bully whose aim is to crush everyone into the ground. **2** *see* GRAVEL-CRUSHER *under* GRAVEL *n.* ▫ **mud-fat** *adj.* [the thickness and density of mud] [1920s+] (*Aus.*) very fat. ▫ **mudflaps** *n.* **1** [1950s+] (*US black*) noticeably large feet. **2** [1970s] (*Aus.*) large ears. **3** [2000s] the female breasts. ❑ **mudfuck/fucker/fucking** *see* separate entries. ❑ **mudguard** *n.* [2000s] (*N.Z.*) a bald head; thus ext. as *shiny on top, all shit beneath*. ❑ **mudguts** *n.* [1960s+] (*N.Z.*) a fat person. ❑ **mud-head/-headed** *see* separate entries. ❑ **mud honey** *n.* **1** [late 19C–1910s] street mud and slush. **2** [1910s] beer. ❑ **mudhook** *see* separate entry. ❑ **mudkicker/kicking** *see* separate entry. ❑ **mudlark** *n. see* separate entry. ❑ **mudlocks** *n.* [1930s–50s] (*US black*) shoes. ❑ **mud-plunging** *n.* [mid-19C–1900s] (*tramp*) walking through muddy streets and lanes in the hope of securing hand-outs; thus *mud-plunger*, one who does this. ❑ **mudsling/slinger/slinging** *see* separate entries. ❑ **mud-stomper** *n.* [1960s+] (*US black*) a second-rate, impoverished prostitute.

IN PHRASES

❑ **blow mud** *v.* [coarse use of SE] [1990s+] to defecate loudly. ❑ **bring mud** *v.* [1920s] (*US black*) to let down, to disappoint. ❑ **cut mud** *v.* [image of car wheels moving through mud] [1930s–50s] (*US*) to move very fast. ❑ **poor as mud** *see* POOR AS WOOD *under* WOOD *n.*^{1}. ❑ **up to mud** *adj.* [the innate worthlessness of mud] [1930s+] (*Aus.*) unsatisfactory.

IN EXCLAMATIONS

❑ **here's mud in your eye!** *see* separate entry.

mud! *excl. see* HERE'S MUD IN YOUR EYE! *excl.*

mud and ooze *n.* [rhy. sl. = BOOZE *n.*] [20C+] (*Aus.*) alcohol.

mudder *n.* [20C+] (*Aus./US*) a horse or human runner who is at their best on a muddy course or track.

mudding-face *n.* [MUD *n.* + play on SE *pudding-face*] [late 19C–1910s] a fool, a weakling.

muddle *n.* [MUDDLED *adj.*] [1910s–30s] a state of slight drunkenness.

IN PHRASES

❑ **on the muddle** *adj.* [1930s] on a spree.

muddle *v.* **1** [late 17C] to continue drinking although already drunk. **2** [19C] to have sexual intercourse.

muddled *adj.* (*also* **muddy**) [late 17C+] drunk.

muddlefug *n.* [1960s] (*US black*) a euph. for MOTHERFUCK *n.* (1).

muddlefugging *adj.* [1960s] (*US black*) a euph. for MOTHERFUCKING *adj.*

muddle on *v.* [late 17C–18C] to carry on drinking despite one's gradually increasing drunkenness.

muddy *adj.* **1** [20C+] (*Aus.*) euph. for BLOODY *adj.* **2** *see* MUDDLED *adj.* (1).

based on MUD n. (4), i.e. excrement

IN COMPOUNDS

❑ **muddy fuck** *n.* [MUD *n.* (4) + FUCK *n.*] [1970s] (*gay*) anal intercourse with a partner whose anus has not been properly cleaned. ❑ **muddy funster** *n.* **1** [1960s+] euph. for MOTHERFUCKER *n.*[initial letters]. **2** [2000s] a homosexual [MUD *n.* (4)].

SE in slang uses

IN COMPOUNDS

❑ **muddy-headed** *adj.* [mid-18C] drunk. ❑ **muddy waters** *n.* [ety. unknown; ? the softness of mud] [1970s+] (*US black*) the loss of a man's erection before or during sex.

IN PHRASES

❑ **get one's feet muddy** *v.* [1960s+] to be in criminal trouble. ❑ **Old Muddy** *n.* [mid-19C+] (*US*) **1** the Missouri River. **2** the Mississippi River.

muddy trench *adj.* [rhy. sl.] [1910s+] French.

mudfuck *n.* [MUDFUCKER *n.*] [1980s+] (*US*) synon. for MOTHERFUCK *n.* (1).

mudfuck *v.* [MUDFUCKER *n.*] [2000s] (*US*) synon. for MOTHERFUCK *v.*

mudfucker *n.* [1970s+] (*US*) synon. for MOTHERFUCKER *n.*

mudfucking *adj.* [MUDFUCKER *n.*] [1990s+] (*US*) synon. for MOTHERFUCKING *adj.*

mudger *n.* [? dial. *nudge*, to crush or bruise] [early 19C] a weakling, a 'milksop'.

mud-head *n.* **1** [mid-19C+] (*US*) a native of Tennessee. **2** [20C+] (*W.I.*) a native of Guyana, the majority of whom live in the muddy coastal areas of the country. **3** [late 19C–1950s] (*also* **mudbrain**) a fool [backform. f. MUD-HEADED *adj.*].

mud-headed *adj.* [late 18C] stupid.

mud hook *n.* [note 1885 *Bulletin* (Sydney) 31 Jan. 14/4: To men who sailed in the good old days [...] it is galling to see the manner in which the amateurs are dragging open boat sailing in the mire, by limiting such boats as the Rosetta [...] to five hands, maybe to suit some old mudhooker with a ton of ballast in her] (*orig. Aus./US*) **1** [early 19C+] an anchor. **2** [mid-19C+] (*also* **mud-hopper, -masher, -splasher, -splitter, -squasher**) a foot, a heavy shoe or boot. **3** [1920s+] a finger or hand.

mud in your eye *n.* [rhy. sl.; playing on the popular toast, HERE'S MUD IN YOUR EYE! *excl.*] [1940s+] a tie.

mud in your eye(s)! *excl. see* HERE'S MUD IN YOUR EYE! *excl.*

Mud Island *n.* [late 19C–1900s] Southend, the popular Cockney resort, which is sited at the seaward end of the Thames estuary.

mud-kicker *n.* [racetrack jargon *mud-kicker*, a slow racehorse that gets stuck in the mud; however, note positive use in sense 3] [1930s+] (*orig. US black*) **1** a prostitute who robs rather than has sex with her clients. **2** a prostitute, esp. later, a second-rate prostitute, one who fails, either through laziness or lack of appeal, to make enough money for her pimp. **3** a dedicated, very hard-working prostitute.

mud-kicking *adj.* [MUD-KICKER *n.* (3)] [1960s] (*US black*) of a prostitute, hard-working.

Mudland *n.* [MUD-HEAD *n.* (2)] [20C+] (*W.I.*) Guyana.

mudlark *n.* **1** [late 18C–1920s] a hog. **2** [late 18C–1950s] a waterside thief, who picks up packages thrown to them by a ship's crew-member. **3** [19C–1900s] a barge boy. **4** [19C; 1990s+] one who scavenges items from the Thames mud. **5** [early 19C] a duck. **6** [early 19C] a scavenger for scrap-iron. **7** [mid-19C] a collector for a bank. **8** [mid-19C] one who steals copper and other items from boats moored in the Thames. **9** [mid-19C] a sewerman. **10** [mid-19C–1910s] a street child, a 'gutter urchin'. **11** [1910s–20s] (*UK, WW1*) a soldier who sings in the trenches. **12** [20C+] (*Aus.*) a resident or native of Victoria, Australia. **13** [20C+] (*Aus./US*) a racehorse that enjoys muddy going.

mud pies *n.* [rhy. sl.] [20C+] (*Aus.*) the eyes.

Mud-salad Market *n.* [late 19C] Covent Garden Market.

mudsling *n.* [SE colloq. *sling mud*] [1950s] a slander, a malicious piece of gossip.

mudslinger *n.* [SE colloq. *sling mud*] [1910s+] one who slanders, talks maliciously about somebody.

mud-slinging *n.* (*also* **shit-slinging**) [SE colloq. *sling mud*] [late 19C+] slandering, talking maliciously behind someone's back.

mud-up *n.* [1990s+] (*W.I.*) **1** menstruation. **2** of a man, his state after sexual intercourse.

mud-up *v.* [1990s+] (*W.I.*) to be seen wearing the same outfit more than once.

muff *n.*^{1} [its supposed resemblance] **1** [17C+] the vagina. **2** [mid-17C+] the pubic hair. **3** [mid-19C] a cat. **4** [20C+] (*US*) a woman. **5** [1910s–50s] (*US*) a prostitute. **6** [1910s–50s] (*US*) a beard, a toupee. **7** [1970s] (*gay*) the anus [camp ext. of sense 1].

IN COMPOUNDS

❑ **muff-dive/-diver/-diving** *see* separate entries. ❑ **muff job** *n.* [JOB *n.*^{2} (2)] [1970s] (*US*) cunnilingus. ❑ **muff merchant** *n.* [1960s+] (*US*) **1** a prostitute. **2** a pimp. ❑ **muff muncher** *n.* [MUNCH *v.*^{1} (2)] [2000s] one who performs cunnilingus, usu. a lesbian; thus *muff-munching*, pursuing lesbian sex. ❑ **muff-nosh** *v. see* MUFF-DIVE *v.*

IN PHRASES

❑ **dive a muff** *v. see* DIVE *v.*

muff *n.*^{2} (*also* **muffer**) **1** [17C; late 19C–1910s] a fool, albeit an amiable one [like the SE *muff*, the fool is SOFT *adj.* (1) in the head, and note MUFF *n.*^{1} (1) and the use of CUNT *n.* (1) and other terms for the vagina as synons. for a fool]. **2** [early 19C–1920s] (*orig. sporting*) an incompetent, one who is awkward [MUFF *v.*^{1}; despite Vaux's use in 1812 *OED* claims that this sense 'has not been found earlier than the second quarter of the 19th C. (being unrecorded even in the slang dictionaries)'; note, however, Nares, who cites Warner *Albion's England* c.1600: 'Those stiles to him weare strange, but thay / Did feofe them on the bace-borne muffe, and him as king obay', which suggests that sense 2 could come from sense 1, although it is generally perceived to be the other way around]. **3** [early 19C–1910s] a blunder, an error; esp. in phr. *make a muff of oneself*, to act in an incompetent, foolish manner. **4** [2000s] a police officer.

DERIVATIVES

▫ **muffish** *adj.* [mid-19C–1950s] foolish or bungling; thus *muffishness*, the state of being a bungler; *muffism*, foolishness.

muff *adj.* [MUFF *n.*^{2}] [late 19C] second-rate, 'amateur'.

muff *v.*^{1} [ety. unknown; ? image of keeping one's hands in a SE *muff* rather than using them properly] **1** [early 19C] (*orig. sporting*) to die. **2** [mid-19C+] (*orig. sporting*) to make a blunder, to make a mess, to trip up. **3** [late 19C] to fail an examination. **4** [1910s] of a bill, to suffer a default.

DERIVATIVES

▫ **muffed** *adj.* [late 19C+] spoilt, bungled, failed. ▫ **muffing** *n.* [mid-19C+] clumsiness, clumsy failure. ▫ **muffing** *adj.* [mid-19C+] bungling, blundering.

muff *v.*^{2} **1** [1940s+] (*US*) to perform cunnilingus [abbr. MUFF-DIVE *v.*]. **2** [1990s+] to have sexual intercourse with [MUFF *n.*^{1} (1)].

muff *v.*^{3} [? MUFF *n.*^{1} (7) or MUFF *v.*^{1} (2)] [1990s+] (*UK juv.*) to fart.

muff-dive *v.* (*also* **muff-nosh**) [MUFF *n.*^{1} (1) + SE *dive*/DIVE *v.* (2)/NOSH *v.* (2)] [1940s+] (*orig. US*) to perform cunnilingus.

muff-diver *n.* [MUFF-DIVE *v.*] (*orig. US*) **1** [1930s+] one who performs cunnilingus. **2** [1930s+] a lesbian. **3** [1940s+] a contemptible person.

muff-diving *n.* (*also* **muff-noshing**) [MUFF-DIVE *v.*] [1930s+] performing an act of cunnilingus.

muff-diving *adj.* [MUFF-DIVER *n.* (3)] [1930s+] used derog., despicable.

muffed *adj. see under* MUFF *v.*^{1}.

muffer *n.* [MUFF *v.*^{2}] [1960s+] (*US*) a lesbian; i.e. a woman who performs cunnilingus.

muffin *n.*^{1} **1** [mid-19C] (*also* **muffincap**) a fool [? play on FLAT *n.*^{2} (1), i.e. the muffin is a small *flat* cake or link to MUFF *n.*^{2}/MUFF *v.*^{1} (2)]. **2** [mid–late 19C] (*also* **muffin-cap**) a 'pill-box' hat or cap, as worn by charity-school boys [resemblance]. **3** [mid-19C–1900s] (*Can./US*) a female companion who accompanies a bachelor on his round of social amusements. **4** [mid-19C–1930s] (*US*) a male chaperone. **5** [mid-19C+] an incompetent, one who is awkward. **6** [1960s+] (*US gay*) in pl., the buttocks. **7** [1970s] in pl., small female breasts. **8** [1970s+] (*US campus*) an admirable person; usu. in combs, such as *STUD-MUFFIN under* STUD *n.*

SE in slang uses

IN COMPOUNDS

▫ **muffin-head** *n.* [SE *muffin* + -HEAD *sfx* (1)] [late 19C; 1990s+] a fool. ▫ **muffin-top** *n.* [2000s] a roll of midriff flesh bulging over tight clothing. ▫ **muffin-walloper** *n.* [joc. use of WALLOPER *n.*^{1} (2)] [late 19C–1900s] a gossipy woman who enjoys dissecting her friends and acquaintances over a cup of tea and a muffin.

muffin *n.*^{2} [ext. of var. defs of MUFF *n.*^{1}] **1** [1940s–50s] (*US gay*) an anal virgin. **2** [1940s–70s] (*US*) a young woman, a sweetheart. **3** [1960s] (*US gay*) an attractive youth. **4** [1960s+] the vagina.

IN PHRASES

▫ **butter the muffin** *v.* [the moistened vagina represents the *butter*] [1990s+] of a woman, to masturbate.

muffin baker *n.* [rhy. sl. = QUAKER *n.*; orig. misunderstood by Hotten and entered in early edn as a 'Quaker' in religious meaning] [mid-19C+] excrement when hard and retained.

muffin-face *n.* (*also* **muffin-countenance**) [supposed resemblance] [mid-18C–19C] **1** a hairless (or expressionless) face. **2** a foolish or childish face.

DERIVATIVES

▫ **muffin-faced** *adj.* [mid-18C–19C] **1** having a foolish or expressionless face. **2** having a fat face or a face with protruding muscles.

muffing *n. see under* MUFF *v.*^{1}.

muffing *adj. see under* MUFF *v.*^{1}.

muffin-struggle *n. see BUN-STRUGGLE under* BUN *n.*^{3}.

muffin-worry *n.* (*also* **muffin-fight**) [ety. unknown] [mid-19C–1920s] an old ladies' tea-party.

DERIVATIVES

▫ **muffin-worrier** *n.* [late 19C] (*Aus.*) one who attends a tea party (and by implication dislikes alcohol).

muffler *n.* [early–mid-19C] **1** in pl., boxing gloves, esp. heavily padded gloves used for sparring. **2** a blow to the mouth or face.

muffling-cheat *n.* [SE *muffle* + CHEAT *n.* (1)] [mid-16C–early 19C] (*UK Und.*) a napkin.

muf fuh *n. see* MUHFUH *n.*

muffy *n.*^{1} [the frill or 'muff' around its neck] [20C+] (*Aus.*) a frill-necked lizard.

muffy *n.*^{2} [proper name *Muffy*, the stereotypical name of such young women] [1980s+] (*US campus*) a young woman who has the look of a typical sorority member, with bleached blonde hair, an alice band, heavy make-up and conventional clothes.

muffy *n.*^{3} [MUFF *v.*^{3}] [1990s+] (*UK juv.*) an act of breaking wind.

mufki pufki *n. see* MIFKY-PIFKY *n.*

mufti *n.* [SE post-1900. Orig. Ind. army slang, according to Y&B f. the *Mufti*, a religious leader and expounder of Islamic law; thus the word 'was perhaps originally applied to the attire of dressing-gown, smoking-cap, and slippers, which was like the Oriental dress of the Mufti, who was familiar in Europe from his appearance in Molière's *Bourgeois Gentilhomme*'; note the Fr. equivalent, *en Pekin*, Peking-style] **1** [19C+] (*orig. milit.*) ordinary clothes worn by someone who usu. wears a uniform to work. **2** [late 19C] (*Aus.*) informal clothes.

mufugly *adj.* [MOTHERFUCKING *adv.* + SE *ugly*] [1980s+] (*US campus*) extremely ugly.

mug *n.*^{1} (*also* **mugg**) [apparently from the 18C drinking *mugs*, bearing a grotesque human face] **1** in context of physical features. (**a**) [late 18C] (*US Und.*) the nose. (**b**) [late 18C+] the human face. (**c**) [early 19C] by metonymy, the individual. (**d**) [early 19C+] the mouth. (**e**) [mid-19C] the head. (**f**) [mid-19C] (*UK Und.*) a coin (which bears a monarch's face on one side). (**g**) [mid-19C–1960s] a grimace. (**h**) [late 19C+] a picture of a person, esp. in police records; thus MUG BOOK below. **2** a fig. container [i.e. one into whom one can 'pour' any nonsense]. (**a**) [early 19C+] a fool, a dupe, orig. the victim of a corrupt card-game; thus MUG'S GAME *n.* (**b**) [1910s+] anyone not directly involved in the underworld, thus, *de facto*, a gullible fool, a (potential) victim. **3** a lit. container. (**a**) [mid-19C] a pipe. (**b**) [mid-19C–1950s] (*US*) a chamberpot [abbr. *MEMBER MUG under* MEMBER *n.*^{1}]. **4** in context of violence. (**a**) [mid-19C–1960s] (*US Und.*) a strong hold placed on a victim when robbing them, usu. an arm lock or a chokehold. (**b**) [mid-19C+] (*US*) (*also* **mugg, mug man**) a thug, a violent person, a crude loutish person [MUG *v.*^{1} (3a)]. **5** as a person. (**a**) [late 19C+] a person, irrespective of character. (**b**) [20C+] used affectionately as a direct address. (**c**) [1980s] (*US black/campus*) a very attractive person. (**d**) [1980s+] (*US black*) a euph. for MOTHERFUCKER *n.* (**e**) [1990s+] (*Irish*) a sulky person. (**f**) [1990s+] (*US campus*) a friend, partner or acquaintance. **6** [1900s–50s] (*US*) (*also* **fly mug**) a police officer or detective; a railroad police officer.

DERIVATIVES

▫ **muglet** *n.* [sfx *-let*] [late 19C] a young victim of a confidence trick.

IN COMPOUNDS

▫ **mug aleck** *n.* [SMART ALECK *n.*] [1930s+] (*Aus.*) an unpleasantly conceited, smug person. ❑ **mug book** *n.* **1** [20C+] (*US police/Und.*) (*also* **mug file, mug list**) a book of pictures used to help police in keeping records of known criminals. **2** [1930s+] a reference book used for casting purposes in theatre, TV and films, containing pictures of actual and aspirant stars. **3** [1930s+] a collection of photographs of prominent people. ❑ **mug-catcher** *n.* [late 19C] (*UK Und.*) a confidence trickster. ❑ **mugfaker** *n.* [FAKER *n.*] [1930s–50s] a street photographer. ❑ **mug-grappler** *n.* *see* GRAPPLER *n.* ❑ **mug-hunter** *n.* [late 19C] one who tours the streets late at night in search of drunken men who can be robbed. ❑ **mug john** *n.* (*also* **mug cop, mug copper**) [JOHN *n.*[1]/ COP *n.*[1] (1)/ COPPER *n.* (3)] [1930s–50s] (*Aus.*) a police officer. ❑ **mug lair** *n.* [LAIR *n.*] [1940s+] (*Aus.*) a contemptuous description, i.e. a stupid, gullible, flashy show-off. ❑ **mug-mapped** *adj.* [1910s] plain, unattractive. ❑ **mug punter** *n.* [PUNTER *n.* (1)] [mid-19C+] a sucker in any game of chance or at a racecourse. ❑ **mug's game** *n.* *see* separate entry. ❑ **mug shot** *n.* *see* separate entry. ❑ **mug-shoot** *v.* [1930s+] (*orig. US*) to take a picture of a prisoner for identification; thus *mug-shooter*, a police photographer. ❑ **mug's ticker** *n.* *see under* TICKER *n.*[1]. ❑ **mug-trap** *n.* [late 19C] a con-man, one who tricks gullible victims.

IN PHRASES

❑ **cop a mug** *v.* [late 19C] of a confidence trickster, to ensnare a victim. ❑ **cut a mug** *v.* [early–mid-19C] to make faces, e.g. of a clown or comedian; as n., *mug-cutter*. ❑ **damp one's mug** *v.* [mid-19C] to take a drink. ❑ **hold one's mug** *v.* *see* HOLD ONE'S GOB *under* GOB *n.*[1]. ❑ **polish one's mug** *v.* [1920s–60s] (*US tramp*) to wash one's face. ❑ **put the mug on** *v.* [mid-19C–1940s] to throttle. ❑ **shut one's mug** *v.* [1910s] to be quiet, esp. as imper. ❑ **square mug** *n.* [mid-19C] (*UK Und.*) a 'straight' or (supposedly) guileless face. ❑ **stall one's mug** *v.* [mid-19C] to run off, to leave quickly; esp. as excl. *stall your mug!* go away! ❑ **throw one's mug away** *n.* [mid-19C] (*UK Und.*) to let anyone see one's face, to reveal oneself.

IN EXCLAMATIONS

❑ **mugs away!** [1940s+] an excl. used in sporting matches when the winners of the previous game tell the losers to start the next contest or game.

SE in slang uses

IN COMPOUNDS

❑ **mughouse** *n.* [SE *mug* + *house*; best known in comb. *mughouse clubs*, political clubs (of Hanoverian sympathies) which met at 'mug-houses' early in the 18C] [early 18C] a cheap tavern.

mug *n.*[2] [MUG (UP) *v.*[2]] **1** [mid-19C] an examination, a test. **2** [late 19C–1900s] a schoolchild or student who works hard.

mug *n.*[3] [1930s–50s] (*US black*) 'the act of putting on a shadow dance' (Durst, *The Jives of Dr Hepcat*, 1953).

mug *adj.* [MUG *n.*[1] (2a)] [late 19C+] foolish, stupid.

mug *v.*[1] **1** [early 18C–mid-19C] to refuse food. **2** in sense of grimace. (**a**) [mid-18C+] to pout, to grow sullen. (**b**) [mid-19C+] to make a face, to make people laugh by one's antics and grimaces; thus fig. to play around. **3** as a physical or verbal attack. (**a**) [19C–1900s] to fight, to punch, to strangle. (**b**) [early–late 19C] (*also* **mug up**) to ruin, to interfere in, to make a mess of. (**c**) [mid-19C] to chastise. (**d**) [mid-19C+] to rob, to assault, usu. in the street and often with violence; orig. to garrotte; thus MUGGER *n.*[1] (2). **4** in sexual senses. (**a**) [early 19C+] (*UK/Aus./US campus*) (*also* **mug down, mug up**) to kiss, to cuddle, to neck. (**b**) [1950s–60s] (*US black*) to have sexual intercourse with. **5** [mid-19C; 2000s] (*UK Und.*) to trick, to fool. **6** [mid-19C–1980s] to bribe, usu. by plying with liquor. **7** [late 19C] to speak. **8** with ref. to MUG *n.*[1] (1). (**a**) [late 19C] to take a photo, e.g. for a newspaper. (**b**) [late 19C+] (*US police*) to take identification pictures for prison/court use; thus *mug room*, a room in which such pictures are taken or stored. (**c**) [1900s–20s] (*US Und.*) to arrest, esp. for purposes of identification. **9** [late 19C+] to act like a fool. **10** *see* MUG (UP) *v.*[1]. **11** *see* MUG (UP) *v.*[2] (1).

IN PHRASES

❑ **mug behind five** *v.* [1930s–40s] (*US black*) to speak with one's hand shielding one's lips. ❑ **mug off** *v.* [2000s] to cause trouble for, to fool or deceive someone. ❑ **mug oneself** *v.* **1** [mid-19C] to get drunk. **2** [late 19C–1900s] to make oneself comfortable.

mug *v.*[2] [? dial. *muggle*, a mess, a confusion, a disorder] [late 19C–1940s] to huddle together in a confined space; to associate with.

mugg *n.* *see* MUG *n.*[1].

mugger *n.*[1] [MUG *n.*[1] (1)] **1** [early–late 19C] a blow in the mouth. **2** [mid-19C+] a street robber, orig. a garrotter.

mugger *n.*[2] [MUG (UP) *v.*[2]] [late 19C] one who studies hard.

mugger *n.*[3] [1940s–60s] euph. for BUGGER *n.*[1].

muggered *adj.* [MUGGER *n.*[3]] [1940s–60s] euph. for BUGGERED *adj.*[2].

mugger-fugger *n.* [1930s] euph. for MOTHERFUCKER *n.*

muggie *n.* *see* MUGGLES *n.*

muggill *n.* [ety. unknown; ? anecdotal f. a beadle named *McGill*] [late 16C–early 17C] (*UK Und.*) a beadle.

mugging *n.*[1] [MUG *v.*[1]] **1** [mid-19C+] in senses of violence. (**a**) a beating, a fight. (**b**) garrotting. (**c**) the act of street robbery and assault. **2** with ref. to MUG *n.*[1] (1). (**a**) [late 19C+] making faces. (**b**) [late 19C+] (*US police*) taking photographs of people, usu. for identification purposes. **3** [1920s+] (*US*) (*also* **mugging up**) kissing, love-making.

mugging *n.*[2] [MUG (UP) *v.*[2]] [mid-19C+] learning, working hard, memorizing.

mugging *n.*[3] [1930s–40s] (*US black*) standing around.

mugging *n.*[4] [1930s–50s] (*US black*) 'the act of doing a shadow dance' (Durst, *The Jives of Dr Hepcat*, 1953).

mugging *adj.* **1** [1960s] euph. for 'fugging'. **2** [1970s] annoying.

mugging up *n.* *see* MUG *v.*[1] (1).

muggins *n.*[1] [MUG *n.*[1] (1)] **1** [19C+] (*also* **Charlie Muggins, Joe Muggins**) a fool, a simpleton. **2** [mid–late 19C] a kind of card-game. **3** [1950s+] oneself, a rueful self-description; the implication is one of being a fool to take on a given task; often in phr. *muggins here*.

IN PHRASES

❑ **talk muggins** *v.* [late 19C] to talk nonsense.

muggins *n.*[2] [MUG (UP) *v.*[1]] **1** [mid-19C] (*US*) a bottle of bourbon. **2** [1930s–40s] (*US prison/tramp*) food.

muggle *n.* (*also* **miggle, miggles, muggie, muggles**) **1** usu. in pl., marijuana. **2** [1920s+] (*orig. US drugs*) a marijuana cigarette; often a real cigarette with marijuana (occas. hashish) substituted for some of the tobacco and packed back inside it.

IN COMPOUNDS

❑ **mugglehead** *n.* (*also* **muggle-smoker**) [-HEAD *sfx* (4)] [1920s–70s] (*US drugs*) a marijuana smoker. ❑ **muggleheaded** *adj.* [1930s] (*US drugs*) under the influence of marijuana.

IN PHRASES

❑ **muggled up** *adj.* [1940s] (*US drugs*) under the influence of marijuana.

muggler *n.*[1] [early 19C] (*Anglo-Irish*) a drink of beer.

muggler *n.*[2] [MUGGLE *n.*] [1930s] (*drugs*) a smoker of marijuana.

muggles *n.* *see* MUGGLE *n.*

muggsy *n.* [1930s] (*US*) a derog. term of address, i.e. stupid.

muggy *adj.*[1] (*also* **muggered**) [SE *muggy*, damp, close] **1** [early 19C+] drunk. **2** [1970s] (*drugs*) causing unpleasant feelings of sweatiness and stupor.

muggy *adj.*[2] [MUG *n.*[1] (1)] [late 19C+] stupid.

IN COMPOUNDS

❑ **muggy-cunt** *n.* [2000s] a general term of abuse. ❑ **muggy-cunt** *adj.* [2000s] disgusting, repellent, stupid.

mug in and mug out, be *v.* [dial. *muggle*, to live haphazardly, to muddle along] [mid-19C] to dawdle, to prevaricate, to fail to make up one's mind.

mug man *n.* *see* MUG *n.*[1] (4a).

mug's game *n.* (*also* **mug's lark**) [MUG *n.*[1] (1)] [late 19C+] a foolish endeavour, a pointless effort.

mug shot *n.* (*also* **mug, mug picture, mug photo**) [MUG *n.*^{1} (1)] **1** [1930s+] a picture taken by the police and used for criminal records. **2** [1970s+] synon., in non-police work, e.g. a publicity photograph.

mugster *n.* [MUG (UP) *v.*^{2} (1)] [late 19C] (*school*) a hard worker.

mugu *adj. see* MOEGIE *adj.*

mug-up *n.* [MUG (UP) *v.*^{1}] [1910s–70s] a snack, a meal, a drink.

mug (up) *v.*^{1} [SE *mug* / MUG *n.*^{1} (1)] [mid-19C+] (*US*) to eat or drink heartily, to have a good meal.

mug (up) *v.*^{2} [orig. theatrical use, MUG UP *v.*^{1}, i.e. paint one's face, as part of preparing to perform a role] [mid-19C+] to study hard, to learn, to memorize, esp. a specific lesson for a specific test or examination; thus *mugging (up)*, studying hard.

mug up *v.*^{1} [MUG *n.*^{1} (1)] **1** [mid–late 19C] to apply theatrical make-up. **2** [late 19C] in fig. use, to prepare for, to dedicate oneself to. **3** [1950s+] (*US black*) to put on one's hat, to leave. **4** *see* MUG *v.*^{1} (1).

mug up *v.*^{2} [late 19C] to praise, to indulge.

mug up *v.*^{3} [late 19C] to be trapped.

mugwump *n.* [SE *mugwump*, 'one who holds more or less aloof from party-politics, professing disinterested and superior views. In 1884, spec. applied to Republicans who refused to support the nominee of their party for president. Also, a person who withdraws his support from any group or organization' (*OED*)] (*orig. US*) **1** [mid-19C] an impotent man [from sex]. **2** [mid-19C+] a person in authority, a self-important person. **3** [late 19C+] an obnoxious, foolish person. **4** [late 19C+] in political terms, one whose vote may go either way and is thus untrustworthy, thus *Mugwumpery*, the attitude of such voters.

(DERIVATIVES)

❑ **mugwumping** *adj.* [late 19C+] foolish.

muh *n. see* MOTHER *n.* (5).

muh-fugger *n. see* MOTHERFUCKER *n.*

muhfuh *n.* (*also* **muf fuh, muhfuck, muh-fuh**) [US black pron.] [1960s+] synon. for MOTHERFUCKER *n.*

muhfuh *adj.* (*also* **muh-fuhn**) [2000s] (*orig. US*) abbr. MOTHERFUCKING *adj.*

muhfuhkuh *n.* (*also* **muh fuck**) [ext. of MUHFUH *n.*] [1960s+] synon. for MOTHERFUCKER *n.*

muke mouth *n.* [1980s] (*US black*) an ugly female.

mul *n.* (*also* **muller**) [MULL *n.* (2)] [1920s+] (*Irish*) a fool, a useless object.

mula *n.* [Mex. Sp. *mula*, female mule] [1970s+] a male homosexual who prefers to take the passive role in sex.

mulat *adj.* [abbr. SE *mulatto*] [1980s] (*US black*) of a black person, light-skinned.

muldoon *n.* **1** [19C; 1970s] (*US, later use US black*) a police officer [a typical Irish name; US police were stereotypically Irish]. **2** [late 19C] (*US*) the truth, the real thing; something or someone dependable [abbr. 'the solid *Muldoon*', popularized by 'Muldoon the Solid Man', a vaudeville song by Harrigan and Hart (1874)].

mule *n.* **1** [mid-17C; 19C+] a fool, a stubborn person [on model of ASS *n.*]. **2** [20C+] any small motor-powered vehicle. **3** as a form of alcohol [the alcohol 'kicks like a *mule*']. (**a**) [1920s+] (*US*) (*also* **white mule**) homemade bourbon made from grain alcohol. (**b**) [1950s] (*US drugs*) marijuana soaked in bourbon. **4** in drug uses. (**a**) [1920s+] (*drugs*) a carrier of drugs, typically across international borders, and in many cases an otherwise 'innocent' person who has no other contact with the drugs trade. (**b**) [1930s+] a drug runner, operating within a given city or prison; on a local scale, the runner who brings supplies from an adjacent hiding place to a street dealer as demand requires. (**c**) [1960s+] (*US prison*) (*also* **packhorse**) a smuggler, usu. a visitor or prison warder. (**d**) [1990s+] any form of carrier, e.g. of weapons for a gang. **5** [1920s+] (*US*) the penis [earlier quotes are doubles entendres]. **6** [1940s+] as a derog. description. (**a**) an unattractive woman. (**b**) (*US campus*) an unattractive man. (**c**) an impotent man. (**d**) (*W.I.*) an infertile woman, who therefore suffers from *mule-belly*. **7** [1960s] (*US*) vodka.

(IN PHRASES)

❑ **corn mule** *n.* [1920s–60s] (*US*) illicitly distilled corn whisky. ❑ **gray mule** *n.* [1900s–10s] (*US*) corn whisky or gin. ❑ **lope the mule** *v.* (*also* **lope, lope one's mule, lope the pony**) [1950s+] (*US*) to masturbate. ❑ **ride the mule** *v.* [1990s+] to have sexual intercourse. ❑ **water the mule** *v.* (*also* **water one's horse, water one's mule, water one's pony**) [1970s+] (*US*) to urinate.

SE in slang uses

(IN COMPOUNDS)

❑ **mule breakfast** *n.* [1920s–40s] (*US*) a straw hat. ❑ **muledick** *v.* [1970s] (*US*) of a man, to copulate aggressively, violently. ❑ **mule-mouth** *n.* [1970s+] (*US black*) one who works regularly as a police informer. ❑ **mule whacker** *n.* (*also* **mule-puncher**) [WHACK *v.*^{1} (1)] [late 19C–1920s] (*US*) a mule-driver.

(IN EXCLAMATIONS)

❑ **mule shit!** [var. on BULLSHIT *n.*] [1920s+] (*US*) a mild oath, used to express disbelief or surprise.

mule *v.* [MULE *n.* (1)] [1960s+] (*US Und./police/prison*) to act as a courier of contraband, esp. illicit drugs.

mulenyam *n.* (*also* **moulenjam, moulonjam, moulonjohn**) [Ital. *melenzana*, an aubergine, which is deep purple in colour] [1960s+] (*US/Ital.*) a black person.

muley-grubs *n. see* MULLIGRUBS *n.*

mulga *n.* (*also* **Mulgaland**) [SAusE *mulga*, one of various plants of the genus *Acacia* found in the dry inland of Australia; thus the dry inland itself. The Aus. term comes from Yuwaalaraay *malga*] [late 19C+] (*Aus.*) an uninhabited, sparsely populated or inhospitable region; thus used attrib. in combs: *mulgaland*; *mulga madness*, mental decay that can overtake those spending long periods alone in such regions; *mulga scrubbers*, stock that have run wild and deteriorated in condition; *Mulga Bill*, generic for a bushman.

(IN COMPOUNDS)

❑ **mulga wire** *n.* [late 19C+] **1** a 'bush telegraph', the 'grapevine'. **2** (*also* **mulga**) a rumour, a lie.

(IN PHRASES)

❑ **go mulga** *v.* [1950s+] (*Aus.*) to take to the bush, thus to go off by oneself.

mull *n.* [? SE *mull*, to grind, to pulverize or SE *muddle*] **1** [19C] a mess; usu. in phr. *make a mull of*, make a mess of. **2** [mid–late 19C] a simpleton, a clumsy person. **3** [1980s+] (*Aus. drugs*) marijuana, esp. when prepared (cleaned, sieved) for smoking.

(IN COMPOUNDS)

❑ **mullhead** *n.* [1980s+] (*Aus. drugs*) a regular smoker of marijuana.

mull *v.* [SE *mull*, to grind, to pulverize] (*orig. US*) **1** [mid-19C] to work steadily without accomplishing much. **2** [mid-19C] (*UK Und.*) to spend money. **3** [late 19C+] to think about, to cogitate upon, to work over in one's mind. **4** [1980s+] (*Aus drugs*) (*also* **mull up**) to chop and mix cannabis finely for consumption [but note MOULI *v.*].

mulla *n. see* MOOLA *n.*

mullah *v.* (*also* **muller**) [SE *mull*, to grind to powder, to pulverize to crumble] **1** [1950s+] (*orig. UK prison*) to beat up severely. **2** [1990s+] to defeat resoundingly.

mullahed *adj.* (*also* **mullered**) [MULLAH *v.*] **1** [1950s+] (*orig. UK prison*) beaten severely. **2** [1990s+] defeated comprehensively, broken, destroyed. **3** [1990s+] drunk, absolutely intoxicated.

mullahing *n.* (*also* **mullering**) [MULLAH *v.*] [1990s+] a beating.

mullarkey *n. see* MALARKEY *n.*

mulled (up) *adj.* [abbr. SE *mulled* (*ale*) or *muddled*] [1930s–70s] drunk.

muller *n.*^{1} [MULL *v.* (4)] [1980s+] (*Aus. drugs*) one who chops and mixes marijuana.

muller *n.*^{2} *see* MUL *n.*

mullered *adj. see* MULLAHED *adj.*

mullet *n.*[1] [abbr. MULLETHEAD *n.*] [1950s+] (*US*) a fool.

IN PHRASES

❑ **like a stunned mullet** *adj.* (*also* **like a baffled mullet**) [1950s+] (*Aus./N.Z.*) dull, stupefied.

mullet *n.*[2] (*also* **ape drape, hockey head, mud flap**) [1970s+] a hairstyle, popularized in the 1970s.

mullethead *n.* [MULLETHEADED *adj.*] [late 19C+] (*US*) a fool.

mulletheaded *adj.* [the freshwater fish the *mullet* has a notably large head] [mid-19C+] stupid, foolish, ignorant.

mullhead *n. see under* MULL *n.*

mulliegrums *n. see* MULLIGRUBS *n.* (1).

mulligan *n.* **1** as a generic Irish name *Mulligan*. (**a**) [late 19C–1940s] (*US*) an Irish person. (**b**) [1930s+] (*US prison*) a prison guard. (**c**) [1930s+] (*US Und.*) a police officer, usu. male. (**d**) [1960s] a part-time, 'amateur' criminal. **2** [late 19C+] (*orig. US tramp*) (*also* **mulligan stew**) a stew made of whatever meats and vegetables are available [either proper name *Mulligan*, an otherwise forgotten cook, or *Mulligan* as a generic for Irish and thus an Irish stew; note army jargon *mulligan battery*, the cook wagon]. **3** [1920s–50s] (*US*) a high-powered rifle. **4** [1940s–60s] (*US black*) a tramp [backform. f. *mulligan stew*, the consumers of which were mainly vagrants]. **5** [1940s–50s] (*Aus.*) in pl., playing cards.

IN COMPOUNDS

❑ **mulligan car** *n.* [20C+] (*US*) a restaurant car on a railway. ❑ **mulligan joint** *n.* [JOINT *n.* (1)] [20C+] (*US*) a cheap restaurant. ❑ **mulligan mixer** *n.* [20C+] (*US, Western*) a cook.

mulligatawney *adj.* [rhy. sl. = HORNY *adj.*] [1960s–70s] sexually aroused or arousing.

mulligrubber *n.* [MULLIGAN *n.* (2) + GRUBBER *n.*[2] (1)] [late 19C] (*US*) a tramp, a vagrant.

mulligrubs *n.* (*also* **grubbs, mollygrubs, muley-grubs, mullygrubs**) [*OED*: 'a grotesque arbitrary formation'; ? SE *mull*, to grind, to pulverize + *grub*, an insect] **1** [late 16C+] (*also* **mulliegrums**) a feeling of unease, not an illness that can be diagnosed, but a general sense of not being fully well [note US regional uses: stomach pains, diarrhoea]. **2** [17C–mid-19C] colic, diarrhoea [note US regional use: menstruation]. **3** [mid-17C] as a nickname.

Mullingar heifer *n.* (*also* **Munster heifer**) [the supposed characteristic of *Mullingar/Munster* women; note Ned Ward, *The London Spy* (1699) 'A *Bouncing beldam*, who had as much Flesh on her Bones as a *Lincolnshire Heifer*'] [19C+] (*Irish*) a woman with thick ankles; thus *beef to the heels/knees, like a Mullingar heifer*; occas. used of men, to describe them as brawny, stalwart.

mullion *n.* [? SE *melungeon*, a member of a racially mixed group of people – half black, half Native American – centred in the Appalachians, ult. Fr. *mélange*, mixture] [1950s–70s] (*US black*) an unattractive woman or ugly person.

mullipuff *n. see* MOLLYPUFF *n.*

mullock *n.* [dial. *mullock*, rubbish; also SAusE *mullock*, the earth taken from a mine and piled at its mouth] (*Aus.*) **1** [mid-19C+] rubbish, a worthless object; thus *mullock-seller*, a con-man who sells worthless goods; as adj., *mullocky*. **2** [late 19C+] an ignorant and generally useless person. **3** [1910s] in fig. use, something unpleasant.

IN PHRASES

❑ **in the mullock** [1980s] in difficulties. ❑ **poke mullock** *v.* [20C+] (*Aus.*) to mock, to tease, to deride.

mullyfogging *adj.* [1960s+] (*US*) synon. for MOTHERFUCKING *adj.*

mullygrubs *n. see* MULLIGRUBS *n.*

mullypuff *n. see* MOLLYPUFF *n.*

mullywhambles *n.* [mid-19C] (*UK Und.*) indigestion.

multa *adj. see* MULTY *adj.*

multa bona fakement *n.* [MULTA *adj.* + BONA *adj.* + FAKEMENT *n.*] [early 19C] (*Polari*) a well-executed confidence trick.

multee kertever *adj.* (*also* **multicattivo**) [Ital./Ling. Fr. *molto cattivo*, very bad] [mid–late 19C] very bad.

multi *adj. see* MULTY *adj.*

multi-culti *adj.* [abbr.] [1980s+] (*US*) *multi-cultural*.

multie *adj. see* MULTY *adj.*

multy *adj.* (*also* **multa, multi, multie**) [Ital. *multo*, many; later use mainly Aus.] [late 19C–1910s] (*orig. Ling. Fr./Polari*) **1** of people and things, bad, unpleasant. **2** criminally obtained.

mulvather *v.* [Sp. *malvader*, to knock down, to stun] [mid–late 19C] (*Irish*) to confuse.

DERIVATIVES

❑ **mulvathered** *adj.* [mid–late 19C] (*Irish*) drunk.

mum *n.*[1] [late 14C SE *mum*, an inarticulate sound made through the closed lips. Such a sound indicates an unwillingness to speak out loud] [mid-16C+] a refusal to speak, silence; the state of being dumb; latterly in phr. *MUM'S THE WORD under* MUM *adj.*

mum *n.*[2] [abbr.] [20C+] a chrysanthe*mum*.

mum *n.*[3] [var. on MOTHER *n.* (1)] [1930s+] (*UK Und.*) one's mistress of many years or one's wife, but not one's actual mother.

mum *adj.* [MUM *n.*[1]] [late 18C+] silent, quiet.

IN COMPOUNDS

❑ **mum-tip** *n.* [early 19C] a bribe to ensure one's silence, 'hush-money'.

IN PHRASES

❑ **keep mum** *v.* [19C+] to keep quiet; thus 1940s exhortation to secrecy, *be like Dad, keep Mum*. ❑ **mum's the word** [18C+] be quiet, say nothing about this.

mum, be *v. see BE MOTHER under* MOTHER *n.*

mum! *excl.* [MUM *n.*[1]] [mid-16C–1900s] an excl. demanding silence.

IN EXCLAMATIONS

❑ **mum your dubber!** [DUBBER *n.*[2]] [late 18C–mid-19C] be quiet! shut up!

mum and dad *adj.*[1] [rhy. sl.] [20C+] (*Aus./N.Z.*) **1** mad. **2** bad.

mum and dad *adj.*[2] [1990s+] (*Aus.*) conventional, respectable, and thus, by criminal standards, naïve.

mum and daddo *n.* [rhy. sl.] [20C+] (*Aus.*) a shadow.

mumble *v.*

SE in slang uses

IN COMPOUNDS

❑ **mumble-crust** *n.* [SE *mumble*, to chew softly, as with toothless gums] [mid-16C–early 17C] a toothless person. ❑ **mumble-matins** *n.* [mid-16C–early 17C] a priest. ❑ **mumble-turd** *n.* [late 16C] a term of abuse.

mumble and moan *n.* [rhy. sl.] [1930s] a telephone.

mumble and mutter *n.* [rhy. sl.] [20C+] butter.

mumble-peg *n.* [SE *mumble-the-peg; mumblety-peg*, a game in which each player in turn throws a knife from a series of positions, continuing until they fail to make the blade stick in the ground] [late 19C–1960s] **1** the vagina. **2** the female pubic hair.

mumbler *n.* [late 18C–early 19C] (*UK Und.*) a beggar pretending to be a failed tradesman.

mumbling cove *n.* [COVE *n.* (1)] [late 18C–mid-19C] (*UK Und.*) a shabby person; an unpleasant, deceitful landlord.

mumbly pegs *n.* (*also* **mumblety-pegs**) [rhy. sl.] [1920s–50s] (*US*) the legs.

mumbojumbo *v.* [colloq. *mumbo-jumbo*] [20C+] to talk meaningless nonsense.

mum-glass *n.* [SE *mum-glass*, a glass used for the drinking of *mum* beer, a type of beer originating in Brunswick in Germany and imported into the UK in the 17C–18C. The Monument presumably resembles such a glass] [late 17C–early 19C] the Monument, a 95m (311ft) column erected in 1671–77 in memory of the Great Fire of London (1666) at the junction of what is now Monument Street and Fish Street Hill.

mummer *n.* [SE *mummer*, one who mutters and murmurs and thus an actor in a dumb-show] **1** [late 18C–mid-19C] the mouth. **2** [19C–1920s] an actor.

IN PHRASES

❑ **dub one's mummer** *v. see* DUB *v.*[1].

mummery-cove *n.* [SE *mummery*, over-acting + COVE *n.* (1)] [mid–late 19C] an actor.

mummick *v.* [? dial. *mammock*, to break into pieces, crumble, tear] [late 19C] (*US*) to handle or feel an object or person.

mummy *n.* [SE *mummy*, a wrapped, embalmed corpse, orig. Egyptian] [1900s–10s] (*US*) an incompetent.

IN COMPOUNDS

❑ **mummyhead** *n.* [-HEAD *sfx* (1)] [1990s+] (*US black gang*) a fool. ❑ **mummy pussy** *n.* [PUSSY *n.* (2)] [1970s+] (*US black*) a woman who does not respond during sexual intercourse.

mummy *v.* [1970s+] (*US black*) to beat a person to death, thus making them into an Egyptian-style mummified corpse.

mump *n.* [MUMPER *n.* (2)] [early 18C] a beggar, a scrounger.

mump *v.* [? Du. *mompen*, to cheat, dial. *mump*, to mutter, to speak indistinctly] **1** [late 16C+] to beg, to visit a house in the course of one's travels as a beggar. **2** [mid-17C–mid-18C] to cheat (out of); to deceive. **3** [late 17C–1910s] to obtain by begging. **4** [early–mid-18C] to disappoint. **5** [late 18C] to eat. **6** [mid-19C] to talk seriously.

IN PHRASES

❑ **on the mump** *adj.* [early 18C; 1910s] begging for one's living.

mumper *n.* [MUMP *v.*] **1** [mid-17C] a prostitute. **2** [mid-17C+] (*UK Und.*) a genteel beggar, a scrounger, 'a Gentiler sort of Beggars, for they scorn to beg for food, but money and cloaths' (Head, *The Canting Academy*, 1673). **3** [mid-19C+] a half-breed gypsy, a 'second-rate' gypsy, i.e. one who has no van. **4** [20C+] a tramp.

IN COMPOUNDS

❑ **mumper's brass** *n.* [BRASS *n.*[1] (1)] [early 18C] money. ❑ **mumper's hall** *n.* [late 17C–early 19C] (*UK Und.*) a low-class ale-house, frequented by beggars, who will be 'very Merry, Drunk and Frolicksome' (B.E.).

mumper *v.* [MUMP *v.* (1)] [20C+] (*US black*) to travel around, to partner someone on their travels.

mumping *n.* [MUMP *v.*; note police jargon *mumping*, of a police officer, accepting cheap or free goods and services from friendly tradespeople] [late 17C+] begging.

mumpins *n.* [predates MUMP *v.* (1) and MUMPER *n.* (2) so poss. SE although not in *OED*] [mid-15C] alms.

mumps *n.* [dial. *mump*, to complain, to speak querulously] [late 16C–19C] constructed with *the*, low spirits, 'the sulks'; thus adj. *mumpish*, depressed, sulky.

IN COMPOUNDS

❑ **mumps-crokery** *n.* [mid-19C] (*UK Und.*) persistent whining and complaining.

mumpy *adj.* [? MUMP *v.*] [1990s+] impoverished.

mums *n.* [var. on MUNS *n.*] [late 18C–late 19C] the mouth, the jaws, the face, the lips.

mum-tip *n. see under* MUM *adj.*

mun *n.*[1] (*also* **mund, munn, munne**) [northern dial.] [late 17C] a member of a band of London street thugs.

mun *n.*[2] *see* MON *n.*[1].

munch *n.* [abbr. MUNCHIE *n.*[1]] [1980s+] (*orig. US teen*) a snack.

munch *v.*[1] **1** [17C; 19C; 1980s+] to eat, esp. enthusiastically. **2** [1960s+] (*also* **munch the box**) to perform oral sex. **3** [1980s] (*US campus*) to kiss.

IN COMPOUNDS

❑ **munching house** *n.* [1910s+] a cheap restaurant or café. ❑ **munch-present** *n.* [he fig. 'eats' the money] [mid-16C–early 17C] one who takes bribes.

IN PHRASES

❑ **munching the truncheon** *n.* [TRUNCHEON *n.*] [1990s+] fellatio. ❑ **munch out** *v.* **1** [1970s+] (*orig. US campus*) to eat voraciously, esp. as a result of smoking cannabis. **2** [1980s+] (*US campus*) to kiss passionately. ❑ **munch the carpet** *v. see under* CARPET *n.*[1]. ❑ **munch the trunch** *v.* [TRUNCHEON *n.*] [1990s+] (*UK juv.*) to fellate.

munch *v.*[2] [1970s+] (*US*) **1** to make a blunder, to perform badly. **2** to crash, as from a surfboard or a vehicle.

munchie *n.*[1] (*also* **munchies, munchy**) [1950s+] (*orig. US*) **1** a snack, snacks or small meal. **2** usu. in pl., the craving for food, often sweet or in an otherwise unlikely combination of flavours, that afflicts smokers of hashish or marijuana. **3** a snack eaten to assuage this craving.

IN PHRASES

❑ **munchied up** *adj.* [1990s+] experiencing the pangs of hunger that accompany the smoking of cannabis or (occas.) heavy drinking.

munchie *n.*[2] [2000s] (*Irish*) a derog. term for a country person.

munchkin *n.* [the *Munchkins*, diminutive characters who featured in the book by L. Frank Baum, *The Wizard of Oz* (publ. 1900, filmed 1939)] [1950s+] a child, a small person.

munch-out *n.* [MUNCH OUT *under* MUNCH *v.*[1]] [1970s+] (*US campus*) a large meal.

munchy *n. see* MUNCHIE *n.*[1].

mund *n. see* MUN *n.*[1].

munds *n. see* MUNS *n.*

mung *n.* [note computer jargon *mung*, to destroy maliciously, to ruin] [1940s+] (*US campus*) filth or dirt of any kind, anything disgusting.

mung *adj.*[1] [SE/dial. *mong*, a mixture, a confusion] [mid–late 19C] (*US*) untrue, false, usu. in journalistic context.

mung *adj.*[2] [MUNG *n.* (1)] [1960s] (*US campus*) spoiled.

mung *v.*[1] [Rom. *mang*, to beg; note also dial. *munge*, to whine in low tones] [19C] (*UK tramp/Und.*) to beg.

DERIVATIVES

❑ **munging** *n.* [mid-19C] begging.

mung *v.*[2] [MUNG *n.* (1)] [1960s+] (*US campus*) to spoil, to ruin.

munga *n. see* MUNGER *n.*

mungare *n. see* NUMGARE *n.*

mungaree *n.* (*also* **mungee, mungy, munjari, munjary, mongee, mongoree**) [Ital. *mangiare*, to eat; 20C+ use also Aus.] **1** [mid-19C–1940s] food. **2** [20C+] (*UK tramp*) begging.

mungarly *n.* [Polari, thence Ital. *mangiare*, Fr. *manger*, to eat. Note Grose, *Provincial Glossary* (1787) *mung*, food for chickens] [mid–late 19C] food.

IN COMPOUNDS

❑ **mungarly-casa** *n.* [CASA *n.*[1]] [mid–late 19C] a baker's shop.

mungas *n.* (*also* **munja**) [Ital. *mangiare*, to eat] [1910s+] (*N.Z.*) food, a meal, esp. lunch.

munge *n.* (*also* **muns, munns**) [ety. unknown] [late 17C–early 18C] (*UK Und.*) the dark.

mungee *n. see* MUNGAREE *n.*

munger *n.* (*also* **manga, munga**) [MUNGARLY *n.*] [20C+] (*Aus./N.Z.*) **1** food. **2** a smoke taken during a rest period.

munging *n. see under* MUNG *v.*[1].

mungo *n.*[1] [generic use of given name] [mid-18C–mid-19C] a black person.

mungo *n.*[2] [definition is queried in *OED*, as also is label 'slang'] [late 18C] ? a person of position, a 'swell'.

mungo *n.*[3] [? SE *mungo*, a tough material, made from recycled rags, ? used for old rugby shirts] [1990s+] (*Aus.*) a fan of Rugby League.

mungous *adj.* [abbr. HUMONGOUS *adj.*] [1990s+] (*UK juv.*) huge.

mungy *adj.* [MUNG *n.* (1)] [1960s] (*US*) dirty, filthy.

muni *n.* (*also* **muny**) [abbr.] **1** [1930s+] (*US tramp*) a *muni*cipal lodging house. **2** [1970s+] (*US*) a *muni*cipal bond. **3** [1980s] a bus conveying prisoners to prison.

munitions *n.* [play on *WARPAINT under* WAR *n.*] [1920s] (*US*) cosmetics.

munja *n. see* MUNGAS *n.*

munjari/munjary *n. see* MUNGAREE *n.*

munjay *n.* [Fr. *manger*, to eat] [1940s] (*W.I.*) a large dumpling.

munn/munne *n. see* MUN *n.*[1].

munns *n. see* MUNS *n.*

munnu *n.* [? MUUNA *n.*, but ? Fr. *mon amour*, my love] [1940s] (*W.I.*) romance.

munpins *n. see* MOMPYNS *n.*

muns *n.* (*also* **munds, munns**) [dial. *mun*, the face; thus mid-19C street cry 'One a penny, two a penny, hot cross buns, / Butter them and sugar them and put them in your muns'; Grose (1785) traces it to Ger. *mund*, mouth] **1** [mid-17C–19C] the mouth, the jaws, the face, the lips. **2** [mid-18C] in ext. use, the whole person.

IN PHRASES

❑ **black muns** *n.* [17C–18C] hoods and scarves made of lutestring (a glossy silk fabric) or alamode (a thin, light, glossy black silk). ❑ **rum muns** *n.* a handsome man. ❑ **suck one's muns** *v. see* SUCK ONE'S FACE *under* SUCK *v.*[1].

muns *v.* [MUNS *n.* (1)] [mid-18C] (*UK Und.*) to kiss.

Munster heifer *n. see* MULLINGAR HEIFER *n.*

Munster plums *n.* [proper name of the Irish county *Munster* and thus a synon. of the stereotype IRISH *adj.*] [late 18C–1900s] potatoes.

munt *n.* (*also* **muntu**) [Bantu *umuntu*, sing. of *abantu*, a person, black person, servant] [1930s+] (*orig. S.Afr.*) derog. term for a black person.

munta *n. see* MUNTER *n.*

munted *adj.* [? MUNTER *n.*] **1** [1990s+] (*Aus. teen*) a general negative description, ugly, unpleasant. **2** [1990s+] very drunk. **3** [2000s] (*N.Z.*) destroyed, defeated, wiped out.

munter *n.* (*also* **munta**) [? MOUNT *n.* (3)] [1990s+] (*UK juv.*) a very ugly, poss. also promiscuous woman.

muny *n. see* MUNI *n.*

muppet *n.* [the puppets created by Jim Henson and featured on TV's *Muppet Show* (1976–80)] **1** [1970s+] a child, a small person. **2** [1980s] a police officer or magistrate. **3** [1990s+] an unattractive person, a fool, poss. one who is mentally retarded; a term of abuse.

mur *n.* (*also* **myrrh**) [backsl.] [mid-19C–1950s] rum.

murdelize *v.* (*also* **murderize**) [? play on fig. use of SE *murder*] [1960s+] (*US teen*) to trounce, to drub.

murder *n.* **1** [mid-19C+] something (or someone) unbearable, extremely difficult or infuriating. **2** [20C+] (*orig. US black*) an excellent or marvellous person or thing.

IN PHRASES

❑ **get murders off** *v.* [1990s+] to be severely chastised or punished.

SE in slang uses

IN COMPOUNDS

❑ **murder house** *n.* [1960s+] (*N.Z., juv.*) a school dental clinic. ❑ **murder-mouth** *v.* [1970s] (*US black*) **1** to talk insincerely, to lie, esp. when pursuing sex. **2** to make threats that one couldn't or wouldn't ever back up with action. ❑ **murder rap** *n.* [1920s+] (*orig. US*) a charge of murder.

IN PHRASES

❑ **blue murder** *n.* see separate entry. ❑ **bloody murder** *n. see* BLUE MURDER *n.* ❑ **get away with murder** *v.* **1** [1910s+] to flout all proprieties with absolute success, to achieve the otherwise unacceptable; occ. with *blue*. **2** *see* separate entry. ❑ **holler (bloody) murder** *v.* (*also* **scream bloody murder, yell (bloody) murder**) [mid-19C+] (*US*) to raise an outcry, to make a fuss. ❑ **murder on** *adj. see* DEATH ON *adj.* ❑ **screaming bloody murder** *adj. see* SCREAMING BLUE MURDER *under* BLUE MURDER *n.*

IN EXCLAMATIONS

❑ **murder in Irish!** [mid-18C] a general excl.

murder *v.* **1** [early 17C; mid-19C–1940s] (*US*) to exasperate, to infuriate, e.g. *that just murders me*. **2** [mid-19C+] (*orig. US*) to consume or desire, greedily and enthusiastically, e.g. *I could murder a roast duck noodle soup*. **3** [1910s+] (*orig. US*) to defeat totally or conclusively, esp. at a game or sport; to ruin. **4** [1970s+] (*US*) to cause pain.

SE in slang uses

IN PHRASES

❑ **murder the bishop** *v. see* BANG THE BISHOP *under* BISHOP *n.*[2].

murder! *excl.* (*also* **murderation!**) [SE *murder!*, 'As a cry or exclamation uttered by one who thinks or pretends to think himself or someone else in danger of murder' (*OED*)] [17C+] an excl. used to express annoyance, pain or surprise.

murderation *n.* [ext. of SE *murder*] [20C+] (*W.I.*) a severe beating, esp. of a woman or child.

murderation! *excl.* [ext. of MURDER! *excl.*] [mid-19C; 1980s+] (*later use UK black*) a general excl.

murdering *adj.* [19C] an intensifier.

murderize *v. see* MURDELIZE *v.*

murder one *n.* [US legal jargon *murder one*, first degree or premeditated murder] **1** [1950s+] (*US drugs*). (**a**) heroin and cocaine. (**b**) a strong variety of heroin. **2** [1980s+] (*US black*) in pl., dark glasses [the wearing of dark glasses is equated with a murderous image].

IN PHRASES

❑ **murder one dun** [ety. unknown] [1990s+] a general greeting.

murder one *adj.* [1990s+] (*US*) very aggressive, murderous.

murerk *n.* [? corruption of BURERK *n.*] [mid-19C] (*tramp*) the mistress of the house.

murk *n.* [its consistency] [1930s–80s] (*US*) coffee.

murkarker *n.* (*also* **murkauker**) [proper name *Jacky Macauco*, a celebrated fighting monkey set against against a variety of canine opponents at the Westminster Pit, *c.*1820; he beat all comers until vanquished by a pit bull. Note Port. *macaco*, a macaque monkey] [mid-19C] (*London*) a monkey.

murky *n.* [the darkness of skin] [20C+] (*Aus.*) an Aborigine.

murotugora *n. see* MOROTGARA *n.*

Murphia *n.* [*Murph(y)*, a common Irish surname + SE (*Maf*)*ia*] [1990s+] the expatriate Irish people living in the UK, esp. those who have prospered.

Murphy *n.* [*Murphy*, a common Irish surname] **1** [mid-19C–1930s] (*orig. UK*) an Irish person. **2** [1960s] (*US*) a police officer. **3** [1960s] (*orig. US Und.*) a victim of MURPHY (GAME), THE *n.*

IN COMPOUNDS

❑ **Murphy land** *n.* [mid-19C–1940s] (*US*) Ireland. ❑ **Murphy's countenance** *n.* (*also* **Murphy's face**) [stereotyped relationship between the Irish and the pig] [early–mid-19C] a pig's face.

Murphy *adj.* [late 19C] (*Aus.*) pertaining to Ireland or the Irish; ext. to the Catholic church.

murphy *n.*[1] [the common Irish surname and the assumption that potatoes are the supreme Irish staple] [early 19C+] a potato, usu. pl.; thus *(short-order) murphy with his coat on*, an unpeeled boiled potato.

murphy *n.*[2] [? stereotyping of an Irish person as foolish or risible] [1980s+] (*US campus*) a condition of having one's underwear caught between the buttocks; thus *have a murphy*.

murphy *v.* [MURPHY (GAME), THE *n.*] **1** [1960s+] (*US Und.*) to swindle by promising some variety of illegal pleasure, usu. sex, then taking the money and failing to deliver the promised 'goods'. **2** [2000s] in a non-criminal sense, to leave without fulfilling a promise.

murphydyke *n. see* MORPHODITE *n.*

Murphy (Game), the *n.* [? orig. practitioners promised the victim a meeting with 'a lovely woman called Mrs Murphy'. The *murphy* can be extended to drug 'deals' and other illicit commerce] **1** [1950s+] (*orig. US Und.*) of a prostitute, luring a client either to a room or a deserted alley, hallway etc. and then, instead of having sex, the client is beaten and robbed by a male accomplice, who may just strike, but may also pose as an aggrieved father, lover, brother etc. **2** [1960s+] (*US*) a swindle in general.

IN COMPOUNDS

❑ **Murphy dog** *n.* [DOG *n.*[2] (1)] [1990s+] a swindler. ❑ **Murphy man** *n.* [1960s+] a man who specializes in the *Murphy game*.

Murrumbidgee *n.* [proper name *Murrumbidgee*, a river in southern New South Wales]

IN COMPOUNDS

❑ **Murrumbidgee jam** *n.* [1900s–40s] (*Aus.*) brown sugar moistened with cold tea and spread on a damper. ❑ **Murrumbidgee oyster** *n.* [1940s] (*Aus.*) a raw egg plus vinegar and seasoning. ❑ **Murrumbidgee whaler** *n.* (*also* **Bidgee whaler, whaler**) [SE *whaling*, implying movement] [mid-19C–1940s] (*Aus.*) an itinerant tramp whose 'beat' focuses on the rivers of New South Wales; thus *Murrumbidgee whaling*, tramping; also as *Darling whaler*; *Murray whaler*.

muscadoodle *n.* [1950s+] (*US*) cheap muscatel wine.

muscateer *n.* [pun on SE *musketeer*] [1930s+] (*Aus.*) a drinker of cheap muscat wine.

muscle *n.* [MUSCLE *v.*] **1** [late 19C+] pressure, threats or coercion. **2** [20C+] (*orig. US*) strength, courage. **3** [1920s+] a thug, esp. as a group of thugs hired to intimidate by using violence. **4** [1930s+] political influence, power, usu. based on threats or intimidation.

IN COMPOUNDS

❑ **muscle boy** *n.* **1** [1930s+] (*US*) a thug. **2** [1950s+] (*also* **muscle bum**) a (homosexual) body builder; thus *Muscle Beach*, a beach that such bodybuilders frequent for display and exercise; thus *muscle magazine* [SE *muscle* + *boy*/BUM *n.*[3] (10)]. ❑ **muscle car** *n.* (*also* **muscle machine**) [1960s+] (*orig. US*) a motor vehicle that is specially modified to give high power and speed. ❑ **muscle fuck** *n.* [FUCK *n.* (1)] [1970s+] (*US*) **1** the rubbing of the penis between a woman's breasts. **2** sexual intercourse in which the woman uses her vaginal muscles to intensify the experience. **3** (*gay*) sexual intercourse where one man's penis is resting between the other man's buttocks while he flexes his buttock muscles. ❑ **muscle gay** *n.* [GAY *n.*[1] (1)] [1960s–70s] (*US*) a homosexual bodybuilder; thus *muscle bitch*, the lesbian equivalent; *muscle movie*, a film featuring bodybuilders. ❑ **musclehead** *n.* [-HEAD *sfx*] **1** [1920s+] (*US*) a stupid if brawny man. **2** [1960s+] (*US*) of an automobile, or motor cycle, speed, power. **3** [1960s+] (*US*) (*also* **muscle missile**) the penis [abbr. *LOVE MUSCLE under* LOVE *n.*; + SE *missile*]. ❑ **muscleman** *n. see* separate entry. ❑ **muscle Mary** *n.* [MARY *n.*] [1980s+] (*gay*) a gay man devoted to bodybuilding and the resultant musculature. ❑ **muscle shirt** *n.* (*also* **muscle T, muscle tee**) [1970s+] (*US*) a T-shirt with very short sleeves or no sleeves, thus displaying the wearer's physique. ❑ **muscle-uncle** *n.* [2000s] an ostentatiously 'masculine' homosexual.

IN PHRASES

❑ **bet on the muscle** *v.* [1950s] (*US Und.*) to make wagers without any financial resources; if one loses one must face a fight or even a knifing. ❑ **on the muscle** (*US*) **1** [mid-19C+] quarrelsome, ready or poised to fight. **2** [1940s] (*US*) for free, provided by someone else. **3** [1940s+] (*US*) using a threat of violence. **4** [1950s+] working as protection for a top gangster. **5** [1960s+] nervous, edgy. ❑ **put the muscle on** *v.* [1940s+] (*US Und.*) to coerce, to threaten with violence.

muscle *adj.* [MUSCLE *v.*] [1930s+] (*US*) physically violent.

muscle *v.* **1** [mid-19C+] (*orig. US*) to put pressure on, to coerce with threats of violence, poss. to beat up. **2** [1910s+] (*US*) to move something by force, to use one's strength to achieve something. **3** [1920s–30s] (*US*) to bluff.

IN PHRASES

❑ **muscle around** *v.* [1930s] to search energetically. ❑ **muscle in** *v.* [1920s+] (*orig. US*) **1** to force an entrance, to use violence to gain something one desires. **2** to gain admission to, to get oneself involved.

muscleman *n.* [note Hughes, *Tom Brown at Oxford* (1861): 'I must call the persons in question "musclemen," as distinguished from muscular Christians'; his ref. is to those who celebrate physical strength but have no religious faith; note 1945 Minnesota Univ. use *muscle moll*, a strong man] [1920s+] (*orig. US*) **1** a thug, usu. as employed by a gangster for purposes of intimidation; any strong, aggressive man. **2** (*also* **muscle freak**) a man with an outstanding physique.

muscler *n.* [MUSCLE *v.* (2)] [1940s+] (*US*) a thug.

mush *n.*[1] [SE *mush*, anything soft and pulpy] **1** [late 18C] (*US Und.*) a thief's girlfriend. **2** [mid-19C+] (*US*) (*also* **mush-talk**) sentimental nonsense. **3** [late 19C+] (*Aus./US*) (*also* **moosh**) prison food, often porridge. **4** [1910s] rubbish, nonsense.

IN COMPOUNDS

❑ **mushbelly** *n.* [1950s+] (*US*) a weak spineless person. ❑ **mushbrain** *n.* (*also* **mushball**) [1980s+] (*US*) a dolt, a mawkishly sentimental person. ❑ **mush-brained** *adj.* [1980s+] stupid, sentimental, nonsensical. ❑ **mush-eater** *n.* [1910s] (*US*) one who speaks in an affected manner. ❑ **mush-face** *n.* [1920s–30s] a fool, a sentimental idiot. ❑ **mush-faced** *adj.* [1910s–30s] stupid, foolish. ❑ **mushhead** *adj. see* separate entry. ❑ **mushmouth** *n.* [SE *mush*] [1930s+] (*US*) **1** indistinct speech. **2** (*also* **mush jib**) a person who mumbles. ❑ **mush-worker** *n.* [SE *worker*/WORKER *n.*[1] (1)] [1920s–70s] (*US Und./police*) a woman or a prostitute who obtains money from men by playing on their sympathy, giving them a 'sob story'.

IN PHRASES

❑ **mush, lush and gush** *n.* [MUSH *n.*[1] (2) + SE *gush* + LUSH *n.*[1] (1)] [late 19C–1900s] favourable criticisms that are written in return for cash or food and drink.

mush *n.*[2] (*also* **moosh, moush-houser**) [orig. boxing; it rhymes with 'push' and was something that was 'pushed' by a blow] [late 18C+] (*orig. Aus./US*) the face or mouth.

mush *n.*[3] **1** as abbr. MUSHROOM *n.* (**a**) [early 19C–1940s] (*Und.*) (*also* **mush-toper**) an umbrella. (**b**) [1940s] (*US Und.*) a confidence game played at a ball park where the confidence trickster poses as a bookmaker, taking bets, then raises an umbrella and disappears into the area where everybody is holding umbrellas. **2** [1990s+] in pl., mushrooms.

IN COMPOUNDS

❑ **mush-faker** *n.* (*also* **mush-fakir, mush-rigger, mushroom-faker, mush toper feeker**) [/FAKER *n.*/RIGGER *n.*/SE *fakir*/TOPER *n.*] [early 19C–1940s] one who advertises themselves as a mender of umbrellas, or pedlar, but may well use this respectable job as a cover for more fraudulent pursuits; also as v., to work as above.

mush *n.*[4] [? Rom. *moosh*, a man] **1** [20C+] (*US*) a fool. **2** [1930s+] (*also* **moosh**) a man, a 'chap'; thus as a term of address or greeting, e.g., *Oi! Mush!* **3** [1980s] (*Liverpool*) a prostitute's client. **4** [2000s] an outsider.

mush *n.*[5] (*also* **moosh**) [abbr.] [1960s+] a *moustache*.

mush *n.*[6] [MUSH *v.*[3]] [2000s] a fight.

mush *v.*[1] [dog sledders' *mush*, to cross snow on a dog sled; ult. Fr. *marchez*/*marchons*, march, let's march!] (*US*) **1** [1900s–30s] to go, to leave. **2** [1990s+] to urge forward.

mush *v.*[2] [MUSH *n.*[1] (2)] **1** [1920s–70s] (*US*) to kiss and cuddle, also as *mush it up*. **2** [1920s–70s] (*US*) to court a woman in a sentimental manner, to 'chat up'. **3** [1940s] (*US black*) to kiss.

mush *v.*[3] **1** [1940s] (*US*) to crash. **2** [1980s+] (*US black/P.R.*) to beat up, to hit.

mushe *n.* [Fr. *monsieur*, a term of address; Syria had been under Fr. control, and thus its expatriates might speak the language, but the link to Chinese people is unclear, perhaps on basis of all foreigners being generically 'French'] [1940s+] (*W.I.*) a Syrian or a Chinese.

mushe-man *n. see* MOOSHE-MAN *n.*

musher *n.*[1] [1900s] (*US*) **1** one who moves from place to place [MUSH *v.*[1] (1)]. **2** an itinerant fakir [abbr. *MUSH-FAKER under* MUSH *n.*[3]].

musher *n.*[2] [MUSH *v.*[2] (1)] [1940s] (*US*) one who kisses and cuddles.

musher *n.*[3] [? ext. of MUSH *n.*[4] (2) or MUSH *v.*[3]] [2000s] a thug, a villain.

mush-head *n.* [SE *mush*, anything soft and pulpy + -HEAD *sfx* (1)] [late 19C+] (*orig. US*) a fool.

DERIVATIVES

❑ **mush-headed** *adj.* (*also* **mush-head**) [late 19C+] stupid, foolish.

mushie *n.* **1** [1930s+] (*orig. Aus.*) a mushroom. **2** [1960s+] (*drugs*) usu. in pl., psilocybin, 'magic mushrooms'.

mushroom *n.* **1** [late 16C–early 19C] a contemptible person [the propensity of the fungus to grow 'in the dark']. **2** [late 16C–mid-19C] a *nouveau riche* individual or an *arriviste* family [the propensity of the fungus to 'spring up overnight']. **3** [19C] the vagina. **4** with ref. to its shape. (**a**) [mid-19C–1910s] a low-crowned circular hat, esp. a lady's straw hat with a down-curving brim. (**b**) [mid-19C–1940s] an umbrella. (**c**) [late 19C–1900s] a tavern clock. (**d**) [1930s+] the head of the penis. **5** [1960s+] (*drugs*) in pl., psilocybin/psilocin. **6** [1980s+] (*US*) a person who is unwittingly caught in crossfire between criminals.

mush-toper *n. see* MUSH *n.*[3] (1a).

mushy *adj.*[1] [MUSH *n.*[1] (2)] [late 19C+] romantic, sentimental.

mushy *adj.*[2] [Zulu *mu* + *hle*, good for one; orig. Zimbabwean use] [1970s+] (*S.Afr.*) nice, pleasant.

mushy *adv.* [MUSHY *adj.*[1]] [1910s] sentimentally.

music *n.* **1** [17C–early 19C] (*UK Und.*) a term used among highwaymen to signify that an individual is a friend and must not be hindered on their journey; usu. in phr. *the music's paid*. **2** [late 18C–early 19C] (*Irish*) the 'tail' of a coin [the 'tail' or reverse side of an Irish halfpenny or farthing bore the image of a harp]. **3** [mid-19C] (*UK Und.*) a verdict of 'not guilty'. **4** [mid-19C+] (*US*) amusement, fun, lively speech. **5** [mid-19C+] (*US*) gunfire. **6** [late 19C–1970s] talking, esp. complaints or nagging.

IN PHRASES

❑ **face the music** *v.* [mid-19C+] **1** to deal stoically with a problem or difficult situation. **2** to take one's punishment. ❑ **read the music** *v.* [1940s] (*US gay/prison*) to know what is going on.

SE in slang uses

IN COMPOUNDS

❑ **music box** *n.* **1** [mid-19C–1940s] a piano. **2** [1940s] a guitar. ❑ **music-duffing** *n.* [DUFF *v.*[1] (3)] [1910s–20s] the reconditioning of musical instruments.

musical *adj.* [late 19C–1900s] used of a horse that suffers from respiratory problems.

IN COMPOUNDS

❑ **musical fruit** *n.* (*also* **musicos**) [1910s+] any fruit or vegetables, esp. beans or Jerusalem artichokes, that produce flatulence.

Music City *n.* (*also* **Musical City, Music Town**) [the city's association with country music] [1970s+] (*US*) Nashville, Tennessee.

musicos *n. see* MUSICAL FRUIT *under* MUSICAL *adj.*

musket *n.* [note mid-17C MUSKET AND BANDELIERS *n.*] [mid-19C;1930s–1970s] (*US*) the penis.

musket and bandeliers *n.* [appearance] [mid-17C] the male genitals.

muski *n.* (*also* **musky**) [abbr. *muscatel*] [1960s+] (*US*) muscatel, thus any cheap wine.

muskin *n.* [mid-18C; 1920s] an eccentric.

musk-rat *n.* [mid-19C+] (*US*) a resident of the state of Delaware, or anywhere flat.

musky *n. see* MUSKI *n.*

muslin *n. see* BIT OF MUSLIN *under* BIT *n.*[1].

muso *n.* [abbr.] [1960s+] a *mus*ician, usu. in a rock band.

muso *adj.* [MUSO *n.*] [1960s+] musical.

muss *n.* [dial.] [early 19C–1960s] (*US*) a fight, a dispute, a commotion.

IN PHRASES

❑ **no muss, no fuss** *n.* (*also* **no fuss, no muss**) [1920s+] (*US*) no problems, either practically or emotionally. ❑ **on the muss** [mid-19C] (*US*) looking for a fight, acting provocatively. ❑ **raise a muss** *v.* (*also* **kick up a muss**) [mid-19C] to start a fight, to cause a commotion.

muss *v.* [SE *muss*, to rumple, to untidy] [mid-19C–1940s] (*US*) **1** to pick a fight. **2** to argue. **3** to have sexual intercourse.

musser *n.* [MUSS *v.* (1)] [mid-19C–1920s] (*US*) someone who picks fights.

muss up *v.* [SE *muss*, to rumple, to untidy (or ext. of MUSS *v.* (1))] **1** [1900s] to spend or waste money [opposite of CLEAN UP *v.* (1)]. **2** [1920s+] (*US*) to treat roughly, to beat up.

mussy *adj. see* MUZZY *adj.* (3).

mustache *n.* and combs, *see* MOUSTACHE *n.*

mustang *n.* [SE *mustang*, note US milit. jargon *mustang*, an officer who has been commissioned from the ranks] [1970s+] (*US black*) an independent woman who is 'hard to ride'.

mustard *n.* **1** in senses of 'hotness' of SE *mustard*. (**a**) [early 17C; 20C+] (*US*) spirit, zest, courage, esp. in adversity. (**b**) [20C+] one who is keen or the best, outstanding, excellent at a task or occupation; the best; often in phr. *proper mustard*, the genuine article. (**c**) [1920s+] a woman who is sexually enthusiastic; something, e.g. a play, that is sexually overt [note the comment, in T.R.G. Lyell, *Slang, Phrase & Idiom* (1931) 'It must never be used of the female sex']. **2** [1930s–40s] (*US*) an Asian person, usu. Chinese [their skin is 'yellow'].

IN COMPOUNDS

❑ **mustard seed** *n.* [colour] [1920s–30s] (*US black*) a light-skinned black person.

SE in slang uses

IN COMPOUNDS

❑ **mustard plaster** *n.* [coined in a music-hall comic song, written by E.L. Blanchard (1820–89) and premiered at Drury Lane] [late 19C–1920s] an unpopular but persistent young man. ❑ **mustard pot** *see* separate entries. ❑ **mustard road** *n.* [1970s+] (*US*) the anus; thus *go up the mustard road*, to sodomize.

IN PHRASES

❑ **cut the mustard** *v. see* separate entry. ❑ **pack the mustard** *v. see under* PACK *v.*[1].

mustard *adj.* [MUSTARD *n.*] [1900s–50s] excellent, very good, often with *at/on/to* (i.e. very good at something).

mustard *phr.* [MUSTARD *adj.*] [1980s] an expression of approval.

mustard (and cress) *n.* [rhy. sl.] [1990s+] a dress.

mustard-and-cress *n.* [19C] the pubic hair.

mustard (pickle) *n.* [rhy. sl.] [1990s+] a cripple.

mustard pot *n.* **1** as a part of the body. (**a**) [late 16C–17C; late 19C+] (*also* **mustard bowl, mustard box, mustard-jar**) the vagina. (**b**) [1940s–50s] (*US*) the anus. **2** [19C–1900s] a carriage with a light yellow body. **3** [1930s] (*US prison*) a passive homosexual.

mustard (pot) *adj.* [rhy. sl. + the quality of mustard] [1930s+] **1** of weather, hot. **2** angry, HOT *adj.* (4a).

mustee *n.* (*also* **mestee**) [Sp. *mestizo*, a half-caste] [late 18C+] (*W.I., Bdos/ Guyn.*) the offspring of a white and a mulatto parent.

must job *n.* [colloq. *must*] [late 19C+] a job that one must take when funds are otherwise unavailable.

mustn't-mention-'ems *n.* [mid-19C–1900s] trousers.

mut *n. see* MUTT *n.* (3).

muta *n.* (*also* **mutah**) *see* MOOTA *n.*

mutant *n.* [1980s+] (*US campus*) a social outcast.

mutcher *n.* [var. on MOOCHER *n.* (3)] [mid–late 19C] a thief who steals from drunks.

mute *n.* [synon. with DUMB GLUTTON *n.*] [1960s+] (*gay*) the vagina.

mutha *n.* **1** *see* MOTHER *n.* (5). **2** *see* MOTHER *n.* (6).

muthafucka *n. see* MOTHERFUCKER *n.*

muthafucken *adj. see* MOTHERFUCKING *adj.*

mutile *n.* [SE *mutilated* or Fr. *mutilé*] [1980s+] (*US campus*) an incapacitated, immobile person, usu. from drink or drugs.

mutt *n.* [abbr. MUTTON-HEAD *n.*] (*orig. US*) **1** [late 19C+] a dog, usu. a mongrel. **2** [late 19C+] a second-rate racehorse, i.e. a DOG *n.*[2] (1). **3** [late 19C+] (*US*) (*also* **mut**) a fool, a bungler, an ignoramus; thus used as a general term of abuse. **4** [1910s] any animal. **5** [1970s+] an unattractive person of the opposite sex.

IN COMPOUNDS

□ **mutthead** *n.* [-HEAD *sfx*] [1910s+] (*US*) a stupid or contemptible person.

IN PHRASES

□ **mutt's game** *n.* [1910s] a foolish endeavour, a pointless exercise. □ **mutt's nuts** *n.* [NUTS *n.*[2] (1); var. on DOG'S BALLOCKS *n.*] [1990s+] anything excellent, admirable, first-rate. □ **mutt up** *v.* [1930s–40s] (*US Und.*) to keep a guard dog, to be guarded by a dog.

mutt and jeff *n.* [the US cartoon characters, *Mutt and Jeff*, introduced by H.C. 'Bud' Fischer in 1907] **1** [1910s–40s] the King George V Silver medal Jubilee and the Edward VIII Coronation medals or ribbons or the 1918 Victory and Overseas medals or ribbons, which are invariably worn together. **2** [1910s+] (*orig. US*) a pair of stupid, bungling men. **3** [1930s] (*US*) foolish conversation. **4** [1960s+] (*US Und.*) a pair of (usu. police) interrogators who work as 'nice' and 'nasty', in order to elicit information.

mutt and jeff *adj.* (*also* **mutton**) [rhy. sl.; see prev.] [1930s+] deaf.

mutt and jeff *v.* [MUTT AND JEFF *n.* (4)] [1980s+] (*US police/Und.*) of police interrogators, to take the parts of the 'good/sympathetic' and 'bad/potentially violent' officers when attempting to gain information from a suspect. Such 'roles' are assumed only for the situation in hand.

mutter and stutter *n.* [rhy. sl.] [20C+] butter.

mutt-eye *n.* (*also* **mutt-eyes**) [ety. unknown; ? Aboriginal language] [1940s+] (*Aus.*) corn (as a food).

mutton *n.* [*OED* suggests 'food for lust', but prob. simply an old sheep as opposed to a young lamb] **1** with ref. to women. (**a**) [early 16C–mid-19C] a promiscuous woman; a prostitute. (**b**) [17C–early 19C] a woman. (**c**) [17C–19C] the vagina; thus sexual intercourse, sexual pleasure; [19C] *in her mutton*, having sexual intercourse with a woman. (**d**) [1910s] (*Aus.*) a girlfriend. **2** in self-referential senses. (**a**) [late 18C–1910s] (*US*) one's person, self, body or flesh. (**b**) [late 19C–1980s] (*orig. US*) one's preference, one's liking; usu. in pl. **3** [mid-19C; 1960s+] (*later use is Aus./N.Z.*) (*also* **mutton tail**) the penis. **4** [1960s+] (*US*) cowardice [the timorousness of sheep].

IN COMPOUNDS

□ **mutton-cove** *n.* **1** [mid-19C] the Coventry Street end of Windmill Street, London, once well-known for its prostitutes [*cove*, abbr. *Coventry*]. **2** [mid–late 19C] a womanizer [COVE *n.* (1)]. □ **mutton dagger** *n.* [1960s+] the penis. □ **mutton-faced** *adj.* [early 19C] fat-faced. □ **mutton-fed** *adj.* [1910s–20s] large, fat and well fed. □ **muttonflaps** *n.* **1** [1960s+] (*N.Z.*) (*also* **muttonflap**) the stomach. **2** [1980s+] (*N.Z.*) the labia majora. □ **mutton gun** *n.* [it 'shoots' MUTTON *n.* (1)] [1940s–50s] (*Aus.*) the penis. □ **mutton merchant** *n.* [MERCHANT *n.*] [1960s–70s] a sexual pervert, an exhibitionist. □ **mutton musket** *n.* (*also* **mutton bayonet**) [1990s+] the penis. □ **mutton-shunter** *n.* [late 19C] a policeman, esp. in his role of harrying street prostitutes. □ **mutton-tugger** *n.* [late 16C–early 17C] a degenerate; a pimp. □ **mutton walk** *n.* [early–mid-19C] **1** the saloon at the Drury Lane Theatre, Covent Garden; often as *the Mutton Walk*. **2** any street where one finds prostitutes, esp. the junction of Coventry Street and Windmill Street in the West End of London.

IN PHRASES

□ **bit of mutton** *n.* [SE *bit* + MUTTON *n.*] [19C] **1** a woman, esp. a prostitute. **2** sexual intercourse; thus *have a bit of mutton*. **3** the vagina. □ **come one's mutton** *v.* [1960s+] to masturbate. □ **flog one's mutton** *v.* (*also* **thump one's mutton**) [late 19C+] to masturbate. □ **fond of his mutton** *adj.* [mid-19C] given to womanizing. □ **give mutton for beef** *v.* [MUTTON *n.* + BEEF *n.*[1] (3)] [19C] of a woman, to have sexual intercourse. □ **hawk one's mutton** *v.* [mid-19C+] of either sex, to work as a prostitute. □ **hook your mutton** [1900s–10s] (*Aus.*) in a dancehall, the invitation to 'take your partners'. □ **in her mutton** [late 18C–early 19C] of a man, having sexual intercourse. □ **in someone's mutton** [early 19C] irritating, 'getting under someone's skin'. □ **make mutton out of** *v.* [mid-19C–1900s] to kill, to murder. □ **mutton in long coats** *n.* [late 17C–19C] women. □ **piece of mutton** *n.* [MUTTON *n.*] [late 17C–early 19C] a woman, seen as a sex object. □ **unbutton the mutton** *v.* [1960s+] (*N.Z.*) to urinate.

SE in slang uses

IN COMPOUNDS

□ **mutton-bird** *n.* *see* separate entry. □ **mutton-brained** *adj.* *see* MUTTON-HEADED *adj.* □ **mutton-chopper** *n.* [late 19C] 'mutton-chop' whiskers. □ **mutton-chops** *n.* [the similarity of fleece to mutton-chop whiskers, and pun on SE *mutton chops*. Note milit. jargon *the Mutton Chops* or *Mutton Lancers*, the Royal West Surreys, whose emblem is a lamb and flag] [mid-19C] a sheep's head. □ **mutton dummies** *n.* [ety. unknown; ? *mutton cloth*, a type of cloth used to wrap meat + DUMMY *n.*[1] (1); i.e. their relative silence, compared to the noise of leather soled shoes] [20C+] (*Ulster*) plimsolls, trainers. □ **mutton-fist** *n.* [late 17C–19C] a large, coarse red hand, usu. in pl. □ **mutton-head/-headed** *see* separate entries. □ **mutton-minded** *adj.* *see* MUTTON-HEADED *adj.* □ **mutton-monger** *n.* *see* separate entries. □ **muttonpuncher** *n.* [play on SAmE *cowpuncher*] [1930s+] (*US, mainly West/N.Z.*) a sheep-herder.

IN PHRASES

□ **dead as mutton** *adj.* (*also* **cold as mutton**) [late 18C–1950s] completely dead, certainly dead; of a place, quiet, deserted. □ **mutton dressed as lamb** *n.* (*also* **mutton dressed lamb-fashion, mutton done up as lamb, old ewe dressed as lamb**) [late 18C+] a woman who dresses younger than her years. □ **sure as mutton's mutton** *see under* SURE AS… *phr.*

mutton *adj.* *see* MUTT AND JEFF *adj.*

mutton-bird *n.* (*also* **mutton(bird)-eater**) [SE *mutton-bird*, an edible species of puffin, found on the Bass Strait (between Tasmania and the mainland)] [20C+] (*Aus.*) a native of northern Tasmania.

DERIVATIVES

□ **muttonbirdy** *adj.* [1970s] old-fashioned, unworldly.

Muttonburg *n.* *see* MUTTONTOWN *n.*

muttoner *n.*[1] [late 17C–early 19C] a womanizer, a promiscuous man.

muttoner *n.*[2] [2000s] (*N.Z.*) a knockout punch that leaves the recipient as 'dead as mutton'.

mutton-head *n.* [MUTTON-HEADED *adj.*] [19C+] a fool, thus *mutton-headed*, stupid, foolish.

mutton-headed *adj.* (*also* **mutton-brained, muttonhead, mutton-minded**) [SE *mutton*] [mid-18C+] stupid, foolish.

mutton-monger *n.*[1] [MUTTON *n.* (1) + SE *monger*, ult. Lat. *mango*, a dealer or trafficker] [mid-16C–19C] a promiscuous man.

IN PHRASES

□ **go mutton-mongering** *v.* [late 19C+] to have sexual intercourse.

mutton-monger *n.*[2] [SE *mutton* + *monger*, ult. Lat. *mango*, a dealer or trafficker] **1** [late 16C–17C] a notable eater of mutton. **2** [mid–late 17C] a sheep-stealer.

mutton-pies *n.* [rhy. sl.] [late 19C–1960s] the eyes.

Muttontown *n.* (*also* **Muttonburg, Muttonjerk, Muttonville**) [1950s+] (*US*) a small, out-of-the-way town or settlement.

muuna *n.* [? link to MOON *n.* (1a)] [1950s] (*W.I.*) the female genitals.

muv *n.* [? SE *my*] [2000s] (*US black*) one's personal space, spec. a twenty-foot radius surrounding one.

muz *n.* (*also* **muzz**) [f. Westminster School jargon *muz*, to study hard] [late 18C–19C] one who works hard at their books.

muz *v.*[1] (*also* **muzz**) [? SE *muss*, to rumple, to untidy] [mid–late 18C] to loiter aimlessly, to 'hang about'.

muz *v.*[2] (*also* **muzz**) [dial. *muzzle*, to drink to excess, to make drunk] [late 18C–1900s; 1970s] to render 'muzzy', to bemuse; usu. through drink.

DERIVATIVES

□ **muzzed** *adj.* [late 18C–19C] tipsy, befuddled by drink.

muzzie man *n.* [MUSCLEMAN *n.* (1)] [2000s] a thug, a stolid, stupid person.

muzzle *n.*[1] [SE *muzzle*, the nose and mouth of an animal] **1** [15C+] the face, the nose or the mouth [orig. SE]. **2** [late 17C–early 19C] a beard, '(usually) long and nasty' (B.E.).

IN COMPOUNDS

❑ **muzzle-chops** *n.* [CHOPS *n.*[1] (1)] [early 17C] nickname for a man with a prominent nose and mouth. ❑ **muzzlejinks** *n.* [mid-19C] (*UK Und.*) toothache.

IN PHRASES

❑ **put the muzzle on** *v.* **1** [20C+] (*US*) to silence, e.g. an informer. **2** [1900s–10s] to stop talking, also as excl.

muzzle *n.*[2] [MUZZLE *v.* (5)] [1900s–30s] (*US Und.*) a trick whereby the tricksters pose as outraged citizens or police officers in order to obtain bribes from homosexuals in toilets.

muzzle *n.*[3] [ety. unknown, ? SE *muzzle*, to silence, a ref. to the immediate effects of an injection, rendering the user comatose] [1950s+] (*drugs*) heroin.

muzzle *v.* [SE *muzzle*, to put a muzzle on; to restrain (usu. speech)] **1** [late 17C–early 18C; 1930s+] (*later use US*) to kiss and fondle, esp. in a rough manner. **2** [mid–late 19C] to fight, to thrash. **3** [mid–late 19C] to hit in the face. **4** [mid–late 19C] to throttle, to garrotte. **5** [mid–late 19C] (*orig. US*) to obtain, to take, to steal. **6** [mid–late 19C] to drink heavily [dial. *muzzle*, to drink to excess].

muzzler *n.* [MUZZLE *n.*[1] (1)] **1** [early–late 19C] a drink. **2** [early–late 19C] a blow to the mouth or face. **3** [mid-19C; 1930s] (*US*) a crook, a strong-arm robber. **4** [1920s–60s] (*US, esp. prison*) a homosexual, spec. a fellator. **5** [1920s+] (*US*) a contemptible person.

muzzle rails *n. see* HEAD RAILS *under* HEAD *n.*

muzzling *n.* [MUZZLE *v.* (2)] [mid-19C] a beating, a thrashing.

muzzling cheat *n.* [MUZZLE *n.*[1] (1) + CHEAT *n.* (1)] [late 17C] a napkin.

muzzy *n.*[1] [abbr.] **1** [1990s+] a moustache. **2** [2000s] a Muslim.

muzzy *n.*[2] [ety. unknown] [2000s] (*Irish*) a rascal, a naughty child.

muzzy *adj.* [SE *bemused* or dial. *mosey*, befuddled with drink] **1** [early 18C–early 19C] of places or weather, dull, gloomy. **2** [early 18C–1950s] (*also* **mussy**) of people, vague, befuddled, confused. **3** [late 18C+] (*also* **mussy**) drunk. **4** [mid–late 19C] blurred, indistinct.

myall *n.* [Abor. *miall*; *myall*, an Aborigine who has had little or no contact with whites; a stranger] [1980s+] one who is out of their usual environment; a fool?

my bloody oath! *excl. see* BLOOD OATH! *excl.*

my bollix! *excl. see* MY BOLLOCKS! *under* BALLOCKS *n.*

my cabbage-tree! *excl.* [*cabbage-tree hat*, a hat made of woven cabbage-tree or cabbage-palm leaves] [mid-19C–1950s] (*Aus.*) a mild excl., synon. with MY HAT! *excl.*

my colonial oath! *excl. see under* MY OATH! *excl.*

my dirty cousin *phr.* [late 17C–mid-18C] a pej. form of address, usu. aimed at one who is judged to be affecting modesty.

my eye! *excl.* [ALL MY EYE *phr.*] [early 19C+] **1** (*also* **in my eye! my eyes!**) a dismissive excl., nonsense! rubbish! **2** (*also* **my eyes! my eyes and limbs!**) a general excl.; often of astonishment.

IN EXCLAMATIONS

❑ **my eye and a bandbox!** [late 19C+] nonsense!

my foot! *excl.* [euph. var. on *my arse!*] [20C+] an excl. used to imply one's contemptuous rejection of the previous speaker's assertion, sometimes as *your foot!*

my fuck! *excl.* [2000s] an excl. of amazement.

my gawd *n.* [rhy. sl.] [late 19C+] a sword.

my gogga! *excl.* [1980s+] (*S.Afr.*) an excl. of surprise.

my gun *n.* [1980s+] (*US black*) one's best friend.

my hat! *excl.* (*also* **in my hat!**) [late 19C+] a general excl.

IN EXCLAMATIONS

❑ **my hat to a halfpenny!** [late 16C] a general excl.

my Jimmy! *excl.* [1900s] (*Aus.*) a mild oath.

my 'king oath! *excl.* [euph. for 'my FUCKING *adj.* oath!'; MY OATH! *excl.*] [1910s+] (*Aus.*) a mild excl.

myla *n. see* MILER *n.*

my left foot! *excl.* (*also* **my left knacker! my left tit!**) [ext. of MY FOOT! *excl.*] [1920s+] an excl. used to imply one's contemptuous rejection of the previous speaker's assertion.

myliers *n. see* MAULEY *n.* (1).

my man *n.* [1950s+] an intimate; a very important person.

IN PHRASES

❑ **my man!** [1950s+] (*orig. US black*) a term of endearment and address between two men.

my mother's away *phr.* [rhy. sl.] [20C+] (*Aus.*) the other day.

my myrtle *n.* [SE *myrtle*, a sweet-scented plant, used in perfumery and sacred to Venus] [early 19C] (*Cockney*) my friend.

my name is Haines *phr.* (*also* **my name is Hanes**) [an encounter between President Thomas Jefferson (1743–1826) and one *Haines* or *Hanes*, a fanatical opponent. Haines, not knowing the identity of his companion, vilified Jefferson in extreme tones as the two men rode side-by-side near Jefferson's home in Virginia. When they arrived at Jefferson's home, the president, affronted but still courteous, invited Haines in. Only then did Haines ask his putative host for his name: 'Thomas Jefferson'. 'Well, my name is Haines,' replied his opponent, before riding promptly away] [mid–late 19C] (*US*) a phr. used on leaving a place or party suddenly.

my name is Twyford *phr.* [proper name of Josiah *Twyford* (1640–1729), whose secret process for glazing provided the basis for his creation of a successful firm of sanitary potters; presumably his response to those who wished to elicit his secret] [late 17C–19C] I know absolutely nothing about it.

my name is Walker *phr.* [pun on *Walker*/SE *walker*] [mid-19C–1950s] I'm leaving, I'm off.

mynheer *n.* [late 18C] generic for the Dutch.

mynt *n. see* MINT *n.*[1] (2).

my oath! *excl.* (*also* **bloody oath! flaming oath! fucking oath!**) [late 19C+] (*Aus./N.Z.*) a mild excl.; often as an affirmation.

IN EXCLAMATIONS

❑ **my colonial oath!** (*also* **my colonial!**) [mid-19C+] (*Aus./N.Z.*) a mild excl. ❑ **my 'kin(g) oath!** *see* separate entry.

m.y.o.b. *phr.* [abbr.] [20C+] (*US*) mind your own business; also extended to *p.m.y.o.b., please...*

my old boots! *excl.* [late 19C] an excl. of disbelief or amazement.

my Prussian blue *phr.* [SE *Prussian blue*, a colour; Dickensian use as synon. for SE *true blue*] [mid-19C] a term of endearment.

Myrmidons *n.* ['Myrmidon [...] a member of a warlike people inhabiting ancient Thessaly, whom Achilles led to the siege of Troy' *OED*] [late 17C–early 19C] a constable's assistants.

Myrna Loy *n.* [rhy. sl.; ult. US film star *Myrna Loy* (1905–93)] [1930s+] a saveloy.

myrrh *n. see* MUR *n.*

myrtle *n.* [ety. unknown; ? link to MUDDLE *v.*] [20C+] (*Aus.*) sexual intercourse.

mystall crikey! (*also* **myst all critey!**) [20C+] (*Aus.*) joc. reverse of CHRIST ALMIGHTY! *under* CHRIST! *excl.*

my stars! *excl.* (*also* **my stars alive! ye stars!**) [late 17C+] a mild oath.

my stars and garters! *excl.* (*also* **my stars and bars! my stars and turnips!**) [joc. ref. to orders of merit that are worn by those entitled] [early–mid-19C] a general excl. of astonishment or shock.

mysteries *n. see* BAG OF MYSTERY *under* BAG *n.*[1].

mystery *n.* **1** as food. (**a**) [late 19C+] (*US short-order*) a plate of corned beef hash. (**b**) [1930s] (*US*) a chocolate and vanilla sundae. (**c**) *see* BAG OF MYSTERY *under* BAG *n.*[1]. **2** [1910s] (*UK Und.*) ? counterfeit money. **3** [1930s+] of a young woman.

(**a**) an unknown young woman, often one recently arrived in London from the provinces. (**b**) a young prostitute. (**c**) any young girl.

IN COMPOUNDS

❑ **mystery punter** *n.* [PUNTER *n.* (5)] [1950s+] any man who prefers his sex and/or relationships with young, naïve women or young prostitutes; thus *mystery mad*, very keen on sex with young women.

SE in slang uses

IN COMPOUNDS

❑ **mystery bags** *n. see* BAG OF MYSTERY *under* BAG *n.*[1]. ❑ **mystery meat** *n.* (*also* **canned mystery, mystery balls**) [note Lancaster (Ohio) Boys' Industrial School (1947) *mystery soup*, a combination of all kinds of vegetables and meats mixed together to form a soup] [late 19C+] (*US*) low-grade meat as used in sausages, hash, hamburgers etc, usu. as served in institutions. ❑ **mystery parcel** *n.* [2000s] (*N.Z.*) a meat pie.

Mystic Meg *n.* [rhy. sl.; ult. *Mystic Meg*, a UK astrologist, made famous in the 1990s by her appearances on the National Lottery TV show] **1** [1990s+] usu. in pl., the human legs. **2** [2000s] the penis, as in 'third leg'.

my winky! *excl.* [late 19C] a mild excl.

my word *n.* [rhy. sl. = TURD *n.*[1] (1)] [20C+] a piece of excrement.

my worries! *excl.* [1940s+] (*Aus.*) a dismissive excl. 'don't worry about me!', 'I don't care!'.

myzzledumper *n.* [mid-19C] (*UK Und.*) a pocket pistol.

N

N *n.* [abbr.] **1** [1970s+] (*US*) a black person [NIGGER *n.*[1] (1)]. **2** [1980s] pertaining to drugs. (**a**) narcotics. (**b**) a painkiller, Darvocet-*N*.

N! *excl.* [abbr.] [1980s+] (*US campus*) *no!*

naai *n.* [NAAI V.] [1990s+] (*S.Afr.*) **1** a prostitute. **2** a despicable person.

DERIVATIVES

❑ **naaier** *n.* [1990s+] (*S.Afr.*) a despicable person.

naai *v.* [Du. *naaien*, to have carnal knowledge of] [1990s+] (*S.Afr.*) **1** to have sexual intercourse. **2** thus in fig. use, synon. with FUCK ABOUT V., FUCK WITH V., etc; also naaier, a FUCKER *n.* (3).

naar *adj.* [synon. Afk.] (*S.Afr.*) **1** [late 19C+] unpleasant, nauseating. **2** [1960s+] sick, queasy.

naar *v.* [Afk. *naar*, nauseated, nauseating] [1980s+] (*S.Afr.*) to stink, to smell foul.

naartjie *n.* [S.Afr.Du. *naartjie*, a variety of tangerine or mandarin orange; ? f. Tamil *narattai*, citrus] [1970s+] (*S.Afr.*) a fool, an idiot.

IN COMPOUNDS

❑ **Naartjie Republic** *n.* [1970s+] (*S.Afr.*) a banana republic.

nab *n.*[1] (*also* **nabe**) [ety. unknown; ? link to dial. *nab*, a projecting lump of rock, a promontory] **1** [mid-16C–17C] (*UK Und.*) the head. **2** [early 17C] (*UK Und.*) the head of a stick or penis. **3** [early 17C–mid-19C] (*UK Und.*) a hat. **4** [late 17C–mid-18C] (*UK Und.*) a coxcomb, a fop. **5** [early 19C] (*UK Und.*) an important person. **6** [1990s+] (*Irish*) the devil. **7** [1990s+] (*Irish*) the joker (cards).

IN COMPOUNDS

❑ **nab cheat** *n.* (*also* **nabchet, nob chete**) [CHEAT *n.* (1)] [16C–early 19C] (*UK Und.*) a hat, a cap. ❑ **nab girder** *n.* (*also* **nab garder, nob girder**) [SE *gird*] [late 17C–mid-19C] (*UK Und.*) a bridle.

IN PHRASES

❑ **nabs on** *adj.* [late 19C] (*UK Und.*) signifying the hallmark, i.e. proof of quality, on a silver or gold object.

nab *n.*[2] [NAB *v.*[1] (2)] **1** [early 19C+] (*also* **the Nabs**) a police officer. **2** [1940s–50s] (*US*) an arrest, a police raid. **3** [1950s] (*US*) a railroad security man.

nab *v.*[1] [ety. unknown, but cf. NAP *v.*[1] (2)] **1** [mid-17C+] (*also* **nib**) to snatch, to steal, to seize. **2** [late 17C+] (*UK Und.*) (*also* **knab**) to catch or capture a person unawares, to apprehend and arrest; to catch, in sense of to hit. **3** [late 18C; 1930s] to bite. **4** [late 18C+] (*also* **nib**) to catch someone out, esp. if cheating. **5** [mid-19C+] (*US*) to obtain for oneself, to grab; in sexual terms, to seduce. **6** [1920s–30s] (*tramp*) to steal a ride on a train.

IN COMPOUNDS

❑ **nabman** *n.* (*also* **nabbing-cull**) [SE *man*/CULL *n.*[1] (3)] [late 18C–early 19C] a policeman. ❑ **nab-cramps** *n.* [mid-19C] (*UK Und.*) handcuffs.

IN PHRASES

❑ **nab in the hock** *v.* [HOCK *n.*[1]/HOCK *n.*[2]] [late 19C] (*US Und.*) to catch in the act. ❑ **nab it on the dial** *v.* [DIAL *n.*] [mid–late 19C] to take a blow on the face. ❑ **nab the bib** (*also* **nab one's bib**) *see* NAP ONE'S BIB *under* NAP *v.*[1]. ❑ **nab the cramp** *v.* [late 18C–mid-19C] (*UK Und.*) to receive a death sentence. ❑ **nab the regulars** *v.* (*also* **nap the regulars**) [REGULARS *n.*] [mid-19C–1900s] (*UK Und.*) to take one's usual share of a robbery's proceeds. ❑ **nab the rust** *v.* [SE *rusty*, refractory (of horses)] [late 18C–mid-19C] **1** orig. of horses, to be ill-tempered, sullen. **2** to be punished. **3** (*UK Und.*) to receive money. ❑ **nab the snow** *v.* [SNOW *n.*[1]] [late 18C–early 19C] (*UK Und.*) to steal linen that has been put out to bleach or dry. ❑ **nab the stifles** *v.* [SE *stifle*, the condition of being choked] [19C–1900s] (*UK Und.*) to be hanged. ❑ **nab the stoop** *v. see* KNAP THE STOOP *under* KNAP *v.* ❑ **nab the teize** *v.* (*also* **nab the tease, ...teaze, nap the teaze, ...teize**) [TEASE *v.*[1]; whippings were often public] [late 18C–early 19C] for a prisoner to be flogged as a punishment while in prison, rather than in public.

nab *v.*[2] [var. on NAP *v.*[1] (1)] [late 17C–early 18C] to cheat with dice.

nab-all *n.* [? var. on SE *nab-all*, a miser, an unpleasant person; lit. 'snatch-all'] [early 17C] a fool.

nabber *n.* [NAB *v.*[1]] **1** [19C] a thief. **2** [early 19C] a bailiff, a constable. **3** [1940s–60s] (*US*) a police officer.

nabbing cheat *n.* [NAB *v.*[1] (2) + CHEAT *n.* (1)] [early 19C] the gallows.

nabbing-cull *n. see* NABMAN *under* NAB *v.*[1].

nabbing-ken *n.* [NAB *v.*[1] (2) + KEN *n.*[1] (1)] [late 17C] (*UK Und.*) a court.

nabble *v.* [NAB *v.*[1] (1)] [mid-19C] (*UK Und.*) to steal.

nabblers *n.* [NAB *v.*[1] (1)] [mid-19C] (*UK Und.*) the fingers (in the context of stealing).

nabe *n.*[1] [abbr. SAmE *neigh*bourhood] (*US*) **1** [1930s+] a local cinema, usu. in pl. **2** [1940s+] a *neighb*ourhood. **3** [1970s+] a local bar.

nabe *n.*[2] *see* NAB *n.*[1].

nabob *n.* [Urdu *nawwab*; ult. Arabic *na'ib*/Port. *nababo*, deputy governor, thus transferred to a merchant who has made his fortune trading in/with India; the sl. use has no India-specific connotations] [late 18C+] a capitalist.

IN PHRASES

❑ **come the nabob** *v. see* COME THE NOB *under* NOB *n.*[2].

nab on *v.* [1980s] (*US*) to abuse, to criticize.

Nabs, the *n. see* NAB *n.*[2] (1).

nabs *n.* (*also* **knabs**) [northern dial.] [late 18C–1950s] a person, usu. in phrs. below.

IN PHRASES

❑ **his nabs** *n.* (*also* **his knabs, ...knobs, ...nobs**) [late 18C–1930s] himself. ❑ **my nabs** *n.* [late 18C–1950s] myself; also used indirectly.

n.a.b.u. *n. see* S.A.B.U. *n.*

nace *adj. see* NASE *adj.*

nach *adv. see* NATCH *adv.*

nackerball *n.* [ety. unknown] [2000s] (*S.Afr.*) a sycophant, a 'teacher's pet'.

nackers *n.* (*also* **nakers**) [var. on KNACKERS *n.*] [mid-19C+] the testicles.

nacky *see* NAUKY *adj.*

nada *n.* [synon. Sp.] [1910s+] (*US*) nothing.

nadger *n.* [ety. unknown] [late 19C+] (*Ulster*) **1** a young boy. **2** a sulky, bad-tempered person.

nadgers *n.* [abbr. SE *gonads*] [1950s+] testicles.

(IN PHRASES)

□ **put the nadgers on** *v.* [1950s+] to jinx, to cause trouble for.

nads *n.* [abbr. SE *gonads*] **1** [1960s+] (*orig. US*) the testicles. **2** [1970s+] (*US*) courage.

(IN COMPOUNDS)

□ **nad-bag** *n.* [BAG *n.*[1] (1)] [1990s+] the scrotum. □ **nad-jam** *n.* [JAM *n.*[2] (4)] [2000s] semen.

nael *adj. see* NALE *adj.*

naf *n.*[1] (*also* **naff**) [? abbr. backsl. FANNY *n.*[1]; but note Scot. *nyaph*, the female genitals] [mid-19C] **1** the buttocks. **2** the vagina.

naf *n.*[2] (*also* **naff**) **1** [1940s+] nothing [coined in prostitute use]. **2** [1960s+] (*S.Afr.*) a fool, a weakling, an ineffectual person.

naff *adj.*[1] (*also* **naph**) [? north. dial. *naffhead, naffin, naffy*, a simpleton; a blockhead; an idiot or *niffy-naffy*, inconsequential, stupid or Scot. *nyaff*, a term of contempt for any unpleasant or objectionable person; however note Polari etymologist WS Wilcox in a letter 25/11/99: 'I have long believed that *naff* may well derive from Romany *naflo*, a form of *nasvalo* – no good, broken, useless. Since several other Parlary words derive from Romany this is not impossible'; in this context note also 16C Ital. *gnaffa*, a despicable person] **1** [1960s+] in poor taste, unappealing, unfashionable, bad. **2** [1990s+] second-rate, workaday.

(IN PHRASES)

□ **naff omee** *n.* [OMEE *n.* (3), lit. an 'unappealing man'] [1960s+] (*gay*) a heterosexual.

naff *adj.*[2] [abbr. *n*ot *a*vailable *f*or *f*ucking/*f*un; pun on NAFF *adj.*[1] (1)] [1980s+] (*gay*) heterosexual.

naff *v.* as quasi-euph. for uses of FUCK *v.*

(DERIVATIVES)

□ **naffing** *adj.* [euph. for FUCKING *adj.*] [1950s+] a general intensifier.

(IN PHRASES)

□ **naff-all** *n.* [1970s+] euph. for FUCK ALL *n.* (1). □ **naffed off** *adj.* [euph. for *fucked off* under FUCKED *adj.*[1]] [1990s+] fed up, annoyed. □ **naff up** *v.* [euph. for FUCK UP *v.*] [1980s+] to make a mess, to blunder.

(IN EXCLAMATIONS)

□ **naff off!** [euph. for FUCK OFF! *excl.*] [1950s+] go away!

nafka/nafkeh *n. see* NOFFKA *n.*

nag *n.* [fig. uses of SE *nag*, a saddle horse] **1** pertaining to a woman. (**a**) [late 16C–early 17C] a term of abuse; spec. a promiscuous woman, a prostitute. (**b**) [19C; 1970s] an ageing prostitute. (**c**) [mid-19C–1900s] a woman, with no pejorative implication. (**d**) [1960s+] (*US*) of a prostitute, one who takes her time over making her daily money from her clients. (**e**) [1980s] (*US*) a queen in cards. **2** [mid-17C–mid-18C] the penis. **3** [mid-18C] a case of venereal disease. **4** [1940s+] in pl., horses, in the context of horseracing.

(IN PHRASES)

□ **tether one's nags on** *v.* (*also* **tip the nags**) [19C] (*Scot.*) to have sexual intercourse. □ **water one's nag** *v.* [sense 2 above] [late 17C] **1** to urinate. **2** to have intercourse.

nagah *n.* [NIGGER *n.*[1] (1); but note Thelwell (1980) '*Nagah*: either a corruption of the old *Nago*, referring to a Yoruba person or custom, or, in the dialect, a version of 'nigger, from the plantocracy's pejorative description of the slaves dance'] [1950s+] (*W.I. Rasta*) a derog. name for a black person.

nag-drag *n.* [DRAG *n.*[1] (5)] [mid-19C–1900s] (*UK Und.*) a three-month period of imprisonment.

naggie *n.* (*also* **naggy**) [NAG *n.* (1) + dimin. *-ie*; note SE *naggie*, a pony, which can be 'ridden'] [19C–1900s] the vagina.

nag (it) *v.* [? abbr. of SE *snag*, to grab hold of] [1930s] (*US*) of a train, to jump on, to ride.

nago *n.* [*Nago*, a person born in Nago, a Yoruba-speaker; many such people were transported from Africa as slaves] [1940s+] (*W.I.*) a very stupid, ugly or notably dark-complexioned person.

nags *n.* [? KNACKERS *n.*] [19C–1900s] the testicles.

nah! *excl.* (*also* **nah, G!**) [pron.] [1920s+] (*US*) no!

nahpoo/nah poo *adj. see* NAPOO *adj.*

nail *n.*[1] **1** (*also* **dead nail, nailing rascal, nails**) based on pun on SHARP *adj.* (1)/SE *sharp*. (**a**) [early 19C] a shrewd, imposing criminal, 'a person of an over-reaching, imposing disposition' (Vaux). (**b**) [early 19C] a gambler who cheats and/or refuses to pay his losses. **2** [1910s–70s] (*US*) a venereal infection [the sharp pain in the penis when urinating]. **3** abbr. COFFIN NAIL *n.*[2]. (**a**) [1910s+] a cigarette. (**b**) [1970s+] (*drugs*) a marijuana cigarette. **4** [1930s+] (*US drugs*) a hypodermic syringe.

(IN PHRASES)

□ **down as a nail** *see* DOWN AS A HAMMER/NAIL/TRIPPET *under* DOWN *adj.*[1]. □ **nail in one's coffin** *n.* [early–mid-19C] a drink of liquor. □ **pick up a nail** *v.* [the way in which venereal disease can lead to a sharp pain in the penis when urinating] [20C+] (*W.I.*) to contract venereal disease. □ **put another nail in one's coffin** *v.* (*also* **add a nail/peg to one's coffin, drive a nail/peg into one's coffin**) [pun on the sealing of a coffin + the pegs that once marked off alcoholic measures in a tankard] [19C+] to drink heavily, to get drunk.

SE in slang uses

(IN COMPOUNDS)

□ **nail bender** *n.* [1920s+] (*US*) a carpenter, a blacksmith. □ **nail-biter** *n. see* BITE *v.* □ **nail can** *n.* [the shape of the cylindrical hat] [late 19C–1950s] (*Aus.*) a top hat. □ **nail groper** *n.* (*also* **grubber**) [mid-19C] one who scours the streets in search of old nails and similar saleable pieces of lost or discarded metal. □ **nail keg** *n.* [the hat resembles the shape of a SAmE *nail keg*, a small barrel in which nails are shipped] [mid-19C–1900s] (*US*) a top hat. □ **nailrod** *n.* (*also* **nail-rod**) [resemblance to SE *nailrod*, a rod of metal from which nails are cut] [late 19C–1920s] (*Aus./N.Z.*) **1** a stick of 'Two Seas' tobacco. **2** any dark tobacco.

(IN PHRASES)

□ **eat one's nails** *v.* [ety. unknown] [early 18C] to do something foolish. □ **give someone a bent nail** *v.* [1950s] (*US*) to make an unclear, misleading statement. □ **go off at the nail** *v.* [the image of two parts of a pair of scissors flying apart when the nail that links them snaps or falls out] [early 18C+] (*Ulster*) to become confused or flustered. □ **off the nail** *adj.* [phr. *go off at the nail*, to behave strangely] [early 19C] tipsy, slightly drunk.

nail *n.*[2] [punning antonym of HAMMA *n.*] [1960s+] (*US black*) a man.

nail *n.*[3] [abbr. *n*ice *a*ss *i*n *L*evi's] [1990s+] (*US campus*) a well-built male, esp. a sportsman.

nail *n.*[4] [? the image of being held together by nails] [2000s] (*N.Z.*) a run-down car.

nail *v.* (*also* **nail down**) [the image in all is of putting a nail through, or nailing down] **1** [mid-18C+] (*orig. UK Und.*) to get hold of, to secure; lit. and fig. **2** [mid-18C+] to steal; to rob. **3** [mid-18C+] to catch someone out, to take advantage of, to get the better of, to cheat. **4** [late 18C+] to punch, to hit hard or squarely. **5** [late 18C+] to shoot someone, to kill someone (occas. an animal or bird). **6** [19C+] to apprehend and arrest. **7** [late 19C+] to corner or defeat, esp. an opponent. **8** [late 19C+] (*US*) to seduce, to secure someone's affections, to have sexual intercourse with. **9** [20C+] (*US*) to identify, to recognize. **10** [1910s+] to put an end to. **11** [1910s+] to approach, to address. **12** [1960s+] to charge with a debt. **13** [1960s+] (*US*) to reprimand. **14** [1970s+] to do something well, to master something, to deal with successfully. **15** [1980s+] to link someone with a person or thing.

(DERIVATIVES)

□ **nailed** *adj.* **1** [mid-19C+] (*orig. US drugs*) arrested. **2** [1950s] (*US campus*) emotionally disturbed. □ **nailing** *adv.* [note NAILER *n.* (3)] [late 19C] exceptionally.

(IN PHRASES)

□ **nail a rattler** *v.* [RATTLER *n.* (1)] [late 19C–1960s] (*US tramp*) to steal a ride on a moving train. □ **nail a strike** *v.* [STRIKE *n.* (2)] [late 19C–1900s] (*UK Und.*) to steal a watch. □ **nailed up** *adj.* [mid-19C] (*US*) drunk. □ **nail 'em and jail 'em** *n.* [1970s+] (*US black*) the police. □ **nailing good** *adv.* [see NAILING above] [mid-19C–1910s] exceptionally. □ **nail jell-o to a tree** *v.* [SAmE jelly product, *Jell-O*] [1980s+] (*US campus*) to do the impossible.

❑ **nail someone's hide to the wall** *v.* (*also* **nail someone's hide to the barn door, ...ass to the barn door, ...ass to the wall**) [late 19C+] (*orig. US*) **1** to punish severely. **2** to beat up comprehensively, to kill. ❑ **nail someone to the cross** *v.* (*also* **nail someone to the mast, ...barn door**) [late 19C+] (*orig. US*) to punish, to defeat in a decisive act, to castigate. ❑ **nail two wames together** *v.* [Scot. *wame*, the belly] [18C–19C] to have sexual intercourse.

nailer *n.* [lit. and fig. uses of NAIL *v.*] **1** [19C] a clincher, a 'knockout'. **2** [mid-19C] a policeman. [NAIL *v.* (6)] **3** [late 19C] a general term of excellence, applied to people, animals or objects. **4** [late 19C–1920s] an extortionist.

nailhead *n.* [her tightly curled hair supposedly resembles a collection of SE *nail heads*] [1960s+] (*US black*) an unattractive woman, esp. one with short, nappy hair.

nailheaded *adj.* [the hardness of a SE *nail head*] [early 18C; 1930s–40s] (*US*) stupid, stubborn.

nails *n.* [SE phr. *hard as nails*] **1** [1980s+] (*UK juv.*) an aggressive person, a 'hard' man. **2** *see* NAIL *n.*[1] (1).

nails! *excl.* (*also* **by nails!**) [abbr. SE *God's nails!*, spec. the nails used to crucify Christ] [late 14C–17C] an oath.

nails and screws *n.* [rhy. sl.] [20C+] (*Aus.*) news.

nair *n.* [backsl.] [late 19C] rain.

naked *adj.* [fig. use of SE; note 14C SE *naked*, without armour or weapons] [20C+] (*US black*) without a gun, without possessions or money, generally at a disadvantage.

IN COMPOUNDS

❑ **naked dance** *n.* [1940s–50s] (*US black*) a sexually provocative dance.

SE in slang uses

IN PHRASES

❑ **get naked** *v.* [1970s+] (*US*) to enjoy oneself uninhibitedly.

naked *adv.* [note *get naked* at NAKED *adj.*] [1970s+] (*US campus*) in an extreme manner.

naked! *excl.* [1970s+] (*US campus*) a general excl. of affirmation, often as a direct response to a previous statement.

nakers *n. see* NACKERS *n.*

nale *adj.* (*also* **nael**) [backsl.] [mid–late 19C] lean.

nallion *n.* [ety. unknown] [20C+] (*Ulster*) a lump, a bump.

Nam *n.* [abbr.] [1960s+] (*US, orig. milit.*) Vietnam.

nam *n.* [backsl.] [mid-19C] **1** a man. **2** a policeman.

namas *v.* (*also* **namase, namaze**) *see* NAMMOUS *v.*

namaser *n.* [NAMMOUS *v.*] [mid-19C] (*UK Und.*) **1** an absconder; one who has run away. **2** something that has vanished, e.g. one's money.

name *n.*

SE in slang uses

IN PHRASES

❑ **bite someone's name** *v.* [the payer has fig. 'signed' for the food] [20C+] (*Aus.*) to eat a meal for which someone else has paid. ❑ **give it a name** *v.* **1** [20C+] (*Aus./US black*) to speak with absolute candour, honesty. **2** [1990s+] (*US black*) a general phr. of affirmation. ❑ **have one's name on** *v.* (*also* **have one's number on it**) [1910s+] to be destined or intended for someone; orig. of a bullet. ❑ **name-it-not** *n.* (*also* **nameless, the**) [19C] the vagina. ❑ **name of the game** *n.* [? the practice of naming the card game when claiming a winning hand] [1910s+] the most important aspect of a situation, whatever matters most, the end, the finish. ❑ **put a name up** *v.* [1950s+] (*UK Und.*) to inform against someone, often to save one's own skin.

IN EXCLAMATIONS

❑ **give it a name!** (*also* **name it! put a name to!**) [mid-19C–1950s] a phr. used when one stands a round of drinks and asks the company what they would like.

na mean? *phr. see* KNOW WHAT I MEAN? *under* KNOW *v.*

namesclop *n.* [backsl.] [mid-19C] a policeman.

name your poison! *excl. see* POISON *n.* (1).

namhus *v. see* NAMMOUS *v.*

nammo *n.* (*also* **namo, namow, nemmo**) [backsl.] [mid-19C+] a woman.

nammous *v.* (*also* **namas, namase, namaze, namhus, nammas, nammus, namous, nommus**) [? Sp. *vamos*, let's go, but cf. NAMUS! *excl.*] (*UK Und.*) [mid–late 19C] **1** to leave, to run off, to slip away quietly. **2** to run, to hurry, to come towards.

namus! *excl.* (*also* **namous! nommus!**) [backsl. *namus* = someone (is coming)] [mid–late 19C] a warning cry on sighting a policeman, meaning 'be off!'; ext. just to mean 'go away!'.

nana *n.* [abbr. SE *banana*, a soft (punning on SOFT *adj.* (1)) fruit] **1** [1920s+] a banana. **2** [1940s+] the head. **3** [1960s] a headmaster[from sense 2]. **4** [1960s+] (*also* **narna**) a fool, an idiot, an incompetent. **5** [1990s+] (*US black*) the vagina.

IN COMPOUNDS

❑ **nana cut** *n.* [1940s+] (*Aus.*) a haircut in which the back of the head is closely shaved.

IN PHRASES

❑ **do one's nana** *v.* [1940s+] to lose one's temper. ❑ **gnaw the nana** *v.* [1960s+] to perform fellatio. ❑ **off one's nana** *adj.* [1940s+] eccentric, mad. ❑ **right nana** *n.* [1960s+] a complete idiot.

nan boy *n.* (*also* **nan**) [the girl's name *Nan*, then synon. with colloq. *nan*, a serving-maid] [late 17C–late 19C] an effeminate or homosexual male.

nance *n.* [NANCY *n.* (1)] [1910s+] an effeminate man, a homosexual.

nance *adj.* [NANCE *n.*] [1920s+] effeminate; homosexual.

nance *v.* [NANCE *n.*] [1940s+] (*US*) to act or speak in an effeminate or homosexual manner.

DERIVATIVES

❑ **nancing** *adj.* [1940s+] effeminate or homosexual in manner.

nancy *n.* **1** [19C] the buttocks, the posterior [? joc. use of proper name]. **2** [early 19C+] (*orig. US*) implying weakness or effeminacy [the female name, but note sense 1]. (**a**) an effeminate male homosexual. (**b**) an effeminate or weak-willed person. **3** [2000s] (*S.Afr. gay*) nothing.

DERIVATIVES

❑ **nancified** *adj.* [1910s+] effeminate, acting in a homosexual manner. ❑ **nancifully** *adv.* [1930s+] effeminately. ❑ **nancitude** *n.* [1930s+] effeminacy.

IN EXCLAMATIONS

❑ **ask my nancy!** [early 19C] go to hell!

nancy *adj.* [NANCY *n.*] [20C+] effeminate, usu. homosexual.

nancy *v.* [1980s+] often constr. with *about*, *around*, to act in an effeminate manner.

nancy boy *n.* [NANCY *n.* (1)] [1910s+] an effeminate man, a homosexual.

Nancy Dawson *n.* [NANCY *n.* (1) + proper name *Nancy Dawson*, a legendary 18C prostitute (d. 1767), about whom a sailor's hornpipe was written; Fraser & Gibbons cite her as 'a celebrated former hornpipe dancer of Covent Garden and Drury Lane Theatres'] [late 19C] an effeminate youth, a homosexual.

nancy lee *n.* [rhy. sl.] [20C+] **1** a flea. **2** (*also* **tancy lee**) tea.

Nanette *n.* (*also* **Natalia, Natalie**) [2000s] (*S.Afr. gay*) a black homosexual man.

nang *n. see* NYANGA *n.*

nang *adj.* [NYANGA *n.*] [2000s] (*UK black*) first-rate, excellent.

nann *adj.* [SE *none*] [2000s] (*US black*) no, nothing.

nan nan *n.* [? NANCY *n.* (1)] [late 19C–1940s] (*Aus.*) **1** a straw hat; also attrib, straw hat wearing. **2** a dandy. **3** one of a gang of youths who sported straw hats as their 'colours'.

nanny *n.*[1] (*also* **nannie**) [generic use of female proper name] [late 17C–19C] a prostitute.

IN COMPOUNDS

❑ **nanny-house** *n.* [HOUSE *n.*[1] (1)] [late 17C–mid-19C] a brothel. ❑ **nanny-shop** *n.* [SHOP *n.*[1] (3)] [mid–late 19C] a brothel.

nanny *n.*^{2} [ety. unknown] [late 18C–19C] (*UK Und.*) the head.

IN PHRASES

❑ **lose one's nanny** *v.* [1900s] to lose one's head. ❑ **off one's nanny** *adj.* [late 19C] mad.

nanny *n.*^{3} [abbr.] [late 19C–1900s] a banana.

nanny *n.*^{4} [NANCY *n.*] [1940s+] (*US*) an effeminate man.

nanny *n.*^{5}

SE *nanny (goat),* in slang uses

IN PHRASES

❑ **get someone's nanny** *v.* [var. on *get someone's goat* under GOAT *n.*^{1}] [1900s–40s] to annoy someone, to infuriate someone.

nanny (goat) *n.* [rhy. sl.] **1** [1920s+] the Totalizator [TOTE *n.*]. **2** [1930s+] a boat. **3** [1940s+] a coat. **4** [1960s+] the throat.

nanny goat *n.*^{1} [ety. unknown; ? rhy. sl. TOT *n.*^{1} (3)] [mid-19C] (*Aus.*) a drink.

nanny goat *n.*^{2} [mispron./semi-rhy. sl.] [mid–late 19C] an anecdote.

nanny goat *n.*^{3} [1900s] (*US*) a style of side-whiskers.

nanny goating *n.* [rhy. sl., albeit imperfect rhyme] [20C+] courting.

nanny-goat sweat *n.* [1940s+] (*US*) rough or inferior liquor.

nantee *n.* (*also* **nante, nanti, nantois, nantoisette, nanty, nenti**) [Ling. Fr. *nantee*, none or not; ult. Ital. *niente*, nothing] [mid-19C+] nothing, none, no, esp. as synon. for phr. *I have none.*

IN COMPOUNDS

❑ **nantee narking** *n.* (*also* **nanti narking, nanty narking**) [NARK *v.*^{1} (4); lit. 'nothing irritating'] [early–mid-19C] great fun. ❑ **nanty crackling** *n.* [CRACKLING *n.*] [late 19C–1920s] (*Polari*) the vagina. ❑ **nanty handbag** *n.* [1990s+] (*UK gay*) no money. ❑ **nanty worster** *n.* [late 19C–1900s] (*Polari*) something that is 'no worse'.

IN EXCLAMATIONS

❑ **nantee palaver!** (*also* **nantee parlaree!**) [PALAVER *n.* (1)] [mid-19C+] shut up! be quiet!

nantee! *excl.* (*also* **nanti! nanty!**) [NANTEE *n.*] [mid-19C+] stop! beware!

nantes *n. see* NANTZ *n.*

nanti *see under* NANTEE.

nantois/nantoisette *n. see* NANTEE *n.*

nanty *see under* NANTEE.

nantz *n.* (*also* **nantes, nants, nantzy**) [proper name *Nantes* in France, a centre of cognac production] [late 17C–late 19C] brandy; see also *COLD NANTZ under* COLD *adj.* and *COOL NANTZ under* COOL *adj.*

Nap *n. see* NAP TOWN *n.* (1).

nap *n.*^{1} [lit. and fig. uses of NAP *v.*^{1}] **1** [late 17C–early 18C] a dose of venereal disease. **2** [late 17C–early 18C] an instance of cheating while playing dice. **3** [mid–late 19C] (*orig. theatrical*) a blow or hit, esp. a pretend hit.

IN PHRASES

❑ **nap (it)** *v.* [late 17C–early 19C] to catch venereal disease.

nap *n.*^{2} [SE *nap*, (woollen) cloth that has a nap surface on it] **1** [late 17C–18C] a sheep, only in phr. *napper of naps* (see NAPPER *n.*^{1}) [note *knapper's poll*]. **2** [late 19C+] (*Aus.*) in senses of bed or covering [SE *knapsack*; but note SE *nap*, a short sleep]. (**a**) a sleeping bag. (**b**) blankets or some other covering used by a sleeper in the open-air, a pack (as used in Northern Territory).

nap *n.*^{3} [NAB *v.*^{1} (1)] [18C] an arrest.

nap *n.*^{4} [NAB *n.*^{1} (3)] [18C–19C] a hat.

nap *n.*^{5} [abbr. proper name *Napoleon III*, whose visit to London in 1855 made the style fashionable] [mid–late 19C] a moustache, of which the two points form a long line that 'cuts' the face.

nap *n.*^{6} [backform. SE *nappy*, i.e. tight, curly hair] [1900s–60s] (*US black*) a black person.

nap *n.*^{7} [abbr.] [1940s+] (*N.Z.*) a *nappy* or diaper.

nap *v.*^{1} [NAB *v.*^{1} or related to Swedish/Norwegian *nappa* or Danish *nappe*, to snatch, snap] **1** [mid-17C–early 19C] (*UK Und.*) (*also* **nap on**) to cheat at dice. **2** [mid-17C–19C] (*also* **nap on**) to seize, to catch, to lay hold of (a person or thing); to arrest. **3** [late 17C–mid-18C] to take into custody. **4** [late 17C–late 18C] to consume. **5** [late 17C–19C] to suffer punishment; to receive a blow. **6** [late 17C–1950s] to steal.

IN PHRASES

❑ **nap a winder** *v.* (*also* **nap the winder**) [WINDER *n.*^{1}] **1** [early–mid-19C] (*also* **nap the winding post**) to be transported for life. **2** [early–mid-19C] to be hanged. **3** [mid-19C–1930s] to receive an unpleasant shock. ❑ **nap it** *v.* (*also* **knap it**) [late 17C–early 19C] to receive severe punishment, esp. in a boxing-match. ❑ **nap it at the nask** *v.* [NASK *n.*] [late 17C–early 18C] to receive a judicial flogging at Bridewell. ❑ **nap one's bib** *v.* (*also* **nab one's bib, nab the bib, nap..., nob...**) [NAP *v.*^{1}/NAB *v.*^{1} + SE bib, to weep] [late 18C–mid-19C] to weep, esp. for effect, i.e. to get one's way, to put across one's point. ❑ **nap the pad** *v.* [PAD *n.*^{2} (1)] [mid-18C] (*UK Und.*) to go to bed. ❑ **nap the regulars** *v. see NAB THE REGULARS under* NAB *v.*^{1}. ❑ **nap the stoop** *v. see KNAP THE STOOP under* KNAP *v.* ❑ **nap the teize** *v.* (*also* **nap the teaze**) *see NAB THE TEIZE under* NAB *v.*^{1}.

nap *v.*^{2} [dial. *knap*] **1** [mid–late 19C] to break, to hit with a hammer. **2** [1990s+] (*Irish*) to knock softly.

nap and double *n.* [rhy. sl.] [1930s+] trouble.

napfry *n. see* FRY *n.*

naph *adj. see* NAFF *adj.*^{1}.

naphead *n. see* NAPPY HEAD *n.*

napkin *n.*

IN PHRASES

❑ **make a napkin out of a dishclout** *v. see under* DISHCLOUT *n.*

napkin ring *n.* [1970s+] (*US gay*) a penis ring.

napkin snatching *n.* [early 19C] stealing handkerchiefs.

Naples canker *n.* (*also* **Naples pox, ...scab**) [racial stereotyping] [17C–mid-18C] syphilis.

Napoleon *n.* [the clichéd image of the mad believing that they are Napoleon or some other world figure] [1930s–50s] (*US black*) a madman, an eccentric.

napoo *n.* [NAPOO *adj.*] [1910s–1920s] a form of termination, e.g. death, disaster.

napoo *adj.* (*also* **nahpoo, nah poo, napoo fini, narpoo**) [Fr. *il n'y a plus*, there is no more; orig. used by French shopkeepers as stock reply to importuning soldiers] [1910s–50s; 2000s] finished, ended, dead, no more; as n. a form of termination, e.g. death, disaster.

napoo *v.* [NAPOO *adj.*] [1910s–20s] **1** (*milit.*) to kill. **2** to die.

napper *n.*^{1} [NAP *v.*^{1}] **1** [mid-17C–19C] (*UK Und.*) (*also* **knapper**) a thief. **2** [18C] a false witness. **3** [mid-18C–early 19C] (*UK Und.*) a cheat.

IN PHRASES

❑ **napper of naps** *n.* [late 17C–late 18C] a sheep stealer.

napper *n.*^{2} **1** [late 17C–19C] a hat [? NAB *n.*^{1} (3)]. **2** [early 18C+] (*also* **knapper, napper tandy, nopper**) the head. **3** [early 19C] a nose. **4** [late 19C–1920s] a face. **5** [late 19C–1920s] the mouth.

IN PHRASES

❑ **do on one's napper** *v.* [late 19C] to achieve something easily. ❑ **go off one's napper** *v.* [late 19C] to go mad.

napper *n.*^{3} [Yorks. dial. *nap*, expert] [late 19C+] (*Ulster*) anything large or outstanding of its type.

nappers' poll *n.* (*also* **knapper's poll, nappers' noll**) [NAP *n.*^{2} + SE *poll*/NOLL *n.*] [early–mid-18C] a sheep's head, as food.

napper tandy *n.* **1** [2000s] (*Aus.*) a shandy (beer and lemonade) [rhy. sl.]. **2** *see* NAPPER *n.*^{2} (2).

nappie *n. see* NAPPY (ALE) *n.*

napping *n.*

IN PHRASES

❑ **catch someone napping** *v.* (*also* **take someone napping**) [20C+ use is SE] [19C+] to take someone by surprise, to catch someone off their guard.

napping bull *n.* [NAP *v.*^{1} (1) + ? BULL *n.*^{5} (1)] [mid-18C] (*UK Und.*) a bailiff.

napping cove *n.* [NAP *v.*[1] (2) + COVE *n.* (1)] [mid-19C] (*UK Und.*) a watchman; by ext. a hue and cry.

napping gear *n. see* NAPPY (ALE) *n.*

napping jigger *n.* see KNAPPING-JIGGER *n.*

nappy *adj.* [SE *nappy*, of hair, tightly curled; i.e. the natural state of many black people's hair] **1** [1970s+] (*US teen*) disgusting, irritating, unpleasant, worthless [derog.]. **2** [1980s+] (*US campus*) bizarre but not unattractive [derog.]. **3** [1990s+] (*US black*) proud to be black; honest, natural ideologically sound [with pride].

SE in slang uses

IN PHRASES

❑ **nappy-ass** *adj.* (*also* **nappy-assed**) [-ASS *sfx*] [1970s+] (*US black teen*) referring to one who has nappy hair. ❑ **nappy dugout** *n.* (*also* **dugout**) [baseball imagery; the dugout where black players, i.e. those with nappy hair which is typically black, wait to bat] [1990s+] (*US black*) the female genitals.

nappy (ale) *n.* (*also* **nappie, napping gear, noppy**) [NAP *n.*[4]; it goes to one's head] [early 16C–mid-19C] drink in general, esp. strong ale.

nappy head *n.* (*also* **naphead**) [backform. *nappy-headed*] [late 19C+] (*US black*) **1** [late 19C+] (*US black*) someone with kinky hair. **2** [late 19C+] (*US black*) an unsophisticated black person [ext. of sense 1 in an era when fashionable blacks straightened their hair]. **3** [1990s+] (*US campus*) unkempt hair.

IN PHRASES

❑ **nappy-headed** *adj.* (*also* **nappy-head**) [late 19C+] (*US black*) having kinky hair.

nappy-tag *n.* [NAP A WINDER *under* NAP *v.*[1] + SE *tag* or 'moral' added to the end of a play] [mid-19C] (*UK Und.*) prayers offered at a judicial hanging.

nappy valley *n.* [SE *nappy* + play on *Happy Valley*] [1970s+] (*Aus./N.Z.*) a dormitory suburb, mainly populated by families with young babies.

naps *n.* [abbr. SE *nappy*, of hair, tightly curled] [late 19C+] (*US black*) kinky hair.

Nap Town *n.* (*also* **Nap**) [abbr.] [1920s+] (*US*) India*napolis*, Indiana.

narangy *n.* [Dharak *narang*, little; applied to those with authority who rank immediately lower than a station manager] [late 19C–1900s] (*Aus.*) a dandy, a 'swell'.

narbo *n.* [ety. unknown] [1990s+] (*US*) an insignificant, boring person.

narc *n.* (*also* **nark**) [abbr. SE *narcotics*] [1960s+] (*orig. US*) **1** *narc*otics. **2** a *narc*otics agent. **3** any informer [note NARK *n.* (1)]. **4** in ext. use, any unpleasant person.

narc *v.* [NARC *n.* + NARK *v.*[1]] [1970s+] to betray someone to the police, spec. a drug dealer or user to the narcotics police.

narco *n.* [abbr.] [1950s+] **1** (*US*) a *narco*tics officer. **2** (*US*) the *narco*tics department of a police station or hospital. **3** (*drugs*) narcotics. **4** (*drugs*) a drug addict or drug dealer.

IN COMPOUNDS

❑ **narco squad** *n.* (*also* **narco man**) [1950s+] (*US drugs/Und.*) the *narco*tics *squad*.

narcotic bull *n.* see BULL *n.*[5] (6).

nard *n.* [ety. unknown; 20C use var. on NERD *n.* but note NARDS *n.*] [mid-19C; 1960s] (*US*) an obnoxious person.

nards *n.* **1** [1960s+] (*US*) male genitals [? SE *gonads*]. **2** [1990s+] (*US*) the female breasts.

narg *n.* [ety. unknown; ? Hindi] [1980s+] (*N.Z.*) derog. term for an Indian.

nark *n.* (*also* **knark**) [Rom. *nak*, nose] **1** [mid-19C+] (*also* **narko**) a police informer. **2** [mid-19C+] (*mainly Aus./N.Z.*) an irritating person, a spoilsport, a badly behaved person. **3** [late 19C+] a police officer. **4** [20C+] (*Aus.*) spite, rancour, umbrage. **5** [20C+] one who reports to the authorities, a telltale. **6** [1910s+] any annoying or disagreeable situation. **7** [1920s–30s] (*tramp*) a beggar who works part-time and lives permanantly in a common lodging house, thus having a privileged relationship with the owner. **8** [1960s] an agent, a go-between. **9** see NARC *n.* (2).

IN PHRASES

❑ **get the nark** *v.* [20C+] (*Aus.*) to become angry. ❑ **get the narkies on** *v.* [20C+] to become domineering, arrogant and bossy. ❑ **give someone the nark** *v.* [20C+] to anger, to annoy.

nark *v.*[1] [NARK *n.*] **1** [mid-19C–1910s] to watch, to survey, to notice. **2** [late 19C+] to inform to the police. **3** [late 19C+] to betray someone; to inform upon. **4** [late 19C+] (*mainly Aus./N.Z.*) to annoy, to irritate. **5** [1930s+] to complain, to nag.

IN COMPOUNDS

❑ **narking dues** *n.* [late 19C] an arrest made on the evidence of an informer.

IN PHRASES

❑ **nark the lurk** *v.* [1930s] (*Aus. Und.*) to betray a plan.

nark *v.*[2] [late 19C+] to stop, to terminate, to desist, esp. to stop talking, to spoil.

IN PHRASES

❑ **I'll nark you** [1910s+] (*Aus.*) I'll ruin your plan. ❑ **put the nark on** *v.* [20C+] to put off, to ruin (a plan), to discourage.

IN EXCLAMATIONS

❑ **nark it!** (*also* **knark it!**) [mid-19C+] stop it!, shut up!

narked *adj.* [NARK *v.*[1] (4)] [late 19C+] annoyed.

narker *n.* [NARK *v.*[1] (2)] **1** [1930s+] an informer. **2** [1950s] a police officer.

narko *n.* see NARK *n.* (1).

narky *adj.* (*also* **narkey, narkie**) [NARK *v.*[1] (4)] [late 19C+] irascible, bad-tempered, sarcastic.

narly *adj.* see GNARLY *adj.* (3).

narna *n.* see NANA *n.* (4).

nar-nar *adj.* [? late 19C *nana* (from Emile Zola's supposedly indecent novel *Nana* (1880)) outrageous, indecent or NANA *n.* (4)] [1910s–50s] (*Aus.*) of a man, over-dressed, often effeminately so.

nar nar goon *n.* [*Nar Nar Goon*, a small town southeast of Melbourne] [20C+] (*Aus.*) a generic name for any small, insignificant, out-of-the way place.

narp *n.* [synon. Scot.] [mid-19C] a shirt.

narpoo *adj.* see NAPOO *adj.*

narrish *adj.* [SE *narrow*] [late 19C] (*UK society*) thrifty, mean.

narrow *adj.* [? SE *nary*, no, not (a)] [mid–late 18C] never a, not a, not one.

narrow-assed *adj.* (*also* **narrowgutted**) [SE *narrow* + ASS *n.* (2)/ SE *gut*] [1910s–70s] (*US/UK*) slim, skinny; thus narrow-minded.

narrowback *n.* [? their stereotyped physique or Ulster dial. *narrow*, mean, miserly] **1** [late 19C] a supporter of political reform. **2** [1950s+] (*US*) an Irish person, esp. a second-generation immigrant. **3** [1950s+] (*US*) a Protestant. **4** [1950s+] (*Irish*) an immigrant who returns from the US to live in Ireland.

narrow lane *n.* [mid-16C] the throat.

narrow place in the road *n. see* BAD PLACE IN THE ROAD *under* BAD *adj.*

narsum *n.* (*also* **narsey-parsey**) [ARSE *n.* (1)] [mid–late 17C] (*Irish*) the buttocks, the behind.

nasal *adv.* [pun on *na(sal)/nay*] [1980s+] (*US campus*) no.

IN PHRASES

❑ **nasal on that** [1980s+] (*US campus*) forget it, no chance.

nase *adj.* (*also* **nace**) [ety. 'obscure' (*OED*) but B&L suggest Ger. *nass*, wet; given the trad. association of red noses and drunkards there might be a link to obs. 14C SE *nase*, nose] [mid-16C–early 17C] (*UK Und.*) drunken, intoxicated.

IN COMPOUNDS

❑ **nase nab** *n.* (*also* **nazie nab, nazy nab**) [above/NAZIE *adj.* + ? NEB *n.*[1] (3) although predates this] [17C–early 19C] **1** (*UK Und.*) a drunkard, drunkenness. **2** a red nose.

nash *n.* [Carib.E. *nash*, soft, effeminate; ult. Eng. dial. *nesh*, juicy, succulent, tender] [1950s+] (*W.I. Rasta*) the female genitalia.

nash *v.*[1] [Rom. *nash, nasher,* to run] [19C; 1980s+] to leave, to rush off.

IN PHRASES

❑ **do a nash** *v.* [2000s] to run off. ❑ **Mr Nash is concerned** [early 19C] used of someone who is absent, having run off.

nash *v.*[2] *see* NOSH V.

nash gab *n.* [Rom. *nash,* to run + GAB *n.*[1]] [19C] insolent speech.

nasho *n.* [abbr. *national (service)* + -O *sfx* (3); Aus. national service was discontinued in 1972; post-70s use is historical] [1950s–70s] (*Aus.*) **1** national service. **2** a national serviceman.

Nashville *n.* [*Nashville,* Tennessee, with its links to country music as the epitome of middle-American values] [1970s+] (*US black*) any unsophisticated, suburban, middle-American town or person.

nask *n.* (*also* **naskin, nass**) [late 17C–mid-19C] a prison, (spec. in London, the *Old Nask,* the City Bridewell, the *New Nask,* the Clerkenwell prison and *Tuttle Nask,* in Tothill Fields).

nasous *n.* [distorted pron. of SE + note SE *nasal,* referring to the nose] [mid-18C] (*UK Und.*) the nose.

nast *adj.* [abbr. SE *nasty*] [1990s+] (*US teen*) unpleasant.

nasties *n.* **1** [20C+] (*US black*) sexual desire, lust. **2** [1930s–40s] the Nazis. **3** [1930s+] (*US*) any unpleasant, disgusting, threatening or scary things or persons. **4** [1980s] (*drugs*) drugs, of any variety.

nasty *n.* [in sexual contexts an acknowledgment, if not an agreement, with the Western ambivalence as regards sexuality; note Williams (1994) for 17C use of *nasty* as 'bedfellow'] **1** [mid-19C; 1960s] the vagina. **2** [1930s+] anything or anyone unpleasant, varying as to context. **3** [1930s+] sexual intercourse. **4** [1960s+] the penis.

IN PHRASES

❑ **do (someone) a nasty** *v.* [1980s+] to do something unpleasant (to someone), to cause (someone) trouble or problems. ❑ **do the (big) nasty** *v.* **1** [1960s+] (*orig. US*) to have sexual intercourse. **2** [1960s+] (*US black*) to perform cunnilingus. ❑ **flash one's nasty** *v.* [2000s] (*N.Z.*) to expose one's genitalia. ❑ **have a bit of (old) nasty** *v.* [1930s–40s] to have sexual intercourse.

nasty *adj.* [on bad = good model or fig. use of SE *nasty*] **1** [mid-19C+] (*orig. US*) first-class, exciting, particularly enjoyable or admirable. **2** [mid-19C+] (*orig. US*) attractive, sexy; often in negative sense, i.e. promiscuous, amoral. **3** [mid-19C+] (*orig. US*) aggressive, hostile, bad-tempered. **4** [1980s+] (*orig. US*) difficult. **5** [1990s+] (*W.I./UK black*) dirty.

IN COMPOUNDS

❑ **nasty-ass** *adj.* [1960s+] (*US*) **1** of a person, unpleasant. **2** of a place, thing or animal, dirty, disgusting. ❑ **nasty-behind** *adj.* [1960s] (*US black*) of a female, promiscuous. ❑ **nastygram** *n.* [1960s+] (*US, orig. milit.*) an unpleasant note or letter or a communication that brings bad news. ❑ **nastyman** *n.* **1** [mid–late 19C] the member of the garrotting team who actually does the choking. **2** [late 19C] (*UK Und*) a thief's assistant. **3** [1950s–60s] (*US black*) a sexual pervert. ❑ **nasty-mouthed** *adj.* [20C+] (*W.I.*) foul-mouthed, given to using obscene language. ❑ **nasty nigger** *adj.* [1990s+] (*W.I.*) ill-mannered, boorish.

IN PHRASES

❑ **nasty up** *v.* [20C+] (*W.I.*) to make a mess of, to dirty.

nasty *v.* [1960s+] to have sexual intercourse.

nasty *adv.* **1** [1900s] (*Aus.*) fast. **2** [1970s+] (*US teen*) extremely (whether pleasant or unpleasant), e.g. *nasty cool,* very cool indeed. **3** [1990s+] (*US*) of language, obscenely.

nasty bit of work *n.* (*also* **nasty bit of goods, ...piece of work**) [1910s+] an unpleasant person.

nat *n.*[1] [? SE *gnat*] [late 19C+] (*Ulster*) a small person.

nat *n.*[2] *see* NATURAL *n.* (4a).

Natalia *n. see* NANETTE *n.*

Natalie *n. see* NANETTE *n.*

natarnal *adj.* (*also* **netarnal**) [pron. SE *eternal,* infinite, in the sense of wearisome, tedious, loathsome] [20C+] (*Irish*) used to express disgust.

natch *n.* [abbrev.] [late 19C–1900s] one's natural life.

natch *adv.* (*also* **nach**) [abbr.] [1940s+] (*orig. US*) naturally.

IN PHRASES

❑ **on the natch** [1960s+] (*drugs*) not using any drugs or other stimulants.

natchie *n. see* NATURAL *n.* (6).

nathan *n.* [? pron. of SE] [1980s+] (*US black teen*) nothing.

nation *n.* [-NATION *sfx*] [20C+] (*W.I.*) a disreputable or unpleasant person.

nation *adv. see* TARNATION *adv.*

'nation *adv.* [abbr. DAMNATION! *excl.*; Grose (1785) attributes it to 'Kent, Sussex and the adjacent counties'] [late 18C–1930s] very much, exceedingly.

nation, the *excl. see* TARNATION *n.*

-nation *sfx* [? trans. of Hind. *jaat,* class, kind, race] [20C+] (*W.I.*) a general sfx used widely to define, usu. derog., various sub-groups in the Caribbean. *See* CHINEE NATION *under* CHINEE *adj.*; COOLIE NATION *under* COOLIE *n.*[1]; HIGH NATION *under* HIGH *adj.*[1], LOW NATION *under* LOW *adj.*; used alone as NATION *n.*

national anthem *n.* [? seen as representing 'stars' and 'stripes' (the US national anthem being 'The Stars and Stripes')] [1940s] (*US*) sauerkraut and spare-ribs.

national death *n. see* NEW ZEALAND DEATH *under* NEW ZEALAND *n.*

national front *n.* [rhy. sl. = CUNT *n.* (4); ult. the UK Far Right movement *National Front* (est. 1967)] [1960s+] a general term of abuse.

national hunt *n.* [rhy. sl. = FRONT *n.*[1] (1)] [20C+] audacity, cheek.

native *n.* [? abbr. *native brew*] [late 18C–early 19C] (*Irish*) illicitly distilled whisky, poteen.

native cavalry *n.* [early–mid-19C] unbroken horses, used by country people, as opposed to those ridden by townsmen.

Nat King Cole *n.* [rhy. sl., ult. US singer *Nat King Cole* (1919–65)] [1940s+] **1** the dole. **2** (*Aus.*) a foal. **3** a mole (on the skin). **4** a bread roll. **5** (*Irish/Scot.*) sexual intercourse [= HOLE *n.*[1] (1e)].

natomy *n.* (*also* **nattermy**) [abbr. SE *anatomy*] [19C–1900s] a small, thin and/or deformed person.

nattum *n.* [? *up and at 'em*] [20C+] (*Aus.*) sexual intercourse.

natty *n.*[1] [NATTY *adj.* (1)] [early 19C] a spruce, smart person; a dandy.

natty *n.*[2] (*also* **natty congo, ...dread, knotty**) [SE *natural* + the *Congo*/DREAD *n.*[2]] [1950s+] (*W.I. Rasta*) **1** dreadlocks. **2** a person with dreadlocks.

natty *adj.* [all SE by late 19C] [late 18C+] **1** well-dressed, smart. **2** neat, spruce. **3** adept with the hands; skilful in any manner.

IN COMPOUNDS

❑ **natty lad** *n.* (*also* **natty, natty kid**) [late 18C–mid-19C] a young thief or pickpocket.

natural *n.* **1** when pertaining to a 'state of nature'. (**a**) [mid-16C+] an idiot; one who is untutored or unsophisticated; often the potential victim of a confidence trick. (**b**) [late 17C–early 19C] a mistress; a prostitute. (**c**) [late 17C–early 19C] an illegitimate child. **2** pertaining to gambling [abbr. SE *natural winner*]. (**a**) [mid-18C; late 19C–1960s] (*gambling*) a winning combination, esp. in craps. (**b**) [1900s–30s] thus fig. good luck (**c**) [1930s–40s] (*US prison*) as ext. of sense 2a, a 7-year sentence. **3** [mid-18C; 1920s+] (*orig. US*) one who is naturally suited to a job or skill; one who is naturally talented. **4** when pertaining to 'one's *natural* life'. (**a**) [late 19C+] (*also* **nat**) one's life. (**b**) [1930s] (*US*) a life sentence. **5** [1920s+] (*US*) something certain to succeed, a winner; something inevitable. **6** [1960s+] (*US black*) (*also* **natch, natchie**) a bushy hairstyle, in which one's hair is allowed to grow naturally rather than being subjected to straightening or similar styling **7** [1970s+] (*US black*) one's 'natural-born' self.

IN COMPOUNDS

❑ **natural pick** *n.* (*also* **pick**) [SE *pick,* a pointed tool, here a comb] [1960s+] (*US black*) a large comb used spec. for tidying an AFRO *n.* (1) or 'natural' hairstyle.

(IN PHRASES)

❑ **all one's natural** [abbr. SE phr. *all one's natural born days*] [late 19C+] all one's life. ❑ **for one's natural** as if one's life depended on it. ❑ **get off the natural** *v.* [1960s] (*US drugs*) to become intoxicated. ❑ **not on your natural** [abbr. SE *natural life*, thus var. on *not on your life* (see under LIFE *n.*)] [20C+] absolutely not. ❑ **throw a natural** *v.* [sense 1b above] [1900s] to experience good luck.

natural-born man *n.* (*also* **natural man**) [the premise is that a 'natural' person is not hidebound by social conditioning etc] [1930s+] (*US black*) a 'real' (i.e. heterosexual) man, a good lover, an honest, unpretentious person.

natural draft *n.* [SE *natural* + *draft*, a plan or sketch] [20C+] (*Ulster*) someone or something identical, the 'living image'.

natural woman *n.* [1930s+] (*US black*) the female version of NATURAL-BORN MAN *n.*

nature *n.* **1** [late 18C–19C] a euph. for the vagina. **2** [mid-19C; 1970s] the penis; semen. **3** [1910s+] (*US black*) one's libido, one's sex-drive [note *Cleland* (1748-9): 'After playing repeated prizes of pleasure, nature overspent, and satisfy'd, gave us up to the arms of sleep'].

terms associated with sexuality

(IN COMPOUNDS)

❑ **nature's duty** *n.* [18C–19C] sexual intercourse. ❑ **nature's founts** *n.* [literary euph.] [19C] the female breasts. ❑ **nature's privy seal** *n.* (*also* **Dame Nature's privy seal**) [mid-17C–19C] the hymen. ❑ **nature's scythe** *n.* [mid-18C–19C] the penis. ❑ **nature's treasury** *n.* (*also* **nature's workshop, treasury of love**) [mid-17C–19C] the vagina. ❑ **nature's tufted treasure** *n.* [19C] the vagina.

(IN PHRASES)

❑ **lose one's nature** *v.* [1960s] to lose one's sex-drive, typically as a result of narcotic addiction.

SE in slang uses

(IN PHRASES)

❑ **give nature a fillip** *v.* [late 17C–18C] to indulge in hedonistic pleasures, notably women and wine.

Naughton and Gold *adj.* [rhy. sl.; ult. Charlie *Naughton* (1887–1976) and Jimmy *Gold* (1886–1967), music-hall stars and members of the Crazy Gang (1935–62)] [1930s+] cold.

naughty *n.* **1** [mid-19C–1900s] the vagina. **2** [mid–late 19C; 1950s+] (*mainly Aus./N.Z.*) sexual intercourse. **3** [1970s] (*Aus.*) a crime. **4** [1970s+] an injury. **5** [1980s+] usu. in pl., sexual liaisons, intercourse.

(IN COMPOUNDS)

❑ **naughty house** *n.* [SE *house*/HOUSE *n.*[1] (1)] [late 16C–mid-19C] a brothel.

(IN PHRASES)

❑ **do oneself a naughty** *v.* [1970s+] to injure oneself. ❑ **do the naughty** *v.* [mid-19C+] to have sexual intercourse. ❑ **work for one's living and do the naughty for one's clothes** *v.* [mid-19C+] to be an amateur prostitute, who has a legitimate day-job but still goes out whoring to make extra money.

naughty *adj.* **1** [late 17C–early 18C] of money, counterfeit. **2** [mid-19C–1900s] flashy, vulgarly over-dressed. **3** [1910s+] (*UK Und.*) criminal, violent, corrupt. **4** [1950s–60s] malfunctioning, sick. **5** [1970s+] problematic, disturbing.

(IN COMPOUNDS)

❑ **naughty bits** *n.* [this quite deliberate euph. was coined *c.*1969 by the Monty Python's Flying Circus comedy team] [1970s+] the genitals, of either sex. ❑ **naughty dickey-bird** *n.* [ext. BIRD *n.*[1] (1a)] [19C] a prostitute. ❑ **naughty pack** *n.* [SE *pack*] [mid-16C–mid-18C] a person of low and worthless character, usu. a woman.

(IN PHRASES)

❑ **Naughty Half Mile** *n.* the redlight district of King's Cross, Sydney.

naughty *v.* [NAUGHTY *n.* (2)] [1950s+] to have sexual intercourse.

nauky *adj.* (*also* **knackety, knacky, knawky, nacky, nawky**) [Scot. *knaw*; ult. SE *know*] [late 18C+] cunning, resourceful.

naus *n.* (*also* **norz**) [pron. as abbr. of SE *naus*(*eating*) and commonly used with a derog. implication, but in fact rhy. sl. *Noah's* = *Noah's Ark* = NARK *n.* (2)] [1950s+] an unpleasant person.

nause *n.* [abbr. SE *nausea*/*nauseating*] [1950s+] the problem, the difficulty, the annoying thing.

nause *v.* (*also* **noorse**) [NAUSE *n.*] [1950s+] to cause problems, to annoy, to ruin a plan.

(IN COMPOUNDS)

❑ **naused off** *adj.* [1950s+] furious, annoyed.

nausie *n.* (*also* **naussie**) [SE *new* + AUSSIE *n.*] [1950s+] (*Aus.*) a recently arrived immigrant.

nautch *n.* (*also* **nautchery, nautch house, nautch joint**) [Urdu/Hind. *nāch*, dancing, usu. as an exhibition of Indian dancing, thus a *nautch girl*, a dancing girl; the image of the 'exotic' East led inevitably to assumptions of sexual licence + HOUSE *n.*[1] (1)/JOINT *n.* (1)] [late 19C–1940s] (*US*) a brothel.

(IN COMPOUNDS)

❑ **nautch broad** *n.* [BROAD *n.*[2] (2)] [1940s] (*US*) a prostitute working in a brothel.

nautical miles *n.* (*also* **nauticals**) [rhy. sl. = piles] [20C+] haemorrhoids.

nav *n. see* NAVIGATOR *n.*

Navajo time *n.* [racist stereotyping] [20C+] (*US*) unpunctuality.

naval depôt *n.* (*also* **naval department**) [a pun on SE *navel*] [mid-19C] the stomach.

naval engagement *n.* (*also* **engagement**) [pun on SE *naval*/*navel*] [20C+] (*orig. milit.*) sexual intercourse.

navel *n.* [play on GUTSER *n.*[2] (1), i.e. the navel is placed near the stomach or 'guts'] [1910s] (*Aus.*) a misfortune.

navigator *n.* (*also* **nav**) [rhy. sl.; the connection with the predominantly Irish *navigators*, builders of Victorian Britain's railways and canals, whose stereotype consumed many potatoes, may or may not be coincidental] [mid-19C–1910s] a potato.

(IN COMPOUNDS)

❑ **navigator scot** *n.* [i.e. potatoes *hot*] [mid-19C] baked potatoes.

navigator of the windward passage *n. see under* WINDWARD PASSAGE *n.*

Navvy *n.* (*also* **navvy**) [abbr.] [1910s+] (*US, mainly southwest*) **1** a Navaho Indian. **2** a Navaho pony.

navvy *n.*

SE *navvy*, a labourer, in slang uses

(IN COMPOUNDS)

❑ **navvy's piano** *n.* [1920s+] a pneumatic drill. ❑ **navvy's prayer book** *n.* [SE *prayer-book*; the 'prayerful' posture the shoveller has to adopt] [late 19C–1900s] a shovel.

navy *n.* [*Navy* Cut, a brand of tobacco] [1900s–60s] a cigar or cigarette end left burning on the pavement.

Navy Office *n.* [pun on *fleet*/*Fleet*; the prison name refers to the Fleet River, itself f. OE *fléot*, a tidal inlet] [early–mid-19C] the Fleet Prison.

nawky *adj. see* NAUKY *adj.*

nawleed *n.* [ety. unknown] [2000s] (*US black*) the police.

naybo! *excl.* (*also* **nayboo! nayo! neighbo! neigho!**) [? SE *nay*, *no* + BO *n.*[1] (1)] [1930s+] (*US black*) used to express disagreement.

naygah *n.* (*also* **nyaga**) [NIGGER *n.*[1] (1)] [20C+] (*W.I.*) a derog. term for a person, oft. with combs.

(IN PHRASES)

❑ **white nayguh** *n.* [1960s] (*W.I.*) an albino.

naygar *n. see* NIGGER *n.*[1].

naygur *n. see* NIGGER *n.*[1].

nay-nay *adj.* [Scot./Irish *nig-nay*, a trifle, a plaything; but note Igbo *neni*, to disregard, to despise] [20C+] (*W.I.*) insignificant, worthless.

nay nays *n.* [NINNIES *n.*] [1950s+] the female breasts.

nayo! *excl. see* NAYBO! *excl.*

Nazarene foretop *n.* [SE *Nazarene*, a synon. for Christ + *foretop*, the lock of hair (whether real or in a wig) that covers the crown of the head] [late 18C–early 19C] an ornamental wig made in imitation of Christ's head of hair, as represented by painters.

nazie *adj.* (*also* **nazy, nazzy**) [for ety. *see* NASE *adj.*] [late 17C–mid-19C] drunk.

IN COMPOUNDS

▫ **nazie cove/mort** *n.* (*also* **nazzy..., nazy...**) [COVE *n.* (1)/MORT *n.*] [late 17C–early 19C] a drunken man (*cove*) or woman (*mort*). ▫ **nazie nab** *n. see* NASE NAB *under* NASE *adj.*

Nazi spy *n.* [rhy. sl.] [1940s+] (*Aus.*) a meat pie.

nazold *n.* [SE *nazzard*, an insignificant or feeble person] [early 17C] a silly, vain or weak-minded person.

nazy *adj. see* NAZIE *adj.*

nazy cove/mort *n. see* NAZIE COVE/MORT *under* NAZIE *adj.*

nazy nab *n. see* NASE NAB *under* NASE *adj.*

nazzy *adj. see* NAZIE *adj.*

nazzy cove/mort *n. see* NAZIE COVE/MORT *under* NAZIE *adj.*

n.b. *adj.* [*n*ot a *b*ean + pun on SE *N.B.*, *nota bene*, i.e. beware of such a pauper] [1900s–10s] penniless, impoverished.

n.b.a. *phr.* [abbr. *no balls at all*; BALLS *n.* (1)] [2000s] (*US black*) cowardly.

n.b.d. *phr.* [abbr. *no big deal*] [1980s+] (*US campus*) a general expression of nonchalance.

n.b.g. *phr.* [abbr.] [20C+] *no bloody good*.

n.c. *phr.*[1] [abbr. NUFF CED *phr.*; 'a certain theatrical manager spells the words, it is said, in this style' (Hotten, 1864)] [mid-19C–1900s] (*US*) enough said, it is possible to infer all the facts from what has already been stated.

n.c. *phr.*[2] [abbr. *no class*] [1980s+] (*US campus*) said of a boorish person.

n.c.a.a. *phr.* [abbr. *no class at all* + a jibe at the sporting *NCAA*, National Collegiate Athletic Assoc.; pron. 'NC double-A' based on N.C. *phr.*[2]] [1980s+] (*US campus*) said of a very boorish person.

nchonalanga *n.* [ety. unknown; presumably an African language] [2000s] (*S.Afr. prison*) prison gang lore.

Neapolitan favour *n.* (*also* **Neopolitan, Neapolitan bone-ache, ...button, ...court, ...disease, ...running-nag, ...scab, ...scurf**) [contemporary stereotyping of Italians as POX *n.*[1] (1) ridden] [late 16C–early 18C] syphilis; thus *Neapolitan*, a person who has syphilis.

near *adj.* (*also* **nearbegone**) [northern dial. *near*, grasping, covetous] [mid-19C+] miserly, cheap.

DERIVATIVES

▫ **neardy** *n.* [mid-19C] a boss, a master, an overseer. ▫ **nearness** *n.* [1900s] miserliness.

SE in slang uses

IN COMPOUNDS

▫ **near enough** *n. see* NIGH ENOUGH *n.* ▫ **near go** *n.* (*also* **near one**) [SE *near* + GO *n.*[1] (3)] [early 19C–1930s] a near thing a 'close shave'. ▫ **near-sighted** *adj.* [1920s+] (*US gay*) uncircumcised, esp. of an uncircumcised penis with its tip protruding slightly above the foreskin.

IN PHRASES

▫ **nearer my God to thee** *n.* [ironic use, the *God* in question being white and the subject's aspirations disapproved of by more politically motivated black peers] [1930s–40s] (*US black*) straight, silky hair, seen as a badge of whiteness.

near and far *n.* [rhy. sl.] **1** [late 19C+] a (public house) bar. **2** [1940s+] (*Aus.*) a motorcar.

neat *adj.* **1** [early–late 19C] in ironic use, rare, fine, delightful. **2** [20C+] (*orig./mainly US*) a term of general approval, pleasant, satisfactory, attractive.

IN COMPOUNDS

▫ **neat article** *n.* [early 19C] one who deliberately makes visits at mealtimes, so as to cadge a free meal. ▫ **neat thing** *n.* [mid-19C] good liquor.

neat *adv.* [late 19C–1900s] (*US Und.*) skilfully.

neatnik *n.* [SE *neat* + -NIK *sfx*] [1950s+] (*US*) someone devoted to neatness and order.

neato *adj.* [SE *neat* + -O *sfx* (5)] [1950s+] (*US teen*) good, excellent, a general term of approbation; often as excl.

IN EXCLAMATIONS

▫ **neato jet!** (*also* **neato torpedo!**) [1980s+] (*US teen*) extremely excellent! absolutely wonderful!

neb *n.*[1] [SE *neb*, a bird's beak; the term dates back to the *Ancren Riwle*, a devotional work composed *c.*1225] **1** [17C–19C] the mouth. **2** [late 17C–early 19C; 1960s] (*also* **nib**) a woman's face. **3** [late 19C+] (*Ulster*) the nose.

IN PHRASES

▫ **black neb** *n.* [20C+] (*Ulster*) a Presbyterian.

neb *n.*[2] [abbr. NEBBISH *n.*] [1920s–40s] (*US*) a nobody.

neb *v.* [NEB *n.*[1] (3)] [late 19C+] (*Ulster*) to interfere, to 'poke one's nose in'.

nebbie *n.* (*also* **neb**) [abbr.] [1960s+] *Nembutal*, a barbiturate.

nebbish *n.* (*also* **nebbich, nebich, nebish, neblish**) [synon. Yid. *nebech*] [late 19C+] a harmless eccentric, a born loser, a nobody; also attrib.

DERIVATIVES

▫ **nebbishy** *adj.* [1980s+] eccentric, insignificant, pitiful.

nebby *adj.*[1] [NEB *n.*[1] (3)] [late 19C+] (*Ulster*) nosy, inquisitive.

nebby *adj.*[2] [NEBBISH *n.*] [1990s+] (*US*) very unsophisticated.

nebich/nebish/neblish *n. see* NEBBISH *n.*

nebo *n.* [abbr. SE *inebriated* + -O *sfx* (3)] [1960s] (*Aus.*) a drunkard.

nebruary (morning) *n.* [SE *ne(ver)* + *(Fe)bruary*] [20C+] (*W.I.*) never.

nebuchadnezzar *n.* [*Nebuchadnezzar* II, (*c.*630–*c.*562 BC) King of Babylon; play on GREENS *n.*[1] and the King's madness, during which period he ate grass] **1** [19C] the penis. **2** [mid-19C–1900s] a vegetarian. **3** [mid-19C–1950s] (*Aus.*) a salad.

IN PHRASES

▫ **take Nebuchadnezzar out to grass** *v.* [19C] of a woman, to have sexual intercourse.

nec *n. see* CONNECTION *n.* (2).

necessaries *n.* [euph.] **1** [17C] the lavatory. **2** [1940s+] the genitals. **3** [1990s+] a condom.

necessary *n.* [all plays on the supposed necessity of such items] **1** [early 17C–early 19C] a bedfellow, usu. a female one [post mid-19C use is US]. **2** [early 17C–mid-19C] an outhouse, a privy. **3** [late 19C+] money. **4** [1990s+] what is required, e.g. intelligence.

necessary house *n.* [early 17C–1930s] an outhouse, a privy.

neck *n.* [lit. and fig. uses of SE *neck*] **1** [mid-19C+] the throat [NECK *v.* (1)]. **2** in fig. senses [orig. northern dial.; note also BRASS NECK *n.*]. (**a**) [late 19C+] (*also* **hard neck**) audacity, daring, impudence. (**b**) [1990s+] one who speaks impudently. **3** (*US*) in senses of stupidity. (**a**) [1900s] a fool. (**b**) [1960s–70s] foolishness, nonsense. **4** [1940s+] (*US campus*) in senses of physical sexuality [NECKING *n.*[1] (1)]. (**a**) the act of kissing and cuddling. (**b**) one with whom one kisses and cuddles. **5** [1960s+] [abbr. REDNECK *n.* (1)]. (**a**) (*US*) a poor farmer, usu. Southern and presumably racist and unsophisticated. (**b**) (*US campus*) a term of abuse. **6** *see* PENCIL-NECK *n.*

DERIVATIVES

▫ **neckful** *n.* [late 19C+] a quantity, usu. of a drink.

IN COMPOUNDS

▫ **neck-basting** *n.* [SE *baste*, to moisten, usu. in culinary context] [late 19C–1900s] drinking.

SE in slang uses

IN COMPOUNDS

▫ **neck bone** *n.* [BONE *v.*[2] (1)] [2000s] (*US black*) fellatio

❑ **neck cloth** *n.* (*also* **neck squeezer**) [late 18C–mid-19C] a hangman's rope. ❑ **neck oil** *n.* [note NECK *v.* (1)] [mid-19C+] alcohol, usu. beer. ❑ **neck stamper** *n.* [? he 'stamps' around carrying bottle by the 'neck'] [late 17C–early 19C] a tavern pot-boy. ❑ **neck verse** *n.* [anyone claiming benefit of clergy, and thus exemption from the gallows, was obliged to read in Lat. the first verse of Psalm 51, beginning *Miserere mei* (Have mercy upon me, o God...); the aim was to weed out false clergymen] [mid-16C–early 19C] a Lat. verse recited as a means of escaping the gallows. ❑ **neckweed** *n.* [mid-16C–early 19C] **1** hemp, the basic constituent of the rope used for the gallows. **2** the hangman's rope itself.

IN PHRASES

❑ **break one's neck** *v.* [1930s+] to make a special effort. ❑ **break one's neck for** *v.* (*also* **break one's neck after**) [late 19C+] to yearn for, to be desperate for. ❑ **break one's (own) neck** *v.* [? the weight of matrimonial responsibilities that form a yoke across one's neck] [1960s–70s] (*US*) to get married. ❑ **break the neck of** *v.* [synon. of SE *break the back of*] [late 19C] to commence, to set events in motions. ❑ **breathe down someone's neck** *v.* **1** [1930s+] to be physically close. **2** [1940s+] to be in hot pursuit or in competition. ❑ **dead neck** *n. see under* DEAD *adj.* ❑ **get it down one's neck** *v.* [20C+] to consume food or drink. ❑ **get it in the neck** *v.* see separate entry. ❑ **get one's neck wet** *v.* [1930s] (*US*) to become nervous. ❑ **get under one's neck** *v.* [horse-racing] [1930s+] (*Aus.*) to defeat or outwit someone. ❑ **go under one's neck** *v.* [horse-racing imagery] [1950s+] (*Aus.*) to take someone else's prerogative, to steal someone's idea, to stop someone else's intended actions. ❑ **neck it** *v.* [mid–late 19C] to stand, to exhibit moral courage. ❑ **neck over nozzle** [late 19C] head over heels. ❑ **no neck** *n.* [boxing jargon *no neck*, one who cannot take a punch; note sense 2a above] [1950s+] (*black*) a weakling, a coward. ❑ **on someone's neck** [1910s+] pressurizing or persecuting someone. ❑ **pull in one's neck** *v.* [the image of a tortoise] [1920s+] (*US*) to mind one's own business. ❑ **put it down one's neck** *v. see* WASH ONE'S NECK *under* WASH *v.* ❑ **rest one's neck** *v.* [2000s] (*US prison*) to be quiet, esp. as an imper. ❑ **shut one's neck** *v. see* SHUT ONE'S HEAD *under* HEAD *n.* ❑ **stick one's neck out** *v.* (*also* **put one's neck out, stick out one's neck**) [1920s+] (*orig. US campus*) to exceed one's brief, to interfere in affairs in which one is not directly concerned and often, having stuck out one's neck, fig. to have one's head cut off; in opposite sense, *wind in one's neck*, to modify one's behaviour. ❑ **swallow one's neck** *v. see under* SWALLOW *v.* ❑ **talk out of the side of one's neck** *v.* (*US black*) **1** [1950s+] to talk nonsense. **2** [1970s+] to talk surreptitiously to ensure that one's conversation remains unheard by eavesdroppers. **3** [1990s+] (*US prison*) (*also* **come out of the side of one's neck**) to talk disrespectfully. ❑ **talk through the back of one's neck** *v.* (*also* **talk out of the back of one's neck/head, ...the top of one's skull, ...through a hole in the back of one's neck, ...through one's neck**) [late 19C+] to talk nonsense, to talk rubbish. ❑ **talk through the top of one's neck** *v.* [1900s] (*Aus.*) to talk in an aristocratic manner.

IN EXCLAMATIONS

❑ **my neck!** [euph. var. on *MY ARSE! under* ARSE *n.*)] [late 19C+] (*Irish*) excl. of surprise or disbelief.

neck *v.* **1** [16C; mid-19C+] to swallow, either alcohol or (latterly) drugs. **2** pertaining to violence, lit. or fig. to the neck. (**a**) [mid-19C–1900s] (*US Und.*) to seize by the neck; by ext. to drag away. (**b**) [mid-19C–1900s] (*US*) to apprehend and arrest. (**c**) [late 19C+] (*Aus./US*) to garrotte. (**d**) [1940s+] (*Aus.*) to kill oneself by hanging. **3** [1910s–60s] (*US*) to stare [abbr. RUBBERNECK *v.* (3)]. **4** [1920s+] (*orig. US*) to pursue sexual pleasure that stops short of intercourse; usu. teen use and practice [orig. UK dial. *neck*, to court; i.e. to put one's arm around someone's neck]. **5** [1960s] (*US campus*) to work very hard [? one's neck is bent over the books].

DERIVATIVES

❑ **necking** *n.* [1910s] (*US*) an act of scrutiny or staring.

IN COMPOUNDS

❑ **neck job** *n.* [1940s+] a hanging; strangulation.

necker *n.* [NECK *v.* (4)] [1920s+] (*US*) one who engages in NECKING *n.*[1] (1).

necking *n.*[1] [NECK *v.* (4)] **1** [1920s+] kissing and cuddling. **2** [1940s] (*US Und.*) hanging. **3** [1960s] (*Aus.*) a means of pickpocketing whereby the thief puts one arm around his victim's neck and the other into his pocket.

IN COMPOUNDS

❑ **necking party** *n.* [1920s–50s] a session of embraces short of intercourse between a single couple.

necking *n.*[2] *see under* NECK *v.*

neckinger *n.* [it goes round the SE *neck*] [mid–late 19C] a cravat.

necklace *n.* **1** [17C] the neck. **2** [mid-17C–1960s] a hangman's noose. **3** [1940s+] (*Aus.*) a garrotter. **4** [1980s+] (*S.Afr.*) (*also* **necklacing**) the act of placing a petrol-soaked tyre around a victim's neck and setting it on fire [NECKLACE *v.*].

IN COMPOUNDS

❑ **necklace artist** *n.* (*also* **necktie artist**) [NECKLACE *n.* (3)/NECKTIE *n.* (1) + -ARTIST *sfx*] [1940s+] (*Aus.*) a garrotter.

necklace *v.* [1980s+] (*orig. S.Afr.*) to murder by placing a petrol-soaked tyre around a victim's neck and setting it alight.

necklaced *adj.* ['laced by the neck'] [1970s+] (*US black*) extremely sophisticated, worldly.

necklacing *n. see* NECKLACE *n.* (4).

necktie *n.* **1** [mid-19C–1950s] the hangman's noose. **2** [mid-19C–1950s] the gallows. **3** *see* COLOMBIAN NECKTIE *under* COLOMBIAN *n.*

necktie party *n.* (*also* **necktie frolic, ...sociable, ...social**) [NECKTIE *n.* (1)] **1** [late 19C+] (*US*) a hanging, usu. an illicit, impromptu lynching. **2** [1990s+] in fig. use.

nectar *n.* [SE *nectar*, popularly, albeit incorrectly known as the food of the gods (which is in fact *ambrosia*)] **1** [mid-18C+] alcohol; a drink [note use of *amber nectar* in adverts for Foster's (Aus.) lager]. **2** [1980s+] (*US campus*) anything exceptionally wonderful. **3** [1990s+] (*W.I.*) semen [note Williams (1994) for fig., use of *nectar* as vaginal secretions].

nectarine *n.* **1** [1910s] (*US*) a pretty young woman. **2** [2000s] (*S.Afr. gay*) a smooth, hairless anus. **3** *see* PEACH *n.*[1].

nectar pot *n. see* HONEYPOT *n.* (2).

nec ultra *n.* [Lat. *nec ultra*, and not beyond; the line beyond which one might not go was Temple Bar, the line between the West End and the City] [mid–late 19C] (*UK society*) the West End of London, thus the fashionable world.

Ned *n.* [generic uses of proper name] **1** [late 17C–1960s] the Devil. **2** [1910s] (*Aus.*) a term of address to a stranger.

IN PHRASES

❑ **raise Ned** *v.* (*also* **...merry Ned, ...old Harry, ...old Ned, ...Old Nick, ...promiscuous Ned**) [mid-19C+] to cause a disturbance, to make trouble.

ned *n.*[1] [ety. unknown; ? joc. use of proper name on pattern of JEMMY O'GOBLIN *n.*] **1** [mid-18C–mid-19C] a guinea. **2** [mid-19C–1930s] (*US*) a $10 gold piece.

IN PHRASES

❑ **half-a-ned** *n.* (*also* **half-ned**) **1** [late 18C–19C] ten shillings (50p). **2** [mid–late 19C] (*US*) a $5 gold piece.

ned *n.*[2] [orig. Ozark use *ned*, boar and thus generic for any pig] **1** [mid–late 19C] (*US*) a soldier, whose diet is mainly pork [from sense 2]. **2** [mid-19C–1950s] (*US*) salt pork or bacon, usu. constructed with *old*. **3** [1960s] (*US black*) a black person who curries favour with white society [? the image of such a figure being effectively a PIG *n.* (1a)].

ned *n.*[3] [? rhy. sl.] [1910s+] **1** (*orig. Aus.*) the head. **2** (*Aus.*) in a game of two-up, the *head* side of the coin.

ned *n.*[4] [orig. probation service abbr. *non-educated delinquent*] [1970s+] a hooligan, a thug, a petty criminal.

DERIVATIVES

❑ **neddy** *adj.* [2000s] pertaining to the hooligan underclass.
❑ **nedette** *n.* [2000s] a female ned.

ned *n.*[5] [ety. unknown] [2000s] (*Irish*) excrement.

nedash *n.* [Rom. *nastis*, I cannot] [early 19C] nothing.

neddie *n.* see NEDDY *n.*[4].

neddy *n.*[1] **1** [mid-17C–1960s] a donkey. **2** [early 19C+] a fool, a simpleton. **3** [late 19C+] a horse, esp. a racehorse.

(IN PHRASES)

❑ **the neddies** *n.* [20C+] (*Aus.*) the sport of horseracing.

neddy *n.*[2] [ext. NED *n.*[1] (1)] [mid-18C–mid-19C] a guinea.

neddy *n.*[3] [ety. unknown] [mid–late 19C] (*Irish*) a good deal, a considerable amount.

neddy *n.*[4] (*also* **neddie**) [abbr. KENNEDY *n.* (1)] [mid-19C+] (*UK Und.*) a cosh, blackjack or life-preserver.

neddy *n.*[5] [? play on use of MATILDA *n.* for the swag itself, to which the tucker-bag is tied, i.e. it dangles 'from her apron-strings' (*AND*)] [late 19C–1910s] (*Aus.*) the tucker-bag carried by an itinerant tramp.

neddy *v.* [NEDDY *n.*[4] (1)] [mid–late 19C] to hit with a cosh or blackjack.

neden *n.* [? SE *needing*, i.e. the woman's presumed desire for sex] [2000s] (*US black*) the female genitals.

ned fool *n.* [generic use of proper name *Ned* + SE *fool*] [late 16C–early 17C] a noisy fool, a simpleton.

Ned Kelly *n.*[1] [*Ned Kelly*, the bushranger (1855–80)] (*Aus.*) **1** [20C+] an unscrupulous businessman. **2** [1920s+] a 'blood-and-thunder' romance. **3** [1930s+] a poker machine.

(IN PHRASES)

❑ **Kelly gang** *n.* [20C+] an unethical business, a tax-grabbing government.

Ned Kelly *n.*[2] [rhy. sl.; ult. bushranger *Ned Kelly* (1855–80)] **1** [1920s+] (*Aus.*) the stomach [*belly*]. **2** [1970s] the television [*telly*].

Ned Kelly *v.* [see NED KELLY *n.*[1]] **1** [1900s] to bushrange. **2** [1950s] to kill a bird or any other game unsportingly.

ned skinner *n.* see JIMMY SKINNER *n.*

ned stokes *n.* [ety. unknown; ? anecdotal] [late 18C–mid-19C] the four of spades.

needful *n.* **1** [late 18C–1940s] money [the necessity of money or of money to life]. **2** [mid–late 19C] (*US*) whisky [thus fig. from sense 1, the necessity of alcohol].

(IN PHRASES)

❑ **do the needful** *v.* [1900s] to pay a bill.

Needham's shore *n.* (*also* **Needham's cross**) [play on SE *need 'em* and the Suffolk town of Needham Market] [late 16C] a state of great poverty.

needing a reef taken in *phr.* [19C] (*orig. naut.*) drunk.

needle *n.* **1** [17C+] the penis [later usage US]. **2** [late 18C–early 19C] (*also* **rank needle**) a confidence trickster [play on SE *sharp*/SHARP *n.*[1] (1); SE *rank*, extreme]. **3** [late 19C+] (*orig. tailoring jargon*) resentment, bitterness, irritation. **4** pertaining to drugs. (**a**) [1900s–50s] the shaking and twitching that accompanies withdrawal from heavy cocaine usage [one's reactions equate with those of one who has been jabbed with a needle]. (**b**) [1910s+] a hypodermic, a syringe, thus constr. with *the*, generic for narcotic use/addiction. (**c**) [1930s+] a narcotics addict. (**d**) [1950s] the immediate sensation, equivalent to an electric shock, that follows an injection of a drug. (**e**) [1990s+] (*US prison*) constr. with *the*, a lethal injection, as used in legal executions. **5** [1910s+] a knife. **6** [1930s+] (*US*) repetitious nagging and complaining; aggressive teasing.

(IN PHRASES)

❑ **get the needle** *v.* [late 19C+] to become annoyed.

pertaining to the penis

(IN COMPOUNDS)

❑ **needlecase** *n.* [SE *case*] [19C] the vagina. ❑ **needle-stuff** *n.* see STUFF *n.* (5b). ❑ **needle woman** *n.* [SE *woman*] [19C] a prostitute. ❑ **needlework** *n.* [SE *work*] [19C] sexual intercourse.

(IN PHRASES)

❑ **pick a needle without eye** *v.* [a SE *needle* without an eye is useless] [20C+] (*W.I.*) of a young woman, to give oneself in marriage to a man whom one knows will be of no use as a sexual partner. ❑ **thread the needle** *v.* (*also* **play at thread the needle**) [mid-16C–late 19C] to have sexual intercourse.

pertaining to narcotics

(IN COMPOUNDS)

❑ **needle artist** *n.* (*also* **needle fiend, ...jabber, ...knight, ...pumper**) [-ARTIST *sfx*] [1920s+] (*US drugs*) **1** an intravenous drug addict. **2** one who fetishizes the needle and the mechanics of injection. ❑ **needle freak** *n.* [-FREAK *sfx*] **1** [1960s+] (*US drugs*) an intravenous drug user who is as stimulated by the act of injection as by the action of the drug. **2** [1970s+] a prostitute's sadistic client who derives pleasure from hiring a woman with large breasts and paying her for every needle she permits him to stick into her flesh. ❑ **needlehead** *n.* [-HEAD *sfx* (4)] [1980s+] (*US drugs*) a narcotics addict. ❑ **needle man** *n.* (*also* **needleman**) [the use of a hypodermic syringe in both occupations] **1** [1920s+] (*drugs*) a drug addict. **2** [1960s+] (*US*) a doctor. ❑ **needle neddie** *n.* [? NEDDY *n.*[1] (3), a horse, with pun on HORSE *n.* (7)] [1980s+] (*Aus. prison*) the spoon in which one heats the heroin/water mixture prior to making an injection. ❑ **needle-nipper** *n.* [1950s] (*US drugs*) an intravenous narcotic addict. ❑ **needle palace** *n.* (*also* **needle house**) [1990s+] (*US drugs*) anywhere that narcotics drug users congregate to inject themselves. ❑ **needle park** *n.* [orig. the traffic island at Broadway and 71st Street; the term was popularized by James Mills's 1966 book *The Panic In Needle Park*] [1960s+] (*drugs*) a variety of locations in New York City, small oases of grass in the larger world of streets and buildings, frequented by heroin users. ❑ **needle pusher** *n.* **1** [1920s–30s] (*US drugs*) an addict who injects narcotics. **2** [1960s+] (*US*) a doctor or nurse. ❑ **needle shooter** *n.* see SHOOTER *n.*[2]. ❑ **needle shy** *adj.* [1930s–50s] (*US drugs*) of an addict, phobic of needles. ❑ **needleworker** *n.* [SE *worker*] [1910s] (*US*) a narcotics addict.

(IN PHRASES)

❑ **bend the needle** *v.* [1950s] to make a futile attempt to withdraw from addiction. ❑ **break the needle** *v.* **1** [1940s] to use up all the available drugs. **2** [1950s–70s] to attempt to end one's addiction to narcotics. ❑ **hit the needle** *v.* [1920s+] (*drugs*) to inject a drug. ❑ **needled up** *adj.* [1940s] (*US*) addicted to narcotics. ❑ **on the needle** [1940s+] (*drugs*) using narcotic drugs.

pertaining to irritation

(IN PHRASES)

❑ **cop the needle** *v.* [mid-19C+] to be annoyed. ❑ **get the needle** *v.* [mid-19C+] to be annoyed. ❑ **give someone the needle** *v.* (*also* **put the needle in**) **1** [late 19C+] to irritate. **2** [1920s] (*US*) to cuckold. **3** [1940s–60s] (*US*) to criticize. **4** [1990s+] (*US*) to kill. ❑ **have the needle** *v.* (*also* **have the dead needle, carry a needle**) [20C+] to be angry, irritated. ❑ **put in the needle** *v.* [1950s] to tease. ❑ **take the needle** *v.* [late 19C+] (*Irish*) to get angry.

SE in slang uses

(IN COMPOUNDS)

❑ **needle dick** *n.* see separate entry. ❑ **needle dodger** *n.* [mid-19C–1920s] a dressmaker. ❑ **needle-dodging** *n.* [1900s] dress-making. ❑ **needle jerker** *n.* [early 19C] a tailor. ❑ **needle-nose/-nosed** *n.* see separate entry. ❑ **needle-point/-pointing** *n.* see separate entry. ❑ **needle puncher** *n.* (*also* **needle queen**) [-PUNCHER *sfx* (1)/QUEEN *n.* (1)] [1960s+] (*US*) a doctor or nurse. ❑ **needle pusher** *n.* [1920s–40s] (*US*) a tailor.

needle *v.* **1** [early 19C] to haggle, esp. if one takes advantage of the other person. **2** [late 19C+] to annoy, to tease maliciously. **3** [late 19C+] to become annoyed. **4** [late 19C+] (*Irish*) to scrounge. **5** [1940s] to find one's way. **6** [1920s–60s] (*US*) to add alcohol or ether to a non-alcoholic beer or drink, usu. by injection through the cork. **7** [1970s] (*US Und.*) to drill a hole, e.g. in a safe.

(DERIVATIVES)

❑ **needled** *adj.* **1** [late 19C+] upset, annoyed. **2** [1920s] (*US*) intoxicated. **3** [1930s–50s] adulterated.

(IN COMPOUNDS)

❑ **needle beer** *n.* (*also* **needled beer, ...brew, shot beer**) [1920s+] (*US*) beer that has been strengthened by pure alcohol or ether. ❑ **needle-man** *n.* [1930s] (*US Und.*) one who adulterates beer.

needle and cotton *adj.* [rhy. sl.] [20C+] rotten.

needle (and pin) *n.* [rhy. sl.] [1910s+] gin.

needle and pin *adj.* [rhy. sl.] [1930s+] thin.

needle and thread *n.* [rhy. sl.] [mid-19C; 1960s+] bread.

needle dick *n.* [SE *needle* + DICK *n.*[1] (5); but note NEEDLE *n.* (1)] [1960s+] (*US*) a particularly small penis; thus the man who has one.

needle-nose *n.* [? backform. f. NEEDLENOSED *adj.*, as a stereotypical Jewish occupation] [1930s] a lawyer.

needlenosed *adj.* [occas., but not invariably, used of Jews] [1920s–70s] (*US*) having a pointed nose; thus *needlenose*, one who has such a nose.

needle point *n.* (*also* **needle pointer**) [like a *needle*, he is 'sharp'; ? an added ref. to the pricking of cards to mark them for cheating purposes] **1** [late 17C–mid-19C] a card-sharp or dice cheat. **2** [early–late 19C] an aggressive person.

needle-pointing *adj.* [NEEDLE POINT *n.* (1)] [mid-19C] (*UK Und.*) cheating.

needles and pins *n.* [rhy. sl.] [1990s+] twins.

needless mark-up *n.* [pun on name and the prices of its luxury goods] [1990s+] (*US*) a Neiman-Marcus department store.

need like a hole in the head *v. see under* HOLE IN ONE'S HEAD *n.*

needmore *n.* [the people *need more*] [1960s+] (*US*) a poor, usu. black, section of town.

needy *n.* [mid-19C–1920s] a tramp, a vagrant.

needy mizzler *n.* [NEEDY *n.* + MIZZLE *v.* (1)] [early–mid-19C] **1** a shabby beggar. **2** a tramp who leaves without paying for his lodging.

(IN COMPOUNDS)

❑ **needy-mizzling** *n.* [early–mid-19C] begging in rags to elicit more money.

neeger *n. see* NIGGER *n.*[1].

neener *n. see* NINA *n.*

neergs *n.* [backsl.] [mid-19C] greens, green vegetables.

neetewif *n.* (*also* **netewif**) [backsl.] [mid-19C] 15.

neetewif gens *n.* (*also* **netewif gens**) [backsl.; NEETEWIF *n.* + GEN *n.*[1]] [mid-19C] 15 shillings (75p).

neetexis *n.* (*also* **netexis**) [backsl.] [mid-19C] 16.

neetexis gens *n.* (*also* **netexis gens**) [backsl.; NEETEXIS *n.* + GEN *n.*[1]] [mid-19C] 16 shillings (80p).

neetrith gens *n.* [backsl.; GEN *n.*[1]] [mid-19C–1900s] 13 shillings (65p).

neetrouf *n.* (*also* **netrouf**) [backsl.] [mid-19C] the number 14.

neetrouf gens *n.* [backsl.; NEETROUF *n.* + GEN *n.*[1]] [mid-19C] 14 shillings (70p).

nef *n.* [abbr. of NEPHEW *n.* (2)] [2000s] (*US black*) term of address to any male.

neg *adj.* [abbr. SE *negligent*] [1960s] (*Aus.*) careless, incompetent.

neg! *excl.* (*also* **negat! negs!**) [abbr. SE *negative*] [1960s+] (*US, orig. milit.*) no! no to...!

negative! *excl.* [orig. in radio messages] [1940s+] no! no to...!

negative perspiration! *excl.* [play on colloq. *no sweat*] [1970s+] (*US*) no problem!

negatory *adv.* (*also* **negatrix, negatron**) [SE *negative*] [1950s+] (*US, orig. milit.*) no, negative.

negatory! *excl.* [NEGATORY *adv.*] [1950s+] no! absolutely not!

neger *n. see* NIGGER *n.*[1].

neggle *v. see* NIGGLE *v.*

nego *n.* [SE *negative* or Lat. *nego*, I deny] [1960s–70s] (*US campus*) a student with a negative or objectionable attitude.

negress *n.* [SE *negress* coined in late 18C but abandoned as prob. racist by 1960s for *black* and latterly *African-/Afro-American* or *person of color*, thus 21C slang use is consciously ironic] [2000s] (*US black*) a black woman.

negro head *n. see* NIGGERHEAD *n.*[1].

negs! *excl. see* NEG! *excl.*

neighbo!/neigho! *excl. see* NAYBO! *excl.*

Nell Gwyn *n.* [rhy. sl.; ult. *Nell Gwyn* (1650–87), mistress of Charles II] [20C+] gin.

nellie *n.* (*also* **nell, nelly**) [the female name, but note NELLIE (DUFF) *n.* (2); Puxley, *Cockney Rabbit: A Dick 'n' Arry of Rhyming Slang* (1992), suggests rhy. sl. *nellie dean* (a popular song) = QUEEN *n.* (2)] **1** [1910s+] an overtly homosexual, effeminate man. **2** [1960s] as a term of address between homosexual men. **3** [1960s+] a general term of disparagement, a fool. **4** [1970s+] (*US campus*) a lesbian.

(IN COMPOUNDS)

❑ **nelly-assed** *adj.* [-ASSED *sfx*] [1960s–70s] (*US gay*) effeminate.

(IN PHRASES)

❑ **nellie (out)** *v.* (*also* **nelly (out)**) [2000s] to act in an effeminate manner.

nellie *adj.* (*also* **nelly**) [NELLIE *n.* (1)] [1960s+] very effeminate.

nellie *v.* (*also* **nelly**) [2000s] (*S.Afr. gay*) to have sexual intercourse.

Nellie Bligh *n. see* NELLY (BLIGH) *n.*

nellie (deans) *n.* (*also* **nelly (deans)**) [rhy. sl.; ? popular song 'Nellie Dean'] **1** [20C+] vegetables, i.e. greens. **2** [1940s] (*S.Afr. drugs*) marijuana.

nellie (duff) *n.* (*also* **nelly (duff)**) [rhy. sl.] [20C+] **1** one's breath [PUFF *n.* (1)]. **2** a male homosexual [PUFF *n.* (3a)].

Nellie Pope *n.* [rhy. sl. = DOPE *n.*[1] (6)] [2000s] (*S.Afr.*) marijuana.

nelly *see also under* NELLIE and its combs.

nelly *n.* (*also* **nelly's death, nellie's downfall**) [generic use of fem. name; its effects] **1** [1940s–50s] (*Aus.*) cheap wine. **2** [1970s] (*Aus.*) semen.

Nelly (Bligh) *n.* (*also* **Nellie ..., Nelly Bly**) [rhy. sl.; ult. *Nellie Bly*, the pseudonym of Elizabeth Cochran Seaman (1864–1922), famous pioneering feminist newspaper reporter, who acquired her pen name from the title of a popular song at the time] [1910s+] **1** a tie. **2** (*Aus.*) a meat pie. **3** an eye, usu. in pl. **4** the trousers' fly. **5** a fly; often in pl. **6** a lie.

nelly kelly *n.* [rhy. sl.] [20C+] (*Aus.*) the belly.

Nelson Eddies *n.* [rhy. sl. = READIES *n.*; ult. US singer/actor *Nelson Eddy* (1901–67)] [1930s+] money, cash.

Nelson Eddy *adv.* [rhy. sl.; for ety. see NELSON EDDIES *n.*] [1930s+] ready.

Nelson (Mandela) *n.* [rhy. sl. = *Stella*; ult. former S.Afr. President Nelson *Mandela* (b.1918)] [1990s+] Stella Artois lager.

Nelson (Riddle) *n.* [rhy. sl. = PIDDLE *n.* (2); ult. US composer/arranger *Nelson Riddle* (1921–85)] [1980s+] (*Aus.*) an act of urination.

nembie *n.* (*also* **nemmie**) [abbr.] [1940s+] (*drugs*) Nembutal, a barbiturate.

nemish *n.* [abbr.] [1960s–70s] (*drugs*) Nembutal, a barbiturate.

nemmo *n. see* NAMMO *n.*

nenne *n.*

(IN PHRASES)

❑ **live at your nenne** *v. see live at your aunt* at AUNT *n.*

nennen *n.* [? NAY-NAY *adj.* or redup. of Twi *ne*, to defecate] [20C+] (*W.I.*) backside, buttocks.

neo maxi zoom dweebie *n.* [ext. of DWEEB *n.*; popularized/coined? by 1985 film *The Breakfast Club*] [1980s+] (*US*) an inconsequential or obnoxious person.

neon *n.* [it shines] [1970s] (*US*) an eye.

Nep *n.* (*also* **Nepalese**) [abbr.] [1960s+] (*drugs*) Nepalese hashish.

nephew *n.* [generic use of SE *nephew* as a euph. for NIGGA *n.*] **1** [1950s] (*US Und.*) a young homosexual boy (cf. AUNTIE *n.*[2] (1)). **2** [2000s] (*US teen*) a friend, thus as a term of affectionate address.

nephy *n. see* NEVVY *n.*

Neptune's daughter *n.* [rhy. sl.] [1930s–70s] (*US*) water.

nerd *n.* (*also* **nurd**) [? euph. for TURD *n.*[1] or infl. by 'Mortimer Snerd' a dummy used by US ventriloquist Edgar Bergen (1903–78), or f. line in *If I Ran a Zoo* (1950) by the children's author Dr Seuss (Theodore Seuss Geisel, 1904–91): 'And then, just to show them,/ I'll sail to Ka-Troo/And Bring Back an It-Kutch, a Preep and a Proo,/ a Nerkle, a Nerd, and a Seersucker, too!'] **1** [1950s+] (*orig. US*) an unpleasant, insignificant or dull person. **2** [1960s+] (*campus/teen*) (*also* **nerdbomber**) anyone outside a peer group and who thus fails to fit in with 'the gang', esp. a studious individual who eschews drink, drugs and similar teen pleasures.

DERIVATIVES

❑ **nerdy** *adj.* (*also* **nurdy**) [1960s+] (*orig. US*) **1** used of any form of speech or behaviour that is judged to be socially unacceptable by the speaker(s). **2** obsessive; the image is of a train-spotter. ❑ **nerdiness** *n.* [1960s+] the quality of being a nerd.

IN COMPOUNDS

❑ **nerd magnet** *n.* [1980s] (*US campus*) a young woman or girl who attracts boring, unattractive men. ❑ **nerd pack** *n.* [1980s+] (*US*) a plastic, sectioned liner for the breast pocket that keeps pens from soiling the cloth.

nerd *v.* [NERD *n.* (2)] [1980s+] (*US campus*) to study hard.

nerf *v.* [? SE *nerve*, i.e. one has to have strong nerves to perform the manoeuvre] [1940s+] (*US, orig. drag-racing*) to bump another vehicle slightly with one's own car.

nerf- *pfx* [brandname of a line of foam-rubber toys] [1980s+] (*US*) used to express stupidity e.g. *nerf-brained*, stupid.

nerf bar *n.* (*also* **nerfing bar**) [NERF *v.*] [1940s+] (*US*) a bumper fitted to a customized car.

nerk *n.* [? var. on BERK *n.*] [1950s+] a fool, a yob, a generally unappetizing, unacceptable person.

nerts *n.* [var. on NUTS *n.*[2] (1)] [1930s–40s] (*US*) the testicles.

nerts *adj.* (*also* **nertz**) [var. on NUTS *adj.*] [1910s+] (*US*) crazy, foolish.

nerts! *excl.* (*also* **gnerts! nertz!**) [var. on NUTS! *excl.*] [1920s+] (*US*) nonsense!

nerver *n.* [it strengthens one's nerves] [late 19C–1920s] a bracing drink, a 'pick-me-up'.

nerver-up *n.* (*also* **nerver, nerve-up**) [they 'have a nerve' to appear uninvited] [1900s–30s] (*US*) a gate-crasher.

nervo and knox *n.* [rhy. sl. *nervo and knox*; ult. Jimmy *Nervo* (1890–1975) and Teddy *Knox* (1896–1974), music-hall comedians and members of the Crazy Gang (1935–62)] **1** [1940s+] socks. **2** [1940s+] venereal disease, esp. syphilis [POX *n.*[1]]. **3** [1960s+] television [the BOX *n.*[1] (4)].

nervous *adj.* [1920s+] (*US, orig. jazz*) excellent, thrilling; strange.

SE in slang uses

IN COMPOUNDS

❑ **nervous burger** *n.* [2000s] (*N.Z.*) a cigarette. ❑ **nervous finger** *n.* [? 'he can't keep his hands still'] [1940s] (*US Und.*) one given to small-time criminality. ❑ **nervous nellie** *n.* (*also* **nervous nelly**) [orig. used of Frank B. Kellogg, Secretary of State (1925–29)] [1920s+] (*US*) a fearful, foolish and timid person. ❑ **nervous pudding** *n.* (*also* **nervous salad**) [it shakes] [1930s–40s] (*US*) a dish made with gelatine or aspic.

nervous wreck *n.* (*also* **I'm a wreck, total wreck**) [rhy. sl.] [1940s+] a cheque.

Nescafé *n.* [the gesture, based on the shaking of a jar of coffee, imitates that of male masturbation and thus means WANKER *n.* (2); ? also rhy. sl. *Gareth Hunt* (the star of the Nescafé adverts who shook the coffee) = CUNT *n.* (4)] [1990s+] a hand gesture used to indicate one's contempt.

nest *n.* **1** [late 16C+] the vagina [20C+ usage US]. **2** [1940s+] (*Aus.*) sexual intercourse. **3** [1960s+] (*US*) the women who make up a pimp's collection of prostitutes.

IN PHRASES

❑ **nest in the bush** *n.* [late 17C–19C] the vagina. ❑ **on the nest** [1940s+] **1** (*US*) pregnant. **2** (*Aus.*) of a man, having sexual intercourse.

nest *v.* [1910s–30s] (*US*) to squat, to make a homestead.

nester *n.* [SE *nest*/NEST *v.*] [late 19C–1950s] (*US West*) a squatter, a homesteader, a farmer, a small rancher; thus *Nestersville*, a small, out-of-the-way settlement.

nestlecock *n.* (*also* **nestcock**) [SE *nestle* + COCK *n.*[3] (1)] [mid-17C–19C] a prostitute.

nest of sparrows flying out of one's backside *phr. see under* SPARROW *n.*

net *n.*[1] [backsl.] [mid-19C] the number ten.

net *n.*[2]

SE in slang uses

IN PHRASES

❑ **drop a net on** *v. see under* DROP *v.*[1]. ❑ **get the net** [the image of the 'men in white coats' brandishing a net with which they capture the 'mad' person] [1980s+] a joc., teasing comment aimed at someone whose behaviour is seen as strange or eccentric.

netarnal *adj. see* NATARNAL *adj.*

netenin *n.* [backsl.] [mid-19C] 19.

netenin gens *n.* [backsl.; NETENIN *n.* + GEN *n.*[1]] [mid-19C] 19 shillings (95p).

netewif *see under* NEETEWIF and combs.

netexis *see under* NEETEXIS and combs.

net-gen *n. see* GEN NET *n.*

netheg *n.* (*also* **net-theg**) [backsl.] [mid-19C] 18.

nether *adj.* used in combs. pertaining to the female genitals.

IN COMPOUNDS

❑ **nether end** *n.* [mid-18C–9C] the vagina. ❑ **nether eye** *n.* [19C] the vagina. ❑ **nether eyebrow** *n.* (*also* **nether lashes ...whiskers**) [18C–19C] the pubic hair. ❑ **nether lips** *n.* [mid-17C–19C] the vagina. ❑ **nether mouth** *n.* [mid-18C] the vagina.

Netherlands *n.* **1** [late 16C–18C] the vagina. **2** [late 18C–early 19C] the buttocks.

nethers *n.* [NETHERSKEN *n.*] [mid–late 19C] lodging-house charges

nethersken *n.* [SE *nether*, used in names of places to mea[n] lower, low + KEN *n.*[1] (1)] [mid–late 19C] a cheap lodging house frequented by beggars, criminals and the very poor.

netnevis *n.* [backsl.] [mid-19C] 17.

netnevis gens *n.* [backsl.; NETNEVIS *n.* + GEN *n.*[1]] [mid-19C] 1[7] shillings (85p).

netrouf *n. see* NEETROUF *n.*

net-theg *n. see* NETHEG *n.*

net-theg gens *n.* [backsl.; NETHEG *n.* + GEN *n.*[1]] [mid-19C] 1[8] shillings (90p).

nettle bed *n.* [early 18C–mid-19C] (*juv.*) the vagina.

netty *v.* [? NUTTY *adj.*[2] (2)] [1940s] (*W.I.*) to be funny.

net-yeneps *n.* [backsl.; NET *n.*[1] + YENNEP *n.*] [mid-19C] te[n] pence.

neuck *n. see* NYUCK *n.*

neuf-soixante *n. see* SIXTY-NINE *n.*

neuk *v.* [Du. *neuken*, to knock] (*S.Afr.*) **1** [1910s+] to beat u[p]. **2** [1980s+] to interfere, to mess with.

nevele *n.* (*also* **nevel**) [backsl.] [mid-19C] the number 11.

nevele gens *n.* [backsl.; NEVELE *n.* + GEN *n.*[1]] [mid-19C] 1[1] shillings (55p).

nevele yeneps *n. see* LEVEN YENNEPS *n.*

never, the *n.*

IN PHRASES

❑ **on the never** **1** [late 19C–1950s] (*Aus.*) taking advantage [of] luck; looking after one's own interests. **2** [late 19C] (*Aus. Und.*) working a form of confidence trick.

never *adv.*

SE in slang uses

IN COMPOUNDS

❑ **never-out** *n.* [it is 'inside' the body] [19C] the vagin[a].

❑ **never-ready morning** *n.* [var. on NEBRUARY (MORNING) *n.*] [20C+] (*W.I.*) never. ❑ **never-see-come-see** *n.* [ext. of SE] **1** [20C+] (*W.I.*) an unsophisticated person, seeing the sophisticated world for the first time. **2** [1990s+] anyone showing off their new status or possessions. ❑ **never-sweat** *n.* *see under* SWEAT *n.* ❑ **never-wag (man of war)** *n.* [WAG *v.* (1)] [late 18C–19C] the Fleet prison, London. ❑ **never-was** *n.* (*also* **never-waser, never-wozzer, never-wuzzer**) ['he *never was* any good'; as opposed to a *has-been*] [late 19C+] (*US*) one who never rose above mediocrity.

IN PHRASES

❑ **never been kissed** *n.* (*also* **never had it**) [the supposed sexual innocence of a 17-year-old girl] [1940s+] (*bingo*) the number 17. ❑ **never hachi** (*also* **never hotchie**) [play on SE *never* + mispron.] [1950s+] (*US*) (it will) never happen. ❑ **never happen** [1950s+] used to dismiss any idea that the speaker cannot support or wishes to deny.

never again *n.* [rhy. sl. *never again* = Ben (Truman), a beer brewed in East London] [20C+] beer.

never better *n.* [rhy. sl.] [20C+] (*Aus.*) a letter.

never fear *n.* [rhy. sl.] [mid-19C] a pint of beer.

never-never, the *n.* (*also* **never-never country, the, never-never land, the, never, the**) [coined *c.*1830, the name gained wide popularity with the book *We of the Never-Never* (1908) by Mrs Aeneas Gunn; despite the logic of the English term, it may in fact come from Comderoi *nievah vahs*, unoccupied land, although this equally may be pure coincidence; on either count it precedes J.M. Barrie's coinage in *Peter Pan* (1904) by more than half a century; note Aborigine use as 'heaven' in Boldrewood (1888): 'I want to die and go up with him to the never-never country parson tell us about'] [mid-19C+] (*Aus./N.Z.*) the deep, deserted interior of Australia.

never-never (land) *n.* (*also* **Peter Pan's Never-Never Land**) [one *never* finishes paying for one's purchase] [late 19C+] the hire purchase system.

IN PHRASES

❑ **on the never-never** (*also* **on the never**) [late 19C+] bought on hire purchase.

never stand still *n.* (*also* **can't-keep-still**) [rhy. sl., accentuated by the endless movement of the machine] [19C] a prison treadmill.

Neville Nobody *n.* [1990s+] (*Aus.*) an insignificant individual.

nevis *n.* (*also* **neves**) [backsl.] **1** [mid-19C+] the number seven. **2** [late 19C+] (*UK prison*) a seven-year sentence. **3** [1950s+] £7.

IN COMPOUNDS

❑ **nevis gens** *n.* [GEN *n.*[1]] [mid-19C] 7 shillings (35p). ❑ **nevis stretch** *n.* [STRETCH *n.* (1c)] [mid-19C] a seven-year sentence. ❑ **nevis yeneps** *n.* (*also* **neves-yenep**) [YENNEP *n.*] [mid-19C] seven pence.

nevvy *n.* (*also* **nephy, nevoy, nevy**) [abbr.; post mid-19C use mainly UK public schools] [early 19C–1930s] a nephew.

new *n.* [note 19C RN training ship jargon *news*, the latest recruits] [1920s] (*US tramp*) a novice within the hobo community.

new *adj.* **1** [mid-19C–1950s] (*US*) cheeky, insolent. **2** [late 19C–1900s; 1990s+] (*US*) naïve and gullible.

SE in slang uses

IN COMPOUNDS

❑ **new boot** *n.* [BOOT *v.*[1] (1a)] [2000s] (*US prison*) a new prison officer. ❑ **new booty** *n.* [BOOTY *n.*[2] (3)] [1990s+] (*US black gang*) a new member of a gang. ❑ **new bran** *adj.* [inversion] [1990s+] (*W.I./UK black teen*) brand new. ❑ **new chum** *n.* *see* separate entry. ❑ **new cock** *n.* [COCK *n.*[2]] [mid-19C–1960s] (*UK prison*) a new inmate. ❑ **new double-six** *n.* (*also* **next double six**) [*double six* = 12 (months)] [1940s–70s] (*US black*) the New Year. ❑ **new hand** *n.* [HAND *n.*[1] (1)] [late 19C–1910s] **1** (*Aus.*) a newly arrived immigrant. **2** a first-time prisoner. ❑ **new hat** *n.* [? the price of such an object] [late 19C] a guinea. ❑ **new iniquity** *n.* [play on *old identity* under OLD *adj.*] [mid–late 19C] (*Aus./N.Z.*) an immigrant. ❑ **new jack** *n.* *see* separate entry. ❑ **new jill** *n.* *see* NEW JACK *n.* ❑ **new light** *n.* *see* separate entries. ❑ **new magic** *n.* [its 'magical' effects] [1970s+] (*drugs*) phencyclidine. ❑ **new meat** *n.* [MEAT *n.* (5)] **1** [1930s+] (*US prison*) a new inmate. **2** [1960s+] (*US campus*) a freshman. **3** [1980s] (*US*) a new army recruit. ❑ **new nayga** *n.* (*also* **new nigger**) [fig. use of NAYGAH *n.*/NIGGER *n.*[1] (1)] [1940s] (*W.I.*) a parvenu, a nouveau riche. ❑ **new school** *adj.* *see under* SCHOOL *n.*

IN PHRASES

❑ **what else is new?** [1950s+] (*orig. US*) deprecating comment on anything the previous speaker has said, esp. if that speaker had intended to make a big impression; a general dismissive rejoinder, often prefaced with *so*… ❑ **what's new?** (*also* **what's the new?**) [1910s+] a general greeting.

newbie *n.* (*also* **newbee, newby**) [? SE *new boy*] **1** [1970s+] (*orig. US milit.*) a new member, a recruit, a novice. **2** [2000s] (*US black*) a neophyte prostitute.

newbie *adj.* [NEWBIE *n.* (1)] [1970s+] (*US*) new, uninitiated, novice.

new chum *n.* [SE *new* + CHUM *n.*] **1** [early 19C–1950s] (*Aus./N.Z./UK Und.*) (*also* **chum, chummy**) a prisoner just arrived in gaol, on the hulks or in Aus. or N.Z.; later an immigrant to Aus. or N.Z. **2** [mid-19C+] a newly arrived immigrant, a novice, an inexperienced person.

new-chum *adj.* [NEW CHUM *n.*] [mid-19C+] (*Aus./N.Z.*) inexpert, raw.

DERIVATIVES

❑ **new-chum-ish** *adv.* [mid-19C] in an inexpert, raw manner.

IN COMPOUNDS

❑ **new-chum gold** *n.* [a newly arrived 'digger' might be fooled into thinking he had discovered the real metal] [mid-19C+] (*Aus.*) iron pyrites, 'fool's gold'.

New College *n.* [? its function as one of the sites where, trad., a new sovereign is proclaimed] [late 17C–early 19C] the Royal Exchange, London.

New Delhi *n.* [rhy. sl.] [20C+] the stomach, the belly.

IN PHRASES

❑ **New Delhi belly** *n.* *see* DELHI BELLY *n.*

Newf *n.* (*also* **Newfie**) [abbr.; *Newfies* are the 'Irish' or 'Poles' of Canada, rural, isolated and thus considered backward and stupid] **1** [1940s+] (*orig. Can.*) a *Newf*oundlander, also attrib. **2** [1940s+] (*US*) *Newf*oundland. **3** [1970s+] (*US*) a *Newf*oundland dog.

Newgate *n.* [the first *Newgate* prison was built near the New Gate in the old City Wall in the 12C, poss. earlier. A gaol stood on the site until the last one was demolished to make way for the Old Bailey in 1901. The original prison was rebuilt by Richard 'Dick' Whittington; this one was burned down during the Great Fire (1666) and rebuilt again in 1672 (it included a statue of Whittington plus cat in its ornamentation). This in its turn was demolished and again rebuilt in 1770–1. This version was destroyed during the Gordon Riots of 1780, and a final *Newgate* was put up in 1781. Public hangings took place in the street outside until 1868] **1** [16C–early 19C] any prison. **2** [1930s] (*UK Und.*) the inside jacket pocket.

IN COMPOUNDS

❑ **Newgate bird** *n.* [BIRD *n.*[1] (1)] [early 17C–19C] a prisoner, esp. a sharper (not necessarily imprisoned in Newgate). ❑ **Newgate collar** *n.* (*also* **Newgate frill, …fringe**) [its being fancifully reminiscent of the hangman's noose] [19C; 2000s] a collar-like beard worn under the chin. ❑ **Newgate fringe** *n.* [mid–late 19C] a moustache and beard, but no side-whiskers. ❑ **Newgate hornpipe** *n.* [hangings were conducted outside Newgate prison; the victim would DANCE *v.* (2) as they choked to death] [early 19C] a hanging. ❑ **Newgate knocker** *n.* [joc. use of SE + ? implication that those who sported such a style tended to criminality] [mid-19C–1900s] a lock of hair shaped like the figure 6 and twisted from the temple back towards the ear. ❑ **Newgate nightingale** *n.* [play on BIRD *n.*[1] (1)] [16C] a novice criminal. ❑ **Newgate nob** *n.* (*also* **Newgate stallion**) [NOB *n.*[1] (1)] [18C–mid-19C] a criminal type of person. ❑ **Newgate saint (canonized at the Old Bailey)** *n.* [18C–19C] a prisoner under sentence of death. ❑ **Newgate solicitor** *n.* [early 18C–19C] a second-rate lawyer who hangs around prisons (including but not invariably Newgate) in the hope of picking up work.

IN PHRASES

❑ **black/dark as Newgate** *adj. see* BLACK AS… *adj.* ❑ **dance the Newgate hornpipe** *v. see under* DANCE *v.* ❑ **do the Newgate frisk** *v.* [19C] to be hanged.

Newgate gaol *n.* [rhy. sl.] [late 19C] a tale, esp. of the 'hard-luck' variety.

newie *n.* (*also* **newy**) **1** [mid-19C–1970s] (*US campus*) a new student, a newcomer. **2** [20C+] (*Aus.*) a new immigrant; a new arrival. **3** [1950s+] (*Aus.*) anything new or hitherto unknown.

newington butts *n.* (*also* **newingtons**) [rhy. sl. = GUT *n.* (1); ult. *Newington Butts* a south London thoroughfare] [20C+] the stomach.

new jack *n.* [SE *new* + JACK *n.*[2] (3)] **1** [1980s+] (*mainly US black*) a newcomer or novice, esp. to the fast life of the ghetto streets. **2** [2000s] (*US black*) a sophisticate, someone who has succeeded in the ghetto culture; the female equivalent is *new jill*.

new jack *adj.* [NEW JACK *n.*] [1980s+] (*US black*) **1** superficial, flashy, meretricious. **2** in tune with the contemporary young black culture.

IN COMPOUNDS

❑ **New Jack City** *n.* [1990s+] (*US black*) Detroit, New York City or any other city with a thriving ghetto lifestyle.

newk *n.* [orig. milit.] [1970s+] (*US campus*) a newcomer, a novice.

newky (brown) *n.* [orig. Newcastle only, but gradually adopted throughout the UK] [1970s+] Newcastle Brown Ale.

newlicks *n. see* NOOLUCKS *n.*

new light *n.*[1] [16C SE *new light*, novel religious views or doctrines; the term covered a variety of 18C Protestant sects in the UK and US] [mid-18C–19C] a Methodist.

new light *n.*[2] [LIGHT *n.* (3)] [mid-19C] (*UK Und.*) newly coined money.

Newman's *adj.* [SE *New(gate)* + -MANS *sfx*] [19C] pertaining to Newgate prison.

IN COMPOUNDS

❑ **Newman's (college)** (*also* **Newman's hotel, …tea-gardens**) [SE *college*/HOTEL *n.* (2)/pun on SE *tea-gardens*] [19C] Newgate prison. ❑ **Newman's lift** *n.* [early–mid-19C] the gallows, erected outside Newgate prison.

Newmarket Heath commissioner *n.* [*Newmarket Heath* was a popular site for highway robbery] [19C] a highwayman.

Newmarket pound *n.* [the use of guineas (£1.05p) rather than pounds for transactions at Newmarket, a centre of horseracing and breeding] [18C] a guinea, one pound and one shilling.

New River Head *n.* [the *New River Head*, a group of reservoirs at Clerkenwell, North London] [late 18C–early 19C] tears.

news *n.*

SE in slang uses

IN COMPOUNDS

❑ **news bug** *n.* [dial. *news-bug*, a wood-boring beetle, the appearance of which is supposed to portend coming news] [1950s] (*W.I.*) a gossip. ❑ **news butcher** *n.* [late 19C+] (*US*) a seller of newspapers, sweets etc on a train. ❑ **news hawk** *n.* (*also* **newshog, newshound**) [SE *news* + SE *hawk*/-HOUND *sfx*] **1** [1910s+] (*orig. US*) a newspaper reporter. **2** [1950s–70s] (*US*) a newspaper seller. ❑ **news hen** *n.* [SE *news* + HEN *n.* (1)] [1940s–70s] (*US*) a female journalist.

newsie *n.* (*also* **newsy**) [abbr. SE *newsboy*] **1** [late 19C+] (*US*) a seller of newspapers in the street; orig. boys and girls only, the term spread, as did the job, to include adults. **2** [1950s+] (*US*) a news broadcaster or journalist. **3** [2000s] a newsagent's.

news of the day *n.* [where people exchange news and gossip] [late 19C] (*UK Und.*) a public house.

News of the Screws *n.* (*also* **Screws**) [assonance + SCREW *n.*[1] (1), punning on its propensity for sex stories] [1990s+] nickname for the UK Sunday paper, the *News of the World*.

new south *n.* [rhy. sl.; ult. *New South Wales*] [1990s+] (*Aus.*) the mouth.

newspaper *n.* **1** [1900s] (*US*) marked cards. **2** [1920s–40s] (*US Und.*) 30 days in prison [the time it supposedly takes an illiterate person to read one].

Newstralian *n.* [1950s] (*Aus.*) a New Australian, i.e. any immigrant, usu. from continental Europe, whose first language is not English.

newsy *n. see* NEWSIE *n.*

newt *n.* [SE *neuter* or *neutral*] [1920s+] (*US campus*) a stupid, unsophisticated or socially inadequate person.

newted *adj.* [backform. f. *pissed as a newt* (see PISSED *adj.*[1])] [1970s+] drunk.

Newton and Ridley *adj.* [rhy. sl.; = TIDDLY *adj.*; ult. the fictional beer/brewery of the TV soap opera *Coronation Street*, which features in its pub 'Rovers Return'] [1990s+] tipsy, drunk.

newy *n. see* NEWIE *n.*

New York *n.*

SE in slang uses

IN COMPOUNDS

❑ **New York City silver** *n.* (*also* **New York City white**) [1970s+] (*drugs*) an imaginary brand of marijuana, silver/white because its seeds have grown in darkness, after being flushed away into the sewer system. ❑ **New York minute** *n.* (*also* **city minute, New York second**) [the city's non-stop energy] [1920s+] (*US*) an instant. ❑ **New York nippers** *n.* [rhy. sl.] [1930s+] kippers. ❑ **New York tubesteak** *n.* [late 19C+] (*orig. US*) a spiced, heated sausage or frankfurter, served on a split roll and garnished, trad., with 'rags and paint' (sauerkraut and mustard).

New York *v.* [the supposed similarity between the sound of *york* and that of retching] [1950s] (*W.I.*) to retch, to vomit.

New Zealand *n.*

SE in slang uses

IN COMPOUNDS

❑ **New Zealand death** *n.* (*also* **national death**) [its contemporary commonness] [mid-19C+] (*N.Z.*) drowning. ❑ **New Zealand green** *n.* [2000s] (*N.Z.*) indigenously grown marijuana. ❑ **New Zealand mutton** *n.* [there is no mutton in New Zealand because lamb is so popular there] [late 19C] (*N.Z.*) pork.

Newzie *n.* [abbr.] [1940s] (*N.Z.*) a *New* Zealander.

next cab off the rank *n. see FIRST CAB OFF THE RANK under* FIRST *adj.*

next (to) *phr.* [late 19C+] (*US*) **1** aware, knowledgeable, informed, sophisticated; as n. a state of being thus informed, etc. **2** close, friendly.

IN PHRASES

❑ **get next to** *v.* (*also* **get next**) **1** [late 19C–1910s] (*US*) to get for oneself. **2** [late 19C–1950s] to become suspicious, to work something out. **3** [late 19C–1970s] (*US*) to make a good impression, to curry favour with, to win over. **4** [1920s+] (*US black*) to become lovers, to seduce. **5** [1950s–70s] (*US black*) to feel friendly towards, to tolerate. **6** [1970s] to become business partners with. **7** [1970s+] (*US black*) to embarrass, to annoy, to anger. ❑ **put next to** *v.* [late 19C+] (*US*) **1** to introduce, to direct towards. **2** to warn, to inform.

nexus *n.* (*also* **bromo, spectrum, 2CB**) [one of a large number of psychoactive substances first isolated by the American libertarian pharmacologist Dr Alexander Shulgin (b.1925), including DOM, STP, DOB, DOI and MDMA] [1980s+] (*drugs*) 2C–B, a hallucinogen similar to LSD but without some of its more extreme side effects; most potent when used in conjunction with MDMA.

n.f. *n.* [abbr.] **1** [late 19C–1900s] *no fool*. **2** [1970s] (*US campus*) *no fun*.

n.f.g. *phr.* [abbr.] [1970s+] (*US*) *no fucking good*.

n.f.w.! *excl.* [abbr.] [1970s+] (*US*) *no fucking way!*

n.g. *n.* [abbr. *no good*] [late 19C+] (*US*) a person or thing that is bad or inferior.

n.g. *adj.* [abbr.] **1** [mid–late 19C] (*orig. US*) *no go*, unsuccessful. **2** [late 19C+] (*orig. US*) *no good*.

n.g.b. *n.* [abbr. *nice guy but*] [1980s+] (*US campus*) a pleasant person, but not one with whom one wishes to have a sexual relationship.

Nguyen *n.* [the widespread use of the name *Nguyen*] [1960s–70s] (*US*) a generic term for a Vietnamese native.

n.h. *n. see* NORFOLK HOWARD *n.*

Niagara Falls *n.* (*also* **niagaras**) [rhy. sl.] **1** [1930s] (*US*) meat balls. **2** [1940s] rubbish, nonsense [BALLS *n.* (4)]. **3** [1940s+] the testicles [BALLS *n.* (1)].

Niagara pineapple *n. see* PINEAPPLE *n.*[1] (1).

niam *v. see* NYAM *v.*

nias *n.* [NIZZIE *n.*] [17C–19C] a simpleton, a fool.

nib *n.*[1] [SE *nib*, the beak or bill of a bird] **1** [late 18C–19C] the mouth or face. **2** [late 19C] a die.

nib *n.*[2] [var. on NOB *n.*[2] (1)] **1** [early 19C–1950s] a gentleman. **2** [late 19C–1920s] a smartly dressed young man.

DERIVATIVES

❑ **niblike** *adj.* [mid-19C] smart, fashionable. ❑ **nibsome** *adj.* [early–mid-19C] gentlemanly.

IN COMPOUNDS

❑ **nib cove** *n.* [COVE *n.* (1)] [early–mid-19C] a gentleman.

IN PHRASES

❑ **half-nibs** *n.* [early–mid-19C] one who apes a gentleman.

nib *v. see* NAB *v.*[1].

nibbed *adj.* [NAB *v.*[1] (2)] [early–mid-19C] arrested.

nibble *n.* [NIBBLE *v.* (3)/SE *nibble*] **1** [early–mid-19C] a petty thief. **2** [mid-19C] (*UK Und.*) an opportunity for gain or theft. **3** [1960s+] a non-committal enquiry, casual conversation.

IN PHRASES

❑ **have a nibble** *v.* [late 19C] **1** to have the best of a bargain. **2** to have a good job. **3** (*UK Und.*) to score a success, whether with a bet or a crime.

nibble *v.* **1** [17C–19C] to catch, to take. **2** in sexual contexts. (**a**) [17C–19C] (*also* **do a nibble, have a nibble**) to have sexual intercourse. (**b**) [1920s+] to peform fellatio or cunnilingus. **3** [early–mid-19C] to pilfer, to work as a petty thief. **4** [late 19C–1940s] (*US*) to take a drink. **5** [late 19C+] to assess a possible purchase. **6** [1930s] to make a purchase. **7** [1980s+] (*US campus*) to have a mild argument.

DERIVATIVES

❑ **nibbling** *n.* [17C] sexual intercourse.

nibbler *n.* [NIBBLE *v.*] **1** [early–mid-19C] a petty thief. **2** [1950s] (*US Und.*) a fellator.

nibbling *adj.* [1980s+] (*US campus*) of weather, chilly, slightly cold.

nibbling cull *n.* [NIBBLE *v.* (3) + CULL *n.*[1] (3)] [18C–19C] a petty thief.

niblike *adj. see* NIB *n.*[2].

nibs *n.* [NIB *n.*[2] (1)] **1** [early 19C+] oneself. **2** [early 19C+] an important, esp. a self-important person. **3** [mid-19C] a shabby, genteel person, 'with no means but high pretensions' (Hotten 1859). **4** [late 19C–1910s] (*US*) as a term of address.

IN PHRASES

❑ **his nibs** *n.* (*also* **her nibs, his knibbs, his niblets, his nobs**) **1** [mid-19C+] himself (or herself). **2** [late 19C+] an employer, a superior. **3** [late 19C+] an important, impressive person. **4** [late 19C+] (*also* **his nabs, his nobs, his royal nobs**) a self-important person. ❑ **my nibs** *n.* [mid-19C–1910s] oneself. ❑ **your nibs** *n.* [19C] yourself.

nibshit *n.*[1] [? Eng. dial. *nib*, a very small amount + SHIT *n.* (1a)] [1940s] (*US*) nil, nothing.

nibshit *n.*[2] [SE *nib*, the beak of a bird + SHIT *n.* (2a)] [1960s+] (*US*) a nosey, inquisitive person.

nibshit *adj.* [NIBSHIT *n.*[2]] [1980s+] meddlesome, interfering.

nibshit *v.* [NIBSHIT *n.*[2]] [1960s+] to meddle, to interfere.

nibso *n.* [NIBS *n.* (1)] [late 19C–1910s] oneself.

nibsomest crib *n.* [mid-19C] (*UK Und.*) a gentleman's house, thus potentially good for begging.

n.i.c. *n.* [abbr. *nigger in charge*] [1960s+] (*US black*) a sarcastic ref. to any black authority figure.

nic *v.* [abbr. SE *nicotine*] [1980s+] to crave nicotine.

nice *adj.*[1] [1940s+] (*US black*) feeling well, happy, at one with the world, esp. as a result of taking drugs or drink.

IN PHRASES

❑ **make nice** *v.* [trans. of Yid./Ger. usage] (*US*) **1** [1950s+] often as admonition, to be friendly or considerate, to behave oneself. **2** [1990s+] to curry favour, to act in a friendly manner (whether or not one means it). **3** [2000s] to caress.

SE in slang uses

IN COMPOUNDS

❑ **nice bit** *n. see under* BIT *n.*[1] (3b). ❑ **nice car** *n.* [1980s+] (*US campus*) a good-looking man or woman. ❑ **nice egg** *n. see* GOOD EGG *n.* ❑ **nice girl** *n.* [1960s] (*US campus*) used ironically by men, a sexually permissive woman. ❑ **nice joint** *n.* [SE *joint*, a piece of MEAT *n.* (1)] [late 19C–1900s] an attractive, if over-made up and over-dressed young woman. ❑ **nice people** *n. see* GOOD PEOPLE *under* PEOPLE *n.*

IN PHRASES

❑ **nice pair of eyes** *n. see under* EYE *n.* ❑ **nice up** *v.* **1** [20C+] (*W.I.*) to improve, dress up esp. to ingratiate oneself. **2** [2000s] (*UK black*) to improve, to make things good for.

nice *adj.*[2] [16C SE *nice*, foolish, trifling] **1** [1950s+] (*W.I.*) compliant, unwilling to make a fuss or cause trouble. **2** [1980s] (*US campus*) boring.

nice *v.* [NICE *adj.*[1]] [1980s+] to get drunk.

nice and handy *n.* [rhy. sl.] [1940s] brandy.

nice enough *n.* [rhy. sl. = PUFF *n.* (3a)] [20C+] a male homosexual.

nicely(, thank you) *phr.* [response to the question, 'how are you feeling/doing?'] [1920s+] drunk.

nice nellie *n.* [SE *nice* + *Nelly*, a generic term for a respectable woman] [1930s+] (*US*) a respectable or fastidious person (not necessarily a woman), also used ironically.

DERIVATIVES

❑ **nice-nellyism** *n.* [1930s+] (*US*) prudishness, excessive gentility, puritanical behaviour or attitudes.

nice-nellie *adj.* (*also* **nice-nelly**) [NICE NELLIE *n.*] [1950s+] prudish, puritanical.

nice nellie *v.* [NICE NELLIE *n.*] [1950s] (*US*) to act in a respectable manner, often excessively and interferingly so.

nice-nellyism *n. see* NICE NELLIE *n.*

nice one *n.* [1930s+] something exceptional, e.g. a blow, a success, esp. referring to a robbery or a large payment.

nice one! *excl.* [1960s+] a general excl. of approval or admiration referring either to an action or to the report of something already carried out; also used ironically.

IN EXCLAMATIONS

❑ **nice one, Cyril!** [football chant created to praise *Cyril* Knowles (1944–91), a Tottenham Hotspur player] [1970s+] a general term of approval.

nice one, Cyril *n.* [rhy. sl.; ult. *NICE ONE, CYRIL! under* NICE ONE! *excl.*] [1990s+] a squirrel.

nicey-nice *adj.* [SE *nice*, fastidious, dainty, hard to please] [1930s+] (*US*) affected, prissy.

nic fit *n.* [abbr. SE *nicotine* + *fit*] [1980s+] a state of withdrawal or craving for cigarettes.

niche cock *n.* [SE *niche* + COCK *n.*[3] (1)] [late 18C–late 19C] the vagina.

nicht *n. see* NISHT *n.*

Nick *n.* (*also* **Nicholas**) [abbr. of proper name *Nicholas*, but no specific reason; ? link to NICK *v.*[1] (2), i.e. the Devil snatches his victims] [mid-17C+] the Devil; often as OLD NICK *n.*

nick *n.*[1] [SE *the nick/very nick*, the critical moment] **1** [mid-17C–early 19C] the winning throw at dice. **2** [late 18C–19C] as *the nick*, the proper thing, the fashionable thing, the best of health.

IN PHRASES

❑ **in the nick** [late 17C–18C] fashionable, in the height of fashion.

nick *n.*[2] [SE *nick*, a notch, a groove, a slit] **1** [18C–19C] the vagina. **2** [late 19C] the cleft of the buttocks.

SE in slang uses

IN COMPOUNDS

❑ **nick-pot** *n.* [the placing of a *nick* or dent in the bottom of the pot] [17C–18C] **1** a false measure in a pot of beer. **2** a publican.

IN PHRASES

❑ **nick and froth** *n.* [a dent in the bottom of the pot and an excess of frothy head on top] [early 17C–mid-18C] **1** a false measure in a pot of beer. **2** by metonymy, a landlord. ❑ **nick and go** *n.* [20C+] (*Ulster*) a 'narrow squeak', a 'close shave'. ❑ **nick in the notch** *n.* [19C] the vagina.

nick *n.*[3] **1** [mid-19C] a low-class casino. **2** (*orig. Aus.*) with ref. to imprisonment, capture [milit. use *nick*, the guard-room]. (**a**) [late 19C+] a prison. (**b**) [1910s+] a police station, esp. its cells. (**c**) [1950s] the police. (**d**) [1980s] an arrest. (**e**) [1980s] an institutional home.

IN PHRASES

❑ **on the nick** [late 19C] taking into custody, arresting.

nick *n.*[4] [abbr. SE *nickel*, a five-cent piece] **1** [mid-19C+] (*US*) a *nick*el coin. **2** [late 19C+] (*US*) generic for money. **3** [1960s+] (*US*) $5 or $5 worth, as in a gambling chip. **4** [1990s+] (*US drugs*) a $5 worth bag of marijuana.

nick *n.*[5] [orig. dial.]

IN PHRASES

❑ **in bad nick** (*also* **in poor nick**) [20C+] in a bad state or condition. ❑ **in good nick** (*also* **in decent nick, in nick**) [20C+] of a person or thing, in good condition.

nick *n.*[6] [NICK *v.*[1] (3)] [1900s–50s] (*US*) the proceeds of a crime, a haul.

nick *n.*[7]

IN PHRASES

❑ **in the nick** [? SE *naked*] [1940s+] (*N.Z.*) naked, esp. in the context of swimming.

nick *n.*[8] [abbr.] [1980s] (*US*) a *nick*name.

nick *v.*[1] [Rom., thus note Caló *nicabar*, to steal; ? underpinned by SE *nick*, to catch, to seize, to take advantage of an opportunity; ult. ety. fig. use of SE *nick*, to mark, i.e. to mark for oneself] **1** [mid-16C–19C] to win at gambling, orig. dice or cards (esp. by cheating). **2** [17C+] to catch, take unawares; to 'get', to understand. **3** [17C+] (*UK Und.*) to rob, to steal. **4** [late 17C+] to cheat, to swindle. **5** [mid-18C+] to apprehend, to arrest. **6** [late 18C] in fig. use of sense 1, to win other than in gambling. **7** [early 19C] to comprehend. **8** [late 19C] to appeal to, to capture one's interest. **9** [late 19C–1960s] (*orig. US*) to demand, to beg. **10** [1910s–30s] a weak form of the senses of to rob and to cheat above, to charge, with implication of excessive price. **11** [1970s] (*US*) to find fault with someone.

DERIVATIVES

❑ **nickable** *adj.* [1990s+] worth stealing. ❑ **nickings** *n.* [1970s] (*US*) criticisms.

IN PHRASES

❑ **nick it** *v.* **1** [early 17C–19C] to win, usu. by good fortune or cheating. **2** [mid-17C–early 18C] (*also* **nick the pin**) to drink fairly, i.e. not taking more than one's share of the tankard (which was marked by pins). ❑ **out on the nick** [1970s] going stealing.

nick *v.*[2] [SE *nick*, to cut a notch in] **1** [18C–1930s] of a man, to have sexual intercourse [note NICK *n.*[2] (1)]. **2** [1910s–50s] (*US*) to shoot.

IN EXCLAMATIONS

❑ **nick me!** [thus euph. for FUCK ME! *excl.*, although it predates the latter] [mid-18C] a mild oath.

nick *v.*[3] [ety. unknown; ? link to SE *nick of time*] [19C+] to avoid, to slip away, to leave on the spur of the moment, often as *nick away*, *nick down/down to*, etc.

IN PHRASES

❑ **do a nick** *v.* [20C+] (*Aus.*) to run off. ❑ **give the nick** *v.* [NIT-NIT! *excl.*] [1940s–50s] to alert someone to the approach of an authority. ❑ **keep nikko** *v.* (*also* **keep nick, keep the nick**) [i.e. be prepared to run off] [1940s+] (*Irish*) to keep a lookout. ❑ **nick off** *v.* (*also* **nick out**) [late 19C+] (*orig. Aus.*) to leave, to depart, to go from one place to another.

Nick Butts *n.* (*also* **Nicky Butts**) [rhy. sl.; ult. *Nicky Butt* (b. 1975), UK footballer] [1990s+] **1** nuts (edible). **2** the testicles [= NUTS *n.*[2] (1)].

nicked *adj.*[1] [NICK *v.*[1] (5)] **1** [late 19C+] arrested. **2** [1940s+] (*UK prison*) put on report to the governor for an infringement of prison rules.

nicked *adj.*[2] [? NICK *v.*[2] (1)] [1960s+] (*Aus.*) a euph. for FUCKED *adj.*[1], e.g. *go and get nicked!*

nickel *n.* [SAmE *nickel*, a five-cent coin] **1** [1930s–40s] a very small amount (not monetary); eg. *not like it a nickel*. **2** [1940s+] (*US*) a $5 bill, $5. **3** [1950s+] (*US prison*) a five-year prison sentence. **4** [1960s+] (*US drugs*) a $5 packet of marijuana, heroin or cocaine. **5** [1970s+] (*US*) the number five. **6** [1970s+] (*US*) $500, esp. in gambling. **7** [2000s] (*US*) the general name for the SKID ROW *n.* (1) area of downtown Los Angeles that is focused on East Fifth Street.

IN COMPOUNDS

❑ **nickel deck** *n.* [DECK *n.*[4] (1)] [1960s+] (*drugs*) $5 worth of heroin. ❑ **nickel dump** *n.* [DUMP *n.*[3] (2); derog. synon. of SE *nickelodeon*] [1900s–50s] (*US*) a cheap cinema, charging only a nickel or 5 cents admission. ❑ **nickel grabber** *n.* **1** [1950s] an insignificant person. **2** *see* NICKEL SNATCHER below. ❑ **nickel-grinder** *n.* [1930s] (*US*) a miser, a 'penny-pincher'. ❑ **nickel hop** *n.* [HOP *n.*[1] (3); although the women worked for 10 cents or 'a dime a dance' they split this half and half with the management] [1910s–30s] (*US*) a taxi-dance. ❑ **nickel-hopper** *n.* [1910s–30s] (*US*) a taxi-dancer. ❑ **nickel note** *n.* [20C+] (*US*) a $5 bill. ❑ **nickel nurser** *n.* [lit. one who 'has a passion for seeing that his nickels don't stray' (Maines & Grant, *The Wise-Crack Dict.*, 1926)] [1910s–70s] (*US*) a miser. ❑ **nickel plate** *n.* [the use of *nickel plate* to counterfeit silver] [late 19C–1900s] (*US*) a fraud, a deception. ❑ **nickel rat** *n.* [1950s] (*US*) a second-rate, small-time criminal. ❑ **nickel shot** *n.* [SHOT *n.*[1] (5b)] [1990s+] (*US black teen*) a five-storey public housing building in the Fillmore area of San Francisco. ❑ **nickel snatcher** *n.* (*also* **nickel grabber**) [1910s–50s] (*US*) a streetcar conductor. ❑ **nickel squeezer** *n.* [1920s–30s] (*US*) a mean, miserly person. ❑ **nickel-plated** *adj.* [paradoxically opposite to NICKEL PLATE above; ? var. on SE *gold-plated*] [late 19C+] (*US*) first-class, thorough. ❑ **nickel-slick** *adj.* [SLICK *adj.* (1); the low value of the coin undermines the slickness] [1970s+] (*US black*) petty, insignificant, esp. in the context of attempting to do something beyond one's abilities (and thus failing in the effort).

IN PHRASES

❑ **don't take any wooden nickels** (*also* **...rubber nickels, ...wooden money**) [1920s+] (*orig. US*) beware of being defrauded or hoaxed. ❑ **have a nickel in that dime** *v.* [i.e. to invest 5 cents (a *nickel*) in a larger investment of 10 cents (a *dime*)] [1970s+] (*US black*) to have an interest in a state of affairs. ❑ **on one's nickel** [1990s+] (*US*) at one's own expense.

nickel *adj.* [the low value of the coin] [late 19C+] (*US*) second-rate, inferior, trivial.

nickel and dime *n.* [rhy. sl.] [1930s+] (*US*) time.

nickel-and-dime *adj.* (*also* **nickel-dime**) [the low value of the coin] [1920s+] (*US*) petty, small-time, insignificant.

nickel-and-dime *v.* [SE *nickel* + *dime*, i.e. the low value of the coins] **1** [1910s+] (*US*) to treat others meanly and miserly, thus to be petty and irksome, to eat away at. **2** [1940s+] (*US*) to carry on a small, cash-starved business, to manage with little money, oft. as to *nickel-and-dime it*. **3** [1940s+] (*UK Und.*) to beg on the street.

nickel-and-dimer *n.* [NICKEL-AND-DIME *adj.*] [1930s+] (*US*) a mean, contemptible or insignificant person.

nickel bag *n.* [NICKEL *n.* (2) + BAG *n.*[1] (7)] [1960s+] (*drugs*) $5 worth of drugs, the quantity varies as to the drug, more marijuana, less heroin.

IN COMPOUNDS

❑ **nickel-bagger** *n.* [1970s] (*US Und.*) a second-rate, minor drug dealer.

nickel-dime *adj. see* NICKEL-AND-DIME *adj.*

nickelnose *n.* [? var. on NEEDLENOSED *adj.* + stereotypical ref. to money] [1970s+] (*US*) a Jewish person.

nicker *n.*[1] [NICK *v.*[1]] **1** [late 17C; late 19C–1950s] a thief, a cheat, a confidence trickster. **2** [1960s] (*Aus.*) a child.

nicker *n.*[2] (*also* **nick**) [ety. unknown] **1** [late 19C+] £1. **2** [1950s+] money in general.

IN COMPOUNDS

❑ **nicker bit** *n.* [1980s+] the pound coin.

IN PHRASES

❑ **half-a-nicker** (*also* **half a nick, half-nicker**) [1930s+] a ten-shilling note (50p).

nicker bits *n.* [rhy. sl. = SHITS, THE *n.*] [20C+] diarrhoea.

nickery *n.* [abbr.] [late 17C–early 19C] a *nick*name.

nickie cakes! *excl.* [Scot. *nickit bake*, a small biscuit with indentations on the top] [20C+] (*Ulster*) easy!

nickin *n.* (*also* **nikey, nikin**) [fig. use of NICK *n.*[2] (1); Grose (1785) suggests 'a diminutive of Isaac'] [late 17C–early 19C] a fool, a simpleton.

nicking *n.* [NICK *v.*[1] (5)] [1970s+] an arrest.

nicklette *n.* [it costs a *nickel* a play] [1930s–40s] (*US black*) an automatic record player.

nick-nack *n.* [SE *nick-nack*, a curious or pleasing trifle, a trinket] **1** [18C–19C] in pl., the testicles. **2** [mid–late 19C] the vagina. **3** [1960s+] (*US*) a male homosexual, esp. a promiscuous one. **4** [1970s] (*US prison*) a man who is raped frequently in prison. **5** [2000s] (*US prison*) (*also* **knick-knack, nic-nac**) one who does not fit in with the group; an outsider.

nick-nick! *excl. see* NIT-NIT! *excl.*

nick-ninny *n.* [? abbr. NICKIN *n.* + SE *ninny*] [late 17C–early 19C] a fool, 'a meer Cod's head' (*B.E.*).

nicks *n.*[1] *see* KNICKS *n.* (3).

nicks *n.*[2] *see* NIX *n.* (1).

nickser *n. see* NIXER *n.*

nicks my doll *phr. see* NIX MY DOLL *under* NIX *n.*

nickum *n.* [NICK *v.*[1] (1)] [late 17C–early 18C] **1** a card sharp or dice fraud. **2** a cheating landlord (although the aspersion can extend to any dishonest retailer).

nickumpoop *n. see* NINCOMPOOP *n.*

Nicky *n. see* OLD NICK *n.*

nicky-hooky *see* NOOKIE *n.*

nic-nac *n. see* NICK-NACK *n.* (5).

nic-stick *n.* [abbr. SE *nicotine* + STICK *n.* (6a)] [1970s+] (*Aus.*) a cigarette.

nidget *n. see* NIGIT *n.*

niece *n.* [linked to AUNT *n.* (1)] [mid–late 17C] (*UK Und*) a euph. for a prostitute.

niegor *n. see* NIGGER *n.*[1].

niem *n.* [2000s] (*US black*) none, nothing.

nieve *n.* [Sp. *nieve*, snow, thus SNOW *n.*[1] (2)] [1970s+] (*drugs*) white powdered drugs, i.e. heroin or cocaine.

niff *n.* [? SE *sniff*; note WW1 milit. *niffy*, a strong, unpleasant smell] [late 19C+] an unpleasant smell, a stink.

DERIVATIVES

❑ **niffy** *adj.* **1** [20C+] smelly, malodorous. **2** [1940s] in fig. use, dubious, questionable.

niff, the *n.* [? SE *naked* + BUFF *n.*[1] (1)] [1960s] bare flesh.

niff *v.* [NIFF *n.*] **1** [late 19C+] (*also* **miff**) to smell unpleasantly, to stink. **2** [20C+] to smell something, usu. an unpleasant smell.

niffkins bridge *n.* [NIFF *n.* + dimin. sfx *-kins* + SE *bridge*] [1990s+] the female perineum.

niffy *adj. see* NIFF *n.*

niffy-naffy fellow *n.* [Yorks. dial. *niff-/niffy-naffy*, trifling] [late 18C–early 19C] a trifler, an unimportant person.

niftik *n.* [NIFTIK *adj.*] [1910s–30s] (*US*) an attractive young woman.

niftik *adj.* (*also* **niftic**) [NIFTY *adj.* (1) + 'European/Slav' sfx *-ik*] [1910s–30s] (*US*) stylish, neat.

nifty *n.* [NIFTY *adj.* (1)] **1** [1910s] something attractive. **2** [1910s+] (*US*) a joke, a funny story, a clever plan. **3** [1930s] something useful, convenient. **4** [1930s+] (*also* **bit of nifty**) a pretty young woman; an attractive object. **5** [1960s] (*US campus*) a well-dressed man. **6** [1980s+] (*also* **bit of nifty**) sexual intercourse. **7** [2000s] a commission.

nifty *adj.* [ety. unknown; according to US author Bret Harte, quoted in *OED*, abbr. *magnificat*; Partridge dismisses this as 'a joke' and suggests SE *magnificent*] **1** [mid-19C+] neat, smart. **2** [20C+] attractive, pretty. **3** [20C+] (*orig. US*) clever, skilful, agile. **4** [20C+] (*US*) cheeky, insolent, disrespectful of authority. **5** [1910s+] amusing.

nifty *v.* [NIFTY *n.* (2)] [1930s–40s] to quip, to joke.

nifty *adv.* [NIFTY *adj.* (3)] [1920s] (*US*) competently.

nifty! *excl.* (*also* **nifty beans! nifty keen!**) [NIFTY *adj.*] [1960s+] (*US teen*) terrific!, splendid!, wonderful!

nifty fifty *n.* [NIFTY *adj.* (1)] [1980s+] (*Irish/US*) a 50 c.c. scooter.

nig *n.*[1] [? Essex dial. *nig*, a piece or SE *nick*] [late 17C–mid-19C] (*UK Und.*) the clippings from doctored gold coins.

nig *n.*[2] (*also* **nige**) [abbr. NIGGER *n.*[1] (1)] **1** [early 19C+] a derog. term for a black person, ext. in Aus. to Asians. **2** [mid-19C+] (*US black*) used non-pejoratively; as a nickname. **3** [1930s] as a term of address. **4** [1960s–70s] a derog. term for an East Asian.

IN COMPOUNDS

❑ **nig-bo** *n.* [on model of SAMBO *n.*[1] (1)] [1990s+] a derog. term for a black person. ❑ **nig-mag** *n.* [sense 1 + SE *magnet*] [2000s] (*US black*) a white woman who is popular among black men.

nig *n.*[3] [backsl.] [mid-19C] gin.

nig *n.*[4] *see* NIG-NOG *n.*[1].

nig *v.*[1] [? Essex dial. *nig*, a piece] [late 17C–early 19C] to clip money.

DERIVATIVES

❑ **nigging** *n.* [late 17C–early 19C] clipping coins.

nig *v.*[2] [abbr. NIGGLE *v.* (1)] [18C–19C] to have sexual intercourse.

nig *v.*[3] [NICK *v.*[1] (5)] [mid-18C] to arrest.

nig *v.*[4] [abbr. NIGGER *n.*[1] (1); racist stereotyping; but also semi-abbr. of SE re*nege*] [early 19C–1950s] (*US*) to renege on one's debts.

nig *v.*[5] [abbr. SE *niggle*] [1990s+] (*UK juv.*) to annoy.

nig-bo *n. see* NIG *n.*[2].

nige *n. see* NIG *n.*[2].

nigel *n.* [proper name *Nigel* seen as quintessentially upper-class and vapid] [1990s+] (*Aus.*) a friendless male.

niger *n. see* NIGGER *n.*[1].

Nigerian *n.* [generic use of specific nationality] [1960s+] (*gay*) a black man.

IN COMPOUNDS

❑ **Nigerian lager** *n.* [its blackness] [1970s+] Guinness stout.

nigette *n.* [NIGGA *n.* + sfx *-ette*] [1990s+] (*US*) a black woman or girl.

nigga *n.* [NIGGER *n.*[1] (1); the sp. is now exclusive to the world of GANGSTA *adj.* rap where the SE sfx *-er* is transposed to *-a*, a foreshortening that is regularly found in black sl. as a means of intensifying a term (cf. PLAYER *n.* (2)/PLAYA *n.*)] [1970s+] (*US black*) a black person; thus pl. *niggaz*.

DERIVATIVES

❑ **niggalicious** *adj.* [-LICIOUS *sfx*] [2000s] (*US black*) of a black woman, heavily built.

IN COMPOUNDS

❑ **nigga beater** *n.* [adopted from white terms such as *nigger knocker*, *nigger stick*, etc (see under NIGGER *n.*[1])] [2000s] (*US black*) any blunt instrument. ❑ **nigga chops** *n.* [CHOPS *n.*[1] (1)] [2000s] (*US black*) a fellow black person. ❑ **nigga town** *n. see* NIGGERTOWN *n.*

IN EXCLAMATIONS

❑ **nigga please!** [2000s] (*US black*) an excl. of disbelief, dismissal.

nigger *n.*[1] (*also* **naygar, naygur, neeger, neger, niegor, niger, nigga, niggah, niggar, niggur, nigra**) [ult. Lat. *niger*, black in colour, thence Early Mod. Eng. (later dial.) *niger*; thus advocated by *HDAS*, although the *OED* and *DSUE* prefer Sp. *negro*, black. *Nigger* has been used in a variety of combs. since 19C; both *Webster III* and the *OED* list a number of these, usu. referring to birds, animals and crops, without comment – the assumption being that, for better or worse, they are an accepted (if local) usage; while they are also based on stereotypes, it is more that of colour than of racist assumptions. Those combs. listed here, usu. unlisted in the standard dictionaries, may well have been colloq. in the 19C, but by their intrinsic hostility are, *de facto*, sl.; otherwise, *nigger* implies the usual derog. stereotypes as allotted to blacks: poverty, laziness, stupidity, lasciviousness, a propensity to mindless hedonism and violence] **1** [17C+] a derog. term for a black person, a Negro slave, by extension any non-white. **2** [19C] of a white person, a slave. **3** [early 19C+] (*US*) a general derog. term applicable to anyone regardless of race/skin colour, used by blacks as well as whites; thus, any foreigner. **4** [mid-19C+] used as a derog. term between blacks, aping the derog. term in sense 1. **5** [mid-19C+] any dark-skinned foreign person. **6** [mid-19C+] an Aborigine, a Maori. **7** [late 19C] (*Aus.*) a Chinese person. **8** [late 19C–1910s] a 'nigger minstrel', i.e, a white person performing in blackface. **9** [late 19C+] a subservient person, a servant. **10** [late 19C+] anything coloured black, e.g. the black numbers of roulette. **11** [1910s+] (*US black*) in a reverse racism, taking pride in such epithets, used by radical blacks of each other. **12** [1950s+] (*US black*) a close male or female friend, companion, boyfriend or husband, usu. constructed with possessive pronoun, as in *my* (*main*) *nigger*, my (best) friend. **13** [1960s+] (*US*) a fellow human being, of any race or skin colour. **14** [1970s+] (*US black*) a non-black person who is considered to act in a very positive manner in relation to black culture or who identifies strongly with it.

DERIVATIVES

❑ **niggerish** *adj.* [early 19C+] (*US*) **1** lazy, couldn't-care-less. **2** selfish. ❑ **niggeritis** *n.* [sfx *-itis*] [20C+] **1** (*W.I.*) the urge to lie down and take a nap after a heavy meal. **2** (*US*) a fig. disease, based on a racist attitude to black people. ❑ **niggerize** *v.* [1970s+] (*US*) to be politically marginalized, i.e. to be rendered 'black' and *de facto* unimportant. ❑ **niggerology** *n.* [sfx -OLOGY *n.*] [1950s–60s] (*US*) a derog. term for a black studies course at college or school. ❑ **niggerville** *n. see* NIGGERTOWN *n.*

IN COMPOUNDS

❑ **nigger and halitosis** *n.* [the brown colour of liver + the effect of (raw) onions on the breath] [1940s–50s] (*US*) liver and onions. ❑ **nigger baby** *n.* **1** [mid-19C] (*US*) a cannon-ball [coined by Confederate General Hardee (1815–73) during the siege of Charleston; the cannons from which the missiles were fired were known as *swamp angels*]. **2** [late 19C+] (*US*) a small liquorice or chocolate sweet or candy shaped like a baby. ❑ **nigger bait** *n.* [1950s–60s] an excess of chrome accessories on an automobile. ❑ **nigger ball** *n.* [SE *ball*, i.e. the colour and shape] [1960s+] (*S.Afr.*) a large, round, black aniseed flavoured sweet, which gradually changes as one sucks away successive layers. ❑ **nigger bankroll** *n. see* NIGGER'S BANKROLL below. ❑ **nigger box** *n.* [BOX *n.*[1] (4); negative stereotyping] [1950s+] (*US black*) television. ❑ **nigger catcher** *n.* [captured runaway slaves were roped to this flap and forced to run home alongside their master on his horse] [mid-19C] (*US*) a small slotted flap on a saddle. ❑ **nigger chaser** *n.* **1** [late 19C+] (*US*) a firework that once lit leaps around along the ground [in UK, a *jumping jack*]. **2** *see* NIGGER SHOOTER below. ❑ **nigger day** *n.* [the one day of rest permitted to slaves] [1930s+] (*US*) Saturday. ❑ **nigger daytime** *n.* [the time at which slaves were allowed their rest] [19C+] (*US*) night time. ❑ **nigger dick** *n.* [DICK *n.*[1] (5); the shape and colour] [2000s] (*US black*) a large cigar. ❑ **nigger driver** *n. see* separate entry. ❑ **nigger-drunk** *adj.* [1940s–60s] (*US*) very drunk. ❑ **nigger fishing** *n.* [the implication is of the lazy black fisherman] [1940s–60s] (*US*) leisurely fishing for catfish or carp. ❑ **nigger flicker** *n.* [SE *flick knife*] [1950s+] (*US black*) a weapon, usu. a small knife or a razor blade with one side heavily taped to preserve the user's fingers. ❑ **nigger-foot** *n. see* NIGGERHEAD *n.*[1] (1). ❑ **nigger fronts** *n.* [NIGGER *adj.* + FRONT *n.*[1] (11)] [1970s+] (*US black*) extreme stylishness in dress. ❑ **nigger gallery** *n. see* NIGGER HEAVEN below. ❑ **nigger gin** *n.* [1900s–30s] (*US*) inferior or synthetic gin. ❑ **nigger golf** *n.* [1910s] (*US*) the game of craps. ❑ **niggergram** *n.* (*also* **nigger-mouth**) [SE (*tele*)*gram*/sfx *-mouth*] [20C+] (*W.I.*) a stupid rumour, demeaning gossip. ❑ **nigger ham** *n.* [both are pink] [1940s–60s] (*US*) a water melon. ❑ **niggerhead** *n. see* separate entries. ❑ **nigger heads** *n.* [SE *head*, alleged resemblance] [1940s–50s] (*US prison*) prison-cooked prunes. ❑ **nigger heaven** *n.* (*also* **nigger gallery**) **1** [mid-19C–1940s] (*US*) the top gallery of a theatre [this gallery was the only one that black theatregoers could afford]. **2** [1900s] (*US*) a state of enjoyment that is derived from vulgar activities. **3** [1920s–60s] a black neighbourhood. ❑ **nigger-heel** *n. see* NIGGER TOE below. ❑ **nigger hill** *n. see* NIGGERTOWN *n.* ❑ **nigger joint** *n.* [JOINT *n.* (3b)] [20C+] (*US*) a cheap bar, saloon or restaurant. ❑ **nigger juke** *n.* (*also* **nigger jook**) [JUKE *n.*[1] (1)] [1930s–40s] (*US*) a cheap bar, saloon or restaurant. ❑ **nigger kickers** *n.* (*also* **nigger stompers**) [SE *kick/stomp*] [1960s+] (*US*) large boots. ❑ **nigger killer** **1** [mid-19C–1940s] (*US*) a yam [the supposed results of over-eating them]. **2** as a weapon. (**a**) [1940s–70s] a slingshot. (**b**) [1940s–70s] a revolver. (**c**) [1960s] a large pocket-knife. ❑ **nigger knocker** *n.* [1960s+] (*US*) a stick or club for use esp. against blacks. ❑ **nigger knots** *n.* [SE *knots*; used as an insult between black people] [20C+] (*W.I.*) thick, tough black hair. ❑ **niggerlip** *v.* **1** [1940s+] to moisten the end of a cigarette while smoking it. **2** [2000s] to slobber on a bottleneck or can when drinking straight from the container. ❑ **nigger liquor** *n.* [1920s+] (*US*) any form of bad liquor, esp. when illicitly distilled. ❑ **nigger logic** *n.* [the black person stereotyped as child-like and simple] [20C+] (*US*) any form of reasoning considered erroneous, over-simplistic, based in fantasy, i.e. totally illogical. ❑ **nigger-lover** *n. see* separate entry. ❑ **nigger luck** *n.* (*US*) **1** [mid-19C–1940s] good luck, the implication is of unfairness. **2** [1940s] bad luck, which one must make the best of, come what may. ❑ **nigger-meat** *n.* [MEAT *n.* (1)] [1980s] a white woman who associates with black men. ❑ **nigger mess** *n.* [1990s+] (*US black*) problems within the black community, which should be solved within that group. ❑ **nigger minstrel** *n. see* MINSTREL *n.* ❑ **nigger-mouth** *n. see* NIGGERGRAM above. ❑ **nigger news** *n.* [mid-19C–1960s] (*US*) gossip; not necessarily about or from black people. ❑ **nigger night** *n.* [1920s+] (*US black*) Saturday night. ❑ **nigger pancake** *n.* [SE *pancake*; alleged resemblance] [1960s] (*US*) a lump of manure. ❑ **nigger pool** *n.* [1930s] (*US*) a derog. name for NUMBERS, THE *n.* (1). ❑ **nigger pot** *n.* [1900s–60s] (*US, mainly Southern*) illicitly distilled whisky. ❑ **nigger-rich** *adj.* [1930s+] (*US*) very poor or deeply in debt but loaded down with flashy material status symbols. ❑ **nigger-rig(ged)** *see* separate entries. ❑ **nigger rigger** *n.* [? NIGGER RIG *v.*] [1980s] (*US prison*) a white inmate who is seen as overly friend to black ones. ❑ **nigger row** *n.* [late 19C–1900s] (*US*) the black area of a town or city. ❑ **nigger's bankroll** *n.* (*also* **nigger bankroll, … roll**) [SE *bankroll*/ROLL *n.*; thus negative stereotyping] [1920s–80s] (*US*) a roll of $1 bills or a wad of small denomination notes inside one larger denomination note. ❑ **niggers' duel** *n.* [late 19C–1900s] (*US*) an argument, a set-to in which no blows are actually struck. ❑ **nigger shooter** *n.* (*also* **nigger-chaser**) [late 19C+] (*US*) a slingshot. ❑ **nigger spit** *n.* [late 19C] the lumps in Demerara sugar. ❑ **nigger steak** *n.* [SE *steak*; it is particularly dark] [1940s–50s] (*US black*) liver. ❑ **nigger stick** *n.* [1970s+] (*US*) an oversized baton, used by policemen and prison officers. ❑ **nigger sticker** *n.* [1960s+] a large pocket-knife. ❑ **nigger stompers** *n. see* NIGGER KICKERS above. ❑ **nigger talk** *n.* [SE *talk*] [mid-19C–1940s] (*US*) chatter, irresponsible gossip. ❑ **nigger tip** *v.* [1940s] (*US*) to tip badly. ❑ **nigger tobacco** *n.* (*also* **nigger twist**) see NIGGERHEAD *n.*[1] (1). ❑ **nigger toe** *n.* [SE *toe*; alleged resemblance] (*US*) **1** [mid-19C–1940s] a type of potato. **2** [late 19C+] (*also* **nigger-heel**) Brazil nut, walnut. ❑ **niggertown** *n. see* separate entry. ❑ **nigger war** *n.* [mid–

late 19C] (*US, Southern*) the US Civil War (1861–5). ◻ **nigger work** *n.* [mid-19C+] (*US*) menial work; ill-performed work. ◻ **nigger yard** *n.* [Carib.E, *negro-yard*, that area on a plantation where the slaves were quartered] [20C+] (*W.I.*) any notably rough area in the slums.

IN PHRASES

◻ **act the nigger** *v.* [mid-19C+] **1** (*US*) a derog. term meaning to play the fool. **2** (*US black*) to act in a manner white racists expect of black people, i.e. foolish, subservient, clownish. ◻ **big nigger** *n.* [the blackness of the spade suit] [20C+] (*US*) in poker, a game in which the high spade splits the pot. ◻ **black nigger** *n.* [19C–1950s] (*US black*) a derog. term of address used by one black man to another. ◻ **dark as a nigger's pocket** *adj. see under* DARK *adj.* ◻ **get one's nigger up** *v.* [20C+] (*US*) to lose control, to lose one's temper. ◻ **I'm a nigger** *see* separate entry. ◻ **keep-a-nigger** *adj.* [1990s+] (*US black*) intended to maintain a relationship, e.g. used of a child deliberately conceived by a woman with the intention of keeping a lover who had only desired a brief relationship. ◻ **let off a little nigger** *v.* [late 19C+] (*US*) a derog. phr. meaning to act in a crazy, uninhibited way, to let off steam. ◻ **my nigger** *n.* (*also* **my nigga**) [1960s+] (*US black*) **1** a major influence, a role-model, a close friend. **2** a general term of address. ◻ **nigger in a blanket** *n.* [SE *blanket*; alleged resemblance] [1930s–40s] (*US, Western*) a pudding made with dark fruits rolled inside pastry. ◻ **nigger in charge** *n.* [for ety. *see* HEAD NIGGER IN CHARGE *under* HEAD *n.*] [1930s+] (*US black*) a sarcastic ref. to any black authority figure. ◻ **nigger it** *v.* [the social situation of many US blacks] [mid-19C+] (*US*) to live in poverty. ◻ **nigger out** *v.* [stereotype of blacks as incompetent farmers] **1** [mid-19C–1940s] to exhaust land by using it constantly without fertilization. **2** [late 19C+] (*US*) to back out, renege on. ◻ **nigger up** *v.* [1950s+] (*US*) to decorate in a vulgar manner. ◻ **prairie nigger** *n.* [2000s] (*US black*) derog. term for a Native American. ◻ **red nigger** *n.* **1** [mid-19C] (*US*) a red Indian. **2** [20C+] (*US/W.I.*) a person both of whose parents are of mixed-African/white descent. ◻ **street nigger** *n.* **1** [late 19C] a burnt cork artiste, who plays and sings for a living. **2** [1970s] a sophisticated 'streetwise' black man. ◻ **sweat like a nigger (at election)** *v. see under* SWEAT *v.*[2].

nigger *n.*[2] [NIG *v.*[1]] [late 18C–mid-19C] (*UK Und.*) a clipper of gold coins.

nigger *adj.* (*also* **nigra**) [NIGGER *n.*[1] (1)] [early 19C+] (*orig. US*) a derog. phr. indicating something or someone associated with black culture; thus as derog., contemptible, odd, inferior.

nigger *v.*[1] [NIGGER *n.*[1] (1)] **1** [early 19C+] (*US*) to do menial work. **2** [late 19C] (*UK Und.*) to work as a nigger minstrel.

nigger *v.*[2] [SE *niggard*, a miser] [mid-19C] (*UK Und.*) to withhold money, to refuse payment.

nigger-driver *n.* [fig. use of NIGGER *n.*[1] (1)] [late 19C–1940s] an employer who works his men excessively hard.

DERIVATIVES

◻ **nigger-driving** *n.* [mid-19C+] (*orig. US black*) **1** the working of blacks to exhaustion by white bosses. **2** any boss–employee relationship characterized by poor treatment. ◻ **nigger-driving** *adj.* [mid-19C–1900s] highly exploitative.

niggerhead *n.*[1] [all fig. uses of NIGGER *n.*[1] (1) + SE *head*; alleged resemblance] **1** [19C–1940s] (*also* (*US*) negro head, nigger, nigger-foot, (*Aus.*) nigger tobacco, nigger twist) cheap, dark tobacco designed for smoking and chewing. **2** [mid-19C+] (*US*) any outcrop of dark, rough, rounded or lumpy rock, stones or boulders. **3** [mid-19C+] any clump or hummock of thick vegetation, swamp grass, ferns, grass etc. **4** [late 19C–1960s] (*US*) a dark raincloud. **5** [20C+] (*also* **negro-head**) peaks of coral that jut above the surface of the sea. **6** [1900s] an ox-eye daisy (with a large black centre). **7** [1900s] (*US campus*) hard black candy. **8** [1910s] a piece of stone, a small boulder. **9** [1930s] (*US*) a shoe-nailing machine. **10** [1930s–60s] (*US Und.*) a type of round wall safe. **11** [1950s+] (*W.I.*) a black person's naturally kinky hair.

IN COMPOUNDS

◻ **niggerhead rum** *n.* [1910s–30s] (*US*) strong, dark rum.

niggerhead *n.*[2] [NIGGER *n.*[1] (1) + -HEAD *sfx* (1)] [mid–late 19C] (*US*) a pro-black civil rights agitator.

niggerican *n.* [NIGGER *n.*[1] (1) + SE *American*] [1970s] (*US*) a black American (incl. a Puerto Rican).

nigger-lover *n.* (*also* **nigger lover, niggerlover**) [NIGGER *n.*[1] (1) + SE *lover*] [mid-19C+] (*orig. US*) a term of abuse, aimed at a white who is seen as overly friendly towards blacks.

DERIVATIVES

◻ **nigger-loving** *n.* [late 19C+] (*US*) a derog. term for the refusal of whites to take a racist attitude to blacks. ◻ **nigger-loving** *adj.* (*US*) **1** [late 19C+] used of any white person showing favour to black people. **2** [1960s+] used as a general derog. epithet, usu. by Southerners, irrespective of the object's actual racial opinions.

nigger rig *v.* [NIGGER *n.*[1] (1) + SE *rig*] [1950s+] (*US*) to perform second-rate, sloppy work.

DERIVATIVES

◻ **nigger rig** *n.* [1950s+] (*US*) a bodged job, a piece of do-it-yourself assembly. ◻ **nigger-rigged** *adj.* [1950s+] (*US*) characterized by bad workmanship.

niggers noggers! *excl. see* 'SNIGGERS! *excl.*

niggertown *n.* (*also* **nigga town, nigger hill, nigger town, niggerville**) [NIGGER *n.*[1] (1) + SE *town/hill/-ville*; note W.I. dial. *negro-town*, a community of runaway slaves or *maroons* who would use them as bases for raids on the plantations] [mid-19C+] (*US*) a black neighbourhood.

nigging *n. see* NIG *v.*[1].

niggle *v.* (*also* **neggle, nigle**) [ety. unknown; probable link to SE *niggle*, to trifle, to play with, although OED first citation (1616) is 50 years subseq. to the sl. use in *Harman* (1567); the use of *tonygle* in Harman is a misprint] [mid-16C–early 19C; 1930s] to have sexual intercourse.

DERIVATIVES

◻ **niggling** *n.* (*also* **nigling**) [17C–early 19C] sexual intercourse.

niggled *adj.* [SE *niggle*] [1950s+] annoyed, irritated, tetchy.

niggler *n.*[1] [NIGGLE *v.*] [17C–late 18C] **1** a prostitute. **2** (*also* **nigler**) a promiscuous man.

niggler *n.*[2] (*also* **nigler**) [NIG *v.*[1]] [late 17C–early 19C] (*UK Und.*) a clipper of coins.

niggling *n. see* NIGGLE *v.*

niggling *adj.* [SE *niggle*] [mid-19C+] irritatingly petty, intrinsically unimportant but time and energy consuming.

niggly *adj.* [SE *niggle*] [1950s+] ill-tempered, obsessed with irrelevancies and petty problems.

niggur *n. see* NIGGER *n.*[1].

niggy *n.* [NIGGER *n.*[1] (1)] [2000s] **1** (*US black*) a white person who acts like a black person. **2** (*UK juv.*) a dark tan.

nigh enough *n.* (*also* **near enough**) [rhy. sl. = PUFF *n.* (3a)] [1930s+] a homosexual male prostitute.

night *n.*

SE in slang uses

IN COMPOUNDS

◻ **nightbird** *n.* (*also* **bird of the night, night fowl**) [they 'fly at night'; note SE *night bird*, one who goes about at night, esp. a thief] **1** [17C; mid-19C+] a prostitute. **2** [early 19C] a wandering vagabond. ◻ **night bull** *n. see* BULL *n.*[5] (3). ◻ **nightcap** *n. see* separate entries. ◻ **night clothes** *n.* [20C+] (*US Und.*) dark, close-fitting clothes used when committing a burglary at night. ◻ **night crawler** *n.* **1** [1950s+] (*US*) someone who socializes or works late at night. **2** [1950s+] (*US Und*) a prisoner who steals from other inmates. **3** [1960s] (*US gay*) a homophobic thug. **4** [1970s] (*US*) the penis. ◻ **night fighter** *n.* [SE *night fighter* planes are painted black] [1940s+] (*US*) a black person. ◻ **night fowl** *n. see* NIGHTBIRD above. ◻ **night glass** *n.* [1940s] (*W.I.*) a euph. for a chamberpot. ◻ **nightgown lady** *n.* [euph.] [late 17C] a prostitute. ◻ **night hack** *n.* [HACK *n.*[3] (1)] [1910s–30s] (*US Und.*) a night watchman. ◻ **nighthawk** *see* separate entries. ◻ **night hunter** *n.* [19C–1910s] a thief who prefers to work at night; a prostitute. ▫ **nightliner** *n.* [late 19C–1900s] (*US*) a street robber who works at night. ▫ **night magistrate** *n.* [late 17C–early 19C] a constable. ▫ **nightman** *n.* **1** [late 17C–mid-19C] a collector of nightsoil, i.e. the contents of cesspools, removed at night. **2** [1920s+] a thief who prefers to work at night, rather than in the daytime. ▫ **night-owl** *see* separate entries. ▫ **night physic** *n.* [late 16C–early 18C] sexual intercourse. ▫ **night poacher** *n.* [19C] **1** a prostitute. **2** a thief who works at night. ▫ **nightshade** *n.* [17C–9C] a prostitute. ▫ **night-shark** *n. see* NIGHTHAWK *n.* ▫ **night sneak** *n.* [SNEAK *n.*[1] (1b)] **1** [18C] robbery by night. **2** *see* EVENING SNEAK *under* EVENING *adj.* ▫ **night stick** *n.* **1** [1910s+] (*US*) the penis [play on SE *nightstick*/STICK *n.* (1a)]. **2** [1950s+] (*US black*) anyone who lives their life in clubs and bars and generally indulges themselves as a 'night person'. ▫ **night trader** *n.* [17C–19C] a prostitute. ▫ **night walker** *n. see* separate entry. ▫ **night work** *n.* [late 16C–mid-19C; 1950s+] sexual intercourse.

IN PHRASES

▫ **dirty night at sea** *n. see under* DIRTY *adj.* ▫ **night on the rainbow** *n.* [1940s+] (*drugs*) a night spent under the influence of drugs.

night and day *n.* [rhy. sl.] [mid–late19C] a play.

night and day *adj.* [rhy. sl.] [20C+] gray, grey.

night and day *v.* [rhy. sl.] [mid-19C] to see a play.

nightcap *n.*[1] [SE *night* + *capture*] **1** [early 17C] a bully who specializes in finding victims at night. **2** [19C–1910s] a thief who prefers to work at night. **3** [19C–1910s] a prostitute. **4** [1940s] (*US Und.*) a night watchman.

nightcap *n.*[2] [SE *nightcap*, a bed hat or a final drink before bedtime] **1** [1910s] (*Aus.*) a condemned prisoner's head mask worn when being hanged. **2** pertaining to culmination. (**a**) [1910s+] (*US*) the final race or contest of a day's sports, esp. the second game in a baseball 'double-header'. (**b**) [1950s+] the last portion of a drug prior to bed. **3** [1970s–80s] (*US black*) a small skull-cap worn by many black men.

SE in slang uses

IN PHRASES

▫ **have one's nightcap on** *v.* [fig. use of SE *nightcap*, a hat worn in bed; note predates SE *nightcap*, a final drink before bed] [18C] to be drunk.

nighthawk *n.* (*also* **night-shark**) **1** [early 19C+] anyone who likes to stay up late, usu. for reasons of criminality. **2** [mid-19C+] (*US*) a worker on a night shift. **3** [mid-19C+] (*US*) a taxi that plys for trade at night; also its driver. **4** [20C+] (*Aus./US*) a thief, esp. one who works at night. **5** [20C+] (*Aus.*) a prostitute.

nighthawk *v.* [NIGHTHAWK *n.*] [late 19C+] (*US*) **1** to work or socialize at night. **2** to drive a cab at night.

nightie *n.*[1] [abbr.] [1900s–50s] a nightwatchman.

nightie *n.*[2] [abbr. SE *nightmare*] [1980s+] (*US campus*) a very bad situation, esp. one over which one has no control.

nightingale *n.* **1** [19C] a prostitute. **2** [late 19C–1910s] (*US*) a singer. **3** [1930s+] (*UK Und.*) an informer [they SE *sing*/SING *v.* (4); note 18C milit. *nightingale*, a soldier who cries out during a flogging].

night owl *n.* **1** [mid-19C+] (*US*) a taxi that plys for trade at night. **2** [mid-19C+] anyone who is habitually out and about at nighttime. **3** [late 19C+] late customers of cafés and restaurants. **4** [1920s] a night-soil worker. **5** [1980s+] one who stays up late (but does not necessarily go out).

night-owl *adj.* (*also* **owl**) [NIGHT OWL *n.*] [late 19C+] being open late at night, or being active late at night.

night-owl *v.* [NIGHT OWL *n.*] [1930s] to be active at night.

night walker *n.* **1** [mid-16C–19C] a thief or rogue. **2** [17C–1930s] (*also* **night-trader**) a prostitute. **3** [late 17C–mid-18C] a bellman or town crier.

DERIVATIVES

▫ **night-walking** *n.* [mid-17C–late 19C] working as a prostitute (at night).

nigit *n.* (*also* **nidget**) [play on SE *an eejit, an idiot*] [17C–18C] a fool, an idiot.

nigle *v. see* NIGGLE *v.*

nigler *n.* **1** *see* NIGGLER *n.*[1] (2). **2** *see* NIGGLER *n.*[2].

niglet *n.* [NIGGER *n.*[1] (1) + dimin. sfx *-let*] [1990s+] (*US black*) a black child.

nigling *n. see* NIGGLING *under* NIGGLE *v.*

nig-mag *n. see* NIG *n.*[2].

nigmenog *n.* (*also* **nimenog**) [? link to dial. *nigmanies*, a trifle] [late 17C–early 19C] a fool, an idiot.

nig-nog *n.*[1] (*also* **nig**) [*The Times* (30 November 1967) claims the term was used 'long before coloured immigrants appeared...' but the greater likelihood is that the stereotype of the incompetent black labourer was the real origin, although note NIGMENOG *n.* + Scot. *nig-nag*, a worthless, useless thing] [1950s–70s] **1** (*orig. railway*) a novice, an unskilled person. **2** a fool, a simpleton.

nig-nog *n.*[2] [abbr. NIGGER *n.*[1] (1) + redup.] [1950s+] any non-white, whether black, Asian or East Asian.

nig-nog *v.* [abbr. and redup. of NIGGLE *v.*] [mid-17C] to copulate with.

-nik *sfx* [the Rus./Yid. sfx *-nik*; already in use but hugely popularized by the first *Sputnik* space craft, launched 1957; the orig. such term was *beatnik*, coined derisively by columnist Herb Caen of the *San Francisco Chronicle*] [1910s+] (*orig. US*) used to denote the involvement or association of a person or thing with the thing or quality described.

nikey/nikin *n. see* NICKIN *n.*

Niki Lauda *n.* [rhy. sl. = POWDER *n.*[1] (2); ult. *Niki Lauda* (b. 1949), Austrian F1 racing driver] [1990s+] (*drugs*) cocaine.

nil *n.* [ety. unknown] [mid-19C] half; thus half-profits.

nilly-dilly *adj.* [? rhy. sl.] [1970s] (*US black*) silly, foolish.

nim *n.* (*also* **nimmer, nym**) [NIM *v.*] [17C–19C] a thief.

nim *v.* (*also* **nym**) [9C–16C SE *nim*, to take from; Grose (1785) cites 'German, *nemen*, to take'] [17C–19C; 1970s+] (*UK Und.*) to steal.

DERIVATIVES

▫ **nimming** *n.* [17C–19C] theft.

IN PHRASES

▫ **nim a tatler** *v.* [TATLER *n.*] [19C] to steal a watch.

nimbie *n.* (*also* **nimby**) [abbr.] [1960s+] (*US drugs*) *Nembutal*.

nimbles *n.* [SE *nimble-fingered*] [early 17C] fingers.

nimble-wimble *n.* [SE *nimble* + *wimble*, a gimlet, an auger] [mid-17C] the penis.

nimby *n. see* NIMBIE *n.*

nimenog *n. see* NIGMENOG *n.*

nimgimmer *n.* [ety. unknown] [late 17C–early 19C] (*UK Und.*) a surgeon or physician, esp. a specialist in venereal diseases.

nimmer *n. see* NIM *n.*

nimrod *n.* [biblical proper name *Nimrod*, the 'mighty hunter' of Gen.] **1** [19C] the penis [pun on ROD *n.* (1)]. **2** [1930s+] (*orig. US campus*) a socially inept person, someone not attuned to the group norms [popularized by 1940s Warner Bros. cartoon character Elmer Fudd (a rabbit-hunter), called 'poor little Nimrod' by Bugs Bunny].

nimshi *n.* [? dial. *nimshie*, a flighty girl] [mid-19C–1950s] (*US*) a fool.

nimshod *n.* [? Nimrod 'a mighty hunter' or NIM *n.* + Rom. *shosho*, a rabbit] [late 19C] a cat.

nimwit *adj.* [NIMROD *n.* (2) + SE *dimwit*] [1990s+] (*US*) stupid.

nina *n.* (*also* **neener**) [the 9mm barrel] [1980s+] (*US black*) a handgun.

nina (with her hair down) *n.* (*also* **Carolina nine, nina from Argentina, ...Carolina, ...Palestina, ...Pasadena**) [1910s+] (*US gambling*) the point of 9 in craps dice.

nincom *n.* (*also* **nincum**) [abbr. NINCOMPOOP *n.*] [late 18C–19C] a fool.

nincompoop *n.* (*also* **nickumpoop, ninc, nincumpoop, nink-a-poop, ninkompoop, ninny-cum-poop**) ['one who never saw his wife's CUNT *n.* (1)' (Grose 1785); Hotten (1860) suggests 'corruption of *non compos mentis*'] [late 17C+] a fool, a simpleton; a suitor who lacks self-confidence; a hen-pecked husband.

(DERIVATIVES)

❑ **nincompoopery** *n.* [1920s] foolishness.

nincum noodle *n.* [NINCOMPOOP *n.* + NOODLE *n.*[1] (2); punning on a SE *noodle* with *no income*] [early 19C] a penniless fool.

nincumpoop *n. see* NINCOMPOOP *n.*

nine *n.* **1** [1920s+] (*Aus.*) (*also* **niner**) a 9-gallon (41-litre) keg of beer. **2** [1980s+] (*US*) (*also* **milly, 9, 9-millie, nines**) a 9mm pistol.

SE in slang uses

(IN COMPOUNDS)

❑ **nine-spot** *n. see under* -SPOT *sfx.*

(IN PHRASES)

❑ **nine o'clock town** *n.* [1930s] (*US*) a town in which all sources of entertainment shut down early. ❑ **nine to never** *n.* [1970s+] (*S.Afr. prison*) an indeterminate sentence.

nine *adj.*

SE in slang uses

(IN COMPOUNDS)

❑ **nine corns** *n.* [Lincolnshire/Salop. dial.] [mid-19C] a pipeful of tobacco. ❑ **nine-eyed** *adj.* [1970s] (*US campus*) intoxicated. ❑ **nine-inch knocker** *n.* [17C+] the penis. ❑ **ninepins** *n.* [it can be easily knocked over] [late 19C] the body. ❑ **nine-tail bruiser** *n.* (*also* **nine-tail mouser**) [18C–19C] the cat-o'-nine-tails. ❑ **nine winks** *n.* [var. on colloq. *forty winks*] [early–mid-19C] a very brief nap.

(IN PHRASES)

❑ **nine ways from breakfast** *adv.* (*also* **nine ways for next Sunday, nine ways to Sunday, three ways (and Sunday)**) [1910s+] in all sorts of ways; comprehensively.

nine *v.* [bowling imagery i.e. one knocks the nine pins] [1930s] to take advantage of.

nine-bob note *n.* [the UK's pre-decimal currency included a '10-bob', i.e. 10-shilling note, but not a 'nine-bob' one] [1960s+] anyone or anything fake, spurious, esp. in phr. *BENT AS A NINE-BOB NOTE under* BENT *adj.* or *...A NINE-BOB NOTE under* QUEER AS... *adj.*

nine-dollar bill *n.* [there is no *nine-dollar bill*] [1940s+] (*US*) **1** a fake, a second-rate imitation. **2** a homosexual.

(IN PHRASES)

❑ **three times as queer as a three dollar bill** *see* under THREE *adj.*

nine-eight *n.* (*also* **98**) [1990s+] (*US*) a 98 Oldsmobile. A very limited make of Oldsmobile, usu. considered to be the company's best model of car, in any given year and thus a real status symbol.

9-millie *n. see* NINE *n.* (2).

911 *n.* [US telephone code for emergencies, the equivalent of the UK 999] [2000s] (*US prison*) a warning that an officer is approaching.

ninepence *n.* [? SE phr. 'nice as nicepence'] [late 19C+] (*mainly UK juv.*) the vagina.

ninepence short of a shilling *phr. see under* ...SHORT OF... *adj.*

ninepennyworth *n.* [1940s–50s] a nine-month prison sentence.

niner *n.* **1** [late 19C] a convict serving a nine-year sentence. **2** [1930s+] (*Aus.*) a woman in her ninth month of pregnancy. **3** [1980s+] a Tech Nine automatic gun. **4** *see* NINE *n.* (1).

nines *n. see* NINE *n.* (2).

nine shillings *n.* [joc. mispron. of SE *nonchalance*] [late 18C–mid-19C] audacity, calmness.

nineteen canteen *adv.* [assonance] [1940s+] (*S.Afr.*) a very long time ago.

nineteen-carrot *adj. see* EIGHTEEN-CARAT *adj.*

nineteener *n.* [? one who talks 'nineteen to the dozen' or the cribbage score of 19, an impossibility to achieve] [late 19C–1940s] (*Aus./N.Z.*) an untrustworthy, unpleasant person.

nineteenth hole *n.* [a golf course has 18 holes] [20C+] the bar at a golf club; esp. used by golfers but understood more widely.

nine-to-five *n.* (*also* **nine-till-five**) [the hours most usu. worked] [1960s+] (*orig. US*) a regular, routine, uninspiring job.

nine-to-five *adj.* [NINE-TO-FIVE *n.*] [1960s+] working in a routine job.

nine-to-five *v.* [NINE-TO-FIVE *n.*] [1960s+] to lead a regular, routine (working) life.

nine-to-fiver *n.* [NINE-TO-FIVE *n.*] **1** [1960s+] (*orig. US*) an office worker. **2** [1970s+] an office job.

ninety *n.* (*also* **90 dog**) [the curled tail, which resembles the number 9] [late 19C–1900s] a pug.

SE in slang uses

(IN COMPOUNDS)

❑ **ninety-nine** *n.* [a play on the usu. SIXTY-NINE *n.* (1)] [1940s–70s] (*Aus./US gay*) anal intercourse. ❑ **ninety-six** *n.* [var. on prev.] [1920s–50s] (*US gay*) homosexual anal intercourse.

ninety *adj.*

SE in slang uses

(IN COMPOUNDS)

❑ **ninety days** *n.* [ref. to SE *90 days*, the standard sentence for petty crime] [1910s+] (*US gambling*) in craps, the point of nine. ❑ **ninety-day wonder** *n.* [orig. milit., a junior officer who has completed the 90-day officer training programme] [1940s+] (*US*) an inexperienced employee or one employed for temporary work.

98 *n. see* NINE-EIGHT *n.*

ning-ning *n. see SEE NING-NING under* SEE *v.*

ning-nong *n.* (*also* **ning-nang**) [note horse-coopers' jargon *ning-nang*, a worthless thoroughbred] [mid-19C+] (*Aus./N.Z.*) a stupid, foolish person.

ninihammer *n. see* NINNYHAMMER *n.*

ninja *adj.* [SE *ninja*, a Japanese warrior] [1990s+] secretive.

ninnies *n.* [SE *ninny*, a child] [20C+] (*orig. US*) the female breasts.

ninnihammer *n. see* NINNYHAMMER *n.*

ninny *n.*[1] [SE *ninny*, a fool; ? ult. SE *innocent*] [late 17C–mid-18C] (*UK Und.*) a 'canting, whining beggar' (B.E.).

SE in slang uses

(IN COMPOUNDS)

❑ **ninny-broth** *n.* [i.e. 'real men' drink beer or wine] [late 17C–early 18C] coffee. ❑ **ninny-broth house** *n.* [early 18C] a coffee house. ❑ **ninny-gut** *n.* [1930s] (*US*) a weakling.

ninny *n.*[2] [abbr. SE *pickaninny*] [1990s+] (*US*) a black person.

ninny *n.*[3] [? SE *ninny*, a fool; reversing the model of terms like PRICK *n.*] [2000s] a penis.

ninnyhammer *n.* (*also* **ninihammer, ninnihammer, ninny**) [? NINNY *n.*[1] or SE *ninny*, a fool + dial. *hammer*, n. a clumsy person or v. to stammer] [late 16C–1910s] a fool, a simpleton; by ext. a cuckold.

ninny jugs *n.* [NINNIES *n.* + SE *jug*] [1960s–70s] (*US*) the female breasts.

ninth part of a man *n.* (*also* **tenth part of a man**) [pvb 'nine tailors make a man'] [mid-17C–19C] a tailor.

Nip *n.* (*also* **Nipper, Nippo**) [abbr. SE *Nipponese*, ult. Jap. *ni(chi)* the sun + *pon, hon*, source] (*orig. US*) **1** [1940s+] a Japanese person. **2** [1940s+] the Japanese language. **3** [1980s+] any East Asian person.

Nip *adj.* [NIP *n.*] (*orig. US*) **1** [1940s+] pertaining to Japan, the Japanese or Japanese culture. **2** [1980s+] pertaining to East Asia, East Asians or East Asian culture.

nip *n.*[1] [NIP *v.*[1] (1)] (*UK Und.*) **1** [late 16C–17C] a cutpurse. **2** [late 17C–early 19C] (*UK Und.*) (*also* **nipps**) in pl., shears used to clip coins. **3** [late 17C–mid-19C] a cardsharp, a cheat. **4** [1920s] (*UK Und.*) in pl., a thief's device for unlocking locked doors.

nip *n.*[2] [? dial. *nip*, a good bargainer, 'just honest and no more'] [early 19C] 'Passengers who are taken up on stage coaches by the collusion of the guard and coachman, without the knowledge of the proprietors, are called nips' (De Quincey, *King of Hayti*, 1823).

nip *n.*[3]

IN PHRASES

❑ **in one's nip** (*also* **in the nip**) [? SE *nip in the air*, i.e. one suffers from the cold] [20C+] (*Irish*) stark naked.

nip *n.*[4] [NIP *v.*[1] (8)] [1930s–40s] (*Aus.*) one who responds favourably to cadgers, a 'soft touch'.

nip *n.*[5] [abbr.] [1930s+] the nipple.

IN COMPOUNDS

❑ **nip-slip** *n.* [2000s] the involuntarily display of a nipple, usu. via an already revealing garment. ❑ **nip tease** *n.* [1990s+] a woman who is not wearing a bra under her top.

nip *n.*[6] [SE *nip* to move quickly] [1950s] an escape from prison.

nip *n.*[7]

SE, meaning a portion of alcohol, in slang uses

IN COMPOUNDS

❑ **nip joint** *n.* [JOINT *n.* (3b)] [1950s+] (*US*) an illegal drinking establishment where drink is sold in *nips* or small (orig. half-pint) measures. ❑ **Nip Shop** *n.* (*also* **nyp shop**) [late 18C–early 19C] the Peacock Tavern in Gray's Inn Lane, London, where Burton ale was sold in *nips* or half-pint measures.

nip *v.*[1] [SE *nip*, to cut, to snip] **1** [mid-16C–1910s] (*UK Und.*) to cut a purse or pick a pocket. **2** [mid-16C–1960s] (*UK Und.*) to arrest. **3** [mid-16C+] to steal, to snatch, to shoplift. **4** [mid–late 19C] (*US*) to shoot someone. **5** [late 19C+] (*US*) to defeat. **6** [1900s–20s] (*US Und.*) to obtain, to get hold of. **7** [1910s–20s] of a man, to have sexual intercourse. **8** [1910s+] (*Aus.*) to borrow, to cadge, to wheedle (money) out of. **9** [1930s–40s] (*US*) to cheat, to take advantage of. **10** [1980s] (*US black*) to scratch to give a superficial wound. **11** [2000s] (*Irish*) to pick up (a woman).

IN PHRASES

❑ **nip a bung** *v.* (*also* **bung-nip, nip a boung** *v.*) [sense 1 above + BUNG *n.*[1] (1)] [mid-16C–mid-18C] (*UK Und.*) to cut a purse. ❑ **put the nips in(to)** *v.* (*also* **get the nips into, put in the nips**) [1910s+] (*Aus./N.Z.*) to cadge from.

SE in slang uses

IN COMPOUNDS

❑ **nip louse** *n.* [his removal of lice from the seams of clothes] [mid-19C–1920s] a tailor. ❑ **nip lug** *n.* [LUG *n.*[1]] [19C] (*Scot.*) a teacher. ❑ **nip shred** *n.* [SE *shred* of cloth] [mid-17C–mid-18C] a tailor.

IN PHRASES

❑ **nip it** *v.* [abbr. SE phr. *nip (it) in the bud*] [1980s+] (*US campus*) to stop something.

nip *v.*[2] [SE *nap*] [1910s] (*Aus.*) to sleep.

nip *v.*[3] [? the fig. tightening of the sphincter muscles] [1960s+] (*S.Afr.*) to be scared, terrified.

nipcheese *n.* [NIP *v.*[1] (3) + SE *cheese*; lit. 'one who steals the cheese'] [late 18C–late 19C] **1** a ship's purser. **2** a mean, miserly person.

nipitate *n.* (*also* **nipitaty, nippitato, nippitatum**) [SE *nip*, a drink] [16C–17C] strong drink in general.

nippels *n.* [? SE *nipples*] [2000s] (*US black*) a sophisticated black man.

Nipper *n. see* NIP *n.*

nipper *n.*[1] [NIP *v.*[1]] **1** [late 16C–19C] (*UK Und.*) (*also* **nypper**) a cutpurse or pickpocket. **2** [mid–late 19C] (*US*) a policeman. **3** [late 19C] a miser, a tight-fisted person. **4** [late 19C–1900s] (*US/Aus.*) a thief or swindler.

nipper *n.*[2] [NIP *v.*[1]; 20C+ use mainly US] **1** [early 19C–1920s] (*US*) in pl., fingers or hands. **2** [early 19C–1950s] in pl., handcuffs. **3** [late 19C–1920s] (*US*) in pl., pince-nez [their 'nipping' the bridge of the nose to gain a purchase on the face]. **4** [1960s] (*US campus*) in pl., the female breasts.

nipper *n.*[3] (*also* **nip**) [children 'nip around'] **1** [mid-19C+] a baby; a young boy (pre-teenage). **2** [mid-19C–1960s] a boy who hires himself out to a costermonger or market greengrocer. **3** [1950s] a small, short person.

nipper *n.*[4] [SE *nip*, to pinch] [late 19C+] (*Aus.*) a prawn.

nipper *v.* [NIP *v.*[1] (2)] [early 19C] to arrest.

nipping Christian *n.* [NIP *v.*[1] (1) + joc. generic use of SE *Christian*] [early 17C–mid-19C] a cut-purse.

nipping jig *n.* [SE *nip*, to pinch + *jig*, a dance] [19C] (*US*) **1** a gallows. **2** a hanging.

nippitato/nippitatum *n. see* NIPITATE *n.*

nipple *n.* **1** [1950s] (*W.I.*) a small finger-shaped dumpling. **2** *see* TIT *n.*[2] (3).

IN PHRASES

❑ **up to one's nipples** *see* UP TO ONE'S ARMPITS *under* ARMPIT *n.*

nipply *adj.* [pun on SE *nippy* cold + the fact that cold weather makes women's nipples erect and thus visible] [1990s+] cold, chilly.

Nippo *n. see* NIP *n.*

nipps *n. see* NIP *n.*[1] (2).

nippy *n.*[1] [? PEE *n.*[1]] [mid-19C] the penis.

nippy *n.*[2] [SE nip, to hurry; the original *nippies*, waitresses at Lyons Corner Houses, whose name was trademarked by the firm and came from their speed; later use is historical] [1920s–50s] a waitress.

nire *n.* [backsl.] [mid-19C] rain.

nisey *see under* NIZZIE.

nish! *excl.* [ext. SE *shhh!*] [mid-19C] (*UK Und.*) be quiet, be still.

nisht *n.* (*also* **nicht, nish, nishte**) [synon. Yid.; *nish* is UK black use] [1910s+] nothing.

nisty *adj.* [? SE *nasty*] [1980s+] (*US campus*) very unattractive.

nit *n.*[1] [SE *nit*, a louse; the implication is perhaps more of its insignificance than of its verminous qualities] **1** [late 16C+] a fool. **2** [1910s] (*Aus. milit.*) a police officer.

SE in slang uses

IN COMPOUNDS

❑ **nit-head** *n.* [-HEAD *sfx* (1)] [1990s+] an idiot, a fool. ❑ **nit squeeger** *n.* [lit. 'louse-squeezer'] [late 18C–early 19C] a hairdresser.

IN PHRASES

❑ **nit's tits** *n.* [1900s] (*Aus.*) an excellent and admirable person or thing.

nit *n.*[2] [ety. unknown; ? SE *nit*, louse] [late 17C–18C] 'Wine that is brisk, [i.e. agreeable to the taste] and pour'd quick into a Glass' (B.E.).

nit *v.* [? NICK *v.*[3] or SE *nit*, a louse] [late 19C+] (*Scot./Aus.*) to escape, to decamp, to hurry away.

nit! *excl.*[1] [var. on SE *not*] [late 19C–1940s] (*US*) used as an emphatic *no*, also added to positive assertions to give a negative meaning e.g., 'I should say nit!'.

nit! *excl.*[2] (*also* **nito!**) [NIT *v.*] [late 19C–1950s] (*orig. Aus.*) a term used to indicate that someone is coming and that one must stop what one is doing and run away.

IN COMPOUNDS

❑ **nit-keeper** *n.* [1930s+] (*Aus.*) one who keeps watch while a companion performs some form of illegal activity.

IN PHRASES

❑ **keep nit** *v.* [var. on *KEEP NIX under* NIX! *excl.*] [20C+] (*Aus.*) to act as lookout.

nite nurse *n.* [the reggae song by Gregory Isaacs 'Night Nurse' (1982)] [1990s+] (*W.I.*) **1** a woman who treats her boyfriend well. **2** cocaine.

niterie *n.* (*also* **nitery**) [latterly SE] [1930s+] (*orig. US*) a nightclub.

nit-nit! *excl.* (*also* **nick-nick!**) [NIT! *excl.*[1]/NIT! *excl.*[2]] [1930s–50s] shut up!

nito *v. see* NITTO *v.*

nito! *excl. see* NIT! *excl.*[2].

nitraph *n.* [backsl.] [mid-19C] a farthing.

nitro *n.* [abbr.] **1** [20C+] (*orig. US*) *nitro*glycerine, as used in blowing up safes. **2** [1950s] (*US*) a strong alcoholic drink.

(IN COMPOUNDS)

❑ **nitro man** *n.* [1950s] a safe-breaker.

nitro *adj.* [fig. use of NITRO *n.*] [1980s+] (*US*) excellent, wonderful.

nits and lice *n.* [rhy. sl.] [20C+] a price, esp. in gambling.

nitshit *n.* [NIT-SHIT *adj.*] [1970s] (*US*) nonsense, trivial matters.

nit-shit *adj.* [SE *nit*, a louse + SHIT *adj.* (1)] [1960s+] (*US*) second-rate, insignificant, trivial.

nit-shit *v.* [NIT-SHIT *adj.*] [1960s–70s] (*US*) to talk in an irritating manner.

nitski! *excl.* [NIT! *excl.*[1] + -SKI *sfx*] [1900s–20s] (*US*) an emphatic 'no!'.

nitto *v.* (*also* **nito**) [NIT-NIT! *excl.*] [1950s–70s] (*UK Und.*) to stop.

(IN EXCLAMATIONS)

❑ **nitto!** [1950s–70s] stop it!

nitty *n.* [abbr. NITTY-GRITTY *n.*] [1970s+] (*US*) the essentials, the fundamentals.

nitty *adj.* (*also* **knitty**) [lit. suffering from SE *nits*, lice] [late 16C–18C] a general epithet of abuse.

nitty-gritty *n.* (*also* **gritty, knitty-gritty**) [ety. unknown; redup. of SE *gritty*, composed of minute particles] [1950s+] (*orig. US black*) the basics, the essentials, the grass roots.

(IN PHRASES)

❑ **get down to the nitty-gritty** *v.* [1960s+] (*orig. US black*) to get down to essentials, to basics.

nitty-gritty *adj.* [NITTY-GRITTY *n.*] [1960s+] (*orig. US black*) fundamental, basic.

nitwit *n.* [SE *nit*, a louse + *wit*] [1910s+] (*orig. US*) a fool.

nitwitted *adj.* (*also* **nitwit**) [NITWIT *n.*] [1920s+] stupid, foolish; a term of abuse.

nix *n.* [colloq. Du./Ger. *nix*; ult. Ger. *nichts*, nothing] **1** [late 18C+] (*also* **nicks**) nobody, no one, nothing. **2** [late 19C–1900s] (*US*) nowhere. **3** [1910s] (*US*) a good-for-nothing. **4** [1980s+] (*drugs*) a stranger among the group.

(IN PHRASES)

❑ **for nix** *adv.* (*Aus.*) to any extent, not at all. ❑ **nix my doll** (*also* **nicks my doll, nix my dolly**) [thus the sl. verse: 'In the box of a stone jug I was born,/Of a hempen widow and a kid forlorn;/And my noble father, as I have heard say,/Was a famous merchant of capers gay;/Nix my dolly, pals, fake away!'; written by William Ainsworth as 'Jenny Junipers' chant in *Rookwood* 1834; he claimed it as the 'first flash song' but was some 300 years late. Farmer (1896) cites Copland's *Rhymes of the Canting Crew* c.1536] [late 18C–19C] nothing, never mind, it doesn't matter.

nix *adj.* [NIX *n.*] **1** [mid-19C–1950s] (*US*) worthless or damaged. **2** [20C+] (*also* **nixie**) no, none, negligible.

nix *v.* (*also* **nix off**) [NIX *n.*] **1** [mid-18C; 20C+] (*US*) to forbid, to veto, to reject, to cancel or eliminate. **2** [1940s] (*US black/Harlem*) to leave, to depart (from).

(IN PHRASES)

❑ **nix on it!** [1940s+] (*Aus.*) no more of that, stop it. ❑ **nix out (on)** [1930s–50s] (*orig. US black*) **1** to throw away, to get rid of a person or object. **2** to go; thus, fig., to die.

nix *adv.* [NIX *n.*] [mid-19C+] no, certainly not.

(IN PHRASES)

❑ **nix on** [20C+] (*US*) enough of, no more of.

nix! *excl.* [NIX *adv.*] **1** [mid-19C+] a warning of someone's approach. **2** [late 19C+] (*orig. US*) an emphatic 'no!', 'stop that (at once)!'.

(IN PHRASES)

❑ **keep nix** *v.* [mid-19C+] to keep a lookout. ❑ **put the nix on** *v.* [mid-19C] to negate, to make unavailable.

(IN EXCLAMATIONS)

❑ **nix deberr!** [*deberr*, a perversion of Rus. *tovarich*, a friend] [early 19C] no, my friend!

nixer *n.* (*also* **foxer, nickser**) [NIX *v.* (1)] [1950s+] (*Irish*) work undertaken in one's free time, as part of the 'black economy'.

nixey *n.* (*also* **nixies**) [NIX *n.* (1)] [20C+] nothing.

nixey! *excl.* (*also* **nixie! nixy!**) [NIX! *excl.*] [mid-19C–1910s] (*US*) an emphatic 'no!'.

nixie *n.* [abbr.] [1920s–30s] in pl., women's knickers.

nixie *adj.* see NIX *adj.* (2).

nixie! *excl.* see NIXEY! *excl.*

nixies *n.*[1] [1990s+] (*UK juv.*) the hidden crossing of one's fingers that allows one to exclude oneself from a task/game.

nixies *n.*[2] see NIXEY *n.*

Nixon *n.* [the corruption of US President Richard M. *Nixon* (1913–94)] [1960s+] (*drugs*) inferior marijuana sold fraudulently as being of high quality.

nixy! *excl.* see NIXEY! *excl.*

nizzie *n.* (*also* **nisey, nizy**) [? 13C SE *nice*, foolish, senseless; ? ult. Lat. *nescius*, ignorant] [late 17C–1920s] (*UK Und.*) a fool, a dunce.

nizzie *adj.* (*also* **nisey, nizy**) [NIZZIE *n.*] [early 18C] foolish, dull.

n.m.c. *n.* [abbr. *no mates club*] [1990s+] (*UK juv.*) a metaphorical 'club' whose members are the least popular children at school.

n.n. *n.* [abbr. *n*ecessary *n*uisance] [late 19C–1900s] (*UK society*) a husband.

N.O. *n.* [abbr.] [1960s] (*US*) New Orleans.

no-account *n.* (*also* **no count**) [NO-ACCOUNT *adj.*] [late 19C+] a worthless person.

no-account *adj.* (*also* **no-count**) [abbr. SE *of no account*] [mid-19C+] (*orig. US black*) a general pej., worthless, insignificant, undependable, untrustworthy, criminal.

(IN COMPOUNDS)

❑ **no-account nigger** *n.* [NIGGER *n.*[1] (1)] [late 19C+] (*US black*) **1** a black who rejects the second-class role offered by the dominant white society. **2** an untrustworthy person.

Noah *n.* [their relation with water] **1** [mid-19C] (*US Und.*) a flat-bottomed boat. **2** [1900s] (*US*) a poached egg.

Noah's (ark) *n.*[1] [rhy. sl.] **1** [19C] a lark, a game; crime. **2** [late 19C] a lark (the bird). **3** [20C+] a park. **4** [20C+] an informer [NARK *n.* (1)]. **5** [20C+] dark. **6** [20C+] (*Aus.*) a dullard, a fool [NARK *n.* (2)]. **7** [1940s+] (*Aus.*) a shark. **8** [1950s] a prostitute [unusual in that it rhymes on the first word, *Noah's* = [wh]'ores, in a Cockney pron.]. **9** [1960s] (*Aus.*) a moneylender [SHARK *n.* (3a)].

Noah's (ark) *n.*[2] [early 19C] a gathering of beggars.

Noah's ark *n.* [coined by *Punch*, the term supposedly reflected the similarity of the coat to those worn by Noah and his children in toy *Noah's arks*] [mid-19C] a long, closely buttoned overcoat, fashionable at the time.

no-ass *adj.* [ASS *n.* (2)] [1980s+] (*US black*) a general term of derision.

nob *n.*[1] [var. on KNOB *n.*] **1** [late 17C+] (*orig. UK Und.*) (*also* **nobb**) the head. **2** [late 18C–19C] (*UK Und.*) a hat. **3** [early 19C] in fig. use to mean first or front. **4** [early 19C] a blow on the head. **5** [mid-19C] (*UK Und.*) a young boy prisoner who bullies weaker ones. **6** [mid-19C] a sovereign. **7** [mid-19C+] the penis [var. of KNOB *n.* (1c)]. **8** [late 19C–1910s] (*Aus.*) in two-up, a double-headed coin. **9** [1920s–30s] (*Aus.*) a go, an item. **10** [1970s+] a socially inept person [fig. use of sense 7].

(IN COMPOUNDS)

❑ **nob artist** *n.* see KNOB ARTIST *under* KNOB *n.* ❑ **nob jockey** *n.* see KNOB-JOCKEY *under* KNOB *n.* ❑ **nob rails** *n.* see HEAD RAILS *under* HEAD *n.* ❑ **nob stilton** *n.* [elaboration of COCK CHEESE *under* COCK *n.*[3]] [1990s+] smegma. ❑ **nob thatch** *n.* [mid 19C] human hair. ❑ **nob-thatcher** *n.* (*also* **knob-thatcher**) [late 18C–mid-19C] a wig-maker; a hat-maker. ❑ **nob-work** *n.* [early 19C] (*UK Und.*) ingenuity.

(IN PHRASES)

❑ **keep one's nob squared** *v.* [1900s] to keep calm. ❑ **off one's nob** *adj.* [1950s+] **1** eccentric, insane. **2** drunk.

nob *n.*[2] [? abbr. SE *nobility* or *nobleman*, but 18C Scot. use suggests an alternative – if unknown – ety.; according to Jon Bee (1823), 'the swell ... makes a show of his finery ... the nob, relying upon intrinsic worth, or bona fide property, or intellectual ability, is clad in plain-ness'] **1** [18C+] a nobleman, a gentleman. **2** [1910s] (*Aus.*) an expert [from sense 1].

DERIVATIVES

❑ **nobbery** *n.* [1990s+] the elite. ❑ **nobbish** *adj.* [mid-19C] aristocratic; showy.

IN PHRASES

❑ **come the nob** *v.* (*also* **come the duke, ...nabob**) [early 19C+] to give oneself airs. ❑ **flash the nob** *v.* [mid-19C] (*UK Und.*) to pose as an aristocrat to defraud tradesmen. ❑ **nob in the fur trade** *n.* [mid-19C] a judge. ❑ **nob it** *v.* [early 19C] (*UK Und.*) to use brains rather than brawn to succeed in the world. ❑ **nobs' houses** *n.* [mid-19C] the Houses of Parliament.

nob *n.*[3] [ety. unknown] [mid-18C–mid-19C] the game of prick-the-garter, a form of swindling game, in which one pricked a belt with a large needle; presumably betting on the odds of hitting a given target.

IN COMPOUNDS

❑ **nob pitcher** *n.* [early 19C] (*UK Und.*) a specialist in prick-the-garter, usu. working at fairs, races and similar open-air events.

nob *n.*[4] [? dial. *nob*, an interloper] [mid–late 19C] in cribbage, the knave of trumps.

nob *v.* [NOB *n.*[1]] **1** [early–mid-19C] to hit on the head. **2** [mid-19C–1930s] (*also* **knob**) to collect money; to make a collection after a sporting contest, a performance etc. **3** [1980s+] of a man, to have sexual intercourse.

DERIVATIVES

❑ **nobber** *n.* [1990s+] a copulator.

nob-a-nob *adj.* [NOB *n.*[1] (1)] [mid–late 19C] intimate, close, friendly.

nobb *n. see* NOB *n.*[1] (1).

nobba *n.* (*also* **nobber**) [Ital. *nove*, nine; 'introduced by the "organ-grinders" from Italy' (Hotten, 1867)] [mid-19C] nine.

IN COMPOUNDS

❑ **nobba saltee** *n.* [mid-19C] ninepence.

nobber *n.* [NOB *v.*] **1** pertaining to violence. (**a**) [early–mid-19C] a blow on the head. (**b**) [early–late 19C] a boxer skilled at delivering such blows. (**c**) [1930s] (*US Und.*) a thug who knocks out his victim before robbing them. **2** [late 19C–1930s] a collector of money, esp. when serving as the assistant to a street performer.

nobbies *n. see* NOBBY STILES *n.*

nobbing *n.* [NOB *v.*] **1** [mid–late 19C] collecting money, 'passing the hat round'. **2** [mid–late 19C] in pl., a collection of money, esp. money tossed into a boxing ring after an amateur or boys' fight. **3** [1980s+] sexual intercourse.

nobbing *adj.* [NOB *v.* (3)] [1990s+] euph. for FUCKING *adj.*

nobbish *adj. see* NOB *n.*[2] (1).

nobble *v.*[1] [NOB *n.*[1] (1)] **1** [mid-19C] to strike, to hit on the head. **2** [1970s+] to kill.

nobble *v.*[2] [ety. unknown; ? NAB *v.*[1]] **1** [mid-19C] to discover. **2** [mid–late 19C] to steal, to take illicitly. **3** [mid–late 19C] to cheat, to over-reach. **4** [mid-19C+] to use illicit methods to obtain a person's help, to swindle, to influence or to corrupt. **5** [mid-19C+] (*racing*) to interfere with a horse in order to spoil its chance of victory, occas. ext. to human competitors. **6** [mid-19C+] to get hold of, to seize, to catch. **7** [late 19C+] to ruin anything deliberately; esp. to impede a rival; to discover (a plot). **8** [1920s+] to kidnap. **9** [1930s+] to recognize. **10** [1990s+] (*US*) to obtain for oneself undeservedly.

IN PHRASES

❑ **jury nobbling** *n.* [1960s+] the interference with the impartiality of a jury (through threats or bribes) either by a defendant or their friends.

nobbler *n.*[1] [orig. boxing but note NOBBLE *v.*[1] (1)] [mid-19C] (*orig. boxing*) a knockout blow.

nobbler *n.*[2] [NOBBLE *v.*[2]; note northern dial. *nobbler*, a low cunning lawyer] **1** [mid–late 19C] a man who runs a game o 'find-the-lady' or THREE-CARD MONTE *n.*; also his accomplice **2** [mid–late 19C] one who lames, drugs or otherwise tamper with horses.

nobbler *n.*[3] (*also* **nobler**) [fig. use of NOBBLE *v.*[2] (6); it 'gets hold o you'] [mid-19C–1950s] (*Aus.*) a small measure of spirits; thu the drink itself.

DERIVATIVES

❑ **nobblerize** *v.* [mid-19C–1950s] (*Aus.*) to drink spirits, usu. a part of a group.

nobbly *adj. see* NOBBY *adj.* (1).

nobby *n.* [? var. on BOBBY *n.* (1)] [1950s] (*UK juv.*) a police officer.

nobby *adj.* [NOB *n.*[2] (1)] **1** [late 18C+] (*also* **knobby, nobbly** extremely smart or elegant, aristocratic. **2** [19C+] showy extravagant. **3** [mid-19C–1900s] as *the nobby*, the smart thing **4** [late 19C] first-rate. **5** [late 19C] smart, clever. **6** [late 19C arrogant. **7** [late 19C–1900s] (*also* **knobby**) (*US*) wonderful.

DERIVATIVES

❑ **nobbily** *adv.* [late 19C] **1** elegantly or aristocratically **2** vulgarly, showily.

nobby *adv.* [NOBBY *adj.* (1)] [late 19C] in a smart manner.

nobby halls *n.* [rhy. sl. = BALLS *n.* (1); ult. *Nobby Halls*, th mono-testicled 'hero' of a music-hall song] [20C+] the testicles

Nobby Stiles *n.* (*also* **nobbies**) [rhy. sl.; ult. 1960s UK socce star *Nobby Stiles* (b. 1942)] [1990s+] haemorrhoids, piles.

nob chete *n. see NAB CHEAT under* NAB *n.*[1].

no beads *phr.* [i.e. 'beads' of sweat; pun on *NO SWEAT under* SWEA *v.*[2]] [1950-60s] (*US teen*) don't worry.

no-beyond jammer *n. see under* JAM *n.*[3] (1).

nob girder *n. see NAB GIRDER under* NAB *n.*[1].

Nob Hill *n.* [NOB *n.*[2] (1) + SE *hill*; note New York's *Nob Hill*, a ro of fine houses built c.1815 near Bowling Green and *Nob's Hill*, a area of San Francisco colonized by wealthy veterans of th California Gold Rush] [early 19C+] (*orig. US*) the most sociall exclusive and/or richest area of a town or city.

no big deal *phr.* (*also* **no biggie, no big thing, no big whoop** [SE *no* + BIG DEAL *n.* (2)/BIGGIE *n.* (1)] [1970s+] (*orig. US teen* don't worry, it's all right etc.

noble *n.* **1** [1910s] (*Aus.*) a friend. **2** [1910s+] (*US*) a ma hired as a guard to protect strike-breakers. **3** [1910s+] (*US*) th boss of a gang of such guards. **4** [1960s–70s] (*US prison*) a inmate considered to be reliable, trustworthy by the guards.

nobler *n. see* NOBBLER *n.*[3].

noble weed *n.* [SE *noble* + WEED *n.*[1] (4)] [1960s] (*drugs* marijuana.

nobody home *phr.* (*also* **nobody home upstairs and room to rent**) [1910s+] (*orig. US*) used of someone who is dull c stupid.

no bon *adj.* [pidgin Fr. *no* + *bon*, good; coined during WW [1910s–20s] no good.

nob onto *v.* [? NOB *n.*[2]] [1910s] to associate with; t accompany.

no bottle *phr.*[1] [the refusal of further drinks by a bar-tende [mid-19C] impossible, not allowed, out of the question.

no bottle *phr.*[2] [rhy. sl. *no bottle and glass*] **1** [mid-19C+] (*als* **not much bottle**) lacking quality or style, no good [= no CLA *n.* (1)]. **2** [1940s+] cowardly [= no ARSE *n.* (7c)].

nob pitcher *n. see* NOB *n.*[3] (1).

no-brainer *n.* [no SE *brain* is required] [1970s+] (*orig. U* **1** anything that requires no intellectual effort. **2** an eas decision. **3** a foolish person or thing.

no-brand cigarette *n.* (*also* **cigarette with no name, n name (brand) cigarette**) [one rolls such cigarettes oneself; there no commercial packaging] [1970s+] (*drugs*) a marijuan cigarette.

nobrow *adj.* [pun on SE *lowbrow*] [1990s+] (*US*) vulga tasteless.

nobs *n.* [NOB *n.*[2] (1); var. of NIBS *n.* (2)] [mid-19C–1950s] (*US*) an important person.

(IN PHRASES)

❑ **his nobs** *see HIS NIBS under* NIBS *n.* ❑ **with nobs on** *see WITH KNOBS ON under* KNOB *n.*

nob-spinner *n. see* SPINNER *n.*[3] (1).

nobstick *n. see* KNOBSTICK *n.*

no burner of navigable rivers *phr.* [play on colloq. phr. *set the Thames on fire*, to accomplish a noteworthy feat] [late 18C–early 19C] a phr. used to describe an unexceptional person, one who will make no mark on the world.

no can tell *n.* [1940s] (*US Und.*) a silencer; a gun armed with a silencer.

no cash, no Swiss *phr.* (*also* **no money, no Swiss**) [the trad. role of the *Swiss* as mercenary soldiers; note 17C whores' demand: 'No money, no cony' (lit. vagina) and the proverbial *no penny, no paternoster*, i.e. no pay, no prayers offered] [mid-19C+] no help without payment in advance.

n.o.c.d. *phr. see* N.Q.O.C.D. *phr.*

no chance *phr.* [20C+] a general term of dismissal or negation, no hope or possibility whatsoever.

no chop *phr.* [Hind. *chhaap*, a print, and thus a seal, notably that which is placed on first-rate merchandise] [late 19C+] (*Aus.*) no class, second-rate.

(IN PHRASES)

❑ **not much chop** [1920s+] of no great value.

nochy *n.* [Ital. *notte*/Sp. *noche*, night] [mid-19C+] (*Ling. Fr./Polari*) night.

nock *n.* [SE *notch* or *see* NOCKANDRO *n.*] **1** [mid-16C–19C] the anus. **2** [late 16C–17C] the vagina [Cotgrave (1611) suggests backslang: 'Noc. Con, Turned backward (as our Tnuc) to be the lesse offensive to chast eares.'].

nock *v.* [NOCK *n.*] [late 16C–late 18C] to have sexual intercourse.

nockandro *n.* (*also* **nockandrow**) [Early Mod.E *nock*, the cleft of the buttocks] [17C] the buttocks.

nocks *n.* [abbr. SE *narcotics*] [1940s–50s] (*US Und.*) narcotics.

nocktress *n.* [NOCK *n.* (1) + fem. sfx *-tress*] [19C] a prostitute.

nocky *n.* [Suffolk dial.; ? f. the fool's *knock*ing on or knuckling of his forehead] [late 17C–18C] a fool, a simpleton.

(IN COMPOUNDS)

❑ **nocky boy** *n.* [late 18C–early 19C] (*UK Und.*) a dullard, a simpleton.

no cool *n.* [joc. use of sl. + ref. to the status of that part of the state] [1980s+] (*US campus*) northern California.

no count *see under* NO-ACCOUNT.

nocturne *n.* [joc. use of painting jargon *nocturne*, a night-piece] [late 19C–1910s] a prostitute.

nod *n.*[1] **1** [late 17C+] (*20C+ use US black*) a sleep. **2** [1930s+] (*orig. US drugs*) (*also* **nodding out**) the drug-induced stupor or semi-sleep that follows an injection of heroin.

(IN COMPOUNDS)

❑ **nod-box** *n.* [1940s] (*US black*) a bedroom.

(IN PHRASES)

❑ **collar a nod** *v.* [1940s] (*US black*) to sleep, to take a nap. ❑ **cop a nod** *v.* (*also* **cop a snooze**) **1** [1930–70s] (*US*) to have a nap, to go to sleep. **2** (*US drugs/prison*) to become intoxicated and initially comatose after injecting a narcotic. ❑ **go on the nod** *v.* [1950s] (*US*) to die. ❑ **knock a nod** *v.* [1930–40s] (*US black*) to have a sleep. ❑ **on the nod** [1950s+] (*drugs*) **1** succumbing to a sleepy stupor after smoking opium or taking an injection of heroin. **2** dozing off after smoking cannabis. **3** falling sleep, exhausted from excess of any sort. ❑ **play the nod** *v.* [1930s–50s] (*drugs*) to doze off as a result of injecting a narcotic drug.

SE in slang uses

(IN PHRASES)

❑ **on the nod** [the shop-owner *nods* his assent to one's request] **1** [late 19C+] on credit. **2** [late 19C+] without argument, typically of Parliamentary or local government business which 'goes through' or 'passes on the nod'. **3** [1910s–20s] for free.

nod *n.*[2] (*also* **noddy, noddy man**) [? from the policeman in the *Noddy* books (cf. PLOD *n.*[2]), created by author Enid Blyton (1897–1968)] [1960s+] a police officer, usu. male.

(IN COMPOUNDS)

❑ **noddy bike** *n.* [1980s] a police motorcycle.

nod *n.*[3] [1970s+] (*US black*) the human hair.

nod *n.*[4] *see* NODDLE *n.* (1).

nod *n.*[5] *see* NODDY *n.* (1).

nod *v.* **1** (*also* **nod off, nod out**) pertaining to drugs [NOD *n.*[1] (2)]. (**a**) [1950s+] to become temporarily comatose following the immediate effects of an injection of heroin or any other opiate drug. (**b**) to suffer the same effects when the drug is cannabis. **2** [1980s+] (*Aus. prison*) to plead guilty [the affirmative SE *nod* to one's crimes].

(DERIVATIVES)

❑ **nodding** *adj.* [1960s+] comatose.

SE in slang uses

(IN PHRASES)

❑ **nod the nut** *v. see under* NUT *n.*[1].

nod cock *n. see* NODGECOCK *n.*

nodder *n.* **1** [1950s] the head [SE *nod*]. **2** [1970s+] (*drugs*) one who becomes comatose immediately following a narcotic injection, hence a narcotics addict [NOD *v.* (1)].

nodding out *n. see* NOD *n.*[1] (2).

noddipol *n.* (*also* **noddy pate, noddy-peake, noddy-pole**) [NODDY *n.* + SE *poll/pate*, head] [16C–early 19C] a simpleton, a fool.

noddle *n.* [15C SE *noddle*, the back of the head] **1** [16C+] (*also* **nod**) the head. **2** [late 16C+] used fig. to denote the head as a seat (or not) of intelligence. **3** [late 18C–mid-19C] an empty, foolish head; thus stupid, a fool.

(DERIVATIVES)

❑ **noddleheaded** *adj.* [late 19C+] confused, forgetful.

(IN COMPOUNDS)

❑ **noddle-case** *n.* [18C] a wig. ❑ **noddle-thatcher** *n.* [18C] a wig-maker.

(IN PHRASES)

❑ **use your noddle** [1950s+] use your head, act sensibly.

noddy *n.* **1** [early 16C–19C] (*also* **nod**) a fool, a simpleton [the foolish wagging of his head]. **2** [late 18C+] (*Irish*) a one-horse conveyance [its 'nodding' from side-to-side]. **3** [1950s+] a weakling [revivial of sense of a fool, influenced by the children's character *Noddy*, created by author Enid Blyton (1897–1968)]. **4** [1990s+] (*US black*) a heroin addict [NOD *v.* (1)].

noddy *adj.* [NOD *v.*] [1990s+] (*drugs*) comatose in the immediate aftermath of injecting heroin or morphine.

noddy head *n.* [NODDY *n.* + SE *head*/-HEAD *sfx* (1)] [mid-19C–1910s] a fool.

(DERIVATIVES)

❑ **noddy-headed** [the nodding of the drunkard's head] [20C+] drunk.

noddy pate/-peake/-pole *n. see* NODDIPOL *n.*

nodgecock *n.* (*also* **nod cock**) [the foolish nodding of their head] [16C–19C] a fool, a simpleton.

no dice *n.* [NO DICE *phr.*] [1930s+] (*orig. US*) nothing, esp. with inferences of a rejection.

no dice *adj.* [NO DICE *phr.*] [1930s+] insignificant, worthless, pointless.

no dice *phr.* [the refusal of a casino proprietor to allow a gambler to start or continue playing] [1930s+] (*orig. US*) impossible, out of the question, on no account.

no diggety! *excl.* (*also* **no dig! no diggity!**) [? var. on HOT DIGGETY (DOG)! *excl.*] [1990s+] (*US teen*) a general excl. implying 'without question!'.

no-do *n.* [1920s–30s] (*US*) a woman who is not interested in sex, or will not have sex with a given male.

no doubt! *excl.* [emphatic var. on SE] [1980s+] (*US campus*) a general expression of agreement.

no down! *excl.* [early 19C] carry on! don't stop!

no earthly *phr.* (*also* **not an earthly**) [EARTHLY *n.*] [late 19C+] no hope whatsoever, no possible chance.

no eyes *phr.* [opposite of *HAVE EYES FOR under* EYE *n.*] [1940s+] I'm not interested.

no fear! *excl.* **1** [early 19C+] absolutely not! not a chance! **2** [late 19C+] absolutely! without any doubt!

noffka *n.* (*also* **nafka, nafkeh, noffgur**) [synon. Yid.] [late 19C+] a prostitute.

no flies (about)! *excl.* [NO FLIES ON *phr.*] [mid-19C–1940s] (*Aus.*) emphatic interj.: no problem! no fuss! no doubt about it!

no flies on *phr.* (*also* **no flies about, no potato bugs on**) [? cattle that were so active that no fly could settle on them] [mid-19C+] as in *no flies on me/her* etc, implying the smartness and imperviousness to trickery of the speaker or subject.

no fooling *phr.* [SE *fool*] [1920s+] **1** don't be silly, don't tease. **2** an excl. meaning 'Honest!'.

no freak *n.* [SE *no* + FREAK *n.*[1] (7)] [1970s] a client who wishes a prostitute to simulate the role of a rape victim, screaming 'No!' and 'struggling' before he overpowers her.

no fuss, no muss *phr. see under* MUSS *n.*

nog *n.* [abbr. NIG-NOG *n.*[2]] [1960s+] (*Aus.*) **1** a Vietnamese, orig. a North Vietnamese or Viet Cong soldier. **2** an Asian.

noge *n.* [ety. unknown] [late 18C–early 19C] (*UK Und.*) a guinea.

noggin *n.*[1] [? SE *noggin*, a small drinking vessel, a mug; orig. US, but migrated to the UK in mid-19C] **1** [mid-19C+] the head. **2** [1930s+] a hangover.

IN PHRASES

❑ **off one's noggin** *adj.* [1950s+] mad, crazy. ❑ **use the noggin** *v.* [early 19C+] (*orig. US*) to act intelligently, to be aware.

noggin *n.*[2] [? NOGGIN *n.*[1] (1), i.e. the head engraved on one side of the coin or SE *noggin*, a quarter (or less) of a pint] [1940s] (*W.I.*) a farthing.

noggy *n.* [abbr. NIG-NOG *n.*[2]] [1950s+] (*Aus.*) an Asian, orig. a N. Korean or N. Vietnamese soldier, subseq. an Asian immigrant to Australia.

no go *n.* [NO GO *adj.* (1)] [mid-19C+] a failure, an impossibility, that which cannot be done or happen.

no go *adj.* **1** [early 19C+] impossible, out of the question. **2** [1970s+] dangerous, off limits, out of bounds.

no-good *n.* [NO-GOOD *adj.*] [20C+] an unappealing, unpleasant, untrustworthy person.

no-good *adj.* [late 19C+] (*orig. US*) a general term of abuse, unpleasant, untrustworthy, dishonest etc.

IN COMPOUNDS

❑ **no-good-ass** *adj.* [-ASS *sfx*] [1970s] general term of disparagement.

IN PHRASES

❑ **no good to gundy** [ety. unknown; ? the Welsh dial. *gundy*, to steal, thus 'not worth stealing'; a relict of the great flood of 1852 that devastated *Gundagai*; a comment by an Aborigine, one *Gundy*, when rejecting a proffered drink of whisky; a rebuttal of a temperance preacher, attempting to force his views on the populace of Gundagai] [20C+] (*Aus.*) no good at all, definitely bad.

no-gooder *n.* [NO-GOOD *adj.*] [1930s+] (*US*) a bad person, a good-for-nothing.

no-goodnik *n.* [NO-GOOD *n.* + -NIK *sfx*] [1940s+] (*orig. US*) a general pej., an unpleasant or unreliable person.

no-goodnik *adj.* [NO-GOODNIK *n.*] [1930s+] a general pej., unpleasant or unreliable.

no great *adv.* [mid-19C–1900s] (*US*) not very much, not particularly, e.g. *I don't care no great.*

nohi *adj.* [JACK NOHI *n.* (1)] [2000s] (*N.Z.*) very inquisitive.

no hide, no Christmas box *phr.* [SE *no* + HIDE *n.* (3) + SE *Christmas box*] [1930s+] (*Aus.*) no hope of that, not a chance.

no-hoper *n.* [horseracing jargon *no-hoper*, an outsider, a horse that has no hope of winning] [1940s+] **1** (*orig. Aus.*) (*also* **no-hope**) a useless or incompetent person, one from whom no good can be expected. **2** (*Aus.*) a recidivist.

DERIVATIVES

❑ **no-hoping** *adj.* (*also* **no-hope**) [1960s+] (*Aus.*) of a person, hopeless, useless.

no-horse *adj.* [ext. of *ONE-HORSE under* ONE *adj.*] [1950s+] (*US*) absolutely insignificant.

noid *n.* [abbrev.] [1990s+] a para*noid*.

noid *adj.* [abbr.] [1980s+] para*noid*.

noise *n.*[1] **1** [mid-19C] (*UK Und.*) a row. **2** [mid-19C+] (*US*) chatter, gossip, empty, foolish talk. **3** [mid-19C+] (*Aus.*) a complaint. **4** [1900s–20s] (*US*) the world of the city (as opposed to the supposed quaintness of the countryside). **5** [1900s–30s] a (self-)important person. **6** [1920s+] (*US*) information, the know. **7** [1960s+] (*US/W.I.*) serious trouble.

DERIVATIVES

❑ **noisy** *adj.* [late 19C+] (*US*) of clothes, showy, 'loud'.

IN PHRASES

❑ **be in noise** *v.* [1960s+] (*US/W.I.*) to be in trouble. ❑ **make a noise** *v.* [1960s] (*Aus.*) to buy a round of drinks. ❑ **make a noise like...** *v.* (*also* **make like a...and**) [the original (perfectly serious) use apparently came in Baden-Powell's *Scouting for Boys* (1908), in which scouts in danger of detection are advised to take cover and 'make a noise like a (say) thrush'; the *Bismark* (ND) *Daily Tribune* cite refers to an incident in 1906 where Capt. Lyons emphasized the necessity of clear commands and overheard a private telling his friends, 'make a noise like an officer'; if true, this appears to predate Baden-Powell] [20C+] pretend to be, a command that is rendered humorous through its impossibility, e.g. *go into the changing room and make a noise like a cricket bat.* ❑ **make noises** *v.* [1950s+] to discuss, with the implication that one wishes to take some form of action. ❑ **real noise** *n.* [1900s] (*US*) the height of fashion.

SE in slang uses

IN EXCLAMATIONS

❑ **bring the noise!** (*US black*) **1** [1970s+] play music. **2** [1990s+] turn up the volume. ❑ **fuck that noise!** [fig. use of FUCK *v.*] [1980s+] (*US*) forget it! rubbish! what a bore! ❑ **hold your noise!** (*also* **hold your din, ...row**) [mid-19C+] to stop talking, esp. as imper. *hold your noise!* shut up!

noise *n.*[2] [? play on SE *nose*] [1920s+] (*drugs*) heroin.

noise *v.*

SE in slang uses

IN PHRASES

❑ **noise around** *v.* (*also* **noise about, ...abroad, ...round**) [mid-19C+] to tell. ❑ **noise (off)** *v.* [1930s+] (*US black*) to boast, to brag, to indulge in foolish talk. ❑ **noise up** *v.* [1990s+] to talk to.

noisola *n.* [SE *noise* + -OLA *sfx*; on model of *pianola*, the jukebox's predecessor] [1930s–40s] (*US black*) a jukebox, a record-player

noisy *adj. see* NOISE *n.*[1].

SE in slang uses

IN COMPOUNDS

❑ **noisy pegs** *n.* [late 19C] (*UK Und.*) boots.

IN PHRASES

❑ **noisy dog racket** *n.* [early 19C] (*UK Und.*) stealing brass knockers from doors. ❑ **noisy racket man** *n.* [mid-19C] a person who steals china or glass from a china shop.

no Jonas tip played on me *phr.* [ety. unknown; ? anecdotal] [1950s–60s] (*US black*) no one is going to take me for a fool.

nokes *n.* [*John-a-Nokes* was, with Tom-a-Stiles, the precursor of John Doe and Richard Roe in legal jargon as generic names for otherwise anonymous plaintiffs and defendants; Also *James Nokes* a comic actor of the Duke's Company in 1660s who was celebrated for his portrayal of solemn fools, incl. *Sir Nicholas Cully* in Ethrege's *The Comical Revenge; or, Love in a Tub*] [late 17C–early 19C] a fool, a dullard.

nol *adj.* [backsl.] [mid-19C] long.

nola *n.* [the female name] [1930s+] (*US*) a (passive) homosexual male.

noli me tangere *n.* [Lat. *noli me tangere*, don't touch me] [17C–19C] (*Scot.*) venereal disease.

noll *n.* [OE *noll*, the crown of the head] [mid-18C–mid-19C] (*UK Und.*) a wig.

nolle pros *v.* (*also* **nolle, nolle pross, nolle prosse, nol-pros**) [legal Lat. *nolle prosequi*, 'to be unwilling to pursue'] [mid-19C+] (*orig. US*) to abandon a trial because the plaintiff or prosecutor has given up the suit, usu. because there is insufficient hard evidence, a key witness has backed down etc.

no-manners *n.*

IN PHRASES

❑ **do one's no-manners** *v.* [1980s] **1** to defecate. **2** to break wind.

no mercy *phr.* [joc. use SE] [1910s] (*Aus.*) a phr. written on the back of a pay cheque and handed to a publican when a man wanted to spend his entire season's wages in a single binge.

nominate your poison! *excl. see* NAME YOUR POISON! *excl.*

nommus *v. see* NAMMOUS *v.*

nommus! *excl. see* NAMUS! *excl.*

no money, no Swiss *phr. see* NO CASH, NO SWISS *phr.*

no more than ninepence in the shilling *phr.* [a shilling (5p) had 12 pence] [late 19C+] referring to one considered a simpleton, a fool.

non *n.* [? SE *non-performer*] [1970s+] (*US black*) a physically unco-ordinated person; a poor athlete.

no-name *n.* [1990s+] (*US*) an insignificant person; one who has no public 'name'.

no-name (brand) cigarette *n. see* NO-BRAND CIGARETTE *n.*

no-nation *n.* [SE *no* + -NATION *sfx*] [20C+] (*W.I.*) a usu. dark-skinned person of more than two racial mixtures.

no-nation *adj.* [NO-NATION *n.*] [20C+] (*W.I.*) despicable, worthless.

nonce *n.* [? dial. *nonce*, a good-for-nothing, thus image of a 'nothing', a 'non-person'; the *Police Review* (18 May 1984) suggests orig. in NANCY BOY *n.*] **1** [1970s+] sexual offender, spec. of young children. **2** [1990s+] a general term of (usu.) abuse. **3** [1990s+] *nonsense*, rubbish.

DERIVATIVES

❑ **noncey** *adj.* [1990s+] stupid, ineffectual, useless.

nonce *v.* [NONCE *n.*] [2000s] to subject to child abuse.

DERIVATIVES

❑ **noncing** *adj.* [2000s] child-abusing.

non-com *n.* (*also* **non-comish**) [abbr.] [mid-19C+] a *non-commissioned* officer in the army.

non compos *adj.* [Lat. *non compos mentis*, not of sound mind] **1** [early 17C+] eccentric, crazy. **2** [18C+] (*also* **non-com, non-compos poo-poo**) drunk. **3** [1940s] (*Aus.*) unconscious.

DERIVATIVES

❑ **noncompusser** *n.* [early–mid-19C] a crazy person.

non-con *n.* [abbr. SE *non-conformist*] [late 17C–mid-19C] a religious dissenter, typically a non-conformist or Presbyterian.

nondy *adj.* (*also* **nondi**) [SE *nondescript*] [1990s+] inferior, second-rate.

no neck *n. see under* NECK *n.*

none of your beeswax *phr. see* BEESWAX *n.*[2].

non est *adj.* [Lat. *non est*, it is not] [mid-19C–1950s] non-existent, absent.

nonesuch *n. see* NONSUCH *n.*

non-event *adj.* [SE *non-event*, an unimportant event] [1990s+] (*Aus.*) insignificant, irrelevant.

nong *n.* (*also* **nong nong**) [Lat. *non compos*; Seal (1999) suggests UK dial. *ning nang*, a fool] [1940s+] (*Aus.*) an idiot, a fool, a general derog. description.

nongie *n.* [2000s] (*S.Afr. prison*) an aggressive prison homosexual.

nongy *n.* [mispron./abbr. of SE *condom*] [1990s+] (*UK juv.*) a condom.

nonny no *n.* (*also* **nonny-nonny, nony-nony**) [SE *nonny no*, the refrain of a song, thus a trifle, a nothing] [17C] **1** the vagina; the vulva. **2** sex in general.

no-no *n.* [SE *no* + redup.] [1940s+] an impossibility, something forbidden.

nonsense *n.* **1** [late 18C–mid-19C] 'melting butter in a wig' (Grose, 1796) [presumably Grose's own joke definition]. **2** [early–mid-19C] money. **3** [1930s+] a fiasco, a farce.

IN PHRASES

❑ **stand the nonsense** *v. see* STAND THE RACKET *under* RACKET *n.*[1].

non-skid *n.*[1] [she doesn't 'skid' in the 'wet'] [1920s] (*US*) a woman who can hold her drink.

non-skid *n.*[2] [rhy. sl. *non-skid* = YID *n.*[1]] [1930s+] a Jew.

nonsuch *n.* (*also* **nonesuch**) [SE *nonesuch*, an unmatched, unrivalled thing] **1** [18C–19C] the vagina. **2** [mid-19C–1900s] as *Mr Nonsuch*, a conceited person.

non-toucher *n.* [the opposite of a TOUCHER *n.*[1] (4)] [1980s+] (*drugs*) a smoker of crack cocaine who recoils from physical contact while experiencing the drug's effects.

nony-nony *n. see* NONNY NO *n.*

noodge *n. see* NUDGE *n.*

noodle *n.*[1] [ety. unknown; ? SE *nod* or SE *noodle*, a fool or var. of NODDLE *n.*] **1** [mid-18C+] the human head. **2** [20C+] used fig. to denote intelligence, the mind [fig. use of sense 1].

IN COMPOUNDS

❑ **noodle bowl** *n.* [2000s] the brain. ❑ **noodlehead** *n.* (*also* **noodlebrain**) [-HEAD *sfx* (1)] [1910s+] (*US*) a dull, stupid person. ❑ **noodle juice** *n.* [1920s] (*US*) tea.

IN PHRASES

❑ **house of noodles** *n.* [mid-19C] the House of Lords. ❑ **out of one's noodle** [1940s+] (*orig. US*) experiencing the effects of a drug.

noodle *n.*[2] [its supposed resemblance, when flaccid, to a cooked noodle] [1970s+] (*US black*) the penis.

SE in slang uses

IN COMPOUNDS

❑ **noodle dick** *n.* [DICK *n.*[1] (5)] [1990s+] (*US*) a general term of abuse; the over-riding image is of impotence, i.e. a penis limp as a cooked noodle. ❑ **noodle soup** *n.* [1920s] (*US Und.*) nonsense.

IN PHRASES

❑ **noodle soup drinker** *n.* [racial stereotyping] [1900s–30s] (*US*) a Jew.

noodle *v.*[1] [? SE *doodle*] **1** [late 18C] to kiss and cuddle. **2** [1930s+] (*US*) to tune a musical instrument, to warm up or improvise musically. **3** [1960s+] to warm up, excite.

noodle *v.*[2] [SE *noodle*, a fool] [early 19C] to fool, to trick.

noodle *v.*[3] [NOODLE *n.*[1] (2)] [1940s+] (*US*) **1** to think, to brainstorm. **2** usu. constructed as *noodle out/up*, to mull something over, to work something out.

noodley *adj.* [SE *noodle*, a fool] [1900s] (*US*) eccentric, crazy.

noodnik *n. see* NUDNIK *n.*

noogie *n.* (*also* **nuggie**) [? corruption of SE *knuckle*] [1970s+] (*US*) the act of rubbing one's knuckles hard across one's victim's skull; also used on other parts of the body.

noogie *v.* (*also* **nuggie**) [NOOGIE *n.*] [1970s+] (*US*) to rub one's knuckles hard across one's victim's skull; also used on other parts of the body.

noogies *n.* [ety. unknown] **1** [1970s] (*US teen*) nasal mucus [? var. on BOOGIE *n.*[1]]. **2** [1980s] (*US*) the testicles.

nook *n.* [ety. unknown] [1910s–30s] a penny.

nook and cranny *n.* [rhy. sl. = FANNY *n.*[1] (3)] [1970s] the buttocks.

nookie *n.* (*also* **nicky-hooky, nook, nookey, nooky, nucky, nukky**) [? NUG *v.* or Du. sl. *neuken*, to fuck] **1** [1920s+] (*orig. US*) sexual intercourse. **2** [1920s+] (*orig. US*) (*also* **piece of nookie**) a woman seen as no more than an object of possible seduction. **3** [1960s+] (*orig. US*) (*also* **nooker**) the vagina. **4** [1970s+] (*US gay*) the anus.

DERIVATIVES

□ **nooking** *n.* [1920s] (*US*) petting.

IN COMPOUNDS

□ **nookie bookie** *n.* [1940s+] (*US*) a pimp or a madam. □ **nookie house** *n.* [HOUSE *n.*[1] (1)] [1980s] (*US*) a brothel.

nookie *adj.* [? Maori *noke*, small] [1910s–30s] (*N.Z.*) tiny, little; thus a nickname for a small boy or short person.

nooky *adj.* [NOOKIE *n.*] [1950s] (*US*) female, pertaining to women.

noolucks *n.* (*also* **newlicks**) [a nonce-word, ety. unknown] [mid-19C] an imaginary person.

noom *n.* [backsl.] [mid-19C] the moon.

nooner *n.* [SE *noon*] **1** [1940s+] a midday alcoholic drink. **2** [1970s+] sexual intercourse, often adulterous, enjoyed around lunchtime.

noorse *v. see* NAUSE *v.*

noose, the *n.* [mid-17C–1950s] marriage.

noose *v.* [lit. and fig. uses of SE *noose*; note synon. in James Joyce *Dubliners* (1914): 'I'm going to have my fling first and see a bit of life and the world before I put my head in the sack'] **1** [late 17C–mid-19C] (*also* **nooze**) to hang. **2** [early 17C–mid-19C] to marry.

DERIVATIVES

□ **noosed** *adj.* (*also* **noozed**) [late 17C–mid-19C] married.

nope *n.* [15C northern dial. *nawp, noup, nope*, a blow; ult. a supposed Scandinavian v. *nawpe*, to strike down] [18C–early 19C] a blow to the head.

nope! *excl.* (*also* **nop, nup**) [late 19C+] (*US*) no!

no place *n.* [1930s+] (*orig. US*) nowhere.

no potato bugs on *phr. see* NO FLIES ON *phr.*

nopper *n. see* NAPPER *n.*[2] (2).

noppy *n. see* NAPPY (ALE) *n.*

no problem *phr.* (*also* **no problemo**) [1960s+] (*orig. US*) don't worry, it's all right.

no probs *phr.* [abbr.] [1970s+] *no problems*.

nora *adj.* [SE *ignorant*] [2000s] (*S.Afr. gay*) stupid.

IN COMPOUNDS

□ **nora nesbit** *n.* [2000s] (*S.Afr. gay*) a stupid person.

Norfolk *adj.*

IN COMPOUNDS

□ **Norfolk capon** *n. see* YARMOUTH CAPON *n.* □ **Norfolk dumpling** *n.* [the typical local foodstuff] **1** [early 17C] a dupe. **2** [mid-17C–19C] (*also* **Norfolk turkey**) a native of Norfolk. **3** [19C] (*Aus.*) a prisoner on Norfolk Island or the act of imprisoning someone there ['Conditions on Norfolk Island... were appalling; Norfolk dumplings lie heavy on the stomach—fair 'settlers', as was a term on the Island' (*DSUE*)].

Norfolk Howard *n.* (*also* **n.h.**) [in cruel memoriam of one Joseph (or Joshua) Bug who, in 1862, changed his name to *Norfolk Howard*, despite popular derision at what was seen as affectation. *The Times* came to his aid, publishing a list of other risible/unpleasant names. Among them were 'Asse, Beaste, Belly, Boots, Cripple, Cheese, Clodd, Dunce, Fatt, Frogge, Hagg, Humpe, Jelly, Kneebone, Lazy, Mudd, Honeybum, Piddle, Paswater, Pisse, Pricksmall, Quicklove, Rottengoose, Swette, Sheartlifte, Silly, Spittle, Teate and Vittels'] [mid-19C–1900s] a bedbug.

no risk *phr.* [1920s+] (*Aus.*) **1** no chance (of). **2** no doubt (about).

norks *n.* (*also* **norgies, norgs, norkers**) [the *Norco* Co-operative Ltd, butter manufacturer of NSW, featured a cow's udder on its labels] [1960s+] (*Aus.*) the breasts.

norm *n.* [SE *normal*] **1** [1970s] (*US gay*) (*also* **norma**) a heterosexual male. **2** [1970s+] (*Aus.*) a generic term used to describe the average Aus. male, beer-drinking, television-watching, over-weight and inactive [the character, created by Victoria's Minister for Sport, Brian Dixon, was launched as part of a 'get fit' campaign in 1975]. **3** [1980s+] (*US campus*) (*also* **normal, Norman Normal**) a dull conventional person.

norma *adj.* [2000s] (*S.Afr. gay*) normal, whether as emotionally stable or sexually, i.e. heterosexual.

norma jean nicotine *n.* [real name of Marilyn Monroe, *Norma Jean* Baker (1926–62) + SE *nicotine* + assonance] [1950s–70s] (*camp gay*) a smoker.

normal *n.* [usu. with ironic overtones] **1** [1950s–70s] (*gay*) a heterosexual male. **2** *see* NORM *n.* (3).

Normandy Beach *n.* [rhy. sl.; ult. ref. to D-Day and the Normandy landings on 6 June 1944] [1980s+] a speech.

Norman Normal *n. see* NORM *n.* (3).

Normanton cocktail *n.* [pun on GIN *n.*[1] (1)/SE *gin*; further racist stereotyping in ref. to Normanton, Queensland, a small cattle town with a population of 50% native Australians] [1950s–60s] (*Aus.*) an Aboriginal woman and two blankets.

no-roast *n.* [? ROAST *v.*] [1970s] (*Aus. Und.*) a positive or neutral statement by the police.

no Robin Hood *phr. see* ROBIN HOOD *adj.* (1).

Norski *n.* (*also* **Norske**) [Scandinavian *Norsk*, Norse + sfx *-ski*] [20C+] (*US*) a person of Norwegian origin; thus a Scandinavian.

Norski *adj.* (*also* **Norsky**) [NORSKI *n.*] [20C+] Norwegian or other Scandinavian.

north *adj.* [stereotype of northerners, esp. Yorkshiremen, as grasping, cheating and cunning] [late 17C–19C] clever, cunning.

SE in slang uses

IN COMPOUNDS

□ **north castle** *n.* [its position in north London and the 'castellated' architecture of its original gateway] [late 19C–1900s] Holloway prison. □ **northpaw** *n.* [the opposite of SOUTHPAW *n.* (1); the term is essentially artificial and rarely used] [1960s+] (*US*) a right-handed person.

IN PHRASES

□ **he's too far north for me** [mid-18C–19C] he's too cunning for me. □ **north end of a southbound horse** (*also* **...bus, ...southbound mule**) [euph./play on HORSE'S ASS *n.*] [1960s+] (*US*) a general term of abuse, used joc. as in *you look like the north end ...* □ **north or south?** [1970s+] (*US gay*) a question implying is someone circumcised or not.

north *adv.* [the image of going 'upwards'] **1** [1970s+] (*US*) increasing in value, improving. **2** [2000s] upwards.

IN PHRASES

□ **go due north** *v.* [the purpose-built debtor's prison, Whitecross Street Prison, is sited in what was then north London; its site is now covered by the Barbican development] [mid-19C] to become bankrupt. □ **go north** *v.* [1970s] (*US black*) to leave.

Northallerton *n.* [the quality of spurs made in *Northallerton*, Yorks.] [late 18C–late 19C] a spur.

north and south *n.* [rhy. sl.] [mid-19C+] the mouth.

north and south, the *n.* [1910s–20s] a quick visual inspection, a look up and down.

North Carolina *n.*

IN PHRASES

□ **get one's North Carolina up** *v. see* GET ONE'S AFRICAN UP *under* AFRICAN *n.*

North Country compliment *n.* [negative stereotyping of the north of England] [late 19C] a gift that is neither desired by the recipient nor of any value to him or to the donor.

North Dakota rice *n.* [1940s] (*US milit.*) warm breakfast cereals.

Northern Territory champagne *n.* [drunk by many Aborigines in the *Northern Territory*] [1970s] (*Aus.*) methylated spirits mixed with health salts, which give a fizzy head.

north pole *n.* [rhy. sl. = ARSEHOLE *n.*] [20C+] the anus.

North Sea rabbit *n.* [1910s] (*N.Z.*) a herring.

north Sydney *n.* [rhy. sl.] [20C+] (*Aus.*) the kidney.

Northumberland arms *n.* (*also* **Lord Northumberland's arms**) [the red and black spectacle-like badge that is the basis of the Percy, i.e. Lord Northumberland's arms] [late 17C–early 19C] a black eye.

Norway neckcloth *n.* [it was often made from *Norway* fir] [late 18C–mid-19C] the pillory.

Norwegian *n.* [their pale complexion and blond hair] [1950s] (*W.I.*) an albino.

IN COMPOUNDS

❑ **Norwegian steam** *n.* [the physical strength of Norwegian immigrants] [1940s+] (*US*) manpower.

N.O.R.W.I.C.H. *phr.* [abbr.] [1940s+] (k)*n*ickers *o*ff *r*eady *w*hen *I* *c*ome *h*ome; an amorous acronym, usu. found on the back of envelopes of love letters (orig. by soldiers).

norwicher *n.* [ety. unknown; Partridge suggests stereotyping, as in the rhyme 'Essex stiles, Kentish miles, Norfolk wiles, many men beguiles'] [mid–late 19C] more than one's fair share; esp. one who drinks more than half of a shared tankard before passing it on.

norz *n. see* NAUS *n.*

nose *n.* **1** [late 18C+] a police spy, an informer [20C+ use is US prison]. **2** [mid-19C+] a detective. **3** [1960s+] (*drugs*) heroin or cocaine [one can inhale them through the *nose*].

IN COMPOUNDS

❑ **nose around** *n.* [1980s+] a search. ❑ **nose burner** *n.* [1960s+] (*drugs*) the butt of a marijuana cigarette. ❑ **nose candy** *n.* [*candy*/CANDY *n.* (5b)] [1920s+] (*orig. US drugs*) **1** cocaine. **2** heroin. ❑ **nose habit** *n.* [HABIT *n.* (1)] [1960s+] (*drugs*) taking narcotic drugs by sniffing them through the nose rather than by injection. ❑ **nose hit** *n.* [HIT *n.* (3e)] [1970s] (*drugs*) a puff of a marijuana cigarette taken through the nose rather than the lips. ❑ **nose powder** *n.* (*also* **nose stuff**) [POWDER *n.*[1] (2)] [1930s+] (*drugs*) heroin, cocaine, morphine. ❑ **nose-up** *n.* [2000s] the inhalation of cocaine.

SE in slang uses

IN COMPOUNDS

❑ **nosebag/baggery** *see* separate entries. ❑ **nosebleed** *see* separate entries. ❑ **nosecone** *n.* [the shape] [1980s+] (*drugs*) a large cannabis cigarette rolled with a rosebud-shaped twist of paper on the end. ❑ **nosedive/diver** *see* separate entries. ❑ **nose-ender** *see* NOSER *n.* (2). ❑ **nosegay** *n.* **1** [early 19C] a blow on the nose. **2** [1980s] (*UK prison*) tobacco. ❑ **nose job** *n.* [JOB *n.*[2] (2)] **1** [1960s–70s] (*US black*) a sexual obsession with some object of desire. **2** [1960s+] a rhinoplasty, cosmetic plastic surgery on one's nose. ❑ **nose music** *n.* [1910s] (*US*) snoring. ❑ **nose paint** *n.* [it turns the nose red; note Shakespearian use of *nose-painting* (e.g. *Macbeth* III iii) refers to sexual rather than alcoholic excess] [late 19C–1970s] (*US*) alcohol. ❑ **nose picker** *n.* (*US*) **1** [1940s] a child or person with offensive habits. **2** [1970s] a rustic, a peasant. ❑ **nose-pinchers** *n.* [literal translation] [late 19C] pince-nez. ❑ **nose-powder** *n.* [1930s+] cocaine. ❑ **nose rag** *n.* **1** [mid-19C–1950s] a handkerchief. **2** [late 19C] an unpopular person. ❑ **nose trouble** *n.* [1930s–80s] (*Aus./US*) a propensity for interfering. ❑ **nose warmer** *n.* **1** [late 19C] a short pipe. **2** [1930s] (*US*) consommé in a cup. ❑ **nose wipe** *n.* [early 19C+] a handkerchief. ❑ **nose wiper** *n.* **1** [mid-19C+] a handkerchief. **2** [1920s] a toady [lit. image, but note ASS-WIPER *n.*].

IN PHRASES

❑ **get it in the nose** *v.* [1910s] to be punished, lit. and fig. ❑ **get nose with** *v.* [BROWN-NOSE *v.*] [1980s+] to curry favour. ❑ **get one's nose cold** *v.* [the drug has a numbing quality, esp. if, as more than likely, it has been adulterated with procaine or Novocaine] [1970s+] (*drugs*) to sniff cocaine. ❑ **get one's nose wet** *v.* [1910s] (*US*) to get drunk. ❑ **get someone's nose** *v.* [var. *HAVE ONE'S NOSE OPEN* below] [1990s+] (*US black*) to have another person utterly dependent on oneself, typically in a one-sided love relationship. ❑ **get up someone's nose** *v.* [1910s+] (*orig. US*) to annoy, to irritate. ❑ **give someone one on the nose** *v. see GIVE SOMEONE ONE IN THE EYE under* EYE *n.* ❑ **have a dirty nose** *v.* [late 16C–mid-17C] to be a good drinker. ❑ **have a good nose** *v.* [late 17C–early 18C] to arrive at a house in time for a meal. ❑ **have a nose of wax** *v.* [SE *nose of wax*, an impressionable person] [19C] to be gullible, to be impressionable. ❑ **have a nose on** *v.* [1900s–70s] (*Aus./N.Z*) to bear a grudge against someone, to take offence. ❑ **have one's nose in parenthesis** *v.* [SE *parenthesis*, an interlude, a hiatus] [late 18C–early 19C] to have one's nose pulled. ❑ **have one's nose open** *v.* (*also* **get one's nose open**) [all uses imply heavy breathing] [1950s+] (*US black*) **1** to produce sexual excitement in another person. **2** to be infatuated with another person. **3** to be under someone's control (other than sexually). **4** to be excited – in a non-sexual context. **5** to be angry. **6** to anger. ❑ **have one's nose up someone's ass/arse** *v.* [1970s+] to act sycophantically, to toady. ❑ **keep one's nose clean** *v.* **1** [mid-19C–1940s] (*orig. milit.*) to avoid alcohol. **2** [late 19C+] (*also* **keep one's snout clean**) to lead a law-abiding, upright life. **3** [1920s+] to resist interfering in things that are not one's business. **4** [1930s+] of a criminal, to avoid being implicated in something illegal. ❑ **keep one's nose in someone's ass** *v.* [1960s+] (*US*) to toady to. ❑ **make a bridge of someone's nose** [late 17C–early 19C] to miss out a person during the passing of a bottle around the table. ❑ **make a long nose** *v.* [note *PULL BACON under* BACON *n.*[1]] [late 19C–1950s] to thumb one's nose. ❑ **nose wipe** *v.* [early 17C–mid-18C] to cheat, to deceive. ❑ **one's nose is always brown** *see under* BROWN NOSE *n.* ❑ **on the nose** **1** [19C] (*UK Und.*) on the watch, on the lookout; thus phr. *beaks (out) on the nose*, magistrates peforming their evening rounds. **2** [1920s+] (*gambling*) a wager on the winning horse, e.g. *£5 on the nose*. **3** [1940s] of a criminal, a reward offered for information leading to capture. **4** [1940s+] (*Aus./N.Z.*) foul-smelling. **5** [1940s+] in fig. use of this, unpleasant, and thus offensive morally or aesthetically as well to the nostrils. ❑ **open someone's nose** *v.* [*HAVE ONE'S NOSE OPEN* above] [1960s+] (*US black*) to provoke sexual excitement in someone.

nose *v.* **1** [mid-17C–early 18C] to make a fool of, to fool, to dupe, to sneer at [? SE phr. *lead by the nose*]. **2** to 'put one's nose into'. (**a**) [mid-17C+] to pry into someone else's proceedings. (**b**) [19C] to inform against, esp. in phr. *nose upon*. **3** in senses of violence. (**a**) [late 18C–early 19C] to bully. (**b**) [late 19C–1900s] to hit on the nose. **4** [1910s+] (*US*) to curry favour [abbr. BROWN-NOSE *v.*].

IN PHRASES

❑ **nose around** *v.* (*also* **nose, nose about**) **1** [mid-19C+] to search, to look over, to survey; thus also as n. **2** [1920s+] to interfere (in). **3** [1970s] to spread rumours, to gossip about. ❑ **nose for** *v.* [late 19C–1900s] (*US*) to pursue, to hunt down. ❑ **nose in** *v.* [1930s] (*US*) to appear, to arrive. ❑ **nose on** *v.* [NOSE *n.* (1)] [late 18C+] to inform against.

nose and chin *n.* [rhy. sl.] **1** [mid-19C] a penny [= WIN *n.*]. **2** [late 19C–1900s] gin. **3** [20C+] a win (on a wager).

nosebag *n.* [SE *nosebag*] **1** [mid-19C–1910s] (*also* **nosebagger**) a day-tripper to the seaside who takes their own provisions and thus makes no useful contribution to the local economy. **2** [mid-19C–1910s] a veil. **3** [late 19C] a handbag. **4** [late 19C] a hospitable hotel or lodging-house. **5** [late 19C–1930s] (*Aus.*) a bag in which an itinerant or SWAGMAN *n.*[2] carries his provisions. **6** [20C+] food, spec. as served in a restaurant. **7** [1910s] a gasmask. **8** [1910s+] a bag of food, a lunch box, a (take-away) meal.

IN PHRASES

❑ **put on the nosebag** *v.* (*also* **get the nosebag on, put the nosebag on**) [mid-19C+] to eat. ❑ **the nosebag crowd** *n.* [1900s] holiday-makers who take their own provisions to a resort.

nosebag *v.* [NOSEBAG *n.* (8)] [1960s+] (*US*) to eat.

nosebaggery *n.* [NOSEBAG *n.* (8)] [1920s] (*US*) a restaurant.

nosebleed *n.* [play on DRIP *n.* (2)] [1950s] an idiot, esp. a weakling.

nose-bleed *adj.* (*also* **nosebleed**) [also used fig.; the nosebleeds that can accompany oxygen deprivation] [1970s+] (*US*) of seating, very high up, esp. in an auditorium or sports stadium.

nosedive *n.* [1930s+] **1** (*US tramp*) a false show of religious belief or action to gain handouts from a religious mission. **2** (*US*) a loss of emotional or mental control. **3** (*orig. US*) a fainting spell or a fall. **4** (*orig. US*) fig. a fall; a rejection.

nosedive *v.* [NOSEDIVE *n.* (1)] [1930s–70s] (*US tramp*) to make a false show of religious belief or action to gain handouts from a religious mission.

nosediver *n.* [NOSEDIVE *v.*] [1930s–70s] (*US tramp*) a vagrant who frequents charitable missions, looking for handouts.

nose 'em *n.* [NOSEY-MY-KNACKER *n.*] [mid-19C] tobacco.

no-see-um *n.* [lit. 'no see them'] [mid-19C+] (*US*) a tiny biting fly, a midge.

noseful *n.*

(IN PHRASES)

▫ **get a noseful** *v. see* HAVE A SNOOTFUL *under* SNOOTFUL *n.*^{2}.

nosegent *n.* [? Fr. *à genou*, kneeling; Ribton-Turner, *A History of Vagrants* (1887), suggests Gaelic *nuas*, 'from on high' + *gean*, a woman] [mid-16C–early 19C] a nun.

nosenheimer *n.* [they have their 'nose in the air' + abbr. WISENHEIMER *n.*] [1940s+] (*US*) an important person or one who poses as such.

noser *n.* **1** [mid–late 19C] a bloody nose [NOSE *v.* (3b)]. **2** [mid–late 19C] (*also* **nose-ender**) a blow on the nose [NOSE *v.* (3b)]. **3** [mid-19C+] (*US Und.*) an informer [NOSE *n.* (1)].

nosey bob *n.* [R.R. Howard (*c.*1836–1906) the New South Wales hangman from *c.*1874–1904; he earned his nickname from a facial disfigurement] [late 19C–1930s] (*Aus.*) **1** a hangman. **2** an inquisitive person, a 'nosey parker'.

nosey-my-knacker *n.* (*also* **nose-my, noser my knacker**) [rhy. sl.] [mid–late 19C] tobacco.

nosh *n.* [NOSH *v.*] **1** [1910s] a delicatessen. **2** [1940s+] food, esp. a snack. **3** [1990s+] an act of fellatio.

(IN COMPOUNDS)

▫ **nosh-up** *n.* [1950s+] a feast; a meal.

nosh *v.* (*also* **knosh, nash**) [Yid. *nosh*, to snack and Ger. *naschen*, to nibble, to eat surreptitiously; mainly US but note *The Nosh Bar*, a long lived delicatessen/cafe in Great Windmill Street, Soho, London] **1** [1930s+] to eat, esp. to snack, to eat between meals; occas. to drink. **2** [1970s+] to practise oral sex [pun on sense 1].

nosher *n.* **1** [1960s+] one who snacks or eats between meals [NOSH *v.* (1)]. **2** [1970s+] a fellator/fellatrix [NOSH *v.* (2)].

noshery *n.* [NOSH *n.* (2) + sfx. *-ery*, or Yid. *nasherei*, snacks] [1950s+] (*orig. US*) a snack-bar.

no-shit *adj.* [NO SHIT! *excl.*] [1950s+] (*US*) genuine.

(DERIVATIVES)

▫ **no-shitter** *n.* [1990s+] a true statement.

no shit! *excl.* [SHIT *n.* (4a)/CRAP *n.*^{1} (4)] [1930s+] **1** an excl. of (usu.) ironic surprise; 'you don't say!' 'goodness me!'. **2** (*also* **no crap!**) an excl. of affirmation, I mean it, this is the truth.

no shit, Sherlock! *excl.* (*also* **NS^2! n.s.s.!**) [*Sherlock* is a pun on HOLMES *n.*, which itself puns on HOMES *n.* + ironic use of the fictional detective *Sherlock* Holmes] [1970s+] (*orig. US*) ext. of NO SHIT! *excl.*

no sir! *excl.* (*also* **nossir!**) [mid-19C+] an emphatic rejection.

no siree (bob)! *excl.* (*also* **no siree bobtail! no siree hoss! no sirree! no sirree-bob-tailed-rooster!**) [NO SIR! *excl.* + *-ee* (+ BOB *n.*^{2} (1))] [mid-19C+] (*orig. US*) an excl. of absolute denial.

no slouch *n.* [late 18C+] something or someone good, acceptable, enterprising, energetic.

no-soap *adj.* [NO SOAP *phr.*] [1920s] hopeless.

no soap *v.* [NO SOAP *phr.*] [1960s] to reject, to dismiss.

no soap *phr.* [SE *no* + SOAP *n.*^{1} (2); or f. rhy. sl. *soap* = DOPE *n.*^{3} (1)/SE *hope*] [1920s+] (*orig. US*) 'nothing doing', not a chance, no hope of that.

nosper *n.* [backsl.] [late 19C–1900s] **1** a person. **2** a stranger [from sense 1].

no spiffing *phr.* [ety. unknown; ? link to SPOOF *v.* (1)] [1920s] (*US juv.*) for sure, no fooling.

nosrap *n.* [backsl.] [mid-19C] a parson.

nossir *excl. see* NO SIR! *excl.*

no stress *phr.* [1990s+] (*US campus*) no problems, don't worry.

no sweat off one's balls *phr. see* NO SKIN OFF ONE'S BALLS *under* SKIN *n.*^{1}.

not! *excl.* [coined at Princeton University in the 1890s, internationally popularized via the film *Wayne's World* (1992)] [late 19C+] (*orig. US*) used at the end of a declaratory sentence to reverse everything that has gone before, e.g. *the Home Secretary is a liberal, tolerant and sophisticated person – not!*

not able to... *phr. see* COULDN'T... *phr.*

not a feather to fly with *phr.* [orig. university use, where to be *plucked* was to have failed one's examinations] [mid-19C–1900s] ruined, penniless.

not a half! *excl. see* NOT HALF! *excl.*

no talent *n.* [1960s+] (*US*) a useless person.

not all there *adj.* (*also* **elsewhere, not quite there**) [the root phr. of many synons., all commenting adversely on the subject's intelligence, e.g. all those at ...SHORT OF... *adj.*; *ELEVATOR DOESN'T REACH THE TOP FLOOR under* ELEVATOR *n.*; NOT PLAYING WITH A FULL DECK *phr.*; *ROW WITH ONE OAR (IN THE WATER) under* ROW *v.*^{2}] **1** [mid-19C+] eccentric, insane, crazy. **2** [1930s] drunk.

not a man jack *phr. see EVERY MAN JACK under* EVERY *adj.*

not an earthly *phr. see* NO EARTHLY *phr.*

not a word of the pudding! *excl. see under* PUDDING *n.*

not bat an eye(lid) *v.* [20C+] (*orig. US*) to show no emotion, to remain imperturbable.

not be able to speak a threepenny bit *v.* [? image of *threepenny bit* as an insignificant sum] [late 19C] to be speechless, struck dumb.

not bloody likely! *excl. see* NOT LIKELY *phr.*

not care a... *v.* (*also* **not give a...**) [examples are listed alphabetically rather than by date and the dating for these combinations can be anything from mid-16C to 1990s+] [mid-16C+] in addition to the most popular combs. listed separately below, there are a number of less common phrs., all stating one's absolute lack of interest in the topic.

(IN PHRASES)

▫ **...a bean** (*also* **...a row of beans, ...beans**) ▫ **...a blast** ▫ **...a blow** ▫ **...a button** ▫ **...a chip** (*also* **...two chips**) ▫ **...a continental** ▫ **...a copper** ▫ **...a damn** ▫ **...a dash** ▫ **...a dodkin** ▫ **...a dot** ▫ **...a dump** ▫ **...a farthing dip** (*also* **...a twopenny dip**) ▫ **...a fly** ▫ **...a groat** ▫ **...a hair** ▫ **...a halfpenny** ▫ **...a mag** ▫ **...a pease** ▫ **...a pinch of snuff** ▫ **...a quinch** ▫ **...a rag** ▫ **...a sixpence** ▫ **...a snuff** ▫ **...a sod** ▫ **...a sou(s)** ▫ **...a splinter** ▫ **...a stiver** ▫ **... a traneen** (*also* **...thraneen, ...three thrawneens**) ▫ **...a turd** ▫ **...a whit**

not care a.../not give a... *v.* combs. are listed under either not care a... or not give a... depending on the most common use found in the citations, however, most can be used with both verbs and alternatives are given throughout, unless no citation has been found.

not care a (brass) farthing *v.* [late 17C+] to not care at all.

not care a cent *v.* (*also* **...a dime, ...a dime a dozen, ...a ten cent piece, ...a thin dime, ...two cents, not give a cent**) [mid-19C+] to not care at all.

not care a curse *v.* (*also* **...a cuss, ...a God's curse, ...a tuppenny cuss, not give a curse**) [mid-19C+] to not care at all.

not care a fart *v.* (*also* **...a cold fart, ...a fartful, ...a fart in a whirlwind, ...a good fart, ...a tuppenny fart, ...two farts in hell, not give a fart**) [FART *n.* (1)] [mid-16C+] to not care at all.

not care a fouter *v.* (*also* **...a footer, not give a footer, ...fouter**) [Fr. sl. *foutre*, to FUCK *v.* (1)] [early 17C–late 19C] to not care at all.

not care a jot *v.* [mid-18C+] to not care at all.

not care a louse *v.* (*also* **...three steps of the louse, not give a louse**) [mid-16C–18C] to not care at all.

not care a pin *v.* (*also* **...a pin's head, ...a row of brass pins, not give a pin**) [mid-16C+] to not care at all.

not care a rush *v.* (*also* **not give a rush**) [? BUM'S RUSH *n.*] [mid-16C–1920s] to not care at all.

not care a straw *v.* (*also* **...a jackstraw, ...three straws, ...two straws, not give a straw**) [16C+] to not care at all.

not care a tinker's (curse) *v.* (*also* **...cuss, ...damn, ...darn, ...fart, ...fiddler's damn, not give a tinker's (curse)**) [the lack of importance one gives a curse thrown over the shoulder of a departing tinker who has been unable to sell anything or find work; note letter 08/02/1999 from Mr George Shaw: 'I learnt my trade as a Tinker and Plumber, and I used a tinkers cuss many, many times. When the copper kettle was heated on the open fire, the fire would burn a hole in the bend at the bottom of the spout. The tinker would take a piece of bread and ram it into the spout blocking up the hole. He would then proceed to solder a patch onto the hole. The bread would dam up the hole, hence a tinker's cuss. This was also a way the plumber would use to soak up the water in the lead pipe (if there was a small seepage of water) whilst he wiped a joint. On both occasions, once the jobs were finished, the water would wash out the bread; the OED, however, dismisses a similar ety. for *tinker's dam(n)* as 'ingenious but baseless'] [mid-18C+] to not care at all.

not care twopence *v.* (*also* **...four-pence ha'penny, ...sixpence, ...tuppence, not give twopence**) [early 17C+] to not care at all.

notch *n.*[1] **1** [17C–late 19C] the vagina. **2** [1920s+] (*US*) (*also* **notch girl**) a prostitute or sexually promiscuous woman.

(IN COMPOUNDS)

❑ **notch house** *n.* (*also* **notch-joint**) [HOUSE *n.*[1] (1)/JOINT *n.* (1)] [1920s–60s] (*US*) a brothel. ❑ **notch moll** *n.* (*also* **notch girl**) [MOLL *n.* (2)/SE *girl*] [1920s–40s] (*US Und.*) a prostitute.

notch *n.*[2] [NOTCH *adj.*] [1990s+] (*W.I./UK black teen*) a high- or top-ranking villain.

notch *adj.* [SE *top notch*] [1980s+] (*black*) first-rate, excellent.

notch *v.* [ety. unknown] [2000s] (*S.Afr. gay*) to look at.

note *n.*[1] **1** [mid-19C] (*UK Und.*) a singer [meton.]. **2** [late 19C–1940s] (*US*) a joke [? it 'strikes a chord' in the hearer].

note *n.*[2] (*also* **notes**) **1** [mid-19C+] (*orig. Aus.*) a one pound note, usu. in pl. **2** [1970s+] (*US*) a cash payment.

(IN COMPOUNDS)

❑ **note layer** *n.* [1940s] a short-change swindler. ❑ **note shaver** *n.* [SHAVE A NOTE *v.*] [early 19C–1920s] (*US*) a promoter of bogus financial companies, a usurer.

(IN PHRASES)

❑ **lay the note** *v.* [1920s–70s] (*US Und.*) **1** to swindle, to short-change. **2** to pay a prostitute.

no-tell hotel *n.* (*also* **no-tell motel**) [the discretion of the staff] [1950s+] (*US*) a cheap hotel which rents out its rooms by the hour to prostitutes and their clients or to illicit lovers.

not even *phr.* [1980s+] (*US campus*) not at all, in no way.

not fucking likely! *excl. see* NOT LIKELY *phr.*

not give a... *v.* [examples are listed alphabetically rather than by date and the dating for these combinations can be anything from mid-16C to 1990s+] **1** [mid-16C+] in addition to the most popular combs. listed separately below, there are a number of less common phrs., all stating one's absolute lack of interest in the topic. **2** *see also* NOT CARE A... *v.*

(IN PHRASES)

❑ **...a crap** ❑ **...a doggone** ❑ **...a 4X** ❑ **...a frig** ❑ **...a hurrah** ❑ **...a kitty** ❑ **...a piss** ❑ **...a rassclot** ❑ **...a rip** ❑ **...a stuff** ❑ **...a sugar** ❑ **...a toot/tootle**

not give a bugger *v. see under* BUGGER *n.*[3].

not give a damn *v.* (*also* **...a (black) dam, ...a D, ...a damn, ...a dang, ...a darn, ...a dern, ...a domn, ...a drat, ...a durn, ...a good damn, ...a good goddamn, ...a twopenny damn, not care a damn, ...a nigger's damn**) [DAMN *n.*] [late 18C+] to not care at all.

not give a fiddler's fuck *v. see under* FIDDLER *n.*[3].

not give a flying fuck *v. see under* FLYING FUCK *n.*

not give a fuck *v.* (*also* **...a cockeyed fuck, ...a fat fuck, ...a good fuck, ...a monkey's fuck, ...a motherfuck, ...a ratfuck, ...a red fuck, ...a royal fuck, ...two fucks, not care a fuck**) [note, however, one-time late 18C use in a poem 'The Discontented Student'; the word is not spelt out, but the rhyme and the context ensure that the absentee can only be 'fuck'] [1910s+] (*orig. US*) to not care at all.

not give a (good) goddam *v.* (*also* **...a good doggone, ...a good goddurn, ...a greased goddam**) [GODDAM *n.*] [1910s+] to not care in the slightest.

not give a rat's arse *v.* (*also* **...a fat rat's ass, ...a rat's ass, ...a rat's fart, ...a rat's fuck, ... a rat's ring**) [1950s+] to not care at all.

not give a rush *v. see* NOT CARE A RUSH *v.*

not give a shit *v.* (*also* **...a crap, ...a dab of wombat shit, ...a good shit, a living shit, ...a pinch of dried-out shit, ...a shite, ...a stiff shit, ...a tin shit, ...two shits, not care two shits**) [SHIT *n.*] [1910s+] to not care at all.

not give a tuppenny damn *v.* (*also* **...a tuppenny cuss, ...a tuppenny dump, ...a tuppenny fuck, ...two tuppeny turds, not matter a tuppenny dam**) [for ety. *see* NOT GIVE A DAMN *v.*] [late 19C+] to not care at all.

not give someone the steam off one's turds *v. see under* STEAM *n.*

not give someone the steam on one's piss *v. see under* STEAM *n.*

not go three rounds with a revolving door *phr.* [i.e. SLOW *adj.* (3); pun on SE boxing *round*] [1960s–70s] very stupid.

not half *phr.* [i.e. a whole, a complete; earlier use is literal, ie not enough] [early 19C+] a mild intensifier, e.g. *she hadn't half made a mess.*

(IN PHRASES)

❑ **not half a one** *n.* [ONE *n.*[1] (5a)] [20C+] a card, a character, usu. in phr. *you ain't half a one!*

not half! *excl.* (*also* **not a half!**) [NOT HALF *phr.*] [mid-19C+] certainly! really! absolutely!

not have a bear's chance of shitting in a swinging jug *phr.* [1970s] (*US*) no chance at all.

not have both oars in the water *v. see* ROW WITH ONE OAR (IN THE WATER) *under* ROW *v.*[2].

not have enough sense to eat peas out of a bottle *v.* (*also* **...to pour piss out of a boot, ...a tin can**) [20C+] (*US*) to be very stupid.

not having any *phr.* (*also* **not taking any**) [20C+] wanting no part in something, rejecting a suggestion or an overture of friendship, refusing to tolerate a situation.

nothin'-ass bitch *n. see under* BITCH *n.*[1] (1).

nothing *adj.* [1950s+] (*orig. US*) insipid, dull, boring, insignificant.

nothing! *excl.* [late 19C+] (*orig. US*) not at all, in no respect.

nothing doing *phr.* (*also* **nothing stirrin'**) [early 19C+] absolutely not, not a hope, not a chance; thus anton. *something doing.*

notice box *n.* [1990s+] (*Irish*) one who is keen to attract attention.

(IN PHRASES)

❑ **Miss Notice Box** *n.* [1990s+] a 'forward' woman.

notice to quit *n.* [Egan (1821): 'A cant phrase, applied to any individual who appears to be in a state fast approaching towards dissolution.'] [early–mid-19C] intimations of one's imminent death.

not in it *phr.* [IN IT *adj.* (3); i.e. fig. *not in* the contest] [late 19C+] (*orig. sporting*) an absolute failure, lacking any chance.

not in the race *phr.* [1990s+] (*Aus.*) very stupid.

not in the same compartment/street/town with *phr. see under* SAME *adj.*

notion *n.* [SE *notion*, an inclination, disposition or desire] [late 19C+] (*Irish*) amorous inclinations, usu. in phr. *have a notion of*, to be sexually attracted by.

not know... *v.* in phrs. below implying one's confusion and/or ignorance.

(IN PHRASES)

❑ **not know a sparrow's shit about** *v.* [1970s] to know

nothing whatsoever. ❑ **not know from a bar of soap** *v.* [2000s] (*N.Z.*) to be totally ignorant of. ❑ **not know if one is Arthur or Martha** *v.* [20C+] **1** a phr. used to describe a man who is still ambivalent about his own sexuality. **2** a phr. used after swimming, to describe a man whose genitals have shrunk dramatically on contact with the cold water. **3** to be confused as to one's aims and intentions. ❑ **not know if it's Christmas or Brazil** *v.* [2000s] (*S.Afr. gay*) to be in a state of confusion. ❑ **not know if it's Piccadilly or Wednesday** *v.* [1910s] to be in a state of confusion. ❑ **not know if one's arsehole is bored or punched** *v. see under* ARSEHOLE *n.* ❑ **not know one's butt from a gourd** *v.* (*also* **not know one's butt from a bear's ass**) [BUTT *n.*[1] (1a)] [1940s+] (*US*) to be very stupid. ❑ **not know Queen Street from Christmas** *v.* [2000s] (*N.Z.*) to be ignorant. ❑ **not know shit from apple butter** *v.* (*also* **...from beans, ...clay, ...salami, ...tunafish, not know dung from honey**) [1940s+] **1** to not have any idea about a topic. **2** to be particularly wrong in an opinion. ❑ **not know shit from Shinola** *v.* [SHIT *n.* (1a) + *Shinola*, a black shoe-polish; orig. 'doesn't know shit from shinola and thinks they are both fat meat.'] [1940s+] (*US*) **1** (*also* **not know shit from shine, ...toothpaste**) to not have any idea about a topic. **2** to be particularly wrong in an opinion. **3** in phr. *not say shit about Shinola*, to say nothing. ❑ **not know where one's behind hangs** *v. see under* BEHIND *n.* ❑ **not know whether to shit or go blind** *v.* (*also* **...pee or go blind, ...shit or buy gas**) [1950s+] (*US*) to be utterly stupid, to be totally confused. ❑ **not know which side is up** *v.* [1960s+] (*US*) to be completely ignorant, deluded.

not know someone from... *v.* to proclaim one's ignorance of a person or their face, in var. combs. other than the main ones listed separately below; can be used with any n. that springs to mind, e.g.

IN PHRASES

❑ **...a bag of assholes** [1970s] ❑ **...a load of coal** [1940s–50s] (*US*) ❑ **...a pisshole in the snow** [1970s] ❑ **...four and sixpence** [late 19C] ❑ **...the next guy's asshole** [1970s]

not likely *phr.* [late 19C+] a phr. implying absolute reluctance, 'in no way will I do that'; usu. in excls. below.

IN EXCLAMATIONS

❑ **not bloody likely!** [popularized by George Bernard Shaw's *Pygmalion* (1913), in which the Cockney flowergirl Eliza Doolittle shocked audiences with her then taboo excl. 'Not bloody likely!'] [1910s+] an emphatic negative. ❑ **not fucking likely!** [FUCKING *adj.* (4)] [20C+] an emphatic negative. ❑ **not Pygmalion likely!** [for ety. see above] [1910s+] a euph. for NOT BLOODY LIKELY! *excl.*

not make head (n)or tail *v.* [early 18C+] to fail to understand, to find incomprehensible.

not much *phr.* (*also* **by much**) **1** [mid-19C–1900s] far from it, 'not likely'. **2** [late 19C+] in ironic use, very much, very likely.

not much bottle *phr. see* NO BOTTLE *phr.*[2] (1).

not much chop *phr. see* NO CHOP *phr.*

not much cop *phr. see* NO COP *under* COP *n.*[2].

not much frocks *n.* [rhy. sl.] [late 19C–1900s] socks.

not nominated *phr.* [horseracing jargon] [1930s+] (*Aus.*) without any chance of success.

not on *adj.* [billiards use, of shots that are 'not on' the table; ? also milit. use, when a proposed operation was 'not on' through unforeseen circumstances] [1930s+] socially unacceptable, impossible.

not on your nannie *phr.* (*also* **not on your nanny**) [? var. on NOT ON YOUR NELLIE *phr.*] [1950s+] (*Anglo-Irish.*) no chance, not a hope.

not on your nellie *phr.* (*also* **not on your nelly**) [rhy. sl. *not on your Nellie Duff* = PUFF *n.* (1c), thus var. on *NOT ON YOUR LIFE under* LIFE *n.*] [1940s+] not a chance, absolutely impossible.

not on your tintype *phr.* [SE *tintype*, an old-fashioned type of photograph, ie a 'life portrait' thus var. on *NOT ON YOUR LIFE under* LIFE *n.*] [late 19C+] (*orig. US*) a general term of derision and dismissal.

not playing with a full deck *phr.* (*also* **have only fifty cards in one's deck, play with 44 cards to the deck**) [1920s+] (*orig. US*) not very intelligent, slightly eccentric, odd.

IN PHRASES

❑ **play with a full deck** *v.* [1960s+] to be very intelligent.

not plump currant *phr.* [a plump currant would be fig. 'happy'] [late 18C–early 19C] out of sorts.

not Pygmalion likely! *excl. see* NOT LIKELY *phr.*

not quite there *phr. see* NOT ALL THERE *adj.*

no troubs *phr. see* NO WORRIES (MATE) *phr.*

not sixteen annas to the rupee *phr. see FIVE ANNAS SHORT OF THE RUPEE under* ...SHORT OF... *adj.*

not so cold *phr.* [late 19C] (*US*) rather good.

not take a blind bit of notice *v. see* BLIND *adj.*[2] (2).

not taking any *phr. see* NOT HAVING ANY *phr.*

not the full... *phr.*

IN PHRASES

❑ **...cup of tea** (*also* **not the full bottle**) [synon. for NOT ALL THERE *adj.*] [1980s+] not very intelligent, slightly eccentric, odd. ❑ **...dollar** (*also* **only ninety-nine cents out of the dollar**) [mid-19C+] (*US/Aus.*) not very intelligent, slightly eccentric, odd. ❑ **...shilling** *see under* SHILLING *n.* ❑ **...two bob** [1960s–70s] not up to standards, not as promised or advertised.

not the half of it *phr.* [1910s+] a phr. implying that there is much more to come, to be recounted.

not the only... *phr.*

IN PHRASES

❑ **...fish in the sea** (*also* **plenty more fish in the sea**) [20C+] used of someone who, whatever they may believe, is not unique (esp. in the context of love affairs). ❑ **...onion in the stew** (*also* **...in the hash, ...in the soup**) [not – as *OED* claims – only in PG Wodehouse] [20C+] not alone, not the only person who is equally qualified. ❑ **...pebble on the beach** (*also* **...turd on the road**) [late 19C+] used of someone who, whatever they may believe, is not unique (esp. in the context of love affairs). ❑ **...silver fish in the pond** (*also* **...sardine in the tin**) [1910s] (*Aus.*) used of someone who, whatever they may believe, is not unique (esp. in the context of love affairs).

not there *phr.* [1960s] (*US black*) boring.

nottie *n.* [pun on SE *not* + HOTTIE *n.*[2]] [1990s+] one who sees themselves as more attractive/sexier than they really are.

nottub *n.* [backsl.] [late 19C–1900s] a button.

not up *adj.* [abbr. *not up to standard*] [20C+] (*Aus.*) second-rate.

not up to Dick *phr. see UP TO DICK under* DICK *n.*[3].

not want to know *v.* [1940s+] a phr. implying a refusal to acknowledge some unpalatable fact or piece of information.

not worth a... *phr.* [examples are listed alphabetically rather than by date and the dating for these combinations can be anything from mid-16C to 1990s+] [14C+] in addition to the most popular combs. listed separately below, there are a number of less common phrs., all meaning worthless, useless (and occas. used without 'not' to mean the opposite), e.g. *that's worth a whoop in hell*.

IN PHRASES

❑ **...a cracker** ❑ **...a dam** ❑ **...a dodkin** (*also* **...doit, ...dotkin**) ❑ **...a farthing** ❑ **...a Flanders pin** ❑ **...a fly** ❑ **...a gnat** ❑ **...a hang** ❑ **...a hoot** ❑ **...a leek** (*also* **...two leeks**) ❑ **...a louse** ❑ **...a mag** ❑ **...an oyster** ❑ **...a plum** (*also* **...two plums**) ❑ **...a preen** ❑ **...a rush** (*also* **...a bulrush, ...two rushes**) ❑ **...a snap (of one's fingers)** ❑ **...a tinker's cuss/damn** ❑ **...a turd** ❑ **...a whoop (in hell)** ❑ **...shucks** ❑ **...three skips of a louse**

not worth a cent *phr.* (*also* **...a red cent, ...two cents**) [19C+] (*US*) worthless, useless.

not worth a curse *phr.* (*also* **...a cobbler's curse, ...a cuss, ...a fiddler's curse, ...a tinker's curse, ...a tinker's dam/damn, not matter a tinker's curse**) [for ety. *see* NOT CARE A TINKER'S (CURSE) *v.*] [mid-14C; mid-19C+] worthless, useless.

not worth a damn *phr.* (*also* **...a continental dam, ...a D, ...a dam, ...a darn, ...a drat, ...a twopenny dam/damn**) [DAMN *n.*]

1 [mid-19C+] a negative phr. used to imply uselessness or incompetence, e.g. *He can't fight worth a damn*. **2** [1980s+] as an intensifier.

not worth a fart *phr.* (*also* **...a fart in a breeze, ...a fart in a gale, ...a fart in a hurricane, ...a fart in a storm, ...a roasted fart, ...a (two-bob) fart in a bottle**) [FART *n.* (1)] [mid-16C+] worthless, useless.

not worth a fuck *phr.* (*also* **not worth a tuppenny frig**) [FUCK *n.* (1a)] [20C+] absolutely worthless.

not worth a good goddam *phr.* (*also* **not worth a good damn, ...a good gosh-damn**) [1910s+] (*US*) absolutely worthless.

not worth a pinch of coonshit *phr.* (*also* **...a pinch of cat's piss, ...a pinch (of shit)**) [SE *racoon* + SHIT *n.* (1a)] [20C+] (*Can.*) worthless, useless; also with vars. on the word *shit*.

not worth a plugged nickel *phr.* (*also* **...a lead nickel, ...a plugged dime, ...a plug nickel**) [1910s+] (*US*) valueless.

not worth a pound of piss *phr.* [1960s] (*US*) utterly worthless, despicable.

not worth a tuppenny frig *phr. see* NOT WORTH A FUCK *phr.* (1).

not wrapped too tight *phr. see under* TIGHT *adj.*

nouce *n. see* NOUS *n.*

'nough said *see* NUFF CED *phr.*

nought and carry one *n.* [var. on DOT AND GO ONE *n.*] [20C+] (*Irish*) a lame person.

noughts and crosses *n.* [1950s–60s] (*UK Und.*) criss-crossing slashes with a razor.

nouns! *excl. see* 'SNOUNS! *excl.*

nous *n.* (*also* **nouce, nouse**) [Gk *nous*, the mind] [18C+] instinct or common sense, as opposed to actual learning.

IN COMPOUNDS

❑ **nous-box** *n.* (*also* **nouse-box**) [early 19C] the head.

nous *v.* [NOUS *n.*] [mid-19C] to understand or learn.

no-user *n.* [SE *no use* + sfx *-er*] [1980s+] (*Irish*) a failure, a 'loser'.

novel *n.* [1970s–80s] (*UK black*) an elaborate story, a piece of information.

Novy *n.* [abbr.] [late 19C+] a native of *Nova Scotia*.

— now (and) — later *phr.* [the *locus classicus* is the film *Live Now, Pay Later* (1962), satirizing the 'hire-purchase' boom of the late 1950s–early 1960s; its screenwriter Jack Trevor Storey publ. a novel of the same name in 1963] [1960s+] used in various phr. implying that someone can act (usu. pleasurably) now and take responsibility, usu. in the form of payment, in due course.

now and never *adj.* (*also* **now or never**) [rhy. sl.] [late 19C] clever.

no way! *excl.* (*also* **no way José! no ways!**) [SE *no way*, in no way whatsoever] **1** [1960s+] (*orig. US*) absolutely not! you must be joking! you can't fool me! **2** [1990s+] used in rejoinder to a story that, however bizarre, is true; 'Surely not!' 'Really, that's amazing!'. The usu. affirmative reply is WAY! *excl.*

nowhere *adj.* **1** [mid-18C–19C] hopelessly beaten, esp. in a race. **2** [mid-19C+] (*orig. US*) utterly confused, very mixed up. **3** [mid-19C+] (*orig. US*) useless, pointless, stupid, unimpressive.

DERIVATIVES

❑ **nowherian** *n.* (*also* **nowhereian**) [Carib.E. *nowherian*, one who has no religious affiliation] [1960s] (*W.I.*) anyone deemed unrespectable; a layabout, an unkempt-looking person who is characterized as a tramp.

IN COMPOUNDS

❑ **nowhere city** *n.* (*also* **nowheresville**) [-CITY *sfx*/-VILLE *sfx*[1]] [1960s+] a situation, place or person who/which is seen as irrelevant, pointless, of no use at all.

nowig *n.* [SE *no* + WIG *v.*[1] (8)] [2000s] (*US black*) a state of calmness, sanity.

no worries (mate) *phr.* (*also* **no troubs, no worries on me**) [1960s+] (*orig. Aus.*) a common phr. of assurance; usu. ext. by *she'll be all right*.

now you're shouting *phr.* [emphatic var. on *NOW YOU'RE TALKING under* TALK *v.*] [late 19C–1910s] (*US*) now you're saying something meaningful or relevant.

n.o.y.b. *phr.* [abbr.] [1910s+] (*US*) *n*one *o*f *y*our *b*usiness.

nozzle *n.* **1** [mid-18C+] the nose or a nostril. **2** [1990s+] (*US*) the penis.

nozzler *n.* [NOZZLE *n.* (1)] [early 19C] a blow on the nose.

n.q.o.c.d. *phr.* (*also* **n.o.c.d.**) [abbr. *n*ot *q*uite *o*ur *c*lass, *d*ear] [1980s+] (*UK/US society*) used of one who is deemed socially unacceptable.

n.s. *phr.* [abbr. NUFF *adj.* + SE *said*] [mid-19C] (*US*) enough said, it is possible to infer all the facts from what has already been stated.

n.s.g. *phr.* [abbr.] [1950s] (*US*) *n*ot *s*o *g*ood.

n.s.h. *phr.* [abbr. *NOT SO HOT under* HOT *adj.*] [1950s] (*US*) a general negative phr., unattractive, unimpressive etc.

n.s.i.t. *phr.* [abbr. *n*ot *s*afe *i*n *t*axis] [1930s+] (*UK society*) a note attached to the name of a prospective male escort by a debutante or her mother.

n.s.s.! *excl. see* NO SHIT, SHERLOCK! *excl.*

NS²! *excl. see* NO SHIT, SHERLOCK! *excl.*

n.t.o. *phr.* [abbr. *n*ot *t*he *o*ne] [1990s+] (*US campus*) a date who does not come up to expectations.

n.t.s. *n.* [abbr. *n*ame *t*ag *s*haker] [1970s+] (*US campus*) an attractive man that makes a woman's heart beat so fast that her name tag shakes.

nub *n.*[1] [ety. unknown; ? SE *nub*, a protuberance, a lump] (*UK Und.*) **1** [late 17C–early 18C] the gallows. **2** [late 17C–early 19C] the neck. **3** [1940s+] (*US*) an ugly or repulsive person. **4** [1950s] a cigarette.

nub *n.*[2] [? dial. *nub*, to jog, to shake] **1** [18C–early 19C] (*also* **nubbing**) sexual intercourse. **2** [late 18C–mid-19C] a husband.

nub *v.* [NUB *n.*[1] (1)] [late 17C–mid-19C] to hang.

DERIVATIVES

❑ **nubbed** *adj.* [late 17C–mid-19C] hanged.

nubbie *n.* [SE *nubs* of hair, but note NEWBIE *n.* (1)] [1960s+] (*W.I./Rasta*) a young Rastafarian with short hair.

nubbies *n.* [SE *nub*, a protuberance, a lump] [late 19C+] (*Aus.*) the female breasts.

nubbin *n.* [play on SE *nubbin*, the remains of something that has been worn away, e.g. a pencil; ult. a dwarfed or imperfect ear of maize] **1** [20C+] (*US black*) the penis. **2** [1930s+] (*US black*) a fool, a simpleton.

nubbing *n.*[1] [NUB *v.*] [mid-17C–19C] hanging.

IN COMPOUNDS

❑ **nubbing cheat** *n.* (*also* **nubbing chit, nubbling cheat**) [CHEAT *n.* (1); lit. 'the hanging thing'] [late 17C–19C] the gallows. ❑ **nubbing cove** *n.* (*also* **nubbing cull**) [COVE *n.* (1)/CULL *n.*[1] (3)] [late 17C–19C] the hangman. ❑ **nubbing ken** *n.* [KEN *n.*[1] (1); lit. 'the hanging house'; one's trial there might well lead to the gallows] [late 17C–19C] the Sessions house. ❑ **nubbing post** *n.* [late 17C–mid-18C] (*UK Und.*) the gallows.

nubbing *n.*[2] *see* NUB *n.*[2] (1).

nubbin-head *n.* (*also* **nubbin**) [NUBBIN *n.* + -HEAD *sfx* (1)] [1930s+] (*US black*) a fool, a simpleton.

nubbling cheat *n. see NUBBING CHEAT under* NUBBING *n.*[1].

nubian *n.* [SE *nubian*, a member of a North African people living near what is now Egypt] [1970s+] **1** (*US campus*) a socially unacceptable person, used of whites and blacks despite obvious racist base. **2** (*US gay*) a black man.

nuck *n. see* KNUCK *n.* (1).

nuckel-head *n. see* KNUCKLEHEAD *n.*

nucker *n.* (*also* **nukka**) [? KNUCKLEHEAD *n.*] [1990s+] (*US black*) a fool; also used as affectionate term of address.

nuckle sandwich *n. see KNUCKLE SANDWICH under* KNUCKLE *n.*

nucks *n. see* KNUCK *n.* (3).

nucky *n. see* NOOKIE *n.*

nuclear *adj.* [1970s+] (*orig. US*) enraged.

nuclear sub *n.* [rhy. sl.] [2000s] a *pub*lic house.

nuddikin *n.* [NOODLE *n.*[1] (1) + KEN *n.*[1] (1)] [mid-19C] the head.

nudes for dudes *n.* [1980s] (*US campus*) a course in art.

nudge *n.* (*also* **noodge, nudzh**) [Yid.] [1960s+] (*US*) a nag, a pest.

SE in slang uses

IN PHRASES

❑ **give it a (bit of) a nudge** *v.* [1950s+] (*Aus.*) to drink to excess. ❑ **nudge the turps** *v.* [1970s+] (*Aus.*) to drink heavily, often with a specified drink, e.g. *nudge the nelly*, to drink too much cheap wine.

nudge *v.*[1] [17C–19C] of a man, to have sexual intercourse.

SE in slang uses

IN PHRASES

❑ **nudge, nudge, wink, wink, know what I mean, say no more** [popularized by Eric Idle in *Monty Python's Flying Circus*, BBC2 TV *c.*1969; Idle was dressed as a SPIV *n.* and was making heavily sexual innuendoes] [1960s+] used, heavy-handedly, to make a sexual or otherwise dubious innuendo, usu. abbr. to *nudge, nudge, wink, wink* or *say no more*.

nudge *v.*[2] (*also* **nudgy**) [NUDGE *n.*] [1960s+] to bother, to irritate.

nudger *n.* [NUDGE *v.*[1]] **1** [1960s+] the penis. **2** [1960s+] (*Irish*) a term of abuse. **3** [1990s+] (*US*) a male homosexual.

nudgy *adj.* [NUDGE *n.*] [1960s+] (*US campus*) nagging, whingeing.

nudie *n.* (*orig. US*) **1** [1930s+] a striptease show or burlesque. **2** [1930s+] in combs. pertaining to naked or semi-naked women. **3** [1950s+] a nude performer. **4** [1960s+] a picture featuring naked or semi-naked flesh.

IN COMPOUNDS

❑ **nudie book** *n.* [1970s] a pornographic magazine. ❑ **nudie pic** *n.* [1930s+] an 'adult' cinema or film.

nudnik *n.* (*also* **noodnik, nudnick**) [synon. Yid.; ? ult. Rus. *nudna*] [1920s+] (*US*) a pest, a fool, an insignificant person.

nudzh *n. see* NUDGE *n.*

nuff *adj.* [mis-sp.] [mid-19C+] enough, plenty, abundant; usu. as NUFF CED *phr.*

DERIVATIVES

❑ **nuffness** *n.* [1980s+] (*W.I.*) showiness, ostentation, vulgarity, precocity.

IN PHRASES

❑ **get one's nuff** *v.* (*also* **have one's nuff**) [late 19C–1910s] (*orig. milit.*) to be drunk. ❑ **nuff respect** [1980s+] (*orig. W.I.*) a general phr. of approval/admiration.

nuff ced *phr.* (*also* **'nough said, nuf ced, nuff said, nuff sed, nuf sed**) [NUFF *adj.* + pron. of SE *said*; the mis-sp. only works, of course, when printed] [mid-19C+] (*orig. US*) enough said, it is possible to infer all the facts from what has already been stated.

nug *n.*[1] [NUG *v.*] **1** [late 17C–19C] a term of affection, e.g. *my dear nug*. **2** [1990s+] (*US campus*) a young woman.

nug *n.*[2] [abbr. NUGGET *n.* (1)] [1980s+] (*US drugs*) high quality, dense, small hydroponically grown marijuana.

nug *n.*[3] [abbr. NUGGIE *n.*] [1990s+] (*US*) in pl., a woman's breasts.

IN PHRASES

❑ **fresh nugs** *n.* [1990s+] a woman with large breasts.

nug *v.* [dial. *nug*, to jog with the elbow, to strike or Lat. *nugae*, trifles] [16C–19C; 1980s] to fondle, to indulge in sexual foreplay, to have sexual intercourse.

IN COMPOUNDS

❑ **nugging dress** *n.* [late 17C–19C] **1** an old-fashioned or out of the ordinary style of dress. **2** a loose dress, denoting a courtesan. ❑ **nugging house** *n.* (*also* **nugging ken**) [HOUSE *n.*[1] (1)/KEN *n.*[1] (1)] [late 17C–early 19C] a brothel.

nugget *n.* [SE *nugget*, a lump] **1** [mid-19C+] (*Aus.*) a small, compact, stocky animal or person, a runt. **2** [late 19C–1900s] in pl., money. **3** [1920s+] (*Aus.*) a very attractive woman. **4** [1960s+] (*US*) (*also* **gold nuggets**) in pl., the testicles. **5** [1970s+] in pl., the female nipples. **6** in drug uses. (**a**) [1970s+] amphetamine. (**b**) [1980s+] in pl., cocaine crystals. (**c**) [1980s+] in pl., crack cocaine. (**d**) [1980s+] in pl., high strength, hydroponically grown cannabis. **7** [1980s+] (*US campus*) a fool, an idiot [synon. with BONEHEAD *n.*[1] (1), LUNKHEAD *n.* and similar terms that equate hardness (of head) with stupidity].

nugget *v.* [brandname, but note NUGGET *n.* (4)] [1960s+] (*N.Z.*) a male 'game' in which a victim's trousers and underpants are removed and his genitals blackened with *Nugget* black shoe polish.

nuggety *adj.* [NUGGET *n.* (1)] [late 19C+] (*Aus.*) chunky, squat, thickset.

nuggie *n.* [? NUBBIES *n.*] [1970s+] (*US*) a woman's breast.

nuggie *v. see* NOOGIE *n.*

nuh? *excl.* (*also* **nuh true?**) **1** [1980s+] (*W.I./UK black teen*) a general interrog., i.e. 'Isn't that so?'. **2** [1990s+] a ridiculing retort.

nuke *n.* [abbr.] **1** [1950s+] a *nu*clear bomb. **2** [1960s+] (*US*) a *nu*clear power station. **3** [1960s+] (*US*) a *nu*clear powered weapon or ship, or one capable of firing nuclear missiles. **4** [1980s] a *nu*clear family or a member of a nuclear family. **5** [1980s+] (*US drugs*) marijuana which has been adulterated with especially dangerous and/or toxic substances.

nuke *v.* [NUKE *n.* (1)] **1** [1960s+] to attack with a *nu*clear bomb. **2** [1960s+] (*orig. US*) to punish severely, to destroy completely, to ruin. **3** [1980s] (*US campus*) to end a relationship with a girl or boyfriend. **4** [1980s+] (*US campus*) of food, to warm up in a microwave, to cook well. **5** [1980s+] (*US campus*) (*also* **nuke oneself**) to get a tan in a tanning booth. **6** [1980s+] of hair, to blow dry or spray excessively. **7** [1990s+] (*US*) to electrocute.

IN COMPOUNDS

❑ **nuke and puke** *n.* [1990s+] (*US campus*) a microwave meal.

nuker *n.* [NUKE *v.* (4)] [1980s+] (*US campus*) a microwave oven.

nukka *n. see* NUCKER *n.*

nukky *n. see* NOOKIE *n.*

null *v.* [? SE *annul*] [late 18C–mid-19C] to beat.

null-groper *n.* [? perversion of SE *nail*] [early 19C] (*UK Und.*) one who searches the streets for nails, bits of iron etc.

nulling cove *n.* [NULL *v.* + COVE *n.* (1)] [early 19C] a prize-fighter.

numans *n.* [corruption of *New* + sfx -MANS *sfx*; it was a general market which burned down in the Great Fire (1666)] [17C] Newgate Market.

numb *n.* [? SE *number*, i.e. of coins] [mid-19C] money.

numb *adj.* **1** [1910s+] (*US*) (*also* **numbs**) blind drunk; occas. intoxicated by drugs. **2** [1960s+] (*US*) (*also* **numbass, numbfuck**) stupid.

SE in slang uses

DERIVATIVES

❑ **numby** *n.* [abbr. *NUMBHEAD* below] [1940s+] (*US*) a fool, a simpleton.

IN COMPOUNDS

❑ **numbhead** *n.* [-HEAD *sfx* (1)] [mid-18C+] (*US*) a fool. ❑ **numbheaded** *adj.* [mid-18C+] (*US*) stupid. ❑ **numbheadedness** *n.* [1960s+] (*US*) stupidity. ❑ **numbnut** *adj.* [*NUMBNUTS* below] [1990s+] (*Aus.*) foolish, stupid. ❑ **numbnuts** *n.* [NUTS *n.*[2] (1)] [1960s+] (*US*) an idiot, a fool; usu. as a term of address. ❑ **numbwit** *n.* [var. on *dimwit*] [1950s+] a fool.

number *n.* **1** of an individual or individuals. (**a**) [late 19C+] (*orig. US*) a person, usu. a young woman, usu. in a sexual context; esp. as *HOT NUMBER* below. (**b**) [1930s+] a person, in a non-sexual context. (**c**) [1960s+] (*US gay*) a potential or actual partner for casual sex, picked up from the street, bar or baths. (**d**) [1970s+] (*US*) a romantically involved couple. **2** [late 19C+] an item of clothing, e.g. a *dainty pink number*. **3** in fig./abstract senses. (**a**) [20C+] in general, a thing, place or situation, defined by context. (**b**) [20C+] a performance; a scene, a display of excessive emotion. (**c**) [1910s+] a job or task, esp. in phr. *cushy number/little number*, an easy job. (**d**) [1920s] belief, commitment. (**e**) [1930s–50s] (*US black*) a jail sentence, a life sentence. **4** [20C+] as a *number* on a door. (**a**) a bedroom in a hotel or boarding house. (**b**) one's house. **5** [1950s] a reputation. **6** [1960s+] (*drugs*) a marijuana or hashish cigarette. **7** [1970s+] a style, a way of living, a pose, e.g. *the ageing rocker number*.

IN PHRASES

❑ **do a number** *v.* [1960s+] (*drugs*) **1** to make and smoke a marijuana or hashish cigarette. **2** of cannabis, to take effect. ❑ **do a number (on)** *v.* **1** [1960s+] to make a fuss, to become emotional; thus *do a number on*, to subject someone to emotional blackmail or at least some form of moral, friendship or ethical pressure. **2** [1970s+] to have sexual intercourse. **3** [1970s+] to manipulate emotionally, esp. through sexuality. **4** [1970s+] to beat savagely. **5** [1980s] (*US*) to get married. **6** [1990s+] to break, to cause harm (other than through deliberate, person-to-person violence). ❑ **have someone's number** *v.* (*also* **get someone's number**) (*orig. US*) **1** [mid-19C+] to understand another person absolutely, for all their possible evasions and excuses. **2** [1920s+] to be aware, to be alert, to see through someone's pretences. ❑ **heavy number** *n.* [HEAVY *adj.* (5c)] [1970s+] anything or anyone seen as serious, important etc. ❑ **hot number** *n.* [HOT *adj.* (1c) + pun on telephone number] [late 19C+] a sexually attractive woman or in gay use man, also her or his telephone number, esp. if written on the wall of a phone booth. ❑ **kill a number** *v.* [1990s+] (*US prison*) to finish one's sentence. ❑ **know one's number** *v.* [1910s+] to understand another person, to assess a situation. ❑ **number is up** (*also* **number comes up, ...turns up**) **1** [late 19C+] a phr. meaning that one dies. **2** [20C+] a phr. meaning that one is in trouble or has reached a point from which one cannot escape. ❑ **on the numbers** [1990s+] (*UK prison*) voluntary solitary confinement for the sake of a prisoner's safety; child molesters, rapists etc choose this in preference to the natural justice of their peers. ❑ **pull a number** *v.* [1970s+] (*orig. US*) **1** to trick, to deceive. **2** with a n., to act in a given manner, usu. in order to deceive. ❑ **roll a number** *v.* [1960s+] (*drugs*) to prepare a marijuana cigarette. ❑ **soft number** *n.* [SOFT *adj.* (4)] [1910s+] (*orig. milit.*) an easy job.

SE in slang uses

IN COMPOUNDS

as specific numbers, written out or in digits as found in source material

❑ **number 8** *n.* [*H* is the eighth letter of the alphabet] [1950s+] (*US drugs*) heroin. ❑ **number eight** *n.* [1980s+] (*N.Z.*) the best; the strongest; the most likely to succeed. ❑ **number fifteens** *n. see* NUMBER TEN *n.* ❑ **number 9** *n.* [early–mid-19C] the Fleet prison, situated at 9 Fleet Market, London. ❑ **number one** *see* separate entries. ❑ **number one thousand** *adj.* [pidgin, imported by veterans of the Vietnam War] [1970s+] (*US*) very bad. ❑ **number six** *n.* **1** [mid–late 19C] a lock of hair shaped like the figure 6 and twisted from the temple back towards the ear. **2** [early–mid-19C] (*US*) (*also* **number 6**) Thomson's Compound Tincture of Myrrh and Capsicum, a popular household remedy [it was regularly listed as the sixth medicine in the firm's catalogue]. ❑ **number ten** *see* separate entries. ❑ **number 13** *n.* [*M* is the 13th letter of the alphabet] [1950s] (*drugs*) morphine. ❑ **number 3** *n.* [*C* is the third letter of the alphabet] [1950s+] (*drugs*) cocaine. ❑ **number three** *n.* [on model of NUMBER ONE *n.* (5a), NUMBER TWO *n.* (1), although in adult use] [20C+] masturbation, whether by oneself, a partner, or as 'executive relief' i.e. from a 'masseuse' or prostitute. ❑ **number two** *n. see* separate entry.

general uses

❑ **number-chaser** *n.* [1930s] (*US*) an accountant. ❑ **number-cruncher** *n.* [computer jargon *number-cruncher*, a large, sometimes slow machine which is used for calculations that would defeat, by quantity rather than complexity, mere human efforts] [1970s+] (*US*) **1** an accountant or statistician. **2** a person lacking creativity or imagination. ❑ **number nip** *n.* [? SE *number*, a thing + *nip*; i.e. the image of the vagina as 'biting' the male] [19C] the vagina.

IN PHRASES

❑ **when the numbers are up** (*also* **when the numbers go up**) [the raising of a board carrying the numbers of the winning horses after a horserace] [late 19C+] (*Aus.*) when the result is known.

number fifteens *n. see* NUMBER TEN *n.*

number one *n.* **1** [18C+] oneself, one's own interests. **2** [mid-19C+] the best, the finest quality. **3** [20C+] (*orig. US*) one's best friend or lover. **4** [20C+] (*S.Afr. black*) refined, white mealie meal. **5** [20C+] (*also* **number ones**) as juv. euph. (**a**) the act of urination. (**b**) urine. (**c**) a chamberpot. **6** [1910s+] an extremely short 'skinhead' hair-style [from the setting of the hair-clippers at '1']. **7** [1930s–50s] (*UK prison*) the punishment diet of bread and water. **8** [1950s+] (*US Und.*) first degree (i.e. pre-meditated) murder.

IN PHRASES

❑ **look after number one** *v.* (*also* **look out for..., mind...**) [19C+] to take care of oneself, irrespective of others.

number one *adj.* (*also* **No 1**) [widely popularized after its importation by veterans of the Korean (1950–3) and Vietnam (1964–75) Wars] [mid-19C+] (*orig. US*) first-rate, excellent, important, influential, the best.

number ones *n. see* NUMBER ONE *n.* (5).

number-one squeeze *n. see* MAIN SQUEEZE *under* SQUEEZE *n.*[1].

numbers, the *n.* [the SE *numbers* upon which one bets] [late 19C+] (*US gambling*) a popular form of street gambling that involves predicting a combination of the winning numbers (between 000-999) at a racetrack, esp. widespread in US black community.

IN COMPOUNDS

❑ **numbers-banker** *n.* (*also* **numbers-baron, ...king, ...man**) [1930s+] one who runs a numbers lottery. ❑ **numbers house** *n.* [1970s] the office where the numbers 'racket' is run. ❑ **numbers racket** *n.* [1940s+] laying odds and betting on numbers. ❑ **numbers runner** *n.* [1950s+] one who takes the money from individual bettors and who delivers any payouts.

IN PHRASES

❑ **hit the number** *v.* (*also* **hit the numbers**) [1930s+] **1** to make a successful bet on the numbers game. **2** to be successful, in a non-gambling context.

numbers game *n.* [the combination of SIXTY-NINE *n.* (1) and SIXTY-SIX *under* SIXTY *n.*] [1960s] (*US gay*) an uninhibited and extended session of sexual activity.

number ten *n.* (*also* **...fifteen, ...tens, size ten**) [ref. to shoe size] [late 19C+] (*US*) a shoe or foot.

number ten *adj.* (*also* **number sixty-nine**) [pidgin, imported by veterans of the wars in Korea (1950–3) and Vietnam (1964–75)] [1950s+] (*orig. US milit.*) very bad, the worst.

number ten thou *adj.* (*also* **number ten thousand**) [for ety. *see* NUMBER TEN *adj.*] [1970s+] (*US*) extremely bad, dire, the very worst.

number two *n.* [euph.] **1** [late 19C+] (*mainly juv.*) (*also* **number twos**) defecation. **2** [1950s] (*W.I.*) a large round dumpling [it is indented around its circumference to facilitate splitting it in half, but note sense 1]. **3** [1950s+] (*orig. milit.*) second-in-command, second in rank. **4** [1990s+] (*US black*) anything considered bad, unpleasant, underhand or deceptive.

numbfuck *adj. see* NUMB *adj.* (2).

numbs *adj. see* NUMB *adj.* (1).

numero uno *n.* [Sp. *numero uno*] **1** [1940s+] the best, whether of objects or persons [NUMBER ONE *adj.* (1)]. **2** [1960s+] (*US*) an important person, the boss. **3** [1970s+] (*orig. US*) oneself [NUMBER ONE *n.* (1)].

numerous *adj.* [mid–late 19C] (*US*) superior, notable.

numgare *n.* (*also* **mungare**) [Ital. *mangiare*, to eat] [mid-19C] food, a meal.

nummer *n.* [ety. unknown] [mid-19C] a vagabond.

numms *n.* [ety. unknown; ? link to SE *nominal*] [late 17C–early 19C] a false, detachable collar, to be worn over a dirty shirt.

num-nums *n.* [echoic of sucking] [1970s+] **1** (*Aus./US*) a woman's breasts. **2** (*US*) a nipple. **3** (*S.Afr.*) food.

nun *n.* **1** [16C–early 19C] a prostitute. **2** [1980s+] a prude, a woman who is uninterested in sex.

IN PHRASES

❑ **in more strife than a pregnant nun** *adj. see* IN MORE STRIFE THAN A PORK CHOP AT A SYNAGOGUE *under* PORK CHOP AT A JEWISH WEDDING *phr.*

nunga-muncher *n.* [Aboriginal *nyoongah*, a man] [1960s–70s] (*Aus.*) a fellatrix.

nungers *n.* [echoic of sucking] [1960s+] (*Aus.*) the female breasts.

nunky *n.* (*also* **nunk, nunkey, nunks**) [late 16C–mid-18C SE *nuncle*, an uncle] **1** [17C–1950s] an uncle, whether lit. or as an address to/description of an older man [UNCLE *n.* (1)]. **2** [1920s–30s] a pawnbroker. **3** [1920s–30s] a Jew, esp. when a money-lender [from sense 2].

nunnery *n.* [NUN *n.* (1); note synon. ref. to a *religious house* in *Coryat's Crudities* (1611)] [late 16C–19C] a brothel.

nunno! *excl.* [1900s–40s] not likely! definitely not!

nunny-bunny *n.* [the nun depicted on the note + ? rhy. sl. = *money*] [2000s] (*Irish*) £5.

nunquam *n.* [Lat. *numquam*, never] [mid-16C–early 17C] (*UK Und.*) a dawdling messenger.

nun with a price on her head *n.* [its design] [1990s+] (*Irish*) a £5 note.

nup *n. see* NOPE! *excl.*

nupson *n.* [ety. unknown] [17C–late 18C] a fool.

nurd *n. see* NERD *n.*

nurdy *adj. see* NERDY *under* NERD *n.*

nurembergs *n.* [rhy. sl. *Nuremberg trials* = SE *piles*] [1940s+] haemorrhoids.

nurgle *n.* [? var. on NERD *n.*] [1990s+] (*N.Z. juv.*) a fool.

nurk *n.* [var. on NERD *n.*] [1990s+] (*UK juv.*) a fool.

nurse *n.* [early 18C] a common name for a homosexual barber.

nurse *v.* **1** [late 18C–19C] to cheat or swindle. **2** [mid-19C–1900s] for one omnibus to follow a rival closely so as to poach its passengers.

IN PHRASES

❑ **at nurse** [late 18C–early 19C] for a person to be in the hands of (dishonest) trustees. ❑ **nurse the iron baby** *v.* [late 19C] (*UK Und.*) to be in prison.

nursery *n.* [its role in procreation] **1** [mid-17C–mid-18C] a brothel, or a place frequented by prostitutes. **2** [19C] the vagina.

nursery rhyme *n.* [rhy. sl.] [2000s] a crime.

nursery rhymes *n.* [rhy. sl.] [1990s+] the *Times* newspaper.

nusslap *v.* [NUTS *n.*[2] (1) + SE *slap*] [2000s] (*US black*) to cause trouble for someone, to harm both lit. and fig.

nut *n.*[1] **1** in senses meaning 'head'. (**a**) [mid-16C+] the head of the penis. (**b**) [mid-19C+] the head. (**c**) [late 19C+] brains, intelligence. (**d**) [1940s+] the head, as used to butt someone in a fight. (**e**) [1990s+] (*Aus.*) in a game of two-up, the *head* side of the coin. **2** [early–mid-19C] an action that is intended to give pleasure, something positive [the pleasant flavour of a *nut* or NUTS *n.*[1] (1)]. **3** with ref. to a person. (**a**) [mid-19C+] a person, a fellow [ext. use of sense 1, often constrained by an unspoken 'tough']. (**b**) [late 19C+] a daredevil. (**c**) *see* KNUT *n.* **4** [late 19C+] (*Aus.*) a horse that is hard to break in [abbr. HARD NUT *n.*]. **5** with ref. to money [SE *nut*, as being the heart of the fruit; such money is at the heart of a project, a relationship etc]. (**a**) [20C+] (*US (orig. entertainment)*) the initial outlay, overheads, expenses; the break-even sum, as in a theatre production or film, after which profit starts. (**b**) [20C+] (*US*) any required sum, a pay-off. (**c**) [1920s+] (*US Und.*) protection money paid to corrupt policemen. (**d**) [1970s] (*US*) a fund used for bribery and other illegal activities, esp. by police. (**e**) [1970s+] the sum of money actually borrowed, as opposed to the interest that accrues on it.

IN COMPOUNDS

❑ **nut-cut** *adj. see* separate entries. ❑ **nut ducker** *n.* [note Aus. cattleman use *duck his nut*, of a horse, to (put its head down and) buck] [1960s+] (*Aus.*) one who deliberately ignores a friend in the street. ❑ **nut worker** *n.* [the use of one's brain to do this] [1910s+] (*Aus.*) one who works out ways of avoiding hard work; thus ext. as a white-collar worker.

IN PHRASES

❑ **do one's nut** *v.* (*also* **...lolly, do the nut**) [1910s+] to lose one's temper, to lose emotional control, to get worked up. ❑ **duck the nut** *v. see* DUCK *v.*[1] (2). ❑ **get someone's nut** *v.* [2000s] to tease, to 'wind up'. ❑ **give someone the nut** *v.* (*also* **put a head on, put the nut on**) [NUT *n.*[1] (1b)] [mid-19C+] to hit with one's head. ❑ **go off one's nut** *v.* [late 19C+] to go mad, to lose emotional control. ❑ **lose one's nut** *v.* [20C+] to lose emotional control; to act without thinking. ❑ **make the nut** *v.* [1950s+] (*US*) to achieve a target, to have a sufficiency. ❑ **nod the nut** *v.* (*also* **give it the nod, nod one's head**) [1930s+] (*Aus./N.Z.*) to plead guilty. ❑ **nut (it) out** *v.* [1910s+] (*Aus.*) to think it over, to work out. ❑ **nut on** *v.* (*US*) **1** [20C+] to attack physically; to abuse verbally. **2** [1960s–70s] (*also* **nut up**) to ignore; to be silent. ❑ **nut out** *v.* [1960s+] (*US black*) to go mad, whether literally or metaphorically. ❑ **nut up** *v.* [1970s+] to lose one's temper completely, to go berserk. ❑ **off one's nut** [mid-19C+] **1** drunk. **2** mad. **3** infatuated, obsessive, very enthusiastic. **4** angry. ❑ **off the nut** [1930s+] (*US*) free from debt. ❑ **on one's own nut** [mid-19C] (*UK Und.*) on one's own. ❑ **on the nut** [20C+] (*US*) **1** in debt. **2** unemployed. ❑ **out of one's nut** [note earlier *OFF ONE'S NUT* above] **1** [1930s+] crazy. **2** [1960s+] intoxicated, either through drink or, later, drugs. ❑ **put the nut in** *v.* [1960s] (*Irish*) to headbutt. ❑ **put the nut on** *v. see* *GIVE SOMEONE THE NUT* above. ❑ **use one's nut** *v.* [1930s+] to think, to act intelligently, to work things out.

nut *n.*[2] [NUTS *adj.*] **1** [mid-19C+] (*orig. US*) (*also* **nuts**) an insane person. **2** [20C+] (*US campus*) an unpopular student. **3** [20C+] (*orig. US*) a fan, an enthusiast, an obsessive; usu. in defining comb., e.g. *cricket nut, computer nut*. **4** [20C+] (*orig. US*) a course of action, an obsession. **5** [1930s] (*US Und.*) a beggar who is insane, or poses as such.

IN PHRASES

❑ **be a nut about** *v.* (*also* **...at, ...for, ...on**) [1920s+] to be enthusiastic about or expert in. ❑ **have a nut on** *v.* [20C+] to be obsessed with.

pertaining to madness or eccentricity, of people

IN COMPOUNDS

❑ **nutbag** *n.* [2000s] (*US*) a mentally unstable person. ❑ **nutball** *see* separate entries. ❑ **nutbar** *n.* (*also* **nutbag, nutbasket, nutbucket**) [joc. uses of SE *bar/basket/bucket*] [1970s+] (*US*) a lunatic. ❑ **nut-boy** *n.* [1990s+] (*US*) a madman, an eccentric. ❑ **nutburger** *n.* [SE *(ham)burger*] [1980s+] (*US*) a lunatic. ❑ **nutcake** *n.* [SE *cake*] [1960s+] (*US*) a fool, a lunatic, an eccentric. ❑ **nutcase** *see* separate entries. ❑ **nut doctor** *n.* [SE *doctor*] [1930s+] (*US*) a psychiatrist. ❑ **nuthead** *n.* [-HEAD *sfx* (1)] [1910s+] (*orig. US*) a fool, a simpleton. ❑ **nuthouse** *n. see* separate entry. ❑ **nut-job** *n.* [JOB *n.*[2] (2)] [1970s+] (*US*) a lunatic or very eccentric person. ❑ **nut-nut** *n.* [redup.] [2000s] an insane, eccentric person. ❑ **nut role** *see* separate entries. ❑ **nut roll** *n.* [pun on the sweet] [1990s+] (*US black*) an eccentric or mad person. ❑ **nut wagon** *n.* (*also* **nut train**) [SE *wagon*] [1960s] (*US*) a state of madness, psychosis.

pertaining to madness or eccentricity, of institutions

IN COMPOUNDS

❑ **nut alley** *n.* [SE *alley*] [1930s] (*US prison*) the prison insane ward. ❑ **nut bin** *n.* [*LOONY BIN under* LOONY *n.*] [1950s–60s] a psychiatric institution. ❑ **nutbox** *n.* [joc. use of SE *box*] [1960s+] (*US*) a psychiatric institution. ❑ **nut college** *n.* [late 19C–1960s] (*US*) a lunatic asylum/psychiatric institution. ❑ **nut factory** *n.* [SE *factory*] [late 19C+] (*Aus./US*) a psychiatric institution. ❑ **nut farm** *n.* [SE *farm*] [1930s–70s] (*US*) a psychiatric institution. ❑ **nut foundry** *n.* [SE *foundry*] [1930s–40s] (*US*) a psychiatric institution. ❑ **nut hatch** *n.* [? underpinned by the well-known asylum at Colney Hatch near London, opened in 1851] [1940s+] (*orig. US*) a psychiatric institution. ❑ **nut hut** *n.* [SE *hut*] [1990s+] a psychiatric institution. ❑ **nut place** *n.* [SE *place*] [1960s+] (*US*) a psychiatric institution. ❑ **nut ward** *n.* [SE *ward*] [20C+] (*US*) a psychiatric unit. ▫ **nut wing** *n.* [SE *wing*] [1990s+] (*US prison*) the psychiatric wing.

IN PHRASES

▫ **nuts and sluts** *n.* [1970s+] (*US campus*) a course in abnormal psychology. ▫ **on the nut** [1960s] being insane, or posing as such.

nut *n.*^{3} [ext. use of NUTS *n.*^{2} (1)] **1** [1930s+] (*orig. US*) an orgasm. **2** [1960s+] (*orig. US*) sexual intercourse. **3** [1970s] (*orig. US*) the vagina. **4** [1980s+] (*orig. US*) in fig. and non-sexual use, a sense of pleasure. **5** [1990s+] (*US*) semen.

IN PHRASES

▫ **bust a nut** *v.* (*also* **...one's nut**) [1930s+] (*orig. US*) **1** to reach orgasm. **2** (*also* **...one's nuts**) to work hard, to strain oneself. **3** to have sexual intercourse. **4** to masturbate. ▫ **get a nut** *v.* (*also* **get (off the) nut, get one's nut off, get one's nuts**) **1** [1950s+] to have an orgasm. **2** [1970s] in fig. use, to experience a catharsis. ▫ **pop a nut** *v.* [1950s+] **1** to masturbate. **2** to reach orgasm; thus by ext. to feel happy, satisfied. **3** to bring someone to orgasm.

nut *n.*^{4} [abbrev./pron.] [2000s] (*US black*) nothing.

nut *n.*^{5} *see* KNUT *n.*

nut *n.*^{6} for testicles and combs. *see under* NUTS *n.*^{2}.

nut, the *n.* (*also* **the nuts**) [abbr. NUTS AND BOLTS *n.*] [1960s+] (*US*) the basic facts, the core.

nut *adj.* [NUT *n.*^{2} (1)] [20C+] crazy; pertaining to the insane.

nut *v.*^{1} **1** [early–mid-19C] (*orig. UK Und.*) in senses of something unpleasant. (**a**) to curry favour, to toady to [NUT *n.*^{1} (2), i.e. one offers something unpleasant]. (**b**) to stare at [NUT *n.*^{1} (2), i.e. one receives something unpleasant]. **2** in senses of violence [NUT *n.*^{1} (1d)]. (**a**) [mid-19C+] (*also* **put in the nut, stick the nut on**) to butt one's opponent in the face, usu. the bridge of his nose, using one's own forehead. (**b**) [2000s] to hit on the head. **3** [1910s+] (*orig. Aus.*) to think [NUT *n.*^{1} (1c)]. **4** [1940s–50s] (*US Und.*) to share out the profits of a confidence trick [NUT *n.*^{1} (5)]. **5** [1940s–50s] (*Aus.*) to give [NUT *n.*^{1} (5)].

IN PHRASES

▫ **nut out** *v.* [1910s+] (*orig. Aus.*) to work out, to analyse.

nut *v.*^{2} [NUTS *n.*^{2} (1)] [1910s+] (*US*) to castrate, also used fig.

nut *v.*^{3} [NUT *n.*^{1} (5)] [1960s] (*US*) to renege.

nut *v.*^{4} [NUT *n.*^{3}] **1** [1970s+] (*US*) to have sexual intercourse. **2** [1990s+] (*US black*) to reach orgasm, to ejaculate.

nutball *n.* [NUT *n.*^{2} (1) + SCREWBALL *n.*] [1960s+] (*US*) an idiot.

nutball *adj.* [NUTBALL *n.*] [1960s+] (*US*) eccentric.

nutcase *n.* [NUT *n.*^{2} (1) + SE (*mental*) *case*] [1950s+] an eccentric, an odd person, a lunatic.

nut-case *adj.* [NUTCASE *n.*] [1990s+] crazy, insane.

nutcracker *n.* (*also* **nutcrackers**) [despite logical links, both NUT *n.*^{1} (1) head and NUTS *n.*^{2} (1), testicles post-date this usage] **1** [late 17C–19C] (*UK Und.*) usu. in pl., the pillory. **2** from NUT *n.*^{1} (1). (**a**) [mid-19C–1940s] (*orig. US*) a blow to the head. (**b**) [late 19C–1900s] the head. (**c**) [late 19C–1900s] in pl., the fists. (**d**) [1920s] (*US*) a nightstick. (**e**) [1910s] (*US Und.*) a police raid. (**f**) [1950s+] (*US*) a psychiatrist [SE *cracker*]. (**g**) [1970s+] a martinet, a disciplinarian. **3** [late 19C–1900s] in pl., teeth, esp. false or prominent teeth. **4** [1940s+] (*US*) (*also* **nutcruncher, nutcrusher**) something difficult, impossible or dangerous [NUTS *n.*^{2} (1)].

DERIVATIVES

▫ **nutcracking** *adj.* [1960s+] (*US*) relating to psychiatry.

nutcrackers *n.* [rhy. sl.; = KNACKERS *n.*] [1990s+] the testicles.

nutcut *n.* (*also* **nutcutting, nutgut**) [NUTS *n.*^{2} (1); the implication is of castration] [1960s+] (*US*) the fundamental basics, usu. of a ruthless nature, dirty work.

nut-cut *adj.* [NUT *n.*^{1} (1b)] [mid-19C] (*Anglo-Ind.*) roguish, mischievous.

nutcutter *n.* [NUTS *n.*^{2} (1); var. on NUTCRACKER *n.*] **1** [1970s+] (*US*) something difficult, impossible or dangerous. **2** [1980s+] (*US*) a ruthless individual.

nutcutting/nutgut *n.* *see* NUTCUT *n.*

nuthatch *n.*

IN PHRASES

▫ **naked as a nuthatch** *see* NAKED AS A JAYBIRD *under* JAYBIRD *n.*^{1}.

nut house *n.* (*also* **nut hospital, nut-house, nuthouse**) [NUT *n.*^{2} (1) + SE *house*] **1** [1920s] (*US*) a mad person. **2** (*orig. US*) [1920s+] a psychiatric institution. **3** [1930s+] (*US*) a chaotic place or situation, a fig. madhouse.

nutmeg-grater *n.* [mid-19C] (*UK Und.*) a beard.

nutmeg (maker) *n.* (*also* **nutmegger**) [SE *wooden nutmeg*, anything false or fraudulent, a fraud, a cheat, a deception. New Englanders have the image of being deceitful, esp. as businessmen. Note the Nutmeg State, Connecticut, where wooden nutmegs are supposedly manufactured for export] [early–late 19C] (*US*) a white New Englander.

nutmegs *n.* [predates NUTS *n.*^{2} (1)] [late 17C–early 19C; 1980s+] the testicles.

nut 'n' berry *n.* [the preference for vegetarianism associated with the HIPPIE *n.*^{2} (3) and early conservationists] [1990s+] (*US campus*) a latter-day hippie.

nut role *n.* [NUT *n.*^{2} (1) + SE *role*] [1960s+] (*US black*) a pretence of insanity or stupidity, usu. to avoid something.

IN PHRASES

▫ **play the nut role** *v.* [1960s+] (*US black*) **1** to pose as a shambling incompetent in order to swindle or otherwise trick a possible victim. **2** to pretend to madness.

nut role *v.* (*also* **nut roll**) [NUT ROLE *n.*] [1960s+] (*US*) to act (deceptively) in an eccentric or stupid manner.

nuts *n.*^{1} ['Prob. ex C.16 *nuts to*, an enticement to' (*DSUE*)] **1** [17C–1920s] anything agreeable, satisfactory, an acceptable situation, usu. as *nuts for/to* a person. **2** [1930s+] (*US*) *the nuts*, a strategic advantage, esp. in gambling, as in a winning hand in cards.

IN PHRASES

▫ **for nuts** *adv.* [the relative insignifance of a *nut*] [late 19C+] at all, in no way, e.g. *she can't cook for nuts*.

nuts *n.*^{2} [SE *nut*, i.e. the shape; Partridge suggests NUT *n.*^{1} (1a)] **1** [mid-19C+] the testicles. **2** [20C+] (*US black*) the female genitals. **3** [1900s–10s] (*US Und.*) the game of THREE-CARD MONTE *n.*; lit. the shells that are used to hide the pea. **4** [1930s] female sexual desire. **5** [1970s+] (*US*) manly courage.

IN COMPOUNDS

▫ **nutbag** *n.* *see* NUTSACK below. ▫ **nutbuster** *n.* (*US*) **1** [1940s] a mechanic or machinist. **2** [1970s+] an insoluble difficulty, the last straw. ▫ **nut-butter** *n.* [BUTTER *n.*^{1} (1)] [1990s+] **1** semen. **2** (*US black*) an enthusiastic and skilful fellatrix. ▫ **nut-chokers** *n.* [1960s+] male underwear. ▫ **nutcut/cutter** *see* separate entries. ▫ **nut-nuzzler** *n.* [1970s+] (*US gay*) a homosexual. ▫ **nut-nuzzling** *adj.* [*NUT-NUZZLER* above] [1970s+] (*US gay*) homosexual. ▫ **nutsack** *n.* (*also* **nutbag**) [SACK *n.* (1c)] **1** [1970s+] (*US*) the scrotum. **2** [1990s+] (*US*) a derog. description. ▫ **nutshot** *n.* [SHOT *n.*^{2} (7)] [2000s] (*US*) a blow to the testicles. ▫ **nut-sucking** *adj.* *see* COCKSUCKING *adj.*

IN PHRASES

▫ **bust one's nuts** *v.* *see* BREAK ONE'S BALLS *under* BALLS *n.* ▫ **crack one's nuts** *v.* [1940s+] (*US*) of a man, to achieve orgasm. ▫ **get one's nuts in an uproar** *v.* [1990s+] (*US*) to lose emotional control. ▫ **get one's nuts off** *v.* [GET OFF *v.*^{2} (5)] **1** [1930s+] (*orig. US black*) to achieve orgasm, poss. through masturbation. **2** [1990s+] to excite. ▫ **get one's nuts rattled** *v.* [1950s] (*US*) of a man, to have sexual intercourse. ▫ **give one's left nut** *v.* (*also* **...left leg, ...right nut**) [1950s+] (*US*) to yearn for, to desire. ▫ **have fat nuts** *v.* [1980s+] (*US black*) to use violence, to be a violent person. ▫ **have one's nuts in a knot** *v.* (*also* **...nose in a knot, ...nuts in the door jamb**) [1990s+] to be in a state of confusion and worry. ▫ **have someone/something by the nuts** *v.* *see* HAVE SOMEONE BY THE BALLS *under* BALLS *n.* ▫ **have someone's nuts in a knot** *v.* [1960s] (*US*) usu. of a woman, to have someone completely under one's control. ▫ **have someone's nuts in a sling** *v.* *see under* SLING *n.*^{2}. ▫ **knock one's nuts out** *v.* [1960s+] (*US*) to make an overwhelming impression, to have a notable effect. ❑ **pop one's nuts** *v.* (*also* **pop off, pop one's nut**) [1940s+] (*orig. US*) to achieve orgasm, usu. male; thus by ext. to feel exhilarated. ❑ **run one's nuts off** *v.* [1960s–70s] to move at high speed, esp. in the context of searching. ❑ **scare the nuts off** *v.* [1970s+] to terrify. ❑ **work one's nuts off** *v.* [1960s+] to work very hard. ❑ **you gotta let yer nutz hang** [1990s+] (*US black teen*) be yourself, don't let anybody dictate to you.

IN EXCLAMATIONS

❑ **Gawd pickle me nuts!** [2000s] (*N.Z.*) excl. of surprise.

nuts *n.*³ *see* NUT *n.*² (1).

nuts, the *n.*¹ [1910s+] (*US*) **1** the best, the superlative. **2** something bad or objectionable.

nuts, the *n.*² *see* NUT, THE *n.*

nuts *adj.* [Partridge suggests *sweet as a nut*, thus 'sweet on'] **1** [late 18C+] fond of, fascinated by, earlier usage usu. *NUTS UPON* below/NUTS ON *adj.*, 20C+ usage usu. *NUTS ABOUT, NUTS OVER* below and influenced by crazy sense below. **2** [mid-19C+] insane, mad, crazy.

IN PHRASES

❑ **drive someone nuts** *v.* [1930s+] to drive crazy, insane. ❑ **go nuts** *v.* [1940s+] to lose emotional control; to make a fuss. ❑ **like nuts** *adv.* [1950s+] hysterically. ❑ **nuts about** *adj.* (*also* **nuts for, nuts over**) [later chronology means it was strongly influenced by sense 2 and the SE phr. *crazy about*] [1910s+] obsessed with, usu. in the context of love. ❑ **nuts around** *v.* (*also* **nuts about**) [1940s–60s] (*US*) **1** to wander around aimlessly. **2** to mess about, to fool around. ❑ **nuts upon** *adj.* [late 18C–19C] obsessed with, in love with. ❑ **nuts upon oneself** *adj.* [late 18C–19C] extremely pleased with one's own actions.

nuts! *excl.* [1920s+] (*orig. US*) a mild excl., nonsense! rubbish! not a chance!

nuts and bolts *n.* [1960s+] the basics of a situation, the fundamental issues.

IN COMPOUNDS

❑ **nuts and bolts man** *n.* [1960s+] an uncomplicated 'hands-on' type of person.

nuts-and-bolts *adj.*¹ (*also* **bolts-and-nuts**) [ext. of NUTS *adj.* (2)] [1920s–40s] (*US*) crazy, insane.

nuts-and-bolts *adj.*² [NUTS AND BOLTS *n.*] [1960s+] basic, practical.

nutso *n.* [NUTS *adj.* (2)] [1970s+] (*orig. US*) a stupid, unstable or eccentric person.

nutso *adj.* [NUTSO *n.*] [1970s+] (*orig. US*) stupid, unstable, eccentric.

nuts on *adj.* (*also* **dead nuts on, filberts on**) [NUTS *adj.* (1); SE *filbert*, a type of nut] [early 19C+] obsessed with, in love with; very pleased by/about.

nuts to *phr.* (*also* **nuts on**) [NUTS *n.*² (1)] **1** [1920s+] (*US*) a retort to express rejection, derision etc, to hell with. **2** *see* NUTS *n.*¹ (1).

nutsy *adj.* [NUTS *adj.* (2)] [1910s+] (*orig. US*) mad, insane, eccentric, occas. used as a nickname; as a n.

nutted *adj.* [NUTS ON *adj.*] [mid-19C] fooled by the claims of one who poses as being an obsessive admirer.

nutten-chops *n. see WIND-PIES under* WIND *n.*².

nutter *n.* **1** [1950s+] a lunatic, an eccentric [NUT *n.*² (1)]. **2** [1960s] the head [NUT *n.*¹ (1b)].

IN COMPOUNDS

❑ **nutter butter** *n.* [redup.; note brandname *Nutter Butter*, a form of peanut-filled biscuit] [1990s+] (*US campus*) someone who is unaware or inattentive.

nuttery *n.* [NUT *n.*² (1); on model of SE *nunnery*] [1910s–50s] (*US*) a psychiatric institution.

nutting *n.* [NUT *v.*¹ (2a)] [1930s+] using the top of one's head to butt an opponent during a fight; such a blow can often end the fight instantly.

nutty *adj.*¹ [? SE phr. *sweet as a nut*] **1** [late 18C–1910s] smart, spruce, attractive. **2** [late 19C] piquant, spicy.

nutty *adj.*² [NUTS *adj.*] **1** [19C+] very fond of, obsessed with. **2** [late 19C+] (*orig. US*) crazy, eccentric; esp. in punning phr. *nutty as a fruit cake, nutty as a peach orchard boar*.

IN PHRASES

❑ **nutty about** *adj.* (*also* **nutty for**) [sense 1 above; heavily influenced by sense 2 on model of SE phr. *crazy about*] [1910s+] (*orig. US*) fond of, keen on. ❑ **nutty upon** *adj.* (*also* **nutty on**) [19C] amorous, fond of, obsessed by.

nutty *adj.*³ [the person/object in question makes the speaker go NUTS *adj.* (2)] [1930s+] (*US black*) excellent, first-rate.

nutty *adv.* [NUTTY *adj.*¹ (1)] [mid-19C] (*UK Und.*) smartly, fashionably.

-nutty *sfx* [NUTTY *adj.*²] **1** [1940s+] rendered insane or unstable by. **2** [1960s+] obsessed with.

nux *n.*¹ [northern dial; ? ult. Lat. *nux*, a nut] [mid-19C] (*UK Und.*) the object in question; the 'game'.

nux *n.*² [abbr. medical Lat. *nux vomica*, the fruit from which strychnine is produced] [1910s–50s] (*US prison*) prison-cooked tea.

nuxyelper *n.* [medical Lat. *nux vomica*, the fruit from which strychnine is produced, i.e. it would induce vomiting + SE *yelp*] [mid-19C] (*UK Und.*) a confidence trickster who fakes a fit in order to gain money from bystanders.

nyaams *n.* [fig./ext. use of NYAM *v.*, i.e. one who thinks of nothing but eating; thus cf. W.I. *coco-head*, a fool, itself the fig. use of *coco-head*, the rhizome of the coco-plant] [1950s+] (*W.I.*) foolishness, nonsense, esp. as an excl.

IN COMPOUNDS

❑ **nyaamshead** *n.* [-HEAD *sfx* (1)] [1950s] (*W.I.*) an absolute fool.

nyafflin' *n.* [onomat.; note Beds. dial. *nyaffle*, to eat in a hasty, gluttonous manner] [20C+] (*Ulster*) eating noisily with an open mouth.

nyam *n.* (*also* **nyam-nyam**) [var. on YAM *n.*¹] [early 19C+] (*orig. W.I.*) food.

nyam *v.* (*also* **niam**) [var. on YAM *v.*] **1** [early 18C+] (*orig. W.I.*) to eat. **2** [1950s] (*orig. W.I.*) to taste. **3** [1970s+] (*UK black*) in fig. use, to attack, to arrest.

IN COMPOUNDS

❑ **nyam dog** *n.* [SE *dog*; the Chinese predilection for cooking dog] [1940s] (*W.I.*) a Chinese person.

nyami nyami *n.* [NYAM *v.*] [1940s+] (*W.I.*) a greedy, omnivorous person; thus also as adj.

nyams *n.* (*also* **nyamps**) [? Twi *nyamma*, small or NYAM *n.*, in context of being 'a vegetable'] [20C+] (*W.I.*) a weakling, a useless idiot.

nyanga *n.* (*also* **nang, nyang, yanga**) [Mende *nyanga*, showing off] [20C+] (*W.I.*) ostentation, esp. in one's dress, ext. to stylish.

nying'i-nying'i *adj.* [? fig. use of NYANGA *n.*] [1920s+] (*W.I. Rasta*) nagging, whining.

nylon *n.* (*S.Afr.*) **1** [1960s+] a police van [its mesh-covered sides]. **2** [1980s+] a virtuous, well-bred young woman [? her 'smoothness'].

SE in slang uses

IN COMPOUNDS

❑ **nylon road** *n.* [1950s+] (*W.I.*) a good, smooth road, better than the average island road.

nym *see under* NIM.

nymph *n.* [SE *nymph*, a semi-divine being, imagined as a beautiful maiden inhabiting the sea, rivers, fountains, hills, woods or trees, thence a young and beautiful woman] **1** [mid-17C+] (*euph.*) a prostitute. **2** [1910s+] a *nymph*omaniac, an allegedly sexually insatiable woman. **3** [1960s] (*US campus*) an effeminate male.

IN PHRASES

❑ **nymph of darkness** *n.* (*also* **...of the shade**) [18C] a prostitute. ❑ **nymph of delight** *n.* [early 18C] a prostitute. ❑ **nymph of the pave** *n. see* separate entry.

nymphette *n.* [SE *nymphette*, a sexually alluring pubescent girl] [1960s–80s] (*US gay*) an attractive gay male youngster.

nympho *n.* (*also* **nympha**) [abbr.] [1910s+] (*orig. US*) a *nympho*maniac, an allegedly sexually insatiable woman.

nympho *adj.* (*also* **nymphy**) [abbr.] [1910s+] *nympho*maniacal.

nymph of the pave *n.* (*also* **girl..., nymph of the pavé, ...pavement**) [NYMPH *n.* (1) + SE *pave*(*ment*)] [early 19C–1930s] a prostitute, a street-walker.

nypper *n. see* NIPPER *n.*[1] (1).

nyp shop *n. see Nip Shop under* NIP *n.*[7].

nyuck *n.* (*also* **neuck**) [? fig. use of SE *nook*] [20C+] (*Ulster*) an unimportant person.

O

O *n.* (*also* **oh**) [abbr.] **1** [1930s+] (*US drugs*) an ounce of a narcotic. **2** [1930s+] (*drugs*) opium. **3** [1980s+] (*Aus. drugs*) an ounce of cannabis. **4** [1980s+] (*US drugs*) a $50 rock of cocaine.

IN COMPOUNDS

❑ **O-head** *n.* [-HEAD *sfx* (4)] [1960s] (*drugs*) an opium addict.

-o *sfx* **1** [mid-17C; late 19C+] used variously to create extended nouns, often as terms of address, e.g. BOYO *n.* (1); BUCKO *n.*[1] (2); KIDDO *n.* (1). **2** [mid-19C+] used variously to create nouns from adjs., e.g. BERSERKO *n.*; PINKO *n.*; WEIRDO *n.*, WIDO *n.* **3** [late 19C+] (*mainly Aus.*) added to a variety of nouns (often occupational) to create sl. forms, usu. abbreviated, e.g. ARVO *n.*; BOMBO *n.*[1]; COMMO *n.*; COMPO *n.*; DERO *n.*; ETHNO *n.*; GARBO *n.*; JOLLO *n.*; JOURNO *n.*; LESO *n.*; MADDO *n.*; METHO *n.*; MILKO *n.*; NASHO *n.*; PLONKO *n.*; RABBIT-O *n.*; REFFO *n.*; SANNO *n.*; SECKO *n.*; SHEEPO *n.*; SUSSO *n.*; SYPHO *n.* [? f. the *-o* sfx in street cries such as *milko!* or in the familiarization of names, e.g. *Johno*]. **4** [20C+] (*mainly Aus.*) less commonly added to adjs. to create shortened sl. forms, e.g. BERKO *adj.*; PREGGO *adj.*; TROPPO *adj.* **5** [20C+] used variously to create extended adjs., e.g. CHEAPO *adj.*, NEATO *adj.* **6** [20C+] used variously to create general shortened forms, mostly of nouns, e.g. AGGRO *n.*; AMMO *n.*; COMBO *n.*[2]. **7** [20C+] used as a meaningless ending, e.g. BILLY-O *n.*; SE *cheerio*.

o.a. *n.* [abbr. OVERAMP *v.*] [1970s] an overdose of Methedrine or methamphetamine.

oafo *n.* [SE *oaf* + -O *sfx* (1)] [1950s–60s] a ruffian, an oaf.

oafo *adj.* [OAFO *n.*] [1950s–60s] thuggish.

oak *n.* (*also* **oke**) [playing on the tree's 'oaken' qualities] **1** [late 16C–early 17C] (*UK Und.*) in a team of confidence tricksters, the one who keeps a watch. **2** [17C–mid-19C] a rich man, a man of substance.

oaken towel *n.* (*also* **oaken cudgel, ...plant, ...sapling, ...staff**) [18C–mid-19C; 1920s] a cudgel.

IN PHRASES

❑ **rub-down with an oaken towel/cudgel** *n.* [18C–mid-19C; 1920s] a thrashing, a beating.

Oakey *n.* *see* OKIE *n.*

oakey dokey *adj.* *see* OKEY-DOKE *adj.*[1].

Oakie *n.* *see* OKIE *n.*

oakie *n.* *see* OKIE *n.*

Oakley *n.* [abbr. ANNIE OAKLEY *n.*] [1920s–60s] (*US*) a free pass, orig. to a circus, but latterly to the theatre.

oak towel *n.* [note OAKEN TOWEL *n.*] [late 18C–1930s] a police truncheon.

Oaktown *n.* [1990s+] (*US black*) Oakland, California.

o.a.o. *n.* [abbr. *one and only*] [1920s+] (*orig. US*) one's steady girlfriend.

oars (and rollocks) *n.* [rhy. sl. = BALLOCKS *n.* (3); note Williams for 17C fig. use of *oar*, penis] [1990s+] nonsense, rubbish.

oary-eyed *adj.* *see* ORY-EYED *adj.*

oat *n.*[1] [? SE *iota*] **1** [mid–late 19C] an atom, the tiniest amount. **2** [late 19C–1900s] a penny, a halfpenny, the smallest amount of money.

DERIVATIVES

❑ **oats** *n.* [late 19C–1900s] money.

IN PHRASES

❑ **have not an oat** *v.* [late 19C–1900s] to be penniless.

SE in slang uses

IN COMPOUNDS

❑ **oat opera** *n.* (*also* **oats opera**) [the horses and the oats they eat] [1930s–40s] (*orig. US*) a Western film. ❑ **oat stealer** *n.* [pun + derog. ref. to the stereotypically corrupt ostler] [late 18C–1900s] an ostler.

oat *n.*[2] [backsl.] [mid-19C+] two.

oater *n.* [abbr. OAT OPERA *under* OAT *n.*[1]] [1940s+] (*orig. US*) a Western film.

oatmeal *n.* [SE phr. *sow one's wild oats*] **1** [17C] an urban rowdy, usu. in a gang [note 'No trace of this odd appellation has yet been found except that the author of a ludicrous pamphlet has taken the name of Oliver Oat-meale' (*Nares Gloss.*, 1822)]. **2** [1940s] corruption, criminality.

oats *n.*[1] [mid-19C] (*UK Und.*) a lumbering, awkward man.

oats *n.*[2] [SE phr. *feel one's oats, sow one's wild oats*; note *double entendre* in D'Urfey, *Pills to Purge Melancholy* (1719): 'Sow your wild Oats, / And mind not her wild Notes'] [1920s+] sexual satisfaction.

IN PHRASES

❑ **get one's oats** *v.* [1920s+] to gain sexual release. ❑ **off one's oats** [late 19C+] feeling unwell, esp. if this diminishes one's appetite.

oats *n.*[3] [rhy. sl.; *oats and barley* = CHARLIE *n.*[8] (1); for an earlier use, playing simply on the proper name, note Binstead & Wells, *A Pink 'Un and a Pelican* (1898): 'Bob and his particular chum Oats (which is short rhyming slang for Charley. "Oats-and-barley" it is in full, but the true art of it lies in the abbreviation.'] [1990s+] (*drugs*) cocaine.

oats *n.*[4] *see* ASH BEANS AND LONG OATS *n.*

oats and barley *n.* [rhy. sl. = CHARLIE *n.*[1] (1)/SE *Charlie/Charley*] **1** [mid-19C] a watchman; shortened to 'Oats'. **2** [late 19C+] the name Charlie/Charley.

oats and chaff *n.* [rhy. sl.; Northern pron.] [mid-19C] a footpath.

O.B. *n.* [abbr.] **1** [late 19C–1900s] (*UK Und.*) the Old Bailey in London, the Central Criminal Court of England. **2** *see* OBIE *n.*

ob *adj.* [abbr.] (*US campus*) **1** [1960s] *ob*noxious. **2** [1980s+] *ob*vious.

Obadiah *n.* [the popularity of that name among the sect] [mid-17C–mid-19C] a Quaker.

obbo *n.* [SE *observation* + -O *sfx* (6)] [1960s+] (*UK Und./police/prison*) police observation; prison observation room.

obbs *n.* *see* OBS *n.*

o-be-joyful *n.* (*also* **oh-be-cheerful, oh-be-joyful, oh-be-rich-an'-happy**) [orig. naut. jargon] **1** [early 19C] brandy. **2** [early 19C+] (*US*) liquor in general. **3** [mid-19C–1900s] rum.

IN COMPOUNDS

❑ **oh-be-joyful house** *n.* (*also* **o-be-joyful works**) [19C] a public house.

IN PHRASES

❑ **I'll make you sing o-be-joyful on the other side of your mouth** [late 18C–19C] a general threat of violence ['o-be-joyful' implies hymn-singing; phr. mimics but appears to antedate 'I'll make you laugh on the wrong/other side of your face'].

obelisk *n.* [SE *obelisk*, a tapering shaft of stone] [19C] the penis.

obese *adj.* [play on SE *obese*, very fat/FAT *adj.* (1c)] [1990s+] excellent, extremely admirable.

obey *n. see* OBIE *n.*

obfuscated *adj.* [mid-19C–1910s] drunk.

obfusticated *adj.* [ext. of OBFUSCATED *adj.*] [mid-19C–1960s] (*US*) bewildered, confused, excited.

obie *n.* (*also* **O.B., obey**) [ety. unknown; Irwin (1931) suggests: 'Originated by the old yeggmen, who merely reversed the initials, "P.O.," to lessen the public's understanding of their conversation, and from carelessness in speech corrupted to its present form'] [1920s–80s] (*US Und.*) a post office.

obies *n.* [pron. of O.B.'S, tradename *Old Brown* sherry] [1970s+] (*S.Afr. campus*) sherry (cf. O.B.'s *n.*).

obituary notice *n.* [1920s] (*US*) a letter from a creditor.

object *n.* [SE *object of pity, object of mirth*] [early 19C–1950s] a person or thing that appears ridiculous or pitiable.

obliterated *adj.* [1980s+] extremely intoxicated by a drug or alcohol.

obno *n.* (*also* **obnoc, obnoxo**) [OBNO *adj.*] [1970s+] (*US campus*) a crude, obnoxious person.

obno *adj.* [abbr.; pron. 'obe-know'] [1970s+] (*US campus*) *obno*xious.

oboe *n.* [1990s+] the penis.

O'Brien's dog *n.* [he goes 'a little way with everyone'; presumably a lost anecdote] [20C+] (*Irish*) one who is all things to all people.

O.B.'s *n.* [abbr.] [1980s+] (*S.Afr.*) Old Brown sherry (cf. OBIES *n.*).

obs *n.* (*also* **obbs**) **1** [1910s–20s] *ob*ligations. **2** [1940s+] a lookout, usu. in phr. *keep obs*, to keep a lookout [abbr. SE *observation*]. **3** [1950s+] (*Aus./US prison*) (*also* **obso**) an observation wing of a prison [abbr. SE *observation*].

obscrophulous *adj. see* OBSTROPOLOUS *adj.*

obsocky *adj.* [? Yoruba *obo*, monkey + *so*, to break wind + *ki*, to greet] [20C+] (*W.I.*) **1** of objects (esp. clothes), ill-fitting, misshapen. **2** of people, ungainly, overweight. **3** of events, absurd, ridiculous [note MONKEY FART *under* MONKEY *n.*].

obsquatulate *v. see* ABSQUATULATE *V.*

obstroculous *adj.* [var. on OBSTROPOLOUS *adj.*] [1930s] (*Aus.*) obstreperous.

obstropolous *adj.* (*also* **obscrophulous, obstriperous, obstroperous, obstropolis**) [mid-18C–1910s] a corruption of SE *obstreperous*.

o.c. *n.* (*also* **o.o.c**) [abbr. *o*ut of *c*ontrol] [1990s+] (*US black/campus/teen*) 'out of control'; ext. use to the public housing projects in the Fillmore district of San Francisco.

occabot *n.* [backsl.] [mid–late 19C] tobacco.

occifer *n. see* OSSIFER *n.*

occupant *n.* [she works in an *OCCUPYING HOUSE under* OCCUPY *V.*] [16C] a brothel prostitute.

occupation *n.* [OCCUPY *V.* (1)] [17C–18C] sexual intercourse.

occupy *v.* [listed as a synon. for copulation in Florio, *Worlde of Wordes* (1598): '*Fottere*, to iape, to sard, to fucke, to swive, to occupy.' Like many taboo terms it moved from SE (it is used ten times in the *Authorized Version*) once it had been perceived as vulgar. Shakespeare notes this in *Henry IV part II* (1597), 'A captaine? Gods light these villaines wil make the word as odious as the word occupy, which was an excellent good worde before it was ill sorted'] [late 16C–early 19C] of a man, to have sexual intercourse.

DERIVATIVES

❑ **occupying** *n.* [late 17C] an act of sexual intercourse.

IN COMPOUNDS

❑ **occupying house** *n.* [HOUSE *n.*[1] (1)] [16C] a brothel.

ocean floor *n.* [rhy. sl.] [1900s] (*Aus.*) the floor.

ocean liner *n.* [rhy. sl. = CLINER *n.*] [20C+] (*Aus.*) a girl, a girlfriend.

ocean pearl *n.* [rhy. sl.] [20C+] a girl, a girlfriend.

ocean wave *n.* [rhy. sl.] [1920s–60s] a shave.

ochive *n. see* OSCHIVE *n.*

ochorboc *n.* [Ital. *bocca*, mouth; popularized by Italian organ-grinders] [late 19C–1900s] beer.

ochre *n.* [SE *ochre*, a pale brownish yellow] [mid–late 19C] money, gold.

ock *n.* [OCKER *n.* (2)] [1970s+] (*Aus.*) a boorish, loutish, unsophisticated, ultra-nationalistic Australian.

ocker *n.* [the character *Ocker* orig. portrayed by actor Ron Frazer (1924–83) in the TV series *The Mavis Bramston Show* (1965–8)] (*Aus.*) **1** [1910s+] a nickname for anyone called Oscar. **2** [1970s+] a boorish, loutish, unsophisticated, ultra-nationalistic Australian, whose rise, and celebration, coincided with Gough Whitlam's Labour government (1972–5). **3** [1970s+] anyone seen as boorishly nationalistic. **4** [1970s+] Australian English.

DERIVATIVES

❑ **ockerdom** *n.* [1970s+] (*Aus.*) the world of the ocker. ❑ **ockerism** *n.* [1970s+] (*Aus.*) boorish behaviour; oafish self-satisfaction. ❑ **ockerization** *n.* [1970s+] (*Aus.*) vulgarization. ❑ **ockerized** *adj.* [1970s+] (*Aus.*) vulgarized.

ocker *adj.* [OCKER *n.* (2)] [1970s+] (*Aus.*) boorish, loutish, ultra-nationalistic.

ocker *v.* [1970s+] (*Aus.*) to behave in a boorish, loutish, ultra-nationalistic manner.

ockerina *n.* [OCKER *n.* (2) + fem. sfx *-ina*; a pun on the musical instrument, an *ocarina*] [1970s+] (*Aus.*) a female OCKER *n.* (2).

ock it! *excl.* [? mispron.] [1970s+] (*US campus*) stop it!

ocky *n.* [abbr.] [1960s+] (*Aus.*) an octopus.

O cry! *excl.* [late 19C–1900s] a euph. for *O Christ!*

octane *n.* [1980s+] **1** (*US*) verve, zest. **2** (*drugs*) phencyclidine laced with gasoline.

octo *n.* [abbr.] [1910s] (*Aus.*) an *octo*pus.

October *n.* [SE *October ale*, a strong beer brewed in October] [mid-19C] blood.

octopus *n.* [his 'eight' hands] [1930s+] (*US*) a man who proves more sexually enthusiastic, thus keen to fondle, than his girlfriend or date might wish.

O.D. *n.* (*also* **o.d.**) [abbr.] [1950s+] (*drugs*) **1** an *o*ver*d*ose. **2** one who has taken an overdose.

O.D. *v.* (*also* **o.d., oh-dee**) [O.D. *n.*] **1** [1960s+] (*drugs*) to overdose (fatally or otherwise) on a given drug. **2** [1960s+] (*drugs*) to give someone a drug overdose. **3** [1970s+] a fig. synon. in non-drug contexts: to act excessively, without restraint, to be greedy.

o.d. *n.* (*also* **o.d.v.**) [pun on pron. of Fr. *eau-de-vie*] [mid-19C–1920s] brandy.

od! *excl.* (*also* **odd! ond!**) [late 16C+] a general euph. oath, meaning God, e.g. *OD ROT IT!* below; usu. found in a variety of possessive combinations (see ODS *n.*).

IN PHRASES

❑ **od rot it!** (*also* **add rabbit! ...rot it! odd rot it! od rabbit! ...rat it! ...rut it! ord rot it!**) [mid-18C–1900s] a mild oath, lit. *God rot it!*

oday *n.* (*also* **O-day**) [pig Lat. *oday* = DOUGH *n.* (1)] [1920s–80s] (*US*) money.

odd *n.* [ety. unknown] [1930s–80s] **1** a police officer. **2** a police car.

IN COMPOUNDS

❑ **odd lot** *n.* [1930s–80s] a police car.

odd *adj.*

SE in slang uses

IN COMPOUNDS

❑ **odd bod** *n.* [SE *odd* + BOD *n.* (1)] [1940s+] (*orig. milit.*) **1** an odd man out. **2** any non-specific person. ❑ **odd fish** *n.* [SE *odd* + FISH *n.*[1] (5)] [mid-17C+] an eccentric person. ❑ **odd-mark firm** *n. see under* FIRM *n.*

oddball *n.* [SE *odd* + fig. use of *ball*] [1940s+] (*orig. US*) an eccentric, unusual person.

oddball *adj.* [ODDBALL *n.*] [1950s+] peculiar.

odd-come short *n.* [var. on ODD-COME-SHORTLY *phr.*] [mid-19C–1950s] a day.

(IN PHRASES)

❑ **one of these odd-come shorts** [mid-19C–1950s] one of these days, sooner or later.

odd-come-shortly *n.* [mid-18C–early 19C] a day.

(IN PHRASES)

❑ **one of these odd-come shortlys** [mid-18C–early 19C] one of these days, sooner or later.

oddcum shorts *n.* (*also* **odd-come shorts**) [early–mid-19C] small, nondescript items, 'bits and bobs'.

oddie *n. see* ODDY *n.*

odds *n.*[1] [SE *odds*, i.e. the idea of gambling on a woman being prepared to prostitute herself] [1940s] (*US Und.*) a woman, esp. one who will support her partner through prostitution.

SE in slang uses

(IN PHRASES)

❑ **over the odds** (*also* **above the odds**) [20C+] of people and things, extreme, beyond the normal limits.

odds *n.*[2] *see* ODS *n.*

odds *v.* [SE *odds*, as used in betting] **1** [20C+] to avoid, to 'get out of'. **2** [1950s+] to risk, to take a chance.

odds and sods *n.* [the orig. WW1 milit. use defined as '"details" attached to Battalion Headquarters for miscellaneous offices, batmen, sanitary men, professional footballers and boxers on nominal duties etc' *Brophy & Partridge* (1930)] [1910s+] (*orig. milit.*) odds and ends, but used of both objects and people.

odds, bods and sods *n.* [ext. of ODDS AND SODS *n.* + BOD *n.* (1)] [1950s+] (*Aus.*) people at random.

odds-on *n.* [20C+] (*Aus.*) the odds-on favourite, in a horserace or other sporting contest.

odds on *phr.* [gambling imagery] [20C+] very likely, in all likelihood.

oddy *n.* (*also* **oddie**) [the 'odd halfpenny' in a sum of money or a price] [1900s–50s] (*Aus.*) a halfpenny.

ods *n.* (*also* **odds**) [OD! *excl.*] [late 16C+] (*orig. US*) a mild euph. for *God's*, used in comb. in various excl. oaths; the major ones being listed below (cf. ADS *n.*).

(IN EXCLAMATIONS)

❑ **odsbobs!** (*also* **odds bob! odds bobs! odds bodikins! odsbodlikins! odsbuds!**) [late 17C–1900s] a general oath, lit. 'God's body!' and vars. ❑ **ods blood!** (*also* **odd's bud! odd's but!**) [late 17C–1900s] a general oath, lit. 'God's blood!'. ❑ **od's fish!** [lit. 'God's flesh!', with overtones of the miracle of the loaves and fishes] [late 17C–1910s] a general oath, one of many ways of euphemizing God. ❑ **odsflesh!** [late 17C–early 19C] a mild euph. excl., lit. 'God's flesh!'. ❑ **ods heart!** [18C–early 19C] a general oath, lit. 'God's heart!'. ❑ **ods my life!** (*also* **ods life!**) [17C–mid-19C] a general oath, lit. 'God's life!'. ❑ **ods nigs!** (*also* **ods niggers!**) [lit. ety. unknown] [mid-17C–early 19C] a general oath. ❑ **odso!** (*also* **od zaws! udso!**) [late 16C–early 19C] a mild euph. excl., lit. 'God's oath!'. ❑ **ods pity!** (*also* **ods pitlikins! ods pittikins!**) [17C] a general oath, lit. 'God's pity!'. ❑ **ods precious!** [late 16C–early 18C] a general oath, lit. 'God's precious (life)!'. ❑ **od zounds!** (*also* **ods harty wounds! ods nouns! ods swoons!**) [late 16C–mid-19C] a general oath, lit. 'God's wounds!'. ❑ **odzooks!** (*also* **odsooks! odzookers!**) [late 17C–mid-19C] a general oath, lit. 'God's hooks!'.

o.d.v. *n. see* O.D. *n.*

o.e. *n.* [abbr.] [1980s+] (*US black*) Old English malt liquor.

oedipus rex *n.* [rhy. sl.; ult. Greek tragedy, *Oedipus Rex* by Sophocles (?496–406 BC)] [1970s+] sex.

oes *adj.* [Afk. *oes*, feeble] [20C+] (*S.Afr.*) seedy, run down, 'under the weather'.

ofaginzy *n.* [? OFAY *adj.* + GINZO *n.*; note Cohen (ed.), *Studies in Slang* (1997) suggestions that if ofay = Fr. *au fait*, then ofaginzy = (*c'est*) *au fait ainsi*] [1940s–50s] (*US black*) a white person.

ofay *n.* (*also* **fay, fey, ofey, oofay**) [ety. unknown. Links to Fr. *au fait*, aware, have been dismissed (though Cohen (ed.), *Studies in Slang* (1997), sees this as the proper ety.), and doubts are also cast on Yoruba *ofe*, 'a charm that lets one jump so high as to disappear', thus trouble (the cause of such vanishing), thus a white man (the essence of trouble); note Mezzrow & Wolfe, *Really the Blues* (1946): '*Ofay*, of course, is pig Latin for *foe*.' (Cohen rejects this – 'there is no indication of blacks ever engaging in the Pig Latin type of word play')] [late 19C+] (*US*) a usu. derog. term for a white person.

(IN PHRASES)

❑ **black fay** *n.* [1960s] (*US black*) a black person considered subservient to whites.

ofay *adj.* (*also* **fay, oofay**) [OFAY *n.*] [late 19C+] (*US*) of a person, white; relating to white culture.

(IN COMPOUNDS)

❑ **ofay trash** *n. see* WHITE TRASH *n.*

off *n.*[1] [sporting jargon *off*, the start of any race, esp. that of horses or dogs] [1950s+] the start.

off *n.*[2] [abbr. SE *day/time off*] [1960s+] (*S.Afr.*) free time.

off *n.*[3] [the idea that things KICK OFF *v.*[2] (1)] [1990s+] (*UK Und.*) a fight.

off *adj.*[1] **1** [18C+] uninterested in, not wanting. **2** [late 19C] (*US Und.*) untrusworthy within the criminal code. **3** [late 19C+] unfashionable, unattractive. **4** [late 19C+] feeling or looking unwell, despondent, unenthusiastic. **5** [late 19C+] stale, in poor condition, out of date. **6** [20C+] of food, unavailable on a menu. **7** [1910s] forbidden. **8** [1950s+] aloof, withdrawn. **9** [1980s] in a trance. **10** [1980s+] (*Aus.*) in poor taste; unfair.

off *adj.*[2] **1** [mid-19C] (*UK Und.*) of a crime, successfully achieved. **2** [1930s] (*UK Und.*) of an arrest, successful.

off *adj.*[3] [mid–late 19C] (*US Und.*) gone, stolen.

off *adj.*[4] [abbr. OFF ONE'S HEAD *adj.*] **1** [late 19C+] mad, very foolish. **2** [1960s+] happy, elated, enjoying the positive effects of drugs or drink.

off *adj.*[5] [1910s+] (*drugs*) not using an addictive drug, usu. narcotic; also of alcohol.

off *adj.*[6] [SE *off*, no longer happening, cancelled] [1990s+] (*Aus. Und.*) dead, dying.

off *v.*[1] [abbr. SE *make off, send off, go off*] **1** [late 19C+] to leave, to go off. **2** [late 19C+] to get rid of, to reject, to dismiss. **3** [1920s–30s] to die. **4** [1960s+] (*US*) to dispose of, to sell. **5** [1970s] to humiliate.

off *v.*[2] [abbr. relevant uses of KNOCK OFF *v.*] **1** [1950s+] (*orig. US black*) to kill or murder. **2** [1960s+] (*orig. US*) of a man, to have sexual intercourse. **3** [1960s+] (*US Und.*) to rob, usu. with violence. **4** [1960s+] (*US black*) to beat up someone. **5** [1970s] (*US police*) to apprehend and arrest someone.

off *prep.* [1960s+] (*orig. US*) by means of, e.g. *Sarah was grooving off Belle and Sebastian.*

off and on *adj.* [mid-19C+] indecisive, variable, vacillating.

off-brand *n.* [OFF-BRAND *adj.*] **1** [1960s] an inferior brand. **2** [1990s+] (*US*) a black person. **3** [1990s+] (*US black gang*) a rival gangster.

off-brand *adj.* [SE *off-brand*, not a mainstream or *brand*name product] [1960s+] (*orig. US black*) **1** of a person, odd, peculiar, inferior – outside the group norm. **2** unfashionable, esp. when wearing too many (clashing) colours. **3** of a child, illegitimate. **4** second-rate.

(IN COMPOUNDS)

❑ **off-brand cigarette** *n.* [1970s+] (*drugs*) a marijuana cigarette.

off-breed *n.* [1960s+] (*US*) a person or animal of mixed or indeterminate ancestry, a mongrel.

off-colour *adj.* [SE *off-colour*, unwell] [1940s–70s] (*US Und.*) homosexual.

offee kay *n.* [backsl.] [1930s] coffee.

offer someone out *v.* [late 19C+] (*Aus.*) to challenge to a fight.

off-go *n.* see GO-OFF *n.*

office *n.* **1** [late 17C+] the place one works; 'His Office, any Man's ordinary Haunt, or Plying-place, be it Tavern, Ale-house, Gaming-house' (B.E.) [this use has been sustained into 20C+, found outside the SE business context in a wide range of occupations, from pimping to commercial flying, in all of which the speaker terms their place of work, whether the street or an aircraft cockpit, the *office*]. **2** [early 18C–1960s] a toilet, a privy [abbr. *HOUSE OF OFFICE under* HOUSE *n.*[1]]. **3** [mid-18C+] a hint, a warning, a 'tip-off', usu. in phrs. *get the office*, *GIVE SOMEONE THE OFFICE* below [SE *office*, a duty to another, a service, i.e. the lookout's duty is to give a warning]. **4** [19C+] information (with no inference of secrecy). **5** [mid-19C+] (*UK/US prison*) a signal.

IN PHRASES

❑ **give someone the office** *v.* [19C+] **1** to tip off, to give a warning. **2** to inform, to tell, with no inference of warning. **3** (*UK prison*) to initiate a new prisoner into the rules and regulations, official and unofficial, of prison life. ❑ **sling the office** *v.* [mid-19C] (*UK Und.*) to give some form of sign, usu. a warning. ❑ **tip the office** *v.* [1900s] to betray a secret.

SE in slang uses

IN COMPOUNDS

❑ **office piano** *n.* [1940s+] (*US*) a typewriter. ❑ **office sneak** *n.* [SNEAK *n.*[1] (1c)] [mid–late 19C] one who enters and steals from an office or business; e.g. coats and/or umbrellas.

office *v.* [OFFICE *n.* (3)] [early 19C–1980s] (*esp. Und.*) to warn, to tip off, to indicate.

officer-toed *adj.* [the stance of police officers on parade] [20C+] (*Ulster*) with one's toes turned out.

office worker *n.* [rhy. sl.] [20C+] a shirker.

offie *n.* (*also* **offy**) [orig. a counter in a public house over which alcohol could be sold for consumption off the premises. The off-licence proper declined during the 1970s–80s but the term is still used for wine merchants and similar stores] [1950s+] an off-licence.

offish *adj.* [abbr. SE *stand-offish* but note OFF *adj.*[1] (1)] [mid-19C+] reserved, distant, aloof.

DERIVATIVES

❑ **offishness** *n.* [mid-19C+] reserve, coolness.

off it *adj.* **1** *see* OFF ONE'S HEAD *adj.* **2** *see* OFF THE WALL *adj.*

off-jiving *n.* [1940s] (*US black*) distasteful behaviour.

off like a... *phr.* [SE *off*, away + pun on *off*, stale]

IN PHRASES

❑ **off like a bride's nightie** (*also* **off like a prom dress, up and down like a bride's nightie**) [1950s+] (*Aus./US campus*) leaving or acting extremely fast, very speedily. ❑ **off like a bucket of prawns in the (hot) sun** [pun on SE *off*, stale] [1960s+] (*Aus.*) leaving very quickly.

offmans *n.* [SE *off*/OFF *v.*[1] (1) + -MANS *sfx*] [1990s+] (*UK Und.*) the advanced preparation of a means of escape.

off one's head *adj.* (*also* **off it, off one's bonce, ...onion, ... thatch**) **1** [mid-19C+] (*also* **off at the head**) insane, out of one's mind. **2** [1960s+] (*drugs*) intoxicated by a drug. **3** [1960s+] drunk.

off-ox *n.* [lit. the 'offside' ox of a pair, presumably linked to such characteristics] [mid-19C+] (*US*) a stubborn or headstrong person.

off-setter *n.* see *ONE FOR THE ROAD under* ONE *n.*[1].

offside *adj.* [sporting imagery] [1910s+] (*Aus./N.Z.*) **1** in poor taste, socially unacceptable. **2** as *offside with*, out of favour, in bad odour with.

IN PHRASES

❑ **play offside** *v.* [1910s] to act excessively.

off-side *v.* [OFFSIDER *n.*] [1920s+] (*Aus./N.Z.*) to assist.

offsider *n.* [SE *off-sider*, an animal positioned on the off-side of a team] [mid-19C+] (*Aus./N.Z.*) an assistant, helper.

off tap *adj.*[1] [1990s+] (*US campus*) excellent.

off tap *adj.*[2] [1990s+] (*Aus.*) **1** acting in an unacceptable manner; thus condemned to death. **2** eccentric, mad.

off the wall *adj.* (*also* **off it**) [? the skewed bouncing of a ball thrown against a wall] [1950s+] **1** (*orig. US*) difficult, obstreperous, strange. **2** (*orig. US*) bizarre, peculiar. **3** (*US black*) unimportant, uninteresting. **4** (*US campus*) excellent, first-rate.

off the wall *adv.* [OFF THE WALL *adj.*] [1970s] (*US*) spontaneously, unconventionally.

off-time *adj.* [1930s+] (*US*) **1** badly timed, at the wrong time, therefore unacceptable. **2** unfashionable.

IN PHRASES

❑ **off-time jive** [JIVE *n.*[1] (2)] [1930s–40s] (*US black*) a weak excuse.

off-trail *adj.* [1950s] (*US*) unconventional, out of the ordinary.

offy *n.* see OFFIE *n.*

ofter *n.* [SE *often*] [late 19C] (*sporting*) a regular attender, usu. at the races, the music-hall etc.

o.g. *n.* **1** [late 19C–1970s] (*US black*) a woman, esp. one's mother or wife [abbr. *old girl*]. **2** (*US black*) in context of street gangs [abbr. *original gangster*. The term allegedly appeared with the formation of the Original Gangster Crips, a breakaway group of Los Angeles' West Side Crips. Both gangs were a sub-group or SET *n.*[1] (1b) of the larger gang, the Crips. One theory suggests that only proven killers qualify as true *o.g.s*]. (**a**) [1980s+] a street-smart person, a leading member of a gang. (**b**) [1990s+] a close male friend. (**c**) [1990s+] a veteran of the streets.

og *n.* (*also* **ogg**) [HOG *n.* (1)] [1900s–50s] (*Aus./N.Z.*) a shilling.

o.g.b. *n.* [O.G. *n.* (2a) + BLOOD *n.*[2] (1)] [1980s+] (*US black gang*) original ghetto blood.

oggins *n.* see HOGGINS *n.*

oggy *n.* [1990s+] (*UK juv.*) a supposed 'disease' contracted by boys through physical interaction with girls.

ogle *n.* [SE *ogle*, to leer, appraise] **1** [late 17C+] usu. in pl., an eye. **2** [late 17C+] an amorous glance, a frankly sexual stare. **3** [mid-19C] a scarf.

IN COMPOUNDS

❑ **ogle-fakes** *n.* [1980s+] (*Polari*) **1** false eyelashes. **2** spectacles.

ogler *n.* [OGLE *n.* (1)] **1** [late 18C–early 19C] an eye. **2** [early 19C] a punch in the eye.

ogles *n.* see OGLE *n.* (1).

oh *n.* see O *n.*

oh-be-cheerful/oh-be-joyful *n.* see O-BE-JOYFUL *n.*

oh boy! *excl.* [1910s+] (*orig. US*) a general excl.

oh, by heck *n.* [rhy. sl.] [1930–40s] (*US*) the neck.

oh-dee *v.* see O.D. *v.*

O-head *n.* see *under* O *n.*

ohmadaun *n.* see OMADHAUN *n.*

oh mamma! *excl.* [late 19C+] (*US*) an excl. of wonder.

oh, my dear *n.* [rhy. sl.] [20C+] beer.

-oholic *sfx* see -AHOLIC *sfx*.

oh shimmy! *excl.* [2000s] (*W.I.*) an excl. of astonishment.

oh shocks! *excl.* [1960s] (*W.I.*) an excl. of disappointment.

oh, you —! *excl.* [KID *n.*[1] (4)] [20C+] (*US*) an excl. of affection; esp. as *oh, you kid!*

oh-zee *n.* see O.Z. *n.*

oi! *excl.* [note the brief 1980s *Oi music*, geared to the sensibilities of a SKINHEAD *n.* (3)/football fan audience and featuring such bands as Sham 69 and Cockney Rejects. Such music mutated into the racist/nationalist songs of Europe's hardcore right-wing music business] [1960s+] a general excl. of address, synon. with earlier *hoy!*, come here! pay attention! etc.

-oid *sfx* [abbr. SE *android*] [20C+] (*orig. US*) used in a nominal or adjectival form to express a brainless or automatic quality, e.g. *zomboid*.

oik *n.* (*also* **oick**) [orig. school use, a working man, then an unpopular pupil or any member of a rival school] [1930s+] an unpleasant youth, usu. as described by a social superior.

DERIVATIVES

□ **oikish** *adj.* (*also* **oiky**) [1930s+] unpleasant, crude, vulgar; usu. of a youth.

oil *n.* **1** as a bodily fluid. (**a**) [17C] vaginal secretions. (**b**) [17C–1900s] semen. **2** in fig. senses, i.e. that which 'greases the wheels'. (**a**) [mid-19C; 1910s+] (*US*) flattery, sweet talk. (**b**) [late 19C+] graft, bribery, and the money for paying it. (**c**) [20C+] (*Aus./N.Z.*) information, which *oils* the wheels of communication. (**d**) [1910s] facility, ability. (**e**) [1930s] lies, misinformation. **3** in senses of drink or drugs. (**a**) [mid-19C+] (*later US black*) alcohol, esp. wine. (**b**) [1920s–40s] (*Irish*) a drink. (**c**) [1940s–70s] (*US*) coffee. (**d**) [1960s+] (*drugs*) hashish oil or purified hashish. (**e**) [1980s+] (*drugs*) heroin. (**f**) [1980s+] (*drugs*) phencyclidine. **4** [1900s–40s] (*US Und.*) nitroglycerin; gelignite.

IN COMPOUNDS

□ **oil merchant** *n.* [MERCHANT *n.*] [1930s–60s] (*US*) a flatterer or a swindler.

IN PHRASES

□ **know one's oil** *v.* [1920s] (*US tramp*) to be aware, to know what is going on. □ **oiled (up)** *adj.* [mid-18C+] (*orig. US*) drunk. □ **oil of barley** *n.* **1** [mid-17C–early 19C] strong ale. **2** [mid-19C] whisky. □ **oil of joy** *n.* [1900s–60s] (*US*) alcohol. □ **old oil** *n.* [OIL *n.* (2a)] [1910s+] (*US*) flattery, insincere charm. □ **on the oil** [1910s–20s] on a drinking bout. □ **pour on the oil** *v.* [1930s+] to flatter. □ **straight oil** *n.* [STRAIGHT *adj.*[1] (2)] [1930s+] (*Aus.*) the honest truth, the facts. □ **swim in golden oil** *v. see* SWIM IN GOLDEN GREASE *under* SWIM *v.*

SE in slang uses

IN COMPOUNDS

□ **oil bags** *n.* [1960s] (*US black*) the buttocks. □ **oil can** *n.* **1** [1920s–30s] (*US*) a useless person, a good-for-nothing. **2** [1940s] (*US*) a derog. term for an automobile.

IN PHRASES

□ **put the oil act on** *v.* [1940s] (*US black*) to beat up; to kill. □ **strike oil** *v. see under* STRIKE *v.*

oil *v.* [SE *oil*/OIL *n.* (1)] **1** [mid-17C; 1920s+] (*later use US*) to persuade in some deceitful manner; to bribe. **2** [late 18C; 1920s+] (*later US black*) (*also* **oil up**) to beat, to whip. **3** [late 19C+] to drink; to become drunk; to render drunk. **4** [1920s+] to move quietly, stealthily or in an underhand, surreptitious manner, also in combs. with various adv. *around, in, out, through.* **5** [1940s+] to pay. **6** [1980s+] to inject oneself with a drug, usu. heroin.

IN COMPOUNDS

□ **oiled behind** *n.* [1930s–40s] (*US black*) the buttocks, after a beating. □ **oiled head** *n.* [1930–40s] (*US black*) a head that has been beaten, usu. by the police.

IN PHRASES

□ **oil in** *v.* [1920s+] to enter, to intrude. □ **oil it** *v.* [SE phr. *burn the midnight oil*] [20C+] (*US campus*) to stay up late studying. □ **oil out (of)** *v.* [1920s+] **1** to escape one's responsibility, to escape from an onerous duty or similar situation. **2** to slide away as if well-lubricated. □ **oil the hand** *v.* (*also* **oil the fist, ... palm**) [17C; 1930s] to bribe. □ **oil the knocker** *v.* [mid-19C–1910s] to tip or bribe a doorman or porter. □ **oil the machinery** *v.* [late 19C] to have a drink. □ **oil the tonsils** *v.* [20C+] to have a drink. □ **oil up** *v.* **1** [late 19C+] (*Aus.*) to drink, to have a drink. **2** [late 19C+] to bribe someone. **3** [20C+] (*Aus.*) to impart information. **4** [1940s] to render drunk.

oil-burner *n.* **1** [1920s–40s] (*US*) a tobacco chewer [US Navy *oil*, chewing tobacco]. **2** [1920s+] (*US*) an exceptionally able or hard-working person [SE phr. *burn the midnight oil*]. **3** [1930s+] (*US drugs*) in drug uses. (**a**) (*also* **oil-burner habit, oil-burning habit**) an extremely heavy level of heroin addiction [predates OIL *n.* (3e), hence prob. SE phr. *burn the midnight oil* or play on the oil lamps that were used to heat opium + HABIT *n.* (1)]. (**b**) an addict with a very high intake of narcotics. **4** [1930s+] a vehicle which, through a malfunctioning or dirty engine, uses up a disproportionate quantity of oil.

oiler *n.*[1] [SE *oil*] **1** [late 19C–1950s] an oil well. **2** [late 19C+] (*orig. US*) an oilskin or oilcloth coat and/or trousers. **3** [1900s–60s] (*US*) a Mexican [var. on GREASER *n.*[1] (1a)].

oiler *n.*[2] [OIL *v.* (2)/OIL *v.* (3)] **1** [1910s+] (*also* **oil**) a heavy drinker. **2** [1930s–40s] (*US black*) one who regularly gets involved in fights.

oiler *n.*[3] [OIL *n.* (3d)] [1980s] (*drugs*) a cannabis cigarette mixing tobacco and hashish oil.

oil leak *n.* [rhy. sl.] [1990s+] a Sikh.

oil of... *n.* **1** money, always in combs. as listed below. **2** a beating, always in combs. as listed below [note parallel usage in Jamaican herbalism and religious cults, some refer to religious beliefs, others to the wishes that are invested in the oil itself; terms include *oil of Calvary; oil of Virgin Mary; oil of power; oil of dead-man; oil of kill-him-dead; oil of bound-to-win*].

IN PHRASES

meaning money

□ **oil of angels** *n.* (*also* **angel's oil**) [predates OIL *n.* (1) so more likely fig. use of SE *oil* + *angel*, 'an old English gold coin, called more fully at first the angel-noble, being originally a new issue of the Noble, having as its device the archangel Michael standing upon, and piercing the dragon' (*OED*). Initially worth 6s 8d, it was worth 10s when last minted under Charles I] [late 16C–17C] money used for bribery. □ **oil of argentum** *n.* [Lat. *argentum*, white money, silver] [early 18C] money. □ **oil of palms** *n.* [used to 'grease the palm'] [early 17C; 19C+] money, usu. in the form of a bribe.

meaning a beating

□ **oil of baston** *n.* [SE *baston*, a cudgel, club or truncheon] [early 17C] a severe beating. □ **oil of birch** *n.* [early 19C–1940s] a beating. □ **oil of gladness** *n.* [late 18C–early 19C] a beating; often in phrs. *I will anoint you with the oil of gladness*, I will beat you. □ **oil of hazel** *n.* (*also* **hazel oil**) [a variety of sap supposedly contained in a green hazel rod, which adds vigour to a beating] [late 17C–19C] a beating, often as phr. *anoint with oil of hazel*, to beat. □ **oil of holly** *n.* [17C] a beating administered with a stick cut from a holly bush. □ **oil of stirrup** *n.* [late 18C–early 19C] a beating. □ **oil of strap'em/strappem** *n. see* STRAP-OIL *n.* □ **oil of whip** *n.* (*also* **oyl of rope**) [mid-17C–early 18C] a severe beating.

oil rigger *n.* [rhy. sl. = NIGGER *n.*[1] (1)] [2000s] (*Irish*) a black person.

oil slick *n.* [rhy. sl. = SPIC *n.*] [1910s+] a Spaniard, a Greek.

oil tanker *n.* [rhy. sl. = WANKER *n.* (2)] [20C+] a general term of abuse.

oily (rag) *n.* [rhy. sl.= FAG *n.*[4] (2)] [1930s+] a cigarette.

oily soil *n.* [likeness] [2000s] human excrement.

oingo boingo! *excl.* [nonsense words, echoic of surprise] [1990s+] (*S.Afr./US teen*) an exclamation of surprise.

oink *n.* [*oink*, onomat. for a pig's grunt, var. on PIG *n.* (2a)] [1960s+] (*orig. US black*) a police officer.

oinker *n.* [*oink*, onomat. for a pig's grunt, plays on PIG *n.* (1), PIG *n.* (2)] [1980s+] (*US*) **1** a glutton, a fat person. **2** an unappealing man. **3** an ugly young woman. **4** a police officer.

oink out *v.* [*oink*, onomat. for a pig's grunt, var. on *PIG OUT under* PIG *v.*[1]] [1980s+] (*US*) to overeat.

oint-jay *n.* [pig Lat./backsl. for JOINT *n.* (1)] [1930s] (*drugs*) the equipment used for injecting a narcotic.

ointment *n.* **1** [15C–17C] money [its use in 'soothing' life's problems]. **2** [late 18C–late 19C] semen. **3** [mid-19C] butter.

oi yoi yoi *n.* [the sounds of Yid.] [1900s–30s] (*US*) a Jew.

O.J. *v.* [the former football and film star *O.J.* Simpson (b.1947), controversially acquitted of murder in 1995] [1990s+] (*US black*) to act violently, to murder.

o.j. *n.* [abbr.] **1** [1930s+] (*orig. US*) orange juice. **2** [1960s+] (*US drugs, orig. milit.*) marijuana laced with opium [O *n.* (2) + J *n.* + pun on sense 1]. **3** [1980s] (*US black*) a large car, typically a Ford or Lincoln [proper name *O.J.* Simpson (b.1947), the former football hero turned film star who advertised such cars for Hertz c.1980, prior to his 1995 murder trial].

OK *n.* (*also* **okay**) [OK! *excl.*] [mid-19C+] agreement, go-ahead, approval.

OK *adj.* (*also* **okay, okey**) [OK! *excl.*] (*orig. US*) **1** [mid-19C+] good, fine, satisfactory, acceptable, occas. splendid. **2** [mid-19C+] safe, unharmed. **3** [mid-19C+] up to date, fashionable, e.g. *it's the OK thing to do*. **4** [late 19C+] of a person, good, decent, e.g. *an OK guy*. **5** [1970s+] constructed with 'with' or 'about', comfortable, at ease with. **6** [1990s+] well supplied with, usu. money.

OK *v.* (*also* **okay**) [OK! *excl.*] **1** [late 19C+] (*orig. US*) to pass, to approve, to 'give the go-ahead'. **2** [1940s–50s] (*US*) to pay someone's bill.

OK *adv.* (*also* **okay**) [OK *adj.* (1)] [mid-19C+] well; in a satisfactory manner, all right.

OK! *excl.* (*also* **okay! okey!**) [corrupted abbr. of SE *all correct*, via its pron. as 'orl korrect'. It dates from 1839 in the US; Hotten (1864) has it (correctly etymologized) without ref. to US origins. The term was used in the election campaign of US president Martin Van Buren in 1840, when it conveniently suited his nickname 'Old Kinderhook', based on the town of his birth Kinderhook, New York. It was further popularized by the *OK* Club, founded in 1840, whose members were Democrats who backed Van Buren] [early 19C+] (*orig. US*) a statement of agreement: all is fine, everything is in order, I agree, go ahead etc; also used interrog. *OK?*, do you agree?

IN COMPOUNDS

❑ **OK sign** *n.* [orig. a visual symbol used, or popularized by 1947 Penzoil motor oil advertisement and, subseq., in used car outlets; 1980s+ SE] [1940s+] (*US*) a hand sign made of a circle with thumb and forefinger, and other fingers upright, to indicate approval, good quality or excellence.

okapi *n.* (*also* **ou kappie**) [the tradename, itself based on the *okapi*, a rare mammal of the *Giraffidae* family] [1960s+] (*W.I./S.Afr.*) a single-bladed knife with a pattern of three stars on the handle.

okapi *v.* [OKAPI *n.*] [1980s] to stab someone.

okay *see under* OK.

okay-doke! *excl. see* OKEY-DOKE! *excl.*

OK coakley *adv.* (*also* **OK koakley**) [1920s] (*US*) fine, satisfactory.

oke *n.*^{1} [abbr. Afk. *outjie*, little chap] [1960s+] (*S.Afr.*) **1** a fellow, a chap. **2** a friend. **3** a general term of address.

oke *n.*^{2} *see* OAK *n.*

oke *adj.* [OK *adj.*] [1920s–50s] (*orig. US*) all right.

oke! *excl.* [OK! *excl.*] [1930s] all right!

okedoke! *excl. see* OKEY-DOKE! *excl.*

okely-dokely! *excl. see* OKEY-DOKE! *excl.*

okey *see under* OK.

okey-doke *n.*^{1} [rhy. sl. = POKEY *n.*^{2} (1)?] [1950s] (*US*) a prison.

okey-doke *n.*^{2} (*also* **o-ke-doke, okey-dokey, okey-pokey, okle-dokle**) [OK *adj.*; underpinned by an image of gratuitous acquiescence] (*US black*) **1** [1960s+] white values and opinions. **2** [1960s+] (*also* **okey-dok**) a swindle, a confidence trick. **3** [1960s+] stupidity, foolish talk. **4** [1990s+] a confidence trick. **5** [1990s+] the best, the utimate.

okey-doke *adj.*^{1} (*also* **hokey-dokey, oakey dokey**) [OKEY-DOKE! *excl.*] [1930s+] (*US*) good, acceptable.

okey-doke *adj.*^{2} [OKEY-DOKE *n.*^{2} (2)] [1970s] (*US Und.*) deceitful, swindling.

okey-doke *v.* (*also* **okey-dokey, okey-pokey**) [OKEY-DOKE *n.*^{2} (2)] [1990s+] (*US black*) to swindle.

okey-doke! *excl.* (*also* **hokey-dokey! okay-doke! okedoke! okel-dokel! okely-dokely! okey-dokey! okey-dokey artichokey! okey-pokey! okie doke! okle-dokle! okydoke!**) [1930s+] (*orig. US*) all vars. of OK! *excl.*

Okie *n.* (*also* **Oakey, Oakie**) **1** [1910s+] (*US*) a derog. term for a migrant worker, orig. from Oklahoma, forced off his land during the Great Depression during the 1930s [abbr. *Oklahoma*]. **2** [1970s+] (*S.Afr.*) a vagrant, a tramp [loan f. US use].

Okie *adj.* [OKIE *n.*] [1910s+] pertaining to Oklahoma or emigrants from that state.

okie *n.* (*also* **oakie, oukie**) [abbr. Afk. *outjie*, little chap] [1940s+] (*S.Afr.*) a boy or man, also used as a form of address.

okie doke! *excl. see* OKEY-DOKE! *excl.*

Okker *n. see* OSCAR (ASCHE) *n.*

OK koakley *adv. see* OK COAKLEY *adv.*

Oklahoma *adj.* used in combs. pertaining to the state, usu. implying social and material backwardness.

IN COMPOUNDS

❑ **Oklahoma credit card** *n.* [1960s+] (*US*) a siphon tube for stealing gasoline. ❑ **Oklahoma guarantee** *n.* [1960s] (*US*) no guarantee. ❑ **Oklahoma rain** *n.* [1910s+] (*US*) a dust storm.

okle-dokle! *excl. see* OKEY-DOKE! *excl.*

okokay *n.* [backsl.] [1930s] cocoa.

okole *n.* [Hawaiian *okole*, the buttocks] [1930s+] (*US*) the buttocks or rear of anything.

okra *n.* [resemblance] [1920s–50s] (*US*) the penis.

IN COMPOUNDS

❑ **okra and prunes** *n.* [coined by Gore Vidal (b.1925) for his novel *Duluth* (1983)] [1980s+] (*US*) the male genitals.

okydoke! *excl. see* OKEY-DOKE! *excl.*

-ola *sfx* [the original use is in *pianola* (1901), although in that context it worked as a diminutive. It was greatly popularized in the *payola* scandals in the US pop music industry during the late 1950s, although *payola* itself had been a recognized part of the business for 20 years.] [1910s+] (*US*) combined with a noun and used as an intensifier of that noun, e.g. BOFFOLA *n.*; CASHOLA *n.*; CRACKOLA *n.*; DRUGOLA *n.*; HOPOLA *n.*; NOISOLA *n.*; PAYOLA *n.*; SCHNOZZOLA *n.*; STACKOLA *n.*

old *n.* **1** [mid-19C] (*UK Und.*) death. **2** constr. with *the*. (**a**) [mid-19C–1900s] a master, a boss. (**b**) [late 19C–1960s] money (usu. owed from gambling), esp. in the phr. *a bit of the old*.

old *adj.* **1** [late 16C; mid-19C+] used affectionately of a person, occas. animal. **2** [mid-17C+] used in combs. to refer to the Devil; other than those listed below, there are a number of other terms e.g. *...boots, ...boy, ...chap, ...child, ...dad, ... Davy, ...fellow, ...hangie, ...hooky, ...Mahoun, ...man, ... Sanners/Sanny/Saunders, ...Scrat/Scratchem, ...Smith, ...smoke, ...scooty, ...soss, ... thief*. For a full discussion *see* Partridge, 'The Devil and His Nicknames' in *World of Words* (1939); *see also* combs. below and separate entries, e.g. OLD NICK *n.* **3** [18C–early 19C] (*UK Und.*) ugly [? OLD NICK *n.*, OLD BOY *n.* and similar devil-related terms; the Devil is assumed to be ugly]. **4** [early 18C+] clever, cunning e.g. *come the old soldier*. **5** [mid-19C+] used as an expression of familiarity, e.g. the *old gaff*, the *old boozer*. **6** [mid-19C+] (*orig. US*) tiresome, usu. constructed with get, e.g. *too much of a good thing gets old*.

meaning the Devil

IN COMPOUNDS

❑ **old bendy** *n.* [18C] the Devil. ❑ **old billy** *n.* [late 19C–1900s] the Devil, usu. in the phr. *like old billy*, very hard, very energetically. ❑ **old clootie** *n.* (*also* **old cloots**) [dial. *cloot*, a cloven leaf] [mid-18C–1900s] (*usu. Scot.*) the Devil. ❑ **old clubfoot** *n.* [mid-19C] (*US*) the Devil. ❑ **old driver** *n.* [late 18C–19C] the Devil. ❑ **old hairy toe** *n.* [var. on OLD HARRY *n.*; but note the Devil's depiction as half-goat] [1930s] the Devil. ❑ **old harrington** *n. see* OLD HARRY *n.* (1). ❑ **old hornie** *n.* (*also* **old horney, old horny**) [HORNS *n.*/the devil's trad. *horns*] [mid-19C+] the Devil. ❑ **old lad** *n.* [late 19C] (*Aus.*) the Devil. ❑ **old Mr Grim** *n.* [late 18C–19C] the Devil. ❑ **old Ned** *n.* [1920s–40s] (*US*) the Devil; thus *raise Old Ned*, to cause a commotion, to cause trouble. ❑ **Old One, the** *n.* [late 18C–19C] the Devil. ❑ **old poker** *n.* (*also* **old poger**) [late 18C–early 19C] the Devil. ❑ **old roger** *n.* [popular use of SE *roger* as nickname for a bull] [late 17C–19C; 1970s] (*later use Irish*) the Devil. ❑ **old sam** *n.* [mid-19C–1930s] (*US black*) the Devil. ❑ **old Scratch** *n.* (*also* **Old Scratcher**) [mid-18C+] the Devil; thus *raise old Scratch*, to cause a disturbance. ❑ **old splitfoot** *n.* [19C] the Devil.

SE in slang uses

IN COMPOUNDS

❑ **old abram** *n.* [mid-19C] (*UK Und.*) a notorious thief. ❑ **old adam** *n.* [SE *old Adam*, original sin] [19C] the penis. ❑ **old-ass** *adj.* [1960s+] (*US*) run-down, dilapidated, old. ❑ **old bads** *n.* (*also* **old broke**) [SE *old* + Shetland dial. *bad*, an article of clothing/SE *broke* or dial. *brock*, rubbish, refuse, remnants] [1950s+] (*W.I.*) old clothes. ❑ **old beeswing** *n.* [SE *beeswing*, the crust that forms on vintage port] [late 19C] a genial drinker. ❑ **old Bet** *n. see* BETSY *n.* ❑ **old blind bob** *n.* [18C] the penis. ❑ **old Boney** *n.* [18C] death. ❑ **old brown Windsor** *n.* [play on *Brown Windsor* soup/BROWN *n.* (3)] [1920s+] (*Aus.*) the anus. ❑ **old buba** *n.* [dial. *buba*, a dry leaf, of cabbage, coconut or any plant] [1950s] (*W.I.*) an old person who acts younger than their age. ❑ **old bundle** *n. see* DIRTY BUNDLE *under* DIRTY *adj.* ❑ **old cheese** *n.* [affectionate nickname] [1970s+] (*Aus.*) one's (occas. someone else's) mother. ❑ **old chip** *n.* [late 19C] a term of endearment. ❑ **old chook** *n.* [CHOOK *n.*] [1910s+] (*Aus.*) a general term of intimate affection; lit. 'old chicken'. ❑ **old cockalorum** *n.* [ext. of OLD COCK *n.*] [late 19C–1900s] a man, esp. as a term of affectionate address. ❑ **old cole** *n.* [mid-16C] (*UK Und.*) a veteran dice cheat. ❑ **old crow** *n.* [late 19C+] **1** a generally misogynistic ref. to an old woman. **2** a general term of abuse, not spec. of a woman. ❑ **old curiosity** *n.* [late 19C–1930s] one's wife. ❑ **old dampa** *n.* [ety. unknown] [20C+] (*W.I.*) old clothes. ❑ **old ding** *n.* [? SE *ding*, to hit, to knock] [19C] the vagina. ❑ **old dirt road** *n. see* DIRT ROAD *n.* ❑ **old Ebenezer** *n.* [? anecdotal] [late 19C] (*US*) a grizzly bear. ❑ **old faithful** *n.* [1950s+] (*US*) menstruation. ❑ **old flint** *n.* [SKINFLINT *n.*] [mid-19C] a miser. ❑ **old flower** *n.* [20C+] (*Irish*) an affectionate term of address esp. as *my old flower*. ❑ **old-foot** *adj.* [1990s+] (*W.I.*) describing older people. ❑ **old fowl** *n.* [20C+] (*Aus./W.I.*) an ageing, unattractive and prob. over-dressed woman. ❑ **old fragment** *n.* [1900s] an old(er) man. ❑ **old frizzle** *n.* [SE *frizzle*, crisp, curly hair] [18C–late 19C] **1** in cards, the ace of spades [the shape of the spade could resemble a beard]. **2** someone wearing a wig e.g. a liveried servant. **3** the vagina [ref. to pubic hair]. ❑ **old gadget** *n.* [1920s] a foolish, second-rate man. ❑ **old gager** *n.* [18C] (*UK Und.*) a rich old man. ❑ **old gang** *n.* [late 19C+] a group or clique of friends or colleagues. ❑ **old gent** *n.* **1** [1900s–30s] (*US*) one's father. **2** [1940s] a husband. ❑ **old glory** *n.* [SE *Old Glory*, nickname for the US flag. The implication is of the stylelessness of trad. white values] [late 19C–1940s] (*US black*) anything seen as unfashionable, out of date. ❑ **old gold** *n.* [late 18C] human excrement. ❑ **old gown** *n.* [ety. unknown; the label placed on the tea-chest for the purpose of deception] [mid-19C] smuggled tea. ❑ **old Grim** *n.* [late 19C] (*US*) death. ❑ **old haggums** *n.* [mid-19C] (*UK Und.*) an old prostitute. ❑ **old hannah** *n.* [1930s+] (*US black*) the sun. ❑ **old haricot** *n. see* OLD BEAN *under* BEAN *n.*[2]. ❑ **old hen** *n.* [HEN *n.* (1)] [20C+] a woman, esp. an old one. ❑ **old hickory** *n.* [it carries the picture of President Andrew 'Old Hickory' Jackson (1767–1845)] [1960s] (*US*) a $20 bill. ❑ **old hige** *n.* [SE *hag* + dial. *old hige*, an old witch] [1940s+] (*W.I.*) a nagging old woman. ❑ **old hornie** *n.* (*also* **old horney, old Hornington, old horny**) [18C–19C] the penis. ❑ **old huddle (and twang)** *n.* [he 'huddles' around his money; the use of *twang*, usu. a prostitute (*see* TWANG *n.*[1] (1)), has no obvious explanation] [mid-16C–mid-17C] a miser. ❑ **old identity** *n.* (*also* **identity**) [mid-19C–1950s] **1** a person, usu. an eccentric, a 'character'. **2** (*Aus./N.Z.*) anyone who has lived in the same place for a long time, a regular resident. ❑ **old Ireland** *n.* [1980s+] (*UK bingo*) the number 17. ❑ **old joe** *n.* [orig. US Navy] [1910s+] (*US*) syphilis. ❑ **old lad** *n.* **1** [late 16C+] a man, esp. as an affectionate term of address. **2** [1970s] a father. ❑ **old Mary** *n.* [1970s] an old woman, or anyone behaving like one. ❑ **old Mr Gory** *n.* [*Fort Goree*, on the Gold Coast] [late 17C–early 19C] gold. ❑ **old Mr Grim** *n.* [late 18C–19C] death. ❑ **Old Mo** *n.* [abbr. of *The Great Mogul*, the original name for the place] [late 19C–1900s] the Middlesex Music Hall. ❑ **old ned** *n.* [orig. regional use] [mid-19C–1930s] (*US black*) salt pork or bacon. ❑ **old net** *n.* [both are torn and are mainly made up of holes] [1950s] (*W.I.*) ragged work-clothes. ❑ **old nigger** *n.* [NIGGER *n.*[1] (1)] [1950s] (*W.I.*) a disreputable, down-at-heel person. ❑ **old north pole** *n.* [mid-19C] (*UK Und.*) burglary. ❑ **old one-two, the** *n.* [the rhythmic movements] **1** [late 19C] masturbation. **2** [20C+] sexual intercourse. **3** [20C+] a lit. or fig. knockout blow. ❑ **old one-two-three, the** *n.* [1970s+] (*US*) insincere, effusive talk. ❑ **old oyster** *n.* [late 19C–1920s] a general term of address, esp. to a reserved, uncommunicative person. ❑ **old pair** *n.* [2000s] (*Irish*) one's parents. ❑ **old patrol** *n.* [1940s] (*US*) an old prostitute. ❑ **old poke** *n.* [POKE *n.*[3] = a stiff, starched collar, c.f. STUFFED SHIRT *n.*] [1930s] (*US*) a spoilsport. ❑ **old pot** *n.* [abbr. POT AND PAN *n.*] [late 19C+] (*orig. Aus.*) an old man, esp. one's father. ❑ **Old Probabilities** *n.* (*also* **Old Prob, Old Probs, probabilities**) [late 19C–1950s] (*US*) the weather bureau or its staff. ❑ **old queer** *n.* (*also* **queer stuff**) [1940s] (*S.Afr. drugs*) marijuana. ❑ **old rail** *n.* (*also* **old ral, old rall, rall**) [? dial. *rail*, to stagger, to reel. The development of the disease gradually impairs mobility] [late 19C–1960s] (*US*) syphilis. ❑ **old raspberry** *n.* [1910s–20s] one who has a notably red nose, presumably a drunkard. ❑ **old red socks** *n.* [the identification of Catholicism with red; e.g. the 'the scarlet woman of Rome'] [20C+] (*Ulster*) the pope. ❑ **old rip** *n.* [1970s+] (*US gay*) the anus. ❑ **old root** *n. see* ROOT *n.*[1] (1a). ❑ **old rowley** *n.* (*also* **old slimey**) [SE *Old Rowley*, the Devil, or *rowley*, alternative sp. for SE *rolly*, thus the shape/SE *slimey*, of the semen it ejaculates] [mid-17C–19C] the penis. ❑ **old sack** *n. see* BAG *n.*[1] (3b). ❑ **old school** *adj. see under* SCHOOL *n.* ❑ **old settler** *n.* [1940s] (*US black*) a woman in her thirties or older. ❑ **old shot** *n.* [late 19C] (*Aus.*) an old, crafty person. ❑ **old smokey** *n.* [1920s+] (*US prison*) the electric chair; thus *ride old Smokey*, to be electrocuted. ❑ **old socks** *n.* (*also* **old sock, old stock, old stockings**) [mid-19C+] (*Aus./US*) a term of address to a man. ❑ **old sol** *n.* [*Sol*, abbr. Solomon is a stereotypical Jewish name] [late 19C] (*US*) a pawnbroker. ❑ **old son** *n. see* OLD MAN *n.* (1d). ❑ **old steve** *n.* [ety. unknown; ? a well-known dealer] [1930s–50s] (*drugs*) any form of narcotic in powder form. ❑ **old strike-a-light** *n.* [his cry of *strike a light!* when asked for yet another 'loan'] [late 19C] one's father. ❑ **old stripes** *n.* (*also* **stripes**) [late 19C–1960s] a tiger. ❑ **old trot** *n.* [mid-14C–1930s] an old woman. ❑ **old 'un** *n.* [mid-19C+] an old person, esp. a parent. ❑ **old whiskers** *n.* [mid-19C–1900s] **1** a working man with long, unkempt, greying whiskers, usu. shouted out by impudent children. **2** an old man. ❑ **old wigsby** *n.* [such a man would still be likely to sport a wig, seen as an 18C affectation] [late 19C–1900s] (*middle class*) an ill-tempered, narrow-minded, elderly man. ❑ **old wives' paternoster** *n.* [SE *paternoster*, the Lord's Prayer] [late 16C–early 17C] grumbling, nagging.

IN PHRASES

❑ **if they're big enough, they're old enough** [1910s+] a phr. used among men to suggest that, whatever actual age a girl is, if she has reached puberty biologically (menstruation, body shape etc), she is old enough for intercourse. ❑ **if they're old enough to bleed, they're old enough to fuck** (*also* **...to breed, ...to butcher, if they're big enough...**) [1960s+] a phr. used among men to suggest that if a girl is old enough to menstruate she is old enough for intercourse; similarly used by homosexuals of young boys. ❑ **old enough to sit at the table, old enough to eat** [the implication of EAT *v.* (4) is oral sex, but the larger usage is general] [1980s+] (*US*) a phr. used to suggest that an underage girl is still a feasible target for seduction. ❑ **old friend and shamrock** *n.* [late 19C] (*US*) an order of corned beef and cabbage. ❑ **old in the tooth** *adj.* (*also* **up in the tooth**) [the use of a horse's teeth to ascertain its age, the older a horse, the more faded the distinguishing marks in their teeth] [mid–late 19C] aged, esp. of old women.

IN EXCLAMATIONS

❑ **old mackinaw!** *see* HOLY MACKINAW! *under* HOLY...! *excl.*

old-age pension *n.* [the age of male retirement] [1940+] (*bingo*) the number 65.

Old Bailey underwriter *n.* [a pun on SE *underwriter* + ref. to his probable destination] [early–mid-19C] a small-scale forger.

Old Bill *n.* [milit. *old Bill*, a veteran, ult. *Old Bill*, the character created by the WW1 cartoonist Bruce Bairnsfeather (1888–1959)] [1950s+] **1** the police; thus *Bill from the Hill*, officers serving at Notting Hill police station in London W11 (cf. BILL, THE *n.* **2** the police force as an institution. **3** a police station.

old bill *n.*[1] [1910s] (*US*) corned beef.

old bill *n.*[2] [2000s] the penis.

old bird *n.* [SE *old* + BIRD *n.*[1] (3a)] **1** [mid–late 19C] (*UK prison*) a veteran prisoner, a recidivist. **2** [mid-19C+] a person who has become knowing through experience, esp. an experienced thief; thus *wily/cunning old bird*. **3** [late 19C+] (*also* **old birdie**) as a form of address. **4** [1910s+] a person, usu. old.

old black joes *n.* [rhy. sl.] [20C+] (*Aus.*) the toes.

old boy *n.* **1** [17C+] (*also* **old cove**) an old or older man, esp. as *the old boy*, one's father; often as a term of familiar address. **2** [late 18C+] (*US/Irish*) constr. with *the*, the Devil. **3** [mid-19C] the stuffing, the 'daylights', e.g. *I'll knock the Old Boy out of him*. **4** [1920s+] (*US*) (*also* **old chap**) the penis [BOY, THE *n.*[1] (1)].

old chap *n.* [SE *old* + CHAP *n.* (1)] **1** [early 19C+] (*also* **old chappie**) a man; also as term of address. **2** [mid-19C–1930s] one's father.

old clo *n.* [lit. SE *old clothes*; the stereotyping of Jews and the second-hand clothes trade] **1** [mid-19C–1900s] old clothes. **2** [mid-19C–1920s] a derog. term for a Jew. **3** [late 19C] ext. of sense 2 as an intellectual.

old clo *adj.* [the street cry *old clo!*, old clothes] [mid–late 19C] worn out, exhausted, out of date, etc.

old cock *n.* (*also* **old cocker, old cock-sparrow**) [COCK *n.*[2] (1), underpinned by COCK *n.*[3] (1)] **1** [mid-17C; late 18C+] a man, esp. as a term of affectionate address. **2** [1950s–60s] (*US prison*) a veteran prisoner.

old cocker *n.* [Yid. *alte cacka*, old man] [1940s+] (*orig. US*) an old man, usu. a disreputable one.

old cove *n. see* OLD BOY *n.*

Old Dart *n.* [? SE *old dirt* (on model of OLD SOD *n.*)] [mid-19C+] (*Aus./N.Z.*) England, or Ireland.

old dear *n.* **1** [late 19C+] one's wife. **2** [late 19C+] an old person, usu. but not invariably a woman. **3** [1900s–20s] an affectionate term of address, irrespective of sex. **4** [2000s] (*chiefly Irish*) one's mother.

old dog *n.* [affectionate use of SE *dog*] **1** [late 16C+] an expert in a given field; usu. with *at*. **2** [mid-18C+] a man, usu. with overtones of admiration for his less than conventional lifestyle; also used fig. of an object. **3** [1930s–60s] (*US*) (*also* **the dog**) constr. with *the*, syphilis [? the disease 'bites' the sufferer]. **4** [1930s+] (*orig. US black*) a direct term of affectionate address.

IN PHRASES

❑ **old dog at common prayer** *n.* [late 17C–18C] a mediocre clergyman who could read the prayers, but had no skill at preaching.

Old Doss, the *n.* [DOSS *n.*[1] (1); the prison, on the site of Henry VIII's palace of Bridewell, flourished 1556–1855] **1** [19C] the Bridewell prison, sited on the banks of the Fleet River. **2** [mid-19C] (*US Und.*) the Tombs prison, NYC.

old-fashioned *adj.* **1** [mid-19C+] of sexual intercourse, performed in the conventional manner, the missionary position. **2** [late 19C–1930s] (*Irish*) precocious, forward. **3** [20C+] of a look or glance, disapproving. **4** [1930s] obscene.

old fellow *n.* **1** [early 19C] the Devil. **2** [early 19C+] a man; also used as a term of address. **3** [mid-19C–1900s] God. **4** [late 19C] an object, a thing. **5** [late 19C+] (*also* **old fulla**) the penis. **6** [20C+] one's father; esp. Irish and often written as *oul fella*, to emphasize the Dublin pron. **7** [1980s] a husband.

old fogey *n.* [rhy. sl. = BOGEY *n.*[3] (1)] [1990s+] nasal mucus.

old gal *n.* (*also* **old girl, ole girl**) **1** [late 18C+] any woman, usu. old but not necessarily so, often as *the old girl*. **2** [mid-19C+] a general term of address to a woman or a female dog or horse. **3** [mid-19C+] one's wife or regular female companion. **4** [late 19C+] one's mother. **5** [1910s–40s] (*US*) used of a non-human object. **6** [1940s] a mother-in-law. **7** [1940s] (*US black campus*) a college boy's roommate. **8** [1980s] (*gay*) a term of address to a homosexual friend.

old gentleman (in black) *n.* **1** [late 17C–1920s] the Devil. **2** [early 19C–1930s] (*also* **old gent**) in gambling, a card that is slightly longer than the rest of the pack and thus identifiable by cheats. **3** [1900s–30s] (*US*) one's father.

IN PHRASES

❑ **old gentleman's bed-posts** *n.* (*also* **old gentleman's four-poster**) [sense 1 above; var. on *devil's bedposts* under DEVIL *n.*] [mid–late 19C] the four of clubs, considered an unlucky card.

old gooseberry *n.* [late 18C–late 19C] the Devil.

IN PHRASES

❑ **like old gooseberry** *adv.* [late 18C–late 19C] very fast. ❑ **play old gooseberry** *v.* [late 18C–late 19C] to cause trouble, to 'play the devil', 'play the deuce'. ❑ **play up old gooseberry with** *v.* [late 18C–mid-19C] to deal with in a peremptory manner, to shut (someone) up.

Old Harry *n.* [*give old Harry* is still current in W.I. use; Nares (1822) defines the phr. as 'formerly applied satirically to Henry the Eighth'] **1** [mid-17C+] (*also* **Lord Harry, old Harrington, old Henry, old Hornie**) the Devil. **2** [late 17C–early 19C] a form of unspecified adulterant used in wine.

IN PHRASES

❑ **like old Harry** *adv.* [mid-19C; 1970s] to a great (lit. 'devilish') extent. ❑ **play old Harry (with)** *v.* (*also* **give old Harry**) [19C–1900s] to 'play the Devil' (with), to make mischief, to tease or scold.

old hat *n.* **1** [late 17C–19C] the vagina ['because frequently felt' (Grose, 1796)]. **2** [1900s–10s] (*Aus.*) sexual intercourse.

old hat *adj.* [1910s+] out of date, old-fashioned.

old head *n.* **1** [mid-19C+] (*US*) an old-timer, an old person; a veteran, esp. a veteran convict [fig. use of SE]. **2** [1950s+] (*drugs*) a long-time marijuana smoker; also attrib. [fig. use of SE, boosted by HEAD *n.* (3a)].

old Henry *n. see* OLD HARRY *n.* (1).

Old Horse, the *n. see* HORSE, THE *n.*

old horse *n.* (*also* **old hoss**) (*orig. US*) **1** [mid-19C–1910s] a man. **2** [mid-19C–1930s] salt beef. **3** [mid-19C+] a term of address by one man to another.

oldie *n.* (*also* **oldy**) **1** [late 19C; 1930s+] (*usu. teen or youth*) an old person; more recently generic for anyone old, esp. those over 40, or at least those who fail to share or appreciate the nuances and delights of the current version of the rebellious youth culture. **2** [1930s+] anything old, esp. an old joke, saying, record or song.

IN PHRASES

❑ **oldie but (a) goodie** *n.* [1950s+] (*US*) something or someone that is old or no longer fashionable or chic but still beloved by its owner/wearer/user, esp. an old song.

oldies *n.* see OLDS *n.*

old iron and brass *n.* [rhy. sl.] [20C+] grass.

old Jamaica rum *n.* [rhy. sl.] [20C+] the sun.

old King Cole *n.* [rhy. sl.] [1930s+] the dole.

old kit bag *n.* [rhy. sl. = FAG *n.*[4] (2)] [1990s+] a cigarette.

old lady *n.* **1** [early 19C] in gambling, a card that is slightly wider than the rest of the pack and thus identifiable by cheats. **2** [mid-19C+] one's mother. **3** [mid-19C+] (*orig. US*) a wife (actual or common-law). **4** [late 19C] the vagina. **5** [1910s+] (*orig. US*) a girlfriend or regular partner, whether heterosexual or homosexual. **6** [1920s–50s] (*US campus*) of the same sex, a roommate. **7** [1930s+] (*US prison*) a passive partner in a homosexual relationship, male or female. **8** [1930s+] of a man, a weakling, a sentimentalist. **9** [1960s+] (*US black*) a member of a pimp's stable of whores; a single whore.

old lady white *n.* **1** [1900s–50s] a drug dealer, presumably in white powders, i.e. narcotics. **2** [1940s–50s] any powdered drug, e.g. cocaine, heroin.

old lag *n.* [SE *old* + LAG *n.*[2] (2). Although the original *lag* was destined for the penal colonies of Australia, the *old lag* can have served his time in any prison] [19C+] a habitual prisoner, a recidivist, orig. a returnee from transportation to Australia.

DERIVATIVES

❑ **old lagdom** *n.* [1900s] the world of convicts.

old madge *n.*[1] [note late 19C SE *madge*, a leaden hammer covered thickly with stout woollen cloth, used in solder plating] [mid-17C–mid-18C] a cudgel.

old madge *n.*[2] [ety. unknown; ? woman's name, note cocaine is a 'feminine' drug, see GIRL *n.*[2]] [20C+] (*drugs*) cocaine.

old man *n.* **1** of a male. (**a**) [late 17C+] a woman's husband. (**b**) [mid-18C; late 19C+] (*also* **man**) the penis. (**c**) [early 19C+] a father. (**d**) [mid-19C+] (*also* **old son**) general greeting or form of address given to a man (usu. one whom one knows), occas. to a woman. (**e**) [1940s+] (*Can./US*) a boyfriend or lover, incl. a homosexual one. (**f**) [1950s+] (*US*) a pimp. **2** [early 19C+] (*Aus.*) a mature kangaroo. **3** constr. with *the*. (**a**) [early 19C+] (*orig. US*) any senior figure, the boss, a commanding officer; a headmaster. (**b**) [late 19C] in cards, the King. (**c**) [1900s–50s] (*US*) God; also as *Old Bloke*. **4** [1930s] (*US*) a piece of piping used as a weapon.

IN COMPOUNDS

❑ **old man Mose** *n.* [abbr. *Moses*; biblical imagery, via spirituals/hymns] [1940s] (*US black*) **1** time. **2** death. ❑ **old man red eye** *n. see* RED-EYE *n.* (1a). ❑ **old man's milk** *n.* **1** [early 19C] wine. **2** [mid-19C+] whisky.

IN PHRASES

❑ **give the old man his supper** *v.* [19C+] of a woman, to make herself available for sex. ❑ **old man has his Sunday clothes on** (*also* **in one's Sunday best**) [freshly laundered Sunday clothes were stiff with starch] [19C] a phr. used of the penis, when erect.

old man *adj.* [mid-19C+] (*Aus./N.Z.*) large, important, of lengthy duration etc, e.g. an *old man kangaroo*, an *old man sand storm*.

old max *n. see* MAX *n.*

old mick *adj.* (*also* **pat and mick**) [rhy. sl.] [late 19C+] sick.

old nag *n.* [rhy. sl. = FAG *n.*[4] (2)] [20C+] a cigarette.

Old Nask *n.* (*also* **Old Nass**) [18C–19C] Bridewell prison, Totillfields, London.

Old Nick *n.* (*also* **Nicky, old Nicholas, old Nicker, old Nickie ben**) [? ref. to *Nic*colo Machiavelli (1469–1527), or abbr. SE *iniq*uity] **1** [mid-17C+] the Devil. **2** [late 19C] (*Anglo-Irish*) the joker in a pack of cards. **3** [1920s] in fig. use.

IN PHRASES

❑ **Old Nick's footsteps** *n.* [1920s] (*UK Und.*) the broad arrows printed on convict uniforms during 19C/early 20C.

oldo *n.* [1950s] an old or, in context, older person.

Old Oak *n.* [rhy. sl. = SMOKE, THE *n.* (1)] [20C+] London.

old one *n.* (*also* **ould wan, oul' one**) **1** [early 19C; 1930s+] (*Irish*) an old woman, esp. as *the old one*, one's mother or wife. **2** [late 19C+] (*Aus.*) a father.

Old Reekie *n.* (*also* **Auld Reikie**) [the smoke and smog that often covered it] [late 18C+] the old town and subseq. the whole town of Edinburgh.

Olds *n.* [abbr.] [1930s+] (*US*) an *Olds*mobile car.

olds *n.* (*also* **oldies**) [late 19C+] old people, parents.

old sherbert *n. see* SHERBET *n.*

Old Slop *n.* [Fr. *salope*, a tart; applied to the newspaper when, *c.*1840–50, it was seen as abandoning its role as the impartial 'thunderer' and currying favour wherever it could] [mid-19C–1900s] *The Times* newspaper.

Old Sod *n.* (*also* **Green Sod, ould sod, sod**) [late 18C+] Ireland.

old soldier *n.* [contrasting images of SE] **1** of a person. (**a**) [early 18C+] an experienced, but somewhat cunning man. (**b**) [mid-19C+] a simpleton, a naïve person. **2** of an empty, a discard. (**a**) [mid–late 19C] (*US*) the stub of a cigar or cigarette; well-chewed tobacco. (**b**) [late 19C+] an empty bottle. **3** [1960s–70s] (*US*) the penis.

Old Start, the *n.* [START, THE *n.* (1), the Old Bailey was erected on the site of Newgate prison] **1** [late 18C–early 19C] Newgate prison. **2** [20C+] the Old Bailey.

oldster *n.* [on model of SE *youngster*] **1** [mid-19C+] (*orig. and mainly US*) an old person, or a more experienced person. **2** [1950s] a veteran.

old-style *adj. see* OLD-TIME *adj.*

old talk *n.* [? OLD *adj.* (6) or SE *old people's talk*] [20C+] (*W.I./UK black*) chatter, gossip, rhetoric, empty boasting.

old-talk *v.* [OLD TALK *n.*] [20C+] (*W.I./UK black*) to chatter, to gossip, to make empty promises.

old thing *n.* **1** [mid–late 19C] (*Aus.*) a meal of salt beef and damper, i.e. a form of unleavened bread, baked in the ashes of a fire. **2** [mid-19C+] a person, often as a term of address or as *funny old thing* etc. **3** as euph. (**a**) [mid-19C+] the vagina. (**b**) [1930s] (*US Und.*) syphilis. (**c**) [1960s+] the penis.

old-time *adj.* (*also* **old-style, old-timer, old-timey**) [OLD TIMER *n.*] [late 19C+] veteran, old-fashioned.

old timer *n.* [SE from 1900] [mid-19C+] a veteran.

old toast *n.* **1** from the drinking of *toasts*. (**a**) [late 17C–early 18C] a drunkard. (**b**) [late 18C–mid-19C] (*UK Und.*) a lively old man. **2** [late 17C–19C] the Devil [the heat of hell, in which sinners are *toasted*].

old tom *n.* [according to Brewer, *Dict. of Phrase and Fable* (1894), the proper name of *Thomas Norris*, who was employed at Hodges' distillery and who opened a gin palace in Great Russell Street, Covent Garden. The drink in which he specialized was concocted by another Hodges' employee, Thomas Chamberlain, who christened his brand in honour of Mr Norris] [early 19C–1930s] gin.

old top *n.* (*also* **old tops**) **1** [mid-19C–1950s] a general form of address to a man, or woman, one knows. **2** [1980s] (*S.Afr.*) a father.

old woman *n.* [reverse of OLD MAN *n.*] **1** [late 18C+] a wife, a regular female partner. **2** [19C] the vagina. **3** [mid-19C] as a term of address to a woman, age is irrelevant. **4** [mid-19C+] one's mother. **5** [late 19C] (*UK prison*) a member of the stocking knitting gang in Dartmoor Prison. **6** [late 19C] the queen, in cards. **7** [20C+] any fussy or complaining person.

oldy *n. see* OLDIE *n.*

ole girl *n. see* OLD GAL *n.*

Ole-Mas *n.* [Carib.E. *Ole-Mas*, the masquerade festival that opens Carnival] [20C+] (*W.I.*) a shambles, chaos, confusion.

IN PHRASES

❑ **turn Old-Mas** *v.* [20C+] to collapse into confusion.

olga *adj.* [2000s] (*S.Afr. gay*) **1** organized. **2** old and ugly.

Olive *n.* [2000s] (*S.Afr. gay*) a beautiful young man.

olive oil *n. see* SOFT SOAP *n.* (1).

olive oil *phr.* [mispron. of Fr. *au revoir*, goodbye] [late 19C–1970s] (*orig. music-hall*) goodbye.

oliver *n.* **1** [mid-18C–1920s] the moon [? the 'O' shape] **2** [late 19C] (*US*) the nose. **3** *see* OLIVER (TWIST) *n.*

IN PHRASES

❑ **oliver is in town** [mid-18C–1920s] (*UK Und.*) the moon is full, and thus the nights are too light for stealing safely. ❑ **oliver's nightcap** *n.* [mid-18C–1920s] the hour the moon goes down. ❑ **oliver's up** [mid-18C–1920s] the moon has risen. ❑ **oliver whiddles** [mid-18C–1920s] the moon is shining.

Oliver (Cromwell) *v.* [rhy. sl. (pron. 'crummle') = TUMBLE *v.*[2] (1)] [late 19C+] to understand, usu. in phr. *do you oliver?*, do you understand?

Oliver's skull *n.* [originating in the Restoration's hatred of the Commonwealth's Lord Protector, *Oliver* Cromwell (1599–1658)] [late 17C–19C] a chamberpot.

oliver's summons *n.* [anecdote of one *Oliver*, a Limerick landlord, who impounded the goods of those who worked for him until the job was properly done] [19C] (*Irish*) an idle person who is forced to work for lack of any alternative means of making money.

oliver (twist) *n.* [rhy. sl.] **1** [mid-19C+] a fist. **2** [late 19C+] (*Aus.*) the wrist. **3** [1930s–70s] a deliberately incorrect entry in a ledger, usu. bookmaker use; usu. as *put the oliver on* [the use of the *fist* to write]. **4** [1960s] (*Aus. prison*) an indeterminate length of prison sentence, known as 'The Oliver'.

oliver twist *adj.* [rhy. sl. = PISSED *adj.*[1]] [1990s+] drunk.

ollapod *n.* [SE *ollapodrida*, a hotchpotch, a mixture, i.e. his mixing of remedies; from Ollapod, a character in G. Colman the Younger's play *The Poor Gentleman* (1802)] [mid-19C] a country apothecary.

'oller, boys, 'oller *n. see* HOLLER BOYS, HOLLER *n.*

olli compolli *n.* [? Sp. *olla*, a jar, and thus a dish containing a great variety of ingredients, a hotchpotch; thus, suggests Partridge, 'the Jack-of-all-trades'; the term is cited in Dekker's *O per se O* (1612) as a nickname, indicating that he is the chief of a given order of rogues, rather than a designation as such] [late 17C–mid-19C] (*UK Und.*) 'the name of one of the principal rogues of the canting crew' (Grose 1785).

ollie beak *n.* [rhy. sl.; ult. 'Ollie Beak', a glove puppet star of the 1960s BBC Children's Show Five O'clock Club] [1990s+] a Sikh.

ollies *n.* [1970s] testicles.

olly *n.* [rhy. sl.; ult. UK actor *Oliver Reed* (1938–99)] **1** [1960s+] marijuana [WEED *n.*[1] (4)]. **2** [1980s] amphetamines [SPEED *n.* (6)].

-ology *n.* [early 19C+] an abstract, a theory, an '-ism'.

olympic pool *n.* [? where one does the 'breast-stroke'] [1950s+] (*Aus.*) an outdoor cinema.

omadhaun *n.* (*also* **amadáin, amadan, amadaun, ohmadaun, omadawn**) [Irish *amadán*, a fool: a form of *onmitán*; from *oń*, a fool] [mid-19C+] (*Irish*) a fool.

Omahog *n.* [late 19C–1960s] (*US*) a resident of Omaha, Nebraska.

O'Malley *n.* [use of Irish surname O'Malley as a generic] [1990s+] a police officer, usu. male.

Omar Sharif *n.* [rhy. sl. = GRIEF *n.*[1] (1); ult. film actor *Omar Sharif* (b.1932)] [2000s] unpleasantness, unhappiness.

-o-matic *sfx* ['technological' sfx *-omatic*] [1970s+] (*US campus*) a sfx indicating intensity or repetition, e.g. CRAM-O-MATIC *under* CRAM *v.*

ombrey *n. see* HOMBRE *n.*

omee *n.* (*also* **omer, omey, omi, homa, homee, homer, homey, homie**) [Polari, Ital. *uomo*, a man] **1** [mid-19C] a landlord. **2** [mid–late 19C] a master, a boss. **3** [mid-19C+] a man; often (*gay*) a heterosexual man.

omee-polone *n.* (*also* **homi-polone, omee-paloney, omipalone**) [OMEE *n.* + POLONE *n.*] [1960s+] (*Ling. Fr./Polari*) a male homosexual.

omer/omey *n. see* OMEE *n.*

o.m.h. *n.* [2000s] (*US*) another man's girlfriend or partner, lit. other men's hos.

omi *n. see* OMEE *n.*

omipalone *n. see* OMEE-POLONE *n.*

omnibus *n.* [anyone can buy a 'ride'] [mid–late 19C] **1** a prostitute. **2** the vagina.

omo *n.* [fr. *Omo* brand of washing powder] [1960s] a derog. name for a black person.

on *adj.* **1** terms of intoxication [Hotten (1864) suggests that the intoxicated person is 'on the road', presumably to collapse]. (**a**) [19C+] tipsy, slightly drunk. (**b**) [1930s+] intoxicated on a drug of any kind; compare ON *prep.* (7a). **2** involved in, part of. (**a**) [early 19C+] involved in a wager; thus *get on*, to place a bet; [1930s+] phr. *you're on*, your bet has been taken. (**b**) [late 19C+] (*orig. US*) in favour of, or willing to take part in something, ready to do something, e.g. *I'm on*, I agree with that, *you're on*, accepting a challenge or a bet. **3** positive terms. (**a**) [mid-19C–1950s] (*US*) fully comprehending or well aware of. (**b**) [late 19C+] (*later use US black*) sophisticated, informed, at an advantage, fashionable. (**c**) [late 19C+] (*US*) good, positive [as opposed to OFF *adj.*[1] (4)]. (**d**) [1930s+] (*Aus.*) alert, keeping one's eye on someone. **4** [1910s–50s] of a cigarette etc, alight, e.g. *with a fag on*. **5** [1930s+] available on a menu [as opposed to OFF *adj.*[1] (6)]. **6** [1930s+] in love with, having a (sexual) relationship. **7** [1960s+] (*US*) being the focus of attention, performing, needing to impress [entertainment industry, as if *on stage*]. **8** [1970s+] menstruating [*on the rag* under RAG *n.*[1]]. **9** [1980s] pregnant. **10** [1990s+] sexually excited [SE *on heat*].

on *adv.* [backsl.] [mid-19C+] no.

on *prep.* **1** [mid-19C–1920s] (*UK Und.*) concentrating or focused on. **2** [mid-19C+] to the disadvantage or detriment of someone, so as to affect or disturb, e.g. *pass out on*, *have a joke on*. **3** [late 19C+] debited to, paid for by, e.g. *lunch is on me*. **4** [20C+] pitted against, attacking. **5** [1910s] due, owed. **6** [1920s+] playing a given musical instrument. **7** terms of consumption. (**a**) [1930s+] (*orig. US drugs*) in a general sense, using or addicted to a given drug, usu. combined with the drug's name, e.g. *on acid, on smack*; compare ON *adj.* (1b). (**b**) [1960s+] consuming a given drink, e.g. *on shorts, on rum*. (**c**) [1960s+] (*US campus*) using the contraceptive pill. **8** [1940s+] doing, having the responsibility for, taking the job of, e.g. *Sally's on nights this week.* **9** [1940s+] destined to secure a seduction. **10** [1970s+] up to, the responsibility of, a person's choice. **11** [1990s+] facing, destined for. **12** [1990s+] sentenced for. **13** [2000s] (*UK black*) (sexually) attracted to.

IN PHRASES

❑ **put someone on** *v.* **1** [1940s–60s] (*drugs*) to give or sell drugs. **2** [2000s] (*US black*) to recruit someone into a criminal organization, thus allowing them to start enjoying the financial and social benefits of membership.

on a ay yo trip *phr. see under* TRIP *n.*[4].

on about *phr.* [1950s+] interested in, talking about.

on all fours with *v.* [late 19C–1920s] to square with, to conform, agree, fit.

on and off *n.* [rhy. sl.] [1990s+] a cough.

on appro *adv.* [abbr. SE *on approval*] [mid-19C+] on sale or return.

on board *adv.* [naut. imagery] [19C+] referring to drink that has been consumed.

once *n.*[1] [SE *on!*, advance, go forward] [late 19C] vigour, energy, cheek.

once *n.*[2] **1** [late 19C–1900s] in pl., wages [they come *once* a week]. **2** [1930s+] a £1 note; one pound sterling [ONCER *n.* (2)].

once *n.*[3] *see* ONCE-OVER *n.*

once a week *n.*[1] [rhy. sl.] **1** [late 19C] a magistrate [= BEAK *n.*[1] (1)]. **2** [20C+] cheek.

once a week *n.*[2] [1920s] (*US Und.*) a regular (weekly) bribe paid to a local official or law officer.

once-a-week man *n.* [debtors, who could not be arrested on a Sunday, hid indoors for the rest of the week] [early 19C] a debtor, one who goes out only once a week.

once-over *n.* (*also* **once**) (*orig. US*) **1** [1910s+] a quick glance of appraisal; usu. in phr. *give the once-over*, to look over, to assess. **2** [1920s+] a search, of a place or at customs. **3** [1930s+] a quick treatment or superficial job, such as a quick clean-up.

once-over *v.* [ONCE-OVER *n.*] [1920s+] to glance at, to survey.

oncer *n.* **1** of a single action. (**a**) [late 19C–1910s] a person who only goes to church once on Sunday; thus *twicer*, one who goes to both matins and evensong. (**b**) [1920s+] (*Aus.*) anything that happens only once. (**c**) [1930s] (*US*) a girl who has many very brief affairs. (**d**) [1940s+] (*gay*) a homosexual who never repeats a sexual encounter with any one partner but continues to seek new people. (**e**) [1960s] (*US*) a man who can only have one orgasm during one session of sexual activity. **2** [1930s+] a £1 note; a A$1 bill.

DERIVATIVES

❑ **oncing** *n.* [1940s+] (*gay*) the refusal to commit a second sexual act with the same partner.

once-round *n.*

IN PHRASES

❑ **give (someone) once-round** *v.* [1900s] (*Aus.*) to scold.

oncus *adj.*[1] (*also* **ongkus, onkiss, onkus**) [ety. unknown; ? link to HONK *v.*[2]] [20C+] (*Aus./N.Z.*) **1** of people, upset, out of sorts, disagreeable. **2** of an inanimate object or situation, out of order, problematic. **3** of food or drink, stale.

oncus *adj.*[2] (*also* **ongkus**) [ety. unknown; Baker (1941) sees this as 'occasional' use only; *AND* cites only ONCUS *adj.*[1]; *DNZE* only this] [1910s+] (*Aus./N.Z.*) good, profitable, pleasant.

ond! *excl.* see OD! *excl.*

on doog *adj.* [backsl.; ON *adv.* + DOOG *adj.*] [mid-19C+] no good.

one *n.*[1] (*orig. US*) **1** terms pertaining to violence. (**a**) [mid-19C+] (*also* **one-er**) a blow with the fist; occas. ext. to *two, three, four*, etc. (**b**) [20C+] a punishment, a beating e.g. *I'll give you one*, also fig. use, a bad turn. (**c**) [1900s] an unpleasant look. (**d**) [1910s+] a bullet, a gunshot. **2** terms pertaining to communication. (**a**) [mid-19C+] a joke on, an act of teasing; a hoax. (**b**) [late 19C] a derog. name, a word of abuse. (**c**) [late 19C+] an anecdote, an amusing story, a joke, e.g. *have you heard the one about …?* (**d**) [late 19C+] a 'line', a persuasive if mendacious story, a lie. (**e**) [1950s+] an excuse. **3** terms pertaining to the body and sexual intercourse. (**a**) [late 19C+] the penis. (**b**) [late 19C+] any act of bodily eructation; see LET ONE GO below. (**c**) [1940s+] an act of sexual intercourse. (**d**) [1960s] an act of defecation. (**e**) [1970s] the vagina. **4** terms pertaining to consumption. (**a**) [late 19C+] a drink, usu. in the phr. *come and have one*, join me for a drink; often comb. as *big one, stiff one*, etc. (**b**) [1920s] (*US*) an inhalation of cocaine. (**c**) [1940s+] a state of drunkenness. (**d**) [1960s+] a cannabis cigarette. (**e**) [1970s+] constr. with *the*, cannabis oil, THC. (**f**) [1980s+] a hangover. (**g**) [1990s+] a heroin injection. (**h**) [1990s+] an adventure, a time, a spree. **5** terms pertaining to individuals. (**a**) [late 19C+] an eccentric or amusing person. (**b**) [late 19C+] one who stands out in some way, either for impudence, expertise etc, esp. as *a one for*. (**c**) [1930s–60s] a male homosexual [? old US Army joke, Sergeant, counting off, 'Are you one?' Soldier, 'Yeth, are you one too?'; Trimble labels this as 'Conv.(entional)']. (**d**) [1960s] an unpleasant person, i.e. a CUNT *n.* (**e**) [1980s] a fool, a dupe. (**f**) [1990s+] a friend. **6** [1910s+] (*UK Und.*) a crime.

IN PHRASES

pertaining to violence

❑ **deal someone one** *v.* [1980s+] (*N.Z.*) **1** to attack someone, to give someone a blow or a beating. **2** to pay someone back (for an injury or slight). ❑ **give someone one** *v.* (*also* **hand someone one**) **1** [mid-19C+] to hit. **2** [late 19C+] to have sexual intercourse, to kiss etc. ❑ **hang one on** *v.* **1** [20C+] to hit someone, to have a fight; also in fig. use. **2** [1910s] to impose a task or burden. **3** [1970s] (*US*) to have an affair. ❑ **lay one on someone** *v.* [1930s+] (*US*) to hit or beat someone. ❑ **pass someone one** *v.* [1900s–10s] (*Aus.*) to hit someone. ❑ **put one on** *v.* (*also* **put one in, …over**) [the *one* is a blow] **1** [1910s+] (*orig. Aus.*) to hit. **2** [2000s] (*N.Z.*) to confront (without violence). ❑ **stick one on** *v.* (*also* **stick one into**) [1910s+] to hit.

pertaining to communication

❑ **go into one** *v.* [1980s+] **1** to lose one's temper, to lose emotional control. **2** to launch into a speech or diatribe. ❑ **put one over (on)** *v.* (*also* **get one over (on), put all over on, put something over on, slip one over, sneak one over on**) [late 19C+] (*orig. US*) to cheat, to deceive. ❑ **throw one** *v.* [1990s+] to lose one's temper, to have an emotional outburst.

pertaining to the body

❑ **get one on** *v.* (*US*) **1** [1910s] to become very excited. **2** [1970s] of a man, to have an erection. ❑ **give her one** *v.* **1** [late 19C+] of a man, to have sexual intercourse. **2** [1940s] to kiss. ❑ **have one up** *v.* [1960s] of a woman, to be pregnant. ❑ **knock one out** *v.* [1990s+] to masturbate. ❑ **let one go** *v.* (*also* **let one fly, …off, …rip**) [mid-17C; late 19C+] to break wind; to burp. ❑ **one off the wrist** *n.* [1960s+] the act of masturbation. ❑ **throw one into** *v.* [1970s] of a man, to have sexual intercourse.

pertaining to consumption

❑ **get one in** *v.* (*also* **get them, get them in**) [20C+] to order and pay for a round of drinks, esp. as excl. *get them in!* ❑ **have one on the city** *v.* [the city-run water supply] [19C+] (*US*) to have a drink of water. ❑ **have one too many** *v.* [euph.] [20C+] to be drunk. ❑ **high one** *n.* [late 19C–1910s] (*US*) a large drink. ❑ **one for the bitumen** *n.* (*also* **one for the street**) [*the bitumen*, a tarred road, esp. the road from Darwin to Alice Springs] [1950s+] (*Aus.*) a last drink, before starting a journey or leaving. ❑ **one for the ditch** *n.* [1960s+] (*US*) a final drink, but, rather than the trad. *one for the road*, this var. acknowledges the perils of drunken driving. ❑ **one for the road** *n.* (*also* **off-setter**) [virtually SE by 1950] **1** [20C+] a final drink before departure; extended to a measure of drugs, i.e. cocaine. **2** [1990s+] in fig. use. ❑ **get one going** *v.* [late 19C+] to drink heavily. ❑ **hang one on** *v.* [1940s+] to be drunk. ❑ **have one or two** *v.* [late 19C+] to be drunk. ❑ **stop one** *v.* **1** [20C+] (*also* **stop it**) to be wounded. **2** [1900s–30s] (*Aus.*) to have a drink.

general uses

❑ **make one** *v.* ['one' is either an escape, a plan, a drink or a murder] **1** [1970s] (*UK prison*) to plan and effect an escape, also as phrs. *make one out, make one with*, to commit a crime or to escape in partnership with one or more other people. **2** [1970s] (*UK Und.*) to put together plans for a crime, esp. a robbery, and then carry out that crime. **3** [1970s] to join in with, e.g. for a drink. **4** [2000s] to commit a murder. ❑ **put one in** *v.* [the *one* is a bullet] [1980s] (*US*) to shoot dead. ❑ **put one together** *v.* [1970s+] (*UK Und.*) to plan a crime.

IN EXCLAMATIONS

❑ **do one!** [1990s+] a general term of dismissal.

SE in slang uses

IN COMPOUNDS

❑ **one-a-man** *n.* [one of these dumplings will satisfy a man's appetite] [1950s] (*W.I.*) a large, round dumpling, using a pound of flour. ❑ **one-and-a-half** *n.* [1980s] £150. ❑ **one-away** *adv.* [1990s+] (*W.I.*) intimately, on a one-to-one. ❑ **one-fifty-one** *n.* (*also* **151**) [ety. unknown; ? Calif. or NY penal code number] **1** [1980s+] (*drugs*) crack cocaine. **2** (*also* **one-five-o**) heroin. ❑ **one-off** *n.* [1980s] (*US*) an act of (casual) sexual intercourse (with a stranger). ❑ **one on** *n.* [late 19C] (*US*) a portion of oyster stew.

IN PHRASES

❑ **do one** *v.* [1910s+] to leave, to run away. ❑ **go up one** [school use, whereby the successful pupil goes up a place or class] [late 19C] a general compliment. ❑ **make someone one** *v.* [the image of the woman and the embryo being 'two' people] [1960s] (*US*) to give someone an abortion. ❑ **one for the book** *n.* [the *record book*] [1920s+] (*US*) anything noteworthy, remarkable or incredible, something worthy of long-term record. ❑ **one in ten** *n.* [the tithes paid by his parishioners] [late 17C–mid-19C] a parson. ❑ **one in the dark** *n.* [opposite of ONE IN THE LIGHT below] [1900–30s] (*US*) a cup of black coffee. ❑ **one in the light** *n.* [opposite of ONE IN THE DARK above] [1900s] (*US*) a white coffee, a coffee with cream. ❑ **one of 'em** *n.* [mid–late 19C] (*US*) a remarkable or admirable person. ❑ **one on someone's tibby** *n.* [? ON ONE'S TIBBY DROP *under* TIBBY DROP *n.*] [mid-19C] (*UK Und.*) 'I owe you one' (Kent). ❑ **one over the eight** (*also* **one over the nine, two over the eight**) [the *eight* being pints, a supposed 'safe' amount of beer] [1910s+] (*orig. UK milit.*) drunk. ❑ **one-percenter** *n.* [the supposed 1% of motorcycle users who refuse to abide by legal and societal rules] [1950s+] (*orig. US*) an outlaw bike rider.

one *n.*[2] [1940s+] (*orig. US*) nothing, not a single one, usu. with qualifying negative, e.g. *He won't get dime one out of me* etc

one *adj.* [early 19C+] used with a n. to emphasize a comment e.g. *one serious boy, one angry young man*; esp. as abbr./euph for *one hell of a*.

SE in slang uses

IN COMPOUNDS

❑ **one-bagger** *n.* [such an individual is so ugly one would need to put a bag over their head before having sexnote Urquhart, *The Complete Works of Rabelais* (1653): 'To be short, they occupied [i.e. had sex with] all like good souls; only, to those that were horribly ugly and ill-favoured, I caused their head to be put within a bag to hide their face'] [1980s+] (*US campus*) a very ugly person. ❑ **one-cheek squeak** *n.* [1990s+] an instance of breaking wind. ❑ **one-finger(ed) salute** *n.* [1960s+] (*US*) an obscene gesture of contempt. ❑ **one-finger exercise** *n.* [pun] [1920s+] manual stimulation of the vagina or clitoris. ❑ **one foot** *n.* see TWELVE INCHES *under* TWELVE *adj.* ❑ **one-hand magazine** *n.* [1960s+] a pornographic magazine, used as an aid to masturbation. ▫ **one-horse** *adj.* (*also* **one-mule, one-pub**) [18C SE *one-horse*, drawn or worked, by a single horse] [mid-19C+] **1** (*orig. US*) of places, insignificant, esp. as in *one-horse town*, a small town of no importance. **2** of individuals, second-rate, petty; usu. of politicians, minor officials. ▫ **one-legged race** *n.* [1970s+] masturbation. ▫ **one-leg trouser** *n.* [resemblance] [late 19C] a style of skirt, tight and straight, popular in the 1890s. ▫ **one-lunger** *n.* **1** [20C+] (*US*) a single-cylinder vehicle, usu. a motorcycle. **2** [1930s] (*US Und.*) a consumptive. **3** [1940s+] (*US*) any small or inferior set-up or device. **4** [2000s] (*US*) an eccentric. ▫ **one-piece overcoat** *n.* [1950s+] a condom.

IN PHRASES

▫ **one brick short of a load** *adj. see under* …SHORT OF… *adj.* ▫ **one eye and a winkle** *n.* [1950s] a blind person or a person with one eye. ▫ **one fat lady** *n.* [resemblance to her opulent curves] [1950s+] (*bingo*) the number eight. ▫ **one good woman** *n.* [1970s+] (*US black*) the ideal soulmate, considerate, sympathetic and prob. sexy too. ▫ **one sandwich short of a picnic** *adj. see under* …SHORT OF… *adj.* ▫ **one sausage short of a B.B.Q.** *adj. see under* …SHORT OF… *adj.* ▫ **one-skinner** *n. see under* SKIN *n.*[1]. ▫ **one stop short of East Ham** *adj. see under* …SHORT OF… *adj.*

one *phr.* [2000s] (*US teen*) goodbye, 'see you later'.

on e *phr.* [*on* empty] [1990s+] (*US black*) lacking, usu. but not invariably money.

one alone *n.* [rhy. sl.] [20C+] (*Aus.*) a moan.

one and eight *n.* [rhy. sl.] [20C+] a plate.

one and elevenpence three farden *n.* [rhy. sl.] **1** [late 19C+] a garden. **2** [1940s] I beg your pardon.

one and half *n.* [rhy. sl.] [20C+] a scarf.

one and nine *n.* [rhy. sl.] [1980s] a line.

one-and-one *n.*[1] (*also* **wan and wan**) [? early Italian immigrant chip-shop owners, whose lack of English meant that one signalled with one finger for chips and added another for fish] [1910s+] (*Irish*) a portion of fish and chips.

one-and-one *n.*[2] *see* ONE-ON-ONE *n.* (2).

one and one *v.* [ONE-ON-ONE *n.* (2a)] [1970s+] (*drugs*) to inhale cocaine or heroin.

one and other *n.* [rhy. sl.] [2000s] (*Irish*) brother.

one and t'other *n.* [rhy. sl.] **1** [1910s+] a brother. **2** [1930s+] a mother.

one and two *n. see* ONES AND TWOS *n.*[2].

one another *n.* [rhy. sl.] **1** [late 19C+] a brother. **2** [20C+] a mother.

one-arm *adj.* (*also* **one-armed**) [backform. f. ONE-ARM (JOINT) *n.*] [1950s+] (*US*) of a shop, police post etc, run by one person.

one-arm (joint) *n.* (*also* **one-arm lunch(room), one-arm restaurant**) [SE *one arm* + JOINT *n.* (1)/SE *restaurant/lunchroom*; such a café provided food one could eat with one hand] [late 19C–1970s] (*US*) a fast-food café.

one-eight *n. see* EIGHTH *n.*

one-eight-seven *n.* (*also* **one eighty seven, 187**) [used generically, based on the actual California penal code for homicide] **1** [1940s+] a homicide. **2** [1990s+] in fig. use any form of crisis or drama. **3** [1990s+] (*US prison*) targeted for assassination.

one-eight-seven *adj.* [ONE-EIGHT-SEVEN *n.* (1)] [1990s+] (*US*) murdered, dead.

one-eight-seven *v.* (*also* **one eighty seven, 187**) [ONE-EIGHT-SEVEN *n.*] [1990s+] (*US black gang*) to murder; thus gang slogan used by the Crips of Los Angeles *B187*, 'we kill Bloods'.

one-eighty *n.* [a 180° turn] **1** [1950s+] (*US, orig. milit.*) a complete reversal of plans, thoughts, action. **2** [1990s+] a 180° turn in an automobile.

one-eighty *v.* (*also* **make a one-eighty**) [a 180° turn] [1980s+] (*US*) to reverse, esp. of a vehicle.

one-er *n.* **1** *see* ONE *n.*[1] (1). *see* ONER *n.* (1).

one-eyed *adj.* **1** [mid-19C+] (*US*) of a person, crooked, dishonest. **2** [mid-19C+] (*orig. US*) (*also* **one-eye**) of a place or object, inferior, inadequate, unimportant. **3** [1910s+] (*orig. US/Aus.*) used in a variety of combs. as the penis; other than those listed below, *one-eyed bob, one-eyed guardsman, one-eyed pants python, one-eyed rocket.*

IN COMPOUNDS

▫ **one-eyed brother** *n.* [BROTHER *n.* (2)] [1990s+] (*US black*) the penis. ▫ **one-eyed Cyclops** *n.* (*also* **hairy Cyclops**) [SE *Cyclops*; tautological, since all Cyclops are one-eyed (Gr. *kuklops*)] [1990s+] the penis. ▫ **one-eyed monster** *n.* [1960s+] (*US*) **1** the penis. **2** a television set. ▫ **one-eyed stag** *n.* [late 18C] the penis. ▫ **one-eyed trouser-snake** *n.* (*also* **one-eyed bed snake, one-eyed trouser mouse, tan trouser snake, trouser serpent**) [mid-19C;1940s+] (*orig. US/Aus.*) the penis. ▫ **one-eyed (wonder) worm** *n.* (*also* **one-armed trouser worm**) [WORM *n.*] [1980s+] the penis. ▫ **one-eyed zipper fish** *n.* [1990s+] the penis.

IN PHRASES

▫ **have a conversation with the one-eyed trouser snake** *v.* [1990s+] to masturbate. ▫ **one-eyed boy with his shirtsleeves rolled up** *n.* [1960s+] a circumcised penis. ▫ **slay the one-eyed monster** *v.* [1960s+] to masturbate.

one-eyed scribe *n.* **1** [mid–late 19C] (*US*) a revolver, a pistol. **2** [1970s+] (*US black*) a monumental liar, an insignificant person, poss. because they cannot be trusted to tell the truth.

one for his nob *n.* [rhy. sl. = BOB *n.*[3] (2)] [20C+] a shilling (5p).

one-hitter *n. see under* HIT *n.*

180 *n.*

IN PHRASES

▫ **do a 180** *v.* [1970s+] (*orig. US campus*) to change one's life radically.

one hundred pounds to a China orange *phr. see* LOMBARD STREET TO A CHINA ORANGE *phr.*

one hundred smackers *n.* [fig. use of *one hundred* SMACKERS *n.*, £100] [1990s+] (*US prison*) a prison sentence of 100 years.

onener *n.* [? SE *one and a*, i.e. ext. of ONE *n.*[1] (1)] [mid–late 19C] a heavy blow.

one-nighter *n.* (*US*) **1** [1910s+] of a musician, band or show, a single performance in one place only. **2** [1940s+] an affair or sexual relationship of one night's duration; the person with whom this occurs.

one-night stand *n.* [entertainment jargon *one night stand*, the giving of only one performance in a specific venue before moving on] **1** [late 19C+] (*US*) a small rural town. **2** [20C+] an affair that lasts only a single night, thus a person with whom one has such a relationship.

one of… *phr.*

SE in slang uses

IN PHRASES

▫ **one of King John's men** *n.* [late 18C–early 19C] a small person, often as *one of King John's men, eight score to the hundred.* ▫ **one of my cousins** *n.* [euph. used presumably when the man accidentally meets a friend and has to make an introduction] [late 17C–early 19C] a prostitute. ▫ **one of the faithful** *n.* [SE *one of the faithful*, a member of a religious sect] **1** [17C] a drunkard. **2** [late 18C–early 19C] a tailor who gives extended credit. ▫ **one of the knights, to be** *v.* [the disease attacks one's SWORD *n.* (1)] [1940s–70s] (*gay*) to have syphilis. ▫ **one of the livery** *n.* [*livery* companies, military or city bands distinguished by their uniforms and badges, in the cuckold's case the 'badge' he 'wears' is that of the HORNS *n.*] [late 17C] a cuckold. ▫ **one of them** *n.* [euph.] **1** [19C+] a prostitute. **2** [late 19C–1900s] a shilling (5p) [ety. unknown; ? sense 1, i.e. the cost of a cheap prostitute]. **3** [1970s+] a male homosexual. ▫ **one of those** *n.* [euph.] **1** [late 19C+] a male homosexual. **2** [1970s+] (*US gay*) a heterosexual woman, any woman. ▫ **one of us** *n.* **1** [late 18C–early 19C] a prostitute. **2** [1930s+] a male homosexual.

one-on-one *n.* **1** [1960s+] (*orig. US*) a fight between two individuals (as opposed to a gang fight or an unequal competition). **2** [1980s+] (*drugs*) (*also* **one-and-one**). (**a**) cocaine, a line of cocaine. (**b**) a dose of one tablet of

Talwin (a painkiller) + one tablet of Pyribenzamine (an antihistamine).

IN PHRASES

❑ **one-on-one house** *n.* [1980s+] (*drugs*) a place where cocaine and heroin can be purchased.

one-on-one *adj.* [1960s+] (*orig. US*) person-to-person, intimate or confrontational, e.g. a fight.

one-on-one *adv.* [1970s+] in an intimate, person-to-person manner.

IN PHRASES

❑ **go one-on-one** *v.* [1960s+] (*orig. US*) to have a direct confrontation with another person.

one or the other *n.* [rhy. sl.] [1990s+] one's mother.

one out *n.* [ONE OUT *adj.*] [1980s+] (*Aus. prison*) a prisoner who prefers his own company.

one out *adj.* [1940s+] (*Aus.*) alone; thus *two-out*, with a single accomplice or helper; *ten out*, in a team or gang of ten etc.

one-out fight *n.* [one person comes *out* of the group] [1920s+] (*Aus. teen*) a fight between the two champions of a pair of rival teen gangs.

one out of the bag *n.* (*also* **one out of the box**) [1930s+] (*Aus.*) a surprising person; an unexpected piece of good luck or pleasant event.

IN PHRASES

❑ **out of the bag** *adj.* [1950s+] (*Aus.*) surprising, remarkable.

one-pot screamer *n.* (*also* **middy screamer, pint screamer, schooner screamer, two-pot screamer**) [1960s+] (*Aus.*) **1** one who cannot hold their liquor without becoming obstreperously drunk; *one-* or *two-pot* refer to the need for only one or two drinks before they lose all control; *middy*, *pint* and *schooner* refer to glass sizes and denote the (small) amount of alcohol required for this effect. **2** in fig. use, one who panics easily.

oner *n.* **1** [mid-19C–1910s] (*also* **one-er**) a remarkable or outstanding person or event [predates ONE *n.*[1] (5a) hence poss. Cockney pron. of SE *wonder* = *wunner*]. **2** [mid-19C–1920s] a knockout blow [ONE *n.*[1] (1)]. **3** (*also* **one-er**) in monetary uses. (**a**) [late 19C–1900s] a shilling (5p). (**b**) [late 19C+] £1. (**c**) [1950s+] £100. **4** [1950s+] (*Aus.*) an amusing or eccentric person, or joke.

IN PHRASES

❑ **do one's one-er** *v.* [only one life to live] [1940s+] to die.

onery *adj. see* ORNERY *adj.*

ones *n.* [1940s+] the female breast, usu. pl. and qualified by an adj. e.g. *big ones*, large female breasts; *nice ones*, attractive breasts.

ones and twos *n.*[1] [rhy. sl.] [1920s+] (*Aus./US*) shoes.

ones and twos *n.*[2] (*also* **one and two**) [1990s+] (*rap music*) two turntables, as used by a hip-hop DJ.

...one's tits off *phr. see under* TIT *n.*[2].

one thousand miles *n. see* THOUSAND-MILER *n.*

one-time *n.* [ety. unknown; ? warning 'I'll tell you just one more time...'] [1980s+] (*US black*) a police officer or the police as an institution.

one time! *excl.*[1] [1990s+] (*US black*) exactly! you're quite right! indeed!

one time! *excl.*[2] [ONE-TIME *n.*] [2000s] (*US prison*) a shout of warning: an officer has appeared.

one-two *n.* [? boxing jargon *one-two*, two quick punches or jabs] **1** [19C+] in fig. use, a knockout blow; often ext. as *old one-two, the* under OLD *adj.* **2** [1900s–40s] (*US*) a speedy exit, a quick departure. **3** [1940s] a quick survey. **4** [1960s] an act of male masturbation.

one-two checker *n.* [the trad. *one-two, one-two* used to check a microphone or PA system] [1990s+] (*rap music*) a cautious person, one who assesses a given situation.

one, two, three, be *v.* [late 19C–1910s] (*US*) to stand out, to succeed (in comparison with).

one way *n.* [play on SE *one way trip*/TRIP *n.*[4] (1)] [1960s+] (*drugs*) LSD.

one-way *adj.* **1** [1930s–40s] (*US*) honest, e.g. a *one-way guy*, an honest man; thus a *two-way guy*, a crook. **2** [1940s+] (*US*) narrow- or close-minded; obsessive; self-interested. **3** [1960s] (*US gay*) heterosexual.

one-way girl *n.* [SE *one way* + *girl*] [1930s] (*US Und.*) a prostitute who offers only 'straight' intercourse.

one-way kid *n.* [one who takes but does not give] [1920s] (*US*) a greedy person.

one-way man *n.* [1960s] (*US gay*) **1** a male prostitute. **2** a male homosexual who is passive but not active.

one-way pockets *n.* [money enters but never leaves] [1910s+] a miser's pockets.

one-way ride *n.* [the victim is driven away by his killers but only they will return] [1930s–50s] (*US Und.*) a gangland murder.

one with, be *v.* [mid-19C] to get even with.

one with t'other *n.* [mid-17C–19C] an act of sexual intercourse.

on fire *adj.* [1980s+] doing very well, typically of a rock band, a sportsperson or some similar achiever.

on for *phr.* **1** [late 19C] keen on. **2** [late 19C+] destined for, promised to have.

IN PHRASES

❑ **on for a tater** *adj.* (*also* **on for a tatur**) [SE *on* + Fr. *tête à tête*, an intimate conversation] [late 19C–1900s] obsessed, fascinated, usu. used of a man who is desperate to talk to a woman he is attempting to pick up. ❑ **on for young and old** *n.* [1940s+] (*Aus.*) complete disorder, utter chaos, a free-for-all.

on full *adj.* [car fuel gauge imagery] [1990s+] (*US black*) well supplied with a given commodity, usu. (but not always) money.

ongkus *adj. see under* ONCUS.

on half cock *adj.* [SE *half cock* + COCK *n.*[3] (1)] [late 19C] of the penis, semi-erect.

on heat *adj.* (*also* **in heat**) [SE *on heat*, usu. applied to female animals, esp. bitches] [late 19C+] of a woman, sexually excited; occas. of a man.

onicker *n.* [her price, one NICKER *n.*[2] (1)] [late 19C] a prostitute.

onion *n.*[1] **1** from the shape. (**a**) [early–mid-19C] (*UK Und.*) a watch-seal; thus *bunch of onions*, a number of seals worn on one ring; *onion hunter*, one who steals such seals. (**b**) [late 19C+] the head. (**c**) [1920s–40s] (*US Und.*) a watch or clock. (**d**) [1930s+] (*also* **bunion**) in pl., the testicles. (**e**) [1940s] in pl., the eyes. (**f**) [1950s] a ball. (**g**) [1990s+] (*US campus*) the buttocks. **2** one or that which fig. 'stinks'. (**a**) [1900s–40s] (*US*) an idiot. (**b**) [1930s–40s] (*US Und.*) of a crime, a failure. **3** as a sum of money [play on CABBAGE *n.*[2] (1); KALE *n.* (1); POTATO *n.* (5) etc]. (**a**) [1900s–50s] (*US*) $1. (**b**) [1980s+] (*US campus*) $100. **4** [1930s–40s] (*US Und.*) a tear-gas bomb.

IN COMPOUNDS

❑ **onion act** *n.* (*also* **onion action**) [? like an onion, it reduces one to tears + the use of onions to create fake 'tears'] [1940s+] (*US black*) an unacceptable, offensive act or situation. ❑ **onion money** *n.* [1970s] a fine. ❑ **onion peeler** *n.* [play on SE, but note sense 1b above] [1940s–60s] (*orig. US black*) a switchblade knife. ❑ **onion skin** *n.* [1960s+] (*US gay*) a long foreskin.

IN PHRASES

❑ **off one's onion** *adj.* [late 19C+] crazy.

SE in slang uses

IN PHRASES

❑ **give someone onions** *v.* [one's watering eyes] [late 19C–1900s] to attack physically.

onion *n.*[2] [pron. 'on-i-on', i.e. 'on and on'] [1960s+] (*Aus.*) **1** mass sexual intercourse with a single woman. **2** the woman who has sex with two or more men in such a session.

onion *n.*[3] [ety. unknown] **1** [1980s+] (*US drugs*) 28g (1oz) of marijuana. **2** [1990s+] 28g (1oz) of cocaine.

onionhead *n.* **1** [1910s–50s] (*US*) a stupid person [-HEAD *sfx* (1)]. **2** (*US*) in senses of a smooth, peeled onion. (**a**) [1930s–70s] a bald-headed person [SE *head*]. (**b**) [1990s+] a close, shaved haircut.

onions! *excl. see* WEE BUNS! *under* WEE *adj.*

on it *phr.*[1] [ON *adj.* (2a)] **1** [mid-19C] (*US Und.*) involved in criminality. **2** [mid-19C+] ready, prepared, capable of, skilled in, in control; thus (*US black*) *to be on it like a hornet*. **3** [1980s] (*US campus*) good, likeable.

on it *phr.*[2] [ON *adj.* (1)] **1** [late 19C+] (*Aus.*) indulging (poss. to a noticeable excess) in drugs or drink. **2** [1950s] having sexual intercourse. **3** [1950s+] (*US*) addicted, whether to a drug or to a person or experience.

IN PHRASES

❑ **get on it** *v.* [1950s+] (*orig. N.Z.*) to go out on a drinking spree.

onk *n.* [pron.] [1910s] (*Aus.*) a franc.

onka *n.* (*also* **onkaparinga**) [rhy. sl., ult. *Onkaparinga*, the brandname of a make of woollen blanket; note Charleston (W.Va.) *Daily Mail* 20/1/1935: 'Onkapringa – More Chinese, or something. Means "good".'] [1960s+] (*Aus.*) a finger.

onkiss/onkus *adj. see* ONCUS *adj.*[1].

onky *adj.* [ONCUS *adj.*[1] or HONK *v.*[2] (1)] [1920s+] (*Aus.*) stinking, stale.

only ninety-nine cents out of the dollar *phr. see* … DOLLAR *under* NOT THE FULL… *phr.*

only one and ninepence in the florin *phr.* (*also* **…in two bob, …in two shillings**) [1910–70s] of someone who is not very intelligent, slightly eccentric, odd.

on my pratt *phr. see* IN MY BOLLOCKS *phr.*

on my sammy say-so *phr.* [assonant ext. of SE *say-so*] [18C–1910s] on my word of honour.

on offer *phr.* [1940s+] liable to problems.

on one *phr.* **1** [1980s+] (*US campus*) having a positive time. **2** [1990s+] behaving crazily.

on one's ownio *phr.* (*also* **on one's owny-o**) [cod Italian] [20C+] by oneself.

on one's ownsome *phr.* [1920s+] by oneself.

on plush *adv.* [SE *plush*, a type of cloth, softer than velvet, used for expensive garments, seat covers etc] [1920s–40s] in luxury.

IN PHRASES

❑ **sit in the plush** *v.* [1910s] to live in luxury.

onswoggled *adj. see* HORNSWOGGLED *adj.*

on swole *adj.* [SE *swollen*] [1990s+] (*US black teen*) **1** swollen, large, usu. of a penis, erect. **2** relaxed and free of stress [f. sense 1].

on tag *phr.* [2000s] wearing an electronic tag on one's ankle as a condition of parole.

on the cripple and crutch *phr.* [rhy. sl. = TOUCH *n.*[1] (5)] [1950s] looking for a loan.

on the G *adv.* [SE *genuine*] [2000s] (*US black*) honestly, sincerely.

on the go *phr.* **1** [late 17C–early 18C] on the verge of destruction. **2** [early 18C–1900s] in a state of decline. **3** [early 19C] slightly drunk, tipsy. **4** [early 19C+] active, lively. **5** [1940s] nervous. **6** [1950s+] happening, going on.

on the line *phr.* [gambling use] **1** [20C+] of money, either put at stake or, e.g. in the case of a drug deal, advanced as a loan. **2** [20C+] honest, straightforward. **3** [1940s–50s] (*US*) prepared, in the offing. **4** [1970s] under interrogation. **5** [1980s] (*Aus.*) under police observation. **6** [2000s] (*US prison*) for sale.

IN PHRASES

❑ **put one's ass on the line** *v.* (*also* **put one's balls on the line**) [ASS *n.* (4)/BALLS *n.* (3)] [1980s+] (*US*) to put oneself into a position of responsibility, to take risks; to face punishment. ❑ **put someone on the line** *v.* [1990s+] to place someone in a difficult or challenging position.

on the Murray cod *phr.* [rhy. sl. = *on the nod* under NOD *n.*[1]] **1** [1960s+] (*Aus.*) in gambling, betting on credit. **2** [1980s+] (*Aus. prison*) with an unspoken arrangement.

on the wagon *phr.* (*also* **on the cart, …water-cart, …water-wagon**) [SE *water-wagon*] **1** [late 19C+] voluntarily refraining from alcohol. **2** [1970s+] thus, by ext. adopting any form of self-denial, e.g. celibate, abandoning one's use of drugs.

IN PHRASES

❑ **climb the water-wagon** *v.* (*also* **ride the water-wagon**) [1900s–20s] to abstain from alcohol.

on tick *adv.* (*also* **on tic**) [the tick against one's name made on a slate or list] [mid-17C+] on credit.

IN PHRASES

❑ **go on/upon tick** *v.* [mid-17C+] to fall into debt.

on time *adv.* (*also* **on T**) [1940s+] (*US black*) at the emotionally or psychologically apposite moment (rather than the chronologically prompt one); of good quality.

IN PHRASES

❑ **get on time** *v.* [1940s+] (*US black*) to have fun.

onto *adj.* [late 19C+] aware of, esp. of someone's supposedly secret or underhand plans.

IN PHRASES

❑ **be onto** *v.* (*also* **get onto**) [late 19C+] to harrass, to nag. ❑ **put someone onto** *v.* **1** [late 19C+] (*orig. US*) to introduce a topic, to point out, esp. to point out a chance of possible social or financial gain etc. **2** [20C+] to introduce someone, to give access to someone.

on with *phr.* [mid-19C+] having a relationship with.

on you! *excl.* **1** [1920s+] (*Aus.*) hello! an excl. of welcome and support. **2** [1960s+] a general excl. of rejection.

o.o. *n.* [ONCE-OVER *n.*] [1910s–50s] (*US*) a brief glance, a visual assessment.

oobtay *n.* [backsl. *tube*] [1990s+] (*UK juv.*) a cigarette.

o.o.c. *adj.* [abbr. out of control] [1980s+] (*US campus*) drunk, high on drugs, acting crazy.

oochie *n.* [? baby-talk *coochie-coo*] [1980s+] (*US campus*) a charming, adorable person.

oochie-coochie *n.* [2000s] a child.

oodle *n.* [OODLES *n.*] [1940s–50s] (*Aus./N.Z.*) money.

oodles *n.* (*also* **oodlins, oudles**) [ety. unknown, though suggestions include a shortening of *the whole boodle* (Partridge), a *huddle* or close-packed group (Webster), which presumes that the var. *oodlins* comes from *huddling*, pressing together in a group. Cohen (1985) rejects these: such *huddle/huddling* refer mainly to animals, *oodles/oddlins* to people, and suggests a simple abbr. of *scadoodles/scadoodlin'*] [mid-19C+] (*orig. US*) a large amount, a great quantity (occas. in sing.).

Oodnagalahbi *n.* (*also* **Oodnawoopwoop**) [*Ooodna(datta)*, a small town in Western Australia + GALAH *n.* (1)] [1960s+] (*Aus.*) an imaginary, out-of-the-way, 'uncivilized' place.

oof *n.* (*also* **ooftish, uff**) [Ger. *auf tische*, on the table. The term originated c.1850 and, according to the *Sporting Times* 'the aristocracy of Houndsditch, being in the habit of refusing to play cards, unless the money were "on the table"'; thus Grey, *Hoods* (1952): 'Tauchess offen tisch, boyus. What's my cut?'] [late 19C–1930s] money.

DERIVATIVES

❑ **oofless** *adj.* [1900s–10s] impoverished. ❑ **oofy** *adj.* [note Wodehouse's wealthy character *Oofy Prosser* (lit. 'Rich Scrounger'] [late 19C–1920s] rich, wealthy.

IN COMPOUNDS

❑ **oof-bird** *n.* (*also* **oof-bag**) [late 19C–1910s] a source of money, one who can supply money.

IN PHRASES

❑ **pad the oof** *v.* [1900s] (*Aus. Und.*) to present a roll of banknotes folded in such a way that each one is counted twice.

oofay *see* OFAY *n.*

oofterpa *n.* [pig Lat. form of POOFTER *n.*] [1940s+] a male homosexual.

ooftish *n. see* OOF *n.*

oofus *n.* [? DOOFUS *n.* + SE *oaf*] [1930s+] (*US black*) a fool, a simpleton.

oofy *adj. see under* OOF *n.*

ooga-booga land *n.* [the racist imagery of chanting Africans] [1980s+] all-purpose term for any unspecified African state.

oogie *n.* [abbr. BOOGIE *n.*[2] (1)] [1970s+] (*US Southern campus*) a derog. ref. to black students.

oogle *v.* [SE *ogle*] [1930s+] (*US*) to stare at, to ogle.

(DERIVATIVES)

❑ **oogley** *adj.* [1930s+] worth staring at.

oogle eyes *n. see* GOO-GOO EYES *n.*

oo-gotz *n.* [? Ital. *ugasita*, dislike] [1970s] (*US*) a general term of dismissal: BULLSHIT! *excl.*, to hell with.

ooh-la-la *n.* [Fr. excl. *ooh-la-la!*] [1920s+] **1** French sexuality, which, in Anglo-Saxon eyes, is 'spicy' and 'naughty'. **2** a young woman, usu. French, who possesses those qualities.

ooh-wee *n.* [the excl. made when smoking it] [2000s] (*US black*) very high quality marijuana.

oojah *n.* (*also* **oojah-capiff, oojah capivvy, ooja-ka-piv, ooja-ka-pivi, ooja-ka-pivvy, oojiboo**) [note 1940s milit. use *oojah*, sauce, custard] [1910s+] a term used when one cannot find the correct description for an object or person.

oojah-cum-spiff *adj.* [OOJAH *n.* + SPIFF *adj.* (2)] [1920s–70s] all right, as required, in order.

ook *n.* [the sound of disgust that indicates the discovery of such a thing] [1960s+] anything unpleasant, esp. something slimy and/or viscous.

ook *v.* [echoic + OOK *n.*] [1990s+] (*US campus*) to vomit.

ookey *adj.* [ety. unknown] [1950s–60s] (*US*) dangerous, difficult.

ooky *adj.* [OOK *n.*] [1960s+] (*US*) disgusting, esp. sticky, slimy.

oolfoo *n.* [backsl.] [late 19C–1900s] a fool.

oomph *n.* (*also* **umph**) [imitative] **1** [1930s+] (*orig. US*) enthusiasm, vitality, energy, esp. as sex appeal. **2** [1940s] a sexy, vivacious young woman.

(DERIVATIVES)

❑ **oomphy** *adj.* [1950s+] (*US*) lively, energetic or sexy.

(IN COMPOUNDS)

❑ **oomph girl** *n.* [1930s–40s] a sexy, vivacious girl.

-ooney *sfx see* -EROONIE *sfx.*

oons! *excl.* (*also* **ounds! ouns! owns!**) [late 16C–19C] a euph. oath, *God's wounds!*

(IN EXCLAMATIONS)

❑ **oons and thunder!** *see* THUNDER AND OUNS! *under* THUNDER *n.*

oont *n.* [Hind. and Urdu *unt*, a camel] (*Aus./Anglo-Ind.*) **1** [late 19C+] a camel. **2** [1920s+] a person, a fellow.

oonu *pron.* [abbr. SE *you now*] [1980s+] (*W.I./UK black teen*) you, you all, y'all.

oony *n.* [? cries of 'oh my stomach!'] [20C+] (*Aus.*) sea-sickness.

oopizootics *n.* (*also* **ooperzootics**) [? SE the disease *epizootic*, a plague among cattle] [late 19C–1910s] a fit of eccentricity, craziness.

oops! *excl.* (*also* **ooph! oopadoop!**) [1920s+] an excl. used on dropping something, tripping over, bumping into someone or something, making a mistake, being surprised etc.

oops-a-daisy! *excl. see* UPSADAISY! *excl.*

oorie *adj.* (*also* **oorey, oory**) [Scot. *oorie*, sickly-looking, weakly] [20C+] (*Ulster*) hungover.

ooroo! *excl. see* HOOROO! *excl.*

007 *n.* [ref. to 'James Bond *007*'] [1980s+] **1** (*US*) a large folding knife with a wooden handle [also a brandname]. **2** (*US*) a doctor. **3** (*Aus. prison*) a bond that ensures one's good behaviour.

oosh *v.* [? SE *usher* or HOOSH *v.*] [1960s+] to remove, to send away, to eject.

oot *n.* [? LOOT *n.*[1] (2)] [1900s–40s] (*Aus.*) money.

ootz *v.* (*also* **ootch**) [? link to CHUTZPAH *n.*] [1940s+] (*US*) to cheat or trick.

oo-wop *n.* [? echoic of noise of firing] [1990s+] (*US*) a gun.

ooze *v.* [SE *ooze*, to slide and slither around] **1** [20C+] (*US*) to walk or to leave, either casually or furtively. **2** [1930s–40s] (*US black*) to walk the streets in search of sexual conquest [+ CRUISE *v.* (1)].

oozer *n. see* BOOZER *n.* (2).

oozle *v.* [SE *ooze*, to slide and slither around] **1** [1910s+] (*Aus./N.Z.*) to steal, to obtain illicitly. **2** [1920s] (*US*) to arrive surreptitiously.

oozy *adj.* [SE *ooze*] [1920s+] of a person, or thing, unpleasant, 'slimy'.

o.p. *n.* [abbr.] [late 19C+] (*US*) other people's things, usu. money or alcohol; ext. to *o.p.p.*, other people's property (cf. O.P.'S *n.*).

o.p. *adj.* [abbr.] [1960s+] (*Can. prison*) restricted, off privilege.

op *n.* [abbr.] **1** [1910s+] an operation, i.e. an activity. **2** [1920s+] (*US*) a private investigator [abbr. SE *operative*; thus Dashiell Hammett's (1894–1961) fictional detective the 'Continental Op']. **3** [1920s+] a surgical operation. **4** [1920s+] (*US*) an operator of any kind, e.g. a telephone or telegraph operator.

o.p.b. *n.* **1** [late 19C–1940s] (*Aus.*) a cheap cigar [abbr. *old pickled bumpers*]. **2** [1910s–50s] (*US black*) a hypothetical brand of cigarette; used by one who rarely purchases their own [abbr. *other people's brand*].

ope *n.* [abbr.] [1920s+] (*drugs*) opium.

open *adj.* [abbr. *have one's nose open* under NOSE *n.*] [1950s+] (*US black*) **1** sexually excited, obsessed. **2** thus in general excited by something.

SE in slang uses

(IN COMPOUNDS)

❑ **open-arse** *n.* [ARSE *n.*] **1** [11C–19C] a medlar; occas. euph. as the anus [the fruit's large open disk between the persistent calyx-lobes]. **2** [late 16C–18C] a prostitute [a coarse ref. to her stock-in-trade]. ❑ **open charms** *n.* (*also* **open C, wide C**) [19C] the vagina. ❑ **open game** *n.* [SE *open* + GAME *n.* (1c)] [1960s+] (*US*) a prostitute with no specific affiliation to one pimp. ❑ **open go** *n. see* FAIR GO *n.* ❑ **open high** *n.* [HIGH *n.* (1)] [1990s+] (*drugs*) the intoxication one gets from breathing in ambient cannabis or crack cocaine smoke in a room, rather than actually smoking the drug directly. ❑ **open slather** *n.* [SE *open* + UK dial./SAmE *slather*, to squander, to use in large quantities] [1910s+] (*Aus.*) a situation with no restrictions or limits to one's wishes. ❑ **open swinging** *n. see* SWINGING *n.*[2] (1). ❑ **open work** *n.* [1930s–40s] (*US Und.*) safe-breaking.

open *v.*

(IN PHRASES)

❑ **open one's face** *v. see* SHUT ONE'S FACE *under* FACE *n.* ❑ **open out** *v.* [i.e. to open out the throttle of an engine] **1** [20C+] (*Aus.*) to act unrestrainedly; to lose one's temper. **2** [1950s] (*also* **open (it) up**) to accelerate, to drive fast. ❑ **open to** *v.* [mid 19C–1900s] (*UK Und.*) to confess. ❑ **open up** *v.* **1** [mid-19C+] of a woman, to have sexual intercourse. **2** [late 19C+] to confess, to speak intimately. **3** [1900s–30s] to berate. **4** [1970s+] (*US gay/prison*) to sodomize a prisoner. ❑ **open up (on)** *v.* **1** [20C+] (*US*) to start firing (at); also fig., to attack verbally. **2** [1950s] to interrogate, to question.

open and shut *n.* [SE *open and shut*, adj.] **1** [late 19C] an expert. **2** [late 19C–1900s] (*US*) an unarguable, inescapable situation.

opener *n.* [17C–18C SE] **1** [1900s–30s] (*US*) in pl., aperient pills or medicines, used to cure constipation. **2** [1930s–40s] (*US*) a jemmy.

open the door *n.* [rhy. sl.] [20C+] (*bingo*) the number 44.

opera *n.* [1930s] (*US dancehall*) a burlesque show.

opera cape *n.* [1960s+] (*US gay*) a long foreskin.

opera queen *n.* [SE *opera*, as synon. for melodrama + -QUEEN *sfx*] [1980s] (*US gay*) a male homosexual who enjoys verbally abusing his partners.

operator *n.* **1** [early 18C+] a thief or swindler. **2** [early–mid 19C] (*UK Und.*) a pickpocket. **3** [late 19C+] (*orig. US*) (*also* **operative**) a person who pursues success, often ruthlessly or manipulatively. **4** [1920s–40s] the controller of a gambling game. **5** [1920s+] a major criminal. **6** [1940s] (*US*) a private detective. **7** [1940s+] a successful seducer of women.

o per se o *n.* [Lat.; Nares (1822) suggests link to SE *a per se a*, pre-eminent excellence; note Thomas Dekker [title] *O per Se O, or a new crier of lanterne and candle-lights* (1612)] [early–mid-17C

(*UK Und.*) a town crier; the phr. became used as a popular chorus.

o.p.h. *adv.* [joc. mis-sp. of SE *off*; note O.R.P.H. *adj.*] [mid-19C–1900s] off, on one's way.

o.p.m. *n.* [orig. US Und. and used by confidence tricksters of various types, it was a staple of City or Wall Street jargon by the 1980s] [20C+] *o*ther *p*eople's *m*oney, the ideal commodity for a risky investment.

O Pollaky! *excl.* [proper name of Ignatius 'Paddington' *Pollaky*, a celebrated contemporary private detective, with an office on Paddington Green, whose exploits, and surname, entered the common language; W.S. Gilbert also found room for him in a lyric, 'the keen penetration of Paddington Pollaky' (*Patience*, 1881). That said, note the euph. for coarser excl. *oh bollocks!*] [late 19C] nonsense! rubbish! don't make such a fuss!

opossum *n.* see POSSUM *n.* (3).

opossum-trap *n.* [late 19C] (*Aus.*) the mouth.

o.p.p. *n.* [abbr.] [1990s+] (*US black/campus*) **1** *o*ther *p*eople's *p*roperty, usu. their wife, husband or partner, esp. in the context of their being 'off limits' to new sexual approaches. **2** *o*ther *p*eople's *p*ussy, the wives and girlfriends of other men [PUSSY *n.* (1)].

IN PHRASES

❑ **you down with o.p.p.?** [DOWN *adj.*[1] (1)] [1990s+] (*US black teen*) do you respect other people's property?

oppo *n.* [abbr.] **1** [1920s+] one's *opp*osite number, best friend. **2** [1980s+] *opp*osition. **3** [2000s] *opp*ortunity.

o.p.'s *n.* (*also* **opp**) [O.P. *n.*] [1920s+] (*US black*) *o*ther *p*eople's, usu. in ref. to an unspoken commodity, e.g. cigarettes, alcohol or clothes.

ops *v.* [? SE *opposed/opposite*; i.e. one gives the item to one's opposite number] [20C+] (*S.Afr., usu. juv.*) to swap.

op shop *n.* [abbr. *op*portunity *shop*] [1970s+] (*Aus./N.Z.*) a second-hand clothes shop.

o.p.t. *n.* [abbr.] **1** [20C+] *o*ther *p*eople's *t*obacco, always popular among poverty-stricken smokers. **2** [2000s] (*US black*) speed, punctuality [*O*riental *P*eople *T*ime].

optic *n.* [SE until late 19C] **1** [early 17C+] usu. in pl., an eye. **2** [1910s+] (*Aus./US*) a look.

IN PHRASES

❑ **cast an optic** *v.* [late 19C+] to look at.

optic (nerve) *n.* [rhy. sl. = PERV *n.* (5)] [1960s+] (*Aus.*) a man who ogles (usu.) women.

racle *n.* **1** [18C] a watch [it 'tells', i.e. predicts, the time]. **2** [late 18C–late 19C] the vagina [the initial 'O' + the 'o' shape; the 'mouth piece of the deity'].

orama *sfx* (*also* **-arama, -erama**) [Gk *orama*, a view and orig. used as the second syllable of *panorama, diorama, cosmorama*, and other London shows created for mass entertainment during the early 19C. This association with large-scale entertainment has persisted in its modern, sl. use] [1960s+] (*orig. US teen*) used to indicate a considerable size, quality or expanse, e.g. *babe-orama*, a very attractive woman (or man) or a large number of attractive women (or men), *fun-orama*, a great deal of enjoyment.

range *n.* [1960s+] (*drugs*) a variety of LSD, in orange-coloured capsules, usu. in combs., e.g. *orange barrels, orange cubes, orange haze, orange micro, orange Owsley, orange sunshine, orange wedges*.

range banana *n.* *see under* BANANA *n.*

range juice *n.* [rhy. sl. = *deuce*] [1980s] (*Aus.*) in cards, a two.

range pip *n.* [rhy. sl. = NIP *n.* (1)] [1940s+] a Japanese person.

ranges *n.* [the colour of the pills] [1960s+] (*drugs*) amphetamine.

range squash *n.* [rhy. sl. = DOSH *n.*] [2000s] money.

range sunshine *n.* (*also* **orange wedges**) [1960s+] (*drugs*) a variety of LSD that was packaged in bright orange pills.

rangutan *n.* [20C+] (*US*) a derog. term for a black person.

ration-box *n.* [play on SE] [early 19C] the mouth.

oration-trap *n.* [TRAP *n.*[1] (4)] [early–mid-19C] the mouth.

orbit *n.* [SE *orbital rave* + play on the drug's sending one *into orbit*] [1980s+] (*drugs*) MDMA.

IN PHRASES

❑ **go into orbit** *v.* [1960s] (*S.Afr.*) to tour the criminal underworld.

orbs *n.* [1970s+] (*Aus.*) the testicles.

orch *n.* *see* ORK *n.*

orchard *n.* **1** [17C; 19C; 1990s+] the vagina; the female genital area. **2** [1920s] (*US gay*) a place where homosexuals meet.

orchestra stalls *n.* (*also* **orchestra falls**) [rhy. sl. = BALLS *n.* (1) + link between Gk. *orchis*, the testicles and orchestra, although SE *orchestra* is f. Gk. *orchestra*, the space on which the chorus danced] [20C+] the testicles.

orchestration *n.* [music jargon *orchestration*, which 'wraps around' the individual scores] [1930s–40s] (*US black*) an overcoat.

orchid-crusher *n.* [SE *orchid*, i.e the equation of the delicate flower with girlhood] [1910s] (*US*) a womanizer.

orchids and turnips *n.* [early 19C–1920s] important and commonplace people; occas. used separately.

order *n.*

SE in slang uses

IN COMPOUNDS

❑ **order-racket** *n.* [SE *order* + RACKET *n.*[1] (1)] [early 19C] (*UK Und.*) obtaining goods by ordering them from a shopkeeper, whose bill will never be paid.

IN PHRASES

❑ **out of order** *adj.* **1** [1930s+] of events, behaviour or people, unacceptable, excessive, in bad taste. **2** [1970s] (*US teen*) menstruating. ❑ **tall order** *n.* (*also* **big order, large order**) [TALL *adj.* (4c)] [late 19C+] an excessive or extreme demand.

order of... *n.*

IN PHRASES

❑ **order of the boot** *n.* (*also* **order of the push**) *see under* BOOT, THE *n.*/PUSH *n.* ❑ **order of the hempen riband** *n.* [play on SE *hemp*, from which the rope is made] [mid-17C–mid-18C] a judicial hanging, esp. at Tyburn. ❑ **order of the rag** *n.* [*rag* = flag] [early 18C–1900s] the military life. ❑ **order of the sack** *n. see under* SACK *n.* ❑ **order of the street** *n.* [late 19C] an act of ejection from a house. ❑ **order of the wooden cross** *n.* [1910s] death in battle.

ordinary *n.* **1** [late 19C–1900s] one's wife. **2** [1970s+] (*US black*) one's regular female companion.

ord rot it! *excl. see* OD ROT IT! *under* OD! *excl.*

ore *n.* [1960s] (*S.Afr.*) the police.

Oregon boot *n.* [its original use in Oregon prisons] [1900s–40s] (*US prison*) a heavy lead collar or shackle fitted around a prisoner's ankle; in pl., handcuffs.

O'Reilly *n.* [*O'Reilly* was apparently a real person, poss. a trade-unionist on the Liverpool docks] used as an intensifier in general excls. as below.

IN EXCLAMATIONS

❑ **blimey O'Reilly!** [1920s+] a general excl., presumed to be an intensifier of BLIMEY! *excl.* ❑ **blind O'Reilly!** [1910s+] **1** a general excl. of surprise, excitement etc. **2** used as an intensifier. ❑ **God blind old Reilly!** [1940s–50s] a general oath of annoyance, incredulity, etc.

Oreo (cookie) *n.* [brandname *Oreo Cookie*, a popular US biscuit, which is black on the outside, with a white filling] **1** [1960s+] (*US black*) a derog. description of a fellow black whose opinions, attitudes and goals are taken from white society; thus *Oreolized*. **2** [1980s] in fig, non-racial use. **3** [1990s+] (*orig. US gay*) (*also* **Oreo sex**) sex between two black men and a white man; sex between two black men and a white woman.

IN COMPOUNDS

❑ **Oreo queen** *n.* [QUEEN *n.* (2)/-QUEEN *sfx* (3)] [1960s+] (*US gay*) a black homosexual who engages in sexual activity with white men.

IN PHRASES

□ **go Oreo** *v.* [1990s+] to adapt oneself to whites mores and culture, to sell out one's blackness.

-orexia *sfx* [1980s+] (*US campus*) a sfx based on SE *anorexia* (compulsive, excessive dieting) combined with a given noun to mean too much, excessive, e.g. TALKOREXIA *n.*

orey-eyed *adj. see* ORY-EYED *adj.*

org *n.* [abbr.] **1** [1910s] (*US*) an *organ*. **2** [1930s+] an *organization*.

organ *n.* [pun on SE *pipe-organ*] [late 18C–mid-19C] a pipe.

IN PHRASES

□ **cock one's organ** *v.* [late 18C–mid-19C] to smoke a pipe.

organ grinder *n.* **1** [1910s+] an Italian, spec. an immigrant [the domination of the occupation by Italians]. **2** [1920s–60s] (*US*) the penis [SE *organ* + GRIND *v.* (1)].

organic *adj.* [acknowledgement of 'green' politics] [1970s+] (*US campus*) fashionable.

organize *v.* [1930s+] (*orig. milit.*) **1** to steal, to loot. **2** to arrange at short notice, to 'fix up'.

DERIVATIVES

□ **organized** *adj.* [1920s+] (*orig. milit.*) **1** acquired illicitly, by underhand methods. **2** drunk.

SE in slang uses

IN PHRASES

□ **organize the family jewels** *v. see under* FAMILY JEWELS *n.*

organ-pipe *n.* [mid-19C–1920s] the windpipe, the throat, the voice.

orie-eyed *adj. see* ORY-EYED *adj.*

orifice *n.* [conscious mispron.] [1970s+] an office.

original *n.* [ext. use of SE] [1920s+] (*US black*) a black person.

IN PHRASES

□ **all-originals** *adj.* [1970s+] involving black people only, as in *all-originals scene*, a blacks-only party etc.

originals *n.* [1950s+] the Levi jeans and jacket (with sleeves cut off) worn at the initiation ceremonies of outlaw bikers clubs. Liberally soiled and 'worn in', the rider wears them until they fall to pieces.

orinoko *n.*[1] (*also* **oronoko**) [? Aphra Behn's play *Oroonoko* or *The Royal Slave* (1688)] [late 17C–early 18C] tobacco.

orinoko *n.*[2] [rhy. sl.] [mid-19C–1920s] **1** cocoa. **2** a poker [pron. 'orinoker'].

orioide *adj.* [? SE *awry*] [late 19C] (*US tramp*) drunk.

o'river *phr.* [play on Fr. *au revoir*, goodbye] [1990s+] (*US campus*) a farewell, goodbye.

ork *n.* (*also* **orch**) [abbr. SE *orch*estra] [1930s+] (*orig. US*) an orchestra, usu. a jazz or dance band.

orlando *n.* [? Orlando, Florida] [1990s+] (*US black, mainly East Coast*) a rural black person, esp. one who does not keep up with the 'gangsta' styles of music or clothing.

ornament *v. see* DECORATE *v.*

ornery *adj.* (*also* **ornary, onery**) [SE *ordinary*, A.W. Read has suggested its origins were as a coarse synon. for *lewd*, which was described in 1869 as a 'shocking' word that should 'never pass the lips of anyone' (quoted in *Maledicta* 12, p.40)] **1** [early 19C+] (*US*) commonplace, of poor quality. **2** [mid-19C+] (*US*) coarse, unpleasant. **3** [late 19C] illiterate. **4** [late 19C+] low, mean, cantankerous.

DERIVATIVES

□ **orneriness** *n.* [late 19C+] meaness, cantankerous behaviour.

ornery *adv.* [ORNERY *adj.*] [mid–late 19C] (*US*) unkindly.

ornythorhynchus *n.* [SE *ornithorhynchus*, a duck-billed platypus, i.e. the punning 'beast with a bill'] [late 19C] (*Aus.*) a creditor.

oronoko *n. see* ORINOKO *n.*[1].

-oroonie *sfx see* -EROONIE *sfx.*

o.r.p.h. *adj.* [pron. of *off* as 'orf'; note O.P.H. *adv.*] [1900s–60s] beneath consideration; thus excl. *off you go!*

orphan *n.* **1** [1930s] (*US Und.*) a prostitute who works without a pimp. **2** [1930s–60s] (*US*) a discontinued model of a motor vehicle, a run-down, dilapidated motorcar.

DERIVATIVES

□ **orphaned** *adj.* [1930s–60s] (*US*) of a motor vehicle, discontinued.

Orphan Annie *n.* [rhy. sl. = FANNY *n.*[1] (1)] [1990s+] the vagina.

orphan paper *n.* [1940s–60s] (*US Und.*) counterfeit money.

ort *n.* [ety. unknown, ? dial. *orts*, odds and ends] [1950s+] (*Aus.*) the anus, the backside.

ory-eyed *adj.* (*also* **oary-eyed, orey-, orie-, orry-**) [SE *awry* + *eyed*, but note Scot. *oorie*, of persons and things, dismal, gloomy 'having a debauched or dissipated look'] **1** [late 19C+] (*US*) very drunk, or looking as if one were. **2** [1920s] very angry.

o.s. *adj.* [abbr. over-seas] [20C+] (*Aus.*) abroad, anywhere other than Australia.

Oscar *n.* [the playwright and epigrammatist *Oscar* Wilde (1854–1901), imprisoned for his homosexuality] **1** [late 19C+] a male homosexual; thus *oscar*, to sodomize. **2** [1900s–50s] (*US*) a stupid or unpleasant man; esp. when narrow-minded [? negative stereotype of sense 1]. **3** [1940s] (*US black*) a man, irrespective of character.

oscar *n.* [ety. unknown; ? play on *Oscar* Wilde + the 'wild' activity of sex or violence; or brandname *Oscar Meyer*, a popular US weiner (thus punning on WEENIE *n.*[1] (4))] **1** [1930s+] (*US black*) the penis. **2** [1940s+] (*US prison*) a handgun.

oscar *v.* [ety. unknown; ? corruption of SE *scurry*] [1920s–30s] (*US*) to move quickly.

Oscar (Asche) *n.* (*also* **Okker, Oscar Nash**) [rhy. sl. = cash; ult. actor *Oscar Asche* (1871–1936)] [20C+] (*Aus./N.Z.*) money.

oscar hock *n.* [rhy. sl.] [1920s+] (*US*) usu. in pl., a sock.

Oscar Joes *n.* [rhy. sl.] [1920s–40s] (*US*) the toes.

Oscar Nash *n. see* OSCAR (ASCHE) *n.*

oscars *n.* [late 19C] (*US campus*) whiskers.

oschive *n.* (*also* **ochive**) [Rom. *o chiv*, the knife; or ? Lat. *os*, bone + CHIVE] [early 18C–mid-19C] (*UK Und.*) a bone-handled knife.

osifer *n. see* OSSIFER *n.*

osmosis amoebas *phr.* [a play on the more common *adios amigos*] [1980s+] (*US campus*) a farewell, goodbye.

osnaburg *n.* [proper name *Osnabrück* (in later Eng. corrupt. *Osnaburg*), a town and district in north Germany noted for its manufacture of linen, thus a kind of coarse linen orig. made in Osnabrück. In W.I. it was orig. used for the garments issued to slaves and later prisoners] [1950s] (*W.I.*) **1** rough, ill-cut clothes. **2** first-rate clothes, the product of the best tailoring.

ossifer *n.* (*also* **occifer, osifer**) [deliberate mispron.] [mid-19C+] a joking, slightly offensive ref. to a police (in 19C also army) officer.

ossified *adj.* [pun on STONED *adj.* (2)] [20C+] highly intoxicated on alcohol or a given drug.

osso *n.* [ety. unknown] [2000s] (*US black*) one's house or home

ostrobogulous *adj.* [coined by the writer Victor B. Neuburg (1883–1940). It can be 'translated' in a variety of ways, e.g. 'mischievous but gorgeous' (of children) or 'indecent or pornographic' (words or pictures). Neuburg's own ety. mixed 'full of (Lat. *ulus*) rich (Greek, *ostro*) dirt (schoolboy, *bog*)] [1910s+] bizarre, unusual, interesting.

otamy *n.* [SE *anatomy*] [18C–19C] a skeleton.

otay! *excl.* [var. on OK! *excl.*] [1990s+] (*US teen*) fine! good! agree!

other, the *n.* [note *Merry Drollery* (1661) 'As much as this a ma[n] may kiss / His sister or his mother; / He that will speed must giv[e] with need / A little o'th' t'on with t'other'] [1930s+] sexu[al] intercourse, esp. in the phr. *a bit of the other*, usu. hetero- b[ut] sometimes homosexual.

other *adj.*

SE in slang uses

IN COMPOUNDS

□ **other half** *n.* [the *half* is presumed to be a half-pint] **1** [la

19C+] (*orig. naut.*) a second drink, a drink bought in return for another. **2** see BETTER HALF *n.* ❑ **other man** *n.* [1930s–60s] (*US black*) a white person, esp. the owner of a neighbourhood store in a black area. ❑ **other side** *n.* **1** [mid-18C–late 19C] (*UK Und.*) Southwark, south of the River Thames; or from south London, north of the Thames. **2** [late 18C+] either America or Britain depending on which side of the Atlantic one is; thus *this side*; also England when used in Ireland, also Britain when in Australia. **3** [late 19C–1900s] (*N.Z.*) Australia, i.e. the other side of the Tasman Sea. **4** [late 19C–1920s] (*Aus.*) depending on the speaker's home, Tasmania or Sydney, the 'other side' of Australia. ❑ **other way** *n.* **1** [1960s+] (*also* **other side, the**) of sexual intercourse, anal rather than vaginal. **2** [2000s] homosexual.

IN PHRASES

❑ **go the other way** *v.* **1** [1960s+] (*US*) to be bisexual or homosexual. **2** [1970s] to alter one's position, to back down on a promise. **3** [1970s] of a judicial verdict, to find against the plaintiff.

othersider *n.* see T'OTHER SIDER *n.*

otis *adj.* [the town drunk in the US TV comedy *The Andy Griffith Show* (orig. shown 1960–8)] [1980s+] (*US campus*) drunk.

otium dig *n.* see DIG *n.*[3].

o.t.l. *adj.* [abbr. OUT TO LUNCH *adj.*] [1950s+] (*US campus*) not in touch with reality, inattentive, unaware.

otomy *n.* see OTTOMY *n.*

O-Town *n.* [abbr.] [2000s] (*US*) Orlando, Florida.

o.t.r. *phr.* [abbr. *on the rag* under RAG *n.*[1]] [1960s+] (*US campus*) **1** menstruating. **2** thus (of either sex) irritable, in a bad mood, tetchy.

o.t.t. *adj.* [abbr. *over the top* under TOP *n.*] [1980s+] extravagant, beyond the usual bounds of taste, behaviour etc.

otter *n.*[1] [early 18C] a sailor.

otter *n.*[2] (*also* **otto**) [Ital. *otto*, eight] [mid–late 19C] (*Ling. Fr./Polari*) the number eight; thus eightpence.

Otto *n.* [a popular Ger. name] [20C+] a derog. name for a German, with an implication of stolidity; thus generic for a stolid, unimaginative person.

ottomized *adj.* [SE *anatomized*] [late 18C–early 19C] dissected, subjected to a post-mortem.

ottomy *n.* (*also* **otomy**) [SE *anatomy*; OTAMY *n.*] [mid-18C–mid-19C] a skeleton; a very thin person.

ou *n.* [Afk. *ou*, a fellow + Du. *ouwe*, old man] (*S.Afr.*) **1** [mid-19C+] a form of address, often in combs. *ou china*, *ou maat*, *ou pellie*, old mate, old pal. **2** [1940s+] a fellow, a chap; occas. of a woman. **3** [1960s+] (*township*) a friend.

Oubaas *n.* [Afk. *ou*, old + *baas*, boss, governor] [1900s–50s] (*S.Afr.*) a nickname for the Roeland Street prison, Cape Town.

ou-di-du-dat *n.* [lit. 'how does he do that?', ? a question frequently asked by these individuals] [1950s] (*W.I.*) an East Indian.

oudish *adj.* [ety. unknown] [2000s] (*UK teen*) amazing, wonderful.

oudles *n.* see OODLES *n.*

ought *n.* [SE *nought*, i.e. 'an ought'] [mid-19C+] zero, nothing, esp. as the number 0. The modern *noughts and crosses* was *oughts and crosses* c.1850.

oui-oui *n.* see WEE-WEE *n.*[1].

ou kappie *n.* see OKAPI *n.*

oukie *n.* see OKIE *n.*

oulap *n.* [Afk. *ou*, old + *lap*, rag, thus a valueless old rag] [1910s] (*S.Afr.*) a penny.

ould sod *n.* see OLD SOD *n.*

ould wan/oul' one *n.* see OLD ONE *n.*

ouman *n.* [Afk. *ou*, old + SE *man*] [1970s+] (*S.Afr.*) a veteran, an 'old hand'; an experienced soldier, esp. a national serviceman who has completed six or more months of his enlistment or who has completed his entire time.

ounce *n.* [the valuation of silver at five shillings an ounce] [early 18C–early 19C] a silver coin.

ounce-brain *n.* [i.e. a LIGHTHEAD *n.*] [1940s] (*US*) a fool.

ounce-brain *adj.* [OUNCE-BRAIN *n.*] [1940s] stupid, foolish.

ounce man *n.* [SE *ounce* + SE *man*/MAN *n.*[1] (1)] [1950s+] (*US drugs*) a small- or medium-time drug dealer.

ounce of baccy *n.* (*also* **ouncer**) [rhy. sl. = PAKI *n.* (1)] [1960s+] an Asian immigrant, esp. the owner of a corner shop.

ouncer *n.* [abbr.; poss. misprint for BOUNCER *n.*[1] (9)] [1990s+] a bouncer at a club or bar.

ounds!/ouns! *excl.* see OONS! *excl.*

oupa juice *n.* [Afk. *oupa*, an old Afrikaans man + JUICE *n.*[1] (3)] [1990s+] (*S.Afr.*) **1** liquor. **2** opium.

our friend with the talking brooch *n.* [the walkie-talkie radio, clipped to the front of the uniform] [1980s+] (*gay*) a police officer.

our Miss Brooks *n.* [the name of the eponymous star of the 1950s TV sitcom] [1950s–70s] (*camp gay*) a teacher.

oussie *adj.* [ety. unknown] [20C+] (*Ulster*) over-inquisitive.

out *n.* **1** in senses of lit. or fig. movement. (**a**) [mid-18C–19C] an outing, an excursion, a holiday. (**b**) [20C+] (*orig. US*) a means of escape, avoidance. (**c**) [1920s+] an excuse; an alibi. (**d**) [1930s] (*US prison*) an escape. (**e**) [1960s] (*US Und.*) constr. with *the*, often in pl., life outside prison; see phrs. below. **2** [early 19C–1930s] a dram measure of gin or a dram glass; thus *three-out*, a glass holding a third of a measure of a liquor [three such glasses will pour *out* a full quartern measure]. **3** [mid-19C] an outside passenger on a coach. **4** [mid-19C] (*US*) an ex-officer. **5** [late 19C–1910s] a defect, a blemish, a disadvantage. **6** [late 19C–1940s] a loss. **7** [1940s+] (*US*) in pl., disagreements, arguments.

IN PHRASES

❑ **at (the) outs** [late 19C–1930s] arguing or angry with someone. ❑ **on the outs** **1** [early 19C+] out of luck, money, favour, popularity etc. **2** [early 19C+] (*US*) (*also* **at outs**) arguing or angry with someone; estranged. **3** [1950s+] (*UK/US Und.*) (*also* **on the out**) out of prison.

out *adj.*[1] **1** in senses of being unwanted. (**a**) [17C; 1930s+] unfashionable. (**b**) [1920s+] (*orig. US*) banned, prohibited. (**c**) [1920s+] (*orig. US*) unfeasible, undesirable; usu. in phr. *that's out*, I won't accept that. (**d**) [1930s] of a lover, unwanted. **2** in senses of lit. or fig. movement. (**a**) [mid-19C+] (recently) released from prison. (**b**) [1930s+] (*gay*) openly homosexual [i.e. no longer *IN THE CLOSET under* CLOSET *n.*]. **3** in a state of physical or mental 'absence'. (**a**) [late 19C] tipsy. (**b**) [late 19C–1940s] dead. (**c**) [late 19C+] (*orig. US*) knocked out, unconscious. (**d**) [1990s+] (*US black*) crazy. **4** [late 19C+] in debt, poor, penniless [abbr. *out of pocket*]. **5** [1910s+] bereft of supplies.

IN PHRASES

❑ **out for the count** *adj.* see *under* COUNT *n.*[3].

out *adj.*[2] [1950s] good, excellent.

out *v.*[1] [OUT *n.* (1a)] [mid-19C–1920s] to go out, esp. on an excursion.

out *v.*[2] **1** [late 19C–1950s] to knock out, to disable. **2** [late 19C–1950s] to dismiss from a job, to discharge. **3** [late 19C–1960s] to kill. **4** [20C+] (*Aus.*) to throw out of a meeting. **5** [1900s] to outdo, to surpass. **6** [1970s] to free from a criminal charge.

DERIVATIVES

❑ **outed** *adj.* [20C+] **1** (*orig. Aus.*) killed, dead. **2** attacked, knocked out. **3** (*orig. Aus.*) dismissed from employment.

IN PHRASES

❑ **outing dues** *n.* [SE *dues*, one's deserts] [late 19C–1910s] execution for murder. ❑ **out someone's light** *v.* (*also* **out the light for someone**) [20C+] (*W.I.*) to cripple or maim someone, to put out of action.

out *v.*[3] [OUT *adj.*[1] (2b); the victim is pushed *out of the closet*. A tactic pioneered by the New York gay magazine *Outweek* and usu. in the form *outing*; thus the converse 'inning', the deliberate masking of homosexuality when a celebrity is known to be gay but the gay/lesbian community finds them (or more likely their politics) so reprehensible that it denies the fact] [1980s+] **1** to expose someone as a homosexual against their will. **2** to reveal negative or personal information about an individual, group or organization.

DERIVATIVES

▫ **outed** *adj.* [1990s+] (*orig. US*) revealed as a homosexual. ▫ **outing** *n.* [1990s+] the exposure of someone as a homosexual against their will.

out *adv.*^{1} [mid-19C–1960s] (*US*) in existence, e.g. *he is the craziest person out.*

out *adv.*^{2} [late 19C] on bad terms.

out *adv.*^{3} **1** [1920s+] refusing to partake in or uninterested in a given plan or scheme or game, e.g. of cards. **2** [1950s+] ejected from a group.

-out *sfx* [1950s+] (*orig. US*) completely, e.g. *clapped-out, drugged-out, stressed-out.*

out and down *adj. see* DOWN-AND-OUT *adj.*

out and in *n.* [rhy. sl.] [1920s] (*US*) the chin.

out and out *n.* [OUT-AND-OUT *adj.* (1)] **1** [mid-19C] strong beer. **2** [mid-19C] (*UK Und.*) a drinking spree. **3** [20C+] (*US black*) a totally unacceptable person.

out-and-out *adj.* **1** [early 19C+] complete, thorough-going, unqualified. **2** [mid-19C+] excellent, first-rate.

out-and-out *adv.* [late 18C+] completely, absolutely, utterly.

out-and-outer *n.* [OUT-AND-OUT *adj.* (1)] **1** [early 19C+] (*also* **outer**) one who is seen as reaching extremes of behaviour, both good and bad and defined according to context [SE after 1880; note Egan's 1821 definition: 'A phrase in the sporting world for *goodness*; a sort of climacteric – the *ne plus ultra*']. **2** [mid-19C] something exceptional. **3** [mid-19C–1920s] a notable lie. **4** [late 19C+] (*US*) (*also* **out-and-out**) a brawl, fistfight.

outasight/outasite *adj. see* OUT OF SIGHT *adj.* (2).

out box *n.* [*OUT OF THE BOX* **under** BOX *n.*^{1} or office jargon *out box*, a box into which out-going mail is placed] [1990s+] (*US black*) the start, the beginning.

outdoor library *n. see* LIBRARY *n.* (2).

outed *adj.* **1** *see under* OUT *v.*^{2}. **2** *see under* OUT *v.*^{3}.

outen sight *adj. see* OUT OF SIGHT *adj.* (2).

outer *n.*^{1} [OUT *v.*^{2} (1)] [late 19C–1900s] a knockout punch.

outer *n.*^{2} [1950s] (*UK Und.*) a pocket.

outer *n.*^{3} [OUT *adj.*^{1} (1)] [1980s+] (*Aus. prison*) the 'free world' outside prison.

outer *n.*^{4} *see* OUT-AND-OUTER *n.* (1).

SE in slang uses

IN PHRASES

▫ **on the outer** *adj.* [SE *outer*, the part of a racecourse outside the enclosure] [1920s+] (*Aus../N.Z*) unpopular, out of favour, penniless or destitute.

outer of three *n.* [mid-19C] (*UK Und.*) ? a meal (of three courses).

outers *n.*^{1} [OUT *n.* (1b)] [1970s+] (*UK Und.*) a lit. or fig. means of escape.

outers *n.*^{2} [SE *outdoors*] [1970s+] (*S.Afr.*) anywhere a vagrant, homeless person finds to sleep, such as a cardboard box, doorway etc.

outers *adj.* [OUT OF ORDER *adj.*] [1970s+] unacceptable, distasteful.

outfit *n.*^{1} ['to cross the plains, or go to the mountains, every one must get an outfit; and having outfitted, you become yourself an outfit' J. F. Meline *Two Thousand Miles on Horseback* (1867)] **1** as a lit. or fig. piece of equipment. (**a**) [mid-19C+] any object or device. (**b**) [late 19C–1920s] (*UK Und.*) a burglar's or safe-breaker's equipment. (**c**) [1940s–50s] (*UK prison*) whatever is needed for attempting a given escape. (**d**) [1970s] (*US Und.*) a weapon. **2** of a collection of individuals. (**a**) [mid-19C+] a travelling party or a party in charge of herds of cattle. (**b**) [late 19C+] any group of people; and their possessions. (**c**) [late 19C+] an organization, a business; a sports team. (**d**) [late 19C+] a criminal organization, a gang. (**e**) [20C+] a person or their possessions. (**f**) [1920s+] (*US Und.*) constr. as *The Outfit*, a specific criminal organization, usu. the US Mafia or Italian gangs in US prisons. **3** in drug uses. (**a**) [late 19C+] equipment for the preparation and smoking of opium. (**b**) [1920s+] (*also* **bang outfit, fit**) the equipment (needle, spoon, cotton etc) used for narcotic injection.

IN PHRASES

▫ **whole outfit** *n.* [1910s+] the lot, everything.

outfit *n.*^{2} [SE *out* + *fit*] [1970s+] (*US campus*) anyone seen as odd or eccentric, who fails to fit in.

outfit *v.* [OUTFIT *n.*^{1} (3)] [1930s] (*US drugs*) to obtain a supply of narcotics.

out front *adj. see* UP FRONT *adj.*

outhouse *n.* [OUT *adj.*^{1} (2a) + SE *house*] [20C+] (*US prison*) a 'half-way house' or hostel, in which newly released prisoners or parolees can learn to reacclimatize themselves to the 'real' world.

outie *n.*^{1} [SE *outdoors*] **1** [1970s] (*S.Afr.*) a vagrant, a tramp. **2** [1980s] a gangster.

IN PHRASES

▫ **on the outies** [2000s] (*S.Afr.*) living as a vagrant.

outie *n.*^{2} [1970s+] a protruding navel, as opposed to an INNIE *n.*

outie *adv.* (*also* **outtie**) [abbr./pron. of OUT OF HERE *phr.* (1)] [1990s+] (*US teen*) leaving, usu. as *I'm outie.*

outing *n. see under* OUT *v.*^{3}.

outing dues *n. see under* OUT *v.*^{2}.

outjie *n.* [Afk. *ou*, a fellow + dimin. sfx *-tjie*] [1950s+] (*S.Afr.*) little fellow, used either of a child or derog. of an adult.

outlaw *n.* **1** [late 19C–1960s] (*Aus./US*) a wild and unmanageable horse. **2** [1920s+] (*US*) a person who flouts conventional practices and regulations (whether in a respectable or criminal context). **3** [1930s+] (*US black*) a prostitute without a regular pimp, or any independent prostitute.

outlaw *adj.* [OUTLAW *n.* (1)] **1** [1900s–40s] (*Aus./US*) of a horse, wild and unmanageable. **2** [1920s+] (*W.I.*) wild, barbarous crude.

outlaw *v.* [OUTLAW *n.* (3)] [1930s+] of a prostitute, to operate independently of a pimp.

out-mouthed *adj.* [20C+] (*Ulster*) having protruding teeth.

out of here *adj.* **1** *see* OUT OF IT *adj.*^{2} (1). **2** *see* OUT OF IT *adj.*^{2} (4).

out of here *phr.* (*also* **outta here**) **1** [1970s+] having left, esp to leave suddenly; thus *I'm out of here!* a phr. of farewell. **2** [1990s+] not wanted, excluded. **3** *see* OUT OF IT *adj.*^{2} (1). **3** *see* OUT OF IT *adj.*^{2} (4).

out of it *adj.*^{1} **1** [late 19C+] (*orig. US*) excluded from one' usual participation in something. **2** [1910s] dead. **3** [1940s+ (*orig. US*) out of touch, behind the times, not au fait with current affairs and interests. **4** [1950s+] (*orig. US black*) unfashionable. **5** [1950s+] fortunately having escaped from something; as in *well out of it.*

out of it *adj.*^{2} ['it' is one's head] (*orig. US*) **1** [1910s; 1960s+ (*also* **out of here**) unable to function adequately because o one's intoxication by drugs or alcohol. **2** [1950s] (*US campus* elated. **3** [1950s+] tired, exhausted, ill. **4** [1960s+] (*also* **out of here, outta there**) crazy, insane, in a daze.

out of order *adj. see under* ORDER *n.*

out of sight *adj.* [note Dalzell (1996): 'Like *far out* out-of-sight can point to serious literary roots. As Richard H. Peck of the University of Virginia noted in *AS* (1966, pages 78–79), *out-of sight* was Bowery slang for astonishingly excellent in the 1890s and was used by Stephen Crane at least four times in *Maggie: A Girl of the Streets* (1893). Visiting a museum, our heroine utters "Dis is outa sight." She could have been speaking 70 years late Lester V. Berrey and Melvin Van den Bark identified out-of-sight as a slang synonym for five categories – beyond comparison, ver superior, excessive, completely, and expensive – in the *America Thesaurus of Slang* (1942), but I found little other evidence of th term's use until the early 1960s'] **1** [late 19C–1920s] (*US* unattainable. **2** [late 19C+] (*orig. US*) (*also* **outasight, outasite outen sight**) excellent, first rate, exceptional; thus ext. as *clea out of sight.* **3** [1960s+] (*US*) extraordinary, esp. bad, insane c deranged.

IN PHRASES

❑ **put out of sight** *v. see under* PUT *v.*[1].

out of sight *adv.* (*US*) **1** [mid-19C+] utterly, thoroughly. **2** [late 19C–1900s] extremely well.

out of there *phr.* [OUT OF HERE *phr.* (1)] [1970s+] (*US*) having left, esp. having left suddenly.

outpost *n.* [1980s+] (*US campus*) someone who is out of touch with reality, a daydreamer.

out-psych *v.* [SE *out* + *psych* (*out*) under PSYCH *v.*] [1960s+] (*US*) to confuse, manipulate or brainwash someone by psychological means.

outrageous *adj.* [on bad = good model] [1950s+] (*US*) excellent, worthy of admiration.

outrun the constable *v.* [late 17C–mid-19C] **1** (*also* **overrun the constable, run a match against the constable**) to spend more than one can afford; to live beyond one's means. **2** to go too far, whether physically or fig. **3** to change the subject.

outs and ins *n. see* IN-AND-OUT *n.*[1] (2).

outside *n.* **1** [late 18C–19C] a passenger who rides on top of a coach. **2** [late 19C+] (*US prison*) the world outside prison, occas. the army [OUTSIDE *adv.*]. **3** [late 19C+] (*US milit.*) the civilian world. **4** [1940s–60s] (*US*) the world beyond one's home and domestic life.

SE in slang uses

IN PHRASES

❑ **at the outside** *adv.* [mid-19C+] at the limit, to the fullest extent.

outside *adj.* [i.e. *outside* the primary relationships or the (fig.) house] [late 19C+] (*US black*) illegitimate; e.g. (W.I.) *outside daughter/son, outside kid/child*, an illegitimate child, *outside man*, a woman's lover, *outside woman*, a man's lover.

SE in slang uses

IN COMPOUNDS

❑ **outside girl** *n.* [1930s] a street prostitute. ❑ **outside job** *n.* [JOB *n.*[2] (1a)] [1920s+] a crime committed in a house etc by a person not connected or associated with the household or building concerned. ❑ **outside pal** *n.* [PAL *n.* (1)] [mid-19C] (*UK Und.*) a lookout for a gang of thieves. ❑ **outside plant** *n.* [PLANT *n.* (1)] [mid-19C] (*UK Und.*) a place where a criminal receiver keeps his stock.

outside *adv.* [late 19C+] out of prison, out of the services; out of a psychiatric hospital.

IN COMPOUNDS

❑ **outside time** *n.* [SE *time*/punning on TIME *n.* (1)] [2000s] (*US prison/Und.*) parole.

SE in slang uses

IN PHRASES

❑ **get outside (of)** *v.* (*also* **get on the outside of, put oneself outside**) **1** [mid-19C+] (*orig. US*) to consume, to swallow, esp. a drink, e.g. *get outside a pint*. **2** [late 19C+] (*US*) to understand, to learn, to master. **3** [late 19C+] of a woman, to have sexual intercourse.

outside! *excl.* [abbr. *come outside and fight!*] [20C+] a challenge.

outside Eliza! *excl.* (*also* **outside Liza!**) [according to Ware, from the evidence given in a specific court case] [late 19C–1900s] go away! be off!, esp. used to a woman considered drunk.

outside man *n.* [SE *outside*] **1** [mid-19C+] (*also* **outsider**) (*UK Und.*) a lookout. **2** [mid-19C+] (*also* **outsideman**) (*orig. US*) that member of a confidence trick team who locates potential victims, lures them deeper into the hoax, and helps to fleece them; the 'steerer' for a brothel.

outsider *n.* **1** [mid-19C] (*UK Und.*) a lookout, one who does not go inside the burgled house. **2** [mid-19C+] (*US Und.*) in pl., a device for unlocking a door by manipulating the key through the keyhole. **3** [late 19C+] a person who is considered socially inferior, esp. as *rank outsider*, a complete and utter inferior. **4** [1900s–20s] (*Irish*) a mentally deficient person. **5** [1910s] (*US Und.*) an outside pocket. **6** [1980s+] (*US*) an act of sexual intercourse performed out of doors.

outslick *v.* [SLICK *v.* (2)] [1940s+] (*US black*) to outwit, outsmart.

outs with *adj. see* OUT WITH *adj.*

outta here *phr. see* OUT OF HERE *phr.*

outta there *adj. see* OUT OF IT *adj.*[2] (4).

out the monk *adj.* [ety. unknown; ? rhy. sl. = drunk] [1940s+] (*N.Z.*) **1** defeated, finished. **2** unconscious, asleep, often the result of drunkenness. **3** disabled through illness or lack of some essential.

IN PHRASES

❑ **be out the monk with** *v.* [1940s] to have fallen out with.

out there *adj.* **1** [1970s+] under the influence of drugs. **2** [1980s+] bizarre, extreme. **3** [1990s+] important, fashionable, 'in the swing'. **4** [1990s+] (*US black*) involved in gang life; 'there' being the street. **5** [1990s+] (*US black*) in a subservient, victimized position.

IN PHRASES

❑ **out there bad** *adv.* [2000s] (*US prison*) in the wrong.

outtie *adv. see* OUTIE *adv.*

outtie 5000 *phr. see* AUDI (5000) *phr.*

out to it *adj.* ['it' being the world] [1940s+] (*Aus.*) extremely drunk, unconscious; also from physical violence.

out to lunch *adj.* [i.e. 'not all there'] (*orig. US campus*) **1** [1950s+] crazy, eccentric, weird. **2** [1950s+] in a daze, stupid, naïve. **3** [1960s–70s] one who is seen as alien to the peer group. **4** [1970s] absent, unavailable. **5** [2000s] intoxicated by drink or drugs; feeling very happy.

out to pasture *phr.* [animals put out to pasture have 'retired' from everyday productive life] [20C+] (*US Und.*) serving time in prison.

out with *adj.* (*also* **outs with**) [ON THE OUTS *under* OUT *n.*] [mid-19C+] on bad terms with, quarrelling, disenchanted with, opposed to.

ovaries *n.*

IN PHRASES

❑ **drop one's ovaries** *v. see under* DROP *v.*[1].

oven *n.* **1** [early 16C–19C; 1980s] the vagina. **2** [late 18C–mid-19C] a large mouth. **3** [1950s+] the womb; usu. in phrs. below.

IN PHRASES

❑ **have a bun in the oven** *v.* (*also* **have a bun in the club, ...a bun in one's tin, ...a pudding in the oven, ...a scone in the oven, ...bread in the oven, ...one in the oven**) [SE *bun/one/* PUDDING *n.* (5)/PUDDING CLUB *n.* (1)] [1950s+] **1** to be pregnant. **2** of a man, to impregnate one's partner.

oven-dodger *n.* [the implication that those who escaped the crematorium ovens of Auschwitz and other Nazi death camps were somehow doing it deceitfully] [1980s+] a derog. term for a Jew.

over *n.* [SE *over*, an extra, a remainder; note mid-19C banking jargon *overs*, odd money remaining after the daily accounts are made up, and which is divided among the clerks] [1970s+] (*UK Und.*) in pl., proceeds of a theft that can, if not carefully disposed of, become vulnerable themselves to further theft, poss. by one of the gang.

over *adj.*[1] **1** [1980s] (*US campus*) bored with. **2** [1990s+] (*US*) out-of-date.

IN PHRASES

❑ **over, be** *v.* [1970s+] (*US campus*) to dislike intensely, to be angry. ❑ **overs-cadovers** *adv.* [1970s+] a long time ago.

over *adj.*[2] [GET OVER *v.*[1] (3)] [1990s+] (*US black*) successful.

over *v.* [abbr. SE *get over*] [20C+] (*Ulster*) to survive.

over *adv.*

IN PHRASES

❑ **have someone over** *v.* [abbr. of HAVE SOMEONE OVER A BARREL *under* BARREL *n.*[1]] [1970s+] **1** to deceive, to defraud, to trick. **2** to seduce [fig. use of sense 1].

over! *excl.* *see* OVER THE LEFT (SHOULDER)! *excl.*

overamp *v.* [SE *over* + AMP *n.* (1)/SE *amp*/abbr. SE *amphetamine*] [1960s+] (*drugs*) to overdose on cocaine or amphetamine.

DERIVATIVES

□ **overamped** *adj.* [1980s+] (*US*) in fig. use, overwrought, over-excited.

over-and-under *n.* [i.e. an UPPER *n.*[2] (1) and a DOWNER *n.*[5] (1)] [1970s+] (*drugs*) a combination of a stimulant and a depressant drug.

overboard *adj.* [1920s+] (*orig. US*) over-enthusiastic, very keen.

overcharged *adj.* [ext. of CHARGED (UP) *adj.* (2)] [1930s–50s] (*US*) overdosed on narcotics.

overcoat *n.* **1** [late 19C+] a coffin. **2** [1910s–40s] (*US*) a pie crust. **3** [1920s–70s] (*also* **Dunlop overcoat**) a condom. **4** [1930s] (*US*) a high value currency note around a bankroll. **5** [1930s] (*US*) a straight jacket. **6** [1940s] (*US*) a parachute.

IN COMPOUNDS

□ **overcoat maker** *n.* [20C+] an undertaker.

over-do *n.* [1920s] (*W.I.*) showing off, ostentation.

IN PHRASES

□ **do the over-do** *v.* [20C+] (*W.I., Guyn.*) to take things too far.

overdraw one's badger *v.* [pun on SE *badger-drawing*, badger-baiting] [mid-19C] to overdraw one's bank account.

overdue *adj.* **1** [1960s+] of a woman, not having had a menstrual period at the expected time. **2** [1970s+] of a criminal, ripe for arrest.

over-eye *v.* [SE *run one's eyes over*] [late 19C–1900s] to watch, to survey.

overheat one's flues *v.* *see under* FLUE *n.*[1].

overjolt *n.* *see under* JOLT *n.*

overlander *n.* [SE *overlander*, one who herds cattle from one Aus. state to another] [late 19C+] (*Aus.*) **1** a tramp. **2** a large mosquito.

overland trout *n.* (*US*) **1** [late 19C] roast pork. **2** [1900s–60s] bacon.

over-ripe fruit *n.* *see under* FRUIT *n.*

over-run the constable *v.* *see* OUTRUN THE CONSTABLE *v.* (1).

overseen *adj.* [17C–19C] tipsy.

overseer of the (new) pavement *n.* *see under* PAVEMENT *n.*

over shoes, over boots *phr.* (*also* **over the ankles**) [? water pouring over the top of one's footwear] [late 16C–18C] totally, recklessly committed.

overshot *adj.* [17C+] tipsy, drunk.

overtaken *adj.* [mid-17C–19C] drunk.

over the ankles *phr.* *see* OVER SHOES, OVER BOOTS *phr.*

over the dam *adj.* *see* *OVER THE BAY under* BAY *n.*

over the left (shoulder)! *excl.* (*also* **over! over the left eye!**) [the term is often accentuated by gesturing over the left shoulder with the thumb. Note the superstitious throwing of spilled salt over one's left shoulder, thus one takes such dubious information 'with a pinch of salt'] [late 17C+] a general term of disbelief, absolutely not! impossible! etc.

over-the-shoulder boulder-holder *n.* *see BOULDER-HOLDER under* BOULDER *n.*

over the stile *adv.* [rhy. sl.] [mid-19C–1900s] committed for trial.

ow *n.* [? abbr. + O *n.* (2); although it predates this] [late 19C–1930s] (*US drugs*) the bowl of an opium pipe.

Owen Nares *n.* [rhy. sl.; ult. UK actor *Owen Nares* (c.1888–1943)] [1910s+] chairs.

owie *n.* [the excl. *ow!* on having one's flesh pierced] [1990s+] **1** (*US*) a bruise or minor injury. **2** (*US black*) any jewellery that requires the piercing of one's flesh, usu. an earlobe.

owl *n.* **1** [late 17C; late 19C+] a prostitute who works nights only. **2** [20C+] the late-night customers of bars, cafés and restaurants. **3** [1900s–40s] (*Aus./US*) a thief, esp. one who works at night.

SE in slang uses

IN COMPOUNDS

□ **owl-eyed** *adj.* (*also* **owly, owly-eyed**) **1** [mid-19C–1960s] (*US*) very drunk. **2** [1900s] cunning. □ **owl-gal** *n.* [like the owl she's 'out all night'] [1940s] (*W.I.*) a promiscuous young woman. □ **owl-hooter** *n.* (*also* **owlhoot**) [? US West *hear the owl hoot*, to travel by night] [1940s+] (*US*) a contemptible person, esp. a fugitive or outlaw.

IN PHRASES

□ **like an owl in an ivy-bush** [18C–19C] used of a narrow-faced man who has a large wig or very bushy hair, or of a woman with frizzy hair. □ **owl's bowels** *n.* *see* BEE'S KNEES *n.*

owl *adj.* [mid-19C+] (*orig. US*) working, operating or open at night, e.g. *owl shift*, the night shift, *owl car*, a late-night streetcar.

owl *v.* [late 19C] (*US campus*) to stay late on a social visit.

owl crap/dung *n.* *see* OWL SHIT *n.*

owled *adj.* [1920s] (*US*) drunk.

owler *n.* [in an attempt to curtail smuggling the transportation of wool by night was forbidden in 1674, therefore those who still carried on the illicit trade were known as *owlers*, because, like the bird, they worked at night] [late 17C–mid-19C] one who smuggles wool or sheep from England to France.

owl feathers *n.* *see* OWL SHIT *n.*

owlhead *n.*[1] (*also* **owl's head**) [? a brandname] [1920s–60s] (*US*) a short, heavy revolver with a feature enabling it to double as a knuckleduster.

owlhead *n.*[2] [1990s+] (*US*) a person.

owl shit *n.* (*also* **owl crap, ...dung, ...feathers, ...milk**) [SE *owl* + SHIT *n.* (1a)/CRAP *n.*[1] (2)/SE *dung/feathers/milk*] **1** [mid-19C+] (*US*) excrement, usu. constructed with 'sour', used fig., shit; also in euph. forms. **2** [1970s] in fig. use, anything distasteful.

IN COMPOUNDS

□ **Owlshit Junction** *n.* [1970s] (*US*) the 'back of beyond'.

owly/owly-eyed *adj.* *see under* OWL *n.*

own *v.* [slave-era imagery] [1910s+] (*US black*) to surpass, to overcome; to dominate.

owner's job *n.* *see* CONSENT JOB *n.*

owns! *excl.* *see* OONS! *excl.*

own the corn *v.* *see* ACKNOWLEDGE THE CORN *v.*

Owsley acid *n.* (*also* **Owsley, Owsley's acid, white Owsley's**) [Augustus *Owsley* Stanley III (b.1935), the best known of all LSD chemists. His 'own-brand' drugs were considered the very best] [1960s+] (*drugs*) LSD.

owt *n.* [backsl.] [mid-19C–1950s] two.

owt gens *n.* [backsl.; OWT *n.* + GEN *n.*[1]] [mid–late 19C] two shillings.

owt yeneps *n.* [backsl.; OWT *n.* + YENNEP *n.*] [mid–late 19C] two pence.

ox *n.* **1** [1930s+] (*US*) a large, thuggish man. **2** [1960s] (*US teen*) an unattractive, overweight female. **3** [1990s+] (*US black*) a razor blade.

oxen-persuader *n.* *see COW-PERSUADER under* COW *n.*[1].

Oxford *n.* [brandname of *Oxford* shoe polish] [1940s] (*US black*) a particularly dark-skinned person.

Oxford bag *n.* [rhy. sl. = FAG *n.*[4] (2)] [1990s+] a cigarette.

Oxford (scholar) *n.* [rhy. sl.] **1** [late 19C+] a crown, 5s (25p); also as a dollar [DOLLAR *n.*[1] (1)]. **2** [1930s] a collar. **3** [1930s+] (*Aus.*) A$1.

IN PHRASES

□ **half-Oxford** *n.* [late 19C] half-a-crown, 2s 6d (12½p).

oxo *n.* [maths notation *0 x 0*] [late 19C–1930s] zero, nothing.

Oxo cube *n.* [rhy. sl. = TUBE *n.*[1] (3); ult. Oxo cube, the brand of stock cube] [20C+] the London Underground.

oxter *n.* (*also* **oxer**) [ety. unknown; *OED* suggests poss. link to rare Norwegian regional use *oster*, the throat, the hollow above the collarbone] [mid-16C+] (*Irish/Scot.*) an armpit.

oxter *v.* [OXTER *n.*] [19C+] (*Irish*) to lift or move a person by holding them under the armpits.

oxy *n.* [abbr.] [2000s] (*US drugs*) *Oxy*contin, a painkiller based on synthetic morphine.

oxy *adj.* [the charity *Oxfam*, esp. its second-hand goods and clothes shops] [1990s+] (*UK juv.*) impoverished-looking.

oxygen thief *n.* [1990s+] (*Aus.*) a completely worthless person.

oyl of rope *n. see* OIL OF WHIP *under* OIL OF... *n.*

oyster *n.* **1** in senses of a woman or her genitals as a FISH *n.*[1] (1) [note D'Urfey, *Pills to Purge Melancholy*(1719): 'And now she has learnt the pleasing Game, / [...] / She daily ventures at the same, / And shuts and opens like an Oyster']. (**a**) [mid-17C+] the vagina. (**b**) [early 18C] a prostitute. (**c**) [late 18C+] a girl, a young woman. **2** as bodily fluid. (**a**) [late 17C+] a gob of phlegm. (**b**) [late 19C; 1970s+] semen. **3** [mid-18C] in pl., the testicles. **4** with ref. to the bivalve's 'closed mouth'. (**a**) [late 19C–1950s] (*also* **sealed oyster**) a close-mouthed person; occas. as adj. (**b**) [1930s–70s] an odd or stupid person. (**c**) [1960s] the mouth. **5** [1910s–50s] a pearl; thus *real oysters*, genuine pearls. **6** [1970s] (*UK Und*) a society woman who is paid to wear stolen pearls, hoping to entice an offer of purchase.

IN COMPOUNDS

❑ **oyster-catcher** *n.* [late 19C] the vagina. ❑ **oyster-faced** *adj.* [the oyster's beard] [late 19C–1910s] unshaven.

IN PHRASES

❑ **catch an oyster** *v.* [19C] of a woman, to have sexual intercourse. ❑ **dumb as an oyster** *adj.* (*also* **close as an oyster**) [1900s–10s] (*Aus.*) silent, secretive. ❑ **inhale the oyster** *v.* [1970s+] (*US gay*) to fellate. ❑ **oyster (up)** *v.* [1960s–70s] to shut up, to be quiet.

SE in slang uses

IN PHRASES

❑ **oyster's eye-tooth** *n. see* CAT'S WHISKERS *n.*

oysterics *n.* [a pun on the SE, intensified by the worries generated after bad oysters allegedly created a typhoid epidemic c.1900] [1900s] (*middle class*) hysterics.

Oz *n.* [pron. of *Aus*(*tralia*) + pun on *The Wonderful Wizard of Oz* (1900)] [20C+] Australia.

o.z. *n.* (*also* **oh-zee, OZ**) [1oz; pron. of the abbr.] [1930s+] (*drugs*) an ounce (28g) of a drug.

oz *n.* [it sends you to the land of *Oz*] [1980s+] (*drugs*) amyl nitrite.

ozard *adj.* [a play on the book/film *The Wizard of Oz*; i.e. the opposite of *Wizard* is *Ozard*; poss. found only in Buckeridge] [1950s] (*juv.*) ghastly.

ozone *n.*[1] (*orig. US*) **1** [1900s–70s] air. **2** [1920s–40s] a dismissal [ext. of GET THE AIR *under* AIR *n.*].

DERIVATIVES

❑ **ozoned** *adj.* [i.e. one is HIGH *adj.*[1] (2)] [1970s+] (*US*) intoxicated by drugs.

IN COMPOUNDS

❑ **ozone ranger** *n.* [i.e. their head is 'in the clouds'] [1970s+] (*US campus*) someone who is out of touch with reality.

IN PHRASES

❑ **in the ozone** *adj.* [SE *ozone* + pun on 0 = zero] [1970s+] (*US*) dazed; or intoxicated by drugs or drink. ❑ **lost in the ozone** *adj.* [1980s] out of touch, alienated.

ozone *n.*[2] [ety. unknown; ? ref. to inhaling] **1** [1970s+] (*drugs*) phencyclidine. **2** [2000s] marijuana.

ozoner *n.* [SE *ozone*, fresh air] [1940s+] (*US*) a drive-in cinema.

Ozzie *n.* [Oz *n.*] [1910s+] an Australian.

Ozzie *adj.* [OZZIE *n.*] [1910s+] Australian.

ozzie *n.* [1 oz] [1980s+] (*Aus./Can. drugs*) 1oz (28g) of marijuana.

ozzimangerum *n.* [? SE *ox* + Fr. *manger*, to eat] [mid-19C] (*UK Und.*) soup made from a leg of beef.

ozzy *n.* [abbr.] [2000s] a hospital.

P

P *n. see* PINK *n.*

IN PHRASES

□ **throw the P** *v. see under* PUSSY *n.*

p *n.* [abbr.] **1** [mid-17C] syphilis [POX *n.*[1] (1)]. **2** [mid-19C] the penis [note also PRICK *n.* (1)]. **3** [1920s–30s] a *p*once, a *p*imp. **4** in drug uses. (**a**) [1960s+] *p*eyote. (**b**) [1970s] heroin, lit. '*p*ure'. (**c**) [1970s+] *p*hencyclidine. **5** [1990s+] a *p*romise (to deliver something). **6** [1990s+] the *p*rice. **7** [2000s] money [*p*ennies/*p*ounds]. **8** [2000s] rejection, dismissal [PUSH *n.* (3)]. **9** [2000s] (*US black*) a parent. **10** *see* PEA *n.*[1] (1).

p *adj.* [abbr.] [1970s+] *p*ure, unadulterated, esp. of drugs.

PA *n. see* PRINCE ALBERT *n.*

pa *n.*[1] [SE *papa*] [early 19C+] (*mainly juv.*) one's father; thus *pa-in-law*, father-in-law.

pa *n.*[2] [abbr.] [late 19C] the *p*arish relieving officer, who distributed money to the poor.

p.a.b.a.c.a.b. *phr.* [abbr. *pack a* BOWL *n.* (2) and *catch a* BUZZ *n.* (3c)] [1980s+] (*US drugs*) an exhortation to smoke cannabis.

pabble-blinkers *n. see under* BLINK *n.*[1].

pac *n.* [backsl.] [mid-19C] a cap.

pace *v.* [1970s] (*US black*) to live a fast, exciting and varied life.

pacer *n.* [late 19C] (*US*) anything or anyone that goes at a great pace.

pachuco *n.* (*also* **pachook**) [Mex. Sp. *pachuco*, flashily dressed, vulgar] [1940s+] (*US*) a Mexican-American, esp. a young man who joins a street gang; thus *pachuca*, his female counterpart.

pachuco *adj.* (*also* **pachook**) [PACHUCO *n.*] [1940s+] (*US*) pertaining to Mexican-Americans (esp. street gang members) or their culture.

pack *n.*[1] [? PACK *v.*[1] (2)] [mid–late 19C] a night lodging for the very poor.

pack *n.*[2]

SE in slang uses

IN PHRASES

□ **gone to the pack** *adj.* [SE *pack of hounds*; thus var. on colloq. phr. *gone to the dogs*] [1910s+] (*Aus./N.Z.*) **1** in social decline, run-down, dirty; poss. turned into a tramp. **2** drunk. □ **go to the pack** *v.* [SE *pack of hounds*; thus var. on colloq. phr. *go to the dogs*] **1** [1910s+] (*Aus.*) to decline socially, economically etc. **2** [1960s] (*Aus.*) to give up. **3** [1980s] (*N.Z.*) to fail continually.

pack *n.*[3] [1950s+] (*drugs*) **1** a packet of heroin. **2** a packet of pills. **3** a packet of marijuana. **4** a packet of cigarettes.

SE in slang uses

IN COMPOUNDS

□ **packhorse** *n. see* MULE *n.* (4c). □ **packrat** *n.* [SE *pack rat*, the US bushy-tailed woodrat, known for its collecting of objects] [20C+] (*US*) **1** an obsessive hoarder. **2** a hotel bellboy.

IN PHRASES

□ **pack of poo tickets** *n.* [punning on POO *n.*[1] (2)/*LIKE A PAKAPOO TICKET under* LIKE A... *phr.*] [1990s+] (*Aus.*) a lavatory roll. □ **pack of rockets** *n.* (*also* **pack of rocks**) [1940s–50s] (*drugs*) a packet of marijuana cigarettes. □ **pack, shack and stack** *n.* [STACK *n.*[1] (1)] [1940s–60s] (*orig. US black*) one's entire belongings: clothes, home and money.

pack *n.*[4] [abbr./pron. PECKERWOOD *n.*] [1990s+] (*US black*) a white person.

pack *n.*[5] *see* PACKER *n.*

pack *n.*[6] *see* PACKET *n.* (3).

pack *adj.* [Scot.] [1960s+] (*Irish*) friendly.

pack *v.*[1] **1** [19C+] (*US*) to carry, also in fig. use. **2** [late 19C+] (*US*) to live as a tramp, travelling the country [the SE *pack* that is carried]. **3** [late 19C+] (*US*) to carry a weapon, usu. a gun or knife; also to wear. **4** [1920s+] (*US*) to carry money, to be in funds. **5** [1940s] (*US drugs*) to carry drugs for a dealer. **6** in sexual uses. (**a**) [1940s] (*US*) of a man, to have sexual intercourse. (**b**) [1960s+] (*US campus*) of male homosexuals, to have anal sex. **7** [1960s+] (*US prison*) to carry contraband in and out of a prison; to carry a concealed weapon. **8** [1970s+] (*US*) to reject a lover [*PACK IN* below]. **9** [1990s+] in drug uses. (**a**) (*Aus. drugs*) to fill a cigarette with marijuana; thus *packer*, one who makes marijuana cigarettes. (**b**) (*US drugs*) to fill a crack cocaine pipe. (**c**) (*US drugs*) to be a major drug dealer, making up the packs of a drug which are then sold on to the dealers who trade on the street.

DERIVATIVES

□ **packing** *adj.* (*also* **packed**) **1** [late 19C+] (*US*) carrying a gun or knife. **2** [1980s+] (*US*) performing anal intercourse [SE *pack in*, to fill]. **3** [1990s+] (*US black*) of a man, having sexual intercourse [SE *pack in*, to fill]. **4** [1990s+] (*US black*) having a large penis. **5** [1990s+] (*US gay*) of a lesbian, wearing a strap-on dildo, usu. under one's clothes, or wearing other padding in the genital area to look as if one has a penis. **6** [2000s] (*US prison*) having weapons for sale.

IN PHRASES

□ **pack a sad** *v.* [1980s+] (*N.Z.*) to be depressed. □ **pack chitlins** *v.* [SE *chitlins*, pig's intestines (which are *de facto* soft)] [1990s+] (*US black*) of a man, to be unable to maintain an erection during intercourse. □ **packing death** *adj.* [1950s] (*Aus.*) terrified, frightened. □ **packing it** *adj.* [1990s+] making a large amount of money. □ **pack peanut butter** *v.* [the colour of the spread] [1970s+] (*US*) to engage in anal intercourse. □ **pack the mustard** *v.* [the colour of the mortar in the hod] [1930s] (*US tramp*) working as a brick layer or labourer. □ **pack the pillow** *v.* [use of *pillow* = menstrual pad] [2000s] (*US*) to menstruate. □ **pack (the) shit** *v.* (*also* **pack one's shit, pack them**) [SHIT *n.* (1a)/SHIT *n.* (4a)] **1** [1940s+] (*Aus.*) to be frightened [image of holding back fear-induced diarrhoea]. **2** [2000s] (*N.Z.*) to talk nonsense. □ **peanut-packer** *n.* [*PACK PEANUT BUTTER* above] [1970s+] (*US*) a male homosexual.

SE in slang uses

IN PHRASES

□ **pack in** *v.* **1** [20C+] to stop, to cease to function, to give up, to die. **2** [1950s+] (*US Und.*) to leave. **3** [1950s+] to end a relationship. □ **pack it in** *v.* (*also* **pack it up**) [SE *pack*, to put away] [1930s+] to stop doing something, usu. as a command. □ **pack off** *v.* [mid-18C–19C] to go away; also as imper. □ **pack the trail** *v.* [SE *pack*, a rucksack] [late 19C+] (*Aus.*) to journey along a trail, on foot or horseback. □ **pack up** *v.* **1** [1910s+] (*orig. milit.*) to tire, to abandon one's efforts, to stop doing something. **2** [1920s–40s] of a person, to die. **3** [1920s+] of machinery, or of anything that works mechanically, e.g. the human heart, to stop working; usu. as *packed up*, occas. *packed*. **4** [1970s] to reject. □ **pack up one's alls and be gone** *v.* (*also* **pack up one's awls and be**

gone) [SE *alls*, everything, or *awls*, tools] [mid-17C–1920s] to leave for good.

pack *v.*[2] [? SE *send packing*] [1920s+] (*Aus.*) to surpass, to beat, to be more enjoyable than something.

package *n.* **1** [late 19C–1930s] a drink. **2** [1910s+] (*US*) a police record; a jail sentence. **3** [1920s+] (*US*) a man, a person; thus (*US Und.*) a kidnap victim. **4** [1930s+] (*US drugs*) a supply of a given drug. **5** [1940s+] an attractive and usu. small, neat woman. **6** [1950s] (*US Und.*) a (long) prison term. **7** [1960s] (*US*) a baby, a pregnancy. **8** [1970s+] (*US*) the male genitals. **9** [1980s+] (*US*) the vagina. **10** [1990s+] (*US prison*) a positive report on a prisoner [the package of papers on which it is written]. **11** [1990s+] (*US black*) a lot, very much, a great deal. **12** [2000s] AIDS.

IN PHRASES

❑ **prize package** *n.* [1920s+] (*US*) a fool.

packer *n.* (*also* **pack**) **1** [late 19C–1940s] (*Aus.*) a *pack*horse [abbr.]. **2** [1990s+] (*drugs*) a thin stick, typically a chopstick, or a piece of metal coat hanger, used to pack a cocaine pipe. **3** *see* FUDGE-PACKER *under* FUDGE *n.*

packet *n.* [SE *packet*, a bundle of letters; thus lit. a 'packet of lies'] **1** [late 18C–mid-19C] a false report; thus *sell one a packet*, to hoax, to deceive, to lie. **2** [1910s+] (*orig. milit.*) a bullet or missile; *see* COP A PACKET below. **3** [1910s+] (*also* **pack, package**) a large sum of money; esp. in phr. *make/win a packet*. **4** [1930s–50s] trouble. **5** [1950s+] (*usu. gay*) the genitals, male or female. **6** [1980s+] constr. with *the*, everything, the lot. **7** [1990s+] (*US prison*) a long sentence.

IN PHRASES

❑ **cop a packet** *v.* (*also* **get a packet, have..., stop...**) [COP *v.* (3a); Brophy & Partridge, *Songs and Slang of the British Soldier* (1930), suggest the 'packet' of gauze and lint that comprised the First Field Dressing that would be applied to a wound] [1910s+] **1** to be killed or wounded, to get into trouble. **2** to suffer a dose of venereal disease. **3** to gain a great deal, poss. more than one bargained for; this can either be good (more money than expected) or bad (a longer prison sentence than feared). ❑ **cost a packet** *v.* [1930s+] to cost a great deal; thus joc. *Costa Packet*, any tourist resort in Spain popular with British working classes. ❑ **drop a packet** *v.* [1930s] to give birth.

IN EXCLAMATIONS

❑ **packets!** [late 19C] a general expression of disbelief.

packet from Paris *n.* (*also* **parcel from Paris**) [? clichéd identification of France with sex, though not usu. with procreative intercourse] [20C+] (*Aus./N.Z.*) a baby.

packie *n.* [abbr. N.Z. SE *pack*man] **1** [1940s+] (*N.Z.*) one who transports supplies by pack animal; also works as the cook. **2** *see* PACKY *n.*[2].

packing *n.*[1] [SE *pack*, i.e. the stomach] [late 19C–1910s] food, esp. of poor quality.

IN COMPOUNDS

❑ **packing-house** *n.* (*also* **packing-ken**) [late 19C–1910s] an eating house, a café; thus *packing house quail*, spare ribs; *packing-house rules*, no rules at all.

packing *n.*[2] *see under* PACK *v.*[1].

packy *n.*[1] [dial. *packy*, the calabash fruit, which resembles the human head] [1940s+] (*W.I.*) the skull, the head.

IN PHRASES

❑ **open packy** *v.* [1940s] (*W.I.*) to reveal one's innermost thoughts.

packy *n.*[2] (*also* **packie**) [the liquor is *packed up* to take away] [1970s+] (*US*) a liquor store.

pad *n.*[1] [Du. *pad*, and OHG *pfad*, the cant equivalent of the SE *path*] **1** [mid-16C–mid-19C] (*UK Und.*) the road. **2** [mid-17C] a villain's female companion. **3** [mid-17C–19C] (*UK Und.*) a highway robber, a footpad (but not a mounted highwayman). **4** [late 17C] a prostitute. **5** [late 17C–19C] an easy-paced horse. **6** [mid-18C–mid-19C] a tramp. **7** [mid-18C–19C] (*UK Und.*) highway robbery. **8** [mid-19C; 1950s] a walk. **9** [1940s] (*Aus.*) a foot.

DERIVATIVES

❑ **paddist** *n.* [late 17C–18C] (*Scot.*) a highwayman.

IN COMPOUNDS

❑ **pad borrower** *n.* [ironic use of SE *borrow*] [late 18C–early 19C] a horse thief. ❑ **pad-nag** *n.* [late 17C] a horse.

IN PHRASES

❑ **go out on the pad** *v.* [18C] (*UK Und.*) to go out to commit a robbery. ❑ **hoof the pad** *v.* [HOOF *v.* (1)] [mid-19C–1920s] (*Aus.*) to live as a tramp, to go on the tramp. ❑ **on the pad** **1** [late 17C–early 19C] going out to commit a robbery, usu. on the highway. **2** [17C; mid-19C–1910s] living as a tramp. ❑ **stand pad** *v.* (*also* **sit pad**) [SE *stand*/SE *sit*] [mid-19C–1900s] to beg at the roadside, usu. with a small piece of paper attached to one's jacket, declaring 'I am hungry'; also displaying deformities or handicaps.

pad *n.*[2] [SE *pad*, a mattress; best known in 20C+ in drug context, it was orig. used for the bed or couch on which an opium smoker could recline; it was then applied to an opium den, and was subseq. a beatnik term for a place where one could smoke cannabis] **1** [18C+] a bed. **2** [1930s+] a place, house or apartment, e.g. a prostitute's room. **3** [1930s+] (*also* **pads**) a padded cell. **4** [1940s+] (*US Und.*) a cell. **5** *see* PADDING KEN *under* PAD *v.*[1].

IN COMPOUNDS

❑ **padhouse** *n.* [1930s–40s] (*US black*) one's house, one's home. ❑ **pad money** *n.* (*also* **pad dough**) [1900s–50s] (*US*) money for a night's lodging or for admission into an opium den. ❑ **pad monster** *n.* *see* RACK MONSTER *under* RACK *n.*[2]. ❑ **pad room** *n.* [note carnival jargon *pad room*, a waiting room for performers] [1930s–50s] (*drugs*) a room in which drug users can gather and use their drugs.

IN PHRASES

❑ **pad down** *v.* (*also* **pad out**) [1930s+] (*US*) to go to bed, to sleep. ❑ **pad of cold cream** *n.* [1940s] (*US black/Southern*) an ice-cream parlour. ❑ **pad of dry scarfs** *n.* [SCARF *n.*] [1940s] (*US black/Southern*) a grocery store. ❑ **pad of galloping snapshots** *n.* [1940s] (*US black/Southern*) a cinema. ❑ **pad of stiffs** *n.* [STIFF *n.*[1] (2)] [1940s] (*US black*) a funeral parlour. ❑ **pad of stitches** *n.* [SE (*surgical*) *stitches*] [1940s–70s] (*US black*) a hospital. ❑ **pad of togs-in-the-rough** *n.* (*also* **pad of togs-in-rough**) [TOGS *n.* (1) + SE *in the rough*, unfinished] [1940s] (*US black/Southern*) a tailor's shop. ❑ **pad of wet scarfs** *n.* (*also* **pad of wet scarf**) [SCARF *n.*] [1940s] (*US black/Southern*) a restaurant. ❑ **pad out** *v.* *see* PAD DOWN above. ❑ **repent pad** *n.* [a woman who visits may 'repent of her sins' later] [1940s–70s] (*US black*) a bachelor's apartment. ❑ **squat pad** *n.* [SQUAT *v.* (1)] [1940s] (*US black*) **1** a lobby, a lounge. **2** a stool; a chair.

pad *n.*[3] [abbr. PADDY *n.*] **1** [late 18C+] an Irishman. **2** [mid-19C+] a nickname or intimate form of address for an Irishman.

pad *n.*[4] [SE *pad* (of paper), on which the payments are listed] [1940s+] (*US Und.*) **1** an establishment that pays bribes to the local police. **2** the regular bribes paid to members of a US police department.

IN PHRASES

❑ **on the pad** [1940s+] (*US Und.*) of the police, accepting bribes; of a villain, paying bribes.

pad *v.*[1] (*also* **pad it**) [PAD *n.*[1] (1)] **1** [early 17C–1930s] to travel as a tramp, thief or vagrant. **2** [mid-17C–mid-18C] to work as a highway robber on foot or on horseback. **3** [mid-17C–1910s] to walk, to wander.

IN COMPOUNDS

❑ **padding crib** *n.* [CRIB *n.*[1] (1)] **1** [mid-19C] (*Aus./UK Und.*) (*also* **padden crib**) a lodging house. **2** [1980s] (*US Und.*) a place to hide or to rest. ❑ **padding ken** *n.* (*also* **pad, padden-can, padden-ken**) [KEN *n.*[1] (1)] [mid-19C–1930s] (*Aus./UK Und.*) a lodging house frequented primarily by vagrants or thieves; thus *padding-ken keeper, padding-ken ranger*.

IN PHRASES

❑ **pad it** *v.* (*also* **pad one's beaters**) [BEATERS *n.*] [early 17C+] to travel on foot, to walk, esp. as a vagrant or person seeking work, or a prostitute. ❑ **pad the hoof** *v.* [HOOF *n.* (1)] **1** [late

18C+] to walk, to travel on foot; thus *hoof-padder*, a pedestrian. **2** [mid-19C] to leave in a hurry.

pad *v.*[2] [one 'pads' or fills the brain with information] [1950s] (*US black*) to inform, to tell.

SE in slang uses

(IN PHRASES)

▫ **pad (a bill)** *v.* [1930s+] fraudulently to add items to a bill or to an expense account statement in order to obtain money that one is not actually owed. ▫ **pad one's skull** *v. see under* SKULL *n.*[1]. ▫ **pad the bricks** *v. see* HIT THE BRICKS *under* BRICKS *n.*

pad *v.*[3] (*also* **pad down**) [PAD *n.*[2] (2)] [1950s–70s] (*US black*) to live somewhere.

padded *adj.* [1910s+] (*US Und.*) concealing contraband (stolen articles, drugs etc) on one's body for removal from a shop, deceiving customs men etc.

padden-can *n. see* PADDING KEN *under* PAD *v.*[1].

padden crib *n. see* PADDING CRIB *under* PAD *v.*[1].

padden-ken *n. see* PADDING KEN *under* PAD *v.*[1].

padder *n.*[1] [PAD *n.*[1] (1); Rowlands, *Martin-Mark-all* (1610), differentiates between the types of highway thief: 'Such as robbe on horse-backe were called high lawyers, and those who robbed on foote...called Padders'] [17C–mid-18C] one who robs on the highway, but does not work from a horse.

padder *n.*[2] [PAD *v.*[1] (3)] [19C] **1** in pl., the feet. **2** in pl., boots or shoes.

paddies *n.* (*also* **patties**) [? SE *pads*] [1970s+] (*US gay*) the buttocks.

padding *n.*[1] [PAD *v.*[1] (2)] (*UK Und.*) **1** [mid-17C–mid-19C] highway robbery. **2** [late 17C] working as a highway robber. **3** [late 17C] confidence trickery, swindling [ety. unknown; ? the conversation that accompanies walking].

(IN PHRASES)

▫ **go a-padding** *v.* [late 18C–early 19C] to rob on the highway.

padding *n.*[2] [2000s] (*UK police*) the practice of planting extra amounts of drugs to ensure a conviction.

Paddington *n.* [Tyburn, the site of London's main 18C gallows, was in the then village of *Paddington*]

pertaining to judicial execution

(IN COMPOUNDS)

▫ **Paddington fair (day)** *n.* [also a pun on the actual Paddington Fair] [late 17C–early 19C] (*UK Und.*) the hanging day, the day of execution. ▫ **Paddington spectacles** *n.* [early 19C] the hood that is pulled over the condemned man's head before the hanging.

(IN PHRASES)

▫ **dance/do the Paddington frisk** *v. see under* DANCE *v.* ▫ **go in the road to Paddington** *v. see under* DANCE *v.*

paddirappery *n.* [PADDY *n.* + RAP *v.*[1]] [mid-19C] (*UK Und.*) smooth talk, 'blarney'.

paddist *n. see under* PAD *n.*[1].

paddle *n.* [mid-19C+] **1** the hand. **2** a foot.

paddle *v.*[1] [SE *paddle*, to walk with short, uncertain steps, to toddle] [mid-19C] to run away, to leave.

paddle *v.*[2] [? SE *paddle*, to walk in shallow water] [late 19C] to drink strong liquor.

paddlefoot *n.* [he 'paddles about'] [1940s+] (*US*) an infantryman.

paddler *n.* [SE *paddle*, to beat] [1940s+] (*Aus.*) a police officer.

paddle the pickle *v. see under* PICKLE *n.*

Paddo *n.* [abbr. + -O *sfx* (3)] [1940s+] (*Aus.*) the suburb of *Padd*ington, Sydney.

paddock lice *n.* (*also* **pasture lice**) [2000s] (*N.Z.*) sheep.

Paddy *n.* (*also* **paddy, patty**) [common Irish name, *Patrick*; all race-related usages are derog.; the occupations are those considered to be stereotypically Irish] **1** [mid-18C+] an Irishman. **2** [19C+] a nickname or intimate form of address to an Irishman. **3** [mid-19C–1900s] (*US/Aus.*) a Chinese person [use of *Paddy* as generic for any foreigner]. **4** [1940s] (*US black*) a police officer, usu. male. **5** [1940s+] (*US black*) (*also* **paddy boy, paddy girl**) a white person, though not always Irish. **6** [1970s] (*US*) a bricklayer. **7** [1970s–80s] (*US black*) a white person, often derog. **8** [1970s+] (*Irish*) Irish whisky. **9** see PADDY WAGON below.

(IN COMPOUNDS)

▫ **Paddy-bashing** *n.* [BASH *v.* (1); on the pattern of *PAKI-BASHING under* PAKI *n.*] [2000s] beating up Irish people, usu. used of soldiers in Northern Ireland. ▫ **paddy boy** *n. see* sense 5 above. ▫ **paddy fever** *n.* (*also* **white fever**) [1960s] (*US black*) the desire for sex with white men or women. ▫ **paddy funeral** *n.* (*also* **paddy's funeral**) [20C+] any boisterous occasion, not necessarily a wake. ▫ **paddy girl** *n. see* sense 5 above. ▫ **paddy land** *n.* (*also* **Paddy's Isle, paddy's land**) [19C+] Ireland; thus *Paddy-lander*, an Irish person. ▫ **paddy-row** *n.* [early 19C–1910s] a fight that entails more verbal than physical aggression. ▫ **Paddy's apples** *n.* [stereotyping of potatoes as Ireland's staple food] [2000s] (*N.Z.*) potatoes. ▫ **Paddy's eyewater** *n.* [SE *eyewater* but note *EYEWATER under* EYE *n.*] [late 19C+] (*Irish*) illicitly distilled whisky, poteen. ▫ **paddy's funeral** *n. see* PADDY FUNERAL above. ▫ **Paddy's Goose** *n. see* separate entry. ▫ **paddy's lantern** *n.* [? a ref. to the lack of electricity in rural Ireland] [1930s+] the moon. ▫ **paddy's market** *n.* [note WW2 milit. use, the market in Cairo where Australian troops sold illegally manufactured goods, black market commodities etc; a similarly named market, frequented by Irish immigrants, existed in late-19C Glasgow] [late 19C–1950s] (*Aus.*) **1** the weekly market for cheap or secondhand goods held in the late 19C near Haymarket Square in Melbourne. **2** any kind of cheap market. ▫ **Paddy's toothache** *n. see IRISH TOOTHACHE under* IRISH *adj.* ▫ **paddy's watch** *n. see* PADDYWHACK ALMANAC *under* PADDYWHACK *n.* ▫ **paddy wagon** *n.* (*also* **paddy**) [? abbr. SE *padlock*, or with the implication that most US police (? or criminals) would be Irish] [20C+] (*orig. US*) the vehicle in which arrested people are transported to the local police station or prison. ▫ **paddywood** *n.* [PECKERWOOD *n.*] [1980s] (*US black*) a derog. term for a white person; also. ext. to Chicanos and Latinos.

(IN PHRASES)

▫ **come (the) Paddy (over)** *v.* [early 19C] to bamboozle, to confuse, to 'blarney'. ▫ **ignorant as Paddy's pig** *adj.* [1970s+] (*N.Z.*) very stupid. ▫ **what Paddy gave the drum** *n.* [i.e. a PADDYWHACK *n.* (4)] [mid-19C+] (*orig. milit.*) a thrashing, a beating.

paddy *n.*[1] [abbr.] [mid-19C+] (*UK Und.*) a padlock.

paddy *n.*[2] [pun on PAD *n.*[1] (5) = horse, i.e. a hobby horse] [late 19C] a hobby, a fad, a pastime.

paddy *n.*[3] [the stereotyped temperamental instability of an Irishman, i.e. PADDY *n.* (1)] [late 19C+] a tantrum, a fit of temper.

paddy *n.*[4] [PAD *n.*[2] (3)] [1940s–50s] (*UK prison*) a padded cell for mentally disturbed prisoners.

paddy *adj.* [PADDY *n.*] **1** [20C+] Irish. **2** [1940s+] (*US black*) (*also* **patty**) white.

paddy and mick *n.* [20C+] **1** stupid [rhy. sl. = THICK *adj.* (1a); stereotyping of Irish names]. **2** a pick (axe) [rhy. sl.].

Paddy O'Rourke *n.* [rhy. sl.] [1990s+] talk, conversation.

paddy quick *n.* [rhy. sl.] **1** [mid–late 19C] a stick. **2** [1960s] a kick.

paddy quick *adj.* [rhy. sl. = THICK *adj.* (1a)] [mid-19C] stupid.

Paddy's Goose *n.* [? its Irish landlord, thus PADDY *n.* (1). Mayhew, *London Labour and the London Poor*, (1861) IV 230/2: 'During the Crimean war, the landlord, when the Government wanted sailors to man the fleet, went among the shipping in the river, and enlisted numbers of men. His system of recruiting was very successful. He went about in a small steamer with a band of music and flags, streamers and colours flying. All this rendered him popular with the Admiralty authorities, and made his house extensively known to the sailors, and those connected with them.'] [mid-19C] the White Swan public house in High Street, Shadwell, the best known seaman's pub in mid-19C London.

Paddy Ward's pig *n.* [anecdotal] [mid-18C–mid-19C] a lazy person, one who is relaxing.

paddywax *n.* [var. on PADDYWHACK *n.* (4); but note PADDY *n.* (1) + WAX *v.*[2] (2)] [1910s–20s] a severe beating.

paddywhack *n.* [PADDY *n.* (1) + WHACK *n.*[2] (1) + negative stereotyping] **1** [late 18C–1910s] an Irishman, esp. when large and brawny. **2** [late 19C] a rage, a passionate outburst of temper. **3** [late 19C+] (*Irish*) stage or 'professional' Irishism, e.g. much use of 'Sure an' beggorrah, sorr…'. **4** [late 19C+] a severe beating.

IN COMPOUNDS

❑ **paddywhack almanac** *n.* (*also* **paddy's watch, paddywhack**) [*COME (THE) PADDY (OVER) under* PADDY *n.*, i.e. such an almanac confuses its user] [late 19C] an unlicensed almanac.

IN PHRASES

❑ **paddywhack the drumstick** *n.* [late 19C+] (*Aus.*) a spanking, a thrashing.

paddywhack *v.* [PADDYWHACK *n.* (4)] [late 19C+] to beat severely.

padiddle *n.* [ety. unknown; the term is used in a synon. travelling game whereby one shouts out 'Padiddle' when seeing such a vehicle; other players suffer a forfeit] [1990s+] (*US*) a vehicle with one burned-out headlight; thus any old or run-down vehicle.

padlock *n.*[1] [rhy. sl. = COCK *n.*[3] (1)] [1960s–70s] the penis.

padlock *n.*[2] *see* LOCK *n.*[1] (1a).

pa-dow! *excl.* [2000s] (*US black*) an excl. of approval, pleasure.

padraic *adj.* [rhy. sl. = *Padraig Pearse* (1879–1916), politician and revolutionary] [1980s] (*Irish*) fierce, strong.

padre *n.* [Sp. *padre*, father, thus a priest] [late 18C+] a (usu. milit.) chaplain.

padroller *n.* [ety. unknown] [1910s] (*US Und.*) a dice cheat.

pads *n.*[1] [affixed to the front and back, they 'pad' the car] [1930s–50s] (*US*) car licence plates.

pads *n.*[2] *see* PAD *n.*[2] (3).

paffle *n.* [ety. unknown] [mid-19C] (*UK Und.*) water; thus *paffle-broth*, water gruel; *jump-paffle*, spring-water; *Thames paffle*, water from the river Thames.

pag *n.*[1] [Ulster dial. *paughle*, a fat, lazy person] [20C+] (*Ulster*) a useless individual.

pag *n.*[2] *see* PAYOL *n.*

pagan *n.* **1** [late 16C–mid-17C] a prostitute [the idea of a paganic, i.e. Greek/Roman, worship of physical beauty, epitomized in the celebrated attractiveness of the Greek *hetairai*, mistresses, concubines or courtesans]. **2** [1980s] (*UK black*) a white person.

page *n.*

SE in slang uses

IN PHRASES

❑ **have a few of one's pages stuck together** *v.* [20C+] to be stupid, to be foolish.

pagger *n.* (*also* **pagga**) [Lowland Scot. *peg*, a blow or thump with the fist] [1990s+] (*Scot.*) a fight.

pagger *v.* [PAGGER *n.*] [1990s+] (*Scot.*) to fight.

pagnol *n. see* PAYOL *n.*

pahtner *n. see* PARTNER *n.* (2).

paid *adj.* [obs. SE *paid*, satisfied, content] **1** [mid-17C] drunk. **2** [1990s+] (*US campus*) wealthy. **3** [2000s] (*US prison*) the favourable outcome of a parole hearing.

paik *v.* [Scot. + northern UK dial. *paik*, to beat] [20C+] (*Ulster*) to beat up, to thrash.

pail *n.* [1940s] **1** (*US black*) the stomach. **2** (*US*) a car.

pail of lard *n. see* BUCKET OF LARD *under* BUCKET OF… *n.*

pain in the arse *n.* (*also* **pain in the ass, …asshole, …backside, …balls, …bum, …butt, …can, …clinkers, …hole, …pants, …tail, …whoozis, p.i.t.a.**) [ARSE *n.* (1)/ASS *n.* (2)/ASSHOLE *n.* (1)/BACKSIDE *n.* (1)/BALLS *n.* (1)/BUM *n.*[1] (1)/BUTT *n.*[1] (1a)/CAN *n.*[1] (1b)/CLINKERS *n.* (4)/HOLE *n.*[1] (1a)/SE *pants*/TAIL *n.* (2)/WHOOZIS *n.* (2)] [1930s+] **1** an annoying person. **2** (*also* **pain in the breakfast**) an annoying object, situation or circumstance.

IN PHRASES

❑ **give someone a pain in the arse** *v.* (*also* **give (someone) a pain in the tail**) [TAIL *n.* (2)] [1930s+] to irritate.

pain-in-the-ass *adj.* (*also* **pain-in-the-arse**) [PAIN IN THE ARSE *n.*] [1930s+] (*US*) infuriating.

pain (in the neck) *n.*[1] (*also* **pain in the arm, …ear, …face, …guts, …head**) [late 18C; 1910s+] **1** an annoying person, a bore, a euph. for PAIN IN THE ARSE *n.* **2** an annoying situation, anything considered unpleasant, typically a task one does not wish to perform. **3** (*Aus.*) a general insult.

IN PHRASES

❑ **give someone a pain in the neck** *v.* (*also* **give someone an ache, …a pain in the guts**) [late 19C+] to irritate.

pain (in the neck) *n.*[2] [rhy. sl.] [20C+] a cheque.

pain in the plaster *n. see under* PLASTER OF PARIS *n.*

pain in the puku *n.* [Maori *puku*, the stomach] [1940s+] (*N.Z.*) a stomach-ache; lit. and fig.

paint *n.* [spec. the colour red] **1** [1910s–20s] (*Aus.*) jam. **2** [1920s+] (*US tramp*) playing cards, usu. the royal cards. **3** [1930s+] (*Aus.*) cheap red wine. **4** [1940s] (*US*) ketchup/catsup.

IN COMPOUNDS

❑ **paint job** *n.* [1970s+] (*US*) one's skin colour. ❑ **paint remover** *n.* [20C+] (*orig. US*) **1** cheap, strong whisky or another drink. **2** strong, bitter coffee. ❑ **paint stripper** *n.* [20C+] an alcoholic drink of inordinate strength and fierceness.

IN PHRASES

❑ **dab the paint** *v. see* DAB *v.* ❑ **in full paint** *adj.* [1900s] (*Aus.*) dressed up. ❑ **up in the paints** *adj.* (*also* **up in the paint cards**) [gambling jargon *paints* = high (royal) cards] [1930s+] (*US*) a general intensifier; depending on context, extremely old, high, superior etc.

paint *adj.* [phr. *as exciting as watching paint dry*] [2000s] (*US black*) stupid; a waste of time.

paint *v.* **1** [mid–late 19C] to drink. **2** [1980s+] (*US gay*) to have a bowel movement during anal intercourse.

IN PHRASES

❑ **paint one's tonsils** *v.* [1930s] (*US*) to drink alcohol.

SE in slang uses

IN PHRASES

❑ **paint someone's eye for them** *v.* [late 19C–1910s] to give someone a black eye. ❑ **paint the pavement** *v. see under* PAVEMENT *n.* ❑ **paint the town pink** *v.* [1900s–40s] (*orig. US*) to go on a (modest) spree. ❑ **paint the town red** *v. see* separate entry. ❑ **paint the walls** *v.* [1990s+] to vomit forcefully.

painted peeper *n. see under* PEEPER *n.*

painters *n.*

SE in slang uses

IN PHRASES

❑ **have the painters in** *v.* [euph.] [20C+] of a woman, to be menstruating.

paint the town red *v.* (*also* **paint the town, paint the town purple, …scarlet, …vermillion, paint the place red**) [? the excesses of the Marquis of Waterford and a bunch of aristocratic vandals who on the night of 5–6 April 1837 literally painted Waterford red, daubing the buildings with paint; given the US origin, poss. linked to the image of turning an entire town into a 'red light district'] **1** [late 19C+] (*orig. US*) to go on a spree. **2** [1960s+] to vomit.

paipsey *adj.* [? UK dial. *papes*, a flour and water gruel, also a foolish youth; ult. SE *pap*, soft or semi-liquid food for infants or invalids] [20C+] (*W.I.*) insipid, weak, unattractive.

pair *n.* **1** [late 19C+] the female breasts. **2** [1960s+] (*US*) the testicles; usu. in phr. *have a pair*, to be macho, manly.

SE in slang uses

IN PHRASES

❑ **give someone a pair of gloves** *v.* [late 18C–early 19C] to give someone a bribe. ❑ **pair of pants** *n. see* PANTS *n.* (3). ❑ **pair of spectacles** *n.* [late 19C] two black eyes. ❑ **pair of tongs** *n.* [late 19C–1900s] a very thin person. ❑ **pair of wheels** *n.* [early 17C] a two-wheeled vehicle. ❑ **pair of wings** *n. see under* WING *n.*[1].

pair of braces *n. see* AIRS AND GRACES *n.* (2).

pair o' round-mys *n. see* ROUND ME HOUSES *n.*

paisa *n.* (*also* **piesa, pisa**) [Hind. *paisa*, the lowest denomination of coin, 100 to the rupee] [1940s–50s] (*W.I.*) money.

paisan *n.* (*also* **paisano**) [Ital. *paisan*, a peasant] **1** [20C+] an Italian, usu. used by fellow members of that race in an affectionate and congratulatory manner. **2** [1950s] a fool.

pajonk *n.* (*also* **pajawonk**) [? echoic of penile thrusts] [1940s–70s] (*US*) a penis.

Pak *n.* [abbr.] [1950s+] **1** *Pak*istan. **2** a derog. term for a *Pak*istani.

IN PHRASES

❑ **black Pak** *n.* [its dark colour] [1960s+] (*drugs*) a variety of hashish produced in Pakistan.

pakalolo *n.* [Hawaiian] [1980s+] (*US drugs*) marijuana.

pakeha *n.* [Maori *pakeha*, a European, poss. link to *pakepakeha*, 'imaginary white-skinned thing', is 'the least unlikely [theory] of those suggested' (*DNZE*)] **1** [early 19C+] (*N.Z.*) a white person; also as adj. **2** [1960s] the English language.

IN COMPOUNDS

❑ **pakeha time** *n.* [2000s] (*N.Z.*) disciplined time-keeping.

Paki *n.* (*also* **pakki**) [abbr. *Paki*stani; sometimes not derog. but merely abbr.] **1** [1960s+] a derog. term for any British Asian or East African Asian immigrant. **2** [1970s+] as *the Paki, the Paki's*, a corner shop, a small supermarket, latterly regardless of the race of the owner. **3** [2000s] as self-appropriated by second-generation UK Pakistanis.

IN COMPOUNDS

❑ **Paki-basher** *n.* [BASH *v.* (1)] [1970s+] a racist who beats up Asians. ❑ **Paki-bashing** *n.* [1970s+] racially motivated attacks on the UK Asian community, usu. by white youths. ❑ **Paki pox** *n.* [SE *pox*; its supposed prevalence, in racist eyes, among the era's Pakistani (in fact more likely Bangladeshi or East African Indian) immigrants] [1960s] a derog. term for smallpox.

Paki *adj.* (*also* **Pakki**) [1970s+] used derog. with ref. to any British Asian or East African Asian immigrant.

pal *n.* (*also* **pall, pal-pal, pell**) [Rom. *pal*, a brother] **1** [mid-18C+] a friend, an accomplice. **2** [mid-19C+] a term of familiar, usu. affectionate address.

IN PHRASES

❑ **pal in** *v.* [mid-19C–1910s] **1** to become friendly with. **2** of a man, to cohabit with a woman. **3** to live with another man. **4** (*UK Und.*) to work with, e.g. a pickpocketing gang. ❑ **palled-in** *adj.* [1900s–30s] of a man, living with a woman. ❑ **palling-in** *n.* [mid-19C] (*UK Und.*) a sexual relationship between a male and female thief. ❑ **pal off** *v.* [late 19C] to travel as friends. ❑ **pal with** *v.* (*also* **pal around, ...in, ...onto, ...out, ...up (with)**) [late 19C+] to befriend, to associate with.

palace of pleasure *n.* [19C] the vagina.

palam-pam *n. see* PAMPER *v.*

palarie *v.* [Ital. *parlare*, to talk] [mid-19C+] (*UK tramp/carnival*) to talk, to speak.

palatic *adj.* (*also* **pallatic**) [PARALYTIC *adj.*] [late 19C+] drunk.

palava *n.* [PALAVER *n.*] [1970s] (*W.I.*) an argument, a row.

palaver *n.* (*also* **perlaver**) [Port. *palabra*, speech, talk; used by Port. traders on the West Coast of Africa, where it was picked up by British sailors, incorporated into their jargon and thence to mainstream sl.] **1** [mid-18C+] chat, talk, conversation. **2** [mid-18C+] wearisome, idle or insincere talk. **3** [20C+] (*also* **palaverment**) business, concern, goings-on; thus *none of your palaver*, no business of yours. **4** [20C+] fussiness, a fuss; thus *what a palaver*, what a fuss. **5** [1930s] (*Scot.*) a fussy, ostentatious person; usu. as *old palaver*. **6** [1980s] (*UK black*) an argument, a fight.

IN COMPOUNDS

❑ **palaver-house** *n.* [mid-19C] any form of social centre.

palaver *v.* [PALAVER *n.*] **1** [mid-18C+] (*also* **pallaber**) to talk, to converse. **2** [mid-18C+] to ask (someone) for something, to beg from, to wheedle out of; thus n. *palaverer*, one who wheedles and flatters. **3** [1970s–80s] (*UK black*) to go around, to wander about.

DERIVATIVES

❑ **palavering** *n.* [19C–1920s] chatter, discussion.

pale *n.* **1** [mid-19C] brandy. **2** [1900s–40s] (*US black*) a white person.

pale about the gills *phr. see* GREEN ABOUT THE GILLS *under* GILLS *n.*

paled (out) *adv.* [one's complexion; ? PALEFACE *n.* (1)] [1960s+] (*Can. teen*) intoxicated by drink or drugs.

paleface *n.* [SE *paleface*, supposedly used by Native Americans to describe white settlers, but rarely found other than in fiction] **1** [mid-19C] (*US*) whisky. **2** [mid-19C+] (*orig. US black*) a white person.

palefaced *adj.* [PALEFACE *n.* (2)] [20C+] a derog. term describing a white person.

paleface nigger *n.* [PALEFACE *n.* (2) + NIGGER *n.*[1] (1)] [1940s+] (*US black*) a highly unpopular white person, whose skin does not save them from the opprobrium usu. heaped on blacks.

Palestine in London *n.* [play on the HOLY LAND *n.*] [early–mid-19C] St Giles, Bloomsbury, mainly occupied by the poor Irish and a well-known criminal slum.

palings *n.* [mid-19C] (*boxing*) the ribs.

Pal Joey *n.* [the book *Pal Joey*, by John O'Hara (1938–40)] [1940s–60s] (*orig. US*) a kept man; a pimp.

pall *n. see* PAL *n.*

pall *v.*[1] [ety. unknown; ? link to SE *paw*, to handle] [mid-19C] to detect.

pall *v.*[2] [orig. naut. jargon *pawl*, a short bar that locks the windlass or capstan and stops it from unwinding] [mid-19C] to stop, to cease; thus *pall that!* stop that!; *you pall me*, you confound me.

pallaber *v. see* PALAVER *v.* (1).

pallatic *adj. see* PALATIC *adj.*

pallbearers *n.* [fig. use of SE, but why?] [late 19C] (*US*) an order of crackers.

palled-in *adj. see under* PAL *n.*

palliard *n.* [Fr. *paille*, straw, upon which the beggars slept as they wandered the country, taking nightly refuge in barns or outhouses. The antithesis of the UPRIGHT MAN *n.*, palliards dressed in rags and adorned themselves with faked but still convincingly hideous sores and wounds. The term emerged *c.*1484, alongside its SE definition, 'a low or dissolute knave; a lewd fellow, a lecher, a debauchee' (*OED*)] **1** [late 15C–late 18C] (*UK Und.*) a professional beggar, born into a begging family. **2** [mid-19C] (*UK/US Und.*) a beggar-woman who uses a child, either her own or one borrowed for the purpose, to excite the pity of passers-by (this pity often increased by the child's piteous cries, created by judicious pinches and prods).

palliasse *n.* [SE *palliasse*, a straw bed or mattress] [19C] a prostitute.

palling-in *n. see under* PAL *n.*

pallish *adj. see* PALLY *adj.*

pall mall *n.* [rhy. sl. = GAL *n.* (1)] [late 19C] a woman.

pally *n.*[1] [PAL *n.* (2)] [late 19C+] a direct term of address; intimacy is not mandatory.

pally *n.*[2] [*Palais de Dance*] [1920s+] a dancehall.

pally *adj.* (*also* **pallish**) [PAL *n.* (1)] [late 19C+] friendly, affectionate.

palm *n.* [PALM *v.* (2)] [late 19C] (*US*) a bribe.

palm *v.* **1** [18C; 19C+] to pass counterfeit money, or anything fake. **2** [19C+] to pass over money as a bribe; thus *palmed*, used of one who has been bribed.

DERIVATIVES

❑ **palmistry** *n.* [play on SE] **1** [early 18C] theft. **2** [1910s–20s] bribery.

IN PHRASES

❑ **Mr Palmer is concerned** [early 19C] the matter involves bribery.

palmer *n.* [SE *palm*, to conceal in the palm of one's hand] **1** [late 17C–19C] a cheat who palms cards, dice etc. **2** [mid-19C] a shoplifter [also pun on SE *palmer*, an itinerant monk, bound by vows of eternal poverty]. **3** [mid-19C] a beggar who visits shops and claims to be collecting halfpence engraved with a harp, offering the shopkeeper 13 pence for a shilling's worth and persuading them to empty all their coppers on the counter. While they search the pile, the palmer hides as many coins as possible.

palmer house *v.* [the walking done by the hard-working waiters of Chicago's *Palmer House* Hotel] [1930s–40s] (*US black*) to walk flat-footed; thus *palmer houses*, flat feet.

palm-grease *n. see* PALM OIL *n.*

palming *n.* [PALMER *n.* (2)] [mid-19C] (*UK Und.*) the robbery of a shop by a pair of thieves, one engaging the shopkeeper in banter, the other committing the robbery.

palming-racket *n.* [SE *palm*, to conceal in one's palm + RACKET *n.*[1] (1)] [early 19C] (*UK Und.*) the concealing of money in one's palm.

palmistry *n. see under* PALM *v.*

palm oil *n.* (*also* **palm-grease, palm soap**) [used to GREASE *v.*[1] (1) someone's palm] [early 17C; 19C+] money, usu. in the form of a bribe.

palm-oil *v.* [PALM OIL *n.*] [late 19C] to bribe; to pay off.

paloma *n. see* POLONE *n.*

palomino *n.* [SE *palomino*, 'a light brown or cream-coloured horse with pale mane and tail, believed to have been developed from Arab stock' (*OED*)] [1930s–60s] (*orig. US black*) an attractive female.

palone/paloney *n. see* POLONE *n.*

palooey *n. see* BALOOEY *n.*

palooka *n.* (*also* **palook, palooker, palooko**) [coined by Jack Conway (d.1928) of *Variety* magazine, and given wide currency by Ham Fisher's comic strip 'Joe Palooka' (launched 1930)] [1920s+] (*US*) **1** a boxer, occas. wrestler, usu. one who is both large and stupid. **2** a large and stupid person. **3** a person, irrespective of size or intelligence. **4** a bodyguard; a thug.

DERIVATIVES

❑ **Palookaville** *n.* [-VILLE *sfx*[1]] [1950s] a metaphorical 'home' for second-rate boxers.

pal-pal *n. see* PAL *n.*

pal squad *n.* [proprietory name *Pal*, a dog-food] [1980s+] (*Aus. prison*) a dog squad used for searching cells.

palsy *n.* (*also* **palsie, palsy-walsy**) [ext. of PAL *n.* (1); redup.] [1930s+] (*orig. US*) a friend, esp. as a form of address.

palsy *adj.* (*also* **palsy-walsy**) [PALSY *n.*; redup.] [1930s+] overly friendly.

pam *n.* [Fr. *pamphile*, a card-game in which the knave of clubs is the highest card, trumping all opposition; ult. Gk *pamphilos*, beloved of all. The Fr. game was imported to Scot., where *pamphie* and *pawnie* were popular alternatives, both meaning knave of clubs, and to England, where *pam* became the term of choice] **1** [late 17C–1910s] the knave of clubs; also in fig. use. **2** [18C–early 19C] a popular card-game.

Pam and her five sisters *n.* [pun on *Pam*/SE *palm*] [1990s+] the hand as an agency of masturbation.

Pamela *adj.* [initial letter] [2000s] (*S.Afr. gay*) pathetic.

pam-pam *n.* [echoic; but note Twi *pam*, to chase away, and *pam-pam*, to persecute, to drive away] [1940s] (*W.I.*) **1** a flogging. **2** an argument, a fuss, a noisy disorder.

pamper *v.* (*also* **palam-pam**) [? W.I. *pam-palam*, a child's term, used to register their amusement of another child's punishment] [20C+] (*W.I., Bdos*) to feel the sting of a lashing.

Pamper pirate *n.* (*also* **Pamper sniffer**) [*Pampers*, brandname of a line of disposable nappies or diapers + SE *pirate/sniffer*] [1990s+] (*US Und.*) a child molester.

pampoen *n.* [Cape Du. *pampoen*, pumpkin] [1940s+] (*S.Afr.*) a fool (sometimes used affectionately).

pampootie *n.* [Irish *pamúpta*, a basic leather shoe, but note Fr. *pantouffle*, a slipper] [1900s–60s] (*Irish*) a slipper.

pan *n.*[1] [SE *pan*, as something round or a container] **1** [late 17C+] the female genital area. **2** [mid-19C+] (*US*) the mouth. **3** [1910s] the head. **4** [1910s+] the human face. **5** [1970s+] (*US gay*) the anus.

IN PHRASES

❑ **shut one's pan** *v.* [late 18C–1920s] to be quiet; esp. as imper. *shut your pan!*

SE in slang uses

IN COMPOUNDS

❑ **panhead** *n.* [the resemblance of their badge to a pan-lid] [1940s] (*W.I.*) a district constable. ❑ **panwit** *n.* [1990s+] (*UK juv.*) a fool. ❑ **pan-wrestler** *n.* [1940s] (*US*) a cook.

IN PHRASES

❑ **down the pan** *see under* DOWN *adv.*[2]. ❑ **go down the pan** *v. see* GO DOWN THE TOILET *under* TOILET *n.* ❑ **in the pan** [i.e. the SE *lavatory pan*; thus euph. for IN (THE) SHIT *under* SHIT *n.*] [1930s–60s] (*US*) in difficulties, facing problems.

pan *n.*[2] [PAN *v.*[1] (1)] [1900s–20s] a criticism.

pan *n.*[3] [SE *brainpan*] [1920s] (*US*) talent.

IN PHRASES

❑ **get the pan** *v.* [1900s] (*US*) to be criticized, denigrated. ❑ **on the pan** [1900s–10s] (*US Und.*) facing criticism, under verbal attack. ❑ **put someone on the pan** *v.* [1900s–10s] (*US*) to subject someone to criticism.

pan, the *n.*[1] [abbr. St *Pancras*] [mid–late 19C] the workhouse, esp. the St Pancras workhouse.

pan, the *n.*[2] [20C+] (*Ulster*) a frying pan of food, a fry-up.

pan *v.*[1] [the blow is lit. or fig. given with a SE *pan*] **1** [20C+] (*orig. US*) to criticize severely, to denigrate. **2** [1940s+] to hit in the face.

pan *v.*[2] *see* PANHANDLE *v.* (1).

Panama red *n.* (*also* **Panama cut, ...gold, red**) [1960s+] (*drugs*) a variety of marijuana, grown in Panama.

Panamite *n. see* PENNEMITE *n.*

panatella *n.* [Am. Sp. *panatella*, a long slender cigar tapering at the sealed end] [1930s–60s] (*drugs*) **1** high-grade marijuana, esp. that imported from South or Central America. **2** a large marijuana cigarette, resembling a cigar.

pancake *n.* [play on the SE comestible, with ref. to being 'good enough to eat' or 'flipped'] **1** [19C+] the vagina. **2** [late 19C–1940s] (*US black*) a black person viewed as overly friendly towards, or imitative of whites [a *pancake* is cooked brown on the outside but is white within]. **3** [1930s+] (*US*) an attractive young woman, esp. with overtones of promiscuity. **4** [1950s] (*US gay*) one who engages in homosexual intercourse and takes both the dominant and passive roles [he or she is 'flipped' from being sexually 'on top' or 'underneath']. **5** [1970s+] (*US gay*) a heterosexual woman [from a gay perspective, she is 'flipped' into the missionary position for sex].

pancake *v.* [making the object 'flat as a pancake'] **1** [1910s] (*US*) to crash. **2** [1950s] to flatten. **3** [1970s] (*US*) to knock down and run over. **4** [1980s+] (*US black/teen*) to lower the body of an automobile.

pancakes! *excl.* [1910s–20s] an excl. used to convey one's derision for what has just been said, e.g. *She's a pretty girl. Pretty? Pancakes!*

pancake(s) and syrup *n.* [1990s+] (*drugs*) a combination of glutethimide and codeine cough syrup.

Pancho *n.* [the stereotypical Mexican name] [1960s+] (*US*) **1** a derog. form of address to an anonymous Mexican man. **2** a Puerto Rican.

pancho *adj.* [the stereotypical Mexican name] [1940s–60s] (*US*) pertaining to a Mexican or to Mexican lifetsyle, fashions etc.

pancoot *n.* [? W.I. *pan cart*, a wheelbarrow, i.e. something large and inelegant] [2000s] (*UK black*) a very unattractive woman.

pancrack *n.* [ety. unknown; ? fig. link to Dev. dial. *pancrock*, a skirt with folds] [1980s+] the social security or the dole office.

pancridge parson *n.* [corruption of St *Pancras*, London, where the clergy were presumably held in low esteem] [early 17C–mid-19C] a general term of contempt.

pancrocked *adj.* [ety. unknown; ? link to CROCKED *adj.* (2)] [20C+] (*Ulster*) exhausted.

p and q *n.* [abbr. *p*eace *and q*uiet] [1990s+] (*US prison*) solitary confinement.

pane *n. see* WINDOWPANE *n.*[1].

panel *n.*[1] *see* PANEL THIEF *under* PANEL *adj.*

panel *n.*[2] *see* PARNEL *n.*

panel *adj.* in combs. below referring to a confidence game carried out in a brothel, supplied with false panels that permitted access to the prostitute's room so that the client could be robbed or beaten up; note James D. McCabe, *Secrets of a Great City* (1868): 'PANEL THIEVING. This method of robbery is closely connected with street walking. The girl in this case acts in concert with a confederate, who is generally a man. She takes her victim to her room, and directs him to deposit his clothing on a chair, which is placed but a few inches from the wall at the end of the room. This wall is false, and generally of wood. It is built some three or four feet from the real wall of the room, thus forming a closet. As the whole room is papered and but dimly lighted, a visitor cannot detect the fact that it is a sham. A panel, which slides noiselessly and rapidly, is arranged in the false wall, and the chair with the visitor's clothing upon it is placed just in front of it. While the visitor's attention is engaged in another quarter, the girl's confederate, who is concealed in the closet, slides back the panel, and rifles the pockets of the clothes on the chair. The panel is then noiselessly closed. When the visitor is about to depart, or sometimes not until long after his departure, he discovers his loss'.

IN COMPOUNDS

❑ **panel crib** *n.* (*also* **panel den, ...house, ...joint, ...store**) [CRIB *n.*[1] (3) /DEN *n.* (2)/ HOUSE *n.*[1] (1)/ JOINT *n.* (3b)/SAmE *store*] [mid-19C–1950s] a brothel, esp. one which specializes in robbing the clients. ❑ **panel game** *n.* [GAME *n.* (6)] **1** [mid-19C] (*US Und.*) the robbing of a prostitute's client by stealing his possessions while he is having sex. **2** [late 19C] (*US Und.*) (*also* **panel trick**) a form of confidence trick involving the passing of counterfeit money. ❑ **panel thief** *n.* (*also* **panel, panel dodger, ...worker**) [SE *thief/dodger*/WORKER *n.*[1] (1)] [mid-19C–1940s] (*US*) a thief, usu. the accomplice of a prostitute, who takes advantage of her client's preoccupation to rob him, using a special panel to enter her room.

panel *v.*[1] [mid-19C–1920s] to pursue the *PANEL GAME under* PANEL *adj.*

panel *v.*[2] [SE *panel-beat*] [1990s+] to attack, to beat up.

DERIVATIVES

❑ **panelling** *n.* [2000s] a beating.

panem *n. see* PANNAM *n.*

pane of glass *n. see* WINDOW *n.*

pang *v.* [Scot.] [20C+] (*Ulster*) to cram full.

pangonadalot *n.* [ety. unknown] [1970s+] (*drugs*) heroin.

panhandle *n.* **1** [mid-19C+] (*US*) the act of begging; thus the *panhandle beat*, the world of beggary [SE *pan*, into which the charitable donor placed money, or the goldfields, where hopefuls panned for gold, washing earth and rocks in perforated 'pans']. **2** [1990s+] an erect penis [resemblance]. **3** [1990s+] a fool, an unpleasant person [fig. use of sense 2].

IN PHRASES

❑ **work the panhandle** *v.* [1900s] to beg.

panhandle *v.* [PANHANDLE *n.* (1)] **1** [late 19C+] (*US*) (*also* **pan**) to beg. **2** [1970s] in fig. use, to elicit.

panhandler *n.* [PANHANDLE *v.* (1)] [late 19C+] (*orig. US*) a professional beggar.

pani *n. see* PARNEY *n.* (2).

pania *n.* [*Spania*rd; such individuals are seen as setting themselves aside from mainstream Belize society and culture] [20C+] (*W.I., Belize*) a Belizian of Spanish descent.

panic *n.* **1** [1910s+] (*drugs*) a period when drugs are hard to purchase; thus *panic man*, a dealer or a drug addict who is desperate for supplies. **2** in fig. uses. (**a**) [1920s–50s] (*US black*) someone or something outstanding, exceptional. (**b**) [1940s+] (*Irish*) someone or something ridiculous, amusing.

panicky *adj.* [1940s] (*US black*) extremely elated, ecstatically happy, highly excited.

pan kibba *n.* [SE *pan cover*] [1940s] (*W.I.*) a district constable.

pan-loaf *adj. see* UPPER CRUST *adj.*

pannam *n.* (*also* **panem, pannum, panum, pennam, pinum**) [Lat. *panis*/Fr. *pain*, bread; note 1573 edn of Harman reads 'yannam'] **1** [mid-16C–19C] (*UK Und.*) bread; thus (mid-19C) *pannam-fencer*, a street pastry-seller. **2** [late 19C–1930s] (*Aus.*) any form of food.

IN COMPOUNDS

❑ **pannam bound** *v.* [mid-19C] (*UK prison*) to stop the issue of rations to a prisoner. ❑ **pannam-struck** *adj.* [mid-19C] (*UK Und.*) very hungry.

panney *n.*[1] (*also* **panny**) [ety. unknown; ? Rom.] [mid-18C–mid-19C] the highway.

panney *n.*[2] (*also* **panny**) [? SE *butler's pantry*, the repository of the silverware and similar valuables] [late 18C–mid-19C] (*UK Und.*) **1** a house. **2** a burglary; thus *do a panny*, to rob a house.

IN COMPOUNDS

❑ **panney-lay** *n.* (*also* **panny-lay**) [LAY *n.*[3] (1)] [early 19C–1910s] burglary, house-breaking.

pannikin *n.* [SE *pannikin*, a small iron drinking vessel] [late 19C–1930s] (*Aus.*) the head.

IN COMPOUNDS

❑ **pannikin boss** *n.* (*also* **panno**) [SE *boss*; abbr. *pann*ikin + -O *sfx* (3); the image is of one who was allowed to serve water to a gang of convicts] [late 19C+] (*Aus.*) a minor official, a 'jack-in-office'.

IN PHRASES

❑ **off one's pannikin** *adj.* [late 19C–1930s] (*Aus.*) eccentric, crazy; thus *go off one's pannikin*, to lose one's temper, to lose emotional control.

panning *n.* [PAN *v.*[1]] **1** [1920s] (*US Und.*) a beating. **2** [1930s+] very harsh criticism, e.g. a very bad review.

pannum *n. see* PANNAM *n.*

panny *n. see under* PANNEY.

pannyman *n.* [PANNEY *n.*[2] + SE sfx *-man*] [19C] a housebreaker, a burglar.

panorama *n.*[1] [corruption of SE *paramour*] [late 19C] a lover.

panorama *n.*[2] [rhy. sl.; pronounced with a short 'a'] [late 19C] a hammer.

pansy *n.* (*also* **pansie**) **1** [late 19C–1900s] (*US*) an admirable person. **2** [1910s+] (*also* **pansy-wansy, panz**) an effeminate and/or homosexual man [redup.; abbr.]. **3** [1920s] (*US black*) a woman, one's girlfriend. **4** [1930s+] a contemptible cowardly person.

DERIVATIVES

❑ **pansified** *adj.* [1930s+] effeminate, homosexual.

IN PHRASES

❑ **pansy up** *v.* [1930s–70s] **1** of a man, to titivate oneself in an effeminate manner. **2** of a homosexual, to flirt.

pansy *adj.* [PANSY *n.* (2)] [1920s+] effeminate, homosexual.

pansy *v.* [PANSY *n.* (2)] [1960s–70s] (*US*) of a homosexual man, to act in an overtly effeminate manner.

pansy-wansy *n. see* PANSY *n.* (2).

panter *n.*[1] [the line 'As pants the hart for cooling streams/When heated in the chase' (Nahum Tate and Nicholas Brady, *New Version of the Psalms*, 1696); ult. f. Ps. 42:1, 'As the hart panteth after the water brooks so panteth my soul after thee, O God'. The pun indicates, as does B.E., that sense 2 is the general use. However, Grose (1785) cites 'the animal' and in 1796 adds 'the human heart, which temporarily pants in times of danger'] **1** [late 17C–mid-19C] the human heart. **2** [late 18C–early 19C] (*UK Und.*) a hart or male deer.

panter *n.*[2] [1940s] underwear.

panters *n.* [their motion when breathing] [late 19C–1900s] the female breasts.

panther piss *n.* (*also* **panther, panther blood, ...milk, ... purge, ...sweat**) [PISS *n.* (4b)/PURGE *n.*] **1** [1920s+] strong home-brewed or cheap liquor, usu. gin. **2** [1950s] nonsense.

panties *n.* **1** [mid-19C] pantaloons. **2** [1970s+] (*US prison*) abbreviated underwear worn by a prison homosexual; also in general homosexual use.

IN PHRASES

❑ **get one's panties in a bunch/...up one's crack** *v. see* GET ONE'S KNICKERS IN A TWIST *under* KNICKERS *n.*

pantile *n.* (*also* **pantiler**) [SE *pantile*, a tile in an ogee shape, often used as a roofing tile] **1** [late 18C–mid-19C] a religious dissenter; thus *pantile-house, pantile-shop*, a dissenters' meeting house [the meeting houses of rural dissenters were often roofed with pantiles]. **2** [mid-19C] a hat. **3** [mid-19C] a hard biscuit, sometimes with jam spread on it.

pantile *adj.* [PANTILE *n.* (1)] [18C] dissenting.

pantomime cow *n. see* BULL AND COW *n.*

pant python *n. see* PYJAMA PYTHON *n.*

pantry *n.* **1** [1910s–20s] (*US*) the stomach. **2** [1920s] (*US black*) the vagina.

pants *n.* **1** [late 19C–1910s; 1990s+] nonsense, rubbish; early use in phr. *one's name is pants* [var. on KNICKERS! *excl.*]. **2** [1910s+] constr. with *the*, the essence; usu. with a v. in phr. — *the pants off*, to do something to excess, e.g. KID THE PANTS OFF *under* KID *v.* **3** [1930s–40s] (*US black*) (*also* **pair of pants**) a man [meton.].

IN PHRASES

❑ **bore the pants off** *v.* (*also* **bore the knickers off**) [1930s+] to bore completely and totally. ❑ **bust one's pants** *v. see* BUST ONE'S ASS *under* BUST *v.*[1]. ❑ **scare the pants off** *v.* (*also* **scare the slacks off**) [1930s+] to terrify. ❑ **have one by the seat of one's pants** *v. see* HAVE SOMEONE BY THE BALLS *under* BALLS *n.* ❑ **take the pants off** *v.* (*also* **lick the pants off, slug..., thrash...**) [LICK *v.*[1] (2)/SLUG *v.*[2] (2)] [1930s+] to beat convincingly, to overwhelm.

SE in slang uses

IN COMPOUNDS

❑ **pants man** *n.* [1960s+] (*Aus.*) a womanizer. ❑ **pants rabbit** *n.* (*also* **pants rat**) [1910s+] (*US*) a body louse.

IN PHRASES

❑ **get into someone's pants** *v.* (*also* **get inside someone's pants, get into someone's drawers, ...knickers**) [1940s+] to seduce. ❑ **get some pants** *v.* [1960s] (*US black*) of a man, to have sexual intercourse. ❑ **give someone pants** *v.* [1960s] (*US black*) of a woman, to allow sexual intercourse. ❑ **in short pants** *adj.* [i.e. what children wear] [1960s] (*US*) impoverished; out of work. ❑ **keep one's feet in one's pants** *v.* [1960s] (*US black*) to keep calm, to restrain one's emotions. ❑ **pull up one's pants** *v.* [1940s] (*US*) to stop talking and interfering. ❑ **wear the pants** *v.* (*also* **pull on the pants**) [coined in an era when only men were thought to wear pants (trousers)] [late 19C+] (*orig. US*) to be the dominant member of a heterosexual partnership. ❑ **wet one's pants** *v.* (*also* **spot one's pants, wet one's knickers**) [the image is of involuntary urination, whether through fear or excitement] **1** [1930s+] to panic, to lose control, to get over-excited. **2** [1960s+] to find extremely exciting or attractive.

IN EXCLAMATIONS

❑ **keep your pants on!** (*also* **hold your pants on! keep your britches on! ...diaper on! ...drawers on! ...knickers on!**) [1920s+] (*orig. US*) calm down! don't lose (emotional) control!

pants *adj.* [PANTS *n.* (1)] [1990s+] rubbish, second-rate, inferior.

pants *v.* [1940s+] (*mainly juv.*) to remove someone's trousers whether they like it or not.

pants! *excl.* [PANTS *n.* (1)] [1990s+] nonsense! rubbish!

pantsula *n.* [? S. Sotho *patsola*, to split open (referring to links with violent crime) or ? S. Sotho *pasola*, to slap, to strike sharply (with a whip) (referring to elements of typical dance styles)] [1970s+] (*S.Afr.*) a township dandy whose life is dedicated to the purchase of expensive, fashionable clothes.

pant-worm *n.* [1990s+] (*US prison*) the penis.

panty-assed *adj.* [PANTIES *n.* (2) + -ASSED *sfx*] [1970s] (*US*) effeminate, homosexual.

pantyman *n.* [the image of his wearing women's *panties*; note PANTIES *n.* (2)] [20C+] (*W.I.*) an effeminate man, a homosexual.

pantywaist *n.* [the image of his wearing women's *panties*] [1930s+] (*orig. US*) a weak, effeminate man.

pantywaisted *adj.* (*also* **pantywaist**) [PANTYWAIST *n.*] [1930s+] (*orig. US*) weak, effeminate.

panum *n. see* PANNAM *n.*

panya *adj.* [mispron. of *Spanish*] [1940s+] (*W.I.*) Spanish.

panz *n. see* PANSY *n.* (2).

panzer head *n.* [the German *Panzer*, lit. 'Panther', armoured units (and tanks) of WW2] [1980s] a term of abuse used of someone who is or resembles a German.

panzy *n.* [? PANNEY *n.*[2]] [mid-19C] (*UK Und.*) a burglar; a burglary.

pap *n.*[1] [abbr.] **1** [mid-19C+] *pap*er money [orig. UK but by mid-20C Aus. only]. **2** [1900s] (*US*) a news*pap*er.

pap *n.*[2] [abbr.] [1990s+] a *pap*parazzo.

pap *n.*[3] **1** *see* PAPA *n.* (1). **2** *see* POP *n.*[3].

pap *adj.* (*also* **pappy**) [Afk. *pap*, soft] [1910s+] (*S.Afr.*) of persons or objects, weak, feeble.

pap *v.* [SE *paparazzi*] [2000s] to take a (snatched) photograph of a celebrity.

papa *n.* [SE *papa*, father] (*US*) **1** [late 19C+] (*also* **pap**) an affectionate name used by a woman to her husband, lover or pimp. **2** [1920s+] oneself. **3** [1930s–40s] (*US Und.*) a Lincoln automobile. **4** [1940s+] a masculine lesbian. **5** [1950s+] an older homosexual man.

IN PHRASES

❑ **hot papa** *n.* (*also* **red-hot papa**) [HOT *adj.* (1a)] [20C+] (*US Und.*) a womanizer; a dandy. ❑ **real papa, the** *n.* [cognate with DADDY *n.* (6)] [late 19C] the best, the ultimate. ❑ **sweet papa** *n. see under* SWEET *adj.*[1].

IN EXCLAMATIONS

❑ **sweet papa!** *see under* SWEET *adj.*[1].

papa! *excl.* (*also* **poopa! pupa!**) [? Twi *papa*, very well, very much] [1960s+] (*W.I.*) **1** a general expression of surprise and approval. **2** an emphasis placed at the end of a sentence, the equivalent of SE *sir!*; esp. in excl. *no, papa!*

papa-tree-top-tall *n.* [1930s–40s] (*US black*) an extremely tall man.

papbroek *n.* [Afk. *pap*, soft + *broek*, trousers, breeches] [1930s+] (*S.Afr.*) a coward, a weakling.

pape *n.* [SE *papist*] [20C+] a Roman Catholic.

paper *n.* (*also* **papers**) **1** [late 18C; late 19C+] (*orig. US black*) money, usu. notes. **2** [late 18C+] any form of money order, IOU, promissory note or financial document other than actual cash. **3** [late 18C+] free passes of admission to a theatre or other entertainment. **4** [late 18C+] those who use free passes. **5** [mid-19C] (*UK Und.*) counterfeit banknotes. **6** [mid-19C] (*US*) playing cards. **7** [mid-19C] (*US*) an admission ticket, e.g. to a dance; also a forged ticket. **8** [late 19C–1920s] (*US*) marked cards. **9** [late 19C–1940s] (*US*) posters or similar publicity material. **10** [20C+] (*US*) a forged or useless cheque or other financial instrument. **11** [1910s+] (*drugs*) cigarette papers, esp. when used for rolling marijuana cigarettes. **12** [1910s+] any form of legal or similarly authoritative documentation, e.g. a marriage certificate, prison documentation, a search warrant. **13** in drug uses. (**a**) [1920s–40s] a sheet of paper impregnated with a drug in solution or any other form of smuggling drugs into prison. (**b**) [1920s+] a measure of heroin, contained in a folded square of paper; hence a *quarter paper*, $25 worth of a narcotic. (**c**) [1960s–70s] a drug prescription. (**d**) [1990s+] crack cocaine. (**e**) [2000s] a small amount of methamphetamine. **14** [1930s–60s] (*US tramp*) a railroad ticket. **15** [2000s] (*US prison*) proof that a prisoner is an informer.

IN COMPOUNDS

❑ **paperback** *n.* [1930s] (*US*) a dollar bill. ❑ **paper chaser** *n.* [2000s] (*US black*) one who is looking for money, usu. a drug dealer. ❑ **paper fiend** *n.* [FIEND *n.* (2)] [1940s–50s] (*drugs*) one who sucks the amphetamine-impregnated strips from an amphetamine inhaler. ❑ **paper hanger** *n. see* separate entry. ❑ **paper-layer** *n. see* PAPER HANGER *n.* ❑ **paper marriage** *n.* [the banknotes employed in funding such a wedding; there may be an added implication of *paper*, spurious, i.e. the marriage is for social convenience rather than love] [late 19C] a society wedding. ❑ **paper pusher** *n.* [PUSHER *n.* (3b)] **1** [1920s–80s] (*US Und.*) one who passes counterfeit notes. **2** *see also* SE compounds below. ❑ **paperwork** *n.* [pun on SE *paperwork*, documents] [1990s+] money.

IN PHRASES

❑ **big paper** *n.* (*also* **tall paper**) [SE *big*/TALL *adj.* (4c)] [1990s+] (*US black*) a great deal of money. ❑ **burn paper** *v.* [1970s] (*US Und.*) to pass counterfeit cheques, money orders or other financial instruments. ❑ **hang paper** *v.* [1930s+] (*US Und.*) to pass counterfeit cheques or similar financial documents. ❑ **hold paper on** *v.* [1960s+] to stand as a creditor to someone. ❑ **hot paper** *n.* [HOT *adj.* (5)] [1940s–50s] (*US Und.*) any form of fraudulent document, esp. of a financial nature, e.g. a fake cheque. ❑ **lay paper** *v.* (*also* **sling paper**) [20C+] (*US Und.*) to pass counterfeit money or stolen cheques. ❑ **pass paper** *v.* [1970s] to use forged cheques, stolen credit cards. ❑ **tall paper** *n. see* BIG PAPER above.

SE in slang uses

DERIVATIVES

❑ **paperer** *n.* [late 19C] one who issues or receives free passes to a theatre or other entertainment.

IN COMPOUNDS

❑ **paper boy** *n.* [pun on SE *paper boy*] **1** [1960s] (*drugs*) a heroin peddler [sense 13b above]. **2** [1990s+] a male who has had sex with a lot of people in his area; i.e. they HAVE BEEN AROUND *v.* (2). ❑ **paper-fake** *v.* [FAKE *v.*[1] (3)] [mid-19C] to sell ballads on the street. ❑ **paper maker** *n.* [mid–late 19C] **1** a gatherer of rags and other saleable rubbish from the streets and gutters. **2** a beggar who poses as an agent of a paper-mill and is thus given cast-off rags, which are then sold for profit. ❑ **paper man** *n.* [mid-19C] (*Aus.*) a convict holding a ticket of leave. ❑ **paper mill** *n.* [mid-19C] (*US*) a small, unstable bank. ❑ **paper pusher** *n.* **1** [1940s+] a bureaucrat or clerk of the lowliest rank, the implication being that they never write on, only push around, paper; thus as v. *push paper*. **2** *see also* sl. compounds above. ❑ **paper stainer** *n.* [SE *paper-stainer*, an author] [mid–late 19C] a clerk. ❑ **paper whip** *v. see* PENCIL-WHIP *under* PENCIL *n.* ❑ **paper worker** *n.* [mid-19C] a street-seller of broadsides.

IN PHRASES

❑ **have paper(s) on** *v.* [one's marriage certificate] [1940s+] (*US black*) to be legally married. ❑ **make paper** *v.* [MAKE *v.* (1f)] [1990s+] (*US prison*) to be granted parole. ❑ **on paper** [one's paper 'ticket-of-leave'] [1990s+] (*US Und.*) on parole. ❑ **peddle one's paper** *v.* [1930s+] (*US*) to go about one's business. ❑ **square paper** *n.* [1940s] (*US Und.*) an honest, respectable person.

paper *adj.*

SE in slang uses

IN COMPOUNDS

❑ **paper mushrooms** *n.* [the hallucinogenic qualities of certain mushrooms, i.e. PAPER *n.* (13a)] [1980s+] (*drugs*) LSD, esp. that which has been dropped onto blotting-paper. ❑ **paper-collar** *adj.* [SE *paper collar*, as worn by clerks pretending to superior elegance] [mid–late 19C] (*N.Z.*) used to imply social superiority, real or otherwise. ❑ **paper skull** *n.* (*also* **paper scull**) [lit. 'one with a paper-thin skull'] [late 17C–early 19C] a fool; thus *paper-skulled/-sculled*, foolish, simple. ❑ **paper yabber** *n.* [YABBER *n.*] [late 19C–1930s] (*Aus.*) a letter.

paper *v.* [PAPER *n.*] **1** [late 19C+] to boost an audience by giving out free passes to a show or entertainment; thus *papered/papery*, filled by means of free passes. **2** [1920s+] (*US*) to pass bad cheques or any other form of fraudulent money-related document.

paper bag *v.* [rhy. sl.] [20C+] to nag.

paper doll *n.* [rhy. sl. = MOLL *n.* (1)] [1970s+] a promiscuous, sexually available woman.

paper doll *v.* [pun on SE *cut out*/CUT OUT *v.*[3] (1)] [1940s] (*US*) to play truant; thus phr. *make like a paper doll and cut*, go away.

paper hanger *n.* (*also* **paper-layer**) [PAPER *n.* (10) + pun; note Sutherland, *The Professional Thief* (1937), claims that this is a term used only by amateurs, never by professional thieves] [early 19C; 1910s+] (*US Und.*) one who habitually passes bad cheques; thus *paper-hanging*, passing dud cheques.

DERIVATIVES

❑ **paperhanging** *n.* [1920s–50s] passing bad cheques, forgery.

paper hat *n.* [rhy. sl. = PRAT *n.*[1] (6)] [1960s+] a fool.

papers *n. see* PAPER *n.*

papes *n.* [abbr.] **1** [1920s] (*US*) news*papers*. **2** [1990s+] (*orig. US black*) money [PAPER *n.* (1)].

pap feeder *n.* [SE *pap*, liquefied food given to babies and invalids] [mid-19C] a spoon.

paphian *n.* [*Paphos*, the city in south-western Cyprus, where it is claimed that Aphrodite, goddess of love, was born] [late 16C–mid-17C; 19C–1900s] a prostitute; thus the *Paphian game*, prostitution.

IN PHRASES

❑ **dance the Paphian jig** *v.* [mid-17C] to have sexual intercourse.

papi *n.* [P.R. *papi*, father] [2000s] (*US black*) a black person or a Puerto Rican.

papiyot *n.* [Fr. *papillon*, a butterfly] [20C+] (*W.I.*) a weakling, a frail person, a useless opponent in a game.

paplar *n. see* POPLARS *n.*

pappy *n.* **1** [mid-18C+] (*US juv.*) father, papa. **2** [1920s–40s] (*US black*) a male lover. **3** [1930s+] an old man.

pappy *adj.*[1] [1930s–60s] (*US*) old, esp. exhibiting the signs of the old.

IN COMPOUNDS

❑ **pappy guy** *n.* (*also* **papy guy, poppa guy**) [GUY *n.*[2] (1)] [1900s–20s] (*US tramp*) an old man.

pappy *adj.*[2] *see* PAP *adj.*

pappy-show *see under* POPPY-SHOW.

paps *n.*[1] [16C; 1960s+] breasts.

paps *n.*[2] [1970s–80s] (*UK black*) a father.

papy guy *n. see* PAPPY GUY *under* PAPPY *adj.*[1].

par *v.* [abbr. SE *party*] [1990s+] (*W.I.*) to relax with, to associate with.

para *n.* [abbr.] [2000s] *para*noia.

para *adj.* [abbr.] [1980s+] *para*noid.

IN PHRASES

❑ **on a para** *adj.* [1990s+] feeling nervous, paranoid.

parachute *n.* **1** [mid-19C] a parasol; an umbrella. **2** in drug uses. (**a**) [1940s] (*US black/drugs*) a marijuana cigarette [it gets one HIGH *adj.*[1] (2)]. (**b**) [1980s+] (*drugs*) a mixture of crack plus heroin or phencyclidine [the 'slowness' of the heroin or phencyclidine reduces the 'speed' of the crack].

paracki *n.* [abbr.] [1950s+] (*drugs*) paraldehyde, a polymer of aldehyde ($C_6H_{12}O_3$) used both as a narcotic and a legitimate treatment for insomnia.

paradise *n.* [Fr. sl. *paradis*, the gods] [mid-19C] the upper gallery of a theatre, the 'gods'.

paradise (white) *n.* [its effects] [1980s+] (*drugs*) cocaine.

paraffin *n.*[1] [rhy. sl.] [20C+] (*S.Afr.*) gin.

paraffin *n.*[2] [rhy. sl.; *paraffin oil*, pron. 'ile' = style] [1920s+] (*Scot.*) style.

paraffin lamp *n.* [rhy. sl.] **1** [20C+] a tramp. **2** [2000s] a sexually promiscuous woman [TRAMP *n.* (2)].

DERIVATIVES

❑ **lampish** *adv.* [2000s] like a tramp.

parakeet *n.* [their stereotyped noisiness and love of bright colours; note WW1 Aus. milit. *parakeet*, 'Staff Officer [...] So called from the red gorget tabs and the red band around the hat of a Staff Officer' (Pretty, *Glossary Of Slang [...] in the A.I.F.*, 1924)] [1960s] (*US*) a Puerto Rican.

parallel parking *n.* [1980s+] (*orig. US preppie/campus*) sexual intercourse.

paralysed *adj.* (*also* **handicapped, paralyzed**) **1** [late 19C–1900s] (*US*) knocked out, incapable; also in fig. use, stunned, shocked; thus *paralyzer*, that which has such effects. **2** [late 19C+] drunk; thus *paralyse*, to make drunk; also intoxicated by drugs.

paralyser *n.* [PARALYSED *adj.* (2)] [1910s] (*Aus.*) a strong drink.

paralytic *adj.* [PARALYSED *adj.* (2)] [mid-19C+] extremely drunk, to the point of passing out cold.

paralytic *adv.* [ext. of PARALYTIC *adj.*] [1900s] (*orig. Aus.*) completely.

paralyzed *adj. see* PARALYSED *adj.*

parangles *n.* [UK dial. *peramble*, a rigmarole, ult. SE *preamble*. Legal papers, wills and similar material tend to begin with a summary preamble before moving to the detailed clauses] [1940s] (*W.I.*) bustle and confusion, trouble and worry, any bothersome, complicated situation.

paranoid *adj.* [all non-clinical uses originated in 1960s HIPPIE *n.*[2] (3) era, often occasioned by an excess of drug use; ult. SE *paranoia*, 'functional psychosis characterized by delusions of grandeur and persecution, but without intellectual deterioration' (C. Rycroft, *A Critical Dict. of Psychoanalysis*, 1968)] [1960s] frightened, worried, disturbed.

parapetted *adj.* [equation of the gallows' drop with a parapet] [mid-19C] (*UK Und.*) executed by hanging.

parate/parater/paratie *n. see* PRATIE *n.*

parcel *n.* **1** [late 16C+] (*US*) a small group, amount or collection. **2** [late 19C] a young woman. **3** [late 19C] a British woman sold into a foreign brothel. **4** [late 19C–1920s; 1990s+] a substantial sum of money, esp. when won or lost in gambling. **5** [20C+] (*Ulster*) a difficult, troublesome person; a term of abuse. **6** [1910s] (*Aus. tramp*) a rolled blanket which contains one's possessions. **7** [2000s] a bulk consignment of drugs.

parcel from Paris *n. see* PACKET FROM PARIS *n.*

parcel post *n.* [they are labelled and travel to their destination like a parcel being sent through the mail] [1930s–50s] (*Aus., Northern Territory*) a person who is newly arrived and thus inexperienced.

parchment *n.* [mid-19C] (*UK Und.*) a ticket-of-leave; thus *parchment-cove*, a man who has a ticket-of-leave.

parchment dab *n.* [SE *parchment* + *dab*, a mark] [early 18C] a writ.

pard *n.* (*also* **pardner, podna, podner, potna**) [a classic 'Wild West' term, its 20C+ use is exclusively fictional, mainly in films] [late 18C; mid-19C+] (*US*) partner, esp. as a term of address.

pardon my French *phr. see* EXCUSE MY FRENCH *under* FRENCH *n.*

parental units *n.* [originating in the 'Coneheads' sketches on the TV show *Saturday Night Live*] [1980s+] (*US campus*) parents.

parings *n.* [Partridge suggests it is only a specific use of SE *paring*, a thin portion pared off the surface of anything, usu. as refuse or superfluous matter; a shaving] [late 17C–mid-19C] the clippings of money.

Paris *n.*

proper name in slang uses

IN COMPOUNDS

❑ **Paris brothers** *n.* [play on stereotyped views of French sexuality] [1950s–60s] (*gay*) homosexuals, esp. twins. ❑ **Paris bun** *n.* [rhy. sl. = HUN *n.* (2)] [1990s+] a Protestant. ❑ **Paris model** *n.* [1980s+] (*Aus. prison*) an attractive woman.

IN PHRASES

❑ **in Paris** *adj.* [Paris was a popular destination for such romantic flights] [late 19C–1900s] (*UK society*) eloped.

parish *n.* [late 19C+] one's own area or neighbourhood; the area in which one has influence and/or does business.

SE in slang uses

IN COMPOUNDS

❑ **parish bull** *n.* (*also* **parish prig**) [SE *bull*/PRIG *n.*[1] (2)] [18C–mid-19C] (*UK Und.*) a parson. ❑ **parish lantern** *n.* [mid–late 19C] the moon. ❑ **parish pick-axe** *n.* [late 19C] a prominent nose. ❑ **parish rig** *n.* [SE *parish-rigged*, cheaply rigged] [late 19C] (*orig. naut.*) a badly rigged ship; thus an ill-dressed man. ❑ **parish soldier** *n.* [the hiring of substitutes by the parish in which the orig. chosen militia-men lived] [late 18C–mid-19C] a militia-man. ❑ **parish stallion** *n.* [late 19C] a parson.

parisheen *n.* [SE *parish* + Irish dimin. sfx *-een*] [late 19C–1910s] (*Irish*) a child brought up by the parish.

park *n.* [early–mid-19C] a prison.

park *v.*[1] **1** [1910s+] to place, to put down. **2** [1920s+] to sit. **3** [1920s+] to place oneself. **4** [1920s+] (*US*) of a (usu.) teenage couple, to park in a secluded spot for petting and, perhaps, intercourse. **5** [1940s–50s] to get rid of someone or something; to knock someone out. **6** [1960s–70s] to give.

IN PHRASES

❑ **park a custard** *v.* [1930s+] (*UK society*) to vomit. ❑ **park a leopard** *v.* (*also* **park a tiger**) [the 'spotted' or 'striped' nature of the material that is vomited up] [1960s+] to vomit. ❑ **park in the same lot** *v.* [1990s+] (*orig. US*) to agree. ❑ **park one's ear** *v.* [1940s] (*N.Z.*) to hear. ❑ **park one's fudge** *v. see under* FUDGE *n.* ❑ **park one's mouth** *v.* [1970s] (*US*) to stop talking. ❑ **park the pink cadillac** *v.* [1990s+] to have sexual intercourse. ❑ **park your carcass** *v.* (*also* **park your arse, ...biscuit, ...fanny, ...frame, ...puku, ...stern**) [SE *carcass*/ARSE *n.* (1)/BISCUIT *n.*[1] (2d)/FANNY *n.*[1] (3)/FRAME *n.*[1] (1)/Maori *puku*, the stomach/STERN *n.* (1); note US radio comedian Harry Einstein (1904–58) used the pseudonym 'Parkyakarkus'] [1940s+] (*orig. US*) to sit down, esp. as an invitation. ❑ **pull a quick park** *v.* [1970s+] (*US black*) to make a quick pick-up of a sexual partner.

park *v.*[2] [Ital. *parlare*, to speak] [1960s–70s] (*Ling. Fr./Polari*) to ask, to speak, to beg.

park ape *n. see under* APE *n.*

parkee *n. see* PARKY *n.*

parker *n.*[1] [his strolling in the fashionable London *parks*] [mid–late 19C] a well-dressed man, a dandy.

parker *n.*[2] [1920s–40s] (*US*) one (of a couple) who uses a parked car as a venue for sex, intercourse or otherwise.

parker *v.*[1] [Ital. *partire*, to pay out] [late 19C] (*Ling. Fr./Polari*) to pay; thus *parker from/with dinarly*, to pay one's debts.

parker *v.*[2] [Ital. *parlare*, to speak] [late 19C+] (*Ling. Fr./Polari*) to ask, to speak, to beg.

parkering ninty *n.* [PARKER *v.*[1] + NANTEE *n.*] [mid–late 19C] wages.

parkie *n. see* PARKY *n.*

parking *n.* [PARK *v.*[1] (4)] [1950s+] (*US*) of a teenage couple, parking a car in a discreet spot for petting and possible intercourse.

parking lot *n.* [play on PARK *v.*[1] (4)] **1** [1960s–70s] (*US teen*) the vagina. **2** [1980s] (*US campus*) a place where men congregate.

park-palings *n.* (*also* **park railings**) [SE *park* + *palings*, a fence/*railings*] **1** [early–mid-19C] the teeth. **2** [late 19C] a neck of mutton.

Parktown prawn *n.* [*Parktown*, an upper-class Johannesburg suburb + SE *prawn*; the cricket, which grows to 7cm (2¾in), can seem to resemble an outsize prawn] [1980s+] (*S.Afr.*) the king cricket (*Libanasidus vittatus*).

parky *n.* (*also* **parkee, parkie**) [1940s+] a park-keeper.

parky *adj.* [Midland dial; ? ult. SE *perky*, sharp] [late 19C+] chilly.

parlatic *adj. see* PALATIC *adj.*

parlay *v.* [Ital. *paroli*, a cast at dice, which was taken up by faro and other card-players to mean to leave one's winnings on the table and then to stake double the sum already staked] **1** [early 19C+] (*orig. US*) to improve one's position, esp. by taking what one already has, material or otherwise, and using it as the basis of one's next move. **2** [1990s+] (*US black*) to calm down, to relax.

DERIVATIVES

❑ **parlaying** *n.* [1990s+] (*US black*) partying, enjoying oneself.

parleyvoo *n.* (*also* **parlay-voo**) [PARLEYVOO *v.* (1)] **1** [mid-18C+] the French language. **2** [early 19C+] (*also* **parly**) a French person.

parleyvoo *adj.* [PARLEYVOO *n.*] **1** [early 19C+] French. **2** [late 19C+] foreign.

parleyvoo *v.* (*also* **parleyvou, parley-vous**) [Fr. *parlez-vous?* do you speak?] **1** [mid-18C+] to speak a foreign language, esp. to speak French. **2** [1910s+] to talk, esp. to chatter meaninglessly.

parliamentary *adj.* [1900s–20s] (*Irish*) respectable; esp. in phr. *the parliamentary side of one's arse*.

parliamentary whisky *n.* (*also* **parliament whiskey**) [late 18C–19C] (*Irish*) whisky on which duty has been paid, as opposed to contraband or home-distilled.

parlor *n.*

SE in slang uses

IN COMPOUNDS

❑ **parlor girl** *n.* (*also* **parlor house girl, parlor queen**) [mid-19C–1900s; 1990s+] (*US*) a prostitute who works in a sophisticated, up-market brothel. ❑ **parlor golf** *n.* [1940s] (*US*) dice. ❑ **parlor house** *n.* [HOUSE *n.*[1] (1)] [mid-19C–1960s] (*US*) a high-class brothel, situated in what appears to be a fashionably furnished middle-class house, and run by a complaisant 'aunt' whose bevy of attractive 'nieces' gather in the front parlour to meet, and make themselves available to visitors (cheaper brothels had little more than bedrooms in which one had sex). ❑ **parlor lizard** *n.* (*also* **parlor athlete, ... ornament, ...rat, ...snake**) [-LIZARD *sfx* / -SNAKE *sfx*] [1910s–30s] **1** (*US*) a poor or miserly man who would rather court a woman in her own house than take her out on the town. **2** (*US*) (*also* **parlor pink**) a womanizer. ❑ **parlor man** *n.* [1910s] (*US Und.*) the safebreaker who lights the fuse on a charge of nitroglycerine.

IN PHRASES

❑ **decorate the parlor** *v.* [1940s] (*US Und.*) to tip.

parlour *n.* [late 17C–early 19C] the vagina; thus *let out one's parlour and lie backwards*, to work as a prostitute.

parlour-jumper *n.* [late 19C–1910s] (*UK Und.*) a thief who robs private rooms or houses; thus *parlour-jumping*, practising such a form of robbery.

parlour pink *n.* [SE *parlour* + PINK *n.* (4); an earlier form was *parlour Bolshevik*] [1920s+] a socialist whose activism is limited by the confines of their dinner table and does not extend on to the streets, let alone the barricades.

parlous *n.* [SE *parlous*, dangerously cunning, mischievous, capable of causing harm] [late 17C–early 18C] a notably shrewd individual.

parly *n. see* PARLEYVOO *n.* (2).

parm! *excl.* [1930s+] an abbr. of SE *pardon me!*

parnel *n.* (*also* **panel**) [SE *parnel*, a priest's concubine or mistress, a wanton young woman] [17C] a prostitute who works in a brothel rather than walking the streets.

Parnell shout *n.* [*Parnell*, a run-down suburb of Auckland + SHOUT *n.* (1a)] [1910s–40s] (*N.Z.*) shared payment for food or drinks.

parney *n.* [Rom. *pani*, water; ult. Hind. *pani*, water] **1** [mid-19C+] (*Anglo-Ind.*) (*also* **parny**) a shower of rain. **2** [late 19C–1950s] (*also* **pani, pawnce, pawni**) water. **3** [20C+] (*Ling. Fr./Polari*) tears (in the eyes).

paro *adj.*[1] [PARALYTIC *adj.*] [2000s] extremely drunk or intoxicated by a drug.

paro *adj.*[2] *see* PARRO *adj.*

parole dust *n.* [1970s+] (*US prison*) fog (which aids in escapes).

Parra *n.* [abbr. *Parramatta*, one of the suburbs in question] [1950s+] (*Aus.*) an inhabitant of the western suburbs of Sydney.

Parrie *n.* [abbr.] [2000s] (*N.Z. Und.*) Paremoremo prison.

parro *adj.* (*also* **paro**) [abbr.] [1980s+] *paranoid*.

parrot *n.* [brandname] [1910s] (*Aus.*) a flask of whisky.

parrot and monkey time *n.* (*also* **parrotty time**) [late 19C] (*US*) an unhappy marriage, in which the two partners fight continually.

parsley *n.* **1** [mid-19C] the female pubic hair [? resemblance]. **2** [1900s–10s] nonsense, rubbish [? the insignificance of the herb]. **3** [1940s] (*US black*) money [it is green]. **4** in drug uses. (**a**) [1970s+] phencyclidine [the use of parsley as a base for smoking phencyclidine]. (**b**) [2000s] marijuana.

IN PHRASES

❑ **take a turn among the parsley** *v.* [19C] to have sexual intercourse.

parsley bed *n.* [esp. as the answer to the question 'where do babies come from'; trad. the *parsley bed* brings girls, while boys come from the less appealing nettle bed or from beneath the gooseberry bush] **1** [early 17C–19C] the vagina; both in the context of copulation and as a euph. used to children. **2** [late 19C] the female pubic hair.

parsnip *n.* [visual 'resemblance'] [1960s] (*Aus.*) a penis.

parson *n.* [the parson supposedly 'sets people in the right way'] [late 18C–early 19C] a signpost, esp. a finger-post.

DERIVATIVES

❑ **parsoned** *adj.* [late 19C] married.

IN COMPOUNDS

❑ **parson Palmer** *n.* [a real-life, if forgotten, clergyman] [mid-18C–early 19C] anyone who stops the communal glass circulating by talking before passing it on. ❑ **parson's barn** *n.* [late 18C–early 19C] a place that is 'never so full but there is still room for more' (Grose, 1788). ❑ **parson's face** *n. see* MINISTER'S FACE *n.* ❑ **parson's mousetrap** *n.* [the role played by a clergyman in solemnizing the wedding ceremony + MOUSETRAP *n.* (1)] [late 17C–early 19C] marriage. ❑ **parson's nose** *n.* (*also* **deacon's nose**) [the religious official varies according to one's faith, so *POPE'S NOSE under* POPE *n.* is usu. Protestant use] [mid-19C+] the rump of a chicken, duck, goose or other poultry; usu. in Catholic use (cf. BISHOP'S NOSE *n.*). ❑ **parson's week** *n.* [irrespective of other duties, the clergyman's trad. 'working day' is Sunday] [late 18C+] Monday to Saturday, esp. a holiday that lasts from Monday to Saturday. ❑ **parson's wife** *n.* [pun on SE *vicar's/Vicker's* + GIN *n.*[1] (1)/SE *gin*] [1920s+] (*Aus.*) gin, esp. Vicker's Gin. ❑ **parson Trulliber** *n.* ['the pig-feeding and the pig-headed' (Hotten, 1873); note epon. character in Fielding's *Joseph Andrews* (1742)] [mid-19C] a rude, vulgar country clergyman.

part *v.* [SE *part with*] [mid-19C–1960s] to give up, to hand over, to restore (usu. of money).

IN PHRASES

❑ **part up** *v.* [1900s–50s] (*Aus.*) to pay money.

SE in slang uses

IN PHRASES

❑ **part one's head with a towel** *v.* [late 19C] (*US*) to be bald. ❑ **part someone's hair** *v.* [late 19C+] (*US*) **1** to shoot at someone, to kill someone. **2** to hit someone on the head. ❑ **part the red sea** *v. see under* RED SEA *n.* ❑ **part the whiskers** *v. see SPLIT THE BEARD under* BEARD *n.*

partake of His/Her Majesty's hospitality *v.* [joc. var. on SE *at His/Her Majesty's pleasure*] [late 19C–1930s] to spend time in prison.

parter *n.* [PART *v.*] [mid–late 19C] a generous person, one who pays up without complaint.

partial *adj.* **1** [late 18C] inclining more to one side than another; crooked. **2** [mid-19C] (*UK Und.*) picking a pocket [? one chooses one pocket over another].

Partick Thistle *n.* [rhy. sl.; the Scot. football team] [20C+] a whistle.

particular *n.* [19C–1910s] one's special choice, e.g. *a glass of my particular*.

particulars *n.* **1** [1940s] (*Irish*) the male genitals. **2** [1970s+] (*US prison*) any member of the authorities who has an immediate effect on a prisoner's life: a warder, the sentencing judge, the parole board etc.

partner *n.* **1** [19C] the penis. **2** [1940s+] (*US*) (*also* **pahtner**) a friend.

partridge *n.* [mid-17C–18C] a prostitute.

parts of shame *n.* [trans. of Lat. *pudendum*, lit. 'that which is shameful'] [19C] the vagina.

part that goes over the fence last *n.* (*also* **last part over the fence**) [euph.] [late 19C] (*US*) the buttocks.

party *n.*[1] [obs. SE *party*, a person] **1** [19C+] a man or woman; still found in *old party*, and the basis of such legal terms as *the guilty party*, and *being a party to*. **2** [1940s] a girlfriend.

party *n.*[2] **1** [1920s+] any form of sex act, usu. provided by a prostitute; often used in the prostitute's question: *What kind of party would you like?* What speciality would you prefer? **2** [1940s–50s] non-commercial heterosexual intercourse. **3** [1960s+] a sexual encounter involving two or more women and one man. **4** [1960s+] an orgy. **5** [1960s+] a sexual encounter between two homosexual men. **6** [1960s+] a difficult, demanding situation.

IN COMPOUNDS

❑ **party boy** *n.* [1960s+] (*US*) a male homosexual prostitute. ❑ **party girl** *n.* [1920s–60s] a promiscuous young woman, not necessarily a prostitute, a 'good-time girl'.

SE in slang uses

IN COMPOUNDS

❑ **party animal** *n.* [1980s+] anyone notably devoted to going out and having a good time. ❑ **party balloon** *n.* **1** [1970s] a breathalyser. **2** [1990s+] (*US*) a condom. ❑ **party favors** *n.* [1980s+] (*US campus*) drugs. ❑ **party hat** *n.* **1** [1970s+] (*US*) the flashing light on top of a police car. **2** [1980s+] (*orig. US campus*) a condom. ❑ **party hop** *v.* [HOP *v.*[1] (7)] [1980s+] (*orig. US*) to move from one party to the next and so on during the course of a single evening and night. ❑ **party pills** *n.* [2000s] (*N.Z. drugs*) pills taken for a desired effect, usu. at a 'rave' to give increased energy for all-night dancing. ❑ **party pooper** *n.* (*also* **party poop**) [POOP *v.*[3] (3)] [1950s+] (*orig. US*) a spoilsport, one who sabotages the pleasures and enjoyments of their companions, whether at a party or other amusement. ❑ **party tits** *n.* [TIT *n.*[2] (1)] [1990s+] artificially enlarged breasts, esp. as adopted by young and famous women, which are then displayed at social and other occasions.

party *adj.* [1980s+] (*US teen*) hedonistic.

party *v.* **1** [1930s+] (*also* **party time, party up**) to enjoy oneself. **2** [1940s+] to have sex; often used in the prostitute's opening line: *Would you like to party?* **3** [1960s+] to partake in an orgy. **4** [1960s+] to drink or take drugs. **5** [1960s+] to offer sex to another person.

IN PHRASES

❑ **party down** *v.* [1970s+] (*orig. US black*) to enjoy oneself very much. ❑ **party foul** *v.* [1980s+] (*US campus*) to behave in a socially unacceptable manner at a party, esp. to vomit or spill alcohol; also as n. or excl. *party foul!* that was a blunder! how embarrassing! ❑ **party hearty** *v.* [1980s+] (*US teen*) to have a good time at a party. ❑ **party out** *v.* [1990s+] (*orig. US*) to outlast one's fellow-celebrants in one's ability to consume drink and/or drugs (and to become exhausted thereby). ❑ **party time** *v. see* sense 1 above. ❑ **party up** *v. see* sense 1 above.

IN EXCLAMATIONS

❑ **party on!** [popularized by the film *Wayne's World* (1992)] [1980s+] (*US teen*) a general excl. of approval, either party-orientated, meaning 'enjoy yourself!' 'have a good time!' or, more broadly based, meaning 'good job!'.

parve *n.* [abbr.] [1980s] (*Aus.*) a *parvenu*.

pasa *v.* [ety. unknown] [1970s] (*S.Afr.*) to attack.

pasadeno *phr.* [play on PASS *v.* (1)] [1940s+] a phr. of rejection/ignorance: I don't know, don't ask me.

pasata grin *n. see* MEXICAN LIPSTICK *under* MEXICAN *adj.*

pash *n.* [SE *passion*] **1** [1910s+] an infatuation, usu. between junior and senior pupils of girls' schools or between a schoolgirl and a female teacher. **2** [1910s+] passion. **3** [1930s] a lover. **4** [1950s+] (*Aus.*) a session of sexual fondling.

IN COMPOUNDS

❑ **pash-off** *n.* (*also* **pash-on**) [1990s+] (*Aus.*) a session of kissing, heavy petting. ❑ **pashpie** *n.* [1950s] (*US teen*) a beloved member of the opposite sex. ❑ **pash show** *n.* [1950s+] (*Aus.*) **1** a film that includes candid sex scenes. **2** (*also* **pasho session**) enthusiastic love-making.

IN PHRASES

❑ **pash on** *v.* (*also* **pash off, pash up**) [1920s+] (*US/Aus.*) to flirt, to indulge in heavy petting or even intercourse.

pash *adj.* [abbr.] [1920s] passionate, obsessive.

pashed up *adj.* [PASH *n.* (2)] [1930s] (*US*) sexually obsessed.

pashing *n.* [PASH *n.* (2)] [1960s+] (*Aus.*) kissing.

pas op! *excl.* (*also* **passop!**) [Afk. *oppassen*, to be on guard] [early 19C+] (*S.Afr.*) be careful! look out!

pass *n.*

IN PHRASES

❑ **give a pass** *v.* [1970s–80s] to reject, to ignore. ❑ **make a pass** *v.* (*also* **throw a pass**) [note Asbury, *Sucker's Progress* (1938) 16: An extraordinary number of the terms, technical and otherwise, which were employed by Faro players [...] have passed into the language [...] Making a pass—Putting the two parts of a pack of cards back as they were before the cut] (*orig. US*) **1** [20C+] to attempt to harm or attack. **2** [1920s+] to approach with amorous intentions. **3** [1940s+] to approach, usu. with some form of business proposition. **4** [1940s+] to approach, to go near. ❑ **put a pass** *v. see* PASS *v.* (1).

pass *v.* **1** [late 19C+] (*also* **pass up, put a pass**) to ignore, to have no interest in; esp. in phr. *I'll pass*, as a response to an offer or suggestion [SE *pass by*]. **2** in senses of SE *pass as/for*. (**a**) [20C+] of a light-skinned black person, to pose as white. (**b**) [1930s+] of a Jew, to pretend to be a Christian. (**c**) [1950s] of a police officer, to masquerade as a 'citizen'. (**d**) [1950s+] of a homosexual, to appear heterosexual to those one encounters; similarly of a transsexual, to 'pass' as a woman or man. **3** [1910s] (*Aus.*) to pawn stolen goods [SE *pass on/over*]. **4** [1960s] (*S.Afr.*) to deal illicit drugs. **5** [1980s] (*US campus*) to become unconscious (from drink or drugs) [SE *pass out*].

IN PHRASES

❑ **pass a sham saint** *v.* [early 18C] to play the hypocrite. ❑ **pass for grass** *v.* [the 'invisibility' of grass] [20C+] (*W.I., Guyn.*) to be treated disrespectfully, to be someone who does not matter. ❑ **pass in** *v.* [PASS IN ONE'S CHECKS *under* CHECK *n.*[1]] [1900s] (*Aus.*) to die. ❑ **pass oneself** *v.* [? abbr. SE *surpass*] [20C+] (*Ulster*) to behave as expected. ❑ **pass oneself out** *v.* [1900s] (*Aus.*) to commit suicide. ❑ **pass out** *v.* **1** [late 19C–1940s] to die. **2** [1900s] (*Aus.*) to disqualify. **3** [1900s–10s] (*Aus.*) to knock out. **4** [1920s+] to fall asleep, usu. as a result of drink or drugs. ❑ **pass the bone** *v.* [1990s+] (*US campus*) to share experience, to pass on information. ❑ **pass the compliment** *v.* [late 19C–1900s] to give a tip. ❑ **pass the pikes** *v.* [SE *turnpike*, a toll gate; villains who had passed this barrier might presume themselves free of effective pursuit] [mid-17C–18C] to be out of danger. ❑ **pass the sleep medicine** *v.* [1910s] (*US*) to knock out. ❑ **pass up** *v. see* sense 1 above.

pass-bank *n.* (*also* **passage-bank**) [gaming jargon *pass-bank*, the pool of money in a game of 'passage'] [late 17C–early 19C] a gaming ground.

passenger *n.* **1** [mid-19C+] one who, while nominally one of a group, team, crew etc, takes no active or useful part in the general efforts. **2** [late 19C–1930s] (*US*) a passenger train; thus *passenger stiff*, a tramp who rides passenger or fast freight trains. **3** [2000s] (*US prison*) a friend [i.e. one who is in the CAR *n.* (1)].

passenger on the Cape Ann stage, to be a *v.* [ety. unknown; ? anecdotal] [mid-19C] (*US campus*) to be drunk.

passer *n.* [1920s–80s] one who passes counterfeit money.

SE in slang uses

IN PHRASES

❑ **take a passer** *v.* [1970s] (*US*) to pass out, to faint.

passion *n. see* PASSION STICK below.

SE in slang uses

IN COMPOUNDS

❑ **passion cramps** *n.* [1940s] of a man, the physical signs of sexual frustration. ❑ **passion flaps** *n.* [1990s+] the labia. ❑ **passion fruit** *n. see under* FRUIT *n.* ❑ **passion gap** *n.* (*also* **love gap**) [1950s+] (*S.Afr.*) the space between the front teeth; such spaces are created by the extraction of up to four teeth. ❑ **passion-killers** *n.* (*also* **passion-busters**) [1940s+] (*orig. milit.*) any article of women's underwear deemed to reduce the chances of (male) exploration; also in homosexual use. ❑ **passion pit** *n.* **1** [19C] the vagina. **2** [1930s+] (*US*) a drive-in cinema. **3** [1960s] (*Aus.*) anywhere that sex takes place. ❑ **passion plug** *n.* [2000s] (*S.Afr.*) the vagina. ❑ **passion stick** *n.* (*also* **passion**) [STICK *n.* (1a)] [1950s] (*Aus.*) the penis. ❑ **passion wagon** *n.* (*also* **kiss wagon**) [note 1940s+ milit. use, the truck taking men for a day's, or part of a day's, leave, into a town or place of entertainment] [1950s+] any vehicle, often a van, in which teenage boys or young men hope to seduce young women.

passop! *excl. see* PAS OP! *excl.*

passremarkable *adj.* [SE *pass a remark*, to comment] [1980s+] (*Irish*) **1** worthy of comment. **2** prone to making tactless remarks.

pasta-breath *n.* [the stereotypical Ital. food] [1980s] (*US*) a derog. term for an Italian or Italian-American.

paste *n.*[1] (*also* **man-paste, population paste**) [resemblance] [mid-19C; 1980s+] semen.

paste *n.*[2] [PASTE *v.*] [1910s–50s] a hit or blow.

paste *v.* [var. on SE *baste*, to beat, to thrash] [mid-19C+] to hit hard.

DERIVATIVES

❑ **pasted** *adj.* **1** [1950s+] (*US*) intoxicated by drink or drugs. **2** [1990s+] (*US campus*) defeated.

IN PHRASES

❑ **paste away at** *v.* **1** [late 19C+] to keep on hitting someone. **2** [1940s] in fig. use, to maintain an effort, to struggle on.

pasteboard *n.* [SE *pasteboard*, a thin card made of pasting together three or more sheets of paper] **1** [mid-19C] an invitation. **2** [mid–late 19C] a visiting card; thus v. *pasteboard*, to leave one's card; also *lodge one's pasteboard*. **3** [mid–late 19C] a playing card. **4** [mid-19C–1900s] a railway ticket. **5** [late 19C–1910s] a betting ticket, issued by a bookmaker. **6** [late 19C–1930s] a ticket to the theatre, cinema etc.

paste eater *n.* [? one who has fig. eaten poisonous wallpaper paste] [1980s] (*US campus*) a socially inept person.

paste-horn *n.* [SE *pastehorn*, a cow's horn used to hold paste] [19C] the nose.

paste in *v.* [? SE *pass in*] [late 19C–1900s] (*US*) to pawn.

pastel *n.* **1** [1900s] a slim person [the shape of artists' colour pastels]. **2** [1980s] (*US police*) an unmarked police car [the usual colouring].

pasties *n.* [? PASTED *under* PASTE *v.* or ? Sp. *pasto*, marijuana, lit. 'a pasture'] [1980s+] (*US drugs*) dryness in the mouth after smoking cannabis.

pasting *n.* [PASTE *v.*] **1** [mid-19C+] a violent assault, a beating up. **2** [1940s–70s] in fig. use, e.g. of a critically negative review.

past it *adj.* **1** [mid-19C+] of animate and inanimate objects, too old or worn-out to be of use; thus of a man, impotent. **2** [1960s+] dead.

past oneself *adj.* [1990s+] (*Irish*) acting crazily, silly.

pastry *n.* **1** [late 19C–1930s] a generic term for pretty young women [i.e. 'good enough to eat']. **2** [1900s] (*Aus.*) flattery, praise [it is 'sweet'].

pastry *v.* [play on SE *roll*/ROLL *v.* (2a)] [1970s–80s] (*UK black*) to roll a cannabis cigarette.

pasture lice *n. see* PADDOCK LICE *n.*

pasture pie *n.* [1980s] (*US*) a cow dropping.

pasty face *n.* [1940s–50s] (*US drugs*) a narcotics addict.

pat *n.*[1] [var. on PADDY *n.*; the two senses, while of differing national origins, are both immigrants] **1** [late 18C+] a generic term for an Irishman. **2** [1900s] (*Aus.*) a Chinese person.

IN COMPOUNDS

❑ **Patland** *n.* [mid-19C–1900s] Ireland. ❑ **Patlander** *n.* [early 19C–1900s] an Irish person. ❑ **pat wagon** *n.* (*also* **patty wagon**) [negative stereotyping] [1900s–30s] (*US*) a vehicle in which prisoners are conveyed to a police station.

pat *n.*[2] [? misspelling of POT *n.*[3]] [1960s] (*drugs*) marijuana.

pat *adj.* [SE *pat*rician] [mid-19C–1900s] (*US campus*) aristocratic, upper-class.

pata-kyat *n.* [dial. *pata*, a kitchen shelf + *kyat*, cat] [1940s] (*W.I.*) a thief.

pat and mick *n.* [rhy. sl. = DICK *n.*[1] (5) or PRICK *n.* (1)] [20C+] the penis.

pat and mick *adj.* [rhy. sl.] [2000s] sick.

pat and mick *v.* [rhy. sl. = LICK *v.*[1] (1)] [20C+] (*Aus.*) to lick, lit. or fig.

pat and mike *n.*[1] (*also* **Irish mike**) [rhy. sl. = SE *bike*] [20C+] a bicycle.

pat and mike *n.*[2] [two generic Irish names, used in many jokes, 'There were two Paddies, Pat and Mike...'] [1970s] (*US*) two men having sex with one woman.

pata-pata *n.* (*also* **phata-phata**) [Xhosa/Zulu *phatha*, to touch, to feel; thence the popular dance *pata-pata*, a highly suggestive dance characterized by the way in which pairs of dancers touch each other] [1970s] (*S.Afr. township*) sexual intercourse.

Pat Cash *v.* [rhy. sl.= SLASH *v.* (2); ult. Aus. tennis star *Pat Cash* (b.1965)] [1990s+] to urinate.

patch *n.* **1** in the context of the genitals. (**a**) [late 18C+] the pubic hair. (**b**) [late 19C] the vagina. **2** [1940s+] (*US Und.*) a go-between who 'arranges' security for criminals in a given area; a 'fixer'. **3** [1950s+] (*orig. US*) any form of insignia as worn by criminal or youth gangs, e.g. the Hell's Angels, US prison gangs, N.Z. street gangs etc.

IN PHRASES

❑ **patch up** *v.* [1970s+] **1** (*N.Z.*) to become a full gang member [one is awarded a *patch* (sense 3 above)]. **2** (*US gay*) to dress fashionably; to apply make-up.

patch *v.* [PATCH *n.* (2)] [1960s+] (*Can. prison*) to arrange for bribes to be paid, deals to be made etc.

patent coat *n.* [? its patented design] [mid-19C] a coat with the pockets on the inside, making it harder to pick.

patent-digester *n.* [its supposedly beneficial effects on the digestion; ? corruption of *Papin's digester*, a vessel designed for dissolving bones etc] [mid-19C] brandy.

patent gentry *n.* [ety. unknown; ? pun on SE] [mid-19C] (*US*) cheating gamblers.

patent leather *n.* [late 19C] (*US short order*) a steak.

pater *n.* [Lat. *pater*, father; 20C+ use is ironic] [early 18C; 19C+] (*school or facetious*) one's father; esp. as *the pater*; thus *grandpater*, grandfather.

pater cove *n.* [PATRICO *n.*] [late 17C–19C] (*UK Und.*) a priest, a wandering beggar posing as a priest; the 15th rank of the underworld.

patess *n.* [PAT *n.*[1] (1) + SE fem. sfx -*ess*] [early–mid-19C] an Irishwoman.

pat malone *n.*

IN PHRASES

❑ **on one's pat (malone)** *adj.* (*also* **on one's mike malone, ... pat maloney**) [rhy. sl.] [1930s+] (*Aus./UK*) alone, on one's own.

pato *n.* [Sp. *pato*, a duck, i.e. he 'ducks' down for sex] [1960s+] (*US/P.R.*) a male homosexual.

patootie *n.* (*also* **patoot**) [? SE *potato*, esp. *sweet potato*] **1** [1910s+] (*US*) an attractive young woman. **2** [1920s] (*US*) the penis. **3** [1920s+] (*US*) (*also* **tootie**) the buttocks; the anus. **4** [1950s] an effeminate man.

(IN PHRASES)

□ **hot patootie** *n.* [1920s+] (*US*) an attractive young woman.
□ **sweet patootie** *n.* [1910s+] a woman, a girlfriend.

(IN EXCLAMATIONS)

□ **sweet patootie!** [1900s–20s] (*US*) a general excl.

pat out *v.* [SE *pat*, appositely, directly to the point] [1920s] to speak openly, honestly.

patriarch co *n.* (*also* **patriarke co**) [poss. punning on SE *patriarch* (although *see* PATRICO *n.* (1) + *co*, abbr. COVE *n.* (1)] [mid-16C] (*UK Und.*) a fake priest, specializing in performing illegal marriage ceremonies.

patricia *adj.* [2000s] (*S.Afr. gay*) **1** pregnant. **2** delicious.

Patrick *n.* [the stereotypical Irish name] **1** [late 19C; 1940s–50s] an Irishman; thus *Patrick O'Flynn*, a beggar who imitates a stereotypical Irishman. **2** [2000s] (*US black*) a red-haired man, usu. in context of a prostitute's client [pun on PAT *n.*[1] (1) + play on TRICK *n.*[1] (3)].

Patrick Cox *v.* [rhy. sl.; ult. shoe designer *Patrick Cox* (b.1963)] [2000s] a box, a hit.

patrico *n.* (*also* **patring-cove, patter-cove, pattering-cove**) [either Lat. *pater*, father, or PATTER *v.* (1) + *co*, abbr. COVE *n.* (1): 'strolling priests that Marry under a Hedge without a Gospel or Common-prayer Book, the Couple standing on each side a Dead Beast, are bid to live together till Death them do's Part, so shaking Hands, the Wedding is ended' (B.E.)] (*UK Und.*) **1** [mid-16C–late 19C] a priest, or a wandering beggar posing as one; the 15th rank of the underworld; such priests officiated in the marriage of beggars. **2** [late 18C–early 19C] any legitimate clergyman.

(IN COMPOUNDS)

□ **patrico's kinchin** *n.* [KINCHIN *n.*, lit. 'the (fake) priest's child'] [mid-16C] (*UK Und.*) a pig.

patri-cove *n.* [var. on PATRICO *n.*] [early 18C] (*UK Und.*) a priest, or a wandering beggar posing as one; the 15th rank of the underworld.

patsy *n.*[1] [the popular Irish name *Patrick;* hence negative stereotyping] [late 19C+] a fool, a dupe, a scapegoat; also as adj.

patsy *n.*[2] [*Patsy Riggir*, N.Z. country music singer (fl.1980s), whose surname sounds like RIGGER *n.*] [2000s] (*N.Z.*) a jar or jug of beer.

patsy *adj.* [ety. unknown; ? lost rhy. sl.] **1** [1930s–50s] (*US*) satisfactory, all right. **2** [2000s] (*S.Afr. gay*) odd.

Patsy Cline *n.* [rhy. sl.; ult. US country music singer *Patsy Cline* (1932–63)] [1990s+] a LINE *n.*[1] (5d) of cocaine.

Patsy Palmer and her five daughters *n.* [var. on *MRS PALM (AND HER FIVE DAUGHTERS) under* MRS *n.*; the ref. is to the soap opera actress *Patsy Palmer* (b.1972), famous for her role as Bianca in UK BBC TV soap opera *EastEnders*] [1990s+] (*UK juv.*) the hand, as used for masturbation.

patten-ken *n.* (*also* **ken**) [var. on *PADDING KEN under* PAD *v.*[1] + ? underpinning by SE *patten*, the sort of shoe worn by the poor] [1910s–20s] (*UK Und.*) a lodging house frequented primarily by vagrants or thieves.

patter *n.* [PATTER *v.*] **1** [mid-18C–mid-19C] (*UK Und.*) a trial, verdict and sentence [the *patter* is that of the judge, counsel, witnesses etc, dismissed as such by the prisoner]. **2** [mid-18C+] (*also* **patter-clatter**) any form of speech or speechifying, e.g. a street seller's sales talk, a judge's summing up. **3** [late 18C–1900s] underworld slang, cant. **4** [19C+] talk considered as empty chatter. **5** [late 19C] a (foreign) language. **6** [2000s] in fig. use, attitude, lifestyle.

(IN COMPOUNDS)

□ **patter-clatter** *n. see* sense 2 above. □ **patter-crib** *n.* [CRIB *n.*[1] (3)] [mid-19C] a criminal public or lodging house.

(IN PHRASES)

□ **flash patter** *n.* [1920s] criminal slang. □ **flash the patter** *v.* [late 18C–19C] **1** to talk fast and meaninglessly. **2** to talk in cant. □ **in for patter** [mid-19C] facing trial. □ **tip the patter** *v.* [early 19C] to flatter, to 'shoot a line'.

patter *v.* [SE *patter*, to mumble one's prayers at speed and without note of their meaning; ult. the *Paternoster*, 'Our Father'] **1** [early 15C–early 19C] to talk rapidly, fluently or glibly, to chatter, to prattle. **2** [mid–late 18C] (*UK Und.*) to sing on the streets. **3** [late 18C–early 19C] (*UK Und.*) to talk in a manner designed to confuse a potential victim of a confidence trick. **4** [late 18C–mid-19C] to put on trial. **5** [19C] to talk the cant of thieves, beggars etc; to talk slang. **6** [mid-19C] to speechify as a cheapjack does in extolling wares, or a conjurer while performing tricks. **7** [mid-19C] to sell broadsides, ballads etc in the streets. **8** [mid-19C+] (*UK Und.*) to talk, to speak. **9** [late 19C] (*Aus. Und.*) to beg. **10** [1960s] to tell tales. **11** [1960s] (*Scot.*) (*also* **patter up**) to talk so as to encourage criminality; to chat up.

patter-cove *n. see* PATRICO *n.*

patterer *n.* [PATTER *v.*; self-proclaimed, according to Mayhew, *London Labour and the London Poor* (1861–2), as 'the aristocracy of the street sellers'] [mid-19C] **1** a street seller, a hawker. **2** a street seller who specializes in last dying speeches, true confessions and similar melodramas. **3** a mouth, a voice.

pattering *n.* [PATTER *v.* (1)] [late 17C–19C] overly 'smart' or irritatingly vague responses made by a servant.

pattering-cove *n. see* PATRICO *n.*

pattern *adj.* [abbr. SE *pattern fair*, mispron. of *patron fair*, ult. *patron saint's fair*] [19C] (*Irish*) excellent, first-rate, brilliant.

patter (the) flash *v. see under* FLASH *n.*[1].

Pattie *n. see* PATTY HEARST *n.*

patties *n. see* PADDIES *n.*

pattin' leather *phr. see under* LEATHER *n.*

patty *see also under* PADDY.

Patty Hearst *n.* (*also* **Pattie**) [rhy. sl. = SE *first*; ult. US heiress-cum-urban terrorist *Pattie Hearst* (b.1954)] [1990s+] a first-class degree.

patty wagon *n. see PAT WAGON under* PAT *n.*[1].

patu *n.* [dial. *patu*, used of an owl or a nightjar; the bird's mouth gapes hugely – out of proportion to its relatively small beak] [late 19C+] (*W.I.*) an ugly or foolish person.

patu-eye *n.* [PATU *n.* + SE *eye*] [1950s] (*W.I.*) an albino.

patzer *n.* (*also* **potzer**) [? Ger. *patzen* to bungle, but note derog. PUTZ *n.* (2)] [1940s+] an inferior chess-player.

paugh! *excl. see* FAUGH! *excl.*

paula *v.* [initial letter] [2000s] (*S.Afr. gay*) passed out, usu. through drink or drugs.

Paul Revere *phr.* [play on Fr. *au revoir*/US revolutionary hero *Paul Revere* (1735–1818)] [1980s+] (*US campus*) farewell, goodbye.

paul's work *n.* [SE *poor work* or ref. to a *Paul's man*, anyone who frequented St Paul's Cathedral, London, for gossip, confidence trickery etc] [17C] a badly done job, a mess.

pauly *n.* [*Paul* Kruger (1825–1904), the Boer leader + pun on SE *poor lies*] [late 19C–1900s] during the Boer war, a derog. term for a pro-Boer.

paut *v.* [Scot. *paut*, to move in a leisurely manner] [20C+] (*Ulster*) to walk around in stockinged feet.

Pav *n.* (*also* **pavvy, P.V.**) [abbr.] [mid-19C–1920s] the *Pavilion* Theatre, London; thus any theatre or cinema called the *Pavilion*.

pav *n.* [abbr.; named/created for the ballerina Anna *Pavlova* (1885–1931)] [1960s+] (*Aus./N.Z.*) a pavlova, Australia's 'national dessert', a large, soft-centred meringue topped with whipped cream and passion-fruit; thus *pavs and savs*, pavlovas and saveloys, typical N.Z. picnic food.

pave *n.* [synon. Fr. *pavé*] [mid-19C] (*UK Und.*) the pathway, the pavement.

(IN PHRASES)

□ **on the pave** *see ON THE PAVEMENT under* PAVEMENT *n.*

pave *v.*[1] [*paving*, i.e. smoothing the 'road' of Latin and Greek study] [late 19C–1930s] (*UK school*) to add marginal or interlinear translations to a classical text.

pave *v.*[2] [ety. unknown] [2000s] (*Irish*) to steal.

pavee *n.* (*also* **pavey**) [? their walking the pavements] [1940s+] (*Irish*) an itinerant Jewish pedlar.

pavement *n.*

SE in slang uses

IN COMPOUNDS

❑ **pavement artist** *n.* [1980s] (*UK Und.*) one who robs security vans delivering money to banks. ❑ **pavement pizza** *n. see under* PIZZA *n.* ❑ **pavement pounder** *n.* **1** [1900s] (*US*) a walker, a marcher. **2** [1910s–50s] (*orig. US*) a police officer. **3** [1940s] a prostitute. ❑ **pavement princess** *n.* (*also* **pavement pretty**) [20C+] (*US*) a prostitute.

IN PHRASES

❑ **across the pavement** [1960s+] (*UK Und.*) a phr. used of any crime committed in the street. ❑ **hit the pavement** *v.* [1930s+] **1** to be ejected, esp. from a nightclub or other place of entertainment. **2** to be released from prison. **3** to be dismissed from one's job. ❑ **inspector of (the) pavements** *n.* **1** [late 18C–mid-19C] (*also* **surveyor of the pavement**) one who stands in the pillory. **2** [1940s] (*US Und.*) a tramp. ❑ **on the pavement** **1** [mid-19C] (*also* **on the pave**) in prostitution. **2** [mid-19C+] (*UK Und.*) (*also* **on the pave**) working as a professional criminal, usu. an armed robber. **3** [1940s+] (*US Und.*) set free from imprisonment. ❑ **overseer of the (new) pavement** *n.* [late 18C–mid-19C] a man standing in a pillory. ❑ **paint the pavement** *v.* [1990s+] to vomit forcefully. ❑ **pound the pavement** *v. see under* POUND *v.*[2]. ❑ **princess of the pavement** *n.* [1940s+] a prostitute. ❑ **slap the pavement** *v.* [1920s+] (*orig. US black*) to walk around. ❑ **superintendent of the pavement** *n.* (*also* **supervisor of the pavement, sidewalk superintendent, superintendent of the sidewalk**) [1950s+] **1** (*Aus.*) anyone, other than those employed at the site, who enjoys standing staring at buildings under construction. **2** (*US*) any unofficial critic or observer.

paviour's workshop *n.* (*also* **pavier's workshop, pavior's workshop**) [SE *paviour*, a layer of paving stones] [late 18C–19C] the street.

pavvy *n. see* PAV *n.*

paw *n.* [SE *paw*, used only of animals] **1** [17C+] the human hand, usu. in pl. **2** [18C–1900s] handwriting, esp. a signature. **3** [late 18C–mid-19C] the foot.

IN COMPOUNDS

❑ **paw-case** *n.* [mid-19C] a glove. ❑ **pawing-match** *n.* [late 19C] (*Aus.*) a fist-fight.

paw *adj.* [? excl. *pah!*, nasty! horrible!] [mid–late 17C] improper, naughty, obscene.

paw *v.* [PAW *n.* (1)] **1** [mid-19C+] to fondle sexually (esp. when the recipient is unwilling). **2** [1930s] to hand over.

pawn *n.* [abbr.] [mid-19C] a *pawn*broker.

pawn *v.*[1] [mid–late 17C] to leave an inn or tavern, forcing one's companion to pay the bill.

pawn *v.*[2] [? PAW *v.* (1)] [1990s+] (*W.I.*) to take hold of someone.

pawnce *n. see* PARNEY *n.* (2).

pawned *adj.* [1940s] (*UK Und.*) imprisoned.

pawni *n. see* PARNEY *n.* (2).

paw-paw *adj.* [PAW *adj.*] [late 18C–early 19C] naughty, improper; thus *paw-pawness*, naughtiness, impropriety.

IN COMPOUNDS

❑ **paw-paw tricks** *n.* **1** [late 18C–19C] any form of naughty, childish trick; orig. used by nurses to children. **2** [19C] masturbation.

pax! *excl.* [Lat. *pax*, peace] [mid-19C+] (*UK juv.*) a cry used to call a truce in a (fighting) game; thus *pax*, a friend; *good pax*, good friends.

pax on —! *excl.* [Lat. *pax*, peace, i.e. enough! leave it in peace!] [mid-17C–mid-18C] confound it! the hell with it!

pay *n.*

SE in slang uses

IN PHRASES

❑ **give out the pay** *v.* [1940s+] (*Irish*) to make a fuss. ❑ **give someone a pay** *v.* [1970s–80s] (*N.Z. prison*) to reprimand, to criticize harshly.

pay *v.* [early 16C–1930s; 1990s+] to beat, to punish; to suffer.

IN PHRASES

❑ **pay as Paul paid the Ephesians** *v.* [? invented by Grose] [late 18C–early 19C] to beat severely. ❑ **pay into** *v.* [late 19C] to attack, to lay into. ❑ **pay out** *v.* (*also* **pay up**) [mid-19C+] to take revenge upon, to give (someone) their deserts, to punch. ❑ **pay over face and eyes, as the cat did to the monkey** *v.* [late 19C] to give someone a serious beating about the head. ❑ **pay someone's coat** *v.* [19C] to thrash, to beat severely.

SE in slang uses

IN COMPOUNDS

❑ **pay-hole** *n.* [late 19C] (*Aus.*) a ticket-office.

IN PHRASES

❑ **get paid** *v.* [1980s+] **1** (*US campus*) to have sexual intercourse. **2** (*US black*) to obtain money, not necessarily by working for it. **3** (*US black*) to get what one deserves, e.g. professional success. ❑ **pay a bill at sight** *v.* [early 19C] to be ready at any time to have sex. ❑ **pay and lay** *v.* [LAY *v.*[1] (1)] [1960s] (*US*) to use the services of a prostitute. ❑ **pay away** *v.* [naut. jargon *pay away*, to let rope run out of a vessel] **1** [late 17C; mid-19C] to continue, to go on with, esp. of a story that is being told. **2** [late 18C–early 19C] to fight manfully. **3** [late 18C–early 19C] to eat voraciously. ❑ **pay back** *v.* [early 18C] (*UK Und.*) to return stolen goods. ❑ **pay off** *see* separate entries. ❑ **pay out the slack of one's gammon** *v. see under* GAMMON *n.*[2]. ❑ **pay the freight** *v.* [1950s+] (*US*) to pay, to bear the expense. ❑ **pay (too much) for one's whistle** *v.* (*also* **pay too dear for one's whistle**) [the whistle of emphasis that acknowledges one's interest] [late 18C–1910s] to pay over the odds for something one desires. ❑ **that won't pay the old woman her ninepence** [coined at the Bow Street Police Court in London] [late 19C–1900s] used to describe an evasive act or statement.

payaka *adj.* [? link to PAYOL *n.*] [1950s+] (*W.I. Rasta*) heathen.

payaso *n.* (*also* **payass**) [Port. *palhaço* or Sp. *payaso*, jester, clown] [20C+] (*W.I.*) fooling around, buffoonery.

payback *n.* (*also* **paybacks**) [SE *pay back*] [1960s+] (*US*) revenge, retaliation.

pay me rent *n.* [rhy. sl.] [20C+] (*Aus.*) a tent.

payoff *n.* (*also* **pay-off game**) **1** [1910s+] (*US Und.*) a confidence trick whereby the victim is encouraged to wager a large sum of money, having been lured into the trick when a smaller wager, also suggested by the trickster, seems to have paid off satisfactorily. **2** [1920s+] (*UK/US Und.*) the division of criminal spoils. **3** [1920s+] (*US Und.*) a bribe. **4** [1920s+] (*orig. US*) the end result, the outcome, the conclusion (whether positive or negative). **5** [1920s+] a (final) payment for services rendered. **6** [1920s+] (*US prison*) a prisoner's hand-out or release from prison. **7** [1920s+] (*US Und.*) a confidence trickster. **8** [1920s+] winnings on a wager or some form of gambling. **9** [1940s] a ransom. **10** [1940s] a gang killing. **11** [1940s] the denouement of a book, film or play. **12** [1940s+] (*US black*) a generous person. **13** [1950s+] a reward, a recompense, other than financial. **14** [1960s] one's deserts.

IN COMPOUNDS

❑ **pay-off joint** *n.* [JOINT *n.* (3b)] [1900s–50s] (*US Und.*) a fake gambling club or broker's office, in which the victim is swindled. ❑ **payoff man** *n.* (*also* **pay-off guy**) [GUY *n.*[2] (1)] [1920s+] (*US Und.*) **1** a confidence trickster. **2** the cashier for a criminal gang. **3** a middleman or fellow-criminal who passes on bribes from criminals to the authorities. **4** one who pays off bets made at a bookmaker's or other gambling organization. **5** a police officer who accepts bribes. ❑ **pay-off mob** *n.* [MO *n.*[2]] [1930s] a team of confidence tricksters.

pay off *v.* [PAYOFF *n.*] **1** [early 18C–1900s] to take revenge upon. **2** [1920s+] (*orig. US*) to bribe. **3** [1920s+] (*orig. US*) to recompense, to pay one's debts; also fig. use. **4** [1940s] (*US*) to get one's deserts.

IN COMPOUNDS

❑ **payoff queen** *n.* [QUEEN *n.* (2a)/-QUEEN *sfx* (3)] [1940s–70s] (gay) a homosexual who prefers to pay for sex.

(IN PHRASES)

□ **pay off in gold** *v.* [i.e. he displays his gold badge as identification] [1930s–50s] (*US drugs*) for a Federal agent to arrest an addict.

payol *n.* (*also* **pag, pagnol**) [Sp. *español.* The word is equated with NIGGER *n.*[1] (1) or COOLIE *n.*[1] in terms of offensiveness. Payols thus call themselves 'Spanish' or, in Sp., *venezolanos*] [20C+] **1** (*W.I., Trin.*) a mixed-race person who retains traces of Spanish ancestry and culture. **2** (*W.I., Gren.*) a Spanish-speaking person, esp. a Venezuelan.

payola *n.* [SE *pay* + -OLA *sfx*; esp. common in the record business where disc jockeys are offered massive inducements to push a certain record or artist. Major scandals in the US *c.*1959 supposedly ended payola, but some believe that the practice persists] [1930s+] (*orig. US*) the practice (ostensibly illegal and generally denied by its practitioners) of bribing (with cash or kind) those with access to the public to tout a product.

paz *n.* [Sp. *paz*, peace] [1980s] (*drugs*) phencyclidine.

pazazz *n. see* PIZZAZZ *n.*

p.c. *n.* [abbr.] **1** [late 19C] (*UK society*) the *p*oor *c*lasses. **2** [late 19C+] (*UK society*) a *p*ost*c*ard. **3** [20C+] a police constable. **4** [1950s] (*US*) the *P*olice *c*ommissioner. **5** [1950s+] (*US drugs/gambling*) a *p*er*c*entage. **6** [1980s+] (*UK Und.*) a *p*revious *c*onviction. **7** [1980s+] (*US teen*) a *p*rivate *c*onversation. **8** [1980s+] (*drugs*) a *p*iece of *c*rack cocaine. **9** [1990s+] (*US prison*) *p*rotective *c*ustody.

(IN PHRASES)

□ **p.c. up** *v.* [1990s+] (*US prison*) to request or be incarcerated in protective custody.

p.c. *adj.* [abbr.] [1980s+] *p*olitically *c*orrect, ideologically pure.

PCP *n.* (*also* **PCE, PCPA**) [abbr. PEACE PILLS *under* PEACE *n.*] [1960s+] (*drugs*) phencyclidine.

p.d. *n.* [abbr. *p*ants *d*own] [1930s+] an embarrassing situation; thus *caught p.d.*, caught in an embarrassing situation.

p.d.a. *n.* [abbr. *p*ublic *d*isplay of *a*ffection] [1960s+] (*US*) kissing and cuddling in public.

p.d.k. *n.* [abbr. *p*olyester *d*ouble-*k*nit, the epitome of unfashionable tailoring] [1980s+] (*US campus*) someone who is out of fashion.

p'd off *adj. see* PISSED OFF *adj.*

p.d.q. *phr.* [abbr.] **1** [late 19C+] *p*retty *d*amn *q*uick(ly). **2** [1920s] fast, lively.

P.E. *n.* [abbr.] [late 19C+] (*S.Afr.*) Port Elizabeth.

pea *n.*[1] **1** [late 19C+] (*Aus.*) (*also* **p**) in fig. uses [horseracing *pea*, the favourite; ult. from the pea in the game of thimble-rig, played with three inverted thimbles and a pea]. (**a**) (*orig. racing*) the ideal, the perfect choice, the favourite. (**b**) someone in a favourable position; a superior person. (**c**) in weak use, a man. **2** [1920s+] (*US Und.*) a bullet [? resemblance].

(IN COMPOUNDS)

□ **pea-rigger** *n.* (*also* **pea-man**) [RIG *v.*[2] (2)] [19C] a 'find-the-lady' man, betting against the likelihood of a player calling correctly as to under which thimble a pea will be found.

SE in slang uses

(IN COMPOUNDS)

□ **peabrain** *n. see* separate entry. □ **pea-dodger** *n.* [ety. unknown] [1930s] (*Aus.*) a bowler hat. □ **peahead** *n. see* PEABRAIN *n.* □ **peapicker** *n. see* separate entry. □ **peashooter** *n. see* separate entry.

pea *n.*[2] *see* PEASOUP *n.*[1] (2).

pea and thimble *n.* [mid-19C+] (*Aus.*) a version of the three-card trick; thus *pea and thimble man*, one who conducts the game.

peabrain *n.* (*also* **peahead**) [SE *pea* + sfx *-brain*/-HEAD *sfx* (1)] [1950s+] (*orig. US*) a fool, a simpleton.

(DERIVATIVES)

□ **peabrained** *adj.* [1950s+] stupid, foolish.

peace *n.* **1** [1970s+] in drug uses. (**a**) STP; 'a hallucinogenic chemical produced by the Dow Chemical Company. The initials are said to represent "serenity, tranquility, and peace," or "scientifically treated petroleum"' (Spears, *Slang and Jargon of Drugs and Drink*, 1986). (**b**) LSD. (**c**) phencyclidine. **2** [2000s] (*US black*) a place where one is happy and secure.

(IN COMPOUNDS)

□ **peace pills** *n.* (*US drugs*) **1** [1960s+] phencyclidine. **2** [1970s+] a mixture of LSD and Methedrine. □ **peace tablets** *n.* [the association of LSD with 'love and peace'] [1970s+] (*US drugs*) LSD. □ **peace weed** *n.* [SE *weed*/WEED *n.*[1] (4)] [1970s+] (*drugs*) phencyclidine.

SE in slang uses

(IN COMPOUNDS)

□ **peacemaker** *n.* **1** [mid-19C+] (*US*) a pistol or revolver, esp. the Colt .45. **2** [1950s] (*W.I.*) a male lover. **3** [1950s] (*W.I.*) (*also* **peaceman**) a police officer. **4** [1970s] (*US black*) the penis [just poss. from the ironic nickname accorded the nuclear arsenal's MX missile].

peace *phr.* [popularized by hippies; mostly in ironic or historical use since] [1950s+] (*orig. W.I.*) farewell, goodbye, a greeting.

peace and quiet *n.* [rhy. sl.] [20C+] a diet.

peacemake *n. see* MATRIMONIAL PEACEMAKER *n.*

peace (out) *v.* [ext. PEACE *phr.*] [1990s+] (*US campus*) to leave.

peace out *phr.* (*also* **peace up**) [1990s+] (*US black/campus/teen*) goodbye.

peach *n.*[1] **1** [mid-18C; mid-19C+] (*also* **nectarine**) a pretty young woman [*see* Williams for fig. uses of *peach* in 16C–17C]. **2** [mid-19C+] (*also* **peony**) someone or something of exceptional worth, quality or desirability. **3** [late 19C+] in ironic use of sense 2. **4** [1900s] (*US campus*) a promiscuous woman. **5** in pl., in sexual uses. (**a**) [1920s] (*US black*) the vagina. (**b**) [1920s+] (*US black*) the male genitals. (**c**) [1960s] (*US black*) (*also* **peach tree**) a hermaphrodite. (**d**) [1970s] a term of affection. (**e**) [1980s+] (*US gay*) the buttocks. **6** [1960s+] (*drugs*) in pl., dexedrine [the colour of the capsules].

(DERIVATIVES)

□ **peacherino** *n.* (*also* **peacherine, peachermaroot**) [-ERINO *sfx*] [20C+] (*orig. US*) something of exceptional worth, quality or desirability, e.g. an attractive young woman.

(IN COMPOUNDS)

□ **peach tree** *n. see* sense 5c above.

(IN PHRASES)

□ **all to the peaches** *adj.* [1900s] very good, very enjoyable.

peach *n.*[2] [PEACH *v.* (1)] [mid–late 19C] a detective, esp. as employed by a stage-coach or omnibus company to check receipts.

peach *adj. see* PEACHY *adj.*

peach *v.* [SE *impeach*] **1** [late 16C+] to betray, to inform against. **2** [mid-19C] to confess, to admit.

peacher *n.* [PEACH *v.* (1)] [mid-16C+] an informer.

peacherino *n. see under* PEACH *n.*[1].

peaches *adj.* [PEACH *n.*[1] (1)] **1** [late 19C–1910s] (*US teen*) attractive, sexually alluring. **2** [1910s–40s] (*US*) fine, excellent.

peach-fuzz *n.* [SE *peach fuzz*, an adolescent male's light facial hair] [1950s–70s] (*gay*) an attractive teenager.

peachy *adj.* (*also* **peach, peachie**) [PEACH *n.*[1] (2)] [20C+] wonderful, excellent, delightful.

(IN COMPOUNDS)

□ **peachy-clean** *adj.* [1990s+] absolutely innocent, untainted. □ **peachy-keen** *adj.* [KEEN *adj.*] [1960s+] (*US*) **1** excellent, first-rate. **2** (ironically) not good enough to warrant enthusiasm but adequate.

peacock *v.* **1** [late 19C] (*Aus.*) to buy up the best sections of land, thus making the adjoining territory worthless [the speculator 'picks out the eyes' of the land]. **2** [late 19C] (*Aus.*) to outwit. **3** [late 19C] to pay morning calls. **4** [late 19C+] (*orig. Anglo-Ind.*) to promenade up and down in one's best clothes [the bird's characteristic display].

peacock horse *n.* [such horses are bedecked in mourning black, with plumes, and step in a very ceremonial way] [late 19C] a horse that pulls a hearse.

pea-eye *n. see* P.I. *n.*

peak *n.*[1] (*also* **peake**) [? link to SE *picot*, needlework that forms the edging of a piece of lace] [mid-17C–early 19C] (*UK Und.*) lace.

peak *n.*[2] **1** [19C] the human nose. **2** [1960s+] (*drugs*) the central two hours or so of an LSD trip when the hallucinogen is at its most powerful.

peak *v.*[1] [PEAK *n.*[2] (2)] [1960s+] **1** (*drugs*) to reach the most extreme point of an LSD trip. **2** to reach the limit of a particular experience.

peak *v.*[2] *see* PEEK *v.*

peake *n. see* PEAK *n.*[1].

peaked *adj.* (*also* **peeked**) [SE *peak*, to look sickly] [mid–late 19C] looking ill, tired.

peaky *adj.* (*also* **peeky**) [SE *peak*, to look sickly] [mid-19C+] feeble, weak.

DERIVATIVES

❑ **peakedy** *adj.* [1950s] weak, ill. ❑ **peakyish** *adj.* [mid-19C] ill, 'under the weather'.

peal *n.* [ety. unknown] [mid-19C] (*UK Und.*) a ball.

peamey *n.* (*also* **peamy**) [SE *pea-merchant*] [mid-19C] a pea-seller.

peanut *n.* **1** [1910s+] (*also* **pretzel**) in pl., anything (occas. anyone) insignificant, petty, esp. money, wages. **2** of a person. (**a**) [1940s] (*US black*) a white man [abbr. *MR PEANUT under* MR *n.*]. (**b**) [1960s] (*US*) a young person, a child. (**c**) [1960s] (*Aus.*) a slightly foolish person. **3** [1960s+] (*drugs*) a barbiturate [the shape of the pill]. **4** [1990s+] (*UK juv.*) one who has an oval, peanut-shaped head; one who has recently received a haircut.

IN COMPOUNDS

❑ **peanut alley** *n.* (*also* **peanut row**) [the consumption of peanuts in this row] [1950s+] (*Aus./US*) the front row of the stalls in a cinema. ❑ **peanut buffer** *n.* [SE *buff*, to polish] [1990s+] a male homosexual. ❑ **peanut factory** *n.* [1980s] (*Aus.*) a psychiatric institution. ❑ **peanut farm** *n.* [the broken stones resemble peanuts] [1930s] (*US tramp*) a workhouse where the inmates are made to break stones. ❑ **peanut flier** *n.* [? the idea of the ridiculous job of flying a peanut] [1950s–60s] (*UK Und.*) a criminal who will take on any job, however small. ❑ **peanut gallery** *n.* [the consumption of peanuts by the occupants of these seats] **1** [late 19C+] the top gallery, the 'gods' in a theatre. **2** [late 19C+] ignorant, vociferous spectators. **3** [1940s+] (*Aus./US*) the front row of the stalls in a cinema. **4** [1990s+] a person who exhibits the characteristics of sense 2. ❑ **peanut politics** *n.* [late 19C–1920s] (*US*) underhand, clandestine politicking, aimed at the securing of minor personal gains; thus *peanut politician*, one who indulges in such tactics. ❑ **peanut roaster** *n.* [joc. resemblance] [1910s+] (*US*) a small locomotive; an old or ramshackle automobile. ❑ **peanut row** *n. see* PEANUT ALLEY above. ❑ **peanut smuggler** *n.* [the 'peanuts' are her nipples, visible through the cloth] [1990s+] (*Aus. juv.*) a girl or young woman who is not wearing a brassiere under her clothing.

IN PHRASES

❑ **peanut butter pussy** *n.* (*also* **peanut butter legs**) [PUSSY *n.* (1); it is 'smooth, brown and easy to spread'] [1970s+] (*US black*) a complimentary term for a black or Hispanic woman's vagina, or legs, and thus the woman who possesses it. ❑ **that ain't/isn't peanuts** *see* THAT AIN'T HAY *under* HAY *n.*

peanut *adj.* [mid-19C+] (*orig. US*) second-rate, 'small-time'.

peapicker *n.* [1970s] (*US*) a derog. term for a peasant.

pea-picking *adj.* [PEAPICKER *n.*] [1970s] (*US*) in the manner of a peasant, hence insignificant.

pear *v.* [? play on PEACH *v.* (1)] [mid-19C] (*UK Und.*) to supply officers with information about a robbery and then warn the thieves to get away.

pear and quince *n.* [rhy. sl.] [20C+] (*Aus.*) a prince.

pearl *n.*[1] **1** [1900s] (*Aus.*) an attractive woman. **2** [1920s+] the clitoris or vagina; usu. in combs. below. **3** [1960s+] semen; usu. in combs. below. **4** [1970s] (*US black*) an attractive white woman.

IN COMPOUNDS

❑ **pearl dive** *v.* **1** [1920s+] (*US*) to perform cunnilingus [DIVE *v.* (2)]. **2** [1970s] (*US gay*) to prefer offering fellatio to receiving it. ❑ **pearl (drop)** *n.* [resemblance and colour] [1960s+] (*US gay*) a drop of semen. ❑ **pearl-fisher** *n.* [1930s] (*US*) a cunnilinguist. ❑ **pearl necklace** *n.* [supposed resemblance] [1990s+] the drops ('pearls') of semen ejaculated onto a partner's neck after fellatio. ❑ **pearl tongue** *n.* [1980s+] (*US black*) the vagina; one who practises cunnilingus.

IN PHRASES

❑ **dive for black pearls** *v. see under* DIVE *v.*

SE in slang uses

IN COMPOUNDS

❑ **pearl dive** *v.* [20C+] to work as a dishwasher. ❑ **pearl diver** *n.* [20C+] (*US*) a dishwasher in a hotel or restaurant; thus *pearl-diving*, washing up. ❑ **pearl handle** *n.* [the image is of luxury compared to a hand-rolled cigarette] [1940s+] (*US prison*) a factory-made cigarette.

IN PHRASES

❑ **dive for pearls** *v. see under* DIVE *v.* ❑ **like a pearl in a half-storm** [late 19C] impossible to find.

pearl *n.*[2] *see* PURLER *n.* (3).

pearl *adj.*[1] [on pattern of DIAMOND *adj.* (1)] [1940s+] (*Aus.*) first-rate, excellent.

pearl *adj.*[2] [? Japanese attack at Pearl Harbor, 6/12/1941] [2000s] (*S.Afr. gay*) untrustworthy.

pearler *n. see* PURLER *n.* (3).

Pearl Harbor *n.* [play on NIP *n.* (1), i.e. there's a nasty 'nip' in the air] [2000s] cold weather.

Pearl Harbor *v.* [the Japanese attack on the US fleet in Pearl Harbor, 6/12/1941] [1970s] to make a surprise attack.

pearlies *n.* **1** [mid-19C+] pearl buttons, esp. found on a costermonger's clothes. **2** [mid-19C+] costermongers as a class. **3** [late 19C+] (*also* **pearls**) the teeth.

pearls *n.* **1** [1960s] (*US black*) a woman's eyes. **2** [1960s+] (*drugs*) amyl nitrite [resemblance of amyl nitrite vials]. **3** *see* PEARLIES *n.* (3).

pearly gate *n.* [rhy. sl.] [20C+] a plate.

pearly gates *n.* **1** [1960s–70s] the teeth. **2** [1970s+] (*drugs*) LSD [the drug can offer visions of heaven, i.e. the 'pearly gates'].

pearly king *n.* [rhy. sl. = RING *n.* (1b)] [20C+] the anus.

pearly whites *n.* [1930s–70s] (*orig. US*) teeth.

pear-making *n.* [dial. *pear*, appear, i.e. one makes an appearance, but does not stay] [19C] (*UK Und.*) enrolling in a regiment, taking the offered bounty and then deserting; the process can be repeated several times.

pear-shaped *adj.* [the image of a solid rectangle 'slipping down' into a pear shape, hence 'the bottom drops out'] [2000s] out of order, going badly or wrong.

IN PHRASES

❑ **go pear-shaped** *v.* (*also* **turn pear-shaped**) [1990s+] of plans or schemes, to fail, to collapse.

peasant *n.* [16C–17C SE use had derog. overtones, initially used for 'the subjects of France'] **1** [1930s+] a general term of abuse, implying stupidity, boorishness, a lack of sophistication. **2** [1960s–70s] (*US gay*) a heterosexual male.

pease pudding hot *n.* [rhy. sl. = SNOT *n.*[1] (1)] [20C+] nasal mucus.

peashooter *n.* **1** [20C+] (*orig. Aus./US*) a small, low-powered firearm [note WW1 Aus. milit. *pea-shooter*, a German anti-tank gun; UK WW1 *pea-shooter*, a rifle]. **2** [1920s] the penis.

peas in the pot *n.* [rhy. sl. = SNOT *n.*[1] (1)] [2000s] (*N.Z.*) nasal mucus.

peas (in the pot) *adj.* [rhy. sl.] [late 19C+] hot; lit. or fig.

peasoup *n.*[1] (*also* **peasouper**) [the stereotyping of pea soup as a French-Canadian staple] **1** [19C+] (*US*) a French-born immigrant. **2** [late 19C+] (*US*) (*also* **Johnny Peasoup, pea, souper**) a French-Canadian; thus *talk peasoup*, to talk in French-Canadian patois. **3** *see* PEASOUPER *n.* (2).

peasoup *n.*^{2} [ety. unknown] [1950s] (*US Und.*) something worthless; an informer.

pea soup *adj.* [PEASOUP *n.*^{2}] [1930s] (*US prison*) bad; of a person, untrustworthy.

peasouper *n.* **1** [mid-19C–1900s] (*Aus.*) a newly arrived British immigrant. **2** [mid-19C+] (*also* **peasoup**) a very dense fog [orig. the pollution-based London fogs, but since the Clean Air legislation of 1950s, any exceptionally impenetrable fog]. **3** [late 19C] (*N.Z.*) a teetotaller [? their preferred diet]. **4** *see* PEASOUP *n.*^{1}.

peasy *adj.* [PEAS (IN THE POT) *adj.* = HOT *adj.* (5a)] [1950s] dangerous for criminal activity.

peazy *n.* [ety. unknown; ? SE *easy-peasy*] [2000s] (*US black*) a telephone.

peb *n.* [abbr. PEBBLE *n.* (2)] [1900s–50s] (*Aus.*) a youthful gangster.

pebble *n.* [the hardness of the SE *pebble*] **1** [17C; 19C] in pl., the testicles [play on STONE *n.*^{1} (1)]. **2** [early 19C+] (*orig. boxing, then Aus.*) anyone seen as hard to deal with, e.g. a youthful ruffian. **3** [late 19C] a monocle. **4** [1980s+] (*drugs*) a small piece of crack cocaine [play on ROCK *n.* (4d)].

(DERIVATIVES)

❑ **pebbly** *adj.* [1910s] hard, challenging.

(IN PHRASES)

❑ **game as a pebble** *adj.* [SE *game*, enthusiastic, keen, 'up for'] [early 19C–1900s] ready for anything, up to any challenge.

pebble-beached *adj.* [fig. 'cast away'] **1** [late 19C–1910s] (*also* **pebbly beach**) penniless, destitute. **2** [1930s] dazed, absent-minded.

pebble-dash *v.* [1990s+] (*Irish*) to have diarrhoea, hence to splatter the lavatory with faeces.

Pebble Mill *n.* [rhy. sl.; ult. UK TV show *Pebble Mill at One*] [1990s+] (*drugs*) any form of pill, i.e. an amphetamine.

pebbles *n.* [the young girl character *Pebbles* in the TV show *The Flintstones*] [1990s+] an underage, sexually active girl.

pebbly beach *adj. see* PEBBLE-BEACHED *adj.* (1).

pec *n.* (*also* **peck**) [abbr.] [1960s+] usu. in pl., a *pec*toral muscle, the development of which is popular among body-builders.

peck *n.*^{1} [SE *peck*, to eat (of a bird); the concepts of food and business are closely allied here] **1** [mid-16C+] (*orig. UK Und.; later use US black/gang*) (*also* **pecks, pek**) food, often meat. **2** [late 19C] an apppetite. **3** [late 19C–1900s] a business, a concern.

(DERIVATIVES)

❑ **peckage** *n.* (*also* **peckadge, peckeridge, peckidge**) [17C–mid-19C] (*UK Und.*) food, esp. scraps. ❑ **peckings** *n.* [1940s–50s] (*US black*) food.

(IN COMPOUNDS)

❑ **peck alley** *n.* [mid-19C] the throat. ❑ **peck and booze** *n.* (*also* **peck and tipple**) [BOOZE *n.* (1)/TIPPLE *n.* (1)] [18C–mid-19C] meat and drink. ❑ **peck and perch** *n.* [early 19C] board and lodging.

(IN PHRASES)

❑ **on the peck** *see* ON THE PROD *under* PROD *n.*^{3}. ❑ **off one's peck** [late 19C–1900s] having no appetite.

peck *n.*^{2} [abbr. PECKERWOOD *n.*] [1930s+] (*US black*) a white person.

peck *n.*^{3} *see* PEC *n.*

peck *n.*^{4} *see* PECKER *n.*^{2} (2).

peck *v.*^{1} **1** [early 16C+] (*orig. UK Und.; later use US black*) to eat. **2** [17C] to bite. **3** [mid-19C] (*UK Und.*) of a pickpocket, to put one's hand into a victim's pocket [image of a bird 'pecking' at the pocket].

peck *v.*^{2} [? image of a bird pecking until one capitulates] [1900s] (*Aus.*) to give in, to surrender.

pecker *n.*^{1} [PECK *v.*^{1} (1)] [mid–late 19C] **1** an eater. **2** the appetite [B&L suggest -ER *sfx*].

pecker *n.*^{2} [SE *pecker*, that which pecks, i.e. a beak, a bill] **1** [mid-19C+] courage. **2** [late 19C+] (*orig. US*) (*also* **peck**) the penis; a generic term for sex. **3** [1940s–80s] a general term of abuse. **4** [1980s] (*US/Can.*) a young child. **5** *see* PECKERHEAD below.

(IN COMPOUNDS)

❑ **pecker check** *n.* [1980s] a health check, looking for symptoms of VD. ❑ **pecker cheese** *n.* [CHEESE *n.*^{1} (2a)] [1990s+] (*US*) smegma. ❑ **peckerhead** *n.* (*also* **pecker**) [-HEAD *sfx* (1)] [1940s+] (*US*) an objectionable, aggressive person. ❑ **pecker palace** *n.* [2000s] (*US prison*) a room set aside for conjugal visits. ❑ **pecker snot** *n.* [SNOT *n.*^{1} (5)] [1990s+] (*US*) semen. ❑ **pecker tracks** *n.* [1950s+] (*US*) sperm left on a sheet or other similar object after intercourse or, usu., masturbation.

(IN PHRASES)

❑ **dead pecker** *n. see under* DEAD *adj.* ❑ **keep one's pecker up** *v.* (*also* **hold one's pecker up**) [sense 1 above; despite chronological impossibility, popular ety. usu. links phr. to sense 2 above] [mid-19C+] to stay cheerful, despite possible adversity; often as imp. *keep your pecker up!* ❑ **stick one's pecker in** *v.* [1990s+] (*US*) to interfere; to become involved.

peckeridge *n. see* PECKAGE *under* PECK *n.*^{1}.

peckerwood *n.* (*also* **pecker, woodpecker**) [the red *woodpecker*, symbol of whites, rather than the black crow, symbol of blacks] [1920s+] (*orig. US black*) a white person, usu. a working-class Southerner; also ext. to Chicanos and Latinos.

(IN COMPOUNDS)

❑ **Peckerwood Town** *n.* [1950s] (*US black*) the area inhabited by poor white people.

peckerwood *adj.* [PECKERWOOD *n.*] [1920s+] (*US*) pertaining to the (working class) rural South.

Peckham *n.* [pun on PECK *v.*^{1} (1) + SE *ham*] used in phrs. pertaining to food, as below.

(IN PHRASES)

❑ **all holiday at Peckham** **1** [late 18C–mid-19C] all over, finished, hopeless. **2** [early–mid-19C] a lack of food. ❑ **go to Peckham** *v.* [early–mid-19C] to sit down to eat. ❑ **take a holiday at Peckham** *v.* [18C–mid-19C] to have nothing to eat.

Peckham (Rye) *n.* [rhy. sl.; ult. *Peckham Rye*, south London] [1910s–80s] a tie.

peckidge *n. see* PECKAGE *under* PECK *n.*^{1}.

peckie *n. see* PEKKIE *n.*

pecking and necking *n.* [SE *peck*, to nibble at + NECK *v.* (4)] [1970s] (*US black*) foreplay, kissing and cuddling.

peckings *n. see under* PECK *n.*^{1}.

peckish *adj.* (*also* **pecky**) [PECK *n.*^{1} (1); 20C+ use is SE] [18C+] hungry.

pecks *n. see* PECK *n.*^{1} (1).

Peck's bad boy *n.* [the name of a fictional character created by George Wilbur *Peck* (1840–1916) in *Peck's Bad Boy and his Pa* (1883)] [late 19C+] (*US*) a mischievous child.

pecnoster *n.* [PECKER *n.*^{2} (2) + pun on SE *paternoster*, our father] [late 19C] the penis.

pecos *v.* [the *Pecos* River] [1920s–40s] (*US Western*) to shoot someone and roll their body in the river.

peculiar *n.* [SE *peculiar*, private] **1** [early 17C] a wife. **2** [late 17C–19C] a mistress; occas. a male lover.

peculiar *adj.* [euph.] **1** [late 19C+] deranged, eccentric. **2** [20C+] homosexual.

ped *n.* [usu. dial.: 'chiefly in use in the Eastern Counties from Northants to Essex, and in Devon and Somerset' (*OED*)] [late 17C–mid-19C] (*UK Und.*) a basket.

pedal *n.* [1900s] (*US*) a foot.

(IN PHRASES)

❑ **get the pedal** *v.* [1930s] to be dismissed from a job. ❑ **put the pedal to the metal** *v.* (*also* **push the pedal to the metal**) **1** [1960s+] (*orig. US*) to accelerate an automobile; thus adv. *pedal to the metal*, very fast, fig. very intense. **2** [2000s] in fig. uses, implying energy.

SE in slang uses

(IN COMPOUNDS)

❑ **pedal and crank** *n. see* CHAIN AND CRANK *n.* ❑ **pedal-pusher** *n.* [1910s–30s] (*US*) a cyclist, esp. a racing cyclist.

pedal one's dogs *v. see under* DOGS *n.*[1].

peddle *v.*

SE in slang uses

IN PHRASES

▫ **peddle one's paper** *v. see under* PAPER *n.* ▫ **peddle out** *v.* [1920s–30s] (*US*) to sell one's possessions, esp. to a second-hand store. ▫ **peddle one's ass** *v.* **1** [1930s+] (*also* **peddle one's arse, ...butt, ...gash, ...hips, ...hump, ...shape, ...stuff**) to work as a prostitute, of either gender; to be very promiscuous [ASS *n.* (2)/ARSE *n.* (1)/BUTT *n.*[1] (1a)/GASH *n.*[1] (1)/SE *hips*/HUMP *n.*[1] (3a)/SE *shape*/STUFF *n.* (8a)]. **2** [1990s+] in fig. use, to prostitute oneself. ▫ **peddle pussy** *v.* (*also* **peddle one's pussy, sell pussy**) [PUSSY *n.* (1)] [1960s+] to work as a prostitute; thus n. *pussy-peddling*. ▫ **peddle someone's ass** *v.* [1960s] to send a prostitute out to work.

IN EXCLAMATIONS

▫ **go peddle your fish!** (*also* **go peel a grape!**) [1930s] (*US*) an excl. of disdainful dismissal.

peddler *n.* (*also* **pedlar, pedler**) **1** [late 19C] (*US*) a seller of counterfeit money. **2** [20C+] a male prostitute. **3** [1920s+] (*also* **dope peddler**) a drug seller. **4** [1930s] (*US tramp*) a freight or goods train, a stopping train. **5** [1960s] (*US prison*) one who provides any form of contraband within the prison.

IN PHRASES

▫ **dick/prick peddler** *n. see* DICK PEDDLER *under* DICK *n.*[1].

peddler's French *n. see* PEDLAR'S FRENCH *n.*

pedestal *n.* [late 17C–early 18C] in pl., the feet.

pedigree *n.* [1910s+] (*US prison*) **1** a criminal record; thus *pedigreed*, having a criminal record; *pedigree-man*, a recidivist. **2** thus, a 'track record', a reputation.

Pedigree Chum *n.* [rhy. sl. = COME *n.* (2); ult. the brand of dogfood *Pedigree Chum*] [1990s+] semen.

pedlar *n. see* PEDDLER *n.*

pedlar's French *n.* (*also* **peddler's French**) [the image is of alien foreignness rather than of France itself] **1** [mid-16C–mid-19C] cant, criminal slang. **2** [late 19C] any incomprehensible language.

pedlar's pack *n.* [rhy. sl. = SACK *n.* (2a)] [1970s+] dismissal from one's job.

pedlar's pony *n.* [late 18C] a walking stick.

pedler *n. see* PEDDLER *n.*

Pedro *n.* [Sp. name *Pedro*, Peter] **1** [1940s+] (*US*) any Spanish-speaking person. **2** [1990s+] cocaine [ref. to S. American origins of cocaine].

IN PHRASES

▫ **friend of Pedro** *n.* [1990s+] a cocaine user.

pee *n.*[1] [PEE *v.* (1)] **1** [20C+] urine. **2** [1930s+] an act of urination.

IN COMPOUNDS

▫ **pee hard** *n.* [HARD-ON *n.* (1)] [1980s+] (*Aus. prison*) an erection on waking up in the morning. ▫ **pee-pot** *n. see* PISSPOT *n.*

IN PHRASES

▫ **beat the pee out of** *v.* (*also* **kick the pee out of**) [1970s] to attack violently. ▫ **scare the pee out of** *v.* [1960s] to terrify.

pee *n.*[2] [abbr.] [1970s] pure heroin.

pee *v.* [abbr./euph. PISS *v.* (2)] **1** [late 18C; mid-19C+] (*also* **pee-pee**) to urinate; thus *pee-er*, one who urinates. **2** [1970s] to do something very well. **3** [1980s] (*US campus*) to do well [fig. use or abbr. SE *perform*]. **4** [1980s+] to rain (hard).

IN PHRASES

▫ **pee between two heels** *v.* (*also* **straddle a chamberpot**) [the position of a woman when urinating] [1940s–60s] (*US black*) a phr. used when referring to a woman, or to female qualities, e.g. *the finest bitch that ever peed between two heels.* ▫ **pee (in) one's pants** *v.* [1960s+] to be terrified. ▫ **pee in the same pot** *v. see* PISS IN SOMEONE'S POCKET *under* PISS *v.* ▫ **pee (it) off** *v.* [semi-euph. var. on *PISS AWAY under* PISS *v.*] [1920s] (*US*) to waste, to squander. ▫ **pee off** *v.* [abbr./euph. PISS OFF *v.*] **1** [1940s] to leave, to depart. **2** [1950s] to annoy, to irritate. ▫ **pee on** *v.* [1990s+] **1** to treat harshly, to bully. **2** to ignore, to dismiss, to treat contemptuously, as in *I would not pee on.* ▫ **pee (oneself)** *v.* **1** [late 18C; 1960s+] to urinate on oneself, esp. in the context of being utterly terrified. **2** [1940s+] to laugh uproariously. ▫ **think it's just to pee through** *v.* (*also* **think it's just to piss through**) [PISS *v.* (2)] [20C+] a phr. denigrating an unsophisticated, inexperienced youth who supposedly has yet to appreciate the alternative function of his penis; also used of a similarly unsophisticated young woman.

peeble *v.* [Scot.; note Yorks. dial. *peeagle*, to do something badly] [20C+] (*Irish*) to whistle out of tune.

peece *n. see* PIECE *n.* (2a).

peed *adj. see* PISSED *adj.*[1].

peedie *n.* [PEE *n.*[1] (1)] [20C+] (*Ulster*) a small boy's penis.

peed off *adj.* [euph. for PISSED OFF *adj.*] [1940s+] (*US*) angry, irritated.

pee-eye *n. see* P.I. *n.*

pee-gee *adj. see* P.G. *adj.*

peehole *n.* (*also* **P hole**) [PEE *n.*[1] (1)] [1930s–60s] (*US*) the vagina.

IN COMPOUNDS

▫ **peehole pirate** *n.* [1960s] (*US*) a rapist.

peek *n.* [SE *peek*] **1** [1940s] (*US*) a peephole, e.g. in a brothel. **2** [1940s–50s] (*UK prison*) an observation cell, into which prisoners are placed if, for instance, they have smashed up their cells or shown other signs of instability.

IN COMPOUNDS

▫ **peek freak** *n.* [FREAK *n.*[1] (7)] [1960s+] a homosexual voyeur who watches two other men during sex. ▫ **peek show** *n.* [2000s] a live sex show.

peek *v.* (*also* **peak**) [? SE *peek*, in the context of children's games] [1910s+] (*Aus.*) to surrender, to give in.

SE in slang uses

IN PHRASES

▫ **peek out** *v.* [1990s+] (*US black*) to appraise someone sexually. ▫ **peek through one's liquor** *v.* [1930s–40s] (*US black*) to pose as sober when one is in fact drunk.

peeked *adj. see* PEAKED *adj.*

peeker *n.* [SE *peek*] [1920s–40s] (*US black*) in pl., the eyes.

peekish *adj.* [? SE *peeky*, i.e. pale] [2000s] (*US black*) homosexual, effeminate.

peeks, the *n. see* BLOCK GAME *under* BLOCK *n.*[8].

peeky *adj. see* PEAKY *adj.*

peel *v.* **1** [mid-19C+] to extract money from a wallet surreptitiously. **2** [1960s+] (*US Und.*) to break into a safe. **3** [1980s] (*also* **peel a can**) to drink. **4** [2000s] to rob someone of their valuables.

SE in slang uses

DERIVATIVES

▫ **peeled** *adj.* **1** [mid-16C] with a shaven head. **2** [19C+] naked. **3** [2000s] (*S.Afr. gay*) circumcised. ▫ **peeler** *n.* [1940s–50s] (*US*) a striptease or burlesque artist.

IN COMPOUNDS

▫ **peeled egg** *n.* [20C+] (*Ulster*) anything easy or simple. ▫ **peel-head** *adj.* (*also* **peely**) [1920s+] (*W.I.*) bald, esp. as a description of certain species of chickens or vultures.

IN PHRASES

▫ **peel a can** *v. see* sense 3 above. ▫ **peel a fine green banana** *v.* [BANANA *n.* (3a)] [1940s] (*US black*) to seduce an attractive, light-skinned woman. ▫ **peel caps** *v.* [lit. 'to peel the flesh from someone's skull'] [1990s+] (*US black/teen*) to attack violently. ▫ **peel it** *v.* [var. on SE *peel off*] [mid-19C] (*US*) to run at full speed. ▫ **peel off** *v. see* PEEL RUBBER *under* RUBBER *n.*[2]. ▫ **peel off a mass** *v.* [MASS *n.*] [1990s+] (*W.I./UK black teen*) to hand out money. ▫ **peel one's (best) end** *v.* [the sliding back of the foreskin] [late 19C–1910s] to enter a woman's vagina. ▫ **peel someone's knob** *v.* [KNOB *n.* (1a)] [1930s] (*US*) to beat someone up. ▫ **peel someone's potatoes** *v.* [i.e. to 'peel' someone's testicles] [2000s] (*US black*) to beat up, to harm badly. ▫ **peel the banana** *v.* [BANANA *n.* (2a)] [1990s+] to masturbate. ▫ **peel the bark** *v.* [BARK *n.*[1] (1)] [mid-19C] in boxing, to draw blood.

peel(e) garlic *n.* *see* PILGARLIC *n.*

peeler *n.*[1] [19C] (*US*) **1** something exceptional, usu. in terms of strength. **2** someone exceptional.

peeler *n.*[2] (*also* **Mr Peeler**) [proper name Sir Robert *Peel* (1788–1850), founder of the Metropolitan Police. The term is now obsolete except in Northern Ireland] [mid-19C+] a policeman, a police officer; orig. the Irish constabulary.

peeler *n.*[3] *see under* PEEL *v.*

peely *adj.* *see* PEEL-HEAD *under* PEEL *v.*

pee-man *n.* [abbr.] [1910s–30s] (*UK Und.*) a policeman in civilian clothes.

peenie *n.* (*also* **peen, peeny, penie**) [dimin. of SE *penis*] [1940s+] (*US juv.*) the penis; thus *pound one's peenie*, to masturbate.

peeny *adj.* [play on SE, on model of *teeny-weeny*] [1910s+] (*US*) tiny.

p.e.e.p. *n.* [abbr. *p*erfectly *e*legant *e*ating PUSSY *n.* (1)] [1970s] the vagina; thus ext. as a very attractive woman.

peep *n.*[1] **1** [mid-18C–1930s] an eye. **2** [1990s+] a look.

IN COMPOUNDS

▫ **peep freak** *n.* [FREAK *n.*[1] (7)] [1960s+] (*US*) a voyeur. ▫ **peep joint** *n.* [JOINT *n.* (3b)] [1960s] (*US*) a striptease club.

IN PHRASES

▫ **on the peep** *adv.* [1900s] (*US*) at a glance. ▫ **peel one's peeps** *v.* *see* PEEL ONE'S PEEPERS *under* PEEPER *n.* ▫ **peeps dig the range** *v.* [DIG *v.*[3] (5) + SE *range*] [1930s–40s] (*US black*) to look around one's immediate environs.

peep *n.*[2] [ety. unknown] [mid-19C] (*US*) a fool.

peep *n.*[3] [pron. of the two 'P's in PCP] [1970s+] (*drugs*) phencyclidine.

peep *n.*[4] *see* PEE-PEE *n.* (2).

peep *v.*[1] [rhy. with SE *sleep*] [late 17C–early 18C] (*UK Und.*) to sleep.

peep *v.*[2] [SE *peep*, a word] [late 19C–1960s] (*US*) to talk, esp. to the authorities.

peep *v.*[3] [PEEP *n.*[1] (1)] **1** [1930s+] to put someone or something under surveillance; in weak use, to watch, to look at. **2** [1950s+] (*US black*) to discover something that was meant to be kept secret. **3** [1990s+] to pay close attention, to listen to what somebody is saying.

IN PHRASES

▫ **peep someone's hole-card** *v.* *see under* HOLE CARD *n.* ▫ **peep things out** *v.* [1990s+] (*US black*) to see what is going on.

pee-pee *n.* **1** [1920s+] (*mainly US juv.*) urination; usu. in phr. *go pee-pee, make pee-pee* [redup. PEE *n.*[1] (2); euph. for PISS *n.* (2)]. **2** [1920s+] (*mainly US juv.*) (*also* **peep, peepee meat**) the penis. **3** [1970s] a male homosexual prostitute. **4** [1970s] the vagina.

IN COMPOUNDS

▫ **pee-pee lover** *n.* [1940s–70s] (*gay*) one who prefers the youngest boys for sex.

IN PHRASES

▫ **pull some pee-pee** *v.* [1970s+] (*US gay*) to fellate.

pee-pee *v.* *see* PEE *v.* (1).

peepee meat *n.* *see* PEE-PEE *n.* (2).

peeper *n.* [SE *peep*, to look at] **1** [mid-16C+] an eye, usu. in pl. **2** [late 17C–19C] a looking-glass, a mirror. **3** [early 18C] glass, e.g. a window. **4** [late 18C–mid-19C] a telescope, a spy-glass. **5** [early 19C] in pl., spectacles. **6** [late 19C+] a police officer; a security officer, e.g. in a hotel. **7** [20C+] (*US*) sunglasses. **8** [1940s] a private investigator, with implications of voyeurism. **9** [1970s+] a Peeping Tom, a voyeur.

IN PHRASES

▫ **painted peeper** *n.* [19C–1940s] a black eye; in pl., a pair of black eyes. ▫ **peel one's peepers** *v.* (*also* **peel one's peeps**) [1900s–10s] to keep a lookout; to look wide-eyed. ▫ **peeper in mourning** *n.* [19C] a black eye; usu. in pl.

peeping *adj.* *see* PEEPY *adj.*

peep in the heater *v.* [coarse use of SE] [1930s] (*US*) to perform cunnilingus.

peep o' day boy *n.* (*also* **peep o' day companion**) [early 19C] (*UK Und.*) one who stays up all night carousing.

peeps *n.* [SE *people*] [1980s+] (*US black/campus*) **1** parents, relatives, family. **2** friends, people in general.

peepy *adj.* (*also* **peeping**) [PEEP *v.*[1]; one's eyes are opening and closing; note *Peepy*, the name of a small child in Dickens's *Bleak House* (1852–3)] [late 17C–mid-19C] (*UK Und.*) sleepy.

peer *v.* [late 18C–mid-19C] to act cautiously.

peer queer *n.* [SE *peer* + QUEER *n.* (4)] [1960s–70s] (*gay*) a gay voyeur, or one who participates in homosexual activity only for money.

peery *adj.* [SE *peer*, to look around suspiciously] **1** [mid-17C–mid-18C] shy, fearful. **2** [late 17C–early 19C] (*UK Und.*) sly. **3** [18C–19C] suspicious. **4** [late 18C–mid-19C] inquisitive.

pee-the-bed *n.* *see* PISSABED *n.*

peeve *n.* (*also* **peeva**) [? BEVVY *n.*; Rus. *peevo*, beer, Rom. whisky] [20C+] alcohol, beer; thus *peeve artist*, a regular drinker.

Pee-Wee *n.*

IN PHRASES

▫ **pull a Pee-Wee** *v.* [the entertainer *Pee-Wee* Herman (b.1952), who poses as a foolish, child-like figure] [1990s+] (*US teen*) to make a fool of oneself or say something stupid.

pee-wee *n.*[1] [PEE-WEE *v.*] [late 19C] an act of urination.

pee-wee *n.*[2] [orig. dial. *pee-wee*, diminutive, tiny] **1** [late 19C+] the penis, usu. of a small boy [PEE-WEE *v.*]. **2** [1900s–50s] (*drugs*) a very thin marijuana cigarette. **3** [1910s+] (*Aus.*) a bowler hat. **4** [1910s+] a nickname for any noticeably small or short person. **5** [1980s+] (*US drugs*) crack cocaine, esp. $5 worth (i.e. very little). **6** [1990s+] (*UK black*) a very junior member of a gang. **7** [1990s+] (*US campus*) a socially insecure young man.

pee-wee *adj.* [redup. SE *wee*, tiny; subseq. reinforced by PEENY *adj.* (1)] [late 19C+] small, unimportant, junior.

pee-wee *v.* [redup. of PEE *v.* (1) but poss. predate of WEE *n.* (1)] [late 19C+] (*UK juv.*) to urinate.

pee-willy *n.* [? PEE-WEE *n.*[2] (1)/PEE-WEE *adj.* + WILLIE *n.*[4]] [1920s+] (*Can.*) an effeminate man.

peeyem *n.* *see* P.M. *n.*

Peg, the *n.* [abbr.] [1930s] (*Can.*) Winnipeg.

peg *n.*[1] **1** [17C+] the penis. **2** pertaining to the human leg [abbr. SE *pegleg*]. (**a**) [late 18C+] usu. in pl., a leg. (**b**) [19C] a wooden leg; one who wears one. (**c**) [1910s–60s] (*US tramp*) a one-legged person. **3** [1900s] (*UK tramp*) anywhere a free meal may be found [? play on SPIKE *n.*[2] (1)]. **4** [1930s–60s] (*US black*) in pl., trousers that taper sharply [mid-19C SE *peg-top trousers*, very wide in the hips and correspondingly narrow at the ankles].

IN COMPOUNDS

▫ **peg-boy** *n.* [1960s–70s] a male homosexual prostitute. ▫ **peg-house** *n.* [SE *peg* + HOUSE *n.*[1] (1); the East Indian brothels where the boys allegedly sat on wooden pegs to maintain a well-distended anus] **1** [1930s+] a male brothel. **2** [1950s] (*US Und.*) a prison with a high level of homosexuality.

IN PHRASES

▫ **play (at) mumble-de-peg** *v.* [MUMBLE-PEG *n.*] [early 17C; late 19C] to have sexual intercourse. ▫ **pull one's pegs** *v.* [gold-mining imagery] **1** [1920s] to leave. **2** [1930s–40s] (*Aus.*) to die.

SE in slang uses

IN PHRASES

▫ **do one's pegs** *v.* [1940s] (*Aus.*) to become angry, excited or anxious.

peg *n.*[2] [early 17C–19C] **1** a blow, esp. a straight-armed jab; thus *peg in the daylight*, a blow in the eye; *peg in the victualling* *office*, a blow in the stomach; *peg in the haltering place*, a blow under the ear. **2** in fig. use, a metaphorical blow, a verbal attack.

peg *n.*^{3} (*also* **peg stick**) [Scot. *peg*, one shilling; mainly Aus. use after mid-19C] [late 18C–19C] (*orig. UK Und.*) a shilling (5p).

peg *n.*^{4} [? each drink was seen as a 'peg [i.e. nail] in one's coffin'; but note 17C SE *peg*, 'one of a set of pins fixed at intervals in a drinking vessel as marks to measure the quantity which each drinker was to drink' (*OED*)]] [early 19C+] (*orig. Anglo-Ind.*) a drink, esp. of brandy and soda.

IN COMPOUNDS

❑ **peg-house** *n.* [1920s–30s] a public house.

IN PHRASES

❑ **go a peg lower** *v.* [19C] to drink heavily. ❑ **king's peg** *n.* [late 19C+] a champagne cocktail, champagne mixed with brandy. ❑ **put in the peg** *v.* (*also* **put on the peg**) [late 19C–1920s] (*Aus.*) **1** to stop doing something, esp. to stop drinking. **2** to cut off someone's credit.

peg *n.*^{5} [PEG *v.*^{4}] [20C+] (*Aus. Und.*) a look, a survey.

peg *n.*^{6}

IN PHRASES

❑ **it's a peg** [ety. unknown] [1930s+] (*Aus.*) a phr. used to indicate pleasure, that's wonderful, excellent etc. ❑ **strip a peg in Plunket Street** *v. see under* STRIP *v.*

peg *n.*^{7} [ety. unknown; ? link to opium jargon or PEG *n.*^{4}] [1940s+] (*drugs*) heroin; a capsule of heroin.

peg *v.*^{1} [SE *peg*, to target or aim at with a peg] **1** [18C+] to throw (at), to pitch (at); thus [20C+] (*Aus.*) *peg a gooly*, to throw a stone; *pegger*, thrower. **2** [1950s] (*US*) to shoot at.

IN PHRASES

❑ **peg it into** *v.* [mid–late 19C] to hit.

peg *v.*^{2} [orig. UK northern dial.] **1** [late 18C–19C; 2000s] (*also* **peg it**) to run, to move fast. **2** [early–mid-19C] to drive, esp. a cab [? pun on SE *peg*, to drive in a peg]. **3** *see* PEG OUT *v.*^{1}.

IN PHRASES

❑ **peg along** *v.* [mid-19C+] to persist. ❑ **peg away** *v.* **1** [19C] (*also* **peg along, peg off**) to move off quickly. **2** [19C+] (*also* **peg in**) to do something (usu. work, but also e.g. eating) hard and energetically for a long period; often in form *peg away at* [the hammering in of tent pegs]. **3** [1960s] to shoot at. ❑ **peg it** *v.* **1** *see* sense 1 above. **2** *see* PEG OUT *v.*^{1}.

peg *v.*^{3} [PEG *n.*^{4}] [mid–late 19C] to drink.

peg *v.*^{4} (*also* **peg for**) [? the image of placing a *peg* to mark that which is surveyed etc] **1** [mid-19C+] to look at, to stare; thus *pegged off*, under surveillance. **2** [1910s+] (*orig. US*) to recognize, to work out, to analyse. **3** [1920s–60s] to survey. **4** [1980s] (*Aus./N.Z.*) to search.

IN PHRASES

❑ **have someone pegged** *v.* [1910s+] (*US*) to categorize (properly), to form an (accurate) opinion of.

peg *v.*^{5} [SE *peg*, to drive a peg into the ground; or *peg away*, to 'hammer away' at] [mid-19C+] to have sexual intercourse; usu. as *peg up/down*.

peg *v.*^{6} [? one has *put the peg* into one's stomach, i.e. blocked it off; ? var. on SE *beg*] [late 19C+] (*Aus.*) to starve; thus *pegging for*, desperate for.

pegged *adj.* [? fig. use of PEG *v.*^{1} (1)] **1** [20C+] (*Ulster*) angry. **2** [1980s] (*US campus*) disparaged.

pegger *n.* [PEG *n.*^{4}] [late 19C] a regular or heavy drinker, a person who 'constantly stimulates themselves by means of brandy and soda-water' (Hotten, 1873).

peggers *n.* [2000s] (*US black*) peg-top trousers.

pegging-crib *n.* [PEG *v.*^{5} + CRIB *n.*^{1} (3)] [mid-19C] a brothel.

peggy *n.*^{1} [PEG *n.*^{1} (2)] **1** [mid-19C–1920s] a thin poker used to facilitate the raking out of fireplaces. **2** [late 19C–1920s] a tooth. **3** [late 19C+] a one-legged person. **4** [20C+] a wooden leg, a peg-leg; one who has such a leg. **5** [1970s+] (*Aus.*) an unskilled worker who makes tea, sweeps up and takes on similar undemanding tasks [naut. jargon *peggy*, a ship's mess-steward or menial; ult. *peg-leg*, a one-legged man who was often given such duties].

peggy *n.*^{2} [? anecdotal or ? fig. use of SE *peg-leg*, i.e. she has only one sexual 'leg' to stand on] [1990s+] (*W.I.*) a woman with sexual passion for a particular group of men.

Peggy Dell *n.* [rhy. sl.; ult. Irish pianist and entertainer *Peggy Dell* (*c.*1905–79)] [2000s] (*Irish*) a smell.

peggy's leg *n.* [dial. *peggy*, an implement for stirring washing; presumably a supposed resemblance] [1920s+] (*Irish juv.*) a type of boiled sweet on a stick.

peg-legger *n.*^{1} [SE *peg-leg*, one who has a wooden leg] [1930s–40s] a one-legged man.

peg-legger *n.*^{2} [rhy. sl.] [1930s–40s] a beggar; thus *peg-legging*, begging.

peglegs *n.* [PEG *n.*^{1} (2a)] [1950s–60s] (*US*) tapered trousers.

pego *n.* (*also* **Don Pego**) [? Gk *pege*, spring or fountain; this 'classical' aspect made the term esp. popular in 19C pornography] [mid-17C–19C] the penis.

peg out *v.*^{1} (*also* **peg, peg it**) [cribbage use + ? the image of taking down a tent] [mid-19C+] **1** to die. **2** to be financially ruined. **3** to lose one's energy, esp. during a strenuous exercise or sport.

peg out *v.*^{2} [1920s] (*US Und.*) to mark the traffic in and out of a building that has been targeted for robbery by placing a peg in the door jamb and seeing if/when it falls any time after the building has supposedly shut for the night.

peg puff *n.* [? generic use of *Peg*, Margaret + *puffed up*] [19C] an older woman dressed younger than her years.

Peg Trantum's *n.*

IN PHRASES

❑ **go to Peg Trantum's** *v.* [note East Anglian dial. *peg trantum*, a tomboy] [late 17C–mid-19C] to die; thus *pegtrantum(s)*, dead.

pek *n. see* PECK *n.*^{1} (1).

pekkie *n.* (*also* **peckie, pek**) [? Zulu *umpheki*, a cook] [1960s+] (*S.Afr.*) a black person.

pekoe *n.* [SE *pekoe*, a superior variety of Chinese tea] [1950s] (*drugs*) top-quality opium.

pelf *n.* [SE *pelf*, stolen property] [16C+] money.

pelfry *n.* [SE *pelf*, stolen property; *pelf* and *pelfry* are both SE in 14C–15C] [16C–early 17C] (*UK Und.*) stolen goods, esp. the booty gained by those who pick locks.

pelile *adj.* [Nguni *ukuphela*, to finish] [20C+] (*S.Afr.*) exhausted, absolutely finished.

pell *n. see* PAL *n.*

pellet *n.* [1960s–70s] **1** (*drugs*) a capsule of LSD. **2** (*UK drugs*) a capsule of amphetemines.

pellicle *n.* [? Lat. *pellis*, the skin; the ref. is to the slashing of the skin of the poppy-heads to release opium] [1950s] (*drugs*) high-quality opium.

pellie *n.* [PAL *n.* (1)] [1950s+] (*S.Afr., mainly Western Cape*) a friend, a pal; thus *ou pellie*, old friend; *pellie blou*, a 'real pal', a 'bosom-buddy' (the *blou* means blue, as in 'true blue').

pellock *n.* [ety. unknown] [late 18C] (*US Und.*) sugar.

peloothered *adj. see* POLLUTED *adj.*

pelt *n.* **1** [17C+] the human skin; thus *in one's pelt*, naked. **2** [1970s] a human being.

pelt back *v.* [2000s] (*N.Z.*) to be beaten.

pelter *n.* **1** [mid-19C] lit. or fig., anything conspicuously large; a strong blow [SE *pelt*, to beat violently]. **2** [mid-19C–1910s] (*also* **pelterer**) a drenching downpour [SE *pelt*, to beat violently]. **3** [mid-19C–1930s] a horse, esp. a slow, old one [ironic use of SE *pelt* (*along*) or 16C *pelter*, a paltry or peddling person]. **4** [late 19C] something that goes fast, including a horse; thus *in a pelter*, in a hurry [SE *pelt*, to move rapidly].

IN PHRASES

❑ **out for a pelter** *adj.* [dial. *pelter*, a bad temper] [late 19C–1900s] in a very bad temper.

elter *adj.* [SE *pelt*, to throw hard] [mid-19C] (*UK Und.*) sharp; thus *pelter-caleb*, a sharper; *pelter-glazes*, sharp eyes; *pelter-skraked*, sharp-stomached; *pelter-whids*, sharp works.

elting-irons *n.* [SE *pelt*, to throw hard, i.e. the aggressive image of intercourse] [mid-17C] the testicles.

elt your skin! *excl.* [SE *pelt*, to move fast] [20C+] (*W.I.*) be off! go away!

en *n.* [abbr.] [1900s] (*Aus.*) *Pentridge* Jail.

en *n.*[1] **1** [mid-16C–1940s] the penis [resemblance]. **2** [mid-19C–1900s] the vagina [in dial., used of a sow]. **3** *see* PENMAN below.

IN COMPOUNDS

❑ **penwiper** *n.* [19C] the vagina.

IN PHRASES

❑ **have no ink in one's pen** *v.* [mid-16C] to be impotent.

SE in slang uses

IN COMPOUNDS

❑ **pen-driver** *n. see* PENCIL-PUSHER *n.* ❑ **penman** *n.* **1** [mid-19C+] (*UK Und.*) (*also* **pen**) a forger of counterfeit notes. **2** [20C+] (*US*) a student who signs their parent's name to excuse notes. **3** [1930s] (*US prison*) an inmate who writes letters to the authorities, presumably informing on his fellows. **4** [1930s+] (*US*) a forger of false signatures etc on cheques and credit cards. ❑ **pen-pusher** *n. see* PENCIL-PUSHER *n.* ❑ **pen-pushing** *see under* PENCIL-PUSHING. ❑ **penwiper** *n.* **1** [1900s] (*UK juv.*) a scholastic gown, coat ['The "pen-wiper", a small piece of folded silk which is attached to the back of the proctor's gown [at Oxford]' (*OED*)]. **2** [1900s–40s] a handkerchief.

IN PHRASES

❑ **put one's pen to the wind** *v.* [2000s] (*US prison*) of a prisoner, to tell an officer to file a disciplinary report; of officers, to tell a prisoner to file a grievance.

en *n.*[2] **1** [early 19C+] a *pen*itentiary [abbr.; 20C+ use mainly US]. **2** [1970s] (*US*) a holding cell in a police station.

IN COMPOUNDS

❑ **pen shot** *n. see* PENITENTIARY SHOT *under* PENITENTIARY *adj.*

en *n.*[3] [ety. unknown] [late 19C–1940s] (*Aus.*) a threepenny piece.

enal *n.* [abbr.] [1910s–40s] (*UK Und./police*) *penal* servitude.

enance board *n.* (*also* **pennance-board**) [late 17C–mid-19C] the pillory.

en (and ink) *n.* [rhy. sl.] **1** [mid-19C+] lit. and fig., a stink. **2** [1950s] a mink. **3** [1960s+] (*orig. Aus./N.Z.*) a drink.

en (and ink) *v.* [rhy. sl.] [late 19C+] **1** to stink. **2** to cause problems, to complain, to 'kick up a stink'.

en and inker *n.* [rhy. sl. = STINKER *n.*[1] (1)] [1940s+] a suspicious person, esp. a possible informer.

ence *n. see* PENNY *n.* (2).

encil *n.* [resemblance] **1** [1930s] (*US prison*) a revolver. **2** [1930s+] the penis, usu. that of a small boy; thus [1940s] *pencil and tassel*, a small boy's penis and testes.

IN COMPOUNDS

❑ **pencil dick** *n. see* separate entry. ❑ **pencil prick** *n.* [PRICK *n.* (1)] [1970s] a term of abuse. ❑ **pencil sharpener** *n.* [1990s+] (*UK juv.*) the vagina. ❑ **pencil-squeezer** *n.* [1980s] a masturbator. ❑ **pencil-whipping** *n.* [2000s] (*US*) a general term of abuse, the implication is of masturbation.

IN PHRASES

❑ **black pencil** *n.* [1970s] a black man's penis. ❑ **grip the pencil** *v. see under* GRIP *v.*[2]. ❑ **have lead in one's pencil** *v.* [1920s+] (*orig. US*) **1** to be potent. **2** to have an erection. **3** in fig. use, to feel emotionally/physically strong. ❑ **have no lead in one's pencil** *v.* [1920s+] to be impotent. ❑ **put lead in one's pencil** *v.* (*also* **put lead in one's pistol**) [1920s+] (*orig. Aus.*) to cheer one up, to strengthen, esp. in a sexual context; thus *this will put lead in your pencil/here's lead in your pencil*, a toast used to accompany the offer of a drink, food or even drug – any of which is cited as a presumed adjunct to potency. ❑ **sharpen one's pencil** *v.* [1990s+] (*UK juv.*) to have sexual intercourse.

SE in slang uses

DERIVATIVES

❑ **penciller** *n.* **1** [mid–late 19C] a bookmaker's clerk. **2** [late 19C] (*US*) a journalist. **3** [late 19C+] (*Aus.*) a bookmaker or their clerk.

IN COMPOUNDS

❑ **pencil geek** *n.* [GEEK *n.*[1] (4)] [1970s+] (*US campus*) anyone who works more devotedly than their peers see fit. ❑ **pencil head** *see* separate entries. ❑ **pencil-neck/-necked** *see* separate entries. ❑ **pencil-pusher/-pushing** *see* separate entries. ❑ **pencil-whip** *v.* **1** [1960s+] (*US*) to falsify a report. **2** [1990s+] (*US*) to criticize severely. **3** [1990s+] (*US prison*) of a guard, to give a written reprimand. **4** [1990s+] (*US prison*) (*also* **paper whip**) of a prisoner, to file a lawsuit or a grievance.

pencil (and chalk) *v.* [rhy. sl.] [1910s] (*Aus.*) to walk.

pencil dick *n.* [SE *pencil* + DICK *n.*[1] (5)] **1** [1970s+] (*US gay*) a long, thin penis. **2** [1980s+] (*US*) a general term of abuse, the implication being that the person in question has a small penis.

IN COMPOUNDS

❑ **pencil-dicked** *adj.* [1990s+] having a small penis, hence a term of abuse.

pencil head *n.* [-HEAD *sfx* (1)] [1970s] an extremely diligent student.

pencil-head *adj.* [PENCIL HEAD *n.*] [1990s+] academic, studious (the over-riding inference is of an inability to function in the 'real' world).

pencil-neck *n.* (*also* **neck**) [1960s+] an intellectual, or one who is considered (negatively) as one.

pencil-necked *adj.* [PENCIL-NECK *n.*] [1960s+] intellectual.

pencil, open, lost and found *n.* [rhy. sl.] [late 19C] £1.

pencil-pusher *n.* (*also* **pen-driver, pen-pusher**) **1** [late 19C+] (*orig. US*) a clerk, a white-collar worker; thus *push a pencil/pen*, to perform office work. **2** [late 19C+] a journalist; a hack writer. **3** [1920s] a letter-writer.

pencil-pushing *n.* (*also* **pen-pushing**) [late 19C+] writing, esp. office work.

pencil-pushing *adj.* (*also* **pen-pushing**) [20C+] pertaining to bureaucracy, clerking, paperwork.

pendejo *n.* [Sp. *pendejo*, pubic hair; used in Sp. contexts as a synon. for 'dumb fuck' or 'dickhead'] [2000s] (*W.I.*) a pervert.

pendulum *n.* [it 'swings'] [19C] the penis.

penelope *n.* (*also* **penelopes**) [initial letters] **1** [1990s+] (*US*) a police officer, usu. male; the police. **2** [2000s] (*S.Afr. gay*) the penis.

penguin *n.*[1] [the trad. black and white habit or clothing] [20C+] (*US, mainly juv.*) a nun or priest.

penguin *n.*[2] [the black and white pill] [2000s] (*drugs*) a variety of LSD.

penguin suit *n.* (*also* **penguin gear**) [1960s+] a dinner jacket.

penie *n. see* PEENIE *n.*

peninsular *n.* [? play on SE *peninsular*, a projecting strip of land, i.e. she sticks out a finger either for thieving or for emphasis] **1** [mid-19C] a female pickpocket. **2** [1950s+] a very inquisitive woman.

penis wrinkle *n.* [1980s+] (*US campus*) an unpleasant, unsophisticated man.

penitentiary *adj.*

SE in slang uses

IN COMPOUNDS

❑ **penitentiary agent** *n.* [1930s+] (*US Und.*) a lawyer who seems to be working more for the courts and police than for the defence of their client. ❑ **penitentiary bait** *n. see* JAILBAIT *n.* (2). ❑ **penitentiary dispatcher** *n.* [the professional inadequacies of court-appointed lawyers, whose clients often end up in the penitentiary] [1960s+] (*US Und.*) a public defender. ❑ **penitentiary highball** *n.* [HIGHBALL *n.*[1] (1)] [1930s] (*US prison*) home-brewed prison alcohol, based on strained shellac and milk. ❑ **penitentiary punk** *n. see* PUNK *n.*[1] (2). ❑ **penitentiary shot** *n.* (*also* **pen shot**) [PEN *n.*[2] + SHOT *n.*[1] (6b)] [1930s–50s] (*US drugs/prison*) an injection achieved by using a rudimentary 'needle', in fact a pin and a medicine dropper; the pin is pushed into the vein and the dropper, filled with a solution of heroin and water, pushed over it. ❑ **penitentiary turn-out** *n. see* TURN-OUT *n.*[4] (2).

pennam *n. see* PANNAM *n.*

pennance-board *n. see* PENANCE BOARD *n.*

Pennemite *n.* (*also* **Panamite, Pennamite, Pennite**) [late 18C+] a native or inhabitant of Pennsylvania.

pennif *n.* [backsl. = FINNIP *n.*] [mid–late 19C] **1** a £5 note. **2** any banknote.

penn'orth of bread *n.* [rhy. sl.] [late 19C+] the head.

penn'orth (of chalk) *n.* [rhy. sl.] [20C+] a walk; also as a term of dismissal.

penn'orth o' treacle *n.* [late 19C] a pretty woman.

Pennsy *n.* [abbr.] [1920s+] *Pennsylvania*, the *Pennsylvania* rail route.

Pennsylvania *adj.*

IN COMPOUNDS

❑ **Pennsylvania diet** *n.* [1910s] (*US prison*) bread and water diet given to a prisoner in the punishment cell. ❑ **Pennsylvania salve** *n.* [SALVE *n.* (2)] [late 19C–1930s] (*US tramp*) apple butter.

penny *n.* **1** [mid-19C+] (*Can./US*) one cent. **2** [late 19C+] (*also* **pence**) in pl., money. **3** [1940s–60s] (*US*) one dollar.

SE in slang uses

IN COMPOUNDS

❑ **penny ante** *adj. see* separate entry. ❑ **penny-boy** *n.* [such a boy would presumably be tipped a penny] **1** [late 19C–1910s] 'a boy who haunted the cattle markets on the chance of driving beasts to the slaughter-house' (F&H). **2** [20C+] (*Ulster*) anyone seen as being at the beck and call of someone else. ❑ **penny-buster** *n.* [it 'busts' one's stomach or appetite for the price of one penny] [mid-19C–1900s] a small loaf. ❑ **penny-catcher** *n.* [1940s+] (*W.I./UK black*) one who is willing to work for derisory pay. ❑ **penny dreadful** *n.* (*also* **penny awful, ... horrible, ...shocker**) [mid-19C+] a sensationally written 'true crime' story, sold for one penny. ❑ **penny gaff** *n. see under* GAFF *n.*[1]. ❑ **penny gush** *n. see under* GUSH *n.*[2]. ❑ **penny hang** *n.* [19C–1930s] (*orig. naut.*) a cellar or basement which features ropes strung from side to side on which drunken or exhausted clients, orig. sailors, drape themselves for a fitful sleep; in the morning one end of the rope is untied and the sleepers are dumped on the floor. ❑ **penny lattice-house** *n.* [RED LATTICE *under* RED *adj.*] [18C–early 19C] a poor alehouse. ❑ **pennyline** *n.* [? ext. of SE *penny-a-liner*, a freelance literary or journalistic hack, from the rate of pay offered to such writers] [1960s+] (*S.Afr. black*) a cheap prostitute. ❑ **penny loaf** *n.* [one who would rather live on a penny loaf than make a greater effort and steal beef] [late 19C] (*UK Und.*) a coward. ❑ **penny number** *n. see* separate entry. ❑ **penny pots** *n.* [mid-19C–1920s] pimples found on a heavy drinker's face. ❑ **penny puzzle** *n.* [its dubious ingredients are 'never found out'] [late 19C] a sausage. ❑ **penny rush** *n. see* separate entry. ❑ **penny shocker** *n. see* PENNY DREADFUL above. ❑ **penny starver** *n.* **1** [mid–late 19C] a penny roll. **2** [late 19C] the cheapest brand of cigars, three for twopence. ❑ **penny stinker** *n. see under* STINKER *n.*[1]. ❑ **penny swag** *n. see under* SWAG *n.*[1]. ❑ **penny toff** *n. see under* TOFF *n.* ❑ **pennyweight(er)** *see* separate entry. ❑ **penny-white** *adj.* [lit. 'one who has been rendered *white*, i.e. beautiful, by her possession of (silver) pennies'] [late 17C–early 18C] usu. of a woman, rich but unattractive.

IN PHRASES

❑ **penny-a-liar** *n.* [pun on SE *penny-a-liner*, a freelance literary or journalistic hack, from the rate of pay offered to such writers] [late 19C] a hack journalist. ❑ **spend a penny** *v.* (*also* **pay a penny**) [the 1d (pre-decimalization) charge in public lavatories] [1930s+] to urinate.

penny *v.* [SE *penetrate*] [1990s+] (*W.I.*) to observe closely.

penny-a-mile *n.* [rhy. sl.] **1** [late 19C–1920s] a hat [= TILE *n.*]. **2** [late 19C–1920s] the head [ext. of sense 1]. **3** [20C+] a smile.

penny ante *adj.* (*also* **penny**) [poker jargon; an *ante* is a deposi that entitles a player to join a round of play; thus an ante of only one penny is *de facto* insignificant] [mid-19C+] (*orig. US* insignificant, unimportant.

penny (a pound) *n.* (*also* **penny the pound**) [rhy. sl.] [20C+ the ground.

penny banger *n.* [rhy. sl. = CLANGER *n.*[1] (1)] [20C+] a mistake a blunder.

penny black *n.* [rhy. sl.; the *penny black*, the UK's first postag stamp, issued 1840] [20C+] the back.

penny brown *n.* [rhy. sl.] [20C+] (*Aus.*) a town.

penny bun *n.* [rhy. sl.] [1920s+] **1** one; one penny. **2** the sun. **3** a son.

penny-come-quick *n.* [rhy. sl.] [late 19C+] (*UK Und.*) a confidence trick.

penny dips *n.* [rhy. sl.] [1960s–80s] (*Aus.*) lips.

penny for the guy *n.* [rhy. sl.] [1990s+] a pie.

penny locket *n.* [rhy. sl.] [late 19C] a pocket.

penny number *n.* [the price of the magazines] **1** [mid-19C-1900s] a sensational story, serialized in weekly penny magazines. **2** [1950s+] in pl., very small, insignifican numbers.

IN PHRASES

❑ **by/in penny numbers** *adv.* [late 19C] in instalments.

penny rush *n.* [1910s–20s] (*Irish*) cheap children's matinées a the cinema; thus (reflective of changing prices): [1930s–40s *twopenny rush*; [1940s–50s] *fourpenny rush*; [1950s–60s *sixpenny rush*.

penny the pound *n. see* PENNY (A POUND) *n.*

pennyweight *n.* **1** [mid-19C] (*UK Und.*) jewellery. **2** [1920s (*Aus.*) small gold pieces, in terms of prospecting.

pennyweight *v.* [SE *pennyweight*, a measure used to state th fineness of silver] [1950s] (*Aus.*) to prospect for small gol pieces.

pennyweighter *n.* [SE *pennyweight*, a measure used to stat the fineness of silver] [late 19C–1960s] (*US*) **1** one who steal jewellery or precious stones or metals, esp. by entering a shop asking to inspect the stock and, using an adhesive substance o their hands, picking up certain items; thus *pennyweighting pennyweight job*, performing this variety of theft. **2** one wh steals by substituting paste gems for the real ones.

penocha *n.* [synon. Sp. sl.] [1960s+] (*US black/Sp.*) the vagina

pension *n.* [1970s] (*UK Und.*) that sum of money paid over fo 'protection'.

IN PHRASES

❑ **on a pension** [1970s+] (*UK Und.*) used of a police office receiving regular bribes.

pensionary miss *n.* [late 17C] a prostitute who works for pimp or in a brothel rather than as an independent.

pensioner (at the petticoat) *n.* (*also* **pensioner to th petticoat**) [note 1920s US theatrical jargon *pensioner*, th husband of an actress] [late 17C–19C] a pimp.

pensioner of the placket *n.* [PENSIONER (AT THE PETTICOAT) *n.* PLACKET *n.* (1)] [17C] a pimp.

pensioner's leg *n.* [resemblance] **1** [1990s+] a thin, pal knobbly, veiny penis. **2** [2000s] a thin kebab.

pensioner to the petticoat *n. see* PENSIONER (AT TH PETTICOAT) *n.*

Pent, the *n.* [abbr.] [mid-19C–1910s] *Pent*onville Prison London N1.

penthouse-nab *n.* (*also* **pentice-nab**) [SE *penthouse*, a small building (often with a sloping roof) attached to the main structu + NAB *n.*[1] (3)] [17C–mid-19C] a large, high hat.

pen yen *n.* (*also* **ah-pen-yen, pen yan, ...yang, pin yen, . yenz, pinyon**) [Chinese *nga pun-yin*, opium] [late 19C+] (*drug* opium.

peola *n.* [Bantu *peula*, skin] [1930s+] (*US black*) a light-skinne black woman.

peony *n. see* PEACH *n.*[1] (2).

people *n.* **1** [mid-19C–1930s] one's relatives, one's family; usu. qualified as *my people, her people* etc. **2** [late 19C+] (*US*) one's group, e.g. fellow players in a company of actors. **3** [late 19C+] (*orig. US*) an admirable person, a trustworthy individual; equally applicable, in context, to criminals as to the law-abiding. **4** [1930s+] a type of person. **5** (*US black/drugs*) in drug uses. (**a**) [1950s–60s] narcotics agents; police. (**b**) [1960s+] as *the people*, high-level drug dealers.

IN PHRASES

❑ **good people** *n.* **1** [late 19C+] (*also* **fine people, nice...**) an admirable individual; a member of one's peer group; less common is the antithetical *bad people*. **2** [20C+] (*US Und.*) spec. former criminals who have retired from their various specialities. **3** [1920s+] a leading criminal, irrespective of speciality. ❑ **my people** *n.* [1950s+] **1** (*US black*) one's fellow gang members. **2** any fellow members of a group or minority, usu. used ironically. **3** (*US campus*) one's family or friends. ❑ **real people** *n.* [1910s–70s] (*US*) one's peers; trustworthy people; equally aplicable to criminals as to the law-abiding; also as adj.

SE in slang uses

IN EXCLAMATIONS

❑ **some people!** [20C+] a derisory or critical comment by the speaker on the opinions or more likely the activities of others; the details are unspoken but will be a condemnation of what *some people* are doing.

Peoria *n.*[1]

IN PHRASES

❑ **play in Peoria** *v.* [*Peoria*, Illinois, as an emblematic small stop on theatrical/vaudeville tours] [20C+] to succeed in rural, provincial areas.

Peoria *n.*[2] (*also* **Peoria water, Peory water**) [mispron. of Fr. *(soupe) purée* + derog. ref. to the city of *Peoria*; note Irwin, *American Tramp and Und. Slang* (1931): 'perhaps so called from a similar article of food served in the Illinois State Prison at the city of the same name, perhaps from the fact that much of the State provides poor pickings for tramps who must get along as best they can on scant rations'] [1920s–30s] (*US tramp*) a thin, meagre soup; also a 'mess' of potatoes, boiled then fried.

pep *n.* see PEP PILL *n.*

pep-'em-up *n.* [their effects] [1970s+] (*drugs*) amphetamine.

pepped out *adj.* [colloq. *pep*, energy] [1920s] (*US*) exhausted.

pepper *n.* **1** [early–mid-19C] hard blows, e.g. in a prizefight; n. *pepperer*, a fighter or boxer. **2** [late 19C] serious trouble. **3** [20C+] zest, vitality. **4** [1940s–50s] (*US black/teen*) an attractive young woman.

SE in slang uses

IN COMPOUNDS

❑ **pepper alley** *n.* [*Pepper Alley*, a landing place on the Southwark side of the Thames, equated with crime, violence and debauchery; PEPPER *v.* (2)] [early 19C] a state of being beaten up. ❑ **pepper belly** *n.* (*also* **hot pepper belly**) [the stereotyped Mexican love of hot food] [1960s+] (*US*) a derog. term for a Mexican or Mexican-American; thus adj., *pepper-bellied*. ❑ **pepper-box** *n.* [resemblance] **1** [mid-19C] (*US*) the head. **2** [1900s] a pistol. ❑ **pepper-castor** *n.* (*also* **pepper-caster**) [? resemblance] **1** [late 18C] the head. **2** [late 19C] (*US*) a revolver. ❑ **pepper-fly** *n.* [dial. *pepper-fly*, a sand-fly, which can give a painful sting] [1950s] (*W.I.*) an irascible, quick-tempered person. ❑ **pepper gut** *n.* [SE (*chili*) *pepper*, a main constituent of Mexican cooking] [1920s+] (*US*) a Mexican-American. ❑ **pepperhead** *n.* [1950s] (*US*) a show-off.

pepper *v.* **1** [late 16C+] to infect with venereal disease. **2** [late 16C+] to hit hard; to shoot dead. **3** [late 17C–1920s] to tease, to deceive [SE *throw pepper in someone's eyes*].

IN COMPOUNDS

❑ **pepper-proof** *adj.* [late 17C–18C] (temporarily) free of venereal disease.

pepper and salt *n.*[1] **1** [mid-19C] (*US*) in pl., striped dress trousers. **2** [1960s–70s] (*US black*) black and white people running together in the street, presumably in the civil rights, anti-Vietnam and other demonstrations of the era.

pepper and salt *n.*[2] [late 19C] (*US*) a severe telling-off.

pepper and salt *n.*[3] [rhy. sl. = BALT *n.*[2]] [1980s] (*Aus.*) a Baltic immigrant.

peppered *adj.* **1** [early 17C–18C] dead, badly hurt [PEPPER *v.* (2)]. **2** [mid-17C–early 19C] (*also* **peppered off**) very badly infected with venereal disease; occas. crab-lice [PEPPER *v.* (1) + play on HOT *adj.* (6a)].

pepper-kissing *n.* [euph. for ASS-KISS *v.*] [1970s+] (*US black*) attempting to put the best face on bad news.

pepper-kissing *adj.* [euph. for MOTHERFUCKING *adj.*] [1970s+] (*US black*) a negative intensifier meaning no good, useless etc.

peppermint drops *n.*

IN PHRASES

❑ **give someone the peppermint drops** *v.* [play on SE *drop/drops*] [1900s] to trip someone up.

peppermint rocks *n.* (*also* **peppermints**) [rhy. sl.] [20C+] socks.

pepper-pot *n.*

IN PHRASES

❑ **in a pepper-pot** *see* IN A PICKLE *under* PICKLE *n.*

pepper-upper *n.* [colloq. *pep up*] **1** [1930s] (*also* **pepper-up**) an amphetamine. **2** [1930s+] alcohol. **3** [1950s] a cheerleader.

pep pill *n.* (*also* **pep**) [colloq. *pep up*] [1940s+] (*drugs*) an amphetamine.

Pepsi *n.* [their drinking of *Pepsi-Cola*, rather than more potent 'men's drinks'] [1970s–80s] (*Can.*) **1** a modern, young French-Canadian (as opposed to their older forebears). **2** an English-Canadian.

Pepsi(-Cola) habit *n.* (*also* **Pepsi-Cola kick**) [*Pepsi-Cola*, a soft rather than alcoholic drink + HABIT *n.* (1)/KICK *n.*[5] (1)] [1960s+] (*drugs*) a limited or occasional use of drugs.

pepst *adj.* [ety. unknown] [late 16C] drunk.

perc *n.* (*also* **perk**) [abbr.] [1930s–50s] **1** (*orig. US cowboy, then tramp*) percolated coffee, as opposed to that boiled up in a pan. **2** (*US*) a coffee *perc*olator.

perc *v.* *see* PERCOLATE *v.* (1).

perch *n.*[1] **1** [mid-19C] a bed; thus *off to perch*, going to bed. **2** [late 19C] death [ext. of DROP OFF THE PERCH below].

IN PHRASES

❑ **drop off the perch** *v.* (*also* **fall off..., tip off..., trip off..., pitch over the perch, tip over..., turn over...**) **1** [16C–18C; 1990s+] to die. **2** [18C+] to climb down, to adopt a less arrogant or condescending manner.

perch *n.*[2] [SE *perch*, a common freshwater fish] [1970s+] **1** (*Aus.*) a glass of beer. **2** (*US campus*) a pint of liquor.

perch *v.* [PERCH *n.*[1] (2)] [late 19C] to die.

percher *n.* **1** [early 18C] a dying person [PERCH *v.*]. **2** [1970s+] UK Und. uses [the victim is 'perched' in innocent vulnerability]. (**a**) a gullible victim for a swindle or con-game. (**b**) a simple arrest [the victim is 'perched' in innocent vulnerability].

percolate *v.* **1** [20C+] (*US*) (*also* **perc, perculate, perk**) to stroll, to wander around; thus *percolating*, walking around looking for sexual conquests [misuse of SE *perambulate*]. **2** [1920s+] (*US*) uses of SE. (**a**) to run smoothly, esp. of an engine. (**b**) to penetrate the mind. (**c**) to do something well. (**d**) to happen.

percolator *n.* [1930s–50s] **1** a party. **2** (*US black*) a party held so that the host can collect money from their guests so as to pay the rent [? the money *percolates* through from the guests to the host].

percs *n.* (*also* **perks**) [abbr.] [1970s+] *perc*odan.

perculate *v.* *see* PERCOLATE *v.* (1).

percy *n.*[1] **1** uses based on the effeminate male proper name. (**a**) [20C+] (*orig. US*) (*also* **percy-boy, percy-pants**) an effeminate man, a weakling; one who appears exhausted. (**b**) [1940s] a masculine woman, poss. a lesbian. **2** [1960s+] the penis [initial letter of proper name].

IN COMPOUNDS

❑ **percy-purse** *n.* [SE *purse*; PURSE *n.* (1) is prob. coincidental] [1980s] the vagina.

IN PHRASES

❑ **point percy at the porcelain** *v.* (*also* **poke percy at the porcelain**) [SE *porcelain*, i.e. the lavatory bowl] [1960s+] to urinate; thus *point percy at the pavement*, to urinate on the street.

percy *n.*[2] *see* PERSY *n.*

Percy Thrower *n.* [rhy. sl. = BLOWER *n.*[2] (4); ult. UK gardening expert *Percy Thrower* (1913–88)] [1940s+] the telephone.

perf! *excl.* [abbr.] [1970s] (*Aus./US campus*) *perfect*! also as adj.

perfectamundo *adj.* [SE *perfect* + -AMUNDO *sfx*] [1990s+] absolutely perfect; also as excl.

perfect lady *n.* (*also* **real lady**) [late 19C] (*US*) a drunken woman; by implication a prostitute.

perfecto! *excl.* [cod-Sp.] [1980s+] wonderful! excellent! perfect!

perfesh *n.* **1** [late 19C–1930s] (*Aus.*) the profession, usu. that of the theatre [pron. of abbr. SE *profession*]. **2** [1930s] (*US tramp*) a veteran tramp [pron. of abbr. SE *professional*].

perforate *v.* **1** [mid-19C+] (*US*) to shoot, to wound. **2** [1930s] of a man, to have sexual intercourse with, esp. to take a woman's virginity.

perform *v.* **1** in sexual uses. (**a**) [17C; late 19C+] to have sexual intercourse. (**b**) [1970s+] (*US gay*) to fellate. **2** [20C+] (*Aus.*) to display extreme anger or bad temper, to swear loudly, to make a great fuss. **3** [1940s+] (*UK Und.*) to commit a crime, esp. when it involves violence.

IN PHRASES

❑ **perform on** *v.* [19C] **1** of a man, to have sexual intercourse. **2** to cheat, to deceive.

performer *n.* [PERFORM *v.*] **1** [late 19C–1900s] a philanderer, a promiscuous man. **2** [20C+] (*orig. naut.*) one who makes a fuss or a good deal of noise. **3** [1940s] an expert. **4** [1960s+] a sexually active woman.

perfume *v.* [1940s] (*US black*) to put the best possible face on otherwise unpalatable facts.

perger *n. see* PURGER *n.*

perhapser *n.* [1910s] (*Aus.*) a risk.

perico *n.* [Sp. *perico*, parakeet] [1970s+] (*drugs*) cocaine.

periin *n.* [? SE *peering*; albinos stereotypically suffer from poor eyesight] [1940s] (*W.I.*) an albino.

period *n.* [play on SE *period*, menstruation] [2000s] (*S.Afr. gay*) anal bleeding following anal intercourse.

SE in slang uses

IN PHRASES

❑ **have a period** *v.* [1980s+] to become emotional, agitated.

period *phr.* [SAmE *period* = SE *full stop*] [1930s+] (*US*) that is that, there is no more to be said.

period hitter *n. see under* HITTER *n.*

periodical *n.* [? one does it *periodically*] [late 19C–1900s] (*US*) a drinking bout.

perish *n.*

IN PHRASES

❑ **do a perish** *v.* [late 19C+] (*Aus.*) to suffer extreme privation, esp. for want of a drink.

perish *v.* [late 19C+] **1** (*orig. S.Afr.*) to suffer a state of deprivation. **2** (*Aus.*) to be homeless, to sleep out at night. **3** (*Aus.*) to cadge. **4** (*mainly Aus.*) to attack, to punish, to kill.

IN EXCLAMATIONS

❑ **perish me!** (*also* **perish me blind! ...pink!**) [mid-19C–1900s] a general excl. of surprise, shock, amazement.

perisher *n.*[1] [one 'perishes' of the cold] **1** [late 19C–1920s] a short coat. **2** [20C+] a spell or day of very cold weather.

IN PHRASES

❑ **do a perisher** *v.* [1900s–20s] (*Aus.*) to feel very cold. ❑ **go in a perisher** *v.* [i.e. to the extent that one might SE *perish*] **1** [mid–late 19C] (*Aus.*) to pursue one's course of action with maximum enthusiasm. **2** [late 19C] to suffer physical harm.

perisher *n.*[2] [late 19C+] a person, often in a derog. sense, and often, as *little perisher*, applied to a child.

periwinkle *n.* [the supposed resemblance to the shellfish] **1** [late 17C–early 19C] a peruke or wig. **2** [mid-19C] a small penis. **3** [mid-19C–1900s] the vagina.

perk *n.*[1] (*also* **perq**) [SE *perquisite*] [late 19C+] a bonus, esp. that which comes with a job; usu. in pl.

DERIVATIVES

❑ **perky** *adj.* [1980s] productive of bonuses.

perk *n.*[2] (*also* **purko**) [? PERK UP *v.* or PERKINS *n.*] [late 19C+] (*Aus.*) beer.

DERIVATIVES

❑ **perked** *adj.* (*also* **perk**) [20C+] (*Aus./N.Z.*) drunk.

perk *n.*[3] [PERK *v.*[1]] [1940s] (*Aus.*) an act of vomiting.

perk *n.*[4] *see* PERC *n.*

perk *adj. see* PERKED *under* PERK *n.*[2].

perk *v.*[1] [echoic or PERK *n.*[2]] [1910s+] (*Aus.*) to vomit, usu. after excessive drinking.

perk *v.*[2] *see* PERCOLATE *v.*

perked *adj. see under* PERK *n.*[2].

perker *n.* [late 19C] one who benefits from a PERK *n.*[1].

perker-upper *n. see under* PERK UP *v.*

perkin *n.* [? SE *perry*, a drink made from pears + dimin. sfx *-kin*] [late 18C–mid-19C] weak cider; the washings from a cider barrel.

perking *n.* [PERK UP *v.*] [late 17C–early 18C] 'any pert, forward, silly fellow' (B.E.).

perkins *n.* [abbr. BARCLAY (AND) PERKINS *n.*] [mid-19C] beer.

perkmeister *n.* [PERK *n.*[1] + -MEISTER *sfx*] [1990s+] (*US*) an official, typically in a company or in government, who can offer favours, jobs etc.

perks *n. see* PERCS *n.*

perk up *v.* [SE *perk*, to thrust oneself forward, to act in a brisk or jaunty manner] [mid-17C+] to cheer up, to improve one's spirits.

DERIVATIVES

❑ **perker-upper** *n.* [20C+] (*orig. US*) one who cheers others up.

perky *adj.* [PERK UP *v.*] **1** [mid-19C+] jolly, cheerful. **2** [1960s] cheeky.

perlaver *n. see* PALAVER *n.*

perm *n.*

IN PHRASES

❑ **give someone a perm** *v.* [SE *permanent wave*, a hairstyle + pun on BLOW JOB *n.*] [1980s+] (*US campus*) to perform oral sex.

perma- *pfx* [abbr. SE *permanent*] [1980s] (*US campus*) a pfx indicating permanence, continuity.

permanent pug *n. see under* PUG *n.*[4].

pernicated dude *n.* [? SE *pernickety* + DUDE *n.*[1] (2)] [late 19C–1910s] (*Can.*) a swaggering dandy.

perp *n.* [abbr. SE *perpetrator*] [1980s+] **1** (*orig. US*) a perpetrator, an accused criminal. **2** (*US black*) one who is pretending or faking. **3** (*US drugs*) fake crack cocaine made of candle wax and baking soda [ext. of sense 2].

perp *v.* **1** [1990s+] (*US campus*) to pretend [PERPETRATE *v.*]. **2** [2000s] (*US*) to commit a crime (against someone) [PERP *n.* (1)].

perpendicular *n.* **1** [mid-19C+] sexual intercourse in which the partners are standing up. **2** [late 19C] a meal taken standing up, a party at which the guests stand rather than sit in a formal 'placement'.

IN PHRASES

❑ **do a perpendicular** *v.* [1940s+] to have sexual intercourse while standing upright.

perpetrate *v.* (*also* **purp**) [SE *perpetrate*, to perform (usu. a crime or other reprehensible act)] [1980s+] (*US black teen/campus*) to pretend to be something that one is not.

perpetrator *n.* [PERPETRATE *v.*] [1980s+] (*US campus*) one who pretends to greater attainments, social position or popularity than they actually have.

perpetual staircase *n.* [late 19C–1900s] the prison treadmill.

perq *n. see* PERK *n.*[1].

perry *n.* [abbr.] [1960s] (*US drugs*) *Percodan.*

Perry Como *n.* [rhy. sl. = HOMO *n.*[2] (1); ult. singer *Perry Como* (1912–2001)] [1950s+] a homosexual.

pers *adj.* [abbr. PERSONAL *n.* (2)] [1990s+] (*drugs*) one's own supply of drugs.

Persian *adj. see* GREEK *adj.* (2).

persian rug *n.* [rhy. sl.] [1960s] (*Aus.*) a bug.

persimmon *n.*

IN PHRASES

❑ **rake up persimmons** *v.* (*also* **knock persimmons, shake down the persimmons**) [mid-19C–1900s] to succeed, to win, to make a profit. ❑ **that's persimmon** (*also* **that's the ripe persimmon, ...the real persimmon**) [late 19C–1940s] (*US*) that's fine, that's satisfactory. ❑ **there ain't no persimmons** *see* THAT AIN'T HAY *under* HAY *n.*

personal *n.* **1** [1960s] a close friend. **2** [1990s+] (*UK drugs*) drugs kept for one's own consumption (as opposed to those which one sells).

persp *n.* [abbr.; all uses in the works of P.G. Wodehouse (1881–1975)] [1920s+] *perspiration.*

persuader *n.* **1** [late 18C–early 19C] usu. in pl., a spur. **2** [mid-19C+] (*also* **persuasive**) a cudgel or bludgeon. **3** [mid-19C+] a revolver. **4** [late 19C] the penis. **5** [1910s] (*US Und.*) safe-breaker's tools.

persy *n.* (*also* **percy**) [abbr. SE *personal*] [1980s+] (*US drugs*) one's own supply of drugs.

pertish *adj.* [SE *pert*] [mid-18C–early 19C] tipsy, quite drunk.

Peruvian *n.*[1] [? pun on initials of the *P*olish and *R*ussian *U*nion, an organization that facilitated the immigration of Jews from Russia and Eastern Europe] [late 19C–1900s] (*S.Afr.*) **1** a Jew, esp. an East European Jew who retains their accent, mannerisms and general culture. **2** a fellow Jew who fails to meet the community's ethical and moral standards. **3** a member of Tammany Hall.

Peruvian *n.*[2] (*also* **Peruvian flake, ...lady**) [its origin] [1980s+] (*drugs*) cocaine.

Peruvian doughnuts *n.*

IN PHRASES

❑ **real Peruvian doughnuts** *n. see* REAL JAM *under* JAM *n.*[2].

perv *n.* (*also* **perve, pervy**) [abbr. SE *pervert*] **1** [1940s+] (*orig. Aus.*) one who is categorized as a sexual pervert, esp. a child-molester; also in joc. use. **2** [1950s+] a male homosexual. **3** [1960s] pornography, usu. featuring what is considered 'bizarre' sex. **4** [1960s] (*Aus.*) a general term of abuse. **5** [1960s+] a voyeur; also non-sexual use. **6** [1980s+] the male act of watching passing women; similarly looking at pornographic or sexy pictures. **7** [1990s+] any form of 'deviant' sex act.

IN PHRASES

❑ **have a perv (at)** *v.* (*also* **have a perve (at)**) [1990s+] to stare at in a sexual manner.

perv *adj.* (*also* **perve**) [PERV *n.*] [1940s+] pornographic, e.g. *perv film, perv book, perv show,* a strip show.

perv *v.* (*also* **perve**) [PERV *n.*] [1940s+] (*orig. Aus./N.Z.*) **1** to behave in a sexually perverted manner, esp. used of child-molesters. **2** to stare at, to watch, usu. in a prurient manner. **3** to read or watch pornography. **4** to act in an effeminate/homosexual manner.

IN PHRASES

❑ **perv about** *v.* (*also* **perve about**) [the use is facetious rather than an actual ref. to any sexual eccentricity] [1940s+] (*orig. Aus.*) to search for potential sexual conquests. ❑ **perv at** *v.* (*also* **perve at**) [1950s+] to stare at, to watch, usu. in a prurient manner. ❑ **perv on** *v.* (*also* **perve on**) [1960s+] to stare at, to watch, usu. in a prurient manner.

perve *see under* PERV.

pervin' *adj.* [? fig. use of PERV *v.*] [1990s+] (*US black teen*) intoxicated, drunk.

pervo *n.* [PERV *v.* (1) + -O *sfx* (3)] [1980s+] (*Aus.*) a pervert.

pervy *n. see* PERV *n.*

pervy *adj.* [PERV *n.*] [1940s+] **1** (*orig. Aus.*) sexually perverted. **2** pornographic, smutty.

pesh *n.* [Sp. *peso,* a coin of low denomination or Fr. *pièce,* a coin] [20C+] (*W.I.*) money.

peso *n.* [Mex. Sp. *peso,* a coin approx. equivalent to $1] [19C+] (*US*) a dollar.

pester *n.* [apparently a nonce-word created by James Curtis] [1930s] to pay for (someone else).

pestilence *adv.* [lit. 'plaguey'] [early–mid-17C] a general intensifier, unpleasantly, unappealingly.

pestle *n.* [often in *double entendres*] **1** [late 16C–19C] the penis; thus the *burning pestle* is suffering from venereal disease. **2** [early 17C] a constable's staff.

pestle *v.* [PESTLE *n.* (1)] [late 19C–1900s] of a man, to have sexual intercourse.

pestlehead *n.* [SE *pestle* + -HEAD *sfx* (1)] [19C] a fool.

pestle of pork *n.* [SE *pestle,* the leg of certain animals used for food, esp. the ham or haunch of the pig] [late 19C–1900s] the leg.

petar *n. see* PETER *n.*[3].

Pete *n.*[1] [1920s+] used in a variety of phrs. as a euph. for Christ/God.

IN PHRASES

❑ **glory be to Pete** [1920s+] (*Can.*) a mild oath. ❑ **honest to Pete** *adv.* [1910s+] (*US*) honestly, sincerely; also as adj. ❑ **in the name of Pete** [1930s–50s] a mild oath. ❑ **what the Pete** [1950s] a phr. used to indicate one's incomprehension.

IN EXCLAMATIONS

❑ **for the love of Pete!** [1920s–30s] a euph. excl. of exasperation or surprise, for goodness' sake!

Pete *n.*[2] *see* SNEAKY PETE *n.* (1).

pete *n.*[1] [PETER *n.*[2] (2)/PETER *n.*[5] (2)] **1** [1910s–50s] (*also* **pete-box**) a safe. **2** [1930s–40s] (*US*) nitroglycerine, used to open safes. **3** *see* PETE-MAN below.

IN COMPOUNDS

❑ **pete-box** *n. see* sense 1 above. ❑ **pete-busting** *n.* [BUST *v.*[1] (1a)] [1950s] (*US Und.*) safe-cracking. ❑ **pete job** *n.* [1910s–20s] safe breaking. ❑ **pete-man** *n.* (*also* **pete**) [1910s+] (*US Und.*) a safebreaker.

pete *n.*[2] **1** *see* PETER *n.*[2] (6). **2** *see* PETER *n.*[4]. **3** *see* PETER *n.*[5].

pete *n.*[3] *see* SNEAKY PETE *n.* (1).

peted *adj. see under* PETER OUT *v.*

Pete Murray *n. see* RUBY MURRAY *n.*

peter *n.*[1] [abbr. PETER SEE ME *n.*] [early–mid-17C] a form of Spanish wine.

peter *n.*[2] (*UK/US Und.*) **1** [mid-17C–1930s] (*also* **petter, pitter**) a trunk, a bundle, a bag or parcel of any kind. **2** [late 18C+] a safe or cash-box, a cash register, a till. **3** [mid-19C] (*US Und.*) a receiver of stolen property. **4** [late 19C] (*US tramp*) a safebreaker. **5** [late 19C+] (*Aus.*) a witness box; thus *mount the peter,* enter the witness box. **6** [1930s+] (*also* **pete**) a cell, whether in jail, a police station or elsewhere, thus also a prison. **7** [1980s+] (*N.Z.*) a half-gallon jar [? fig. use of proper name *Peter,* based on its ety., Gk *petros,* a stone].

IN COMPOUNDS

❑ **peter-biter** *n.* [BITE *v.* (1)] **1** [mid-19C] (*UK Und.*) one who steals luggage. **2** [1990s+] (*UK Und.*) (*also* **peter blower**) a safe-blower. ❑ **peter-boatman** *n.* [late 18C–mid-19C] a thief who operates on the river. ❑ **peter-claimer** *n.* [CLAIM *v.* (1)] [late 19C] (*UK Und.*) one who steals unguarded parcels and bags from railway stations. ❑ **peter-claiming** *n.* [CLAIM *v.* (1)] [late 19C] stealing unguarded parcels and bags from railway stations. ❑ **peter-cutter** *n.* (*also* **petter-cutter**) [mid-19C] an implement used to break into safes. ❑ **peter-drag** *n.* [DRAG *n.*[1] (1b)] [19C] the stealing of boxes, parcels, bags etc, esp. from carriages. ❑ **peter-gee** *n.* [GEE *n.*[3] (1)] [1940s] (*US Und.*) a safecracker. ❑ **peter-hunting** *n.* [19C] (*UK Und.*) the stealing of baggage and boxes. ❑ **peter lay** *n.* [LAY *n.*[3] (1)] [early 18C–early 19C] (*UK Und.*) the stealing of baggage and boxes. ❑ **peterman** *n.* **1** [early 19C+] a safecracker. **2** [mid-19C] a thief who specializes in stealing goods from the back of vans and carts. ❑ **peter-nicking** *n.* [NICK *v.*[1] (3)] [1900s–10s] (*Aus.*) stealing from tills. ❑ **peter school** *n.* [*DNZE* claims 'unknown'; ? the casino's cash-box] [1900s–30s] (*Aus./N.Z.*) a gambling den. ❑ **peter-screwing** *n.* [SCREW *v.* (4a)] [mid-19C+] breaking open safes. ❑ **peter thief** *n.* [1980s+] (*Aus. prison*) one who steals from a fellow prisoner's cell. ❑ **peter work** *n.* [1930s] safe-breaking.

IN PHRASES

❑ **bite the peter** *v.* [BITE *v.* (1)] [late 17C–19C] to steal suitcases or portmanteaux. ❑ **black peter** *n.* [1920s+] (*Aus.*) a cell for solitary confinement. ❑ **nap a peter** *v.* [NAP *v.*[1] (2)] [late 19C] (*UK Und.*) steal luggage from a carriage. ❑ **on the peter** [1940s] (*US Und.*) working as a safebreaker. ❑ **shoot a peter** *v.* [1940s] (*US Und.*) to blow open a safe.

peter *n.*[3] (*also* **petar**) [? SE *petard*, upon which the loser is 'hoist'] [late 17C–mid-18C] (*UK Und.*) a variety of loaded dice, used for cheating.

peter *n.*[4] (*also* **pete, petey**) [joc. use of proper name + initial letters] [mid-19C+] the penis, esp. of a young boy.

IN COMPOUNDS

❑ **peter-beater** *n.* [1980s+] (*US*) a masturbator. ❑ **peter-eater** *n.* [EAT *v.* (4)] [1920s+] (*US*) a male homosexual fellator; a heterosexual fellatrix. ❑ **peter-meter** *n.* [popularized by *Screw* magazine in the late 1960s, when it was used as part of reviews to assess the degree to which a pornographic film or book was arousing] [1960s+] (*US*) a notional means of measuring the size of a penis, or the excitement it is experiencing. ❑ **peter-pitching** *adj.* [1930s] of a man, sexually active. ❑ **peter puffer** *n.* [SE *puff*, to blow, i.e. BLOW *v.*[2] (1c)] [20C+] (*US*) one who performs oral sex. ❑ **peter-puller** *n.* [late 19C+] a masturbator. ❑ **peter-pusher** *n.* [1960s] (*US black*) a man who has sexual intercourse.

IN PHRASES

❑ **peddle one's peter** *v.* [1970s] to work as a homosexual male prostitute. ❑ **pitch the peter** *v.* [1930s] of a man, to have sexual intercourse.

peter *n.*[5] (*also* **pete, peter-drop**) **1** [late 19C+] (*US tramp*) drugged or adulterated liquor, derived from nitroglycerine; a 'knockout' drug; thus *peter-thrower*, a thief who uses 'knockout drops'. **2** [1920s–30s] (*UK Und.*) nitroglycerine.

IN COMPOUNDS

❑ **peterman** *n.* [late 19C–1900s] one who uses knockout drops to facilitate a robbery. ❑ **peter player** *n.* (*also* **peter-thrower**) [mid–late 19C] (*US*) one who uses knockout drops to facilitate a robbery.

peter *v.*[1] [? PETER OUT *v.* but it appears to be earlier; ? Fr. *peter*, to explode weakly] **1** [mid-18C+] (*also* **petre, petter**) to stop, to cease; in fig. use, to die. **2** [mid-19C] to tire, to feel exhausted.

IN EXCLAMATIONS

❑ **peter that!** [19C] shut up! be quiet!

peter *v.*[2] [PETER *n.*[5] (1)] [1920s–60s] (*US*) to use knockout drops on a victim.

peter *v.*[3] [PETER *n.*[5] (2)/ PETER *n.*[2] (2)] [1920s+] to blow open a safe with nitroglycerine.

Peter and Lee *n. see* PETERS AND LEE *n.*

peter-drop *n. see* PETER *n.*[5].

peterer *n.* (*also* **peteree, peteress**) [PETER *n.*[2] (1)] [late 18C–mid-19C] a thief who specializes in stealing goods from the back of vans and carts; thus fem. *peteress*.

Peter Funk *n.* (*also* **Funk, Peter Funker**) [a generic proper name, orig. Ger./Du.] [mid–late 19C] (*US*) a fraudulent salesman, often operating in the guise of an auctioneer, who augments the appeal of their third-rate merchandise by intimating that it had in some way been acquired illegally.

DERIVATIVES

❑ **Peter Funkism** *n.* [mid-19C] a form of swindling.

peter grievous *n.* (*also* **peter grievance**) [mid-19C–1900s] a whiner, a complainer, a whinging child.

peter gunner *n.* [a supposed name but note *peter*, saltpetre (used in bullets)] [17C–early 19C] a poor shot; thus [19C] *Peter Gunner who will kill all the birds that died last summer.*

peter jay *n.* [ety. unknown] [1980s+] (*US black/Los Angeles*) a police officer.

peterman *n.* [SE *peterman*, a fisherman, ult. after the apostle Simon Peter, a fisherman] [mid-17C–early 18C] one who poaches fish from the River Thames.

Peter O'Toole *n.* [rhy. sl.; ult. Irish-born actor *Peter O'Toole* (b.1932)] [1990s+] a (bar) stool.

peter out *v.* (*also* **petter out**) [orig. US mining jargon, but note PETER *v.*[1]; note Michael Quinion, *World Wide Words* 14/4/01: 'There are two possibilities for where it came from. One is the *saltpetre* (US spelling *saltpeter*) that was a component of the blasting power that miners used (the second part comes from Greek '*petros*', a rock); this sounds a bit of a stretch, but you never know. The other is French '*peter*', which literally means "to fart", but which I believe has been used figuratively to mean "to fizzle out" (and which famously appears in the English '*petard*' for a medieval military explosive device, from which we get "hoist by his own petard").'] **1** [mid-19C+] to give out, to fade away. **2** [late 19C+] to tire, to feel exhausted. **3** [1900s–30s] to die. **4** [1910s] to reject, to scapegoat.

DERIVATIVES

❑ **peted** *adj.* [mid-19C+] (*Can./US*) exhausted.

Peter Pan *n.* [rhy. sl.; ult. J. M. Barrie's *Peter Pan* (1904)] **1** [1940s] (*US*) a chamberpot [SE *pan*]. **2** [1990s+] a van. **3** [2000s] a suntan.

Peter Pan's Never-Never Land *see* NEVER-NEVER (LAND) *n.*

Peters and Lee *n.* (*also* **Peter and Lee**) [rhy. sl.; ult. singing duo Lennie *Peters* (1939–92) and Dianne *Lee* (b.1950)] [1990s+] **1** a cup of tea. **2** an act of urination [PEE *n.*[1] (2)/WEE *n.*].

peter see me *n.* [*peter* = *Pedro*, a famous grape + Cardinal *Ximenes* (1436–1517)] [early–mid-17C] a Spanish wine, properly named *Pedro Ximenes*.

pete tong *adj.* [rhy. sl.; ult. UK dance DJ *Pete Tong* (b.1960)] [1980s+] wrong.

petey *n. see* PETER *n.*[4].

peth *n.* [abbr.] [1980s+] (*drugs*) *peth*idine.

petre *v. see* PETER *v.*[1] (1).

petrified *adj.* [lit. 'turned to stone'; logically a pun on STONED *adj.* but predates it by 50 years] **1** [20C+] very drunk; thus *petrification*, a state of drunkenness. **2** [1950s] under the influence of a drug.

petro *adj.* [P.R. Sp. *petro*, scared] [1980s+] (*US*) terrified, fearful paranoid; thus *petrolyze*, to render paranoid.

petrol *n.* [? its role as a 'fuel'] **1** [1950s] (*Irish*) alcohol **2** [1980s+] (*Aus. prison*) heroin.

petrol-head *n.* [SE *petrol* + -HEAD *sfx* (3)] [1980s] (*Aus.*) a devotee of motor-racing.

petrols *n.* [rhy. sl. on *petrol bowsers*] [1970s] (*Aus.*) trousers.

petrol tank *n.* [rhy. sl. = WANK *n.*] [1990s+] masturbation.

petronel *n.* [SE *petronel*, a kind of large pistol or carbine, used in the 16C and early 17C] [late 16C–early 17C] a braggart, a blusterer, a bully.

petter *see also under* PETER.

petter *n.* [SE *pet*, to fondle] [1930s–40s] (*US*) one who enjoys indulging in sexual fondling and caresses.

pet the poodle *v. see under* POODLE *n.*

petticoat *n.* [metonymy] **1** [17C] a woman; thus *Petticoat lane* the vagina. **2** [late 17C+] attrib., pertaining to women and female culture; usu. in combs. below. **3** [mid-19C] in coin tossing, the tail. **4** [1950s] (*US*) a general derog. term for a man.

IN COMPOUNDS

❑ **petticoat government** *n.* (*also* **petticoat rule**) [late 17C–1910s] a domestic relationship in which the wife dominates her husband, or a mother her child. ❑ **petticoat hold** *n.* [SE *hold*, freehold, tenure] [late 18C–early 19C] a husband's interest in his wife's estate, limited to his lifetime only. ❑ **petticoat hunter** *n.* [late 18C–early 19C] a womanizer. ❑ **petticoat merchant** *n.* [MERCHANT *n.* (1)] [late 19C] a pimp. ❑ **petticoat-peer** *n. see* SQUIRE OF THE PETTICOAT *under* SQUIRE *n.* ❑ **petticoat pension** *n.* [17C] the money a prostitute gives her pimp, or a woman gives her 'kept' lover. ❑ **petticoat pensioner** *n.* (*also* **petty-coat pensioner**) [late 16C–mid-19C] a kept man. ❑ **petticoat pet** *n.* [1900s] (*Aus.*) one who is beloved by women. ❑ **petticoat-preacher** *n.* [early 18C] a domineering wife. ❑ **petticoat rule** *n. see* PETTICOAT GOVERNMENT above.

SE in slang uses

IN PHRASES

❑ **go under-petticoating** *v.* [19C] to have sexual intercourse. ❑ **go up her petticoats** *v.* (*also* **raise her petticoats**) [late 19C] of a man, to have sexual intercourse. ❑ **take a turn up her petticoats** *v. see* TAKE A TURN AMONG HER FRILLS *under* TAKE *v.*

Petticoat Lane *n.* [rhy. sl.; ult. the East London street market, *Petticoat Lane*] [20C+] a pain.

Pettigo *n.*

IN EXCLAMATIONS

❑ **go to Pettigo!** *see* GO TO PUTNEY (ON A PIG)! *under* PUTNEY *n.*

petty *n.* [SE *pet*] [1910s+] a term of endearment.

petty-coat pensioner *n. see* PETTICOAT PENSIONER *under* PETTICOAT *n.*

petty (house) *n.* [lit. 'small house'] [late 19C] the lavatory.

petunia *v.* [initial letter of PISS *v.* (2)] [2000s] (*S.Afr. gay*) to urinate.

pew *n.* **1** [late 19C+] a seat. **2** [1930s] (*US Und.*) the electric chair.

IN PHRASES

❑ **take a pew** *v.* (*also* **grab a pew**) [late 19C+] an invitation to sit down.

pewk *v. see* PUKE (IT) OUT *under* PUKE *v.*

pewter *n.* **1** [19C–1940s] money, esp. silver. **2** [1910s] a pewter drinking pot, esp. as given as a prize.

IN PHRASES

❑ **unload pewter** *v.* [mid-19C] to drink from a pewter tankard.

peysle *v.* (*also* **picell, pisel**) [Scot. *peist*, to work feebly] [20C+] (*Ulster*) to work lazily or half-heartedly.

Peyton Place *n.* [rhy. sl.; ult. the bestselling novel (and later film and TV series) *Peyton Place* (1956) by Grace Metalious (1924–64)] [1990s+] (*US*) the human face.

pez *n.* [ety. unknown; ? link to Yid. *peyes*, sidelocks] [1940s–50s] (*US black*) facial hair, the hair on one's head.

Pez-head *n.* [*Pez*, a brand of children's sweets packaged in a tube with a comical animal head top] [1990s+] (*Aus./teen*) a mildly derog. affectionate term.

pfat *adj.* [var. on PHAT *adj.*] [1990s+] (*US black*) very wise, sophisticated.

pfft *adj.* [PHUT *adv.*] [1930s–50s] (*orig. US*) finished, terminated, over.

IN PHRASES

❑ **go pfft** *v. see* GO PHUT *under* PHUT *adv.*

pfinif *n. see* FIN *n.*[2] (2).

pfiz *n. see* FIZZ *n.*[1] (3).

pfotz *n.* [? euph. for FUCK *n.* (1a)] [20C+] the vagina.

pfui! *excl. see* PHOOEY! *excl.*

p.g. *n.*[1] [abbr.] **1** [late 19C] (*US campus*) a post-graduate. **2** [1900s] (*US campus*) a pretty girl. **3** [1920s+] a paying guest.

p.g. *n.*[2] [abbr.; a cough medicine based on opium linctus, which heroin addicts use when no stronger drugs are available; William Burroughs, *Junkie* (1953): '*P.G.* ...Paregoric. A weak, camphorated tincture of opium, two grains to the ounce. Two ounces will fix a sick addict. It can be bought without prescription in some states. P.G. can be injected intravenously after burning out the alcohol and straining out the camphor'] [1930s–60s] (*drugs*) paregoric.

p.g. *adj.* (*also* **pee-gee**) [abbr.] [1970s+] pregnant.

p.g. *phr.* [abbr. *past gone*] [1950s] (*US black*) of time, last, just happened, e.g. *four o'clock p.g.*

P.G. tips *n.* [rhy. sl.; ult. the popular brand of tea] [20C+] the lips.

P.H. *n. see* PLAYER-HATER *under* PLAYER *n.*

p.h. *n.* [abbr.; PURPLE HEARTS *under* PURPLE *adj.*] [1960s] (*drugs*) amphetamine pills.

phantom *n. see* GHOST *n.* (5).

pharaoh *n.*[1] [abbr. the brandname *Old Pharaoh*; ? the power attributed to the Egyptian kings] [late 17C–18C] a particularly strong malt beer.

pharaoh *n.*[2] [Kanuri (an African lang. of northeast Nigeria) *fero*, a girl] [19C–1920s] (*US black*) a young woman.

Pharaoh's revenge *n. see* MONTEZUMA'S REVENGE *n.*

phar lap *n.* [proper name *Phar Lap*, flash of lightning, Australia's most famous racehorse, fl. 1930s] (*Aus.*) **1** [1930s+] a very slow person. **2** [1950s] a wild dog, with its hair burnt off, trussed up and cooked in the ashes.

IN COMPOUNDS

❑ **phar lap gallop** *n.* [1930s–40s] (*Aus.*) a foxtrot.

pharmacist *n.* [1990s+] (*W.I.*) a major drug dealer.

pharm party *n.* (*also* **pharming party**) [abbr. SE *pharm*aceuticals] [2000s] (*US drugs*) the taking by teenagers of prescription drugs – usu. high-strength opioid painkillers – as found at home; thus *pharming*, stealing drugs from the family medicine cabinet.

phase out *v.* (*also* **phaze**) [1980s+] (*US campus*) to become unaware, as if asleep.

phat *adj.* [deliberately skewed sp. of FAT *adj.* (1c); but also popularly linked to a variety of suggested acronyms, e.g. *ph*ysically *a*ttractive or *p*retty *h*ips *a*nd *t*highs or *p*retty *h*ips, *a*ss and *t*its, or *p*retty *h*ot *a*nd *t*empting, or *p*ussy, *h*ips, *a*ss and *t*highs etc] **1** [1960s+] (*orig. US black/campus*) used to describe an attractive woman. **2** [1990s+] (*also* **phat-ass, phatman sweet**) a general term of approval, admiration; also in phrs., e.g. *phat 2 death*.

IN COMPOUNDS

❑ **phat-cat** *n.* [1990s+] (*US campus*) a very fashionable person. ❑ **phat pocket** *n.* [1990s+] (*US black*) a wealthy person. ❑ **phat tape** *n.* (*also* **fat tape**) [1990s+] (*US black teen*) an exceptionally good mix tape.

phata-phata *n. see* PATA-PATA *n.*

phatty *adj.* (*also* **phattie**) [PHAT *adj.* (2)] [1990s+] (*US black*) excellent.

phaze *v.* [? SE *faze* or ? SE *phase* (out)] **1** [1990s+] (*US campus*) to ignore. **2** see PHASE OUT *v.*

Ph.D. *v. see* PILE IT HIGHER AND DEEPER *under* PILE *v.*

p.h.d. *n.* [2000s] **1** (*US teen*) a fig. 'degree' held by a teacher who dislikes students who espouse 'gangsta' culture; thus used of one who undermines the activities of a 'player' [abbr. PLAYER-HATER *under* PLAYER *n.* + SE *degree*]. **2** (*US black*) a large penis [abbr. *p*retty *h*uge *d*ick, i.e. DICK *n.*[1] (5)].

p.h.d. *phr.* [*p*etticoat *h*anging *d*own] [1930s] (*US*) a warning to a woman that her slip is showing.

pheasant *n.* [note naut. jargon *Spithead pheasant*, a bloater or kipper] **1** [early 17C] a term of abuse. **2** [late 17C–early 19C] a promiscuous woman. **3** [late 19C] a herring.

pheasantry *n.* [PHEASANT *n.* (2)] [19C–1900s] a brothel.

pheeny *n. see* PHENNIE *n.*

pheeze *see under* FEEZE.

phenagle *v. see* FINAGLE *v.*

phennie *n.* (*also* **pheeny, phenal**) [abbr.] [1950s+] (*drugs*) *pheno*barbitol, a depressant.

pheno *n.* (*also* **phenobob, phenos**) [abbr.] [1940s–70s] *pheno*barbital, *pheno*barbitone (a soporific drug best known by the US tradename Luminol).

phenogler *n. see* FINAGLER *n.*

phenom *n.* [abbr. SE *phenomenon*] [late 19C–1950s] (*US*) an outstanding person or thing, a prodigy.

phenomy *n.* (*also* **phenomony**) [abbr. SE *phenomenon*] [early 19C] an outstanding person or thing, a prodigy.

phenos *n. see* PHENO *n.*

phet *n.* [1990s+] (*drugs*) am*phet*amine.

Phil/Phila *n. see* PHILLY *n.*

Philadelphia lawyer *n.* [negative stereotyping] [late 18C+] (*US*) a shrewd or unscrupulous lawyer, an expert in exploiting the minutiae of the law.

philander *v.* [play on SE] [mid-19C–1900s] 'to ramble on incoherently, to write discursively and weakly' (Hotten, 1873).

philharmonic *n.* [rhy. sl.] [20C+] tonic water; gin and tonic.

phililoo *n. see* FILLALOO *n.*

philip! *excl.* [? the shared initial letter] [late 19C] (*UK Und.*) an excl. that indicates the approach of the police.

philip and cheyney *n.* (*also* **philip, hob and cheyney**) [the contemporary commonness of these names] [mid-16C–early 17C] a collective generic term for average people, the mass.

philiper *n.* (*also* **philliper**) [? dial. *philip*, a sparrow] [mid-19C] a thief's accomplice.

philistines *n.* [Judg. 16:20, 'The Philistines be upon thee, Samson'] **1** [late 17C–mid-19C] bailiffs. **2** [late 17C–mid-19C] (*also* **philistians**) a group of drunkards.; thus *have been among the Philistines*, to be drunk. **3** [19C] the police.

philliper *n. see* PHILIPER *n.*

Philly *n.* (*also* **Phil, Phila, Phillie**) [abbr.] **1** [late 19C+] (*US*) *Phil*adelphia. **2** [1900s] a native of Philadelphia; a player for a local sports team. **3** [1980s+] (*US black/drugs*) a marijuana cigarette made of buds rolled in a tobacco leaf taken from the wrapper of a *Phillies* Blunt cigar.

IN COMPOUNDS

□ **Philly blunt** *n. see* BLUNT *n.*[3] (1).

Phil McBee *n.* [rhy. sl.] [19C] a flea.

phil the fluter *n.* [rhy. sl. = SHOOTER *n.*[1] (1)] [20C+] a gun.

phinney *n. see* FINNY *n.*[1].

phiz *n.*[1] (*also* **fiz, fizzog, phis, phizz, phizzog, physimiog, physiog, physog, phyz, phyzog**) [abbr. SE *physiognomy*] **1** [late 17C+] the face. **2** [1910s] (*UK WW1*) a photograph.

phiz *n.*[2] *see* FIZZ *n.*[1] (3).

phizgig *n.*[1] [SE *fizgig*, a frivolous woman] [late 19C] an old woman dressed younger than her years.

phizgig *n.*[2] *see* FIZGIG *n.*[2].

phizz *n. see* PHIZ *n.*[1].

phizzer *n. see* FIZZER *n.*[3].

phizzing *n. see* FIZZING *adj.*

phizzog *n. see* PHIZ *n.*[1].

phizz water *n. see* FIZZ *n.*[1] (3).

phlegm-cutter *n.* (*also* **phlegm-disperser, phlegm-splitter**) [19C+] **1** a drink of whisky or other strong liquor. **2** the first drink of the day, usu. that taken by an alcoholic soon after waking up; thus *cut the phlegm*, to take a first drink.

phlip *n. see* FLIP *n.*[1].

phoby *n.* [abbr. SE *hydrophobia*] [mid-19C] a dread or horror of water; thus in general, madness.

Phoebe *n.* (*also* **little Phoebe**) **1** [late 19C+] (*US gambling*) the point of five in craps dice. **2** *see* FEEB *n.*

phoenix *n.* [it 'rises'] [1920s] the penis.

phoenix nest *n.* (*also* **phoenix alley**) [? it makes the penis 'rise again'] [17C–mid-19C] the vagina.

pho(h)! *excl. see* FAUGH! *excl.*

P hole *n. see* PEEHOLE *n.*

phone *n.* [2000s] (*US prison*) a makeshift communications system created by emptying a toilet.

SE in slang uses

IN COMPOUNDS

□ **phone booth** *n.* [supposed resemblance] [1930s] (*US*) a double-bass. □ **phone freak** *n.* (*also* **phone phreak**) [-FREAK *sfx*] **1** [1970s+] (*US*) a person who uses special equipment to obtain free calls from the telephone system. **2** [1970s+] a client who arranges to phone up a prostitute and listen while she runs through a pornographic monologue and he masturbates. **3** [2000s] (*US*) one who makes obscene phonecalls for sexual arousal. □ **phone ho** *n.* [HO *n.* (1)] [1990s+] (*US black*) a woman, not necessarily a working prostitute, who offers 'telephone sex' to credit-card paying clients.

IN PHRASES

□ **hold the phone** *v.* [telephone imagery] [1970s+] (*US*) to wait, to delay, to 'hang on'; esp. as imper. *hold the phone!* □ **phone's off the hook** [2000s] (*US prison*) a warning that a guard is listening.

phones *n.* [abbr.] [1910s+] head*phones*.

phoney *n.*[1] (*also* **phony**) [PHONEY *adj.*] **1** [20C+] anything fake, counterfeit, untrustworthy. **2** [1910s+] an insincere, untrustworthy, 'fake' person. **3** [1940s+] (*gay*) a mean or cheap client for a gay prostitute. **4** [1950s] a male homosexual; a man who pursues underage girls [implies a 'fake' man, lacking in 'masculinity'].

IN COMPOUNDS

□ **phoney stiff** *n.* [STIFF *n.*[1] (4i)] [1910s–20s] (*US tramp*) a tramp who sells fake jewels.

phoney *n.*[2] [abbr. SE *telephone*] [1980s+] (*US campus*) a crank telephone call.

phoney *adj.* (*also* **phony**) [? *fawney-rig* under FAWNEY *n.* and allied terms (proposed by Partridge but disputed by Simes, *A Dict. of Australian Und. Slang* (1993); for link to *fawney see* P. Tamony in *American Speech* XII:2 108–10] [late 19C+] (*orig. US*) fake, counterfeit, insincere; thus *phoney as a three-dollar bill/ nine-dollar bill*.

phoney *v.* (*also* **phony, phoney up**) [PHONEY *adj.*] [1930s+] (*US*) to counterfeit, to falsify, to make up.

phoney-baloney *adj.* [PHONEY *adj.* + BALONEY *n.* (1a)] [1910s+] (*US*) absurd, nonsensical.

DERIVATIVES

□ **phoney-baloneyness** *n.* [1990s+] absurdity, insincerity.

IN COMPOUNDS

□ **phoney-baloney bit** *n.* [BIT *n.*[1] (3b)] [1950s] (*US Und.*) a clearly unjust or discriminatory prison sentence, esp. one based not on sound legal principles but on a technicality. □ **phoney-baloney life** *n.* [i.e. a 'fake' life sentence] [20C+] (*US prison*) an ostensible life sentence which can be appreciably shortened by parole.

phonus balonus *n.* (*also* **phoney-baloney**) [PHONEY-BALONEY *adj.* in cod-Lat. format] [1920s+] (*US*) rubbish, nonsense; a stupid false person.

phony *see also under* PHONEY.

phooey! *excl.* (*also* **fooey! foy! pfui!**) [synon. Ger. *pfui!*] [mid-19C+] (*orig. US*) an excl. of disdain or dismissal, rubbish! nonsense!; thus ext. as *phooey on that!*

phos *n.* (*also* **foss, phoss**) [abbr.] **1** [early 19C] *phos*phorus, used by burglars for illumination; thus *ding the phos*, throw away the bottle of phosphorus. **2** [late 19C] *phos*phorus necrosis.

photie *n.* (*also* **fotie, photy**) [abbr.] [1960s+] a photograph.

photo finish *n.* [rhy. sl.] [1950s+] (a pint of) Guinness (stout)

photog *n.* (*also* **fotog, photogger**) [abbr.] [1910s+] (*orig. US*) a *photog*rapher.

photy *n. see* PHOTIE *n.*

phreak *n.* (*also* **phreaker**) [abbr. of *PHONE FREAK under* PHONE *n.*] [1970s+] (*US*) a person who uses special equipment to obtain free calls from the telephone system.

phreak *v.* [PHREAK *n.*] [1970s+] (*US*) to use a variety of special equipment ('black boxes', 'blue boxes') to obtain free calls from the telephone system.

phukk *n.* [1990s+] a euph. sp. of FUCK *n.*; thus *muthaphukka* MOTHERFUCKER *n.*

phunbaba *n.* [ety. unknown] [2000s] (*US black*) a large piece of excrement.

hungky *adj.* [1990s+] (*US*) a deliberate mis-sp. of FUNKY *adj.*[3].

hunt *n. see* FUNT *n.*

hut *adv.*

IN PHRASES

❑ **go phut** *v.* (*also* **go pfft**) [echoic of the noise of air escaping rom a deflated, popped balloon] [late 19C+] to come to an ıbrupt end; spec., of a couple, to divorce.

hutten *adj.* [1960s] (*Aus.*) a euph. for FUCKING *adj.*

hutz *see under* FUTZ.

huza *n.* (*also* **poosa, pusa, puza**) [Xhosa/Zulu *phuza*, a drink, a ip] [20C+] (*S.Afr. township*) liquor; thus *phuza-face*, a face bearing the marks of prolonged heavy drinking.

IN COMPOUNDS

❑ **phuza-buddy** *n.* [BUDDY *n.* (1)] [1980s] a companion with whom one drinks phuza. ❑ **phuza-cabin** *n.* (*also* **phuza-joint**) OINT *n.* (3b)] [1980s] a form of 'shebeen' devoted to selling huza.

huza *v.* (*also* **poosa, pusa, puza**) [PHUZA *n.*] [20C+] (*S.Afr. ownship*) to drink.

hy *n.* [abbr.; both forms of synthetic heroin] [1960s] (*drugs*) hyceptone, methadone.

hysic *n.* [play on SE *physic*, medicine] [late 17C–early 18C] exual intercourse.

hysic *v.* [SE *physic*, to give a dose of medicine] [early–mid-19C] o punish, either physically or through depriving of money.

hysics for poets *n.* [1970s+] (*US campus*) a course in basic hysics for arts specialists; thus also vars. for other similarly easy' courses.

hysimiog/physiog/physog *n. see* PHIZ *n.*[1].

hyssie *n.* [SE *physical culturist*] [1970s] (*W.I.*) a keen body-uilder.

hyz/phyzog *n. see* PHIZ *n.*[1].

I. *n.* [1950s+] a Private *I*, i.e. eye.

i. *n.* (*also* **pea-eye, pee-eye**) [abbr.] [1920s–60s] (*US black*) a imp.

adj. [abbr.] [late 19C+] (*orig. juv.*) pious, always in a derog. ense of self-righteous, unctuous, poss. hypocritical.

ano *n.* **1** [1930s+] (*also* **piana**) a cash register [abbr. JEWISH ANO *under* JEWISH *adj.*]. **2** [1940s+] (*US black*) spare ribs; thus *iano on a platter*, barbecued ribs on a plate [perceived esemblance to piano keys].

N COMPOUNDS

piano leg *n.* [1940s] (*US*) a woman with stout legs. ❑ **piano layer** *n.* [he makes the accounts 'dance'] [1970s] (*US Und.*) a criminal) accountant.

N PHRASES

piano player in a brothel *n.* (*also* **pianist in a brothel**) 970s+] (*Aus.*) one who is involved in a situation, but damantly refuses to take any responsibility for it. ❑ **play the iano** *v.* [1970s] to rob the till, e.g. as a barmaid or waiter.

ano *v.* [? one's hands are tapping at the floor in the hope of eeling a tiny piece] [1980s+] (*drugs*) to search on hands and nees for any small pieces of crack cocaine that may have fallen the floor.

ano wire *n.* [rhy. sl.] [1980s+] (*Aus. prison*) a buyer.

aster *n.* (*also* **piastre**) [SE *piastre, piaster*, used for a small-enomination coin in various currencies] [1900s] (*US*) a dollar.

i.b. *n.* [abbr. *people in black*] [1990s+] (*US campus*) a rooding, gloomy adolescent who wears dark clothes and stens to gloomy alternative music.

c *n.* [abbr.] **1** [late 19C+] a *pic*ture. **2** [1910s+] a film. [1930s–40s] (*orig. US black*) (*also* **piccolo**) a jukebox, a ecord-player [SE *piccolo pianoforte*, a small piano]. **4** [1980s] in ., constr. with *the*, the cinema.

ca *n.* [? Sp.] [2000s] (*US prison*) a knife.

canniny *n. see* PICCANINNY *n.*

caroon *n.* (*also* **picardo, picaro, picarre**) [SE *picaroon*, a ogue, ult. synon. Sp. *picaro*] [early 17C–mid-19C] a rogue; thus *the picaro*, looking for easy opportunities for money-making.

DERIVATIVES

❑ **picarooning** *adj.* [early 19C] villainous.

piccadill *n. see* TYBURN PICCADILL *under* TYBURN *n.*

Piccadilly *adj.*[1] [rhy. sl.; ult. *Piccadilly*, area in central London] [20C+] **1** silly. **2** chilly.

Piccadilly *adj.*[2] in combs. below, mostly based on the reputation of this area in central London as a focus for prostitution in the 19C and early 20C, before the Street Offences Act of 1959 took prostitutes off the streets.

IN COMPOUNDS

❑ **Piccadilly bushman** *n.* [1920s–40s] (*Aus.*) a wealthy Australian who has left their native land for London. ❑ **Piccadilly cramp** *n.* [early 18C] venereal disease. ❑ **Piccadilly crawl** *n.* [late 19C] an affected style of walking adopted by society during the 1880s. ❑ **Piccadilly daisy** *n.* [note WW2 army *Piccadilly commando*, a prostitute] [1900s–50s] a prostitute. ❑ **Piccadilly fringe** *n.* [the style allegedly originated in Paris *c.*1870] [late 19C] a popular women's hairstyle in which the hair is cut short into a fringe and curled over the forehead. ❑ **Piccadilly weepers** *n.* [mid–late 19C] long side whiskers, worn without a beard and temporarily fashionable. ❑ **Piccadilly window** *n.* [affected by the fashionable men promenading in *Piccadilly*] [late 19C–1900s] a monocle.

Piccadilly percy *n.* [rhy. sl.] [1970s] mercy.

piccalilli *n.* [rhy. sl. = WILLIE *n.*[4]] [1990s+] the penis.

piccaninny *n.* (*also* **picanniny, pickanine, pickaninny, pikkie**) [adopted in W.I. f. Sp./Port. *pequeño*, small or Port. *pequenino*, tiny. The term was seen as neutral, as it was used mainly of children, but is now generally seen as patronizing and thus derog.; note vaudeville jargon *pick*, a black child who danced and sang onstage with a white headliner] [mid-17C+] (*orig. W.I.*) a black child, occas. any black person; any child, when spoken by a black person.

piccaninny *adj.* (*also* **pickaninny**) [PICCANINNY *n.*] **1** [mid-19C+] (*Aus.*) tiny; in senses of time, just prior to, e.g. *piccaninny dawn*, a false dawn. **2** [1930s–70s] (*US*) black, usu. derog.

IN COMPOUNDS

❑ **piccaninny kaya** *n.* (*also* **piccaninny kia, p.k.**) [Nguni *kia*, house] [1960s+] (*S.Afr.*) an outdoor privy.

piccie *n. see* PICCY *n.*

piccolo *n.* **1** [1960s+] the penis. **2** *see* PIC *n.* (3).

IN COMPOUNDS

❑ **piccolo-player** *n.* [1920s] a fellator or fellatrix.

piccolo and flute *n.* [rhy. sl.] **1** [20C+] a suit. **2** [1930s+] in pl., boots.

Piccy *n.* [abbr.] [1960s] *Piccadilly*.

piccy *n.* (*also* **piccie, pickie, picky, pikkie**) [abbr.] [20C+] a picture.

picell *v. see* PEYSLE *v.*

pick *n.*[1] [abbr.] **1** [late 19C] a third-rate cigar [the type of cigar smoked by 'Mr *Pick*wick' in Charles Dickens's *Pickwick Papers* (1836)]. **2** [late 19C] a tooth*pick*. **3** [late 19C+] (*also* **picks**) a lock*pick*, the tool; a person who uses it. **4** [20C+] (*UK/US Und.*) a *pick*pocket, usu. the one who removes the victim's wallet or jewellery.

IN PHRASES

❑ **penny pick** *n.* [mid-19C] a cheap cigar.

pick *n.*[2] [SE colloq. *pick on*, to criticize] **1** [20C+] (*Anglo-Irish*) a quick-tempered person. **2** [1900s] (*US Und.*) a girlfriend.

pick *n.*[3] **1** [1930s+] an ice *pick* or a weapon that resembles one. **2** [1980s+] (*Aus. prison*) a hypodermic syringe.

pick *n.*[4] *see* NATURAL PICK *under* NATURAL *n.*

pick *v.*[1] **1** [late 16C–early 19C] to pilfer, to commit petty larceny. **2** [18C–19C] to eat [SE *pick*, to eat daintily]. **3** [early 19C+] (*US Und.*) to pickpocket. **4** [1920s+] (*Aus.*) to guess [SE *pick out*]. **5** [1990s+] (*drugs*) to search on hands and knees for any small pieces of crack cocaine that may have fallen to the floor.

SE in slang uses

IN COMPOUNDS

▫ **pick-mouth** *n.* [mid–late 19C] (*W.I.*) one who sets out to pick a quarrel. ▫ **pick-penny** *n.* [SE *pick-penny*, one who greedily collects or steals money] [18C] a card-sharp.

IN PHRASES

▫ **pick a berry** *v.* [euph.] [1940s–50s] (*US*) to rob a clothes-line. ▫ **pick and cut** *v.* [one *picks* up or holds the purse, then *cuts* it] [late 16C] to work as a cut-purse. ▫ **pick at** *v.* (*also* **have a pick at**) [1910s+] (*Aus.*) to irritate, to nag at, to annoy. ▫ **pick daisies** *v. see* PUSH UP (THE) DAISIES *v.* ▫ **pick meat for dead goats** *v.* [20C+] (*W.I.*) to waste one's time on fruitless tasks. ▫ **pick one's hole** *v.* [HOLE *n.*[1] (1a)] [1990s+] to be at a loose end, idle. ▫ **pick one's teeth (with)** *v.* (*also* **pick one's mouth**) [20C+] (*W.I.*) to gossip with. ▫ **pick straws** *v. see* DRAW STRAWS *under* STRAW *n.*

pick *v.*[2] [SE colloq. *pick on*, to criticize] [1950s+] (*Aus.*) to victimize.

pickadilly *n.* [brandname *Piccadilly*] [2000s] (*US black*) a cigarette, usu. a cheap brand.

pick and choose *n.*[1] [rhy. sl. = BOOZE *n.* (1)] [20C+] alcohol, liquor.

pick and choose *n.*[2] [1920s] (*W.I.*) fastidiousness, esp. if taken to irritating extremes.

pick-and-choose *adj.* [PICK AND CHOOSE *n.*[2]] [1950s] (*W.I.*) hard to satisfy, pernickety.

pick and shovel chauffeur *n.* [1920s] (*US*) a labourer.

pickanine/pickaninny *see under* PICCANINNY.

pick-axe *n.* [its effects] [late 19C] (*S.Afr.*) a drink composed of whisky or rough brandy, Pontac (a sweet red dessert wine) and ginger-beer.

IN PHRASES

▫ **I'll be pick-axed** [1910s] (*Aus.*) a strong expression of denial or refusal.

picked-hatch *n.* (*also* **pick-hatch, pickthatch, picthatch**) [SE *picked*, spiked + *hatch*, a half door, designed to prevent unauthorized entrance; commonly used as a brothel-sign. The original such address was a tavern-cum-brothel in Turnmill Street, Clerkenwell, London; later uses are historical] [late 16C–17C] a brothel, orig. one situated either in Turnmill Street, a notorious 'red-light' district, or between Old Street and Goswell Road – both in Clerkenwell, London; thus *picked-hatch captain*, a pimp.

IN COMPOUNDS

▫ **picked-hatch vestal** *n.* (*also* **pickthatch vestal**) [ironic use of *Vestal* virgin] [17C–early 19C] a prostitute.

IN PHRASES

▫ **go to the manor of picked hatch** *v.* (*also* **go to the manor of pickt hatch, go to picket hatch grane**) [late 16C] to visit a brothel.

picker *n.* (*also* **picker-up**) [SE *pick* (up)] **1** [mid-19C; 1940s] (*later use US black*) a hand; usu. in pl. **2** *see* ROPER *n.*[2] (2).

pickers and stealers *n.* [16C catechism, 'To keep my hands from picking and stealing'] [17C–mid-19C] the hands.

picker-up *n.* **1** [late 18C–19C] that member of a confidence trick team who first meets and lures the victim into the plot. **2** [late 19C] (*UK Und.*) a prostitute [PICK UP *v.* (1a)]. **3** *see* PICKER *n.*

pick-hatch *n. see* PICKED-HATCH *n.*

pickie *n. see* PICCY *n.*

picking up the vibrations *n.* [1940s–70s] (*gay*) watching other men perform a sex show, all-male voyeurism.

pickle *n.* **1** [late 18C–19C] a difficult, troublesome person, often a child but by no means invariably; 'an arch, waggish fellow' (Grose, 1785); also of an amusing individual. **2** [mid–late 19C] (*also* **dead pickles**) in pl., nonsense, rubbish. **3** [1940s+] (*orig. US*) the penis; thus *pickle lugger*, as a term of abuse, a masturbator [resemblance to a *pickled* gherkin]. **4** [1950s–70s] a woman of a sour, unpleasant disposition [play on SE *pickle*, i.e. something/someone 'sharp'].

IN COMPOUNDS

▫ **pickle-chugging** *n.* [CHUG *v.*[1] (1)] [1990s+] (*US gay*) ma homosexual fellatio; thus *pickle-chugger*, a fellator. ▫ **pickle jar** *n.* [the *yellow* colour of some pickles] [mid-19C–1900s] coachman with a yellow uniform. ▫ **pickle-kisser** *n.* [1990s+ a male homosexual.

IN PHRASES

▫ **and no pickles** [late 19C] without a doubt. ▫ **in a pickl** *adj.* **1** [17C+] (*also* **in a pepper-pot**) in a predicament, difficulties. **2** [18C–early 19C] drunk. ▫ **in pickle** *adj.* [th contemporary cure for VD, which involved sitting in a 'sweatir tub'] [late 16C–18C] venereally diseased. ▫ **paddle the pick** *v.* [SE *paddle*, to beat with a paddle] [1960s+] to masturbat ▫ **pump one's pickle** *v.* [1970s–80s] to masturbate.

pickle *v.* **1** [late 18C–19C] to tease, to hoax, to deceiv **2** [20C+] (*US*) to spoil, to wreck, to kill.

IN EXCLAMATIONS

▫ **pickle it!** [1910s+] (*Aus./US*) a general excl. of dismiss forget it! be quiet! ▫ **pickle me bloody agates!** (*also* **pick me daisies! ...nut! ...tit!**) [AGATES *n.*/SE *daisy*/NUT *n.*[1] (1b)/TIT *n* (1)] [1960s+] (*N.Z.*) a general excl. of surprise or disbelief.

pickle and pork *n. see* PICKLED PORK *n.* (3).

pickled *adj.* **1** [late 17C–18C] waggish, roguish [play on *pickle*, i.e. someone who is 'sharp']. **2** [mid-19C+] drunk.

pickled onion *n.* [rhy. sl.] [1980s+] a bunion.

pickled pork *n.* [rhy. sl.] [late 19C+] **1** talk, conversatio **2** chalk. **3** (*also* **pickle and pork, pickling pork**) a walk.

pickle-herring *n.* [ext. of PICKLE *n.* (1)] **1** [17C–mid-19C] a amusing companion, a 'wag'. **2** [18C–mid-19C] (*also* **pick her-ring**) a professional clown, usu. one who accompanies a itinerant quack doctor.

picklepuss *n.* [SE *pickle*, a sour gherkin + PUSS *n.*[2] (1)] [1930s- (*US*) a sour-faced individual.

pickles! *excl.* [PICKLE *n.* (2)] [mid-19C–1900s] a general excl. disbelief: nonsense! rubbish!

pickling pork *n. see* PICKLED PORK *n.* (3).

pickling tub *n.* [visual resemblance] **1** [mid-19C] in pl., high Wellington boots. **2** *see* POWDERING TUB *n.*

picklock *n.* [play on LOCK *n.*[1] (1a)] [17C–19C] the penis.

pick-me-up *n.* **1** [mid-19C+] any form of drink that reliev the physical and mental state of the imbiber, esp. used f those concoctions advertised as curing hangovers. **2** [la 19C+] a person, object or place that has a similar effe **3** [1900s] (*Aus./S.Afr.*) an ambulance. **4** [1920s+] a dr having the same effect as sense 1. **5** [1940s+] (*S.Afr.*) (*a* **pick-up**) a police van, a black maria.

pickney *n.* (*also* **picknee, picknie, picney, picny**) [PICCANIN *n.*] [20C+] (*W.I./UK black*) a young child.

IN COMPOUNDS

▫ **pickney father** *n. see* BABY-FATHER *under* BABY *n.*

pick of the basket *n.* (*also* **pick of the bunch**) [market-st imagery; SE in 20C+] [mid–late 19C] the best, the choicest offer.

picks *n.*[1] [abbr. colloq. SE *the pictures*] [1910s] (*Aus.*) the cinem

picks *n.*[2] *see* PICK *n.*[1] (3).

pickthank *n.* [lit. one who 'picks a thank', i.e. 'curries favour w another, esp. by informing against someone else' (*OED*)] [16 early 19C] a flatterer, a sycophant; a tale-bearer, a tell-tale.

pickthatch *n. see* PICKED-HATCH *n.*

pick-up *n.* **1** in senses of an encounter, sexual or otherwi (**a**) [mid-19C] a confidence trick in which a prostitute lure client to a room or deserted place, where, instead of havi sex, the client is robbed by a male accomplice. (**b**) [mid-19C a casual sex partner, met and seduced without previo introduction. (**c**) [20C+] an arrest but no subsequent crimi charge; thus (*S.Afr.*) *pick-up van*, a police van. (**d**) [1920s someone met in informal circumstances; sex may be involve but not invariably. (**e**) [1930s+] the act of meeting someone informal circumstances, usu. with a sexual relationship in mi **2** in Und. uses. (**a**) [1920s–60s] robbery, theft; thus *at the pi* *up*, working as a professional thief. (**b**) [1920s+] an arrest; an arrest warrant. (**c**) [1930s] payment for undertaking a criminal job. (**d**) [1940s] (*UK Und.*) a criminal who specializes in taking unguarded luggage, e.g. at railway stations. **3** [1920s+] as a stimulant. (**a**) (*drugs*) a dose or injection of narcotics; the feeling that follows. (**b**) a restorative drink. **4** *see* PICK-ME-UP *n.* (5).

pick-up *adj.* [PICK UP *v.* (1a)] [1950s+] referring to a place or a person who is used for casual sex.

pick up *v.* **1** to meet or encounter. (**a**) [mid-17C+] to accost for possible sex; also *pick up a cull*. (**b**) [18C+] (*UK/US Und.*) to accost or enter into conversation with the intention of practising a hoax or confidence trick on someone. (**c**) [19C–1940s] to meet, with no sexual overtones involved. **2** in Und. uses. (**a**) [late 18C–1920s] to rob, to steal. (**b**) [early–mid-19C] to cheat, to deceive; to rob by deception. (**c**) [mid-19C+] to arrest. (**d**) [20C+] (*UK police*) to spot and shadow a suspect. **3** in fig. senses. (**a**) [mid-19C–1950s] to find fault with, to criticize. (**b**) [mid-19C+] (*US*) to tidy or clean up, to put in order. (**c**) [1910s–20s] to be stimulated or enlivened. (**d**) [1940s+] to resume where one has left off. (**e**) [1950s+] to stimulate, to invigorate. **4** (*US*) in senses of intellectual activity. (**a**) [1910s–20s] to set in motion, to start. (**b**) [1940s+] to understand. (**c**) [1940s+] to do, to act, to perform. (**d**) [1950s+] to notice. **5** [1930s+] in drug uses. (**a**) to use narcotics or cannabis. (**b**) to give someone else drugs. (**c**) to buy or sell drugs. (**d**) to resume taking narcotics after a period of abstinence.

(IN COMPOUNDS)

❑ **picking-up lay** *n.* (*also* **pick-up lay**) [LAY *n.*[3] (1)] [mid-19C] (*UK Und.*) posing as a prostitute but actually luring a victim into the hands of a male companion, who would beat and rob him. ❑ **picking-up moll** *n.* [MOLL *n.* (2)] [mid–late 19C] (*UK Und.*) a woman who poses as a prostitute only to rob or lure a victim into the hands of her male companion, who would beat and rob him.

(IN PHRASES)

❑ **pick up a flat** *v.* [FLAT *n.*[2] (1)] **1** [late 18C–19C] of a prostitute, to meet a client. **2** [19C] to accost the potential victim of a confidence trick. ❑ **pick up on** *v.* (*orig. US*) **1** [1940s+] to notice, to understand. **2** [1950s] to get hold of, esp. drugs; to visit. ❑ **pick up one's crumbs** *v.* [mid-19C] **1** to recover from an illness, esp. to begin eating after a period of fasting. **2** to begin enjoying improved circumstances. ❑ **pick up pennies** *v.* [1970s+] (*US gay*) of a male prostitute, to accept a minimal sum for one's services. ❑ **pick up the soap for** *v.* [the posture necessarily adopted for both activities] [1940s+] (*gay*) to permit oneself to be sodomized. ❑ **pick up with** *v.* [1960s] (*Aus.*) to establish a relationship.

pick up sticks *n.* [rhy. sl.] [20C+] the number six.

pick up yourself! *excl.* [20C+] (*W.I.*) get up and get out!

picky *n. see* PICCY *n.*

picky-picky *adj.* [SE *picky* + redup.] [1950s] (*W.I. Rasta*) **1** finicky or choosy, esp. in eating. **2** used of uncombed hair just starting to turn into dreadlocks.

picky-picky head *n.* (*also* **picky head**) [1960s] (*W.I.*) very short hair growing close to the scalp in small balls of fluff.

picney/picny *n. see* PICKNEY *n.*

pics *n. see* PIC *n.* (4).

picthatch *n. see* PICKED-HATCH *n.*

picture *n.* **1** [mid-17C–19C] a face. **2** [early 19C+] (*also* **movie**) anything or anyone considered very pleasing, shocking or amusing to the viewer, e.g. *you look a picture, she looks a picture, a picture of good health*. **3** [mid-19C] (*US Und.*) in pl., counterfeit notes. **4** [mid-19C] in pl., playing cards. **5** [1920s+] (*orig. milit.*) a situation. **6** [1990s+] (*US*) a currency note, money [the pictures of US presidents printed on the different denominations of dollar bills].

(IN PHRASES)

❑ **get one's pictures** *v.* [? a picture on an identity card] [1920s–40s] to be dismissed from a job. ❑ **lawful picture** *n.* [the engraving on coins or picture on notes] [17C–18C] a coin; usu. in pl., money.

(IN EXCLAMATIONS)

❑ **take a picture!** [1980s+] (*US campus*) stop staring!

picture of... *n.*

SE in slang uses

(IN PHRASES)

❑ **picture of Abe (Lincoln)** *n.* [the face of *Abraham Lincoln* (1809–65), 16th president of the US, printed on the bills] [1950s+] (*US*) a $5 bill. ❑ **picture of George** *n.* [the face of *George Washington* (1732–1799), 1st president of the US, printed on the bills] [1960s] (*US*) a $1 bill. ❑ **picture of ill-luck** *n.* [the ill luck comes since 9d is 'not the whole shilling'] [late 18C–early 19C] ninepence. ❑ **picture of the Queen** *n.* [the face of *Elizabeth II* (b.1926), printed on banknotes] [2000s] paper money.

piddle *n.* [PIDDLE *v.* (1)] **1** [mid-19C+] urine; thus adj. *piddly*, redolent of urine. **2** [mid-19C+] an act of urination. **3** [1910s] nonsense. **4** [1980s] weak beer.

(IN PHRASES)

❑ **all piddle and wind like the barber's cat** *see* ALL PISS AND WIND (LIKE THE BARBER'S CAT) *under* PISS *n.*

piddle *v.* [mid-16C SE *piddle*, to trifle, to work or act in a petty or insignificant way. The ext. to urination began as a childish expression (? implying the insignificant amount of urine produced). The phrs. below therefore refer back to the 16C use, even if the assumption is of the later one] **1** [late 18C+] to urinate. **2** [late 19C+] to rain, with an implication of drizzle rather than heavy rain.

(IN PHRASES)

❑ **piddle about** *v.* (*also* **piddle around**) [*see* main ety. above] [20C+] **1** to waste time, to mess about. **2** to waste, to squander. ❑ **piddle along** *v.* [*see* main ety. above] [1930s+] lit. or fig., to wander, to go. ❑ **piddle away** *v.* [*see* main ety. above] [1950s+] to waste, to squander.

piddly-squat *n. see* DIDDLY-SQUAT *n.*[1].

pie *n.* **1** in sexual contexts, like the foodstuff as 'sweet' and 'good enough to eat'. (**a**) [mid-16C–17C; 1930s+] (*orig. US*) the vagina. (**b**) [mid-16C–18C] a woman. (**c**) [1960s] a term of affection. (**d**) [1960s+] (*US campus*) an attractive, sexually desirable woman; also used derog. **2** in sense of a 'pie' that can be cut up or distributed. (**a**) [late 18C–1910s] political or other patronage or favours. (**b**) [mid-19C+] (*orig. US*) a treat, a bribe, something highly desirable. (**c**) [20C+] money. **3** [late 19C+] (*orig. US*) that which is easy or enjoyable. (**a**) anything easy or simple; often as *easy as pie, good as pie, sweet as pie*. (**b**) something to be appreciated; usu. in phr. *as pie*. **4** [1990s+] (*US black/drugs*) 1kg of cocaine [the dealer will most likely 'slice it up' into smaller weights].

SE in slang uses

(IN COMPOUNDS)

❑ **pie-back** *n. see* SWEETBACK (MAN) *n.* ❑ **pie-can** *n.* [1900s–40s] **1** a fool, a simpleton. **2** a second-rate object. ❑ **pie-card** *n.* (*US*) **1** [1900s–20s] a ticket that entitles one to a meal from a *pie card mission*. **2** [1920s–60s] one who begs for a meal. **3** [1920s–60s] a union-card, esp. when used as a credential for begging. **4** [1920s–60s] the holder of a union-card. ❑ **piechopper** *n.* [1950s] (*US black*) the mouth. ❑ **pie-eater** *n.* (*also* **pie-biter**) [the negative stereotype of a greedy person who sees no further than immediate gratification] [late 19C+] (*mainly Aus.*) **1** an insignificant person. **2** one who is greedy for material possessions. **3** a fool, a simpleton. **4** a small-time criminal. ❑ **pie-eyed** *adj.* [one's wide eyes supposedly resemble a circular *pie*] **1** [20C+] drunk. **2** [1920s] exhausted. **3** [1940s] astonished, amazed. **4** [1980s+] under the influence of drugs. ❑ **pie floater** *n. see* FLOATER *n.*[1] (1d). ❑ **pie hole** *n.* [var. on CAKEHOLE *under* CAKE *n.*[1]] [1980s+] (*US teen*) the mouth. ❑ **pie out** *v.* [PIE-EYED above] [1970s] (*US campus*) to become drunk. ❑ **pie shop** *n.* [the popular belief that when in 1842 one Blauchard opened a pie shop in London, he used dead dogs as meat] [mid–late 19C] a dog. ❑ **pie wagon** *n.* **1** [20C+] (*US*) a police van, used to transport villains. **2** [1900s] a prison. **3** [1920s–30s] (*US*) a wagon used as sleeping quarters for chaingang workers.

IN PHRASES

❑ **all pie and velvet** *n.* [1910s] (*Aus.*) total pleasure or enjoyment; usu. in negative. ❑ **like pie** *adv.* [? enthusiastic eating] [late 19C] energetically, vigorously. ❑ **pie in the sky** *n.* [the line 'There'll be pie in the sky when you die', in the song 'The Preacher and the Slave' (1911) penned by Joe Hill, leader of the Industrial Workers of the World, a prototype US union] [1910s+] (*orig. US*) fantasies, fond hopes and illusions.

pie *adj.*[1] (*also* **old pie**) **1** [late 19C] (*US*) experienced. **2** [late 19C–1900s] (*Aus./US*) small-time, insignificant, second-rate. **3** [late 19C+] very easy [abbr. of EASY AS PIE *under* EASY AS… *adj.*].

pie *adj.*[2] [Maori *pai*, good] [1940s+] (*N.Z.*) good at, expert in.

pie and liquor *n.* [rhy. sl.; SE *liquor*, the green parsley gravy that accompanies pie and mash] [20C+] a vicar.

pie and mash *n.* [rhy. sl.] **1** [1970s+] money [SE *cash*]. **2** [1990s+] an act of urination [SLASH *n.* (2a)].

pie and mash *adj.* [rhy. sl.] [1990s+] showy, ostentatious [FLASH *adj.* (1a)].

pie and one *n.* [rhy. sl.] [20C+] **1** a son. **2** the sun.

piebald *n.* [1900s–50s] (*Aus.*) a half-caste.

IN COMPOUNDS

❑ **piebald pony** *n.* [1920s+] (*Aus.*) a half-caste white/Aboriginal child.

piebald *adj.* [1900s] (*Aus.*) using blacks and whites as fellow-workers.

piebald *v.* [late 19C] to give a black eye; thus *piebald eye*, a black eye.

piece *n.* **1** as an individual. (**a**) [mid-16C+] a woman, esp. when appraised sexually [i.e. a 'piece of meat']. (**b**) [late 18C+] a man. (**c**) [1950s+] (*gay*) a man, in a sexual context. (**d**) [1960s+] one's body, in the context of violence. **2** in financial or commercial senses. (**a**) [17C+] (*also* **peece, pieces**) a sum of money, a coin worth £1 and 2 shillings. (**b**) [late 19C+] a share. (**c**) [1920s+] a commission, a percentage. **3** as a lit. or fig. weapon or tool. (**a**) [mid-19C+] a gun [SE late 16C–mid-19C, then sl.]. (**b**) [mid-19C+] (*also* **fowling piece**) the penis. (**c**) [1910s] (*US*) a hypodermic syringe [play on GUN *n.*[1] (5)]. (**d**) [1970s+] a knife. **4** abbr. SE *masterpiece*. (**a**) [late 19C] a tattoo. (**b**) [1980s+] (*orig. US*) a major work of graffiti, typically as displayed on a New York City subway train. **5** [20C+] (*Irish/Scot.*) as food. (**a**) a piece of bread and butter. (**b**) a sandwich, a worker's packed lunch; thus *piece-plate*, a sandwich plate; *piece-time*, lunchtime. **6** [1920s+] an act of sexual intercourse. **7** in drug uses. (**a**) [1920s+] (*also* **piece of stuff**) a quantity of heroin, cocaine or morphine, approx. 28g (1oz). (**b**) [1960s+] (*also* **piece of stuff**) an unspecified quantity of drugs. (**c**) [1980s+] a marijuana pipe. **8** [1960s+] something or someone undesirable [abbr. PIECE OF SHIT below]. **9** [1970s] (*US black*) an automobile. **10** [1970s+] (*US black*) in pl., clothes [? SE piece of goods]. **11** [1980s+] (*US campus*) a hairdo [abbr. SE *hairpiece*]. **12** [1990s+] (*US prison*) a jail sentence. **13** see PIECE OF THE ACTION below.

DERIVATIVES

❑ **pieced** *adj.* [1990s+] deflowered.

IN COMPOUNDS

❑ **piece man** *n.* [1970s] (*US*) a gunman, an armed bodyguard.

IN PHRASES

referring to people in general, as *piece of…*

❑ **piece of cancer** *n.* [1980s+] (*US*) a despicable person. ❑ **piece of chickenshit** *n.* (*also* **piece of camelshit**) [CHICKENSHIT *n.* (2)] [1980s+] (*US campus*) a coward, a weakling. ❑ **piece of entire** *n.* [they are 'entirely' excellent] [mid–late 19C] an admirable person. ❑ **piece of garbage** *n.* (*also* **piece of rot**) [1960s+] (*US*) a despicable person. ❑ **piece of goods** *n.* **14** [late 18C+] a person. ❑ **piece of jab** *n.* [SE *jabber*] [1930s] a talkative person. ❑ **piece of meat** *n.* [MEAT *n.*] **1** [late 19C+] (*also* **hunk of meat, piece of pie-meat**) anyone regarded as no more than a physical object, esp. in a sexual context. **2** [1920s] (*US gay*) a penis. ❑ **piece of one's ass** *n.* [ASS *n.* (2)] [1950s+] (*US*) a beating, a thrashing, a punishment. ❑ **piece of piss** *n.* [PISS *n.* (1)] [1920s] a term of contempt. ❑ **piece of poop** *n.* [POOP *n.*[2] (3)] [1980s+] (*Aus.*) a term of contempt. ❑ **piece of rot** *n.* see PIECE OF GARBAGE above. ❑ **piece of shit** *n.* (*also* **piece of crap**) [fig. use of SHIT *n.* (1a)/CRAP *n.*[1] (2)] [1940s+] (*orig. US*) anything or anyone unpleasant, disgusting, of poor quality, e.g. a disliked person, a piece of gross hypocrisy etc. ❑ **piece-of-shit** *adj.* [fig. use of SHIT *n.* (1a)] [1980s+] a general derog. term: disgusting, unattractive, unkempt. ❑ **piece of stockfish** *n.* [early 17C] a contemptible person. ❑ **piece of work** *n.* **1** [mid-19C] a fuss, a 'to-do'. **2** [20C+] a person; usu. qualified by an adj., e.g. *nasty piece of work*, an unpleasant person. **3** [1960s+] a formidable person. **4** [1970s+] one who is considered odd or eccentric by the speaker. **5** [2000s] an attractive woman.

referring to objects, as *piece of…*

❑ **piece of cake** *n.* (*also* **piece of meat, lump of cake, …duff, slice of cake**) [1930s+] anything seen as simple, lucky, easily achieved, no bother. ❑ **piece of iron** *n.* see IRON *n.* (3b). ❑ **piece of piss** *n.* [PISS *n.* (1)] [1940s+] (*orig. RAF*) anything seen as supremely easy. ❑ **piece of pudding** *n.* [late 19C] an example of good luck; a welcome change in circumstances. ❑ **piece of resistance** *n.* [a pun on SE *resistance*/Fr. *pièce de résistance*, the supreme example, esp. the best dish in a meal] [1930s+] (*Aus.*) constipation. ❑ **piece of seven** *n.* [1970s] (*US black*) any one of the seven days of the week. ❑ **piece of stuff** *n.* see senses 7a and 7b above. ❑ **piece of the action** *n.* (*also* **piece**) [ACTION *n.* (4)] [1960s+] (*orig. US*) a share in what is going on, usu. monetary, criminal or gambling. ❑ **piece of thick** *n.* [late 19C] a cake of pressed tobacco. ❑ **piece of work** *n.* see WORK *n.* (1).

meaning a woman, usu. promiscuous, as *piece of…*

❑ **piece of ass** *n.* (*also* **piece of arse, …butt, …cock, …cunt, …gash, …hump, …pussy, …snatch, …trim, chunk of fanny, hunk of arse, …ass, …butt**) [ASS *n.* (5)/ARSE *n.* (2b)/BUTT *n.*[1] (1d)/COCK *n.*[4] (3)/CUNT *n.* (2)/GASH *n.*[1] (3)/HUMP *n.*[1] (3c)/PUSSY *n.* (2)/SNATCH *n.* (1d)/TRIM *n.* (2)/FANNY *n.*[1] (5)] **1** [1910s+] a woman, not necessarily derog. but invariably from a sexual point of view and usu. dismissive; occas. a man. **2** [1930s+] heterosexual sexual intercourse. **3** [1930s+] hetero- or homosexual anal intercourse [ASS *n.* (2)/ARSE *n.* (1)]. **4** [1950s] (*US Und.*) a passive male homosexual [ASS *n.* (2)/ARSE *n.* (1)]. ❑ **piece of beef** *n.* see BEEF *n.*[1]. ❑ **piece of business** *n.* [1920s] a woman. ❑ **piece of calico** *n.* [CALICO *n.*[1]] [mid–late 19C] an attractive woman. ❑ **piece of femme** *n.* [FEMME *n.* (1)] [1930s] (*US*) sexual intercourse with a woman. ❑ **piece of flesh** *n.* (*also* **piece of honey, piece of skin**) [mid-16C–17C; 20C+] (*US black/W.I.*) a woman, esp. an attractive woman. ❑ **piece of furniture** *n.* (*also* **bedroom furniture, house furniture**) [mid-19C; 1930s+] (*orig. US black*) a woman or girl (in sexual context). ❑ **piece of gash** *n.* see PIECE OF ASS above. ❑ **piece of goods** *n.* (*also* **bale of goods, piece of trade goods**) [late 18C+] a young woman; a flighty young woman who has 'abandoned the proprieties' (Ware). ❑ **piece of hump** *n.* see PIECE OF ASS above. ❑ **piece of magnolia** *n.* [1960s+] (*Can.*) **1** a sexually available woman. **2** sexual intercourse. ❑ **piece of muslin** *n.* see BIT OF MUSLIN *under* BIT *n.*[1]. ❑ **piece of mutton** *n.* see *under* MUTTON *n.* ❑ **piece of pussy** *n.* see PIECE OF ASS above. ❑ **piece of sin** *n.* (*also* **lump of sin**) [early 17C] a young sexually appealing woman. ❑ **piece of skin** *n.* see PIECE OF FLESH above. ❑ **piece of skirt** *n.* [metonymy] [1930s+] a woman, seen as a sex object. ❑ **piece of snatch** *n.* see PIECE OF ASS above. ❑ **piece of strange** *n.* [STRANGE *n.*] [1950s+] an unknown woman, usu. in a sexual context. ❑ **piece of stuff** *n.* [17C–18C] a young woman. ❑ **piece of tail** *n.* [TAIL *n.* (7)] (*US*) **1** [1920s+] a woman, a girl, not necessarily derog. but invariably from a sexual point of view and usu. dismissive. **2** [1920s+] an act of sexual intercourse. **3** [1960s] (*US gay*) a sexual partner [TAIL *n.* (2)]. ❑ **piece of trade** *n.* [TRADE *n.* (1)] [1930s+] **1** a prostitute. **2** (*gay*) a sexual partner. ❑ **piece of trade goods** *n.* see PIECE OF GOODS above. ❑ **piece of trim** *n.* see PIECE OF ASS above.

pertaining to sexual intercourse

❑ **beg for a piece** *v.* (*also* **chase…, get…, look for…**) [20C+] (*W.I.*) to pursue a woman for sex. ❑ **get a piece** *v.* (*also* **get a piece of ass, …of tail**) [PIECE OF ASS above] [1940s+] of a man, to seduce a girl or woman, to have sexual intercourse. ❑ **give**

someone a piece *v.* [1940s+] (*W.I.*) of a woman, to permit casual sexual intercourse. ❑ **have a piece (of)** *v.* [1940s+] of a man, to seduce a woman, to have sexual intercourse. ❑ **house piece** *n.* [mid-19C–1910s] a servant who doubles as a lover. ❑ **ill piece** *n.* [1950s+] (*gay*) an unattractive and therefore unpopular homosexual. ❑ **knock (off) a piece** *v.* [1940s] (*US black*) to have sexual intercourse.

pertaining to money

❑ **light piece** *n.* [the silver, i.e. light colour, of the coins] [late 19C–1920s] (*US tramp*) a dime (10 cents) or quarter (25 cents). ❑ **piece off** *v.* [1920s+] (*US*) to bribe, to pay off, to give out a 'piece' of cash. ❑ **piece up** *v.* **1** [20C+] (*US Und.*) to divide up the spoils of a robbery. **2** [1950s+] (*drugs*) to divide a large amount of a drug into smaller, saleable pieces. **3** [1990s+] to give someone a share. ❑ **pull in the pieces** *v.* [mid-19C–1920s] to make a good wage.

SE in slang uses

IN PHRASES

❑ **do a piece of work** *v.* [20C+] (*US*) to murder, to kill. ❑ **take a piece out of** *v.* [1940s+] (*Aus.*) **1** to scold, to reprimand severely. **2** to tease. ❑ **this piece** *n.* [2000s] (*US teen*) a place.

pieces of eight *n.* [rhy. sl.] [20C+] weight.

pie-face *n.* **1** [late 19C+] a person with a round or blank face, a stupid person. **2** [1980s] (*Aus.*) an Asian [the cuts in a pie-crust that supposedly resemble slanted Asian eyes].

pie-faced *adj.* (*also* **dish-faced**) [PIE-FACE *n.*] [20C+] a general insult: stupid and unattractive.

piel *n.* [Afk. *piel*, the penis] [2000s] (*S.Afr.*) the penis.

pieman *n.*[1] [PIE *n.* (1a)] [mid-17C] a lecher.

pieman *n.*[2] [the pieman's cry 'Hot pies, toss or buy! Toss or buy!'] **1** [mid-19C+] the player who shouts out in pitch and toss. **2** [1900s] the game of pitch and toss.

piepiejoller *n.* (*also* **pippiejoller**) [Afk. sl. *piepie*, a penis + JOL *v.* (4) + sfx *-er*, lit. 'one who has fun with his penis'] [1970s+] (*S.Afr.*) an adolescent.

pierce the hogshead *v.* [early 17C] to have sexual intercourse, esp. to deflower a virgin.

pies *n.* [? rhy. sl.] [1940s] (*US black*) the eyes.

piesa *n. see* PAISA *n.*

piffed *adj.* (*also* **piffled**) [? one's drunken spluttering] [20C+] (*US*) drunk.

piffin bridge *n.* [ety. unknown; ? link to Lancashire dial. *piff*, a puff of wind] [1990s+] the perineum on a man.

piffle-jaw *n. see* PI-JAW *n.*

pifflicated *adj.* [colloq. *piffle*, to talk nonsense + SPIFLICATE *v.*] [1900s–30s] drunk.

pig *n.* **1** as an insult, based on negative stereotyping. (**a**) [mid-16C; 19C+] a general insult denoting unpleasantness, esp. to one who is fat, ugly and/or greedy. (**b**) [1920s–30s] (*US horseracing*) a slow or otherwise useless horse, not to be betted on. (**c**) [1920s+] (*also* **pig stuff**) a fat, unattractive woman. (**d**) [1920s+] (*US campus*) a woman considered to be drunken, promiscuous and sexually available. (**e**) [1950s–70s] (*Can./US*) a prostitute. (**f**) [1960s+] (*drugs*) a greedy consumer of a given drug. **2** as an authority figure. (**a**) [19C+] (*orig. UK Und.*) (*also* **pigman**) a police officer; thus *pigs*, the police as a group; a watchman [Egan's Grose (1823) suggests that a pig's rooting for food is the image behind the TRAP *n.*[1] (3) who 'roots up' the haunts of the PRIG *n.*[1] (2)]. (**b**) [mid-19C–1940s] an informer. (**c**) [1930s+] any conventional person, a member of the Establishment or authorities. (**d**) [1970s+] a prison warder. (**e**) [1980s] (*US black*) a white person. **3** [20C+] a venereal ulcer. **4** a vehicle. (**a**) [20C+] (*US*) a discontinued model of motorcar, a run-down, dilapidated motorcar, a car that looks good but has a small, low-powered engine. (**b**) [1930s] (*US tramp*) a railroad engine. (**c**) [1950s+] (*US black*) a Cadillac. (**d**) [1950s+] (*US*) a large motorcycle, esp. a Harley-Davidson. **5** [1910s] (*US Und.*) a hardware store; the goods it sells [joc. abbr. of SE *pig iron*]. **6** [1920s] (*US prison*) any form of meat. **7** [1930s] (*US Und.*) a dollar. **8** [1930s] (*US tramp*) a hot water bottle. **9** [1980s+] (*N.Z.*) a flagon of beer. **10** *see* BLIND PIG *n.*

IN COMPOUNDS

❑ **pig brother** *n.* [BROTHER *n.* (2)] [1960s+] (*US black*) any black who informs against their own people to the (white) police. ❑ **pig heaven** *n.* **1** [1960s+] a fantasy paradise that would delight the gross rather than the fastidious. **2** [1970s+] (*US black*) a police station. ❑ **pigman** *n. see* sense 2a above. ❑ **pig-out** *n.* [PIG OUT *under* PIG *v.*[1]] [1990s+] (*orig. US*) an orgy of eating. ❑ **pigpen** *n.* **1** [20C+] (*US*) any dirty, unpleasant place. **2** [1970s] a police station. ❑ **pig stuff** *n. see* sense 1c above. ❑ **pig wagon** *n.* [1990s+] a police van.

IN PHRASES

❑ **dance in the pig trough** *v. see under* DANCE *v.* ❑ **make a pig of oneself** *v.* (*also* **make a hog of oneself**) [1920s+] (*orig. US*) to act in a gluttonous manner, to be extremely greedy.

SE in slang uses

IN COMPOUNDS

❑ **pig-eater** *n.* [19C] a general term of affection. ❑ **pigface** *n.* [1940s] a general term of abuse; the assumption is of ugliness. ❑ **pig-fucker** *n.* [FUCKER *n.* (3)] [1930s+] (*US*) a worthless, very unpleasant person. ❑ **pig-fucking** *adj.* [1980s] worthless, unpleasant. ❑ **pig iron** *n.* [joc. use; note the low value of SE *pig iron*] **1** [late 18C] (*US*) an order of sausages. **2** [1920s] alcohol, often cheap and unpleasant. **3** [1980s+] (*Irish*) fun, devilment, amusement; usu. as *for the pig-iron*, for the fun of it. ❑ **pig-iron** *adj.* [the low value of SE *pig iron*] [1960s] terrible, useless, rubbish, a general negative. ❑ **pig-iron dump** *n.* [1920s] (*US*) a hardware store. ❑ **pig jump** *v.* [late 19C–1940s] (*Aus.*) of a horse, to jump with all four legs in the air at once; ext. to a jumping human. ❑ **pig meat** *n.* [MEAT *n.* (1)] (*US black*) **1** [1920s–30s] sexual intercourse. **2** [1920s+] a young woman, esp. an attractive one; a sexually attractive young man. **3** [1930s+] a promiscuous woman; a prostitute. **4** [1970s+] (*US gay*) an underage boy. ❑ **pigmouth** *n. see* PIGGER *n.* ❑ **pig-muck** *n.* [1950s] a general derog.; euph. for CRAPPY *adj.* (5) or SHITTY *adj.*[1] (2). ❑ **pig party** *n.* [1950s–80s] an orgy, a gang-rape. ❑ **pigpen Irish** *n.* [1910s–30s] (*US*) lower-class, poor Irish. ❑ **pig puncher** *n.* [on pattern of COW-PUNCHER *n.*] [1900s] (*US*) a pig farmer. ❑ **pig room** *n.* [? PIG OUT *under* PIG *v.*[1]] [1970s+] (*US gay*) an orgy room. ❑ **pig root** *v.* [SE *pig-root*, for a horse to buck violently with its hind legs] [1900s–10s] (*Aus.*) to ride. ❑ **pig's arse** *n.* [ARSE *n.* (1)] [1970s+] **1** a difficult or messy situation. **2** (*Irish*) (*also* **pig's ass, pig's behind**) a contemptible person [ASS *n.* (2)/BEHIND *n.* (1)]. ❑ **pig's breakfast** *n. see* DOG'S DINNER *n.* ❑ **pig sconce** *n.* [SE *sconce*, the head] [mid-17C–19C] a stubborn fool, a 'pig-headed' person. ❑ **pig's ear** *n.* (*also* **pig's diddy**) [? euph. for PIG'S ARSE above/DIDDY *n.*[3]] [1950s+] a mess, chaos; usu. as *make a pig's ear of*. ❑ **pig's eye** *n.* **1** [mid-19C] in cards, the ace of diamonds. **2** [late 19C] (*also* **pig's-eye-in-a-bottle**) a term of abuse. **3** [1930s–50s] (*Can.*) *the pig's eye*, something excellent, outstanding, first-rate. ❑ **pig's foot** *n.* [the forked end resembles a pig's foot] [mid-19C] (*US Und.*) a forked crowbar. ❑ **pig-sick** *adj.* [1960s+] furious, enraged; thus *pig-sick of*, infuriated by, incapable of tolerating. ❑ **pigskin** *n. see* separate entry. ❑ **pig's scream** *n. see* BEE'S KNEES *n.* ❑ **pigsticker** *n. see* separate entry. ❑ **pigsticking** *n. see* separate entry. ❑ **pig strip** *n.* [1930s] (*US*) bacon. ❑ **pigstyle** *adv.* [1980s+] (*US black*) living in filthy circumstances. ❑ **pig sweat** *n.* [20C+] (*US*) **1** beer. **2** inferior 'rotgut' bourbon. ❑ **pig's whiskers** *n. see* CAT'S WHISKERS *n.* ❑ **pig's whisper** *n. see* separate entry. ❑ **pig's whistle** *n.* [mid-19C] a very short time. ❑ **pigswill** *n.* [20C+] nonsense, rubbish; thus excl. *pigswill!* rubbish! ❑ **pigtail** *n. see* separate entry. ❑ **pig town** *n.* [1960s] (*US*) the slums. ❑ **pig tranquilizer** *n. see* HORSE TRANQUILIZER *under* HORSE *n.*

IN PHRASES

❑ **all around the pig's arse there is pork** [1980s] (*N.Z.*) a phr. of resignation, acceptance. ❑ **drive (one's) pigs to market/the pigs home** *v. see under* DRIVE *v.*[1]. ❑ **go to pigs and whistles** *v.* [Scot. *pigs and whistles*, 'a mass of foolish, inconvenient furniture or nick-nacks' (*EDD*)] [late 18C–mid-19C] (*Scot.*) to be ruined financially. ❑ **have boiled pig at home** *v.*

[according to Grose (1785), an allusion to a 'well-known' (but unspecified) poem and story] [late 18C–early 19C] to be the master in one's own home. ❑ **have pigs in one's belly** *v.* [early 18C] to be incompetent. ❑ **in pig** *adj.* [joc. use of SE, which refers only to swine] [1940s+] pregnant. ❑ **in the pig's a.h.** *see* A.H. *n.* ❑ **is a pig's pussy pork?** (*also* **is a pig's ass pork?**) [1960s+] (*US*) the response to a question to which the answer is definitely in the affirmative. ❑ **on the pig's back** (*also* **on the pig's ear**) [trans. of Erse *ar mhuin na muice*, referring to an amulet shaped like a pig, supposedly a source of good luck] [late 19C+] (*Irish/Aus./N.Z*) living in luxury, living well, in good fortune; thus *home on the pig's back*, very contented, happily or successfully placed, having arrived at a successful conclusion. ❑ **pig between the sheets** *n.* [1940s] (*US*) a ham sandwich. ❑ **pig's-eye-in-a-bottle** *n. see* PIG'S EYE above. ❑ **pig's vest with buttons** *n.* [1930s] (*US tramp*) sow belly, or any fat bacon. ❑ **stuff a fat pig in the arse** *v. see* GREASE A FAT SOW IN THE ARSE *under* GREASE *v.*[1].

IN EXCLAMATIONS

❑ **pig's arse!** *see* separate entry. ❑ **pig's ear!** *see* PIG'S ARSE! *excl.*

pig *adj.* [PIG *n.* (2)] **1** [1970s+] pertaining to the police. **2** [1980s] (*US*) pertaining to the the white Establishment.

pig *v.*[1] **1** [late 17C+] to live in a slovenly manner. **2** [1950s] to provide food. **3** [1970s+] to overeat.

IN PHRASES

❑ **pig down** *v.* [1980s] to eat hurriedly and greedily. ❑ **pig in** *v.* **1** [late 17C+] to share a home; usu. as *pig in with*. **2** [20C+] to gorge oneself; often as exhortation *pig in!* ❑ **pig it** *v.* **1** [1900s–30s] to renege. **2** [2000s] to prosper. ❑ **pig out** *v.* (*also* **pig it**) **1** [mid-19C; 1930s] to die. **2** [mid-19C+] (*also* **pig up**) to overeat massively; ext. as *pig out on* (a food or drink). **3** [1970s+] (*also* **pig up**) to overindulge in anything. **4** [1990s+] to treat someone to a (large) meal.

pig *v.*[2] [? due to the arrival of a PIG *n.* (2a)] [mid-19C+] (*US Und.*) to run off.

pig- *pfx* [late 19C+] a general intensifier, usu. implying extremes of ignorance, dirt etc.

pig and roast *n.* [rhy. sl.] [1940s+] toast.

Pig and Tinder-box *n.* [a former smithy, it was converted to a tavern in 1760 and was a major 19C London coaching terminus] [mid-19C] the Elephant and Castle tavern in south London.

pi-gas *n. see* PI-JAW *n.*

pigeon *n.*[1] **1** as a woman. (**a**) [late 16C+] a young woman. (**b**) [1990s+] (*US black*) a woman who trades sex for drugs. (**c**) [1990s+] (*US campus*) a lazy, worthless woman. (**d**) [2000s] (*US teen*) a promiscuous young woman. (**e**) [2000s] a woman's breast. (**f**) [2000s] (*US teen*) an unattractive young woman. **2** in Und. uses. (**a**) [late 16C+] (*orig. UK Und.*) one who is susceptible to a confidence trick or other variety of fraud. (**b**) [late 18C–mid-19C] (*UK Und.*) 'Pigeons – sharpers who, during the drawing of the lottery, wait ready mounted, near Guildhall, and as soon as the first two or three numbers are drawn, which they receive from a confederate, ride, i.e. 'fly', with them to some distant insurance office where there is another of the gang, commonly a decent looking woman; to her he secretly gives the numbers, which she insures for a considerable sum' (Grose, 1796). (**c**) [mid–late 19C] (*UK/US Und.*) a professional gambler. **3** [mid-19C+] (*orig. US*) an informer [abbr. STOOL-PIGEON *n.*[1] (1)]. **4** [1950s–70s] (*US*) a person, esp. as a target for murder. **5** *see* BLUE PIGEON *n.* (2). **6** *see* YARDBIRD *n.*[2].

IN COMPOUNDS

❑ **pigeon artist** *n.* [ARTIST *n.* (1)] [1960s] (*US Und.*) a confidence trickster. ❑ **pigeon-cracking** *n.* [CRACK *v.*[2] (2c)] [mid-19C] stealing lead from the roofs of buildings. ❑ **pigeon drop** *n. see* separate entry.

IN PHRASES

❑ **blue pigeon** *n. see* separate entry. ❑ **dead pigeon** *n. see under* DEAD *adj.* ❑ **fly the pigeon** *v. see* FLY A BLUE PIGEON *under* BLUE PIGEON *n.*

SE in slang uses

IN COMPOUNDS

❑ **pigeon-livered** *adj.* [17C–early 19C] cowardly. ❑ **pigeon pair** *n.* [the pigeon's brood is usu. one male, one female] **1** [late 19C] a family whose children are a boy (born first) and a girl. **2** [late 19C+] any male and female pair. ❑ **pigeon's milk** *n.* **1** [mid-19C–1900s] the subject of a fool's errand which apprentices are sent on, trad. on 1 April. **2** [2000s] (*N.Z.*) good liquor. ❑ **pigeon-'tomach** *n.* [play on SE *pigeon-chested*] [20C+] (*W.I.*) a woman with larger than average breasts.

IN PHRASES

❑ **pigeon on** *v.* [the image of a flying pigeon defecating on the unsuspecting human] [1940s] (*Aus.*) to drop something on (someone) from above.

pigeon *n.*[2] [corruption of SE *pidgin*, concern, affair] **1** [20C+] one's concern, a problem. **2** [1940s] one's choice or preference.

IN PHRASES

❑ **mind one's own pigeon** *v.* [20C+] (*Aus./N.Z.*) to mind one's own business.

pigeon *v.*[1] [PIGEON *n.*[1] (2a)] [late 17C–mid-19C] to trick, to hoax, to deceive.

pigeon *v.*[2] [PIGEON *n.*[1] (3)] [1950s–60s] (*US*) to act as an informer.

pigeon and doves *n.* [rhy. sl.] [20C+] gloves.

pigeon drop *n.* [PIGEON *n.*[1] (2a)] [mid-19C+] (*US Und.*) a confidence trick that involves dropping a wallet where a victim can find it or a scheme in which the con-man tells the victim that they have found a large sum of money and, if the victim will advance some money as a show of good faith, they can have a share in the 'windfall'.

IN COMPOUNDS

❑ **pigeon dropper** *n.* [1940s] (*US Und.*) a confidence trickster. ❑ **pigeon dropping** *n.* [1940s] (*US Und.*) playing any form of confidence trick.

pigeonhole *n.* [SE *pigeonhole*, a small hole or recess] **1** [late 16C–17C] (*UK Und.*) the stocks. **2** [late 19C–1900s] the vagina.

piggen de wiggen *n. see* PIG WIDGEON *n.*

pigger *n.* (*also* **pigmouth**) [PIG *n.* (1)] [20C+] (*US black*) a very fat woman.

piggery *n.* **1** [mid-19C+] (*US*) a squalid drinking establishment. **2** [late 19C+] a room that is rarely cleaned or tidied but which is very much the private concern of its occupant.

pigging *adj.* [20C+] **1** an intensifier; euph. for FUCKING *adj.* (1). **2** (*Irish*) filthy.

piggot *n. see* PIGOT *n.*

piggy *n.* [1980s+] (*Aus. prison*) one who has been jailed for bestiality.

piggy *adj.* **1** [late 19C–1950s] (*Aus.*) unpleasant. **2** [1970s+] (*US gay*) sexually abandoned [stereotype of porcine sexuality].

piggybacking *n.* **1** [1980s] the occupation by a dealer of several floors in a building; when one is raided others are still available. **2** [2000s] (*US drugs*) the simultaneous injection of two drugs.

piggy bank *n.* [rhy. sl. = WANK *n.* (1)] [1960s+] masturbation.

pig in the middle *n.* [rhy. sl. = PIDDLE *n.* (2)] [20C+] an act of urination.

Pig Island *n.* [the introduction of pigs to New Zealand by Captain Cook] [20C+] (*Aus./N.Z.*) New Zealand.

DERIVATIVES

❑ **Pig Islander** *n.* [20C+] (*Aus./N.Z.*) a New Zealander.

Pigopolis *n. see* PORKOPOLIS *n.*

pigot *n.* (*also* **piggot**) [proper name of Richard *Pigott* (c.1828–89), the forger of the Parnell papers] [late 19C] a flagrant lie; usu. as *piggotted*, cheated, fooled.

p.i.g.s. *n.* [abbr.] [1990s+] (*US*) *Poles*, *Italians*, *Greeks* and *Slavs*.

pigs *n.* see PIG'S (EAR) *n.*

pigs! *excl.* see PIG'S ARSE! *excl.*

pig's arse *n.*[1] [rhy. sl.] [20C+] (*Aus.*) a glass.

pig's arse *n.*[2] *see under* PIG *n.*

pig's arse! *excl.* (*also* **pigs! pig's ass! pig's bum! pig's ear!**) [ARSE *n.* (1)/ASS *n.* (2)/BUM *n.*[1] (1)/SE *ear*] [1910s+] a contemptuous excl.

IN EXCLAMATIONS

❑ **in a pig's arse!** (*also* **in a pig's! in a pig's butt! ...ear! ...eye! ...gizzard! ...hole! ...kapooch! ...navel! ...neck! ...patrot! ... pink pyjamas! ...poke! ...prick! ...snout! ...tit! ...tonsil! ... valise! ...wig!**) [US rural catchphrase *in the pig's ass*, referring to bestiality and, as such, the subject of a variety of coarse jokes, which depend on the mistaken orifice (the anus rather than the vagina) and the mistaken object of affection (the pig rather than the woman); ARSE *n.* (1)/BUTT *n.*[1] (1a)/HOLE *n.*[1] (1a)/PRICK *n.* (1)/TIT *n.*[2] (1)] [mid-19C+] (*orig. US*) completely impossible, absolutely not! I don't believe you! go away!

pig's Christmas parcel! *excl.* [rhy. sl. = *pig's* ARSEHOLE *n.* (1)] [1940s+] (*N.Z.*) a general excl. of annoyance.

pig's (ear) *n.* [rhy. sl.] **1** [late 19C+] beer. **2** [1960s] (*Aus.*) a year.

pig's fry *n.* [rhy. sl.] [1930s+] a tie.

pig's fry *v.* [rhy. sl.] [1930s+] to try.

pigskin *n.* **1** [late 19C] a saddle; thus horseracing. **2** [20C+] (*US campus*) a football.

IN COMPOUNDS

❑ **pigskin artist** *n.* [-ARTIST *sfx*] [1940s] (*Aus.*) a jockey.

pigsnyes *n.* (*also* **birdsnies, pinckany**) [SE *pig's eyes*, small eyes; ? the implication is of a pig, greedy, in this case, for sex] [late 14C–early 19C] a coarse term of endearment used to a woman.

pigsticker *n.* [note WW1 Aus. milit. *pigstabber*, a bayonet] **1** [late 19C–1940s] a pig-butcher. **2** [late 19C+] (*also* **pig stabber**) any form of sharpened, stabbing weapon, e.g. a lance, a bayonet, a large knife etc. **3** [1970s] a general term of abuse.

pigsticking *n.* [1920s+] (*Can.*) sodomy.

pig's trotter *n.* [rhy. sl.] [1990s+] a squatter.

pig's whisper *n.* [note SE *cockstride*, a very short space of time; lit. 'the length of a cock's pace'] **1** [mid-19C] a nearly inaudible whisper, a grunt. **2** [mid-19C+] a very short space of time.

IN PHRASES

❑ **in a pig's whisper** *adv.* [late 18C+] very quickly, immediately.

pigtail *n.* **1** [late 17C–1930s] a roll of coarse tobacco [resemblance]. **2** [early–mid-19C] an old man [a ref. to the fact that some old men still wore their hair in a pigtail, an 18C affectation]. **3** [mid-19C] the penis. **4** [mid-19C–1940s] (*US Und.*) (*also* **John Pigtail**) a Chinese man [the wearing of pigtails by the Chinese]. **5** [mid-19C–1950s] (*Aus.*) a Chinese immigrant, mainly to Australia [the wearing of pigtails by the Chinese].

pigtail *adj.* [late 19C] wearing a pigtail, thus generic for Chinese, e.g. *pigtail brigade, pigtail land, pigtail party*.

IN COMPOUNDS

❑ **pigtail alley** *n.* (*also* **pigtail town**) [late 19C] (*US*) Chinatown in New York City, centred on Mott Street.

pig widgeon *n.* (*also* **piggen de wiggen, pig widgin, pig-wiggen**) [*pig* is used as an intensifier; presumably f. SE *pigwidgen, pig-widgeon*, 'of obscure origin and meaning' (*OED*), although it is either a proper name, as used of a constable by sl. collector Robert Greene (1558–92) or that of a 'fairy knight' as suggested by the writer Michael Drayton (1563–1631); however, note WIDGEON *n.*] [late 17C–early 19C] a fool, a simpleton.

pi-jaw *n.* (*also* **piffle-jaw, pi-gas**) [PI *adj.* + JAW *n.* (2)/GAS *n.*[1] (1a)/SE *piffle*] [late 19C–1940s] (*orig. UK juv.*) an earnest, moralizing lecture, esp. as delivered by parents or teachers; occas. v.

pike *n.*[1] [SE *pike*, a pointed weapon] [late 16C–19C] the penis.

pike *n.*[2] [abbr. SE *turnpike*, initially a toll-gate, thence the 'high road'] **1** [mid-18C–19C] a toll-gate. **2** [mid–late 19C] the toll paid on one; thus *pike, pike-keeper*, one who takes the tolls; *bilk a pike*, cheat the toll-gate keeper. **3** [mid-19C+] a road, a highway.

IN COMPOUNDS

❑ **pike-man** *n.* [mid–late 19C] a toll-keeper.

IN PHRASES

❑ **collar the pike** *v.* [late 19C] (*US*) to walk (from town to town). ❑ **come down the pike** *v.* (*also* **come over the pike**) [late 19C+] (*US*) **1** to appear, to arrive, to happen. **2** in fig. use, implying the passing of time, progression of events. ❑ **give someone the pike** *v.* see GIVE SOMEONE THE BAG *under* BAG *n.*[1]. ❑ **hit the pike** *v.* [1900s] (*US*) **1** to leave. **2** to leave one's job. ❑ **take (someone) down the pike** *v.* [1930s] to defraud; to beat up.

pike *n.*[3] [PIKE *v.*[3]] [1910s–50s] a look.

pike *v.*[1] [fig. uses of SE *turnpike*] **1** [mid-17C–1920s] (*also* **pike off**) to leave, to run off quickly; often as *pike it, pike over*; also to move forward. **2** [late 17C–18C] (*UK Und.*) to die. **3** [2000s] to beg, cadge.

IN PHRASES

❑ **pike on the been** *v.* (*also* **pike on the bene, ...on the Leen**) [BENE *adj.*; ? *Leen* a misprint] [mid-17C–mid-18C] (*UK Und.*) to run away at top speed. ❑ **pike out** *v.* [1980s+] (*Aus.*) to leave an event or a party early.

pike *v.*[2] (*also* **pike out**) [backform. f. PIKER *n.* (2)] [late 19C+] (*US*) to hold back, to shirk, to act cautiously, often in gambling.

IN COMPOUNDS

❑ **pike bet** *n.* [1900s] a small bet.

IN PHRASES

❑ **pike on** *v.* [1980s+] (*N.Z.*) to let down, to disappoint.

pike *v.*[3] [orig. Notts. dial. *pike*; ult. SE *peek*] (*US*) **1** [1900s–40s] (*also* **pike around**) to ask questions. **2** [1900s–50s] (*also* **pike off, pike the eye**) to look at.

piked off *adv.* [PIKE *v.*[1] (1)] [late 17C+] safely escaped.

piker *n.* [PIKE *n.*[2] (3); lit. 'one who walks the turnpikes'. But note *Promptuarium Parvulorum* (1440): *pikar*, a little thief; also note N.Z. agricultural *piker*, a wild bull; all senses fig. uses of sense 1] **1** [mid-19C–1900s] a vagrant, a tramp, a gipsy. **2** [mid-19C+] (*US*) a small-time gambler. **3** [late 19C+] (*orig. US*) a mean, grasping person, one who will not take the least risk, esp. to help others. **4** [late 19C+] an insignificant person. **5** [1900s–20s] (*orig. US*) a lazy person. **6** [1910s–20s] a small-time burglar. **7** [1930s+] a cheat. **8** [1940s] (*Aus.*) a confidence trickster. **9** [1950s] (*Aus.*) an unpleasant, unpopular person; a bore, a 'party pooper'.

DERIVATIVES

❑ **pikish** *adj.* [1950s] (*US*) mean, stingy.

IN COMPOUNDS

❑ **piker joint** *n.* [JOINT *n.* (3b)] [late 19C+] (*US*) a casino or gambling house specializing in the small-time gambler.

piker *adj.* [PIKER *n.* (2)] [1920s–60s] (*US*) esp. in gambling, small-time, petty.

pikestaff *n.* [late 17C–1900s] the penis.

pikey *n.* (*also* **piky, pyky**) [PIKER *n.* (1)/Kentish dial.; ult. PIKE *n.*[2] (3)] **1** [mid-19C+] a vagrant. **2** [2000s] a working-class person, considered loutish and tasteless by their middle-class counterparts.

pikish *adj.* see *under* PIKER *n.*

pikkie *n.*[1] see PICCANINNY *n.*

pikkie *n.*[2] see PICCY *n.*

piky *n.* see PIKEY *n.*

pil *n.* see PILLETIJIE *n.*

pilch *n.* [? 11C–16C SE *pilch*, an outer garment, a wrapper] [1930s–40s] (*US black*) one's residence, a house, a home, an apartment.

pilcher *n.* [? 'one who wears a pilch or leathern jerkin or doublet' or 'one who pilches, a thief' (*OED*); ult. SE *pilchard*] **1** [early–mid-17C] a general term of abuse. **2** [mid-19C] (*UK Und.*) a thief, esp. of handkerchiefs.

pile *n.*[1] **1** [mid-18C+] a large amount of money; thus *make a/one's pile*, to become rich. **2** [mid-19C+] a large amount.

IN PHRASES

❑ **go the whole pile** *v.* [mid-19C] (*US*) to bet all one's assets on a single wager.

SE in slang uses

IN PHRASES

❑ **pile of bricks** *n.* (*also* **pile of stone**) [1940s–60s] (*US black*) a building. ❑ **pile of shit** *n.* (*also* **pile of crap**) [fig. use of SHIT *n.* (1a)/CRAP *n.*[1] (2)] [1950s+] (*orig. US*) anything or anyone unpleasant, disgusting, of poor quality, e.g. a disliked person, a piece of gross hypocrisy etc.

pile *n.*[2] [ROCKPILE *n.* (1)] [1970s] (*US prison*) a prison.

pile *v.* **1** [late 19C] to cost, to amount to [SE *pile up*]. **2** [1910s+] usu. constr. with a prep., to move fast, e.g. *pile off/on, pile in/out*. **3** [1930s+] (*US black/campus*) to have sexual intercourse [one 'makes a heap']. **4** [1970s] (*US campus*) to laze about [one 'makes a heap'].

IN PHRASES

❑ **pile in** *v.* (*also* **pile into, pile on(to)**) (*orig. US*) **1** [late 19C] to attack verbally. **2** [late 19C+] to attack physically, to crash into, to get to work on, to take part in. ❑ **pile up (at)** *v.* [late 19C+] (*US*) to end up (at), esp. of an evening out.

SE in slang uses

IN PHRASES

❑ **pile it higher and deeper** *v.* (*also* **Ph.D., shovel it higher and deeper**) [1970s] (*US*) to boast, to lie. ❑ **pile it on** *v.* **1** [mid-19C–1900s] to perform an act with greater intensity. **2** [late 19C+] to charge a high price. ❑ **pile up some Zs** *v. see* BUST SOME *Z's under* Z *n.*[1].

piled (for French velvet) *phr.* [FRENCH *adj.* (1)] [early 17C] suffering from a venereal disease.

pile drive *v.* [PILE-DRIVER *n.* (1)] [1960s–70s] (*gay*) to have sex with someone.

DERIVATIVES

❑ **pile-driving** *adj.* [1970s] sexually potent.

IN PHRASES

❑ **go pile-driving** *v.* [late 19C] to have sexual intercourse.

pile-driver *n.* [play on SE *piledriver*] **1** [19C; 2000s] the penis. **2** [1930s] (*US tramp*) strong coffee. **3** [1960s–70s] a male homosexual [play on SE *piles*].

pilgarlic *n.* (*also* **peele garlic, peel garlic, pillgarlick**) [SE *peel garlic*, a peeled, thus smooth, garlic clove, and thence a bald-headed man; seen presumably as an outcast] **1** [late 15C–mid-18C; 1990s+] an outcast; often as *poor pilgarlick*, poor me. **2** [16C; 1990s+] (*Irish*) a bald head, a bald-headed man. **3** [1990s+] (*Irish*) a shabbily dressed, sickly-looking person.

pilgrim *n.*[1] **1** [mid-19C] (*Can./N.Z./US*) an early immigrant from Britain to New Zealand. **2** [late 19C+] a person, usu. in the context of a place or country other than their own; also as a term of address. **3** [1920s+] a conventional person.

IN COMPOUNDS

❑ **pilgrim salve** *n.* (*also* **pilgrim's salve**) [16C SE *pilgrim's salve*, an ointment, made mainly of swine's grease and isinglass] [late 17C–early 19C] human excrement. ❑ **pilgrim's staff** *n.* [18C] the penis.

pilgrim *n.*[2] (*also* **advertising pilgrim**) [play on SE + ADVERTISE *v.* (2)] [1960s] (*US gay*) a well-dressed, attractive heterosexual, unaware of the reaction he gains from watching gay men.

pill *n.* **1** as a pill-shaped, i.e. round, object. (**a**) [early 17C+] a cannon-ball, bomb or shell; thus [1950s] *big pill*, the atomic bomb. (**b**) [late 17C; late 19C+] in pl., the testicles. (**c**) [mid-19C] (*US Und.*) a counterfeit coin. (**d**) [late 19C–1900s] in pl., billiards. (**e**) [late 19C+] a bullet. (**f**) [20C+] (*orig. US*) any form of ball, esp. a basketball. **2** [mid-19C] (*UK Und.*) a knife [? when used on a victim/enemy it achieves a 'cure' for one's problem]. **3** in senses of pills being generically unpleasant. (**a**) [mid-19C–1910s] anything unpleasant; suffering, punishment; the term is 'endless in application' (Ware). (**b**) [mid-19C+] an unpleasant person, a weakling, a bore. (**c**) [late 19C] something unfashionable. (**d**) [late 19C; 1950s] a man, a person. (**e**) [1900s] (*US campus*) a hard-working student; a teacher who makes the students work hard. **4** (*drugs*) a portion or measure of a drug. (**a**) [mid-19C–1960s] (*drugs*) a 'pill' of opium. (**b**) [1900s] morphine. (**c**) [1930s+] a pill of heroin. (**d**) [1950s+] (*drugs*) a generic term for any form of barbiturate or amphetamine drug capsule. (**e**) [1950s+] (*orig. US drugs*) a marijuana cigarette. **5** [mid-19C–1920s; 1990s+] (*orig. milit.*) (*also* **pills**) a doctor, a surgeon; one who deals with or dispenses medicines. **6** in sense of 'curing' one's ills. (**a**) [late 19C–1930s] a drink. (**b**) [1910s–60s] a cigarette or cigar; thus *pill mill*, a cigar factory; *pill-smoker*, a cigarette smoker.

DERIVATIVES

❑ **pilled (up)** *adj.* [1960s+] (*drugs*) under the influence of amphetamines or barbiturates. ❑ **pilling** *adj.* [1980s+] (*drugs*) experiencing the effect of some form of pill, e.g. an amphetamine or barbiturate.

IN COMPOUNDS

❑ **pill cooker** *n.* [COOK *v.* (5b)] [1920s–50s] (*drugs*) an opium smoker. ❑ **pill freak** *n.* [-FREAK *sfx*] [1960s+] (*drugs*) a heavy user of pills, e.g. amphetamines, barbiturates. ❑ **pillhead** *n.* [-HEAD *sfx* (4)] [1960s+] (*drugs*) a regular user of amphetamine or barbiturate drugs. ❑ **pill man** *n.* [1960s] (*drugs*) a drug dealer. ❑ **pill mill** *n.* [MILL *n.*[1] (4b)] [1980s+] (*US*) a doctor's surgery, usu. in a ghetto area, in which the bulk of prescriptions are written for drugs which are then sold in the street. ❑ **pill-pad** *n.* [PAD *n.*[2] (2)] [late 19C+] an opium den, a place where opium users can gather to smoke. ❑ **pill-popper** *n.* [POP *v.*[1] (4c)] [1960s+] (*drugs*) a regular user of any drugs in pill form. ❑ **pill-popping** *adj.* [POP *v.*[1] (4c)] [1960s+] (*drugs*) **1** taking pills. **2** addicted to pills. ❑ **pill-shooter** *n.* (*also* **pill-slinger**) [1910s–60s] a doctor. ❑ **pill shop** *n.* [1900s] an opium den.

IN PHRASES

❑ **black pill** *n.* (*also* **green pill**) [the colour of the drug; opium is rolled into a pill for smoking] [20C+] (*drugs*) an opium pill. ❑ **pill up** *v.* [1960s+] (*UK drugs*) to take amphetamines.

IN EXCLAMATIONS

❑ **all pills!** [play on sense 1b above, i.e. BALLS *n.* (1)] [late 19C+] rubbish! nonsense!

SE in slang uses

IN COMPOUNDS

❑ **pill-box** *n. see* separate entry. ❑ **pill driver** *n.* (*also* **pill-monger**) [mid-18C; mid-19C–1900s] a travelling apothecary. ❑ **pill-grinder** *n.* **1** [late 19C] a doctor. **2** [20C+] a pharmacist. ❑ **pill-peddler** *n.* [1920s–30s] a doctor. ❑ **pill-pusher** *n.* (*also* **pill-thrower, pill-twister**) [PUSH *v.* (2c)] [1900s–10s] a doctor. ❑ **pill-roller** *n.* [late 19C+] **1** a pharmacist. **2** a doctor.

IN PHRASES

❑ **drop the pill on** *v. see under* DROP *v.*[1].

pill *v.* [PILL *n.* (1e)] **1** in senses of rejecting or failing someone. (**a**) [mid-19C–1910s] to blackball. (**b**) [1900s–20s] to fail a candidate in an examination. **2** [1910s] (*Aus.*) to shoot dead.

IN PHRASES

❑ **pill up** *v.* [PILL *n.* (3b); image is of ostentation, showiness] [mid-19C] (*US campus*) to get dressed up.

pill and poll *v.* [SE *pillage* + *poll*, to plunder, to despoil] [16C–early 17C; mid-19C] (*UK Und.*) to cheat one's accomplice or partner in crime.

pillar *n.* [1930s–40s] (*US black*) in pl., the human legs.

pillar and post *n.* [rhy. sl.] [20C+] a ghost.

pill-box *n.* **1** joc. use of SE *pill-box* for anything small, circular and box-like. (**a**) [mid-19C] a coffin. (**b**) [mid–late 19C] a pulpit. (**c**) [late 19C–1900s] a soldier's hat. (**d**) [late 19C+] a small brimless hat. **2** [mid–late 19C] (*US*) a revolver, a pistol [PILL *n.* (1e)]. **3** in medical contexts [PILL *n.* (5)]. (**a**) [mid–late 19C] a small carriage [such carriages were typically used by doctors]. (**b**) [late 19C] a doctor [note pre-WW2 London taxi-driver jargon *The Pill-box*, Harley Street, site of many private consulting rooms].

pilletijie *n.* (*also* **pil**) [lit. 'a little pill'; note PILL *n.* (4e)] [1960s+] (*S.Afr. drugs*) a marijuana cigarette.

pillgarlick *n. see* PILGARLIC *n.*

pillicock *n.* (*also* **pillcock, pillie, pillock**) [northern dial.; ult. Norwegian dial. *pill*, the penis + COCK *n.*[3] (1)] **1** [early 14C–19C] the penis. **2** [late 16C–mid-17C] a term of affection for a young boy.

pillion pussy *n.* [SE *pillion* + PUSSY *n.* (2)] [1950s] (*N.Z.*) a young woman who accompanies a motorbike-riding young social outlaw.

pillock *n.* [PILLICOCK *n.* (1)] **1** [1960s+] a general term of abuse. **2** [1970s+] a fool, a simpleton. **3** *see* PILLICOCK *n.*

pillocks *n.* [PILL *n.* (1b) + BALLOCKS *n.* (3)] [late 19C+] nonsense; thus *talk pillocks*, to talk nonsense; *pillocky*, stupid, nonsensical.

IN PHRASES

❑ **pillox around** *v.* [1980s] to annoy, to mess around with.

pillory *n.* [? the placing of bakers who were caught giving false measure in the pillory; the profession was often synon. with fraud] [late 17C–18C] a baker.

pillow *n.* [its padding] [late 19C] (*US*) a boxing glove.

SE in slang uses

IN COMPOUNDS

❑ **pillowcase** *n.* [play on HORSEFEATHERS *n.*] [1920s] (*US*) one who talks nonsense. ❑ **pillow-mate** *n.* [note Hindley, *The Old Book Collector's Miscellany* (1873) 'Serving [...] as a little Side *Pillow*, to render the Yoke of *Matrimony* more easy'] [19C] a prostitute. ❑ **pillow pigeons** *n.* [1940s] (*US black*) bedbugs.

pillow-biter *n.* (*also* **pillow chewer**) [the supposed agonies of anal intercourse] [1960s+] (*orig. Aus.*) **1** a homosexual, usu. the passive partner. **2** (*US prison*) one who has been subjected to homosexual rape. **3** a general term of abuse, irrespective of actual sexual preference.

pillox around *n. see under* PILLOCKS *n.*

pill-pate *n.* [14C–17C SE *pill*, to shave + *pate*, head; f. the tonsure adopted by friars] [mid-16C] a friar.

pills *n. see* PILL *n.* (5).

pilot *n.* **1** [early–mid-19C] a watchman. **2** [late 19C–1930s] (*US*) a cabdriver. **3** [20C+] (*US*) a jockey. **4** [1930s] (*W.I.*) a procurer. **5** *see* SKYPILOT *under* SKY *n.*[2].

IN COMPOUNDS

❑ **pilot cove** *n.* (*also* **pilot bloke**) [COVE *n.* (1)/BLOKE *n.* (3)] [1910s] (*Aus.*) a clergyman.

pimgenet *n.* (*also* **pimginet, pimginnit, pimpgennet**) [? SE *pomegranate*, a fruit that might be seen as being covered in 'pimples'. Halliwell, *Dict. of Archaic and Provincial Words* (1847), cites the 'old saying': 'Nine pimgenets make a pock royal'] [late 17C–early 18C] a prominent, red pimple.

pimp *n.* [? Fr. *pimpreneau*, a scoundrel; *pimpant*, alluring or seducing in outward appearance or dress; or *pimpesouée*, a pretentious woman] **1** [17C] a procurer [began life as sl. but entered SE late 17C]. **2** [early 18C] a prostitute's customer. **3** [18C–early 19C] a piece of wood used for lighting a fire [? play on FIRE *n.* (1)]. **4** one who tells tales. (**a**) [late 19C+] (*Aus./N.Z./S.Afr.*) a police informer. (**b**) [20C+] (*Aus.*) a sneak, a tell-tale. **5** [1940s] a general term of abuse, esp. of a man who does not work for his living. **6** [1940s–70s] (*Aus./US black*) a male prostitute. **7** [1960s] (*US black*) a style of walking, supposedly reminscent of a pimp [but note McCall, *Makes Me Wanna Holler* (1994): 'My Aunt Iris [...] said it [i.e. the pimp] was handed down through generations from the slavery days. [...] Some slaves were forced to walk with a ball and chain attached to one ankle. When they walked they took a regular step with the free leg and sort of hopped on the other to drag the heavy ball and chain']. **8** [1960s+] (*US black/campus*) a fashionable, stylish person. **9** [1980s+] (*US campus*) a man who sustains several relationships at the same time; a womanizer. **10** *see* PIMP DUST below.

DERIVATIVES

❑ **pimpable** *adj.* [2000s] (*US black*) a woman who is a potential prostitute. ❑ **pimping** *adj.* [PIMP *adj.*] **1** [1970s+] (*US campus*) well-dressed. **2** [1970s+] (*US campus*) doing well. **3** [1990s+] a general term of approval. ❑ **pimpish** *adj.* [1970s+] (*US teen*) stylishly dressed. ❑ **pimpmobile** *n.* (*also* **pimpillac**) [-MOBILE *sfx*] [1970s+] a flashy, ostentatious car, potentially the choice of a pimp, but not restricted to such drivers. ❑ **pimptastic** *adj.* [-TASTIC *sfx*] [2000s] (*US black*) fantastic; self-aggrandizing. ❑ **pimpy** *adj.* (*also* **pimpo**) [1940s] (*US*) having the characteristics or personality of a pimp.

IN COMPOUNDS

❑ **pimp-ass** *adj.* [-ASS *sfx*] (*US black*) **1** [1960s+] contemptible. **2** [1990s+] on bad = good model, excellent. ❑ **pimp-boots** *n.* [1970s+] (*US gay*) ankle boots, 'Beatle boots'. ❑ **pimp cane** *n.* [2000s] (*US black*) a cane used orig. by pimps to discipline their prostitutes; latterly in general use to describe a cane used as a weapon, but also purely as a fashion accessory. ❑ **pimp car** *n. see* PIMP RIDE below. ❑ **pimp crazy** *adj.* [-CRAZY *sfx*] [1950s–70s] (*US*) of a prostitute who goes from one sadistic, abusing pimp to another, apparently unable to break the habit. ❑ **pimp dust** *n.* (*also* **pimp**) [SE *dust*/DUST *n.* (6b), based on the assumption that this is the pimp's drug of choice] [1970s] (*US black/drugs*) cocaine. ❑ **pimp fronts** *n.* [FRONT *n.*[1] (11)] [1950s+] (*US black*) a particular style of dress associated with pimps. ❑ **pimp hand** *n.* [2000s] (*US black*) the skills that go to making a successful pimp. ❑ **pimping shoes** *n. see* PIMP SHOES below. ❑ **pimping stick** *n. see* PIMP STICK below. ❑ **pimp kiss** *v.* [2000s] to make a false show of affection. ❑ **pimp oil** *n.* [2000s] (*US black*) a strong perfume. ❑ **pimp playa** *n.* [PLAYER *n.* (2)] [2000s] (*US black*) a man who adopts the trad. pimp style, but may not actually be selling women. ❑ **pimp post** *n.* (*also* **pimp rest**) [1970s+] (*US black*) the arm-rest between driver and passenger in a car. ❑ **pimp ride** *n.* (*also* **pimp car, ...wagon**) [RIDE *n.* (2a)] [1970s+] (*US black*) an expensive car, suitable for a pimp. ❑ **pimp roll** *n.* **1** [1970s+] (*US Und.*) a strutting style of walk affected by US black pimps. **2** *see under* ROLL *n.* ❑ **pimp shades** *n.* (*also* **pimp tints**) [SHADE *n.*[1] (7)/TINTS *n.*] [1960s+] a style of dark glasses affected by pimps. ❑ **pimp shoes** *n.* (*also* **pimping shoes**) [1970s+] whatever fashion in shoes is currently favoured by black pimps. ❑ **pimp slap** *n.* [1970s+] (*US black*) an open-handed slap across the face. ❑ **pimp slap** *v.* (*also* **pimp smack**) [1990s+] (*US black*) to hit in the face, either with the fist or a weapon. ❑ **pimp socks** *n.* [1950s–70s] (*US black*) ultra-thin nylon socks, usu. with a pattern of vertical stripes. ❑ **pimp steak** *n.* [? its phallic dimensions] [1940s+] (*US black*) a frankfurter. ❑ **pimp stick** *n.* **1** in the context of smoking [STICK *n.* (6d)]. (**a**) [1920s+] (*Can./US*) a cigarette. (**b**) [1950s+] (*Can./US drugs*) a marijuana cigarette. (**c**) [1960s–70s] (*US prison*) a cigarette holder. **2** (*US black*) in senses of a weapon. (**a**) [1930s+] (*also* **pimping stick**) two wire coat hangers twisted together to make an improvised and vicious whip. (**b**) [2000s] a cane used by a pimp both as part of his 'uniform' and for beating up his whores. ❑ **pimp stride** *n.* (*also* **pimp stroll, ...strut, ...walk**) [1970s+] (*orig. US black*) a strutting style of walking, intended to emphasize one's pride, independence and masculinity. ❑ **pimp stride** *v.* (*also* **pimp strut, ...walk**) [1970s+] (*US*) to walk in the strutting manner associated with a black pimp. ❑ **pimp's turban** *n.* [1920s–30s] (*US*) a derby hat. ❑ **pimp talk** *n.* (*US black*) **1** [1950s–70s] the 'line' used by a pimp when attempting to persuade a new young woman to join his group of prostitutes. **2** [1950s–70s] the bantering, self-aggrandizing conversations between a group of pimps. **3** [1970s+] the jargon of pimps. ❑ **pimp-talk** *v.* [1970s] (*US black*) to talk in a bantering, self-aggrandizing manner. ❑ **pimp tints** *n. see* PIMP SHADES above. ❑ **pimp wagon** *n. see* PIMP RIDE above. ❑ **pimp walk** *see* PIMP STRIDE above. ❑ **pimp whisk** *n.* (*also* **pimp-whiskin, pimp-whisking**) [WHISK *n.*] **1** [17C–early 19C] a first-rate pimp [although *whisk* usu. means the derog. *whipper-snapper*]. **2** [late 17C–early 19C] a mean-spirited, bigoted man.

IN PHRASES

❑ **pimped down** *adj.* (*also* **pimped out, pimped up**) [1970s+] (*US black*) **1** of a person, fashionably or smartly dressed. **2** of an object, ostentatious, flashy. ❑ **pimp on** *v.* (*also* **pimp off**) [weak form of SE *pimp*, to run prostitutes] [1940s] (*US black*) to take advantage of, to scrounge off.

pimp *adj.* [PIMP *n.* (1); the enviable status of the pimp in black street culture; 'this one little syllable represents a job, a mindset, a way of life, a way of walking, a way of talking, a way of dressing, a pejorative, and a high compliment' (Touré, *The Portable Promised Land*, 2002)] [1960s+] (*US black*) **1** stylish, expensive. **2** (*also* **the pimp, the pimpiest, pimpalicious**) the best, the ultimate.

pimp *v.* [PIMP *n.*] **1** [17C] (*UK Und.*) to work as a procurer [later use is SE]. **2** [mid-19C] (*US campus*) to toady, to curry favour by performing petty actions [SE *pimping*, petty]. **3** [1940s+] (*Aus./N.Z.*) (*also* **pimp on**) to tell tales; to inform on someone. **4** [1960s+] (*US black*) to strut (in the supposed manner of a pimp). **5** [1970s] (*US black*) to play on human emotions to obtain money. **6** [1970s+] (*US campus*) (*also* **pimp up**) to dress up, of a person and of an object; to promote. **7** [1970s+] to seduce, to flirt with. **8** [1980s] (*US campus*) to steal. **9** [1980s] (*US*) to nag, to harass. **10** [1980s] (*US*) to deceive.

pimper *n.* [PIMP *n.* (1)] [1990s+] (*US black*) one who adopts the *PIMP STRIDE* under PIMP *n.*

pimpgennet *n. see* PIMGENET *n.*

pimple *n.*[1] [ety. unknown; ? link to PIMP *n.*] [late 17C–early 18C] a boon companion.

pimple *n.*[2] **1** [early 19C–1940s] the head. **2** [late 19C+] a baby's penis. **3** [1980s] (*US*) a fool.

IN COMPOUNDS

❑ **pimple cover** *n.* (*also* **pimple coverer**) [19C] a hat.

IN PHRASES

❑ **like a pimple on a cow's arse** (*also* **...bull's arse, ...pig's bum**) [20C+] utterly insignificant.

pimple and blotch *n.* [rhy. sl.] [20C+] Scotch (whisky).

pimple and wart *n.* [rhy. sl.] [late 19C–1900s] **1** a quart. **2** port wine.

pimple in a bent *n.* [SE *pimple* + *bent*, a grass-stalk] [late 16C–mid-17C] something infinitesimally small.

pin *n.* **1** in ext./fig. uses of SE. (**a**) [mid-15C+] the penis. (**b**) [1920s+] (*drugs*) a hypodermic syringe (or a makeshift alternative), used for injecting narcotic drugs. (**c**) [1960s+] (*drugs*) a very thin marijuana cigarette. **2** [16C+] almost always in pl., a leg; thus *pin-ends*, feet. **3** [1980s+] a drug dealer [? abbr. SE *kingpin*]. **4** [1990s+] (*US prison*) a female inmate acting as a lookout.

IN COMPOUNDS

❑ **pin box** *n.* [late 17C] the vagina. ❑ **pin case** *n.* [mid-16C] the vagina. ❑ **pin-cushion** *n.* [19C] the *mons veneris*; thus the vagina. ❑ **pin gun** *n.* [GUN *n.*[1] (5)] [1950s–70s] (*US drugs*) an improvised hypodermic syringe, using a medicine dropper and a pin. ❑ **pin-jabber** *n.* [JAB *v.* (1)] [1920s+] (*drugs*) a drug user who injects their preferred drug. ❑ **pin joint** *n.* [JOINT *n.* (5c)] [1970s] (*drugs*) a very thin marijuana cigarette. ❑ **pinroll** *n. see* PINNER *n.*[3].

SE in slang uses

IN COMPOUNDS

❑ **pin artist** *n.* [-ARTIST *sfx*] [1930s–60s] (*US tramp*) an abortionist. ❑ **pin basket** *n.* [SE *pin-basket*, a large ornamented pin-cushion with pins of varying lengths arranged to resemble a basket; such a pin-cushion was trad. given to a mother after the birth of a child] [late 18C–early 19C] the youngest child. ❑ **pin-grease** *n. see* AXLE GREASE *n.* (1). ❑ **pinhead** *n. see* separate entries. ❑ **pin work** *n.* [1930s–40s] (*US Und.*) pinpricks on cards, used to aid cheating.

IN PHRASES

❑ **hang a pin** *v.* [1930s] (*US*) to give one's girlfriend one's fraternity pin to wear as a sign of engagement or exclusive dating relationship. ❑ **pull the pin** *v.* [the pulling of the connecting pin between two railroad wagons] **1** [1920s+] (*US*) to resign, to retire, to quit, to be fired from a job; to go on strike. **2** [1930s–60s] (*US Und.*) to leave, to go (away). **3** [2000s] (*US prison*) to call for help. ❑ **put in the pin** *v.* [*PUT IN THE PEG* under PEG *n.*[4]] [mid-19C] to stop drinking during a session, or to give up drinking completely.

pin *v.* **1** in senses of 'pricking'. (**a**) [mid-16C; 20C+] of a man, to have sexual intercourse; thus *take the pin*, of a woman, to have sexual intercourse [note PIN *n.* (1a)]. (**b**) [1950s] (*US teen*) to stab. **2** in senses of *pin down*. (**a**) [mid-18C–mid-19C] to snatch, to steal. (**b**) [late 18C–1930s] to seize, to catch, to arrest. (**c**) [mid-19C] to obtain something from someone. **3** [late 19C–1930s] to pawn clothes [? SE *pawn*]. **4** in senses of 'keeping one's eyes pinned'. (**a**) [1920s+] (*Aus.*) to target someone for one's (often amatory) attentions. (**b**) [1930s+] to mark down visually, to notice. (**c**) [1950s+] (*US black*) to stare at (aggressively). (**d**) [1970s] (*US black*) to draw someone else's attention to, to point out. (**e**) [1970s–80s] (*US*) to identify. (**f**) [1990s+] (*US prison*) of a female prisoner, to act as a lookout. **5** [1930s–40s] (*Aus./US*) to cause trouble for, to 'do down'. **6** [1940s–70s] (*US*) to knock out [? wrestling imagery]. **7** [1950s–70s] (*US*) to come to terms with, to work out. **8** [1950s+] (*US campus*) to state one's commitment to a person of the opposite sex by giving them one's fraternity pin.

SE in slang uses

IN PHRASES

❑ **pin a can on** *v. see GET A CAN ON under* CAN *n.*[1]. ❑ **pin a rose** *v.* [1930s] (*US short order*) to put a slice of onion on a hamburger. ❑ **pin back one's ears** *v. see under* EAR *n.*[1]. ❑ **pin back one's lugholes** *v. see under* LUGHOLE *n.* ❑ **pin on** *v.* [SE *pin on*, to attach] [1930s+] to accuse, to lay the blame on someone. ❑ **pin one on** *v.* (*also* **pin a few on**) [1910s–50s] (*US/Aus.*) to have a drink. ❑ **pin them** [1980s] (*US campus*) an instruction to stop talking.

pinch *n.* **1** [late 17C–1900s] a certainty, something easily achieved [? SE *pinch*, the critical point]. **2** in Und. uses. (**a**) [mid-18C+] a theft, esp. short-changing; an act of stealing or plagiarism; also in fig. use. (**b**) [mid-19C+] (*orig. US*) an arrest. (**c**) [1900s] (*Aus.*) a prison. (**d**) [1920s] (*US*) an arrested person. **3** [1960s+] in drug uses. (**a**) a small amount of marijuana, enough for perhaps two cigarettes. (**b**) a small amount of a narcotic drug.

IN COMPOUNDS

❑ **pinch-box** *n.* [1900s–10s] **1** (*Aus./US*) a police station. **2** (*US*) a police call-box.

IN PHRASES

❑ **hang a pinch on** *v.* [1930s–50s] (*US*) to arrest, to have someone arrested. ❑ **make a pinch** *v.* (*also* **make the pinch**) [20C+] to arrest. ❑ **put the pinch on** *v.* [in both one 'feels the pinch'] **1** [1940s+] (*US*) to reduce to poverty. **2** [1970s] to put pressure on. ❑ **take a pinch** *v.* (*also* **get a pinch**) [1920s+] to be arrested.

pinch *v.* [orig. Und., mainstream sl. from mid-19C] **1** [late 16C–19C] to rob. **2** [late 17C+] to steal. **3** [mid-18C–early 19C] spec. to rob a shopkeeper by confusing them while asking for change. **4** [late 18C+] to arrest. **5** [mid-19C] to pass counterfeit money in exchange for goods. **6** [late 19C–1950s] to raid. **7** [1900s] to capture. **8** [1950s] to charge with a crime.

DERIVATIVES

❑ **pinching** *adj.* [mid-19C] (*UK Und.*) pertaining to an arrest.

IN COMPOUNDS

❑ **pinch-back** *n.* (*also* **pinch-belly**) [they *pinch* someone else's *back* by refusing to pay them enough to buy enough clothes] [17C–early 19C] a miser. ❑ **pinch-bottom** *n.* [19C] a pimp. ❑ **pinch-buttock** *n.* [19C] a pimp. ❑ **pinch-commons** *n.* [SE *commons*, provisions that are provided in common for a group] [17C–early 19C] a miser. ❑ **pinch-cunt** *n.* [CUNT *n.* (1)] [19C] a pimp. ❑ **pinch-fart** *n.* [FART *n.* (1)] [late 16C–early 17C] a miser. ❑ **pinch-fist** *n.* [SE *fist*] [late 16C; late 19C–1900s] a miser. ❑ **pinch-gloak** *n.* [GLOAK *n.*] [19C] a petty thief who specializes in stealing small articles from jewellers. ❑ **pinch-gut** *see* separate entries. ❑ **pinch-prick** *n.* [PRICK *n.* (1)] [late 19C] a prostitute. ❑ **pinch-wife** *n.* [late 19C–1900s] a mean, boorish husband, who does not trust his wife.

IN PHRASES

❑ **at the pinch** [late 18C–early 19C] (*UK Und.*) working as a thief, esp. petty theft from shops, carried out during a purchase, giving short change or passing counterfeit money in exchange for good. ❑ **pinch a bob** *v.* [thus cited by Greenwood (*Seven Curses of London*, 1869), but the *bob* may either be generic for money, or a mishearing of LOB *n.*[1] (2)] [mid-19C] to rob a till. ▫ **pinch a loaf** *v.* [1990s+] (*US*) to defecate. ▫ **pinch one off** *v. see* separate entry. ▫ **pinch on the parson's side** *v.* [late 17C–early 19C] to cheat a parson of their tithes. ▫ **pinch the cat** *v.* [joc. use of SE] [1960s–70s] of a man, to fondle one's genitals through one's trouser pocket.

IN EXCLAMATIONS

▫ **pinch it off!** *see* separate entry.

pincher *n.*[1] [PINCH *v.*] **1** [mid-18C–early 19C] a rogue specializing in short-changing. **2** [19C] a policeman. **3** [19C+] a shoplifter, a thief.

IN PHRASES

▫ **put a pincher on** *v.* [mid-19C] (*UK Und.*) to arrest.

pincher *n.*[2] **1** [1900s] (*Aus.*) a baby. **2** [1920s–40s] (*US black/Und.*) in pl., shoes [their tightness].

IN PHRASES

▫ **pinchers up** *adj.* [1990s+] (*US prison*) dead.

pincher *n.*[3] [quarrying jargon *pincher*, one who uses a crowbar or pincher (a tool for grasping large objects)] [1900s–10s] (*Aus.*) a navvy.

pinch-gut *n.* [they constantly 'tighten their belt'; note naut. *pinch-gut money*: 'allow'd by the King to the Seamen, [...] on Bord the Navy [...], when their Provision falls Short' (B.E. *c.*1698)] [mid–late 17C] a miser.

pinch-gut *adj.* [PINCH-GUT *n.*] [late 17C; 1900s] miserly, impoverished.

pinch hit *v.* [baseball jargon *pinch-hit*, to substitute for a batter, esp. at a crucial point in the game] [1910s+] to act as a substitute, esp. in an emergency.

pinch hitter *n.* [*see* PINCH HIT *v.*] **1** [1910s+] a temporary worker. **2** [1980s] (*drugs*) one who is hired to inject an addict too ill to do it themselves.

pinching *adj. see under* PINCH *v.*

pinching-do *n.* [PINCH *v.* (4)] [mid-19C] (*UK Und.*) an arrest.

pinching lay *n.* [PINCH *v.* (2) + LAY *n.*[3] (1)] [late 18C–early 19C] a variety of petty crimes involving cash, passing counterfeit money, stealing from shops, giving short change.

pinch it off! *excl.* [fig. use of PINCH ONE OFF *v.*] [1920s+] (*Aus.*) hurry up!

pinch one off *v.* ['one' is a piece of excrement; the phr. reflects the basic meaning of TURD *n.*[1] (1), something that is 'torn off' from the body] [1940s+] (*US*) to defecate.

pinckany *n. see* PIGSNYES *n.*

pinckle *n. see* PINTLE *n.*

pine *adj.*

SE in slang uses, pertaining to a coffin

IN COMPOUNDS

▫ **pine-box parole** *n.* (*also* **pine-box release**) [1940s+] (*US prison*) an inmate's death in prison. ▫ **pine-box suit** *n.* [1960s] a coffin. ▫ **pine drape** *n.* (*also* **pine outfit, ...overcoat**) [DRAPE *n.* (1)/SE *outfit/overcoat*] [mid-19C–1940s] (*Aus./US*) a coffin. ▫ **pine liner** *n.* [late 19C] (*Aus.*) a coffin.

pineapple *n.*[1] **1** [1910s+] (*also* **Niagara pineapple, pineapple bomb**) a bomb, a grenade [the shape]. **2** [1960s–70s] a male homosexual [play on FRUIT *n.* (2)]. **3** [1980s] (*US*) a Puerto Rican [the jungle associations]. **4** [2000s] (*US campus/drugs*) heroin [ety. unknown].

SE in slang uses

IN COMPOUNDS

▫ **pineapple bomb** *n. see* sense 1 above. ▫ **pineapple cut** *n.* [1940s] (*Aus.*) a rough haircut, leaving the hair shaggy and irregular. ▫ **pineapple head** *n.* [-HEAD *sfx* (2); the jungle associations] [1990s+] a derog. term for a Samoan American. ▫ **pineapple princess** *n.* (*also* **pineapple queen**) [SE *pineapple*, Hawaii's state fruit + PRINCESS *n.* (2b)/QUEEN *n.* (2a)] [1960s+] (*gay*) a homosexual person from Hawaii.

pineapple *n.*[2] [rhy. sl.] [1960s–70s] (*Scot.*) a chapel.

pineapple chunk *n.* [rhy. sl.] **1** [20C+] departure, escape [BUNK *n.*[1]]. **2** [1990s+] semen [SPUNK *n.* (5)].

piner *n.* [late 19C] (*Aus.*) a coffin.

pine-top *n.* [? the wood used in its barrels] [mid-19C–1940s] (*US*) cheap or illicitly distilled bourbon.

Ping *n.* [*Ping* as a 'typical' Chinese name] [1980s+] (*N.Z.*) a derog. name for an Asian person.

ping *n.* [SE *ping*, echoic of a sudden high-pitched noise] [1980s+] **1** (*Aus.*) a try, an attempt. **2** (*N.Z. drugs*) an injection of a narcotic drug [PING *v.* (3)].

ping *v.* **1** [1930s+] (*Aus.*) to penalize. **2** [1940s+] (*Aus./N.Z.*) to hit, to shoot; also in fig. use, as in *have a go at* [the pinging noise of a musket]. **3** [1980s+] (*N.Z. drugs*) to inject narcotics [ext. of sense 1, i.e. SHOOT *v.* (6a)].

pinga *n.* [Sp.] [1970s+] (*US*) the penis.

ping-in-wing *n.* (*also* **ping-in-the-wing, ping-wing**) [PING *n.* (2) + WING *n.*[1] (2)] [1940s–50s] (*drugs*) an injection of a narcotic.

ping off! *excl.* [1970s–80s] (*Aus. teen*) go away!

ping-pong *n.*[1] [not a 'real' photo; *see* PING-PONG *v.*] [20C+] (*W.I., Bdos*) a passport-sized photograph of one's face.

ping-pong *n.*[2] [play on brandname] [1940s–60s] (*drugs*) Pantopon, a synthetic opiate.

ping-pong *adj.* [rhy. sl.] [2000s] strong.

ping-pong *v.* [the image of *ping-pong* or table-tennis as not being a 'serious' sport] [1940s+] (*W.I.*) to play at something, not to take one's commitments seriously.

ping-wing *n. see* PING-IN-WING *n.*

pinhead *n.* [SE *pin* + -HEAD *sfx*] **1** in US drug uses. (**a**) [late 19C–1930s] a small pill of opium, costing 25 cents. (**b**) [1920s–40s] one who injects narcotics, esp. when using a rudimentary syringe based on a pin and medicine dropper. (**c**) [1960s] an amphetamine user. (**d**) [1960s+] a very thin marijuana cigarette. **2** [late 19C+] (*orig. US*) a stupid person. **3** [late 19C+] (*orig. US*) a person with a small head.

pinhead *adj.* (*also* **pinheaded**) [PINHEAD *n.* (2)] [late 19C+] stupid, with a small brain.

Pink *n.* (*also* **P., Pinkerton, Pinkie**) [abbr.] **1** [mid-19C+] (*US*) a member of Pinkerton's Detective Agency; thus *the Pinks*, the Agency as a whole. **2** [1920s+] in fig. use, a detective or a sharp person.

pink *n.* **1** in sexual contexts. (**a**) [17C; 1950s] a prostitute. (**b**) [late 19C] naked (female) flesh. (**c**) [1970s+] the open vagina, esp. as in pornography. (**d**) [1990s+] sexual intercourse. **2** as a synon. for excellence [SE *in the pink*]. (**a**) [late 17C–1900s] constr. with *the*, something of the highest fashion, the best. (**b**) [19C–1920s] a fashionable, well-dressed person. **3** [1920s+] (*US black*) a white person; thus [1960s+] *pink boy*, a white man of any age [the actual skin colour of a 'white' person]. **4** [1920s+] (*orig. US*) one whose politics are left of centre, but who is certainly not a communist (sometimes with an implication of insincerity) [a 'paler' version of RED *n.* (8)]. **5** [1960s+] in pl., in drug uses [the colour of the tablets]. (**a**) (*S.Afr. drugs*) Wellconal tablets, a form of synthetic heroin. (**b**) (*US drugs*) Seconal, barbiturates. (**c**) (*US drugs*) Dexytal capsules, i.e. amphetamines and barbiturates. **6** [1970s–80s] (*US*) the *pink* slip that confirms ownership of a vehicle. **7** *see* DUTCH PINK *under* DUTCH *adj.*[1].

IN COMPOUNDS

▫ **pink chaser** *n.* [late 19C+] (*US black*) a black person who pursues the company and friendship of whites.

IN PHRASES

▫ **get some pink** *v.* [1990s+] (*US*) to have sexual intercourse.

pink *adj.* **1** [early 19C; 1910s] fashionable, exclusive [SE in 16C]. **2** [mid-19C+] (*also* **pink pretty**) left-wing, socialist (rather than Communist, ie. RED *adj.* (2)). **3** [late 19C–1940s] violent, extreme, absolute; esp. as (*not*) *a pink thing*. **4** [late 19C+] slightly indecent, violent or vulgar, mildly 'blue'. **5** [20C+] homosexual [use predates Gay Liberation days]. **6** [1920s+] (*US black*) white.

IN COMPOUNDS

▫ **pink finger** *n.* [1900s] (*US*) an effeminate, poss. homosexual man. ▫ **pink pretty** *adj. see* sense 2 above. ▫ **pinktea** *see* separate entries. ▫ **pink whoogie** *n.* [WHOOGIE *n.*] [20C+] (*US*) a derog. term for a white person. ▫ **pink widow** *n.* [such 'widows' are known to move from one such relationship to the next as funeral follows funeral] [1990s+] (*US gay*) an HIV-negative man who forms a relationship with an HIV-positive man on the understanding that he will become his partner's sole heir.

IN PHRASES

▫ **pinked up** *adj.* [late 19C–1900s] (*US*) fashionably dressed.

SE in slang uses

IN COMPOUNDS

▫ **pink cigar** *n. see* PINK PANATELLA below. ▫ **pink champagne** *n.* [1990s+] (*drugs*) **1** a mixture of cocaine and heroin. **2** amphetamine sulphate [the colour of the powder]. ▫ **pink-eye** *n. see* separate entry. ▫ **pink hearts** *n. see* PURPLE HEARTS *under* PURPLE *adj.* ▫ **pink lady** *n.* [the colour of the capsules] [1950s+] (*drugs*) a barbiturate, usu. Seconal/Darvon. ▫ **pinkmail** *n.* [1960s+] (*US prison*) secret notes of a romantic or sexual nature passed between inmates; as n., *pink, pink kite.* ▫ **pink oboe** *n. see* separate entry. ▫ **pink owsley** *n.* (*also* **pink panther, ...robot**) [OWSLEY ACID *n.*/SE *panther/robot*; ? the colour of the capsules + play on *Pink Panther* films (1964–78)] [1960s+] (*drugs*) LSD. ▫ **Pink Palace, the** *n. see* separate entry. ▫ **pink panatella** *n.* (*also* **pink cigar**) [resemblance (if white)] [1990s+] the penis. ▫ **pink slip** *n.* [also note the *pink slip* that, in the US, proves ownership of a car] [1910s+] (*US*) **1** a notice of dismissal [the *pink* paper on which it is written/printed]. **2** a brush-off, a rejection [fig. use of sense 1]. **3** in prison, the notice that permits one's parole. ▫ **pink spiders** *n.* [one supposedly 'sees' them] [late 19C] delirium tremens. ▫ **pink starfish** *n. see* BROWN STAR *under* BROWN *adj.*[2]. ▫ **pink steel** *n. see under* STEEL *n.* ▫ **pinktoe** *n. see* separate entry. ▫ **pink-tongue** *n.* [1980s] (*US*) a derog. term for a black person. ▫ **pink torpedo** *n.* [2000s] a penis. ▫ **pink trumpet** *n.* [2000s] the penis. ▫ **Pink 'Un** *n. see* separate entry.

IN PHRASES

▫ **go for pink slips** *v.* [the *pink slip* that is proof of ownership] [1950s+] (*US*) to race cars with the winner gaining the loser's vehicle. ▫ **on one's pink** *adj.* [late 19C] (*Aus.*) drunk. ▫ **see pink elephants** *v.* [1910s+] to have hallucinations from alcoholism.

Pinkerton *n. see* PINK *n.*

pinkey *n. see* PINKY *n.*[1].

pink-eye *n.* **1** in the context of alcohol or drinking [pron. of PINKIE *n.* (2)]. (**a**) [20C+] (*Aus./Can.*) the cheapest red wine, methyl alcohol. (**b**) [20C+] (*Aus.*) a regular drinker of methylated spirits or 'pinkie'. (**c**) [1920s+] (*Aus./Can.*) a drinking bout, a party; thus *go pink-eye*, to get drunk. (**d**) [1950s] (*US*) cheap, 'rotgut' bourbon. **2** [20C+] (*US*) the vagina.

Pinkie *n. see* PINK *n.*

pinkie *n.* **1** in the context of skin tone. (**a**) [late 19C+] a very light-coloured black person. (**b**) [1960s+] (*orig. US black*) a white person. **2** (*Aus.*) (*also* **pinky**) as a form of (cheap) drink. (**a**) [late 19C+] cheap red wine; thus *pinky-shop*, a store specializing in such wine; *pinkyite*, a drinker of such wine. (**b**) [20C+] methylated spirits mixed with cheap red wine or Condy's crystals. **3** [20C+] in pl., the fingers. [Scot. dial.]. **4** as a colour. (**a**) [1990s+] (*US black*) a pink automobile, esp. a Cadillac. (**b**) [2000s] (*UK black*) a £50 note. **5** *see* PINKO *n.* **6** *see* PINKY *n.*[1]. **7** *see* PINKY *n.*[2].

pinkindindies *n.* (*also* **pinking-dindees**) [lit. 'a turkey-cock given to pinking with a rapier'] [mid–late 18C] (*Irish*) a gang of dissolute, rich young men who cut off the bottom few inches of their scabbards and prod or 'pink' with their exposed sword point those whom they encounter and with whom they can start an argument.

pinkle-twister *n.* [? PINTLE *n.* (1)] [1980s] a male homosexual.

pink lint *adj.* [rhy. sl. = SKINT *adj.*] [20C+] penniless, very poor.

pinko *n.* (*also* **pinkie**) [PINK *n.* (4) + -O *sfx* (2)] [1930s+] (*orig. US*) a communist, socialist or even mildly liberal sympathizer (depending on the speaker's viewpoint).

pinko *adj.* **1** [1920s–40s] (*Aus.*) drunk, esp. on methylated spirits. [PINK-EYE *n.* (1)]. **2** [1920s+] left-wing [PINKO *n.*].

pink oboe *n.* [1980s+] the penis.

IN PHRASES

▫ **play the pink oboe** *v.* (*also* **perform on the pink oboe**) [1980s+] to fellate.

Pink Palace, the *n.* [its original colour scheme] [1990s+] (*Aus. prison/Und.*) Risdon prison, Tasmania.

pinktea *n.* [the orig. *Pink Tea* was held in 1886 by the US Women's Christian Temperance Union; men wore pink ties and women pink caps] **1** [late 19C+] (*US/Can.*) a very formal or exclusive tea party; thus, as v., to attend such an event. **2** [1960s–70s] (*gay*) an upper-class homosexual, usu. 'in the closet' and insulated from active homophobia by social privilege.

pinktea *adj.* [as one who frequents a PINKTEA *n.* (1)] **1** [1900s–30s] (*US*) weak, effeminate. **2** [1930s] second-rate.

pinktoe *n.* (*also* **pink-toes, pinky**) [1930s+] (*US black*) **1** a light-skinned black woman. **2** a white woman, esp. a black man's white girlfriend; occas. a white man. **3** a generic term for the white race.

pinktoe *adj.* [1960s] (*US black*) white.

Pink 'Un, the *n.* [the colour of the newsprint, and, in the case of the *Sporting Times*, to distinguish it from the *Sportsman's Guide to the Turf* (cf. BROWN 'UN, THE *n.*)] **1** [late 19C–1900s] a reporter or writer for *The Sporting Times* (esp. such 'stars' as Arthur Binstead (1861–1914), nicknamed 'The Pitcher', William Farn Goldberg, 'The Shifter', and Nathaniel Newnham-Davies, 'The Dwarf of Blood'). **2** [late 19C–1910s] a reader of *The Sporting Times*. **3** [late 19C–1930s] *The Sporting Times*. **4** [1910s+] the *Financial Times*.

pinky *n.*[1] (*also* **pinkey, pinkie**) **1** [19C+] (*orig. Scot.*) the little finger; thus [20C+] (*US*) *pinky-crooker*, an affected person, a poseur. **2** [1970s+] (*US gay*) the erect penis [resemblance to sense 1]. **3** [1970s+] (*US gay*) a small penis [resemblance to sense 1].

pinky *n.*[2] (*also* **pinkie**) [the image of SE *pink* as a 'feminine' colour] [1960s+] a passive or 'feminine' lesbian.

pinky *n.*[3] **1** *see* PINKIE *n.* (2). **2** *see* PINKO *n.* **3** *see* PINKTOE *n.*

pinky and perky *n.* [rhy. sl.; ult. *Pinky and Perky*, popular characters from children's TV] [1950s] a turkey.

pinnace *n.* [SE *pinnace*, a light vessel in attendance upon a larger one; the implication is that she is aged between the juvenile punk and older bawd or 'madam'] [late 16C–early 19C] a prostitute.

pinned *adj.* [in both senses, the effect of the drugs is to shrink the pupils] **1** [1950s+] (*drugs*) used of eyes in which the pupils are reduced, irrespective of the light available, to pinpricks. **2** [1980s+] (*US campus, drugs*) under the influence of a drug, usu. cocaine.

pinner *n.*[1] [SE *pin*, v.] [late 18C] (*Irish*) a gaoler, a policeman.

pinner *n.*[2] [SE *pin*] [1980s+] (*US campus*) a thin person.

pinner *n.*[3] (*also* **pinroll**) [PIN *n.* (1c) + ROLL-UP *n.*[2] (1)] [1990s+] (*drugs*) a very small marijuana cigarette.

pinner *adj.* [PINNER *n.*[2]] [1980s+] (*US campus*) thin.

pinnie *n.* [abbr.] [1990s+] (*N.Z.*) a *pin*ball machine; thus *pinnie joint*, an amusement arcade.

pins and needles *n.* [rhy. sl.] [20C+] beetles.

pint *n.* [i.e. half a QUART *n.*[2]] [1950s] (*W.I.*) a six-month prison sentence.

IN PHRASES

▫ **pint screamer** *n. see* ONE-POT SCREAMER *n.*

pinta, la *n.* [Sp.] [1960s+] (*US*) prison.

pintle *n.* (*also* **pinckle, pintie**) [OE *pintel*, the penis] **1** [late 16C–19C] the penis. **2** [20C+] (*Ulster*) a small, irritating person.

IN COMPOUNDS

▫ **pintle-bit** *n.* (*also* **pintle-maid**) [BIT *n.*[1] (2a)/SE *maid*] [19C–1900s] a mistress. ▫ **pintle-blossom** *n.* [joc. use of SE *blossom*] [18C–1900s] a bubo, the result of syphilis. ▫ **pintle-case** *n.* [19C] the vagina. ▫ **pintle-fancier** *n.* (*also* **pintle-ranger**) [SE *fancier*/RANGER *n.* (2)] [early 19C–1900s] a promiscuous woman.

❑ **pintle-fever** *n.* [19C–1900s] any form of venereal disease. ❑ **pintle-keek** *n.* [Scot. *keek*, a glance] [19C–1900s] a sexually inviting look, a leer. ❑ **pintle-maid** *n. see* PINTLE-BIT above. ❑ **pintle-merchant** *n.* (*also* **pintle-monger**) [MERCHANT *n.*/-MONGER *sfx*] [late 18C–1900s] a prostitute. ❑ **pintle-smith** *n.* (*also* **pintle-tagger**) [SE sfx *-smith*/SE *tag*, to stitch together] [late 18C–1900s] a surgeon.

pintle-de-pantledy *adj.* [ety. unknown; ? echoic of nervous fidgeting] [mid-17C–early 19C] frightened, scared.

pinto *n.* [PINTA, LA *n.*] [1960s+] (*US*) a former convict.

pinto bean *n.* [derog. use of SE] [1960s] (*US campus*) a derog. name for a Mexican or Mexican-American.

pint of mahogany *n. see under* MAHOGANY *n.*

pint-pot *n.* **1** [late 16C] a beer-seller. **2** [late 19C+] (*Aus.*) a tin can, holding a pint, which is used for boiling water. **3** [1940s] (*US*) a drunk.

pinum *n. see* PANNAM *n.*

pinurt pots *n.* [backsl.] [mid-19C] turnip tops.

pin yen *n. see* PEN YEN *n.*

pin-yen toy *n. see* TOY *n.*[2] (1).

pin yenz *n. see* PEN YEN *n.*

pinyon *n. see* PEN YEN *n.*

pioneer (of nature) *n.* [mid-17C] the penis.

piong *n.* [16C Fr. *pion*, excessive drinking, thus modern Fr. sl. *pion*, a hard drinker] [20C+] (*W.I.*) an enthusiast, esp. for a food or game.

pious *adj.* [mid-19C] (*UK Und.*) drunk.

p.i.p. *n.* [abbr. *p*arty *i*n *p*ower] [20C+] (*W.I.*) a toady, a sycophant.

pip *n.*[1] [SE *pip*, 'a disease of poultry and other birds, characterized by the secretion of a thick mucus in the mouth and throat, often with the formation of a white scale on the tip of the tongue' (*OED*)] [mid-16C+] **1** ill humour or poor health. **2** syphilis.

(DERIVATIVES)

❑ **pippish** *adj.* [1910s+] irritated, out of sorts. ❑ **pippy** *adj.* [1920s+] (*Aus.*) irritated, out of sorts.

(IN PHRASES)

❑ **get the pip** *v.* **1** [mid-19C+] to feel depressed, out of sorts, ill. **2** [1910s] to become obsessed with. **3** [1920s–80s] to be fed up. ❑ **give someone the pip** *v.* [late 19C+] to annoy or to infuriate someone, or to be so annoyed oneself.

pip *n.*[2] [abbr. PIPPIN *n.* (2)] **1** [late 19C+] (*orig. US*) the very best, the finest example. **2** [1900s] (*US*) a negative, bad example. **3** [1920s–30s] (*US*) an innocent. **4** [1950s] an attractive woman.

pip *v.*[1] [? fig. uses of SE *pip*, a spot on a die, card or domino] **1** [late 19C] to blackball. **2** [late 19C] (*UK campus*) to be fined. **3** [20C+] to defeat, to beat. **4** [1900s] to fail (a candidate) in an examination. **5** [1900s–30s] to die. **6** [1910s–30s] to hit with a shot. **7** [1960s] (*W.I./US*) to have sexual intercourse.

pip *v.*[2] (*also* **pip off**) [backform. f. PIP-PIP! *excl.* (2)] [1920s–30s] to leave.

pip! *excl.* [1960s] nonsense!

pipe *n.*[1] **1** with ref. to the reproduction of sound [ext. of SE *pipe*, the voice, as used in singing]. (**a**) [late 16C–mid-19C] a voice. (**b**) [17C] a song. (**c**) [1900s] (*US*) a story. (**d**) [1910s; 1960s] (*also* **pipes**) a telephone. (**e**) [1930s+] (*US*) a saxophone. **2** with ref. to the pipe's tubular shape [the *double entendres* cover tobacco pipes, bag-pipes and water pipes]. (**a**) [17C+] (*also* **standpipe**) the penis [note D'Urfey, *Pills to Purge Melancholy* (1719): 'Next came a smug Physician [...] He was so us'd to Glisters, she told him to his face, / He would always be bobbing his Pipe at the wrong place']. (**b**) [late 18C–early 19C] (*also* **quill-pipes**) in pl., top boots [? the tubular shape, or cleaning with pipe-clay]. (**c**) [mid-19C+] the vagina. **3** in drug uses. (**a**) [mid-19C] a cigar. (**b**) [late 19C+] an opium pipe; thus *pipe, the pipe*, the smoking of opium; *pipe fiend*, an addict. (**c**) [1930s–50s] (*also* **pipey, pipie**) an opium addict. (**d**) [1950s+] a marijuana or hashish pipe. (**e**) [1950s+] a vein into which a drug can be injected. (**f**) [1960s+] (*S.Afr.*) enough marijuana to fill a pipe. (**g**) [1970s+] a marijuana smoker. (**h**) [1980s+] (*also* **rock pipe**) a pipe for smoking base cocaine or crack cocaine; thus, by metonymy, the drug itself. **4** [late 19C+] (*US*) anything that is easily accomplished; a certainty; thus (*US campus*) *pipe course*, an easy academic course [abbr. LEAD-PIPE CINCH *under* LEAD *n.*]. **5** [1950s–70s] constr. with *the*, a euph. for hell [? H.E. Bates nonce use]. **6** [1950s+] any form of clubbing weapon [SE *lead pipe*]. **7** [2000s] constr. with *the*, the River Thames.

in terms pertaining to drugs

(DERIVATIVES)

❑ **pipey** *adj.* [1930s–50s] (*US drugs*) under the influence of opium.

(IN COMPOUNDS)

❑ **pipe fiend** *n.* [FIEND *n.*] [1910s–30s] (*US*) a regular opium user. ❑ **pipe head** *n.* [-HEAD *sfx* (4)] [1980s+] (*drugs*) a regular user of crack cocaine. ❑ **pipe man** *n.* [1980s+] a seller of crack cocaine. ❑ **pipe smoker** *n.* [1900s–30s] (*drugs*) an opium user. ❑ **pipe talk** *n.* [late 19C–1900s] (*US*) fantasizing; nonsense.

(IN PHRASES)

❑ **hit the pipe** *v.* (*US drugs*) **1** [late 19C+] to smoke opium; thus *pipe-hitter*, an opium smoker [note Burnett, *Little Caesar* (1929): 'Hit the pipe, drinking'; presumably an authorial error]. **2** [1950s] to smoke cannabis. **3** [1980s+] (*also* **crack the pipe**) to smoke crack cocaine. ❑ **on the pipe** (*drugs*) **1** [1920s–50s] using opium on a regular basis. **2** [1980s+] using crack cocaine on a regular basis. ❑ **ride the pipe** *v.* [1950s] to smoke opium.

in terms relating to the penis

(IN COMPOUNDS)

❑ **pipe job** *n.* [JOB *n.*[2] (2)] [1970s–80s] (*US*) an act of sexual intercourse or fellatio. ❑ **pipe smoker** *n.* [SMOKE *v.*[3]] [1990s+] a gay man.

(IN PHRASES)

❑ **blow someone's pipe** *v.* (*also* **blow the pipe**) [BLOW *v.*[2] (1c)] [1910s] (*US*) to fellate. ❑ **clamp the pipe** *v.* [1990s+] to masturbate. ❑ **clean one's pipes** *v.* [2000s] (*US*) to release sexual tension, spec. to masturbate. ❑ **clean someone's pipe** *v.* (*also* **clean the pipe**) [20C+] (*US*) to perform oral sex on a man. ❑ **lay (some) pipe** *v.* [1930s+] (*US*) to have sexual intercourse, whether vaginal or anal. ❑ **on pipe** [2000s] (*US prison*) living as a jail homosexual.

SE in slang uses

(IN COMPOUNDS)

❑ **pipe cinch** *n. see* LEAD-PIPE CINCH *under* LEAD *n.* ❑ **pipe-layer** *n. see* separate entry. ❑ **pipestem** *n.* [1910s] (*US*) an arm.

(IN PHRASES)

❑ **get up someone's pipe** *v.* [BROWN PIPE *under* BROWN *adj.*[2] or the idea of fig. close pursuit in a car, i.e. up someone's exhaust pipe] [1990s+] to annoy, to infuriate, to provoke. ❑ **on the pipe** [1990s+] (*US prison*) using the waterpipes to communicate between cells. ❑ **put someone's pipe out** *v.* [mid-19C] **1** to ruin someone's plans. **2** to shock, to disgust. ❑ **run some water through one's pipe** *v.* [1970s] (*US*) of a man, to urinate. ❑ **take the pipe** *v.* [ety. unknown] [1960s+] (*US*) to fail to act or achieve under pressure, esp. in sports; thus to be punished.

(IN EXCLAMATIONS)

❑ **put that in your pipe and smoke it!** [early 19C+] an excl. meaning deal with that, whether you like it or not. ❑ **strike me up a pipe!** *see under* STRIKE ME...! *excl.* ❑ **up your pipe!** [1930s+] a euph. synon. of UP YOUR ARSE! *excl.*

pipe *n.*[2] [PIPE *v.*[3] (2)] **1** [mid-19C+] a glance, a look (at). **2** [1960s] a dream.

(IN PHRASES)

❑ **have a pipe** *v.* [1900s–80s] to glance at. ❑ **lay pipes** *v.* [1910s] to survey, to reconnoitre. ❑ **on the pipe** [mid-19C] (*UK Und.*) keeping a lookout; conducting a surveillance.

pipe *v.*[1] [SE *pipe*, to play a pipe] **1** [early 17C; early 19C+] to talk; esp. as *pipe out*, to start talking, to interrupt; *hit the pipe*, to inform. **2** [late 18C–19C] to weep. **3** [early–mid-19C] to breathe heavily, through exertion, e.g. in a prizefight.

IN PHRASES

▫ **pipe the stem** *v.* [STEM *n.* (1)] [1920s–40s] (*US*) to beg in a city's main street. ▫ **stretch a pipe** *v. see* separate entry. ▫ **take a pipe** *v.* [late 19C] to cry.

pipe *v.*[2] **1** [mid-19C] (*US*) to smoke a pipe. **2** [1990s+] (*drugs*) (*also* **pipe up**) to smoke crack cocaine.

pipe *v.*[3] [? SE *peep*] **1** [mid-19C–1900s] orig. of a detective, to follow, to pursue; to spy on. **2** [mid-19C+] to look over, to inspect. **3** [1900s] to understand, to work out.

IN PHRASES

▫ **pipe down** *v.* [mid-19C] (*US Und.*) to track down and arrest a criminal. ▫ **pipe off** *v.* **1** [mid-19C] to recognize. **2** [mid-19C–1940s] to survey, to assess. **3** [late 19C] to leave, to depart. **4** [late 19C] to dismiss. **5** [1910s–30s] to make jokes. **6** [1920s–40s] to inform, to explain. **7** [1930s] to 'pump' a person for information.

pipe *v.*[4] [PIPE *n.*[1] (2a); note Fr. argot *une pipe*, fellatio] [1980s] (*US*) to perform fellatio.

pipe and drum *n.* [rhy. sl. = BUM *n.*[1] (1)] [20C+] the buttocks.

piped *adj.*[1] **1** [1900s–20s] (*US*) drunk [SE *pipe*, a large barrel]. **2** (*also* **piped up**) in drug uses [PIPE *n.*[1] (3)]. (**a**) [1920s–50s] under the influence of drugs. (**b**) [1990s+] under the influence of crack cocaine.

piped *adj.*[2] [? mis-reading of PIP *v.*[1] (3)] [1980s+] (*US campus*) defeated, humiliated.

pipe-layer *n.* [for extensive ety. *see* Bartlett, *Dict. Americanisms* (1848) pp.251–2] [mid-19C–1910s] (*US*) 'one who schemes to procure corrupt votes' (*OED*).

pip emma *n.* [1910s] the evening, i.e. p.m.

piper *n.*[1] [? SE *pipes*, the lungs and the wheezing noise they make] **1** [late 18C–early 19C] a broken-down horse. **2** [mid-19C] a human who is out of breath.

piper *n.*[2] [PIPE *v.*[3] (1)] **1** [mid-19C] (*US*) a private detective. **2** [mid-19C–1900s] a spy, esp. one employed on an omnibus. **3** [late 19C] (*US Und.*) a lookout.

piper *n.*[3]

IN PHRASES

▫ **what the piper?** [1900s] (*US*) a phr. used to express surprise or irritation.

IN EXCLAMATIONS

▫ **by the piper (that played before Moses)!** (*also* **by the piper that shook the Giant's Causeway!**) [19C] a mild excl.

piper *n.*[4] [PIPE *n.*[1] (1)] [1990s+] (*drugs*) a smoker of crack cocaine.

piper fou *adj.* [SE *piper* + FOU *adj.*[1]] [late 18C–19C] very drunk, lit. 'drunk as a piper'.

piperheidsick *v.* [PIPE *v.*[3] (2); play on the brand of champagne] [1920s] (*US*) to look, to see.

pipero *n.* [Sp. 'a pipe-er'] [1980s+] (*drugs*) a smoker of base cocaine or crack cocaine.

piper's news *n.* [? the piper trad. receives the news last] [19C] (*Scot.*) stale news.

piper's wife *n.* [derog. stereotyping] [late 18C] (*Scot.*) a prostitute.

pipes *n.*[1] **1** [mid-16C+] the voice. **2** [18C+] the lungs, esp. of a singer. **3** [early 19C+] the throat. **4** [1990s+] (*US campus*) the upper arms. **5** [2000s] the vocal chords. **6** *see* PIPE *n.*[1] (1d).

IN PHRASES

▫ **clear one's pipes** *v.* [early 18C; 1980s] to loose one's emotions, to 'let off steam'. ▫ **get one's pipes cleaned** *v.* [2000s] to gain sexual release. ▫ **knock one's pipes out** *v.* [1980s] to work oneself to exhaustion. ▫ **open one's pipes** *v.* [18C+] to sing. ▫ **put up one's pipes** *v.* (*also* **pack up one's pipes, poke up one's pipes**) [mid-16C–mid-18C] to cease from an action; to stop talking. ▫ **set up one's pipes** *v.* [17C] to yell, to scream. ▫ **stretch a pipe** *v.* [early 19C] to cry.

pipes *n.*[2] [abbr. SE *drainpipes*] [1970s+] (*US gay*) very tight trousers.

pipes *adj.* [ety. unknown] [1900s] (*US*) crazy; thus *pipe-house*, a psychiatric institution.

pipey *n. see* PIPE *n.*[1] (3c).

pipey *adj. see under* PIPE *n.*[1].

pipie *n. see* PIPE *n.*[1] (3c).

pipieri *n.* [dial. *pipieri*, the tyrant flycatcher, a small fighting bird] [mid-19C+] (*W.I.*) an aggressive person.

piping *n.*[1] [PIPE *v.*[1] (2)] [late 18C–19C] crying.

piping *n.*[2] [PIPE *v.*[2] (2)] [1980s+] smoking crack cocaine.

pipkin *n.*[1] [SE *pipkin*, a small, earthenware pot] **1** [17C–18C] the female genitals; thus *cracked pipkin*, a vagina that has been deflowered. **2** [early–mid-19C] the stomach. **3** [early–mid-19C] the head.

IN PHRASES

▫ **crack a pipkin** *v.* (*also* **crack one's pipkin, ...a pitcher, ... one's pitcher**) [SE *crack*/CRACK *v.*[2] (2a)/SE *pitcher*] [17C–early 18C] **1** to take a woman's virginity. **2** to lose one's virginity.

pipkin *n.*[2] *see* PIPPIN *n.* (2).

pipped *adj.*[1] [PIP *v.*[1] (3)] **1** [1910s] drunk. **2** [1910s–20s] wounded. **3** [1910s+] beaten.

pipped *adj.*[2] [PIP *n.*[1] (1)] [1910s+] annoyed, irritated.

pipper *n.* [the 'pips' of rank on their shoulders] [1980s+] (*Aus. prison*) a senior prison officer.

pippiejoller *n. see* PIEPIEJOLLER *n.*

pippin *n.* [SE *pippin*, the name of various types of apple] **1** [mid-17C–early 18C; 1900s–10s] a pej. term of address or description. **2** [mid-17C+] (*also* **pipkin, pippins**) a term of approval or congratulation, applied to a person; thus affectionate term of address *my pippin*. **3** [late 19C+] a perfect example of whatever is under discussion; usu. as *it's a pippin*. **4** [1900s] a loved one. **5** [1920s–40s] the female breast.

pippin-squire *n.* [play on *APPLE SQUIRE under* APPLE *n.*[1]; i.e. SE *pippin*, used in the names of various types of apple] [early–mid-17C] a pimp.

pip-pip *adj.* [PIP-PIP! *excl.* (2)] [1930s] (*US*) Anglicized; in an English manner.

pip-pip! *excl.* [the noise of the cyclist's horn] **1** [late 19C] a street cry, often launched at passing cyclists (still a novelty in late 19C). **2** [20C+] goodbye! hello! **3** [1940s+] a toast.

pippish *adj. see under* PIP *n.*[1].

pippy *adj. see under* PIP *n.*[1].

pippy-poo *adj.* [20C+] (*US*) extremely small, tiny.

pirate *n.* **1** [20C+] (*Aus.*) a man who wanders around looking for a casual pick-up; thus *on the pirate*, looking for a casual pick-up. **2** [1930s] (*US*) a promiscuous woman, a prostitute. **3** [1940s] (*US Und.*) a pimp who steals a prostitute from a fellow-pimp. **4** [1990s+] (*W.I.*) an oppressor.

pirate *v.* **1** [20C+] (*Aus.*) to pick up in the hope of seduction [PIRATE *n.* (1)]. **2** [1930s] (*US*) to be a criminal.

pirate's dream *n.* [she has a 'sunken chest'] [1980s+] (*US campus*) a flat-chested woman.

pisa *n. see* PAISA *n.*

pisel *v. see* PEYSLE *v.*

pish *n.* [SE *pish!* expressing disgust or impatience; plus var. on PISS *n.* (6)] **1** [1940s+] rubbish, nonsense. **2** [1940s+] (*Irish/Scot.*) a var. on PISS *n.* in various phrs. **3** *see* PISS *n.* (4b).

pish *v.* [1940s+] **1** to urinate [PISS *v.* (2)]. **2** (*Ulster*) to rain heavily [PISS *v.* (3)].

pisher *n.*[1] (*also* **pishkeh**) [synon. Yid.] [1940s+] an insignificant person.

pisher *n.*[2] *see* PISSER *n.* (2b).

pishery-pashery *n.* [SE *pish!* nonsense! rubbish!] [late 16C–early 17C] nonsense, rubbish.

pish-posh *n.* (*also* **pish-tush**) [SE *pish!*, nonsense! rubbish!] [1910s–30s] (*US*) rubbish, nonsense.

pish-tosh *v.* [PISH-POSH *n.*] [1940s] to deride, to mock.

pisk *n.* [? a Yiddishised version of PUSS *n.*[2] (1)] [1930s] the human face.

piss *n.* [PISS *v.* (2)] **1** [late 14C+] urine. **2** [mid-18C+] an act of urination. **3** [mid-19C; 1970s] vaginal fluid. **4** as a drink. (**a**) [1910s+] any sort of weak or otherwise unpalatable drink, whether alcoholic or non-alcoholic. (**b**) [1910s+] (*also* **pish**) an alcoholic drink. (**c**) [1920s+] beer. **5** [1930s+] constr. with *the*, a general intensifier; the essence, the 'daylights'. **6** [1940s+] rubbish, nonsense, anything or anyone unappealing, worthless. **7** [1960s] in fig. use, high spirits.

DERIVATIVES

❑ **pissless** *adj. see* separate entry.

IN COMPOUNDS

adjectival or adverbial uses

❑ **piss-ache** [1940s+] appalling, unpleasant, distasteful. ❑ **piss-ass** *see* PISSY-ARSED *under* PISSY *adj.*[1]. ❑ **pissballing** *see* separate entry. ❑ **piss-burned** [late 17C–early 19C] discoloured, esp. of a grey wig which has turned yellow. ❑ **piss-faced** *see* separate entry. ❑ **piss-proud** [late 18C+] of a man, having an erection on waking. ❑ **piss-scared** [1980s] terrified. ❑ **piss-taking** *see* separate entry.

general uses

❑ **piss-all** *n.* [var. on FUCK ALL *n.*] [1990s+] nothing at all. ❑ **piss and punk** *n.* [PUNK *n.*[3]] [20C+] (*orig. US prison*) bread and water. ❑ **piss artist** *n.* [-ARTIST *sfx*] **1** [1940s+] a regular drunk. **2** [1990s+] a general term of abuse. ❑ **piss-bag** *n.* [-BAG *sfx*] [1980s] a despicable person. ❑ **piss-barrel** *n. see* PISSPOT *n.* ❑ **piss britches** *n.* [i.e. one who 'wets their pants'] [1960s] (*US black*) a general term of abuse. ❑ **piss bucket** *n.* [2000s] (*US*) a contemptible person. ❑ **piss-call** *n.* [1950s+] a break – during work or on a journey – for urination. ❑ **pisscan** *n.* [CAN *n.*[1] (4c)] [1940s–50s] (*US prison*) a prison. ❑ **piss-cutter** *n.* [? the sharpness, whether seen as positive or negative] [1940s+] (*US*) **1** a generally obnoxious person. **2** an admirable or exceptional person. **3** an outstanding or excellent thing. **4** a drunken spree, a binge. **5** a major confrontation. ❑ **pissface** *n. see* separate entry. ❑ **piss-factory** *n.* [late 19C–1940s] a public house. ❑ **pissfart** *n.* [2000s] (*N.Z.*) an insignificant person. ❑ **pissflaps** *n.* (*also* **piss-flappers**) **1** [1970s+] the labia [FLAP *n.*[1] (7)]. **2** [2000s] a term of abuse. ❑ **piss freak** *n.* [FREAK *n.*[1] (7)] [2000s] a person who derives sexual satisfaction from being urinated on. ❑ **piss hard-on** *n.* (*also* **piss-horn**) [HARD-ON *n.* (1)/HORN *n.*[2] (1c)] [1960s+] the erection with which a man awakes, due to the need to urinate as much as the desire for sex. ❑ **piss-head** *n. see* separate entry. ❑ **pisshole** *see* separate entries. ❑ **pisshouse** *n.* **1** [mid-17C; 1940s+] a lavatory. **2** [1930s–40s] (*US Und.*) a police station. **3** [1960s] an unpleasant place. ❑ **piss-kitchen** *n.* [SE *kitchen*, i.e. where she (fig.) urinates] [mid-18C] a kitchen maid. ❑ **piss-maker** *n.* [the results of alcohol consumption] [late 18C–early 19C] a heavy drinker. ❑ **piss pipe** *n.* [SE *pipe*/PIPE *n.*[1] (2a)] [1990s+] the male urinary tract. ❑ **pisspot** *see* separate entries. ❑ **piss prophet** *n.* (*also* **pisspot-peeper**) [PISSPOT *n.* + SE *prophet/peeper*] [late 17C–early 19C] a physician who makes all their diagnoses on the basis of inspecting the patient's urine. ❑ **piss stop** *n.* [pun on SE *pit stop*, motor-racing jargon] [1980s+] a visit to the lavatory, esp. during a drive or drinking session. ❑ **piss-take/-taker/-taking** *see* separate entries. ❑ **piss-tank** *n.* [20C+] a drunkard. ❑ **piss test** *see* separate entries. ❑ **piss-walloper** *n.* [1900s] (*US*) something remarkable, impressive. ❑ **piss-water** *n.* [2000s] (*US*) a weak drink. ❑ **piss-willie** *n.* [1970s] (*US*) a coward, an insignificant person; also attrib.

IN PHRASES

pertaining to (weak) drink

❑ **buffalo piss** *n.* [1970s+] (*US*) weak beer. ❑ **bull piss** *n.* [1910s+] (*US*) very low quality, cheap liquor. ❑ **cat's piss** *n.* [1940s+] any form of weak drink. ❑ **dogpiss** *n.* [1990s+] any weak or diluted drink. ❑ **gnat's piss** *n. see* separate entry. ❑ **horse piss** *n. see* separate entry. ❑ **monkey piss** *n.* [1970s] (*US*) weak beer or bad wine. ❑ **panther piss** *n. see* separate entry. ❑ **shark's piss** *n.* [1900s] weak beer or other alcohol. ❑ **snake's piss** *n.* [1960s–70s] (*Aus.*) beer.

pertaining to the 'essence' in the context of violence

❑ **beat the piss out of** *v.* (*also* **mangle the piss out of, pound..., whop..., beat the holy piss out of, ...the living piss out of, stomp the pissin' out of**) [WHOP *v.* (1)] [1930s+] (*orig. US*) to beat severely. ❑ **kick the piss out of** *v.* [1930s] to beat severely. ❑ **knock the piss out of** *v.* [1970s] to beat up, to assault. ❑ **rip the piss out of** *v.* [2000s] to tease aggressively. ❑ **scare the piss out of** *v.* [1970s+] to terrify. ❑ **take the piss (out of)** *v.* (*also* **piss-take**) **1** [1930s+] to tease, esp. aggressively. **2** [1930s+] to attack verbally, to sneer or jeer at. **3** [1980s+] to make something up, to say something ludicrous, to make grand claims, to joke; e.g. *he must be taking the piss*, he must be joking (because what he is saying is so ridiculous or unfair etc). **4** [1990s+] of a person, to act absurdly, to play the fool. **5** [1990s+] of a man, to have sexual intercourse. ❑ **whip the piss (out of)** *v.* [1990s+] to beat severely. ❑ **whop the piss out of** *v. see* BEAT THE PISS OUT OF above.

general uses

❑ **all piss and wind (like the barber's cat)** (*also* **all piddle and wind like the barber's cat, all wind and piss**) **1** [20C+] a phr. describing a loudmouth, a braggart, all talk and no action. **2** [1920s+] empty talk. **3** [1940s+] (*Aus./N.Z.*) a phr. describing a very thin person. ❑ **arse-piss** *n.* [ARSE *n.* (1)] [1990s+] diarrhoea. ❑ **can of piss** *n.* [2000s] (*Irish*) a term of abuse. ❑ **feel one's piss** *v.* [1940s] to become infatuated with one's own importance. ❑ **he would drink the piss from a brewer's horse** [2000s] (*N.Z.*) a phr. used of a dedicated drinker. ❑ **hit the piss** *v.* [1970s] to get drunk. ❑ **like a snob's cat – all piss and tantrums** [SE *snob*, a bootmaker] [early–mid-19C] a general phr. of derision or disdain. ❑ **make a piss stop** *v.* [pun on SE *pit stop*, motor-racing jargon] [1980s+] to visit the lavatory, esp. to stop drinking in order to do so. ❑ **not enough sense to pour piss out of a boot** [20C+] (*US*) a phr. used of one who is very stupid. ❑ **not give someone the steam on one's piss** *v.* [1980s+] to hold in absolute contempt. ❑ **on the piss** [1910s+] out drinking, usu. with friends; usu. in phr. *go/get on the piss*. ❑ **piece of piss** *n.* **1** [1920s] a term of contempt. **2** [1940s+] (*orig. RAF*) anything seen as supremely easy. ❑ **piss-in-the-face** *n.* [1970s] a despicable person. ❑ **piss in the hand** *n.* [1970s+] (*N.Z.*) anything considered very easy. ❑ **piss in the wind** *n.* [PISS IN(TO) THE WIND *under* PISS *v.*] [1960s+] a waste of time. ❑ **piss-in-the-wind** *adj.* [1990s+] pointless, time-wasting. ❑ **piss over teakettle** [var. on ARSE OVER TEAKETTLE *under* ARSE *n.*] [1990s+] head-over-heels. ❑ **poor as piss** *adj. see* PISS-POOR *under* PISS- *pfx.* ❑ **puddle of piss** *n.* [1950s] a contemptible person, object or circumstance.

piss *adj.* [PISS *n.* (6)] [1950s] rubbish, second-rate.

piss *v.* [? echoic] **1** [late 17C] to issue vaginal secretions. **2** [mid-18C+] to urinate [prior use is SE dating back to 13C]. **3** [1920s+] to rain heavily; usu. in phr. *piss down*. **4** [1930s+] in ext. use, to exude liquid, other than urine; also in fig. use. **5** [1940s+] (*orig. US*) to complain, to whinge. **6** [1960s+] in fig. use, to deride, to attack, to disdain. **7** *see* PISS-TEST *v.* (1).

IN COMPOUNDS

❑ **piss-making** *adj.* [it makes one want to *piss*] [1990s+] (*US black*) infuriating. ❑ **piss-parade** *v.* [PISS ON SOMEONE'S PARADE *under* PISS ON *v.*] [1970s+] (*W.I.*) to shatter illusions, to ruin an otherwise satisfactory situation. ❑ **piss-quick** *n.* [its resemblance to urine or ? its micturative effect] [early 19C] gin mixed with marmalade topped up with boiling water.

IN PHRASES

❑ **good as ever pissed** [mid-17C–18C] of a person, as good as there has ever been. ❑ **he looks like he wouldn't piss if his pants were on fire** [20C+] a phr. used of an especially dull, stupid-looking person. ❑ **I'll be pissed** [1970s] a phr. implying impossibility. ❑ **make someone piss** *v.* **1** [late 17C] to annoy, to infuriate, to disgust. **2** [1980s] (*Aus.*) to beat up, to defeat. ❑ **piss about** *v. see* separate entry. ❑ **piss all over** *v. see* PISS ON *v.* ❑ **piss all over someone and tell them it's raining** *v. see* PISS IN SOMEONE'S EAR AND TELL THEM IT'S RAINING below. ❑ **piss and moan** *v.* [1950s+] (*orig. US*) to complain, to whinge. ❑ **piss around** *v. see* PISS ABOUT *v.* ❑ **piss-arse about** *v.* [ext. PISS ABOUT *v.* (1)] [1920s+] (*orig. milit.*) to mess about. ❑ **piss away** *v.* [fig. use of sense 2 above] [20C+] to waste. ❑ **piss-ball about** *v. see* separate entry. ❑ **piss blood** *v.* **1** [late 19C+] to work extremely hard. **2** [1960s+] to worry excessively, to make a great fuss. **3** [1960s+] to suffer a great deal. ❑ **piss bones** *v.* (*also* **piss children, ...hard**) [late 19C–

1900s] to go into labour, to give birth. ◻ **piss broken glass** *v.* (*also* **piss razor blades**) [the pain experienced when urinating during a bout of VD] [1960s+] to have venereal disease, esp. gonorrhoea. ◻ **piss bullets** *v. see* SHIT BULLETS *under* SHIT *v.* ◻ **piss down someone's back** *v.* (*also* **piss up someone's back**) [late 18C–early 19C] to flatter someone. ◻ **piss in** *v. see* separate entry. ◻ **piss in a quill** *v.* [the narrowness of a quill and the need to bend the flow of urine to achieve the feat] [late 17C–mid-18C; 1950s] to agree on a plan. ◻ **piss (in) one's pants** *v. see* separate entry. ◻ **piss in someone's ear and tell them it's raining** *v.* (*also* **piss all over someone and...**) [1990s+] to deceive. ◻ **piss in someone's pocket** *v.* (*also* **piss in the same pot, pee...**) [1920s+] (*Aus.*) to curry favour, to be extremely close to someone, to ingratiate oneself. ◻ **piss in(to) the wind** *v.* [the futility thereof] [1960s+] to waste one's efforts or time. ◻ **piss it** *v.* [fig. use of sense 2 above] [1970s+] to succeed with no difficulty whatsoever, to win very easily. ◻ **piss it up** *v.* [PISSED *adj.*[1]] [1960s+] to drink. ◻ **piss it up the wall** *v.* (*also* **piss it against the wall, ...on the wall, ...out of the window**) [var. on next] [late 15C+] to waste money on drink; thus to waste money in general. ◻ **piss (money) against the wall** *v.* [the cost of a drink lost through urinating afterwards] [late 15C+] to waste money, usu. on drink. ◻ **piss off** *see* separate entries. ◻ **piss on** *v. see* separate entry. ◻ **piss one's breeches** *v. see* PISS (IN) ONE'S PANTS *v.* (1). ◻ **piss oneself** *v. see* separate entry. ◻ **piss one's tallow** *v.* [SE *piss one's grease/tallow*, said of a deer becoming lean in rutting-time] **1** [late 16C–17C] of a man, to be sufficiently sexually excited as to ejaculate (without actual intercourse). **2** [late 17C] to sweat. ◻ **piss on ice** *v.* [1920s] (*US*) to live well, esp. to visit an upmarket restaurant (where blocks of ice are placed in the urinals). ◻ **piss on someone's parade** *v. see under* PISS ON *v.* ◻ **piss or get off the pot** [1940s+] (*orig. US*) either make a decision or let someone else do it. ◻ **piss out of a dozen holes** *v.* [i.e. the rotting of one's penis] [late 19C+] of a man, to be infected with syphilis. ◻ **piss pins and needles** *v.* [pain during urination can be one of the symptoms of venereal disease] [late 18C–early 19C] to have venereal disease, esp. gonorrhoea. ◻ **piss razor blades** *v. see* PISS BROKEN GLASS above. ◻ **piss through** *v.* [fig. use of sense 2 above] [1910s+] to do something with no difficulty. ◻ **piss up** *see* separate entries. ◻ **piss up a rope** *v.* [1980s] (*US*) to be engaged in a futile exercise. ◻ **piss up a storm** *v.* **1** [20C+] (*US*) to complain strongly, to make a major fuss. **2** [1990s+] to urinate for a relatively long time. ◻ **piss up someone's back** *v. see* PISS DOWN SOMEONE'S BACK above. ◻ **piss up someone's leg** *v.* [1990s+] (*US*) to lie, to deceive. ◻ **piss when one cannot whistle** *v.* [the loss of bladder control that results from being hanged] [late 18C–early 19C] to be hanged. ◻ **think it's just to piss through** *v. see* THINK IT'S JUST TO PEE THROUGH *under* PEE *v.* ◻ **wouldn't piss on someone if they were on fire** [1960s+] a phr. implying the speaker's absolute contempt or loathing for the person thus decried.

IN EXCLAMATIONS

◻ **go (and) piss up a rope!** (*also* **go piss up a flagpole! ... pipe! ...shutter! ...your leg!**) [1930s+] (*orig. US*) a general excl. of dismissal. ◻ **piss around a pretzel!** [1970s] (*US*) a dismissive excl.

piss! *excl.* **1** [late 17C–early 18C] constr. with *a*, a general excl. of disgust or annoyance. **2** [1950s+] a general excl.

piss- *pfx* [1940s+] (*orig. US*) a general intensifier, usu. derog. but not always.

IN COMPOUNDS

◻ **piss-awful** *adj.* [1970s+] very bad, very unpleasant. ◻ **piss-easy** *adj.* [1980s+] (*orig. N.Z.*) very easy. ◻ **piss-elegance/-elegant** *see* separate entries. ◻ **piss-poor** *adj.* (*also* **poor as piss**) **1** [1940s+] third-rate, incompetent, useless. **2** [1960s+] totally lacking in finances. ◻ **piss-rotten** *adj.* [1940s+] appalling, unpleasant, distasteful. ◻ **piss-sick** *adj.* [SE *sick* (and tired)] [1990s+] utterly contemptous. ◻ **piss-ugly** *adj.* [1980s+] (*orig. US*) very ugly.

pissabed *n.* (*also* **pee-the-bed**) [PISS *v.* (2)] **1** [mid-17C+] a bed-wetter. **2** [mid-18C; 1920s] a general derisive epithet.

piss about *v.* (*also* **piss around**) [fig. use of PISS *v.* (2)] **1** [20C+] to waste time, to mess about. **2** [1930s+] to wander, to go. **3** [1980s+] to irritate or tease someone.

pissant *n.* [SE *pissant*, an ant] [1930s+] an insignificant person, a 'nobody'; thus *drunk as a pissant*, very drunk; *game as a pissant*, very brave.

IN PHRASES

◻ **pissant (around)** *v.* [1940s+] (*Aus.*) **1** to mess around. **2** to defeat, to outwit.

pissant *adj.* (*also* **pissy-ant**) [PISSANT *n.*] [1960s+] insignificant, trifling.

piss-ball about *v.* [1920s+] to mess about, to idle.

pissballing *adj.* [PISS-BALL ABOUT *v.*] [2000s] mean, contemptuous.

pissed *adj.*[1] (*also* **peed**) [PISS *n.* (1)] [20C+] drunk; thus *half-pissed*, tipsy.

IN PHRASES

◻ **pissed as...** *adj.* [20C+] in combs. with a n., very drunk; for expressions other than those listed below *see* DRUNK AS (A)... *adj.* ◻ **...a chook** [CHOOK *n.* (1)] [1980s+] (*N.Z.*) ◻ **...a fart** [fig. use of FART *n.* (1)] [1960s+] ◻ **...a newt** [1950s+] ◻ **...a parrot** [1970s+] (*Aus.*) ◻ **...a rat** [1980s+] ◻ **...arseholes** [fig. use of ARSEHOLE *n.* (1)] [1940s+] ◻ **...a sparrow** [1980s] (*Aus.*) ◻ **pissed to...** *adj.* [1960s+] in combs. with a n., very drunk. ◻ **...the ears** [1960s+] ◻ **...the eyeballs** [1990s+] (*Aus.*) ◻ **...the gills** [TO THE GILLS *under* GILLS *n.*] [1970s+] (*US*)

pissed *adj.*[2] [abbr. PISSED OFF *adj.*] [1950s+] (*US*) annoyed; thus *pissedness*, anger.

pissed off *adj.* (*also* **p'd off**) [? US var. on BROWNED OFF *adj.*] [1940s+] (*orig. US*) furious, very annoyed; bored.

pissed-out *adj.* **1** [1950s] (*US*) useless, third-rate. **2** [1960s+] (*US*) exhausted, finished.

pissed up *adj.* [PISSED *adj.*[1]] [1910s+] very drunk.

IN PHRASES

◻ **all pissed up and nothing to show** [1910s–60s] a general phr. of discontent, based on the premise that one has drunk away one's wages and there's nothing left to show for a week's work.

piss-elegance *n.* (*also* **piss-elegant**) [PISS-ELEGANT *adj.*] [1970s+] extreme elegance, used lit. and ironically.

piss-elegant *adj.* [PISS- *pfx* + SE *elegant*] [1940s+] extremely elegant (usu. used ironically or deprecatingly).

pisser *n.* [PISS *n.* (1)/PISS *v.* (2)] **1** in concrete uses. (**a**) [late 19C+] a urinal. (**b**) [late 19C+] the penis. (**c**) [late 19C+] the vagina. (**d**) [1920s+] one who urinates. (**e**) [1950s–60s] a very unpleasant place. (**f**) [1970s] (*US prison*) solitary confinement. (**g**) [1980s] a public house. (**h**) [1980s] a drunkard. (**i**) [2000s] (*Irish*) a heavy drinking session. **2** [1940s+] (*US*) in fig. uses [used here in the sense of 'that which makes one (fig.) *piss*']. (**a**) (*also* **pisseroo**) an extraordinary person or thing. (**b**) (*also* **pisher**) a difficult or distasteful event or task, an unpleasant person. (**c**) a bloke, a chap, esp. one who is tough and purposeful. (**d**) something or someone considered hilariously funny.

IN PHRASES

◻ **pull someone's pisser** *v.* [1920s+] to tease, to deceive.

pissface *n.* [PISS *n.* (1)] [1990s+] (*UK juv.*) a general term of abuse.

piss-faced *adj.* [PISS *n.* (4b)] [2000s] (*Aus.*) very drunk.

piss-head *n.* **1** [1950s+] a heavy drinker [PISS *n.* (4b) + -HEAD *sfx* (4)]. **2** [1980s+] an obnoxious person [PISS *n.* (1) + -HEAD *sfx* (4)].

pisshole *n.* [PISS *n.* (1) + SE *hole*] [1950s+] **1** the vagina. **2** a urinal, a lavatory. **3** any very dirty or unpleasant house, room or place. **4** the urethra.

IN PHRASES

◻ **not worth a pisshole in the snow** [1960s+] worthless, useless. ◻ **pisshole bandit** *n.* **1** [1960s+] a minor criminal [-BANDIT *sfx* (1)]. **2** [1970s] a male homosexual who solicits in lavatories [-BANDIT *sfx* (2)]. ◻ **pissholes in the snow** *n.*

[1960s+] eyes which are bloodshot, shrunken and showing signs of excess.

pisshole *adj.* [PISSHOLE *n.* (3)] [1950s+] second-rate, inferior, disgusting.

piss in *v.* [PISS *v.* (2), the natural ease of urination] [1980s+] (*N.Z.*) to achieve with ease; thus n.

pissing *adj.* [PISS *v.* (2)] **1** [mid-16C+] urinating. **2** [1950s+] a general adj. of abuse. **3** [1960s+] in fig. use, implying short.

pissing *adv.* [PISS *v.* (2)] [1950s] extremely.

pissing contest *n.* [fig. use of PISS *v.* (2) + SE *contest*; the image of two small boys urinating against a wall, each attempting to aim the flow of urine higher] [1970s+] (*mainly US*) any form of competition in which the participants are motivated more by the need to assert their superiority than by any desire to attain an accurate or positive conclusion.

pissing fou *adj.* [PISS *v.* (2) + FOU *adj.*[1]; the idea of urinating through drunkenness] [19C] very drunk.

pissing place *n.* [mid-17C] the vagina.

pissing-pot *n. see* PISSPOT *n.*

pissing-tail *adj.* (*also* **piss'n'tail, pissy-tail**) [PISS *v.* (2) + TAIL *n.* (2); the image is of a toddler still wetting itself] [20C+] (*W.I.*) **1** esp. of a young person, disrespectful, bumptious. **2** officious but impoverished and socially unimportant.

piss (in) one's pants *v.* [fig. use of PISS *v.* (2)] **1** [late 18C; 1960s+] (*also* **piss one's breeches**) to be terrified. **2** [1920s+] (*US*) to be very excited, in a state of suspense. **3** [1950s+] to be irritable or angry. **4** [1960s+] to laugh hysterically. **5** [1970s+] to make a fool of oneself. **6** [1990s+] to be very keen.

pissless *adj.*

(IN PHRASES)

□ **scare pissless** *v.* [1910s] to terrify.

piss'n'tail *n. see* PISSING-TAIL *adj.*

pisso *n.* [PISSED *adj.*[1] + -O *sfx* (3)] [1960s] (*Aus.*) a drunkard; a general term of abuse.

piss-off *n.* [PISS OFF *v.* (2)] [1980s+] something or someone annoying.

piss-off *adj.* [PISS OFF *v.* (2)] [1990s+] annoying, irritating.

piss off *v.* [PISS *v.* (2)] **1** [1910s+] to leave. **2** [1950s+] (*also* **piss up**) to annoy; thus *pissed-offness*, a state of anger; euph. *wee-wee off*.

piss off! *excl.* [PISS OFF *v.* (1)] [1950s+] an excl. of rejection, dismissal.

pissoliver *n.* [? SP. *pistolero*] [20C+] (*US*) a pistol, a revolver.

piss on *v.* (*also* **piss all over, piss up**) [fig. use of PISS *v.* (2)] **1** [17C+] to treat contemptuously. **2** [1950s+] to be drenched with rain.

(IN PHRASES)

□ **piss on...** [1930s+] to hell with; thus excl. *piss on it!* who cares! □ **piss on a nettle** *v.* [mid-16C–mid-18C] to be annoyed, uneasy, tetchy; thus *on nettles*, anxious, uneasy. □ **piss on one's shoe** *v.* [1980s] to blunder, to fail in a task. □ **piss on someone's chips** *v.* [1980s] (*Can.*) to spoil someone's plans. □ **piss on someone's parade** *v.* (*also* **rain on someone's parade, shit on...**) [fig. use of SE *rain*/SHIT *v.*] [1970s+] (*orig. US*) to shatter illusions, to ruin an otherwise satisfactory situation. □ **piss on someone's shoe** *v.* [1970s] (*US*) to humiliate.

(IN EXCLAMATIONS)

□ **piss on you!** [1950s+] a general insult.

piss oneself *v.* [fig. uses of PISS *v.* (2)] **1** [late 18C; 1960s+] to urinate on oneself, esp. in the context of being utterly terrified. **2** [1940s+] to laugh uproariously.

pisspot *n.* (*also* **pee-pot, piss-barrel, pissing-pot**) [PISS *n.* (1) + SE *pot*/PEE *n.*[1] (1)] **1** [mid-16C+] a chamberpot. **2** [late 16C+] an unpleasant person or contemptible place. **3** [1960s+] a drunkard. **4** [1970s+] a lavatory bowl. **5** [1990s+] anywhere unpleasant, dirty, smelly etc.

(IN COMPOUNDS)

□ **Piss Pot Hall** *n.* [Dr Henry Sacheverell (c.1674–1724) was a High Church and high Tory cleric, who preached two sermons in 1709 that resulted in his impeachment on charges of seditious libel. He was condemned, but received so light a punishment as to claim victory. His supporters were as vehement as the unknown potter. The Rector of Whitechapel commissioned an altarpiece in which the figure of Judas Iscariot was represented by that of the Dean of Peterborough, one of the Doctor's most virulent critics] [late 18C] 'a house [? a tavern] at Clapton, near Hackney [in northeast London] built by a potter chiefly out of the profits of chamberpots, in the bottom of which the portrait of Dr Sacheverell, preacher, was depicted' (Grose, 1796). □ **pisspot-peeper** *n. see* PISS PROPHET *under* PISS *n.*

(IN PHRASES)

□ **know the pisspot from the handle** *v.* [1990s+] (*US tramp*) to be wise.

pisspot *adj.* [PISSPOT *n.* (1)] [17C; 1930s+] third-rate, incompetent.

piss-take *n.* (*also* **piss-taking**) [PISS-TAKE *v.*] [1970s+] a tease, a hoax, a practical joke.

piss-take *v. see* TAKE THE PISS (OUT OF) *under* PISS *n.*

piss-taker *n.* [PISS-TAKE *v.*] [1990s+] a teaser, a joker, a mocker.

piss-taking *n. see* PISS-TAKE *n.*

piss-taking *adj.* [PISS-TAKE *v.*] [1940s+] teasing, mocking, fooling.

piss test *n.* [PISS *n.* (1) + SE *test*] [1970s+] (*drugs*) a urine analysis, carried out to check for drug use.

piss-test *v.* [PISS TEST *n.*] **1** [1990s+] (*drugs*) (*also* **piss**) to carry out a urine analysis. **2** [2000s] to take a urine test.

piss-up *n.* [PISSED *adj.*[1]] [1950s+] a drunken party; a drunken spree.

piss up *v.* **1** [1960s–70s] (*US*) to vomit. **2** *see* PISS OFF *v.* (2). **3** *see* PISS ON *v.*

pissy *adj.*[1] [PISS *n.*] **1** [1930s+] redolent of urine. **2** [1950s+] drunken. **3** [1960s+] unpleasant. **4** [1960s+] weak, ineffectual, trifling.

(IN COMPOUNDS)

□ **pissy-ant** *adj. see* PISSANT *adj.* □ **pissy-arsed** *adj.* (*also* **piss-ass, pissy-assed**) [ARSE *n.* (4)/-ASS *sfx*/-ASSED *sfx*] **1** [1940s+] extremely drunk. **2** [1950s+] (*also* **pissy pants**) (*US*) insignificant, useless, juvenile. **3** [1960s] a synon. for BLOODY *adj.* (1), FUCKING *adj.* etc. **4** [1960s+] unpleasant. □ **pissy-eyed** *adj.* **1** [1960s+] (*US*) extremely drunk. **2** [1980s+] (*N.Z.*) (mildly) drunk. □ **pissy-tail** *adj. see* PISSING-TAIL *adj.* □ **pissy weed** *n.* [WEED *n.*[1] (4)] [2000s] (*US black/drugs*) marijuana that burns with a slightly urinous smell.

pissy *adj.*[2] **1** [1950s+] cocky, arrogant [PISS OFF *v.* (2)]. **2** [1970s+] irritated, angry; also as *in a pissy* [PISSED OFF *adj.*].

pistakle *n.* (*also* **pistarckle**) [? PISS ABOUT *v.* + SE *spectacle*] [20C+] (*W.I.*) **1** a foolish confusion. **2** a confused, foolish person, one who makes a fool of themselves in public.

pistareen *n.* [? Irish] [mid-19C] (*US Und.*) a thief who claims, presumably fraudulently, to be of good family, to have never committed a crime before etc.

pistol *n.* **1** [late 16C+] the penis; also occas. the vagina [thus Shakespeare's double pun 'Pistol's cock is up' (*Henry V*, 1599)]. **2** [1930s+] (*US*) anything or anyone seen as remarkable, exemplary etc [underpinned by phr. 'hot as a pistol']. **3** [1940s] (*US black*) in pl., the trousers of a ZOOT SUIT *n.* [they 'shoot forward']. **4** [1950s] a thug. **5** [1980s] a sexual athlete. **6** *see* POCKET PISTOL *under* POCKET *n.*

(IN COMPOUNDS)

□ **pistol local** *n.* [1950s] (*US*) a trade union local run by corrupt bosses; any rebels are suborned by physical violence. □ **pistol pocket** *n.* [1930s] the buttocks.

(IN PHRASES)

□ **put lead in one's pistol** *v. see* PUT LEAD IN ONE'S PENCIL *under* PENCIL *n.*

pistol *v. see* GUN *v.*[2] (2).

pistol-shot *n.* [mid-19C–1940s] a drink, a shot of liquor.

piston *n.* [1960s+] the penis.

pit *n.* **1** [mid-17C+] (*also* **sawpit**) the vagina. **2** [late 17C–early 19C] (*UK Und.*) the common grave, beneath the gallows, in which those who fail to pay a burial fee of 6s 8d are buried after their remains have been cut down. **3** [early 19C+] a breast pocket; thus (*UK Und.*) *pit-worker*, a pickpocket who specializes in robbing inside pockets. **4** [late 19C+] (*UK Und.*) a wallet [from sense 3]. **5** [1940s+] as a place, usu. untidy, dirty. (**a**) a bed. (**b**) a real mess, esp. a room that is untidy. (**c**) an unattractive, unpleasant place. **6** [1950s+] (*orig. US*) in fig. use, as *the pits*. (**a**) a situation, object or person who is totally undesirable. (**b**) the depths of despair; thus *in the pits*, very depressed. **7** [1950s+] an armpit, with an implication of body odour; usu. in pl., thus *the pits*, body odour. **8** [1960s] (*drugs*) the place on the inside of the elbow that is often used for injections. **9** [1960s+] (*orig. US*) a pit bull terrier [abbr.].

DERIVATIVES

▫ **pitty** *adj.* [1970s+] (*US campus*) messy, untidy, disgusting.

IN COMPOUNDS

▫ **pit-hole** *n.* **1** [17C] hell; a grave. **2** [19C] (*also* **pit mouth, pit of darkness**) the vagina. ▫ **pit job** *n.* [JOB *n.*[2] (2)] [1960s] intercourse *in axilla*, i.e. beneath the armpit.

IN PHRASES

▫ **hit the pit** *v.* **1** [1960s] (*N.Z.*) to go to bed. **2** [2000s] to inject a drug.

p.i.t.a. *n. see* PAIN IN THE ARSE *n.*

pitch *n.*[1] [fig. uses of SE *pitch*, to throw] **1** [mid-19C; 1910s+] (*orig. US*) any plan that should benefit its maker, a scheme, esp. a piece of trickery or deceit. **2** [mid-19C+] sales talk, esp. when inflated; also in fig. use. **3** [late 19C–1910s] a conversation, a chat. **4** [1930s+] the line of talk used by a swindler. **5** [1940s+] an area conducive to crime. **6** [1940s+] (*US*) a situation.

pitch *n.*[2] [? one 'pitches camp'] [late 19C–1900s] a nap, a short sleep.

pitch *n.*[3] [SE *pitch camp*; although Mayhew, *London Labour and the London Poor* (1861–2), apostrophizes it; *pitch*, 'a spot in a street or other public place at which a stall for the sale or display of something is pitched or set up, or at which a street performer, a bookmaker, etc stations himself' (*OED*) has been SE since late 17C] [20C+] (*Aus.*) a camp.

pitch *v.* [fig. use of SE *pitch*, to throw] **1** [mid-19C–1910s] (*UK Und.*) to pass counterfeit coins. **2** [mid-19C+] to tell a tale, to speak persuasively. **3** [1930s+] (*drugs*) to sell drugs. **4** in sexual uses [baseball imagery; ult. fig. use of SE *pitch*, to throw]. (**a**) [1960s+] (*gay*) to be the active partner in anal sex or in sado-masochism. (**b**) [1980s+] (*Aus. prison*) to act in an ostentatiously homosexual manner. (**c**) [1990s+] (*US campus*) to ejaculate.

IN PHRASES

▫ **pitch a ball** *v.* (*also* **pitch a party**) [BALL *n.*[3] (1)/play on SE] [1930s] (*US black*) to host or enjoy oneself at a party. ▫ **pitch a bitch** *v. see under* BITCH *n.*[1]. ▫ **pitch a fork** *v.* (*also* **pitch the fork**) [? play on SE *pitch*, throw / *pitchfork*] [mid-19C–1930s] to tell a story, esp. a sad or romantic one. ▫ **pitch a tent in one's shorts** *v.* [1990s+] (*orig. US*) to get an erection. ▫ **pitch a yarn** *v. see under* YARN *n.* ▫ **pitch boogie** *v.* [BOOGIE *n.*[3] (3)] [1950s] (*US*) of a man, to seduce a woman. ▫ **pitch it strong** *v.* (*also* **pitch it high, ...hot, ...into, ...warm**) [STRONG *adv.* (1)/SE *high*/HOT *adv.* (1)/WARM *adv.*] [mid-19C+] to speak forcefully, to state a case with feeling or enthusiasm, to exaggerate. ▫ **pitch on** *v.* **1** [late 17C–19C] to target. **2** [1930s+] (*Aus.*) to nag, to attack verbally, to tell off. ▫ **pitch the crack** *v.* (*also* **crack the pitch**) [SE *crack*, a break / to break] [mid-19C] (*UK Und.*) to stop doing something. ▫ **pitch the cuffer** *v.* [SE *cuffer*, a yarn or story; ult. *cuff*, to discuss, to tell a story] [late 19C–1900s] to tell exaggerated stories, esp. as a confidence trickster. ▫ **pitch the dirt** *v.* [DIRT *n.* (6)] [1950s] (*US*) to gossip (maliciously), to slander. ▫ **pitch the fork** *v. see* PITCH A FORK above. ▫ **pitch the nob** *v. see* PRICK THE GARTER *under* PRICK *v.*[2]. ▫ **pitch the tale** *v.* [mid-19C+] to tell exaggerated stories, esp. as a confidence trickster. ▫ **pitch the woo** *v.* [1930s+] (*Aus./US*) to utter affectionate pleasantries. ▫ **straight pitching** *n.* [mid-19C] (*UK Und.*) working without accomplices.

pitch and fill *n.* [rhy. sl.] [mid-19C] the proper name Bill, ult. William.

pitch and toss *n.* [rhy. sl.] **1** [1940s+] the boss. **2** [1980s] (*Aus.*) King's Cross, the 'bohemian' area of Sydney.

pitcher *n.*[1] [SE *pitcher*, a jug] **1** [late 16C–1900s] the vagina. **2** [early 19C] a prison, esp. Newgate in London [play on JUG *n.*[1] (2a)].

IN PHRASES

▫ **crack a pitcher** *v. see* CRACK A PIPKIN *under* PIPKIN *n.*[1].

pitcher *n.*[2] [SE *pitch*, the place in the street where such an individual works] **1** [late 19C] (*UK Und.*) a person who passes counterfeit coins. **2** [late 19C+] a street vendor. **3** [20C+] a member of a three-card monte team. **4** [1980s+] (*drugs*) a drug dealer, esp. when working on the street and actually handing over the drugs to the buyer.

IN COMPOUNDS

▫ **street pitcher** *n.* [mid-19C] anyone who makes a living from declaiming ballads or songs (with or without accompanying sheet music), selling 'true confessions', posing as a 'nigger minstrel' etc.

pitcher *n.*[3] [PITCH A YARN *under* YARN *n.*; note Arthur Binstead (1861–1914), a late 19C sporting journalist and *bon viveur*, whose fund of stories, retailed to cronies as well as to the readers of *The Sporting Times* (cf. PINK 'UN, THE *n.*), earned him the nickname *Tale-Pitcher*, usu. abbr. to *Pitcher*] [20C+] (*Aus.*) a chatterbox.

pitcher *n.*[4] [PITCH *v.* (4a)] **1** [1960s+] (*gay*) the dominant partner in male homosexual intercourse. **2** [1980s] (*US*) the male partner in heterosexual intercourse.

pitcher-bawd *n.* [SE *pitcher*, a jug + *bawd*] [late 17C–early 18C] a worn-out or semi-retired prostitute who runs errands in a tavern, either bringing drinks or providing customers with her more alluring peers.

pitch-fingers *n.* [SE *pitch*, a sticky substance used, *inter alia*, for sealing ships' timbers + *fingers*] [19C] a thief.

pitch fly *n.* [SE *pitch*, a street seller's site + fig. use of *fly*, an insect which has settled on one's spot] [1970s] someone who takes over another's street-selling position without permission.

pitching and catching *n.* [baseball imagery] [1960s+] the two opposed and complementary sides of any form of physical sex, esp. sado-masochism, bondage and discipline or coprophilia.

pitch-kettled *adj.* [? the image of black pitch being poured over a person, obscuring their vision] [mid-18C–mid-19C] utterly puzzled, nonplussed.

pitchman *n.* [SE *pitch*, a street-seller's site + sfx *-man*] [1920s+] a street-seller of cheap articles.

pitchy-man *n. see* DOLLY-MAN *n.*

pitchy-patchy *n.* [SE *patch* + redup.] [1940s] (*W.I.*) **1** ragged old work-clothes. **2** one who is wearing them.

pit-man *n.* [PIT *n.* (3)] **1** [19C] a small pocket-book, worn in the inside pocket of a jacket. **2** [1900s] (*US Und.*) a front trouser pocket.

pits *n.* **1** *see* PIT *n.* (6). **2** *see* PIT *n.* (7).

pit stop *n.* [joc. use of motor-racing jargon] **1** [1960s+] (*orig. US*) a visit to the lavatory; a stop on a car journey, usu. for passengers to relieve themselves; usu. as *make a pit stop*. **2** [1980s+] a stop on a journey or a rest from an activity to have a drink.

pitter *n. see* PETER *n.*[2] (1).

Pittsburgh feathers *n.* [coal that is being transported to the steel mills of Pittsburgh] [1910s–30s] (*US tramp*) coal, as slept on in a freight train.

Pitt's picture *n.* [in order to help finance the war against the American colonists, Prime Minister William *Pitt* (1759–1806) increased the tax on windows, charging householders for each one they owned. This was generally disliked and the poor and mean preferred to brick up windows rather than pay the tax] [late 18C–early 19C] a bricked-up window.

Pitt Street farmer *n.* (*also* **Pitt Street bushman, ...drover, ... stockman**) [*Pitt Street*, the financial centre of Sydney] [1920s]

(*Aus.*) a business person who owns or shares a farm from which they take annual profits but which they rarely visit.

pitty *adj. see under* PIT *n.*

pity fuck *n. see* CHARITY FUCK *under* CHARITY *n.*

pitzu *n.* [? Sp.] [1980s+] (*drugs*) impure morphine base.

pivot *v.* [their pivoting on their feet] [1910s–60s] (*US Und.*) of a beggar, to solicit for alms; of a street prostitute, to attract customers.

pix *n.* [abbr./pron.] [1930s+] (*orig. US*) pictures, whether still or motion.

pixie *n.* **1** [1930s–40s] (*Aus.*) a slender beer glass, with an 'hour-glass' shape; the drink served in such a glass [used fig. to reflect the size of the glass]. **2** [1930s–70s] (*also* **pix**) a homosexual man [var. on FAIRY *n.*[1] (3)]. **3** [1950s+] (*US black*) as haircuts [SE *pixie*, a sprite; the styles supposedly resemble illustrations of such figures]. (**a**) a short hairstyle for a woman. (**b**) straightened hair on a man.

IN COMPOUNDS

❑ **pixie stick** *n.* [play on *FAIRY'S WAND under* FAIRY *n.*[1]] [1960s–70s] (*US gay*) any phallic object carried by a cruising gay man, e.g. a cigarette holder, a rolled umbrella (on a dry day), a long-stemmed rose.

pixillated *adj.* (*also* **pixielated, pixilated, pixolated**) [SE *pixie*, a sprite, thus lit. 'having been taken over by pixies'] **1** [mid-19C+] confused. **2** [1930s+] drunk.

pizaro *n.* [? the Sp. conquistador *Francisco Pizarro* (*c.*1475–1541), who 'discovered' Peru and founded Lima] [1900s] (*US*) a fad, a discovery.

pizazz *n. see* PIZZAZZ *n.*

pizz *adj.* (*also* **pizicato**) [euph. for PISSED *adj.*[1]] [1930s] tipsy.

pizza *n.*

SE in slang uses

IN COMPOUNDS

❑ **pizzahead** *n.* [1990s+] **1** (*Aus. teen*) a general insult. **2** (*US campus*) greasy, dirty hair. ❑ **pizza toppings** *n.* [1980s+] (*drugs*) psilocybin/psilocin 'magic' mushrooms.

IN PHRASES

❑ **pavement pizza** *n.* (*also* **street pizza**) [1980s+] (*Aus.*) a pile of vomit; thus *deliver a street pizza*, to vomit.

pizza face *n.* (*also* **pizza features**) [1960s+] (*US/UK teen*) one who suffers from a severe case of acne.

pizza-faced *adj.* [PIZZA FACE *n.*] [1960s] suffering from a severe case of acne.

pizzazz *n.* (*also* **bezazz, pazazz, pizazz**) [ety. unknown; but note RAZZLE *n.* (1); RAZZMATAZZ *n.* (1)] **1** [1910s] (*US*) an expert, an exemplar. **2** [1930s+] (*orig. US*) style, glamour, ostentation. **3** [1930s+] energy, zest.

IN PHRASES

❑ **on the pizzazz** *adj.* [1910s] (*US*) outlawed.

pizzle *v.* [SE *pizzle*, a bull's penis] [mid-17C; 18C–19C] of a man, to have sexual intercourse.

p.j. *n.* [2000s] (*US*) a housing *project*.

p.k. *n. see* PICCANINNY KAYA *under* PICCANINNY *adj.*

plaasjapie *n.* [Afk. *plaas*, farm + JAAP *n.* (2)] [1950s+] (*S.Afr.*) a country bumpkin.

plaba *n.* (*also* **ploba**) [Carib.E. *plaba*, a stew, but note PALAVER *n.* (6)] [1950s] (*W.I.*) an argument.

plabbery *adj.* [Irish *plab*, a person who is easily taken in] [1920s] (*Irish*) foolish.

placa *n.* [Sp.] **1** [1960s+] (*US*) one's 'street' or gang name; thus a prison nickname. **2** [1990s+] (*US prison*) the police; prison officers.

placcy *adj. see* PLACKY *adj.*

place, the *n.* [euph.] **1** [late 17C–19C] the vagina. **2** [early 19C] the life of prostitution. **3** [late 19C–1950s] a lavatory.

placebo *n.* [Lat. *placebo*, I shall please; popularized as the name commonly given to Vespers in the Office for the Dead, from the first word of the first antiphon (*Placebo Domino in regione vivorum*, Ps. cxiv. 9)] [mid-14C–mid-17C] a toady or sycophant.

IN PHRASES

❑ **hunt a placebo** *v.* [mid-14C–16C] to be a toady or sycophant. ❑ **make (a) placebo** *v.* (*also* **dance a placebo, sing...**) [mid-14C–17C] to be a toady or sycophant. ❑ **play with a placebo** *v.* [late 15C–17C] to be a toady or sycophant.

place of convenience *n. see* CONVENIENCE *n.*

place of sixpenny sinfulness *n.* [costing less than its equivalent in the London's West End] [early 17C] a suburban (i.e. outside London's wall) brothel.

placer *n.* [1960s+] a middle-man who places stolen goods with a purchaser.

placido *n.* [ult. *Plácido Domingo* (b.1941), one of the 'three tenors', i.e. TENNER *n.* (1)] [2000s] £10.

plack *n.* [SE *plack*, either a small 15C–16C Flemish coin or a contemporary Scot. coin, worth 4d] **1** [mid-16C–early 19C] (*Irish*) anything of small value. **2** [19C+] (*Ulster*) a mouthful.

plack *v.* [SE *plack*, a small amount (of money)] [early 19C] (*UK Und.*) to defraud a victim of their money.

placket *n.* [SE *placket*, the slit at the top of an apron or petticoat, facilitating dressing and undressing; note Shakespearian uses of *placket* as a *double entendre*, e.g. in *Love's Labours Lost*, *The Winter's Tale* and *Troilus and Cressida*] [late 16C–18C] **1** (*also* **placket-box, placket-hole**) the vagina. **2** (*also* **placket-lady**) a woman considered only as a sex object, a prostitute.

IN COMPOUNDS

❑ **placket-broaker** *n. see* BROKER *n.*[1]. ❑ **placket-racket** *n.* [SE *racket*, an implement for hitting balls] [17C] the penis. ❑ **placket-stung** *adj.* [mid-17C–mid-18C] suffering from a venereal disease.

IN PHRASES

❑ **search the placket** *v.* [early 18C] to have sexual intercourse, esp. with a prostitute or mistress. ❑ **tear one's placket** *v.* [17C] of a woman, to lose one's virginity.

placky *adj.* (*also* **placcy, plakky**) [abbr.] [1970s+] *plastic*; esp. in *placky bag*, a polythene carrier bag.

plague, the *n.* [note Williams for 17C use of *plague* as synon. for venereal disease] **1** [1960s] (*US*) mass consumption of heroin in the urban black community. **2** [1990s+] AIDS.

plagued *adj.* [PLAGUE, THE *n.* (2)] [1990s+] (*US*) suffering from AIDS.

plaguer *n.* [PLAGUE, THE *n.* (2)] [1990s+] (*US*) a person with AIDS.

plain *n.* [1930s+] (*Irish*) Guinness stout, seen as the basic Irish drink.

plain and jam *n.* [rhy. sl.] [1900s–20s] a tram.

plainie *n.* [1940s] (*US*) a plain-clothes police officer, a detective.

plain people *n.* [a deliberate play on the SE white term, *coloured people*] [mid-19C] (*US black*) white people.

plain-turkey *n.* (*also* **plains-turkey, turkey**) [SE *plains-turkey*, the Australian bustard, *Ardeotis australis*] [1930s–50s] (*Aus.*) a tramp, a vagrant living in the Great Plains of Western Queensland.

plain vanilla *adj. see* VANILLA *adj.*

plaister of warm guts *n.* (*also* **plaister of hot guts, plaster of warm guts**) [i.e. 'one warm Belly clapt to another' (B.E.)] [late 17C–early 19C] sexual intercourse.

IN PHRASES

❑ **do a plaster of warm guts** *v.* [late 17C–early 19C] to have sexual intercourse.

plak *v.* [Du. *plakken*, to glue] [1960s+] (*S.Afr.*) **1** to stick on, to slap on, to glue on. **2** to plaster, to paint.

plakkies *n.* [PLAK *v.* (1); they 'stick' to one's feet] [1960s+] (*S.Afr.*) thongs, flip-flops.

plakky *adj. see* PLACKY *adj.*

plank *n.*[1] [? PLANK *v.* (1) or the SE *planks* beneath which it is hidden, or the wooden box in which it is kept] [1950s+] (*Irish*) a cache of money.

plank *n.*[2] [SE *plank*, both lit. and fig. uses based on ... *TWO SHORT PLANKS under* THICK AS... *adj.*] **1** [1960s+] (*Aus.*) a surf board.

2 [1980s+] (*also* **plankbrain**) a fool. **3** [2000s] (*S.Afr.*) an Afrikaner. **4** *see* STICK *n.* (8).

IN PHRASES

❑ **make the plank** *v.* [i.e. to lie down flat] [1960s] (*US gay*) to take the passive role in anal sex. ❑ **slap the plank** *v.* [var. on *SLAP FIVE under* FIVE *n.*[2]] [1930s+] (*US black*) exchanging ritualized slaps of greeting, congratulation etc.

plank *n.*[3] [1990s+] the penis; usu. in combs. below.

IN COMPOUNDS

❑ **plankspanker** *n.* [SPANK *v.*[2] (3)] [2000s] a masturbator.

IN PHRASES

❑ **yank the plank** *v. see under* YANK *v.*[1].

plank *v.* [fig. uses of SE *plank*, to lay a floor] **1** [19C+] (*also* **plink**) to place, to put, to deposit, to plant. **2** [19C+] to pay money down, to lay out money, esp. when done without quibbling. **3** [1950s] to bury. **4** [1950s+] to have sexual intercourse [additional pun on *lay*/LAY *v.*[1] (1)].

IN PHRASES

❑ **plank down** *v.* **1** [mid-19C+] (*also* **plank on, ...out, ...up**) to pay money down, to lay out money, esp. when done without quibbling. **2** [1910s+] to place, to put down. ❑ **plank it** *v.* [ety. unknown] [2000s] (*Irish*) to be anxious.

plant *n.* [PLANT *v.*[1] (1)] **1** [late 18C+] (*orig. UK Und.*) a hiding place for stolen goods; thus the goods themselves. **2** [late 18C+] a swindle, a fraudulent trick. **3** [early 19C–1930s] any form of criminal activity. **4** [mid-19C] a hiding place for burglary tools. **5** [mid-19C] a hiding place, e.g. for one's legally earned money. **6** [mid-19C] a person targeted for robbery; a building targeted for burglary. **7** [mid-19C+] a detective, a spy, a decoy, esp. one who works under cover in a criminal gang; also any undercover police activity. **8** [mid-19C+] (*UK/US Und./police*) a trap; often in the form of an item that is deliberately left vulnerable and under surveillance, e.g. a briefcase, in the hope that a thief will pick it up. **9** [late 19C–1900s] (*US*) one's home. **10** [1900s] (*US*) a venue, e.g. to display one's wares. **11** [1900s] a site where a street-seller is established. **12** [1900s–40s] (*US Und.*) a place targeted for a crime, e.g. a bank. **13** [1910s] a hiding place for a person. **14** [1910s–40s] (*UK Und.*) the manufacture and selling of counterfeit money. **15** [1920s–50s] a trick, a tease. **16** [1920s+] (*orig. US*) someone or something who has been deliberately placed in an environment, typically an audience, where they respond (ostensibly as just another punter) to a call from the stage for 'volunteers'. **17** [1920s+] (*drugs*) a hiding place for drugs or drug-taking equipment; thus the drugs or equipment thus hidden. **18** [1990s+] the act of placing incriminating evidence on a suspected person, or in their room, car etc.

IN PHRASES

❑ **in plant** *adj.* [early–mid-19C] (*Aus.*) hidden away. ❑ **prime plant** *n.* [PRIME *adj.*] [mid-19C] (*UK Und.*) a potential victim, as assessed by a villain. ❑ **rise a plant** *v.* [early 19C] (*UK Und.*) of a thief, to unearth some loot from where it has been hidden by them or by another thief. ❑ **spring a plant** *v.* [SPRING *v.* (2)] [19C] (*UK Und.*) to uncover a hiding place, usu. one which another villain uses for their plunder. ❑ **take a plant** *v. see* PLANT *v.*[1] (4).

plant *v.*[1] **1** [17C+] (*mainly Aus. mid-19C+*) to hide an object, usu. stolen. **2** [late 18C+] to bury a body. **3** [19C+] (*also* **plant upon**) usu. of the police, to hide evidence in the clothes, home or car of a suspected person in order to ensure they have something with which to charge their victim. **4** [19C+] (*also* **plant upon, take a plant**) to post a spy, a detective or any individual, or listening device, for the purposes of surreptitious surveillance. **5** [mid-19C] to mark out a potential victim for robbery. **6** [mid–late 19C] (*UK Und.*) to pass counterfeit coins or notes; thus *planter*, one who undertakes this. **7** [late 19C] to 'salt' a gold-field in the hope of attracting investors. **8** [late 19C+] to abandon, to leave. **9** [1920s–40s] to hide oneself. **10** [1930s] to swindle, to deceive; to play a trick.

IN PHRASES

❑ **plant the whids and stow them** *v.* [SE *plant*, lay down + WHID *n.* (1) + STOW *v.* (1)] [17C–mid-18C] (*UK Und.*) to talk carefully, to guard one's tongue. ❑ **plant you now, dig you later** *see under* DIG *v.*[3].

plant *v.*[2] **1** [17C+] of a man, to have sexual intercourse. **2** [early 19C+] (*Irish*) to hit. **3** [late 19C–1940s] (*Irish*) to kill, to shoot dead.

plantain leaf *n.* [like the note, it is green] [1940s+] (*W.I.*) a £1 note.

planter *n.* [PLANT *v.*[1] (1)] **1** [mid-19C] (*UK Und.*) one who hides stolen property. **2** [late 19C+] (*Aus.*) one who steals and then hides cattle.

planter's medicine *n.* [administered every Monday to slaves who complained of ulcers and went to the plantation hospital. The punishment was meted out until the ulcers healed] [mid-19C] (*W.I.*) a flogging.

planting *n.* [PLANT *v.*[1]] **1** [late 18C+] the hiding of stolen items, esp. (*Aus.*) horses, and then 'discovering' them as soon as a reward is offered. **2** [20C+] (*Aus./US*) a funeral.

planting beets *n.* [1980s] (*Aus.*) the act of vomiting.

plants *n.* [17C–18C] the feet.

plant upon *v. see* PLANT *v.*[1].

plaque *n.* [1940s] (*Irish*) the human face.

plarry *n.* [Scot. *plorie*, a piece of ground that has been trodden into mud; ult. SE *plough*] [20C+] (*Ulster*) an unappealing mess of food.

plasma *n.* [its importance in maintaining life] [1980s] (*US campus*) coffee.

plaster *n.* **1** in financial/monetary senses [the rectangular shape + its efficacy in 'curing' financial ills]. (**a**) [mid-19C+] (*US*) a banknote. (**b**) [1920s] (*US Und.*) the paper on which an injunction or court order is printed. (**c**) [1920s+] (*Can.*) a mortgage; thus *plaster*, to pay money towards a mortgage. (**d**) [1930s+] (*Aus.*) a bill, an account. **2** [late 19C] an outsize collar [resemblance, though Partridge suggests Fr. *plastron*, a stiff shirt-front; the style was popularized by the Duke of Clarence (1864–92)]. **3** in senses of 'sticking'. (**a**) [20C+] (*US*) a follower, a TAIL *n.* (10a). (**b**) [20C+] (*Irish*) an encumbrance, a burden. (**c**) [20C+] (*Irish*) (*also* **sticking-plaster**) one's wife. (**d**) [1930s] (*US tramp*) butter. (**e**) [1930s+] (*Irish*) an unpleasant person or creature.

SE in slang uses

IN PHRASES

❑ **have a plaster for every sore** *v.* [20C+] (*W.I.*) to have an excuse ready for any situation.

plaster *v.* **1** [late 19C–1930s] to bet (heavily) on. **2** [1910s+] to hit. **3** [1960s+] (*Irish*) to persuade. **4** [1970s+] (*US black*) to flatter. **5** [1970s+] (*US black*) to shoot someone.

plastered *adj.*[1] [joc. use of PLASTER *v.* (2)] [20C+] (*orig. milit.*) drunk.

plastered *adj.*[2] [1900s] a euph. for DAMNED *adj.* (1).

plasterer's trowel and seringapatam *n.* (*also* **seringapatam**) [rhy. sl.; *Seringapatam*, apparently used purely for assonance, was the former capital of the Indian state of Mysore] [late 19C] a fowl and ham.

plaster of Paris *n.* [rhy. sl. = ARRIS *n.* (2)] [1990s+] the buttocks.

IN COMPOUNDS

❑ **pain in the plaster** *n.* [1990s+] a bore, a nuisance, an irritation.

plaster of warm guts *n. see* PLAISTER OF WARM GUTS *n.*

plastic *n.* [1970s+] **1** any form of credit card; thus (*US*) *work plastic*, to obtain goods using a stolen credit card. **2** (*UK Und.*) plastic explosive, used for safe-breaking.

IN PHRASES

❑ **on the plastic** [1970s+] (*UK Und.*) using stolen credit cards for a variety of frauds and swindles.

plastic *adj.* [1960s+] synthetic, false, insincere.

IN COMPOUNDS

❑ **plastic hippie** *n.* [HIPPIE *n.*[2] (3)] [1960s] a part-time or uncommitted HIPPIE *n.*[2] (3), more interested in the hedonistic and clothes-wearing side of the movement than in its philosophies. ❑ **plastic paddy** *n.* [PADDY *n.* (1)] [1980s+] the children of first-generation Irish immigrants to the UK. ❑ **plastic people** *n.* [1960s] conventional people, characterized by their rejection (and fear) of alternative modes of thought or action. ❑ **plastic screw** *n.* [SCREW *n.*[1] (2c)] [1990s+] (*UK Und.*) a security guard employed by the courts and prison services.

IN PHRASES

❑ **plastic out** *v.* [1970s+] (*US campus*) to assume temporarily an artificial mode of behaviour or personality.

SE in slang uses

IN COMPOUNDS

❑ **plastic cow** *n.* [COW *n.*[1] (5)] [1980s] (*US campus*) non-dairy creamer. ❑ **plastic job** *n.* [SE *plastic* (*surgery*) + JOB *n.*[2] (2)] [1940s+] (*orig. US*) **1** plastic surgery. **2** one who has had plastic surgery.

plastic surgeon *n.* [rhy. sl.] [2000s] a virgin.

plat *n.* [Fr. *plat*, flat; ? thus play on FLAT *n.*[2] (1)] [1920s+] (*Aus.*) a fool, an 'easy mark'.

plate *n.*[1] **1** [late 18C–1910s] (*orig. UK Und.*) money. **2** [1930s+] (*orig. US*) a gramophone record [resemblance]. **3** [1960s] a record deck [resemblance].

SE in slang uses

IN COMPOUNDS

❑ **plate-face** *n.* [the perceived 'flatness' of some Asian faces] [1980s+] (*Aus.*) a derog. term for an Asian, orig. Vietnamese.

IN PHRASES

❑ **dirty a plate with** *v.* [late 18C; 1930s–60s] to eat (with), to have a meal (with). ❑ **drop plates (on this mother)** *v.* [fig. use of SE + abbr. MOTHERFUCKER *n.*] [1970s] (*US black*) to lose one's temper, to get sufficiently annoyed to resort to physical violence. ❑ **foul a plate with** *v.* [SE *foul*, to dirty] [late 18C–early 19C] to share a meal with. ❑ **in for the plate** [laboured derivation f. horseracing jargon: horses that qualify for the *plate* (the main race) have first won the *heat*; symptoms of VD include inflammation, i.e. *heat*] [late 18C–early 19C] suffering from venereal disease. ❑ **plate of straight** *n.* [? SE *straight*, no trimmings] [1950s] (*W.I.*) a dish of boiled bananas. ❑ **put it over the plate** *v.* [baseball imagery] [late 19C] (*US*) to achieve a success, a coup.

plate *n.*[2] [PLATE *v.*[1]] [1960s+] an act of oral sex, usu. fellatio.

plate *v.*[1] [rhy. sl.; *plate of ham* = GAM *v.*[2] (1) or *plate of meat* = EAT *v.* (4)] [1960s+] to fellate; thus *plater*, a fellator or fellatrix.

plate *v.*[2] [1990s+] (*UK Und.*) to change the number plates of a stolen car.

plate and dish *n.* [rhy. sl.] [1990s+] a wish.

plate-fleet *n.*

IN PHRASES

❑ **when the plate-fleet comes in** [SE *Plate fleet*, the fleet that brought home the annual yield of silver from the Indies to Spain] [late 17C–early 19C] when one finally makes a fortune, 'when one's ship comes in'.

plate it *v.* [PLATES (OF MEAT) *n.*] [late 19C–1900s] to walk.

plate of ham *n.* [rhy. sl. = GAM *n.*[4]] **1** [1950s+] fellatio. **2** *see* BEEF AND HAM *n.*

plate of meat *n.* [rhy. sl.] [mid-19C] the street.

plate-rack *n.* (*also* **plater**) [rhy. sl. = SE *hack*, a horse for everyday riding] [late 19C+] a horse.

plates and dishes *n.* [rhy. sl.] **1** [1930s+] kisses. **2** [1950s+] the wife, 'missus'.

plates (of meat) *n.* (*also* **blades of meat**) [rhy. sl.] [mid-19C+] the feet.

plating *n.* (*also* **tongue-plating**) [PLATE *v.*[1]] [1960s+] oral sex, fellatio, cunnilingus.

platinum *adj.* [on pattern of DIAMOND *adj.*] **1** [1950s–60s] having a big heart, generous. **2** [1980s+] (*US*) excellent, special.

plato *n.* [Mex. Sp.] [1960s+] (*US*) a fight, a problem, an argument.

Plato to NATO *n.* [1980s] (*US campus*) a course in European civilization.

plats *n.* [abbr.] [2000s] (*US black*) *plat*form heeled shoes.

platsak *adj.* [Du. *plat*, flat + *sak*, pocket] [1950s+] (*S.Afr.*) out of funds, impoverished.

platter *n.*[1] [? SE *plates* + *clatter*] [late 19C] broken crockery.

platter *n.*[2] [resemblance] [1930s–90s] (*orig. US black*) a vinyl record.

platter-faced *adj.* [20C use appears to be Irish] [late 17C–1940s] plain, broad-faced.

platters (of meat) *n.* [rhy. sl.] [1920s+] the feet.

plausy *adj.* (*also* **plausey, plazy, plossey**) [SE *plausible*] [mid-19C] (*Anglo-Irish*) smooth-tongued, overly polite, apparently weak.

play *n.* **1** [early 16C+] sexual activity; flirtation. **2** [late 18C+] any form of action, plan or scheme. **3** [late 19C+] the situation, the state of affairs. **4** [late 19C+] (*orig. US*) a show of interest, patronage, publicity; a chance; thus *give (it/one) a play*, to try out, to give a chance. **5** [20C+] (*US Und.*) the performance of a single confidence trick, esp. one which requires substantial preparation, props etc. **6** [1930s] (*US*) way of life, well-being. **7** [1970s] (*US black*) a form of greeting that involves the slapping of palms [note 9C–14C SE *play*, to clap the hands].

IN PHRASES

❑ **back someone's play** *v.* [gambling jargon] [1970s] (*US*) to support one's own statement or action or back up those of another person. ❑ **give someone a play** *v.* [1930s+] (*US black*) **1** to express sexual interest in, to flirt with. **2** to give someone a chance; to make a deal with. **3** in fig. use, to frequent (and spend money). ❑ **give the man the play** *v.* [MAN *n.*[1] (4a)] [1970s+] (*US black*) to inform. ❑ **make a play** *v.* [20C+] **1** to act in a demonstrative, theatrical manner. **2** to pretend, esp. in an 'obvious' manner. ❑ **make a play for** *v.* (*also* **give a play to, make a play at/with**) **1** [late 19C+] to make sexual advances towards someone, to attempt seduction. **2** [1900s–20s] as sense 1, but in a non-sexual manner. ❑ **pull a play** *v.* [1950s] to perform an action, usu. constr. with descriptive adj.

IN EXCLAMATIONS

❑ **that's the play!** *see* THAT'S THE SHOT! *under* SHOT *n.*[1].

play *v.* **1** [16C+] to trick, to deceive. **2** [16C+] (*also* **play turnabout**) to pursue sexually; to seduce. **3** [mid-19C+] to be involved in an affair outside one's primary relationship. **4** [late 19C+] to conduct oneself; to approach a situation. **5** [late 19C+] to manipulate, to exploit, to 'use' someone. **6** [late 19C+] to mock, to make fun of, to tease; thus *to play oneself*, to act in a humiliating way. **7** [1900s] (*Aus.*) to bet, to gamble (at a horserace). **8** [1930s–60s] (*US*) to treat someone as. **9** [1930s+] (*orig. US*) to cooperate, to comply, to accept, to tolerate, to make sense; usu. as negative *I don't play that, that doesn't play*. **10** [1980s] (*US drugs*) to adulterate. **11** *see* PLAY OFF below.

IN COMPOUNDS

❑ **play-white** *n.* [1950s+] (*S.Afr.*) one who attempts to 'pass' as white.

IN PHRASES

❑ **play along** *v.* (*orig. US*) **1** [1920s+] to agree, to cooperate. **2** [1930s+] to deceive gradually, to 'take for a ride'. ❑ **play around** *v.* (*orig. US*) **1** [1910s+] to indulge in sexual play. **2** [1920s+] to have a number of affairs, lovers, entanglements. **3** [1920s+] to seduce. **4** [1930s+] to play mental or emotional 'games' with someone. ❑ **play a store** *v.* [1950s] (*US*) to go shoplifiting. ❑ **play away** *v.* [sporting imagery] [1970s+] **1** to philander, to commit adultery. **2** to do something outside one's experience. ❑ **play bad** *v.* [20C+] (*W.I.*) **1** of a child, to behave badly, rudely. **2** of an adult, to put on a show of defiance. ❑ **play both sides of the street** *v.* (*also* **play both sides of the game, ...ends in the middle**) *see* WORK BOTH SIDES OF THE STREET *under* WORK *v.* ❑ **play chaneys** *v.* [? SE *Chinese*, so far as the racial stereotype is concerned, the Chinese person is 'not straight'] [late 19C] (*Aus.*) to exert influence; thus *play at chaneys*, to bribe. ❑ **play diddle-diddle** *v.* [pun on SE *diddle-diddle*, a fiddle/SE *to fiddle*] [16C] to play tricks, to importune. ❑ **play dirt** *v.* [late 19C–1930s] (*US*) to deceive. ❑ **play down on** *v.* [mid-19C] to take a mean or unfair advantage of. ❑ **play Fourteenth Street** *v.* [the cheap shops of New York's 14th St] [1940s] (*US black*) to disparage, to treat in a condescending manner. ❑ **play it on (someone)** *v.* (*also* **play it off on**) [late 19C–1900s] (*Aus./UK*) to deceive, to trick. ❑ **play low** *v.* (*also* **play low down**) [LOWDOWN *adv.*] [late 19C–1910s] (*US*) to act meanly. ❑ **play off** *v.* **1** [late 16C–early 17C; late 19C–1910s] (*also* **play, play off one's dust**) to finish a drink, to toss off a glass. **2** [mid-19C] to commit adultery. ❑ **play Old Harry (with)** *v. see under* OLD HARRY *n.* ❑ **play on** *v.* **1** [19C+] (*also* **play off on**) to trick, to fool. **2** [1950s+] to cheat on sexually, to cuckold. ❑ **play oneself** *v.* [1950s+] (*US black*) to delude oneself as to one's success, sexuality, character etc, to aggrandize oneself. ❑ **play out** *v.* **1** [mid-19C+] (*orig. US black*) to wear out, to lose usefulness, interest, value. **2** [1930s] (*US campus*) to use so much that it will eventually fade out. **3** [1950s+] to go along with something for the sake of appearance, until it loses its interest or value. ❑ **play someone against the wall** *v.* [*UP AGAINST THE WALL under* UP AGAINST *phr.*] [20C+] (*US Und.*) to practise a confidence trick. ❑ **play someone off** *v.* [mid-19C+] (*US*) to avoid someone's attentions through guile. ❑ **play staff** *v. see RIDE STAFF under* RIDE *v.* ❑ **play turnabout** *v. see* sense 2 above. ❑ **play white** *v.* [1960s] (*S.Afr.*) for a 'coloured' person to 'pass' as white.

SE in slang uses

IN COMPOUNDS

❑ **play brother** *n.* [1960s+] (*US black*) an extremely close friend, one who resembles a brother; thus also *play cousin, play mother, play sister*. ❑ **playground** *n.* (*also* **chippy's playground**) [1940s+] (*orig. US black*) the stomach. ❑ **playhouse** *n. see* separate entry.

IN PHRASES

❑ **not playing with a full deck** *see* separate entry. ❑ **play a-cross** *v.* (*also* **play across**) [early 19C] (*UK Und.*) to lose deliberately, so as to lure one's victim deeper into the game. ❑ **play a full hand** *v.* [poker imagery] [1900s] (*US*) to act from a position of strength. ❑ **play a game at loll-tongue** *v.* [late 18C–early 19C] to have one's saliva checked for traces of syphilis. ❑ **play a good stick** *v.* [mid-18C–mid-19C] of a fiddler, to perform competently. ❑ **play a record** *v.* [1950s] to boast, to brag. ❑ **play at up and down** *v.* [mid-19C] (*UK Und.*) to serve time on the treadmill. ❑ **play billy with** *v.* [? BILLY BARLOW *n.*[1] or fig. use of Scot. *billy-blind*, blind man's buff] [late 19C–1930s] to tease, to 'mess someone about'. ❑ **play both sides of the fence** *v. see WORK BOTH SIDES OF THE STREET under* WORK *v.* ❑ **play cagey-cannon** *v.* [SE *cagey*; ety. of *cannon* unknown] [1940s] (*Irish*) to act cautiously. ❑ **play close** *v. see* separate entry. ❑ **play dirty** *v.* [1910s+] (*orig. US*) to behave reprehensibly, to cheat. ❑ **play doggo** *v. see LIE DOGGO under* LIE *v.*[1]. ❑ **play ducks and drakes with** *v.* (*also* **make ducks and drakes of**) [SE *ducks and drakes*, a game based on the tossing of flat stones across a pond; thus in a financial context one is idly tossing away one's money] [17C–mid-19C] to squander one's fortune, to spend money unwisely. ❑ **play for** *v. see* separate entry. ❑ **play for both teams** *v.* [1990s+] (*US gay*) to be bisexual. ❑ **play for the other team** *v.* [2000s] to be homosexual. ❑ **play from the pavilion end** *v. see BOWL FROM THE PAVILION END under* BOWL *v.* ❑ **play hooky** *v. see* separate entry. ❑ **play it...** *v. see* separate entry. ❑ **play it by ear** *v.* (*also* **play it by skyhook**) [a musician who has no score as a guide/*skyhook*, an imaginary contrivance that keeps one 'flying'] [1960s+] to act in an ad hoc spontaneous manner. ❑ **play it close to one's chest** *v.* (*also* **play it close to one's vest**) [card-playing imagery: the player holds their cards close to their body in order to stop any opponent seeing them] **1** [late 19C] to conserve one's funds. **2** [1940s+] to act in a reserved, secretive manner. ❑ **play it off** *v.* [1980s+] (*US campus*) to dismiss something, to not care. ❑ **play jip** *v.* [GYP *v.*/dial. *jip*, to trick, to cheat] [1940s] (*Aus.*) to irritate. ❑ **play least in sight** *v.* [late 18C–early 19C] to hide, to keep out of the way. ❑ **play on a wet wicket** *v.* [1900s–10s] (*Aus.*) to be drunk. ❑ **play past** *v.* [1960s] (*US black*) **1** to circumvent obstacles, mental as well as physical. **2** to lose an opportunity. ❑ **play scared pool** *v.* [1970s] (*US*) to act over-cautiously. ❑ **play stickers (with)** *v.* [1930s] (*UK Und.*) to steal money which one is supposedly passing on to a confederate. ❑ **play the iggie** *v.* [abbr.] [1960s–70s] (*US*) to ignore. ❑ **play the mouth organ** *v.* [1960s+] (*drugs*) to smoke heroin with a rolled-up matchbook cover substituted for the usual roll of tinfoil, which is used to suck up the heated, smoking heroin. ❑ **play the old soldier** *v. see COME THE OLD SOLDIER under* COME THE... *v.* ❑ **play the part of the strong man** *v.* [one is 'pushing' the cart] [late 18C–early 19C] to be whipped at the cart's tail. ❑ **play up** *v. see* separate entry. ❑ **play upon the prick** *v.* [play on SE] [mid-16C] (*UK Und.*) to mark cards with pinpricks. ❑ **play with 44 cards to the deck** *v. see* NOT PLAYING WITH A FULL DECK *phr.*

playa *n.* [PLAYER *n.* (2); part of the general sp. changes used by GANGSTA *n.* (1) rappers] [1990s+] (*US black*) **1** anyone who uses wit, charm, intelligence to gain objectives, whether honestly or (more usu.) dishonestly. **2** a womanizer.

IN COMPOUNDS

❑ **playa hata** *n. see PLAYER-HATER under* PLAYER *n.*

IN PHRASES

❑ **playa from the Himalaya** *n.* [assonance, plus the importance/size of the mountain range] [2000s] (*US black*) one who is popular with the opposite sex.

play-around *n.* [*PLAY AROUND under* PLAY *v.*] [1980s] (*Liverpool*) an act of masturbation, as provided by a prostitute.

play (at)... *v.* [16C+] a phr. used in various combs. as synons. for having sexual intercourse, e.g. *play at brangle, ...bouncy-bouncy, ...buttock, ...cock in cover, ...mumble-peg, ...prick the garter, ...pully-hauly, ...put in all, ...stable my naggie, ... thread the needle, ...tops and bottoms, ...top sawyer, ...where the Jack takes Ace, ...pyrdewy*; *see also* below and at individual nouns for more phrs.

IN PHRASES

❑ **play a game single-hand** *v.* [early 16C; mid-18C] to have sexual intercourse. ❑ **play a little five-on-one** *v.* [*five* fingers, *one* penis or vagina] [20C+] to masturbate. ❑ **play a mouth organ** *v.* (*also* **play a piccolo**) [1960s+] (*US*) to perform oral sex. ❑ **play at Adam and Eve** *v.* [18C–19C] to have sexual intercourse. ❑ **play at all fours** *v.* [note Cotton's description in *The Compleat Gamester* (1674): 'This game [...] is called All-Fours from *Highest*, *Lowest*, *Jack* and *Game*', all of which terms can be taken as *double entendres*] [late 17C–19C] to have sexual intercourse. ❑ **play at belly-to-belly** *v.* (*also* **turn belly to belly**) [late 16C–1960s] to have sexual intercourse. ❑ **play at blindman's buff** *v.* [17C] to have sexual intercourse. ❑ **play at bo-peep** *v.* [SE *bo-peep*, a nursery game in which one amuses a child by hiding (usu. the face), revealing, then repeating the process] **1** [late 16C–early 18C] to have sexual intercourse. **2** [mid-17C–early 19C] to keep watch, to lie hidden. **3** [late 18C] to live alternately hidden and then appearing in public. ❑ **play at buttock and leave her** *v.* [late 17C–mid-18C] to have sexual intercourse. ❑ **play at cherry pit** *v.* [SE *cherry pit*, the chewy stone] [17C–19C] to have sexual intercourse. ❑ **play at couch quail** *v.* [16C] to have sexual intercourse. ❑ **play (at) cuddle my cuddie** *v.* [SE *cuddle* + dial. *cuddy*, a woman] [mid-17C–early 18C] to have sexual intercourse. ❑ **play (at) fathers and mothers** *v.* (*also* **play (at) dads and mums, ...doctors and nurses, ...mothers and fathers, ...mummies and daddies**) [the adult version of children's sex games, the main one being playing doctors and nurses] [late 19C+] to have sexual intercourse. ❑ **play at grapple-my-belly** *v.* [late 19C–1900s] to have sexual intercourse. ❑ **play at handie dandie** *v.* [Scot./SE *handie-dandy*, a children's game based on the rapid moving of an object from one hand to another, then back] [16C] (*Scot.*) to have sexual intercourse. ❑ **play at hooper's hide** *v.* (*also* **play at hoop and hide**) [SE *hooper's hide*, hide-and-seek] [late 17C] to have sexual intercourse. ❑ **play at houghmagandie** *v.* [SE/Scot. *hough* = hock = back of the knee + Scot. *canty*, cheerful, active] [late 18C+] to have sexual intercourse. ❑ **play (at) in**

and in *v.* (*also* **throw in and in**) [Nares: 'in-and-in. A gambling game, played by three persons with four dice, each person having a box. It was the common diversion at ordinaries, and places of inferior resort [...] it appears that *in* was, when there was a doublet, or two dice alike out of the four; *in and in* when there were either two doublets, or all four dice alike, which swept the stake'] [late 16C–19C] to have sexual intercourse. ❑ **play (at) itch-buttocks** *v.* [late 16C–19C] to have sexual intercourse. ❑ **play (at) level-coil** *v.* [SE *level-coil*, any form of rough game, spec. that once played at Christmas (an embryo form of musical chairs) in which each player is in turn driven from their seat and replaced by another; Fr. (*faire*) *lever la cul* (*à quelqu'un*), to make someone raise their buttocks, properly 'arse'; also found in Ital. as *levaculo*] [late 16C–17C] to have sexual intercourse. ❑ **play at mothers and fathers/mummies and daddies** *v.* *see* PLAY (AT) FATHERS AND MOTHERS above. ❑ **play at potfinger** *v.* [one sticks one's finger in her 'pot'/POT *n.*[1] (1); the vagina sense is slightly later, but the generic *pot*, a woman, fits the chronology] [late 16C] to stimulate the vagina with the fingers. ❑ **play at push-pin** *v.* (*also* **play at push-pike, ...put-pin**) [PUSH *v.* (1) + PIN *n.* (1a); + pun on children's game *push-pin* or *put-pin*, in which each player pushes or fillips their pin with the object of crossing that of another player] [17C–mid-19C] to have sexual intercourse. ❑ **play at the close-buttock game** *v.* (*also* **play at the brangle-buttock game**) [BRANGLE *v.*] [mid-17C–19C] to have sexual intercourse. ❑ **play (at) two-handed put** *v.* [pun on *put* = Fr. *putain*, prostitute] [18C–early 19C] to have sexual intercourse. ❑ **play carnival** *v.* ['guess-my-weight' competitions were a fairground attraction] [1940s+] of a woman, to position one's vagina directly above one's partner's mouth, either literally sitting or squatting above their face, in order to facilitate cunnilingus. ❑ **play checkers** *v.* [the movements in checkers (UK: draughts)] [1940s+] (*US gay*) to move from seat to seat in a cinema in search of a receptive sex partner. ❑ **play chopsticks** *v.* [joc. use of 'Chopsticks', a basic piece learnt by a novice piano-player] [1940s+] (*orig. gay*) to indulge in mutual masturbation. ❑ **play cock in cover** *v.* [pun on SE *play cock*, to display oneself/COCK *n.*[3] (1)] [late 19C] to have sexual intercourse. ❑ **play couple your navels** *v.* (*also* **play wriggle your navels**) [18C] to have sexual intercourse. ❑ **play fast and loose with a woman's apron-strings** *v.* [17C] to have sexual intercourse. ❑ **play hey gammer cook** *v.* (*also* **play hey gaffer cook**) [? dial. *gammocks*, wild play] [late 17C–mid-18C] to have sexual intercourse. ❑ **play hide the salami** *v.* (*also* **play hide the banana, ...sausage**) [SALAMI *n.*/BANANA *n.* (2a)/SAUSAGE *n.* (2)] [1930s+] (*US*) to have sexual intercourse. ❑ **play hoop-snake with** *v.* [1940s–70s] (*gay*) for two homosexual men to indulge in mutual fellatio. ❑ **play night baseball** *v.* [1960s+] to have sexual intercourse. ❑ **play nug a nug** *v.* [NUG *v.*] [early 17C] to caress, to fondle; to have sexual intercourse. ❑ **play one's ace** *v.* [RED ACE *under* ACE *n.*] [late 19C+] of a woman, to have sex with a man. ❑ **play pickle-me-tickle-me** *v.* [mid-17C–early 18C] to have sexual intercourse. ❑ **play solitaire** *v.* [1930s–70s] to masturbate. ❑ **play the first game ever played** *v.* [19C] to have sexual intercourse. ❑ **play three to one (and sure to lose)** *v.* [*three*, the penis and testes, and *one*, the vagina; what the man is *sure to lose* is semen] [late 18C–19C] of a man, to have sexual intercourse. ❑ **play tickle-tail** *v.* [1940s] to have sexual intercourse. ❑ **play tickle the pickle** *v.* [20C+] (*US*) to have sexual intercourse. ❑ **play touchy-touchy** *v.* [1980s] (*US*) to indulge in sexual fondling. ❑ **play with oneself** *v.* [late 19C+] to masturbate. ❑ **play wriggle your navels** *v.* *see* PLAY COUPLE YOUR NAVELS above.

play close *v.* [1980s+] (*US black*) to become intimate with, esp. with the aim of using one's supposed friend for one's own purposes.

IN PHRASES

❑ **play someone too close** *v.* **1** [1980s+] (*US black*) to involve oneself too intimately and without invitation in another person's life. **2** [2000s] to tease or intimidate someone.

played *adj.* [PLAY *v.*] [1990s+] (*US black*) **1** insulted. **2** cheated on by one's girlfriend or boyfriend.

played (out) *adj.* [PLAY OUT *under* PLAY *v.*] [mid-19C+] (*US*) exhausted, worn-out, finished.

player *n.* **1** [late 19C+] a participant. **2** [1950s+] (*orig. US black*) anyone who uses intelligence, wit, brains to gain objectives, whether a businessman, politician, womanizer or criminal. **3** [1950s+] (*orig. US black*) a pimp. **4** [1950s+] (*orig. US black*) a man who is a gambler by nature, who makes friends easily, and never gives up trying. **5** [1960s+] (*US campus*) a promiscuous person; a sexual cheat. **6** [1960s+] (*N.Z.*) a woman, occas. a man, who is seen as enthusiastic about sex [SE *play* or PLAY AROUND *under* PLAY *v.*]. **7** [1970s+] (*US drugs*) a drug user.

IN COMPOUNDS

❑ **player-hate** *v.* [1990s+] **1** to resent the achievements and extravagant lifestyle of a ghetto success, whether gained legally or otherwise. **2** (*US campus*) to interfere in someone else's life or business. ❑ **player-hater** *n.* (*also* **hater, P.H., playa hata, player hata**) [PLAYA *n.* (1) + SE *hater* or 'gangsta' sp. *hata*] [1990s+] (*US black*) one who resents the achievements and extravagant lifestyle of a ghetto success, whether gained legally or otherwise; thus ext. into non-ghetto environments.

play for *v.* **1** [20C+] (*US Und.*) to treat with contempt or as a fool; to subject to a confidence trick. **2** [1930s] to pose as.

IN PHRASES

❑ **play for a chump** *v.* (*also* **play for a clown, ...duffer, ...mug**) [CHUMP *n.*[1] (3)/CLOWN *n.* (1)/DUFFER *n.*[2] (1)/MUG *n.*[1] (2a)] [late 19C+] (*orig. US black*) to treat like a fool. ❑ **play for a sucker** *v.* [SUCKER *n.*[1] (3b)] [late 19C+] (*US*) to deceive a gullible victim.

play hooky *v.* (*also* **play hookey**) [SE *play* + ? Du. *hoekje* (*spelen*), to play hide-and-seek] [mid-19C+] (*US*) **1** to play truant from school. **2** in fig. use, to be absent, missing. **3** to be adulterous.

playhouse *n.* **1** [late 17C] a brothel. **2** [1920s] (*US Und.*) a prison known for its liberal regime. **3** [1930s] (*US prison*) a small prison. **4** [1940s] (*US Und.*) ext. to non-prison contexts, e.g. a town with little law and order. **5** [1970s+] (*US gay*) a room filled with implements to augment sado-masochistic sex.

play it... *v.* [1920s+] to act in a given manner, defined by an adj.

play-play *n.* [1940s+] (*S.Afr.*) a pretence, insincerity.

play-play *adj.* [PLAY-PLAY *n.*] [1940s+] (*S.Afr./W.I., Bdos*) fake, make-believe.

play-play *v.* [PLAY-PLAY *n.*] [1940s+] (*S.Afr.*) to pretend.

play-three *n.* [ety. unknown] [1990s+] (*W.I.*) death; dying.

play up *v.* **1** [mid-19C+] of people or animals, to irritate, to 'mess around'. **2** [mid-19C+] to break the rules, esp. sexually. **3** [late 19C+] of a wound or disease, to cause discomfort, e.g. *my bad arm's playing me up today*. **4** [1900s] (*Aus.*) to bet, to gamble (at a horserace). **5** [1920s+] of machinery, or a thing, to malfunction.

IN PHRASES

❑ **play up a drip** *v.* [1900s] (*Aus.*) to buy a round of drinks. ❑ **play up to** *v.* [early 19C+] to indulge, to humour.

plazazus *n.* *see* BEJAZUS *n.*

plazy *adj.* *see* PLAUSY *adj.*

plazzy *adj.* [abbr.] [1960s+] **1** plastic. **2** in fig. use, false, second-rate.

plea at the bar *n.* [mid-19C] (*US*) a drink in a tavern.

plea-cop *v.* *see* COP A PLEA *v.*

pleader *n.* [? euph. for BLEEDER *n.* (6)] [1910s–20s] a person, a fellow, a 'bloke'.

pleading *adj.* [1900s] a euph. for BLEEDING *adj.*

plea out *v.* [1980s+] (*US Und.*) to plead guilty in the hope of getting a lighter sentence.

pleasant *adj.* [euph.] [mid-19C] drunk, tipsy.

please *v.* [mid-16C–18C] to have sexual intercourse with; lit. to gratify sexually.

pleased as a dog with two cocks *phr.* (*also* **pleased as a dog with two choppers, ...tails, pleased as a pup...**) [COCK *n.*[3] (1)/CHOPPER *n.*[1] (3)] [20C+] very pleased, delighted.

pleaser *n.* [SE, but note PLEASE *v.*] [1960s] (*US campus*) an indiscriminately promiscuous young woman.

pleasure *n.* [late 17C; late 19C] an orgasm.

SE in slang uses

IN COMPOUNDS

❑ **pleasure boat** *n.* (*also* **pleasure conduit, ...girth, ...ground, ...pit, ...place**) [late 16C–19C] the vagina. ❑ **pleasure-lady** *n.* (*also* **pleasurable lady**) [mid-17C; 19C] a prostitute (cf. LADY OF PLEASURE *under* LADY *n.*). ❑ **pleasure-pivot** *n.* [mid-18C] the penis.

pleasure *v.* [early 18C; 1950s+] to have sexual intercourse with.

pleasure and pain *n.* [rhy. sl.] [20C+] rain.

plenty *adj.* [1930s+] (*US*) excellent.

plenty *adv.* [mid-19C+] (*US*) abundantly, very much.

plenty more fish in the sea *phr. see* ...FISH IN THE SEA *under* NOT THE ONLY... *phr.*

plenty of guts, but no bowels *phr. see under* GUT *n.*

pleuro *n.* (*also* **pleura, ploorer**) [abbr.] [late 19C–1910s] (*Aus.*) contagious bovine *pleuro*-pneumonia, a disease of cattle.

plex *n.* [PLEX *v.*] [1990s+] (*US black*) threats, aggression.

plex *v.* **1** [1960s+] (*US prison*) to get psychologically prepared to start a (gang) fight [? SE *flex*]. **2** [1990s+] (*US*) to show disrespect, to slander [ety. unknown]. **3** [1990s+] (*US prison*) to be anxious or nervous [? SE *perplex*].

plier *n.* (*also* **plyer**) [SE *ply one's way*; *ply one's trade*] **1** [late 17C–early 18C] a prostitute. **2** [late 17C–early 19C] (*UK Und.*) a crutch. **3** [late 18C–early 19C] a tradesman. **4** [mid–late 19C] a hand.

pliers *n.* [because of its toughness, it would need a pair of pliers to break it] [1950s] (*W.I.*) a small, finger-shaped dumpling.

pliff *v. see* FLIP *v.*[3] (2).

plimsoll *n.*

SE in slang uses

IN PHRASES

❑ **over the plimsoll** *adj.* [the SE *plimsoll line*, marking the limit of loading a ship] [1920s+] (*N.Z.*) drunk.

pling *v.* [? abbr. SE *pleading*] [1920s–30s] (*US tramp*) to beg.

plinger *n.* [PLING *v.*] [1910s–40s] (*US Und.*) a street beggar.

plink *n.* [PLONK *n.*[1] (1) + PINK-EYE *n.* (1a); or abbr. PLINKITY PLONK *n.*] [1910s+] (*Aus.*) cheap or second-rate wine.

plink *v. see* PLANK *v.* (1).

plinker *n.* [the 'plinking' noise it makes] [1980s+] (*US*) **1** an airgun. **2** a cheap, low-calibre weapon. **3** one who owns and uses such weapons.

plinkity plonk *n.* (*also* **plink plonk**) [rhy. sl. = *vin blanc*, white wine; orig. WW1 milit.] [1910s+] (*Aus.*) white wine; cheap or second-rate wine.

plizzow *v.* [PLOUGH *v.* (1) + -IZ- *infix*] [2000s] (*US black*) of a man, to perform sexual intercourse in an aggressive manner.

ploba *n. see* PLABA *n.*

plocker *n.* (*also* **plugher**) [Irish *plúch*, to choke; *plúchadh*, asthma] [20C+] (*Ulster*) **1** a bad throat, a clearing of the throat. **2** a smoky atmosphere.

plod *n.*[1] [Cornish dial. *plod*, a short story, a lying tale] (*Aus.*) **1** [1920s+] a story, a piece of information. **2** [1940s+] a work sheet giving information about the ground worked by a miner; thus *pitch the plod*, for miners to gossip as they come off and on shift. **3** [1940s+] a specific piece of ground worked by a miner [what is accounted for in sense 2].

plod *n.*[2] (*also* **Mister Plod, Mr Plod**) [children's story character *PC Plod*, created by Enid Blyton (1897–1968) in her *Noddy* books] [1970s+] a police officer, usu. male.

plongkas *n.* (*also* **pluncas**) [echoic *plonk*, the noise it makes hitting a plate or the floor] [1940s] (*W.I.*) **1** a heavy cake or dumpling. **2** a heavy shoe.

plonk *n.*[1] [? mispron. of Fr. *vin blanc*, white wine, picked up by Anglophone soldiers during WWI; the brandname 'Plonque' was merchandised in the early 1970s] **1** [1910s+] cheap or second-rate wine. **2** [1950s+] (*Aus.*) attrib. use, e.g. *plonk bar*, a wine bar; *plonk shop*, an off-licence/liquor store; *plonk waiter*, a wine waiter. **3** *see* PLONKO *n.*

IN PHRASES

❑ **go on the plonk** *v.* [1950s] to go out drinking.

plonk *n.*[2] *see* PLONKER *n.* (3).

plonk *v.* [PLONK! *excl.*] **1** [1930s+] to put down. **2** [1940s+] to have sexual intercourse.

DERIVATIVES

❑ **plonking** *n.* [2000s] sexual intercourse.

IN PHRASES

❑ **plonk oneself down** *v.* [1940s+] to sit down, often as an invitation.

plonk *adv.*

IN PHRASES

❑ **go plonk** *v.* [1910s] (*Aus.*) to fall, thus to fail.

plonk! *excl.* (*also* **plonkety-plonk!**) [1910s+] echoic of the sound of an object hitting the ground.

plonker *n.* [fig. use of SE *plonk*, to hit or strike with a plonking noise] **1** [mid-19C+] anything large or substantial. **2** [1910s+] the penis [note PLONK *v.* (2)]. **3** [1980s+] (*also* **plonk**) a general term of abuse [widely popularized by the 1980s BBC TV series *Only Fools and Horses*].

IN PHRASES

❑ **pull one's plonker** *v.* (*also* **pull one's plonk**) **1** [1910s+] to masturbate. **2** [1990s+] to fool, to mislead.

plonkie *n.* [PLONK *n.*[1] (1)] [1980s+] a wine-drinking alcoholic.

plonko *n.* (*also* **plonk**) [PLONK *n.*[1] (1) + -O *sfx* (3)] [1960s+] (*Aus.*) one who is addicted to cheap wine, an alcoholic.

plook *n. see* PLUKE *n.*

ploorer *n. see* PLEURO *n.*

ploot *n.* [ety. unknown] [1960s] (*S.Afr.*) a young woman.

plop *v.* [1920s] (*US*) to hit.

plossey *adj. see* PLAUSY *adj.*

plot *n.* [SE *plot* (of land)] [1970s+] (*UK Und.*) the place where street-sellers or confidence tricksters operate, e.g. the street, an alley or a doorway.

IN PHRASES

❑ **plot up** *v.* [1960s+] (*UK Und.*) **1** of a gang or group, to seek out and establish territory, e.g. in a soccer stadium, club, crowded place etc. **2** of an individual or group, to make a base.

plot, the *n.* [1920s+] the situation, the facts, the real meaning.

IN PHRASES

❑ **lose the plot** *v.* [1980s+] **1** to lose one's way in a situation, to miss the meaning or point. **2** to become incoherent or incapacitated through drugs or drink. ❑ **plot up** *v.* (*also* **plot on**) [1970s+] (*UK Und.*) to make a plan, e.g. for an escape from prison, a robbery. ❑ **what's the plot?** [1920s] what is happening?

plotz *n.* [PLOTZ *v.* (1)] [1960s] a fool.

plotz *v.* [Yid. *plotzen*/Ger. *platzen*, burst, split] [1920s+] (*orig. US*) **1** to lose emotional control. **2** to collapse physically; to do nothing; to relax after taking marijuana.

plotzed *adj.* [PLOTZ *v.*] [20C+] drunk.

plough *n.* [PLOUGH *v.* (1)] [late 16C–18C] the penis.

plough *v.* (*also* **plow**) **1** [mid-16C+] (*US*) to have sexual intercourse. **2** [mid–late 19C] to reject a candidate as not reaching the pass standard in an examination [SE *plough under*]. **3** [1940s+] to beat up.

IN PHRASES

❑ **plough into** *v.* [1900s–20s] to begin eating enthusiastically. ❑ **plough the back forty** *v.* (*also* **plow the back forty**) [SE *plough* + BACK FORTY *under* BACK *adj.*[2]] [1950s+] **1** to have sexual intercourse. **2** (*US*) to waste time. ❑ **plough the deep** *v.* (*also* **plow the deep**) [fig. use of SE; ? reinforced 20C+ by rhy. sl.] [late 18C+] to (go to) sleep; also as euph. for sexual intercourse.

ploughed *adj.* (*also* **plowed**) [? PLOUGH *v.* (2)] [mid-19C; 1960s+] drunk.

ploughshare *n.* [PLOUGH *v.* (1)] [mid–late 19C] the penis.

plouter *v. see* PLOWTER *v.*

plover *n.* [fig. uses of the bird's name] [17C] **1** a victim, a dupe. **2** a promiscuous woman, a prostitute.

plow *v. see* PLOUGH *v.* and its combs.

plowed *adj. see* PLOUGHED *adj.*

plowhandle *n.* [metonymy] [1930s] (*US*) a peasant, a farmer.

plow jockey *n.* (*also* **plow-jogger**) [SAmE *plow* = SE *plough* + JOCKEY *n.*[2] (3b)] [mid-19C+] (*US*) a farmer, a rustic.

plowter *v.* (*also* **plouter**) [northern dial. *plowter*, to splash about in mire or water] [19C] to have sexual intercourse.

p.l.u. *n.* [abbr.] [1980s+] (*UK society*) people *like us*.

pluck *n.*[1] [SE *pluck*, the intestines of an animal that are plucked out during its cleaning. The term began as early boxing jargon, then moved into sl. Despite its apparent neutrality, the term was not used by women before the 1860s; 20C+ use is SE] **1** [late 18C–1900s] courage. **2** [late 19C] (*US*) an order of beef stew.

DERIVATIVES

❑ **plucked** *adj.* [late 19C] brave.

IN COMPOUNDS

❑ **plucked 'un** *n.* [mid-19C–1920s] a brave person, a 'stout fellow'; usu. with preceding adj., such as *rare, bad, good, real, hard etc.*

IN PHRASES

❑ **against the pluck** *adv.* [late 18C–early 19C] reluctantly, 'against the grain'. ❑ **pluck up** *v.* [early 19C] to be brave, also as imper.

pluck *n.*[2] [SE *pluck*, to pick up] **1** [1950s] (*Aus.*) a stone [? one *plucks* it from the ground]. **2** [1960s+] (*US black*) wine, esp. cheap wine [? SE *pluck*, to harvest grapes]. **3** [1960s+] (*US black*) an attractive woman [she is 'plucked' from the bunch; or ? ref. to fig. use of SE *pluck*, offal, i.e. the vagina].

pluck *v.* **1** [mid-17C–mid-18C; 1960s+] to have sexual intercourse. **2** [late 17C+] to rob. **3** [mid-19C+] (*US campus*) to find lacking, deficient. **4** [20C+] (*US*) to arrest. **5** [1900s] (*US campus*) to expel. **6** [1900s] (*US campus*) to reprimand. **7** [1940s] (*US*) to cashier or retire a military officer. **8** [1980s+] (*US black*) to choose one's woman.

DERIVATIVES

❑ **plucking** *n.* [1960s] robbery, theft.

IN COMPOUNDS

❑ **pluck-up fair** *n.* [SE *pluck up*, to gather, to grab] [late 16C–mid-17C] 'a general scramble for booty or spoil' (*OED*).

IN PHRASES

❑ **pluck a pigeon** *v.* [PIGEON *n.*[1] (2a)] **1** [late 18C+] to fleece a victim. **2** [1910s] in weak use, to conclude a business deal. ❑ **pluck a rose** *v.* (*also* **pull a rose**) [euph.] **1** [17C–early 19C] to visit the lavatory. **2** [mid-17C] to have sexual intercourse. ❑ **pluck Sir Onion** *v.* [? the round 'onion-shape' of a tavern knocker] [late 17C–early 18C] to knock on the tavern door. ❑ **pluck the riband** *v.* (*also* **pluck the ribbon**) [SE *riband*, ribbon, presumably the tavern bell-pull] [late 17C–mid-19C] to ring the bell at a tavern.

plucked *adj.*[1] [PLUCK *v.* (1) or euph. for FUCK *v.* (1)] [1960s+] (*US black*) enjoying a feeling of mental and physical contentment following sexual intercourse.

plucked *adj.*[2] *see under* PLUCK *n.*[1].

plucker *n.* [PLUCK *v.* (2)] [early–mid-19C] (*US*) a robber; a confidence trickster.

pluck that! *excl.* [euph. for *FUCK THAT! under* FUCK *v.*] [1990s+] (*US campus*) an excl. of rejection.

plucky *adj.* (*also* **pluckey**) [PLUCK *n.*[1] (1)] **1** [mid-19C+] brave, courageous; thus adv. *pluckily*; n. *pluckiness*. **2** [late 19C–1900s] a negative intensifier.

plug *n.*[1] **1** [late 18C–1900s] a blow, a punch; a bullet wound. **2** [1900s] (*US*) a prizefighter.

plug *n.*[2] [? lit. or fig. plays on SE *plug*, i.e. it 'fills a gap'] **1** [early 19C] of alcohol. (**a**) a draught of beer. (**b**) wine, esp. cheap wine. **2** [mid–late 19C] a translation, a 'crib' [? it 'plugs up' the gaps in one's knowledge]. **3** [late 19C] (*US*) of money [ext. use of SE *plug*, a small piece of solid material used to stop up a hole]. (**a**) a silver dollar. (**b**) a counterfeit coin.

plug *n.*[3] [Du. *plug*, a worn-out horse] **1** [mid-19C] (*Aus./N.Z.*) a sturdy horse, standing about 15 hands high, that does the work required. **2** [mid-19C–1940s] (*US*) an incompetent or undistinguished person. **3** [mid-19C–1940s] (*US*) a damaged or malfunctioning object, e.g. an old car. **4** [mid-19C+] (*US*) a worn-out old horse. **5** [mid-19C+] (*US*) a fellow, a person, a chap. **6** [1900s] (*US campus*) a hard-working student. **7** [1900s] (*Can.*) an unpleasant person. **8** [1910s] (*US*) a hard-working but materially unsuccessful person. **9** [1930s] a worn-out racing greyhound.

plug *n.*[4] [abbr. PLUG-HAT *n.* (1)] [mid-19C–1920s] a top-hat.

plug *n.*[5] [PLUG *v.*[3] (2)] [20C+] (*orig. US*) **1** an advertisement, a puff, esp. when filtered through a TV or radio programme. **2** a self-aggrandizing or promoting statement.

plug *n.*[6] [? PLUG *v.*[1] (1a) or SE *plug a hole* (in one's life)] [2000s] (*US black*) a woman with whom one is having an affair (in addition to one's primary relationship).

plug *v.*[1] **1** in transitive senses. (**a**) [late 18C+] to have sexual intercourse. (**b**) [mid-19C+] to strike, either with the fist or with a missile, usu. a bullet. (**c**) [1920s] (*US black*) to damage oneself. (**d**) [1940s+] (*gay*) to perform anal intercourse. (**e**) [1980s] (*S.Afr.*) to fail. (**f**) [2000s] (*drugs*) to hide sealed packets of illegal drugs in the rectum. **2** (*also* **plug along, plug at, plug away, plug on**) in senses of lit. or fig. movement. (**a**) [mid-19C+] to persist, to struggle hard against whatever odds. (**b**) [1920s] to continue moving.

DERIVATIVES

❑ **plugging** *n.* [late 19C–1920s] persistence; effort.

IN PHRASES

❑ **plug in the neon** *v.* [the drug 'brightens up' one's senses] [1970s] (*US gay*) to inhale amyl nitrite at the moment of orgasm. ❑ **plug it** *v.* [2000s] (*UK drugs*) to hide drugs in the cleft of the buttocks. ❑ **plug the mug** *v.* [MUG *n.*[1] (1d)] [1940s] (*US black*) to be quiet, to stop talking. ❑ **plug up** *v.* [2000s] to hide something.

plug *v.*[2] [SAmE *plug*, to hinder another person's plans] [late 19C] (*US*) to experience problems, to get into trouble, to fail.

plug *v.*[3] **1** [late 19C] (*US*) to wager, to lay a bet. **2** [late 19C+] to advertise, to promote something, esp. when filtered through a TV or radio programme.

IN COMPOUNDS

❑ **plug money** *n.* [1940s] an illicit payment for promoting a record or song.

IN PHRASES

❑ **plug for** *v.* [20C+] to act in support of, to make favourable statements about.

plug *adv.* [var. on PLUM *adv.*] [1900s] (*Aus.*) directly.

plugged in *adj.* [electrical imagery] [1960s+] **1** abreast of the times, fashionable. **2** involved, connected.

plugger *n.*[1] [PLUG *v.*[1] (1b)] [mid-19C+] a person who shoots, a killer.

plugger *n.*[2] [PLUG *v.*[1] (2a)] [20C+] (*US/Aus.*) one who does not give up; a hard worker.

plugger *n.*[3] [PLUG *v.*[3] (2)] [1900s] (*US*) a promoter.

plugging *n. see under* PLUG *v.*[1].

plug-hat *n.* [the head supposedly fits the hat like a plug] **1** [mid-19C–1940s] a top hat, a silk hat. **2** [1940s] (*Aus.*) a bowler hat.

plugher *n. see* PLOCKER *n.*

plugola *n.* [PLUG *v.*[3] (2) + -OLA *sfx*] [1950s+] (*orig. US*) an illicit payment or favour given for mentioning a commercial product in a non-commercial context.

plug-tail *n.* [SE *plug* + TAIL *n.* (4)] [late 18C–mid-19C] the penis.

plug-ugly *n.* [proper name *Plug-Uglies*, a New York (and Baltimore) street gang of the period. The origin of the name is debatable. One suggestion is that they were named after the large PLUG-HAT *n.* (1), stuffed with paper, that each member wore for protection from the clubs of such opponents as the Dead Rabbits or the Bowery Boys; alternatively f. SE *ugly* + *plug*, a face, or, as a correspondent of *The Times* (4 Nov. 1876), writing of the Baltimore variety, suggested, 'it was derived from a short spike fastened in the toe of their boots, with which they kicked their opponents in a dense crowd, or, as they elegantly expressed it, "plugged them ugly"'] [mid-19C+] (*orig. US*) **1** (*also* **pug-ugly**) a thug, a violent person. **2** a professional boxer. **3** an extremely unattractive person. **4** a carnival float.

plug-ugly *adj.* [PLUG-UGLY *n.* (3)] [20C+] (*orig. US*) extremely unattractive.

pluk *n.* [ety. unknown] [2000s] (*S.Afr. drugs*) a psychedelic experience.

pluke *n.* (*also* **plook**) [Scot. dial. *plook, pluke*, a pimple, a spot] [1960s+] **1** a spot, a pimple, a boil. **2** a general term of abuse [fig. use of sense 1].

DERIVATIVES

❑ **pluky** *adj.* [1990s+] spotty.

IN COMPOUNDS

❑ **pluke-face** *adj.* (*also* **plukey-faced**) [1990s+] a general term of abuse, lit. 'spotty, acne-faced'.

plum *n.*[1] [resemblance] [17C; 20C+] in pl., the testicles; thus *long plum*, the penis.

plum *n.*[2] (*also* **plumb**) [SE *plumb*, a lump of lead; note Egan, *Book of Sports* (1832): '*City Slang*. — A man worth 100,000'] **1** [late 17C–19C] a fortune of £100,000, usu. as a legacy or as the possession of an heiress; thus *half a plum* £50,000. **2** [mid-19C] a rich man. **3** [mid-19C] a member of the upper classes. **4** [late 19C–1950s] a fortune; that which will yield one. **5** [late 19C–1950s] a political office that is lucrative, esp. when it has been obtained by bribery or influence of some kind.

IN PHRASES

❑ **worth a plum** *adj.* [mid-19C] wealthy.

plum *n.*[3] [SE *plum*, excellent] (*Aus.*) **1** [late 19C] a good horse. **2** [1900s] an attractive (young) woman.

plum *n.*[4] [? var. on PRUNE *n.* (2)] [1990s+] a repressive puritan.

plum *adv.* (*also* **plumb, plump**) [SE *plum-ripe*; primarily US since mid-19C, esp. in such clichés as *plumb loco*, utterly crazy] [17C+] a general intensifier, completely, entirely, absolutely, quite, e.g. *plumb loco*, totally mad.

plumb *n. see* PLUM *n.*[2].

plumb *v.*[1] [? SE *plumb someone's depths* + prior gambling jargon] [mid-19C–1900s] to fool, to deceive.

plumb *v.*[2] [1920s+] to have sexual intercourse.

plumb *adv. see* PLUM *adv.*

plumber *n.*[1] [note the political 'plumbers' of the 1972–4 US Watergate Scandal, similarly deputed to 'plug leaks'] [1950s] (*US Und.*) a hired killer.

plumber *n.*[2] [PLUMBING *n.* (1)/PLUMB *v.*[2]] [1970s+] (*US black*) a man with a frequent and varied sex life.

plumber *v.* [? negative stereotype of the occupation] [1930s] (*US*) to blunder, to make a mistake.

plumber's crack *n. see* BUILDER'S BUM *n.*

plumbing *n.* **1** [1920s+] (*orig. US*) the excretory tract, the urinary system; the genitals. **2** [1930s–50s] (*US*) a trumpet, trombone, or similar wind instrument. **3** [1950s] fillings in teeth. **4** [1990s+] (*Aus.*) the lungs.

plum jam *n.* [rhy. sl.] [1980s+] (*N.Z.*) a lamb.

plummy *adj.* [SE *plum*] **1** [late 18C–19C] good, excellent. **2** [mid-19C–1900s] round, sleek, fat, jolly. **3** [late 19C+] (*also* **plummy-voiced**) of a voice, affected or upper-class [SE *have a plum in the mouth*]. **4** [1920s–30s] (*Scot.*) dull.

plummy *adv.* [PLUM *adv.*] **1** [early 19C] excellently. **2** [mid–late 19C] nicely, satisfactorily, pleasantly.

plump *n.* [mid-18C–early 19C] a blow; thus *plump in the bread-basket*, a blow to the stomach; *plump in the peepers*, a blow to the eyes.

plump *v.* [PLUMP *n.*] [late 18C–1900s] to hit, to shoot; also fig. use.

IN PHRASES

❑ **plump someone up to** *v.* [they are 'plumped up' with the information] [1910s–20s] to tell someone something secretly.

plump *adv. see* PLUM *adv.*

plump currant *n.* [late 18C–early 19C] used of one who is ir good health, usu. in negative, e.g. *Charles is not the plump currant*.

plumper *n.*[1] [lit. and fig. uses of PLUMP *n.*] **1** [mid-17C–mid-18C] a whore. **2** [early 18C] a (large) female breast. **3** [late 18C–19C] a heavy blow; also fig. use. **4** [early–mid-19C] a major lie. **5** [late 19C] an unusually large version of its type.

plumper *n.*[2] [SE *plump for*, to commit wholeheartedly] **1** [late 18C–1910s] a single vote at an election. **2** [late 19C+] a heavy bet.

plumpies *n.* [SE *plump*/PLUMPER *n.*[1] (2)] [1990s+] large female breasts.

plump in the pocket *adv.* [late 17C–early 19C] satisfactorily well-off.

plump-pate *n.* [var. on FAT-HEAD *n.*[1]/BLOCKHEAD *n.*[1]] [19C] a fool.

plum pud *adj.* [rhy. sl.] [20C+] (*Aus.*) good.

plum-pudding (dog) *n.* [the spots resemble the plums] [mid-19C] a variety of the dog Dalmatian, with notable dark spots.

plumpy *n.* [var. on FAT *n.* (3)] [2000s] (*US*) the (erect) penis.

plum tree *n.* **1** [mid-16C–17C] the vagina; thus *plum tree shaker*, the penis. **2** [early 17C] the penis [? PLUM *n.*[1] (1)] **3** [20C+] (*US*) the spoils of political office; thus *shake the plum tree*, to extract graft from one's office [one shakes the fig. 'tree' to gain the PLUM *n.*[2] (5)].

pluncas *n. see* PLONGKAS *n.*

plunge *n.* (*also* **plunger**) **1** [late 19C–1920s] a (heavy) be [PLUNGE *v.* (1a)]. **2** [1910s] (*US tramp*) the act of street begging esp. with a specific sum in mind. **3** [1920s] (*US tramp*) mone obtained by begging. **4** [1950s] (*US drugs*) a narcotic injection. **5** [1990s+] an act of sexual intercourse.

plunge *v.* **1** in fig. uses. (**a**) [mid-19C+] to spend money o bet recklessly, to speculate heavily, to run into debt. (**b**) [2000s to perform anything intensely. **2** [1990s+] in lit. uses. (**a**) to kill, to murder. (**b**) to stab.

plunger *n.* **1** as a lit. or fig. gambler [PLUNGE *v.* (1a); the 'plunge' deep into the game; but note milit. jargon *plunger*, cavalryman; post WW2 use is historical]. (**a**) [mid–late 19C+] reckless gambler. (**b**) [late 19C] in fig. use, anyone who take risks. (**c**) [1990s+] (*US campus*) a spendthrift. **2** in sexua uses. (**a**) [1930s+] the penis; thus *plunger-pumping*, sex (**b**) [1970s+] (*US gay*) an energetic, speedy copulator **3** [1940s] (*US black/Harlem*) a bathtub. **4** [1950s] (*US drugs* a hypodermic syringe. **5** *see* PLUNGE *n.*

plunk *n.* [ety. unknown; predates *PLUNK DOWN under* PLUNK *v.* **1** [mid-18C–mid-19C] a large sum, a fortune. **2** [early 19C 1930s] (*also* **plunker**) (*US*) a dollar; thus in pl., money in general. **3** [1900s] a blow, a hit.

plunk *v.* [echoic of the sound of a blow] **1** [late 19C] (*orig. Aus* to hit someone. **2** [late 19C+] in fig. use, to attack, to produce **3** [20C+] (*Ulster*) to fail an examination.

IN PHRASES

❑ **plunk down** *v.* [20C+] (*orig. US*) **1** to wager. **2** to lay mone down forcibly. **3** (*also* **plunk**) to sit down, to put down. **4** to s someone down. ❑ **plunk for** *v.* [1940s] (*US*) to opt for, to giv one's support to.

plunk *adv.* [fig. use PLUNK *v.* (1)] [late 19C] (*US*) directly.

plunk a baby *v.* [the Royal New Zealand *Plunket* Societ founded 1907, the N.Z. version of the UK Royal Society for th Protection of Women and Children; ult. Lady *Plunket*, wife of th then governor of N.Z., an early patron] [1930s+] (*Aus./N.Z.*) t have a baby; thus *get plunked*, to be pregnant.

plunker *n. see* PLUNK *n.* (2).

plurry *adj.* [Maori mispron.; but note McGill, *Dict. of Kiwi S* (1988): 'Partridge says it is from Aboriginal's natural use of th word, OEDS says NZA slang, Turner thinks it a convention journalists rather than Maori, in support of which was th slanguage of the character Hori in the bestselling book *The Hal Gallon Jar*'] [late 19C+] (*Aus./N.Z.*) a synon. for BLOODY *adj.*

plush *n.* [the texture; note Ital. *peluccio, peluzzo*, a little hair, so down, fine hair] **1** [19C] female pubic hair. **2** [1910s] (*U* profit, money.

SE in slang uses

IN PHRASES

❑ **on the plush** *see* ON THE CUSHIONS *under* CUSHION *n.*

plush *adj.* (*also* **plushy**) [SE *plush*, a type of soft material] [20C+] luxurious, expensive, stylish, thus also snobbish.

plushery *n.* [PLUSH *adj.*] [20C+] (*orig. US*) a luxurious hotel, expensive restaurant, smart nightclub etc.

plush horse *n.* [1910s–20s] (*US*) a socially conservative, rigid person; usu. upper-class and over-dressed.

plush-horse *adj.* [PLUSH HORSE *n.*] [1920s] (*US*) wealthy, privileged.

plushite *n.* ['James Yellowplush', the fictional servant of Thackeray's *Yellowplush Papers* (1837)] [1900s] a servant.

plushy *adj. see* PLUSH *adj.*

plute *n.* (*also* **plut, plutess**) [abbr. SE *plutocrat*] [20C+] (*US/Aus.*) the very rich, the social elite; thus *plutish*, elitist; *pluty*, wealthy and consciously elitist.

plyer *n. see* PLIER *n.*

Plymouth Argyll *n.* [rhy. sl.; name of a soccer team] [20C+] a file.

Plymouth blade *n.* (*also* **Plymouth cloak**) [the violence of the naval town] [17C] a cudgel.

ply the acid *v. see* PUT THE ACID ON *under* ACID *n.*[2].

ply the toby *v. see* TOBY *v.* (1).

p.m. *n.* (*also* **peeyem**) [SE *p.m.*, *post meridiem*, used in chronological notation] [mid-19C+] the afternoon.

p-maker *n.* [abbr. PISS *n.* (1)-*maker*] [mid-19C–1900s] the vagina.

p.m.s. *v.* [abbr. *pre-menstrual syndrome*, or *putting up with men's shit*] [1990s+] (*US campus*) of a woman, to feel irritable, anxious.

p.m.s. monster *n.* [abbr. *pre-menstrual syndrome* + -MONSTER *sfx*] [1980s+] (*US campus*) a menstruating woman.

pneumonia blouse *n.* [the style of the blouse was seen as rendering the wearer susceptible to diseases of the lungs] [1900s–20s] a transparent blouse of muslin and lace with next to no collar and thus, for some puritan contemporaries, a shockingly low neckline.

p-nut *n.* [PRICK *n.* (1)] [2000s] (*US black*) the outline of the male genitals visible through very tight trousers.

p.o. *n.* [abbr.] **1** [late 19C+] a postal order. **2** [1910s+] (*US*) a post office. **3** [1950s+] (*US*) a parole or probation officer. **4** [1990s+] a police officer.

p.o. *adj.* (*also* **p.o.'d, p.o.'ed**) [abbr. PISSED OFF *adj.*] [1950s+] (*orig. US*) angry.

p.o. *v.* **1** [1910s] (*Aus.*) to go away; also as imper. [PISS OFF *v.* (1)]. **2** [1940s+] (*US*) to annoy [PISS OFF *v.* (2)].

po *n.* (*also* **poe, poh**) [abbr. SE *chamberpot* + 'affected' abbr. of Fr. *pot de chambre*] **1** [late 19C+] a chamberpot; a commode. **2** [1920s+] the lavatory.

IN PHRASES

❑ **after you with the po, Jane** [late 19C–1920s] a ref. to the need to take turns in using an outdoor privy; transferred in joc. usage to indoor facilities.

poach *v. see* POOCH *v.*

poached egg *n.* [1930s–40s] (*Aus.*) a yellow speed bump placed in the centre of an intersection.

poag *n. see* POGUE *n.*[3].

po'chaise *n.* (*also* **po'chay, pochay, post-chay, post-shay**) [abbr. SE *post-chaise*] [18C–19C] a travelling carriage seating two or four, with the coachman or postilion riding one of the horses.

pock *v. see* POKE *v.* (1).

pocket *n.*

SE in slang uses

pertaining to genitals

IN COMPOUNDS

❑ **pocket billiards** *n.* [1910s+] playing with one's genitals through a trouser pocket, hence masturbating. ❑ **pocket pinball** *n.* [1930s+] (*orig. US*) playing with one's genitals through a trouser pocket, hence masturbating. ❑ **pocket pool** *n.* [1940s+] playing with one's genitals through a trouser pocket, hence masturbating. ❑ **pocket rocket** *n.* [1990s+] (*UK juv.*) the erect penis.

pertaining to money

IN COMPOUNDS

❑ **pocket cabbage** *n.* (*also* **pocket lettuce**) [CABBAGE *n.*[2] (3a)/ LETTUCE *n.*[1]] [1920s+] (*US*) money. ❑ **pocket roll** *n.* [ROLL *n.* (2)] [1960s+] (*US black*) a roll of paper money kept in the pocket.

IN PHRASES

❑ **deep pockets** *n.* [1950s+] (*US*) a person who can always be counted on to provide cash. ❑ **have death adders in one's pockets** *v.* (*also* **have mousetraps..., have scorpions..., have snakes...**) [one dare not, therefore, put one's hand in one's pocket to extract money] [1920s+] (*Aus.*) to be extremely mean. ❑ **have fish-hooks in one's pockets** *v.* [one's pockets are lined with SE *fish-hooks* so one cannot put one's hand in; but note FISH-HOOK *under* FISH *n.*[1]] [1910s+] (*US*) to be particularly mean and miserly. ❑ **have long pockets and short arms** *v.* [1970s] (*Aus./N.Z.*) to be miserly, mean. ❑ **have one's hand in someone's pocket** *v.* [1920s–40s] to be in receipt of bribes. ❑ **make a pocket** *v.* [mid-19C] to make money, e.g. as a street-seller. ❑ **pocketful of rocks** *n. see* ROCKS *n.* (1). ❑ **pockets to let** *adj.* [mid-19C] out of money, impoverished. ❑ **pull one's pocket** *v.* [one must pull out the pocket's lining to find the necessary coins] [20C+] (*W.I.*) to pay with difficulty.

general uses

IN COMPOUNDS

❑ **pocket-book** *n.* **1** [1950s] (*W.I.*) a large, flat, fried dumpling [resemblance]. **2** [1970s] (*US black*) the vagina [var. on PURSE *n.* (1)]. ❑ **pocket pistol** *n.* (*also* **pistol**) **1** [mid-18C–1900s] a dram flask, a hip-flask [it gives one a 'shot in the arm']. **2** [1970s] (*W.I.*) a roasted corn on the cob [resemblance of shapes]. ❑ **pocket rocket** *n.* [it gets you 'high'] [1980s+] (*drugs*) marijuana.

IN PHRASES

❑ **out of (the) pocket** [pool jargon, an *out of pocket* shot causes a player to miss a turn] **1** [1970s+] (*US black*) acting in an unacceptable, tasteless manner. **2** [1990s+] (*US black gang*) using a gun.

pockily *adv. see* POCKY *adv.*

pock-pudding *n.* (*also* **pock-pud, poke-pudding**) [Scot. *poke-pudding*, a bag-pudding, hence a glutton] **1** [early 18C–19C] (*Scot.*) an Englishman. **2** [1910s] a foolish person.

pocky *adj.* (*also* **pockey, pockified**) [SE *pocky*, covered in syphilitic sores] [16C–mid-19C] a general term of abuse, lit. 'syphilitic'.

pocky *adv.* (*also* **pockily**) [POCKY *adj.*] [17C] negative intensifier, lit. 'syphilitically'.

p.o.'d *adj. see* P.O. *adj.*

p.o.d. *adj.* [abbr. *passed overdose*] [1990s+] (*US black/drugs*) extremely intoxicated by a given drug, usu. marijuana.

pod *n.*[1] [orig. dial.] [late 19C–1910s] a large stomach.

IN PHRASES

❑ **in pod** *adj.* [late 19C+] pregnant.

pod *n.*[2] [POT *n.*[3]] [1940s+] (*US drugs*) marijuana.

pod *n.*[3]

IN PHRASES

❑ **pull one's pod** *v. see* PULL ONE'S PUD *under* PUD *n.*[1].

poddy *n.* [? dial. *poddinger*, an earthenware pot, orig. used for porridge] [late 19C–1950s] (*Aus.*) a bottle of alcohol.

poddy *adj.*[1] [POD *n.*[1]] [mid-19C–1900s] corpulent, obese.

poddy *adj.*[2] [PODDY *n.*] [1900s–10s] drunk.

poddy calf *n.* [rhy. sl.; ult. *see* next] [20C+] (*Aus.*) *half*-a-crown, 2s 6d (12½p).

poddy dodger *n.* [SAusE *poddy*, an unbranded calf + *dodge*, to steal (cattle)] [1910s–50s] (*Aus.*) one who steals unbranded cattle, a cattle rustler; as v., *poddy-dodge*.

DERIVATIVES

❑ **poddy-dodging** *n.* [1940s+] cattle-rustling.

podger *n.* [dial. *podge*, to hit] **1** [early–mid-19C] a hard blow. **2** [late 19C] (*Irish*) a cudgel.

podgy *adj.* [Ital. *poco acqua*, a little water, or Rom. *pogado*, crooked, thus the way one walks, or POGY *adj.*] [mid-19C] drunk.

podna/podner *n. see* PARD *n.*

pod people *n.* [film *Invasion of the Body-Snatchers* (1956, 1978), in which aliens spawn in pods] [1980s+] stupid or robotic people; fundamentalist Christians; thus *podspeak*, meaningless talk.

podunk *n.* [Algonquin *podunk*, a marshy meadow, used esp. by a small tribe of Indians formerly inhabiting an area around the Podunk River in Hartford County, Connecticut. When the word was used (on the grounds of its amusing sound) in a series of letters featuring the supposed small town of Podunk, published in the US in 1846, it gained a greater currency and took on the meaning it has retained ever since. A secondary ety. notes the 'po-dunk' croak of a bullfrog, *podunker* in dial.; thus such towns are out where the bullfrogs can croak undisturbed] **1** [mid-19C+] (*US*) a generic term for a small town. **2** [2000s] a provincial, a peasant.

podunk *adj.* [PODUNK *n.*] [1960s+] (*US campus*) worthless, insignificant; lost.

poe *n. see* PO *n.*

p.o.'ed *adj. see* P.O. *adj.*

poefte *n. see* POOFTER *n.*

poegaai *adj.* (*also* **poeg-eyed**) [Du. *pooien*, to tipple + sfx *-eyed*] [1940s+] (*S.Afr.*) **1** drunk. **2** exhausted.

poep *n.* [Afk. *poep* = FART *n.* (1)] (*S.Afr.*) [1960s+] **1** breaking wind. **2** faeces. **3** a fool.

IN EXCLAMATIONS

❑ **poep!** [1970s] an excl. of annoyance.

poep *adj.* [POEP *n.*] [1960s+] (*S.Afr.*) bad, unpleasant.

poep *v.* [POEP *n.* (1)] [1960s+] (*S.Afr.*) to break wind.

poephol *n.* [Afk. sl. *poep-hol* = ARSEHOLE *n.*] (*S.Afr.*) [1960s+] **1** a general term of abuse, fool, idiot. **2** the anus.

poep-scared *adj.* (*also* **poop-scared**) [POEP *n.* (2); note Afk. *poepbang*, dead scared] [1970s+] (*S.Afr.*) terrified, lit. 'shit-scared'.

poes *n.* [synon. Afk. sl.] [1960s+] (*S.Afr.*) **1** the vagina; hence generic for sexual intercourse. **2** the buttocks. **3** a general term of abuse.

IN COMPOUNDS

❑ **poes-boekie** *n.* [Afk., lit. 'cunt book'] [1980s] a pornographic book or magazine. ❑ **poesface** *n.* (*also* **poeshead, poes-licker**) [2000s] an insult. ❑ **poesplaas** *n.* [lit. 'cunt place'] [2000s] a reformatory. ❑ **poes-tiefie** *n.* [2000s] (*S.Afr.*) a slut, lit. 'cunt-thief'. ❑ **poeswyn** *n.* [2000s] (*S.Afr.*) cheap wine, 'rotgut'.

poet's day *n.* [abbr. *p*iss *o*ff *e*arly, *t*omorrow's *S*aturday] [1970s+] Friday.

po-faced *adj.* [? PO *n.* (1) or SE *poh!* + sfx *-faced*] [1930s+] arrogant, stand-offish, humourless.

p. off! *excl.* [abbr. PISS OFF! *excl.*] [1960s+] go away!

poge *n. see under* POGUE.

pogee *n.* (*also* **pogey, pogie**) [? POKE *v.* (1)] [1970s] (*US/P.R.*) a passive male homosexual; thus n. *pogie bait*, a homosexual who pursues young men.

poger *n.* (*also* **pogey**) [? POKE *v.* (1)] [1950s–70s] (*orig. US tramp*) an active male homosexual.

pogey *n.*[1] (*also* **poggie, pogie, pogy**) [? POKE *n.*[2] (2), i.e. something in which one is 'put away'; dial. *poghole*, a boggy hole or Fr. *poche*, a pocket] **1** [late 19C–1960s] (*US tramp*) a workhouse; a relief centre. **2** [1920s–70s] a prison hospital. **3** [1930s] a prison cell. **4** [1930s–60s] a house of correction, a prison.

pogey *n.*[2] **1** *see* POGEE *n.* **2** *see* POGER *n.*

pogey *adj.* [Ital. *poco*, little] [20C+] (*Ling. Fr./Polari*) small, insignificant.

pogey acqua! *excl.* (*also* **pogy acqua!**) [Ital.; lit. *poco acqua*, little water] [early 19C] make the drink strong!

pogey bait *n. see* POGY BAIT *n.*

poggie *n.* **1** *see* POGEY *n.*[1]. **2** *see* POGUE *n.*[3].

poggle *n.* (*also* **puggle, puggly**) [Hind. *pagal*, a madman] [late 19C–1930s] a fool, an eccentric.

poggled *adj.* (*also* **poggle, puggareed, puggled**) [POGGLE *n.*] **1** [20C+] mad, drunk, crazy; thus *poggle-khana*, a picnic, lit. a 'fool's dinner'. **2** [1960s+] drunk.

poggler *n.*[1] [? POKE *n.*[2] (2)] [1970s] **1** a pocket. **2** a wallet or purse.

poggler *n.*[2] [POGUE *n.*[3] (2)] [1970s+] a male homosexual.

poggy *adj. see under* POGY.

pogh! *excl. see* FAUGH! *excl.*

pogie *n. see* POGEY *n.*[1].

pogo stick *n.* [rhy. sl. = PRICK *n.* (1)] [1960s+] (*Aus./US*) the penis.

pogram *n.* [proper name *Pogram*, a well-known dissenting preacher of the time] [mid-19C] a dissenter.

pogue *n.*[1] [POKE *n.*[1] (1)] **1** [early 18C] an act of copulation. **2** [mid-19C+] (*Irish*) a kiss.

pogue *n.*[2] (*also* **poge**) [? POKE *n.*[2] (2) or 9C SE *pough*, a bag, a sack] [early 19C+] (*UK Und.*) a purse, a wallet, a pocket.

IN COMPOUNDS

❑ **poge-hunter** *n.* [late 19C–1900s] a purse-snatcher or pickpocket who specializes in taking purses.

pogue *n.*[3] (*also* **poag, poge, poggie**) [Ital. *poco*, small; note US Military Corps *poge*, any non-combatant member of the Corps] **1** [1930s+] a young boy; in ext. use, an inexperienced person. **2** [1950s+] (*US gay*) the passive partner in anal intercourse.

pogue *v.* [POKE *v.* (1) + note POGUE *n.*[3] (2)] [1940s–70s] to have anal intercourse, also in fig. use.

Pogue Mahone *phr.* [Gaelic *pogue mahone*, 'kiss my arse'] [20C+] (*Irish*) a dismissive retort, lit. 'kiss my arse'.

pogue the hone *v.* [*see* prev.; ? or 'Irish' pron. of 'poke the hole'] [early 19C] (*Irish*) to copulate.

pogy *n. see* POGEY *n.*[1].

pogy *adj.* (*also* **poggy**) [? Rom. *pogado*, crooked] [late 18C–19C] drunk.

pogy acqua! *excl. see* POGEY ACQUA! *excl.*

pogy bait *n.* (*also* **pogey bait, poggy bait**) [POGUE *n.*[3] (1)] [1910s+] (*orig. US milit.*) snack foods, occas. cigarettes, money; underlying image of the use of such snacks as a lure by child-molesters.

poh *n. see* PO *n.*

poh-poh *n. see* PO-PO *n.*

poindexter *n.* [play on POINTED-HEAD *n.*] [1980s] (*US teen*) a derog. term for an intellectual, bookish person.

Point, the *n.* **1** [early 19C+] (*US*) West *Point*, properly the United States Military Academy at West Point, New York [abbr.]. **2** [1930s] San Quentin prison [? misreading]. **3** [1990s+] (*US black teen*) Hunter's *Point*, San Francisco [abbr.].

point *n.* **1** [late 19C–1940s] the chin, the face, the nose. **2** [1930s+] (*drugs*) a hypodermic syringe. **3** [1940s+] (*US*) anyone standing guard or leading the way [milit. jargon *point*, the man walking at the head of a patrol; ult. ranching jargon *point*, the front of a herd]. **4** [1960s] a nipple. **5** [1960s–70s] (*gay*) any form of writing implement.

IN PHRASES

❑ **keep point** *v.* [1990s+] (*US prison*) to keep a lookout.

SE in slang uses

IN PHRASES

❑ **get points** *v.* (*also* **have points**) [late 19C+] to have an advantage. ❑ **give points** *v.* [late 19C] to permit an advantage to. ❑ **on point** *adj.* [milit. *point*, the lead man of a patrol] **1** [1970s+] standing guard, keeping a lookout. **2** [1990s+] alert, sharp, aware. ❑ **work a point** *v.* (*also* **work points**) [late

19C+] (*Aus.*) to live by one's wits, to take advantage by trickery and deception.

point *v.* [SE *score points*] (*Aus.*) **1** [mid-19C–1910s] to take unfair advantage of. **2** [1950s+] to waste time, to malinger.

point blank *n.* [Fr. *vin blanc*] [1910s] (*UK/Aus. milit.*) white wine.

pointed-head *n. see* POINTY-HEAD *n.*

pointer *n.*[1] **1** [mid-18C–19C] the penis. **2** [mid-19C] (*UK Und.*) an informer. **3** [late 19C+] (*orig. US*) a hint, a suggestion. **4** [1930s] (*W.I.*) a knife. **5** [1950s–60s] (*US*) in pl., the female breast.

pointer *n.*[2] [POINT *v.* (1)] (*Aus./N.Z.*) **1** [mid–late 19C] a confidence trickster, a card-sharp. **2** [mid-19C+] an idler, a loafer, a malingerer. **3** [late 19C+] one who takes an unfair advantage, esp. by trickery; an informer. **4** [1930s] in pl., crooked dice.

pointhead *n. see* POINTY-HEAD *n.*

point percy at the porcelain *v. see under* PERCY *n.*[1].

point shot *n. see under* SHOT *n.*[1].

point the bone *v.* [Aborigine practice of pointing a bone (the 'death bone') at one whose death is desired] [1940s+] (*Aus.*) to betray a friend and leave them in the lurch; thus *bone-pointer*, *bone-pointing*.

pointy-head *n.* (*also* **pointed-head, pointhead**) [both senses are derog. and suggest that an excess or an absence of brain lead to a 'pointed' head] **1** [1960s+] (*US*) a fool. **2** [1970s+] an intellectual.

pointy-headed *adj.* (*also* **pointy-head**) [POINTY-HEAD *n.*] [1960s+] (*US*) intellectual, cultured.

poison *n.* **1** [mid-17C; 19C+] (*also* **rat poison**) an ironic term for drink in general. **2** in senses of someone or something harmful. (**a**) [mid-19C+] an unpleasant person, best to be avoided; also used semi-affectionately. (**b**) [1910s–30s] something that one should avoid, i.e. something suspicious. (**c**) [1930s–50s] (*US drugs*) a doctor who refuses to prescribe narcotics. **3** in drug uses. (**a**) [1920s] cocaine. (**b**) [1950s+] (*drugs*) heroin, esp. in its pure state. (**c**) [1980s] (*S.Afr.*) marijuana. (**d**) [2000s] fentanyl.

IN COMPOUNDS

❑ **poison people** *n.* [1960s–70s] (*US black*) heroin addicts, taken as a group. ❑ **poison shop** *n.* (*Aus.*) **1** [1910s+] a public house. **2** [1950s] a brothel.

IN PHRASES

❑ **name your poison** (*also* **nominate your poison, pick...**) [late 19C+] (*orig. US*) an invitation to a fellow drinker to make a choice of drink at a party or in a bar. ❑ **put in the poison** *v.* [1920s] to slander, to malign a person's character, esp. in court. ❑ **what's your poison?** *see* separate entry.

SE in slang uses

IN COMPOUNDS

❑ **poison joint** *n.* [JOINT *n.* (3b)] [1930s–40s] (*US Und.*) a pharmacy; a drug store. ❑ **poison-pate** *n.* [SE *red* being a symbolically 'dangerous' colour + *pate*] [late 17C–early 19C] a redhead; thus *poison-pated*, red-haired.

poison *adj.* [on bad = good model] [1960s+] (*S.Afr.*) excellent, admirable, first-rate.

poisoned *adj.* [the swelling that often follows actual poisoning; 20C+ use is US black] [17C+] pregnant.

poisoner *n.* [1900s–40s] (*Aus./N.Z.*) a cook, esp. one serving a team of sheep shearers; thus v., *poison*, to cook.

poison oneself *v.* [POISON *n.*] [late 19C] to take a drink.

poke *n.*[1] **1** [18C; mid-19C+] sexual intercourse. **2** [late 18C+] a blow; thus *TAKE A POKE AT* below. **3** [late 19C+] a woman seen as a partner in sexual intercourse; often as *good poke*, *lousy poke*; occas. of a man. **4** [1950s+] usu. of cars or motorcycles, speed, horsepower. **5** in drug uses. (**a**) [1950s+] a puff on a marijuana cigarette. (**b**) [2000s] a puff on a crack cocaine pipe.

IN PHRASES

❑ **take a poke at** *v.* **1** [20C+] (*orig. US*) to assault, to aim a blow at. **2** [1930s+] to have a try, to attempt. **3** [1950s] to attack verbally, to cause problems for.

poke *n.*[2] [SE *poke*, a bag; ult. Fr. *poche*, pocket] **1** [mid-19C–1900s] stolen property. **2** [mid-19C+] (*US*) a wallet, a purse. **3** [mid-19C+] a bag of food handed out to a beggar. **4** [20C+] (*Irish/US*) a cone-shaped bag, esp. for sweets or chips, or an ice-cream cornet; thus *poke man*, an ice-cream seller; *poke van*, an ice-cream van. **5** [1910s+] a roll of banknotes, money in general. **6** [1940s] (*US Und.*) a variety of confidence trick.

IN COMPOUNDS

❑ **poke-getter** *n.* [1900s–20s] (*US Und.*) a pickpocket. ❑ **poke-lifter** *n.* (*also* **poke-picker**) [1930s] (*UK Und.*) a pickpocket. ❑ **poke-out** *n.* **1** [late 19C–1930s] food given to a tramp who begs at the door. **2** [1940s] (*S.Afr. prison*) a bag of tobacco or similar smuggled into prison. **3** [1950s–60s] (*US*) food cooked outdoors; a gathering to eat such food; a long trek that involves eating outdoors. ❑ **poke-shakings** *n.* [SE *shaking*, i.e. the image of turning out one's wallet] [20C+] (*Irish*) **1** the last pig in a litter. **2** the last child of a family.

SE in slang uses

IN PHRASES

❑ **get the poke** *v.* [SE *poke*, a small bag or sack] [late 19C+] (*Scot.*) to be dismissed from one's job.

poke *n.*[3] [? abbr. SE *poke bonnet*, which had a projecting rim] [1900s–20s] (*US*) a shirt collar.

poke *n.*[4] *see* POKEY *n.*[2] (1).

poke *v.* **1** [17C+] (*also* **pock**) of a man, occas. woman, to have hetero- or homosexual intercourse. **2** [20C+] (*orig. US*) to hit, to strike. **3** [1970s] (*US*) to drive fast.

DERIVATIVES

❑ **pokeable** *adj.* [1970s] sexually appealing/available. ❑ **poked** *adj.* [euph. for FUCKED *adj.*[1] (1)] [1970s+] (*N.Z.*) exhausted.

IN COMPOUNDS

❑ **poke-hole** *n.* (*also* **poking-hole**) [late 19C+] the vagina. ❑ **poking-stick** *n.* [*double entendre*; a SE *poking stick* was used to iron a ruff] [early 17C] the penis.

IN PHRASES

❑ **you don't look at the mantelpiece when you're poking the fire** [20C+] a phr. meaning that a woman's looks are irrelevant if she's sexually available.

SE in slang uses

IN COMPOUNDS

❑ **poke-nose** *n.* [1910s] an interfering person.

IN PHRASES

❑ **poke along** *v.* (*also* **poke about**) [mid-19C+] to walk slowly; to do anything slowly. ❑ **poke bogey (at)** *v.* [SE *bogus*] [late 19C–1900s] to trick, to fool, to deceive. ❑ **poke borack** *v. see under* BORAK *n.* ❑ **poke borax/poke it** *v. see* POKE (THE) BORAK *under* BORAK *n.* ❑ **poke-in-the-arse** *adj.* [1970s] (*N.Z.*) backward, insignificant.

poke a smipe *v.* [joc. reversal] [mid-19C] to smoke a pipe.

poke-pudding *n. see* POCK-PUDDING *n.*

poker *n.*[1] **1** [late 17C–mid-19C] a sword. **2** [early 19C+] the penis. **3** [mid-19C] a womanizer, a 'sexual athlete' [POKE *v.* (1)]. **4** [1980s] (*US Und.*) a single-barrelled shotgun. **5** [1990s+] (*US*) a knife.

IN COMPOUNDS

❑ **poker-breaker** *n.* [19C–1900s] one's wife.

poker *n.*[2] [POKE ALONG *under* POKE *v.*] [mid-19C] (*UK Und.*) an idler, a casual labourerer.

poker talk *n.* [late 19C] **1** a fireside chat. **2** exaggerated talk, boasting, bragging [CHANT THE POKER *under* CHANT *v.*].

pokey *n.*[1] [POKE *v.* (1)] **1** [20C+] (*orig. W.I. teen*) the vagina. **2** [1960s] (*US*) a penis.

pokey *n.*[2] [? POGEY *n.*[1] (1) or the 'poky' conditions] **1** [1910s+] (*also* **poke**) a prison, usu. small and local. **2** [1940s] a turnkey, a jailer. **3** [1990s+] a prison cell.

pokey *n.*[3] *see* POKIE *n.*[1].

pokey *adj.* (*also* **poky**) [POKE ALONG *under* POKE v.] [mid-19C–1950s] (*US*) slow, boring.

pokey stiff *n.* [POKE-OUT *under* POKE *n.*[2] + STIFF *n.*[1] (4a)] [1910s–30s] (*US tramp*) a tramp who subsists on nothing but handouts.

pokie *n.*[1] (*also* **pokey**) [abbr.] [1960s+] (*Aus.*) an electronic *poker* machine, used in casinos; also as *pokie bandit*.

pokie *n.*[2] [POKE ALONG *under* POKE v.] [1980s] a person or vehicle that travels slowly.

poking *n.* [POKE v. (1)] [mid-19C+] sexual intercourse.

poky *adj. see* POKEY *adj.*

pol *n.*[1] [abbr.] **1** [1920s] (*US Und.*) an illegal racket based on a *pol*itical project. **2** [1930s+] (*US*) a *pol*itician.

pol *n.*[2] [abbr. *polly parrot*] [1940s+] (*UK prison*) a talkative person, a chatterer or gossip.

pol! *excl.* [abbr. *by Pollux*, one of the twins of the Gemini constellation] [late 16C–early 17C] a general excl.

Polack *n.* (*also* **Polac, Polacker, Polacki, Polak, Pollacky, Pollock, Pullack**) [early 17C; late 19C+] **1** a Pole. **2** (*mainly Jewish*) a Jew whose family come from Poland.

Polack *adj.* (*also* **Polock**) [early 17C; mid-19C+] pertaining to Poles or Polish culture.

IN COMPOUNDS

❑ **Polack town** *n.* [20C+] (*US*) the Polish community within an urban area.

polboron *n.* (*also* **pulboron**) [Sp. *polboron*, 'big powder'; a dry powdered candy] [1970s] (*drugs*) heroin.

polcat *n. see* POLECAT *n.*

pole *n.* [17C+] the penis.

IN COMPOUNDS

❑ **pole hole** *n.* [1970s+] the vagina. ❑ **pole pleaser** *n.* [1990s+] (*US*) a (passive) homosexual man. ❑ **pole sitter** *n.* [2000s] (*US black*) a homosexual man. ❑ **polesmoker** *n.* [SMOKE *v.*[3]] [2000s] a term of abuse, lit. 'fellator'. ❑ **pole work** *n.* [mid-19C+] sexual intercourse.

IN PHRASES

❑ **get one's pole varnished** *v.* [1980s+] to have sexual intercourse. ❑ **varnish one's pole** *v.* [1980s+] to masturbate.

SE in slang uses

IN PHRASES

❑ **have a pole up one's ass** *v. see under* ASS *n.* ❑ **up the pole** *adj. see* separate entries.

IN EXCLAMATIONS

❑ **get up your pole!** [1900s] (*Aus.*) an excl. of dismissal.

pole *v.* **1** [mid-19C–1910s] (*US campus*) to work hard. **2** [1900s] (*Aus.*) to arrive, to appear [SE *pole*, the shaft fitted to a vehicle to permit the harnessing of draft animals; thus the image of movement]. **3** [1960s+] in sexual senses [POLE *n.*]. (**a**) usu. of a man, to perform sexual intercourse. (**b**) (*Irish*) to rape. (**c**) to make pregnant. **4** [1990s+] (*US prison*) to stab.

IN PHRASES

❑ **pole on** *v.* [bullock-driving use; *polers*, the pair of bullocks nearest the wagon's pole, seen as most likely to 'take things easy'] **1** [20C+] (*Aus./N.Z.*) (*also* **pole in**) to take advantage of someone, to impose or sponge off. **2** [1930s+] (*Aus.*) to steal; thus *poled*, stolen.

pole-axe *n.* [mispron. + ? allusion to police violence] [mid-19C] a policeman.

polecat *n.* (*also* **polcat**) [SE *polecat*, a notoriously aggressive, foul-smelling animal] **1** [late 16C–18C] a woman. **2** [17C] a lecherous man. **3** [late 19C–1960s] an untrustworthy, violent, dangerous man. **4** [1950s+] (*US black*) a dirty, untrustworthy woman.

poler *n.*[1] [POLE *v.* (1)] [mid-19C–1910s] (*US campus*) a very diligent student.

poler *n.*[2] [POLE ON *under* POLE *v.*] [1900s–50s] (*Aus.*) a cadger, a sponger, one who shirks work; thus *poling*, doing less than a fair share of work.

poles *n.* [1960s] (*S.Afr.*) the legs.

poley *adj.* [colloq. *poley*, one-horned (of cattle) or broken (of a utensil's handle), thus a pun on CROPPIE *n.* (1), a convict who has lost their 'horns', i.e. hair] [mid–late 19C] (*Aus. Und.*) wanted by the police.

police *n.* **1** [mid-19C+] (*Scot./US*) a *police*man [abbr.]. **2** [1990s+] (*US prison*) a prison guard.

police *v.* [POLICE *n.* (2)] [1910s+] (*US prison*) to maintain prison discipline and rules.

police clothes *n.* [1930s] (*Irish*) free second-hand clothes distributed to the poor by the police.

policed *adj.* [1950s] (*US black*) aware, knowledgeable.

police dog *n.* [? he follows you around and offers protection] [1920s] (*US*) one's fiancé.

policeman *n.* **1** [mid-19C] a bluebottle fly [play on BLUEBOTTLE *n.* (2)]. **2** [mid-19C] 'among the dangerous classes, a man who is unworthy of confidence, a sneak or mean fellow' (Hotten, 1873). **3** [1920s] (*US prison*) a term of abuse. **4** [1920s+] an informer.

policeman's helmet *n.* [resemblance to UK *police helmets*] [1930s+] the glans penis.

police pimp *n.* [1940s+] (*Aus. Und.*) an informer.

policy *n.* [SE *policy certificate*; the original game may date to the lotteries of early 18C UK, although it is now US and esp. widespread in the black community; although *policy* is usu. synon. with NUMBERS, THE *n.*, Carlson, *Argot of Number Gambling* (1947), defines it: 'A number game in which players wager on numbers within a range of 1–78. Winning wagers are determined by a drawing. Capsules or balls numbered from 1 to 78 are placed in a container. From these twelve, twenty-four, or thirty-six numbers are drawn, depending on the type of house.'; for details and history *see* Asbury, *Sucker's Progress* (1938), pp.88–106] [mid-19C+] (*US*) a popular form of street gambling that involves predicting a combination of the winning numbers at a racetrack; thus *policy runner*, one who acts as a go-between between bettors and the policy 'banker'; *policy king*, one who controlled a network of *policy shops*.

Polish *adj.* used in combs. as an indicator of peasant stupidity and poor hygeine [racial stereotyping].

IN COMPOUNDS

❑ **Polish airlines** *n.* [1960s] (*gay*) walking. ❑ **Polish handball** *n.* [1970s] (*gay*) dried nasal mucus. ❑ **Polish shower** *n.* (*also* **English shower**) [2000s] a cursory wash or the application of deodorant to unwashed armpits.

polish *n.* **1** [1900s] (*US*) a fool, a synon. for SHINE *n.*[2] (3); a failure. **2** [1900s] effrontery, arrogance. **3** [1980s+] (*N.Z.*) fellatio. **4** [1990s+] an act of masturbation.

SE in slang uses

IN PHRASES

❑ **boot polish** *n.* [which is *black*] [1950s] (*UK Und.*) blackmail. ❑ **brown polish** *n.* [late 19C–1900s] (*orig. US*) **1** a black person. **2** a mulatto. ❑ **shoe-polish** *n.* (*also* **floor-polish, furniture polish**) [1900s] (*US*) whisky; thus *shoe-polish shop*, a saloon.

polish *v.* **1** [mid-19C] to hoodwink, to exploit. **2** [mid-19C–1900s] to beat, to thrash.

SE in slang uses

IN PHRASES

❑ **polish it up** *v.* ['it' is the proverbial 'apple for teacher'] [1960s] (*US campus*) to toady, to act sycophantically. ❑ **polish off** *v. see* separate entry. ❑ **polish one's arse on the top sheet** *v. see under* ARSE *n.* ❑ **polish the apple** *v.* (*also* **polish apples**) [APPLE-POLISHER *n.*] [1920s–60s] to curry favour, to act the sycophant. ❑ **polish the king's iron with one's eybrows** *v.* [late 18C–mid-19C] to look through one's prison bars; thus [20C+] (*Aus.*) *polisher*, a gaolbird.

polish... *v.* [1970s+] used in combs. to mean to masturbate, e.g. *polish Charlie Brown*, *...one's antlers*, *...one's bayonet*, *... one's knob*, *...one's sword*, *...percy*, *...the lighthouse*, *...the penguin*, *...the pole*, *...the rocket*, *...the sword*, *...the viper*.

IN PHRASES

❑ **polish a bone** *v. see under* BONE *n.*[1]. ❑ **polish someone's gun** *v. see under* GUN *n.*[1].

polish and gloss *v.* [rhy. sl. = TOSS (OFF) *v.* (1)] [20C+] to masturbate.

polish and shine *n.* [1990s+] (*W.I.*) fellatio.

polish off *v.* [mid-19C+] **1** to attack. **2** to complete or finish, esp. of a meal or a job of work. **3** to defeat. **4** to kill (clandestinely).

politic *v.* [the empty verbosity of politicians] **1** [1990s+] (*US campus*) to lie. **2** [2000s] (*US black*) to talk rather than act.

political *adj.* [the racial politics that underpin US prison gangs] [1990s+] (*US Und.*) concerning prison gang life and activities.

IN COMPOUNDS

❑ **political tats** *n.* [TAT *n.*[3]] [1990s+] (*US Und.*) specialized tattoos that refer to one's membership of a gang.

politician *n.* [both senses take a dim view of the SE use] **1** [20C+] a flatterer, a clever talker. **2** [1910s–70s] (*US prison*) one who gains good jobs and maximum privileges.

IN PHRASES

❑ **give birth to a politician** *v.* [2000s] (*N.Z.*) to defecate.

poll *n.*[1] [SE *poll*, the head, ult. ME *poll*, the nape of the neck] **1** [mid-16C+] the hair. **2** [18C–early 19C] a wig.

IN COMPOUNDS

❑ **poll talk** *n.* [one is 'talking through the back of one's neck'] [mid–late 17C; 20C+] (*Irish*) slander, tale-telling.

poll *n.*[2] [the proper name *Polly*] [late 18C–1900s] a prostitute, a loose woman.

IN PHRASES

❑ **poll up** *v.* [mid–late 19C] to court, to live with without being married; thus *polled up*.

poll *v.* [fig. uses of SE *poll*, to plunder, to fleece; ult. to cut hair] **1** [16C–17C; late 19C] (*UK Und.*) to rob, by trickery rather than violence. **2** [mid-19C] (*UK Und.*) to cheat one's accomplice in crime. **3** [late 19C–1900s] to ignore, to snub. **4** [1910s] (*Aus.*) to take advantage of someone's good nature.

DERIVATIVES

❑ **polling** *n.* **1** [17C; late 19C] robbery. **2** [mid-19C] one thief robbing another.

IN PHRASES

❑ **polling and pilling** *n.* [SE *pillage*] [16C–early 17C] robbery.

Pollacky *n. see* POLACK *n.*

poll axe *n.* [pun on SE *poleaxe*/POLL *n.*[2] (though antedating)] [late 16C; 19C] the penis.

polled off *adj.* [UP THE POLE *adj.*[1] (2)] [late 19C–1930s] drunk.

poller *n.* [SE *poller*, plunderer, extortionist] [late 17C] a pistol.

pollie *n. see* POLLY *n.*[3] (2).

pollo *n.* [Sp. *pollo*, a chicken] **1** [1970s] (*US/P.R.*) a woman, usu. pretty and young; thus phr. *tremendos pollos*, good-looking (lit. 'tremendous') women. **2** [1980s] (*US*) an illegal Mexican immigrant.

Pollock *n. see* POLACK *n.*

pollock *v.* [? POLL *v.* (1) or racist allusion to a Pole, i.e. a POLACK *n.*] [mid–late 18C] (*Irish*) to trick, to hoax, to defraud.

pollone *n. see* POLONE *n.*

poll parrot *n.* [mid-19C+] a talkative, gossipy woman; as v., to repeat, to copy.

polluted *adj.* (*also* **peloothered**) [joc. use of SE; ? the state of one's bloodstream] **1** [20C+] extremely drunk. **2** [1930s+] (*drugs*) intoxicated by a drug. **3** [1940s–60s] (*Aus.*) a term of abuse.

Polly *n.* [abbr.] [2000s] (*N.Z.*) a *Polynesian*.

polly *n.*[1] [POLL *n.*[2] or *Polly*, nickname for *Mary* = MOLL *n.* (1)] [19C–1900s] **1** a mistress, a prostitute who lives with a man. **2** a woman.

polly *n.*[2]

IN PHRASES

❑ **doing polly** [ety. unknown] [mid-19C] (*UK prison*) picking oakum.

polly *n.*[3] [abbr.] **1** [1910s] an *apology*. **2** [1930s+] (*Aus./US*) (*also* **pollie**) a *politician*; thus *pollies*, politicians, esp. when corrupt.

polly *n.*[4] [ety. unknown] [1950s] a bathroom.

polly *n.*[5] (*also* **pretty polly**) [rhy. sl. = LOLLY *n.*[4]] [1970s+] money.

polly flinder *n.* [rhy. sl. both with Cockney pron.; ult. the nursery rhyme, 'Little Polly Flinders sat among the cinders'] [late 19C+] **1** a window. **2** a cinder.

polly parrot *n.* [rhy. sl.] [20C+] a carrot.

polly waffle *n.* [rhy. sl.] [1980s] (*Aus.*) a brothel.

pollywogger *n.* [SE *pollywog*, tadpole] [2000s] a penis.

polo! *excl.* [1990s+] a lover's acronym used in letters or on envelopes, meaning '*p*ants *o*ff, *l*egs *o*pen'.

Polock *adj. see* POLACK *adj.*

polo mint *n.* [rhy. sl. = BINT *n.* (1)] [2000s] a woman.

polo mint *adj.* [rhy. sl. = SKINT *adj.*] [1990s+] penniless, impoverished.

polone *n.* (*also* **paloma, palone, paloney, pollone, polony**) [Ital. *pollone*, chick; however, note Polari etymologist WS Wilcox in a letter 25/11/99: 'On the origins of *polone* I venture to suggest an alternative to previous ideas: Mayhew, *London Labour and the London Poor* (1861–2), gives the cant term *hay-bag* (a hay or straw mattress) for woman, very insulting, but *paglione* is an almost exact Italian translation of this. One of the possible suggested sources, *pollone* – plant-shoot, I feel unlikely, since in Italy it also has the slang meaning of penis'] [late 19C+] (*Ling. Fr./Polari*) **1** a young woman. **2** an effeminate man.

polone-omee *n.* (*also* **polone-homi**) [1960s+] a lesbian, opposite of OMEE-POLONE *n.*

polony *n.*[1] [Ital. *Bologna* sausage] **1** [late 18C+] a sausage, a salami. **2** [1910s] a silly person.

polony *n.*[2] *see* POLONE *n.*

polter *v.* (*also* **poulter, powter**) [synon. Scot. *pouter/powter*] [late 19C+] (*orig. Ulster*) **1** to work carelessly. **2** to potter about.

polvo *n.* [Sp. *polvo*, powder, dust; *polvo de angel*, angel powder] **1** [1970s+] (*drugs*) heroin. **2** [1980s+] (*also* **polvo de angel**) phencyclidine.

poly *n.* (*also* **polynesian**) [abbr. SE *Polynesian*, generic for a far-away place] [1990s+] (*UK drugs*) marijuana of no particular origin or quality.

poly *adj.* [abbr.] [1990s+] (*gay*) *poly*gamous, open to or preferring to have two or more partners at once.

polyester *n.* [1990s+] (*US campus*) something out of style or fashion; thus *polyester princess*, a woman who dresses in out-of-date fashions.

polynesian *n. see* POLY *n.*

pom *n.* [abbr.] **1** [20C+] a *Pom*eranian dog. **2** *see* POMMIE *n.*

pom *adj. see* POMMIE *adj.*

pomegranate *n.* (*also* **pommygranate, pommygrant**) [play on the similarity of the sound of *pomegranate* and *immigrant*] [1910s–20s] (*Aus.*) an immigrant from Britain.

Pomgolia *n.* (*also* **Pongolia**) [POMMIE *n.* + play on *Mongolia*] [1970s+] (*N.Z.*) Britain.

pommie *n.* (*also* **pom, pommey, pommy**) [abbr. POMEGRANATE *n.*; but note Aus. writer Henry Lawson, in a short story (1921): 'An' the Pommy he says "Pom-me-word" [i.e. 'pon my word] — and that's how I think Pommies got their name'] [1910s+] (*Aus.*) a British person, usu. an immigrant.

IN COMPOUNDS

❑ **pommie-bashing** *n.* (*also* **pommy-bashing**) [BASH *v.* (7)] [1970s+] (*Aus./N.Z.*) verbal abuse of the British (incl. immigrants) (occas. affectionate). ❑ **Pommieland** *n.* (*also* **Pomland, Pommyland**) [1910s+] (*Aus.*) Britain. ❑ **pommy's breakfast** *n.* [1990s+] (*Aus.*) a cup of tea and a cigarette.

pommie *adj.* (*also* **pom, pommy**) [POMMIE *n.*] [1910s+] (*Aus.*) British, English.

pommy *see under* POMMIE.

pommygranate/pommygrant *n. see* POMEGRANATE *n.*

Pomp *n. see* POMPEY *n.* (1).

pomp *n.*[1] [abbr.] [1910s+] (*US*) a *pomp*adour hairstyle, esp. worn by 'rockers', Teddy Boys etc.

pomp *n.*[2] [abbr. SE *pompous*] [1940s+] (*US campus*) someone who acts as if they are better than others; thus *pomp up*, v., to give someone false praise.

pomp *v.* [Afk. *pomp*, to pump] [20C+] (*S.Afr.*) to have sexual intercourse; thus as n. *pomp*, sexual intercourse, a sexual partner.

Pompey *n.* **1** [mid-19C] (*US*) (*also* **Pomp**) a generic name for a black slave, thus a servant [the use of classical names for slaves, e.g. Cassius]. **2** [late 19C+] (*orig. naut.*) Portsmouth; also used in expressions such as *Pompey Royal*, a Hampshire-brewed beer [ety. unknown; poss. a ref. to the French vessel *Pompée*, captured in 1793 and moored at Portsmouth].

IN COMPOUNDS

❑ **Pompey's hole** *n.* [HOLE *n.*[1] (2a)] [mid-19C] (*UK prison*) the punishment cell, solitary confinement.

IN PHRASES

❑ **Pompey's pillar to a stick of sealing-wax** *n.* [early–mid-19C] long odds.

pompey *n.*

IN PHRASES

❑ **dodge pompey** *v. see* DODGE *v.*

Pompey whore *n.* [rhy. sl.] [1910s+] (*bingo*) the number four.

pompkin *n. see* PUMPKIN *n.* (1b).

Pompkinshire *n. see* PUMPKINSHIRE *under* PUMPKIN *n.*

pom-pom *n.*[1] [? imitative of the rhythm of intercourse] [1950s] the vagina; thus sexual intercourse; a sexually attractive woman; thus *pom-pom girl*, a prostitute; *pom-pom house*, a brothel; *pom-pom man*, a brothel owner, a pimp.

pom-pom *n.*[2] [milit. *pom-pom*, a quick-firing gun] [1970s+] (*US Und.*) a pump-action shotgun.

pom-pom *n.*[3] *see* PUM-PUM *n.*[2].

ponce *n.* [ety. unknown. *OED* suggests SE *pounce*. Hancock, 'Shelta and Polari' (1984), notes Fr. argot *pont* (*d'Avignon*) or *pontonnière*, a prostitute (who works from the arches of a bridge); Partridge offers Fr. *pensionnaire*, a lodger and thus poss. link to earlier PENSIONER (AT THE PETTICOAT) *n.* Note that many 'ponce' usages show the very different status of such a man in the UK compared with the US pimp] **1** [mid-19C+] one who lives off the earnings of one or more prostitutes. **2** [1930s+] a derog. epithet for any man or woman, incl. the police. **3** [1970s+] (*Aus.*) a male homosexual. **4** [2000s] one who lives off beggars' collections.

ponce *adj.* [PONCE *n.* (2)] [1970s+] second-rate, unpleasant; lit. having the characteristics of a ponce.

ponce *v.* [PONCE *n.*] [1930s+] **1** to work as a pimp or ponce. **2** to sponge (although with no implication of 'immoral earnings'). **3** to act in an affected, effeminate manner.

DERIVATIVES

❑ **poncing** *adj.* [1960s+] a general term of abuse.

IN PHRASES

❑ **ponce about** *v.* (*also* **ponce around, ponce in**) **1** [1950s+] to act in a pretentious, affected manner. **2** [1970s+] to wander aimlessly, to live as a good-for-nothing. **3** [1970s+] to waste time. **4** [1970s+] to tease, to be impudent. ❑ **ponce it up** *v.* [1980s] to act in an affected manner. ❑ **ponce off** *v.* (*also* **ponce on**) [1930s+] **1** to live off immoral earnings. **2** to scrounge (money) from someone. ❑ **ponce up** *v.* [1920s+] (*orig. milit.*) to decorate (an object), to dress up (a person), usu. with some ostentation and flashiness.

ponce shicer *n. see* POUNCE-SHICER *n.*

poncey *adj. see* PONCY *adj.*

ponch *n.* [? the character nicknamed *Ponch* in the 1980s TV police show *C.H.I.P.S.*; Eble's suggestion of *Poncho* refers in fact to the character *Pancho* and is thus less feasible] [1980s+] (*US campus*) a term of address for a man.

poncy *adj.* (*also* **poncey**) [PONCE *n.* (3); although this predates but there is no actual link to a pimp or procurer] [1930s+] affected, ostentatiously 'artistic', poss. homosexual.

DERIVATIVES

❑ **poncified** *adj.* [1960s] affected, 'done up'.

pond, the *n.* [deliberate understatement] **1** [late 18C+] (*also* **fish-pond, the**) the Atlantic Ocean. **2** [1910s–20s] the English Channel. **3** [1960s] (*US*) the Pacific Ocean. **4** [2000s] (*N.Z.*) the Tasman Sea.

IN PHRASES

❑ **big pond** *n.* [mid-19C+] (*orig. US*) the Atlantic Ocean.

pondlife *n.* [1990s+] a term used to describe someone seen as unintelligent, simple.

pond scum *n. see* SHOWER SCUM *under* SCUM *n.*

pong *n.*[1] [ety. unknown; ? ext. of SE *pong*, the sound of a blow, or negative stereotyping of PONG *n.*[2] (1), i.e. a Chinese person; usu. reserved for use in mass-market children's comics or by society speakers who retain much juv. vocabulary from school] [20C+] a smell.

pong *n.*[2] [the *ong* sound in Chinese speech] **1** [1910s–40s] (*Aus.*) a Chinese person. **2** [1950s] a Japanese person.

pong *n.*[3] *see* PONGELO *n.*

pong *v.*[1] [PONGELO *n.*] [mid-19C–1900s] to drink.

pong *v.*[2] (*also* **ponk**) [PONG *n.*[1]] [20C+] to stink, to smell bad.

pongelo *n.* (*also* **pong, ponge, pongellorum, pongelow, ponjello**) [ety. unknown; given origins of the word in the Indian Army there may be a link to the Tamil festival of Pongol, the festival of the new rice, and which if so may pun on BOILED *adj.* (1), since *pongal* means 'boiled', albeit of rice] [mid-19C–1930s] beer, esp. pale ale or half-and-half.

pongo *n.* [Angola or Loango *mpongo*, a large anthropoid ape, the chimpanzee or gorilla; this 17C use was in late 18C transferred to the orang-utan of Borneo and Sumatra] **1** [1900s] (*US*) a black person, esp. an African. **2** [1910s+] (*Aus./N.Z.*) a marine, a soldier. **3** [1940s+] (*Aus./N.Z.*) a British person.

Pongolia *n. see* POMGOLIA *n.*

pongy *adj.* [PONG *n.*[1]] [1930s+] smelly.

ponjello *n. see* PONGELO *n.*

ponk *n.* **1** [20C+] (*mainly N.Z.*) a stench. **2** [1970s] (*US*) a smelly, contemptible person.

ponk *v. see* PONG *v.*[2].

'pon my life *n.* [rhy. sl.] [late 19C] a wife.

'pon my sivvy! *excl. see* UPON MY SIVVY! *excl.*

ponte *n.* [Ital. *pondo*, a weight] [mid-19C] (*Ling. Fr./Polari*) £1 sterling.

Pontius Pilate *n.* [his supposed venality] [late 18C–mid-19C] a pawnbroker.

pontoon *n.* [card use, the game of *pontoon* or '21'] [1950s+] (*UK prison/Und.*) a 21-month sentence.

ponum *n.* [Yid. *punim*, the face] [late 19C] (*Aus.*) the face or head.

pony *n.* **1** in monetary senses [? relatively small sums, as a pony is a small horse; Bee claims 'the one [i.e. the bet] being derived from the other [i.e. the horse]']. (**a**) [late 18C–mid-19C] money in general. (**b**) [late 18C+] £25, orig. 25 guineas. (**c**) [late 19C+] a double-headed coin. (**d**) [1910s] (*N.Z.*) a £5 note; £5. (**e**) [1960s+] (*Aus.*) A$25; A$50. **2** [19C] a bailiff, esp. one who accompanies a debtor on a day out from prison [? he carries people off]. **3** US campus uses. (**a**) [early 19C+] (*also* **automobile**) a literal translation of a classical text, a 'crib' ['So called, it may be, from the fleetness and ease with which a skilful rider is enabled to pass over places which to a common plodder present many obstacles' (Hall, *College Words and Customs*, 1856)]. (**b**) [1950s] one who offers illicit help with an examination. **4** fig. use of SE *pony* in its sense of a *small* horse. (**a**) [mid-19C+] (*orig. US*) a small glass of beer or other liquor; thus *pony-glass*, a small glass, with a capacity of approx. 6ml (2fl oz). (**b**) [1900s–50s] (*US*) a (small) dancer or chorus girl. (**c**) [1940s–50s] (*US drugs*) a weak measure of heroin [play on HORSE *n.* (7)]. **5** [late 19C+] (*US*) a racehorse; thus *the ponies*, horseracing. **6** one who is 'ridden'. (**a**) [1940s] (*US black*) a young woman, a lover. (**b**) [1960s+] (*also* **pony girl**) a prostitute or promiscuous woman. **7** [1980s+] (*drugs*) crack cocaine. **8** [1990s+] a *pony*tail hairstyle.

IN COMPOUNDS

❑ **pony boy** *n.* [sense 6a above] [2000s] (*US*) a young male homosexual. ❑ **pony girl** *n. see* sense 6b above.

IN PHRASES

❑ **play the ponies** *v.* (*also* **play the horse(s)**) [20C+] to bet on horseracing. ❑ **push ponies** *v.* [1960s+] of a pimp, to promote prostitutes. ❑ **string of ponies** *n. see* STRING *n.* (5).

SE in slang uses

IN PHRASES

❑ **feeding the pony** *n.* [? the shape/movement of the hands] [1990s+] the digital stimulation of a woman's genitals. ❑ **off one's pony** [i.e. fallen over] [1960s] (*US*) in a state of collapse from excessive drinking. ❑ **ride the white pony** *v.* (*also* **ride the baloney pony**) [1980s+] (*US*) of a woman, to have sexual intercourse astride the man.

ony *v.*[1] [PONY *n.* (3a)] **1** [mid-19C–1900s] (*US campus*) to use any form of translation as an aid to work. **2** [1990s+] (*US teen*) to understand.

ony *v.*[2] [? one whips the pony] [1900s] (*US campus*) to pressurize, to urge.

ony (and trap) *n.* [rhy. sl. = CRAP *n.*[1] (6)] [1930s+] **1** an act of defecation; a piece of excrement. **2** in fig. use, nonsense, rubbish. **3** difficulties, problems. **4** silver items [the inference is the relative worthlessness of such items as compared with gold]. **5** imitation jewels. **6** loaded dice.

IN PHRASES

❑ **walk the pony** *v.* [1980s] to visit the lavatory.

ony (and trap) *v.* [PONY (AND TRAP) *n.* (1)] [late 19C+] to defecate.

ony (up) *v.* [PONY *n.* (1a)] [early 19C+] (*orig. US*) to pay one's debts or one's dues.

oo *n.*[1] [1930s+] **1** the vagina. **2** (*usu. juv.*) (*also* **pooh, poo-poo**) excrement [SE *poo!* excl. announcing an unpleasant smell or expressing disbelief]. **3** in fig. use, rubbish, nonsense.

IN COMPOUNDS

❑ **poo-hammer** *n.* [2000s] (*US black*) a male homosexual. ❑ **pooh-butt** *n.* (*also* **poo-butt**) [BUTT *n.*[1] (1a)] [1980s+] a weakling; a general derog. term. ❑ **pooh-chute** *n.* [1990s+] the anus. ❑ **poo-head** *n.* (*also* **pooh-brain**) [-HEAD *sfx* (1); euph. for SHITHEAD *n.*] [1980s+] (*US campus*) an irritating person. ❑ **poo-hole** *n.* [1980s+] (*Aus.*) **1** the anus. **2** an unpleasant place. ❑ **poo-jabber/-jammer** *n. see* POO-STABBER below. ❑ **poo-packer** *n.* [1990s+] a male homosexual. ❑ **poo palace** *n.* [2000s] (*N.Z.*) a homosexual bar. ❑ **poopants** *adj.* [2000s] stupid. ❑ **poo percolator** *n.* [1990s+] a male homosexual. ❑ **poo-pipe pirate** *n.* [1990s+] a male homosexual. ❑ **poo pirate** *n.* [1990s+] (*Aus.*) a male homosexual. ❑ **poo pusher** *n.* [1980s+] a male homosexual. ❑ **poo-stabber** *n.* (*also* **poo-jabber, poo-jammer, poo-puncher, poo-shooter**) [1990s+] a male homosexual; the active partner in homosexual anal intercourse.

IN PHRASES

❑ **in the poo** (*also* **in the pooh**) [1960s+] (*Aus.*) in difficulties. ❑ **poos and wees** [2000s] (*N.Z.*) a mild phr. expressing disapproval or disgust.

oo *n.*[2] [abbr. SHAMPOO *n.*] [1980s+] champagne.

oo *v.* (*also* **pooh**) [POO *n.*[1] (2)] [1970s+] to defecate.

oo-bah *n. see* POOH-BAH *n.*

ooch *n.* [? Ger. *Putzi*, a popular name for a lap-dog] **1** [20C+] a small) dog; thus *pooch-flop*, dog excrement. **2** [1990s+] (*US* een) a Greyhound bus [play on DOG, THE *n.*[1]].

ooch *v.* (*also* **poach, pouch**) [SE *poke*] **1** [1920s+] (*Irish*) to poke around, to laze about. **2** [1980s] to seduce. **3** [2000s] to tick out.

ood *n.*[1] (*also* **poodle, poodle-dink**) [? abbr. PUDDING *n.* (2)] [late 19C–1950s] (*US*) the penis.

ood *n.*[2] [abbr. SE *poodle*, seen as an 'effeminate' species of dog] 1910s+] (*Aus.*) an effeminate young man.

oodle *n.* **1** [late 19C–1900s] any breed of dog. **2** [1900s–50s] (*also* **French poodle**) a sausage [play on HOT DOG *n.*[1] (1)]. **3** [1930s+] an act of wandering [POODLE *v.*]. **4** with ref. to a woman. (**a**) [1940s] the female genitalia; the vagina. (**b**) [1970s+] (*US black*) a sexy or sophisticated woman [positive image of the over-groomed pedigree French poodle]. (**c**) [2000s] an unattractive woman [var. on DOG *n.*[2] (9)]. **5** [1950s] any animal or person viewed with contempt. **6** *see* POOD *n.*[1].

IN PHRASES

❑ **pet the poodle** *v.* [1970s+] of a woman, to masturbate.

poodle *v.* [the image of the strolling dog; note WW2 N.Z. milit. *on poodle*, relaxing] [1930s+] to move or travel in a leisurely manner; often as *poodle around, poodle down, poodle off.*

poodle-dink *n. see* POOD *n.*[1].

poodle-faker *n.* [the role of a *poodle* as a fashionable pet] [1900s–40s] (*orig. milit.*) **1** one who cultivates women's society, esp. for social advancement; thus n. *poodle-faking.* **2** one who interferes. **3** a womanizer, a 'ladies' man'.

pooey *adj.* (*also* **poohy**) [SE *poo(h)!* an excl. of disgust] **1** [1930s+] (*orig. Aus.*) used of anything unpleasant, smelly; thus excl. *pooey!* that's rubbish! that's disgusting! **2** [1980s] of a person, hostile, snobbish.

poof *n.* (*also* **poove, pouf, pouffe**) [? PUFF *n.* (3a)] **1** [mid-19C; 1910s+] a homosexual. **2** [late 19C; 1960s+] an effeminate man.

IN COMPOUNDS

❑ **poof-rorting** *n.* (*also* **poof-wroughting**) [RORT *v.* (1)] [1930s–40s] beating and robbing male prostitutes.

IN PHRASES

❑ **poof about** *v.* [1930s+] to act in an ostentatiously homosexual manner. ❑ **put someone on the poof** *v.* [2000s] (*Aus. prison*) to challenge, poss. physically, a fellow inmate's masculinity.

poof *adj.* [POOF *n.* (1)] [1950s+] homosexual.

poof *v.*[1] [SE *puff*] [1970s] (*US campus*) to kiss.

poof *v.*[2] [? to vanish in a 'puff of smoke'] [1990s+] (*US campus*) to leave.

poof out *v.* [SE *puff* (of air)] [1930s] to vanish, to fade away, to evaporate.

poofter *n.* (*also* **boofter, poefte, poofdah, poofta, pooftah, poufter**) [POOF *n.*; note WW2 RN jargon *poofter*, a flashy civilian suit, supposedly indicative of homosexual tastes] [1910s+] (*orig. Aus.*) **1** a homosexual man. **2** an effeminate-looking but not necessarily gay man, often a derog. term of address. **3** anyone considered to have 'unmanly' interests, e.g. art, reading.

DERIVATIVES

❑ **poofterish** *adj.* (*also* **poofta**) [1980s+] (*Aus.*) effeminate, weak; the subject may or may not be actually homosexual. ❑ **poofterism** *n.* [1970s+] homosexuality.

IN COMPOUNDS

❑ **poofter-basher** *n.* [BASH *v.* (1)] [1970s+] (*Aus.*) one who beats up homosexuals. ❑ **poofter-bashing** *n.* [1980s+] beating homosexuals. ❑ **poofter-rorter** *n.* [RORT *v.* (1)] (*Aus.*) **1** [1940s] a procurer for male homosexuals. **2** [1960s+] one who beats up homosexuals; thus *poofter-rorting*, assault on a homosexual for robbery or pleasure.

poofy *adj.*[1] [SE excl. *poof!* what an unpleasant smell!] [1940s+] (*UK juv.*) smelly.

poofy *adj.*[2] (*also* **poofta, poovey, poovy, poufy, puffy**) [POOF *n.*] [1950s+] effeminate, pertaining to homosexuality.

poogie *n.* [POKEY *n.*[2] (1)] [20C+] (*US Und.*) prison.

pooh *n. see* POO *n.*[1] (2).

pooh *v. see* POO *v.*

pooh-bah *n.* (*also* **poo-bah, pooh-ba**) [Gilbert and Sullivan's Savoy Opera, *The Mikado* (1885), in which 'Ko-Ko' is 'Lord High Executioner of Titipu' and 'Poo-Bah' is 'Lord High Everything Else'] [late 19C+] an important person.

poohed (out) *adj.* [var. on POOPED (OUT) *adj.*] [1930s+] (*US*) exhausted, tired out.

pooh-pooh *see also under* POO-POO.

poohpooh *n.* [echoic] [1910s+] (*N.Z.*) a rifle; a large gun.

poohy *adj. see* POOEY *adj.*

pookie *n.* [ety. unknown] [2000s] (*US black*) an obsessive drug user.

Pool, the *n.* [abbr.] [1960s+] Liver*pool*.

pool *v.* [? the image of tossing someone into a swimming pool; SAmE *pool*, to place resources in a common stock or fund] [1910s+] (*Aus.*) to involve someone in, to implicate, to inform against.

IN PHRASES

❑ **in the pool** [1960s] in trouble.

pooley *n.* (*also* **poolie**) [SE *pool* (of liquid)] **1** [1920s+] (*Irish*) urination; usu. as *do pooley*, to urinate. **2** [1990s+] (*Irish*) sexual intercourse.

pooloo *n.* [? Fr. *poilu*] [1930s] (*US*) ? a soldier.

pool shark *n. see under* SHARK *n.*

poom-poom *n. see* PUM-PUM *n.*^{2}.

poon *n.*^{1} [abbr. POONTANG *n.*] **1** [1920s+] (*also* **pooney, poonie, poononny**) the vagina; also the male genitals. **2** [1950s+] (*also* **poonie**) a woman or women in general when seen purely in a sexual context. **3** [1970s+] (*US gay*) the anus. **4** [1980s+] sexual intercourse. **5** [2000s] a general term of abuse.

IN COMPOUNDS

❑ **poon hound** *n.* [-HOUND *sfx*] [1980s+] (*US*) a dedicated womanizer.

poon *n.*^{2} [ety. unknown; note Northamptonshire dial. *pun*, a slow, dreamy, inactive person] [1940s+] (*Aus.*) **1** one who lives alone in the outback. **2** a simpleton, a fool, a useless person.

poon *v.* [ety. unknown; ? link to POONTANG *n.*] [1940s+] (*Aus.*) usu. constr. with *up*, to dress up in a showy manner; thus *pooned up*, dressed up.

poona *n.* [SE *pound*] [mid-19C] (*Ling. Fr./Polari*) a sovereign, £1 sterling.

poonce *n.* (*also* **punce**) [Yid. *punse*, the vagina] **1** [late 19C+] the vagina. **2** [1930s+] (*Aus.*) a procurer; thus a general insult. **3** [1970s+] (*Aus.*) a catamite; a male homosexual prostitute.

pooner *n.* [POONTANG *n.*] [1960s] (*US campus*) a male sexual athlete; a womanizer.

pooney/poonie *n. see* POON *n.*^{1}.

poonj *v.* [allegedly Ojibwe *poonjegay*, to dip meat in grease] [1990s+] to have sexual intercourse.

poononny *n. see* POON *n.*^{1} (1).

poontang *n.* [? Fr. *putain*, a prostitute] **1** [1920s+] sexual intercourse; thus *on a poontang trip*, obsessed with seducing women; usu. hetero- but occas. homosexual. **2** [1920s+] (*also* **pune, puntang**) the vagina. **3** [1920s+] a woman or women in general, when seen purely in a sexual context. **4** [1990s+] in a homosexual context, the penis. **5** [1990s+] semen.

IN COMPOUNDS

❑ **poontang juice** *n.* [2000s] (*US*) vaginal secretions. ❑ **poontang magnet** *n. see under* -MAGNET *sfx*.

poontang *v.* [POONTANG *n.* (2)] [1990s+] to perform cunnilingus.

poontanger *n.* [POONTANG *n.* (2)] [1960s+] (*US*) the penis.

poonts *n.* [? SE *font* or *fountain*] [late 19C] the female breasts.

poop *n.*^{1} [SE *poop*, the stern or highest stern deck of a boat] **1** [late 16C–17C] the vagina. **2** [17C–early 18C] the 'dickey' or rear seat of a coach. **3** [mid-17C+] the buttocks.

IN COMPOUNDS

❑ **poop-noddy** *n.* (*also* **pup noddy**) [SE *nod*, to bob up and down] [16C] sexual intercourse.

IN PHRASES

❑ **get it up the poop** *v.* [1960s] to suffer; to be exploited.

poop *n.*^{2} [SE *poop*, echoic of the report of a gun and thus the sound of defecation] **1** [mid-18C; 1930s+] the act of breaking wind. **2** [late 18C; 1940s+] (*orig. US*) rubbish, tripe, nonsense. **3** [1920s+] (*also* **poopee, poopy**) excrement. **4** *see* POOP-CHUTE below.

IN COMPOUNDS

❑ **poop-bag** *n.* [2000s] a colostomy bag. ❑ **poopbutt** *n. see* separate entry. ❑ **poop-catchers** *n. see* SHIT-CATCHERS *under* SHIT *n.* ❑ **poop-chute** *n.* (*also* **poop, poophole, poopshoo**[...] [1970s+] the anus. ❑ **poophead** *n.* [-HEAD *sfx* (1)] [1970s+ (*US campus*) a fool, a dullard. ❑ **poop-scared** *adj. see* POEP SCARED *adj.* ❑ **poop stick** *n.* [STICK *n.* (2c)] [1930s] a[...] unpleasant person.

IN PHRASES

❑ **poop-for-brains** *n. see* SHIT-FOR-BRAINS *n.* ❑ **take a poop** [...] [1960s] to defecate.

poop *n.*^{3} [? abbr. NINCOMPOOP *n.*] [late 19C+] a fool.

poop *n.*^{4} [*OED* suggests ety. unknown, but ? fig. use of POO[...] *n.*^{2} (3) as synon. for SHIT *n.* (3h)] [1940s+] (*orig. US*) **1** news information, gossip. **2** (*also* **straight poop**) the facts, th[...] situation.

IN COMPOUNDS

❑ **poop sheet** *n.* [1940s+] (*orig. US milit.*) any form [...] information posted on a noticeboard or distributed to students

IN PHRASES

❑ **hot poop** *n.* [HOT *adj.* (2c)] [1940s+] the latest news [...] gossip.

poop *adj.* [? POOP *n.*^{2} (3)] [2000s] out of date, dead.

poop *v.*^{1} [? SE *poop*, to deceive, to cheat] [18C] of a man, to hav[...] sexual intercourse.

poop *v.*^{2} [SE *poop*, onomat. for the report of a gun/POOP *n.*[...] **1** [early 18C+] to break wind. **2** [1910s–40s] to shoot [...] weapon. **3** [1920s+] to shoot someone. **4** [1920s+] t[...] defecate; also fig. use. **5** [1940s] (*US*) to give, to hand ou[...] **6** [1950s] (*US*) to urinate.

IN PHRASES

❑ **poop around** *v.* [1960s] (*US*) to socialize. ❑ **poop one'**[...] **pants** *v.* [2000s] to be terrified.

poop *v.*^{3} [ety. unknown] **1** [1900s–30s] to malfunction, t[...] destroy. **2** [1930s+] (*orig. US*) to tire, to exhaust, to wast[...] **3** [1950s+] to ruin someone's enjoyment. **4** [1960s] (*U*[...] *campus*) to fill in, to explain.

IN PHRASES

❑ **poop out** *v. see* separate entry.

poop! *excl.* [1980s] (*US*) an excl. of annoyance [...] disappointment.

poopa *n. see* POOPER *n.* (1).

poopa! *excl. see* PAPA! *excl.*

poopbutt *n.* (*also* **pootbutt**) [POOP *n.*^{2} (3)/POOT *n.*^{2} (2) + BUTT *n*[...] (1a)] [1960s+] (*US black*) **1** a lazy person. **2** an uninforme[...] unsophisticated, immature person. **3** a general term of abuse

poopbutt *adj.* [POOPBUTT *n.* (1)] [1970s] lazy, inefficient.

pooped (out) *adj.* [POOP *v.*^{3} (2)] [1920s+] (*orig. US*) exhauste[...] tired out.

IN PHRASES

❑ **too pooped to pop** *adj.* [1960s+] totally exhausted.

poopee *n. see* POOP *n.*^{2} (3).

pooper *n.* **1** [late 19C; 1940s+] (*also* **poopa, poopy**) th[...] posterior, the buttocks; the anus [POOP *v.*^{2} (1)]. **2** [20C+] th[...] penis [POOP *n.*^{1} (1)].

pooper-scooper *n.* [POOP *n.*^{2} (3) + SE *scoop*] [1970s+] (*ori*[...] *US*) a small scoop used by dog owners to remove a dog excreta from urban pavements or parks.

poopie *n.* [POOP *n.*^{2} (3)] [1980s] (*juv.*) an act of defecation.

poopie-plops *n.* [ext. of POOP *n.*^{2} (3)] [1950s+] (*UK ju*[...] excrement.

poop off *v.* **1** [1920s] to leave, to finish. **2** [1960s] (*US*) [...] spend.

poo-poo *n.*^{1} (*also* **pooh-pooh**) [POO-POO *v.*^{1}] [mid-18C+] [...] act of dismissal, derision; also as excl.

poo-poo *n.*^{2} (*also* **pooh-pooh**) [POO *n.*^{1} (2) + redu[...] **1** [1970s+] (*US gay*) the anus. **2** *see* POO *n.*^{1} (2).

IN COMPOUNDS

❑ **poo-poo head** *n.* [-HEAD *sfx* (1)] [1980s] (*juv.*) general term [...] abuse.

poo-poo *v.*[1] (*also* **pooh-pooh, po-po**) [SE *poo!* + redup.] [late 19C+] to deride, to dismiss.

poo-poo *v.*[2] (*also* **pooh-pooh**) [POO-POO *n.*[2] (2)] [1960s+] to defecate.

poop-out *n.* [POOP OUT *v.* (2)] [1930s–50s] a mechanical failure.

poop out *v.* [POOP *v.*[3] (2)] [1920s+] (*US*) **1** to fail. **2** to have a breakdown; mental or physical; also of a machine, to go wrong. **3** to die. **4** to faint; to collapse; to be excessively drunk.

poopy *n.* **1** *see* POOP *n.*[2] (3). **2** *see* POOPER *n.* (1).

poopy *adj.* [POOP *n.*[2] (3)] [1960s–70s] (*US*) pertaining to excrement, i.e. SHITTY *adj.*[1].

poor *adj.*

SE in slang uses

IN COMPOUNDS

❑ **poor-ass** *adj.* (*also* **poor-arse, poor-assed**) [-ASS *sfx*/-ASSED *sfx* (2)/-ARSE *sfx*] [1960s+] (*US*) wretched, lousy, unpleasant. ❑ **poor creatures** *n.* [mispron. + ref. to their role as poverty food] [early 19C] potatoes. ❑ **poor-great** *adj.* [20C+] (*W.I.*) proud but impoverished, unwilling to take charity, however much it might be needed. ❑ **poor john** *n.* [late 16C–early 19C] dried, salted hake. ❑ **poor man's...** *adj. see* separate entry. ❑ **poormouth** *adj. see* separate entry.

IN PHRASES

❑ **poor as wee-wee** *adj. see under* WEE *n.* ❑ **poor blind Nell** *see* AND DID HE MARRY POOR BLIND NELL? *phr.* ❑ **poor boy it** *v.* [1990s+] (*US*) to be extremely poor, to be severely deprived.

poorly *adj.* [SE *poorly*, unwell] [late 19C] menstruating.

DERIVATIVES

❑ **poorliness** *n.* [late 19C] menstruation.

IN COMPOUNDS

❑ **poorly time** *n.* [late 19C] the menstrual period.

poor man's... *adj.* used in combs. denoting the second-rate, a substitute.

IN COMPOUNDS

❑ **poor man's alcohol** *n.* [2000s] (*US black*) cough syrup. ❑ **poor man's blessing** *n.* [sex being ostensibly free of charge] [19C] the vagina. ❑ **poor man's cocaine** *n.* [one enjoys similar effects for less expenditure] **1** [1980s+] isobutyl nitrite. **2** [1990s+] (*drugs*) methamphetamine. ❑ **poor man's diggings** *n.* [late 19C–1940s] (*Aus.*) alluvial gold deposits, which can be mined far more easily than reef-gold that requires capital to develop; and fig. uses. ❑ **poor man's goose** *n.* [19C] baked liver with sage and onions. ❑ **poor man's oyster** *n.* [late 19C] a mussel. ❑ **poor man's piano** *n.* [the wind-inducing, 'musical' effect it has on one's stomach] [mid-19C] (*Can.*) a meal of dried beans. ❑ **poor man's sugar** *n.* [play on BROWN SUGAR *n.*[2] (2)/SE *brown sugar*, i.e. seen as 'poorer' than white sugar] [2000s] (*US black*) heroin. ❑ **poor man's treacle** *n.* [not sweet, but flavoursome] **1** [17C] garlic. **2** [19C] onions.

poor-me-one *n.* [20C+] (*W.I.*) a miserable-looking person, desperate for sympathy.

poor-me-one *adj.* [POOR-ME-ONE *n.*] [20C+] (*W.I.*) miserable-looking.

poormouth *adj.* [1940s+] (*US*) weary, depressed, 'down in the mouth', whether or not genuinely so.

IN PHRASES

❑ **talk poor mouth** *v.* [20C+] (*US*) to deny one's assets or advantages.

poor mouth *v.* [early 19C+] to belittle oneself or others; to pose as impoverished; thus (*Irish*) *make/play/put on the poor mouth*, to complain, to whinge, to slander.

poor relation *n.* [rhy. sl.] [20C+] a railway station.

poosa *see under* PHUZA.

pooshey/pooshie/pooshy *n. see* PUSHIE *n.*

poot *n.*[1] [Hind. *poot*, a shilling, coined by East London's many Indian beggars] [late 19C] a shilling (5p).

poot *n.*[2] [POOT *v.* (1)] [1950s+] **1** a fart. **2** (*US, usu. juv.*) soft excrement. **3** (*US*) an unpleasant person; sometimes used affectionately. **4** the anus, the buttocks.

poot *v.* [a US southernism, from the Fr. *péter*, to fart] [1950s+] (*US*) **1** to break wind. **2** to defecate.

IN PHRASES

❑ **poot about** *v.* (*also* **poot around**) [var. on FART ABOUT *under* FART *v.*] [1930s+] to dawdle, to mess around.

poot! *excl.* [1940s+] (*US*) an excl. of disgust, annoyance.

pootbutt *n. see* POOPBUTT *n.*

pootenanny *n.* [PUNAANY *n.* + HOOTENANNY *n.*] [1970s+] (*US black*) the vagina.

pootie *n.* (*also* **pootie-tootie**) [? var. on BOOTY *n.*[2]] [1970s+] the vagina.

poove *n. see* POOF *n.*

poove *v.* (*also* **poove about, ...around**) [POOVE *n.*] [1960s] to act in an ostentatiously homosexual manner.

poovey/poovy *adj. see* POOFY *adj.*[2].

poozle *n.* [? PUSSY *n.* (1)] [late 19C+] the vagina, hence sexual intercourse.

poozle *v.* [ety. unknown; ? SE *puzzle*, to search out (mentally)] [1970s+] (*N.Z.*) to scavenge for collectible objects.

pop *n.*[1] **1** with ref. to an explosion. (**a**) [18C+] (*also* **popp**) a pistol, usu. in pl. (**b**) [mid-19C] a bullet. (**c**) [mid-19C+] an orgasm, usu. male. (**d**) [1960s+] a single instance of sexual intercourse. **2** with ref. to drink [the *pop* of a cork]. (**a**) [early 19C+] (*usu. US juv.*) a fizzy, non-alcoholic drink [note WW1 milit. *pop wallah*, a teetotaller]. (**b**) [mid-19C–1930s] champagne. (**c**) [late 19C] in fig. use of sense 2a, i.e. something insubstantial, meaningless. (**d**) [1970s–80s] (*US*) any form of alcoholic drink. **3** as a lit. or fig. blow. (**a**) [early 19C+] a try, an attempt, a 'go'; hence *first pop*, the first try, the first time. (**b**) [mid-19C+] as *a pop*, a go, an item, each. (**c**) [late 19C] a proposal. (**d**) [late 19C+] (*also* **pop on**) a hit at, also in fig. use. **4** with ref. to drink or drugs. (**a**) [1930s+] (*drugs*) an injection of a narcotic drug. (**b**) [1960s+] a sip or swig of a drink; a drink. (**c**) [1970s] (*drugs*) any variety of amphetamine in pill form; any pill. **5** [1940s–70s] an arrest, a criminal charge [POP *v.*[1] (1j)].

IN COMPOUNDS

❑ **pop on** *n. see* sense 3d above. ❑ **popgun** *n. see* separate entry. ❑ **pop-squirt** *n. see* SQUIRT *n.* (2b).

IN PHRASES

❑ **not a fair pop** *adj.* [1920s+] (*N.Z.*) unfair, not a fair chance. ❑ **Polish pop** *n.* [1940s] vodka. ❑ **sure pop** *n.* [mid-19C+] (*US*) a certainty, an absolute fact; as adj., competent. ❑ **take a pop at** *v.* **1** [mid-19C] to fire a gun, to shoot at. **2** [1920s+] to make an attempt (at). **3** [1930s+] to hit (someone). **4** [1990s+] to attack verbally.

pop *n.*[2] [POP *v.*[2]] [mid-19C+] **1** the act of pawning; thus *in pop*, in pawn. **2** the pawnbroker's.

pop *n.*[3] (*also* **pap, poppa, poppy**) [SE *papa*] **1** [mid-19C+] one's father. **2** [mid-19C+] an older, respected man. **3** [late 19C+] a term of address to or nickname for an old(er) man. **4** [1950s–60s] (*US gay/prison*) a masculine lesbian.

pop *n.*[4] [2000s] (*S.Afr.*) a dupe, a weakling.

pop *n.*[5] *see* LOLLIPOP *n.*[1] (2c).

pop *v.*[1] **1** in transitive senses, implying lit. or fig. aggression. (**a**) [17C; mid-19C; 1950s+] (*US*) (*also* **pop in**) to seduce, to have sexual intercourse. (**b**) [18C+] (*also* **pop away**) to fire a gun; to shoot at. (**c**) [late 18C; late 19C+] (*orig. US*) to hit, to punch. (**d**) [early 19C] in weakened form of sense 1c, to abuse. (**e**) [mid-19C+] to set off, to set in motion. (**f**) [mid-19C+] (*also* **pop off, pop out, pop over**) to murder someone, to kill someone. (**g**) [1920s] (*US*) to execute by a firing squad. (**h**) [1920s] to bring to a conclusion. (**i**) [1920s+] (*US*) to hit with a bullet. (**j**) [1950s+] to arrest, to catch. (**k**) [1960s] to identify. **2** in intransitive fig. senses, of someone who or something that 'explodes'. (**a**) [mid-19C+] of things, to come to a head, to suddenly start happening, to be energized. (**b**) [1950s+] (*orig. US black*) to live well. (**c**) [1960s] (*US black*) to live a full social life. (**d**) [1970s+] to feel elated, extremely pleased, enthusiastic. **3** [1930s+] to give birth; to be born. **4** in drug uses. (**a**) [1930s+] to inject a drug; thus SKINPOP *v.*, to inject under the skin rather than into a vein. (**b**) [1950s] to inject oneself with a narcotic. (**c**) [1960s+] to swallow a pill. (**d**) [1960s+] (*US campus*) to take amphetamines spec. for staying up and working all night. (**e**) [1960s+] to take a drink. (**f**) [1980s] to smoke a drug. (**g**) [1980s+] (*US campus*) to initiate someone into drug use. (**h**) [1990s+] to inhale cocaine. **5** in speech. (**a**) [1940s+] (*US black/W.I.*) to tell, to reveal, to gossip. (**b**) [1950s+] (*US black*) to lie, to cheat, to manipulate. (**c**) [1980s] to extol, to promote. **6** in senses of entering, opening. (**a**) [1950s+] (*orig. US black*) to steal; thus *pop a car*, to steal an automobile. (**b**) [1950s+] to break. (**c**) [1990s+] to take, to extract from. (**d**) [1990s+] to open. (**e**) [2000s] to free from prison. **7** in sexual senses. (**a**) [1960s+] (*also* **pop off**) to ejaculate; to reach orgasm. (**b**) [1960s+] to bring someone to orgasm. (**c**) [1980s] (*US*) to make pregnant.

IN COMPOUNDS

❑ **pop-off** *n. see* separate entries. ❑ **pop-out** *n. see* separate entry. ❑ **pop shot** *n.* [1990s+] in a pornographic film, the shot in which a male actor ejaculates. ❑ **pop visit** *n.* [one 'just pops in' for a moment] [early 17C] (*UK society*) a brief visit.

IN PHRASES

❑ **how are you popping (up)?** [late 19C–1940s] (*Aus.*) a general phr. of greeting, how are you doing? how are you feeling? ❑ **pop a...** *v. see under* relevant nouns. ❑ **pop around (with)** *v.* [1950s] (*US*) to associate (with). ❑ **pop away** *v. see* sense 1b above. ❑ **pop for** *v.* (*also* **pop to**) **1** [1950s–60s] (*US black*) to pay (for), to treat. **2** [1970s] to provide without payment. ❑ **pop in** *v. see* sense 1a above. ❑ **pop it** *v.* [1950s] to ask a question. ❑ **pop it in** *v.* [mid-19C+] to enter a woman or in gay use a man, to have sexual intercourse. ❑ **pop it in the toaster** *v.* [the toaster makes white bread 'brown'] [1980s+] (*US gay*) to have anal intercourse. ❑ **pop it on** *v.* [SE *pop on*, to place on] **1** [late 19C+] to ask for more, esp. when raising a commodity's price. **2** [1900s] to make a bet. ❑ **pop junk** *v. see under* JUNK *n.*[1]. ❑ **pop off** *v.* **1** *see* sense 1f above. **2** *see* sense 7a above. **3** *see* separate entries. ❑ **pop off (at the mouth)** *v. see* separate entry. ❑ **pop one's...** *v. see also under* relevant nouns. ❑ **pop one's bubble** *v.* [1920s–30s] (*US*) to go mad. ❑ **pop one's collar** *v.* [2000s] (*US black*) to have a conversation. ❑ **pop one's cork** *v.* **1** [1950s+] to lose one's temper, to lose patience. **2** [1960s+] to surrender sexually, to come to orgasm. **3** [1960s+] to masturbate. ❑ **pop one's drawers** *v.* [1970s] to have an orgasm, lit. or fig., i.e. to get very excited. ❑ **pop out** *v. see* sense 1f above. ❑ **pop over** *v. see* sense 1f above. ❑ **pop shit** *v. see under* SHIT *n.* ❑ **pop someone's cork** *v.* [1970s+] (*US gay*) to deflower anally. ❑ **pop style** *v.* [1950s+] (*W.I.*) of a woman, to walk in a provocative manner or to act stylishly. ❑ **pop the bud** *v.* [1920s] to administer a judicial whipping. ❑ **pop to** *v. see* POP FOR above. ❑ **pop tops** *v.* [SE *pop open* + *top* (of a beer can)] [1980s+] (*US campus*) to drink beer. ❑ **pop up** *v.* [1930s] to create, to make happen, to cause. ❑ **what's popping?** [2000s] (*US teen*) a phr. of greeting, enquiry.

SE in slang uses

IN COMPOUNDS

❑ **pop-nine** *n.* [1990s+] a 9mm pistol. ❑ **pop quiz** *n.* (*also* **pop test, shotgun quiz**) [it 'pops up' or 'explodes'] [1960s+] (*US campus*) a surprise test; also as v. ❑ **popskull** *n. see* BUSTSKULL *under* BUST *v.*[1].

pop *v.*[2] [SE *pop something in*] [late 18C+] to pawn.

IN COMPOUNDS

❑ **pop shop** *n.* [SE *shop*] [late 18C+] a pawnbroker's shop.

IN PHRASES

❑ **pop one's clogs** *v.* [SE *clogs*] [1970s+] to die.

pop *adv.*

IN PHRASES

❑ **go pop** *v.* [1900s–10s] **1** to die. **2** to lose one's temper.

popcorn *n.*[1] [rhy. sl. = HORN *n.*[2] (1c)] [20C+] an erection.

popcorn *n.*[2] [POPCORN *adj.* + CORNY *adj.*] **1** [1940s–50s] (*US prison*) a fool, a dullard. **2** [1950s] one with a legitimate job, rather than a criminal or a confidence man. **3** [2000s] anything mediocre and lightweight. **4** *see* POPCORN PIMP *n.*

popcorn *adj.* [the banality of the foodstuff] **1** [late 19C+] (*orig. US Und.*) foolish, slow-witted, lightweight, second string. **2** [1950s] (*US*) respectable, law-abiding.

popcorn pimp *n.* (*also* **popcorn**) [POPCORN *adj.* (1) + SE *pimp*] **1** [1960s+] (*US black*) a small-time, ineffectual pimp; thus anyone of little or no importance. **2** [1980s] a man who claims to be, but is not, a pimp.

pope *n.* [1970s] (*US*) an Irish (and Roman Catholic) person.

SE in slang uses

IN COMPOUNDS

❑ **pope-head** *n.* [-HEAD *sfx* (2)] [1990s+] (*Ulster*) a Roman Catholic. ❑ **pope's eye** *n.* [earlier use is SE] [mid-19C] the lymphatic gland surrounded with fat, found in a leg of mutton. ❑ **pope's nose** *n.* [var. on PARSON'S NOSE *under* PARSON *n.*; usu. in Protestant use] [late 18C+] the rump of a chicken or turkey.

IN PHRASES

❑ **is the pope a guinea?** *see* DOES A BEAR SHIT IN THE WOODS? IS THE POPE A CATHOLIC? *phr.*

pope *v.* [? obs. SE *poop*, to deceive, cheat; ? ult. Du. *poep*, a clown] [20C+] (*W.I.*) to get in without paying, to 'crash' a party.

Pope (of Rome) *n.* [rhy. sl.] [mid-19C+] home.

poperin pear *n.* (*also* **poperine pear**) [*Poperinghe*, in west Flanders. The word comes in Shakespeare's *Romeo and Juliet* (1594), that repository of so much innuendo. 'O Romeo, that she were/An open et-caetera/Thou a poperin pear!' says Mercutio. Partridge, in *Shakespeare's Bawdy* (1947), suggests a pun on 'pop her in'; Nares complains that 'it seems that there is much attempt at wit on this pear, in some old dramas; but such as it is not worthwhile to repeat, or attempt explaining'] [late 16C–mid-17C] the penis.

popeyed *adj.* [SE *pop-eyed*, with bulging eyes] **1** [1930s] drunk. **2** [1950s] regrettable, bad [fig. use of sense 1].

popeye the sailor *n.* [rhy. sl.; ult. cartoon character *Popeye*] [1990s+] a tailor.

pop goes the weasel *n.* [rhy. sl.] [20C+] diesel.

popgun *n.* [late 18C–1940s] a small-calibre weapon, e.g. a .22; thus used derog. for any unimpressive gun.

popla *n.* (*also* **poplar**) [ety. unknown] [1970s+] (*S.Afr. township*) beer.

poplars *n.* (*also* **paplar, poplar, poplers, poppelars**) [SE *pap*, infant food] [mid-16C–mid-19C] (*UK Und.*) porridge.

po-po *n.* (*also* **Mister Bobo, poh-poh**) [abbr. + redup.] [1980s+] **1** (*US black*) the police. **2** (*US prison*) a prison officer.

po-po *v. see* POO-POO *v.*[1].

popo *n.* [abbr. + redup. of SE *posterior*] [1950s+] (*US*) the buttocks.

IN PHRASES

❑ **pound someone's popo** *v.* [1970s+] (*US gay*) to sodomize.

pop-off *n.*[1] [POP OFF (AT THE MOUTH) *v.*] [1930s+] (*US*) **1** a brash or boastful statement. **2** a brash or boastful person. **3** an informer. **4** any form of comment.

pop-off *n.*[2] [1940s+] (*W.I.*) the proceeds of some form of illegal deal or racket, a reduction in price, e.g. on stolen goods.

pop-off *n.*[3] [POP *v.*[1] (1f)] [1950s] (*US*) a death, a killing.

pop-off *n.*[4] [1990s+] (*W.I.*) reaching for a firearm.

pop off *v.*[1] [SE *pop*, to move] **1** [mid-18C+] to die. **2** [19C+] to depart. **3** [1990s+] to happen, to start.

IN PHRASES

❑ **pop off at the handle** *v.* [mid-19C] (*US*) to reject, to dismiss. ❑ **pop off at the hooks** *v.* **1** [19C+] to die. **2** [1930s+] (*US*) to exit, to vanish.

pop off *v.*[2] **1** *see* POP *v.*[1] (1f). **2** *see* POP *v.*[1] (7a).

pop off (at the mouth) *v.* (*also* **pop off at**) [SE *pop*, to explode sharply] **1** [19C+] to make a fuss about. **2** [1920s] to confess, to tell the truth. **3** [1930s–50s] to joke. **4** [1930s+] to talk in an enthusiastic or aggressive, threatening manner. **5** [1960s+] to brag, to boast. **6** [1980s] to criticize.

pop-out *n.* [1920s] a jeer, a ridicule.

popp *n. see* POP *n.*[1] (1a).

poppa *n.* (*also* **popper**) [SE *papa*] **1** [late 19C+] (*orig. US*) a father. **2** [1920s] a boyfriend. **3** [1940s+] a term of address between men. **4** [1970s+] (*US gay*) a fellow lesbian. **5** *see* POP *n.*[3].

IN COMPOUNDS

❑ **poppa guy** *n. see* PAPPY GUY *under* PAPPY *adj.*[1]. ❑ **poppa large** *n.* [LARGE *adj.* (2)] [1990s+] (*US black teen/East coast*) an important, influential figure. ❑ **poppa-stoppa** *n.* (*also* **poppa-loppa**) [1930s–40s] (*US black*) **1** a man; also as intimate term of address. **2** an older man who still possesses his faculties and strength [i.e. his ability to 'stop' an opponent]. **3** a euphemistic reverse of MOTHERFUCKER *n.* (1)[i.e. 'stopper' used like 'plug'].

popped *adj.* [POP *v.*[1]] **1** [20C+] shot. **2** [1960s+] arrested. **3** [1970s] caught out. **4** [1980s] (*US campus*) in a difficult situation.

popped out *adj.* [POP *v.*[1] (4a)] [1940s–50s] intoxicated with a drug.

popped up *adj.* [1960s] **1** drunk [POP *v.*[1] (4e)]. **2** (*US*) intoxicated with amphetamines [POP *v.*[1] (4d)].

poppelars *n. see* POPLARS *n.*

popper *n.*[1] **1** [mid-18C+] (*US black 20C+*) usu. in pl., a pistol, a gun [POP *v.*[1] (1b)]. **2** [1940s] (*US black*) in pl., the fingers [? one 'pops' them in time to music]. **3** [2000s] a gunman.

popper *n.*[2] [POP *v.*[1]] (*drugs*) **1** [1930s+] an intravenous drug user. **2** [1930s+] an injection. **3** [1960s+] a pill-taker. **4** [1960s+] amyl or (iso)butyl nitrite, usu. in pl. [SE *pop*, to explode, i.e. the necessity of breaking open the ampoule that contains the drug].

popper *n.*[3] *see* BODY POPPER *under* BODY *n.*

popper *n.*[4] *see* POPPA *n.*

popping *n.* [1940s] (*US black*) spending money recklessly and enthusiastically.

pop-pop *n.* [echoic] **1** [1990s+] (*US black teen*) the noise of a gun being fired. **2** *see* POPPY *n.*[2] (1).

poppsie *n. see* POPSIE *n.*[1].

poppy *n.*[1] **1** [mid-19C+] (*drugs*) opium [prior 17C–19C use was literary SE, e.g. Shakespeare's 'Not Poppy, nor Mandragora' in *Othello* (1604)]. **2** [1990s+] heroin.

DERIVATIVES

❑ **poppied** *adj.* [1900s] under the influence of opium.

IN COMPOUNDS

❑ **poppyhead** *n. see* separate entry.

IN PHRASES

❑ **picking the poppies** *adj.* [1950s] addicted to opium.

poppy *n.*[2] (*Irish*) **1** [1940s+] (*also* **pop-pop**) a hole in one's sock or stocking [? one's flesh 'pops out']. **2** [1990s+] a potato [the flesh 'pops out' when baked].

poppy *n.*[3] [? SE *popular*] [1970s+] money.

poppy *n.*[4] *see* POP *n.*[3].

poppyhead *n.* [POPPY *n.*[1] (1) + -HEAD *sfx* (4)] [1950s] (*US drugs*) an opium addict.

poppy love *n.* [? POPPA *n.* (1)] [1980s+] (*US black*) an elderly Jewish man.

poppy-show *n.*[1] [SE *poppy* + *show*] [late 19C–1900s; 1950s+] (*later use N.Z.*) an inadvertent display of one's underclothes, orig. those made of red or brown flannel.

poppy-show *n.*[2] (*also* **pappy-show, puppy-show**) [dial. *poppy-show*, a puppet show] [20C+] (*W.I.*) **1** foolishness, showing off. **2** one who makes a stupid exhibition of themselves.

poppy-show *adj.* (*also* **pappy-show, puppy-show**) [POPPY-SHOW *n.*[2]] [20C+] (*W.I.*) foolish, ridiculous.

poppy-show *v.* (*also* **pappy-show, puppy-show**) [POPPY-SHOW *n.*[2]] [20C+] (*W.I.*) to make a fool of someone.

pops *n.* [POP *n.*[3]] [1920s+] **1** one's father; thus *grandpops*, grandfather. **2** (*orig. US black*) a term of address, usu. from a younger man to an older one. **3** (*US*) an old man.

popsee *n. see* POPSIE *n.*[1].

popsicle *n.* [SAmE *popsicle* = SE *lollipop*] [1980s+] (*US gay*) the penis.

popsicle stand *n.* [1970s+] (*US campus*) wherever one is currently situated.

popsie *n.*[1] (*also* **poppsie, popsee, popsy**) [SE *pop/poppet*, a term of endearment for a woman + sfx *-sy*, as in Betsy, Topsy etc] [mid-19C+] a woman, usu. one who is young and attractive; also occas. of a baby.

popsie *n.*[2] [POP *n.*[3] (1)] [1910s] (*US*) a SUGAR DADDY *n.*

popskull *n.* [SE *pop*, to explode + *skull*] **1** [mid-19C+] (*US*) illicitly distilled whisky. **2** [1940s] any form of strong drink.

popsy *n. see* POPSIE *n.*[1].

popsy-wopsy *n.* [POPSIE *n.*[1] + redup.] [late 19C–1920s] 'a smiling, doll-like attractive girl' (Ware); a term of affection, esp. by a father to a daughter.

popular *adj.* (*US*) **1** [mid–late 19C] conceited. **2** [late 19C] good, e.g. *a popular pie*.

population paste *n. see* PASTE *n.*[1].

p.o.(q.)! *excl.* [PISS OFF! *excl.* + SE *quick/quickly*] [1910s+] (*Aus.*) go away!

porangi *adj.* [Maori *porangi*, beside oneself, out of one's mind, mad] [mid-19C+] (*N.Z.*) mad; eccentric; stupid.

porcelain god *n.* (*also* **porcelain goddess, enamel god, … goddess**) [1970s+] (*US campus*) joc. terms for a lavatory, in the context of vomiting.

IN PHRASES

❑ **kiss the porcelain god** *v.* (*also* **kiss the porcelain goddess, bow to the porcelain god, …goddess, hug the porcelain god, …goddess, make love to the porcelain god, …goddess, pray to the porcelain god, …goddess, worship the porcelain god, …goddess, pray on the porcelain altar, pray to the enamel god, hug the throne, worship…**) [1970s+] (*US campus*) to vomit.

porch *n.* [1980s+] (*US gay*) the buttocks.

SE in slang uses

IN COMPOUNDS

❑ **porch climber** *n.* (*also* **window climber**) [20C+] (*US*) a burglar; thus *porch-climbing*. ❑ **porch monkey** *n.* [MONKEY *n.* (4a); the stereotyped image of black laziness, i.e. sitting on the porch] [1980s+] (*US*) a derog. term for a black person.

porcupine *n.* [corruption of PORKY *n.*[2] (1)] [1980s] a lie.

pork *n.* **1** in senses of flesh. (**a**) [18C+] a generic term for a woman or women viewed as sex objects. (**b**) [mid-19C; 1950s+] (*also* **purple pork, spicy pork roll**) the penis. (**c**) [1920s+] (*US tramp*) (*also* **dead pork**) a corpse. (**d**) [1980s] the vagina. (**e**) [1980s] (*UK black*) a white person. **2** in senses of monetary 'fat'. (**a**) [late 19C+] (*US*) federal funds obtained for particular areas or individuals on the basis of political patronage. (**b**) [1970s] (*US black*) money. **3** [1970s] a fool. **4** [2000s] (*US*) the police [play on PIG *n.* (2a)]. **5** *see* PORKY *n.*[1] (2).

IN COMPOUNDS

❑ **pork barrel** *n.* [late 19C+] (*US*) a political 'slush' fund; also as v.; also as attrib., corrupt. ❑ **pork chop** *n. see* separate entry. ❑ **pork chopper** *n.* [1960s] (*US*) the penis. ❑ **pork chops** *n.* [1920s–60s] (*US*) material or sensual gratification, often referring to sex. ❑ **pork leg** *n.* [1970s] (*US*) the penis. ❑ **pork puller** *n.* [PULL *v.* (6)] [1970s] one who masturbates. ❑ **pork sword** *n.* [1950s+] the penis.

IN PHRASES

❑ **bit of pork** *n.* [18C–1900s] the vagina. ❑ **dead pork** *n. see* sense 1c above. ❑ **do the pork sword jiggle** *v.* [1990s+] to masturbate. ❑ **have a bit of pork** *v.* [18C+] to have sexual intercourse. ❑ **pound one's pork** *v.* (*also* **flog one's pork**) [1970s+] to masturbate. ❑ **pour the pork** *v.* [1950s+] (*orig. US*) to have sexual intercourse, hetero- or male homosexual.

❑ **purple pork** *n.* see sense 1b above. ❑ **spicy pork roll** *n.* see sense 1b above. ❑ **walk one's pork** *v.* [1910s] (*Aus.*) to swagger.

SE in slang uses

IN COMPOUNDS

❑ **pork-and-beaner** *n.* see separate entries. ❑ **pork and beans** see separate entries. ❑ **pork fritz** *n.* see FRITZ *n.*[1]. ❑ **porkhead** *n.* [-HEAD *sfx* (1)] [1980s+] a stupid, thuggish person.

IN PHRASES

❑ **on the pork** see *ON THE HOG (TRAIN) under* HOG *n.* ❑ **pork chop at a Jewish wedding** see separate entry.

pork *v.* **1** [1960s] (*US*) to shoot dead, to kill [fig. use of sense 2]. **2** [1960s+] of a man, to have sexual intercourse; thus *porker*, n., a male sexual partner; *porkee*, n., a female sexual partner; *pork pit*, a place used for intercourse; *pork time*, sexual intercourse [PORK *n.* (1b)].

IN PHRASES

❑ **pork out** *v.* [mid-19C+] to overeat massively.

pork and bean *n.* [rhy. sl. = QUEEN *n.* (2a)] [1960s+] (*Aus.*) a male homosexual.

pork-and-bean *adj.* see PORK-AND-BEANS *adj.*

pork-and-beaner *n.*[1] [PORK-AND-BEANS *adj.*] [1910s+] (*US*) a second-rater.

pork-and-beaner *n.*[2] [the stereotypical ingredients of cowboy food] [1920s] (*US*) a cowboy.

pork and beans *n.* **1** [1910s–40s] a Portuguese [joc. pron.]. **2** [1960s] (*US black*) a means of living, one's livelihood.

pork-and-beans *adj.* (*also* **pork-and-bean**) [the banality of the dish] [late 19C–1950s] (*US*) basic, unenterprising.

pork chop *n.*[1] [rhy. sl. = COP *n.*[1] (1) + pun on PIG *n.* (2a)] [20C+] a police officer.

pork chop *n.*[2] **1** [1920s+] (*US*) an attractive young woman [? *PORK CHOPS under* PORK *n.*; or she is 'good enough to eat']. **2** [1940s] (*US*) a dollar [image of money as a staple of life]. **3** [1970s+] (*US*) a black person who, despite supposed advances in equality, is willing to accept an inferior position to that of whites [the stereotype of pork chops as a staple black food].

pork chop at a Jewish wedding *phr.* [the prohibition on pork in orthodox Judaism] [1930s+] used in various phrs. below.

IN PHRASES

❑ **as popular as a pork chop at a Jewish wedding** unpopular. ❑ **as useless as a pork chop at a Jewish wedding** (*also* **as useless as a slice of bacon at a Jewish wedding**) irrelevant, superfluous, useless. ❑ **as welcome as a pork chop at a Jewish wedding** unwelcome, completely superfluous or unwanted. ❑ **go down like a pork chop at a Jewish wedding** to make a gross social faux pas, to behave inappropriately. ❑ **in more strife than a pork chop at a synagogue** (*also* **in more strife than a pregnant nun**) (*Aus.*) in very great difficulties, in a most embarrassing situation. ❑ **like a pork chop at a Jewish wedding** superfluous, inappropriate.

porker *n.*[1] [? POKER *n.*[1] (1), but cf. PIGSTICKER *n.* (2)] [late 17C–mid-18C] (*UK Und.*) a sword.

porker *n.*[2] **1** [late 18C+] a Jew [SE *porker*, a pig; the Jewish laws of *kashrut*, which forbid the consumption of pig flesh]. **2** [mid-19C] (*UK Und.*) a saddle [the pigskin used for saddles]. **3** [late 19C+] a fat person [SE *porker*, a pig, when raised for its meat]. **4** [1980s+] a police officer [var. on PIG *n.* (2a)].

porking *n.* [PORK *v.* (2)] [1980s+] (*US black*) sexual intercourse.

Porklander *n.* [? ironic; N.Z. is a land of sheep-farming not pigs] [2000s] (*N.Z.*) a New Zealander.

Porkopolis *n.* (*also* **Hogopolis, Pigopolis**) [both centres of the meat trade] (*US*) **1** [mid–late 19C] Cincinnati; thus adj. *Porkopolitan*; also as n., a resident of Cincinnati. **2** [mid-19C–1900s] Chicago.

porky *n.*[1] **1** [late 19C] a pork-butcher. **2** [1900s–40s] (*also* **pork**) a Jew. **3** [1920s+] an obese person, often in direct address.

porky *n.*[2] (*also* **pork pie, porky pie**) [rhy. sl. on *porky pie*] **1** [1940s+] a lie. **2** [1990s+] an eye.

porky *adj.* **1** [mid-19C+] fat, even obese. **2** [1900s] (*US*) second-rate, inferior. **3** [1920s] (*US*) dissatisfied.

porky pig *adj.* [rhy. sl.] [1990s+] big, esp. in sense of generous.

porny *adj.* [abbr.] [1960s+] *porn*ographic, though usu. only mildly so.

pornzine *n.* [abbr.] [1960s+] a *porn*ographic *magazine*.

porpus *n.* [? joc. use of SE *porpoise*, i.e. an *ODD FISH under* ODD *adj.*] [mid-18C] (*UK Und.*) a stupid pompous fellow.

Porra *n.* [? mispron. of SE *Portuguese* or Port. *porra!* a coarse excl.] [1970s+] (*S.Afr.*) a derog. term for a person of Portuguese descent.

porridge *n.* **1** [20C+] imprisonment [the staple morning diet of such establishments in the UK + pun on STIR *n.*[1] (1)/SE *stir*]. **2** [1920s+] (*Irish*) based on SE *porridge*, a hotch potch. (**a**) a confusion, e.g. a traffic jam. (**b**) nonsense; usu. as *you have your porridge*, you are talking nonsense.

IN COMPOUNDS

❑ **porridge bird** *n.* [1980s+] (*S.Afr. gay*) **1** a flaccid penis. **2** an impotent man. ❑ **porridge gun** *n.* [the supposed similarity of semen to porridge] [1990s+] the penis. ❑ **porridge hole** *n.* [late 19C] (*Scot.*) the mouth. ❑ **porridge stuffer** *n.* [stereotypical Scot. food] [late 19C] (*Aus.*) a Scotsman. ❑ **porridge wog** *n.* [WOG *n.*[1] (3)] [1990s+] a derog. term for a Scottish person.

IN PHRASES

❑ **dish out the porridge** *v.* see *DISH OUT THE GRAVY/PORRIDGE under* DISH OUT *v.* ❑ **stir the porridge** *v.* [1980s+] (*orig. Aus.*) to have sexual intercourse with a woman immediately after she has had sex with another man, esp. used of the final man in a gang rape.

SE in slang uses

IN PHRASES

❑ **wouldn't know (someone) if (they) stood up in my porridge** [2000s] (*N.Z.*) to profess complete ignorance of someone.

Porsche *n.* [alleged resemblance to *Porsche* cars] [1970s+] (*US black*) a woman whose body is small, rounded, compact and stylish.

port *n.* [abbr.] [20C+] (*Aus.*) *port*manteau; a school satchel.

Portagee *n.* (*also* **Portugee, Portygee**) **1** [mid-19C+] a Portuguese person. **2** [1900s–10s] the Portuguese language.

IN COMPOUNDS

❑ **Portagee colonial** *n.* (*also* **Portagee chic, Portugee chic, ... colonial, immigrant chic**) [racial stereotyping] [1980s] (*US*) cheap furniture, touted as ultra fashionable and peddled mainly to gullible recent immigrants. ❑ **Portagee lawnmower** *n.* (*also* **Portugee lawnmower**) [racial stereotyping] [1980s] a goat used to keep the grass down. ❑ **Portagee lift** *n.* (*also* **Portugee lift**) [racial stereotyping; orig. used on US docks] [late 19C+] one who carries less than their share of a load. ❑ **Portagee overdrive** *n.* [the stereotyped poverty of Portuguese immigrants] [1980s] (*US*) freewheeling down hills to save petrol.

port and brandy *adj.* [rhy. sl. = SE *randy*] [20C+] sexually excited.

port and sherry *adj.* [rhy. sl.] **1** [1930s] fine, well [= JERRY *adj.* (2)]. **2** [1940s] wise [= JERRY *adj.* (1)].

portcullis *n.* [the SE *portcullis* engraved on one side of the silver coin] [late 16C–17C] a halfpenny.

porter-without-froth *n.* [SE *porter*, a dark beer, so called from its being preferred by market porters. Porter, e.g. Guinness, should have a head or 'froth' if poured properly] [1950s] (*W.I.*) a layabout, a ne'er-do-well.

porthole *n.* [17C] **1** the anus. **2** the vagina.

portie *adj.* [abbr. SE *port*able] [2000s] a mobile phone.

portion *n.* [late 17C; 1990s+] an act of sexual intercourse.

Port Melbourne Pier *n.* [rhy. sl.] [1940s+] (*Aus.*) an ear.

porto *adj.* [pron. of *Puerto*] [1960s–70s] (*US*) Puerto Rican.

portrait *n.* **1** [mid-19C] a sovereign [the monarch's face on the coin]. **2** [1940s] (*US black*) one's face.

portrait of Madison *n.* [the face of *James Madison* (1751–1836), 4th President of the US, is printed on $5000 bills] [1940s+] (*US*) a $5000 bill.

Port Saint Peter *n.* [Port Saint Peter/Saint Peter Port in Guernsey (Channel Islands) was a popular destination for fleeing UK debtors] [mid-19C] (*UK Und.*) a suitcase, a portmanteau.

portsammy *n.* (*also* **sammy**) [joc. mispron.] [20C+] (*N.Z.*) a portmanteau, a travelling bag.

port-sider *n.* [naut. imagery; *port*, the left-hand side of the boat] [20C+] (*US*) a left-hander.

Portugee *n. see* PORTAGEE *n.* and combs.

Portuguese *adj.*

IN COMPOUNDS

❑ **Portuguese parliament** *n.* [negative stereotyping; orig. naval jargon] [late 19C+] a meeting at which everyone gathers but no one listens to anyone else. ❑ **Portuguese pump** *n.* [late 19C–1900s] masturbation. ❑ **Portuguese time** *n.* [negative stereotyping] [1980s] any time later than that set up for an appointment.

port wine *n.* [mid-19C] in boxing, blood.

Portygee *n. see* PORTAGEE *n.*

p.o.s. *n.* [abbr. *PIECE OF SHIT under* PIECE *n.*] [2000s] (*US black*) something bad, useless or undesirable.

pos *adj.*[1] (*also* **pozz**) [abbr.] **1** [early 18C–1900s] *positive*. **2** [late 19C] inflexible [i.e. *positive* in a dogmatic way].

pos *adj.*[2] *see* POSS *adj.*

pose off *v.* (*also* **pose up**) [1950s] (*W.I./UK black/US gay*) to strike an exaggerated pose.

posey *adj.* [SE *pose*] [1990s+] (*orig. US*) pretentious.

posh *n.*[1] [despite the links in sense, the n. and adj. uses come apparently from different origins. Partridge suggests link to POSH *n.*[2], i.e. one who is rich, while *OED* prefers a completely discrete word] [mid-19C–1900s] a dandy.

posh *n.*[2] (*also* **posher, poshery**) [Rom. *posh*, a half] [mid-19C–1910s] a coin or money, usu. a halfpenny.

posh *n.*[3] [SE *piffle* + *tosh*] [1950s] nonsense, rubbish.

posh *n.*[4] [POSH *adj.* (1), i.e. the drug's image] [1990s+] (*drugs*) cocaine.

posh *adj.* (*also* **posho**) [ety. unknown. The *OED*, like most modern authorities, rejects the trad. '*p*ort *o*ut, *s*tarboard *h*ome' derivation. *DSUE* and J.P. Mayer (in Cohen (ed.), *Studies in Slang* I (1985), opt for a contraction of *polished*, well turned out, smart, sophisticated (note US milit. use in *You Chirped a Chinful!!* (c.1943), *posh*: bright and polished); M. Quinion in *Port Out, Starboard Home* (2004) prefers a link to POSH *n.*[2]; the novelist P.G. Wodehouse uses *push* in 1903, which *OED* sees as a synon., but this may be linked to PUSH *n.* (2a), a clique] [20C+] (*orig. milit.*) smart, pertaining to the upper classes.

DERIVATIVES

❑ **poshery** *n.* [1960s] upper-class airs.

IN PHRASES

❑ **all poshed up** *adj.* [1920s] dressed up. ❑ **bit of posh** *n.* [var. on BIT OF ROUGH *n.*[2]] [1970s+] an attractive young woman who is also considered intelligent or upper class. ❑ **do the posh** *v.* [1940s–50s] (*Aus.*) to spend to excess, to do something in style. ❑ **posh (up)** *v.* [1910s+] of a person, to smarten one's clothes, house etc.

posh *adv.* [POSH *adj.*] [1950s+] in an aristocratic, upper-class manner.

posher/poshery *n. see* POSH *n.*[2].

posh horri *n.* (*also* **poshero**) [Rom. *posh*, half + *horri*, penny] [mid-19C] a halfpenny.

poshie *see under* POSHY.

posh korona *n.* (*also* **posh-korauna**) [Rom. *posh*, half + *korona*, crown] [mid–late 19C] half-a-crown, 2s 6d (12½p).

posho *adj. see* POSH *adj.*

poshy *n.* (*also* **poshie, posho**) [POSH *adj.*] [1950s+] an upper-class person.

poshy *adj.* (*also* **poshie**) [POSHY *n.*] [2000s] smart, upper-class.

posie *n.* [ext. of PO *n.* (1)] [20C+] (*W.I.*) a chamberpot.

posilutely *adv.* [comb. of SE *absolutely* + *positively*; inverse of ABSOTIVELY *adv.*] [1920s+] (*US*) without a doubt, irrefutably.

posish *n.* [abbr.] [mid-19C+] (*orig. US*) a *posi*tion, a situation.

poss *n.* **1** [1940s] a *poss*ibility. **2** [1940s+] (*Aus.*) a fool, esp. a trickster's victim [abbr. POSSUM *n.* (6)].

poss *adj.* (*also* **pos**) [abbr.] [early 18C+] *poss*ible.

posse *n.* [SE *posse*, an armed band recruited to pursue law-breakers] [1980s+] **1** (*orig. US black*) a gang, usu. teenage. **2** (*orig. US campus*) one's own circle of friends. **3** (*orig. US black*) oneself, as described in the third person, e.g. *the posse can't dig this*, I am unhappy. **4** an in-group. **5** a band.

IN PHRASES

❑ **posse (down)** *v.* [1980s+] (*orig. US black*) to move in a gang or group. ❑ **posse up** *v.* [1980s+] (*US black/teen*) of a gang, to move together as a group.

posse mobilitatis *n.* [play on Lat. *posse comitatus*, force of the county, a band of citizens summoned by the sheriff to deal with outbreaks of rioting and similar disorder] [late 17C–early 19C] the mob.

possesh *n.* [abbr. SE *possession*] [1920s–40s] a homosexual boy who is used for sex by the tramp he accompanies.

IN PHRASES

❑ **in one's possesh** [1910s] on one's person, in one's possession.

possible *n.* **1** [early 19C–1900s] a coin, money [which makes things possible]. **2** [mid-19C–1940s] in pl., necessities, supplies.

IN COMPOUNDS

❑ **possible sack** *n.* [late 19C+] (*orig. US*) **1** a bag for personal belongings. **2** a bag containing items that can be taken to the pawnbroker.

SE in slang uses

IN PHRASES

❑ **not have a possible** *v.* [1900s] (*Aus.*) not have a chance.

possie *n.* (*also* **possy, pozzie, pozzy**) [abbr.] **1** [1910s+] (*Aus.*) a position, usu. an advantageous one. **2** [1910s+] (*Aus./S.Afr.*) a seat. **3** [1920s–70s] a job. **4** [1940s+] (*S.Afr.*) a room, a home.

IN COMPOUNDS

❑ **pozzie walloper** *n.* [1910s] an idler.

posso-de-luxe *n.* [POSSUM *n.* (6)] [1930s+] (*Aus.*) an extremely rich fool, esp. when used as a confidence trickster's victim.

poss (out) *v.* [Irish *poss*, to dash or shake violently in water; ult. may be Fr. *pousser*, to push] [1920s+] (*Irish*) to wash; thus adj., *possing*, very wet; n., *posser*, one who gets wet.

possum *n.* **1** [mid-19C] (*US*) a friend. **2** [late 19C] (*US*) a coward [one of the animal's characteristics is feigning death when threatened]. **3** [late 19C+] (*Aus.*) (*also* **opossum**) a person (used either affectionately or derog.). **4** [20C+] (*Aus.*) a fraudulent substitution. **5** [1900s] (*US*) a black person. **6** [1930s+] (*Aus.*) a fool, esp. a trickster's victim; sometimes intensified as POSSO-DE-LUXE *n.* **7** [1940s+] (*Aus.*) a thief.

SE in slang uses

IN COMPOUNDS

❑ **possum-belly** *n.* [thus used for similar arrangements on livestock and circus wagons] **1** [19C–1940s] 'a baggy, dried cowhide fastened horizontally beneath the wagon box and used for carrying a reserve of fuel' (P.A. Rollins, *Gone Haywire*, 1939); also as a term of abuse. **2** [1920s–40s] (*US tramp*) to ride under a railroad car. ❑ **possum-eater** *n.* [their supposed diet] [1900s–60s] (*Aus.*) a peasant, a country bumpkin; thus *possum-eating*, countrified. ❑ **possum fucker** *n.* [FUCKER *n.* (1)] [2000s] (*Aus.*) a country-dweller, a peasant. ❑ **possum-guts** *n.* [reflecting a low opinion of the animal] **1** [mid–late 19C] (*Aus.*) a general term of abuse. **2** [1950s–60s] (*Aus.*) a coward; thus *possum-gutted*, cowardly. ❑ **possum-rider** *n.* [1990s+] (*US* *campus*) a promiscuous person. ❑ **possum-scoffer** *n.* [SCOFF *v.* (1)] [late 19C] a Native Australian.

IN PHRASES

❑ **have possums in one's top paddock** *v. see* HAVE KANGAROOS IN ONE'S TOP PADDOCK *under* KANGAROO *n.*². ❑ **like a possum up a gum-tree** *adv.* [late 19C–1950s] (*Aus.*) absolutely contentedly, perfectly happyily. ❑ **stir the possum** *v.* (*also* **rouse the possum**) [the animal's habit of keeping quite still for long periods] [20C+] (*Aus.*) to create a disturbance, to start things moving, to jolt the general apathy.

possum *v.* [SE *possum* + POSSUM *n.* (2), i.e. the habits of the animal] [early 19C+] to dissemble; to feign sickness; thus *possum trick*, a feigning of injury to lure an intended robbery victim.

IN PHRASES

❑ **possum-foot** *v.* [1960s] to tread quietly. ❑ **possum up** *v.* [1950s] to be quiet.

possy *n. see* POSSIE *n.*

post *n.* [abbr.] [1900s–30s] (*US*) a *post*-graduate.

post *v.*¹ [SE *post*, a trading station, or Ital. *posta*, a stake + COLE *n.* (1)/NEDDY *n.*²/PONY *n.* (1a)/TIN *n.* (1a)] **1** [late 18C+] to lay down or stake money, esp. to put up bail; thus [late 18C] *post the cole*; [late 18C] *post the neddies*; [early 19C] *post the pony*; [mid-19C] *post the tin*. **2** [early 19C] (*UK Und.*) to swear on oath.

post *v.*² [? *posting* accounts in a ledger or nailing announcements to a *post*] [mid-19C+] (*orig. US*) to inform; thus *keep someone posted*, keep someone up to date.

IN PHRASES

❑ **post a flyer** *v.* [1970s+] (*gay*) to advertise one's sexual availability. ❑ **post bills** *v.* [pun on SE] [1940s] (*US Und.*) to pass counterfeit money; thus *bill-poster*, a forger, a counterfeiter, a passer of bad cheques. ❑ **post up** *v.* **1** [mid–late 19C] (*US*) to supply with the latest information, to learn the latest news; usu. as passive *posted up*, informed. **2** [1990s+] (*US black*) to frequent a popular meeting-place with one's friends.

post *v.*³ [SE *post*, to hurry] [1950s+] (*Aus.*) to abandon, to 'leave in the lurch'.

post *v.*⁴ [SE to take up a *post*] [1990s+] **1** (*US*) to appear, to make oneself available. **2** (*W.I.*) to miss an appointment.

postage stamp *n.* [rhy. sl. = RAMP *n.*³] [20C+] a bar.

postal *adj.* [coined to reflect a spate of mass killings (of fellow workers) by disgruntled postal employees] [1990s+] (*US*) crazy, psychotic.

IN PHRASES

❑ **go postal** *v.* [1990s+] (*US teen*) to lose one's temper, to lose control of one's emotions.

post-and-rail *n.*¹ [the resemblance to a *post-and-rail* fence] [late 19C–1940s] (*Aus.*) a wooden match.

post-and-rail *n.*² [rhy. sl. = *fairy tale* (*see* FAIRY-STORY *under* FAIRY *n.*¹)] [1940s+] (*Aus.*) a lie, a (fairy) tale.

post-and-rail (tea) *n.* (*also* **post-and-rails**) [the idea of chunks of wood floating in it] [mid-19C–1940s] (*Aus.*) poor quality tea, with particles of stalk and other impurities floating on its surface; such impurities may have been deliberately added to bulk out a grocer's measure.

post-chay *n. see* PO'CHAISE *n.*

posted *adj.*¹ (*also* **posted up**) [POST *v.*²] [mid-19C+] (*orig. US*) aware, in the know, shrewd.

posted *adj.*² [? image of a horse or dog left tied to a post] [1960s+] (*Aus.*) abandoned.

postern gate *n.* (*also* **postern passage**) [SE *postern*, a backdoor or gate] [18C] that part of a pair of trousers, or other clothing, that fits over the buttocks.

post-horn *n.* [one blows it] [19C] the nose.

postie *n.* [abbr.] **1** [1910s+] (*orig. Aus.*) a *post*man. **2** [1990s+] a *post* office clerk. **3** [2000s] a *post* office.

postilion *v.* [SE *postilion*, a swift messenger; thus the practice makes one 'COME *v.*¹ faster'] [19C+] to insert and manipulate a finger in the anus of a sexual partner as a means of increasing sexual excitement.

postilion of the gospel *n.* [late 18C–early 19C] a parson who rushes through the service.

post-knight *n. see* KNIGHT OF THE POST *n.*

postman's knock *n.* (*also* **knock**) [rhy. sl.] [20C+] clock.

post nointer *n.* [he 'anoints' the door posts] [late 18C–early 19C] a house painter.

post office *n.* [1930s] (*US Und.*) one who receives or delivers letters to criminals.

SE in slang uses

IN PHRASES

❑ **there's a letter in the post office** (*US*) **1** [mid-19C+] a phr. used to warn a man his fly is undone or his shirt is out; also used to a woman when her slip is showing. **2** [late 19C–1910s] said of a woman who is menstruating.

post-op *n.* [abbr.] [1990s+] (*gay*) a *post-op*erative transsexual.

post-op *adj.* [abbr.] [1970s+] *post-op*erative, having recently undergone an operation; usu. of *transsexuals*.

post-shay *n. see* PO'CHAISE *n.*

post toasties *n.* [brandname of a US breakfast cereal] [1970s] (*US camp gay*) the mailman.

posture moll *n. see under* MOLL *n.*

posy *n.*¹ [SE *posy*, a small bunch of flowers] [late 19C] (*US campus*) an attractive person.

posy *n.*² [SE *poser*, something that poses problems] [late 19C] (*US campus*) a general term of abuse.

pot *n.*¹ **1** based on the idea of the vagina as a 'container'. (**a**) [mid-16C–mid-19C; 1930s] (*orig. UK Und.*) a woman. (**b**) [17C–18C; 1940s–60s] (*later use US black*) the vagina. **2** in the context of drinking. (**a**) [mid-16C+] a generic term for alcohol; thus *potter*, a drink. (**b**) [18C; 1910s+] a glass of beer, irrespective of measure. (**c**) [mid-19C] sixpence [the contemporary price of a quart pot of *half-and-half*, a mixture of ale and porter]. (**d**) [1980s] (*Aus.*) in Queensland, a 10oz (285ml) beer glass. **3** based on the idea of a 'pot' belly. (**a**) [late 18C; 1920s+] (*also* **pot gut**) an enlarged stomach, usu. developed through excessive drinking; also occas. used of the stomach in general. (**b**) [1950s] a plump person. **4** in monetary senses. (**a**) [early 19C+] a large sum of money; often in pl.; thus *put on the pot*, to bet heavily. (**b**) [late 19C–1900s] the favourite in a horserace, upon whom 'pots of money' have been wagered. **5** of a person [abbr. BIG POT *n.*]. (**a**) [late 19C–1910s] an important person [later use is SE]. (**b**) [1910s] (*Aus.*) a person, irrespective of status. (**c**) [1930s] (*US*) an obnoxious person. **6** [late 19C+] a lit. or fig. prize. (**a**) a prize, esp. a cup given to a sporting victor. (**b**) (*UK Und.*) the rewards of a crime or a bet. **7** *see* POT HAT below.

IN COMPOUNDS

❑ **pot-eyed** *n.* [1900s] drunk. ❑ **pot gut** *n. see* sense 3a above. ❑ **pot-gutted** *adj.* [sense 3a above] [mid-19C+] (*US/Aus.*) pot-bellied. ❑ **pot-jostler** *n.* [1910s] (*Aus.*) a barman; thus v., *pot-jostle*, to serve drinks. ❑ **pot-jostling** *adj.* [late 19C] (*Aus.*) drunken. ❑ **pot-polisher** *n.* [1910s] (*Aus.*) a barmaid. ❑ **pot-shaken** *adj.* [17C] drunk. ❑ **pot-shot** *adj.* [one has been fig. *shot* by drinking a *pot* of beer] [mid-17C] drunk. ❑ **pot-sick** *adj.* [early 17C] drunk. ❑ **pot-valiant** *n.* [early 17C] a drunkard. ❑ **pot-valiant** *adj.* [17C–1910s] exhibiting the bravado that comes from imbibing alcoholic drink.

IN PHRASES

❑ **get (a bit of) a pot** *v.* [1920s+] to become obese. ❑ **go on the pots** *v.* [1960s] (*Aus.*) to go on a drunken spree. ❑ **have a pot in the pate** *v.* [lit. a 'tankard in the head'] [mid-17C–mid-18C] to be drunk. ❑ **have a pot on** *v.* [1920s] to be drunk. ❑ **have one's pots on** *v.* [19C–1940s] to be drunk. ❑ **hit the pot** *v.* [1900s–30s] (*US*) to drink excessively. ❑ **in one's pots** *adj.* [1960s] drunk. ❑ **sling a pot** *v.* [late 19C] to drink heavily.

SE in slang uses

DERIVATIVES

❑ **potless** *adj. see* separate entry.

IN COMPOUNDS

❑ **pot burst** *adj.* [the pot breaks under the relationship's stress] [20C+] (*W.I.*) a phr. used of a friendship to indicate that it has come to an end. ❑ **pot convert** *n.* [SE *pot*, a container for food or drink] [late 18C–early 19C] a convert to Roman Catholicism who is won over by the free provision of food and drink. ❑ **pot-faker** *n.* [FAKER *n.* (4)] [mid-19C] a hawker of crockery, a cheap-jack. ❑ **pot hat** *n.* (*also* **pot**) **1** [late 18C–19C] a bowler hat. **2** [late 19C] a low-crowned hat, as opposed to the more common top hat of the period. ❑ **pothead** *n. see* separate entry. ❑ **pot-hunter** *n. see* separate entries. ❑ **pot-lick/-licker** *see* separate entries. ❑ **pot rassler** *n.* [SE *wrestler*] [1930s] (*US black*) a cook. ❑ **pot slinger** *n.* [20C+] (*US*) a cook. ❑ **pot-wallop/-walloper** *see* separate entries. ❑ **pot-wrestler** *n.* [19C+] a scullion, a kitchen-hand.

IN PHRASES

❑ **get off the pot** *v.* [1970s] (*US*) to calm down. ❑ **go to the pot** *v.* [18C–1900s] to die; also as dismissive excl. ❑ **have the pot on** *v.* [? cooking imagery based on the 'heat' of intercourse] [1960s] (*US prison*) to have (homosexual) sexual intercourse. ❑ **in the pot** [early 19C] in trouble. ❑ **make a pot with two ears** *v.* (*also* **make the pot with two ears**) [resemblance] [late 17C] to set one's arms akimbo. ❑ **make pots and pans** *v.* [? the selling of pots and pans by a tinker] [19C] to spend heavily, to use up one's money and start begging. ❑ **not have a pot to piss in (or a window to throw it out of)** *v.* (*also* **not have a pot to pee in, without a pot to pee in, ...piss in**) [PISS *v.* (2)/PEE *v.* (1)] (*orig. US*) **1** [1930s+] to be very poor. **2** [1970s] to be stupid. **3** [1980s+] to be completely destroyed. ❑ **off one's pot** *adj. see* OUT OF ONE'S BOX *under* BOX *n.*[3]. ❑ **put on one's pot** *v.* [20C+] (*W.I.*) to take care of oneself; thus *not put on the pot for, not make one's pot bubble*, to refuse to help someone. ❑ **put someone's pot on** *v.* [i.e. putting a pot or saucepan on their hopes or activities] [20C+] (*Aus./N.Z.*) **1** (*also* **put someone's pot away**) to tell tales, to inform against, to destroy the hopes of. **2** to catch someone out in wrong-doing. ❑ **sweeten (the pot)** *v. see under* SWEETEN *v.*

pot *n.*[2] [backsl.] [mid-19C] the top.

pot *n.*[3] [Mexican Sp. *potiguaya*, marijuana leaves; thus Algren, *Walk on the Wild Side* (1956): 'Byron smoked too much potiguaya bush for a lunger'] [1930s+] (*drugs*) marijuana, occas. hashish; thus *pot party*, a gathering of people to smoke marijuana.

IN COMPOUNDS

❑ **pothead** *n. see* separate entry. ❑ **pot liquor** *n.* (*also* **potlikker**) [play on SE *pot liquor*, the liquid derived from boiling greens] [1960s+] (*drugs*) a drink derived from brewing marijuana leaves and stalks. ❑ **pot-pig** *n.* [PIG *n.* (1f)] [2000s] one who smokes more than their share of a cannabis cigarette. ❑ **pot stick** *n.* [1970s] a marijuana cigarette.

IN PHRASES

❑ **pot out** *v.* [1960s+] (*drugs*) to smoke marijuana.

pot *v.* [all other senses are fig. use of sense 2, where the food goes in the SE *pot*] **1** [mid–late 19C] to outdo, to outwit, to deceive. **2** [mid-19C+] to shoot, esp. food for eating; thus n., *potting*. **3** [late 19C] to punish. **4** [late 19C–1910s] to take from, to extort. **5** [20C+] (*Aus./N.Z.*) to throw a stone. **6** [20C+] (*US*) to hit, to strike. **7** [1900s] to appropriate. **8** (*Aus./N.Z.*) in Und. uses. (**a**) [1900s–10s] to arrest; to charge. (**b**) [1900s–50s] to inform against, to hand over for trial. **9** [1940s] to render drunk. **10** [1970s] (*S.Afr.*) to drink. **11** [1990s+] of a man, to seduce, to have sexual intercourse with.

IN PHRASES

❑ **pot off** *v.* [1950s] (*US*) to kill. ❑ **pot pork for** *v. see* separate entry. ❑ **take a pot at** *v.* [1910s] to shoot at.

-pot *sfx* [SE *pot*, container. In such combs. the person is seen as a container for a characteristic] [20C+] a person; usu. found in combs., e.g. BARMPOT *n.*; BIG POT *n.*; CRANKPOT *n.*; FUSSPOT *n.*; SEXPOT *under* SEX *n.*

pot and pan *n.* [rhy. sl.] **1** [late 19C+] a man; esp. as *old pot and pan*, often abbr. to *OLD POT under* OLD *adj.* **2** [20C+] a husband, or father; often as *old pot and pan*.

potash and perlmutter *n.* [rhy. sl.; ult. a play by Montague Glass, first performed in 1914] [1910s–50s] butter.

potato *n.* **1** [mid-18C; late 19C+] a person, often as an insult with a negative adj. **2** [mid-19C] constr. with *the*, the right thing, the apposite thing; usu. as *quite the potato*; thus negative, *not quite the potato*. **3** [mid-19C+] (*also* **spud**) a large hole in a sock or stocking through which the flesh shows [? the shape + the dirt that accrues to the bare flesh]. **4** senses based on the shape. (**a**) [1920s] (*US*) the head. (**b**) [1930s] (*US*) a bump, a swelling. **5** [1920s+] (*also* **potato chip**) a dollar; money; usu. in pl. [on the 'vegetable' pattern of CABBAGE *n.*[2] (3a), KALE *n.*, LETTUCE *n.*[1] etc although unlike them not green]. **6** [1950s] (*Can.*) a native of New Brunswick [the province grows many potatoes; the implication is one of rural stolidness and stupidity]. **7** [1970s] (*US*) a severely disabled person. **8** [2000s] (*N.Z.*) a Polynesian (regarded as being brown on the outside but white on the inside).

SE in slang uses

IN COMPOUNDS

❑ **potato-box** *n.* [late 19C] the mouth. ❑ **potato chip** *n. see* sense 5 above. ❑ **potato-eater** *n.* (*also* **potato-consumer, -head, pratie-machine, spud-eater, tater-eater**) [stereotyping; -HEAD *sfx* (2)/PRATIE *n.*/SPUD *n.*[3] (1)/TATER *n.* (1)] [19C+] (*mainly US*) an Irishman. ❑ **potato-face** *n.* (*also* **spud face**) [SPUD *n.*[3] (1)] [mid-19C; 1980s] (*US*) a mild term of abuse. ❑ **potato-finger** *n.* [the shape + the supposed aphrodisiac quality of the sweet potato] [17C] **1** a long, thick finger. **2** the penis. **3** a dildo. ❑ **potato-fingered Irishman** *n.* [negative stereotyping] [20C+] a clumsy person. ❑ **potato-grabler** *n.* [GRABBLE *v.*] [mid-19C] (*US*) the hand. ❑ **potato-head** *n. see* separate entry. ❑ **potato jack** *n.* [JACK *n.*[13] (1)] [1970s+] (*US prison*) illicit liquor distilled from potatoes. ❑ **potato jaw** *n.* [its use in consuming the vegetable] [late 18C] the mouth. ❑ **potato masher** *n.* [resemblance] [1920s] a drum stick. ❑ **potato queen** *n.* [? a quintessential Western food + -QUEEN *sfx* (3)] [1980s+] (*US gay*) an East Asian gay man who prefers Western partners. ❑ **potato-stealer** *n.* [mid-19C] (*US*) a hand. ❑ **potato-trap** *n.* (*also* **pratee-trap**) [SE *trap*/TRAP *n.*[1] (4)/PRATIE *n.*] [late 18C–1900s] the mouth.

IN PHRASES

❑ **have one's potatoes** *v.* [2000s] (*N.Z.*) to be ruined. ❑ **hold your potato** *v.* [mid-19C+] (*orig. US*) to slow down, to show restraint. ❑ **sweet potato** *n. see SWEET POTATO PIE under* SWEET *adj.*[1]. ❑ **sweet potato pie** *n. see under* SWEET *adj.*[1].

IN EXCLAMATIONS

❑ **potato is cooked!, one's** *see EGGS ARE COOKED! under* EGG *n.*[1].

potato *v.* [? *COUCH POTATO under* COUCH *n.*] [1980s+] (*US campus*) to lie around doing nothing.

potatoes (in the mould) *adj.* [rhy. sl.] [1910s+] cold.

potato-head *n.* [SE *potato* + -HEAD *sfx* (1)] [mid-19C+] (*US*) a fool, a simpleton.

DERIVATIVES

❑ **potato-headed** *adj.* (*also* **tatur-headed**) ['TATUR *n.*] [mid-19C; 1990s+] stupid.

potato (peeler) *n.* [rhy. sl. = SHEILA *n.*[1] (1)] [1950s+] (*Aus.*) a woman, a girlfriend.

potato-pillin' *n.* [rhy. sl.; pron. of SE *peeling*] [1930s] a shilling.

potch *n.* [Yid./Ger. *Patsch*, a smack, a splash] [20C+] a slap, a smack, usu. given to a child.

potch *v.* [POTCH *n.*] [20C+] to slap, to smack, usu. a child.

potcharooney *n. see HOT POCKAROO under* HOT *adj.*

potchky *v.* (*also* **potchkie, potskie**) [fig. use of POTCH *v.*] [20C+] (*US*) to mess about.

pot-cover love *n.* [? Jam. *pot-cover*, a species of flat-fish, thus play on FISH *n.*[1] (1a) = vagina] [1990s+] (*W.I.*) lesbianism.

poted *adj. see* POTTED *adj.*[1].

pothead *n.*[1] [SE *pot* + -HEAD *sfx* (1)] [mid-19C] a fool; thus *potheaded*, stupid.

pothead *n.*[2] [POT *n.*[3] + -HEAD *sfx* (4)] [1950s+] (*drugs*) a smoker of marijuana or hashish.

pothooks and hangers *n.* [SE *pothooks and hangers*, the curved strokes used in writing, which supposedly resemble the hooks and hangers found in a kitchen] [19C] shorthand.

pothouse *n.* [POTTY *adj.*[1] (4)] [2000s] a madman, one who goes to excessive lengths, esp. criminal.

pot-hunter *n.*[1] [SE *pot*, a tankard, i.e. the pose as a drunkard + *hunter*] [late 16C–early 17C] a confidence trickster, one of a team but posing as an independent person, often drunk, who befriends a potential victim and lures them into a swindle.

pot-hunter *n.*[2] [SE *pot*/POT *n.*[1] + SE *hunter*] **1** [late 18C–1910s] one who hunts for food rather than pleasure. **2** [mid-19C] an unwelcome guest who carefully arrives just in time for dinner. **3** [late 19C–1920s] in punning use of sense 1, one who pursues medals and/or prizes; thus *pot-hunting*, such a pursuit. **4** [20C+] (*US*) a scavenger.

potion *n.* [SE *potion*, a measure (usu. of liquid), thus phr. plays on PIECE *n.* (6)] [1990s+] (*W.I.*) a large quantity.

SE in slang uses

IN PHRASES

❑ **have a potion** *v.* [2000s] to have sexual intercourse.

potless *adj.* [NOT HAVE A POT TO PISS IN (OR A WINDOW TO THROW IT OUT OF) *under* POT *n.*[1]] [2000s] impoverished.

pot-lick *v.* [backform. f. POT-LICKER *n.* (1)] [1920s–60s] to toady to, to curry favour.

pot-licker *n.* [fig. use of SE] **1** [mid-19C+] a sycophant, a contemptible person; thus *pot-licking*, toadying. **2** [1930s–50s] (*US/W.I.*) a mongrel, kept as a watchdog and allowed to forage for its food.

potlikker *n. see* POT LIQUOR *under* POT *n.*[3].

potna *n. see* PARD *n.*

pot of glue *n.* [rhy. sl.] [20C+] **1** a Jew. **2** a queue.

pot of honey *n.* [rhy. sl.] [late 19C+] money.

pot of jelly *n.* [rhy. sl.] [1940s+] the belly.

pot of O *n.* [rhy. sl.; *pot of* OH, MY DEAR *n.* = beer] [mid–late 19C] a glass or tankard of beer.

pot pork for *v.* [20C+] (*W.I.*) **1** of a young woman, to cook special meals for the object of one's affections. **2** to get a husband through deliberate scheming.

pots *adj.* (*also* **potsy**) [POTTY *adj.*[1] (4)] [1920s–30s] insane, eccentric.

pots and dishes *n.* [rhy. sl.] [1970s] wishes.

potskie *v. see* POTCHKY *v.*

potsy *n.* [the tin (used for *pots*) that is allegedly made into badges; also note *potsy*, a flat stone used for the game of *potsy* (UK: *hopscotch*)] [1930s+] (*US*) a police badge, an identification card.

potsy *adj. see* POTS *adj.*

potted *adj.*[1] (*also* **poted, potted off, potted out**) [SE *pot*, a container for drink] [20C+] (*US*) drunk.

potted *adj.*[2] [2000s] (*Aus.*) pregnant.

potted bush *n.* [SE *potted*, confined in a small space + BUSH *n.*[1] (5a)] [1950s+] (*drugs*) hashish.

potted head *adj.* [rhy. sl.] [1990s+] dead.

potted off *adj. see* POTTED *adj.*[1].

potted (out) *adj.*[1] [gardening imagery] **1** [mid–late 19C] confined. **2** [mid–late 19C] dead and buried. **3** [late 19C] snubbed, suppressed.

potted (out) *adj.*[2] [POT *n.*[3] (1)] [1960s+] (*drugs*) intoxicated by marijuana.

potted out *adj. see* POTTED *adj.*[1].

potter-carrier *n.* [mispron.] [mid-18C] an apothecary.

potting *n.*[1] [SE *pot*] [mid-19C] drinking.

potting *n.*[2] *see* POT *v.* (2).

potty *n.*[1] [SE *pot*, which they mend] [late 19C] a tinker.

potty *n.*[2] [POTTY *adj.*[1] (4)] [1950s] a fool.

potty *adj.*[1] [SE *pot*, a tankard, thus lit. 'drunken'] **1** [mid-19C+] usu. of a plan or scheme, dubious, indifferent. **2** [mid-19C+] insignificant, feeble. **3** [late 19C+] easy to manage, simple. **4** [20C+] crazy, eccentric; thus *potty about*, madly in love with, obsessed by. **5** [1900s] (*Aus.*) drunk.

IN COMPOUNDS

❑ **potty house** *n.* [1900s–30s] a lunatic asylum.

potty *adj.*[2] [POT *n.*[1] (3)] [1950s] (*US*) chubby.

potty mouth *n.* [colloq. *potty*, a chamberpot] [1960s+] (*US*) one who uses a great deal of obscenities.

potty watch *n.* [colloq. *potty*, a chamberpot] [2000s] (*US prison*) the special duty of checking a prisoner's body waste for contraband.

pot wallop *v.* [POT-WALLOPER *n.*] **1** [mid-19C] to drink heavily. **2** [1920s–50s] to wash dishes.

pot-walloper *n.* [a pun on SE *pot-walloper*, lit. 'the boiler of a pot'. 'The term applied in some English boroughs, before the Reform Act of 1832, to a man qualified for a parliamentary vote as a householder (i.e. tenant of a house or distinct part of one) as distinguished from one who was merely a member or inmate of a householder's family; the test of which was his having a separate fire-place, on which his own pot was boiled or food cooked for himself and his family' (*OED*)] **1** [mid-19C+] a scullion, a kitchen servant. **2** [late 19C] (*US*) a slovenly person. **3** [late 19C] a heavy drinker.

potz *n. see* PUTZ *n.*

potzer *n. see* PATZER *n.*

pouch *n.* [mid-19C; 1940s+] **1** the vagina. **2** women considered purely as sex objects.

pouch *v.*[1] [SE *pouch*, to place in a bag] **1** [early 19C–1920s] to steal, to grab. **2** [mid-19C] to give a gift of money. **3** [late 19C] to eat. **4** [1910s] (*Aus.*) to drink.

pouch *v.*[2] *see* POOCH *v.*

pouf/pouffe *n. see* POOF *n.*

poufter *n. see* POOFTER *n.*

poufy *adj. see* POOFY *adj.*[2].

pough! *excl. see* FAUGH! *excl.*

poulain *n.* [synon. Fr., which also means the penis] [mid-17C–early 19C] a venereal bubo.

poule *n.* [adoption of Fr. sl. *poule*, a prostitute (lit. 'a chicken')] [1920s+] a prostitute; thus *poule-de-luxe*, a high-class prostitute, a courtesan.

poulter *v. see* POLTER *v.*

poulterer *n.* [he 'guts' the letters] [early 19C] a thief who specializes in removing the contents of letters; thus *poultry-rig*, the crime thus performed.

poultice *n.* **1** [late 19C] (*UK society*) a high stiff collar, which resembles a medical poultice. **2** [late 19C] (*UK society*) a fat woman. **3** [late 19C] a Bohemian. **4** [20C+] (*Aus.*) a large sum of money; a bribe. **5** [20C+] (*Ulster*) an unpleasantly persistent person. **6** [1900s] (*UK Und.*) a heavy blow. **7** [1920s] (*US Und.*) a story designed to deceive. **8** [1920s–60s] (*US tramp*) a dish of bread and gravy. **9** [1930s] (*US prison*) a sandwich spread with butter and jam or any other two ingredients. **10** [1930s–50s] a mortgage. **11** [1940s] (*US Und.*) a money belt. **12** [1980s+] (*Aus.*) a large number. **13** [1980s+] (*N.Z.*) a very large sandwich with multiple ingredients.

IN PHRASES

❑ **poultice over the peeper** *n.* [PEEPER *n.* (1)] [late 19C] a blow on the eye. ❑ **sling a poultice** *v.* [1950s+] (*Aus.*) to offer a bribe.

poultry *n.* [play on CHICKEN *n.* (1)] [17C] **1** women in general. **2** prostitutes; thus *poulter* a pimp.

poultry dealer *n.* [play on CHICKEN *n.* (4d)] [1950s+] (*US gay*) a pimp who trades in young homosexuals.

pounce *n.* [PONCE *n.* (1)] [2000s] a pimp; thus a general term of abuse.

SE in slang uses

IN PHRASES

❑ **get the pounce** *v.* [1910s] (*US*) to be sponged upon.

pounce-shicer *n.* (*also* **ponce shicer**) [PONCE *n.* (1) + SHICER *n.* (3)] [19C] a pimp.

pound *n.*[1] [rhy. sl.; *pound of lead* = head] [late 19C–1910s] the human head.

pound *n.*[2]
SE in slang uses
IN PHRASES
❑ **you don't get many of those to the pound** [20C+] a phr. used by leering men observing a woman with large breasts.

pound *n.*[3] [an era when the *pound* sterling equalled $5] **1** [1920s+] (*US*) money, esp. $1 or $5. **2** [1950s+] (*US Und.*) a five-year sentence.
IN COMPOUNDS
❑ **pound note** *see* separate entries.
IN PHRASES
❑ **pounds to peanuts** *adv.* [20C+] (*Aus./UK*) for sure, certainly.

pound *n.*[4] [SE *pound*, an enclosure] [1960s+] (*Aus. Und.*) the punishment cells.

pound *n.*[5] [1990s+] **1** an act of sexual intercourse [POUND *v.*[2] (1)]. **2** (*US black*) the hitting together of fists or a slap on the back used as a greeting [SE *pound*, to hit].

pound *n.*[6] [? link to a weight] [1990s+] (*US*) a .357 handgun.

pound *v.*[1] (*also* **pound it**) [the cockfighting practice of offering £10 to 5s, a very extravagant bet which was known as *pounding a cock*. If no one took it the match was automatically off] [early–mid-19C] to place a bet that one is sure one will win.
DERIVATIVES
❑ **poundable** *adj.* [early 19C] certain, definite, inevitable, esp. as regards the result of a wager.

pound *v.*[2] **1** [1920s+] (*US*) of a man, to perform sex vigorously. **2** [1970s+] (*US black/campus*) to drink beer quickly.
SE in slang uses
IN COMPOUNDS
❑ **pound-text** *n.* [his thumping of the Bible] [late 18C–19C] a parson.
IN PHRASES
❑ **go pound salt (up one's ass)** *v.* [20C+] (*US*) a euph. for GO TO HELL! *under* HELL *n.* ❑ **pound a cotton** *v. see under* COTTON *n.* ❑ **pound brass** *v.* [1910s] (*US*) to work as a telegraph operator. ❑ **pound off** *v.* [1970s+] (*orig. US*) to masturbate. ❑ **pound one's...** *v. see also under* relevant nouns. ❑ **pound one's ear** *v.* (*also* **pound one's pillow, ...the bell**) [tramps attempting to sleep in the boxcars of US railroads as they bumped over the rails] [late 19C–1960s] (*US*) to sleep; thus n. *ear-pounding*. ❑ **pound sand in a rathole** *v.* [late 19C+] (*US*) to be reasonably intelligent; usu. in phr. *not enough sense to pound sand in a rat hole*. ❑ **pound sand up one's ass** *v.* [1970s] (*US*) to suffer. ❑ **pound someone's name** *v.* [20C+] (*W.I.*) to denigrate someone, to criticize someone behind their back. ❑ **pound the...** *v. see also under* relevant nouns. ❑ **pound the headboard** *v.* (*also* **pound the mattress, ...the springs**) [1940s+] (*US campus*) to have sexual intercourse. ❑ **pound the pavement** *v.* (*also* **pound the asphalt, ...streets**) **1** [19C+] (*US Und.*) (*also* **walk the pavement, ...pave, pound the blocks, trudge the street**) to work as a street prostitute; thus adj. *pavement-pounding*, street-walking. **2** [20C+] (*US*) to walk the streets, esp. in search of a job. **3** [1900s–30s] of a police officer, to walk the streets. **4** [1990s+] (*US drugs*) to search for drugs, which can often require hours of walking. ❑ **pound the rails** *v.* (*also* **pound the ties**) [1910s] (*US*) to travel by train, esp. as a hobo. ❑ **pound the shit out of** *v. see* BEAT THE SHIT OUT OF *v.*

poundage cove *n.* [SE *poundage*, 'an impost, duty, or tax of so much per pound sterling on merchandise' (*OED*) + COVE *n.* (1)] [mid-19C] (*UK Und.*) 'a fellow who receives poundage for procuring customers for damaged goods' (Kent, *Modern Flash Dict.*, 1835); the share of a prostitute's fee which is given to the madam of a brothel.

poundcake *n.* **1** [1930s+] (*US*) an attractive woman. **2** [1970s+] (*US gay*) the buttocks. **3** [1990s+] (*US*) pornographic writing or magazines.
IN PHRASES
❑ **make poundcake** *v.* [1980s+] (*US gay*) to have anal intercourse.

pounded *adj.* [SE *pound*, an enclosure where animals are kept/*impound*, to lock up] [early–mid-19C] caught out in some form of (? homosexual) impropriety.

pounder *n.* **1** [17C] in pl., the testicles [? their knocking together]. **2** [1930s–60s] (*US black*) a police officer [abbr. *BEAT POUNDER under* BEAT *n.*[1]].

pounding match *n.* [mid-19C] a boxing match, a fight.

pound it *v. see* POUND *v.*[1].

pound note *n.*[1] [rhy. sl.] [20C+] a coat.

pound note *n.*[2] **1** [1930s–40s] (*US*) $5 [the contemporary exchange rate of $5 = £1]. **2** [1920s–70s] an upper-class person [i.e. rich]. **3** [1950s] any sum of money.

pound-note *adj.* (*also* **pound-noteish**) [POUND NOTE *n.*[2] (2)] [1920s–70s] pompous, affected, pretentious; upper-class.

pound of butter *n.* [rhy. sl. = NUTTER *n.* (1)] [1980s+] an eccentric, a mad person.

pound of lead *n.* (*also* **pound o' lead**) [rhy. sl.] [late 19C–1900s] the head.

poundrel *n.* [SE *poundrel*, scales] [17C] the head.

pounds and pence *n.* [rhy. sl.] [20C+] sense.

pour it on *v.* **1** [1930s+] (*orig. US*) to make a great effort; to intensify one's efforts; of a vehicle, to accelerate. **2** [1950s+] (*also* **pour it to**) to punish harshly. **3** [1960s] (*US*) to seek a verbal or physical confrontation. **4** [1960s] to have sexual intercourse. **5** [1980s] to speak in any form of extreme manner – flattery, telling a 'hard-luck story' – in order to gain money or emotional advantage.

pour-man *n.* [pun] [1940s] (*US black*) a bartender.

pour (on) the coal *v.* [railroad use] **1** [1940s+] (*US*) of a person or a vehicle, to accelerate. **2** [1950s] to punish severely.

pour the pork *v. see under* PORK *n.*

pout *n.* [SE *pullet*, a young hen] [mid-18C] a mistress.

pouter *n.* [i.e. 'that which pouts'] **1** [late 18C–19C] the vagina; in pl., the labia. **2** [1910s] (*Aus.*) the male chest.

pov *n.* (*also* **povvo**) [SE *pov*erty-stricken/im*pov*erished] [1990s+] (*UK juv.*) an impoverished person.

poverty *n.* [its effect and/or its drinkers] [early–mid-18C] gin.

poverty-basket *n.* [early 19C] a wicker cradle.

Poverty Row *n.* [late 19C] (*US*) a metaphorical 'street' denominating a state of impoverishment.

poverty-truck *n.* [no absolute definition is available (*see* Cassidy & LePage, *Dict. of Jamaican English*, 1967, 1992)] [1920s] (*W.I.*) ? a small hand-cart.

povvo *n. see* POV *n.*

powder *n.*[1] **1** [1910s–60s] (*US*) a drink of liquor [joc. use of SE *powder*, a medicine or a dose of medicine]. **2** [1920s+] (*drugs*) any form of powdered drug, e.g. heroin, cocaine, amphetamine.
IN COMPOUNDS
❑ **powder factory** *n.* [1970s] a wholesale distribution centre for narcotics. ❑ **powder puff** *n. see* separate entry.
IN PHRASES
❑ **powder one's nose** *v. see* separate entry. ❑ **powder up** *v.* [1930s–60s] (*US*) to drink alcohol; to become drunk.

powder *n.*[2]
IN PHRASES
❑ **take a powder** *v.* (*also* **do a powder, pull a powder**) [abbr. RUN-OUT POWDER *n.*] **1** [1910s+] to escape, to run away; also as imper. **2** [1940s+] to leave without paying one's rent. **3** [1940s+] of a boxer, to lose deliberately.

powder *v.*[1] [the explosive qualities of powder; 20C+ ety. more likely abbr. POWDER *n.*[2]] [mid-17C–mid-19C; 20C+] to move fast, to run off.
IN COMPOUNDS
❑ **powder car** *n.* [1940s] (*US Und.*) a car used by criminals to flee from the scene of the crime.

powder *v.*[2] [fig. to reduce to powder] (*Aus./US*) **1** [1900s] to hit very hard. **2** [1930s–80s] to kill, to murder.

powdered chalk *n.* [rhy. sl.] [late 19C+] a walk; thus *take a powdered chalk*, to take a walk.

powdering tub *n.* (*also* **pickling tub**) [SE *powdering/pickling tub*, the tub in which the flesh of dead animals was pickled or 'powdered'] **1** [late 16C–early 19C] the sweating tub used for the cure of venereal disease. **2** [late 17C–early 19C] the hospital for sexual diseases, near Kingsland, London. **3** [mid-19C] (*UK Und.*) shoes or boots.

powder one's nose *v.* (*also* **powder one's schnoz**) [SCHNOZZLE *n.*; pun on SE euph. for visiting the lavatory] [1970s+] (*drugs*) to take cocaine.

powder puff *n.* **1** [1920s+] an effeminate male homosexual [the term was notoriously used to attack the silent film god Rudolph Valentino (1895–1926)]. **2** [1950s] a cautious fighter. **3** [1990s+] (*W.I.*) a special woman.

powderpuff *adj.* [POWDER PUFF *n.*/SE *powder puff*] (*US*) **1** [1930s–60s] of a man, weak. **2** [1960s] of a woman, pampered.

powder wagon *n.* [like SE *powder-wagon* it carries an explosive charge] [1920s] (*US Und.*) a sawn-off shotgun.

power *n.* **1** [mid-19C+] the penis. **2** [late 19C–1930s] (*US black*) money. **3** [1920s] (*US Und.*) nitroglycerin. **4** [1990s+] (*US prison*) constr. with *the*, the authorities.

SE in slang uses

(IN COMPOUNDS)

❑ **power dance** *n.* *see* BLACK POWER DANCE *n.* ❑ **powerhouse** *n.* [1910s+] a strong, important, energetic and influential person. ❑ **power point** *n.* [play on SLANT *n.* (3); ety. offered by a respondent to Moore, *Lexicon of Cadet Language* (1993), 'So called because in a power point, that is the socket in the wall, the two top holes for the plug are on a slant and look like slanting eyes, and the bottom hole is vertical and looks like a nose, so the whole power point is said to resemble an Asian face '] [1990s+] (*Aus.*) a derog. term for an Asian. ❑ **power sludge** *n.* [1980s] (*US campus*) coffee. ❑ **power tool** *see* separate entries. ❑ **power trip** *see* separate entries.

(IN PHRASES)

❑ **more power to your elbow** (*also* **more power to your small clothes, more speed to your elbow**) [early 19C+] an excl. of encouragement.

power *v.* [SE *power*, to move with speed or force] **1** [1980s] (*US*) to persuade through threats and/or violence. **2** [1980s+] (*US campus*) to drink beer quickly.

(IN PHRASES)

❑ **power on** *v.* (*also* **power through**) [1980s+] (*US campus*) to do well, to succeed.

power *adv.* [SE *powerfully*] [1980s+] (*US campus*) extremely.

power tool *n.* [SE *power*, supreme, outstanding + TOOL *n.*[1] (1c)] **1** [1960s+] (*US campus*) a very annoying person. **2** *see* TOOL *n.*[1] (2g).

power tool *v.* [POWER TOOL *n.* (2)/SE *power* + TOOL *n.*[1] (2g)] [1980s] (*US campus*) to study hard.

power trip *n.* [SE *power* + TRIP *n.*[4] (2a)] [1970s+] (*orig. US*) a show of personal power, esp. if blatant.

power-trip *v.* [POWER TRIP *n.*] [1970s+] (*orig. US*) to exercise one's personal power, esp. at the expense of others.

powo *adj.* [exaggerated pron. of SE *poor*] [2000s] (*Aus.*) impoverished.

powter *v.* *see* POLTER *v.*

pow-wow *n.* [POW-WOW *v.*] **1** [19C+] a meeting. **2** [mid–late 19C] a noise, a commotion. **3** [late 19C] a fight. **4** [late 19C+] a chat, a conversation.

pow-wow *v.* [Algonkin (Narragansett) *pow'waw* or *po'wah*, a priest, a medicine man; thus the ceremonies over which such figures officiated and thus any gathering or conference] [mid-19C+] (*orig. US*) to chat, to converse with, to talk to.

pox *n.*[1] [the SE *pocks* or eruptive pustules on the skin that are a sign of syphilis; SE *pox* is smallpox; syphilis was also called the *great* or *grand* pox, to distinguish it from 'lesser' venereal diseases] **1** [16C+] syphilis. **2** [17C–18C] constr. with *the*, a synon. for *fuck/hell* etc, esp. in interrog. phrs., e.g. *who the…*, *how the…* **3** [17C+] any venereal disease.

(DERIVATIVES)

❑ **poxed** *adj.* [17C+] venereally diseased, esp. suffering from syphilis; also used fig.

(IN COMPOUNDS)

❑ **pox bottle** *n.* *see* POXHEAD *n.* ❑ **pox doctor** *n.* [mid-18C; 1930s+] a doctor specializing in venereal diseases. ❑ **pox-doctor's clerk** *n.* *see* separate entry. ❑ **pox-eaten** *adj.* (*also* **pox-rotten**) [1930s–50s] a general negative. ❑ **pox-eyed** *adj.* *see* POXY-FACED *under* POXY *adj.* ❑ **poxhead** *n.* *see* separate entry. ❑ **pox hospital** *n.* [1930s–40s] a hospital or clinic specializing in sexually transmitted diseases.

(IN PHRASES)

❑ **get the pox out (of)** *v.* [1970s] a euph. for *GET THE FUCK OUT under* FUCK *n.*

(IN EXCLAMATIONS)

❑ **pox!, a** (*also* **pocks! pox!**) [mid-16C+] a general excl. of annoyance, irritation. ❑ **pox on —!** (*also* **pox of —! pox to —!**) [20C+ use is historical] [late 16C–early 19C] a general oath. ❑ **pox take —!** [17C–18C] a general oath of dismissal. ❑ **what a pox!** (*also* **with a pox!**) [late 16C+] a general excl. of annoyance, irritation.

pox *n.*[2] [? abbr. *YEN POK under* YEN *n.*[1]] [1930s–50s] (*drugs*) opium.

pox *v.* [POX *n.*[1] (1)] [late 16C–mid-19C] to infect with syphilis.

pox-doctor's clerk *n.*

(IN PHRASES)

❑ **done/dressed/mockered up like a pox doctor's clerk** [1930s+] (*UK/Aus.*) flashily dressed, overdressed. ❑ **got up like a pox-doctor's clerk** [SE *got up*, dressed up] [1930s+] describing someone who is very smartly (too smartly) dressed.

poxer *n.* [POX *n.*[1] (1)] [2000s] a term of abuse.

poxhead *n.* (*also* **pox bottle**) [POX *n.*[1] (1) + -HEAD *sfx* (1)] [1980s+] (*Aus./Irish*) a general term of abuse.

poxy *adj.* [POX *n.*[1] (1)] **1** [1920s+] unpleasant, dirty, disgusting. **2** [1950s+] piffling.

(IN COMPOUNDS)

❑ **poxy-faced** *adj.* (*also* **pox-eyed, poxy-puss**) [PUSS *n.*[2] (1)] [1930s–60s] a general term of abuse, lit. 'syphilitic-faced'.

pozz *adj.* *see* POS *adj.*[1].

pozzie/pozzy *n.* *see* POSSIE *n.*

p.p. *n.* [abbr.] **1** [late 19C; 1930s] a *p*ick*p*ocket. **2** [1900s] a beggar who encases his legs in *p*laster of *P*aris soaked bandages to counterfeit a serious illness. **3** [1920s+] (*Irish*) a *p*arish *p*riest.

p.p.c. *n.* [abbr. Fr. *pour prendre congé*, to take leave, written on a visiting card] [late 19C] (*UK society*) a curt, barely polite farewell; thus as v., *p.p.c.*, to fall out, to quarrel, to 'cut'.

p.p.d. *n.* [abbr. *p*ossible/*p*otential *p*rom *d*ate] [1980s+] (*US campus*) an attractive person of the opposite sex.

PP9-ing *n.* [2000s] (*UK prison*) an act of coshing another prisoner with a sock or similar loaded with PP9 batteries.

p.q. *n.* [abbr. *p*olyester *q*ueen] [1980s+] (*US campus*) someone who is out of date, unfashionable.

P.R. *n.* [abbr.] (*US*) **1** [20C+] *P*uerto *R*ico. **2** [1950s+] a *P*uerto *R*ican.

p.r. *n.* [abbr.] **1** [19C] the *p*rize *r*ing, a generic term for the world of prize-fighting and pugilism. **2** [1960s+] (*drugs*) marijuana [abbr. *P*anama *R*ed].

prad *n.* (*also* **praddle, pred**) [Du. *paard*, a horse; ult. Lat. *paraveredus*, which gives the SE *palfrey*, a riding horse as opposed to a war-horse] [18C–1930s] (*20C use Aus./N.Z. only*) a horse; thus *pradback*, horseback.

(IN COMPOUNDS)

❑ **prad borrower** *n.* [late 18C] (*UK Und.*) one who steals a horse, but (sometimes) returns him. ❑ **prad cove** *n.* [COVE *n.* (1)] [mid-19C] (*UK Und.*) a horse dealer. ❑ **pradholder** *n.* [early 19C] a bridle. ❑ **prad lay** *n.* [LAY *n.*[3] (1)] [18C–mid-19C] the stealing of bags from horses. ❑ **prad layer** *n.* [18C] one who steals baggage from horses, taking advantage of the darkness to cut the bindings. ❑ **prad-napper** *n.* [NAP *v.*[1] (6)] [late 18C] a horse-thief. ❑ **prad-napping** *n.* (*also* **pred-napping**) [19C] horse-stealing. ❑ **prad prigger** *n. see* PRIGGER OF PRANCERS *under* PRIGGER *n.*[1].

prag *n.* [var. on PRIG *n.*[1] (2)] [late 16C] (*UK Und.*) a thief.

prairie nigger *n. see under* NIGGER *n.*[1].

prairie wool *n.* [1930s] (*US*) grass.

pram *n.*[1] [synon. Du. *praam*] [1910s] (*S.Afr.*) the female breast.

pram *n.*[2] **1** [1920s–30s] (*Scot.*) in pl., the legs. **2** [1940s] (*UK Und.*) a large car.

SE in slang uses

IN COMPOUNDS

❑ **pram-face** *n.* [2000s] a derog. term for a working class, council-estate dwelling young woman and single mother.

IN PHRASES

❑ **get out of one's pram** *v.* (*also* **jump out of one's pram**) [1950s+] to lose one's temper. ❑ **out of one's pram** *adj.* [1960s] (*Aus.*) reacting in an extreme manner.

pram! pram! *excl.* [echoic] [1980s+] (*W.I./UK black teen*) a sound made by the mouth, simulating gun shots fired in appreciation of something, such as a dancehall song etc.

prancegagger *n.* [SE *prancer*, a mettlesome, spirited horse] [mid-18C] (*UK Und.*) a bridle.

prancer *n.* (*also* **prauncer**) [SE *prancer*, a mettlesome, spirited horse] [mid-16C–mid-19C] (*UK Und.*) **1** a horse. **2** a highwayman. **3** a horse thief. **4** a cavalry officer.

IN COMPOUNDS

❑ **prancer's nab** *n.* (*also* **prancer's nob, ...poll**) [NAB *n.*[1] (1)/NOB *n.*[1] (1)/SE *poll*, head] [late 17C–early 19C] (*UK Und.*) a horse's head seal, when used for counterfeiting documents. ❑ **prancer's poll** *n.* [late 17C–early 19C] (*UK Und.*) a horse's head, usu. in ref. to the popular public house name, 'The Nag's Head'.

prancers *n.* [one *prances* up them] [mid-18C] (*UK Und.*) stairs.

prang *n.* [? echoic; ? mispron. of SE *prank*] **1** [1940s+] a crash. **2** [1950s] a joke or prank.

prang *adj.* [? PRANG *n.* (1)] [1990s+] (*black*) extremely intoxicated, esp. by crack cocaine.

prang *v.* [PRANG *n.* (1); orig. WW2 RAF use; note 1960s US Air Force Academy *prang in*, to make a very serious mistake] [1940s+] **1** (*also* **prang in**) to attack, to crash one's car, or plane. **2** to break, e.g. an arm, a leg. **3** to have sexual intercourse.

pranker *n.* [PRANCER *n.* (1)] [late 16C] (*UK Und.*) a horse.

prannet *n.* [PRANNIE *n.*] [1970s] a fool, an idiot.

prannie *n.* (*also* **pranny**) [? Scot. *pran/prann*, to squeeze, to crush] **1** [late 19C+] the vagina. **2** [1980s+] a general term of contempt [fig. use of sense 1].

pra-pra *adj.* [PRA-PRA *v.*] [20C+] (*W.I.*) cheating, mixed up.

pra-pra *v.* [Twi *pra*, to carry away] [20C+] (*W.I.*) to snatch, to steal.

prat *n.*[1] (*also* **pratt, pratte, praty**) [? echoic of the buttocks hitting a hard surface; subseq. senses are fig. uses of sense 1] **1** [16C+] (*orig. UK Und.*) a buttock, the buttocks. **2** [late 17C–early 19C] a tinder-box. **3** [19C+] the vagina. **4** [20C+] a young woman. **5** [1910s+] (*US*) a hip pocket; thus *prat-digger*, a pickpocket; *prat frisk*, the theft of a wallet from a hip pocket; *prat leather*, a wallet kept in the hip pocket; *prat poke*, a wallet stolen from the hip pocket. **6** [1960s+] a general term of abuse; mainly a fool, an idiot. **7** [1970s] (*US*) a young homosexual man.

DERIVATIVES

❑ **pratful** *n.* [1970s] a tiny or insignificant amount. ❑ **prattish** *adj.* [1990s+] stupid.

IN COMPOUNDS

❑ **prat-boy** *n.* (*also* **pratt-boy**) **1** [1940s–50s] (*US*) a catamite. **2** [2000s] (*US*) one who takes the punishment for another's crime, a FALL GUY *n.* (1). ❑ **pratfall** *n.* [orig. theatre jargon *pratfall*, a fall onto the buttocks, usu. as part of a slapstick routine] [1950s+] (*orig. US*) **1** a humiliating defeat, a sudden failure. **2** a danger, a pitfall. ❑ **prat-kick** *n.* [KICK *n.*[4]] [1910s–40s] (*US Und.*) the back pocket of one's trousers.

IN PHRASES

❑ **get someone's pratt** *v.* [1950s] (*US prison*) to annoy someone, to drive someone to lose their temper.

prat *n.*[2] [survival of AS *prat*, a piece of trickery] [1960s] (*US black*) a hoax, a deception, a confidence trick.

prat *v.*[1] [Rom. *praster*, to run] **1** [16C+] to beat. **2** [late 19C–1910s] to go.

prat *v.*[2] (*also* **pratt**) **1** Und. uses [PRAT *n.*[1] (1)]. (**a**) [mid-19C] (*UK Und.*) to eject, to throw out. (**b**) [mid-19C] (*UK Und.*) to sit down, to make someone sit down. (**c**) [mid-19C+] (*UK/US Und.*) in pickpocketing, to back gently into the victim, pushing them against the primary pickpocket (WIRE *n.*[2]) who actually takes the wallet, money etc. **2** as lit. or fig. teasing [PRAT *n.*[1] (1) or PRAT *n.*[2]]. (**a**) [1930s–50s] (*US black*) of a woman, to play sexually hard to get, to tease physically [note PRAT *n.*[1] (3)]. (**b**) [1940s–60s] (*US*) of a confidence trickster, to play with the potential victim. **3** [1950s] (*US Und.*) to have sexual intercourse; esp. homosexual anal intercourse. **4** [1960s] (*Aus.*) to place.

IN PHRASES

❑ **prat about** *v.* (*also* **prat around**) [PRAT *n.*[1] (6)] [1960s+] to act foolishly, to act in an irritating manner. ❑ **prat for** *v.* (*also* **pratt for**) [PRAT *n.*[1] (1)] **1** [1940s–50s] (*US drugs*) in weak use of sense 2, to work for in an subordinate role. **2** [1940s+] (*gay*) to indulge, actively or passively, in anal intercourse. ❑ **prat in** *v.* (*also* **prat oneself in, prat one's frame in**) [PRAT *n.*[1] (1)/FRAME *n.*[1] (1)] [20C+] (*Aus.*) to push oneself forward, to barge in. ❑ **prat someone in** *v.* [PRAT *n.*[1] (1)] [20C+] (*US Und.*) for a pickpocket's assistant to push the victim so as to place them in the correct position for the theft.

prat *v.*[3] [abbr. SE *prattle*] [1910s+] (*Aus.*) to talk to someone.

prate/pratee *n. see* PRATIE *n.*

prater *n.*[1] [SE *prater*, an obnoxious or idle talker] **1** [mid-16C–18C] a boaster. **2** [late 17C–19C] an itinerant, bogus preacher. **3** [19C] the mouth.

prater *n.*[2] *see* PRATIE *n.*

prate-roast *n.* [SE *prate*, chatter] [late 17C–mid-19C] a talkative boy.

pratie *n.* (*also* **parate, parater, paratie, prate, pratee, prater, praty**) [pron.] [late 18C+] (*Anglo-Irish*) a potato.

IN COMPOUNDS

❑ **pratee-trap** *n. see* POTATO-TRAP *under* POTATO *n.* ❑ **pratie-machine** *n. see* POTATO-EATER *under* POTATO *n.*

prating cheat *n.* (*also* **pratling chete, prattling cheat**) [SE *prate*, to talk, to chatter + CHEAT *n.* (1)] [mid-16C–mid-19C] (*UK Und.*) the tongue.

pratt *see under* PRAT.

pratte *n. see* PRAT *n.*[1].

pratter *n.* [PRAT *v.*[2] (3)] [1920s] (*US*) a homosexual who takes the passive role in sodomy.

pratting-ken *n.* [PRAT *n.*[1] (1) + KEN *n.*[1] (1), i.e. a place one can rest one's buttocks] [mid–late 19C] a cheap lodging house.

prattle-box *n.* [mid-17C–mid-18C] a chatterer, a gossip.

prattle-broth *n.* [the stereotypical chattering women supposed to gather around a tea-table] [late 18C–mid-19C] tea.

prattling-box *n.* [early 18C–early 19C] a pulpit.

prattling-cheat *n. see* PRATING CHEAT *n.*

prattling parlour *n.* [mid-19C] a private apartment.

prat whids *v.* [SE *prate*/PRAT *n.*[1] (1) + WHID *n.* (1), lit. 'speak buttock words'] [17C] to break wind.

praty *n.* **1** *see* PRAT *n.*[1]. **2** *see* PRATIE *n.*

prauncer *n. see* PRANCER *n.*

prawn *n.* [the image of the SE *prawn* as a 'humorous' or 'stupid' fish] [late 19C+] (*Aus.*) a fool.

prawnhead *n.* [PRAWN *n.* + -HEAD *sfx* (1)] [1960s+] (*Aus.*) a fool, a simpleton.

DERIVATIVES

❑ **prawn-headed** *adj.* [1960s+] (*Aus.*) foolish, stupid.

prawnie *n.* (*also* **prawny**) [1940s+] (*Aus.*) a fisher or seller of prawns.

prayer *n.*

SE in slang uses

IN COMPOUNDS

❑ **prayer-bones** *n.* (*also* **prayer-handles**) [one's genuflection] [late 19C–1940s] (*US black*) the knees. ❑ **prayer book** *n.* **1** [late 18C] (*UK Und.*) a small piece of stolen lead, which can be carried in a pocket. **2** [mid-19C+] (*US*) a pack of rolling papers. **3** [late 19C] *Ruff's Guide to the Turf*, the racing man's 'Bible'. ❑ **prayer-dukes** *n.* [DUKE *n.*[3] (1); they are clasped in prayer] [1920s–40s] (*US black*) the hands. ❑ **prayer-factory** *n.* [1930s–50s] (*Irish*) a convent. ❑ **prayer meeting** *n.* [the prayers are for good luck] [1940s] (*US gang*) a game of dice, a crap game.

IN PHRASES

❑ **at her last prayers** [late 17C–early 19C] a phr. used to typify an old maid.

pray to the porcelain god/goddess *v. see* KISS THE PORCELAIN GOD *under* PORCELAIN GOD *n.*

pray with one's knees upwards *v.* [i.e. in the 'missionary position'] [late 18C–early 19C] of a woman, to have sexual intercourse; the implication is of promiscuity.

pre *n.* [SE *pre-*, before, i.e. the age of consent] [2000s] a young (underage) sex object, male or female, seen as suitable for exploitation.

preach at Tyburn cross *v. see under* TYBURN *n.*

preach on Tower Hill *v.* [ironic use of SE *preach*, referring, perhaps, to the criminal's last words on the scaffold + *Tower Hill*, the site of many London executions] [16C] to be hanged.

preachy-preachy *adj.* [colloq. *preachy* + redup.; 20C+ use is W.I.] [early 19C+] tediously moralizing.

precheck *n.* [1970s+] an inspection of a client's penis made by a prostitute before intercourse.

precious juice *n.* [1980s+] (*US campus*) any alcoholic drink.

pred *n. see* PRAD *n.*

preem *n.* [abbr.] [1930s+] (*orig. US*) a theatrical or cinematic *premi*ère; thus *preem*, to have a première, a first night.

preemie *n.* (*also* **preemy, premie**) [abbr.] [1920s+] (*US*) a *pre*mature baby.

preesh! *excl.* [abbr. SE *appreciation*] [1980s+] (*US campus*) an expression of approval; thanks!

preg *adj.* (*also* **pregged**) [abbr.] [1950s+] (*US*) *preg*nant.

preggers *adj.* (*also* **preggars**) [abbr. SE *pregnant* + -ER *sfx*] [1940s+] pregnant.

preggo *adj.* (*also* **prego**) [abbr. + -O *sfx* (4)] [1950s+] (*Aus.*) pregnant.

preggy *adj.* [abbr. + sfx *-y*] [1930s+] pregnant.

pregnant *adj.* [1980s+] (*US drugs*) referring to a marijuana cigarette that is rolled badly, usu. with a bulge of cannabis in the middle.

prego *n.* [abbr. SE *pregnant*] [1950s+] (*US*) a pregnant teenager.

prego *adj. see* PREGGO *adj.*

preke *n.* (*also* **preky**) [Sp. *pereque*, an intolerable person] [1940s+] (*W.I.*) **1** a fool, a gullible person. **2** a low-class prostitute. **3** a good-for-nothing, an ill-kempt, dirty, slovenly man.

prekkah *v.* [PREKE *n.* (1)] [1990s+] (*W.I.*) to be exploited, to be 'put-upon'.

premie *n. see* PREEMIE *n.*

premises *n.* [euph.] **1** [late 17C–1900s] the vagina. **2** [19C] a brothel.

premiums *n.* [1990s+] (*US prison*) brandname, commercially produced cigarettes.

premmie *n.* [abbr. + sfx *-ie*] [1990s+] a *prem*ature ejaculator.

premo *adj.* [? abbr. SE *premium* + -O *sfx* (4)] [1990s+] amazing, excellent, attractive.

prems *n.* [abbr.] [1900s] *premises*, buildings.

pre-op *n.* [abbr.] [1990s+] (*US gay*) a *pre-op*erative transsexual.

prep *v.* (*also* **prep up**) [abbr.] **1** [20C+] (*US*) to *prep*are, to get ready. **2** [1980s] (*US campus*) (*also* **prep out**) to get dressed up, esp. over-dressed, or elaborately made up.

prepared *adj.*

IN PHRASES

❑ **are you prepared?** (*also* **are you ready?**) [1960s+] (*orig. US gay*) a phr. implying amazement or shock, both approving and disapproving.

preppie *n.* (*also* **prep, prepette, preppy, prepster**) [1950s+] (*US campus*) one who attends one of the major US 'prep' schools (St Paul's, Choate, Groton, Miss Porter's, Dana Hall etc), the equivalent of the UK's public (i.e. fee-paying, private) schools. The graduates of such schools are the children of the US establishment and share similar codes, styles, language and society.

preppie *adj.* (*also* **preppy**) (*US*) **1** [1900s] silly, immature [SAmE *prep* school]. **2** [1950s+] mainstream in style and thought, as a result of having been to a major US prep school [PREPPIE *n.*].

preppie *adv.* [1970s+] (*US/Can.*) in a manner pertaining to a PREPPIE *n.*

preppy *see under* PREPPIE.

pre-pre *v.* [dial. *pre-pre*, to lose control, to become hysterical] [1960s] (*W.I.*) to suffer from diarrhoea.

prepster *n. see* PREPPIE *n.*

pres *n. see* PREZ *n.*

presbo *n.* [abbr. SE + -O *sfx* (3)] [1950s+] (*Aus.*) a *Presb*yterian.

prescott *n. see* CHARLIE PRESCOTT *n.*

prescription *n.* **1** [1970s+] (*drugs*) any drug that comes primarily in pill form, barbiturates, amphetamines etc; thus *prescription reds*, Seconal [the SE *prescription* that is issued for it]. **2** [1980s+] (*drugs*) a marijuana cigarette [? 'just what the doctor ordered'].

presents *n.* [play on synon. SE *gift*] [late 19C+] white spots on one's fingernails, supposedly auguring good luck.

presh *adj.* [abbr. SE *precious*] [1980s+] (*US campus*) favourable, enjoyable.

preshun *n. see* PRUSHUN *n.*

president *n. see* DEAD PRESIDENT *under* DEAD *adj.*

President Franklin *n. see* BEN FRANKLIN *n.*

press *v.*

SE in slang uses

IN PHRASES

❑ **press blankets** *v. see* BEAT THE SHEETS *under* BEAT *v.* ❑ **press ham** *v. see under* HAM *n.*[1]. ❑ **press one's hair** *v.* [1960s–70s] (*US black*) to straighten one's hair. ❑ **press someone's button** *v. see under* BUTTON *n.*[1]. ❑ **press the bricks** *v. see under* BRICKS *n.* ❑ **press the button** *v. see under* BUTTON *n.*[1]. ❑ **press the ether** *v.* [1950s] (*US black*) to play music. ❑ **press the flesh** *v.* [1920s+] (*orig. US*) usu. of a politician on a campaign tour to meet the electors, to shake hands; thus *press-the-flesh*, ingratiating, insincere, oleaginous. ❑ **press the sheets** *v. see* BEAT THE SHEETS *under* BEAT *v.*

press and scratch *n.* [rhy. sl.] [19C] a safety-match.

press button *n.* (*also* **pressie**) [joc. mispron.; usu. Catholic use] [20C+] (*Aus./N.Z.*) a Presbyterian.

pressed *adj.* **1** [1950s+] (*US black*) very well dressed. **2** [1980s] (*US black*) used of hair that has been chemically straightened.

pressie *n.*[1] [abbr.] [1960s+] a gift, a *pres*ent.

pressie *n.*[2] *see* PRESS BUTTON *n.*

pretender to the throne *n. see under* THRONE *n.*

pretty *n.* **1** [mid-18C+] a pretty woman. **2** [1900s–50s] (*US*) usu. in pl., an attractive object, e.g. an item of jewellery or clothes. **3** [1970s+] an innocent, hitherto untouched young sex object, either male or female.

pretty-boy *n.* **1** [late 19C+] an effeminate-looking young man, though not necessarily a homosexual. **2** [1960s] (*S.Afr.*) a criminal who uses violence.

IN COMPOUNDS

❑ **pretty-boy clip** *n.* [late 19C] a hairstyle for men in which the hair is brushed straight forward over the forehead and cut in a straight line from ear to ear.

pretty horse breaker *n.* (*also* **horsebreaker**) [the way such women showed themselves off in a horse and trap, mixing with society as it too paraded in Hyde Park in London and similar places. Their riding costume was often known as ABANDONED HABITS *n.*] [mid-19C] a high-class prostitute; orig. a woman hired to ride in Hyde Park.

pretty police *n.* [1990s+] a policeman or police squad specializing in the entrapment of gay men.

pretty polly *n. see* POLLY *n.*[5].

pretty up *v.* [ironic reverse of SE] [1950s+] (*Aus.*) to disfigure.

pretzel *n.* [the shape] **1** [1930s–40s] (*US jazz*) a French horn; thus *pretzel bender*, a French horn player. **2** [1940s] a German [the stereotypically Ger. foodstuff].

SE in slang uses

IN PHRASES

❑ **do the naked pretzel** *v.* [supposed resemblance to a SE *pretzel*, a crisp biscuit, baked in the form of a knot] [1990s+] (*US campus*) to have sexual intercourse.

pretzels *n. see* PEANUT *n.* (1).

prevert *n.* [deliberate mispron. of SE] [1970s+] a pervert.

previous *n.* **1** [1930s+] (*UK Und./police*) previous convictions. **2** [2000s] (*Aus.*) a previous appointment.

previous *adj.* (*orig. US*) **1** [late 19C+] arriving or occurring too soon, hasty, premature. **2** [late 19C+] forward, cheeky, unacceptable or in poor taste; often as *that's a bit previous*. **3** [20C+] (*US*) usu. of clothing, tight, snug.

previous *adv.* [PREVIOUS *adj.* (1)] [late 19C–1900s] hastily, quickly.

previousness *n.* [PREVIOUS *adj.* (1)] [late 19C] (*US*) anything seen as coming too soon, too hastily or prematurely; the state of being too hasty or premature.

prexy *n.* (*also* **prex**) [mispron.] [early 19C+] (*orig. US college*) the *President* (i.e. of a college, a corporation or firm, but also of America).

prey *n.* [i.e. what one 'preys upon'] [late 17C–18C] (*UK Und.*) money.

prez *n.* (*also* **pres**) (*US*) **1** [late 19C+] a president, whether of a college or organization, or America itself. **2** [1950s+] (*US black*) an important, influential individual [note tenor saxophonist Lester Young (1909–59) was so nicknamed by Billie Holiday]. **3** [1950s+] a term of address, genuinely respectful or ironic.

prezzie *n.* (*also* **prezzo**) [abbr.] [1930s+] (*orig. Aus.*) a *present*.

price of... *n.* [20C+] (*Irish*) all one is worth, one's due desserts, one's fate; esp. as *the price of me*.

prick *n.* [SE *prick*, a pointed weapon or implement. Although the *OED*, with its first citation in 1592, labels it unequivocally as 'coarse slang', Partridge suggests that *prick* was SE before becoming taboo *c.*1700. The *OED*'s citation – 'The pissing Boye lift up his pricke' ('R.D.', *Hypnerotomachia*) – may appear coarse to modern ears, but it should be noted that *piss*, certainly, was still SE at the time. In 1540, *prick* denoted 'a pert, forward, saucy boy or youth; a conceited young fellow', thus sense 2. The term is defined as 'humorous or contemptuous', but not indecent; it might have referred simply to the lad's 'sharpness'. That said, a sexual interpretation is possible] **1** [mid-16C+] the penis. **2** [late 16C–17C] a woman's term of endearment for a man. **3** [1920s+] (*orig. US*) (*also* **pricker**) a general derog. term: an idiot, a fool, an incompetent. **4** [1950s] (*US drugs*) a hypodermic syringe. **5** [1970s] anything phallic, e.g. a flagpole. **6** [1970s] aggression, attacks.

DERIVATIVES

❑ **pricknic** *n.* [pun on SE *picnic* + EAT *v.* (4)] [1980s+] (*US gay*) fellatio. ❑ **pricky** *adj.* (*also* **prickish**) [1960s+] (*US*) obnoxious.

IN COMPOUNDS

❑ **prick-arsed** *adj.* (*also* **prick-nosed**) [-ARSED *sfx*/SE *nose*] [1980s] a term of abuse. ❑ **prick cheese** *n. see* COCK CHEESE *under* COCK *n.*[3]. ❑ **prick-chinking** *n.* [CHINK *n.*[2]] [18C] having sexual intercourse. ❑ **prick-ear/-eared** *see* separate entries. ❑ **prickface** *n.* [1960s+] a general term of abuse, lit. 'penis face'. ❑ **prickhead** *n.* [-HEAD *sfx* (1)] **1** [1980s+] a fool, a simpleton; used both derog. and affectionately. **2** [1990s+] a bald-headed man. ❑ **prick-holder** *n.* (*also* **prick-purse, -scourer, -skinner**) [19C] the vagina. ❑ **prick hole** *n.* [late 19C] the vagina. ❑ **prick-lick** *v.* [1920s+] (*US*) to perform fellatio; thus *prick-lick, prick-licker*, a fellator. ❑ **prick-nosed** *adj. see* PRICK-ARSED above. ❑ **prick office** *n.* [note OFFICE *n.* (1)] [mid-17C] either a brothel staffed by heterosexual male prostitutes or a group of regular brothel patrons. ❑ **prick peddler** *n. see* DICK PEDDLER *under* DICK *n.*[1]. ❑ **prick-pride** *n.* [late 19C] an erect penis. ❑ **prick-purse/-scourer** *n. see* PRICK-HOLDER above. ❑ **prickshaft** *n. see* SHAFT *n.* (1a). ❑ **prick-skinner** *n. see* PRICK-HOLDER above. ❑ **prick sucker** *n.* [late 19C+] one who performs fellatio, whether male or female. ❑ **pricksucking** *adj.* [1960s] of a woman, performing oral sex on a man. ❑ **pricktease/-teaser** *see* separate entries.

IN PHRASES

❑ **act the prick** *v.* [1980s+] to behave foolishly. ❑ **all prick and breeches** *n.* [1920s+] all talk and no action, a braggart, a fake. ❑ **all prick and no pence** *n.* [1920s] all talk and no action, a braggart, a fake. ❑ **all prick and ribs like a drover's dog** *adj.* (*also* **all prick and ribs like a shearer's dog, ...like a swaggie's dog**) [SWAGGIE *n.*] [1960s+] (*Aus.*) lean and eager. ❑ **do on one's prick** *v. see* DO SOMETHING ON ONE'S DICK *under* DICK *n.*[1]. ❑ **get on someone's prick** *v.* [1940s+] to annoy, to infuriate someone. ❑ **go prick scouring** *v.* [SCOUR *v.*[2] (3)] [late 19C] of a man, to have sexual intercourse. ❑ **like a spare prick at a wedding** *adv.* (*also* **like a spare dick on a honeymoon**) [the assumption is that only the bridegroom is necessary] [1930s+] absolutely uselesslessly; often preceded by *standing around*. ❑ **may your prick and purse never fail you** (*also* **may the two Ps never fail you, may your purse never fail you**) [early 18C–mid-19C] a popular toast. ❑ **more pricks than a second-hand dartboard** (*also* **more pricks than a pin-cushion, ...than a second-hand primus**) [1940s+] used of a promiscuous woman; usu. as *she's had more pricks...* ❑ **pour the prick** *v.* [1930s] (*US*) of a man, to have sexual intercourse. ❑ **prick around** *v.* [synon. FUCK ABOUT *v.* (1)] [1980s] to mess about. ❑ **pull one's prick** *v.* **1** [1960s–70s] to masturbate [PULL *v.* (6)]. **2** [1970s] to tease, to deceive. **3** [1980s] (*US*) to promote oneself. ❑ **put some flick in one's prick** *v.* [1940s–60s] (*Aus.*) of a man, to increase one's potency. ❑ **step on one's prick** *v. see* STEP ON ONE'S DICK *under* DICK *n.*[1].

prick *adj.* [PRICK *n.* (3)] [1960s+] (*US*) a general term of abuse: wretched, damnable.

prick *v.*[1] [PRICK *n.* (1)] [17C–mid-19C] to enter a woman.

prick *v.*[2]

SE in slang uses

IN COMPOUNDS

❑ **prickamouse** *n.* [1940s] (*US*) an insignificant, paltry person.

IN PHRASES

❑ **prick in the wicker for a dolphin** *v.* [ext. image based on SE *wicker*, i.e. the basket] [late 18C–mid-19C] to steal loaves from a baker's basket. ❑ **prick the garter** *n.* (*also* **prick (in) the belt, prick the girdle, pitch the nob**) [mid-18C–1930s] (*UK Und.*) a gambling and cheating game, in which a garter or belt is folded and held out to the punter, who bets that by pricking with a pin they can hit the place where the material is folded; almost inevitably they fail and lose their money. ❑ **prick-(the-)louse** *n.* [SE *prick*, i.e. the needlework + the lice that accrued to clothing] [early 16C–early 19C] a tailor; thus *prick a louse*, to work as a tailor. ❑ **prick the master vein** *v. see under* MASTER VEIN *n.*

prick-ear *n.* (*also* **prick-ears**) [PRICK-EARED *adj.* (2); the Roundheads and Puritans were typified by their tight-fitting black skullcaps, which sat above the ears] [mid-17C] a Roundhead, a Parliamentarian, 'a Crop, whose Ears are longer than his Hair' (B.E.).

prick-eared *adj.* [fig. use of SE] **1** [16C; 1980s] a term of abuse. **2** [mid-16C–18C] crop-headed, thus generic for a puritan.

pricker *n.*[1]

(IN PHRASES)

❑ **get the pricker** *v.* [SE *pricker*, that which pricks or pierces] [1940s–60s] (*Aus./ N.Z.*) to get angry, to lose one's temper.

pricker *n.*[2] *see* PRICK *n.* (3).

pricktease *n.* [PRICKTEASE *v.*] [1950s+] **1** a woman (or man in a homosexual context) who appears to be offering unrestrained sexual favours but stops short of intercourse, leaving the male partner frustrated. **2** in fig. use, any person or thing that keeps people wanting more.

pricktease *v.* [PRICK *n.* (1) + SE *tease*] [1940s+] to lead on sexually but to stop short of intercourse.

prickteaser *n.* [PRICKTEASE *v.*] [1940s+] a woman who allows some physical intimacies but who, no matter how daring, will always stop short of intercourse.

pride (and joy) *n.* [1930s–40s] (*Aus./US*) the penis.

pride and joy *n.* [rhy. sl.] [1930s–70s] (*Aus./US*) a boy.

pride-and-pockets *n.* [he has much pride, but empty pockets] [late 19C–1910s] a half-pay officer.

pride of the morning *n.* (*also* **morning pride**) [late 19C] an early morning erection, more due to the need to urinate than actual sexual desire.

priest-linked *adj.* [late 17C–early 19C] married.

priest of the blue bag *n.* [the trad. colour of the bag in which they carry their gown and wig] [mid-19C] a barrister.

priest's share *n.* [late 19C–1910s] (*Irish*) one's soul.

prig *n.*[1] (*also* **prigg, prigman**) [either Lat. *pregare*, to pray, or SE *prig* = prick = sting = rob or cheat. SE *prig*, meaning a carping know-all, may have similar roots, but may be based on the divine Richard Baxter (1615–91), who in 1684 associated it with the initial letters of *pr*oud *ig*norance] (*UK Und.*) **1** [16C–19C] a ne'er-do-well who, accompanied by his woman, wanders the country, mixing villainy and legitimate work, pursuing neither, it appears, with particular enthusiasm (sometimes known as the DRUNKEN TINKER *n.*). **2** [mid-16C–19C] a thief, esp. a mendicant villain who specializes in stealing clothes from hedgerows where they are left to dry, or poultry from the farmyard. **3** [late 17C–mid-19C] a dandy, a fop. **4** [18C–mid-19C] a cheat.

(DERIVATIVES)

❑ **priggish** *adj.* [late 17C–mid-19C] (*UK Und.*) having the characteristics of a thief. ❑ **prigster** *n. see* separate entry.

(IN COMPOUNDS)

❑ **prig-napper** *n.* (*also* **prigger-napper**) [NAP *v.*[1] (3)] [late 17C–early 19C] (*UK Und.*) a thief-taker, thus a policeman.

(IN PHRASES)

❑ **prince prig** *n.* [17C–early 19C] (*UK Und.*) **1** a leading thief, esp. one who acts as a receiver for the robberies of colleagues. **2** the King of the Gypsies.

prig *n.*[2] [? it is 'pricked' with spurs] [late 16C–mid-19C] a horse.

(IN COMPOUNDS)

❑ **prig-napper** *n.* [NAP *v.*[1] (6)] [late 17C–18C] (*UK Und.*) a horse-thief.

prig *v.*[1] [SE *prick*, to urge a horse forward] **1** [mid-16C–early 19C] to ride; thus n., *prigger*, a rider. **2** [17C–early 19C] to have sexual intercourse [i.e. RIDE *v.* (1a), but note PRICK *v.*[1]].

(IN COMPOUNDS)

❑ **prig-beard** *n.* [BEARD *n.* (1)] [late 16C–early 17C] a degenerate, a seducer.

prig *v.*[2] (*also* **prigg**) [? SE *prick*, to skewer] (*UK/US Und.*) **1** [mid-16C–1910s] to steal; thus *priggism, priggery, priggyism*, theft. **2** [mid-18C–mid-19C] to cheat, to swindle, to haggle.

(IN PHRASES)

❑ **prig and buzz** *n.* [BUZZ *v.*[1] (3a)] [late 18C] the act of pickpocketing; thus v., *work upon the prig and buzz*.

prigg *see also under* PRIG.

prigg *n.* [rhy. sl.; *Wally Prigg* = GIG *n.*[11] (3)] [1940s–50s] (*Aus.*) a busybody.

prigger *n.*[1] [PRIG *v.*[2] (1)] **1** [mid-16C–mid-19C] a thief; thus *priggery, priggism*, theft. **2** [late 17C] a highwayman.

(IN COMPOUNDS)

❑ **prigger-napper** *n. see* PRIG-NAPPER *under* PRIG *n.*[1].

(IN PHRASES)

❑ **prigger of prancers** *n.* (*also* **prad prigger, prigger, prigger of paulfreys, ...prainers**) [PRANCER *n.* (1)/PRAD *n.*] [mid-16C–early 19C] (*UK Und.*) a horse-thief. ❑ **prigger of (the) cacklers** *n.* [CACKLING-CHEAT *n.*] [late 17C–mid-19C] (*UK Und.*) a chicken stealer.

prigger *n.*[2] [PRIG *v.*[1] (2)] [early 19C] a fornicator, a womanizer.

prigging *n.*[1] [PRIG *v.*[1]] **1** [mid-16C–18C] (*UK Und.*) riding. **2** [late 16C–18C] having sexual intercourse.

prigging *n.*[2] [PRIG *v.*[2] (1)] **1** [late 16C–17C] horse-stealing; thus *prigging law*, horse-stealing as a criminal profession. **2** [18C–19C] (*also* **prigging lay, ...rig**) pilfering, small-time thieving [LAY *n.*[3] (1)/RIG *n.*[2] (1)].

prigster *n.* (*also* **prigstar**) [ext. of PRIG *n.*[1]] **1** [16C–19C] (*UK Und.*) a thief. **2** [late 17C–early 18C] a rival in love. **3** [late 17C–18C] a general pej.

prim *n.* [SE *prim*, 'consciously or affectedly strict or precise; formal, stiff, demure' (*OED*)] [16C–17C] 'a silly, empty, starcht fellow' (B.E.).

prima donna *n.* [Ital. *primadonna*, the first or principal female singer in an opera] **1** [mid-19C] the second rank of superior prostitutes, immediately below that of kept mistresses. **2** [1930s+] one who behaves in a self-important or temperamental manner.

prime *adj.* [mid-17C+] excellent, first-rate.

(IN COMPOUNDS)

❑ **prime cut** *n.* [SE *prime cut*, a superior cut of meat] [1970s+] the vagina. ❑ **prime flat** *n. see under* FLAT *n.*[2]. ❑ **prime plant** *n. see under* PLANT *n.*

(IN PHRASES)

❑ **in prime twig** *adv. see* IN FINE TWIG *under* TWIG *n.*[1].

prime *v.* [fig. use of SE *prime*, to load a gun] [1950s] (*US teen*) to hold up and rob.

SE in slang uses

(IN PHRASES)

❑ **high prime** *v.* [late 19C–1920s] (*US black*) to show off. ❑ **prime one's pump** *v. see under* PUMP *n.*

prime *adv.* (*also* **primely**) [mid-18C–1900s] excellently.

primed *adj.* [SE *prime*, to prepare a gun for firing; all imply a readiness to 'explode into action'] **1** [19C+] stimulated rather than intoxicated by drink. **2** [late 19C+] prepared, ready. **3** [1940s–50s] intoxicated by drugs.

primo *n.* [the intensified effects] (*drugs*) **1** [1970s+] any top quality drug. **2** [1980s+] (*also* **primo square**) a marijuana cigarette laced with cocaine and/or heroin.

primo *adj.* [Sp. *primo*, first] [1960s+] first-rate, excellent; usu. referring to the quality of a drug.

primpy-primpy *adj.* [SE *primp*, to preen, to show off] [20C+] (*W.I.*) affected, over-dressed.

prinado *n.* [ety. unknown; Sp. *prenada*, pregnant (as cited in the *OED*) is hard to justify. Partridge opts for *primada*, first and thus most skilful, but the feminine '-a' ending makes this link unlikely] [mid-17C] a card-sharp.

prince *n.* **1** [early 19C; 1910s+] a general term of approval, an admirable or generous person. **2** [1970s–80s] (*US black*) a charismatic man.

Prince Albert *n.* (*also* **Albert, PA**) [? Victoria's consort, *Prince Albert* (1819–61), was pierced] [1990s+] a body piercing performed on the penis, usu. a small bolt through the glans.

Prince Alberts/Alfreds *n. see* ALBERTS *n.*

princess *n.* **1** [1950s+] a general form of (affectionate) address to a woman. **2** [1960s] in sexual contexts. (**a**) a prostitute. (**b**) (*gay*) an effeminate and relatively youthful male homosexual or lesbian. (**c**) (*gay*) as *princess of the Nile*, a black homosexual or lesbian.

Princess Di *n.* [rhy. sl.] [1990s+] a pie.

princess of the pavement *n. see under* PAVEMENT *n.*

Princeton rub *n.* (*also* **college fuck, Princeton first-year**) [a practice attributed to freshmen at Princeton University; note Rodgers, *The Queen's Vernacular* (1972), 'It was alleged that college men, wanting to explore homosexuality, would refuse to actually penetrate one another for fear of turning queer; so, they turned to a position which most resembled heterosexual coitus'] [1950s+] (*US gay*) body-to-body rubbing; intercrural intercourse; thus adv. *Princeton style.*

princock *n.* (*also* **princocks, princox, prinkockes, prinkox**) [? SE *prime cock* (as suggested by John Florio in *World of Wordes*, 1598) or Lat. *praecox*, early, precocious] **1** [mid-16C–early 19C] a dandified, conceited young man. **2** [19C] the vagina [may be error by F&H, more likely link to PRINCOD *n.*].

princod *n.* [Scot. *preencod*, a pincushion] [late 18C–early 19C] a plump man or woman.

prink *v.* [SE *prank*, to dress oneself up in a bright or showy manner; ult. Du. *pronk*, show, finery, ornament] [mid-16C+] to dress up, to spruce oneself up; thus *prinked (up)*, spruced up, dressed in one's best clothes; *prinking*, sprucing oneself up.

prinkockes/prinkox *n. see* PRINCOCK *n.*

prinkum-prankum *n.* (*also* **princum-prancum**) [redup. of SE *princome*, a prank, ult. SE *prank*; also *prinkum-prankum*, 'a round dance, formerly danced at weddings, in which the women and men alternately knelt on a cushion to be kissed' (*OED*)] [late 16C–mid-17C] **1** a trick, a game, a prank. **2** sexual intercourse.

IN PHRASES

❑ **play at princum-prancum** *v.* [mid-17C] to have sexual intercourse.

print *n.* [abbr.] **1** [late 19C] (*UK Und.*) in pl., boots [abbr. foot-print]. **2** [1920s+] finger*print*, usu. in pl.

SE in slang uses

IN PHRASES

❑ **all in print** *adj.* [late 18C–early 19C] neat, exact, set in place.

print *v.* [PRINT *n.* (2)] [1930s+] to take someone's fingerprints.

prior *n.* [1930s+] a prior conviction, a criminal record; often in pl. *priors.*

Priscilla *n.* [initial letter] [2000s] (*S.Afr. gay*) a police officer, usu. male.

prison whites *n.* [2000s] expensive trainers favoured by rap stars and their acolytes; the implication is that such shoes are worn by young black men, who are de facto criminals.

prison wolf *n.* [SE *prison* + WOLF *n.* (4)] [1960s+] (*Can. prison*) a prisoner who prefers women when free, but turns to men when imprisoned.

prison-yard queen *n.* [SE *prison-yard* + QUEEN *n.* (2a)] [1980s+] (*US Und.*) a prison homosexual.

priss *n.* [colloq. *prissy*, prim, priggish] **1** [1920s+] a weakling; a 'kill-joy'. **2** [1960s] (*US campus*) an effeminate man.

prisspants *n. see* PRISSY-PANTS *n.*

prissy *n.* [*Prissy*, the black maid in the book/film *Gone With The Wind* (1936/1939)] [1940s–60s] (*camp gay*) a black homosexual.

prissy-pants *n.* (*also* **Miss Prissy-pants, prisspants, prissy**) [colloq. *prissy*, prim, priggish] [1920s–70s] a person who is prim, prudish, often also effeminate, esp. when old.

prit *adj.* [abbr.] [1990s+] (*US campus*) pretty.

prittle-prattle *n.* [redup. of SE *prattle*] [mid-16C–early 19C] idle chatter, gossip.

private *n.* **1** (*also* **privities**) in sexual senses, usu. in pl. [abbr. euph. SE *private parts*]. (**a**) [17C+] the female genitals. (**b**) [late 18C+] the male genitals. **2** [1900s–20s] (*US tramp*) a private house. **3** [2000s] (*S.Afr. prison*) a handrolled cigarette.

private *adj.*

SE in slang uses

IN COMPOUNDS

❑ **private dick** *n.* (*also* **private D**) [DICK *n.*[5] (1)/D *n.*[2] (1)] [1910s+] (*orig. US*) a private detective. ❑ **private eye** *n.* [the orig. *eye* was that displayed as a badge of the Pinkerton's National Detective Agency (founded 1852)] [1930s+] (*orig. US*) a private detective. ❑ **private property** *n.* (*also* **private concern, ... passage, ...person**) [mid-17C; mid-19C; 1970s] the genitals. ❑ **private star** *n.* [a star-shaped badge of identification] [1950s] (*US*) a private detective.

privateer *n.* [SE *privateer*, 'a volunteer soldier, a free-lance, a guerrilla' (*OED*)] [late 17C; late 19C–1910s] an amateur, part-time prostitute.

privateer *v.* [SE *privateer*, 'a volunteer soldier, a free-lance, a guerrilla' (*OED*)] [mid-19C] (*US*) to cause trouble, to act as a rowdy.

privities *n. see* PRIVATE *n.* (1).

privy *n. see* PRIVY PARADISE below.

SE in slang uses

IN COMPOUNDS

❑ **privy council** *n.* [1950s] (*US*) a privy, an outhouse. ❑ **privy-counsel** *n.* [mid-17C; mid-19C] the vagina. ❑ **privy paradise** *n.* (*also* **privy, privy hole**) [18C] the vagina. ❑ **privy-queen** *n.* [QUEEN *n.* (2a)/-QUEEN *sfx* (3)] [1940s+] (*gay*) a homosexual who seeks sex in or around public lavatories.

prize *adj.* [i.e. worthy of a SE *prize*] [20C+] absolute, complete, utter; often as *prize package*, a mildly derog. description of an individual.

IN COMPOUNDS

❑ **prize packet** *n. see under* PACKET *n.*

prize of the poor *n.* [2000s] (*US prison*) capital punishment.

prizey *adj.* [i.e. worthy of a SE *prize*] [1990s+] (*US campus*) very good.

pro *n.* [abbr.] **1** [mid-19C+] a *pro*fessional, an expert in a field; esp. as *the pro*, the professional employed by a golf club. **2** [1930s+] a prostitute, male or female [abbr. is of *pro*fessional woman, not *pro*stitute]. **3** [1940s–50s] (*US*) a condom [SE *pro*phylactic]. **4** [2000s] one's *pro*file, one's appearance. **5** *see* PROBIE *n.* **6** *see* PROHI *n.*

pro *adj.* [abbr.] [1920s+] *pro*fessional.

pro *v.* [abbr.] [1940s–60s] (*N.Z.*) to take out a *pro*hibition order against a heavy drinker.

pro *adv.* [abbr.] [1950s+] *pro*fessionally.

prob *n.* [abbr.] [1930s+] (*US*) often in pl., a *prob*lem.

probabilities *n. see* OLD PROBABILITIES *under* OLD *adj.*

probably *adv.* [ironic use] [1980s+] (*US campus*) probably not.

probie *n.* (*also* **pro**) [abbr.] **1** [1970s–80s] (*N.Z. prison*) a *prob*ation officer. **2** [2000s] a *prob*ation order. **3** [2000s] one who is 'on *prob*ation' to become a full member of a gang.

process *n.* [the straightening *process*] [1960s+] **1** (*US black*) straightened hair; a hairstyle that involves effort to achieve. **2** the chemical-based product used to achieve the process.

process *v.* [the straightening *process*] [1960s+] (*US black*) to straighten one's hair.

IN COMPOUNDS

❑ **processed mind** *n.* [fig. use] [1960s] (*US black*) a black person who appears to prefer to see things from a white perspective.

Prod *n.* [abbr.] [late 19C; 1940s+] a Protestant, esp. in Northern Ireland.

Prod *adj.* [PROD *n.*] [1940s+] pertaining to a Northern Ireland Protestant or to their culture.

prod *n.*[1] [var. on PRAD *n.* (1)] [mid-19C] **1** (*Aus.*) a horse. **2** (*UK Und.*) a cart, a wagon, a coach.

prod *n.*[2] [abbr. SE *prod*igy] [late 19C] (*US campus*) an outstanding student.

prod *n.*[3] [SE *prod*, a pointed implement] **1** [late 19C+] the act of sexual intercourse. **2** [1930s–50s] (*US drugs*) an injection. **3** [1950s+] the penis.

SE in slang uses

IN PHRASES

❑ **give someone the prod** *v.* [1950s] (*Aus.*) to warn, to give an order. ❑ **on the prod** (*also* **on the peck**) [SE *prod*, to poke at] [20C+] (*US*) on the attack, on the offensive, angry.

prod *v.* [SE *prod*, to push at] **1** [late 19C+] usu. of a man, to engage in sexual intercourse. **2** [1920s–50s] (*US drugs*) to inject a narcotic.

prodder *n.* [1920s–30s] (*drugs*) one who injects narcotics.

Proddie *see under* PRODDY.

Proddo *n.* [PROD *n.*+ -O *sfx* (3)] [1910s+] (*Aus.*) a *Prot*estant.

Proddy *n.* (*also* **Proddie, Proddy dog, Proddywoddy**) [PROD *n.*] [1910s+] (*usu. Anglo-Irish*) a Protestant, as used by Roman Catholics.

Proddy *adj.* (*also* **Proddie**) [PRODDY *n.*] [1940s+] pertaining to a (Northern Ireland) Protestant or to their culture.

proddyhopper *n.* [PRODDY *n.*] [1960s+] (*N.Z.*) a derog. term (mainly juv.) for a Protestant.

Proddywoddy *n. see* PRODDY *n.*

produce *v.* [20C+] to produce good results, to 'come up with' (money).

product *n.* **1** [1930s+] (*drugs*) a quantity of a drug, usu. as described by a dealer. **2** [1940s+] (*Irish*) a bottle of Guinness stout. **3** [2000s] crack cocaine.

profesh *n.* [abbr.] (*US*) **1** [late 19C–1930s] (*US tramp*) a *profess*ional, fulltime vagrant. **2** [late 19C+] a *profession*, esp. the criminal or theatrical profession.

professor *n.* (*also* **prof**) **1** [late 18C+] anyone considered particularly clever or even educated; also in ironic use. **2** [mid-19C–1940s] (*US*) a pianist in a bar, cabaret or brothel; by ext. any musician [stereotyped identification of piano-playing with 'long-hair music']. **3** [late 19C] (*UK Und.*) a sophisticated criminal, preferring confidence trickery to violence. **4** [1920s] a bartender [from sense 2].

profile *v.* [1960s+] (*US black/teen*) to show off, to act in an exhibitionistic manner; thus *profiling for the fans*, showing off for an audience.

Prog *n.* [abbr.] [1960s+] (*S.Afr.*) a member of the *Prog*ressive Party (1959–75) and its successors the *Prog*ressive Reform Party (1975–7), *Prog*ressive Federal Party (1977–89) and the Democratic Party (from 1989).

prog *n.*[1] (*also* **proggery**) [PROG *v.* (1); note Carib.E. *prag*, to beg for, to forage] [mid-17C–19C] (*orig. UK Und.*) food, esp. supplies that have been secreted away for later use, e.g. on a journey; thus *rum prog*, high-quality food.

prog *n.*[2] [abbr.] **1** [1920s; 1970s+] a *prog*ramme, a plan. **2** [1950s+] a radio or TV *prog*ramme, e.g. *the J.Y. prog*, the Jimmy Young programme.

prog *v.* [*OED* citations suggest non-food uses and states 'it is not certain whether all the senses belong to one word'; Nares has poss. link to *progue*, to steal, although *OED* only has this as alt. sp. of *prog*] **1** [mid-17C–1900s] to poke about for food or to scavenge; thus *on the prog*, scavenging. **2** [1900s] to poke.

progger *n.* [PROG *v.* (1)] [1900s] (*Irish*) a scavenger.

proggery *n. see* PROG *n.*[1].

progging day *n.* [PROG *n.*[1]] [late 19C] (*W.I.*) market day.

program *n.* (*also* **programme**) [the recovery techniques of Alcoholics Anonymous/Narcotics Anonymous and other groups that offer their variously habituated members a twelve-point *program* of self-help] (*mainly US*) **1** [1900s; 1960s+] the established routine of an institution. **2** [1960s+] any form of verbal plan or stratagem whereby one can deal with circumstances, one's preferred way of conducting one's life.

IN PHRASES

❑ **dis di program** *v. see under* DIS *v.* ❑ **have one's program together** *v. see* HAVE ONE'S GAME TOGETHER *under* GAME *n.* ❑ **jump on someone's program** *v.* [1970s] to harass, to castigate, to cause trouble for. ❑ **not with the programme** *adj.* [reverse of WITH THE PROGRAM below] [2000s] (*UK teen*) not aware, not up to date with the current culture. ❑ **out of one's program** *adj.* [1970s] out of one's depth, acting beyond one's actual capabilities. ❑ **with the program** *adj.* (*also* **with the programme**) (*orig. US*) **1** [1970s+] in tune with the prevailing situation in a positive manner; usu. as imper. *get with the program*, pay attention, wise up. **2** [1980s+] accepting the majority rules.

program *v.* **1** [1960s+] (*US*) to look after one's own interests. **2** [1980s+] (*US prison*) to follow the prison rules in the hope of gaining time off for good behaviour [PROGRAM *n.* (1)].

progressive rope *n.* [the tie is seen as a sign of upward mobility, i.e. progress] [1990s+] (*W.I.*) a tie.

Prohi *n.* (*also* **pro, prohy**) [abbr.] [1920s–30s] (*US Und.*) a *Prohi*bition agent.

prole *v. see* PROWL *v.* (1).

prom date *n.* [SAmE *prom date*; the implication being that no one fashionable or sophisticated would attend such a dance] [1980s+] (*US campus*) an unattractive person of the opposite sex.

promise *n.*

SE in slang uses

IN PHRASES

❑ **on a promise** [1960s+] (*UK Und.*) awaiting a promised event, a bribe, a tip-off etc.

promise land *n.* [1950s] a promise.

promo *n.* [abbr.] [1960s+] **1** *promo*tion, publicity, public relations etc. **2** *promo*tion in rank. **3** *promo*tional copy, esp. of records.

promote *v.* **1** [1920s–50s] (*Aus./US*) to borrow, to exploit someone else for one's own advantage. **2** [1920s+] (*US Und./tramp*) to obtain; to survive by theft, begging or persuasion. **3** [1930s–70s] (*US*) to seduce; to flatter.

promoted pimp *n.* [1970s+] (*US black*) **1** a pimp who gives advice to other pimps or to their prostitutes. **2** a method of getting money, i.e. the way a pimp would set about using his brains/mouth to get funds.

promoter *n.* [the fraudulent schemes he 'promotes'; note Holyoake, *Dict.* (1617): 'A *promotour*, which, having part of the forfeit, bringeth men into trouble'; Nares defines *promoter* as 'an informer'] [early 17C; late 19C–1910s] a confidence trickster.

prong *n.* (*also* **pronger**) **1** [mid-19C; 1940s+] the penis, esp. when erect. **2** [1930s] (*drugs*) a hypodermic syringe.

IN COMPOUNDS

❑ **prong-on** *n.* [1960s+] an erection.

prong *v.* [PRONG *n.* (1)] **1** [1940s+] to have sexual intercourse. **2** [1940s+] (*US black*) to enjoy oneself [poss. euph. for sense 1]. **3** [1990s+] (*US gay*) to have anal intercourse.

pronk *n.* [? PRAT *n.*[1] (6) + PONCE *n.* (2) + WANK *n.* (1)] [1940s+] a fool, an idiot.

prop *n.*[1] [abbr.] **1** [18C; 1920s] a *prop*rietor. **2** [20C+] *prop*erty. **3** [1910s+] a *prop*ellor. **4** [1950s–60s] (*US Und.*) as abbr. SE *proposition/proposal*. (**a**) a suggestion, made by the police, that one turns informer in return for a lighter sentence or reduction in charges; thus *shoot someone a prop*, to make such a suggestion. (**b**) a suggestion, a plan. (**c**) a sexual proposition.

IN PHRASES

❑ **do someone a prop** *v.* [SE *prop*, support] [1990s+] (*US teen*) to do someone a favour.

prop *n.*[2] **1** [late 18C–19C] usu. in pl., the arm, esp. when extended in a boxing match. **2** [late 18C–1910s] usu. in pl. the hand, esp. as a fist. **3** [late 18C–1940s] usu. in pl., a crutch. **4** [mid-19C] the gallows [it 'holds one up']. **5** [mid-19C] a blow esp. an upper-cut. **6** [mid–late 19C; 1940s–60s] (*Aus./US*) usu. in pl., the legs, esp. a woman's legs, if attractive. **7** [1930s] (*UK tramp*) trousers.

prop *n.*[3] [Du. *proppe*, a brooch, a skewer] **1** [mid–late 19C] a scarf- or tie-pin. **2** [late 19C] a woman's brooch. **3** [20C+] a diamond or other valuable piece of jewellery.

IN COMPOUNDS

❑ **prop-getter** *n.* **1** [1900s] a pickpocket in general. **2** [1900s–30s] (*also* **stone getter**) a stealer of diamond and other brooches. ❑ **prop-man** *n.* [1930s–40s] (*US*) a thief specializing in small pieces of personal jewellery. ❑ **prop nailer** *n.* [NAIL *v.* (2)] [mid–late 19C] a thief who steals scarf- or tie-pins, brooches and similar small pieces of jewellery. ❑ **prop worker** *n.* [WORKER *n.*[1] (1)] [1940s] (*UK Und.*) a thief specializing in tie-pins or other pieces of small jewellery.

prop *v.*[1] **1** [mid–late 19C] to hit, to knock down [PROP *n.*[2] (5)]. **2** [late 19C–1950s] (*Aus./N.Z.*) to stop, i.e. to come to a halt. **3** [1960s+] (*Aus./N.Z.*) to stop, i.e. remain. **4** [1970s] to die. **5** [1980s] (*N.Z. prison*) to hold a sit-down strike or similar protest.

prop *v.*[2] [abbr. SE *propose/proposition*] [1950s–70s] to suggest or propose; to proposition sexually.

(IN PHRASES)

❑ **prop up** *v.* [1970s] (*UK Und.*) **1** to make a proposition. **2** to arrange, to suggest, to fabricate a story.

propel *v.* [mid-19C] (*US*) to drink (heavily).

propeller *n.* [SE *propel*] [mid-19C] a leg.

propeller head *n.* [the SAmE *propeller beanie*, a small hat, like a skullcap, with a propeller fixed to the top, worn by children] [1990s+] a fool.

proper *n.* [1980s] (*US drugs*) a large lump of cocaine.

proper *adj.* [SE 14C–17C] **1** [mid-16C+] a general intensifier, e.g. a *proper idiot*. **2** [mid-19C+] correct, first-rate, often used ironically.

(IN COMPOUNDS)

❑ **proper crowd** *n.* (*also* **proper bunch, ...mob**) [1920s+] (*Aus.*) one's intimates, one's best friends. ❑ **proper charlie** *n.* *see* CHARLIE *n.*[5] (1).

proper *adv.* **1** [mid-19C+] a general intensifier, e.g. *proper stupid*. **2** [late 19C+] properly, correctly.

(IN PHRASES)

❑ **talk proper** *v.* [20C+] to talk Standard English.

propers *n.*[1] ['Meaning refused – but thoroughly comprehended by the costermonger classes. Erotic' (Ware); ? abbr. of a *proper seeing-to*] [late 19C] ? sexual intercourse.

propers *n.*[2] *see* PROPS *n.*[2].

prophet *n.* [mid–late 19C] a racing tipster.

propho *n.* [abbr.] [1910s–20s] (*US milit.*) the regimental *prophy*laxis clinic, issuing contraceptives and dealing with venereal disease.

proposition cheat *n.* [20C+] a ruthless card-sharp who never gives victims even the slightest chance of winning, but takes 100% of the pots.

props *n.*[1] [SE *props*, i.e. accessories] [mid-19C] (*UK Und.*) dice.

props *n.*[2] (*also* **propers**) [abbr. SE *proper respect*] [1980s+] (*US black/campus*) respect, admiration.

(IN PHRASES)

❑ **get props** *v.* [1990s+] (*US black*) to gain respect, admiration. ❑ **give props** *v.* (*also* **give propers**) [1970s+] (*US black*) to applaud, to praise, to acknowledge as good.

propvol *adj.* [Afk. *propvol*, stuffed] [1970s+] (*S.Afr.*) full to bursting.

pros *n.* **1** [20C+] (*also* **pross**) a *prostitute*; *prostitution* [abbr.]. **2** *see* PROSS *n.*[1] (2).

proslang *n.* [PROSLANG *adj.*] [2000s] (*US black*) an articulate person.

proslang *adj.* [PRO *adj.* + SE *slang*] [2000s] (*US black*) first-rate, esp. in the context of lyrics or speech.

prospect *n.* **1** [1940s] (*gay*) a potential client for a street prostitute. **2** [1950s+] (*orig. US*) a recruit to an outlaw motorcycle gang before any initiation rites. **3** [1960s–70s] (*gay*) one who may prove a fellow homosexual. **4** [1970s] a suspect.

pross *n.*[1] **1** [mid-19C] one who can be sponged on or is good for a loan [PROSS *v.*[1] (1)]. **2** [mid–late 19C] (*also* **pros**) a sponger, a cadger; thus *on the pross*, sponging [abbr. PROSSER *n.* (1)].

pross *n.*[2] [PROSS *v.*[2]] [1930s] (*UK Und.*) a person with previous convictions.

pross *n.*[3] *see* PROS *n.* (1).

pross *v.*[1] [ety. unknown; ? SE *prose*] [mid–late 19C] to sponge on one's acquaintances, to cadge, usu. drinks or money.

(IN PHRASES)

❑ **on the pross** [late 19C] sponging. ❑ **pross about** *v.* [late 19C–1900s] to hang around, to mooch about.

pross *v.*[2] [abbr.] [1930s] (*UK Und.*) to *pros*ecute.

pross *v.*[3] [PROS *n.* (1)] [1960s] (*US*) to be sexually promiscuous; to have sexual intercourse.

prosser *n.* [PROSS *v.*[1] (1); note the celebrated *Prossers' Avenue* in London's Gaiety Theatre, the theatre bar where the more raffish elements of society were wont to promenade; also the P.G. Wodehouse (1881–1975) character *Oofy Prosser*, lit. 'rich sponger'] [mid–late 19C] **1** an idler or sponger. **2** a pimp.

prossie *n.* (*also* **prosso, prossy, prozzy**) [abbr.] [1910s+] (*orig. Aus.*) a *pros*titute.

prostie *n.* (*also* **prost, prosty**) [abbr.] **1** [1930s+] (*orig. US*) a *prostit*ute. **2** [1980s] (*US juv.*) a term of abuse.

prostie *adj.* (*also* **prosty**) [PROSTIE *n.* (1)] [1930s+] (*US*) pertaining to prostitution.

protected *adj.* [? the protection is that of the gods] [1910s+] (*Aus./N.Z.*) lucky, fortunate.

Protestant herring, a *n.* [mid-19C+] (*Irish*) **1** a bad, stale herring. **2** any form of stale or unpleasant food. **3** anything second-rate, inferior.

proud *adj.* [a man's penis, which 'stands erect'; ? underpinned in 19C by SE *proud*, slightly raised or projecting. See *Dialect Notes* III v. 360 *proud*, of a female dog, to be in heat] [late 16C–early 19C] sexually aroused, 'desirous of Copulation' (B.E.).

prough *n.* (*also* **pruck, prugh**) [Scot. *pruch*, a perquisite; ult. PROG *v.* (1)] [20C+] (*Ulster*) anything gained for free, a perquisite, esp. when illicitly come by.

provender *n.* [SE *provender*, provisions, food] (*UK Und.*) **1** [17C–mid-19C] the victim of highway robbery. **2** [mid-18C] the money that is stolen in such a robbery.

proverbial, the *adj.* (*also* **a proverbial**) [1910s+] archetypal, typical, e.g. *the proverbial lovelorn lad*.

provide one's chump *v. see* GET ONE'S CHUMP *under* CHUMP *n.*[1].

Provie *n.* (*also* **Provvie**) [abbr.] [1970s+] a member of the *Provi*sional IRA.

provincial *n.* [SE *provincial*, the chief of a religious order in a district or province] [mid-17C] a procuress, a brothel-keeper.

Provo *n.* [abbr.] [1950s+] a member of the *Provi*sional IRA.

provo *n.* [abbr. SAmE *provost*] **1** [late 18C–mid-19C] a temporary prison of the military police. **2** [1960s–70s] (*N.Z.*) a military police officer.

Provvie *n. see* PROVIE *n.*

prowl *n.* **1** [1910s–50s] (*US Und.*) (*also* **prowl job**) a burglary. **2** [1910s–60s] (*US Und.*) a survey of somewhere that is to be robbed; a search of a place or individual. **3** *see* PROWLER *n.* (2).

(IN COMPOUNDS)

❑ **prowl job** *n. see* sense 1 above.

(IN PHRASES)

❑ **on the prowl** **1** [1930s–60s] (*US Und.*) working as a housebreaker, committing or planning a robbery; living on one's wits. **2** [1980s] working in prostitution.

prowl *v.* **1** [late 17C–18C] (*also* **prole**) to wander around in search of seducible women. **2** [1900s–60s] (*US Und.*) to rob a place. **3** [1910s+] to inspect either a potential victim or the site of a possible robbery before carrying out the robbery. **4** [1930s–40s] (*US*) to search a person, to frisk someone.

prowl car *n.* (*also* **prowl, prowler, prowl heap**) [1930s+] (*US*) a police car that patrols the streets.

(IN COMPOUNDS)

❑ **prowl cop** *n.* [COP *n.*[1] (1)] [1960s] a police officer using a patrol car.

prowler *n.* **1** [mid-19C+] a petty thief; a sneak thief. **2** [1910s+] (*US*) (*also* **prowl**) a housebreaker.

prowly *n.* [1940s] (*US*) a police officer who drives a PROWL CAR *n.*

prozzie *n.* [abbr.] [1990s+] *Prozac*.

prozzy *n. see* PROSSIE *n.*

pruck *n. see* PROUGH *n.*

prude *v.* [SE *prude*] [1900s] (*Aus.*) to act as a chaperon(e).

prugge *n.* [? PUG *n.*^{3} (1)] [17C] a street-walker.

prugh *n.* see PROUGH *n.*

prune *n.* **1** as a physical feature [supposed resemblance]. (**a**) [late 19C] the face. (**b**) [1920s–50s] (*US*) a black person's head. (**c**) [1960s–70s] (*US prison*) the anus. **2** [late 19C+] a disagreeable, odd or irritable person. **3** [20C+] a simpleton, a fool [note WW2 RAF jargon *P.O.* (Pilot Officer) *Prune*, the personification of stupidity and incompetence. The character was created by Squadron Leader Anthony Armstrong and the artist 'Raff' (L.A.C. W. Hooper) to teach pupils and other flying personnel how things should not be done]. **4** [1900s] (*US campus*) a mistake, a blunder. **5** [1920s+] a person. **6** [1930s+] (*US prison*) in pl., a black person. **7** [1970s+] an unattractive, prudish woman.

SE in slang uses

IN COMPOUNDS

❑ **pruneface** *n.* [1960s+] (*US*) a plain or miserable-looking person. ❑ **prunehead** *n.* [-HEAD *sfx* (1)] [1980s] (*Aus.*) a general term of abuse. ❑ **prune-juice** *n.* [? SE *prune-juice*, i.e. its laxative effects on the stomach; thus euph. for BULLSHIT *n.* (1)] [1920s–60s] (*US*) nonsense. ❑ **prune-picker** *n.* [the prevalence of the crop] [1910s–50s] (*US*) a native-born Californian. ❑ **prune-pusher** *n.* [his predilection for anal intercourse] [1950s–60s] (*gay*) a male homosexual.

IN PHRASES

❑ **full of prunes** (*also* **full of prune juice**) [? the laxative powers of prunes; thus euph. for FULL OF SHIT *phr.*] [late 19C–1930s] (*US campus*) mistaken. ❑ **stewed prune** *n.* **1** [1920s+] in pl., nonsense, rubbish [on the lines of APPLE SAUCE *n.*^{1} (1)]. **2** [1950s+] a tune [rhy. sl.].

prune and plum *n.* [rhy. sl. = BUM *n.*^{1} (1)] [1990s+] the buttocks, the behind.

pruned *adj.* [horticultural imagery] [1990s+] (*UK black*) well dressed, turned-out.

pruney *n.* [ety. unknown; ? PEACH *v.* (1)] [2000s] (*US black*) a prostitute working for the narcotics squad.

pruning *n.* [equation of the testicles with SE *prunes*] [1990s+] (*Irish*) the act of grabbing someone by the testicles to inflict pain and humiliation.

pruno *n.* [*The Other Side of the Wall: A Prisoner's Dict.* (2000): 'Pruno: Homemade alcohol, fermented juice, the classic prison drink. It is made by putting fruit juice, fruit, fruit peelings in a plastic bag with bread and/or sugar. The yeast in the bread along with the sugar helps ferment the fruit juice, fruit, or peelings. The plastic bag is usually placed down the toilet and secured so that it is not detected'] [1910s+] (*US prison*) illegally distilled liquor.

prushun *n.* (*also* **preshun, prushon, Prussian**) [late 19C+] a tramp's young companion; 'PRUSHUN.-A boy enslaved by an older tramp or "jocker." The boy is forced to beg and at times to steal for the jocker, and is often forced into unnatural practices. Those "prushuns" who stay with their "jockers" for any length of time find themselves absolutely at a loss when the older tramp dies, unable to think or act for themselves. On the other hand, if the "jocker" fears that the "prushun" may betray him to the law, or if the boy grows so large that he is a danger to the older man, the "jocker" has little compunction about "losing" [i.e. murdering] the luckless "prushun."' (Irwin, *American Tramp and Und. Slang*, 1931).

prussian guard *n.* **1** [1910s] (*UK WW1*) a flea [anti-German var. on SCOTCH GREYS *under* SCOTCH *adj.*]. **2** [1940s+] a card, esp. a bingo card [rhy. sl.].

p.s. *n.* [abbr.] **1** [20C+] (*US prison*) *p*rotective *s*egregation; thus those who seek protective segregation: *p*unks and *s*nivellers. **2** [1910s–20s] *p*enal *s*ervitude.

p.'s *n.* [abbr.] [1980s+] (*US campus*) *p*arents.

psalm *n.*

SE in slang uses, pertaining to religion

IN COMPOUNDS

❑ **psalm-singer** *n.* **1** [mid-19C] a soft-hearted, pious person. **2** [1910s] (*US prison*) an informer, a prison trusty. ❑ **psalm-slinger** *n.* [1940s] (*US*) a clergyman. ❑ **psalm-smiter** *n.* [their thumping of their text] [mid-19C–1910s] a non-conformist, a street preacher. ❑ **psalm-snuffling** *n.* [late 19C] (*Aus.*) religiosity.

p's and q's *n.* [rhy. sl.] [1910s–60s] shoes.

pseud *n.* (*also* **pseudo**) [abbr.] [1960s+] a *pseudo*-intellectual; a derog. description, often of quite genuine, if pretentious, intellectuals, who offend their perhaps less academic critics.

pseudie tudie *adj.* (*also* **pseudo-tudo**) [SE *pseudo* + *Tudor*] [1950s+] an architectural style popular in the UK Home Counties, featuring fake beams and the other appurtenances of (Hollywood-style) Elizabethan and Tudor England.

psych *n.* (*also* **psyc**) [abbr.] **1** [late 19C+] (*US campus*) *psych*ology or *psych*iatry, as a course. **2** [1940s] (*Aus.*) superstition [abbr. SE *psychic*]. **3** [1960s+] (*orig. US*) a *psych*iatrist. **4** [1970s+] *psych*ology. **5** [1990s+] (*US*) a *psych*iatric patient.

DERIVATIVES

❑ **psychey** *adj.* [1960s] (*Scot. gang*) crazy, mad.

IN COMPOUNDS

❑ **psych jockey** *n.* [JOCKEY *n.*^{2} (3b)] [1950s+] (*US*) one who hosts a radio/TV programme or phone-in on emotional and sexual problems.

psych *adj.* [abbr.] [1960s+] **1** *psych*iatric. **2** *psych*ological. **3** (*US drugs*) *psych*edelic.

psych *v.* [abbr.] **1** [1920s] (*also* **psyche**) to *psych*oanalyse, to undergo *psych*ological testing. **2** [1930s+] to work out. **3** [1980s+] (*US campus*) to fool, to trick, to tease.

IN COMPOUNDS

❑ **psych-up** *n.* [1990s+] (*US*) an act of emotional self-energizing prior to undertaking something challenging.

IN PHRASES

❑ **psych (out)** *v.* [SE *psychologize*] **1** [1930s+] to frighten or at least perturb someone else by playing on their inner fear; to break someone down psychologically. **2** [1960s] to work out. **3** [1960s–70s] to lose emotional control, to break down. **4** [1970s] in weak use, to astonish, to amaze. ❑ **psych (up)** *v.* [SE *psychologize*] **1** [1960s] to feel tense or nervous. **2** [1960s+] to put oneself or another person into a confident, aggressive etc frame of mind as preparation for dealing with a situation; to energize or persuade.

psych! *excl.* (*also* **psyche! sike!**) [abbr. PSYCH (OUT) *under* PSYCH *v.*] [1980s+] (*US campus/teen*) fooled you! just kidding!

psychedelic to the bone *phr.* [fig. use of SE *psychedelic* + TO THE BONE *under* BONE *n.*^{1}] [1970s+] **1** (*US black drugs*) extremely intoxicated by a drug, but not necessarily a hallucinogen. **2** of clothes, very colourful.

psyched (up) *adj.* (*also* **psyched out**) [PSYCH (UP) *under* PSYCH *v.*] [1960s+] (*orig. US*) **1** extremely excited; a more extreme version is *psyched to death*. **2** emotionally ready. **3** very happy. **4** insane.

psycho *n.* [abbr.] (*orig. US*) **1** [1920s+] *psycho*analysis or *psych*ology. **2** [1940s+] (*also* **psychey**) a *psycho*path, or the act of a mad person. **3** [1940s+] an insane, strange or eccentric person. **4** [1940s+] a *psych*iatrist, *psycho*logist, *psycho*analyst. **5** [1970s+] a *psych*iatric ward.

IN PHRASES

❑ **take a psycho** *v.* [1950s–60s] (*US*) to feign madness, in order to avoid one's responsibilities.

psycho *adj.* [abbr.] [1920s+] (*orig. US*) **1** *psycho*logical, *psych*iatric; thus *psycho doc*, *psycho ward* etc. **2** *psycho*tic, violent, threatening. **3** weird, eccentric, bizarre, mad.

psycho *v.* [SE *psychoanalyse*] **1** [1930s–40s] (*Aus.*) to work out a person's state of mind. **2** [1990s+] to suspend or dismiss a person from work for psychological reasons.

IN PHRASES

❑ **psycho (off)** *v.* [1990s+] (*UK prison*) to be sent to a psychiatric prison. ❑ **psycho out** *v.* [1960s] to subject to psychiatric tests.

psychobabble *n.* [coined by R.D. Rosen in his book *Psychobabble* (1977)] [1970s+] (*orig. US*) the jargon of the New Age and the New Therapy, esp. when used by lay people to aggrandize (discussions of) their own condition.

DERIVATIVES

❑ **psychobabbly** *n.* [1990s+] pertaining to New Age jargon.

psycho hosebeast *n. see under* HOSE *n.*[1].

psychopathic *n.* [rhy. sl.; Cockney pron. 'psychopaffic'] [1990s+] traffic.

psyl *n.* [abbr.] [1970s] (*drugs*) *psil*ocybin, *psil*ocin.

p.t. *n.* [abbr. PRICKTEASER *n.*] [1940s+] (*orig. US*) **1** a woman (or man in a homosexual context) who appears to be offering unrestrained sexual favours but stops short of intercourse, leaving the male partner frustrated. **2** an attractive, desirable woman.

p.t.a. *n.* [*p*ussy, *t*its and *a*rmpits; *p*its, *t*its and *a*ss] [1970s+] (*US black*) the washing by a woman of only the genital area, the breasts and armpits, all of which are most likely to smell.

P-town *n.* [abbr.] [1970s+] (*US*) **1** *P*hiladelphia. **2** *P*ortland.

pub *v.* (*also* **pub it**) [colloq. n. *pub*] [late 19C+] to visit a public house.

pubby *n.* [abbr. colloq. *pub* + sfx *-y*] [1900s] (*Aus.*) a publican.

pube *n.* [abbr.] **1** [1960s+] (*US*) a *pube*scent. **2** *see* PUBES *n.*

pube *adj.* [abbr.] [1990s+] *pube*scent.

pubehead *n.* [PUBES *n.* + SE *head*] [1980s+] (*US teen*) a person with short, curly hair.

pubes *n.* (*also* **pube, pubeys, pubies**) [abbr.] [1950s+] the pubic hair.

pubickers *n.* [1990s+] (*Irish*) the pubic hair.

pub it *v. see* PUB *v.*

public *adj.*

SE in slang uses

IN COMPOUNDS

❑ **public convenience** *n.* [pun] [20C+] a prostitute. ❑ **public ledger** *n.* ['like that paper, she is open to all parties' (Grose, 1796). The newspaper *The Public Ledger* was founded in 1760] [late 18C–early 19C] a prostitute. ❑ **public man** *n.* [? the publication of his name in the newspapers] [early 19C] a bankrupt. ❑ **public patterer** *n.* [PATTERER *n.*] [mid-19C] a confidence trickster who poses as a dissenting preacher, thus attracting a crowd who can be robbed by the 'preacher's' confederates.

published *adj.* [play on BOOKED *adj.*[2]] [1990s+] (*US campus*) very ugly.

pub pet *n.* [1980s+] (*N.Z.*) a two-litre plastic beer flagon or the beer it contains.

pub-stiff *n. see under* STIFF *n.*[1].

puce *n.* [ety. unknown] [1980s+] (*Aus. prison*) a gun.

puck *n.*[1] [Irish *poc*, bag] [1950s–60s] (*Irish*) a large quantity.

puck *n.*[2] [? PUCKEY *n.* or euph. for FUCK *n.* (4)] [1970s+] (*US campus*) anyone deemed socially unacceptable.

puck *n.*[3] [resemblance/colour] [2000s] a lump of hashish.

pucker *n.* [ext. of SE use; 19C+ use is Irish/US] [mid-18C+] a state of fear or excitement, a fuss, a panic.

DERIVATIVES

❑ **puckery** *adj.* [early 19C] tense, nervous.

IN COMPOUNDS

❑ **pucker-assed** *adj.* [-ASSED *sfx*] [1960s+] (*US*) timid, fearful.

IN PHRASES

❑ **in a pucker** [one's face puckers up when expressing excitement] [mid-18C–1900s] in a state of excitement.

pucker *adj. see* PUKKA *adj.*

pucker *v.* [SE *pucker*, to draw the lips tightly together] **1** [mid–late 19C] to speak incomprehensibly. **2** [mid-19C; 1930s] to talk privately.

IN PHRASES

❑ **pucker up** *v.* [the facial expression] [mid-19C+] to get into a bad temper, to become tense.

puckering *n.* [PUCKER *v.* (2)] [mid-19C] talking privately.

puckering string *n. see* FARTING STRINGS *under* FARTING *adj.*

puckeroo *n.* [var. on BUCKAROO *n.* (3)] [1950s] a young man.

puckeroo *adj.* (*also* **buckeroo, pukaroo, pukaru, pukeroo, pukkaroo**) [Maori *pakaru*, broken] [1910s+] (*N.Z.*) useless, broken; thus as v., to ruin.

pucker-water *n.* [late 18C–early 19C] water mixed with alum or a similar astringent, used to tighten the vaginal muscles by those who wish to counterfeit virginity.

puckey *n.* (*also* **pucky**) [? similarity to SE *puck*, a disk of hard rubber, used in hockey; or ? POO *n.*[1] (2)] [1950s+] excrement.

puckfist *n.* (*also* **puckfoist**) [SE *puckfist*, the Puff-ball, *Lycoperdon Bovista*] [late 16C–mid-17C] a braggart.

pud *n.*[1] (*also* **pudd**) **1** as a term of description/address [abbr. of SE *pudding*]. (**a**) [late 19C–1900s] (*US*) a term of abuse; a fool. (**b**) [1910s] (*Aus.*) a fat person. (**c**) [1940s] (*US*) a young girl. **2** [1910s+] a *pud*ding [abbr.]. **3** [1930s+] (*US teen/campus*) an easy job, an easy course at college; thus *pud course*, an easy course [abbr. PUDDING *n.* (7a)]. **4** [1940s+] (*US*) as the genitals. (**a**) the penis [abbr. PUDDING *n.* (2)]. (**b**) the vagina [abbr. PUDDING *n.* (1)].

IN COMPOUNDS

❑ **pud-puller** *n.* [PULL *v.* (6)] [1970s+] (*US*) a masturbator. ❑ **pud water** *n.* (*also* **pud juice**) [2000s] semen. ❑ **pud-whacker** *n.* [WHACKER *n.*[4]] [1980s] (*US teen*) a masturbator; thus a general term of abuse.

IN PHRASES

❑ **in the pud** *adj.* [abbr. of PUDDING CLUB *n.*] [1960s] pregnant. ❑ **pound one's pud** *v.* [1960s] to masturbate. ❑ **pull one's pud** *v.* (*also* **pull one's pod, ...pudding**) [PULL *v.* (6) + PUDDING *n.* (2)] [1910s+] (*orig. US*) to masturbate. ❑ **pull someone's pud** *v.* [PULL *v.* (6) + PUDDING *n.* (2)] [1910s+] (*orig. US*) **1** to masturbate someone else. **2** (*also* **pull someone's pudding**) to tease, to hoax.

pud *n.*[2] *see* PUDSEY *n.*

pudden *v.* [PUDDING *n.* (6)] [mid-19C] to drug a dog in order to silence it during the carrying out of a burglary.

pudding *n.* [SE *pudding*, guts, entrails] **1** [mid-16C–mid-19C] the vagina. **2** [mid-16C–19C] (*also* **white pudding**) the penis; thus *pudding-bag*, the vagina; *pudding prick*, the penis. **3** [late 16C–early 19C] (*also* **puddings**) the stomach. **4** [late 17C–19C] sexual intercourse. **5** [mid-18C] an unborn child, a foetus. **6** [mid-19C] (*UK Und.*) meat, usu. liver, that has been impregnated with drugs or poison, used by a thief to silence a house dog. **7** in fig. senses [var. on PIE *n.* (3a)]. (**a**) [late 19C+] (*US*) anything easily accomplished. (**b**) [1940s+] of a person, esp. a victim, a weakling, a 'pushover'. **8** [1960s+] (*US*) an affectionate term of address. **9** [1970s] semen.

IN COMPOUNDS

❑ **pudding club** *n. see* separate entry. ❑ **pudding-pie** *n.* [euph.] [17C] the vagina.

IN PHRASES

❑ **black pudding** *n.* **1** [mid-19C+] a black man's penis. **2** [1990s+] (*US black*) the vagina; thus sexual intercourse. ❑ **dead pudding** *n. see under* DEAD *adj.* ❑ **have hot pudding for supper** *v.* [late 19C] of a woman, to have sexual intercourse. ❑ **pudding in the oven** *see* HAVE A BUN IN THE OVEN *under* OVEN *n.* ❑ **pull one's pudding** *v. see* PULL ONE'S PUD *under* PUD *n.*[1]. ❑ **pull someone's pudding** *v. see* PULL SOMEONE'S PUD *under* PUD *n.*[1].

SE in slang uses

DERIVATIVES

❑ **puddingy** *adj.* [late 19C] stupid.

IN COMPOUNDS

❑ **pudding-brain** *n. see* PUDDING-HEAD *n.* ❑ **pudding-eater** *n.* [1980s] a pimp. ❑ **pudding-head/-headed** *see* separate entry. ❑ **pudding-house** *n.* **1** [late 16C–early 19C] the stomach. **2** [mid-19C] (*UK Und.*) the workhouse. ❑ **pudding sleeves** *n.* [the voluminous sleeves of his vestments] [mid-18C–early 19C] a parson. ❑ **pudding-snammer** *n.* (*also* **snammer**) [SNAM *v.*] [mid-19C] one who robs a cook-shop.

IN PHRASES

❑ **not a word of the pudding** [? simply the idea of not revealing the 'surprise' of the final course] [late 17C–early 18C] keep quiet about it, say absolutely nothing about it. ❑ **put a bit of pudding on** *v.* [1950s] (*Aus.*) to put on weight.

IN EXCLAMATIONS

❑ **my pudding!** [1930s] (*US*) a general excl. of dismissal, contempt, negation.

pudding and gravy *n.* [rhy. sl.] [1940s+] the Royal Navy.

pudding chef *adj.* [rhy. sl.] [1990s+] deaf.

pudding club *n.* [PUDDING *n.* (5)] [late 19C+] the state of pregnancy, usu. in phrs. e.g. *in the pudding club*, pregnant; *put in the pudding club*, to make pregnant; *join the pudding club*, to become pregnant.

pudding-head *n.* (*also* **pudding-brain**) [backform. f. PUDDING-HEADED *adj.*] [mid-19C+] a fool, a simpleton.

pudding-headed *adj.* (*also* **pudding-faced, pudding-head**) [mid-18C–1920s] stolid, stupid.

puddings *n. see* PUDDING *n.* (3).

puddings and pies *n.* [rhy. sl.] [mid-19C; 1930s+] the eyes.

puddle *n.* (*also* **big puddle**) [late 19C+] the sea, esp. the Atlantic Ocean; thus *this/the other side of the puddle*, the UK or the US.

SE in slang uses

IN COMPOUNDS

❑ **puddlejumper** *n. see* separate entry.

IN PHRASES

❑ **puddle of piss** *n. see under* PISS *n.* ❑ **puddle of shit** *n. see under* SHIT *n.* ❑ **real puddle, the** *n.* [play on 'a big fish in a small pond' and its antithesis] [late 19C–1900s] (*US*) New York City.

puddle *v.* [SE *puddle*, to poke about in mud or shallow water] [late 18C–early 19C] to have sexual intercourse.

puddled *adj.* [? Scot. *puddle*, to drink] [1930s–70s] eccentric, insane.

puddlejumper *n.* **1** [1910s] (*US*) an excitable person. **2** [1920s+] (*US*) any form of small, speedy transport, e.g. a fast small car, a light aeroplane or lightweight truck. **3** [1950s] (*US*) a farmer, an unsophisticated rustic. **4** [2000s] a homosexual.

puddy *n.* [abbr.] [1990s+] (*US campus*) **1** a pudding. **2** the vagina [PUDDING *n.* (1)].

pudenany *n. see* PUNAANY *n.*

puderhead *n.* [? PUD *n.*[1] (1a) + -HEAD *sfx* (1)] [1980s+] (*US campus*) a disappointment, a person who fails to come up to one's expectations.

pudge *n.* (*also* **pudgy**) [orig. dial.] [late 19C+] a short squat person, occas. a thing.

IN COMPOUNDS

❑ **pudge patrol** *n.* [1960s] a group of obese people.

pudsey *n.* (*also* **pud, pudsy**) [? Du. *poot*, a paw] **1** [17C] the hand. **2** [late 18C+] a foot. **3** [late 18C+] a term of affection for a child.

puella *n.* [Lat. *puella*, a girl] [1940s] (*US*) a prostitute, occas. a lesbian.

Puerto Rican Pendleton *n.* [derog. ref. to the poverty of Puerto Rican labourers, for whom an expensive Pendleton shirt would be an impossible dream] [1960s] (*US*) an old workshirt.

puff *n.* **1** in senses of a lit. or fig. puff of air. (**a**) [18C+] breath, a breaking of wind. (**b**) [mid-18C] (*UK Und.*) an informer. (**c**) [late 19C+] (*also* **puff-puff**) life, esp. as *in my puff, on my puff*. **2** [mid-18C; 1950s] a house player in a gambling house, one who decoys victims into a crooked game [SE *puff*, to praise to excess and for one's own interest; Grose (1785) notes auction jargon *puff* or *puffer*, one who bids at auctions, not with an intent to buy, but only to raise the price of the lot, for which purpose many are hired by the proprietor of the goods on sale]. **3** in senses of insubstantiality of one's character. (**a**) (*also* **puffo**) [early 19C+] a male homosexual [mid-20C+ uses are indistinguishable from POOF *n.* (1)]. (**b**) [1970s+] a general term of abuse; the object's actual sexuality is irrelevant. **4** with ref. to the 'puff' that accompanies the explosion. (**a**) [1900s–60s] (*US Und.*) dynamite. (**b**) [1910s] the explosion caused by 'blowing' a safe. **5** in drug uses [SE puff, an emission of smoke]. (**a**) [1940s–50s] an opium user. (**b**) [1970s] tobacco. (**c**) [1980s+] cannabis.

IN COMPOUNDS

❑ **puff artist** *n.* [ARTIST *n.* (1)] [20C+] (*US*) one who flatters or praises insincerely, esp. in the commercial world. ❑ **puffhead** *n.* [-HEAD *sfx* (4)] [2000s] a (regular) cannabis smoker. ❑ **puffwad** *n.* [-WAD *sfx*] [2000s] (*US*) a weakling; an effeminate man.

IN PHRASES

❑ **all one's puff** [1920s+] all one's life. ❑ **have a puff** *v.* [1990s+] (*drugs*) to smoke cannabis. ❑ **in full puff 1** [late 18C] in a state of enthusiasm, energy. **2** *see* IN FULL FEATHER *under* FEATHER *n.* ❑ **on one's puff** (*also* **in one's puff**) [20C+] on one's own.

puff *v.* **1** [mid-17C+] to break wind [SE *puff*, to discharge a puff of air]. **2** [mid-18C] (*UK Und.*) to impeach, to inform against. **3** [late 19C] (*US Und.*) to speak, to tell. **4** in drug uses [PUFF *n.* (5)]. (**a**) [1920s+] to smoke opium. (**b**) [1950s+] to smoke cannabis. **5** [1930s] (*US Und.*) to open a safe with an explosive charge [PUFF *n.* (4a)]. **6** [1950s] (*US black*) to ride, walk or fly.

IN COMPOUNDS

❑ **puff box** *n.* [1920s] (*US*) an old car.

puff and dart *n.* [rhy. sl.] [late 19C–1930s] a start; thus *make a puff and dart*, to begin, to make a start.

puff and drag *n.* [rhy. sl. = FAG *n.*[4] (2)] [20C+] a cigarette.

puff daddy *n.* [SE *puff* + DADDY *n.* (11)] [2000s] (*US black*) a pimp whose girls specialize in oral sex.

puffer *n.* [PUFF *v.* (4)] **1** [late 19C] (*US*) a cigar. **2** [1970s+] (*drugs*) an opium smoker. **3** [1980s+] (*drugs*) a smoker of crack cocaine. **4** [1980s+] (*drugs*) a smoker of cannabis or hashish.

puff lye *v.* [SE *puff* + LYE *n.*] [1990s+] (*US black drugs*) to smoke marijuana.

puffo *n. see* PUFF *n.* (3a).

puffoon *n. see* BAFOON *n.*

puff-puff *n. see* PUFF *n.* (1c).

puffy *n.*[1] [one 'puffs' it] [1980s] (*drugs*) phencyclidine.

puffy *n.*[2] [2000s] (*US black*) fellatio.

puffy *adj.*[1] [SE *puff*, to extol] [2000s] (*US*) adulatory.

puffy *adj.*[2] *see* POOFY *adj.*[2].

pug *n.*[1] [? SE *pug*, a demon, an imp] **1** [mid-16C–19C] a pet name for an animal, usu. a dog or monkey, and also for a person, usu. a woman or child. **2** [19C] (*also* **puggy**) a fox. **3** [mid-19C] an upper servant in a great house; thus *pug's hole/parlour*, the housekeeper's room in such a house [fig. use of PUG *n.*[1] (1), i.e. their role as the master's 'pet'].

pug *n.*[2] [? SE *pug*, to pull, to tug] [late 16C–early 17C] a bargee; thus *western pugs*, those who navigate barges down the Thames to London.

pug *n.*[3] [PUNK *n.*[1] (1); but note PUG *n.*[1] (1)] [17C–early 18C] **1** a prostitute or courtesan. **2** an unpleasant woman, esp. one who is regarded as sexually immoral.

IN COMPOUNDS

❑ **pugnasty** *n.* [SE *nasty*] [late 17C–early 18C] an unpleasant woman, esp. one who is cast as sexually immoral.

pug *n.*[4] [abbr. SE *pugilist*] **1** [mid-19C+] a prize-fighter, a boxer, esp. one who relies more on savagery than skill. **2** [late 19C+] (*also* **pugger**) a thug, a hoodlum.

IN PHRASES

❑ **permanent pug** *n.* [orig. journalistic jargon, a man employed to stand at a newspaper office to head off any complainers] [late 19C] a man employed by a public house to keep order or eject troublesome customers.

pug *n.*[5] [ety. unknown] [1930s] (*Aus.*) a lift on a horse.

pug *n.*[6] [ety. unknown] [1940s–50s] (*US drugs*) a narcotics addict, esp. one who is attempting to give up their addiction.

pug *n.*[7] [PUD *n.*[1] (4a)] [1980s] the penis.

pug *n.*[8] [? PUNK *n.*[1] (10)] [1990s+] (*US black*) a homosexual.

pug *v.* [PUG *n.*[4] (1)] [1930s–40s] (*US*) to fight as a professional boxer.

pug drink *n.* [dial. *pug*, the pulp of apples after they have been pressed for cider, which is presumably used to make this] [late 18C–early 19C] watered-down cider.

puggard *n.* [SE *pug*, to pull, to tug, thus to steal from + sfx *-ard*] [early 17C] (*UK Und.*) a thief.

puggareed *adj. see* POGGLED *adj.*

pugger *n. see* PUG *n.*[4] (2).

puggle/puggly *n. see* POGGLE *n.*

puggled *adj.* **1** *see* POGGLED *adj.* **2** *see* PUGGY-DRUNK *adj.*

puggy *n.* [PUG *n.*[1] (1)] **1** [17C–early 18C] a term of affection used to women or children. **2** [19C] (*Scot.*) a monkey. **3** *see* PUG *n.*[1] (2).

puggy-drunk *adj.* (*also* **puggled**) [? POGY *n.*/POGGLE *n.* + pun on PUG *n.*[1] (2), thus on FOXED *adj.*] [late 19C+] very drunk.

pugh! *excl. see* FAUGH! *excl.*

pug-nancy *n.* [PUG *n.*[3] (1) + SE *nasty* or var. on *PUGNASTY under* PUG *n.*[3]] [early 18C] a bawd.

pug-ugly *n. see* PLUG-UGLY *n.* (1).

pukacker *n.* [ety. unknown] [1900s] (*Aus.*) a lazy, shiftless person.

pukaroo/pukaru *adj. see* PUCKEROO *adj.*

puke *n.*[1] (*also* **puker**) [apparently but not definitely linked to late 17C+ SE *puke*, vomit (ety. unknown), although it may be an abbr. of unrecorded *spuke*; this would lead logically to the Indo-European root *spu-*, *speu-*, which underpins OE and OHG *spiwan*, to spew, spit, and Lat. *spuere*] **1** [mid-19C] a person from Missouri [from the declaration by early Californians that immigrants from Missouri had been 'vomited forth' from that state]. **2** [mid-19C+] (*US*) an obnoxious person or thing, a pest. **3** [20C+] a college freshman. **4** [1970s+] an insignificant person. **5** [1980s+] (*Scot.*) nonsense, rubbbish. **6** [2000s] any form of disgusting drink.

IN COMPOUNDS

▫ **pukeface** *n.* [1990s+] a term of abuse.

puke *n.*[2] [Irish *pioc*, to pick at food] [20C+] (*Ulster*) a supercilious person, a picky eater, an unhealthy-looking, poor person.

puke *v.*

SE in slang uses

IN PHRASES

▫ **puke (it) out** *v.* (*also* **pewk, puke (it) up, puke one's guts**) [SE *puke*, to vomit] [1920s+] to speak unrestrainedly. ▫ **puke one's ring** *v. see SPEW ONE'S RING under* RING *n.* ▫ **puke someone off** *v.* [1960s] to attack, to cause trouble for.

puke-in *n.* [fig. use of SE *puke* on model of BE-IN *n.*] [2000s] a meeting or public occasion at which participants express their strong, usu. antagonistic, feelings about a topic.

puker *n. see* PUKE *n.*[1].

pukeroo *adj. see* PUCKEROO *adj.*

pukey *adj. see* PUKY *adj.*

puking/pukish *adj. see* PUKY *adj.*

pukka *adj.* (*also* **pucker**) [Hind. *pakka*, substantial, initially used in the Raj, of buildings] **1** [late 18C+] genuine, correct, honest. **2** [20C+] the best, the highest class.

pukka *adv.* [PUKKA *adj.* (1)] [1920s] correctly, properly.

pukkaroo *adj. see* PUCKEROO *adj.*

puky *adj.* (*also* **pukey, puking, pukish**) [SE *puke*, to vomit] [20C+] disgusting, 'sick-making'.

pulboron *n. see* POLBORON *n.*

pull *n.* **1** as a power over someone/something. (**a**) [16C; late 18C+] influence, advantage. (**b**) [early 17C–19C] a trick, a fraud, a knack. (**c**) [mid-19C] a physical advantage. (**d**) [late 19C] an ulterior motive, a hidden agenda. **2** in senses of fig. 'taking away'. (**a**) [mid-19C] (*UK Und.*) a successful theft or the profits it brings. (**b**) [late 19C–1900s] (*US*) a police raid. (**c**) [late 19C+] (*also* **pulley**) an arrest. (**d**) [20C+] an object of sexual conquest; one who can be seduced. (**e**) [1960s] (*Aus.*) that which has been earned. **3** [1900s–50s] an anxious or worrying moment that 'tugs at one's heartstrings'. **4** as a physical act. (**a**) [1920s] (*US Und.*) the act of drawing a gun. (**b**) [1940s+] a (puff on a) cigarette.

IN PHRASES

▫ **get the pull on** *v.* [1910s] to have at a disadvantage. ▫ **give someone a pull** *v.* [1950s+] **1** to tell off, to reprimand. **2** to arrest.

pull *v.* **1** [mid-18C–mid-19C] to drink. **2** in senses meaning lit. or fig. to 'move'. (**a**) [early–mid-19C] to pilfer, to steal. (**b**) [19C+] to arrest, to stop and search on the street. (**c**) [late 19C+] to accuse, to have someone arrested. (**d**) [1910s+] of a club doorman, a 'steerer', to attract clients. (**e**) [1920s+] to pick up for sexual purposes, to seduce. (**f**) [1920s+] of a prostitute, to attract a client. (**g**) [1950s+] (*US black*) of a pimp, to enlist a new prostitute. (**h**) [1960s+] to lure a woman away from another man, esp. of a pimp. **3** to get hold of, to obtain. (**a**) [late 19C+] (*Aus.*) (*also* **pull off**) to obtain money. (**b**) [20C+] (*US campus*) to obtain, to achieve. (**c**) [1920s] to earn a wage. (**d**) [1920s+] (*US campus*) to earn a grade in an examination. (**e**) [1930s+] to be allotted. (**f**) [1940s+] (*US Und.*) to receive a jail sentence; to serve a jail sentence. **4** [late 19C+] (*orig. US Und.*) to draw a gun or other weapon. **5** [1910s+] to leave, to go away [SE *pull out*, to leave]. **6** [1910s+] to masturbate; usu. in comb. with a n. meaning penis. **7** [1950s+] to remove, to censor. **8** *see* PULL DOWN *v.* (3). **9** *see* PULL OUT *v.* (3).

IN COMPOUNDS

▫ **pull dude** *n.* [DUDE *n.*[1] (1)] [1990s+] (*US black*) an informer. ▫ **pulling party** *n.* [1970s] (*US*) group masturbation.

IN PHRASES

▫ **in pull** [early–mid-19C] under arrest. ▫ **Mr Pullen is concerned** [pun on *PULL IN* below] [early 19C] an arrest has been made. ▫ **on the pull** [1980s+] looking for a sexual encounter. ▫ **pull a...** *v. see also* separate entry. ▫ **pull (a/the bag) away** *v.* [mid-19C] to pick a pocket or purse. ▫ **pull down on** *v. see* separate entry. ▫ **pull for tall timber** *v. see TAKE TO THE TALL TIMBER(S) under* TALL TIMBERS *n.* ▫ **pull in** *v.* (*also* **pull up**) [early 19C+] (*orig. Und.*) to arrest. ▫ **pull it** *v.* **1** [early 19C] to run off as fast as one can. **2** [1960s] (*US*) to leave. ▫ **pull off** *v.* **1** [mid-19C–1900s] (*UK/US Und.*) to steal. **2** [1900s] (*Aus.*) to stop doing something [? SE *pull up*]. **3** *see* sense 3a above. ▫ **pull one's duff** *v.* [DUFF *n.*[2]] [1930s+] (*US*) to masturbate. ▫ **pull (oneself) off** *v.* [20C+] to masturbate, oneself or another person. ▫ **pull one's taffy** *v. see TUG ONE'S TAFFY under* TUG *v.* ▫ **pull the chain** *v.* [lavatory imagery] **1** [1990s+] (*US*) to masturbate. **2** *see* SE phrs. below.

SE in slang uses

IN COMPOUNDS

▫ **pull-down** *n. see* separate entry. ▫ **pullout** *n. see* separate entry. ▫ **pull-through** *n. see* separate entry.

IN PHRASES

▫ **I could pull her on like an old gumboot** [1960s+] a phr. used of a sexually alluring woman by the man who desires her. ▫ **pull about** *v.* [19C] **1** to masturbate. **2** to handle roughly or unceremoniously, esp. of a man abusing or harassing a woman. ▫ **pull caps** *v.* [they tear at each other's headgear] [mid-18C–early 19C] of women, to fight, to squabble, esp. over a man. ▫ **pull down** *v. see* separate entry. ▫ **pull for** *v.* [late 19C+] to support, to back up. ▫ **pull on** *v. see* separate entries. ▫ **pull one off (on)** *v.* (*also* **pull one on, pull one over**) [1920s+] (*US*) to hoax, to trick to 'pull a fast one' (on someone). ▫ **pull oneself over** *v.* [late 19C] to eat. ▫ **pull one's handkerchief** *v.* [late 19C] (*US teen*) to make (sexual) advances. ▫ **pull one's plum** *v.* [? nursery rhyme 'Jack Horner': Little Jack Horner sat in a corner / [...] He put in his thumb, and pulled out a plum, / And said, 'What a good boy am I!'] [2000s] (*Irish*) to be idle. ▫ **pull out** *v. see* separate entry. ▫ **pull shoe strings** *v.* [ext. of colloq. *pull strings*] [1930s–40s] (*US black*) to exert influence, esp. surreptitiously. ▫ **pull someone's chain** *v.* [1940s+] **1** to annoy someone, to agitate. **2** to lie, to deceive. ▫ **pull someone's coat** *v.* (*also* **pull, pull someone's coattails, ...jacket, tug someone's/the coat**) [Mezzrow & Wolfe, *Really the Blues* (1946): 'The phrase pulling my coat [...] refers to what a man does when he grabs your coat-tail and tugs it two or three times, as a warning or hint or cue when he can't speak up directly; the sort of thing someone might do when you're in a group of people and he wants to call your attention to something; a variation on the nudge'] [late 19C+] (*orig. US black*) to draw attention, to point out, to nag, to give information on. ❑ **pull someone's string** *v.* [1990s+] (*US*) to amuse, to excite, to stimulate. ❑ **pull the chain** *v.* [lavatory imagery] **1** [1930s+] (*orig. US*) to bring to a conclusion, to make a decisive move to end a period of uncertainty. **2** [1950s] (*S.Afr. gang*) to abduct people from a public place, robbing the men and/or raping the women. **3** *see* sl. phrs. above. ❑ **pull the chain on** *v.* [20C+] (*US*) **1** to murder, to kill. **2** to dismiss, to abandon, e.g. an idea. ❑ **pull the coat** *v.* [the image is of being held back by a hand pulling one's coat] [1970s] (*Aus.*) to make little effort. ❑ **pull the other one (it's got bells on)** (*also* **pull the other leg, ...tit**) [TIT *n.*[2] (1)] [1960s+] a derisive rebuttal of an improbable statement. ❑ **pull the plug** *v.* [electrical imagery] **1** [20C+] to commit suicide. **2** [1930s–40s] (*US Und.*) to set things going. ❑ **pull the plug on** *v.* [electrical imagery] **1** [1940s+] to terminate, to bring to an end, usu. abruptly; to murder. **2** [1990s+] to treat very harshly. ❑ **pull the string (of the shower bath)** *v.* **1** [mid-19C–1930s] to cause something to be released or made common knowledge, to reveal something previously hidden. **2** [late 19C] to die. ❑ **pull up** *v.* **1** [early–mid-19C] to work as a highwayman; thus *pull up a jack*, to stop a coach in order to rob it. **2** *see* PULL IN above.

(IN EXCLAMATIONS)

❑ **pull the chain!** [1920s] (*US*) shut up! stop talking (rubbish)!

pull a... *v.* in fig. uses, denoting forms of action. (**a**) [mid-19C+] to act in a way that is calculated to shock, amuse or deceive, e.g. *pull a gag, pull some dirty stuff, pull a stunt* (see phrs. below and under individual nouns). (**b**) [1940s+] (*orig. US*) used with a proper name to mean to imitate or act in the manner of, esp. when the proper name is almost synon. with a certain type of extreme or easily identifiable behaviour, e.g. *pull a Daniel Boone*, to act drunkenly; *pull a Lindbergh*, to act in a heroic manner; *see under* individual proper names.

(IN PHRASES)

❑ **pull a bootsie** *v.* [BOOT *n.*[2] (2)] [1930s] (*US black*) to act in a deliberately stupid manner. ❑ **pull a fast one** *v. see under* FAST ONE *n.* ❑ **pull a fast shuffle/switch** *v. see* PULL A FAST ONE *under* FAST ONE *n.* ❑ **pull a G** *v. see* G *n.* (3). ❑ **pull a head** *v.* [1970s] (*Aus. Und.*) to divert a bystander's attention from a crime. ❑ **pull a jones** *v.* [generic use of *Jones*] [1990s+] (*US teen*) to scrounge constantly from one's friends; thus *Mr/Mrs Jones*, one who scrounges constantly. ❑ **pull a kite** *v.* [? dial. *kite-nipped*, suffering from stomach cramps] [late 19C] to make a face, to grimace. ❑ **pull a rose** *v. see* PLUCK A ROSE *under* PLUCK *v.* ❑ **pull a will** *v.* [ety. unknown; ? echoic; or ? SAmE *pull a will*, to shoot a basket in basketball] [1980s+] (*drugs*) to vomit after excessive drug consumption.

Pullack *n. see* POLACK *n.*

pull-down *n.* [one pulls on its ends] [mid–late 19C] a style of moustache with long extensions to the sides that became fashionable *c.*1870–90.

pull down *v.* **1** [mid–late 19C] (*Aus./UK Und.*) to steal. **2** [mid-19C+] to provide (with). **3** [late 19C+] (*also* **pull**) to earn, usu. money, e.g. *I pulled down £500.* **4** [late 19C+] to win money.

pull down on *v.* [ext. PULL *v.* (4)] [1980s+] (*US Und.*) to threaten with a gun or weapon.

pull down the shutter *n.* [rhy. sl.] [20C+] butter.

pulled *adj.* (*also* **pulled in, pulled up, pullied**) [*PULL IN under* PULL *v.*] **1** [early 19C+] arrested (and taken before a magistrate) or caught and taken before any authority figure. **2** [1980s] (*US campus*) stopped by the police for a driving offence.

pullemaside *n.* [SE *pull them aside*] [1960s+] (*Aus.*) a racecourse tout.

puller *n.* **1** [1930s] (*US*) a smuggler (of liquor) [they 'pull in' contraband]. **2** [1940s] (*UK Und.*) that member of a smash-and-grab team who pulls the merchandise from a shop window. **3** [1940s] (*US Und.*) a pickpocket. **4** in drug uses [SE *pull*, to puff on a pipe or cigarette]. (**a**) [1950s] (*US drugs*) a marijuana smoker. (**b**) [1960s] (*US drugs*) one who lures addicts to buy and non-addicts to try heroin; like a PUSHER *n.* (3a). (**c**) [1990s+] a crack cocaine user who pulls at parts of their body when intoxicated.

puller-in *n.* (*also* **puller-inner**) [mid-19C–1950s] (*US*) an employee of a shop or saloon or other place of recreation and entertainment whose task is to lure passers-by in from the street; also used of a specific feature of the place which serves as an attraction.

pullers *n. see* COME-ALONG *n.* (2).

Puller's of Perth *n.* [rhy. sl.] [1940s] worth.

pullet *n.* [SE *pullet*, a young fowl, thus precursor of CHICKEN *n.* (1a)] **1** [mid-16C+] an adolescent girl; thus *pullet-party*, a party for teenage girls (and boys). **2** [17C] (*UK Und.*) a young woman who accompanies a RUFFLER *n.*, i.e. a vagrant posing as a discharged soldier as a disguise for robbery. **3** [early 18C] an effeminate male homosexual.

(IN COMPOUNDS)

❑ **pullet-squeezer** *n.* [mid–late 19C] a womanizer who prefers younger partners.

pulley *n.*[1] [Fr. *poulet*, chicken] [mid-19C] a thief's accomplice, usu. a female one.

SE in slang uses

(IN PHRASES)

❑ **off one's pulley** *adj.* [? fallen off] [1990s+] insane, eccentric.

pulley *n.*[2] *see* PULL *n.* (2c).

pulleys *n.* [1940s] (*US black*) suspenders (UK: braces).

pullied *adj. see* PULLED *adj.*

pull on *v.*[1] [20C+] (*Aus.*) to marry a woman.

pull on *v.*[2] [the image of trying on a garment] **1** [20C+] (*Can./US*) to adopt something as an excuse. **2** [1920s+] (*Aus.*) to deal with, to test, to tackle. **3** [1930s] (*US black*) to flirt.

pullout *n.* [one pulls it out of the car, house etc] [1990s+] (*UK black*) any item that can be stolen and carried away, e.g. car stereos, jewellery, computer games etc.

pull out *v.* **1** [mid-19C] to extend oneself, to make a great effort. **2** [mid-19C] to exaggerate. **3** [late 19C+] (*also* **pull**) to leave; of a person or an object, to withdraw.

(IN PHRASES)

❑ **pull out, the dogs are pissing on your swag** [1960s] (*Aus.*) a phr. used to advise someone who finds themselves in a no-win position that the only sensible course of action is retreat.

pull-through *n.*[1] [SE *pull-through*, a piece of cloth attached to a string used to clean rifle barrels] [1910s–20s] a tall thin person.

pull-through *n.*[2] [rhy. sl.; ult. *see* prev.] [1970s] a Jew.

pully-hawly *n.*

SE in slang uses

(IN PHRASES)

❑ **have a game at pully-hawly** *v.* (*also* **play at pully-hawly**) [colloq. *pully-hawly*, a rough and tumble, ult. the *pulling* and *hauling* of sails] [late 18C–19C] to have sexual intercourse.

pulp *n.* [1920s] nonsense, extreme sentimentality.

pulpit *n.* [17C] the vagina.

SE in slang uses

(IN COMPOUNDS)

❑ **pulpit-banger** *n.* (*also* **pulpit-cackler, ...comedian, -cuffer, -drubber, -drummer, ...hector, -smiter, -thumper**) [his thumping of the Bible] [late 17C+] a ranting parson. ❑ **pulpit-face** *n.* [late 17C] a pious look.

pulver *n.* [Sp. *polvo*, powder] [1980s+] (*drugs*) amphetamines.

pulverized *adj.* [mid-19C] (*US*) drunk.

puma *phr.* [*p*anties *u*p *m*y *a*rse] [1990s+] a phr. used when one has one's underwear caught between the buttocks.

pummeled *adj.* [mid-18C; 1990s+] (*US campus*) drunk.

pump *n.* **1** in senses of an engine or machine. (**a**) [18C; 1920s+] the penis. (**b**) [early 18C] the vagina. (**c**) [19C] in pl., the eyes [they *pump* out tears]. (**d**) [late 19C–1900s] (*Scot.*) a public house [metonymy f. the beer *pumps*]. (**e**) [1910s+] the heart. (**f**) [1940s+] a promiscuous woman, usu. 'localized', e.g., *town pump, village pump*. (**g**) [1960s] (*Aus.*) an act of sexual intercourse. (**h**) [1970s+] a gun, esp. a *pump*-action shotgun [abbr.]. (**i**) [1990s+] a nose. **2** [mid-18C] an indirect question. **3** with ref. to pumped air. (**a**) [19C] a pompous fool. (**b**) [late 19C+] (*Scot.*) a breaking of wind.

IN COMPOUNDS

❑ **pump dale** *n.* [17C] the vagina. ❑ **pump-handle** *n.* **1** [18C; 1970s] the penis. **2** [1910s] the hand. **3** [1910s] (*Aus.*) an arm. ❑ **pump-handle** *v.* [late 19C–1900s] to shake hands vigorously, as if wielding a pump-handle; thus *pump-handler*, a handshake of this nature. ❑ **pump jockey** *n.* [JOCKEY *n.*[2] (3b)] [1940s+] (*US*) a petrol pump attendant. ❑ **pump-pump** *n. see* separate entry. ❑ **pump-sucker** *n.* [they fig. 'suck' the water-*pump*] [late 19C–1920s] a teetotaller. ❑ **pump-thunder** *see* separate entries.

IN PHRASES

❑ **prime one's pump** *v.* [1990s+] to masturbate. ❑ **prime someone's pump** *v.* **1** [1940s+] to fellate. **2** [1950s+] to excite sexually.

pump *v.* (*also* **pump at, pump out, put on the pump**) **1** [mid-17C+] to ask questions, to cross-examine, esp. [20C+] to interrogate in a police station; thus *your pump is good but your sucker is dry*, your questions are good, but I have nothing to offer; *pumping*, questioning, interrogation. **2** [late 17C–19C] to duck someone under the *pump*, as a punishment. **3** in sexual contexts [SE *pump*, to move vigorously up and down]. (**a**) [mid-18C+] to have sexual intercourse. (**b**) [1980s+] (*US teen*) to excite sexually. **4** [19C; 1980s+] to break wind. **5** [mid-19C] to weep [SE *pump*, to raise up water]. **6** [mid-19C] to exploit, to extort from. **7** [1950s+] (*US teen*) to ride pillion on a motorcycle or scooter [ety. unknown]. **8** [1970s] (*W.I.*) to catch a free ride. **9** [1980s+] (*drugs*) to sell crack cocaine [one 'pumps' it out]. **10** [1990s+] (*US black*) to play music loudly [one 'pumps up the volume']. **11** *see* PUMP SHIP below.

DERIVATIVES

❑ **pumpage** *n.* [-AGE *sfx*; but poss. a nonce-word coined for the novel *King's Road* (1971) by Mariella Novotny] [1960s–70s] sexual intercourse. ❑ **pumping** *adj.* [2000s] usu. of music, hard-hitting, energetic, with a heavy bass line.

IN PHRASES

❑ **pump iron** *v. see under* IRON *n.* ❑ **pump off** *v.* [1950s+] to masturbate. ❑ **pump out** *v.* [1930s] (*US Und.*) to kill by shooting. ❑ **pump ship** *v.* [naut. jargon *pump ship*, to pump the ship dry of water] **1** [late 18C–early 19C] to vomit. **2** [late 18C+] to urinate; also as n., an act of urination. ❑ **pump the stump** *v.* [1940s] (*US black*) to shake hands. ❑ **pump up** *v.* **1** [1970s+] to exaggerate. **2** [1980s+] (*US black/campus*) to make livelier, to fill with energy. **3** [1990s+] to lift weights, to bodybuild. ❑ **up to pumpery** [mid-19C] (*UK Und.*) resistant of questioning.

pumped *adj.* **1** [mid-19C–1900s] out of breath, exhausted [one's heart is *pumping* fast]. **2** [1950s] exhausted from a surfeit of sexual intercourse [one's heart is *pumping* fast]. **3** [1990s+] (*orig. US*) having well-developed muscles [*PUMP IRON under* IRON *n.*].

IN COMPOUNDS

❑ **pumped nuts** *n.* [NUTS *n.*[2] (5)] [1990s+] (*US*) temporary courage.

pumped (up) *adj.* **1** [1970s+] (*US*) excited, full of something, usu. oneself. **2** [2000s] (*US campus*) drunk.

pumper *n.* **1** [mid-19C–1920s] a questioner, esp. when very boring [PUMP *v.* (1)]. **2** [late 19C] anything exhausting, e.g. a running race [one's pounding heart]. **3** [1930s–40s] (*Aus.*) the heart [PUMP *n.* (1e)].

pumpernickel *n.* [SE *pumpernickel*, dark wholemeal rye bread] [1920s] a black prostitute, esp. a mulatto.

pumpkin *n.* (*also* **punkin**) **1** as a person. (**a**) [mid-18C+] a fool, a rustic. (**b**) [late 18C–early 19C] (*also* **pompkin**) a native of Boston, Massachusetts [the popularity of the *pumpkin* as a crop and a foodstuff; an alternative ety. suggests the use of a hollowed-out pumpkin as a form of template for Puritan haircuts]. (**c**) [mid-19C+] (*US*) an important person or object. (**d**) [20C+] a term of affectionate address, usu. by a man to a woman. **2** in senses of the shape. (**a**) [mid-19C+] (*also* **punkin-piece**) the head. (**b**) [1940s] (*US black*) the sun, the moon. (**c**) [1950s] a breast, usu. in pl. (**d**) [1980s] (*W.I.*) a pregnant stomach; a foetus.

DERIVATIVES

❑ **Pumpkinshire** *n.* (*also* **Pompkinshire**) [late 18C] Boston, Massachusetts.

IN COMPOUNDS

❑ **pumpkin-face** *n.* [late 19C] (*US*) a round, expressionless face. ❑ **pumpkin head/-headed** *see* separate entries. ❑ **pumpkin pate** *n. see* PUMPKIN HEAD *n.* (2). ❑ **pumpkin pie** *n.* [1960s] (*US gay*) an underage boy; thus *pumpkin-eater*, an older man who prefers sex with such boys. ❑ **pumpkin-roller** *n.* (*also* **pumpkin husker, punkin-roller**) [20C+] (*US*) a rustic, a farmer. ❑ **pumpkin-seed** *n.* (*also* **pumpkin-skin**) [19C–1920s] (*US black*) a light-coloured person.

IN PHRASES

❑ **some pumpkins** *n.* (*also* **some punkins**) [SOME *adj.* (1)] [mid-19C+] (*US*) anything or anyone of importance. ❑ **think pumpkins of oneself** *v.* [i.e. a fig. ref. to the size of the vegetable] [late 19C–1900s] to admire oneself.

pumpkin head *n.* (*also* **punkin-head**) [SE *pumpkin* + SE *head*/-HEAD *sfx* (1)] **1** [19C+] a fool. **2** [mid-19C; 1970s+] (*also* **pumpkin pate**) a person with an abnormally large head. **3** [1970s+] as a term of address.

pumpkin head *v.* [2000s] (*US prison*) to beat up a victim using a pillowcase containing some form of hard object.

pumpkin-headed *adj.* [PUMPKIN HEAD *n.* (1)] [mid-19C; 1950s] (*US*) stupid.

pump-pump *n.* [echoic] [1990s+] (*US black teen*) an imitation of the sound of gunfire.

pump-thunder *n.* [PUMP *n.* (3a) + SE *thunder*] [19C] a braggart, a boaster.

pump-thunder *v.* [PUMP-THUNDER *n.*] [late 19C–1900s] to bluster.

pumpulum *n.* [? SE *pumpum yam*, a round, lumpish tuber] [2000s] (*W.I.*) a large protruding stomach.

pum-pum *n.*[1] [the 'pum-pum, pum-pum' of the tunes] [18C–mid-19C] a fiddler.

pum-pum *n.*[2] (*also* **pom-pom, poom-poom**) [? Krio *pumbe*, the female vulva] [1980s+] (*W.I./UK black*) the vagina; thus *pum-pum-pum*, a fool.

punaany *n.* (*also* **pudenany, punani, punny**) [ety. unknown; ? link to PUM-PUM *n.*[2]; also note PUNDU *n.* (2)] [1980s+] (*US/W.I./UK black teen*) **1** the female genitals. **2** women regarded as sex objects. **3** sexual intercourse. **4** something good.

punce *n. see* POONCE *n.*

punch *n.* (*also* **punch date**) [PUNCH *v.* (1)] [1960s+] (*orig. US campus*) a promiscuous woman.

SE in slang uses

IN PHRASES

❑ **lose one's punch** *v.* [1940s] (*Aus.*) to reach one's limit, to exhaust oneself. ❑ **make a punch** *v.* [1900s–10s] (*Aus.*) to make a killing in the goldfields, stock market etc; thus *punch*, a killing, a coup. ❑ **punch in the mouth** *n.* [pun on SE *punch*/PUNCH *v.* (1)] [1960s] cunnilingus.

punch *v.* **1** [mid-17C; 1940s+] to engage in sexual intercourse. **2** [late 17C–early 19C] to deflower. **3** [1930s] (*US campus*) to give a failing grade. **4** [1940s+] (*US Und.*) to break open a safe using a steel punch and a hammer to knock out the combination. **5** [1990s+] (*US*) to accelerate a car.

DERIVATIVES

❑ **punchable** *adj.* [late 17C–early 19C] a woman considered ripe for seduction; thus *punchable nun*, a prostitute.

IN COMPOUNDS

❑ **punchboard** *n.* (*also* **punchcard**) [pun on SE *punchboard*/*punchcard*] [1940s+] (*US*) a promiscuous woman; a cheap prostitute. ▫ **punch date** *n. see* PUNCH *n.* ▫ **punch house** *n. see* separate entry.

SE in slang uses

IN COMPOUNDS

▫ **punch-on** *n.* [1960s+] (*Aus.*) a fight, esp. in a street or public house; thus *punch-on artist*, a street fighter. ▫ **punch-out** *n. see* separate entry. ▫ **punch-up** *n.* [1950s+] **1** a fight, usu. in the street, a pub etc. **2** a beating.

IN PHRASES

▫ **punch a dark one** *v.* (*also* **punch a nougat, ...steamer**) [2000s] (*N.Z.*) to defecate. ▫ **punch cows** *v. see* separate entry. ▫ **punch gun** *v. see under* GUN *n.*[5]. ▫ **punch in** *v.* [the *punching* of a time clock] [1940s+] to arrive at work. ▫ **punch it** *v.* **1** in senses of movement [one's feet 'punch' the street]. (**a**) [late 18C–early 19C; 1970s] (*UK/US Und.*) to run away, to escape. (**b**) [early 19C] to walk; also as *punch outsides*, to go outside. (**c**) [1980s] (*US campus*) to hurry, to make a vehicle go fast. **2** [1970s+] (*US gay*) to take the passive role in anal intercourse. ▫ **punch out** *v. see* separate entry. ▫ **punch over** *v.* [2000s] (*N.Z.*) to beat up, to thrash with the fists. ▫ **punch someone's ticket** *v.* (*also* **punch someone's time-card**) [the image of 'cancelling' the victim's life] [1930s+] (*US*) **1** to murder, to kill. **2** to beat comprehensively. ▫ **punch the...** *v. see also under* relevant nouns. ▫ **punch the bundy** *v.* [ety. unknown] [1930s+] (*Aus.*) to work hard, less from choice than from the desire to make more money. ▫ **punch the clock** *v.* [SE *punch* + *(time)clock*] **1** [1920s+] to 'clock on' or 'clock off' for work. **2** [1930s+] to be employed, to go to work. **3** [1990s+] in fig. use, to die [implies 'clocking off' at the end of the day]. ▫ **punch the wind** *v.* [1920s–30s] (*US tramp*) to ride on the outside of a train.

punch and judy *n.*[1] [ety. unknown; ? a brandname; ? weak use of SE *punch*, an alcoholic cocktail] [late 19C–1910s] lemonade.

punch and judy *n.*[2] [? rhy. sl.; ? the policeman in the trad. *Punch and Judy* puppet show] [1930s] a school inspector.

punch and judy *adj.* [rhy. sl. = SE *moody*] [20C+] sulky, ill-tempered.

punch cows *v.* (*also* **punch bulls, ...cattle**) [COW-PUNCHER *n.*] [late 19C+] to be a cowboy.

-puncher *sfx* **1** in combs. meaning a ranger or driver, e.g. *BULL-PUNCHER under* BULL *n.*[1]; *BULLOCK-PUNCHER under* BULLOCK *n.* **2** in combs. meaning a homosexual, e.g. *BUM-PUNCHER under* BUM *n.*[1]; *DATE-PUNCHER under* DATE *n.*[3]; *DUNG-PUNCHER under* DUNG *n.*; *FRECKLE-PUNCHER under* FRECKLE *n.* **3** *see* COW-PUNCHER *n.*

punch house *n.* [HOUSE *n.*[1] (1); orig. the provision of alcoholic *punch* at such establishments but underpinned by PUNCH *v.* (1)] **1** [late 17C–mid-19C] a brothel, or a tavern that doubles as such. **2** [1920s–40s] (*US black*) a spontaneous get-together, a party. **3** [1970s] (*US black*) a party frequented by pimps and their women, usu. an orgy.

punchie *n.* [1950s] a boxer.

punching bag *n.* [boxing jargon *punching bag*, a fighter who has no real abilities and is useful only as the recipient of a fortunate opponent's punches] [late 19C+] one who is constantly beaten up, e.g. an abused woman; also in fig. use.

punch-out *n.* [1940s+] (*US*) a fight.

IN COMPOUNDS

▫ **punch-out artist** *n.* [ARTIST *n.* (1)] [1960s+] (*US*) anyone who enjoys and is expert in beating up their opponents with their fists.

punch out *v.* [note US Air Force slang *punch out*, to eject from an aircraft] (*US*) **1** [1940s+] to leave work, i.e. to punch the timeclock. **2** [1940s+] (*US*) to beat up, to assault with the fists. **3** [1960s–70s] (*US campus*) to fail in one's studies. **4** [1970s] in fig. use, to reject, to turn against. **5** [1980s] to crash. **6** [2000s] to die.

punchy *adj.* [boxing jargon *punchy*, abbr. *punch drunk*, used of a boxer who has taken too many punches and is becoming eccentric] [1930s+] **1** disorientated, eccentric, out of control. **2** looking like a boxer, e.g. with broken nose, 'cauliflower' ears etc. **3** aggressive. **4** exhausted.

punda *n.* (*also* **pundah**) [PUNDU *n.*] [1980s+] (*S.Afr.*) women, seen collectively as sex objects.

pundu *n.* [Xhosa *impundu*, buttocks] [1970s+] (*S.Afr.*) **1** the buttocks, the posterior. **2** the vagina.

pune *n. see* POONTANG *n.* (2).

pung *n. see* PUNK *n.*[1] (1).

punga *n.* [Maori *ponga*, a tree fern] [1960s+] (*N.Z.*) the penis.

IN PHRASES

▫ **how's your punga?** [1960s+] (*N.Z.*) a phr. of greeting.

pungie *n.* [? Cheshire dial., *pungow*, to bother, to harrass] [mid-19C] (*US*) a shop tout.

pungle *v.* (*also* **pungle down, pungle up**) [Sp. *póngale* put it down; ult. *poner* put, give] [mid-19C+] (*US*) to hand over money.

punish *v.* **1** [early 19C] to hurt badly in a boxing match or a fight. **2** [early 19C] to make inroads into, esp. a stock of food or wine. **3** [mid-19C+] to attack, esp. in sports. **4** [1940s+] to use something vigorously. **5** [1960s+] to play a musical instrument badly, thus 'abusing' it. **6** [1970s] (*W.I., Bdos*) to desire intensely.

IN PHRASES

▫ **punish one's teeth** *v.* [1920s] (*US tramp*) to eat.

punisher *n.* **1** [19C] a heavy hitter; thus *punishing*, hard-hitting. **2** [early 19C] a demanding, laborious task; thus *punishing*, difficult, laborious. **3** [late 19C] a heavy user. **4** [1950s+] a long-winded bore.

punishment *n.* **1** [early 19C+] physical or emotional pain, damage or loss. **2** [1940s+] (*gay*) taking an extra-large penis either in the mouth or the anus.

punk *n.*[1] [? SE *punch*, to pierce and linked to PUNCH *v.* (1); note Sp. *punto, puto*, a male prostitute] **1** [late 16C–1920s] (*also* **pung, punque, punquetto**) a young female prostitute. **2** [20C+] (*US prison*) (*also* **penitentiary punk, punkie**) a young inmate used for sex by older, stronger peers; thus an inmate's 'boyfriend' or 'wife'; thus *punkfucker*, the active partner in such a relationship; *punk tank*, a segration zone for punks in a prison; similarly used by US tramps. **3** [20C+] (*US*) a tramp's younger companion; usu. a catamite. **4** [20C+] a general term of disparagement. **5** [1900s] (*US*) a person, irrespective of character. **6** [1910s+] (*US*) (*also* **punkie, punky**) a young criminal or street gang member. **7** [1910s+] an adolescent boy. **8** [1930s–40s] a youngster, a child. **9** [1930s+] (*US/W.I.*) a coward, a weakling. **10** [1940s+] (*US*) a male homosexual. **11** [1950s] (*US*) a sexually forward teenage girl. **12** [1960s–70s] (*US*) (*also* **punkie**) a male prostitute.

DERIVATIVES

▫ **punkish** *adj.* **1** [17C–18C] showy, flashy. **2** [1960s+] (*US*) weak, effeminate.

IN COMPOUNDS

▫ **punk-ass** *n.* [-ASS *sfx*] [1970s+] (*US*) a general term of abuse. ▫ **punk-ass** *adj.* [-ASS *sfx*] [1970s+] (*US*) **1** of a person, object or situation, useless, second-rate, worthless. **2** young, immature. ▫ **punk jacket** *n. see under* JACKET *n.* ▫ **punk-master** *n.* [early 17C] a pimp. ▫ **punk-out** *n. see* separate entry. ▫ **punk pills** *n.* [i.e. their creation of artificial courage] [1960s–70s] (*drugs*) any form of tranquillizer. ▫ **punk-simple** *adj.* [-SIMPLE *sfx* (1)] [1950s] (*US prison*) obsessed with young homosexual boys. ▫ **punk's run** *n.* [pun on SE *chicken run*] [1980s+] (*US prison*) the protective custody unit for those whose lives would be at risk if they were kept with the prison population as a whole.

punk *n.*[2] [? US *punk*, rotten wood or a fungus growing on it] [mid-19C+] nonsense, rubbish.

punk *n.*[3] [ety. unknown] [late 19C+] (*US*) bread; thus *yellow punk*, bread and butter.

IN COMPOUNDS

▫ **punk and gut** *n.* [1920s–60s] (*US tramp*) a bread and bologna/cheese sausage sandwich. ▫ **punk and plaster** *n.* [late 19C–1930s] (*US*) bread and butter.

punk *n.*[4] [2000s] (*UK drugs*) 'skunk' cannabis.

punk *adj.* [PUNK *n.*[1]] **1** [late 19C+] (*US*) (*also* **punko**) of people and things, second-rate, inferior, distasteful, worthless, unimportant. **2** [late 19C+] weak, effeminate. **3** [1920s+] unwell, out of sorts. **4** [1930s+] young. **5** [1960s] as an intensifier.

punk *v.* [PUNK *n.*[1]] **1** [early 18C] to work as a prostitute. **2** [1940s+] to engage in anal intercourse; to sodomize. **3** [1960s+] to beat up severely. **4** [1980s+] (*US black*) to criticize, to insult. **5** [2000s] (*US campus*) to trick, to tease. **6** [2000s] (*US teen*) to steal. **7** *see* PUNK (OUT) *v.*

punk! *excl.* [PUNK *n.*[2]] [1920s] (*US juv.*) an excl. of annoyance, disappointment.

punkawn *n.* [Irish *poncán*, an American, esp. a Yankee] [mid-19C+] (*Irish*) a talkative, self-assertive person.

punked-out *adj. see under* PUNK (OUT) *v.*

punker *n.* **1** [late 17C–18C] one who pursues prostitutes [PUNK *n.*[1] (1)]. **2** [1960s] (*US prison*) a male homosexual who takes the active role in anal intercourse [PUNK *n.*[1] (2)].

punkie *n. see* PUNK *n.*[1].

punkin *n. see under* PUMPKIN and combs.

punk jacket *n. see under* JACKET *n.*

punko *adj. see* PUNK *adj.* (1).

punk-out *n.* [PUNK (OUT) *v.* (1)] [1950s–60s] (*US*) a coward.

punk (out) *v.* [PUNK *n.*[1]] **1** [1920s+] (*US*) to display cowardice. **2** [1960s+] (*US prison*) (*also* **ride**) to force or persuade someone to have homosexual anal intercourse. **3** [1960s+] (*US campus*) to cause trouble for; to intimidate. **4** [1990s+] to make someone into an acquiescent weakling.

(DERIVATIVES)

❑ **punked out** *adj.* [1980s] (*US campus*) furious.

punky *n. see* PUNK *n.*[1] (6).

punky *adj.* **1** [20C+] (*US*) cowardly, weak; second-rate [PUNK *n.*[1] (9)]. **2** [1900s] broken, malfunctioning. **3** [1980s] (*US*) strong and unpleasant.

punny *n. see* PUNAANY *n.*

punque/punquetto *n. see* PUNK *n.*[1] (1).

punse *n.* [Yid.] [late 19C+] the vagina.

punt *n.*[1] [PUNT *v.*[1] (1)] **1** [early 18C] one who bets in a gambling game. **2** [late 19C+] a bet, lit. or fig.

(IN PHRASES)

❑ **take a punt** *v.* [1940s+] (*orig. Aus.*) to have a try at something, to make a bet on.

punt *n.*[2] [? SE *peasant*] [1970s] (*US gay*) a heterosexual male.

punt *v.*[1] [ety. unknown; orig. SE use in certain card-games, to bet against the bank; note also faro jargon, *punt*, a point] **1** [18C+] to gamble, to wager; lit. and fig. **2** [1930s] to pay up. **3** [1980s+] to sell, to promote. **4** [2000s] to make an investment in.

punt *v.*[2] [US football imagery; the team that fails to score within four downs is forced to punt the ball to the opposition] [1960s+] (*US campus*) to give up, esp. one's work.

(IN PHRASES)

❑ **punt off** *v.* [1970s+] (*US campus*) to forget, to put to the back of one's mind.

punta *n.*[1] [? cod-Ital.] [mid-19C] (*Ling. Fr.*) £1 sterling.

punta *n.*[2] [POONTANG *n.* (2)] [2000s] (*US black*) the odour of vaginal secretions.

puntang *n. see* POONTANG *n.* (2).

punt around *n.* [PUNT AROUND *v.*] [1970s] an attempt to find someone or something.

punt around *v.* [1970s+] to try one's luck, esp. when looking for a person.

punter *n.* [? Sp. *ponto*, a point, or *ponte*, the player against the bank] **1** [18C+] a gambler, on cards, dice, horses, dogs etc. **2** [1900s] (*Aus.*) a small-time, cautious gambler. **3** [1930s–40s] (*N.Z.*) a pickpocket's assistant. **4** [1930s+] the victim of a confidence trickster's schemes. **5** [1930s+] a generic term for a member of the general public, particularly when in the role of customer, esp. of a prostitute, a casino and other slightly 'shady' enterprises. **6** [1960s–70s] (*Scot. gang*) a gang member.

punting-shop *n.* [PUNT *v.*[1] (1) + SHOP *n.*[1] (1)] [mid-19C] a casino, a gambling house.

pup *n.* [abbr. PUPPY *n.* (1)] **1** of a person. (**a**) [mid-19C+] a youthful, inexperienced person; esp. as *young pup*. (**b**) [1930s+] a child. **2** [1930s–40s] (*US*) a spiced, heated sausage, served on a split roll [play on HOT DOG *n.*[1] (1)]. **3** [1950s+] (*US*) a four-wheeled trailer drawn by a tractor, lorry or other road vehicle. **4** *see* HOT DOG *n.*[1] (2).

SE in slang uses

(IN PHRASES)

❑ **beat the pup** *v.* [1940s–50s] (*US*) to masturbate. ❑ **have pups** *v. see HAVE KITTENS under* KITTEN *n.* ❑ **sell a pup** *v. see under* SELL *v.*

pup *v.* [reverse anthropomorphism] [mid-19C+] to experience childbirth; thus *pupped*, born; also in fig. use.

pupa! *excl. see* PAPA! *excl.*

pupa-lick *n.* (*also* **pupperlick**) [Carib.E. *pupa*, father + LICK *v.*[1] (1); the image is of being turned over the father's knees, buttocks in the air, for a spanking] [late 19C+] (*W.I.*) a somersault.

pup noddy *n. see POOP-NODDY under* POOP *n.*[1].

puppet-head *n.* [SE *puppet* + -HEAD *sfx* (1)] [1960s+] (*US teen*) a gullible, conventional person, esp. one who permits hearsay to 'pull their strings' in matters of current taste.

puppies *n.* **1** (*also* **pups**) in the context of the feet [play on DOGS *n.*[1] (1); thus the brandname Hush Puppies, supposed to comfort one's feet]. (**a**) [1920s+] the feet. (**b**) [1980s] shoes. **2** [1940s+] (*Aus.*) constr. with *the*, racing greyhounds. **3** [1960s+] the female breasts [their 'snuggling' together]. **4** [1970s] nipples.

(IN PHRASES)

❑ **puppies in a haystack** *n. see DOGS IN THE GRASS under* DOG *n.*[2]. ❑ **two puppies fighting in a bag** *n.* [coined to describe the actress Elizabeth Taylor (b.1932)] [1970s+] very large, poorly contained and mobile breasts; also of buttocks.

puppy *n.* (*also* **puppy dog**) **1** [late 16C+] a socially or sexually inexperienced man [reverse anthropomorphism]. **2** [18C] the penis [play on SE, but note DOG *n.*[2] (3)]. **3** [mid-19C–1900s] a blind man [the blindness of new-born puppies]. **4** [1930s] cowardice [var. on DOG *n.*[2] (1)]. **5** in the context of the small size. (**a**) [1930s+] (*US black*) a half-pint bottle of fortified wine. (**b**) [1980s+] (*US black*) a small penis. (**c**) [1980s+] (*US campus*) an otherwise unspecified and nameless object. **6** [1940s] (*US Und.*) a stolen car that has been painted prior to resale. **7** [1960s+] a love-sick young man. **8** [1980s] an idea, a suggestion [used as a generic]. **9** [1990s+] (*US*) a handgun.

(IN COMPOUNDS)

❑ **puppy boy** *n.* [1990s+] (*US teen*) a young man who is deeply in love. ❑ **puppy-eyed** *adj.* [1990s+] lovesick. ❑ **puppy-foot** *n.* (*also* **puppy-dog foot**) [the similarity to a small paw-print] [20C+] in cards, any of the club suit, esp. the ace. ❑ **puppy-match** *n.* (*also* **puppy-snatch**) [late 17C–mid-18C] a trap, a snare. ❑ **puppy paws** *n.* [2000s] (*US*) the throw of double-five in craps dice. ❑ **puppy-prick** *n.* [PRICK *n.* (1)] [1940s] (*US*) a lipstick so made that once uncapped the lip-rouge slowly 'erects' itself to protrude from the container. ❑ **puppy's mamma** *n.* [late 18C] a euph. for BITCH *n.*[1] (1a).

puppy-show *see under* POPPY-SHOW.

pups *n. see* PUPPIES *n.* (1).

purch *n. see* PURSE *n.* (1).

purchase *n.* [late 16C–18C] (*UK Und.*) money procured by a confidence trickster team.

pure *n.* **1** [17C–early 19C; 1990s+] a mistress, a prostitute [ironic use of SE]. **2** [1910s+] top quality, unadulterated drugs. **3** [1960s+] (*drugs*) the best heroin.

(IN PHRASES)

❑ **purest pure** *n.* [late 17C–18C] the highest class of prostitute, a courtesan.

pure *adj.* [late 17C–19C] fine, jolly, splendid, esp. when ironic.

SE in slang uses

IN COMPOUNDS

▫ **pure glassy, the** *n.* [GLASSY (ALLEY), THE *n.*] [1900s] (*Aus.*) someone of superlative qualities. ▫ **pure love** *n. see under* LOVE *n.* ▫ **pure silk** *n. see under* SILK *n.*

pure-d *adj.* (*also* **pure dee, pure idee, pure-t**) [SE *pure* + ? D *adj.*] [1950s+] (*US*) complete, absolute, utter.

pure merino *n.* [*Merino sheep*, a variety of sheep with especially fine wool, introduced from Spain to England in the late 18C and used for the improvement of the fleece-bearing sheep of Britain and the colonies. *AND* notes 'one who finds in this a basis for social pretension'] [early 19C+] 'an early immigrant to Australia with no convict origins; a member of a leading family in Australian society; a person of fine breeding or good character' (*OED*); a person with good manners.

pure merino *adj.* (*also* **pure wool**) [PURE MERINO *n.*] [mid-19C+] first-class, well-bred, excellent.

pure-t *adj. see* PURE-D *adj.*

purge *n.* [SE *purge*, an aperient; 20C+ use is only N.Z.] [late 19C+] any form of alcoholic liquor.

purger *n.* (*also* **perger**) [negative image of teetotallers] [mid-19C–1930s] **1** a teetotaller. **2** a general pej.

puritan *n.* [? the hypocrisy of Puritans or play on PURE *n.* (1)] [17C] an ironic term for a prostitute.

purko *n. see* PERK *n.*[2].

purl *n.*[1] [? link to SE *purl*, a rill or whirl of water] [mid-17C–mid-19C] beer warmed nearly to boiling, mixed with gin or wormwood (the basis of absinthe), sugar and ginger; a later version substituted gin for the wormwood. Both were considered suitable for a morning pick-me-up; thus *purl-royal*, a glass of Canary wine with a dash of wormwood; *purl-man*, a seller of purl.

purl *n.*[2] [PURL *v.*] [mid-19C] **1** a heavy fall. **2** whirling or pitching head-first or head-over-heels.

purl *v.* [SE *purl*, often of a top, to spin round and round; an earlier version was *pirl*] [mid-19C] to turn upside down, to overturn, to upset, to turn a somersault.

purler *n.* [PURL *v.*] **1** [mid-19C+] a crash, an accidental fall. **2** [mid-19C+] a knockout blow. **3** [20C+] (*Aus./N.Z.*) (*also* **pearl, pearler, purl**) something of outstanding excellence or perfection [fig. use of sense 2].

IN PHRASES

▫ **come a purler** *v.* (*also* **come a pearler**) [mid-19C+] to fall down, to trip over an obstacle, usu. sustaining some form of injury; often in fig. use.

purp *n.* (*also* **purple drink, ...stuff**) [1990s+] (*US drugs*) prescription cough syrup, containing codeine.

purp *v. see* PERPETRATE *v.*

purple *n.* [the colour of the pills] (*drugs*) **1** [1960s+] amphetamine. **2** [1960s+] LSD. **3** [1980s+] ketamine.

IN PHRASES

▫ **purple down** *v.* [the purple colour of the Xanax tranquillizer] [1990s+] (*US drugs*) to calm down, thanks to tranquillizers.

purple *adj.* **1** [late 19C–1920s] splendid, regal [from the image of purple as a royal colour]. **2** [1910s] a euph. for BLOODY *adj.* **3** [1940s–50s] homosexual [the image of purple as a 'royal' colour, thus of a QUEEN *n.* (2)].

SE in slang uses

IN COMPOUNDS

▫ **purple death** *n.* [its colour and possible effect; mainly N.Z. use] [1940s+] cheap Italian wine. ▫ **purple drank** *n. see* DRANK *n.* ▫ **purple drink** *n. see* PURP *n.* ▫ **purple haze** *n.* [the Jimi Hendrix song title (1967)] (*drugs*) **1** [1960s+] LSD. **2** [1990s+] a strong variety of cannabis. ▫ **purple hearts** *n.* (*also* **pink hearts**) [the colour of the pills] [1960s+] (*drugs*) **1** amphetamines. **2** (rarely) barbiturates. ▫ **purple microdots** *n.* (*also* **purple dot, ...dragons, ...flats, ...owsley, ...wedges**) [the colour of the capsules + SE *dragons*, i.e. the stamp on the pill/*FLAT BLUES under* FLAT *adj.*[3]/MICRODOT *n.*/OWSLEY ACID *n.*/WEDGE *n.*[4]] [1970s+] (*drugs*) LSD. ▫ **purple para** *n.* [abbr. SE *paraffin*] [1960s+] (*Aus.*) cheap, unpleasant port wine. ▫ **purple pork** *n. see* PORK *n.* (1b). ▫ **purple stuff** *n. see* PURP *n.*

IN PHRASES

▫ **purple-veined junket gun/porridge gun/yoghurt gun** *n. see BLUE-VEINED JUNKET PUMP under* BLUE-VEINED *adj.*

purple and mauve *n.* [rhy. sl.] [2000s] (*Aus.*) the stove.

purr-tongue *n.* [play on PUSSY *n.* (1)] [1990s+] (*US black*) the clitoris.

purse *n.* [var. on BAG *n.*[1] (1)] **1** [early 16C+] (*also* **purch**) the vagina [underpinned by the commercial potential of the vagina]. **2** [18C+] the scrotum.

SE in slang uses

DERIVATIVES

▫ **pursie** *adj.* (*also* **pursed-up**) [SE *pursy*] [1940s–60s] (*Aus.*) well-off, 'in funds'.

IN COMPOUNDS

▫ **purse-bouncer** *n.* [1900s] a swindler. ▫ **purse-catcher** *n.* [early 17C] a pickpocket. ▫ **purse-emptier** *n.* **1** [early 17C] a swindler. **2** [late 19C] a highwayman. ▫ **purse-finder** *n.* [play on SE *money-bag*] [19C] a prostitute. ▫ **purse-lifter** *n.* [1900s] a pickpocket. ▫ **purse-milking** *n.* [note MILK *v.* (1a)] [early 17C] swindling, robbery; also as adj. ▫ **purse-snatcher** *n.* [1900s] a pickpocket. ▫ **purse-trick man** *n.* (*also* **purse-fakir**) [presumably involving the selling of supposedly money-bearing purses] [1900s–30s] (*UK/Aus.*) a confidence trickster; a swindler.

IN PHRASES

▫ **may your purse never fail you** *see MAY YOUR PRICK AND PURSE NEVER FAIL YOU under* PRICK *n.* ▫ **open one's purse** *v.* [1990s+] (*gay*) to break wind.

purse *v.* [late 16C–early 17C] to steal purses.

purse-net *n.* [SE *purse-net*, a bag-shaped net, the mouth of which can be drawn together with cords; used esp. for catching rabbits, also used as a fishing net] **1** [late 16C–early 19C] a small purse. **2** [late 16C–mid-19C] in pl., goods sold to a gullible young person at vastly inflated prices and on credit.

pusa *see under* PHUZA.

pus-bag *n.* (*also* **bag of pus, pus brain, pushole, pus-nuts, puss-bag**) [NUTS *n.*[2] (1); the use of SE *pus* may offer a link to earlier derog. terms relating to venereal diseases] [1960s+] (*US*) a contemptible person.

pus-gut *n.* (*also* **pustle-gut**) [pron. SE *purse*, i.e. a full purse + GUT *n.* (1a)] [mid-19C+] a fat stomach; one who has a fat stomach; thus *pus-gutted, pusley-gutted*, fat-stomached.

push *n.* **1** in fig. senses, that which 'pushes' or can be 'pushed'. (**a**) [mid-17C+] sexual intercourse; thus *do a push*, to have sexual intercourse [the thrusting movements of the man, but note PUSH IN THE TRUCK *n.*]. (**b**) [late 18C] a robbery, a swindle. (**c**) [mid-19C; 1980s] influence [var. on PULL *n.* (1a)]. (**d**) [late 19C] money [? fig. use of SE, i.e. it lets one 'push forward' in life]. (**e**) [20C+] (*Irish*) help, encouragement. (**f**) [1900s] (*Irish*) a problem, a difficult situation. (**g**) *see* PUSHOVER *n.* (2). **2** in senses of a crowd or gang. (**a**) [late 17C–early 19C] a crowd, a 'press' of people. (**b**) [mid-19C] (*UK Und.*) a small gang who mask the activities of a pickpocket by surrounding the victim. (**c**) [late 19C+] (*Aus.*) a criminal gang, a gang of tramps; a prison work gang; thus *upper-ten push*, upper-class criminals and prisoners, also a tramp gang; *pushism*, the world of such gangs; *pushite*, a gang member. (**d**) [late 19C+] (*US/Aus.*) a crowd, thence a clique, a set, among the most celebrated of which was the *Sydney Push*, or Sydney University Libertarian Society of the early 1960s; thus *pushite*, a member of a gang or 'crowd'. (**e**) [1930s] (*US*) a family. (**f**) (*US*) a street fight between gangs. **3** [late 19C+] constr. with *the*, an act of ejection, dismissal. (**a**) dismissal from a job; usu. as *get/give the push*, to be dismissed, to dismiss; also of a lover. (**b**) ejection from a place, e.g. a public house.

IN COMPOUNDS

▫ **pushman** *n.* [1900s] a member of a criminal gang. ▫ **push money** *n.* [1930s+] (*US*) commission paid to a salesperson on each item sold. ◻ **push-note** *n.* [1940s] **1** (*US Und.*) a one-dollar bill. **2** a person who looks like someone else. ◻ **push-push** *n.* [Trimble, *5,000 Adult Sex Words & Phrases* (1966), suggests orig. pidgin use by 'Americans in foreign countries'] [20C+] (*US*) sexual intercourse.

IN PHRASES

◻ **give someone the order of the push** *v.* [late 19C–1900s] to dismiss from a job. ◻ **in the push** [1900s–10s] (*US*) moving in fashionable circles. ◻ **make a push** *v.* [1910s] (*Aus.*) to leave. ◻ **push in the bush** *n. see under* BUSH *n.*[1]. ◻ **stand the push** *v.* (*also* **do the push**) [late 19C] of a woman, to have sexual intercourse.

SE in slang uses

IN PHRASES

◻ **another push and you'd have been a nigger** (*also* **another push and you'd have been a chink**) [NIGGER *n.*[1] (1)/ CHINK *n.* (1)] [20C+] a general insult; the implication (in this context a slur) is that one's mother was happy to have sex with all races. ◻ **do a push** *v.* **1** [mid-19C–1920s] to run away. **2** [late 19C+] of a man, to have sexual intercourse [*PUSH IN THE BUSH under* BUSH *n.*[1]]. ◻ **when push comes to shove** [SE *push* is seen as less aggressive than *shove*] [1940s+] (*orig. US*) in the final assessment, when all other alternatives have been exhausted.

push *v.* **1** [late 17C+] to have sexual intercourse [PUSH *n.* (1a)]. **2** in commercial senses [SE *push*, 'to advance or try to advance or promote' (*OED*)]. (**a**) [20C+] (*orig. US*) to sell, to promote, to advertise. (**b**) [1930s–50s] to distribute counterfeit money. (**c**) [1930s+] (*drugs*) to sell drugs. (**d**) [1940s] to smuggle. (**e**) [1940s+] to sell any item. **3** [1910s+] to go [abbr. *PUSH OFF* below]. **4** [1960s+] (*US black*) to drive a vehicle [one pushes the accelerator].

SE in slang uses

IN COMPOUNDS

◻ **push-foot** *n.* [on this car low gear was engaged by pressing a foot-pedal] [1920s–40s] (*W.I.*) a Ford Model T automobile. ◻ **pushover** *n. see* separate entry. ◻ **push-up** *adj. see* separate entry.

IN PHRASES

◻ **push along** *v.* [1910s+] to leave. ◻ **push a pike** *n.* [SE *push of pike*, close combat, fighting at close quarters] [early 18C] sexual intercourse. ◻ **push clouds** *v.* [one's ascent to heaven] [late 19C–1930s] (*US*) to die; to be dead. ◻ **push fire** *v.* [one 'fans the flames'] [20C+] (*W.I.*) to urge others into a fight, with no intention of participating oneself. ◻ **push in one's cut-off** *v.* [1910s] (*Aus.*) to stop talking. ◻ **push it** *v.* [1950s+] to approach a limit, often in one's conduct; esp. as *don't push it*, don't go too far (or you will face the consequences). ◻ **push off** *v.* **1** [mid-18C+] (*also* **push on**) to leave; esp. as imper. *push off!* go away! **2** [20C+] to start, esp. to start a game [SE *push off*, to push a boat off from its mooring]. **3** [1910s+] (*also* **push on**) to go somewhere. **4** [1920s–30s] to kill. ◻ **push one's...** *v. see also under* relevant nouns. ◻ **push one's own barrow** *v.* [1910s+] (*Aus.*) **1** to brag. **2** to look out for one's own interests first. ◻ **push someone's face (in)** *v.* [20C+] to hit someone in the face. ◻ **push someone's key** *v.* [1990s+] (*US prison*) to irritate someone, to tease someone. ◻ **push the...** *v. see also under* relevant nouns. ◻ **push the boat out** *v.* **1** [1910s+] to spend heavily, usu. on pleasure, eating, drinking etc, often treating others. **2** [1910s+] to do something to excess. **3** [1960s] to exaggerate. ◻ **push the bottle** *v.* (*also* **push the glass about**) [late 18C] to drink. ◻ **push the cart up Holborn Hill** *v. see WALK BACKWARDS UP HOLBORN HILL under* HOLBORN HILL *n.* ◻ **push up on** *v.* [1980s+] (*US black*) **1** to make romantic moves towards someone, usu. in the hope of seduction. **2** to frighten, to intimidate. ◻ **push up (the) daisies** *v. see* separate entry. ◻ **what are you pushing?** [1970s] (*US black*) what sort of car do you drive?

IN EXCLAMATIONS

◻ **push me pink!** [1930s] (*Aus.*) a dismissive retort.

pushed *adj.* (*also* **pushed out**) [one of many words associating physical violence with drunkenness] [mid-19C–1930s] drunk.

pusher *n.* **1** in commercial senses. (**a**) [late 19C] (*US*) a salesman. (**b**) [1900s] (*US Und.*) a bank teller; a cashier. (**c**) [1920s+] (*US tramp*) the foreman on a construction site. (**d**) [1930s] any form of salesperson. **2** [1910s–40s] a young woman, esp. a flirt or a prostitute; *see also SQUARE PUSHER* below. **3** in Und. uses. (**a**) [1920s+] (*drugs*) (*also* **pusherman**) one who sells drugs; usu. in his 'small-time' or 'retail' role as opposed to the wholesale DEALER *n.* (2). (**b**) [1930s+] (*US Und.*) a distributor of counterfeit money. (**c**) [1950s] (*US gay*) a man who runs a string of homosexual male prostitutes. **4** [1950s+] (*Aus.*) a pushchair. **5** [1980s+] (*drugs*) as an implement. (**a**) a thin stick, typically a chopstick, used to pack a cocaine pipe. (**b**) a metal hanger or umbrella rod used to scrape residue in crack cocaine stems.

IN PHRASES

◻ **square pusher** *n.* [SQUARE *adj.* (1)] **1** [1910s–30s] a young woman, usu. respectable; thus *square-pushing*, courting. **2** [1920s] a boyfriend.

pushie *n.* (*also* **pooshey, pooshie, pooshy**) [1960s+] **1** a coward; also as adj., cowardly, effeminate [PUSSY *n.* (10)]. **2** (*Ulster*) an over-sensitive person [SE *push*].

pushing school *n.* [PUSH *v.* (1) + SE *school*. Note SE *pushing school*, a fencing school, thus link to the sl. uses of DAGGER *n.*[1] and other synons. meaning the penis] [late 17C–early 19C] a brothel.

pushing tout *n. see under* TOUT *n.*[1].

push-in job *n.* [SE *push-in* + JOB *n.*[2] (1a)] [1970s+] a mugging that takes place on the victim's doorstep.

push in the truck *n.* [rhy. sl. = FUCK *n.* (1a)] [1930s+] sexual intercourse.

pushover *n.* **1** [late 19C+] (*orig. US*) a situation that presents no difficulties or problems. **2** [1910s+] (*orig. US*) (*also* **push**) one who is easily overcome, convinced or imposed upon. **3** [1920s+] one, esp. a woman, who is easily seduced. **4** [1930s] (*US*) a trick, a hoax.

push-up *adj.* [1990s+] (*W.I.*) presumptuous, arrogant.

push-up man *n.* [1910s–30s] (*Aus.*) a pickpocket's accomplice who *pushes up* the arm of the victim to facilitate access to their wallet; thus *push-up mob*, a gang of pickpockets specializing in this; *at the push-up*, working as a pickpocket.

push up (the) daisies *v.* (*also* **kick up (the) daisies, pick..., shove up..., push up the poppies**) [1910s+] **1** to die; thus *pushing (up the) daisies*, dead. **2** in fig. use, to waste time, to lead a pointless existence.

pus-nuts *n. see* PUS-BAG *n.*

pus pocket *n. see* PUSSBUCKET *n.*

puss *n.*[1] **1** [late 16C+] (*also* **pussy**) a hare [orig. dial.]. **2** in senses of 'femininity' [SE *puss*; the association of women and cats]. (**a**) [17C+] a (young) woman. (**b**) [mid-17C] a prostitute, a madame. (**c**) [mid-17C+] the vagina. (**d**) [1970s+] the 'feminine' partner in a lesbian couple. (**e**) [1970s+] (*US gay*) the buttocks. (**f**) [1970s+] (*US gay*) an underage boy. **3** (*W.I.*) with ref. to the cat's silent walk. (**a**) [1940s] rubber-soled canvas shoes. (**b**) [1950s] a thief. **4** *see* PUSSY *n.* (4). **5** *see* PUSSY *n.* (10).

DERIVATIVES

◻ **pussery** *n.* (*W.I.*) **1** [1940s] trickery. **2** [1950s] theft.

IN COMPOUNDS

◻ **puss-boots** *n.* [the quietness of one's steps + ? ref. to the folktale 'Puss-in-Boots'] [1940s] (*W.I.*) rubber-soled canvas shoes. ◻ **puss gentleman** *n.* [PUSSY *n.* (10)] [1960s+] (*US black*) a weak man. ◻ **puss pelmet** *n. see PUSSY-PELMET under* PUSSY *n.*

IN PHRASES

◻ **puss out** *v. see PUSSY OUT under* PUSSY *n.*

puss *n.*[2] [Irish *pus*, the mouth, a sulky expression] **1** [late 19C+] a face. **2** [1910s+] the mouth. **3** [1910s+] (*Irish*) a sulky look; also as v., to pout or sulk.

DERIVATIVES

◻ **pussful** *n.* [1970s] (*US*) a sufficiency, esp. of drink.

IN PHRASES

◻ **have a puss on** *v.* [1950s+] to display a sulky or ill-humoured face. ❑ **shut one's puss** *v.* [1950s] (*US*) to be quiet, to stop talking; also as imper.

puss *n.*[3] [abbr. PUSS-EYE *n.*] [1950s] (*W.I.*) an albino.

puss-bag *n. see* PUS-BAG *n.*

pussbucket *n.* (*also* **pus pocket**) [the use of *puss*, i.e. pus, may offer a link to other derog. terms relating to venereal diseases] [1950s+] (*orig. US*) a general derog. term.

puss-eye *n.* [? SE *pus* + *eye*; the stereotype of short-sighted albinos] [1950s] (*W.I.*) an albino.

puss-in *n.* [var. on PUSSY *n.* (2)] [20C+] (*W.I.*) a young woman.

pussing *n.* [PUSS *n.*[2] (3)] [1990s+] (*Irish*) crying, whingeing.

pussle-gutted *adj. see* PUSSY-GUTTED *adj.*

pussy *n.* [SE *pussy*, an affectionate name for a cat] **1** [18C+] the vagina; thus, by metonymy, sexual intercourse. **2** [mid-19C+] women in general, with an implication of their being sexually available. **3** [late 19C+] the female pubic hair. **4** [1900s–40s] (*also* **puss**) the cat-o'-nine-tails. **5** [1920s] in fig. use, one who is gentle, kind. **6** [1920s+] an old woman, usu. a spinster, who is inquisitive and meddling. **7** [1930s+] (*Aus.*) a rabbit. **8** [1930s+] a fur garment; thus *pussy-hoisting*, stealing furs; *pussy mob*, a gang of fur thieves; *pussy-shop*, a furrier's. **9** [1940s+] a male homosexual; or a man judged to be or teased as being so. **10** [1950s+] (*also* **puss**) a coward, a weakling, with an implication of homosexuality. **11** [1960s–70s] (*gay*) the anus, i.e. a play on sense 1. **12** [1970s] cowardice. **13** [1980s] in fig. use of sense 1, the 'real thing', i.e. as opposed to masturbation. **14** *see* PUSS *n.*[1] (1).

DERIVATIVES

❑ **pussified** *adj.* [1990s+] effeminate.

IN COMPOUNDS

❑ **pussy-ass** *adj.* [-ASS *sfx*] [1970s+] (*US*) cowardly, weak. ❑ **pussy-bait** *n.* [1970s] (*US black*) money. ❑ **pussy bandit** *n.* [-BANDIT *sfx* (3)] [1950s+] (*US*) a man who is obsessed with sex and seduction. ❑ **pussyboy** *n.* **1** [1950s+] a passive male homosexual, a catamite. **2** [1980s+] a general insult, implying cowardice or homosexuality. ❑ **pussy-bully** *n.* [1990s+] (*W.I.*) a male sexual athlete. ❑ **pussy bumper** *n.* [SE *bumper*] [1940s–70s] **1** (*US Und.*) a male homosexual. **2** thus, an effeminate whipping boy. **3** a lesbian [BUMPER *n.*[7]]. ❑ **pussycat** *see* separate entries. ❑ **pussy claat** *n.* (*also* **pussyclaht, pussyclot**) [SE *cloth*, i.e. a sanitary towel] [1960s+] (*W.I./UK black*) a general pej., a coward, an informer; also as adj. ❑ **pussy eater** *n.* [EAT *v.* (4)] [1970s+] (*orig. US*) a cunnilinguist. ❑ **pussy-eating** *n.* [EAT *v.* (4)] [1980s] (*orig. US*) cunnilingus. ❑ **pussyfoot/footing** *see* separate entries. ❑ **pussyfur** *n. see* FUR *n.* (1). ❑ **pussy game** *n.* [GAME *n.* (6)] [1960s+] (*US*) the world of prostitution. ❑ **pussy glommer** *n.* [GLOM *v.* (1)] [1920s] (*Can. tramp*) a hand. ❑ **pussy hair** *n.* **1** [1970s+] the female pubic hair. **2** *see* CUNT HAIR *under* CUNT *n.* ❑ **pussy hole** *n.* [1980s+] (*UK/US black/W.I.*) the vagina. ❑ **pussy-hound** *n.* [-HOUND *sfx*] [1970s+] a man who is obsessed with the pursuit of sex. ❑ **pussy juice** *n.* (*also* **pussy-liquids**) [JUICE *n.*[1] (2a)] [1960s+] vaginal secretions. ❑ **pussy-kisser** *n.* [1960s] (*US*) a general insult, lit. a cunnilinguist. ❑ **pussylicker** *n.* (*also* **pussy-lapper**) [1960s] (*US*) a general term of abuse, lit. a cunnilinguist; thus adj. *pussylick*. ❑ **pussy magnet** *n. see under* -MAGNET *sfx*. ❑ **pussy-parlor** *n.* [1980s] (*US*) a striptease club. ❑ **pussy-pelmet** *n.* (*also* **puss-pelmet**) [1960s+] a very short miniskirt. ❑ **pussy picture** *n.* [1940s] (*US*) a pornographic photograph of a woman. ❑ **pussy posse** *n.* (*also* **pussy patrol**) [1970s+] (*US police/Und.*) the Vice Squad, esp. those members who deal with prostitutes. ❑ **pussy-printer** *n.* [1990s+] (*W.I.*) shorts so tight they outline the genital area. ❑ **pussy prober** *n.* [1980s] (*US*) a gynaecologist. ❑ **pussy pusher** *n.* [fig. use of PUSHER *n.* (1a)] [1970s] (*US gay*) a heterosexual. ❑ **pussy queer** *n.* (*also* **pussy queen**) [QUEER *n.* (4)/QUEEN *n.* (2a)] [1960s–80s] (*US*) a lesbian. ❑ **pussy-struck** *adj.* [1920s+] obsessed by sex. ❑ **pussy sucker** *n.* [1990s+] a cunnilinguist. ❑ **pussy tickler** *n.* [1940s+] (*orig. US black*) a moustache. ❑ **pussy whip** *v.* [1950s+] (*orig. US*) of a woman, to dominate one's husband or partner. ❑ **pussy-whipped** *adj.* (*also* **hen-whipped, p.w.'ed, p-whipped**) [fig. used of SE *whip*] **1** [1960s+] (*orig. US*) dominated by a woman, esp. a wife or girlfriend. **2** [1980s] (*US black/campus*) besotted with, infatuated by.

IN PHRASES

❑ **bump pussies** *v.* **1** [1940s+] (*gay*) of male homosexuals or lesbians, to have sexual intercourse. **2** [1960s–70s] of male homosexuals, to find themselves too similar in their sexual preferences (e.g. both passive or both active) to have satisfactory sex. ❑ **fan one's pussy** *v.* [FAN *v.*[2] (2)] [1960s+] (*US black*) of a woman, to flaunt oneself sexually. ❑ **feed one's pussy** *v.* (*also* **feed one's pussycat**) [19C+] of a woman, to have sexual intercourse. ❑ **fuck up someone's pussy** *v.* [FUCK UP *v.* (1)] [20C+] (*US black*) to interfere with a rival, a companion's efforts at seducing a woman. ❑ **get some pussy** *v.* (*also* **do the pussy**) [1950s+] (*US/Aus.*) of a man, to have sexual intercourse. ❑ **give up pussy** *v.* [1980s] of a woman, to have sexual intercourse. ❑ **peddle pussy** *v. see under* PEDDLE *v.* ❑ **play pussy and get fucked** *v.* [play on PUSSY *n.* (1)/PUSSY *n.* (10) + FUCK *v.* (1)/FUCK *v.* (2a)] [1990s+] (*US black*) to act weakly and to suffer as a result. ❑ **poke one's pussy** *v.* [POKE *v.* (1)] [1960s+] of a woman, to masturbate. ❑ **pop pussy** *v.* [2000s] to work as a prostitute. ❑ **pussy in a can** *n.* [the derog. association of the smell of the vagina with the smell of fish] [1960s+] (*US prison*) sardines sold in a can at a prison commissary. ❑ **pussy out** *v.* (*also* **puss out**) [PUSSY *n.* (10)] [1960s+] (*orig. US*) to act in a cowardly manner, to give up under pressure. ❑ **sell pussy** *v. see* PEDDLE PUSSY *under* PEDDLE *v.* ❑ **sling pussy** *v.* [1960s+] to work as a prostitute. ❑ **throw the P** *v.* [1980s+] (*US black*) of a woman, to have sexual intercourse.

SE in slang uses

IN PHRASES

❑ **not while pussy's a cat** [20C+] (*Ulster*) never. ❑ **see which way the pussy jumps/how the pussy jumps** *v. see* SEE WHICH WAY THE CAT JUMPS *under* CAT *n.*[1]. ❑ **up to pussy's bow** *see* UP TO DOLLY'S WAX *under* DOLLY *n.*[1].

pussy *adj.* [PUSSY *n.*] **1** [mid-19C–1910s] fat, corpulent. **2** [20C+] easy, undemanding (the inference being not worthy of a 'real man)'. **3** [1950s+] (*orig. US*) scared, cowardly. **4** [1960s+] effeminate, implying homosexuality. **5** [1970s+] female. **6** [1970s+] (*US*) pertaining to sex; pornographic. **7** [1980s+] useless, insignificant.

pussy *v.* [SE *pussy*, i.e. like a cat] **1** [1910s+] (*Aus.*) to move (in) quietly or unobtrusively. **2** [1960s+] (*Scot./US*) (*also* **pussy around**) of a man, to play sexual games, to have sexual intercourse.

pussycat *n.* **1** [19C+] (*orig. US black*) the vagina; by metonymy, a woman [ext. PUSSY *n.* (1)]. **2** [1950s+] a weak or at least amiable and passive person [ext. PUSSY *n.* (10)].

IN PHRASES

❑ **feed one's pussycat** *v. see* FEED ONE'S PUSSY *under* PUSSY *n.*

pussycat *adj.* (*also* **pussy-kitten**) [PUSSYCAT *n.* (2)] [1900s–20s] (*US*) weak, effeminate.

pussyfoot *n.* [PUSSYFOOT *v.*] **1** [1910s] (*US Und.*) a detective. **2** [1930s] (*also* **pussyfooter**) a coward, a weakling; someone sly or underhand; a general derog. term of address.

pussyfoot *adj.* [PUSSYFOOT *n.* (2)] **1** [1910s+] cowardly, weak; general term of abuse. **2** [1920s] teetotal.

pussyfoot *v.* (*also* **pussyfoot around**) [the animal's cautious movements] [1920s+] to compromise, to act in a cowardly or weak manner.

pussyfooter *n. see* PUSSYFOOT *n.* (2).

pussyfooting *adj.* [PUSSYFOOT *v.*] [1920s+] weak, dithering, ineffectual.

pussy-gutted *adj.* (*also* **pussle-gutted**) [SE *purse* + GUT *n.* (1a)] [1900s] (*US*) fat, with a large stomach; thus n. *pussy guts*, a fat person.

pussy-kitten *adj. see* PUSSYCAT *adj.*

pustle-gut *n. see* PUS-GUT *n.*

put *n.*[1] [ety. unknown; ? one who is easily 'put upon'] **1** [late 17C–mid-19C] a peasant, a countryman. **2** [mid-18C–1910s] a general term of derision.

IN PHRASES

❑ **old put** *n.* [mid-18C–19C] a pretentious old gentleman.

put *n.*[2] [Fr. *putain*, a prostitute] [19C] a prostitute.

put *v.*[1] [SE *put* oneself in motion] [mid–late 19C] (*US*) to make off, to be off, to 'clear out'.

SE in slang uses

IN COMPOUNDS

❑ **put and take** *n.* *see* separate entry.

IN PHRASES

❑ **put a churl upon a gentleman** *v.* [the supposed links of social class and drinking habits] **1** [late 17C–early 19C] to drink beer or malt liquor after drinking wine. **2** [18C] to drink ale immediately after drinking wine. ❑ **put an egg in your shoe and beat it** *v. see under* BEAT IT *v.* ❑ **put away** *see* separate entries. ❑ **put back** *v.* [var. on PUT AWAY *v.* (3)] [1970s+] to drink, esp. a large amount. ❑ **put down** *see* separate entries. ❑ **put-em-up** *n.* [the hold-up man's command of 'Put 'em up!'] [1910s] (*US Und.*) a violent, potentially homicidal criminal. ❑ **put foot** *v.* [abbr. of 'put one's foot on the accelerator'] [1980s+] (*S.Afr.*) to drive fast. ❑ **put for tall timber** *v. see* TAKE TO THE TALL TIMBER(S) *under* TALL TIMBERS *n.* ❑ **put in** *see* separate entries. ❑ **put it about** *v. see under* IT *n.*[1]. ❑ **put it across** *v.* [20C+] **1** (*also* **put one across**) to beat, to get the better of. **2** to hoax, to trick, to defraud. **3** to punish. ❑ **put it around** *v.* [1970s] to circulate information. ❑ **put it down** *v. see under* IT *n.*[1]. ❑ **put it in and break it** *v. see under* IT *n.*[1]. ❑ **put it in cruise mode** *v.* (*also* **put it in overdrive**) [automobile imagery] [1990s+] (*US campus*) to seek a partner for romance or sex. ❑ **put it on a bullet (and put it in your brain)** [1990s+] (*US black teen*) remember that, don't forget. ❑ **put it on (someone)** *v. see* separate entry. ❑ **put it over** *v.* [late 19C+] (*orig. US*) **1** to cheat or confuse. **2** to defeat, to surpass. **3** (*Aus.*) to be a success at something, e.g. singing. ❑ **put (it) round** *v.* [mid-19C] (*UK Und.*) to divide up spoils. ❑ **put it to** *v.* (*US*) **1** [1920s+] to beat up, to put under pressure, e.g. of the police. **2** *see under* IT *n.*[1]. ❑ **put it to the wood** *v.* [i.e. press the accelerator to the floor of the car] [1970s] (*US campus*) to accelerate an automobile. ❑ **put it up** *v. see under* IT *n.*[1]. ❑ **put off** *v.* **1** [mid-18C–1900s] (*Aus./US Und.*) to distribute counterfeit money. **2** [1930s] (*Aus.*) to lay off from work, to dismiss. **3** [1990s+] (*Aus.*) to kill, to murder. ❑ **put on** *see* separate entries. ❑ **put one across** *v. see* PUT IT ACROSS above. ❑ **put one over (on)** *v. see under* ONE *n.*[1]. ❑ **put oneself about** *v.* [1970s+] **1** to lead an active social or sexual life. **2** to go into action. ❑ **put oneself away** *v.* [1930s] to pretend, to hoax. ❑ **put oneself outside of** *v. see* GET OUTSIDE (OF) *under* OUTSIDE *adv.* ❑ **put on the pump** *v. see* PUMP *v.* ❑ **put on the third degree** *v. see* THIRD DEGREE *v.* ❑ **put out** *see* separate entries. ❑ **put out of sight** *v.* **1** [mid-19C] to drink. **2** [late 19C] to eat. ❑ **put over** *v.* [mid-19C–1910s] to knock over with a gunshot. ❑ **put someone back** *v.* [var. on SET BACK *under* SET *v.*] [20C+] to cost; often as *how much did that put you back?* ❑ **put someone in** *v.* (*also* **put someone in it, put someone in with**) ['one' is the report or the person thus 'put in' prison] **1** [1920s+] (*orig. Aus.*) to inform against. **2** [1950s] to ruin someone's reputation, to talk maliciously behind someone's back. **3** [1950s+] to incriminate. ❑ **put someone on** *v.* (*also* **put someone upon**) [19C–1900s] (*US*) to inform, to explain. ❑ **put someone on the linger** *v.* [1940s] (*US black*) to abandon someone. ❑ **put someone through** *v.* [mid-19C–1900s] (*US/Aus.*) to play a trick on someone, to overcome. ❑ **put something down** *v.* [1950s+] (*US black*) to stop what one is doing. ❑ **put something on** *v.* [1920s+] to accuse, to find evidence against. ❑ **put (something) on (someone)** *v.* [1960s] (*US black*) to present (something or someone) to someone. ❑ **put the…** *v. see* separate entry. ❑ **put them up** *v.* ['them' are the fists or arms] [mid-19C+] to get ready to fight. ❑ **put this reckoning up to the Dover wagoner** [a pun on the contemporary Dover wagoner, one *Owen*, i.e. 'owing'] [early–mid-19C] put this (usu. tavern bill) on credit. ❑ **put through** *see* separate entries. ❑ **put under** *v.* (*also* **put under the sod**) [SE *sod*, a lump of earth] [late 19C+] to kill, to murder. ❑ **put up** *see* separate entries.

IN EXCLAMATIONS

❑ **put another record on!** [1920s] an excl. used in the hope of silencing a nagging or critical person. ❑ **put it there!** (*also* **put her there! put it there if it weighs a ton!**) ['there' being the speaker's outstretched hand and 'it'/'her' being the hand of the person spoken to] [mid-19C+] shake hands! esp. in the context of sealing a deal or affirming a friendship. ❑ **put that on!** [2000s] (*US teen*) an excl. used to intensify a statement.

put *v.*[2] [echoic] [1900s] (*US campus*) to vomit.

puta *n.* [synon. Sp.] (*US Hisp.*) **1** [1930s+] a prostitute; a very promiscuous woman. **2** [1960s+] a general term of abuse.

put and take *n.*[1] [the 'backwards-and-forwards' movement of intercourse] [1920s+] **1** sexual intercourse. **2** homosexual intercourse.

put and take *n.*[2] [rhy. sl.] [1920s+] a cake.

put-away *n.* [PUT AWAY *v.* (2)] **1** [late 19C–1900s] imprisonment. **2** [1910s+] (*Aus.*) an informer. **3** [1930s] (*Aus.*) an object or piece of information that gives something away.

put away *v.* **1** in fig. senses implying violence. (**a**) [late 16C+] to kill, to murder. (**b**) [late 19C+] to bury. (**c**) [late 19C+] to knock out. (**d**) [late 19C+] (*orig. US*) to defeat an opponent; lit. and fig. **2** in senses meaning to confine or deposit. (**a**) [mid-19C+] to imprison. (**b**) [mid-19C+] (*orig. UK Und.*) to inform against someone and thus be instrumental in having them imprisoned. (**c**) [late 19C–1920s] to pawn. (**d**) [1910s+] to put in a lunatic asylum or old people's home. **3** [mid-19C+] to eat or drink, esp. a large amount. **4** in senses of performing, acting. (**a**) [1930s–40s] (*US Und.*) to pose as someone important. (**b**) [1940s] (*orig. US black*) to perform. (**c**) [1960s] of a man, to seduce a woman. (**d**) [1960s+] of an entertainer, to score a resounding success with one's audience, to impress greatly. **5** [1940s] to praise.

put-down *n.* [PUT DOWN *v.*[1] (2a)] [1950s+] a verbal attack, criticism, condemnation.

put down *adj.* [1960s] depressed, disappointed.

put down *v.*[1] **1** [mid-19C+] to eat, to drink. **2** in senses implying aggression, hostility. (**a**) [late 19C+] to deride, to slander, to attack verbally, to tease. (**b**) [1950s] to imprison. (**c**) [1950s+] to attack physically, to kill. **3** (*US*) in lit. and fig. senses of SE *put down*, to set down. (**a**) [20C+] of an activity, to abandon. (**b**) [1910s] (*UK Und.*) to successfully cash a forged cheque at a bank; to pass counterfeit money; thus *putter-down*, one who passes counterfeit cheques. (**c**) [1940s+] to act, to do, to say. (**d**) [1950s+] of a person, to reject, to give up. (**e**) [1970s] of a place, to leave. **4** in senses of SE *put down for*. (**a**) [1990s+] to involve someone, i.e. in a crime. (**b**) [2000s] (*US black*) to enlist a candidate in a gang or similar group.

IN PHRASES

❑ **put down shoe leather** *v.* [1960s] to run fast.

put down *v.*[2] *see under* DOWN *adj.*[1] (1).

pu the elop *adj.* [backsl. UP THE POLE *adj.*[2]] [20C+] pregnant.

put-in *n.* **1** [mid–late 19C] of a man, an act of sexual intercourse. **2** [mid-19C+] (*US*) one's turn to speak, one's affair [poker imagery].

IN PHRASES

❑ **have a put-in** *v.* [19C] to have sexual intercourse.

put in *v.* **1** [mid-19C+] of time, to expend, to serve, usu. referring to a job. **2** in senses of SE *put in a word*. (**a**) [late 19C] (*US*) to introduce. (**b**) [1920s+] (*Aus./US*) to get someone into trouble, esp. to inform on (to the police). (**c**) [1930s+] to give information. (**d**) [1980s+] to put someone forward for a job.

IN PHRASES

❑ **put in the bucket** *v.* (*also* **put in the garden, …hole, …well**) [BUCKET *v.* (1); the image is of hiding away the partner's share; only *hole* is 20C+] [early 19C+] (*UK Und.*) to deceive, to cheat, to swindle, to ruin, esp. to rob an accomplice of their share of a robbery.

put it on (someone) *v.* **1** [mid-19C–1900s] to extort money, with or without menaces; to charge to someone else's account.

2 [late 19C+] to assault, to beat someone up, to murder. **3** [20C+] to show off. **4** [20C+] to overcharge. **5** [1910s+] (*Aus.*) to make a suggestion, to propose. **6** [1950s] to demand, to extort, to persuade. **7** [1950s] (*US gang*) to declare war. **8** [2000s] (*US black*) to excite sexually.

Putney *n.*

IN EXCLAMATIONS

❑ **go to Putney (on a pig)!** (*also* **go to Pettigo!**) [*Putney* S.W. London; *Pettigo* village, Co. Donegal] [mid-19C; 1990s+] a dismissive excl., as in GO TO JERICHO! *under* JERICHO *n.*

puto *n.* [masc. version of Sp. *puta*, a prostitute] [1950s+] **1** a male homosexual. **2** a male prostitute. **3** the penis. **4** a general derog. term.

put-on *n.* [PUT ON *v.* (2b)] **1** [mid-19C+] a joke, a hoax. **2** [late 19C] an old female beggar who specializes in *putting on* a look that makes her look as pitiful as possible.

IN COMPOUNDS

❑ **put-on artist** *n.* [ARTIST *n.* (1)] [1930s+] (*US*) a hoaxer, a tease.

put-on *adj.* [PUT ON *v.* (1)] [late 19C+] (*US*) affected, pretentious.

put on *v.* **1** [early 18C; late 19C+] (*also* **put up**) to affect airs; thus n., *put-on*, one who puts on airs. **2** in senses based on speech. (**a**) [mid–late 19C] (*UK/US Und.*) to inform. (**b**) [mid-19C+] to tease, to joke with, to deceive for one's own gain. (**c**) [1910s+] (*Aus. Und.*) to arrest and/or charge on the basis of concocted evidence, to 'frame up'. (**d**) [1960s] to annoy, to irritate. (**e**) [1960s] to request. **3** in senses of consumption. (**a**) [1930s+] (*US*) to eat, e.g. *put on the chicken pie* [abbr. PUT ON THE FEED BAG *under* FEED BAG *n.*]. (**b**) [1940s] to smoke a cigarette. **4** [1960s] (*orig. US black*) to do to, to make happen to.

IN PHRASES

❑ **put on roll** *v.* **1** [1910s] (*UK juv.*) to put on airs, to swagger. **2** [1930s] (*US black*) to fight. ❑ **put on (the)...** *v.* [1980s+] (*Aus. prison*) used with a pertinent n. to indicate that an individual is being labelled, e.g. *put on the dog*, to be branded as an informer. ❑ **put on the bloomy** *v.* [late 19C] to dress oneself up. ❑ **put on the Fair Persian** *v.* [? stereotyped image of Persian women lying around in the harem] [late 19C] (*Aus.*) of a woman, to act lazily. ❑ **put on the skid** *v.* [SE *skid*, a block used to retard a wheel] [late 19C] to speak or act cautiously.

put out *adj.* [PUT OUT *v.* (1b)] [late 19C+] murdered, killed.

put out *v.* **1** in senses of violence [abbr. SE *put out*, to extinguish; poss. also SE *put out of one's misery*]. (**a**) [mid-19C+] to knock out, to assault. (**b**) [late 19C+] (*also* **put out of the way**) to murder, to kill. **2** in senses of handing over or displaying. (**a**) [late 19C+] to pay money. (**b**) [1910s] (*US prison*) to offer in exchange, or as a bribe or reward. (**c**) [1930s] to make an effort. (**d**) [1930s+] (*US*) to offer oneself for sex.

putsy *n. see* PUTZ *n.* (2).

putter-up *n.* [SE *put up* (*a plan*)] [early 19C–1940s] (*UK Und.*) one who plans a robbery or tips off thieves as to where a robbery might profitably be committed, e.g. a servant in a great house, a bank clerk etc.

put the... *v.*

IN PHRASES

❑ **put the bit on** *v.* [SE *bit*, the mouthpiece of a horse's bridle, used to restrain the animal] [1950s] (*Aus.*) to extort, to blackmail, to force someone to do something they would rather avoid. ❑ **put the bleed on** *v. see* BLEED *v.*[1] (1). ❑ **put the box on** *v. see* PUT THE BLOCK ON *under* BLOCK *n.*[6]. ❑ **put the clamps on** *v.* [i.e. one SE *clamps* hold of the stolen item, villains or spouse-to-be] [20C+] **1** (*US*) to steal. **2** (*US Und.*) of the police, to clamp down on crime. **3** (*US*) to make somebody into one's spouse. ❑ **put the comether on** *v.* (*also* **put the come-hither on**) [SE *come hither*] [mid-19C+] (*Aus./Irish*) to coax, to wheedle, to impress. ❑ **put the devil into hell** *v.* (*also* **put the Pope into Rome**) [a euph. coined by Boccaccio in a ribald story in the *Decameron* (1358), in which a hermit seduces a virgin by persuading her of the necessity of letting him 'put the devil into hell'] [17C+] to have sexual intercourse. ❑ **put the leg-rope on** *v.* [SE *leg-rope*, a rope used to tether or control an animal] [20C+] (*Aus.*) to curb a person who is acting in a hysterical or very bad-tempered manner. ❑ **put the maginnis on** *v.* (*also* **put the macginnis on, ...mcginnis...**) [SE *mcginnis*, a wrestling hold] [1900s–40s] (*Aus.*) to put in a position from which there is no escape, to pressurize; thus *crooked maginnis*, an unfair form of control, e.g. (moral) blackmail. ❑ **put the nuts on** *v.* [i.e. one 'turns a screw'] [1940s–50s] (*US prison*) to threaten or intimidate, physically and/or verbally.

put through *adj.* [i.e. PUT THROUGH A/THE WRINGER *under* WRINGER *n.*] [1900s] (*Aus.*) suffering, abused.

put through *v.* [abbr. PUT THROUGH A/THE WRINGER *under* WRINGER *n.*] [1960s] (*Aus.*) to cheat someone.

puttock *n.* [SE *puttock*, a kite or buzzard, hence the human version of a 'bird of prey'] [17C] **1** an unpleasant person. **2** a prostitute.

putt-putt *n.* [the sound of its mechanism] **1** [20C+] (*orig. US*) a small vehicle or motor-boat. **2** [1920s] (*UK Und.*) a machine-gun.

putty *n.* **1** [mid–late 19C; 1970s] (*mainly US*) money [i.e. it 'fills in the cracks']. **2** [1980s+] (*Aus. prison*) second-rate hashish.

SE in slang uses

IN COMPOUNDS

❑ **putty-brained** *adj.* (*also* **putty-faced, putty-nosed**) [late 19C+] stupid. ❑ **putty-cove** *n.* (*also* **putty-covess**) [COVE *n.* (1)/COVESS *n.*] [mid-19C] (*UK Und.*) an unreliable person. ❑ **putty-head** *n.* (*also* **putty-brain**) [-HEAD *sfx* (1)] [mid-19C+] (*US*) a fool. ❑ **putty medal** *n.* [a proper medal would be made of metal] [late 19C–1900s] a fig. award given to someone who has botched a job or in some other way failed to do what is required. ❑ **putty pusher** *n.* [image of anal intercourse] [1990s+] a homosexual man.

IN PHRASES

❑ **up to putty** *adj.* [the innate worthlessness of putty] [1910s+] (*Aus.*) worthless, ineffectual.

putty *adj.* [play on putty's flexible consistency and on SOFT *adj.* (1)] [1910s–20s] stupid, foolish.

putty and soap *n.* [mid-19C] (*UK Und.*) bread and cheese.

put up *n.* [PUT UP *v.* (2)] [mid-19C–1920s] (*UK Und.*) a planned act of robbery/burglary.

put up *v.* **1** [early 19C] to plan in advance, esp. a crime or some form of deception. **2** [early 19C+] to propose, to put forward. **3** [mid-19C] (*N.Z./US Und.*) to hold up and rob. **4** [late 19C+] to pay out money in advance, esp. on a bet or for the purchase of drugs. **5** [20C+] (*US black*) to explain, to 'put in the picture'. **6** [1900s] (*Aus.*) to set aside. **7** [1960s] (*N.Z.*) to report a crime to the authorities. **8** *see* PUT ON *v.* (1).

IN COMPOUNDS

❑ **put-up man** *n.* [1900s–50s] (*US Und.*) one who points out or sets up a victim for the thief.

IN PHRASES

❑ **put up or shut up** [gambling imagery] [late 19C+] (*orig. US*) a challenge; back your big talk with a genuine commitment.

put-up job *n.* (*also* **put-up affair, ...go, ...thing**) [PUT UP *v.* (1) + JOB *n.*[2] (1); variants tend to disappear by late 19C] [19C+] a pre-arranged, and usu. criminal or at least deceptive, plan.

putz *n.* (*also* **potz, putzo**) [Yid. *putz*, the penis; ult. Ind.-Eur. *puts*, a swelling, thus in Lat. *praeputium*, the prepuce or foreskin] [1930s+] **1** the penis. **2** (*also* **putsy**) an idiot, a fool, a simpleton.

IN PHRASES

❑ **putz around** *v.* (*also* **putz**) [1930s+] to act like a fool, to mess around.

puxsey-mot *n.* [? PUDDING *n.* (5) + MOT *n.* (2)] [mid-19C] (*UK Und.*) a pregnant woman.

puza *see under* PHUZA.

puzzey-baubled *adj.* [? var. on SE *fuzzy-headed*] [mid-19C] (*UK Und.*) embarrassed; confused.

puzzle *n.*[1] [dial. *puzzle*, a slut; ult. Fr. *pucelle*, a virgin; the tricks played by young girls, esp. when fresh from the country, of presenting themselves as virgins (and thus demanding higher prices)] [late 16C–17C] a prostitute.

IN PHRASES

□ **dirty puzzle** *n.* [late 17C–early 19C] a slatternly woman.

puzzle *n.*[2]

SE in slang uses

IN COMPOUNDS

□ **puzzle-cause** *n.* [SE *cause*, a legal suit] [late 18C–early 19C] an ignorant, incompetent lawyer. □ **puzzle-cove** *n.* [COVE *n.* (1)] [mid–late 19C] a lawyer. □ **puzzle factory** *n.* [2000s] (*US*) a psychiatric institution. □ **puzzle-text** *n.* (*also* **martext**) [late 18C–early 19C] an uneducated clergyman.

IN PHRASES

□ **fifteen puzzle** *n.* [SE *fifteen puzzle*, a popular puzzle, *c.*1879; like a prototype Rubik's cube, it required players to arrange a set of numbered, moveable squares in rows, each of which had to add up to 15] [late 19C] absolute chaos, utter confusion.

puzzlegut *n.* [var. on PUSTLE-GUT *n.*] [1900s–40s] (*US black*) an exceptionally large stomach.

puzzling sticks *n.* [the criminal fig. 'puzzles' the crimes while being punished] [early 19C] a triangle to which a criminal is tied to receive a judicial whipping.

P.V. *n. see* PAV *n.*

p.v. *n.* [abbr.] [1960s+] (*US prison*) **1** *parole violator.* **2** *parole violation.*

p.w'd/p-whipped *adj. see* PUSSY-WHIPPED *under* PUSSY *n.*

p.w.t. *n.* [abbr. SE *poor* + WHITE TRASH *n.*] [1990s+] (*US*) the poor white population of the Southern states of the US.

pyaka *adj.* [Carib.E. *pyaka-pyaka*, messy, dirty; ult. unknown Afr. language's *poto-poto*, muddy] [1950s+] (*W.I. Rasta*) tricky or dishonest.

p.y.c. *phr.* [abbr.] [1930s+] (*Aus.*) *pay your cash.*

pye *v.* (*also* **py**) [SE *pie*, a magpie; the bird was used as a synon. for the penis in 17C] [mid-17C] of a man, to have sexual intercourse.

IN COMPOUNDS

□ **py-man** *n.* (*also* **pyeman**) [mid-17C] (*UK Und.*) a womanizer, a lecher. □ **py-woman** *n.* [mid-17C] (*UK Und.*) a prostitute.

pyjama python *n.* (*also* **pant python**) [1960s–80s] the penis.

py korry *n.* [fig. use of PY KORRY! *excl.*] [1940s] (*N.Z.*) a Maori.

py korry! *excl.* (*also* **by korry!**) [mispron.] [late 19C+] (*N.Z.*) by golly!

pyky *n. see* PIKEY *n.*

p.y.t. *n.* [abbr. *pretty young thing*] [2000s] (*S.Afr. gay*) an attractive young man.

python *n.* [1970s+] (*Aus./S.Afr.*) the penis.

pyu *v.* [SE *spew*, to vomit] [1950s+] (*W.I. Rasta*) of a running sore etc, to drip or ooze.

p.y.w. *n.* [abbr. *pretty young whore*] [2000s] a trophy wife.

Q *n.*[1] [abbr.] **1** [late 19C–1930s] (*US tramp*) the Chicago, Burlington and Quincey Railroad. **2** [late 19C+] (*US Und.*) San Quentin prison, in California. **3** [1920s] (*Aus.*) The Queensland Railway.

SE in slang uses

IN PHRASES

❑ **go on the letter Q** *v.* [synon. for ON *THE* BILLIARD SLUM *under* SLUM *n.*[2] and thus a pun on *Q*/(billiard) cue] [early 19C] (*UK Und.*) to work as a confidence trickster.

Q *n.*[2] [abbr.] [1940s–50s] (*US black*) barbecued ribs.

Q *n.*[3] [abbr. brandname *Q*uaalude] [1970s] (*drugs*) methaqualone.

q *n.* [abbr.] **1** [1960s–70s] (*US*) a male homosexual [QUEER *n.* (4)]. **2** [1990s+] (*UK drugs*) a quarter ounce of hashish.

q *adj.* (*also* **queue**) [QUEER *adj.* (4)] [1940s+] homosexual.

IN PHRASES

❑ **go queueing** *v.* [1940s] to live as a homosexual.

Q.E. *n.* [abbr.] [1950s+] (*UK prison*) Queen's Evidence, i.e. giving evidence against one's fellow criminals.

Q.H.B. *n. see* HIS MAJESTY'S BAD BARGAIN *n.*

q.p. *n.* (*also* **QP**) [abbr.] [1980s+] (*US drugs*) a *q*uarter *p*ound of cannabis.

q.q. *n.* [abbr.] [1950s] (*W.I.*) a *q*uarter-*q*uart (of rum).

q.s. *n.* [abbr. QUEER STREET *n.*] [late 19C–1900s] any difficult situation.

Q.T. *n.* [abbr. *quiet*]

IN PHRASES

❑ **do the Q.T.** *v.* [late 19C] to lead a quiet life. ❑ **on the Q.T.** **1** [late 19C+] surreptitiously, on the quiet; also ext. as *on the strict Q.T.* **2** [1910s] living quietly, soberly.

Q.T. *adj.* [ON *THE* *Q.T. under* Q.T. *n.*] [late 19C+] surreptitious.

q.t. *n.* [abbr. *q*uality *t*ime] [1990s+] (*US*) proper care and attention.

qua *n.*[1] [? QUOD *n.* (1)] [early 19C] (*US Und.*) a prison; thus *qua keeper*, a warden.

qua *n.*[2] [abbr. brandname *Qua*alude] [1970s] (*drugs*) methaqualone.

quaabs *n.* (*also* **quabs**) [? link to SE *squab*, a fledgling] [1970s+] (*W.I.*) socially equal, thus friends.

quack *n.*[1] **1** in senses of charlatanry [abbr. of SE *quacksalver*, one who 'quacks' mendaciously about the quality of their medicines and salves]. (**a**) [late 16C+] an incompetent medical charlatan; thus adj. *quacky*. (**b**) [late 17C+] (*orig. Aus./N.Z.*) a doctor, irrespective of their abilities. (**c**) [mid-18C+] a charlatan (other than in a medical context). **2** [late 19C–1910s] (*also* **quacker**) a duck. **3** [1960s+] (*US black*) a homosexual [? he 'ducks down' for sex]. **4** [1980s] (*US drugs*) a habitual cocaine user [ref. to their constant verbal 'quacking']. **5** [1990s+] an act of breaking wind.

quack *n.*[2] [initial letter] [1970s–80s] (*US drugs*) a quaalude.

quack *adj.* [QUACK *n.*[1] (1a)] [late 18C+] pertaining to a charlatan doctor or his medicines; occas. ext. to other professions.

quack *v.* **1** in senses of charlatanry [QUACK *n.*[1] (1a)]. (**a**) [late 17C–mid-19C] to be an incompetent doctor, to work as an itinerant doctor. (**b**) [mid-19C] to promote one's business through fraudulent claims. **2** in senses of sound. (**a**) [1940s+] to complain. (**b**) [1990s+] to break wind noisily.

quacker *n.*[1] [? noise during sexual intercourse] [2000s] (*Aus.*) the female genital area.

quacker *n.*[2] *see* QUACK *n.*[1] (2).

quacking cheat *n.* (*also* **quaking cheat**) [SE *quack* + CHEAT *n.* (1)] [mid-16C–early 19C] (*UK Und.*) a drake or duck.

quacktail *n.* [her hairstyle, either a ponytail or a DUCK'S ARSE *n.*] [1960s–70s] (*S.Afr.*) the girlfriend of a township gangster; also attrib.

quaco *n.* [Twi *kwacu*, a boy who is born on a Wednesday] [1940s+] (*W.I.*) an unsophisticated, ignorant person, a countrified person.

quad *n.* [abbr.] **1** [late 18C–mid-19C] a prison [abbr. SE *quadrangle*]. **2** [mid-19C] a horse [SE *quadriped*]. **3** [late 19C] a *quad*ricycle. **4** [1970s+] (*US campus*) a very clumsy person [? f. *quad*riplegic]. **5** [1970s+] (*US drugs*) methaqualone [brandname *Qua*alude]. **6** [1990s+] a *quad*riplegic. **7** *see* QUOD *n.*

IN COMPOUNDS

❑ **quad-cull** *n. see* DUB-CULL *under* DUB *n.*[1].

quaecall *n.* [var. on QUOD CULL *under* QUOD *n.*] [late 18C] (*US Und.*) a turnkey.

quaedam *n.* [Lat. *quaedam*, one of those, thus a euph.] [late 17C] a prostitute.

quaggot *n.* (*also* **quag**) [QUEER *adj.* (4) + FAGGOT *n.*[1] (3)] [1930s+] (*US gay*) a male homosexual.

quail *n.* [SE *quail*, a supposedly amorous bird] **1** [17C+] a prostitute. **2** [mid-19C; 1920s–30s] (*US tramp*) an 'old maid'. **3** [mid-19C+] a young woman, poss. under the age of consent. **4** [late 19C] (*US*) an order of chicken stew. **5** [1960s–70s] (*US gay*) an attractive young man.

quailer *n.* [ety. unknown; ? link to dial. *quail*, to frighten] [20C+] (*Aus.*) a stone.

quail pipe *n.* [SE *quail pipe*, a pipe or whistle that imitates the notes of the female quail and lures birds into a net] **1** [17C–mid-19C] a woman's tongue, esp. as the seducer of foolish men. **2** [late 17C–18C] the throat.

quaint *n.* (*also* **quainter, quent, queynte**) [CUNT *n.* (1)] [late 14C–19C] the vagina.

quake breach *n.* (*also* **quake buttock**) [lit. 'fear-anus', 'fear-buttock'] [late 16C–early 17C] a coward.

quaker *n.* [it is long and thin, hard and 'wears brown'] [mid-19C] a hard, and poss. lengthy, piece of excreta.

IN PHRASES

❑ **bury a quaker** *v.* [mid-19C] to defecate.

Quaker oat *n.* (*also* **Quaker oats**) [rhy. sl.] [1930s+] a coat.

Quaker's bargain *n.* [play on YEA AND NAY (MAN) *n.*] [late 17C–early 18C] a 'take it or leave it' bargain.

quaker's meeting *n.* [pun on SE, since quakers' meetings are silent] [late 18C] noise, uproar.

quaking cheat *n.* [SE *quake*, to tremble + CHEAT *n.* (1)] **1** [mid-16C–mid-19C] a sheep. **2** [late 17C–early 19C] a calf. **3** *see* QUACKING CHEAT *n.*

Quaky Isles *n.* [i.e. the islands' earth*quakes*] [20C+] (*Aus.*) New Zealand.

qualified *adj.* [1960s+] (*US black*) of a prostitute, experienced.

qualify *v.* [1970s] (*US Und.*) of a confidence trickster, to assess the potential of a possible victim.

qually *n.* [? SE *cloudy* or *squally*] [late 17C–early 18C] cloudy, sour wine.

quamin *n.* (*also* **quarmin**) [Twi *kwamé*, a boy who is born on a Saturday] [1940s+] (*W.I.*) an unsophisticated, ignorant person, a countrified person.

quams *n.* [SE *qualms*] [2000s] (*US black*) problems, worries.

quandary *n.* [SE f. 1800; ? f. Fr. *qu'en dirai-je*, what shall I say of it?, but the pron. militates against this; 'possibly a corruption of some term of scholastic Latin' (*OED*)] [mid-16C–18C] a dilemma, a state of extreme uncertainty.

quandary *v.* [QUANDARY *n.*] [mid–late 17C] to be in a dilemma, to be uncertain, to wonder.

quandong *n.* [SE *quandong*, a fruit which is soft on the outside but hard inside] (*Aus.*) **1** [late 19C+] stupidity, softness; in phr. below. **2** [1910s+] ext. use of sense 1, personified as a country bumpkin. **3** [1930s+] a disreputable figure, living on their wits. **4** [1960s+] a young woman who accepts any amount of gifts but still refuses to cede her sexual favours.

IN PHRASES

❑ **have the quandongs** *v.* [late 19C+] (*Aus.*) to behave stupidly, to be stupid.

quanger *n.* [initial letter] [1960s+] (*Aus. teen*) a quince.

quantum *n.* [Lat. *quantum*, enough] [late 18C–mid-19C] a drink.

quare *adj.* [Irish pron. of SE *queer*] [mid-19C+] (*Irish*) **1** good, excellent, very; also as general intensifier. **2** odd, eccentric, 'queer'.

IN COMPOUNDS

❑ **quare place** *n.* [1960s+] (*Irish*) **1** hell. **2** somewhere unpleasant. ❑ **quare stuff** *n.* [1960s+] (*Irish*) constr. with *the*, illicitly distilled whisky, poteen. ❑ **quare thing** *n.* [1970s] (*Irish*) constr. with *the*, an act of sexual intercourse.

IN PHRASES

❑ **quare man, m'da** [lit. 'odd man, my father'] [20C+] (*Ulster*) a general expression of disbelief.

quarm *n.* (*also* **quarmburger**) [? QUEER *n.* (4)] [1990s+] (*UK juv.*) a male homosexual.

quarmin *n.* *see* QUAMIN *n.*

quarrel picker *n.* [pun on SE *quarrel*, a small, usu. diamond-shaped pane of glass, used for lattice-windows; ult. Fr. *carreau*, pane + SE *picker*] [late 17C–early 19C] a glazier.

quarrel with one's bread and butter *phr. see under* BREAD AND BUTTER *n.*[1].

quarrom *n.* (*also* **quarren, quarrome, quarromes, quarroms, quarron, quarrons**) [Ital. *carogna* or Fr. *charogne*, flesh] [mid-16C–mid-19C] (*UK Und.*) a body, a person.

quarry *n.* [SE *quarry*, a pit + ? *quarry*, that which is hunted] [18C] the vagina.

quarry cure *n.* (*also* **rockpile cure**) [Maurer, 'Lang. of the Underworld Narcotic Addict', Pt.2 (1938), notes 'Restricted to the Chicago Bridewell and to addicts who have done time there'] [1930s–60s] (*US drugs*) a 'cure' for drug addiction that involves being imprisoned and working in the rock quarry.

quart *n.*[1] [abbr.] **1** [late 19C–1900s] (*Aus.*) a quart pot, used for drinking; thus *quart-pot tea*, tea made in the open air and in a quart. **2** [1990s+] in drug uses. (**a**) a *quarter* of an ounce of cannabis. (**b**) a *quarter* of a gram or ounce of any given drug.

quart *n.*[2] [a double PINT *n.*] [1950s] (*W.I.*) a one-year prison sentence.

quarter *n.* **1** as a sum of money. (**a**) [mid-18C–mid-19C] five shillings (25p), $5. (**b**) [20C+] £25. (**c**) [1970s] (*US*) $25. **2** in drug and tobacco uses. (**a**) [mid-19C–1900s] (*UK prison*) a quarter inch of tobacco. (**b**) [1960s+] a quarter ounce (7g) of a narcotic drug. (**c**) [1980s+] $25 worth of a given drug. **3** as a jail sentence. (**a**) [late 19C–1900s] (*UK Und.*) a three-month's prison sentence. (**b**) [20C+] (*US Und.*) a 25-year prison sentence.

IN COMPOUNDS

❑ **quarter bag** *n.* (*also* **quarter sack**) [BAG *n.*[1] (7a)/SACK *n.* (3c)] [1960s+] (*drugs*) $25 worth of a given drug. ❑ **quarter house** *n.* [1970s] (*US drugs*) a place where drug users can obtain quarter-ounces of narcotics. ❑ **quarter piece** *n.* [PIECE *n.* (7a)] [1930s–50s] (*US drugs*) a quarter-ounce (7g) of drugs (cf. HALF-PIECE *under* HALF *n.*

IN PHRASES

❑ **half-quarter** *n.* [1980s+] (*US drugs*) one-eighth of an ounce (5g) of cannabis.

SE in slang uses

IN PHRASES

❑ **white quarter** *n. see* RED CENT *n.* ❑ **who put the quarter in your slot?** [1980s+] (*US campus*) a sarcastic admonition to mind one's own business.

quarter *adj.*

SE in slang uses

IN COMPOUNDS

❑ **quarter-mast** *n. see* AT HALF-MAST *under* MAST *n.* ❑ **quarter-pint** *adj. see* HALF-PINT *adj.* (2).

IN PHRASES

❑ **quarter flash and three parts stupid** *see under* FLASH *adj.*

quartereen *n.* [? Ital. *quattrino*; a farthing was a quarter of a penny] [mid-19C] a farthing.

quartern o'Bry *n.* [SE *quartern* + BRIAN O'FLYNN *n.*] [mid-19C] a quarter-pint of gin.

quartern of bliss *n.* [SE *quartern* + *bliss*] [late 19C] a short, attractive woman.

quartern o'finger *n.* [SE *quartern* + FINGER AND THUMB *n.* (1)] [mid-19C] a measure of rum.

quarter to two *n.* [rhy. sl.] [20C+] a Jew.

quart mania *n.* [19C] a hangover, delirium tremens.

quartz *n.* [late 19C–1900s] (*US*) money.

quashiba *n.* [Twi *akwasiba*, a girl born on a Sunday] **1** [late 18C] a white man's black or coloured mistress. **2** [late 18C–early 19C] a mistress in a non-sexual sense, i.e. of a house. **3** [1940s+] (*W.I.*) a foolish, uncultivated woman.

quashie *n.* [Twi *kwasi*, a boy born on a Sunday] **1** [late 18C–mid-19C] (*also* **quashy**) generic for a black person. **2** [mid-19C+] (*20C+ W.I.*) (*also* **quashee**) a country bumpkin, a peasant, a stupid person; thus generic for the lower classes *en masse*. **3** [1970s] (*W.I.*) a coward.

quasimodo *n.* [rhy. sl.; Cockney pron.] [20C+] soda.

quat *n.* [SE *quat*, a pimple] [early 17C] a derog. term used for a young man.

quattie *n.* (*also* **quatty**) [? a *quarter* of 6d] [20C+] (*W.I.*) 1½d (post-1969 value 25 cents).

quaver *n.* [SE *quaver*, a note, equal in length to half a crotchet or one-eighth of a semibreve] [mid-19C–1950s] a musician.

quaw *n.* (*also* **quawy**) [Twi *kwaw*, a boy who is born on a Thursday] [mid-19C+] (*W.I.*) **1** a stupid, ugly person, a peasant or bumpkin. **2** an albino.

quay *n.* (*also* **quee**) [? QUOD *n.* (1)] [mid-18C–mid-19C] (*US Und.*) prison.

quean *n.* [11C SE *quean*, woman (with no pej. aspect); Nares suggests AS *cwean*, a barren cow] **1** [early 16C–19C] a strumpet, a prostitute. **2** [1910s+] a (passive) homosexual. **3** [1960s] an afficionado of sado-masochism.

DERIVATIVES

❑ **queanish** *adj.* (*also* **queenish**) [early 17C] promiscuous.

IN PHRASES

❑ **quean up** *v.* (*also* **queen up**) [1930s+] (*Aus.*) to dress carefully, though not always effeminately; usu. in phr. *all queaned up*.

queanie *n.* [ext. of QUEAN *n.* (2)] [1930s+] a homosexual.

queanie *adj.* (*also* **queany**) [QUEANIE *n.*] [1930s+] (*Aus.*) effeminate.

quee *n. see* QUAY *n.*

queeb *n.* [ety. unknown; ? SE *quibble* n.] [1960s] (*US teen*) any small problem, esp. mechanical.

queef *n.* [QUEEF *v.*] [1990s+] a vaginal fart.

queef *v.* [QUIFF *n.*[1] (1) + ? SE *whiff*] [1990s+] (*US*) of a woman, to make a vaginal fart (usu. noisy rather than malodorous).

queen *see also under* QUEAN.

queen *n.* **1** as a heterosexual woman. (**a**) [18C+] (*US*) a pretty girl, a beauty. (**b**) [late 19C+] a woman. (**c**) [20C+] (*US*) the best, usu. used with a suitable n. or v., e.g. *queen of maths*. (**d**) [1910s–40s] a woman, usu. categorized by her job, e.g. *candy counter queen*. (**e**) [1940s+] (*S.Afr.*) a woman who runs an illicit township bar or shebeen [abbr. *SHEBEEN QUEEN under* SHEBEEN *n.*]. **2** as a male homosexual [16C SE *quean*, a woman; this sp. is still occas. used to distinguish it f. SE use (cf. QUEAN *n.* (2))]. (**a**) [late 19C+] an effeminate (older) homosexual male. Popular culture offers a number of variations based on words and phrases including *queen*, e.g. *Queen for a day*; *Queen Mother*; *Queen of All the Fairies*. The variety of homosexual tastes is often denoted by a comb. of adj.+ *queen* (see -QUEEN *sfx*). (**b**) [1960s] (*gay*) used ironically by a homosexual of a heterosexual. (**c**) [1970s+] (*US prison*) an attractive, effeminate young prison homosexual; as such, much sought after and fought over. (**d**) [1980s+] (*Aus. prison*) a transsexual.

IN COMPOUNDS

❑ **queen drag** *n. see* DRAG QUEEN *n.* ❑ **queen Mary** *n.* [MARY *n.* (2a)] [1970s+] (*US gay*) an obese gay man. ❑ **queen mother** *n.* [1970s] (*US gay*) an older homosexual man. ❑ **Queens' Row** *n.* [ref. to 1941 film *King's Row*, starring Ronald Reagan] **1** [1950s+] (*US gay*) the Public Gardens, Boston, Massachusetts. **2** [1960s+] (*US prison*) a section of the prison where homosexual inmates have their cells.

IN PHRASES

❑ **queen for a day** *n.* [2000s] (*S.Afr. gay*) an ostensibly heterosexual married man, who has sex with men and then returns home. ❑ **queen of Scotch** *n.* [pun on *Mary Queen of Scots* + *Scotch* whisky] [1970s] (*US gay*) an alcoholic gay man. ❑ **queen of spades** *n. see under* SPADE *n.*

SE in slang uses

IN COMPOUNDS

❑ **queen's head** *n.* [the monarch's head on the stamp] [mid-19C] a postage stamp. ❑ **queen's pictures** *n.* (*also* **queen's portrait**) [the pictures of the reigning monarch, in this case Queen Anne and Queen Victoria, on one side of the coin] [early 18C; mid–late 19C] money. ❑ **queen's tears** *n.* [? ref. to the tears Queen Victoria supposedly shed after the defeat at Isandhlwana] [1940s+] (*S.Afr. Zulu*) alcohol, usu. gin.

IN PHRASES

❑ **draw the queen's picture** *v. see under* DRAW *v.*[4]. ❑ **queen of tarts** *n. see under* TART *n.* ❑ **queen's bad bargain/shilling** *n. see* HIS MAJESTY'S BAD BARGAIN *n.* ❑ **queen's hard bargain** *n. see* HIS MAJESTY'S BAD BARGAIN *n.* ❑ **queen's gold medal** *n.* [the monarch's head on the coin] [late 19C–1900s] a shilling (5p). ❑ **where the queen goes on foot** *n.* (*also* **where the queen sends nobody**) [note Urquhart, *Gargantua & Pantagruel* (1653): '*Cagar*. Spanish. To do that which the king himself can't get another to do for him'] [20C+] the lavatory.

queen *v.* (*also* **queen it up**) [QUEEN *n.* (2)] [1970s+] to act in an effeminate manner; to pose ostentatiously.

-queen *sfx* [SE *queen*/QUEEN *n.* (2a)] **1** [1940s+] a combining form indicating that a woman is the best at something (cf. -KING *sfx*). **2** [1940s+] a combining form indicating a female enthusiast. **3** [1940s+] (*orig. US gay*) a combining form indicating a male homosexual enthusiast.

Queen Anne's fan *n.* (*also* **Anne's fan**) [the spread fingers resemble a fan] [early 18C–mid-19C] thumbing one's nose.

queen bee *n.* [play on SE] **1** [1950s–70s] in gay uses [QUEEN *n.* (2a) + SE *bee* but ? abbr. *b*itch)]. (**a**) a woman who likes to surround herself with young men, who may or may not be homosexual. (**b**) as sense 1a but of a man, usu. homosexual himself. **2** [2000s] (*US black*) the woman with the largest breasts in a group.

Queen Bess *n.* ['perhaps because that queen (Elizabeth I), history says, was of a swarthy complexion' (Hotten, 1867)] [late 18C–mid-19C] in cards, the queen of clubs.

Queen Dick *n.*

IN PHRASES

❑ **in the days of Queen Dick** (*also* **in the reign of Queen Dick**) [*Dick*, i.e. Richard, being a man there could not be a *Queen Dick*] [late 18C+] never.

queenie *n.* **1** [late 19C] an affectionate nickname used of 'a fat woman trying to walk young' (Ware) [the line 'Queenie, come back, sweet', from the 1884 Drury Lane pantomime in which it was addressed to 'Mr H. Campbell, one of the heaviest men on the stage, and then playing "Eliza" a cook' (Ware)]. **2** [1910s–70s] (*US*) a derog. name for an effeminate male homosexual [QUEEN *n.* (1)]. **3** [1950s] (*Aus.*) a prostitute.

queenie *adj. see* QUEENY *adj.*

queening *n.* [2000s] (*S.Afr. gay*) sitting on a man's face, so that his mouth and nose are covered with one's anus.

queen mama *n.* [1990s+] (*US teen*) the very best of a person, place or thing; the female counterpart of *KING DADDY under* KING *n.*

Queen Mum *n.* [rhy. sl. = BUM *n.*[1] (1)] [2000s] the buttocks.

queen of the south *n.* [rhy. sl.; ult. a Scot. soccer team] [20C+] the mouth.

queen pin *n.* [1960s+] the female equivalent of KINGPIN *n.*, i.e. a woman who heads an institution or arranges an event.

Queensland salute *n. see BARCOO SALUTE under* BARCOO *n.*

Queen's Park Ranger *n.* [rhy. sl.; ult. the West London football club] [1960s+] a stranger.

Queen Street cocky *n.* (*also* **Queen Street bushie, ...farmer**) [*Queen Street*, the business/financial centre of Auckland + COCKY *n.*[2] (1)] [1950s+] (*N.Z.*) a businessman who owns a farm as an investment.

Queen Street yank *n.* [*Queen Street*, the business/financial centre of Auckland + YANK *n.* (1)] [1950s] (*N.Z.*) a New Zealander who apes American styles etc.

queen's woman *n.* [mid-19C] 'a prostitute who received medical attention under the terms of the Contagious Diseases Acts of the 1860s' (*OED*).

queeny *n.* [QUEEN *n.* (2a)] [1960s] a derog. term of address to a male homosexual.

queeny *adj.* (*also* **queenie**) [QUEEN *n.* (2a)] [1930s+] (*gay*) flamboyant and effeminate; also as adv.

queer *n.* [SE *queer*, odd/QUEER *adj.*] **1** [mid-18C–1910s] a hoax, a confidence trick; thus phr. *play the queer*, to hoodwink. **2** [mid-18C+] (*also* **queer stuff**) counterfeit money. **3** [late 19C] a look (on one's face); a look (at something). **4** [1910s+] a homosexual, usu. male, occas. female. **5** [1940s] an eccentric. **6** [1950s] (*US Und.*) a heterosexual who enjoys non-standard sexual practices. **7** [1950s] (*Aus.*) a fool, a simpleton. **8** [1960s] (*US campus*) one who works (overly) hard.

IN COMPOUNDS

❑ **queerbait** *n.* [1950s+] an effeminate young boy who attracts, or is supposed to attract older male homosexuals; thus as v., to seek out a homosexual encounter for money. ❑ **queer-basher** *n.* [1960s+] one who specializes in beating up (and usu. robbing) male homosexuals. ❑ **queer-bashing** *n.* [1960s+] the beating up (and usu. robbing) of male homosexuals. ❑ **queer-rolling** *n.* [ROLL *v.* (3a)] [1960s+] the beating up (and robbery) of homosexual men; thus *queer-roller*, one who does this. ❑ **queer shover** *n.* [late 19C+] (*UK Und.*) a passer of counterfeit money. ❑ **queersman** *n.* [late 19C] one who makes or distributes counterfeit money.

IN PHRASES

❑ **push the queer** *v.* [1930s–50s] (*US Und.*) to pass counterfeit money. ❑ **shove the queer** *v.* [mid-18C–1950s] to pass counterfeit money.

queer *adj.* [Ger. *quer*, oblique, skewed; the line between SE *queer*, strange, odd, peculiar, eccentric, and the Und. use is both semantically and chronologically slim; the SE slightly predates (at least in printed citations) the cant, but as the *OED* remarks, some examples of the one may in fact equally well serve for the other. Only the context gives any real clue, the most obvious of which occur in such undeniably Und. combs. as QUEER COVE below; QUEER CUFFIN below etc. Ribton-Turner, *A History of Vagrants* (1887), suggests Welsh *chwired*, craft, deceit or cunning. The use as a pej. description of homosexuals does not emerge until *c.*1915; like NIGGER *n.*[1], it has been repossessed by some homosexuals as an affirmative] **1** [mid-16C+] (*UK Und.*) (*also* **queerish, quer, quire**) an all-purpose negative, the antonym of RUM *adj.* (1). **2** [18C+] (*UK Und.*) fake, counterfeit, esp. of money, jewellery, official papers etc; e.g. *queer peg*, a 'bad' shilling. **3** in senses of being 'out of order', of malfunctioning. (**a**) [late 18C+] ill, out of sorts; esp. in phr. *feel queer, look queer*. (**b**) [late 19C] of machinery etc, out of order. (**c**) [1920s] in difficulties. **4** [1910s+] homosexual; thus *queerness*, homosexuality; also of women, lesbian. **5** [1930s–40s] (*orig. US Und.*) of a heterosexual male, sexually unorthodox.

as a general negative

(IN COMPOUNDS)

❑ **queer beak** *n.* [BEAK *n.*[1] (1)] [mid-18C–mid-19C] (*UK Und.*) an incorruptible magistrate. ❑ **queer belch** *n.* [BELCH *n.* (1)] [mid-19C] sour beer. ❑ **queer bird** *n.* (*also* **choir bird, quire bird**) [BIRD *n.*[1] (3a); by 18C the term referred to any unreformed villain] **1** [mid-16C–mid-19C] (*UK Und.*) (*also* **choir bird**) a mendicant villain who, recently released from prison, returns to robbery, specializing in stealing horses. **2** [late 18C–early 19C] (*also* **choir bird**) a recidivist. **3** *see also* SE compounds below. ❑ **queer blowing** *n.* (*also* **queer blowen**) [BLOWEN *n.* (1)] [early–mid-19C] (*UK Und.*) an ugly woman. ❑ **queer bluffer** *n.* (*also* **queer buffer**) [BLUFFER *n.*[1] (1)] [late 17C–mid-19C] a 'sneaking, sharping, Cut-throat Ale-house or Inn-keeper' (B.E.). ❑ **queer booze** *n.* (*also* **queer bowse, quire bowse**) [BOOZE *n.* (1)] [mid-16C–mid-19C] sour or inferior beer, 'small and naughtye drynke' (Harman). ❑ **queer bub** *n.* [BUB *n.*[1] (1)] [18C–mid-19C] second-rate or sour beer. ❑ **queer buffer** *n.* [mid-19C] (*UK Und.*) a cur, a valueless dog. ❑ **queer bung** *n.* [BUNG *n.*[1] (1)] [late 17C–early 19C] (*UK Und.*) an empty purse (viewed as an object of robbery). ❑ **queer chum** *n.* [CHUM *n.* (1)] [early–mid-19C] a suspicious companion. ❑ **queer clout** *n.* [CLOUT *n.*[1] (1)] [late 17C–18C] (*UK Und.*) a cheap, prob. cotton, handkerchief that as such is not worth stealing. ❑ **queer cove** *n.* (*also* **choir cove, quire cove**) [COVE *n.* (1)] **1** [late 16C–mid-19C] (*UK Und.*) a villain. **2** [mid-18C] (*also* **quer cove**) a poor man. **3** [mid-19C] a turnkey. ❑ **queer cramp-ring** *n. see* CRAMP-RINGS *n.* ❑ **queer cuffin** *n.* (*also* **queer cuffen, quire cuffin**) [CUFFIN *n.* (1)] **1** [mid-16C–mid-19C] (*UK Und.*) a Justice of the Peace. **2** [late 17C–early 19C] a peasant. ❑ **queer cull** *n.* [CULL *n.*[1] (3)] [late 17C–mid-18C] **1** a foolish dandy, a fop. **2** a poor, ill-dressed person. **3** (*UK Und.*) a passer of counterfeit money. ❑ **queer degen** *n.* [DEGEN *n.* (1)] [late 17C–mid-19C] (*UK Und.*) a brass, iron or steel-hilted sword, with no special ornamentation. ❑ **queer diver** *n.* [DIVER *n.* (3)] [late 17C–early 19C] (*UK Und.*) a bungling, incompetent pickpocket. ❑ **queer doxy** *n.* [DOXY *n.* (2)] [late 17C–mid-19C] (*UK Und.*) a slatternly woman. ❑ **queer drawers** *n.* [SE *drawers*] [late 17C–18C] (*UK Und.*) yarn, coarse worsted, ordinary or old stockings. ❑ **queer duke** *n.* [DUKE *n.*[1] (2)] [late 17C–18C] (*UK Und.*) **1** an impoverished gentleman. **2** a lean, half-starved person. ❑ **queer figure** *n.* [mid-19C] (*UK Und.*) a deformed man. ❑ **queer flash** *n.* [late 17C–early 19C] (*UK Und.*) a poor quality, worn out wig. ❑ **queer flicker** *n.* [FLICKER *n.*[1]] [late 17C–18C] (*UK Und.*) a poor quality or 'ordinary' glass. ❑ **queer fun** *n.* [FUN *n.*[2]] [late 17C–18C] (*UK Und.*) a cheat or trick that does not work out as intended. ❑ **queer gill** *n.* [GILL *n.*[1] (2)] [19C] **1** a shabby fellow. **2** in fig. use, an untrusting, suspicious person. ❑ **queer ken** *n.* (*also* **quier-ken, quirken**) [KEN *n.*[1] (1)] (*UK Und.*) **1** [mid-16C–17C] a prison. **2** [mid-18C–mid-19C] (*also* **quer ken**) a house not worth robbing. ❑ **queer ken hall** *n.* [early 17C] a prison. ❑ **queer kicks** *n.* [KICKS *n.*[1] (1)] [late 17C–early 19C] (*UK Und.*) old, worn-out trousers; trousers of coarse material. ❑ **queer lap** *n.* [LAP *n.*[2] (2)] [late 18C–mid-19C] (*UK Und.*) bad liquor. ❑ **queer lully** *n.* [LULLY *n.*[2]; despite citations, Partridge is suspicious of validity] [early–mid-19C] (*UK Und.*) a deformed child. ❑ **queer mort** *n.* [MORT *n.* (1)] **1** [mid-17C–19C] (*UK Und.*) a woman suffering from venereal disease; 'a dirty Drab, a jilting Wench, a Pockey jade' (B.E.). **2** [mid-18C] (*also* **quer mort**) a poor woman. ❑ **queer nab** *n.* [NAB *n.*[1] (3)] [late 17C–early 19C] (*UK Und.*) a cheap, shabby hat, thus one that is not worth stealing; 'a felt, Carolina, Cloth or ord'nary Hat, not worth whipping off a man's head' (B.E.). ❑ **queer nantz** *n.* [NANTZ *n.*] [early–mid-19C] (*UK Und.*) bad brandy. ❑ **queer nicks** *n.* [? mis-reading of KICKS *n.*[1] (1)] [early–mid-19C] (*UK Und.*) worn-out breeches. ❑ **queer ogles** *n.* [OGLE *n.* (1)] [early–mid-19C] (*UK Und.*) cross eyes; thus *queer-ogled*, squinting. ❑ **queer patter** *n.* [PATTER *n.* (2)] [early–mid-19C] (*UK Und.*) a foreign language. ❑ **queer peeper** *n.* [PEEPER *n.* (2)] [late 17C–18C] a badly made, thus distorting mirror. ❑ **queer peepers** *n.* [PEEPER *n.* (1)] [18C–19C] (*UK Und.*) squinting or short-sighted eyes. ❑ **queer people** *n.* [1940s] (*UK Und.*) criminals. ❑ **queer place** *n.* [poss. implication of sense 2 above] **1** [1920s–30s] prison. **2** [1940s–50s] a lavatory. ❑ **queer plunger** *n.* [SE *plunger*, a diver] [late 18C–mid-19C] a confidence trickster who plunges into water and is saved from 'drowning'. Conveniently pre-assembled 'rescuers' then claim money for saving the person. ❑ **queer prancer** *n.* [SE *prancer*/PRANCER *n.* (1)] (*UK Und.*) **1** [late 17C] an ageing prostitute. **2** [late 17C–mid-19C] a second-rate and/or worn-out horse. **3** [18C–early 19C] a cowardly horse stealer. ❑ **queer rooster** *n.* [SE *rooster*] [late 18C–19C] a police spy who frequents thieves' haunts, often feigning sleep in order to listen to their conversations. ❑ **queer rotan** *n.* [ROTAN *n.*] [early–mid-19C] (*UK Und.*) a run-down coach. ❑ **queer rums** *n.* [RUM *adj.* (1), lit. 'bad good things'] [early 19C] confusing talk. ❑ **queer skin** *n. see* SKIN *n.*[1] (1a). ❑ **Queer Street** *n. see* separate entry. ❑ **queer thimble** *n.* [THIMBLE *n.* (1)] [early–mid-19C] (*UK Und.*) a watch of no value. ❑ **queer timber** *n.* [late 18C] a wooden leg. ❑ **queer tol** *n.* [TOL *n.*[1]] [late 17C–18C] a brass or steel- (rather than silver-) hilted sword. ❑ **queer topping** *n.* [late 17C–18C] (*UK Und.*) a second-rate or worn-out wig. ❑ **queer vinegar** *n.* [VINEGAR *n.* (1)] [early–mid-19C] (*UK Und.*) a worn-out woman's cloak. ❑ **queer wedge** *n.* [WEDGE *n.*[1] (1)] **1** [late 18C–early 19C] a large belt or shoe buckle. **2** [early 19C] pointed shoes. **3** [mid-19C] adulterated gold or silver.

meaning fraudulent

(IN COMPOUNDS)

❑ **queer bail** *n.* [late 18C–mid-19C] fraudulent bail. ❑ **queer beer** *n.* [1970s] (*US*) 'near bear', beer with a low alcohol content. ❑ **queer bit** *n.* [BIT *n.*[1] (1a)] [late 18C–19C] counterfeit money. ❑ **queer bit-maker** *n.* [late 18C–19C] (*UK Und.*) a coiner, a counterfeiter. ❑ **queer blunt** *n.* [BLUNT *n.*[1]] [mid–late 18C] (*UK Und.*) counterfeit money. ❑ **queer cole** *n.* (*also* **quer cole**) [COLE *n.* (1) + -FENCER *sfx*] [late 17C–19C] (*UK Und.*) counterfeit money; thus *queer cole fencer*, the distributor of counterfeit money; *queer cole maker*, a counterfeiter. ❑ **queer lambs** *n.* [LAMB *n.*[2]] [late 18C–mid-19C] (*UK Und.*) false dice. ❑ **queer money** *n.* [19C+] (*UK Und.*) counterfeit money. ❑ **queer paper** *n.* [mid–late 19C] **1** counterfeit paper money. **2** in fig. use, something dubious, unreliable. ❑ **queer rag** *n.* [RAG *n.*[1] (1a)] [early–mid-19C] (*UK Und.*) counterfeit money. ❑ **queer ridge** *n.* [RIDGE *n.* (1)] [mid-19C] (*US Und.*) counterfeited gold coins. ❑ **queer screens** *n.* [SCREEN *n.*[1]] [19C] (*UK Und.*) forged banknotes. ❑ **queer soft** *n.* [SOFT MONEY *n.* (1)] [mid-19C] counterfeit notes. ❑ **queer stuff** *n. see* QUEER *n.* (2). ❑ **queer tats** *n.* [TATS *n.* (1)] [late 18C–mid-19C] (*UK Und.*) false dice.

(IN PHRASES)

❑ **on the queer** [20C+] acting dishonestly.

meaning homosexual

(IN COMPOUNDS)

❑ **queer-faced** *adj.* [1980s+] a general pej.; lit. 'looking like a homosexual'. ❑ **queer street** *n.* [+ pun on QUEER STREET *n.*] [1960s] (*US*) the world of homosexuality.

(IN PHRASES)

❑ **queer as...** *adj. see* separate entry.

SE, meaning odd/eccentric, in slang uses

(IN COMPOUNDS)

❑ **queer bird** *n.* **1** [mid-19C+] an odd, eccentric person. **2** [1960s] (*US gay*) a heterosexual who dabbles in homosexuality. **3** *see also* slang compounds above. ❑ **queer bitch** *n.* [BITCH *n.*[1] (3a); despite appearances, there is no hint of homosexuality] [late 18C–early 19C] 'an odd out of the way fellow' (Grose 1785). ❑ **queer card** *n.* [CARD *n.*[2] (2)] [mid-19C–1940s] an odd, eccentric person. ❑ **queer customer** *n.* (*also* **queer merchant**) [SE *customer*/MERCHANT *n.*] [mid-19C+] an odd or eccentric person. ❑ **queer fellow** *n.* **1** [early 18C+] an odd, eccentric person. **2** [1980s] a prisoner condemned to hang [ref. to Brendan Behan play *The Quare Fellow*]. ❑ **queer fish** *n.* [FISH *n.*[1] (5)] [late 18C+] an odd or eccentric person. ❑ **queer gum** *n.* [GUM *n.*[1] (1)] [mid-19C] (*UK Und.*) strange talk. ❑ **queer hawk** *n.* (*also* **quare harp, queer harp, ...hawk**) [SE *queer*/QUARE *adj.* (2) + ? HARP *n.*[1] (3) or fig. use of the *harp* as a symbolic Irish artefact, thus person] [20C+] (*Irish*) an odd person. ❑ **queer put** *n.* [PUT *n.*[1] (2)] [early–mid-19C] an odd simple person. ❑ **queer start** *n.* [START *n.*[1]] [19C] a strange affair, an odd situation. ❑ **queer stick** *n.* [STICK *n.* (2c)] [late 19C+] an odd person, an eccentric. ❑ **Queer Street** *n. see* separate entry. ❑ **queer stuff** *n.* **1** [1940s] (*S.Afr.*) methylated spirits. **2** *see* OLD QUEER *under* OLD *adj.*

IN PHRASES

❑ **queer about the gills** *adj. see* GREEN ABOUT THE GILLS *under* GILLS *n.* ❑ **queer as...** *see* separate entry. ❑ **queer in the attic** *adj.* [ATTIC *n.* (1)] [19C] mad and/or drunk. ❑ **queer in the garret** *adj.* (*also* **queer in the upper storey**) [GARRET *n.* (1)/UPPER STOREY *under* UPPER *adj.*] [late 18C–19C] eccentric, mad. ❑ **queer in the nut** *adj.* [NUT *n.*[1] (1b)] [1950s] mad, eccentric.

queer *v.* **1** [late 18C–mid-19C] to quiz or ridicule, to puzzle. **2** [late 18C–1930s] to impose on, to swindle, to cheat; thus *queer a flat*, to hoodwink a gullible victim. **3** [late 18C+] to spoil, to put out of order. **4** [early 19C; 1970s] to act in an odd manner. **5** [mid-19C+] of a person, to spoil the reputation of, to spoil someone's efforts or opportunities. **6** [1910s] (*US*) to cause trouble for. **7** [1970s+] to sexually abuse.

IN PHRASES

❑ **queer someone's/the act** *v. see under* ACT *n.* ❑ **queer someone's ogle** *v.* (*also* **queer someone's ogles**) [OGLE *n.* (1)] [late 18C–mid-19C] to get or give a black eye. ❑ **queer someone's pitch** *v.* (*also* **queer the pitch**) [SE *pitch*, a stall; music-hall use, where it dealt with one actor stealing a scene from the others, and in turn from street patterers, whose open-air *pitch* would be *queered* by an over-officious policeman] **1** [mid-19C+] to spoil someone else's efforts, usu. deliberately; occas., to ruin an object or place. **2** [1920s] (*Aus.*) as *queer the...*, to behave badly, to 'go off the rails'. ❑ **queer the game** *v.* [GAME *n.* (6)] [late 19C–1910s] to cause trouble for someone. ❑ **queer the quod** *v.* [QUOD *n.* (1)] [late 18C] (*US Und.*) to break out of jail. ❑ **queer the stifler** *v.* [STIFLER *n.* (1)] [early 19C] to escape the gallows.

queer *adv.* [QUEER *adj.* (1)] [late 19C] in a problematic, difficult manner.

queeralities *n.* [SE *queer*] [20C+] (*Ulster*) eccentricities, peculiarities.

queer as... *adj.* [QUEER *adj.* (4)/SE *queer*, odd]

IN PHRASES

❑ **...a chorus boy's backside** [1990s+] undeniably homosexual. ❑ **...a clockwork orange** **1** [1950s+] extremely odd. **2** [1970s] ostentatiously homosexual. ❑ **...a coot** [1940s+] undeniably homosexual. ❑ **...a nine-bob note** (*also* **queer as a two-quid note, ...three-pound note**) [NINE-BOB NOTE *n.*] [1960s+] unusual, particularly suspicious; the phrase survives the demise of the currency. ❑ **...a three-dollar bill** (*also* **queer as a four-dollar bill, ...nine-dollar bill, ...six-bit coin**) [1950s+] (*orig. US*) ostentatiously homosexual. ❑ **...beer** [1990s+] (*Aus.*) extremely odd; outrageously homosexual. ❑ **...Chloe** [1980s+] (*N.Z.*) ostentatiously homosexual. ❑ **...Dick's hatband** (*also* **odd as Dick's hatband**) [the proper name *Dick*, some long-dead eccentric figure + SE *hatband*, a band or narrow ribbon that runs around a hat just above the rim; the dial. phr. is *as queer as Dick's hatband that went nine times round and wouldn't meet*] **1** [18C+] odd, eccentric. **2** [18C+] referring to something comical. **3** [18C+] referring to something one cannot recognize or identify; thus *I wouldn't know him from Dick's hatband*. **4** [late 18C] out of sorts, dispirited, 'under the weather'. ❑ **...duck soup** [1940s] (*US*) ostentatiously homosexual or effeminate.

queered *adj.* [QUEER *adj.* (1)] [early–mid-19C] tipsy.

queer 'em *n.* (*also* **queer'm, queerum**) [QUEER *v.* (3)] [early 19C] the gallows.

queer for *adj.* [the origin is QUEER *adj.* (4), but there need be no actual homosexuality involved] [1940s+] obsessed with, sexually or otherwise.

queerie *n.* (*also* **queery**) (*US/N.Z.*) **1** [1930s+] a male homosexual. **2** [1970s+] a fool.

queerly *adv.* [QUEER *adj.* (1)] **1** [late 17C–mid-19C] in a criminal manner. **2** [late 18C] (*UK Und.*) badly.

queer'm *n. see* QUEER 'EM *n.*

queer on *adj.* [QUEER *adj.* (4)] [1940s+] (*orig. Aus.*) homosexually attracted towards.

queer out *v.* [QUEER *adj.* (4)] [1960s] (*US*) to subject to homosexual advances.

queers, the *n.* [QUEER *adj.* (3a)] [late 19C] sea-sickness.

Queer Street *n.* [QUEER *adj.* (1) + SE *street*] [early 19C+] any difficult situation; usu. in phr. below.

IN PHRASES

❑ **in Queer Street** [*Queer Street* begins as a fig. 'place' where the only 'dwellers' are problems and difficulties; the financial aspect, now dominant, was added in mid-19C] [early 19C+] in trouble, esp. financial.

queerum *n. see* QUEER 'EM *n.*

queervert *n.* [QUEER *n.* (4) + SE *pervert*] [1950s] (*US*) a homosexual.

queery *n. see* QUEERIE *n.*

queery *adj.* [SE *queer*] [mid-19C] shaky.

quegg *n.* [? QUEER *n.* (4)] [2000s] a male homosexual.

Quego *n.* [? Fijian greeting *ko iko*] [1980s+] (*N.Z.*) a Pacific Islander.

quencher *n.* [SE *quench*] [mid-19C–1900s] a drink; when quenching one's thirst; esp. as *modest quencher*.

quent *n. see* QUAINT *n.*

Quentin *n.* [abbr.] [1920s+] (*US Und./prison*) San *Quentin* Prison, California.

que pasa? *phr.* [Mexican Sp. *que pasa?* what's happening?] [1980s+] (*US campus*) a greeting.

quer(e) *see under* QUEER and combs.

querier *n.* [they *query* householders] [mid-19C] a chimney sweep who goes from house to house offering their services.

question lay *n.* [SE *question* + LAY *n.*[3] (1)] [18C] (*UK Und.*) 'To knock at a Door early in the Morning and ask for the Master of the House, and if he's a Bed, to desire the Servant not to disturb him, for you'll wait till he rises, and so you take an Opportunity of stealing something.' (Tyburn Chron., 1768).

queue *adj. see* Q *adj.*

queueing *n.*

IN PHRASES

❑ **go queueing** *v. see under* Q *adj.*

queynte *n. see* QUAINT *n.*

quick *n.* [1950s+] (*US black*) instantly available money.

quick *adj.* [late 19C] (*UK society*) well-dressed and clever.

SE in slang uses

DERIVATIVES

❑ **quicksville** *adv.* [-VILLE *sfx*[1]] [1960s+] (*US*) fast, quickly.

IN COMPOUNDS

❑ **quick buck** *n. see* FAST BUCK *n.* ❑ **quick one** *n. see* separate entry. ❑ **quick quid** *n. see under* QUID *n.* ❑ **quickshit** *n.* [2000s] (*Aus.*) absolute nonsense. ❑ **quicksilver** *n.* **1** [1970s–80s] (*drugs*) LSD when combined with another drug. **2** [2000s] isobutyl nitrite. ❑ **quick starts** *n.* [1970s+] (*US campus*) rubber-soled sneakers; popular for those who need to make a speedy exit. ❑ **quick step** *n.* [the need to 'dance' fast towards the lavatory] [1900s] (*US*) diarrhoea. ❑ **quick sticks** *adv. see* separate entry. ▫ **quick worker** *n. see* FAST WORKER *under* FAST *adj.*[1].

IN PHRASES

▫ **on the quick** (*UK Und.*) **1** [mid-19C] in private, surreptitiously. **2** [1980s] of goods, stolen, obtained by theft. ▫ **quick and dirty** *see* separate entries. ▫ **quick as bunny fucks** *adj.* [1990s+] (*US*) very fast. ▫ **quick on the draw** (*also* **quick on the buzzer, ...trigger**) [gunfighting imagery] **1** [19C+] bright, intelligent, quick to act. **2** [late 19C+] impetuous. **3** [1930s+] suffering from premature ejaculation. ▫ **quick on the zipper** *see under* ZIPPER *n.*

quick and dirty *n.* [the standard of the service, the hygiene and the food] [1960s–70s] (*orig. US*) a cheap café.

quick-and-dirty *adj.* [1970s+] used of any kind of instant remedy, poss. not the best one for long-term dependence.

quickie *n.* (*also* **quicky**) [SE/abbr. QUICK ONE *n.*] **1** [1920s+] a spontaneous and brief act of sexual intercourse, esp. with a prostitute; thus the person with whom one has that intercourse; also attrib. **2** [1940s+] a quick drink. **3** [1940s+] a quick, 'dirty' story, retailed at the end of a party or drinking session. **4** [1970s+] (*US gay*) fellatio. **5** [1990s+] beer. **6** [2000s] (*N.Z.*) an act of deception.

quick one *n.* **1** [20C+] a spontaneous and brief act of sexual intercourse. **2** [20C+] a quick drink, usu. of alcohol. **3** [1910s+] an act of urination. **4** [1940s] a brief act of masturbation. **5** [1950s] a trick, a deception.

quick sticks *adv.* [mid-19C+] hurrying, evading, hurriedly.

IN PHRASES

▫ **in quick sticks** *adv.* [mid-19C+] speedily, hurriedly.

quicky *n. see* QUICKIE *n.*

quicumque vult *n.* (*also* **quicunque vult**) [Lat. *quicumque vult*, whomsoever wants; ? ref. in *quicunque* to CUNT *n.* (1)] [late 18C] a prostitute.

quid *n.* [? Lat. *quid*, what (one needs) or *quid pro quo*, lit. 'something for something'] **1** [late 17C–mid-19C] a guinea. **2** [late 18C+] in pl., money; thus phr. *not for quids*, not for anything. **3** [19C+] a pound sterling; thus *half-a-quid*, ten shillings (50p). **4** [mid-19C] (*US Und.*) $5. **5** [late 19C] the vagina. **6** [1960s] (*US black*) a dollar bill.

IN COMPOUNDS

▫ **quid fishing** *n.* [SE *fish*] [late 19C] (*UK Und.*) first-class, expert thieving.

IN PHRASES

▫ **for quids** [1920s+] (*N.Z.*) for anything in the world, e.g. *I wouldn't miss your birthday for quids.* ▫ **half-a-quid** *n.* (*also* **half-quid**) [early 19C+] half a guinea; then ten shillings; latterly 50p. ▫ **quick quid** *n.* [1920s+] (*Aus./N.Z.*) money that is earned quickly and, poss., illicitly. ▫ **quids in** (*also* **quids, quids up**) [the image of making a successful bet and the money thus gained] **1** [1910s+] doing well, financially or otherwise. **2** [1950s] (*UK Und/prison*) first-class, excellent; of a person, reliable. ▫ **quid to a bloater** [lit. 'a sovereign to a herring'] [late 19C–1900s] a certain bet; esp. in phr. *it's a quid to a bloater.* ▫ **smoke a quid** *v.* [image of 'burning money' + SMOKE *v.*[2] (7) with implications of 'killing' or 'beating', i.e. getting rid of the money] [mid-19C] (*UK Und.*) to spend money hedonistically.

quiddish *adj.* [ety. unknown] [mid-18C] good-natured.

quidlet *n.* [QUID *n.* + dimin. *-let*] [1900s–10s] £1 sterling.

quien *n.* [Fr. *chien*, or a Fr. dial.] [mid-19C–1900s] a dog.

quier-ken *n. see* QUEER KEN *under* QUEER *adj.*

quiet *n.* [2000s] (*N.Z.*) a drink taken on one's own.

quiet *adj.*

SE in slang uses

IN COMPOUNDS

▫ **quiet-clothes boy** *n.* [1930s] (*US Und.*) a plain clothes policemen. ▫ **quiet mouse** *n. see* LONE DUCK *n.* ▫ **Quiet Village** *n.* [? the relative peacefulness compared to a ghetto] [1980s+] (*US black, Los Angeles*) Venice, California. ▫ **quiet woman** *n. see* GOOD WOMAN *under* GOOD *adj.*[1].

IN PHRASES

▫ **quiet is kept** [2000s] (*US black*) a phr. used to request secrecy after making a revelation.

quiet down *v.* [euph.] [1970s] (*US*) to kill, to murder.

quiff *n.*[1] (*also* **quoiff**) [on pattern of QUAINT *n.* etc, thus ult. CUNT *n.* (1)] **1** [18C+] the vagina. **2** [1930s+] (*also* **quif**) women, esp. sexually available ones. **3** [1950s–70s] (*US*) a homosexual.

quiff *n.*[2] [ety. unknown] [late 19C–1910s] a smart trick or clever dodge, esp. one that makes a task easier.

quiff *adj.* [fig. use of QUIFF *n.*[1]] [1960s] (*US*) second-rate, lightweight.

quiff *v.*[1] [QUIFF *n.*[1] (1)] [late 17C–19C] to have sexual intercourse.

quiff *v.*[2] [QUIFF *n.*[2]] [late 19C] to come up with a cunning dodge or trick; to go or do well, to get along pleasantly.

qui-hi *n.* (*also* **qui-hai, qui-hy**) [Urdu *koi hai*, is anyone there?, the usual summons to a servant; note E.F. Benson's character, the ex-Indian Army Major Flint, in the *Lucia* stories, whose catchphrase this is] (*Anglo-Ind.*) **1** [19C+] as *old qui-hi*, a former colonial administrator or Indian Army soldier. **2** [mid–late 19C] an English resident of Calcutta.

quill *n.*[1] **1** [17C–early 18C] the penis. **2** [mid-19C] (*US*) in pl., money.

SE in slang uses

IN COMPOUNDS

▫ **quill-driver** *n.* (*also* **quillpusher**) **1** [late 18C–1900s; 2000s] (*US*) a clerk. **2** [mid-19C–1910s] (*Aus.*) a journalist; thus *quill-driving*, working as a journalist. ▫ **quill-pipes** *n. see* PIPE *n.*[1] (2b).

IN PHRASES

▫ **pure quill** *n.* (*also* **clear quill, the quill**) [? a perfect SE *quill* or feather] [late 19C+] (*US*) something that is excellent or flawless.

quill *n.*[2] [senses 1 and 2 ext. of SE; others ety. unknown other than in their relationship to the earlier senses] (*drugs*) **1** [1910s+] a folded-over matchbook cover that hides a narcotic drug. **2** [1960s+] anything, e.g. a dollar bill, rolled up to make a 'straw' through which to sniff a powdered narcotic. **3** [1980s+] methamphetamine. **4** [1980s+] heroin. **5** [1980s+] cocaine.

quill *n.*[3] [backform. f. PURE QUILL *under* QUILL *n.*[1]] [1920s–30s] (*US*) **1** first-rate whisky, the genuine thing as opposed to the 'bathtub' or 'rotgut' versions producing during Prohibition. **2** first-rate opium.

quiller *n.* [one who 'sucks up' (i.e. through a *quill*, the precursor of the modern straw)] [mid-19C] a toady, a parasite.

quilt *n.* [the making of quilts being a trad. female occupation] **1** [mid-19C] (*US*) a wife. **2** [20C+] (*Irish*) a petulant, pedantic, pernickety man. **3** [20C+] a timid, effeminate man. **4** [20C+] (*Irish*) a fool, someone who acts against their own interests.

quilt *v.* (*also* **put the quilt on**) [Scot./Cumberland dial.] [early 19C+] (*Aus./Irish/US*) to thrash, to beat, to flog; thus n., *quilting*, a beating.

quilting *n.* [QUILT v.] [early 19C–1940s] a thrashing, a beating.

quilty *adj.* [1960s] (*US black*) of clothes, luxurious.

quim *n.* [? play on Celtic *cwm*, a valley; ult. CUNT *n.* (1); Williams notes *queme*, 'which not only means pleasure, but in the sense of joining or fitting closely, or slipping in'] **1** [early 18C+] (*also* **queam, quin, whim**) the vagina. **2** [20C+] a woman; women collectively, viewed in a sexual context. **3** [1930s+] (*US gay*) the anus. **4** [1970s+] (*US gay/prison*) a heterosexual inmate, subjected to homosexual rape. **5** [1990s+] a general derog. term of abuse.

IN COMPOUNDS

▫ **quim bush** *n.* [BUSH *n.*[1] (2a)/SE *bush*] [late 18C+] the female pubic hair. ▫ **quimfill** *n.* [1990s+] having one's penis fully embedded in the vagina. ▫ **quimling** *n.* [1990s+] manipulation of a woman's body in an attempt to produce orgasm, generally regarded as genital manipulation by the tongue, but not limited to such. ▫ **quim nuts** *n.* [NUTS *n.*[2] (1)] [1990s+] (*US*) notably large and pendant labia. ▫ **quimstake** *n.* (*also* **quim-stick, quimwedge**) [19C] the penis. ▫ **quim-**

sticker *n.* [19C] a womanizer. ❑ **quimwedge** *v.* (*also* **go quim-wedging**) [late 19C+] to have sexual intercourse. ❑ **quim whiskers** *n.* (*also* **quim wig**) [19C] the female pubic hair.

IN PHRASES

❑ **go quim-sticking** *v.* [19C] of a man, to have sexual intercourse. ❑ **have a bit of quimsy** *v.* [19C] to have sexual intercourse.

quim *adj.* [Scot. *queem*, pleasant] [20C+] (*Ulster*) **1** prim, affectedly 'nice'. **2** moving easily, precisely.

quim *v.* [QUIM *n.* (1)] [early 18C+] to have sexual intercourse; usu. as *quimming*.

quimp *n.* [? QUEER *n.* (4) + WIMP *n.*[1] (2); note WW1 milit. *quimp*, slack, unsoldierly] [1970s] (*US campus*) a socially inept person.

quimsby *n.* [ext. of QUIM *n.* (1)] [early 18C+] the vagina.

quince *n.* [puns on SE *quince*, a SOFT *adj.*FRUIT *n.* (1)/FRUIT *n.* (2)] **1** [20C+] (*Aus./US*) a weakling, a fool; thus *quince-head*. **2** [1900s–20s] (*US*) of a situation/object, a failure. **3** [1960s+] (*Aus./US*) a homosexual, esp. one who can be both active and passive. **4** [1990s+] (*Aus.*) the buttocks.

IN PHRASES

❑ **get on someone's quince** *v.* [1920s+] (*Aus.*) to annoy.

quinine *n.* (*also* **strychnine**) [play on SE *nine*] [20C+] (*US gambling*) the point of nine in craps dice.

quinsey *v.* [backform. f. *HEMP-STRING under* HEMPEN *adj.*] [mid-19C] (*US Und.*) to choke, to garotte.

quips *n.* [? SE *quip*, an odd or whimsical trifle] [1950s+] (*W.I. Rasta*) a tiny piece or amount.

quire *see under* QUEER and combs.

quirk *n.* [synon. Scot. *quirk*] [20C+] (*Ulster*) an untrustworthy individual.

quirken *n. see QUEER KEN under* QUEER *adj.*

quirley *n.* (*also* **quirly**) [SE *quirl*, to twist, to twirl] [1930s+] (*Aus./US*) a hand-rolled cigarette.

quisby *n.* [ext. of QUIZ *n.* (1)] [early–mid-19C] an idler; thus *doing quisby*, not working, idling.

quisby *adj.* [QUISBY *n.*] [mid–late 19C] **1** (*also* **quisby snitch**) of people, unwell; out of sorts. **2** of events, objects or people, unpleasant or malfunctioning. **3** bankrupt, poverty-stricken.

quit *v.* [ext. SE] [1930s+] (*orig. US*) to die.

quitam *n.* (*also* **qui tam**) [Lat. *qui tam*, to whom so much] [late 18C–mid-19C] a solicitor who takes an informer's fee for their prosecution of the case.

quit it! *excl.* [SE *quit*] [1980s] (*US campus*) shut up! an expression of disdain.

quitsest *n.* [Lat. *quietus est*, it is discharged, thus modern SE *quits*] [late 16C–17C] a release, a discharge.

quitter *n.* [SE *quit*] [1950s+] (*drugs*) one who has abandoned drug use.

quiver *n.* [lit. translation of Lat. *vagina*] [mid-16C–mid-18C] the vagina.

quiver and shake *n.* [rhy. sl.] [20C+] (*Aus.*) a steak.

quiz *n.* [? Lat. *quis?* who?] **1** [late 18C–mid-19C] an eccentric person, thus an odd-looking thing; orig. university sl. for a hard-worker who eschews undergraduate amusements. **2** [19C] a monocle [abbr. SE *quizzing-glass*]. **3** [1920s–40s] (*US Und.*) a question.

quiz *v.* [SE *quiz*, to interrogate, to find out] [late 18C–1900s] to watch, to spy on; as n., *quiz*, a look.

quizzer *n.* [SE *quizzing-glass*] **1** [early 19C] a monocle. **2** [late 19C] (*US*) in pl., spectacles.

quizzy *adj.* [abbr.] [1950s+] (*Aus./N.Z.*) inquisitive.

quockerwodger *n.* [SE *quockerwodger*, a wooden puppet which can be made to 'dance' by pulling its strings] **1** [mid-19C] an imitation of a person. **2** [mid–late 19C] a politician acting in accordance with the instructions of an influential third party, rather than properly representing their constituents.

quod *n.* (*also* **quad**) [abbr. SE *quadrangle*; the original was Newgate, but the term became general] **1** [late 17C+] prison; also attrib. **2** [early 19C] a prisoner. **3** [mid-19C–1900s] a police-station.

IN COMPOUNDS

❑ **quod cove** *n.* [COVE *n.* (1)] [early 19C] (*UK Und.*) the governor of a prison; a turnkey. ❑ **quod cull** *n.* (*also* **quad cull**) [CULL *n.*[1] (3)] [mid-18C–mid-19C] a prison warder, a turnkey.

quod *v.* [QUOD *n.* (1)] **1** [19C+] to imprison. **2** [late 19C] to serve a prison sentence.

DERIVATIVES

❑ **quodded** *adj.* [19C] imprisoned.

IN PHRASES

❑ **quodding dues are concerned** [early 19C] (*UK Und.*) it is a matter that will involve imprisonment.

quodling *n.* [QUOD *n.* (1) + sfx *-ing*, a child of] [mid-19C] (*UK Und.*) a criminal.

quoiff *n. see* QUIFF *n.*[1].

quoit *n.* [it is 'round with a hole in it'] [1940s+] (*Aus./N.Z.*) the anus, the buttocks; thus *go for one's quoit(s)*, to hurry.

IN PHRASES

❑ **go for one's quoits** *v.* (*also* **go for a lick of one's coit**) [? fig. use of QUOIT *n.*] [1920s+] (*Aus.*) to run fast, to work hard, to make one's best effort.

quollecackle *n.* [? Lat. *quo*, which + CACKLE *v.* (2)] [mid-19C] (*UK Und.*) a criminal who betrays his associates.

quoniam *n.* [Lat. *quoniam*, whereas, or one of the CUNT *n.* (1)/QUAINT *n.* group] [late 14C–early 18C] the vagina.

quot *n. see* COT *n.*

quota *n.* [late 17C–early 19C] (*UK Und.*) a share of plunder.

quotquean *n. see* COTQUEAN *n.*

quoz *n.*[1] [var. on QUIZ *n.* (1)] [late 18C–early 19C] an absurd person.

quoz *n.*[2] (*also* **quozzie**) [*Quasimodo*, the hunchback in Hugo's novel *The Hunchback of Notre Dame*] [1990s+] (*UK juv.*) a disabled person.

quoz! *excl.* [late 18C–mid-19C] an all-purpose excl. in which the speaker, according to context, makes fun of the subject of the excl.

qwasha *n.* [Zulu ideophone for a crunching noise; in this context echoic of the sound of the explosive click that is made when the gun is fired] [1980s+] (*S.Afr. township*) a homemade gun, made from piping, springs and rubber tubing.

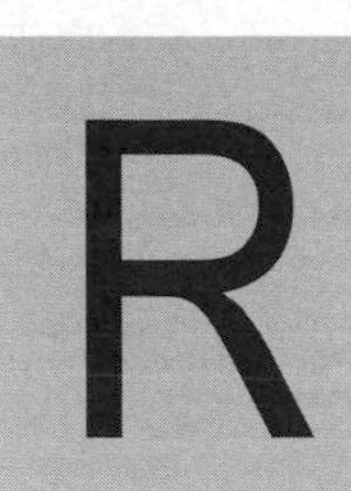

r. *adv.* [abbr.] [1900s] right, correct.

r.a. *n. see* RED ASS *n.*

ra, the *n.* [abbr.] [1980s+] (*orig. Ulster*) the provisional *IRA*.

raany *n.* (*also* **ranny**) [Irish *ranaí*, thin] [20C+] (*Ulster*) an emaciated, stunted or delicate looking person.

raas *n.* (*also* **rarse, rass**) [RAAS! *excl.*] [1950s+] (*W.I./UK black*) **1** the buttocks, thus fig. the whole person, esp. as a target for violence. **2** nonsense, rubbish. **3** a derog. description of a person. **4** a synon. for '(the) hell', '(a) fuck', '(a) shit' etc. **5** anything. **6** a Rastafarian.

raas *adj.* (*also* **raass, rarse, rass**) [RAAS *n.* (1)] [1950s+] (*W.I./UK black*) **1** a general negative epithet, the equivalent of FUCKING *adj.* **2** as infix.

raas *v.* [RAAS *n.* (1)] [1950s+] (*W.I.*) **1** to thrash. **2** to rush about, to rush away. **3** (*also* **rass up**) to stir up, to excite.

raas! *excl.* (*also* **rarse! rass!**) [? f. phr. *your arse* or Du. *raas*, to rage, to rave; one of the most taboo words in the W.I., it has been banned from public use in the majority of islands] [1950s+] (*W.I./UK black*) an all-purpose abusive term.

(IN EXCLAMATIONS)

❑ **raas to you! 1** [1950s+] go to hell! **2** [1990s+] as a pun on sense 1, see you later!

raasclat *n.* (*also* **rassclat, rass-cloth**) [lit. *arse/ass cloth*, i.e. a sanitary towel] [1940s+] (*orig. W.I., Jam.*) **1** an extreme derog. term. **2** as infix.

raasclat *adj.* (*also* **raas cloth, raas klaat, rarse claat, rass-clot**) [RAASCLAT *n.* (1)] [1950s+] (*W.I.*) a general negative epithet.

raasclat! *excl.* (*also* **raascloth!**) [RAASCLAT *n.* (1)] [1950s+] **1** a general exclamation. **2** (*also* **rass claat!**) used as an intensifier.

raashole *n.* (*also* **rasshole**) [1950s+] (*orig. W.I.*) **1** nonsense, rubbish. **2** a great fool, an absolute idiot. **3** a synon. for '(the) hell', '(a) fuck', '(a) shit' etc.

raashole *adj.* [1960s+] (*orig. W.I.*) worthless, contemptible.

raas klaat *adj. see* RAASCLAT *adj.*

raass *adj. see* RAAS *adj.*

raatid *n.* (*also* **rhatid**) [1950s+] (*W.I.*) an excl. of anger, annoyance, amazement etc.

raatid *adj.* (*also* **rahtid, rarted, wrated**) [? SE *wrath/wrathed*; used as euph. for RAAS *adj.* (1)] **1** [1940s+] (*W.I./UK black*) furious, very angry; stupid. **2** [1970s+] (*UK black*) used as a general intensifier; thus *to rarted*, for the hell of it.

raatid! *excl.* (*also* **rahtid! rawtid!**) [RAATID *adj.* (2)] [1940s+] an excl. implying great anger, surprise, amazement, envy, etc.

rab *n.*[1] [SE *rabble*] [20C+] (*W.I./UK black*) a lawless, rowdy person.

(IN PHRASES)

❑ **make rab** *v.* [1950s] (*W.I.*) to make a fuss, to complain.

rab *n.*[2] [1930s+] (*UK Und.*) a cash register.

rabbi *n.* (*also* **angel**) [1930s+] (*US, orig. police*) an influential sponsor or patron.

rabbit *n.*[1] **1** in sexual senses. (**a**) [late 16C] a prostitute. (**b**) [1900s–50s] (*Aus.*) a girl. (**c**) [1940s+] (*S.Afr.*) a male homosexual. (**d**) [1960s+] a client who ejaculates quickly and thus leaves the prostitute free to carry on her trade. (**e**) [1970s+] (*US gay*) a fellator. **2** [late 16C] a term of abuse. **3** [late 18C–early 19C] a newborn baby. [an affectionate nickname, but ? ref. to one Mary Tofts (c.1701–63) who, in 1726, allegedly (but fraudulently) 'gave birth' to a litter of rabbits]. **4** [the animal's nervousness]. (**a**) [late 19C+] a coward. (**b**) [late 19C+] (*US*) the desire to run away. (**c**) [late 19C+] (*also* **rabbit blood**) one who makes or wishes to make an escape. (**d**) [1970s] (*US*) a runaway. **5** [late 19C+] a coat made of, or lined with, rabbit fur. **6** in senses of weakness, inadequacy. (**a**) [20C+] (*Aus.*) a simpleton, a victim. (**b**) [1910s] (*US*) a youngster, a naive individual. (**c**) [1920s+] a poor player, esp. in golf or tennis; thus *rabbitry*, a state of being such a player. **7** [1940s–50s] (*Aus.*) a native-born Australian. **8** [1970s+] (*US black*) a white person.

(IN COMPOUNDS)

❑ **rabbit blood** *n. see* sense 4c above. ❑ **rabbit-catcher** *n.* [late 18C–early 19C] a midwife. ❑ **rabbit fever** *n.* [20C+] (*US Und.*) **1** the compelling desire to run off whenever things get difficult. **2** the compulsion to attempt escapes from any form of imprisonment. ❑ **rabbit foot** *n.* **1** [1920s] (*US black*) a coward, a timid person. **2** [1920s–40s] (*US*) an escaped convict. **3** *see also* SE compounds below. ❑ **rabbit-snatcher** *n.* [1950s] (*US Und.*) an abortionist. ❑ **rabbit-sucker** *n.* **1** [late 16C–early 19C] (*UK Und.*) a rich young man who is gulled into running up large bills by confidence tricksters who later dun him for his debts. **2** [early 18C] one who lends at exorbitant rates, thus rendering impoverished those to whom they extend credit.

(IN PHRASES)

❑ **pull a rabbit** *v.* [1950s] (*US prison*) to make an escape.

SE in slang uses

(IN COMPOUNDS)

❑ **rabbit-ass** *n.* [1950s] (*US black*) insignificant, inferior. ❑ **rabbitchoker** *n.* [1950s] (*US*) a farmer, an unsophisticated peasant. ❑ **rabbit ears** *n.* [1950s+] (*orig. US*) a V-shaped television antenna. ❑ **rabbit food** *n.* (*also* **rabbit's food, rabbit tucker**) [20C+] vegetables or salad greens considered unfit for consumption, esp. by a carnivore. ❑ **rabbit foot** *n.* [the trad. wearing of a rabbit's foot as a good-luck charm] [late 19C–1930s] (*US black*) **1** attention. **2** good luck. **3** *see also* sl. compounds above. ❑ **rabbit killer** *n.* (*also* **rabbit-chop, rabbit-punch**) [the blow used by farmers etc to dispatch rabbits] [1940s+] (*Aus.*) a chopping blow to the back of a neck. ❑ **rabbit trap** *n.* [SE *rabbit* + SE *trap*/TRAP *n.*[1] (4)] [1910s] (*Aus.*) the mouth.

(IN PHRASES)

❑ **brr rabbit** *v.* [SE *brr*, an echoic acknowledgement of cold weather + pun on the character *Br'er Rabbit*, the creation of Joel Chandler Harris (1848–1908)] [1970s] (*US campus*) to complain about the cold. ❑ **buy the rabbit** *v.* (*also* **buy the rabbits**) [a rabbit is presumably the lesser bargain in this hypothetical deal. Note 16C proverb 'who will change a rabbit for a rat?'] [early 19C–1930s] (*orig. US*) to conclude a deal unfavourably, to do badly. ❑ **don't pay no rabbit (foot)** [Mezzrow & Wolfe, *Really the Blues* (1946): 'When you don't pay a man no rabbit, you're not paying him any more attention than would a rabbit's butt as it disappears hurriedly over the fence'] [1900s–40s] (*US black*) an exhortation to ignore a person or situation. ❑ **go like a rabbit** *v.* (*also* **go like a herd of turtles**) [1940s+] of a woman, to copulate enthusiastically. ❑ **have some rabbit in one** *v.* [the alleged obsession of rabbits] [1980s] (*US black/Und.*) to be sexually active. ❑ **have the rabbits** *v.* [the assumed stupidity of rabbits] [late 19C+] (*Aus.*) to be exceptionally stupid. ❑ **rabbit died, the** [the test formerly used to determine pregnancy]

[1940s+] I am pregnant. ❑ **stab the rabbit** *v.* [2000s] (*Aus.*) to have sexual intercourse.

IN EXCLAMATIONS

❑ **rabbit foot!** [1920s] (*US black*) an excl. of annoyance.

rabbit *n.*[2] **1** [late 17C–early 19C] a wooden drinking vessel. **2** [1910s–50s] (*US/Aus.*) (*also* **bunny**) a bottle of beer.

IN PHRASES

❑ **run the rabbit** *v.* [1910s–50s] (*Aus.*) **1** to bring home liquor from a public house; thus *rabbit-runner*, one who carries out this errand. **2** to obtain liquor illegally.

rabbit *n.*[3] [? Irish *ráibéad*, a big, hulking person] [mid-19C] (*US*) a rowdy.

rabbit *n.*[4] [rhy. sl.; *rabbit-and-pork* = talk] [1920s+] **1** a talk, a conversation. **2** audacity, cheek.

rabbit *n.*[5] [1950s] an informer.

rabbit *v.*[1] [note *DOD RABBIT IT! under* DOD *n.*[1]] [mid-18C] a euph. for 'damn', esp. as an oath (e.g. *rabbit it!*).

rabbit *v.*[2] (*also* **play rabbit, turn rabbit**) **1** [20C+] to scrounge [naut. jargon *rabbit*, a smuggled/stolen article; note N.Z. use (post 1950) which comes from the image of a *rabbit* attacking the tops of root crops]. **2** [1930s+] to leave quickly, to run away.

rabbit (and pork) *v.* [RABBIT *n.*[4]] [1930s+] to talk; thus *rabbit away, rabbit on*, to chatter, to grumble, to complain; as n., a chat.

rabbiter's breakfast *n.* [2000s] (*N.Z.*) smoking a cigarette while defecating.

rabbit hutch *n.* [rhy. sl.] [20C+] **1** the crotch. **2** a crutch.

rabbit in the thicket *n.* [rhy. sl.] [1980s] (*Aus.*) **1** a ticket. **2** cricket. **3** a wicket.

rabbit-o *n.* (*also* **rabbit-oh**) [the cry, but note Aus. -O *sfx* (3); thus *The Rabbit-Os*, derog. nickname for the South Sydney Rugby Club, whose fortunes suffered so much in the 1930s Depression that its officials were reduced to raffling and selling rabbits] [20C+] (*Aus.*) an itinerant seller of rabbits as food; also attrib.

rabbit pie *n.* [LIVE RABBIT *n.*] [19C] a prostitute.

IN COMPOUNDS

❑ **rabbit-pie shifter** *n.* [? RABBIT PIE *n.* or ref. to his appetite] [19C] a policeman.

rabbit-proof fence, the *phr.* [the rabbit-proof fencing erected in Aus. to protect crops]

IN PHRASES

❑ **beyond the rabbit-proof fence** **1** [late 19C+] (*Aus.*) the wilds, the back of beyond, the edge of 'civilization'; also in fig. use. **2** [2000s] in fig. use, absurd, incomprehensible.

rabbit's paw *n.* [var. on RABBIT *n.*[4]] [1990s+] talk, conversation.

rabblings *n.* [SE *rabble*] [mid-19C] (*UK Und.*) the lowest class of thieves.

rabbo *n.* [abbr.] [1900s–1940s] **1** a *rabbit*; *rabbits* as a group, thus *rabbo!* the street-cry of a seller of rabbits. **2** a street-seller of rabbits.

racan *n.* [Irish *racán*, a rake] [20C+] (*Irish*) a lanky, raw-boned person.

race *n.* [16C SE *race*, a journey] [20C+] (*Ulster*) a short visit or journey.

IN PHRASES

❑ **go to the races** *v.* [euph.] [20C+] to die.

racehorse *n.* **1** [1950s+] (*Aus./N.Z*) in sense of something sleek and lean. (**a**) a very thin roll-up cigarette. (**b**) a thin pack. **2** [1960s+] (*US*) an up-market prostitute [on pattern of THOROUGHBRED *n.*].

racehorse charlie *n.* [var. on HORSE *n.* (7); though note CHARLIE *n.*[8]] [1930s–70s] (*drugs*) **1** any narcotic drug. **2** a morphine user.

race man *n.* (*also* **race woman**) [i.e. one who is conscious of their SE *race*] [1920s–60s] (*US*) a culturally conscious black person, esp. one who advocates black civil rights.

race off *v.* (*also* **whiz off, whizz off**) [1940s+] (*Aus.N.Z.*) to seduce, to go off with a woman in the hope of achieving seduction.

race one's motor *v.* (*also* **rev one's motor**) **1** [1940s+] (*US*) to become over-excited. **2** [1970s+] to excite sexually.

race woman *n.* *see* RACE MAN *n.*

racial *adj.* [i.e. characteristic of the black race] [1940s] (*W.I.*) generous, open-handed.

rack *n.*[1] [Irish *raca*, a comb] [mid-19C+] (*Irish*) **1** coarse hair. **2** a comb.

rack *n.*[2] **1** [late 19C] (*US*) an omnibus. **2** [1930s+] (*US*) the female breasts, esp. when large and firm. **3** [1940s+] (*orig. US milit.*) a bed; thus sleep. **4** [1970s+] (*US black*) a card holding bubble-packed birth control pills. **5** [1970s+] (*US drugs*) a quantity of drugs, e.g. pills, vials of crack cocaine, etc. **6** [2000s] (*US black*) of money, a large quantity. **7** [2000s] a hotel.

DERIVATIVES

❑ **racked** *adj.* [1960s+] tired out, exhausted.

IN COMPOUNDS

❑ **rack attack** *n.* [1970s+] (*US campus*) a sudden onset of sleepiness. ❑ **rack monster** *n.* (*US campus*) **1** [1960s+] (*also* **pad monster**) sleepiness, the result either of boredom or exhaustion. **2** [1980s+] a bed. ❑ **rack time** *n.* [1990s+] sleep; a nap.

IN PHRASES

❑ **hit the rack** *v.* **1** [1960s+] to go to bed. **2** [1960s+] (*US/US gay*) by ext., to have sexual intercourse.

SE in slang uses

IN COMPOUNDS

❑ **rack man** *n.* [he deals with the *racks* of coins] [1930s+] an official in a crap game who deals with making change, paying winners, etc. ❑ **rack pick** *n.* [SE *rack*, i.e. the widely spaced teeth resemble objects hanging from a rack + *pick*, a pronged instrument] [1960s+] (*US black*) a comb designed spec. for use on a NATURAL *n.* (6) or an AFRO *n.* (1) hairstyle.

IN PHRASES

❑ **rack (it)** *v.* [SE *book rack*] [1940s] (*US campus*) to work hard.

rack *v.*[1] [RACK *n.*[1]] [mid-19C+] (*Irish*) to comb.

rack *v.*[2] [RACK *n.*[2] (3)] **1** [1940s–60s] (*orig. US black*) to go to sleep. **2** [1950s+] (*US*) (*also* **rack in**) to sleep, thus *racked out*, asleep. **3** [1950s+] (*also* **rack with**) to seduce a woman, to make love.

IN COMPOUNDS

❑ **rack date** *n.* [1970s] a seducible female.

IN PHRASES

❑ **rack out** *v.* [1960s+] (*US*) to fall asleep, to go to bed.

rack *v.*[3] [1960s+] **1** to beat up. **2** to admonish. **3** to kick in the testicles.

SE in slang uses

IN PHRASES

❑ **rack back** *v.* *see* RACK UP *v.*[1] (4). ❑ **rack off** *see* separate entries. ❑ **rack on** *v.* *see* RACK UP *v.*[1] (2). ❑ **rack one's soul-case** *v.* *see BURST ONE'S SOUL-CASE under* SOUL-CASE *n.* ❑ **rack (the bars)** *v.* (*also* **rack the doors**) [1990s+] (*US prison*) to open or close the cell doors. ❑ **rack up** *v.* *see* separate entries.

rackaback *n.* [for Grose's explanation, *see* GORMAGON *n.*] [late 18C–early 19C] a man on horseback with a woman behind him riding side-saddle.

racked *adj.* *see under* RACK *n.*[2].

racked out *adj.* [1940s–50s] (*US teen*) frustrated, let down.

racked up *adj.* [pool/snooker jargon *rack up*, to place the balls in order preparatory to a game] [1950s] neat, smartly turned out.

racket *n.*[1] **1** [early 19C+] any form of deception, criminal trickery, hoaxing; also attrib. **2** [late 19C] a theory, an idea. **3** [late 19C+] a job, an occupation; not necessarily illegal. **4** [late 19C+] a story, a 'line'. **5** [late 19C+] in combs., with a defining n. **6** [1900s–20s] (*US*) a plan, a scheme. **7** [1900s–20s] in weak use, any form of activity. **8** [1920s] (*US*) an easy job or situation, esp. a sinecure. **9** [1920s+] (*US*) as *the rackets*, organized crime. **10** [1950s–60s] (*US prison*) the world of homosexual relationships. **11** [1960s] (*US*) *the racket*, prostitution.

IN COMPOUNDS

❑ **racket man** *n.* **1** [mid-19C] a thief. **2** [1930s+] (*US*) (*also* **racket boy, racket ghee, racket guy**) a member of an organized crime syndicate.

IN PHRASES

❑ **lay one's racket** *v.* [1930s–40s] (*US black*) **1** to reveal one's real agenda, usu. a confidence trick or hoax. **2** to tease. **3** to show off. ❑ **stand the racket** *v.* [STAND *v.*[2] (2)] **1** [late 18C–1930s] (*also* **stand the nonsense**) to pay the bill, to treat one's companions. **2** [early 19C–1910s] to take the blame for the crimes of one's confederates. **3** [mid-19C–1940s] to put up with a situation; to overcome a challenge [SE *stand*, to suffer].

racket *n.*[2] [SE *racket*, a noise, a disturbance; SAmE *racket*, a type of waltz] (*US*) **1** [late 19C+] an organized social event, designed to make money for the sponsor. **2** [20C+] a large party. **3** [1900s–60s] an organized dance, held in a dancehall and frequented by lower-class young people.

IN COMPOUNDS

❑ **racket jacket** *n.* [1930s–40s] (*US black*) a ZOOT SUIT *n.*

IN PHRASES

❑ **on the racket** [1910s] (*Aus.*) on a spree.

rackety *adj.* [RACKET *n.*[1] (1) + ? pun on SE *rackety*, noisy] [mid–late 19C] insalubrious.

rack-off *n.* [mid-19C] an act of sexual intercourse.

rack off! *excl.* [SE *rack*, to move, to travel] [1970s+] (*Aus./N.Z.*) go away! be off!

racks *n.* (*also* **racks of meat**) [rhy. sl.; *racks of meat* = *teat*/TIT *n.*[2] (1)] [20C+] the female breasts.

rackumbub *n.* [mid-19C] (*UK Und.*) medicine.

rack up *v.*[1] **1** [mid-19C; 1960s+] to go to bed [presumably similar to ety. at sense 2, the idea of putting oneself 'on the rack'; the link to RACK *n.*[2] (3) is coincidental]. **2** [1940s–50s] (*also* **rack on**) to retire, to abandon an occupation or action [pool imagery: one puts one's cue in the *rack*]. **3** [1950s+] to stop doing something. **4** [1960s+] (*also* **rack back**) to accumulate, to register or to achieve [pool imagery: one *racks up* the balls].

rack up *v.*[2] [SE *rack*, to strain, to stretch] **1** [1950s+] (*US*) to damage, to wreck, to harm. **2** [1980s+] to steal.

rack up *v.*[3] [1990s+] (*drugs*) to cut up lines of a narcotic, usu. cocaine.

raclan *n.* [Rom. *rakli*, a girl] [mid-19C] (*tramp*) a married woman.

rad *n.* *see* RADICATION *n.*

rad *adj.* (*also* **rad-o**) [abbr. RADICAL *adj.*] [1970s+] (*orig. US teen*) a general intensifier; extreme, excessive, very much, excellent, the best.

rada *n.* [abbr.] [1960s–70s] (*US black*) a Cadillac Eldorado.

radar! *excl.* [1990s+] (*US drugs/teen*) a cry of warning at the arrival of the police.

raddie *n.* **1** [20C+] an Italian living in London, orig. spec. in Clerkenwell [? image of Italians as anarchistic, i.e. SE *radical*]. **2** [1930s+] a radical.

raddled *adj.* [play on SE] [late 17C+] drunk.

radge *n.* [orig. northern dial., ult. SE *rage*] [1990s+] **1** (*also* **radgehead**) a psychotic. **2** a temper tantrum.

radge *adj.* (*also* **radgy**) [RADGE *n.*] [1990s+] **1** of a person or situation, mad, furious, insane. **2** of an idea, a situation, foolish, absurd. **3** in fig. use, 'crazy', i.e. wonderful.

radge *v.* [RADGE *n.*] [1990s+] to lose one's temper.

radgehead *n.* *see* RADGE *n.* (1).

radgy *n.* [RADGE *n.* (1)] [1990s+] a psychotic.

radgy *adj.* *see* RADGE *adj.*

radical *n.* [so called from its being the favourite breakfast of the *radical* Henry 'Orator' Hunt (1773–1835)] [mid-19C] roasted corn.

radical *adj.* [SE use of *radical* as 'basic, essential, from the roots' and eschewing political overtones; like a number of other terms, the word moved from surfer jargon, to 'Valley Girls' use and thence, via the 1990s *Teenage Mutant Ninja Turtles* craze, to general use] [1970s+] (*US campus*) a term of utmost approval.

radication *n.* (*also* **radics, radix**) [SE *eradication*; the Metropolitan Police's violent and racist attitude towards black youth] [1970s–80s] (*UK black*) the police.

radio *n.* [? pun] [1960s] a toasted tuna fish sandwich on white bread.

SE in slang uses

IN PHRASES

❑ **put something on the radio** *v.* [i.e. to 'broadcast'] [1960s] to publicize something.

radio! *excl.* [the two-way radios carried by guards; the term initially used to warn of an approaching *radio* or guard, widened into a general imper. implying 'Shut up and listen to your radio!'] [1960s+] (*US prison*) be quiet! stop that!

radio (rental) *adj.* [rhy. sl. = MENTAL *adj.* (1)] [1960s+] insane, mad.

radish *n.* [late 19C–1900s] the penis.

radishes! *excl.* [1970s+] (*US campus*) a general excl. of disgust and annoyance.

radix *n.* *see* RADICATION *n.*

radjy *adj.* [? Scot.] [1930s] delightful.

rado *n.* [abbr.] [1970s+] (*US black*) a Cadillac Eld*orado*.

rad-o *adj.* *see* RAD *adj.*

r.a.f. *adj.* [abbr. *rough as fuck*] [1990s+] used of a very unattractive woman.

rafe *n.* (*also* **ralph**) [? Suffolk dial. *rafe/ralph*, a fool] [mid-19C] a pawnbroker's ticket.

raff *n.* [SE *riff-raff*] [early–mid-19C] (*UK campus*) a vulgar, worthless person.

Rafferty's rules *n.* (*also* **Rafferty rules**) [despite use of capital 'R', which implies a proper name, the term comes f. mispron. of SE *refractory*; note Seal, *The Lingo* (1999): 'RAFFERTY'S RULES, meaning no rules at all, seems to be an Australianization of a British dialect term for confusion or mess, RAFF or RAFFETY'] [1920s+] (*Aus./N.Z.*) no rules whatsoever, anything goes.

raffle ticket *n.* [rhy. sl. = RICKET *n.*] [20C+] a mistake.

raff off *n.* [? var. *naff off!* under NAFF *v.*] [1980s] to leave, to go.

raffry *n.* [RAFF *n.*] [mid-19C] (*UK Und.*) rowdiness; thus *raffryroister*, one who stages a fake fight in a public house, talking advantage of the confusion to commit a robbery.

raft *n.*[1] **1** [early 19C+] (*US*) a large number; a large amount. **2** [late 19C+] (*US*) a piece of toast.

raft *n.*[2] [synon. Norwegian dial. *raft*] [20C+] (*Ulster*) a tall, thin person.

rag *n.*[1] **1** with ref. to money [SE *rag*, a small amount, extended to a small amount and then any sum of money, thus sense 1b the minimally valuable farthing; the mid-19C introduction of banknotes adds secondary ref. to *rag*, a piece of cloth]. (**a**) [late 16C–1920s] money in general. (**b**) [late 17C–early 19C] a farthing. (**c**) [late 18C–1940s] usu. in pl., a banknote, paper money. (**d**) [mid-19C–1900s] (*US Und.*) in pl. counterfeit notes. (**e**) [1940s–50s] (*US Und.*) a confidence game based on stocks and shares [ext. of sense 1c, banknote, to any monetary document]. **2** as ext. versions of SE. (**a**) [late 18C+] a flag. (**b**) [19C+] an article of clothing, esp. a dress, thus *raggery*, clothes. (**c**) [mid-19C–1910s] a theatre curtain. (**d**) [mid-19C+] a pocket handkerchief. (**e**) [1900s] a towel. (**f**) [1910s] (*US*) a necktie. (**g**) [1920s] a wig. (**h**) [1950s] a baby's nappy. (**i**) [1960s+] a bandana. (**j**) [1990s+] (*US black*) by metonymy from sense 2i, a gang member. (**k**) [1990s+] (*W.I./UK black*) the semi-uniform clothes worn by a RAGAMUFFIN *n.* **3** with ref. to speech [RED RAG *n.*]. (**a**) [early 19C+] the tongue. (**b**) [mid-19C+] abuse, teasing, talk; usu. as *ragging*. **4** [late 19C+] a newspaper or magazine [derog. ref. to its worthlessness, but note the use of *rags* in paper-making]. [1940s] (*US black*) a magazine. **5** in cards. (**a**) [20C+] (*US*) a playing card. (**b**) [1930s–40s] (*N.Z.*) a low playing card in a suit. **6** with ref. to menstruation. (**a**) [1920s+] a sanitary towel. (**b**) [1990s+] a menstrual period. **7** as a derog. [abbr. WET RAG *under* WET *adj.*[1], but ? ult. 16C–19C SE *rag*, a derog. description of a person, a 'rag of a man']. (**a**) [1960s]

(*N.Z.*) a derog. term for a man. (**b**) [1960s+] a fool. (**c**) [1970s+] (*US campus/teen*) an unpleasant person. **8** [1980s+] (*US*) a second-rate, run-down car. **9** *see* RAG HOUSE below. **10** *see* RAG TOP below.

IN COMPOUNDS

❑ **rag-alley** *n. see* RAG TRADE below. ❑ **rag baby** *n.* [mid-19C] a dollar bill. ❑ **rag box** *n. see* separate entry. ❑ **rag carrier** *n.* [late 18C–early 19C] an ensign, charged with carrying the flag. ❑ **rag chewer/chewing** *see* separate entries. ❑ **rag gorger** *n.* (*also* **rag gorgy**) [Rom. *gorgio*, a (non-gypsy) man] [early 19C] a wealthy man. ❑ **rag-out** *n.* [1970s] (*US campus*) a person who plays tricks; something unpleasant. ❑ **rag shop** *n.* [SHOP *n.*[1] (2)] [early–mid-19C] a bank; thus *rag-shop boss*, a banker, *rag-shop cove*, a banker, a cashier. ❑ **rag splawdger** *n.* (*also* **rag splawger**) [SPLODGER *n.*[2]] [mid–late 19C] a wealthy man. ❑ **rag trade** *n.* **1** [mid-19C] the purchasing of counterfeit banknotes and the subsequent passing them off to innocent victims. **2** [mid-19C+] (*also* **rag-alley, rag fair**) the garment industry. ❑ **rag week** *n.* [punning link to university *rag weeks*] [1980s+] the menstrual period.

IN PHRASES

❑ **dead rag** *n. see under* DEAD *adj.* ❑ **drop the rag** *v. see under* DROP *v.*[1]. ❑ **flash one's rags** *v.* [mid–late 19C] to show off one's bankroll. ❑ **get one's rag out** *v.* [late 19C+] **1** (*also* **get one's rag up, let one's rag out**) to lose one's temper. **2** to make someone else angry. ❑ **give rag** *v.* [1980s] (*W.I.*) to tease and joke aggressively and competitively. ❑ **have the rag on** *v.* **1** [1940s+] of a woman, to be menstruating. **2** [1960s+] to act foolishly or eccentrically, to be annoyed. ❑ **hold one's rag** *v.* [1990s+] to keep one's temper. ❑ **lose one's rag** *v.* (*also* **lose the rag**) [1950s+] to lose one's temper. ❑ **off one's rag** *adj.* [1990s+] (*UK juv.*) extremely angry, in a furious temper. ❑ **on the rag** **1** [1930s+] menstruating; thus *off the rag*. **2** [1960s+] irritated, testy, bad-tempered; thus *share the rag*, to be hostile, to place blame on someone else. ❑ **rag out** *v.* **1** [mid-19C; 1950s–70s] (*US*) to dress up, to wear one's best clothes. **2** [1980s+] (*US/Can.*) to be in a bad mood. ❑ **rag up** *v.* [1900s] (*US Und.*) to dress oneself up. ❑ **ride the rag** *v. see under* RIDE *v.* ❑ **share the rag** *v.* [1970s+] (*US gay*) to be hostile, to pass responsibility onto another. ❑ **take the rag out** *v.* [1990s+] (*US*) in fig. use, to control one's temper, to cheer up.

IN EXCLAMATIONS

❑ **get off the rag!** [1970s] a dismissive excl.; the implication is that the addressee is lit. or fig. suffering from menstrual ill temper.

SE in slang uses

IN COMPOUNDS

❑ **rag-ass** *n.* [SE *rag* + -ASS *sfx* (1)] [1990s+] (*US black*) an impoverished person. ❑ **rag baby** *n.* [20C+] (*US black*) a poor, ill-clothed woman, who is nonetheless attractive. ❑ **rag bag** *n. see* separate entry. ❑ **rag-cat alley** *n.* [1900s] (*US*) a backstreet, the poor, run-down part of a city. ❑ **rag head** *n. see* separate entry. ❑ **rag house** *n.* (*also* **cot house, rag shanty**) [the canvas sides or roofs that such buildings often had] (*US*) **1** [mid-19C–1920s] a cheap rooming house or 'hotel', esp. in a town based on an oil-drilling camp. **2** [late 19C–1930s] (*also* **rag**) a tent. ❑ **rag-mannered** *adj.* [SE *rag* adj., a general derog. term] [late 17C] aggressively uncouth, very badly mannered. ❑ **rag mob** *n.* [MOB *n.*[2] (3)] [1960s] (*US Und.*) a team of confidence men working 'the rag', a trick based on a persuading the victim that they can profit from a fixed stock swindle. ❑ **rag stick** *n.* [SE *rag*, a piece of cloth + *stick*] [late 19C] an umbrella, esp. one that is not rolled up. ❑ **rag top** *n.* (*also* **ragger**) (*US*) **1** [1950s+] a car with a 'convertible' soft top. **2** [1970s] a truck that has an open back, which, when loaded, is covered with a tarpaulin. **3** [1970s+] (*also* **rag**) the car or truck's soft top. ❑ **rag water** *n.* [the effect of over-indulgence, 'these liquors seldom failing to reduce those that drink them to rags' (Grose, 1796)] [late 17C–early 19C] spirits, esp. gin. ❑ **ragweed** *n.* [WEED *n.*[1] (4)/SE *ragweed*, a form of hardy weed, of the genus *Ambrosia*] **1** [1960s+] (*drugs*) inferior quality marijuana. **2** [1980s+] heroin.

IN PHRASES

❑ **have a rag on every bush** *v.* [mid-19C+] (*Irish*) of a man, to pursue a number of women at the same time. ❑ **take the rag off the bush** *v.* (*also* **take the rag off the hedge, take the rag off all creation**) [mid-19C–1950s] (*US*) to surpass, to excel, to outdo.

rag *n.*[2] ['The familiar name of the *Rag*, by which it is generally known, was invented by Captain William Duff, of the 23rd Fusiliers. Coming in to supper late one night, the refreshment obtainable appeared so meagre that he nicknamed the club the *Rag and Famish*' (Nevill & Jerningham, *Piccadilly to Pall Mall*, 1908); note also the less well-known *Rag*: the Raglan Music Hall in Leather Lane, off Holborn WC2] [mid-19C+] an abbr. of the *Rag and Famish*, the Army and Navy Club, London.

rag *n.*[3] [derog. use of SE; + ? link to HAVE A RAG ON EVERY BUSH *under* RAG *n.*[1]] **1** [late 19C+] (*US*) a girlfriend, a female companion. **2** [1960s] (*US campus*) an unattractive female. **3** [1970s] (*Aus.*) a promiscuous woman.

rag *n.*[4] [1910s] anything physically energetic, a party; a fight, a battle.

rag *n.*[5] *see* DO-RAG *n.*

rag *adj.* [2000s] (*N.Z.*) no good, useless.

rag *v.* **1** in senses of verbal or physical harassment [despite chrono., presumably link to RAG *n.*[1] (3b); ? abbr. BULLYRAG *v.*]. (**a**) [mid-18C+] to scold, to talk severely to. (**b**) [19C+] (*also* **rag off, rag on**) to annoy, to tease (esp. in context of school or university). (**c**) [20C+] to attack, to cause trouble; in context, to rob. (**d**) [1900s] (*US campus*) to talk nonsense. (**e**) [1910s] to fight, to beat up; to manhandle. (**f**) [1910s] (*juv.*) to create disorder. (**g**) [1910s] to argue over a topic, to wrangle. (**h**) [1970s] (*US*) to gossip. (**i**) [1970s+] to complain. (**j**) [2000s] to question closely, to interrogate. **2** [mid-19C] to share, esp. to divide up the proceeds of a crime; thus *go rags*, to share out [? SE *rag*, to tear in pieces]. **3** with ref. to menstruation. (**a**) [1960s+] to menstruate. (**b**) [1970s+] to be irritable. **4** [1990s+] (*US black*) to dress (fashionably).

IN PHRASES

❑ **rag off** *v. see* sense 1b above. ❑ **rag on** *v.* **1** [1980s+] (*US*) to nag, to criticize. **2** *see* sense 1b above. ❑ **rag out** *v.* [1980s] to abuse verbally. ❑ **rag talk** *v.* [2000s] to threaten.

ragamofi *n.* (*also* **ragamorfi**) [SE *ragamuffin*] [1950s] (*W.I.*) ragged clothes.

ragamuffin *n.* (*also* **raga, ragga, raggamuffin**) [SE *ragamuffin*, orig. the name of a demon, latterly a ragged, dirty, disreputable man or boy; like a number of teen terms, this pej. is used as a term of approval] [1990s+] **1** (*UK black*) a hooligan, a lout. **2** (*US black*) an unaffected, down-to-earth person. **3** (*W.I./UK black*) a lover of modern dancehall reggae.

IN COMPOUNDS

❑ **ragamuffin tip** *n.* [TIP *n.*[7]] [1990s+] (*US black*) a down-to-earth situation.

rag and bone *n.*[1] [rhy. sl. = THRONE *n.* (1)] [20C+] the lavatory.

rag-and-bone *n.*[2] [? lost rhy. sl.] [1930s] a woman.

raga-raga *adj.* (*also* **ragga-ragga**) [SE *rags, ragged*] [1940s+] (*W.I.*) ragged, worn-out, usu. of clothes.

rag bag *n.* (*also* **ragbag, rag doll**) **1** [mid-19C+] a miscellaneous collection of anything. **2** [late 19C+] a sloppily-dressed woman, a slattern [play on SE + BAG *n.*[1] (3)/DOLL *n.*[1] (2)]. **3** [1920s–40s] the lowest category of touring carnival. **4** [1920s+] (*Aus./US*) (*also* **rag-bunch**) a messy, unkempt person. **5** [1930s+] a general derog., the implication is of unkempt slovenliness. **6** [1990s+] a person who relinquishes sex or money easily.

rag box *n.* (*also* **rag shop**) [RAG *n.*[1] (3a) + SE *box/shop*] **1** [late 19C] the mouth. **2** [1970s+] (*US black*) in ext. use of sense 1, the vagina [? also BOX *n.*[1] (1a)].

IN EXCLAMATIONS

❑ **shut your rag-box!** [late 19C] shut up! be quiet!

rag chewer *n.* [CHEW THE RAG *v.*] [1900s] a story.

rag chewing *n.* [CHEW THE RAG *v.*] [late 19C+] (*US*) talking, esp. chatting or arguing.

rage *n.* (*also* **rage up**) [1970s+] (*Aus./N.Z.*) a noisy, exciting party; a good time, thus *ragey*, exciting, boisterous.

rage *v.* [SE *rage*/RAGE *n.*] [1970s+] (*Aus./N.Z./US campus*) **1** to have a great time, do something well. **2** to look fashionable. **3** to have sexual intercourse.

rager *n.* [RAGE *v.* (1)] [1970s+] (*Aus./N.Z./US campus*) **1** a particularly good party. **2** (*also* **rage**) a person, or animal, known for wild behaviour.

rage up *n.* see RAGE *n.*

ragga/raggamuffin *n.* see RAGAMUFFIN *n.*

ragga-ragga *adj.* see RAGA-RAGA *adj.*

ragg-arsed/-assed *adj.* see RAGGED-ARSED *adj.*

ragged *adj.* **1** [mid-18C] drunk. **2** [late 18C+] of a person or object, second-rate, inferior. **3** [late 19C] of an era, unfortunate, ill-fated. **4** [1930s+] (*orig. Aus.*) nervy, out of sorts, 'under the weather,' tired.

ragged-arse *n.* (*also* **ragg-arse, raggedy-arse, raggedy-ass, raggedy-pants**) [1930s] a disreputable, seedy, run-down person.

ragged-arsed *adj.* (*also* **ragg-arsed/-assed, raggedy-arsed/-assed**) [SE *ragged* + -ARSED *sfx*] **1** [late 19C+] of clothes, tattered. **2** [late 19C+] of people, disreputable, seedy, run-down. **3** [1940s+] of things, worthless.

ragged down (heavy) *adj.* (*also* **ragged out**) [RAG OUT *under* RAG *n.*[1] + HEAVY *adv.* (1)] [1950s+] (*US black*) (very) well-dressed.

IN PHRASES

▫ **ragged to the bone** *adj.* (*also* **clean to the bone**) [BONE *n.*[1]] [1950s+] (*US black*) exceptionally well dressed.

ragged out *adj.* **1** [1970s+] (*US campus*) tired out [SE *ragged*]. **2** [2000s] (*US teen*) appalling, unattractive etc [RAG *n.*[3] (2)].

raggedy *adj.* (*also* **ragidy, raggety, raggly**) [1930s+] (*US black*) run-down, second-rate, dilapidated; of emotions and objects.

raggedy Ann *n.* [play on *Raggedy Ann*, a children's doll] [1980s] (*US black*) an untidy, unkempt woman.

raggedy-arse *n.* see RAGGED-ARSE *n.*

raggedy-arsed/-assed *adj.* see RAGGED-ARSED *adj.*

raggedy-ass *n.* see RAGGED-ARSE *n.*

raggedy-ass ride *n.* [RAGGED-ARSED *adj.* (3) + RIDE *n.* (2a)] [1950s+] (*US black*) an old car, any form of motor vehicle that has become run down and dilapidated.

raggedy-pants *n.* see RAGGED-ARSE *n.*

ragger *n.* see *RAG TOP under* RAG *n.*[1].

raggety *adj.* see RAGGEDY *adj.*

ragging *n.* [RAG *v.* (1)] **1** [late 18C] scolding, abuse. **2** [20C+] teasing, an act of teasing.

raggly *adj.* see RAGGEDY *adj.*

raggy *adj.* [RAG *v.* (1b)] [late 19C–1900s; 1960s] irritated.

raggy-arsed *adj.* [1990s+] (*Aus.*) very poor.

rag-head *n.* [the cloth that each wears as a head-covering] **1** [20C+] (*US*) a gypsy. **2** [1920s] (*US*) a Hindu. **3** [1920s+] (*Aus./US*) an Arab native of the Middle East. **4** [1920s+] (*UK/US*) a Sikh. **5** (*US black*) with ref. to the bandanna or DO-RAG *n.* worn by old ladies and latterly gang members. (**a**) [1960s+] one who wears a scarf or bandanna tied round the head. (**b**) [1980s+] anyone who is not absolutely up to date with current information, gossip, style etc.

ragidy *adj.* see RAGGEDY *adj.*

raging *adj.* [RAGE *v.* (1)] [1980s+] (*US campus/teen*) of a party, of a drug, wild, fantastic, very enjoyable.

rag order *n.*

IN PHRASES

▫ **in rag order** (*also* **in rags**) [SE *ragged*] [1940s+] (*Irish/Aus.*) in dire straits, in a mess.

rag out *v.*[1] [? *RACK OUT under* RACK *v.*[2]] [1970s] (*US campus*) to become tired.

rag out *v.*[2] **1** *see under* RAG *n.*[1]. **2** *see under* RAG *v.*

rags *n.* (*orig. US*) **1** [mid-19C+] clothes, usu. pl. **2** [1960s+] (*US black*) stylish, fashionable clothes. **3** [1990s+] (*US Und.*) clothing and insignia that indicate one's membership of a (prison) gang.

IN EXCLAMATIONS

▫ **dash my rags!** see *DASH MY BUTTONS! under* DASH! *excl.*

rags and bones *n.* [1970s] (*US black*) the corpse of a poor person.

rag shop *n.* **1** *see under* RAG *n.*[1]. **2** see RAG BOX *n.*

rag, tag and bobtail *n.* (*also* **bobtail; tag, rag and bobtail; tag rag and longtail**) [later uses are SE] [mid-16C+] **1** the rabble, the masses. **2** everyone, the whole lot.

rah! *excl.* [abbr. RAATID! *excl.*] [2000s] (*UK black*) a general excl., used for anger, surprise, amazement, approval, envy, etc.

rah-rah *n.* [earlier uses, the encouraging cries of *rah! rah!*] **1** [1940s–60s] (*US black*) clothes fashionable among students in black colleges. **2** [1960s–70s] (*US campus*) one who is imbued with college (esp. sporting) spirit. **3** [1980s+] (*Aus.*) a fan of Rugby Union; hence the game itself [implying the educated, middle-class image of rugby union, i.e. the *rah-rah* accents of the fans]. **4** [1990s+] (*US*) enthusiastic speech; a pep-talk. **5** [1990s+] (*US prison*) a female inmate who fraternizes with the authorities.

IN PHRASES

▫ **give someone the rah-rah** *v.* [late 19C] (*US*) to mock (on the grounds of supposed snobbishness).

rah-rah *adj.* [used slightly disparagingly, as are other sl. refs. to US college students, e.g. *JOE COLLEGE under* JOE *n.*[1]] **1** [late 19C+] (*usu. US*) enthusiastic, excited, esp. in the context of college students cheering a team; thus *rah-rah boy*, *rah-rah girl*, over-excited students, *rah-material*, a freshman. **2** [1910s+] upper class, esp. British.

rahtid see RAATID.

rahzoo *n.* see RAZOO *n.*[1].

raifield *v.* (*also* **rayfield**) [? dial. *raffle*, an idle vagabond] [1950s–70s] (*US black*) to steal without concealment or regard for the consequence, to break the law in a contemptuous manner.

rail *n.* **1** [1920s] (*US tramp*) an employee of a railroad. **2** [1970s] (*US*) an erection; thus *get a rail on*, to get an erection. **3** [1980s+] (*US drugs*) a thin line of a powdered narcotic [such lines tend to be cut in a parallel pair, one per nostril].

SE in slang uses

IN PHRASES

▫ **off the rails** [railway imagery] **1** [mid-19C+] emotionally stressed; usu. in phr., *go off the rails*. **2** [late 19C+] errant, mistaken, esp. in phr. *go off the rails*, to blunder, to make a mistake. **3** [2000s] exceptional.

railbird *n.* (*gambling*) **1** [late 19C+] a racetrack fan who stands next to the rails to get as near as possible to the racing. **2** [1940s+] a fan or spectator who crowds round the rails that surround a big game in a casino, or other place of entertainment.

railings *n.* [resemblance] [1910s+] the teeth.

railroad *n.* **1** [mid-19C] (*US*) rough whisky [? as drunk by railroad workers and tramps]. **2** [1970s+] (*drugs*) the scars that accompany repeated injections of narcotics into one's veins [TRACKS *n.* (1)].

railroad *adj.*

SE in slang uses

IN COMPOUNDS

▫ **railroad bible** *n.* [note Wink Martindale's country/pop hit 'Deck of Cards' (1959) in which the cards are reinterpreted along religious lines] [late 19C] (*US*) a pack of cards. ▫ **railroad bull** *n.* see BULL *n.*[5] (2). ▫ **railroad dick** *n.* see *YARD BULL under* YARD *n.*[2]. ▫ **railroad Irish** *n.* [their living on 'the wrong side of the tracks'] [1910s] (*US*) a generic for the poor Irish working class. ▫ **railroad weed** *n.* [WEED *n.*[1] (4); ? it grows at the side of the tracks] [1970s] (*drugs*) marijuana. ▫ **railroad whisky** *n.* [Santa

Fe wine, based on the name of a US railroad] [1970s+] (*US black*) cheap wine, esp. Santa Fe Tokay.

railroad *v.* **1** [mid-19C] (*US*) to enforce a mild punishment by dragging the victim up and down along the floor until the seat of their trousers is worn through. **2** [late 19C–1930s] to hurry or rush somewhere. **3** [1920s] (*US tramp*) to ride a train. **4** [1920s] (*US*) to throw someone out of a city or town (on the railroad). **5** [1970s] (*US campus*) to use influence in the pursuit of personal interests.

railsplitter *n.* [mid-19C–1950s] (*US/Aus.*) a farmer, an unsophisticated rustic.

rail up *adj.* [SE *riled up*] [1970s–80s] (*UK black*) angry.

rain *n.* [mid-19C] (*UK Und.*) gin.

SE in slang uses

IN COMPOUNDS

❑ **raincoat** *n.* **1** [1930s+] a contraceptive sheath. **2** [1940s] a dutch cap contraceptive. **3** [1990s+] (*UK Und.*) an Ingram Mac-10 machine pistol. ❑ **rain drain** *n.* [a var. of the DUCK'S ARSE *n.* (1); the image being that the rain runs off it] [1950s+] (*US*) a 1950s youth hair style. ❑ **rainjuice** *n.* [1950s] (*US*) water. ❑ **rain maker** *n.* [20C+] (*US*) an extremely successful member of a firm, often a lawyer, who commands high fees and is thus a lucrative asset to their employer; thus *rainmaking*, promoting trade. ❑ **rain napper** *n.* [SE *rain* + NAP *v.*[1] (2)] [mid–late 19C] an umbrella. ❑ **rain water** *n.* [1930s] (*US prison*) coffee.

rain *v.*

SE in slang uses

IN PHRASES

❑ **if it were raining pea soup, I'd get hit on the head by a fork** [1920s+] (*Aus.*) a general expression of continual bad luck. ❑ **rain curtain-/stair-rods** *v. see* COME DOWN STAIR-RODS *under* STAIR *n.* ❑ **rain Duke Georges** *v.* (*also* **rain like a dunken dog**) [1930s+] (*N.Z.*) to rain heavily. ❑ **rain on** *v.* [1920s+] (*US*) **1** to kill. **2** to make suffer, to beat up, to lose one's temper with. ❑ **rain on someone's parade** *v. see* PISS ON SOMEONE'S PARADE *under* PISS ON *v.*

rain and pour *v.* [rhy. sl.] [20C+] to snore.

rainbow *n.* [its colourfulness, usu. in context of clothes] **1** [early 19C] a large, discoloured bruise, gained through boxing. **2** [early 19C] a pattern book. **3** [early–mid-19C] a footman, abbr. (late 18C) *knight of the rainbow*, a footman in livery. **4** [early–mid-19C] a mistress, a whore. **5** [mid-19C] a golden guinea [its shape; Partridge suggests link to RHINO *n.*[1] (1)]. **6** [mid-19C] a young man about town. **7** [1950s] (*W.I.*) a tall, thin person. **8** [1960s+] in drug uses. (**a**) Tuinal, a barbiturate. (**b**) LSD. (**c**) any form of pill (usu. the barbiturates Amytal and Seconal which have red-and-blue capsules) in a coloured jacket. **9** [1970s+] (*US black*) one who dresses in gaudy bad taste.

IN COMPOUNDS

❑ **rainbow kiss** *n.* [SE *rainbow* + *kiss*] [1990s+] (*US*) a passionate kiss, which follows an orgasm reached through reciprocal oral sex between a man and a menstruating woman, and thus involves mixing the semen and vaginal secretions/blood in the mouth. ❑ **rainbow necker** *n.* [NECK *v.* (1)] [1990s+] a person who has oral sex with a women while she is menstruating. ❑ **rainbow queen** *n.* [SE *rainbow* (*coalition*), a campaign involving a variety of races + -QUEEN *sfx* (3)] [1970s+] **1** (*US black/gay*) anyone who is involved in a black/white sexual relationship. **2** (*US gay*) a gay man who prefers inter-racial sex and/or relationships.

rainy day woman *n.* [ety. unknown; popularized and poss. coined by Bob Dylan in the song 'Rainy Day Women Nos. 12 and 35' (1966)] [1960s] (*drugs*) marijuana.

raise *n.* **1** [mid-19C] (*UK Und.*) a substanial amount of (stolen) money. **2** [mid-19C+] a tip or monetary contribution, whether given voluntarily or extorted. **3** [mid-19C; 1990s+] an opportunity to pick up some money, legal or otherwise. **4** [late 19C+] an increase in salary or wages. **5** [1940s+] (*US black*) an arm; thus *on your left raise*, on your left-hand side. **6** [1940s+] (*US black*) a pocket. **7** [1950s–70s] (*US black*) constr. with *the*, the police. [? they *raise* the alarm/a hue and cry]. **8** [1950s+] (*UK black*) robbery. **9** [1970s+] (*US black/campus*) one's parents.

IN PHRASES

❑ **make a raise** *v.* **1** [19C] (*US Und.*) to pick a pocket; to rob. **2** [mid-19C] (*US gambling*) to fund a fellow-gambler who has lost all his money. **3** [mid-19C–1930s] (*US*) to obtain money, in a non-criminal manner; to secure something.

raise *v.* [RAISE *n.*/SE *raise money*] **1** [20C+] to obtain, to get hold of. **2** [1940s] (*US Und.*) to steal. **3** [1940s–50s] (*US Und.*) to make a signal by raising one's hat. **4** [1940s+] (*W.I.*) to get hold of some money (legally or otherwise). **5** [1950s] (*UK Und.*) to forge cheques. **6** [1960s] (*US black*) to stop, to pause. **7** [1960s] to put up bail for. **8** [1960s+] (*US*) to go, to leave. **9** [1960s+] (*US*) to escape, to get out of, to be released from prison. **10** [1980s] (*US campus*) to have a good time.

IN PHRASES

❑ **raise up** *v.* **1** [1970s+] (*US black*) to leave a place. **2** [1970s+] (*US prison*) to be given leave or parole to leave a prison. **3** [1990s+] (*US black teen*) to get out of the way. **4** [1990s+] (*US black*) to prepare oneself, e.g. for a fight. **5** [1990s+] (*US black*) to keep watch; to give a warning.

SE in slang uses

IN COMPOUNDS

❑ **raise-up** *n.* [pun on HOLD-UP *n.* (1)] [1940s] (*US Und.*) an armed robbery or hold-up.

IN PHRASES

❑ **raise...** *v. see under* relevant n. ❑ **raise ants' nests** *v.* [the effect on ants when one breaks open their nest] [20C+] (*W.I.*) to make trouble, to foster an argument. ❑ **raise Cain** *v.* [Adam's wicked son, *Cain*, here used as synon. for *hell*] [mid-19C+] (*orig. US*) to cause as much trouble as one can. ❑ **raise dust** *v.* [1910s] (*US*) to hurry, to go quickly. ❑ **raise Hob** *v.* [SE *raise* + SE *Hob*, the Devil] [late 19C+] (*US*) to cause as much trouble as one can. ❑ **raise jack** *v. see* CUT UP JACK *v.* ❑ **raise the ante** *v. see* UP THE ANTE *under* ANTE *n.* ❑ **raise the colour** *v.* [the *colour* being gold; 20C+ use is historical] [mid–late 19C] (*Aus.*) to discover gold. ❑ **raise the elbow** *v. see* LIFT ONE'S ELBOW *under* LIFT *v.* ❑ **raise the flag** *v. see* FLY THE FLAG *v.*[2] (1). ❑ **raise the wind** *v.* **1** [late 18C+] (*also* **raise the breezes, whistle up a breeze**) to obtain money, to obtain a loan; thus *wind-raising*, obtaining a loan. **2** [late 19C–1920s] to create a rumour, to make up stories.

raise-my-thoughts *n.* [its effects] [1900s] (*W.I.*) a drink of rum.

raiser *n.* [1990s+] (*US black*) a lookout, e.g. for a street drug dealer.

raisin *n.* **1** [1970s–80s] (*US*) derog. term for a black person. **2** [2000s] (*N.Z.*) an old person.

raisin bag *n.* [BAG *n.*[1] (1); play on NUTSACK *under* NUTS *n.*[2]] [1990s+] (*Can.*) the scrotum.

raisin-brain *n.* [1990s+] (*US black*) a fool, a term of abuse.

raj *n.* [? SE *rogue*] [1940s+] (*W.I.*) a villain, a trickster.

Rajah, the *n.* [mid–late 19C] the Mogul, a well-known centre of entertainment on Drury Lane, London.

rajah *n.* [1940s+] (*N.Z.*) an erection.

raj-ma-taj *n. see* RAZZMATAZZ *n.*

rake *n.*[1] **1** [mid-19C+] a comb, thus *bug-rake*, *garden-rake*. **2** [1950s] (*W.I.*) in fig. uses [i.e. that which 'smooths over']. **3** [1950s] (*W.I.*) a hunch. **4** [1950s] (*W.I.*) any form of trickiness, e.g. a duplicitous answer that hides the true situation.

rake *n.*[2] [SE *rake up*, a fabrication, a concoction] **1** [1950s] (*W.I.*) a piece of gossip. **2** [1960s] a betting tip.

rake *n.*[3] [Irish *reic*, lavish spending] [1960s+] (*Irish*) a large number.

rake *n.*[4] **1** *see* RAKE-OFF *n.* (1). **2** *see* RAUGE *n.*

rake *v.*[1] [SE *rake*, 'a man of loose habits and immoral character; an idle dissipated man of fashion' (*OED*)] **1** [late 17C–18C] of a man, to have sexual intercourse. **2** [18C–19C] (*also* **come upon the rake**) to live in a rakish manner.

rake *v.*^{2} **1** [mid-19C] (*UK Und.*) to divide (loot). **2** [1960s] (*Scot.*) to search. **3** *see* RAKE (IT) IN *v.*

rake *v.*^{3} [RAKE *n.*^{1}] [1910s+] (*Irish*) to comb.

raked *adj.* [SE *raked over the coals*] [1980s+] (*US campus*) **1** humiliated. **2** emotionally or intellectually exhausted. **3** having suffered a horrific experience. **4** having lost in a competition. **5** drunk.

rake down *v.* [? the croupier's *rake* at a casino] [mid-19C+] (*orig. US*) to win money at gambling, esp. cards.

rake (it) in *v.* (*also* **rake, rake together, rake up**) [mid-19C+] to make a great deal of money.

rake-off *n.* [the croupier's *rake* in a casino] **1** [late 19C+] (*orig. US*) (*also* **rake, rake-in**) a commission, esp. on some form of illegal deal. **2** [20C+] a profit.

rake on *v.* [1980s+] (*US campus*) to humiliate, to criticize.

rake-out *n.* [SE *rake out*, to clean out, e.g. a boiler, a grate] [late 19C–1900s] a pipeful of tobacco.

raker *n.*^{1} [mid-19C] a comb.

raker *n.*^{2} [SE *rake*, a 'fast' man-about-town] [mid–late 19C] **1** a heavy bet. **2** a very fast pace.

IN PHRASES

❑ **go a raker** *v.* [late 19C] (*Aus.*) **1** to place a heavy bet. **2** to fall heavily.

rake together/up *v. see* RAKE (IT) IN *v.*

rake-up *n.* [one 'rakes up' the tobacco] [1940s] a hand-rolled cigarette.

rakker *v. see* ROCKER *v.*

raleigh bike *n.* (*also* **village bike**) [rhy. sl. = DYKE *n.*; ult. the popular UK bicycle maker *Raleigh*] [20C+] a lesbian.

rall *n. see* OLD RAIL *under* OLD *adj.*

rally *v.* [? SAmE *pep rally*; but note 18C SE *rally*, to banter with, to tease with pleasantry] [1960s+] (*US campus*) to have a good time; to act utterly madly, drunkenly, obstreperously.

rally up *n.* [1960s] (*Aus. prison*) a prison riot.

Ralph *n.* [echoic of the noise of vomiting] [1950s+] (*US/Aus.*) used in phrs. pertaining to vomiting.

IN PHRASES

❑ **cry Ralph** *v.* (*also* **call Ralph, cry Ruth**) [1960s+] to vomit.
❑ **call (for) Ralph** *v.* [1960s+] to vomit.

ralph *n.*^{1} **1** [mid–late 17C; 1920s] a country bumpkin; a simpleton [stereotyping of *Ralph* as a peasant]. **2** [1950s–60s] (*camp gay*) an effeminate, timid or plain and undistinguished man [stereotyping as a 'sissy' name].

ralph *n.*^{2} [so-called in Judy Blume's *Forever* (1975)] [1980s] (*US/UK campus/teen*) the penis.

ralph *n.*^{3} *see* RAFE *n.*

ralph *v.* (*also* **bob, rauf, rolf**) [1960s+] (*US campus*) to vomit.

ralphie *n. see* REGGIE *n.*^{2}.

ralph lynn *n.* [rhy. sl.; ult. UK actor *Ralph Lynn* (1882–1964), best-known in the Ben Travers farces of 1920s] [1920s–40s] gin.

ralph spooner *n.* [Suffolk dial.] [late 17C–early 19C] a fool.

ram *n.*^{1} [animal imagery] **1** [early 17C–1900s] a penis. **2** [mid-17C+] a virile and/or promiscuous man; often as *OLD RAM* below. **3** [1980s+] an act of sexual intercourse.

DERIVATIVES

❑ **rammish** *adj.* (*also* **rammy**) [17C–early 19C] of either gender, sexually enthusiastic.

IN PHRASES

❑ **old ram** *n.* [RAM *n.*^{1} (2)] [19C+] an old or middle-aged man who still pursues women.

ram *n.*^{2} **1** [mid-19C] (*US campus*) a practical joke. **2** [1950s] (*US*) something unpleasant.

ram *n.*^{3} [RAMP *v.*^{2} (2) + image of the animal's horns, pushing at the victim] [1940s+] (*Aus.*) a trickster's confederate who encourages the public to lose their money in a con-game.

ram *n.*^{4} [ety. unknown] [1980s+] (*drugs*) alkyl nitrites.

ram *adj.* (*also* **rammed, rammers, ram up**) [SE *ram*, to force] [1980s+] (*UK black*) full.

ram *v.*^{1} [RAM *n.*^{1}] [17C; mid-19C+] to have sexual intercourse.

IN EXCLAMATIONS

❑ **ram it!** (*also* **ram it up your arse/ass!**) **1** [1930s+] (*orig. US*) an excl. of dismissal, 'go to hell!'. **2** [1980s+] (*UK black*) an expression of praise, encouragement.

ram *v.*^{2} [RAM *n.*^{3} (1)] [1950s+] (*Aus.*) to work as a confidence trickster's accomplice.

ram! *excl.* [orig. Irish/Kent dial.] [mid-19C; 1930s+] damn!; thus *rammed*, DAMNED *adj.*

rama *n.* [Sp. *rama*, a branch] [1970s] (*drugs*) marijuana.

-rama *sfx see* -ORAMA *sfx.*

ram and dam *n.* (*also* **ram and damn**) [one *rams* in the charge and *damns* the target] [mid–late 19C] a muzzle-loading gun.

ramatracks *n.* [? SE *ramble* + *track*; Share suggests 'nonce-wd.' but note Shetland Islands dial. *rammatrack*, a rabble] [20C+] (*Ulster*) purposeless wandering.

ram, bam, thank you ma'am *phr. see* WHAM-BAM-THANK-YOU-MA'AM *phr.*

ramble *v.* [early 17C–mid-19C] to go out looking for sex; also as n.

rambler *n.* [RAMBLE *v.*] **1** [early 17C–early 19C] a person who goes out looking for sex. **2** [1910s–60s] (*US tramp*) (*also* **rambler wolf**) a tramp who travels on passenger trains.

rambling *adj.* [1920s+] (*US tramp*) fast, e.g. a *rambling freight*.

rambustious *adj. see* RUMBUSTIOUS *adj.*

ram cat *n.* (*also* **ram-cat cove**) [SE *ram-cat*, a tomcat + COVE *n.* (1)] [mid–late 19C] a man wearing furs.

Ram Chundur *n.* (*also* **Chunder**) [stereotypical Hindu name] [1900s–10s] (*Aus.*) generic for any Indian (Hindu) immigrant.

ramfeezled *adj.* [Scot.] [late 19C] exhausted.

ram it! *excl. see under* RAM *v.*^{1}.

ramjam *n.* [1970s–80s] (*UK black*) a crowd.

ram jam *v.* **1** [late 19C+] to stuff with food. **2** [1970s–80s] (*UK black*) to fill up, to cram.

ram-jam full *adj.* [RAM JAM *v.*] [late 19C] absolutely stuffed.

rammaged *adj.* [SE *ramage*, wildness, high spirits] [18C] drunk.

rammed *adj. see* RAM *adj.*

rammer *n.* **1** [late 17C+] (*also* **cunt-rammer**) the penis. **2** [late 18C–19C] (*UK Und.*) the arm. **3** [mid-19C] the leg. **4** [1970s+] (*US gay*) an enthusiastic, energetic copulator.

rammers *adj. see* RAM *adj.*

rammies *n.* [Malay *rami*, a Chinese and East Indian plant of the nettle family (*Boehmeria nivea*); thus the fine fibre of this plant, extensively employed in weaving; note RAMMY ROUSERS *n.*] **1** [1910s–60s] (*Aus./S.Afr.*) trousers. **2** [1950s] knickers.

ramming *adj.* [early 19C] forcible, 'go-ahead'.

rammish *adj. see under* RAM *n.*^{1}.

rammy *n.* [SE *rampant*/Scot. *rammish*, violent, untamed] [1920s+] (*Scot. juv.*) a fight.

rammy *adj.* **1** [1950s–70s] (*US prison*) suffering from delirium tremens. **2** [1960s] (*US*) drunk. **3** [1970s] (*US*) eccentric, over excited. **4** *see* RAMMISH *under* RAM *n.*^{1}.

rammy rousers *n.* (*also* **ripsy rousers**) [rhy. sl. + link to RAMMIES *n.* (1)] [20C+] (*Aus.*) trousers.

ramp *n.*^{1} [SE *rampant*, exhibiting fierceness or high spirits] [mid-15C–19C] a high-spirited, independent woman, usu. synon. with a prostitute; thus *ramping*, high-spirited, promiscuous.

ramp *n.*^{2} [RAMP *v.*^{2}] **1** [early 19C] robbery with violence. **2** [mid-19C] a racecourse swindler; thus ext. to any type of swindler. **3** [mid-19C+] any form of swindle or fraud. **4** [late 19C] a spree, a boisterous good time. **5** [1910s–20s] a spurious argument or similar commotion intended to disguise a swindle or confidence trick. **6** [1980s] (*Aus.*) a search.

ramp *n.*^{3} [the long wooden bar] [1930s+] a public house or its bar.

IN PHRASES

❑ **on the ramp** **1** [late 19C–1920s] out on a spree [? abbr. SE *rampage*; note RAMP *n.*^{2} (4)]. **2** [late 19C] noticeable, active.

ramp *v.*[1] [mid-16C–17C] of a woman, to act in a promiscuous manner; to work as a prostitute.

DERIVATIVES

□ **ramping** *adj.* [mid-16C–17C] rampant, extreme.

ramp *v.*[2] [SE *ramp*, to act in a threatening manner] **1** [early–mid-19C] to rob with violence; thus *done for a ramp*, convicted of a violent crime. **2** [19C–1900s] to swindle. **3** [late 19C] to force someone to pay their debts. **4** [1910s+] (*Aus.*) to search a prisoner and/or their cell. **5** [1930s+] (*Aus./W.I.*) to play around, lit. or fig; also as adj. **6** [1980s] (*UK black*) to tease, to banter, to trick.

rampacious *adj.* (*also* **rampageous**) [SE *rampageous*, violent; unruly; boisterous] [mid-19C–1920s] crazy, eccentric.

rampallian *n.* [SE *ramp*, to act in a threatening manner] [late 16C–early 19C] a ruffian, scoundrel, villain.

ramped *adj.* [SE *ramage*; high spirits or *rampage*, a state of boisterous excitement] [1990s+] (*US campus*) **1** drunk. **2** tired.

ramper *n.* [RAMP *v.*[2]] **1** [early 19C] (*UK prison*) one who initiates a new prisoner by robbing them of their possessions. **2** [late 19C] a racehorse swindler. **3** [late 19C–1900s] a street thug, a hooligan.

ramping *adj. see under* RAMP *v.*[1].

ramping *adv.* [SE *rampant*] [early 19C–1910s] extremely, very much, esp. phr. *ramping mad*, very drunk.

rampsman *n.* [RAMP *v.*[2] (1)] [mid-19C] a robber with violence.

ramraid *n.* (*also* **ramrod**) [RAMRAID *v.*] [1990s+] a method of stealing from shops that have erected blinds, shutters, bars etc, whereby the thief steals a car, then drives at high speed into the shop-front, smashing the way through any defences; the car is filled with loot, then driven away.

ramraid *v.* [SE *ram* + *raid*] [1990s+] to perform a RAMRAID *n.*

ramraider *n.* (*also* **ramrodder**) [RAMRAID *v.* (1)] [1990s+] **1** one who carries out a RAMRAID *n.* **2** (*UK drugs*) amphetamine sulphate [its harsh, immediate effect].

ramrod *n.* [fig. use SE *ramrod*, 'a rod used for ramming down the charge of a muzzle-loading fire-arm' (*OED*)] **1** [mid-18C+] the penis [ROD *n.* (1)]. **2** [early 19C+] (*also* **rod**) a manager or leader, usu. a tough person or harsh disciplinarian. **3** [mid-19C–1900s] a landlord.

ramrod *v.* [RAMROD *n.* (2)] [1940s+] to be the boss, to run or lead, esp. in a tough or disciplinarian way; to act aggressively in pursuit of a project.

ramrodder *n. see* RAMRAIDER *n.*

rams *n.* [ety. unknown] [20C+] delirium tremens.

ramscootrify *v.* [Scot. *ramscooter*, to induce panic] [20C+] (*Ulster*) **1** to defeat verbally. **2** to beat up.

ramsgate sands *n.* [rhy. sl.; ult. *Ramsgate* (coastal town) Kent, UK] [20C+] the hands.

ram-shackled *adj.* [pun on SE *ramshackled*/RAM *n.*[1] (1) + SE *shackle*] [1990s+] subjected to anal intercourse, usu. by a person with a large penis.

ram's horn *n.* [1910s–20s] someone who speaks very loudly; as adj., noisy.

ramsies *n.* [mid-19C] (*UK Und.*) leather breeches.

ram skin *n.* [their willingness to take any and all possessions, even a *ram skin* mat] [early 19C] (*Anglo-Irish*) a bailiff.

ramsquaddle *v.* [mid-19C] (*US*) **1** to overcome, to 'use up'. **2** to drink heavily, thus as adj., drunk.

ram up *adj. see* RAM *adj.*

ram (up) *v.* [1970s–80s] (*UK black*) to fill up, to crowd.

ranch *n.*

IN PHRASES

□ **go to the ranch** *v.* [the ranch style 'homosexual healing centres' advocated by anti-gay campaigner Anita Bryant] [1990s+] (*US gay*) to go crazy.

ranch *v.* [? RAUNCH *v.* (1)] [1990s+] (*US*) **1** to ejaculate. **2** to bring to orgasm, to make ejaculate.

ranchy *adj.* [? *OED* suggests var. on *raunchy*, but impossible given cited chronology; ref. to a SE *ranch* and the conditions associated with it] [early 19C+] (*US*) dirty, disgusting, indecent.

rancid *adj.* **1** [1900s] infatuated. **2** [1980s+] (*US teen*) ugly, unattractive.

rancy-tancy *adj.* [1950s] (*Aus.*) fancy, refined.

randal's man *n.* [its being favoured by the prize-fighter Jack *Randall* 'The Nonpareil' (1794–1828)] [mid-19C] a silk handkerchief with a green base and white spots.

randan *n. see* RANTAN *n.* (2).

randem tandem *n.* (*also* **random tandem**) [mid–late 19C] three horses driven in tandem.

r. & i. *phr.* [abbr. radical (i.e. RADICAL *adj.*) and *i*ntense] [1980s+] (*US campus*) extremely exciting or enjoyable.

randle *n.* [the verses varied as to area. In Cumberland: 'The offender is seized by the ear or by the back hair, whilst the following is repeated "Rannel me! Rannel me! Grey goose egg/Let every man lift up a leg./By the hee (high) by the low, by the buttocks of a crow; Fish, cock or hen." If "cock" was the reply then the other said, "Hit him a good knock" and did so. If "fish" was the answer, the other said, "Spit in his face". (*EDD*)] [late 18C–19C] a set of nonsense verses that a schoolchild was forced to recite, to the accompaniment of pinching, hair-pulling and similar juvenile tortures, if they were caught breaking wind in public; thus *randling*, punishing a child in this way; *randle*, to punish with a randle.

Randolph Scott *n.* [rhy. sl.; ult. film star *Randolph Scott* (1903–87)] [20C+] a spot.

random *n.* (*also* **randomer**) [1960s+] (*orig. US campus*) a stranger; someone who does not fit in.

random *adj.* [1980s+] (*US campus/teen*) **1** ordinary, run-of-the-mill. **2** eccentric, bizarre, odd. **3** spontaneous, unexpected.

IN COMPOUNDS

□ **random joe** *n.* [JOE *n.*[1] (1b)] [1980s+] (*US campus*) an unspecified person.

random tandem *n. see* RANDEM TANDEM *n.*

randy *n.*

IN PHRASES

□ **on the randy** *see* ON THE RANDAN *under* RANTAN *n.*

randy *v.* [SE *randy*] [late 19C] to make sexually excited.

randy-arsed *adj.* (*also* **randy-assed**) [SE *randy* + ARSE *n.* (2a)] [late 19C+] sexually voracious.

randyvoo *n.* [earlier uses milit. jargon *randyvoo*, a tavern frequented by recruiting sergeants; all ult. Fr. *rendezvous*, meeting (place)] **1** [late 19C] noise, arguments. **2** [1910s] (*Aus.*) a tavern. **3** [1940s] a sexual encounter [SE *randy*].

ranfla *n.* [Sp.] [1980s+] (*US*) a car that has been lowered and otherwise customized for teen use.

Range *n.* [abbr.] [2000s] a *Range*-Rover.

range *n.* [1910s+] (*Can./US prison*) the open area outside a row of cells.

IN PHRASES

□ **flash the range** *v.* (*also* **flash the gallery**) [1950s+] (*US prison*) to scan the area outside one's cell by using a hand mirror to catch any reflections of approaching warders etc.

range *v.* [SE *range*, to wander around] **1** [late 16C–early 18C] (*UK Und.*) (of either sex) to live promiscuously. **2** [late 17C] to live or work as a prostitute.

DERIVATIVES

□ **ranging** *adj.* [mid-17C–early 19C] of a man, pursuing women, philandering.

ranger *n.* [SE *ranger*, a wanderer; earlier uses + RANGE *v.*] **1** [17C] the penis. **2** [17C] a prostitute. **3** [late 19C–1900s] (*Aus.*) a bushranger.

ranggatan *n. see* RANTANRANGATANG *n.*

ranging *adj. see under* RANGE *v.*

Rangitoto yank *n.* (*also* **Rangitoto yankee**) [*Rangitoto*, an island in Auckland harbour + *yank*; i.e. the supposedly Americanized city] [1980s+] (*N.Z.*) a derog. term for an Aucklander.

rango *n. see* RANTANRANGATANG *n.*

rangoon *n.*[1] [rhy. sl.] [20C+] a prune.

rangoon *n.*^{2} (*also* **rangood**) [ety. unknown; ? wild marijuana is common in *Rangoon*] [1960s] (*drugs*) marijuana grown wild.

Rangoon runs *n.* [proper name *Rangoon* + RUNS, THE *n.*] [1940s+] diarrhoea, esp. contracted on foreign holidays.

ranikaboo *n. see* RANNYGAZOO *n.*

rank *n.*^{1} [RANK *adj.*^{1} (2)] [1920s–60s] (*US Und.*) a failed crime, esp. when foiled by the authorities; thus *in the rank*, arrested, captured while committing a crime.

rank *n.*^{2} [1990s+] (*W.I./UK black*) a criminal, a gangster.

rank *adj.*^{1} [ext. uses of SE *rank*, rancid, rotten, coarse or indecent] **1** [late 17C+] (*also* **ranky**) foul-smelling. **2** [mid-18C+] (*also* **rank-ass**) second-rate, inferior, disgusting; also as intensifier. **3** [20C+] (*W.I.*) impertinent, extremely cheeky.

rank *adj.*^{2} [SE *rank*, stout, strong] [1970s+] (*UK black*) excellent, first-rate, admirable.

rank *v.*^{1} [SE *rankle* or dial. *rank*, to lead a dissipated life] **1** [mid-19C] to cheat. **2** [1920s–60s] (*US*) to catch in the act of committing a crime. **3** [1920s+] (*US*) to betray, to let down.

rank *v.*^{2} (*also* **rank on, rank out**) [RANK *adj.*^{1} (2) + SE *rank*, to assign a rank, in this case low and thus to put someone 'in their place'] **1** [1920s–40s] (*US Und.*) to fail, esp. in the commission of a crime. **2** [1930s+] (*US*) to disdain, to disparage. **3** [1930s+] to lower; to lose status or job seniority. **4** [1940s+] (*orig. US black*) to cause problems for another person's plans or actions. **5** [1950s+] to insult, often by ritual insults directed at the other person's mother; as n., an insult. **6** [1990s+] (*US campus*) to ridicule.

IN PHRASES

❑ **rank a joint** *v.* [JOINT *n.* (4a)] [1940s] (*US Und.*) to blunder in the operation of a confidence trick. ❑ **rank out** *v.* [i.e. to abandon one's aggressive posture (on model of COP OUT *v.*^{2} etc)] [1980s+] (*US black*) to beg for help, to surrender to pressure, to behave badly or weakly. ❑ **rank someone's game** *v.* (*also* **rank someone's action, ...play, ...style**) [GAME *n.* (6) / ACTION *n.* (4) / PLAY *n.* / SE *style*] [1930s+] (*US black*) to obstruct deliberately another's sexual advances.

rank *v.*^{3} [SE *rank*, to assign a rank, in this case high] [1950s+] (*UK black*) to admire, to respect.

IN PHRASES

❑ **rank one's hand** *v.* [1960s] (*US black*) to overestimate one's abilities or position.

rank and ritches *n.* (*also* **rank and riches**) [rhy. sl.] [late 19C] trousers, breeches.

rank and smell *n.* [a pun on SE *rank*, (high) class and *swell*] [late 19C] a common person.

rank-ass *adj. see* RANK *adj.*^{1} (2).

ranked *adj.* [? RANK *adj.*^{1} (1), thus ? play on STINKING *adj.*^{2} (1)] [1990s+] (*US campus*) drunk.

ranker *n.* [abbr. SE *rank* + DUFFER *n.*^{2} (1)] [mid-19C] an absolute idiot.

ranking *n.*^{1} [RANK *v.*^{2} (2)] [1960s+] (*US black*) the act of insulting, usu. one's family and esp. one's mother.

ranking *n.*^{2} *see* RANKS *n.*

rank needle *n. see* NEEDLE *n.* (2).

rank rider *n.* [SE *rank rider*, a reckless rider, ult. Danish *rank*, upright, erect and thence proud, headstrong] **1** [17C–early 19C] (*UK Und.*) a highwayman. **2** [late 17C] a jockey.

ranks *n.* (*also* **ranking**) [RANK *v.*^{3}] [1980s+] (*W.I./UK black teen*) a highly regarded (and revered) person; thus adj., admirable, excellent.

ranky *adj. see* RANK *adj.*^{1} (1).

ranky dank *n.* [? RINKY-DINK *adj.*^{2} (2) + RANK *adj.*^{1} (2)] [1960s–70s] (*US black*) an unsophisticated, unworldly person.

rannicaboo *n. see* RANNYGAZOO *n.*

ranny *n.*^{1} [abbr. *ranahan*] [1930s–60s] (*US, West*) a top cowhand.

ranny *n.*^{2} *see* RAANY *n.*

rannygazoo *n.* (*also* **ranikaboo, rannicaboo**) [ety. unknown; ? links to ? dial. *ranny*, rash, giddy + Fr. sl. *gazouiller*, to sing, to speak] [late 19C+] nonsense; irrelevant, irritating activity.

rant *n.* [Scot./dial. *rant*, boisterous merry-making] [mid-17C] a spree.

rant *v.* [RAMP *v.*^{2} (1)] [late 19C] to take by violence.

rantallion *n.* [late 18C–early 19C] 'one whose scrotum is relaxed as to be longer than his penis' (Grose, 1785).

rantan *n.* [echoic, but note SE *randan*, riotous behaviour; thus mid-19C SAmE *rantankerous*, 'a row, a drunken frolic, means given to quarrelling' (Schele De Vere, 1872)] **1** [mid-17C–mid-19C] a loud, banging noise. **2** [mid-19C+] (*also* **randan**) a drinking bout, a spree, a riot.

IN PHRASES

❑ **on the randan** (*also* **on the randy**) [SE *ran-dan*, a spree, lit. 'random (behaviour)'] [mid-17C+] on a spree. ❑ **on the rantan** [mid-19C+] out on a spree, drunk.

rantanrangatang *n.* (*also* **ranggatan, rango**) [SE *orang-utang*] [20C+] (*W.I.*) a belligerent, aggressive, coarse person.

rantipole *n.* (*also* **rantipoll**) [SE *rantipole*, a wild, abandoned woman] **1** [mid-17C–early 19C] sexual intercourse with the woman taking the superior position; thus *ride a rantipole*, to have intercourse in this position; as adj., sexually ardent. **2** [late 17C–mid-19C] a 'rude, romping boy or girl' (Grose, 1785); also as adj. **3** [18C–early 19C] a prostitute.

rantum scantum *n.* [SE *rantum-scantum*, chaos, a disorderly situation] **1** [mid-18C–early 19C] (*also* **rantie-tantie**) sexual intercourse. **2** [late 18C–early 19C] a noisy argument.

IN PHRASES

❑ **play at rantum-scantum** *v.* (*also* **play rantum**) [late 17C–early 19C] to have sexual intercourse.

rap *n.*^{1} [ext./fig. uses of SE *rap*, a blow, a stroke] **1** [mid-18C] the theft of a purse. **2** in senses of speech. (**a**) [late 18C+] (*orig. US*) a rebuke, the blame. (**b**) [20C+] (*US*) an official complaint or reprimand; thus *rapper*, n., one who makes a complaint. (**c**) [1920s+] a lecture, a reprimand. (**d**) [1920s+] speech or conversation, esp. the spontaneous wise-cracking repartee of street life. (**e**) [1940s+] (*orig. US black*) a 'line' used for seduction or picking up members of the opposite sex. (**f**) [1970s] the received opinion. (**g**) [1970s] a partner in conversation. (**h**) [1980s+] a set speech, e.g. that used by a street salesman. (**i**) [2000s] talk designed to persuade or deceive. **3** in Und. uses. (**a**) [mid-19C+] (*mainly US*) an arrest. (**b**) [late 19C–1900s] (*US*) confinement to an institution, other than a prison. (**c**) [20C+] a criminal charge. (**d**) [1910s] the identification of somebody as a murder target. (**e**) [1910s–60s] (*US*) an identification by the police. (**f**) [1910s+] (*US*) a jail sentence; also as v. (**g**) [1930s] (*US prison*) a one-year sentence. (**h**) [1930s+] (*Aus.*) congratulations, a commendation, praise. (**i**) [1930s+] a situation. (**j**) [1990s+] (*US Und.*) a criminal speciality.

pertaining to criminal charges

IN COMPOUNDS

❑ **rap buddy** *n.* [BUDDY *n.* (1), lit. a friend with whom one suffers an arrest] [1990s+] (*US black*) a close friend. ❑ **rap partner** *n.* [1960s+] (*US Und.*) someone who is on the same charge sheet as oneself; someone who is jailed for the same crime. ❑ **rap sheet** *n.* [1950s+] (*US*) a criminal record.

IN PHRASES

❑ **bad rap** *n.* **1** [1940s+] (*US*) a serious criminal charge. **2** [1960s+] the state of being criticized unfairly. **3** [1970s+] an unfair criminal charge or sentence. **4** [1970s+] a sentence of 20 years or more. ❑ **beat (a) rap** *v.* **1** [1920s+] to be found not guilty in a court. **2** [1940s] (*US*) in non-judicial context, to extricate oneself from difficult circumstances. ❑ **beat the rap** *v.* [1920s+] (*US*) to be found innocent of a charge in court; also attrib. ❑ **get the rap** *v.* [1970s+] to be scolded, to be told off, to be blamed. ❑ **give someone the rap** *v.* [SE *rap*, a blow] [1930s+] (*US*) **1** to murder, to kill. **2** to blame. ❑ **hang a rap on** *v.* (*also* **hang the rap on, tie the rap on**) [1920s–50s] (*US Und.*) of police or other authorities, to charge a criminal (fairly or otherwise). ❑ **lay a rap on** *v.* [LAY ON *v.* (2)] [1970s+] (*orig. US*) to persuade. ❑ **pin the rap on** *v.* [1930s+] to impute a crime (to a criminal) (whether or not they are actually implicated). ❑ **square a rap** *v.* [SQUARE *v.* (1)] [1940s+] to have a criminal charge dropped. ❑ **stand the rap** *v.* [1920s–30s] (*US Und.*) to take the blame, sometimes on behalf of another; to face criminal charges. ❑ **take the rap** *v.* (*also* **take a rap**) [1920s+] (*US Und.*) **1** to take a punishment, often a prison sentence, that is actually due to someone else. **2** to take the blame when one is not the guilty party. ❑ **tie the rap on** *v.* *see* HANG A *RAP* ON above.

pertaining to speech

(IN COMPOUNDS)

❑ **rap attack** *n.* [1980s+] (*US black*) extended, emotional, aggressive talk. ❑ **rap club** *n.* (*also* **rap studio**) [1970s] (*US*) an ostensible club that supposedly provides conversation but actually doubles as a brothel. ❑ **rap game** *n.* [GAME *n.* (6)] [1990s+] (*US black*) the ability to talk persuasively in pursuit of sexual conquest. ❑ **rap group** *n.* [1960–70s] (*US*) a discussion or encounter group. ❑ **rap parlor** *n.* [SAmE *rap parlor*, 'any establishment advertising, offering or selling the service of engaging in or listening to conversation, talk or discussion between an employee of the establishment and a customer, regardless of whether those other goods or services are also required to be licensed'] [1970s+] (*US*) a euph. for a massage parlour, itself a cover for a store-front organization behind which, while legitimate massage may be available, men pay for a variety of sexual services from 'relief' or 'executive' massage' (masturbation) to full intercourse. ❑ **rap session** *n.* **1** [1970s] (*US*) a police interrogation. **2** [1970s+] an intense conversation; by ext., in new therapy use, an encounter group.

rap *n.*[2] [Ger. penny engraved with an eagle that had been drawn so crudely that it was known as a *Rabe*, a raven. The coin was presumably introduced to Ireland by Ger. mercenaries] **1** [mid-18C–1900s] a halfpenny; thus in US a cent. **2** [late 18C–early 19C] (*orig. Irish*) a counterfeit halfpenny, circulated 1700–50. **3** [late 19C] money in general.

(DERIVATIVES)

❑ **rapless** *adj.* [late 19C–1900s] penniless.

(IN PHRASES)

❑ **not care a rap (for)** *v.* (*also* **not give a rap (for)**) [mid-19C+] to not care at all. ❑ **not matter a rap** *v.* [late 19C+] not to matter whatsoever. ❑ **not worth a rap** [19C–1900s] worthless, useless.

rap *v.*[1] **1** in intransitive senses pertaining to speech. (**a**) [late 16C+] to curse. (**b**) [mid-18C–mid-19C] to swear a false oath, to perjure oneself; thus as n. a false oath. (**c**) [mid-19C] (*UK Und.*) to stand accused, to appear guilty. (**d**) [mid-19C+] to inform, esp. to the police. (**e**) [late 19C+] to talk, to converse. (**f**) [1960s+] to have any form of impromptu dialogue. (**g**) [1960s+] (*US black*) to speak lines in the DOZENS *n.* (1). **2** in transitive senses pertaining to speech. (**a**) [mid-18C–mid-19C] to swear (evidence) against someone; or for someone. (**b**) [late 19C+] to attack verbally, to criticize, to say sharply. (**c**) [20C+] (*US*) to charge; to prosecute, to arrest with a view to prosecution. (**d**) [1920s] (*US Und.*) to recognize. (**e**) [1940s] (*US*) to persuade, to trick out of. (**f**) [1950s+] (*Aus.*) (*also* **rap up, wrap, wrap up**) to praise, esp. to praise to excess. (**g**) [1960s+] to indulge in repartee, street-talk, to have a rapport with. (**h**) [1970s+] (*US black*) to talk with the aim of seduction. **3** [late 19C+] (*orig. Aus.*) to knock out, to kill.

(IN PHRASES)

❑ **bad rap** *v.* [1960s+] (*orig. US*) to malign, to criticize unfairly. ❑ **rap on the real** *v.* [ON THE REAL *under* REAL, THE *n.*] [1980s+] (*US black*) to speak sincerely, honestly. ❑ **rap to** *v.* (*US*) **1** [late 19C] to own up to; to declare. **2** [1920s] to recognize; to work out; to discover. ❑ **rap up** *v.* *see* sense 2f above.

rap *v.*[2] [? SE *rap*, to seize or snatch] [late 17C–early 19C] to swap, to exchange, to barter.

rape *n.* [backsl.] [mid-19C] a pear.

rape *v.* [weak uses of SE] (*US campus*) **1** [1970s] to abuse. **2** [1980s] to diminish the effects of; to reduce someone's pleasure; thus n., *raper*. **3** [1990s+] to misuse, to steal. **4** [1990s+] to defeat.

rape artist *n.* (*also* **rape hound**) [SE *rape* + -ARTIST *sfx*] [1960s] a rapist.

rape-o *n.* (*also* **rapo**) [1940s+] (*US Und.*) a rapist.

rape someone's buzz *phr. see under* BUZZ *n.*

rape wagon *n.* [1960s] (*US*) a flashy car belonging to a pimp.

rapid! *adj.* [1980s+] (*Irish*) a general term of approval, excellent! wonderful!

rapper *n.*[1] [SE *rap*, a blow] [late 17C–early 19C] a major lie.

rapper *n.*[2] [RAP *v.*[1]] **1** [late 18C–1900s] a professional perjurer. **2** [1900s–60s] (*US*) a plaintiff, a prosecutor. **3** [1920s–30s] (*US Und.*) an informer. **4** [1920s–40s] (*US Und.*) a judge. **5** [1940s] (*US*) one who takes or is given the blame for a crime, even if they are not actually guilty. **6** [1960s+] (*US*) a chatterer, a talker. **7** [1960s+] (*US*) the voice. **8** [1970s+] (*US black*) one who talks articulately and persuasively.

rappie *n.* [both men have faced or would face the same charge or RAP *n.*[1] (3c); they would also talk or RAP *v.*[1] (1e) together when plotting] [1920s+] (*US prison*) a confederate.

rapping *n.*[1] [RAP *v.*[1] (1b)] [mid-18C–mid-19C] perjury.

rapping *n.*[2] [RAP *v.*[1] (1e)] [1960s+] (*orig. US black*) talking.

rapping *adj.* [SE *rap*, a blow] [mid-19C] enormous, huge.

rapt *adj.* [SE *enraptured*] [1960s+] (*Aus.*) **1** overjoyed with, carried away, delighted. **2** emotionally and/or sexually excited by.

Raquel Welch *n.* [rhy. sl.; ult. film star *Raquel Welch* (b.1940)] [1960s+] a belch.

rare *v.* [the injected drug must first be 'cooked'] [1940s–70s] to inhale narcotics.

rare as rocking horse manure, as *phr.* (*also* **rare as a pregnant nun, rare as fairies**) [1940s+] (*Aus.*) a phr. used of anything extremely rare.

rare-lapper *n. see* LAPPER *n.* (1).

rark *v.* [2000s] (*N.Z.*) to drive around in an ostentatious manner.

rark up *v.* [2000s] (*N.Z.*) to scold severely, to argue.

rarse *see under* RAAS.

rarse *v.* [1990s+] (*UK black*) to sodomize.

rarted *adj. see* RAATID *adj.*

rarzer/rarzo *n. see* RASPBERRY TART *n.* (2).

rascal *n.* [SE *rascal*, a young or inferior deer, whose antlers have yet to grow properly; Grose (1785) also suggests Ital. *rascaglione*, a eunuch] [late 18C–early 19C] a man without genitals.

rash *v.* [1990s+] (*US teen*) to go to a party.

rash act *n.* [SE *rash*, foolhardy, precipitous] [1910s] (*Aus.*) suicide.

rasher *n.* [ety. unknown; ? SE *rash* which results from rubbing or VERTICAL BACON SANDWICH *under* BACON *n.*[1]] [1990s+] (*Irish*) the vagina, sexual intercourse; thus ext. as *rub of a rasher*.

rasher and bubble *n.* [rhy. sl.] [1970s] in darts, a 'double'.

Rasherhouse *n.* [RASHER *n.* + SE *house*] [1990s+] (*Irish*) the Mountjoy women's prison.

rasher of bacon *n.* [ety. unknown] [mid-18C] a fiery drink.

rasher of wind *n.* (*also* **rasher of bacon**) [mid-19C–1940s] **1** a very thin person. **2** a weak, spineless person. **3** anything of little or no account.

rasher wagon *n.* [it cooks SE *rashers* of bacon] [mid–late 19C] a frying pan.

rashing *n.* [SE *thrashing* + *harassing*] [1970s] (*US black*) an assault, violence.

rasp *n.* [SE *rasp*, a file, that which rubs] **1** [late 19C–1900s] the vagina. **2** [1940s–50s] a shave.

(IN PHRASES)

❑ **do a rasp** *v.* [late 19C–1900s] to have sexual intercourse.

rasp *v.* [SE *rasp*, to rub against; 20C+ use mainly Aus.] [late 19C+] to have sexual intercourse.

raspberries! *excl.* [RASPBERRY *n.* (1)] [1910s–20s] (*US*) an excl. used to express disbelief or defiance.

raspberry *n.* (*also* **raspo, razzberry**) [rhy. sl.; *raspberry tart* = FART *n.* (1), the noise of which this resembles] **1** [late 19C+] a coarse, dismissive, jeering noise. **2** with ref. to the colour. (**a**) [1910s] the nose [? one that is reddened from drink]. (**b**) [1960s–70s] (*drugs*) an abscessed injection site. (**c**) [1980s]

(*US campus*) a bloody wound. **3** [1910s+] a rejection, dismissal. **4** [1980s+] (*drugs*) a woman who trades sex for crack cocaine or money to buy the drug [? var. on STRAWBERRY *n.* (5) or pun on abbr. *raspberry tart*, i.e. TART *n.* (2)].

IN PHRASES

□ **blow a raspberry** *v.* [20C+] to make an obscene noise with one's lips, usu. intended to imply derision; also in fig. use. □ **flip one's raspberry** *v. see* FLIP ONE'S BANANAS *under* BANANAS *adj.* □ **get on someone's raspberry** *v.* [1960s] to irritate. □ **give someone the raspberry** *v.* [20C+] to deride or dismiss, to escape from.

raspberry *v.* [RASPBERRY *n.*] [1900s–40s] to deride, to dismiss.

raspberry-jam *n.* [mid-19C] (*UK Und.*) black eyes and a bleeding nose.

Raspberry-land *n.* [? the raspberry is a common plant there] [20C+] (*Aus.*) Tasmania; thus *Raspberry-landers*, Tasmanians.

raspberry (ripple) *n.* [rhy. sl.; ult. a type of ice cream] [1970s+] **1** a nipple. **2** (*also* **vanilla ripple**) a disabled person [= *cripple*].

raspberry tart *n.* (*also* **strawberry tart, cherry tart, gooseberry tart**) [rhy. sl.] **1** [late 19C+] the heart. **2** [1950s+] (*also* **rarzer, rarzo, razzo**) an act of breaking wind [= FART *n.* (1)].

rasper *n.* [SE *rasp*, to rub roughly] **1** [mid-19C+] a person or thing of an unpleasant character. **2** [mid-19C+] anything remarkable or extraordinary. **3** [20C+] a noisy breaking of wind.

raspin *n.* [? Scot. *rasp-house*, ult. Du. *rasphuis*, house of correction in which prisoners were employed in rasping wood] [early 19C] a prison.

rasping gang *n.* [SE *rasp* or RASPIN *n.* + SE *gang*] [mid-19C] toughs and thieves who attend prize-fights.

raspo *n. see* RASPBERRY *n.*

raspy *adj.* (*also* **rasty**) [SE *rasp*, to grate upon, to irritate] **1** [late 19C+] (*US black*) unattractive, unkempt. **2** [2000s] (*US teen*) excellent, wonderful (on bad = good model).

rass *see under* RAAS and its combs.

rasta *n.* [the *Rasta*farian use of marijuana as a sacrament] [2000s] (*US black*) one who takes drugs obsessively.

Rastus *n.* [popular mid-19C slave name *Erastus*; depending on context, as much patronizing as actively derog.] [late 19C+] **1** a derog. term for a black man. **2** as a term of address.

rasty *adj. see* RASPY *adj.*

rat *n.*[1] **1** with ref. to negative stereotypes of the animal which in nature possesses none of these characteristics. (**a**) [late 16C+] an unpleasant person. (**b**) [19C+] a person who changes allegiance out of self-interest. (**c**) [19C+] an informer; also attrib. (**d**) [late 19C] (*US*) a worker who undercuts standards established by unionized labour. (**e**) [late 19C] a cunning, deceitful person. (**f**) [late 19C+] (*orig. Aus.*) a street urchin. (**g**) [20C+] a person, esp. an enthusiast. (**h**) [1900s] (*US Und.*) a thieving prisoner. (**i**) [1900s] (*Aus.*) a bus inspector. (**j**) [1940s] (*US*) the quality of being an informer. (**k**) [1970s] (*Aus. Und.*) an incompetent. **2** [17C–mid-19C] a clergyman. **3** [17C–mid-19C] a drunkard who has been (breaking street lamps and) arrested and taken to the cells; thus *Rat's Castle*, the Poultry Counter prison [DRUNK AS A RAT *adj.*]. **4** (*Aus.*) in pl., usu. constr. with *the*, in context of emotions. (**a**) [mid-19C–1920s] tetchiness, bad temper. (**b**) [1910s+] a hangover, delirium tremens; usu. as *in the rats*. (**c**) [1950s] mad. **5** with ref. to the rat's fur. (**a**) [late 19C+] (*US*) a hair-pad with tapering ends used as the base of the elaborate pompadour hairstyles affected by women in the late 19C [also the shape of its tail]. (**b**) [1930s] (*US black*) a wig. (**c**) [1990s+] the pubic hair. (**d**) [1990s+] the vagina. **6** f. backform. RATTY *adj.* (2). (**a**) [1910s] (*UK juv.*) a bad temper. (**b**) [1920s] (*Aus.*) a bout of madness. (**c**) [1920s] an obsession, an eccentricity. **7** [1990s+] (*US campus*) a promiscuous, attractive woman [SE but ? Fr. *rat*, a young woman, esp. a young ballet dancer aged 7–14; cited as a young whore in Balzac *A Harlot High and Low* (1839–47)].

SE in slang uses

IN COMPOUNDS

□ **rat-and-fowl** *n. see* separate entry. □ **rat-arse** *n.* (*also* **rat-ass**) **1** [1950s+] (*orig. US*) a general term of abuse; also as adj. [ARSE *n.* (1)/-ASS *sfx* (1)]. **2** [1990s+] a drunk [backform. f. RAT-ARSED below]. □ **rat-arsed** *adj.* [-ARSED *sfx*; note DRUNK AS A RAT *adj.*] [1980s+] drunk. □ **rat-assed** *adj.* (*also* **ratty-ass, ratty-assed**) [1980s+] (*US*) dirty, untidy. □ **rat back clip** *n.* [the supposed similarity to a rat's fur] [mid-19C] a short haircut. □ **ratbag** *see* separate entries. □ **rat bastard** *n.* [1920s+] (*orig. US*) a general term of abuse; also as adj. □ **ratboy** *n.* **1** [1980s] (*US drugs*) a street chemist, testing illicit drugs for purity. **2** [1990s+] a young boy exploited by a paedophile. □ **rat-brained** *adj.* [1970s] cunning, duplicitous. □ **rat castle** *n.* (*also* **rat's castle**) [its population of vermin] [early 18C] a prison, esp. the Poultry Counter, a prison in London. □ **rat-drawn** *adj.* [? a rat's pointed nose] [1960s] (*US black*) of shoes, pointed; such shoes were part of the pimp's 'uniform'. □ **rat face** *n.* [1910s+] (*orig. US*) a contemptible person, esp. if treacherous or cunning; also as a derog. term of address. □ **rat-faced** *adj.* (*also* **rat-face**) [1910s+] a general term of abuse. □ **rat fink** *see* separate entries. □ **rat fuck/fucker/fucking** *see* separate entries. □ **rathole** *see* separate entries. □ **rathouse** *n.* [RATTY *adj.* (2a)/BANDHOUSE *n.*] **1** [1920s+] (*Aus.*) (*also* **rat-factory**) a psychiatric institution. **2** [1940s–50s] any situation that drives one crazy. **3** [1980s+] (*Aus. prison*) a prison. □ **rat jacket** *n. see under* JACKET *n.* □ **rat joint** *n.* **1** [1910s] (*Aus.*) a psychiatric institution [RATTY *adj.* (2a) + JOINT *n.* (3i)]. **2** [1970s] (*US*) a second-rate, unpleasant establishment [RATTY *adj.* (1) + JOINT *n.* (3b)]. □ **rat muncher** *n.* [1980s+] a general term of abuse. □ **rat-off** *n.* [*RAT OFF (ON) under* RAT *v.*)] [1950s] a betrayal, an act of informing. □ **rat-on** *n.* [2000s] (*N.Z.*) an erection. □ **ratpack** *see* separate entries. □ **rat poison** *n. see* POISON *n.* (1). □ **rat prick** *n.* [PRICK *n.* (3)] [1940s+] a general term of abuse. □ **rat-prick** *adj.* [1970s] a general abusive epithet. □ **rat shagger** *n.* [SHAGGER *n.*[1] (1)] [1980s+] a general term of abuse. □ **rat's ass** *n. see* separate entry. □ **rat's castle** *n. see* RAT CASTLE above. □ **ratshit** *see* separate entries. □ **rat's piss** *n.* [2000s] weak beer. □ **rat's tail** *n.* [the fashion – as part of the MULLET *n.*[2] – and thus the word, re-emerged in 1980s] **1** [early 18C] a pig-tail, as fashionable as a man's hairstyle. **2** [1920s–60s] (*US black*) a straight-haired wig. □ **rat-tail** *adj.* (*also* **rat-tailed**) [19C+] a general term of disapproval, disdain. □ **rat trap** *see* separate entries.

IN PHRASES

□ **do a rat** *v. see* RAT *v.* (3). □ **drunk as a rat** *adj. see* separate entry. □ **get a rat** *v.* (*also* **have a rat**) [1900s–20s] (*Aus./N.Z.*) to act crazily in an eccentric manner; thus *give a rat*, to drive someone crazy. □ **get rats** *v.* (*also* **have rats, see rats**) (*Aus./N.Z.*) **1** [mid–late 19C] to feel unwell, 'out of sorts'. **2** [mid-19C+] to be very drunk. **3** [1900s] to act in a cowardly manner. □ **give green rats** *v.* [the link of *green* to envy/jealousy] [19C] to slander someone in their absence, to backbite. □ **give someone rats** *v.* [late 19C–1910s] (*Aus.*) to drive someone mad. □ **go the rat** *v.* [1990s+] (*Aus.*) to act without restraint. □ **have the rats** *v.* [1910s] (*Aus.*) to suffer the delirium tremens. □ **like a rat up a drainpipe** *adv.* (*also* **like a rat up a rope**) [1940s+] (*orig. Aus.*) very quickly, usu. used in a sexual context. □ **make rat** *v.* (*also* **rat in**) [Fr. Creole *faire* (*le*) *rat*, to act like a rat; ult. the negative stereotype of the rat] [20C+] (*W.I.*) to sneak into without paying, to gatecrash. □ **no rats** *n.* ['it being supposed that a Scot is always associated with bagpipes, and that no rat can bear the neighbourhood of that musical instrument' (Ware)] [late 19C–1900s] a Scotsman. □ **not give a rat's tit** *v. see NOT GIVE A FISH'S TIT under* TIT *n.*[2]. □ **rat out** *v.* [20C+] (*W.I.*) of a woman, to work as a prostitute. □ **rats in the attic** *adj.* (*also* **rats in the garret, ...loft, ...upper storey**) [var. on SE *have bats in the belfry*] [late 19C+] insane, mad. □ **rat track whisky** *n.* [1920s] (*drugs*) very strong whisky. □ **see rats** *v. see GET RATS* above. □ **street rat** *n.* [20C+] (*US*) a street child, usu. the homeless offspring of Irish immigrants.

IN EXCLAMATIONS

□ **rat's claws!** *see* RATSHIT! *excl.* □ **ratshit!** *see* separate entry.

rat *n.*[2] [abbr. RATTLER *n.*] **1** [1910s–50s] (*US Und.*) a train; thus *rat stand*, a railway station. **2** [1940s+] (*US*) a near-derelict but just driveable second-hand car.

IN COMPOUNDS

□ **rat crusher** *n.* [CRUSH *v.*[1] (3)] [1910s–60s] (*US Und.*) a thief who specializes in robbing railroad boxcars.

IN PHRASES

□ **on the rats** [1940s–50s] (*US Und.*) breaking into and stealing from freight-cars.

rat *adj.* [RAT *n.*[1] (1)] [1910s+] (*orig. US*) unpleasant, untrustworthy, generally despicable.

rat *v.* [RAT *n.*[1]] **1** [18C] to damn. **2** [early 19C+] (*also* **rat against, rat out**) to betray one's own party or cause; to let someone down. **3** [early 19C+] (*also* **do a rat**) to change sides. **4** [1910s+] (*orig. US*) to inform on, to betray. **5** [1910s+] (*Aus./N.Z.*) to steal, to ransack; esp. as *ratted*, (of people) robbed or (of objects) stolen [note mining jargon *ratter*, one who steals one's finds]. **6** [1990s+] (*US campus*) to tease, to ridicule. **7** [2000s] (*US black*) to go out in pursuit of women.

IN PHRASES

□ **rat against** *v. see* sense 2 above. □ **rat around** *v.* [20C+] (*US*) to loaf about, to idle. □ **rat off (on)** *v.* [1950s+] (*US*) to betray, to inform against. □ **rat on** *v.* [1910s+] to betray, whether as an informer, or morally and ethically. □ **rat one's hair** *v.* [the resulting style resembles a 'rat's nest'] [1950s] to backcomb one's hair in order to create the once popular 'beehive' style. □ **rat out** *v.* **1** [1910s+] to act like a RAT *n.*[1] (1c), to abandon one's responsibilities or friends. **2** [1930s+] to betray, to inform against. **3** *see* sense 2 above.

-rat *sfx* [1910s+] (*US*) constructed with a noun to indicate someone's habit or particular preference e.g. *arcade rat, gym rat*, MALL RAT *n.*

rat-and-fowl *n.* [? the images engraved upon it] [1910s] (*Aus.*) an Aus. shilling.

rat and mouse *n.* [rhy. sl.] **1** [1910s+] a house. **2** [1970s+] fig. a louse, an unpleasant person.

ratbag *n.* **1** [late 19C; 1930s+] (*orig. Aus./N.Z.*) a general term of abuse, a rogue, an eccentric; thus *ratbaggery*, acting in such a manner. **2** [1960s] (*US*) an unpleasant situation or job.

ratbag *adj.* [RATBAG *n.*] [1950s+] (*Aus.*) a general negative adj.

ratcatcher's daughter *n.* [rhy. sl.] [20C+] water, as drunk rather than sailed on or swum in.

ratch *adj. see* RATSHIT *adj.*

ratchet mouth *n.* (*also* **rachet jaw**) [SE *ratchet*, a notched wheel used in a machine + *mouth/jaw*] [1970s] a chatterer.

ratchet mouth *v.* (*also* **ratchet jaw**) [RATCHET MOUTH *n.*] [1970s+] to talk nonsense, to talk for the sake of hearing oneself talk.

ratepayers' hotel *n.* [paid for by the ratepayers] [1920s–30s] (*tramp*) a workhouse.

rat fink *n.* (*also* **r.f.**) [SE *rat*/RAT *n.*[1] + FINK *n.* (4)] [1960s+] an unpleasant person, with overtones of working as an informer.

rat fink *v.* [RAT FINK *n.*] [1980s+] (*US campus*) to play a practical joke on.

rat fuck *n.*[1] [SE *rat* + FUCK *n.* (1a); the rat is stereotyped as a 'bad' animal] **1** [1920s+] (*US*) a general term of personal abuse. **2** [1970s+] (*US*) a damn, e.g. *who gives a rat fuck*. **3** [1970s+] (*US campus*) a term of approval (on bad = good model).

rat fuck *n.*[2] [note political jargon *rat fuck*, to sabotage an opponents' campaign by whatever means (usu. illegal) necessary; the original *rat fuckers* learned their trade in college politics and were later recruited to Richard Nixon's national campaign team; it was their techniques that would lead to Watergate] [1950s+] (*orig. US campus*) **1** a prank, a practical joke. **2** a difficult examination.

rat fuck *v.* [RAT FUCK *n.*[2] (1)] [1960s+] (*US, mainly campus*) **1** to blunder, to make a (stupid) mistake. **2** (*also* **r.f.**) to play a practical joke on someone, to outwit, to trick. **3** to break off a relationship. **4** (*N.Z.*) to cause (serious) problems for.

rat fucker *n.*[1] [FUCKER *n.* (7)] [1950s–60s] (*US campus*) a home-made tool, which approximates a car's starting-handle.

rat fucker *n.*[2] [1960s+] a general term of dislike.

rat fucking *n.* (*also* **rat kissing**) [RAT FUCK *v.* (2); SE *kiss* is euph.] [1920s+] (*US*) any form of destructive, negative activity, esp. on campus or in the forces.

rather! *excl.* [later uses are historical or satirical] [mid-19C+] a general term of agreement, indeed! I agree! very much so!

rathers *n. see* DRUTHERS *n.*

rathole *n.* **1** [mid-19C+] (*orig. US*) a dirty or unpleasant place or room; also attrib. **2** [1940s] (*US black*) a pocket.

rathole *v.* [RATHOLE *n.*] **1** [1930s] (*US*) to palm money during a gambling game. **2** [1970s] to hide away, to save up money, to hoard.

rations *n.* **1** [1930s] a cache of drugs. **2** [1930s–50s] (*drugs*) a dose or injection of drugs. **3** [2000s] (*N.Z.*) sexual entitlement.

rat kissing *n. see* RAT FUCKING *n.*

ratler *n. see* RATTLER *n.* (1a).

rat me! *excl.* (*also* **rat it!**) [SE *rot*] [late 17C–19C] a general excl.

rat pack *n.* [best known of such gangs are Hollywood's *Holmby Hills Rat Pack* whose members included not juveniles but such stars as Humphrey Bogart and its successor, the *Rat Pack*, led by Frank Sinatra, Dean Martin et al. (which group had formerly been known as *The Clan*] [1940s+] **1** (*US*) a juvenile or prison gang. **2** a group of sycophants, hangers-on.

rat pack *v.* (*also* **wolfpack**) [RAT PACK *n.* (1)] [1960s+] (*orig. US prison*) to attack in a group.

rats! *excl.* [late 19C+] (*orig. US*) a general excl. of disgust or disbelief.

rats and mice *n.* [rhy. sl.] **1** [20C+] a (game of) dice. **2** [1960s+] rice.

rat's ass *n.* (*also* **rat's, rat's arse, ...backside**) [SE *rat* + ARSE *n.*] **1** [1950s+] a general pej. implying anything bad or insignificant, small or trivial e.g. *not worth a rat's ass*; also attrib. **2** *see* CAT'S WHISKERS *n.*

IN PHRASES

□ **give a rat's arse** *v.* (*also* **give a rat's ass**) [1950s+] usu. in negative, to care, to bother. □ **not mean a rat's ass** *v.* [1970s–80s] (*US*) unimportant, to not matter.

IN EXCLAMATIONS

□ **I'll be rat's ass!** [1960s–70s] a general excl. of surprise, amazement, delight, etc.

ratshit *n.* (*also* **r.s.**) [RATSHIT *adj.* (1)] [1970s+] (*orig. US*) **1** a very unpleasant person. **2** rubbish, something annoying.

ratshit *adj.* (*also* **r.s., ratch**) [SE *rat* + SHIT *n.* (1a)] [1970s+] (*orig. Aus.*) **1** unpleasant, disgusting, annoying. **2** malfunctioning, useless.

ratshit! *excl.* (*also* **rat's claws!**) [RATSHIT *adj.* (1)] [1960s+] a general excl. of annoyance or distaste.

ratta *n.* [dial. *ratta*, a rat, thus the supposed resemblance to a large rat] [1940s–50s] (*W.I.*) a bulging bicep.

ratta castle *n.* [dial. *ratta*, a rat; ? link to the Anancy folktale in which Rat lives in a castle] [1940s–50s] (*W.I.*) a run-down old house filled with idling inhabitants.

rattat *n.* (*also* **rutat**) [backsl. = TATER *n.* (1)] [mid-19C] a potato.

ratted *adj.* [*RAT-ARSED under* RAT *n.*[1]] [1980s+] (*UK society*) drunk.

ratter *n.* [RAT *v.* (4)] [1930s+] (*US*) an informer.

rattle *n.* **1** in senses of speech. (**a**) [mid-17C+] the tongue, the voice; thus noise. (**b**) [early 18C] a dispute, a quarrel. (**c**) [late 19C] a person who talks a lot. (**d**) [1970s] (*US prison*) petty grievances. **2** [late 18C–early 19C] a dicebox. **3** [late 18C–early 19C] a coach. **4** in pl., constr. with *the* [abbr. SE *death-rattle*]. (**a**) [late 18C–19C] the croup. (**b**) [19C] the death-rattle. (**c**) [mid-19C–1900s] nerves, anxiety, esp. as *case of (the) rattles*. **5** [mid-19C–1910s] money, cash; thus phr. *have a bit of rattle*, to be well-off. **6** [late 19C] spirit, ebullience. **7** [1930s–40s] an opportunity, a chance [play on sense 2]. **8** [1960s+] an act of sexual intercourse. **9** [2000s] (*UK drugs*) withdrawal from narcotics addiction [the aches and pains that *rattle* the body].

IN COMPOUNDS

□ **rattle and pad** *n.* [PAD *n.*[1] (5)] [late 18C–early 19C] a coach and horses. □ **rattle bollocks** *n.* [SE *rattle* + BALLOCKS *n.* (2)]

[18C] the vagina. ❑ **rattle-box** *n.* **1** [1940s] a machinegun. **2** [1960s] (*Irish*) the male genitals. **3** *see* RATTLE-HEAD *n.* ❑ **rattle can** *n.* [20C+] (*Ulster*) a noisy child. ❑ **rattle-cap** *n.* [SE *cap*, head] [mid-19C] a volatile, unsteady person.

IN PHRASES

❑ **have a rattle** *v. see* RATTLE *v.* (3).

rattle *v.* **1** [early 17C] to send away. **2** [mid-17C+] to unnerve, to frighten. **3** [mid-17C+] (*also* **have a rattle**) to have sexual intercourse [note the *double entendre* in Burns c.1800: 'But it's in among the blankets that I like best, / To get a jolly rattle at the cuckoo's nest']. **4** [late 17C+] (*also* **rattle along, rattle away, rattle off, rattle one's hocks**) to leave, to move off, usu. quickly and noisily; to send away. **5** [mid-19C+] to move about, to act with energy. **6** [20C+] (*Ulster*) to work energetically. **7** [1910s–20s] to hit someone, thus *rattle the ivories*, to hit someone in the teeth. **8** [1940s] (*US Und.*) to blackmail. **9** [1990s+] (*drugs*) to tremble, from heroin addiction.

IN PHRASES

❑ **rattle along/away** *v. see* sense 1 above. ❑ **rattle off** *v.* **1** [late 17C–early 19C] (*also* **rattle up**) to scold, to tell off. **2** *see* sense 1 above. ❑ **rattle one's...** *v. see also under* relevant n. ❑ **rattle one's cage** *v.* **1** [1960s+] to annoy, to irritate; to nag. **2** [2000s] to make a fuss. ❑ **rattle one's hocks** *v. see* sense 1 above. ❑ **rattle someone's chain** *v.* [var. on *JERK SOMEONE'S CHAIN under* JERK *v.*[2])] [1960s+] (*orig. US*) to annoy, to distract forcefully, to taunt. ❑ **rattle the cup on** *v.* [1930s–50s] (*US*) to betray, to inform against. ❑ **rattle up** *v. see RATTLE OFF* above.

rattle and clank *n.* [rhy. sl.] [20C+] a bank.

rattle and hiss *n.* [rhy. sl. = PISS *n.* (2)] [20C+] an act of urination.

rattle and jar *n.* [rhy. sl.] [1920s+] (*US*) a car.

rattled *adj.* [mid-19C+] **1** anxious, unnerved. **2** drunk.

rattle-head *n.* (*also* **rattle-bladder, -box, -brain(s), -pate, -skull**) **1** [mid-17C+] an excitable, foolish person, a fool; thus adj. *rattle-pated, rattle-headed*, foolish, chattering. **2** [19C+] a gossip.

rattler *n.* **1** as a vehicle. (**a**) [early 17C–19C] (*UK Und.*) (*also* **ratler**) a coach. (**b**) [19C] a cab. (**c**) [mid-19C+] a passenger train or carriage of the train, esp. in phr. *the rattlers*. (**d**) [mid-19C+] (*Aus./US*) a freight train or carriage of a train. (**e**) [1900s–60s] (*US*) the Manhattan elevated railway, cable cars or streetcars. (**f**) [1910s–20s] (*US Und.*) a tramp who rides on freight cars. (**g**) [1910s–20s] any tram. (**h**) [1920s] (*US*) an automobile. (**i**) [1920s] a bicycle. (**j**) [1920s+] the New York or London underground railway. **2** in fig. uses. (**a**) [19C] a blow. (**b**) [late 19C] something serious or impressive. (**c**) [late 19C] an admirable person. **3** [mid-19C; 1920s] an amorous man; a promiscuous woman.

IN PHRASES

❑ **battle the rattler** *v.* [1920s+] (*Aus.*) to travel on the railways without paying. ❑ **jump the rattler** *v.* (*also* **jump a rattler, hop a rattler, jump the train**) [late 19C+] (*orig. Aus.*) to travel on the railway without paying. ❑ **mace the rattler** *v.* [1920s] to defraud the railway, to travel for free.

rattlesnake canyon *n.* [20C+] the vagina.

rattlesnakes *n.* [rhy. sl. = SHAKES, THE *n.* (1)] [20C+] delirium tremens.

rattletrap *n.* **1** with ref. to speech [TRAP *n.*[1] (4)]. (**a**) [early 19C] the mouth. (**b**) [late 19C+] a gossip, a chatterer. **2** in senses of physical collapse. (**a**) [mid-19C] anything run-down, dishevelled. (**b**) [1910s–50s] (*also* **clap-trap, trap**) a rundown vehicle or other form of transport.

rattletrap *adj.* [RATTLETRAP *n.*] **1** [late 19C] insubstantial, untrustworthy. **2** [1920s+] (*US*) run-down, seedy.

rattlie *n.*

IN PHRASES

❑ **get someone's rattlie up** *v.* [dial. *rattlie*, a child's rattle] [20C+] (*Ulster*) to infuriate.

rattling *adj.* pertaining to a RATTLER *n.* (1a).

IN COMPOUNDS

❑ **rattling-cove** *n.* [COVE *n.* (1)] [late 17C–mid-19C] (*UK Und.*) a coachman. ❑ **rattling-lay** *n.* [LAY *n.*[3] (1)] [early–mid-18C] (*UK Und.*) stealing goods from a moving coach. ❑ **rattling mumper** *n.* [MUMPER *n.* (2)] [late 17C–mid-19C] (*UK Und.*) a beggar who specializes in approaching those who ride in coaches.

rattling-gloak *n.*[1] (*also* **rattling-gloke**) [GLOAK *n.*] [mid-18C–mid-19C] (*UK Und.*) a coachman.

rattling-gloak *n.*[2] [SE rattle, to chatter] [late 18C–mid-19C] a foolish chatterer.

rat trap *n.*[1] **1** [mid-19C+] a shabby or ramshackle building or dwelling. **2** [1920s–50s] a vehicle, esp. as *rolling rat trap*.

rat trap *n.*[2] [SE *rat* + SE *trap*/TRAP *n.*[1] (4)] [late 19C+] the mouth.

rat trap *n.*[3] [rhy. sl. = JAP *n.* (1)] [1940s+] a Japanese person.

ratty *adj.* **1** in senses of dilapidation. (**a**) [mid-19C+] (*orig. US*) run-down, ramshackle, unkempt. (**b**) [20C+] (*US*) drunk. (**c**) [1960s] (*US*) of a person, run down, exhausted. (**d**) [1960s] unkempt, disordered. **2** in context of emotions. (**a**) [late 19C+] (*Aus./N.Z.*) mad, eccentric; thus *ratty on/over*, infatuated with. (**b**) [late 19C+] irritated, annoyed, obstreperous.

IN COMPOUNDS

❑ **ratty-ass(ed)** *adj. see RAT-ASSED under* RAT *n.*[1].

IN PHRASES

❑ **ratty on** *adj.* (*also* **ratty over**) [2000s] (*N.Z.*) infatuated with.

rauf *v. see* RALPH *v.*

rauge *n.* (*also* **rake**) [mid-19C] (*UK Und.*) a share of plunder.

raughty *adj. see* RORTY *adj.*

raunch *n.* [backform. f. RAUNCHY *adj.* (1)/RAUNCHY *adj.* (3)] [1960s+] (*orig. US*) **1** vulgarity, grubbiness, shabbiness. **2** obscenity, pornography. **3** a sexual obsessive.

raunch *v.* [backform. f. RAUNCHY *adj.*] [1940s+] (*US*) to have sexual intercourse.

raunch out *v.* [backform. f. RAUNCHY *adj.* (3)] [1970s+] (*US campus*) to offend by making sexual remarks or using offensive language.

raunchy *adj.* (*also* **ronchie**) [ety. unknown; Partridge suggests SE *rancid* or fig. use of dial. *raunch*, of vegetables, uncooked, i.e. 'raw'] **1** [1930s+] (*orig. US*) sordid, sloppy, contemptible, excessive, seedy. **2** [1940s+] (*US campus/teen*) inferior, cheap. **3** [1960s+] (*orig. US*) suggestive, sexually provocative, smutty, salacious. **4** [1970s] (*US campus*) ill, unwell. **5** [1970s] (*US*) drunk. **6** [1990s+] (*US*) violent.

raus mit 'em! *excl.* [Ger. *heraus mit ihm!* out with him!] [20C+] (*US*) get out! away with you!

rave *n.* **1** in senses of praise or enthusiasm. (**a**) [20C+] a sudden display of enthusiasm, a 'craze'. (**b**) [1900s] (*US*) talk, conversation. (**c**) [1900s–40s] an obsession with someone or something. (**d**) [1920s+] (*orig. US*) an extremely favourable review of a show, film, book etc. (**e**) [1920s+] (*orig. US*) any strong, negative or positive, opinion. **2** [1950s+] in senses of enjoyment, pleasure. (**a**) (*also* **rave-up**) in the late 1950s/early 1960s, a party; the term was revived in the 1980s, with much the same meaning, although the parties concerned were often held in clubs or, in the case of the much-vilified *ACID HOUSE PARTY under* ACID *n.*[1], in disused warehouses, hangars etc. (**b**) in ext. use, anything pleasurable, amusing, exciting. (**c**) an admirable individual.

DERIVATIVES

❑ **ravey** *adj.* [1950s] party-going, pleasure-seeking.

rave *adj.* [RAVE *n.*] [1950s+] **1** usu. of a critical review, ecstatic, hugely positive. **2** fashionable.

rave *v.* **1** [mid-19C+] to praise enthusiastically. **2** in senses of seeking enjoyment. (**a**) [1960s+] to have or go out in search of a good time. (**b**) [1980s+] to attend a club or larger gathering to listen to music and, almost invariably, to take MDMA. **3** [1970s] (*Aus. Und.*) of a shoplifter, to make a fuss so as to cause a distraction while his accomplices work.

ravel *v.*

SE in slang uses

IN PHRASES

▫ **ravel up one's ball of yarn** *v. see* WIND ONE'S BALL OF YARN *under* WIND *v.*

ravellavern *n.* [ety. unknown; ? SE *unravel*] [mid-19C] (*UK Und.*) a person who steals luggage from travelling coaches.

raven *n.* **1** [early 19C] an undertaker [SE *raven*, a carrion-eating bird]. **2** [late 19C] a small portion of bread and cheese. [the Biblical story of ravens taking small portions of food to the prophet Elisha].

raver *n.* [RAVE *v.* (2)] **1** [1950s+] anyone devoted to having an energetically good time with variations of 'dope, sex and rock 'n' roll' as to individual taste and situation. **2** [1950s+] esp. in *right little raver*, a hedonistic woman who is also presumed to be sexually available; also a homosexual man. **3** [1960s+] a fan of dixieland jazz. **4** [1990s+] a devotee of *rave* music.

rave-up *n. see* RAVE *n.* (2a).

ravey *adj. see under* RAVE *n.*

raving *adj.* [SE *raving*, insane, crazed] [mid-19C] utmost, excellent, very much, extreme.

raw *n.* **1** [mid-19C] (*UK Und.*) neat gin. **2** [mid-19C] whisky. **3** [mid–late 19C] in pl., the bare fists, as used in street-fighting. **4** [1980s+] (*drugs*) crack cocaine that has not been adulterated or 'cut'. **5** *see* JOHNNY RAW *n.*

raw *adj.* [SE *raw*, in a natural, unadorned and undiluted state] **1** [mid-18C+] inexperienced, unsophisticated. **2** [late 19C+] angry, upset. **3** [20C+] unfair. **4** [20C+] (*US*) honest, candid, unadorned. **5** [1900s–60s] (*US*) harsh, inhospitable. **6** [1910s] suggestive, smutty. **7** [1910s+] (*US*) uncouth, bold, brazen; also as adv. **8** [1940s+] naked. **9** [1960s+] (*US black*) excellent, powerful, impressive. **10** [1990s+] (*US*) used of sexual intercourse without a condom. **11** [1990s+] (*W.I.*) hungry. **12** [2000s] (*UK black*) very bad.

IN COMPOUNDS

▫ **raw deal** *n.* (*also* **rough deal**) [sense 3 above + DEAL *n.*[1] (3)] [1910s+] (*orig. US*) unfair, harsh treatment, particularly poor luck; usu. from the point of view of the victim. ▫ **rawskin** *n.* [sense 1 above + SKIN *n.*[1] (3b)] [1940s+] (*Aus.*) an inexperienced criminal.

SE in slang uses

IN COMPOUNDS

▫ **raw lobster** *n.* (*also* **blue lobster**) [SE *raw* + LOBSTER *n.*[1] (1b); i.e. the blue uniform, which resembles an unboiled or raw lobster] [early 19C] a policeman. ▫ **raw meat** *n.* **1** [18C; 1970s] (*also* **raw sausage**) the penis [MEAT *n.* (2)/SAUSAGE *n.* (2)]. **2** [late 19C–1900s] a woman who partakes, naked, in sex shows. **3** [1900s] a prostitute caught *in flagrante*; thus *raw-meat business*, prostitution. ▫ **raw meat man** *n.* [late 19C] (*Aus.*) a bare-knuckle boxer. ▫ **raw ones** *n. see* RAWS *n.* ▫ **raw prawn** *n.* [the foodstuff and the concept are both 'hard to swallow'] [1940s+] (*Aus.*) **1** an unfair action or circumstance, anything far-fetched; thus *come the raw prawn*, to act resentfully or unpleasantly; to be rude. **2** someone who is easy to deceive, a dupe. ▫ **raw sole** *n.* [pun on *sole*/SOUL *n.*[2] (2)] [1950s+] (*US black*) a virgin black woman. ▫ **raw 'uns** *n.* [late 19C–1930s] the fists, esp. as used in a fight.

raw *v.* [*RAW DEAL under* RAW *adj.*] [1990s+] (*US*) to treat badly, unfairly.

rawalpindi *adj.* [rhy. sl.] [1940s+] of the weather, windy.

raw and ripe *n.* [rhy. sl.] [20C+] a tobacco pipe.

raw chaw *n.* [SE *raw* + *chaw* (*chew*), to chew coarsely] **1** [mid-19C] a drink of spirits. **2** [1940s+] (*W.I.*) an uncouth, ill-mannered person. **3** [1940s+] (*W.I.*) the unvarnished truth.

raw-chaw *adj.* [RAW CHAW *n.*] [1950s+] (*W.I.*) coarse, vulgar; unadorned.

rawdog *n. see* RAW DOGG *n.*

rawdog *adj.* [RAW *adj.* (7) + play on HOT DOG *n.*[2] (4)] [1990s+] (*US campus*) outrageous, exciting.

raw dog *v.* [1980s] (*US black*) to humiliate horribly, to treat someone with utter contempt.

raw dogg *n.* (*also* **rawdog**) [RAW *adj.* (8) + *DOG OUT under* DOG *v.*[1]] [1990s+] (*US black teen*) sexual intercourse (without a condom); also as v., to have sexual intercourse.

rawhide *n.* (*also* **rawhider**) [metonymy; i.e. his *rawhide* whip] [1900s–60s] (*US*) **1** a cowboy. **2** a hard worker; a hard taskmaster.

rawhide *v.* [*see* prev.] **1** [1910s] (*US*) to beat. **2** [1930s–60s] (*US tramp*) to work hard; to make others work hard.

raw-jaw *adj.* (*also* **raw-jawed**) [1930s+] (*US*) tough, 'strong-arm', also as n.

raw jaw *v.* [SE *raw* + JAW *v.*[1] (1)] (*US prison*) **1** [1970s] to scold, to criticize. **2** [1990s+] to ignore, to refuse to speak to.

raw jaws *n.* [RAW *adj.* (1) + SE *jaws*] [1970s+] (*US gay*) someone who is still a novice as a fellator; thus an inexperienced street prostitute.

raws *n.* (*also* **raw ones**) [one's bare skin] [mid–late 19C] the bare fists, as used in street-fighting.

rawser *n. see* ROZZER *n.*[1].

rawted *adj.* [RAATID *adj.* (2)] [1970s] (*W.I.*) damned.

rawtid! *excl. see* RAATID! *excl.*

rawurawu *n.* [1970s] (*S.Afr. township*) a gangster.

rax (up) *v.* [? RAZZ *v.*[1] (1)] [1940s+] (*W.I.*) to abuse.

ray *n.* [? obs. SE *ray*, a small piece of gold or gold-leaf] [mid-19C] one shilling and sixpence.

rayfield *v. see* RAIFIELD *v.*

Ray Milland *n.* [rhy. sl.; ult. US film star *Ray Milland* (1907–86)] [1980s] (*Aus.*) the hand.

rays *n.*

IN PHRASES

▫ **catch (some) rays** *v.* (*also* **bag some rays, cop..., get..., grab..., lap..., soak..., take..., catch sun, catch sunrays**) **1** [1960s+] to sunbathe. **2** [2000s] (*US teen*) goodbye, a feasible alternative farewell in sun-drenched California.

razmataz *see* RAZZMATAZZ.

razoo *n.*[1] (*also* **rahzoo**) [*AND* says 'unknown origin'; Partridge suggests Maori *rahu*; but note *Ozwords* April 2000 in which for *not worth...* a correpondent suggests a bowdlerization of *arse razoo*, a fart (abbr. of an *arse raspberry*; this seems feasible, although *brass razoo* is not noted till 1960s while *razoo* by itself is cited from 1919+] [1910s+] (*orig. N.Z., then Aus./N.Z.*) a small amount of money.

IN PHRASES

▫ **not a brass razoo** [1930s+] (*Aus./N.Z.*) nothing at all, esp. money, i.e. absolutely penniless. ▫ **not worth a brass razoo** [1930s+] (*Aus./N.Z.*) lit. and fig., utterly worthless.

razoo *n.*[2] **1** *see* RAZZ *n.* **2** *see* RAZZLE *n.*

razor *n.*[1] **1** [mid-19C] (*US campus*) a pun. **2** [1980s+] a notably 'sharp' person.

razor *n.*[2] (*also* **razor-blade**) [rhy. sl.; *razor blade* = SPADE *n.* (1)] [1960s+] a black person.

razor *v.* [one is feeling 'sharp'; note 19C Westminster School jargon *razor*, 'a defiant, quarrelsome or bad-tempered person' (Ware)] [1980s+] (*Irish*) to be spoiling for a fight.

razorback *n.* [SAmE *razorback*, a breed of hog found in the Southern states] [late 19C–1960s] (*US*) **1** a manual labourer, thus, adj., *razorbacked*, uncouth. **2** a circus roustabout.

razor-blade *n. see* RAZOR *n.*[2].

razor-legged *adj.* [1950s] (*US black*) duplicitous.

razorridge *n.* [SE *razor* + sfx *-age*] [early 18C] shaving.

razz *n.* (*also* **razoo, razzoo**) [abbr. RASPBERRY *n.* (1)] **1** [20C+] (*US*) a scolding, a telling-off; constr. with *the*, mocking insults, rude noises. **2** [1930s] (*US Und.*) the sales pitch used by a financial swindler. **3** *see* RAZZLE *n.*

IN PHRASES

▫ **all that razz** *n.* [2000s] (*orig. US*) that sort of thing, usu. following a list of proper nouns ... *and all that razz.* ▫ **big razoo** *n.* [1930s+] a gesture of extreme contempt or scorn. ▫ **get the razz** *v.* (*also* **get the razoo**) [1900s–50s] to suffer insults, catcalls. ▫ **give someone the razz** *v.* [20C+] to tease.

razz *v.*[1] [RAZZ *n.* (1)] [1910s+] (*orig. US*) to tease, to heckle, to barrack, to scold.

razz *v.*[2] *see* RAZZLE *v.*[1].

razzamataz *n. see* RAZZMATAZZ *n.*

razzberry *n. see* RASPBERRY *n.*

razzed up *adj.* [1990s+] (*Aus.*) enthusiastic.

razzer *n. see* ROZZER *n.*[1].

razzing *n.* [RAZZ *v.*[1] (1)] [1920s+] (*orig. US*) **1** a scolding, a telling off. **2** a teasing.

razzle *n.* (*also* **razoo, razz**) [abbr. RAZZLE-DAZZLE *n.* (2)] **1** [20C+] a spree, a good time. **2** [1900s] (*Aus.*) a problem, a contretemps.

IN COMPOUNDS

❑ **razzle mag** *n.* [note actual mag. title *Razzle* (1973–)] [1990s+] a pornographic magazine.

razzle *v.*[1] (*also* **razz**) [? SE *rustle*] [20C+] (*Aus.*) to steal.

razzle *v.*[2] [1900s] (*US*) to harass.

razzle-dazzle *n.* [ety. unknown; redup. of SE *dazzle* + ? link to fig. use of Yorks. dial. *razzle*, to scorch, to burn] (*US*) **1** [late 19C–1930s] (*US carnival*) a merry-go-round. **2** [late 19C+] enjoyment, pleasure, celebration. **3** [20C+] confusion, chaos, often deliberately engineered to 'blind' the onlooker. **4** [20C+] showy nonsense, boasting. **5** [1900s] in fig. use, e.g. a bad situation. **6** [1920s–40s] as ext. of sense 1 above, a form of confidence trick. **7** [1970s+] extravagant publicity.

IN PHRASES

❑ **on the razzle** (*also* **on the raz, on the razz, on the razzle-dazzle**) [late 19C+] indulging in a series of parties, binges and general self-indulgent excesses.

razzle-dazzle *adj.* [RAZZLE-DAZZLE *n.*] [late 19C+] **1** (*US*) spectacular, dazzling. **2** (*Aus./US*) showing off, ostentatious, boastful.

razzle-dazzle *v.* [RAZZLE-DAZZLE *n.*] **1** [late 19C+] (*US*) to dazzle, to deceive. **2** [1920s] to harass, to pressurize. **3** [1980s] (*US black*) to hang around, to loiter. **4** [1980s] (*US black*) to pretend something has happened or is happening when in fact nothing is.

razzle-dazzled *adj.* [RAZZLE-DAZZLE *v.* (1)] [late 19C] (*US campus*) confused.

razzle-dazzler *n.* [RAZZLE-DAZZLE *n.* (4)] [late 19C] a very brightly patterned sock.

razzler *n.* [RASPBERRY *n.* (1)] [2000s] a loud fart.

razzmatazz *n.* (*also* **raj-ma-taj, razmataz, razzamataz**) [jazz use *razzmatazz*, a variety of old-fashioned, trad. jazz; ult. echoic of the brassy, syncopated music] (*orig. US*) **1** [20C+] a garish, meretricious display, an event or occasion surrounded by such excesses. **2** [1930s–40s] anything old-fashioned, corny, out-of-date.

razzmatazz *adj.* (*also* **razmataz**) [RAZZMATAZZ *n.*] [late 19C] (*US*) showy, high-class.

razzmatazz! *excl.* (*also* **razmataz!**) [RAZZMATAZZ *n.*] [1930s–40s] (*US*) an excl. of delight or pleasure.

razzo *n.*[1] [var. on SE colloq. *rarzo*, a red-nosed man] [late 19C–1930s] a nose.

razzo *n.*[2] *see* RASPBERRY TART *n.* (2).

razzoo *n. see* RAZZ *n.*

razzy *adj.* [1970s] (*W.I.*) shabby, shoddy, of behaviour and of appearance.

r.b. *n.* **1** [2000s] (*US prison*) a rich inmate [*r*ich *b*itch]. **2** *see* RUGGER BUGGER *n.*

R.C. *n. see* ROCKCHOPPER *under* ROCK *n.*

RD *n. see* RED DEVIL *under* RED *adj.*

rea *n.* (*also* **ree**) [SE *rea, ree*, female bird of the ruff family] [mid-17C] the female genitals.

reach *n.* [? they are *reaching* for the stars] [1980s+] (*US campus*) someone who is out of touch with reality.

reach *v.* **1** [20C+] (*US*) to bribe or otherwise suborn. **2** [1970s] (*US black*) to help. **3** [1970s+] (*UK/US black*) to go somewhere.

SE in slang uses

IN PHRASES

❑ **reach for the moon/roof/sky/stars/stratosphere** *v. see* GRAB SKY *under* GRAB *v.*

reach-around *n.* **1** [1990s+] during inter-male anal intercourse, the reaching round by the active partner to masturbate the passive partner's penis. **2** [2000s] similarly of a female sitting on a man's lap, facing away from his erect penis.

reach-me-down *adj.* [SE *reach-me-down*, a ready-made new or second-hand garment, often trousers; ult. any garment that is hung up on display and must be 'reached down'] **1** [late 19C+] (*UK Und./US*) inferior, shoddy. **2** [1910s–20s] thrown together, improvised.

read *v.* **1** in senses of comprehension. (**a**) [1910s+] to understand. (**b**) [1980s] (*US campus*) to appraise, to look over. **2** in senses of condemnation [READ THE RIOT ACT below]. (**a**) [1930s+] (*Irish*) of a priest, to censure [the practice of Catholic priests of reading out names of alleged sinners from the altar]. (**b**) [1950s+] (*US black/campus*) (*also* **read off, read out, read up**) to reprimand.

IN PHRASES

❑ **read braille** *v.* [SE *braille*, the written language of the blind which is accessed by touch] [1970s] (*US gay*) to grope someone's genitals through their clothing. ❑ **read 'em and weep** (*also* **read them and weep**) [gambling jargon, to acknowledge/announce a winning hand] [1910s+] (*US*) some unwelcome or distressing news or information, the truth; often as an imper., either delivered on retelling bad news or as a confirmation of the speaker's superiority. ❑ **read one's shirt** *v.* [1910s–30s] (*orig. milit.*) to check the seams of someone's shirt for lice. ❑ **read the maker's name** *v. see* LOOK AT THE MAKER'S NAME *under* LOOK *v.* ❑ **read the riot act** *v.* (*also* **read the (riot) law**) [the practice, before its repeal in 1973 but effectively abandoned in 19C, of reading the Riot Act (1715) to unruly crowds before attacking with police or troops if they refused to calm or disperse] [mid-19C+] to tell off severely and threateningly. ❑ **you wouldn't read about it** (*also* **you wouldn't know about it**) [1940s+] (*orig. Aus.*) a phr. describing anything amazing or unbelievable and proving that nature is infinitely more bizarre than mere art.

read and write *n.* [rhy. sl.] **1** [mid-19C] a flight, an escape. **2** [1930s+] a fight.

read and write *v.* [rhy. sl.] [mid-19C+] to fight; thus *reader and writer*, a fighter.

reader *n.* **1** [18C–1900s] (*UK Und.*) a wallet or pocket-book. **2** [mid–late 18C] (*UK Und.*) a book. **3** [mid-19C+] (*also* **luminous reader**) a marked card; thus (gambling) *readers*, a crooked deck of cards that a cheat can read from the backs. **4** [1910s–40s] (*US Und.*) a permit, e.g. to beg, to street-sell. **5** [1930s] a newspaper. **6** [1930s] (*US Und.*) a small-time thief who follows postmen or delivery men to their destination, having sneaked a look at the label, then claims to be the official recipient. **7** [1930s–40s] (*UK Und.*) a 'wanted' poster. **8** [1930s+] (*US Und.*) a warrant for arrest. **9** [1930s+] (*drugs*) a drug prescription; thus *reader with a tail*, an illegally issued prescription which had been traced by narcotics agents. **10** [1940s+] (*UK prison*) any form of reading matter, books, magazines, comics etc. **11** [1960s] a pornographic novel, without pictures.

IN COMPOUNDS

❑ **reader hunter** *n.* [early 19C] (*UK Und.*) a pickpocket specializing in stealing wallets and pocket-books. ❑ **reader merchant** *n.* [MERCHANT *n.*] [late 18C–early 19C] a pickpocket specializing in the theft of wallets and pocket-books.

IN PHRASES

❑ **draw a reader** *v.* (*also* **nail a reader, nap a reader**) [late 18C–mid-19C] (*UK Und.*) to steal a pocketbook.

readies *n.* [READY *n.*] [1930s+] cash, rather than cheques etc.

reading room *n. see* LIBRARY *n.* (2).

read of tripe *n.* [rhy. sl.; SE *read*, the stomach of an animal (from which comes *tripe*) + the '*tripe*' that is *read* out in court] [mid-19C] transportation for life.

ready *n.* (*also* **reddy**) [abbr. *ready money*] **1** [mid-17C+] (*orig. UK Und.*) cash in hand, usu. as *the ready*. **2** [1910s+] (*Aus.*) a swindle; a lie [SE *ready*, to prepare, in this case the victim]. **3** *see* READY ROCK *under* READY *adj.*

ready *adj.* **1** [1930s+] (*US black*) aware, sophisticated, prepared to deal with the real world. **2** [1930s+] (*US black*) esp. of musicians, excellent, first-rate, mature, fully competent. **3** [1930s+] (*W.I./UK black teen*) sexually attractive. **4** [1940s] (*US*) drunk. **5** [1980s] (*US black*) well-dressed.

IN PHRASES

❑ **not ready** *adj.* [1960s+] (*US/W.I.*) naive, unaware. ❑ **not ready for people** [1970s+] (*US black*) describing someone who acts stupidly, childishly, who calls attention to their own idiocies.

SE in slang uses

pertaining to money, i.e. READY *n.*

IN COMPOUNDS

❑ **ready gelt** *n.* (*also* **ready gilt**) [GELT *n.*/GILT *n.*[1]] [mid–late 19C] cash in hand. ❑ **ready john** *n.* [JOHN DAVIES, THE] [mid-17C; late 19C–1900s] (*orig. US*) money. ❑ **ready rhino** *n.* [RHINO *n.*[1] (1)] [late 18C–19C+] (*UK Und.*) money.

general uses

IN COMPOUNDS

❑ **ready-come-at** *n.* [20C+] (*Irish*) any form of skimpy woman's garment. ❑ **ready Hedy** *n.* [film star *Hedy* Lamarr (1913–2000)] [1940s] (*US teen*) an attractive young woman. ❑ **ready-made** *n.* **1** [1900–1910s] (*US*) shop clothing. **2** [1930s+] (*US tramp/prison*) a handmade, pre-rolled cigarette. **3** [1940s–50s] (*N.Z.*) a factory-made cigarette. ❑ **ready rock** *n.* (*also* **ready, redi rock**) [*READYWASH* below + ROCK *n.* (4d)] [1980s+] (*drugs*) crack cocaine; ext. to cocaine and heroin. ❑ **readywash** *n.* [the process of chemical purification that is used when making the drug] [1980s+] (*drugs*) crack cocaine.

IN PHRASES

❑ **ready for Freddie** *adj.* (*also* **ready as (Mister) Freddie**) [redup.] [1940s+] (*US*) ready and eager. ❑ **ready for the cleaners** *adj. see under* CLEANERS *n.* ❑ **ready to spit** *adj. see under* SPIT *v.*

ready *v.* [SE *ready*, to prepare] **1** [late 19C–1900s] to bribe. **2** [late 19C+] to contrive, to manipulate, to 'wangle'. **3** [1910s+] to drug someone so as to knock them out.

IN PHRASES

❑ **ready up** *see* separate entries.

ready-eye *n.* [READY EYE *v.*] [2000s] a police officer or other offical conducting a surveillance.

ready eye *v.* [20C+] (*UK Und.*) **1** to plan, to scheme; to know something in advance. **2** to conduct a surveillance.

ready-eyed *adj.* [READY EYE *v.* (1)] [20C+] fully aware of a situation in all its ramifications, both obvious and hidden.

ready-up *n.* [READY UP *v.* (1)] [1900s–60s] (*Aus.*) a conspiracy or swindle; a fake.

ready up *v.* **1** [late 19C–1930s] (*Aus.*) to manipulate events or a person so as to achieve an improper or illegal end, usu. a fraud or swindle. **2** [1910s+] (*Aus.*) to find or hand over some money. **3** [1910s+] (*Aus.*) to hand on information, to 'put someone in the picture'. **4** [1990s+] (*US campus*) to prepare oneself: wash, dress etc, to get ready to go out.

real *n.* [2000s] (*US prison*) a commercially branded cigarette (rather than the cheap, generic substitutes usu. distributed to inmates).

real, the *n.* [abbr. REAL THING *n.*] [late 19C+] the genuine article, esp. in the phr. *what's the real?*, what's going on? what's the meaning?

IN PHRASES

❑ **on the real** *adv.* [1980s+] (*US black teen*) honestly, sincerely, truthfully.

real *adj.* [1940s+] used by a succession of teen generations as an all-embracing term of approbation.

IN PHRASES

❑ **for real** *see* separate entries. ❑ **get real** *v.* [1960s+] (*orig. US*) to face facts, to abandon one's unreal fantasies. ❑ **keep it real** *v.* (*also* **keep one's shit real**) [1990s+] to maintain one's honesty, to stick to one's roots. ❑ **keep-it-real** *adj.* [prev.] [1990s+] honest, dedicated to one's roots.

IN EXCLAMATIONS

❑ **get real!** (*also* **be real!**) [1970s+] (*US campus*) an admonition to be serious, act maturely.

SE in slang uses

IN COMPOUNDS

❑ **real...** *n. see also under* relevant n. ❑ **real article** *n. see* REAL THING *n.* ❑ **real A.V.** *n.* [ante-Volstead Act] [1920s–30s] (*US*) pre-Prohibition liquor, thus 'pure' liquor. ❑ **real deal** *see* separate entries. ❑ **real lady** *n. see* PERFECT LADY *n.* ❑ **real-for-sure** *see* FOR SURE *adv.* ❑ **real McCoy, the** *n. see* separate entry. ❑ **real Maginnis** *n.* [*Maginnis* whisky] [late 19C] (*Aus.*) the genuine article, the 'real thing'. ❑ **real man** *n.* [1960s+] **1** (*US prison*) a prisoner well respected by his peers. **2** (*US campus*) a macho male. ❑ **real pietro** *n.* [? play on STONE *adv.*] [1900s] (*US*) an absolute certainty. ❑ **real raspberry jam** *n.* [var. on *BIT OF RASPBERRY under* BIT *n.*[1]] [late 19C] an extremely attractive woman. ❑ **real thing** *see* separate entries. ❑ **real-time** *adj.* [SE *real time*, the actual time during which a process or event occurs; i.e. nothing has been faked or otherwise altered] [1990s+] (*US black*) honest, candid. ❑ **real woman** *n.* [1970s+] (*US black*) a heterosexual woman.

real Ally Daly, the *n.* (*also* **the real Ally Dooley, ...Annie Daly**) [*Alice Daley* (*fl.* early 19C), a noted producer of butter] [late 19C–1960s] (*Irish*) the real thing, the ultimate example.

real deal *n.* [SE *real* + DEAL *n.*[1] (4)] [1970s+] (*orig. US black*) the end result, the final assessment, the absolute truth.

real deal *adj.* [REAL DEAL *n.*] [1970s+] (*orig. US black*) genuine, trustworthy.

real McCoy, the *n.* (*also* **the real Mackay, ...McKay, ...McKie, ...McKoy, McCoy, the McCoy, the M'Coy**) [a variety of popular etymologies have focused on the fighting name of Norman Selby 'Kid' *McCoy* (1873–1940), welterweight champion (1898–1900) and sometime strike-breaker or 'scab-herder' for the Ford Motor Co. Ironically, Selby was not in fact the *real McCoy*, this was another, slightly older welterweight, Peter *McCoy*, who toured with John L Sullivan *c.*1885 and who killed himself after a bad loss. However the *Scot. National Dict.*, (1870) notes that the saying, albeit spelt 'McKay' was adopted in 1856 by Messrs G Mackay and Co, whisky distillers of Edinburgh, as their advertising slogan. A further citation, as the 'real Sandy McKay' is found in 1871 – both are substantially earlier than the boxing attribution, although this may well have broadened the usage] **1** [mid-19C+] (*orig. US*) the genuine article, the 'real thing'. **2** [1900s] (*US*) money.

real thing *n.* (*also* **real stuff, real article**) constr. with *the* **1** [19C+] of people, circumstances or objects, the genuine article. **2** [mid-19C+] (*Irish*) the finest whisky, often with a suggestion that it has been obtained illicitly; fine brandy. **3** [1940s–50s] (*US drugs*) heroin. **4** [1970s] marijuana.

real-thing *adj.* [REAL THING *n.* (1)] [1900s] of people, circumstances or objects, genuine.

ream *n.* [backform. f. *REAM (OUT) under* REAM *v.*] [2000s] (*N.Z.*) the anus.

ream *adj.* [var. on RUM *adj.* (1)] [mid-19C] good; thus *ream bloak*, a good man.

ream *v.* [SE *ream*, to stretch, to tear in pieces] **1** [1910s+] (*US*) to cheat, to swindle. **2** [1940s+] (*US*) (*also* **ream out**) to scold, to reprimand. **3** [1970s+] (*US campus*) (*also* **reem**) to treat unfairly.

IN COMPOUNDS

❑ **ream job** *n.* [JOB *n.*[2]] **1** [1960s–80s] the licking and sucking of the anus, orig. gay use. **2** in fig. use.

IN PHRASES

❑ **ream (out)** *v.* [SE *ream*, to enlarge or widen a hole] [1930s+] (*orig. US gay*) to penetrate the anus either with the tongue or penis; also used fig., to cause harm to or trouble for.

reamer *n.* **1** [1930s] (*US Und.*) a cheat, a swindler [REAM *v.* (1)]. **2** in sexual senses [SE *ream*, to enlarge a hole *REAM (OUT) under* REAM *v.*]. (**a**) [1930s–40s;1980s] (*also* **reemer**) a sodomite. (**b**) [1940s+] the penis.

reaming *n.* [REAM *v.* (2)] [1970s+] a telling-off, a scolding.

reaper *n.* [REEFER *n.*[1] (1)] [1960s] (*US drugs*) a marijuana cigarette.

rear *n.* **1** [mid-18C+] the buttocks. **2** [20C+] (*orig. campus*) (*also* **rears**) a lavatory [the position in the rear of a college or ref. to sense 1].

rear *v.* (*also* **do a rear, have a rear**) [REAR *n.*] [late 19C+] to defecate.

rear-admiral *n.* [play on SE/REAR *n.*] [1990s+] a male homosexual.

rear end *n.* [1920s+] (*orig. US*) the backside or buttocks.

(IN COMPOUNDS)

❑ **rear-end loader** *n.* [pun on SE *rear end*] [1980s+] (*N.Z.*) a male homosexual.

(IN EXCLAMATIONS)

❑ **my rear end!** [late 17C+] a general excl. of disdain, dismissal, arrogant contempt.

rear end *v.* **1** [1970s+] of a vehicle, to run into the back of another. **2** [1990s+] to have sexual intercourse in the rear entry position.

rear-ender *n.* [REAR END *v.* (1)] [1970s+] a crash in which one vehicle hits the back of that in front.

rearrange someone's face/teeth *v. see* BREAK SOMEONE'S FACE *V.*

rear rank *n.* [rhy. sl.] [1940s] a bank.

rears *n. see* REAR *n.* (2).

rear (seat) gunner *n.* [the image of sodomy] [1990s+] a male homosexual.

rear up *v.* [1910s+] to become very angry; thus *rear-up*, an argument.

reat (and compleat) *adj. see* REET *adj.*

Reb *n.* [the Confederate, i.e. Southern, 'Rebels' who triggered the US Civil War (1861–5)] [mid-19C+] (*US*) a white Southerner, orig. spec. a fighter for the Confederacy; also attrib.

Rebecca *n.* (*also* **Rebekah**) [1900s] (*Aus.*) generic for a Jewish girl or woman.

rebel *n.* [the role of the South during the US Civil War] [20C+] (*US*) a derog. term for a native of the Southern states.

rebop *n.* [SE *rebop*, an echoic nonsense syllable used by jazz musicians, coined *c.*1945 as a description for the music of Dizzy Gillespie and Charlie Parker and ult. derived from Sp. *Arriba!* (up!) as used by rhumba bands to accompany a sudden shift in tempo] [1940s–60s] (*US*) nonsense.

rebore *n.* [SE *rebore*, the re-boring of one or more cylinders of an internal-combustion engine when it is worn out from use] [1980s+] (*Aus. prison*) used of a woman who is sexually active and is thought to have an enlarged vagina.

recavey *v.* [play on SE *recall*] [mid-19C] (*UK Und.*) to recollect, to remember.

recce *n.* (*also* **recco, reccy, reckie, recon**) [abbr.] [1940s+] (*orig. milit.*) reconnaissance; orig. milit. use, now a general term for making a preliminary exploration, assessment etc.

recce *v.* [RECCE *n.*] [1940s+] to look around, to explore.

receipt of custom *n.* [for ety. *see* CUSTOM HOUSE *n.*] [late 18C] the vagina.

receiver *n.* [baseball terminology] [1960s] a passive male homosexual.

receiver general *n.* [pun; i.e. she 'receives' such lovers as pay their money] [early 19C] a prostitute.

receive the canvas *v.* [play on *GET THE SACK under* SACK *n.*, which was often made of canvas; but note this significantly predates] [17C] to be dismissed from a job.

Recent Incision, the *n.* [pun; running from Waterloo Road to Great Charlotte Street, the New Cut was one of the busiest and most notorious Victorian street markets, as well known for its pickpockets and con-men as for the wide range of goods on sale] [mid-19C] the New Cut, London SE1.

receptacle *n.* [1900s] vagina.

reck *n.* [1980s+] (*N.Z.*) something second-rate, useless.

reckie *n. see* RECCE *n.*

reckless eyeballing *n.* [20C+] (*US*) shameless ogling of the opposite sex.

reckon *v.* (*also* **reck**) [ext. use of SE *reckon*, to count, to ascertain] **1** [17C+] to consider, to think, to suppose, to be of the opinion [mainly US since mid-19C]. **2** [mid-19C+] to esteem, to value, usu. as negative, *I don't reckon that lot*. **3** [1990s+] to know, to be aware of.

(IN PHRASES)

❑ **reckon oneself** *v.* [1940s+] to think a great deal of oneself, to be arrogant.

reckon! *excl.* [RECKON *v.* (1)] [1940s+] **1** a general excl. of affirmation, you bet! absolutely! **2** a challenging excl. of disbelief: do you really think so?

recluse *n.* [1980s+] (*US prison*) someone who has been inside a prison for five years or more without hearing from anyone in the free world.

recognize *v.* [2000s] (*US teen*) to give respect.

recompress *v.* (*also* **reconstitute**) [1980s] (*US drugs*) to change the shape of cocaine flakes so they resemble 'rock'.

recon *n. see* RECCE *n.*

recorder's nose *n.* [unlike the usual refs. to clergyman, this phr. depends on the Recorder, a legal official appointed by the Mayor and aldermen of London as the guardian of the City's customs and of their own legal proceedings; thus ? an underlying ref. to ALDERMAN *n.* (1)] [early 19C+] the rump of a chicken, duck, goose or other poultry.

recoup *v.* [SE *recoup* (one's losses)] [1970s+] (*US Und./black*) to start off fresh and determined on one's release from prison, undeterred by a few years' absence from the world.

recroots *n. see* DAISY ROOTS *n.*

recruit *v.* [RECRUITS *n.*] [late 18C–early 19C] to obtain a new supply of money.

recruiting service *n.* [RECRUITS *n.* + play on SE] [early 19C] highway robbery.

recruits *n.* [late 17C] (*UK Und.*) money, esp. when expected; thus the punning phr. *raise the recruits*, to obtain money.

rectal ranger *n.* (*also* **rectum ranger**) [1990s+] a male homosexual.

rectify *v.* [pun on SE *rectify/rectum*] [1970s+] (*US gay*) to have anal intercourse.

rector *n.* [late 19C–1920s] **1** the bottom half of a sliced teacake, which received the most butter [the *rector* was given (and expected) the best part of the cake]. **2** a poker kept only for show [such a poker was brought out when the rector was visiting].

rector of the females *n.* [SE *rector*, ruler + ? pun on *erection*] [17C] the penis.

rectum ranger *n. see* RECTAL RANGER *n.*

Red *n.* [late 19C+] a red-headed person, esp. as a nickname or as a direct address; of black people, one with reddish-brown skin colouring.

red *n.* **1** [18C–19C] a soldier [abbr. SE *redcoat*]. **2** [19C] a smoked herring. **3** [mid-19C–1930s] (*UK Und.*) gold, thus money, i.e. sovereigns. **4** [mid-19C+] (*US*) a cent, a penny [abbr. RED CENT *n.*]. **5** [late 19C] in pl., constr. with *the*, the menstrual period. **6** [late 19C] blushes. **7** [late 19C] (*US*) chops. **8** [20C+] a Bolshevik, a Communist, a socialist or anyone considered to have left-wing leanings; often generically as *the reds* [RED *adj.* (2)]. **9** [20C+] (*US/Texas*) chilli. **10** [1900s] (*UK Und.*) a gold watch. **11** [1960s+] (*drugs*) usu. in pl., barbiturates, usu. Seconal [the colour of the capsules]. **12** [1990s+] (*W.I.*) a difficult or problematic situation. **13** *see* PANAMA RED *n.* **14** *see* REDNECK *n.* (1).

(IN PHRASES)

❑ **bit of red** *n.* [his uniform] [18C–19C] a soldier. ❑ **red and blue** *n. see* separate entry. ❑ **red, white and blue** *see* separate entries.

red *adj.* **1** [17C+] golden, made of gold. **2** [mid-19C+] communist, socialist, left-wing [*red* has been synon. with communism since its birth in 1848 and has been thus used as a synon. adj.; its mass and thus slangier use came after the Russian Revolution of 1917; a handy right-wing insult, it is often used of anything that frightens a conservative speaker]. **3** [late 19C–1900s] in cash (rather than paper) money. **4** [1930s] (*Aus.*) having red or ginger hair. **5** [1940s+] (*US black*) (*also* **red-ass, redskin**) light-skinned [SE *red* + -ASS *sfx*/SE *skin*]. **6** [1960s–70s] (*US*) used of an impoverished, bigoted white Southerner [abbr. REDNECK *n.* (1)]. **7** [1970s] (*US campus*) conservative, strait-laced. **8** [1990s+] (*W.I.*) intoxicated by drugs [? one's red eyes].

IN COMPOUNDS

pertaining to gold

❑ **red clock** *n.* [late 19C] a gold watch. ❑ **red jerry** *n.* [JERRY *n.*^{6}] [late 19C] (*UK Und.*) a golden watch chain. ❑ **red kettle** *n. see* RED TOY below. ❑ **red lot** *n.* [late 19C] a gold watch and chain. ❑ **red rogue** *n.* [early 17C] a gold coin. ❑ **red slang** *n.* [SLANG *n.*^{2} (2)] [mid-19C–1910s] (*UK/US Und.*) a gold watch chain. ❑ **red stuff** *n.* [SE *stuff*] **1** [1900s–20s] money, presumably golden sovereigns. **2** [1920s+] (*UK Und.*) gold; esp. jewellery. ❑ **red super** *n.* [SUPER *n.*^{2} (1)] [mid-19C–1950s] (*US Und.*) a gold watch. ❑ **red tackle** *n.* [TACKLE *n.*^{1} (6)] [late 19C–1930s] (*UK Und.*) a gold chain. ❑ **red toy** *n.* (*also* **red kettle**) [TOY *n.*^{1} (5)/KETTLE *n.*^{1} (3a)] [late 19C–1930s] a gold watch. ❑ **red 'un** *n.* (*also* **red thing**) **1** [late 19C–1900s] a gold coin, a sovereign. **2** [late 19C–1930s] a gold watch.

other uses

❑ **red fed** *n.* [RED *adj.* (2) + abbr. SNZE *Federation of Labour*] [1910s+] (*N.Z.*) a left-winger, an agitator, a militant. ❑ **Redland** *n.* [1940s+] Communist Russia, the USSR.

SE in slang uses

IN COMPOUNDS

❑ **red...** *n. see also* under relevant n. ❑ **red 'Arry** *n.* [the colour + ? the signature on the note] [1930s–60s] (*Aus.*) a £10 note. ❑ **red ass** *see* separate entries. ❑ **redball** *n.* (*also* **redball freight**) [on early railroads such trains mounted a red ball on the engine as a signal calling for priority; note US police jargon *redball*, a high priority, high-pressure case] [1920s] (*US*) a fast freight train. ❑ **red beard** *n.* [the implied youthfulness, thus energy of a *red beard*, as opposed to the 'white hair' of an older man] [early 17C] a watchman, a constable, poss. a young man. ❑ **red birds** *n.* [the colour of the pills] [1950s+] (*US drugs*) barbiturates, esp. Seconal. ❑ **red bob** *n.* (*also* **red quid**) [play on RED SHILLING below] [1940s+] (*Aus.*) a pimp, thus the money he extorts. ❑ **redbone** *see* separate entries. ❑ **red boots** *n.* (*also* **red tennis shoes**) [var. on RED BIRDS above] [1980s] (*drugs*) secobarbital (Seconal). ❑ **redbreast** *n. see* ROBIN REDBREAST *n.* ❑ **redcap** *n. see* separate entry. ❑ **red card** *n.* [1920s] (*US*) a membership card of the Industrial Workers of the World. ❑ **red carpet** *n.* [1970s+] (*US gay/prison*) the tongue. ❑ **red cent** *n. see* separate entry. ❑ **red centre** *n.* [the predominantly *red* soil] [20C+] (*Aus.*) the central areas of Australia. ❑ **red chenke** *n. see* REDLEG below. ❑ **red chicken** *n.* [SE *red*, i.e. the brown colour and/or packaging] [1960s+] (*drugs*) Chinese heroin. ❑ **redcoat** *n.* [the uniform] [20C+] a member of the Royal Canadian Mounted police. ❑ **red-collar** *adj.* [late 19C] (*UK Und.*) of a prisoner, privileged. ❑ **red copper** *n. see* RED CENT *n.* ❑ **red cross** *n.* [? its efficacy as a painkiller] **1** [1920s–60s] (*drugs*) morphine. **2** [1980s+] marijuana. ❑ **red death** *n.* [1970s+] (*US prison*) **1** prison-cooked barbecue beef or pork. **2** jam (jelly in the US). ❑ **red deener** *n. see* RED SHILLING below. ❑ **red devil** *n.* (*also* **RD**) [the colour of the capsules] **1** [1950s+] (*drugs*) any form of barbiturate available in a red capsule, e.g. Seconal. **2** [1980s+] (*Aus. prison*) amphetamines. **3** [1980s+] phencyclidine. ❑ **red dime** *n. see* RED CENT *n.* ❑ **red dirt** *n.* [SAmE *dirt*, earth] [1950s+] (*US drugs*) marijuana that is or has been growing in the wild. ❑ **red disturbance** *n.* [the colour and the effects] [mid–late 19C] (*US*) whisky. ❑ **red dog** *see* separate entries. ❑ **red eel** *n.* [late 19C] a general term of derision. ❑ **red-eye** *see* separate entries. ❑ **red flag day** *n. see* RED-LETTER DAY below. ❑ **red fustian** *n.* [SE *fustian*, a coarse cloth; thus note the contrast with 'smooth' SATIN *n.* (1a), denoting gin] **1** [late 17C–early 19C] port or claret. **2** [late 19C] porter. ❑ **red grate** *n. see* RED LATTICE below. ❑ **red gravy** *n.* [1940s] (*US black*) blood. ❑ **redgut** *n. see* GUT *n.* (1e). ❑ **red head/redheaded** *see* separate entries. ❑ **red herring** *n.* [play on LOBSTER *n.*^{1} (1a)] [mid-19C] a soldier. ❑ **red horse** *n.* [mid-19C] (*US*) an inhabitant of Kentucky. ❑ **red hot** *see* separate entries. ❑ **red house** *n.* [? a particular institution] [1900s] (*US milit.*) a psychiatric institution. ❑ **red ink** *n. see* separate entry. ❑ **red jackets** *n.* [packaging] [1960s–70s] (*drugs*) Seconal, a barbiturate. ❑ **red lady** *n. see* RED MAN below. ❑ **red lamp** *n.* [such a lamp hung outside] [1910s] a brothel. ❑ **redlands** *n. see* separate entry. ❑ **red lane** *n. see under* LANE *n.*^{1}. ❑ **red lattice** *n.* (*also* **red grate**) [a *red lattice* or grate was a popular tavern sign and thence, if the tavern was thus inclined, could also indicate a brothel; at one time an actual *Red Lattice* inn stood at Butcher's Row, off the Strand] [late 16C–mid-17C] an inn; often doubling as a brothel; also attrib. ❑ **red lead** *n.* **1** [1910s+] (*US*) jam, jelly (US). **2** [1920s+] tomato ketchup, catsup (US). **3** [1990s+] (*Irish*) luncheon meat. ❑ **redleg** *n.* **1** [late 19C–1940s] (*US milit.*) an infantryman [the red stripe on his uniform trousers]. **2** [20C+] (*W.I., Bdos*) (*also* **red chenke, red-leg johnny, red shanks**) a poor white [SE *red* + *leg/chenke/shank*; i.e. their skin tone; *chenke* is pron. of *shank*]. ❑ **red-letter day** *n.* (*also* **red flag day**) [1960s+] (*US*) menstruation. ❑ **red-letter man** *n.* [SE *red letter day*, a saint's day or church festival indicated in the calendar by *red letters*] [late 17C–early 19C] a Roman Catholic. ❑ **red light** *see* separate entries. ❑ **red line** *see* separate entries. ❑ **red lizzie** *n.* (*also* **red liz**) [var. on RED BIDDY *under* BIDDY *n.*^{2})] [1930s–50s] cheap red wine. ❑ **red man** *n.* (*also* **red lady**) [1980s] (*drugs*) secobarbital (Seconal). ❑ **red mare** *n.* (*also* **red steer**) [late 19C+] (*Aus.*) a bush fire. ❑ **red mary** *n.* [1970s+] (*US black*) a menstrual period. ❑ **red mike** *n. see* separate entry. ❑ **redneck** *see* separate entries. ❑ **red ned** *n.* ['masculine' var. on RED BIDDY *under* BIDDY *n.*^{2}] [1940s+] (*Aus./N.Z.*) cheap red wine. ❑ **red nightcap** *n.* [mid-19C] (*US*) a scalping. ❑ **rednose** *n.* **1** [mid-17C; 20C+] a drunkard. **2** [1910s] (*US*) cheap whisky. ❑ **red nugget** *n.* [ety. unknown; ? the name of a specific saloon] [1930s] (*US*) an illicit saloon. ❑ **red oil** *n.* [1970s–80s] (*US drugs*) hashish oil. ❑ **red one** *n.* **1** [2000s] (*UK black*) a £50 note [its colouring]. **2** *see* REDCAP *n.* (1). ❑ **red paint** *n.* [1900s–30s] (*US*) tomato ketchup. ❑ **red pants** *n.* [euph. RED ASS *n.* (2)] [20C+] irritation, bad temper. ❑ **red penny** *n.* **1** *see* RED CENT *n.* **2** *see* RED SHILLING below. ❑ **red petticoat** *n.* [early 17C] a prostitute. ❑ **red quid** *n. see* RED BOB above. ❑ **red rag** *n. see* separate entries. ❑ **red ribbon** *n.* [RIBBON *n.*^{1}] [early 19C–1900s] brandy. ❑ **red rock** *n.* [the brown grains of the cheap Chinese heroin] [1960s+] (*drugs*) **1** heroin. **2** methadone. ❑ **red sail-yard docker** *n.* [? the identification of such goods with a *red* mark] [late 18C–early 19C] a criminal dealer who specialized in goods and stores stolen from the Royal Navy's dockyards. ❑ **red sea/Red Sea pedestrian** *n. see* separate entries. ❑ **redshank** *n. see* separate entry. ❑ **red shanks** *n. see* REDLEG above. ❑ **red shilling** *n.* (*also* **red deener, red penny**) [ety. unknown; ? fig. use of SE *red*, i.e. scarlet meaning sinful + SE *shilling*/DEENER *n.*/PENNY *n.*] [1940s+] (*Aus.*) money that has been earned by a prostitute and passed to her pimp; thus *red penny man*, a pimp. ❑ **red shirt** *see* separate entries. ❑ **redskin** *adj. see* separate entry. ❑ **red snapper** *n.* [play on the fish name (FISH *n.*^{1} (1a)) + ref. to the mythical *vagina dentata*] [1990s+] (*US*) the vagina. ❑ **red steer** *n.* **1** *see* RED MARE above. **2** *see also* separate entries. ❑ **red stuff** *n.* **1** [late 19C–1920s] (*US*) red wine. **2** [1900s] blood. ❑ **red tag** *v.* [2000s] (*US prison*) to confine an inmate to their cell. ❑ **red tape** *n.* [TAPE *n.* (1)] **1** [18C] gin. **2** [late 18C–mid-19C] brandy. **3** [mid-19C] red wine. ❑ **red tennis shoes** *n. see* RED BOOTS above. ❑ **red tide** *n.* [1990s+] (*US*) the menstrual flow. ❑ **red top** *n.* **1** [1940s] a redhead. **2** [1950s–60s] (*US gay*) a lesbian who prefers blondes. **3** [1990s+] a tabloid newspaper [the logo is usu. printed white reversed out of a red block]. ❑ **red 'un** *n.* [1930s] a match with a red tip. ❑ **red-up** *adj.* [one's *red* eyes] [1990s+] (*W.I.*) intoxicated by marijuana. ❑ **red wagon** *n. see* LITTLE (RED) WAGON *under* LITTLE *adj.* ❑ **red wings** *n.* [orig. Hell's Angels, where those who achieved this were awarded a patch in the shape of a pair of red wings] [1960s+] cunnilingus with a menstruating woman.

IN PHRASES

❑ **red knight on a white horse** *see* RED DOG ON A WHITE HORSE *n.* ❑ **red sails in the sunset** [the 1935 song 'Red Sails in the Sunset', a hit for Bing Crosby, Nat King Cole etc; however nothing in the lyrics implies a link to menstruation, other than the *red* of menstrual blood] [20C+] menstruation. ❑ **reds are playing at home** [2000] to be menstruating.

redaa *adj.* [pron. of *red eye*] [1950s+] (*W.I. Rasta*) extremely intoxicated by marijuana.

red and blue *n.* [the colour of the pills] [1960s–70s] (*drugs*) Tuinal, a barbiturate.

red ass *n.* (*also* **r.a., red arse**) **1** [1940s] (*N.Z.*) an incompetent person. **2** [1940s+] bad temper, irritation. **3** [1970s] a scolding.

DERIVATIVES

❑ **red-assed** *adj.* [1960s] (*US*) very angry.

IN PHRASES

❑ **get the red ass** *v.* [1950s+] (*orig. US*) to bear a grievance, to be in a bad temper. ❑ **give the red ass** *v.* [1960s+] to infuriate.

red ass *adj. see* RED *adj.* (5).

red ass *v.* [RED ASS *n.* (3)] [1970s] (*US*) to tell off, to scold.

redbone *n.* [Fr. *os rouge* (lit. 'red bone'), one who has native American blood] [1930s+] (*US black*) a pale skinned black person, esp. one who has Native American blood.

redbone *adj.* [REDBONE *n.*] [2000s] (*US black*) of a light-skinned woman, attractive.

redbreast *n. see* ROBIN REDBREAST *n.*

redcap *n.* **1** [1900s–60s] (*also* **red one**) the penis. **2** [1910s+] (*orig. milit.*) (*also* **cherry-nob**) a military police officer. **3** [1910s+] (*US*) a railway porter; an airline porter. **4** [1980s+] (*drugs*) in pl., generic for crack cocaine [the *red-capped* vial in which the drug is often sold].

red cent *n.* (*also* **blue cent, red copper, red dime, red penny, white quarter**) [the copper colour of a cent; the blue cent may refer to the blue cardboard ration tokens issued in US during WWII as payment for processed foods (meat tokens were red)] [mid-19C+] (*US*) a trivial amount of money, usu. in the phr. *not a/one red cent*, absolutely nothing.

reddener *n.* [2000s] a blush.

redding *n.* [var. pron. of *RED 'UN under* RED *adj.*] [mid–late 19C] a gold watch.

red dog *n.* [the stamping of certain NY State banknotes, which proved worthless, with a large red stamp] [mid–late 19C] (*US*) a short-lived, unstable bank; thus the money it issues.

red dog *adj.* [RED DOG *n.*] [mid-19C–1910s] (*US*) of a bank, its money or financial affairs generally, unstable, dubious etc.

red dog on a white horse *n.* (*also* **red knight on a white horse**) [1970s+] (*US black*) a woman having her menstrual period.

reddy *n.*[1] [var. of RADDIE *n.*, but note Ital. *red* wine] [20C+] an Italian living in London.

reddy *n.*[2] [1930s] (*US*) a person with red hair.

reddy *n.*[3] *see* READY *n.*

red-eye *n.* **1** with ref. to food or drink. (**a**) [early 19C+] (*US*) (*also* **old man red-eye, old red-eye**) strong, poor quality whisky [the after-effects on the hungover drinker]. (**b**) [1920s–60s] (*US*) tomato ketchup. (**c**) [1970s+] (*Can.*) a drink made from mixing beer and tomato juice; a hangover cure. **2** [1960s+] the anus [-EYE *sfx*]. **3** [1960s+] (*orig. US*) with ref. to transport [abbr. SE *red-eye special*]. (**a**) any air flight that deprives the traveller of proper sleep, due to take-off times, arrival times or differences in time zones. (**b**) of other forms of transport, e.g. an overnight long-distance bus. **4** [1970s–80s] (*UK black*) jealousy [one's eyes supposedly *redden*, although the usu. colour of envy is green]. **5** [1980s+] (*US drugs*) the telltale redness of the eyes when smoking cannabis. **6** [1980s+] (*US black*) a long, hard, aggressive stare.

IN PHRASES

❑ **have red-eye for** *v.* (*also* **red one's eye, red-eye after**) [the red eyes that are trad. associated with madness] [20C+] (*W.I.*) to become obsessed with at first sight and thus to desire to possess immediately.

red-eye *adj.* [RED-EYE *n.* (4)] [1980s+] (*W.I./UK black teen*) jealous, envious.

red-eye *v.* [1990s+] (*US campus*) to stay up all night (working).

IN PHRASES

❑ **red-eye after** *v. see HAVE RED-EYE FOR under* RED-EYE *n.*

redge *n.* [var. on RIDGE *n.* (1)] [late 17C–19C] gold, thus money.

red head *n.* [1950s+] (*US prison*) a match.

redheaded *adj.* [the red face of an angry person] [1900s–20s] (*US*) angry.

red hot *n.* [its flavour and temperature] **1** [late 19C+] (*US*) a frankfurter, a hot dog. **2** [1910s+] a small, cinnamon-flavoured sweet. **3** [1920s–40s] (*US*) a gangster. **4** [1930s+] (*US black*) a highly aggressive, volatile person. **5** *see* HOT MAMA *n.*

red-hot *adj.* [ext. of HOT *adj.*] **1** [late 18C+] very keen on. **2** [mid-19C+] obsessive; utterly dedicated. **3** [mid-19C+] (*US campus*) excellent, perfect. **4** [late 19C] (*US*) furious, enraged. **5** [late 19C+] of a bet, very likely, certain. **6** [late 19C+] (*US*) erotic, sexy, provocative. **7** [late 19C+] (*Aus.*) unfair, unreasonable. **8** [1900s] lively, entertaining. **9** [1930s] in a relationship, intense, devoted. **10** [1930s–40s] (*US prison*) tense, nervous, on edge. **11** [1930s+] (*US Und.*) extremely suspect; intensely pursued by the law.

red-hot! *excl.* [RED-HOT *adj.* (3)] [1900s] (*Aus.*) excellent! wonderful!

red hot cinder *n. see* BURNT (CINDER) *n.*

red-hot mama *n. see* HOT MAMA *n.*

red-hot papa *n. see HOT PAPA under* PAPA *n.*

red-hot poker *n.* [HOT *adj.* (1a) + POKER *n.*[1] (2)] [late 19C+] the penis.

red hots *n.* [rhy. sl.] [1950s+] (*Aus.*) **1** trotting races [TROTS *n.* (4)]. **2** dysentery [TROTS *n.* (1)].

red ink *n.* **1** as a red liquid. (**a**) [mid-19C–1920s] blood. (**b**) [mid-19C–1940s] (*US*) cheap red wine. (**c**) [1930s] (*US*) whisky. **2** [20C+] tomato ketchup. **3** [1920s+] (*orig. US*) in financial senses [in pre-computing days debts were written in *red*, credits in black]. (**a**) the debit side of an account. (**b**) (*US*) a financial loss.

IN COMPOUNDS

❑ **red ink joint** *n.* [JOINT *n.* (3b)] [20C+] (*US*) a cheap Italian restaurant.

redi rock *n. see READY ROCK under* READY *adj.*

redlands *n.* [1980s] (*US drugs*) Ritalin, as used by drug addicts.

red light *n.*[1] [the use of a *red light* as a warning signal] [late 19C–1930s] a supervisor, a manager.

red light *n.*[2] (*also* **red-light house**) [late 19C+] a brothel; thus *red-light girl*, a prostitute; also attrib.

red light *v.* [the red rear-lights of the train or car recede into the distance] [1930s+] (*US*) **1** to kill someone by pushing them from a moving train. **2** to throw someone out of a car or other vehicle and force them to walk home, often over a great distance. **3** to ambush and rob couples in parked cars by flashing a red light and pretending to be a police officer.

red lighter *n.* (*also* **red light sister**) [RED LIGHT *n.*[2] (1)] [1910s; 1940s] (*US*) a prostitute.

redline *v.* [1970s+] **1** (*US*) to drive a vehicle at top speed. **2** in fig. use.

red liner *n.* (*also* **red lioner**) [when a boy was caught begging his name was noted down, with a *red line* drawn beneath it] [mid-19C] an officer of the Mendicity Society, a mid-Victorian society devoted to the suppression of street beggars.

red mike *n.* **1** [1900s] (*US milit.*) canned salmon. **2** [1930s] corned beef.

IN PHRASES

❑ **red mike and (a bunch of) violets** *n.* [1920s] (*US*) corned beef and cabbage.

redneck *n.* [note 19C Lancs. dial. *redneck*, a Roman Catholic] **1** [late 19C+] (*orig. US*) (*also* **red**) a derog. term for a country dweller, a peasant, esp. a southern US poor farmer who is stupid and racist; strictly *rednecks* came from swampy areas while *hillbillies*, their peers, came from the mountains [their sunburn; orig. a Presbyterian, then transferred to all poor whites]. **2** [20C+] (*Irish*) a yokel [borrows f. sense 1 above]. **3** [20C+] (*S.Afr.*) an English immigrant. [Boer War era *redneck*, a British soldier, f. his uniform and the sunburn]. **4** [1950s] (*US*) an Irish immigrant.

IN COMPOUNDS

❑ **redneck cocaine** *n.* [2000s] (*US drugs*) methamphetamine. ❑ **redneck foreplay** *n.* [1960s+] the complete absence of any preliminary physical contact prior to intercourse. ❑ **redneck stew** *n.* [2000s] stew based on squirrel and similar small game.

redneck *adj.* (*also* **rednecked**) [REDNECK *n.* (1)] **1** [1920s+] (*orig. US*) pertaining to a country dweller, a peasant, esp. a southern US poor farmer who is stupid and racist. **2** [1940s] (*US*) Irish.

red-necked *adj.* [one's neck blushes with emotion] [late 19C+] (*US*) angry.

red one's eye *v. see* HAVE RED-EYE FOR *under* RED-EYE *n.*

red rag *n.* **1** [late 17C–late 19C] the tongue; thus *too much red rag*, speaking too long and too loud, *give the red rag a holiday*, be quiet, stop talking, *wag the red rag*, to talk to excess [its colour and its 'flapping']. **2** [late 19C+] a menstrual cloth or sanitary towel.

IN PHRASES

❑ **flash the red rag** *v.* [early 19C–1900s] to menstruate. ❑ **mount the red rag** *v.* (*also* **mount the red flag**) [19C] to blush.

red-ragger *n.* [the red flag/RAG *n.*[1] (2a), the symbol of the revolutionary left] [1910s+] (*Aus.*) a left-winger, a socialist; also attrib.

redraw *n.* [backsl.] [late 19C] a warder.

red rum *adj.* [rhy. sl.; ult. the triple Grand National winning horse *Red Rum*] [1970s+] dumb.

red sea *n.* **1** [late 18C+] the throat. **2** [1990s+] the vagina, usu. in phr. below.

IN PHRASES

❑ **part the red sea** *v.* [1990s+] to masturbate a woman.

Red Sea pedestrian *n.* [the exploits of the Hebrews during their Exodus from Egypt, among them the crossing of the Red Sea, temporarily dried up with divine assistance] [late 19C+] (*Aus.*) a Jew.

redshank *n.* **1** (*UK Und.*) of poultry [dial., the *redshank* gull (*Totanus calidris*) of the snipe family (Scolopacidae)]. (**a**) [mid-16C–early 19C] a duck. (**b**) [early 18C] a turkey. **2** with ref. to bare, wind-reddened legs [the kilted Highlander's or the woman's bare legs, coloured through exposure to the elements]. (**a**) [18C] a derog. term for a Scottish Highlander. (**b**) [mid-19C–1910s] (*Irish*) a woman wearing no stockings.

red shirt *n.* **1** [mid-19C] a back that has been scarred by a judicial flogging. [the colour of the blood and subseq. the scars]. **2** [mid-19C; 1930s–60s] (*US*) a troublemaker; latterly mainly prison use, a recalcitrant, tough prisoner [in mid-20C US prisons' known inmate troublemakers were issued red shirts; they thus became an easy target during a riot].

red shirt *v.* [*see* REDSHIRTED *adj.*] [1960s] (*US campus*) to miss a class or examination.

redshirted *adj.* [college sports jargon *redshirt*, an athlete taking a year off from playing sport to extend their eligibility as a 'student'] [1990s+] (*US campus*) jilted.

redskin *adj. see* RED *adj.* (5).

red steer *n.* [rhy. sl.] [1940s+] (*US*) beer.

red, white and blue *n.*[1] **1** [late 19C] (*US*) corned beef hash. **2** [1900s] (*US*) a plate of mixed flavour ice-cream.

red, white and blue *n.*[2] [rhy. sl.] [1970s] a shoe.

ree *n.*[1] [abbr.] [1980s] (*US prison*) respect.

ree *n.*[2] *see* REA *n.*

reeb *n.*[1] [backsl.] [mid-19C+] beer.

reeb *n.*[2] [? var. on DWEEB *n.*] [1980s+] (*US campus*) a socially inept person, an outsider.

Reebs *n.* [1990s+] a *Reebok* trainer.

reebs *n.* [? play on HERB *n.*[1] (1)] [1980s] (*US campus/drugs*) marijuana.

reed horn *n.* [1940s] (*US*) a saxophone.

reed-roof'd-cot *n. see* THATCHED HOUSE (UNDER THE HILL) *n.*

reef *n.*[1] [REEF *v.*] [mid-19C] (*UK Und.*) the act of pulling up the lining of a pocket until the purse it contains is within reach.

reef *n.*[2] *see* REEFER *n.*[1].

reef *v.* [SE *reef*, to roll up and secure all or part of a sail] **1** [mid-19C–1950s] (*orig. pickpocket jargon*) to steal money; thus (*US/Aus. Und.*) *reef a leather*, to steal a wallet by pulling out the lining of the pocket that contains it. **2** [20C+] (*Irish*) to gouge out, to attack, to remove forcibly; as n., a kick. **3** [1940s] (*Irish*) to criticize, to tell off. **4** [1940s–70s] (*gay*) to fondle someone's genitals.

IN PHRASES

❑ **reef it off in lumps** *v.* [LUMP *n.* (1)] [1920s+] (*Aus.*) to obtain large sums of money.

reefed up *adj.* [REEFER *n.*[1] (1)] [1950s] (*US drugs*) intoxicated by marijuana.

reefer *n.*[1] (*also* **reef**) [abbr. GREEFO *n.*] [1920s+] (*drugs*) **1** marijuana; also attrib. **2** a marijuana cigarette, esp. (1980s) a large and slender version. **3** someone who smokes marijuana; also attrib.

DERIVATIVES

❑ **reefered** *adj.* [1980s] (*US drugs*) intoxicated by marijuana.

IN COMPOUNDS

❑ **reefer-head** *n.* [-HEAD *sfx* (4)] [1930s] (*US drugs*) a smoker of marijuana. ❑ **reefer man** *n.* [1920s+] (*drugs*) a marijuana seller. ❑ **reefer pad** *n.* (*also* **reefer den, reefer flat, reefer joint**) [JOINT *n.* (3b)/PAD *n.*[2] (2)] [1930s–60s] (*drugs*) a house, apartment or room where cannabis users can gather to smoke. ❑ **reefer rat** *n.* [1930–50s] (*US black/drugs*) a marijuana smoker. ❑ **reefer weed** *n.* [WEED *n.*[1] (4)] [1940s] marijuana. ❑ **reefing man** *n.* [1930s–50s] (*US drugs*) a marijuana smoker.

IN PHRASES

❑ **bang a reefer** *v.* [1950s] to smoke marijuana.

reefer *n.*[2] [REEF *v.* (1)] [1930s–40s] (*Aus./UK/US Und.*) **1** a pickpocket. **2** a pickpocket's accomplice.

reef up *v.* [1950s] (*W.I.*) to bring up, to remember.

reek *n.* [1930s] (*US*) lewd language.

reeking *adj.* [var. STINKING *adj.*[2] (3)] [20C+] drunk.

reeler *n.*[1] [they *reel in* the criminal; ? var. PEELER *n.*[2] (1)] [late 19C] a policeman.

reeler *n.*[2] [SE *reel*, stagger] [1930s–50s] (*US*) a spree, a drunken carouse.

reeling and rocking *n.* [rhy. sl.] [1950s–60s] a stocking.

reel in the biscuit *v. see under* BISCUIT *n.*[1].

reels of cotton *adj.* [rhy. sl.] [1960s+] rotten.

reem *v. see* REAM *v.* (3).

reemer *n. see* REAMER *n.* (2a).

re-entry *n.* [spaceflight jargon *re-entry*, a space vehicle returning to the pull of Earth's gravity] [1970s+] returning to the 'normal' world after a period spent taking drugs, esp. a hallucinogen.

reesbin *n.* [Shelta] [mid–late 19C] (*UK tramp*) a prison.

reesch *adj.* [SE *retch*, or echoic] [1980s+] (*US campus*) disgusting, unpleasant.

reestie *n.* [? Scot. *reest*, to smoke (fish)] [1990s+] (*US*) an unpleasant odour, object or person.

reet *adj.* (*also* **eat, reat and compleat; root**) [mispron. SE *right*] [1930s+] (*orig. US black*) ideal, perfect, excellent quintessential.

reet? *phr.* [mispron. SE *right*] [1960s] right?

reet pleat *n.* [mispron. of SE *right* + the large *pleats* that distinguish the suit trouser] [1930s–40s] (*US black*) a sharply pleated ZOOT SUIT *n.*

reffo *n.* (*also* **refo**) [abbr. *refugee* + -O *sfx* (3)] [1930s+] (*Aus.*) a derog. term for any European (esp. Italian, Greek, Yugoslav) immigrant to Australia.

refreshed *adj.* [euph.] [early 19C] drunk.

refrigerator *n.* [late 19C] (*US*) a local jail.

refujew *n.* [1930s–40s] (*US*) a Jewish refugee from Germany or Central Europe.

reg *n.* [abbr.] **1** [1900s] (*US milit.*) a *reg*ular soldier. **2** [1970s] (*drugs*) *reg*ular strength marijuana. **3** [2000s] a *reg*ular, e.g. regular customer.

regemaker *n. see* REGMAKER *n.*

regent *n.* [pun] [mid-19C] half a sovereign.

rege-rege *n.* [Yoruba *rege-rege*, rough, in a rough manner or Hausa *rega*, to shake] [1950s+] (*W.I.*) **1** rags, ragged old clothes. **2** a quarrel.

reggie *n.*[1] [ety. unknown] [1970s] the buttocks.

reggie *n.*[2] (*also* **ralphie**) [initial letter *r* of the name; cf. LOUIE *n.*[2]] [1990s+] in driving, a right turn.

reggie and ronnie *n.* [rhy. sl. = JOHNNY *n.*[1] (12); ult. UK gangsters *Reggie* Kray (1933–2000) and his brother *Ronnie* (1933–95); they offered 'protection'] [1960s+] a condom.

reggin *n.* [despite origin in backsl. NIGGER *n.*[1] (1), there are no racist overtones] [1950s+] (*US prison*) a black person.

reggo *n.* (*also* **rego**) [abbr. SE *registration* + -O *sfx* (3)] [1960s+] (*Aus./N.Z.*) registration, usu. of a motor vehicle; thus as v. *reggo*, to register; also attrib.

reg grundys *n.* (*also* **reggys, reginalds**) [rhy. sl. = UNDIES *n.*; ult. Aus. entrepreneur Reg Grundy (b.1923)] [1990s+] (*Aus.*) underwear.

regimentals *n.* [SE *regimentals*, a uniform] **1** [mid-19C] (*UK prison*) prison uniform. **2** [1900s] (*US police*) police uniform. **3** [1940s] any uniform.

register *n.* **1** [late 19C] the human face. [it *registers* the emotion]. **2** [1960s] the vagina [abbr. *cash register*].

register *v.* [1930s+] (*drugs*) to draw up blood into an eyedropper or syringe while injecting a vein; thus n. *register*, the mix of heroin/water/blood drawn up into the syringe.

regjegs *n.* [? SE *rags* + *jags*, rags, tatters] [1940s] (*W.I.*) rags, old clothes.

regmaker *n.* (*also* **regemaker**) [Du. *recht*, right + SE *maker*, the word is also used as the title of the house magazine of the S.Afr. Alcoholics Anonymous and for a brand of caffeine tablets, supposed to cure hangovers] [1950s+] (*S.Afr.*) a drink taken in the hope of curing a hangover, a drink of the same alcohol that caused the hangover.

rego *n. see* REGGO *n.*

regroup *v.* [1960s–70s] (*US black/campus*) to recover from an unpleasant surprise.

regs *n. see* REGULARS *n.*

regular *n.* **1** [early–mid-19C] one who keeps regular hours and thus pursues a dull life. **2** [mid-19C+] one's usual or habitual drink or order in a pub, bar etc. **3** [late 19C+] (*US*) a close friend, a boy or girlfriend, a lover. **4** [20C+] one who frequents the same public house, or bar, on a regular basis. **5** [1930s+] (*US Und.*) an admirable person (in criminal sense); a career criminal.

regular *adj.*

SE in slang uses

(IN COMPOUNDS)

❑ **regular crow** *n.* [SE *regular* + CROW *n.*[3]] [19C–1920s] a big success. ❑ **regular guy** *n.* (*also* **regular fellow, regular folks, regular kid**) [1910s+] (*US*) a thoroughly good person; in the speaker's opinion their peer, intellectually, in sense of humour, opinions, politics etc, also used adjectivally; used of a woman. ❑ **regular Indian** *n.* [racist stereotyping] [20C+] (*Can.*) a habitual drunkard. ❑ **regular oner** *n.* [late 19C] an incorrigible rogue, 'one who is past praying for' (Ware); by no means invariably derog. but often implying a sneaking admiration.

regulars *n.* (*also* **regs**) [19C–1900s] a share of criminal booty; thus *go regulars*, to share profits.

regulate *v.* [mid-19C; 2000s] (*US teen*) to take an action of enforcement; to punish or hurt.

regulator *n.* [? it stops men getting 'over-heated'] [19C] the vagina.

rehab *n.* [abbr.] [1940s+] **1** *rehab*ilitation, from drug or alcohol abuse; thus extended to emotional or non-drug-related physical problems. **2** the ward or hospital in which *rehab*ilitation takes place. **3** the state of being *rehab*ilitated.

rehab *v.* [1970s+] **1** to rehabilitate, e.g. a broken-down house. **2** to undergo rehabilitation.

rehabilitative conversation *n.* [ironic ref. to the prison system's claim to *rehabilitate* criminals] [1980s+] (*Aus. prison*) a beating from prison officers.

rehap *v.* [1980s] (*US black*) to reappear.

reimburse *v.* [play on SE *reimburse*, to pay back a debt] [1970s] (*US black*) to lose one's life for the refusal or inability to pay off a debt or favour.

reindeer dust *n.* [play on SNOW *n.*[1] (2a)] [1930s–50s] (*drugs*) any powdered narcotic.

rel *n. see* RELLIE *n.*

relation *n.* [play on UNCLE *n.* (1)] [mid-19C] a pawnbroker.

release a chocolate hostage *v.* (*also* **release some hostages**) [1990s+] to defecate.

relief *n.* [1990s+] (*US prison*) anything sent in to a prisoner from the outside world.

reliefer *n.* [1930s–40s] (*US black*) someone who exists on welfare *relief*.

reliever *n.* [the garments or footwear *relieve* suffering] **1** [mid-19C] a coat that is kept in a variety of public places, that can be lent to anyone who does not possess one. **2** [20C+] (*Irish*) slippers. **3** [1920s–60s] (*US tramp*) in pl., shoes.

relieving officer *n.* [SE *relieving officer*, an officer appointed by a parish or union to administer relief to the poor] [mid–late 19C] one's father.

religious *adj.* [pun] [late 18C–early 19C] of a horse, one that is always on its knees.

religo *n.* [abbr. + -O *sfx* (3)] [1940s] (*N.Z.*) one who objects to war on *relig*ious grounds.

Relish, the *n.* [also known as *The House*, according to Weinreb and Hibbert, *London Encyclopedia* (1983)] [late 18C–early 19C] the Cheshire Cheese tavern, in Wine Office Court, off Fleet Street; frequented by such figures as Johnson, Garrick and later Dickens.

relish *n.* [early 19C] sexual intercourse.

rellie *n.* [abbr.] (*also* **rel, rello, relo**) [1990s+] (*orig. Aus.*) a family *rel*ative; also attrib.

reload *v.* [1940s+] **1** (*US Und.*) to trick a person for a second time. **2** (*UK Und.*) to ensnare a victim in a confidence game, e.g. three-card monte, by allowing them small victories, thus increasing their confidence (and bets) prior to taking their money.

reltney *n.* [ety. unknown] [20C+] (*US*) the (erect) penis.

rem *n.* (*also* **remhead**) [abbr. *rem*edial classes] [1990s+] (*UK juv.*) a stupid, poss. mentally deficient person.

remedy *n.* [pun on SE phr. *sovereign remedy*] [18C] a sovereign.

remedy critch *n.* [SE *remedy*, ease + *critch*, an earthenware vessel; ult. *cratch*, a stable hayrack and thus a *crèche*; the term is used as such in early descriptions of Christ's birth] [late 18C–early 19C] a chamberpot.

remember Parson Malham! *excl.* (*also* **remember Parson Mallum! ...Meldrum!**) [? the proper name of a once celebrated toping cleric; presumably, since B.E. adds 'Norfolk', from that county] [late 17C–early 19C] drink up! finish your glass!

r.e.m.f. *n.* [abbr.] [1960s+] (*orig. US milit.*) rear echelon motherfuckers; used by combat troops and brought into civilian life by veterans; also as term of address and attrib.

remhead *n. see* REM *n.*

Remington *n.*

(IN PHRASES)

❑ **give a Remington** *v.* [a *Remington* double-barrelled shotgun] [1970s] to have two penises in one's mouth.

remish *n.* [abbr.] [1950s] of a prison sentence, *remission*.

remo *n.* [? SE *remedial* + -O *sfx* (2)] [1980s+] (*US campus*) a fool, an incompetent.

remove one's digit *v.* see PULL ONE'S FINGER OUT *under* FINGER *n.*

Remuera rocket *n.* [*Remuera*, an upmarket suburb in Auckland] [2000s] (*N.Z.*) a four-wheel drive vehicle.

renee *n.* [the popular working-class name] [1980s] a girlfriend.

renk *adj.* [RANK *adj.*[1] (3)] [1950s+] (*W.I., Rasta*) out of order, impudent, as in a *rank-imposter*; thus *yu too renk!* your behaviour is unacceptable!

renk *v.* [SE *rank*, foul] [1970s–80s] (*UK black*) to stink; to render stinking; also as adj.

renking meat *n.* [lit. 'stinking meat'] [1990s+] (*W.I.*) the vagina.

rent *n.* **1** [late 18C–mid-19C] loot, booty. **2** [early 19C–1930s] money. **3** [20C+] protection money; thus *rent-collector*, a thug who gathers in such payments. **4** [1920s–50s] blackmail; thus *renting*, obtaining money either by criminal means (blackmail) or by offering homosexual favours. **5** [1960s+] a male homosexual prostitute [note that the website Gaymart.com 'Queer Slang in the Gay 90s' claims use throughout 19C]. **6** [1990s+] (*Aus. police/Und.*) bribes paid to policemen, and the division thereof.

IN COMPOUNDS

❑ **rent boy** *n.* [1960s+] a young male homosexual prostitute; also attrib. ❑ **rent collector** *n.* [late 18C–early 19C] a highwayman, esp. one who prefers cash to jewels etc. ❑ **rent rag** *n.* [late 19C+] (*orig. US black*) a party where the guests buy their refreshments to help pay the rent.

rent *v.* **1** [late 19C+] to obtain money by criminal means, e.g. blackmail (apparently specific to Oscar Wilde and his circle). **2** [1960s+] to work as a homosexual prostitute, to take money in return for sexual favours.

rent-a- *pfx* [a play on the care-hire firm *Rentacar*, a US proprietary name, dating from 1921] [1960s+] (*orig. US*) a general pfx used to demean whatever noun it is attached to by implying a monetary rather than emotional basis for its existence, e.g. *rent-a-crowd, rent-a-mob*, a group of demonstrators who, it is inferred, will turn up purely to demonstrate, irrespective of the actual event; thence in general use e.g. *rent-a-nigger*, a black private security guard, seen as protecting white interests against black individuals; *rent-a pig, rent-a-cop*, a security guard.

rental units *n.* (*also* **rentals, rents, units**) [abbr. PARENTAL UNITS *n.* or SE *parents*] [1960s+] (*US campus*) parents.

renter *n.* [ext. RENT *n.* (5)] [late 19C+] a young male homosexual prostitute.

renuncles *n.* [SE *ranunculus*, a species of plant, often with bright flowers] [mid-19C] (*UK Und.*) a heavily made-up prostitute.

rep *n.* [abbr.] **1** based on SE *reputation*. (**a**) [18C+] *rep*utation; thus *no-rep*, one who has no reputation. (**b**) [1950s+] (*orig. US teen*) a member's standing and status in a street gang. **2** based on SE *reprobate*, underpinned by *reputation*. (**a**) [late 18C] something worthless. (**b**) [late 18C–mid-19C] a man or woman who has a (usu. bad) reputation. **3** based on SE *representative*. (**a**) [mid-19C+] a *rep*resentative, e.g. of a trade union. (**b**) [1910s+] (*US*) a member of a state or national House of *Rep*resentatives. (**c**) [1930s+] a commercial traveller, a sales *rep*resentative. **4** [1920s+] a *rep*ertory theatre.

IN PHRASES

❑ **make one's rep** *v.* [1950s] (*US Und.*) to establish oneself as a successful, respected criminal.

rep *adj.* [SE *reputed, reputable*] [1910s] (*Aus.*) well-respected.

rep *v.* (*US black*) **1** [1970s+] to represent [abbr. REPRESENT *v.*]. **2** [1990s+] to maintain a reputation as [REP *n.* (1a)].

repap *n.* [backsl.] [mid-19C+] paper.

repeater *n.* **1** [mid-19C] a second (third, fourth etc) drink after one's first. **2** [late 19C–1920s] (*US tramp*) a veteran tramp. **3** [late 19C+] (*Can./US*) a recidivist. **4** [20C+] (*Aus.*) in pl., belching after rich or 'windy' food; also as v. **5** [20C+] (*US gambling*) loaded dice [they keep coming up with the same numbers]. **6** [1920s] a college student who is retaking a whole year. **7** [1930s–40s] (*US*) in pl., beans.

repentance curl *n.* [? the lock of hair hanging over the heart signified *repentance*] [mid–late 19C] (*UK society*) a woman's hairstyle, pioneered by the Princess of Wales (later Queen Alexandra; 1844–1925), in which a single lock of the back–hair was brought forward over the left shoulder and allowed to hang over the left breast.

repent pad *n. see under* PAD *n.*[2].

repo *n.* [abbr.] [1970s+] **1** (*Aus./US*) the *repo*ssession of items bought on hire purchase, but not paid for. **2** (*US*) a car which is *repo*ssessed for non-payment of instalments.

IN COMPOUNDS

❑ **repo man** *n.* [1970s+] (*US*) a *repo*ssession man, one who is employed by finance companies to repossess goods on which the owner is defaulting as to his payments.

repo *v.* [abbr.] [1950s+] to *repo*ssess.

repository *n.* [late 18C–early 19C] a lock-up, a prison.

reppock *n.* [backsl. COPPER *n.* (3)] [mid-19C+] a police officer.

represent *v.* [1990s+] (*orig. US black*) to act positively, to perform as required, to do (something) well, to behave authentically.

reptile *n.* [the skins used for many popular styles] [1970s] (*US black*) in pl., shoes.

republic of letters *n.* [pun on SE *republic of letters*, the world of literature] [early 19C] the post office.

res *n.* [abbr. SE *residue*] [1980s+] (*drugs*) an oily deposit left in a pipe after smoking crack cocaine.

rescue station *n.* [ironic var. on SE *rescue mission*, a centre for alcoholics and other down-and-outs] [1970s+] (*US black*) a liquor store.

reservation *n.*

SE in slang uses

IN PHRASES

❑ **off the reservation** *adj.* **1** [late 19C–1900s] (*US*) absent, away. **2** [1930s] in fig. use, drunk. ❑ **off one's (mental) reservation** *adj.* [late 19C–1900s] insane, out of touch with reality.

residenter *n.* [SE *resident*] [20C+] (*Irish*) **1** an old inhabitant, an old creature. **2** a fixture.

respeck/respect *see under* RISPECK.

rest *n.* [note theatrical euph. *resting*, out of work] **1** [late 19C–1950s] (*Aus.*) a year's imprisonment; thus *resting*, in prison. **2** [1990s+] (*US campus*) one's home.

SE in slang uses

IN PHRASES

❑ **at rest** *adj.* [19C] tipsy, drunk. ❑ **give someone/something a rest** *v.* [late 19C+] (*orig. Aus.*) to leave someone or something alone; to abandon an obsession or interest.

IN EXCLAMATIONS

❑ **give it a rest!** (*also* **give us a rest!**) [late 19C+] shut up! stop talking!

rest and be thankful *n.* [19C] from a male perspective, the vagina.

resthouse *n.* **1** [1900s] (*UK Und.*) a prison or police station. **2** [1930s] (*US Und.*) any prison where the discipline is lax and the work undemanding.

resting *adj.* [UK theatrical *resting*, out of work] [2000s] (*S.Afr. gay*) not interested in sex.

rest of it *n.* [1950s] life imprisonment.

rest one's neck *v. see under* NECK *n.*

rests *n. see* CABMAN'S RESTS *n.*

rest stop *n.* [1960s–70s] (*US*) the navel, in the context of oral sex.

result *n.* [1950s+] (*orig. UK Und.*) **1** a successful outcome to an endeavour, a sporting victory; an arrest for policemen, a lucrative robbery for villains etc. **2** a verdict of not guilty.

resurrection-cove *n.* (*also* **resurrection man/woman, resurrectionist**) [SE *resurrection* + COVE *n.* (1)] [late 18C–19C] a body snatcher, who robbed (usu. fresh) graves to sell the corpses to a surgeon for dissection.

resurrection jarvey *n. see under* JARVEY *n.*

resurrection pie *n.* **1** [mid-19C+] any dish made from yesterday's left-overs which have thus 'risen from the dead'; thus *resurrection bolly*, a beefsteak pudding. **2** [1900s] in fig. sense.

resurrection rig *n.* [SE *resurrection* + RIG *n.*[2] (1); the dissection of human corpses was then illegal] [late 18C–early 19C] (*UK Und.*) body-snatching; the corpse is then sold to a surgeon.

resurrection woman *n. see* RESURRECTION-COVE *n.*

reswort *n.* [backsl.] [mid-19C] trousers.

ret *n. see* RETTE *n.*

retard *n.* (*also* **retardo**) [1960s+] (*orig. US*) derog. ref. to a mentally retarded person, whether actually or fig.

retarded *adj.* [1990s+] **1** (*US*) a general negative; stupid, bad, inferior. **2** (*US black*) intoxicated by a drug or drunk.

retchus *adj. see* RIGHTEOUS *adj.*

retired *adj.* [2000s] (*US prison*) serving a life sentence.

retread *n.* [SE *retread*, a tyre that has been reprocessed, with a new tread, to extend its practical life; orig. 1940s Aus. milit. jargon *retread*, a WW1 soldier who re-enlists for WW2] [1940s+] (*orig. Aus.*) **1** anything or anyone old that has been given a new lease of life, esp. someone who has been retrained for a new job. **2** an ex-lover, someone who has recently been divorced. **3** a retired schoolteacher who is still teaching; also attrib.

retriever *n. see* VERSER *n.*

retsio *n.* [backsl.] [mid-19C] an oyster.

rette *n.* (*also* **ret**) [abbr.] [1960s–70s] (*US campus*) cigarette.

reub *see under* RUBE.

reuben *n.* [the 'rustic' proper name] **1** [19C+] (*US*) a country bumpkin, a farmer; also generically. **2** [1900s] a fool, a gullible person, irrespective of geography.

re-up *n.* [RE-UP *v.* (2)] [1970s+] (*US black*) a dealer's fresh supply of drugs.

re-up *v.* **1** [20C+] (*orig. US milit.*) to re-enlist, to join up again. **2** [1970s+] (*US drugs*) to replenish one's stocks of a drug. **3** [1990s+] (*US drugs*) to take another dose of a drug. **4** [1990s+] to replenish one's energy.

rev *n.*[1] [abbr. SE *Reverend*] **1** [20C+] a clergyman; also as a term of address. **2** [2000s] (*US prison*) a religious inmate.

rev *n.*[2]

(IN PHRASES)

❑ **give someone a rev** *v.* [? abbr. of SE *revelation*] [1990s+] (*Aus. Und.*) to warn, to inform.

rev *adj.* [abbr.] [1990s+] disgusting, *rev*olting.

Reverend Ronald Knox *n.* [rhy. sl. = POX *n.*[1] (1); ult. the Catholic clergyman *Ronald Knox* (1888–1957)] [1950s] syphilis.

reverse *v.* [late 17C–early 19C] (*UK Und.*) to turn someone upside down and shake them until the money falls out of their pockets.

reverse cowboy *n.* (*also* **reverse cowgirl, ...western**) [1970s+] a position of heterosexual intercourse (vaginal or anal) whereby the woman straddles the man; also as v.

reverse English *n.* [billiards/pool imagery] [1900s–50s] (*US*) the opposite; thus as adj. negative, oppositional.

reverse game *v. see under* GAME *v.*

reverse gears *v.* [1980s+] (*US teen*) to vomit.

reverse western *n. see* REVERSE COWBOY *n.*

rev-head *n.* [SE *revup* + -HEAD *sfx* (3)] [1970s+] (*Aus.*) a young man dedicated to driving fast as well as drinking heavily and getting sex whenever possible; also attrib.

review of the black cuirassiers *n.* [late 18C–early 19C] a gathering of black-garbed clergymen.

reviver *n.* [mid-19C+] a stimulating drink.

revlis *n.* [backsl.] [mid-19C] silver.

revolver *n.* **1** [mid-19C–1930s] (*US*) a recidivist. **2** [late 19C–1920s] (*US tramp*) a veteran tramp or criminal.

rev one's motor *v. see* RACE ONE'S MOTOR *v.*

rev-out *adj.* [1990s+] (*W.I.*) prematurely past one's sexual prime.

revved (up) *adj.* [SE *revup*] [1960s+] excited, tensed up, emotionally intense.

revving *adj.* [from the 'revolutions' of an aeroplane engine] [1910s] (*Aus.*) very busy.

rewired *adj.* [electrical imagery + WIRED *adj.*[1] (3)] [1970s] (*drugs*) of an addict, returning to drug use after abstention.

Rex Hunt *n.* [rhy. sl. = CUNT *n.* (4); ult. Aus. television and radio personality *Rex Hunt* (b.1949)] [1990s+] (*Aus.*) a fool.

rey *adj.* [2000s] (*US teen*) important.

rez *n.* [abbr.] [1980s+] (*US drugs*) cannabis *res*in.

r.f. *n.* **1** [1960s] a general term of personal abuse. **2** *see* RAT FINK *n.* **3** *see* ROYAL FUCKING *under* ROYAL *adj.*

r.f. *v. see* RAT FUCK *v.* (2).

r.f.d. *adj.* abbr. *r*ural *f*ree *d*elivery, used in combs. below to indicate rural naïvety.

(IN COMPOUNDS)

❑ **r.f.d. boob** *n.* [BOOB *n.*[2]] [1920s] a country bumpkin, simpleton. ❑ **r.f.d. dopehead** *n.* (*also* **r.f.d. gowster, r.f.d. junker**) [DOPEHEAD *under* DOPE *n.*[1]/GOWSTER *n.*[1]/JUNKER *n.*] [1930s–50s] (*US drugs*) a drug addict who travels between small towns, hoping to persuade sympathetic or naïve doctors to write narcotics prescriptions. ❑ **r.f.d. queen** *n.* [QUEEN *n.* (2a)] [1940s–70s] (*US*) a homosexual living in a rural area, outside the main gay world.

r.g. *n. see* ARGEE *n.*

rhatid *n. see* RAATID *n.*

rheumatism *n.*

SE in slang uses

(IN PHRASES)

❑ **have rheumatism in the shoulder** *v.* [the pain engendered by the hand that grasps one's shoulder] [early 19C] to be arrested.

rheumatiz *n.* (*also* **rheumatis, rheumatize, rumatiz**) [abbr.] [mid-18C–1950s] rheumatism.

rhino *n.*[1] (*also* **rhine, rhyno, rino, ryno**) [ety. unknown; one suggestion, that it refers to the rhinoceros, then a fabulous creature 'worth its weight in gold', implies a certain lexicographical desperation; the term moved f. Und. to general sl., in mid-19C] [late 17C+] (*orig. UK Und.*) money; thus (19C) *rhino-fat*, wealthy.

rhino *n.*[2] [abbr.] [1980s] a *rhino*plasty.

rhinocerical *adj.* (*also* **rhinoceral**) [RHINO *n.*[1]] [late 17C–mid-19C] well-off, wealthy.

Rhoda *n.* [2000s] (*S.Afr. gay*) drugs.

rhode *n.* [ety. unknown; too early for *ROAD DOG under* ROAD *n.*] [1940s] (*US black*) one's best friend.

Rhodes scholar *n.* [the *scholarships* established by Cecil *Rhodes* (1853–1902), sending students born and educated in the then British colonies (incl. the US) to Oxford University] [1950s] (*Aus. Und.*) **1** a derog. description of someone the speaker feels is trying to set themselves above the mass. **2** a non-derisive phr. of thanks for a favour done, *you're a Rhodes scholar, mate.*

Rhodie *n.* [abbr. *Rhodesia*] [1980s+] (*S.Afr.*) a white southern Rhodesian who emigrated to South Africa (and Australia) when the country became Zimbabwe in 1980 and black rule was instituted.

rhoid *n.* [abbr. SE *haemorrhoid*] **1** [1970s] (*US black*) anyone or anything that makes one's life less easily manageable. **2** [1990s+] (*US*) in pl., haemorrhoids.

rhubarb *n.*[1] [a mix of uses, e.g. theatrical, the actors' trad. muttering of *Rhubarb* to provide background in crowd scenes; and sporting, baseball fans' term to describe a disturbance. The term was popularized *c.*1943 by the US baseball commentator 'Red' Barber, whose memoirs were entitled *Rhubarb in the Catbird Seat*

(1968); for detail see Cohen (ed.), *Studies in Slang* IV, pp.52–55] **1** [mid-19C+] nonsense, rubbish. **2** [1940s+] (*orig. US*) an argument, a noisy dispute, esp. one that takes place on the field of play at a sporting event.

IN PHRASES

❑ **like rhubarb** *adv.* [1880s] intensely.

rhubarb *n.*[2] [20C+ use is US] [late 19C+] the genitals, of either sex; thus the coarse query, *How's your rhubarb, Missus?*

rhubarb *n.*[3] [rhy. sl.; *rhubarb* = SUB *n.*[1] (4); (Cockney pron. 'roobub')] [20C+] an advance on one's wages.

rhubarb pill *n.* [rhy. sl.] [late 19C] **1** a bill [pun on both requiring a 'giving out']. **2** a hill.

rhubarbs, the *n.* [play on rhy. SE *rhubarbs/suburbs* + pun on STICKS *n.*[3]/SE *sticks* of rhubarb STICKS *n.*[3]] [20C+] (*US*) the suburbs, the provinces.

rhygin *adj. see* RYGIN *adj.*

rhyme *v.* [1950s+] **1** (*W.I.*) to tell funny stories, to joke; thus *rhymer*, a teller of jokes or amusing tales. **2** (*US black/teen*) to compete with ritualized insults.

rhyme slinger *n.* (*also* **rhyme thumper**) [late 19C–1910s] a poet.

rhynie *n.* [ety. unknown] [1940s] (*US black*) a term of ridicule.

rhyno *n. see* RHINO *n.*[1].

rhythm *n.* [play on BLUE *n.*[1] (4a)/SE *rhythm* and blues] [1960s–70s] (*drugs*) amphetamine.

SE in slang uses

IN PHRASES

❑ **give up rhythm** *v.* [1960s+] (*US black*) for a woman, using body language, to indicate her sexual availability to a man with whom she is walking or dancing.

rhythm and blues *n.* [rhy. sl.] [1980s+] shoes.

'ria *n.* [abbr. proper name *Maria*] [mid-19C–1950s] the generic name for a costermonger's woman, often a coster herself.

riah *n.* (*also* **riha**) [backsl. but note Sp. *raya*, a parting in the hair] [mid-19C+] (*orig. Ling. Fr./Polari*) hair; thus *riah-zshumpah*, a hairdresser.

rial *n.* [SE *rial*, a coin of low value] [1940s+] (*W.I.*) a half-caste, the offspring of an East Indian woman and a black man; usu. combs. e.g. *Chiney-rial, Indian-rial*.

Rialto *n.* [proper name *Rialto*, that quarter of Venice in which the Exchange was situated, thus the centre of commercial life; actors presumably picked up the ref. from Shakespeare's use of the name in *The Merchant of Venice* (1596); like the STROLL *n.* (1), the *Rialto* moved, as did the activities it denoted. In 1890 it meant the stretch of Broadway between Union and Madison Squares, in 1905 it centred on Herald Square, by 1910, during theatrical Broadway's heyday it meant the stretch between 34th and 47th Streets, centring on Times Square; its last gasp was the blocks along W. 42nd Street] [mid-19C–1920s] (*US*) the centre of New York's theatrical life; spec. the south side of Union Square, on 14th Street; thus extended to local equivalents; also attrib.

rib *n.*[1] [the creation myth of the first woman, Eve, being made from Adam's *rib*] **1** [17C–19C] a wife. **2** [late 19C–1900s] in pl., a fat person. [ironic use of SE; 'the ribs' are unlikely to be visible]. **3** [1910s–60s] (*US black*) a woman.

SE in slang uses

DERIVATIVES

❑ **ribby** *adj.* [1930s+] **1** short of money [one is 'on one's ribs']. **2** second-rate, poor quality, dirty, run-down [fig. the 'ribs are showing'].

IN COMPOUNDS

❑ **rib baste** *v.* [late 16C–mid-17C] to thrash, to beat up. ❑ **rib bender** *n.* (*also* **rib-winder**) [boxing jargon] [mid–late 19C] a blow to the ribs. ❑ **rib joint** *n.* **1** [1940s+] (*US*) in commercial sexual contexts [JOINT *n.* (3b)]. (**a**) a brothel. (**b**) any form of sex show which permits the customers to watch, but definitely not to touch. **2** [1940s+] (*US*) a restaurant featuring spare ribs [SE (*spare*) *rib* + JOINT *n.* (3b)]. ❑ **rib roast** *see* separate entries. ❑ **rib shirt** *n.* [late 19C] a false shirt-front, covering only the ribs and chest, worn over an otherwise dirty garment. ❑ **rib stickers** *n.* [1940s] (*US Und.*) beans. ❑ **rib tickle** *v.* (*also* **tickle someone's ribs**) [mid-19C+] to thrash, to beat.

IN PHRASES

❑ **get into one's ribs** *v.* [one's wallet is carried in a pocket near the ribs] **1** [1900s] to lay a bet on credit. **2** [1920s] to borrow money. ❑ **on the ribs** *adj.* [poverty has emptied one's stomach + one's skin thus rests *on the ribs*] [1930s+] short of money. ❑ **ribbed-up** *adj.* [one's full wallet, sitting next to one's ribs] [late 19C–1900s] (*Aus./US*) (financially) secure.

rib *n.*[2] [RIB *v.* (2)] **1** [1910s+] (*US*) a joke, a trick, an act of teasing. **2** [1920s] (*US Und.*) an act of setting up an innocent person.

IN PHRASES

❑ **give someone the rib** *v.* [1950s–60s] to tease. ❑ **put someone on the rib** *v.* [1960s] to tease.

rib *n.*[3] [ety. unknown] [1950s] (*US black*) a shoe.

rib *v.* [one lit. or fig. 'tickles' or pokes the *ribs*] **1** [late 17C–early 19C] to hit someone in the ribs; as n., a boxer. **2** [1910s+] (*US*) to tease, to make fun of; thus n. *ribber*. **3** [1910s+] (*Aus./US Und.*) (*also* **rib up**) to prepare a victim for being swindled; to cheat. **4** [1920s–30s] (*US*) (*also* **rib up**) to discredit, to incriminate. **5** [1920s–30s] (*US*) to annoy or threaten, to pressurize (someone).

IN PHRASES

❑ **rib oneself up** *v.* [1930s] to convince onself, to pluck up one's courage.

riband *n. see* RIBBON *n.*[2].

ribband *n. see* RIBBIN *n.*

ribben *n.* [SE *ribbon*] [late 18C] (*UK Und.*) a whip.

ribber *n.* [early 19C] a blow, esp. one to the body.

ribbery-plague *n.* [mid-19C] (*UK Und.*) a domineering wife.

ribbin *n.* (*also* **ribband, ribbon**) [? SE *ribbon*; the image is of the richness of ribbon-bedecked packages] [late 17C–mid-19C] (*UK Und.*) money; thus *the ribbin runs thick, the ribbin runs thin*, implying the availability or otherwise of cash.

ribbing *n.* (*also* **ribbing-up**) [RIB *v.* (2)] [1910s+] the act of teasing.

IN COMPOUNDS

❑ **ribbing hand** *n.* [1940s] (*US Und.*) a member of a team of card cheats who distracts the victim with a flow of witticisms.

ribbon *n.*[1] [19C] gin; spirits in general [var. on SATIN *n.* (1a) and like it implying the smoothness of good gin].

IN PHRASES

❑ **pluck the ribbon** *v. see* PLUCK THE RIBAND *under* PLUCK *v.*

ribbon *n.*[2] (*also* **riband**) [19C–1910s] in pl., reins, esp. in the phr. *handle the ribbons*.

ribbon *v.* [1900s] (*Aus.*) to whip.

ribbon and curl *n.* [rhy. sl.] [20C+] a little girl.

ribbon clerk *n.* **1** [1950s] (*US*) generic for a small-time trader, esp. in the stock market. **2** [1950s+] (*US gay*) a gay man who has a desk job. **3** [1990s+] (*US gay*) a heterosexual woman who prefers the company of gay men.

rib roast *n.* **1** [late 16C–17C; mid-19C] (*also* **rib-roasting**) a beating [pun]. **2** [1930s–40s] (*US Und.*) an infant, a young child.

rib roast *v.* [RIB ROAST *n.* (1)] **1** [17C–mid-19C] to thrash, to beat up. **2** [mid-19C] of a wife, to scold her husband.

rib roaster *n.* [RIB ROAST *v.* (1)] [mid–late 19C] a body-blow, especially one to the ribs.

ribston *n.* (*also* **ribstone**) [the *Ribston pippin*, a dessert apple orig. introduced from Normandy *c.*1707] [late 19C] a general term of affection, admiration.

ribuck *see* RYEBUCK.

ribuck! *excl. see* RYEBUCK! *excl.*

rib-up *n.* [1930s–60s] (*US Und.*) a pre-arranged deal; the concoction of criminal guilt or charges.

rib up *v.* [1910s] (*US*) **1** to dress, to provide an outfit of clothes. **2** to create, to flesh out, to embellish.

Rican *n.* [abbr.] [1960s+] (*US*) a Puerto Rican.

rice *n.*

SE in slang uses

pertaining to East Asia

(DERIVATIVES)

❑ **ricer** *n.* [SE *rice*, the predominant Asian staple] [1980s+] a derog. term for an Asian person.

(IN COMPOUNDS)

❑ **riceball** *adj.* [2000s] (*US*) East Asian. ❑ **rice-burner** *n.* **1** [1980s] (*US campus*) a Japanese manufactured motorcycle. **2** [2000s] a Japanese automobile. ❑ **rice Christian** *n.* [the use continued in East Asia to 1960s] [late 19C–1910s] (*Aus./UK society*) an inhabitant of a rice-growing country who volunteered for conversion less through religious fervour and more through a desire to gain food from gullible missionaries. ❑ **rice-eater** *n.* [1990s+] (*Aus.*) a derog. term for a Chinese or Asian person. ❑ **rice man** *n.* [1940s] (*US black*) an East Asian man. ❑ **rice paddy Hattie** *n.* [joc./assonant use of the female name, a nickname for Harriet] **1** [1940s] rural Chinese prostitutes. **2** [1980s+] (*US gay*) one who has a penchant for East Asian men. ❑ **rice picker** *n.* [2000s] (*US black*) a Chinese person. ❑ **rice queen** *n.* [-QUEEN *sfx* (3)] [1970s+] (*gay*) someone who favours Asian partners. ❑ **rice rocket** *n.* [1990s+] **1** (*orig. US black*) a Japanese-made car (usu. a four-wheel drive Jeep clone, e.g. a Shogun) or motorcycle. **2** a cheap or old automobile, usu. owned by someone of Hispanic descent.

general uses

(IN COMPOUNDS)

❑ **ricebags** *n.* [late 19C–1900s] trousers. ❑ **rice crispies** *n.* (*also* **rice krispies**) [the cereal's slogan, 'Snap, crackle and pop'] [1970s] (*drugs*) amyl nitrite. ❑ **rice dog** *n.* [20C+] (*W.I.*) a mongrel, fed on scraps (mainly rice) and useless as a watchdog.

(IN PHRASES)

❑ **like white on rice** (*also* **like gravy on rice**) [rice is white itself] [1930s+] (*US black/P.R.*) very closely. ❑ **not for all the rice in China** see NOT FOR ALL THE TEA IN CHINA *under* TEA *n.*

rice *v.* [the role of SE *rice* as a staple] [20C+] (*W.I.*) to maintain financially, look after, to feed; thus *rice at (one)*, to be supported as a servant, a kept woman etc.

rice-and-bean *adj.* [the stereotyped P.R. diet] [1970s–80s] (*US*) **1** Puerto Rican. **2** Mexican.

rice and beaner *n.* [the popular staple macrobiotic diet of the era] [1990s+] (*US campus*) someone who identifies with the styles and concerns of the 1960s.

rice-and-beans *adj.* [SE/RICE-AND-BEAN *adj.*; the poverty of the foodstuff and/or racist stereotyping] [1970s] second-rate, impoverished, unimpressive.

rice and sago *n.* [rhy. sl. = DAGO *n.* (1)] [1980s] (*Aus.*) a Greek or Italian immigrant.

rice-belly *n.* [20C+] **1** (*W.I.*) a stomach swollen from malnutrition and eating only rice. **2** (*W.I.*) a child who has such a stomach. **3** (*US*) a derog. term for a Chinese person.

rich *adj.* **1** [early 19C+] surprising, highly unlikely; usu. *that's rich*. **2** [mid-19C–1910s] (*US*) pornographic. **3** [mid-19C+] very funny.

SE in slang uses

(IN COMPOUNDS)

❑ **rich face** *n.* (*also* **rich nose**) [seen as the product of a diet of *rich* food] [late 17C–early 19C] a red and/or heavily acned face or nose. ❑ **rich friend** *n.* [euph.] [early 19C] a prostitute's keeper; i.e. a wealthy man rather than a pimp. ❑ **rich one** *n.* [the term was used by upmarket prostitutes with ref. to the wives that their clients dared not leave altogether] [late 19C] a wealthy, but unloved wife.

(IN PHRASES)

❑ **strike it rich** *v. see under* STRIKE *v.*

Richard *n.* **1** [mid-19C] (*US Und.*) a hunchback [the hunchbacked King Richard III]. **2** [1910s–30s] (*US Und.*) (*also* **Mr Richard**) a detective [play on DICK $n.^{5}$ (1)].

(IN PHRASES)

❑ **bop Richard** *v.* [BOP *v.* (1) + SE *Richard*, i.e. DICK $n.^{1}$ (5)] [1990s+] to masturbate. ❑ **have the Richard** *v.* (*also* **have the dick**) [theatrical rhy. sl.; *Richard III* = BIRD $n.^{2}$ (4)] [1960s+] (*Aus.*) to be finished or exhausted, to be irreparably damaged. ❑ **swinging Richard** *n. see* SWINGING DICK *under* SWINGING $adj.^{2}$.

Richard Burton *n.* [rhy. sl.; ult. UK actor *Richard Burton* (1925–84)] [20C+] a curtain.

richard snary *n.* (*also* **richard, richardanary**) [play on abbr. *dick*; 'A country lad, having been reproved for calling persons by their Christian names, being sent by his master to borrow a dictionary, thought to show his breeding by asking for a *Richard Snary*' (Grose, 1796)] [late 18C–19C] a dictionary.

Richard (the Third) *n.* [rhy. sl.] **1** [late 19C+] a piece of excrement; thus fig. an unpleasant person [= TURD $n.^{1}$]. **2** [late 19C+] a word. **3** [late 19C+] booing, barracking [= BIRD $n.^{2}$ (1)]. **4** [1940s+] a young woman, a girlfriend [= BIRD $n.^{1}$ (1b)]. **5** [1960s+] a bird. **6** [1980s+] a *third* class degree.

rick *n.* [? RICKET *n.* or bookmakers' jargon *rick*, a spurious bet] [1950s+] an error, a mistake.

rickaticks *n.* [UK dial. *rickmatick*, a (rowdy) affair] [20C+] (*W.I.*) a very bad temper; thus *get in one's rickaticks*, to lose one's temper and stay furious for some time.

ricket *n.* [ety. unknown; link to the disease SE *rickets*] [1950s–70s] a mistake, a blunder.

rickets *n.* [2000s] (*US black*) an infestation of pubic lice.

SE in slang uses

(IN PHRASES)

❑ **have the rickets** *v.* [mid-19C] (*UK Und.*) to have no money.

rickety kate *n.* [rhy. sl.] [20C+] (*Aus.*) a gate.

ricky-tick *adj.* (*also* **ricky-tick-tock, ricky-ticky**) [jazz use *ricky-tick*, old fashioned jazz] [1930s+] **1** (*orig. US*) old-fashioned, predictable, monotonous. **2** (*US*) cheap and shabby.

ricockulous *adj.* [SE *ridiculous* + ? COCK $n.^{5}$ (2)] [1990s+] (*US black*) ludicrous, absurd, worthy of verbal denigration.

riddle-me-ree *n.* [rhy. sl.] [1980s+] **1** an act of urination [PEE $n.^{1}$ (2)]. **2** the number three.

ride *n.* **1** in sexual contexts [RIDE *v.* (1a)]. (**a**) [late 15C; mid-19C+] sexual intercourse. (**b**) [late 19C+] (*orig. Irish*) a woman when regarded as a (potential) partner in intercourse. (**c**) [1920s] an act of sodomy. (**d**) [1960s+] (*Scot.*) a term of abuse, syn. with FUCKER *n.* (**e**) [1990s+] (*Irish*) an attractive man. **2** anything that one rides. (**a**) [1920s+] (*US*) an automobile. (**b**) [1980s+] (*US campus*) a bicycle or motorcycle. (**c**) [1990s+] (*US black*) a skateboard. **3** [1940s–60s] (*US prison*) a jail sentence. **4** [1960s+] (*US prison*) a companion, esp. a fellow gang-member [a member of the same group or CAR *n.* (1)]. **5** [1980s] (*US drugs*) a state of intoxication; thus v. to become intoxicated by a drug [play on TRIP $n.^{4}$ (1a)].

(IN PHRASES)

❑ **do a ride** *v.* [mid-19C+] to have sexual intercourse. ❑ **dry ride** *n. see under* DRY $adj.^{1}$. ❑ **get a ride** *v.* [1950s] to be taken by car to one's execution. ❑ **take for a ride** *v.* **1** [1920s+] (*US Und.*) (*also* **take for an airing, take for a trip**) to assassinate, usu. by taking the victim out in a car and killing them at some stage, then dumping the body far from one's base; thus *go for a ride*, to suffer this form of death. **2** [1920s+] (*orig. US*) (*also* **give a ride, take for a trot**) to deceive, to fool, to trick, usu. for financial gain. **3** [1930s–40s] (*US Und.*) (*also* **ride, take for a walk**) to arrest.

ride *v.* **1** in sexual senses. (**a**) [16C+] of a man, to have sexual intercourse. (**b**) [17C+] of a woman, to have sexual intercourse. (**c**) [1920s] to sodomize. (**d**) [1930s–50s] (*US*) to play an instrument with rhythm and competence. (**e**) [1990s+] (*US prison*) to trade sexual favours for immunity from physical attack by fellow inmates. **2** [late 19C–1930s] (*US campus*) to use a translation in an examination or when preparing classwork [pun]. **3** in verbal or emotional senses; to 'get on someone's back'. (**a**) [20C+] to pressurize. (**b**) [1900s–50s] (*US campus*) to reprimand, to scold. (**c**) [1910s+] to annoy, to irritate. (**d**) [1910s+] to tease, to taunt. (**e**) [1950s] to pursue closely. **(f)** [1960s] to overcome. **4** [20C+] (*US Und.*) to move from a local gaol to prison proper. **5** [1930s+] (*US*) to endure, to suffer, to experience. **6** see PUNK (OUT) *v.* (2). **7** *see RIDE THE LIGHTNING* below. **8** *see TAKE FOR A RIDE under* RIDE *n.*

IN PHRASES

pertaining to sexual intercourse

❑ **ride a blind piece** *v.* [BLIND *adj.*[1] (2) + PIECE *n.* (3b)] [1940s–60s] (*gay*) to fellate an uncircumcized penis. ❑ **ride a St George** *v.* [illustrations of a mounted St George slaying the Dragon; note Lat. use, translated as 'mounting the Hectorean horse'] [mid-18C–19C] to have sexual intercourse with the woman on top of the man. ❑ **ride bareback** *v.* [BAREBACK *adv.* (1)] [1950s+] to have sexual intercourse without a condom. ❑ **ride below the crupper** *v.* [SE *crupper*, the hind-quarters or rump of a horse; also the human buttocks] [mid-17C–18C] of a man, to have sexual intercourse. ❑ **ride in another man's boots** *v.* (*also* **to ride in another's/anyone's old boots, ride in old shoes**) [mid-17C–early 19C] to marry another man's ex-wife or widow, or to start keeping his former mistress. ❑ **ride someone's leg** *v.* [the image of a dog rubbing itself amorously against one's leg] [2000s] (*US prison*) to befriend officers in the hope of gaining favours. ❑ **ride tantivy** *v.* [SE *tantivy*, a gallop at full tilt] [18C] as a euph. for sexual intercourse, i.e. to gallop. ❑ **ride the arse off** *v. see FUCK THE ARSE OFF SOMEONE under* FUCK *v.* ❑ **ride the deck** *v.* [DECK *n.*[1] (2)] [1910s+] (*US prison*) to perform anal intercourse. ❑ **ride the hobby horse** *v.* [it is unlikely that the ref. to HOBBY HORSE *n.* (2) is more than coincidental] [1980s+] (*US campus*) to have sexual intercourse. ❑ **ride the tan track** *v.* [TAN TRACK *n.*] [1990s+] to have homosexual anal intercourse.

meaning to attack

❑ **ride down** *v.* [image of a 'Wild West' posse] [1990s+] (*US prison*) to attack in a group. ❑ **ride down to the ground** *v.* [image of a 'Wild West' posse] **1** [1970s+] (*US black*) to attack verbally, to criticize heavily. **2** [1980s+] to get down to the facts. ❑ **ride in** *v.* [1940s] (*US Und.*) to ensnare a victim into a confidence trick. ❑ **ride someone's ass** *v.* [2000s] (*US*) to scold, to reprimand.

SE in slang uses

IN PHRASES

pertaining to menstruation

❑ **ride a cotton horse** *v.* (*also* **ride a white horse, ride the white horse**) [cotton sanitary towels; cf. *RIDE THE RED HORSE* below] [1960s+] to be menstruating. ❑ **ride the cotton pony** *v.* [1990s+] (*US*) to menstruate. ❑ **ride the rag** *v.* (*also* **wear the rag**) [RAG *n.*[1] (6a)] [1960s+] (*US black/campus*) to have a menstrual period. ❑ **ride the red horse** *v.* [1990s+] (*US*) to be menstruating.

pertaining to walking

❑ **ride Bayard of ten toes** *v.* [proper name Bayard, a horse that featured in various medieval romances; the name itself comes from Fr. *bayard*, bay-coloured; Henke, *Gutter Life and Language* (1988) notes a one-off use in *A Hundred Merry Tales* (1526) in which Bayard is synon. with a young woman's buttocks, the cleft of which is 'Bayard's mouth', a play between the brown horse and the brown anus] [late 16C–18C] to walk. ❑ **ride by the marrowbone stage** *v.* (*also* **ride in the marrowbone stage, ride in/by the Marylebone stage, go in/by the marrowbone stage, go in/by the Marylebone stage**) [*Marylebone* is simply a mispron. of SE *marrowbone*, itself metonymic for the legs] [mid-19C] to walk. ❑ **ride shank's mare** *v.* (*also* **ride shank's pony, take shank's mare**) [SHANKS'S PONY *n.*] [mid-18C+] to walk. ❑ **ride the shoe leather express** *v.* (*also* **go by...**) [1920s] (*US tramp*) to walk.

pertaining to drugs

❑ **ride the E-train** *v.* [play on the New York subway *E-train*/E *n.*] [1990s+] (*US campus/drugs*) to be under the influence of MDMA. ❑ **ride the horse** *v.* [HORSE *n.* (7)] [1940s–70s] (*drugs*) to take heroin; thus *horseriding, on horseback*, using heroin. ❑ **ride the mainline** *v. see under* MAINLINE *n.* ❑ **ride the poppy train** *v.* [1950s–60s] (*drugs*) to smoke opium. ❑ **ride the white horse** *v.* (*also* **ride the wave**) [*WHITE HORSE under* WHITE *adj.*] [1950s+] (*US black*) to be intoxicated with drugs.

general uses

❑ **ride a desk** *v.* [play on *DESK JOCKEY under* DESK *n.*] [2000s] (*US*) to work as a clerk or any otherwise deskbound occupation. ❑ **ride a jock** *v.* [JOCK *n.*[1] (5)] [1980s+] (*US campus*) of a woman, to attempt to get to know a man of her own peer group with the intentions of ultimately having a relationship with that person because of his personality, not his material possessions. ❑ **ride backwards up Holborn Hill/in a cart up Holborn Hill** *v. see WALK BACKWARDS UP HOLBORN HILL under* HOLBORN HILL *n.* ❑ **ride bitch** *v.* (*also* **ride the bitch's seat, ride punk, ride pussy**) [BITCH *n.*[1]/PUNK *n.*[1]/PUSSY *n.* (2), i.e. the supposed 'woman's seat'] [1970s+] (*US black/teen*) to ride in the middle of the back seat or pillion on a motorbike. ❑ **ride blind baggage** *v. see RIDE THE BLINDS* below. ❑ **ride booty** *v. see PLAY BOOTY under* BOOTY *n.*[1]. ❑ **ride grub** *v.* [SE *grub*, an unpleasant person] [late 18C] to be bad-tempered or sulky. ❑ **ride herd on** *v.* [cowboy imagery] [late 19C+] (*US*) to control or manage someone or something, to admonish, to beat. ❑ **ride one's thumb** *v.* [1960s] to hitchhike. ❑ **ride out** *v.* [20C+ uses are cowboy imagery] **1** [early 17C–18C] to be a highwayman. **2** [1950s+] (*US black/teen*) to leave; also as imper. **3** [2000s] (*US prison*) to move to another prison. **4** [2000s] (*US black*) an excl. of dismissal, disbelief. ❑ **ride Pegasus** *v.* [the flying horse *Pegasus* of Greek mythology] [mid-19C] (*UK Und.*) to work on the prison treadmill. ❑ **ride plush** *v.* [PLUSH *adj.*+ the lit. *plush*-covered seats] [20C+] (*US tramp*) to pay for one's seat (and thus travel in comfort). ❑ **ride punk/pussy** *v. see RIDE BITCH* above. ❑ **ride rusty** *v.* [SE *rusty*, refractory (of horses)] [late 18C–mid-19C] to be ill-tempered or sullen. ❑ **ride shotgun** *v.* (*also* **ride shottie, sit shotgun**) [orig. the shotgun-wielding assistant who sat next to the driver] [1950s+] **1** (*orig. US*) to sit in the seat next to the driver in a car, also fig. use. **2** (*US*) to act as a security guard, esp. on a vehicle. ❑ **ride staff** *v.* (*also* **play staff**) [Zulu sl. *ukubamb' istuff*, to board a moving train, ult. ? f. *staff*, the pole in the doorway of railway carriage, which is grasped by those jumping aboard when the train is already moving] [1960s+] (*S.Afr.*) to cling to the outside, or stand on the roof, of a moving train, having boarded it while in motion. ❑ **ride the beams** *v.* see *RIDE THE RODS* below. ❑ **ride the beef** *v.* [BEEF *n.*[2]] [20C+] (*US Und.*) to take the blame. ❑ **ride the bitch's seat** *v. see RIDE BITCH* above. ❑ **ride the black donkey** *v.* [mid-19C] to be in a bad temper. ❑ **ride the blinds** *v.* (*also* **ride blind baggage**) [BLIND *n.*[2] (2)] [late 19C+] (*US tramp*) to ride for free in the closed baggage compartment of a train. ❑ **ride the broom** *v.* [the trad. witch on her broomstick] **1** [1970s+] (*US prison*) to threaten or intimidate another inmate; to prophesy. **2** [1950s–70s] (*US drugs*) (*also* **ride the broomstick, ...the witch's broom**) to participate in drug taking. ❑ **ride the bumpers** *v. see RIDE THE RODS* below. ❑ **ride the cushions** *v.* [the upholstered seats] [1910s+] (*US tramp*) **1** to ride in a passenger car rather than in a boxcar. **2** in fig. use, to prosper, to be comfortable. ❑ **ride the Erie** *v.* (*also* **ride the earie**) [*ON THE ERIE under* ERIE *n.* + play on the *Erie* railroad] [1940s] (*US*) to eavesdrop. ❑ **ride the goat** *v.* [the fantasy that initiate Masons have to ride a live goat] [1900s–20s] (*US campus*) to be initiated into a secret society. ❑ **ride the grub line** *v.* [*GRUB-LINER under* GRUB *n.*[2]] [1900s–40s] (*US*) of an out-of-work cowboy, to travel around seeking work while subsisting on hand-outs. ❑ **ride the gun** *v.* [*RIDE SHOTGUN* above] [1970s+] (*US teen*) to ride in the front passenger seat of a car. ❑ **ride the handcar** *v.* [from the up-and-down movement of a handle with which one drives the vehicle] [1940s+] (*US*) to masturbate. ❑ **ride the horse foaled by an acorn** *v.* (*also* **... foaled of an acorn**) [i.e. the oak tree gallows] [mid-17C–mid-19C] to be hanged. ❑ **ride the lightning** *v.* (*also* **ride**) [1930s+] (*US*) to be executed in the electric chair. ❑ **ride the odno** *v.* [backsl. *odno* = nod, thus 'on the nod'] [late 19C] to travel by train without paying a fare. ❑ **ride the pilot** *v.* [1930s] (*US tramp*) to ride on the cowcatcher of the locomotive. ❑ **ride the pine** *v.* [the *pine* bench] [1980s] (*US campus*) to sit on the bench during an athletic event, esp. when one wants desperately to play. ❑ **ride the plush** *v.* [1920s–40s] (*US tramp/Und.*) **1** to ride inside a passenger train. **2** in fig. use, to be well provided with material comforts. ❑ **ride the porcelain bus** *v.* (*also* **ride the porcelain Honda, ride the porcelain pony**) [i.e. the porcelain lavatory bowl] [1960s+] (*orig. US campus*) **1** to vomit. **2** to have diarrhoea. ❑ **ride the rap** *v.* [RAP *n.*[1] (3a)] [1980s+] (*US*) to accept the consequences of one's crimes, such as arrest and imprisonment, and deal with them as well as possible. ❑ **ride the rods** *v.* (*also* **ride the beams, ...bumpers, ...rod**) [late 19C+] (*US tramp*) to ride on the steel bars beneath a freight car; fig. to be a tramp. ❑ **ride the rumble** *v.* [RUMBLE *n.*[2] (2)] [1950s] (*US Und.*) to take responsibility for a crime. ❑ **ride the toby** *v.* [TOBY *n.*[2] (2)] [early–mid-19C] to practise highway robbery. ❑ **ride the wagon** *v.* [the image of lying on a hay-laden wagon as it moves through the fields] [1970s] (*US black*) to enjoy a pleasant experience on a drug. ❑ **ride to Romford** *v.* (*also* **ride to Rumford**) [proper name *Romford*, Essex, esteemed for the quality of its leather breeches] **1** [mid-18C] to be blunt, properly, *you may ride to Romford on this knife*. **2** [late 18C–early 19C] to get a new pair of breeches or to get a new bottom put in an old pair. ❑ **ride with** *v.* [fig. use of SE, but note CAR *n.* (1)] [1960s+] (*US prison*) **1** to side with (in a fight). **2** to be friends with.

IN EXCLAMATIONS

❑ **ride-on-your-back!** [1910s] (*Aus.*) a general term of abuse; the implication is that the subject is 'a goat'.

ride-by *n. see* DRIVE-BY *n.* (1).

rideman *n.* [1920s–40s] (*US jazz*) a soloist.

rider *n.* **1** in sexual senses. (**a**) [17C+] a womanizer; thus, a male copulator. (**b**) [1970s] (*US gay*) a male homosexual who takes the active role in anal intercourse. **2** [mid-18C–mid-19C] (*UK Und.*) a cloak. **3** [late 18C–early 19C] someone who receives part of the salary for a job through an agreement with the job's actual appointee or with their patron; the rider is said to be 'quartered' on the job's possessor and a single possessor may have several riders in tow [SE *rider*, one who rides + legal jargon, an additional clause tacked on to a document after its first drafting]. **4** [1920s] (*US prison/Und.*) a prosecutor. **5** [2000s] (*US drugs*) free heroin provided to a purchaser of bulk cocaine, e.g. 5 kilos of heroin for every 100 kilos of cocaine.

riders *n.* [1970s+] (*US gay*) very tight trousers.

ridge *n.* [the term vanished in the UK during the 19C but reappeared in Aus. in the mid-20C+] **1** [late 17C–mid-19C; 1920s+] (*also* **rige**) gold, thus money, a guinea. **2** [mid-19C+] (*UK/US Und.*) coins, rather than notes.

IN COMPOUNDS

❑ **ridge cove** *n.* [COVE *n.* (1)] [late 18C–mid-19C] (*UK Und.*) a goldsmith. ❑ **ridge cully** *n.* [CULLY *n.*[1] (4)] [mid-17C–early 19C] (*UK Und.*) a goldsmith. ❑ **ridge montra** *n.* [MONTRA *n.*] [19C] (*UK Und.*) a gold watch. ❑ **ridge-super** *n.* [SUPER *n.*[2] (1)] [mid-19C] (*UK Und.*) a gold watch. ❑ **ridge thimble** *n.* [mid-19C] (*UK Und.*) a gold watch.

ridge *adj.* [RIDGE *n.* (1)] **1** [mid-19C] (*UK Und.*) golden. **2** [1930s+] (*Aus.*) valuable, good.

ridgerunner *n.* [orig. f. Arkansas only] [1910s+] (*US*) a southern mountain farmer, a hillbilly.

ridgey-didge *n.* [rhy.sl.] [1980s] (*Aus.*) a refrigerator.

ridgie-didgie *adj.* (*also* **ridgey-the-didge, ridgie-didge, ridgy-dig, ridgy-dite, rigi-dig**) [RIDGE *adj.* (2) + redup.] [1950s+] (*Aus.*) genuine, honest.

ridic *adj.* [abbr.] [1910s+] (*US campus*) *ridic*ulous.

riding *n.* [RIDE *v.*] [1920s–30s] (*orig. US*) annoying, irritating, teasing.

riding academy *n.* [RIDE *v.*] [1930s–60s] (*orig. US black*) a brothel; a hotel where one can go with a whore.

riding a thorn *phr.* [i.e. the needle] [1950s–70s] (*drugs*) injecting narcotics.

riding the donkey *phr.* [mid-19C] cheating when assessing weights or measures.

riding the wave *phr.* (*also* **riding a wave**) [surfing imagery] [1920s–50s] (*drugs*) under the influence of drugs.

riff *n.* [jazz use *riff*, a simple musical phrase repeated over and over] **1** [1940s+] (*orig. US black*) one's personal style. **2** [1950s+] (*US black*) a theme, a cause. **3** [1960s] (*US*) information. **4** [1960s] a sudden action. **5** [1970s] (*US*) a joke, a line. **6** [1970s] (*US*) an argument. **7** [1970s+] (*orig. US black*) familiar or habitual words, or music. **8** [1980s+] (*US campus*) one who takes advantage of another person. **9** [2000s] a rumour.

IN PHRASES

❑ **riffs and rills** *n.* [SE *rill*, to sing with liquid notes] [1940s] (*US black*) ideas, plans.

riff *v.* [RIFF *n.*] **1** [1940s+] (*orig. US black*) to chatter, to talk. **2** [1970s] (*US campus*) to boast or exaggerate; also as n. **3** [1980s+] (*US*) to complain. **4** [1980s+] (*US campus*) (*also* **riff on**) to take advantage of someone. **5** [1990s+] to inform on; to reveal facts about. **6** [1990s+] to offend.

riffle *n.* [SE *riffle* the notes] [mid–late 19C] (*US Und.*) a large amount of money acquired by deceit or trickery.

IN PHRASES

❑ **make the riffle** *v.* [mid-19C–1940s] (*US tramp*) to acquire money; in general, to succeed.

riffle *v. see* RIFLE *v.*

riff-raff *n.* [rhy. sl.] **1** [20C+] a Welsh person [= TAFF *n.* (1)]. **2** [1990s+] a café, i.e. 'caff'.

riffs and rills *n. see under* RIFF *n.*

rifle *v.* (*also* **riffle**) [SE *rifle*, of a hawk, to tread the hen; + overtones of SE *rifle*, to despoil, to plunder] [mid-16C–mid-19C] to have sexual intercourse; thus *rifler*, n., a prostitute's customer.

rifler *n. see* TOLLER *n.*

rifle range *n.*[1] [play on SHOOTING GALLERY *n.*] [1960s–70s] (*drugs*) **1** a house, apartment or room in which addicts gather to inject drugs. **2** a detoxification ward.

rifle range *n.*[2] [rhy. sl.] [2000s] **1** change (monetary). **2** a change.

rift *n.* [echoic] [1960s+] (*Irish*) a belch.

rig *n.*[1] [? SE *rig*, to play the wanton, to romp about; ult. ety. unknown] **1** [late 16C–mid-19C] a wanton, promiscuous woman. **2** [mid-19C] a smart, 'sharp' young man.

DERIVATIVES

❑ **riggish** *adj.* [late 16C–19C] lecherous, amorous, lascivious.

rig *n.*[2] [? dial.] **1** [mid-18C+] (*also* **rigg, rigging**) a dodge, a confidence trick. **2** [late 18C–mid-19C] ridicule, mockery. **3** [late 18C–1900s] a prank or game.

IN COMPOUNDS

❑ **rig sale** *n.* [19C] a false sale, a mock auction.

IN PHRASES

❑ **run one's rig upon** *v.* [late 18C–mid-19C] to ridicule. ❑ **run the rig on** *v.* [late 18C–early 19C] to deceive, to trick.

rig *n.*[3] [RIG *v.*[1] (1)] **1** [late 18C+] one's clothing, one's style of dress. **2** [early 19C] in fig. use, one's personal style.

rig *n.*[4] **1** [20C+] (*orig. US*) a vehicle [early 19C SE *rig*, a horse and its vehicle; ult. the 'rigging' or harness]. (**a**) an automobile. (**b**) a truck. **2** in lit. or fig. senses of SE *rig*, equipment. (**a**) [20C+] the male genitals. (**b**) [1930s+] (*drugs*) the equipment needed to inject narcotics. (**c**) [2000s] (*US*) a gun.

rig *n.*[5] [dial. *rig*, a half-castrated ram] [1930s] (*Irish*) a man with one testicle.

rig *v.*[1] (*also* **rig out, rig up, trig up**) [naut. imagery] [17C+] **1** to clothe; thus *rigged out* or *rigged up*, dressed (up). **2** in fig. use, to 'patch up'.

rig *v.*[2] [? link to RIG *n.*[1] (2)] **1** [late 17C–mid-19C] to play tricks on, to fool. **2** [mid-19C+] to manipulate illegally.

IN PHRASES

❑ **rig a jig** *v.* [1970s] (*US black*) **1** of a pimp, to set up a potential customer with a woman [JIG *n.*[4] (2)]. **2** of a confidence man, to set up a victim for deception [JIG *n.*[2] (1)].

rige *n. see* RIDGE *n.* (1).

rigg *n. see* RIG *n.*[2] (1).

rigged *adj.* [RIG *v.*[2]] [20C+] of a contest, manipulated or set-up.

rigger *n.* [? SE *square-rigger*] [1940s] (*Aus./N.Z.*) a quart bottle of beer, esp. a quart of draught beer in a square-faced gin bottle.

rigging *n.*[1] [RIG *v.*[1] (1) + naut. *rigging*, the various ropes that are used on a sailing ship] **1** [17C+] (*UK Und.*) clothes; thus *rum rigging*, fashionable, expensive clothes; *under-rigging* underclothes. **2** [1960s] a party, an event. **3** [1980s] (*US*) the male genitalia.

rigging *n.*[2] *see* RIG *n.*[2] (1).

riggish *adj. see under* RIG *n.*[1].

right *adj.* [note Williams refs. to the 17C use of *right* to mean whorish, immoral] **1** [mid-19C+] (*Und.*) reliable, trustworthy, (from the criminal's point of view); thus corrupt (i.e. of a police officer). **2** [late 19C+] (*Aus./N.Z.*) safe, secure; lit. and fig. **3** [20C+] (*US Und.*) justifiable, e.g. an arrest that follows a crime one actually did commit. **4** [1900s] sober. **5** [1910s+] sane, mentally balanced; usu. in negative to mean insane, e.g. *not right*, and usu. in combs. e.g. *right in the wits*, *right in the head*. **6** [1910s+] (*US*) respectable, honest, dependable. **7** [1930s+] (*US*) drunk or intoxicated [the inference is that the sober/drugless state is 'wrong']. **8** [1970s] (*US*) good, in good spirits. **9** [1980s+] of a confidence trickster's victim, thoroughly ensnared.

DERIVATIVES

❑ **rightness** *n.* [1950s] (*US Und.*) defiance of authority.

IN COMPOUNDS

❑ **right copper** *n.* (*also* **right cop**) [COPPER *n.* (3)/COP *n.*[1] (1)] [1930s+] a corrupt police officer. ❑ **right croaker** *n.* [CROAKER *n.*[5] (1)] [1920s–50s] (*US*) a doctor who is willing to write prescriptions for narcotic drugs, patch up wounded villains and perform other illegal services. ❑ **right grift** *n.* [GRIFT *n.* (2)] [1900s–20s] (*US Und.*) working confidence tricks after bribing the police and thus without fear of arrest. ❑ **right guy** *n.* [GUY *n.*[2] (1)] **1** [20C+] (*US, usu. Und.*) a trustworthy person, esp. in criminal terms. **2** [1950s+] (*US prison*) a popular prisoner, respected by his peers. ❑ **right joint** *n.* [JOINT *n.*] [20C+] (*US Und.*) **1** a safe criminal haunt or establishment. **2** a prison, esp. one considered to treat prisoners fairly. ❑ **right oil** *n.* [OIL *n.* (2c)] [1920s+] (*Aus.*) the honest truth, true facts. ❑ **right one** *n.* **1** [early 19C; 1930s+] something that is an exceptional example of its type, usu. humorous or bizarre. **2** [late 19C–1940s] an admirable person (or animal). **3** [20C+] (*Ulster*) an unpredictable person. ❑ **right screw** *n.* [SCREW *n.*[1] (2c)] [late 19C+] a corrupt prison warder. ❑ **right sort** *n. see* separate entry. ❑ **right stuff** *n. see* separate entry. ❑ **right town** *n.* [1910s–40s] (*US Und.*) any town or small city where the authorities – police, local politicians – have been bribed into allowing criminal activity to flourish. ❑ **right twirl** *n.* [TWIRL *n.* (2)] [late 19C] a corrupt prison warder.

IN PHRASES

❑ **get one's head right** *v.* [1950s+] **1** to get drunk or intoxicated by drugs. **2** *see* sl. phr. below. ❑ **get right** *v.* **1** [1930s+] (*US black*) to become drunk or intoxicated by drugs. **2** *see* SE phr. below. ❑ **have someone right** *v.* [1940s] (*US Und.*) to buy protection from an official. ❑ **make (one) right** *v.* (*also* **make oneself right**) [1950s+] (*US black*) to feel good, esp. as a result of drug use.

SE in slang uses

IN COMPOUNDS

❑ **right bower** *n.* [Ger. *bauer*, peasant, which can be seen as a 'knave'; orig. used in the card-game euchre for the two highest cards – the knave of trumps, and the knave of the same colour, called *right* and *left bower* respectively] **1** [late 19C–1920s] in cards, the knave of trumps; also fig. use. **2** [1900s] in fig. use: a preferred suitor. **3** [1900s–80s] (*US*) a deputy or second in command. ❑ **right charlie** *n. see* CHARLIE *n.*[5].

IN PHRASES

❑ **get one's head right** *v.* **1** [1950s+] to come to one's senses. **2** *see* sl. phr. above. ❑ **get right** *v.* **1** [late 19C+] (*US*) to pull oneself together. **2** [1980s] (*US campus*) to get ready. **3** *see* sl. phr. above. ❑ **right and fly** *adj.* [early 19C] all in order, completed. ❑ **right as a bank** *adj. see under* BANK *n.*[1].

IN EXCLAMATIONS

❑ **right arm!** [1970s] (*US campus*) a parody of the 1960s slogan RIGHT ON! *excl.*

right *v.* (*also* **right up**) [1940s] (*US Und.*) to corrupt, to make someone, e.g. a police officer, a politician, amenable to bribery and thus the permitting of criminal activity.

right *adv.* **1** [late 16C+] (*also* **rightly, right smart**) totally, completely. **2** [mid-19C+] (*also* **rite**) used for emphasizing how good or bad someone or something is, e.g. *a right bastard*, *a right good 'un*. **3** [1900s–20s] (*US Und.*) of a criminal, under protection from corrupt authorities. **4** [1910s+] (*US*) properly; thus *get (one) right*, to capture 'dead to rights'.

IN PHRASES

❑ **do it up right** *v.* [ext. of DO IT UP *under* DO IT *v.*[1]] [20C+] to carry out fully and correctly, to achieve a set objective. ❑ **do up right** *v.* [1970s] to look after.

right *phr.* (*also* **yeah, right**) [1980s+] a dismissive, sarcastic phr. 'sure, I (don't) believe you'.

right down *adv.* [early 19C–1920s] a general intensifier: completely, utterly, absolutely.

right enough *phr.* [late 19C+] indeed, certainly.

IN PHRASES

❑ **that's right enough** [late 19C+] that's satisfactory, within its limits, as far as you may be concerned (but not me).

righteo! *excl. see* RIGHTO! *excl.*

righteous *n.* [joc. mispron.] [1900s–10s] (*Aus.*) riotous behaviour; also as *adj.*

righteous *adj.* [from SE, with undertones of the Biblical sense of 'God on one's side'] **1** [late 19C] (*UK Und.*) legitimate. **2** [late 19C] honest, the truth. **3** [1930s+] (*orig. US black*) honest, trustworthy, honourable. **4** [1930s+] of things, esp. drugs, excellent, first-rate. **5** [1930s+] attractive, beautiful. **6** [1960s+] ideologically pure. **7** [1970s] (*UK black*) respectable. **8** [1970s] extreme, very great. **9** [1980s] as an intensifier.

IN COMPOUNDS

❑ **righteous bush** *n.* [BUSH *n.*[1] (5a)] [1940s+] (*drugs*) marijuana. ❑ **righteous jones** *n.* [JONES *n.*[1] (1)] [1950s+] (*drugs*) a severe drug addiction. ❑ **righteous man** *n.* [mid-19C] (*UK Und.*) a housebreaker. ❑ **righteous moss** *n.* (*also* **righteous grass**) [MOSS *n.* (2b)/GRASS *n.*[1] (2)] [1940s+] (*US black*) white people's hair. ❑ **righteous nod** *n.* [NOD *n.*[1] (1)] [1940s] (*US black*) a good night's sleep. ❑ **righteous rags** *n.* [RAGS *n.* (2)] [1940s] (*US black*) expensive, well-cut, fashionable clothes. ❑ **righteous riff** *n.* [RIFF *n.* (1)] [1940s] (*US black*) good conversation, inspiring, intelligent talk. ❑ **righteous yellow** *n.* [YELLOW *n.* (4)] [1920s–40s] (*US black*) an attractive, light-skinned young woman.

IN PHRASES

❑ **do righteous** *v.* [1950s+] (*US*) to do good (to).

righteous *adv.* [RIGHTEOUS *adj.*] [1960s+] (*US black*) absolutely, completely.

righteous! *excl.* [RIGHTEOUS *adj.* (4)] [1990s+] an affirmative excl., absolutely!, sure!

righteously *adv.* [RIGHTEOUS *adj.*] **1** [1940s+] openly, undisguisedly, intensely. **2** [1970s+] honestly, dependably, with integrity.

right-ho *v.* [RIGHT-HO! *excl.*] [1940s] to agree.

right-ho! *excl. see* RIGHTO! *excl.*

rightid *adj.* [1990s+] sensible.

rightie *n.* (*also* **righty**) (*US*) **1** [1910s+] a person who has lost one or both their limbs on their right side (arm and leg). **2** [1940s] right-handedness. **3** [1940s+] a right-hander.

rightly *adv. see* RIGHT *adv.* (1).

righto *adj.* [1910s] (*Aus.*) excellent, admirable.

righto! *excl.* (*also* **rhighty-o! righteo! right-ho! rightio! right-oh! righty-ho!**) [late 19C+] certainly! yes!

right on *adj.* [RIGHT ON! *excl.*] [1960s+] **1** absolutely correct. **2** politically correct, ideologically pure.

right on *adv.* [RIGHT ON *adj.*] [1950s] absolutely, completely, unreservedly.

right on! *excl.* [abbr. earlier *right on T/right on time*; the later use implied movement/progress rather than chronology] [1910s+] an excl. of encouragement, approval: excellent! perfect! exactly right! orig. black use but taken up by white hippies, radicals etc.

rights and wrongs *n.* [rhy. sl.] [1980s] (*Aus.*) a pair of thongs, i.e. footwear.

right sort *n.* [play on SE] [early–mid-19C] an alcoholic drink, esp. gin.

right stuff *n.* **1** [late 19C+] any alcoholic drink, esp. in phr. *a drop of the right stuff.* **2** [late 19C+] an admirable person. **3** [1920s–30s] money. **4** [1930s] attractive women.

righty *n. see* RIGHTIE *n.*

righty-ho!/righty-o! *excl. see* RIGHTO! *excl.*

right you are! *excl.* (*also* **right you got! right you is!**) [mid-19C+] a general excl. of agreement.

rigid *adj.* [1960s+] drunk and passed out.

rigi-dig *adj. see* RIDGIE-DIDGIE *adj.*

rig-out *n.* (*also* **rig-up**) [ext. RIG *n.*[3] (1)] [early 19C+] a suit of clothes, an outfit.

rig out *v. see* RIG *v.*[1].

rigsby *n.* [RIG *n.*[1] (1)] [mid-16C–early 17C] a wanton, promiscuous woman.

rig-up *n.*[1] [RIG *n.*[2] (1)] [1990s+] (*US black*) an unpleasant, intolerable situation.

rig-up *n.*[2] *see* RIG-OUT *n.*

rig up *v. see* RIG *v.*[1].

riha *n. see* RIAH *n.*

Rikki Lake *adj.* [rhy. sl.; ult. US tabloid talk show host *Rikki Lake* (b.1968)] [2000s] counterfeit, fake.

riley *n. see* LIFE OF RILEY *n.*

rileyed *adj.* [typical Irish surname *Riley* (plus *Reilly* and *O'Reilly*) and thus the stereotyping of the Irish as drunkards; the spec. source is the stage production of *The Mulligan's Silver Wedding* 'a low life comedy' in Feb. 1881, in which was featured a song 'John Riley's Always Dry' which listed the eponymous Riley's prodigious drinking] [late 19C–1930s] (*US*) drunk.

rily *phr.* [1940s] (*US*) affectionate acronym used in telegrams: *remember I love you.*

rim *n.* [2000s] (*US*) an automobile tyre.

rim *v.* [REAM *v.*] [1940s+] (*US*) **1** to cheat, to swindle. **2** to cause failure, to ruin someone's chances, esp. by deception. **3** (*usu. gay*) to stimulate the anus with the lips and tongue; thus *rimming*, the action of this licking [var. *REAM (OUT) under* REAM *v.*/SE *ream*, to stretch, to scrape out].

IN COMPOUNDS

❑ **rim job** *n.* (*also* **rimming job**) [JOB *n.*[2] (2)] [1970s+] an act of anilingus. ❑ **rim queen** *n.* [-QUEEN *sfx* (3)] [1950s+] a homosexual who enjoys anilingus.

rimadona *n.* [puns on SE *primadonna*/RIM *v.* (3)] [1960s] (*gay*) a sodomite, a male homosexual.

rimble-ramble *n.* [late 17C; 1910s] nonsense, thus *rimble-ramble*, nonsensical, absurd.

rimmer *n.* [RIM *v.* (3)] [1970s+] someone who stimulates another's anus with their tongue.

rimming *n.* [RIM *v.* (3)] [1970s+] (*orig. US*) anilingus.

rim slide *n.* [the fart *slides* from the *rim* of the anus] [1960s+] (*US prison*) a silent but foul-smelling fart.

rince *v.* (*also* **rinse**) [19C] to drink.

rinctum *n.* (*also* **rinktum**) [US regional *rinctum*, a gadget, something that has no name or which one prefers not to name] [1970s+] (*US black*) the rectum, the anus.

rind *n.* [play on CRUST *n.*[2] (1)] **1** [late 19C+] cheek, impudence, effrontery. **2** [1920s–40s] (*US black*) the human skin.

ring *n.* **1** as a 'circular' part of the body. (**a**) [late 16C–18C] the vagina. (**b**) [late 19C+] the anus, the buttocks; thus *ring-snatcher*, a sodomite, *ring-snatching*, sodomy. (**c**) [1940s] anal intercourse, sodomy. (**d**) [2000s] the mouth. **2** (*UK Und.*) with ref. to money [? SE *ring*, thus an object worth money, or the ringing noise the cash makes as it is thrown from the coach/into the begging bowl]. (**a**) [17C] the money that is stolen by a highwayman. (**b**) [late 17C–early 19C] money that is procured by begging. **3** [1910s+] (*Aus.*) the site of a two-up game. **4** [1990s+] (*W.I.*) in pl., firearms [? the circular barrels]. **5** *see* RINGER *n.* (2a). **6** *see* RINGER *n.* (2b).

IN COMPOUNDS

❑ **ringbark** *v. see* separate entry. ❑ **ringburner** *n.* [RING *n.* (1b) + SE *burner*] [1960s+] (*UK society*) diarrhoea, or very painful defecation. ❑ **ring jerk** *n. see* CIRCLE JERK *n.* ❑ **ring master** *n.* [1990s+] a male homosexual. ❑ **ringpiece** *n.* [RING *n.* (1b)] **1** [1930s+] the anus; thus (1990s+) *ringpiece licker*, an anilinguist. **2** [2000s] a general term of abuse. ❑ **ring raider** *n.* [1990s+] a male homosexual, a sodomite. ❑ **ring snatcher** *n.* [1960s–70s] a sodomite; thus *ring-snatching*, sodomy. ❑ **ring-sting** *n.* (*also* **ring-stinger**) [1990s+] a painful act of defecation, attributed to a meal with an excess of hot spices.

IN PHRASES

❑ **ask for the ring** *v.* [1950s+] to perform anal intercourse. ❑ **bit of ring** *n.* [1930s+] anal intercourse. ❑ **black ring** *n.* [19C] the vagina. ❑ **bring one's ring up** *v.* [1970s+] to vomit violently. ❑ **buy the ring** *v.* [1980s+] to perform anal intercourse. ❑ **cracked in the ring** *adj.* [note Williams: 'Gold coins were very thin, so liable to fracture [...] The inscription around the coin's circumference was enclosed within two rings. When a crack extended past the inner ring, the coin lost currency'] [late 16C–19C] deflowered. ❑ **lose one's ring** *v.* [late 19C–1900s] of a woman, to lose one's virginity. ❑ **put a ring around** *v.* [image of *ringing* important dates on a calendar] [1950s+] (*N.Z.*) to be sure of, to be certain of, esp. in phr, *you can put a ring around that one.* ❑ **ring-dang-do** *n.* [RING *n.* (1a)] **1** [1930s+] (*also* **ringadangdoo, ring-a-rang-roo**) the vagina. **2** [1950s+] (*Aus.*) a spree, a party. **3** [1950s+] (*US*) a complicated affair, a rigmarole. ❑ **running at the ring** *n.* [SE *run at the ring*, to compete for a circlet of metal suspended from a post which each of a number of riders endeavoured to carry off on the point of his lance] [late 16C–17C] (adulterous) sexual intercourse. ❑ **spew one's ring** *v.* (*also* **puke one's ring, throw up one's ring**) [1960s+] **1** to be violently sick. **2** in fig. use, to talk openly, candidly.

SE in slang uses

IN COMPOUNDS

❑ **ring chopper** *n.* [mid-16C] (*UK Und.*) a swindler who sells counterfeit gold rings. ❑ **ring dropper** *n. see* RING FALLER *n.* ❑ **ring dropping** *n. see* separate entry. ❑ **ring faller** *n. see* separate entry. ❑ **ring pigger** *n.* [ety. unknown] [mid–late 16C] a drunkard.

IN PHRASES

❑ **have a ring through one's nose** *v.* **1** [1960s] (*US gambling*) to bet heavily when losing badly, hoping to get even. **2** [1960s+] (*US black/campus*) to be obsessed, to the point of foolishness, with one other person, usu. a lover, by whom one can be led.

ring *v.* **1** in senses of change, alteration [fig. use of abbr. SE phr. *ring the changes*]. (**a**) [mid-18C] (*UK Und.*) to change a good coin for a counterfeit. (**b**) [mid-18C+] to change, to alter; thus *ringing castors*, changing hats, typically by going to some public place, stealing an expensive hat from where it has been deposited and leaving a cheap one; *ring togs*, to change clothes. (**c**) [mid-19C] to desert, i.e. a lover. (**d**) [mid-19C] (*UK Und.*) used of individuals or groups, to substitute, to swap. (**e**) [mid-19C] to substitute cards. (**f**) [mid–late 19C] (*UK Und.*) to be disturbed in the act of a robbery, and thus having to flee without the goods. (**g**) [late 19C+] to cheat. (**h**) [late 19C+] (*US*) to illegally substitute a horse for another in a horserace. (**i**) [1900s] to substitute crooked dice. (**j**) [1910s] (*US Und.*) as *ring up*, to assume a disguise. (**k**) [1940s+] to alter a car for the purposes of using it as a getaway vehicle, hold-up van etc, or for reselling it to an unsuspecting customer. **2** [late 19C+] (*Aus.*) to be the most successful shearer in a shed. [RINGER *n.* (1a); ult. SE *ring the bell*, to win a victory]. **3** [1960s] to open and then steal the contents of a cash register [the ring of the 'no change' key on an old-fashioned till].

IN COMPOUNDS

❑ **ring job** *n.* [JOB *n.*[2] (2)] [1990s+] (*UK Und.*) a car that has been 'ringed', i.e. has had its identification changed for illicit resale.

IN PHRASES

□ **ring in** *see* separate entries. □ **ring it on** *v. see* separate entry. □ **ring the changes** *v. see* separate entry.

SE in slang uses

IN COMPOUNDS

□ **ring-stiff** *n. see under* STIFF *n.*[1].

IN PHRASES

□ **ring a peal (in a man's ears)** *v.* [late 18C–early 19C] to scold, usu. of a wife scolding her husband. □ **ring a tatt into** *v. see under* TAT *n.*[2]. □ **ring one's chimes** *v.* [1970s+] (*orig. US*) **1** to excite one's attention, to enthuse. **2** to have an orgasm. **3** to pressurize. □ **ring one's tail** *v.* [RINGTAIL *n.*[2] (1)] [20C+] (*Aus.*) in a game, to surrender, to give in. □ **ring someone's bell** *v. see under* BELL *n.*[1]. □ **ring the bell (on)** *v. see under* BELL *n.*[1].

ring-a-ding *n.* [pun] [1980s] a Bell's whisky.

ring-a-ding *adj.* (*also* **ring-a-ding-ding**) [the image of celebratory bell-ringing] **1** [1950s–60s] a term of approval for a beautiful woman. **2** [1990s+] perfect, ideal.

ring-a-rang-roo *n. see* RING-DANG-DO *under* RING *n.*

ring around the rosy *n.* [the children's game] **1** [1920s–60s] (*US*) a waste of time, a lightweight matter. **2** [1960s+] (*US gay*) an orgy.

ringbark *v.* [2000s] (*N.Z.*) to break wind.

ringbarked *adj.* [SE *ringbark*, to kill a tree by removing a ring of bark from the trunk] **1** [1980s+] (*N.Z.*) circumcised. **2** [2000s] worn out.

ringbolt *v.* [the use of SE *ringbolts* on ships] [1960s+] (*N.Z.*) to obtain a free ship voyage by posing as a crew member.

ring-ding *n.*[1] (*W.I.*) **1** [1900s] hilarity, lively entertainment. **2** [1940s] a quarrel.

ring-ding *n.*[2] [? a punch-drunk boxer who has 'bells ringing' in his head] [1950s+] (*US*) a fool, a second-rate person, a no-hoper.

ringdinger *n.* [1910s] (*US*) a person or object of excellence.

ring dropping *n.* **1** [late 18C–19C] a swindle whereby some valuable object is dropped in the road, where it is found by a potential victim. This leads to an encounter, after which the victim is either lured into a fixed game or, in the case of the (fake) valuable, persuaded by the trickster to buy it, claiming that while they should share the profits, he, the con-man, will sell his share and let the victim have the whole benefit. **2** [late 19C] a term of scorn, 'equivalent to "tell your grandmother to suck eggs"' (Ware); so common had sense 1 above become that anyone could spot a ring-dropper.

ringer *n.* **1** (*Aus.*) in senses of excellence. (**a**) [late 19C+] (*also* **wringer**) the fastest and best shearer in a shed. (**b**) [late 19C+] an expert; anything or anyone outstanding or superlative of its/their kind. **2** with ref. to counterfeiting, faking. (**a**) [mid-19C+] (*orig. US*) (*also* **ring, ringer-in, wringer**) a fake; someone posing as a person they are not; esp. a pool or bowling hustler who pretends not to be an expert. (**b**) [late 19C+] (*also* **ring**) a simulacrum; someone who looks exactly like another, also of an object. (**c**) [late 19C+] a horse or dog (occas. other animal) substituted either for a better or a worse animal for the purposes of those betting either for or against it. (**d**) [late 19C+] someone who illegally substitutes a horse or animal in a race. (**e**) [1940s] one who uses a number of disguises (of themselves and their cars) during the committing of a crime. **3** [1910s] (*Aus.*) a coward. **4** [1920s] (*US Und.*) one who inteferes in another criminal's activities. **5** [1920s–40s] (*US tramp*) a doorbell. **6** [1960s] (*S.Afr.*) an accomplice. **7** [1960s+] with ref. to car dealing. (**a**) a second-hand car made up to look better than it is. (**b**) someone who specializes in stealing then improving second-hand cars for sale in the UK or Europe. (**c**) a false registration plate attached to a stolen motor vehicle; thus the thief who uses one, and the car itself.

ringerangeroo *n.* [nonce-word, but ? ref. to RING *n.* (1a)] [1930s+] (*US*) the vagina.

ring faller *n.* (*also* **ring dropper**) [RING DROPPING *n.*] [mid-16C–mid-19C] a con-man who plays a trick of dropping a fake valuable object in the road and offering to let their victim buy it so they can have all the supposed profit.

ringie *n.* [1940s+] (*Aus./N.Z.*) the keeper of the RING *n.* (3) in a game of two-up (a gambling game played by tossing two coins, bets being laid on the showing of two heads or two tails).

ring-in *n.* [RING IN *v.*[1]] [1920s+] (*Aus./N.Z.Und.*) **1** anything that has been fraudulently substituted for something else, typically a racehorse or dog. **2** a stacked deck of cards.

ring in *v.*[1] [ext. RING *v.* (1b)] **1** [early 19C+] to substitute fraudulently, e.g. one racehorse for another. **2** [mid-19C+] (*US*) to gain admission, to force one's way in, to impose. **3** [late 19C–1920s] to tell lies, to deceive. **4** [20C+] (*Aus./US*) (*also* **ring on**) to involve someone in something fraudulent; to subject someone to fraudulent acts. **5** [1900s] to involve.

ring in *v.*[2] **1** [late 19C] (*US Und.*) to attract, to ensnare. **2** [late 19C–1920s] (*US Und.*) to join, to associate with. **3** [1900s] (*US*) to obtain. **4** [1910s] (*US*) to use.

ring it *v.* [RINGTAIL *n.*[2] (1)] [1910s+] (*Aus.*) to act in a cowardly way.

ring it on *v.* [ext. RING *v.* (1b)] [1910s+] (*orig. Aus./N.Z.*) to outwit, to fool.

ring neck *n.* (*also* **wring neck**) [SE *wring a neck*] [20C+] (*W.I., Guyn.*) a tough, brawling person, esp. a woman.

ring off *v.* **1** [late 19C] (*US*) to tell someone to be quiet. **2** [1910s–20s] to stop talking (other than on a telephone).

ring off! *excl.* [telephone imagery] [late 19C–1920s] be quiet! shut up! stop doing that!

ring on *v. see* RING IN *v.*[1] (4).

Ringsend handshake *n.* (*also* **Ringsend uppercut**) [Ring's End – a rough area of Dublin] [1920s+] (*Irish*) a kick in the testicles.

ringside *n.* [boxing imagery] [1920s+] (*orig. US*) the tables nearest to the stage in a nightclub or similar establishment.

ringtail *n.*[1] [RING *n.* (1b) + TAIL *n.* (2)] **1** [20C+] the anus. **2** [1920s+] (*also* **ring tail wife**) a tramp's young homosexual companion.

ringtail *n.*[2] [SAusE *ringtail*, a possum, known for 'playing dead' when threatened] [1910s+] **1** (*Aus.*) a coward. **2** (*US*) an irritable, unpleasant person. **3** (*US*) a tramp (who is seen as inevitably ill-tempered). **4** (*US tramp*) a tramp who is a poor beggar and sponges off his peers or takes temporary employment. **5** (*US prison*) an informer.

ringtailed *adj.* [19C+] describing a person or thing that is superlative, unique, extraordinary, usu. positive but occas. negative.

ringtailed snorter *n.* (*also* **ringtailed roarer, ...peeler, ... squealer, ...tooter, ...whizzer, ringtail snorter**) [RINGTAILED *adj.* (1) + SE *snorter*, perhaps of dragon-like fire; a fantasy creature] [early 19C+] (*US*) an impressive person, usu. physically aggressive.

ring tail wife *n. see* RINGTAIL *n.*[1] (2).

ring the changes *v.* (*UK Und.*) **1** [19C+] to defraud, to deceive, esp. by passing counterfeit money or substituting a worse article for a better one; thus *change-ringer*, one who practises this form of fraud. **2** [early 19C] in fig. use; to manipulate facts and figures. **3** [early 19C] to use deceptive language (in a non-criminal context). **4** [late 19C] (*UK prison*) of a prisoner, to move surreptitiously from one companion to another in the exercise yard. **5** [late 19C–1920s] to adopt a series of variant disguises with the intention of confusing, thus *ringer*, one who practises this form of deception.

ring-ting *n.* [? the *ring* of a glass that indicates it is pure crystal] [1940s] (*W.I.*) the genuine article, the real thing.

ringy *adj.* [RINGTAIL *n.*[2] (2)] [1920s+] (*US*) ill-tempered, tetchy.

rinkle *n. see* WRINKLE *n.* (1).

rinktum *n. see* RINCTUM *n.*

rinky dink *n.* (*also* **rinky-do**) [ety. unknown] **1** [20C+] (*US*) a swindle, a deception; often as *GIVE SOMEONE THE RINKY-DINK* below. **2** [20C+] (*US*) an insignificant person. **3** [1960s] (*US campus*) an easy course. **4** [1960s] a second rate object. **5** *see* DINK *n.*[2] (4).

IN PHRASES

□ **give someone the rinky-dink** *v.* [1900s–40s] (*US*) to cheat, to swindle.

rinky-dink *adj.*[1] [rhy. sl.] [20C+] pink.

rinky-dink *adj.*[2] (*also* **rinky-dinky**) [ety. unknown; *OED* suggests link to jazz use *ricky-tick*, old-fashioned, monotonous rhythms] (*US*) **1** [1910s+] cheap, second-rate. **2** [1940s+] outdated, unfashionable.

IN COMPOUNDS

□ **rinky-dink joint** *n.* [JOINT *n.* (3b)] [1930s+] (*US black*) a cheap tavern or inn.

rino *n. see* RHINO *n.*[1].

rinse *n.* [RINSE *v.* (1)] [1980s] (*Aus.*) an ejaculation of semen.

rinse *v.* **1** [1980s+] (*Aus. prison*) to fellate; occas. to masturbate. **2** [1990s+] (*UK black*) to have sexual intercourse. **3** [2000s] (*W.I*) to exploit. **4** [2000s] to play a record. **5** [2000s] to reprimand. **6** *see* RINCE *v.*

rinsing *n.* [2000s] a reprimand, a telling-off.

rinsings *n.* [1930s–50s] (*US drugs*) the residue of the narcotic/water solution that remains after it has been strained through a cotton filter.

Rin Tin Tin *n.* [rhy. sl.] [1980s] (*Aus.*) gin.

riotpack *n.* [2000s] (*N.Z.*) a carton of wine or beer.

rip *n.*[1] **1** in senses of inferiority, worthlessness. (**a**) [late 18C–1910s] an exhausted, worn-out horse. (**b**) [late 18C+] a worthless person, a rake; usu. used of a (young) man, (Irish) occas. of a woman. **2** [1910s+] (*Aus. Und.*) a blow, a punch. **3** [1970s] (*US Und.*) a scar [SE *rip*, a tear]. **4** [2000s] with ref. to smoking [? one *rips* a cigarette paper from a pack to roll the cigarette]. (**a**) (*US prison*) a hand-rolled cigarette. (**b**) (*US drugs*) marijuana. **5** *see* RIP-OFF *n.*

DERIVATIVES

□ **rippish** *adj.* [? SE *rebrobate*] [late 18C] of a person, worthless.

IN PHRASES

□ **take the rip out of** *v.* [1990s+] to mock, to criticize, to attack verbally.

SE in slang uses

IN PHRASES

□ **from the rip** [1960s] (*N.Z.*) from the start.

rip *n.*[2] [1990s+] one pound sterling.

rip *v.* **1** in transitive uses [SE *rip*, to tear (off)]. (**a**) [20C+] (*US*) to steal, to rob. (**b**) [1940s+] (*orig. Aus.*) to annoy intensely; thus *wouldn't it rip you?* wouldn't it drive you mad? (**c**) [1970s] to kill, to murder. **2** [1920s+] to do without restraint [SE rip, to move fast]. **3** [1980s] (*US campus*) to fail. **4** [1980s+] to do very well, to be successful.

IN COMPOUNDS

□ **rip job** *n.* [JOB *n.*[2] (2)] [1990s+] (*US*) a negative attack, e.g. via a piece of critical journalism. □ **rip snorter** *n. see* separate entry. □ **ripstaver** *n. see* RIP SNORTER *n.* (1).

IN PHRASES

□ **rip and run** *v.* [1900s–70s] (*US black*) to move restlessly, to act in an aimless but frenzied manner. □ **rip her guts down** *v.* [1970s+] (*US black*) to copulate aggressively, sadistically, but with implication that both partners achieve mutual satisfaction. □ **rip into** *v.* (*also* **rip it into**) **1** [late 19C+] to start a fight; to attack physically. **2** [1910s+] (*also* **rip it off**) to criticize harshly. **3** [1960s+] to do something energetically, enthusiastically. **4** [1970s] (*Aus.*) of a man, to have sexual intercourse. □ **rip it up** *v.* [1950s+] to have a good time. □ **rip on** *v.* [1980s+] **1** (*US campus*) to criticize (behind someone's back), to nag. **2** (*US black*) to harass, to insult. □ **rip out** *v.* [mid-19C] (*US*) to talk without restraint, to swear. □ **rip shit** *see* separate entries. □ **rip, shit or bust** (*also* **rip, split or bust**) [ext. of *SHIT OR BUST under* SHIT *v.*] [1940s+] (*N.Z.*) a phr. describing a situation in which one forges on, irrespective of the consequences. □ **rip someone a new ass** *v. see* TEAR SOMEONE A NEW ASS *v.* □ **rip the rug** *v.* [var. on CUT THE RUG *v.*] [1970s] (*US campus*) to dance. □ **rip up** *v.* **1** [20C+] (*US Und.*) to rob on a large scale. **2** [1900s–60s] (*also* **rip someone up**) to abuse verbally, to tease.

IN EXCLAMATIONS

□ **rip me!** [mid-19C–1900s] a general excl. of anger, surprise.

rip and tear *n.* [RIP *v.* (1a)] [1940s] (*US Und.*) robbery without forethought or planning.

rip and tear *adj.* [RIP AND TEAR *n.*] [1900s–30s] (*US Und.*) unplanned, unsophisticated.

rip and tear *v.*[1] [20C use is rhy. sl.] [mid-19C; late 20C] to swear.

rip and tear *v.*[2] [1940s] (*US Und.*) of a confidence man, to operate at will, without fear of interference from the authorities; also as adj.

ripcord *n.* [1960s+] the small loop attached to the back of some men's shirts.

ripe *adj.* **1** [early 17C; 19C–1950s] drunk. **2** [mid-19C+] excessive, in poor taste, beyond the bounds of acceptability, e.g. phr. *a bit ripe, ripe old time.* **3** [mid-19C+] thoroughgoing, complete; esp. in phr. (*you*) *ripe bastard.* **4** [mid-19C+] appealing, sensible. **5** [mid-19C+] (*US campus*) attractive. **6** [20C+] (*W.I.*) old, esp. too old to work. **7** [20C+] of food, over-cooked, stale, poss. smelling bad; thus of people, places. **8** [1960s] angry, irritated.

IN COMPOUNDS

□ **ripe banana** *n. see under* BANANA *n.* □ **ripe fruit** *n. see under* FRUIT *n.*

rip-off *n.* (*also* **rip, ripoff**) [1970s+] **1** (*orig. US*) a fraud, a cheat, a disappointment. **2** an act of theft or robbery. **3** something stolen or plagiarized. **4** (*US prison*) a physical attack. **5** a thief.

IN COMPOUNDS

□ **rip joint** *n.* [JOINT *n.* (3b)] [1970s+] (*US campus*) any store that charges exorbitant prices to students.

rip off *v.* [SE *rip off*, to tear off] **1** [1910s] (*US*) to create, to make. **2** [1960s] to take, to secure (with no implication of theft). **3** [1960s+] (*US black*) to have sexual intercourse. **4** [1960s+] (*US black/prison*) to rape. **5** [1960s+] to steal (from). **6** [1960s+] (*orig. US*) to cheat, to defraud, esp. in drug deals. **7** [1970s] to raid. **8** [1970s+] to kill, to assassinate. **9** [1970s+] to beat up, to attack physically. **10** [1970s+] to satirize. **11** [1970s+] to copy, to plagiarize. **12** [1970s+] to exploit financially. **13** [1980s+] (*US black*) usu. of whites, to exploit, socially or economically, to place at a disadvantage.

IN COMPOUNDS

□ **rip-off artist** *n.* (*also* **rip-off merchant**) [ARTIST *n.* (1)/MERCHANT *n.* (1)] [1970s+] **1** a thief. **2** a prostitute who specializes in robbing her clients and as such is more thief than purveyor of commercial sex. **3** any form of cheat, emotional as well as material.

IN PHRASES

□ **rip off a piece** *v.* (*also* **rip off a hunk**) [SE *rip off*/RIP OFF *v.* (3) + PIECE *n.* (6)] [1930s+] (*US*) to seduce, to have sexual intercourse.

ripped *adj.*[1] [SE *ripped*, torn] [1960s+] **1** (*also* **rip, ripped off, ripped up**) (*orig. US*) extremely intoxicated by drink, drugs or a mixture. **2** unhappy, furious. **3** very unattractive.

IN PHRASES

□ **ripped out of one's gourd** *adj.* [GOURD *n.* (2)] [1970s+] (*US campus*) drunk. □ **ripped to the tits** *adj.* (*also* **ripped off one's ass, ripped to the gills**) [ASS *n.*/*TO THE TITS under* TIT *n.*[2]/*TO THE GILLS under* GILLS *n.*] [1970s+] (*orig. US*) very intoxicated by drink, drugs or a combination.

SE in slang uses

IN EXCLAMATIONS

□ **get ripped!** [1940s+] (*Aus.*) a general excl. of dismissal, be quiet! go to hell!

ripped *adj.*[2] [1980s+] (*orig. US campus*) well-built, muscled.

ripped off *adj.* [RIP OFF *v.* (6)] [1970s+] of people, exploited, stolen from.

ripper *n.*[1] **1** as a superlative [SE rip, to tear open, i.e. all uses 'tear open' the usual standards]. (**a**) [mid–late 19C] a very great lie. (**b**) [mid-19C+] an attractive young woman. (**c**) [mid-19C+] a first-rate man or woman, an excellent article, or thing. **2** in senses of violence [late 19C criminal Jack the *Ripper*, thus christened by the contemporary press]. (**a**) [late 19C+] a murderer who specializes in mutilation, often for sexual purposes. (**b**) [2000s] (*US prison*) a rapist. **3** [late 19C+] (*US Und.*) a tool used in the opening of a safe; thus the safebeaker who uses such a tool.

ripper *n.*^{2} [ext. RIP *n.*^{1} (1b)] [late 19C] a person who behaves recklessly.

ripper *n.*^{3} [RIPPED *adj.*^{1} (1)] [1960s–70s] (*drugs*) in pl., amphetamine.

ripper *adj.* [RIPPER *n.*^{1} (1a)] [1980s+] (*Aus.*) excellent, wonderful, perfect, first-class.

ripper! *excl.* [RIPPER *adj.*] [1980s+] (*N.Z.*) excellent! amazing!

ripperty man *n.* [1930s+] (*Aus.*) a confidence trickster.

ripping *adj.* [mid-19C+] excellent, first-rate, wonderful; thus adv. *rippingly*.

ripping *adv.* [RIPPING *adj.* (1)] **1** [mid-19C] wonderfully, in an excellent manner. **2** [1970s+] a general intensifier, completely, utterly.

ripping! *excl.* [RIPPING *adj.* (1)] [late 19C+] excellent! wonderful!

ripping-iron *n.* [1970s] (*W.I.*) a jacket with a back vent.

rippish *adj. see under* RIP *n.*^{1}.

ripple *n.* [? one fig. 'ripples' the surface] [1960s] (*US*) a try, an attempt.

rippling *n.* [1970s] (*US black*) enjoying oneself.

rip rap *v.* [rhy. sl. = TAP *v.*^{2} (3b)] [1930s+] to borrow money, thus *the rip-rap*, the act of obtaining such a loan.

rip-shit *adj.* [*RIP SHIT OUT OF* ***under*** RIP SHIT *v.*] **1** [1980s] afraid. **2** [1990s+] angry.

rip shit *v.* [SE *rip* + SHIT *n.*] (*also* **rip shit up**) [1980s+] **1** to have a party, to act energetically, to make a disturbance. **2** to excel, to do something really well or intensely.

IN PHRASES

❑ **rip shit and bust** *v.* [1980s+] (*N.Z.*) to make a big effort. ❑ **rip shit out of** *v.* [1980s+] (*orig. US*) to assault physically.

ripskated *adj.* [ety. unknown] [1990s+] (*US campus*) drunk.

rip snorter *n.* [SE *rip* + SNORTER *n.*^{2} (3)] **1** [mid-19C+] (*orig. US*) (*also* **ripstaver**) a remarkable or wonderful person or thing of which the speaker approves. **2** [1940s+] a very loud breaking of wind.

rip-snorting *adj.* (*also* **rip-staving, rip-sneezing**) [RIP SNORTER *n.* (1)] [mid-19C+] wonderful, very enjoyable.

ripsy rousers *n. see* RAMMY ROUSERS *n.*

rip van winkle *v.* [rhy. sl. = TINKLE *v.*] [20C+] to urinate.

rise *n.* **1** [late 19C+] an erection; thus *get/have a rise*, to get an erection, *give a rise*, of a woman, to give a man an erection. **2** [1940s+] in fig. use, a stimulus, excitement.

SE in slang uses

IN PHRASES

❑ **give someone a rise in the world** *v.* [pun] [1920s+] (*Aus.*) to kick someone's buttocks.

rise *v.*

SE in slang uses

IN PHRASES

❑ **rise a barney** *v. see under* BARNEY *n.*^{2}. ❑ **rise a plant** *v. see under* PLANT *n.* ❑ **rise up** *v.* [1990s+] (*US teen*) to go away, to leave alone.

rise and shine *n.* [rhy. sl.] [20C+] wine.

rise and shine! *excl.* [20C+] a joc. wake-up call; sometimes preceded by 'wakey-wakey!'; also as v.

riser *n.* **1** [1910s–60s] (*US Und.*) a surprise, a scare, an 'eye-opener'. **2** [1940s] (*US tramp*) an artificial sore.

rising *n.* [one stays in jail until the next *rising* of the sun] [1900s] (*Aus.*) a sentence of one night in jail.

rising blowback *n. see under* BLOWBACK *n.*

rising damp *n.* [rhy. sl.] [20C+] cramp.

risk cubes *n. see* CUBE *n.*^{1} (1).

risk it for a biscuit *v.* [1980s+] (*Irish*) to take a chance, esp. in a sexual context.

risky *adj.* **1** [late 19C] (*UK society*) clandestinely adulterous. **2** [1910s] (*W.I.*) flirtatious, bold, cheeky.

rispeck *v.* (*also* **respeck, respect**) [1980s+] (*W.I./UK black teen*) to hold someone or something in high esteem; also used as a greeting.

rispeck due *phr.* (*also* **respeck, respeck due, respect, respect due, rispeck due**) [1970s+] (*W.I./UK/US black teen*) a phr. used to accord the subject the respect they have earned on the basis of earlier positive or praiseworthy actions.

rispin *n.* [mid–late 18C] (*UK Und.*) a hangman.

risto *adj.* [1990s+] (*W.I.*) aristocratic, upper-class.

rit *n.* [abbr.] [1980s+] (*drugs*) a tablet of *Rit*alin.

rita *n.* [gay icon Hollywood star *Rita* Hayworth (1918–87)] [1940s–70s] (*S.Afr. camp gay*) a male prostitute.

rite *adv. see* RIGHT *adv.* (2).

rith *n.* [backsl.] [1910s–20s] the number three.

ritie *n.* [abbr.] [1980s+] (*drugs*) *Rit*alin (methylphenidate hydrochloride, a central nervous system stimulant related to amphetamine).

RITP *excl.* [*r*ip *i*nto *t*he *p*iss] [2000s] (*N.Z.*) drink up!

ritsy *adj. see* RITZY *adj.*

ritz *n.* [the chain of hotels established by César *Ritz* (1850–1918), esp. the *Ritz-Carlton* in New York City] [1920s+] glamour, elegance, wealth, sophistication; thus phr. *in the ritz*, living well; *this ain't the Ritz*, don't expect anything special; *ritz it*, v., to live luxuriously.

IN PHRASES

❑ **put on the ritz** *v.* [popularized by Irving Berlin's song 'Putting on the Ritz' (1929)] **1** [1920s+] (*orig. US*) to make a display of wealth or luxury, to dress stylishly. **2** [1930s] (*US*) to snub.

ritz *adj. see* RITZY *adj.*

ritz *v.* [RITZ *n.* (1)] [1920s–30s] (*US Und.*) to snub.

ritzy *n.* [RITZ *n.* (1)] [1950s] a smart, fashionable person.

ritzy *adj.* (*also* **ritsy, ritz**) [RITZ *n.* (1)+ sfx *-y*] [1920s+] **1** smart, chic, fashionable; wealthy, affluent. **2** pretentious, posturing, esp. in phr. *don't get ritzy with me.*

Riv *n.* (*also* **rivie, rivie hog**) [abbr.] [1970s+] (*US black*) a Buick *Riv*iera.

river *n. see* RIVER OOZE *n.*

SE in slang uses

IN COMPOUNDS

❑ **river rat** *n. see* separate entry.

IN PHRASES

❑ **down the river** **1** [late 19C+] serving time in prison [var. on *UP THE RIVER* below; *see also* *GO DOWN THE RIVER* below]. **2** [late 19C+] (*also* **down the Swanny**) finished, over and done, used up [a boat that has gone *down the river* has vanished from sight]. **3** [1920s] in debt. ❑ **go across the river** *v.* (*also* **go over the river, go over the Styx, ride old Charon's Ferry-Boat**) [the mythological River Styx across which dead Greeks were supposedly ferried by Charon on their way to Hades] [19C+] to die; thus *gone across*, dead. ❑ **go down the river** *v.* [the practice of selling an errant slave to a Mississippi sugar-cane plantation. The journey to the plantation, where work was especially hard, meant a trip 'down the river'] [1900s–40s] (*US, Southern*) to go to the state prison in Mississippi. ❑ **go up the river** *v.* [the Hudson *River*, which leads to Sing-Sing, New York State's main prison] [mid-19C+] to go to prison; thus phr. to get oneself into trouble. ❑ **over the river** [1910s] (*US Und.*) at Blackwell's Island prison, New York. ❑ **up the river** (*also* **up the big stream**) [orig. the penitentiary at Ossining ('Sing-Sing'), which is sited *up the river* from New York City] [late 19C+] (*orig. US*) in prison; sometimes ext. as *sanitarium/summer hotel up the river*.

riverina *n.* [rhy. sl. = DEANER *n.*] [1940s+] (*Aus.*) one shilling.

River Lea *n.* [rhy. sl.] **1** [mid-19C] tea. **2** [late 19C–1900s] the sea.

River Murray *n.* [rhy. sl.] **1** [20C+] (*Aus.*) a curry. **2** [1990s+] (*Aus.*) in pl., phr. of affirmation, assurance, encouragement [*River Murrays* = NO WORRIES (MATE) *phr.*].

River Nile *n.* [rhy. sl.] [20C+] a smile.

river ooze *n.* (*also* **river, river Ouse**) [rhy. sl. = BOOZE *n.* (1)] [20C+] alcohol, liquor; thus as phr. *on the ooze*, drinking or drunk.

IN PHRASES

❑ **on the (river) ooze** [1960s–80s] drinking.

river rat *n.* **1** [19C] a thief who specializes in stripping the corpses of those who drowned in London's River Thames. **2** [1920s–40s] (*US Und.*) a thief who steals on the river front. **3** [1930s] (*US*) a dock labourer.

River Tyne *n.* [rhy. sl.] [20C+] wine.

riveted *adj.* **1** [early–mid-18C; 1930s] married. **2** [1970s+] (*UK society*) fascinated by; thus *riveting*, absolutely fascinating.

rivets *n.* (*also* **iron rivets, rivits**) [fig. use of SE on pattern of BRAD *n.*[1] (2); *HORSE-NAILS under* HORSE *n.*] [mid-19C–1930s] money.

rivie/rivie hog *n. see* RIV *n.*

riz *adj.* [SE *rise*] [mid-19C+] (*Irish/US*) annoyed.

rizolin *n.* [ROLL *v.* (4b) + -IZ- *infix*] [1930s–50s] (*US drugs*) a term meaning 'the drugs are on their way'.

roach *n.* [joc. uses of SE *cockroach*] **1** as a negative descriptor. (**a**) [1900s] (*US*) an inferior racehorse. (**b**) [1920s] (*US Und.*) a prostitute. (**c**) [1930s+] (*US*) a pej. term for a police officer; a prison guard. (**d**) [1950s+] (*US campus*) an unattractive and/or unpopular man or woman. **2** [1930s+] in drug uses. (**a**) marijuana. (**b**) a marijuana cigarette. (**c**) the unsmoked, final portion of a marijuana or hashish cigarette. (**d**) the cardboard 'filter' of a cannabis cigarette, often made of a rolled up piece of a Rizla packet. (**e**) a marijuana smoker. (**f**) the unsmoked portion of a cigarette.

IN COMPOUNDS

❑ **roach bender** *n.* [1940s] (*drugs*) a marijuana smoker. ❑ **roach clip** *n.* (*also* **roach holder, roach pick**) [1950s+] (*drugs*) a small spring clip or pair of tweezers used to hold the last fragments of a marijuana cigarette, which is otherwise too hot to hold in one's fingers. ❑ **roach hotel** *n.* [1980s+] (*US drugs*) a collection of cannabis cigarette stubs that can be recycled [pun on US *Roach Motel*, a patented cockroach trap].

IN PHRASES

❑ **blast a roach** *v.* [1950s+] (*drugs*) to inhale deeply on a marijuana cigarette.

SE in slang uses

IN COMPOUNDS

❑ **roach coach** *n.* (*US*) **1** [1970s–80s] the 'coach' or economy section of a passenger aircraft. **2** [1980s+] a food service wagon. ❑ **roach hotel** *n.* [1980s+] (*US*) (*also* **roach trap, roach motel, roach palace**) a cheap, dilapidated, dirty hotel. ❑ **roach killers** *n.* [abbr. COCKROACH KILLERS *n.*] [1960s] highly pointed shoes. ❑ **roach-palace** *adj.* [2000s] (*US*) infested with cockroaches. ❑ **roach stompers** *n.* [2000s] (*US*) heavy, unfashionable shoes.

IN PHRASES

❑ **put roach on one's bread** *v.* [SE *cockroach*] [20C+] (*W.I.*) to be sexually unfaithful, to cuckold.

roach *v.* [SAmE *roach*, to cut (a horse's mane) short, so that it stands up like the bristles of a hog] [1900s] (*US*) to cut one's hair very short.

roach and dace *n.* [rhy. sl.] [20C+] the face.

roaches/roachies *n. see* ROCHE *n.*

road *n.* **1** in sexual senses, playing on RIDE *v.* (1a). (**a**) [late 16C] a prostitute. (**b**) [17C] the vagina. **2** [2000s] (*UK black*) the 'real world', which exists on the streets, rather than in the protected environments of home, office, family etc [var. on STREET, THE *n.*].

SE in slang uses

DERIVATIVES

❑ **roadster** *n.* [late 19C+] (*Aus.*) a tramp, someone who has no fixed abode.

IN COMPOUNDS

❑ **road-agent** *n.* [late 19C–1900s] (*US West*) a highway robber. ❑ **road apple** *n.* [APPLE *n.*[4]] [20C+] horse manure. ❑ **road brew** *n.* (*also* **roadies, road sauce**) [BREW *n.*[1] (4)/dimin. sfx *-ies*/SAUCE *n.*[1] (6)] [1970s+] (*US campus*) beer. ❑ **road bull** *n. see* BULL *n.*[5] (9). ❑ **road dog** *n.* (*also* **roadie**) [DOG *n.*[2] (2c)] [1980s+] (*US black/prison*) an extremely intimate friend. ❑ **road dope** *n.* [DOPE *n.*[1] (6); the drug's use during long-distance driving] [1980s+] (*drugs*) amphetamines. ❑ **roadhog** *n.* [SE *roadhog*, a careless, selfish driver] **1** [1920s–30s] (*US tramp*) a tramp who is perpetually riding the trains. **2** [2000s] a girl or young woman who follows rock bands and offers herself for sex. ❑ **road kid** *n.* [late 19C–1940s] (*US*) a young tramp; the (catamitic) companion of an older JOCKER *n.*[1] (2). ❑ **roadkill** *n.* (*also* **road kill, road pizza**) (*orig. US*) **1** [1970s+] any form of creature (usu. small animals or birds) killed by a vehicle on the roads and used for food. **2** [1970s+] a person or object that is considered absolutely useless, i.e. 'dead meat'; also attrib. **3** [1990s+] a recently shaved vagina. ❑ **road louse** *n. see under* -LOUSE *sfx.* ❑ **road maggot** *n.* [1980s] (*US campus*) a camper van or recreational vehicle. ❑ **road making** *adj.* (*also* **road up for repairs**) [mid–late 19C] used of a woman who is menstruating. ❑ **road man** *n.* [1920s–50s] (*US*) an itinerant thief. ❑ **road queen** *n.* [-QUEEN *sfx*] [1970s+] (*US gay*) a gay hitch-hiker, looking for sex with those who pick him up. ❑ **road rash** *n.* [1970s+] (*orig. US*) cuts, scratches and grazes that come with falling off a motor-cycle or skateboard. ❑ **road roller** *n.* [1900s–30s] (*N.Z.*) an unsophisticated country person, a bushman; an itinerant worker. ❑ **road sauce** *n. see* ROAD BREW above. ❑ **road sister** *n.* [1920s] (*US tramp*) a female tramp. ❑ **road smart** *adj.* [1990s+] (*US tramp*) experienced as a tramp. ❑ **road stake** *n.* [1920s–60s] (*US tramp*) money. ❑ **road starver** *n.* [the pockets would be used to hold food for a journey] [late 19C] (*UK tramp*) a long coat made without pockets. ❑ **road whore** *n.* [1980s+] (*US campus*) a promiscuous woman. ❑ **roadwise** *n.* [-WISE *sfx*] [1930s–40s] (*US*) of a tramp, 'wise' in the ways of travelling. ❑ **road work** *n.* [WORK *n.* (1)] [1920s–50s] (*US*) crimes committed by an itinerant thief.

IN PHRASES

❑ **down the road** *adj.* [Mile End *Road*, London, a favoured costermongers' market] [mid–late 19C] **1** stylish, fashionable. **2** vulgar, showy. ❑ **give someone the road** *v.* [1910s+] (*US/US black*) to avoid, to ignore. ❑ **hit the road** *v. see* separate entry. ❑ **on the road** [2000s] (*N.Z.*) unemployed. ❑ **over the road** (*also* **up the road**) [late 19C–1930s] in prison. ❑ **road-bums' Coronas** *n.* [a *Corona* is an expensive Cuban cigar] [1930s] tobacco that is extracted from discarded 'fag-ends' and recycled in a pipe or 'roll-up'. ❑ **road less travelled** *n.* [play on new age book title *The Road Less Traveled*: A New Psychology of Love, Traditional Values and Spiritual Growth by M. Scott Peck (1979)] [1990s+] the female anus as a hosting place for a penis. ❑ **road to a christening** *n.* (*also* **road to heaven, way to heaven**) [19C] the vagina.

roader *n.* [abbr. Mile End *Road*] [late 19C] (*UK/East End*) a young man who disports himself on the Mile End Road, London, in his finest clothes, usu. with his woman, on a Sunday.

roadie *n.* **1** [1960s+] a member of a rock band's support unit who sets up and dismantles stage, equipment etc [they go 'on the road' with the band]. **2** [1980s+] (*N.Z.*) one employed in road maintenance [they lit. work on it]. **3** *see* ROAD DOG *under* ROAD *n.*

roadie *v.* [1970s+] to be a ROADIE *n.* (1).

roadies *n. see* ROAD BREW *under* ROAD *n.*

Roadwatch accent *n. see* DART ACCENT *n.*

roaf *n. see* ROUF *n.*

roak *v.* [? abbr. CROAK *v.*[2] (2)] [1970s] (*US black*) to beat savagely about the head.

roapies *n. see* ROCHE *n.*

roar *n.* [late 19C–1960s] (*US*) **1** an uproarious joke. **2** a complaint.

roar *v.* **1** [17C–mid-19C; 1950s] to riot; to act in a riotous manner. **2** [1900s–40s] to complain; to inform.

IN PHRASES

❑ **roar like a town bull** *v.* [TOWN BULL *under* TOWN *n.*[2]] [late 18C–early 19C] to make a good deal of noise. ❑ **roar up** *v.* **1** [1910s] to talk loudly, to abuse. **2** [1910s+] (*Aus.*) to scold, to tell off, to reprimand.

roaration *n. see* RORATION *n.*

roaratorious *adj. see* RORTORIOUS *adj.*

roarer *n.* **1** [late 16C–19C] a riotous hooligan, a roisterer; an outstanding performer [SE *roar*, to riot, to behave in a boisterous manner; Griffiths, *Chronicles of Newgate* (1884), quotes an indictment of 1311 and adds that: 'The term "roarer" and "roaring boy", signifying a riotous person, was in use in Shakespeare's day, and still survives in slang.']. **2** [19C–1940s] a broken-down horse [the sound of its breathing]. **3** [mid-19C] in fig. senses. (**a**) (*US*) something superlatively good. (**b**) something notably large. **4** [1940s] (*US*) a noisy argument. **5** [1950s] a riotous good time.

roaring *adj.* [ROAR *v.* (1)] **1** [17C+] boisterous, exuberant. **2** [mid-19C+] a general intensifier, extreme, uncompromising.

IN COMPOUNDS

❑ **roaring fou** *see* separate entries. ❑ **roaring horn** *n.* (*also* **roaring jack**) [HORN *n.*[2] (1b)/JACK *n.*[3] (2)] [late 19C] (*Aus.*) an erection, esp. one that feels very demanding.

roaring *adv.* [ROARING *adj.*] [late 17C; mid-19C+] extremely, very, often in comb. *roaring drunk.*

roaring boy *n.* (*also* **roaring blade, ...girl, ...ruffian**) [ROARING *adj.* (1) + SE *boy*/BLADE *n.* (2a)/SE *girl/lad/ruffian*] [17C–19C] a riotous hooligan, a roisterer; of a girl or young woman, promiscuous, tom-boyish.

Roaring Forties *n.* (*also* **Forties**) [joc. use of ROARING *adj.* (1) + naut. jargon *Roaring Forties*, exceptionally rough seas that occur between latitudes 40° and 50° south, where strong westerly winds blow; formerly also applied to the part of the Atlantic Ocean between latitudes 40° and 50° north] [1920s–40s] (*US*) Broadway, New York City, in the area immediately around Times Square, spec. 40th Street to 49th Street.

roaring fou *n.* [FOU *adj.*[1]] [17C+] a drinking spree.

roaring fou *adj.* [FOU *adj.*[1]] [19C] extremely drunk, lit. roaring drunk.

roaring horsetails *n.* [rhy. sl.] [20C+] (*Aus.*) Aurora Australis.

roaring rain *n.* [rhy. sl.] [20C+] (*Aus.*) a train.

roaring ruffian *n. see* ROARING BOY *n.*

roart *n. see* RORT *n.*

roast *n.*[1] **1** [late 18C–1920s] a criticism. **2** [1900s] (*US campus*) a joke. **3** [1900s] (*US campus*) something that can be easily accomplished. **4** [1900s] (*US*) a disappointing entertainment. **5** [1950s+] (*Aus.*) a piece of information, usu. accusatory. **6** [1960s] (*US campus*) a difficult examination.

roast *n.*[2] [ROAST COCO *v.*] [1950s+] (*W.I.*) a second job, kept secret and thus part of the 'black economy'.

roast *n.*[3] *see SPIT ROAST under* SPIT *n.*[1].

roast *v.* [? play on *roast*, 'a roast', or as v. to give the subject 'a hot time'; according to Hotten, 1867 one can only be *roasted* by 'the whole company', when the teasing comes from one person only, it is *quizzing*] **1** [late 17C–early 19C; 1990s+] to arrest. **2** [mid-18C+] to jeer, ridicule or banter. **3** [mid-18C+] to criticize aggressively. **4** [mid-19C+] to give someone a tough questioning, to interrogate. **5** [late 18C; 1900s] to put at a disadvantage. **6** [late 19C] (*US*) to renege on one's debts or bills. **7** [1930s] to beat up. **8** [1940s] (*US Und.*) to die in the electric chair.

IN EXCLAMATIONS

❑ **roast me!** [late 19C] (*Aus.*) a general excl.

roast a time *v.* [20C+] (*W.I.*) to enjoy oneself thoroughly.

roast beef *n.* [rhy. sl.; Cockney pron. 'teef'] [20C+] teeth.

roast beef curtains *n. see BEEF CURTAINS under* BEEF *n.*[1].

roast coco *v.* [the habit of roasting coco-yams as the conclusion of the meal; thus fig. waiting for something desirable] [1950s] (*W.I.*) to plot, to scheme, to bide one's time.

roasted *adj.* [var. on BAKED *adj.*] [1990s+] intoxicated, usu. with drugs, sometimes drink.

roasted duck *n.* [rhy. sl. = FUCK *n.* (1a); unmentioned by Partridge or Franklyn, *Dict. of Rhyming Slang* (1960), this may be a nonce-word, invented by Isherwood and Auden in their play *The Dog beneath the Skin* (1935), *O how I cried when Alice died / The day we were to have wed! / We never had our Roasted Duck / And now she's a Loaf of Bread*] [1930s] sexual intercourse.

roastie *n. see* ROAST POTATO *n.*

roasting *n.* [ROAST *v.*] **1** [mid-19C+] a thorough criticism; verbal hostility. **2** [late 19C] (*US Und.*) police surveillance. **3** [1940s] (*US Und.*) the 'third degree'. **4** [2000s] a state of being held in suspense; also attrib. **5** [2000s] group sex, spec. the simultaneous penetration of a woman by two men, one by the mouth, one by the vagina; she is thus 'on the spit'.

roasting jack *n.* [pun on SE/JACK *n.*[3] (1)] [19C] the vagina.

roast joint *n.* [rhy. sl.; Cockney pron.] [20C+] a pint of beer.

roast me! *excl. see under* ROAST *v.*

roast meat *n.*

SE in slang uses

IN COMPOUNDS

❑ **roast-meat clothes** *n.* [the meat in question being the 'Sunday roast' and the clothes one's 'Sunday best' outfit; note naval jargon *roast-beef dress*, full uniform] [late 17C–early 19C] one's best clothes.

IN PHRASES

❑ **give roast meat and beat with the spit** *v.* [late 17C–18C] to offer an apparent compliment and then to abuse its recipient.

roast plantain for someone *v.* [1920s+] (*W.I.*) **1** to get ready to benefit from someone else's misfortune. **2** to plot actively to bring about this downfall.

roast pork *n.*[1] [rhy. sl.] **1** [1910s+] a talk; also as v. **2** [1940s+] a table fork.

roast pork *n.*[2] [1940s] (*W.I.*) a variety of cactus whose leaves resemble chunks of meat; such leaves can be roasted for medicinal use.

roast potato *n.* [rhy. sl.; pron. 'pertater'] [20C+] a waiter.

rob *n.* [abbr.] [1990s+] (*Aus. Und.*) a robbery.

rob *v.* [one's victim is 'robbed' of speech] [1980s+] (*US campus*) to silence with a witty remark or rejoinder.

SE in slang uses

IN PHRASES

❑ **rob blind** *v. see under* BLIND *adv.*[1]. ❑ **rob the cradle** *v.* [1920s+] (*orig. US*) to have a relationship with someone much younger than oneself. ❑ **rob the mail** *v.* [1930s] (*US tramp*) to steal food delivered to people's doorsteps early in the morning. ❑ **rob the ruffian** *n.* [BELLY RUFFIAN *under* BELLY *n.*] [19C] the vagina. ❑ **who's robbing this coach?** [a joke based on the bush-ranging era, cited at length in *DSUE*] [1930s+] (*Aus.*) mind your own business.

robardsmen *n. see* ROBERDSMEN *n.*

robberdy *n. see* RUBBEDY *n.*

robbo *n.* [the late 19C Sydney costermonger-turned-liveryman 'Four Bob *Robbo*' who specialized in undercutting his rivals] [late 19C–1900s] (*Aus.*) a cab; thus *robbo man*, a cab-driver.

rob-davy *n.* (*also* **roberdavy, rob-o'-davy**) [? SE *rob* + *Davy*, the Welsh name *Dafyyd*, anglicized as *Taffy*] [17C] metheglin or spiced mead.

roberdsmen *n.* (*also* **robardsmen, roberts men**) [early 14C SE *Roberdsmen*, a type of marauding vagabond, who were outlawed under an act of 1331; Ribton-Turner, *A History of Vagrants* (1887), notes the coincident 15C *Roberts men* who followed one Hugh Roberts, a former soldier and one of the leaders, with the better known Jack Cade (a.k.a. Jack Mendall) of the Peasants' Revolt; Roberts fled after the revolt and lived as an outlaw with one hundred other 'rakehells and vagabonds' until he was killed, as a follower of Edward IV, during the Wars of the Roses] [late 17C–early 19C] (*UK Und.*) 'the third (old) rank of the CANTING CREW *n.*', outlaw thieves who act, according to B.E., like real-life Robin Hoods.

·obert *n.* (*also* **roberto**) **1** [late 19C–1910s] (*Aus.*) a shilling [play on BOB *n.*[3] (2)]. **2** [late 19C–1950s] a police officer, usu. male [elaboration of BOBBY *n.* (1)].

Roberta Flack *n.* [rhy. sl.; ult. disco diva *Roberta Flack* (b.1937)] [1970s] (*Aus.*) **1** the bed; thus *hit the Roberta*, to go to bed [SACK *n.* (4)]. **2** dismissal from one's job [SACK *n.* (2a)].

·obert dinero *n.* [pun on DINERO *n.*/film star *Robert de Niro* (b.1943)] [1990s+] (*US teen*) money.

·obert e. *n.* [rhy. sl.; ult. *Robert E.* Lee, Confederate general (1807–70)] [20C+] **1** a knee. **2** an act of urination [= PEE *n.*[1] (2)].

·oberto *n. see* ROBERT *n.*

·oberts men *n. see* ROBERDSMEN *n.*

Robertson and Moffatt *n.* [rhy. sl.; the epon. Melbourne firm] [1940s+] (*Aus.*) a profit.

Robert Young *n.* [rhy.sl.; ult. US film/TV actor *Robert Young* (1907–98)] [1960s–80s] (*Aus.*) the tongue.

·obin *n.* **1** [mid-17–19C; 1950s+] the penis [20C+ use is US; note *robin* is the pet name for a servant's penis in the late 19C pornographic classic *The Modern Eveline* (the heroine's incestuous brother is named *Percy*)]. **2** [late 19C] a child beggar, 'standing about like a starving robin' (Ware) [a philanthropic clergyman, the Rev. Charles Bullock, organized a series of 'Robin dinners', at which he fed thousands of such unfortunate children]. **3** [late 19C–1910s] a penny [ety. unknown; perhaps mis-definition: the robin was engraved on a *farthing* rather than a penny].

(IN PHRASES)

❑ **pull one's robin** *v.* [1950s] to masturbate.

·obin hog *n.* [ety. unknown; ? simply derog. since PIG *n.* (2a) is not coined until early 19C] [early 18C] a constable.

Robin Hood *adj.* [rhy. sl.] [1910s–70s] good; thus as *no Robin Hood*, no good.

·obin hoods *n.* [rhy. sl.] [20C+] **1** (material) goods. **2** the woods.

·obin redbreast *n.* (*also* **redbreast**) [Charles Dickens, letter (18 April 1862): 'The Bow Street runners...had no other uniform than a blue dress-coat, brass buttons...and a bright red cloth waistcoat. The waistcoat was indispensable and the slang name for them was "red-breasts" in consequence'; founded in 1750 the Runners, London's first organized constables, were replaced by the Metropolitan Police in 1829] [early 19C] a Bow Street runner.

·obin ruddock *n. see* RUDDOCK *n.*

Robinson and Cleaver *n.* [rhy. sl.; ult. the defunct London department store] [20C+] a fever.

Robinson Crusoe *v.* [rhy. sl.] [late 19C–1950s] to do so, often as imper.

·ob my pal *n.* [rhy. sl. = GAL *n.* (1)] [1950s+] a woman.

·obo *n.* [abbr.] [1970s] (*US drugs*) *Robi*tussin.

·ob-o'davy *n. see* ROB-DAVY *n.*

·obot *n.* [1940s+] (*W.I.*) a privately owned vehicle, used to provide public transport when the usual drivers of such transport are on strike; as v. to drive.

Rob Roy *n.* [rhy. sl.; ult. Scot. hero *Rob Roy* McGregor (d.1734)] [19C] a boy.

·obustious *adj.* [SE mid-16C–mid-18C, thereafter condemned by Dr Johnson as 'low'] [mid-18C–late 19C] violent, boisterous, noisy, strongly self-assertive, pompous.

·oby douglas *n.* ['with one eye and a stinking breath' (Grose 1785); presumably f. a real person] [late 18C–early 19C] the posterior, the buttocks.

·oche *n.* (*also* **roaches, roachies, roapies, rochas dos**) [the manufacturer, *Roche*] [1990s+] (*drugs*) Rohypnol, better known as the 'date-rape' drug, as it is allegedly given to people to knock them out and facilitate their rape.

·ochester portion *n.* [orig. use is in a Kentish pvb] [late 17C–early 19C] the vagina, lit. 'two torn smocks and what Nature gave' (B.E.).

·ock, the *n.* **1** [mid-19C] (*UK Und.*) the prison at Gibraltar, used for transported UK felons. **2** [1930s–70s] (*also* **Big Rock**) Alcatraz Federal prison on Alcatraz Island, California. **3** [1950s] (*US Und.*) Florida State Penitentiary, Raiford. **4** [1960s+] Rikers Island prison, New York City.

rock *n.* **1** in monetary senses. (**a**) [mid-19C+] (*US*) one dollar; thus *half a rock*, 50 cents. (**b**) [1990s+] (*US prison*) one carton of prison cigarettes, the equivalent of $1 in a barter economy. **2** [20C+] a diamond. **3** [20C+] a man who is sturdy and solid both emotionally, physically and in his character. **4** in drug uses. (**a**) [1920s] opium. (**b**) [1940s–50s] a piece of hashish. (**c**) [1960s+] (*also* **rock cocaine**) cocaine, when in uncrushed form. (**d**) [1980s+] (*also* **rock crack**) crack cocaine; a piece of crack cocaine. (**e**) [1990s+] heroin, prior to being crushed to powder. (**f**) [2000s] methamphetamine, when in uncrushed form. **5** [1950s] (*US teen*) a large, tough person. **6** [1960s+] (*US prison*) a cellblock. **7** [1970s+] (*S.Afr.*) an Afrikaner. [abbr. ROCK SPIDER *n.*]. **8** [1980s+] (*US black*) a basketball. **9** [1990s+] (*US*) in fig. use, the essence, the 'bottom line'.

(IN COMPOUNDS)

❑ **rock attack** *n.* [1980s+] (*drugs*) a desire for crack cocaine. ❑ **rock cocaine** *n. see* sense 4c above. ❑ **rock crack** *n. see* sense 4d above. ❑ **rock crank** *n.* [CRANK *n.*[2] (4)] [1980s+] (*drugs*) methamphetamine. ❑ **rock fiend** *n.* [FIEND *n.* (2)] [2000s] (*US drugs*) a habitual user of crack cocaine. ❑ **rock head** *n.* [-HEAD *sfx* (4)] [1990s+] (*drugs*) a consumer of crack cocaine. ❑ **rock ho** *n.* [HO *n.* (1)] [2000s] (*US black*) a woman who takes crack cocaine; thus a general derog. ❑ **rock house** *n.* [1980s+] (*drugs*) a place where crack cocaine is sold and smoked. ❑ **rock kid** *n.* [KID *n.*[1] (4)] [1990s+] (*UK black/drugs*) a smoker of crack cocaine. ❑ **rock monster** *n.* [MONSTER *n.* (6)/SE *monster*?] [1980s] (*US drugs/campus*) an addict who is desperate for a dose of rock or crack cocaine; one who may steal to support their habit. ❑ **rock pipe** *n. see* PIPE *n.*[1] (3h). ❑ **rock star** *n.* [1980s+] (*drugs*) a smoker of crack cocaine, esp. a woman who trades sex for crack cocaine or money to buy crack cocaine.

(IN PHRASES)

❑ **rock out** *v.* [1980s+] (*drugs*) to collapse through an excessive consumption of crack cocaine.

SE in slang uses

pertaining to prison

(IN COMPOUNDS)

❑ **rock college** *n.* [COLLEGE *n.* (3)] [1980s+] (*N.Z.*) a prison. ❑ **rock crusher** *n.* **1** [20C+] (*US*) in prison uses [hard labour in the rock quarry]. (**a**) a convict. (**b**) a prison. **2** as a form of machine. (**a**) [1920s] (*US*) an automobile. (**b**) [1930s] (*orig. US black*) an accordian. ❑ **rockpile (cure)** *n. see* separate entries.

(IN PHRASES)

❑ **big rock** *n.* [1960s] (*US*) a prison.

general uses

(IN COMPOUNDS)

❑ **rock ape** *n. see under* APE *n.* ❑ **rock candy** *n.* [1920s–40s] (*US tramp/black*) diamonds. ❑ **rockchopper** *n.* (*also* **chopper, R.C.**) [used by Protestants as a derog. ref. to the original Irish immigrants, who were mainly convicts and, as such, condemned to hard labour; the common initials 'r.c.' are strengthening, but not the origin] [1940s+] (*Aus.*) a derog. term for a Roman Catholic. ❑ **rockhead** *n.* [-HEAD *sfx* (1)] [1920s+] (*US*) a stupid person, thus adj., *rock-headed*, very stupid. ❑ **rockhound** *n.* (*also* **rock sharp**) [-HOUND *sfx*/SHARP *n.*[1] (2)] [late 19C+] (*orig. US*) **1** a geologist. **2** an amateur mineralogist. ❑ **rock worker** *n.* [WORKER *n.*[1] (1)] [1940s] (*US Und.*) a seller of cheap jewellery.

(IN PHRASES)

❑ **rock of ages** *n. see* separate entry.

rock *adj.* **1** [1940s+] excellent, outstanding. [i.e. it knocks one off-balance]. **2** [2000s] very firm, adamant, uncompromising [SE *rock-hard*].

rock *v.*[1] **1** in senses of aggression. (**a**) [mid-19C–1940s] (*mainly US*) to throw rocks or stones at. (**b**) [1930s+] (*US black*) to trouble emotionally; to amaze. (**c**) [1980s+] (*US campus*) to fight with, to beat up. (**d**) [1980s+] (*US campus*) to suffer badly. **2** [2000s] (*drugs*) to make pure cocaine into crack cocaine.

rock *v.*[2] [Rom. *roker*, to talk] [late 19C+] to talk.

rock *v.*[3] [SE *rock*, to tremble, to move; orig. US black uses cognate with the sexual v. JAZZ *v.* (1) – the word *rock* works both as a style of music and a term for intercourse; e.g. in the 1922 song title 'My man rocks me (with one steady roll)'; for further details on sexual imagery of rock/blues *see* Cohen (ed.), *Studies in Slang* V (1997), pp.127 ff] **1** [20C+] to get drunk [one's unsteadiness]. **2** [1920s+] (*orig. US black*) to have sexual intercourse. **3** [1930s+] (*orig. US black*) of music and dancing, to make one move in a rhythmical manner. **4** in fig. uses. (**a**) [1930s+] to delight, to bring excitement to. (**b**) [1940s+] of a place, to be carried away with emotion, usu. through a performance. (**c**) [1940s+] to be active. (**d**) [1940s+] to perform, to offer up. (**e**) [1980s] to do well in something. (**f**) [1990s+] to display, to indulge oneself in, esp. of clothes. (**g**) [2000s] to move, to travel.

DERIVATIVES

❑ **rocking** *adj.* [1980s+] (*US campus/teen*) a general term of approval.

IN PHRASES

❑ **rock along** *v.* [20C+] (*orig. US*) to proceed, to go on with life in one's usual manner. ❑ **rock and roll** *v. see* separate entry. ❑ **rock in** *v.* **1** [1910s] (*Aus.*) to eat heartily. **2** [1940s–50s] (*Aus.*) to intensify, to accelerate, esp. in the phr. *rock it in!* hurry up! make it snappy! **3** [1970s+] (*S.Afr.*) (*also* **rock over, rock up**) to arrive without prior announcement or appointment, to 'roll up'. ❑ **rock it** *v.* **1** [1930s–50s] to fight. **2** [1950s] (*Aus.*) to hurry up. ❑ **rock it in** *v.* [one is throwing verbal 'rocks'] [1940s] **1** (*Aus./N.Z.*) to boast. **2** (*Aus./N.Z.*) to tease. **3** (*N.Z.*) to upset, to hurt. ❑ **rock on** *v.* [1960s+] (*US*) to enjoy oneself, esp. by playing or dancing to rock music. ❑ **rock out** *v.* **1** [1960s+] (*US*) to enjoy oneself, esp. by playing or dancing to rock music. **2** [1980s] (*US black*) to collapse, to be exhausted. ❑ **rock someone's world** *v.* [1970s+] **1** (*US campus*) to have sexual intercourse. [note the now clichéd description of love-making – 'make the earth move' – from Ernest Hemingway's *For Whom the Bell Tolls* (1940)]. **2** (*US*) to beat up, render unconscious. **3** to amaze; to move emotionally.

IN EXCLAMATIONS

❑ **rock out!** *see* separate entry.

rockalow *n.* (*also* **rock-a-low**) [Fr. *roquelaure*, an overcoat] [mid-19C] an overcoat.

rock and lurch *n.* [rhy. sl.] [20C+] (*Aus.*) a church.

rock and roll *n.* (*also* **rock 'n' roll**) [rhy. sl.] **1** [1980s+] the dole. **2** [1980s+] a hole. **3** [2000s] sexual intercourse [HOLE *n.*[1] (1e)].

rock and roll *v.* [fig. use of SE] **1** [1930s+] to have sexual intercourse. **2** [1980s+] to fight, to shoot, to fire a grenade. **3** [1990s+] (*US campus*) to leave.

rocked *adj.* [i.e. they have 'rocks in the head'] **1** [early 19C] forgetful, esp. used of an ex-prisoner whose mental state has been affected by their punishment, whether prison or transportation. **2** [1980s+] (*US campus*) drunk or drugged. **3** [1990s+] (*US campus*) in a state of excitement.

rocked in a stone kitchen *phr.* [someone who has been thus rocked will have had their brain injured] [late 18C–early 19C] foolish, stupid.

Rockefeller bid *n.* [the sentence instituted by Nelson *Rockefeller*, as governor of New York state + BID *n.*[2]] [1980s+] (*US Und./prison*) a sentence of ten years to life.

rocker *n.*[1]

IN PHRASES

❑ **off one's rocker** (*also* **off one's rock**) [SE *rocker*, a rocking-chair] **1** [late 19C+] crazy; occas. antithesis, *on one's rocker*. **2** [1950s+] in fig. use, acting excessively (though not necessarily madly).

rocker *n.*[2] [ROCK *v.*[1] (1a)] [1900s–50s] a stone-thrower.

rocker *n.*[3] [1960s] (*US*) a painful blow.

rocker *n.*[4] [SE *rock 'n' roll*] [1960s+] **1** a member of a youth cult whose members wear leather, ride powerful motorcycles and fight their ritual rivals, the 'Mods'; latterly the hardcore rockers developed into a UK version of the US Hell's Angels. **2** a fan of rock music.

rocker *v.* (*also* **rakker, roker, rokker**) [Rom. *roker*, to talk] **1** [mid-19C–1950s] to speak, esp. to speak tramps' jargon. **2** [1900s–10s] to understand.

rockers *n.* [1970s+] (*W.I. Rasta*) reggae music, esp. the latest sound.

rocket *n.* **1** [1940s+] (*orig. milit.*) a severe reprimand or telling off; thus *get a rocket, give a rocket*. **2** [1940s+] (*drugs*) a marijuana cigarette [one 'blasts' off]. **3** [1960s+] (*US black*) a bullet. **4** [1990s+] in pl., the female breasts.

IN PHRASES

❑ **off one's rocket** *adj.* [pun on OFF ONE'S ROCKER *under* ROCKER *n.*[1]] [1910s–50s] crazy.

rocket *v.* [ROCKET *n.*] **1** [1940s+] (*orig. milit.*) to scold severely, to reprimand. **2** [1990s+] (*drugs*) to suddenly become extremely intoxicated when smoking cannabis.

rocket fuel *n.* **1** [1970s+] (*drugs*) phencyclidine. **2** [1990s+] cocaine. **3** [2000s] (*N.Z.*) alcohol mixed with a soft drink in a plastic bottle, as drunk by teenagers in an attempt to get drunk quickly.

rockin' *n.* [SE *rock*, to shake] [20C+] (*US prison*) a prison riot.

rocking chair *n.* [1930s–40s] (*US black*) sexual intercourse, esp. as used metaphorically in blues lyrics.

rocking horse *n.* [rhy. sl.] [1960s+] **1** sauce (condiment). **2** sauce (cheek).

rocking-horse manure *n.* [1950s+] (*orig. Aus.*) something extremely hard, if not impossible to find.

rock 'n' roll *n. see* ROCK AND ROLL *n.*

rock of ages *n.*[1] [1920s] (*US*) an older woman.

rock of ages *n.*[2] (*also* **rocks**) [rhy. sl.] [1930s+] wages.

rock out! *excl.* [1980s] keep enjoying yourself! have a great time!

rockpile *n.* [note naut. use *rockpile*, a ship on which the work is especially demanding] **1** [late 19C+] (*also* **pile**) (*US prison*) the prison quarry, in allusion to the convict's task of breaking stones; thus fig. the prison. **2** [1940s] (*US black*) any tall building; thus *topside of the rockpile*, the top flat, the penthouse. **3** [1950s] (*US*) one's home.

rockpile cure *n. see* QUARRY CURE *n.*

rocks *n.* **1** [mid-19C+] (*US*) money; usu. in the phr. *pocketful of rocks*. **2** [late 19C] (*US*) (*also* **rocksy**) as a term of address. **3** [20C+] the teeth. **4** [20C+] precious stones, jewels, esp diamonds. **5** [1940s] (*US Und.*) a variety of confidence trick based on fake diamonds. **6** [1940s–50s] (*US drugs*) withdrawa symptoms. **7** [1940s+] (*orig. US*) ice-cubes. **8** [1940s+] the testicles [play on STONE *n.*[1] (1)]. **9** [1950s–70s] in fig. use, courage, bravery. **10** in drug uses. (**a**) [1960s+] a form of crystallized, smokeable heroin. (**b**) [1970s+] cocaine (**c**) [1980s+] crack cocaine. **11** *see* ROCK OF AGES *n.*[2].

IN PHRASES

❑ **blow one's rocks** *v.* [1960s] to ejaculate. ❑ **bust someone's rocks** *v.* [1960s] (*US campus*) to vilify. ❑ **get one's rocks off** *v.* [1940s+] **1** of either sex, to have sexua intercourse, to experience orgasm. **2** to enjoy oneself. **3** to obtain any form of satisfaction or to satisfy, to please. **4** to masturbate. **5** (*drugs*) to binge pleasurably on drugs. ❑ **pop one's rocks** *v.* (*also* **pop the rocks**) [1970s+] (*US*) to become excited; to lose emotional control, lit. to ejaculate. ❑ **shoot one's rocks** *v.* [1970s+] of a man, to reach orgasm, to ejaculate.

SE in slang uses

IN PHRASES

❑ **give someone big rocks to hold** *v.* [20C+] (*W.I., Bdos*) for a woman to make a date with a man when she has no intention of keeping it, thus to trick a suitor in any way. ❑ **give someone rocks** *v.* [fig. use of sense 8 above; see also *GET ONE'S ROCKS OF* above] [1950s+] (*US*) to excite sexually, spec. to make a man have an erection. ❑ **have rocks in the head** *v.* (*also* **have stones in the head**) [20C+] (*Aus./US*) to be stupid. ❑ **hold big rocks** *v.* [20C+] (*W.I.*) to be left waiting for someone who doe not turn up. ▫ **on the rocks** **1** [late 19C+] in trouble, facing problems. **2** [late 19C+] in great need of. **3** [1990s+] in fig. use, to the greatest extent. ▫ **rocks for jocks** *n.* (*also* **rocks**) [JOCK *n.*[1] (3)] [1960s+] (*US campus*) an undergraduate course in 'introductory geology'.

rocks! *excl.* [1920s] nonsense! rubbish!

rocks and boulders *n.* [rhy. sl.] [1910s–70s] the shoulders.

rocks of Gibraltar *n.* [1950s] (*mainly juv.*) roast potatoes.

rock someone's frame *v. see* CLIMB SOMEONE'S FRAME *under* FRAME *n.*[1].

rock someone's mic *v. see under* MIC *n.*[1].

rock spider *n.* [in Aus. senses, in nursery rhyme 'Little Miss Muffet': 'There came a big spider / And sat down beside her'] **1** [1930s+] (*Aus.*) (*also* **spider**) a thief who robs courting couples in parks or at the seaside when their attention is elsewhere. **2** [1950s+] (*S.Afr.*) an Afrikaner. **3** [1990s+] (*also* **rocky, spider**) (*Aus.*) a sexual offender, usu. a paedophile or child molester.

rocksy *n. see* ROCKS *n.* (2).

Rocky *n.* (*also* **Rocky III**) [ROCK *n.* (4d) + play on the *Rocky* films of 1980s] [1990s+] (*drugs*) crack cocaine.

rocky *n.* [1990s+] **1** (*UK drugs*) a variety of hashish. **2** (*UK juv.*) the erect penis [it is 'rock-hard']. **3** (*UK juv.*) a scavenger. **4** *see* ROCK SPIDER *n.* (3).

rocky *adj.* [SE *rock*, to sway] **1** [mid-18C+] drunk. **2** [mid-19C+] (*orig. US*) difficult, problematical. **3** [late 19C] unfair, cruel. **4** [late 19C+] (*orig. US*) unwell, 'off-colour'. **5** [1910s–60s] (*US*) crazy. **6** [1920s] (*orig. US*) penniless, impoverished.

IN PHRASES

▫ **go rocky** *v.* [late 19C+] to go wrong.

Rocky Mountain canary *n.* [the noise of its braying, the antithesis of that of a mellifluous bird] [late 19C+] a donkey, an ass.

rocky road *n.* [? an ice-cream variety, which features lumps of *chocolate*, punning on CHOCOLATE *adj.* (2)] [1990s+] (*US*) the anus.

Rocky III *n. see* ROCKY *n.*

rod *n.* **1** [17C+] (*also* **hot rod, love rod, rod of correction, rod-pole**) the penis, erect penis. **2** [20C+] (*US*) a gun, a pistol. **3** [1900s–40s] (*US tramp*) usu. in pl., the metalwork – struts, supports etc – found underneath a railroad coach or wagon. **4** [1930s–50s] (*US*) a gunman. **5** [1930s+] an overcoat [ety. unknown; ? play on phr. *a rod for one's back*]. **6** [1950s] (*US*) an automobile. **7** *see* HOT-ROD *n.* (2). **8** *see* HOT-RODDER *n.* **9** *see* RAMROD *n.* (2).

pertaining to sex

IN COMPOUNDS

▫ **rod-pole** *n. see* sense 1 above. ▫ **rod walloper** *n.* [1960s+] (*orig. Aus.*) a masturbator; lit. or fig.

IN PHRASES

▫ **get a rod on** *v.* [1960s] to get an erection. ▫ **get some rod** *v.* [1990s+] (*US campus*) of a woman, to have sexual intercourse. ▫ **lay the rod** *v.* [LAY *v.*[1] (1)] [1980s+] (*W.I.*) to have sexual intercourse. ▫ **rod of correction** *n. see* sense 1 above.

general uses

IN COMPOUNDS

▫ **rod man** *n.* **1** [1920s+] (*US*) (*also* **rodman**) a gunman. **2** [1930s–40s] (*US tramp*) (*also* **rodsman, rod rider**) a tramp who travels by clinging onto the metalwork beneath a coach or wagon.

IN PHRASES

▫ **hit the rods** *v.* (*also* **hop the rods**) [1920s–50s] (*US*) **1** to ride freight trains as an itinerant worker or tramp. **2** to leave, to run off. ▫ **long rod** *n.* [1930s–80s] (*US Und.*) a rifle. ▫ **pack a rod** *v.* [PACK *v.*[1] (3)] [1920s+] (*US*) to carry a gun. ▫ **ride the rods** *v. see under* RIDE *v.* ▫ **rod up** *v.* **1** [1920s+] (*US Und.*) to arm oneself with a gun. **2** [1970s+] (*US*) to convert a car by giving it a very powerful engine to make it go fast.

SE in slang uses

IN PHRASES

▫ **rod in pickle** *n.* (*also* **rod in lye, rod in piss**) [from the toughening of rods by marinating them in lye] **1** [late 16C–1910s] a punishment in prospect. **2** [early 19C] any agent of revenge or aggression that has been put aside for use at the right time. **3** [1940s] (*Aus.*) in horseracing, a certainty.

rod *v.* [ROD *n.*] **1** [late 19C+] of a man, to have sexual intercourse. **2** [1910s] (*US Und.*) to hold up with a gun. **3** [1920s–30s] (*also* **rod off**) to shoot dead. **4** [1920s+] to arm oneself with a gun.

rodda *n.* [? ROD *n.* (7)] [1960s] (*US black*) a Cadillac.

rodded *adj.* (*also* **rodded up**) [ROD *n.* (2)] [1920s+] carrying a gun.

rodder *n.* [ROD *n.* (7)] [1950s+] (*US*) one who drives a customized 'hot rod'.

rodeo *n.*[1] [? play on SE *road*] [1920s] (*US tramp*) a vagrant, a traveller.

rodeo *n.*[2] [the image of a rodeo bronco-rider] **1** [1990s+] (*US black teen*) a style of sexual intercourse, where the man 'rides' the woman; usu. anal intercourse, while pulling her hair and slapping her buttocks. **2** [1990s+] a form of sexual 'game' whereby the male of a couple arranges for his friends to jump out from hiding while he he is having intercourse; they sound an air horn and he 'wins' if he can continue for eight seconds longer before the horrified girl 'bucks' him off her body.

rodge *n.* [airforce jargon, *roger* = message received and understood] [1970s] (*US campus*) a fact, anything that's true.

rodney *n.*[1] [dial. *rodney*, an idler, a loafer, a fool] [late 19C+] (*Irish*) a fool.

rodney *n.*[2] [ROD *n.* (1)] [1960s–70s] the penis.

Rodney King *n.* [*Rodney King*, a black man, was severely beaten by the police during his arrest. A videotape of the beating led to the trial of the officers involved and, after their controversial acquittal, to the Los Angeles riots of 1992] [1990s+] (*US black*) an arrest, esp. one involving brutality; thus *pull a Rodney King*, to initiate police brutality.

Rod's *n.* [abbr.] [1970s+] (*UK society*) Harrods.

rodsman *n. see* ROD MAN *under* ROD *n.*

rody *n. see* RUDE BOY *n.*

roe *n.* [SE *roe*, fish eggs] [mid-19C–1900s] semen.

rofe *n.* [backsl.] [1940s–50s] (*UK prison*) a four-year sentence.

rofefil *n.* (*also* **rouf-efil**) [backsl.; lit. 'for life'] [mid-19C] a life sentence.

rogan gosh *n.* [rhy. sl. = DOSH *n.*; ult. an Indian dish] [2000s] money.

roger *n.*[1] [despite the 'e' the g was pronounced hard, thus ? corruption of SE *rogue*; Ribton-Turner, *A History of Vagrants* (1887), notes Gaelic *ruaigair*, a pursuer, a hunter, Erse *ruaigaur* and Lowland Scot. *rugger*, an outlaw] [mid-16C] a wandering beggar who pretended to be a poor scholar from Oxford or Cambridge.

roger *n.*[2] [generic use of human name] **1** [mid-16C–early 19C] a goose. **2** [mid-17C–18C] a country simpleton. **3** [late 17C+] (*also* **rogero**) the penis, an erect penis. **4** [mid–late 19C] an act of sexual intercourse. **5** [1920s] a police officer, usu. male. **6** [1970s] an erection.

IN PHRASES

▫ **roger the lodger** *n. see* separate entry.

roger *n.*[3] [? dial. *roger*, the paunch of a pig] [mid-17C–mid-19C] (*UK Und.*) a suitcase.

IN PHRASES

▫ **bite the roger** *v.* [18C] to steal a portmanteau.

roger *n.*[4] [18C] (*UK Und.*) a thief-taker.

roger *v.*[1] [ROGER *n.*[2] (3)] [early 18C+] to have sexual intercourse, to seduce; also as *do a roger*.

IN COMPOUNDS

▫ **rogering iron** *n.* [18C–19C] the penis.

roger *v.*[2] [ROGER THE LODGER *n.*] [1940s–50s] (*Aus.*) of a man, to be betrayed sexually by one's wife or partner during one's absence.

Roger Hunt *n.* [rhy. sl. = CUNT *n.* (1); ult. the former Liverpool and England footballer *Roger Hunt* (b.1938)] [1990s+] the vagina.

rogering *n.* [ROGER *v.*[1]] [19C+] sexual intercourse.

rogering iron *n. see under* ROGER *v.*[1].

Roger Moore *n.* [rhy. sl.; ult. UK film star *Roger Moore* (b.1927)] [1990s+] **1** a whore. **2** a door.

rogero *n. see* ROGER *n.*[2] (3).

roger the lodger *n.* [rhyme, but also pun on ROGER *n.*[2] (3)] [1920s+] a lodger who seduces his landlady, or the wife of his landlord; thus used of anyone who seduces a woman while her partner is absent.

rogue *n.* [the term is an original cant coinage and refers to a specific order of villain, the Fourth Order of Canters; its absorption into SE, meaning a general-purpose rascal, ran in parallel, albeit slightly later by some 20 years] **1** [mid-16C–18C] (*UK Und.*) a professional villain, 'neither as stout or hardy as the upright-man' (Harman). **2** [late 18C–early 19C] a corn chandler [his trad. negative image]. **3** [1960s+] (*US black*) a ladies' man, a sexually active man [SE *rogue male*; note Urquhart, *The Complete Works of Rabelais* (1653), in list of names for the penis: 'my lusty live sausage, my crimson chitterlin, [...] my pretty rogue'].

IN COMPOUNDS

❑ **rogue's walk** *n.* [late 19C] (*UK society*) a stroll along Piccadilly from the Circus to Bond Street.

IN PHRASES

❑ **arch-rogue** *n.* **1** [early 17C–late 18C] the leader of a gang of thieves. **2** [mid-17C–late 19C] a confirmed villain. ❑ **rogue and pullet** *n.* [PULLET *n.* (1)] [mid-19C+] (*UK Und.*) a man and woman working together as a criminal team. ❑ **rogue in grain** *n.* [late 17C–early 19C] a very great rogue [the poor reputation of millers]. ❑ **rogue in spirit** *n.* [pun] [late 18C–mid-19C] a distiller or brandy merchant. ❑ **rogue with one ear** *n.* [the 'ear' is the handle] [late 17C–early 18C] a chamberpot.

rogue *v.* [ROGUE *n.* (1)] **1** [mid-16C–mid-17C] (*UK Und.*) to live as a professional beggar; thus *roguing*, living in this way, *roguishness*, being a rogue. **2** [1980s+] (*US campus*) to steal.

rogue and villain *n.* [rhy. sl.] [mid–late 19C] a shilling.

roguing Joe *n.* (*also* **roguing Tom**) [mid-16C–mid-17C SE *rogue*, to wander as a rogue or vagrant] [1950s] (*W.I.*) **1** a wandering scrounger or pilferer. **2** the bag into which such a person places their finds.

Rohie *n.* (*also* **Rohy**) [abbr.] [1990s+] (*drugs*) the sedative Rohypnol.

roid *n.* [abbr. SE *steroid*] [1980s+] (*US*) in pl., steroids.

IN COMPOUNDS

❑ **roid-head** *n.* [-HEAD *sfx* (1)] [2000s] a stupid thug. ❑ **roid rage** *n.* [play on *road rage*] [1980s+] (*drugs*) aggressive behaviour caused by excessive steroid use.

roister *n.* (*also* **roisterer, royster, roysterer**) [Fr. *rustre*, a ruffian, a royster, a hackster, a swaggerer; ult. Lat. *rusticus*, a peasant] [mid-16C+] (*UK Und.*) a swaggering, blustering bully, a noisy reveller; also as adj., *roistering*; as v., *roist*, to swagger.

roker *n.* (*also* **rooker**) [Du. *roken*, to smoke] [late 19C+] (*S.Afr.*) a marijuana smoker; also as v.

roker *v. see* ROCKER *v.*

rokker *v. see* ROCKER *v.*

Roland Young *n.* [rhy. sl.; ult. British actor *Roland Young* (1887–1953)] [1990s+] the tongue.

rolf *v. see* RALPH *v.*

rolie *n.* [abbr.] [1980s+] (*N.Z. drugs*) a *Rohy*pnol.

roll *n.* **1** in sexual senses. (**a**) [mid-19C; 1940s] the penis. (**b**) [1930s–40s] (*US*) the vagina [abbr. JELLY ROLL *n.*]. (**c**) [1940s+] (*orig. US*) sexual intercourse; thus v. *roll ass*, to have sexual intercourse [abbr. ROLL IN THE HAY *n.* (1)]. (**d**) [1970s+] (*US gay*) in pl., the buttocks. **2** [mid-19C+] a bank*roll*. **3** [1950s–60s] (*US black*) a suit jacket. **4** in drug uses. (**a**) [1960s] a small package of heroin. (**b**) [1960s] (*US drugs*) a roll of benzedrine tablets. (**c**) [1960s] (*UK drugs*) a small measure of hashish. (**d**) [1970s+] (*US black*) a month's supply of contraceptive pills. (**e**) [1980s+] three barbiturates, as sold by a dealer. (**f**) [2000s] (*US campus*) a tablet of MDMA. **5** [1970s–80s] (*UK black*) a fight. **6** *see* ROLL-UP *n.*[2] (1).

IN COMPOUNDS

❑ **roll of tarpaper** *n.* [1950s–70s] (*US*) a black man's penis.

IN PHRASES

❑ **drop a roll** *v. see under* DROP *v.*[6]. ❑ **flash one's roll** *v.* [20C+] to display one's money. ❑ **gambler's roll** *n.* [1980s] (*US*) a roll of money with a high-value note visible on the outside, hiding only small denominations. ❑ **pimp roll** *n.* [2000s] a large roll of money. ❑ **pop a roll** *v.* [1970s+] (*drugs*) to swallow a number of pills at one go. ❑ **roll Jack Rice couldn't jump over** *n.* (*also* **roll a kangaroo couldn't jump over, roll big enough to choke a bullock, ...the tunnel, roll that would choke a mule**) [proper name of the racehorse *Jack Rice*, Aus. champion hurdler] **1** [1910s–70s] (*Aus.*) a large quantity of money. **2** in fig. use.

SE in slang uses

IN COMPOUNDS

❑ **rollover** *n. see* separate entry. ❑ **roll-up** *n. see* separate entries.

IN PHRASES

❑ **have a roll on** *v.* [late 19C–1910s] (*UK teen*) to swagger to put on airs. ❑ **on a roll** [SE *roll*, the roll of a dice] [1970s+] (*orig. US gambling*) on a winning streak, enjoying a period of success, whether lit. or fig. ❑ **roll in the hay** *n. see* separate entry. ❑ **slow your roll** *v.* [1990s+] (*US black*) to slow down whatever one is doing.

IN EXCLAMATIONS

❑ **go and have a roll!** [1940s+] go away! get lost!

roll *v.* **1** [mid-19C; 1920s+] to have sexual intercourse [orig. meaning work, it was extended in blues songs to mean intercourse i.e. the physical effort involved]. **2** in drug uses. (**a**) [late 19C; 1960s+] (*drugs*) (*also* **roll up**) to roll a marijuana cigarette (**b**) [1990s+] to take MDMA. (**c**) [1990s+] of a vein, to move away from the syringe when one is attempting to inject onesel with narcotics. **3** to assault [one *rolls* the victim over]. (**a**) [late 19C+] to rob; usu. a drunk or any helpless person; thus *roll a stiff*, LUSH ROLL *under* LUSH *n.*[1]. (**b**) [20C+] to attack. **4** in senses of movement. (**a**) [late 19C–1920s; 1990s+] (*US*) to walk (**b**) [1910s+] (*US*) (*also* **roll off**) to start moving; lit. or fig., thus the phr. *let's roll*, let's go, let's leave. (**c**) [1920s] (*US*) to drive a car. (**d**) [1980s+] (*US campus*) to leave, to avoid a class (**e**) [1990s+] (*US*) to leave home. (**f**) [2000s] in fig. use, to exist to conduct one's life. (**g**) [2000s] (*US black*) to perform, e.g. as a rapper. **5** in fig. uses ['roll with the punches']. (**a**) [1950s+ (*US*) (*also* **roll high**) to prosper, to do well, to succeed (**b**) [1980s+] (*US black*) to survive, to live, to conduct oneself **6** [1980s+] in context of laughter [abbr. SE *rolling in the aisles*] (**a**) to laugh hysterically. (**b**) to make someone laugh. **7** *see* ROL IN *v.*

IN COMPOUNDS

❑ **roll dog** *n.* [DOG *n.*[2] (2c)] [1990s+] (*US black*) someone wit whom one drives around. ❑ **roll job** *n.* [JOB *n.*[2] (2)] [1950s] (*U. Und.*) a street robbery, a mugging. ❑ **roll right** *n.* [2000s] (*U. prison*) a generically branded cigarette.

IN PHRASES

❑ **get one's roll on** *v.* [2000s] (*US teen*) to drive an expensiv car. ❑ **roll a lush** *v. see* LUSH ROLL *under* LUSH *n.*[1]. ❑ **roll a number** *v. see under* NUMBER *n.* ❑ **roll hard** *v.* [HARD *adv.* (4 [2000s] (*US black*) to be very aggressive, fearless. ❑ **roll high** *v see* sense 5a above. ❑ **roll in** *v. see* separate entry. ❑ **roll i one's ivories** *v. see under* IVORY *n.* ❑ **roll in one's marbles** *v see* PASS IN ONE'S MARBLES *under* MARBLES *n.*[4]. ❑ **roll in the hay** *v see* separate entry. ❑ **roll into** *v.* [ext. of ROLL IN *v.*] **1** [19C+] t arrive. **2** [late 19C–1900s] (*Aus.*) to attack. ❑ **roll me in th kennel** *n. see under* KENNEL *n.*[2]. ❑ **roll off** *v. see* sense 4b above ❑ **roll on** *v. see* separate entries. ❑ **roll one's bones** *v.* (*als* **roll one's trail**) [20C+] (*US*) to get into action, to move onesel ❑ **roll one's hoop** *v.* **1** [late 19C–1920s] to do well, t succeed. **2** [1900s–30s] (*US*) (*also* **roll one's tail**) to leave, es as an excl. of dismissal *go roll your hoop!* ❑ **roll out** *v.* **1** [lat 19C+] to get out of bed, to get up. **2** [mid-19C+] (*US black* *campus*) to leave, to depart. **3** [1990s+] (*US prison*) to release from jail. **4** [2000s] (*US prison*) to move to a new cell. ◻ **roll over** *see* separate entries. ◻ **roll stuff** *v.* [STUFF *n.* (5b)] [1930s] (*US drugs*) to move around wholesale quantities of narcotics. ◻ **roll the bars** *v.* [1990s+] (*US prison*) to open a row of cell doors using a remote mechanism that opens every door simultaneously. ◻ **roll the bones** *v. see under* BONES *n.*[1]. ◻ **roll the log** *v.* (*also* **roll the boy**) [1930s–40s] (*drugs*) to smoke opium. ◻ **roll up** *v.* **1** *see* sense 2a above. **2** *see also* separate entry. ◻ **roll up on** *v.* [1990s+] (*US black*) **1** to approach sexually. **2** to attack. ◻ **roll up the sidewalk** *see under* SIDEWALK *n.* ◻ **roll with** *v.* [1960s+] (*US black*) **1** to agree with, to accept. **2** to associate with.

IN EXCLAMATIONS

◻ **go roll in it!** [abbr. of *go roll in the shit!*] [1970s] (*US*) a dismissive retort. ◻ **go roll your hoop!** [abbr. of *go roll in the shit!*] [1970s] (*US*) a dismissive retort. ◻ **roll on!** *see* separate entry.

oll and lurch *n.* [rhy. sl.] [1900s] (*Aus.*) a church.

oll and rind *n.* [mid-19C] (*Aus.*) bread and cheese.

oll-around *n. see* ROLL IN THE HAY *n.*

olled up *adj.* [mid-19C] (*UK Und.*) imprisoned for debt.

Roller *n.* [abbr.] **1** [1970s+] a *Rolls* Royce car. **2** *see* HOLY ROLLER *n.* (1).

oller *n.* **1** [early 19C] in pl., a nightly patrol, on both horse and foot, that covered London in the hope of preventing robberies. **2** in drug uses. (**a**) [late 19C–1940s] someone who rolls opium into smokeable pellets. (**b**) [1920s–40s] a drug user or addict. (**c**) [1930s] a tobacco cigarette. (**d**) [1970s+] a vein that rolls as one attempts to insert a needle. (**e**) [1990s+] a drug seller, thus *rolling*; dealing drugs. **3** [20C+] (*US black*) someone who keeps moving continuously; thus a hard worker. **4** as a vehicle. (**a**) [1900s] (*US*) a hansom cab. (**b**) [1950s+] (*US*) (*also* **rollo**) a police car. **5** [1910s+] (*US*) a robber, esp. one who robs drunks and other defenceless people; a blackmailer. **6** [1950s+] (*US black*) (*also* **roller boys**) in pl., the police, occas. in sing., a police officer. **7** [1960s+] (*US prison*) (*also* **live roller**) a prison guard.

ollerskate *n.* [note 1940s UK hauliers' slang *roller skate*, a small, light wagon] **1** [1960s+] (*US*) a small foreign-made car. **2** [2000s] (*S.Afr. prison*) in pl., handcuffs.

ollick *v.* [euph. BALLOCKS *v.*] [1930s+] to tell off, to reprimand; thus *a good rollicking*.

ollicking *n.* [1930s+] a telling off, a reprimand.

ollicking *adj.* [BOLLICKING *adj.*] [1990s+] nonsensical.

ollicks! *excl. see* ROLLOCKS! *excl.*

ollie *n.* [1940s+] (*orig. US prison*) a hand-rolled cigarette.

oll-in *n.* [1990s+] (*US gang*) the rolling of a dice by a female recruit to a gang to ascertain how many members will have sex with her.

oll in *v.* **1** [late 18C+] (*also* **roll**) of people, to arrive, to come home. **2** [late 19C–1920s] (*US*) to go to bed. **3** [20C+] of objects, to appear, to arrive.

olling *n.*[1] [ROLL *v.* (1); *DSUE* and the *OED* both have v. *roll*, to rob, esp. of a drunk, as 19C; but Copeland, *Hye-Way to the Spittel House* (c.1531) offers 'Taverners that keep bawdry and polling/ Marring wine with brewing and *rolling*', thus poss. earlier, though equally poss. it means simply rolling the barrels and over-fermenting the wine] [late 19C+] a robbery; note *QUEER-ROLLING under* QUEER *n.*

olling *n.*[2] [ety. unknown] [1980s+] (*drugs*) MDMA.

olling *n.*[3] **1** [1980s+] (*US black teen*) driving around very slowly [ROLL *v.* (4b)]. **2** [2000s] being associated either with an individual or a larger group [*ROLL WITH under* ROLL *v.*].

olling *adj.*[1] [late 18C–mid-19C] clever, sophisticated.

IN COMPOUNDS

◻ **rolling joe** *n.* [JOE *n.*[1] (1b)] [mid–late 19C] a smart, fashionable person. ◻ **rolling kiddy** *n.* [KIDDY *n.* (1)] [early–mid-19C] (*UK Und.*) a dandified thief.

olling *adj.*[2] [SE *roll*, to tumble] **1** [20C+] very drunk. **2** [2000s] under the influence of MDMA.

rolling billow *n.* [rhy. sl.; later joc. use in Borough market, S.E. London, for sacks of potatoes] [late 19C–1950s] a pillow.

rolling deep *n.* [rhy. sl.] [20C+] (*Aus.*) sleep.

rolling-pin *n.* [late 17C+] the penis.

rollin' ome *n.* [rhy. sl.] [1940s] a comb.

roll in the hay *n.* (*also* **roll-around, toss in the hay, tumble in the hay**) [SE *roll*/TUMBLE *n.* (2) + SE *hay*] [1940s+] (*orig. US*) **1** sexual intercourse, with the implication of spontaneity, adultery or the open air. **2** a person viewed as a possible sexual partner.

roll in the hay *v.* [ROLL IN THE HAY *n.*] [1940s+] to have sexual intercourse.

roll me (in the dirt) *n.* [rhy. sl.] [late 19C] a shirt.

roll (me) in the gutter *n.* [rhy. sl.] [20C+] (*Aus.*) butter.

rollo *n. see* ROLLER *n.* (4b).

rollock *n. see* TOMMY ROLLOCKS *n.*

rollocking *n.* [euph. for BALLOCKING *n.*[2]] [1930s+] a scolding, a reprimand; thus v. *rollock*, to reprimand.

rollocks! *excl.* (*also* **rollicks!**) [euph. for BALLS! *excl.* (1); BALLOCKS! *excl.*; TOMMY ROLLOCKS *n.*] [1960s+] nonsense! rubbish!

roll on *v.* **1** [late 19C+] used to introduce a variety of wishes, usu. referring to escaping the environment that one is in, e.g. *roll on payday, roll on Friday* etc. **2** (*US*) in transitive uses, *roll on someone*. (**a**) [1970s] to address, to talk to. (**b**) [1980s–90s] to attack. (**c**) [2000s] to betray; to inform on.

roll on! *excl.* [1950s+] a general excl. of dismissal, resignation, amazement, surprise etc, often intensified as *fucking roll on!*

rollover *n.* **1** [1910s–50s] (*US prison*) the last night of a prison sentence [one wakes up, rolls out of bed, and the sentence is over]. **2** [1980s] (*US Und.*) a confession; a plea of guilty [ROLL OVER *v.* (1)].

roll over *v.* [1970s+] **1** to give up, to acquiesce, to surrender [the way in which a dog *rolls over* on its back to indicate surrender]. **2** to betray, to inform against, as in the phr. *roll over on*. **3** (*US black*) to attack.

rolls *n.* [1970s+] (*US gay*) the buttocks.

Rolls Canardly *n.* (*also* **Rolls Can-hardly**) [it *rolls* down the hills but *can hardly* get up them + ref. to the antithetical *Rolls* Royce; note the letter once sent to the manufacturers of Rolls Royces by Sir W.S. Gilbert (1836–1911): 'your car rolls but it will not royce'] [1950s+] (*orig. Aus.*) a run-down old car.

rolls royce *n.* [rhy. sl.] [20C+] the voice.

roll-up *n.*[1] [ROLL UP *v.*] **1** [late 19C–1910s] (*Aus.*) assembly, 'get-together'. **2** [late 19C–1910s] (*Aus.*) in spec. use, an unofficial trial, held in the goldfields. **3** [1990s+] (*US prison*) of an inmate, the act of leaving the prison, whether temporarily (for a court appearance) or permanently (after completing a sentence or moving to a new prison).

roll-up *n.*[2] **1** [1940s+] (*orig. UK prison*) (*also* **roll**) a handmade cigarette of papers and tobacco. **2** [1980s+] (*N.Z.*) an illicit smoke. **3** [1990s+] a hand-rolled marijuana/tobacco cigarette.

roll up *v.* **1** [late 19C+] (*orig. US*) to congregate, to assemble. **2** [late 19C+] (*orig. US*) to arrive, to appear. **3** [late 19C+] (*Aus.*) to pack one's belongings before leaving [the rolling up of one's pack]. **4** [1940s+] to die. **5** [1970s+] (*US prison*) of an inmate, to leave the prison, whether temporarily (for a court appearance) or permanently (after completing a sentence or moving to a new prison); to move from one cell to another [the old practice of rolling up one's mattress on every occasion of leaving one's cell]. **6** [2000s] (*US black*) to prepare to fight [i.e. *roll up* one's sleeves].

rollux *v. see* BALLOCK *v.*[2].

roly-poly *n.*[1] [play on PUDDING *n.* (2) + ? SE *roly-poly*, stout, podgy] [19C+] the penis.

roly-poly *n.*[2] (*also* **rowly-powly**) [? the same game as that noted by Johnson, *Dictionary* (1755): 'a sort of game, in which, when a ball rolls into a certain place, it wins'] [early 19C] a game known as 'un-deux-cinq'.

roly-poly *n.*[3] [late 19C] (*Irish/US*) money.

Roman *n.* [late 19C–1950s] a Roman Catholic.

Roman *adj.* [in the taxonomy of international sexual stereotypes, Rome is identified with orgies] [1950s+] in the world of gay sex, used to describe group sex.

IN COMPOUNDS

❑ **Roman culture** *n.* (*also* **Roman history**) [1960s+] orgies, group sex. ❑ **Roman engagement** *n.* [1960s+] (*gay*) anal intercourse with a virgin woman. ❑ **Roman fountains** *n.* [1960s+] (*gay*) urinals. ❑ **Roman historian** *n.* [1960s+] (*gay*) an enthusiast of orgies. ❑ **Roman night** *n.* [1960s+] (*gay*) an orgy.

SE in slang uses, pertaining to Catholicisim

IN COMPOUNDS

❑ **Roman collar** *n.* [SE *Roman collar*, a priest's white collar] [1960s+] (*Irish*) a generous head on a glass of stout. ❑ **Roman roulette** *n.* [1960s] contraception using no other system than the notoriously hit-and-miss 'rhythm method' as ordained by conservative popes.

Roman candle *n.*[1] **1** [mid-19C; 1970s+] (*UK/US gay*) a penis. **2** [1940s+] a Roman Catholic. **3** [1970s+] an Italian.

Roman candle *n.*[2] [rhy. sl.] [20C+] a sandal.

romance boy *n.* [1950s] (*W.I.*) a young man who chases women.

romantic ballad *n.* [rhy. sl.] [1990s+] salad.

Romany rye *n.* [Rom. *rai*, a gentleman; best-known through George Borrow's book *Romany Rye* (1857)] [mid-19C] a non-gypsy gentleman who associates with gypsies.

romboyle *n.* (*also* **rumboyle**) [ety. unknown] [late 17C–early 19C] the watch (an early form of policing).

romboyle *v.* (*also* **rumboyle**) [ety. unknown] [17C–early 19C] (*UK Und.*) **1** to seek out by hue and cry. **2** to arrest on a warrant; thus *romboyled*, wanted by the watch.

rombustical *adj. see* RUMBUSTIOUS *adj.*

rome *adj. see under* RUM *adj.* (1) and its combs.

Rome-ville/-vyle *n. see* RUM VILLE *n.*

Romford lion *n.* (*also* **Rumford lion**) [joc. ref. to *Romford*, Essex, then a market town] [late 17C–early 19C] a calf.

Rommel *n.*

IN PHRASES

❑ **pull a Rommel** *v.* [the about-turn made by Nazi General Erwin *Rommel* (1891–1944) as he began to face defeat in the North African desert] [1940s; 2000s] (*US black*) to turn back, to reverse direction (physically or fig.).

rommel *v.* [Afk. *rommel*, to rumble] [1960s] (*S.Afr.*) to flirt, to have sexual intercourse.

romoner *n.* [late 18C–mid-19C] (*UK Und.*) a fortune-teller.

romp *v.* **1** [1930s+] (*US*) to have sexual intercourse [note the coincidental UK tabloid press use of *romp* n., a sexual entanglement, *e.g.*, 'three-in-a-bed romp']. **2** [1950s–60s] (*US*) of street gangs, to fight, to beat up.

IN COMPOUNDS

❑ **rompworthy** *adj.* [1930s+] of a woman, ripe for sexual conquest.

IN PHRASES

❑ **romp home** *v.* (*also* **romp in**) [late 19C+] (*orig. racing*) to win easily. ❑ **romp it** *v.* [1970s+] (*US campus*) to accelerate in a car.

romper room *n.* (*also* **romping room**) [1960s+] (*US campus*) a place where one can enjoy oneself in an uninhibited manner.

ronald rich *n.* [rhy. sl. = BITCH *n.*[1] (1a)] [1990s+] an extremely unpleasant woman.

ronchie *adj. see* RAUNCHY *adj.*

roni *n.* [cod Ital. *tenderoni*] [1990s+] (*US black teen*) a sweet woman.

ronnie *n.* [? SE *round*, i.e. their shape] [early 19C] (*Scot*) usu. in pl., potatoes.

Ronnie Biggs *n.* [rhy. sl. = DIGS *n.*[1] (1); ult. *Ronald Biggs* (b.1929), one of the Great Train Robbers of 1963] [20C+] lodgings.

ron randell *n. see* JACK RANDALL *n.*

ronson *n.* [rhy. sl.] **1** [1950s] a pimp [*rons*(*on*) = PONCE *n.* (1)] **2** [1990s+] the anus; thus dismissive excl. *up your ronson* [*ronson lighter* = SHITER *n.*].

roody-poo *adj. see* ROOTIE-POOT *adj.*

roof *n.* **1** [mid-19C] (*US campus*) a hat; thus *drop one's roof*, tc lose one's hat. **2** [mid-19C–1940s] the human head.

IN PHRASES

❑ **blow one's roof** *v.* [1950s] (*US*) **1** to act hysterically, to ac irrationally. **2** to lose one's temper. ❑ **your roof is leaking** [1940s] a phr. used of an eccentric, an unstable person.

SE in slang uses

IN PHRASES

❑ **fall off the roof** *v.* **1** [1950s+] to be menstruating **2** [1970s] (*US gay*) to be in a nervous, irritable state. ❑ **out or the roof** [1940s] (*US*) out on a drunken spree.

roof *v.*[1] **1** [1910s] (*US Und.*) to travel on the roof of a railwa passenger carriage. **2** [1960s] (*US Und.*) to break into building via the roof.

roof *v.*[2] [? SE *rough* or phr. *knock him through the roof*] [1940s+ (*Aus.*) to kick or punch.

roofer *n.* **1** [mid-19C+] (*orig. US*) a hat [20C+ use is Aus.] **2** [1900s] (*US Und.*) a country gentleman [they have 'a roof ove their head']. **3** [1910s–20s] a third-rate, run-down theatre **4** [1910s–40s] (*US Und.*) a tramp who travels on the roofs c passenger carriages.

roofie *n.*[1] [? Afk. *roof*, scab] [1970s+] (*S.Afr.*) a junior Nationa Servicemen, part of the latest intake.

roofie *n.*[2] (*also* **roofies, rophies, rophy, ruffies, ruffles, wolfies** [the drug, which causes users to appear drunk, is allegedly popula as a new form of knockout drop, prob. used to facilitate a numbe of rapes] [1990s+] (*drugs*) Rohypnol; a strong sedative.

roogodoo *n.* [? SE *ruckus*] [20C+] (*W.I.*) a commotion, a nois uproar.

roogodung *adj.* (*also* **rukadung**) [? ROOGODOO *n.* + SE *dowr* [20C+] (*W.I.*) tumble-down, dilapidated.

rooibaard *n.* [Afk. *rooibaard*, red beard] [1990s+] (*S.Afr. drug* very strong marijuana, with tiny red hairs.

Rooihell *n.* [Afk. 'red hell'] [1960s–70s] (*S.Afr. Und.*) North En Jail, Capetown.

rooinek *n.* (*also* **rooi neker**) [Afk. *rooinek*, redneck; the effect c the sun] [late 19C+] (*S.Afr.*) an Englishman; also attrib.

rook *n.*[1] [the allegedly larcenous character of the bird] **1** [la 16C+] (*UK Und.*) a cheat or swindler. **2** [late 18C–early 19C (*UK Und.*) a small crow bar•[pun; a reverse of nature, where th rook is larger than the crow]. **3** [mid-19C] a clergyman [the blac clothes or, according to Hotten (1864) f. the nursery rhyme 'Wh Killed Cock Robin?', 'I, says the Rook, / With my little book, / I'll b the parson'.]. **4** [1930s+] a swindle.

rook *n.*[2] *see* ROOKIE *n.*

rook *v.*[1] [ROOK *n.*[1] (1)] [late 16C+] to cheat, to swindle, to stea thus *rooking*, an act of cheating.

rook *v.*[2] [1960s–80s] (*S.Afr. drugs*) to smoke marijuana.

rooked *adj.* [? ext. of ROOK *v.*[1]] [1920s] (*US*) impoverished.

rooker *n. see* ROKER *n.*

rookery *n.* [note milit. jargon *rookery*, that part of the barrac occupied by the subalterns] **1** [mid-18C–mid-19C] a gamblir den. **2** [19C+] a criminal slum 'inhabited by dirty Irish an thieves' (Hotten, 1860); the best known was the *St Gil Rookery* (now occupied by the Centre Point tower) in centr London. **3** [early 19C] a brothel. **4** [early 19C–1940s] a ro disturbance. **5** [1960s] in ext. use, any centre of the lik minded but marginal.

rookery nook *n.* [rhy. sl.; ult. the Ben Travers farce *Rooke Nook* (1926)] **1** [1920s+] a book. **2** [1960s] a cook.

rookie *n.* (*also* **rook, rooky**) [? SE *recruit* or children's use *rook* a lookout, if one considers that a lookout would be the least acti and thus newest/youngest member of a gang; note *crow-boy*, lookout, used in Southwark in the late 19C and derived f. the ru term for the boy who scared birds away from growing crop **1** [late 19C+] (*mainly US*) a novice, a beginner, a new recru esp. in milit., police, sports use. **2** [1960s] (*US black*) an outsider; one who is outside the group norms.

rookie *adj.* [ROOKIE *n.* (1)] [1910s+] (*mainly US*) newly recruited, unfledged, unsophisticated.

rookus juice *n. see* RUCKUS JUICE *n.*

rooky *adj.* [ROOK *n.*[1] (1)] [mid–late 19C] rascally, roguish.

rooled up *adj.* [SE *ruled up*] [mid-19C] (*UK Und.*) placed in the watchman's lockup.

room *adj. see* RUM *adj.*

roombelow *n.* [i.e. she offers 'room below'] [early 17C] (*UK Und.*) a prostitute.

roomie *n.* (*also* **roomy**) [abbr.] [1910s+] (*US*) **1** a *room*-mate, one who shares an apartment or other dwelling. **2** a prison cell mate.

rooms *n.* [on pattern of HOMES *n.*] [1990s+] (*US campus*) a *room*-mate.

room to rent *n.* [their brain is 'vacant'] [1980s] (*US teen*) a stupid person.

roomy *n. see* ROOMIE *n.*

rooney *n.* [joc. mispron. + abbr. of SE] [1950s–60s] (*US black*) marijuana.

roosevelt *n. see* F.D.R. *n.*

Rooshian/Roosian *n. see* RUSSIAN *n.*

Rooski *adj. see* RUSSKI *n.*

roost *n.* **1** [mid-19C+] a bed, thus go to roost, to go to bed. **2** [1900s–50s] one's home, one's house. **3** [1910s] (*US*) the upper gallery or 'gods' in a theatre.

roost *v.* **1** [17C–1900s] to sleep. **2** [19C+] to sit down.

rooster *n.* **1** [early 19C+] (*US*) a person. **2** in sexual senses. (**a**) [mid-19C–1900s] the vagina. (**b**) [late 19C+] the penis. (**c**) [late 19C+] (*US*) a sexually active man. (**d**) [1910s] (*Aus.*) a man, with derog. implications. (**e**) [1950s] the buttocks. **3** [1940s] (*US*) a chair, a seat [ROOST *v.* (2)]. **4** [1950s–60s] (*UK Und.*) a lookout [ext. use of ROOST *v.* (2)]. **5** [1980s+] (*drugs*) crack cocaine [play on CLUCK *n.*[4]].

rooster brand *n.* [ety. unknown; ? packaging] [late 19C–1940s] (*US drugs*) ashes from smoked opium, sold for recycling by poor but desperate users.

roostered *adj.* [fig. use of SE *rooster*] **1** [mid-19C–1900s] (*US*) drunk. **2** [2000s] (*N.Z.*) exhausted, esp. sexually.

roosting ken *n.* [ROOST *v.* (1) + KEN *n.*[1] (1)] [19C] a lodging house.

roost lay *n.* [SE *roost* + LAY *n.*[3] (1)] [early 19C] poultry-stealing.

root *n.*[1] **1** in sexual contexts. (**a**) [mid-16C+] (*also* **old root**) the penis. (**b**) [mid-18C] the female genitals. (**c**) [late 19C+] an erection, thus the phr. *get/have the root*, to get an erection. (**d**) [1950s+] (*Aus.*) the act of sexual intercourse. (**e**) [1970s+] (*orig. Aus.*) the person with whom one has intercourse, usu. the woman, thus a *weekend root*, a casual sexual partner. (**f**) [1990s+] (*Aus. teen*) a good-looking (and thus sexually attractive) male. **2** [mid-19C] a person, a man. **3** [late 19C–1900s] money. [the '*root* of all evil']. **4** [20C+] a kick [ROOT *v.* (1a)]. **5** [1910s] (*US*) a nose.

IN PHRASES

❑ **dry root** *n. see under* DRY *adj.*[1].

root *n.*[2] [? SE *cheroot*] **1** [1900s–30s] a cigarette. **2** [1950s+] (*drugs*) marijuana.

root *adj. see* REET *adj.*

root *v.* **1** in senses of aggression. (**a**) [late 19C–1950s] to kick a ball or a person. (**b**) [1910s] (*US*) to attack. (**c**) [1930s] (*Aus.*) to throw off. **2** [mid-19C] (*US campus*) to act as a sycophant in the hope of favours and career advancement. **3** [mid-19C–1920s] (*US campus*) to work hard. **4** [1920s+] (*US Und.*) to steal. **5** in sexual contexts. (**a**) [1930s+] to have sexual intercourse; thus *root/shag like a rattlesnake*, to have very vigorous sex; also used as euph. for FUCK *v.* in a variety of similarly negative uses, e.g. to outwit, to baffle, to exhaust, to utterly confound (someone); thus excl. *get rooted!* go to hell!; *root my old boot!* I don't believe you! I am very surprised!; *wouldn't it root you?* would you believe it?! (**b**) [1970s+] (*US gay prison*) to fellate.

DERIVATIVES

❑ **rooty** *adj.* **1** [1910s+] (*US*) (*also* **rooting**) sexually aroused. **2** *see also under* ROOT (FOR) *v.*

IN COMPOUNDS

❑ **root-rat** *n.* [-RAT *sfx*] [1980s+] (*N.Z.*) an active heterosexual.

IN PHRASES

❑ **root (for)** *v. see* separate entry. ❑ **root like a rattlesnake** *v. see* FUCK LIKE A RATTLESNAKE *under* FUCK *v.*

IN EXCLAMATIONS

❑ **get rooted!** [1950s+] (*Aus.*) a strongly dismissive excl., euph. FUCK OFF! *excl.*, GET FUCKED! *excl.* ❑ **root my boot!** (*also* **root my boot and shag my shoe!**) [1960s+] (*Aus.*) a general expression of exasperation.

rooted *adj.* [ROOT *v.* (5a)] **1** [1940s+] (*Aus.*) exhausted, crippled, out of action. **2** [1960s] deficient.

rooter *n.*[1] [the hair appeared to be throwing out a root] [mid-19C] a form of pony-tail, worn by men.

rooter *n.*[2] [SE *root*, meaning the basis, the ultimate] [mid-19C–1910s] **1** anything considered excellent, first-class. **2** anything extreme, violent, highly aggressive.

rooter *n.*[3] [ROOT (FOR) *v.*] [late 19C+] (*US*) **1** a sports fan, esp. a baseball fan. **2** an enthusiast, a supporter, in non-sports context.

rooter *n.*[4] [1930s] (*US Und.*) an armed robber.

rooter *n.*[5] [ROOT *v.* (5a)] [1940s+] a sexually active person.

root-faced *adj.* [a face carved into the hard twists of a tree root] [20C+] humourless, sanctimonious, censorious.

root (for) *v.* [ety. unknown; Cohen (ed.), *Studies in Slang* II (1989), pp.67–8, suggests *root* = SE *dig*, and thus an image of cheering and stamping so hard that one 'digs a hole' in the grandstand] [late 19C+] (*US*) **1** to cheer and urge on. **2** to support a cause.

DERIVATIVES

❑ **rooty** *adj.* **1** [late 19C] (*US*) of a sporting contest, well- and fervently supported. **2** *see also under* ROOT *v.*

root, hog or die *n.* [1920s–40s] (*US*) as a euph. for ROOT *n.*[1] (1a), the penis.

root, hog or die *v.* (*US*) **1** [early 19C+] to work extremely hard, or face inevitable failure; also used as an excl. of resignation; also attrib. **2** [1920s+] as a euph. for ROOT *v.* (5a), to have sexual intercourse.

rootiepoot *n.* [var. on POOPBUTT *n.*] (*also* **rootypoop, rootypoot**) [1960s+] (*US black*) an uninformed, unsophisticated person; as adj., out of date.

rootie-poot *adj.* (*also* **roody-poo**) [ROOTIEPOOT *n.*] [1960s+] (*US black*) inferior, superficial.

rooting *n.*[1] [ROOT (FOR) *v.*] [late 19C+] (*US*) cheering, encouraging, supporting one's sports team.

rooting *n.*[2] [ROOT *v.* (5a)] [1920s+] (*mainly Aus.*) the act of copulation.

rooting and tooting *n.* (*also* **rooting-tooting**) [ROOTING-TOOTING *adj.*] [1940s–50s] (*US black*) violent behaviour; as n., *rooting-tooter*, a violent person.

rooting-tooting *adj.* (*also* **rootin'-tootin', rootytoot**) [? orig. Lancs. dial.; SE *root around* + *toot*] [mid-19C+] noisy, boisterous, rip-roaring.

rootle *v.* [SE *rootle*, to rummage about] [mid-19C–1920s] to have sexual intercourse, thus the phr. (late 19C–1920s) *do a rootle*.

root-on *n.* [ext. of ROOT *n.*[1] (1c); on the pattern of HARD-ON *n.*] [1990s+] an erection.

rootrat *n. see under* ROOT *v.*

roots *n.* [abbr. DAISY ROOTS *n.*] [20C+] (*Aus.*) boots.

roots *adj.* (*also* **rootsy**) [1960s+] (*orig. W.I. then US/UK black*) authentic, culturally sound (by Rastafarian standards); thus *roots people*, those who feel they belong in Africa, rather than in the W.I. or the black diaspora; *rootsheads*, fans of roots music.

roots *phr.* [1960s+] (*W.I./Rasta*) used as a greeting to a fellow Rastafarian.

rooty *adj.* **1** *see under* ROOT *v.* **2** *see under* ROOT (FOR) *v.*

rootypoot/rootypoop *n. see* ROOTIEPOOT *n.*

rooty-toot *adj. see* ROOTING-TOOTING *adj.*

ropable *adj.* (*also* **ropeable**) [the image of an enraged horse or bull] [mid-19C+] (*Aus./N.Z*) in a very bad temper, infuriated.

rope *n.* **1** [late 16C–1950s] constr. with *the*, execution by hanging; also attrib. **2** [1900s–40s] (*US*) in senses of something smokable [the similarity of some cigars to a piece of tarry rope]. (**a**) a cigar, esp. a foul-smelling one. (**b**) tobacco. **3** [1930s–60s] (*US*) money [? it 'holds one together']. **4** [1940s+] in drug uses [? the use of hemp in rope-making or rhy. sl. *rope* = DOPE *n.*[1] (6)]. (**a**) marijuana. (**b**) a marijuana cigarette. **5** [1940s+] (*drugs*) a vein [resemblance]. **6** [1960s] (*US Und.*) a form of confidence game. **7** [1970s+] (*S.Afr.*) a derog. term for Afrikaner.

IN COMPOUNDS

❑ **ropehead** *n. see* separate entry. ❑ **rope walk** *n.* [London's major court; one might *walk* thence to the gallows] [mid–late 19C] the Old Bailey.

IN PHRASES

❑ **dance in/on a rope** *v. see under* DANCE *v.* ❑ **for the rope** *adj.* [late 19C–1910s] due to be hanged. ❑ **get in the ropes with** *v.* [boxing imagery] [20C+] (*W.I.*) to start a quarrel, an argument. ❑ **look through a rope** *v.* [16C] to be hanged. ❑ **over the ropes** *adj.* [boxing imagery] **1** [1900s] (*US*) in a state of confusion, surprise. **2** [1950s] subjected to a robbery. ❑ **stretch rope** *v.* [1940s] (*US*) to be hanged. ❑ **take a rope** *v.* [1940s] (*US Und.*) to hang oneself.

rope *adj.* [2000s] (*US black*) good, remarkable.

rope *v.* **1** [mid-19C–1960s] (*US Und.*) of a confidence man, to gain a victim's trust and thus lure him deeper into the 'game'. **2** [1920s] (*US tramp*) to spy on criminals.

IN COMPOUNDS

❑ **roped game** *n.* (*also* **roping-in game**) [mid–late 19C] (*US*) a crooked gambling game, e.g. of faro or poker, into which victims have been 'roped-in' by confidence tricksters who take a share of the profits.

IN PHRASES

❑ **rope in** *v. see* separate entry.

ropeable *adj. see* ROPABLE *adj.*

ropehead *n.* [such hair resembles ropes] [2000s] (*N.Z.*) a Rastafarian, a (white) person wearing dreadlocks.

rope-in *n.* [ROPE IN *v.* (2)] [1990s+] (*W.I.*) an invitation to join in.

rope in *v.* [Schele de Vere, *Georgia Scenes* (1872): '*Rope in*, to, in the sense of gathering in, enlisting, is a bold metaphor derived from the common practice of gathering the cut hay of a meadow by means of a long rope, drawn by a horse'] [mid-19C+] (*orig. US*) **1** to swindle or cheat; to ensnare a victim into a (crooked) gambling game; thus *the rope*, the snare that is used. **2** to involve, to include, to force someone to be involved [post-1920 use is SE]. **3** as *rope in the pieces*, to make money. **4** to arrest.

IN COMPOUNDS

❑ **roping-in game** *n. see* ROPED GAME *under* ROPE *v.*

roper *n.*[1] [ROPE *n.* (1)] [mid-17C–mid-18C] constr. with *the*, the hangman.

roper *n.*[2] (*also* **roper in**) [ROPE IN *v.*] **1** [mid-19C–1960s] (*US*) a detective. **2** [mid-19C+] that member of a confidence trick team who first meets and lures the victim into the plot. **3** [mid-19C+] (*US Und.*) (*also* **picker-up**) an employee of a dancehall or gambling house whose task was to entice passers-by into the establishment; some ropers worked from hotel lobbies, where they paid the clerk a fee to introduce them to wealthy or gullible tourists.

ropey *adj.* (*also* **ropy, roupy**) [? SE *roup*, a form of catarrh, orig. a disease of poultry, thence Scot. *roupy*, husky, hoarse] **1** [late 18C+] of an object or person, second-rate, inadequate, unwell, run-down etc. **2** [1940s–50s] of a person, unpopular.

rophies/rophy *n. see* ROOFIE *n.*[2].

ropper *n.* [Scot. *roppin*, to wrap + SE *wropper*] [19C] a scarf.

ropy *adj. see* ROPEY *adj.*

roration *n.* (*also* **roaration**) [SE *roar* + *oration*] [late 18C] a speech given in a 'loud, unmusical voice' (Grose, 1785).

rorf *v.* [ety. unknown] [1950s+] (*S.Afr.*) to indulge in horseplay.

roritorious *adj. see* RORTORIOUS *adj.*

roro *n.* [? Fr. *ronron*, whirring, buzzing] [20C+] (*W.I.*) slander, malicious gossip; thus *put one in roro*, to slander, to cause trouble for.

rort *n.* (*also* **roart, wrought**) [RORT *v.*] (*Aus./N.Z.*) **1** [1920s+] any form of trick or deception, usu. qualified by a relevant noun, e.g. 'New Labour election rort'. **2** [1920s+] anything exceptionally good. **3** [1940s+] a crowd, a wild, noisy party. **4** [1970s+] an act of sexual intercourse. **5** [1970s+] a woman seen as a sex object.

rort *adj.* [SE *rort*, i.e. wrought] [1990s+] (*Aus.*) tricky, deceptive.

rort *v.* (*also* **wrought**) [? RORTY *adj.* (3); RORT *n.* appears to be later] (*Aus./N.Z.*) **1** [1910s+] to deceive, to defraud, to hoax. **2** [1930s+] as *rort at*, to shout, to complain loudly, to shout abuse. **3** [1940s+] to have sexual intercourse. **4** [1950s+] to go out on a spree. **5** [1980s+] to manipulate ballots or any form of record; thus *rorted*, rigged.

rorter *n.*[1] (*also* **wroughter**) [RORT *v.* (1)] **1** [1910s] (*UK Und.*) that member of a confidence trickery team who jostles, and thus attracts the attention of the victim. **2** [1980s+] (*Aus.*) someone who engages in a form of fraudulent manipulation.

rorter *n.*[2] [RORT *n.* (2)] [1920s+] something exceptionally good.

rorting *n.* [RORT *v.* (1)] [1910s+] confidence trickery; in weak sense, any form of 'sharp practice'.

rortorious *adj.* (*also* **roaratorious, roritorious, rorytorious**) [RORATION *n.*] [early-19C; 1910s] happily, triumphantly noisy.

rorty *adj.* (*also* **raughty**) [? Yid., *rorität*, anything choice or f. rhy. sl. *rorty* = naughty] **1** [mid-19C–1900s] fine, splendid, jolly. **2** [late 19C] of drinks, intoxicating. **3** [late 19C+] boisterous, rowdy, noisy; also as a nickname, also as adv., and *rortily*. **4** [late 19C+] of behaviour, speech etc, coarse, earthy, crudely comic.

DERIVATIVES

❑ **rortyness** *n.* [late 19C] energy, vitality.

IN COMPOUNDS

❑ **rorty bloke** *n.* (*also* **rorty dasher, rorty toff**) [BLOKE *n.* (3)/DASHER *n.* (2)/TOFF *n.* (2); the *bloke* is seen (according to Ware) as a superior being to the *toff* (? because the *toff* had pretensions while the *bloke* was down to earth)] [late 19C] a good fellow, an engaging companion, a fashionable upper-class gentleman.

IN PHRASES

❑ **do the rorty** *v.* [late 19C] to enjoy oneself.

Rory (O'Moore) *n.* [rhy. sl.; note St Vincent Troubridge, *Some Notes on Rhyming Argot* (1946): 'Probably derived from the tremendously popular song of that name, sung by Madame Vestris in the 1830's and 1840's'] **1** [mid-19C+] (*also* **Georgie Moore**) the floor; also in fig. use, in a bad way. **2** [late 19C+] prostitute, i.e. a *whore*. **3** [late 19C+] a door. **4** [1980s+] (*Aus.*) the number four.

IN PHRASES

❑ **on the rory** *adj.* [1930s+] penniless.

rorytorious *adj. see* RORTORIOUS *adj.*

rosa *n.* [Sp. *rosa*, red] [1980s+] (*drugs*) amphetamine.

rosa maria *n.* [play on MARY JANE *n.*[2] (1)] [1930s] (*US drugs*) marijuana.

rosary *n.* [the SE *rosary* is made of *decades* of prayers] **1** [1930s] (*US prison/Und.*) a thirty-day sentence. **2** [1950s+] (*US prison*) a sentence to be served for the remainder of one's natural life.

IN PHRASES

❑ **do the rosary** *v.* [1950s–70s] (*US Und.*) to serve a sentence of imprisonment for the rest of one's natural life.

rosary man *n.* [SE *rosary*, but why?] [1940s] (*UK Und.*) a confidence man who ensnares a victim by the fortuitous 'dropping' of a wallet.

roscoe *n.* (*also* **John Roscoe, rosca, rosco**) [? anecdotal] **1** [1910s+] (*US*) a handgun. **2** [1910s] (*US*) a man.

roscoe *v.* [ROSCOE *n.* (1)] [1970s] (*US*) to hold up with a gun.

rose *n.*[1] [literary euph.] [late 16C–17C; late 19C] the vagina, esp. of a virgin; thus *pluck a rose*, to deflower.

rose *n.*[2] [? the pleasant smell] [mid-19C] an orange.

SE in slang uses

IN PHRASES

❑ **gather a rose** *v.* [late 17C] euph., to urinate.

Roseanne (Barr) *n.* [rhy. sl.; ult. US comedienne and TV star *Roseanne Barr* (b.1953)] [1990s+] a *brassiere*.

rosebowl *n.* [ironic comment on the smell] [1940s–50s] (*Aus. milit.*) a latrine.

rosebud *n.*[1] [supposed resemblance] **1** [1910s] the mouth. **2** [1960s–70s] (*drugs*) a distended, inflamed rectum after passing a painful stool, the result of extended opium or heroin use. **3** [1960s+] (*US gay*) the anus.

rosebud *n.*[2] [rhy. sl. = SPUD *n.*[3] (1)] [1910s+] a potato.

rose-coloured *adj.* [1920s] a euph. synon. for BLOODY *adj.* (1).

roseleaf *v.* [? synon. Fr. *faire feuille de rose*, 'to do the rose-leaf'; note ROSEBUD *n.*[1] (3)] [mid-19C+] to perform anilingus.

roses *n.* **1** [early–mid-19C] (*UK Und.*) members of the aristocracy ['the flowers of society']. **2** [mid-19C–1920s] the menstrual period [pun on FLOWERS *n.* (1)]. **3** [1960s+] (*drugs*) amphetamine [play on RED *n.* (11)].

roses (are) red *n.* [rhy. sl.] [1910s+] (*Aus./US*) a bed.

rosey *n.* [ROSEBUD *n.*[1] (3)] [1970s+] (*US gay*) the buttocks, the rectum.

IN EXCLAMATIONS

❑ **up someone's rosey!** [1960s] (*US*) an excl. of aggressive dismissal.

rosey lee *n. see* ROSIE (LEA) *n.*

rosie *n.* [ironic comment on the smell] [1920s] (*US*) a garbage can.

rosie *v.* [ROSEBUD *n.*[1] (3)] [2000s] (*S.Afr. gay*) to perform anilingus.

rosie (lea) *n.* (*also* **rosey lee, rosy, rosy lea, rosy lee**) [rhy. sl.] [1910s+] **1** (*orig. milit.*) tea. **2** a flea.

rosie loader *n.* (*also* **rosie loder, rosy loader, rosy loder**) [rhy. sl.] [20C+] a whisky and soda.

Rosie O'Grady's *n.* [rhy. sl.] [1990s+] the ladies (lavatory).

rosin *n.* [? SE *rosin*, a sticky material that is smeared on a violin string or bow, to facilitate its playing; fiddlers were assumed to be drinkers; or Irish *raisín*, a snack] **1** [mid-18C] liquor. **2** [early–mid-19C] beer or other drink given to the musicians who entertain at a dance or party; thus *rosin*, to supply the musicians with drink. **3** [mid–late 19C] a fiddler, a violinist, also *rosin-the-bow*.

rosin chewer *n. see* ROSIN HEEL *n.*

rosin-drunk *adj.* (*also* **rosinned**) [? ROSIN *n.* (1) or the rosy pinkness of the drunkard's cheeks and nose] [20C+] drunk.

rosiner *n.* (*also* **rosner, rossiner, rozener, rozner, rozziner**) [Irish 20C+; Aus. 1930s+; ROSIN *n.* (1) + sfx *-er*] [20C+] (*Aus./Irish*) any form of stiff drink, a pick-me-up.

rosin heel *n.* (*also* **rosin chewer**) [ety. unknown; ? play on TARHEEL *n.*] **1** [19C] (*US*) a native of Florida. **2** [1980s] (*US black*) a derog. term for a white peasant.

rosinned *adj. see* ROSIN-DRUNK *adj.*

rosser *n. see* ROZZER *n.*[1].

rosy, the *n.* **1** [mid-19C–1900s] (red) wine [? Fr. *rosé*]. **2** [late 19C] blood. **3** [late 19C] the good life. **4** *see* ROSIE (LEA) *n.*

IN COMPOUNDS

❑ **rosy god** *n.* [late 19C] (*Aus.*) red wine.

IN PHRASES

❑ **do the rosy** *v.* [? ROSY, THE *n.* (2) or SE *rosy*, pleasant, enjoyable, positive] [mid–late 19C] to enjoy oneself, to have a good time.

rosy *adj.* [one's pink face] [1900s–40s] drunk, tipsy.

rosy lea/lee *n. see* ROSIE (LEA) *n.*

rosy loader/loder *n. see* ROSIE LOADER *n.*

Rosy Palm and her five (little) sisters *n.* (*also* **...her five (little) daughters**) [1950s+] the hand, as used in masturbation.

IN PHRASES

❑ **have a big date with Rosy Palm** *v.* (*also* **date Rosy Palm and her (five) sisters, entertain Rosy Palm, get off with..., go on a date with..., visit...**) [1990s+] to masturbate.

rosy-red *n.* [rhy. sl.] [1900s] (*Aus.*) the head.

rot *n.*[1] **1** [mid-19C+] rubbish, nonsense; esp. in *talk rot*, to talk nonsense. **2** [1910s] an unfortunate situation.

rot *n.*[2] **1** *see* ROTGUT *n.* (3). **2** *see* ROTTIE *n.*

rot *v.* **1** [late 19C] to talk nonsense [ROT *n.*[1]]. **2** [late 19C–1930s] to spoil, to interfere with, to ruin [i.e. to render SE *rotten*]. **3** [late 19C+] to tease heavily, to abuse, to denigrate [ROT *n.*[1]].

IN PHRASES

❑ **rot about** *v.* (*also* **rot along**) [late 19C–1920s] (*UK society*) to laze around, to idle, to fool around. ❑ **rot the socks off** *v.* [1950s+] to defeat comprehensively.

IN EXCLAMATIONS

❑ **rot off!** [1960s] a dismissive retort.

rot! *excl.*[1] [abbr. *God rot!*] [late 16C–19C] a general excl. of irritation, disbelief, dismissal; usu. as *rot it! rot 'em! rot on!*

IN EXCLAMATIONS

❑ **rot you!** [late 17C; mid-19C–1900s] a general excl. of derision, dismissal, synon. with 'to hell with you!'.

rot! *excl.*[2] [ROT *n.*[1]] [mid-19C+] nonsense! rubbish!

rotan *n.* [? Lat. *rota*, a wheel] [18C–mid-19C] (*UK Und.*) a wheeled vehicle, esp. a cart.

rotary (ho)! *excl.* [rhy. sl. RIGHTEO! *excl.* + pun on SE *rotary hoe*] [1960s] (*Aus./N.Z.*) fine! OK!

rotgut *n.* [its effects; cf. *GUT-ROT under* GUT *n.*] **1** [late 16C+] cheap or inferior beer. **2** [18C+] cheap wine. **3** [early 19C+] (*also* **rot**) (*US*) cheap whisky. **4** [mid-19C+] cheap alcohol in general; also attrib. **5** [1950s+] illicitly distilled alcohol.

rotic *adj.* [abbr. SE *romantic*, lit. without the 'man'] [1990s+] (*US campus*) romantic, without the 'man' and thus used in a non-sexual context.

roti ou *n.* [Hind. *roti*, bread (in the form of a chapatti) + OU *n.*] [1970s+] (*S.Afr.*) a Hindi speaker.

ro' tow *v.* [ROLL *v.* (4c) + TORE UP *adj.* (3)] [2000s] (*US black*) to drive under the influence of drink or drugs.

rots *adj.* [1980s] (*US campus*) bad.

rott *n. see* ROTTIE *n.*

rotted *adj.* [1990s+] (*US campus*) inferior, undesirable.

rotten *adj.* **1** [late 16C+] in a very poor state, of a very bad quality, quite worthless; by ext. venereally diseased; dead. **2** [mid-19C+] a general intensifier, e.g. *rotten luck, rotten bastard* etc. **3** [1940s+] (*Aus.*) very drunk; thus *get rotten*, to become very drunk.

SE in slang uses

IN COMPOUNDS

❑ **rotten apple** *v.* [the throwing of rotten fruit] [late 19C] (*US*) of an audience, to boo, hiss and generally give the actors a hard time. ❑ **rotten guts** *n.* [SE *rotten* + GUT *n.* (1a)] [1910s–20s] a person who has bad breath. ❑ **rotten orange** *n.* [pun on SE *rotten*, stale/*rotten*, unpleasant; William had been Prince of *Orange* before ascending the English throne] [late 17C] a pejorative term for a follower of King William III (r.1688–1702).

IN PHRASES

❑ **rotten with** *adj.* [20C+] usu, of money, well-supplied with.

rotten *adv.* [mid-19C+] a general intensifier, e.g. appallingly, disgustingly, extremely.

rotten row *n.* [rhy. sl.; *Rotten Row* is a riding track around London's Hyde Park, used by 19C fashionable society; promenading on horseback 'in the Row' was a daily necessity for the smart] **1** [late 19C+] a bow. **2** [20C+] a blow.

rotter *n.*[1] [ROT *v.*] **1** [late 19C+] a 'bad lot', a socially unacceptable person. **2** [1910s] (*Aus.*) a half-trained horse.

rotter *n.*[2] [in sceptical eyes a talker of ROT *n.*[1] (1)] [1930s+] (*Aus.*) an expert.

rottie *n.* (*also* **rot, rott, rotty**) [abbr.] [1980s+] a *Rott*weiler dog.

IN PHRASES

❑ **have a rottie** *v.* [2000s] (*N.Z.*) to be in a very aggressive mood.

rotto *adj.* [ROTTEN *adj.*] [late 19C–1950s] (*Irish*) drunk.

rouf *n.* (*also* **roaf**) [backsl.] **1** [mid-19C+] the number four. **2** [1940s–70s] four pence; four shillings. **3** [1940s+] £4, £400. **4** [1950s+] a four-year prison term etc.

IN COMPOUNDS

❑ **rouf gens** *n.* [GEN *n.*[1]] [mid-19C] 4 shillings. ❑ **rouf yeneps** *n.* [YENNEP *n.*] [mid-19C] 4 pence.

rouf-efil *n. see* ROFEFIL *n.*

rouge *n.* [the red jam that 'makes up' the plain bread] [2000s] (*S.Afr. prison*) bread.

rough *n.* [1960s+] rough cider.

rough *adj.* **1** [mid–late 19C] of foodstuffs, coarse, stale, 'off', decaying. **2** [mid-19C+] unfair, unreasonable. **3** [mid-19C+] a general pejorative; the inference is physically or mentally run-down or depressed. **4** [20C+] exhausting, demanding. **5** [1930s+] (*US black/campus*) excellent, admirable, very good. **6** [1940s–50s] (*US*) sexually unrestrained. **7** [1940s+] (*Aus.*) promiscuous.

IN PHRASES

❑ **a bit rough** *adj.* [1940s+] (*Aus.*) unreasonable, unfair. ❑ **bit of rough** see separate entries. ❑ **feel rough** *v.* [1910s+] to feel very bad, whether emotionally or physically. ❑ **on the rough** [1920s] (*US*) in difficulties. ❑ **rough as…** *adj.* see separate entry. ❑ **rough end of the pineapple** *n.* (*also* **rough end of the stick, wrong end of the pineapple**) [1960s+] (*Aus.*) hostile or unfair treatment.

SE in slang uses

IN COMPOUNDS

❑ **rough-ass** *adj.* [-ASS *sfx*] [20C+] (*US*) crude, coarse. ❑ **rough bananas** *n. see under* BANANA *n.* ❑ **rough deal** *n. see* RAW DEAL *under* RAW *adj.* ❑ **rough-dried hair** *n.* [as opposed to blow-dried hair and thus neatened or even straightened] [1930s–40s] (*US black*) very kinky hair. ❑ **rough fam** *n.* (*also* **rough-fammy**) [FAM *n.*[1] (1); ? f. one's putting one's thumbs into the waistcoat pockets and the rubbing this entails] [early 19C] (*UK Und.*) a waistcoat pocket. ❑ **rough-guts** *n.* [1940s+] (*N.Z.*) a hooligan, an uncouth person. ❑ **rough-headed** *adj. see* ROUGHNECK *adj.* ❑ **roughhouse** *see* separate entries. ❑ **rough malkin** *n.* [MALKIN *n.*] [mid-16C] the vagina. ❑ **roughneck(ed)** *see* separate entries. ❑ **rough nut** *n. see* TOUGH NUT *n.* ❑ **rough spin** *n. see under* SPIN *n.*[3]. ❑ **rough stuff** *n. see* separate entry. ❑ **rough trade** see separate entries. ❑ **rough trot** *n. see under* TROT *n.*[2]. ❑ **rough work** *n. see* ROUGH STUFF *n.* (1).

IN PHRASES

❑ **rough on rats** *n.* [brandname *Rough on Rats*, a US proprietary rat poison] [late 19C] (*Aus.*) bad luck.

rough *v. see* ROUGH UP *v.*

rough *adv.* [mid-19C+] badly, unpleasantly.

IN PHRASES

❑ **cut up rough** *v. see* separate entry. ❑ **play rough** *v.* [1950s+] (*orig. US*) to be tough or ruthless, to not act fairly.

rough and ready *n.* (*also* **rough and tumble**) [mid-19C] the vagina.

rough as… *adj.*

IN PHRASES

❑ **…a badger's arse** (*also* **rough as a badger, rough as a badger's behind, rough as a badger's bottom, rough as a bear's arse, rough as a rat's back**) [early 18C+] bristly, straggly, coarse, also fig. use. ❑ **…a bag** (*also* **rough as bags**) [abbr. SE *sandbag*] [1910s+] (*Aus./N.Z.*) uncouth, ill-mannered. ❑ **…a cob** [the use of corn *cobs* as toilet paper in country districts] [1940s+] (*US*) very rough. ❑ **…a pig's breakfast** (*also* **rough as a dog's breakfast**) [1940s+] (*Aus./N.Z.*) uncouth, ill-mannered. ❑ **…a soojee bag** [Hind. *suji*, a flour based on Indian wheat, thus the bag that held it] [mid-19C] (*N.Z.*) very rough. ❑ **…guts** (*also* **rough as old guts**) [1960s+] (*Aus./N.Z.*) **1** lacking in refinement (usu. fig. but also lit.). **2** a phr. of admiration, praising the 'rough diamond' who may be vulgar but remains tough and ingenious and ultimately successful. ❑ **…sacks** [1940s+] (*N.Z.*) very rough. ❑ **…sandbags** [1910s] (*Aus.*) guilty of performing an offensive action or telling exaggerated stories.

roughey *n. see* ROUGHIE *n.*[1].

roughhouse *n.* [late 19C+] (*orig. US*) **1** boisterous behaviour, usu. harmless. **2** physical violence, a fight. **3** unpleasant behaviour.

roughhouse *adj.* (*also* **roughhousy**) [20C+] **1** of a person, violent, emotionally unrestrained. **2** usu. of a fight, violent. **3** of a place, or situation, tough, rough.

roughhouse *v.* **1** [late 19C+] (*orig. US*) to fight, to beat up; as n., *rough-houser*, a fighter. **2** [20C+] (*orig. US*) to behave in a rowdy, boisterous manner. **3** [1990s+] (*US*) to enjoy the sleazier aspects of sex; to be a devotee of sado-masochism.

roughie *n.*[1] (*also* **roughey, roughy**) [ROUGH *adj.*] **1** [20C+] (*orig. Aus./N.Z.*) any person or animal considered tough and intractable. **2** [1910s] (*Aus.*) an unpleasant place or situation. **3** [1910s] (*Aus./N.Z.*) an unqualified or incompetent worker. **4** [1910s+] (*Aus.*) an implausible story. **5** [1930s+] (*Aus.*) a fraud, a deception, esp. in the phr. *put a roughie over*, to cheat. **6** [1930s+] (*Aus.*) in horse and dog racing, an outsider. **7** [1980s] (*US black*) a person looking for trouble, wanting to start a fight. **8** [2000s] (*N.Z.*) a quick act of sexual intercourse.

roughie *n.*[2] *see* ROUGHNECK *n.* (3).

rough it *v.* **1** [late 18C+] to live deprived of life's material comforts; not simply to be poor, but to volunteer oneself, as in camping, the forces etc, for such hardy existence; thus *rough-un* n., a good spot for sleeping out of doors. **2** [1910s] (*US*) to treat roughly. **3** [1910s–20s] to fight.

roughneck *n.* **1** [mid-19C+] (*orig. US*) a thug, a hoodlum, a fighter. **2** [20C+] (*US*) an unmannered, informal person. **3** [1910s+] (*also* **roughie**) a labourer, usu. on an oil rig. **4** [1990s+] (*W.I.*) a dancehall enthusiast.

roughneck *adj.* (*also* **rough-headed, roughnecked**) **1** [1910s–20s] (*US*) aggressive, tough. **2** [1910s+] a general pejorative. **3** [2000s] excellent, admirable, very good [on bad = good model].

rough-o *n.* [var. on ROUGH AND READY *n.*] [late 19C] the vagina.

rough stuff *n.* [SE *rough*] **1** [20C+] (*also* **rough work**) physical violence. **2** [1900s–30s] severe criticism; intense teasing. **3** [1910s–20s] (*Aus./US*) a disrespectful, reckless, indecent or disorderly person; disrespect, recklessness, indecency. **4** [1970s+] (*orig. US*) sado-masochistic sex. **5** [1970s+] (*drugs*) marijuana that contains a lot of unsmokeable debris [STUFF *n.* (5b)].

rough trade *n.* **1** [1910s+] (*gay*) a violent sexual partner; often a man who is, or poses as, a construction worker, serviceman, truck driver, motorcyclist etc, with appropriate costumes, often of leather. **2** [1960s] a male heterosexual who has intercourse with a male homosexual. **3** [1960s] (*US*) anyone seen as tough.

rough-trade *adj.* [ROUGH TRADE *n.*] [1920s+] pertaining to sex with a violent, aggressive partner.

rough-up *n.* [ROUGH UP *v.* (2)] **1** [late 19C–1940s] a street-fight, a violent fracas; also in fig. use. **2** [1910s] an aggressive or violent person.

rough up *v.* (*also* **rough, rough around**) **1** [late 19C] to act aggressively; to cause a fuss. **2** [late 19C+] (*US*) to beat up, to injure, esp. to intimidate.

roughy *n. see* ROUGHIE *n.*[1].

round *n.* **1** [17C+] a walk; a spree. **2** *see* ROUNDS *n.*[1].

round *adj.*

SE in slang uses

IN COMPOUNDS

❑ **roundball** *n.* [1970s+] (*US black*) basketball (as opposed to football, played with an oval ball). ❑ **round brown** *n. see* BROWN *n.* (3a). ❑ **round file** *n.* (*also* **round filing cabinet**) [1970s+] (*orig. US*) a wastepaper basket. ❑ **roundman** *n.* [the *round* coin] [1920s] (*US*) a dollar. ❑ **round mouth** *n.* [abbr.

BROTHER ROUND-MOUTH *under* BROTHER *n.*] [early 19C] the anus. ❑ **round o** *n.* [the *oh!* of disbelief it elicits] [early 17C] a great lie. ❑ **round pussy** *n.* [SE *round* + PUSSY *n.* (1)] [1990s+] (*US*) the anus. ❑ **round steak** *n. see under* STEAK *n.*

round *v.* [abbr. GET ROUND *v.*] **1** [mid-19C] to elicit information from someone by trickery. **2** [1900s] (*UK Und.*) to confess, to tell the truth. **3** [1900s–40s] to obtain information about someone by questioning a third party.

roundabout *n.* **1** [early 19C] (*UK prison*) the treadmill. **2** [mid-19C] (*US*) a prize-ring.

roundakin *n. see* ROUNDY-KEN *n.*

roundem *n.* [ext. of SE *round*] **1** [mid-19C–1900s] a button. **2** [1910s–20s] the head.

rounder *n.* **1** in senses of SE *do the rounds/know one's way around*. (**a**) [mid-19C] (*US Und.*) a sponger, a parasite on gamblers. (**b**) [mid-19C–1900s] (*US*) a rich, fashionable man-about-town, a playboy. (**c**) [late 19C+] (*Can. prison*) anyone familiar with the underworld. (**d**) [1920s] (*US*) a pimp, a procurer. (**e**) [1990s+] (*US prison*) a member of a prison gang, esp. of an Italian gang. **2** [late 19C] a tight, short jacket [it *goes around* the body]. **3** in senses of SE *move around, go round and round*. (**a**) [late 19C–1930s] (*US*) a vagrant. (**b**) [1900s] (*US Und.*) a recidivist. **4** [late 19C+] (*US Und.*) an informer. [SE round on, to turn against].

rounders *n.* [events have fig. 'turned around' on the sufferer + the image of the running in a game of SE *rounders*] [20C+] (*W.I.*) confusion, trouble.

(IN PHRASES)

❑ **give rounders** *v.* [20C+] (*W.I., Trin.*) to be evasive, to deceive, to deal with in an annoying manner.

roundeye *n.* [1950s+] **1** the anus [SE *round* + -EYE *sfx*]. **2** anal intercourse. **3** a male homosexual [metonymy]. **4** a white person, as opposed to an East Asian person; usu. of women; also attrib [as opposed to SLANT *n.* (3)].

round-eyed *adj.* (*also* **roundeye**) [1960s+] (*US*) Caucasian.

roundhead *n.* **1** [late 19C+] (*US*) an immigrant from northern Europe, esp. a Swede [? physiognomy]. **2** [20C+] (*usu. teen*) a circumcised penis; thus the boy or man who has one [the antonym of CAVALIER *n.*]. **3** [1970s+] (*drugs*) any drug contained in a capsule with curved ends.

roundheel *n.* (*also* **roundheeler, roundheels**) [all fall over easily; the image is of pivoting on the rounded heel] **1** [1920s+] (*US*) an inferior prize-fighter, also fig. use. **2** [1920s+] a promiscuous woman. **3** [1970s+] (*US gay/prison*) a victimized young inmate, forced into homosexuality.

roundheeled *adj.* [ROUNDHEEL *n.*] [1920s+] (*US*) **1** easily defeated. **2** of a woman or gay man, promiscuous.

roundhouse *n.* [1910s+] a blow delivered with a wide sweep of the arm, usu. in comb., e.g. *roundhouse punch, roundhouse right*.

roundhouse *v.*[1] [ROUNDHOUSE *n.*] [1920s+] to hit someone with a wide sweep of the arm.

roundhouse *v.*[2] [1960s+] (*US*) of a prostitute, to lick, suck and otherwise stimulate every orifice and erogenous zone her client has to offer.

roundie *n.* [1940s+] (*N.Z.*) a factory-made cigarette.

round me houses *n.* (*also* **pair o' round-mys, round mys, rounds, round the houses**) [rhy. sl.] [mid-19C+] trousers.

round (on) *v.* [SE *round on*, to turn against, to attack] [mid-19C–1900s] to inform against, to betray; to become an informer.

round robin *n.* [SE *round robin*, a document, typically a complaint or petition, in which the signatories place their names in a circle, thus hiding any form of hierarchy] **1** [mid 16C–mid-17C] the host (in communion). **2** [mid-16C+] a complainant, a petitioner. **3** [late 19C] a swindle.

round-robin *v.* [SE *round robin*, a sports tournament, e.g. tennis, in which each competitor plays all the rest] [1960s+] to have sex on a single occasion with a succession of partners.

rounds *n.*[1] [abbr. *all rounds, all rounders*, trade names of fashionable collars] [mid-19C] shirt collars; occas. sing.

rounds *n.*[2] *see* ROUND ME HOUSES *n.*

rounds of the kitchen *n. see under* KITCHEN *n.*[1].

round the... *phr.*

SE in slang uses

(IN PHRASES)

❑ **round the bend** *adj.* (*also* **around the bend**) [the image is of one who is 'not straight'] [1920s+] (*orig. naut.*) eccentric, crazy, insane; ext. as [1950s+] *round the bend – and back again; round the bend – and halfway down the straight*. ❑ **round the clock** *n.* [1940s] (*Aus. Und.*) a sentence of twelve months. ❑ **round the horn** *adj.* [ety. unknown] **1** [mid-19C] drunk. **2** [20C+] (*US Und.*) detained on a minor criminal charge but suspected of a more serious crime. **3** [1920s] (*US Und.*) used of a suspect who is moved between police stations to keep them from legal advice. ❑ **round the twist** *adj.* [var. on ROUND THE BEND above] [1960s+] mad, eccentric, insane. ❑ **round the world for a dollar** *adj.* [1960s] (*Aus.*) inferior, as of wine, usu. laced with methylated spirits. ❑ **round the world for threepence** (*also* **...fourpence, ...ninepence**) [the effects and cheap price] [1980s+] (*N.Z.*) drinking methylated spirits, or cheap wine.

round the houses *n. see* ROUND ME HOUSES *n.*

round-up *n.* **1** [1900s] (*US Und.*) dismissing the victim after a confidence trick has been concluded successfully [SE *round up*, to conclude]. **2** [1920s+] a get-together, an assembly, a collection of bits, e.g. food left on a plate [ROUND UP *v.*].

round up *v.* [Western imagery] [1920s+] (*orig. US*) to assemble, to get together.

roundy-ken *n.* (*also* **roundakin**) [lit. 'round-house'] [early–mid-19C] a lock-up, an early police station.

roupy *adj. see* ROPEY *adj.*

rouse *n.* [? SE *carouse*, or Ger. *rausch*, intoxication, drunken fit] [mid-16C–mid-19C] a large glass; a full glass.

rouse *v.* (*also* **rouse on, roust**) [Scot. *roust*, to roar, bellow] [mid-18C; 20C+] (*Aus.*) to scold, to berate; thus *get roused on*, to be scolded.

rouser *n.* **1** [mid-19C] (*US*) an outstanding individual; an exceptional creature; a startling event. **2** [late 19C–1930s] the first drink of the day, used as a 'pick-me-up'. **3** [1940s] a womanizer [? SE *arouse*]. **4** [1970s+] (*drugs*) any type of amphetamine or stimulant drug which 'gets one up'.

rousie *n.* (*also* **rouser, rousey**) [SE *rouseabout*] [late 19C+] (*Aus.*) a general hand on a rural property.

roust *n.*[1] [ROUST *v.*[1]] [late 16C–early 17C] sexual intercourse.

roust *n.*[2] **1** [1930s] a kick [SE *roust*]. **2** [1960s+] (*orig. US Und.*) an arrest [ROUST *v.*[2] (3)].

roust *v.*[1] [SE *roust*, to roar, to bellow] [late 16C–early 17C] to have sexual intercourse.

roust *v.*[2] [SE *roust*, to stir, to wake up, to arouse] **1** [early 19C; 1940s+] (*US black*) to steal; to rob. **2** [1900s–60s] (*UK Und.*) to jostle, as in picking a pocket. **3** [1910s+] (*US*) to harass, esp. of the police. **4** [1920s+] to awaken. **5** [1930s+] to raid an establishment. **6** [1950s] (*US*) to beat up. **7** [1960s+] to arrest. **8** [1980s+] (*US campus*) to tease, to harass.

roust *v.*[3] *see* ROUSE *v.*

rout *v.* [SE *rout*, to poke about] [1970s] (*US campus*) to engage in sexual intercourse.

route *n.*

(IN PHRASES)

❑ **go the route** *v.* **1** [20C+] (*US*) to commit oneself completely. **2** [1950s] to live a hedonistic life.

routine *n.* [show business jargon *routine*, a carefully rehearsed act] [1930s+] (*US*) **1** an evasive or contrived response. **2** a fraudulent scheme, esp. as practised by confidence tricksters.

(IN PHRASES)

❑ **put down a routine** *v.* [SE *put down* + show business *routine*, a regularly performed sketch, song, dance etc] [1950s+] (*US*) to hoax or otherwise persuade someone with a clever story.

Rover *n.* [ety. unknown] [late 19C+] (*US*) an inhabitant of Colorado.

rover *n.* [2000s] (*S.Afr. gay*) the penis.

Rover Boy *n.* [1950s] (*US*) a policeman.

Row, the *n.* **1** [early 17C] Goldsmith's Row. **2** [late 17C–mid-19C] Paternoster Row, EC4 the centre of London publishing. **3** [late 18C] (*Irish*) New Row, Dublin, the site of the prison. **4** [19C] Rotten Row. **5** [mid-19C] as *Booksellers Row*, euph. for Holywell St, WC, the contemporary centre of pornographic publishing. **6** [late 19C] Club Row, London E1. **7** [1930s+] (*US prison*) the condemned cells, i.e. DEATH ROW *n.* **8** [1980s+] (*US campus*) fraternity or sorority row, i.e. the line of adjacent fraternity or sorority houses on a campus.

row *n.*[1] [virtually SE today, *row* began as sl. and is cited as 'a very low expression' in Todd's revision of Johnson's *Dict.* (1818)] [mid-18C+] a disturbance, a noisy quarrel; thus *what's the row?*, what's all the noise about?; *hold your row*, be quiet.

IN PHRASES

❑ **kick up a row** *v.* [late 18C+] to cause trouble, to create a disturbance. ❑ **row up** *v.* [mid–late 19C] **1** to wake up someone roughly and noisily. **2** to scold, to criticize. ❑ **shut one's row** *v.* (*also* **shut one's noise**) [late 19C+] to be quiet, esp. as imper.

row *n.*[2] [var. LINE *n.*[1] (5d)] [1970s+] (*US drugs*) a small quantity of a narcotic, esp. cocaine.

SE in slang uses

IN PHRASES

❑ **row of beans/pins** *n. see* HILL OF BEANS, A *phr.*

row *v.*[1] [ROW *n.*[1]] **1** [late 18C] to rouse up by making a noise. **2** [late 18C–mid-19C] to attack or assail a person in a rough manner. **3** [late 18C+] to make a row or disturbance, to quarrel noisily or heatedly. **4** [late 18C+] to scold or criticize a person angrily or severely, to take sharply to task.

row *v.*[2]

SE in slang uses

IN PHRASES

❑ **row in the (same) boat** *v. see under* BOAT *n.*[1]. ❑ **row (someone) up Salt River** *v. see under* SALT RIVER *n.* ❑ **row with one oar (in the water)** *v.* (*also* **not have both oars in the water**) [1980s+] (*US*) to be irrational or stupid.

row-de-dow *n.* (*also* **row-dow**) [ext. of ROW *n.*[1]] [mid–late 19C] (*Irish*) an argument, a row, a set-to; thus v. *row-de-dow*, to argue, to make a disturbance.

row-de-dow *adj.* [ROW-DE-DOW *n.*] [late 19C] boisterous, noisy.

rowdy *n.* (*also* **rowdie**) [note Thackeray's fictitious bankers, *Rowdy and Stump*, a firm who can also be found in Cuthbert Bede's *Adventures of Mr Verdant Green* (1853)] [mid–late 19C] money; the word implies the efforts involved in obtaining money.

rowdy-dow *n.* [ROW-DE-DOW *n.*] **1** [late 18C] disturbance, noise. **2** [late 19C–1900s] a socially unacceptable person, who is vulgar, noisy or reprobate.

rowdy-dow *adj.* [redup. of SE *rowdy*, rough, disorderly] [mid-19C+] socially unacceptable, vulgar, noisy, rough.

rowdy-dowdy *adj.* [redup. of SE *rowdy*, but note ROWDY-DOW *adj.*] [mid-19C–1920s; 2000s] aggressive, antagonistic; also as n.

rowdy-dows *n.* [? rhy. sl.] [1900s] (*US*) trousers.

row in *v.* (*UK Und.*) **1** [late 19C+] to allow someone to join a scheme, a conspiracy. **2** [1910s+] to implicate a suspect in a crime; thus *row out*, to exonerate a suspect from a crime. **3** [1910s+] to include.

IN PHRASES

❑ **row in the (same) boat** *v. see under* BOAT *n.*[1].

rowly-powly *n. see* ROLY-POLY *n.*[2].

row oneself onto *v.* [ROW IN *v.*] [1940s+] to associate oneself with a group.

row out *v.* [anton. of ROW IN *v.* (1)] [1960s+] to exclude someone from a deal or organization.

Rowton Houses *n.* [rhy. sl.] [1900s–50s] trousers; usu. *Rowtons*.

rox *n.* (*also* **roxanne**) [ROCK *n.* (4)] [1980s+] (*drugs*) **1** cocaine. **2** freebase, later crack cocaine.

roxmellow *n.* [mid-19C] (*UK Und.*) a drunken woman.

roy *n.*[1] **1** [1960s–70s] (*Aus.*) a chic, sophisticated, 'trendy' Australian [a stereotypically 'smart' name]. **2** [1990s+] (*US black*) a stupid white boy [a stereotypically 'white' name].

roy *n.*[2] [Romani] [1980s] a gentleman.

royal *n.*[1] [? fig. use of Sp. *real*, a coin of very low value and considered inferior to UK sterling; such individuals have low social status; the US use is prob. ignorant of such overtones] [20C+] **1** (*W.I., Jam.*) any black person from a race other than West Indian; thus in combs. *coolie royal* (East Indian) and joc./derog. *jackass-royal, monkey-royal*. **2** (*W.I.*) (*also* **Chiney-Royal**) a mixed black/Chinese person. **3** (*US black*) a West Indian. **4** (*W.I., Trin.*) the buttocks [fig. use of sense 1 above; in this case the physical 'lowness' of the buttocks].

IN PHRASES

❑ **catch one's royal** *v.* [1950s] (*W.I.*) to have no money. ❑ **in one's royal** *adj.* [? Carib.E *royal/rial*, arrogant, high and mighty] [20C+] (*W.I.*) very drunk.

royal *n.*[2] (*also* **boss's royal**) [SE *royal*, i.e their privileged position in the working hierarchy] [1930s–60s] (*N.Z.*) a management stooge.

royal *adj.* [SE *royal*, pertaining to a royal family] [mid-19C+] (*orig. US*) a general intensifier, often used before so-called taboo terms, e.g. *a royal screwing, a royal shafting*.

IN COMPOUNDS

❑ **royal fucking** *n.* (*also* **r.f.**) [FUCKING *n.* (2)] [1950s+] (*US*) harsh or very bad treatment. ❑ **royal screw** *n. see under* SCREW *n.*[1]. ❑ **royal shaft** *n.* (*also* **king's elevator, royal shafting**) [SHAFT *n.* (2)/SHAFTING *n.* (2)/pun on SE *elevator shaft*] [1950s+] an act of extreme harshness or unfairness, as meted out on oneself or to another person.

SE in slang uses

IN COMPOUNDS

❑ **royal Alberts** *n. see* ALBERTS *n.* ❑ **royal blues** *n.* [the uniform/pills are blue] **1** [mid-19C] the police force. **2** [1970s] (*drugs*) LSD. ❑ **royal bob** *n. see under* BOB *n.*[3]. ❑ **royal game** *n.* [2000s] (*S.Afr. gay*) an underage boy. ❑ **royal order, the** *n.* [abbr. *royal order of the sack/boot*] [1920s+] (*Aus.*) dismissal from one's job. ❑ **royal poverty** *n.* [gin may be drunk when one is 'feeling right royal' but it will lead to poverty] [mid–late 18C] gin. ❑ **royal scamp** *n. see under* SCAMP *n.*

IN PHRASES

❑ **royal palace of Holloway** *n. see* HOLLOWAY CASTLE *n.*

royal *adv.* [1920s+] completely, comprehensively.

royal docks *n.* [rhy. sl. = POX *n.*[1] (3)] [20C+] venereal disease.

royal mail *n.* [rhy. sl.] [20C+] (*mainly UK Und.*) bail.

royal navy *n.* [rhy. sl.] [20C+] gravy.

royalty *n.* [its superior ranking in the hierarchy of drugs] [1980s+] (*drugs*) cocaine.

Roy Castle *n.* [rhy. sl. = ARSEHOLE *n.* (1); ult. UK comedian *Roy Castle* (1932–94] [1990s+] the anus.

roy rodgers *n.* [rhy. sl. = *bodgers*; ult. film cowboy *Roy Rogers* (1912–98)] [20C+] second-rate builders.

royster *n. see* ROISTER *n.*

rozener *n. see* ROSINER *n.*

rozner *n. see* ROSINER *n.*

rozzer *n.*[1] (*also* **rawser, razzer, rosser, roz**) [? Rom. *roozlo*, strong or *roast*, a villain] [late 19C+] a police officer.

rozzer *n.*[2] [? SE *arouser/rouser*] [1970s] (*US black*) a rubber contraceptive with small protrusions for extra stimulation of the vagina.

rozzinelly *n.* [mid-19C] (*UK Und.*) a drunken woman.

rozziner *n. see* ROSINER *n.*

r.s. *see* RATSHIT.

r/s *phr.* [abbr.] [1970s+] used in sex contact advertisements, rough stuff, i.e. sado-masochism, urolagnia, piercing and rubberwear.

rub *n.*[1] [abbr. SE *rubber*] [late 18C–19C] a round or rubber of a card-game, usu. whist.

rub *n.*[2] **1** [1900s–10s] (*US*) a dance, typified by the overt sexuality and physical proximity of the partners; a dancing party; *rub club*, *rub joint*, a dancehall where such dancing occurs. **2** [1950s] (*W.I.*) (*also* **rub-up**) a dance or dancing party.

IN COMPOUNDS

❑ **rub joint** *n.* [JOINT *n.* (3b)] [1910s–40s] a low dancehall, which features dances such as the *lovers' two-step*, the *bunny hug* and the *turkey trot*, all of which permit much more physical intimacy than those on offer at more staid establishments.

SE in slang uses

IN COMPOUNDS

❑ **rub parlour** *n.* [SE *rub*/RUB OFF *v.*[1] (2)] [1960s+] (*US*) a massage parlour.

IN PHRASES

❑ **rub of the relic** *n.* (*also* **rub of the rasher**) [1970s+] (*Irish*) sexual intercourse. ❑ **give someone the rub** *n.* (*also* **give someone a rub**) [1940s] to tease.

rub *n.*[3] [1960s] (*US black*) a successful confidence trick.

rub *n.*[4] *see* RUB(-OUT) *n.*

rub *v.*[1] [mid-16C–early 19C] (*UK Und.*) to run away.

rub *v.*[2] **1** [1920s+] (*US*) to steal, to burglarize. **2** [1950s] (*US*) to lose one's temper. **3** [1970s] (*US black*) to criticize.

SE in slang uses

IN PHRASES

❑ **rub a sentence** *v.* [1990s+] (*W.I.*) to serve a prison sentence. ❑ **rub bellies** *v. see under* BELLY *n.* ❑ **rub in** *v.* **1** [mid-19C+] to emphasize, often with malicious pleasure; thus [late 19C] (*UK Und.*) *rub it in well*, to give (true or false) evidence that will certainly lead to a conviction. **2** [1910s] (*US*) to treat harshly. ❑ **rub the grub** *v.* [SE *rub*/RUB OFF *v.*[1] (2)] [1990s+] (*Aus.*) to masturbate. ❑ **rub (to)** *v.* [SE *rub*, to go] [late 17C–early 18C] (*UK Und.*) to carry off to gaol, to imprison. ❑ **rub to the whit** *v.* [WHIT *n.*] [late 17C–mid-19C] (*UK Und.*) to send to prison.

rub *v.*[3] *see* RUB OUT *v.*

rub-a-dub *n.* (*also* **rubadub, rub-a-dub-dub, rubbity-dub, rubbledebub, ruddity dub**) [rhy. sl.] **1** [late 19C+] a pub or public house. **2** [1930s] a 'sub' or advance on wages. **3** [1930s+] a drinking club, a social club.

IN COMPOUNDS

❑ **rub-a-dub soldier** *n.* [Carib. E. *rub-a-dub*, heavy instrumental music, also a type of dance] [1990s+] (*W.I.*) a dancehall music enthusiast.

rub-a-dub(-dub) *n.* [SE *rub-a-dub*, the beat of a drum] [1950s+] (*orig. US*) sexual intercourse; esp. quick and spontaneous.

rub-a-tug shop *n.* (*also* **rub and tug shop**) [RUB-A-DUB(-DUB) *n.*/RUB OFF *v.*[1] + TUG *v.* + SHOP *n.*[1] (3);] [1980s+] a cheap brothel, an 'escort agency'.

rubbed *adj.* [RUB OUT *v.* (1)] [20C+] murdered, killed.

rubbed off *adj.* [RUB *v.*[1]] [late 17C–mid-19C] (*UK Und.*) bankrupt and thus run away.

rubbed out *adj.* [sense 1 has no implication of foul play, one has simply been erased from the 'Book of Life'] **1** [mid-19C+] dead. **2** [20C+] murdered.

rubbedy *n.* (*also* **robberdy, rubberdy, rubbidy, rubbity, rubby, ruppery**) [RUB-A-DUB *n.* (1)] [late 19C+] (*Aus.*) a public house.

rubber *n.*[1] [? SE *rub* (*up against*); ? link to the sporting use, coined in the 16C, meaning a match, adopted in the 17C as a quarrel or fight] **1** [mid-16C] (*UK Und.*) a member of a team of confidence tricksters who works as a back-up to those running the fraud; if the victim realizes they are being tricked, the rubber swiftly causes a disturbance, usu. by picking a fight with the earnest bystander, thus allowing their confederates to grab the stakes and run. **2** [early 17C; 1900s–50s] any form of deception or trick.

rubber *n.*[2] **1** [1930s] (*US*) a cosh. **2** [1930s–40s] (*US black*) a car; thus *on rubber*, to be driving a car. **3** [1930s+] (*orig. US*) a contraceptive sheath. **4** [1950s+] a fake or forged cheque, thus *drop rubber*, to pass such a cheque. **5** [1970s] (*US*) a set of tyres. **6** *see* RUBBER CHEQUE *n.*

IN COMPOUNDS

❑ **rubber shop** *n.* [sense 3 above; in a puritan era, such shops were a primary source of contraceptives] [1930s–50s] a sex shop.

IN PHRASES

❑ **burn rubber** *v. see* separate entry. ❑ **get rubber** *v. see* LAY RUBBER *under* LAY *v.*[1]. ❑ **lay rubber** *v. see under* LAY *v.*[1]. ❑ **peel rubber** *v.* (*also* **catch rubber, peel off**) [the smoking tyres that accompany acceleration] [1950s+] to drive a car very fast. ❑ **screech/smoke/tear rubber** *v. see* BURN RUBBER *v.*

SE in slang uses

IN COMPOUNDS

❑ **rubber queen** *n.* [SE *rubber* + -QUEEN *sfx*] [1970s+] (*orig. gay*) a rubber fetishist.

IN PHRASES

❑ **where the rubber meets the road** *n.* [1950s] (*US*) in fig. use, the desired place.

rubber *n.*[3] [RUB OUT *v.* (1)] [1930s–40s] (*US Und.*) a professional killer.

rubber *n.*[4] [rhy. sl.; abbr. *rubber and plastic*] [2000s] a spastic.

rubber *n.*[5] *see* RUBBERNECK *n.*

rubber *adj.*

SE in slang uses

IN COMPOUNDS

❑ **rubber boot** *n.* [1970s+] a contraceptive sheath. ❑ **rubber check** *n. see* RUBBER CHEQUE *n.* ❑ **rubber cheque** *n. see* separate entry. ❑ **rubber-chicken circuit** *n.* (*also* **mashed potato circuit**) [the poor quality of the food (almost invariably chicken) on offer] [1930s+] (*US*) the after-dinner-speaking circuit; esp. as followed by political hopefuls. ❑ **Rubber City** *n.* [tyre-making, its primary industry] [1970s+] (*US*) Akron, Ohio. ❑ **rubber dollies** *n.* [dial. *dollies*, rags] [1970s+] (*Irish*) plimsolls, gymshoes, trainers. ❑ **rubber drink** *n.* [it 'bounces back'] [1920s] (*US*) a drink which causes vomiting. ❑ **rubber gash** *n. see* GASH *n.*[1] (1). ❑ **rubber guts** *n.* [? the image of a pompous individual with a large stomach that appears to have been blown up] [1910s] (*Aus./N.Z.*) a clumsy or pompous person. ❑ **rubberhead** *n.* [1990s+] (*Aus.*) a fool; a jocular form of address. ❑ **rubber johnny** *n.* [SE *rubber*/RUBBER *n.*[2] (3) + JOHNNY *n.*[1] (12)] [1950s+] a contraceptive sheath. ❑ **rubber kite** *n. see* RUBBER CHEQUE *n.* ❑ **rubber pill** *n.* [1950s–70s] (*drugs*) a condom or the finger of a rubber glove used to store or transport narcotics. ❑ **rubber room** *n.* (*also* **rubber palace**) [1930s+] a padded cell. ❑ **rubber sock** *n.* [? the limpness of such a supposed garment] [1930s–40s] (*US tramp*) a timid person. ❑ **rubber sole** *n.* [1980s] (*US*) a police officer. ❑ **rubber tramp** *v.* [? image of bouncing from place to place + pun on SE *rubber-stamp*] [1920s] (*US*) to live as a vagrant. ❑ **rubber tyre** *n. see* SPARE TYRE *under* SPARE *adj.* ❑ **rubberwrist** *n.* [his stereotypically limp wrist] [1970s+] an effeminate male homosexual; thus *rubber-wristed*, effeminate.

IN PHRASES

❑ **don't take any rubber dimes** *see under* DIME *n.*

rubber *v.*[1] [1900s] (*US campus*) to annoy; to deceive or trick; to put at a disadvantage, to question.

rubber *v.*[2] *see* RUBBERNECK *v.*

rubber (around) *v.* **1** [1890s] (*US*) to wander about. **2** *see* RUBBERNECK *v.*

rubber cheque *n.* (*also* **inner tube, rubber, rubber check, rubber kite**) [SE *rubber* + *cheque*/SAE *check*/KITE *n.* (3a); it 'bounces'] [1920s+] a cheque that is not honoured by the writer's bank; thus *rubber checkbook*; *rubber check artist*, one who passes such cheques.

rubber duck *n.* [rhy. sl. = FUCK *n.* (1a)] **1** [1980s+] (*Aus. prison*) fellatio. **2** [1990s+] sexual intercourse.

rubberdy *n. see* RUBBEDY *n.*

rubberer *n.* [RUBBERNECK *v.*] [1900s] (*US*) an inquisitive person.

rubber glove *v.* [rhy. sl.] [2000s] to love, i.e. to enjoy.

rubber heel *n.* [note police jargon *rubber heels*, Special Branch, the internal investigations department of Scotland Yard, policing the police] **1** [1920s+] (*also* **rubberglue, soft heel**) (*US*) a private detective; a store detective; a railway detective. **2** [1920s+] someone who spies on their fellow employees; thus *rubber heel boy, rubber heel inquiry, rubber-heel mob.* **3** [1940s] (*US prison*) in pl., meatloaf [negative comment on the dish's consistency/flavour].

rubberneck *n.* (*also* **rubber, rubbernecker**) [RUBBERNECK *v.*] [late 19C+] (*orig. US*) **1** a tourist, esp. to New York City. **2** a very inquisitive, curious person, usu. naïve. **3** (*S.Afr.*) a nagging woman.

IN COMPOUNDS

❑ **rubberneck wagon** *n.* (*also* **rubberneck, rubberneck auto, rubberneck buggy, rubberneck bus, rubberneck car, rubberneck coach**) [late 19C–1940s] (*US*) a sightseeing bus or similar vehicle; thus *rubberneck ride, rubberneck tour.*

rubberneck *v.* (*also* **rubber, rubber around**) [visitors to New York City craning their necks to view the high buildings] **1** [late 19C–1950s] (*also* **rubber in**) to eavesdrop on someone else's conversation (feasible in the era of party line telephones). **2** [late 19C+] to act as an obvious tourist, thus *rubbernecking,* staring, peering. **3** [late 19C+] to stare at, to peer, to gaze around. **4** [1910s] to search for. **5** [1920s] to investigate, e.g. as a reporter.

rubber out *v.* [RUBBERNECK *v.* (5)] [1900s] (*US*) to work out, elucidate.

rubber the bitumen *v.* [1960s] (*Aus.*) to drive along a highway.

rubbidy *n. see* RUBBEDY *n.*

rubbish *n.* **1** [late 18C–early 19C] money. **2** [late 19C+] (*orig. S.Afr.*) an unpleasant person.

rubbish *adj.* (*also* **rubbishing**) [1960s+] inferior, second-rate.

rubbish *v.* [i.e. to talk *rubbish* about, to treat like *rubbish*] [1950s+] (*orig. Aus.*) **1** to attack verbally, to slander. **2** to treat badly, with disrespect. **3** to beat up. **4** to wipe out, to destroy. **5** to tease.

rubbity *n. see* RUBBEDY *n.*

rubbity-dub/rubblededub *n. see* RUB-A-DUB *n.*

rubby *n. see* RUBBEDY *n.*

rubby-dub *n.* (*also* **rubby, rubby-dubby**) [joc. ref. to SE *rubbing alcohol*] [1920s+] (*Can./US*) a drinker of cheap alcohol, or some substance, e.g. paint-thinner, bay-rum, that can substitute; the liquids themselves.

rubby-dubby *n.* [? echoic of its underpowered engine] [1910s] (*Aus.*) a small, under-powered car.

rubdown *n.* **1** [1930s+] a search of a person's clothes and body, either for security reasons or as a preliminary to picking their pocket; also *rub-down dippy,* n. a prison guard who searches new prisoners. **2** [1940s–60s] (*orig. US black*) a beating.

IN PHRASES

❑ **rub-down with an oaken towel** *n. see under* OAKEN TOWEL *n.*

rub down *v.* [ext. of SE] **1** [late 19C–1920s] to scold, to reprimand. **2** [early 19C+] to search a person's clothes and body, either for security reasons or as a preliminary to picking their pocket. **3** [1970s+] (*UK black*) to dance very close, rubbing one's body against one's partner.

rube *n.*[1] (*also* **hay rube, reub**) [abbr. REUBEN *n.*] [late 19C+] (*US*) **1** a rustic, a farmer. **2** a fool, an unsophisticated person. **3** a general term of abuse/disdain.

rube *n.*[2] [? SE *ruby*] [1920s+] (*Aus.*) something seen as exceptional, first-rate etc.

rube *adj.* (*also* **reub**) [late 19C–1970s] (*US*) pertaining to a small town or the country and the supposedly unsophisticated inhabitants thereof.

rubia (de la costa) *n.* [Sp. *rubia*, blonde] [1980s+] (*US drugs*) light-coloured Colombian marijuana.

rubies *n.* [? film star *Ruby* Keeler (1909–93)] [1940s–70s] (*US black*) the lips, esp. large or full lips.

rubigo *n.* [? Lat. *ruber*, red] [late 16C] (*Scot.*) the penis.

rubik's (cubes) *n.* [rhy. sl. = PUBES *n.*] [1990s+] the pubic hair.

rub-off *n.* [RUB OFF *v.*[1]] **1** [17C] sexual intercourse. **2** [19C+] masturbation.

rub off *v.*[1] **1** [late 17C] to have sexual intercourse. **2** [19C] to masturbate.

rub off *v.*[2] *see* RUB OUT *v.*

rub(-out) *n.* [RUB OUT *v.* (1)] [1930s–60s] (*orig. US Und.*) a murder, esp. an assassination.

IN PHRASES

❑ **give somone the rub** *v.* [1960s] (*US*) to murder, to assassinate.

rub-out *n.* [SE *rub out*, to erase] [1970s] a failure, a disappointment.

rub out *v.* (*also* **rub, rub off**) **1** [early 19C+] (*orig. US*) to murder, to assassinate, to kill. **2** [late 19C+] (*Aus.*) to reject an idea or a suggestion. **3** [20C+] (*Aus.*) to debar, to ban (a person). **4** [1900s–30s] (*Aus.*) to destroy something. **5** [1910s–30s] (*US*) to leave.

IN COMPOUNDS

❑ **rub-out guy** *n.* [GUY *n.*[2] (1)] [1960s] (*US*) an assassin, a murderer.

rub-up *n.*[1] [RUB UP *v.* (1)] **1** [mid-17C; 19C+] an act of sexual intercourse. **2** [19C+] stimulating another's genitals. **3** [19C+] masturbation.

rub-up *n.*[2] *see* RUB *n.*[2] (2).

rub up *v.* [the image of cleaning something tarnished] **1** in sexual contexts. (**a**) [mid-17C+] to stimulate the penis to erection using the hands. (**b**) [late 18C+] to stimulate the vagina. (**c**) [19C+] to masturbate. (**d**) [1970s] to have sexual intercourse. **2** [late 17C+] to revise, to refresh one's memory.

ruby *n.*[1] [mid-19C–1900s] blood; also as *adj.*

SE in slang uses

IN PHRASES

❑ **hit the ruby** *v.* [SE *ruby* wine or port] [late 19C] (*US*) to drink heavily, to be drunk.

ruby *n.*[2] [? film star *Ruby* Keeler (1909–93)] [1950s–70s] (*black/camp gay*) a man with large, prominent lips.

ruby-dazzler *n.* [var. on BOBBY-DAZZLER *n.*] [1940s+] (*Aus./N.Z.*) something exceptional.

rubyfruit *n.* [the colour and supposed appearance; best known as title of novel *Rubyfruit Jungle* (1973) by Rita Mae Brown (b.1944)] [1960s+] the female genitals.

Ruby Murray *n.* (*also* **Arthur Murray, Pete Murray**) [rhy. sl.; the popular singer *Ruby Murray* (1935–96)] [1980s+] a curry.

ruby red *n.* [rhy. sl.] [1910s] the head.

ruby rose *n.* [rhy. sl.; note 17C–18C *ruby*, a carbuncle on the nose, thus Ned Ward (1707): 'a Man who always lugg'd about with him at least two pounds of Nose, beset as thick with magnificent Rubies, as the Gills of a Turkey-Cock going to Battle'] [20C+] the nose.

ruca *n.* [Sp. *ruca*, old lady] **1** [1950s–60s] (*US teen gang*) a female gang-member. **2** [1990s+] (*US prison*) an inmate's wife or girlfriend.

ruck *n.*[1] [SE *ruck*, the general run of things, the undistinguished crowd] **1** [late 19C] (*US*) nonsense, rubbish. **2** [1920s] a cigarette end.

ruck *n.*[2] (*also* **ruckery**) [? SE *ruckus* or *ruck*, a crowd] [1950s+] **1** an argument, a fight, esp. a gang fight. **2** in fig. use.

IN PHRASES

❑ **in the ruck** [1980s+] (*Aus. prison*) involved.

ruck *v.* [? SE *ruck*, to disturb, orig. clothes and thence tempers] **1** [late 19C–1960s] to get angry with; in fig. use, to pain. **2** [late 19C+] to lay information against, to inform on. **3** [1950s+] to scold, to tell off. **4** [1950s+] to involve oneself in a fight, esp. a gang fight. **5** [1960s–70s] to masturbate. **6** [2000s] to fight.

IN PHRASES

❑ **ruck in** *v.* [late 19C] to join in a group. ❑ **ruck on** *v.* **1** [late

19C] to betray, to abandon one's loyalty to, to go back on. **2** [1930s] to quarrel with.

ruck and row *n.* [rhy. sl. = COW *n.*[1] (1)] [20C+] an unpleasant woman.

rucker *n.* [RUCK *n.*[2] (1)] **1** [1950s+] an arguer, a combative person. **2** [1970s+] a fighter.

ruckery *n. see* RUCK *n.*[2].

rucking *n.* (*also* **rucky-up, ruggy-up**) [RUCK *v.* (1)] [1920s+] (*Irish*) a fight.

ruckus juice *n.* (*also* **rookus juice, rukus juice**) [SE *ruckus*, a commotion + JUICE *n.*[1] (3a)] [1920s–60s] (*US*) alcohol; prob. cheap and potent and thus liable to inflame one's passions.

rudder *n.* **1** [mid-16C–mid-19C] the penis. **2** [20C+] an animal's, usu. a dog's tail.

ruddity dub *n. see* RUB-A-DUB *n.*

ruddling *n.* [? dial. *ruddle*, to smear] [late 19C] sexual intercourse.

ruddock *n.* (*also* **robin ruddock**) [SE *ruddock*, a robin redbreast, i.e. the 'red' colour of the golden money] [mid-16C–mid-17C] a gold coin; in pl. money; often ext. as [early 17C] *red ruddock, golden ruddock*.

ruddy *adj.* [play on SE *ruddy*, red in colour] **1** [late 19C+] a general intensifier, a euph. synon. for BLOODY *adj.* (1). **2** [1930s] of a person, unpleasant, unacceptable, crooked.

rude *adj.* [ext. of SE] **1** [20C+] (*W.I.*) sexually aggressive. **2** [1930s] wild, uncontrolled, openly hostile to authority. **3** [1950s+] sexual. **4** [1960s+] (*orig. US campus*) unfair, distasteful, offensive, generally poor, flagrantly bad. **5** [1980s+] (*orig. US campus*) excellent, admirable.

(IN COMPOUNDS)

❑ **rude girl** *n.* (*also* **rude gal**) [1960s+] (*W.I./UK black teen*) the female equivalent of the RUDE BOY *n.*

SE in slang uses

(DERIVATIVES)

❑ **rudesby** *n.* [SE *rude* + sfx *-by*] [late 16C–early 17C] an unpleasant, boorish person.

(IN COMPOUNDS)

❑ **rude-ass** *n.* [1990s+] (*US campus*) a dislikeable, rude person. ❑ **rude parts** *n.* [euph.] [1970s+] the genitals, both male or female (in the latter case extended to breasts also).

rude! *excl.* [1980s+] (*US campus*) how rude!

rude boy *n.* (*also* **rody, rude bwai, rude bwoy, rudey, rudie**) [ext. use + W.I. pron. of SE *rude boy*] **1** [1960s+] (*orig. W.I.*) 'a young, Black Jamaican male who is an aggressive social drop-out; he may be a ghetto type, a gang type or one who adopts some Rastafarian cultist habits' (Allsopp, *Dict. Caribbean English Usage*, 1996); also a term of address. **2** [1960s+] someone who poses as such a 'drop-out' but is in fact more middle class. **3** [1970s+] a young person, of any race, who likes W.I. music, typically blue-beat, rock-steady and ska; the term was revived in the early 1980s for fans of two-tone music (itself reviving the old blue-beat etc); also attrib.

rudeness *n.* [1960s] (*W.I.*) sexual intercourse; thus *do rudeness*, to have sex.

rudeness! *excl.* (*also* **how rudeness!**) [1980s+] (*US campus*) how rude!

rudey *n. see* RUDE BOY *n.*

rudie *n.*[1] [1970s] (*Aus.*) a coarse comment, an obscenity.

rudie *n.*[2] *see* RUDE BOY *n.*

rudipoop *n.* [2000s] (*US prison*) one who does not fit in with the group; an outsider.

rudolph *n.* [the Christmas song 'Rudolph, the red-nosed reindeer' by Johnny Marks] [1950s] a red nose, gained through drinking; thus, a habitual drunkard.

Rudolph (Hess) *n.* [rhy. sl.; ult. Nazi leader *Rudolph Hess* (1894–87); note ephemeral 1940s (US black) *Rudolph Hess*, to leave, to disappear, echoing the Nazi's flight to Scotland during WW2] [1990s+] a mess.

ruff *n.* [ety. unknown; ? link to ROUF *n.*] [1930s–40s] (*US black*) 25 cents, a quarter.

ruffelar/ruffeler *n. see* RUFFLER *n.*

ruffer *n.*[1] [18C; late 19C] a rough person, a thug.

ruffer *n.*[2] [? modern adoption of RUFFMANS *n.* = bushes, undergrowth, or SE *rough sleeping*] [1930s] (*UK tramp*) a bed in a bush, thus with no overhead protection.

Ruffian, the *n. see* RUFFIN, THE *n.*

ruffian *n.*[1] [mid-16C–early 19C] an assassin, a (murderous) thug; a bouncer for a brothel.

ruffian *n.*[2] (*also* **ruffin**) [mid-17C–early 19C] a justice of the peace.

ruffian *n.*[3] *see* BELLY RUFFIAN *under* BELLY *n.*

Ruffian's Hall *n. see* RUFFIN'S HALL *n.*

ruffies *n. see* ROOFIE *n.*[2].

Ruffin, the *n.* (*also* **old Ruffian, the Ruffian, the old Ruffin**) [SE *ruffian*, rogue + 13C SE *Ruffin*, the name of a specific demon] [mid-16C–early 19C] the Devil.

(IN PHRASES)

❑ **to the Ruffian** (*UK Und.*) **1** [16C] as an interj. meaning 'to the Devil'. **2** [19C] to the utmost perfection.

(IN EXCLAMATIONS)

❑ **Ruffin cly thee!, the** [CLY *v.* (1)] [mid-16C–mid-19C] (*UK Und.*) an excl. meaning 'the Devil take thee!'.

ruffin *n. see* RUFFIAN *n.*[2].

Ruffin's Hall *n.* (*also* **Ruffian's Hall**) [mid-17C–mid-19C] [late 16C–17C] that area of London, now Smithfield, where trials of skill were held among 'ordinary, Ruffianly people, with Sword and Buckler' (T. Blount, *Glossographia*, 1674), thus phr. *he is only fit for Ruffian's Hall*, used of an over-dressed apprentice.

rufflar *n. see* RUFFLER *n.*

ruffle *n.*[1] **1** [1900s] (*US*) a girl, a woman [SE *ruffle*, as adorning a dress]. **2** [1960s+] (*gay*) the passive partner in a lesbian relationship [? RUFUS *n.* (1)].

ruffle *n.*[2] [1970s] (*US black*) a fight.

ruffle *v.* [RUFFLES *n.*[1]] [mid-19C] (*UK Und.*) to place in handcuffs.

ruffler *n.* (*also* **ruffelar, ruffeler, rufflar, ruffleer, rufler**) [SE *ruffle it*, to swagger; it is linked to the idea of a bird ruffling up its feathers] [mid-16C–mid-19C] (*UK Und.*) a villain, of the 'first rank of canters', who posed as a discharged soldier (and might indeed have been one, though equally likely might have been a former servant), but actually worked as an itinerant.

ruffles *n.*[1] (*also* **ruffs**) [? ironic use of SE *ruff*, which is worn round the neck] [late 18C–1900s] (*UK Und.*) handcuffs.

ruffles *n.*[2] [? their appearance] [1940s+] (*US black*) chitterlings.

ruffles *n.*[3] *see* ROOFIE *n.*[2].

ruffmans *n.* [SE *rough* (as in ground) + -MANS *sfx*] [mid-16C–early 19C] (*UK Und.*) the woods or bushes.

ruff neck *n.* [deliberate mis-sp. of ROUGHNECK *n.*] [1980s+] (*W.I./UK black teen*) a rebellious person; a bohemian; a person with a couldn't-care-less attitude.

ruff peck *n.* [SE *rough* + PECK *n.*[1] (1); lit. 'rough food'] [mid-16C–mid-18C] (*UK Und.*) bacon.

ruffs *n. see* RUFFLES *n.*[1].

rufler *n. see* RUFFLER *n.*

rufus *n.* [Lat. *rufus*, red] **1** [19C] the female genitals. **2** [1900s–50s] (*US*) a country person, a peasant [the 'rustic' name]. **3** [1950s] a red-head.

rug *n.*[1] **1** [20C+] (*orig. US*) a wig, a toupee, a hairpiece, esp. in show business [it lies on/covers one's head/bald patch]. **2** [1930s+] the pubic hair, usu. female. **3** [1940s+] the hair. **4** [1970s+] (*US prison*) a black prisoner. **5** *see* *RUGHEAD* below.

(IN COMPOUNDS)

❑ **rug-muncher** *n.* [MUNCH *v.*[1] (2)] [1980s+] (*orig. US campus*) a lesbian; thus *rugmunching*, cunnilingus.

(IN PHRASES)

❑ **get one's rug beat** *v.* [1940s] (*US black*) to have a haircut.

SE in slang uses

(IN COMPOUNDS)

❑ **rug ape** *n.* (*also* **drape ape**) [1960s+] (*US*) a small child. ❑ **rug**

beat *n.* [1920s–50s] (*US black*) a noisy, festive party where the dancing 'beats the rug'. ◻ **rug cut/cutter** *see* separate entries. ◻ **rughead** *n.* (*also* **rug**) [the texture of black hair] [1960s+] a derog. name for a black person. ◻ **rug joint** *n.* [JOINT *n.* (3b); such restaurants were as distinguished by the splendours of their interior decoration as by their menus] **1** [late 19C+] (*US*) an elegant, expensive restaurant, patronized by the wealthy. **2** [1960s+] (*US*) an upmarket, luxury casino. ◻ **rug peddler** *n.* [negative stereotyping] [1920s] (*US*) an Arab. ◻ **rug rat** *n.* (*also* **rug-muncher**) [1960s+] a small child who is still crawling on the carpet. ◻ **rug shaker** *n. see* RUG CUTTER *n.*

IN PHRASES

◻ **at rug** *adj.* [early–mid-19C] asleep, in bed. ◻ **cut the rug** *v. see* separate entry. ◻ **rug's the word** [? the security of a *rug*] [early 18C] everything is fine, all is safe; thus [late 19C–1900s] *ruggy*, safe. ◻ **rug up** *v. see* separate entry.

rug *n.*[2] [? RAG *n.*[1] (1a)] **1** [1940s] (*US*) a dollar. **2** [1940s–80s] (*Aus.*) a £1 note.

rugby team *n.* [the 15 members of a rugby team] [1940s+] (*bingo*) the number 15.

rug cut *v.* (*also* **rug**) [CUT THE RUG *v.*] [1920s+] to dance; thus *rug-cutting*, dancing.

rug cutter *n.* (*also* **rugcutter, rug shaker**) [CUT THE RUG *v.*] [1920s–50s] (*US black*) a good and energetic dancer.

rugged *adj.* **1** [mid-18C+] of people, tough. **2** [1940s+] of activity, tough, difficult.

rugged up *adj.* [SE *rug*] [1990s+] (*Aus.*) wearing warm clothes.

rugger bugger *n.* (*also* **r.b.**) [SE *rugger*, rugby + BUGGER *n.*[1] (1)] [1950s+] a dedicatedly masculine man, whose lack of sensitivity/intelligence is more than compensated for by his enthusiasm for all forms of sport.

ruggins *n.* (*also* **ruggins's**) [one is under the SE *rug*] [early 19C] in bed.

IN PHRASES

◻ **go to ruggins** *v.* to go to bed.

ruggy *adj.* [the warmth and cosiness of being wrapped in a *rug*] [mid-19C] fusty, frowsy.

ruggy-up *n. see* RUCKING *n.*

rug up *v.* [1990s+] (*Aus.*) to dress warmly.

rugy *adj.* [? elision of *rude guy*] [1970s+] (*US black*) unattractive; ill-tempered.

ruin *n.* [its effects] **1** [19C] cheap, inferior gin. **2** [1910s] (*UK juv.*) a despised schoolboy.

ruin *v.* [1960s+] (*gay*) to deliberately exaggerate one's effeminacy as a shock tactic.

ruin and spoil *n.* [rhy. sl.] [20C+] oil.

ruined *adj.* (*also* **ruint**) [1960s+] (*orig. US black*) **1** beaten, injured. **2** drunk, under the influence of drugs.

Ruins, the *n.* [late 19C] (*UK Und.*) an area of wasteland between Farringdon Road and Saffron Hill, London, where bookmakers, touts, thieves and tipsters congregated.

ruin't *adj.* **1** [1940s] (*US black*) pregnant. **2** [1960s–80s] (*US black*) of a person, unattractive.

rukadung *adj. see* ROOGODUNG *adj.*

rukus juice *n. see* RUCKUS JUICE *n.*

rule *n.*

IN PHRASES

◻ **run the rule over** *v.* **1** [mid-19C–1900s] of a pickpocket, to check all a person's pockets. **2** [late 19C–1910s] to search. **3** [1900s–10s] to give someone a medical examination; thus in fig. use, to subject to any form of examination. **4** [1940s+] of police, to interrogate a suspect.

rule *v.* **1** [1980s+] (*US campus*) to do well or be something admirable, good. **2** [1990s+] (*US black*) to be in control.

rule of three *n.* [SE *rule* + *three*, i.e. the penis and testicles; note Williams: 'This alludes to the golden rule whereby a fourth number is deduced from a given three numbers'] **1** [18C] the male genitals. **2** [19C] sexual intercourse.

Rules *n.* [abbr.] [1940s+] (*Aus.*) Australian *Rules* Football.

— **rules/rules OK** *phr.* [SE *rule*] [1960s+] the text of a graffitto proclaiming the excellence of a star, a local gang etc, e.g. *Eric rules OK.*

ruly *adj.* [2000s] (*N.Z.*) excellent, first-rate.

Rum, the *n.* [late 19C] (*Aus.*) a Sydney newspaper.

rum *n.*[1] [abbr. RUMMY *n.*[1] (2)/RUM *adj.* (2)] **1** [1900s] (*US*) an eccentric. **2** [1900s–70s] (*US black*) a fool, a dupe, a victim. **3** [1950s–60s] a drunkard.

rum *n.*[2]

SE in slang uses

IN COMPOUNDS

◻ **rum bump** *n.* [1950s] (*W.I.*) **1** the adam's apple. **2** a swelling in the throat supposedly caused by excessive rum drinking. ◻ **rum dragger** *n. see* DRAGGER *n.*[1]. ◻ **rum factory** *n. see* BOOZE FACTORY *under* BOOZE *n.* ◻ **rumhead** *n.* [-HEAD *sfx* (4)] [late 19C+] a drunkard, esp. a rum-drinker. ◻ **rum-hole** *n.* (*also* **rum-joint**) [HOLE *n.*[1] (2b)/JOINT *n.* (3b)] [early 19C–1920s] (*US*) orig. a cheap tavern, specializing in rum; a bar. ◻ **rum hound** *n.* [-HOUND *sfx* (1)] [1910s–50s] a heavy drinker. ◻ **rum-jar** *n.* [late 19C] (*Aus.*) a heavy drinker; a drunkard. ◻ **rum repository** *n.* [late 19C–1900s] (*US*) a bar. ◻ **rum row** *n.* [SE, on the lines of agglomerations of similar enterprises, e.g. *Publishers' Row*, *Restaurant Row* etc] [1920s] (*US Und.*) a bootlegger's fleet, held in international waters and thus beyond US jurisdiction. ◻ **rum slim** *n.* [SE *rum* + var. on SAmE *sling*, a form of cocktail; ? ult. SLING *n.*[1]] [late 18C–mid-19C] rum punch. ◻ **rum-sucker** *n.* [mid-19C] (*US*) a heavy, habitual drinker.

IN PHRASES

◻ **have in (some) rum** *v. see* HAVE IN SOME LIQUOR *under* LIQUOR *n.*

rum *adj.* (*also* **rome, room**) [most prob. from SE *Rome* (and indeed could be spelled 'rome' until the 18C), which, as a city, meant glory and grandeur. Other origins include the Romany *rom*, a male gypsy, or the Turkish *Röm*, a gypsy, many of whom passed through the Ottoman Empire. Reversing the process, the Lat. *Roma* (Rome) is cognate with the Teutonic root *hruod* (fame) (as found in the names Roger and Roderick) which appears in the German *Ruhm* (fame)] (*orig. UK Und.*) **1** [mid-16C–1920s] excellent, first-rate. **2** [mid-18C+] odd, peculiar, strange, thus *rummily*, oddly; *rummish*, strange, odd. **3** [19C] illicit, illegal, criminal. **4** [mid-19C] drunk, tipsy.

pertaining to excellence

DERIVATIVES

◻ **rumly** *adv.* **1** [early 17C] nimbly. **2** [mid-17C–early 19C] (*also* **rumley**) excellently; well. **3** [late 17C] honestly. **4** [late 17C–18C] bravely.

IN COMPOUNDS

◻ **rum beak** *n.* (*also* **rum-beck**) [BEAK *n.*[1] (1)] [late 18C–mid-19C] (*UK Und.*) a corruptible magistrate. ◻ **rum beck** *n.* [BECK *n.*[1]] [early 17C–mid-19C] (*UK Und.*) **1** a justice of the peace. **2** a magistrate who is susceptible to corruption. ◻ **rum bing** *n.* [BUNG *n.*[1] (1)] [mid-19C] (*UK Und.*) a full purse. ◻ **rum bite** *n.* [BITE *n.*[1]] **1** [late 17C–early 19C] (*UK Und.*) a clever trick, a cunning ploy. **2** [late 18C–early 19C] a clever fraud or confidence trickster. ◻ **rum-bleating cheat** *n.* [*BLEATING CHEAT under* BLEAT *v.*] [late 17C–early 19C] (*UK Und.*) a very fat wether or castrated ram. ◻ **rum blowen** *n.* (*also* **rum blower, rum blowing**) [BLOWEN *n.* (1)/BLOWER *n.*[1]] [late 17C–18C] (*UK Und.*) a good-looking woman, esp. an attractive mistress or kept woman. ◻ **rum bluffer** *n.* [BLUFFER *n.*[1]] [late 17C–early 19C] (*UK Und.*) an honest, jovial, accommodating alehouse-keeper or publican. ◻ **rum bob** *n.* (*UK Und.*) **1** [late 17C–early 19C] a sharp, fly trick [BOB *v.*[1] (1)]. **2** [late 17C–early 19C] (*also* **bob**) a neat, short wig [SE *bobbed hair*]. **3** [late 18C–mid-19C] a smart young apprentice [BOB *n.*[2]]. **4** [early–mid-19C] a shop till. ◻ **rum booze** *n.* (*also* **Rome bowse, Rom-bouse, rum bouse, rum bouze, rum bues, rum buse, rum buze**) [BOOZE *n.* (1)] [mid-16C–19C] good drink, esp. good wine. ◻ **rum-boozing welts** *n.* [SE *welt*, a ridge or raised portion] [late 17C–early 19C] (*UK Und.*) bunches of grapes. ◻ **rum bub** *n.* [BUB *n.*[1]] [late 17C–mid-19C] excellent liquor. ◻ **rum bubber** *n.* [BUBBER *n.*[1] (3)]

[late 17C–18C] a thief who specializes in stealing silver tankards from taverns. ❑ **rum buffer** *n.* [BUFE *n.*] [late 18C–mid-19C] (*UK Und.*) a valuable and attractive dog. ❑ **rum bughar** *n.* (*also* **rum bugher**) [BUGHER *n.*] [late 17C–early 19C] (*UK Und.*) a valuable and attractive dog. ❑ **rum bung** *n.* [BUNG *n.*[1] (1)] [late 17C–mid-19C] (*UK Und.*) a full purse. ❑ **rum buse/buze** *n. see* *RUM BOOZE* above. ❑ **rum chant** *n.* [CHANT *n.* (1)] [late 17C–mid-19C] (*UK Und.*) a song. ❑ **rum clank** *n.* [CLANK *n.* (1)] [18C–early 19C] (*UK Und.*) a gold or silver cup or tankard. ❑ **rum clout** *n.* [CLOUT *n.*[1] (1)] [late 17C–mid-19C] (*UK Und.*) a handkerchief made of silk or other high-quality material. ❑ **rum cly** *n.* [CLY *n.* (2)] [late 18C–mid-19C] (*UK Und.*) a full pocket, i.e. of money. ❑ **rum cod** *n.* [COD *n.*[3] (3)] [late 17C–early 19C] a full purse; a round sum of money. ❑ **rum cole** *n.* (*also* **rum gelt, rum ghelt, rum gilt**) [COLE *n.* (1)/GELT *n.*/GILT *n.*[1]] [late 17C–mid-19C] (*UK Und.*) **1** new money. **2** 'Medals, curiously Coyn'd' (B.E.), presumably counterfeit. ❑ **rum-cove** *n.* [COVE *n.* (1); lit. a 'good man'] **1** [17C] (*UK Und.*) a leading beggar, whether through strength or intelligence. **2** [17C–mid-18C] a rich man. **3** [17C–early 19C] a successful villain. **4** [late 17C–mid-18C] (*UK Und.*) the hangman. **5** [late 18C–mid-19C] (*UK Und.*) a good-natured landlord. **6** [early 19C] an attractive man. **7** [mid-19C+] an odd or eccentric character. ❑ **rum covey** *n.* [mid-19C] **1** an attractive man. **2** a sharp fellow. ❑ **rum cull** *n.* (*also* **rum cully**) [CULL *n.*[1]/CULLY *n.*[1]; note mid-19C theatrical jargon *rum cull*, the manager] (*UK Und.*) **1** [mid-17C–early 19C] a gullible, rich fool, open to fraud. **2** [late 17C] a man who is very generous to his mistress. **3** [18C–19C] (*also* **rum coll**) an intimate friend; a good man. ❑ **rum cuttle** *n.* (*also* **room cuttle**) [CUTTLE *n.*; SE *cuttle*, a knife; ult. OF *coutel*] [16C–early 17C] a sword. ❑ **rum dab** *n.* [DAB *n.*[1]] [late 17C–early 18C] (*UK Und.*) a very successful sharper, pickpocket and thief. ❑ **rum degen** *n.* (*also* **ram dagen, rum job, rum tilter, rum tol**) [DEGEN *n.*/SE *jab*/TILTER *n.*/TOL *n.*[1]] [late 17C–mid-19C] (*UK Und.*) a sword with a silver hilt or a hilt or blade inlaid with silver. ❑ **rum diver** *n.* [DIVER *n.* (3)] [late 17C–early 19C] (*UK Und.*) an accomplished pickpocket. ❑ **rum doxy** *n.* (*also* **rum dell**) [DOXY *n.* (2)/DELL *n.* (1)] [late 17C–early 19C] (*UK Und.*) a beautiful woman or attractive whore. ❑ **rum drag** *n.* [DRAG *v.*[1] (1a)] [late 18C] (*UK Und.*) a thief who poses as a drunkard and persuades a carter to let him lead his horse while he gets some sleep; the 'drunkard' then re-addresses the parcels that are on the wagon, which will therefore be delivered to houses where his confederates can collect them. ❑ **rum drawers** *n.* [DRAWERS *n.*] [late 17C–18C] (*UK Und.*) stockings made of silk or some similar quality material. ❑ **rum dropper** *n.* [SE *drops* of liquor] (*UK Und.*) **1** [late 17C–mid-19C] (*also* **dropper**) a vintner. **2** [early 18C] a landlord. ❑ **rum dubber** *n.* [DUBBER *n.*[1]] [late 17C–early 19C] (*UK Und.*) an expert pick-lock. ❑ **rum duchess** *n.* [DUCHESS *n.*[1] (1)] [late 17C–mid-18C] (*UK Und.*) a jolly, buxom woman. ❑ **rum duke** *n.* [generic use of SE *duke*] (*UK Und.*) **1** [late 17C–early 19C] a notably handsome man. **2** [late 17C–early 19C] a tough villain who is sent by a bankrupted individual to guard their possessions, while they leave home and take refuge from arrest in a criminal rookery. **3** [late 18C–early 19C] an odd, eccentric, showy man. ❑ **rum fam** *n.* (*also* **rum fem**) [FAMBLE *n.* (2)] **1** [early 18C] (*UK Und.*) a gold ring. **2** [late 19C] (*UK Und.*) a diamond ring. ❑ **rum feeder** *n.* [FEEDER *n.* (1)] [late 18C–mid-19C] (*UK Und.*) a large silver spoon. ❑ **rum file** *n.* [FILE *n.* (2)] [late 17C–early 19C] (*UK Und.*) an expert pickpocket. ❑ **rum flash** *n.* [FLASH *n.*[1] (2)] [late 17C–early 19C] (*UK Und.*) a large wig. ❑ **rum fun** *n.* [FUN *n.*[1]] [late 17C–mid-19C] (*UK Und.*) a clever trick, a cunning fraud. ❑ **rum gagger** *n.* [GAGGER *n.*[1] (1)] [late 18C–mid-19C] (*UK Und.*) a confidence trickster who raises money on the basis of telling fraudulent tales of supposed suffering at sea, at the hands of the pirates of the Barbary Coast and so on. ❑ **rum gelt/ghelt** *n. see* *RUM COLE* above. ❑ **rum gill** *n.* [GILL *n.*[1] (2)] [late 18C–mid-19C] (*UK Und.*) a well-off man who thus presents a target for robbery. ❑ **rum gilt** *n. see* *RUM COLE* above. ❑ **rum glimmer** *n.* (*also* **rum glymmar**) [GLIMMER *n.* (1)] [late 17C–mid-19C] (*UK Und.*) the head of the link-boys, who were employed to carry a link to light passengers along the street. ❑ **rum gloak** *n.* [GLOAK *n.*] [late 18C–mid-19C] (*UK Und.*) a well-dressed man. ❑ **rum gutlers** *n.* [SE *guzzle*] (*UK Und.*) **1** [late 17C–mid-19C] Canary wine. **2** [18C] good eating. ❑ **rum hopper** *n.* [SE *hopper*, one who moves quickly and efficiently, who 'hops to it'] [late 17C–mid-19C] (*UK Und.*) someone who draws ale or wine at a tavern. ❑ **rum job** *n. see* *RUM DEGEN* above. ❑ **rum ken** *n.* [KEN *n.*[1] (1)] **1** [mid–late 18C] (*UK Und.*) a large, substantial house. **2** [mid–late 19C] (*UK Und.*) a well-known criminal public house or brothel. ❑ **rum kicks** *n.* [KICKS *n.*[1]] [late 17C–mid-19C] (*UK Und.*) breeches that have been adorned with silver or gold embroidery. ❑ **rum kiddy** *n.* [KIDDY *n.* (1)] [late 18C–early 19C] (*UK Und.*) a popular, successful young thief. ❑ **rum lap** *n.* [LAP *n.*[2] (2)] [late 18C–mid-19C] (*UK Und.*) good liquor. ❑ **rum mizzler** *n.* (*also* **mizzler**) [MIZZLE *v.* (1)] **1** [late 18C–mid-19C] (*UK Und.*) someone who is clever at escaping difficult situations, whether physically or through words; thus *tip someone the rum mizzle*, to give someone the slip. **2** [mid-19C] a general derog. term. ❑ **rum mort** *n.* (*also* **rome mort, rum mot**) [MORT *n.* was orig. coined for Elizabeth I] **1** [mid-16C–early 19C] (*UK Und.*) a queen. **2** [early 17C–mid-19C] a great lady; an attractive woman. **3** [mid-17C–mid-19C] a prostitute. **4** [mid-18C] a rich woman. ❑ **rum-muns** *n.* [MUNS *n.* (1)] [mid-18C] (*UK Und.*) a good-looking man. ❑ **rum nab** *n.* [NAB *n.*[1] (3)] [late 17C–early 19C] (*UK Und.*) a well-made, fashionable hat, a beaver hat. ❑ **rum nantz** *n.* [NANTZ *n.*] [late 17C–mid-19C] (*UK Und.*) the best quality French brandy. ❑ **rum ned** *n.* [NEDDY *n.*[1] (2)] [late 17C–early 19C] (*UK Und.*) a very foolish rich man. ❑ **rum ogles** *n.* [OGLES *n.*] [late 17C–early 19C] (*UK Und.*) bright, clear eyes. ❑ **rum one** *n. see* separate entry. ❑ **rum pad** *n.* [PAD *n.*[1]] [mid-17C–mid-19C] (*UK Und.*) **1** (*also* **rom pad, rome pad**) the highway. **2** a highwayman. ❑ **rum padder** *n.* (*also* **rom-padder**) [PADDER *n.*[1]] **1** [late 17C–mid-18C] a horse. **2** [late 17C–mid-19C] (*UK Und.*) a highwayman. ❑ **rum patter** *n.* [PATTER *n.* (3)] [late 18C] (*UK Und.*) criminal slang, cant. ❑ **rum peck** *n.* [PECK *n.*[1] (1)] [late 17C–early 19C] (*UK Und.*) good food. ❑ **rum peeper** *n.* [PEEPER *n.* (2)] **1** [late 17C–mid-19C] (*UK Und.*) a silver mounted looking glass. **2** [late 18C–mid-19C] in pl. bright eyes. ❑ **rum prad** *n.* [PRAD *n.* (1)] [late 19C–mid-19C] (*UK Und.*) a highwayman's horse. ❑ **rum prancer** *n.* [PRANCER *n.* (1)] [late 17C–early 19C] (*UK Und.*) a beautiful, well-made horse. ❑ **rum quids** *n.* (*also* **rum quidds**) [QUID *n.*] (*UK Und.*) **1** [late 17C–early 19C] a large amount of stolen money, or a share thereof. **2** [late 18C–mid-19C] a 'good', i.e. not counterfeit guinea. ❑ **rum ruff peck** *n.* [RUFF PECK *n.*; Westphalia ham was considered to be of the best quality] [late 17C–mid-19C] (*UK Und.*) Westphalia ham. ❑ **rum screen** *n.* [SCREEN *n.*[1] (1)] [late 18C] (*UK Und*) a banknote. ❑ **rum snitch** *n.* [SNITCH *n.*[1] (2)] [late 17C–early 19C] (*UK Und.*) a hard blow on one's nose. ❑ **rum snooze** *n.* [SNOOZE *n.* (1)] [late 18C] **1** (*UK Und.*) a sleep induced by alcohol. **2** one who sleeps soundly. ❑ **rum snoozer** *n.* [late 18C] (*UK Und.*) one who falls asleep in a tavern and is robbed. ❑ **rum speaker** *n.* [SPEAK *v.*] [late 18C–mid-19C] (*UK Und.*) a good haul of booty. ❑ **rum squeeze** *n.* [SE *squeeze*] (*UK Und.*) **1** [late 17C–mid-19C] a good measure of drink distributed among the fiddlers at a wedding or similar event [a few drops squeezed out]. **2** [late 18C] a crush at the theatre; its members are susceptible to pickpockets [a crush]. ❑ **rum strum** *n.* [late 17C–early 19C] **1** a pretty young strumpet [STRUM *n.*[1]]. **2** a long wig [STRUM *n.*[2]]. ❑ **rum swag** *n.* [SWAG *n.*[1] (1)] [late 17C–early 19C] (*UK Und.*) a shop full of expensive goods and thus worth robbing. ❑ **rum tilter/tol** *n. see* *RUM DEGEN* above. ❑ **rum Tom Pat** *n.* [TOM PAT *n.*[1]] [late 18C–mid-19C] (*UK Und.*) a clergyman. ❑ **rum topping** *n.* [SE *topping*] [late 17C–early 19C] (*UK Und.*) a first-rate or brand-new wig. ❑ **rum twang** *n.* [late 18C] (*UK Und*) a silver stock buckle. ❑ **rum wipe** *n.* (*also* **rum wiper**) [WIPE *n.* (3)/WIPER *n.* (1)] [late 17C–19C] (*UK Und.*) a handkerchief made of silk or other high-quality material.

pertaining to eccentricity

(DERIVATIVES)

❑ **rumminess** *n.* (*also* **rumness**) [mid-19C] oddness, eccentricity.

(IN COMPOUNDS)

❑ **rum bow** *n.* [SE *bowline*] [late 18C–mid-19C] (*UK Und.*) rope stolen from a royal dockyard. ❑ **rum bug** *n.* [BUG *n.*[1] (1)] [late 19C] (*Aus.*) an important (or self-important) person. ❑ **rum**

flicker *n.* [FLICKER *n.*[1]] [late 17C–18C] (*UK Und.*) a poor quality or 'ordinary' glass. ▫ **rum maund** *n.* (*also* **rum mawnd, rum maunder**) [MAUND *n.* (2)] [late 17C–mid-19C] (*UK Und.*) a beggar who poses as more stupid than they really are to encourage donations. ▫ **rum one** *n. see* separate entry. ▫ **rum phiz** *n.* (*also* **rum phyz**) [PHIZ *n.*[1] (1)] [late 18C–early 19C] an odd-looking face. ▫ **rum touch** *n.* [RUM *adj.* (2) + SE *touch*, with the implication of someone against whom one brushes up] [early 19C] an odd, eccentric person; a strange affair.

rum *adv.* [RUM *adj.*] (*UK Und.*) **1** [mid-18C] well. **2** [mid-19C] smartly. **3** [mid-19C] strangely, eccentrically.

rumatiz *n. see* RHEUMATIZ *n.*

rumba *n.* (*US*) **1** [1930s] a spree, a celebration, a party. **2** [1950s] a fight, esp. a gang fight.

rumba *v.* [RUMBA *n.* (2)] [1950s] (*US*) to fight with.

rumble *n.*[1] [RUMBLE *v.*[2] (1)] **1** [1900s–60s] the act of discovery, usu. in the context of a crime. **2** [1910s–50s] an alarm (during the course of a crime). **3** [1910s+] a warning, a piece of information. **4** [1920s] (*US Und.*) an accident, a problem. **5** [1960s+] (*US*) a rumour.

rumble *n.*[2] [RUMBLE *v.*[1]; but note 14–18C SE *rumble*, a commotion, an uproar] **1** [1920s–60s] sexual intercourse. **2** [1940s+] (*US*) a street gang fight. **3** [1940s+] a fight; an argument. **4** [1950s+] (*US drugs*) a police drug raid. **5** [1960s] (*US campus*) a wild party.

rumble *n.*[3] [the sound of the engine] [1930s–40s] (*US*) a car.

rumble *v.*[1] **1** [early 19C] (*UK Und.*) to pickpocket, to steal. **2** [early–mid-19C] to handle roughly, to rule out without any discussion. **3** [1910s] (*Aus.*) to obtain through deception; to deceive. **4** [1910s] (*US prison*) to create a disturbance to distract one's accomplices. **5** [1910s–20s] (*UK army/US Und.*) to spoil, to upset. **6** [1920s] (*US tramp*) to betray a friend. **7** [1940s+] to hit, to fight; esp. of teen gangs; thus adj. *rumbling*, ready to fight. **8** [1950s+] (*US*) to steal, esp. from an aeroplane. **9** [1950s+] (*drugs*) to be searched by the police.

rumble *v.*[2] [? modern ext. of ROMBOYLE *v.*] **1** [late 19C+] to discover, to find out, to unmask. **2** [1940s] (*US Und.*) to reveal one's plans, to make a potential victim aware of one's criminal intentions.

rumbler *n.* **1** [late 18C–early 19C] a cart (e.g. as used in a hanging). **2** [early 19C] a hackney carriage. **3** [mid-19C] a four-wheeled cab; thus *rumbler's flunkey*, a footman who runs for cabs in return for tips.

rumble-tumble *n.* [note Anglo-Indian use *rumble-tumble*, scrambled eggs] [early–mid-19C] a stage-coach.

rumbo *n.*[1] (*also* **rumbo-ken**) [? ironic use of RUM *adj.* (1) + KEN *n.*[1] (1)] [18C–mid-19C] Newgate, thus any prison.

rumbo *n.*[2] [SE *rum*] [mid-18C–late 19C] a mixture of rum, water and sugar.

rumbo *n.*[3] [Sp. *rumbo*, liberality, generosity] [late 19C] a sufficiency, a plenitude.

rumbo *adj.* [RUMBO *n.*[3]] [mid–late 19C] **1** plentiful, sufficient. **2** elegant, fashionable.

rumbo! *excl.* [Sp. *carambo* and ? adopted f. gypsy use] [mid-19C] (*middle class*) an excl. of congratulation, i.e. *splendid! excellent!* used (exclusively) by two men.

rumbo dick *n.* [mid-19C] (*UK Und.*) a shabby, dirty man.

rumbo-ken *n.* **1** [early 18C] a pawnshop [KEN *n.*[1] (1)]. **2** *see* RUMBO *n.*[1].

rumboyle *see* ROMBOYLE.

rumbumtious *adj.* (*also* **rumbumptious**) [vars. on SE *rambunctious*] **1** [late 18C–early 19C] obstreperous. **2** [mid-19C] haughty.

rumbusticate *v.* [RUMBUSTIOUS *adj.* + sfx *-ate*, e.g. in SPIFLICATE *v.*] **1** [mid-19C] (*US*) to be (fig.) knocked down, to be confused. **2** [late 19C–1900s] as euph. use of sense 1 above, of a man, to have sexual intercourse.

rumbustious *adj.* (*also* **rambustious, rombustical, rumbustical**) [late 18C–19C] boisterous, noisy, unruly, turbulent.

rumdadum *n.* [? rhy. sl. = BUM *n.*[1] (1)] [1910s–20s] the buttocks.

rum-dum *n.* (*also* **rum-dumb, rumdummy, rundum**) [SE *rum* + redup.] (*US*) **1** [late 19C+] a heavy drinker. **2** [1930s] an insane person. **3** [1960s] an inferior or worn out thing.

rum-dum *adj.* (*also* **rum-dumb**) **1** [late 19C–1960s] drunk. **2** [1930s–70s] stupid.

rum factory *n. see* BOOZE FACTORY *under* BOOZE *n.*

Rum File *n. see* RUM VILLE *n.*

rumfoozeled *adj.* [RUMFOOZLE *n.*] [mid-19C] untidy, disarrayed.

rumfoozle *n.* [early 19C] a muddle, a surprising occurance.

Rumford lion *n. see* ROMFORD LION *n.*

rumgumption *n.* (*also* **rumgumshus, rummelgumption**) [? abbr. Scot. *rumblegumption*, common sense] [mid-18C–mid-19C] knowledge, ability; thus *rumgumptious*, knowing, positive, blunt, pert.

rumly/rumley *adv. see under* RUM *adj.*

rummage *v.* [late 17C–19C] of a man, to have sexual intercourse.

rummarian *n. see* RUMMER *n.*

rummed up *adj.* (*also* **rummied**) [1920s–40s] tipsy, drunk.

rummelgumption *n. see* RUMGUMPTION *n.*

rummer *n.* (*also* **rummarian**) [SE *rum*] [1940s] (*W.I.*) a rum drunkard.

rummery *n.* [mid-19C–1910s] a saloon.

rummie *n.* **1** *see* RUMMY *n.*[1]. **2** *see* RUMMY *n.*[2].

rummied *adj. see* RUMMED UP *adj.*

rum-mill *n.* [var. on GIN-MILL *n.* (1)] [mid–late 19C] (*US*) a cheap tavern or saloon, selling primarily rum.

rummy *n.*[1] (*also* **rummie**) [SE *rum*] (*US*) **1** [mid-19C–1920s] a rum seller; a bootlegger. **2** [mid-19C+] a drunkard. **3** [1950s] attrib., i.e. dealing with drunkards.

rummy *n.*[2] (*also* **rummie**) [RUM *adj.* (2)] [1900s–30s] a fool, an eccentric, a dupe.

rummy *adj.*[1] [RUM *adj.*] **1** [18C+] odd, peculiar, bizarre, thus adv. *rummily*. **2** [mid–late 19C] first-rate, excellent.

rummy *adj.*[2] [1910s–60s] drunken.

IN COMPOUNDS

▫ **rummy stiff** *n.* [STIFF *n.*[1] (4a)] [1910s] (*US tramp*) an alcoholic tramp.

rum one *n.* (*also* **rum 'un**) [RUM *adj.*] **1** [late 18C–mid-19C] an admirable person or object. **2** [late 18C–1920s] anything considered odd or eccentric, whether animate, inanimate or theoretical.

rump *n.* [SE *rump*, the buttocks] **1** [17C] a prostitute. **2** [1990s+] sexual intercourse.

SE in slang uses

IN COMPOUNDS

▫ **rump butter** *n.* [mid-19C] (*UK Und.*) a whipping. ▫ **rump ranger** *n.* (*also* **rump wrangler**) [1980s+] a male homosexual. ▫ **rump shaker** *n.* [1990s+] (*US*) an act of sexual intercourse. ▫ **rump-splitter** *n.* (*also* **split-rump**) **1** [mid-17C] the penis. **2** [19C–1900s] a lecher, a womanizer.

IN PHRASES

▫ **not know one's rump from a hole in the ground** [1930s] to be stupid.

rump *v.* [SE *rump*, the buttocks] **1** [late 18C–mid-19C] to turn one's back on. **2** [late 18C+] to copulate. **3** [early 19C] to flog. **4** [20C+] (*US*) to have anal intercourse. **5** [1990s+] also used fig. for FUCK *v.* (2a).

rump and a dozen *n.* **1** [late 18C–19C] an orig. Irish wager, a rump of beef and a dozen of claret. **2** [1920s] (*also* **rump and dozen**) a whipping, twelve lashes.

rump-and-kidney men *n.* [their payment in kind, they were given the leftovers] [late 17C–early 19C] fiddlers who play for weddings, feasts, fairs and similar festivities.

rumper *n.* [SE *rump*] **1** [mid-17C] (*also* **cully-rumper**) a pimp, a prostitute's customer. **2** [19C] a prostitute.

rumping *n.* [RUMP *v.* (2)] [1970s] sexual intercourse.

rumpo *n.* [RUMP *v.* (2)] [1950s+] sexual intercourse.

rumpot *n.* [1930s+] a drunkard.

rumpty *adj.* [1910s+] (*Aus.*) excellent, first-rate.

rumpty (dooler) *n.* [RUMPTY *adj.*] [1940s+] (*Aus./N.Z.*) **1** anything excellent, first-rate. **2** something broken down, unattractive, disreputable. **3** (*also* **rumpty dollar**) a fuss, an uproar.

rumptyvump *n.* (*also* **rump-tee-vump**) [initial letters of radio, motion pictures and TV – i.e. *rumptyvump*] [1980s+] (*US campus*) a course in radio-television-motion pictures.

rumpy-pumpy *n.* (*also* **humpy-pumpy, rumptypumpty, rumty tumty**) [SE *rump* + HUMP *v.*[1]/PUMP *v.* (3a)] [1970s+] sexual intercourse.

rum-ti-tum *n.* [mid-19C] (*UK Und.*) a bull kept for baiting.

rumtitum *n.* [echoic of the chatter] [1900s] enthusiastic, if ultimately empty talk.

rumtitum *adj.* (*also* **rum-ti-tum**) [mid–late 19C] in excellent condition, usu. of a bull or a pimp; intensified as *rum ti tum with the chill off.*

rumtowzle *n.* [? SE *tousle*] [late 19C] boisterousness.

rumty *n.* [ety. unknown] [1980s+] (*N.Z.*) an admirable person or object.

rumty tumty *n. see* RUMPY-PUMPY *n.*

rum 'un *n. see* RUM ONE *n.*

Rum ville *n.* (*also* **Rome-ville, Rome-vyle, Rum File, Rumville**) [RUM *adj.* (1) + SE *vill*, village] **1** [mid-16C–mid-19C] (*UK Und.*) London. **2** [mid-19C] (*US Und.*) New York City.

rumy *n.* [Rom. *romeni*, a wife, a bride] [mid-19C] a good woman.

run *n.* **1** [1920s] (*UK/US Und*) time spent out of prison. **2** [1950s+] among outlaw motorcyclists, a full-scale club outing involving all the members of a given chapter or gang and devoted to maximum excess in all possible areas of activity. **3** in drug uses. (**a**) [1950s+] (*drugs*) the immediate and intense feeling that follows the injection of heroin into a vein; or that follows the ingestion of any drug. (**b**) [1960s+] (*drugs*) an extended period of drug use. (**c**) [1990s+] (*drugs*) a search for drugs, often qualified by the drug's name. **4** [1990s+] (*US Und.*) the walkway that runs the length of a line of cells. **5** *see* RUNAROUND *n.* (3).

SE in slang uses

IN COMPOUNDS

❑ **runaround** *n. see* separate entry. ❑ **rundown** *see* separate entries. ❑ **run-in** *n. see* separate entry. ❑ **run out** *see* separate entries.

IN PHRASES

❑ **dry run** *n. see under* DRY *adj.*[1]. ❑ **getting run** *see HIT A HOME RUN under* HOME RUN *n.* ❑ **get the run** *v.* [late 19C–1910s] to be dismissed from employment. ❑ **get the run on** *v.* [mid-19C] (*US*) to have at a disadvantage, to be in a position to laugh at. ❑ **give someone a run for their money** *v.* (*also* **give someone a run for it, give someone a run for their marbles**) [note earlier racing sl. *have a run for one's money*, to have some kind of return or satisfaction for one's expenditure or exertions] [late 19C+] to provide satisfaction, to give someone their 'money's worth', usu. fig. ❑ **give someone the run** *v.* [1900s] to get rid of. ❑ **make a run** *v.* **1** [1950s+] to go out to buy a commodity, esp. drugs, but also groceries, liquor etc. **2** [1970s] to attempt to seduce, to approach with amorous intentions. ❑ **take a run at someone** *v.* [20C+] (*US*) to attempt to capture, assault or seduce someone.

IN EXCLAMATIONS

❑ **take a run!** [late 19C+] a general expression of contempt, dismissal. ❑ **take a run at yourself!** [1920s+] (*Aus.*) a general phr. of dismissal, dislike, i.e. go to hell!

run *v.* **1** [mid-19C] to understand, to comprehend. **2** [mid-19C–1920s] (*Aus./US*) to harass verbally, to tease; thus *running*, teasing, scolding. **3** [1900s–40s] (*Aus.*) to cover the expenses of [SE *run to*, to cover, to extend sufficiently, usu. of money]. **4** in senses of association. (**a**) [1910s] to go out with someone, usu. a boyfriend or girlfriend, on a regular basis. (**b**) [1910s+] of a partner, usu. a man, to dominate and control the other partner's life. (**c**) [1980s+] to go around together, to play together. **5** in drug uses. (**a**) [1930s+] to sell drugs. (**b**) [1970s+] to be a habitual drug user; to inject narcotics. (**c**) [1990s+] to work as a drug dealer's assistant. (**d**) [2000s] to steal drugs. **6** [1970s+] (*US Und.*) to use stolen credit cards; to pass any form of false document, e.g. a traveller's cheque [one 'runs up' debts or 'runs' the card 'by' the victim]. **7** *see* RUN IN *v.* (1).

SE in slang uses

IN PHRASES

❑ **run...** *v. see also under* relevant n. or adj. ❑ **run a banker** *v.* [SE *banker*, a river with its water level with or over-running its banks] [late 19C–1940s] (*Aus.*) to be intense; usu. of emotions or feelings. ❑ **run a boat** *v.* [the multi-person crew required to sail a boat] [1990s+] (*W.I.*) to pool resources to buy a meal. ❑ **run a buck** *v.* [ety. unknown] [late 18C–early 19C] (*Anglo-Irish*) to register an invalid vote. ❑ **run a hooligan on** *v.* [1920s] (*US*) to play tricks on, to defraud. ❑ **run a match against the constable** *v. see* OUTRUN THE CONSTABLE *v.* (1). ❑ **run around** *v.* (*orig. US*) **1** [late 19C–1970s] to have a relationship; also friendship. **2** [1920s+] to carry on sexual affairs, deceiving one's primary partner. ❑ **run around like a blue-arsed fly** *v. see BUZZ AROUND LIKE A BLUE-ARSED FLY under* BUZZ *v.*[1]. ❑ **run around like a cut cat** *v.* [SE *cut*, castrated] [1950s+] (*Aus.*) to be very angry, thus comparative *meaner than a cut cat*. ❑ **run a saw on** *v.* [obs. SE *saw*, a tale] [mid–late 19C] (*US/Aus.*) to deceive, to hoax. ❑ **run a temperature** *v.* [i.e. one is HOT *adj.* (5c)] [1990s+] (*US*) to be wanted, usu. by the police. ❑ **run down** *v. see* separate entry. ❑ **run in** *v. see* separate entry. ❑ **run it down/to** *v. see under* RUN DOWN *v.* ❑ **run it out** *v.* [1920s] (*US campus*) to behave in a socially unacceptable manner, esp. when acting 'above one's station' as stated by the larger group. ❑ **run it up the flagpole (and see if anyone salutes)** *v.* (*also* **run something up the flagpole...**) [1950s+] (*US*) to test a reaction to a new idea or concept, usu. as *let's run it up...* ❑ **run like a hairy goat** *v.* (*also* **run like a hairy dog**) (*Aus./N.Z.*) **1** [1940s+] of a racehorse, to run very badly; occas. to run fast. **2** [1960s+] of a motor vehicle, to run badly. ❑ **run off** *v.* [SE *run off*, of water, to flow away] **1** [mid-19C+] (*US*) to talk excessively, to talk rubbish. **2** [1970s] to masturbate. ❑ **run off at** *v.* [SE *run*, to function] [1970s+] (*US black*) to be sustained by something, esp. a drug. ❑ **run off (at) the mouth** *v.* (*also* **run off at the chin, ...head, ...jaw, ...jibs, ...lips**) [SE *chin/jaw/*JIB *n.*[1] (5)] [20C+] (*orig. US*) to talk to excess and to the irritation of one's audience, to lose one's temper or launch into a diatribe. ❑ **run off one's mouth** *v.* [1940s+] (*US*) to be annoyed, to talk angrily. ❑ **run on** *adj.* **1** [1960s] (*US Und.*) arrested. **2** *see* RUN IN *v.* (1). ❑ **run on dim lights** *v.* [1960s] (*US*) to be unintelligent. ❑ **run one's final** [1910s] (*Aus.*) to die. ❑ **run one's mouth** *v.* (*also* **fly one's mouth, run one's gab, run one's gums, run one's jaws**) [one's *mouth runs* like an engine] [1930s+] (*orig. US/W.I.*) **1** to gossip, to tell tales. **2** to give advice. **3** to talk without restraint. **4** as *run up one's mouth*, to brag, to boast, to fantasize. **5** as *run up one's mouth*, to stop talking, to be quiet. ❑ **run over** *v.* [mid-19C+] to treat contemptuously, to victimize; to defeat. ❑ **run sly** *v.* [late 18C] to escape or evade. ❑ **run someone ragged** *v.* (*also* **run one's ass/can ragged**) [1920s+] (*orig. US*) **1** to exhaust or wear out someone or something. **2** to beat. **3** to subject to censure and punishment. ❑ **run something up the flagpole (and see if anyone salutes)** *v. see RUN IT UP THE FLAGPOLE (AND SEE IF ANYONE SALUTES)* above. ❑ **run taper** *v.* [SE *run* + *taper*, to grow thinner] [mid–late 19C] of money, to run short. ❑ **run the cutter** *v.* [Scot. *cutter*, a small whisky bottle, but note phr. *run the cutter*, to smuggle liquor ashore, avoiding the customs' cutter] [late 19C–1940s] (*Aus./N.Z.*) to buy beer in bulk, to be brought home and drunk there. ❑ **run the gears** *v.* [1990s+] (*US prison*) to eviscerate. ❑ **run through** *v.* [one 'runs through' their pockets] [late 19C–1920s] to rob someone, to defraud. ❑ **run to** *v.* **1** [mid-19C] to understand; as phr., *run to tick*, to be acceptable. **2** [late 19C] to be able to afford, usu. in negative [SE in 20C+]. ❑ **run up on** *v.* **1** [1940s+] (*US*) to meet (a person). **2** [1970s] (*US*) in fig. use, to encounter (an idea, a situation). **3** [1990s+] (*US black*) to challenge, attack physically. ▫ **run with** *v.* [mid-19C+] (*orig. US black*) to associate with, to be friends with.

runabout *n.* [var. on RUNDOWN *n.*] [1970s] (*US black*) the facts of a situation.

runaround *n.* **1** [mid-19C–1910s] (*US*) (*also* **run-round**) a suppurative inflammatory sore or swelling in a finger or thumb. **2** [1900s–40s] (*US prison*) an area of confinement that is outside the cells proper. **3** [1910s+] (*orig. US*) (*also* **the run**) usu. constr. with *the*, an attempt to deceive, to delay, to put off, to avoid – usu. in order to give oneself some form of advantage, breathing space etc; usu. as *give someone the runaround*. **4** [1950s+] (*orig. US*) a short trip, an excursion.

runcible *adj.* [play on Edward Lear's nonsense word, coined in 1871 to describe a spoon with three broad prongs, thus ? pun on SPOON *v.*[1]] [1920s–30s] of women, sexually attractive.

rundown *n.* (*also* **run-down**) [RUN DOWN *v.* (3)] [1910s+] (*orig. US*) an explanation, a summary, a brief list of the most important facts or points on which to act.

run down *v.* **1** [mid-18C+] to denigrate someone, to slander someone. **2** [1940s] (*W.I.*) to seduce someone, to persuade them to become one's lover. **3** [1940s+] to rehearse, to practise, to explain. **4** [1960s] to verbalize.

IN PHRASES

▫ **run it down** *v.* (*also* **run it to**) [1950s+] (*mainly US black*) to explain, to point out facts. ▫ **run down game** *v. see under* GAME *n.* ▫ **run down some lines** *v. see under* LINE *n.*[1].

rundum *n. see* RUM-DUM *n.*

rung *adj.* [RING *v.* (1k)] [1950s+] of cars, supplied with false plates, documents etc for use in a robbery.

run goods *n.* [SE *run*, to smuggle; smuggled goods 'have never been entered' (in the customs' ledger)] [late 18C–early 19C] a woman's virginity.

run-in *n.* [1920s] (*US tramp*) of a beggar, obtaining a free meal from someone whom one solicits for a donation.

run in *v.* **1** [mid-19C+] (*also* **run, run on**) to arrest, to run in to prison, to set aside for punishment, to report to the police. **2** [1900s–10s] in fig., non criminal use. **3** [1910s] to report on, to inform against, to betray.

run mouth *n.* [20C+] (*W.I., Gren.*) a gossip, a rumour-monger.

runner *n.* **1** (*UK Und.*) as a thief. (**a**) [late 17C–18C] a sneak thief, esp. one who specializes in entering houses and taking furs, cloaks and coats. (**b**) [late 19C] a dog-stealer. **2** in senses of an intermediary, a go-between. (**a**) [mid-18C] an employee of a casino who keeps track of police activity. (**b**) [mid-18C; 1920s+] (*US Und.*) often with defining n. comb.; someone engaged in conveying prohibited goods (such as drugs, liquor), or illegal immigrants, secretly. (**c**) [mid-19C+] (*US Und.*) an employee of a dancehall or gambling house whose task was to entice passers-by into the establishment; some runners worked from hotel lobbies, where they paid the clerk a fee to introduce them to wealthy or gullible tourists [see Williams for 17C use of *runner* as a brothel errand-boy]. (**d**) [late 19C] one who lures victims into a confidence trick. (**e**) [1930s+] a bookmaker's clerk or assistant. (**f**) [1940s+] (*US*) in numbers gambling, one who picks up bets and takes the money to the central operator/operators. (**g**) [1950s] (*US drugs*) one who recruits new customers for a narcotics dealer. (**h**) [1950s+] (*drugs*) a drug dealer's assistant, who ferries drugs from seller to buyer. **3** [1910s] (*US*) a commercial traveller. **4** in pl. (**a**) [1920s] (*US Und*) a foot. (**b**) [1930s+] (*Aus./Can./Irish*) track shoes, training shoes. **5** [1930s] (*US*) a soda to take out. **6** in senses of physical running. (**a**) [1970s+] someone who is on the run from the police. (**b**) [1980s+] (*Aus. prison*) an escapee.

IN PHRASES

▫ **do a runner** *v.* [1970s+] (*UK Und.*) to abscond from the police or to be on the run, before possible capture by the police, or simply to run away.

runner and rider *n.* [rhy. sl.] [20C+] cider.

runners *n. see* RUNS, THE *n.*

running *adj.*

IN COMPOUNDS

▫ **running bawd** *n.* [mid-17C] a prostitute, or one who sets up a client with a prostitute, who uses an establishment, such as a tavern, which provides rooms to be used on a freelance basis for prostitution. ▫ **running glazier** *n.* [late 18C] (*UK Und.*) a criminal who poses as a window cleaner/mender so as to find empty houses that can be robbed. ▫ **running patterer** *n.* (*also* **running stationer**) [SE *running* + PATTERER *n.* (2)/SE *stationer*] [late 17C–19C] a street-hawker of books, pamphlets, ballads and similar printed material. ▫ **running rambler** *n.* [late 18C] (*UK Und.*) one of a team of pickpockets who rolls a large grindstone down the street; when pedestrians move out of his way, the attendant pickpockets rob them. ▫ **running smoble** *n.* (*also* **running smabble, running smobble, running-smobbler**) [SMABBLE *v.* (1)] [18C–early 19C] (*UK Und.*) a shop-thief. ▫ **running snavel** *n.* [SNAFFLE *v.* (2)] [late 18C] (*UK Und.*) one who robs children on their way to school.

running belly *n.* [1990s+] (*W.I.*) diarrhoea.

running buddy *n. see* RUNNING PARTNER *n.*

running for Sweeney *phr.* [? the idea of running for help from a stereotypically Irish policeman, i.e. 'Sweeney'] [1900s] (*US*) running away from something threatening or dangerous.

running horse *n.* (*also* **running nag**) [SE *running*, oozing + *HORSE-POX under* HORSE *n.*/NAG *n.* (1c) (HORSE *n.* (11) appears to be too late)] [mid-17C–early 19C] a venereal discharge.

running orders *n.* [1940s] (*US*) an order of wheatcakes and coffee.

running partner *n.* (*also* **running buddy, running man, running mate**) [20C+] (*US*) a close friend with whom one pursues most of one's daily activities.

running range *n.* [? SE *running* + Fr. *reins*, kidneys] [1920s–50s] (*US black*) the discharge from the penis or vagina that accompanies gonorrhoea.

runnings *n.* [1980s+] (*UK black*) **1** what is going on, the situation, 'the score', a plan. **2** business.

running shoes *n.*

IN PHRASES

▫ **give someone (their) running shoes** *v.* [1930s+] (*orig. Aus./N.Z.; later US*) to dismiss from a job, as a lover etc.

run out *n.* [1910s–30s] (*UK Und.*) a mock auction of cheap goods.

runout *n.* **1** [mid-19C] (*UK Und.*) a pickpocketing expedition. **2** [1950s] an escape, an evasion.

run-out powder *n.* [a fig. SE *powder* that inspires speed; note POWDER *v.*[1]]

IN PHRASES

▫ **take a run-out powder** *v.* (*also* **take a run-out**) [20C+] to escape, to run away.

run-round *n. see* RUNAROUND *n.* (1).

runs, the *n.* (*also* **runners, the**) [the diarrhoea runs from one's body; one runs to the lavatory] **1** [1930s+] diarrhoea. **2** [1980s] in fig. use, an image of uncontrolled excess.

IN PHRASES

▫ **on the run** *adj.* [1950s] (*US*) suffering from diarrhoea.

runt *n.* [weak use of SE *runt*, the smallest of a litter] [early 17C+] a short person, thus a contemptible person.

runty *adj.* [1940s–60s] (*US*) short, 'sawn-off'.

rupert *n.* [the stereotypical 'classiness' of the name] **1** [1910s+] (*orig. milit.*) a generic name for any young male aristocrat. **2** [1960s–70s] the penis.

rupert bears *n.* [rhy. sl.] [1980s+] (business) shares.

rupperty *n. see* RUBBEDY *n.*

ruption *n.* [SE *eruption*] [1990s+] (*W.I.*) a disturbance.

rupture a gut *v. see BUST A GUT under* GUT *n.*

ruptured duck *n.* [orig. US Air Force jargon for a damaged aircraft; the 'ruptured' presumably indicates the fact that one wing of the eagle is underneath and extends beyond the circular design of the button] [1940s+] (*US milit.*) the lapel pin or pocket insignia worn by an honourably discharged US serviceman; thus the honourable discharge itself.

rural *n.*

IN PHRASES

❑ **do a rural** *v.* **1** [20C+] to have sex in the open-air. **2** [1980s] to urinate or defecate in the open.

rush *n.* **1** in senses of lit. or fig. overwhelming. (**a**) [late 18C–early 19C] (*UK Und.*) robbery with violence; if *the rush*, then usu. of a single item, e.g. a cloak hanging outside a shop; if a *rush*, an assault by a number of men on a house with the intent of robbing the owners of their money and valuables. (**b**) [mid–late 19C] a swindle. (**c**) [mid-19C–1910s] (*US campus*) a mass confrontation, groups of students against each other. (**d**) [mid-19C+] (*Aus./US*) a stampede. (**e**) [20C+] the lavishing of attention on someone, usu. a woman, in the hope of gaining their affections; thus *put on the rush*, to attempt to impress. (**f**) *see* BUM'S RUSH *n.* **2** in US campus uses. (**a**) [mid-19C] a poor recitation. (**b**) [mid-19C–1900s] a perfect recitation. **3** [1930s] a winning streak. **4** in drug uses. (**a**) [1950s+] the immediate effect of any drug. (**b**) [1960s+] the immediate and intense feeling that follows the injection of heroin into a vein. (**c**) [1960s+] a rush of adrenalin. (**d**) [1970s+] amyl or isobutyl nitrite, which produces an instant effect.

IN COMPOUNDS

❑ **rush act, the** *n.* **1** [20C+] (*US*) the seduction of a woman. **2** [1920s] an attempt to befriend somebody. **3** [1930s] (*US*) any fast move. **4** [1980s] (*UK Und.*) impersonating the police in order to extort bribes from fellow criminals.

IN PHRASES

❑ **do it on the rush** *v.* [mid-19C] to run away; to make an escape. ❑ **give it one upon the rush** *v.* [early–mid-19C] to make an intense effort to leave or escape a place. ❑ **give someone the rush** *v.* [mid-19C–1910s] to sponge off someone for a lengthy period and top it off by successfully requesting a loan.

rush *adj.* [RUSH *v.* (1f)] [late 19C+] (*US campus*) describing objects, people or activities that are to do with paying court to a student with the hope of having them join a fraternity, e.g. *rush party*.

rush *v.* **1** in senses of lit. or fig. assault. (**a**) [late 18C–early 19C] (*UK Und.*) to rob; 'A number of villains assemble at the door of a house, and as soon as opened rush in, bind the family, and plunder the house' (*Gentleman's Magazine*, LV, 1785). (**b**) [mid-19C+] (*Aus./US*) to charge, to assault. (**c**) [late 19C] to make advances toward, of a non-sexual nature. (**d**) [late 19C+] (*US campus/W.I.*) to make a pass at, to court, to make sexual advances towards. (**e**) [late 19C+] to cheat, to overcharge, the victim is not given time to think. (**f**) [late 19C+] (*US campus*) to pay court to a student with the hope of having them join a fraternity; also fig. (**g**) [late 19C+] (*US campus*) to confront, esp. groups of students against each other. (**h**) [late 19C+] (*US black*) to jump on someone, to beat someone up. (**i**) [20C+] to show intense interest in something or someone. (**j**) [1980s+] (*US campus*) to gang up on a particular person. **2** [mid–late 19C+] (*US campus*) to make a perfect recitation. **3** [1900s–30s] to charge money, to obtain from someone. **4** [1910s] (*Aus.*) to eat. **5** [1960s+] in drug uses. (**a**) (*drugs*) of a drug, to take effect, to work on the user. (**b**) of a person, to experience the immediate effects of a drug, esp. heroin or cocaine.

IN COMPOUNDS

❑ **rush buckler** *n.* [SE *rush*, to force violently + *buckler*, a shield] [mid-16C] a thug, a bully. ❑ **rushing business** *n.* [late 19C] (*UK Und.*) robbery through confidence tricks and hoaxes.

IN PHRASES

❑ **rush a beat** *v.* [1950s] (*US black*) to get very excited. ❑ **rush the can** *v. see under* CAN *n.*[1]. ❑ **rush the growler** *v. see under* GROWLER *n.*[3]. ❑ **rush the kip** *v. see under* KIP *n.*[3]. ❑ **rush up the frills** *v.* (*also* **rush up the petticoats**) [mid–late 19C] to have sexual intercourse while virtually fully clothed.

rusher *n.* **1** [late 18C–early 19C] a thief, as in 'Thieves who knock at the doors of great houses in London, in summer time, when the families are gone out of town, and on the door being opened by a woman, rush in and rob the house' (Grose, 1785). **2** [late 18C–early 19C] a house-breaker who specializes in breaking into secluded houses. **3** [mid-19C–1900s] (*US*) a 'go-ahead', fashionable person.

rushlight *n.* [SE *rushlight* which 'blazes up'] [mid-18C] a fiery drink.

Ruski/Rusky *n. see* RUSSKI *n.*

Russ *n. see* RUSSKI *n.*

russell harty *n.* [rhy. sl.; ult. TV personality *Russell Harty* (1934–88)] [2000s] a party.

russia *n.* [made of *Russia* leather, a durable leather often used in bookbinding] [late 19C] (*UK Und.*) a pocket-book.

Russian *n.* (*also* **Rooshian, Roosian**) **1** [early 19C+] (*Aus.*) a wild horse, wild cattle. [? pun on *rush around*]. **2** [1930s–50s] (*US black*) a newly arrived southern black who has moved to the north. [pun on *rush-in*; many blacks moved north during WW2 to work in war-related manufacturing industries]. **3** [1940s+] in S.Afr. use [negative image of Russia during the Cold War]. (**a**) any of the gangs from the south townships in South Soto known for their violence and terror from 1940s. (**b**) any south Sotans. **4** [1980s] (*US*) intercrural intercourse whereby the man rubs his penis between his partner's thighs but does not enter the vagina.

IN PHRASES

❑ **high Russian** *n.* [1960s+] (*gay*) simultaneous anal and oral sex.

Russian *adj.*

SE in slang uses

IN COMPOUNDS

❑ **Russian coffeehouse** *n.* [the bear is a 'Russian' animal] [late 18C–early 19C] the Brown Bear public house in Bow Street, Covent Garden, a popular haunt for both thieves and thief-takers. ❑ **Russian high** *n.* [? assumptions of Russian sexual preferences] [1950s–60s] (*gay*) simultaneous fellatio and anal intercourse. ❑ **Russian law** *n.* [a trad. Russian punishment] [mid-17C] a punishment of one hundred blows on the shins. ❑ **Russian neckcloth** *n.* [mid-19C] (*UK Und.*) the hangman's noose.

IN PHRASES

❑ **Russian salad party** *n.* [SE *Russian salad*, a mix of chopped or shredded vegetables and mayonnaise] [1950s–70s] (*gay*) an orgy in which all participants are covered in baby oil.

Russian duck *n.* [rhy. sl.] **1** [1910s–20s] dirt [SE *muck*]. **2** [1970s] sexual intercourse [FUCK *n.* (1a)].

Russian Turk *n.* [rhy. sl.] [late 19C] work.

Russki *n.* [orig. Crimean War milit.] (*also* **Rooski, Ruski, Rusky, Russ, Russky**) **1** [1910s+] a derog. term for a Russian; also attrib. **2** [1960s] the Russian language.

rust *n.* **1** [mid-19C] money. **2** [late 19C] old metal.

SE in slang uses

IN COMPOUNDS

❑ **rust bucket** *n.* **1** [1940s+] (*US*) a rusty old ship. **2** [1960s+] (*Aus./N.Z./US*) a car that is noticeably and dangerously rusty. **3** [1990s+] an old plane. ❑ **rust eater** *n.* [1920s–30s] (*US tramp*) a construction worker.

IN PHRASES

❑ **take the rust out of** *v.* [mid-19C] (*US*) to discomfit, to deflate.

rustiness *n.* [mid-19C–1900s] irritability, bad temper.

rustle *n.* [RUSTLE *v.* (1)] **1** [late 19C–1920s] (*US*) bustle, hustle; thus *get a rustle on*, to hurry up. **2** [1940s] (*US black*) an orphan, esp. one whose parents are unknown [such a child is the product of a quick, brief relationship]. **3** [2000s] (*US prison*) a riot or lesser disturbance.

rustle *v.* **1** [mid-19C+] (*US*) to rush around, to bustle about; thus ext. as (US) *rustle one's bustle*, also n. *rustler*, a busy, active person. **2** [1950s] to make available, to round up.

rustler *n.* [RUSTLE *v.*; a *rustler* of cattle is SAmE] **1** [mid-19C–1900s] (*US*) a busy, active person. **2** [late 19C] (*Aus./US*) one who enjoys a good time. **3** [2000s] (*US prison*) a sexual predator.

rustling *n.* [RUSTLE *v.*] [late 19C] (*US*) energetic, bustling activity.

rustling *adj.* [RUSTLE *v.*] [late 19C–1900s] bustling, energetic, active.

rustskellum *n.* [mid-19C] (*UK Und.*) an ageing thief, no longer capable of active criminality.

rusty *n.*[1] [? backform. *CUT UP RUSTY under* CUT UP *v.*[1]] [mid-19C] **1** an informer. **2** a fight, a skirmish.

rusty *n.*[2] [the colour] [20C+] a nickname for anyone with red or auburn hair.

rusty *n.*[3] *see* RUSTY-DUSTY *n.*

rusty *adj.*[1] [one who lacks the 'polish' to make a successful path in the world] **1** [17C–1920s] ill-tempered. **2** [1960s+] anti-social.

IN PHRASES

❑ **run rusty** *v.* [mid-19C] to misbehave, to act counter to discipline.

SE in slang uses

IN COMPOUNDS

❑ **rusty bullet wound** *n.* (*also* **rusty starfish**) [supposed resemblance] [1990s+] the anus. ❑ **rusty gun** *n.* [their weapon has rusted in its holster] **1** [1960s+] (*US*) a veteran police officer. **2** [2000s] (*UK Und.*) an armed robber who has retired from his profession. ❑ **rusty guts** *n.* (*also* **rusty-guts**) [SE *rustic*, countrified, rough, boorish + SE *guts*, the intestines, used fig. as a man; Hotten (1874) prefers 'Corruption of RUSTICUS'] [late 17C–early 19C; 1930s–50s] a surly, unpleasant old man. ❑ **rusty nails** *n.* [mid-19C] (*UK Und.*) diamond jewellery.

rusty *adj.*[2] [? Somerset dial. *rusty*, gross, obscene] [17C; 20C+] (*Aus.*) lecherous, amorous.

rusty-dusty *n.* (*also* **rusty**) [1930s+] (*US*) the buttocks, esp. with the implication that someone has been sitting around doing nothing; thus they are *rusty* and *dusty* from lack of movement.

IN PHRASES

❑ **shake one's rusty-dusty** *v.* [1940s] (*orig. US*) to hurry up.

IN EXCLAMATIONS

❑ **up your rusty!** *see UP YOUR BROWN! under* BROWN *n.*

rutabaga *n.* [SAmE *rutabaga* = SE *swede*] **1** [1920s] a poor (Southern) peasant. **2** [1930s+] an ugly woman. **3** [1950s] (*US*) a dollar.

rutat *n. see* RATTAT *n.*

Ruth *n.*

IN PHRASES

❑ **cry Ruth** *v. see CRY RALPH under* RALPH *n.*

Ruth Buzzy *n.* [proper name *Ruth Buzzi* (b.1936), the actress best known for her work on *Rowan & Martin's Laugh-In* (1967–73)] [1960s–70s] (*US black*) a plain-looking woman.

ruthers *n. see* DRUTHERS *n.*

ruttat *n.* [backsl. *ruttat* = *tatur* = potato] [mid–late 19C] a potato.

IN COMPOUNDS

❑ **ruttat pusher** *n.* [late 19C] the owner of a potato-cart.

rutter *n.* [? SE *router*, a lawless person, a robber, a ruffian] [late 16C–early 17C] (*UK Und.*) one of a team of four swindlers operating the *BARNARD'S LAW under* BARNARD *n.*; their task was to stand at the door and keep watch.

rutting *adj.* [1940s] (*Aus.*) a euph. for FUCKING *adj.* (1).

Ruud Gullit *n.* [rhy. sl.; ult. Dutch football player and manager *Ruud Gullitt* (b.1962)] [2000s] a bullet.

r.w.v. *n.* [abbr.] [1940s+] (*UK Und.*) robbery with violence.

RX *n.* [the *Rx* notation placed on prescriptions, meaning *recipe*, i.e. of the medical preparation] [1950s+] (*US drugs*) a prescription.

ryache *n.* [backsl.] [mid-19C+] a chair.

Ryan Giggs *n.* [rhy. sl. = DIGS *n.*[1]; ult. Manchester United and Wales footballer *Ryan Giggs* (b.1973)] [1990s+] lodgings.

rybeck *n.* [? Yid.] [mid-19C] a share.

rybuck *see* RYEBUCK.

ryder *n.* [? Rom. *ruder*, to clothe] [late 18C–mid-19C] a cloak.

rydim *n.* [SE *rhythm*, i.e. that of the moving buttocks] [1940s] (*W.I.*) the buttocks.

ryebuck *n.* (*also* **ribuck, rybuck**) [RYEBUCK *adj.*] [mid-19C+] (*Aus.*) something good, worthwhile, the 'real thing'.

ryebuck *adj.* (*also* **ribuck, rybuck**) [ety. unknown; ? Ger. *Reibach*, var. of *rebbach*, profit, ult. synon. Yid/Heb. *revach*] [mid-19C–1960s] (*orig. UK Und.*) good, excellent, first-rate.

ryebuck *adv.* [RYEBUCK *adj.*] [mid-19C] (*UK Und.*) admirably, excellently; in pleasant circumstances.

ryebuck! *excl.* (*also* **ribuck! rybuck!**) [RYEBUCK *adj.*] [mid-19C–1960s] (*Aus./US*) a general expression of agreement or approval.

rye mort *n.* (*also* **rye mush**) [Rom. *rei*, a gentleman + MORT *n.*/MUSH *n.*[4] (2)] [1930s] a lady, a gentleman.

rygin *adj.* (*also* **rhygin**) [SE *rage* + RAG *v.* (1); the locus classicus is the epon. *Rygin*, the name adopted by the RUDE BOY *n.* hero of the film *The Harder They Come* (1972)] [1940s+] (*W.I.*) **1** angry. **2** vigorous, lively, spirited. **3** first-class, excellent.

ryno *n. see* RHINO *n.*[1].

rype *v.* [mid-19C] (*Scot.*) to search (a person).

's *abbr.* (*also* **'z**) [16C–18C] an abbr. of 'God's', as found in a number of oaths.

s.a. *n.* [abbr.] [1920s–50s] *s*ex *a*ppeal.

saali *adj.* [SE *salty*] [1940s+] (*W.I.*) attractive, well-dressed.

s.a.b. *n.* [abbr.; SE *social* + AIRHEAD *n.* (1) + BITCH *n.*[1] (1a)] [1980s+] (*US campus*) *s*ocial *a*irhead *b*itch.

sab *n.* [the film star *Sabu* (Dastagir) (1924–63), 'the Elephant Boy', whose hair was thus cut] [1950s] (*W.I.*) a haircut in which the back of the hair is rounded rather than tapered.

sabana *n.* [Sp.] [1990s+] (*US prison/Hisp.*) a white person.

sabbe/sabby *n. see* SAVVY *n.*

Sabé *n.* [SAVVY *v.*] [late 19C–1900s] (*US*) an immigrant of French origin.

sabe *n. see* SAVVY *n.*

sable maria *n.* [SE *sable*, black, i.e. var. on BLACK MARIA *n.*] [late 19C–1910s] a police or prison van.

s.a.b.u. *n.* (*also* **n.a.b.u., t.a.b.u.**) [abbr. *s*elf-*a*djusting *b*alls–*up* or *n*on-*a*djusting *b*alls–*up* or *t*ypical *a*rmy *b*alls–*up*; BALLS-UP *n.*] [1940s] (*orig. US milit.*) a complete disaster.

Sac *n.* [abbr.] [1930s–60s] (*US tramp/Und.*) Sacramento, California.

sac *n. see* ZAC *n.*

sach *n.*[1] *see* SATCH *n.*[2].

sach *n.*[2] *see* STASH *n.*[2].

sacherea *n.* [SE *sashay*, to move or walk ostentatiously; to strut or parade] [2000s] (*US black*) the state of being outrageously homosexual.

sacht *n. see* SATCH *n.*[2].

sack *n.* **1** as a container or receptacle. (**a**) [late 17C–early 18C] the vagina. (**b**) [late 17C–mid-19C] a pocket. (**c**) [late 19C+] the scrotum; often in combs. such as *NUTSACK under* NUTS *n.*[2]. (**d**) [2000s] (*US black*) attractive female buttocks. **2** constructed with *the*, in senses of dismissal, expulsion [one is given one's possessions, lit. or fig., in a *sack*; current in Fr. f. 17C: '*On luy a donné son sac*, hee hath his pasport giuen him (said of a seruant whom his master hath put away)' (Cotgrave, *Dict. French and English Tongues*, 1611). Note Du. *iemand den zak geven*, to give someone the sack (already in MDu.), *den zak krijgen*, to get the sack]. (**a**) [early 19C+] (*also* **the bag**) rejection or dismissal from one's job. (**b**) [mid-19C] expulsion from school. **3** in drug uses. (**a**) [1910s+] (*US prison*) a sack of tobacco, used as prison 'currency'. (**b**) [1980s+] (*drugs*) heroin. (**c**) [1990s+] a bag of drugs, usu. marijuana or crack cocaine. **4** [1920s+] a bed. **5** in negative terms describing people [? SAD SACK OF SHIT *n.*]. (**a**) [1950s] (*US*) a pitiable, downtrodden person. (**b**) [1960s] (*US campus*) an unattractive woman. (**c**) [1980s+] (*US black/campus*) a second-rate athlete. **6** [1960s+] (*US black*) an overcoat, a jacket [mid-19C SE *sack*, a loose-fitting coat]. **7** [1980s] (*US black*) one's home.

IN COMPOUNDS

❑ **sack artist** *n.* [-ARTIST *sfx*] [1940s+] (*US*) a chronic idler. ❑ **sack-chaser** *n.* [as sense 1b above, i.e. a wallet] [1990s+] (*US black*) a woman (but not a prostitute) who pursues a man, bartering her sexual favours for his financial status. ❑ **sack-diver** *n.* [late 17C–mid-19C] a pickpocket. ❑ **sack drill** *n.* [1940s–50s] (*orig. US milit.*) sleep, time spent in bed. ❑ **sack duty** *n.* [1940s+] (*orig. US milit.*) sleep, time spent in bed. ❑ **sack lunch** *n.* [1960s+] cunnilingus. ❑ **sack rash** *n.* [2000s] (*N.Z.*) a rash from vigorous sexual activity. ❑ **sack rat** *n.* [-RAT *sfx*] [1940s+] (*US*) a chronic idler. ❑ **sack time** *n.* [1940s+] (*orig. US milit.*) time spent in bed, time to go to bed.

IN PHRASES

❑ **dive into the sack** *v.* [late 17C–early 19C] to pick a pocket. ❑ **get the sack** *v.* **1** [mid-19C+] to be dismissed from a job. **2** [1930s+] to be rejected by one's lover or sweetheart. ❑ **give someone the order of the sack** *v.* (*also* **bestow the order of the sack, confer the order of the sack**) [joc. amplification of SACK *v.* (2a)] [mid-19C+] to dismiss, to relieve of one's job, to throw out. ❑ **give someone the sack** *v.* **1** [early 19C+] to dismiss from a job. **2** [mid-19C–1920s] to reject (as a former lover or sweetheart). ❑ **hit the sack** *v.* **1** [1920s+] to go to sleep. **2** [1960s+] (*US/US gay*) by ext., to have sexual intercourse. ❑ **in the sack** *adj.* **1** [1940s+] in bed for the purpose of sex. **2** [1950s] (*US*) in trouble. ❑ **sack o' nuts** *n.* [NUTS *n.*[2] (1)] [1970s+] (*US black*) the scrotum.

SE in slang uses

IN COMPOUNDS

❑ **sack mouth** *see* separate entries. ❑ **sack-shaker** *n.* [the sacks that were filled with cotton] [late 19C–1930s] (*US black*) a cotton-picker.

IN PHRASES

❑ **sack of lard** *n. see TUB OF LARD under* TUB *n.*[1]. ❑ **sack of shit** *n. see* separate entry. ❑ **sack of wind** *n. see BAG OF WIND under* BAG *n.*[1].

sack *v.* **1** in senses of taking or placing 'in a sack'. (**a**) [late 18C+] to rob, to steal, to take possession of, to pocket. (**b**) [19C] to put in one's pocket. (**c**) [1940s] (*US Und.*) to sort out, to arrange. **2** in senses of dismissal. (**a**) [mid-19C+] to dismiss someone from a job. (**b**) [mid-19C+] to reject or dismiss something or someone. (**c**) [mid-19C+] to expel from school or university. (**d**) [1970s+] to end a relationship, esp. in an abrupt, brutal manner. (**e**) [1980s] (*US campus*) to humiliate someone. (**f**) [1980s+] (*Aus. prison*) to ostracize. **3** [1930s–50s] (*UK Und.*) to tie someone up with the cord round their limbs and throat; they are then placed in a sack and when they struggle to get free they will asphyxiate themselves.

IN PHRASES

❑ **sack (down)** *v.* [1940s+] to go to bed, to sleep. ❑ **sacked out** *adj.* [1940s+] fast asleep. ❑ **sack in** *v.* **1** [1940s+] (*US*) to go to bed, to sleep. **2** [1960s] to lie in, to stay in bed. ❑ **sack it up** *v.* [1970s–80s] (*US black*) to terminate, to bring to a conclusion. ❑ **sack out** *v.* [1940s+] to fall asleep, to go to bed. ❑ **sack up** *v.* [1920s+] (*US*) to go to bed.

SE in slang uses

IN PHRASES

❑ **sack 'em up man** *n.* [the corpse is placed in a *sack* before its delivery to a hospital] [mid-19C] a resurrectionist or grave-robber. ❑ **sack up** *v.* **1** [1990s+] (*US campus*) to survive a challenging situation [? one places it in a fig. SE *sack*]. **2** [2000s] (*drugs*) to divide up and place bulk drugs into separate bags prior to sale.

sacking *n.* [SACKING LAW *n.*] [late 16C–early 17C] prostitution.

sacking law *n.* [SE *sack*, to plunder, to lay waste + LAW *n.* (1); the object of such 'sacking' is the client; or ? OE *sæccing*, a bed] [16C–early 17C] (*UK Und.*) the occupation of a prostitute.

sack mouth *n.* [joc. resemblance to an open, spilling SE *sack*] [1980s] (*US black*) a chatterer, a gossip.

sack mouth *v.* [SACK MOUTH *n.*] [1980s] (*US black*) to talk nonsense, to talk for the sake of it.

sack of shit *n.* [SE *sack* + SHIT *n.*] [1940s+] a general term of abuse, usu. of a person; esp. as SAD SACK OF SHIT *n.*

sacks of rice *n.* [rhy. sl.] [1990s+] mice.

sacrament *n.* [the placing of the pill or the blotter on the tongue, reminiscent of a Communion wafer] [1960s–70s] (*drugs*) LSD.

sad *n.*[1] [abbr. SE *sadist*] [1920s] (*US*) one who leads a supposedly 'degenerate' sex life.

sad *n.*[2] [SE *sad*] [1990s+] a general term of abuse for someone perceived as dull and unfashionable.

sad *adj.* [note paradoxically that the earliest use of *sad*, *c.*1000, is wholly positive, meaning satisfied or sated and thence settled, firmly established in purpose or condition, steadfast, valiant, orderly, trustworthy etc. The negative connotation emerges only in the mid-14C; the positive use is found in W.I. (1920s–50s) where *sad* = excellent, first-class] **1** [17C–mid-18C] mischievous, troublesome, corrupt; often of a place. **2** [late 19C+] a general term of abuse, esp. for someone who is unfashionable by current teen standards. **3** [late 19C+] very bad (of quality). **4** [1990s+] (*US campus*) very good.

DERIVATIVES

▫ **saddo** *n.* [1990s+] a pathetic individual.

IN COMPOUNDS

▫ **sad apple** *n. see under* APPLE *n.*[1]. ▫ **sad-ass** *see* separate entries. ▫ **sad bird** *n. see* SAD APPLE *under* APPLE *n.*[1]. ▫ **sad case** *n.* [1940s+] (*US teen/Aus.*) one who tells unamusing jokes. ▫ **sad cattle** *n.* [late 17C–early 19C] (*UK Und.*) prostitutes, viewed as a group; gypsies. ▫ **sad dog** *n.* [early 18C–late 19C] a wicked, debauched fellow. ▫ **sadfuck** *adj.* [FUCK *n.* (4)] [1990s+] a general term of abuse. ▫ **sad sack** *see* separate entries. ▫ **sad sack of shit** *n. see* separate entry. ▫ **sad vulgar** *n.* [late 19C] (*UK society*) a common, vulgar person.

IN PHRASES

▫ **sadder than a map** *adj.* [1930s–40s] (*US black*) very bad, terrible, disgusting.

sad and sorry *n.* [rhy. sl.] [20C+] a lorry.

sad-ass *n.* [deliberate mispron.; thus ref. to ASS *n.* (2)] [1960s+] (*US gay*) a sadist.

sad-ass *adj.* (*also* **sad-assed**) [SE *sad* + -ASS *sfx*] [1960s+] (*US*) depressing, depressed, miserable.

Saddam Hussein *n.* [rhy. sl.; ult. Iraqi dictator *Saddam Hussein* (1937–2006)] [1990s+] a pain.

saddity *n.* (*also* **sadit**) [SADDITY *adj.*] [1960s+] (*US black*) a stuck-up, conceited, snobbish person.

saddity *adj.* (*also* **sadiddy, seddity, siditty, sidity**) [SIDE *n.* (1)] [1960s+] (*US black*) **1** arrogant, haughty, snobbish, conceited. **2** elegant, high-class, sophisticated.

saddle *n.* **1** [mid-16C–mid-18C; 2000s] the vagina, in fig. sense of 'that which is ridden'. **2** [mid–late 19C] a loaf. **3** [late 19C] (*UK tramp*) an overcoat.

SE in slang uses

DERIVATIVES

▫ **saddler** *n.* [late 19C–1940s] (*US*) a saddle-horse.

IN COMPOUNDS

▫ **saddleback** *n.* [its shape] [mid–late 19C] a louse. ▫ **saddlebag** *n.* [play on RIDE *v.* (1a)] [1990s+] (*UK juv.*) a promiscuous girl. ▫ **saddlebags** *n.* **1** [1960s+] the excess flesh around the upper thighs. **2** [1990s+] the labia majora; the scrotum. ▫ **saddle blanket** *n.* **1** [1990s+] (*US*) a sanitary towel. **2** *see* HORSE BLANKET *under* HORSE *n.* ▫ **saddle-leather** *n.* [mid–late 19C] the skin of the buttocks. ▫ **saddle-sick** *adj.* [late 18C–early 19C] tired or injured through excessive riding. ▫ **saddle tramp** *n.* (*also* **saddle bum, saddle stiff**) [SE *tramp*/BUM *n.*[3] (1)/STIFF *n.*[1] (4a)] [20C+] (*US*) a cowboy who moves from ranch to ranch, dependent for survival on local hospitality.

IN PHRASES

▫ **in the saddle** *adj.* **1** [mid-18C; 20C+] engaged in sexual intercourse. **2** [1950s+] in charge, in control. **3** [1990s+] menstruating. ▫ **saddle and bridle** *n.* [1930s–50s] (*US drugs*) the equipment used for smoking opium.

saddle *v.*

SE in slang uses

IN PHRASES

▫ **saddle one's nose** *v.* [late 18C–mid-19C] to wear spectacles. ▫ **saddle the spit** *v.* [SE *saddle a spit*, to put meat upon a spit] [late 18C–early 19C] to host a dinner or supper. ▫ **saddle up** *v.* [play on RIDE *v.* (1a); note SADDLE *n.* (1)] [1970s+] **1** to engage in mutual fellatio and cunnilingus. **2** to have sexual intercourse. **3** (*US gay*) to have anal intercourse. ▫ **saddling paddock** *n.* (*Aus.*) **1** [mid–late 19C] the bar of the Theatre Royal, Melbourne, generally accepted as a place to pick up prostitutes. **2** [late 19C–1950s] any place of assignation.

sadiddy *adj. see* SADDITY *adj.*

sadie (and) maisie *n.* [euph. + initial letters] [1960s+] *sado-masochism.*

sadistics *n.* [joc. mispron.] [1980s] (*US campus*) a statistics course.

sado-maso *n.* [abbr.] [1960s+] (*US*) a *sado-masochist.*

sado-maso *adj.* [SADO-MASO *n.*] [1960s+] (*US*) sado-masochistic.

sad sack *n.* [abbr. SAD SACK OF SHIT *n.*, and thus the eponymous cartoon, created by George Baker (1915–75) in the US Army's *Yank* magazine] [1940s+] (*orig. US milit.*) a miserable, depressed (and depressing) person, usu. thus singled out in an institution, such as prison or the army.

sad sack *v.* [SAD SACK *n.*] [1970s] (*US*) to act or move in a miserable or depressed manner.

sad sack of shit *n.* [SE *sad*/SAD *adj.* (2) + SACK OF SHIT *n.*] [1940s+] (*orig. US*) a miserable, pessimistic, morale-lowering person.

safe *n.* **1** [late 19C+] (*US*) a condom [SE *safe* adj.]. **2** [1990s+] (*US prison*) as a container [the image of the SE *safe*, into which things can be placed for security]. (**a**) the anus. (**b**) the vagina, when used for hiding contraband.

SE in slang uses

IN PHRASES

▫ **safe-and-loft man** *n.* [1950s] (*US Und.*) a thief who specializes in breaking into and stealing from stores, factories etc.

safe *adj.* **1** [mid-19C] relevant to membership of the sporting fraternity. **2** [late 19C+] denoting approval, the overall implication is of being socially acceptable to a given peer group. **3** [1950s+] satisfactory, pleasant. **4** [1960s] (*US Und.*) untraceable, e.g. of an unlicensed gun. **5** [1980s+] used in sex contact advertisements to mean the man advertising has had a vasectomy.

DERIVATIVES

▫ **safeness** *n.* [1990s+] the state of excellence.

SE in slang uses

IN COMPOUNDS

▫ **safe card** *n.* [CARD *n.*[2] (2)] [mid-19C–1920s] a trustworthy person.

IN PHRASES

▫ **safe as...** *adj. see* separate entry.

safe! *excl.* [1960s+] (*US/UK teen*) an all-purpose term of approval.

safe and sound *n.* [rhy. sl.] [20C+] the ground.

safe as... *adj.* used in phrs. meaning extremely safe or sure.

IN PHRASES

▫ **...a bank** [1960s] ▫ **...a church** (*also* **safe as a minister in a church**) [1910s+] ▫ **...a cock in a jock** [1990s+] ▫ **...a convent** [1950s] ▫ **...a crow in a gutter** (*also* **safe as a sow in a gutter**) [mid-17C–mid-18C] ▫ **...a horse in the pound** [late 18C] ▫ **...a mouse in a malt-heap** [mid–late 17C] ▫ **...a mouse in a mill** [early–mid-17C] ▫ **...a thief in a mill** [the thief is the miller, trad. seen as a cheat] [early 17C–18C] ❑ **...a vault in hell** [1980s] ❑ **...coons** [mid-19C–1910s] ❑ **...eggs** [mid-19C] ❑ **...houses** (*also* **safe as a house**) [mid-19C+] ❑ **...mutton** [mid-19C] ❑ **...rats in a hole** [1900s] ❑ **...Sunday** [1980s] ❑ **...the bank** [late 18C–early 19C] ❑ **...the bellows** [mid-19C]

safe as Kelsey *adj. see under* KELSEY'S NUTS *n.*

safety *n.* **1** [1930s+] (*US black*) a condom. **2** [1940s–50s] (*US black*) a bed. **3** [1950s] (*US drugs*) a safety pin used as a hypodermic needle.

safety pin mechanic *n.* [1950s] (*US drugs*) a narcotics user who is forced to resort to an improvised syringe.

sag *n.* [SAG *v.*[1]] [1930s] (*US tramp*) a police truncheon.

sag *v.*[1] [? fig. use of SE *sag*] [1920s–30s] (*US tramp*) to beat with a truncheon.

sag *v.*[2] [1990s+] (*US black*) to wear one's trousers hanging low, exposing the top of one's underwear.

saga *adj.* (*also* **sagger**) [SE *swagger*] [1950s] (*W.I.*) fashionable, showy, garish, over-dressed.

IN COMPOUNDS

❑ **saga-boy/girl** *n.* [1950s] (*W.I.*) a young person who adopts a particular style of dressing, e.g. tight-waisted jackets and peg-top trousers.

sagaciate *v.* [? SE *sagacious*] [mid-19C–1940s] (*US*) to get along; to endure; to work out.

sage hen *n.* [? the state's abundance of prairie fowl] [late 19C+] (*US*) an inhabitant of Nevada.

sagger *adj. see* SAGA *adj.*

sagging deuce *n.* [SE *sagging* + DEUCE AND A QUARTER *under* DEUCE *n.*[1]] [1990s+] (*US black*) a lowered Cadillac automobile.

sago *n.* [their stereotyped diet] [1950s+] (*Aus.*) a Pacific Islander.

sag (off) *v.* [? fig. use of SE *sag*] **1** [1950s] (*US*) to leave. **2** [1990s+] (*UK juv.*) to truant from school.

Sahara *n.* [? they look as if they have walked across the *Sahara* desert] [1940s] (*S.Afr.*) a very tall, thin person.

sail *n.* [resemblance] [1940s] (*US black*) in pl., the human ears.

SE in slang uses

IN PHRASES

❑ **have one's sails high** *v.* [1940s+] (*US black*) to be drunk.

sail *v.*[1] [SE *set sail*] [mid-19C] (*UK Und.*) to leave.

SE in slang uses

IN PHRASES

❑ **sail about** *v.* [late 17C–early 18C; 1910s] to saunter. ❑ **sail in** *v.* (*also* **sail into**) [mid-19C+] **1** (*orig. US*) to attack, physically or verbally. **2** to launch oneself headlong on a course of action. **3** to arrive, to enter, esp. in a slow and measured manner. ❑ **sail up Holborn Hill** *v. see* WALK BACKWARDS UP HOLBORN HILL *under* HOLBORN HILL *n.*

sail *v.*[2] [SAIL CLOSE TO THE WIND *v.*] [1930s–50s] (*US drugs*) of a doctor or dentist, to write prescriptions for narcotics.

sail close to the wind *v.* [naut. imagery] [mid-19C+] to take risks, esp. with a set of rules and regulations.

sailor's farewell *n.* [late 19C+] any form of goodbye that is essentially a curse.

sailors on the sea *n.* [rhy. sl.] [20C+] tea.

saint *n.* **1** [early 19C] a hypocrite. **2** [early–mid-19C] (*US campus*) a notably religious student.

saint and sinner *n.* [rhy. sl.] [20C+] dinner.

St Bernard *n.* [the size and hairiness of the breed of dog] [2000s] (*S.Afr. gay*) a very large, hairy penis.

St George (a-horseback) *n.* [RIDE A ST GEORGE *under* RIDE *v.*] **1** [17C–19C] sexual intercourse in which the woman takes the superior position. **2** [1990s+] sexual intercourse from the rear-entry position.

St Giles *n.* [late 18C–mid-19C] the criminal slum, in the parish of St Giles, at the junction of Oxford Street and Tottenham Court Road, London, destroyed when New Oxford Street was cut through in 1847.

IN COMPOUNDS

❑ **St Giles buzzman** *n.* [BUZMAN *under* BUZ *n.*] [mid-19C] (*UK Und.*) a pickpocket who specializes in stealing handkerchiefs. ❑ **St Giles's breed** *n.* (*also* **Giles's breed, St Giles's company**) [18C–early 19C] criminals as a class. ❑ **St Giles's carpet** *n.* [late 19C] (*London*) a sprinkling of sand on the street. ❑ **St Giles's Greek** *n.* [GREEK *n.* (2)] [late 18C–mid-19C] slang, cant.

St Grotlesex *n.* [1980s+] (*US*) a portmanteau description of the East coast preparatory schools *St* Marks, *St* Paul's, *Grot*on and Midd*lesex*.

St Hugh's bones *n.* [given that the trad. patron saints of shoemakers are St Crispin and St Crispinian, the link to sense 1 is not obvious; whether the Hugh in question was St Hugh (*c.*1140–1200) or Hugh of Lincoln (d.1255), supposedly murdered in a race libel against the city's Jews, is unknown] **1** [17C] shoemaker's tools. **2** [mid-19C] dice.

St Joe *n.* (*also* **St Jo**) [abbr.] [mid-19C+] (*US tramp*) Saint Joseph, Missouri.

St Johnstone's tippet *n.* (*also* **tippet**) [? a hanging judge or prison governor] [mid-16C; early 19C] the noose.

St John's Wood dona *n.* [*St John's Wood*, the home of many courtesans + DONA *n.*] [late 19C] an up-market prostitute or kept woman.

St Looie *n.* (*also* **St Loo**) [abbr./pron.] [late 19C+] (*US*) Saint Louis, Missouri.

St Louis blues *n.* [rhy. sl.] [1960s+] (*Aus.*) shoes.

St Louis flats *n.* [1900s–30s] (*US black*) flat, moccasin-like shoes with a design on the toe – often a club, diamond or other card suit – a style of shoe popular among jazz musicians and gamblers.

St Lubbock *n.* [the invention in 1871 of the August and other bank holidays by Sir John *Lubbock*, 1st Baron Avebury (1834–1913)] [late 19C] a drunken riot.

IN COMPOUNDS

❑ **St Lubbock's day** *n.* (*also* **feast of St Lubbock**) [late 19C] a bank holiday.

St Luke's bird *n.* [pictures of St Luke always feature him with an ox] [late 18C–early 19C] an ox.

St Margret's ale *n.* (*also* **St Marget's ale**) [ety. unknown; ? anecdotal] [early 17C] water.

St Martin's lace *n.* (*also* **St Martin's rings, ...stuff, ...ware**) [16C SE *St Martin's*, 'the parish of St Martin's-le-Grand, London, formerly celebrated as the resort of dealers in imitation jewellery' (*OED*)] [early 17C] respectively, fake gold lace, imitation gold rings and counterfeit goods of any sort.

St Martin's (le Grand) *n.* (*also* **Martin-le-Grand, Martin's**) [rhy. sl.; *St Martin's le Grand* was a monastery and college founded *c.*1050; Its bells rang the nightly curfew, and prisoners on their way from Newgate to Tyburn regularly passed it; those who managed to escape were able to claim sanctuary within its walls – thieves and coiners were accepted, Jews and traitors were barred. It was suppressed in 1540, and its only memory is a street name] [mid-19C–1960s] a hand.

St Mary *n.* [rhy. sl. = FAIRY *n.*[1] (3) + joc. ref. to MARY! *excl.*] [1980s] (*Aus.*) a homosexual male.

St Monday *n.* [the workman's incapacity following a weekend's drinking. The phr. mocks the trad. SE *saint's day*, a religious holiday] [late 18C–19C] a day off.

IN PHRASES

❑ **keep St Monday** *v.* [late 18C–19C] to take a day off work.

Saint Moritz *n.* [rhy. sl. = SHITS, THE *n.*] [1990s+] diarrhoea.

St Nicholas's clergyman *n.* (*also* **St Nicholas's clerk**) [? mis-reading of OLD NICK *n.*; i.e. the Devil] [late 16C] a highwayman.

St Peter *n.* [he 'keeps the keys of Paradise'] [19C] the penis.

St Peter's sons *n.* (*also* **St Peter's children**) [proper name *St Peter*, 'the greatest fisherman' and disciple of Christ; such thieves 'having every finger a fish-hook' (Grose, 1785)] [18C–early 19C] petty thieves, who take anything they can lay their hands on.

St Tibb's eve *n.* (*also* **St Tib's eve, tib's eve**) [defined as 'the evening of the last day, or day of judgment' (Grose 1785)] [late 18C–1940s] never.

St Vitus's dance *n.* [20C+] **1** nerves, jitters, shakes [weak use of SE *St. Vitus's dance*, chorea (Lat. a dance), which promotes spasmodic convulsions of the limbs]. **2** (*Aus.*) pants [rhy. sl.].

sakes! *excl.* (*also* **my sakes! sakes alive!**) [i.e. *for Lord's/God's sake!*] [mid-19C+] (*US*) a mild oath.

sakes alive *n.* [rhy. sl.] [1990s+] the number five.

Sal *n.* **1** see AUNT SALLY *n.* (1). **2** see SALLY *n.*

sal *n.* **1** [mid-18C–early 19C] a form of treatment for syphilis [abbr. SE *salivation*]. **2** [mid-19C] a *sal*ary. **3** [1930s] a young woman. **4** [1970s] (*W.I.*) a friend. **5** see SALTING *n.*

IN PHRASES

❑ **in a high sal** [mid-18C–early 19C] undergoing treatment for syphilis.

salad *n.* [1980s+] (*US drugs*) a mixture of different varieties of cannabis.

SE in slang uses

IN COMPOUNDS

❑ **salad basket** *n.* [trans. of Fr. sl. *panier à salade*, lit. 'salad basket'; so called from the iron grating or trellis that covered the rear of the original 'baskets', horse-drawn carts in which prisoners were transported] [1950s] a police van. ❑ **salad dodger** *n.* [1990s+] a fat person. ❑ **salad oil** *n.* [1910s–20s] hair oil. ❑ **salad queen** *n.* [TOSS SALAD below] [2000s] (*US gay*) a man who enjoys anilingus.

IN PHRASES

❑ **buy a salad** *v.* [1990s+] (*W.I.*) to be rendered stupid. ❑ **eat salad** *v.* [2000s] to indulge in anilingus. ❑ **tossed salad** *n.* [TOSS SALAD below] [1990s+] **1** (*US black teen*) anilingus embellished by an application of jam or syrup. **2** (*gay*) anilingus and anal intercourse. ❑ **toss salad** *v.* [? the general mixing of flesh and embellishments] [1970s+] (*US prison*) to engage in anilingus, seen by otherwise heterosexual participants as a 'clean' non-homosexual form of quick and easy gratification.

IN EXCLAMATIONS

❑ **toss my salad!** [1970s+] (*US prison*) an insulting excl.

Salada crackers *n.* [rhy. sl. = KNACKERS *n.*] [1980s+] (*Aus. prison*) the testicles.

Salamanca wedding *n.* [? anecdotal] [late 19C] the marriage of an old man to a (rich) young woman.

salamander *n.* [SE *salamander*, a mythical lizard-like animal, once thought to be capable of living in fire; Williams notes used in the 17C to invoke sexual coldness (i.e. the cold-blooded lizard)] [mid–late 19C] a fire-eating juggler.

salami *n.* [1960s+] the penis.

IN COMPOUNDS

❑ **salami slapper** *n.* [1990s+] **1** a masturbator. **2** a general pej. term.

IN PHRASES

❑ **play hide the salami** *v. see under* PLAY (AT)… *v.* ❑ **slap the salami** *v.* (*also* **stroke the salami**) [1990s+] to masturbate.

salamon *n.* (*also* **salmon, saloman, salomon**) [? Fr. *serment*, a sermon (*OED*), or cant term for an altar (Harman)] [mid-16C–early 19C] (*UK Und.*) the Mass; usu. in the beggars' oath *by salamon!* by the Mass!

sale *n.*

SE in slang uses

IN PHRASES

❑ **make a sale** *v.* [1930s+] (*Aus.*) to vomit.

sales lady *n.* [as in SALESMAN *n.* (2)] [1920s–70s] (*US*) a prostitute.

salesman *n.* (*US Und.*) **1** [1920s] a confidence trickster. **2** [1940s–60s] a pimp.

salesman's dog *n.* [pun on BARKER *n.*[1] (2)] [late 17C–mid-18C] a shop tout.

Salisbury Crag *n.* [rhy. sl. = SCAG *n.*[2] (2)] [1990s+] (*drugs*) heroin.

Sallenger's/Sallinger's dance/round *n. see under* DANCE *v.*

Sally *n.* (*also* **Sal, Sallie**) **1** [late 19C] as *Salvation Sally*, a Salvation Army girl. **2** [1910s] (*Aus./US/UK*) constr. with *the*, a Salvation Army hostel. **3** [1910s] (*US prison*) a homosexual prostitute. **4** [1910s+] (*Aus./US/UK*) (*also* **Sally's, the Sallies**) the *Sal*vation Army. **5** see AUNT SALLY *n.* (1).

Sally *adj.* [SALLY *n.* (4)] [1950s+] (*US*) pertaining to the Salvation Army.

Sally *v.* [initial letter of SUCK *v.*[1] (1)] [2000s] (*S.Afr. gay*) to practise male-to-male fellatio.

sally *n.* [film *When Harry Met Sally* (1989)] [1980s+] (*US campus*) **1** a person who is punctilious to an absurd, near-certifiable degree. **2** a likeable person.

Sally Ann *n.* (*also* **Sally Army**) [abbr.] [1920s+] **1** the *Sal*vation *Army*. **2** (*Aus.*) a female Salvationist.

sally fairy ann *phr.* see SAN FAIRY ANN *phr.*

Sally Gunnell *n.* [rhy. sl.; ult. UK athlete *Sally Gunnell* (b. 1966)] [1990s+] the Blackwall Tunnel.

salmon *n.*[1] **1** [late 19C] (*UK Und.*) the drowned corpse of a wealthy person. **2** see SALAMON *n.*

SE in slang uses

IN COMPOUNDS

❑ **salmon belly** *n.* [the colour] [1920s] (*US Und.*) a high-denomination bill. ❑ **salmon canyon** *n.* [equation of the female genitals with SE *fish*] [1990s+] the female genitals.

IN PHRASES

❑ **dried salmon** *n.* [mid-19C] (*UK Und.*) an old maid, no longer marriageable. ❑ **half a salmon** *n.* [mid-19C] (*UK Und.*) 2/6d [12.5p.]. ❑ **salmon-tot retriever** *n.* [Carib.E. *salmon-tot*, a salmon-tin + mockery of the pedigree *retriever* breed] [20C+] (*W.I.*) a mongrel, kept as a watch-dog and allowed to forage for its food.

salmon *n.*[2] [? rhy. sl.] [1980s] (*Aus.*) the anus.

salmon (and) trout *n.* [rhy. sl.] **1** [mid–late 19C] the mouth [Cockney pron. of *trout* as *traaht*]. **2** [1910s+] the nose [= SE *snout*]. **3** [1930s–60s] (*also* **mountain trout**) a bookmaker's tout. **4** [1930s–80s] gout. **5** [1950s+] stout beer. **6** [1970s+] (*also* **salmon**) tobacco, esp. prison use [= SNOUT *n.*[2] (1)].

saloman/salomon *n.* see SALAMON *n.*

salop *n.* [Fr. *salope*, a slut, a prostitute] [20C+] (*W.I.*) a dirty, grubby person, esp. a woman or child.

sal slappers *n.* [SE *Sal*, abbr. *Sarah* + the *slapping* of her feet on the pavement; ? SLAPPER *n.*[2] (1) but if so, a lengthy predate] [late 19C] (*costermonger*) a prostitute or promiscuous woman.

salt *n.*[1] [SE *salt*, lecherous] [mid-17C–early 18C] sexual intercourse.

IN COMPOUNDS

❑ **salt-bitch** *n.* [SE *salt bitch*, a bitch in heat] [late 17C] a homosexual. ❑ **salt-cellar** *n.* [19C] the vagina. ❑ **salt-cunted** *adj.* [CUNT *n.* (1)] [late 19C] sexually voracious.

salt *n.*[2] [abbr. colloq. *old salt*] as a veteran, an exemplar. (**a**) [mid-19C] in non-naval contexts, a fine example. (**b**) [mid-19C+] a veteran sailor. (**c**) [1960s+] a veteran of any experience or discipline.

salt *n.*[3] [SE *salt*] **1** [late 19C–1900s] money [generic use of *salt* as a necessity of life, as is money]. **2** [20C+] (*US black/W.I.*) trouble, annoyance, difficulties [the image of oversalting one's food]. **3** [1970s] (*drugs*) heroin.

IN PHRASES

❑ **get salt** *v.* [1990s+] (*US black/W.I.*) to be thwarted, to encounter misfortune. ❑ **suck salt** *v.* [20C+] (*W.I.*) to suffer hardship.

SE in slang uses

IN COMPOUNDS

❑ **salt bomb** *n.* [2000s] (*US black*) personal vilification. ❑ **salt-box** *n.* [? its dimension; the salt tears shed within it] [19C] the condemned cell at Newgate prison. ❑ **salt cellar** *n.* **1** [late 19C] the cavity above a woman's collar-bone. **2** [1950s+] (*nursery*) the navel. ❑ **salt creek** *n.* [var. on *UP SHIT('S) CREEK*

(*WITHOUT A PADDLE*) *under* SHIT CREEK *n*.] [1910s–20s] (*US Und.*) execution in the electric chair. ❑ **salt eel** *n*. [early 17C–early 19C] a rope's end, used for flogging. ❑ **salt horse** *n*. [mid-19C–1940s] salt beef. ❑ **salt junk** *n*. *see* JUNK *n*.[1] (1a). ❑ **salt water** *n*. *see* separate entry.

IN PHRASES

❑ **have a salt eel (for supper)** *v*. [early 17C–early 19C] to be flogged. ❑ **salt and pepper** *see* separate entries. ❑ **salt-box cly** *n*. [supposed resemblance of the pocket to a SE *salt-box*, which has a flap] [early 19C] (*UK Und.*) the outside coat pocket, with a flap. ❑ **want salt** *v*. [SE *salt*, that which enhances flavour] [late 19C] (*US*) to be a weakling, to be lacking strength of character.

salt *adj*. **1** [early 18C–19C] costly, expensive, esp. over-expensive. [the 'salting' of mines, thus the padding of bills]. **2** [1950s+] (*W.I. Rasta*) unlucky, in a bad state; impoverished, empty-handed, low on food.

salt *v*. **1** in senses of initiation. (**a**) [late 16C–early 17C] (*UK student*) to initiate new students by a variety of rituals, esp. making them drink salt water or swallow dry salt. (**b**) [1940s] (*UK prison*) to initiate a new prisoner. **2** in senses of SE *salt away*. (**a**) [mid-19C–1900s] (*US*) to shoot (dead). (**b**) [late 19C–1900s] to ignore, to not bother. **3** [mid-19C+] (*orig. US*) in senses of artificial improvement. (**a**) to 'improve' the apparent quality of a mine by planting specimens of the ore it supposedly yields. (**b**) in ext. or fig. use.

IN PHRASES

❑ **salt the books** *v*. [mid-19C+] to improve the state of a firm's accounts by judicious, if illicit, alterations to the figures.

SE in slang uses

IN PHRASES

❑ **salt down** *v*. **1** [mid-19C+] to put by, to store away. **2** [1900s–10s] (*US*) to tell off, to reprimand. **3** [1930s] in fig. use, to kill, to quieten. ❑ **salt up** *v*. [1980s+] (*US campus*) to cause trouble for, to place in a difficult or embarrassing situation [? the image of 'adding flavour' to the situation].

salt and pepper *n*. **1** [1940s–50s] (*drugs*) marijuana, esp. of poor quality. **2** [1950s+] (*US black*) as a synon. for black and white, usu. in racial contexts. (**a**) an inter-racial couple. (**b**) friends or colleagues of different races. (**c**) a police team, usu. operating from a squad car, that consists of one black and one white police officer. (**d**) a black and white squad car. **3** [1960s] (*US black*) courage, cheek, audacity.

salt-and-pepper *adj*. [1950s+] (*US*) **1** of a person, mixed-race. **2** segregated. **3** of a place, frequented by both blacks and whites, e.g. *salt-and-pepper neighbourhood*. **4** involving both blacks and whites, e.g. a pair of TV anchors. **5** of hair, black and grey/white. **6** of two men, having sex with one woman.

IN COMPOUNDS

❑ **salt-and-pepper queens** *n*. [QUEEN *n*. (2)] [1970s+] (*gay*) a mixed-race gay couple.

salted *adj*. [SE *salted*, of a horse, having survived a disease] [mid–late 19C] experienced, esp. after overcoming some form of problem.

salted (down) *adj*. [mid-19C] drunk.

saltee *n*. (*also* **soldi**) [Ital. *soldi*, pl. of *soldo*, one-twentieth of a lira. Combs. are based on Ital. numbers one to ten, *uno, due, tre, quattro, cinque, sei, sette, otto, nove, dieci*] [mid-19C] (*Ling. Fr./Polari*) one penny; thus *oney saltee*, one penny; *dooe saltee*, twopence; *tray saltee*, threepence; *quarterer saltee*, fourpence; *chinker saltee*, fivepence; *say saltee*, sixpence; *setter saltee* or *say oney saltee*, sevenpence; *otter saltee* or *say dooe saltee*, eightpence; *nobba saltee* or *say tray saltee*, ninepence; *dacha saltee* or *say quarterer saltee*, tenpence; *dacha oney saltee* or *say chinker saltee*, elevenpence; *oney beong*, one shilling; *beong say saltee*, one shilling and sixpence.

salting *n*. (*also* **sal**) [fig. use of Carib.E. *salting*, i.e. 'salt thing', or *salt food*, dishes cooked with salt fish or meat] [1950s+] (*W.I. Rasta*) the vagina.

salt junk *adj*. [rhy. sl.] [late 19C–1900s] drunk.

Salt River *n*. [? *Salt River roarer*, a backwards, unsophisticated country dweller (poss. from Kentucky, where there is an actual Salt River); note J. Inman in *Bartlett* (1848): '*To row up Salt River* has its origin in the fact that there is a small stream of that name in Kentucky, the passage of which is made difficult and laborious as well by its tortuous course as by the abundance of shallows and bars. The real application of the phrase is to the unhappy wight who has the task of propelling the boat up the stream; but in political or slang usage it is to those who are *rowed up* – the passengers, not the oarsman']

IN PHRASES

❑ **go up Salt River** *v*. [? the salty tears of the mourners and/or the bitterness of death] [1920s–40s] (*US black*) to die. ❑ **row someone up Salt River** *v*. [mid–late 19C] (*US*) to defeat (a political opponent); to overcome, to send to oblivion. ❑ **row up Salt River** *v*. **1** [mid-19C–1910s] (*US*) (*also* **row up Salt Creek, go to Salt River**) to suffer a political defeat. **2** [mid-19C–1940s] (*US*) (*also* **soak one's head in Salt River**) to become drunk, i.e. to send oneself 'to oblivion'.

salt water *n*. **1** [late 17C–early 18C] urine. **2** [mid-19C] tears. **3** [mid-19C] a sailor. **4** [1920s] (*US black*) alcohol.

salt-water negro *n*. [note *salt-water Creole*, a black person born during the voyage from Africa; to be a full Creole it is necessary to be born on the islands] [early 19C] (*W.I.*) an African-born black person, so called by the Creoles, who were born in the West Indies.

salt-water taffy *n*. [play on SAmE *salt-water taffy*, which one licks and sucks] [1970s] (*US gay*) a sailor's penis as an object for fellatio.

salty *adj*. (*also* **saltyback**) [? US navy jargon *salty*, tough, aggressive; Dillard suggests link to UK dial. *salty*, 'of a bitch, *maris appetens* [desirous of a male]' (*EDD*)] **1** [1920s+] (*US*) irritated, annoyed, feeling sour, supercilious. **2** [1920s+] (*US*) (*also* **salty-ass**) tough, aggressive, used of a veteran of a particular environment, e.g. a prison. **3** [1920s+] (*US teen*) a general pej., unpleasant, uncouth, crude; of language, obscene. **4** [1980s+] of a garment, well-worn, 'lived-in'.

IN COMPOUNDS

❑ **salty dog** *n*. [DOG *n*.[2]] (*US black*) **1** [late 19C–1930s] something or someone very exceptional. **2** [1970s] one who uses an excess of obscene language.

salty bananas *n*. [rhy. sl.] [20C+] (*Aus.*) sultanas.

salubrious *adj*. [SE *salubrious*, conducive to good health] [19C] drunk.

Salvador Dali *n*. [rhy. sl. = CHARLIE *n*.[8] (1); ult. Span. surrealist *Salvador Dali* (1904–89)] [2000s] cocaine.

salvage *v*. [1910s+] (*Aus./US*) to steal, to pilfer.

salvation *n*. [rhy. sl.] [late 19C–1910s] a station.

Salvation Army *adj*. [rhy. sl. = BARMY *adj*.] [late 19C] **1** crazy, eccentric. **2** drunk.

salvation juggins *n*. (*also* **salvation rotter, …soul-sneaker**) [SE *salvation* + JUGGINS *n*./ROTTER *n*.[1] (1)/SE *soul-sneaker*; all these negative nicknames came from many people's dislike of the Army's heavy-handed religiosity, esp. its attacks on drinking and similar pleasures, which undermined its charitable reputation] [late 19C] a member of the Salvation Army.

salve *n*. **1** [mid-19C–1940s] (*US*) praise, flattery; any form of 'line' that facilitates a confidence trick. **2** [late 19C+] (*US tramp*) butter. **3** [20C+] (*US*) money, esp. as a reward for something difficult. **4** [1910s] (*US campus*) exaggeration. **5** [1910s–20s] (*US/US tramp*) a bribe. **6** [1920s] (*US tramp*) a complaint.

IN COMPOUNDS

❑ **salve-eater** *n*. [late 19C–1930s] (*US*) an immigrant from northern Europe, esp. a Swede.

IN PHRASES

❑ **spread the salve** *v*. (*also* **give the salve, shoot the salve**) [1900s–70s] (*US*) to talk in a conciliatory, soothing manner.

salve *v*. [SALVE *n*. (3)] [20C+] (*US*) to pay, usu. a bribe or reward.

Salvo *n.* (*also* **Salv', salvarmy**) [abbr. + -O *sfx* (3)] [late 19C+] (*Aus.*) the *Salv*ation Army or one of its members.

SAM *n.* [*s*mart-*a*ssed *m*asochist] [1990s+] (*US gay*) a masochist who is rude in order to receive punishment.

Sam *n. see* UNCLE SAM *n.*

sam *n.* **1** [mid-19C] a fool, a simpleton [abbr. SAMMY (SOFT) *n.*]. **2** [mid-19C–1930s] a familiar nickname/generic term used to address black men [*Old Black Sam* or SAMBO *n.*[1] (1)]. **3** [1930s–70s] (*US black*) a black man who willingly conforms to white stereotyping. **4** [1950s–60s] a generic used when the proper name has been forgotten, esp. of women.

sam *v.* **1** [late 19C] to pay for a drink [abbr. *STAND SAM under* STAND *v.*[2]]. **2** [1960s–70s] to cheat, to deceive [? SAMMY (SOFT) *n.*].

Sam and Dave *n.* [soul singers *Sam* Moore (b.1935) and *Dave* Prater (1937–88)] [1980s+] (*US black*) the police, when working in a team of two.

sambo *n.*[1] (*also* **sambie, zambo**) [Sp. *zambo*, used to describe those of mixed Negro and Indian or European blood. The word also describes a breed of yellow monkey. The US use, which emerged during the era of slavery, may have a different root; the Foulah *sambo*, uncle or Hausa *sambo*, second son, or name of the spirit. The suggestion by F&H of a third root, an African tribe, the Samboses (for whom they claim an appearance in a text of 1558) has no validity. *Sambo* began as a neutral term, but as slavery fell into increasing disrepute, so did its terminology. The word was widely popularized by Helen Bannerman's best-selling children's book *The Story of Little Black Sambo* (1923), but the term, and that book, have long since been considered unacceptable] **1** [late 17C+] a derog. term for a black man, strictly the offspring of a mulatto and a black. **2** [early 19C; 1950s+] (*W.I.*) the colour between brown and black; someone who is a cross between a mulatto (brown) and a full black. **3** [1960s+] a direct term of address to any coloured person. **4** [1980s] (*US black*) an obsequious black person.

IN COMPOUNDS

❑ **sambo backra** *n.* [BACKRA *n.* (2)] [1950s] (*W.I.*) a person of mixed race, usu. three-quarters black.

sambo *n.*[2] (*also* **sambie**) [abbr. + -O *sfx* (3)] [1970s+] (*Aus./Irish*) a *san*dwich.

sambo *v.* [SAMBO *n.*[1] (1)] [1940s+] (*US*) of a black person, to act subserviently.

sambolio *n. see* SIMOLEON *n.*

same *adj.*

SE in slang uses

DERIVATIVES

❑ **samey** *adj.* [1920s+] boring, tedious, undistinguished.

IN COMPOUNDS

❑ **same again** *n.* **1** [1930s] the third drink of a session. **2** [1930s+] a general response to an offer of another drink, usu. in a public house setting; as a query *same again?* it can be the offer. ❑ **same o.b.** *n.* [SE *same old* + BOB *n.*[3] (2)] [late 19C] one shilling (5p), esp. in the context of the charge for most contemporary places of entertainment.

IN PHRASES

❑ **not in the same street** *adj.* (*also* **not in the same compartment, ...town**) [late 19C+] utterly unequal to, not to be compared with. ❑ **same old same old** (*also* **same ol' same ol, 'same-o same-o**) [SE *same old thing*] [1970s+] (*orig. US black*) a general expression to imply that nothing has changed in one's life, used in response to a question as to one's current health or feelings. ❑ **same old three and four** *n.* (*also* **same old 3 and 4**) [late 19C] a weekly wage, six days at three shillings and fourpence a day gives £1 for a six-day week. ❑ **same shit, different day** (*also* **s.s.d.d.**) [SHIT *n.* (3)] [1980s+] (*orig. US black*) life goes on as normal, with no surprises, good or bad.

samfie *n.* [Twi *asumanfo*, a sorcerer, *asumangfa*, a magician] **1** [20C+] (*W.I.*) a confidence trick. **2** *see* SAMFIE-MAN below.

DERIVATIVES

❑ **samfieism** *n.* [20C+] deceit, trickery.

IN COMPOUNDS

❑ **samfie-man** *n.* (*also* **samfie**) [20C+] (*W.I.*) a confidence trickster.

samfie *v.* (*also* **samfai, samfi**) [SAMFIE *n.*] [20C+] (*W.I./UK black teen*) to trick, to deliberately deceive.

s.a.m.f.u. *n.* [abbr.; var. on S.A.B.U. *n.* and S.N.A.F.U. *n.*] [1940s+] (*orig. milit.*) *s*elf-*a*djusting *m*ilitary *f*uck-*u*p.

Sam Hill! *excl.* (*also* **Sam Houston! Sam Patch! Sam Scratch!**) [euph., via the initial 'h' of *WHAT THE HELL! under* HELL *n.*; note AK Sokol in *American Speech* XV:1 (1940) who suggests the name *Samael*, 'the prince of the demons', which appeared, as *Samiel* in the opera *Der Freischütz*, premiered in the US in 1825] [early 19C+] (*orig. US*) a euph. for HELL! *excl.*

IN EXCLAMATIONS

❑ **what the Sam Hill!** [early 19C+] (*US*) an excl. of surprise, shock, alarm or resignation etc.

Sami *n.* [abbr.] [1980s+] (*N.Z.*) a *Sam*oan.

sammie *n.* [abbr.] [2000s] (*N.Z.*) a sandwich.

sammo *n.* [abbr.] [1930s+] (*Aus./US*) a sandwich.

Sammy *n. see* UNCLE SAM *n.*

sammy *n.* **1** [19C–1940s] (*S.Afr.*) a generic name for any Hindu, esp. Indian people living in South Africa [abbr. SE *ramsammy*]. **2** [1910s] (*US*) a US soldier during WW1 [UNCLE SAM *n.*]. **3** [1990s+] (*US milit.*) (*also* **skinny**) a derog. name for a Somali. **4** *see* PORTSAMMY *n.*

IN COMPOUNDS

❑ **sammy lunchmeat** *n. see WILLIE LUNCHMEAT under* WILLY *n.*[1].

sammy *adj.* [SAMMY (SOFT) *n.*] [early 19C–1930s] foolish, dull.

Sammy Lee *n.* [rhy. sl. = PEE *n.*[1] (2) / WEE *n.*; poss. ult. the US diver *Sammy Lee* (b.1920)] [1990s+] an act of urination.

sammy (soft) *n.* [orig. dial. *sammy*, a simpleton, compounded by SOFT *adj.* (1)] [mid–late 19C; 1930s+] a fool.

samoleon *n. see* SIMOLEON *n.*

sample *n.* [1990s+] (*W.I.*) unique; of a man, mild-mannered.

sample *v.* **1** [19C–1910s] to caress or fondle a woman sexually. **2** [mid-19C–1900s] to drink [? backform. f. SAMPLE ROOM *n.*].

sampler *n.* [SE *sampler*, a piece of embroidery, which is worked with a NEEDLE *n.*] [19C] the vagina.

sample room *n.* ['Sometimes the bar is at the side, screened off, and genteelly disguised under the name of "sample room". You enter ostensibly to purchase cherries, and immediately "put yourself outside" a "tot" of Bourbon' (G.A. Sala, *My Diary in America*, 1865)] [mid-19C–1930s] (*US*) a bar, often as attached to a grocery, in which one can purchase liquor by the glass.

samson *n.* (*also* **sampson**) [the biblical strongman *Samson*; ? either the strength of the drink or the strength it imparts to the drinker] [mid-19C–1900s] a drink combining brandy, cider, sugar and water.

Samuel Pepys *n.* [rhy. sl. = SE *creeps*; ult. British diarist *Samuel Pepys* (1633–1703)] [1980s+] a sense of uneasiness or distaste, a nervous feeling.

san *n.* [abbr.] [20C+] a *san*itarium, esp. at a boarding school.

San Bardoo/Berdoo *n. see* BERDOO *n.*

Sancho *n.* [generic use of Hisp. proper name] [1980s+] (*US prison*) used by Hisp. inmates for the new boyfriend/lover who takes one's place while one is incarcerated.

sancocho *v.* [Sp. 'to cut up into little pieces and stew'] [1980s+] (*drugs*) to steal.

sand *n.*[1] [fig. uses of SE] **1** [early 19C+] (*now mainly US prison or short order*) sugar, e.g. *Joe with cow and sand*, a cup of coffee with milk and sugar [Vaux glosses 'moist sugar']. **2** [mid-19C] (*US*) courage, firmness of purpose, determination. **3** [late 19C–1900s] (*orig. US*) money [refers to money not as a 'staff of life' but as dirt].

DERIVATIVES

❑ **sandies** *n.* [abbr.] [1980s] (*Aus.*) *sand* flies. ❑ **sandiness** *n.* [late 19C] (*US*) the quality of having courage or 'guts'.

SE in slang uses

IN COMPOUNDS

❑ **sandbag/sandbagger** *see* separate entries. ❑ **sand-duster** *n.* [1950s] (*US*) a short person. ❑ **sand-grope/-groper** *see* separate entries. ❑ **sand-hog** *n.* (*also* **sand-hogger**) [late 19C+] a caisson worker, working under compressed air, digging and laying the foundations of bridges etc. ❑ **sandman** *n.* [they SANDBAG *v.*[2] (1) their victim] [1910s+] (*Aus.*) a footpad, a mugger. ❑ **sand scratcher** *n.* [note 19C Aus. *sandscratcher*, a gold miner] [2000s] (*US*) a derog. term for a Syrian, an Indian (from India).

IN PHRASES

❑ **dance in the sandbox** *n. see under* DANCE *v.* ❑ **have sand in one's craw** *v.* (*also* **have sand in one's gizzard**) [sense 2 above] [1910s] (*US*) to act courageously. ❑ **kick sand** *v.* [? the famous 'Charles Atlas' advert, in which the bully kicks sand into the weakling's face] [1950s–60s] (*US black*) to make a fuss, to complain. ❑ **raise sand** *v.* [image of kicking sand in someone's face or blowing up a sand storm] **1** [late 19C+] (*US*) to cause a stir, a commotion. **2** [1920s] (*US black*) to have a good time. **3** [1930s+] to complain. **4** [1980s] (*US Und.*) to fight.

sand *n.*[2] [1970s+] used in the following combs. as a derog. for a Middle-Easterner.

IN COMPOUNDS

❑ **sand coon** *n.* [COON *n.* (5)] [2000s] an Arab from the Middle East. ❑ **sand hopper** *n.* [1970s] an Arab. ❑ **sand-jockey** *n.* [JOCKEY *n.*[2] (1)] [2000s] an Arab from the Middle East. ❑ **sand nigger** *n.* [NIGGER *n.*[1] (1)] [1980s+] (*US*) an Arab or any other native of the Middle East (except Israelis). ❑ **sand toad** *n.* [1990s+] (*US*) an Arab, a Middle Easterner. ❑ **sand wog** *n.* [WOG *n.*[1] (1)] [1990s+] an Arab or Middle Eastern person.

sandbag *n.* [SANDBAG *v.*[1] (1)] [1900s] (*US*) a confidence trick.

sandbag *v.*[1] [the use in war of SE *sandbags* as a protective wall from which one can then emerge] (*US*) **1** [late 19C–1920s] to cheat. **2** [20C+] to feign weakness in order to mislead an opponent; to evade one's responsibilities. **3** [1940s+] (*poker*) to resist raising the bet immediately in the hope of making a larger raise later on.

sandbag *v.*[2] [i.e. to hit with a SE *sandbag*] **1** [late 19C+] (*orig. US*) to ambush, to take by surprise. **2** [20C+] to trick. **3** [1910s+] to get rid of. **4** [1920s+] (*US*) to intimidate. **5** [1930s] to extort.

sandbag and jemmy *adv.* [a villain's tools] [1900s] (*Aus.*) completely.

sandbagger *n.* [SANDBAG *v.*[2] (1)] (*US*) **1** [late 19C–1920s] a street robber, a 'mugger'; one who wins. **2** [1960s] one who is believed to win unfairly in a betting game.

sand-grope *v.* [SE *sand-grope*, to walk in soft sand] [late 19C] (*Aus.*) to bungle.

sand-groper *n.* [SE *sand-grope*, to walk through soft sand. Western Australia encompasses a large area of sandy desert] [late 19C+] (*Aus.*) an inhabitant of Western Australia; thus *sand-groper land*, Western Australia.

S and M *n.* (*also* **S&M, S/M, S-M**) [abbr.] [1960s+] **1** sado-masochism. **2** a sado-masochist.

S and M *adj.* (*also* **S&M, S/M, S-M**) [abbr.] [1960s+] pertaining to sado-masochism.

sandoz *n.* [the discovery of the drug by Dr Albert Hofmann of *Sandoz* Pharmaceuticals, Switzerland] [1960s+] (*drugs*) LSD.

sandpaper suit *n.* [the roughness of the material] [1930s–40s] (*N.Z.*) a school cadet uniform.

Sandra Bullocks *n.* [the film star *Sandra Bullock* (b.1966); play on *sweaty bollocks*] [1990s+] itching, uncomfortable testicles.

sandwich *n.* **1** [mid–late 19C] a sandwich man, carrying a pair of advertising boards around the streets ['the doleful broken-down men employed at one shilling a day to carry pairs of advertisement boards, tabard-fashion, one on the unambitious chest, the other on the broken back' (Ware)]. **2** [1960s+] (*also* **triple-decker sandwich**) a sexual threesome, involving any permutation of the sexes. **3** [1980s+] (*drugs*) two layers of cocaine with a layer of heroin in the middle.

IN COMPOUNDS

❑ **sandwich man** *n.* [1970s+] (*US black*) a man having sex with two women at the same time.

IN PHRASES

❑ **make a sandwich** *v.* [1970s+] to make a sexual position in which two men are having simultaneous vaginal and anal intercourse with a woman.

SE in slang uses

IN COMPOUNDS

❑ **sandwich lane** *n.* [one is sandwiched between the fast and slow lanes] [1970s+] (*US*) the middle lane of a three-lane highway.

IN PHRASES

❑ **a sandwich short of a picnic** *adj. see under* ...SHORT OF... *adj.* ❑ **open the sandwich box** *v.* [1990s+] (*Aus.*) to break wind.

sandwich *v.* [1950s] (*W.I.*) to kiss.

Sandy *n.* [abbr. common Scot. name *Alexander*] [late 18C+] a generic name for any Scot.

sandy *n.* (*US*) **1** [late 19C] a drunken spree of which one has no memory [may be gambling jargon or fig. use of SANDBAG *v.*[1]]. **2** [1930s] a trick, trickery [SE phr. *throw sand in someone's eyes*].

sandy blight *adj.* [rhy. sl.] [1970s] (*Aus.*) dead right.

Sandy Macnab *n.* (*also* **Sandy McNab**) [rhy. sl.] **1** [1910s] (*Aus.*) the stomach [SE *flab*]. **2** [1910s+] a crab, a body louse, usu. in pl. **3** [1920s+] (*Aus.*) a scab. **4** [1940s+] a taxi-cab.

Sandy Powell *n.* [rhy. sl.; ult. the northern radio/music-hall comedian Albert *'Sandy' Powell* (1898–1982)] [1940s–50s] a towel.

sane *n.* (*also* **sein**) [Ger. *zehn*, ten] [1930s+] (*Aus.*) ten, in a variety of contexts, e.g. a ten-shilling note, a ten-year prison sentence, ten ounces of tobacco.

san fairy ann *phr.* (*also* **sally fairy ann, san ferry ann, send for mary ann**) [pron. of synon. Fr. *ça ne fait rien*] [1910s+] (*orig. milit.*) no matter, forget it.

San Fran *n.* [abbr.] [20C+] (*US*) *San Francisco*.

San Francisco *n.*

SE in slang uses

IN PHRASES

❑ **have a San Francisco accent** *v.* [the city's stereotyped identification with an active gay movement] [1990s+] (*US gay*) to be homosexual.

San Francisco Bay, one small boat half sunk *n.* [late 19C] (*US*) a cocktail.

sangaree *n.* [SE *sangaree*, spiced wine, diluted with water; ult. Sp. *sangria*] [early–mid-19C] a drinking bout.

sanger *n.* (*also* **sanga, sango**) [abbr.] [1940s+] (*Aus./Irish*) a sandwich.

sanguinary *adj.* (*also* **sanguineous**) [late 19C–1940s] a euph. for BLOODY *adj.* (1).

IN COMPOUNDS

❑ **sanguinary doubles** *n.* [? the site of much bloodshed] [mid-19C] the Piccadilly Saloon, at 222 Piccadilly, London. ❑ **sanguinary james** *n.* [play on *BLOODY JEMMY under* BLOODY *adj.*] [mid-19C] an uncooked sheep's head.

sanitize *v.* [euph.] [1960s–70s] (*US*) to shoot dead, to kill.

San Juan Hill *n.* [the Battle of San Juan Hill (1898) in which many black troops were involved] [1900s–10s] (*US*) an area of New York City with a predominantly black population, covering those blocks between Tenth and Eleventh Avenues, between 59th Street and the low 60s.

sank *n.* [SANK WORK *n.*] [late 18C–19C] a tailor employed to make soldiers' clothes.

sankey *n.* [Ira David *Sankey* (1840–1908), who, with his partner Dwight Lyman Moody (1837–99), was the best known evangelist of the mid-19C] [1920s–50s] (*W.I.*) a hymn; a hymn book.

sank work *n.* [? Fr. *sang* (thus Norman *sanc*), blood, referring either to the scarlet uniform or the blood-letting that comes with soldiering] [late 18C–19C] the making of soldiers' clothes.

san lo *n.* (*also* **son lo**) [Chinese or fake Chinese] [1930s–50s] (*US drugs*) cheap, refined opium residue.

sanno *n.* (*also* **sano**) [abbr. + -O *sfx* (3)] [1930s+] (*Aus.*) a *san*itary carter or inspector; a sewage disposal worker.

sanny *n.* [abbr.] **1** [late 19C+] (*Aus.*) a *san*itary man, who removes sewage. **2** [1940s+] a *san*itary towel. **3** [1990s+] (*Scot.*) a *san*dwich.

San Q *n.* [abbr.] [1930s–60s] (*US Und.*) *San Quentin* prison, California.

San Quentin *adj.*

IN COMPOUNDS

□ **San Quentin briefcase** *n.* [the suggestion that those who carry such pieces of equipment are, *de facto*, criminals; accentuated by the racist stereotyping of the original users, young black men] [1990s+] (*US*) a large, portable tape-recorder-cum-radio. □ **San Quentin cross** *n.* [CROSS *n.*[1] (2)] [1970s] (*US prison*) blackmail of one inmate by another, who desires homosexual favours. □ **San Quentin quail** *n.* (*also* **San Quentin**) [QUAIL *n.* (3); the illegality of sex with such a girl] [1930s+] (*US*) a girl still under the age of consent who sleeps with an older man. □ **San Quentin strawberries** *n.* [1910s] (*US prison*) beans.

sansy *adj.* see SONSY *adj.*

Santa Claus *n.* [the popular image of the Christmas figure as both generous and gaudy] **1** [20C+] (*US*) a generous benefactor. **2** [1960s+] an older man who is willing to provide the various material wants of a younger mistress or, if gay, a younger male lover. **3** [1980s] (*US black*) a vulgar, gaudy and tasteless dresser.

santar *n.* (*also* **senter**) [SE *sanctuary*/SE *sent*] [late 16C–early 17C] (*UK Und.*) that member of a team of parcel thieves who actually removes the stolen goods and takes them to a hideout.

san toys *n.* [rhy. sl. = BOYS, THE *n.* (2); ult. *San Toy*, brandname of a small cigar] [1900s–30s] villains, criminals.

sap *n.*[1] [Lat. *sapiens*, wise] **1** [late 18C+] (*UK school*) (*also* **sapper**) a hard worker. **2** [mid–late 19C] a derog. term for an intellectual.

sap *n.*[2] (*also* **john sap, sapadillo, sapolio, sapolo, sapper, sappo**) [SE *sap*, the vital juice of a plant; the image is of one who is thus 'green'] [19C+] a fool, a dupe.

IN COMPOUNDS

□ **sap-happy** *adj.* [in main sense above or meaning JUICE *n.*[1] (3a) + sfx *-happy* + pun on SLAP-HAPPY *adj.*] [20C+] (*US*) drunk. □ **sap-head/-headed** see separate entries. □ **sap-pate** *n.* [late 17C–early 18C] a fool. □ **sapscull** *n.* [mid-18C–1910s] a fool. □ **sapsucker** *n.* see SAP-HEAD *n.*

sap *n.*[3] [SE *sapling*, from which the weapons were orig. made] **1** [late 19C–1930s] (*US tramp*) an act of clubbing. **2** [late 19C+] (*US*) a small club, orig. of wood, latterly a small leather 'bag' filled with sand, lead shot or similar material. **3** [1900s] (*US*) a beggar on crutches.

sap *v.*[1] [SAP *n.*[1] (1)] [late 18C–19C] (*UK school*) to work overly hard.

sap *v.*[2] (*also* **sap down, sap up**) [SAP *n.*[3] (2)] **1** [late 19C+] to attack using a blunt instrument. **2** [1920s] (*US Und.*) to hit with any implement, e.g. a whip.

IN COMPOUNDS

□ **sapping-down** *n.* (*also* **sapping-up**) [1950s] (*US*) a beating.

sapadillo *n.* see SAP *n.*[2].

s.a.p.f.u. *phr.* [abbr.] [1940s+] (*US milit.*) surpassing all previous fuck-ups.

sap-head *n.* (*also* **sapsucker**) [SAP *n.*[2] (1)+ -HEAD *sfx* (1)/directly f. the earlier SAP-HEADED *adj.*] [late 18C+] a fool.

sap-headed *adj.* (*also* **sap-head**) [fig. use of SE *sap*, liquid, juice] [mid–late 17C; mid-19C–1920s] foolish.

DERIVATIVES

□ **sapheadism** *n.* [1900s] foolishness.

sapient *n.* [SE *sapient*; ult. Lat. *sapiens*, wise man] [mid-16C] (*UK Und.*) a travelling quack.

sapolio/sapolo *n.* see SAP *n.*[2].

sapper *n.*[1] [a line sung by the Parisian music-hall star Theresa, who visited London c.1866, 'Rien est sacré pour un s–s–sapeur!', although note Fr. cant *sapeur*, a judge] [mid–late 19C] a man-about-town, a 'gay dog'.

sapper *n.*[2] see SAP *n.*[2].

sapphire *n.* [? she makes one BLUE *adj.*[1] (1) (like the jewel); or f. the character Sapphire in the radio (later TV) show *Amos 'n' Andy* (late 1920s–50s), a portrait, as stereotyped as the rest of the cast, of a complaining, emasculating, unpleasant black woman. Note the use of the name as the pseudonymous author of the 1996 novel *Push*, a story of poverty and abuse in the ghetto] [1940s–70s] (*US black*) an unpopular woman.

sappho *n.* [proper name *Sappho* (c.600 BC), the poetess of the island of Lesbos] [mid-18C; late 19C+] a lesbian.

DERIVATIVES

□ **sapphic** *adj.* [late 19C+] a code-word to describe female homosexuality.

IN COMPOUNDS

□ **sappho-daddy-o** *n.* [DADDY-O *n.* (2)] [1990s+] (*US gay*) a heterosexual man who socializes extensively with lesbians.

sapping-down/sapping-up *n.* see under SAP *v.*[2].

sappo *n.* see SAP *n.*[2].

sappy *adj.* [SAP *n.*[2] (1)/SE *sap*, which is SOFT *adj.* (3)] **1** [mid-17C+] foolish, stupid. **2** [late 19C+] (*US*) sentimental and mawkish.

DERIVATIVES

□ **sappiness** *n.* [mid-19C+] (*US*) stupidity.

IN COMPOUNDS

□ **sappyhead** *n.* [-HEAD *sfx* (1)] [mid-19C–1920s] a fool. □ **sappyheaded** *adj.* [mid-19C] foolish.

sarah soo *n.* [rhy. sl.] [1920s+] a Jew.

sarajevo *phr.* ['see you later'] [1980s+] (*US campus*) goodbye.

sarc *n.* (*also* **sark**) [abbr.] [1900s–10s] *sarc*asm.

sard *v.* [10C when the *Lindisfarne Gospel* used it in its translation of Matt. 5:27, 'Ye have heard that it was said by them of old time, Thou shalt not commit adultery'. By the 17C it was the basis of a Nottingham proverb, 'Go teach your Grandma to sard', but vanished soon afterwards. It is one of Florio's synons. for Ital. *fottere*] [16C–17C] to copulate.

sardine *n.* **1** [mid-19C–1910s] (*US*) a general term of abuse, a fool. **2** [mid-19C–1930s] (*US*) a person. **3** [1910s–20s] (*US campus*) a young woman. **4** [1940s] a run-down prostitute.

sardine box *n.* [the close-packing of the prisoners] **1** [late 19C–1940s] (*also* **sardine can**) a prison or police van. **2** [late 19C+] (*Aus.*) (*also* **sardine tin**) any extremely small dwelling. **3** [1910s] a small railway compartment.

sarge *n.* (*also* **sarg, sargie, sargy, sarj, serg**) [abbr.] [mid-19C+] *serg*eant; esp. as a familiar term of address.

sark *n.*[1] [? Scot. *sark*, a woman's undergarment] [1980s+] (*N.Z.*) a sanitary towel.

sark *n.*[2] see SARC *n.*

sarmie *n.* (*also* **sarmy**) [abbr.] [1960s+] (*S.Afr.*) a sandwich.

sarnie *n.* (*also* **sarney, sarny**) [abbr.] [1960s+] a *san*dwich.

sarse *n.* (*also* **sarpidilly**) [abbr.] [1920s+] (*Aus.*) *sars*parilla, the dried root of *Smilax officinalis*, at one time used as a tonic.

sarve out *v.* see *SERVE OUT under* SERVE *v.*

sarvo *n.* [abbr. SE *this* + ARVO *n.*] [1940s+] (*Aus./N.Z.*) this afternoon.

sasfras *n.* see SASSAFRAS *n.*

sashay *n.* [SASHAY *v.*] [1900s–30s] a walk that is casual and yet confident.

sashay *v.* (*also* **sasshay**) [Fr. *chassé*, a gliding step in dancing] **1** [mid-19C+] (*US*) to walk or travel in a casual manner; to saunter. **2** [20C+] (*US*) to hurry; to move briskly. **3** [1900s] to strut, to parade, to walk in an ostentatious or provocative manner.

sass *n.* [SE *sauce*, cheek, impudence] [mid-19C+] (*orig. US*) cheek, impertinence, rudeness.

DERIVATIVES

□ **sassiness** *n.* [1940s+] cheek.

IN COMPOUNDS

□ **sass-box** *n. see* SASSY BOX *under* SASSY *adj.* □ **sass-talking** *n.* [2000s] (*US*) talking in a cheeky manner.

sassafras *n.* (*also* **sasfras, sassfras**) [SE *sassafras* tree] **1** [1930s] (*US*) a beard [facial hair supposedly resembles the leaves of the tree; cognate with SPINACH *n.*[2] (1)]. **2** [1960s+] (*drugs*) marijuana [*sassafras* leaves are used for tea, thus link to TEA *n.* (4a)].

sasshay *v. see* SASHAY *v.*

sassiger *n.* (*also* **sassenger, sassinger, saussenger, saussinger, sossinger**) [mispron.] [19C] a sausage.

sass (out) *v.* [SASS *n.*] [mid-19C+] (*US*) to answer back, to cheek; to tease.

sassy *adj.* [SE *saucy*/SASS *n.* (1)] **1** [mid-19C+] (*orig. US*) cheeky, spirited, back-talking. **2** [late 19C+] smart, fashionable.

IN COMPOUNDS

□ **sassy-ass** *adj.* [-ASS *sfx*] [1960s] (*US black*) used as derog. intensifier. □ **sassy box** *n.* **1** [late 19C+] (*US*) (*also* **sass-box**) a saucy young woman. **2** [1980s] the vagina [BOX *n.*[1] (1)].

IN PHRASES

□ **sling sassy** *v.* [mid-19C+] (*US black*) to show sudden contempt or cheekiness.

sassy *adv.* [SASSY *adj.* (1)] [1900s] (*US*) cheekily, with impudence.

sata *v.* (*also* **satta**) [ety. unknown] [1950s+] (*W.I. Rasta*) to rejoice, to meditate, to give thanks and praise.

IN PHRASES

□ **go sata** *v.* [1950s+] (*W.I. Rasta*) to claim how spiritual one is.

Satan *n.* [late 19C] a euph. for HELL, THE *phr.* (3) or *the devil.*

Satan's bones *n.* [early 18C] dice.

Satan's scent *n.* (*also* **Satan's secret**) [1980s] (*drugs*) any inhalant.

satch *n.*[1] [abbr. SE *satchel*] [1900s–60s] **1** (*US black*) a notably large mouth; thus a person with a large mouth. **2** (*US*) a talkative person.

satch *n.*[2] (*also* **sach, sacht**) [SE *saturate*] [1930s–60s] (*drugs*) paper or clothing that is saturated with a drug solution (usu. used to smuggle drugs into prisons or hospitals).

IN COMPOUNDS

□ **satch cotton** *n.* [COTTON *n.* (1)] [1960s] (*drugs*) fabric used to filter a solution of narcotics before injection; the cotton may be boiled later and the drug residue used.

satch *n.*[3] [? SACK *n.* (6)] [1940s–50s] (*US black*) a jacket.

satchel *n.* [note WW2 US milit. *satchel*, a fat person] **1** [1930s] (*US Und.*) a prison. **2** [1930s–50s] (*US*) the vagina. **3** [1940s+] (*US*) the anus or buttocks. **4** [2000s] (*US*) the scrotum. **5** [2000s] (*US*) thus used as a term of abuse. **6** *see* SATCHEL-MOUTH *n.*

satchel *v.* [it is thus *IN THE BAG under* BAG *n.*[1]] [20C+] (*US*) to pre-arrange the outcome of a contest, race or fight.

satchel-arsed *adj.* (*also* **satchel-arse, satchel-ass**) [SE *satchel* + -ARSED *sfx* (1)/ASS *n.* (2)] [18C+] a general term of abuse, often ext. to e.g. *satchel-arsed fellow, …son of a whore.*

satchel-mouth *n.* (*also* **satchel**) [note the jazz musician Louis 'Satchmo' (*Satchel-Mouth*) Armstrong (1900–72)] [1930s–40s] (*US black*) anyone with a large mouth.

satchel-mouthed *adj.* [SATCHEL-MOUTH *n.*] [1930s–60s] (*orig. US black*) **1** used of someone who has a large mouth. **2** in fig. use, used of someone who talks a great deal, eg. an informer.

satin *n.* **1** in the context of alcohol [its supposed smoothness]. (**a**) [mid-19C–1930s] gin. (**b**) [1970s+] (*US black*) Italian Swiss Colony Silver *Satin* wine mixed with lemon juice. **2** [2000s] (*US black*) death [the SE *satin* that lines a coffin].

satin and lace *n.* [rhy. sl.] **1** [late 19C–mid-20C] His Grace, i.e. a Duke. **2** [1990s+] the human face.

satin and silk *n.* [rhy. sl.] [20C+] milk.

sativa *n.* [abbr. botanical name *Cannabis sativa*] [1970s+] (*drugs*) cannabis.

satta *v. see* SATA *v.*

saturated *adj.* [metaphorical, but also a lit. description of the bloodstream; its 1980s resurgence emerged in US campuses] [late 19C–1940s; 1980s+] very drunk.

Saturday *n.*

SE in slang uses

IN COMPOUNDS

□ **Saturday gangster** *n.* [1990s+] (*Aus. Und.*) an aspirant gangster. □ **Saturday-night** *n.* [late 19C] wages.

IN PHRASES

□ **Saturday morning quarterback** *n. see* MONDAY MORNING QUARTERBACK *n.* □ **Saturday-to-Monday** *n.* [1900s–10s] a mistress whom one sees only at weekends. □ **shitten Saturday** *n.* [mispron. of SE *shut-in Saturday*, referring to the day on which Christ's body was enclosed in his tomb] [mid-19C] (*mainly school/provincial*) Easter Saturday.

Saturday-night *adj.*

IN COMPOUNDS

□ **Saturday night butch** *n.* [BUTCH *n.*[1] (5)] [1950s–60s] (*US gay*) a lesbian who dresses butch only at weekends. □ **Saturday night habit** *n.* [HABIT *n.* (1)] [1930s–50s] (*US drugs*) an occasional (perhaps literally weekly) use of narcotics. □ **Saturday night palsy** *n.* (*also* **Saturday night-itis, …paralysis**) [? one has passed out drunk on Saturday night] [1920s+] (*US*) the temporary paralysis of the arm, esp. a weakness in the wrist, after it has rested on a hard edge for a long time, as during sleep following a bout of drinking. □ **Saturday night pistol** *n.* [1920s–30s] (*US*) a small handgun. □ **Saturday night smile** *n.* [1940s] (*US*) an enthusiastic smile. □ **Saturday night special** *n.* [1960s+] (*US*) a small handgun, often used in the many fracas that occur over Saturday night in big US cities.

satyr *n.* [SE *satyr*, a mythological Greek woodland demon, usu. pictured with the ears and tail of a horse. 'Men living wild in the Fields, that keep their Holds and Dwellings in the Country and forsaken Places, stealing Horses, Kine, Sheep, and all other sort of Cattle' (A. Smith, *Lives of the Highwaymen*, 1714)] [mid-18C] (*UK Und.*) a professional horse thief.

sauce *n.*[1] **1** [late 17C–early 19C] a venereal disease. **2** [late 17C; 1930s] vaginal fluids. **3** [mid-18C] money. **4** [1910s] (*US*) petrol, gasoline. **5** [1930s+] (*orig. US*) alcohol, (rarely) drugs. **6** [1970s] (*US campus*) beer. **7** [1970s+] (*US gay*) semen.

IN COMPOUNDS

□ **saucehound** *n.* [-HOUND *sfx* (1)] [1940s+] (*US*) a drunkard, an alcoholic.

IN PHRASES

□ **hit the sauce** *v.* [1920s+] (*orig. US*) to drink to excess. □ **on the sauce** [1970s+] (*orig. US*) drinking heavily and consistently. □ **sauced (up)** *adj.* [1960s+] drunk, tipsy.

sauce *n.*[2] [fig. use of SE, but why?] [1990s+] (*US campus*) something bad or inferior.

DERIVATIVES

□ **saucy** *adj.* [1990s+] bad or inferior.

IN PHRASES

□ **drink of sauce's cup** *v. see under* DRINK *v.*

sauce *v.*[1] [SE *sauce*, cheek, impudence] [mid-19C+] to cheek, to tease.

sauce *v.*[2] [SAUCE *n.*[2]] [1990s+] (*US campus*) to ruin.

saucebox *n.* [SE *sauce*, cheek] [mid–late 19C] the mouth.

saucepan *n.* [early 19C] a male servant.

saucepan handle *n.* [2000s] the penis.

saucepan lid *n.* [rhy. sl.] **1** [late 19C] money, esp. in pl. [= DIBBS *n.* (1)]. **2** [late 19C+] a tease, a 'leg-pull' [= KID *n.*[2] (2)]. **3** [1950s+] a Jew [= YID *n.*[1]]. **4** [1950s+] a child [= KID *n.*[1]]. **5** [1950s+] one pound [= QUID *n.* (3)].

saucer *n.* [SE phr. *eyes like/as big as saucers*, coined 14C] [mid-19C–1910s] an eye.

SE in slang uses

IN PHRASES

❑ **off one's saucer** *adj.* **1** [mid-19C–1900s] (*Aus.*) disinclined, dispirited, 'out of sorts' [the image is of a pet refusing its food]. **2** [20C+] (*Aus.*) mad, eccentric [the image is of a spinning 'flying saucer'].

saucy *adj. see under* SAUCE *n.*[2].

sauerkraut *n.* (*also* **sauerkraut eater, sauerkrauter, sourcrout, sourkrout**) [the popular German dish] (*mainly Aus./US*) **1** [mid-18C+] a derog. term for a German. **2** [mid-19C] a cantankerous person; a term of abuse.

saunsy *adj. see* SONSY *adj.*

sausage *n.* **1** [mid-19C] in pl., fetters [resemblance]. **2** [mid–late 19C] in pl., side-whiskers. **3** [mid-19C+] the penis. **4** [late 19C+] a German. **5** [late 19C+] in joc. uses. (**a**) an ineffectual, easily imposed-upon person, esp. in teasing phr. *silly sausage/old sausage.* (**b**) an affectionate term of address to an animal. **6** [1930s] (*US*) a prize-fighter, esp. one with a swollen, bruised face. **7** [1970s] (*UK prison*) a cannabis or cannabis/tobacco cigarette. **8** [1990s+] (*US campus*) a man, the male domain; only in combs. such as *SAUSAGE PARTY* below.

IN COMPOUNDS

❑ **sausage cockpit** *n.* [*COCK PIT under* COCK *n.*[3]] [2000s] the vagina. ❑ **sausage-eater** *n.* (*also* **sausage mangler, -meat, -spoiler**) [1910s+] a German. ❑ **sausage-eating** *adj.* [1910s+] German. ❑ **sausage jockey** *n.* [JOCKEY *n.*[2] (1)] **1** [1980s+] (*US*) a male homosexual. **2** [2000s] (*N.Z.*) a woman who prefers the superior position in heterosexual intercourse. ❑ **sausage party** *n.* (*also* **sausage fest**) [1990s+] a social gathering where men outnumber women. ❑ **sausage sandwich** *n.* [1990s+] **1** intercourse between the breasts. **2** sex between two men and one woman. ❑ **sausage smuggler** *n.* [1990s+] a male homosexual. ❑ **sausage walloper** *n.* [1910s] a German.

IN PHRASES

❑ **eat sausage** *v.* [1980s+] (*N.Z.*) of a woman, to fellate. ❑ **have a live sausage for supper** *v.* (*also* **have a live sausage for breakfast**) [19C] of a woman, to have sexual intercourse. ❑ **hide the sausage** *v.* [1940s+] (*Aus.*) to have sexual intercourse. ❑ **live sausage** *n.* [mid-17C+] the penis. ❑ **sink the sausage** *v. see under* SINK *v.* ❑ **slap the sausage** *v.* [2000s] to masturbate. ❑ **string of sausages** *n.* [mid-19C] a chain.

SE in slang uses

IN COMPOUNDS

❑ **sausage dog** *n.* [its German origins and its roughly tubular shape] [1910s+] a dachshund. ❑ **sausage wrapper** *n.* [late 19C+] (*Aus.*) a newspaper.

IN PHRASES

❑ **not a sausage** (*also* **without a sausage**) [1930s+] absolutely nothing; a derisory amount. ❑ **not have a sausage** *v.* [1930s] to be penniless.

sausage *v.* [rhy. sl. SAUSAGE AND MASH *n.* (1)] [1920s+] to cash (a cheque).

IN PHRASES

❑ **sausage a goose's** *v.* [GOOSE'S NECK *n.*[2]] [1920s–60s] to cash a cheque.

sausage and mash *n.* [rhy. sl.] **1** [late 19C+] cash. **2** [1950s+] a smash, a car crash.

sausage roll *n.* [rhy. sl.] **1** [1920s+] the dole. **2** [1940s+] a Pole. **3** [1960s+] (*Aus.*) a goal.

sausie *n.* (*also* **sossie**) **1** [1910s+] (*N.Z.*) a *sausage* [abbr.]. **2** [2000s] (*N.Z.*) the penis.

sauskee *n.* [pron. of *sawski* at SAWBUCK *n.*; ? misunderstanding] [1940s] (*US carnival*) $15.

saussenger/saussinger *n. see* SASSIGER *n.*

sav *n.*[1] [abbr.] [late 19C+] a saveloy.

IN PHRASES

❑ **battered sav** *n.* [1960s+] (*Aus.*) a saveloy covered in a flour and water paste, impaled on a lollipop stick and then deep fried.

sav *n.*[2] *see* SAVVY *n.*

savage *n.* [1930s–40s] (*US*) a keen young police officer eager to make arrests.

savage *adj.* [weak use of SE] **1** [late 18C+] extremely annoyed, furious. **2** [1940s+] strong, intense.

savage as a meat axe *adj. see MAD AS A MEAT AXE under* MEAT AXE *n.*

save-alls *n.* [SE *save-all*, 'a kind of candlestick used by our frugal forefathers to burn snuffs and ends of candles' (Grose, 1785)] [late 18C–early 19C] (*Anglo-Irish*) 'boys running about gentlemen's houses in Ireland, who are fed on broken meats that would otherwise be wasted' (Grose, 1785).

save it! *excl.* [1930s+] (*US*) be quiet! shut up!

save it for Sweeney! *excl. see TELL IT TO SWEENEY! under* SWEENEY *n.*

saveloy *n.* [rhy. sl.] [20C+] a boy.

Saveloy Square *n.* [as a centre of London's East End Jewish community, no pork sausages, only beef *saveloys* were to be found there] [late 19C] Duke Place, Aldgate.

save one's ass *v. see under* ASS *n.*

save one's groats *v.* [university custom, those taking their finals deposit nine groats (= 36 old pennies) with an academic officer; if they pass with honours the groats are returned] [late 18C–19C] to succeed, to do well.

save-reverence *n. see* SIR-REVERENCE *n.*

savey *see under* SAVVY.

savez *n. see* SAVVY *n.*

saving chin *n.* [it supposedly catches the food that drops from the mouth when its owner is eating badly] [late 18C] a protruding chin.

savoury rissole *n.* [rhy. sl. = PISSHOLE *n.*] [1990s+] **1** a lavatory. **2** anywhere dirty or unpleasant.

savvy *n.* (*also* **sabbe, sabby, sabe, sav, savey, savv, savve, savvey, scavey**) [SAVVY *v.*] [late 18C+] understanding, intelligence, awareness.

savvy *adj.* [SAVVY *n.*] [late 19C+] bright, knowledgeable, aware.

savvy *v.* (*also* **sabe, savey, savez, savvey, scavey**) [Fr. *savoir*, to know, to understand] **1** [late 18C+] to understand, to be aware of. **2** [20C+] as interrog.; often as *do you savvy?*

saw *n.*[1] [abbr. SAWBUCK *n.* (1)] [mid-19C+] (*US*) $10.

IN PHRASES

❑ **half-saw** *n.* [mid-19C+] (*US Und.*) five (dollars).

saw *n.*[2] [? their 'rough/sharp edges'] [1940s] (*US black*) **1** a woman, esp. when a nag. **2** the landlady of a cheap rooming house.

SE in slang uses

IN COMPOUNDS

❑ **sawbones** *n.* [mid-19C+] a doctor, a surgeon. ❑ **sawbox** *n.* [1930s–60s] (*orig. US black*) a cello.

IN PHRASES

❑ **hand-saw** *n.* [Partridge suggests that -FENCER *sfx*, i.e. seller, should be assumed] [mid-19C] a street seller of cutlery, razors and knives. ❑ **old saw** *n.* [? her nagging *saws* away at a man] [late 19C–1940s] (*US black*) one's wife.

saw *v.*

SE in slang uses

IN PHRASES

❑ **saw away** *v.* [early 19C] to talk incessantly, to chatter on. ❑ **saw gourds** *v.* [mid-19C+] (*orig. US*) to snore loudly. ❑ **saw off** *v.* **1** [1900s–40s] (*US*) to stop talking, usu. as imper. **2** [1940s–60s] to berate; to reprimand. ❑ **saw them off** *v.* [1930s–40s] to snore. ❑ **saw wood** *v.* **1** [late 19C–1930s] (*US*) to carry on as normal, to get on with one's work, to keep to oneself [the mundane act of sawing wood]. **2** [20C+] (*US*) (*also* **saw logs**) to snore.

sawbuck *n.* (*also* **sawski, sawsky, sawzie**) [SE *sawbuck*, an X-shaped sawhorse; the X of the sawhorse is equated with the

Roman numeral *X*, 10 + BUCK *n.*[3] (1)/joc. use of 'Slavic' sfx *-ski*] (*US*) **1** [mid-19C+] $10. **2** [1920s+] a ten-year prison sentence.

IN PHRASES

▫ **double sawbuck** *n.* (*also* **double saw, double sawski**) **1** [mid-19C+] (*US*) $20. **2** [1930s+] (*US/Can. prison*) a 20-year prison sentence. **3** [1970s] (*US prison*) a 25-year prison sentence.

sawder *see under* SOFT SAWDER.

sawdust *n.*[1] (*also* **the sawdusty**) [? SOFT SAWDER *n.*] [late 19C] flattery, insincerity.

sawdust *n.*[2] **1** [20C+] (*US Und.*) dynamite. **2** [1900s] (*US campus*) sugar. **3** [1940s] (*US*) cheap tobacco, used for rolling cigarettes.

IN COMPOUNDS

▫ **sawdust game** *n.* [late 19C–1930s] (*US*) a confidence trick based on the passing of bad banknotes; thus *sawdust man/swindler*.

SE in slang uses

IN COMPOUNDS

▫ **sawdust joint** *n.* (*also* **sawdust parlor, ...place, ...saloon**) [JOINT *n.* (3)/SE *parlour/saloon*; such places lacked smart interiors and their plank floorboards were covered only by sawdust] [20C+] (*US*) a down-market restaurant or bar, or gambling saloon.

IN PHRASES

▫ **lose one's sawdust** *v.* [1950s] (*US*) to become drunk.

sawed *adj.* [mid-19C] (*US*) drunk.

sawed-off *n.* (*also* **sawn-off**) **1** [late 19C–1910s] a short person. **2** [1920s+] (*US*) a sawn-off shotgun.

sawed-off *adj.* (*also* **sawn-off**) [mid-19C+] of a person or occas. object, short; or legless.

saweer *v.* [SE *see-er*, one who sees] [mid-18C] (*UK Und.*) of a gang member, to keep watch.

sawn *n.* [abbr. SAWNEY *n.*[1] (1)] [1950s+] (*Aus.*) a simpleton.

Sawney *n.* [proper name *Sawney*, an abbr. of the common Scot. name Alexander] [late 17C–19C] a generic term for a Scotsman.

sawney *n.*[1] (*also* **sawny**) [SE *zany*, a fool, a laughing stock] [late 17C+] **1** a fool. **2** a clumsy person, a thug.

sawney *n.*[2] [? SE *sawn*, i.e. the 'sawing off' of bacon into rashers, or the cannibalistic *Sawney* Beane (*fl.*15C), who killed people, smoked their corpses and ate them] [early 19C–1900s] bacon.

IN COMPOUNDS

▫ **sawney-hunter** *n.* [mid-19C] one who steals bacon or cheese from grocers' shops. ▫ **sawney-hunting** *n.* [mid-19C] stealing bacon from where it hung on shop doors.

sawney *n.*[3] [? mis-reading/generic use of SAWNEY *n.* (1)] [mid-19C] (*US Und.*) a soldier.

sawney *adj.* [SAWNEY *n.*[1]] [late 17C–19C; 1940s] foolish.

sawn-off *see under* SAW-OFF.

sawpit *n. see* PIT *n.* (1).

sawski/sawsky *n. see* SAWBUCK *n.*

sawyer *n.* [1940s] (*US Und.*) a sawn-off shotgun.

sawzie *n. see* SAWBUCK *n.*

sax *n.* [abbr.] **1** [1920s–70s] (*Aus./N.Z.*) *six*pence [mispron.]. **2** [1920s+] a saxophone. **3** [1960s] a saxophone player.

saxa *n.* [abbr.] [1930s] (*Aus.*) a saxophone.

saxophone *n.* (*also* **Chinese saxophone**) [1930s–50s] (*US drugs*) an opium pipe.

IN COMPOUNDS

▫ **saxophone player** *n.* [1930s] a smoker of opium.

say *n.* (*also* **sei, sey**) [Ital. *sei*, six] [mid-19C+] (*Ling. Fr./Polari*) the number six.

IN COMPOUNDS

▫ **say-dooe** *n.* (*also* **sey-dooe**) [DOOE(E) *n.*] [1990s+] the number eight. ▫ **say-oney** *n.* (*also* **sey-oney**) [SE *one* + sfx *-y*] [1990s+] the number seven. ▫ **say-tray** *n.* (*also* **sey-tray**) [TRAY *n.*[1] (1)] [1990s+] the number nine.

say *v.* [1900s] (*US Und.*) to rob; to break into.

SE in slang uses

IN PHRASES

▫ **ain't saying nothing** [1970s] (*US black*) a dismissive phr. suggesting that nothing you say is of the slightest importance. ▫ **he-say-she-say** *n.* (*also* **he-said-she-said**) [1960s–80s] (*US black*) gossip, chatter, loose talk. ▫ **I bet you say that to all the boys/girls** [1930s+] a teasing phr. orig. used by women to men but latterly by either sex; it follows a compliment or 'line'; thus fig. ext. to any person. ▫ **I'll say (so)** [1910s+] (*orig. US*) absolutely, definitely, I couldn't agree more. ▫ **I'm saying doe** [2000s] (*US black*) a phr. of agreement, affirmation. ▫ **say a mouthful** *v.* (*also* **say an armful, ...speak an armful, ...a mouthful**) (*orig. US*) **1** [1910s+] to say something important and true. **2** [1920s+] to talk at length, esp. critically. **3** [1940s–70s] (*gay*) to reprove a fellow homosexual in detail and at great length. ▫ **say calf-rope** *v. see* HOLLER CALF-ROPE *under* HOLLER *v.* ▫ **say it like it is** *v. see* TELL IT LIKE IT IS *under* TELL *v.* ▫ **say nothing** *v.* [1950s–60s] (*US black*) to talk trivially. ▫ **say something** *v.* [1910s+] (*US*) to make an important statement, to say something profound; lit. or fig. ▫ **say uncle** *v. see* CRY UNCLE *under* UNCLE *n.* ▫ **say what?** (*also* **say which? says which?**) [20C+] (*US*) an expression of mock disbelief, e.g. what did you say? are you telling the truth? ▫ **say when** [late 19C+] a formula used when pouring someone else a drink, i.e. say when you want me to stop pouring. ▫ **what do you say?** [1920s+] (*US*) how are you? ▫ **what-I-might-say** *n.* [20C+] (*US black*) a euph. for an obscenity. ▫ **what say?** [early 19C+] (*orig. US*) what did you say? what was that? what do you think? ▫ **you can say that again** [1940s+] (*orig. US*) a phr. underlining the speaker's agreement with the previous statement. ▫ **you don't say** (*also* **you don't say so, you don't say that, you don't tell**) [early 19C+] a heavily sarcastic response to a statement of the obvious.

IN EXCLAMATIONS

▫ **say my name!** [1990s+] (*US teen*) an excl. used to intimidate or used for celebration. ▫ **says you!** (*also* **sez you!**) [mid-19C+] a general excl. of contempt and disbelief, dismissing as beneath argument the previous speaker's words. ▫ **say word!** *see* WORD UP! *excl.*

say *adv.* [backsl.] [mid-19C] yes.

sazeech *n.* [SAUSAGE *n.* (2)] [1960s] (*US*) the penis.

s.b. *n.* [abbr. *s*our *b*osom/*b*elly] **1** [mid-19C–1910s] (*US*) bacon. **2** [late 19C+] (*US*) a euph. for son of a *b*itch.

s.b.d. *n.* [abbr. *s*ilent *b*ut *d*eadly] [1960s+] the breaking of wind silently and with a foul smell.

'sblood! *excl.* (*also* **'sbleed! 'sblud! 'sbud! 'slud! 'zbud!**) [late 16C–mid-19C] a euph. oath, lit. 'God's blood'.

'sbody! *excl.* (*also* **'sbobs!**) [mid-17C–mid-19C] a euph. oath, lit. 'God's body'.

S.C. *n.* [abbr.] [1990s+] (*US black teen*) South-Central Los Angeles.

scab *n.*[1] (*also* **scab neck**) **1** [late 16C] a sheriff's officer, a constable. **2** [late 16C+] an unpleasant person. **3** [17C] a prostitute. **4** [late 18C+] (*also* **scalie**) a strike-breaker or anyone who stands out against a mass action. **5** [1950s] an amateur [ext. of sense 4]. **6** [1960s+] (*US black/campus*) an unattractive man or woman. **7** [1970s–80s] (*N.Z. prison*) an inmate who curries favour with the authorities. **8** [1990s+] (*UK juv.*) one who attempts to beg money or food.

scab *n.*[2] [mid-19C] (*UK Und.*) a sixpence.

scab *adj.* [SCAB *n.*[1] (4)] **1** [late 19C+] pertaining to strike-breakers or strike-breaking. **2** [1960s] thus in fig. use, illegal, e.g. of an after-hours drinking club.

scab *v.* (*also* **scab it**) [SCAB *n.*[1] (4)] **1** [early 19C–1920s] to brand a company or fellow worker as a strike-breaker. **2** [early 19C+] to break a strike, refuse to join a union or any form of mass action; ext. to 'letting down the side' in non-work contexts. **3** [1920s+] to take a job without belonging to the relevant union. **4** [1970s–80s] (*N.Z. prison*) of an inmate, to curry favour with the authorities. **5** [1980s] (*Aus.*) to cadge.

scabbado *n.* [a 'Spanished' version of SE *scab*, syphilis] [mid-17C–early 18C] syphilis.

scabbard *n.* [a trans. of Lat. and euph. for SE *vagina*] [17C–19C] the vagina.

scabbed *adj.* [weak use of SCAB v.] [1960s–70s] (*drugs*) cheated in a deal.

scabbery *n.* [SCAB v. (2)] [20C+] (*Aus./US*) the betrayal of one's fellow workers, the breaking of a strike.

scabby *n.* [SCAB *n.*[1] (4)] [1910s+] (*Aus.*) a non-union worker.

scabby *adj.*[1] [SE *scab*, a variety of skin diseases, incl. syphilis, which is the most likely ref. in a sl. context] **1** [mid-17C+] of a person or thing, unpleasant, contemptible, generally distasteful. **2** [2000s] mean, grasping.

IN COMPOUNDS

❑ **scabby-neck** *n.* [orig. naut. use] [mid-19C] a native of Denmark. ❑ **scabby sheep** *n.* [SE *scabby sheep*, a sheep that has a diseased mouth; thus a moral leper, a corrupt person; *sheep* also puns on the popular religious use of the word] [mid-19C] a person tainted by their association with dubious society or undue influences.

scabby *adj.*[2] [SCAB *n.*[1] (4)] [late 19C+] (*Aus.*) non-union.

scad *n.*[1] [? Cornwall/Devon dial. *scad*, a brief shower of rain] [early 17C] semen.

scad *n.*[2] [ety. unknown] **1** [19C–1940s] (*US*) $1. **2** [mid-19C+] (*also* **scadoodles, skadoodles, skads**) in pl., large quantities, usu. of money.

scadger *n.* [SE *cadger* + ? Cornish *scadgan*, a tramp] [mid–late 19C] a general term of abuse, a mean, contemptible person, one who always wants a loan.

scadoodle *v.* [SKEDADDLE v. + SCOOT v. (2)] [mid-19C] to run off, to leave in a hurry.

scady *adj. see* SCODY *adj.*

scaffe *n.* [ety. unknown] [1970s] (*Aus. drugs*) a smoke of marijuana.

scag *n.*[1] (*also* **skag**) [? elision of SE *cigar*(*ette*)] [1900s–40s] (*US*) a cigarette, a cigar, a cigarette butt.

scag *n.*[2] (*also* **skag**) [ety. unknown; note Smitherman, *Black Talk* (1994): 'low-grade heroin that has been diluted'] **1** [1940s] bad liquor. **2** [1960s+] (*drugs*) heroin.

IN COMPOUNDS

❑ **scag hag** *n.* (*also* **skag hag**) [1990s+] **1** one who enjoys associating with heroin addicts. **2** a female heroin addict. ❑ **scaghead** *n.* [-HEAD *sfx* (4)] [1990s+] a heroin addict. ❑ **scag jones** *n.* (*also* **skag jones**) [JONES *n.*[1] (1)] [1960s+] (*US drugs*) a heroin addiction. ❑ **scag town** *n.* (*also* **skag town**) [1960s+] (*drugs*) an area of a city or town where addicts live and heroin is easily available.

IN PHRASES

❑ **scagged (out)** *adj.* (*also* **skagged**) [1970s+] (*drugs*) addicted to heroin. ❑ **skaggy-bawed** *adj.* [Scot. *baw*, to sleep] (*Scot.*) [1990s+] comatose or impotent as a result of taking heroin.

scag *n.*[3] [var. on SKAG *n.* (1)] [1960s+] (*US campus/black*) an unattractive female.

DERIVATIVES

❑ **scaggy** *adj.* [1960s+] unattractive.

scag-nasty *n.* (*also* **skag-nasty**) [? var. on *shag-nasty* at SHAG v.[1]] [1990s+] (*UK juv.*) an unpleasant person.

scal *n. see* SCALLY *n.*

scalawag *n. see* SCALLYWAG *n.*[1].

scald *n.* (*also* **scaldings**) [Irish *scal*, hot tea] [20C+] (*Irish*) tea or coffee.

scald *adj.* [obs. 16C dial. *scald*, scabbed, afflicted with the 'scall' (any scaly or scabby disease of the skin, esp. of the scalp; *dry scall* was psoriasis, *humid* or *moist scall* was eczema)] [mid-16C–mid-17C] suffering from venereal disease.

scald *v.*[1] [SCALD *adj.*] [late 16C–17C] to infect with venereal disease.

IN COMPOUNDS

❑ **scalding-house** *n.* [late 16C–17C] a brothel.

scald *v.*[2] [Irish *scall*, to scald; thus fig. to grieve bitterly] [late 19C+] (*Irish*) **1** to be mortified. **2** to reprimand, to scold.

scald *v.*[3] [SCALD *n.*] [20C+] (*Irish*) to make tea.

scalded *adj.*[1] [ext. of SCALD *adj.* (1)] [17C] suffering from venereal disease.

scalded *adj.*[2] [fig. use of SE *scald*] [1980s] (*US campus*) rejected.

scalder *n.*[1] **1** [early 19C] venereal disease [SCALD *adj.*]. **2** [late 19C] tea.

scalder *n.*[2] [SCALD *n.*] [late 19C] tea.

scalding *n.* [mid-19C] (*US*) a beating.

scaldings *n. see* SCALD *n.*

scaldrum dodge *n.* [SE *scald*, burn + DODGE *n.* (1)] [mid-19C–1900s] (*UK Und.*) the practice of deliberately burning the body with a mixture of acids and gunpowder in order to simulate scars and wounds that should soften the hearts of those from whom one begs.

IN PHRASES

❑ **scaldrum scoldrum** *n.* [mid-19C–1900s] a beggar who adopts the above ploy.

scaldy *n.* [ON *scalle*, a bald head; Irish *scalltán*, a fledgling] [20C+] (*Irish*) **1** a bald-headed, or very short-haired, person, thus a baby. **2** a mean, cadging person.

scaldy *adj.* [SCALDY *n.*] [20C+] (*Irish*) stingy.

scale *n.*[1] (*also* **shadscale**) [SE *scale*, a thin piece of metal, used in scale-armour] [late 19C–1920s] (*US*) money.

scale *n.*[2] [SE *scale*, on a reptile/fish; or ? a form of skin disease] [1910s+] (*US prison*) a louse.

IN PHRASES

❑ **scale-backed 'un** *n.* [1910s–20s] a louse.

SE in slang uses

IN PHRASES

❑ **have scales (on one's belly)** *v.* [idea of being a snake or fish that crawls, i.e. CRAWL v.[1] (1)] [1910s] (*Aus.*) to be a sycophant.

scale *n.*[3] [13C–16C SE *scale*, drinking vessel and/or synon. Du. *schaal*; hence Sintu *sekale*, a large container for beer or other liquor, a measure of liquor] [1980s] (*S.Afr. township*) an alcoholic drink.

scale *v.*[1] **1** [early 16C; 1960s] of a man, to enter a woman and commence intercourse [SE *scale*, to climb; thus synon. with MOUNT v.[1]]. **2** [late 19C] to impress, to astonish [? SE phr. *scale the heights*].

scale *v.*[2] [SE *scale*, to strip the scales from] (*Aus./N.Z./S.Afr.*) **1** [1910s–20s] to leave surreptitiously or speedily; esp. as *scale off*. **2** [1910s+] to steal, to defraud; thus *scale a train/tram*, to board and ride without paying.

DERIVATIVES

❑ **scaler** *n.* [1910s+] (*Aus./N.Z.*) **1** a fraud, anyone who betrays a financial trust. **2** one who rides illegally for free on public transport. ❑ **scaling** *n.* [1910s+] (*Aus./N.Z.*) the act of riding for free on public transport.

scale *v.*[3] [1990s+] (*drugs*) to weigh a measure of a drug.

IN COMPOUNDS

❑ **scale boy** *n.* [1990s+] (*drugs*) one who weighs and measures out portions of a drug.

scallawag *n. see under* SCALLYWAG.

scallowag *n. see* SCALLYWAG *n.*[1].

scally *n.* (*also* **scal**) [abbr. SCALLYWAG *n.*[1] (2); coined in Liverpool, where it is tinged with a degree of admiration] [1960s+] a hooligan youth.

scally *adj.* [1990s+] pertaining to a hooligan.

scallybip *v. see* BIPE *v.*

scallywag *n.*[1] (*also* **scalawag, scallawag, scallowag, skalawag, skally wag**) [? link to Scot. *scurryvaig*, a vagabond or *scalrag*, a raggedly dressed person, ? ult. Lat. *scurra vagas*, a wandering fool] **1** [mid–late 19C] (*US*) a white Southerner who was willing to accept the terms of Reconstruction after the US Civil War (1861–5). **2** [mid-19C+] (*orig. US*) a ne'er-do-well, a disreputable person. **3** [late 19C–1930s] (*orig. US*) a political intriguer, a corrupt politician. **4** [1990s+] (*US*) the penis.

DERIVATIVES

❑ **scallywaggery** *n.* (*also* **scallywaggism**) [late 19C–1930s] (*orig. US*) roguery, political opportunism. ❑ **scallywagging** *n.* [late 19C–1930s] (*orig. US*) the act of behaving in a corrupt manner.

scallywag *n.*[2] (*also* **scallawag**) [ext. use of SCALLYWAG *n.*[1]] [mid-19C–1900s] undersized or ill-conditioned cattle.

scalp *v.*[1] [orig. Stock Exchange use, to buy shares very cheap, then sell below the prevailing price; *theatre scalpers* look for greater profits] **1** [mid-19C+] to tout tickets (orig. for railroads) at above face-value price. **2** [1930s] (*gambling*) to take a commission on a bet. **3** [1940s+] to re-sell any item for a profit.

DERIVATIVES

❑ **scalper** *n.* (*orig. US*) **1** [mid-19C+] a ticket tout. **2** [late 19C] one who buys the unused portions of long-distance railroad tickets in order to sell them at a profit. **3** [late 19C+] one who ruthlessly pursues financial deals. **4** [1950s+] (*gambling*) one who bets in such a way as never to lose. ❑ **scalping** *n.* [late 19C+] (*orig. US*) working as a ticket tout.

IN COMPOUNDS

❑ **scalp ticket** *n.* [1940s] (*Aus.*) the unused half of a return ticket.

IN PHRASES

❑ **ticket-scalper** *n.* [late 19C+] (*orig. US*) a ticket tout, who sells tickets to popular events at greatly inflated prices.

scalp *v.*[2] [play on HEAD PLAY *under* HEAD *n.*] [1970s] (*US black*) to perform cunnilingus.

scalp *v.*[3] [SE *scalp*, to remove the enemy's scalp as a trophy] [1990s+] (*N.Z.*) to capture the insignia or PATCH *n.* (3) of a rival gang-member.

scalp hunter *n.* [1960s–70s] (*US gay*) a homosexual who likes to seduce otherwise heterosexual males.

scaly *n.* [1930s+] (*Aus.*) a crocodile.

scaly *adj.* [SE *scaly*, suffering from a skin disease, typically ringworm] **1** [late 18C–mid-19C] sick, run-down. **2** [late 18C–1910s] mean, miserly. **3** [late 18C–1950s] despicable. **4** [mid-19C–1920s] shabby. **5** [mid-19C+] unpleasant.

IN COMPOUNDS

❑ **scaly bloke** *n.* [BLOKE *n.* (1)] [1930s] (*N.Z.*) a thin man. ❑ **scaly fish** *n.* [late 18C–early 19C] a rough but honest sailor. ❑ **scaly-leg** *n.* [1960s+] (*US*) a promiscuous woman. ❑ **scaly-leg** *adj.* [1960s+] (*US*) promiscuous. ❑ **scalyleg** *v.* [1960s+] (*US*) to work as the cheapest level of prostitute.

scam *n.*[1] [? SE *scheme*] **1** [1940s+] (*also* **scamus**) a plan, a scheme. **2** [1950s] (*US*) nonsense. **3** [1960s–70s] (*US*) information. **4** [1970s+] a large-scale plan to smuggle and distribute illegal drugs. **5** [1970s+] a confidence trick.

DERIVATIVES

❑ **scamster** *n.* [1970s+] a confidence trickster.

IN COMPOUNDS

❑ **scam artist** *n.* [-ARTIST *sfx* (1)] a confidence trickster. ❑ **scamhead** *n.* [-HEAD *sfx* (1)] [1980s+] a trickster, anyone who can get 'something for nothing', someone who is cunning but not necessarily criminal.

IN PHRASES

❑ **crocodile scam** *n.* [SE *crocodile*; the amphibian opens its jaws to embrace its victims] [1980s] (*US*) the ensnaring of a client by a girl, often a prostitute, and his subsequent robbery, either by the woman herself or, more often, by her pimp, posing as an 'outraged boyfriend', who emerges, while the pair are *in flagrante*, from a hidden door or panel in the bedroom wall. ❑ **what's the scam?** [1970s+] (*US*) what's happening? what's going on?

scam *n.*[2] [abbr. SCAMMISH *n.*] [2000s] (*US prison*) heroin.

scam *adj.* [1950s] (*US*) fake, fraudulent.

scam *v.* [SCAM *n.*[1] (5)] **1** [1950s+] (*also* **scam out**) to defraud, to trick. **2** [1960s+] to carry out any form of scheme, usu. dubious or illegal. **3** [1980s] (*US Und.*) to escape. **4** [1980s+] (*US campus*) to go in search of and look over the opposite sex for casual sex.

DERIVATIVES

❑ **scammed** *adj.* [1990s+] subjected to a confidence trick. ❑ **scammer** *n.* **1** [1970s+] a confidence trickster. **2** [1980s+] (*US campus*) a flirt. ❑ **scamming** *n.* [1970s+] practising confidence tricks and similar schemes.

IN PHRASES

❑ **scam in** *v.* [1960s+] to gain entry to a concert, performance etc without paying for a ticket. ❑ **scam on** *v.* [1980s+] (*US campus*) to flirt.

scamander *v.* [the classical river *Scamander*, ult. SE *meander*; note Yorks. dial. *skimaundering*, hanging or hovering about] [mid-19C] of persons, to wander about, to take a devious or winding course.

scammer *v.* see SCUMMER *v.*

scammered *adj.*[1] [? dial. *scammed*, injured or Somerset dial. *scammish*, rough, untidy] [mid–late 19C] drunk.

scammered *adj.*[2] [? fig. use of SCAM *v.* (1), the image of deception] [1930s+] (*US prison*) homosexual.

scammery *adj.* [var. on SCAMMERED *adj.*[1]] [mid-19C] drunk.

scammish *n.* [ety. unknown] [1910s] (*US drugs*) the acquiring and preparation of unadulterated opium.

scammy *adj.* [SCAMMISH *n.*] [1930s] (*US drugs*) under the influence of opium.

scamp *n.* [Scot. *scamp*, to wander, to shirk; note late 16C *scampant*, a burlesque 'coat-of-arms', modelled on SE *rampant* and illustrating 'a roge in his ragges' (*OED*)] **1** [mid-18C–early 19C] highway robbery. **2** [mid-18C–mid-19C] a highwayman. **3** [early 19C–1910s] a cheat, a swindler. **4** [mid–late 19C] (*UK Und.*) a footpad; a thief.

DERIVATIVES

❑ **scamperer** *n.* (*also* **scamper**) [early 18C–mid-19C] a street thug.

IN COMPOUNDS

❑ **scampsman** *n.* [late 18C–mid-19C] a highwayman.

IN PHRASES

❑ **foot-scamp** *n.* [late 18C–mid-19C] (*UK Und.*) a highway robber. ❑ **foot scamper** *v.* [mid-18C] (*UK Und.*) to work as a highway robber. ❑ **foot scamperer** *n.* [18C] (*UK Und.*) a highway robber who works on foot. ❑ **on the scamp** [mid-18C–early 19C] working as a highwayman. ❑ **royal scamp** *n.* [the highwayman of romantic fiction rather than of the recorded type] [late 18C–mid-19C] a highwayman who specializes in robbing rich victims and in causing them no physical harm.

scamp *v.* [SCAMP *n.* (2)] **1** [mid–late 18C] (*UK Und.*) to work as a highwayman. **2** [mid-19C–1930s] to give short measure, to cheat generally.

DERIVATIVES

❑ **scamping** *adj.* [early–mid-19C] dishonest.

IN COMPOUNDS

❑ **scamping blade** *n.* [late 18C–mid-19C] a highwayman.

IN PHRASES

❑ **scamp upon the lay/panney** *v.* [LAY *n.*[3] (1)/PANNEY *n.*[1]] [mid-18C–mid-19C] to go out robbing on the highway.

scamper *v.* [SE since early 19C] [late 17C–18C] to run, to run off.

SE in slang uses

IN COMPOUNDS

❑ **scamper juice** *n.* [1970s] (*US*) whisky.

Scan *n.* (*also* **Scand**) [abbr.] [1930s+] a *Scand*inavian.

scan *v.* [mid-16C; 19C–1900s] to see, to notice.

IN COMPOUNDS

❑ **scan on** *v.* [1960s–70s] (*US black*) to watch closely, to look closely, esp. at something one intends stealing.

Scandahoovian *n.* (*also* **Scandanoovian**) [joc. mispron.] [late 19C+] (*US*) a Scandinavian person.

Scandahoovian *adj.* (*also* **Scandahoofian, Scandanoovian, Scandihoovian**) [SCANDAHOOVIAN *n.*] [late 19C+] (*US*) Scandinavian.

scandal-broth *n.* (*also* **scandal-soup, scandal-water**) [image of old ladies gossiping over tea] [mid-19C+] tea.

scandalize *v.* [1990s+] (*US*) to behave badly.

scandalous *n.* [? one 'hides' one's head beneath it] [late 17C–18C] (*UK Und.*) a wig.

scandalous *adj.* [17C–18C SE *scandalous*, 'guilty of grossly disgraceful conduct, infamous' (*OED*)] [1980s+] (*orig. US black*) **1** extremely bad. **2** excellent, first-rate [on bad = good model].

scandalously *adv.* [1990s+] (*US teen*) in a totally unacceptable manner (on the basis of a group's standards).

scandal-proof *adj.* [late 17C–18C] of a professional thief, so hardened as to be beyond shame.

scandal-soup/-water *n. see* SCANDAL-BROTH *n.*

scanderbeg *n.* (*also* **scanderbag**) [Turk. proper name *Iskander*, Alexander, thus xenophobic equation of Turks as rascally] [late 16C] a term of abuse, a rascal.

Scandie *n.* (*also* **Scandy**) [abbr.] [late 19C+] (*orig. N.Z.*) a *Scandi*navian.

Scandie *adj.* (*also* **Scandy**) [late 19C+] (*orig. N.Z.*) *Scandi*navian.

scanger *n.* (*also* **skanger**) [ety. unknown] [2000s] (*Irish*) **1** a silly woman. **2** a lout.

scank *see under* SKANK.

scankie *adj. see* SKANKY *adj.*

scanmag *n.* [legal jargon *scandalum magnum*, the 'scandal of magnates', coined in a statute of King Richard II (*2 Ric. II* stat. 1 c. 5), which forbade anyone from publishing a malicious report against any person holding a position of dignity] [early 18C; 19C–1910s] chatter, gossip, scandal.

scanmag *v.* [SCANMAG *n.*] [early 18C; 19C–1910s] to chatter, to gossip.

scant *n.* [1970s+] (*UK juv.*) in pl., underwear.

scanting *n.* [SCANT *n.*] [1990s+] (*UK juv.*) the action of tugging the victim's underwear upwards, in order to give them a painful shock.

scapa *v.* [abbr. SCAPA FLOW *v.*] [1950s+] to go, esp. to run off.

Scapa Flow *v.* [rhy. sl.; ult. British naval anchorage in the Orkney Islands used in both WW1 and WW2] [1910s+] to go, esp. to run off.

scapali *v. see* SCARPER *v.*

scapegallows *n.* [late 18C–mid-19C] a dedicated villain who has (so far) escaped the gallows.

scapper *v.* [SCAPA FLOW *v.*] [1960s+] (*Irish*) to go, to run off.

Scarborough Fair *n.* [rhy. sl.] [1990s+] hair.

scarce-o-fat *n.* [SCARCE-O-FAT *adj.*] [1950s] (*W.I.*) a nickname for a thin person.

scarce-o-fat *adj.* [1950s] (*W.I.*) thin.

scare *n.*

SE in slang uses

IN COMPOUNDS

❑ **scaredy-cat** *n.* (*also* **scarecat, scaredy, scaredy shite, scary cat**) [20C+] (*mainly juv.*) anyone who is, or appears to be, frightened; also attrib. ❑ **scarehead** *n.* **1** [1900s] (*UK Und.*) a puritanical religious preacher. **2** [1910s] (*US*) a sensational newspaper headline, thus any sensational writing. ❑ **scare party** *n.* [the ghost motif] [1940s–50s] (*US black*) a Halloween party.

scare *v.*

SE in slang uses

IN PHRASES

❑ **scared green** *adj.* [1970s+] terrified. ❑ **scared shitless** *adj.* (*also* **scared fartless, ...pissless, ...shit, ...titless**) [SHIT *n.* (1)] [1930s+] **1** extremely frightened. **2** in a state of terror. ❑ **scare seven bells out of** *v. see* KNOCK SEVEN BELLS OUT OF *under* BELL *n.*[1]. ❑ **scare someone green** *v.* (*also* **scare someone pink, ...white**) [1970s+] to terrify. ❑ **scare someone shitless** *v.* [backform. f. SCARED SHITLESS above] [1960s+] to terrify. ❑ **scare someone spitless** *v.* (*also* **scare someone witless**) [1970s+] a euph. for prev. ❑ **scare the — out of** *v. see under* relevant n. ❑ **scare up** *v.* (*also* **scare together**) [SE *scare up*, to frighten game out of cover] [mid-19C+] (*US*) to obtain, usu. with some difficulty and poss. by threatening the supplier.

scarecrow *n.* [? his visibility resembles that of a scarecrow standing in a field] [mid-19C] (*UK Und.*) a pickpocket's young assistant, who is disposable and can be turned over to the police.

scarf *n.* [SCOFF *n.* (1)] [1930s+] (*US*) food.

IN PHRASES

❑ **knock a scarf** *v.* [1940s–50s] (*US black*) to eat.

scarf *v.* (*also* **scarf down, scarf up, skarf**) [SCOFF *v.*] **1** [20C+] (*orig. US*) (*also* **scorf**) to eat, esp. to gobble up, to eat aggressively. **2** [1960s+] (*US campus*) to pilfer, to steal. **3** [1960s+] (*US*) to perform cunnilingus. **4** [1970s] (*US campus*) to throw away, to abandon. **5** [1970s+] to consume, esp. in an aggressive manner. **6** [1970s+] (*US gay*) to fellate. **7** [1980s] (*US campus*) to borrow. **8** [1990s+] to obtain, to get hold of.

scarlet *n.* [a synon. for BLOOD *n.*[1] (1)] [mid-19C] an upper-class ruffian.

scarp *v.* [SCARPER *v.* (1)] [1910s+] (*Aus.*) to escape, to run off.

scarper *n.* [SCARPER *v.*; note WW1 Aus. milit. *scarperer*, a runner, a front-line messenger] [late 19C–1970s] an escape, an act of running way.

scarper *v.* (*also* **scapali, scarpa, scarpy, skarper**) [Ital. *scappare*, to escape, to get away] **1** [mid-19C+] (*orig. Ling. Fr./Polari*) to escape, to run off. **2** [1920s] to run.

scars *n.* (*also* **whore scars**) [1940s–60s] (*US black*) the scars left from continuous injections of narcotics.

scat *n.*[1] [var. on *-skey* ending of SAmE sp.] [1910s–40s] (*US Und.*) whisky, esp. of poor quality.

IN COMPOUNDS

❑ **scat joint** *n.* [1910s–40s] (*US Und.*) a bar.

scat *n.*[2] (*also* **scate**) [var. on SCAG *n.*[2] (2)] [1940s+] (*drugs*) heroin.

scat *n.*[3] [ety. unknown] [1970s+] (*US black*) the vagina.

scat *n.*[4] [abbr.; SE is properly 'filthy writing'] [1980s+] **1** faeces, excrement. **2** *scat*ology, defecation for sexual purposes.

IN COMPOUNDS

❑ **scatman** *n.* [1990s+] a male homosexual.

scat *n.*[5] [? abbr. obs. SE *scatterling*, a vagrant, or Billingsgate fish market jargon *scat*, a man employed to push barrows] [1980s+] an itinerant, a tramp.

scat *v.* (*also* **go like scat, scat off, scat up, skat**) [echoic of hissing at a cat: 'Ssss! cat!] [mid-19C+] to leave, to go away, esp. as a command.

IN PHRASES

❑ **get scat of** *v.* [mid-19C+] to get rid of. ❑ **quicker than scat** *adj.* [mid-19C+] very fast.

scate *n.*[1] [SE *scat*, a skate; thus ref. to equation of the vagina with a fish (cf. FISH *n.*[1] (1))] [17C] **1** the vagina. **2** a prostitute.

scate *n.*[2] *see* SCAT *n.*[2] (1).

scats *adj. see* SCATTY *adj.*

scatter *n.* [? SE *scatter*, i.e. one's money in senses 2–5] **1** [mid-19C] (*US Und.*) a musket [? the shot *scatters* once it leaves the weapon]. **2** [1910s–50s] anywhere that addicts frequent in order to buy drugs and socialize. **3** [1920s–40s] (*US*) a bar, saloon, nightclub or speakeasy where one can purchase alcoholic drinks; similarly used of a drug centre. **4** [1930s–40s] a place; a room.

IN COMPOUNDS

❑ **scatter man** *n.* [1930s–40s] a saloon-keeper.

SE in slang uses

IN PHRASES

❑ **get a scatter on** *v.* [SE *scatter*, to become dispersed] [1940s+] (*Aus.*) to lose touch with someone.

scatter *v.* **1** [20C+] to leave, to go away. **2** [1980s+] (*US black*) to shoot dead.

scatter! *excl.* [20C+] go away! leave!

scattered *adj.* **1** [1940s] (*Irish*) drunk. **2** *see* SCATTY *adj.*

scatter-eye *n.* [1950s] (*US*) a derog. nickname for a cross-eyed or squinting person.

DERIVATIVES

❑ **scatter-eyed** *adj.* [1950s] (*US*) cross-eyed.

scatting *n.* [SCAT *n.*[4] (2)] [1980s+] the sexual practice of defecating on one's partner's face.

scatty *adj.* (*also* **scats, scattered, scatty-arsed**) [SE *scatter-brained*] [20C+] incapable of logical thought or speech, feather-brained, eccentric.

scav *n.* (*also* **scavvy**) [1990s+] (*UK juv.*) a *scavenger*; used as a general insult.

scavenge *v.* [1940s+] (*Aus.*) to pilfer.

scavey *n. see* SAVVY *n.*

scavvy *n. see* SCAV *n.*

scavvy *adj.* [i.e. only of interest to a SCAV *n.* or scavenger] [1990s+] (*UK juv.*) second-rate.

scene *n.* **1** [late 19C+] any situation. **2** [20C+] a place, esp. a party. **3** [1920s+] the fashionable world, usu. of the young, as defined by the current trends. **4** [1940s+] (*drugs*) the drug-taking environment. **5** [1960s+] (*orig. US black*) choice, preference; usu. as *NOT ONE'S SCENE* below. **6** [1960s+] (*gay*) a lengthy sexual encounter; often paid-for. **7** [1970s+] a sexual relationship. **8** [1990s+] (*US gay*) a situation created as a backdrop to a given sexual fantasy. **9** [2000s] (*S.Afr. gay*) the meeting places and relationships of the gay community.

IN COMPOUNDS

❑ **scene queen** *n.* [-QUEEN *sfx* (3)] [1980s+] (*gay*) one who frequents the world of bars, restaurants and streets equated with the gay lifestyle.

IN PHRASES

❑ **cut the scene** *v.* [1940s–60s] (*US*) to leave. ❑ **make the scene** *v.* **1** [1950s+] to understand, to appreciate a situation, to experience something. **2** [1950s+] to go somewhere. **3** [1950s+] to be involved in a particular situation, esp. one that features fashionable, smart people. **4** [1960s–70s] to appear, to be present. **5** [1960s–70s] (*US gay*) to have sexual intercourse. ❑ **not one's scene** [1960s+] (*orig. US*) **1** describing an unpleasant or unacceptable situation. **2** describing anything not to one's taste. ❑ **quit the scene** *v.* [1950s] (*US black*) to die. ❑ **scene on** *v.* [1970s+] (*US black*) **1** to belittle. **2** to attempt to gain an advantage over someone by out-talking them. **3** to show off, to attempt to impress. ❑ **split the scene** *v.* [SPLIT *v.* (2b)] [1950s+] (*orig. US*) to leave, to depart.

scene! *excl.* [SCENE *n.*] [1990s+] (*US campus*) understand! understood!

sceneries *n.* [1910s] (*US Und.*) spectacles or pince-nez.

scenery *n.*[1] **1** [late 19C–1930s] (*US*) clothing or uniform. **2** [1930s] (*US Und.*) an impressive board of directors, used to bolster the credibility of a financial fraudster. **3** [1930s] (*US Und.*) fake dividend cheques, used to reassure the potential victim of a financial swindler. **4** [1950s–60s] the female body.

SE in slang uses

IN COMPOUNDS

❑ **scenery skirt** *n.* [SKIRT *n.* (1)] [1940s] (*UK Und.*) a young woman used as a decoy for a brothel, nightclub etc. ❑ **scenery stiff** *n.* (*also* **scenery bum**) [STIFF *n.*[1] (4a)/BUM *n.*[3] (1)] **1** [1920s–30s] (*US tramp*) a tramp who loves nature. **2** [1940s] a tourist.

scenery *n.*[2] [play on SE + SCENE *n.* (3)] [1970s+] (*US gay*) **1** sexually attractive individuals in a particular environment, e.g. the baths or a club. **2** anyone in whom one is interested but who does not share your sexual orientation.

IN PHRASES

❑ **have lots of scenery** *v.* [1970s+] (*US gay*) to be filled with sexually available men.

scent-bottle *n.* [late 19C] a lavatory.

scent-box *n.* [early–mid-19C] the nose.

sceptre *n.* (*also* **scepter**) [joc. resemblance] [mid-17C+] the penis.

IN COMPOUNDS

❑ **sceptre and jewels** *n.* [mid-17C+] the male genitals.

sces *n.* [pron. 'sess'; SENSIMILLIA *n.*] [1980s+] (*US drugs*) cannabis.

scew *n. see* SKEW *n.*[1].

sch... *see also under* SH....

scharn *n.* [dial. *scharn*, cowdung] [1910s] excrement.

sched *n.* [abbr.] [1950s+] a *sched*ule.

scheisty *adj. see* SHYSTY *adj.*

scheme *n.* [2000s] (*S.Afr. township*) a major criminal gang.

scheme *v.* **1** [1930s+] (*Irish*) to play truant. **2** [1970s+] (*S.Afr.*) to think, to 'reckon'.

DERIVATIVES

❑ **schemish** *adj.* (*also* **schemey**) [1980s+] (*US black/P.R.*) cunning.

IN PHRASES

❑ **scheme (on)** *v.* [1960s+] (*orig. US black*) **1** to make sexual designs on. **2** to make plans (for someone/something). ❑ **scheme out** *v.* [1930s] (*US*) **1** to deceive, to trick. **2** to plan.

schemie *n.* [20C+] a person who lives on a Scot. *scheme* or council estate.

schemozzle *see under* SHEMOZZLE.

schfatzer *n. see* SCHWARTZE *n.*

schicer *n. see* SHICER *n.*

schickery *adj.* [SHICER *n.*] [mid-19C] shabby, bad.

schickery *adv.* [SCHICKERY *adj.*] [mid-19C] shabbily, badly.

schicksie *n. see* SHIKSA *n.*

schiest *v.* [backform. f./var. on SHICER *n.*] [2000s] (*US*) to rob.

Schindler's List *adj.* [rhy. sl. = PISSED *adj.*[1]; ult. the film *Schindler's List* (1993) directed by Steven Spielberg] [1990s+] drunk.

schism-shop *n.* [the theological *schisms* debated there] [late 18C–mid-19C] a nonconformist meeting house.

schitzy *adj. see* SCHIZZY *adj.*

schiz *n.* (*also* **schitz, skitz, skiz**) [abbr. SE *schizophrenic*] **1** [1950s+] (*orig. US*) an eccentric, a mad person; one who has a split personality. **2** [1990s+] (*US black/drugs*) stimulation from crack cocaine.

schiz *adj. see* SCHIZZY *adj.*

schizo *n.* (*also* **schizoid, shizo**) [abbr. SE *schizophrenic*] [1940s+] (*orig. US*) an eccentric, a mad person.

schizo *adj.* (*also* **shizoid**) [abbr. SE *schizophrenic*] [1950s+] **1** of a person, eccentric, insane, disorientated; esp. when demonstrating two extreme forms of behaviour. **2** of an event, bizarre.

schiz (out) *v.* (*also* **schitz, schiz, schizz out, skiz out**) [SCHIZO *n.*] [1960s+] **1** (*orig. US*) to go mad, to exhibit the signs of insanity. **2** (*US drugs*) to hallucinate from crack cocaine use. **3** (*US*) to become emotional, tense.

schizzed *adj.* [SE *schizophrenic*; pron. 'skizzed'] [2000s] drunk.

schizz out *v. see* SCHIZ (OUT) *v.*

schizzy *adj.* (*also* **schitzy, schiz, schizy, skitzy**) [SE *schizophrenic*, having schizophrenia, 'a mental disorder [...] characterized by a breakdown in the relation between thoughts, feelings and actions, usu. with a withdrawal from social activity and the occurrence of delusions and hallucinations' (*OED*)] **1** [1940s+] of a person, eccentric, insane, disorientated; esp. when demonstrating two extreme forms of behaviour. **2** [1960s+] of an event, bizarre.

schlacky *adj. see* SCHLOCKY *adj.*

schlag *adj. see* SCHLOCK *adj.*

schlamming *n. see* SLAMMING *n.*[1] (1).

schlang *n. see* SCHLONG *n.*

schlap *n. see* SLAP *n.*[2] (2).

schlap *v. see* SCHLEP *v.*

schlapper *n. see* SCHLEPPER *n.*

schleinter *n. see* SLANTER *n.*[1].

schlemazel *n.* (*also* **schlemasel, shlemozzle**) [Western Yid. *schlimm Masel*, bad luck] [late 19C+] a fool, esp. an unfortunate, an incompetent.

schlembo *n.* [cod-Yid.] [2000s] a fool.

schlemiel *n.* (*also* **schlemihl, schlemmil, shlemiel**) [Yid. *schlemiel*, a bungler, a simpleton; ? the proper name *Shelumiel*, cited in Num. 25:8, as meeting an unfortunate end. He is generally equated with Zimri, whose fornication with a pagan, as recounted in the Talmud, led to his being killed *in flagrante delicto* by Phinehas. The details of the execution were suppressed by pious Jewish historians, but when *schlemiel* entered Yid. it meant anyone in 'an unfortunate (if unspecified) predicament' and thence, by phonetic confusion with Western Yid. *schlimm Masel*, a luckless fellow (cf. SCHLEMAZEL *n.*), it took on the 20C+ popular meaning] [mid-19C+] a fool, a clumsy person, a misfit, a gullible person etc.

schlemozzle *n. see* SHEMOZZLE *n.*

schlenter *n. see* SLANTER *n.*[1].

schlenter *adj.* (*also* **slenter, slinter**) [Du. *slenter*, a trick] [late 19C+] (*Aus./S.Afr.*) counterfeit, spurious, fake; thus (mining jargon) *schlenter*, a fake diamond sold as the real thing.

schlenter *v.* [SCHLENTER *adj.*] **1** [late 19C] to pretend (for criminal purposes); to defraud. **2** [1970s+] (*S.Afr.*) to obtain by underhand means.

DERIVATIVES

▫ **schlenterer** *n.* [1970s+] (*S.Afr.*) a devious, untrustworthy person.

schlep *n.*[1] [Yid. *schlep*] [1930s+] (*orig. US*) **1** a general term of abuse. **2** an ordinary working person.

DERIVATIVES

▫ **schleppy** *adj.* [1970s] (*US*) awkward, clumsy, stupid.

schlep *n.*[2] (*also* **shlap, shlep**) [SCHLEP *v.*] [1960s+] a long and unappealing distance.

schlep *v.* (*also* **schlap, schlepp**) [Yid. *schlep*, Ger. *shleppen*, to drag] [1920s+] **1** to carry an inconvenient weight for an equally inconvenient distance. **2** to travel further than one might prefer. **3** to take someone somewhere; to drag physically. **4** to drag off something for one's own benefit. **5** to travel, to walk wearily or slowly.

IN COMPOUNDS

▫ **schlepalong** *n.* [1920s+] one who is dragged along.

schlepper *n.* (*also* **schlapper, shlepper**) [Yid. *schlep*] [1940s+] **1** (*orig. US*) an insignificant person, a second-rater. **2** (*US*) a miserly person who wants something for nothing. **3** (*orig. US*) a tout.

schlinter *n. see* SLANTER *n.*[1].

schliver *n.* [CHIV *n.*[1] (1)] [19C] a clasp-knife.

schlock *n.* (*also* **schlocker, shlock**) [Ger. *Schlag*, a blow; thus merchandise that has been 'knocked about'] **1** [1910s+] cheap, inferior merchandise; anything, concrete or abstract, e.g. a piece of popular culture, defective or in poor taste. **2** [1930s] a large amount. **3** [1930s–50s] (*drugs*) narcotics, usu. heroin. **4** [1990s+] nonsense, rubbish.

IN COMPOUNDS

▫ **schlockmeister** *n.* [-MEISTER *sfx*] [1960s+] (*US*) a successful seller of cheap, meretricious goods. ▫ **schlock shop** *n.* (*also* **schlockhouse, schlock joint, schlock store**) [SE *shop*/JOINT *n.* (1)/*store*] [1910s+] a store selling flashy but cheap clothes.

schlock *adj.* (*also* **schlag, shlock**) [SCHLOCK *n.* (1)] [1910s+] cheap, inferior; in poor taste, e.g. a *schlock movie*.

IN PHRASES

▫ **non-schlock** *adj.* [1980s+] (*US campus*) avant-garde.

schlocked *adj.* [Ger. *Schlag*, a blow] [1930s] (*US*) badly beaten, punched.

schlocky *adj.* (*also* **schlacky, shlocky**) [SCHLOCK *n.* (1)] [1960s+] in poor taste, vulgar, second-rate.

schloep *n.* (*also* **schloop, shloep, shloop**) [? SCHLUB *n.* or onomat. for a sucking 'slurping' noise] [1960s+] (*S.Afr.*) a sycophant, a toady.

DERIVATIVES

▫ **schloepy** *adj.* [1960s+] (*S.Afr.*) ingratiating.

schloep *v.* [SCHLOEP *n.*] [1960s+] (*S.Afr.*) to ingratiate oneself.

schlog it on *v.* (*also* **slog it on**) [? Ger. *auf den Preis schlagen*, 'clap the price on', or SCHLOCK *n.* (1)] [1930s+] (*Aus.*) to raise a price extortionately.

IN PHRASES

▫ **get schlogged** *v.* (*also* **get slogged**) [1930s+] (*Aus.*) to be charged an excessive price.

schlong *n.* (*also* **schlang, schlontz, schlorger, shlang, shlong, shlontz**) [Yid. *schlang*, snake] **1** [1950s+] the penis. **2** [1970s] an idiot. **3** [1990s+] an important, worthwhile person.

schloomp *n.* (*also* **schlump, shloomp, shlump**) [Ger. *Schlumpe*, a slovenly woman] [1940s+] (*US*) a stupid person.

schloop *n. see* SCHLOEP *n.*

schlorger *n. see* SCHLONG *n.*

schlossed *adj. see* SLOSHED *adj.*

schlub *n.* (*also* **shlub, shlubbo, zhlob, zhlub**) [Yid. *schlub*, ult. Slavic *zhlob*, a coarse fellow] [1950s+] **1** a fool, a moron. **2** a coarse bumpkin. **3** in non-judgemental use, a person.

DERIVATIVES

▫ **schlubby** *adj.* [1950s+] awkward and unsophisticated. ▫ **schlubette** *n.* [SCHLUB *n.* + fem. sfx *-ette*] [1990s+] a stupid young woman.

schlub *v.* [SCHLUB *n.*] [1980s+] (*US campus*) to fight.

schlump *n. see* SCHLOOMP *n.*

schlunk *n.* [var. Yid. *schlump*, a slattern] [1970s] (*US*) a boring, stolid person.

schm- *pfx see* SHM- *pfx*.

schmack *n. see* SCHMECK *n.*

schmaltz *n.* (*also* **schmalz, schmultz, shmaltz, smaltz**) [fig. + lit. uses of Yid. *schmaltz*, (animal) fat] [1930s+] **1** anything mawkish, over-emotional, esp. in show business use. **2** sentimental nonsense. **3** (*US*) any viscid substance.

schmaltzy *adj.* (*also* **schmalzy, shmaltzy, smaltzy**) [SCHMALTZ *n.* (1)] [1930s+] sentimental, mawkish.

schmangle *n.* [ety. unknown] [2000s] (*S.Afr. gay*) cocaine.

schmatte *n.* (*also* **schmattah, schmatteh, shmatte, shmotte**) [Pol. *szmata*, a rag] **1** [1960s+] (*US*) a shabby or unfashionable garment. **2** [1970s+] (*US gay*) a sanitary napkin.

schmear *see under* SCHMEER.

schmeck *n.* (*also* **schmack, schmeek, schmock, shmeck, smeck**) [Yid./Ger. *schmecken*, a taste; Yid. *schmeck*, to sniff] **1** [1930s+] (*drugs*) heroin. **2** [1960s+] cocaine.

DERIVATIVES

▫ **schmecker** *n.* (*also* **shmecker, smecker**) [1930s+] (*drugs*) a heroin user.

IN COMPOUNDS

▫ **schmeck biz** *n.* [1950s] heroin dealing.

schmeck *v.* (*also* **schmack, schmeek, schmock, shmeck, smeck**) [SCHMECK *n.*] [1930s+] (*drugs*) to take heroin.

schmeckel *n.* [Yid. sl. *schmeckel*, a small penis; ult. Yid./Ger. *schmecken*, a taste, i.e. a small amount] [1990s+] (*US*) a fool, a second-rater.

schmeen *n. see* SCHMO *n.*

schmeer *n.*[1] (*also* **schmeer, shmear**) [mispron. of SE *smear*] **1** [1940s] (*US police*) something of little consequence. **2** [1950s] (*US Und.*) flattery. **3** [1950s+] (*US*) a slander, a slur.

schmeer *n.*[2] (*also* **schmear, shmear**) [lit. and fig. uses of Yid. *schmir*, to apply ointment, to lubricate] (*US*) **1** [1950s+] a daub or spread of butter, cream cheese etc. **2** [1950s+] a bribe. **3** [1960s+] political or other influence.

IN PHRASES

▫ **whole schmeer** *n.* (*also* **whole shmear, ...shmeer, ...shmier, ...smear**) [SE *whole* + fig. use of sense 1 above; despite ety. of v., authorities claim that *whole schmeer* is not Yid.; Nathan Süsskind (Cohen, 1991) suggests Ger. *Schmiere*, a small, insignificant and third-rate piece of art or performance. Extended to the artist or theatre company that produces it, and thence to the company, its props, and everything it possesses; thus *whole schmeer* = WHOLE KIT AND CABOODLE *under* WHOLE KIT *n.* = everything; note Rosten, *The Joys of Yiddish* (1968), who includes v. but does not mention n.] [1910s+] (*US*) everything, the whole lot; everyone.

schmeer *v.* (*also* **schmear, shmear, smear**) [Yid. *schmir*, to apply ointment, to lubricate] **1** [1930s+] to bribe; to flatter and cajole someone. **2** [1940s] to spend money.

schmegegge *n.* (*also* **schmegeggy, shmegeggy, smegeg**) [US Yid.] [1930s+] (*US*) **1** an unpleasant, petty person. **2** an inept, incompetent person. **3** a sycophant, a toady. **4** nonsense.

schmegma *n.* [a 'Yiddishizing' of SE *smegma*] [1990s+] (*US campus*) any slimy substance.

schmendrick *n.* (*also* **shmendrick, shmendrik**) [the name of a character in an operetta by Abraham Goldfaden (1840–1908); cited as Yid. by Rosten, *The Joys of Yiddish* (1968), but no further/previous ety. given] [1940s+] a contemptible, foolish or immature person, an upstart, a dupe.

schmiel *n.* (*also* **schmele, shmielage**) [cod-Yid.] [1980s+] (*US campus*) a woman.

IN PHRASES

□ **schmiel on** *v.* [1980s+] (*US campus*) to act pleasantly in order to pick up a woman.

schmo *n.* (*also* **schmeen, schmoe, schmoo, schmooh, shmo, shmoe**) [*schmo* is not a Yid. word *per se*, but was invented as a deliberate euph. for the taboo SCHMUCK *n.*] [1930s+] (*orig. US*) a fool.

IN COMPOUNDS

□ **schmoehopper** *n.* [1940s] a young woman who only goes out with weak, spineless men.

schmock *n.* **1** *see* SCHMECK *n.* **2** *see* SCHMUCK *n.*

schmoos *see under* SCHMOOZE.

schmoose *n. see* SMOUS *n.* (2).

schmooz *n.* [SCHMOOZ *v.*] [1990s+] (*US campus*) a person who behaves in a calm, relaxed manner.

schmooz *v.* [SCHMOOZE *v.*] [1990s+] (*US campus*) to behave in a calm, relaxed manner.

schmooze *n.* (*also* **schmoos, shmooze**) [SCHMOOZE *v.*] [1930s+] **1** a chat, a long and intimate conversation. **2** inconsequential words. **3** flattering talk.

schmooze *v.* (*also* **schmoos, shmooze**) [Heb. *schmuos*, rumours, idle talk, lit. 'things heard'] [late 19C+] **1** to flatter, to butter up. **2** to act in a romantic, seductive manner. **3** to chatter inconsequentially. **4** to gossip about. **5** to pretend, to pose.

DERIVATIVES

□ **schmoozer** *n.* (*also* **schmooser**) [late 19C+] a liar, a BULLSHITTER *n.*; a flatterer. □ **schmoozefest** *n.* [-FEST *sfx*] [1980s+] any gathering devoted to mutual (if momentary and insincere) congratulation.

schmotzing *n.* [? SCHMOOZE *v.*] [1940s–50s] (*US teen*) necking.

schmozzle *n. see* SHEMOZZLE *n.*

schmuck *n.* (*also* **schmock, schmuch, schmucko, shmuck**) [Yid. *schmuck*, the penis; play on *schtekele*, a little stick, on *sh-/sch-* pattern, thus *shteckele/schmekele*] [1930s+] **1** the penis. **2** (*also* **schmuckette, schmuckhead**) a fool, an unpleasant person.

schmucky *adj.* (*also* **schmuck**) [SCHMUCK *n.* (2)] [1950s+] stupid.

schmultz *n. see* SCHMALTZ *n.*

schmutter *n.* (*also* **schmuter**) [Yid. *shmatte*, rags, ult. Polish *szmata*, a piece of cloth, a rag] [1930s+] clothes, usu. cheap.

schmutz *n.* [synon. Ger.] **1** [1960s+] filth, dirt. **2** [1990s+] heroin [on the pattern of DIRT *n.* (10b)].

schmutzig *adj.* [SCHMUTZ *n.*] [1960s+] dirty.

schnack *n.* [cod. Yid. sp. of SE *snack*, i.e. 'I like you so much I could eat you'] [1990s+] (*US campus*) affection.

schnazzy *adj. see* SNAZZY *adj.*

schneider *n.* [Ger. *schneider*, a butcher, a cutter] **1** [19C] a tailor. **2** [1980s] a Jew.

schnicky-schnacky *n.* [redup. of SCHNACK *n.*] [1990s+] (*US campus*) physical affection in public.

schnide *n.* [SNIDE *n.* (2)] [1940s+] an unpleasant, despicable person.

schnifter *n. see* SNIFTER *n.*[2].

schnip *n.* [Yid.] [1960s] an insignificant person.

schnitz *n.* [SCHNITZEL *n.* (1), i.e. the destroyed object has been FUCKED *adj.*[1] (2) or given the SHAFT *n.* (2)] [1960s–70s] (*US*) an act of destruction.

schnitzel *n.* [Ger. *schnitzel*, a veal cutlet] [1950s+] **1** the penis. **2** a term of abuse.

IN PHRASES

□ **dip the schnitzel** *v.* [1950s+] (*US*) of a man, to have sexual intercourse.

schnob *n.* [var. on SCHNOZZLE *n.* (1)] [1930s] the nose.

schnockered *adj. see* SNOCKERED *adj.*

schnoink *n.* [a deliberately faked 'Yiddish' word] [1970s] used by a non-Jew, a derog. term for a Jew.

schnook *n.* (*also* **schnookle, schnoorp, shnook**) [US Yid.; there is no orig., i.e. European Yid., equivalent] [1930s+] a fool, a naïve or ineffectual person, esp. as a victim.

schnookered *adj. see* SNOCKERED *adj.*

schnorrer *n.* (*also* **shnurrer**) [Yid. *schnorrer*, a beggar, itself Ger. sl. *schnurren*, to go out begging, and poss. related to *schnarchen*, to snore, a ref. to the beggar's supposed 'whining' (cf. CANTER *n.* (1))] [late 19C+] **1** a beggar, esp. one who lives by his wits. **2** a person, i.e. a BEGGAR *n.* **3** a cheat, a mean person. **4** a tramp, a drifter. **5** a compulsive bargain-hunter, a haggler.

schnozzed *adj.* [ety. unknown] [1980s] (*US campus*) drunk.

schnozzle *n.* (*also* **schnoz, schnozz, schnozzer, shnoz, shnozzle**) [Ger. *Schnauze*, a snout] [1920s+] the nose.

schnozzola *n.* (*also* **shnozolla**) [ext. of SCHNOZZLE *n.*] [1930s+] the nose.

schofel-pitcher *n. see* SHOFUL-PITCHER *under* SHOFUL *n.*

schoful *n. see* SHOFUL *n.*

schonk/schonky *n. see* SHONK *n.*

school *n.* **1** in terms meaning a group or gang. (**a**) [early 16C; mid-19C–1910s] a gang of beggars or thieves (usu. pickpockets) working as a team. (**b**) [early 19C+] a group of gamblers gathered for a game. **2** [early 19C+] prison [i.e. a *school* of crime]. **3** [1990s+] any specific era in the history of hip-hop/rap music; usu. in phrs. OLD SCHOOL and NEW SCHOOL below [the exact division between the two remains a source of much debate among fans].

DERIVATIVES

□ **schooling** *n.* **1** [mid-19C] a criminal gambling party. **2** [late 19C] a term of confinement in a reformatory.

IN COMPOUNDS

□ **schoolman** *n.* [early–mid-19C] a fellow member of a gang.

IN PHRASES

□ **big school** *n.* [as compared to LITTLE SCHOOL below] [1920s–60s] (*US tramp*) a state prison. □ **little school** *n.* [in contrast to BIG SCHOOL above] [1920s–40s] (*US Und.*) a juvenile reformatory. □ **new school** *adj.* [1990s+] in rap music use, of anything recent or new, not OLD SCHOOL below. □ **old school** *adj.* (*also* **old skool**) [SE *old school*, n. and adj. describing old-fashioned things] [1980s+] (*orig. US black*) **1** in rap music use, used of anything pertaining to the early days of the musical style, esp. the work of such performers as Grandmaster Flash (b.1958) or Afrika Bambaataa (b.1957); also as n. **2** used of anything typical of the fashions, music and general styles of a previous era; orig. of the 1960s–70s, now of the 1980s and even 1990s.

SE in slang uses

DERIVATIVES

□ **schoolie** *n.* [abbr.] **1** [late 19C+] (*Aus.*) a schoolteacher. **2** [1970s+] a schoolgirl. □ **schooly** *n.* [1980s+] (*US black*)

1 anyone who wishes to go to school and further their education. **2** a naïve, unsophisticated person, a conformist.

IN COMPOUNDS

❑ **schoolboy** *n.* **1** [1960s–80s] (*drug*) codeine, cough syrup, even cocaine, anything seen (by heroin users) as a drug for 'beginners'. **2** [1970s+] (*US black*) a neophyte in the street life, an apprentice criminal. ❑ **school-butter** *n.* [late 17C–early 19C] a whipping. ❑ **schoolcraft** *n.* [? its popularity among teenagers + *see* SCHOOLBOY above] [1980s+] (*drugs*) crack cocaine.

IN PHRASES

❑ **come to school** *v.* [1940s] (*US black*) to be educated (in 'street' terms). ❑ **go to school at Bromley** *v.* [the celebrated 1920s Bromley dance band, based in Bridgetown and named for its leader, and its association with hedonistic fun] [1920s] (*W.I.*) not to go to school at all and thus to become a rough, ignorant person. ❑ **go to school in August** *v.* [*August* is a school holiday] [20C+] (*W.I.*) to be uneducated, to display one's ignorance. ❑ **hot school** *n.* [1910s] (*Aus.*) a dramatic, challenging environment. ❑ **schoolbook chump** *n.* [1970s+] (*US black*) one who is academic, but not very sophisticated or worldly-wise. ❑ **schoolboy scotch** *n.* [1970s+] (*US black*) cheap wine. ❑ **take to school** *v.* [1990s+] (*US black*) to educate (in 'street' terms). ❑ **teach school** *v.* [1970s+] (*US gay*) to initiate someone into the world of homosexuality.

school *v.* **1** [1930s+] to gamble in a group. [SCHOOL *n.* (1)]. **2** [1940s+] (*orig. US black*) to explain a situation or a plan to someone else, to teach. **3** [1980s+] (*US campus*) to defeat (in a game).

DERIVATIVES

❑ **schooled** *adj.* [1960s+] (*US black*) intelligent, sophisticated.

school of hard knocks *n.* (*also* **college of hard knocks, university..., school of hard fact**) [1910s+] (*orig. US*) a hard life, seen as a means of education.

school of placebo *n.*

IN PHRASES

❑ **be at the school of placebo** *v.* (*also* **go to the school of placebo**) [SE *placebo*, the Vespers for the Dead, ult. Lat. *placebo*, I shall please] [mid-14C–17C] to be a toady or sycophant.

school of Venus *n.* **1** [mid-17C–early 19C] (*UK Und.*) a brothel. **2** [early 18C] a synon. for BUTTOCK-BALL *n.* (1).

schooner *v.* [1970s] (*S.Afr.*) to rob.

schooner screamer *n. see* ONE-POT SCREAMER *n.*

schpritz *n.* [Yid. *schpritz*, a squirt] **1** [1950s+] (*US*) a small bit, a dose. **2** [2000s] a personal view, a version.

schpritz *v.* (*also* **shpritz**) [Yid. *schpritz*, to spray] [1950s+] (*US*) **1** to attack, to slander. **2** to deliver a stand-up monologue, usu. composed of fast one-liners.

schronch *n. see* SCRONCH *n.*

schtarka *n.* (*also* **shtarka, shtarker, shtorikue**) [Yid.] [1950s–70s] **1** a strong, brave man, an important person (esp. used ironically). **2** a thug, a hoodlum.

schtick *n.* (*also* **schtuck, shtick, shtik, stick**) [show business jargon *shtick*, one's stage speciality, one's act, esp. of a comedian's monologue; ult. Ger. *Stück*, a piece] [1950s+] (*orig. US*) **1** an act, a performance. **2** a personal habit or trait; a speciality. **3** a device or gadget.

DERIVATIVES

❑ **schticky** *adj.* [1990s+] artificial, contrived.

schtick *v.* [SCHTICK *n.*] [1960s] to perform, to 'put on an act'; to act in an extreme way.

schtoonk *n.* (*also* **schtunk, shtonk, shtoonk, shtunk**) [Ger. *Stunk*, a scandal, a 'stink'] [1930s+] (*US*) a detestable person.

schtum *adj. see* SHTUM *adj.*

schtup *n.* (*also* **shtup**) [SCHTUP *v.* (1)] [1950s+] sexual intercourse.

schtup *adj.* [SCHTUP *n.*] [1960s] pertaining to sexual intercourse.

schtup *v.* (*also* **shtup, stupp**) [Yid.; euph. 'to stuff, to fill, to fatten up' (thus Yid. *farshtopt*, constipated)] [1930s+] (*orig. US*) **1** to have sexual intercourse; to have anal intercourse. **2** to destroy, to humiliate, to defeat [fig. use of sense 1].

DERIVATIVES

❑ **schtupper** *n.* (*also* **shtupper**) [1960s+] (*US*) one who has sexual intercourse. ❑ **schtupping** *n.* [1960s+] sexual intercourse.

schv... *n. see also under* SCHW...

schvug *n.* (*also* **schvoog, schvugie, shvoogie**) [SCHWARTZE *n.* + BOOGIE *n.*[2] (1)] [1960s+] (*US*) a black person.

schwacked *adj. see* SCHWAGGED *adj.*

schwag *n.* [ety. unknown; ? SE *shag* tobacco] **1** [1980s+] (*US drugs*) inferior quality cannabis. **2** [1990s+] (*US campus*) promotional free gifts.

schwag *adj.* [SCHWAG *n.* (1)] [1990s+] (*US campus*) second-rate, inferior, bad.

schwagged *adj.* (*also* **schwacked**) [SWACKED (UP) *adj.*; ? link to SCHWAG *n.*, although there is no inference of poor quality] [1990s+] (*US black/drugs*) intoxicated by marijuana.

schwah *adj.* (*also* **zhwah**) [2000s] (*S.Afr. gay*) smart, sophisticated, up-market.

schwantz *n.* (*also* **schvantz, schvonce, schvontz, schwanz, shvantz, shvonce, shvuntz**) [Yid. *schwantz*, the tail] **1** [1930s+] (*US*) the penis. **2** [1930s+] a general derog. description. **3** [1960s] (*US gay*) a sexually successful male, assumed to have a large penis.

schwartze *n.* (*also* **schfatzer, schvartza, schvartze, schvartzeh, schvartzer, schwartza, schwartzer, shva, shvartz, shvartze, swartzer**) [Ger. *schwartz*, black] **1** [1950s+] a black person. **2** [1960s+] (*US gay*) one who prefers black partners.

IN COMPOUNDS

❑ **schwartze queen** *n.* [-QUEEN *sfx*] [1970s+] (*US gay*) a white man who prefers black partners.

schwartze *adj.* (*also* **shvartze**) [SCHWARTZE *n.* (1)] [1960s+] black, African-American.

schwassle-box *n. see* SWATCHEL-BOX *n.*

schwoz *n.* [? WAZ *n.* (1)] [1990s+] (*UK juv.*) an act of urination.

schyckle *n.* [Yid. *sheitl*, the wig trad. worn by orthodox Jewish women subsequent to their marriage] [1960s–80s] a wig.

science *n.* **1** constr. with *the*. (**a**) [early 18C] (*UK Und.*) stealing, pickpocketing. (**b**) [early–mid-19C] boxing or fencing, esp. the former; also known as *the sweet science*. **2** [1950s+] (*W.I. Rasta*) obeah, witchcraft. **3** [1980s+] (*US black*) wisdom, skill. **4** [1990s+] information, knowledge.

DERIVATIVES

❑ **scientific** *adj.* [early–mid-19C+] pertaining to boxing. ❑ **scientist** *n.* [1950s+] (*W.I. Rasta*) an occult practitioner.

IN PHRASES

❑ **drop science** *v.* [DROP *v.*[4] (5)] [1980s+] (*US black*) to demonstrate wisdom or skill.

scientist *n.* [SCIENCE *n.* (2)] [1950s+] (*W.I. Rasta*) an occult practitioner.

scillion *n. see* SKILLION *n.*

scissorbill *n.* **1** [mid-19C–1940s] (*US*) a foolish, incompetent, gossipy or objectionable person. **2** [1910s–40s] a wealthy or privileged person. **3** [1920s] (*US tramp*) a railroad detective or police officer. **4** [1920s] (*US tramp*) an itinerant knife-sharpener. **5** [1920s–30s] (*US*) a farmer, a peasant. **6** [1920s+] (*US tramp*) (*also* **scissorsbill**) anyone unwilling to join a union or otherwise improve their lot [from the fig. idea of the worker 'cutting off his nose to spite his face' (P.S. Fromer, *History of the Labor Movement in the US*, 1965)].

scissors *n.* [ety. unknown; ? link to late 19C *scizzors*, a type of firecracker that had to be bent double and stamped on to make it explode; note also HAIRCUT *n.*[2]] [1960s–70s] (*drugs*) marijuana.

SE in slang uses

IN PHRASES

❑ **give someone scissors** *v.* [one fig. 'cuts them up'] [mid-

19C–1900s] to treat someone badly, to pay someone back (for a slight or injury).

scissors! *excl.* [mid-19C+] a mild excl.

sciv *n. see* SKIVVY *n.*[2].

scivvie house *n. see under* SKIVVY *n.*[1].

scoat dog *n.* [2000s] (*N.Z. teen*) an undesirable person.

scode *n.* [ety. unknown] [1980s+] (*N.Z. drugs*) the butt end of a marijuana cigarette that is unwrapped and recycled.

scody *adj.* (*also* **scady**) [derived f. skateboarding sl.] [1990s+] (*N.Z.*) perceived as admirable; thus also its opposite.

scoff *n.* (*also* **scoffings, skauf, skoff**) [SCOFF *v.*] [mid-19C+] food.

(DERIVATIVES)

❑ **scoffless** *adj.* [1960s] deprived of food, starving.

(IN COMPOUNDS)

❑ **scoff jack** *n.* [JACK *n.*[4] (2)] [1930s] (*US tramp*) money for food collected among a group of tramps when they have been unable to beg successfully.

(IN PHRASES)

❑ **cop a scoff** *v.* (*also* **knock a scoff**) [1940s] to eat.

scoff *v.* [Scot. *scaff*, to beg or ask for (food etc) in a mean or contemptible manner, but note S.Afr. *scoff*, food, a meal, f. Du. *schoft*, a quarter of a day, thus each of the day's four meals] **1** [mid-19C+] (*also* **scorf, skoff**) to eat, to gobble up. **2** [late 19C] to give food, to feed. **3** [late 19C+] to grab. **4** [20C+] in fig. use, to defeat or attack. **5** [1930s–50s] (*US drugs*) to take narcotics orally. **6** [1950s+] (*US teen*) to steal, to pilfer. **7** [1960s] (*US campus*) to fellate. **8** [1970s] to drink.

(IN PHRASES)

❑ **scoff fishheads (and scramble for the gills)** *v.* [1940s–50s] (*US black*) to have a difficult time, to encounter problems.

scoldrum *n. see* SCALDRUM DODGE *n.*

scold's cure *n.* [the misogynistic concept that only death would silence a nagging woman] [late 18C–early 19C] a funeral, a coffin.

(IN PHRASES)

❑ **nap the scold's cure** *v.* [late 18C–early 19C] to be placed in one's coffin.

scollogue *v.* [? link to SCALLYWAG *n.*[1] (2)] [mid–late 19C] to live in a debauched, degenerate manner.

scolopendra *n.* [SE *scolopendra*, a centipede or millipede, orig. 'a fabulous sea-fish which feeling himselfe taken with a hooke casteth out his bowels vntill hee hath vnloosed the hooke and then swalloweth them vp againe' (Bullokar, *English Expositour*, 1616)] [mid-17C] a prostitute.

sconce *n.* (*also* **skonce**) [either SE *sconce*, a lantern or *sconce*, a fort or earthwork] **1** [mid-16C–19C] judgement, sense. **2** [mid-16C–1950s] the head, the brain. **3** [late 16C] a person (whose head it is). **4** [late 18C] the penis.

sconce off *v.* (*also* **sconce the reckoning**) [Oxford University jargon *sconce*, to fine someone a tankard of ale, as imposed by undergraduates on each other for various small misdemeanours; also as n., the fine itself] [mid-17C–19C] to run off without paying a bill.

(IN PHRASES)

❑ **build a sconce** *v.* [note the *OED* prefers to link the phr. to SE *sconce*, a small fort or earthwork, but this lacks any drinking ref.] [mid-17C–early 18C] to run up a large bill at a tavern or inn, esp. when one has no intention of paying it. ❑ **sconce one's diet** *v.* [19C] to eat less, to diet.

scone *n.*[1] [rhy. sl.; *hot scone* = JOHN *n.*[1]] [1940s–50s] (*Aus.*) a police officer, a detective.

scone *n.*[2] [joc. resemblance] [1940s+] (*Aus./N.Z.*) the head.

(IN PHRASES)

❑ **do one's scone** *v.* [1940s+] (*Aus./N.Z.*) to lose one's temper (with someone). ❑ **duck the scone** *v.* [1940s+] (*Aus.*) to plead guilty in court. ❑ **gone in the scone** *adj.* [1950s+] eccentric, insane. ❑ **off one's scone** *adj.* [1980s+] (*N.Z.*) mad, eccentric. ❑ **scone-doer** *n.* [1940s+] (*Aus./N.Z.*) an over-emotional person. ❑ **scone-doing** *n.* [1940s+] (*Aus./N.Z.*) a loss of control. ❑ **use one's scone** *v.* [1980s+] (*N.Z.*) to act sensibly.

(IN EXCLAMATIONS)

❑ **pull your scone in!** (*also* **suck your scone in!**) [on basis of PULL YOUR HEAD IN! *under* HEAD *n.*] [1950s] an excl. of annoyance, mind your own business! don't interfere!; an angry retort telling somebody to calm down or suffer the consequences.

SE in slang uses

(IN PHRASES)

❑ **old scone** *n.* [1950s] a generally affectionate address.

scone *v.* [SCONE *n.*[2] (1)] [1940s+] (*Aus./N.Z.*) to hit someone on the head.

scone-hot *adv.* [1930s+] (*Aus.*) an intensive, either positive or negative.

(IN PHRASES)

❑ **go (at someone) scone-hot** *v.* [1930s+] (*Aus.*) to lose one's temper with; to tell off severely.

scoob *n.* [abbr. SCOOBY-DOO *n.*[2] (1)] [1980s+] (*Aus./Can. drugs*) cannabis; a marijuana cigarette.

scoob *v.* [TV cartoon character *Scooby-Doo* and his *Scooby Snacks*] [1980s+] (*US campus*) to eat, usu. to eat snacks.

scoobied *adj.* (*also* **skoobied**) [SCOOBY *v.*] [1990s+] **1** beaten up, defeated. **2** under the influence of drink or drugs. **3** confused.

scoobie snax *n.* (*also* **scooby snacks**) [SCOOBY-DOO *n.*[2] (1) + SE *snacks*] (*US drugs*) **1** [1980s+] food eaten when suffering the hunger-pangs promoted by smoking cannabis. **2** [2000s] MDMA.

scooby *v.* (*also* **skobby**) [rhy. sl.; *scooby-doo* = SCREW *v.* (1); ult. TV cartoon character *Scooby-Doo*] [1990s+] **1** to defeat, to trounce, to outwit. **2** to confuse.

scooby-doo *n.*[1] [rhy. sl.; ult. TV cartoon character *Scooby-Doo*] **1** [1960s+] (*UK prison*) a warder [= SCREW *n.*[1] (2c)]. **2** [2000s] a clue.

scooby-doo *n.*[2] [TV cartoon character *Scooby-Doo*] [1990s+] **1** (*US black/teen*) a large cannabis cigarette. **2** (*US campus*) someone who eats a lot and never gains weight. **3** (*US black*) a firearm.

scooby snacks *n. see* SCOOBIE SNAX *n.*

scooch *n.* [? nonce-word *scootch up*, move over] [1990s+] (*Irish*) a lift in a car.

scooch *v. see* SCRUNCH *v.*

scood *n. see* SCUD *n.* (3).

scoop *n.* **1** in the context of drink or drugs. (**a**) [late 19C–1950s] (*US*) a glass of beer. (**b**) [late 19C+] (*Irish/Scot.*) a drink. (**c**) [1960s] (*drugs*) a folded matchbox cover used to sniff narcotics. (**d**) [2000s] (*drugs*) gamma hydroxybutyrate (GHB). **2** in fig. senses [journalist jargon *scoop*, an exclusive or (as yet) unrivalled story]. (**a**) [late 19C+] an advantage, a lucky result in one's business or similar dealings. (**b**) [1930s+] information, knowledge, intimate details.

(IN PHRASES)

❑ **on the scoop** *adj.* **1** [mid–late 19C] on a spree, on a round of dissipation. **2** [1900s–10s] (*Aus.*) drunk.

SE in slang uses

(IN PHRASES)

❑ **what's the scoop?** [SE *scoop*, a revelatory newspaper story] [1950s] (*US*) a general greeting, what's going on?

scoop *v.* **1** [late 19C–1900s] (*US*) to beat, to defeat. **2** [1950s+] (*US*) to arrest. **3** [1960s] (*drugs*) to sniff cocaine through a SCOOP *n.* (1c). **4** [1970s] to pick up, to seduce. **5** [1970s+] (*US campus*) to obtain, to give a lift to. **6** [1990s+] (*US*) to watch, usu. people in the street.

(IN PHRASES)

❑ **scoop in** *v.* **1** [mid-19C–1910s] to take someone in, to dupe or defeat someone. **2** [mid-19C+] (*orig. US*) to have a stroke of luck, a 'lucky break', usu. in business. **3** [mid-19C+] to gather or gain something, often in large quantities (esp. to the exclusion of others). **4** [1960s] (*US*) to impart information

[SCOOP *n.* (1)]. ▫ **scoop on** *v.* [1980s+] (*US campus*) to pick up, to make advances to. ▫ **scoop the pool** *v.* (*also* **scoop the kitty**) [poker imagery] [late 19C+] to make a major profit; lit. or fig.

scooper *n.*[1] [late 19C] (*UK Und.*) a hasty escape.

scooper *n.*[2] [2000s] (*US prison*) one who eats with a spoon.

scoot *n.*[1] [SCOOT *v.* (2)] **1** [late 19C] a run. **2** [late 19C+] an escape. **3** [1920s] (*US*) an elevator boy. **4** [1920s] (*Aus.*) a prolonged bout of drunkenness. **5** [1990s+] speedy movement.

scoot *n.*[2] [euph. of SHIT *n.* (1)/SHIT *n.* (2)] [late 19C+] diarrhoea; thus a general term of abuse; occas. in pl., *the scoots*.

scoot *n.*[3] [ety. unknown] [1940s+] in pl., dollars.

scoot *n.*[4] [abbr. SE *scooter*] [1960s+] a motorcycle or motorcar.

scoot *v.* [mid-18C–early 19C naut. jargon *scout*, to run off swiftly] **1** [mid-19C; 1920s+] (*US*) of a person or object, to slide. **2** [mid-19C+] (*also* **scoot off**) to run off, to escape; to move suddenly or swiftly. **3** [late 19C] to travel. **4** [1910s] to send (someone), to impel (someone).

IN PHRASES

▫ **on the scoot** *adj.* (*also* **up on the scoot**) [20C+] (*Aus./N.Z.*) on a drunken spree, drunk.

scootch *v.* [var. on SE *scoot*] [1980s+] to move.

scooter *n.*[1] [SCOOT *v.* (2)] [19C] one who leaves quickly, an escapee.

scooter *n.*[2] [1930s–40s] (*US Und.*) **1** an automobile, esp. a car used for the smuggling of rum. **2** a legless tramp who travels on a wheeled platform.

scooter tracks *n.* see SKID MARK *n.*

scope *n.* [abbr. SE *telescope*] **1** [1950s–60s] (*also* **telescope**) the erect penis. **2** [1970s+] (*US black/campus*) a look, a stare, a lookout point.

scope *v.* (*also* **scope down, scope on, scope out**) [abbr. SE *telescope*] **1** [1950s+] (*orig. US*) to look over, to stare at, to investigate. **2** [1970s] (*US campus*) to cheat by copying in an exam. **3** [1970s+] to stare at someone intently, usu. with sexual interest. **4** [1970s+] to look in various public places for a partner for romance or sex. **5** [2000s] (*US*) to ascertain, to work out.

IN PHRASES

▫ **scoped in** *adj.* [1970s] (*US*) focused on.

scorch *n.* [1980s] (*UK Und.*) arson.

scorch *v.* **1** [20C+] (*Aus./US*) to go or move very fast. **2** [1930s] (*US black*) to find, to provide. **3** [1940s] (*US black*) to escort. **4** [1990s+] to arrest.

scorcher *n.* **1** [mid–late 19C] a severe reprimand, a telling-off; thus an unpleasant situation. **2** [mid-19C+] a very hot day. **3** [late 19C] a major problem. **4** [late 19C–1910s] an outspoken or domineering person. **5** [late 19C–1930s] an attractive and/or sexually voracious woman. **6** [late 19C–1940s] one who cycles or motors with above average speed or energy. **7** [late 19C+] anything or anyone exceptional of its type. **8** [1910s] that which is hit or thrown, e.g. a ball, with above-average speed. **9** [1940s+] anything sensational, esp. when seen as risqué or 'naughty'.

IN PHRASES

▫ **real scorcher** *n.* [in non-sexual use of sense 5 above] [late 19C] a very attractive young woman, but also a chaste one.

scorching *adj.* [SCORCHER *n.* (9)] [late 19C+] astounding, sensational, licentious, risqué.

score *n.*[1] [SE *score*, a group of 20; ult. the counting of sheep in 20s, each of which was 'scored' on some form of tally, e.g. by cutting notches in a stick] [early 19C+] 20, in a variety of contexts, e.g. 20 years' prison, a 20-ounce packet of tobacco, $20, £20 etc.

score *n.*[2] [sporting imagery] **1** [mid-19C+] the situation, the facts, what is going on; esp. in phrs. *KNOW THE SCORE* below, *what's the score?* what's going on? **2** [1900s] a successfully made point in an argument.

IN PHRASES

▫ **carve up scores** *v.* [1930s] (*US*) to reminisce with an old friend (cf. *CUT UP OLD SCORES under* SCORE *n.*[3]). ▫ **know the score** *v.* [1930s+] to understand a situation, to know what is going on; often as negative. ▫ **learn the score** *v.* [1960s+] to work out what is going on.

SE in slang uses

IN COMPOUNDS

▫ **score-card** *n.* **1** [1930s] (*US*) a menu. **2** [1970s+] (*US gay*) an address book.

score *n.*[3] [SCORE *v.*] **1** in Und. uses. (**a**) [1910s+] (*US*) the profits from a robbery, fraud or similar criminal act. (**b**) [1930s–70s] (*Can./US*) the site of a robbery or similar crime. (**c**) [1930s+] (*US*) a planned killing. (**d**) [1930s+] (*orig. US*) a success or coup; usu. in criminal activity or gambling. (**e**) [1940s+] (*Can./US*) a robbery. **2** [1940s+] (*drugs*) a purchase of drugs. **3** [1960s+] any form of material gain. **4** [1960s+] (*orig. US*) in context of commercial sex. (**a**) a male or female prostitute's client. (**b**) a potential partner for sex. (**c**) a sexual conquest. (**d**) money gained from commercial sex. **5** [1990s+] (*US prison*) anything sent in to a prisoner from the outside world. **6** [2000s] (*US black*) a cache of illicit goods.

IN COMPOUNDS

▫ **score money** *n.* (*also* **score dough**) [SE *money* / DOUGH *n.*] [1930s–50s] (*drugs*) money set aside or offered for a purchase of drugs. ▫ **score-strung** *adj.* [late 19C] (*Aus.*) in funds.

IN PHRASES

▫ **cut up old scores** *v.* [CUT (IT) UP *v.* + sense 1c above but cf. *CARVE UP SCORES under* SCORE *n.*[2]; note synon. carnival use *cut up jackpots*] [1930s+] (*orig. US Und.*) to reminisce over old successes, major villainies etc. ▫ **cut up the score** *v.* (*also* **cut up the touch, put the shiv in the touch**) [1930s–40s] (*US Und.*) to share out illicit profits. ▫ **hang a score** *v.* [1950s] to perform a robbery. ▫ **run up a score** *v.* [? the old *scoring* of one's debts on some form of tally] [mid-17C; mid-19C] to buy on credit, esp. at a public house.

score *v.* **1** to get hold of. (**a**) [early 18C; 1910s+] to obtain, to get. (**b**) [late 19C] to consume. (**c**) [1910s+] to obtain money. (**d**) [1960s+] (*US campus*) to obtain something desirable, usu. sex. **2** [late 19C+] to succeed, to do well. **3** [late 19C+] (*orig. US*) (*also* **score on**) to seduce, to have sexual intercourse. **4** [1910s+] to commit a robbery, to make a dishonest gain, to filch something from a counter or stall. **5** [1930s+] (*also* **score (for) a connection**) to buy drugs. **6** in context of commercial sex. (**a**) [1960s] to procure sex for a third party. (**b**) [1960s+] (*US gay*) for a male prostitute to secure a client. **7** [1980s+] (*S.Afr.*) to give, to pass over.

IN PHRASES

▫ **score between the posts** *v.* [football imagery] [1960s+] (*Aus.*) of a man, to have sexual intercourse, to seduce a woman. ▫ **score ten** *v.* [SE *score ten*/SCORE *v.* (3)] [1980s] (*Aus.*) to seduce, to have sexual intercourse.

SE in slang uses

IN PHRASES

▫ **score off** *v.* [late 19C+] to make a point at another's expense. ▫ **score on** *v.* [1910s] (*Aus. Und.*) to inform against. ▫ **score someone the ages** *v.* [1980s] (*S.Afr.*) to tell someone the time.

score! *excl.* [SCORE *v.*] [1990s+] an excl. of satisfaction, pleasure.

scorf *v.* see SCARF *v.*

scot *n.* [stereotyping; but ? note Grose 1796 *scot*, a young bull + Jon Bee: 'the small Scots oxen coming to their doom with little resignation to fate'] **1** [early–mid-19C] (*also* **fine Scot**) an ill-tempered person, esp. one who is susceptible to teasing. **2** [mid-19C–1910s] a bad temper, a fit of irritation.

Scotch *adj.* [racial stereotyping] [20C+] mean, miserly.

IN COMPOUNDS

▫ **Scotch bait** *n.* (*also* **Welsh bait**) [*Scotch/Welsh* + *bait*, a snack] [late 18C–mid-19C] a rest taken as one walks along. ▫ **Scotch bum** *n.* [BUM *n.*[1] (1)] [early 17C] a form of dress-bustle. ▫ **Scotch casement** *n.* [SE *casement*, a window frame] [late 18C–mid-19C] the pillory. ▫ **Scotch chocolate** *n.* [late 18C–

mid-19C] brimstone (sulphur) and milk. ▫ **Scotch coffee** *n.* [orig. naut. jargon] [mid-19C] hot water flavoured with burned biscuit. ▫ **Scotch convoy** *n.* [20C+] (*Ulster*) a walk home with a visitor, who then comes back with you. ▫ **Scotch fiddle** *n.* (*also* **Welsh fiddle**) [note that a fiddle or violin also symbolizes the vagina, thus the 17C riddle commencing 'I've two holes in my Belly and none in my Bum / Yet me, with much pleasure, Italians do thrum...'] [late 17C–19C] venereal disease. ▫ **Scotch greys** *n.* (*also* **Scotch grays, Scots greys/grays**) [Hotten (1860), partly eschewing Johnson's prejudice, notes that 'our northern neighbours are calumniously reported, from their living on oatmeal, to be particularly liable to cutaneous eruptions and parasites'] **1** [early 19C–1900s] lice. **2** [late 19C] (*Aus.*) large mosquitoes. ▫ **Scotch hobby** *n.* [SE *hobby*, a small or middle-sized horse] [late 17C–18C] a small, stunted Scottish horse. ▫ **Scotch lick** *n.* [SE *lick*, a hit, a dab] [20C+] (*Irish*) a poorly done cleaning job. ▫ **Scotch louse trap** *n. see* LOUSE TRAP *under* LOUSE *n.* ▫ **Scotch mist** *n.* [note B.E. (c.1698): '*Scotch-mist*, a sober, soaking Rain'] [1940s+] anything insubstantial, mythical, esp. used sarcastically when one wants to imply that the other speaker has failed to grasp the point or, lit., perceive something that is clear and obvious. ▫ **Scotch ordinary** *n.* [SE *ordinary*, an eating house] [late 18C–early 19C] a lavatory. ▫ **Scotch pint** *n.* [early 19C] a bottle holding two quarts (four pints/three litres). ▫ **Scotch polo** *n.* [20C+] (*US*) golf. ▫ **Scotch screw** *n.* [SCREW *n.*[1] (1); the stereotypical Scot is too mean to offer sexual pleasure to anyone but themselves] [20C+] a nocturnal emission. ▫ **Scotch shout** *n. see* YANKEE SHOUT *under* YANKEE *n.*[1]. ▫ **Scotch warming-pan** *n.* (*also* **Scottish warming-pan**) **1** [mid-17C–18C] a complaisant young woman. **2** [19C] (*also* **Scots warming-pan**) the breaking of wind. ▫ **Scotch wine** *n.* [1900s–60s] whisky.

IN PHRASES

▫ **headquarters of the Scots greys** *n.* [early 19C–1900s] a lousy head. ▫ **play the Scotch fiddle** *v.* [19C–1910s] 'to work the index finger of the right hand like a fiddlestick between the index and middle finger of the left. This provokes a Scotchman in the highest degree, it implying that he is afflicted with the itch' (Hotten 1860). ▫ **Scots greys are in full march by the crown office, the** [early 19C–1900s] lice are crawling on one's head.

scotched up *adj.* (*also* **double-scotched**) [*Scotch* whisky] [1930s] (*US*) drunk.

Scotch eggs *n.* [rhy. sl.] [1950s+] legs.

scotches *n.* [abbr. SCOTCH PEG *n.* (1)] [mid-19C+] the legs.

Scotchie *n.* (*also* **Scotchy, Scottie, Scotty**) [mid-19C+] a Scot; a nickname for a Scotsman.

scotchie *n.* (*also* **scotty**) [abbr. SCOTCH PEG *n.* (1)] [late 19C–1930s] a leg; a false leg.

Scotchman *n.*[1] [the story that a Scottish immigrant to S.Afr. fooled his black employees by giving them florins (worth 2s/10p) but calling the coins half-crowns (worth 2s 6d/12½p)] [mid–late 19C] (*S.Afr.*) a florin (a two-shilling/10p piece).

Scotchman *n.*[2] [SCOTCH TAPE *n.*] [1980s+] (*Aus. prison*) a rapist.

Scotchman's shout *n.*

IN COMPOUNDS

▫ **Scotch shout** *n. see* YANKEE SHOUT *under* YANKEE *n.*[1].

Scotch peg *n.* [rhy. sl.] **1** [mid-19C+] usu. in pl., the legs. **2** [20C+] in pl., eggs.

scotch tape *n.* [rhy. sl.] [1980s+] (*Aus.*) rape.

Scotchy *n. see* SCOTCHIE *n.*

scotia! *excl.* [? elision of SE *it's* + KOSHER *adj.* (1)] [1970s] (*US black*) all right! fine!

Scotland (the Brave) *v.* [rhy. sl.] [1990s+] to shave.

Scotland Yard *n.* [? New *Scotland Yard*, the headquarters of the Metropolitan Police in London] [1970s] (*US black*) a plain-clothes police officer.

Scots greys *n. see* SCOTCH GREYS *under* SCOTCH *adj.*

Scotsman's *adj.* used in combs. below to imply meanness, based on negative stereotyping of the Scot.

IN COMPOUNDS

▫ **Scotsman's grandstand** *n.* (*also* **Scotsman's stand, Scotsman's zoo**) [1970s+] **1** a grandstand erected on private property overlooking a sports arena in which seats are available cheaply. **2** a vantage point that allows people to watch an event, usu. sporting, for free. ▫ **Scotsman's half-crown** *n.* [a true SE *half-crown* was worth 2s 6d (12½p)] [1940s–70s] (*N.Z.*) a two-shilling (10p) coin. ▫ **Scotsman's shout** *n.* [1940s+] (*N.Z.*) a round of drinks in which everyone pays for their own.

Scots warming-pan *n. see* SCOTCH WARMING-PAN *under* SCOTCH *adj.*

scott *n.*[1] [? SCAT *n.*[2]] [1970s] (*drugs*) heroin.

scott *n.*[2] [the stereotypical middle-class name *Scott*, and the perceived social inadequacies of such public-school educated young men] [1990s+] (*Aus. teen*) a socially inept male.

scott! *excl. see* GREAT SCOTT! *under* GREAT...! *excl.*

scottie *adj. see* SCOTTY *adj.*

Scottish *adj.* [negative stereotyping] [early–mid-19C] irritable, easily annoyed.

IN COMPOUNDS

▫ **Scottish fleas** *n.* [early 17C] syphilis.

Scottish Football Association *n.* [play on initial letters of SWEET FANNY ADAMS *n.*] [1990s+] absolutely nothing.

Scottish warming-pan *n. see* SCOTCH WARMING-PAN *under* SCOTCH *adj.*

Scotty *n.*[1] [like the character Scotty, in the TV series *Star Trek* (from 1966), it 'makes one's engines run' + BEAM ME UP, SCOTTY! *excl.* (2)] [1980s+] (*drugs*) cocaine; crack cocaine.

Scotty *n.*[2] *see* SCOTCHIE *n.*

scotty *adj.* (*also* **scottie**) [racial stereotyping; note Vaux (1812): '*Scot*, a person of irritable temper, who is easily put in a passion'] [mid-19C+] (*Aus.*) tetchy, irritable.

scour *v.*[1] (*also* **scoure**) [SE *scour*, to rub] [mid-15C–18C] to wear (fetters), thus to sit in the stocks.

IN PHRASES

▫ **scour the cramp-rings** *v.* [CRAMP-RINGS *n.*] [mid-16C–early 19C] to wear chains or fetters. ▫ **scour the darbies** *v.* [DARBIES *n.* (1)] [late 17C–early 19C] to wear chains or handcuffs.

scour *v.*[2] (*also* **scower, scowre**) [SE *scour*, to move around hastily and energetically] **1** [late 16C–early 19C] to travel at speed, to run away. **2** [mid-17C–mid-18C] to roam about at night uproariously, breaking windows, beating the watch and molesting wayfarers. **3** [mid-17C–1940s] of a man, to have sexual intercourse; occas. of a woman.

scourer *n.* (*also* **scowrer**) [SCOUR *v.*[2] (2); the term was used as the title of the play by Thomas Shadwell, *The Scowrers* (1691) 'an excellent but coarse comedy, which gives an interesting picture of the times' (*DNB*)] [17C–18C] (*UK Und.*) a dissolute young man who roams the streets, usu. as one of a gang, beating up passers-by, breaking windows, attacking the watch and generally acting in a hooligan manner.

scouring *n.* [SCOUR *v.*[1]] [early 18C] imprisonment.

Scouse *n.* [after the sailors' dish *lobscouse*, a meat stew totemic of Liverpool] **1** [1940s+] a Liverpudlian; a nickname for a Liverpudlian. **2** [1960s+] the dialect spoken in Liverpool. **3** [1990s+] used a term of direct address.

Scouse *adj.* [SCOUSE *n.* (1)] [1940s+] Liverpudlian.

scouse *n.* [abbr. *lobscouse*] [mid-19C+] cheap, tasteless food, esp. a thin stew.

scouse *v.* [SCOUSE *n.* (2)] [1960s] to speak with a Liverpudlian dialect/accent.

Scouser *n.* [SCOUSE *n.* (1)] [1950s+] a Liverpudlian; thus *Scousers*, a collective name for Liverpudlians.

scout *n.* **1** in derog. senses [late 14C–19C ? SE *scout*, a term of contempt]. (**a**) [late 16C–17C] a bawd, a pimp; one who obtains clients for a prostitute. (**b**) [early 18C+] (*Anglo-Irish*) a bold, forward young woman. (**c**) [mid-18C] a mean person. (**d**) [mid-19C] (*Irish*) a disreputable person. (**e**) [1950s+] (*W.I. Rasta*) a person of inferior status. **2** a person or thing which keeps a lookout. (**a**) [late 17C–early 19C] a pocket watch [a pun on sense 2b]. (**b**) [late 17C–mid-19C] a member of the watch [orig. milit. use]. **3** [1910s+] in positive sense, a person; esp. as *good scout*, an admirable person [the popular image of the Boy Scouts].

IN COMPOUNDS

❑ **scout-cull** *n.* [CULL *n.*[1] (3)] [early 18C] (*UK Und.*) a watchman. ❑ **scout-ken** *n.* [KEN *n.*[1] (1)] [early 19C] a watch-house.

SE in slang uses

IN PHRASES

❑ **girl scout** *n.* [1970+] (*US camp gay*) a soldier on leave, and looking for sex. ❑ **old scout** *n.* [early 19C+] a person, usu. as an affectionate term of address.

scout off *v.* [early 19C] to put off, to ignore.

scowbanker *n.* (*also* **skowbanker, skullbanker**) [dial., lit. one who scours or wanders the banks; Partridge and *OED* offer alt. etys. but the *EDD* ety., used here, seems obvious] [mid–late 19C] (*orig. Aus.*) a rogue, a rascal, one who loiters around in the hope of hand-outs, which will save him from earning a living.

DERIVATIVES

❑ **scowbanking** *n.* [mid–late 19C] (*orig. Aus.*) the state of loafing or idling.

Scowegian *n.* [SE *Scandinavian* + *Norwegian*] [1910s+] (*Aus./Can./US*) a Scandinavian.

Scowegian *adj.* [SCOWEGIAN *n.*] [1920s] (*US*) Scandinavian.

scower/scowre *v. see* SCOUR *v.*[2].

scowrer *n. see* SCOURER *n.*

scrabblers' cram *n.* [ety. unknown] [mid-19C] (*UK Und.*) mud, filth.

scrabbler-strap *n.* [ety. unknown] [mid-19C] (*UK Und.*) a street-sweeper.

scrag *n.*[1] [development of older *crag*, the neck, the throat; ult. synon. terms in Teutonic languages] **1** [mid-18C–19C] the neck. **2** [late 19C] the gallows; the act of hanging.

IN COMPOUNDS

❑ **scrag squeezer** *n.* [early–late 19C] (*UK Und.*) the gallows.

scrag *n.*[2] [? backform. f. SE *scraggy*/SE *scrag-end*, the worst part of anything] **1** [1960s] (*Aus.*) an ill-kempt person. **2** [1980s+] (*US campus*) an unattractive woman. **3** [2000s] (*N.Z.*) anything considered inferior.

scrag *v.* [SCRAG *n.*[1]] **1** [early 18C–mid-19C] to hang (on the gallows). **2** [mid-19C+] (*also* **skrag**) to do harm, to beat up, to kill. **3** [1900s] to throttle, to choke, to garrotte. **4** [1930s] to commit suicide. **5** [1950s] (*also* **skrag**) (*US drugs/gang*) to steal. **6** [1990s+] (*Aus./US*) to have sexual intercourse.

IN COMPOUNDS

❑ **scrag-boy** *n.* [late 18C–mid-19C] a hangman.

IN PHRASES

❑ **scrag a lay** *v.* [SCRAG *v.* (5) is too late; thus fig. use of SCRAG *v.* (1), i.e. to grasp tightly + SE *lay*, to place upon] [late 18C–early 19C] to steal clothes that have been laid out on a hedge to dry. ❑ **scrag 'em fair** *n.* (*also* **scrag-fair**) [late 18C–early 19C] an execution by hanging.

scragged *adj.* [SCRAG *v.* (1)] **1** [early 18C–19C] hanged. **2** [20C+] killed; dead.

IN EXCLAMATIONS

❑ **I'll be scragged!** *see* I'LL BE HANGED! *under* HANGED *adj.*

scragger *n.* [SCRAG *v.* (1)] [late 19C] a hangman.

scragging *n.* [SCRAG *v.* (1)] **1** [19C] a hanging. **2** [mid-19C+] a beating. **3** [1930s] a shooting.

IN COMPOUNDS

❑ **scragging match** *n.* [mid-19C] (*UK Und.*) a judicial hanging. ❑ **scragging post** *n.* [19C] the gallows.

scragg's hotel *n.* [? a lost proper name or SE *scrag-end*, the worst part of anything] [late 19C] (*tramp*) a workhouse.

scram *n.* [SCRAM *v.*] [1920s+] (*US Und.*) money, clothing.

IN COMPOUNDS

❑ **scram-bag** *n.* [1920s+] (*US Und.*) a suitcase packed ready for leaving in a hurry. ❑ **scram money** *n.* [1920s+] (*US Und.*) cash reserved for a sudden departure.

scram, the *n.* [1940s] (*US*) an act of rejection or ejection.

scram *v.* [SE *scramble* or Ger. *schrammen*, to run away] [1920s+] (*orig. US*) **1** (*also* **scram out**) to escape, to run off. **2** as imper. *scram!*

DERIVATIVES

❑ **scramming** *n.* [mid-19C] (*UK Und.*) of a tramp, taking a job of work, then quickly moving on. ❑ **scramsville** *n.* [-VILLE *sfx*[1]] [1950s–60s] desertion, running off.

IN PHRASES

❑ **do the scramming act** *v.* [1930s] (*US*) to disappear, to run off. ❑ **take a scram** *v.* [1940s] (*US Und.*) to run off.

scramble *n.* [i.e. that which one *scrambles* to obtain] [early 19C+] (*US*) money.

scramble *v.* [1960s+] (*US black*) to make one's money by a variety of schemes, not always legal ones.

scrambled eggs *n.*[1] [1940s+] **1** the gold braid that adorns a senior officer's cap. **2** a senior officer.

scrambled eggs *n.*[2] [rhy. sl.] [1990s+] the legs.

scramble grass *n.* [1960s+] (*US*) marijuana.

scrambler *n.* [1990s+] (*US drugs*) a low-level runner for a drug dealer.

scramble someone's eggs *v.* [1930s] (*US black*) to beat someone up, to kill.

scramboose *v.* (*also* **scrambooch**) [SCRAM *v.* (1) + VAMOOSE *v.* (1)] [1940s–60s] (*US*) to leave.

scrammy *n.* [dial. *scram*, withered] [mid–late 19C] (*Aus.*) one who has a withered or defective hand or arm.

IN PHRASES

❑ **chuck a scrammy** *v.* [mid–late 19C] (*Aus.*) to pretend to have a withered arm (so as to shirk work).

scran *n.* [ety. unknown; note RN jargon *scran*, rations] **1** [18C–19C] payment for food at an inn. **2** [early 18C+] (*also* **scrand, scranny, scrano**) food, esp. various bits of food, left-overs, 'broken victuals' etc, thrown together for an impromptu meal or a meal taken onto their job by a labourer.

IN COMPOUNDS

❑ **scran-bag** *n.* (*also* **scran-pocket**) [SE *bag*; note milit. jargon *scran-bag*, a haversack] [mid–late 19C] **1** a beggar's receptacle for the scraps of food they solicit. **2** any form of bag into which bits of food can be placed. ❑ **scran-basher** *n.* [1990s+] (*Aus.*) a cook. ❑ **scran-time** *n.* [early 18C+] a mealtime.

IN PHRASES

❑ **cold scran** *n.* [late 19C] something unappealling, distasteful, lit. 'cold food'.

IN EXCLAMATIONS

❑ **hard scran!** [mid-19C–1940s] (*Aus.*) bad luck (to you)!

scran *v.* [SCRAN *n.* (2)] **1** [mid-18C–mid-19C] to provide with food. **2** [mid-18C–mid-19C] to collect scraps of food to make up a meal. **3** [1990s+] to eat.

DERIVATIVES

❑ **scranning** *n.* [mid-19C] (*Scot.*) begging for scraps of food.

IN PHRASES

❑ **out on the scran** [mid-18C–mid-19C] in the position of begging for scraps of food.

scrap *n.*[1] (*also* **scrapp**) [SE *scrape*] [late 17C–mid-19C] a plot, a villainous scheme.

scrap *n.*[2] [? SE *scrape*] (*orig. boxing*) **1** [mid-19C+] (*also* **scrape, scrap-up**) a fight. **2** [20C+] a heated argument, a quarrel. **3** [1920s–40s] a military encounter.

scrap *v.* [SCRAP *n.*[2] (1)] **1** [mid-19C+] to fight, to box. **2** [late 19C+] to argue heatedly. **3** [1930s] to fight against. **4** [1950s] (*juv.*) to remove someone's trousers against their will.

scrape *n.* **1** [mid-19C–1900s] short shrift. **2** [mid-19C–1920s] a shave; a barber. **3** [mid-19C–1940s] butter. **4** [20C+] (*Irish*) a sexually complaisant woman. **5** [1960s+] (*also* **scraping, scrape job**) an abortion.

IN COMPOUNDS

❑ **scrape clinic** *n.* [1960s+] an abortion clinic. ❑ **scrape doctor** *n.* [1960s+] an abortionist.

IN PHRASES

❑ **bread and scrape** *n.* [mid-19C–1940s] bread and butter, esp. as offered in institutions.

scrape *v.* **1** [mid-19C–1960s] (*also* **scrape off the pavement, scrape the mug**) to shave. **2** [late 19C] (*US*) to vaccinate. **3** [1950s+] (*Aus.*) to have sexual intercourse [SCRAPER *n.* (4) suggests a much earlier use]. **4** [1970s+] (*US black/teen*) to have one's car lowered to such an extent that it scrapes the road and shoots up showers of sparks. **5** [1980s+] (*US*) to perform an abortion.

SE in slang uses

IN COMPOUNDS

❑ **scrape-all** *n.* [they *scrape* everything into their own hands/pocket] **1** [mid–late 17C] an unpleasant person. **2** [late 17C] a miser.

IN PHRASES

❑ **scrape Dixie** *v.* [DIXIE *n.* (1)] [1940s] (*US black*) to walk the streets of a Southern city or town in search of work. ❑ **scrape one's horns** *v. see under* HORN *n.*[2] (1). ❑ **scrape the barrel** *v.* (*also* **scrape the bottom of the barrel**) [20C+] **1** to make do with the most mediocre people, objects etc, simply because no others exist. **2** to utilize the very last of one's resources, irrespective of quality.

IN EXCLAMATIONS

❑ **go and scrape yourself!** [late 19C–1900s] a general excl. of dismissal or contempt. ❑ **go scrape!** [? trans. of Fr. *envoyer au grat*, to dismiss from employment, lit. 'to send grazing'] [early 17C] go away!

scraper *n.* **1** [late 18C–19C] (*also* **three-cornered scraper**) a cocked hat [its shape]. **2** [late 18C; 1920s–40s] (*also* **chin-scraper**) a barber. **3** [late 18C+] (*Irish US*) a foot; a shoe, usu. in phr. *TAKE TO ONE'S SCRAPERS* below. **4** [early 19C] the penis. **5** [mid-19C–1930s] a razor. **6** [late 19C] a cheating beggar, one who shams suffering.

IN PHRASES

❑ **take to one's scrapers** *v.* [late 18C–1960s] (*Irish*) to run off.

scraping castle *n.* [one 'scrapes' oneself clean; but note *CRAPPING CASTLE under* CRAPPING *n.*[2]] [mid-19C] a water closet, a lavatory.

scrap iron *n.* **1** as an alcoholic drink. (**a**) [1940s+] (*US*) homemade whisky, bad liquor. (**b**) [1990s+] (*UK prison*) a drink made of rubbing alcohol, mothballs and chlorine solution. **2** [1960s+] (*US prison*) weights, used for exercising and body-building.

scrapp *n. see* SCRAP *n.*[1].

scrapper *n.* [SCRAP *v.* (1)] **1** [mid-19C+] a fighter, a boxer, a brawler. **2** [late 19C] (*US tramp*) a victim of either tramps or criminals who 'puts up a fight'.

scrappy *adj.* [SCRAP *v.* (1)] [late 19C+] pugnacious, aggressive.

scratch *n.*[1] [mid-18C] (*UK Und.*) one mile.

scratch *n.*[2] [late 18C–mid-19C] a wig, designed to resemble the wearer's own hair.

scratch *n.*[3] [the image of scratching in the dirt for funds, scratching words on a page etc] **1** [mid-19C+] (*also* **scratch spread**) a letter. **2** [late 19C–1900s] the struggle to 'make ends meet'. **3** [1910s–50s] (*US Und.*) a bad cheque. **4** [1910s+] money; sometimes a small amount. **5** [1910s+] (*US*) a loan. **6** [1930s+] (*US*) publicity, a favourable mention in the media. **7** [1940s] an I.O.U. **8** [1940s] (*UK Und.*) silver in quantity. **9** [2000s] (*Irish*) dole; social security.

IN PHRASES

❑ **make a scratch** *v.* [1930s] to improve one's status. ❑ **no great scratch** [i.e. it makes little impression] [mid-19C] (*orig. US*) not much use, of no great importance.

scratch *v.* **1** [mid-19C+] (*Aus./US*) to leave or move at speed [one's tracks are scratched in the ground, but note Aus. cattleman use *scratch*, to rowel a horse with one's spurs]. **2** [mid-19C+] (*US Und.*) to forge banknotes or other documents; thus n. *scratch*, a forger. **3** in senses of SE *scratch*, to remove a horse (or dog) from those running in a given race. (**a**) [mid-19C+] to get rid of, to wipe out, e.g. a police record, a debt. (**b**) [late 19C+] (*US*) to kill, to murder. (**c**) [1960s] (*US prison*) to catch in the commission of a disciplinary offence. **4** in senses of SE *scratch for* (money). (**a**) [1920s+] (*US black*) to work. (**b**) [1940s] (*US black campus*) to hand over. **5** [1960s] of a man, to seduce, to have sexual intercourse.

IN COMPOUNDS

❑ **scratch-ass** *adj.* [-ASS *sfx*] [2000s] (*US*) impoverished. ❑ **scratchman** *n.* [1910s–60s] (*US Und.*) a forger.

IN PHRASES

❑ **on the scratch** [1950s] (*US Und.*) engaged in forgery. ❑ **scratch (around)** *v.* [20C+] (*orig. US*) to search for something, esp. when hard to find. ❑ **scratch gravel** *v.* (*also* **dig gravel, throw gravel**) [the image of wheels spinning furrows in the gravel] [mid-19C+] **1** (*Aus./US*) to work hard; thus n. *gravel-scratcher*, a working man. **2** (*also* **chuck up gravel, throw dust, throw gravel**) to leave hurriedly, to move very fast. ❑ **scratch it** *v.* [1910s–20s] to rush off. ❑ **scratch (off)** *v.* [SE *scratch*, to erase the name of (a person) from a list] [1910s+] (*Aus.*) to accept a resignation from a job. ❑ **scratch one's ass** *v.* (*also* **scratch oneself**) **1** [mid-19C+] to waste time, to daydream. **2** [1970s] (*US black*) to stop doing something.

IN EXCLAMATIONS

❑ **scratch!** [mid-19C+] (*Aus./US*) go away!

SE in slang uses

IN COMPOUNDS

❑ **scratch-cat** *n.* [1910s] (*N.Z.*) a bad-tempered woman. ❑ **scratch-crib** *n.* (*also* **scratch-pad**) [CRIB *n.*[1] (1); one scratches at the bites inflicted by bedbugs] [1940s] (*US black*) a cheap hotel or rooming house. ❑ **scratch house** *n.* [the scratching caused by bedbugs + HOUSE *n.*[1] (1)] **1** [late 19C+] a cheap hotel or lodging house; anywhere suffering an infestation of insects. **2** [1950s] a third-rate musical show, verging on burlesque. ❑ **Scratchland** *n.* [derog. image of Scotland as louse-ridden] [late 18C–early 19C] Scotland. ❑ **scratch-spread** *n.* [mid-19C] (*UK Und.*) a letter.

IN PHRASES

❑ **scratch the monkey** *v. see FEED THE MONKEY under* MONKEY *n.*

scratched *adj.* [early 17C; mid-19C] drunk.

scratcher *n.* **1** [early–mid-19C] (*Anglo-Irish*) a toe. **2** [early–mid-19C] (*Anglo-Irish*) a hand, usu. in pl.; fingers. **3** [early–mid-19C] (*US Und.*) a writer of begging letters. **4** [mid-19C–1940s] (*Anglo-Irish*) a forger, a counterfeiter. **5** [late 19C+] (*Anglo-Irish*) a match [prison use only by 1950s]. **6** [1940s+] (*Irish/Scot.*) a bed. **7** [1960s] (*US*) a writer, a journalist. **8** [1970s+] (*Irish*) a lottery scratch-card.

scratching *n.*[1] [the image is of a hen scratching the ground for food] [1930s+] (*Aus.*) **1** worried, bemused, in a quandary. **2** struggling for a living.

scratching *n.*[2] [SE *scratch*] [1950s–70s] (*US black*) writing.

scratch platter *n.* [SE *scratch*, impromptu + *platter*] [late 18C–early 19C] bread soaked in the dressing in which cucumbers have stood.

scraunched *adj.* (*also* **scronched**) [? dial. *scranched*, crushed or SE *scrunch*] [20C+] (*US*) drunk.

scrav *v.* [? SE *scavenge* + *scrape up*; note dial. *scravvle*, to grope with the hands] [1990s+] (*UK juv.*) to borrow or steal (usu. money); thus as n., the borrower or thief.

scream *n.* (*orig. US*) **1** [1900s–20s] an urgent message. **2** [1900s–50s] someone considered excellent, attractive. **3** [1910s–20s] a success. **4** [1920s] a fuss. **5** [1920s+] a good time. **6** [1920s+] the act of informing on or betraying a criminal accomplice. **7** [1930s+] a complaint, esp. against criminal activities or to the police. **8** [1930s+] an alarm, a hue and cry. **9** [1980s+] an appeal against conviction or sentence.

IN PHRASES

❑ **put the scream out** *v.* [1930s+] to put out an alert for someone.

SE in slang uses

(IN COMPOUNDS)

❑ **scream sheet** *n.* see *under* SHEET *n.*

(IN PHRASES)

❑ **at full scream** *adv.* [20C+] **1** (*US black*) with total commitment, no holds barred. **2** (*UK Und.*) at the highest estimate. ❑ **old scream** *n.* [1920s] a person; usu. as a term of address.

scream *v.* **1** [1920s+] to inform, usu. to the police but occas. against them. **2** [1950s+] to complain. **3** [1960s+] (*US black*) to engage in verbal confrontation. **4** [1970s+] (*US gay*) to be obviously homosexual.

(IN PHRASES)

❑ **scream cold** *v.* (*also* **scream foul, ...hard**) [1980s] (*US black*) to use language that is likely to cause a fight. ❑ **scream (down) some heavy lines** *v.* [HEAVY *adj.* (5c) + LINE *n.*[1] (2b)] [1970s+] (*US black*) **1** to impress with one's smart talk. **2** to debate or argue intensely and emotionally. ❑ **scream on** *v.* **1** [1960s–70s] (*US black*) to betray a confidence, to inform against, to gossip about. **2** [1960s+] (*US black*) to attack verbally. **3** [1970s] to embarrass. **4** [1970s+] (*US gay*) to pick a fight; to be very keen on (something). ❑ **scream out** *v.* [1990s+] to criticize, to tell off, to reprimand.

SE in slang uses

(IN PHRASES)

❑ **make someone scream** *v.* [the screams are of orgasmic bliss] [1980s+] (*US campus*) to have sexual intercourse with someone. ❑ **screaming for it** *adj.* [1960s+] desperate for sexual intercourse, usu. but not invariably of a woman. ❑ **scream oneself into fits** *v.* [mid-19C+] to become hysterical. ❑ **scream the place down** *v.* [1930s+] (*orig. Und.*) to report a burglary.

scream and holler *n.* (*also* **scream and hollar**) [rhy. sl.] [1930s+] (*US Und.*) a dollar.

screamer *n.* **1** in fig. uses, implying something or someone exceptional or egregious. (**a**) [early 19C+] (*orig. US*) anything or anyone exceptional, in size, attractiveness, wit etc. (**b**) [mid-19C] a serious and unpleasant situation. (**c**) [mid–late 19C] (*orig. US*) a thrilling or funny story, a 'screaming' farce. (**d**) [1970s+] (*US campus*) anything exceptionally challenging, difficult, esp. work. (**e**) [1980s+] something horrifying. **2** a person who lit. or fig. 'screams'. (**a**) [mid-19C] a ballad singer. (**b**) [mid–late 19C] (*orig. US*) a teller of exaggerated or very funny stories. (**c**) [1920s+] an informer [SCREAM *v.* (1)]. (**d**) [1940s+] (*also* **screamer and creamer**) a woman who screams or otherwise makes a good deal of noise during intercourse [CREAM *v.* (1)]. (**e**) [1960s+] (*orig. gay*) a flagrant homosexual. **3** an object which lit. or fig. 'screams'. (**a**) [late 19C+] an exclamation mark. (**b**) [late 19C+] a powerful shot in a game, e.g. of cricket, golf, hockey. (**c**) [20C+] (*US*) a sensational newspaper headline or story. (**d**) [20C+] (*US*) a conspicuous advertisement. (**e**) [1900s] a sensational or propagandist piece of writing. (**f**) [1930s–60s] (*US Und.*) an arrest warrant. (**g**) [1960s+] (*US black*) a siren, esp. on a police car.

screaming *adj.* [SE *scream*; note 19C Adelphi Theatre playbills, which advertised a 'screaming farce'] **1** [mid-19C–1940s] first-rate, splendid. **2** [mid-19C+] very funny. **3** [mid-19C+] a general intensifier. **4** [1910s+] (*US black*) fantastic, amazing, extreme. **5** [1920s] (*US*) of clothing, loudly patterned or coloured. **6** [1930s+] (*gay*) blatantly homosexual.

as a general intensifier

(IN COMPOUNDS)

❑ **screaming abdabs** *n.* see *under* ABDABS *n.* ❑ **screaming fairy** *n.* (*also* **screaming faggot, ...queen**) [FAIRY *n.*[1] (3)/FAGGOT *n.*[1] (3)/QUEEN *n.* (2)] [1940s+] an ostentatiously effeminate homosexual man. ❑ **screaming meemies** *n.* see *under* MEEMIES *n.* ❑ **screaming uglies** *n.* [1980s+] (*US campus*) an extremely messy or ugly look.

(IN PHRASES)

❑ **screaming blue murder** *n.* see *under* BLUE MURDER *n.*

(IN EXCLAMATIONS)

❑ **screaming yellow zonkers!** [1970s] a general excl.

SE in slang uses

(IN COMPOUNDS)

❑ **screaming eagle** *n.* [the image engraved on it] [1940s+] (*US*) a GI discharge button, issued after WW2. ❑ **screaming gasser** *n.* [1940s] (*US black*) a police car moving at speed and sounding its siren.

screamy *adj.* [used of something that fig. SE *screams*] **1** [late 19C] extreme, exaggerated, undignified; of colour, glaring, violent. **2** [1970s] (*gay*) pertaining to a flamboyant, effeminate homosexual man.

screave *n.* see SCREEVE *n.*

screech *n.* **1** [20C+] (*US*) cheap, rotgut whisky. **2** [1900s] a hit, a success. **3** [1970s+] (*gay*) the throat, the mouth.

(DERIVATIVES)

❑ **screechers** *adj.* [20C+] (*US*) drunk. ❑ **screeching** *adj.* [1920s] (*US*) drunk.

screecher *n.* [mid-19C] (*Irish*) a jorum of hot punch.

screechie *v.* (*also* **screechy**) [var. on SE *squeak by*] [1950s+] (*W.I. Rasta*) to sneak by; to move stealthily.

screeching *adj.* [play on HOWLING *adj.* (1)] [mid-19C–1900s] (*Aus./US*) extreme, complete.

screemies *n.* see MEEMIES *n.*

screen *n.*[1] [? SCREEVE *n.* (1)] **1** [late 18C–19C] a banknote. **2** [early 19C] (*also* **flash screen**) a counterfeit note.

screen *n.*[2] **1** [1930s] (*US prison*) in pl., constr. with *the*, an isolation cell for psychotic prisoners with a mesh screen. **2** [1960s+] (*US black*) a television.

screeve *n.* (*also* **screave, scrieve, scrive**) [? Scot. *scrieve*, to read or write quickly or continuously; or SCREEVE *v.* (2) although sense 1 here predates] **1** [late 18C–1940s] a letter; a note. **2** [early–mid-19C] (*UK Und.*) a banknote, a guinea or a pound sterling. **3** [mid-19C] a chalk drawing on the pavement. **4** [mid-19C] a begging letter. **5** [mid–late 19C] a counterfeit banknote.

(IN PHRASES)

❑ **fake a screeve** *v.* [FAKE *v.*[1] (1) + SCREEVE *n.* (4)] [19C] to write a (begging) letter.

screeve *v.* [Ital. *scrivere*, ult. Lat. *scribere*, to write] **1** [mid-19C] to draw on the pavement with chalk. **2** [mid-19C–1930s] to write, esp. to write fraudulent documents or letters.

(IN PHRASES)

❑ **screeve a fakement** *v.* [mid-19C] to concoct or write a begging letter or any other document aimed to extract money by trickery.

screever *n.* (*also* **screeve, scriever, scrivener**) [SCREEVE *v.*] **1** [mid-19C] a begging letter. **2** [mid–late 19C] a writer of begging letters. **3** [mid-19C–1940s] a pavement artist, who draws in coloured chalks on the paving stones.

(IN PHRASES)

❑ **shallow screever** *n.* [mid–late 19C] a pavement artist.

screigh *n.* [ety. unknown; ? Scot. *screigh*, screech, cf. SCREECH *n.* (1)] [19C] (*Scot.*) whisky.

screw *n.*[1] **1** in sexual contexts [SCREW *v.* (1)]. (**a**) [18C–early 19C] a prostitute. (**b**) [mid-19C+] an act of sexual intercourse; also in fig. use. (**c**) [mid-19C+] one's partner in intercourse, esp. as a *good screw* or *bad screw*; usu. applied to a woman. (**d**) [1960s] (*US*) a synon. for FUCK *n.* (**e**) [1960s–70s] a swindle. (**f**) [1960s+] a dismissive and pej. ref. to a woman, relegating her to the status of a pure sex object. **2** with reference to a key or lock. (**a**) [late 18C+] (*UK Und.*) (*also* **skeleton screw**) a (skeleton) key. (**b**) [early 19C] a robbery achieved with a skeleton key. (**c**) [early 19C+] (*also* **bull-screw, screwsman**) a turnkey; a prison warder. (**d**) [1980s+] (*US*) a police officer. **3** in terms meaning hard tasks or taskmasters. (**a**) [19C] (*US campus*) a particularly demanding instructor. (**b**) [19C; 1970s] (*US campus*) the essays and examinations they set. (**c**) [mid–late 19C] a miser [? they *screw down* their money or *screw* it out of creditors]. (**d**) [1900s] (*Aus.*) a station overseer. **4** [mid-19C–

1910s] an old and/or broken-down horse [? racing jargon *screw*, to force a horse to the front; thus a horse can be made to gain a better than expected place; note late 19C local New Orleans *screw*, a fool]. **5** in senses of SE *screw out of*, i.e. one's employer. (**a**) [mid-19C+] wages, salary. (**b**) [1900s] pocket money. (**c**) [1960s–70s] a swindle. **6** [late 19C] a pick-me-up, a tonic [it 'pulls one together']. **7** [20C+] (*orig. Aus.*) a look, a stare, a gaze, esp. a challenging one. **8** [1900s] (*Aus.*) an unpleasant old woman.

pertaining to sex

IN COMPOUNDS

❑ **screwdriver** *n.* see separate entry.

IN PHRASES

❑ **dry screw** *n.* see separate entry. ❑ **still-screw** *n.* [1920s] (*US black*) an upright act of sexual intercourse while slow-dancing. ❑ **three screws** *n.* [brandname, *Three Screws* + pun on sense 1b above] [1920s+] (*Can.*) an aluminium container holding three condoms. ❑ **throw someone a screw** *v.* [1940s] to have sexual intercourse with.

pertaining to a key or lock

DERIVATIVES

❑ **screwess** *n.* [1980s+] (*Aus. prison*) a female prison officer.

IN COMPOUNDS

❑ **screwdriver** *n.* see separate entry. ❑ **screwman** *n.* [1930s–50s] a thief, a burglar. ❑ **screwsman** *n.* **1** [19C+] a skilled house-breaker. **2** [mid-19C] (*UK prison*) a warder, a turnkey.

IN PHRASES

❑ **big screw** *n.* [1920s–30s] (*US prison*) the Deputy Warden. ❑ **fake a screw** *v.* [FAKE *v.*[1] (1)] [19C] to make a skeleton key. ❑ **screw on wheels** *n.* [1980s+] (*Aus. prison*) a parole officer. ❑ **superscrew** *n.* [1980s+] (*Aus. prison*) an over-officious warder. ❑ **under the screw** [mid-19C] in prison.

general uses

IN PHRASES

❑ **have a screw at** *v.* (*also* **give a screw at, take a screw at**) [1910s+] **1** to stare, to survey. **2** (*orig. Aus.*) to stare at in aggressive manner. ❑ **royal screw** *n.* [ROYAL *adj.* (1) + SCREWING *n.* (2a)] [1950s–60s] (*US*) an act of extreme harshness or unfairness, as meted out on oneself or to another person.

SE in slang uses

DERIVATIVES

❑ **screws, the** *n.* [SE *screw*; the pains it causes] [late 19C+] rheumatism, sciatica, fibrositis.

IN PHRASES

❑ **have a screw loose** *v.* (*also* **drop a screw, have screws loose**) **1** [19C] to be on bad terms. **2** [early 19C] to be unwell. **3** [early 19C–1920s] to have something wrong in the condition of things; a dangerous weakness in some arrangement; also of a person and their behaviour; usu. as *there's a screw loose somewhere*. **4** [early 19C+] to be eccentric, insane or retarded. ❑ **have someone by the screws** *v.* see *HAVE SOMEONE BY THE BALLS under* BALLS *n.* ❑ **lose a screw** *v.* [1960s] to be insane. ❑ **put a screw into** *v.* [1910s] (*Aus.*) to hit. ❑ **put on the screw** *v.* [SE *screw*, that which tightens] [mid-19C] to set a limit on someone's credit. ❑ **put the screws on** *v.* (*also* **get one's screws into, put on the screws, put the screws to**) [SE *thumbscrews*] [early 19C+] to pressurize. ❑ **put under the screw** *v.* [*PUT THE SCREWS ON* above] [early–mid-19C] to coerce, to compel, to force. ❑ **under the screws** [SE *thumbscrews*] [early 19C] under pressure.

screw *n.*[2] [*HAVE A SCREW LOOSE under* SCREW *n.*[1]] [1950s+] a mad person.

IN COMPOUNDS

❑ **screwball** see separate entries. ❑ **screw factory** *n.* [1970s] a psychiatric hospital.

IN PHRASES

❑ **loose screw** *n.* [early 19C+] an eccentric.

screw *n.*[3] [Afk. *abskroef*, screws; ? i.e. they are part of something larger] [2000s] (*S.Afr. township*) a minor criminal gang.

screw *v.* **1** [mid-17C; late 19C] to render drunk [SCREWED *adj.* (1)]. **2** as a synon. for FUCK *v.* (**a**) [early 18C+] to have sexual intercourse; poss. the most common example of the equation sex = violence. (**b**) [mid-18C+] (*orig. US*) (*also* **screw out of, screw with**) to cheat, to swindle, to take advantage of, to treat badly or unfairly. (**c**) [1930s+] used as a synon./euph. for FUCK *v.* in a variety of senses and parts of speech, e.g. *screw the government! screw you!* (**d**) [1940s+] (*orig. US*) to ruin, to pervert, to upset. (**e**) [1960s+] to hurt. (**f**) [1960s+] (*US*) to sodomize. **3** (*US campus*) in terms based on SE *screw*, to pressurize. (**a**) [19C] to subject a student to an extremely searching examination. (**b**) [1960s] to fail a test or examination. **4** in senses of SCREW *n.*[1] (2). (**a**) [early 19C+] to break into, to rob, orig. with a skeleton key. (**b**) [mid-19C] to lock, e.g. a door, a moneybox. (**c**) [1920s] to escape by unlocking a door. **5** [mid-19C] to act like a miser [SCREW *n.*[1] (3c)]. **6** in the context of movement. (**a**) [late 19C+] (*US*) to run off, to leave; also as imper. *screw*, go away. (**b**) [1980s] to drive, to travel about. **7** [20C+] (*orig. Aus.*) in senses of 'screwing up the eyes'. (**a**) to survey, to look at an object. (**b**) to stare intently at someone. **8** (*W.I./UK black teen*) in senses of facial contortion. (**a**) [1980s+] to crumple up one's face in annoyance, tightly puckering the lips and features into a vexed look. (**b**) [1990s+] to complain, to make a fuss. (**c**) [2000s] to vilify, to humiliate.

pertaining to sex

IN PHRASES

❑ **screw-and-spew movie** *n.* [SE *spew*] [1980s] a pornographic film depicting extreme violence. ❑ **screw around** *v.* [1950s+] (*orig. US*) to act in a promiscuous manner. ❑ **screw off** *v.* [20C+] (*US*) to masturbate. ❑ **screw oneself silly** *v.* [2000s] to indulge in sexual intercourse excessively. ❑ **screw the arse off** *v.* (*also* **screw the ass off, screw the socks off**) [ARSE *n.* (4)] [1940s+] to indulge in aggressive, vigorous copulation.

pertaining to cheating or swindling

IN PHRASES

❑ **get screwed** *v.* [mid-18C+] (*orig. US*) to be swindled or cheated. ❑ **screw out of** *v.* [1970s+] (*orig. US*) to defraud, to cheat, to deceive. ❑ **screw over** *v.* [1970s+] to cheat, to swindle, to treat badly or harshly. ❑ **screw-your-buddy week** *n.* see *FRIG-YOUR-BUDDY WEEK under* FRIG *v.* ❑ **super-screwing** *v.* [SUPER *n.*[2] (1)] [mid-19C] (*UK Und.*) watch-stealing.

negative terms

IN COMPOUNDS

❑ **screwnut** *n.* [SCREW UP *v.* (5) + NUT *n.*[2] (1)] [1990s+] (*UK juv.*) a failure, a blunderer.

IN PHRASES

❑ **screw around** *v.* [1930s+] (*orig. US*) **1** to mess about, to waste time. **2** to annoy someone, to mess someone around; usu. as *screw around with*. ❑ **screw the pooch** *v.* (*also* **screw the dog**) [SE *dog*/POOCH *n.*; *see FUCK THE DOG (AND SELL THE PUPS) under* DOG *n.*[2]] [1960s+] to waste time; to blunder badly. ❑ **screw up** see separate entries. ❑ **screw with** *v.* [1950s] to annoy, to challenge.

IN EXCLAMATIONS

❑ **go screw yourself!** (*also* **go screw!**) [20C+] a general excl. of dismissal. ❑ **screw it!** [euph. for FUCK IT! *excl.*] [1940s+] the hell with it! forget it! ❑ **screw you!** [1950s+] (*US*) an excl. of dismissal, contempt.

pertaining to robbery

DERIVATIVES

❑ **screwable** *adj.* [early 19C+] suitable for a robbery. ❑ **screwer** *n.* [1930s–50s] (*UK Und.*) **1** a thief, a burglar. **2** burglary.

IN PHRASES

❑ **screw a chat** *v.* [CHEAT *n.* (1)] [late 19C] (*UK Und.*) to break into a house.

pertaining to departure

IN PHRASES

❑ **screw off** *v.* **1** [1950s+] to take time off work or duty.

2 [1960s+] to leave, to depart. ❑ **screw out** *v.* [mid-20C+ uses seem to be a euph. for FUCK OFF *v.* (1), but early ones may be autonomous] [late 19C+] (*orig. US*) to leave, to depart.

pertaining to staring

IN PHRASES

❑ **who you screwin'?** [1960s+] an aggressive question aimed at someone who is staring, or perhaps is not, but with whom the speaker wishes to challenge.

pertaining to facial contortion

IN COMPOUNDS

❑ **screwface** *n.* [1980s+] (*W.I./UK black teen*) one whose face is crumpled up in annoyance; thus *Old Screwface*, the devil.

SE in slang uses

IN COMPOUNDS

❑ **screw-lucky** *adj.* [1960s] (*US*) having good fortune, without any hinderances.

IN PHRASES

❑ **come unscrewed** *v.* [ref. to HAVE ONE'S HEAD SCREWED ON below] [1930s+] to go mad. ❑ **have one's head screwed on** *v.* (*also* **have one's head screwed on right, ...the right way, have one's bobbin screwed on, ...cranium..., ...headpiece..., ...nut...**) [early 19C+] to be aware, to understand, to know what's what. ❑ **screw face** *v.* [1990s+] (*US campus*) to pretend. ❑ **screw it on** *v.* [SE *screw*, to tighten] [1960s+] to drive one's car or motorcycle very fast. ❑ **screw one's nut** *v.* [NUT *n.*[1] (1)] **1** [late 19C] to dodge a blow aimed at one's head. **2** [1900s–20s] (*US*) to turn around, to leave, to go. **3** [1930s–70s] to think hard. **4** [1960s] to behave in a crazy, poss. violent, manner. ❑ **unscrew** *v.* [mid-19C] (*UK Und.*) to break, e.g. a trunk, open.

screw! *excl.* [1950s+] a euph. for FUCK! *excl.*

screwball *n.* (*also* **screwbox**) [baseball use *screwball*, a ball pitched with reverse spin against the natural curve] **1** [1930s+] (*orig. US*) an eccentric, an out-of-the-ordinary person. **2** [1950s] nonsense.

screwball *adj.* [SCREWBALL *n.*] [1930s+] (*orig. US*) **1** (*also* **screwballed**) of a person, eccentric, mad, crazy. **2** of a thing or procedure, bizarre, eccentric.

screwdriver *n.* [1970s+] **1** (*Aus./UK prison*) a principal officer who 'drives' his subordinates [SCREW *n.*[1] (2c)]. **2** the penis [SCREW *n.*[1] (1) + pun].

screwed *adj.* **1** [mid-19C+] drunk. **2** in senses of SCREW *v.* (2b). (**a**) [late 19C+] in trouble. (**b**) [1940s+] (*also* **scrod**) cheated, deceived. **3** [late 19C+] (*Aus./US*) (*also* **screwed out**) worn out with hard work.

IN PHRASES

❑ **half-screwed** *adj.* [mid-19C+] tipsy. ❑ **screwed, blued and tattooed** *adj.* (*also* **screwed, jewed and tattooed; stewed, screwed and tattooed**) [SCREW *v.* (1) + ? *blewed*, robbed + SE *tattooed*, to be repeatedly struck] [1940s–70s] **1** (*US*) comprehensively defeated; suffering very great harm. **2** an excl. of delight. ❑ **screwed up** *adj.* [abbr. phr. *screwed up in a corner*] **1** [late 19C] in serious financial difficulties. **2** [late 19C–1910s] (*US*) emotionally stimulated with alcohol, drunk. **3** [20C+] in a mess, out of order, malfunctioning. **4** [1930s+] neurotic, very miserable, anxious. **5** [1960s] absurd, improbable, unlikely.

screwing *n.* **1** [mid-19C+] UK Und. uses [SCREW *v.*]. (**a**) house-breaking. (**b**) (*also* **screwing job**) an act of burglary. **2** as synons. of FUCKING *n.* (**a**) [late 19C+] punishment; harsh or unfair treatment. (**b**) [20C+] sexual intercourse. (**c**) [1940s+] cheating, fooling, deceiving.

screwing *adj.* [1960s] a synon. of FUCKING *adj.*

screwnoodleous *adj.* [ext. of SCREWED *adj.* (1)] [late 19C] drunk.

screw-off *n.* [SCREW OFF *under* SCREW *v.*] [1940s+] (*US*) an idler, a loafer.

Screws, the *n.* see NEWS OF THE SCREWS *n.*

screws me *phr.* [joc. mispron.] [1970s+] (*US campus*) excuse me.

screw-up *n.* [SCREW UP *v.*] **1** [1920s+] of an object, plan or scheme, a disaster. **2** [1960s+] (*orig. US*) of a person, a failure, an incompetent.

screw up *v.* **1** [late 18C–early 19C] to cheat, to defraud; to drive a very hard bargain. **2** [early 19C] to imprison [SCREW *n.*[1] (2)]. **3** [mid-19C; 1940s+] (*orig. US*) to make trouble, to cause difficulties for. **4** [mid–late 19C] to garrotte [SE *screw up*, to tighten]. **5** [1930s+] (*orig. US*) to make a mess, to blunder badly. **6** [1940s] (*US*) to confuse, to perturb. **7** [1950s+] to hurt, to put out of order.

IN PHRASES

❑ **screw up (with)** *v.* [1960s] (*US*) to get involved with, associated with.

screwy *adj.* **1** [mid-19C] drunk [SCREWED *adj.* (1)]. **2** [mid-19C] worn out [SCREWED *adj.* (3)]. **3** [mid–late 19C] mean. **4** (*orig. US*) in senses derived from HAVE A SCREW LOOSE *under* SCREW *n.*[1]. (**a**) [late 19C+] foolish, stupid, insane. (**b**) [1920s+] odd, strange. (**c**) [1930s] (*US*) suspicious, alarmed. (**d**) [1930s+] illegal; counterfeit. **5** [1940s+] weak, malfunctioning.

-screwy *sfx see* -CRAZY *sfx.*

scribble one's teeth *v. see under* TEETH *n.*

scribe *n.* **1** [mid-19C+] a writer. **2** [late 19C+] (*US*) a newspaperman. **3** [1930s–40s] (*UK Und.*) a forger. **4** [1930s–60s] (*US black*) a letter. **5** [1940s] (*US black*) a young woman.

scribe *v.* [1960s+] to write.

scribing-gloak *n.* [GLOAK *n.* (1)] [mid–late 18C] (*UK Und.*) a clerk.

scrieve *n. see* SCREEVE *n.*

scriever *n. see* SCREEVER *n.*

scrilla *n.* (*also* **scrill, skrilla**) [? Sp.] [1990s+] (*US black teen*) money.

IN COMPOUNDS

❑ **scrilla monger** *n.* [2000s] (*US black*) someone who does whatever they can to get money.

IN PHRASES

❑ **gotta get me scrill on** [1990s+] (*US black teen*) I must find some cash.

scrilling *n.* (*also* **skrilling**) [SCRILLA *n.*] [1990s+] (*US black*) **1** wasting time, lounging around with friends. **2** making money.

scrimy *adj.* [? SE *scratchy* (i.e. from fleas/bed-bugs) + *grimy*] [1920s–40s] (*US*) unpleasant, dirty, run-down.

scrip *n.*[1] [SE *scrip*, a scrap of paper or a certificate of indebtedness, as issued to workers in lieu of actual cash] [1900s–40s] (*US*) $1.

scrip *n.*[2] [abbr.] [1920s+] (*drugs*) a pre*scrip*tion.

scripper *n.* (*also* **scrippet**) [? Lat. *scripsit*, he wrote, and poss. referring to written instructions given to this member of the gang] [late 16C–early 17C] (*UK Und.*) the member of a team of highway robbers who keeps a watch.

script *n.* [abbr.] **1** [1920s+] (*drugs*) a pre*scrip*tion for narcotics. **2** [1980s] pre*scrip*tion drugs.

IN COMPOUNDS

❑ **script doctor** *n.* [1920s+] (*drugs*) one who prescribes. ❑ **script mill** *n.* [MILL *n.*[1] (1)] [1990s+] (*US drugs*) a doctor's surgery where, for a price, one can obtain prescriptions for narcotics, painkillers etc.

scripture-tickler *n.* [late 19C] (*Aus.*) a preacher, a clergyman.

scrive *n. see* SCREEVE *n.*

scriveners *n.*

IN PHRASES

❑ **go to the scriveners (and learn to make indentures)** *v.* [mid-17C] to get drunk.

scrob *v.* [SCROBY *n.*] [1910s] to thrash, to beat hard.

scroby *n.* (*also* **scrobe**) [? dial. *scrobble*, a quarrel, a problem, a scratching] [late 18C–19C] (*UK Und.*) a judicial flogging; thus *scrobe*, one who is to be flogged.

scrod *adj. see* SCREWED *adj.* (1).

scrog *n.* [1970s] (*N.Z.*) snacks, food.

scrog *v.* (*also* **scrogg**) [var. on SCREW *v.* (1)] [1980s+] (*US campus*) to have sexual intercourse.

scroll *v.* [mid-19C] (*UK Und.*) to write.

DERIVATIVES

❑ **scroller** *n.* [mid-19C] (*UK Und.*) one who can write.

scronch *n.* (*also* **schronch**) [SCRONCH *v.* (1)] [1920s–30s] a dance.

scronch *v.* [SE *scrunch*, the proximity of the dancers] **1** [1920s–30s] to dance. **2** [1940s] in fig. use, to participate in any activity.

scronched *adj. see* SCRAUNCHED *adj.*

scronchous *adj. see* SCRUMPTIOUS *adj.* (2).

scrooch *v. see* SCRUNCH *v.*

scrooched *adj.* [Yorks. dial. *scrooch*, to crouch] [1920s] (*US*) drunk.

scroodge *v. see* SCROUGE *v.*

scroof *n.* (*Irish*) **1** [17C; 1910s] a crust of bread [16C *scruff*, a thin crust]. **2** [1990s+] dandruff [SE *scurf*]. **3** [1990s+] unpleasant people, scum [SE *scruff*, someone worthless].

scroof *v.* [? SE *scrounge* + *off*] [19C–1920s] to sponge off.

scrooge (up) *v. see* SCROUGE *v.*

scroogie *n.* [abbr.] [1990s+] (*US Und*) a *screw*driver.

scrooly *adj.* [? var. on SCREWY *adj.* (1)] [1940s] (*US*) mad.

scrootch *v. see* SCROUGE *v.*

scrope *n.* [proper name of Sir John *Scrope*, secretary of the Treasury 1724–52] [18C–early 19C] (*UK Und.*) a farthing.

scrote *n.* (*also* **scroat, scrot, scrotum**) [abbr. SE *scrotum*] [1970s+] a general term of abuse.

scroucher *n.* (*also* **scrouger, scrousher, scrowcher**) [? SE *scrounger*, dial. *scringer*, one who pries around looking for trifles or dial. *skreenger*, one who is (negatively) energetic] [20C+] (*Aus.*) a general derog. term for a person.

scrouge *n.* (*also* **scrowge**) [SCROUGE *v.* (1)] [mid-19C] **1** a crowd, a crush. **2** (*US campus*) anything, e.g. a tedious lesson, considered unpleasant.

scrouge *v.* (*also* **scroodge, scrooge (up), scrootch, scrowge, skrowdge**) [? 16C SE *scruze*, to squeeze] **1** [mid-18C+] to encroach on a person's space, to crowd, to push forward in a crowd. **2** [early 19C+] to push something out of the way, to squeeze a thing. **3** [mid-19C] (*US campus*) of a teacher, to impose unpleasant tasks.

scrouged *adj.* (*also* **scrowged**) [SCROUGE *v.* (1)] [mid-18C+] crowded.

scrouger *n.*[1] (*also* **scrouge**) [SCROUGE *n.*] [mid-19C] (*orig. US*) something or someone large or forceful.

scrouger *n.*[2] *see* SCROUCHER *n.*

scrounge *n.* **1** [1910s] a search, a hunt. **2** [1930s+] (*US*) (*also* **scrounger**) a general derog. term; lit. one who scrounges.

scroungy *adj.* (*also* **scroungy-ass**) [colloq. *scrounge*, i.e. something that has been cadged] [20C+] (*US*) inferior, second-rate, grubby.

scrouperize *v.* [SE *scroop*, to rub against] [mid-17C–early 18C] to have sexual intercourse.

scrousher *n.* [? colloq. *scrounge*] (*Aus./N.Z.*) **1** [mid–late 19C] a worn-out prospector. **2** [20C+] a prostitute. **3** *see* SCROUCHER *n.*

scrowcher *n. see* SCROUCHER *n.*

scrowge *v. see* SCROUGE *v.*

scrub *n.*[1] [SE *scrub*, an insignificant, unattractive person] **1** [late 17C+] a general pej. term, a lout, a failure, a dirty or unpleasant person or thing. **2** [18C+] a low-class prostitute. **3** [early 18C] (*UK Und.*) a low-class thief. **4** [mid-18C–early 19C] one who does not pay their share of the tavern bill. **5** [mid-19C+] (*US*) a derog. term for a black person. **6** [late 19C] (*US*) a beggar who is willing to perform occasional paid work, usu. as a 'shabbos goy', performing work that orthodox Jews may not do on the Sabbath. **7** [1910s+] (*US black*) a fool. **8** [1990s+] (*US teen*) a sponger, a parasite. **9** [2000s] (*US teen*) an exploitative womanizer.

DERIVATIVES

❑ **scrubbish** *adj.* [late 17C+] unpleasant.

scrub *n.*[2] (*Aus.*) with ref. to the SAusE *scrub*.

IN COMPOUNDS

❑ **scrub bull** *n.* [SAusE *scrub bull*, a bull that was bred in, or escaped into, the wild] [1950s+] (*Aus.*) a solo prospector, living out in the desert and characterized by surliness, taciturnity and general misanthropy. ❑ **scrub cockie** *n.* (*also* **scrub cocky**) [COCKY *n.*[2] (1)] [20C+] (*Aus.*) a small farmer working tree-covered or otherwise rough land. ❑ **scrub-dangler** *n.* [late 19C–1910s] (*Aus.*) a wild bullock. ❑ **scrub-dashing** *n.* [1940s–50s] (*Aus.*) the act of riding through bush or scrub in pursuit of strayed cattle or horses. ❑ **scrub turkey** *n.* **1** [1950s–70s] (*Aus.*) an itinerant who moves around the Australian bush, whose long absence from urban life may have rendered them slightly eccentric. **2** [1950s+] a contemptible woman.

scrub *adj.* [1900s–50s] (*US*) second-rate.

scrub *v.* [SE *scrub out*] **1** [early–mid-19C; 1940s+] (*orig. US*) to cancel, to wipe out, to forget. **2** [1940s] of a lover, to abandon. **3** [1980s] to kill. **4** [1980s+] (*US campus*) to fail. **5** [2000s] (*US teen*) to trip or fall down.

IN PHRASES

❑ **scrub along** *v.* [mid-19C+] to survive with difficulty.

IN EXCLAMATIONS

❑ **scrub it!** [1940s+] forget it! ignore it! cancel it!

SE in slang uses

IN PHRASES

❑ **scrub up well** *v.* [1980s] (*Aus.*) of a man, to look presentable despite being in the aftermath of a drunken night out; of a woman, to show good dress sense. ❑ **scrub the kitchen** *v. see* *CLEAN UP THE KITCHEN under* KITCHEN *n.*[1].

scrubbado *n.* (*also* **scrubado**) [SE *scrub*, 'the itch' + Sp./Port. sfx *-ado*, thus giving underpinning of racist stereotyping] **1** [mid-17C–early 19C] 'the itch', venereal disease. **2** [late 18C–mid-19C] (*UK Und.*) (*also* **screwbado**) a general term of abuse.

scrubber *n.* [SE *scrub*, heavily wooded country, whether growing small or large bushes and trees; *scrubber*, one who lives in the woods or wooded countryside is SAusE] **1** [mid-19C–1910s] (*Aus./N.Z.*) a rough, unkempt person; by ext. an outsider. **2** [mid-19C+] a cow or horse that has run wild in the scrub and has deteriorated in condition. **3** [1940s+] an unpleasant weakling. **4** in derog. terms for a woman [? SE *scrubber*, a charwoman, one who scrubs; orig. sl. use was in jazz community, where it described 'a girl who slept with a jazzman but for her own satisfaction as much as his' (George Melly, *Owning Up*, 1965). ? link to Aus. term, defined as 'a mare that runs wild in the scrub country, copulating indiscriminately with stray stallions' (quote cited in *OED*)]. (**a**) [1950s+] a promiscuous woman, usu. young. (**b**) [1960s+] (*Irish*) a common working-class woman, with no sexual implications.

scrubbing brush *n.* **1** [mid-19C+] the pubic hair. **2** [late 19C–1920s] (*Aus.*) a loaf of bread made from inferior materials.

scrubby *adj.* [SCRUB *n.*[1]] **1** [19C] (*US campus*) vulgar, ill-bred, mean. **2** [1960s] promiscuous.

Scrubs, the *n.* [abbr.] [20C+] (*UK police/Und.*) Wormwood *Scrubs* prison, London.

scrud *n.* [ext. of CRUD *n.* (1c)] **1** [1930s+] (*US, orig. milit.*) a painful disease, esp. a venereal disease. **2** [1990s+] (*UK juv.*) the junior members of a school.

scrudge *n.* [SCROUGE *v.* (1), from her approaching one in a crowd] [18C] a prostitute.

scruff *n.* [dial. *scruff*, refuse, thus human refuse in dial. use since mid-19C; ult. SE *scurf*] **1** [1950s+] an unkempt, messy person, also a term of abuse. **2** [1990s+] pornographic literature.

IN COMPOUNDS

❑ **scruff-bag** *n.* [1920s+] **1** a down-and-out. **2** a messy, unkempt creature. ❑ **scruff-hound** *n.* [-HOUND *sfx* (1)] [1940s] a rough, tough individual.

scruff *adj.* [SCRUFF *n.* (1)] [1950s] messy, unkempt.

scruff *v.* [dial. *scruff*, the nape of the neck] **1** [19C] to hang. **2** [mid-19C–1940s] (*Aus.*) to grab by the scruff of the neck. **3** [mid-19C–1940s] (*Aus.*) to attack, to manhandle.

scrum *n.* (*also* **scrummy**) [rhy. sl. = THRUMS *n.*] [late 19C–1900s] (*Aus./N.Z.*) a threepenny piece.

scrum *adj. see* SCRUMPTIOUS *adj.* (2).

scrumdolious *adj.* (*also* **scrumbotious**) [1910s–30s] wonderful, excellent, often but not always of food.

scrummy *adj.* [? misreading of CRUMMY *adj.*[2] (1)] [1910s] (*N.Z.*) lice-ridden.

scrump *n.* [SCRUMP *v.*[2]] [1990s+] (*US black/campus*) sexual intercourse.

scrump *v.*[1] [dial. *scrump*, anything withered or dried up; esp. a withered or stunted apple] [mid-19C+] to steal fruit, usu. apples, from orchards.

scrump *v.*[2] [? SCRUMPTIOUS *adj.*] [1980s+] (*US campus*) **1** to have sexual intercourse; to neck. **2** to engage in an adulterous sexual relationship.

DERIVATIVES

❑ **scrumper** *n.* [1980s+] (*US campus*) an adulterer.

scrumplicate *v.* [? var. SPIFLICATE *v.* (2)] [late 19C] to beat up, to totally defeat.

scrumptious *adj.* [dial. *scrumptious*, mean, stingy, close-fisted; although the senses seem totally opposed, cf. SE *nice* for a similar shift in meaning from overly fastidious to attractive and appealing] [mid-19C+] (*orig. US*) **1** fastidious, hard to please. **2** (*also* **scronchous, scrum**) first-rate, excellent. **3** stylish, handsome. **4** (*mainly teen*) delicious, extra-tasty, nearly always of food but occas. of an attractive person.

scrunch *n.* [SE *scrunch*, the noise of crunching] [1920s+] (*Aus.*) food, esp. sweets.

scrunch *v.* (*also* **scooch, scrooch**) **1** [late 19C+] to squeeze. **2** [1920s+] (*US black*) to dance extremely close to someone; to snuggle up.

scrunge *n.* [? GRUNGE *n.*] **1** [1970s+] (*orig. US campus*) filth, mess, dirt. **2** [2000s] (*US*) a filthy, unpleasant person, a 'lowlife'.

scrungy *adj.* (*also* **skrungy**) [echoic; var. on GRUNGY *adj.* or SCRUNGE *n.* (1)] [1970s+] (*orig. US campus*) filthy, messy, dirty, disgusting.

scrunt *v.* [dial. *scrunt*, to scratch + SE *scrounge*] [20C+] (*W.I.*) to eke out a living, to suffer great poverty, to be forced into begging.

scuba *v.* [play on SE *scuba-dive* + DIVE *v.* (2)] [2000s] (*US black*) to perform cunnilingus.

scuba bum *n. see* BUM *n.*[3] (10).

scuba (diver) *n.* [rhy. sl. = FIVER *n.* (1)] [1990s+] a five-pound note.

scud *n.* [Scot. *scud*, a blow] **1** [mid-19C] (*UK school*) a fast runner. **2** [1960s+] (*Ulster*) a jinx. **3** [1960s+] (*also* **scood**) a general term of abuse.

scud *v.* [SE *scud*, to move fast; ? reinforced by the *Scud* missiles used in the Gulf War (1991)] [1990s+] to partake in the act of copulation.

DERIVATIVES

❑ **scuddy** *adj.* [1990s+] pornographic.

IN COMPOUNDS

❑ **scud mag** *n.* [1990s+] a pornographic magazine.

scuddick *n.* (*also* **scuddock**) [dial. *scud*, a wisp of straw] [early–mid-19C] a tiny sum of money.

scuddy *n.* [from 'Scud' missile] [1990s+] (*US campus*) a large marijuana cigarette.

scuddy *adj. see* SCUZZY *adj.* (1).

scudi *n.* [Ital. *scudo*, 'A silver coin and money of account formerly current in various Italian states, usually worth about 4 shillings' (*OED*)] [late 19C–1900s] money; or as a pl. with the amount.

scuff *n.*[1] [late 19C] a crowd of people.

scuff *n.*[2] **1** [1930s+] (*US Und.*) a shoe. **2** [1970s+] (*Aus./US*) a slipper, or a backless shoe.

scuff *v.* [1930s+] (*US Und.*) to walk.

scuffer *n.* (*also* **scufter, skuffter**) [? dial. *scuff*, to strike; Yorks. dial. *scuff*, 'mean, sordid fellow, the scum of the people' (*EDD*); or *scurf*, the back of the neck, and thus one who grabs you by it] [mid-19C+] (*UK, usu. north.*) a policeman.

IN COMPOUNDS

❑ **judy scuffer** *n.* [mid-19C+] (*UK, usu. northern*) a policewoman.

scuffle *n.*[1] [SCUFFLE *v.* (1)] [1920s+] (*US black*) **1** difficult circumstances, poverty. **2** a job.

scuffle *n.*[2] (*also* **skuffle**) [ety. unknown] [1970s+] (*drugs*) phencyclidine.

scuffle *v.* **1** [mid-19C+] (*US, orig. jazz*) to survive with difficulty, to eke out one's bare living, often through unpleasant, degrading methods. **2** [late 19C+] (*US, orig. jazz*) to dance. **3** [1940s+] (*US black/W.I.*) (*also* **scuffle up**) to collect, raise or obtain money or something desirable.

IN COMPOUNDS

❑ **scuffle-hunter** *n.* [they *scuffle around*, hunting for items to steal] [18C] a dockside pilferer.

scuffler *n.* [SCUFFLE *v.* (1)] [1940s+] **1** anyone who ekes out a living, esp. a petty criminal. **2** (*US black*) one who works hard and honestly for their subsistence.

scuff up *v.* [abbr. SE *scuffle*, to struggle confusedly together] [1990s+] (*US prison*) to fight, usu. with fists.

scufter *n. see* SCUFFER *n.*

scug *n.* [public school use *scug*, 'a boy of untidy, dirty, or ill-mannered habits; one whose sense of propriety is not fully developed' (*Everyday Life in Public Schools* (1881)] [1910s] a despicable person.

scull *n.*[1] (*also* **sculler**) [SE *scull*, a light boat rowed by a single oarsman] [late 18C–19C] a one-horse chaise or buggy.

SE in slang uses

IN PHRASES

❑ **scull around** *v.* [1920s+] to wander aimlessly.

scull *n.*[2] *see* SKULL *n.*[1].

scully *n.* [? SE *scullion*] [1980s+] (*US campus*) an unspecified person.

scum *n.* **1** [1940s+] (*US*) semen. **2** *see* SCUMBAG below.

terms of abuse combining SE use with refs. to semen

IN COMPOUNDS

❑ **scumbag** *n.* [SE *bag*; but note BAG *n.*[1] (1a)] [1950s+] (*orig. US*) **1** a contraceptive sheath. **2** (*also* **joe scumbag, scum, scum wad**) a term of general abuse. ❑ **scumbag** *adj.* [1970s+] repellent, disgusting, despicable. ❑ **scumball** *n.* [1980s+] (*US*) an unpleasant person. ❑ **scumball** *adj.* [1980s+] disgusting, repellent. ❑ **scumbelly** *n.* [1990s+] (*US*) a term of abuse. ❑ **scumbucket** *n.* [1980s+] (*US*) **1** an unpleasant person. **2** an unpleasant, dirty place. ❑ **scumbucket** *adj.* [1980s+] (*US*) unpleasant, disgusting. ❑ **scumdog** *n.* [1990s+] (*US*) a term of abuse; also attrib. ❑ **scum fuck** *n.* (*also* **scumfucker**) [1980s+] a general term of abuse. ❑ **scumhead** *n.* [-HEAD *sfx*] [1940s+] a general term of abuse. ❑ **scumpig** *n.* [1990s+] a general term of derision, abuse; sometimes used affectionately. ❑ **scumsucker** *n.* [1960s+] (*orig. US*) **1** a person who performs fellatio. **2** (*also* **scumsnorter**) a derog. term of general abuse. ❑ **scumsucking** *adj.* [1960s+] a derog. epithet. ❑ **scum wad** *n. see* SCUMBAG above.

IN PHRASES

❑ **baththub scum** *n.* [1980s+] (*US campus*) an unpleasant person. ❑ **male scum** *n.* [1990s+] (*US campus*) a man who treats women badly. ❑ **shower scum** *n.* (*also* **pond scum**) [1980s+] (*US campus*) a highly unpleasant person.

scum *v.* [SCUM *n.*] [1990s+] (*US*) to ejaculate.

scumber *n.* (*also* **scummer**) [dial. *scumber*, animal dung or sticky, viscous mud] [mid-17C] excrement.

scumber *v.* [SCUMBER *n.*] [mid-17C] to defecate.

scummer *n.* [SE *scum*] [1980s+] **1** (*US*) an outlaw biker. **2** a despised person.

scummer *v.* (*also* **scammer**) [SCUMBER *n.*] [late 16C–mid-17C] to defecate.

scummy *adj.* [SE *scum*] [mid-19C+] unpleasant, disgusting.

scumpteen *n.* [ext. UMPTEEN *n.*] [1940s] an undetermined but substantial number.

scunge *n.* [Scot. *scunge*, to slink around] **1** [20C+] (*Ulster*) one who is always 'on the make'. **2** [1960s+] (*Aus./N.Z./US*) (*also* **scungeel**) an unpleasant, objectionable person. **3** [1960s+] (*Aus./N.Z.*) dirt, filth, often associated with the body.

scungies *n.* [joc. use of SCUNGY *adj.*; such trunks are seen as too sordid for public display] **1** [1970s] (*Aus.*) men's bikini-style swimming trunks, often worn under surf shorts or 'baggies'. **2** [1990s+] old clothes.

scungy *adj.* (*also* **skungy**) [SCUNGE *n.* or var. on SCRUNGY *adj.*] [1960s+] (*Aus./N.Z.*) filthy, dirty.

IN COMPOUNDS

❑ **scungebucket** *n.* [1960s+] (*Aus./N.Z.*) a filthy person.

scunner *n.* [Scot. *scunner*, an abomination] [20C+] (*US*) extreme dislike, hostility.

IN PHRASES

❑ **take a scunner to** *v.* [1950s] to conceive a dislike for.

scunner *v.* [SCUNNER *n.*] [20C+] (*US*) to arouse hostility.

scunted *adj.* [? Yorks. dial. *scunted*, having lost all one's marbles] [1990s+] (*Aus. teen*) caught out doing something.

scupper *n.* [? SE *scupper*, a boat's drain through which dirty water can run] [1930s–70s] a prostitute.

scupper *v.* [i.e to pour down the SE *scupper*, a drain] [late 19C+] (*orig. milit.*) to defeat, to ruin, to put an end to; to kill.

scurf *n.* [SE *scurf*, a general term referring to a variety of skin diseases] [mid-19C–1900s] **1** an unpleasant person, esp. a miser or skinflint; also as collective noun. **2** an employer who pays less than average wages. **3** a worker who accepts less than the average rate.

scurf *adj.* [SCURF *n.*] [mid–late 19C] of labour, cheap.

scurf *v.* [? SE *scruff*, to seize by the nape of the neck] [early 19C] to arrest.

scurrick *n. see* SKERRICK *n.*

scurryfunging *n.* [Scot. *scurryvaig*, a vagabond] [late 19C] the act of wandering like a tramp.

scurve *n.* [SCURF *n.* (1) + ? SE *scurvy*] [20C+] **1** (*US*) a contemptible person. **2** (*US black*) any form of ugliness or shabbiness.

scurvy *adj.* [1980s] (*US black*) of a woman, unattractive.

scut *n.*[1] [SE *scut*, a rabbit or hare's tail] **1** [late 16C–early 19C] the female genitals, the pubic hair; also the male genitals. **2** [late 17C; 1900s–20s] the buttocks, the posterior. **3** [1990s+] (*UK juv.*) a promiscuous girl, beneath or just at the age of consent.

scut *n.*[2] [? dial. *scutter*, diarrhoea or SCOUT *n.*] **1** [late 19C+] (*also* **scutt, skut**) a contemptible person. **2** [20C+] (*US*) a novice or new recruit.

DERIVATIVES

❑ **scutty** *adj.* [20C+] unpleasant, distasteful.

IN COMPOUNDS

❑ **scut work** *n.* [1950s+] (*US*) menial or routine work.

scut *v.*[1] [1920s+] (*Irish/juv.*) to grab a free ride by hanging on to the rear of a vehicle, unbeknown to the driver.

IN PHRASES

❑ **give a scut** *v.* [1920s] to allow a free ride on the back of vehicle.

IN EXCLAMATIONS

❑ **scut the whip!** [1960s+] a warning to a driver that riders are on his vehicle.

scut *v.*[2] [2000s] (*S.Afr. prison*) to search; also as n.

scutcher *n.* [? SE *scotch*, to kill; thus a 'killer'] [1910s+] (*Aus.*) anything notably large or esp. outstanding.

scutter *n.*[1] [Scot. *scutter*, a slovenly, untidy worker] [20C+] an unpleasant person.

DERIVATIVES

❑ **scuttering** *adj.* [20C+] unpleasant.

scutter *n.*[2] [Irish *sciodar*, diarrhoea] [1960s+] (*Irish*) excrement.

DERIVATIVES

❑ **scutters, the** *n.* [1960s+] (*Irish*) diarrhoea.

IN PHRASES

❑ **tail-scutter** *n.* [1960s+] (*Irish*) a fart.

scutter *v.* [SCUTTER *n.*[2]] [1960s+] (*Irish*) to defecate.

scuttered *adj.* [dial. *scutter*, to expend a great deal of energy in doing nothing constructive + Irish *sciotarálaí*, idle chatter] [1960s+] (*Irish*) tipsy, drunkenly loquacious.

scuttle *n.* [abbr. SE *coalscuttle*] [1900s] (*US*) a derog. term for a black person.

scuttle *v.* [SE *scuttle*, to make a hole in a ship's bottom in order to sink her] **1** [19C] (*also* **scuttle a ship**) to deflower a woman. **2** [mid-19C] (*US Und.*) to slice into a pocket so as to steal the contents. **3** [mid-19C–1900s] to stab. **4** [2000s] of a man, to have sexual intercourse.

DERIVATIVES

❑ **scuttler** *n.* [mid-19C–1900s] a knife-carrying villain; one using a leather belt as a weapon.

IN PHRASES

❑ **scuttle someone's nob** *v.* (*also* **scuttle someone's hull**) [NOB *n.*[1] (1)] [early–mid-19C] to break someone's head.

scuttlebutt *n.* [US Navy *scuttlebutt*, a ship's water barrel, around which sailors gathered and gossiped] **1** [20C+] gossip, rumour. **2** [1960s] a gossip.

scuttler *n.* [Lancashire dial. *scuttle*, a street brawl; ? SE *scuttle*, to run off] [mid–late 19C] (*Manchester*) a young street thug.

scuzz *n.* (*also* **scuz, skuz**) [? SE *disgusting* or SCUMMY *adj.* (1) + SE *fuzzy*] (*orig. US*) **1** [1960s+] any unpleasant person. **2** [1980s+] dirt, mess, any horrible substance. **3** [2000s] a sexually active, thus by sexist definition, promiscuous, woman.

IN COMPOUNDS

❑ **scuzzbag** *n.* (*also* **scuzbag**) [1980s+] **1** (*US campus*) a sexually promiscuous woman. **2** (*US*) a contemptible person. ❑ **scuzzbag** *adj.* [1980s+] disgusting, contemptible. ❑ **scuzzball** *n.* [1980s+] a contemptible person. ❑ **scuzzball** *adj.* [2000s] unpleasant, disgusting. ❑ **scuzzbucket** *n.* [1980s+] an unpleasant person. ❑ **scuzzbucket** *adj.* [1980s] unpleasant, distasteful, repellent. ❑ **scuzz-food** *n.* [1970s+] (*US*) any cheap, greasy or sweet snack foods, e.g. chips, crisps, popcorn. ❑ **scuzzhead** *n.* (*also* **scuzz-brain**) [1990s+] a general term of abuse.

scuzz *v.* [SCUZZ *n.* (2)] [1980s+] **1** to make filthy, to make a mess of. **2** in fig. use, to act in a sordid manner.

IN PHRASES

❑ **scuzzed out** *adj.* [1980s+] (*US teen*) disgusted, nauseated. ❑ **scuzzed-up** *adj.* [1990s+] deliberately filthy.

scuzzy *n.* [SCUZZ *n.* (1)] [1970s] (*US*) an old person, on the verge of death.

scuzzy *adj.* (*also* **skuzzy**) [? SE *disgusting* or SCUMMY *adj.* (1) + SE *fuzzy*] **1** [1960s+] (*US teen*) (*also* **scuddy**) filthy, repellent. **2** [1970s+] unkempt, down at heel, ragged.

'sdeath! *excl.* (*also* **'zdeath!**) [17C+] a euph. oath, lit. 'God's death'.

sea *n.*

SE in slang uses

IN COMPOUNDS

❑ **sea-coal** *n.* [SE *sea-coal*, coal that is exposed at low tide or washed up on the coastline] **1** [mid-18C–19C] smuggled spirits. **2** [19C+] money. ❑ **sea-crab** *n.* [late 18C–19C] a sailor. ❑ **sea dust** *n.* [1930s–40s] (*US milit.*) salt. ❑ **seafood** *n.* **1** [1920s] (*US Und.*) whisky [? the smuggling of whisky by sea during the Prohibition era, 1920–33]. **2** [1930s+] (*gay*) sailors as sex objects; thus *seafood queen*, a homosexual man who prefers sailors for sex [i.e. something to EAT *v.* (4)]. **3** [1930s+] (*US*) cunnilingus; a woman as a partner for cunnilingus [the association of the vagina with FISH *n.*[1] (1a)]. ❑ **seagull** *n.* [like the seagull, they hope to pick up 'scraps', in this case, of work] [1950s+] (*Aus./N.Z.*) a casual wharf labourer. ❑ **sea pie** *n.* ['A dish of meat and vegetables, etc, boiled together, with a crust of paste, or in layers between crusts, the number of which denominate it a two or three decker' (Smyth, *Sailor's Word-book*, 1867); Brendan Behan, *Borstal Boy* (1958): 'a kind of Irish stew with suet instead of potatoes in it'] [mid-19C–1950s] a stew. ▫ **sea pussy** *n.* [SE *sea* + PUSSY *n.* (9); note Dos Passos, *The Big Money* (1936): '"Not too far out, on account of the seapussies" "What?" "Currents, she shouted"'] [1960s+] (*US gay*) a homosexual sailor. ▫ **sea rover** *n.* [late 19C–1910s] a herring. ▫ **seaweed** *n.* [? resemblance or ? its consumption by cartoon hero Popeye the Sailorman] [1930s–40s] (*US milit.*) spinach.

IN PHRASES

▫ **all at sea** *adj.* (*also* **at sea, deep sea**) [losing one's bearings] **1** [mid-19C+] confused. **2** [1930s+] drunk. ▫ **dirty night at sea** *n.* [1940s–50s] (*Aus.*) an all-night drinking session. ▫ **part the red sea** *v.* [1990s+] to masturbate a woman.

seafood plate *phr.* [Fr. *s'il vous plait*, please] [1980s] (*US campus*) please.

seagull's breakfast *n.* [20C+] (*N.Z.*) 'traditional bushman's breakfast of a yawn, a piss and a look around, with the addition of a walk on the beach'.

seal *n.*[1] [coined by John Donne (1572–1631)] **1** [late 16C–mid-17C] the penis. **2** [late 16C–mid-17C] the vagina. **3** [mid-19C] in pl., the testicles.

seal *n.*[2] (*also* **sealskin**) [the smoothness of her skin] [20C+] (*US*) a black woman.

seal *v.* [SEAL *n.*[1]/SE *seal up*] [late 16C–18C] to have sexual intercourse, esp. to impregnate a woman.

sealed oyster *n. see* OYSTER *n.* (4a).

sealer *n.* [SE *sealer*, one who affixes a seal to a document] [late 17C–19C] (*UK Und.*) 'one ready to give bond and judgement for goods or money' (Grose, 1785).

sealing wax *n.* [rhy. sl.] [20C+] (*Aus.*) tax.

sealskin *n. see* SEAL *n.*[2].

seam *n.* [1980s+] (*US drugs*) $10 worth of phencyclidine, wrapped in tinfoil.

SE in slang uses

IN COMPOUNDS

▫ **seam squirrel** *n.* [1910s–50s] (*US*) a body louse.

IN PHRASES

▫ **down on one's back seam** *see* DOWN ON THE KNUCKLE *under* KNUCKLE *n.* ▫ **down to one's seams** *adj.* [the seams of one's empty pockets] [late 19C] (*US*) absolutely impoverished. ▫ **red seam** *n.* [the red seam that runs up the uniform trousers] [1910s+] (*W.I.*) a police officer.

seamster *n. see* SEMPSTRESS *n.*

Seamus *n.* [the common Irish name] [2000s] a generic term for an Irishman.

searchlights *n. see* HEADLAMPS *under* HEAD *n.*

search-my-heart *n.* [its effects] [1900s] (*W.I.*) a drink of rum.

search the placket *v. see under* PLACKET *n.*

Sears Roebuck library *n. see* LIBRARY *n.* (2).

season breast *n.* [1990s+] (*W.I.*) a female breast which has been smeared with vaginal secretions.

seat *n. see* HOT SEAT *n.* (1).

SE in slang uses

IN COMPOUNDS

▫ **seatman** *n.* **1** [1950s+] (*US gambling*) a professional card-dealer. **2** [1980s+] (*Aus.*) a homosexual.

IN PHRASES

▫ **on the anxious seat** *adj. see* ON THE ANXIOUS BENCH *under* BENCH *n.* ▫ **seat of honour** *n.* (*also* **seat of shame, ...vengeance**) [late 18C–19C] the posterior, the buttocks. ▫ **seat of pleasure** *n.* (*also* **seat of love**) [18C] the vagina.

seat *v.* [SE *seat*, the buttocks] (*Aus./N.Z.*) **1** [1950s+] (*orig. prison*) to sodomize. **2** [1980s+] to knock down.

IN COMPOUNDS

▫ **seatman** *n.* [1980s+] a predatory homosexual.

seater *n.* [1960s] (*US*) the buttocks.

sec *n.* [abbr.] **1** [late 19C+] a second. **2** [20C+] (*also* **seck**) a secretary. **3** [1960s] (*drugs*) seconal.

secco *n. see* SECKO *n.*

seccy *n.* (*also* **seggs, seggy**) [abbr.] [1960s+] (*drugs*) Seconal.

secesh *n.* [abbr.] [mid–late 19C] (*US*) a secessionist, i.e. a supporter of the South in the US Civil War.

secesh *v.* [abbr./? SECESH *n.*] [1900s] (*Aus.*) to secede, to break away.

seck *n. see* SEC *n.* (2).

secko *n.* (*also* **secco, sekko**) [SE *sex* + -O *sfx* (3)] [1940s+] (*Aus., usu. prison*) a sexual pervert.

seco *n.* [abbr.] [1960s] (*drugs*) a Seconal pill.

second *n.* [late 19C] (*Aus.*) a girlfriend.

second *adj.*

SE in slang uses

IN COMPOUNDS

▫ **second banana** *n.* [show business use *second banana*, a supporting comedian to the star, a 'straight man'] [1940s+] the second most important person, the second-in-command. ▫ **second base** *n.* [baseball imagery] [1930s+] (*US black/teen*) sexual exploration above the waist (cf. FIRST BASE *n.* (1); THIRD BASE *under* THIRD *adj.*; HOME RUN *n.* (3)). ▫ **second chop** *adj. see* FIRST CHOP *adj.* ▫ **second closet** *n.* [CLOSET *n.* (2)] [1960s+] (*gay*) the hiding of one's specific sexual preferences and practices, even if the basic fact of homosexuality can be admitted; also used of domestic violence within same-sex relationships. ▫ **second line** *v.* [1910s+] (*US*) to follow a leader or someone first-rate, with the hope of advancement or promotion.

IN PHRASES

▫ **second-hand sue** *n.* [SE *second-hand* + assonant use of proper name *Sue*] [1940s–50s] (*Aus.*) **1** a worn-out prostitute. **2** an ageing passive homosexual. ▫ **second hole from the back of the neck** *n.* [2000s] the vagina. ▫ **second-storey job** *n.* (*also* **second-storey trade, ...work**) [JOB *n.*[2] (1a)] [late 19C+] (*US*) a break-in, spec. one that involves climbing above ground level. ▫ **second-storey man** *n.* (*also* **second-storey worker**) [WORKER *n.*[1] (1)] [late 19C+] (*US*) a thief who climbs into buildings above the ground floor.

seconds *n.* **1** [late 18C; 1910s+] a second helping of food or similar; ext. to *thirds*. **2** [late 19C–1900s] opium residue; used fig. to imply that a speaker is talking nonsense, fantasizing. **3** [20C+] (*US*) coffee brewed from used grounds. **4** [1950s+] taking second (or later) place in an act of group sex (usu. forced).

IN PHRASES

▫ **sloppy seconds** *n. see* separate entry. ▫ **take the seconds** *v.* [1930s] (*UK Und.*) to give up, to abandon on second thoughts.

section eight *n.* [1940s+] (*US*) **1** spec. a section eight discharge, discharge from the US army on grounds of mental instability; also as v. **2** insanity, instability. **3** a crazy, neurotic or eccentric person.

seddity *adj. see* SADDITY *adj.*

seducer *n.* [1970s+] (*US black*) one who supplies the means of making fast, poss. illegal, money.

see *n.* [late 18C–early 19C] (*UK Und.*) in pl., the eyes.

IN PHRASES

▫ **sew someone's sees** *v.* [late 18C–mid-19C] to give someone a black eye.

see *v.* **1** [mid-18C–early 19C] to take care to do something, usu. combined with another v., e.g. *see that you get*. **2** in sexual senses. (**a**) [19C] to have sexual intercourse. (**b**) [1950s+] to have a sexual relationship with. **3** [mid-19C+] (*orig. US*) as a mental process. (**a**) to understand, to appreciate the veracity of an idea or statement. (**b**) to consider, to think of doing something. (**c**) as interrog., do you understand? **4** in senses of SE *see to*. (**a**) [mid-19C+] (*orig. US*) to visit a person, esp. a politician, in order to influence them, either legally or, more likely, illegally. (**b**) [1900s] (*orig. US*) to take care of.

SE in slang uses

IN PHRASES

❑ **have seen the French king** *v.* [17C–mid-18C] to be drunk. ❑ **see a dog about a man** *v.* [joc. var. on next] [1920s+] **1** to go out for a drink. **2** to urinate. ❑ **see a man about a dog** *v.* (*also* **see a man about a horse, ...rose, see a cat about a duck, ...horse, ...rose**) **1** [mid-19C–1940s] (*also* **go see a man**) (*orig. US*) to go for a drink; usu. in the form of an excuse before going out for a drink; also when absenting oneself from home in order to visit one's mistress. **2** [mid-19C+] a euph. used to disguise one's need or desire to visit the lavatory. **3** [1910s+] (*also* **write a letter to a man about a dog**) an excuse to leave. ❑ **see a sick friend** *v.* [late 19C+] an excuse used by a married man slipping out to consummate an illicit affair. ❑ **see a thing or two** *v. see* KNOW A THING OR TWO *v.* ❑ **see company** *v.* [euph.] **1** [mid–late 18C] to visit a brothel. **2** [mid-18C–early 19C] to live as a prostitute. ❑ **see foot** *v.* [20C+] (*W.I.*) to see how fast a person runs away. ❑ **see France** *v.* (*also* **see your days, ...your nennen, ...your skin, ...your tail**) [FRANCE *n.* (1)/SE *days*/NENNEN *n.* (1)/SE *skin*/TAIL *n.* (2)] [20C+] (*W.I.*) to endure hardships, esp. in the hope of ultimate success. ❑ **see how the land lies** *v.* [late 17C–early 19C] to check the state of one's tavern bill. ❑ **see if it fucks** *v.* [fig. use of FUCK *v.* (1)] [20C+] to see if something works or runs. ❑ **seeing double** *adj.* [late 18C] drunk. ❑ **seeing-to** *n.* [SE *see to*, to be solicitous towards; note SEE TO below, a backform. f. this n.] [1970s+] **1** referring to a woman, sexual intercourse. **2** referring to a man, a beating up, violence. ❑ **see Mrs Murray** *v.* (*also* **see Mrs. Murphy**) [ult. ref. is to the *Murray* River, Australia's longest] [1930s–50s] (*Aus.*) to visit the lavatory. ❑ **see ning-ning** *v.* [Carib.E. *ning-ning*, dizziness] [20C+] (*W.I.*) to reel from shock, to suffer a spell of dizziness. ❑ **see off** *v.* **1** [1930s+] to deal with, to dismiss, to send away, to defeat. **2** [1980s+] (*Aus. prison*) to murder. **3** [1990s+] to consume. ❑ **see royal** *v.* [fig. use of ROYAL *n.*[1]] [20C+] (*W.I.*) to find it hard to make enough money to live, to subsist, to suffer great hardship. ❑ **see snakes** *v.* **1** [late 19C+] (*US*) to have delirium tremens. **2** [1900s] to be in a state of shock. ❑ **see someone coming** *v.* [the implication is that the swindler saw a 'soft touch' coming before putting the price up or whatever] [late 19C+] to take advantage of someone. ❑ **see stars** *v.* (*also* **see candles, ...spots**) [*candles*, mid-18C–mid-19C; *spots*, mid–late 19C] [mid-18C+] 'to have a sensation as of flashes of light, produced by a sudden jarring of the head, as by a direct blow' (*Century Dict.*, 1891). ❑ **see Steve** *v.* [1940s] (*US drugs*) to take cocaine to the extent that one hallucinates. ❑ **see the lions** *v.* **1** [late 16C] to have some experience of life. **2** [mid-17C] to be drunk. **3** [early–mid-19C+] to see the fashionable 'sights'. ❑ **see them** *v.* (*also* **have them**) ['them' = snakes, pink elephants etc] [late 19C–1900s] (*US*) to suffer delirium tremens. ❑ **see the nose-cheese first** *v.* [ety. unknown] [mid-18C–1900s] to make a refusal rudely or contemptuously. ❑ **see the stars lying upon one's back** *v.* [19C] of a woman, to have sexual intercourse. ❑ **see through a brick wall** *v.* (*also* **see through a stone wall**) [mid-19C+] to be particularly perceptive, to be intelligent, to be aware; sometimes ext. as *see further through a brick wall than most*. ❑ **see through a mill-stone** *v.* [late 16C; 18C] to be aware, to understand what is going on. ❑ **see to** *v.* [backform. f. SEEING-TO above] [1980s+] to have sexual intercourse. ❑ **see two moons** *v.* [mid-18C; 1920s] (*US*) to be drunk. ❑ **see which way the cat jumps** *v. see under* CAT *n.*[1]. ❑ **see ya later alligator** (*also* **later alligator**) [according to *DARE* f. ALLIGATOR *n.* (10); given that alligator is essentially (if not invariably) derog., the phr. certainly began as a dismissal, even if its popular use among those who had no idea of its origin rendered it neutral; an alternative response is 'on the Nile, crocodile'] [1950s+] *See ya later, alligator ... in a while, crocodile*, an all-purpose synon. for 'goodbye', popularized by the 1956 Bill Haley and the Comets' pop hit of the same name and the by then widely publicized use of the phr. by Princess Margaret (1930–2002). ❑ **see you** (*also* **see ya**) [1940s+] goodbye. ❑ **see you around, like a donut** [1960s] (*US*) a general phr. of farewell, 'see you again'. ❑ **see you in court** [1960s+] used as a synon. for goodbye. ❑ **see you in the funny papers** [1920s+] (*US*) goodbye, see you later. ❑ **see you some more** [1940s] (*N.Z.*) goodbye.

IN EXCLAMATIONS

❑ **see ya!** [1980s] (*orig. US campus*) a general excl. of dismissal, shut up! leave me alone! ❑ **seeyabye!** [SEE YOU above + SE *goodbye*] [1980s] (*US teen*) goodbye!

see *adv.* [backsl.] [mid-19C] yes.

seed *n.* **1** in monetary senses. (**a**) [mid-19C–1940s] (*US*) a dollar; money. (**b**) [1900s] a poker chip. **2** [mid-19C+] (*US campus*) a person, esp. when unpopular or notably rowdy. **3** [1960s+] in drug uses. (**a**) marijuana; usu. in pl. (**b**) the butt end of a marijuana cigarette. **4** [1970s+] (*US black*) a child, children [SE *seed* of one's loins].

SE in slang uses

IN COMPOUNDS

❑ **seedbags** *n.* [1970s–80s] (*UK black*) the testicles. ❑ **seed beast** *n.* [2000s] (*N.Z.*) a compulsive male masturbator. ❑ **seed corn** *n. see* CORN *n.*[1] (1).

seedy *n.* [ety. unknown; ? fig. use of SE *seedy*, rundown; or ? play on *c.d.*, standing for cocaine (? orig.) *dealer*] [1980s] (*US black*) a dealer in pills.

seedy *adj.* [SEED *n.*] **1** [late 18C–mid-19C] impoverished. **2** [mid-19C] (*US campus*) rowdy, noisy.

seedy (boy) *n.* [ironic use of Urdu *sidi*, my lord] [mid–late 19C] a derog. term for a black person.

seek *n.*

SE in slang uses

IN PHRASES

❑ **on the seek** [mid-19C] (*UK Und.*) of a prostitute, walking the streets in search of clients.

seek and search *n.* [rhy. sl.] [1990s+] a church.

seek on *v. see* SIC ON *v.*

seen! *excl.* [although the term is used as a synon. for SE *yes*, the implication is one of bearing witness and thus of a more profound agreement with the speaker] [1950s+] (*orig. W.I.*) **1** a general excl. of affirmation. **2** a general excl., 'do you understand?'.

see-o *n.* [backsl.] [mid-19C] shoes.

seer *n.* [lit. 'see-er'] [19C] the eye.

s.e.g. *n.* [abbr. SHIT-EATING GRIN *n.*] [1960s+] (*US campus*) a toadying or hypocritical smile.

seg *n.* [abbr.] [1960s+] **1** (*US*) (*also* **seggie**) a segregationist. **2** (*Can./US prison*) a segregation unit or cell.

seg *v.* [SEG *n.* (1)] [1960s–70s] to segregate, to have a segregationist policy.

seggs/seggy *n. see* SECCY *n.*

segooni *n.* [1980s] (*US black*) a homosexual.

seh one *v.* [1990s+] (*W.I.*) of a woman, to be attractive.

seh-seh seh-seh *n.* [1990s+] (*W.I.*) gossip.

sei *n. see* SAY *n.*

sein *n. see* SANE *n.*

sekko *n. see* SECKO *n.*

seldom see *n.* [rhy. sl.; ult. the initials of the manufacturers *B*radley, *V*oorhees & *D*ay] [1920s] (*US*) in pl., underwear, known as BVDs.

seldom seen *n.* [rhy. sl.] **1** [20C+] the queen. **2** [1940s] (*US*) a limousine.

self-starter *n.* **1** [1930s] (*US drugs*) an addict who volunteers themselves for a cure, taken in prison or a similar institution. **2** [1960s+] one who acts, esp. when employed, on their own initiative rather than await instructions or orders.

Selina Scott *n.* [rhy. sl.; ult. TV personality *Selina Scott* (b.1951)] [1980s+] a spot.

sell *n.* [SELL *v.*] **1** [mid-19C] betrayal to the police. **2** [mid-19C–1900s] a lying joke. **3** [mid-19C–1910s] a disappointment. **4** [mid-19C–1920s] a hoax, a trick, a deception. **5** [late 19C] (*Aus.*) a show-off; an unreliable person. **6** [late 19C–1900s] (*US*) a swindler. **7** [1970s] (*US*) an opportunity to sell something.

sell *v.* **1** [17C+] to deceive, to swindle, to take someone in by promoting something. **2** [19C+] (*UK Und.*) to betray, to inform against. **3** [mid-19C] in sports, to take a bribe to influence the outcome of a contest, usu. by losing deliberately.

IN PHRASES

❑ **sell a bargain** *v.* [Grose (1796) mentions a specific 'bargain', quoted by Swift, as being popular among Queen Anne's courtiers: 'A lady would come into a room full of company, apparently in a fright, crying out, "It is white, and follows me!" On any of the company asking, "What?", she sold him the bargain, by saying, "Mine a–e"'] [late 16C–early 19C] to fool, to hoax. ❑ **sell a boy** *v.* [1940s+] (*gay*) for one man to obtain the services of a boy prostitute at a price and then to offer him to a second man for the actual sex. ❑ **sell a horse** *v.* [play on SELL THE PONY below; one person thinks of, or writes down, a number under ten; the group starts counting down, and the one who gets the chosen number pays] **1** [1910s] as sense 2, in non-bar contexts. **2** [1910s–30s] (*N.Z.*) to play a bar game to determine who buys a round of drinks. ❑ **sell a pup** *v.* [stock market jargon *pup*, a worthless investment] [20C+] to deceive, esp. in business or financial transactions; thus the person deceived *buys a pup*. ❑ **sell a woof ticket** *v.* (*also* **sell a wolf ticket**) [ext. WOOF *v.*[1]] [1960s+] (*US black*) **1** to boast, to brag. **2** to talk nonsense, to lie. **3** to threaten, to intimidate. ❑ **sell body** *v.* [1960s] (*US black*) to work as a prostitute. ❑ **sell buicks** *v. see* RIDE THE BUICK *under* BUICK *v.* ❑ **sell down the river** *v.* (*also* **sell down the drain, sell up the river**) [the practice of selling an errant slave to a Mississippi sugar-cane plantation; the journey to the plantation, where work was especially hard, was lit. 'down the river'] [late 19C+] (*orig. US black*) to betray. ❑ **sell honey for a halfpenny** *v.* [? proverbial] [late 16C–early 17C] to think very badly of someone. ❑ **sell one's crack** *v.* [CRACK *n.*[3]] [1980s+] (*Aus. prison*) to prostitute oneself. ❑ **sell out** *see* separate entries. ❑ **sell someone on** *v.* [1920s+] to convince, to persuade, to convey enthusiasm. ❑ **sell the buick** *v. see* RIDE THE BUICK *under* BUICK *v.* ❑ **sell the pony** *v.* (*also* **sell the lady**) [late 19C–1900s] to toss a coin to determine who pays for a round of drinks; thus *buy the pony/lady*, to pay for that round.

sellary *n.* [Lat. *sellarius*, one who sits upon a *sella*, a couch, i.e. in a brothel] [early 17C] a male homosexual prostitute.

Sellinger's round *n. see under* DANCE *v.*

sell-out *n.* [SELL OUT *v.*] **1** [mid-19C+] an act of betrayal or sacrificing of beliefs and principles for money or position. **2** [1950s+] a person who betrays someone, or who sacrifices their principles for money.

sell out *v.* **1** [mid-19C+] (*orig. US*) in senses of betrayal. (**a**) as *sell someone out*, to betray someone or some external cause, for money or a similar reason. (**b**) to sacrifice one's own beliefs and principles for money or position. **2** [1930s–40s] (*US Und.*) to die in a gunfight rather than surrender to the police. **3** [1930s–50s] (*orig. US black*) to leave, to run away (in terror). **4** [1940s–50s] (*Aus./N.Z.*) to vomit.

selopas *n.* [backsl.] [mid-19C] apples.

s'elp me bob! *excl.* (*also* **s'elp me baub! ...cat! ...crikey! ....davy! ...Hannah! ...James! ...Jemima! ...shicker! ...Susannah! ...ten men! s'elp my bob! s'help me...! so help me bob! s'welp me...! swipe me! swob!**) [SE *so help me* + BOB *n.*[2]; euph. for *so help me God!*] [early 19C+] a general excl. of intensification and affirmation.

s'elp me Dash! *excl.* [SE *dash*, i.e. —] [late 19C–1920s] a laboured euph. of *s'elp me God!*

s'elp me greens! *excl.* (*also* **s'elp my greens! ...my good garden stuff! ...my goodness!**) [mid-19C–1900s] a general excl. of intensification and affirmation, i.e. 'may I lose the attributes of masculine vigour if I am diverging from the line of rectitude' (Ware).

s'elp me never! *excl.* (*also* **so help my never!**) [mid-19C–1910s] a general excl. of affirmation.

s'elp my tater! *excl.* (*also* **s'elp me tater! so help me tater! swelp me taters!**) [mid-19C–1900s] a general oath.

semen demon *n.* [1990s+] (*US*) a (passive) male homosexual, the inference is of a fellator.

semi *n.* **1** [1960s] (*US gay*) of a place, e.g. a club, half-homo- and half-heterosexual in clientele. **2** [1980s+] (*also* **semi-on**) a semi-erection of the penis.

semi *adv.* [1970s+] partly, to some extent.

seminary *n.* [pun on SE *semen*] **1** [mid-17C] a brothel. **2** [19C] the vagina.

semi-on *n. see* SEMI *n.* (2).

semi-pro *n.* [1960s] (*US Und.*) a young woman who occas. works as a prostitute but is not fully committed to the life.

semolia *n.* [? name of a psychiatric institution] [late 19C–1930s] (*US black*) a fool.

semolina *n.* [rhy. sl.] [20C+] a cleaner, a charwoman.

sempstress *n.* (*also* **seamster**) [17C–early 18C] a prostitute.

send *n.*

IN PHRASES

❑ **on the send** **1** [1930s–50s] (*US Und.*) working as a go-between; of the victim of a confidence trick, being sent off to get money; obtaining drugs for an addict from a dealer. **2** [1960s] (*US*) running errands. ❑ **put on the send** *v.* [1900s–70s] (*US Und.*) **1** of a confidence trickster, to persuade the victim to fetch (more) money. **2** thus *send store*; any kind of trick that involves the sending of a victim home to get his money.

send *v.* **1** [1930s–40s] (*US drugs*) to smoke marijuana, or heroin, i.e the effect equates with sense 2. **2** [1930s+] (*orig. US*) to excite emotionally. **3** *see* SEND UP below.

SE in slang uses

IN PHRASES

❑ **send across** *v.* **1** [1900s] to kill. **2** [1920s–40s] (*US*) to send to prison. ❑ **send along** *v.* [late 19C–1910s] **1** (*Aus.*) to have someone arrested, to send to prison. **2** (*Aus.*) to criticize severely. **3** (*US*) to cost, to charge. ❑ **send away** *v.* [1910s+] to imprison, to have someone imprisoned. ❑ **send down** *v.* (*also* **send downstairs**) [either var. on (US) SEND UP THE RIVER below or (UK) walking down the steps from the dock (orig. at the Old Bailey, London) to the cells beneath the court] [mid-19C+] to imprison. ❑ **send down the road** *v.* (*also* **send down the track, put someone down the track**) **1** [1950s+] (*N.Z.*) to dismiss from employment; thus *go/get/be sent down the road/track*, to be dismissed. **2** [1970s] (*US Und.*) to send to prison. ❑ **send her down Hughie** (*also* **send it down Hughie, send her/it down Davey, ...Steve**) [*Hughie*, the mythical deity of surfing and as such invoked by surfers who want suitable waves; note the Bulletin (Sydney) 14/11/1912: 'I believe the Queensland black's word for cloud is 'ugon,' and the shearers and surf-bathers may have misapplied it to the man behind the gun. If that is not the explanation, what in fury is?'; also used as synon. for God by US loggers of Pacific Northwest/*Davey*, ? St David, the patron saint of Wales, the land of 'leeks'/generic use of proper name *Steve*] [20C+] (*Aus./N.Z.*) a general appeal to the gods for rain. ❑ **send in by the servant's entrance** *v.* [SE *servant's entrance*, usu. in the rear or bottom storey of the house] [1960s+] of a man, to have sexual intercourse from the rear position. ❑ **send in one's checks** *v. see under* CHECK *n.*[1]. ❑ **send it in** *v.* **1** [early–mid-19C] to push in, to drive something home. **2** [1960s] (*US gambling*) to make big bets. ❑ **send off** *v.* [1950s+] (*Aus.*) to steal. ❑ **send on a humbug trip** *v.* (*also* **send on a humbug, ...merry-go-round, ...trip**) [1950s+] (*US black*) to send on a wild goose chase, a fool's errand. ❑ **send over** *v.* **1** [1990s+] (*US Und.*) to betray to the authorities. **2** *see* SEND UP below. ❑ **send south** *v.* [1960s] (*US*) to get rid of a person; to terminate a relationship. ❑ **send to Birching Lane** *v.* (*also* **send to Birchen Lane, ...Birchin Lane**) [SE *birch* + *Birchin Lane*, London EC3, once known for its ready-made clothes shops, although the name ? f. OE meaning 'lane of the barbers'] [18C] to administer a flogging. ❑ **send to grass** *v.* [boxing orig. took place on grass] [late 19C–1900s] (*orig. boxing*) to knock down. ❑ **send to graze** *v.* (*also* **send to grass**) [farming imagery] [mid-18C] to dismiss. ❑ **send to Long Beach** *v.* [? the sewer outlets at Long Beach] [1960s–70s] (*US/Los Angeles drugs*) to flush drugs down the lavatory before or during a drugs raid. ❑ **send to pot** *v.* [late 18C] to dispose of, to bring to an end. ❑ **send to the dogs** *v.* [SE *go to the dogs*]

[1930s] to bring down in the world. ❑ **send to the pack** *v.* [1910s–20s] (*Aus./N.Z.*) to discard, to dismiss. ❑ **send up** *v.* (*also* **send, send over**) **1** [mid-19C+] (*US Und.*) to imprison [abbr. SE *send up* for punishment, or SE *send* UP THE RIVER *under* RIVER *n.*]. **2** [1910s] (*Aus.*) to cheat, to defraud. ❑ **send up Green River** *v. see* GREEN RIVER *n.* ❑ **send up the river** *v.* (*also* **send up the hill**) [ext. of SEND UP above + UP THE RIVER *under* RIVER *n.*] [20C+] (*US Und.*) to imprison. ❑ **send up the road** *v.* [2000s] to kill, to murder.

sender *n.* **1** [mid-19C] (*orig. boxing jargon*) a solid, hard blow. [? it *sends* the victim to the floor]. **2** [1920s–40s] (*US black*) a person (usu. a musician) or thing (usu. a record) who or which is emotionally arousing [SEND *v.*].

send for mary ann *phr. see* SAN FAIRY ANN *phr.*

send-in *n.* **1** [1910s] (*US Und.*) an endorsement, a recommendation; as v., to praise or recommend for one's own purposes. **2** [1930s] (*US Und.*) information about a possible crime.

Senegambian *n.* [SE *Senegambian*, a native or inhabitant of Senegambia, former name of the region surrounding the Senegal and Gambia rivers in West Africa] [late 19C–1940s] (*US*) a derog. term for an African-American.

seni *n.* [ety. unknown] [1970s] (*drugs*) peyote; mescaline.

senor-eater *n.* [puns on Sp. *señorita*, miss + *señor*, mister + SE *eater*; i.e. one who indulges in oral sex] [1970s+] (*US gay*) **1** a gay man who prefers Latin or Hispanic partners. **2** a Hispanic homosexual.

sensation *n.* (*also* **slight sensation**) [ironic understatement] **1** [mid-19C] 143ml (¼ pint) of gin. **2** [mid–late 19C] a taste, a small quantity. **3** [mid-19C+] (*Aus.*) a half glass of sherry.

sensimillia *n.* (*also* **sensamilia, sense, senseed, sensi, sinse, sinsemilla**) [lit. 'seedless'] [1970s+] (*W.I./UK black teen*) a variety of extremely potent marijuana; it has no seeds because it is isolated from male pollen during the blooming process; instead, the marijuana plant makes more tetrahydrocannabinol (THC), thus intensifying the effects.

sensitive plant *n.* **1** [mid-18C+] the penis. **2** [early–mid-19C] (*orig. boxing*) the nose.

sensitive truncheon *n.* [19C] **1** the nose. **2** the penis.

sent *adj.* [SEND *v.*] **1** [late 19C] imprisoned. **2** [1930s–50s] (*drugs*) experiencing the effects of alcohol or marijuana. **3** [1930s–60s] emotionally overcome, esp. by a jazz solo.

sentimental *n.* [rhy. sl. *sentimental bloke* = SMOKE *n.* (2a); ult. title of 1915 collection of poems by C.J. Dennis] [1920s–70s] (*Aus.*) a cigar or cigarette.

sent up *adj.* [SEND UP *under* SEND *v.*] [late 19C+] (*orig. US*) imprisoned.

separate *n.* (*also* **separates**) [mid-19C–1920s] (*Aus./UK Und.*) solitary confinement in prison.

seppo *n. see* SEPTIC (TANK) *n.* (1).

seppo *adj.* (*also* **septic**) [2000s] (*N.Z.*) angry.

September morn *n.* [rhy. sl. = HORN *n.*[2] (1); note *September Morn*, a painting by Paul Chabas of a young woman bathing nude, which was first exhibited at the 1912 Salon in Paris. Censors attempted to ban a reproduction of the picture from public exhibition in the US, a farcical effort, which led to the sale of more than seven million reproductions – appearing on dolls, statues, umbrella handles, tattoos and many other places – and the assurance that Chabas need never work again] [1970s+] an erection.

September 10th [i.e. prior to 9/11, the destruction of the World Trade Center, NYC] [2000s] old-fashioned.

septic *n.* [SEPTIC *adj.* (1)] [2000s] (*N.Z.*) any unpleasant person or object.

septic *adj.* [fig. use of SE] **1** [1910s+] unpleasant, rotten, mean. **2** [1970s+] (*Irish*) affected.

septic (tank) *n.* [rhy. sl.] [1960s+] (*orig. Aus.*) **1** (*also* **seppo**) an American [= YANK *n.* (1)]. **2** a bank. **3** a tank.

IN COMPOUNDS

❑ **Seppo-land** *n.* [1990s+] America.

septic (tank) *adj.* [rhy. sl.] **1** [1980s] (*N.Z.*) foolish; self-deluded; incompetent [= WANK *adj.* (1)]. **2** [2000s] American [SEPTIC (TANK) *n.* (1)].

serg *n. see* SARGE *n.*

sergeant *n.* [abbr. TOP SERGEANT *under* TOP *adj.*] [1950s] a 'masculine' lesbian.

Sergeant Kite *n.* (*also* **Sergeant Snap**) [? SE *kite*, a bird of prey/*snap*, the click of a fig. lock or the order, 'Snap to it!'] [mid–late 19C] a recruiting sergeant.

sergeant-major *n.* **1** [late 19C] (*UK Und.*) a burglar's chisel. **2** [1910s–20s] the crown in the gambling game of 'Crown and Anchor' [the NCO's badge of office]. **3** in senses of an enriched or strengthened beverage [trad. preferred by the NCO]. (**a**) [1910s+] strong sweet tea or tea with rum. (**b**) [1920s+] (*US*) coffee with cream or milk and sugar.

sergeant space *n. see under* SPACE *n.*

seringapatam *n. see* PLASTERER'S TROWEL AND SERINGAPATAM *n.*

serious *adj.* **1** [1910s+] an all-purpose intensifier, e.g. *serious drinking*. **2** [1940s+] (*US black*) excellent, first-rate.

seriously *adv.* **1** [1920s; 1980s+] an all-purpose intensifier, e.g. *seriously rich*. **2** [1990s+] an expression of agreement.

serpent *n.* (*also* **silver serpent**) [1960s–70s] a hypodermic syringe and needle.

Serps, the *n.* (*also* **Turpentine, the**) [abbr.; rhy. sl.] [1930s+] the *Serpentine*, Hyde Park, London.

servant *n.* [SE *service*, usu. of an animal, to copulate] [late 16C–mid-17C] a womanizer, a promiscuous man.

serve *n.* [SERVE *v.* (1)] [1960s+] (*Aus.*) **1** negative criticism, a reprimand; verbal abuse. **2** a beating.

IN PHRASES

❑ **give something a serve** *v.* [1990s+] to deal with or consume enthusiastically, e.g. of food or drink; to 'punish'.

serve *v.* **1** in senses of violence. (**a**) [early 16C+] (*UK Und.*) (*also* **serve out**) to injure, to wound; thus *serve out and out*, to murder; also fig., i.e. to treat badly. (**b**) [1990s+] (*US black*) to kill. **2** in sexual contexts [SE *service*, usu. of an animal, to copulate]. (**a**) [mid-16C+] (*also* **serve one's turn**) to have sexual intercourse. (**b**) [1980s+] (*US black/prison*) to assault sexually, to rape. **3** in verbal senses. (**a**) [early 19C] (*UK Und.*) to convict and sentence. (**b**) [1970s+] (*N.Z.*) to abuse. (**c**) [1970s+] (*N.Z.*) to tell lies. (**d**) [1990s+] (*US*) to dominate. **4** [early–mid-19C] (*UK Und.*) to rob. **5** [late 19C+] to serve a term of imprisonment. **6** [1980s+] (*US black teen*) to give someone their due deserts; to take one's revenge.

IN PHRASES

❑ **serve out** *v.* (*also* **sarve out**) [boxing jargon] [19C–1900s] **1** to revenge oneself upon, to retaliate. **2** to punish. ❑ **serve someone a ticket** *v.* [early 19C] (*Anglo-Irish*) to hit someone.

service lay *n.* [SE *service* + LAY *n.*[3] (1)] [18C] (*UK Und.*) a method of thieving whereby someone enters a house posing as a servant later to decamp with whatever they can steal.

service of beef *n.* [SERVE *v.* (1) + BEEF *n.*[1] (3)] [1980s] sexual intercourse.

service station *n.* [play on SE/SERVE *v.* (1)] **1** [1940s] a brothel. **2** [1980s+] (*US gay*) a public lavatory used for sexual assignations.

servo *n.* [SE *service* + -O *sfx* (6)] [1990s+] (*Aus.*) a service station.

sese *n.* [SESE *v.*] [1980s+] (*W.I./UK black teen*) whisperings, rumours, gossip.

sese *v.* [echoic; plus Twi *sise*, to talk a lot] [1980s+] (*W.I./UK black teen*) to whisper.

sesh *n.* [abbr. SESSION *n.*] [1980s+] a session of drinking or taking drugs.

IN PHRASES

❑ **do the full sesh** *v.* (*also* **go full sesh**) [1980s] (*US teen*) to indulge completely, to take to the limit.

sesh *adj.* [the implied excellence of a SESH *n.* (1)] [1990s+] (*UK juv.*) very good, excellent.

sess *n.* (*also* **cess**) [? SENSIMILLIA *n.*] [1980s+] (*US black*) top-grade marijuana.

session *n.* **1** [1910s+] (*Aus./US*) a disturbance, an argument. **2** [1930s] a conversation. **3** [1930s+] (*US teen*) a dance, a party. **4** [1940s+] (*orig. Aus.*) a period of time devoted to drinking. **5** [1950s+] (*drugs*) a period of time devoted to drug taking. **6** [1950s+] a period of time devoted to sex.

Sessions Pie *n.* [1940s] (*UK prison*) a type of pasty based on bully beef, served to prisoners who had to attend the Sessions court.

set *n.*[1] **1** in senses of SE *set*, 'a number, company, or group (of persons) associated by community of status, habits, occupations, or interests' (*OED*). (**a**) [late 19C+] (*US*) a group of friends. (**b**) [1980s+] (*US black/gang*) a local gang, part of the larger gang but working autonomously in its own neighbourhood or area of influence; e.g. the Crips are the larger gang, but *sets* include Eight Trey Gangsters or ETGs, West Side Crips, Compton Santana Block Crips etc; hence a gang hand sign. (**c**) [1990s+] a prison gang. **2** in senses of a SE *set*, pieces of equipment. (**a**) [1950s+] (*US drugs*) a makeshift syringe combining a pacifier (UK *dummy*), an eyedropper and a needle, sealed together with a paper 'collar'. (**b**) [1960s+] (*US drugs*) a dose of two Seconals and one amphetamine. (**c**) [1980s] (*US drugs*) three to ten pills of similar or varying strength or type. (**d**) [1990s+] (*W.I.*) the outsized speakers used in a dancehall sound system. (**e**) [2000s] (*US drugs*) an injection of combined Talwin and Ritalin, the effect of which mimics a mix of heroin and cocaine. **3** in physiological contexts, a pair. (**a**) [1960s+] (*Aus.*) the female breasts. (**b**) [1970s] the male genitals.

SE in slang uses

IN COMPOUNDS

❑ **set trip/tripping** *see* separate entries.

IN PHRASES

❑ **get a set on** *v.* [late 19C–1910s] (*Aus.*) to take against someone, to attack someone. ❑ **have a set on** *v.* (*also* **take a set on**) [SE *set against*] [mid-19C+] to bear a grudge against, to have a score to settle with. ❑ **put a set on** *v.* [fig. use SE *set*, to place in a sitting posture, i.e. no longer moving forward] [1910s] (*Aus.*) to terminate, to bring to an end. ❑ **set of seven brights** *n. see under* BRIGHT *n.* ❑ **set of tits** *n. see under* TIT *n.*[2]. ❑ **set of wheels** *n. see under* WHEELS *n.*

set *n.*[2] **1** in senses of theatre/film jargon *set*, the backdrop to the action. (**a**) [1950s+] (*US black*) wherever the hedonistic, criminal or night life takes place. (**b**) [1950s+] (*US black*) a party, a gathering. (**c**) [1960s+] (*drugs*) a place where drugs are sold. (**d**) [1970s+] (*US black*) a discussion. (**e**) [1980s+] (*US black*) the neighbourhood. **2** *see* DEAD SET *n.* (1).

IN PHRASES

❑ **break to the set** *v.* [1950s+] (*US black*) to move to or arrive at a gathering. ❑ **bust the set** *v.* [1990s+] (*UK black*) to ruin an atmosphere. ❑ **pull to a set** *v.* [1970s+] (*US black*) to attend a party.

set *adj.* [? SE *set back*] [late 19C–1930s] conquered, defeated.

IN PHRASES

❑ **get one set** *v.* [20C+] (*Aus.*) to bear a grudge against someone, to have a score to settle with someone. ❑ **have someone set** *v.* [abbr. SE *set down*] [20C+] (*Aus.*) to have someone marked down for punishment or revenge.

set *v.* [? SE *set upon*] **1** [late 17C–19C] to target a potential victim, to survey before robbing. **2** [late 19C] (*Aus.*) of a (young) woman, to target a man as a potential husband/lover. **3** [1910s+] (*Aus.*) to attack verbally, to think little of.

SE in slang uses

IN PHRASES

❑ **set back** *v.* [late 19C+] (*orig. US*) to cost, e.g. *her coat must have set him back a few quid.* ❑ **set fire** *v.* [1900s–50s] to cause suspicion. ❑ **set going** *v. see* GET GOING *v.* ❑ **set horses** *v.* [i.e. fig. hitching one's horses to the same pole] [1930s+] (*US black*) to get along in a friendly manner. ❑ **set in a crack** *v.* [? the speedy crack of a whip] [late 19C+] (*N.Z.*) to settle something quickly. ❑ **set mouth on** *v. see under* MOUTH *n.* ❑ **set off** *v.* [1980s+] (*US prison*) to deny a prisoner parole. ❑ **set one's child a-crying** *v.* [the watchman's rattle was the predecessor of the policeman's whistle] [early–mid-19C] for a watchman, to 'spring his rattle', i.e. to sound an alarm. ❑ **set oneself back** *v.* [1930s] to spend money. ❑ **set on fire** *v. see under* FIRE *n.* ❑ **set on one's ass** *v.* [ASS *n.* (2)] [1970s+] (*drugs*) to render unconscious from excessive drug consumption. ❑ **set over** *v.* [1920s–40s] (*US Und.*) to kill, to murder. ❑ **set (something) on** *v.* [1930s+] (*US black*) **1** to give, esp. of drugs. **2** to tell, to impose facts upon. ❑ **set the hare's head to the goose's giblets** *v.* [the perceived 'equivalence' of the two foodstuffs] [early 17C] to give as good as one gets, to pay like with like. ❑ **set up** *see* separate entries.

IN EXCLAMATIONS

❑ **set it alight!** [1940s+] (*N.Z.*) get a move on! hurry up!

set-down *n.* [regional pron. of SE *sit*] [early 19C–1940s] (*US*) a sit-down meal, thus a square meal; spec. when a tramp is invited into a house and offered a meal indoors.

set o' sun *n.* [1900s] (*Aus.*) an image of great distance.

set-out *n.* **1** [19C] a person's horse or horses and carriage. **2** [19C] a display of china and plate. **3** [19C] a table full of dishes of food. **4** [mid-19C] a group of people. **5** [mid–late 19C] a person's clothes or way of dressing. **6** [late 19C–1930s] a disturbance, a fuss. **7** [1940s] (*US tramp*) a meal given to a tramp.

setter *n.*[1] [SE *setter*, a species of hunting dog] **1** [mid-16C–18C] the member of a criminal gang who keeps watch or entices a victim into a crooked gambling game. **2** [mid-17C] a pimp. **3** [mid-17C–mid-19C] a bailiff's assistant or serjeant's [i.e. an official authorized to arrest wrongdoers] yeoman. **4** [late 17C–18C] an excise man, whose job is to ensure that brewers do not defraud the Excise. **5** [late 17C–19C] (*UK Und.*) a police spy or informer. **6** [mid-19C] 'a person employed by the vendor at an auction to run the biddings up' (Hotten, 1860).

setter *n.*[2] (*also* **setta**) [Ital. *sette*, seven] [mid-19C] (*orig. Ling. Fr./Polari*) **1** the number seven. **2** sevenpence.

settle *v.* [semi-euph.] **1** [late 18C+] to knock down, to stun; also in fig. use. **2** [mid-19C] to sentence to penal transportation. **3** [mid-19C+] to deal with, get even with. **4** [mid-19C+] to kill, to murder. **5** [late 19C–1950s] to sentence to a term of imprisonment, usu. life.

IN PHRASES

❑ **settle one's coffee** *v.* [mid-19C] (*US*) to resolve one's difficulties. ❑ **settle one's hash** *v. see under* HASH *n.*[1]. ❑ **settle someone's coffee** *v.* [mid-19C] (*US*) to deal with someone who has wronged you, to take revenge. ❑ **settle someone's tater** *v.* [mid-19C] (*US*) to deal with someone who has wronged you, to take revenge.

settled *adj.* (*also* **wind-settled**) [SETTLE *v.* (1)] **1** [mid-19C] sentenced to transportation. **2** [late 19C–1960s] imprisoned. **3** [1900s–10s] (*Aus.*) finished, 'done for'.

IN PHRASES

❑ **settled right** *adj.* [late 19C–1960s] convicted and imprisoned after a fair trial. ❑ **settled wrong** *adj.* [late 19C–1960s] convicted and imprisoned unfairly.

settlement *n.* [pun] [20C+] (*Aus.*) a cemetery.

settler *n.* **1** [mid-18C–19C] a parting drink, 'one for the road' [such a final drink supposedly 'settles' the stomach after an evening's indulgence]. **2** [early 19C+] a knockout blow, esp. in fig. use, i.e. something that brings things to a conclusion.

Aus. uses in context of SE *settler*

IN COMPOUNDS

❑ **settler's clock** *n.* [i.e. it wakes one up] [late 19C+] (*Aus.*) a kookaburra. ❑ **settler's matches** *n.* [late 19C] (*Aus.*) easily lit strips of bark, used to light fires.

set trip *v.* (*also* **trip**) [SET *n.*[1] (1b) + TRIP *v.*[1] (2c)] [1990s+] (*US gang*) to attack another gang.

set tripping *n.* [SET TRIP *v.*] [1990s+] (*US gang*) the attacking of another gang.

set-up *n.*[1] **1** as a position, a place. (**a**) [late 19C–1930s] a person's carriage, deportment or body. (**b**) [20C+] (*US*) a place, esp. one's home, office etc. **2** [20C+] any situation, experience, e.g. *what's the set-up over there?* **3** in senses of planned manipulation or exploitation. (**a**) [1910s+] a situation planned to put a third party in a position of weakness, poss. to be murdered; thus the victim of that situation. (**b**) [1920s+] in sport, a 'fixed' match. (**c**) [1930s+] a criminal scheme. (**d**) [1930s+] an organization, often criminal. (**e**) [1960s+] (*US Und.*) a scheme whereby a criminal is caught red-handed. (**f**) [1980s] (*US*) a person who is easily duped, a 'sucker'. **4** in senses of equipment, kit. (**a**) [1910s+] (*US*) a place setting in a restaurant. (**b**) [1930s+] (*US*) the ice, mixer and other ingredients provided in unlicensed premises, to which patrons must bring their own alcohol, but in which they can then drink. (**c**) [1940s–50s] the preparation of an injection of a drug. (**d**) [1990s+] (*US prison*) the uniform, bedding, washing equipment etc issued to a new prisoner. (**e**) [2000s] (*US*) the makings of a drink, e.g. whisky, ice and a chaser, served in a bar. **5** [1980s] an arrangement.

set-up *n.*[2] [one 'sets' or sits it out] [1920s–40s] (*US Und.*) a one-day prison sentence.

set-up *adj.* [*SET UP (FOR) under* SET UP *v.*] **1** [mid-19C+] successful or comfortable; usu. as *well set-up*. **2** [20C+] (*orig. US*) pleased, happy. **3** [1900s] (*US campus*) drunk. **4** [1900s] (*US campus*) conceited, snobbish. **5** [1930s] physically 'built'.

set up *v.* **1** [late 19C+] to place a potential victim in a position of weakness, esp. a target for murder. **2** [1950s+] of police, to concoct evidence or create a situation whereby an innocent person is charged with a crime. **3** [1950s+] to intoxicate.

IN COMPOUNDS

❑ **set-up man** *n.* [SE *set up*, i.e. a robbery] **1** [1950s+] (*US Und.*) someone who organizes and plans major robberies, recruits those who carry them out, disposes of the loot etc. **2** [1970s] (*US Und*) a criminal who works for the police.

IN PHRASES

❑ **set up (for)** *v.* **1** [mid-19C+] to be well provided with. **2** [late 19C+] (*US*) to treat. ❑ **set up one's ebenezer** *v.* [Heb. *eben ha-ezer*, the stone of help, the memorial stone set up by Samuel (1 Sam. 7:12); i.e. the enduring solidity of such a memorial] [mid-19C–1900s] (*US*) to make up one's mind. ❑ **set up one's pipes** *v. see under* PIPES *n.*[1].

seven *n.* **1** [late 19C+] (*Und.*) a seven-year jail sentence. **2** [1960s] a week. **3** [1970s+] (*Aus.*) a seven-ounce (200ml) glass of beer.

SE in slang uses

DERIVATIVES

❑ **sevener** *n.* [such convicts were lower in the prison hierarchy than those serving longer terms or life sentences] **1** [late 19C] (*Aus.*) a convict sentenced to a seven-year prison sentence. **2** [1920s] (*Irish*) a fainting fit.

IN COMPOUNDS

❑ **seven-eleven** *adj.* [craps imagery] [1930s] (*US*) excellent, first-rate. ❑ **seven-up** *n.* [1940s] (*US Und.*) a general store; the robbery of a general store; thus *seven-up hustler*, a robber of a general store; *seven up hustling*, robbing general stores.

IN PHRASES

❑ **chuck a seven** *v. see* separate entry. ❑ **seven out** *v.* [the losing throw of *seven* in craps] [1950s] (*US black*) to lose, to be defeated. ❑ **throw a seven** *v. see* CHUCK A SEVEN *v.*

seven *adj.*

IN COMPOUNDS

❑ **seven digits** *n.* [1980s+] (*US black*) a telephone number (in the multiple exchanges of the major cities). ❑ **sevenpence** *n.* [early–mid-19C] (*UK Und.*) a sentence of seven years' transportation. ❑ **seven pennorth** *n.* [mid-19C] **1** a sentence of seven years' transportation. **2** seven months in prison. **3** seven years in prison. ❑ **seven single** *n.* [2000s] (*S.Afr. gay*) a person who is comfortable with being both active and passive in anal intercourse.

IN PHRASES

❑ **seven kinds of hell** *n. see under* HELL *n.* ❑ **seven kinds of shit** *n.* (*also* **seven shades of shit**) *see SEVEN KINDS OF HELL under* HELL *n.* ❑ **seven-sided animal** *n.* [late 18C–mid-19C] 'A one-eyed man or woman, each having a right side and a left side, a fore side and a backside, an outside, an inside and a blind side' (Grose, 1796). ❑ **seven-sided son of a bitch** *n.* (*also* **seven-sided son of a so-and-so**) [the US definition was presumably taken direct from Grose, above; 20C uses are only general derog.] [19C–1940s] (*US*) a man or a woman with one eye, having a right side and a left side, a fore side and a backside, an outside, an inside and a blind side; thus as a term of abuse.

seven and a three *n. see* FIVE AND TWO *n.*

seven and eleven *n.* [? winning craps throw, *seven and eleven*] [1930s] (*US black*) of a woman, sitting so as to diplay underwear or genitals.

seven and six *n. see* WAS SHE WORTH IT? *n.*

Seven Dials *n.* [rhy. sl. = SE *piles*] [1970s+] haemorrhoids.

Seven Dials raker *n.* [SE *Seven Dials* + RAKE *v.*[1] (2)] [late 19C–1920s] a prostitute whose home is in Seven Dials and who pursues her trade elsewhere; thus she 'never smiles out of the Dials' (Ware).

sevendible *adj.* [SE *seven double*, seven-fold; thus the severity is fig. multiplied seven-fold] [mid-19C+] (*Ulster*) severe, harsh, esp. of a beating; thus adv. *sevendably*.

seven-fifty-two *adv.* [seven days a week, 52 weeks a year] [2000s] all the time.

714s *n.* [? the digits imprinted into the pill] [1970s+] (*US drugs*) methaqualone.

seventeen-carat *adj. see* EIGHTEEN-CARAT *adj.*

seventeener *n.* [ety. unknown] [20C+] (*Aus. Und.*) a corpse.

730 *adj.* [the official numerical code applied in New York state to persons needing mental health treatment] [20C+] (*US black*) crazy.

seventy-'leven *n.* [20C+] (*US*) an indefinite number of anything.

seventy-one *n.* [a play on SIXTY-NINE *n.*] [1960s] (*Aus./US gay*) anal intercourse.

severe *adj.* **1** [19C–1900s] (*US, Western*) very big or powerful, hard to overcome. **2** [1980s] excellent, first-rate.

severely *adv.* [mid-19C+] to a great or excessive degree, esp. unwisely.

se voet! *excl.* [Afk. *se voet*, my foot] [1970s+] (*S.Afr.*) an excl. of dismissal or disbelief, 'my foot!'.

sew *v.* [the movements of the needle and of the body or hand] **1** [late 19C+] (*also* **sew up**) to have sexual intercourse. **2** [1940s+] (*US black/gay*) to masturbate. **3** *see* SEW UP *v.* (6).

IN PHRASES

❑ **sew someone's sees** *v. see under* SEE *n.* ❑ **sew up** *v. see* separate entry.

sewed up *adj.* [SEW UP *v.*] **1** [mid-19C] cheated, swindled. **2** [mid-19C] ill, sick. **3** [mid-19C–1900s] orig. of horses only, exhausted. **4** [mid-19C–1940s] (*also* **sewn up**) drunk. **5** [late 19C] pregnant. **6** [1920s+] confirmed, unsusceptible to error, esp. of a sporting contest in which the result has already been assured. **7** [1970s] set on a path, committed.

sewer *n.* **1** [late 19C–1900s] the Metropolitan and Metropolitan District Railway [like a *sewer* it runs beneath the London streets]. **2** [1940s–60s] (*drugs*) the median cephalic vein in the arm; thus *go into/hit the sewer*, to inject a narcotic, usu. heroin, into that vein [play on SHIT *n.* (1a)/SHIT *n.* (6a)]. **3** [1960s] (*Aus.*) the mouth.

IN PHRASES

❑ **go down the sewer** *v. see GO DOWN THE TOILET under* TOILET *n.* ❑ **go into a sewer** *v.* [1930s+] (*drugs*) to inject a drug intravenously.

sewer *v.* [2000s] to ruin.

sewermouth *n.* [the image of such language as 'dirty'] [1970s+] (*US campus*) anyone who regularly uses obscenities or profanities.

sewermouth *adj.* [SEWERMOUTH *n.* (1)] [1970s] (*US*) obscene, profane.

sewer trout *n.* [1940s+] (*US milit./prison*) any species of fish served at mealtimes.

sewing machine *n.* [SEW v. (1)] **1** [1950s] the vagina. **2** [1970s] the penis.

sew up *v.* **1** [early 19C+] to make drunk. **2** [early 19C+] (*also* **sow up**) of a person, to render secure, to dominate. **3** [mid–late 19C] to exhaust physically. **4** [mid-19C; 1940s] to surround, to seal off; in lit. and fig. uses. **5** [mid-19C–1950s] to outwit, to cheat, to swindle. **6** [late 19C+] (*orig. US*) (*also* **sew**) of an object/idea, to conclude, to possess completely, to finalize, to place under complete control. **7** [late 19C+] to impregnate; thus *sewn up*, pregnant. **8** [late 19C+] of a person, to tire out, to put at a disadvantage, to nonplus, to bring to a standstill, to put *hors de combat*. **9** [1920s–30s] to bring about the conviction of someone. **10** [1930s–40s] (*US Und.*) to ensure that a victim causes no trouble once they have been defrauded in a confidence trick.

sew up someone's stocking *v.* [mid-19C] to put to silence, to strike dumb.

sex *n.* **1** [mid-18C+] the vagina. **2** [late 19C+] the penis.

IN COMPOUNDS

❑ **sexboat** *n.* [1960s] a very attractive man or (usu.) woman. ❑ **sex-bomb** *n.* [1960s+] a very attractive man or (usu.) woman. ❑ **sex-box** *n. see* BOX *n.*[1] (1a). ❑ **sex fight** *n.* [1990s+] (*US*) a sexual game played between two people (of the same or opposite sex) in which each partner tries to make the other reach orgasm first; thus *sex fighter*, a participant in such a game. ❑ **sex goddess** *n.* (*also* **sex queen**) [1930s+] (*US*) a woman, esp. a film star (and latterly rock star), who is viewed as sexually provocative. ❑ **sex house** *n.* [1990s+] (*US*) anywhere where sex is on sale. ❑ **sex job** *n.* [JOB *n.*[2] (2)] [1930s+] (*US*) a sexually provocative or available person. ❑ **sex kitten** *n.* (*also* **sex bunny**) [coined in the late 1950s for the charms of the young Brigitte Bardot (b.1933)] [1950s+] a young woman with overt sex-appeal. ❑ **sex machine** *n.* **1** [1950s–60s] a promiscuous, sexually eager woman. **2** [1960s+] a sexually virile man, a womanizer. ❑ **sex-pole** *n.* [1970s] (*N.Z.*) a tall, attractive, and prob. promiscuous, man. ❑ **sexpot** *n.* [1950s+] **1** a very attractive man or (usu.) woman. **2** one who is obsessed with sex; a promiscuous woman. ❑ **sex queen** *n. see* SEX GODDESS above. ❑ **sex tank** *n.* [1960s] (*US*) a holding cell used to confine prostitutes or homosexuals. ❑ **sex wagon** *n.* [1960s+] (*US*) a flashy car, esp. as owned by a pimp.

IN PHRASES

❑ **sex on a stick** *n.* [2000s] one who is exceptionally sexually attractive; usu. of a woman. ❑ **sex with Jesus** [1980s+] (*orig. US*) a general phr. of satisfaction, praise, delight, e.g. *that movie – sex with Jesus*.

sex *v.* (*also* **sex down, ...up**) [1950s+] to have sexual intercourse.

IN COMPOUNDS

❑ **sexing-piece** *n.* [1920s+] the penis.

IN PHRASES

❑ **sexed up** *adj.* [20C+] sexually excited. ❑ **sex in** *v.* [1990s+] (*US black/teen*) to gang rape. ❑ **sex on** *v.* [1950s+] (*Aus.*) to indulge in 'heavy petting' or even intercourse. ❑ **sex up** *v.* **1** [1940s+] to increase the sexual content of, e.g. a film script. **2** [2000s] to make the content of something more attractive or exciting.

sexile *n.* [1980s+] (*US campus*) exclusion from a dorm room overnight or temporarily so that a roommate may use the room for sex.

sexo *n.* (*also* **sexoh**) [SE *sex* + -O *sfx* (1)] (*N.Z.*) **1** [1940s+] a sexual offender. **2** [1950s+] someone seen as over-sexed or obsessed with sex.

sexton blake *n.* [rhy. sl.; ult. the fictional detective created by 'Hal Meredith' (Harry Blyth) in *The Halfpenny Marvel* magazine (1893)] **1** [20C+] a cake. **2** [1970s+] a fake.

sexy *adj.* [1960s+] **1** (*orig. media*) used to describe anything that pulls in audiences, readers etc, thus usu. violence, disaster, scandal etc. **2** (*US*) used to describe anything very appealing. **3** used of anything or anybody 'clever' or 'smart'.

sey *n. see* SAY *n.* and its combs.

S.F.A. *n. see* SWEET FANNY ADAMS *n.*

s.f.a. *n.* [abbr. *sweet fuck all*] [1940s+] absolutely nothing at all.

s.f. & t. *phr.* [abbr.] [1990s+] sucked, fucked and tattooed.

S.F.C. *n.* (*also* **s.f.c.**) [abbr.; capitals and lower case letters are interchangeable] [1990s+] (*US black teen*) San Francisco City or sucka-/sucker-free city.

'sfoot! *excl.* (*also* **z'foot!**) [17C; early 19C] a mild oath, lit. 'God's foot!'.

shab *n.* [? SCAB *n.*[1] (2)/SE *scab*, a rascal, a scoundrel or *shabby*] [early 17C–19C] an unpleasant, sneaky person.

DERIVATIVES

❑ **shabster** *n.* [-STER *sfx*] [mid–late 19C] an unpleasant, sneaky person.

shab *v.* [SHAB *n.*] [mid-18C–mid-19C] to cheat, to deceive, to act in an underhand manner.

IN PHRASES

❑ **shab off** *v.* **1** [late 17C–mid-18C] to cheat someone, then to dismiss them without apology or explanation. **2** [late 17C–18C; 1910s] to sneak away.

shabba *v.* [rhy. sl.; *shabba rank* = WANK v. (1); ult. reggae star *Shabba* Ranks (Rextion Gordon, b.1965)] [1990s+] to masturbate.

shabberoon *n.* (*also* **shabaroon, shabroon**) [SE *shabby*; alt. uses are 18C–19C] **1** [late 17C–18C] a shabby, down-at-heel person. **2** [late 18C–early 19C] a mean-spirited person.

shabeen *n. see* CHABEN *n.*

shabers *n.* [? SHAB *n.*] [1940s] (*W.I.*) a disreputable person.

shaboney *n. see* JIBONE *n.*

shab-rag *adj.* [dial. *shab-rag*, a mean beggarly person, a ragamuffin] [mid–late 18C] shabby, damaged, worn.

shabroon *n. see* SHABBEROON *n.*

shabu *n.* [ety. unknown] [1980s+] (*drugs*) methamphetamine.

shack *n.*[1] [SE *shake-rag*, a beggar + dial. *shackle-bag*, a lazy loiterer, a vagabond] (*US tramp*) **1** [mid-18C; 19C–1910s] a tramp, a vagrant. **2** [late 19C–1940s] a railroad brakeman. **3** [1920s] (*US Und.*) a police officer.

IN COMPOUNDS

❑ **shack fever** *n.* [mid-19C] (*US tramp*) weariness, fatigue.

shack *n.*[2] **1** [20C+] (*US*) one's home, one's house. **2** [1920s] any place where tramps congregate. **3** *see* SHACK JOB *under* SHACK v. **4** *see* SHACK-UP *n.* (1).

IN COMPOUNDS

❑ **shack bully** *n.* [1940s–50s] (*US black/teen*) the outstanding person, the 'boss'.

shack *v.* [SHACK *n.*[1]] (*US*) **1** [mid–late 19C] to idle, to loaf. **2** [late 19C+] (*also* **shuck out**) to live alone, to live as a bachelor or single woman. **3** [1940s+] (*also* **shack around, shack out**) to have sexual intercourse; also as *n.* **4** [1940s+] to live with a partner. **5** [1950s] (*US Und.*) to rob a house or apartment when the owner is having dinner in another room; thus *shacker*, a 'dinner burglar'; *shacking touch*, the loot gained from such a burglary or the burglary itself. **6** [1960s+] to stay the night at someone's house, whether sexually or not.

IN COMPOUNDS

❑ **shack job** *n.* [1940s+] **1** the person with whom one lives. **2** a couple or the state of being a couple. **3** (*also* **shack, shack baby**) a casual sex partner. ❑ **shack man** *n.* (*also* **shack rat**) [SE *man*/RAT *n.*[1] (1)] [1940s] (*US*) **1** an adulterous man. **2** a married man.

shackles *n.* [? dial. *shacklebone*, the hind leg of a pig's carcass] [1900s–40s] **1** the off-cuts from a butcher's preparing of meat for sale. **2** (*UK/US tramp*) soup [note Irwin, *American Tramp and Und. Slang* (1931): 'No doubt the word was coined in some prison where the dish was of such a nature as to keep the prisoners near a toilet, or 'shackled' to one place. It is generally used on the road to indicate any article of food that exercises a definite effect upon the elimination']. **3** (*US*) cheese [cheese is trad. 'binding'].

shackle-up *n.* [SHACKLE UP *v.*] [1930s–50s] (*UK tramp*) a midday meal cooked at the roadside.

shackle up *v.* [? SHACKLES *n.*] [1930s–50s] (*UK tramp*) to cook a midday meal.

shacks! *excl.* [var. on SHUCKS! *excl.*] [1980s+] (*US campus*) a mild excl. of surprise, regret, annoyance etc.

shack-stoner *n.* [ety. unknown] [late 19C–1900s] (*Aus./N.Z.*) a sixpence.

shack-up *n.* [SHACK UP *v.*] **1** [1920s+] (*US*) (*also* **shack**) a person with whom one has a sexual relationship. **2** [1950s–70s] an act of sexual intercourse. **3** [1970s] a sexual relationship.

shack up *v.* [SHACK *v.*] [1930s+] (*orig. US*) **1** to live with a sexual partner. **2** to have sex with someone. **3** to pick up, for sexual purposes. **4** to live or reside, usu. temporarily.

shade *n.*[1] [SE *shade*, partial darkness] **1** [mid-18C] (*UK Und.*) a wig. **2** [mid-19C] (*US Und.*) an umbrella or sunshade. **3** [mid–late 19C] in pl., a variety of late-night music-halls and bars on or near the Strand, London; used generically in US [their opening during the 'shady' hours]. **4** in racial contexts. (**a**) [mid-19C–1960s] (*US*) a derog. term for a black person. (**b**) [1960s+] (*US*) a derog. term for a white person. **5** [1920s+] (*US Und.*) a receiver of stolen goods. **6** [1930s+] (*Irish*) a police officer. **7** [1950s+] (*also* **sunshades**) in pl., dark glasses, sunglasses [note 19C *shades*, goggles, e.g. for use during stone-breaking].

IN PHRASES

❑ **in the shade** [1910s] (*US Und.*) in prison.

shade *n.*[2] **1** [mid-19C+] a minute quantity. **2** [1900s–20s] (*US*) a (marginal) advantage.

shade *n.*[3] [SHADE *v.* (1)] [1930s–40s] (*US Und.*) an accomplice who shields a working pickpocket.

shade *v.* [SE *shade*, to protect from the light] **1** [1930s–40s] (*US Und.*) to protect a pickpocket while he/she works. **2** [1950s+] (*US black*) to hide, to conceal. **3** *see* THROW SHADE *under* THROW *v.*

shade-glim *n. see* GLIM *n.* (9).

shadow *n.* **1** [mid-19C+] (*US*) a plain-clothes detective. **2** [late 19C] (*UK Und.*) a pimp, male or female. **3** [late 19C+] (*US*) a derog. term for a black person.

shadow *v.* [SHADOW *n.* (1)] [mid-19C+] (*orig. US.*) of a detective, to follow someone.

shadscale *n. see* SCALE *n.*[1].

shady *adj.* [mid-19C; 1960s+] stupid, strange.

SE in slang uses

IN PHRASES

❑ **keep shady** *v.* [mid–late 19C] (*UK Und.*) to act discreetly; to keep oneself hidden.

shady grove of the evangelist *n. see* GROVE OF THE EVANGELIST *n.*

shady spring *n.* [late 18C] the vagina.

shaft *n.* **1** in physiological senses. (**a**) [17C+] (*also* **prickshaft**) the penis [20C+ use mainly US black; note blaxploitation films of the 1970s, starring macho private eye 'John Shaft']. (**b**) [1930s+] (*US*) a woman's body, considered simply as a sexual object. (**c**) [1920s–50s] (*US*) a (woman's) leg. **2** [1910s+] (*orig. US*) unfair treatment; often as *the shaft*.

IN COMPOUNDS

❑ **shaft job** *n.* [JOB *n.*[2] (2)] [2000s] an example of unfair treatment. ❑ **shaftsman** *n.* (*also* **shaft artist**) [-ARTIST *sfx*] [1970s] a cheat, a deceiver.

IN PHRASES

❑ **get the shaft** *v.* [1950s+] (*orig. US*) **1** to treat unfairly or harshly. **2** to cheat, to deceive. **3** to take advantage of. **4** to slight or reject. ❑ **shaft of delight** *n.* [mid-18C] the penis. ❑ **sink the shaft** *v. see under* SINK *v.*

shaft *v.* [SE *shaft*, to shoot with an arrow] **1** [1950s+] to have sexual intercourse (usu. of a man with a woman). **2** [1950s+] (*orig. US*) to defeat, to defraud, to harm, to treat unfairly. **3** [1990s+] (*US campus*) to steal. **4** [2000s] to stab.

DERIVATIVES

❑ **shaftable** *adj.* [1990s+] of a woman, suitable for and hopefully susceptible to seduction.

shafted *adj.* [SHAFT *v.*] [1950s+] **1** treated unfairly, in serious trouble; usu. as *get shafted*. **2** stood up by one's date. **3** suffering a broken relationship.

shaftesbury *n.* [? proper name of the Dorset town] [late 17C–early 19C] a gallon pot full of wine, with a cock (i.e. tap).

shafting *n.* [SHAFT *v.*] [1960s+] **1** an act of sexual intercourse. **2** unfair treatment. **3** a stabbing.

shag *n.*[1] [SHAG *v.*[1] (1)] **1** [late 18C+] an act of sexual intercourse. **2** [1930s] (*US teen*) a party where teenagers experiment sexually. **3** [1940s–60s] a person in general use. **4** [1960s+] a person, usu. a woman but in 1990s+ also a man, seen simply as a sexual object; thus *good shag, lousy shag*.

IN COMPOUNDS

❑ **shag all** *n.* [var. on FUCK ALL *n.*] [1980s+] nothing at all. ❑ **shag artist** *n.* [ARTIST *n.* (1)] [1960s+] a womanizer, a sexual athlete. ❑ **shag-bag** *n.* **1** [1970s] (*orig. milit.*) a prostitute. **2** [1990s+] (*orig. Aus.*) a general pej. term for a woman; sexual availability is presumed, but not automatic. **3** [2000s] (*US*) the vagina. ❑ **shag magnet** *n. see under* -MAGNET *sfx.* ❑ **shag-pad** *n.* [PAD *n.*[2] (2)] [2000s] an apartment or room where one can bring a casual sex partner. ❑ **shagpit** *n.* [PIT *n.* (5)] [2000s] a bed. ❑ **shag-wagon** *n.* (*also* **shagging station, ...wagon**) [1960s+] a van or car used primarily for sex.

shag *n.*[2] [SHAG *v.*[2] (2)] [1930s–60s] (*US tramp*) a chase, a hue and cry.

shag *n.*[3] [var. SCAG *n.*[2] (2)] [1990s+] (*drugs*) heroin.

shag *n.*[4] [? link to SHAKEDOWN *n.* (3c)] [2000s] (*US Und.*) the patter used to lure victims into a confidence game.

shag *adj.*[1] [? SE *shag*, a rascal, a rogue] [1930s–50s] (*US prison*) worthless.

shag *adj.*[2] [? fig. use SHAG *n.*[1] (1)] [1940s+] (*US teen*) excellent, wonderful.

shag *v.*[1] (*also* **sheg**) [? SE *shake*, hence SHAKE *v.*] **1** [late 17C+] to have sexual intercourse; thus *shag around*, to lead a promiscuous sex-life. **2** [late 19C+] used as a semi-euph. for FUCK *v.* in various non-copulatory uses. **3** [1950s–60s] to assault, to beat up. **4** [1980s+] to masturbate. **5** [2000s] to cheat.

DERIVATIVES

❑ **shagability** *n.* [1990s+] one's sex appeal. ❑ **shaggable** *adj.* [1990s+] sexy, lit. (potentially) available for seduction. ❑ **shagtastic** *adj.* [2000s] extremely sexually alluring.

IN COMPOUNDS

❑ **shag-happy** *adj.* [-HAPPY *sfx*] [2000s] keen on sexual intercourse. ❑ **shag-nasty** *adj.* **1** [20C+] a general pej. name for any unpopular man. **2** [1980s+] (*N.Z.*) used affectionately.

IN PHRASES

❑ **shag ass** *v.* [SE *shake*/SHAG *v.*[2] (5) + ASS *n.* (4)] [1950s+] (*US*) **1** to work hard, to move fast, to expend effort and energy. **2** to depart or leave hurriedly. ❑ **shagged (out)** *adj.* [fig. use of sense 2 above, i.e. euph. for FUCKED *adj.*[1]] **1** [1930s+] exhausted. **2** [1940s+] broken, out of order. ❑ **shag like a rattlesnake** *v. see* FUCK LIKE A RATTLESNAKE *under* FUCK *v.* ❑ **shag out** *v.* **1** [1950s] to exhaust. **2** [1970s] to eject. ❑ **shag the arse off** *v. see* FUCK THE ARSE OFF SOMEONE *under* FUCK *v.*

IN EXCLAMATIONS

❑ **shag me!** [1980s+] (*N.Z.*) an excl. of atonishment and/or resignation; a semi-euph. for FUCK ME! *excl.* ❑ **shag that for a lark!** *see* FUCK THAT/THIS FOR A LARK! *under* FUCK *v.*

shag *v.*[2] [Gloucester dial. *shag*, to make off, to traipse around] **1** [1910s] (*US Und.*) to discover, to identify. **2** [1910s+] (*US*) to chase; lit. and fig. **3** [1920s+] (*US*) to wander around; to walk, esp. slowly, whether through laziness or exhaustion. **4** [1930s–40s] to give someone a false impression. **5** [1940s+] to move fast. **6** [1950s] (*US gang*) to deliver. **7** [1950s] (*US black*) to dance. **8** [1960s+] to deal with. **9** [1960s+] to throw.

10 [1960s+] to obtain. **11** [1980s] (*US teen*) to tease, to harass.

shag *v.*[3] [1940s–50s] (*drugs*) to inject a narcotic.

shag! *excl.* (*also* **shag off!**) [semi-euph. for FUCK OFF! *excl.* (1)] [1960s+] (*US*) go away!

shag-bag *n.* (*also* **shake-bag**) [17C SE *shag*, a rascal] [late 17C+] a worthless, shabby person.

shagger *n.*[1] [SHAG *v.*[1]] **1** [20C+] one who copulates; a sexual enthusiast. **2** [1970s] a nuisance, a lazy, disobedient person. **3** [1970s] any thing or person.

IN COMPOUNDS

❑ **shagger's back** *n.* [1980s+] (*orig. Aus.*) a particularly painful backache, supposedly the result of over-enthusiastic copulation.

shagger *n.*[2] [SHAG *v.*[2] (2)] [1930s] (*US*) a police officer; a person who shadows or follows someone.

shagging *n.* [SHAG *v.*[1] (1)] [mid-19C+] an act of sexual intercourse.

IN COMPOUNDS

❑ **shagging machine** *n.* [late 19C] (*US*) the vagina. ❑ **shagging-station/-wagon** *n.* *see* SHAG-WAGON *under* SHAG *n.*[1].

shagging *adj.* [SHAG *v.*[1] (1)] **1** [1920s+] a semi-euph. for FUCKING *adj.* **2** [1970s+] as an infix.

shagging *adv.* [1920s+] a semi-euph. for FUCKING *adv.*

IN PHRASES

❑ **shagging well** *adv. see* FUCKING WELL *under* FUCKING *adv.*

shagging hell! *excl. see* FUCKING HELL! *excl.*

shag-leg *n.* [anyone who can SE *shake* (a) *leg*] [1930s] (*US black*) a person.

shagrag *n.* [synon. SE *shake-rag*] [late 16C–early 19C] a ragged, disreputable person; a low rascally fellow.

shagroon *n.* [? Irish *seachrán*, wandering] [mid–late 19C] (*N.Z.*) an early settler in Canterbury, New Zealand, from anywhere except Britain, esp. one from Australia.

shaka *n.* [1990s+] (*W.I.*) an unattractive person.

shake *n.*[1] **1** in sexual senses. (**a**) [16C–1900s] an act of sexual intercourse. (**b**) [mid–late 19C] a prostitute or kept woman. **2** [mid-19C] a disreputable man. **3** [mid-19C] (*US*) constr. with *the*, malaria. **4** as a form of entertainment. (**a**) [mid-19C+] (*US*) a dance. (**b**) [1930s+] (*US black*) a party at which the guests pay an admission fee to help pay the rent and pay for the refreshments. (**c**) [1970s] a party. **5** [mid-19C+] a moment, a second. **6** [1910s+] in (*US Und.*) uses [abbr. SHAKEDOWN *n.* (3)]. (**a**) blackmail, extortion, often from homosexuals. (**b**) an arrest; a search by the police or prison guards. **7** in drug uses [note dial. *shake*, the residue of grain after harvesting]. (**a**) [1970s+] marijuana, esp. the residue of a bag of cannabis after the smokeable buds are removed. (**b**) [1980s] diluted cocaine. **8** [1980s+] (*US campus*) constr. with *the*, an undesirable person. **9** *see* FAIR SHAKE *n.*

pertaining to extortion

IN COMPOUNDS

❑ **shake artist** *n.* [-ARTIST *sfx*] [1940s] (*US Und.*) a blackmailer. ❑ **shake man** *n.* [1900s–50s] (*US Und.*) an extortionist. ❑ **shake mob** *n.* [1900s–30s] (*US Und.*) a gang of extortionists.

IN PHRASES

❑ **put the shake on** *v.* [1920s+] (*US Und.*) to blackmail, to extort.

pertaining to drugs

IN COMPOUNDS

❑ **shake-bag** *n.* [BAG *n.*[1] (7)] [2000s] (*US drugs*) a bag of second-rate marijuana.

IN PHRASES

❑ **cold shake** *n.* [1990s+] (*US drugs*) to prepare a drug for injection by shaking a capsule in cold water so as to dissolve the pill and mix the two together (the usual method is to heat the drug/water solution).

other uses

DERIVATIVES

❑ **shakish** *adj.* [sense 1a above] [mid-19C] (*UK Und.*) promiscuous; spec. working as a prostitute.

IN PHRASES

❑ **half-a-shake** *n.* [20C+] (*N.Z.*) a moment, a very short time. ❑ **two shakes** *n.* (*also* **brace of shakes, couple of shakes**) [abbr. of TWO SHAKES OF A LAMB'S TAIL *phr.*; SE *brace*, pair; but note also sense 5 above] [mid-19C+] a very short time; usu. with *in…*, meaning quickly, immediately.

SE in slang uses

IN PHRASES

❑ **asking for a shake** [1950s] (*US*) looking for trouble. ❑ **do fries go with that shake?** [burger bar imagery] [1970s+] (*US black*) a phr. called out by a man to a passing attractive woman (whose buttocks move as she walks). ❑ **even shake** *n.* (*also* **good shake**) [the shaking of dice; FAIR SHAKE *n.*] [1960s+] an equal chance. ❑ **fair shake** *n. see* separate entry. ❑ **give someone the shake** *v.* [abbr. SE *handshake*] [late 19C+] (*US*) to reject someone, to dismiss or get rid of someone, to leave or run off; often as *…cold shake*, *…dead shake*. ❑ **give something the shake** *v.* [1900s] to abandon, to give up. ❑ **great shakes** *n.* (*also* **great shucks, some shakes**) [early 19C+] something very good or admirable; usu. in negative *no great shakes*, *not any great shakes* etc. ❑ **shake of the bag** *n.* (*also* **shakings of the bag, shake-poke**) [the image of shaking the very last crumbs from a bag + BAG *n.*[1]] [mid-19C+] (*Irish*) **1** the youngest child in a family. **2** an unappealing person. ❑ **square the shake** *v.* [1940s] (*US Und.*) to pay a bribe. ❑ **unfair shake** *n.* [reverse of FAIR SHAKE *n.*] [1970s+] bad luck.

shake *n.*[2] (*also* **shaker**) [? SHADE *n.*[1] (1) or play on chocolate milk*shake*] [1900s] (*US*) a derog. term for a black person.

shake *v.* **1** [17C–1960s] to have sexual intercourse; thus *shake oneself*, to masturbate. **2** in Und. uses. (**a**) [early 19C+] (*Aus./UK Und.*) to steal, to run off with [use after mid-19C mainly Aus.]. (**b**) [1950s+] (*Can. Und.*) to serve a prison sentence. **3** (*orig. UK Und.*) in senses of SE *shake off*. (**a**) [mid–late 19C] to abandon. (**b**) [mid-19C–1910s] to leave. (**c**) [mid-19C+] to get rid of, usu. of a person. (**d**) [20C+] to evade a pursuer. **4** [late 19C] (*US Und.*) to divide criminal spoils. **5** [late 19C] (*US*) to win when gambling. **6** in uses implying lit. or fig. movement. (**a**) [1910s] (*US*) as imper., get going, hurry up; to hurry up. (**b**) [1970s] (*US black*) to explain. (**c**) [1950s+] to happen, to start to happen. (**d**) [1990s+] (*W.I.*) to move on. **7** *see* SHAKE DOWN *v.* (2a).

IN COMPOUNDS

❑ **shake-bag** *n.* **1** [18C] a prostitute. **2** [late 19C] the vagina. **3** *see* SHAG-BAG *n.*

SE in slang uses

IN COMPOUNDS

❑ **shake baby** *n.* [BABY *n.* (3) is encouraged to 'shake that thing'] [1920s–30s] (*US black*) a dress that is tight across the hips and has a short, full skirt. ❑ **shake-buckler** *n.* [SE *shake* + *buckler*, a sword] [mid-16C–mid-17C] a bully, a thug. ❑ **shake-em-up** *n.* [its effects] [1970s+] (*US black*) white port and lemon juice. ❑ **shakefoot** *n.* (*also* **shake-up**) [1940s+] (*W.I.*) a party or dance, esp. one to which an invitation is not required; thus *shakefoot*, to dance. ❑ **shake-glim** *n.* [SE *shake*, to wave + GLIM *n.* (7)] [mid–late 19C] a begging letter, based on the fantasy that the writer has lost all their possessions through fire. ❑ **shake-lurk** *n.* [SE *shake*, to wave + LURK *n.* (1)] [mid-19C] a piece of paper, carried by a beggar, which purports (falsely) to give an account of a terrible disaster, usu. a shipwreck, in which the beggar has suffered.

IN PHRASES

❑ **how's it shaking?** *see* WHAT'S SHAKING? below. ❑ **nothing shaking** [1950s+] (*US*) used as a response to the greeting WHAT'S SHAKING? below and meaning things are normal. ❑ **shake a cloth in the wind** *v.* **1** [late 18C–19C] to be hanged in chains [one's flapping clothes]. **2** [1930s] to be slightly drunk [orig. naut. jargon]. ❑ **shake a hoof** *v.* **1** [1910s] to run. **2** [1920s] (*US*) to dance. ❑ **shake a leg** *v.* **1** [late 18C+] (*also* **shake a foot, ...heel, ...toe, ...shoulder, turn a leg**) to dance. **2** [late 19C] to go out on a spree. **3** [20C+] to hurry up, to get a move on (lit. and fig.); often as imper. ❑ **shake along** *v.* [1910s] to move on. ❑ **shake a loose leg** *v.* (*also* **shake a free leg**) [mid-19C] (*UK tramp*) to live wandering as a tramp. ❑ **shake (a man's) back** *v.* [horseriding imagery] [late 16C] of a woman, to copulate enthusiastically. ❑ **shake a sheet** *v.* [early 17C] to have sexual intercourse. ❑ **shake a sock** *v.* [20C+] to urinate. ❑ **shake a tail-feather** *v.* [note Ward, *A Compleat and Humorous Account of all the Remarkable Clubs and Societies* (1709): 'A Set of Dancers were wantonly engaged in their Shake-Tail Exercise'] [1960s+] (*orig. US*) to dance energetically. ❑ **shake a tart** *v.* [TART *n.* (1)] [late 19C+] of a man, to have sexual intercourse. ❑ **shake a wicked leg** *v.* (*also* **shake a wicked calf, ...foot, ...hoof, shake a mean..., shake a nasty...**) [1920s] (*US*) to dance well. ❑ **shake down** *see* separate entries. ❑ **shake hands** *v. see* separate entry. ❑ **shake it up** *v.* (*also* **shake it, shake her up, shake oneself up**) **1** [mid-19C+] (*Aus./US*) to hurry up. **2** [1930s] (*US*) to walk in a provocative manner. ❑ **shake 'n' bake** *n. see* separate entry. ❑ **shake-off** *n.* [1910s–30s] (*US*) the act of dismissing or abandoning someone. ❑ **shake one's arse/fanny** *v. see under* ARSE *n.* ❑ **shake one's heels** *v.* [late 16C] to be hanged. ❑ **shake one's jolt** *v. see under* JOLT *n.* ❑ **shake one's shambles** *v.* [late 17C–18C] to hurry up, to get started. ❑ **shake one's shirt** *v.* [1930s+] (*N.Z./US*) to make an effort, to 'get stuck in'. ❑ **shake one's tail** *v. see under* TAIL *n.* ❑ **shake one's teeva** *v.* [var. BATTY *n.*[2] (1)] [2000s] (*US black*) to dance in an exuberant manner. ❑ **shake one's tree** *v.* [1970s+] to pressurize someone emotionally. ❑ **shake one's trotters** *v. see under* TROTTER *n.* ❑ **shake one's trotters at Beilby's ball** *v. see under* BEILBY'S BALL *n.* ❑ **shake out** *v.* [1950s+] (*W.I. Rasta*) to leave without haste, casually. ❑ **shake the bullet** *v. see under* BULLET *n.*[1]. ❑ **shake the cross** *v. see under* CROSS *n.*[1]. ❑ **shake the daylights out of** *v. see* BEAT THE (LIVING) DAYLIGHTS OUT OF *under* DAYLIGHTS *n.* ❑ **shake the dew off the lily** *v. see under* LILY *n.* ❑ **shake the fleas out** *v.* [1940s] (*US*) to make an effort, to 'get a move on', to stop being lazy. ❑ **shake the lead out (of) one's arse/ass** *v. see under* LEAD *n.* ❑ **shake the tree** *v.* [early 17C] to have sexual intercourse. ❑ **shake up** *see* separate entries. ❑ **what shakes?** [mid-19C] (*UK Und.*) what chance is there of stealing something? ❑ **what's shaking? 1** [1950s+] (*US*) (*also* **how's it shaking?**) a greeting, hello and how are you? **2** [1960s] (*US*) what's the matter?

(IN EXCLAMATIONS)

❑ **shake five!** [1950s+] (*W.I.*) a greeting between two men, lit. 'shake my five fingers'.

shake and shiver *n.* (*also* **stand and shiver**) [rhy. sl.] [20C+] (*Aus.*) a river.

shakedown *n.* **1** [early 19C+] an impromptu bed, somewhere to sleep, not necessarily a proper bed. **2** in senses of extortion or coercion [the image of shaking one's clothes (or cell) until money falls out]. (**a**) [mid-19C] (*US Und.*) a brothel where one is liable to be robbed. (**b**) [mid–late 19C] (*US*) a rough dance. (**c**) [late 19C+] blackmail, extortion. (**d**) [1910s+] a search, either of a person, a place or one's belongings. (**e**) [1910s+] (*US prison*) a search, whether of a cell or of an individual prisoner. (**f**) [1930s+] a payment, a bribe. **3** *see* THROWDOWN *n.*

(IN COMPOUNDS)

❑ **shakedown artist** *n.* (*also* **shakdowner**) [1930s+] an extortionist, a blackmailer.

shake down *v.* **1** in senses of SHAKEDOWN *n.* (1). (**a**) [mid-19C+] to sleep in an impromptu bed. (**b**) [late 19C] to settle into living quarters. **2** (*also* **shake, shake loose, shake out**) in senses of SHAKEDOWN *n.* (3). (**a**) [mid-19C+] to blackmail, to extort money (from). (**b**) [late 19C–1910s] to obtain a financial contribution, e.g. to a political campaign. (**c**) [20C+] of (usu.) police, to search, to raid; also (*prison*) to search the cell. (**d**) [1910s] to pay protection to the police involuntarily. (**e**) [1930s+] to interrogate; to elicit information. (**f**) [1930s+] (*W.I.*) to rob. (**g**) [1950s] to empty out. (**h**) [1980s+] (*US black*) to rape. (**i**) [1990s+] (*US black*) to have sex with. **3** [1990s+] to beat at cards.

(IN PHRASES)

❑ **on the shake** [1930s] of police, raiding, making arrests. ❑ **shake it down** *v.* [2000s] to make an effort, to get to work.

shake hands *v.*

(IN PHRASES)

❑ **shake hands with an old friend** *v.* (*also* **shake hands with him, ...Mr Right, ...the baby, ...the fellow who stood up with me at my wedding**) [1960s+] to urinate. ❑ **shake hands with the governor** *v.* [1990s+] to masturbate. ❑ **shake hands with the unemployed** *v.* [1960s+] **1** to urinate. **2** (*also* **shake hands with the bloke who enlisted with me**) to masturbate. ❑ **shake hands with the wife's best friend** *v.* [WIFE'S BEST FRIEND *under* BEST FRIEND *n.*] [1960s+] (*orig. Aus.*) **1** to masturbate. **2** to urinate.

shake 'n' bake *n.* [brandname of popular US instant food. Note US milit. jargon *Shake 'n' Bake*, a sergeant who attended NCO school and gained rank after only a short time in uniform. This, in turn, has similar synons., *Ready Whip*, *Nestle's Quick*; also N.Z. *shake 'n' bake*, a quickly built kitset suburb] [1970s+] (*US black*) any form of trickery that ensures that one eludes work and/or responsibilities.

shaker *n.*[1] [? dial. *shaker*, a worn-out, shabby garment] [mid-19C] a shirt, coat or waistcoat.

shaker *n.*[2] **1** [mid-19C] a beggar who pretends to have fits. **2** [mid-19C] a hand. **3** [late 19C+] (*Aus.*) a rickety motor vehicle. **4** [1930s] (*US Und.*) in pl. (loaded) dice. **5** [1980s+] (*drugs*) a small glass bottle used for heating and 'cooking' crack cocaine.

shakes, the *n.* (*also* **shivery-shakes**) **1** [mid-19C+] delirium tremens, the shaking associated with an alcoholic who has been deprived of sufficient drink to achieve normality. **2** [1910s+] (*also* **shakeroos**) extreme terror, nervousness. **3** [1930s+] as sense 1 in the context of withdrawal from narcotics. **4** [1940s] a similar effect to sense 1, caused by excess coffee. **5** [1940s] palsy. **6** [1950s+] great excitement.

shakester *n.* (*also* **shickster**) [mispron. of Yid. *shikse*, a gentile female; according to Hotten (1867) a term used by the costers to refer to the women of the class immediately above, i.e. tradesmen's wives/daughters] [mid–late 19C] **1** a gentile woman. **2** a non-Jewish servant-girl. **3** a woman.

shake-up *n.* [SE *shake up*/SHAKE UP *v.*] **1** [late 19C] an unnerving experience. **2** [1900s–50s] the process of 'cleaning up' a city/establishment. **3** [1920s–40s] (*US black*) a form of cocktail, made from a variety of liquors, plus wine. **4** [1940s] (*US black*) cheap corn whisky. **5** *see* SHAKEFOOT *under* SHAKE *v.*

shake up *v.* **1** [19C] to masturbate. **2** [mid–late 19C] to come up with, to contribute. **3** [1960s] (*US*) of police, to raid and search an individual and/or their premises.

shaking *n.* [SHAKE *v.*] [1950s+] (*US black*) what is going on; news; events.

shakings of the bag *n. see* SHAKE OF THE BAG *under* SHAKE *n.*[1].

shaking the sheets *n.*

(IN PHRASES)

❑ **dance to the tune/time of shaking the sheets (without music)** *v. see under* DANCE *v.*

shakish *adj. see under* SHAKE *n.*[1].

shaky *adj.* [1940s –60s] (*US Und.*) of a town or city, unsafe for criminal operations; similarly of a place targeted for a robbery.

Shaky City *n.* [the frequency of earthquakes on the San Andreas Fault] [1960s+] (*US*) **1** Los Angeles, California. **2** San Francisco, California.

Shaky Isles *n.* [the frequency of earthquakes] [1930s+] (*Aus.*) New Zealand.

shaler *n.* [proper name *Sheila*, ult. Irish *caille*, a young girl] [mid–late 19C] (*Aus.*) a woman.

shall-I *n.* [abbr. dial. *shalligonaked*, 'a thin flimsy garment, cloth of an inferior kind' (*EDD*)] [1940s] (*W.I.*) cheap material.

shall I put a bit of hair on it? *phr. see under* HAIR *n.*

shallow *n.* **1** [late 18C–19C] a hat [shape]. **2** [mid-19C] a basket, used by a costermonger [shape]. **3** [1900s] a fool.

shallow *adj.* [mid–late 19C] naked.

IN COMPOUNDS

❑ **shallow cove** *n.* (*also* **shallow, shallow bloke, ...chap, ...covey, ...fellow, ...runner**) [COVE *n.* (1)/BLOKE *n.* (3)/COVEY *n.* (1)] [mid–late 19C] a wandering beggar, adopting tattered clothing and posing as a madman, or shipwreck survivor; thus the *shallow brigade*, a party or group of beggars. ❑ **shallow cove lay** *n.* [LAY *n.*[3] (1)] [mid-19C] (*UK Und.*) acting as a wandering beggar who adopts tattered clothing and poses as a madman. ❑ **shallow dodge** *n.* [DODGE *n.* (1)] [mid–late 19C] the practice of dressing in minimal rags for the purpose of begging. ❑ **shallow mot** *n.* [MOT *n.* (2)] [mid-19C] the female companion of a wandering beggar.

IN PHRASES

❑ **do the shallow** *v.* (*also* **run shallow, work the shallow**) [mid–late 19C] to dress in rags to enhance one's appeal as a beggar. ❑ **on the shallow(s)** [mid–late 19C] going around half-naked (for the purpose of begging); very poorly dressed; usu. as *go on the shallow*.

SE in slang uses

IN COMPOUNDS

❑ **shallow pate** *n.* [SE *shallow*, lacking depth of mind + *pate*, head] [mid-17C–1900s] a fool, a simpleton; thus adj. *shallow pated*, foolish. ❑ **shallow screever** *n. see under* SCREEVER *n.*

IN PHRASES

❑ **live shallow** *v.* [late 19C] of a villain, to live quietly, 'in retirement', when wanted by the police.

shally *n.* [SE *shilly-shally*] [mid-19C] (*UK Und.*) a negative person.

sham *n.*[1] [SE *shame* or *shamed*; thus this anecdote: 'The word Sham is true Cant of the Newmarket Breed. It is contracted of ashamed. The native Signification is a Town Lady of Diversion, in Country Maid's Cloaths, who to make good her Disguise, pretends to be so sham'd! Thence it became proverbial, when a maimed Lover was laid up, or looked meager, to say he had met with a Sham' (R. North, *Examen*, 1740)] (*UK Und.*) **1** [mid-17C–19C] a trick, a hoax, a fraud [subsequent use is SE]. **2** [early 18C] a fake shirtfront. **3** [late 18C–19C] something intended to impose upon, delude or disappoint. **4** [early 19C] in pl., 'false sleeves to put on over a dirty shirt, or false sleeves with ruffles to put over a plain one' (Grose 1785). **5** [late 19C] (*UK Und.*) counterfeit money.

IN PHRASES

❑ **cut a sham** *v.* [late 17C–18C] to hoax, to trick. ❑ **put a sham upon** *v.* (*also* **put upon a sham, ...the sham**) [late 17C–18C] to trick, to hoax, to defraud.

sham *n.*[2] (*also* **shammy**) [abbr.] [mid–late 19C] *cham*pagne.

sham *n.*[3] *see* SHAMUS *n.*

sham *v.*[1] [SHAM *n.*[1] (1)] [late 17C+] to deceive, to hoax, to fool.

IN PHRASES

❑ **sham on** *v.* [1980s+] **1** (*US black*) to cheat, to deceive. **2** (*US campus*) to tease, to make fun of someone.

sham *v.*[2] [SHAM *n.*[2]] [1900s] to ply with, or treat oneself to, champagne.

sham Abraham Newland *v. see under* ABRAHAM NEWLAND *n.*

sham-abram *n.* [SHAM ABRAM *v.*] [mid-19C] a fake.

sham abram *v.* (*also* **sham abraham**) [SHAM *v.*[1] (1) + ABRAM *n.* (1)] **1** [mid-18C–19C] to fake illness. **2** [mid-19C] of a beggar, to travel the country posing as a madman.

shame *adj.* [bad = good model] [1980s+] (*S.Afr./N.Z. teen*) excellent, first-rate.

shamer *n.* [2000s] (*Irish*) something shameful.

sham-legger *n.* [SHAM *n.*[1] (3) + LEGGER *n.*[1] (1)] [late 18C–19C] a seller of second-rate goods at very low prices.

shammus *n. see* SHAMUS *n.*

shammy *n. see* SHAM *n.*[2].

shamos *n. see* SHAMUS *n.*

shamozzle *n. see* SHEMOZZLE *n.*

shampata *n.* [Sp. *zapato*] [20C+] (*W.I. Rasta*) a sandal of wood or tyre rubber.

shampers *n. see* CHAMPERS *n.*

shampoo *n.* [elaboration on CHAMPERS *n.*] [1950s+] champagne.

shamrock *n.* [the stereotyped link between the Irish and the police and drinking] **1** [17C; 1940s] (*US Und.*) an Irishman. **2** [19C+] (*US*) a police officer. **3** [19C+] a mixed drink, esp. whisky and stout. **4** [2000s] (*drugs*) MDMA [the logo on the pills]. **5** [2000s] (*US Und.*) an Irish gang.

Shamrockshire *n.* [early 18C] Ireland.

shamrock tea *n.* ['it has only three leaves in it'] [20C+] (*UK tramp*) weak tea.

shamus *n.* (*also* **sham, shammus, shamos, shommus**) [*Seamus*, the common Irish name of many policemen; but note Heb./Yid. *shames*, a synagogue official] **1** [1920s+] (*US*) a police officer, usu. male. **2** [1930s+] a detective, esp. a private operative. **3** [1930s+] a police informer. **4** [1940s+] any person, also as an affectionate term of address.

shan *n.* [Scot. *shan*, pitiful, paltry, poor] **1** [early 19C] in fig. use, an untrustworthy person. **2** [early 19C; 1900s] (*also* **shand**) (*UK Und.*) counterfeit money.

shan *adj.* [see prev.] [1990s+] unsteady.

shand *n. see* SHAN *n.* (2).

shandah *n.* [Ger. *schande*, shame] [1960s] (*US*) a nuisance, an annoyance.

shandy *n.* [rhy. sl.; SE *chandelier* = QUEER *n.* (4)] [20C+] a male homosexual.

shandygaff *n.* [SE *shandygaff*, a drink composed of beer and ginger-beer, both mixed and alcoholically weak] [late 19C–1930s] (*Aus./N.Z.*) an uneasy compromise, anything that fails to please either party in a dispute; thus adj. *shandygaffy*, prone to compromise; v. *shandygaff*, to mix things up.

shanghai *n.*[1] (*also* **shanghaier**) [SHANGHAI *v.* (1)] [mid-19C; 1920s] a kidnapper, an abuctor.

proper name in slang uses

IN COMPOUNDS

❑ **Shanghai ballast** *n.* [1910s–50s] (*N.Z.*) rice. ❑ **Shanghai smoke** *n.* [late 19C] (*US*) an opium-laced cigar.

shanghai *n.*[2] (*also* **shang, shangeye, shangie, shong**) [? Scot. *shangie*, a cleft stick; note McGill *Dict. of Kiwi Slang* (1988): 'Macquarie suggests a derivation from British dialect word 'shangan', a cleft stick for putting on a dog's tail; the act of shanghai-ing or press-ganging by stupefying victim, although clearly related to the East China seaport of Shanghai, has related merit for the impact of a child's shanghai'] [mid-19C+] (*Aus./N.Z.*) a catapult.

shanghai *n.*[3] [? dial. *shandrydan*, a rickety, old-fashioned vehicle] [20C+] a broken-down old vehicle.

shanghai *v.* [naut. use *shanghai*, to press a man into service at the port of *Shanghai*] **1** [mid-19C+] to kidnap, to abduct; thus *shanghai game*, kidnapping; also in fig. use. **2** [late 19C] in ext. use, to destroy, to remove. **3** [20C+] (*US*) to trick, to cheat. **4** [1960s+] (*Aus. prison*) to transfer to a new prison without prior warning. **5** [2000s] (*US black*) to cut someone. **6** [2000s] (*US black*) to have sexual intercourse very energetically.

DERIVATIVES

❑ **shanghaied** *adj.* [20C+] (*Aus.*) thrown from one's horse.

shangie *n. see* SHANGHAI *n.*[2].

shank *n.*[1] [17C SE *shank*, the tang of a knife or chisel, i.e. the part that is inserted into the handle] (*US prison/Und.*) **1** [1940s+] a stiletto-like weapon, similar to a screwdriver, used by street gangs, prisoners etc. **2** [1960s+] any form of knife.

DERIVATIVES

❑ **shanked** *adj.* [1950s] (*US teen*) carrying a knife.

shank *n.*[2] [var. on SKANK *n.*[1] (1)] [1960s] (*US teen*) an unattractive female.

shank *v.*[1] [abbr. SHANKS'S PONY *n.*] [late 18C; 1990s+] to walk.

shank *v.*[2] [SHANK *n.*[1]] **1** [1950s+] (*US*) to stab with a knife; also fig.; thus *shanking*, a stabbing. **2** [1980s] (*US campus*) to try one's hardest. **3** [1990s+] (*US campus*) to harm.

Shank End, the *n.* [SE *shank*, a shaft or stem] [late 19C+] (*S.Afr.*) the Cape Peninsula; thus *Shankender*, an inhabitant of Cape Peninsula.

shanker *n.* [SE *chancre*, an ulcer arising from venereal disease] **1** [mid-17C–19C; 1930s–50s] a venereal wart [20C use is Aus.]. **2** [mid-19C] a button, as worn by a costermonger to decorate his clothing.

IN COMPOUNDS

❑ **shanker mechanic** *n.* [the disease he treats is not necessarily an STD] [1950s] (*US*) a doctor.

shank-painter *n.* [SE *shank*, a leg + naut. *painter*, a boat's rope] [early 19C] a leg.

shanks's pony *n.* (*also* **shank's, shanks's mare, ...nag, ...naggie**) [SE *shank*, a leg + *pony/mare/nag/naggie*; note synon. US regional *ride one's mother's colt/granny's colt/mother's pony* etc] [late 18C+] walking, on foot; usu. as *ride/take...* (*see* RIDE SHANK'S MARE *under* RIDE *v.*).

Shannon *n.*

IN PHRASES

❑ **dipped in the Shannon** *adj. see* separate entry.

shant *n.* [? Aus./N.Z. *shanty*, a public house, esp. when unlicensed; ult. SE *shanty*, a makeshift dwelling] **1** [mid-18C–19C] a quart pot or a quart of liquor. **2** [mid-19C+] a drink, esp. beer. **3** [late 19C] beer money.

shant *v.* [SHANT *n.* (2)] [1980s] to have a drink.

shants *n.* [SE *shorts* + *pants*, i.e. trousers] [1990s+] (*US teen*) extremely baggy, long shorts.

shanty *n.*[1] [late 19C–1940s] (*US*) a black eye.

IN PHRASES

❑ **hang a shanty on** *v.* [1940s] (*Aus.*) to give someone a black eye.

shanty *n.*[2] *see* SHANT *n.*

shanty Irish *n.* (*also* **shanty Irishman, shanty mick**) [SE *shanty*, a rough cabin, a hut; ? Fr. *chantier*, a woodcutters' hut] [20C+] (*US*) a lower-class Irish person.

shap *n. see* SHAPO *n.*

shape *n.* [his figure] **1** [late 17C] a fop, a dandy. **2** [late 17C–18C] in pl., an ugly, ill-proportioned man. **3** [mid-18C] in pl., 'a nice finikin Lass that goes extream tightly laced' (Dyche & Pardon, *A New General English Dict.*, 1735). **4** [1920s–60s] (*US*) in pl., crooked dice with bevelled faces on some sides of the cube, thus causing an irregular roll.

SE in slang uses

IN PHRASES

❑ **in shape** *adj.* [euph., based on colloq. *in great shape*] [1960s+] in possession of drugs. ❑ **out of shape** *adj.* **1** [late 19C; 1970s+] out of sorts, upset. **2** [1970s+] (*US*) drunk or otherwise intoxicated. ❑ **peddle one's shape** *v. see* PEDDLE ONE'S ASS *under* PEDDLE *v.* ❑ **pushed out of shape** *adj.* [1960s+] (*US*) upset, angry. ❑ **run one's shape** *v. see* RUN (ON) ONE'S FACE (FOR) *under* FACE *n.* ❑ **show one's shapes** *v.* **1** [late 17C–18C] to turn around, to march off. **2** [18C–19C] to make an appearance, to come into view. **3** [late 18C–early 19C] to take off one's clothes, esp. preparatory to a judicial flogging. ❑ **throw shapes** *v.* [200s] to pose.

shape *v.* **1** [late 19C+] (*Irish*) to show off, to display oneself; thus n. *shaper*, one who poses. **2** [1960s] (*US black*) to speak impudently; as in phr. *shape one's mouth*.

IN PHRASES

❑ **shape (up) (to)** *v.* **1** [mid-19C+] of a boxer, to ready himself; ext. to general use. **2** [mid-19C+] of a situation or person, to develop or turn out. **3** [late 19C+] of a person, to improve one's behaviour, activities, attitude etc. **4** [1930s+] to prepare oneself to commit a crime. **5** [1930s+] to achieve a successful outcome. **6** [1940s+] to seem, to appear. ❑ **shape up or ship out** *v.* [*see* SHIP OUT *under* SHIP *v.*] [1950s+] (*orig. milit.*) to do properly what one is supposed to be doing or to simply go away (rather than keep doing it badly).

shapo *n.* (*also* **shap, shappeau, shappo**) [Fr. *chapeau*, a hat] [late 17C–19C] a hat.

share certificate *n.* [she is his 'investment'] [1960s+] (*US*) a pimp's favourite woman.

share lashes *v.* (*also* **share licks**) [20C+] (*W.I.*) **1** to flog a number of people, usu. schoolchildren, at the same time. **2** (*orig. political*) to trounce one's opposition.

sharge *v.* [? dial. *sharge*, to grind] [19C] to have sexual intercourse.

shark *n.* **1** in Und. uses. (**a**) [late 16C+] a confidence trickster, a crooked gambler. (**b**) [late 18C–19C] a pickpocket. **2** [17C] a parasite, a hanger-on. **3** in senses of legalized extortion. (**a**) [17C+] (*also* **sharkie**) a sharp operator, a crooked businessman; hence adj. *sharky*. (**b**) [late 18C–1910s] a custom house officer. (**c**) [early–mid-19C] as *the sharks*, the press gang. (**d**) [mid-19C+] (*orig. US Und.*) a lawyer. (**e**) [1910s+] a supplier of private loans at maximum interest; a LOAN SHARK *n.* (**f**) [1920s] (*US*) a pawnbroker. (**g**) [1920s+] (*US*) an employment agent. (**h**) [1930s] (*US*) a private detective. (**i**) [1940s+] (*Aus.*) a second-hand car salesman. **4** in US campus uses. (**a**) [mid-19C] one who deliberately misses a lesson or similar compulsory attendance; the act of choosing to miss such an attendance. (**b**) [late 19C–1920s] a very intelligent or hard-working student. **5** in senses of expertise. (**a**) [1910s+] (*US*) an expert, an authority. (**b**) [1920s–40s] a womanizer. (**c**) [1940s+] a POOL SHARK (see below). **6** [1980s] (*US black*) a sharkskin suit. **7** [1990s+] (*US prison*) a dangerous, violent person.

IN COMPOUNDS

❑ **shark and taties** *n.* [1980s+] (*N.Z.*) fish and chips. ❑ **shark-bait** *n.* (*also* **shark-baiter**) [1910s+] (*Aus.*) a solitary swimmer swimming too far out at sea. ❑ **shark biscuit** *n.* [on model of SE *dog biscuit*] [1920s+] (*Aus.*) **1** a novice surfer. **2** the victim of a shark attack. **3** a bodyboard. ❑ **shark-hunter** *n.* [1920s] (*US Und.*) a thief who robs a drunk. ❑ **shark-shift** *n.* [SHIFTER *n.*[1] (1)] [16C] a confidence man. ❑ **shark's piss** *n.* [1900s] weak beer or other alcohol.

IN PHRASES

❑ **harbour shark** *n.* [1990s+] (*W.I.*) a greedy person. ❑ **land shark** *n.* **1** [17C] a ruffian, a thug. **2** [19C] a policeman. **3** [19C] a custom house officer. **4** [19C] a lawyer. **5** [19C] (*US*) a wild hog. **6** [mid-19C–1930s] a money-lender, a usurer. ❑ **pool shark** *n.* [20C+] (*US*) an expert pool player, esp. one who makes money by winning at pool.

shark *v.* **1** [late 16C+] to cheat, to defraud, to steal; thus n. *sharker* [SHARK *n.* (1)]. **2** [1960s] to treat unfairly, to victimize [SE *shark*].

sharking *n.* [SHARK *v.* (1)] [1960s+] the practice of a private credit company taking high interest on loans.

sharking *adj.* [SHARK *v.* (1)] **1** [17C+] underhand, cheating. **2** [20C+] (*W.I., Nevis*) greedy, gluttonous.

sharma *n.* [stereotyped Indian surname] [2000s] (*US black*) a person of Indian descent who tries to act black.

Sharon *n.* (*also* **Shaz, Tracey**) [archetypal working-class name] [1980s+] (*UK middle class*) a pej. generic term for a working-class young woman regarded as overly flashy and socially unacceptable; a female KEVIN *n.*

Sharon Stone *n.* [rhy. sl., ult. *Sharon Stone*, US film actress (b.1957)] [1990s+] a (usu. mobile) telephone.

sharp *n.*[1] [SHARP *v.*; note shop assistants' jargon *Mr Sharp*, a known shoplifter or fraud] **1** in Und. uses. [late 18C+] a confidence trickster. **2** [19C–1920s] an expert or connoisseur, a clever person or one who poses as such; also, in comb. with n., a job title, e.g. *doctor sharp, revenue sharp*. **3** in pl., from medical jargon *sharps*, needles, scalpels etc. (**a**) [1900s–30s] household needles. (**b**) [1980s+] (*drugs*) needles. **4** [1960s] (*US campus*) an attractive and/or socially adept person.

IN PHRASES

❑ **book sharp** *n.* [late 19C] (*US western*) an intellectual.

❑ **weather sharp** *n.* [late 19C–1950s] (*US*) a weather-forecaster.

sharp *n.*[2] [mid-19C] (*US Und.*) a rifle.

sharp *n.*[3] [SHARP *adj.*] **1** [1950s] (*US black*) fashionable clothing. **2** [1960s+] (*US*) a second-hand car in excellent condition.

sharp *adj.* [fig. use of SE *sharp*] **1** [late 17C+] cunning, on the lookout for oneself. **2** [18C+] intelligent, perceptive. **3** [1910s+] of a woman, attractive. **4** [1920s+] (*also* **sharpy**) fashionable, good, admirable. **5** [1940s+] good (of quality). **6** [1940s+] used of a person who dresses well and with style, e.g. a *sharp dresser, sharp threads*. **7** [1940s+] (*S.Afr.*) good (of health). **8** [1950s] (*US drugs*) intoxicated by a given drug. **9** [1960s] (*S.Afr.*) promiscuous.

IN COMPOUNDS

❑ **sharping-omee** *n.* (*also* **sharpy**) [OMEE *n.*] [mid-19C] a policeman.

IN PHRASES

❑ **sharp as a mosquito's peter** *adj.* (*also* **sharp as a rat turd**) [pun on SE *sharp* + *mosquito* pron. 'moskeeter' for assonance + PETER *n.*[4] (1)] [1970s+] (*US black*) very smartly and fashionably dressed. ❑ **sharp up** *v.* [1930s+] (*US*) to dress oneself up smartly. ❑ **you're so sharp you'll cut yourself** [20C+] a mocking phr. directed at someone who seems to think themselves exceptionally clever, well-informed etc.

sharp *v.* **1** [late 17C–early 18C] to obtain through trickery. **2** [late 17C–19C] to trick, to defraud.

IN PHRASES

❑ **on the sharp** **1** [18C] fraudulently. **2** [mid-18C–19C] attempting to defraud victims; thus *go on the sharp*. **3** [mid-19C] (*UK Und.*) too alert to be easily cheated.

sharp *adv.* [SHARP *adj.*] **1** [19C+] quickly, speedily. **2** [19C+] intelligently, smartly. **3** [1990s+] fashionably.

sharp and blunt *n.* [rhy. sl. = CUNT *n.* (1)] [late 19C+] the vagina.

IN PHRASES

❑ **have a bit of sharp and blunt** *v.* [late 19C–1900s] of a man, to have sexual intercourse.

sharpener *n.* [it supposedly makes the drinker SHARP *adj.* (2)] [2000s] an alcoholic drink.

sharpen one's pencil *v. see under* PENCIL *n.*

sharper *n.* [SHARP *v.* (2)] **1** [late 17C+] a confidence trickster; a cheating gambler. **2** [late 18C] in a non-criminal context, a trickster. **3** [1940s] someone who sees themselves as 'clever'.

IN COMPOUNDS

❑ **sharper's tools** *n.* [SE *tools*; ostensibly rhy. sl., but given the date, prob. simply metaphorical] [late 17C+] false dice or cards (and a fool with whom to play).

sharpie *n.*[1] (*also* **sharpy**) [SHARP *adj.*] **1** [1920s–30s] (*US*) a devotee of swing music. **2** [1940s+] (*US*) a slick operator, one who lives and hopes to prosper by their wits. **3** [1940s+] a cheat, a liar, a confidence trickster. **4** [1940s+] (*US*) a stylish dresser. **5** [1960s+] (*US*) anything in conspicuously good condition, esp. a motorcar.

sharpie *n.*[2] [the equivalent of the SKINHEAD *n.* (3)] [1960s–70s] (*Aus.*) a member of a crop-haired teen cult.

sharping *n.* [SHARP *v.* (2)] [late 17C–18C] swindling and cheating in its various forms.

Sharp's Alley blood worms *n.* [proper name *Sharp's Alley*, an abattoir near the Smithfield meat market in London] [mid–late 19C] beef sausages or black puddings.

sharps and flats *n.* [the erect penis is 'sharp', the vagina 'flat'] [late 17C] the penis and vagina, in the context of intercourse.

sharpshoot *v.* [backform. f. SHARPSHOOTER *n.*] [1950s] (*US*) to defraud, to cheat out of one's money.

sharpshooter *n.* [play on SE] **1** [19C+] a cheater, a fraudster. **2** [1910s–40s] a professional gambler. **3** [1920s+] (*also* **sharpy**) a womanizer. **4** [1930s–40s] (*US Und.*) a successful criminal. **5** [1930s–50s] (*US*) an expert; one who cannot be fooled. **6** [1950s] (*US drugs*) a narcotics addict.

sharpy *n.* **1** *see* SHARPIE *n.*[1]. **2** *see* SHARPING-OMEE *under* SHARP *adj.*

sharrer *n. see* CHARA *n.*

shassas! *excl. see* YISSUS! *excl.*

shat *n.* [? SE *chat*] [early 18C] a chatterbox, a gossip, a 'tattler'.

shat *adj.* (*also* **shat-off**) [past participle of SHIT *v.* (1a); thus cognate with PISSED *adj.*[2] or PISSED OFF *adj.*] [1940s+] (*Aus./N.Z.*) very angry, furious.

shathead *n. see* SHITHEAD *n.*

shat on *adj.* (*also* **shat upon**) [past participle of SHIT *v.* (1a)] [1940s+] abused, humiliated; ext. as *shat on from a great height*.

shatting on one's uppers *phr.* [late 19C–1930s] (*US*) (to be) completely out of money.

shat up *adj.* [fig. use of SHIT *v.* (1a)] [1990s+] utterly emotionally destroyed.

shat upon *adj. see* SHAT ON *adj.*

shave *n.* **1** [19C] (*US*) an excessive discount on a note [SHAVE A NOTE *v.*]. **2** [mid-19C] a trick, a hoax, a rumour. **3** [mid-19C+] a narrow escape, esp. as *close shave* [SE *shave*, a glancing touch]. **4** [2000s] (*N.Z.*) a crop-haired young man (although not an actual skinhead).

shave *v.* [SE *shave*] **1** [late 16C–18C] to steal. **2** [late 16C–1900s] to defraud, to rob, to overcharge; thus intensified as *shave to the quick* [used in this sense as SE in late 14C–early 16C]. **3** [1930s–50s] (*US drugs*) to reduce the size of a supposed one-ounce cube of morphine. **4** [1950s–60s] (*UK Und.*) to attack with a razor.

shave-and-a-haircut *n.* [the echoic rhythm of the phr.] [20C+] (*orig. US*) a sequence of knocks in the rhythm tum-ti-ti-tum-tum; often as *shave-and-a-haircut – two/six bits*, which has a final tum-tum.

shave a note *v.* [NOTE *n.*[2] (1)] [19C–1900s] (*US*) to discount a promissory note at a very high rate of interest.

shaved *adj.* [SE colloq. *shave*, a drink; ? excuse given as 'I'm just off out for a shave'] [mid-19C] drunk.

IN PHRASES

❑ **half-shaved** *adj.* [early–mid-19C] (*US*) drunk.

shaver *n.*[1] [lit. one who shaves and has thus reached manhood; best known in phr. *young shaver* (usu. referring to a younger person); now used ironically; but note Rom. *chavo*, a boy] **1** [late 16C+] a man; occas. a woman. **2** [17C+] a young or adolescent boy, esp. as *young shaver*; occas. a young girl. **3** [mid-19C] (*US*) an errand boy.

shaver *n.*[2] [SHAVE A NOTE *v.*] **1** [early 17C] a thief. **2** [mid-17C–18C] a roisterer. **3** [late 17C–19C] a cheat, a grasping tradesman. **4** [19C] (*also* **money shaver**) someone who discounts a promissory note at a very high rate of interest. **5** [early 19C] a merchant or shopkeeper who charges high prices. **6** [mid-19C] a bank that issues discounted notes.

shavetail *n.* [milit. use *shavetail*, an untrained pack animal, identified by a shaven tail; thus a newly commissioned second lieutenant] **1** [late 19C–1930s] (*US tramp*) a young mule. **2** [late 19C+] (*US*) an inexperienced person; a new lieutenant.

shavetail *adj.* [SHAVETAIL *n.* (2)] [1950s+] (*US*) inexperienced.

shaving *n.* [SHAVE *v.*] **1** [early 17C–19C] the act of swindling or defrauding. **2** [early–mid-19C] (*US*) discounting bills or promissory notes at a very high rate of interest.

shavings *n.* **1** [late 17C–19C] (*UK Und.*) the clippings from shaved coins. **2** [1950s] (*US Und.*) alcohol.

shavoo *n. see* SHIVOO *n.*

shawl *n.* [SHAWLIE *n.* (2)] [1900s–20s] a prostitute.

shawlie *n.* (*also* **shawly**) [late 19C–1930s] (*Irish*) **1** an Irish, usu. Dublin, fisherwoman. **2** any working-class woman wearing a shawl.

shay *n. see* CHAY *n.*

shaygets *n.* (*also* **sheygets**) [Heb. *sheygets*, a rascal] [late 19C+] **1** a young male gentile, as referred to by a Jew. **2** a mischievous rascal, a 'charming devil', whether Jewish or gentile. **3** an arrogant person. **4** an illiterate, one who lacks education, which in trad. learning-focused Jewish eyes is equated with sense 1.

Shaz *n. see* SHARON *n.*

she *n.* **1** [late 16C+] a girl, a woman. **2** [late 19C+] the vagina. **3** [1920s+] the penis, esp. in phr. *up she rises*. **4** [1930s+] a term used by homosexuals of other homosexuals. **5** [1990s+] (*US*) one's wife.

(IN COMPOUNDS)

▫ **she-boss** *n.* [mid-19C] a female brothel-keeper. ▫ **she-bro** *n.* [BRO *n.*[1] (3)] [2000s] (*US black*) a very attractive woman. ▫ **she-centaur** *n.* [SE *centaur*, 'a fabulous creature, with the head, trunk, and arms of a man, joined to the body and legs of a horse' (*OED*); the play is on *horseriding* and RIDE *v.* (1)] [late 17C] a lesbian. ▫ **she-flunkey** *n.* [late 19C–1910s] a lady's maid. ▫ **she-he** *n.* [note Hindley (1871) 'The She He Barman of Southwark' who 'engaged herself as a barman, / And said her name was Tom'; how much this cross-dressing should be seen as implying lesbianism or transsexuality is debatable] [1940s+] (*US*) **1** a lesbian. **2** a transvestite or trans-sexual. ▫ **she-hobby** *n. see* HOBBY HORSE *n.* (2). ▫ **she house** *n.* [late 18C–19C] a house in which a wife rules her husband. ▫ **she-inmate** *n.* [late 16C] a prostitute of a brothel. ▫ **she-lion** *n.* [a pun on the pron.] [late 18C–19C] a shilling (5p). ▫ **she-male** *n. see* separate entry. ▫ **she-man** *n.* [play on SE *he-man*] [20C+] a homosexual man. ▫ **she-medico** *n. see* MEDICO *n.* ▫ **she-napper** *n.* [NAP *v.*[1] (2)] [late 17C–early 19C] **1** a madam. **2** a female pimp or procuress. **3** a female thief-taker. ▫ **she-oak** *n.* [SE *she-oak*, a tree of the genus *Casuarina*; note Aus. use of *she* for wood to indicate inferior texture, colour etc] [late 19C–1950s] (*Aus.*) beer. ▫ **she-school** *n.* [late 16C] a brothel. ▫ **she-she** *see* separate entries. ▫ **she-spanker** *n.* [SPANKER *n.*[2]] [late 19C] an exceptional woman. ▫ **she-wolf** *n.* [WOLF *n.* (1)] [1940s] a woman who actively pursues men (or women) for sex.

shear *v.* [SE *shear* a sheep] [late 17C; late 19C+] to fool, to trick.

shearer *n.* [play on SHEAR *v.* + SE *sheep*, a sucker] [1900s] (*Aus.*) a bookmaker.

shearer's joy *n.* (*also* **shearer's delight**) **1** [late 19C+] (*Aus./N.Z.*) beer. **2** [1920s] treacle.

'sheart! *excl.* (*also* **'sheartlikins!**) [late 16C–18C] a mild, if blasphemous, oath, lit. 'God's heart'.

sheba *n.* [the Queen of *Sheba*] **1** [1920s–30s] (*US*) an attractive, fashionable woman. **2** [1970s+] (*US gay*) a homosexual black man [play on QUEEN *n.*].

shebang *n.* [SE *shebang*, a hut, a dwelling, one's quarters] **1** [mid-19C–1900s] a vehicle. **2** [mid-19C+] (*US*) a house, a home, a dwelling place, a shop. **3** [late 19C] (*US*) a saloon bar. **4** [late 19C–1900s] (*US*) a thing, an object. **5** [20C+] an event. **6** [1940s–50s] (*US Und.*) a criminal rendezvous. **7** [1940s–50s] (*UK/US Und.*) a prison cell. **8** *see* SHEBEEN *n.*

shebeen *n.* (*also* **sebeen, shab, shebang, shubeen**) [Irish *síbín*, illicit whisky; orig. Irish use, also in Irish immigrant communities in UK/US, ext. to S.Afr. townships and UK W.I. community] [late 18C+] an unlicensed drinking place, an illegal, late-night drinking club.

(DERIVATIVES)

▫ **shebeener** *n.* [late 19C–1900s] a person who frequents an unlicensed drinking place.

(IN COMPOUNDS)

▫ **shebeen house** *n.* [19C] an unlicensed drinking place. ▫ **shebeen queen** *n.* [1940s+] the owner of an unlicensed drinking establishment (cf. QUEEN *n.* (1e)). ▫ **shebeen shop** *n.* [19C] an unlicensed drinking place.

shebeen *v.* [SHEBEEN *n.*] [20C+] (*S.Afr.*) to visit a shebeen.

sheckles *n. see* SHEKELS *n.*

sheckles! *excl.* [? euph. for SHIT! *excl.*] [1900s–10s] a general excl.

shed *n.*[1] **1** [1930s–40s] a solid-top car. **2** [1940s] (*US Und.*) any form of depot or terminus, esp. of trains. **3** [1990s+] a run-down car.

shed *n.*[2] ['something you put your tools/TOOL *n.*[1] (1) in'] [1990s+] an unattractive, promiscuous young woman.

shed *v.* [1980s] (*US campus*) to work very hard, esp. when 'cramming' for an examination or test.

SE in slang uses

(IN PHRASES)

▫ **shed a tear** *v.* [mid-19C] **1** to take a drink, esp. a quick one. **2** to urinate. ▫ **shed ink** *v. see under* INK *n.* ▫ **shed one's skin** *v. see under* SKIN *n.*[1].

shedder *n.* [mid-19C] (*US*) a counterfeit note.

sheeba *n.* [var. on CHEEB *n.*] [1990s+] (*US drugs*) marijuana.

shee-it! *excl.* [20C+] (*US*) a joc. imitation of a Southern pron. of SHIT! *excl.*

sheela *n.* [Irish name *Síle*, but note SHEILA *n.*[1]] [late 19C–1910s] (*Irish*) a man who takes excessive interest in stereotyped 'women's affairs', i.e. housework, gossip, child-rearing.

sheen *n.*[1] [the SE *sheen* of the coins or Ger. *Schein*, a banknote] **1** [mid–late 19C] a counterfeit coin. **2** [late 19C+] (*Aus.*) money.

sheen *n.*[2] [abbr.] [1960s–70s] (*US black*) a machine, either a car or a motorcycle.

sheena *n.* [the cartoon character, *Sheena, Queen of the Jungle*/ QUEEN *n.*] [1950s–60s] (*camp gay*) a black homosexual man.

sheeny *n.* (*also* **sheeney, sheenie, sheney**) [as laid out by Nathan Süsskind (Cohen (ed.), *Studies in Slang II*, 1989), Yid. *shayner Yid*, a pious (lit. 'a beautiful-faced') Jew; the pious, thus old-fashioned and trad. Jew. According to the Talmud such a Jew has a full beard – beauty in this case being spiritual rather than physical. The phr. was used by assimilated German Jews, who had emigrated to England, as a derog. term, meaning 'an old-fashioned Jew', i.e. in habits, clothing and religion, which mocked their less sophisticated successors, who followed them from Germany and clung on (at least initially) to their old-fashioned ways. The first half of the phrase, which the 'uncultured' Jews pronounced *sheena* rather than the more Germanic *schön*, was taken up by gentile Jew-baiters to create *sheeny*; note WW1 milit. *sheeny*, a careful, extra-economical man] **1** [19C+] a derog. term for a Jew. **2** [mid-19C+] a pawnbroker. **3** [1900s] a mean, grasping person. **4** [1930s–40s] a derog. term for a person with dark skin, often of Mediterranean origin.

(IN COMPOUNDS)

▫ **sheeney's fear** *n.* [late 19C] (*UK Und.*) bacon. ▫ **sheeny wagon** *n.* [1950s] (*US*) a pedlar's cart.

sheeny *adj.* (*also* **sheenie, sheeney**) [SHEENY *n.* (1)] **1** [mid-19C+] Jewish; also as a nickname for someone Jewish or having a Jewish appearance. **2** [late 19C] of people, deceitful, dubious, fraudulent. **3** [late 19C] of money, counterfeit [reinforced by SE *sheeny*, shiny].

sheep *n.*

SE in slang uses

(DERIVATIVES)

▫ **shebeepish** *adj.* [1970s] (*US campus*) of men, long-haired.

(IN COMPOUNDS)

▫ **sheep-biter** *n. see under* BITE *v.* ▫ **sheep cocky** *n. see under* COCKY *n.*[2]. ▫ **sheep dip** *n.* **1** [1910s] (*Aus./US*) inferior whisky, or any bad alcohol. **2** [1940s] (*US*) nonsense. **3** [1960s] (*Aus.*) coarse tobacco, issued in prisons. ▫ **sheep-dodger** *n.* [20C+] (*Aus.*) a sheep hand. ▫ **sheep-guts** *n.* [19C] a general term of contempt. ▫ **sheep's arse** *n.* [2000s] nonsense, deception. ▫ **sheep's back** *n.* [the wealth of sheep farmers] [late 19C+] (*Aus./N.Z.*) luxury, indolence, security; usu. in phr. *on the sheep's back*, living very comfortably, securely. ▫ **sheep-shagger** *n.* [SHAGGER *n.*[1] (1); negative racial stereotyping] **1** [1970s] a Scot; orig. a derog. ref. to Scots regiments, esp. the Black Watch. **2** [1970s+] a peasant. **3** [1990s+] a Welshman. **4** [2000s] (*Aus./N.Z.*) an Australian or New Zealander, depending on the nationality of the speaker. ▫ **sheep-shagging** *n.* [SHAG *v.*[1]; reference to the act is often used to mock the Welsh] [1940s+] committing bestiality with a sheep. ▫ **sheep's head** *n.* [the perceived stupidity of sheep, reinforced by subseq. saying, 'like a sheep's head, all jaw'] [late 16C–1910s] a fool, esp. a talkative one; thus adj. *sheepheaded*. ▫ **sheep-shearer** *n.* [pun on SE *fleece*, to rob + SHEAR *v.* (1)]

[16C–mid-18C] a swindler, a confidence trickster, esp. one who works the JACK IN A BOX *n.* confidence trick. ❑ **sheepskin** *n. see* separate entry. ❑ **sheep's piss** *n.* [2000s] weak alcohol, usu. beer. ❑ **sheep-tail** *n.* [1970s] (*W.I.*) **1** a bit of shirt-tail that protrudes through a hole in torn trousers. **2** the person (usu. a boy) who has such a costume. ❑ **sheep-wash** *n.* [20C+] (*Aus./N.Z.*) **1** poor liquor. **2** poor tobacco.

IN PHRASES

❑ **do sheep wear sweaters?** *see* DOES A BEAR SHIT IN THE WOODS? IS THE POPE A CATHOLIC? *phr.* ❑ **keep sheep by moonlight** *v.* [the gibbet was often on a heath or moorland where sheep might be wandering; the corpse provided a fig. 'shepherd'] [late 18C–early 19C] to hang in chains. ❑ **one sheep to the acre** [2000s] (*N.Z.*) used of an unintelligent person.

sheepie *n.* [abbr. + sfx *-ie*] [1990s+] a sheepskin coat or jacket.

sheepo *n.* (*also* **sheep-ho**) [SE *sheep* + -O *sfx* (3)] **1** [late 19C–1900s] (*Aus./N.Z.*) a sheep-shearer, spec. one who works in the catching sheds, filling the catching pens. **2** [1980s] (*N.Z.*) a shepherd, a musterer of sheep into pens.

sheepskin *n.* **1** as a document [the use of sheepskin for parchment]. (**a**) [19C+] (*also* **skin**) a college diploma, received on graduation [such diplomas are trad. made of *sheepskin*-based parchment]. (**b**) [mid-19C–1900s] a document. (**c**) [1930s–60s] (*US prison*) a pardon or discharge certificate. **2** [1990s+] (*US campus*) a condom [sheepskin is an allegedly superior material for contraceptives].

IN COMPOUNDS

❑ **sheepskin fiddle** *n.* [early 19C] a drum; thus *sheepskin fiddler*, a drummer.

sheesh! *excl.* [? popularized through the *Yogi Bear/Huckleberry Hound* TV cartoons] [1950s+] (*US*) a mild oath; euph. for JESUS! *excl.* or SHIT! *excl.*

shee-shee *adj. see* CHEE-CHEE *adj.*

sheet *n.* [abbr. SE *sheet of paper*; note WW1 milit. *on the sheet*, charged with an offence] **1** [mid-18C+] a newspaper, a magazine [mainly US since 20C+]. **2** [1920s+] a single unit of paper currency, e.g. £1, $1, one euro. **3** [1930s–40s] (*US Und.*) a cigarette paper. **4** [1950s+] (*US Und.*) an official police record.

IN COMPOUNDS

❑ **sheet passer** *n.* [1930s–40s] (*US Und.*) one who passes counterfeit notes.

IN PHRASES

❑ **brown sheet** *n.* [1970s–80s] (*UK black*) a £10 note. ❑ **bunk sheet** *n.* [1920s–30s] (*US*) a sensational newspaper. ❑ **grave-sheet** *n.* [1950s] (*US*) a police record. ❑ **scream sheet** *n.* [SCREAMER *n.* (3c)] [1940s+] (*US*) a tabloid newspaper.

SE in slang uses

IN COMPOUNDS

❑ **sheet alley** *n.* (*also* **sheet lane**) [mid-19C–1900s] bed; thus *go down sheet alley into Bedfordshire*, to go to bed. ❑ **sheet-boy** *n.* [1930s] (*Aus.*) a bookmaker. ❑ **sheet-slinger** *n.* [1900s] (*US campus*) a chambermaid.

IN PHRASES

❑ **a sheet in the wind's eye** *see* THREE SHEETS IN THE WIND *phr.* ❑ **cheat sheet** *n.* [1950s+] (*US campus*) notes smuggled into an examination. ❑ **drag through the sheet** *v. see under* DRAG *v.*[1]. ❑ **hit the sheets** *v.* [1960s+] **1** (*US*) to go to bed. **2** (*US*) to have sexual intercourse. **3** (*US gay/lesbian*) to be passive to the overtures of another woman.

sheet *v.* [1980s+] (*Aus. prison*) to charge with a prison misconduct.

IN PHRASES

❑ **sheet it home to** *v.* [? putting a criminal on a charge sheet] **1** [late 19C–1960s] to prove something against someone. **2** [1900s] in non-criminal contexts, to prove something.

sheets *n.* **1** [1960s+] perforated sheets of LSD-impregnated blotting-paper, which can be torn into 100 separate doses of LSD. **2** [1970s+] phencyclidine.

Sheffield handicap *n.* [rhy. sl. = CRAP *n.*[1] (7)] [20C+] an act of defecation.

sheg *v.* [SE *shag*, to shake about] (*W.I./UK black*) **1** [1940s+] to annoy, to provoke. **2** [1950s] to seduce. **3** [1970s] to do badly. **4** *see* SHAG *v.*[1].

shegarry *n.* [SHEG *v.* (1) + ? CARRY-ON *n.* (1)] [1980s] (*UK black*) annoyance, irritation.

sheg round *v.* [ext. of SHEG *v.*] [1940s] (*W.I.*) to work as a petty criminal.

sheg-up *n.* [SHEG ROUND *v.*] (*W.I.*) **1** [1940s] a confidence trickster, whose role is to appear as gullible as the potential victim. **2** [1970s+] an unpleasant attitude.

sheg up *v.* [SE *shake* n.] [1950s+] (*W.I. Rasta*) **1** to be messed up, to be ruined. **2** to bother, as in *all sheg up*, all hot and bothered, or all spoiled, as of work that has been ruined.

she has to cross her legs to keep her guts from falling out *phr. see under* GUT *n.*

sheik *n.*[1] (*also* **sheikh**) [*The Sheik*, a novel by E.M. Hull, publ. 1919 + its film adaptation, released 1921, starring Rudolph Valentino; ult. Arabic *sheikh*, a tribal chieftain, a leader] [1920s+] (*orig. US*) **1** a man who considers himself irresistible to women, a romantic lover. **2** a fashionably dressed young man.

DERIVATIVES

❑ **sheiky** *adj.* (*also* **sheikhy**) [1920s–30s] with the character of or pertaining to a 'lady-killer'.

IN PHRASES

❑ **sheiked out** *adj.* [1920s–30s] (*orig. US*) dressed in a rakish style. ❑ **sheik up** *v.* [1920s] (*US*) to smarten/dress (oneself) up.

sheik *n.*[2] [proprietory name *Sheik*] [1940s+] (*Can.*) a condom.

sheik *v.* [SHEIK *n.*[1] (1)] [1920s+] (*orig. US*) to go out looking for female conquests.

sheikha *n.* [*Sheikha*, an Arab lady or matron of good family; the chief wife of a *sheikh*] [1920s] the female consort of a SHEIK *n.*[1] (1).

sheila *n.*[1] (*also* **sheilah**) [proper name *Sheila*, ult. Irish *caille*, a young girl] **1** [20C+] (*orig. Aus.*) a woman; for 19C uses see SHALER *n.* (1). **2** [1950s+] (*S.Afr.*) a black housemaid. **3** [1960s–70s] (*S.Afr.*) the girlfriend of an urban gangster.

IN COMPOUNDS

❑ **sheila rorter** *n.* [RORTER *n.*[1]] [1980s+] (*Aus. prison*) a prisoner obsessed with women. ❑ **sheila trap** *n.* [1960s–70s] (*Aus.*) a man's flat or house, in which he attempts seductions.

sheila *n.*[2] [initial letter, i.e. SHIT *n.* (1a)] [2000s] (*S.Afr. gay*) excrement.

sheila *v.* [initial letter, i.e. SHIT *v.* (1a)] [2000s] (*S.Afr. gay*) to defecate.

sheila-day *n.* (*also* **sheila's day**) [*Sheila*, generic name for black domestic servants] [1970s+] (*S.Afr. black*) Thursday, the day that most nannies and maids are allowed off work.

sheister *n. see* SHICER *n.*

sheisty *adj.* (*also* **shiesty, shisty**) [SHIT *adj.* (1)/SHICER *n.* + FEISTY *adj.*] [1990s+] (*US black/campus*) underhand, unethical, untrustworthy, criminal.

sheive *n. see* SHIV *n.*

shekel *v.* [SHEKELS *n.*] [1990s+] (*US campus*) to give, to hand out.

shekels *n.* (*also* **sheckles, sheks**) [Heb. *shekel*, a Babylonian, hence Heb. monetary unit; ult. Heb. *shāqal*, to weigh] **1** [mid-19C+] money; thus *rake in the shekels*, to prosper. **2** [2000s] (*US*) dollars.

shelf *n.*[1] [SHELF *v.*] [1920s+] (*Aus./N.Z.*) a police informer.

shelf *n.*[2] [joc. use of SE] **1** [1930s+] (*US prison*) an isolation cell, a holding cell. **2** [1940s+] (*Aus.*) the dress circle in a cinema.

SE in slang uses

IN PHRASES

❑ **lay on the shelf** *v.* [an ironic ref. to SE use, to put away for later] [late 18C–19C] to pawn something. ❑ **on the shelf** **1** [19C] transported. **2** [19C–1930s] dead; thus as phr. *shelf one's ass*, to die. **3** [early–mid-19C] in pawn. **4** [early–mid-19C] past one's best, retired. **5** [mid-19C+] put on one side for unspecified future use. **6** [mid-19C+] of a woman (occas. a man), unmarried and worried about it, feeling that she has been 'put to one side'. **7** [late 19C–1920s] finished, destroyed. **8** [20C+] (*US prison*) in solitary confinement.

shelf *v.* [SE *shelf*, to place something, in this case information, aside] [1910s+] (*Aus./N.Z.*) to inform (on someone) to the police, or any authority.

shelfer *n.* [ext. of SHELF *v.*] [1960s+] (*Aus.*) a police informer.

shell *n.* **1** [mid-18C] the female body. **2** [mid-18C–19C] the vagina. **3** [19C] (*US Und.*) a safe. **4** [late 19C–1910s] (*US*) a portion of opium. **5** [late 19C–1910s] (*Aus.*) a coffin. **6** [1900s] (*Aus.*) a corpse. **7** [1910s–20s] a hearse.

SE in slang uses

IN COMPOUNDS

❑ **shell-back** *n.* [the image of a slow-moving turtle] [late 19C+] an ultra-conservative, slow-witted person. ❑ **shell game** *n.* [late 19C+] **1** a swindling game in which a small object is concealed under a walnut shell or the like; the manipulator then moves the shells round at speed; bets are made on the shell under which the object is found. **2** a generic for any form of confidence trick. ❑ **shell road** *v.* [SAmE *shell road*, a back road having a bed or layer of shells] [1900s–30s] (*US*) to throw a person, often a woman who refuses to have sex, out of a vehicle and thus force them to walk home an inconvenient and poss. embarrassing distance. ❑ **shell worker** *n.* (*also* **shell man**) [WORKER *n.*[1] (1)] [late 19C–1940s] (*US Und.*) one who operates a *SHELL GAME* above.

shell *adj.* **1** [1980s+] (*US campus*) crazy. **2** [2000s] (*US campus*) bad, second-rate.

shell *v.* **1** [mid-19C] to remove some or all of one's clothes, e.g. preparatory to a fight. **2** [1970s] (*W.I.*) to drive fast [Shell Motor Oil]. **3** [1980s+] (*N.Z. drugs*) to remove painkilling drugs from their capsule before making home-produced narcotics.

SE in slang uses

IN PHRASES

❑ **shell out** *v.* (*also* **shell off, shell over**) [the removal of a seed from a shell] **1** [early 19C+] to hand over, usu. money. **2** [1900s–30s] (*US*) to leave, to depart. **3** [1920s] to take an opponent's money when playing cards or dice. **4** [1940s] to do what is required or demanded.

shellac *v.* (*also* **shellack**) [SE *shellac*, to coat or varnish with shellac; note Dennis Wilson on *American Dialect Society List* (Internet, 14/11/02: 'Here are my guesses; I find any of them plausible, or a combination. (1) Derivative of German "schlagen" (= "strike") or equivalent. Cf. supposed etymology of "schlock" (from Yiddish). Cf. "Our team really got clobbered", "I really got hammered on schnapps last night", "They really gave him a pounding". (2) Onomatopoeic (cf. "smack", "whack" etc). (3) [The books seem to favor this one] Shellacking being the last step in finishing something; thus something shellacked is something completed, something which has been "finished off"'] [1920s+] to beat, to thrash, to punish.

shellacked *adj.* [for ety. *see* SHELLAC *v.*] [1920s+] (*US*) drunk.

shellacking *n.* [SHELLAC *v.*] [1920s+] a severe beating or defeat; also fig., a scolding.

she'll be grannies *phr. see under* GRANNY *n.*[1].

she'll be right *phr. see* SHE'S RIGHT *phr.*

shelled *adj.* [? SHELL *n.* (4) or SHELLACKED *adj.* (1)] [2000s] (*US black*) drunk; acting stupidly.

shellmex *n.* [rhy. sl.; ult. *Shell-Mex* brand from the *Shell* oil company] [20C+] sex.

Shells, the *n.* [mid-19C] (*Scot.*) the Glasgow lunatic asylum.

shells *n.* [late 16C–17C; 1990s+] (*UK Und.*) money, esp. as taken from a victim by cut-purses or pickpockets.

shell shock *n.* **1** [1910s–50s] cocoa. **2** [1920s] (*US*) a joc. term of address; the implication is that the subject has an 'explosive' personality. **3** [1920s–30s] (*tramp*) tea served in a casual ward or hostel. **4** [1930s–50s] (*Aus./N.Z.*) a mixed alcoholic drink, usu. very potent, e.g. port and stout.

s'help...! *excl. see under* S'ELP...

she-male *n.* (*also* **shemale**) **1** [19C–1920s] a woman; usu. a feminist or an intellectual. **2** [mid-19C] a female transvestite. **3** [20C+] a male homosexual or transvestite. **4** [1970s+] (*US gay*) a lesbian.

shemale *adj.* [SHE-MALE *n.* (1)] [1900s–20s] (*Aus.*) pertaining to female or feminist concerns.

she-mi-a-play-wid *n.* [lit. 'she plays with me'] [1950s] (*W.I.*) one's female sweetheart.

shemmy *n. see* SHIMMY *n.*[1].

shemozzle *n.* (*also* **chermozzle, chimozzle, schemozzle, schlemozzle, schmozzle, shamozzle, shimozzle, shlemozzle**) [coined in UK and not 'real' Yid.; similar sp. to SCHLEMAZEL *n.*, but with no other links] [late 19C+] **1** a fuss, a disturbance; noise, uproar, excitement. **2** a state of difficulty. **3** bad luck.

shemozzle *v.* [SHEMOZZLE *n.*] [1910s+] to run off, to decamp.

shenanigan *n.* (*also* **shenanigans, shenannigan, shenannigin**) [? Erse *sionnach* (pron. 'shinnuck'), hiding, malingering, 'playing the fox'; East Anglian dial. *nannicking*, playing the fool, 'messing about'] [mid-19C+] trickery, skulduggery, machination, intrigue, teasing, 'kidding', nonsense; (usu. pl.) a plot, a trick, a prank, an exhibition of high spirits, a carry-on.

shent-per-shent(er) *n. see* CENT PER CENT *n.*

Sheol *n.* [Heb. *she'ol*, the underworld, the abode of the dead or departed spirits, translated as 'the pit' or 'hell'] [late 19C–1970s] a joc. euph. for SE *hell*, e.g. *sheol to pay*; *this side of sheol*; *sheol for hides*, hell for leather.

shepherd *v.* **1** [late 19C] (*Und., usu. Aus.*) to follow someone who is a potential target for robbery or fraud. **2** [late 19C+] to watch over carefully, to shadow.

shepherd's bush *n.* [rhy. sl. = PUSH *n.* (3)] [20C+] dismissal.

shepherd's clock *n.* [its sounds punctuate the day] [late 19C+] (*Aus.*) a kookaburra or laughing jackass.

shepherd's pie *n.* [rhy. sl.] [20C+] the sky.

shepherd's (plaid) *adj.* [rhy. sl.] [1930s–50s] bad.

sherbet *n.* (*also* **sherbert**) [Turk. *sherbet* (ult. Arab. *sharbah*, a drink), a cooling drink made of fruit juice and water sweetened, often cooled with snow] **1** [late 19C] grog or any warm, alcoholic drink; also as *old sherbert*. **2** [20C+] (*Aus.*) any form of alcoholic drink; usu. beer. **3** [1950s+] beer. **4** [2000s] cocaine [resemblance to a popular UK sweet, a *sherbet dab*, a bag of sherbet powder with a liquorice 'straw' through which it is sucked up].

sherbet (dab) *n.* [rhy. sl.] [1990s+] a taxi-cab.

sherbet dip *n.* [rhy. sl.] [20C+] a tip.

sherbet(t)y *adj.* [SHERBET *n.* (2)] [late 19C] drunk.

sheriff *n.* [1980s+] (*Aus. prison*) an informer.

SE in slang uses

IN COMPOUNDS

❑ **sheriff's ball** *n.* [late 18C–mid-19C] a hanging. ❑ **sheriff's basket** *n.* [early–mid-17C] a basket or tub placed outside a prison to receive charitable gifts for the prisoners. ❑ **sheriff's bracelets** *n.* [SE *bracelets*/BRACELETS *n.*] [late 18C–19C] handcuffs. ❑ **sheriff's hotel** *n.* [HOTEL *n.* (2)] [late 18C–19C] a prison. ❑ **sheriff's journeyman** *n.* [early 19C] the hangman. ❑ **sheriff's posts** *n.* [late 16C] two painted posts, set up at the sheriff's door, to which proclamations are affixed.

IN PHRASES

❑ **dance at the sheriff's ball** *v. see under* DANCE *v.* ❑ **dangle in the sheriff's picture-frame** *v. see under* DANGLE *v.*

sheriff's picture frame *n.* [late 18C–19C] the gallows or pillory.

IN PHRASES

❑ **nab the picture-frame** *v.* [mid-19C] (*UK Und.*) to be executed by hanging.

sherk *n. see* SHIRK *n.*

sherlock *n.*[1] [for ety. *see* SHERLOCK HOLMES *n.*] **1** [1900s–60s] (*US Und.*) (*also* **sherlocko**) a police officer or detective. **2** [1980s+] (*US campus*) a friend.

sherlock *n.*[2] *see* SHYLOCK *n.* (2).

sherlock *v.* [SHERLOCK *n.*^{1}] [1900s–60s] (*US Und.*) to act as a detective.

Sherlock Holmes *n.* [proper name *Sherlock Holmes*, the private consulting detective invented by Sir Arthur Conan Doyle (1859–1930)] [1950s+] (*US black*) the police.

sherlocko *n. see* SHERLOCK *n.*^{1} (1).

sherm *n.* (*also* **shermans, sherms**) [the smoking of *Sherman* cigarettes laced with phencyclidine] [1980s+] (*US black/drugs*) **1** phencyclidine; thus adj. *shermed*, intoxicated. **2** embalming fluid, formaldehyde [note William Shaw, *Westsiders* (2000): 'It probably acquired the name sherm when users started dipping Sherman cigarettes in the fluid, choosing the brand because its cigarettes are more robustly constructed than most and don't fall apart when steeped in fluid'].

IN COMPOUNDS

❑ **shermhead** *n.* [-HEAD *sfx* (3)] [1990s+] (*US drugs*) one who is addicted to marijuana or plain cigarettes dipped in PCP. ❑ **sherm stick** *n.* [STICK *n.* (6a)] [1980s+] (*US black/drugs*) a plain cigarette or one composed of marijuana, laced with phencyclidine.

sherman (tank) *n.* [rhy. sl.] **1** [1940s+] an American [YANK *n.* (1)]. **2** [1990s+] masturbation [WANK *n.* (1)].

shermed *adj.* [*see* SHERM *n.*] [1980s+] (*US black/drugs*) intoxicated.

sherry *n.*^{1} [abbr.] [mid-19C] a *sheriff*.

sherry *n.*^{2} [late 19C] cheap beer, sold at fourpence a quart (1.14 litres).

sherry (off) *v.* [? SE *sheer off*, to change one's course, to turn] [late 18C+] to run away, to leave.

IN PHRASES

❑ **sherry one's ribs** *v.* [late 19C–1900s] (*US*) to leave in a hurry.

she-she *n.* ['Oriental'-style Pidgin English] [1950s+] (*US*) a young woman.

she-she *adj.* [1920s+] (*W.I.*) effeminate.

IN COMPOUNDS

❑ **she-she talk** *n.* [1920s+] (*US black*) women's talk.

she's right *phr.* (*also* **she'll be right**) [1940s+] (*Aus.*) a phr. used to reject offers of assistance, don't worry, don't fuss, everything will be fine in the end.

shevvle *n.* [Fr. *cheval*, horse] [late 19C] cat's meat.

she wouldn't know if someone was up her *phr. see under* UP *adv.*

sheygets *n. see* SHAYGETS *n.*

shice *n.* (*also* **shise**) **1** [mid–late 19C] counterfeit coins. **2** [mid-19C–1930s] anything worthless; a wash-out.

shice *adj.* (*also* **shise, shish**) [SHICER *n.*] **1** [mid-19C] out of funds; impoverished. **2** [mid–late 19C] of money, counterfeit. **3** [mid-19C+] useless, worthless.

shice *v.* (*also* **shish**) [SHICER *n.*] [mid-19C+] to defraud, to cheat, to betray, to abandon.

shicer *n.* (*also* **schicer, sheister, shiser, shisser, shizer, shyser, skycer**) [? fig. use of Ger. *Scheisse*, shit or SHYSTER *n.*] **1** [mid-19C] one who has no money, i.e. lit. 'worthless'. **2** [mid-19C] (*UK Und.*) a prostitute. **3** [mid-19C+] a worthless, idle person. **4** [mid-19C+] nothing, something worthless. **5** [mid-19C+] counterfeit money. **6** [mid-19C+] (*Aus.*) (*also* **shyster**) a worthless or worked-out mine. **7** [late 19C+] a cheat, one who does not pay their debts. **8** [20C+] (*Aus.*) a criminal. **9** [1900s–20s] (*UK Und.*) a dishonest race course bookmaker.

shicery *adj. see* SHICKERY *adj.*^{1}.

shicked *adj. see* SHICKERED *adj.*

shicker *n.* (*also* **shick, shicka, shikkar, shikker, shikkur**) [SHICKER *adj.*] [20C+] (*usu. Aus./N.Z.*) **1** alcohol; a drink. **2** a drunkard. **3** a drunken spree.

DERIVATIVES

❑ **shickerhood** *n.* [1920s] (*Aus./N.Z.*) drunkenness.

IN COMPOUNDS

❑ **shicker saloon** *n.* [1900s] a public house. ❑ **shicker-up** *n.* [1910s] a drinking session.

IN PHRASES

❑ **on the shicker** *adj.* (*also* **on the shick**) [20C+] (*mainly Aus./N.Z.*) on a drinking spree, drunk.

shicker *adj.* (*also* **shick, shiker, shikka, shikker, shikkur**) [synon. Yid.; ult. Heb. *shikor*, drunk] [late 19C+] (*mainly Aus./N.Z.*) drunk.

shicker *v.* [synon. Yid.; ult. Heb. *shikor*, drunk] [20C+] (*Aus./N.Z.*) to drink, usu. to drunkenness.

DERIVATIVES

❑ **shickering** *n.* [20C+] drinking.

shicker! *excl.* [? euph. for SHIT! *excl.*] [1910s–40s] (*Aus./N.Z.*) a mild oath, e.g. *shicker me grandmother!*

shickered *adj.* (*also* **shicked, shikkared, shikkered (up), shikkured**) **1** [late 19C+] (*mainly Aus./N.Z.*) drunk [SHICKER *n.* (1)]. **2** [1960s] out of funds, impoverished [prob. a nonce-use].

shickery *adj.*^{1} (*also* **shicery**) [SHICE *adj.*; but note dial. *shiggyry*, shaky] [mid–late 19C] **1** bad, fake. **2** shabby, useless.

shickery *adj.*^{2} [SHICKER *n.* (1)] [mid-19C–1900s] drunk.

shickse(h) *n. see* SHIKSA *n.*

shickster *n.*^{1} (*also* **chickster**) [? SHIKSA *n.* (1)] [mid-19C] a promiscuous woman, a good-time girl.

shickster *n.*^{2} *see* SHAKESTER *n.*

shickster *n.*^{3} *see* SHIKSA *n.*

shickster-crabs *n.* [SHAKESTER *n.* (3) + CRABS *n.*^{2} (1)] [mid-19C] (*tramp*) women's shoes.

shield *n.* [the wearer's shield-shaped badge of office] [1910s+] (*US*) **1** the badge as a symbol of being a police officer. **2** by metonymy, a policeman or prison guard.

shiesty *adj. see* SHEISTY *adj.*

shieve *n. see* SHIV *n.*

shiever *n.* [? CHIV *n.*^{1} (1); thus a 'backstabber'] [1920s] (*US Und.*) a traitor.

shif *n.*^{1} [backsl.] [mid-19C] fish.

shif *n.*^{2} *see* CHIV *n.*^{3}.

shife *adj.* [? SHIF-MAN *n.*] [1990s+] pretending to be more experienced than one actually is.

shif-man *n.* [1950s] (*W.I.*) **1** an effeminate man [SE *shift*, the woman's undergarment]. **2** a ne'er-do-well, a lazy idler [SE *shiftless*, lazy].

shift *n.*

SE in slang uses

IN PHRASES

❑ **do a shift** *v.* [euph. corruption of SHIT *n.* (1); one also SE *shifts* or moves one's bowels] [late 19C–1920s] to defecate. ❑ **town shift** *n.* [senses 1 and (poss.) 2, f. his constantly changing his address to keep ahead of the authorities and outraged victims] **1** [mid-17C–mid-18C] a scoundrel, esp. a card-sharp. **2** [early 18C] a male homosexual.

shift *v.* [SE *shift*, to move] **1** [mid-17C+] to have sexual intercourse. **2** [late 19C] to kill, to murder [on model of PUT AWAY *v.* (1a)]. **3** [late 19C+] to consume, esp. to eat or drink a large amount [on model of PUT AWAY *v.* (3)]. **4** [20C+] (*orig. Aus.*) to move fast, to run. **5** [1900s] (*Aus.*) in fig. use, to die. **6** [1970s] to deep kiss. **7** [1980s+] (*Irish*) to pursue women.

IN COMPOUNDS

❑ **shift work** *n.* (*also* **shift service**) [sense 1 above + play on SE *shift*, a female undergarment] [19C] sexual intercourse.

SE in slang uses

IN COMPOUNDS

❑ **shift-round** *n.* [1940s+] movement, a changing of one's place.

IN PHRASES

❑ **shift one's bob** *v.* [? naut. *bobstay*, a rope that keeps the bowsprit steady] [mid-18C–early 19C] to leave, to run off. ❑ **shift someone's ears** *v.* [late 19C] (*Aus.*) to knock someone down. ❑ **shift someone's jaw** *v.* [late 19C] to assault. ❑ **shift the weight** *v.* [20C+] to place the blame on someone else.

shifted *adj.* [? SHAFTED *adj.*] [1990s+] (*UK black*) arrested.

shifter *n.*[1] [SE *shift*, to employ underhand methods, to deceive, also to live by one's wits; note the nickname of the resourceful but impoverished *Sporting Times* journalist William Farn Goldberg, 'The Shifter'] **1** [mid-16C–17C; 1920s] (*UK Und.*) a trickster, a confidence man. **2** [early 19C] (*UK Und.*) a warning from one thief to another. **3** [1920s+] (*US Und.*) a receiver of stolen goods.

shifter *n.*[2] [SHIFT *v.* (3)] [late 19C] a drunkard.

shifting cove *n.* [SHIFTER *n.*[1] (1) + COVE *n.* (1)] [early 19C] (*UK Und.*) a confidence trickster.

shift-monger *n.* [SE *shift*, a large, highly starched shirt-front, sported as part of such a person's evening dress + sfx *-monger*] [late 19C] a young man-about-town.

shifty *adj.* [SE *shifty*, 'full of shifts or expedients; well able to shift for oneself'; this 16C–19C sense has been superseded in SE by the negative 'fond of indirect or dishonest methods; addicted to evasion or artifice; not straightforward, not to be depended on' (*OED*)] [2000s] (*US black*) calm, cool, unruffled.

shigs *n.* [? abbr.] [mid-19C] money, esp. shillings.

shigus *n.* [? early, 'untranslated' use of Heb. *sheygets*, a rascal, i.e. a derog. description] [mid-19C] (*US Und.*) a judge.

shik... *see also under* SHICK...

shiksa *n.* (*also* **schicksie, shickse(h), shiksel**) [Yid. *shikse*, a gentile female; ult. Heb. *sheques*, a blemish; while *goy*, a gentile man, or gentiles in general, is a relatively neutral term, *shicksa*, strictly the fem. of SHAYGETS, always carries pej. overtones] **1** [mid-19C+] (*Jewish*) a gentile woman. **2** [late 19C+] a non-Jewish servant-girl. **3** [1900s–10s] (*Aus.*) a girl(friend), a young unmarried woman.

shill *n.*[1] [abbr. Irish *shillelagh*, cudgel + links of the Irish and the police] **1** [mid-19C] (*also* **shillaluh**) the penis. **2** [late 19C+] (*US*) a police officer's truncheon.

shill *n.*[2] **1** [late 19C+] (*also* **shillaber, shiller, shilliber, shilliver**) any form of criminal who poses as a member of the public to lure victims, usu. into confidence tricks. **2** [1910s] (*US Und.*) an apprentice criminal. **3** [1930s+] (*gambling*) a house player in a casino. **4** [1930s+] a promotion or, used fig., anyone who advocates something enthusiastically; thus also a promotion. **5** [1940s+] a member of the three-card monte team who appears to be another innocent gambler and who lures players into the game. **6** [1980s] a confidence trick. **7** [1990s+] a spokesperson – the implication is of mendacity – for an institution.

IN PHRASES

❑ **shill through** *v.* [abbr. *shillaber*, one who publicizes a circus, carnival etc] [1920s] (*US Und.*) to get in to an entertainment free.

shill *v.* [SHILL *n.*[2]] **1** [1910s+] (*orig. US*) to act as a frontman, either in a casino, where one is a house player, or in ext. senses. **2** [1960s] to act as an 'agent', directing clients to a prostitute.

shillaluh *n. see* SHILL *n.*[1] (1).

shilling *n.*

SE in slang uses

IN COMPOUNDS

❑ **shilling shocker** *n.* (*also* **shilling dreadful, shocker**) [late 19C–1920s] a short sensational novel, published at a shilling (5p). ❑ **shilling sicker** *n. see SIXPENNY SICKER under* SIXPENNY *adj.* ❑ **shilling tabernacle** *n.* [late 19C] a Baptist or Methodist tea-meeting, where refreshment was available at a shilling (5p) a head.

IN PHRASES

❑ **full shilling** *adj.* **1** [1940s+] (*Aus./N.Z.*) sensible, intelligent, aware, trustworthy, 'all there'; esp. in negative phr. *not (quite) the full shilling* etc, not very intelligent, slightly eccentric, odd cf. *FULL QUID, THE under* FULL *adj.*). **2** [1960s] (*Irish*) the proper, complete thing. ❑ **just the shiny shilling** *see JUST THE SHINY BOB under* BOB *n.*[3]. ❑ **shilling in (and the winner shouts)** *n.* [var. on *BOB IN under* BOB *n.*[3]] [late 19C–1900s] (*Aus./N.Z.*) a bar-room dice gambling game in which everyone puts one shilling (5p) in a kitty and the winner pays for the round (and poss. makes a small profit).

shillings *n.* [2000s] money.

shillings and pence *n.* [rhy. sl.] [20C+] sense.

shilliver *n. see* SHILL *n.*[2] (1).

shilly-shally *n.* [SE after 1850; orig. *stand shill I, shall I*; f. *shall I this? shall I that?*] **1** [late 18C–early 19C] one who hesitates, an irresolute, undecided person; also as adj. **2** [late 18C–mid-19C] hesitation, vacillation.

shilly-shally *v.* (*also* **shilly-shamble**) [SHILLY-SHALLY *n.*; SE after 1850] [late 18C–mid-19C] to vacillate.

shim *n.*[1] [ety. unknown ? SE *shimmy*] [1950s] (*US*) a person who does not appreciate rock and roll.

shim *n.*[2] [SE *shim*, a sliver of metal, used to fill the space between parts of machinery that are subject to wear] [1960s+] a piece of plastic used to open a door.

shim *n.*[3] [? SE *shimmy*, to wriggle, or SE *she* + *him*] **1** [1970s+] (*also* **shims**) a male homosexual. **2** [1970s+] (*US black*) a lesbian; a masculine-looking woman. **3** [1990s+] a transsexual.

shim *v.* [SHIM *n.*[2]] [1970s] (*US*) to open a door or lock with a piece of plastic.

shimmy *n.*[1] (*also* **shemmy**) [abbr. SE *chemise*, a shift or smock; the *OED* suggests that this 'vulgar corruption' was the result of people assuming *chemise* was a pl.] **1** [mid-19C+] a woman's undergarment, essentially synon. with a petticoat. **2** [1950s–70s] a man's shirt.

shimmy *n.*[2] (*also* **chimmy**) [abbr.] [1920s+] the gambling game of *chemin de fer*.

shimmy *n.*[3] [it 'shimmies' or wobbles] [1940s] (*US*) jello.

shimozzle *n. see* SHEMOZZLE *n.*

shims *n. see* SHIM *n.*[3] (1).

shim-sham *n.* [? JIM-JAMS *n.* (3)] [1970s+] (*US campus*) feelings of unease, of nervousness.

shim sham *adj.* [redup. SE *sham*] [early 18C] (*UK Und.*) second-rate, fake.

shin *n.*[1] [SHIN *v.*[2] (1)] [late 19C] (*US campus*) velocity.

shin *n.*[2] [? SHIV *n.* (1)] [1930s+] (*US prison*) any contraband gun or knife.

shin *n.*[3]

SE in slang uses

IN COMPOUNDS

❑ **shin battle** *n.* [? one kicks only shins; weapons are not used] [1950s–60s] (*street gang*) a fake, practice battle. ❑ **shinplaster** *adj.* [SE *shinplaster*, a square piece of paper saturated with vinegar etc, used as a plaster for sore legs. The implication is that the 'folk remedy' has no real, or certainly long-term efficacy] [mid-19C] worthless. ❑ **shinrapper** *n.* [SE *rap*, to hit; note SE *shin-rapper*, one who disables horses by striking the splint-bone] [19C] (*UK prison/Und.*) the prison treadmill. ❑ **shinscraper** *n.* [its scraping against the shins of the 'walker'] [mid–late 19C] (*UK prison/Und.*) the treadmill. ❑ **shin stage** *n.* [*stage-coach*] [18C] walking, travelling on foot.

shin *v.*[1] [for ety. *see BREAK SHINS under* BREAK *v.*[1]] [mid–late 19C] (*US*) to borrow money.

IN PHRASES

❑ **shin out** *v.* [mid–late 19C] to pay up (one's share, one's debts).

shin *v.*[2] [mid–late 19C] (*US*) **1** to pay a social visit. **2** to walk off.

IN PHRASES

❑ **shin off** *v.* [late 19C+] (*Aus./US*) to run away, to abscond.

shindig *n.* [SE *shindig*, a noisy party or festivity + SHINDY *n.* (1)] [mid-19C+] an altercation, a violent quarrel, a tremendous fuss.

shindy *n.* (*also* **shindying, shinty**) [naut. jargon *shindy*, a form of dance among sailors; ? ult. SE *shinty*, a game, mainly played in Ireland, that resembles a rougher form of hockey] [mid-19C] a noise, a disturbance, a commotion.

IN PHRASES

▫ **kick up a shindy** *v.* (*also* **cut shindies**) [mid-19C+] to cause trouble, to create a disturbance.

shindykit *n.* (*also* **swindlecat**) [SE *syndicate* + SHINDY *n.*/SE *swindle*] [1900s–10s] (*Aus.*) a business consortium.

shine *n.*[1] [? SHINERS *n.*[1] (1)] [mid–late 19C] money.

shine *n.*[2] **1** [mid-19C–1950s] a noise, a commotion. **2** [late 19C] (*US*) a smile [? one's glinting teeth]. **3** [late 19C–1910s] (*US*) a fool. **4** in uses meaning a black person [the reflection of a blue-black skin; as used in W.I. the term refers to someone with a very dark, smooth complexion and has no derog. connotations]. (**a**) [late 19C+] (*US*) (*also* **chinee, shiner**) a derog. term for a black person. (**b**) [1920s+] (*US*) as used by a black person, thus not derog. **5** [1900s] a noisy person; a show-off. **6** [1900s] (*US*) a fake diamond. **7** [1990s+] (*US black*) jewellery. **8** [1990s+] (*W.I.*) fellatio [play on *POLISH THE KNOB under* KNOB *n.*].

IN PHRASES

▫ **do a shine** *v.* [1910s] to run away and hide. ▫ **kick up a shine** *v.* [mid-19C–1950s] to cause trouble, to create a disturbance.

shine *n.*[3]

IN PHRASES

▫ **take a shine to** *v.* (*also* **take a shindy to, have the shiners for**) [UK dial. *shiner*, a sweetheart; but, given the var. of *take a shindy*, note SHINDY *n.*, cognate with SHINE *n.*[2] (1)] [mid-19C+] (*orig. US*) to find attractive or appealing, to have a fancy or affection for.

shine *n.*[4] [abbr. MOONSHINE *n.* (2)] **1** [1920s+] (*US*) illicitly distilled whisky. **2** [2000s] (*US prison*) homemade prison alcohol.

shine *adj.*[1] (*also* **shyin'**) (*Aus./N.Z./US*) **1** [late 19C+] of objects, excellent, first-rate. **2** [1940s+] of people, likeable.

shine *adj.*[2] [SHINE *n.*[2] (4)] [20C+] (*W.I./US*) black or pertaining to black culture.

IN COMPOUNDS

▫ **shine box** *n.* [BOX *n.*[1] (3c), a nightclub, Fr. sl. *boîte*, a nightclub (lit. 'a box')] [1940s–50s] (*US*) a nightclub featuring entertainment by black jazz musicians; it may also be patronized by a primarily black clientele. ▫ **shine joint** *n.* [JOINT *n.* (3)] [1940s–50s] (*US*) **1** an illicit liquor-selling establishment [SHINE *n.*[4] (1)]. **2** a nightclub patronized by a primarily black clientele. ▫ **Shinetown** *n.* [1940s] (*US*) a derog. name for any predominantly black area of a town or city.

shine *adj.*[3] [1900s] second-rate, crafty.

shine *v.*[1] [SHINE *n.*[1]] [mid-19C] to raise money, to display money.

shine *v.*[2] **1** [late 19C+] (*US campus*) to play truant, to skip classes. **2** [1950s] to impress. **3** [1960s+] (*US black*) (*also* **shine on**) to fool, to delude. **4** [1970s] to get rid of. **5** [1970s] to abandon, to fail. **6** *see SHINE UP TO* below.

SE in slang uses

IN PHRASES

▫ **shine-eye gal** *n.* [1970s+] (*W.I./UK black*) a materialistic young woman. ▫ **shine (in)** *v.* [1920s–50s] (*US*) to appear. ▫ **shine like a diamond in a goat's ass** *v.* (*also* **shine like a dime in a goat's ass**) [1980s+] (*US*) to shine very brightly. ▫ **shine like a shitten barn door** *v.* [SE *shitten*, filthied with excrement; the image of wet ordure glistening on a barn door] [mid-18C–early 19C] to shine brightly. ▫ **shine on** *v. see* sense 3 above. ▫ **shine one's pole** *v.* [1990s+] to masturbate. ▫ **shine someone on** *v.* (*also* **put someone on shine, shine it on**) [euph. SHIT *n.* (1)] [1960s+] (*US black*) to ignore, to disdain. ▫ **shine up** *v.* [2000s] (*US black*) to fellate. ▫ **shine up to** *v.* (*also* **shine**) [? to shine a fig. light on the object of one's admiration] [mid-19C+] (*US*) to flatter someone, to curry favour, to court.

shine! *excl.* [euph. SHIT! *excl.*] [1980s+] (*US campus*) impossible! absolutely not! on no account!

shined *adj.* [SHINE *n.*[4] (1)] [1920s] (*US*) drunk.

shine-on *adj.* [*SHINE SOMEONE ON under* SHINE *v.*[2]] [1950s+] (*US black*) dismissive.

shiner *n.*[1] **1** [mid-17C–19C] a gold coin. **2** [late 18C; 20C+] a black eye. **3** [19C+] (*Und.*) a mirror, esp. as used by card-sharps to spy on otherwise hidden hands. **4** [mid-19C–1920s] a silver dollar. **5** [late 19C–1900s] a silk hat. **6** [late 19C–1930s] a diamond, or other jewel, also in pl. **7** [1910s] (*Aus.*) an attractive person. **8** [1930s] (*US tramp*) a ten-cent piece.

shiner *n.*[2] **1** [19C+] a clever person. **2** [1930s+] (*Aus.*) one who wants the limelight, but is unwilling to work towards gaining it.

shiner *n.*[3] [their job] [1950s+] a window-cleaner.

shiner *n.*[4] [spittle 'shines' the head of the penis] [1990s+] fellatio.

shiners *n.*[1] (*also* **shinery**) [the shininess of coins and the cloth] **1** [early 18C–19C] money, esp. sovereigns, guineas. **2** [1990s+] (*W.I.*) sparkly clothes fabrics.

shiners *n.*[2] [? *SHINE ONE'S POLE under* SHINE *v.*[2]/*POLISH THE KNOB under* KNOB *n.*] [1990s+] (*black*) fellatio.

shines *n.* [SE *shine*, a brilliant display] **1** [mid-19C] (*orig. US*) tricks. **2** [late 19C] sexual intercourse.

shiney *n.* [SHINE *n.*[2] (4)] [late 19C–1930s] (*US*) a black person.

shiney, the *n. see* SHINY, THE *n.* (1).

shingle *n.* [metonymy, f. SE *shingle*, i.e. the small sign o nameplate outside his office] [1950s] (*US*) a lawyer.

SE in slang uses

IN PHRASES

▫ **take a shingle off** *v.* **1** [late 19C] (*N.Z.*) to lose one' temper, i.e. to 'hit the roof'. **2** [1900s–10s] (*Aus.*) to refuse tc drink in a public house.

shingler *n.* [SE *shingler*, a woman who has her hair 'shingled', i.e tapered from the back of the head to the nape of the neck; earl adoptees of the fashion were presumably considered 'fast' and b ext. immoral] [1900s–10s] (*Aus.*) a prostitute.

shingle short *adj.* (*also* **one shingle short**) [var. on NOT AL THERE *adj.*] **1** [mid-19C+] (*Aus.*) eccentric, crazy; thus n. *shingl short*, an eccentric. **2** [1910s] in fig. use, deficient, lacking i (but not mentally deficient).

shingle-splitting *n.* [SAusE *shingle-splitter*, a builder of houses esp. in the outback] [mid–late 19C] (*Aus.*) escaping one' creditors by vanishing into the countryside.

shinie *n.* [SHINE *n.*[2] (4)] [late 19C] (*US Und.*) a black tramp.

Shinkin-ap-Morgan *n.* (*also* **Shon Ap Morgan**) [stereotypical Welsh name, lit. 'Jenkins son of Morgan'] [17C early 18C] a generic nickname for any Welshman.

Shinner *n.* [*Sinn* [pron. 'shin'] *Fein*] [1920s+] a member of th Irish nationalist movement Sinn Fein.

shinner *n.* [? *SHINPLASTER under* SHIN *n.*[3]] [mid-19C] (*US*) merchant who borrows money from his peers in order to mee a note drawn on a bank.

shinnies *n.* [var. SHINERS *n.*[1] (1)] [late 19C] (*US*) money.

shinny *n.* [SHINE *n.*[4] (1)] [1920s+] (*US black*) illegally distille alcohol.

shinny *v.* [1910s] (*US*) to make an effort, to work hard.

shino *n.* [SHINE *n.*[1] (1) + RHINO *n.*[1] (1)] [late 18C] a guinea.

Shinola *n.* [*NOT KNOW SHIT FROM SHINOLA under* SHIT *n.*] [1980s (*US*) nothing.

shinty *n. see* SHINDY *n.*

shiny, the *n.* (*also* **shiney, the**) [glittering coins] [mid–late 19C money.

shiny *adj.* **1** [late 19C] (*also* **shiney**) smart, successful. **2** [lat 19C–1900s] (*US*) (*also* **shinny**) tipsy. **3** [1990s+] happy.

SE in slang uses

IN COMPOUNDS

▫ **shiny Bob** *n.* [BOB *n.*[1]] [1920s+] (*Aus.*) one who has a ve high opinion of themselves. ▫ **shiny-bum** *see* separate entrie ▫ **shiny button** *n. see* BUTTON *n.*[1] (2c). ▫ **shiny ten** *n.* [? la 19C, 'The Shiny Tenth': the 10th Royal Hussars] [20C+] (*bing* the number ten.

shiny and bright *phr.* [rhy. sl.] [20C+] all right.

shiny-bum *n.* (*also* **shiny, shiny-arse, shiny-seat**) [SE *shiny* + BUM *n.*[1] (1); one's bottom polishes the seat] [1940s+] (*orig. Aus.*) one who has a desk job.

IN COMPOUNDS

❑ **shiny-arsed** *adj.* [1940s+] (*orig. Aus.*) working in an office.

shiny-bum *v.* [SHINY-BUM *n.*] [1940s] (*Aus.*) to hold down a desk job.

ship *n.*[1] [1910s–60s] (*US*) an aeroplane.

SE in slang uses

DERIVATIVES

❑ **shippy** *n.* [mid-19C] (*US*) shipmate, also as term of address.

IN COMPOUNDS

❑ **ship-moll** *n.* (*also* **shippie**) [MOLL *n.* (2)] [1970s+] (*N.Z.*) a prostitute who works on docked ships; a descendant of the 19C Maori *ship-girl*. ❑ **shipwreck** *n.* **1** [mid-19C] (*US campus*) (*also* **wreck**) an absolute failure. **2** [late 19C–1950s] (*US*) scrambled eggs. ❑ **shipwreck** *v.* [late 19C–1950s] to scramble eggs. ❑ **ship-wrecked** *adj.* [late 19C–1900s] drunk.

IN PHRASES

❑ **give up the ship** *v.* [Captain James Lawrence's famous dying words, 'Don't give up the ship' at the taking of the *Chesapeake*, 1 Jun. 1813] [late 19C–1930s] to die. ❑ **old ship** *n.* [1910s] (*Aus.*) a term of affectionate address. ❑ **steer the ship** *v.* [1980s] (*Aus.*) to buy a drink.

ship *n.*[2] [abbr.] [1950s] (*US*) a scholar*ship*.

ship *v.* [1930s+] (*US Und.*) to send to prison or to be moved from one prison to another.

SE in slang uses

IN PHRASES

❑ **ship out** *v.* [1930s+] (*orig. milit.*) **1** to leave, to depart; to release from prison. **2** in fig. use, to die.

ship (in full sail) *n.* [rhy. sl.] [mid-19C; 1930s+] a pot of ale.

shipload *n. see* SHITLOAD *n.*

shippie *n. see* SHIP-MOLL *under* SHIP *n.*[1].

ship under sail *n.* [rhy. sl. = SE *tale*] [1930s] a story used for begging or for a confidence trick.

shiralee *n.* [ety. unknown] [late 19C+] (*Aus.*) a bundle of blankets or personal belongings.

shirk *n.* (*also* **sherk**) [SHARK *n.* (2), but cf. 17C SE *shirk*, to practise fraud or trickery, esp. instead of working, to sponge upon others] **1** [mid-17C–18C] a cheating gamester. **2** [mid-17C–19C] a sponger, a parasite.

shirk the roundbottom *v.* [early 19C] (*UK Und.*) to avoid a criminal charge, through bribery.

shirl *n.* [the proper name *Shirley*] [1970s] (*Aus.*) the female counterpart of the OCKER *n.*

shirley *n.* [proper name of US actress and gay icon (esp. in her roles as a 1930s child star) *Shirley Temple* (b.1928)] [1980s] (*US*) a gay man.

Shirley Temple *n.* [the US film actress Shirley Temple (b.1928) whose early career was as a child-star] [1980s] a young girl, poss. below the age of consent; a young effeminate boy.

shirt *n.*

SE in slang uses

IN COMPOUNDS

❑ **shirt-fly** *n.* [they are 'always up the gaffer's arse'] [1990s+] a toady. ❑ **shirtlifter** *n.* [i.e. the lifting of the shirt before sodomy] [1960s+] (*orig. Aus.*) a male homosexual. ❑ **shirtlifterish** *adj.* [1960s+] (*orig. Aus.*) pertaining to homosexuality. ❑ **shirt potato** *n.* [2000s] (*Aus.*) the female breast. ❑ **shirtrat** *n.* (*also* **shirt hound, ...rabbit, ...squirrel**) [1910s–20s] (*US*) a body louse, a bedbug. ❑ **shirt-stretcher** *n.* [1990s+] the female breast; thus a woman with large breasts. ❑ **shirt-tail** *adj.* [one's shirt-tail is (fig.) hanging out] [1920s+] (*US*) impoverished, deprived, mean. ❑ **shirt-tail relation** *n.* [20C+] (*Aus./US*) a distant relation, a family friend.

IN PHRASES

❑ **another clean shirt ought to see you out** [1930s+] (*N.Z.*) you look very ill; i.e. you look as if you'll soon be dead. ❑ **clean shirt** *n.* [1940s] (*UK prison*) a beating administered by warders to a new prisoner on admission. ❑ **clean-shirt day** *n.* [the one day of the week on which even the poorest wore a clean shirt] [mid-19C] Sunday. ❑ **fill one's shirt** *v.* [a full, bulging stomach fills one's shirt] [20C+] (*US*) to eat heartily. ❑ **get one's shirt out** *v.* (*also* **have one's shirt out**) **1** [mid-19C] to become angry or to make another angry [the disarrangement of one's clothes that may follow a fit of arm-brandishing fury]. **2** [mid-19C–1930s] to cause someone to lose all their money (through gambling) [? precursor of *LOSE ONE'S SHIRT* below]. ❑ **get one's shirt-tails cracking** *v.* [1970s] (*N.Z.*) to hurry up. ❑ **have someone's shirt** *v.* [1910s+] to take someone's money. ❑ **lose one's shirt** *v.* **1** [1910s+] to lose a good deal of money, usu. through gambling or other speculation. **2** [1990s+] (*US campus*) to laugh uncontrollably. ❑ **put one's shirt on** *v.* (*also* **have one's shirt on, put one's socks on**) [late 19C+] (*gambling*) to bet heavily. ❑ **take one's shirt off** *v.* [late 19C] to lose one's temper.

IN EXCLAMATIONS

❑ **do as my shirt does!** [pun on KISS MY ARSE! *excl.*] [mid-17C–18C] a euph. but derisive excl. of abuse, rejection. ❑ **hold your shirt!** [20C+] calm down! ❑ **keep your shirt on!** [mid-19C+] calm down! don't lose (emotional) control!

shirt (and) collar *n.* [rhy. sl. = DOLLAR *n.*[1] (1)] [1930s] five shillings (25p).

shirty *adj.* (*also* **shirtey**) [*GET ONE'S SHIRT OUT* **under** SHIRT *n.*] [mid-19C+] irritable, angry, tetchy.

DERIVATIVES

❑ **shirtily** *adv.* [mid-19C+] angrily, tetchily.

shise *see under* SHICE.

shiser *n. see* SHICER *n.*

shish *see under* SHICE.

shisser *n. see* SHICER *n.*

shista *n.* [SHYSTER *n.*] [1990s+] (*US black*) a crooked lawyer.

shisty *adj. see* SHEISTY *adj.*

shit *n.* [OE *scite*/MLG *Schite*, dung + OE *scitte*, diarrhoea; SE 14C–late 17C, henceforth sl.] **1** in context of excrement. (**a**) [mid-17C+] excrement. (**b**) [1920s+] an act of defecation. **2** pertaining to individuals (or objects). (**a**) [late 19C+] a contemptible person; often in combs., e.g. *little shit, dumb shit*. (**b**) [1960s+] (*orig. US black*) constr. with *the*, of things or people, the best, the ideal, the ultimate. (**c**) [1980s+] a person, irrespective of qualities. (**d**) [1990s+] a boastful, pretentious person, a braggart. **3** in fig./abstract uses. (**a**) [late 19C+] fig. anything seen as unpleasant and disgusting. (**b**) [1910s+] an unpleasant situation; usu. as phr. *IN (THE) SHIT* below. (**c**) [1910s+] problems, difficulties. (**d**) [1920s] (*US*) constr. with *the*, something bad. (**e**) [1920s+] any inferior, rubbishy, shoddy or pretentious thing. (**f**) [1930s+] any thing (material or otherwise), irrespective of its actual quality. (**g**) [1930s+] anything, something. (**h**) [1930s+] (*orig. US black*) a general abstract term, a thing, a situation, an opinion or idea; the precise meaning varies as to the context, e.g. *I don't like this shit*, I don't like what's happening. (**i**) [1940s+] nothing; thus *not mean shit*, not matter, not mean anything; *not worth shit*, not worth anything. (**j**) [1950s+] abuse, offensive and contemptuous treatment, e.g. to *take a lot of shit, don't take any shit*. (**k**) [1960s+] in abstract use, one's possessions, one's actions, one's life. **4** in senses of communication. (**a**) [1920s+] nonsense, rubbish, lies, prevarications; often in *TALK SHIT* below. (**b**) [1970s] influence. (**c**) [1990s+] (negative) information. **5** [1930s+] (*also* **the living shit, the shitter, the slop**) constr. with *the*, the essence, the absolute; usu. in phr. *the shit out of*. **6** with ref. to drugs. (**a**) [1940s+] heroin, occas. morphine. (**b**) [1950s+] cannabis. (**c**) [1950s+] (*also* **shite**) any form of drug. (**d**) [1970s+] cocaine; crack cocaine. **7** [1960s] (*US*) money. **8** [1960s+] (*orig. US*) constr. with *the*, a general intensifier, e.g. *who the shit are you? let's get the shit out of here* [note synon. uses of the stronger FUCK *n.* and the milder HELL, THE *phr.*]. **9** [1960s+] as a general negative intensifier, e.g. *would I shit! did she shit!* **10** in Und. or prison uses. (**a**) [1980s+] (*US Und.*) gunfire. (**b**) [1980s+] (*Aus. prison*)

prison food. **(c)** [1980s+] (*Aus. prison*) tobacco. **(d)** [1980s+] (*US*) a criminal. **(e)** [1980s+] (*US Und.*) any form of weapon. **(f)** [1990s+] (*US prison*) violence; a prison riot. **(g)** [2000s] (*US prison*) HIV or AIDS.

DERIVATIVES

□ **shitless** *adj.* *see* separate entry. □ **shitted** *adj.* [1990s+] terrified. □ **Shitville** *n.* [-VILLE *sfx*[1] (1)] [1970s] (*US*) a very out-of-the-way, rural place.

IN COMPOUNDS

□ **shit-all** *n.* (*also* **shite-all**) [var. on FUCK ALL *n.* (1)] [1930s+] nothing at all. □ **shit ass** *see* separate entries. □ **shitbag** *n.* **1** [late 19C–1910s] the stomach; thus *shitbags*, the guts. **2** [1920s+] (*also* **shite-bag**) a general pej. term, whether of people or things. **3** [1990s+] (*US black/teen*) a colostomy bag. □ **shitball** *n.* [1960s+] (*US*) a general term of abuse. □ **shitbird** *see* separate entries. □ **shit-box** *n.* [SE *box*/BOX *n.*[1] (1d)] [1980s+] **1** (*US*) the anus. **2** (*Aus. prison*) a portable latrine. **3** a run-down vehicle. **4** anything bad or inferior. □ **shitbound** *adj. see* SHITCANNED *adj.* □ **shit-brained/shitbrains** *see* separate entries. □ **shit-breeched** *adj.* [mid-17C] a general term of abuse. □ **shit bucket** *n.* [initial letters] [1970s] (*S.Afr.*) the Special Branch. □ **shitbug** *n. see* SHITBIRD *n.*[2]. □ **shitbum** *see* separate entries. □ **shitcan/-canned** *see* separate entries. □ **shit-cart** *n.* [1920s] a nightsoil cart; a refuse lorry. □ **shit-catchers** *n.* (*also* **poop-catchers**) [1930s] (*Aus.*) knickerbockers. □ **shit-chute** *n.* **1** [1960s+] the anus. **2** [2000s] a disgusting, filthy place. □ **shit-coloured** *adj.* [1920s–50s] (*US black*) a derog. term applied to a light-skinned black person who tries to pass as white. □ **shit creek** *n. see* separate entry. □ **shit-cunt** *n.* [CUNT *n.* (4)] [1990s+] (*UK black*) a general term of abuse. □ **shit detail** *n.* [SE *detail*, a job] [1940s+] (*orig. milit.*) any unpleasant or dirty task. □ **shit-disturber** *n.* [20C+] a malicious gossip. □ **shit-eater/-eating** *see* separate entries. □ **shit-eating grin** *n. see* separate entry. □ **shitface/-faced** *see* separate entries. □ **shit factory** *n.* [1990s+] (*US*) the buttocks. □ **shit-farm** *n.* [1980s] (*Aus.*) a unpleasant, worthless place. □ **shit-features** *n.* [2000s] (*N.Z.*) an unattractive person. □ **shit-fight** *n.* [1990s+] a bitterly contested struggle, e.g. a sporting encounter. □ **shitfire** *see* separate entries. □ **shitfit** *n.* [1950s+] (*US*) an emotional outburst. □ **shitfuck** *see* separate entries. □ **shithead** *see* separate entries. □ **shitheap** *n.* [1960s+] **1** a dirty, unpleasant, disgusting place or object. **2** a contemptible person. □ **shit-heel** *n.* (*also* **shithealer, shit-heeler**) **1** [20C+] (*US*) a generally derog. term of abuse; also as adj. **2** [1990s+] (*UK/US Und.*) an informer. □ **shithole** *see* separate entries. □ **shithook** *n.* [note US milit. use *shithook*, CH-47 'Chinook' helicopter] [1960s+] (*orig. US campus*) **1** a foolish, clumsy person. **2** an unpleasant, aggressive individual. □ **shit-hooks** *n.* [SE *hook*/HOOK *n.*[1] (1a)] [1970s] (*US campus*) the hands. □ **shit hot** *see* separate entries. □ **shithouse** *see* separate entries. □ **shit-hunter** *n.* [late 19C–1900s] a sodomite. □ **shit jacket** *n.* [1970s] (*US black*) an outside lavatory. □ **shitkick/kicker/kicking** *see* separate entries. □ **shit-licking** *adj.* [1970s] (*US*) a term of abuse, applied to homosexuals. □ **shit list** *n.* (*also* **s-list**) [1940s+] a list of people one considers distasteful, untrustworthy and otherwise unacceptable; similarly extended to places. □ **shitload** *n. see* separate entries. □ **shit lover** *n.* [SHIT *n.* (1a), i.e. a coprophile] [1960s] (*US*) a term of abuse. □ **shitman** *n.* **1** [1980s] (*Aus.*) one who gossips maliciously. **2** [1980s+] (*Aus. prison*) an unimportant person. **3** [1980s+] (*Aus. prison*) thus, an assistant, one who is low(er) in the hierarchy. □ **shit-packer** *n. see* TURD-PACKER *under* TURD *n.*[1]. □ **shit-pan** *n.* **1** [1940s] a general term of abuse. **2** [1990s+] the anus. □ **shitpaper** *n.* [1970s+] (*Aus./US*) lavatory paper. □ **shit pie** *n.* [1990s+] nothing. □ **shit-pit** *n.* (*also* **shit pen**) [1990s+] **1** a lavatory. **2** any dirty and/or disgusting place. □ **shitpot** *see* separate entries. □ **shitpull** *n.* [2000s] (*US*) a struggle. □ **shit-puncher** *n. see* SHIT-STABBER below. □ **shit-ringer** *n.* [SAusE *ringer*, a stockman] [1940s+] (*Aus.*) a stockman. □ **shitsack** *n. see* separate entry. □ **shit sandwich** *n.* **1** [1960s+] a humbling experience; 'humble pie'. **2** [1980s] (*N.Z.*) homosexual anal intercourse. □ **shit-scared** *adj. see* separate entry. □ **shit-shark** *n.* [mid–late 19C] a night-soil collector. □ **shit-shoe** *n.* (*also* **shit-shod**) [late 19C] one who has trodden in excrement. □ **shit-skin** *see* separate entries. □ **shit-slinging** *n. see* MUD-SLINGING *n.* □ **shit-sniffer** *n.* [1980s] a term of abuse. □ **shit-squirting** *adj.* [1980s] (*US*) dirty, disgusting. □ **shit-stab** *v.* [backform. f. *SHIT-STABBER* below] [1990s+] to have anal intercourse, usu. in a male homosexual context. □ **shit-stabber** *n.* (*also* **shit-puncher, shit-stirrer**) [1960s+] (*orig. gay*) **1** the penis. **2** a male homosexual. □ **shitstain** *n.* [1990s+] (*orig. US*) a fool. □ **shitstem** *n.* [SE *system*] [2000s] (*UK black*) the white power structure. □ **shit-stick** *n.* (*also* **shite-sticks**) [SE *stick*/STICK *n.* (1a)] **1** [late 16C; 20C Aus.] a contemptible person. **2** [1980s] (*US*) the penis, esp. when used for anal intercourse. **3** [1990s+] (*UK prison*) a billy-club. □ **shit-stir** *v.* [late 19C+] to gossip maliciously in the hope of causing trouble. □ **shit-stirrer** *n.* **1** [late 19C+] a malicious gossip. **2** [1930s+] a trouble maker; a political activist. **3** *see SHIT-STABBER* above. □ **shit stompers** *n.* [STOMPERS *n.* (1)] [1970s+] (*US campus*) **1** cowboy boots. **2** cowboys. □ **shit-stopper** *n.* [the image of an event so dramatic or surprising that it suspends one's normal bodily processes] [1960s+] a prank, a funny scene, an escapade. □ **shitstorm** *n.* [1940s+] (*US*) a very confused or frightening situation. □ **shit street** *n. see* separate entry. □ **shit-sucking** *adj.* [1990s+] (*US*) an abusive intensifier. □ **shit-talker** *n.* [1990s+] (*US black*) one who talks nonsense. □ **shit ticket** *n.* [1990s+] (*US juv.*) a sheet of lavatory paper. □ **shitwad** *n.* [2000s] (*US*) an unpleasant person. □ **shitwagon** *n.* [1970s+] (*US*) a second-rate, run-down automobile. □ **shitweasel** *n.* [1990s+] a term of abuse, of a person or an unpleasant thing. □ **shitwork** *n.* [1960s+] unpleasant, unwanted, prob. dirty occupations. □ **shit-worth** *n.* [1920s+] a derisory amount.

IN PHRASES

verbs pertaining to lit. or fig. uses of excrement

□ **do a shit** [mid-19C+] to defecate. □ **eat shit** *see* separate entry. □ **get one's shit blown away** (*also* **get one's shit blown backwards**) [1960s+] (*US*) to be killed. □ **get one's shit hard** [2000s] to make one excited. □ **get up in someone's shit** [*GET UP IN under* GET UP *v.*[1]] [1980s] (*US*) to get angry with someone else. □ **go like shit off a stick** [1970s+] to move very fast, of a person or vehicle. □ **have a shit** [1980s] (*Aus./S.Afr.*) to become enraged. □ **have shit in one's blood** [1970s] (*US*) to be a coward. □ **have shit on one's liver** (*also* **have dirt on one's liver**) [SE *liverish*, testy] [1930s+] (*Aus.*) to be in a bad temper. □ **have someone's shit on a stick** [1960s+] (*US*) to place at an extreme disadvantage. □ **lose one's shit** [1980s+] (*US campus*) to experience something frightening or shocking. □ **pack shit** *see* PACK (THE) SHIT *under* PACK *v.*[1]. □ **push shit uphill** **1** [1980s+] to work, to talk etc unsuccessfully, against the odds. **2** [1980s+] (*US gay*) to have anal intercourse. □ **put the shit up** (*also* **put the shits up**) [1940s+] to terrify. □ **take a shit** **1** [early 17C; 1920s+] to defecate. **2** [1960s–70s] in fig. use, to cause trouble for, to attack. □ **think one's shit smells like ice-cream** [1940s] (*US*) to behave affectedly and in an arrogant manner.

verbs pertaining to trouble or ill treatment

□ **catch shit** (*orig. US*) **1** [1950s+] to be scolded or told off, to get into trouble. **2** [1960s+] to suffer physical harm. □ **drop someone in the shit** *see DROP SOMEONE IN IT under* DROP *v.*[1] □ **drop (the) shit on** [1970s] (*US*) to give someone a difficult time, to persecute. □ **fall in the shit** [mid-19C+] to find oneself in difficulties. □ **get in the shit** **1** [1940s+] to become involved in a situation; spec. (*US milit.*) to join a firefight or arrive on the front line. **2** [1960s+] (*also* **get in the cactus ...crap**) to get into trouble. □ **give someone shit** [1960s+] (*orig. US*) **1** to cause trouble for someone. **2** to nag, to criticize. □ **hit some shit** (*also* **get into shit**) [SE *hit*, to encounter] [1970s+] (*US black*) to encounter problems. □ **kick up shit** [KICK UP *v.* + SHIT *n.* (3c)] [1940s+] to cause a commotion, to cause trouble. □ **land someone in the shit** (*also* **dump someone in it**) [1950s+] to bring trouble to someone else. □ **put shit in the game** *see under* GAME *n.* □ **put (the) shit on** [1960s] **1** (*Aus./US*) to deride, to attack verbally. **2** (*US black*) to take advantage; to trick, to deceive

❑ **raise shit** [1990s+] (*US*) to cause trouble, to make a fuss. ❑ **shovel (the) shit** *see under* SHOVEL *v.* ❑ **start shit** [1950s+] (*US black*) to initiate trouble, to start an argument. ❑ **stir (the) shit** *see under* STIR *v.* ❑ **suck shit** *see under* SUCK *v.*[1]. ❑ **take shit** [1950s+] (*orig. US*) to suffer (and accept) humiliation, annoyance or (in weak form) teasing; often as *take no shit.*

verbs pertaining to the 'essence' in the context of violence

❑ **bash the shit out of** *see* BEAT THE SHIT OUT OF *v.* ❑ **beat the shit out of** *see* separate entry. ❑ **kick the shit out of** (*also* **kick the dog shit out of, ...the living shit out of**) [1920s+] to beat severely. ❑ **knock the shit out of** (*also* **knock the dog shit out of**) [1950s+] to beat severely. ❑ **pound the shit out of** *see* BEAT THE SHIT OUT OF *v.* ❑ **scare the (living) shit(s) out of** [1920s+] (*orig. US*) to terrify. ❑ **slap the shit out of** [1960s+] to beat severely. ❑ **stomp the living shit out of** *see* BEAT THE SHIT OUT OF *v.* ❑ **thump seven kinds of shit out of** (*also* **kick seven kinds of shit out of, knock...**) [1950s+] (*orig. milit.*) to beat up severely. ❑ **thump/whack the shit out of** *see* BEAT THE SHIT OUT OF *v.*

verbs pertaining to objects or situations with negative connotations

❑ **feel like shit** (*also* **feel shit, feel shitty**) [1940s+] to feel very bad, whether emotionally or physically. ❑ **go from sugar to shit** [1960s] of a place and its standards, to decline severely. ❑ **go to shit** [1970s+] to decline, to collapse. ❑ **look like shit** [1970s+] **1** of a person, to appear extremely unwell, whether through actual illness or through the effects of drink or drugs. **2** of an object, to look in very poor condition. ❑ **suck shit** *see under* SUCK *v.*[1]. ❑ **take the shit with the sugar** [1990s+] (*Aus.*) to accept that one must have both bad and good experiences. ❑ **treat like shit** [1970s+] to treat in a very unpleasant manner, deservedly or not.

verbs pertaining to lying or deception

❑ **cut the shit** *see* CUT THE CRAP *v.* ❑ **pop shit** [POP OFF (AT THE MOUTH) *v.* (5)] [1960s+] to boast, to talk nonsense. ❑ **shoot (the) shit** *see under* SHOOT *v.* ❑ **sling (the) shit** *see* SLING THE DIRT (AT) *under* DIRT *n.* ❑ **talk shit** **1** [1940s+] (*US black*) to seduce, to 'chat someone up'. **2** [1960s+] (*orig. US*) to talk nonsense. **3** [1960s+] (*US campus*) to criticize someone behind their back. **4** [1960s+] (*US campus*) to boast, to brag. **5** [1960s+] (*US black*) to talk slang. **6** [1960s+] (*US black*) to talk aggressively, to challenge verbally.

verbs based on a general abstract thing or situation

❑ **cut shit** **1** [1970s+] (*orig. US*) to impress, to influence, to make a difference. **2** [2000s] (*US campus*) to act eccentrically. ❑ **get off someone's shit** [1970s] (*US*) to cease bothering someone; as imper., *get off my shit*, leave me alone. ❑ **get one's shit together** [1970s+] (*orig. US black*) **1** to calm down, to plan sensibly. **2** to be competent. ❑ **have one's shit together** (*also* **have one's shit down, have one's shit in one bag**) [1960s+] (*orig. US black*) to be in full control of a situation. ❑ **hit one's shit up** [1980s] (*US*) to inscribe one's name and gang affiliation on a wall. ❑ **know one's shit** [1990s+] (*US*) to be very competent. ❑ **play that shit** [1950s+] (*US black*) to act in a particular way; usu. in negative as *I don't play that shit*, I don't do that. ❑ **pull shit** [1960s+] (*US black*) to do something devious, underhand, treacherous. ❑ **put shit in the game** *see under* GAME *n.* ❑ **rip shit** *see* separate entry.

general verbs

❑ **get shit of** [20C+] to get rid of something or someone.

comparatives

❑ **as shit** *adv.* (*also* **as shite**) [1960s+] a general intensifer, e.g. *mad as shit.* ❑ **for shit** *adv.* [1940s+] (*orig. US*) **1** whatsoever, at all, in any way. **2** awful, very badly. ❑ **from shit to Shinnecock** [1970s] (*US*) of any sort whatsoever, across the entire spectrum. ❑ **good as shit** *adj.* [1970s] (*US campus*) very good. ❑ **like shit** *adv.* **1** [1940s+] very fast, enthusiastically. **2** [1970s+] badly, very bad. **3** [1980s+] a sarcastic retort of dismissal. **4** [1990s+] very much. ❑ **like shit off a shovel** *adv.* (*also* **like spit on a hot griddle, ...steam on piss**) [1920s+] promptly, immediately, fast. ❑ **like shit on a shoe** *adv.* [1980s+] extremely closely. ❑ **like shit through a goose** *adv.* (*also* **like crap through a goose, ...shit through a tin horn**) [20C+] extremely fast. ❑ **like stink on shit** *adv.* (*also* **like funk on a skunk, ...stank on shit, ...stink on glue**) [1960s+] (*US black*) very close, extremely intimate. ❑ **soft as shit and twice as nasty** [late 19C+] a general pej. phr. used of anyone the speaker dislikes. ❑ **so thin you can smell shit through them** [late 19C+] a phr. used of a very slim person. ❑ **stick as close as shit to a blanket** *v.* [1930s+] to stay very close. ❑ **sure as shit** *adv. see under* SURE AS... *phr.*

proverbial uses

❑ **act like one's shit don't stink** *v.* (*also* **act like one's shit don't smell, act like shit wouldn't melt in one's mouth, think one's shit don't stink**) [Partridge claims that *think one's shit doesn't stink* dates back to 'later C.19' but offers no proof] [1960s+] (*orig. US*) to behave affectedly and in an arrogant manner. ❑ **all over the place like a mad woman's shit** (*also* **...like a mad woman's breakfast, ...knitting, ...lunchbox**) [1950s+] (*Aus.*) confused, extremely messy. ❑ **bet a pound to a pinch of shit** *v.* (*also* **bet a pound to a pinch of poop**) [1940s+] a statement denoting the speaker's absolute confidence, whether in a real bet or merely a point of view. ❑ **break one's shit string** *v.* [instead of excrement, there is blood] [1960s+] (*US gay*) to have violent anal intercourse. ❑ **don't get your shit hot** [20C+] don't get over-excited. ❑ **he wouldn't say 'shit' even if he had a mouth full of it** (*also* **...even if he had his mouth full of it**) [20C+] (*Can.*) a phr. used of an especially mealy-mouthed, hypocritical person. ❑ **I could use her shit for toothpaste** (*also* **I'd crawl three miles over broken glass to use her shit for toothpaste**) [1950s+] a hugely exaggerated phr. implying the extent of one's infatuation. ❑ **I'm so hungry I could eat a shit sandwich – only I don't like bread** [1950s+] (*Aus.*) a phr. implying the intensity of one's starvation. ❑ **same shit, different day** (*also* **s.s.d.d.**) [1980s+] (*orig. US black*) life goes on as normal, with no surprises, good or bad. ❑ **shit comes in piles** [1990s+] (*US black*) problems always come at the same time, rather than one by one. ❑ **shit happens** [1980s+] an all-purpose statement of resignation in the face of life's vicissitudes, i.e. these things happen. ❑ **shit hits the fan, the** [1940s+] the difficulties start to happen, esp. when such problems have been expected to occur sooner or later; usu. used with *when*. Euph. alternatives include *the ca-ca hits the fan, the doo-doo..., the egg..., the omelette..., the excrement/solids hit(s) the air conditioning.* ❑ **ten pounds of shit in a five pound bag** [20C+] (*US*) a phr. describing anything considered ugly, esp. someone obese or overweight. ❑ **think one's shit don't stink** *v. see* ACT LIKE ONE'S SHIT DON'T STINK above. ❑ **think one's shit smells like ice-cream** *v.* [1940s] (*US*) to behave affectedly and in an arrogant manner. ❑ **you don't know whether you want a shit or haircut** [20C+] a phr. used to indicate that a person is very stupid. ❑ **you're all about – like shit in a field** [20C+] you're a useful, alert, efficient person – like hell you are!

negatives

❑ **not a shit show** [1980s+] (*N.Z.*) no chance. ❑ **not fit to shovel shit** *adj.* [1940s+] of a person, absolutely worthless or incompetent. ❑ **not know a sparrow's shit (about)** *v.* [1970s] to know nothing whatsoever. ❑ **not know from shit** *v.* [1970s] to be completely ignorant. ❑ **not know shit from apple butter** *v.* (*also* **...from beans, ...clay, ...salami, ...tunafish**) [1940s+] **1** to have no idea about a topic. **2** to be particularly wrong in an opinion. ❑ **not know shit from Shinola** *v.* [*Shinola*, a brand of black shoe polish] [1940s+] (*US*) **1** (*also* **not know shit from shine**) to have no idea about a topic. **2** to be particularly wrong in an opinion. ❑ **not say shit about Shinola** *v.* [1940s+] (*US*) to say nothing. ❑ **not worth a shit** *adj.* (*also* **not worth shit, ...two shits**) [1920s+] worthless, useless.

fig. general phrases

❑ **ain't shit** [1950s+] (*US black*) used of someone/something useless, worthless or of absolutely no value. ❑ **and shit** [1960s+] (*orig. US black*) a general abstract term, usu. thrown into the end of a sentence, similar to YOU KNOW *phr.* ❑ **bucket of shit** *n. see* CROCK OF SHIT *n.* ❑ **crock of shit** *n. see* separate entry. ❑ **dick shit** *n. see* DICK *n.*[1]. ❑ **in a shit** [2000s] (*N.Z.*) in a bad mood. ❑ **in (the) shit** [1920s+] in serious trouble; extended as *in deep shit*. ❑ **line of shit** *n.* [1920s+] nonsensical talk, usu. intended to persuade. ❑ **my shit** [2000s] (*US black*) an apology, 'my mistake'. ❑ **on one's shit list** [1940s+] a phr. used to describe someone that one dislikes intensely. ❑ **puddle of shit** *n.* [1940s+] (*also* **pish**) rubbish, nonsense, anything or anyone unappealling, worthless. ❑ **shit for brains** *n. see* separate entry. ❑ **shit-for-nothing** *adj.* (*also* **shit for the catfish, shit-for-wage**) [1980s] (*US*) third-rate, of very poor quality. ❑ **shit of a thing** *n.* [2000s] (*N.Z.*) something unacceptable or unpleasant. ❑ **shit on** *adj.* [1960s+] humiliated. ❑ **shit on a string** *n.* [1960s+] something extremely hard or impossible to do. ❑ **shit on a shingle** *n.* (*also* **cream on a shingle, SOS**) **1** [1930s+] (*mainly US milit.*) minced beef on toast. **2** [1980s+] as an excl. of astonishment. ❑ **shit on a stick** *n.* **1** [1950s+] (*US*) someone important. **2** [1980s] (*US black*) a self-appointed tough guy, more words than action. ❑ **shit on wheels** *n.* [1950s+] (*orig. US*) an important person, a person who thinks that they are important. ❑ **to shit** *adv.* [1910s+] a general intensifier. ❑ **up in someone's shit** [2000s] (*US black*) interfering, 'poking one's nose in'. ❑ **up the Dutch shit** [2000s] (*N.Z.*) facing serious trouble. ❑ **up the shit** [1980s] (*US campus*) in large quantities. ❑ **what's the shit?** [1960s] (*US*) what's going on, what's happening?

IN EXCLAMATIONS

❑ **for shit's sake!** [1960s+] an excl., usu. used to indicate one's mild annoyance. ❑ **go plait your shit!** [1960s] a general excl. of dismissal. ❑ **I'll be dipped in shit!** [1960s+] (*US*) an excl. of surprise. ❑ **no shit!** *see* separate entry. ❑ **shit howdy!** [1970s] (*US*) a mild excl. ❑ **shitlaw!** [? SHIT! *excl.* + *Lord!*] [1980s+] (*US campus*) a general excl. of annoyance. ❑ **shit oh dear!** (*also* **shit oh dearie!**) [2000s] (*N.Z.*) an excl. of regret, sorrow.

shit *adj.* [SHIT *n.*] **1** [1920s+] (*orig. US*) applied to any thing or person considered bad, obnoxious, unpleasant, inferior, worthless, e.g. a *shit teacher*. **2** [1960s] untidy, unkempt. **3** [1980s+] on the bad = good model, excellent, first-rate. **4** [2000s] (*UK black*) any.

shit *v.* **1** in context of bodily waste. (**a**) [mid-16C+] to defecate, also fig. (**b**) [late 19C] to vomit. **2** [1930s+] to deceive, to bamboozle, to tell lies, to exaggerate. **3** [1940s] (*US*) to waste time. **4** [1960s+] (*also* **shite, shite out**) to act in a cowardly manner. **5** [1960s+] to respond dramatically, with alarm, fear, anger, e.g. *he'll shit himself when he hears this!* **6** [1960s+] (*Aus.*) to annoy. **7** [1970s] to stop. **8** [1980s] to do something badly, to fail, to make a mess. **9** [2000s] to frighten.

IN PHRASES

pertaining to defecation, in lit. and fig. uses

❑ **I could shit through the eye of a needle** [late 19C+] a phr. used by someone suffering from diarrhoea. ❑ **not know whether to shit or go blind** *v.* (*also* **...whether to pee or go blind, ...shit or buy gas**) [1950s+] (*US*) to be utterly stupid, to be totally confused. ❑ **shit and wish** [8C phr. 'shit in one hand and wish in the other; see which fills up first'; Bridges' *Homer Travestie* (4 edn 1797) offers euph. 'spit' for shit] [20C+] (*US black*) a general retort to anyone who says 'I wish...'. ❑ **shit dimes and quarters** *v.* [DIME *n.* (1) + QUARTER *n.* (2c)] [2000s] (*US black/drugs*) to excrete bags of drugs after swallowing them when facing a police search. ❑ **shit green** *v.* [SE *green* as the image of disturbed stomach, thus emotions] [1960s+] (*US*) **1** to desire. **2** to be extremely shocked. **3** to be enraged. **4** to be afraid. ❑ **shit in high cotton** *v. see under* HIGH COTTON *n.* ❑ **shit in high grass** *v.* [20C+] (*W.I.*) to aim for or reach a higher social class than that to which one was born. ❑ **shit in one's own backyard** *v.* (*also* **shit in one's nest**) [1950s+] (*orig. US*) to do anything that jeopardizes one's life by its proximity to one's personal, social or professional life, e.g. to steal from one's own workplace, to conduct an affair with an in-law. ❑ **shit on one's own doorstep** *v.* (*also* **shit on one's own backdoor**) [late 19C+] used of one who foolishly has adulterous affairs within their circle of friends and acquaintances. ❑ **shit on someone's parade** *v. see* PISS ON SOMEONE'S PARADE *under* PISS ON *v.* ❑ **shit on the dining room table** *v.* [2000s] (*US*) to become involved in a sexual relationship with a friend or employee. ❑ **shit or bust** *v.* (*also* **shit or go blind**) [late 19C+] to make a last, desperate gamble; as an excl. of exasperation. ❑ **shit or get off the pot** *v. see* separate entry. ❑ **shit (someone) up** *v.* [terror makes one shit] [2000s] to disturb, to terrify. ❑ **shit the bed** *v.* [2000s] (*US*) in fig. use, to make a mess. ❑ **shit through one's teeth** *v.* **1** [late 18C+] to vomit. **2** [1970s+] (*also* **shit through one's mouth**) to lie blatantly. **3** [1980s] (*W.I.*) (*also* **shit through one's nose**) to suffer, to be humiliated. ❑ **shit where one eats** *v.* [1980s+] (*orig. US*) to commit a crime in one's own neighbourhood; lit. and fig.

pertaining to fear

❑ **shit a brick** *v. see* separate entry. ❑ **shit bricks** *v. see* SHIT A BRICK *v.* ❑ **shit bullets** *v.* (*also* **piss bullets**) [PISS *v.* (2) + SE *bullets*] [1940s+] (*US*) to be terrified. ❑ **shit it** *v.* (*also* **shite it**) [abbr. SHIT A BRICK *v.*] [1950s+] to be terrified, to act in a cowardly manner. ❑ **shit one's brains out** *v.* [1940s] to be absolutely terrified. ❑ **shit one's load** *v.* [LOAD *n.* (4a)] [1990s+] to be absolutely terrified. ❑ **shit one's pants** *v.* (*also* **shit in one's britches**) [1930s+] to be terrified or extremely excited. ❑ **shit pickles** *v. see* SHIT A BRICK *v.* ❑ **shit tacks** *v.* [2000s] (*N.Z.*) to be very frightened. ❑ **shit up** *v.* [1990s+] to terrify.

pertaining to lying, deception

❑ **do a lot of shitting and one's pants aren't down** [abbr. BULLSHIT *v.* (2)] [1970s] to be talking particularly loudly and foolishly. ❑ **I shit you not** [1930s+] a phr. meaning I am telling the truth, believe me. ❑ **don't shit a shitter** (*also* **don't bullshit a bullshitter**) [1950s+] a phr. meaning one can't fool someone who deals in fooling others. ❑ **would I shit you, you're my favourite turd** [TURD *n.*[1] (1)] [1960s+] (*US*) an assertion of one's sincerity, in answer to the previous speaker's 'Don't bullshit me...'.

pertaining to trouble or ill treatment

❑ **shit on** *v.* **1** [late 19C+] (*also* **shit over**) to abuse, to humiliate. **2** [1970s+] to deal with comprehensively. **3** [2000s] to defeat, e.g. in a sporting fixture. **4** [2000s] to talk tediously. ❑ **shit on from a great height** *v.* [1920s+] (*orig. RAF*) to be extremely unpleasant, to make a great deal of trouble for someone else.

general uses

❑ **go shit** *v.* [1960s+] (*US black*) to dismiss. ❑ **shit about** *v.* [1960s] to waste time, to act halfheartedly. ❑ **shit in** *v.* [1980s+] (*N.Z.*) to win easily. ❑ **shit off** *v.* **1** [20C+] to annoy, to irritate; as adj., annoyed. **2** [1950s+] (*also* **shit**) to run away. ❑ **shit out** *v.* (*also* **shite out**) [1960s+] **1** to behave as a coward, to run away from danger or confrontation. **2** to terrify. **3** to abuse, to scold.

IN EXCLAMATIONS

❑ **go shit in your hat!** (*also* **go crap in your hat! go shit in a pot and duck your head! go shit in your wallet! go spit in your hat! go spit up your trouser leg! shit in it!**) [1940s+] (*US*) a general excl. of abuse; an extended version is *go shit in your hat, pull it over your head and call it flowers!* ❑ **shit and fall back on it!** [1970s] (*N.Z.*) an excl. of amazement. ❑ **shit in your teeth!** [18C–mid-19C] a general excl. of dismissal. ❑ **shit me!** [1990s+] an excl. of surprise, astonishment, resignation. ❑ **shit on...!** [early 17C; 1930s+] an excl. of dismissal, equivalent to *THE HELL WITH IT! under* HELL *n.* ❑ **shit on you!** [1930s+] (*orig. US*) a general term of abuse. ❑ **shit the bed!** [1990s+] an excl. of surprise.

shit *adv.* [1930s+] as an intensifier extremely, very, completely, certainly.

IN COMPOUNDS

❑ **shitsure** *adv.* [1950s+] (*US*) certainly, definitely.

IN PHRASES

❑ **shit out of luck** [20C+] (*US*) at the end of one's good fortune, in serious trouble with no escape.

shit! *excl.* (*also* **shit and onions! shit and piss! shit on toast! shitty! snakeshit!**) [SHIT *n.* (1a)] [mid-19C+] **1** an excl. of fury, irritation, disappointment. **2** nonsense! rubbish! **3** a general excl. of emphasis, usu. implying approval. **4** an excl. of amazement, disbelief.

IN EXCLAMATIONS

❑ **oh shit!** [mid-19C+] (*orig. US*) a general excl. of surprise with undertones of dismay. ❑ **shit and derision!** [20C+] a general excl. of annoyance. ❑ **shit, eh!** [1940s+] (*Aus.*) an excl. of moderate astonishment or irony.

shit a brick *v.* (*also* **shit a giraffe, shit bricks, shit nickels, shit peach pits, shit pickles, shit snowballs, sweat bricks**) [SHIT *v.* (1a) + fig. use of SE *brick/bricks*] **1** [late 19C+] to defecate after a lengthy period of constipation. **2** [1930s+] to tremble with extreme fear. **3** [1960s] to be absolutely delighted. **4** [1960s+] to be furious.

shit a brick! *excl.* (*also* **shit a pebble!**) [SHIT *v.* (1a)] [1950s+] (*orig. Aus.*) an excl. of extreme surprise, annoyance.

shit ass *n.* (*also* **shit-arse, shite-arse**) [SHIT *n.* (1a)/SHITE *n.* + ARSE *n.* (1)/ASS *n.* (2)] [20C+] (*US*) a contemptible person, also attrib.

shit-ass *adj.* (*also* **shitaceous, shit-arse, shit-assed**) [SHIT ASS *n.*] **1** [1960s+] (*orig. US*) very bad. **2** [1960s+] (*US*) annoyed.

shitbird *n.*[1] [SHIT *n.* (6a) + BIRD *n.*[1] (3a)] [1950s+] a narcotic drug abuser, a heroin addict.

shitbird *n.*[2] (*also* **shitbug**) [SHIT *n.* (1a) + BIRD *n.*[1] (3a)] [1950s+] a general term of abuse.

shitbird *adj.* [SHITBIRD *n.*[2]] [1990s+] (*US*) a general term of abuse.

shit-brained *adj.* [SHIT *n.* (1a)] [1970s] stupid, brainless.

shitbrains *n.* [1970s+] (*US*) a stupid person.

shitbum *n.* [SHIT *n.* (1a) + BUM *n.*[1] (1)] [1950s+] a general term of abuse.

shitbum *adj.* [SHITBUM *n.*] [2000s] (*US*) contemptible, unpleasant, worthless.

shitcan *n.*[1] [SHIT *n.* (1a) + SE *can*] **1** [1960s+] a lavatory. **2** [1970s] (*US prison*) the punishment cells.

shitcan *n.*[2] [fig. use of SHIT *n.* (1a) + SE *can*] [1970s] (*US*) a near-derelict but just drivable second-hand car, or motor-bike, one step from the junkyard.

shitcan *v.* [SHIT *n.* (1a) + SE *can*/as intensifier of CAN *v.* (2)] [1950s+] (*Aus./US*) **1** to do someone a wrong. **2** to stop, to abandon a course of action, to toss away; to dismiss from a job. **3** to denigrate.

shitcanned *adj.* (*also* **shitbound**) [1970s+] in a bad way or bad situation.

shit creek *n.* [fig. use of SHIT *n.* (1a) + SE *creek*] [1950s+] an unpleasant, problematic situation; usu. in phr. below.

IN PHRASES

❑ **up shit('s) creek (without a paddle)** (*also* **up salt creek**) [20C+] (*orig. US*) in serious trouble.

shite *n.* [var. on SHIT *n.* (1a) and combs.; before 1990s usu. found in dial. and often put into the mouths of those a writer is attempting to portray as Irish. For no discernible reason it is now often found in place of the more usu. *shit*] **1** [mid-17C+] excrement. **2** [late 18C+] an act of defecation. **3** [1920s+] rubbish, nonsense. **4** [1920s+] an unpleasant person. **5** [1970s+] a derog. form of address. **6** [1980s+] the essence, the 'daylights'. **7** [1990s+] something useless, second-rate, inferior etc. **8** [2000s] anything disgusting.

IN COMPOUNDS

❑ **shite-all** *n. see SHIT-ALL under* SHIT *n.* ❑ **shite-arse** *n. see* SHIT ASS *n.* ❑ **shitehawk** *n.* (*also* **shitehound**) [SE *hawk*/-HOUND *sfx*] [1940s+] a person of little worth. ❑ **shite-poke** see separate entries. ❑ **shite shifter** *n.* [lit. a defecator] [1970s] (*Irish*) a term of abuse.

IN PHRASES

❑ **break one's shite** *v.* [2000s] (*Irish*) to collapse in laughter. ❑ **frighten the shite out of** *v.* [late 19C+] to terrify. ❑ **give out shite** *v.* [GIVE OUT *v.* (9)] [1990s+] (*Irish*) to criticize, to scold. ❑ **have one's shite** *v.* [late 19C+] (*Irish*) to be due to suffer, usu. as an indication of rejection. ❑ **shite-for-brains** *n.* *see* SHIT-FOR-BRAINS. ❑ **sure as shite on your shoe** *see under* SURE AS… *phr.*

IN EXCLAMATIONS

❑ **get to shite off!** [1920s+] a harsh demand to go away. ❑ **you will in your shite!** [late 19C+] (*Irish*) no chance! no possible way!

shite *adj.* [SHITE *n.*] [1940s+] a general negative; something second-rate, unpleasant, distasteful etc.

shite *v.* [SHITE *n.* (1)] [early 17C+] to defecate.

DERIVATIVES

❑ **shiters** *adj.* [one wishes to *shite* with terror] [2000s] terrified.

IN COMPOUNDS

❑ **shitefire** *n.* [lit. trans. of CACAFUEGO *n.* i.e. someone who shits fire] [late 16C–early 18C] a term of abuse applied to a hot-headed person. ❑ **shite-rags** *n.* [late 16C] 'an idle lazie fellow'.

shite! *excl.* (*also* **good shite! my shite!**) [SHITE *n.* (1)] [1920s+] a general excl. of annoyance.

IN EXCLAMATIONS

❑ **shite and onions!** [1920s] an excl. of fury or resignation. ❑ **will it shite!** *see DO I FUCK! under* FUCK! *excl.*

shit-eater *n.* [SHIT *n.* (1a)] [1940s+] a general term of abuse.

shit-eating *adj.* [SHIT-EATER *n.*] [1940s+] **1** a general term of disparagement. **2** sly, duplicitous. **3** toadying, subservient.

shit-eating grin *n.* (*also* **cat-eating-shit grin, crud-eating grin, shit-eating smile**) [SHIT-EATING *adj.*] [1950s+] (*orig. US*) a smug, self-satisfied smile.

shite-poke *n.* [SHITE *n.* (1) + SE *poke*, a bag] **1** [late 18C+] (*Can.*) the bittern [its habit of defecating when frightened]. **2** [1930s] a general term of abuse [synon. with *SHITBAG under* SHIT *n.*].

shite-poke *adj.* (*also* **shitpoke**) [SHITE-POKE *n.* (2)] [1950s] (*US*) a general term of abuse.

shiter *n.* **1** *see* SHITTER *n.*[1] (1). **2** *see* SHITTER *n.*[3].

shitey *adj. see* SHITTY *adj.*[1].

shitface *n.*[1] [SHIT *n.* (1a) + SE *face*] [1950s+] an unpleasant, distasteful person; also directly as term of abuse.

shitface *n.*[2] [backform. f. SHITFACED *adj.* (2)] [1960s+] a drunken party.

shitface *adv.* (*also* **shitfaced**) [SHITFACED *adj.* (2)] [1960s+] extremely, very, completely, totally; usu. as *shitface drunk*.

shitfaced *adj.* (*also* **shite-faced, shitface, shitty**) [fig. uses of SHIT *n.* (1a) + SE *faced*] (*orig. US*) **1** [1930s+] stupid, ignorant. **2** [1960s+] very drunk. **3** [1970s] under the influence of cannabis; occas. other drugs. **4** [1970s+] a general intensifier: total, complete.

shitfire *adv.* [SHITFIRE! *excl.*] [1960s] enthusiastically, energetically.

shitfire! *excl.* [var. on SE *hellfire*] [1940s+] a general excl.

shit-for-brains *n.* (*also* **dick-for-brains, poop-for-brains, shite-for-brains**) [SHIT *n.* (1a) + SE *brains*] [1970s+] an all-purpose insult.

shit-for-brains *adj.* (*also* **shite-for-brains**) [SHIT-FOR-BRAINS *n.*] [1970s+] an all-purpose insult, the implication being of stupidity.

shit-fuck *v.* [SHIT *n.* (1a) + FUCK *v.* (1)] [1980s+] (*US gay*) to have anal intercourse.

shitfuck! *excl.* [SHIT-FUCK *v.*] [1970s+] a general excl.

shithead *n.* (*also* **shathead, shitehead**) [SHIT *n.* (1a) + -HEAD *sfx* (1)] **1** [1940s+] a derog. term of general abuse, also as adj. **2** [1980s] (*US drugs*) a heroin addict. **3** [1990s+] (*US prison*) a prison guard.

shithead *adj.* (*also* **shitheaded**) [SHITHEAD *n.*] [1960s+] an abusive epithet.

shithole *n.* (*also* **shitehole**) [SHIT *n.* (1a) + SE *hole*/HOLE *n.*[1] (1)] **1** [19C+] the anus. **2** [1960s+] a general term of hostility; a term of abuse. **3** [1960s+] a disgusting place, an absolutely worthless place, esp. of a bar or venue [intensifier of HOLE *n.*[1] (2b)]. **4** [1980s+] a lavatory.

shithole *adj.* [SHITHOLE *n.* (3)] [1970s+] usu. of places, the worst, the most disgusting.

shit-hot *adj.* [SHIT *adv.* (1) + SE colloq. *hot*, attractive, pleasurable] [1910s+] **1** excellent, fashionable. **2** first-rate.

shit-hot *adv.* [SHIT-HOT *adj.* (2)] [1910s+] extremely, superlatively, especially.

shit hot! *excl.* [SHIT-HOT *adj.*] [1980s] an excl. of approval.

shithouse *n.* (*also* **shitehouse, slash house**) [SHIT *n.* (1a) + SE *house*] **1** [mid-17C; 1940s+] (*also* **shithouse mouse**) an unpleasant person. **2** [late 18C+] a lavatory. **3** [1940s+] any dirty, messy, disgusting place. **4** [1960s] a jail. **5** [1960s+] (*orig. Aus.*) a bad situation. **6** [1990s+] a coward.

IN PHRASES

❑ **feel like a haunted shithouse** *v.* [2000s] (*N.Z.*) to have a bad hangover. ❑ **out on its own like a country shithouse** *adj.* [1910s+] (*Aus./N.Z.*) unique, unrivalled. ❑ **shithouse full of** *n.* [20C+] (*US*) a very large number or amount. ❑ **to the shithouse** *adv.* [as a euph. for SE *hell*] [1970s] (*Aus.*) to pieces, 'to hell'.

shithouse *adj.* [SHITHOUSE *n.* (3)] **1** [1930s+] unpleasant, disgusting, filthy, messy, second-rate. **2** [1990s+] of a person, ill, exhausted, run down, highly nervous.

shithouse rat *n.* used in comparatives as a (usu. negative) measure.

IN PHRASES

❑ **crazy as a shithouse rat** *adj.* (*also* **crazy as a shit-eating rat**) [1960s+] (*US*) extremely unstable. ❑ **cunning as a shithouse rat** *adj.* (*also* **shifty as a shithouse rat**) [1940s+] (*orig. Aus.*) very cunning; sometimes euph. as ...*sewer rat*, ...*lavatory rat*. ❑ **have eyes like a shithouse rat** *v.* [1910s+] to have shifty, but acute eyes. ❑ **lucky as a shithouse rat** *adj.* [1960s] (*US*) very fortunate. ❑ **ugly as a shithouse rat** *adj.* (*also* **ugly as a rat's ding**) [1990s+] (*Aus.*) extremely unattractive.

shitily *adv. see* SHITTY *adv.*

shitkick *v.* **1** [1960s] (*US*) to work as a street prostitute. **2** [1990s+] (*US*) to beat up, to kill [*see* KICK THE SHIT OUT OF *under* SHIT *n.*].

DERIVATIVES

❑ **shitkicking** *n.* [1960s] working as a prostitute on the street.

shitkicker *n.* [SHIT *n.* + SE *kicker*; the image is either of kicking one's way through animal dung or from KICK THE SHIT OUT OF *under* SHIT *n.*] **1** [1940s+] a shoe or boot, esp. one used for everyday wear or work. **2** [1940s+] (*Aus.*) one who performs menial tasks; an unskilled labourer. **3** [1950s+] (*US*) (*also* **kicker**) a farmer or other country person. **4** [1960s] (*US*) a Western film. **5** [1960s] (*US*) a depressive. **6** [1960s] (*US*) a street prostitute. **7** [1960s+] (*US*) (*also* **crap-kicker, shitkick**) a fool, a person of meagre intelligence. **8** [1960s+] something exceptional and powerful, i.e. that 'kicks shit'. **9** [1970s] (*US drugs*) a stimulant. **10** [1980s+] (*US*) a thug.

shitkicker *adj.* (*also* **kicker, S.K.**) [SHITKICKER *n.* (3)] [1960s+] (*US*) pertaining to rural or stereotypically Western life.

shitkicking *adj.* [SHITKICKER *n.* (3)] [1960s+] (*US*) rough, crude, rural.

IN COMPOUNDS

❑ **shitkicking music** *n.* [1950s+] (*orig. US*) music that makes the hearer want to get up and dance, shout, sing, generally have a good, boisterous time; thus also *shitkicking records*.

shitless *adv.* [1950s+] to an extreme extent.

IN PHRASES

❑ **scare shitless** *v. see under* SCARE *v.*

shitload *n.* (*also* **crapload, shitloads, shitpot**) [SHIT *n.* + SE *load*] [1960s+] a great many, a large amount; usu. as *a shitload of*.

IN PHRASES

❑ **by the shitload** *adv.* [1960s] in large amounts.

shit oneself *v.* (*also* **crap oneself**) [for ety. *see* SHIT ONE'S PANTS *under* SHIT *v.*] **1** [mid-19C+] to defecate in one's underclothes. **2** [1920s+] in fig. use, to be terrified.

IN EXCLAMATIONS

❑ **go and shit yourself!** [late 19C] as a dismissive insult.

shit or get off the pot *phr.* (*also* **crap or get off the hole, get off the pot, get off the pot or shit, shit or git**) [SHIT *v.* (1a) + SE (chamber) *pot*] [1930s+] either make a decision or let someone else do it; esp. as excl.

shitpot *n.* [SHIT *n.* + SE *pot*] **1** [mid-18C+] a chamberpot, a lavatory. **2** [mid-19C+] (*also* **shitepot**) an unpleasant person. **3** [mid-19C+] an unpleasant place, or inferior object.

shitpot *adj.* [SHITPOT *n.*] [1970s+] (*Aus.*) second-rate, inferior.

shits, the *n.* [SHIT *n.*] **1** [1930s+] (*also* **shits**) diarrhoea. **2** [1960s+] terror, fear. **3** [1970s+] anything objectionable or unpleasant. **4** [1990s+] (*Aus.*) a bad temper.

IN PHRASES

❑ **get the shits with** *v.* [1990s+] (*Aus.*) to become annoyed (with someone). ❑ **give someone the shits** *v.* [1960s+] to annoy, to infuriate someone. ❑ **go the shits** *v.* [1970s] (*Aus.*) to sulk.

shitsack *n.* [fig. use of SHIT *n.* + SE *sack*] **1** [late 18C–early 19C] a nonconformist [the term was euphemized in 19C as *shick-shack* (also *shig-shag*; *sic-sac*; *shuck-shack*; *shiff-shack* etc). Orig. a term of abuse for people who were found not wearing the customary oak-apple or sprig of oak before noon on Royal-oak Day (29 May, commemorating Charles II's hiding in an oak tree). Such people would most likely be nonconformists or Puritans. That day became known in dial. as *Shick-sack Day* and the oak-apple or sprig of oak became known as *shick-shack*. If you wore your oak sprig after noon you became a *shick-shack*, a fool]. **2** [late 18C+] (*also* **sack of shit**) a general pej., an unpleasant person.

shit-scared *adj.* [*see* SCARE THE (LIVING) SHIT(S) OUT OF *under* SHIT *n.*] [1950s+] terrified.

shit-skin *n.* [SHIT *n.* (1a) + SE *skin*, i.e. a derog. ref. to colour] [20C+] a derog. term for a black person.

shitskin *adj.* [SHIT-SKIN *n.*] [1960s] (*US black*) a derog. term meaning pertaining to black people.

shit street *n.* [1960s+] a fig. bad place; usu. in phr. below.

IN PHRASES

❑ **in shit street** *adj.* (*also* **up shit street**) [1920s+] (*orig. US*) in difficulties, facing problems, in disgrace.

shitten *adj.* (*also* **beshitted**) **1** [late 14C–mid-18C] covered in excrement; generally filthy. **2** [mid-16C–mid-18C] unpleasant, disgusting; mediocre, second-rate.

IN COMPOUNDS

❑ **shitten cull** *n.* [early 18C] a coprophile. ❑ **shitten Saturday** *n. see under* SATURDAY *n.*

shitten! *excl.* (*also* **shitting!**) [SE *shitten*, fouled with excrement; thus disgusting] [17C; 1930s] a general excl. of derision.

shitter *n.*[1] [SHIT *v.* (1a)] **1** [20C+] (*also* **shiter**) the anus. **2** [1960s] used fig.: a disgusting place or situation. **3** [1960s–70s] (*US prison*) a punishment cell. **4** [1960s+] (*US*) a lavatory, a commode. **5** [1960s+] one who defecates in a public place. **6** [1970s] (*US gay*) in coprophiliac sex, one who defecates on their partner. **7** [1970s+] (*UK Und.*) a thief who likes to excrete inside the places he robs.

IN PHRASES

❑ **down the shitter** *see* DOWN THE PAN *under* DOWN *adv.*[2].

shitter *n.*[2] [abbr. BULLSHITTER *n.*] [1970s+] **1** (*orig. US*) a braggart, a boaster. **2** (*orig. US*) a term of abuse. **3** an exceptional example of something.

shitter *n.*[3] (*also* **shiter**) [SHIT A BRICK *v.*] [2000s] a coward.

shitters *n.* [SHIT *v.* (1a); i.e. the state of the average cowyard] [1940s] (*Aus.*) cattle.

shitters, the *n.* [SHIT *v.* (1a)] [late 19C+] diarrhoea.

shitters *adj.* (*also* **shiters**) [SHIT ONESELF *v.*] [1990s+] terrified.

shitties *n.* [1970s] (*Aus.*) municipal sewage disposal workers.

shitting *adj.* (*also* **shiteing**) [1930s+] **1** cowardly. **2** a general term of abuse. **3** as an intensifier.

shitting! *excl.* see SHITTEN! *excl.*

shittle-cum-shaw! *excl.* (*also* **shittle-cum-shite! shittletidee!**) [SE *shittle*, inconstant, fickle, flighty] [late 19C] a general excl. of annoyance.

shitty *n.* [SHITTY *adj.*[1] (7)] [1970s+] (*Aus./N.Z.*) a fit of temper; a bad mood.

shitty *adj.*[1] (*also* **shitey, shitty-ass, shittypants**) **1** [1920s+] covered in excrement; generally filthy. **2** [1920s+] unpleasant, disgusting; mediocre, second-rate. **3** [1920s+] (*US*) mean, malicious, nasty. **4** [1920s+] (*US*) tedious, futile. **5** [1920s+] (*US*) unwell, ill. **6** [1960s+] depressed, guilty. **7** [1960s+] (*Aus.*) bad-tempered. **8** [1970s] (*US*) dangerous. **9** [1970s] incompetent.

DERIVATIVES

❑ **shittiness** *n.* [1920s+] unpleasantness.

IN COMPOUNDS

❑ **shitty-livered** *adj.* [1980s+] (*N.Z.*) bad-tempered. ❑ **shitty-nosed** *adj.* [1970s] (*US*) sycophantic and contemptible.

IN PHRASES

❑ **feel shitty** *v. see* FEEL LIKE SHIT *under* SHIT *n.* ❑ **shitty end of the stick** *n. see* SHORT END (OF THE STICK) *under* STICK *n.*

shitty *adj.*[2] *see* SHITFACED *adj.*

shitty *adv.* (*also* **shitily**) [SHITTY *adj.*[1] (2)] [1920s+] badly, unsatisfactorily.

shiv *n.* (*also* **schieve, sheive, shieve, shive**) [CHIV *n.*[1]] **1** [late 19C+] a knife. **2** [1910s+] (*US tramp*) a razor. **3** [1940s] (*US Und.*) a form of confidence trick that employs a knife.

IN COMPOUNDS

❑ **shiv man** *n.* [late 19C+] one who uses a knife in crimes of violence.

shiv *v.* (*also* **shive, shive up, shiv up on**) [SHIV *n.* (1)] [1930s+] **1** (*US Und.*) to stab. **2** in fig. use.

shiva *n. see* CHIVA *n.*

shivaree *see also under* SHIVOO.

shivaree *n.* [SHIVOO *n.*; but more likely euph. for SHIT *n.* (4a)/SHIT *n.* (3j)] **1** [1920s+] verbose official talk. **2** [1960s+] abuse.

shive *n.* **1** [late 17C–late 19C] (*UK Und.*) a slice. **2** *see* SHIV *n.*

shive *v.* **1** *see* SHIV *v.* **2** *see* SHUCK AND JIVE *v.* (1).

shiveau *n. see under* SHIVOO.

shiver and shake *n.* [rhy. sl.] [1940s] a (slice of) cake.

shivering dodge *n.* [mid-19C] (*UK Und.*) to pose as a scantily-dressed beggar in cold weather.

shivering James *n.* (*also* **shivering Jemmy, ...Jimmy**) [SE *shivering* + generic *James/Jemmy*] [mid–late 19C] a beggar who parades in rags and tatters in the hope of attracting greater sympathy.

shivers *n.*

IN PHRASES

❑ **all to shivers** *see* ALL TO SMASH *under* SMASH *n.*[1].

shivers, the *n.* [late 19C] (*US Und.*) terror, induced by a fear of arrest.

shivers! *excl.* [1980s] (*N.Z.*) a euph. excl. for SHIT! *excl.*

Shivery Isles *n.* [var. SHAKY ISLES *n.*; the frequency of earthquakes; ? a *Bulletin*-ism] [1930s–50s] (*Aus.*) New Zealand.

shivery-shakes *n. see* SHAKES, THE *n.*

shive up *v. see* SHIV *v.*

shiving *n.* [SHIV *v.*] [1970s] a stabbing.

shivoo *n.* (*also* **cheveaux, chivoo, shavoo, shivaree, shiveau, shivvoo**) [Fr. *chez vous*, at your house] [early 19C+] a party, a celebration.

IN PHRASES

❑ **ginger-beer shivoo** *n.* [early 19C+] a teetotal party.

shivoo *v.* (*also* **shivaree, shivaroo, shiveau**) [SHIVOO *n.*] [mid-19C+] (*Aus.*) to entertain.

shiv up on *v. see* SHIV *v.*

shivver *n.* [SHIV *n.*] [1950s] a knife-wielder, one who stabs.

shivvoo *n. see* SHIVOO *n.*

shizer *n. see* SHICER *n.*

shiznit *n.* (*also* **shiz, shiznet, shiznits**) [ext. of SHIT *n.* + -IZ- *infix*] [1990s+] (*US black/campus*) **1** a euph. for SHIT *n.* (3e), i.e. something rubbish or unimpressive. **2** a euph. for SHIT *n.* (2b); the ultimate, the best – or the worst.

shl... *see also under* SCHL...

shlanter *n. see* SLANTER *n.*[1].

shlemozzle *n. see* SHEMOZZLE *n.*

shlenter/shlinter *n. see* SLANTER *n.*[1].

shm... *see also under* SCHM...

shm- *pfx* (*also* **schm-**) [cod Yid.] [1940s+] a facetious pfx, used to nullify the word (and thus the statement) to which it is appended.

shmear *see under* SCHMEER.

shmeez *v.* [Yid. *schmeiss*, to hit, thus cognate with HIT *v.* (3g)] [1980s+] (*US drugs*) to smoke good cannabis.

shmyes *v.* [? Yid. *schmeiss*, to hit, thus cognate with HIT THE ROAD *v.* (1)] [2000s] to leave.

shn... *see also under* SCHN...

shnide *n.* ['Yiddishized' var. on SNIDE *n.* (2)] [1950s–70s] an unpleasant, underhand person.

shnide *adj. see* SNIDE *adj.*

shock *n.* [the dictum that, after drinking it, 'you get a shock, walk a block and fall in the gutter'] [late 19C–1930s] (*US*) a measure of cheap liquor.

IN COMPOUNDS

❑ **shock house** *n.* (*also* **shock joint**) [SE *house*/JOINT *n.* (3b)] [late 19C–1930s] (*US*) a tavern, catering mainly to black people, in which customers would most likely be given some form of knockout drop in their drink and then robbed.

SE in slang uses

IN COMPOUNDS

❑ **shock-absorbers** *n.* [1950s+] the female breasts. ❑ **shock and sting** *adj.* [1990s+] (*W.I.*) excellent. ❑ **shock-out** *n.* [1990s+] (*W.I.*) anything exceptionally eye-catching.

IN PHRASES

❑ **shocks for jocks** *n.* [JOCK *n.*[1] (3)] [1960s+] (*US campus*) a course in introductory engineering.

shock a broe *phr.* (*also* **shock a brew**) [Hawaiian pidgin *shaka brah*, right on, brother; but note BREW *n.*[1] (4)] [1980s+] (*US campus*) an invitation to have a beer.

shocker *n.* **1** [late 19C+] an appalling person, thing or situation. **2** *see* SHILLING SHOCKER *under* SHILLING *n.*

shocker! *excl.* [1990s+] (*US campus*) an ironic excl. referring to something that is not remotely surprising.

shockerhorsey *n.* [? Fr. *choucroute*] [mid-19C] ? sauerkraut.

shocking *adj.* [mid-18C+] a general intensifier.

shockingly *adv.* (*also* **shocking**) [late 18C+] a general intensifier, e.g. *a shockingly bad hat*, a very unpleasant person.

shod all round *phr.* [SE *shod*, wearing shoes] **1** [18C–19C] *au fait* with the niceties of married life. **2** [late 18C–1900s] a phr. used of a parson at a funeral who receives a hat-band, gloves and scarf.

shoddy *adj.* [SE *shoddy*, woollen yarn obtained by tearing to shreds refuse woollen rags, which, with the addition of some new wool, is made into a kind of cloth; thus, worthless material that is made to appear as if it boasts a higher quality. The term was used of people f. mid-19C. It was underlined after the US Civil War (1861–5), when fortunes were made by the sellers of shoddy, who then attempted to use their money to enter society] [mid–late 19C] (*US*) used of those who either claim a degree of importance to which they have no actual right or of *nouveaux riches*, whose importance is not backed up by breeding or manners.

DERIVATIVES

❑ **shoddydom** *n.* [late 19C] the world of social climbers. ❑ **shoddyite** *n.* [mid–late 19C] a social climber.

SE in slang uses

IN COMPOUNDS

❑ **shoddy dropper** *n.* [post-WW2 use mainly Aus./N.Z.; DROPPER *n.*[3] (2)] [1930s+] a hawker, a pedlar.

shoddy-doo *n.* [? corruption of SE *how do you do*] [1960s–70s] (*US black*) any form of ritual hand-slapping that serves as a greeting or farewell.

shoe *n.* **1** [late 19C] the debtors' ward in Newgate prison [those incarcerated begged by letting down a shoe from the window]. **2** [20C+] (*US Und.*) a private detective [abbr. GUMSHOE *n.* (1)]. **3** [1910s–30s] a tyre. **4** [1940s+] (*Aus.*) a sanitary towel. **5** [1950s+] (*orig. US black*) a smartly dressed person, by ext. one who is smart, sophisticated [orig. jazz use; the quality of the subject's footwear]. **6** [1960s] (*US black*) a black person.

SE in slang uses

IN COMPOUNDS

❑ **shoebox** *n.* [1940s] a prison cell. ❑ **shoedog** *n.* [1950s+] (*US*) a shoe salesman. ❑ **shoe-horn** *v.* [? play on HORN *n.*[1] (1)] [17C] to cuckold. ❑ **shoelaces** *n.* [resemblance] [20C+] (*S.Afr. black*) chicken intestines, as used in cooking. ❑ **shoemaker's pride** *n.* [new leather shoes often creak, thus drawing attention to the maker's handiwork] [19C–1900s] creaking shoes or boots. ❑ **shoemaker's stocks** *n.* [late 17C–early 19C] tight shoes; thus *in the shoemaker's stocks*, wearing tight shoes. ❑ **shoe-polish** *n. see under* POLISH *n.* ❑ **shoe thief** *n. see* HEEL-THIEF *n.*

IN PHRASES

❑ **buy new shoes** *v.* [1920s–50s] (*US Und.*) to jump bail. ❑ **buy the baby (new) shoes** *v.* [20C+] (*US*) to act in a purposeful manner. ❑ **die in one's shoes** *v.* [mid-17C–mid-19C] to be hanged. ❑ **everlasting shoes** *n.* [mid–late 19C] the feet. ❑ **get one's shoes full** *v.* (*also* **get the shoes on**) [the drink 'overflows'] [20C+] to become drunk. ❑ **put the shoe on the left foot** *v.* [1970s+] (*US black*) to put blame where it does not belong. ❑ **put the shoe on the right foot** *v.* [late 19C+] (*US black*) to place blame where it duly belongs. ❑ **shoe it** *v.* [1970s] to walk. ❑ **shoe leather express** *n. see RIDE THE SHOE LEATHER EXPRESS under* RIDE *v.* ❑ **with shoes on** *adj.* [1960s] (*US short order*) of one's food/drink purchase, takeaway.

IN EXCLAMATIONS

❑ **shoe-leather!** [i.e. get one's *shoe-leather* (shoes) moving] [mid-19C] (*UK Und.*) a warning cry uttered by a thief to his confederate on sighting the police.

shoe *adj.* **1** [1950s] smart, fashionable [SHOE *n.* (5)]. **2** [1960s] (*US black*) racially black.

shoe *v.*

SE in slang uses

IN PHRASES

❑ **shoe one's mule** *v.* [mid-17C–early 18C] to embezzle. ❑ **shoe the goose** *v.* [? the impossibility of such a task, other than to a drink-sodden mind] [early 16C] to be drunk. ❑ **shoe the horse** *v.* [1910s–20s] to cheat one's employer.

shoes and sox *n.* [rhy. sl. = POX *n.*[1] (3)] [20C+] venereal disease.

shoful *n.* (*also* **schoful, shofel, shofle, shovel, show-full**) [Ger. thence Yid. *schofel*, worthless stuff, rubbish; ult. the Ger.-Jewish pron. of Heb. *shāphāl*, low; sense 2 although Hotten (1864) and Ware spec. define *showfull/shofel* as a 'Hansom cab' (the name had been patented in 1834) it may be a different word (or their mis-reading of the term) since such cabs were the 'legitimate' vehicle of which sense 5 is the counterfeit; Dickens defines it as 'a hackney cab' in 1853, but offers nothing as to its 'legitimacy'] **1** [mid-19C] a low tavern. **2** [mid-19C] a Hansom cab. **3** [mid–late 19C] counterfeit coins, sham jewellery. **4** [mid–late 19C] a humbug, an impostor. **5** [mid-19C–1910s] a cab other than that patented by Hansom.

IN COMPOUNDS

❑ **shoful-man** *n.* [mid–late 19C] one who passes counterfeit money. ❑ **shoful-pitcher** *n.* (*also* **schofel-pitcher, showful-pitcher**) [PITCHER *n.*[2] (1)] [mid–late 19C] a distributor of counterfeit money; thus *shoful-pitching*, passing counterfeit money. ❑ **shoful-pullet** *n.* [PULLET *n.* (1)] [mid-19C] a prostitute, esp. a spurious 'virgin' prostitute, whose maidenhead is miraculously renewed for each new client.

shoful *adj.* (*also* **showful**) [SHOFUL *n.* (3)] [mid–late 19C] (*UK Und.*) low, inferior, second-rate.

shoke *n.* [ety. unknown] [1930s] (*US*) a derog. term for a black person.

sholl *v.* [ety. unknown; link to SE *shell*, i.e. to turn the hat into a shell for the head] [mid-19C–1900s] to crush someone's hat over their ears.

sho-lo *n.* [*sh*ort on top, *lo*ng in the back] [2000s] (*US*) a 'mullet' hairstyle.

shommus *n. see* SHAMUS *n.*

Shon Ap Morgan *n. see* SHINKIN-AP-MORGAN *n.*

Shone *n.* [supposedly 'Welsh' pron. of stereotypical name *Jones*] [late 17C–early 18C] a generic term for a Welshman.

shoneen *n.* [Irish *seonin*, a person of foreign ways, a poor Protestant] [1910s+] (*orig. Irish*) a would-be gentleman who puts on superior airs; orig. an Irish person aping the English gentry.

shong *n. see* SHANGHAI *n.*[2].

shonk *n.* (*also* **schonk, schonky**) [? SHONNICKER *n.*; note RN *shonky*, a miser whose meanness is typified by their like of drinking but unwillingness to stand a round] **1** [20C+] a derog. term for a Jew or foreigner. **2** [1960s+] the nose. **3** [1980s+] (*Aus.*) a dishonest business person.

shonky *adj.* [SHONK *n.* (1)/SHONNICKER *n.* (2); note WW1 milit. *shanky*, thrifty, close-fisted] [1970s+] (*Aus./N.Z.*) unreliable, dishonest, 'crooked'; hence one who is engaged in irregular or illegal business activities.

shonnicker *n.* (*also* **shonnacker**) [Yid. *shonnicker*, a small trader or pedlar] **1** [1910s] (*US Und.*) a novice criminal. **2** [1910s+] a derog. term for a Jew.

shont *n.* [? SHONK *n.* (1)] [late 19C–1910s] a foreigner.

sho' 'nuff *adj.* [SE *sure enough*] [20C+] (*US*) a general term of approval: genuine, qualified, responsible, trustworthy.

sho' 'nuff *v.* [SHO' 'NUFF *adj.*] [1970s] (*US black*) to be in earnest, to do something seriously.

sho' 'nuff *adv.* (*also* **sure nuff**) [SE *sure enough*] [late 19C+] (*US*) definitely, certainly.

sho' 'nuff *phr.* [SE *sure enough*] [late 19C+] (*orig. US black*) yes indeed.

shoo! *excl. see* SHOOT! *excl.*[1] (1).

shoob *v.* (*also* **shuby**) [1950s+] (*W.I. Rasta*) to shove; hence fig., to have sexual intercourse.

shoobie *n.* [the *shoebox* in which they carry their lunch] [1970s+] (*US*) a passenger on a day-trip excursion.

shoo-fly *n.* [trad. and unattributed song lyrics 'Shoo fly! Don't bother me'] **1** [late 19C+] (*US Und.*) a plain-clothes police officer on observation duty. **2** [20C+] an undercover police officer who spies on his colleagues. **3** [1920s–50s] a drug used to deal with troublesome drinking club customers.

shoo-fly! *excl.* [late 19C] an excl. of denial, disdain: 'get away!' 'get out of here!'

shoofti/shoofty *n. see* SHUFTIE *n.*

shoo-in *n.* [SE *shoo-in*, of a racehorse, an easy winner] [1930s+] a dead certainty, usu. in political use.

shook *adj.* **1** [early 19C+] forgetful, esp. used of an ex-prisoner whose mental state has been affected by prison or transportation. **2** [mid-19C+] (*Irish*) drunk. **3** [late 19C+] (*also* **shooked**) (*US*) highly excited, disturbed, frightened, upset.

IN COMPOUNDS

❑ **shook one** *n.* [1990s+] a person who is scared, upset, emotionally unstable etc.

IN PHRASES

❑ **shook on** *adj.* (*also* **shook after**) [SE *shake*, quiver, tremble (in this case with passion)] [late 19C+] (*Aus./N.Z.*) infatuated with, obsessed with. ❑ **shook up** *adj.* [mid-16C; 20C+] upset, disturbed.

shool *n.* [adapted by Londoners from Yid. *shool*, a synagogue] [late 19C] a place of worship.

shool *v.* (*also* **shoole, shule**) [SE *shoal*, to move as a shoal; thus the meanderings of a shoal of fish or dial. *shool*, to go about begging] **1** [mid-18C] to impose upon someone. **2** [mid-18C–mid-19C] to go begging, to find what one can by chance. **3** [late 18C–early 19C] to skulk around. **4** [early 19C] to carry something as a 'front'.

shooler *n.* (*also* **shoolman, shuiler, shuler**) [SHOOL *v.* (2)] [mid-19C–1930s] a beggar and scrounger, a tramp.

shoon *n.* [ety. unknown] [late 19C–1900s] a fool.

shoop *v.* [? echoic; Eble (*Campus Slang*, Apr. 1997) claims it is f. the song 'Shoop' by Salt-n-Pepa] [1990s+] (*US black*) to have sexual intercourse.

shooper *n. see* SHUPER *n.*

shoosh *n.* [SE *ssh*, quiet, be quiet] [1940s] (*Aus.*) quiet, silence.

shoosh *v.* [echoic] [1920s] to dismiss someone, to send away.

shoo-shoo *v.* [SE *ssh*, quiet, be quiet] [1930s–40s] (*US black*) to whisper; thus *shoo!* be quiet!

Shoot, the *n.* [SE *rubbish-shoot*, both areas were associated with the poor or with menial workers] [late 19C–1900s] **1** Walworth Road station, London. **2** Walthamstow, London.

shoot *n.* **1** [mid-19C] an ejaculation; an act of sexual intercourse. **2** [mid-19C–1900s] (*Aus.*) constructed with *the*, dismissal from a job. **3** *see* SHOUT *n.*

IN PHRASES

❑ **get the shoot** *v.* [1900s] to be dismissed from a job. ❑ **up the shoot** *adj.* **1** *see* UP THE CHUTE *under* CHUTE *n.*[2]. **2** *see* UP THE SPOUT *under* SPOUT *n.*[2]. ❑ **whole bang shoot** *n. see* separate entry.

shoot *v.* **1** in sexual senses. (**a**) [17C+] to ejaculate. (**b**) [mid-17C+] of a man, to have sexual intercourse. (**c**) [late 19C] to have a wet dream. (**d**) [1990s+] (*W.I.*) to be infected with an STD. (**e**) [2000s] (*US prison*) to have sex with an effeminate, younger male prisoner. **2** in senses of movement. (**a**) [19C+] to move, to travel; usu. as *shoot along*, *shoot down*, *shoot for* etc. (**b**) [mid-19C+] to leave, esp. as imper. (cf. SHOOT OFF *v.* (1)). (**c**) [late 19C+] (*also* **shoot in, shoot to**) to send; to convey; to drive. (**d**) [20C+] to hurry someone along, to send someone quickly to a place. (**e**) [1910s–50s] as an order, to fetch, to bring, to send. (**f**) [1990s+] to promote, to propel. **3** in gambling senses. (**a**) [mid-19C–1910s] to (make a) bet. (**b**) [1920s+] to throw dice. **4** in senses of consumption or use. (**a**) [late 19C–1950s] to get rid of, to expend. (**b**) [1900s–20s] (*Aus./US*) to give, to pay for. (**c**) [1900s–60s] to perform, to do. (**d**) [1900s–70s] to consume. **5** [late 19C+] to speak, to sing; to impart. **6** in drug uses. [20C+] (**a**) to inject a narcotic, usu. in comb. with the drug, e.g. *shoot smack*, to inject heroin; *shoot coke*, to inject cocaine. (**b**) to inject someone else with a narcotic. **7** [1920s] (*US Und.*) (*also* **shoot it**) to use explosive to open a safe. **8** [1950s] to cheat someone.

IN PHRASES

meaning to speak

❑ **shoot a good shot** *v.* [1970s+] (*US black*) to have a sophisticated verbal wit; to defeat someone in a verbal contest, e.g. DOZENS *n.* ❑ **shoot a line** *v. see under* LINE *n.*[1]. ❑ **shoot a paper-bolt** *v.* [1910s–20s] to circulate a false or dubious rumour. ❑ **shoot con** *v. see* SHOOT THE CON below. ❑ **shoot jokes (on)** *v.* [1970s+] (*US black*) to belittle, to tease aggressively. ❑ **shoot on** *v.* [1960s+] (*US black*) **1** to mock, to tease, to discredit. **2** to talk seductively. ❑ **shoot one's best mack** *v.* [MACK *n.*[2] (2)] [1970s+] (*US black*) to make an all-out effort at seduction by one's persuasive conversation. ❑ **shoot one's gab** *v. see under* GAB *n.*[1]. ❑ **shoot one's head off** *v.* (*also* **shoot one's face off**) **1** [1910s–50s] to talk, esp. boastfully. **2** *see under* HEAD *n.* ❑ **shoot one's jib off** *v.* [JIB *n.*[1] (1)] [1950s–60s] to talk, esp. arrogantly or boastfully. ❑ **shoot one's mouth off** *v.* (*also* **shoot off one's mouth, shoot one's bazoo off, ...gums off, ...lip off, ...yap off**) [SHOOT OFF *v.* (2) + BAZOO *n.*[1] (1)/YAP *n.*[1] (1a)] (*orig. US*) **1** [mid-19C+] to talk, esp. in a loud or boastful way (cf. *SHOOT OFF (AT THE MOUTH) under* SHOOT OFF *v.*). **2** [1930s+] to betray secrets. **3** [1960s+] to vomit. ❑ **shoot straight** *v.* (*also* **shoot square**) [1910s+] to talk or behave openly, honestly or candidly. ❑ **shoot the baloney** *v. see under* BALONEY *n.* ❑ **shoot the breeze** *v.* (*also* **shoot the jive**) [JIVE *n.*[1] (2)] [1930s+] (*orig. US*) to gossip, to talk idly; thus n. *breeze shooter.* ❑ **shoot the bull** *v. see under* BULL *n.*[6]. ❑ **shoot the con** *v.* (*also* **shoot con**) [CON *n.*[1] (9)] [1930s+] (*US tramp*) to talk nonsense. ❑ **shoot the dozens** *v. see* PLAY THE DOZENS *under* DOZENS *n.* ❑ **shoot the fat** *v. see* CHEW THE FAT *v.* ❑ **shoot the gift** *v.* [SE *gift of the gab*] [1990s+] (*US black*) **1** to gossip, to talk idly. **2** to rap well. ❑ **shoot the regular** *v.* [SHIT *n.* (4a) is unspoken] [1970s+] (*US black*) to chatter on in the usual, predictable manner. ❑ **shoot (the) shit** *v.* [SHIT *n.* (4a)] [1930s+] to gossip, to chat.

meaning to ejaculate or have sexual intercourse

❑ **shoot a bishop** *v.* (*also* **shoot the bishop**) [BISHOP *n.*[2] (2e)] [late 19C+] to have a nocturnal emission, a 'wet dream'. ❑ **shoot blanks** *v. see under* BLANK *n.* ❑ **shoot gravy** *v. see under* GRAVY *n.* ❑ **shoot in the stubble** *v.* [STUBBLE *n.*] [18C–19C] to have sexual intercourse; thus *shoot over the stubble*, to ejaculate prematurely, and outside the vagina. ❑ **shoot in the tail** *v.* [mid-19C+] **1** to have anal intercourse [TAIL *n.* (2)]. **2** to copulate [TAIL *n.* (4)]. ❑ **shoot one's bolt** *v.* **1** [1920s+] to ejaculate, usu. prematurely [SE *bolt* as literary euph. for penis]. **2** *see also* SE phrs. below. ❑ **shoot one's load** *v. see under* LOAD *n.* ❑ **shoot one's milt** *v.* [SE *milt*, seed] [mid-19C–1910s] to ejaculate. ❑ **shoot one's roe** *v.* [SE *roe*, seed] [mid-19C–1900s] to ejaculate. ❑ **shoot over the stubble** *v. see* SHOOT IN THE STUBBLE above. ❑ **shoot the bishop** *v. see* SHOOT A BISHOP above. ❑ **shoot the cat** *v.* [the penis (i.e. the GUN *n.*[1] (2)) shoots the CAT *n.*[1] (2a), i.e. pubic hair] **1** [late 19C+] to have sexual intercourse. **2** *see also* SE phrs. below. ❑ **shoot the owl** *v.* [SE *owl* as synon. for the pubic hair] [1900s] (*US*) to ejaculate outside one's partner's body as a crude form of contraception. ❑ **shoot white** *v.* [the colour of semen] [late 19C] to ejaculate.

other uses

❑ **shoot a pete** *v.* [PETE *n.*[1] (1)] [1920s] (*US Und.*) to break into a safe using explosives. ❑ **shoot in** *v. see* sense 2c above. ❑ **shoot it** *v. see* sense 7 above. ❑ **shoot to** *v. see* sense 2c above. ❑ **will you shoot?** [1900s–50s] (*Aus.*) will you pay for a drink?

SE in slang uses

IN COMPOUNDS

❑ **shoot-out** *n.* **1** [1930s+] a gun battle. **2** [1970s] a decisive confrontation.

IN PHRASES

❑ **I'll be shot (if)** [mid-18C–1920s] a strong expression of denial or refusal; thus synon. *I'll see you shot first!* ❑ **I shot him lightly and he died politely** [1930s–50s] (*US black*) a phr. implying that the speaker has had the better of an opponent, verbally or physically. ❑ **on the shoot** [the equation of sex and violence] [late 19C–1900s] (*Aus./US*) involved in fighting, warfare. ❑ **shoot a beaver** *v. see under* BEAVER *n.*[1]. ❑ **shoot a blank** *v. see under* BLANK *n.* ❑ **shoot a bone** *v. see* FLAG A BONE *under* BONE *n.*[1]. ❑ **shoot a bunny** *v.* [2000s] (*N.Z.*) to break wind. ❑ **shoot a butt** *v.* [BUTT *n.*[1] (2a)] [1910s–30s] (*US*) to extinguish a cigarette. ❑ **shoot a card** *v.* [1900s–20s] to leave a visiting card. ❑ **shoot a cat** *v. see* SHOOT THE CAT below. ❑ **shoot a dog** *v.* [1900s] (*US*) to defecate. ❑ **shoot a moon** *v. see under* MOON *n.* ❑ **shoot at** *v.* [1950s–60s] to make (sexual) advances towards. ❑ **shoot cuffs** *v.* [SAmE *cuffs*, trouser turn-ups (UK)] [1990s+] (*US black*) to grab someone's legs and bring them down, as part of a fight. ❑ **shoot (dead)** *v.* [late 19C] (*Aus.*) to dismiss from a job. ❑ **shoot down** *v.* (*also* **shoot down in flames**) **1** [1940s+] to reject an invitation to dance or go for a date. **2** [1940s+] to humiliate, to ridicule. **3** [1950s+] to reject a line of argument, to overrule an opinion. **4** [1960s+] to place at a disadvantage. **5** [1960s+] (*US prison*) to reject a parole application. ❑ **shoot-'em-up** *n.* [the predominant on-screen/on-page activity] **1** [1930s+] (*orig. US*) (*also* **shootum**) a Hollywood Western film. **2** [1960s] (*US*) a 'Western' book or short story. ❑ **shoot eyes** *v.* [1970s+] (*US gay*) to flirt; to stare; to glower. ❑ **shoot for** *v.* [1910s+] to aim for, to target; often as *shooting for*, e.g. *he's got 50 runs and now he's shooting for a century*. ❑ **shoot for two** *v.* [NUMBER TWO *n.* (1)] [2000s] (*US campus*) to defecate. ❑ **shoot from the hip** *v.* [Western film imagery] [1930s+] (*orig. US*) to attack a problem head-on, to be a tough, purposeful performer. ❑ **shoot in** *v.* [SE *shoot in*, to throw in] [1910s+] (*Aus.*) to put in prison; usu. as *shot in*, imprisoned. ❑ **shoot in the eye** *v.* [late 19C] to do someone a bad turn. ❑ **shoot into** *v. see* THROW (IT) INTO *v.* (2). ❑ **shoot into the brown** *v.* [in rifle practice the outermost part of the target, denoting a 'miss', is brown; but note shooting jargon *into the brown*, an indiscriminate blast into the heart of a covey of passing birds. By extension this was used by sporting officers of firing into a large group of advancing (brown-uniformed) troops] [late 19C–1910s] (*orig. milit.*) to fail. ❑ **shoot London Bridge** *v.* [? a nonce usage in Ned Ward, *London Bridge* (1699), punningly describing a 'buttocking brimstone' who could 'show you how the Watermen shoot London Bridge or how the lawyers go to Westminster'] [early 18C] to have sexual intercourse. ❑ **shoot off** *v. see* separate entry. ❑ **shoot one's best shot** *v. see under* SHOT *n.*[1]. ❑ **shoot one's bolt** *v.* **1** [late 16C+] to give everything one has, to be incapable of further effort. **2** [1950s] (*S.Afr.*) to run off. **3** *see also* sl. phrs. above. ❑ **shoot one's cookies** *v. see under* COOKIE *n.*[1]. ❑ **shoot one's cuff** *v.* (*also* **shoot one's linen**) [the 'shooting' of the cuffs – making them project fashionably beyond the jacket sleeves – that is indulged in by the well-dressed] [late 19C+] to dress up as smartly as one can, or generally present oneself in the most positive way possible. ❑ **shoot oneself in the foot** *v.* [20C+] (*orig. US*) to blunder so that one harms oneself or exposes oneself to further hardship. ❑ **shoot one's star** *v.* **1** [late 19C–1900s] to die. **2** [1970s] (*US black*) senses relating to the anus, based on the shape of the SE *star*. (**a**) to perform anal intercourse. (**b**) to arrest a homosexual. ❑ **shoot over** *v.* [20C+] to go quickly to a place. ❑ **shoot someone out** *v.* [1960s] (*US Und.*) to prepare someone for a given occupation. ❑ **shoot the agate** *v. see under* AGATE *n.* ❑ **shoot the beaver** *v. see SHOOT A BEAVER under* BEAVER *n.*[1]. ❑ **shoot the bird** *v. see under* BIRD *n.*[2]. ❑ **shoot the bone** *v. see FLAG A BONE under* BONE *n.*[1]. ❑ **shoot the boots off** *v.* [20C+] (*Ulster*) to wipe out, lit. or fig. ❑ **shoot the cat** *v.* (*also* **shoot a cat**) **1** [late 18C–mid-19C] to vomit [var. on WHIP THE CAT *v.* (3)]. **2** *see also* sl. phrs. above. ❑ **shoot the chimney** *v.* [*shoot*, to discard, to get rid of + ? SE *chimney* to mean throat] [late 19C] (*US*) to be quiet, to stop talking. ❑ **shoot the crow** *v.* [ety. unknown] **1** [19C–1930s] to leave without paying. **2** [1960s+] (*Scot.*) to leave. ❑ **shoot the curve** *v.* [? fig. use of SE *shoot the curve*, to go round a bend fast, but why?] **1** [1930s] (*US prison*) to negotiate privileges, esp. a drug supply. **2** [1930s–50s] (*US drugs*) to buy narcotics. ❑ **shoot the gulf** *v.* [? according to Daniel Defoe, *A Voyage Round the World*, 1725: 'Such a mighty and valuable thing also was the passing this strait [the Straits of Magellan] that Sir Francis Drake's going through it gave birth to that famous old wives' saying viz., that Sir Francis Drake shot the gulf; [...] as if there had been but one gulf in the world'] [mid-17C–mid-18C] to succeed in a very hard task, to achieve the impossible. ❑ **shoot the lights out** *v.* [fig. marksmanship] [20C+] (*US*) to excel, to perform outstandingly. ❑ **shoot the marbles from all sides of the ring** *v.* [1930s–40s] (*US black*) to be in a position to take action. ❑ **shoot the pill** *v.* (*also* **shoot the peel**) [PILL *n.* (1f)] [1980s+] (*US black/campus*) to shoot baskets, to play a pick-up game of basketball. ❑ **shoot the squirrel** *v. see under* SQUIRREL *n.* ❑ **shoot the thrill** *v.* [1970s] (*US black*) to lead a promiscuous and varied sex life. ❑ **shoot the willie** *v.* [? the single finger represents a WILLIE *n.*[4]] [1960s] (*US campus*) to make a derisory, insulting gesture by raising the middle finger. ❑ **shoot the works** *v.* [WORKS, THE *n.*] (*US*) **1** [1920s] to vomit. **2** [1920s+] (*also* **shoot the roll**) to commit oneself absolutely, to make every effort no matter what the cost. **3** [1920s+] to make a full confession; to speak candidly. **4** [1930s] to die. **5** [1930s] to have an orgasm. ❑ **shoot through** *v.* [1940s+] (*Aus./N.Z.*) to leave, to exit quickly; in milit. context, to go absent without leave. ❑ **shoot through the grease** *v.* [1950s–60s] (*US black/campus*) to let down, to betray, to deceive, to victimize. ❑ **shoot to kill** *v.* [20C+] to aim ruthlessly for a goal without reservation or compromise. ❑ **shoot up** *see* separate entries.

IN EXCLAMATIONS

❑ **go shoot yourself!** *see GO FUCK YOURSELF! under* FUCK *v.*

shoot! *excl.*[1] [euph. for SHIT! *excl.*] [late 19C+] **1** (*also* **shoo! shoot it! shoots!**) an excl. of annoyance or surprise. **2** (*also* **shoots! shoot me!**) a general excl. of intensification, affirmation.

IN EXCLAMATIONS

❑ **shoot that hat!** [mid–late 19C] (*US*) a mild oath.

shoot! *excl.*[2] [SHOOT *v.* (5)] [20C+] (*orig. US*) go on! go ahead! get on with it! esp. as regards telling a story, delivering a piece of gossip etc; often ext. as *shoot – you're faded*.

shooter *n.*[1] **1** [mid-19C+] (*UK/US Und.*) a gun, a revolver. **2** [20C+] (*gambling*) the player currently throwing the dice in a game of craps. **3** [1940s+] one who fires a weapon, an assassin.

shooter *n.*[2] (*also* **needle shooter**) **1** [1930s+] (*US drugs*) a heroin or other narcotics addict. **2** [1990s+] a hypodermic syringe.

shooter *n.*[3] [SHOT *n.*[1] (6a)] **1** [1960s] a martini and pernod cocktail. **2** [1970s+] (*US*) a measure of spirits, esp. whisky; tequila.

shooter's hill *n.* [play on the proper name, but note SHOOT *v.* (1a)] [19C] the vagina.

IN PHRASES

❑ **take a turn on Shooter's Hill** *v.* [late 19C; 1970s+] (*US black*) to have sexual intercourse.

shoot-flier *n.* [SHOOT-FLYING *n.*] [late 19C–1930s] (*UK Und.*) a thief who specializes in snatching wallets, watches and similar small items.

shoot-flying *n.* [? SHOOT OFF *v.* (1) + SE *fly*] [late 19C–1930s] (*UK Und.*) the robbery of watches, wallets and similar small personal items.

shooting *n.* [SE *shoot*/SHOOT *v.* (5)] [1920s–80s] (*US black*) aggressive, provocative talk, often leading to a fight.

IN PHRASES

❑ **sure as shooting** *see under* SURE AS... *phr.*

shooting *adj.* [SHOOT *v.*] [late 19C–1950s] (*Aus.*) verbally aggressive.

shooting gallery *n.* (*also* **gallery**) [pun on SE, the fairground sideshow] **1** [1950s] (*US drugs*) play on sense 3, the hospital ward for drug addicts undergoing withdrawal. **2** [1950s–60s] (*UK Und.*) a venue for burglary, robbery or other crimes. **3** [1950s+] (*drugs*) a place, often an apartment or an abandoned building, used by a number of heroin addicts to take the drug. **4** [2000s] as sense 2 but used for smoking crack cocaine.

shooting iron *n.* [note WW1 Aus. milit. *shooting iron*, 18-pounder field gun] **1** [late 18C+] (*also* **talking iron**) a pistol or gun. **2** [19C] (*US*) the penis.

shooting star *n.* [mid-19C] (*UK Und.*) an itinerant thief, moving from town to town.

shooting stick *n.* **1** [19C] the penis [play on SE + STICK *n.* (1a)]. **2** [mid–late 19C] a gun [play on SE + STICK *n.* (3)].

shoot off *v.* **1** [mid-19C+] to leave quickly (cf. SHOOT *v.* (2b)). **2** [mid-19C+] to talk, as in phrs. below. **3** [1920s+] to ejaculate [ext. of SHOOT *v.* (1a)].

IN PHRASES

❑ **shoot off (at the mouth)** *v.* **1** [late 19C+] (*US*) to talk irresponsibly (cf. *SHOOT ONE'S MOUTH OFF under* SHOOT *v.*). **2** [1960s] to reprimand, to threaten. **3** [1960s+] to lose one's temper. ❑ **shoot off one's face** *v.* (*also* **shoot off one's head, ...pan, shoot with the face**) [PAN *n.*[1] (2)] [late 19C–1950s] (*US*) to talk effusively. ❑ **shoot off one's mouth** *v. see SHOOT ONE'S MOUTH OFF under* SHOOT *v.* ❑ **shoot off the fat** *v.* [ety. unknown] [mid-19C] (*Can.*) to ask for credit.

shoots! *excl. see* SHOOT! *excl.*[1].

shootum *n. see SHOOT-'EM-UP under* SHOOT *v.*

shoot-up *n.*[1] [SHOOT UP *v.*[1]] [1930s–40s] a gun rampage, firing weapons indiscriminately to destroy a place.

shoot-up *n.*[2] [SHOOT UP *v.*[2]] [1960s] the act of injecting a drug.

shoot up *v.*[1] [late 19C+] (*orig. US*) **1** to rampage around firing weapons, to destroy a place with gunfire. **2** in fig. use, to defeat, to destroy.

shoot up *v.*^{2} [ext. of SHOOT *v.* (6a)] [1920s+] (*drugs*) **1** to take narcotic or other drugs by injection. **2** to inject someone with a narcotic or other drug.

Shop, the *n.* [ironic use of SE] **1** [late 19C+] the Royal Military Academy, Woolwich. **2** [1960s+] (*Aus.*) Melbourne University.

shop *n.*^{1} **1** [16C+] a place, a place of business, any place where one pursues one's occupation, e.g. a brothel. **2** [late 17C–1900s] (*UK Und.*) a prison [note that SHOP *v.*^{1} (1) actually predates the n.]. **3** [early 19C–1910s] a public house. **4** [1960s+] an act of shopping.

SE in slang uses

IN COMPOUNDS

❑ **shop bouncer** *n.* [BOUNCER *n.*^{1} (6)] [mid–late 19C] **1** a thief who steals from shops while distracting the merchant's attention with his argumentative bargaining; thus *shop-bouncing*, shoplifting. **2** a thief who poses as a respectable customer and while buying a cheap item, steals a more valuable one. ❑ **shop cop** *n.* [COP *n.*^{1} (1)] [2000s] a security man working in a shop. ❑ **shop-door** *n.* [late 19C+] the fly buttons; thus warning *your shop-door is open*, your flies are undone. ❑ **shop-dropper** *n.* [1950s–60s] (*Aus.*) one who delivers goods, liquor etc from a market or store to retailers. ❑ **shoplift** *n. see* separate entry. ❑ **shop-lobber** *n.* [LOB *v.*, i.e. his langorous pose] [late 18C–mid-19C] a dandified shop assistant. ❑ **shop-masher** *n.* [MASHER *n.* (2)] [late 19C–1900s] a dandified shop assistant. ❑ **shop-pad** *n.* [PAD *n.*^{1} (3)] [18C] a shoplifter. ❑ **shop-sneak** *n.* [SNEAK *n.*^{1} (1b)] [early 18C–mid-19C] (*UK Und.*) a sneak thief who lurks near a shop, waiting a chance to steal some goods. ❑ **shop teeth** *n.* [20C+] (*Irish*) false teeth, dentures.

IN PHRASES

❑ **all over the shop** **1** [late 19C] in chaos, in a mess [SE in 20C+]. **2** [late 19C+] everywhere; thus *knock all over the shop*, to beat severely. ❑ **come to the wrong shop** *v.* (*also* **go to the wrong shop**) [mid-19C+] to make a mistake, esp. in the context of asking the wrong person or going to the wrong place to get one's desires. ❑ **lay back and front shops into one** *v.* [thus described by Grose (1785); presumably, since he refers to 'an operation in midwifery', he means episiotomy, the widening of the vulval orifice to facilitate childbirth] [late 18C–early 19C] to remove the physical division between the vagina and the anus. ❑ **shut up shop** *v.* **1** [mid-16C+] to stop, usu. talking. **2** [late 17C] (*also* **shut up shop-windows**) to go bankrupt. ❑ **shut up someone's shop** *v.* [late 19C–1900s] to kill someone, to murder someone. ❑ **unshop** *v.* [SE *shop*, a workshop, a place of work] [1910s–20s] to dismiss a workman.

shop *n.*^{2} [mid–late 19C] the mouth.

IN EXCLAMATIONS

❑ **shut your shop!** *excl.* [mid–late 19C] be quiet!

shop *v.*^{1} [presumably SHOP *n.*^{1} (2) although this appears to predate] **1** [late 16C+] (*UK Und.*) to imprison; thus n. *shopping*, a jail sentence. **2** [mid-19C+] to inform on and thus cause to be imprisoned, or in trouble; to denounce.

shop *v.*^{2} [fig. use of SE *shop*, as n. or v.] **1** [mid-19C] to dismiss, esp. to dismiss a shop assistant. **2** [1960s–70s] (*US gay*) to look for a sexual partner, whether in the street or in bars, clubs etc.

SE in slang uses

IN PHRASES

❑ **shop around** *v.* [SE *shop around*, to search out the best bargain] [1940s+] to have a number of sexual relationships before choosing one that will serve for marriage or the longer term. ❑ **shop in** *v.* [1940s–60s] (*Irish prison*) for a non-prisoner, usu. a warder, to smuggle contraband goods or letters into/out of the prison.

shoplift *n.* [SE f. 1700] [mid-17C] a shoplifter, one who steals goods from shops while pretending to be a legitimate customer.

shopped *adj.* **1** [late 16C–early 19C] imprisoned [SHOP *v.*^{1} (1)]. **2** [19C] in work [SE]. **3** [mid-19C+] betrayed, informed on [SHOP *v.*^{1} (2)].

shopper *n.* [SHOP *v.*^{1} (2)] [1920s–50s] an informer.

shoppie *n.* (*also* **shoppy**) [abbr.] **1** [1900s–30s] a female *shop* assistant. **2** [1970s+] (*Aus.*) (*also* **shopper**) a *shop*lifter.

shopping *n.*^{1} [SHOP *v.*^{1} (2)] [1930s+] an act of betrayal, of informing.

shopping *n.*^{2} [ironic use of SE] [1990s+] **1** (*US Und.*) shoplifting. **2** (*US prison*) looking for something to steal.

shopping *n.*^{3}

IN PHRASES

❑ **drop off the shopping** *v. see under* DROP OFF *v.*^{1}.

shopping and fucking *adj.* [1980s+] used of a type of blockbusting novel, developed during the materialist 1980s, in which the normal ingredient of a certain type of bestseller – 'procrastinated rape' (V.S. Pritchett, *The Living Novel*, 1947) – is boosted by regular excursions into the world's up-market shopping malls in search of lovingly delineated designer-labelled garments and other consumables. When bowdlerized the term is found as *sex and shopping*.

shoppy *n. see* SHOPPIE *n.*

shoppy *adj.* [SE *talking shop*] [mid–late 19C] wholly engrossed in one's occupation.

shoppying blue *n.* [SHOP *v.*^{1} (2) + BLUE *n.*^{1} (2d)] [1970s] (*Aus. Und.*) a signed confession.

shore dinner *n.* [play on SE *dinner*/EAT *v.* (4); SAmE *shore dinner*, a dinner of seafood] [1970s+] (*US gay*) a homosexual sailor who only takes the passive role in fellatio.

Shoreditch fury *n.* [*Shoreditch*, a notably tough area of East London] [late 16C] an aggressive woman; a harlot.

short *n.* **1** as a vehicle [the comparatively short distance a street car or automobile would travel compared to a railway train; note *Current Slang* III:2 (1968): 'This seems to be derived from the idea that most cars, especially compacts, are short in comparison with the old favorites, especially the Cadillac']. (**a**) [1900s–50s] a street car. (**b**) [1930s+] (*also* **shot**) an automobile. **2** [1930s–40s] (*US*) a *short*-barrelled or sawn-off revolver. **3** [1930s–50s] a short measure of drugs. **4** [1940s+] (*US black/prison*) a cigarette butt; a half-smoked cigarette. **5** [1980s+] a measure of drugs, esp. crack cocaine, that is sold at a reduced price. **6** [1980s+] a child.

IN PHRASES

❑ **crack a short** *v.* [1960s] (*US Und.*) to break into a car; usu. in pl. *crack shorts*. ❑ **on the hot shorts** [1940s] (*US Und.*) stealing automobiles. ❑ **push shorts** *v.* [1930s–50s] (*drugs*) (*also* **shove shorts**) to sell in small amounts; to sell short measure. ❑ **take no shorts** *v.* [SE *short change*] [1980s+] (*US black*) to refuse to be fooled, cheated or put at a disadvantage. ❑ **will you short?** [late 19C] (*Aus.*) will you have a drink of spirits? ❑ **work the shorts** *v.* [1940s] (*US Und.*) to pick pockets on a street car.

short *adj.*^{1} **1** [17C+] impoverished, out of cash. **2** [mid-18C+] insufficient, esp. of money; thus *short bread*, not enough cash. **3** [mid–late 19C] of banknotes, in large denominations [orig. cashiers' jargon; large denominations mean fewer notes, which take a *shorter* time to count]. **4** [1910s+] (*US prison*) of a prisoner, having only a few weeks or days of a sentence to serve. **5** [1950s] (*drugs*) of an injection, weak. **6** [1960s+] (*US milit.*) near the end of a term of duty, spec. the twelve-month tours of Vietnam. **7** [1990s+] (*drugs*) in insufficient quantity for the money paid.

IN COMPOUNDS

❑ **short go** *n.* **1** [1930s–60s] (*US drugs*) short measure on a drug deal; a weak injection. **2** [1960s] a shortage of drugs. ❑ **short on** *adj.* [1940s+] badly supplied, wanting. ❑ **short piece** *n.* [PIECE *n.* (7a)] [1930s–50s] (*US drugs*) a purported ounce of a narcotic that has in fact been shaved or otherwise reduced. ❑ **short pot** *n.* [late 17C–early 18C] a short measure used to cheat drinkers in a tavern.

IN PHRASES

❑ **on the short** [2000s] (*US drugs*) buying drugs without paying the full price. ❑ **run short** *v.* [late 19C+] (*US*) to run out of money. ❑ **suffer with the shorts** *v.* [1940s] (*US black*) to be out of cash, to be impoverished.

SE in slang uses

IN COMPOUNDS

❑ **short arm** *n.* see separate entry. ❑ **short-arse/-arsed** see separate entries. ❑ **short bit** *n.* see *under* BIT *n.*[1]. ❑ **short boy** *n.* [the *Short Boys* gang, *fl.* c.1850 in New York City] [mid–late 19C] (*US Und.*) a thug. ❑ **short-brim** *n.* see STINGY-BRIM *n.* ❑ **short-coat** *v.* [1900s] to circumcise. ❑ **short con** see separate entries. ❑ **short count** *n.* [1950s+] (*drugs*) a short measure. ❑ **short digs** *n.* see SHORT STROKES *n.* ❑ **short dog** *n.* [DOG *n.*[7] (1)] [1960s+] (*orig. US black*) a small bottle of cheap wine. ❑ **short end (of the stick)** *n.* see *under* STICK *n.* ❑ **short eyes** *n.* [for ety. see SHUT EYES *n.*] [1970s+] (*US prison*) a child molester. ❑ **short fuse** *n.* (*also* **short wick**) [1960s+] (*orig. US*) a short temper. ❑ **short hair** *n.* [their shaved heads] [1970s] a convict, esp. a new one. ❑ **short hairs** *n.* see SHORT AND CURLIES *n.* ❑ **short heist** *n.* see separate entry. ❑ **short-histe** *adj.* see separate entry. ❑ **shorthorn** *n.* [agricultural imagery; cf. LONGHORN *n.*] [late 19C–1940s] (*US, mainly western*) **1** a northerner. **2** a newcomer, an innocent. ❑ **short-house** *n.* [euph. SHORT-ARSE *n.*] [1970s+] a short person. ❑ **short john** *n.* see CHEAP JOHN *n.*[2]. ❑ **short-length** *n.* [mid-19C] (*Scot.*) a glass of brandy. ❑ **short-limbered** *adj.* [SE *limber.* 'The detachable fore part of a gun-carriage, consisting of two wheels and an axle, a pole for the horses, and a frame which holds one or two ammunition-chests. It is attached to the trail of the gun-carriage proper by a hook' (*OED*)] [late 19C–1900s] short-tempered. ❑ **short money** see separate entries. ❑ **short-mouthed** *adj.* [1900s] (*W.I.*) verbally agile, good at snappy repartee. ❑ **short nail** *n.* [NAILHEAD *n.*] [1960s–70s] (*US black*) an unkempt, unattractive woman, esp. with messy hair. ❑ **short-nose** *n.* [1960s–70s] (*US*) a .38 revolver, which has a short barrel. ❑ **short sheet** *v.* [SAmE *shortsheet*, the UK 'apple-pie bed'] [20C+] (*US*) to mistreat, to trick someone. ❑ **short short** *n.* [2000s] (*US black*) a very short time, very soon. ❑ **short skate** *n.* see CHEAPSKATE *n.* (2). ❑ **short stop** see separate entries. ❑ **short story** *n.* see separate entry. ❑ **short strokes** *n.* see separate entry. ❑ **short stuff** *n.* **1** [1950s] a short person. **2** [1980s+] (*US Und.*) a quick and spontaneous con trick, thought up on the spur of the moment and workable only while the target is on hand. ❑ **short time** see separate entries. ❑ **short trill** *n.* [? obs. SE *trill*, to trundle, to whirl] [1940s] (*US black*) a short walk. ❑ **short 'un** *n.* [SE *short one*] [late 19C] 285ml (½ pint) of coffee. ❑ **short-weight** see separate entries. ❑ **short wick** *n.* see *SHORT FUSE* above.

IN PHRASES

❑ **short-heeled wench** *n.* (*also* **short heels**) [her 'short heels' mean that she is constantly falling on her back] [mid-16C–early 19C] a promiscuous woman. ❑ **short-order shrimp** *n.* [1970s] (*US gay*) 'a drunk sailor leaned up against an alley wall and quickly sucked off' (Rodgers, *Queens' Vernacular*, 1972). ❑ **short pants court** *n.* [1950s] (*US juv.*) a juvenile court.

short *adj.*[2] [abbr. SHINGLE SHORT *adj.*] [1930s+] (*Aus.*) eccentric, insane.

short *v.*[1] [SHORT *adj.*[1] (2)] **1** [1920s+] to cheat in any form of share-out or distribution, e.g. of food or attention. **2** [1950s+] (*US*) to cheat when dividing the spoils of a robbery or of drug dealing; to underpay.

short *v.*[2] [SHORT *n.* (5)] [2000s] (*US black*) to share a cigarette.

short and curlies *n.* (*also* **curlies, curly fellas, curly hairs, short hairs**) [late 19C+] **1** the pubic hair. **2** fig. use of sense 1; usu. in phr. *HAVE SOMEONE BY THE SHORT AND CURLIES* below.

IN PHRASES

❑ **have someone by the short and curlies** *v.* (*also* **...by the shorts, by the short hair(s), ...by the big brown ones, ...by the slack of someone's pants, ...by the wool, ...where the hair is short, ...where the wool is tight**) [the image of grasping the victim's pubic hair] **1** [late 19C+] to have someone at an extreme disadvantage, to control completely. **2** [1920s+] (*Aus.*) to know a subject extremely well. **3** [1930s+] (*US*) to annoy.

short arm *n.* [similar to *THIRD LEG under* THIRD *adj.* but note G. Williams (1994) who makes a link to 17C milit. metaphor *arms*, the genitals] the penis, usu. found in compounds below.

IN COMPOUNDS

❑ **short-arm bandit** *n.* [-BANDIT *sfx* (2)] **1** [1960s–70s] (*gay*) a male homosexual. **2** see *SHORT-ARM HEISTER* below. ❑ **short-arm heister** *n.* (*also* **short-arm bandit**) [HEISTER *n.*] [1950s+] (*US Und.*) a rapist; thus *short-arm heist*, rape. ❑ **short-arm inspection** *n.* (*also* **short arm, short arm drill**) [1910s+] (*orig. milit.*) medical inspection of the genitals.

short-arse *n.* (*also* **short-ass**) [early 18C; 1940s+] a small person, an insignificant person; thus as a nickname.

short-arsed *adj.* (*also* **short-assed**) [SHORT-ARSE *n.*] [1920s+] a non-specific insult, usu. aimed at a short person.

short con *n.* (*also* **short coin, short money racket**) [abbr. SE *short* (*time*) + CON *n.*[1] (7)] [1930s+] (*US Und.*) any variety of confidence trick that can be performed spontaneously and on the spot, with no elaborate props, preparation etc.

IN COMPOUNDS

❑ **short con artist** *n.* (*also* **short con man, short con worker**) [-ARTIST *sfx*] [1920s–50s] (*US Und.*) a confidence trickster who specializes in spontaneous or short-term trickery.

short con *adj.* [SHORT CON *n.*] [1960s] (*US Und.*) prone to petty dishonesty.

short con *v.* [SHORT CON *n.*] [1930s–50s] to perform such confidence tricks as are known as the SHORT CON *n.*

short end *n.* [abbr. *SHORT END (OF THE STICK) under* STICK *n.*] [mid-19C+] (*US*) the losing end, the bad side of a deal or situation; by ext. the unfavoured option in a bet on sport; thus *short-ender*, a contestant who is expected to lose.

short-end money *n.* [in a bet of twenty to one or nine to four the smaller digit is the 'short' end] [20C+] (*gambling*) money bet on the possibility of a team or individual (esp. in boxing) losing a contest.

short end of the funnel *n.* see *SHORT END (OF THE STICK) under* STICK *n.*

shorter *n.* [mid-19C] a clipper of coins.

short heist *n.* [SE *short* (*time*) + HEIST *n.* (1)] [1950s+] (*US Und.*) petty theft.

short heist book *n.* [SHORT-HISTE *adj.*] [1950s] (*US Und.*) a pornographic book.

short-histe *adj.* [1940s] (*US*) masturbatory, perverted.

short money *n.* [SHORT *adj.*[1] (2)] [1950s–70s] (*US black*) of a prostitute, insufficient money to satisfy her pimp; for a drug dealer or user, insufficient money to make a desired purchase.

short money *v.* [SHORT MONEY *n.*] [1950s–60s] (*US black*) to exploit an unsatisfactory prostitute for as much money as possible.

short-money game *n.* [SHORT MONEY *v.*] [1960s] (*US Und.*) the money that a pimp can make from a prostitute who works for him for only a short period.

short money racket *n.* see SHORT CON *n.*

...short of... *adj.* [var. on NOT ALL THERE *adj.*]

IN PHRASES

❑ **couple of bottles short of a six-pack** [1990s+] unstable, not very intelligent. ❑ **couple of bricks short of the load** see *ONE BRICK SHORT OF A LOAD* below. ❑ **couple of chips short of a fish dinner** (*also* **few chips short of a computer, ...short of a cookie**) [1990s+] not very intelligent. ❑ **couple of tinnies short of a slab** [TINNIE *n.* (1) + SLAB *n.* (11)] [1990s+] (*Aus.*) eccentric, foolish, simple-minded. ❑ **few bob short of the pound** [1960s+] unintelligent, eccentric. ❑ **few snags short of a barbie** [*snag*, a sausage] [1980s+] (*Aus.*) eccentric, crazy. ❑ **few spring rolls short of a banquet** (*also* **few french fries short of a happy meal**) [1990s+] unintelligent, eccentric, mad. ❑ **five annas short of the rupee** (*also* **not sixteen annas to the rupee**) [16 annas make a full rupee] [late 19C–1930s] not very intelligent. ❑ **ninepence short of a shilling** [1980s] stupid, foolish. ❑ **one brick short of a load** (*also* **couple of bricks short of the load, few bricks short/shy of a load, one brick shy of a load, two bricks short/shy of a load**) [1980s+] slightly insane, eccentric. ❑ **one sandwich short of a picnic** (*also* **pork pie short of a picnic, sandwich short of a picnic, two biscuits short of a picnic, two sandwiches short of a picnic**) [1960s+] not very intelligent, slightly eccentric, odd. ❑ **one sausage short of a BBQ** [1990s+] (*US teen*) not very intelligent, slightly eccentric, odd. ❑ **one stop short of East Ham** [pun on London Underground stop *Barking* / BARKING *adj.*] [1990s+] mad, eccentric. ❑ **tenpence short of the full quid** [QUID *n.* (3); the pound sterling had 240 pence] [mid-19C+] not very intelligent, slightly eccentric, odd. ❑ **two pence short of a bob** [a BOB *n.*[3] (2) was composed of 12 *pence*] [20C+] not very intelligent, slightly eccentric, odd. ❑ **two tacos short of a combination plate** [1980s] (*US*) not very intelligent, slightly eccentric, odd. ❑ **two wafers short of a communion** [1960s+] not very intelligent, slightly eccentric, odd.

short of a sheet *phr.* [the *sheets* of bark used to roof early dwellings] [late 19C+] used of someone who is not very intelligent; also as *short of a sheet of bark*.

IN PHRASES

❑ **have a sheet short** *v.* [1910s+] (*Aus.*) to be mentally deficient.

short of change *adj.* [2000s] (*N.Z.*) unintelligent.

shorts *n.* [1970s+] the last few puffs of a discarded cigarette.

shorts, the *n.*[1] [CAUGHT SHORT *adj.* (1)] [1910s+] (*US*) an urgent need to visit the lavatory; the inability to control one's bowels and/or bladder.

shorts, the *n.*[2] [SHORT *adj.*[1] (2)] [1930s+] (*US*) lack of or insufficiency of money.

short stop *n.* [baseball imagery] **1** [1950s–60s] (*US black*) a temporary arrangement, a short period of time. **2** [1950s–70s] a fool, a dupe, a coward. **3** [1960s–70s] of money, a small amount, just enough to carry one over for a short time; thus a gambler with little money. **4** [1980s] a short person.

short stop *v.* [SE *stop short*] [1970s] **1** (*US black*) to abruptly stop someone from moving or carrying on with what they are doing. **2** (*US*) to take food as it is being passed to someone else at a meal.

short story *n.* [1930s–50s] (*US Und.*) a forged cheque.

IN PHRASES

❑ **write short stories** *v.* [1930s–50s] (*US Und.*) to pass bad cheques.

short story writer *n.* [SHORT STORY *n.* + SE *writer*] [1930s–50s] (*US Und.*) one who passes bad cheques.

short strokes *n.* (*also* **short digs, short shoves**) [late 19C+] the final stage of sexual intercourse, immediately preceding male orgasm.

IN PHRASES

❑ **on the short strokes** (*also* **down to the short strokes**) **1** of a man, approaching orgasm. **2** in fig. use, running out of time, approaching the end, nearing a conclusion.

short time *n.* **1** [mid-19C+] of a prostitute, the time spent with one client before taking on a new one, rather than spending a whole night with the same man; the *short time* allows a single copulation. **2** [20C+] (*UK prison*) a short sentence, a short part of one's sentence left to run; thus *short-time pains*, pre-release nerves [TIME *n.* (1)]. **3** [20C+] (*milit.*) a short-service commission, a short period of enlistment. **4** [1920s] in pl., a couple who rent a room for an hour in order to have adulterous sex. **5** [1990s+] (*US prison*) one who has a short sentence or whose sentence is nearing its end [TIME *n.* (1)].

IN COMPOUNDS

❑ **short-time girl** *n.* [1900s] a basic, cheap prostitute who satisfies her client's immediate need and then looks for her next customer.

short-time *v.* [1960s–70s] **1** (*US prison*) to reach the end of one's sentence [TIME *n.* (1)]. **2** in fig. use of sense 1, to take the short view as regards one's lifestyle. **3** to have sex with a prostitute for a short time (rather than a whole night) [SHORT TIME *n.* (1)].

short-timer *n.* [SHORT TIME *n.*] **1** [20C+] (*US prison*) one who is serving a short prison sentence; one whose sentence is nearing its end. **2** [1920s+] one who frequents a prostitute for a brief visit, involving a single act of intercourse. **3** [1940s+] (*US*) one who has only a short period left of his service in the military. **4** [1960s+] one who has only a short time in a given ocupation or institution.

short-weight *n.* [1920s] a fool.

short-weight *adj.* [1920s+] mentally defective, stupid.

shorty *n.* **1** [late 19C+] a short person, often as a term of address or nickname; ironic use for a tall man. **2** [1930s+] (*US black*) a young person. **3** [1970s+] (*US black*) a child. **4** [1990s+] (*orig. US black*) a woman, a girlfriend; occas. a boyfriend. **5** [2000s] (*US black*) a small penis.

sho-sho gun *n.* [? echoic] [1910s–40s] (*US Und.*) a machine gun.

shot *n.*[1] **1** [mid-16C+] money, esp. an amount that is due to be paid or one's share of it, e.g. at a tavern. **2** [early 17C+] an ejaculation; an act of sexual intercourse [SHOOT *v.* (1a)]. **3** in senses of (negative) speech. (**a**) [early 19C+] (*US*) a sneering remark, aimed at another person with the express purpose of wounding them. (**b**) [mid-19C] (*US*) any form of remark. (**c**) [2000s] (*US prison*) a disciplinary report. **4** [mid-19C] a corpse that has been disinterred by body-snatchers for the purpose of selling it to a medical school [spec. ety. unknown]. **5** [SE *shoot* (at a target)] in senses of a chance, attempt, a number. (**a**) [mid-19C+] an opportunity, a chance, an attempt, a guess. (**b**) [late 19C+] anything that has a reasonable chance of success; usu. preceded by a qualifying figure indicating the odds against, e.g. *ten to one shot*. (**c**) [1940s+] (*Aus./US*) one's preference, style or choice. (**d**) [1960s] (*US campus*) attendance at a party, movie, sporting match etc. **6** in senses of measure, amount. (**a**) [late 19C+] a measure of liquor; usu. with the drink specified, e.g. a *shot of rum*. (**b**) [20C+] (*drugs*) an injection, or dose, of a narcotic drug. (**c**) [20C+] (*drugs*) the amount of a drug required to get a user intoxicated. (**d**) [1910s+] any form of injection. (**e**) [1960s+] a fig. injection.

pertaining to drink

IN COMPOUNDS

❑ **shot beer** *n. see* NEEDLE BEER *under* NEEDLE *v.* ❑ **shot-clog** *n.* [mid–late 19C] a fool who is tolerated only because of their willingness to pay their share for drinks. ❑ **shot-house** *n.* [1950s+] (*US*) an illegal drinking establishment where drink is sold in *nips* or small (orig. half-pint) measures.

pertaining to drugs

IN PHRASES

❑ **pin shot** *n.* [1920s–50s] an injection of a narcotic using a rudimentary 'syringe' made of a pin or needle and an eye-dropper. ❑ **point shot** *n.* [1930s–50s] (*US drugs*) an injection using a makeshift 'needle' made of a pin and a medicine dropper. ❑ **shot in the arm** *n.* **1** [1920s+] a narcotics injection. **2** *see also* SE phrs. below. ❑ **skin shot** *n.* [1930s+] (*drugs*) an injection of a narcotic that is made into the skin, rather than a specific vein; thus *skin-shooter*, one who injects.

pertaining to sexual intercourse

IN COMPOUNDS

❑ **shot-locker** *n.* [into which goes or from where comes a *shot*] [20C+] (*US*) **1** the vagina. **2** the penis.

IN PHRASES

❑ **bust a shot** *v.* [1970s+] usu. of a man, to reach orgasm. ❑ **dead shot** *n. see under* DEAD *adj.* ❑ **double-shot** *n.* [1970s+] two ejaculations of semen during a single bout of intercourse. ❑ **get a shot away** *v.* [2000s] (*N.Z.*) to ejaculate. ❑ **give someone a shot** *v.* [19C+] of a man, to have sexual intercourse. ❑ **pay one's shot** *v.* (*also* **pay the shot**) **1** [17C] to have sexual intercourse. **2** *see also* SE phrs. below. ❑ **shot on the swings** *n.* [ety. unknown; ? the movements of the two bodies] [1940s+] (*Scot.*) sexual intercourse. ❑ **straight shot** *n.* [1970s+] (*US black*) sexual intercourse without contraception.

pertaining to a chance or attempt

IN PHRASES

❑ **get a shot of crack** *v. see under* CRACK *n.*[3]. ❑ **get a shot of**

leg *v.* [SE *leg*] [1970s+] (*US black*) to have sexual intercourse.

IN EXCLAMATIONS

❑ **that's the shot!** (*also* **that's the play!**) [1930s+] (*Aus.*) a general excl. of agreement or approval.

SE in slang uses

IN COMPOUNDS

❑ **shot-caller** *n.* [*see* CALL THE SHOTS *under* CALL *v.*] [1960s+] a person who has authority or takes the lead in saying what should happen. ❑ **shot-ging** *n.* [ext. GING *n.*[1]] [1920s+] (*Aus.*) a catapult. ❑ **shotgun** *see* separate entries. ❑ **shot pocket** *n.* [1970s] (*US Und.*) a special pocket adapted for secreting items that have been shoplifted. ❑ **shot-rodder** *n.* [1950s] (*US black*) one who is emotionally unstable [play on HOT-RODDER *n.*].

IN PHRASES

❑ **by a long shot** (*also* **by a long jump**) [mid-19C+] (*orig. US*) by a good distance, by a considerable amount; usu. as a negative, e.g. *too fast by a long shot* or *not by a long shot,* in no way at all, by an extremely unlikely chance. ❑ **call the shots** *v. see under* CALL *v.* ❑ **dead shot** *n. see under* DEAD *adj.* ❑ **do a shot** *v.* [? link to *HAVE A SHOT AT* below] [late 19C] (*S.Afr.*) to cheat, to swindle. ❑ **give it one's best shot** *v.* [20C+] to make one's best efforts. ❑ **have a shot at** *v.* **1** [early 19C+] (*Aus.*) to make a sneering remark in someone's direction, to try to provoke. **2** [late 19C+] to make an attempt, to have a try. ❑ **just the shot** [1940s+] (*Aus./N.Z.*) exactly what one requires. ❑ **like a shot off a shovel** *adv.* [? euph. for *LIKE SHIT OFF A SHOVEL under* SHIT *n.*] [1920s+] (*Irish*) promptly, immediately, fast. ❑ **pay one's shot** *v.* (*also* **pay the shot**) **1** [late 17C+] to pay one's share. **2** *see also* slang phrs. above. ❑ **shot in the arm** *n.* (*also* **shot in the ass**) [lit. an injection] **1** [1910s+] (*orig. US*) anything (verbal, physical, stimulant) that cheers one up, energizes one etc. **2** *see also* slang phrs. above. ❑ **shot in the dark** *n.* [late 19C+] a wild guess, a random try. ❑ **take a shot (at)** *v.* [1970s+] to try, to make an attempt. ❑ **take a shot at** *v.* [late 19C+] to attack, whether physically or verbally. ❑ **take one's best shot** *v.* (*also* **shoot one's best shot**) [ult. boxing imagery] [1960s+] (*orig. US*) to do the best one can, to try one's hardest. ❑ **whole shot** *n. see* WHOLE BANG SHOOT *n.*

shot *n.*[2] [lit. and fig. uses of SE *shot*] **1** [1910s] (*Aus.*) baking powder [play on SE *shot/powder*]. **2** [1910s–20s] a very hard cake [SE *shot*, a cannonball]. **3** [1920s] dried peas [? SE *shot*, the lead shot contained in a shotgun cartridge]. **4** [1920s] anything very hard to understand or believe. **5** [1920s–50s] (*US Und.*) the detonation of an explosive during safe-breaking [SE *shot*, an electrical device for detonating the shot]. **6** [1930s–50s] (*Aus.*) an abortion. **7** [1940s+] a blow, a hit. **8** [1960s–70s] (*US black*) a professional pickpocket; thus *shot broad*, a female pickpocket. **9** [1990s+] (*US prison*) a friend.

shot *n.*[3] *see* SHORT *n.* (2b).

shot *adj.* **1** [mid-19C+] (*US/Aus./N.Z.*) drunk (cf. CUPSHOT *under* CUP *n.*). **2** [1920s–30s] (*US*) nervous, on edge. **3** [1920s+] (*orig. Aus.*) (*also* **all shot**) of a person, exhausted or in bad shape. **4** [1930s+] (*US*) (*also* **shotty**) of a thing, lost, useless, worn out or beyond repair.

IN PHRASES

❑ **get shot** *v.* **1** [1900s] (*Aus.*) to be dismissed. **2** [1970s] (*US prison*) to be punished by loss of privileges. ❑ **get shot in the tail** *v. see under* TAIL *n.* ❑ **half shot** *adj.* [mid-19C+] (*orig. US*) tipsy, mildly drunk. ❑ **shot between wind and water** *n.* (*also* **shot betwixt wind and water**) [naut. jargon *betwixt wind and water*, that part of a ship's side that is sometimes above water and sometimes submerged, in which part a shot is particularly dangerous] [mid-17C–19C] an act of sexual intercourse, from the perspective of the man. ❑ **shot between wind and water** *adj.* (*also* **shot betwixt wind and water**) [see prev.] [mid-17C–19C] infected with venereal disease. ❑ **shot down** *adj.* [1950s+] **1** (*drugs*) under the influence of drink or drugs [SE + play on SHOT *n.*[1] (6b)]. **2** (*US campus*) miserable, useless, distasteful [SE + play on DOWN *adj.*[2] (1)]. ❑ **shot full of holes** *adj.* **1** [1910s+] (*Aus./N.Z.*) drunk. **2** [1940s] (*US*) suffering a nervous breakdown. ❑ **shot in the ass** *adj.* [image of narcotic addiction] [1950s–60s] (*US*) obsessed with, excessively dedicated to. ❑ **shot in the neck** *n.* [mid-19C] a drink. ❑ **shot in the neck** *adj.* [early–mid-19C] (*US*) drunk. ❑ **shot in the tail** *adj.* [SE *shot* + TAIL *n.* (4)] [late 19C–1900s] pregnant. ❑ **shot out** *adj.* [SHOOT *v.* (6a)] [1990s+] (*drugs*) of a narcotics addict, worn out from an excess of drug use. ❑ **shot to hell** *adj.* (*also* **shot to pieces, shot to shit**) [20C+] in a state of utter collapse. ❑ **shot to the curb** *adj.* [2000s] of a person, completely destroyed, useless, having lost everything, usu. with ref. to crack cocaine. ❑ **shot up** *adj.* **1** [1930s+] (*drugs*) experiencing the effect of narcotic drugs [SHOOT UP *v.*[2] (1)]. **2** [1930s+] (*US*) of a person, or limb, severely wounded. **3** [1940s+] of the body, not well. **4** [1950s+] of an object, e.g. a car, damaged by shooting. ❑ **shot up the back** *adj.* [1910s] (*Aus.*) disconcerted; confused.

shot *v.* [SHOTTER *n.*] [2000s] (*black*) to deal drugs.

shotgun *n.*[1] [play on SHOTGUN WEDDING *n.*] [20C+] (*US*) a matchmaker, a marriage broker.

shotgun *n.*[2] **1** [1960s+] (*US drugs*) a type of pipe used for smoking marijuana. **2** [1970s+] (*drugs*) a means of intensifying the effect of cannabis smoke: the cigarette is reversed, the lit end in the mouth, sealed there by the lips; its holder then blows into the cigarette and the resultant powerful stream of smoke passes into a receiver's mouth.

shotgun *n.*[3] [*RIDE SHOTGUN under* RIDE *v.*] **1** [1970s+] (*orig. US*) (*also* **shotgun seat**) the seat next the driver in a vehicle. **2** [1980s+] (*drugs*) a guard who accompanies a drug courier to ensure that all goes well on their trip (and that they do not attempt to abscond with the consignment). **3** [1980s+] any form of guard.

shotgun *v.* **1** [1960s+] to drink a full can of beer in a single swallow, esp. when a hole has been poked through the bottom. **2** [1970s+] (*drugs*) to blow cannabis smoke into someone else's mouth by reversing the cigarette inside one's own mouth and blowing; the other person places their open lips near the stream of smoke and inhales for as long as they can; thus *shotgun, shot-gunning,* the act of doing this [SHOTGUN *n.*[2] (2)].

shotgun! *excl.* [abbr. *RIDE SHOTGUN under* RIDE *v.*] [1980s+] (*US teen*) when choosing seats in a car, 'I want to ride in the front seat next to the driver!'.

shotgun quiz *n. see POP QUIZ under* POP *v.*[1].

shotgun seat *n. see* SHOTGUN *n.*[3] (1).

shotgun wedding *n.* (*also* **shotgun marriage, shotgunner**) [the image of the aggrieved father holding a shotgun to the reluctant groom's back] [20C+] (*orig. US*) a wedding that is forced on the groom through his girlfriend's (soon to be bride's) pregnancy.

shotten herring *n.* [Du. *schoten haringh*, a fish, esp. a herring, that has spawned. Such herrings are 'empty' of their spawn. In a human context, therefore, it also means fig. 'empty'] [late 16C–early 19C] an emaciated, worthless and generally good-for-nothing person.

shotten soul *n.* [lit. an 'empty soul'] [early 17C] an emaciated, worthless and generally good-for-nothing person; thus *shotten-souled*, worthless.

shotter *n.* (*also* **shotta**) [2000s] (*UK black*) a drug dealer.

shottie *n. see* SHOTTY *n.*

shottie *v.* [abbr. SE *shotgun*] [1980s+] (*N.Z. drugs*) to inhale a puff of a marijuana cigarette through a large funnel and then drop from a standing position to a crouch when the lungs are filled to capacity, to force more smoke into the lungs.

shotting (game) *n.* [2000s] (*UK black*) drug-dealing, being a drug dealer.

shotty *n.* (*also* **shottie**) [abbr.] [1990s+] (*orig. US black*) a *shotgun*.

shotty *adj.* **1** [2000s] (*N.Z. teen*) excellent, first-rate. **2** *see* SHOT *adj.* (4).

shoulder *n.*

SE in slang uses

IN COMPOUNDS

❑ **shoulder-boulders** *n. see under* BOULDER *n.* ❑ **shoulder-clapper** *n.* (*also* **shoulder man**) [the physical action that accompanies an arrest for debt] [late 16C–early 19C] a bailiff.

❑ **shoulder-dab** *n.* (*also* **shoulder-dabber**) [their 'dabbing' or tapping their target on the shoulder] [early 19C] a bailiff. ❑ **shoulder-hitter** *n.* (*also* **shoulder-striker**) [lit. 'one who hits from the shoulder'] [mid-19C–1930s] (*US*) a bully, a ruffian. ❑ **shoulder-knot** *n.* [their taking their victim by the shoulder] [mid-19C] a bailiff. ❑ **shoulder-sham** *n.* [SHAM *n.*[1] (1)] [late 17C–early 19C] (*UK Und.*) a partner to a pickpocket. ❑ **shoulder-surfing** *n.* [1990s+] a general term for a variety of 'distraction crimes', i.e. street robberies performed where one member of a team distracts the target by starting an argument, pouring liquid on their clothes etc; while the argument is being resolved or the clothes cleaned, the actual robber has the opportunity to steal. ❑ **shoulder-tapper** *n.* [their taking their victim by the shoulder] **1** [late 18C–mid-19C] a bailiff. **2** [1940s] (*US Und.*) a police officer.

IN PHRASES

❑ **burn one's shoulder** *v.* [? the burn comes from a fire or by falling on the stove] [mid-18C] to be drunk. ❑ **get up off the shoulder** *v.* [1990s+] (*US black gang*) to fight with one's fists. ❑ **on the shoulder** [late 19C] (*US*) involved in fighting.

shoulder *v.* [ety. unknown] **1** [early 19C] of a stage-coachman, to take on (and charge) extra passengers, without informing the coach company; thus *shoulder-stick*, a passenger who takes advantage of such corruption. **2** [mid-19C] of a servant, to cheat or embezzle from their master.

shouse *n.* (*also* **shoush, sh'touse**) [elision of SHITHOUSE *n.*] [1940s+] (*Aus./N.Z.*) a lavatory.

shouse *adj.* [SHOUSE *n.*] [1960s+] (*N.Z.*) a general negative: unpleasant, disgusting etc.

shout *n.* (*also* **call, shoot**) [SHOUT *v.* (1)] **1** [mid-19C+] (*Aus./N.Z.*) in context of public drinking. (**a**) a round of drinks. (**b**) one's turn to order a round of drinks; thus *your shout*; *my shout*; *go on the shout*; *stand the shout*; thus *shout-dodger*, one who avoids his turn. (**c**) a drink. (**d**) in fig. use, a 'turn'. **2** [late 19C+] (*US black*) an act of crying out or 'speaking in tongues', usu. in church, as the apparent result of being possessed by spirits. **3** [1920s+] (*US black*) a party, esp. one where the guests buy their refreshments to help pay the rent. **4** [1920s+] (*US black*) a dance. **5** [1970s] a piece of information, a 'tip-off'.

IN PHRASES

❑ **give someone a shout** *v.* [1970s+] **1** to get in touch with, usu. by telephone. **2** (*W.I./US*) to pay a casual visit.

shout *v.* (*Aus./N.Z.*) **1** [mid-19C+] to buy a round of drinks [one *shouts* to the publican for drink]. **2** [late 19C–1940s] (*US*) of things, to be undeniably important. **3** [late 19C+] (*US black*) to cry out or 'speak in tongues', usu. in church, as the apparent result of being possessed by spirits. **4** [20C+] to treat (other than to liquor).

DERIVATIVES

❑ **shouted** *adj.* [1940s] (*Aus./N.Z.*) used of a drink that is paid for by someone other than the drinker.

IN PHRASES

❑ **on the shout** [late 19C] out drinking. ❑ **shout oneself hoarse** *v.* [pun on the actual shouting – to attract attention to one's generosity and as a result of one's drunkenness] **1** [late 19C–1900s] to get drunk. **2** [late 19C+] to buy a round of drinks for the whole bar.

SE in slang uses

IN PHRASES

❑ **shout at one's shoes** *v.* [1980s+] (*US campus*) to vomit. ❑ **shout for Ruth** *v.* [*Ruth* = echoic] [1980s] (*Aus.*) to vomit. ❑ **shout the odds** *v.* [1910s+] to talk loudly, to boast.

shout and holler *n.* [rhy. sl.] [20C+] a collar.

shouter *n.*[1] [SHOUT *v.* (1)] [mid–late 19C] (*Aus./N.Z.*) one who stands a round of drinks.

shouter *n.*[2] [SE *shouter*, a loud or voluble speaker] **1** [late 19C–1920s] (*US*) a gospel or blues/gospel singer. **2** [late 19C–1920s] (*US*) a black church. **3** [20C+] (*US*) a soapbox or street-corner orator, a fervent preacher. **4** [1920s] (*US Und.*) a criminal's girlfriend.

shout(-out) *n.* [1990s+] as used on (pirate) radio stations, esp. 1990s stations playing jungle music, a greeting, an acknowledgement to a named listener or group of listeners.

shout out *v.* [1990s+] on (pirate) radio stations, to send a greeting or acknowledgement to a named listener or group of listeners.

shout-up *n.* [1960s+] a noisy argument.

shov *n.* [CHIV *n.*[1] (1) + SE *shove*, one 'shoves it in' to the victim] [late 19C] (*UK Und.*) a knife.

shove *n.* **1** [early 18C+] sexual intercourse; thus *give her a shove*, to have sexual intercourse with a woman [SHOVE *v.* (1)]. **2** [mid-19C] (*UK Und.*) a crowd [play on PUSH *n.* (2a)]. **3** [late 19C] energy, high spirits, self-glorification, hollow talk [play on PUSH *n.* (2a)]. **4** [late 19C–1940s] (*US tramp*) a gang of tramps [play on PUSH *n.* (2a)].

IN PHRASES

❑ **shove in the eye** *n.* [late 19C+] a punch in the face. ❑ **shove in the mouth** *n.* [19C] a glass of spirits.

shove, the *n.* [late 19C+] dismissal from one's employment.

IN PHRASES

❑ **get the shove** *v.* **1** [late 19C+] to be dismissed from a job. **2** [1900s] to be rejected by a lover. **3** [2000s] in sports contexts, to be dismissed from the game. ❑ **give someone the shove** *v.* [late 19C+] to dismiss, usu. from a job.

shove *v.* **1** [mid-17C+] to have sexual intercourse. **2** [mid-19C] (*UK Und.*) to deceive, to cheat; to take advantage of. **3** in Und. use. (**a**) [mid-19C+] (*US*) to pass counterfeit money. (**b**) [1920s] (*US*) to sell stolen goods. (**c**) [1930s–50s] (*US drugs*) to sell narcotics. **4** [mid-19C+] to put, to place. **5** [1920s–60s] (*US Und.*) (*also* **shove across**) to kill. **6** [1940s+] a negative intensifier, synon. with FUCK *v.* (3), to stop, to forget; usu. in phr. *you can shove that* or imper. *shove it!* **7** *see* SHOVE ALONG below. **8** *see* SHOVE OFF below.

IN COMPOUNDS

❑ **shove-devil** *n.* [? the trad. joke whereby a monk seduces a virgin by explaining the necessity of 'shoving the devil back into hell'] [mid-17C] the penis. ❑ **shove-straight** *n.* [18C] the penis.

IN PHRASES

❑ **shove across** *v. see* sense 5 above. ❑ **shove-and-let-go** *n.* [on this car low gear was engaged by pressing a foot-pedal] [1920s–40s] (*W.I.*) a Model T Ford. ❑ **shove the queer** *v. see under* QUEER *n.* (2).

SE in slang uses

IN PHRASES

❑ **shove along** *v.* **1** [late 19C–1920s] to move (quietly). **2** [mid-19C+] (*also* **shove**) to leave. **3** [1900s–10s] to go along with, to support. **4** [1940s] to survive. ❑ **shove for** *v.* [late 19C] to move towards, to go to. ❑ **shove in** *v.* [one 'shoves' the pawned item across the pawnbroker's counter] [late 19C] to pawn. ❑ **shove it in and break it** *v.* (*also* **shove it up someone's ass and break it**) [1960s+] to defeat an opponent, to cause a good deal of trouble. ❑ **shove off** *v.* (*also* **shove, shove on, shove out**) [naut. jargon, to push a boat away from the side of another one or off the harbour wall before setting out] [mid-19C+] to leave, to go away; usu. as imper. ❑ **shove one's oar in** *v.* (*also* **stick one's oar in, shove one's blade in**) [19C+] to interfere where one is not wanted. ❑ **shove one's trunk** *v.* [late 18C] to move. ❑ **shove shit uphill** *v.* [SHIT *n.* (1a)] [1960s+] to sodomize. ❑ **shove shorts** *v. see* PUSH SHORTS *under* SHORT *n.* ❑ **shove the brass** *v. see under* BRASS *n.*[1]. ❑ **shove the (flogging) tumbler** *v. see under* TUMBLER *n.*[2]. ❑ **shove the moon** *v.* [such exits are usu. nocturnal] [early–mid-19C] to abscond from a house or flat, taking one's furniture and possessions, but paying no bills. ❑ **shove tumrill** *v. see* SHOVE THE TUMBLER *under* TUMBLER *n.*[2]. ❑ **shove under** *v.* [i.e. to push under the ground] [20C+] (*Aus./N.Z.*) to kill, usu. in passive, i.e. *to be shoved under*, to be killed. ❑ **shove up daisies** *v. see* PUSH UP (THE) DAISIES *v.* ❑ **tell someone where to shove it** *v.* (*also* **tell someone where to stick it, tell someone where to put it**) [20C+] (*orig. US*) to reject something vehemently.

IN EXCLAMATIONS

❑ **go shove yourself!** [1940s] a synon. for GO FUCK YOURSELF! *under* FUCK v.

shove it! *excl.* [abbr. SHOVE IT UP YOUR ARSE! *excl.*] [1940s+] (*orig. Aus.*) a general excl. of dismissal and rudeness.

shove it up your arse! *excl.* (*also* **shove it up your ass! ...hole! jam it up your arse! stick it up your arse! ...ass! ...butt! ...pratt! stuff it up and break if off! stuff it up your arse! ...hole!**) [SE *shove* + ARSE *n.* (1)/ASS *n.* (2)/HOLE *n.*[1] (1a)] **1** [20C+] an excl. of contempt, dismissal. **2** [1970s] as v. in fig. use, to treat badly.

shove it up your nose! *excl.* (*also* **stick it up your nose!**) [euph. of SHOVE IT UP YOUR ARSE! *excl.*] [1920s+] (*orig. US*) a general excl. of dismissal.

shovel *n.*[1] **1** [1930s] (*US*) a banjo. **2** [1970s+] (*US gay/prison*) the penis.

IN COMPOUNDS

❑ **shovelhead** *n.* [SE *shovel* + -HEAD *sfx* (1)] [1980s+] (*Aus./US*) an idiot. ❑ **shovel stiff** *n.* (*also* **shovel bum**) [SE *shovel* + STIFF *n.*[1] (4a)] [1900s–30s] (*US tramp*) a tramp who would beg but does it poorly and will therefore work (at a labouring job) when necessary.

SE in slang uses

IN PHRASES

❑ **shovel of malt** *n.* [SE *malt*, the main constituent of the drink] [early 19C] a pot of porter.

shovel *n.*[2] *see* SHOFUL *n.*

shovel *n.*[3] **1** *see* SHOVEL AND BROOM *n.* **2** *see* SHOVEL AND PICK *n.*

shovel v. [1920s–50s] (*orig. S.Afr.*) to hand over, to pass.

SE in slang uses

IN PHRASES

❑ **shovel guts** v. [20C+] (*US*) to perform menial, distasteful tasks. ❑ **shovel it higher and deeper** v. *see* PILE IT HIGHER AND DEEPER *under* PILE v. ❑ **shovel shit against the tide** v. [SHIT *n.* (1a)] [1930s+] to make one's best efforts, despite overwhelming odds. ❑ **shovel the dirt** v. [1950s] to take a walk. ❑ **shovel (the) shit** v. [1930s+] **1** to gossip, esp. maliciously; to talk nonsense [SHIT *n.* (4a)]. **2** to do an unpleasant job of work [SHIT *n.* (3b)].

IN EXCLAMATIONS

❑ **shovel it!** [1980s+] (*N.Z.*) excl. of dismissal, disbelief.

shovel and broom *n.* (*also* **shovel**) [rhy. sl.] [1920s–50s] (*Aus./US*) a room.

shovel and pick *n.* (*also* **shovel**) [rhy. sl.] [1940s+] **1** a prison [NICK *n.*[3] (2a)]. **2** an Irishman [MICK *n.*[1] (1a)].

shovel and spade *n.* [rhy. sl.] [20C+] a blade, a knife.

shovel and tank *n.* [rhy. sl.] [20C+] a bank.

shovels and spades *n.* [rhy. sl.] [1990s+] AIDS.

shover *n.*[1] (*also* **shuffer**) [mispron.] [1900s–20s] **1** a chauffeur. **2** a driver.

shover *n.*[2] [synon. with PUSHER *n.* (3a)] [1930s–70s] (*US drugs*) a drug dealer.

shover (of the queer) *n.* [SHOVE v. (3a) + QUEER *n.* (2)] [mid-19C–1940s] a passer of counterfeit money.

shove-up *n.* [early 19C] (*UK Und.*) nothing.

shovin' and pushin' *adj.* [1970s] (*US black*) trying as hard as possible to succeed.

shoving *adj.* [1940s] a general intensifier; synon. with FUCKING *adj.* (1).

show *n.* **1** [late 18C+] (*orig. US*) a matter, an event, an affair, e.g. *good show, bad show, poor show, the whole show.* **2** [mid-19C] (*UK Und.*) a facial expression. **3** [mid-19C+] (*Aus./US*) a chance, an opportunity, e.g. *give him a show*, give him a chance. **4** [late 19C+] (*orig. milit.*) a fight, a battle, a military engagement, a war. **5** [1900s–10s] a home. **6** [1910s] (*Aus.*) a business. **7** [1920s–30s] (*UK Und.*) any form of crime. **8** [1940s+] (*Aus.*) a sanitary towel [the blood thereon].

IN PHRASES

❑ **big show** *n.* [late 19C+] (*orig. milit.*) a major campaign, a war. ❑ **give the show away** v. [mid-19C+] to betray a secret, to reveal one's or another's plans. ❑ **no show** (*also* **no show and fisho**) [late 19C; 1960s+] (*US/Aus.*) no hope of success. ❑ **put on show** v. [1980s+] (*Aus. prison*) to humiliate in public. ❑ **run the show** v. [20C+] to take charge, to direct operations or activities. ❑ **sling the show** v. [1910s] (*Aus.*) to leave a place; to abandon a situation. ❑ **stand a show** v. [mid-19C+] (*Aus./US*) have a chance.

IN EXCLAMATIONS

❑ **over goes the show!** [late 19C–1900s] an excl. of dismay when faced by a sudden disaster.

SE in slang uses

IN COMPOUNDS

❑ **showbiz** *see* separate entries. ❑ **showboat** *see* separate entries. ❑ **showdog** *n. see* separate entry. ❑ **showhouse** *n. see* separate entry. ❑ **show pony** *n.* [SE *show pony*, one that looks good in shows but may be less useful in practical life] [1940s+] (*Aus.*) one who cares more for appearance than performance. ❑ **show stopper** *n.* **1** [1950s+] (*camp gay*) a particularly attractive young man. **2** [1980s+] a very attractive woman. ❑ **showtime** *see* separate entries. ❑ **show tunes** *n.* [SE *show tunes*, the songs performed in a musical] [1970s] (*US gay*) noises made during intercourse or fellatio.

show, the *n.* [1960s+] (*US black*) a state of prominence, 'the spotlight'.

show v. (*also* **show up**) **1** [19C] to appear in society [SE *show*, display (rather than 'appear')]. **2** [late 19C] to exhibit oneself for money. **3** [1930s+] of a woman, to be obviously pregnant.

DERIVATIVES

❑ **showing** *adj.* [1930s+] pregnant.

SE in slang uses

IN COMPOUNDS

❑ **showdown** *n. see* separate entry.

IN PHRASES

❑ **show a clean pair of heels** v. (*also* **show a clean pair of legs, show one's heels**) [note Taylor (1619): 'A Sixth, with tongues glib, like the tails of eels / Hath shewed this land and me foul pairs of heels] **1** [mid-17C+] to leave at speed. **2** [late 17C] (*also* **show a fair pair of heels**) to be bankrupt [? sent to debtor's prison]. ❑ **show an Abyssinian medal** v. [the *Abyssinian* War 1893–6] [late 19C] of a man, to have a fly-button undone, to have one's penis sticking inadvertently through one's flies. ❑ **show and prove** v. [1990s+] (*US black*) to demonstrate. ❑ **show and tell** *n.* [play on juv. *show-and-tell* periods at school] [1950s+] (*US*) an elaborate exhibit intended to impress, persuade or inform. ❑ **show a point to** v. (*also* **show a trick to**) [late 19C–1910s] (*Aus./N.Z.*) to swindle, to act dishonourably towards. ❑ **show drink** v. [late 19C] (*US*) to be tipsy, to be drunk. ❑ **showing up** *n.* **1** [mid-19C] (*UK Und.*) that which reveals one's presence to the authorities. **2** [1910s–20s] a shameful predicament. ❑ **show leg** v. *see* SHOW A LEG v. ❑ **show one's ass** v. [1950s+] (*US black*) to appear foolish; to show off, to make an exhibition of oneself. ❑ **show one's cards** v. (*also* **show one's hand, ...hole-card**) [poker imagery; the *hole-card* is that held face-down on the table] [late 19C+] (*orig. US*) to reveal oneself, usu. to a greater extent than desired. ❑ **show one's color** v. [ironic reversal of SE *show one's colours*, to declare one's own standpoint, to act proudly despite any opposition] [1950s–80s] (*US black*) to act in a stereotyped way, to behave in the way whites expect blacks to behave. ❑ **show one's gums** v. [1970s] (*US*) to smile, esp. in a self-satisfied manner. ❑ **show one's hobnails** v. [18C] to be drunk. ❑ **show one's shape** v. [SE *shape*, one's figure] [18C–19C] to make an appearance, to come into view. ❑ **show one's shapes** v. **1** [late 17C–early 18C] to turn around, to march off. **2** [late 18C–early 19C] to take off one's clothes, esp. preparatory to a judicial flogging. ❑ **show out** v. *see* separate entries. ❑ **show shapes** v. **1** [mid-19C] to play pranks, to act in a flighty manner. **2** [1960s+] to dance, esp. at a discotheque. ❑ **show (someone) the ropes** v. [naut. imagery] **1** [mid-19C+] to show someone how to do a task, to explain something to someone. **2** [1910s+] to explain, esp.

to explain the details of a task or operation. ❑ **show the goods** *v. see* DELIVER THE GOODS *under* GOODS *n.* ❑ **show the lions (and tombs)** *v.* (*also* **lionize**) [in the original context of London, the *lions* refer to the Tower of London, the *tombs* to Westminster Abbey] [late 18C–early 19C] to point out the sights. ❑ **show the white feather** *v.* (*also* **show the white rag**) [a white feather in a game-bird's tail is a mark of inferior breeding; note earlier *find a white feather in one's tail, mount the white feather*] [early 19C+] to surrender or act in a cowardly manner. ❑ **show up** *see* separate entries.

show a leg *v.* (*also* **show leg**) [*show a leg*, to make an appearance, is SE] [19C] to run off, to escape; to move at speed.

show a leg! *excl.* [orig. used in institutions to ensure that the leg was masculine and not, illicitly, female; note Fraser & Gibbons *Soldier & Sailor Words & Phrases* (1925): 'In the Navy, it dates from long ago, when women, ostensibly as sailors' wives, were allowed to live on board ship. The usual call was, 'Show a leg or a purser's stocking!' Everybody had to put a leg outside the hammock, a stockinged leg denoting that its occupant was a woman, who was then allowed to remain until the men had cleared out'] [mid-19C+] a wake-up call.

showbiz *n.* (*also* **show bizz**) [1940s+] (*orig. US*) **1** show business, the entertainment industry. **2** in fig. use, ostentation, melodrama, showing-off.

IN PHRASES

❑ **that's showbiz** [1940s+] (*orig. US*) that's how things are (and there's nothing you can do about it).

showbiz *adj.* [SHOWBIZ *n.*] [1940s+] pertaining to show business, entertainment.

IN COMPOUNDS

❑ **showbiz sherbet** *n.* [SHERBET *n.* (4); the image of cocaine as an expensive drug] [2000s] (*drugs*) cocaine.

showboat *n.* [see SHOWBOAT *v.*] **1** [1970s] a flashy car. **2** [2000s] a self-promoting person; a show-off.

showboat *v.* [SE *showboat*, a river steamer on which entertainments are given] [1950s+] (*orig. US*) **1** to show off, esp. by parading oneself in front of an audience. **2** to show someone off, to display, to parade.

DERIVATIVES

❑ **showboating** *n.* [1960s+] (*US*) ostentatious self-promotion.

showcase nigger *n.* [SE *showcase*, a display cabinet + NIGGER *n.*[1] (1)] [1960s+] (*US black*) a token black employee, hired to parade the liberal racial attitudes of a white-owned organization.

showdog *n.* (*also* **shoedog**) [1970s] a high-pressure shop salesman.

showdown *n.* [SE *showdown*, the moment in poker when all the cards are revealed to see who wins the pot] **1** [late 19C+] (*orig. US*) a confrontation. **2** [1970s] (*US prison*) an opportunity to break the prison rules without discovery.

shower *n.* [late 19C+] (*Aus.*) a dust-storm, usu. prefaced by a local name, e.g. *Cobar shower, Darling shower*.

SE in slang uses

IN COMPOUNDS

❑ **shower scum** *n. see under* SCUM *n.* ❑ **shower spank** *v.* [SPANK *v.*[1] (5)] [1980s+] (*US teen*) to masturbate in the shower.

IN PHRASES

❑ **shower of shit** *n.* (*also* **shower of cunts, ...savages, ...shites, ...tom tits, ...whore's bastards**) [SHIT *n.* (1a)/CUNT *n.* (4)/SHITE *n.* (4)] [1940s+] **1** an unimpressive group of people; occas. an individual. **2** a pile of second-rate things. **3** a term of abuse aimed at a single person.

shower bath *n.* [rhy. sl., Cockney pron. of *shower bath*, 'shahr barf' = half] [20C+] (*dog-racing*) ten shillings (50p); thus (sporting) *showers to a shilling*, odds of 10:1.

shower of rain *n.* [rhy. sl.] [20C+] (*Aus.*) a train.

showful *adj. see* SHOFUL *adj.*

show-full *n. see* SHOFUL *n.*

showful-pitcher *n. see* SHOFUL-PITCHER *under* SHOFUL *n.*

showhouse *n.* [1940s+] (*gay*) a brothel, a place where homosexuals can meet openly (sex is usu. performed off the premises).

showie *n.* (*also* **showy**) [abbr.; it is worn for 'show'] [1950s+] (*Aus.*) a display handkerchief, worn in one's top jacket pocket.

show leg *v. see* SHOW A LEG *v.*

show-leg day *n.* (*also* **shulleg-day**) [on such days women accidentally/are forced to raise their long skirts and thus 'show a leg', or at least an ankle] **1** [late 19C] a very windy day. **2** [late 19C–1920s] a very muddy day.

show out *v.*[1] [late 19C] (*Aus.*) to try, to attempt.

show out *v.*[2] [late 19C+] (*US black*) **1** to show off, to flaunt oneself. **2** to lead on, to deceive.

showtime *n.* [SHOWTIME *v.*] [1990s+] (*US black*) a show-off.

showtime *adj.* [SHOWTIME *v.*] [1990s+] (*US black*) ostentatious.

showtime *v.* [1990s+] (*US black*) to show off, to flaunt oneself.

show-up *n.* [SHOW UP *v.*] **1** [mid-19C+] an identification parade. **2** [2000s] an embarrassment.

show (up) *v.* [late 19C+] (*US*) to appear, to arrive.

show up *v.* [mid–late 19C] **1** (*UK Und.*) to identify (and arrest). **2** (*US Und.*) to put in an identification parade. **3** (*UK Und.*) to make a complaint against.

show-up man *n.* [1930s] (*US Und.*) the member of a hijack team who holds up the truck driver.

showy *n. see* SHOWIE *n.*

shpeiler/shpieler *n. see* SPIELER *n.*

shpilkes *n.* [Yid.] [20C+] (*US*) anxiety, nervousness.

shpritz *v. see* SCHPRITZ *v.*

shrap *n.* (*also* **shrape**) [SE *shrape*, bait of chaff or seed laid for birds; hence a snare] [late 16C] (*UK Und.*) wine used to weaken the will of a confidence trickster's victim.

shrapnel *n.* (*also* **shrap**) [SE *shrapnel*, shell or bomb fragments] [1910s+] (*orig. N.Z.*) copper coins, small change.

shreat (of booze) *n.* [BOOZE *n.* (1)] [mid-18C] (*UK Und.*) a pot (of ale or beer).

shred *n.* [the shreds of cloth he discards] [late 17C–early 19C] a tailor.

shred *v.* [1970s+] **1** (*UK/US campus*) to overcome, to conquer. **2** (*US black*) to travel fast.

IN PHRASES

❑ **shred the tube** *v.* [surf jargon *tube*, the top part of the wave, where it starts to curl over, forming a tube] [1980s] (*US teen*) to go surfing.

shredded *adj.* **1** [1980s+] (*US teen*) drunk. **2** [2000s] very upset.

shreddie *n.* [the breakfast cereal *Shreddies*, made of spaced strands of wheat] [1990s+] (*UK juv.*) one who has badly thinning hair but still combs it in attempt to disguise this situation.

shreddies *n.* [1990s+] **1** underpants. **2** (*UK juv.*) a 'game' whereby the victim's underpants are tugged upwards so hard that they tear.

shrewd-head *n.* [SE *shrewd* + -HEAD *sfx* (1)] [20C+] (*Aus./N.Z.*) a cunning person.

shrewdy *n.* (*also* **shrewdie**) [1910s+] (*Aus./N.Z.*) a shrewd person, one who lives on their wits.

IN PHRASES

❑ **pull a shrewdy** *v.* [1960s] (*N.Z.*) to trick, to deceive.

shriek *n.* [1900s–30s] **1** something or someone seen as very funny. **2** something ostentatiously fashionable. **3** an excl. of alarm, annoyance or similar emotion.

shrimp *n.* **1** in senses of diminutive size. (**a**) [15C+] a small, weak, insignificant person. (**b**) [1960s+] a midget. (**c**) [1970s+] (*US gay*) a small penis. (**d**) [1990s+] a baby. **2** [mid-17C] a prostitute [the association of prostitution/women with FISH *n.*[1]]. **3** [late 19C+] a term of address, used affectionately or derisively.

shrimper *n.* [toes are supposed to resemble pink shrimps] [1970s+] a foot fetishist.

shrimping *n.* [for ety. *see* SHRIMPER *n.*] [1970s+] toe-sucking.

shrimps and rice *n.* [1940s] (*US black*) metaphor for whatever it is one wants.

shrimpy *adj.* [SHRIMP *n.* (1a)] [mid-19C; 1950s+] (*US*) small, insignificant, physically slight.

shrine of Venus *n. see* VENUS'S HIGHWAY *n.*

shrink *n.*[1] [*HEAD-SHRINKER* below] **1** [1960s+] (*orig. US*) (*also* **shrinker**) a psychoanalyst, a psychiatrist. **2** [1980s+] (*also* **shrinking**) psychoanalysis.

DERIVATIVES

❑ **shrinkette** *n.* [1970s] a female psychoanalyst or psychiatrist. ❑ **shrinksville** *n.* [-VILLE *sfx*[1] (1)] [1950s+] (*orig. US*) madness; spec. a state of mind that makes it advisable for a person so afflicted to consult a psychoanalyst.

IN COMPOUNDS

❑ **shrink klink** *n.* [CLINK *n.*[1]] [1980s] (*Aus.*) a psychiatric institution.

IN PHRASES

❑ **head-shrinker** *n.* (*also* **headshrink**) **1** [1950s+] (*orig. US*) a psychoanalyst, a psychotherapist, a psychiatrist. **2** [1980s] a session of psychoanalysis. ❑ **headshrinking** *n.* [1950s+] (*orig. US*) psychoanalysis, psychotherapy. ❑ **shrink someone's head** *v.* [1950s+] (*orig. US*) to psychoanalyse.

shrink *n.*[2] [1970s] (*US campus*) a young woman's tight-fitting sweater.

shritter *n.* [ety. unknown] [2000s] (*US black*) the victim of a beating.

shroom *v.* [? SHROOMS *n.*] **1** [1980s] (*US campus*) to act wild, to be madly excited. **2** [1990s+] (*US*) to ambush.

shrooms *n.* [abbr.] [1980s+] psilocybin mus*hrooms*, used as a recreational hallucinogenic drug.

IN COMPOUNDS

❑ **shroom dog** *n.* [DOG *n.*[2] (1)] [1980s+] (*US campus*) someone who uses hallucinogens.

shroud and boiler *n.* [1900s–40s] (*US*) a formal dress suit and starched dress shirt.

shrubbery *n.* **1** [19C] (*also* **shrubs**) the pubic hair. **2** [1900s–40s] (*also* **face shrubbery**) whiskers. **3** [1920s–40s] (*US prison*) sauerkraut.

sht... *see also under* SCHT...

shtorikue *n. see* SCHTARKA *n.*

sh'touse *n. see* SHOUSE *n.*

shtuck *n.*

IN PHRASES

❑ **in shtuck** *adj.* (*also* **in schtook, ...shtook, ...stook**) [Yid. *shtook*, difficulties] [1940s+] in trouble.

shtum *adj.* (*also* **schtum, shtoom, stumm, stumpf**) [synon. Yid.] [late 19C+] quiet, silent, dumb.

IN PHRASES

❑ **keep shtum** *v.* (*also* **keep schtum, ...shtoom, ...stumm**) [1950s+] to keep quiet, to say nothing. ❑ **shtum up** *v.* (*also* **shtoom up, stumm...**) [1950s+] to be quiet.

shubalafa *n.* [ety. unknown] [2000s] (*US black*) a black female who assumes the dominant role in the relationship.

shuby *v. see* SHOOB *v.*

shuck *n.* [SE *shuck*, a husk; thus fig. nonsense, deception] **1** [mid-19C+] (*US, esp. black*) a hoax, a lie, a deceit. **2** [1940s] (*US black*) a theft, a fraud. **3** [1960s] an easy job.

IN COMPOUNDS

❑ **shuckman** *n.* [1960s] a swindler.

IN PHRASES

❑ **cut a shuck** *v.* [1970s] (*US*) to leave. ❑ **put the shuck on** *v.* [1970s+] (*US*) to trick, to deceive, to fool verbally. ❑ **shuck drop** *v.* [DROP *v.*[2] (4)] [1940s] (*US black*) to take advantage of a victim or fool.

shuck *v.* **1** [mid-19C+] (*US, esp. black*) to defraud, to tease, to lie [SHUCK *n.* (1)]. **2** [1960s] (*US black*) to have sexual intercourse with [? SHAKE *v.* (1)]. **3** [1960s+] to do something half-heartedly or deceptively [SHUCK *n.* (1)]. **4** *see SHUCK DOWN* below.

SE, meaning to pod, to strip husks, in slang uses

IN PHRASES

❑ **shuck down** *v.* (*also* **shuck, shuck off, shuck out of**) [mid-19C+] (*US*) to strip off one's clothes, to undress. ❑ **shuck out** *v. see* SHACK *v.* (2). ❑ **shuck the corn** *v.* [20C+] to masturbate.

shuck and jive *n.* [SHUCK *n.* (1) + JIVE *n.*[1] (2)] [1960s+] (*US, esp. black*) deception, play-acting, obfuscation.

shuck and jive *v.* [SHUCK AND JIVE *n.*] [1960s+] (*US, esp. black*) **1** (*also* **shive**) to act deceptively, to confuse. **2** to make a promise one has no intention of keeping.

shucking and jiving *n.* (*also* **shucking and sliding**) [SHUCK AND JIVE *v.*] [1950s+] (*US black*) fooling, playing around.

shucks *n.* [SE *shuck*, shells of peas, husks of corn and similar refuse; thus implying the worthlessness of the Confederate currency] [mid-19C] (*US*) **1** the paper money issued by the Confederate States during the US Civil War. **2** in fig. use, nothing.

IN PHRASES

❑ **sure as shucks** *see under* SURE AS... *phr.* ❑ **to shucks** *adv.* [mid-19C] (*US*) comprehensively.

shucks! *excl.* [SE *not worth shucks*, worthless, useless] **1** [mid-19C+] (*orig. US*) a mild excl. of surprise, regret, annoyance etc; also as phr. *I'll be shucked.* **2** [1970s] (*US campus*) synon. for SUCKS (TO YOU)! *excl.* (1).

shuffer *n. see* SHOVER *n.*[1].

shuffle *n.* [the shuffling walk, along with shiny smiles and 'natural rhythm' are major parts of this image] [1900s–60s] (*US black*) a black man deliberately playing dumb and acting out the white man's stereotyped view of their race; also as v., to play this part.

shuffle *v.* **1** [mid-18C–1960s] to practise a confidence trick, a hoax or a deception. **2** [1950s] (*US street gang*) to have a fist-fight. **3** [1980s] (*US prison*) to play the passive role in a homosexual couple.

IN COMPOUNDS

❑ **shuffleman** *n.* (*also* **shuffle-sharper**) [mid-18C–1960s] a confidence trickster.

SE in slang uses

IN PHRASES

❑ **shuffle (off)** *v.* (*also* **shake off**) [orig. in *Hamlet* (1602) III.i.67: 'When we have shuffel'd [*sic*] off this mortall coile'] [early 17C; 19C+] to die. ❑ **shuffle the deck** *v.* [1990s+] to masturbate.

shuffler *n.*[1] [their shuffling, hesitant demeanour] [mid-17C] one who cadges drinks.

shuffler *n.*[2] [their ability, lit. or fig., to 'shuffle one's deck', i.e. either to perform as a card-sharp or to render the victim confused] [mid-19C+] (*US Und.*) a confidence trickster.

shufflers *n.* [mid-19C] the feet.

shuftie *n.* (*also* **shoofti, shoofty, shufti, shufty**) [Arabic *sufti*, have you seen?; note Aus. milit. *shooftie room*, the viewing room of an Egyptian brothel] [1940s+] a brief glance, a quick look.

shuftie *v.* (*also* **shufty**) [SHUFTIE *n.*] [1940s] to watch, to look at.

shufty *v.* [SHUFTIE *n.*] [1950s] to tell, to assure.

shug *n.* (*also* **sug**) **1** [mid-19C+] (*US black*) an affectionate name, usu. for a woman or homosexual man [abbr. SE *sugar*]. **2** [late 19C+] (*Aus.*) money [SUGAR *n.*[1] (1)].

shuiler *n. see* SHOOLER *n.*

shuks *v.* [SHAKE *v.* (3c) or SE *shuck* (*off*), but note excl. of disappointment, SHUCKS! *excl.*] [1950s] (*W.I.*) to hurt someone's feelings.

shule *v. see* SHOOL *v.*

shuler *n. see* SHOOLER *n.*

shulleg-day *n. see* SHOW-LEG DAY *n.*

shundicknick *n.* [Yid.] [late 19C–1930s] a pimp, a ponce.

shungudgeon *n. see* SLUMGUDGEON *n.*

shunk *v.* [1980s+] (*US teen*) to break a promised appointment.

shunt *n.*[1] [1950s] the vagina; thus attrib.

shunt *n.*[2] [orig. racing driver jargon] **1** [1970s+] a car crash. **2** [1980s] sexual intercourse.

shunt *v.* (*also* **shunt off**) **1** [late 19C] (*Aus.*) to get rid of a thing. **2** [late 19C–1910s] to leave, to run off quickly. **3** [late 19C+] to dismiss, usu. from a job; also as n., 'the sack'. **4** [20C+] (*Aus.*) to be dismissed.

IN PHRASES

❑ **give the shunt** *v.* [late 19C+] to get rid of. ❑ **off-shunt** *n.* [late 19C] (*Aus.*) an act of dismissal.

shunter *n.*[1] [? play on his 'coupling up' or cf. PULL A TRAIN *under* TRAIN *n.*[1]] [1990s+] a male homosexual.

shunter *n.*[2] [rhy. sl. = PUNTER *n.* (5)] [2000s] a member of the public, one who is outside the criminal world.

shunter's pole *n.* [railway jargon *shunter's pole*, a rod used to facilitate the coupling and uncoupling of goods wagons and engines / POLE *n.* (1)] [1980s+] the penis.

shuper *n.* (*also* **shooper, shupper**) [ety. unknown; ? link to SE *super*] [1900s–20s] (*US*) a large beer glass.

shure as shit *phr. see* SURE AS SHIT *under* SURE AS… *phr.*

shurk *n.* [SE *shirk*] [late 17C–18C] (*UK Und.*) **1** a pickpocket. **2** a cardsharp.

shut *n.* [abbr.] [late 18C] a *shutter*.

shut *v.*

SE in slang uses

IN COMPOUNDS

❑ **shut-door** *n.* [2000s] a private conversation. ❑ **shut-eye/ shut eyes** *n. see* separate entries. ❑ **shut-in** *n.* **1** [20C+] one who stays in a lot, esp. due to illness. **2** [1950s] (*US prison*) a prisoner.

IN PHRASES

❑ **shut ass** *v.* [ASS *n.* (4)] [1960s] (*US black*) to keep quiet. ❑ **shut down** *v.* **1** [1960s+] (*US black*) to leave someone bereft of repartee. **2** [1970s] (*US black*) to prove someone wrong. **3** [1970s] to be left by a partner. **4** [1980s] (*US campus*) to go to sleep. ❑ **shut it off** *v.* [1950s] (*US drugs*) to stop doing something, to give up an addiction. ❑ **shut one's…** *v. see also under* relevant n. ❑ **shut one's noise** *v. see* SHUT ONE'S ROW *under* ROW *n.*[1]. ❑ **shut someone down** *v.* [1950s+] (*US*) **1** to beat a rival in a drag race. **2** to gain a victory in any competition. ❑ **shut up** *see* separate entries.

IN EXCLAMATIONS

❑ **shut it!** (*also* **shut! shut it before I slide down it! shut it off!**) ['it' is the mouth] [late 19C+] be quiet! shut up! ❑ **shut off!** [1910s] be quiet!

shut-eye *n.*[1] **1** [late 19C+] sleep, rest. **2** [1920s] (*US tramp*) a victim, a dupe.

IN PHRASES

❑ **go shut-eye** *v.* [late 19C] to go to sleep. ❑ **go to shut-eye land** *v.* [1940s] (*W.I.*) to die. ❑ **play shut-eye** *v.* [1940s] to stop working or shut down for a rest.

shut-eye *n.*[2] [1930s] (*US*) whisky.

shut eyes *n.* [their suggestion, 'Now just shut your eyes…'] [1960s+] (*US police*) a sexual offender.

shutter *n.*

SE in slang uses

IN COMPOUNDS

❑ **shutter-bug** *n.* [BUG *n.*[4] (3c)] [1930s+] (*orig. US*) a photographer; both a professional and an enthusastic amateur. ❑ **shutter clicker** *n.* [1940s] (*US black*) a cinema projectionist. ❑ **shutter-girl** *n.* [1930s] (*US*) a prostitute working from a room with shutters, attracting customers from the street. ❑ **shutter racket** *n.* [RACKET *n.*[1] (1)] [early 19C] a robbery committed by boring through a shutter, removing a pane of glass and reaching through for anything to steal. ❑ **shutter-racket worker** *n.* [WORKER *n.*[1] (1)] [early 19C] one who specializes in such robberies.

shuttered *adj.*[1] [late 19C] taken away on a shutter, esp. of drunkards.

shuttered *adj.*[2] [SE *shutter*, which one pulls down over one's shame] [late 19C] in a state of total ignominy.

shutters *n.* **1** [late 19C+] (*US black*) the eyes. **2** [1940s] in fig. use, the end, finality. **3** [1990s+] the eyelids.

shuttle *n.* [euph.; the weaver's *shuttle* goes backwards and forwards/in and out] [late 17C] the penis.

SE in slang uses

IN COMPOUNDS

❑ **shuttlebutt** *n.* [SE *shuttle*, i.e. its movement backwards and forwards + BUTT *n.*[1] (1a); play on SCUTTLEBUTT *n.*] [1970s+] (*US campus*) a fat woman, esp. referring to the buttocks. ❑ **shuttle-headed** *adj.* (*also* **shuttle-witted**) [mid-17C] (*US*) garrulous.

shut up *adj.* [mid-19C] thoroughly exhausted.

shut up *v.* **1** [mid-17C+] to stop talking. **2** [early 19C+] to bring to an end, to reduce to a state of incapacity, to kill. **3** [mid-19C+] (*also* **shut**) to stop someone else talking, or making a noise.

SE in slang uses

IN PHRASES

❑ **shut up in the parson's pound** *adj.* [late 18C–early 19C] married. ❑ **shut up one's garret** *v. see under* GARRET *n.* ❑ **shut up shop** *v. see under* SHOP *n.*[1]. ❑ **shut up someone's shop** *v. see under* SHOP *n.*[1].

shut up! *excl.* **1** [mid-19C+] be quiet! stop talking! **2** [1980s+] a general excl. of disbelief, you can't fool me! forget it! don't make me laugh!

shuvly-cowss *n.* (*also* **shuvly-kouse**) [the term was popularized when a 'half-witted girl used it […] in a police court' (Ware)] [late 19C] a public house.

shv… *see also under* SCHW…

shvitz *v.* [synon. Yid.] [20C+] to sweat.

shvoogie *n. see* SCHVUG *n.*

shy *see also under* SHYLOCK.

shy *n.* [ety. unknown; *OED* suggests link to SE *shy cock*, a cowardly cock and thus person, but the logic is hard to comprehend – unless one had to throw the cock at its opponent] **1** [late 18C–19C] a quick, jerking or careless throw, as of a stone etc. **2** [mid-19C] an attempt to damage by sarcasm or verbal attack. **3** [mid-19C–1920s] an attempt, a 'go'.

IN PHRASES

❑ **have a shy for** *v.* [1920s+] (*Aus.*) to search for.

shy *adj.*[1] [orig. gambling] [mid-19C+] doubtful in amount or quality.

shy *adj.*[2] [late 19C+] (*orig. US*) short of, esp. short of money.

shyckle *n. see* SCHYCKLE *n.*

shy-cock *n.* [SE *shy-cock*, a fighting cock that will not fight; but ? pun on *Shylock*, one who does not wish to let go of their money] **1** [mid-18C–mid-19C] one who hides from the bailiff. **2** [late 18C–early 19C] a coward.

shyin' *adj. see* SHINE *adj.*[1].

shylock *n.* (*also* **shy**) [the money-lender in Shakespeare's *Merchant of Venice* (1600)] **1** [mid-19C+] one who supplies private loans. **2** [1900s–10s] (*also* **sherlock**) a crooked businessman. **3** [1930s] derog. generic for a Jew.

shylock *v.* (*also* **shy**) [SHYLOCK *n.*] **1** [20C+] to lend money at extortionate rates of interest. **2** [1950s–70s] to offer 'protection'.

shypoo *n.* [SHYPOO *adj.*] [20C+] (*Aus./N.Z*) **1** second-rate liquor; beer. **2** (*also* **shypoo house, …joint, …shanty, …shop**) the place that sells such liquor.

shypoo *adj.* [ety. unknown; ? 'bastard Chinese' (citation in *AND*) for 'soft drink'; ? Canton. *sai po*, a small shop] [20C+] (*Aus./N.Z.*) second-rate, inferior.

shyser *n. see* SHICER *n.*

shyst *adj.* [backform. f. SHYSTY *adj.* (2)] [2000s] (*UK black/teen*) aggressive, promiscuous.

shyster *n.* (*also* **shice, shise, shyster lawyer**) [Ger. *Scheisser*, shitter or Du. *scheidsman* or *schiedsreichter*, an arbitrator, an umpire. Alternatively, f. a New York lawyer named *Scheuster* (pron. *shyster*), whose courtroom antics so infuriated Justice Osborne of the city's Essex Market Court that he began talking of 'scheuster' practices; for full discussion *see* Quinion, *World Wide*

Words (2004)] **1** [mid-19C+] (*orig. US*) a lawyer, usu. a crooked one, or with the implication that any lawyer is innately untrustworthy. **2** [mid-19C+] a general term of abuse. **3** [1920s–30s] a crooked business man. **4** [1930s] (*UK Und.*) one who refuses to pay their debts. **5** *see* SHICER *n.* (6).

shyster *adj.* [SHYSTER *n.*] [mid-19C+] (*US*) crooked, corrupt; fraudulent.

shystering *adj.* [SHYSTER *n.*] [mid-19C+] as a derog. epithet, describing one who tricks money out of someone.

shysty *adj.* (*also* **scheisty**) [SHYSTER *n.*] **1** [mid-19C+] (*US*) tight-fisted. **2** [1990s+] (*orig. US*) a general negative, used of situations, objects and primarily people, in which case a degree of arrogance/cockiness is implied.

Siamese twins *n.* [mid-19C] (*US*) fish balls.

Siberia *n.* [*Siberia*, centre of the Russian *gulag*] [1930s+] (*US prison*) **1** the solitary confinement cells. **2** Sing Sing Penitentiary, New York. **3** Clinton Prison, Dannemora, New York. **4** in fig. use, abandoned, ignored 'sent to Coventry'.

si-buxom *n. see* SYEBUCK *n.*

sice *n.* [14C SE *sice*, the six on a die] [mid-17C–mid-19C] sixpence.

siced *adj.* [2000s] (*US black*) angry.

sices *n.* [14C SE *sice*, the six on a die] [mid-19C] in dice-playing, a throw of six.

sick *n.* (*also* **sickness**) **1** [late 19C] illness. **2** [1930s+] (*drugs*) (*also* **kick-sick**) the illness that accompanies withdrawal from drug addiction.

IN PHRASES

❑ **good sick** *n.* [1950s+] (*drugs*) the short-lived bout of vomiting that can follow an injection of heroin.

SE in slang uses

IN PHRASES

❑ **give someone the sick(s)** *v.* [mid-19C–1950s] to disgust.

sick *adj.*[1] **1** [mid-19C] (*US Und.*) imprisoned. **2** [mid-19C; 1980s+] (*US campus*) a general pej., of poor quality, unfashionable, unappealing, stupid, weak, bizarre. **3** [mid-19C+] annoyed, worried, disgusted, often with undertones of jealousy. **4** [1950s+] (*US*) mentally disturbed, psychopathic, esp. in a sadistic way. **5** [1950s+] (*orig. US*) morbid, depraved, e.g. a sick sense of humour. **6** [1980s+] (*Aus./US campus*) excellent, first-rate [on the bad = good model].

IN COMPOUNDS

❑ **sick-ass** *adj. see* sepaerate entry.

IN PHRASES

❑ **knock someone sick** *v.* [1900s–20s] to amaze, to astonish. ❑ **sick and wrong** *adj.* [1980s+] (*US campus*) a general pej., absolutely impossible, unthinkable, totally disgusting; also used ironically. ❑ **sick as...** *adj. see* separate entry. ❑ **sick in fourteen languages** *adj.* [late 19C] (*US*) very sick.

sick *adj.*[2] [1930s+] (*drugs*) suffering from withdrawal symptoms when addicted to narcotics, esp. heroin.

IN PHRASES

❑ **go sick** *v.* [1980s+] to suffer withdrawal symptoms.

sick-ass *adj.* [SICK *adj.*[1] (5) + -ASS *sfx*] [1990s+] (*US*) unpleasant, crazy.

sick as... *adj.*

IN PHRASES

❑ **...a cat** *adj.* [late 17C; mid-19C+] very sick; also fig. use. ❑ **...a cushion** *adj.* [late 17C–late 18C] very hungry, thus not sick at all. ❑ **...a dog** *adj.* (*also* **dog-sick**) [late 16C+] very sick; also fig. use; thus ext. (*Aus.*) *sick as a blackfellow's dog*. ❑ **...a horse** *adj.* (*also* **...a mule**) [a horse cannot vomit, so such sickness has no immediate relief] [mid-18C–1930s] extremely ill. ❑ **...a parrot** *adj.* [the term became widespread as the clichéd response attributed to many sportsmen, esp. soccer players and managers, after a loss or defeat. Note 17C *melancholy as a parrot*, quoted by Partridge] [1970s+] extremely depressed, usu. mentally rather than physically distressed. ❑ **...a rat** *adj.* [late 19C+] very sick. ❑ **...mud** *adj.* [1930s] very depressed or upset.

sickener *n.* (*also* **sickner**) **1** [19C+] anything depressing, disappointing, frustrating. **2** [late 19C] an excess.

sickie *n.*[1] [SE *sickleave*] [1950s+] (*Aus.*) a day's sick leave.

IN PHRASES

❑ **throw a sickie** *v.* (*also* **chuck..., pull...**) [1970s+] to take the day off sick, esp. when one is perfectly healthy.

sickie *n.*[2] [SICK *adj.*[2]] **1** [1960s] a heroin addict. **2** [1960s] (*US campus*) a homosexual. **3** [1960s+] (*orig. US*) (*also* **sicky**) anyone considered to be 'sick in the head', insane, crazy [SICK *adj.*[1] (4)].

sickle *n.* [1940s–50s] (*US teen*) a motorcycle police officer.

sickner *n. see* SICKENER *n.*

sickness *n. see* SICK *n.*

sicko *n.* (*also* **sicksicksick**) [SICK *adj.*[1] (4)] [1970s+] a mentally unstable person, with overtones of sexual perversion.

sicko *adj.* [SICKO *n.*] [1970s+] perverted, insane.

sick on *v. see* SIC ON *v.*

sickrel *n.* [SE *sick* + sfx *-rel*] [late 17C–early 18C] a puny, weak, sickly person.

sicksicksick *n. see* SICKO *n.*

sicky *n. see* SICKIE *n.*[2] (3).

sic on *v.* (*also* **seek on, sick on**) [SE *sick on*, to set a dog on] [mid-19C+] to set on, to have someone attack a third party, to set someone on another person.

side *n.* **1** [late 19C+] pretentiousness, swagger, conceit; usu. in *put on side*, to give oneself airs [? play on billiards jargon *side*, spin or dial. *side*, proud; post-1940s use tends to be consciously archaic]. **2** in geog. senses. (**a**) [1930s] (*US*) America, as opposed to England. (**b**) [1960s] (*orig. US black*) the black area of town; the original was Chicago's *South Side*. (**c**) [1970s+] an area of a town or city; used (in London) as *West Side*, *South Side*, meaning Shepherd's Bush or Brixton – somewhat romanticized analogies with areas of US cities. **3** [1930s–80s] (*US black*) a gramophone or vinyl record. **4** [1960s+] (*US black*) a woman [ideally she is on or at one's *side* in all circumstances].

DERIVATIVES

❑ **sidey** *adj.* (*also* **sidy**) [late 19C–1940s] conceited.

IN PHRASES

❑ **bung on side** *v.* (*also* **bung on swerve**) [BUNG *v.* (3) + sense 1 above/SE *swerve* + pun on billiards/snooker use] [1950s+] (*Aus.*) to show off. ❑ **more side than a billiard ball** [1950s+] (*Aus.*) very arrogant, snobbish.

SE in slang uses

IN COMPOUNDS

❑ **side-splitter/-splitting** *see* separate entries.

IN PHRASES

❑ **drive on the other side of the road** *v. see under* DRIVE *v.*[1]. ❑ **go off the side** *v.* [1930s–40s] (*UK Und.*) to abscond, e.g. when a criminal runs off with a gang's spoils. ❑ **on the side** **1** [late 19C+] quietly; in secret, esp. in phr. *a bit on the side*, a clandestine lover. **2** of a sexual relationship, illicit, clandestine. ❑ **over the side** [1910s+] away from one's home or place of work. ❑ **side of a funeral** *n.* [late 19C] (*US*) pork chops.

side *adj.* [ON THE SIDE *under* SIDE *n.*] [20C+] surreptitious, clandestine.

IN COMPOUNDS

❑ **side action** *n.* [1990s+] an illicit affair. ❑ **side chick** *n.* (*also* **side-gal**) [1920s+] a woman who is an alternative to a man's wife or regular girlfriend. ❑ **side dish** *n.* [1940s] (*US Und.*) a mistress. ❑ **side money** *n.* [1920s–60s] (*US*) money earned in addition to one's regular job. ❑ **side partner** *n.* [late 19C–1920s] (*US*) an accomplice, an assistant. ❑ **side pen** *n.* [1930s] (*US*) an associate, a partner.

SE in slang uses

IN COMPOUNDS

❑ **sidearms** *n.* [1940s] (*US milit.*) cream and sugar; salt and pepper. ❑ **sideboard** *n.* **1** [mid–late 19C] a stand-up collar. **2** [mid-19C+] side-whiskers. ❑ **side boys** *n.* [1900s] (*US*) a style of side whiskers. ❑ **sidekick/sidekicker** *n. see* separate entries. ❑ **side levers** *n.* [1920s+] sideburns, side-whiskers. ❑ **side-pocket** *n.* **1** [late 18C–early 19C] used in a variety of phrs. implying a lack of need, e.g. *as much need of a wife as a dog of a side-pocket*, of a worn-out old man; *want as much as a toad/dog wants a side-pocket*, does not want/need at all. **2** [late 19C] (*US*) an out-of-the-way drinking saloon. ❑ **side-pork** *n.* [the similarity in colour of the meat and the human skin-tone] [1950s] (*W.I.*) an albino. ❑ **side-sim** *n.* [abbr. *simpleton* or abbr. *Simon*, as in late 16C *Sim subtle*, a cunning fellow] [early 17C] a fool, a simpleton. ❑ **side-scrapers** *n.* [late 19C] (*middle class*) short sideburns, fashionable 1879–8. ❑ **sidetrack** *v.* [1920s–60s] (*US Und.*) to arrest. ❑ **side valve** *v.* [1980s+] (*Aus. prison*) to act the gangster. ❑ **sidewalk** *n. see* separate entry. ❑ **sideways** *see* separate entries. ❑ **side-wheeler** *n.* [20C+] (*US, orig. baseball jargon*) a left-handed person. ❑ **sidewinder** *n.* **1** [mid–late 19C] a powerful blow. **2** [1940s+] a thug, esp. a gangster's bodyguard. **3** [1940s+] in fig. use, something powerful. ❑ **side wings** *n.* [late 19C–1900s] sideburns, side-whiskers.

IN PHRASES

❑ **side-door Pullman** *n.* [from the side-opening doors of the freight wagon. The real Pullman is a luxury passenger coach] [late 19C–1920s] (*US tramp*) a freight car. ❑ **side-hill salmon** *n.* [1950s] (*US*) bacon.

side *v.* [SIDE *n.*] [1910s] to act in a pretentious manner, to put on airs.

IN PHRASES

❑ **sidebust** *v.* [1990s+] (*US black*) to gossip, to tell tales.

sidedywry *adj.* [SE *side* + *awry*] [late 18C–early 19C] crooked.

sidekick *n.*[1] [backform. f. SIDEKICKER *n.*] [20C+] (*Aus./US*) **1** an assistant, a partner, an accomplice. **2** in fig. use; something on which one depends; a regular pleasure.

sidekick *n.*[2] [SE *side* + KICK *n.*[4]] [1910s–50s] (*US Und.*) a side pocket.

sidekicker *n.* [ext. SIDEKICK *n.*[1] (1)] [1900s–30s] (*Aus./US*) an assistant, a partner, an accomplice.

sides *n.* [1920s–40s] (*US black*) padding used by women to enlarge the appearance of the hips.

side-splitter *n.* [mid-19C+] something exceedingly funny.

side-splitting *adj.* [mid-19C+] extremely funny.

sidewalk *n.*

SE in slang uses

IN COMPOUNDS

❑ **sidewalk snail** *n.* [their slow and steady pace] [1930s–50s] (*US*) a police officer. ❑ **sidewalk superintendent** *n. see* SUPERINTENDENT OF THE PAVEMENT *under* PAVEMENT *n.* ❑ **sidewalk surfer** *n.* [1970s+] (*US*) a skate-boarder. ❑ **sidewalk surfing** *n.* [1970s+] (*US*) skate-boarding. ❑ **sidewalk surveyor** *n.* [1920s] (*US*) a drunkard. ❑ **sidewalk susie** *n.* [mid-19C] a prostitute.

IN PHRASES

❑ **dust the sidewalk** *v. see under* DUST *v.*[1]. ❑ **hit the sidewalk** *v.* [20C+] (*US*) to walk the streets searching for a job. ❑ **roll up the sidewalk** *v.* [mid-19C] (*US*) of shops and entertainments in towns or cities, to close down at nightfall. ❑ **superintendent of the sidewalk** *n. see* SUPERINTENDENT OF THE PAVEMENT *under* PAVEMENT *n.*

sideways *n.* [euph.; weak rhy. sl.] [1960s+] (*N.Z. prison/US campus*) suicide.

sideways *adj.* [1990s+] (*US prison*) eccentric.

SE in slang uses

IN PHRASES

❑ **go sideways** *v.* [late 19C] (*UK Und.*) to commit a crime.

sideways *phr.* [1990s+] (*US black*) a general excl. of departure, I'm off, goodbye, see you later.

sidge *n.* [abbr.] [1970s] (*US Und.*) a Sicilian.

sidies *n.* [abbr.] [1960s] *side*burns.

siding *n.* [1980s+] (*US black/Los Angeles*) leaning to the side in an exaggeratedly relaxed manner while driving.

sidity/siditty *adj. see* SADDITY *adj.*

Sidney rocks *n.* (*also* **Charley rocks**) [rhy. sl.] [1920s–30s] (*US*) socks.

siege *n.* [Lat. *sedem*, a seat + 16C *siege*, a privy] [mid-16C–17C] excrement.

sieg heils *n.* [rhy. sl. = piles] [2000s] haemorrhoids.

sies! *excl. see* SIS! *excl.*

Sif *n.* [abbr.] [1970s] (*US*) San Francisco.

sif/siff *n. see* SYPH *n.*

sift *v.*[1] [such that would pass through a sieve] [mid–late 19C] **1** to steal small coins. **2** emptying out a wallet or purse to identify and extract cash and valuables.

sift *v.*[2] [SE *shift*] [20C+] (*US/UK black*) to move, to start moving.

IN PHRASES

❑ **sift in** *v.* [20C+] (*US/UK black*) to arrive.

sifting *n.* [2000s] (*N.Z.*) the act of relaxing.

sig *v. see* SIGNIFY *v.*

sigging *n.* [SIGNIFY *v.*] [1940s] (*US black*) competing in rounds of ritualized mockery.

siggy *n. see* CIGGIE *n.*

sigh *v.* [1960s] (*S.Afr.*) to complain.

sigher *n. see* GROANER *n.*

sighs and tears *n.* [rhy. sl.] [1930s+] (*US Und.*) ears.

sight *n.*[1] [early 18C–mid-19C] a gesture of derision, made by placing the thumb on the tip of one's nose and spreading out the fingers like a fan; thus *double sight*, the same gesture, intensified by joining the tip of the little finger to the thumb of the other hand, which in turn has its fingers extended fanwise.

IN PHRASES

❑ **have a sight on** *v.* [mid-19C] to have a strong negative opinion, to behave in an outrageous manner. ❑ **take a sight at** *v.* (*also* **take double sights**) [mid–late 19C] to place the thumb against the nose and close all the fingers except the little one, which is agitated as a token of derision.

SE in slang uses

IN COMPOUNDS

❑ **sight delight** *n.* [1980s+] (*US campus*) a good–looking man. ❑ **sightseers** *n.* [1970s+] (*UK Und.*) the crowd that gathers round illicit street traders or gamblers.

IN PHRASES

❑ **out of sight** *see* separate entries. ❑ **sight for sore eyes** *n.* (*also* **flap for sore eyes, sight for bum eyes**) [mid-19C+] a welcome appearance, often used as an affectionate greeting, *you're a sight for sore eyes*.

IN EXCLAMATIONS

❑ **darn one's sight!** *see* DAMN ONE'S EYES! *under* DAMN! *excl.*

sight *n.*[2] [early 19C+] a good deal, a large amount, usu. in phr. *a sight more*; usu. prefixed with *darned, bloody, dashed* etc.

IN PHRASES

❑ **by a long sight** *adv.* (*also* **by a considerable sight, by a damn sight, by a darn(ed) sight, by a durn sight**) [early 19C+] (*US*) by a long way, by a good deal; usu. as a negative and thus + pfx *not...*

sight *v.* **1** [1910s+] (*Aus.*) to tolerate, to put up with. **2** [1930s; 1970s+] (*UK Und/UK black*) to observe, to see.

sight? *excl.* [1950s+] (*W.I. Rasta*) do you understand?

sigmunds *n.* [rhy. sl. *sigmund freuds*; ult. Austrian neurologist *Sigmund Freud* (1856–1939)] [1990s+] haemorrhoids.

sign *n.*

SE in slang uses

IN COMPOUNDS

❑ **signboard** *n.* [late 19C–1900s] the human face.

IN PHRASES

❑ **give someone the sign** *v.* [1950s] to make a gesture of recognition, usu. indicating that all is well, 'the coast is clear'. ❑ **sign of a house to let** *n.* (*also* **sign of tenements to let**) [ext. of APARTMENT TO LET *n.* (3)] [late 18C–early 19C] a widow's weeds. ❑ **sign of the five shillings** *n.* [SE *five shillings* (25p), the value of the obsolete crown piece] [late 18C–early 19C] any public house called the Crown; thus the *sign of the ten shillings*, the Two Crowns; …*fifteen shillings*, the Three Crowns.

IN EXCLAMATIONS

❑ **signs on you!** (*also* **sign's on it!**) [1920s+] (*orig. Irish*) bad luck to you! consequences will follow!

signification *n.* [SIGNIFY *v.*] [20C+] (*US black*) negative or hostile talk, criticism, ritualized abuse.

signifier *n.* [SIGNIFY *v.*] [1930s+] (*US black*) one who boasts or makes insulting remarks.

signify *v.* (*also* **sig**) (*US black*) **1** [1920s+] to boast or to pretend to a greater sophistication than one actually possesses. **2** [1930s+] to cause trouble, to stir things up, often purely for fun, whatever the actual results. **3** [1930s+] to recite one of a variety of purpose-written 'tales', usu. recounting the exploits of some mythical gangster-cum-sexual athlete. **4** [1950s] to lure, to talk in a persuasive manner. **5** [1990s+] to chatter, to gossip.

signifying *n.* [SIGNIFY *v.*] [1940s+] (*US black*) boasting, insinuating; esp. in the form of a ritual game of testing a rival's emotional strength by insulting their relatives.

sign on *v.* [1980s+] (*Aus. prison*) to enter into a stable homosexual relationship.

sign up *v.* [1970s] (*Aus. Und.*) to make a written confession.

sigoggling *adj. see* SKYGODLIN *adj.*

Sigourney Weaver *n.* [rhy. sl. = BEAVER *n.*[1] (5); ult. US film star *Sigourney Weaver* (b.1949)] [1990s+] the female genitals, esp. the pubic hair.

sigster *n.* [ety. unknown; ? echoic, thus predecessor of Z *n.*[1]] [mid-19C] a nap, a short sleep.

sike! *excl. see* PSYCH! *excl.*

sil *adj.* (*also* **sill**) [abbr. SE *silly about*] [1930s+] foolish; thus of a homosexual, involved in an affair.

silence *v.* [early 18C+] to stun, to knock down; to kill.

silencer *n.* [SILENCE *v.* (1)] [19C+] a stunning blow.

silent *adj.* [early 18C] murdered.

SE in slang uses

IN COMPOUNDS

❑ **silent beard** *n.* [development of 18C BEARD *n.* (1)] [18C] the pubic hair; the vagina. ❑ **silent beef** *see* separate entries. ❑ **silent city** *n.* [1970s] (*US black*) a graveyard. ❑ **silent cop** *n.* [SE *silent* + COP *n.*[1] (1)] [1930s+] (*Aus.*) a yellow 'sleeping policeman' placed in the centre of road intersections. ❑ **silent flute** *n.* [early 18C–early 19C] the penis. ❑ **silent woman** *n. see* GOOD WOMAN *under* GOOD *adj.*[1].

IN PHRASES

❑ **silent but deadly** (*also* **silent but violent**) [1950s+] describing a silent, but very smelly, breaking of wind.

silent beef *n.* [SE *silent* + BEEF *n.*[2] (4)] [1960s+] (*US Und.*) a note attached to an individual's police record stating that they have been suspected (but not charged due to lack of proof) of committing a crime; the note requests that they be punished to the maximum extent for such lesser charges that can be brought.

silent beef *v.* [1990s+] (*US Und.*) to attach a note to an individual's police record stating that they have been suspected (but not charged due to lack of proof) of committing a crime; the note requests that they be punished to the maximum extent for such lesser charges that can be brought.

silent night *n.* [rhy. sl.] [20C+] light (ale).

Silicon Valley *n.* [the use of silicon in microchip manufacturing; the 'Siliconia' list (1999) includes — SILICON ALLEY New York City [first noted 1995]; SILICON BEACH Santa Barbara, California [1997]; SILICON BOG The midlands of Ireland [1995]; SILICON CITY Chicago [1998]; SILICON DESERT Phoenix, Arizona [1992]; SILICON DITCH M4 Corridor, west of London [1999]; SILICON FEN Cambridge, England [1998]; SILICON FOREST Seattle, Washington [1997]; SILICON GLEN Around Livingston, Scotland [1985]; SILICON GULCH San Jose, California [date not known]; SILICON HILL Around Hudson, Massachusetts [1990]; SILICON ISLAND St. John, Virgin Islands [1998]; SILICON ISLE Ireland [1997]; SILICON NECKLACE Suburbs of Boston [1979]; SILICON PLAIN Kempele, Finland [1996]; SILICON PLAINS Lincoln, Nebraska [1980s]; SILICON PLATEAU Bangalore, India [1995]; SILICON RIVER Area in Missouri, US [1996]; SILICON TUNDRA Area around Ottawa, Canada [c.2002]; SILICON VALLEY Fairfield, Iowa [1997]; SILICON VALLEY OF THE EAST Penang State, Malaysia [1998]; SILICON WADI Israel [1997]; BILLY-CAN VALLEY Arnhem Land, Australia [1996]] [1980s+] Santa Clara County, California, home of the USA's microchip technology industry.

silk *n.* **1** [mid-19C; 1960s+] (*US black*) a white person; also as adj. [the supposed wearing of silk clothes by (rich) whites]. **2** [1910s] (*US*) in fig. use, courage, integrity. **3** [1940s+] (*US black*) in pl., expensive clothing, poss. actually made of silk [SE early 16C–19C]. **4** [1980s] (*US*) an authority figure [the supposed wearing of silk clothes by (rich) whites]. **5** *see* SILK BROAD below.

DERIVATIVES

❑ **silker** *n.* [late 19C–1900s] (*US*) a silk top-hat. ❑ **silkies** *n.* [1980s] (*US*) silk women's underwear.

IN COMPOUNDS

❑ **silk broad** *n.* (*also* **silk**) [BROAD *n.*[2] (3)] [1930s–50s] (*US black*) a white woman. ❑ **silk stocking** *n. see* separate entry. ❑ **silk snatcher** *n.* **1** [early 18C–early 19C] a thief who grabs the bonnets and hats from pedestrians. **2** [mid-18C] (*UK Und.*) a thief who specializes in stealing cloaks by twitching them from the wearer's back. ❑ **silkworm** *n.* **1** [early–mid-18C] a woman who tours clothes shops and examines the goods but never buys. **2** [late 19C–mid-20C] (*US/UK Und.*) a shoplifter who specializes in silk items or jewellery.

IN PHRASES

❑ **hit the silk** *v.* [the silk that makes the parachute canopy] **1** [1940s–50s] (*US*) to bail out of an aeroplane using a parachute. **2** [1940s+] (*orig. US*) thus, to bail out of any situation. ❑ **pure silk** *n.* [an image of softness and smoothness] [1970s] (*US black*) a male homosexual. ❑ **silked (to the bone)** *adj.* (*also* **silked out**) [sense 3 above + *TO THE BONE under* BONE *n.*[1]] [1930s+] (*US black*) dressed in the height of fashion.

silk *adj.* [1920s+] (*US*) admirable, excellent, acceptable.

silk and satin *n.*[1] [1970s+] (*drugs*) any combination of amphetamines and barbiturates or tranquillizers.

silk and satin *n.*[2] [ext. of *SILK BROAD under* SILK *n.*] [1970s+] (*US black*) an attractive white or light-skinned woman.

silk and top *n. see* STRING AND TOP *n.*

silk and twine *n.* (*also* **string and twine**) [rhy. sl.] [1920s–50s] (*US*) wine.

silko *n.* [ety. unknown] [2000s] (*Irish*) a thug, a thief.

silk stocking *n.* (*also* **silk hat, silk stockings**) [SILK STOCKING *adj.*] [late 19C+] (*US; later US black*) a rich person; in pl., the social élite.

silk stocking *adj.* [metonymy; such stockings, as opposed to the more usual cotton stockings, were a luxury item until the invention of nylon *c.*1935] [late 18C+] designating the social élite, pertaining to the wealthy.

sill *adj. see* SIL *adj.*

sillikin *n.* (*also* **silliken**) [SE *silly* + dimin. sfx *-kin*] [mid-19C–1910s] a fool, a simpleton.

silly *n.*[1] [mid-19C+] a foolish person.

silly *n.*[2] [? it makes one 'feel silly'] [1970s] (*N.Z. juv.*) an erection.

silly *adj.*

SE in slang uses

IN COMPOUNDS

❑ **silly-arse** *n.* [1990s+] (*Aus.*) a fool. ❑ **silly-ass** *adj.* (*also* **silly-arse, silly-assed**) **1** [1910s+] a general term of disparagement, the implication is of stupidity. **2** [1940s+] foolish. ❑ **silly billy** *n.* (*also* **silly billie**) [SE *silly billy*, a clown's stooge] [mid-19C+] a fool, a simpleton. ❑ **silly-bollocks** *n. see* BALLOCKS *n.* (5). ❑ **silly-born** *adj.* [1940s–50s] stupid, foolish. ❑ **silly cow** *n.* [COW *n.*[1] (1)] **1** [late 19C+] a derog. ref. to a woman, irrespective of her actual character. **2** [1910s] a man. **3** [2000s] used in a homosexual context. ❑ **silly house** *n.* [1960s] a psychiatric institution. ❑ **silly moo** *n.* [this softened version of SILLY COW above enjoyed a nationwide revival in the UK in the late 1960s with the success of the TV sitcom *Till Death Us Do Part*, in which it was used by Alf Garnett (played by Warren Mitchell) as a knee-jerk description of his put-upon wife] [late 19C+] a stupid woman. ❑ **sillypop** *n.* [late 19C] a fool, esp. a foolish, flighty woman. ❑ **silly putty** *n.* [joc. use of proprietory name of the children's toy] [1960s+] (*drugs*) psilocybin/psilocin. ❑ **silly season** *n.* [note journalists' jargon *silly season*, the summer holiday period, esp. August, when no real news is supposed to happen] [20C+] (*Aus.*) the Christmas holidays. ❑ **silly willy** *n.* [mid-17C–18C; 1960s] a fool, a simpleton.

(IN PHRASES)

❑ **silly as...** *adj.* see separate entry.

(IN EXCLAMATIONS)

❑ **silly grin!** [1910s] (*Aus.*) an ironic excl. on encountering pain or bad luck.

silly *v.* [mid–late 19C] to stun, i.e. to render silly or 'insensible'.

silly as... *adj.* used in phrs., usu. meaning extremely silly or foolish.

(IN PHRASES)

❑ **...a bag** [1930s+] (*Aus./N.Z.*) ❑ **...a chook (with its head cut off)** (*also* **silly as a curlew**) [1940s+] (*Aus./N.Z.*) **1** extremely silly. **2** tipsy, drunk. ❑ **...a cut snake** [1930s+] (*Aus./N.Z.*) ❑ **...a hatful of arseholes** [ARSEHOLE *n.* (1)] [1940s–50s] (*Aus.*) ❑ **...a hatful of worms** [1950s+] (*orig. Aus.*) ❑ **...a two-bob watch** (*also* **crazy as a two-bob watch, mad as..., silly as a Woolworth's watch**) [1940s+] (*Aus.*) ❑ **...a wet hen** [1980s+] (*N.Z.*) **1** extremely foolish. **2** drunk. ❑ **...a wet weekend** [1990s+] (*Aus.*) ❑ **...a wheel** [1950s+] (*Aus.*)

silo *n.* [1910s] (*US*) an alcohol made of fermented vegetables.

silver *n.* [1980s+] (*N.Z. drugs*) aluminium foil, used for smoking heroin.

silver *adj.*

SE in slang uses, based on colour

(IN COMPOUNDS)

❑ **silver bangle** *n.* [1990s+] (*W.I.*) handcuffs. ❑ **silver beggar** *n.* **1** [mid-19C] a counterfeit banknote or forged document. **2** [mid–late 19C] (*also* **silver lurker**) a beggar who claims to have suffered in some disaster or other, e.g. a fire or shipwreck, and asks for money in order to rebuild their life; such pleas are accompanied by a variety of documents, supposedly 'proving' the legitimacy of their claims. ❑ **silver cooper** *n.* [naut. jargon, the press gang, who 'cooped up' men for a payment of silver coins] [19C] a kidnapper. ❑ **silver hell** *n.* [SE *silver*, fig. inferior to gold + HELL *n.* (2c)] [mid-19C] a low-class casino. ❑ **silver jeff** *n.* [the image of Thomas *Jefferson* on the nickel, ? presumably confused with that of George Washington on the quarter] [1950s] (*US*) a quarter or a nickel coin. ❑ **silver-laced** *adj.* [SE *silver-laced*, silver-threaded] [19C] suffering from an infestation of lice. ❑ **silver pearl** *n.* [? the silveriness of this particular strain] [1990s+] (*drugs*) a type of marijuana. ❑ **silver pheasant** *n.* [1920s] a beautiful upper-class woman. ❑ **silver serpent** *n.* see SERPENT *n.* ❑ **silversmith** *n.* [mid-19C] (*UK Und.*) a pawnbroker. ❑ **silvertail** see separate entries. ❑ **silver-wig** *n.* [SE *wig*/WIG *n.*[2] (1)] [1920s] a grey-haired man. ❑ **silver wing** *n.* [the engraving of eagle's wings on the coin] [1950s] (*US*) a 50-cent piece.

silver and gold *n.* [rhy. sl.] [1990s+] a cold.

silver (and gold) *adj.* [rhy. sl.; the image is of ageing hair] [1990s+] old.

silverback riding *n.* [2000s] (*US black*) male homosexual intercourse.

silver plate *phr.* [Fr. *s'il vous plait*; revived in campus use] [1910s–20s; 1990s+] please.

silver spoon *n.* [rhy. sl.] **1** [20C+] (*Aus.*) the moon. **2** [1990s+] a pimp [= HOON *n.* (2)].

silvertail *n.* [SE *silver* + TAIL *n.* (2)] **1** [late 19C+] (*orig. Aus.*) a wealthy or upper-class person. **2** [1940s–50s] one who puts on 'airs and graces', a social climber. **3** [1940s–50s] (*UK prison*) a better-class prisoner. **4** [1980s+] (*Aus. prison*) a prisoner who colludes with the authorities.

silvertail *adj.* (*also* **silver-tailed**) [late 19C+] (*Aus.*) wealthy, upper-class.

silvery moon *n.* (*also* **silvery**) [rhy. sl.] **1** [1950s+] a derog. term for a black person [= COON *n.* (5)]. **2** [1970s+] (*Aus.*) a pimp [= HOON *n.* (2)].

sim *n.* [abbr. SE *simpleton*] [1990s+] (*Aus. Und.*) a fool, a dupe.

simkin *n.*[1] (*also* **simpkin**) [proper name *Simon*, presumably as in the nursery rhyme *Simple Simon*; note 19C theatrical jargon *Simkin* or *Simpkin*, the fool in (usu. comic) ballets] [late 17C+] a fool, a simpleton.

simkin *n.*[2] (*also* **simpkin**) [Ind. pron.] [mid–late 19C] (*Anglo-Ind.*) champagne.

simmer *v.* (*also* **simmer down**) [mid-19C+] to calm down.

simmon *n.* [abbr.] [late 18C+] per*simmon*, esp. in *simmon beer*.

simoleon *n.* (*also* **sambolio, samoleon, simoleum, simolion**) [? SIMON *n.*[1] (2) + SE *Napoleon*, a Fr. coin worth 20 francs] [late 19C+] (*US*) $1.

(DERIVATIVES)

❑ **simoleons** *n.* [late 19C+] (*US*) money.

simon *n.*[1] [for ety. *see* TANNER *n.*] **1** [late 17C–19C] a sixpence. **2** [late 19C+] (*US*) $1.

simon *n.*[2] **1** *see* SIMON PURE *n.* **2** *see* SIMPLE SIMON *n.*[1].

simon! *excl.* [Sp.] [1960s+] (*US*) yes!

simon legree *n.* [the character *Simon Legree*, the stereotypically evil slave-master, in the novel *Uncle Tom's Cabin* (1852) by Harriet Beecher Stowe] [20C+] (*US black*) a cruel overseer or employer.

simon pure *n.* (*also* **simon**) [proper name of a Quaker character in *A Bold Stroke for a Wife* (1718) by Susannah Centlivre; he is impersonated by another character during Act V] **1** [early 19C+] the genuine article, the real thing. **2** [1900s] poteen.

simon-pure *adj.* [mid-19C+] genuine, real.

simon soon gone *n.* [mid–late 16C] a lazy servant; 'He, that when his Mayster hath any thing to do, he will hide him out of the way' (Awdeley, *Fraternitie of Vagabondes*, c.1561).

simp *n.* [abbr.] [20C+] (*orig. US*) a fool, a *simp*leton.

simp *adj.* **1** [1970s] (*US campus*) easy [abbr. SE *simple*]. **2** [1980s+] the best [abbr. SE *simply* the best].

simp *v.* [SIMP *n.*] **1** [1900s] (*Aus.*) to do things in a simplistic manner. **2** [1960s] (*US black*) to act like a fool.

simper like a frumety-kettle *v.* (*also* **simper like a furmity-kettle**) [15C–18C SE *simper*, to simmer + *frumenty*, a dish made of hulled wheat boiled in milk and seasoned with cinnamon, sugar etc] [late 17C–19C] to smile, to look cheerful.

simping *n.* [SIMP *v.* (2)] [1970s] acting like a fool.

simpkin *n.* *see under* SIMKIN.

-simple *sfx* **1** [1920s+] (*US*) used with a variety of nouns to imply obsessiveness. **2** [1990s+] as sfx implying ignorant.

simple animal *n.* *see* ANIMAL *n.*[1] (6).

simple pimp *n.* [1950s–70s] (*US black*) one who barely manages as a pimp and has no hope of transcending that level of employment within the criminal hierarchy.

simpler *n.* [SE *simple*] [late 16C–early 17C] (*UK Und.*) the dupe or victim of a confidence trickster or a prostitute.

simple simon *n.*[1] (*also* **simon**) [the nursery rhyme] **1** [late 18C+] a fool, a simpleton. **2** [1950s] (*drugs*) a non-addict.

simple simon *n.*[2] [rhy. sl.] **1** [1910s–40s] a diamond, usu. a diamond ring. **2** [1970s] (*drugs*) psilocybin/psilocin.

simpson *n.* [one *Simpson*, a dairyman who c.1868 was prosecuted for watering down his milk supply] [late 19C] **1** water used in adulterating milk. **2** adulterated milk. **3** a milkman.

simpy *adj.* [SIMP *n.*] [1940s+] foolish, gullible.

sin *n.* [? his sinfulness] [2000s] (*US black*) a tough, aggressive black man.

SE in slang uses

DERIVATIVES

❑ **sinful** *adj.* [1920s+] excessive, far too much.

IN COMPOUNDS

❑ **sin bin** *n.* **1** [1950s+] (*orig. US; sports*) an enclosure where errant players, e.g. in ice hockey, have to sit for a pre-determined period of time. **2** [1950s+] (*orig. US; education*) a school to which otherwise uneducable pupils, whose activities have disrupted their original school, are sent as a last resort. **3** [1980s+] (*Aus.*) a van or car used primarily for sex. ❑ **sin-buster** *n.* [1930s–40s] (*US*) a clergyman. ❑ **Sin City** *n.* [1970s+] (*orig. US*) any city seen as a centre of vice and corruption, esp. Las Vegas, Nevada. ❑ **sin-hiders** *n.* [? they cover the male genitals] [late 19C] (*UK Und.*) trousers. ❑ **sin hound** *n.* [-HOUND *sfx*] [1920s–40s] (*orig. US black*) a priest. ❑ **sin-shifter** *n.* [? pun on SE *scene-shifter*] [1910s] (*Aus.*) any form of clergyman.

IN PHRASES

❑ **as sin** *adv. see* AS ALL HELL *under* HELL *n.* ❑ **like sin** *adv. see* LIKE HELL *under* HELL *n.*

sincanter *n.* [Fr. *cinquante*, fifty, which in 16C was considered old] [late 16C] a contemptuous or depreciatory term applied to men, usu. as *old...* .

sinch *n. see* CINCH *n.*[1].

sing *v.* [proverbial phr. 'he that sings once, weeps all his life after'; note Shakespearian *sing*, (of a woman) to make advances to; (of a man) to have sexual intercourse)] **1** [early 19C+] to speak. **2** [late 19C] to speak insincerely, hypocritically. **3** [1920s+] to make a confession, usu. to the authorities. **4** [1930s+] to inform against, to betray.

IN PHRASES

❑ **sing (a) placebo** *v. see under* PLACEBO *n.* ❑ **sing dumb** *v.* (*also* **sing dummy**) [SE *dumb*/DUMMY *n.*[1] (1)] [mid-19C] (*UK/US Und.*) to say nothing (esp. under interrogation). ❑ **sing like a canary** *v.* (*also* **...a bird, ...a lark, trill like a canary**) [1930s+] (*UK Und.*) to make a full confession to the police. ❑ **sing more like a whore's bird than a canary bird** *v. see under* WHORE *n.* ❑ **sing out** *v.* [sense 1 above, since it antedates sense 3 above + naut. jargon *sing out*, to call out; in later edns Scott offered a note: 'To sing out, or whistle in the cage, is when a rogue, being apprehended, peaches against his comrades.'] [early–mid-19C] of a villain, on being arrested, to betray their accomplices. ❑ **sing out beef** *v. see under* HOT BEEF! *excl.* ❑ **sing psalms** *v.* var. on SEE STARS *under* SEE *v.* ❑ **sing small** *v.* [mid-18C–1950s] to modify one's speech, esp. when it had previously been arrogant and boastful. ❑ **sing the blues** *v. see under* BLUES *n.*[1].

SE in slang uses

IN PHRASES

❑ **don't sing it** [one 'sings' an exaggerated tale] [late 19C–1900s] don't exaggerate. ❑ **go and sing 'sweet violets'** *v.* [euph.] [late 19C+] to defecate. ❑ **sing o-be-joyful** *v.* (*also* **sing oh-be-easy**) [late 18C–early 19C] to pretend to satisfaction when one wants, in fact, to complain but dare not. ❑ **sing on** *v.* [Carib.E. *sing on*, to sing a song or hymn with the intention of using its lyrics to mock a third party] [20C+] (*W.I.*) to gossip about. ❑ **sing one's song** *v.* [20C+] to make a remark, whether complimentary or otherwise. ❑ **sing the black psalm** *v.* [late 18C–early 19C] usu. of children, to weep. ❑ **sing the hallelujah chorus** *v.* [1990s+] (*US prison*) to be released from prison; to die in prison.

Singapore tummy *n.* [20C+] the diarrhoea that often afflicts travellers in foreign countries.

singer *n.* [SING *v.* (4)] [1930s–60s] (*US Und.*) an informer.

singe someone's eyebrows *v.* [1990s+] (*US gay*) to attack verbally.

singing *n.* [SING *v.* (4)] **1** [1930s+] the act of informing. **2** [1970s] (*US gay*) a sustained verbal attack.

single *n.* **1** [20C+] one cigarette. **2** [1930s+] (*US*) a $1 bill. **3** [1930s+] (*US*) a person, esp. a criminal, who works or lives alone. **4** [1960s] (*US Und.*) for a prostitute, a single act of paid intercourse.

single *adj.*

SE in slang uses

DERIVATIVES

❑ **single-o** *n.* [SE *single*/SINGLE *n.* (3) + -O *sfx* (1)] **1** [1930s] (*US*) an unmarried person. **2** [1930s–40s] (*US tramp*) a tramp who travels alone. **3** [1930s+] (*US Und.*) a criminal who works alone and the crimes they commit; thus also as adj., solo, working alone; also in non-criminal contexts.

IN COMPOUNDS

❑ **single broth** *n.* [17C] small beer. ❑ **single-duke** *v.* [1920s] (*US Und.*) to cheat one's confederates when dividing loot. ❑ **single peeper** *n.* [PEEPER *n.* (1)] [late 18C–early 19C] a one-eyed person. ❑ **single-pennif** *n.* [backsl. on FINNIF *n.*; PENNIF *n.*] **1** [mid–late 19C] a £5 note. **2** [20C+] £1.

single *v.* [SINGLE *n.* (3)] [1930s–40s] (*US*) to work as a criminal by oneself.

singleten *n.* (*also* **singleton**) [? SE *single*, simple or as an elision of a *single ten*; the ten in cards ranks one below the knave, 'he' must therefore be a fool] [late 17C–early 19C] a very foolish person.

singleton *n.*[1] [*Singleton*, a Dublin corkscrew maker, who lived 'in a place called Hell... his screws are famous for their excellent temper' (Grose, 1785)] [late 18C–early 19C] a corkscrew.

singleton *n.*[2] [popularized by Helen Fielding in *Bridget Jones's Diary* (1996)] [1990s+] an unmarried person.

Sinjin's Wood *n.* [the affectedly smart pron. of *St John's* + deliberate puns on the 'sin' and 'gin' available in St John's Wood, then an area of London notorious for its kept women and prostitutes] [late 19C] St John's Wood.

sink *n.* [mid-19C–1910s] a drunkard.

sink *v.* **1** [early 18C–19C] (*US Und.*) to embezzle the takings of an illegal card-game, confidence trick etc. **2** [late 18C+] to drink alcohol, e.g. *sink the amber*, to drink beer [note *Antidote against Melancholy* (1661) 'In a pint there's small heart, Sirah, bring a quart / [...] / Wee'l sink him before sunset']. **3** [late 19C–1900s] (*US*) to bury; also in fig. use. **4** [1900s] to betray, to inform on. **5** [1960s] (*US*) to hit.

IN EXCLAMATIONS

❑ **sink me!** (*also* **sink you!**) [mid-17C–1940s] a general oath.

SE in slang uses

IN COMPOUNDS

❑ **sink-hole** *n.* [mid–late 19C] the throat. ❑ **sink-pocket** *n.* [the winnings *sink* into his *pocket* and are lost there forever] [1910s] (*Aus.*) a winner at cards who leaves the game without offering a chance for his opponents to redeem their losses.

IN PHRASES

❑ **sink the black** *v.* [snooker imagery + ref. to the colour of stout] [1990s+] to drink stout. ❑ **sink the boot in** *v.* [var. on PUT THE BOOT IN *under* BOOT, THE *n.*] [1910s+] (*Aus./N.Z.*) to give a kicking. ❑ **sink the little man in the boat** *v. see under* LITTLE MAN (IN THE BOAT) *n.* ❑ **sink the sailor** *v.* [1960s] of a man, to have sexual intercourse. ❑ **sink the sausage** *v.* (*also* **sink the log, sink the shaft, sink the weenie**) [SAUSAGE *n.* (2)/LOG *n.* (6)/SHAFT *n.* (1a)/WEENIE *n.*[1] (4)] [1960s+] to have sexual intercourse; to have anal intercourse.

sinker *n.*[1] [SINK *v.*] **1** [early 18C–19C] (*US Und.*) one who cheats his partner(s) in crime by embezzling the takings of a scam. **2** [late 18C+] a drunkard [later use Aus.]. **3** [1960s] (*S.Afr.*) a judge.

sinker *n.*[2] **1** [late 18C–mid-19C] (*UK Und.*) in pl., old stockings that, through wear, have developed mis-shapen heels. **2** in monetary senses [SE *sinker*, a small circular lead weight]. (**a**) [mid–late 19C] a counterfeit coin. (**b**) [late 19C–1900s] (*US*) $1. (**c**) [1930s] (*UK tramp*) a shilling (5p). **3** [late 19C+] (*US*) any form of doughy cake, esp. a doughnut [the habit of dunking or 'sinking' a doughnut into one's coffee].

IN PHRASES

❑ **sinkers and** *n. see* COFFEE-AND *n.* (1).

sinks *n.* [Fr. *cinq*, five] [mid-19C] in dice-playing, a throw of five.

sinner *n.* **1** [mid-19C–1920s] a publican [Luke 18:13 'And the publican, standing afar off, would not lift up so much as his eyes unto heaven, but smote upon his breast, saying, God be merciful to me a sinner']. **2** [late 19C+] an affectionate term for an otherwise unnamed man; usu. prefaced by 'old'.

sinse/sinsemilla *n. see* SENSIMILLIA *n.*

sip *n.*[1] [a bee 'sipping' nectar from a flower] [mid-19C–1900s] a kiss.

sip *n.*[2] [1940s–70s] (*US drugs*) a puff of a marijuana cigarette.

sip *v.*[1] [backsl. *sip* = PISS *v.* (2)] [late 19C–1900s; mid-20C+] to urinate.

sip *v.*[2] [1940s–70s] (*US drugs*) to smoke cannabis.

SE in slang uses

IN PHRASES

❑ **sip at the fuzzy cup** *v.* (*also* **drink at the fuzzy cup**) [1970s+] (*US black*) to perform cunnilingus. ❑ **sip from the hairy teacup** *v.* [2000s] to perform cunnilingus. ❑ **sip the syrup** *v.* [1990s+] (*US teen*) to drink (beer or liquor).

siph *n. see* SYPH *n.*

siphon the python *v.* (*also* **syphon the python**) **1** [1960s+] (*Aus.*) to urinate. **2** [2000s] (*US*) to have sexual intercourse. **3** [2000s] (*US*) to masturbate.

sipper *n.*[1] [mid-19C] (*UK Und.*) a teaspoon.

sipper *n.*[2] [SE *sibber-sauce*, ? ult. Lat. *cibarius*, pertaining to food] [late 19C] gravy.

'Sippi *n.* [abbr.] [1960s] (*US black*) Mississippi.

si quis *n.* [the notification of the candidacy begins *si quis*..., if anyone...] [mid-19C] a candidate for holy orders.

Sir Andrew's knot *n.* (*also* **Sir Tristram's knot**) [? notorious hanging judges] [16C] the hangman's noose.

Sir Anthony Blunt *n.* [rhy. sl. = CUNT *n.* (4); ult. UK art historian and traitor *Anthony Blunt* (1907–83)] [1980s+] a highly objectionable person.

Sir Berkeley *n.* [rhy. sl.; *Sir Berkeley Hunt* = CUNT *n.* (1)] [1930s] the vagina; thus by meton., sexual intercourse.

Sir Cloudesley *n.* [orig. a naval speciality, proper name *Sir Cloudesley* Shovel (1650–1707), a notable British admirable who was knighted for his suppression of piracy] [late 17C–18C] a hot drink of small beer mixed with brandy, plus lemon juice, spices and sugar.

Sir Courtly Nice *n.* [the play *Sir Courtly Nice* (1685) by John Crowne (*c.*1640–*c.*1700)] [late 17C–18C] a foolish, foppish dandy.

siretch *n.* (*also* **sirretch**) [backsl.] [mid-19C] cherries.

Sir Garnet *adv.* (*also* **Sir Garny**) [for ety. *see* ALL SIR GARNET *phr.*] [late 19C–1930s] all in order, everything as it should be.

Sir Harry *n.* [euph.] **1** [mid-19C] a close-stool, a commode. **2** [1920s] constipation.

Sir James Cotterel's salad *n.* [for ety. *see* COTTERELL'S SALAD *n.*] [late 18C] hemp.

Sir John *n.* **1** [14C–18C] a country parson. **2** [19C] a close-stool, an enclosed chamberpot. **3** [late 19C] the penis.

Sir Martin Wagstaffe *n.* [play on SE *wag* + *STAFF OF LOVE under* STAFF *n.*] [mid-17C] the penis.

Sir Oliver *n.* (*also* **Sir Olive**) [ext. of OLIVER *n.* (1)] [early–mid-19C] the moon.

Sir Posthumous Hobby *n.* [a pun on SE *hobby*: 'one that Draws on his Breeches with a Shoeing-horn; also a Fellow that is Nice and Whimsical in the set of his Cloaths' (B.E.)] [late 17C–early 19C] an obsessive dandy.

Sir Quibble-Queer *n.* [late 17C–18C] a trifling fool.

sirretch *n. see* SIRETCH *n.*

sir-reverence *n.* (*also* **save-reverence, surreverence**) [14C formal phrase (Nares suggests orig. *save reverence*) meaning 'begging your pardon' and used as 'a kind of apologetical apostrophe, when anything was said that might be thought filthy, or indecent' (Nares). By the late 16C it had taken on this euph. secondary meaning and is the basis of the 20C+ euph. to 'excuse oneself' and the schoolchild's cry of 'Can I be excused?' Thus: '*reverence*, an ancient custom which obliges any person easing himself near the highway or foot-path, on the word *reverence* being given to him by a passenger, to take off his hat with his teeth, and without moving from his station to throw it over his head, by which it frequently falls into the excrement ...' (Grose, 1796)] [late 16C+] faeces, excrement; also used as excl.

sirrocco-sifters *n.* [? rhy. sl.] [late 19C] (*US campus*) whiskers.

Sir Sydney *n.* [ety. unknown] [early–mid-19C] a clasp-knife.

Sir Thomas *n. see* JOHN THOMAS *n.* (1).

Sir Timothy (Treat-all) *n.* [from the play *The City-Heiress, or, Sir Timothy Treat-all* (1682) by Aphra Behn (1640–1689)] [late 17C–18C] a very generous man.

Sir Tristram's knot *n. see* SIR ANDREW'S KNOT *n.* (1).

Sir Walter Scott *n.* [rhy. sl.; ult. Scot. novelist *Sir Walter Scott* (1771–1832)] [mid–late19C] a pot, usu. of beer.

sis *n.* (*also* **cis, siss, sissy, suz**) [abbr. SE] **1** [mid-17C+] a sister. **2** [mid-19C+] used as a term of direct address whether or not to one's actual sister. **3** [late 19C+] (*US*) a young woman [abbr. SISSY *n.*]. **4** *see* SISSY *n.*

sis! *excl.* (*also* **cess! sies!**) [Du.] **1** [mid-19C] (*Aus.*) a call of encouragement. **2** [mid-19C+] (*S.Afr.*) an excl. of disgust, contempt, disappointment, dismay.

siserary *n.* (*also* **siserara**) [popular corruption of a writ of *certiorari*: 'A writ, issuing from a superior court, upon the complaint of a party that he has not received justice in an inferior court, or cannot have an impartial trial, by which the records of the cause are called up for trial in the superior court' (*OED*)] **1** [late 18C–mid-19C] a severe reprimand. **2** [mid-19C] a hard blow.

siss *n.*[1] **1** [early 17C] a large, fat woman. **2** [early 18C] a prostitute.

siss *n.*[2] *see* SIS *n.*

sissy *n.* (*also* **ciss, cissie, cissy, sis, siss, sissie**) [SE *sissy*, a coward; ult. *sis*, *sissy*, a sister] **1** [late 19C+] a weakling, an effeminate man or boy. **2** [1920s+] an effeminate homosexual man. **3** *see* SIS *n.*

IN COMPOUNDS

❑ **sissy-bar** *n.* (*also* **goody-bar**) [1960s+] a metal loop fixed behind the seat of a cycle or motorcycle. ❑ **sissy-boy** *n.* (*also* **sissy's ass**) [20C+] (*US*) a weakling; a male homosexual. ❑ **sissy cure** *n.* [1950s] (*US drugs*) tapering off a narcotic addiction rather than stopping immediately (with the concomitant withdrawal pains). ❑ **sissy pants** *n.* (*also* **sissy britches**) [on model of SMARTIEPANTS *n.*] [1940s+] a weakling, thus an effeminate homosexual man. ❑ **sissy rod** *n.* [ROD *n.* (2)] [1950s] (*US Und.*) a weapon fitted with a silencer. ❑ **sissy soft sucker** *n.* (*also* **soft sucker**) [SISSY *adj.* (1) + SE *soft* + SUCKER *n.*[1] (3a)] [1980s+] (*US black*) a weak, effeminate man (though not necessarily a homosexual).

sissy *adj.* (*also* **cissy, sissie, sissified, sissyish**) [SISSY *n.*] **1** [late 19C+] (*orig. US*) weak or effeminate. **2** [1920s+] homosexual; pertaining to the world of male homosexuality. **3** [1940s] easy, simple.

sister *n.* **1** [1910s+] (*US*) a term of address to any woman whose proper name one does or does not know. **2** [1920s+] a term of address between effeminate male homosexuals; thus self-referential as *your sister*. **3** [1920s+] (*US black*) a black woman; esp. as *the sisters*. **4** [1940s] (*gay*) the platonic gay friend of another gay man; similarly used by lesbians. **5** [1950s–60s] (*camp gay*) in pl., the police, when working in pairs. **6** [1960s+] (*orig. US*) a feminist or fellow woman. **7** in pl., *see SISTERS OF THE SCABBARD* below.

IN COMPOUNDS

❑ **sister act** *n.* [1940s–70s] **1** a homosexual couple. **2** a homosexual man having sex with a heterosexual woman. ❑ **sister hicks** *n. see* JIMMY HIX *n.*

SE in slang uses

IN COMPOUNDS

❑ **sisterfucking** *adj. see* MOTHERFUCKING *adj.* ❑ **sister girl** *n.* [1980s+] (*US campus*) a term of address among female friends. ❑ **sister-in-law** *n.* [1940s+] (*US black*) any woman working for a pimp other than his favourite or *TOP WOMAN under* TOP *adj.*; also used of homosexual prostitutes.

IN PHRASES

❑ **little sister** *n.* [late 19C–1940s] the vagina. ❑ **road sister** *n.* *see under* ROAD *n.* ❑ **sisters of the scabbard** *n.* (*also* **sisters**) [play on *BROTHER (OF THE) BLADE under* BROTHER (OF THE)... *n.*] [17C] prostitutes, as a group.

sit *v.*

SE in slang uses

IN COMPOUNDS

❑ **sit-upons** *n.* [abbr. *SIT-DOWN-UPONS under* SIT-DOWN *n.*] [mid-19C] trousers.

IN PHRASES

❑ **sit a woman** *v.* [trans. use of SE *sit*, to sit someone down] [mid-19C+] (*US black*) to entertain a woman. ❑ **sit bitch** *v.* *see under* BITCH *n.*[1]. ❑ **sit bodkin** *v.* *see* BODKIN *n.*[2]. ❑ **sit chilly** *v.* *see LAY CHILLY under* CHILLY *adj.* ❑ **sit down** *see* separate entries. ❑ **sit eggs** *v.* [the image of a hen awaiting her chicks] [late 19C+] to overstay one's welcome. ❑ **sit-'em-up guy** *n.* [1960s] (*S.Afr. Und.*) a hold-up man. ❑ **sit fat** *v.* *see under* FAT *adj.* ❑ **sit-in-'ems** *n.* [late 19C] trousers. ❑ **sit in the catbird seat** *v.* *see IN THE CATBIRD SEAT under* CATBIRD *n.* ❑ **sit in the garden with the gate unlocked** *v.* [late 19C–1900s] **1** to conceive an illegitimate child. **2** to catch a cold. ❑ **sit in the plush** *v.* *see under* ON PLUSH *adv.* ❑ **sit like a toad on the chopping block** *v.* [late 18C–19C] to sit badly on a horse. ❑ **sit-me-down** *n.* [1920s+] the buttocks. ❑ **sit off** *v.* [1990s+] (*Aus. Und.*) to place under surveillance, to stake out. ❑ **sit on** *v.* *see* separate entry. ❑ **sit pad** *v.* *see STAND PAD under* PAD *n.*[1]. ❑ **sit shotgun** *v.* *see RIDE SHOTGUN under* RIDE *v.* ❑ **sit there with one's finger up one's ass** *v.* *see under* ASS *n.* ❑ **sit up like jacky** *v.* *see under* JACKY JACKY *n.* ❑ **sit upon** *v.* *see* SIT ON *v.*

IN EXCLAMATIONS

❑ **go sit on a tack!** (*also* **go sit on a tap! sit on a tack!**) [1910s+] a derisive response. ❑ **sit on it and rotate!** (*also* **sit on it! sit on it and spin! sit on it and swivel!**) [1950s+] (*US*) a general excl. of abuse suggesting that a hard and painful object be thrust into the subject's anus. ❑ **sit on it, Potsie!** [*Potsie* Weber, a character in the 1970s *Happy Days* TV show; the names of other characters can be substituted] [1990s+] (*US black teen*) a general excl. of dismissal or mockery.

sit beside her *n.* [rhy. sl.; from the nursery rhyme of 'Miss Muffet'] [20C+] **1** cider. **2** a spider.

sitch *n.* [1960s+] (*US campus*) a difficult situation.

sit-down *n.* **1** [1910s–30s] (*US tramp*) a free sit-down meal. **2** [1930s+] (*US black*) a rest. **3** [1970s+] a conference.

SE in slang uses

IN COMPOUNDS

❑ **sit-down money** *n.* [1970s+] (*Aus.*) unemployment benefit. ❑ **sit-down stool** *n.* [1980s] (*US black*) the buttocks. ❑ **sit-down-upons** *n.* [mid-19C] trousers.

sit down *v.* **1** [20C+] (*Aus.*) to settle in a place, to take up a piece of land. **2** [1960s+] (*US teen*) in fig. use, to make a telling, lasting impression, to have a major effect.

SE in slang uses

IN PHRASES

❑ **sit down like Miss Priss** *v.* (*also* **sit down like Miss Queensie**) [the names of fig. lazy women] [20C+] (*W.I.*) to sit around while others are working.

sith-nom *n.* [backsl.] [mid-19C] a month.

sit on *v.* (*also* **sit upon**) [mid-19C+] to squash, to snub.

IN PHRASES

❑ **sit on oneself** *v.* [late 19C] (*US*) to calm down, to quieten down.

SE in slang uses

IN PHRASES

❑ **sit (on) a beast** *v.* *see under* BEAST *n.* ❑ **sit (on) a dago** *v.* *see SIT (ON) A BEAST under* BEAST *n.* ❑ **sit on chrome** *v.* *see under* CHROME *n.* ❑ **sit on dubs** *v.* *see under* DUBS *n.*[3]. ❑ **sit on one's ass** *v.* (*also* **sit on one's arse, ...butt, ...stern, ...tail**) [ASS *n.* (2)/ BUTT *n.*[1] (1a)/TAIL *n.* (2)] [20C+] (*US*) to be idle when one has responsibilities to carry out. ❑ **sit on one's stuff** *v.* [STUFF *n.* (8a)] [1970s] (*US black*) to work as a prostitute. ❑ **sit on someone's face** *v.* **1** [1960s+] for a woman, to position her vagina directly above her partner's mouth, either lit. sitting or squatting above their face, in order to facilitate cunnilingus; also used, as a synon. for enjoying fellatio, by men. **2** [1980s] (*US campus*) as a dismissive retort. ❑ **sit on the penniless bench** *v.* [SE *penniless bench*, a small bench provided for passing poor travellers; the first was at Carfax, Oxford] [late 16C–mid 17C] to be impoverished. ❑ **sit on the throne** *v.* *see under* THRONE *n.*

sitter *n.*[1] [they are all sitting indoors rather than walking the streets] **1** [mid-19C–1900s] a drunk, who sits around in a bar sleeping off the drink or generally wasting time. **2** [late 19C] (*US*) a tramp who, lacking any alternative accommodation, sits in a tenement hallway. **3** [late 19C–1930s] (*US*) a part-time prostitute. **4** [late 19C–1940s] (*US*) a homeless person, employed by a tavern to sit near the fire and shiver in an obvious way so that kind-hearted patrons would buy them drinks (thus profiting the tavern). **5** [1940s+] a woman who frequents certain taverns or nightclubs and who receives a percentage on the drinks they induce male patrons to buy.

sitter *n.*[2] [in shooting, a bird that is *sitting* rather than flying, and thus presents an easy target] **1** [late 19C+] an easy target, both in shooting and in metaphor. **2** [1910s] a certainty. **3** [1920s] a racehorse that is bound to win.

sitter *n.*[3] [1940s] (*UK Und.*) one who takes part in confidence tricks.

sitter *n.*[4] [they do nothing but sit and drink] [1940s+] (*Aus., mainly Sydney*) a regular and heavy drinker in a bar or public house.

sitting duck *n.* [hunting imagery] [1940s+] (*orig. milit.*) an easy target, someone or something vulnerable and defenceless, both lit. and fig.

sitting-pad *n.* [SE *sit* + PAD *n.*[1] (1)] [mid-19C] (*UK Und.*) the cross-legged position adopted by beggars positioning themselves on the pavement.

sitting pretty *adj.* **1** [1920s] (*US*) drunk. **2** [1920s+] secure, safe, enjoying an easy life, esp. as to material things.

situ *n.* [abbr.] [1970s+] a *situation*.

situation *n.* [SE *situation*, a job] [1960s+] (*S.Afr. black*) a member of the black middle class, a black 'white-collar' worker and regarded as a social climber.

siwash *n.* [cowboy jargon *Siwash*, pej. for a Native American, who mounted horses from the right-hand side, and wrestled down cows from the left; whites preferred the left and right sides respectively; thus *siwash outfit*, a second-rate ranch; note *Siwash* n., an Alaskan Indian] **1** [late 19C–1930s] (*US tramp*) a dirty or ill-mannered person. **2** [1930s+] (*US*) any small, archetypal college.

IN COMPOUNDS

❑ **siwash side** *n.* [late 19C+] (*US*) **1** anything done ineptly or clumsily. **2** the right-hand side of a horse. **3** the left-hand side of a cow.

siwash *v.* [ext. of SIWASHED *adj.*; drunkenness was stereotyped as one of many endemic Native American vices] [1910s+] (*US*) to ban someone from buying alcohol.

siwashed *adj.* [*Siwash*, a Native American of the northwest Pacific Coast. The term, ult. Fr. *sauvage*, savage, became a generic pej.; such exclusions were often made when ranchers were seen as being over-friendly to known cattle-rustlers] [19C] (*US, Western*) 'blackballed', i.e. used of a ranch that was barred from sending cowboys to the general round-up or to work on other ranches.

six *n.*[1] [abbr.] **1** [mid-18C] (*UK Und.*) a thirty-*six* shilling piece. **2** [mid–late 19C] *six*penny-worth of a given drink, as sold in a public house. **3** [mid-19C+] a *six*-month prison sentence. **4** [1920s] a *six*-year prison sentence. **5** [1980s+] a *six*-pack of beer.

DERIVATIVES

❑ **sixes** *n.* [its trad. price of 6 shillings (30p) per barrel] [mid-17C–early 19C] small beer.

IN COMPOUNDS

❑ **six-four** *n.* *see SIXTY-FOUR under* SIXTY *n.* ❑ **six-nine** *n.* *see* SIXTY-NINE *n.*

IN PHRASES

❑ **give six** *v. see under* SIX! *excl.* ❑ **old six** *n.* [mid–19C–1910s] old ale priced at sixpence per quart. ❑ **six-and-tips** *n.* [*see* SIXES above] [late 18C–early 19C] whisky and small beer. ❑ **six of everything** *adj.* [used by working families to describe a woman about to be married; her trousseau has six sets of everything necessary] [late 19C] respectable. ❑ **six to four** *n. see* TWO BY FOUR *n.*[2].

IN EXCLAMATIONS

❑ **six up!** [DEEP SIX *v.* (1)] [1980s+] a warning shout to alert drug-users or illicit street vendors to the presence of the police or security guards; the drugs or merchandise should be hidden or even thrown away to prevent problems in a search.

six *n.*[2] [*see* SIX FEET UNDER *under* SIX *adj.*] [1940s] (*US black*) a grave.

six *adj.*

IN COMPOUNDS

❑ **six-bit** *adj. see under* BIT *n.*[1]. ❑ **six bits** *n. see under* BIT *n.*[1]. ❑ **six-bit words** *n. see* TWO-DOLLAR WORDS *under* TWO-DOLLAR *adj.* ❑ **six-cornered oath** *n.* [late 19C] (*US*) a complex and many-worded oath. ❑ **six-foot bungalow** *n.* [1930s] (*US*) a coffin. ❑ **six-foot subway** *n.* [1940s] (*US black*) a grave. ❑ **six-letter word** *n. see* FOUR-LETTER WORD *n.* ❑ **six man** *n.* [ety. unknown] [1960s+] (*Can. prison*) a lookout. ❑ **six monthser** *n.* [late 19C] a severe magistrate, who, whenever they can, gives the longest sentence, six months, that the law allows. ❑ **six-pack** *n. see* separate entry. ❑ **sixpenny** *see* separate entries. ❑ **six pounder** *n.* [her annual wages were for many years set at £6] [late 18C] a maid. ❑ **six shooter** *n.* (*also* **six-man can**) [2000s] (*S.Afr.*) a bottle of cheap wine.

IN PHRASES

❑ **six feet by two** *n.* (*also* **six times three**) [1920s–40s] a grave. ❑ **six feet under** *adj.* (*also* **six feet deep**) [1930s+] (*orig. US*) dead and buried. ❑ **six months in front and nine behind** *adj.* [the resemblance of one's stomach and buttocks to the swelling stomach of a pregnant woman] [1930s–40s] (*US black*) obese. ❑ **six o'clock swill** *n.* [SE *six o'clock* + SWILL *n.* (2)] [1940s+] (*Aus./N.Z.*) the rushed orders of drinks that, between 1916 and 1955 (before a change in the laws), took place in pubs in New South Wales and parts of N.Z. before 'last orders'. ❑ **six times three** *n. see* SIX FEET BY TWO above. ❑ **six ways for/from/to Sunday** (*also* **six sides of Sunday**) *see under* SUNDAY *n.*[1].

six! *excl.* [? link to 6-5 *n.*] [1970s+] (*Can. Und./US prison*) a shout of warning.

IN PHRASES

❑ **give six** *v.* (*also* **keep six**) [SE *give* + *six!*] [1970s+] (*Can. prison*) to keep a lookout.

six-and-eight *n.* [rhy. sl.] [1960s+] an emotional 'state'.

six-and-eight *adj.* [rhy. sl. = STRAIGHT *adj.*[1] (3)] [1930s+] honest.

six-and-eightpence *n.* **1** [late 17C–18C] the accepted fee demanded for the removal of a felon from the gallows and for their burial in sacred ground. **2** [mid-18C–1910s] (*also* **six-and-eight**) a solicitor, whose basic fee usu. came to this amount.

six-and-eightpenny *adj.* [SIX-AND-EIGHTPENCE *n.* (2)] [mid-19C–1900s] legal, pertaining to a solicitor.

six-and-four *n.*[1] [rhy. sl. = SE *whore*] [1950s] (*UK Und.*) a prostitute.

six-and-four *n.*[2] [1960s+] (*drugs*) heroin that has been adulterated and weakened by mixing one part pure heroin to six or four parts sugar.

sixer *n.* **1** [mid-19C] a sixth term of imprisonment of whatever length. **2** [mid-19C+] a six-month prison sentence, six months' hard labour. **3** [late 19C] a 6-ounce (170g) loaf. **4** [1980s+] (*US black/campus*) a six-pack of beer. **5** [1990s+] (*drugs*) six pills.

IN PHRASES

❑ **chuck a sixer** *v. see* separate entry. ❑ **throw a sixer** *v. see* CHUCK A SIXER *v.*

6-5 *n.* [2000s] (*US prison*) code for a correctional officer; thus a warning when one approaches.

six months' hard *n.* [rhy. sl.] [20C+] (*bingo*) a card.

606 *adj.* [? visual pun on fellatio, as a var. of SIXTY-NINE *n.*] [1910s] (*US*) a euph. for homosexual.

six-pack *n.* **1** [1990s+] (*orig. US black*) (*also* **eight-pack**) a tight, flat stomach [the ripples resemble beer cans]. **2** [1990s+] (*Ulster*) a paramilitary punishment involving shots to the knees, ankles and hands.

SE in slang uses

IN COMPOUNDS

❑ **six-pack girl** *n.* [1980s] a very ugly woman whom no man would consider seducing unless he were drunk.

sixpenny *n.* [mid-19C] a pint of beer costing sixpence.

IN COMPOUNDS

❑ **sixpenny dark** *n.* [1960s] a glass of port.

sixpenny *adj.* [late 16C–mid-17C] second-rate, cheap, worthless.

SE in slang uses

IN COMPOUNDS

❑ **sixpenny rush** *n.* [1950s–60s] (*Irish*) cheap admission to children's matinées at the cinema. ❑ **sixpenny sicker** *n.* (*also* **shilling sicker**) [it may make holiday-making 'landlubbers' sick; note local *sixpenny sick*, the Portsmouth to Gosport ferry] [20C+] a seaside pleasure-boat. ❑ **sixpennyworth** *n.* [1940s–50s] a six-month prison sentence.

IN PHRASES

❑ **sixpenny suburb-sinnet** *n.* (*also* **sixpenny damnation**) [SE sixpenny, the prostitute's usual fee + play on SE *sinnet*, a trumpet-blast that introduced actors on the stage/SE *sinner*] [early 17C] a prostitute.

six pennyworth of God help us *n.* [20C+] (*Aus.*) a weakling, an insignificant person.

sixteen-carat *adj. see* EIGHTEEN-CARAT *adj.*

sixteener *n. see* EIGHT-PAGER *under* EIGHT *adj.*

sixteenth *n.* [1950s+] (*drugs*) one 16th of an ounce of a given drug.

sixteen-year-old after shave *n.* (*also* **sixteen-year-old shaving lotion**) [1970s] (*US black*) very cheap and unpleasant wine.

sixth finger *n.* [1950s] a knife.

sixty *n.* [mid-19C] (*UK Und.*) a 60-day (two-month) jail sentence.

SE in slang uses

IN COMPOUNDS

❑ **sixty-eight** *n.* [play on SIXTY-NINE *n.* (1)] [1970s+] fellatio, i.e. 'you suck me and I'll owe you one'. ❑ **sixty-four** *n.* (*also* **six-four, 64**) [1990s+] **1** (*US*) a 64-ounce (9-litre) bottle of malt liquor. **2** a 1964 Chevrolet Impala. **3** *see* TWO BY FOUR *n.*[2]. ❑ **sixty-six** *n.* [play on SIXTY-NINE *n.* (1)] [1940s–70s] (*Aus.*) anal intercourse.

IN PHRASES

❑ **like sixty** *adv. see* separate entry.

sixty *adj.*

SE in slang uses

IN COMPOUNDS

❑ **sixty-minute man** *n.* [1950s+] a sexual athlete, one who can postpone his orgasm for sixty minutes; thus dimin. *sixty-minute boy*. ❑ **sixty-second man** *n.* [play on SIXTY-MINUTE MAN above] [1970s] (*US black*) a premature ejaculator.

IN PHRASES

❑ **sixty-per-cent** *n.* [the exorbitant rate of interest] [mid–late 19C] a money-lender, a usurer, a bill-discounter.

sixty *adv. see* LIKE SIXTY *adv.*

sixty-nine *n.* (*also* **neuf-soixante, six-nine, sixty-niner, soixante-neuf, 69**) [synon. Fr. *soixante-neuf*; the numerals 69 supposedly mimic the head-to-tail bodily positions] **1** [late 19C+] mutual oral-genital stimulation. **2** [1910s; 1960s] (*US* *campus*) a homosexual. **3** [2000s] in fig. use, anything intensely satisfying or pleasurable.

sixty-nine *v.* [SIXTY-NINE *n.*] [1960s+] to perform soixante-neuf.

size *n.*[1] [16C *size*, the portion of bread and beer allowed to undergraduates in Cambridge colleges] [late 18C–early 19C] a half-pint (285ml).

size *n.*[2] [? play on SE *shape*, a jelly mould] [mid-19C] a jelly.

size *n.*[3]
SE in slang uses

IN COMPOUNDS

▫ **size freak** *n.* [-FREAK *sfx* (1)] [1990s+] of either sex, one who is obsessed by the size of a man's penis (which obsession determines their willingness to have sex). ▫ **size queen** *n.* [-QUEEN *sfx* (3)] [1960s+] (*usu. gay*) one who is obsessed by the size of the penis of a potential partner.

sizendizup *n.* [1930s–50s] (*US drugs*) used between a dealer and addict to indicate that the drugs are on their way.

size ten *n. see* NUMBER TEN *n.*

size (up) *v.* (*orig. US*) **1** [mid-19C+] to estimate, to assess, to get to know about. **2** [late 19C–1920s] to amount to. **3** [1930s] to appear, to seem to be.

sizzle *n.* [play on HOT *adj.* (5)] [1960s] (*US black*) narcotics, when carried on the person.

sizzle *v.* **1** [1930s–40s] (*US Und.*) to die or execute in the electric chair [SE *hot*]. **2** [1930s+] (*US drugs*) to be exceptionally prone to arrest, esp. when holding drugs or acting in an outrageous manner [HOT *adj.* (5a)].

IN COMPOUNDS

▫ **sizzle seat** *n.* [1930s+] (*US prison*) the electric chair.

sizzled *adj. see* SOZZLED *adj.*

sizzler *n.* **1** [mid-19C+] (*US*) any exciting thing or person. **2** [1900s–50s] (*US*) (*also* **frizzler**) a very hot day. **3** [1920s] (*US tramp*) a construction camp cook. **4** [1940s] a shot, e.g. from a sling shot. **5** [1940s–60s] (*US*) the electric chair. **6** [1950s–70s] something salacious, risqué, e.g. a book or clothing.

DERIVATIVES

▫ **sizzling** *adj.* [mid-19C+] (*US*) of people or things, exciting.

skaap *n.* [Afk. *skaap*, a sheep] **1** [1920s+] (*S.Afr.*) a country bumpkin, a fool. **2** [1980s+] a derog. name for an Afrikaner.

skaatie *n.* [Afk. *skat, skaatie*, darling, beloved] [1990s+] (*S.Afr.*) a term of affection.

skabenga *n.* [Zulu *isigebengu*, a bandit] [1970s+] (*S.Afr.*) a villain, a rascal.

skag *see also under* SCAG and its combs.

skag *n.* [? dial. *scag*, a putrid herring] **1** [1920s+] (*orig. US black*) an unattractive, slutty-looking woman. **2** [1980s+] a promiscuous woman. **3** [1980s+] a tease.

DERIVATIVES

▫ **skaggy** *adj.* [1980s+] (*US black/campus*) ugly, sluttish.

skainsmate *n.* [ety. unknown. Used in *Romeo and Juliet* (1594–5): 'Scurvie knave! I am none of his flurt-gils; I am none of his skaines mates.' The context seems to indicate a prostitute. ? dial. *skain*, a dagger; thus fig. a penis or *skein* of thread or wool, and thus relates to the 'sewing' imagery of intercourse; Nares is 'inclined to think that the old lady [sc. the nurse] means "roaring or swaggering companions"'] [late 16C] a prostitute.

skaitch *n. see* SKANCH *adj.*

skal *n.* [2000s] (*S.Afr.*) a litre bottle of cheap wine.

skalawag/skally wag *n. see* SCALLYWAG *n.*[1].

skamas *n.* [ety. unknown; ? Yid.] [1930s–50s] (*US drugs*) opium.

skamp *n.* [SKANK *n.*[1] + TRAMP *n.* (2)] [2000s] (*US black*) an unattractive, dirty and promiscuous woman.

skanch *adj.* (*also* **skaintch**) [SKANK *n.*[1]] [1990s+] (*US campus/teen*) anything, or anybody, seen as repulsive, disgusting.

skanger *n.* **1** [2000s] (*Irish*) a derog. term for a member of the working-class. **2** *see* SCANGER *n.*

skank *n.*[1] (*also* **scank**) **1** [1960s+] (*orig. US black*) an unattractive, easily available woman. **2** [1970s+] (*US black*) a female who smells badly. **3** [1970s+] (*US*) a prostitute. **4** [1980s+] (*US campus*) a repulsive person of either sex. **5** [1980s+] (*US*) filth, malevolence, dirtiness. **6** [2000s] an unsatisfactory situation. **7** [2000s] a mean, mercenary person. **8** [2000s] (*also* **skankface**) on bad = good model, an affectionate term of address.

skank *n.*[2] (*also* **scank**) [SKANK *v.* (8)] [1980s+] (*W.I./UK black teen*) a confidence trick, a fraudulent scheme.

skank *n.*[3] (*also* **skankweed**) [1990s+] (*drugs*) marijuana.

DERIVATIVES

▫ **skanked out** *adj.* [1990s+] (*US drugs*) intoxicated by a drug.

skank *adj.* [SKANK *n.*[1]] **1** [1970s+] (*US*) promiscuous. **2** *see* SKANKY *adj.*

skank *v.* [Allsopp, *Dict. Caribbean English Usage* (1996), suggests the dance style is 'derived from the kind of hip-swinging dancing which is both typical of people of generally low social status and reminiscent of the waist movements of a motorcyclist speeding in and out of other traffic'] [1970s+] (*orig. W.I.*) **1** to dance in a style associated with ska, dub or reggae music. **2** in fig. sense, to move rhythmically. **3** to steal and run away. **4** to loaf around. **5** to use deception to get one's way. **6** (*US campus*) to observe members of the opposite sex. **7** (*UK black*) to play truant. **8** to cheat, to 'stab in the back'.

skanker *n.* [SKANK *v.*] **1** [1970s+] (*W.I.*) an untrustworthy, dissolute person. **2** [1970s+] (*W.I.*) someone who dances in a style associated with ska, dub or reggae music. **3** [1990s+] an alcoholic tramp.

skankface *n. see* SKANK *n.*[1] (8).

skanky *adj.* (*also* **scankie, scanky, skank, skank-ass, skanky-ass**) **1** [1970s+] (*orig. US black*) dirty, second-rate, unattractive, cheap-looking, ugly [SKANK *n.*[1] (5)]. **2** [1980s+] of a woman, attractive, sexy; promiscuous [SKANK *n.*[1] (1) on bad = good model].

IN COMPOUNDS

▫ **skanky box** *n.* [BOX *n.*[1] (1)] [1980s+] (*US*) an unpleasant, dirty (physically and ethically) woman.

skarapafet *n.* [ety. unknown] [1970s+] (*S.Afr.*) a prostitute.

skarf *v. see* SCARF *v.*

skarper *v. see* SCARPER *v.*

skat *v. see* SCAT *v.*

skate *n.* [subseq. senses are fig. uses of sense 1] (*US*) **1** [mid-19C+] an inferior horse. **2** [late 19C] a second-rate sportman. **3** [late 19C–1900s] (*US*) in pl., shoes. **4** [late 19C–1920s] a person, irrespective of qualities. **5** [20C+] (*also* **skater**) a mean or contemptible person. **6** [1900s] (*US campus*) a reckless person. **7** [1900s–30s] an old person. **8** [1960s] (*US*) a lazy person, a shirker. **9** [1970s] (*US teen*) a motorcycle. **10** [1970s] (*US campus*) an easy course or task; an opportunity to relax, to be lazy. **11** [1970s+] (*S.Afr.*) 'a disreputable white male (from a working-class background) whose behaviour is uncouth, hedonistic, and irresponsible' (*DSAE*) [note Afk. *skuit*, excreta].

IN COMPOUNDS

▫ **skate rat** *n.* [1980s+] (*US teen*) a fanatical skateboarder. ▫ **skates-lurk** *n.* [? SE *skate*, the fish + LURK *n.* (1). Paul Beale in *DSUE* (1984) suggests that this might 'just poss[ibly]' be the origin of SKATE *n.* (5)] [mid-19C] (*UK Und.*) the practice of posing as a sailor for the purposes of begging.

IN PHRASES

▫ **get a skate on** *v.* [1900s] (*US*) to go fast, to hurry up. ▫ **get one's skates on** *v.* (*also* **have one's skates on, put one's skates on**) [note SKATE *v.*[1]] [late 19C+] (*orig. milit.*) to hurry up, to stop wasting time; often as imper. ▫ **go for a skate** *v.* [1950s+] (*N.Z.*) **1** to fail. **2** to be killed. **3** to be brought up in court. ▫ **on a skate** [orig. RN *skate*, to go in search of liquor and women; ult. fig. use of SE] [late 19C+] drinking heavily.

skate *adj.* [SKATE *n.* (10)] [1970s+] (*US campus*) easy, simple, esp. of work or a course.

skate *v.*[1] **1** [mid-19C+] (*also* **do a skate, skate off, skeete, skite**) to rush off, to leave at speed, to go quickly. **2** [1940s+] (*orig. US black*) to get away with anything, to shirk one's responsibilities, esp. to avoid paying one's debts. **3** [1960s+] to perform or make something, e.g. an essay or a meal, quickly.

4 [2000s] (*US prison*) to be in a forbidden area of the prison.

IN PHRASES

❑ **skate on** *v.* [1970s+] to take advantage of. ❑ **skate off** *v. see* sense 1 above.

skate *v.*^{2} [skating should be on *ice* but this antedates ICE *n.*^{1} (5); thus ? ref. to SNOW *n.*^{1} (2)] [1920s–50s] (*US drugs*) to use morphine or cocaine.

skater *n.*^{1} [1930s–40s] (*US Und.*) a legless person who uses a wheeled board for transportation.

skater *n.*^{2} *see* SKATE *n.* (5).

skatie *n.* [1980s+] (*N.Z.*) a skateboarder.

skating *adj.* [SKATE *v.*^{1} (2)] [1970s] of a despised person, one who shirks their duties.

skating rink *n.* (*also* **flies' skating rink**) [1910s+] a bald head.

skauf *n. see* SCOFF *n.*

skedaddle *n.* [SKEDADDLE *v.*] **1** [mid-19C+] a rush, a hurry; an act of running away or escaping. **2** [1990s+] a fuss, excitement, disturbance.

skedaddle *v.* (*also* **skedoo, skidaddle, skidoodle**) [orig. US milit. jargon *skedaddle*, to flee the battlefield, to retreat quickly; thence 'civilian' uses. Webster (1867) suggests Scand. roots, but *OED* and other authorities reject this. The term may have existed in Eng. dial./Scot. (meaning to scatter, to spill, as of a pail of milk, a bucket of potatoes) slightly earlier than its US use, but that seems merely coincident. Hotten (1864) adds a ref. to 'very fair Greek, the root being that of "skedannumi" to disperse, to "retire tumultuously" ... it was probably set afloat by some professor at Harvard'. A number of other commentators – incl. Cohen in *Studies in Slang* (1985), Wentworth & Flexner and Bartlett – agree. Other theories include a link to the Irish *scegadol*, scattered, which has been disproved, but there may still be one to a variety of other Gaelic words, e.g. *scead*, fright, *sgadarlach*, anything scattered or dispersed, *scaoll*, fright, panic. Cohen, in an extensive analysis (Cohen, 1985, pp.29–63), suggests Scot. *skiddle*, to scatter + ? comb. *jabble*, to scatter. Thus the earlier use must be accepted and the Scot./northern 'spill/scatter' transfers to the US 'flee' through the image of blood and corpses being thus 'spilled and scattered' on the battlefield before the flight of a demoralized army] [mid-19C+] (*orig. US*) of people, to rush off, to scamper, to escape.

skedaddler *n.* [SKEDADDLE *v.*] [mid-19C] (*US*) a fugitive.

skee *n.*^{1} [abbr./pron.] [20C+] (*US, then Aus./N.Z.*) whisky.

IN COMPOUNDS

❑ **skee joint** *n.* [JOINT *n.* (1)] [late 19C] (*US*) a bar or saloon.

skee *n.*^{2} [? SKEE *n.*^{1} (1) or SKAMAS *n.*] [1930s–50s] (*drugs*) opium.

IN COMPOUNDS

❑ **skeed-up** *adj.* [1990s+] (*US drugs*) intoxicated by drugs.

skeedoo, skeedoo! *excl. see* SKIDOO! *excl.*

skeedoodle *v.* [1990s+] (*US drugs*) to sell adulterated or fake drugs.

skeef *adj.* [Afk. *scheef*, askew] **1** [1960s+] (*S.Afr.*) crooked, off-beat; also as adv. **2** [1980s+] (*S.Afr. gay*) thus in fig. use, homosexual.

skeeger *n. see* SKEEZA *n.*

skeek *n.* [? var. SKANK *n.*^{1} (7)] [2000s] (*US*) an unpleasant person.

skeesicks *n. see* SKEEZICKS *n.*

skeet *n.*^{1} [var. on SKATE *n.* (5)] [20C+] a general term of abuse.

skeet *n.*^{2} [? SCAG *n.*^{2} (2) + HIT *n.* (1) or SKEET *v.*] [2000s] (*US prison*) a single injection of heroin.

skeet *v.* [dial. *skeet*, to squirt, to eject fluid] **1** [1970s+] (*drugs*) (*also* **skeeter**) to flush out a hypodermic syringe by using the plunger. **2** [1980s+] (*US black*) to have sexual intercourse. **3** [1980s+] (*US black*) to ejaculate.

skeete *v. see* SKATE *v.*^{1} (1).

skeeter *n.*^{1} (*also* **skeet, skeeto**) [abbr. + Aus./N.Z. pron.] [mid-19C+] (*Aus./US*) a mosquito.

skeeter *n.*^{2} [SKEET *v.* (3)] [1990s+] semen.

skeeter *v. see* SKEET *v.* (1).

skeeve *n.* [SKEEVE *v.*] [1990s+] (*US*) a disgusting person.

DERIVATIVES

❑ **skeevy** *adj.* [1990s+] disgusting.

skeeve *v.* (*also* **skeeve out**) [? Ital. *schifoso*, disgusting] [1990s+] (*US*) to disgust, to repel.

skeeza *n.* (*also* **skeeger, skeez, skeeze, skeezer**) [? SAmE *skeezicks*, a 'mean, contemptible fellow' (Bartlett, *Dict. Americanisms*, 1877); SKEEZE *v.*^{2}] [1980s+] (*orig. US black*) **1** a woman who trades sex for status or for free drugs; her chosen partners are often drug dealers or performers. **2** a person, usu. female, who attempts to have a relationship with a member of the opposite sex only for their material possessions, in order to make an impression on other people. **3** a man. **4** a derog. term for any disliked person.

skeeze *n.* [ety. unknown; ? link to SE *easy*] [1900s] (*US*) something easily acheived.

skeeze *v.*^{1} [ety. unknown] [1920s+] to ogle.

skeeze *v.*^{2} [? Cornish *skeese*, to frisk about + *skicer*, a lamb that kills itself through excess activity] [1980s+] (*orig. US black*) **1** to have sexual intercourse. **2** to seek members of the opposite sex. **3** to have an orgy.

skeezer *n. see* SKEEZA *n.*

skeezicks *n.* (*also* **skeesicks, skeezix, skeezucks**) [mid-19C+] (*US*) a person, usu. a troublemaker.

skeg *n.*^{1} (*also* **skeghead**) [SE *skeg*, the fin beneath a surboard] [1980s+] (*Aus.*) a surfer.

skeg *n.*^{2} (*also* **skeggy**) [dial. *scag*, putrid fish] [2000s] a smelly vagrant or one who resembles such a person.

DERIVATIVES

❑ **skeggy** *adj.* [1990s+] unpleasant, disgusting, the implication being of rotting or faecal matter.

skein of thread *n.* [rhy. sl.] [1920s+] a bed.

skelder *v.* [Du. *skellum*, a rogue, a villain, a pestilence] **1** [late 16C–17C] to work as a professional beggar, esp. to pose as a wounded or discharged soldier. **2** [late 16C–18C] to swindle, to defraud; thus *skeldering*, begging, swindling.

skeleton screw *n. see* SCREW *n.*^{1} (2a).

skell *n.* (*also* **skel**) [SKELDER *v.*] [1960s+] (*US*) a villain, a rogue, esp. a vagrant who lives on the streets.

skelly *n.*^{1} [Scot. *skelly*, a squint, ult. OE *sceolh*, a squint] [20C+] (*Irish*) a glance, a look.

skelly *n.*^{2} [abbr.] **1** [1950s] (*UK Und.*) a *skel*eton key. **2** [2000s] a *skel*eton.

skelly *adj.* [SKELL *n.*] [1960s+] (*US*) seedy, run-down.

skelly *v.* [SKELLY *n.*^{1}] [20C+] (*Irish*) to look.

skelm *adj.* [SKELM *v.*] [20C+] (*S.Afr. Und.*) fake, counterfeit.

skelm *v.* [Afk. *skelm*, a villain, a rascal; note obs. SE *skelm* a rascal, itself f. Du. *schelm*, a rascal] [20C+] (*S.Afr. Und.*) to do something in an underhand way.

skeng *n.* [? Carib.E. *skengay*, a form of music in which the guitar sounds are seen as mimicking those of gunfire] [1970s+] (*W.I./UK black*) a ghetto weapon, e.g. a gun, a ratchet-knife.

skep *n.* [mid-19C] (*UK Und.*) anywhere one deposits money, from a pocket to a bank.

skepper *n. see* SKIPPER *n.*^{1} (2).

skepsel *n.* [1980s+] (*S.Afr.*) a lazy person, often a labourer.

skerrick *n.* [dial. *skewick*, an atom, a fragment] [early 19C+] (*mainly Aus./N.Z.*) **1** (*also* **scurrick, skirrach**) a halfpenny. **2** a small amount, a small fragment, the slightest bit.

sket *n.* [? abbr. SKETEL *n.* (1)] [2000s] (*UK black teen*) a derog. term for a promiscuous young woman.

sketch *n.* [SE *sketch*, an outline] **1** [late 19C] a very small quantity, a single drop. **2** of an individual. (**a**) [20C+] a ridiculous or amusing person or sight. (**b**) [1910s] a couple. (**c**) [1980s+] (*US campus*) (*also* **sketchball, sketcher, sketchmaster**) one who looks or feels confused, unstable, odd; thus adj. *sketchy*, weird. **3** [1980s+] (*US campus*) a male homosexual. **4** [1990s+] (*US drugs*) methamphetamine. **5** [2000s] (*Scot.*) a look at, a view of. **6** [2000s] the rules, the situation.

IN PHRASES

□ **hot sketch** *n.* (*also* **sketch**) [HOT *adj.* (7)] [1900s–30s] (*US*) **1** an attractive person, usu. a young woman. **2** an amusing person or thing. **3** an eccentric person.

sketch *adj.* [? SKETCHY *adj.*] [1970s+] (*US campus*) risky, dangerous.

sketch *v.*^{1} [SE *sketch*, to draw, *i.e.*, on someone's flesh] [1980s] (*UK black*) to slash with a knife or other edged weapon.

sketch *v.*^{2} [SKETCH *n.*] [1980s+] **1** (*US campus*) (*also* **sketch out**) to feel unstable or confused. **2** (*US drugs*) to experience the after-effects of amphetamines.

IN COMPOUNDS

□ **sketched out** *adj.* **1** [1980s+] (*US campus*) bad, bizarre, weird. **2** [1980s+] (*US drugs*) suffering paranoia due to the effects of hallucinogenic or other drugs, e.g. cocaine; thus *sketching*, coming down from a drug-induced high.

sketchball/sketcher/sketchmaster *n. see* SKETCH *n.* (2c).

sketchy *adj.* [a SE *sketch*, rather than an oil painting] **1** [late 19C+] flimsy, insubstantial, vague. **2** [1910s] brief, minimal. **3** [1980s+] (*US campus*) confused, unstable, strange, unsettling. **4** [1990s+] (*US campus*) untrustworthy, suspicious. **5** [1990s+] (*US campus*) second-rate.

sketel *n.* (*also* **sketell, skets, skittle**) [? she falls over like a *skittle*; note Catherine 'Skittles' Walters, mistress of Edward VII, Louis Napoleon, et al.] [1990s+] a promiscuous woman, or one who is judged as such.

skew *n.*^{1} (*also* **scew**) [Lat. *scutella*, a dish; note Harman (c.1566) has *askew*, a cup, and *DSUE* offers an ety. of Fr. *escuelle*, a cup; however, a simple misprint or mishearing of *a skew* is more likely] [mid-16C–19C] a cup or dish.

skew *n.*^{2} [backsl.] [mid-19C] weeks.

skewer *n.* **1** [mid-19C–1910s] a sword. **2** [late 19C–1920s] a pen.

skew-fisted *adj.* [SE *askew*] [late 17C–18C] awkward, ungainly.

skewgee *n.* [SKEWGEE *adj.*] [late 19C–1900s] a squint.

skewgee *adj.* [SE *askew*] [late 19C+] **1** squinting, crooked. **2** mixed-up, confused.

skewings *n.* [SE *skew*, to escape; i.e. money that has 'escaped' from the regular accounts] [mid-19C] extras, bonuses; any form of money, esp. when gained for nothing.

skew-jawed *adj.* [SE *askew*] [mid-19C] (*US*) awkward, ungainly.

skewvow *adj.* [var. on SE *skew-whiff*] [late 18C–19C] askew, out of true, crooked.

skezag *n.* [SCAG *n.*^{2} (2) + -IZ- *infix*] [1970s+] (*drugs*) heroin.

ski *n.*^{1} [1940s–60s] (*US black*) a very large shoe.

SE in slang uses

IN COMPOUNDS

□ **ski bum** *n. see* BUM *n.*^{3} (10). □ **ski bunny** *n. see under* BUNNY *n.*^{1}.

ski *n.*^{2} [? weak rhy. sl.] [1950s+] (*Aus.*) a taxi.

ski *n.*^{3} [play on SNOW *n.*^{1} (2)] [1980s+] (*US drugs*) cocaine.

IN COMPOUNDS

□ **ski-ride** *n.* [1940s–60s] (*orig. US black*) a cocaine binge.

ski *n.*^{4} *see* SKY *n.*^{3}.

-ski *sfx* (*also* **-sky**) [1910s+] (*orig. US campus*) a sfx added to names in humorous imitation of Russian; a general intensifier.

skibby *n.* (*also* **skippy**) [Jap. *sukibei*, randy or lecherous; the word had also meant a courtesan, and the sense was extended to mean 'loose' or 'unchaste'. In US use it tended to refer to a female domestic servant, but the seeming synonymity of the term *skivvy*, also a maid of all work, may be coincidental] (*US*) **1** [1910s+] (*also* **skivvy**) an East Asian prostitute, thus, when addressing a Japanese speaker, any prostitute. **2** [1920s+] a derog. term for a Japanese person.

skibo *n.* **1** [1900s] (*Aus.*) a house-painter. **2** [1950s] (*US Und.*) an East Asian person; occas. an African American [? SKIBBY *n.*].

ski-bunk *n.* [SKIDOO! *excl.* (2) + BUNK *n.*^{1}] [1900s] (*US*) a rejection; an act of dismissal.

IN PHRASES

□ **put the skibunk on** *v.* [var. on *PUT THE KIBOSH ON under* KIBOSH *n.*] [1900s] (*US*) to impose upon, to defraud.

skid *n.*^{1} [var. on *GREASY BAG under* GREASY *adj.*^{2}] [1970s] (*drugs*) heroin, usu. heavily diluted.

IN COMPOUNDS

□ **skid bag** *n.* [BAG *n.*^{1} (7)] [1970s] (*US drugs*) a bag in which heroin is transported and/or sold.

skid *n.*^{2} [? SKID ROW *n.*] [1990s+] one who likes to go out at night; an ill-dressed, dirty, dishevelled person.

skid *n.*^{3} *see* SKIV *n.*^{1}.

skid *adj.* [SKID *n.*^{2}] [1990s+] unattractive, dirty, dishevelled.

skid *v.* (*also* **skids**) **1** [1910s–20s] to leave, to go. **2** [1920s+] (*US*) to blunder, to make a mistake, to decline. **3** [1950s] (*US Und.*) to get rid of someone.

SE in slang uses

IN COMPOUNDS

□ **skid artist** *n.* [the speedily driven car *skids* around corners + -ARTIST *sfx*] [1970s] (*UK Und.*) an expert driver of a get-away car, used on robberies. □ **skid-bid** *n.* [SE *skid*, i.e. off the 'straight and narrow' + BID *n.*^{2}] [1990s+] (*US prison*) a term in prison or in juvenile detention. □ **skid grease** *n.* [1920s–40s] (*US*) butter. □ **skidlid** *n.* [LID *n.*] [1950s+] a crash helmet. □ **skid magazine** *n.* [2000s] a pornographic magazine. □ **skid mark** *see* separate entries. □ **skid row** *see* separate entries.

IN PHRASES

□ **skid-pipe plumber** *n.* [1990s+] a male homosexual. □ **skid the rig** *v.* [fig. use of oil rig jargon *skid the rig*, to move a derrick] [1940s] (*US*) to cuckold.

skidaddle *v. see* SKEDADDLE *v.*

skiddies *n. see* SKID MARK *n.*

skiddoo *v. see* SKIDOO *v.*

skiddy *n.* [? SKID MARK *n.* (1)] [1990s+] (*N.Z.*) something repulsive.

skid mark *n.* (*also* **skiddies, scooter tracks**) **1** [1930s+] usu. in pl., faecal stains on one's underwear; thus adj. *skid-marked*. **2** [1990s+] any form of bodily stain. **3** [1990s+] a general term of abuse.

IN PHRASES

□ **do you see skid marks on my forehead?** [i.e. synon. with 'do you think I'm talking out of my ass?'] [1980s] (*US campus*) do you think I'm a fool?

skid-mark *v.* [SKID MARK *n.*] [1990s+] to stain.

skidoo *n.* [1900s–10s] **1** bad luck [SE *skid*]. **2** an exit [SKIDOO *v.*].

skidoo *v.* (*also* **skiddoo**) [? SKEDADDLE *v.* (1) or SCADOODLE *v.* or SE *skid*] [1900s–50s] (*US*) to leave quickly, to run off.

skidoo! *excl.* (*also* **skeedoo!**) [SKIDOO *v.*; see also TWENTY-THREE SKIDOO! *excl.*] **1** [1900s–10s] an excl. of pleasure or surprise. **2** [1900s–50s] a general term of abuse, scram! go away!

skidoodle *v. see* SKEDADDLE *v.*

skid row *n.* [late 19C logging jargon *skid road*, a prepared track with greased skids over which logs were hauled towards the river that would float them down to the sawmill; by late 19C (poss. earlier, the orig. 'skid road' was Yesler's Way in Seattle, Wash., constructed 1852) the sense had extended to describe a low-class district of drinking and gambling houses, which grew up around the terminuses of skid roads and was extended into sl. to mean that part of a town where loggers spent their free time or lived when they were out of work. It was the latter meaning, with its added implication of a man, rather than a log, who was 'skidding downhill' economically that dominated usage by the 1930s, when *skid road* became *skid row*; hence the use of *row* to denote the concentration of certain businesses or occupations in certain urban streets, e.g. Hollywood's *Poverty Row*, the area where the cheaper studios congregated] **1** [1920s+] (*also* **skid road, the Skid**) the centre, in any town or city, for down-and-outs, alcoholics, tramps and other poor or homeless individuals. **2** [1940s] a dead end for one's career. **3** [1950s] (*US drugs*) the convalescent ward of a drug rehabilitation hospital. **4** [1980s] a down-and-out alcoholic.

skid-row *adj.* [SKID ROW *n.*] [1930s+] (*US*) down and out, alcoholic, tramp-like.

skids *n.* [SE *skid* + SKID ROW *n.* (1)]

DERIVATIVES

❑ **skidsville** *n. see* separate entry.

IN PHRASES

❑ **have the skids under** *v.* [1930s–50s] to be facing decline. ❑ **hit the skids** *v.* [1920s+] (*orig. US*) to suffer problems, whether professional or personal. ❑ **on the skids** (*also* **on the toboggan**) [1920s+] on a social and economic decline. ❑ **put the skids to** *v.* (*also* **put the skids under, slip the skids**) [1910s+] (*orig. US*) **1** to dismiss someone from a job; to end a relationship. **2** to make someone hurry up, usu. in doing their work. **3** (*also* **throw the skids under**) to hasten someone's downfall. **4** to bring to a conclusion. ❑ **shove the skids under** *v.* [1920s] to get rid of.

skids *v. see* SKID *v.*

skidsville *n.* [ON THE SKIDS *under* SKIDS *n.* + -VILLE *sfx*[1] (1)] [1950s+] (*US*) a state of poverty.

skied *adj.*[1] [play on PSYCHED (UP) *adj.*] [1960s+] (*US campus*) ready for anything.

skied *adj.*[2] [pun on SE *sky*/HIGH *adj.*[1] (2)] [1980s+] (*drugs*) extremely intoxicated by a drug.

skiets *n.* [Afk. *skyt*, to defecate] [20C+] (*S.Afr.*) diarrhoea.

skiffle *n.* [SE *scuffle* via dial. *skiffle*; music at such parties was provided by non-professional musicians; thus the *skiffle groups* (who were paid but performed on essentially homemade instruments) of the 1950s] [1930s–40s] (*US black*) a party at which the guests pay a subscription to cover refreshments and to help the host out with the rent.

skiffling and skuffling *n.* [SKIFFLE *n.* and SE *shuffle*] [1940s–60s] (*US black*) any form of frenetic activity.

skilagolee *n.* (*also* **skillagalle, skilligalee, skilligolee**) [ety. unknown; 'prob. a purely fanciful formation' (*OED*)] [19C] **1** (*prison/services/workhouse*) thin, un-nourishing broth, gruel. **2** (*Aus.*) any broth or stew. **3** a small coin of minimal value; usu. in phr. *not worth a skilagolee*; thus *skilagolee*, worthless.

skiley *n. see* SKILLY *n.*

skill *adj.* [1990s+] (*UK teen*) first-rate, very good.

skillet *n.* [SE *skillet*, a cast-iron (black) frying pan] **1** [1930s] an old car. **2** [1930s–70s] (*US black*) a black person.

IN COMPOUNDS

❑ **skillet blonde** *n.* [1920s–30s] (*US black*) **1** a black woman wearing a blonde wig. **2** a very dark-skinned black person.

skilley *n. see* SKILLY *n.*

skilligalee/skilligolee *n. see* SKILAGOLEE *n.*

skillion *n.* (*also* **scillion**) [pattern of SE *trillion* etc] [2000s] (*US*) a very large and indefinite number.

skilly *n.* (*also* **skiley, skilley, skilly-go-lee**) [abbr. SKILAGOLEE *n.*; note London, *People of the Abyss* (1903): '"Skilly" is a fluid concoction of three quarts of oatmeal stirred into three buckets and a half of hot water'] **1** [mid-19C–1950s] (*UK prison/workhouse*) gruel, broth. **2** [1920s–40s] (*US prison*) gravy. **3** [1920s–50s] any weak beverage, e.g. tea or coffee.

IN COMPOUNDS

❑ **skilly and toke** *n.* [fig. use of SKILLY *n.* + TOKE *n.*[1] (3)] [mid–late 19C] anything mild or insipid.

skillz *n.* [deliberate 'hip-hop' mis-spelling] [1990s+] (*orig. US black*) skills, capabilities.

skim *v.* (*orig. US*) **1** [1910s+] of an employee, to hold back a proportion of the profits from their job (usu. in some form of gambling), thus stealing from their employer. **2** [1940s+] to conceal some part of one's earnings in order to avoid paying tax on them. **3** [1980s+] to steal from a store of money, drugs etc. **4** [1980s+] to forge a credit card.

skimish *n.* (*also* **skimmish**) [Shelta *skimis*, to drink, *skimisk*, drunk] [1900s–70s] (*mainly UK tramp*) beer, alcohol; thus *skimisher/skimmisher*, a heavy drinker.

skimished *adj.* (*also* **skimmished**) [SKIMISH *n.*] [1900s–30s] drunk.

skimmer *n.*[1] [SE *skimmer hat*, so called from the potential of skimming it like a frisbee] [mid-19C+] (*US*) a broad-brimmed boater with a very low crown, esp. when made of straw.

skimmer *n.*[2] [SKIM *v.* (1)] [1930s+] (*US*) a financial criminal who withholds money from their firm's profits.

skimming *n.* [SKIM *v.* (1)] [1960s+] stealing from the till, taking money 'off the top', esp. as found in casinos, strip clubs and other places where a degree of criminality is already endemic.

skimmish *n. see* SKIMISH *n.*

skimmished *adj. see* SKIMISHED *adj.*

skimmy *n.* [? she is the 'cream', which has been *skimmed*] [1990s+] (*US black*) an attractive female.

skin *n.*[1] **1** that which is made of SE *skin*. (**a**) [late 18C–1940s] a purse, a pocketbook, a wallet; thus *queer skin*, an empty wallet [the leather of which it is made]. (**b**) [1920s+] (*US black*) a drum [abbr. SE *drumskin*]. (**c**) [1920s+] in pl., a set of drums. (**d**) [1940s–60s] (*US*) a rasher of bacon. (**e**) [1940s+] (*US black*) the hand as in a handshake or a palm-slapping greeting. (**f**) [1950s–70s] a tyre. (**g**) [1950s+] (*US*) a condom. **2** in senses of SE *skin*, something that wraps or contains. (**a**) [mid-19C] (*UK Und.*) a watch case. (**b**) [mid-19C–1910s] (*US Und.*) a shirt. (**c**) [1960s+] a cigarette paper, esp. those used for rolling cannabis joints, usu. in pl. [it provides a *skin* for the tobacco (and cannabis)]. (**d**) [1970s+] (*US gay*) in pl., very tight trousers. **3** by metonymy, in senses pertaining to a human being. (**a**) [mid-19C; 20C+] (*orig. naut.*) a derog. generic for women; the vagina. (**b**) [late 19C+] a person, e.g. in phr. *a decent old skin*. (**c**) [1910s–20s] (*US*) oneself, one's life. (**d**) [1950s] (*US Und.*) a male homosexual. (**e**) [1980s] as a term of address to an unknown person. **4** (*US*) abbr. FROGSKIN *n.*[2]. (**a**) [late 19C+] $1. (**b**) [1940s–70s] in pl. a note. **5** [1910s–40s] (*US/Aus.*) a horse, a mule. **6** [1940s–50s] a painter. **7** [1970s+] abbr. *skin*head.

IN PHRASES

❑ **give some skin** *v.* (*also* **slip some skin, skin**) [the practice is of African origin; thus Temme *botme-der*, put skin and/or Mandingo *i golo don m bolo*, place your hand in my hand; Burley, *Original Handbook of Harlem Jive* (1944), suggests it originated in Chicago in 1944 at the time of the Joe Louis-Tony Galento fight] [1930s+] (*orig. US black*) the ritual palm slapping that forms a greeting between blacks or a black and a knowledgeable white; thus the greeting *give/slip me some skin*. ❑ **knock some skin** *v.* [1940s] (*US*) to shake hands. ❑ **one-skinner** *n.* [1970s+] (*drugs*) a marijuana cigarette using a single rolling paper. ❑ **skin up** *v.* **1** [1960s+] (*drugs*) to roll a cannabis-filled cigarette. **2** [1990s+] in fig. use, to involve oneself with. **3** [1990s+] (*W.I.*) to be on friendly terms [the proximity of human *skin*]. ❑ **slap skins** *v.* (*orig. US black*) **1** [1960s+] to exchange a greeting by slapping each other's hands. **2** [1990s+] (*also* **slap, slap on**) to have sexual intercourse.

IN EXCLAMATIONS

❑ **skin me!** *see* separate entry.

SE in slang uses

IN COMPOUNDS

❑ **skin-and-grief** *n.* [late 19C–1950s] a very thin person. ❑ **skin-beater** *n.* [1930s–50s] a drummer. ❑ **skin boy** *n.* [abbr. SE *foreskin*] [1980s] (*N.Z.*) an uncircumcised male. ❑ **skincoat** *n.* [mid-16C] the vagina. ❑ **skin diver** *n.* [1960s–70s] **1** a male homosexual [his supposed appetite for fellatio; Trimble extends use to practitioners of heterosexual oral intercourse]. **2** a fellatrix. ❑ **skin flute** *n. see* separate entry. ❑ **skin frisk** *n. see under* FRISK *n.*[1]. ❑ **skinhead** *n. see* separate entry. ❑ **skin-heist** *n.* [1950s] (*US Und.*) a rape. ❑ **skin hustling** *n.* [1930s] (*US Und.*) selling fake fur. ❑ **skin merchant** *n.* [ironic use of SE] [late 18C–19C] a military recruiting officer. ❑ **skin-out** *n.* [1990s+] (*W.I.*) sexual abandonment. ❑ **skin pop/popper** *see* separate entries. □ **skin queen** *n.* [-QUEEN *sfx*] **1** [1960s+] (*US gay*) a male homosexual who views his partners as no more than sex objects, a gay sexist. **2** [1990s+] one who prefers uncircumcised penises. □ **skin-roll** *n.* [the resemblance of the penis to a roll of skin; thus cognate with DORK *n.*, PRICK *n.* (3) etc] [1990s+] (*UK juv.*) a totally inadequate, inept person. □ **skin shake** *n.* [1960s] (*US prison*) a body search. □ **skin shooter** *n.* *see* SHOOT SKIN below. □ **skin shot** *n.* *see* SHOT *n.*[1] (6b). □ **skintight** *see* separate entries. □ **skintop** *n.* [1990s+] (*US*) a bald head. □ **skin worker** *n.* [WORKER *n.*[1] (1)] [20C+] (*US Und.*) a shoplifter, usu. of furs.

IN PHRASES

□ **get some skin** *v.* [1930s–40s] (*US*) to have sexual intercourse. □ **get (some) skins** *v.* [1990s+] (*US black*) to have sexual intercourse. □ **hit skins** *v.* [20C+] to have sexual intercourse [note Papua New Guinea Tok Pisin *paitim bun*, to have sex, lit. 'hit bones']. □ **in a bad skin** *adj.* [late 18C–1910s] bad-tempered, 'out of sorts'. □ **in a good skin** *adj.* (*also* **in a whole skin**) [mid-18C–1910s] good-humoured, cheerful. □ **in one's skin** [early–mid-18C] a non-committal answer when asked where someone is. □ **in someone's skin** [20C+] (*W.I.*) harassing, nagging. □ **no skin off one's ass** (*also* **no skin off one's backside, ...tail**) [1930s+] (*orig. US*) no problem, no worries; of no importance. □ **no skin off one's balls** (*also* **no skin off one's dick, ...testicles**) [1930s+] (*orig. US*) of no importance. □ **no skin off one's nose** (*also* **no skin, no skin off one's back, ...ear, ...elbow, ...hide, ...knuckles, ...shonk, ...teeth, no hair off one's brows**) [20C+] a phr. implying one's contemptuous lack of interest; 'I don't care', 'it doesn't bother me'. □ **one's skin is cracking** [play on SE *parched*, dried out, thirsty] [1950s–60s] (*Aus./N.Z.*) desperate for a drink of alcohol. □ **on my skin** [the primary importance of one's skin colour in prison] [20C+] (*US Und.*) a phr. that implies absolute honesty. □ **on the skin** [1940s–50s] stealing furs. □ **skin catch fire** [20C+] (*W.I.*) a phr. meaning one is obsessed with someone at first sight and wants to possess them immediately. □ **skin dive** *v.* [1980s+] (*Aus. prison*) to inject narcotics. □ **shed one's skin** *v.* [1950s] (*Aus.*) to become hysterical with rage. □ **shoot skin** *v.* (*also* **go in the skin**) [SE *skin*] [1930s+] (*drugs*) to inject narcotics into the skin rather than into a vein; thus as n., *skin-shooter*, one who injects in this way.

IN EXCLAMATIONS

□ **dash my skin!** *see* DASH MY BUTTONS! *under* DASH! *excl.* □ **skin off your nose!** [1900s–60s] (*orig. naut.*) a popular toast; often ext. as *here's to the skin off your nose!*

skin *n.*[2] [? SKIN *n.*[1] (4a)] [mid-19C] a sovereign.

IN PHRASES

□ **for skins** *adv.* [20C+] (*Irish*) at all, in any way.

skin *n.*[3] (*US campus*) **1** [mid-19C–1900s] a lesson one has not learned properly; a lesson learned by any form of cheating aid. **2** [late 19C] that which deceives or cheats. **3** [1900s] a cheat; a liar.

skin *n.*[4] [abbr. SKINFLINT *n.*] [late 19C–1900s] (*US*) a mean, avaricious person.

skin *n.*[5] *see* SKINPOP *n.*

skin *adj.*[1] [SKIN *v.*[1] (4)] [1900s] (*US campus*) unfair.

skin *adj.*[2] [1950s+] (*orig. US*) featuring nudity; usu. in the context of pornography.

IN COMPOUNDS

□ **skin flick** *n.* [1960s+] a pornographic film. □ **skin house** *n.* [1970s+] (*US*) an establishment providing pornographic entertainment. □ **skin joint** *n.* [JOINT *n.* (1)] [1990s+] a nightclub or bar with young women employed to entertain customers. □ **skin mag** *n.* (*also* **skin book, ...magazine, ...rag**) [1960s+] a pornographic magazine.

skin *v.*[1] **1** [mid-18C–1960s] (*also* **skin out**) to steal from. **2** [late 18C+] (*US*) of people, to beat, to overcome completely; of objects, to surpass. **3** [early 19C+] (*also* **skin out**) to take all a person's money, esp. in a gambling game. **4** [mid-19C+] (*also* **skin out of**) to cheat or defraud someone of their money or other possessions; thus n. *skinning*; in fig. use, to exploit. **5** [mid-19C+] to lower in price or value. **6** [late 19C] (*US*) to renege on one's bills or debts. **7** [20C+] to thrash. **8** [1900s] to extract money from a wallet surreptitiously. **9** [1910s] to pass off surreptitiously.

IN COMPOUNDS

□ **skin artist** *n.* [-ARTIST *sfx*] [mid–late 19C] (*US Und.*) a cheating gambler, a cardsharp. □ **skin-disease** *n.* [? its deleterious effects or its (relatively) high cost, which will take all of the purchaser's money] [late 19C–1910s] fourpenny ale. □ **skinflint** *n.* *see* separate entry. □ **skin gambler** *n.* [1900s–50s] (*US Und.*) a cheating gambler. □ **skin game** *n.* (*also* **skin**) **1** [mid-19C+] (*US*) any form of gambling that is designed to fleece the uninitiated; also fig. use. **2** [1930s+] (*US black*) a card-game, spec. tonk or coon can. □ **skin house** *n.* [mid-19C–1900s] (*US*) a corrupt gambling establishment. □ **skin joint** *n.* [JOINT *n.* (1)] [1930s] (*US Und.*) a crooked casino or gambling house.

IN PHRASES

□ **skin the lamb** *v.* [a play on SE *fleece*] **1** [mid-19C–1900s] of a bookmaker, to take bets on every horse in a race other than the winner; thus to make a substantial profit. **2** [mid–late 19C] to swindle, to hoax, to blackmail. **3** [1900s] to 'fix' a horserace.

SE in slang uses

IN PHRASES

□ **skin a louse** *v.* (*also* **skin a fart, ...flea, ...fly**) [mid-19C+] (*Aus./Irish*) to be extremely mean and covetous. □ **skin and grin** *v.* [SKIN *n.*[1] (1e) + SE *grin*] **1** [1950s+] (*W.I.*) to laugh foolishly or ingratiatingly, to pretend to be friendly; thus *skinning and grinning*, laughing foolishly, pretending to be friendly. **2** [1990s+] (*US black*) to act in an openly friendly, happy manner. □ **skin one's eels** *v.* [mid–late 19C] to mind one's own business. □ **skin one's own skunk** *v.* [mid-19C] (*US*) in phr. *let every man skin his own skunk*, to keep private matters to oneself. □ **skin (one's) teeth** *v.* (*also* **'kin teet**) [the amount of gum revealed by such a broad, empty smile] **1** [20C+] (*W.I.*) to smile falsely, although one feels furious or embittered, to laugh cynically. **2** [20C+] to bare one's teeth, to smile broadly. **3** [1970s+] (*W.I./UK black teen*) to have a laugh or a joke with someone or at something, to mess around. □ **skin one's thing** *v.* *see under* THING *n.* □ **skin out** *v.* **1** [late 19C] (*US*) to produce, to show. **2** [1990s+] (*W.I.*) to enjoy oneself. **3** *see* sense 1 above. **4** *see* sense 3 above. □ **skin out of** *v.* *see* sense 4 above. □ **skin-teeth** *n.* [1970s+] (*W.I.*) a false smile. □ **skin the cat** *v.* *see under* CAT *n.*[2]. □ **skin the live rabbit** *v.* *see under* LIVE RABBIT *n.* □ **skin-the-pizzle** *n.* [mid-19C–1900s] the vagina. □ **skin through** *v.* [1900s–20s] to slip through, to pass through narrowly, to get through something with a narrow margin. □ **skin up** *v.* [20C+] (*W.I.*) **1** to overturn. **2** of a woman, to expose oneself, esp. one's buttocks, in an indecent manner; also as *skin up one's clothes/dress/oneself*. □ **skin up one's face** *v.* (*also* **skin up one's lip, ...mouth, ...nose**) [the movement of the skin that is part of the grimace] [1950s+] (*W.I.*) to make a grimace of displeasure, scorn or disapproval. □ **skin up with** *v.* [1950s+] (*W.I.*) to laugh foolishly and ingratiatingly.

skin *v.*[2] [? ext. of SKIN *v.*[1] (4)] [mid–late 19C] (*US campus*) to copy, to cheat in an examination.

skin *v.*[3] (*also* **skin out**) **1** [mid-19C–1920s] (*US*) to abscond, to run off. **2** [1900s–10s] to move at speed.

IN PHRASES

□ **give someone the skin** *v.* [1950s] to ignore, to desert.

skin *v.*[4] **1** [late 19C] (*US*) to glance at, to examine [one fig. 'removes their skin']. **2** [1920s] (*US prison*) to shave a prisoner's head. **3** [1920s] (*US*) to remove and put down one's guns, to disarm oneself.

skin *v.*[5] [SE phr. *by the skin of one's teeth*] [1910s] to survive.

skin *v.*[6] *see* SKINPOP *v.*

skin-and-blister *n.* (*also* **blister, water-blister**) [rhy. sl.] [1910s+] a sister.

skinch *n.* *see* CINCH *n.*[1].

skinder *n.* (*also* **skinner**) [Afk. *skinder*, to slander, to gossip, to tattle] [1970s+] (*S.Afr.*) gossip, slander; thus *skinderbek*, a scandalmonger (lit. 'scandal-mouth').

skinflint *n.* (*also* **flint**) [obs. SE phr. *skin a flint*, to be very mean or greedy] [late 17C+] a mean person.

skin flute *n.* [FLUTE *n.*[1] (2)] [1940s+] the penis.

IN PHRASES

❑ **blow the skin flute** *v.* [1940s+] to fellate. ❑ **play the skin flute** *v.* [1980s+] **1** to masturbate. **2** to fellate.

skinful *n.* [lit. a skin full of alcohol] **1** [late 16C+] a very large amount of alcohol; esp. in phr. *have/get a skinful*, to get very drunk. **2** [early 17C] (*also* **skin**) a large amount. **3** [1920s] the state of being drugged.

skinhead *n.* **1** [1950s+] (*orig. US*) a bald person; thus as a nickname. **2** [1960s+] a shaven head. **3** [1960s+] (*also* **skin**) a member of a teen youth cult whose main identifying features are bald heads, large 'bother' boots, turned-up jeans and braces and who provide much of the 'heavy' element of the modern neo-Nazi movements. **4** [1970s] one who resembles sense 3.

skink *n.* [ety. unknown] [1990s+] (*UK black*) a term of abuse for a white person.

skinker *n.* (*also* **skink**) [note UK milit. *skink*, menial tasks performed by the junior officer in the regiment] [early 17C–mid-19C] a waiter, one who pours wine.

skin me! *excl.* **1** [late 19C] (*US Western*) a general oath. **2** [1950s+] (*US black*) a form of greeting involving ritual palm slapping [imper. form of GIVE SOME SKIN *under* SKIN *n.*[1]].

skinned *adj.* [SE *skin*/SKIN *v.*[1]] **1** [mid-19C] empty of, lacking in. **2** [late 19C–1930s] comprehensively beaten, utterly defeated. **3** [late 19C–1940s] (*also* **skinned out**) deprived of one's money, esp. after gambling unsuccessfully. **4** [1950s–60s] (*orig. Aus.*) totally bereft.

skinner *n.*[1] [SKIN *v.*[1]] **1** [late 18C–1950s] one who defrauds another of their money. **2** [mid-19C; 1940s] (*orig. UK Und.*) one who has no money. **3** [late 19C+] a bet that brings large profits to the bookmakers [20C+ use mainly Aus./N.Z.]. **4** [late 19C+] (*Aus.*) a horse that wins despite very long odds; by ext. any form of racing coup. **5** [1940s+] (*N.Z.*) an object that is useless or used up.

skinner *n.*[2] [SE *skin*] [mid–late 19C] a thief, usu. a woman, who waylays young children and strips them of their clothes, which she then sells.

skinner *n.*[3] [abbr. SE *mule-skinner*] [1910s–60s] (*Can./US*) a mule or horse-driver.

skinner *n.*[4] [SE *skin*] **1** [1920s–30s] (*US prison*) a new prison inmate. **2** [1950s+] (*US prison/Und.*) a rapist; a sex offender.

skinner *n.*[5] [? SE phr. *by the skin of one's teeth*] [1920s+] (*Aus.*) an appointment that one has deliberately avoided.

skinner *n.*[6] *see* SKINDER *n.*

skinning *n.*[1] [SKIN *v.*[1] (1)] [mid-19C] (*US Und.*) the theft of cargo from ships by harbour thieves.

skinning *n.*[2] [SKIN *v.*[1] (3)/SE *skin*] **1** [mid-19C+] the fleecing of a victim, e.g. by a confidence trickster. **2** [1920s+] (*US*) a beating, whether physical or verbal.

IN COMPOUNDS

❑ **skinning game** *n.* [mid–late 19C] (*US*) any form of corrupt, crooked gambling, e.g. poker, faro and the establishment where it takes place. ❑ **skinning house** *n.* (*also* **brace house, skinning den, ...joint**) [SKIN *v.*[1] (3) + SE *house*/JOINT *n.* (3)/*den*; BRACE *v.* (1)] [late 19C–1940s] (*US*) a casino or any place of entertainment where confidence tricksters or crooked gamblers operate.

skinning *n.*[3] [SKIN *v.*[6]; ult. abbr. SKINPOP *v.*] [1960s+] the injecting of a narcotic into the skin but not into a vein.

skinny *n.*[1] [? a thin coin] [1940s] (*US Und.*) a ten-cent piece, a dime.

skinny *n.*[2] [SKIN *n.*[1] (3a)] [1940s+] (*Aus./N.Z.*) a woman; a girl.

skinny *n.*[3] [? play on SE *skin*, i.e. 'the naked truth', 'the bare facts'] **1** [1950s+] information; often as *inside skinny, hot skinny*. **2** [1970s+] the truth.

IN PHRASES

❑ **straight skinny** *n.* [STRAIGHT *adj.*[1] (2)] [1960s–70s] (*US*) the truth.

skinny *n.*[4] *see* SAMMY *n.* (3).

skinny *adj.*

SE in slang uses

IN COMPOUNDS

❑ **skinny-ass** *adj.* (*also* **skinny-assed**) [-ASS *sfx*] [1950s+] (*orig. US*) of a person, thin. ❑ **skinny-dipping** *n. see* separate entry. ❑ **skinny Lizzie** *n.* [1950s+] a thin woman. ❑ **skinny worker** *n.* [1940s] (*US Und.*) a sneak thief.

IN PHRASES

❑ **thrilled skinny** *adj.* [20C+] (*Irish*) very excited, very enthusiastic.

skinny as a broom *n.* [rhy. sl.] [20C+] a bridegroom.

skinny-dip *n.* [SKINNY-DIP *v.* (1)] [1960s+] a swim in the nude.

skinny-dip *v.* [1950+] (*orig. US*) to swim in the nude.

skinny-dipper *n.* [SKINNY-DIP *v.* (1)] [1970s+] a person who swims in the nude.

skinny-dipping *n.* [SE *skinny* + DIP *v.*[2]] [2000s] picking pockets on the London Underground; the idea being that the pickpocket has to be thin to work in the crowds.

skinpop *n.* (*also* **skin**) [SKINPOP *v.*] [1940s+] (*drugs*) an injection into the flesh rather than directly into a vein.

skinpop *v.* (*also* **pop, skin**) [SE *skin* + POP *v.*[1] (1)] [1940s+] (*drugs*) to inject a narcotic beneath the skin rather than directly into a vein; the effect of such an injection is less immediate and somewhat weaker.

skinpopper *n.* [SKINPOP *v.* (1)] [1950s+] (*drugs*) a narcotics user who injects into the skin rather into a vein; the assumption is that such a user is less wholly habituated.

skins *n.* [his job] [late 18C] a tanner.

skint *adj.* [SKINNED *adj.* (3)] [1910s+] without money, out of funds; sometimes intensified as *skint stony*; also *skun(t)*, to be made penniless.

skin-the-lamb *n.* (*also* **lamb skin-it**) [pun on pron.] [mid-19C] the card-game *lansquenet*.

skintight *n.* [1900s] a sausage.

skintight *adj.* [pun on SE *skintight* + TIGHT *adj.* (9)] [1960s] really friendly.

skip *n.*[1] [abbr. SKIPPER *n.*[2] (2)] **1** [mid-19C+] the captain. **2** [1920s] (*US prison*) a jailer. **3** [1930s+] as a term of address, esp. to a boss, a manager, a barman etc.

skip *n.*[2] [SKIP *v.* (1)] **1** [late 19C–1930s] (*US*) the act of absconding, running away. **2** [20C+] an act of ignoring, passing by. **3** [1910s+] (*US*) an absconder, esp. one who leaves without paying their debts. **4** [1980s+] (*US campus/teen*) in pl., tennis shoes. **5** *see* SKIP-KENNEL *under* SKIP *v.*

IN COMPOUNDS

❑ **skip tracer** *n.* [SE *tracer*] [1930s+] (*US*) an investigator who tracks down those who default on hotel and other bills; thus *skip-tracing*, the investigation.

IN PHRASES

❑ **on the skip** [late 19C] running away.

skip *n.*[3] [abbr. SKIPPY *n.*[2] (1)] [2000s] (*Aus.*) an Anglo-Australian.

skip *v.* [SE 15C–early 19C] **1** [early 19C+] to leave, to escape, to run off. **2** [late 19C–1900s] to die. **3** [20C+] to avoid, to run away from, e.g. a school lesson. **4** [20C+] to overlook, to forget. **5** [1980s+] to expel.

IN COMPOUNDS

❑ **skip-kennel** *n.* (*also* **skip**) [he *skips* or jumps over the SE *kennel*, *i.e.*, gutter] [mid-17C–mid-19C] a footman. ❑ **skip-out** *n.* [1950s] (*US*) an absconder, e.g. from a hotel bill.

IN PHRASES

❑ **skip on** *v.* [1980s+] (*US campus*) to go away, to leave. ❑ **skip out** *v.* (*also* **skip out on**) [mid-19C+] (*orig. US*) to desert, to abandon, to run off. ❑ **skip the crap** *v. see* CUT THE CRAP *v.* ❑ **skip the tralaloo** *v.* [1940s] to run off without permission.

IN EXCLAMATIONS

❑ **skip it!** *excl.* **1** [20C+] (*orig. US*) forget it! don't bother! etc. **2** [1950s+] (*orig. US*) imper., go away! leave!

skip and jump *n.* [rhy. sl.] [20C+] **1** a pump. **2** the heart [rhy. sl. = PUMP *n.* (1)].

skip-jack *n.* [SE *skip* + *jack*, generic for a man] **1** [mid-16C–1920s] a conceited fop or dandy. **2** [17C] a jockey. **3** [17C–early 19C] (*UK Und.*) a horse-trader's boy, who puts the horses through their paces.

skipper *n.*[1] [Welsh *ysgubor*, a barn] **1** [mid-16C+] (*also* **skypper**) in weak senses of sense 2, a shelter for tramps and other homeless people. **2** [late 16C–1930s] (*also* **skepper**) a barn. **3** [1920s+] one who sleeps in hedges and outhouses.

IN COMPOUNDS

❑ **skipper-bird** *n.* [BIRD *n.*[1] (1)] [mid-19C] one who sleeps in a barn, a tramp, a vagrant.

IN PHRASES

❑ **do a skipper** *v.* [1930s–70s] to sleep rough.

skipper *n.*[2] [SE *skipper*, a ship's captain] **1** [19C] the devil. **2** [mid-19C+] (*also* **skip**) a boss, a manager, a police sergeant or captain etc. **3** [1910s+] a general mode of address. **4** see CAPTAIN *n.* (11).

skipper *n.*[3] [SKIP *v.* (1)] **1** [late 19C; 1930s] one who is retreating or leaving; an absconder. **2** [1990s+] a young woman, esp. promiscuous and under the age of consent [SE *skip*, i.e. from partner to partner].

skippering *n.* [SKIPPER (IT) *v.* (1)] [mid-19C+] sleeping in derelict, empty houses, barns, sleeping rough.

skipper (it) *v.* [SKIPPER *n.*[1]] [mid-19C+] to sleep rough.

skippies *n.* [? SE *skip*, i.e. like a child] [1990s+] (*US*) cheap trainers, rather than those manufactured by major labels.

skippy *n.*[1] [SE *skip*, to jump around] **1** [1930s–40s] (*US black*) an effeminate homosexual man. **2** [1990s+] (*US campus*) an over-energetic person.

skippy *n.*[2] [the TV series *Skippy, the Bush Kangaroo*] [1980s] (*Aus.*) a derog./racist term for a white child; a white youth.

skippy *n.*[3] *see* SKIBBY *n.*

skippy *adj.* [ety. unknown] [1970s+] (*US black*) right, correct.

skirmish *v.* [mid-19C–1910s] (*US*) to look around in search of something.

skirrach *n. see* SKERRICK *n.*

skirt *n.* [late 19C+] **1** a woman, usu. an attractive woman. **2** a generic term for women as a group.

IN COMPOUNDS

❑ **skirt-chaser** *n.* [1920s+] (*orig. W.I/US*) a Don Juan, a habitual and dedicated ladies' man; thus *skirt-chasing*, womanizing. ❑ **skirt duty** *n.* [1920s] of a woman, the practice of acting in a way designed to attract men; of a man, associating with women. ❑ **skirt foist** *n. see under* FOIST *n.*[2]. ❑ **skirt-lifter** *n.* [play on *SHIRTLIFTER under* SHIRT *n.*] [1980s] a lesbian. ❑ **skirtman** *n.* [1970s] (*US black*) a man who is dominated by his female partner. ❑ **skirt patrol** *n.* [1940s] (*US*) the activity of wandering around looking for female companionship.

IN PHRASES

❑ **bit of skirt** *n.* [late 19C+] a woman. ❑ **do a bit of skirt** *v.* (*also* **have a bit of skirt**) [late 19C+] to have sexual intercourse.

IN EXCLAMATIONS

❑ **up your dirty skirt!** [1940s] (*US*) a general excl. of abuse, aimed at a woman.

skirt *adj.* [2000s] (*Aus.*) effeminate.

skish *n.* [? echoic of slurred tones] [1900s] (*US*) a state of drunkenness.

skit *n.*[1] [late 18C+] (*Irish*) a joke, a game.

skit *n.*[2] [mid-19C] (*UK Und.*) a lively young woman or girl.

skit *n.*[3] [? link to Scot. *skit*, a piece of ostentation] [1960s] (*US black*) a garment.

skit *v.*[1] [SE *skit*, to caper or leap around] [late 18C–early 19C] to wheedle.

skit *v.*[2] [Afk. *skut*, to impound] [1950s+] (*S.Afr.*) to steal, to 'pinch'.

skite *n.* [SKITE *v.*[1] (1)] (*Aus./N.Z.*) **1** [mid-19C+] boasting, bragging. **2** [20C+] a braggart, a boaster. **3** [1910s] (*Irish*) a silly, frivolous person. **4** [1910s] a complaint. **5** [1910s] nonsense.

IN PHRASES

❑ **on the skite** *adj.* (*also* **on the skyte**) [Scot. *scit*, a slight shower] [20C+] (*Scot./Irish*) engaged in serious drinking.

skite *v.*[1] [abbr. BLATHERSKITE *n.*] [mid-19C+] (*Aus./N.Z.*) to boast or brag; thus *skite up*, to extol, to praise; *nothing to skite about*, nothing to make a fuss about.

skite *v.*[2] *see* SKATE *v.*[1].

skiter *n.* [SKITE *v.*[1] (1)] [late 19C+] (*Aus./N.Z.*) an incessant talker; a braggart.

skite-the-gutter *n.* [OE *skite*, to defecate] [20C+] (*Ulster*) an unimportant person.

skitey *adj.* [SKITE *v.*[1]] [1940s+] (*Aus./N.Z.*) boastful.

skiting *n.* [SKITE *v.*[1]] [20C+] (*Aus./N.Z.*) boasting, bragging.

skitter *n.* [? SE *skit*, to act skittishly] **1** [1900s–20s] a person. **2** [1940s+] (*Irish*) an unruly child, a disreputable young person.

skitters, the *n.* [dial. *skitter*, ult. OE *scitte*, diarrhoea] [mid-19C+] diarrhoea.

skittle *n. see* SKETEL *n.*

skittles *n.*[1] [i.e. one can 'knock it down' easily; note chess jargon *skittles*, chess played without serious application] [mid-19C–1940s] nonsense, rubbish; also used as excl. *skittles!* rubbish!

skittles *n.*[2] [1950s] food or drink.

skitz *n. see* SCHIZ *n.*

skitzing *n.* [SE *schizophrenia*] [1990s+] (*US black teen*) acting in a bizarre or eccentric manner.

skitzy *adj. see* SCHIZZY *adj.*

skiv *n.*[1] (*also* **skid**) [ety. unknown; 'fashionable slang' (Hotten, 1859)] [mid–late 19C] a sovereign.

skiv *n.*[2] *see* CHIV *n.*[1].

skiv *n.*[3] *see* SKIVVY *n.*[2].

skive *n.* [SKIVE *v.* (1)] [1910s+] an evasion, a way of getting out of one's responsibilities.

skive *v.* (*also* **skive off**) [? dial. *skive*, to move quickly or Fr. *esquiver*, to dodge, to slink away] [1910s+] (*orig. milit.*) to neglect one's duties or work.

skiver *n.* [SKIVE *v.*] [1940s+] a 'lazybones', a shirker.

skivver *v.* [? dial. *skive*, to move quickly] [1940s] (*US black*) to wander around.

skivvies *n.* [ety. unknown] **1** [1910s+] (*US*) (*also* **skivvie drawers, skivvs**) men's underwear, esp. underpants. **2** [1950s] a vest, esp. in the form of a *skivvy shirt*. **3** [1970s] women's underwear.

skivvy *n.*[1] [presumably a var. on SKIBBY *n.* (2), although citations put dates at variance] **1** [late 19C] a derog. term for a Japanese person. **2** [1950s–60s] a Japanese prostitute.

IN COMPOUNDS

❑ **skivvy house** *n.* (*also* **scivvie house**) a brothel.

skivvy *n.*[2] (*also* **sciv, scivvie, skiv, skivy**) [? SLAVEY *n.*; *see also* ety. for SKIBBY *n.* (2)] [late 19C+] a maid of all work.

skivvy *v.* [SKIVVY *n.*[2] (1)] [1910s+] to perform menial tasks.

skiz *see under* SCHIZ.

skizzah *n.* [? ext. of SKEEZA *n.*] [2000s] (*US black*) an unpopular person.

skizzel *n.* [SKIZZLE *v.*] [1930s+] (*US*) a promiscuous woman.

skizzle *v.* [? nonce-word] [1930s+] (*US*) to have sexual intercourse.

skizzy *adj.* **1** [1960s] a general term of approval, admiration [SCHIZZY *adj.* on bad = good model]. **2** [1970s] disgusting, dirty, repellant, a general term of disapproval [var. SCUZZY *adj.* (1)].

sko *n.* [abbr. SKANKY *adj.* + HO *n.*; compare SKOOCHIE *n.*] [1990s+] (*US black/campus*) a disgusting, promiscuous woman.

skob *n.* [ety. unknown] [1940s–50s] (*US teen*) a pretty young woman.

skobby *v. see* SCOOBY *v.*

skobie *n.* (*also* **skobe**) [perceived 'vulgarity' of the given name] [2000s] (*Irish*) derog. term for a member of the working classes.

skoff *n. see* SCOFF *n.*

skoll *v. see* SKULL *v.*[1] (3).

skolly *n.* (*also* **skollie, skolly-boy**) [? Du. *schoelje*, a scavenger, but note *skorriemorrie*, a rascal, riffraff, ult. Yid. *soyrerumoyre*, a rogue, a hoodlum; *DSAE* suggests SE *scullery boy*, 'a very low form of humanity'] [1930s+] (*S.Afr.*) a street thug, a hoodlum, usu. a member of a gang.

skomfaan *n.* [Zulu *isigomfane*, formed on *gomfa*, to bend, crouch or stoop; presumably its effects 'knock down' the drinker] [1960s+] (*S.Afr. township*) a potent illicitly-brewed alcoholic drink.

skommel *v.* [ety. unknown] [1990s+] (*S.Afr.*) to masturbate.

skonce *n. see* SCONCE *n.*

skoobied *adj. see* SCOOBIED *adj.*

skooby *v. see* SCOOBY *v.*

skoochie *n.* [abbr. SKANKY *adj.* + HOOCHIE *n.*[1]; compare SKO *n.*] [1990s+] (*US black/campus*) a disgusting, promiscuous woman; also (derog.) a lesbian.

skoofer *n.* (*also* **skoofus, skroofus, skrufer**) [ety. unknown; ? link to SKUIF *n.*] [1970s+] (*US black/drugs*) a marijuana cigarette.

skookum *adj.* [Chinook jargon *skookum*, strong] [late 19C+] (*Can., mainly west coast*) satisfactory, OK.

skookum house *n.* (*also* **skookum**) [Chinook jargon. *skookum*, strong + SE *house*] [late 19C–1920s] (*Can., mainly west coast/ US*) a prison; often preceded by *strong*.

skop *n.* [Afk. *skop*, a kick; cognate with KICK *n.*[1]] (*S.Afr.*) **1** [1920s+] a kick. **2** [1960s+] a good time, a dance, a party; thus *skop, skiet en donder*, lit. 'kick, shoot and thunder', any rough and tough activity, an action film. **3** [1980s+] a thrill, a kick (from a drink or drug).

skop *v.* [SKOP *n.*] [1960s+] (*S.Afr.*) **1** to enjoy oneself, to 'party'; thus *skop lawaai*, to have a rowdy, noisy good time. **2** to kick something or someone; thus *skop it*, to die.

skorking *n.* [ety. unknown] [2000s] (*US*) sexual intercourse.

skorrie-morrie *n.* [Afk. *skorrie-morrie*, a hooligan, one who is part of the lowest section of the community] [1910s+] (*S.Afr.*) a good-for-nothing.

skosh *n.* [Jap. *sukoshi*] [1940s+] (*orig. US milit.*) a little bit.

skowbanker *n. see* SCOWBANKER *n.*

skr... *see also under* SCR...

skrag *v. see* SCRAG *v.*

skrik *n.* [Du. *schrik*, a fright] [late 19C+] (*S.Afr.*) a fright, a tremor of fear.

skrik *v.* [SKRIK *n.*] [late 19C+] (*S.Afr.*) to be terrified.

skroofus/skrufer *n. see* SKOOFER *n.*

skrunty *adj.* [? SE *runt*] [1970s] (*US*) unpleasant, mean.

skud *n.* [Afk. *skud*, to shake] [1970s] (*S.Afr. prison*) a cell search.

skuffle *n. see* SCUFFLE *n.*[2].

skuffling *adj.* [SCUFFLE *v.* (1)] [1970s+] a derogatory epithet.

skuffter *n. see* SCUFFER *n.*

skuif *n.* (*also* **skuifie, skyf, skyfie**) [Afk. *skuif*, a draw, a puff] [1970s+] (*S.Afr.*) **1** a cigarette. **2** (*also* **boomskuif**) marijuana. **3** (*also* **boomskuif**) a marijuana cigarette. **4** a suck, a taste.

skuif *v.* (*also* **skuyf**) [SKUIF *n.*] **1** [1970s] (*S.Afr.*) to smoke a (marijuana) cigarette. **2** [1970s+] to smoke.

skulk *v.* [1970s] (*US campus*) to steal.

skulker *n.* (*also* **skulk**) [Scand. *skulka*, to lurk, *skolka* to play truant; orig. milit. jargon *skulker*, a soldier who shirks his duties by hiding away; SE from mid-19C] [late 18C+] one who hides themselves to avoid labour.

skull *n.*[1] (*also* **scull**) **1** [early 18C–mid-19C] the head, principal or master of a university college. **2** by metonymy, an individual. (**a**) [1910s] (*US*) a fellow soldier, with derog. implication. (**b**) [1940s] (*Aus.*) a person in authority, e.g. in armed forces. **3** [1910s–40s] (*US*) a free ticket. **4** [1920s] a share, a portion, a 'go'; in phr. denoting price, *so much a skull*. **5** [1940s] (*US black*) a star, an outstanding performer. [i.e. what is within the skull: brains, talent, ability]. **6** [1940s+] (*Aus.*) in the game of two-up, a 'head'. **7** [1960s] (*Aus.*) a bottle top. **8** [1970s+] (*orig. US black*) in senses of oral sex. (**a**) (*also* **skully**) fellatio. (**b**) cunnilingus.

DERIVATIVES

❑ **skulled** *adj.* [OUT OF ONE'S SKULL below] [1950s+] **1** (*also* **skulled out**) intoxicated by a drug or by an excess of alcohol. **2** insane, crazy.

IN COMPOUNDS

❑ **skull book** *n.* [1960s] (*US black*) anything committed to memory; oral tradition. ❑ **skullbust** *v.* [1950s] (*US black*) to talk in a convincing and excessive manner. ❑ **skull-buster** *n.* [BUST *v.*[1]] **1** [1920s+] (*US*) anything seen as especially intellectually challenging, esp. a hard college course. **2** [1930s+] (*US black*) a police officer. ❑ **skullbusting** *adj.* [BUST *v.*[1] (1)] [1940s+] (*US*) intellectually challenging. ❑ **skull-cracker** *n.* **1** [late 19C–1930s] (*US*) very strong alcohol. **2** [1910s–50s] (*US*) a large thuggish person. ❑ **skull-cracking** *n.* **1** [1920s] (*US*) hard physical work. **2** [1930s] (*US*) fighting. ❑ **skulldrag** *n.* [DRAG *n.*[1] (1)] [1940s–60s] (*US black*) any activity that taxes the mind or emotions. ❑ **skull drag** *v.* [note late 19C N.Z. gang, the *Skulldraggers;* Lincoln U. (Oxford, Penn.) use c.1934: 'SKULL-DRAG. To play hard'] **1** [mid-19C+] (*Aus.*) to haul along, to drag by force. **2** [1920s–40s] (*US Und.*) to demand a free drink in a bar. **3** [1960s] (*US teen*) to study. ❑ **skull drive** *v.* [i.e. to drive knowledge into reluctant skulls] [late 19C–1920s] (*Aus.*) to work as a schoolteacher. ❑ **skull file** *n.* [1960s] (*US black*) one's mind, esp. in context of thoughts/memories that are stored there. ❑ **skull-filler** *n.* [1900s] (*Aus.*) a schoolteacher. ❑ **skull fry** *n. see* FRY *n.* ❑ **skull fuck** *n.* [FUCK *n.* (1)] [1990s+] (*US*) heterosexual male-female intercourse whereby the male subsitutes the mouth for the vagina; this differs from fellatio in that the man is active rather than passive. ❑ **skull fuck** *v.* [FUCK *v.*] [1990s+] of a man, to have intercourse with a woman, using her mouth rather than her vagina. ❑ **skull game** *n.* [1970s] an intellectual pursuit. ❑ **skull job** *n.* [JOB *n.*[2] (2)] [1950s+] oral sex, whether fellatio or cunnilingus. ❑ **skullneck** *v.* [one removes the skull from the neck] [20C+] to decapitate. ❑ **skull note** *n.* [1960s] (*US black*) a mental note. ❑ **skull note** *v.* [1960s] (*US black*) to memorize. ❑ **skull orchard** *n.* [1930s–50s] (*US black*) a cemetery. ❑ **skull-popper** *n.* [1950s] (*US*) a very strong drink. ❑ **skull pussy** *n.* [PUSSY *n.* (1)] [1970s+] (*US gay*) a fellator. ❑ **skull session** *n.* [1950s+] (*US*) a discussion, a conference. ❑ **skull-thatcher** *n.* **1** [late 18C–19C] a wig-maker. **2** [mid-19C] a maker of straw bonnets. **3** [mid-19C] a hat. ❑ **skull trouble** *n.* [1900s–30s] (*US*) a blow on the head.

IN PHRASES

❑ **get one's skull swelled** *v. see* HAVE A SWELLED HEAD *under* SWELLHEAD *n.*[2]. ❑ **get skull** *v.* [1990s+] to receive oral intercourse. ❑ **give skull** *v.* [1990s+] to fellate. ❑ **out of one's skull** *adj.* **1** [1950s+] crazy. **2** [1960s+] an intensifer, meaning extremely bored. **3** [1960s+] intoxicated, either through drink or, later, drugs. ❑ **pad one's skull** *v.* [1950s] (*US black*) to pass on information, to render pleasure. ❑ **whip some skull on** *v.* [1970s+] to fellate.

IN EXCLAMATIONS

❑ **pull your skull in!** *see* PULL YOUR HEAD IN! *under* HEAD *n.*

skull *n.*[2] [? SE *skulduggery*] [20C+] (*W.I., Trin.*) a trick, an act of deception; thus *pull a skull on*, to deceive.

skull *v.*[1] **1** [1940s+] (*US/Aus.*) to hit someone on the head. **2** [1970s+] (*orig. US black*) to perform oral sex. **3** [1980s+] (*Aus./N.Z.*) (*also* **scull, skoll**) to drink down a large container of beer in one go [SE *skull*, into which it is poured + *skol!* a toast].

IN PHRASES

❑ **could skull the cap of a can of beer** [2000s] (*N.Z.*) a phr. used to describe someone who is very thirsty.

skull *v.*[2] [? SE *skulk*] [1990s+] (*W.I.*) to play truant.

skull and crossbones *n.* [the acknowledged sign for 'poison'] **1** [1930s] (*US*) blackmail. **2** [1980s] (*US black*) poison. **3** [1980s] (*US black*) anyone who is 'poison', esp. one who disrupts one's plans.

skullbanker *n. see* SCOWBANKER *n.*

skully *n.* **1** [2000s] (*US*) a skull-cap. **2** *see* SKULL *n.*[1] (8).

skunge *v.* [? SE *scrounge*] [2000s] (*N.Z.*) to beg or borrow, e.g. a cigarette.

skunk *n.* **1** [1950s] (*US*) (*also* **skunkie**) a bedwetter. **2** [1960s–80s] a woman, esp. one who smells badly. **3** [1970s] (*US*) a black and white police car. **4** in drug uses. (**a**) [1980s+] (*drugs*) (*also* **skunkweed**) an exceptionally strong variety of marijuana (often grown in the user's home) with up to 30% tetrahydrocannabidinol (THC) content, thus intensifying the effects from the merely stimulating to those of such hallucinogens as LSD; thus *superskunk*, an even stronger variety. (**b**) [2000s] (*US black*) poor quality marijuana. (**c**) [2000s] heroin.

skunk *adj.* [1940s+] (*US black*) second-rate, inferior.

skunk *v.* **1** [mid-19C] (*US campus*) to renege on a bill. **2** [mid-19C+] (*US/W.I. sport*) to beat decisively; also fig. use. **3** [late 19C–1960s] (*US tramp*) to cheat. **4** [1900s–30s] to finish off, to consume.

skunked *adj.* [SKUNK v. (3)] **1** [1920s+] deceived, tricked. **2** [1920s+] very drunk [SE colloq. phr. *drunk as a skunk*]. **3** [1990s+] intoxicated by very strong marijuana [SKUNK *n.* (1)].

skunked! *excl.* [1900s] (*US*) an excl. of surprise.

skunkie *n. see* SKUNK *n.* (1).

skunkweed *n. see* SKUNK *n.* (4a).

skunky *adj.* [SE colloq. *skunk*, a contemptible person] [1920s+] disgusting, contemptible.

skunky *adv.* [SE colloq. phr. *drunk as a skunk*] [1950s] very drunk.

skupter *n.* [SCUFFER *n.*] [mid-19C] (*UK Und.*) a policeman.

skuyf *v. see* SKUIF *v.*

skuz *n. see* SCUZZ *n.*

skuzzy *adj. see* SCUZZY *adj.*

sky *n.*[1] [rhy. sl. = EYETIE *n.*] [1920s+] (*Aus.*) an Italian.

sky *n.*[2] **1** [1930s–40s] (*US black*) a police officer; a prison warder [the blue uniform]. **2** [1940s+] (*US black*) a hat [it is above the head].

SE in slang uses

IN COMPOUNDS

❑ **sky artist** *n.* [-ARTIST *sfx*] [1940s] a psychiatrist. ❑ **skybird** *n.* [1940s] (*US black*) a hallucination. ❑ **sky blue** *see* separate entries. ❑ **sky drummer** *n.* [DRUMMER *n.*[2]] [1900s] (*Aus.*) a missionary. ❑ **sky farmer** *n. see* separate entry. ❑ **sky high** *v. see* BLOW SKY HIGH *v.* (1). ❑ **sky hoot** *v.* [SE *hoot*, i.e. *blow* (*sky high*)] (*US*) [late 19C–1920s] **1** to rise, to increase. **2** to run off, to move fast; to act irresponsibly. ❑ **sky-juice** *n.* [1920s–40s] (*US*) rainwater. ❑ **sky kick** *n. see under* KICK *n.*[4]. ❑ **skylark** *v. see* LARK *v.* (2). ❑ **skylarker** *n. see* separate entry. ❑ **skylight** *n.* [late 18C–mid-19C] the small space between the top of a glass and the drink within it. ❑ **skylights** *n.* **1** [early 19C–1910s] eyes. **2** [1900s] spectacles. ❑ **sky-parlour** *n.* [late 18C–19C] a garret. ❑ **sky-piece** *n.* **1** [1900s–10s] (*US*) the head. **2** [1900s–70s] (*US*) any form of headgear. ❑ **skypilot** *n.* (*also* **kirk pilot, pilot, sky pi, sky scout, sky-sharp, soul aviator**) [he guides one to heaven] [late 19C+] a priest, a prison chaplain, a preacher, a missionary. ❑ **sky-rocket** *n. see* separate entries. ❑ **sky rug** *n.* [RUG *n.*[1] (1)] [1940s+] (*US*) a wig or toupee. ❑ **sky-scraper** *n. see* separate entries. ❑ **sky-topper** *n.* [late 19C–1920s] someone or something very high.

IN PHRASES

❑ **dive into the sky** *v. see under* DIVE *v.* ❑ **in the skies** *adj.* [the image is cognate with FLY *v.* (3)/HIGH *adj.*[1] but antedates both] [1900s] intoxicated by a drug.

sky *n.*[3] (*also* **ski**) [abbr.] [1940s+] (*WW II/Aus.*) whisky.

sky *n.*[4] *see* BLUE SKY *n.*[3].

sky *n.*[5] *see* SKY (ROCKET) *n.*

sky *v.* [SE *sky*] **1** in lit./fig.senses of 'above' or 'upwards'. (**a**) [19C+] to toss into the air. (**b**) [late 19C–1900s] to spend all one's funds, esp. in a carefree, spendthrift manner. (**c**) [late 19C–1920s] of a picture, to hang high on the gallery wall. (**d**) [1970s+] (*US campus*) to jump high. (**e**) [1980s] (*US black*) to wear or have on one's head. **2** (*also* **sky out**) in senses of departure. (**a**) [1930s+] to leave. (**b**) [1970s] (*US prison*) to escape.

IN PHRASES

❑ **sky a copper** *v.* [19C] **1** to toss a coin. **2** to make a noise, to make a nuisance of oneself. ❑ **sky off** *v.* [1970s+] (*US black*) to depart, to exit. ❑ **sky out** *v. see* sense 2 above. ❑ **sky the wipe** *v.* (*also* **sky the rag, ...towel**) [orig. boxing jargon; WIPE *n.* (3)/RAG *n.*[1] (2e)/SE *towel*] [1900s–50s] (*Aus.*) to surrender.

-sky *sfx see* -SKI *sfx.*

sky blue *n.* **1** in senses of drink. (**a**) [mid-18C–mid-19C] gin, esp. second-rate gin. (**b**) [late 18C–19C] 'London milk, much diluted with water, or from which the cream has been too closely skimmed' (Hotten, 1860). (**c**) [mid-19C] (*N.Z.*) a milkman or a nickname for a milkman. (**d**) [1900s–10s] vegetable soup. **2** with ref. to blue uniforms. (**a**) [19C] (*Can.*) an officer of the Hudson's Bay Company, usu. in pl. (**b**) [mid-19C] (*US*) a soldier. (**c**) [20C+] (*S.Afr.*) a long-term prisoner. **3** [1970s] (*drugs*) a brand of LSD.

sky-blue *adv.* [1950s] (*US*) excessively.

skycer *n. see* SHICER *n.*

sky-diver *n.* [rhy. sl. = FIVER *n.* (1)] [20C+] £5.

skyf *n. see* SKUIF *n.*

skyfarmer *n.* ['the isle of Sky(e), or some other remote place [...] or else from their farms being *in nubibus*, "in the clouds"' (Grose, 1785)] **1** [mid-18C–early 19C] (*UK Und.*) a criminal beggar who tours the country posing as a gentleman farmer fallen on hard times, backed by suitably impressive, if counterfeit, papers. **2** [19C–1910s] (*Anglo-Irish*) a farmer with very little, if any, land.

skyfie *n. see* SKUIF *n.*

skyfoozle *v.* [late 19C] to disconcert.

skygodlin *adj.* (*also* **sigoggling, skygoggling**) [? SE *sky* + *goggle*; i.e. one who, instead of looking straight ahead, looks upwards] [mid-19C+] (*US*) askew, slanted.

skyhacking *n.* [CHI-IKE *n.* (2)] [1920s+] (*Aus.*) slandering, talking behind someone's back.

skylark *n.* [rhy. sl.] [20C+] a park.

skylarker *n.* [using the legitimate job to facilitate the villainy, he gets up early – 'with the lark' – to spy out vulnerable houses] [late 18C] a thief who doubles as a journeyman bricklayer.

sky-pocket *n.* [? rhy. sl.; var. on SKY KICK *under* SKY *n.*[2]] [1940s] (*US black*) an inside pocket.

skypper *n. see* SKIPPER *n.*[1] (1).

sky (rocket) *n.* [rhy. sl.] [late 19C+] a pocket.

IN PHRASES

❑ **dive into one's sky** *v.* [late 19C] to put one's hand in one's pocket, esp. to remove money. ❑ **touch one's sky** *v.* [1950s+] (*Aus.*) to pay for a round of drinks.

sky rocket *n.*[1] [mid-19C–1940s] (*US*) a form of college cheer, rounded off with a cry of *sis-boom-bah!*, supposedly that of an ascending and exploding rocket.

sky rocket *n.*[2] [1980s+] (*Aus. prison*) a homosexual.

sky-scraper *n.*[1] [18C naut. jargon *sky-scraper*, a triangular sky-sail, the highest sail on a boat. Such sails were also known as *moon-rakers*. The orig. US use of the term to mean a tall building, began life as sl. (*c.*1888; cited as such in Maitland's *American Slang Dict.*, 1891) but had entered the mainstream by 1920; note *NY Times* 18 Aug. 1837 2/7: [Balloon flights are] so common a business that the people call it nothing more than 'skylarking', or 'sky scraping'; also 1880s baseball jargon *skyscraper*, a 'towering fly ball'] **1** [19C] a tall hat or bonnet. **2** [mid-19C–1900s] a notably tall person. **3** [late 19C] a rider on a 'penny-farthing' cycle. **4** [late 19C] the penis.

sky-scraper *n.*[2] [the horse *Skyscraper*, sired by Highflyer, which won the Epsom Derby in 1789] [19C] a tall horse.

skyscraper *n.* [rhy. sl.] [1960s+] a newspaper.

slaat *n.* [synon. Du.] [20C+] (*S.Afr.*) a blow.

slaat *v.* [SLAAT *n.*] [20C+] (*S.Afr.*) to hit, to beat up; fig., to sell.

slab *n.* **1** [early 19C–1900s] a milestone. **2** [late 19C–1920s] (*Aus.*) a tough(-looking) person or creature [SAusE *slab*, 'a coarse, axe-hewn plank, two or three inches in thickness' (*OED*)]. **3** [late 19C+] a sandwich or bread. **4** [1900s] (*US Und.*) a shop display tray. **5** [1920s+] (*US*) a stretcher, an undertaker's table.

6 [1930s–40s] (*US*) a small town. **7** [1930s+] (*US black*) a bed. **8** [1960s] (*US*) a highway. **9** [1970s+] (*US black*) $1. **10** [1980s+] in drug uses. (**a**) weak or impure crack cocaine [? SE (*mortuary*) *slab*, i.e. it is 'dead']. (**b**) a large piece of crack cocaine, the approximate dimensions of a piece of chewing gum. **11** [1990s+] (*Aus.*) a case of 24 bottles or tins of beer. **12** [1990s+] (*US black*) an automobile.

IN COMPOUNDS

❑ **slab-dabber** *n. see* separate entry. ❑ **slab-sides** *n.* [mid-19C] (*US*) a large, stupid person; thus adj. *slab-sided*.

IN PHRASES

❑ **long slab of misery** *n. see* LONG STREAK OF MISERY *under* STREAK *n.* ❑ **put on a slab** *v.* [20C+] (*US prison*) to fight in private to settle a score. ❑ **whip the slab** *v.* [2000s] to sell crack cocaine.

slab *v.* [i.e. to send to the mortuary/undertaker's *slab*] [1980s+] (*Aus. prison*) to murder.

slabba-slabba *adj.* [dial. *slabby*, sloppy + redup.] [20C+] (*W.I. Rasta*) big and fat, slobby, droopy.

slabbed and slid *adj.* [SE (mortuary) *slab* + *slid*] [1940s–80s] (*UK prison*) dead and gone, or certainly long since departed from the prison and thus the immediate knowledge or interest of those left behind.

slabber *n.* [Du. *slabberen*, muddy ground + SE *slobber*, to dribble saliva] **1** [late 18C–early 19C] a filthy, slobbering person. **2** [1990s+] (*Irish*) talkativeness.

slabber *v.* [1990s+] (*Irish*) to talk nonsense.

slabberdegullion *n.* (*also* **slubberdegullion, slobber-degullion**) [Du. *overslubberen*, to wade through mud + SE *slabber*, to drool] [early 17C–19C] a filthy, slobbering fellow.

slabbering bib *n.* [SE *slobber*, to dribble + *bib*] [late 18C–mid-19C] a neckband as worn by a lawyer or parson.

slabdab *n.* [? SE *slap* + *dab*, i.e. actions involved in making gloves] [late 17C–early 18C] a glover.

slab-dabber *n.* [journalistic jargon *slab*, a lengthy paragraph + SE *dab* (down)] [late 19C] a left-wing hack journalist.

slabs *n.* [backsl. BALLS *n.* (1)] [20C+] the testicles.

slack *n.*[1] [SE *slack*, that which hangs loose] **1** [19C] impertinence, cheek. **2** [mid-19C] a spell of inactivity, idleness. **3** [1940s+] (*W.I.*) a promiscuous woman. **4** [1950s] a prostitute. **5** [1950s+] (*W.I.*) a slovenly person. **6** [1950s+] freedom, leeway, relief of pressure; thus *give some slack*, to let someone relax, to stop pressurizing.

DERIVATIVES

❑ **slackness** *n.* **1** [1950s+] (*W.I.*) sloppiness, incompetence. **2** [1950s+] vulgarity; overt sexiness. **3** [1980s] (*W.I.*) lewd, vulgar lyrics used in popular songs.

IN COMPOUNDS

❑ **slack-jaw** *n.* [SE *jaw*/JAW *n.*] [mid-19C–1910s] cheek or impudence; thus adj. *slack-jawed*.

IN PHRASES

❑ **cut some slack** *v.* (*also* **give some slack, take up slack**) (*orig. US black*) **1** [1960s+] to ease the pressure upon, to permit the subject to relax. **2** [1970s] to hand over money. ❑ **hold onto the slack** *v.* [naut. imagery, holding the slack of a sail requires no real effort] [mid-19C] to be lazy, to skulk around. ❑ **pull some slack** *v.* [1970s] (*US*) to idle, to be lazy.

slack *n.*[2] [1970s] (*US black*) a form of ritualized handshake, intended to imply absolute agreement between the two participants.

slack *adj.* **1** [late 19C+] (*US teen*) of a person, either unmotivated or just plain lazy; intensified as *slack daddy*. **2** [1950s+] of work or performance, below standard. **3** [1970s+] (*Aus./WI/UK black*) sexually available, promiscuous. **4** [1980s] (*US campus*) easy. **5** [1980s+] (*N.Z.*) unsatisfactory or substandard.

SE in slang uses

DERIVATIVES

❑ **slackie** *n.* [a negative ref. to her flesh] [1980s] (*Aus.*) an ageing woman.

IN COMPOUNDS

❑ **slackarse** *n.* [1970s+] (*Aus.*) a general term of abuse; usu. aimed at women, it implies promiscuity, or laziness. ❑ **slack-arsed** *adj.* [1970s] (*Aus.*) of a woman, promiscuous. ❑ **slack-assed** *adj.* [1980s] (*US*) lazy, undisciplined. ❑ **slacked out** *adj.* [1970s] (*US*) inefficient, second-rate, below par.

slackener *n.* [it *slakes* one's thirst] [mid-19C] (*UK Und.*) a (restorative) drink.

slacken your glib! *excl. see under* GLIB *n.*

slacker *n.* [SE *slack*] **1** [late 19C+] one who shirks work or avoids exertion etc. **2** [1990s+] (*orig. US*) a member of the generation in their 20s (*c.* 1995) who, for whatever reason, perhaps cynicism or indolence, sees no point in joining the social mainstream.

slack (off) *v.* [the relaxation of one's bladder] [late 19C+] to urinate.

slacks *n.*

IN PHRASES

❑ **scare the slacks off** *v. see* SCARE THE PANTS OFF *under* PANTS *n.*

slackum yackum *v.* [ety. unknown] [2000s] (*US black*) to have sexual intercourse.

sladder-slabber *n.* [mid-19C] (*UK Und.*) a lamplighter.

slag *n.*[1] [18C *slag*, a coward, f. *slack-mettled*] **1** [18C–early 19C; 1940s+] a worthless, insignificant or objectionable person; frequently used as a term of contempt, e.g. *you slag!* **2** [1930s–60s] a rough or brutal person. **3** [1940s–60s] rubbish, nonsense. **4** [1950s+] a prostitute, a promiscuous woman, a slattern. **5** [1950s+] a vagrant, a petty criminal; thus [1950s–60s] *the slag*, such persons collectively.

DERIVATIVES

❑ **slaggery** *n.* [1960s] the world of villains, layabouts etc. ❑ **slaggy** *adj.* **1** [1940s+] dirty, unpleasant, offensive. **2** [1970s+] promiscuous, immoral.

IN COMPOUNDS

❑ **slagbag** *n.* [ext. of sense 5 above] [1960s+] a promiscuous woman.

slag *n.*[2] [SLANG *n.*[2] (2)] [mid-19C; 1920s–40s] (*UK Und.*) a gold or silver chain; thus *nip the slag*, to cut a watch chain.

slag *adj.* [SLAG *n.*[1]] **1** [1960s+] second-rate, worthless. **2** [1970s+] promiscuous.

slag *v.*[1] [dial. *slag*, to smear] [1960s+] (*Aus.*) to spit.

slag *v.*[2] *see* SLOG *v.* (1).

slag (off) *v.* (*also* **slag off at**) [SLAG *n.*[1]] [1960s+] to criticize, to slander, to attack verbally.

DERIVATIVES

❑ **slagging** *n.* (*also* **slagging off**) [1960s+] criticism, verbal attack.

slam *n.*[1] (*US*) **1** [late 19C+] an insult. **2** [1900s–20s] (*US*) a try, an attempt. **3** [1900s–60s] a violent blow (given to a ball); ? also used fig. **4** [1920s] a disappointment. **5** [1930s] (*US*) a drink of alcohol [one 'slams' the glass on the bar counter or the drink down one's throat]. **6** [1960s+] in pl., prison uses [the sound they make when shut]. (**a**) a cell door. (**b**) a cell. **7** [1980s] (*campus*) of a man, an act of sexual intercourse. **8** [1990s+] (*drugs*) the act of injecting a narcotic. **9** [2000s] (*prison*) the use of force by an officer. **10** *see* SLAM DANCE *n.*

slam *n.*[2] [abbr. SLAMMER *n.*[1] (1)] [1950s+] (*orig. US*) a prison.

slam *v.*[1] **1** in verbal senses. (**a**) [18C–19C] to talk, to boast. (**b**) [late 19C+] (*US*) to insult, to criticize harshly; thus *slamming contest*, a fight in which the contestants criticize each other verbally. **2** [late 19C+] (*orig. US*) to beat up, to hurt badly, to hit; also fig. use. **3** [20C+] (*US*) to hurry off [? the *slamming* of a door behind one or the *slamming* of one's feet on the ground]. **4** [1910s] (*US prison*) to oppose the authorities, to go on strike. **5** [1940s+] (*US black/campus/W.I./UK black teen*) of a man, to have sexual intercourse. **6** [1980s] (*US campus*) to reject someone. **7** [1980s] (*US campus*) to do well. **8** [1980s+] (*US black/campus*) to drink fast, usu. beer; thus *slam a forty*, to drink a 40-ounce (2-litre) bottle of beer. **9** [1990s+] to shut down, to close. **10** [1990s+] in drug uses. (**a**) to sell drugs. (**b**) to use heroin regularly. (**c**) to inject a narcotic, usu. heroin. **11** *see* SLAM DANCE *v.*

IN COMPOUNDS

❑ **slam dance** *see* separate entries. ❑ **slam dunk** *see* separate entries. ❑ **slam-piece** *n.* [PIECE *n.* (1)] [1990s+] (*US campus*) a sexual partner.

IN PHRASES

❑ **slam off** *v.* **1** [1930s+] to die. **2** [1960s] to kill. **3** [1990s+] (*UK juv.*) to play truant. ❑ **slam the clam** *v.* [BEARDED CLAM *n.*] [1960s+] of a woman, to masturbate. ❑ **slam the gate** *v.* [late 19C–1930s] (*US tramp*) to beg from private houses. ❑ **slam the ham** *v.* (*also* **slam the salami, ...salmon, ...spam**) [HAM *n.*[5] (1) / SALAMI *n.* / SE *salmon* / SPAM *n.* (1)] [1950s+] of a man, to masturbate. ❑ **slam the hammer** *v.* (*also* **slam the wapper**) [HAMMER *n.*[1] (1)/WAP *v.* (1)] [1990s+] of a man, to masturbate. ❑ **slam the slats** *v.* [SE *slam* + *slat*, a bar] [1990s+] (*US Und.*) to close a row of cell doors using a remote mechanism that closes every door simultaneously.

IN EXCLAMATIONS

❑ **slam me!** [mid–late 18C] a euph. for *damn me!*

slam *v.*[2] [SLAMMER *n.*[1] (1)] [1970s+] (*US*) **1** to imprison. **2** to place in solitary confinement.

IN PHRASES

❑ **slam down** *v.* [1970s+] (*US prison*) to lock into one's cell as a punishment – no association is permitted. ❑ **slam up** *v.* [1970s+] (*US Und.*) to imprison.

slam bam *adj. see* SLAM-BANG *adj.* (1).

slambam *adv.* [echoic] [1940s+] (*W.I.*) at once, immediately.

slam-bam-thank-you-ma'am *phr. see* WHAM-BAM-THANK-YOU-MA'AM *phr.*

slam-bang *n.* [SE *slam-bang*, rough, aggressive] **1** [late 19C] something exceptional. **2** [1920s] (*US*) a vicious prize-fight.

slam-bang *adj.* [SLAM-BANG *adv.*] **1** [1920s+] (*also* **slam bam**) vigorous, energetic. **2** [1960s+] (*orig. US*) exciting, first-rate, excellent.

slam-bang *adv.* [echoic] **1** [mid-19C+] vigorously, energetically. **2** [mid-19C+] (*US*) exactly, precisely, directly.

slam-bang shop *n. see* SLAP-BANG(-SHOP) *n.*

slam dance *n.* (*also* **slam, slamming, slam-dancing**) [SE *slam* + *dance*; usu. associated with the audiences of punk or THRASH *n.* (3) music] [1970s+] a particularly energetic style of dance that involves physical collision with other dancers; thus *slammer*, an energetic dancer.

slam dance *v.* (*also* **slam**) [SLAM DANCE *n.*] [1970s+] (*US*) to perform a slam dance; thus *slam dancer*, one who dances in this way.

slam-dunk *n.* [*see* next] [1980s+] a certainty.

slam-dunk *v.* [basketball jargon *slam-dunk*, to slam the ball down through the basket, jumping high and using both hands] **1** [1980s+] (*US black*) to make an aggressive, powerful move. **2** [1990s+] to reject a request.

slamkin *n.* (*also* **slammerkin, slammocks, slommack**) [note the slovenly 'Mrs Slammekin' in John Gay's *Beggar's Opera* (1727); however, the name may have reflected the *slammerkin*, a loose gown or dress, rather than the later sl.] **1** [late 18C–mid-19C] a slovenly woman; also as adj., slovenly. **2** [mid-19C] a servant. **3** [late 19C] a run-down animal.

slamkin *adj.* [late-18C–mid-19C] slovenly.

slammack *v.* [SLAMKIN *n.*] [late 19C] to act in a slovenly manner.

slammed *adj.*[1] [SE *slam* the door/SLAM *v.*[1]] [1970s] (*US prison*) locked into one's cell during a crisis, e.g. a prison strike.

slammed *adj.*[2] (*also* **slammered**) [SLAM *v.*[1] (2)] [1980s+] (*US campus*) **1** drunk. **2** intoxicated by drugs. **3** overwhelmed with work.

slammer *n.*[1] **1** [late 19C+] anything or anyone exceptional [SE *slam*, to hit with a bang]. **2** with ref. to a slammed door. (**a**) [1930s+] (*also* **slammers**) prison. (**b**) [1940s–60s] (*US black*) a door. (**c**) [1960s] (*US*) a psychiatric hospital.

slammer *n.*[2] *see* SLAM DANCE *n.*

slammered *adj. see* SLAMMED *adj.*[2].

slammerkin *n. see* SLAMKIN *n.*

slammerkin *adj.* [SLAMMERKIN *n.*] [late 19C] of a woman, slovenly.

slammers *n. see* SLAMMER *n.*[1] (2a).

slamming *n.*[1] [SLAM *v.*[1] (2)] **1** [1950s+] (*US Und.*) (*also* **schlamming**) very violent assault, stopping short of murder. **2** [1980s+] (*US black*) fighting, either with fists or knives; thus *slamming and jamming*, of the Guardian Angels group, raiding a crack house or similar establishment to smash it up, rough up the patrons and take away the drugs.

slamming *n.*[2] *see* SLAM DANCE *n.*

slamming *adj.* [SLAM *v.*[1] (2)] [late 19C–1900s; 1960s+] a general intensifier, overwhelming, extraordinary, the best, the most fashionable, attractive etc; thus synon. *slamminest*.

slamming and jamming *n.* **1** [1980s+] (*US black*) of a disc jockey, playing exciting music. **2** *see* SLAMMING *n.*[1] (2).

slammocks *n. see* SLAMKIN *n.*

slaney *n.* [mid-19C] (*US Und.*) a theatre.

slang *n.*[1] [ety. debatable. Of the various theories the most likely is SE *sling*, to throw; thus fig. 'thrown' language, underpinned by cognates in Norw. *slenja-keten*, sling the jaw etc] **1** [mid-18C] nonsense, rubbish. **2** [mid-18C] (*UK Und.*) things acquired by trickery or pickpocketing. **3** [mid–late 18C] (*also* **slango**) a line of work, an occupation; thus *on/upon the slang*, involved in one's own profession or job. **4** [mid-18C–mid-19C] cant, i.e. the jargon of criminals. **5** [mid-18C–mid-19C] illiterate, 'low' language. **6** [early 19C] banter, teasing. **7** [early 19C] the criminal fraternity. **8** [mid-19C] a travelling show; a single performance or 'house' in a travelling show. **9** [mid-19C] a set of counterfeit scales, as used by cheating costermongers, counterfeit measures; thus the *slang quart*, a measure with a false bottom that actually holds only 1½ pints (855ml); the *slang pint*, ¾ pint (428ml) etc; *work slang*, to use such weights and measures. **10** [mid-19C] a legal warrant. **11** [mid-19C–1930s] a hawker's licence; thus *out on the slang*, working as an itinerant hawker. **12** [late 19C] a salesman's or showman's speech to attract customers; also as *bad slang*, an exagerated but successful speech and performance to attract the public.

IN COMPOUNDS

❑ **slang-boy** *n.* (*also* **boy of the slang**) [late 18C] one who can speak underworld cant. ❑ **slang cove** *n.* (*also* **slang cull**) [COVE *n.* (1)/CULL *n.*[1] (3)] [mid–late 19C] a showman; thus *slang*, a showman's stall, a travelling show. ❑ **slang-madge** *n.* [MADGE *n.* (2)] [mid-18C] (*UK Und.*) the robbery of homosexuals.

IN PHRASES

❑ **slang and pitcher shop** *n.* [PITCHER *n.*[2] (2)] [late 19C–1900s] a cheapjack's stall; thus the stock it holds. ❑ **stand slang** *v.* [mid-18C] to stand by ready to remove stolen articles after a robbery.

slang *n.*[2] [Ger. *Schlange*, a chain, watch-chain or Du. *slang*, a snake] **1** [late 18C–1910s] any form of chains or fetters used to secure a prisoner; usu. in pl.; the noose. **2** [19C–1940s] a watch-chain. **3** [1930s] (*US Und.*) a necklace. **4** [1990s+] (*S.Afr. gay*) the penis.

IN COMPOUNDS

❑ **slang-dipper** *n.* [20C+] one who gilds ordinary metal chains and attempts to pass them off as 'gold'; thus *slang-dropper*, the person who actually does the 'trade', usu. by dropping a chain in the street, picking it up as the victim is passing, then asking them to suggest how much it might be worth; they then get the dupe to buy it, assuring them that they themselves are losing by the deal. ❑ **slangpark** *n.* [1990s+] (*S.Afr. gay*) a public lavatory used for soliciting, a 'cottage'.

IN PHRASES

❑ **double-slangs** *n.* [late 18C–mid-19C] double irons; thus *double-slanged*, fettered on both legs.

slang *n.*[3] [1990s+] (*US drugs*) a measure of drugs.

slang *adj.* [SLANG *n.*[1] (9)] **1** [early–mid-19C] (*UK Und.*) defective or crooked, usu. of weights and measures. **2** [mid-

19C] nouveaux riche, raffish; thus *talk slang*, to talk in a flashy manner.

slang *v.*[1] [SLANG *n.*[1]] **1** [mid-18C–mid-19C] to cheat, to swindle, to defraud. **2** [mid-18C+] to abuse, to banter with. **3** [late 18C] to exhibit at a fair. **4** [19C+] to use slang. **5** [2000s] (*US black*) to pose, to assume a role that one cannot sustain.

IN COMPOUNDS

❑ **slanging match** *n.* [late 19C+] a vituperative argument.

IN PHRASES

❑ **slanging dues concerned** (*also* **there's slanging dues concerned**) [early 19C] (*UK Und.*) a phr. used to imply that one has been cheated. ❑ **slang upon the safe** *v.* [mid-18C] to remove stolen goods from the scene of the crime.

slang *v.*[2] [SLANG *n.*[2] (1)] [early 19C] to chain up, to place in fetters.

slang *v.*[3] [SE *sling* / SLING *v.* (1h)] **1** [1980s+] (*orig. US black*) to sell drugs. **2** [1990s+] in weak use, to give, to sell. **3** [1990s+] in fig. use, to hit.

IN PHRASES

❑ **slang the mauleys** *v. see under* MAULEY *n.*

slanged *adj.* [SLANG *v.*[2]] [early 19C] chained up, fettered.

slanger *n.* [SLANG *v.*[1] (1) or SE *sling*, to throw] [mid-18C] (*UK Und.*) a thief or pickpocket who uses an assistant to carry the stolen goods.

slango *n. see* SLANG *n.*[1] (3).

slangy *adj.* [SLANG *adj.* (2)] [mid-19C+] flashy, vulgar, whether in speech or appearance.

slant *n.* **1** as a scheme or opportunity [naut. jargon *slant*, a favourable wind]. (**a**) [mid-19C–1900s] an opportunity to push forward a plan or stratagem. (**b**) [late 19C–1940s] (*Aus.*) a plan or scheme spec. designed to ensure a favourable result; an exploitable gimmick, an ulterior motive. (**c**) [1920s] (*US*) a sense of, comprehension [var. on ANGLE *n.*]. **2** [1910s–40s] (*US*) a glance, a brief look [i.e. 'out of the corner of one's eye']. **3** [1960s+] (*also* **slanty**) a derog. term for an East Asian person [the shape of East Asian people's eyes].

IN COMPOUNDS

❑ **slanthead** *n.* [-HEAD *sfx*] [1920s–40s] (*US*) a general pej. ❑ **slant-eye/-eyed** *see* separate entries.

IN PHRASES

❑ **do a slant** *v.* [1900s] to run off without paying a bill. ❑ **get a slant on** *v.* (*also* **have a slant**) [1930s+] to form an opinion of/about someone. ❑ **take a slant** *v.* (*also* **cop a slant, get a slant, have a slant**) [1900s–40s] to glance (at).

slant *adj.* [SLANT *n.* (3)] [1960s+] Asian, esp. Vietnamese.

slant *v.* **1** [late 19C–1900s] to run away. **2** [late 19C–1900s] to exaggerate. **3** [1910s–30s] to glance at.

slantendicular *adj. see* SLANTINDICULAR *adj.*

slanter *n.*[1] (*also* **schleinter, schlenter, schlinter, shlanter, shlenter, shlinter, slinter**) [Du. *slenter*, knavery, a trick] (*mainly Aus./S.Afr.*) **1** [late 19C] a counterfeit coin. **2** [late 19C] a counterfeit object. **3** [late 19C+] a fraudulent trick; thus *work a slanter*, to defraud, to hoax, to play a confidence trick on; *run a slanter*, to make no effort to win. **4** [1900s] a third-rate performance, e.g. in a boxing match.

slanter *n.*[2] [the angle at which it projects from the face] **1** [1910s] (*US*) the nose. **2** [1940s] (*US black*) in pl., the eyes. [SLANT *v.* (3)].

slant-eye *n.* (*also* **slanty-eye, slit-eye**) [SLANT-EYED *adj.*] [1920s+] a derog. term for an East Asian person.

slant-eyed *adj.* (*also* **slant-eye, slanty-eyed, slit-eyed**) [the shape of East Asian people's eyes] [mid-19C+] a derog. term meaning East Asian, esp. Japanese.

slantindicular *adj.* (*also* **slantendicular, slantingdicular**) [a play on SE *perpendicular*] [mid-19C] (*orig. US*) oblique, awry.

slanty *n. see* SLANT *n.* (3).

slaoc *n.* [backsl.] [mid-19C] coals.

slap *n.*[1] [late 18C–early 19C] (*mainly Anglo-Irish*) booty, the proceeds of a robbery, 'swag'.

slap *n.*[2] [SE *slap*, a blow] **1** [mid–late 19C] a go, an attempt; thus a bet. **2** [mid-19C+] (*also* **schlap, shlap, slop**) make-up, esp. in theatre use; also as v., *slap up*, to apply make-up [one SE *slaps* it on]. **3** [late 19C+] an attack on someone. **4** [20C+] (*Irish*) a large amount, a quantity.

IN COMPOUNDS

❑ **slap and tickle** *n. see* separate entry. ❑ **slap-happy** *see* separate entries.

IN PHRASES

❑ **have a slap at** *v.* [late 19C+] to make an attempt, to have a try. ❑ **put a slap down on someone** *v.* [2000s] (*US black*) to hit someone when they are behaving in a cowardly manner.

slap *adj.* [SLAP-UP *adj.* (1)] [mid-19C] first-rate, excellent.

slap *v.* (*also* **slap along**) [one's shoes SE *slap* the ground; 20C+ use is UK black] **1** [mid-19C; 1990s+] to move or walk quickly. **2** [late 19C] (*Aus.*) to shoot.

SE in slang uses

IN COMPOUNDS

❑ **slaphead** *see* separate entries. ❑ **slapman** *n.* [SE *slap*; i.e. his violent treatment of suspects] [1920s–30s] (*US Und.*) a policeman.

IN PHRASES

❑ **slap five** *v. see under* FIVE *n.*[2]. ❑ **slap ham** *v. see under* HAM *n.*[1]. ❑ **slap skins** *v. see under* SKIN *n.*[1]. ❑ **slap someone's shit away** *v.* [1980s] (*US black*) to attack, physically or verbally. ❑ **slap tar** *v. see* BEAT TAR *under* BEAT *v.* ❑ **slap the monkey** *v. see under* MONKEY *n.* ❑ **slap the pavement** *v. see under* PAVEMENT *n.* ❑ **slap the salami** *v. see under* SALAMI *n.*

slap *adv.* [SE *slap*, the sound of a sharp blow] **1** [late 17C+] quickly, unexpectedly, suddenly. **2** [mid-18C+] (*also* **slap off**) exactly, perfectly, e.g. *slap in the middle.* **3** [mid-19C+] directly; completely.

IN PHRASES

❑ **slap into** *adv.* [mid-19C+] used with verbs of collision or impact, directly, straight at, e.g. *ran slap into the wall*.

slap and tickle *n.*[1] [rhy. sl.] [20C+] a pickle.

slap and tickle *n.*[2] **1** [1920s+] playful kissing and cuddling. **2** [1980s] empty verbosity. **3** [1980s] physical violence.

IN PHRASES

❑ **bit of slap and tickle** *n.* [in trad. stereotyping, he tickles, she slaps] **1** [1910s+] sexual by-play, necking. **2** [1950s+] sexual intercourse; thus *have a bit of slap and tickle*, to have sexual intercourse.

slap-bang *n.* [mid-19C] **1** the food sold at a SLAP-BANG(-SHOP) *n.* (1). **2** a form of alcoholic drink [used by Benjamin Disraeli in *Sybil* (1845) as 'the Mowbray slap-bang', but otherwise unspecified. Presumably it was tossed off in a single gulp, guaranteed to 'hit the spot' or, like the *tequila slammers* of the present day, the glass was knocked against the table before taking a drink].

slap-bang *adv.* (*also* **smack-bang**) [ext. SLAP *adv.*] **1** [late 18C+] energetically, vigorously, directly. **2** [late 19C] implying closeness. **3** *see* SLAP-DAB *adv.*

slap-bang(-shop) *n.* (*also* **slam-bang shop, slap-dash**) [late 18C–mid-19C] a small eating-house or restaurant where one pays on receipt of the food, rather than eating then receiving a bill.

slapdab *n.* [SLAP-DAB *adv.*] [late 19C] anything put together quickly but not well.

slap-dab *adv.* (*also* **bang-slap, slap-bang**) [echoic] [mid-19C+] directly, straight at, immediately.

slap-dash *n. see* SLAP-BANG(-SHOP) *n.* (1).

slap-dash *adv.* [UK usage became SE in 18C, and the term was taken up by Aus. speakers; the adj. meaning careless, undisciplined is SE] [late 17C+] suddenly, immediately; violently.

slapgat *n.* [1980s+] (*S.Afr.*) a lazy person.

slap-happy *n.* [the use of the jazz jargon *slap bass*] [1940s] (*US black*) a devotee of swing music.

slap-happy *adj.* [SE *slap* + -HAPPY *sfx*; orig. boxing use, someone whose brain has suffered from an excess of fighting] [1930s+] cheery, slightly eccentric.

slap-head *n.* [1980s+] a bald person.

slaphead *adj.* [SLAP-HEAD *n.*] [mid-19C; 1990s+] bald, hairless.

slapper *n.*[1] [early 19C] a hard blow; a fatal wound.

slapper *n.*[2] [? Yid. *schlepper*, a unkempt, untidy person or the 'slapping on' of make-up] [1980s+] **1** a promiscuous woman. **2** a prostitute.

slapping *n.* [1990s+] a beating.

slapping *adj.* [mid-19C+] first-rate, excellent; also as an intensifier.

slapping (the plank) *n. see under* PLANK *n.*[2].

slappy *adj.* [SLAP-HAPPY *adj.*] [1950s] (*US*) deranged.

slapsie maxie *n.* [rhy. sl.; US boxer *Slapsie Maxie* Rosenbloom (1904–76), fought 1920s–30s] [1960s+] (*Aus./N.Z.*) a taxi.

slap-up *adj.* **1** [early 19C+] (*also* **slam up**) fashionable, first-rate, of superior quality; thus *slap-uppish*, smartly, fashionably. **2** [mid-19C] in good spirits, comfortable. **3** [mid-19C] drunk. **4** [late 19C] of a person, honest, honourable.

slap up *v.* **1** [mid-19C+] to assemble or put together in a haphazard, bodged manner. **2** *see* SLAP *n.*[2] (2).

slap-up *adv.* [SLAP-UP *adj.* (1)] [mid-19C; 1930s] excellently, pleasantly, very well.

slash *n.* **1** [mid-19C] an outside pocket [SE *slash*, a slit in a garment that is designed to reveal the colour of the lining]. **2** in context of urination [? SE *slash*, a thin, sloping line, i.e. that of urine; or echoic of the urine hitting the lavatory water]. (**a**) [1930s+] an act of urination. (**b**) [2000s] urine. **3** [1930s–80s] an alcoholic drink [*DSUE* suggests play on PISS-UP *n.*]. **4** [1960s+] (*Aus./US*) the vagina [note Cleland, *Memoirs of a Woman of Pleasure* (1748–49): 'The agreeable interior red of the sides of the orifice came into view, and with respect to the white that dazzl'd round it, give somewhat the idea of a pink-slash in the glossiest of white sattin'].

slash *v.* [SLASH *n.* (2)] **1** in senses of aggression. (**a**) [1940s] (*Aus.*) to beat up. (**b**) [1960s+] (*US black/campus*) to demolish someone verbally. **2** [1960s+] to urinate.

IN COMPOUNDS

❑ **slash house** *n. see* SHITHOUSE *n.*

SE in slang uses

IN COMPOUNDS

❑ **slash job** *n.* [JOB *n.*[2]] [1990s+] (*US prison*) slashing one's own wrists in a suicide attempt.

slashed *adj.* [SLASH *v.* (2), i.e. PISSED *adj.*[1]] [1990s+] very drunk.

slasher *n.*[1] [note the comedian Sid Field's 1940s SPIV *n.* character *Slasher* Green, whose name may have equally referred to the contemporary 'razor gangs' of Soho and the racetrack] **1** [mid-16C–19C] a violent thug, a bully; used positively of a prize-fighter. **2** [19C] anyone or anything seen as exceptional, whether positively or otherwise. **3** [early 19C+] a sword; a knife. **4** [late 19C–1960s] (*Aus.*) a general term of praise, an excellent fellow; thus *slasheroo*, an intensified form. **5** [1920s–30s] (*UK Und.*) a criminal accomplice who cheats on his partners. **6** [1980s+] (*Aus. prison*) a self-mutilator.

IN COMPOUNDS

❑ **slasher-gaff** *n.* [GAFF *n.*[2] (4)] [mid-19C] (*US*) very harsh criticism.

slasher *n.*[2] [SLASH *v.*] [1960s] **1** the testicles. **2** the penis.

slashing *adj.* [SLASHER *n.*[1] (2); 20C+ use mainly Aus.] [19C+] excellent, wonderful, the best.

slashing *adv.* [SLASHING *adj.*] [late 19C] excellently, wonderfully, exceptionally.

slat *n.*[1] [SLATE *n.*[1]] [late 17C–18C] (*UK Und.*) a sheet.

slat *n.*[2] [SLATE *n.*[2]; the term was used by market traders in the 20C until decimalization made the half-crown obsolete] **1** [18C–early 19C] (*UK Und.*) half-a-crown, 2s 6d (12½p); occas. a crown or 5 shillings (25p). **2** [mid-18C] (*UK Und.*) a guinea, 21 shillings (£1.05p); *half a slat*, 10/6d (52.5p). **3** [mid-19C] (*US Und.*) half a dollar. **4** [1950s–60s] (*US black*) $1.

slat *n.*[3] [SE *slat*, a long, thin piece of wood] **1** [late 19C+] (*orig. US*) in pl., the ribs; thus a skinny person. **2** [1900s] (*US*) a thin person. **3** [1920s+] (*US prison*) in pl., the steel mesh that covers the front of a prison cell.

IN PHRASES

❑ **wouldn't that rattle your slats?** [1900s–10s] (*US*) isn't that amazing? wouldn't that give you a shock?

SE in slang uses

IN PHRASES

❑ **hit the slats** *v. see* HIT THE HAY *under* HAY *n.*

slat *n.*[4] [UK dial. *slat*, a (slapping) blow] [1920s] (*US*) a kick, a punch.

slat *n.*[5] [1920s; 1970s] (*US*) a young man.

slat *n.*[6] [? Irish *slat*, a rod or measuring stick] [1940s–70s] (*US black*) used as a term of quantity, esp. in the context of the length of a prison sentence; thus a prison sentence.

slate *n.*[1] [SE *slate*] **1** [mid-16C–mid-19C] a bedsheet. **2** [mid-19C+] one's bill, the credit one has run up; usu. in a public house or bar.

IN PHRASES

❑ **clean the slate** *v.* [mid-19C+] lit. or fig., to pay off one's outstanding debts. ❑ **have a slate loose** *v. see* HAVE A TILE LOOSE *under* TILE *n.* ❑ **on the slate** [the practice of writing public house debts on a slate] [late 19C+] on credit.

slate *n.*[2] [ety. unknown] [late 17C–early 19C] (*UK Und.*) half-a-crown, 2s 6d (12½p).

slate *n.*[3] [SLATE *v.*[1] (2)] [late 19C] an argument, a quarrel; a reprimand, a scolding.

slate *v.*[1] [Scot. *slate*, to attack with a dog, to drive away with abuse; ? Irish *slat mara*, ult. *slad-mhara*, murder and robbery] **1** [17C; mid-19C] (*orig. Irish*) to thrash or beat up. **2** [mid-19C+] to criticize severely. **3** [late 19C] to punish. **4** [1900s] to abuse. **5** [1990s+] to rain hard.

slate *v.*[2] [SE *slate*, a roof-covering] [mid-19C] to knock a man's hat over his eyes.

slate *v.*[3] [SE *slate*, to set down in writing] **1** [late 19C–1900s] to bet heavily against a boxer, a racehorse etc. **2** [20C+] (*orig. milit.*) to assign to a job or other situation.

slated *adj.* [hospital practice of writing the names of those currently likely to die on a *slate*] [late 19C] dead.

slater *n.* [SLATE *v.*[1] (2)] [late 19C] (*Aus.*) a critic.

slater's pan *n.* [proper name *Slater*, the deputy provost-marshal in Grose's era; given the heat of the West Indies, prisoners were presumably 'cooked' in the 'pan'] [late 18C–early 19C] the prison at Kingston, Jamaica.

slather *n.* (*also* **slathers**) [SE *slather*, to squander] [mid-19C+] (*US*) a large amount, e.g. *a whole slather of pretty women*; *slathers of fresh fruit*.

slather *v.* [SE *slather*, to spread, or smear liberally] [1910s+] to defeat utterly, to thrash, to criticize harshly.

slathered *adj.* [? SLATHER *v.* or dial. *slather*, to spill, to slobber] [1920s+] (*Aus.*) tipsy, slightly drunk.

slathers *n. see* SLATHER *n.*

slather-up *n.* [SLATHER *v.* (1)] [1910s] (*N.Z.*) a fight, a brawl.

slat mara *n.* [Ir. *slad-mhara*, murder and robbery; *slad-mharoir*, freebooter] [1920s] (*Irish*) a contemptible person.

slatty *adj. see* SLAT *n.*[3].

slaughter *n.* [abbr. SLAUGHTERHOUSE *n.*[1] (2)] [1950s+] (*UK Und.*) an immediate dumping ground for recently stolen property before it is shared out, also tools and equipment used in a robbery, before being hidden more permanently, e.g. in a hired lock-up.

slaughtered *adj.* **1** [late 19C] heavily overworked, 'sweated'. **2** [1980s+] (*US campus*) drunk.

slaughterer *n.* [such one-sided deals *slaughter* the sellers] [mid-19C] a dealer who buys from small makers at extremely low prices.

slaughter floor *n. see* KILLING FLOOR *n.* (1).

slaughterhouse *n.*[1] [in all cases, the buyer or customer is fig. *slaughtered*] **1** [early 19C] a crooked gambling house or casino.

2 [mid–late 19C] a shop where goods are bought from small makers at very low prices. **3** [late 19C] a factory paying very low wages. **4** [1920s+] a cheap brothel.

slaughterhouse *n.*[2] [play on KILLING FLOOR *n.*] [1970s] (*US black*) anywhere a couple can indulge in sexual intercourse.

slaughtering floor *n. see* KILLING FLOOR *n.* (1).

slaughtering-knife *n.* [late 17C–early 18C] the penis.

slaughter in the pan *n.* [late 19C–1950s] (*US short order*) steak.

slave *n.* **1** [1900s] (*US campus*) a college servant. **2** [1930s+] (*US black/campus*) work, any form of job.

IN COMPOUNDS

❑ **slave market** *n.* (*US*) **1** [mid-19C+] an office, a café or any other meeting place where unemployed actors seek work. **2** [1910s+] cheap employment agencies, offering menial jobs for poor wages. ❑ **slave tip** *n.* [1940s] (*US black*) work.

IN PHRASES

❑ **cop a slave** *v.* (*also* **cop the slave**) [20C+] (*US black*) to work, to go out and find work.

slave *v.* [late 19C+] to work.

slave and Turk *v. see* TERRIBLE TURK *n.* (1).

slavey *n.* (*also* **moll slavey**) [note Egan's Grose (1821): 'A *slang* term for servant maids; being servants of all work; and also in allusion to their laborious employment and hard work'] [late 18C+] a servant, whether male or female; thus [1920s] *slavey market*, an employment agency for servants.

slaving gloak *n.* [SE *slaving* + GLOAK *n.*] [late 19C] a servant.

slawminyeux *n.* [? Du. *ja mynheer*, yes sir] [mid-19C] a Dutchman.

sleaze *n.* (*also* **sleeze**) [backform. f. SLEAZY *adj.*] **1** [1950s+] (*US*) anything considered disgusting, shabby or offensive. **2** [1970s+] (*also* **sleazter**) an unappealing, seedy person. **3** [1970s+] (*US*) (*also* **sleez, sleazebitchlet**) a sexually promiscuous woman.

DERIVATIVES

❑ **sleazo** *n.* (*also* **el sleazo, sleazoid**) [-O *sfx*] **1** [1970s+] (*US*) a disgusting, obnoxious person. **2** [1980s+] a sexually promiscuous woman.

IN COMPOUNDS

❑ **sleazebag** *n.* (*also* **sleazeball, sleazyball, sleezebag**) [-BAG *sfx*/-BALL *sfx*] [1980s+] a distasteful person, with overtones of dirtiness, criminality and sexual excess. ❑ **sleazebitchlet** *n. see* sense 3 above. ❑ **sleazebucket** *see* separate entries. ❑ **sleazehole** *n.* [HOLE *n.*[1]] [1990s+] a seedy, run-down place, a down-market bar or club. ❑ **sleazemonger** *n.* [-MONGER *sfx*] [1960s+] (*US*) a producer or seller of inferior, trashy or pornographic entertainment.

sleaze *v.* **1** [1960s+] to move in a repellent or seedy manner. **2** [1980s] (*US*) to acquire in a underhand manner.

sleazebucket *n.* [SLEAZE *n.*] **1** [1980s+] (*US campus*) (*also* **sleeze bucket**) a sexually promiscuous woman. **2** [1990s+] a revolting, repellent individual.

sleazebucket *adj.* [1960s+] (*US*) revolting, disgusting.

sleazoid *n. see* SLEAZO *under* SLEAZE *n.*

sleazter *n. see* SLEAZE *n.* (2).

sleazy *adj.* (*also* **sleazo, sleazoid, sleazy-ass, sleezy**) [SE *sleazy*, of textile fabrics or materials, thin or flimsy; ult. *sleazy*, of ropes or yarn, rough from projecting fibres] **1** [1930s+] of a person, unpleasant, poss. criminal, generally distasteful. **2** [1930s+] of a thing, dirty, run-down, decayed. **3** [1980s] (*US juv.*) lucky. **4** [2000s] sexually perverse.

sleazyball *n. see* SLEAZEBAG *under* SLEAZE *n.*

sleazycheesin' *n.* [2000s] (*US black*) taking drugs then wandering in pursuit of women willing to have sex.

sled *n.* [1930s+] (*US*) **1** an automobile; occas. second-rate. **2** a motorcycle.

IN PHRASES

❑ **lead sled** *n.* [1950s+] (*US*) a slow vehicle.

sledding *n.*

IN PHRASES

❑ **tough sledding** *n.* (*also* **hard sledding, heavy sledding**) [1920s+] (*US*) a problematic, demanding situation; hard times.

sledge *v.* [2000s] to become bored.

sleek and slum (shop) *n.* [SE *sleek*, i.e. a well-dressed, 'smooth' man + SLUM *n.*[2] (3), i.e. the tricks the woman might play or SLUM *n.*[1] (1)] [early 19C] a public house frequented by 'single men and their wives' (Bee), i.e. prostitutes and their male clients.

sleek lady *n.* [1960s–80s] (*US black*) an extremely attractive woman.

sleek wipe *n. see under* WIPE *n.*

sleep *n.* **1** [1910s+] (*UK/US/Aus.*) a short term in prison [the UK/US versions are somewhat longer, about twelve months, than the Aus., which is three months]. **2** [1940s] (*US black campus*) constr. with *the*, a college lecture.

SE in slang uses

DERIVATIVES

❑ **sleepville** *n.* [-VILLE *sfx*[1]] [late 19C+] (*US*) sleep.

IN COMPOUNDS

❑ **sleepless hat** *n.* [pun on *nap*] [mid-19C–1900s] a hat on which the nap has worn off. ❑ **sleepwalker** *n.* [1940s] (*Aus.*) a sneak-thief.

sleep *v.* [SE *put to sleep*] [2000s] (*US prison*) to knock someone down.

SE in slang uses

IN COMPOUNDS

❑ **sleeping beauty** *n.* [1970s] (*US gay*) an impotent penis, incapable of erection. ❑ **sleeping dictionary** *n.* [1920s+] a foreign woman with whom a man has a sexual relationship and from whom he learns her language. ❑ **sleeping Jesus** *n.* [pun on *creeping Jesus*, a whining, sneaking person] (*US black*) **1** [1920s+] a dull, tedious person. **2** [1980s] a person who is comatose due to the influence of heroin.

IN PHRASES

❑ **sleep at Mrs. Green's** *v.* (*also* **sleep with Mrs Green**) [1930s–50s] (*Aus./N.Z.*) to sleep in the open air. ❑ **sleep in chapters** *v.* [1960s] (*drugs*) to experience broken, fragmentary sleep during withdrawal from heroin. ❑ **sleep like a cow** *v.* [late 18C–early 19C] to sleep like a married man, i.e. with one's back to one's wife [Grose (1785) defines it as 'i.e. with a **** [CUNT *n.* (1)] at one's a–se' and quotes a contemporary rhyme: 'All you that in your beds do lie/Turn to your wives, and occupy [have sex],/And when that you have done your best,/Turn a-se to a-se, and take your rest']. ❑ **sleep off** *v.* [1950s] (*US Und.*) to serve a prison sentence without problems, i.e. as if one were simply talking a nap. ❑ **sleep on** *v.* [1980s+] (*US black*) **1** to ignore. **2** to be unaware or unprepared but otherwise awake. **3** to attack, to criticize negatively. ❑ **sleep upon the queer roost** *v.* (*also* **dorse upon the queer roost**) [QUEER *adj.* (1) / DOSS *v.* (1); the arrangement is 'queer' because it is fraudulent] [late 18C] to live together as man and wife. ❑ **sleep with one's glasses on** *v.* [1940s] (*US black*) to act in an arrogant manner. ❑ **sleep with the fishes** *v.* [invariably associated with the US Mafia thanks to Mario Puzo's book *The Godfather* (1969), although the use only exists in the film] [1960s+] **1** to have been drowned, whether accidentally or as a form of homicide. **2** to die. **3** thus fig., to be over, defeated.

sleeper *n.* **1** in senses of that which has been 'left to sleep'. (**a**) [mid-19C–1930s] (*gambling*) (*also* **snoozer**) a stake that has been left on the table, when neither the croupier/banker nor a winning bettor has realized it is to be picked up. (**b**) [1910s–20s] (*US*) a bar customer who was too drunk to pick up their change when they left; the bartender kept it. **2** in senses of 'awakening' to gradual movement. (**a**) [late 19C–1910s] a potentially successful racehorse that has eluded the eye of the betting public. (**b**) [late 19C+] (*orig. US sport*) any product that gains acceptance and success only slowly. (**c**) [1900s] (*US*) a financial collapse. (**d**) [1950s] a surprise. (**e**) [1980s+] one whose character has yet to be properly developed. **3** [1940s–

50s] (*US Und.*) a short prison sentence [var. SLEEP *n.*]. **4** in drug uses. (**a**) [1960s+] any form of barbiturate sleeping pill. (**b**) [2000s] heroin. **5** [1970s] (*US campus*) a lazy, useless person. **6** [1970s] (*Can. prison*) a means of subduing violent prisoners (and patients in mental hospitals) by strangling them unconscious with a towel.

IN PHRASES

❑ **hang a sleeper on** *v.* [1920s] to cause someone ill luck.

sleeps, the *n.* [late 19C] (*US*) sleep.

sleepy *adj.*[1] [punning remark 'the cloth of your coat must be extremely sleepy, for it has not had a nap this long time' (Grose, 1796)] [late 18C–early 19C] old, worn-out.

sleepy *adj.*[2] [mid-19C] (*US*) a euph. for drunk.

SE in slang uses

IN COMPOUNDS

❑ **sleepy dust** *n.* [early 19C] some form of sleeping draught, used to help in robberies. ❑ **sleepytime girl** *n.* [SAmE *sleepytime*, bedtime] [1950s+] (*US*) a promiscuous woman, a man's mistress.

Sleepy Hollow *n.* [SE *Sleepy Hollow*, a name given to a place with a soporific atmosphere, esp. as title of Washington Irving's story 'The Legend of Sleepy Hollow' (1820)] **1** [mid-19C+] (*N.Z.*) Nelson, New Zealand. **2** [late 19C+] any quiet provincial place. **3** [1940s] (*US Und.*) Trenton Prison, New Jersey. **4** [1940s+] (*S.Afr.*) Pietermaritzburg.

sleestak *n.* [creature in the 1980s TV series *Land of the Lost*] [1980s+] (*US campus*) an unappealing, sexually promiscuous woman.

sleeve *n.* [1990s+] (*US prison*) in pl., tattoos running the full length of one's arms, a sign of one's prison experience.

SE in slang uses

IN PHRASES

❑ **on the sleeve** [the rolling up of a sleeve before the injection] [1940s+] using narcotics. ❑ **put the sleeve on** *v.* [the police officer or borrower grabs the target's sleeve] [1930s] (*US*) **1** to arrest. **2** to borrow money (from); to request favours (from). **3** (*US Und.*) to manhandle a victim for mugging. ❑ **that's another pair of sleeves** [1920s+] (*Aus.*) that's another matter.

sleeve button *n.*[1] [late 19C–1900s] (*US short order*) **1** a dropped egg. **2** codfish balls; fishcakes.

sleeve button *n.*[2] [? SLEEVER *n.*] [20C+] a long drink.

sleever *n.* [abbr. *LONG-SLEEVER under* LONG *adj.*] **1** [late 19C+] (*mainly Aus./N.Z.*) a beer glass holding 369ml (13fl oz). **2** [20C+] (*N.Z.*) a drinking straw.

sleez *n. see* SLEAZE *n.* (3).

sleeze *n. see* SLEAZE *n.*

sleezebag *n. see SLEAZEBAG under* SLEAZE *n.*

sleeze bucket *n. see* SLEAZEBUCKET *n.* (1).

sleezy *adj. see* SLEAZY *adj.*

sleighride *n.* **1** [1910s–60s] in US drug use [pun on SE *snow*/SNOW *n.*[1] (2)]. (**a**) the taking of cocaine. (**b**) rarely, the taking of morphine (which is also white) or heroin. **2** [1920s–30s] (*US Und.*) a deception, a trick [pun on SNOW *v.*].

IN PHRASES

❑ **go for/on a sleighride** *v.* [1920s–50s] to take cocaine. ❑ **take a sleighride** *v.* **1** [1910s–50s] to take cocaine. **2** [1920s–40s] to take morphine (which is also white).

sleighride *v.* [SLEIGHRIDE *n.*] **1** (*US*) in drug uses. (**a**) [1910s–60s] to inhale cocaine. (**b**) [1920s–40s] to take morphine (which is also white). (**c**) [1960s] to give someone cocaine. **2** [1940s–60s] to deceive, to trick [pun on SNOW *v.*].

sleng teng *n.* [ety. unknown] [2000s] (*W.I./Rasta*) marijuana.

slenter *adj. see* SCHLENTER *adj.*

slept on *adj.* [1990s+] (*US black*) attacked, criticized negatively.

slew *v.*[1] (*also* **slue**) [dial. *slew*, to twist around] **1** [19C+] (*Aus.*) to defeat, to 'do for', to 'settle'. **2** [late 19C+] (*Aus.*) to deliver a tale. **3** [1970s] (*Aus. Und.*) to divert a bystander's attention from a crime. **4** [2000s] (*UK teen*) to abuse one's rivals.

slew *v.*[2] [SLOUGH *v.*] [mid-19C] (*UK Und.*) to close, to bar.

slewed *adj.* (*also* **slued**) [dial. *slew*, to twist around, then naut. jargon; note also SLEW *v.*[2]] **1** [19C+] drunk, off-balance. **2** [mid-19C+] confused, baffled. **3** [late 19C+] (*Aus.*) lost, esp. in the bush.

IN PHRASES

❑ **half-slewed** *adj.* [early 19C+] tipsy, half-drunk.

slewfoot *n.* (*also* **sluefoot**) **1** [late 19C+] (*US*) a shambling or clumsy person. **2** [1910s–50s] a police officer.

slice *n.* **1** in sexual senses the equation of women with food, reinforced in sense 1b by pvb 'a slice off a cut loaf is never missed'. (**a**) [mid-18C+] the vagina. (**b**) [1960s+] a generic for women. (**c**) [1980s] an attractive woman. **2** [1940s–70s] (*Aus.*) a £1 note; since decimalization, A$2 [? a single 'slice' of a wad of notes]. **3** [1980s+] (*US campus*) a friend, an intimate [abbr. *HOME SLICE under* HOME *n.*].

IN COMPOUNDS

❑ **slicetown** *n.* [1950s+] (*US*) a 'red-light' area.

IN PHRASES

❑ **carve a slice** *v.* **1** [late 18C; 20C+] to have sexual intercourse. **2** [2000s] to take a portion of the profits. ❑ **cut a slice (off the joint)** *v.* (*also* **knock..., take...**) [late 18C+] of a man, to have sexual intercourse, esp. with a married woman, since proverbially 'a slice off a cut loaf is never missed'. ❑ **slice of cake** *n. see PIECE OF CAKE under* PIECE *n.* ❑ **slice off the legs** *n.* [1960s+] (*Irish*) an act of sexual intercourse. ❑ **slice of life** *n.* (*also* **spice of life**) [20C+] the vagina. ❑ **take a slice** *v.* [1960s+] to have an affair with a married woman. ❑ **take a slice off a cut cake** *v.* [1960s] (*Aus.*) to commit adultery.

slice *v.* [1940s+] to attack, usu. with knife.

IN COMPOUNDS

❑ **slice and dice** *n.* [the fate of the victims] [1950s+] (*US*) a horror film. ❑ **Slice City** *n.* [-CITY *sfx* (1)] [1940s] (*orig. US black*) an assault with a razor or a knife. ❑ **slice job** *n.* [JOB *n.*[2] (2)] [1950s+] (*US*) an attack with an edged or stabbing weapon.

IN PHRASES

❑ **slice one's chops** *v. see under* CHOPS *n.*[1].

sliced *adj.* [1980s+] (*US gay*) circumcised.

slice of ham *n.* [rhy. sl. = GAM *n.*[4]] [20C+] fellatio.

slice of toast *n.* [rhy. sl.] [20C+] a ghost.

slicer *n.* [1940s+] (*US black/Und.*) a knife.

slicing *n.* [SLICE *v.* (1)] [1970s] (*US prison*) a knifing.

slick *n.*[1] [SE *slick*, smooth, plausible, glib] **1** [mid-19C] (*US campus*) an unpopular, unpleasant person. **2** [mid-19C+] (*orig. US black*) a smart, charming, fashionable, sophisticated person. **3** [1930s+] (*US*) a glossy, expensive, middle-class magazine [SE *slick*, i.e. high-quality, glossy paper]. **4** [1940s+] a swindler, a hoaxer. **5** [1990s+] as a term of address.

slick *n.*[2] [1940s] (*US Und.*) silk.

slick *n.*[3] [ety. unknown; ? its effects] [1980s+] (*drugs*) methcathinone.

slick *n.*[4] [1990s+] (*US prison*) a criminal speciality.

slick *adj.* **1** [mid-19C+] (*US, mainly teen*) a general term of approval, clever, sharp; thus n. *slickness*. **2** [1970s] (*US campus*) attractive (of either gender).

IN COMPOUNDS

❑ **slick-ass** *adj.* [-ASS *sfx*] [1970s] smooth, sophisticated, smart. ❑ **slick-boy** *n.* [1990s+] (*US black*) a confidence trickster, a cheat, a liar. ❑ **slick chick** *n.* [CHICK *n.*[1] (2)] [1930s+] (*US black*) a smart, attractive young woman. ❑ **slick citizen** *n.* [CITIZEN *n.* (2)] [1900s–10s] (*US*) an unprincipled individual. ❑ **slickdick** *adj.* [generic use of proper name] [1990s+] cunning, self-promoting, 'smooth'. ❑ **slick duck** *n.* (*also* **slick coot**) [DUCK *n.*[1] (4)] [1900s–10s] (*US*) a cunning, sly person. ❑ **slick shit** *n.* [SHIT *n.* (3h)] [1950s+] (*orig. US black*) any clever stratagem that gets one what is desired. ❑ **slick-leg** *adj.* [1990s+] (*US prison*) innocent of a crime; too clever to get caught, even though guilty. ❑ **slick-leg** *v.* [1960s+] (*gay*) to rub one's penis against the thigh of one's sexual partner.

IN PHRASES

❑ **half-slick** *adj.* [1950s–60s] (*US*) stupid or reckless. ❑ **slick as owl shit** *adj.* (*also* **slick as a biscuit, ...a button, ...a greased pig, ...a greased rope, ...an eel, ...a piece of chalk (o)iled at both ends, ...a ribbon, ...a smelt, ...a whistle, ...cat-shit, ...shit through a goose, ...snot on a door knob**) **1** [mid-19C+] (*US*) very smooth, very slick. **2** [1910s] (*US*) attractive, good.

slick *v.* [SE *slick*] **1** [mid-19C] to get something finished with or disposed of quickly. **2** [mid-19C+] to swindle, to hoax, to cheat.

IN PHRASES

❑ **slick-'em-plenty** *n.* [racial stereotyping both as to ethics and occupation] [1970s] (*US black*) **1** a derog. term for a Jew. **2** a pawnbroker. **3** a smooth-talking confidence trickster. ❑ **slick up** *v.* **1** [mid-19C+] (*US*) to tidy, to make neat. **2** [1910s–50s] in fig. use, to arrange, to defeat, to 'make good'.

slick *adv.* (*also* **slick off**) [mid-19C+] (*US black*) smartly.

slick-a-dee *n.* (*also* **slick-a-die**) [SE *slick* + DEE *n.*[1] (1)] [mid-19C] a pocket-book.

slicker *n.* [SLICK *adj.*] **1** [20C+] (*US*) a cunning or dishonest person, usu. of a businessman, a shrewd and predatory lawyer, a confidence trickster. **2** [1920s+] (*orig. US*) a dandy, a smart dresser. **3** [1920s+] (*US*) ext. of sense 2, a socially sophisticated, wordly individual. **4** [1950s] a smooth, plausible person, esp. in the context of seduction.

slicker *v.* [SLICKER *n.*] **1** [1920s] (*US*) to act in a sophisticated, wordly manner; to be cunning. **2** [1950s] to trick.

slickies *n.* [their 'slick' appearance] [1990s+] (*US campus*) members of a sorority.

slicking *adj.* [SLICK *v.* (2)] [1970s] smooth, plausible, cunning.

slick off *adv. see* SLICK *adv.*

slickster *n.* [SLICK *v.* (2)] [1940s+] (*orig. US black*) a cheat, a smooth talker, a hustler.

slickum *n.* [SE *slick*, to polish] [20C+] (*US*) hair oil.

'slid! *excl.* (*also* **'zlead! 'zleads! z'lid!**) [late 16C–early 18C; mid-19C] euph. oath, lit. 'God's eyelid!'.

slide *n.*[1] **1** [mid-19C] (*UK Und.*) a money box as used in a shop [the user *slides* it off and on a shelf]. **2** [late 19C] (*UK Und.*) a purse [it *slides* in and out of the pocket]. **3** [1920s–60s] (*US black*) in pl., shoes. **4** [1930s+] (*US Und.*) the member of the three-card monte team who keeps an eye out for police and warns the rest so that all can *slide off* in time. **5** [1930s+] (*US black*) a trouser pocket [? SE *side*; or one *slides* things into it]. **6** [1970s+] (*US campus*) an easy course [one *slides* through it]. **7** [1990s+] (*drugs*) a syringe, used for injecting narcotic drugs [the sliding plunger that is part of the syringe].

SE in slang uses

IN PHRASES

❑ **do a slide up the board** *v.* (*also* **do a slide up the straight**) [late 19C] of a man, to have sexual intercourse. ❑ **take the Sabine slide** *v.* [? play on G.T.T. *phr.*; the *Sabine* river is in Texas] [mid-19C] (*US*) to run off, leaving one's debts unpaid.

slide *n.*[2] [1930s–70s] (*UK Und.*) an establishment where transvestites can solicit conventionally dressed men.

slide *v.* **1** in senses of movement. (**a**) [mid-19C+] (*also* **do the slide, slide off, slide out**) to move, to travel; to run away. (**b**) [1900s] as *slide off*, to take someone away. **2** in senses of fig. 'letting go/off'. (**a**) [1920s+] to forgive, to pardon, to let someone off. (**b**) [1970s+] to ignore. (**c**) [1990s+] (*US black*) to give credit, esp. in a drug deal. (**d**) [2000s] (*US*) to escape a criminal charge. **3** [1930s–40s; 1990s+] (*orig. US black*) to dance [the use of smooth parquet dance-floors].

IN PHRASES

❑ **let it slide** *v.* [mid-19C+] to ignore, to dismiss; also as imper., don't bother, it doesn't matter. ❑ **let slide** *v.* [mid-19C+] (*orig. US*) to overlook, to forgive. ❑ **slide by** *v.* [1950s–60s] (*US black*) **1** to drop in uninvited, without previous notice. **2** to fool, to deceive. ❑ **slide off/out** *v. see* sense 1a above.

SE in slang uses

IN COMPOUNDS

❑ **slidewalk** *n. see* separate entry.

IN PHRASES

❑ **slide off a log** *v.* [late 19C] (*Aus.*) to blunder, to make a mistake. ❑ **slide one's jib** *v. see under* JIB *n.*[1].

slide and sluther *n.* [rhy. sl.] [1990s+] a brother.

slider *n.* [Irish *sliodarnach* slithering, sliding, i.e. its potential for sliding out] **1** [1910s+] an ice-cream placed between two wafers. **2** [1940s–60s] (*US*) a small, greasy hamburger [poss. orig. navy slang]. **3** [1950s] (*UK prison*) a hacksaw.

slidewalk *n.* [1940s+] (*US black*) a specific style of walking: one foot takes normal paces, the other drags; one hand is tucked into the side, the other is positioned with the wrist pressed to the waist and the elbow sticking out.

'slife! *excl.* [17C–1920s] a mild oath, lit. 'God's life!'.

'slight! *excl.* [late 16C–mid-17C] a mild oath, lit. 'God's light!'.

slight sensation *n. see* SENSATION *n.*

slim *n.*[1] [ety. unknown] [late 18C–mid-19C] rum or gin.

slim *n.*[2] [? their attempts to be unobtrusive; but note SLIM *adj.* (1)] **1** [1920s–30s] an informer. **2** [1930s–40s] (*US prison*) a police spy.

slim *n.*[3] **1** [1940s–60s] (*US black*) a plain tobacco cigarette, as opposed to a marijuana-filled one [its dimensions, which tend to be leaner than those of a marijuana cigarette]. **2** [1960s] (*US gay*) in pl., very tight trousers [abbr. SLIM JIM *n.* (2)].

slim *n.*[4] [1960s+] (*US black*) a term of address, a friend.

slim *adj.* [Du. *slim*, crafty] [early 19C+] (*S.Afr./US*) clever, crafty, wily.

slim-dilly *n.* [ety. unknown; ? link to DILLY *n.*[3] (1)] [1930s+] (*Aus.*) a young woman.

slime *n.* [its consistency + implication of distaste] **1** [late 17C; 1910s+] semen. **2** [late 19C; 1940s+] (*Aus.*) flattery, ingratiation. **3** [1960s+] an extremely unpleasant person [note the character Chevy *Slime* in Charles Dickens's *Martin Chuzzlewit* (1843–4)].

IN COMPOUNDS

❑ **slimebag** *n.* (*also* **slimeball, slime-mouth**) [1970s+] (*US*) a highly objectionable or offensive person. ❑ **slimebucket** *n.* [1980s+] (*US campus*) a highly objectionable or offensive person.

slime *v.* [SLIME *n.*] **1** [late 19C+] (*Aus.*) to flatter; thus *slimer*, a sycophant. **2** [1990s+] (*Aus.*) to ejaculate.

Slim Jim *n.* (*orig. US*) **1** [late 19C+] a thin person. **2** [1950s] long tapered trousers. **3** [1950s+] a narrow tie, fashionable in the 1950s. **4** [1970s+] (*US Und.*) a small, narrow crowbar used for break-ins. **5** [1980s] (*US black*) the penis.

slimmie *n.* [2000s] (*N.Z.*) a girl or young woman.

slimy *adj.* [SE *slime*] **1** [mid-19C+] deceitful. **2** [1980s+] (*US black/campus*) very unattractive.

sling *n.*[1] [SE *sling*, to throw (back)] **1** [late 18C] a draught, a 'pull' at a bottle or glass. **2** [1940s+] (*Aus.*) in monetary senses. (**a**) (*also* **slingback**) a bribe, a gift. (**b**) a tip.

sling *n.*[2] [1990s+] (*US prison*) a belt with a sharpened buckle, used as an offensive weapon.

SE in slang uses

IN COMPOUNDS

❑ **sling shot** *n. see* separate entry.

IN PHRASES

❑ **get one's ass in a sling** *v.* [ASS *n.* (2)] [1940s+] (*US*) to get into bad trouble, physical or otherwise. ❑ **get one's eye in a sling** *v.* [late 19C+] to be depressed, crushed, defeated; thus *put someone's eye in a sling*, to depress someone. ❑ **have one's head in a sling** *v.* [1940s–60s] (*orig. US black*) to be defeated or depressed. ❑ **have someone's nuts in a sling** *v.* [1990s+] to have someone at one's mercy, lit. or fig. ❑ **in a sling** [1940s–60s] (*US*) in difficulties. ❑ **put someone's ass in a sling** *v.* (*also* **have someone's ass in a sling**) [ASS *n.* (2)] [1940s+] (*US*) to cause trouble for.

sling *v.* [SE *sling*, to throw] **1** in senses of giving, passing. (**a**) [19C+] to throw, cast, hurl, fling; also fig. [SE to late 19C]. (**b**) [19C+] to give. (**c**) [mid–late 19C] to pass from one person to another. (**d**) [mid-19C+] (*Aus.*) to bribe, to pass over a bribe. (**e**) [mid-19C+] (*US*) to work as a waiter or waitress; esp. in phr. *sling hash*, to wait at tables; *sling beer*, to work as a bartender. (**f**) [late 19C+] (*orig. Aus.*) to abandon, to give up, to get rid of; to end a relationship. (**g**) [1960s+] (*US*) to fight with the fists. (**h**) [1980s+] (*drugs*) to sell drugs; usu. modified by a drug name. **2** in senses of communication. (**a**) [mid-19C+] to speak. (**b**) [mid-19C+] (*also* **sling out**) to write, to perform etc. (**c**) [late 19C+] to recount, to tell. (**d**) [1910s+] (*also* **sling off at**) to criticize, to abuse. **3** [late 19C] to do easily. **4** [late 19C] to steal; thus *sling the smash*, to steal tobacco [SE *sling* or SLANG *v.*[1] (1)].

IN PHRASES

❑ **sling (a daddle)** *v.* [DADDLE *n.*] [late 19C] to shake hands. ❑ **sling a deaf 'un** *v.* [1910s–30s] (*UK Und.*) to pretend not to hear (cf. *COP A DEAF 'UN under* COP A… *v.*). ❑ **sling colonial** *v.* [late 19C] (*Aus.*) to talk idiomatic/vernacular Australian (rather than 'English') English. ❑ **sling it** *v.* **1** [1900s] as imper.: 'forget it!'. **2** [20C+] (*Aus.*) to abandon or give up something. **3** [1930s+] (*also* **sling it in**) (*Aus.*) to leave one's job or one's work. ❑ **sling off** *v.* [SLING ONE'S HOOK *v.*] [late 19C+] to leave. ❑ **sling off (at)** *v.* **1** [20C+] (*orig. Aus./N.Z./S.Afr.*) to mock, to tease, to cheek; to berate, to scold. **2** *see* sense 2d above. ❑ **sling out** *v. see* sense 2b above.

SE in slang uses

IN PHRASES

❑ **sling…** *v. see also under* relevant n. ❑ **sling about** *v.* (*also* **sling along**) [mid–late 19C+] to loiter, to hang around with particular intent. ❑ **sling a cat** *v.* (*also* **throw the cat**) [var. WHIP THE CAT *v.* (3)] [19C] to vomit. ❑ **sling for** *v.* [mid-19C] (*UK Und.*) to pay for, to stand treat. ❑ **sling in** *v.* [late 19C] to arrive. ❑ **sling into the middle of next week** *v. see KNOCK INTO THE MIDDLE OF NEXT WEEK under* KNOCK INTO *v.* ❑ **sling one's —** *v.* [mid-19C] to pay admission, qualified by a n. indicating the price paid. ❑ **sling one's bunk** *v.* [naut. imagery] [mid-19C–1900s] to leave, to depart. ❑ **sling one's daniel** *v.* (*also* **take one's daniel**) [ety. unknown; ? lost rhy. sl. referring to some form of pack; given occas. synon. *sling one's dannet* ? link to dial. *donnot/dannet*, a good-for-nothing] [mid-19C] (*US*) to leave. ❑ **sling oneself** *v.* [late 19C] (*US campus*) to show off. ❑ **sling one's hook** *v. see* separate entry. ❑ **sling one's juice** *v. see under* JUICE *n.*[1]. ❑ **sling one's teeth** *v.* [mid-19C] (*US*) to eat. ❑ **sling out** *v.* [1920s+] to eject, to throw out. ❑ **sling someone in the eye** *v.* [late 19C] to punch someone in the eye. ❑ **sling the crap** *v. see SHOOT THE CRAP under* CRAP *n.*[1]. ❑ **sling the hatchet** *v.* **1** [mid-19C] to skulk about. **2** [1920s] to run away, to abscond. ❑ **sling to** *v.* [1920s+] (*Aus./N.Z.*) to pay a bribe or a commission, esp. on one's winnings at gambling. ❑ **sling trout** *v. see under* BROWN TROUT *n.* ❑ **sling up** *v.* [1980s+] (*US campus*) to have sexual intercourse.

IN EXCLAMATIONS

❑ **sling yourself!** [late 19C] an excl. urging immediate action, hurry up! get on with it! ❑ **sling your tross!** *see under* DABTROS *n.*

slingback *n. see* SLING *n.*[1] (2a).

slinge *n.* [ety. unknown] [early 19C] (*UK Und.*) stolen cloth.

slinger *n.* [SLING *v.*] **1** [mid-19C+] (*US*) a waiter or waitress. **2** [1910s+] as sfx, denoting a variety of worker. **3** [1940s–50s] (*UK Und.*) one who passes forged notes. **4** [1980s+] (*US Und.*) a drug dealer; thus (*S.Afr.*) *bum-slinger*, a seller of second-rate drugs.

slingers *n.* [? elision of SE *sailing* or SE *sling*, i.e. one 'throws' the food into the liquid] **1** [late 19C–1910s] (*orig. milit.*) bread or ship's biscuits soaked in tea or coffee. **2** [1930s–40s] sausages.

slingers, the *n.* [SE *sling out*] [1940s+] rejection, dismissal.

IN PHRASES

❑ **get the slingers** *v.* [1950s–60s] to be thrown out, to be dismissed from a job.

sling one's hook *v.* (*also* **take a hook, …one's hook, …the hook**) [? the raising of the anchor (*hook*) before departure or the SE *hook* on which a working miner left his day clothes. When he finished his shift he removed his possessions from the hook and left for home] **1** [mid-19C+] to leave. **2** [late 19C–1900s] to die.

sling shot *n.* **1** [1960s] (*US*) a flick-knife. **2** as a form of under-garment [the shape]. (**a**) [1980s] (*US black*) a sanitary towel. (**b**) [1990s+] (*W.I.*) skimpy underwear; a thong. (**c**) [1990s+] (*US prison*) male underwear, briefs. **3** [1980s] (*US black*) a Cadillac Eldorado [ety. unknown].

slingtail and galena *n.* [mid-19C] (*UK Und.*) a dish of chicken and pickled pork.

slink *n.* [SE *slink*, a premature calf or lamb (thus a human illegitimate child) or *slink*, to creep around] [19C–1910s] a general pej. term, a sneak, a skulker, a cheat; also as adj.

IN COMPOUNDS

❑ **slink-hearted** *adj.* [mid-19C] despicable, unpleasant.

slink *v.* [SE *slink*, of animals, to abort] [1920s+] to abort.

slinky *n.*

IN PHRASES

❑ **dinky one's slinky** *v. see* separate entry.

slinter *n. see* SLANTER *n.*[1].

slinter *adj. see* SCHLENTER *adj.*

slip *n.*[1] [ety. unknown] [late 16C–mid-17C] a counterfeit coin.

IN PHRASES

❑ **nail up for a slip** *v.* [late 16C–early 17C] to be reduced (through poverty) to using counterfeit coins.

slip *n.*[2] [for *slipping* things into] [early 19C] the back pocket of a tail-coat.

SE in slang uses

IN PHRASES

❑ **give someone the slip** *v.* [SE *give the slip*, to elude, to run off] [19C] to die.

slip *n.*[3] [SLIP *v.*[2] (1)] [1960s] (*Aus.*) a loan (from a friend).

slip *v.*[1] [mid-19C] (*UK Und.*) to see, to notice.

slip *v.*[2] **1** [late 19C+] to give, to hand over. **2** [20C+] to pass on information, to tell tales. **3** [1910s+] (*US*) to lose one's competence, to decline. **4** [1980s] (*US black*) (*also* **slip around**) to behave promiscuously. **5** [1990s+] (*US black*) to let one's attention waver, to become too casual, to abandon one's vigilance. **6** [1990s+] (*drugs*) to become somnolent after taking heroin.

SE in slang uses

IN COMPOUNDS

❑ **slip-gibbet** *n.* (*also* **slip-halter**) [SE *slip*, to escape + *gibbet*, the gallows] [mid-17C–early 19C] a thief or pickpocket or one who associates with them.

IN PHRASES

❑ **slip…** *v. see also under* relevant n. ❑ **slip a cog** *v.* [engineering imagery] [1910s–20s] to blunder. ❑ **slip a fast one (over)** *v. see under* FAST ONE *n.* ❑ **slip a gear** *v.* [2000s] to lose emotional control. ❑ **slip a mickey** *v. see under* MICKEY FINN *n.* ❑ **slip around** *v. see* sense 4 above. ❑ **slip five** *v. see SLAP FIVE under* FIVE *n.*[2]. ❑ **slip in Daintie Davie** *v.* (*also* **slip in Willie Wallace**) [late 18C] (*Scot.*) of a man, to have sexual intercourse. ❑ **slip into** *v.* **1** [mid-19C+] to beat; thus *let slip at*, to attack violently. **2** [late 19C] to set about a task enthusiastically. **3** [late 19C+] of a man, to have sexual intercourse. ❑ **slip (it) across** *v.* [1920s] **1** to fool, to 'do down', to upset. **2** to hit, to punch. ❑ **slip it into** *v.* [1920s] to attack verbally. ❑ **slip it to** *v.* (*also* **slip it into, …over**) **1** [1930s+] of a man, to have sexual intercourse with a woman. **2** [1940s] to speak, to inform. ❑ **slip one over on** *v. see PUT ONE OVER (ON) under* ONE *n.*[1]. ❑ **slip one's anchor** *v.* [naut. imagery] [1900s] (*Aus.*) to leave (surreptitiously). ❑ **slip one's cable** *v.* (*also* **part from one's cable**) [naut. imagery] [mid-18C–1910s] to die; to abscond. ❑ **slip one's elbow** *v.* [1990s+] to have an illegitimate child. ❑ **slip one's wind** *v.* [naut. imagery] [late 18C–1910s] to die. ❑ **slip something over (on)** *v.* (*also* **slip something to, slip up**

on) [1910s+] to deceive, to take advantage of in a surreptitious manner. ❑ **slip the calf** *v. see* CAST THE CALF *under* CAST *v.* ❑ **slip up** *v.* (*Aus.*) **1** [late 19C–1900s] to defraud, to swindle. **2** [1910s] in weakened use, to let down, to disappoint.

slip in the gutter *n.* [rhy. sl.] [20C+] butter.

slipped *adj.* [one has 'slipped over the edge of the world'] [1960s] (*US teen*) insane; eccentric.

slipper *n.*[1] [1980s] (*Aus.*) a kicking.

IN PHRASES

❑ **put in the slipper** *v.* [1940s+] (*Aus., orig. prison*) to give a kicking.

slipper *n.*[2] ['Derived from the 'poorer estates' in towns where there are always three shops – a chip shop, a video shop and an offie. People from the estate would shop, rent a video but mostly play the bandit in the chip shop wearing their slippers – never shoes, they'd walk to the shops in their slippers. Slippertown – the part of town would be then named' (*OnLine Dict. of Playground Slang*, 2001)] [1990s+] (*UK juv.*) one who looks much older/younger than they actually are.

slipper *v.* [the SE *slippers* that symbolize a peaceful life] [1920s+] (*US Und.*) to reform and renounce the criminal life.

slippery *n.* [its essential quality] [mid-19C] soap.

SE in slang uses

IN PHRASES

❑ **do a slippery** *v.* [1970s] to absent oneself, usu. for dubious purposes.

slippery-dip *n.* [rhy. sl.] **1** [20C+] (*Aus.*) cheekiness [= LIP *n.*[1] (1)]. **2** [1980s+] (*Aus. prison*) LSD [= TRIP *n.*[4] (1)].

slippery sam *n.* [late 18C; 1970s] an unreliable, evasive, untrustworthy person.

slippery (Sid) *n.* [rhy. sl. = YID *n.*[1]] [1980s+] a Jew.

slippery tit *n.* [1940s] (*US Und.*) a cheap restaurant.

slippin' *adj.* [SE *slipping along nicely*] [1990s+] (*US teen*) a general adj. of approval.

slipping *n.* [SLIP *v.*[2] (3)] [1990s+] (*US black*) not paying attention.

slipping and sliding *n.* [1960s+] (*US black*) sneaking around, acting in a clandestine manner.

slippy tit *n.* [SE *slippy*, cunning + TIT *n.*[3]] [1980s+] (*Ulster*) a sly, untrustworthy person.

slip-slapping *n.* [*see* SLAP FIVE *under* FIVE *n.*[2]] [1970s] a mutual hand-slapping ritual used by blacks (and some whites) for greeting, emphasis, congratulation etc.

slip-slop *n.* [SE *slip-slop*, any form of sloppy mixture, whether food or drink] **1** [early 18C] kissing [echoic of the exchange of spittle]. **2** (*also* **slippy sloppy, slops**) in pl., as a drink. (**a**) [early 18C] a non-alcoholic drink taken for medicinal purposes. (**b**) [late 18C–early 19C] any form of soft drink, esp. tea. (**c**) [mid-19C] any drink. **3** [1960s+] (*S.Afr.*) a thong sandal [the noise it makes as one walks].

slit *n.* **1** with ref. to a woman. (**a**) [early 17C+] the vagina. (**b**) [1940s+] a derog. term for a woman. **2** [1940s+] (*also* **sliteye**) a derog. term for an Asian or East Asian person [the supposed shape of their eye].

slither *n.* (*also* **slitherum**) [it slithers through one's fingers] [1910s–40s] counterfeit money.

slither *v.* (*also* **do a slither**) [SE *slither*, a rush, a hurry; later use is Aus.] [mid-19C+] to hurry away.

sliver-brain *n.* [one has but a 'sliver' of the normal brain] [1930s] a fool.

sliz *n.* [SE *slut* + -IZ- *infix* (1)] [2000s] (*US black*) a promiscuous woman.

sloan *v.* (*also* **Tod Sloan**) [coined and abandoned in 1899; f. the US jockey Tod *Sloan* (1874–1933), who cut his horse Holocaust across those of his rivals in an attempt to win that year's Derby; Sloan had picked up the trick from the British champion Archer, but the sl. gave him the tribute] **1** [late 19C+] to balk, to hinder, to get in the way of, to 'cut up'. **2** [1910s] (*Aus.*) a pun on sense 1, to cut up, as with a knife and fork.

Sloane Ranger *n.* (*also* **Sloane, Sloaney**) [coined by Peter York and Ann Barr in *Harpers & Queen*, October 1975. It puns on *Sloane* Square, London SW3, home of such women + the TV lawman the Lone *Ranger*] [1970s+] a stereotypically conventional, if fashionable British upper-middle-class young woman (occas. man); often abbr. as *Sloane*.

DERIVATIVES

❑ **Sloaney** *adj.* [1980s] pertaining to the world of Sloane Rangers.

slob *n.* [Slavic *zhlub*, a coarse fellow, note also Irish *slaba*, mud; thus a slovenly person] (*orig. US*) **1** [late 19C+] a lazy, dirty, unkempt, good-for-nothing person, usu. a man. **2** [late 19C+] an average person, 'Joe Public'. **3** [20C+] a harmless simpleton, a 'soft', fat fellow. **4** [1900s] in ext. use of sense 1, used of objects. **5** [1990s+] (*US gang*) a derog. term used by Crip gangs for their rivals the Bloods.

DERIVATIVES

❑ **slobhood** *n.* [1990s+] the state of being a slob.

IN COMPOUNDS

❑ **slob-faced** *adj.* [1970s] looking like a slob.

IN PHRASES

❑ **slob out** *v.* (*also* **slob around**) [1990s+] to act lazily, to act in a slovenly manner.

slob *v.* [abbr. SE *slobber*/SLOBBER *n.*] [1900s–70s] (*US black*) to kiss.

IN PHRASES

❑ **slob a knob** *v. see under* KNOB *n.*

slobber *n.* **1** [mid-18C] porter. **2** [late 19C–1920s] nonsensical, sentimental chatter [SLOBBER *v.* (2)]. **3** [late 19C–1950s] a kiss [the swapping of spittle].

IN COMPOUNDS

❑ **slobber-chops** *n.* (*also* **slabber-chops**) [CHOPS *n.*[1] (1); modern use seems primarily for naming a pet] [late 18C–19C] a large-jowled person, a term of ridicule.

IN PHRASES

❑ **chuck a slob** *v.* [1950s] (*US gay*) to kiss. ❑ **sling a slobber** *v.* [late 19C] to throw a kiss, to kiss.

slobber *v.* [orig. UK dial.] **1** [late 16C+] (*also* **slabber**) to kiss. **2** [mid-19C+] to talk sentimental, mawkish nonsense. **3** [20C+] (*US*) to cry. **4** [1970s] to masturbate.

slobberdegullion *n. see* SLABBERDEGULLION *n.*

slobber-slobber *n.* [dial. *slobber*, to work in a slovenly manner] [1950s] (*W.I.*) a slovenly, unkempt, lazy person.

slock *n.* [SLOCK *v.* (1)] [1990s+] (*US prison*) any form of bludgeon-like weapon, e.g. batteries or a padlock in a sock.

slock *v.* [SE *sock* + SLUG *v.*[2] (3)] [1990s+] (*US prison*) to hit someone with a heavy padlock concealed in a sock.

slockdolager/slockdologer *n. see* SOCKDOLAGER *n.*

slog *n.* [SLOG *v.*] **1** [mid-19C] (*UK Und.*) in senses of violence. (**a**) a fight. (**b**) a blow (with a blackjack or cosh). **2** in senses of physical effort. (**a**) [late 19C+] work that is definitely hard and poss. unrewarding. (**b**) [1990s+] an exhausting journey, usu. on foot.

slog *v.* [? Yorks. dial./SE *slug*, to hit hard] **1** [mid-19C+] (*also* **slag**) to hit, to punch. **2** [mid-19C+] to thrash, to beat; also fig. **3** [20C+] to work hard (cf. SLOG ONE'S GUTS OUT below). **4** [20C+] to persist; often as *slog on*. **5** [2000s] (*N.Z.*) to drink alcohol.

IN COMPOUNDS

❑ **slogging match** *n.* [late 19C] a prize-fight.

IN PHRASES

❑ **slog it on** *v. see* SCHLOG IT ON *v.* ❑ **slog it out** *v.* (*also* **slog it through**) **1** [late 19C+] to engage in a (hard and lengthy) fight. **2** [1980s] to work hard. ❑ **slog one's guts out** *v. see under* GUT *n.* ❑ **slog the log** *v. see* FLOG THE LOG *under* LOG *n.*

slogger *n.* [SLOG *v.*] **1** [early 19C+] one who delivers heavy blows, esp. in boxing or cricket. **2** [mid-19C–1950s] a hard, ponderous worker. **3** [late 19C–1900s] a weight attached to a string and used as a weapon. **4** [1980s] a heavy, hard-wearing shoe.

IN PHRASES

□ **sole-slogger** *n.* [SE *sole*] [late 19C] a bootmaker.

slogging *n.* [SLOG *v.*] **1** [mid-19C–1900s] hitting, fighting. **2** [mid-19C+] a beating, a thrashing. **3** [1930s+] working hard; esp. as *slogging away/away at.*

slommack *n. see* SLAMKIN *n.*

sloop of war *n.* [rhy. sl. = *whore*] [mid-19C; 1930s] a prostitute.

sloosh *n.* (*also* **sluish**) [echoic] [late 19C–1910s] a quick wash.

sloosh *v.* [SLOOSH *n.*] **1** [1910s] to have a quick wash, to splash. **2** [2000s] in fig. use, to 'splash' an idea around.

slop *n.*[1] (*also* **slops**) [SE *slop*, liquid or semi-liquid food, esp. as served to invalids] **1** as a drink. (**a**) [mid-18C–19C; 1950s+] (*later use Aus.*) tea. (**b**) [mid-19C+] (*Aus./N.Z./US*) alcohol; usu. beer. (**c**) [late 19C+] (*US*) food in general, usu. second-rate. (**d**) [1960s] (*US prison*) coffee. (**e**) [1960s] (*Aus.*) brandy. **2** in senses of emotional or intellectual weakness. (**a**) [mid-19C+] sentimentality, mawkish emotion. (**b**) [late 19C+] nonsensical talk. (**c**) [1940s] a weak, insignificant person. **3** [1950s] the essence, the 'daylights'.

IN COMPOUNDS

□ **slop and flop** *n.* [FLOP *n.*[5] (2)] [1920s–30s] (*US tramp*) food and accommodation, esp. in transient camps, typically those set up by an oil-drilling company. □ **slopchute** *n.* [note WW2 USN *slop chute*, a chute through which garbage is propelled into the ocean; also a cheap bar] [1960s] (*US gay*) the anus. □ **slop detail** *n.* [1950s] (*US*) a menial task. □ **slop-feeder** *n.* [early 19C] a teaspoon. □ **slophouse** *n.* [play on FLOPHOUSE *n.* (1)] [1940s] (*US Und.*) a cheap restaurant. □ **slop-jaw** *n.* [1950s] a garrulous, self-opinionated talker. □ **slop joint** *n.* [JOINT *n.* (1); note US milit. *slop chute*, the barracks/base canteen] [20C+] a cheap, unappetizing restaurant. □ **slops and slugs** *n.* [SLUG *n.*[1] (1), i.e. the hardness of the doughnut] [1940s] (*US black*) coffee and doughnuts. □ **slop-tubs** *n.* [early 19C] a tea-service.

IN PHRASES

□ **get slops** *v.* [1900s] (*Aus.*) to be punished. □ **slop out** *v.* [SE *slop*, to spill, to pour] **1** [1950s+] (*UK prison*) to empty a chamberpot. **2** [1990s+] to masturbate. □ **slop (over)** *v.* [late 17C SE *slop*, to slobber (over)] [mid-19C–1920s] to treat with exaggerated, mawkish sentiment. □ **slop up** *v.* [SE *slop up*, to absorb] [late 19C+] to drink heavily, to become drunk.

slop *n.*[2] [SE *slop*, a loose outer garment] [mid-19C–1930s] (*UK prison*) a form of smock, in easily distinguishable colours, worn by prisoners on work parties.

IN COMPOUNDS

□ **slop-made** *adj.* [synon. with SE *slop-built*] [late 19C–1900s] (*Aus.*) disjointed; of clothes, badly tailored; also in fig. use; thus *slop-suit*, a badly tailored suit; *slop-tailor*, a second-rate tailor.

slop *n.*[3] [backsl. or rhy. sl. *esclop/slop* = COP *n.*[1] (1)] [mid-19C–1950s] usu. in pl., a police officer, the police.

slop *n.*[4] [1940s] (*US black campus*) a sophomore.

slop *v.* [SE *slop*, to feed an animal with slops] [1900s] (*Aus.*) in fig. use, to feed, to give, to apportion.

slope *n.*[1] [Yorks. dial. *slope*, deception] [mid-19C] (*US*) a trick, a hoax.

slope *n.*[2] (*also* **slopehead, slopie, slopy**) [the supposed 'slope' of East Asian eyes] **1** [1940s+] a derog. term for an East Asian person, esp. Vietnamese, Korean. **2** [1980s] used for any foreigner, not necessarily Asian.

SE in slang uses

IN PHRASES

□ **slope in a cup with the light out** *n.* [late 19C] (*US short order*) black coffee.

slope *adj.* (*also* **slopehead, slopie**) [SLOPE *n.*[2] (1)] [1940s+] (*US*) East Asian, esp. Vietnamese.

slope *v.*[1] [synon. Du.; Rowlands, *Martin-Mark-all* (1610), notes that this replaces Harman's and Dekker's synon. *couch a hogshead* under COUCH *v.*, which is 'like an Almanac that is out of date'] [17C] to sleep.

slope *v.*[2] [SE *let's lope* or *slope*, to move obliquely; note Schele De Vere, *Americanisms* (1872): 'The term came first into use here, when the new State of Texas offered a ready asylum to unfortunate speculators, dishonest creditors, and even escaped criminals, so that the words Gone To Texas (G. T. T.) meant to be gone to the American Alsatia, and the act of going so far "down South," became known as *sloping*. It implied, virtually, that the *sloper* had cheated his creditors, plundered a bank, or robbed his employers. The precise meaning of the word has been elucidated in the statement that "a mean fellow does not slope, he sneaks or slinks away; but the scoundrel, bold and unabashed, when defeated, slopes to parts unknown".'] **1** [mid-19C+] (*orig. US*) to leave, to move off. **2** [1900s–20s] (*US Und.*) to escape from prison. **3** [1900s–50s] to cheat, e.g. a publican, a shopkeeper; to avoid payment. **4** [1950s] to leave one's lodgings without paying.

IN COMPOUNDS

□ **slopeout** *n.* [1960s] (*US*) anything seen as easy to perform.

IN PHRASES

□ **do a slope** *v.* [1900s] to leave, to escape. □ **slope about** *v.* [1910s] to wander around. □ **slope off** *v.* (*also* **slope out**) [mid-19C+] (*orig. US*) to leave, esp. surreptitiously.

slopehead *see under* SLOPE.

sloper *n.*[1] [late 19C] an act of sexual intercourse in which the couple are leaning against something, e.g. a table or the edge of a bed.

sloper *n.*[2] [dial. *sloper*, a trickster + SLOPE *v.*[2] (1)] [late 19C+] (*Aus.*) one who leaves without paying off their debts or bills.

slopie *see under* SLOPE.

slopped *adj.* (*also* **sloppo**) [SLOP *n.*[1] (1); underpinned by SE *sloppy*, weak, feeble, waterlogged] [20C+] drunk.

sloppiness *n.* [SE *slop*, liquid or semi-liquid food] [1910s] some form of liquid-based food, e.g. a stew.

slopping up *n.* [SLOP *n.*[1] (1)] [late 19C–1920s] (*US tramp*) a session of heavy drinking.

sloppo *adj. see* SLOPPED *adj.*

sloppy *adj.* [SE; ult. *slop*, an act of spilling, the liquid thus spilt] **1** [early 19C+] lazy, inefficient, imprecise. **2** [late 19C+] mawkishly sentimental. **3** [1910s+] (*US*) messy. **4** [1920s+] (*US*) (*also* **slip-sloppy**) drunk.

IN COMPOUNDS

□ **sloppy-ass** *adj.* [1950s] (*US*) overcome by drink.

IN PHRASES

□ **get sloppy** *v.* [1980s+] **1** (*US black/campus*) to get drunk. **2** to have sexual intercourse.

sloppy Joe *n.* (*US*) **1** [1940s+] (*also* **sloppy**) a loose, floppy sweater. **2** [1940s+] a multi-decked sandwich (the fillings ooze out when eating it). **3** [1940s+] a slovenly, inefficient person. **4** [1960s+] a type of hamburger in which the meat filling is diluted to a form of sauce.

sloppy joe's *n.* [generic use of a supposed cook + SLOPPY JOE *n.* (2); the orig. Sloppy Joe's was a Havana, Cuba, bar run by Jose (Joe) Abeal Otero (d. 1942), allegedly thus nicknamed for its low standards of hygiene] **1** [1930s+] (*US*) a cheap restaurant or snack bar. **2** [1960s] (*S.Afr.*) a design of shoe favoured by S. Afr. 'teddy girls'.

sloppy seconds *n.* **1** [1960s+] (*also* **slops, sloppy thirds**) sexual intercourse with a woman who has had another partner/partners immediately previously, whether forced or voluntary. **2** [1960s+] the woman who is participating in this sequential sex. **3** [1970s+] (*US gay/prison*) the man who participates second or later in sequential sex.

IN PHRASES

□ **go slops** *v.* [1970s+] (*Aus.*) of a man, to be one of the last to participate in the multiple rape of or intercourse with a woman.

slops *n.*[1] [SE *slop*, an outer garment; dial. the leg(s) of a pair of breeches; ult. ety. unknown] [mid-16C–1910s] wide, baggy breeches or hose; thus *slop-shop*, a clothiers.

slops *n.*[2] **1** *see* SLOP *n.*[1]. **2** *see* SLOPPY SECONDS *n.* (1).

slopy *n. see* SLOPE *n.*[2].

slorch *n.* [? SE *slut* + *whore* + BITCH *n.*[1] (1)] [1990s+] (*US campus*) a promiscuous woman.

slosh *n.*[1] [SE *slosh*, weak, watery, unappetizing drink; ult. *slush*, liquid mud] **1** [mid–late 19C+] a drink, alcoholic or otherwise. **2** [late 19C+] mawkish emotionalism; thus *slosh-bucket*, n., a highly sentimental person. **3** [1920s+] (*Aus.*) coffee.

slosh *n.*[2] [SLOSH *v.*[1]] **1** [20C+] a hit, a blow. **2** [1950s] an attempt at hitting.

slosh *v.*[1] (*also* **sloush**) [mid-19C+] to hit; thus *slosh the burick, slosh the old gooseberry*, to hit one's wife.

(IN PHRASES)

❑ **slosh around** *v.* **1** [late 19C] (*US*) to hit out at random; physically and verbally. **2** [late 19C–1920s] to strut about, to swank.

slosh *v.*[2] [the consumption of SLOSH *n.*[1] (1)] [late 19C+] **1** to swallow carelessly, to eat heartily. **2** to pour out liquid in an abrupt manner.

(IN PHRASES)

❑ **slosh around** *v.* [mid–late 19C] (*US*) to go out drinking.

slosh and mud *n.* [rhy. sl.] [20C+] a (collar or ear) stud.

sloshed *adj.* (*also* **schlossed, slozzo, soshed**) [SLOSH *n.*[1] (1) + SLOSH *v.*[2] (1)] [20C+] drunk.

(IN COMPOUNDS)

❑ **slosh sex** *n.* [1990s+] sexual intercourse at a time when one is very drunk.

slot *n.* **1** in mechanical senses [the slot into which one places money]. (**a**) [late 19C–1950s] (*US*) an Automat [the coin-operated self-service Automats, popularized in New York (although in no other city) by the Horn & Hardart Baking Co.]. (**b**) [1940s] (*orig. US black*) a general term of address [Mezzrow & Wolfe, *Really the Blues* (1946): 'A private inner-racial joke, suggesting a mouth as big and as avaricious as the coin slot in a vending machine, always looking for something to put in it.']. (**c**) [1950s+] (*orig. US*) often as *the slots*, a slot-machine. **2** in physiological senses. (**a**) [late 19C+] the vagina. (**b**) [1970s] (*US gay*) the anus. **3** [1970s+] (*Aus./N.Z.*) a prison cell [into which one is put].

slot *v.* **1** [1950s] to hit, to beat up. **2** [1980s+] (*Aus. prison*) to lock into a cell. **3** [1990s+] to obtain. **4** [1990s+] to kill.

slouch *n.* [SE *slouch*, 'an awkward, slovenly, or ungainly man; a lubber, lout, clown; also, a lazy, idle fellow' (*OED*)] **1** [late 19C+] an indifferent, second-rate or inefficient thing, place, person etc. **2** [1970s] (*US black*) an eccentric, lazy, unprofessional prostitute.

slough *n.*[1] (*also* **cold slough**) **1** [1910s] (*Aus.*) a prison; a state of imprisonment [SLOUGH *v.* (1)]. **2** [1920s–50s] (*US Und.*) a temporarily empty house, thus a target for a robbery; thus *cold slough prowler*, a thief who robs empty houses.

(IN COMPOUNDS)

❑ **slough worker** *n.* [1900s–40s] (*US Und.*) one who robs a house or apartment in the absence of its owners.

(IN PHRASES)

❑ **hot slough** *n.* [HOT *adj.* (1e)] [1920s–60s] (*US tramp*) somewhere that is robbed while the owners are in occupation.

slough *n.*[2] [SE *slough*, a piece of muddy ground] [1920s–50s] the vagina.

slough *v.* (*also* **slough in, slough up, slow**) [SE *slough*, to be swallowed up; ult. *slough*, a piece of soft, muddy ground] **1** [mid-19C–1950s] to lock up, to put in prison. **2** [1900s–60s] (*US Und.*) to throw away, to abandon, to dispose of; to conceal quickly. **3** [1920s–60s] (*US tramp*) to assault. **4** [1950s] (*US*) to ignore, to dismiss. **5** [1960s] (*US Und.*) to steal, to shoplift.

(IN PHRASES)

❑ **unslough** *v.* **1** [mid-19C–1940s] (*UK Und.*) to unlock, to open. **2** [1920s] (*US tramp*) to steal a watch from inside a man's coat.

sloughed (up) *adj.* (*also* **slowed**) [SLOUGH *v.*] [mid-19C+] (*UK/US Und.*) imprisoned, locked up.

(IN PHRASES)

❑ **get sloughed up** *v.* [1940s–50s] (*US Und.*) to move from the general prison population into protective solitary confinement.

slougher *n.* [SLOUGH *v.* (2)] [1910s] (*US Und.*) one who helps a thief dispose of stolen goods.

slough in/up *v. see* SLOUGH *v.*

slour (up) *v.* [ety. unknown] **1** [early–mid-19C] to button up a garment; thus *sloured hoxter*, a buttoned-up inside pocket. **2** [early–mid-19C; 1990s+] (*UK Und.*) to lock up, to fasten, to secure.

sloush *v. see* SLOSH *v.*[1].

slousher *n.* [SE *slouch*] [1900s] (*N.Z.*) a lazy person; usu. in phr. *be no slousher/slousher at.*

slow *adj.* **1** [early–mid-19C] unfashionable. **2** [mid-19C+] of places, events, dull, boring. **3** [mid-19C+] of people, dull, lifeless, insipid. **4** [mid-19C+] sexually timid. **5** [1960s+] (*US black*) unsophisticated, lacking in knowledge.

SE in slang uses

(DERIVATIVES)

❑ **slowie** *n.* [1980s+] a slow dance or song.

(IN COMPOUNDS)

❑ **slow-ass** *adj.* [SE *slow* + sfx SLOUGH *v.* + -ASS *sfx*] [1970s+] (*US black*) slow. ❑ **slowball** *n.* [1950s] (*US*) a slow person, a dawdler. ❑ **slow boat** *n.* [? the song 'I want to get you on a slow boat to China'; the emphasis is on the supposed exoticism of marijuana, although, given 'China', the link should be to opium] [1970s+] (*S.Afr. drugs*) a marijuana cigarette. ❑ **slowcoach** *n.* [SE *slowcoach*, one who acts, works, or moves slowly] [mid-19C] an unfashionable person. ❑ **slow con** *n. see under* CON *n.*[1]. ❑ **slow connecter** *n.* [1930s] (*US Und.*) a second-rate criminal (by criminal standards). ❑ **slow-play** *v.* (*also* **slow-walk**) [1990s+] (*US prison*) to waste time deliberately; to stall someone, e.g. in the payment of a debt. ❑ **slowpoke** *n.* (*also* **poke**) [POKE ALONG *under* POKE *v.*] [mid-19C+] (*US*) a sluggard, a lethargic, lazy person. ❑ **slow track** *n.* [the image of the small town or the West Coast being 'slower' than New York] [1940s] (*US black*) **1** the whoring and high-life centre in a small town or city. **2** the West Coast.

(IN PHRASES)

❑ **go-slow** *n.* [1980s+] (*Aus. prison*) the punishment cells. ❑ **have the slows** *v.* **1** [mid-19C+] to suffer some form of imaginary disease to which one attributes lassitude, inactivity etc. **2** [1970s+] (*drugs*) to be very intoxicated, at which point life outside one's head seems to crawl by. ❑ **slow-em-ups** *n.* (*also* **slow-me-down juice**) [the effects] [1970s+] (*drugs*) any form of barbiturate, tranquillizer or sleeping pill. ❑ **slow on the draw** *adj.* [gun-fighting imagery] [20C+] **1** not very intelligent. **2** (*Irish*) reluctant to stand one's round of drinks. ❑ **slow on the trigger** *adj.* [gun-fighting imagery] [20C+] stupid, dull. ❑ **slow your roll** *v. see under* ROLL *n.* ❑ **slow up** *v.* [1980s+] (*Aus. prison*) to place in isolation.

slow *v. see* SLOUGH *v.*

Slowbart *n.* [the slow pace of its life] [late 19C–1900s] (*Aus.*) Hobart, the capital city of Tasmania.

slowed *adj.* [? SLOUR (UP) *v.* (2)] [mid-19C] (*UK prison*) locked up.

Slow Town *n.* [? its image among hobos, or play on its role as a car manufacturer, i.e. 'slow down'] [1900s] (*US*) Detroit.

slozzo *adj. see* SLOSHED *adj.*

slubber *n.* [late 18C–mid-19C] a stupid drunkard.

slubberdegullion *n. see* SLABBERDEGULLION *n.*

'slud! *see* 'SBLOOD! *excl.*

sludge *n.* [1960s+] (*US black*) the anus.

sludgeball *n.* [SE *sludge* + sfx *-ball*] [1960s+] (*US*) a slovenly person.

slue *v. see* SLEW *v.*[1].

sluefoot *n. see* SLEWFOOT *n.*

sluff *v.* [phonetic sp. of SE *slough (off)*] [1920s–50s] (*US*) to avoid or shirk one's responsibilities or work.

IN COMPOUNDS

❑ **sluff course** *n.* [1960s–70s] (*US campus*) a course that requires little work, a course for which one does little work.

slug *n.*[1] [SE *slug*, a piece of lead (which may ult. refer to SE *slug*, the gastropod; SAmE *slug*, the name of various large gold coins issued privately in California *c.*1850, usu. worth $50] **1** as a projectile. (**a**) [18C+] a bullet. (**b**) [1930s] a shell. **2** in senses of drink and drugs. (**a**) [mid-18C] a fiery drink. (**b**) [mid-18C+] a portion or measure of liquor. (**c**) [1940s+] a portion of a non-alcoholic drink, e.g. coffee. (**d**) [1950s] in non-alcoholic contexts, a portion, a share. (**e**) [1960s] a portion or measure of a drug. **3** as a coin or token. (**a**) [mid-19C+] (*US*) $1.00; thus *half a slug*, fifty cents; thus money, irrespective of amount. (**b**) [1910s+] a token.

IN PHRASES

❑ **chuck a slug** *v.* (*also* **toss a slug**) [1930s] to shoot. ❑ **fire a slug** *v.* [late 18C–early 19C] to drink a dram.

slug *n.*[2] [*OED* suggests the n. comes from SLUG *v.*[2] (3), but n. cites antedate those of the v.; thus ? SLOG *v.* (1)] (*US*) **1** [early 19C+] a blow; lit. and fig. **2** [1920s] (*US Und.*) a blackjack. **3** [1940s+] a thug. **4** [2000s] (*N.Z.*) in fig. use, an excessively high price.

IN COMPOUNDS

❑ **slug-nutty** *adj.* [NUTTY *adj.*[2] (2)] [1930s–50s] (*US*) lit. or fig., punch-drunk.

IN PHRASES

❑ **put the slug on** *v.* **1** [1920s+] to beat up. **2** [1930s] to criticize harshly. **3** [1940s] to deliver an official punishment.

slug *n.*[3] [supposed resemblances to the gastropod] **1** [1910s] (*US*) a piece of nasal mucus. **2** [1940s+] (*orig. Aus. navy*) the penis; thus *slug slewer*, one who watches men in the shower.

IN PHRASES

❑ **tug one's slug** *v.* [TUG *v.* (2)] [1990s+] to masturbate.

slug *v.*[1] (*also* **slug down, slug up**) [mid-19C+] to drink.

slug *v.*[2] [SLUG *n.*[2] (1)] **1** [late 19C] to criticize harshly. **2** [late 19C–1900s] in fig. use, to overcome. **3** [late 19C+] (*orig. Und.*) to hit hard. **4** [late 19C+] in fig. use, to dispute aggressively; often ext. as *slug it out*. **5** [1920s–40s] to shoot. **6** [1930s] to kill, to murder. **7** [1940s+] (*Aus.*) to overcharge. **8** [1940s+] (*US*) to trudge, to move with an effort, to make effort. **9** [1960s] (*US*) to apply, to dose.

DERIVATIVES

❑ **slugfest** *n.* [-FEST *sfx*] [1910s+] (*US*) a rough battle, a hard-hitting contest. ❑ **sluggy** *adj.* [1950s] (*US teen*) violent, aggressive.

slug *v.*[3] [1980s] (*US campus*) to sleep.

slug and snail *n.* [rhy. sl.] [20C+] a (finger)nail.

slugbug *n.* [a supposed resemblance to the SE *slug* + *bug*, the car's popular nickname] [1990s+] (*US campus*) a Volkswagen 'Beetle'.

slugged *adj.* [SLUG *n.*[1] (2b)] [1950s] (*US*) drunk.

slugger *n.* [SLUG *v.*[2] (3)] **1** [late 19C+] a fighter, professional or otherwise, esp. one who relies on brute force rather than skill for their conquests; a thug. **2** [1950s+] used as an affectionate term of address. **3** [1970s+] (*US campus*) a sexual success, a seducer.

sluggers *n.* [SLUG *v.*[2] (3); such whiskers were orig. a sign of a pugnacious fighter, stereotypically Irish] [late 19C+] (*US*) whiskers that extend from the ear to the chin, typically worn by a stage Irishman.

slugging *n.* [SLUG *v.*[2] (3)] **1** [mid-19C+] (*US*) a beating, fatal or otherwise. **2** [1930s] in fig. use, strenuous efforts.

sluice *n.* [SE *sluice*: (1) a channel; a gap, a hole, a gash; (2) a valve for regulating the flow of water; (3) to pour something through a sluice] **1** [late 17C–early 18C] the vagina. **2** [late 17C–mid-18C] the penis. **3** [mid-19C] (*UK Und.*) a drink. **4** [mid-19C–1920s] the mouth. **5** [1950s–70s] sexual intercourse.

IN COMPOUNDS

❑ **sluice-cunted** *adj.* [SE *sluice*, a channel, a run off + CUNT *n.* (1)] [mid-19C+] having a large vagina. ❑ **sluice-head** *n.* [1900s] a drunk. ❑ **sluice-house** *n.* [mid-19C] **1** a public house, a tavern. **2** the mouth.

sluice *v.* [late 16C–early 17C] to have sexual intercourse.

SE in slang uses

IN PHRASES

❑ **sluice the bolt** *v.* [BOLT *n.*[2] (1)] **1** [late 18C–19C] to drink heartily. **2** [early 19C] to ply with drink. ❑ **sluice the dominoes** *v.* [DOMINO *n.*[1] (1)] [19C] to drink heartily. ❑ **sluice the gob** *v.* (*also* **sluice one's chops, ...gob, ...neck, ...whistle**) [GOB *n.*[1] (1)] [mid-18C–1940s] to take a hearty drink.

sluicery *n.* [SE *sluice*, to wash down; note Egan, *Life in London* (1821): '[...] from the lower orders of society, and women of the town, *sluicing* their throats as it were with gin'] [early–mid-19C] a gin-shop or public house.

sluk *n.* [Afk. *sluk*, to swallow] [1970s+] (*S.Afr.*) a gulp, a swallow.

sluk *v.* **1** [1970s+] (*S.Afr.*) to gulp, to swallow down. **2** [2000s] (*S.Afr. Und.*) to betray.

sluker *n.* [such women were considered socially inferior to those who worked in Islington] [late 19C–1900s] a prostitute who works in the City Road, London, itself part of the parish of St Luke's.

slum *n.*[1] [? SE *slumber*] **1** [late 18C–mid-19C] (*UK Und.*) a room; usu. defined by a descriptive n. **2** [mid-19C] a chest or box. **3** [mid-19C] a shop; usu. defined by a descriptive n. **4** [mid-19C] (*UK Und.*) 'a low drinking-place' (Matsell). **5** [late 19C] a back-alley.

slum *n.*[2] [SE *slum*, a run-down, poverty-stricken area; thus a generic negative] **1** [early–mid-19C] nonsensical talk or writing, 'gammon', 'blarney'. **2** [early–mid-19C] the jargon of gypsies. **3** [early–mid-19C] a trick, a hoax. **4** [mid-19C] a professionally written begging letter. **5** [mid-19C] an insinuation, an innuendo. **6** [mid-19C] (*UK Und.*) a letter written from prison. **7** [1910s–40s] (*US*) a disparaging name for a person.

DERIVATIVES

❑ **slummy** *adj.* [1940s] (*US*) socially inferior.

SE in slang uses

IN COMPOUNDS

❑ **slumbox** *n.* [1920s+] a typical example of slum housing. ❑ **slum-dragger** *n.* **1** [1900s] a member of the London working classes. **2** [1970s+] (*US campus*) a course in urban local government. ❑ **slums and bums** *n.* [BUM *n.*[3] (1)] [1970s+] (*US campus*) a course in urban local government. ❑ **slum-scribbler** *n.* [mid-19C] (*UK Und.*) a writer of begging letters, posing as an honest labourer fallen on hard times.

IN PHRASES

❑ **on the billiard slum** [SE *billiards*, i.e. a ball bouncing at various angles + sense 3 above, orig. Und.] [early 19C–1910s] (*Aus.*) working as a confidence trickster; thus *give it them on the billiard slum, go on the billiard slum*, to hoax, to defraud. ❑ **up to slum** *adj.* [early–mid-19C] knowing, aware, on the lookout for tricks.

slum *n.*[3] [ety. unknown] **1** [mid-19C] (*UK Und.*) a bundle of banknotes. **2** [mid-19C] a dollar. **3** [1910s+] (*also* **slump**) cheap or counterfeit jewellery, typically that sold illegally by street vendors. **4** [1930s] stolen jewellery. **5** [1940s+] the virtually worthless prizes offered at fairs, carnivals etc.

IN COMPOUNDS

❑ **slum hustler** *n.* [HUSTLER *n.* (4)] [1920s+] (*UK Und.*) one who sells cheap jewellery or clothing, pretending to the gullible buyer that it is stolen property; thus *slum hustle*, the trick itself. ❑ **slum hustling** *n.* [1930s] (*US Und.*) selling fake jewellery. ❑ **slum joint** *n.* [JOINT *n.* (1)] [1930s–40s] (*US Und.*) a jewellery store. ❑ **slum-worker** *n.* [1950s] (*US Und.*) one who sells cheap or imitation jewellery as its expensive equivalent.

slum *n.*[4] [SLUMGUDGEON *n.*] **1** [mid-19C–1940s] (*US prison/tramp*) stew; thus *slum-slinger, slum-burner*, a cook. **2** [1910s] (*US*) soup. **3** [1930s] (*UK tramp*) anything edible.

slum *n.*[5] [1920s] (*US drugs*) narcotics.

IN COMPOUNDS

❑ **slum dump** *n.* [DUMP *n.*[3]] [1950s] (*US drugs*) anywhere that users take narcotics.

slum *v.*^{1} [18C] (*UK Und.*) to break into.

slum *v.*^{2} [SLUM *n.*^{2}] **1** [mid-19C] to boast; to talk nonsense; to speak criminal cant. **2** [mid-19C] (*UK Und.*) to fake illness. **3** [mid–late 19C] to trick or cheat. **4** [1920s] (*US Und.*) to drink. **5** [1990s+] (*US drugs*) to be sold inferior or fake drugs.

IN PHRASES

❑ **slum the gorger** *v.* [GORGER *n.*^{1}] [mid-19C] **1** to cheat on the sly, to be an eye *servant*, i.e. a servant who works hard only when the master's or mistress's eye is on them. **2** to hide, to pass to a confederate.

slum *v.*^{3} [SE *slum*] **1** [mid-19C+] to saunter about, esp. in poor or 'red–light' areas, poss. with an eye on 'immoral pursuits', also as *do the slums*. **2** [late 19C+] to visit impoverished areas, looking for 'atmosphere' and 'characters', but secure in the knowledge that one's real life is elsewhere, either as a tourist, or for personal reasons, e.g. political support; thus n. *slumming*. **3** [1920s+] in fig. use of sense 2, to do something ostensibly demeaning, while telling oneself that one is really above it.

slumber party *n.* [1930s–40s] (*US drugs*) morphine.

slumgudgeon *n.* (*also* **gullion, shungudgeon, slumgullion**) [ety. unknown; ? SE *slum* + Lancashire dial. *gullion*, a worthless wretch] **1** [mid-19C–1950s] 'any cheap, nasty, washy beverage' or foodstuff (Hotten, 1874). **2** [late 19C] a representative or servant. **3** [1900s] in fig. use, nonsense.

slumgullion *adj.* [fig. use of SLUMGUDGEON *n.*] [1940s] (*US*) second-rate, run-down.

slumguzzle *v.* [SLUM *n.*^{2} + GUZZLE *v.*^{2} (2)] [mid-19C–1910s] (*orig. US*) to trick, to cheat.

slummer *n.* [SLUM *v.*^{3} (2)] **1** [late 19C+] one who plays the tourist in impoverished areas, looking for 'atmosphere' and 'characters', but secure in the knowledge that one's real life is elsewhere. **2** [1950s] an inferior person.

slumming *n.* [? SLUM *v.*^{2} (3)] [mid-19C] **1** (*UK Und.*) the practice of passing counterfeit money. **2** (*US Und.*) the practice of stealing packages of bank bills.

slummock *n.* [SLUMMOCK *v.*] [1910s–1940s] a slovenly person.

slummock *v.* (*also* **slummuck**) [SE *slummocky*, slovenly] **1** [late 19C] to become run-down, slovenly. **2** [late 19C+] to move in a slovenly manner. **3** [1910s–40s] to clean carelessly or half-heartedly.

slummy *n.*^{1} [SE *slum*] **1** [late 19C–1930s] a servant girl. **2** [1920s–60s] a slum-dweller. **3** [1980s] an ill-dressed, unattractive woman.

slummy *n.*^{2} [SLUM *n.*^{3}] [2000s] small change, coppers.

slump *n. see* SLUM *n.*^{3} (3).

slump *v.* [late 19C] (*US*) to defeat thoroughly.

slung *adj.* [SE *get slung off*, to be thrown] **1** [1930s+] (*Aus.*) thrown from one's horse. **2** [1980s] acquitted.

slur *n.* [SLUR *v.*] [17C–early 19C] a cheat.

slur *v.* [? Low Ger. *slurrn*, to drag the feet] [17C–early 19C] (*UK Und.*) to cheat at dice; spec. to slide a dice out of the dice-box without actually letting it roll.

slurb *n.* [SE *slum* + *suburb*] [1970s] (*US*) the dormitory suburbs of a big city, mass-produced, featureless, sprawling and aesthetically null.

slurp *n.* [1960s] (*Aus.*) a drink.

slurp *v.* [SE *slurp*, to make a noise while eating/drinking] [1990s+] to consume, to eat or drink.

slush *n.* [SE *slush*, watery, melted snow; note RN jargon *slush*, the refuse fat from boiled meat, the selling of which was a perk accorded the SLUSHY *n.* or ship's cook] **1** [late 18C] worthless information. **2** [mid-19C+] (*orig. US*) (*also* **slushiness**) blatant sentimentality. **3** in context of potable liquids. (**a**) [mid-19C+] (*UK tramp*) the tea or coffee available in lodging houses. (**b**) [late 19C] (*US*) beer. (**c**) [20C+] any form of sloppy food, e.g. a thin stew. (**d**) [1980s] (*US campus*) a heavy drinker [SLUSH UP below]. **4** [1920s+] (*UK Und.*) forged, counterfeit money. **5** *see* SLUSHY *n.*

DERIVATIVES

❑ **slushed** *adj.* [note SLOSHED *adj.*] [1940s] (*US Und.*) drunk.

IN COMPOUNDS

❑ **slush-bucket** *n.* [late 18C–mid-19C] an ill-mannered eater; one who eats much greasy food. ❑ **slush pile** *n.* [orig. publishing jargon *slush pile*, unsolicited manuscripts, or those unmediated by an agent] [1960s] of things or individuals, the average, the run-of-the-mill. ❑ **slush pump** *n.* [the spittle that collects while playing it] [1930s–50s] (*US*) a trombone.

IN PHRASES

❑ **slush up** *v.* [1900s–40s] (*US Und.*) to drink.

slusher *n.*^{1} [late 19C] a period of (very) wet weather.

slusher *n.*^{2} [SLUSH *n.* (4)] [1910s–20s] a printer and distributor of counterfeit notes.

slush fund *n.* [fig. use of RN jargon *slush*, refuse fat, the sale of which was a cook's perk] [late 19C+] an emergency fund for unforeseen expenditure, esp. that which may be illegal or extra-legal; such funds came into prominence during the Watergate Affair of 1972.

slushiness *n. see* SLUSH *n.* (2).

slushy *n.* (*also* **slusher, slush, slushie**) [orig. naut. jargon *slushy*, a ship's cook, who collected and sold refuse fat or *slush*] **1** [early 19C+] a cook, or assistant cook. **2** [mid-19C–1900s] (*Aus.*) (*also* **slush lamp**) a fat lamp, a wick placed in a dish of fat. **3** [late 19C+] (*Aus./N.Z.*) a cook's assistant, esp. for a shearing gang. **4** [20C+] any unskilled assistant; a servant, thus a derogatory label.

slushy *adj.* [SLUSH *n.* (2)] [1910s+] sentimental.

slushy *v.* [SLUSHY *n.* (1)] [1900s] (*Aus.*) to cook; to work as a cook.

slut *n.* [SE *slut*, a promiscuous woman] **1** [1900s] in cards, the queen. **2** [1980s+] (*US campus*) an affectionate term of address among women. **3** [1990s+] an habitué; usu. in combs.

SE in slang uses

IN COMPOUNDS

❑ **slut hut** *n.* ['homosexualizing' of SE *slut*, usu. applied to women + *hut*] [1980s+] (*US gay*) **1** a gay brothel. **2** anywhere that gay men congregate for sex. **3** (*Aus.*) a van or car used primarily for sex. ❑ **slut (lamp)** *n.* [play on BITCH *n.*^{2}] [late 19C+] (*US, Western*) an improvised lamp made of a twist of rag in a container of grease. ❑ **slut-puppy** *n.* [play on DOG *n.*^{2} (3c)] [1980s+] **1** (*US*) a derog. term for a lesbian. **2** (*orig. US campus*) a promiscuous woman. **3** (*US gay*) a promiscuous or available man.

sly *adj.* [SE *sly*, secretive, underhand] **1** [mid-19C+] (*orig. Aus.*) illicit, illegal. **2** [1950s] (*US teen*) excellent.

IN COMPOUNDS

❑ **sly-bag** *n.* [1940s+] (*Aus.*) a cunning person. ❑ **sly-balls** *n.* [2000s] (*N.Z.*) a derog. term for a man. ❑ **slyboots** *n.* (*also* **sly-cap**) [late 17C+] a cunning, deceptive person, usu. with overtones of affection rather than an expression of outright disapproval. ❑ **sly-grog** *n.* (*also* **sly, slyg**) [sense 1 above + GROG *n.*^{1}] [late 19C+] (*Aus./N.Z.*) liquor sold without a licence, often through a *sly-grog shop*; thus *sly-groggery, sly-grog shanty*, an illicit saloon or liquor store; *sly-grogger, sly-grogster, sly-groggist, sly-grog man*, an illicit liquor seller; *sly-grogging*, selling liquor illegally.

IN PHRASES

❑ **sly, slick and wicked** *n.* [1920s+] (*US black*) an individual who plans to be caught out in a small act of deceit, which exposé will facilitate plans for a larger confidence trick.

smaak *v.* (*also* **smark**) [synon. Afk.] [1960s+] (*S.Afr.*) to like, to enjoy, to 'fancy' someone.

smabble *v.* [echoic or var. on SNABBLE *v.*] **1** [early 18C] to knock down, to plunder. **2** [early 18C] (*UK Und.*) to seize. **3** [19C+] to have sexual intercourse with.

smabbled *adj.* (*also* **snabbled**) [SMABBLE *v.* (1)] [late 18C–mid-19C] killed in battle.

smack *n.*^{1} (*orig. US*) **1** [late 17C; mid-19C+] a try, a 'go'; thus *have a smack at*, to have a go at. **2** [19C–1940s] (*US black*) a kiss [SE 17C–early 19C]. **3** [mid-19C+] a liking for [SE *smack*, enjoyment, appreciation]. **4** [late 19C] a telling-off, a punishment. **5** [20C+] a blow, a slap; also fig. use. **6** in senses of money, which one 'smacks down'. (**a**) [1900s] a pound sterling. (**b**) [1900s–40s] (*US Und.*) a form of confidence trick based on matching pennies. (**c**) [1910s+] (*US tramp*) a dollar. (**d**) [1930s+] (*US Und.*) the use of a specially doctored coin for heads-or-tails gambling [the trickster's smacking his hand on the coin as he catches it]. **7** [1950s–60s] (*US black*) sexual intercourse.

DERIVATIVES

❑ **smacktastic** *adj.* [-TASTIC *sfx*] [2000s] (*US black*) physically violent.

IN PHRASES

❑ **lay the smack down** *v.* [2000s] (*US black*) to hit someone. ❑ **put the smack down** *v.* [1990s+] to hit, to assault. ❑ **smack in the eye** *n. see* separate entry.

IN EXCLAMATIONS

❑ **oh smack!** [1990s+] (*US teen*) a reaction to something astonishing.

smack *n.*[2] (*also* **smock**) [Yid. *schmeck*, to sniff; see also SCHMECK *n.*] **1** [1930s+] (*drugs*) heroin. **2** [1990s+] adulterated cocaine.

DERIVATIVES

❑ **smackster** *n.* [-STER *sfx*] [1990s+] (*US drugs*) a heroin addict.

IN COMPOUNDS

❑ **smack freak** *n.* [-FREAK *sfx*] [1970s+] (*drugs*) a heroin addict. ❑ **smack-head** *n.* (*also* **smackhead**) [-HEAD *sfx* (4)] [1960s+] (*drugs*) a heroin addict. ❑ **smack pack** *n.* [1990s+] (*Aus. drugs*) a 'starter kit' of heroin, containing a potion of the drugs and the equipment for injection.

IN PHRASES

❑ **smacked out** *adj.* (*also* **smacked back, smacked up**) [1980s+] (*drugs*) under the influence of heroin. ❑ **talk smack** *v.* [punning on words like SHIT *n.* (6a), heroin/SHIT *n.* (3j), nonsense, and JUNK *n.*[1] (7a), heroin/JUNK *n.*[1] (4), nonsense] [1980s+] (*US black/teen*) to gossip maliciously; to speak aggressively; thus *smack-talking*, malicious gossip.

smack *n.*[3] [SMACK *v.* (2)] (*US black/teen*) **1** [1960s] flirtatious talk. **2** [1980s+] nonsense; esp. malicious rumours. **3** [1990s+] aggressive talk. **4** [1990s+] (*US campus*) rules, regulations, the 'last word'.

smack *n.*[4] [? they are constantly smacking their head in concentration] [1980s+] (*US campus*) an overly hard-working student.

smack *v.* **1** [late 16C–1960s] to kiss. **2** [late 18C+] (*also* **smack about, smack around**) to hit, to beat. **3** [1930s–50s] to throw (into). **4** [1990s+] (*US black gang*) to act sycophantically, to toady. **5** [1990s+] (*US black*) (*also* **smack ass, smack it**) to criticize someone behind their back [ASS *n.* (2)]. **6** [1990s+] to be very good, to excel.

IN PHRASES

❑ **smack about/around** *v. see* sense 2 above. ❑ **smack ass/it** *v. see* sense 5 above. ❑ **smack the calfskin** *v.* [the SE *calfskin* cover of the Bible] [late 18C–late 19C] (*UK Und.*) to kiss the Bible when taking an oath.

SE in slang uses

IN PHRASES

❑ **smack a blue** *v. see under* BLUE *n.*[4]. ❑ **smack around** *v.* [1920s] (*US*) to travel in an ostentatious manner, to parade. ❑ **smack down** see separate entries. ❑ **smack it** *v.* [1950s] (*Aus.*) to hurry. ❑ **smack one's gums** *v. see* BEAT ONE'S GUMS *v.* ❑ **smack the bit** *v. see under* BIT *n.*[1]. ❑ **smack up** see separate entries.

smack *adv.* (*also* **smacko**) [19C+] [echoic/SMACK *v.* (2)] **1** directly. **2** immediately. **3** see *SMACK-DAB* below.

IN COMPOUNDS

❑ **smack-dab** *adv.* (*also* **smack**) [echoic] [late 19C+] (*US*) exactly, precisely, entirely. ❑ **smack-bang** *adv. see* SLAP-BANG *adv.* ❑ **smack on** *see* separate entry. ❑ **smack-smooth** *adj.* [late 18C–mid-19C] absolutely level, perfectly smooth.

smackarolas *n. see* SMACKEROOS *n.*

smackdown *n.* [SMACK DOWN *v.*] [1990s+] (*US campus*) a (punishment) beating.

smack down *v.* [SMACK *v.* (2)] [late 19C+] (*US*) **1** to hit hard, esp. to hit in the face. **2** to tell off, to reprimand, to put in one's place.

smacker *n.*[1] [the sound] **1** [early 19C] a blow, a slap. **2** [mid-19C+] a kiss. **3** [1920s] (*US*) a boxer. **4** [1920s–50s] (*US Und.*) a year. **5** [1930s+] (*Aus.*) a boy, a young man. **6** [1980s+] (*N.Z.*) the mouth. **7** see SMACKERS *n.* (1).

smacker *n.*[2] [SMACK *adv.* (1)] [1930s] a perfect example.

smackerinos *n. see* SMACKERS *n.*

smackeroo gun *n.* [SMACK *n.*[2] (1) + GUN *n.*[1] (5)] [1980s+] (*Aus. prison*) a hypodermic syringe.

smackeroos *n.* (*also* **smackarolas, smackeroonies, smackolas**) [ext. SMACKERS *n.* + -EROO *sfx*] [1940s+] dollars or pounds sterling.

smackers *n.* (*also* **smackerinos**) [ext. of SMACK *n.*[1] (6a)/SMACK *n.*[1] (6c)] [1910s+] (*orig. US*) rarely in sing., dollars or pounds sterling.

smacking *adj.* [orig. dial.] [mid-18C+] good, excellent.

smacking-cove *n.* [SE *smack*, i.e. his whipping of the horses + COVE *n.* (1)] [late 17C–early 19C] a coachman.

smack in the eye *n.*[1] [rhy. sl.] [20C+] a pie.

smack in the eye *n.*[2] [1940s+] a rebuff, a rejection, a severe and surprising disappointment.

smacko *n.*[1] [it has been *smacked*] [1930s] (*US Und.*) a car that has been rebuilt following a serious crash.

smacko *n.*[2] [SE *smack*, a blow; thus one who either hits or, lit. or fig., is likely to be hit] [1940s] (*US black*) a street person; a thug.

smacko *adv. see* SMACK *adv.*

smackolas *n. see* SMACKEROOS *n.*

smack on *adj.* [SMACK ON *adv.*] [1950s] good, wonderful.

smack on *adv.* [ext. SMACK *adv.* (1)] [late 19C+] accurately, right in the middle of.

smack-up *n.* [SMACK *v.* (2)] (*Aus./N.Z.*) **1** [1900s–10s] a fight. **2** [1950s] (*juv.*) a caning at school. **3** [1950s+] a crash, an accident.

smack up *v.* [SMACK-UP *n.*] **1** [1910s+] to attack physically; thus *smacked up*, bested in a fight. **2** [1930s] to lay a criminal charge on someone.

smag *n.* [Scot. *smag*, a sweet, a tasty titbit] **1** [early 19C] (*UK Und.*) a snack. **2** [1990s+] (*US campus*) a cigarette.

small *adj.*

SE in slang uses

DERIVATIVES

❑ **smaller** *n.* [mid-19C] (*US*) a glass of undiluted spirits.

IN COMPOUNDS

❑ **small and early** *n.* [mid-19C–1910s] (*UK society*) an informal dance (as opposed to a full-scale ball), to which few guests are invited and which starts early and ends before midnight. ❑ **small beans** *n.* (*also* **small bananas**) [20C+] an insignificant thing; usu. in negative. ❑ **small beer** see separate entries. ❑ **small bones** *n. see* separate entry. ❑ **small-bore** *adj.* [SE *small bore*, a small calibre gun barrel] [1900s] (*US*) trivial, insignificant. ❑ **small bread** *n.* [BREAD *n.*[1] (2)] [1940s–50s] (*US black*) anything insignificant, esp. a small amount of money. ❑ **small change** see separate entries. ❑ **small cheque** *n.* [late 19C] a dram; thus to *knock down a cheque*, to spend all one's money on alcohol. ❑ **small coals** *n.* [mid-19C] that which is inferior, worthless, second-rate. ❑ **smallest room** *n.* [1930s+] euph. for the lavatory in a private house. ❑ **small fortune** *n.* [understatement] [20C+] (*orig. US*) a very large sum of money, esp. when paid out for some commodity. ❑ **small gang** *v.* [? the 'gang' requires only one or two people] [mid–late 19C] to rob in the street. ❑ **small meat** *n.* [MEAT *n.* (2)] [1960s+] (*US gay*) a small penis. ❑ **small nickel** *n.* [NICKEL *n.* (6)] [20C+] (*US gambling*) a bet of $50. ❑ **small pipe** *n.* [1940s–50s] (*US*) an alto saxophone. ❑ **small potato/potatoes** see separate entries. ❑ **small shit** *n.* [SHIT *n.* (2a)] [1970s+] (*US*) someone or something insignificant, unimportant. ❑ **small stuff** *n.* [1940s] (*US*) a term of address to a short person, slightly derog. ❑ **small time/-timer** *see* separate entries.

small beer *n.* [SE *small beer*, weak, inferior quality beer] [17C+] inferior things, worthless or second-rate matters; also *chronicle small beer*, to record insignificant events.

IN PHRASES

❑ **think small beer of** *v.* (*also* **think small coals of**) [SE *small coals*, slack, useless for a blazing fire] [19C] to have a low opinion of.

small beer *adj.* [SMALL BEER *n.*] [17C–19C] inferior, insignificant, worthless.

small bones *n.* [late 19C] (*Aus.*) insignificant.

IN PHRASES

❑ **make small bones (of)** *v.* [late 19C] (*Aus.*) to deal with easily.

small change *n.* [monetary imagery] [1940s+] (*US*) **1** an insignificant, weak person. **2** as a term of address to a smaller person.

small-change *adj.* [SMALL CHANGE *n.* (1)] [1970s+] (*US*) insignificant.

small-potato *adj.* [SMALL POTATOES *n.*] **1** [mid–late 19C] (*orig. US*) insignificant, irrelevant. **2** [1900s] (*also* **small potatoes**) selfish, mean.

small potatoes *n.* (*also* **mean potatoes, small potato**) (*orig. US*) **1** [mid-19C+] something, or someone, seen as insignificant, of little worth, irrelevant; ext. as *small potatoes and few in a /the hill.* **2** [1920s+] in fig. use, a hanger-on, one who acts as a parasite on the powerful or influential.

smallpox *n.*

SE in slang uses

IN PHRASES

❑ **have smallpox** *v.* [20C+] (*US Und.*) to be wanted on an arrest warrant.

small time *n.* [SMALL-TIME *adj.*] [1960s] (*US*) a term of insulting address.

small-time *adj.* [theatre jargon *small time*, a vaudeville circuit for second-rate acts] [1920s+] second-rate, inferior.

IN COMPOUNDS

❑ **small-time joint** *n.* [JOINT *n.* (3b)] [1970s+] (*S.Afr.*) the lowest class of shebeen; thus *big-time joint*, a superior shebeen.

small-time *v.* [SMALL-TIME *adj.*] [1970s+] (*orig. US*) to occupy oneself with minor business, usu. in a criminal context.

small-time *n.* [SMALL-TIME *adj.*] [1920s+] a mediocrity, a failure.

smaltz *see under* SCHMALTZ.

smarm *n.* [backform. f. SMARMY *adj.* (1)] [1930s+] an unctuous bearing, flattering or toadying behaviour.

smarm *v.* [backform. f. SMARMY *adj.* (1)] [1930s+] to toady, to ingratiate.

smarmy *adj.* [SE *smarm*, to smooth down with some form of greasy substance] **1** [1920s+] unctuous, ingratiating. **2** [1950s+] smug and self-righteous. **3** [1990s+] of a voice, sonorous, rich. **4** [2000s] unpleasant.

smart *n.* [1900s–60s] used insultingly, a 'clever' person.

smart *adj.*

SE in slang uses

IN COMPOUNDS

❑ **smart aleck** *see* separate entries. ❑ **smart apple** *n. see under* APPLE *n.*[1]. ❑ **smart-arse/-arsed** *see* separate entries. ❑ **smart-ass** *see under* SMART-ARSE. ❑ **smart bucks** *n.* (*also* **smart dollar**) [BUCK *n.*[3] (3)] [1950s] (*US Und.*) money gained through crime. ❑ **smart butt** *n. see* SMART-ARSE *n.* ❑ **smart dick/Elick** *n. see* SMART ALECK *n.* ❑ **smart eye** *v.* [2000s] (*US*) to stare in a challenging manner. ❑ **smart fart** *n.* [FART *n.* (2)] [1960s+] (*Aus./N.Z.*) one who considers themselves clever. ❑ **smart guy** *see under* WISE GUY. ❑ **smart money** *n. see* WISE MONEY *under* WISE *adj.* ❑ **smart mouth** *see* separate entries. ❑ **smartpants** *n. see* SMARTY-BOOTS *n.* ❑ **smart stuff** *n.* [1940s–50s] (*US black*) deceitful, underhand activity.

IN PHRASES

❑ **book smart** *adj.* [1980s+] (*US campus*) academically high-flying, but low on common sense and social skills; also as n., one who reads and studies. ❑ **half-smart** *adj.* [1920s–60s] (*US*) stupid or reckless. ❑ **smart as...** *adj. see* separate entry. ❑ **smart off** *v.* [1960s+] (*US black*) to cheek, to 'backtalk'. ❑ **smart someone up** *v.* (*also* **smarten, smarten up**) [1920s–60s] (*US*) to pass over information, to explain. ❑ **street smart** *adj. see* separate entry.

smart aleck *n.* (*also* **smart alec, ...Alick, ...dick, ...Elick, wise aleck**) [proper name *Alec* Hoag, a celebrated New York City thief of 1840s, who, with his wife Melinda and his accomplice French Jack, specialized in the *PANEL GAME under* PANEL *adj.*; for a detailed account of Hoag and his career, *see* Cohen (ed.), *Studies in Slang* I (1985)] [mid-19C+] (*orig. US*) an unpleasantly conceited, smug person; as v., to act as a smart aleck.

smart-aleck *adj.* (*also* **smart-alec, smart-alecky, smart-alexist, wise-alecky**) [SMART ALECK *n.*] **1** [20C+] cocky, conceited, smug. **2** [2000s] in ext. use, of objects.

smart-arse *n.* (*also* **smart-ass, smart butt**) [SMART-ARSED *adj.*/BUTT *n.*[1] (1c)] [1950s+] **1** one who sees themselves as cleverer than they really are. **2** (*US campus*) a hard-working, academically successful student; a strong, offensive male. **3** self-confidence; cockiness.

IN PHRASES

❑ **come the smart-arse** *v.* [1930s+] to pose as being cleverer than one actually is.

smart-arse *v.* (*also* **smart-ass**) [SMART-ARSE *n.* (1)] [1960s+] to cheek someone, to be impudent to.

smart-arsed *adj.* (*also* **smart-arse, smart-ass, smart-assed**) [SE *smart* + ARSE *n.* (4)/ASS *n.* (4)] [1950s+] self-opinionatedly clever, smug, complacent.

smart as... *adj.*

SE in slang uses

IN PHRASES

❑ **...a carrot (new scraped)** [late 18C–19C] smartly dressed. ❑ **...a rat with a gold tooth** [1970s] (*Aus.*) very smartly dressed. ❑ **...be-damned** [1920s–30s] very well dressed. ❑ **...threepence** [late 19C] very well dressed.

smarten (up) *v. see* SMART SOMEONE UP *under* SMART *adj.*

smartie *n. see* SMARTY *n.*

smartiepants *n. see* SMARTY-BOOTS *n.*

smarties *n.* [fig. resemblance to the confectionery] [2000s] (*UK drugs*) pills.

smartipants *n. see* SMARTY-BOOTS *n.*

smart-mouth *n.* [1960s+] (*US*) **1** (*also* **smarty-mouth**) an insolent person. **2** cheek, insolence.

smart-mouth *adj.* (*also* **smart-mouthed**) [SMART-MOUTH *n.*] [1980s+] (*US*) cheeky, disrespectful.

smart mouth *v.* (*also* **smart off**) [SMART-MOUTH *n.*] [1970s+] (*orig. US black*) to attack verbally, to slander; to be cheeky, to tease.

smarts *n.* [1960s+] (*orig. US*) wit, intelligence.

smarty *n.* (*also* **smartie**) **1** [mid-19C+] (*orig. US*) an unpleasantly conceited, 'clever' person; also, one who is 'too smart to work' and lives by his wits (prob. illegally). **2** [late 19C; 1950s] a fashionable person. **3** [late 19C+] a general, usu. negative form of address. **4** [1950s] an aristocrat. **5** [1960s] (*US campus*) a hard worker; an intellectual success.

IN PHRASES

❑ **pull a smartie** *v.* [1930s] (*US*) to trick, to deceive; to get away with something, usu. a slightly nefarious scheme.

smarty *adj.* [late 19C–1960s] (*US*) clever, esp. in ironic use.

smarty-boots *n.* (*also* **smarty-britches, smarty-drawers, smarty-pants, smartiepants, smartipants, smartpants**) [note the nickname given to essayist and critic Cyril Connolly (1903–74): Smartyboots] **1** [1930s+] (*orig. US*) a general term of usu. light-hearted abuse. **2** [1940s–50s] (*US black*) a young man at the outset of his sexual career.

smarty-mouth *n. see* SMART-MOUTH *n.*

smash *n.*[1] **1** as a mashed root vegetable [note 1960s+ *Smash*, brandname for instant mashed potatoes]. (**a**) [late 18C–mid-19C] mashed turnips. (**b**) [mid-19C] mashed potatoes. **2** [early 19C+] bankruptcy, financial collapse. **3** [mid-19C–1950s] (*UK Und.*) a smash-and-grab raid. **4** in the context of alcohol. (**a**) [mid-19C+] iced brandy and water [abbr. SE *brandy-smash*]. (**b**) [1950s+] (*US black*) wine. **5** [mid-19C+] (*US*) a failure, a disaster; thus *GO TO SMASH* below. **6** [late 19C] (*also* **smash-up**) an argument. **7** [late 19C+] a heavy blow. **8** [1900s] a glamorous social event. **9** [1910s–20s] (*US*) a time, a 'go', each. **10** [1910s+] (*Aus.*) a violent, frightening man, usu. one who is drunk. **11** [1920s+] a great success, a 'smash hit'.

IN PHRASES

❑ **all to smash** *adj.* **1** [mid-18C+] (*also* **into smash, all to shivers**) physically collapsed. **2** [late 18C+] bankrupted, utterly destroyed; usu. in phr. *go all to smash*. ❑ **come a smash** *v.* [late 19C] (*Aus.*) to fall down. ❑ **go to smash** *v.* **1** [late 18C+] to blunder, to err, to fail. **2** [mid-19C+] to ruin one's life; to die. ❑ **play smash** *v.* [mid-19C–1910s] (*US*) **1** to come to grief. **2** to cause trouble for, to 'play hell with'.

smash *n.*[2] **1** [late 18C–1900s] (*UK Und.*) counterfeit money [? it smashes the hopes of those who use it]. **2** [mid-19C+] (*also* **smesh**) cash, usu. change [rhy. sl.]. **3** [late 19C] (*UK prison*) tobacco, in its role as prison 'cash'.

IN COMPOUNDS

❑ **smash-feeder** *n.* [SE *feeder*] (*UK Und.*) **1** [mid-19C] a silver spoon; the best counterfeit coins were made from such spoons. **2** [mid-19C–1900s] a Britannia-metal spoon, made from a metal resembling silver but in fact an alloy of tin and regulus of antimony.

smash *n.*[3] *see* SMASHED *adj.* (2).

smash *v.*[1] **1** [late 17C–early 19C] (*UK Und.*) to kick downstairs. **2** [late 18C+] (*also* **go smash, smash up**) to fail financially, to be ruined, to become bankrupt; thus n. *smashing*, bankruptcy. **3** [mid–late 19C] to beat; also in fig. use. **4** [1900s] (*Aus.*) to spend recklessly. **5** [1900s] (*US campus*) to fail in recitation. **6** [1920s] (*US*) to dismiss from a job. **7** [1960s] to be a smash hit.

IN COMPOUNDS

❑ **smashing-cove** *n.* [COVE *n.* (1)] [mid-19C] (*UK Und.*) a housebreaker.

IN PHRASES

❑ **smash it** *v.* [1960s] (*US campus*) to do well in an examination. ❑ **smash out** *v.* [1970s] (*US*) to leave abruptly. ❑ **smash the teapot** *v.* [late 19C] **1** (*UK prison*) of a prisoner, to forfeit the privilege – gained for good behaviour – of substituting tea for the usual gruel. **2** to abandon one's pledge of abstinence (taken earlier at the urging of the Salvation Army or a similar teetotalist body).

IN EXCLAMATIONS

❑ **smash me!** [mid-19C] (*US*) an excl. of surprise, disbelief. ❑ **smash my glim!** (*also* **smash my apple-cart!**) [GLIM *n.* (6)] [mid-19C] a general excl., synon. with *blast my eyes!* ❑ **smashy!** [mid-19C] (*US*) an excl. of surprise and delight.

smash *v.*[2] [SMASH *n.*[2] (1)] **1** [19C] to pass counterfeit money; thus n. *smashing*. **2** [early 19C+] (*also* **smash up**) to give or obtain change for a note.

smash *v.*[3] [cognate with BOMB *v.*[1] (8)] [1990s+] to paint a piece of graffito on a wall or similar surface.

smash *adv.* [2000s] a general intensifier.

smash and grab *n.* [rhy. sl.] [20C+] a cab.

smashed *adj.* **1** [mid-19C; 1940s+] very drunk. **2** [late 19C] infatuated with; usu. with *on*; also as n., *smash*, an infatuation. **3** [1960s+] intoxicated with a drug, esp. cannabis or LSD. **4** [1980s] very tired. **5** *see* SMASHED-UP *adj.*

smashed out *adj.* [2000s] overwhelmed.

smashed-up *adj.* (*also* **smashed**) [SMASH *n.*[1] (2)] [mid–late 19C] impoverished, broke.

smasher *n.*[1] [SMASH *v.*[2] (1)] (*UK Und.*) **1** [late 18C–1910s] (*also* **bit smasher**) one who makes or passes counterfeit money. **2** [mid-19C] in fig. use, one who commits a libel. **3** [1920s] a receiver of stolen goods. **4** [1940s] a receiver who specializes in buying and recycling stolen money.

smasher *n.*[2] **1** [late 18C+] anything, or anybody, exceptionally large or excellent. **2** [19C] a hard blow, lit. or fig. **3** [mid-19C] a crushing remark, a highly negative review. **4** [1930s+] a pretty woman, or attractive person of either sex. **5** [1940s+] an admirable, likeable person.

smasher *n.*[3] [late 19C–1910s] (*S.Afr.*) a 'wideawake' hat, with a large brim.

smasher *n.*[4] [1920s] (*US Und.*) one who breaks the shop window and extracts the booty during a smash-and-grab raid.

smasher *n.*[5] *see* SNATCHER *n.* (1).

smashing *adj.* (*also* **smasho**) [i.e. it *smashes* all rivals] [mid-19C+] (*usu. teen*) wonderful, delightful, excellent.

smash-on *adj.* [1950s] a general intensifier.

smash-up *n. see* SMASH *n.*[1] (6).

smash up *v.* **1** *see* SMASH *v.*[1] (2). **2** *see* SMASH *v.*[2] (2).

smatter hauling *n.* [SCHMATTE *n.* + SE *haul*] [mid–late 19C] (*UK Und.*) the stealing of handkerchiefs.

smear *n.*[1] [metonymy] **1** [early 18C] (*also* **smeer**) a house-painter. **2** [early 18C–early 19C] a plasterer. **3** [1940s–50s] (*Aus.*) the corpse of a murdered person.

smear *n.*[2] [mid-19C] (*US campus*) food, esp. in context of a formal dinner.

smear *n.*[3] **1** [1920s] something showy, ostentatious. **2** [1920s+] (*orig. US*) a slanderous or defamatory remark; an attempt to defame by slander.

smear *v.* **1** [late 19C+] (*orig. US*) to knock unconscious, to beat up, to hit. **2** [1910s–30s] (*US*) to defeat, to trounce. **3** [1930s–50s] to kill, to murder. **4** [1930s+] (*US*) to bribe. **5** [1930s+] to slander, esp. to cause trouble for someone by discrediting their reputation. **6** *see* SCHMEER *v.*

smear and smudge *n.* [rhy. sl.] [2000s] a judge.

smear-gelt *n.* [Yid. *smiergelt*, a bribe, lit. 'money for greasing' (the palm)] [late 18C–mid-19C] a bribe.

smearies *n.* [2000s] (*S.Afr. prison*) anything one can spread on bread.

smears *n.* [it has been smeared onto paper or tablets] [1970s] (*drugs*) LSD.

smeb *v.* [ety. unknown] [2000s] (*US black*) to adopt the strutting, rolling walk trad. associated with a pimp.

smeck *n. see* SCHMECK *n.*

smeer *n. see* SMEAR *n.*[1] (1).

smeerlap *n.* [Du. *smeerlap*, 'grease cloth'; i.e. a cloth used for wiping spillage, stains etc] [mid-19C+] (*S.Afr.*) a general term of abuse, a 'bastard', a 'swine'.

smeg *n.* [abbr.] [1980s+] **1** *smegma*. **2** a dirty, unkempt person.

DERIVATIVES

❑ **smeggy** *adj.* [1980s+] dirty, unkempt.

IN COMPOUNDS

❑ **smeghead** *n.* [-HEAD *sfx* (1)] [1980s+] a general term of abuse.

IN EXCLAMATIONS

❑ **smeg!** [SE *smegma*, penile secretions. Coined as a deliberate euph. for FUCK! *excl.* by Grant Naylor, scriptwriter of the BBC's *Red Dwarf* science fantasy series, from 1989] [1980s+] a general excl. of annoyance, surprise; thus adj. *smegging*.

smegeg *n. see* SCHMEGEGGE *n.*

smell *v.* **1** [1930s+] to appear, to seem, usu. with negative overtones. **2** [1960s] (*US drugs*) to inhale a narcotic drug. **3** [1990s+] (*US black*) to understand.

SE in slang uses

IN COMPOUNDS

❑ **smell-powder** *n.* [the *powder*-powered pistols that are used in duelling] [early 19C] a duellist. ❑ **smell-smock** *n.* [SMOCK *n.*[1]] **1** [16C] a derog. term for a priest. **2** [late 16C–mid-18C] a pimp; thus *smock-smelling*, pimping. **3** [mid-17C] the penis.

IN PHRASES

❑ **come up smelling of violets** *v.* (*also* **come out smelling of roses, come up smelling of roses**) [20C+] to survive an unpleasant experience not only unscathed, but actually better placed; thus *so lucky that if he fell in shit he'd come up...* ❑ **he who smelt it, dealt it** [1950s+] a phr. used to disclaim all responsibility for having farted; often used as a rejoinder to the query WHO CUT THE CHEESE? *phr.* ❑ **not have a smell** *v.* [1990s+] (*Irish*) to be completely outclassed by. ❑ **smell a mouse** *v.* (*also* **smell a bug, ...a fox, ...a mice, sniff a rodent**) [joc. var. on *SMELL A RAT* below] [mid-19C–1910s] (*US*) to be suspicious. ❑ **smell a rat** *v.* [SE f. 1850] [mid-16C–mid-19C] to be suspicious of people or situations. ❑ **smell garlic** *v.* [? underpinned by xenophobia, i.e. the image of garlic as 'funny foreign food'] [late 19C–1920s] to be suspicious of people or situations. ❑ **smell hell** *v.* [mid-19C+] (*US*) to face danger, punishment. ❑ **smelling of the cork** *adj.* [19C] drunk. ❑ **smell like...** *v. see* separate entry. ❑ **smell of broken glass** *n.* [1900s–30s] a stench of body odour, typically in a sports changing room. ❑ **smell one's hat** *v.* [late 19C] to pray into one's hat on reaching one's pew in church. ❑ **smell trap** *v.* [TRAP *n.*[1] (1)] [late 17C–19C] to sense danger. ❑ **smell you** (*also* **smell you later**) [1990s+] (*US campus*) **1** goodbye. **2** a sarcastic retort.

IN EXCLAMATIONS

❑ **smell your monkey!** (*also* **screw a monkey!**) [1990s+] a general insult, a less injurious version of *SMELL YOUR MOTHER!* below. ❑ **smell your mother!** [1990s+] an insult, usu. accompanied by waving the middle finger under the insultee's nose; the implication is of recent sexual foreplay.

Smellbourne *n.* (*also* **Smellbun, Smellburn**) [coined by *The Bulletin* magazine. The name reflects the city's poor sewage, which was simply dumped into the River Yarra] [late 19C–1910s] (*Aus.*) Melbourne, capital city of Victoria.

smeller *n.* [positive and negative uses of SE *smell* v.] **1** [early 17C] (*UK Und.*) a garden. **2** [late 17C–1940s] the nose; occas. pl. *smellers*, nostrils. **3** [early–mid-19C] a blow on the nose. **4** [late 19C] (*US*) a spy, a prying person. **5** [late 19C–1920s] anything exceptional, esp. very strong, very aggressive etc. **6** [late 19C–1930s] a heavy fall; thus *come a smeller*, to tumble down heavily [one SE *smells* the ground on hitting it]. **7** [late 19C+] (*N.Z.*) an unpleasant person. **8** [1910s] (*Aus.*) a camel.

smellers *n.* [SE *smell* v.] [late 18C–early 19C] a cat's whiskers.

smellerwank *n.* [ety. unknown] [mid-19C] (*UK Und.*) an informer.

smelling-cheat *n.* (*also* **smelling-chete**) [SE *smell* + CHEAT *n.* (1)] **1** [mid-16C–late 17C] the nose. **2** [mid-16C–early 19C] a garden, an orchard. **3** [late 17C–early 19C] a nosegay, a posy.

smell like... *v.*

SE in slang uses

IN PHRASES

❑ **...a badger's touch-hole** [TOUCH-HOLE *n.* (1)] [20C+] to smell very unpleasant. ❑ **...a ram-goat** [20C+] (*W.I.*) to smell disgusting, esp. after one has passed out drunk and urinated down one's legs. ❑ **...a rose** [20C+] (*US*) to appear pure and innocent. ❑ **...a whore's garret** [20C+] to smell strongly of cheap perfume, as applicable to a man or a place as to a woman.

smelly *adj.* [*SMELL A RAT under* SMELL *v.*] [1920s+] dubious, suspicious.

smelly belly *n.* [1990s+] (*UK juv.*) a person who is playing the fool.

smelly welly *n.* [1990s+] (*UK juv.*) a poor person who looks like a tramp.

smelt *n.*[1] [ety. unknown, but Partridge suggests SE *melt*, to melt down; thus a half guinea is a 'melted down' guinea] **1** [late 17C–mid-19C] (*UK Und.*) a half guinea or ten shillings (50p). **2** [mid-19C] (*US*) a five-dollar piece, a 'half-eagle'.

smelt *n.*[2] [mid-19C] (*UK Und.*) a fool.

smezzle *n.* [ety. unknown] [mid-19C] (*UK Und.*) a secret, a personal matter.

smicket *n.* [*double entendre* for SE *smicket*, a woman's smock or chemise] [late 17C–mid-19C] the vagina.

smiddys *n.* [var. on TITTY *n.* (1)] [1990s+] the female breasts.

smidge *n.* [SE *smidgen*] [20C+] a very small amount.

smiflicated *adj. see* SPIFLICATED *adj.*

smifligate *v. see* SPIFLICATE *v.*

smifligated *adj. see* SPIFLICATED *adj.*

smiggins *n.* (*also* **smiggen**) [ety. unknown; ? SE *smidgen*, i.e. the small amount of appetizing meat or vegetables present in the broth] [19C] (*UK Und.*) a poor quality soup served up to convicts, esp. those imprisoned on the hulks.

smile *n.*[1] (*also* **fancy smile**) [i.e. it promotes a smile or one's lips open in a 'smile' as one drinks] [mid-19C–1940s] (*orig. US*) a drink, usu. of whisky.

IN PHRASES

❑ **do a smile** *v.* [mid-19C+] to take a glass of whisky, or any other drink. ❑ **will you try a smile?** [mid-19C] an invitation to drink.

smile *n.*[2] **1** [1910s–40s] the gap of bare flesh between a stocking and a suspender belt. **2** [1950s+] bare flesh appearing between the top of a skirt or pair of trousers and the shirt, blouse etc.

smile *v.* [SMILE *n.*[1]] **1** [mid-19C–1930s] (*orig. US*) to drink, esp. whisky. **2** [late 19C] to buy a drink or round of drinks.

IN PHRASES

❑ **I should smile** [mid-19C–1920s] (*US*) an ironic response to an implausible suggestion. ❑ **I should snicker to smile** [late 19C] (*US teen*) phr. of affirmation: 'you are absolutely right'.

smile and smirk *n.* [rhy. sl.] [20C+] work.

smile and titter *n. see* GIGGLE AND TITTER *n.*

smiler *n.* [? SMILE *v.*] **1** [mid-19C] (*US*) a drinker. **2** [late 19C] a form of shandygaff, a mixture of beer and ginger beer.

smiley *n.* **1** [1980s+] (*US*) a man who is showing a slice of flesh above the top of his trousers [SMILE *n.*[2] (2)]. **2** [1990s+] (*S.Afr.*) a sheep's or goat's head (sometimes split in half), cleaned and grilled or stewed with or without the tongue and brain [the 'grinning' aspect of the cooked head].

smiling faces *n.* [1970s] (*US black*) hypocrites, false friends.

smiller *n.* [ety. unknown] [late 18C–mid-19C] a large glass of alcohol, a 'bumper'.

smim *n.* [? SE *spastic* + *mimic*] [1990s+] (*UK juv.*) one who is both highly conformist and physically unco-ordinated.

smirk *n.* [SE *smirk*, an affected simpering smile] [late 17C–late 18C] 'A finical [finicky], spruce Fellow' (B.E.).

smish *n.* [abbr. COMMISSION *n.*] [mid-18C–19C] a shirt.

smisk *n. see* CAMESA *n.*

smitchy *adj.* [SE *small* + *titchy*] [late 19C] tiny, insignificant.

smiter *n.* [SE *smite*, to hit] [late 17C–mid-19C] the arm.

smithereen *v.* [SMITHEREENS *n.*] [1920s+] to break, to smash into pieces.

smithereens *n.* (*also* **flindereens**) [SMITHERS *n.* + Irish dimin. *-een*. Share suggests Irish *smiodar*, a fragment] [mid-19C+] tiny fragments, atoms; esp. in phr. *smashed to smithereens*, *blow/break/knock/split to/into smithereens*, to shatter into fragments; *all to smithereens*, smashed to pieces, often in fig. use.

smithers *n.* [Lincolnshire dial. *smithers*, fragments, shivers; ult. ? SE *smite*, to smash] [mid-19C] tiny fragments, atoms.

Smithfield *n.* [proper name *Smithfield* market, London's horse and cattle, and later meat market, flourishing on the same site since the 12C]

IN COMPOUNDS

❑ **Smithfield bargain** *n.* **1** [late 18C–mid-19C] a bargain in which the buyer is cheated. **2** [early 18C–mid-19C] a marriage of convenience, based on financial interest. ❑ **Smithfield jade** *n.* [late 17C] an inferior horse which has been smartened up to deceive a prospective buyer; in ext. use, a prostitute.

Smithy *n.* [1990s+] (*US Und.*) a firearm manufactured by Smith & Wesson.

smit smoke *n.* [? SE *smart* + SMOKE *n.* (3a)] [1940s] (*US black*) a highly intelligent black person.

smoak *v.* *see* SMOKE *v.*[1] (1a).

smoaky *adj.* *see* SMOKY *adj.*[1].

smock *n.*[1] [SE *smock*, a chemise or shift; thus generically 'womankind'] [late 16C–early 18C] an immoral woman, esp. when used as a pfx in combs. below.

IN COMPOUNDS

❑ **smock alley** *n.* [the actual Smock Alley, running off Petticoat Lane in London's East End, was well known in 17C for its brothels] **1** [17C–early 18C] those streets occupied by brothels. **2** [late 17C–19C] (*also* **smock castle**) the vagina. ❑ **smock fair** *n.* [SE *fair*] [17C] a gathering place of whores. ❑ **smock hunter** *n.* [SE *hunter*] [17C–early 18C] a womanizer. ❑ **smock merchant** *n.* (*also* **smock agent, ...attorney, ...tearer, ...tenant, smockster**) [MERCHANT *n.*/SE *agent/attorney/tearer/tenant*/-STER *sfx*] [late 16C–early 17C] a pimp. ❑ **smock pensioner** *n.* [SE *pensioner*] [18C] a pimp, a kept man. ❑ **smock piece** *n.* (*also* **smock servant**) [PIECE *n.* (1a)/SE *servant*] [19C] a prostitute. ❑ **smock rampant** *n.* [SE *rampant*] [17C] a promiscuous woman, lit. one who raises her smock. ❑ **smock shop** *n.* [SHOP *n.*[1] (1)] [17C] a brothel. ❑ **smock toy** *n.* [SE *toy*] [late 16C–early 17C] **1** a mistress. **2** a woman's male lover. ❑ **smock vermin** *n.* [SE *vermin*] [17C] prostitutes.

smock *n.*[2] *see* SMACK *n.*[2].

smock *v.* [SE *smock*/SMOCK *n.*[1]] [late 16C–mid-18C] to have sexual intercourse.

smockface *n.* [SE *smockface*, a pale, smooth or effeminate face; thus one who is so endowed] [19C] an effeminate man; a male homosexual; as adj., *smockfaced*, homosexual.

smock-faced *adj.* [SE *smock*, a chemise; thus the smooth whiteness of the garment] [mid-17C–mid-19C] attractive.

smockster *n.* *see* SMOCK MERCHANT *under* SMOCK *n.*[1].

smogged *adj.* [SE *smog*, a dense, toxic fog] [20C+] (*US prison*) executed in the gas chamber.

Smoke, the *n.* [the pall of pollution that, before the clean air legislation of the 1950s, hung over the industrialized city] **1** [mid-19C+] London, as regarded from the provinces, occas. as *Smokes*. **2** [mid-19C+] (*Aus./US*) any big city. **3** [1940s+] (*Aus.*) Sydney, Melbourne.

smoke *n.* **1** in fig. senses. (**a**) [mid-16C] suspicion. (**b**) [mid-16C+] myth, illusion, fantasy, esp. when actively promoted as disinformation or lies; thus *all smoke*, nonsense; *smoky*, deceptive. (**c**) [late 19C] (*US*) a fuss. (**d**) [1970s] nonsense. **2** in lit. uses, pertaining to smoking tobacco or drugs. (**a**) [17C+] (*also* **smoking**) anything smokeable, a cigar, a pipe, a cigarette, tobacco. (**b**) [mid-19C+] the action of smoking a cigarette, cigar or pipe; thus *do a smoke*. (**c**) [late 19C] (*Aus.*) a party [SE *smoker*]. (**d**) [late 19C] (*US*) a portion or share taken from a can or pail of beer [the putting of one's lips to the can and sucking down the beer resembles puffing on a pipe]. (**e**) [late 19C+] (*drugs*) any form of smokeable drug, e.g. marijuana, opium, heroin and, latterly, crack cocaine. (**f**) [1900s–50s] the action of smoking opium. (**g**) [1930s+] marijuana, esp. a marijuana cigarette. (**h**) [1960s+] the action of smoking cannabis. (**i**) [1990s+] crack cocaine. **3** in context of skin colour. (**a**) [late 19C+] a derog. term for a black person. (**b**) [1920s–40s] as used by a black person, thus not derog. (**c**) [1930s] (*US*) a Mexican. **4** [20C+] any cheap, rotgut alcohol, esp. denatured alcohol shaken up with water and drunk by down-and-out alcoholic tramps; thus *smoke bum*, a regular drinker of such alcohol [the liquid turns cloudy when shaken]. **5** [1900s] (*US*) the ideal, the best. **6** [1970s] (*US campus*) $1 [so small a sum 'goes up in smoke']. **7** [2000s] (*US campus*) an attractive female.

pertaining to smoking tobacco or drugs

IN COMPOUNDS

❑ **smoke factory** *n.* (*also* **smoke joint**) [JOINT *n.* (3b)] [1900s–20s] (*US*) an opium den. ❑ **smokehead** *n.* [-HEAD *sfx* (4)] [1980s+] a crack cocaine addict. ❑ **smokehouse** *n.* **1** [1990s+] (*US drugs*) a house or apartment where crack cocaine is sold and used. **2** *see also* separate entry. ❑ **smoke pad** *n.* [PAD *n.*[2] (2)] [1940s–50s] (*drugs*) anywhere that people can gather to smoke opium, later marijuana. ❑ **smoke shop** *n.* (*also* **smoke shack**) [note 18C–19C SE *smoke shop*, a tobacconist's where one could gather to talk and smoke] [1930s+] (*US drugs*) a place or shop where marijuana is sold, esp. somewhat openly. ❑ **smoke wagon** *n.* [2000s] (*US black*) a large and smoky marijuana cigarette.

IN PHRASES

❑ **blow smoke** *v.* [1980s+] **1** (*drugs*) to inhale cocaine. **2** (*drugs*) to smoke crack cocaine. **3** (*US campus*) to smoke marijuana.

pertaining to alcohol

IN COMPOUNDS

❑ **smoke-hound** *n.* [-HOUND *sfx*] [1930s+] (*US*) an alcoholic who drinks rotgut alcohol. ❑ **smoke joint** *n.* [JOINT *n.* (3b)] [1930s] (*US*) a bar that specializes in selling cheap, second-rate liquor.

pertaining to deception

IN PHRASES

❑ **blow smoke up someone's ass** *v.* [1950s+] to confuse, to tell lies to. ❑ **in smoke** [the obscurity cast by a pall of smoke] [1910s+] (*Aus.*) in hiding. ❑ **pass the bottle of smoke** *v.* [mid-19C] to accept conventional untruths, to tell white lies.

SE in slang uses

IN COMPOUNDS

❑ **smoke cheaters** *n.* *see* CHEATERS *n.*[2] (1). ❑ **smoke-eater** *n.* (*US*) **1** [late 19C–1930s] a firefighter. **2** [1920s] a heavy smoker. ❑ **smoke-hole** *n.* [early 18C] the mouth. ❑ **smoke iron** *n.* [1930s] (*US*) a handgun. ❑ **smoke-pole** *see* separate entries. ❑ **smoke screen** *n.* [its masking of body odour] [1940s] (*US black*) underarm deodorant. ❑ **smokestack** *see* separate entries. ❑ **smoke-stick** *n.* [1900s–40s] a firearm. ❑ **smoke-up** *n.* [1960s] a break for smoking. ❑ **smoke wagon** *n.* [1900s–60s] **1** (*US Und.*) a revolver, a pistol. **2** (*US*) a taxicab.

IN PHRASES

❑ **like smoke** *adv.* [mid-19C–1900s] (*Aus.*) very energetically; very quickly; exceedingly.

smoke *v.*[1] **1** fig. uses based on the idea of smoking someone/something out. (**a**) [mid-16C–mid-19C] (*also* **smoak**) to suspect. (**b**) [late 16C] (*UK Und.*) of a member of a pickpocket team, to select a potential victim. (**c**) [late 16C–mid-17C] to be discovered. (**d**) [late 16C–1930s] (*also* **smoke out**) to discover, to unmask. (**e**) [18C–mid-19C] as imper., take notice of. (**f**) [mid-19C] (*US*) to understand. **2** fig. uses based on the idea of blowing smoke into someone's face/eyes. (**a**) [late 17C–mid-19C] to ridicule or attack a stranger verbally as soon as they enter the room. (**b**) [late 17C–mid-19C] to cheat, to deceive; thus n. *smoker*, one who deceives. (**c**) [20C+] (*US*) (*also* **smoke someone's ass**) to fool, to give the wrong idea; thus *smoke up*, to confess, to tell the truth. **3** fig. uses based on the idea of heat. (**a**) [mid–late 19C] (*UK teen*) to blush; thus n. *smoking*, blushing. (**b**) [20C+] (*US*) to get angry. (**c**) [1970s] (*US*) to be dangerous (for criminal activity), i.e. to be HOT *adj.* (1a). **4** [20C+] (*US Und.*) to be executed in a gas chamber.

SE in slang uses

IN PHRASES

❑ **smoke a bowl** *v.* *see under* BOWL *n.* (2). ❑ **smoke a toke** *v.* *see under* TOKE *n.*[2] (2). ❑ **smoke bacon** *v.* [2000s] to work well and enthusiastically. ❑ **smoke it white** *v.* [Mandrax capsules are white] [1960s+] (*S.Afr. drugs*) to smoke a mixture of marijuana and powdered Mandrax (methaqualone). ❑ **smoke like that** [2000s] (*US black*) in phr. 'I can/can't smoke like that', I can/cannot do something. ❑ **smoke one** *v.* [20C+] (*drugs*) to smoke marijuana. ❑ **smoke out** *v.* **1** [1920s+] to get information from someone. **2** [1970s+] (*US black*) to impress, to outdo. **3** [2000s] (*US*) to collapse, to break down [automobile imagery]. **4** *see* sense 1d above. ❑ **smoke over** *v.* [1930s–50s] (*Aus.*) to think over. ❑ **smoke rubber** *v.* *see* BURN RUBBER *v.* ❑ **smoke (someone) over** *v.* [1920s–70s] (*US black*) to stare at, to look over, to assess. ❑ **smoke the habit off** *v.* *see under* HABIT *n.* ❑ **smoke up** *v.* (*US drugs*) **1** [1900s] to smoke opium. **2** [1960s+] to smoke cannabis.

smoke *v.*[2] [SE *smoke*, to move or ride at a rapid pace] **1** [17C] to have sexual intercourse. **2** [18C] to beat, to kill. **3** [early 19C] (*US*) to hang. **4** [late 19C+] (*Aus./N.Z.*) (*also* **smoke one's dot**) to make a hasty departure [SE late 17C–19C]. **5** [20C+] (*US Und.*) to be executed in a gas chamber. **6** [1910s+] to throw very fast, usu. of a ball. **7** [1920s+] to kill, to murder, to shoot at (with a firearm) [the image of smoke coming from the gun]. **8** [1970s] (*US campus*) to perform well. **9** [1970s+] to beat comprehensively (at sport). **10** [1980s+] to beat up.

smoke *v.*[3] [play on PIPE *n.*[1] (2a); note synon. Fr. *faire une pipe*] [1960s+] to perform fellatio.

(IN PHRASES)

❑ **smoke a horn** *v. see under* HORN *n.*[2]. ❑ **smoke someone's bone** *v. see under* BONE *n.*[1]. ❑ **smoke the bald man** *v.* (*also* **smoke the big one, smoke the white owl**) [*WHITE OWL under* WHITE *adj.*] [1990s+] to fellate. ❑ **smoke the White House cigar** *v.* [the Bill Clinton/Monica Lewinsky liaison] [2000s] of a woman, to fellate.

(IN EXCLAMATIONS)

❑ **smoke it!** [1990s+] (*Aus.*) an excl. of dismissal or derision.

smoke! *excl. see* HOLY SMOKE! *excl.*

Smokeburg *n.* [its polluting heavy industry] [late 19C–1900s] (*US*) Pittsburgh.

smoked *adj.*[1] [fig. uses of SE *smoke*/SMOKE *v.*[2]] **1** [mid-19C+] (*US*) drunk. **2** [1920s–30s] emotional. **3** [1970s+] intoxicated by cannabis.

smoked *adj.*[2] (*also* **smoked up**) [SMOKY *adj.*[2]] [1900s] (*Aus./US*) black.

smoked Irishman *n.* [SMOKY *adj.*[2]] [1950s] (*US Und.*) an African American.

smoked out *adj.* (*also* **smoke-out**) [SMOKE *n.* (2e)] [1990s+] (*US black gang*) heavily intoxicated by a drug, usu. marijuana or crack cocaine.

smoked up *adj.*[1] **1** [1960s] (*US*) angry. **2** [1970s+] (*US drugs*) intoxicated with cannabis. **3** [1990s+] (*US drugs*) intoxicated with crack cocaine.

smoked up *adj.*[2] *see* SMOKED *adj.*[2].

smoked Yankee *n.* (*also* **smoked Yank**) [SMOKY *adj.*[2] + SAmE *Yankee*/YANK *n.*] [mid-19C; 1940s–50s] a derog. term for a black person., usu. a freed slave.

smoke-ho *n. see* SMOKO *n.*

smokehouse *n.* **1** *see* SMOKER *n.*[1] (2a). **2** *see* SMOKER *n.*[1] (2e).

smoke-o/smoke-oh *n. see* SMOKO *n.*

smoke-out *adj. see* SMOKED OUT *adj.*

smoke-pole *n.* **1** [20C+] a firearm. **2** [2000s] (*N.Z.*) a cigarette.

smokepole *v.* [play on SMOKE-POLE *n.* (1)/SMOKE *v.*[2] (1) + POLE *n.* (1)] [1980s] (*US campus*) usu. of a man, to have sexual intercourse.

smoker *n.*[1] **1** [late 17C–early 19C] (*UK Und.*) a tobacconist. **2** that which emits smoke or steam. (**a**) [19C] (*also* **smokehouse**) a chamberpot [the steam that rises from hot urine in cold weather]. (**b**) [mid-19C] (*US*) a steamship. (**c**) [1940s] a privy. (**d**) [1960s+] a motor vehicle that emits stronger than average exhaust fumes. (**e**) [late 19C–1950s] (*US*) (*also* **smoke house**) the smoking carriage on a train. **3** in drug uses. (**a**) [late 19C–1930s] (*drugs*) a smoker of opium. (**b**) [1960s+] a smoker of marijuana. (**c**) [1990s+] a smoker of crack cocaine.

smoker *n.*[2] [SMOKE *v.*[1] (3a)] [mid-19C] (*UK teen*) one who blushes.

smoker *n.*[3] [late 19C] a hot day.

smoker *n.*[4] [it fig. makes the brain *smoke* with effort] [1970s+] (*US campus*) something difficult.

smoker *n.*[5] [SMOKE *v.*[3] (1)] [1970s+] a woman or homosexual man who performs fellatio.

smoker *n.*[6] [? SE *smoker*, a social gathering of men, sometimes with organized entertainment; such men-only gatherings might well run a pornographic movie] [1990s+] a pornographic film.

smoker *n.*[7] [the negative effects of smoking, presumably used by non-smokers] [1990s+] (*US campus*) a fool.

smoker's tickers *n.* [ety. unknown] [1940s] (*Aus.*) any variety of dark tobacco.

smokestack *n.* [late 19C+] (*US black*) a black person, esp. when very dark.

smokestack *v.* [one 'blows off steam'] [1970s] (*US*) to talk boastfully.

smokey *n.*[1] [SMOKE *n.* (2e)] [1930s] (*US Und.*) an opium addict.

smokey *n.*[2] [1980s+] (*Aus. prison*) a mysterious or private person; a 'closeted' homosexual.

smokey *n.*[3] *see* SMOKY *n.*

smokey *adj. see* SMOKY *adj.*[2].

smokey the fire bear *n. see* SMOKY *n.* (2).

smoking *n. see* SMOKE *n.* (2a).

smoking *adj.* [orig. jazz use *smoking*, technically skilled] **1** [1960s+] first-rate, excellent. **2** [1970s] (*US campus*) difficult, intense. **3** [1970s+] (*US black*) very urgent, very excited, esp. in a sexual context. **4** [1980s+] (*US black*) attractive, well-dressed, elegant. **5** [2000s] of a place, tense, expectant.

smoking gun *n.* [its powerful effects] [1990s+] (*drugs*) a mixture of heroin and cocaine.

smoking pistol *n.* [late 19C] an opium pipe.

smokkel *v.* [Du. *smokkeln*, to smuggle] [1940s+] (*S.Afr.*) to deal in drugs or in illicit liquor.

(IN COMPOUNDS)

❑ **smokkelhuis** *n.* (*also* **smokkie**) [1950s] an illegal drinking den.

smoko *n.* (*also* **smoke-o, smoke-ho, smoke-oh**) [SE *smoke* + -O *sfx* (3)] **1** [mid-19C+] (*Aus./N.Z.*) a break for smoking; thus *smoko-room, smoko-shed*, a room where one takes a smoking break. **2** [1950s] the cup of tea and/or the food that often accompanies such a break. **3** [1980s+] (*Aus. prison*) marijuana [SMOKE *n.* (2e)].

Smoky *n.* (*also* **Smoky Bear**) [*Smoky the Bear*, a character used in US fire prevention campaigns] [1970s+] a traffic policeman, a Highway Patrolman.

smoky *n.* (*also* **smokey**) **1** [1930s–60s] (*US black*) a black person; esp. as a generic term for blackness or a number of black people gathered together. **2** [1970s+] (*US black*) (*also* **smokey the fire bear**) a derog. term for a dark-complexioned black person. **3** [1970s+] (*US campus*) a policeman. **4** [1980s+] (*N.Z.*) a derog. term for a Maori.

(IN PHRASES)

❑ **mama smokey** *n.* [1970s+] (*US*) a policewoman.

smoky *adj.*[1] (*also* **smoaky**) [SMOKE *v.*[1] (1a)] **1** [late 17C–mid-18C] jealous. **2** [late 17C–late 18C] alert, shrewd. **3** [early 18C–mid-19C] suspicious, inquisitive, suspect.

smoky *adj.*[2] (*also* **smokey**) [1940s–70s] (*US*) black; pertaining to black people or culture.

Smoky Bear *n. see* SMOKY *n.*

smoky beaver *n.* [SMOKY *n.* + BEAVER *n.*[1] (6)] [1970s] (*US*) a female (motorcycle) police officer.

smoky seat *n.* [the smoke that rises from the electrocuted victim] [1930s–60s+] (*US prison*) the electric chair.

smoly hoke! *excl. see* HOLY SMOKE! *excl.*

smooch *n.* (*also* **smooge**) [SMOOCH *v.*[1] (1)] [1930s+] a passionate kiss; a bout of kissing and cuddling; thus adj. *smoochy*.

smooch *v.*[1] (*also* **smooch it up**) [late 16C SE *smouch*, to kiss] **1** [17C; 1910s+] (*Aus./US*) to caress amorously, to kiss. **2** [1980s+] to sing in a mawkish, sentimental way.

smooch *v.*[2] (*also* **smooge, smootch**) [? MOOCH *v.*[1] (1)] [1900s–40s] (*US*) to steal, to pilfer; to borrow.

smooching *n.* [SMOOCH *v.*[1] (1)] **1** [1940s+] (*orig. US*) kissing and cuddling. **2** [1950s] in fig. sense, becoming non-sexually intimate with.

smoodge *v.* (*also* **smooge, smooge up, smooze**) [SCHMOOZE *v.* (1) or SMOOCH *v.*[1] (1) or SE *smudge*, to caress] [20C+] (*Aus.*) to ingratiate oneself, to cuddle up; thus *come the smoodge, do a smoodge; smoodging*, ingratiation.

smoodger *n.* (*also* **smooger**) [SMOODGE *v.*] [20C+] (*Aus.*) **1** a toady, a sycophant, a flatterer. **2** an informer. **3** a lover, one who is 'smoodging'.

smooey *n.* [SMOODGE *v.*] [1940s–80s] (*Aus.*) the vagina; thus by metonymy, sexual intercourse; also in phr. *have a bit of smooey*, to have sexual intercourse.

smooge *see also under* SMOOCH.

smooge *v. see* SMOODGE *v.*

smooger *n. see* SMOODGER *n.*

smoogy *n.* [1910s] (*Aus.*) those who SMOODGE *v.*, i.e. kiss and cuddle.

smoogy *adj.* [SMOODGE *v.*] [1900s–50s] (*Aus.*) affectionate, ingratiating.

smootch *v. see* SMOOCH *v.*[2].

smooth *adj.* **1** [late 19C+] (*orig. US*) (*also* **smoothe**) clever, skilful, superior. **2** [late 19C+] of manners or dress, elegant, fashionable, suave. **3** [late 19C+] (*US campus*) performed well. **4** [late 19C+] (*US campus*) of a situation, pleasant. **5** [1920s+] (*US black*) (*also* **smoothe, smoove**) good, admirable. **6** [1950s] attractive. **7** [1960s] (*US gang*) law abiding, peaceful. **8** [2000s] of an individual, affable, courteous.

smooth article *n.* (*also* **smoothie, smooth operator**) [20C+] a sophisticated, smart person, both mentally and physically.

smoothie *n.*[1] (*also* **smoothy, smoother**) **1** [1920s+] one who is suave or stylish in conduct or appearance, usu. a man; often with unfavourable sense: a slick but shallow or insinuating person. **2** [1980s+] (*Aus.*) a lie.

smoothie *n.*[2] [it smooths clothes] [2000s] (*US black*) an iron.

smoothiechops *n.* [SMOOTH *adj.* (2) + CHOPS *n.*[1] (1)/on model of SMARTY-BOOTS *n.*] [1970s+] **1** a lightweight, affable but pretentious person. **2** (*N.Z.*) (*also* **smoothieboots**) a womanizer.

smoothiepuss *n.* [SMOOTH *adj.* (2) + PUSS *n.*[1] (2a)/PUSS *n.*[2] (1)] [1980s+] (*N.Z.*) an attractive woman.

smooth operator *n. see* SMOOTH ARTICLE *n.*

smooth up *v.* [SMOOTH *adj.* (2)] [1920s] (*US campus*) of a man, to attempt seduction.

smoothy *n. see* SMOOTHIE *n.*[1].

smoove *adj. see* SMOOTH *adj.* (5).

smooze *v. see* SMOODGE *v.*

smother *n.* [SE *smother*, to hide, to cover up] **1** [20C+] a coat, a wrap; thus (*UK Und.*) *smother game*, pickpocketing with the aid of an overcoat for cover [note SCHMATTE *n.*]. **2** [1900s] (*Aus.*) a plan, an undercover stratagem. **3** [1930s] (*UK Und.*) a place used to hide stolen goods.

SE in slang uses

IN PHRASES

❑ **put the smother on** *v.* [SE *smother*] [1960s] (*Aus.*) to censor, to suppress.

smother *v.* **1** [1910s] (*UK Und.*) to stand guard and cover for an accomplice breaking into a premises. **2** [1970s] (*Aus. Und.*) to use some form of object to obscure the shopkeeper's view while a shoplifter abstracts a targeted object; also of a pickpocket.

IN EXCLAMATIONS

❑ **I'll be smothered!** (*also* **you be smothered!**) [mid–late 19C] a general excl.

smother a parrot *v.* (*also* **strangle a parrot**) [translation of Fr. argot *asphyxier un perroquet*, to drink a glass of absinthe] [1900s–10s] to drink off a glass of absinthe in a single gulp.

smouge *v.* (*also* **smouch**) [? derog. generic use of SMOUS *n.* (1)] [mid-19C–1900s] (*US*) to steal.

smous *n.* (*also* **smouch, smouse, smouser, smoutch**) [Du. *smous*/Yid. *schmus*, patter or profit; ult. Heb. *schmuoss*, news or tales] **1** [early 18C–19C] a German Jew. **2** [mid-19C+] (*UK/S.Afr.*) (*also* **schmoose, smouzer**) an itinerant Jewish pedlar.

smous *v.* (*also* **smouch, smouse, smouth**) [SMOUS *n.*] (*S.Afr.*) **1** [mid-19C+] to work as an itinerant Jewish pedlar. **2** [mid-19C+] to solicit business, esp. in a demeaning manner. **3** [1970s+] to obtain in an underhand way. **4** [1990s+] to search out bargains.

smoush *n.* [SMOOCH *n.*] [1960s+] (*Aus.*) a kiss.

smoutch *n. see* SMOUS *n.*

smouth *v. see* SMOUS *v.*

smouzer *n. see* SMOUS *n.* (2).

smuckered *adj.* [SE *smack*] [1970s+] (*US campus*) drunk.

smudge *n.*[1] [SE *smudge*, a dirty mark] **1** [1930s+] a photograph. **2** [1930s+] a (gay) pornographic magazine. **3** [1940s+] (*US*) a derog. term for a black person.

smudge *n.*[2] *see* SNUDGE *n.*

Smudger *n.* [1910s+] an 'inevitable' nickname for someone surnamed 'Smith'.

smudge (up) *v.* [SMUDGE *n.*[1] (1)] [2000s] to photograph.

smug *n.*[1] [? SE *smuggy*, dirty, grimy. The late-20C+ use of *Smugs* for W.H. Smith, the chain of stationers and booksellers, is probably coincidental – the term refers more to the company's reputation as self-appointed guardians of its customers' morals than as any back-ref. to the name *Smith*] [early 17C–early 19C] a blacksmith.

smug *n.*[2] [abbr.] [mid-19C] (*Anglo-Chinese*) *smuggling*.

smug *n.*[3] [SE *smug*, i.e. their self-satisfaction] [late 19C–1910s] **1** (*UK teen*) a hard worker. **2** an intellectual.

smug *adj.* [*OED* accepts *smug* as SE, but its 17C citations – Greene, Dekker, Middleton, Wycherley – are all colloq., if not sl.] [late 16C–early 18C; mid-19C] extremely neat and tidy; thus *smug*, a person who is excessively neat.

IN PHRASES

❑ **smug up** *v.* [17C] to smarten oneself up.

smug *v.* [? SE *smuggle* or dial. *smug*, to hide, to move stealthily] **1** [early 18C; 19C] to snatch another's property and run off with it. **2** [early–mid-19C] to silence, to 'hush up'. **3** [mid–late 19C] to copy, to cheat. **4** [late 19C–1920s] to arrest. **5** [20C+] (*Irish*) to engage in homosexual practices.

IN PHRASES

❑ **smug up** *v.* [late 19C] to hide oneself away; to lead an uneventful life.

smugger *n.* [SMUG *v.* (1)] [late 19C] a thug, specializing in snatch-and-grab thefts; also in fig. use, anyone who steals, e.g. ideas.

smuggings! *excl.* [the excl. used at the end of a game of marbles or spinning tops when the child who shouted thus first was allowed to keep the toy in question] [mid-19C] (*UK teen*) mine!

smuggling-ken *n.* [dial. *smuggle*, to smother with hugs and kisses + KEN *n.*[1] (1)] [early 18C–early 19C] a brothel.

smug-lay *n.* [SE *smuggle* + LAY *n.*[3] (1)] [early–mid-19C] the selling of virtually worthless goods on the pretext that they are actually smuggled contraband.

smurf *n.* [from the *Smurfs*, the animated children's TV characters] **1** [1980s+] (*Aus. prison*) an inexperienced or short prison officer. **2** [1990s+] (*US gay*) a blond young homosexual man. **3** [1990s+] (*Aus.*) a term of abuse.

smush *n.* [? MUSH *n.*[2] (1)] [1910s–30s] (*Irish/US*) the mouth.

smush *v.* [obs. SE] [late 18C–early 19C] to snatch, to seize.

smut *n.* **1** [late 17C+] pornography, obscenity; thus *smut-peddler*, a seller of pornography [SE *smut*, a black stain; i.e. the identification of sexuality and 'dirt']. **2** [early–mid-19C] copper, a copper boiler, lead, a furnace [its smokiness]. **3** [1920s+] (*US black*) a derog. term for a woman. **4** [1970s] (*US campus*) a prostitute.

IN COMPOUNDS

❑ **smut-butt** *n.* [SE *smut* + BUTT *n.*[1] (1a)] [1970s] (*US campus*) a derog. term for a black student. ❑ **smut-hound** *n.* [-HOUND *sfx*; coined by H.L. Mencken (1880–1956) and one of the coinages (along with *bible belter* + *booboisie*), of which he was 'vainest' (letter, 2 December 1927)] [1920s+] one who is obsessed by the tiniest trace of obscenity, esp. in the arts or media; thus a censor.

smutter *n.* [SMUT *n.* (1)] [1980s] (*US*) a maker of or dealer in pornography.

snaaks *adj.* [Du. *snaaks*, droll, comical] [1910s+] (*S.Afr.*) strange, peculiar, bizarre.

snab *adj. see* SNABBY *adj.*

snabble *v.* [? dial. *snabble*, to eat greedily] **1** [18C] to arrest. **2** [mid-18C–early 19C] to knock down, to plunder. **3** [late 18C–early 19C] to kill in battle. **4** [late 19C] to have sexual intercourse with.

snabbled *adj. see* SMABBLED *adj.*

snabby *adj.* (*also* **snab**) [mid-19C] (*US campus*) stylish, fashionable; perfect, excellent.

snack *n.*[1] [SE *snack*, a portion, itself linked to root for sense 3] **1** [mid-17C–mid-19C] (*UK Und.*) a share of booty; also as v. **2** [late 19C] (*US Und.*) a confederate. **3** [late 19C+] a snide remark [SE *snack*, a snap or bite, esp. of a dog].

IN PHRASES

❑ **go snacks** *v.* (*also* **go a snack**) [late 17C–mid-19C] to divide up, to hand over a share of the loot. ❑ **half-snack** *n.* [late 17C–19C] half-shares in something. ❑ **snack (the bit)** *v.* [mid-17C–19C] (*UK Und.*) to divide up, to hand over a share of the loot.

snack *n.*[2] ['a piece of cake'] [1940s+] (*Aus.*) anything simple.

SE in slang uses

IN PHRASES

❑ **snack of thunder** *n.* [early 19C] a small glass of brandy.

snack *n.*[3] [its role in oral sex] [1950s–60s] (*US black*) the penis, often when small.

IN COMPOUNDS

❑ **snackpack** *n.* [SE *pack*; also a proprietory food name] **1** [1970s+] (*US gay*) an athletic supporter, a jockstrap. **2** [1980s+] (*US gay*) the male genitalia, when seen in a jockstrap or bikini briefs.

snack *v.*[1] [SNACK *n.*[1] (3)] [late 19C] to nag, to criticize.

snack *v.*[2] [the couple nibble on each other] [1980s+] (*US campus*) to kiss passionately.

IN COMPOUNDS

❑ **snackbar** *n.* [1990s+] (*US campus*) a girl- or boyfriend.

snaffle *n.* **1** [16C–18C] (*UK Und.*) a successful highwayman [SE *snaffle*, a light bridle + SNAFFLE *v.* (2)]. **2** in senses of incomprehensible or constrained speech, as if subject to a *snaffle*. (**a**) [mid-19C] talk that no one but the speaker either understands or cares about. (**b**) [1910s–20s] secret talk.

snaffle *v.* (*also* **snavvle**) [SE *snaffle*, to place a bridle-bit on a horse] **1** [late 16C; mid-19C–1910s] to arrest. **2** [17C+] to steal. **3** [20C+] to grab, to take hold of; to pilfer (and as such seen as less immoral than stealing); thus n. *snaffler*, one who is miserly.

snaffle-biter *n. see under* BITE *v.*

snaffler *n.*[1] [SNAFFLE *v.* (2)] [18C–early 19C; 1940s–50s] a highwayman.

IN PHRASES

❑ **snaffler of prancers** *n.* [18C–early 19C] (*UK Und.*) a horse-thief.

snaffler *n.*[2] [fig. use of SE *snaffle*, to place a bridle on] [early 19C] a blow, a punch.

snaffling lay *n.* [SNAFFLE *v.* (2) + LAY *n.*[3] (1)] [mid-18C–early 19C] the profession of highway robbery.

s.n.a.f.u. *n.* (*also* **g.a.f.u.**) [abbr. *s*ituation *n*ormal, *a*ll *f*ucked *u*p (*f*ouled *u*p can provide a euph. substitute); also *g*od *a*lmighty *f*uck-*u*p; orig. a WW2 milit. catchphrase, *s.n.a.f.u.* quickly entered mainstream sl. and generated a number of variations, although none has had the same impact (cf. F.I.G.M.O. *phr.*; F.U.B.A.R. *adj.*; F.U.B.B. *phr.*; F.U.B.I.S. *phr.*; F.U.M.T.U. *phr.*; M.F.U.T.U. *phr.*; S.A.M.F.U. *n.*; S.A.P.F.U. *phr.*; S.U.S.F.U. *phr.*; T.A.R.F.U. *phr.*; T.U.I.F.U. *n.*)] [1940s+] (*orig. US milit.*) a mistake, an error, a situation, often within an institution or organization, that has gone awry.

s.n.a.f.u. *adj.* (*also* **snafu**) [S.N.A.F.U. *n.*] [1940s+] messed up, gone wrong.

s.n.a.f.u. *v.* [S.N.A.F.U. *n.*] [1940s+] (*orig. US milit.*) to mess up, to go wrong, esp. in a complex, elaborate manner; thus adj. *snafued*.

snag *n.*[1] [SE *snag*, a jagged or angular projection, a short stump projecting from a tree trunk] **1** [late 17C–mid-19C] (*also* **snagg**) a large tooth. **2** [1940s+] (*Aus./US*) a jagged tooth.

IN COMPOUNDS

❑ **snag-catcher** *n.* [late 19C–1910s] a dentist.

snag *n.*[2] [SE *snag*, an impediment or obstacle] [mid-19C; 20C+] (*Aus./N.Z.*) an adversary worthy of consideration.

snag *n.*[3] [dial. *snag*, a morsel, a snack, i.e. where the tramp keeps such sustenance] [late 19C] (*N.Z.*) a tramp's backpack.

snag *n.*[4] [? dial. *snag*, to carp, to nag] [1950s–60s] (*US black*) an unattractive or unpleasant woman.

snag *n.*[5] [acronym] [1980s+] (*US campus*) a sensitive new-age guy.

snag *n.*[6] **1** *see* SNAGGER *n.* **2** *see* SNAGS *n.*

snag *v.* [SE *snag*, to be caught or pierced by a snag or rough projection] **1** [late 19C+] to grab, to steal. **2** [20C+] to catch or arrest. **3** [1920s] (*N.Z.*) to hunt for bargains, as a means for poor people to survive. **4** [1920s–70s] (*US tramp*) to sodomize. **5** [1940s–80s] (*US black*) to have sexual intercourse. **6** [1950s] (*gang*) to attack an individual without warning. **7** [1950s] to destroy. **8** [1960s+] to woo, to wed, to seduce; to attract in a non-sexual context. **9** [1980s] (*US campus*) to ridicule. **10** [1990s+] to win.

snagg *n.*[1] [Sussex dial. *snag*, a snail] [late 18C–early 19C] (*UK Und.*) a snail.

snagg *n.*[2] *see* SNAG *n.*[1] (1).

snagger *n.* (*also* **snag**) (*Aus./N.Z.*) **1** [late 19C–1900s] an itinerant worker or tramp, esp. one who is lazy, or work-shy. **2** [late 19C–1900s] in ext./fig. use, a parasite. **3** [1930s+] a poor person who seeks cheap bargains.

snaggers/snaggles *n. see* SNAGS *n.*

snagging *n. see* DOZENS *n.*

snaggle-tooth *n.* [SE *snaggle-tooth*, irregular or projecting teeth] [20C+] a person with poor, uneven teeth.

snaggling *n.* [? dial. *snaggler*, an eel-fisher] [mid-19C] the practice of angling for geese with a hook and line, the bait being a worm or snail.

snags *n.* (*also* **snaggles, snaggers**) [dial. *snag*, a morsel, a snack] [1940s+] (*Aus./N.Z.*) sausages; rarely used in sing.

SE in slang uses

IN PHRASES

❑ **half-snags** *n.* [late 17C–19C] half-shares in something; note HALF-SNACK *under* SNACK *n.*[1].

snail *n.* **1** [late 19C] (*Aus.*) a shepherd, a musterer, one who mends boundary fences [? the speed of his progress]. **2** [late 19C] (*US*) a freight train [its (lack of) speed]. **3** [1920s–60s] (*US tramp*) a cinnamon roll or bun [? its shape].

snailer *n.* [resemblance to a snail track] [1990s+] (*Irish*) a trail of mucus running down the face.

snailly *n.* [SE *nail varnish*] [2000s] (*UK drugs*) nail varnish, in the context of sniffing its fumes.

'snails! *excl.* [SE *God's nails* (although the nails in question are those suffered by Christ rather than God)] [16C–early 17C] a mild, if blasphemous, oath.

snail's ankle *n. see* CAT'S WHISKERS *n.*

snail trail *n.* **1** [1990s+] vaginal secretions marking the underwear. **2** *see* HAPPY TRAIL *under* HAPPY *adj.*

snake *n.*[1] [fig. use of SE *snake*, f. its perceived characteristics] **1** [mid-19C+] (*US*) an unreliable, deceptive person [note Urqhart (tr. of *Gargantua & Pantagruel*, 1653): 'Cursed snakes, dissembling varlets, seeming sancts / Slipshop caffards, beggars pretending wants'; Nares defines it as 'a term of reproach, equivalent to a wretch, a poor creature']. **2** [1950s+] (*US gang*) a spy. **3** [1960s] (*US campus*) a promiscuous or ugly young woman. **4** [1970s] (*US black*) a homosexual, whether male or female. **5** [1970s+] (*US campus*) someone who steals something, particularly someone else's date.

IN PHRASES

❑ **fatten frogs for snakes** *v.* [1950s] to prepare a victim (including oneself) for exploitation by a criminal or trickster.

SE in slang uses

IN COMPOUNDS

❑ **snakebit** *adj.* [1970s] (*US*) defeated. ❑ **snakebite** *n. see* separate entry. ❑ **snake-bitten** *adj.* [SE] [1920s+] (*US*) incapacitated. ❑ **snake charmer** *n.* [1930s] **1** (*Aus.*) a railway plate-layer (in Western Australia); also *hairy leg* (New South Wales), *woolly nose* (South Australia) [the prevalence of snakes along the track]. **2** (*US*) an oboe [the image of a snake-charmer luring a snake by playing a flute-like instrument]. ❑ **snake eyes** *n. see* separate entries. ❑ **snake gully** *n.* [*Snake Gully* was the location of the long-running radio serial *Dad and Dave*] [1940s+] (*Aus.*) an imaginary place that is a byword for backwardness and remoteness. ❑ **snake-headed** *adj.* [the negative image of the reptile] **1** [early 19C] (*UK Und.*) quickwitted. **2** [1900s–40s] (*Aus.*) testy, irritated. ❑ **snake juice** *n.* [JUICE *n.*[1] (3c)] [late 19C+] (*orig. Aus.*) any form of liquor, esp. when cheap and potent; thus *snake-juicer*, a drinker of such liquor. ❑ **snake poison** *n.* (*also* **snake medicine, snake water**) [var. on *SNAKE JUICE* above] [late 19C–1940s] (*Aus./US*) whisky. ❑ **snake room** *n.* (*also* **snake ranch**) [1920s–30s] (*US*) a bar, esp. when full of drunkards. ❑ **snake's eyebrows/hips/toenails** *n. see* CAT'S WHISKERS *n.* ❑ **snake's house** *n. see* separate entry. ❑ **snake's piss** *n. see* separate entry. ❑ **snake tart** *n.* [joc. resemblance] [mid-19C–1900s] eel pie. ❑ **snake yarn** *n.* [lit. or fig. involving snakes] [20C+] (*Aus.*) a fantastical tale, a 'tall story'.

IN PHRASES

❑ **above snakes** *adj.* ['a snake's eye view' of life above ground] [mid-19C] (*US*) **1** tall. **2** above the ground. ❑ **could crawl under a snake's belly** [1920s+] (*orig. Aus.*) acting immorally and without the least ethics; sometimes extended as *could crawl under a snake's belly with a top hat/with stilts on*. ❑ **give someone a snake** *v.* [late 19C–1920s] to annoy, to irritate. ❑ **kill a snake** *v.* (*also* **kill a tree**) [the act of urinating in the bush; note also SNAKE *n.*[3]] [20C+] to absent oneself from a group, e.g. to urinate. ❑ **snake (off)** *v.* [the reptile's characteristic movement] [1910s+] (*orig. Aus.*) to slip along, to move stealthily. ❑ **snake out** *n.* [the hunting of deadly snakes] [early–mid-19C] (*US*) to hunt down, to pursue. ❑ **snakes in one's boots** *n. see* separate entry. ❑ **wake snakes** *v.* [mid–late 19C] (*US*) to drive to utmost fury, to start moving; also as adj., fast, intense.

IN EXCLAMATIONS

❑ **snakes alive!** *see* separate entry. ❑ **snakes and sawdust!** *see* separate entry. ❑ **snakeshit!** *see* SHIT! *excl.*

snake *n.*[2] **1** [1910s–30s] (*US Und.*) a railroad switchman. **2** [1940s] (*Aus.*) a non-commissioned officer. **3** [1940s] (*US*) a police officer. **4** [1970s] a non union employment agency.

snake *n.*[3] [abbr. *ONE-EYED TROUSER-SNAKE under* ONE-EYED *adj.*] [1940s+] the penis.

IN COMPOUNDS

❑ **snake charmer** *n.* [1970s+] (*US gay*) a fellator. ❑ **snake gully** *n.* [1960s–70s] the vagina. ❑ **snakepit** *n.* **1** [1950s–70s] (*US gay*) a bar frequented by homosexuals. **2** [1960s] (*US*) the vagina. **3** [1960s] (*US*) a prison. **4** [1960s] a 'red–light' area. **5** [1960s+] (*also* **snake ranch**) a brothel.

IN PHRASES

❑ **burp the snake** *v. see BURP THE WORM under* WORM *n.* ❑ **drain the snake** *v. see DRAIN THE DRAGON/SNAKE under* DRAIN *v.* ❑ **take one's snake for a gallop** *v.* [1940s+] **1** to masturbate. **2** to urinate.

snake *n.*[4] [play on VIPER *n.* (1)] [1950s] (*US drugs*) a regular smoker of marijuana.

snake *v.*[1] [the snake-like whip] [mid-19C] (*US*) to beat, to thrash.

snake *v.*[2] [SNAKE *n.*[1] (1)] **1** [mid-19C] (*US Und.*) to arrest. **2** [late 19C+] to take in a surreptitious manner, to pilfer, to sneak. **3** [1950s+] to steal. **4** [1960s+] to flirt with and/or steal someone else's date [SNAKE *n.*[1] (5)]. **5** [1960s+] to cheat.

snake *v.*[3] [SNAKE *n.*[3]; SNAKE *n.*[1] (5)] [1980s+] **1** to masturbate. **2** to have sexual intercourse.

-snake *sfx* [1920s] (*US*) used in combs. to describe a person with a particular habit or type of behaviour; such as *parlor snake* at *PARLOR LIZARD under* PARLOR *n.*

Snake and Kidney *n.* [rhy. sl.] [1900s] (*Aus.*) Sydney.

snakebite *n.* [its effects] **1** [1920s+] (*US*) a strong alcoholic drink, usu. cheap but strong whisky. **2** [1950s–60s] an injection of heroin and morphine; thus *snakebit*, addicted. **3** [1980s+] a 'cocktail' of cider mixed with lager.

snakebite remedy *n.* [1950s+] (*US*) potassium permanganate, washing with which after sexual intercourse is used as a prophylactic against venereal disease.

snake eyes *n.*[1] [resemblance] [1910s–30s] (*US*) tapioca.

snake eyes *n.*[2] [i.e. a pair of ones; such a throw loses one's bet] **1** [1920s+] (*gambling*) the (losing) point of two in craps dice. **2** [1930s+] thus fig., bad luck; disappointment. **3** [1960s] (*bingo*) number eleven.

snake in the grass *n.* [rhy. sl., either of which might prove a 'treacherous friend'] [mid-19C+] **1** a looking glass, a mirror. **2** a drinking glass.

snake ranch *n. see SNAKEPIT under* SNAKE *n.*[3].

snakes *n.* (*also* **snakes in one's boots**) [from the *snakes*, pink elephants and other wonders one supposedly sees] [mid-19C+] alcoholic hallucinations, delirium tremens.

snake's *n. see* SNAKE'S HISS *n.*

snakes (alive)! *excl.* [mid-19C+] (*US*) a mild excl. often ext. e.g. *snakes and alligators!*

snakes and sawdust! *excl.* [late 19C] (*Aus.*) a mild excl.

snake's hiss *n.* (*also* **snake's**) [rhy. sl. = PISS *n.*] [1960s+] (*Aus.*) **1** an act of urination. **2** urine. **3** a lavatory.

snake's house *n.* [var. SNAKE'S HISS *n.* or SNAKE *n.*[3] + SE *house*] [20C+] (*orig. Aus.*) a lavatory.

snakes in one's boots *n. see* SNAKES *n.*

snakesman *n.* [late 18C–19C] a member of a gang of thieves who is sufficiently small and lithe to enter buildings through any narrow entrance that would otherwise be impassable; once within they unlock a main door through which all can pass.

snake's piss *n.* [1960s–70s] (*Aus.*) beer.

snakey *adj. see under* SNAKY.

snakies *n.* [2000s] snakeskin shoes or boots.

snaky *adj.*[1] (*also* **snakey**) [the biblical story of Eden/SNAKE *n.*[1] (1)] **1** [late 19C+] (*orig. US*) devious, underhand, cunning. **2** [1910s+] (*Aus.*) irritable, tetchy. **3** [1920s+] unpleasant, sinister. **4** [1930s+] (*Aus.*) jealous.

snaky *adj.*[2] (*also* **snakey**) [i.e. 'seeing snakes'] [1920s–70s] (*US*) **1** drunk. **2** suffering from alcoholic hallucinations; crazy.

snaky-bony *n.* [1950s] (*W.I.*) a very thin person; sometimes in comb. with SCARCE-O-FAT *n.*

snaky-bony *adj.* [SNAKY-BONY *n.*] [1950s] (*W.I.*) very thin.

snam *v.* [Scot. *snam*, to snap at greedily. 'That kind of theft which consists in picking up anything lying about, and making off with it rapidly' (Hotten, 1874)] [mid-19C–1900s] to steal, to pilfer.

IN PHRASES

❑ **on the snam** [late 19C] engaged in thieving.

snammer *n. see PUDDING-SNAMMER under* PUDDING *n.*

snap *n.*[1] [SE *snack*, a share or part; synon. with *snatch*, the image is of a grabbed or snatched handful or mouthful] **1** [mid-16C–mid-19C] a share, a portion; thus *snap/go snap*, to share half-and-half. **2** [late 16C–early 17C] (*UK Und.*) a cut-purse's assistant. **3** [late 16C–19C] a pickpocket, cut-purse or card-sharp, spec. an experienced one who demanded a share of his younger peers' profits. **4** [1900s] (*US*) a job.

DERIVATIVES

❑ **snappage** *n.* [early 17C] (*UK Und.*) a share in the booty.

snap *n.*[2] [? a *snap* of the fingers] **1** [late 19C] (*US campus*) a lenient instructor. **2** [late 19C] (*US*) a personal possession, e.g. a lover, a political office. **3** [late 19C–1900s] (*US*) an event, a circumstance; a trick. **4** [late 19C+] (*orig. US*) anything easy, a simple task or achievement. **5** [late 19C+] (*US campus*) an easy course. **6** [1900s] (*US campus*) an advantage; a foregone conclusion. **7** in drugs uses [the energy generated]. **(a)** [1960s amyl nitrite [the snapping of the ampoules in which the drug is packaged]. (**b**) [2000s] amphetamine.

IN PHRASES

❑ **on the snap** [late 19C] (*UK Und.*) on the lookout, waiting a chance of robbery. ❑ **private snap** *n.* [1930s] (*US*) a kept woman, a mistress. ❑ **soft snap** *n.* [SOFT *adj.* (4)] [mid-19C+] (*Aus./US*) an easy, pleasant job, a profitable business or undertaking.

SE in slang uses

IN PHRASES

❑ **give snaps** *v.* [1990s+] (*US teen*) to give (someone) credit. ❑ **give the snap away** *v.* [? the snap of a finger that launches an action] [late 19C] to betray plans, to 'give the game away'. ❑ **have snaps on** *v.* [2000s] (*US black*) to claim for oneself, or claim a share in. ❑ **not care a snap** *v.* (*also* **...two snaps, ...a snap of the fingers, not give...**) [the act of snapping one's fingers] [early 19C–1940s] to not care at all. ❑ **two snaps up** [referring to the snapping of one's fingers, and a play on the phr. 'two thumbs up' used by US TV film critics Roger Ebert and Gene Siskel] [1990s+] (*US campus*) an expression of approval.

snap *n.*[3] [SNAP *v.* (5)] [1980s+] (*US black*) a wisecrack, a witty retort.

snap *adj.*[1] [SNAP *n.*[2] (4)] [1900s–60s] (*US campus*) relatively easy.

snap *adj.*[2] *see* SNAPPY *adj.*[1] (3).

snap *v.* **1** [late 16C–early 18C; mid-19C; 1980s] (*UK Und.*) to arrest [? the *snapping* on of handcuffs]. **2** [late 18C–1920s] to grab. **3** [mid-19C] (*US*) to skip any appointment or duty [SE *snap*, to break]. **4** [1900s] (*US campus*) to skip a recitation [SE *snap*, to break]. **5** [1960s+] (*US black*) to tease. **6** [1960s+] (*US black*) to laugh along with. **7** [1960s+] (*US prison*) to understand, to work out. **8** [1960s+] (*US*) to act more carefully, to stop doing something.

SE in slang uses

IN COMPOUNDS

❑ **snap-and-snarl** *n.* [2000s] (*N.Z.*) one's wife. ❑ **snapcase** *n.* [1960s] (*US*) a mentally unstable person. ❑ **snap house** *n.* [mid-19C] (*US*) a cheap, poss. crooked casino.

IN PHRASES

❑ **snap...** *v. see also under* relevant n. ❑ **snap back** *v.* [1940s+] to make a quick recovery from a setback. ❑ **snap into** *v.* [1910s+] to involve oneself enthusiastically. ❑ **snap one off** *v.* **1** [1950s] (*US*) to fire a shot. **2** [1980s+] (*Aus. prison*) to defecate. **3** [1990s+] to masturbate. ❑ **snap out** *v.* [1910s–60s] (*US*) to lose emotional control. ❑ **snap someone's dick** *v.* [DICK *n.*[1] (5)] [1970s+] (*US*) to hurry someone up. ❑ **snap the rubber** *v.* [1940s–50s] to masturbate. ❑ **snap the whip** *v.* [1950s–60s] to masturbate, to masturbate another person. ❑ **snap to** *v.* [1980s] to work something out. ❑ **snap to (it)** *v.* (*also* **snap up**) [1930s+] (*US*) to get going, to get busy, to hurry up; esp. as imper. *snap to it!* ❑ **snap up** *v.* [1970s] (*US*) to become insane (or pose as such).

snap! *excl.* **1** [1960s+] (*US teen*) an excl. of surprise, apology, esp. after making a mistake or blunder. **2** [1970s+] (*US black*) to convey displeasure by directing a loud fingersnap towards the offending party; or one simply says 'Snap!'.

snapped *adj.*[1] [SNAP *v.* (1)/abbr. SE *snapped up*] [late 17C–18C; 20C+] arrested, caught.

snapped *adj.*[2] [mid-19C] (*US, Southern*) drunk.

snapped *adj.*[3] [late 19C] abrupt, sudden, surprising.

snapped up *adj.* [SNAP *n.*[2] (7a)] [1960s] (*drugs*) under the influence of amyl nitrite.

snapper *n.*[1] [ext. SNAP *n.*[1] (2)] [mid-16C] an assistant or lookout man for a criminal gang or team of fraudsters.

snapper *n.*[2] [SAmE *snapper*, the cracker on the end of a whip] (*US*) **1** [mid-19C+] a caustic remark. **2** [mid-19C+] the point of a story or joke. **3** [late 19C] a braggart. **4** [1920s] (*US*) a sharp-witted person. **5** [1930s+] (*gay*) the foreskin. **6** [1960s] (*Aus.*) a shark.

snapper *n.*[3] [image of penis as aggressor] [late 19C–1900s] the penis.

snapper *n.*[4] [SE *snap*, a photograph] [1910s+] (*orig. US*) a photographer.

snapper *n.*[5] [the clipping of tickets] [1920s–50s] a ticket inspector.

snapper *n.*[6] [one 'snaps' it alight] [1940s] (*US black*) a match.

IN PHRASES

❑ **snap a snapper** *v.* [1940s] (*US black*) to light a match.

snapper *n.*[7] [the image of the vagina as both a fish (FISH *n.*[1] (1a)) and a predator] [1950s+] **1** (*US*) the vagina. **2** (*US black*) excellent sex. **3** (*US campus*) a very attractive girl.

snapper *n.*[8] [abbr. BREADSNAPPER *under* BREAD *n.*[1]] [1950s+] (*Irish*) a baby, a small child.

snappers *n.*[1] [their noise] **1** [late 16C–19C] pistols. **2** [1920s–70s] teeth, usu. false.

snappers *n.*[2] [SNAP *n.*[2] (7a)] [1960s+] (*drugs*) amyl nitrite, isobutyl nitrite.

snapping *adj.* [the finger-snapping that demonstrates one's approval] [1990s+] (*US black teen*) excellent, wonderful.

snapping new *adj.* [the snapping of the notes to emphasize their crisp freshness] [late 19C] (*US*) of notes, absolutely fresh.

snappings *n.* [SE *snap up*] [late 16C–early 17C] (*UK Und.*) goods that are pilfered from stalls or shop windows.

snapping turtle (puss) *n.* [PUSS *n.*[1] (2c)] [1950s+] (*US*) the vagina.

snappish *adj. see* SNAPPY *adj.*[2].

snapps *n.*[1] [var. on SNAP *n.*[1] (1)] [mid-19C] (*UK Und.*) **1** a share, a portion. **2** anything that will serve as a means of making money; thus *looking out for snapps*, waiting for a lucky break or a windfall.

snapps *n.*[2] [mid-19C] Dutch gin, genever.

snappy *adj.*[1] [late 19C+] (*orig. US*) **1** smart, clever, esp. of language; thus *snappier, snappiest*. **2** energetic. **3** (*also* **snap**) neat, elegant. **4** sharply flavoursome. **5** sexy, titillating.

IN PHRASES

❑ **look snappy (about)** *v.* [1920s–40s] to hurry, to 'look smart'. ❑ **make it snappy** *v.* (*also* **make it crisp**) [1910s+] to get on with, to hurry up; usu. as imper. *make it snappy!* ❑ **snappy enough to freeze the plumbing off a brass elephant** *see* COLD ENOUGH TO FREEZE THE BALLS OFF A BRASS MONKEY *phr.*

snappy *adj.*[2] (*also* **snappish**) [SE *snap one's head off*] [late 19C+] (*orig. US*) irritable, irascible.

snaps *n.*[1] [SE *snap*] **1** [late 19C+] (*US*) handcuffs [they *snap* onto the wrist]. **2** [1980s+] (*orig. US black teen*) money [the 'snapping' of a dollar bill]. **3** [2000s] (*orig. US black teen*) praise, congratulations; occas. ironic [a congratulatory snap of the fingers].

snaps *n.*[2] [SNAPPY *adj.*[1] (1)/SE *snap up*] **1** [1970s] (*US black*) someone or something amusing. **2** [1980s] (*US campus*) snack foods.

snaps *n.*[3] *see* SNOPS *n.*

snarbone-red *n.* [ety. unknown] [mid-19C] (*UK Und.*) a City police-officer.

snare *n.* [1900s] (*US*) a house, an apartment, a room.

snare *v.* **1** [late 19C–1920s] (*US tramp*) to entice a boy into tramping. **2** [late 19C; 1940s] (*US tramp*) to arrest. **3** [late 19C+] (*Aus.*) to obtain, to grab, to win.

snarf *n.* [SNARF *v.* (2)] [1950s] something edible.

snarf *v.* [? var. on SCARF *v.* (1)] **1** [1940s+] (*also* **snarvle**) to grab, to take possession of. **2** [1960s+] to eat, to drink; to consume, e.g. a drug. **3** [1960s+] (*US campus*) in fig. use, to pick someone up. **4** [1990s+] to expel liquid (or, more rarely, food) out of one's nose by laughing in the middle of a swallow.

snark *n.* [dial. *snark*, to fret, to grumble] **1** [1960s] an informer. **2** [2000s] a sense of anger, irritation, tetchiness.

snark *v.* [SNARKY *adj.*] [1990s+] (*US campus/gay*) to gossip, usu. maliciously; to criticize, to be grumpy.

snarked off *adj.* [SNARKY *adj.*] [2000s] irritated, upset.

snarky *adj.* [dial. *snark*, to fret, to grumble] [1910s+] **1** (*orig. US*) irritable, touchy. **2** (*US gay*) maliciously gossipy, bitchy.

snarler *n.* [1980s+] (*N.Z.*) a sausage.

snarl(-up) *n.* [SNARL UP *v.*] **1** [mid-19C+] any form of difficulty; a fight. **2** [1930s+] (*orig. US*) a traffic jam.

snarl up *v.* [1910s+] to confuse, to entangle, to impede.

snarvle *v. see* SNARF *v.* (1).

snash *n.* [1950s+] (*Ulster*) nonsense, cheek.

snatch *n.* [Yorks. dial.; ult. SE *snatch*, to grab] **1** in sexual contexts. (**a**) [early 16C+] sexual intercourse, esp. quick or illicit or with a prostitute. (**b**) [mid-19C+] the vagina [negative image]. (**c**) [1940s–50s] (*US prison*) a male homosexual. (**d**) [1940s+] a generic word for women, esp. when viewed in a sexual context. (**e**) [1940s+] (*US gay*) the anus. (**f**) [1970s] (*US campus*) a notably ugly woman. (**g**) [2000s] AIDS. **2** [late 18C–mid-19C; 1940s–50s] an arrest. **3** [late 19C+] (*UK/US Und.*) a robbery, a victim ripe for robbing. **4** [1920s+] (*orig. US*) a kidnapping; thus *put the snatch on*, to kidnap. **5** [2000s] (*US black*) a fight.

pertaining to the vagina

IN COMPOUNDS

❑ **snatch-blatch** *n.* [dial. *blatch*, dirt] [late 19C–1910s] the vagina. ❑ **snatch-box** *n.* [SE *box*/BOX *n.*[1] (1a)] [mid–late 19C] the vagina. ❑ **snatch pad** *n.* [1940s] (*US black*) a house, a home. ❑ **snatch-play** *n.* [PLAY *n.* (2)] [1940s] (*US black*) sexual activity. ❑ **snatch-salami** *n.* [SE *salami*/SALAMI *n.*] [2000s] the penis. ❑ **snatch-thatch** *n.* [THATCH *n.* (2)] [18C] the female pubic hair.

IN PHRASES

❑ **flash one's snatch** *v.* [mid-19C+] to reveal one's genitals.

pertaining to crime

IN COMPOUNDS

❑ **snatch-game** *n.* (*also* **snatch racket**) [GAME *n.* (6)] [1920s+] kidnapping.

IN PHRASES

❑ **on the snatch** (*UK/US Und.*) **1** [1930s] working as a kidnapper. **2** [1970s] working as a street robber. ❑ **put the snatch on** *v.* [1920s+] (*US*) **1** to kidnap, to seize, to take over. **2** to arrest.

SE in slang uses

IN COMPOUNDS

❑ **snatch-back** *n.* [1980s] repossession, e.g. of a car when the buyer defaults on credit payments. ❑ **snatch-up** *n.* [1950s+] (*US black*) an arrest.

IN PHRASES

❑ **snatch one's time** *v.* (*also* **snatch it, snatch one's bit, snatch one's rent**) [i.e. to snatch one's time back for oneself] [1910s+] (*Aus.*) to resign.

snatch *v.* **1** [early 18C; late 19C+] (*US*) (*also* **do a snatch**) to steal, esp. to shoplift. **2** [1930s+] (*mainly US*) to kidnap. **3** [1940s+] (*US black*) to threaten someone by grabbing their lapels and talking menacingly into their face; also fig. use, to critically butt in. **4** [1980s] (*US black*) to forcefully fondle sexually when the recipient is unwilling.

IN COMPOUNDS

❑ **snatch-cly** *n.* [SE *snatch* + CLY *n.* (2)] [late 18C–early 19C] (*UK Und.*) a thief who specializes in stealing from women's pockets.

IN PHRASES

❑ **snatch bald-headed** *v.* (*also* **snatch bald**) *see under* BALD-HEADED *adv.*

snatcher *n.* [SE *snatch*/SNATCH *v.*] **1** [mid–late 19C] (*UK Und.*) (*also* **smasher**) a body-snatcher or 'resurrectionist'. **2** [late 19C] a young and inexperienced pickpocket. **3** [late 19C–1960s] a thief, esp. a pickpocket. **4** [1900s–40s] a police officer, esp. a detective. **5** [1910s] with the pertinent n., a person who arrests a type. **6** [1930s–40s] (*US*) a kidnapper.

snavel *v.* (*also* **snawel**) [dial. *snavel*, to remove slyly; post-19C use mainly Aus.] **1** [late 18C–1920s] to steal, to pilfer; thus *snaveller*, a thief, esp. one who thieves from children. **2** [1910s] to catch, to grab hold of.

snavvle *v. see* SNAFFLE *v.*

snazz *n.* [backform. f. SNAZZY *adj.*] [1930s+] (*US*) style, elegance.

snazz up *v.* [SNAZZ *n.*] [1930s+] (*US*) to enliven by making something smarter and more attractive.

snazzy *adj.* (*also* **schnazzy, snazz, snozzy**) [? SNAPPY *adj.*[1] (3) + JAZZY *adj.*[1] (1)] [1930s+] (*orig. Aus.*) smart, fashionable, brightly coloured; thus *snazzy chassis*, an attractive (female) figure.

sneak *n.*[1] **1** in Und. use. (**a**) [late 17C–1900s] an act of theft. (**b**) [mid-18C+] a thief. (**c**) [mid-19C–1950s] (*US Und.*) a sneak-thief. (**d**) [late 19C–1950s] (*US Und.*) a bank robber (using guile rather than force). **2** [mid–late 19C] an unpleasant person, irrespective of tale-telling. **3** [mid-19C–1930s] (*also* **sneaker**) an escape. **4** [mid-19C+] (*mainly teen*) one who tells tales on their fellows, usu. in the context of school. **5** [late 19C] (*US prison*) a night-guard.

IN COMPOUNDS

❑ **sneak job** *n.* [JOB *n.*[2] (1a)] [1920s–30s] (*US Und.*) house-breaking. ❑ **sneak play** *n.* [baseball imagery or SE *sneak* + PLAY *n.* (2)] [20C+] a surreptitious entrance and exit from a brothel.

IN PHRASES

❑ **do a sneak** *v.* **1** [1900s] (*Aus.*) to inform against, to tell tales on. **2** (*also* **make a sneak, take a sneak**) [late 19C–1920s] to leave, to escape. ❑ **go on the sneak** *v.* [late 17C–late 19C] (*UK Und.*) to go out working as a sneak-thief or petty pilferer. ❑ **on the sneak** *adv.* [late 17C+] surreptitiously, on the sly. ❑ **on the sneak tip** *adv.* (*also* **on a sneak cue**) [1980s+] (*US black*) surreptitiously, deceitfully.

sneak *n.*[2] [abbr. SNEAKER *n.*[3] (1)] **1** [late 19C+] a soft-soled, canvas-topped shoe, often in pl. **2** [1930s] (*US*) a slipper.

sneak *adj.* [SNEAK *n.*[1] (1c)] **1** [mid-19C] (*UK Und.*) working as a sneak-thief. **2** [1960s] (*US*) secret.

sneak *v.* **1** [early 17C+] to rob, to steal. **2** [mid-18C+] to act in a surreptitious manner, esp. when looking for something to steal. **3** [mid-18C+] (*usu. juv.*) to tell tales on one's fellows [SNEAK *n.*[1] (4)]. **4** [early 19C] (*UK Und.*) of a prisoner, to escape surreptitiously. **5** [mid-19C] (*UK Und.*) to seduce someone's wife or lover. **6** [late 19C+] (*US*) to slip away quietly **7** [1960s] (*US black/gang*) to go into another gang's territory usu. to harass or fight. **8** [1990s+] to make a surprise attack **9** [2000s] (*US black*) to hit someone hard in the face.

sneak-a-toke *n. see* TOKE *n.*[2].

sneaker *n.*[1] [SE *sneaker*, a small bowl with a lid or cover] [late 17C–mid-19C] a small bowl of punch.

sneaker *n.*[2] **1** [early 18C] (*UK Und.*) a housebreaker [SNEAK *v.* (1)]. **2** [early–mid-19C] a coward [they *sneak* about]. **3** [1960s] (*S.Afr.*) a smuggler.

sneaker *n.*[3] [SE *sneak*, to move quietly] **1** [late 19C+] (*orig. US*) (*also* **sneaks**) a soft-soled, noiseless slipper or shoe, a gym shoe usu. in pl. **2** [1930s] (*US Und.*) a motorboat [presumably in the context of smuggling liquor]. **3** [1980s+] (*US*) quiet or silent breaking of wind.

IN PHRASES

❑ **beat one's sneaks** *v.* [1930s] (*US tramp*) to leave, to move

sneaker *n.*[4] *see* SNEAK *n.*[1] (3).

sneak go *v.* [2000s] (*Aus.*) to attack without warning.

sneaking budge *n.* [SNEAK *v.* (1) + BUDGE *n.*[1] (1)] [late 17C–late 18C] a sneak thief, esp. one who specializes in entering houses and taking furs, cloaks and coats; also shop-lifting; thus the act of performing this crime.

sneaks *n. see* SNEAKER *n.*[3] (1).

sneaksby *n.* [SNEAK *v.* (2)] [late 18C–early 19C] a term of general disparagement.

sneaksman *n.* [SNEAK *v.* (2)] **1** [mid-18C–mid-19C] the lower order and more contemptible species of thieves who lurk around and grab whatever they can regardless of value. **2** [mid-19C] a shoplifter.

sneaky joe *n.* [play on SNEAKY PETE *n.* (1)] [1950s] cheap brand

sneaky pete *n.* [the effects 'sneak up' on the consumer] **1** [1940s+] (*also* **pete, sneaky**) cheap, rotgut wine. **2** [1950s+] (*US drugs*) marijuana mixed with wine.

sneaky pete *adj.* **1** [1960s] (*US*) confidential, top secret. **2** [1980s] duplicitous.

sneaky pete *v.* [1940s+] (*US*) to creep quietly, to move stealthily.

sneck drawer *n.* [Scot. *sneck*, a latch + SE *drawer*, one who pulls; lit. one who opens a latch (in order to enter surreptitiously)] [early–mid-19C] a sly, cunning, flattering person.

sneck up! *excl.* (*also* **snick up!**) [SE *sneck*, a latch, i.e. draw the latch and go to the other side of the door] [late 16C–mid-17C] an excl. of dismissal, the hell with you!

sned *v.* [dial. *sned*, to prune, to cut off] [20C+] (*Ulster*) of a man, to have sexual intercourse.

sneerg *n.* [backsl.] [mid-19C] greens, green vegetables.

sneeze *n.* **1** [19C–1910s] the nose. **2** [1910s] (*US drugs*) a portion of a powdered narcotic, e.g. cocaine. **3** [1960s+] (*US prison*) pepper, esp. red pepper.

IN COMPOUNDS

▫ **sneeze-box** *n.* [the immediate effects of snuff] [mid-19C] a snuffbox. ▫ **sneeze-lurker** *n.* (*also* **snuff-lurker**) [SE *sneeze* + LURK *n.* (3)] [mid-19C] (*UK Und.*) a thief who temporarily blinds a victim by throwing snuff in their face and then robs them as they stagger around blindly; thus *give it (one) on the sneeze-/snuff-racket*, to attack and rob someone in this way. ▫ **sneeze-machine** *n.* [1960s+] (*S.Afr.*) an appliance for the dispersal of tear gas and other crowd-breaking irritants carried by army and police vehicles. ▫ **sneeze wagon** *n.* [the sounds of the engine] [1900s–40s] (*US Und.*) an automobile.

IN PHRASES

▫ **sneeze in the loins** *n.* [1970s] (*Aus.*) a quick act of sexual intercourse.

sneeze *v.*^{1} (*also* **sneeze at**) [early 19C+] to disdain, to regard as of low worth.

IN PHRASES

▫ **sneeze it out** *v.* [1970s+] to confess.

SE in slang uses

IN PHRASES

▫ **not to be sneezed at** (*also* **not to be grinned at, not to be sniffed at**) [early 19C+] not to be spurned, not to be overlooked. ▫ **sneeze in the cabbage** *v.* (*also* **sneeze in the canyon**) [CABBAGE *n.*^{6} (1)/CANYON *n.* (1)] [1940s+] to perform cunnilingus. ▫ **sneeze it out** *v.* [the sneezing that accompanies withdrawal] [1930s–70s] (*US drugs*) to withdraw from narcotic addiction.

sneeze *v.*^{2} **1** [1910s–40s] (*US Und.*) to arrest; also as n. **2** [1930s] (*US prison*) to kidnap. **3** [1930s–40s] to steal.

IN PHRASES

▫ **put the sneeze on** *v.* [1940s] (*US Und.*) to intimidate, to blackmail, to extort.

sneezer *n.*^{1} **1** [early 18C–late 19C] a snuff-box. **2** [late 18C–mid-19C; 1940s] a pocket handkerchief. **3** [early 19C] a measure of alcohol, a dram. **4** [early–mid-19C] the nose. **5** [mid–late 19C] a blow on the nose. **6** [late 19C] (*UK Und.*) a gag. **7** [1910s–70s] (*US*) a prison, a local jail, the police station cells.

IN PHRASES

▫ **sneezer to breezer** *adv.* see BREEZER TO SNEEZER *under* BREEZER *n.*^{1}.

sneezer *n.*^{2} [dial. *sneezer*, a severe blow] **1** [mid-19C] (*US*) a very hot day. **2** [mid-19C–1940s] something or someone exceptionally good, strong, violent etc.

sneezer *adj.* [SNEEZER *n.*^{2} (2)] [1940s] (*Aus.*) excellent, wonderful.

sneezing coffer *n.* (*also* **sneezing scoop**) [SE *sneeze* + *coffer/scoop*] [early 19C] a snuff-box.

sneezing powder *n.* [1950s] (*US teen*) heroin.

snells *n.* [Scot. *snell*, sharp + ? Somerset dial. *snell*, a short stick pointed at both ends] [mid–late 19C] needles and buttons and other small wares carried by a street-hawker; thus *snell-fencer*, a hawker of such items.

snelt *n.* [? link to SNAVEL *v.* (1)] [20C+] (*Aus./N.Z.*) a sneak-thief.

snib *n.* [Scot. *snib*, to cut into] [early 17C–mid-19C] (*Scot. Und.*) a petty thief; also as v.

snib *v.* [Scot. *snib*, to cut into, to snuff a candle] [19C] **1** (*Scot.*) to have sexual intercourse with a woman. **2** (*Scot. Und.*) to snatch, to pickpocket.

snibbet *n.* [SNIB *v.* (1)] [20C+] sexual intercourse.

snibley *n.* [SNIB *v.* (1)] [20C+] sexual intercourse; often as a *bit of snibley*.

snich *n.* see SNITCH *n.*^{1}.

snicker *n.*^{1} [ety. unknown] [late 18C–early 19C] a horse suffering from glanders, a contagious disease typified by swellings beneath the jaw and discharge of mucus from the nostrils.

snicker *n.*^{2} [ety. unknown] [mid-19C] a drinking glass.

snicket *n.* [? Yorks. dial. *snicket*, a narrow passage; or Lancs. dial. *snicket*, a forward woman] **1** [1940s] a woman as a sexual object; thus sexual intercourse, esp. as *a bit of snicket*. **2** [1990s+] the vagina. **3** [1990s+] (*Irish*) a penis.

snick fadger *n.* [SE *snick*, to cut, snip, clip, nick + FADGE *v.*] [mid–late 19C] a petty thief.

snick up! *excl.* see SNECK UP! *excl.*

snid *n.* (*also* **snide**) [? SNIDE *n.* (1)] [mid-19C] a sixpence.

snide *n.* (*also* **snyde**) [? Ger. *aufschneiden*, to boast, to brag, to show off, or Ger. *schneide*, to cut, i.e. the cutting of fake coins] **1** [mid-19C+] (*orig. US*) spec. counterfeit money; thus *snide lurk*, the passing of counterfeit money; *snide shop*, an agency that organizes the passing of counterfeit money; *snide tickler*, a passer of counterfeit money. **2** [late 19C+] a deceptive, fake person; a confidence trickster. **3** [1910s] worthless goods, touted as valuable. **4** [1940s+] (*UK Und.*) anything counterfeit. **5** [1970s+] (*orig. S.Afr.*) imitation diamonds, fake gold, platinum and silver jewellery.

IN COMPOUNDS

▫ **snide and shine** *n.* [SHEENY *n.* (1)] [late 19C] an East End Jew. ▫ **snide pitcher** *n.* (*also* **snide pusher, snyde-pitcher**) [PITCH *v.* (1)/PUSHER *n.* (3b)] [mid–late 19C] one who passes bad money; thus *snide pitching*, passing counterfeit money. ▫ **snidesman** *n.* (*also* **snider**) [sfx *-man*] [late 19C–1910s] a counterfeiter.

snide *adj.* (*also* **shnide, snydey**) [SNIDE *n.*] **1** [mid-19C+] fake. **2** [mid-19C+] second-rate, useless. **3** [mid-19C+] unpleasant, mean, sneering. **4** [late 19C] smart, aware. **5** [late 19C+] corrupt. **6** [1900s] deemed to have contravened rules.

DERIVATIVES

▫ **snideness** *n.* [a positive use that implies the 'clever' aspects of fakery] [late 19C] astuteness, awareness, mental acuity. ▫ **snidey** *adj.* **1** [late 19C] counterfeit. **2** [late 19C+] bad, unfavourable. **3** [1950s+] sneering, supercilious. ▫ **snidy** *adj.* [2000s] unpleasant, menacing.

IN COMPOUNDS

▫ **snidebox** *n.* [1920s] (*US Und.*) an easily opened safe. ▫ **snide sparkler** *n.* [SPARKLER *n.* (2)] [late 19C] a counterfeit diamond. ▫ **snide 'un** *n.* [late 19C] one who is smart, aware, 'fly'.

snide *v.* [SNIDE *n.* (2)] [late 19C] to deceive, to trick.

snider *n.*^{1} see SNIDESMAN *under* SNIDE *n.*

snider *n.*^{2} see SNYDER *n.*

snidger *adj.* see SNODGER *adj.*

snidget *adj.* [? SNODGER *n.*] [1930s+] (*Aus. teen*) excellent, first-rate.

sniff *n.* [SE *sniff*, i.e. the methods of consumption] **1** [1900s] (*Aus.*) perfume. **2** [1910s+] (*drugs*) narcotics, esp. cocaine. **3** [1970s+] (*drugs*) amyl nitrite, butyl nitrate; thus (*US gay*) *sniff queen*, a devotee of such drugs. **4** [1990s+] (*drugs*) glue, paint thinner and other chemicals used for intoxication.

IN PHRASES

▫ **do a sniff** *v.* [1900s] (*Aus.*) to cry, to weep.

sniff *v.* **1** [1910s+] (*drugs*) to inhale heroin, cocaine, glue or any other intoxicating substance. **2** [1920s+] to drink alcohol.

IN PHRASES

▫ **sniffed up** *adj.* [1980s+] (*US drugs*) intoxicated by a narcotic. ❑ **not to be sniffed at** *see* NOT TO BE SNEEZED AT *under* SNEEZE *v.*[1].

sniff a powder *v.* [var. on *TAKE A RUN-OUT POWDER under* RUN-OUT POWDER *n.*] [1940s] (*US black*) to leave fast, to run away.

sniff a rodent *v. see SMELL A MOUSE under* SMELL *v.*

sniffer *n.* [SE *sniff*] **1** [mid-19C+] the nose. **2** [late 19C] a snob, one with 'their nose in the air'. **3** [20C+] (*drugs*) a cocaine, morphine or heroin user. **4** [1930s] (*US black*) a nervous, excitable mood. **5** [1940s+] any device used to sense gas, radiation etc; thus *sniffer dog*, a dog trained to sniff out drugs or explosives. **6** [1950s] (*US*) an (unpleasant) odour. **7** [1960s+] (*drugs*) one who sniffs glue. **8** [1970s] an investigator from the DHSS/Benefits Agency who checks on the validity of unemployment benefit claims. **9** [1970s+] a prostitute's client who enjoys sniffing her used underwear.

sniffer and snorter *n.* (*also* **sniffer**) [rhy. sl.] [1980s] a newspaper reporter.

sniffler *n.* [late 19C–1930s] (*Anglo-Irish*) an alcoholic drink; usu. in phr. *will you have a sniffler?*

sniffles, the *n.* [SE *sniffles*, weeping, tearfulness] [1900s] (*US*) a fit of depression.

sniffs *n. see* SNIPS *n.* (2).

snifter *n.*[1] [SE *sniff*/SNIFF *v.* (1) + play on SNIFTER *n.*[2]] **1** [19C] the nose. **2** [1920s–50s] (*US drugs*) a cocaine user. **3** [1930s] (*US drugs*) a morphine user. **4** [1930s+] a measure of cocaine, enough for a single inhalation. **5** [1940s] a suspicion, lit. a sniff.

snifter *n.*[2] (*also* **schnifter**) [SE *snifter*, a brandy glass, shaped to be warmed by the hands and for the fumes, so intensified, to be sniffed] **1** [mid-19C+] an alcoholic drink. **2** [1920s] in fig. use, a (small) portion. **3** [2000s] the act of inhaling glue or similar substances.

snifter *n.*[3] [? fig. use of dial. *snifter*, a strong breeze] [late 19C–1910s] **1** anyone or anything seen as especially important, large or powerful. **2** ext., an attractive woman.

snifter *adj.* [SNIFTER *n.*[3] (1)] [1910s] first-rate, the best.

snifty *adj.* **1** [late 19C] having a pleasant smell. **2** [late 19C–1940s] (*US*) haughty, arrogant, disdainful; thus as adv. [var. on SE colloq. *sniffy*, disdainful, arrogant].

snig *v.* [Yorks. dial. *snig*, to chop off, to steal] [late 19C; 1960s] to steal, to pilfer.

'sniggers! *excl.* (*also* **niggers noggers! 'snigs! udsnigs!**) [meaning of *nigs* unknown] [17C] a general oath, lit. 'God's nigs'.

IN EXCLAMATIONS

❑ **I'll be sniggered!** (*also* **I'll be snickered! I'm sniggered!**) [mid-19C–1900s] a general oath; basically a euph. for *I'll be damned!*

sniggle *n.* [? SNIGGLE *v.* or SE *snuggle*] [1930s+] (*Aus.*) a woman seen as a sex object; thus through metonymy, sexual intercourse.

sniggle *v.* [? dial.] [19C] to wriggle, to creep stealthily.

'snigs! *excl. see* 'SNIGGERS! *excl.*

snilch *v.* [ext. of SE *sneck*] [late 17C–early 19C] (*UK Und.*) to look at closely; to spy on.

sninny *n.* [var. on SKINNY *n.*[2]] [1920s+] (*Aus.*) a young woman.

snip *n.* [fig. uses SE *snip*, a single cut of the scissors] **1** [late 16C–1940s] a tailor; also used as a generic proper name, e.g. *Master Snip, Snip the Tailor*. **2** [early 18C–early 19C] a swindle, a deception. **3** [early 18C; 1920s] (*UK Und.*) a cheat. **4** [late 19C+] a certainty. **5** [1920s+] anything simple, an easy task. **6** [1920s+] a bargain. **7** [1960s] (*Aus.*) a bite. **8** [1960s] an insignificant person.

snip *v.* [SE *snip*, to slice, to cut; 20C+ uses Aus.] **1** [early 18C; 1960s+] to swindle, to deceive. **2** [1960s] (*Aus.*) to borrow money. **3** [2000s] (*Irish*) to seduce, to pick up.

SE in slang uses

IN COMPOUNDS

❑ **snip-cabbage** *n.* (*also* **snip-louse**) [CABBAGE *n.*[1] (1)/SE *louse*] [18C; 19C] a tailor.

IN PHRASES

❑ **go snip** *v.* [mid-17C] to share, to divide up. ❑ **snip a dolly** *v.* [ety. unknown] [1940s] (*US black*) to leave, to go away.

snipe *n.*[1] [SE *snipe*, the long-beaked bird or SE *snip*, to cut off; note dial. *snipe*, a mean person] **1** [mid-18C–late 19C] a lawyer, esp. one who has presented a large bill; thus the inflated bill itself [a pun on the bird's long *bill*]. **2** [late 19C] a defaulter on the Stock Exchange. **3** [late 19C+] (*orig. US tramp*) a cigarette or cigar butt; thus *snipe-shooting, snipe-hunting*, picking up cigar or cigarette ends from the gutter. **4** [late 19C+] (*Ulster*) the nose; one who has a long nose. **5** [late 19C+] a derog. term of abuse. **6** [1950s] (*US*) a male prostitute or one who befriends homosexuals to acquire money, esp. by robbing.

snipe *n.*[2] [SE *snipe*, to shoot at] **1** [20C+] (*Aus./US*) a small wall poster, a flyer, usu. political. **2** [1920s–30s] (*US prison*) a newspaper.

snipe *adj.* [SNIPE (ON) *v.*] [1950s] (*US*) aggressive.

snipe *v.*[1] [? image of the bird foraging with its beak] **1** [late 19C+] (*mainly US*) to pick up, to pilfer, to filch. **2** [1900s] to prospect for gold in old diggings. **3** [1980s+] (*Aus. prison*) to request a loan.

snipe *v.*[2] [orig. milit. use] [1970s+] (*US black*) to kill.

snipe (on) *v.* [var. on synon. SE *snipe at*] [1930s+] (*US black*) to malign, to criticize, to gossip about someone.

sniper *n.*[1] [SNIPE *n.*[1] (3)/SNIPE *v.*[1] (1)] [1920s–50s] (*US*) one who picks up cigar or cigarette ends from the gutter or sidewalk.

sniper *n.*[2] [SE *sniper*, i.e. he 'shoots down' available work] [1930s+] (*Aus.*) a non-union wharf worker.

sniper *n.*[3] [SNIPING *n.*[2]] [2000s] (*US black*) one who places illicit fly-posters.

sniper *n.*[4] [2000s] (*US black*) the act of ejaculating in a woman's eye as a climax to fellatio.

snipes *n.* [SE *snip*] [early–mid-19C] a pair of scissors.

snipe shooter *n.* [SNIPE *n.*[1] (3) + SE *shooter*] [late 19C–1970s] (*US*) one who picks up cigarette ends from the gutter; thus v. *shoot snipes*.

sniping *n.*[1] [SNIPE *v.*[1] (2)] [late 19C] (*US*) prospecting for gold in old, abandoned diggings.

sniping *n.*[2] [SNIPE *n.*[2] (1)] [2000s] (*US black*) the illegal flyposting of advertisements on available surfaces, e.g. lamp-posts etc.

snips *n.* **1** [late 19C] handcuffs. **2** [1900s–60s] (*also* **sniffs**) a pair of scissors.

sniptious *adj.* [anything unnecessary has been *snipped* away] [early 19C–1930s] (*US*) neat and elegant.

snit *n.* [? echoic; coined by US writer/diplomat Clare Booth Luce (1903–87)] **1** [1930s; 1960s+] (*orig. US*) an outbreak of temper, generally a children's term; also adj., *snitty*. **2** [1960s] an aloof individual.

DERIVATIVES

❑ **snittiness** *n.* [2000s] ill temper, verbal unpleasantness.

snitch *n.*[1] (*also* **snich, snitcher**) **1** [late 17C–mid-18C] a blow on the nose. **2** [late 17C+] (*UK Und.*) the nose. **3** [late 18C+] an informer [SNITCH *v.* (1)]. **4** [1910s] a contemptible person **5** [1910s] (*US prison*) a prisoner who curries favour.

IN COMPOUNDS

❑ **snitch-ass** *adj.* [-ASS *sfx*] [1980s+] (*US black*) untrustworthy tale-telling. ❑ **snitchball** *n.* [1990s+] (*US prison*) any game played by those inmates, among them informers, who live in protective segregation. ❑ **snitch-box** *n.* [1990s+] (*US prison*) a box used both for institutional correspondence and for passing on messages that accuse fellow inmates of illegal activity. ❑ **snitch game** *n.* [GAME *n.* (6)] [1990s+] (*US prison*) obtaining information from inmates by threatening to falsely expose them as informers. ❑ **snitch jacket** *n. see under* JACKET *n.* ❑ **snitch kite** *n.* [KITE *n.* (3e)] [1960s] (*US prison*) a note passed by a prisoner, giving information to the authorities. ❑ **snitch pad** *n.* [weak uses of SNITCH *v.* (1) + SE *pad*] [1930s–40s] (*US black*) **1** a notebook. **2** a newspaper. ❑ **snitch rag** *n.* [1940s] a handkerchief. ❑ **snitch sheet** *n.* [weak use of SNITCH *v.* (1) + SHEET *n.* (1)] [1930s–40s] (*US black*) a newspaper.

IN PHRASES

❑ **snite someone's snitch** *v. see* separate entry. ❑ **turn snitch** *v.* [late 18C–mid-19C] to become an informer.

snitch *n.*[2] (*also* **snitcher**) [ety. unknown; ? link to SNIT *n.* (1)] [1940s+] (*N.Z.*) a grudge; hostility, bad feeling.

IN PHRASES

❑ **get a snitch on, have..., take..., get a snitcher on, have..., take...** *v.* [1940s+] to bear a grudge towards, to take offence (at).

snitch *n.*[3] *see* SNITCHER *n.*[2] (2).

snitch *n.*[4] *see* SNITCHER *n.*[4].

snitch *v.* (*also* **snitch off, snitch on, snitch out**) [SNITCH *n.*[1] (2), i.e. one sticks one's nose in] **1** [18C+] to inform, to turn King's/Queen's evidence, to betray. **2** [20C+] to steal, to take; lit. and fig. **3** [1990s+] (*Aus.*) to arrest.

IN COMPOUNDS

❑ **snitching-rascal** *n.* [SE *rascal*] [early 19C] an informer. ❑ **snitch-off** *n.* [1950s] (*US Und.*) an act of betrayal.

snitchel *n.* [SNITCH *n.*[1] (2)] [late 17C–early 18C] a blow on the nose.

snitchel *v.* [SNITCHEL *n.*] [late 17C–early 19C] to hit on the nose.

snitcher *n.*[1] [? SNITCH *n.*[1] (1), i.e. their devotion to tweaking or punching people on the nose] [mid-18C] a member of a set of fashionable young men or 'bloods'.

snitcher *n.*[2] [SNITCH *n.*[1] (3)] **1** [late 18C+] an informant, a tell-tale. **2** [mid-19C–1930s] (*Scot.*) (*also* **snitch**) in pl., handcuffs, esp. strings used in place of handcuffs [? addition of SE *snatch*]. **3** [1900s–20s] a detective. **4** [1940s] (*US black*) a newspaper reporter or columnist, a writer.

snitcher *n.*[3] [SNITCH *v.* (2)] [1930s] (*US*) a petty thief.

snitcher *n.*[4] [? SNEEZER *n.*[2] (2)] [1930s+] (*Aus./N.Z.*) any person or thing considered notably excellent, attractive, strong etc.

snitcher *n.*[5] **1** *see* SNITCH *n.*[1] (2). **2** *see* SNITCH *n.*[2] (1).

snitcher *adj.* [SNITCHER *n.*[4]] [1930s+] (*Aus./N.Z.*) first-rate, excellent, attractive.

snitching *n.* [SNITCH *v.*] **1** [early 19C+] informing. **2** [1930s+] (*US*) stealing.

snitchy *adj.* **1** [1910s] (*US*) petty, mean, or stingy [SNITCH *n.*[1] (4)]. **2** [1970s+] (*N.Z.*) tetchy, ill-tempered [SNITCH *n.*[2]].

snite someone's snitch *v.* [SE *snite*, to wipe + SNITCH *n.*[1] (2)] [late 17C–early 19C] to wipe, i.e. hit, someone's nose.

snitzy *adj.* [? SE *snobbish* + RITZY *adj.* (1)] [1930s–40s] (*US*) elegant, smart.

sniv *v.* [SE *snib*, to reprove, to reprimand] [early–mid-19C] (*UK Und.*) to hold one's tongue.

sniv! *excl.* [SNIV *v.*] [early 19C] nonsense! humbug! rubbish!

sniveller *n.* [the propensity of raw onions for causing tears] [mid-19C] an onion.

snizzle *n.* [? SNIFTER *n.*[2] (1)] [1940s] (*US black*) a drink, a can of beer.

snizzle *v.* [? dial. *sniggle*, to wriggle] [1910s–20s] to have sexual intercourse.

snoach *v.* [echoic] [late 18C–early 19C] to snuffle.

snob *n.* [the class-conscious, modern use of SE *snob*, one who despises their inferiors and/or toadies to those seen as superior, began as Cambridge University jargon *c.*1793 as a description of a townsman, as opposed to a university member. This may have been based on the orig. sl. use, implying the desire of tradesmen to flatter custom out of the undergraduates. It was widely popularized through the success of William Thackeray's *Book of Snobs* (1848). Ironically, a parallel use (early–mid-19C) means simply an ordinary person, with no pretensions to superiority, and in mid-19C Aus. *snobs* were tradesmen, while *nobs* were the 'gentlemen'. Similarly, in university use *snobocracy*, in SE the world of the influential upper classes, meant the world of townspeople, as opposed to undergraduates – again the use returns to the orig. sl. meaning] **1** [late 18C+] (*also* **snobber**) a cobbler, a shoemaker; thus *snobbing*, shoemaking or repairing; WW1 Aus. *snob-shop*, the shoemender's. **2** [mid-19C] a strike-breaker. **3** [20C+] (*Aus./N.Z.*) the last, most recalcitrant sheep to be sheared.

IN COMPOUNDS

❑ **snob's duck** *n.* [19C] a leg of mutton stuffed with sage and onions. ❑ **snobstick** *n.* [var. on or misreading of SE *knobstick*, a strike-breaker, ult. *knobstick*, a knobbed stick or cane] [mid-19C] a strike-breaker; one who refuses to join a trade union.

SE in slang uses

IN COMPOUNDS

❑ **snob-nob** *n.* [NOB *n.*[2] (1)] [1900s] (*N.Z.*) the self-appointed rural 'aristocracy'. ❑ **snobshop** *n.* [2000s] (*N.Z.*) an exclusive and expensive private school whose students are taught to consider themselves as being socially superior to public school pupils. ❑ **snob zoning** *n.* [1960s+] (*US*) a method of placing restrictions on specific city areas in a deliberate attempt to make it impossible for low-income families, e.g. non-white, non-middle-class families, to purchase homes there.

IN PHRASES

❑ **like a snob's cat – all piss and tantrums** [early–mid-19C] a general phr. of derision or disdain.

snob *v.* [SE *snob*] **1** [late 19C+] (*US black*) to snub, to ignore, to treat disdainfully. **2** [1960s] (*US*) to associate with upper-class people.

snockered *adj.* (*also* **schnockered, schnookered, snockered out, snookered**) [? dial. *snock*, a blow] **1** [1950s+] drunk or intoxicated by a drug. **2** [1970s] (*US*) assessed, worked out.

sno-cone *n.* [1990s+] (*US*) a frigid woman.

snoddy *n.* [var. on SWADDY *n.*] [late 19C–1910s] a soldier.

snodger *n.* [ety. unknown; *OED* suggests link to Scot/dial. *snod*, smart, neat, comfortable and/or Scot. *snog*, smooth, neat] [1910s+] (*Aus/N.Z.*) an excellent example of something.

snodger *adj.* (*also* **snidger**) [SNODGER *n.*] [1910s+] (*Aus./N.Z.*) excellent, first-rate, very good.

snoek-town *n.* [Du. *snoek*, the European pike (*Esox lucius*), in S.Afr. use usu. the snake mackerel (*Thyrsites atun*) + SE *town*; Cape Town was once the home of the *snoek* fishing and processing industry] [late 19C] (*S.Afr.*) Cape Town.

snoep *adj.* [Afk. *snoep*, greedy] [1960s+] (*S.Afr.*) mean, greedy, selfish, stingy.

snog *n.* [SNOG *v.*] [1940s+] kissing, cuddling; caresses short of intercourse; thus n. *snogging*.

snog *v.* [? SE *snug*; orig. RAF usage] [1940s+] to enjoy sexual preliminaries, stopping short of intercourse, usu. of teenage experimentation; 1980s+ use always implies a minimum of French kissing; thus n. *snogging*.

snollygoster *n.* [? Ger. *schnelle Geister*, lit. 'wild host', and thus a bird of prey that terrorizes man, or *schnelle Geeschte*, lit. 'quick spirits', also defined as a monster. According to Safire (*Political Dict.*, 1978), it was coined during or near the time of the US Civil War (1861–5). There may be a link to the Maryland *snallygaster*, a mythical monster supposedly part reptile and part bird, designed to terrify ex-slaves out of voting] [mid-19C+] (*US*) a shrewd, unprincipled person, esp. a politician.

snoodge *v. see* SNOOZE *v.*

snook *n. see* SNOOKS *n.* (2).

IN PHRASES

❑ **cock a snook (at)** *v. see* COCK A SNOOT *under* SNOOT *n.*

snook *v.* [Yid. *schnook*, a snout, a nose] **1** [1930s] (*Irish*) to sniff out news and gossip. **2** [1950s] (*UK prison*) to look through; thus *snook the Judas*, to look through the observation window or 'Judas hole' in a cell.

snooker *n.* [SNOOKER *v.* (1)] [1970s–80s] (*N.Z. prison*) a hiding place.

snooker *v.* [SE *snooker*, to impede] **1** [20C+] (*Aus.*) to hide. **2** [1980s+] to trick, to cheat.

snookered *adj.* [SE *snooker*, to impede] **1** [1910s+] cheated, hoaxed. **2** [1910s+] trapped in a difficult position. **3** *see* SNOCKERED *adj.*

snooks *n.* [seen as a foolish name] **1** [mid-19C–1920s] 'an imaginary personage often brought forward as the answer to an idle question, or as the perpetrator of a senseless joke' (Hotten, 1860). **2** [1920s+] (*also* **snook**) a term of endearment, either to a child or lover.

snookums *n.* [ext. of SNOOKS *n.* (2), orig. addressed esp. to lap-dogs] [1920s+] a term of endearment.

snookums! *excl.* [1950s] (*US*) an excl. of surprise.

snooky *adj.* [? *cock a snook* at COCK A SNOOT *under* SNOOT *n.*] [1910s–50s] (*Aus.*) critical, fault-finding.

snoop *n.*[1] [SNOOP *v.* (1)] **1** [late 19C+] an inquisitive person, a 'nosey parker'. **2** [1930s+] (*orig. US*) a detective. **3** [1940s] a suspicion, a cause of 'snooping'. **4** [1970s] a spy.

snoop *n.*[2] [ety. unknown] [1990s+] (*US black gang*) a derog. name for a member of the Bloods gang, as used by a Crip.

snoop *v.* [Du. *snoepen*, 'to appropriate and consume dainties in a clandestine manner' (*OED*)] (*orig. US*) **1** [mid-19C+] to pry, to interfere, to listen in. **2** [20C+] to survey (surreptitiously). **3** [1920s–60s] to steal.

(IN PHRASES)

❑ **snoop out** *v.* [1950s] (*US*) to investigate, to uncover.

snoop and pry *n.* [rhy. sl.] [20C+] a cry, an act of weeping.

snoop and pry *v.* [rhy. sl.] [20C+] to cry.

snooper *n.* [SNOOP *v.*] **1** [late 19C+] one who pries, who is inquisitive; often applied to local government officials. **2** [1920s] a thief. **3** [1930s+] (*also* **snooper hound**) a private detective.

snoopy *adj.* [SNOOP *v.* (1)] [1920s] (*US*) inquisitive.

snoos/snoose *n. see* SNOOZE *n.* (1).

snoot *n.* [SE *snout*] **1** [mid-19C+] the nose. **2** [late 19C+] arrogance, superciliousness. **3** [1920s+] a snob, an arrogant person who 'sticks their nose in the air'.

(IN COMPOUNDS)

❑ **snoot-cloot** *n. see* CLOUT *n.*[1] (1).

(IN PHRASES)

❑ **blow one's snoot off** *v.* [1910s–30s] (*US*) to reprimand, to criticise harshly. ❑ **cock a snoot** *v.* (*also* **cock a snoot at, cock a snook, concoct a snoot, make...**) [late 19C+] to disdain, to ignore, to turn up one's nose; thus in adv. form *cocking snooty*, disdainfully.

snoot *v.* [backform. f. SE colloq. *snooty*, snobbish, stand-offish] [1920s+] (*US/Aus.*) to snub.

snooted *adj. see* SNOOTERED *adj.* (1).

snooter *n.* [SNOOT *n.* (1)] [1960s+] (*drugs*) anyone who inhales a narcotic rather than injecting it.

snooter *v.* [SNOOT *n.* (1), i.e. 'shove one's nose in'; ? nonce-coinage by comic writer P.G. Wodehouse (1881–1975); however, note SNOTTER *v.*] [1920s] to cause trouble for someone.

snootered *adj.* **1** [1910s+] (*also* **snooted**) drunk [backform. f. SNOOTFUL *n.*[2]]. **2** [1920s+] troubled [SNOOTER *v.* (1) see prev. note].

snootful *n.*[1] [fig. use of SNOOT *n.* (1)] [mid-19C+] (*US*) an experience, a 'flavour'; sufficiency.

snootful *n.*[2] [SNOOT *n.* (1)] [20C+] (*US*) an alcoholic drink; thus by metonymy, a state of drunkenness.

(IN PHRASES)

❑ **have a snootful** *v.* (*also* **get a snootful, pack a snootful, get a noseful**) [20C+] to be drunk or to get drunk.

snooze *n.* [? SE *snore* + *doze*] **1** [mid-18C+] (*also* **snoos, snoose**) a nap, a brief or light sleep. **2** [early–mid-19C] a lodging, a bed. **3** [1940s+] (*Aus.*) a three-month prison sentence. **4** [1960s+] something or someone considered boring.

(IN COMPOUNDS)

❑ **snooze job** *n.* [JOB *n.*[2] (2)] [1970s+] anything especially boring. ❑ **snooze juice** *n.* [JUICE *n.*[1] (3)] a soporific drug. ❑ **snooze stand** *n.* [1960s] (*S.Afr.*) a bed.

snooze *v.* (*also* **snoodge**) [SNOOZE *n.* (1)] **1** [late 18C–mid-19C] (*UK Und.*) to have sexual intercourse. **2** [late 18C+] to doze, to sleep for a short time; thus *snooze-case*, a pillow-slip.

snooze ken *n. see* SNOOZING KEN *n.* (1).

snoozem *n.* [ext. of SNOOZE *n.* (1)] [mid-19C] a nap, sleep.

snoozer *n.*[1] [SNOOZE *v.* (2) + sfx *-er*] **1** [early 19C+] a person, a 'chap', a woman. **2** [1910s] as a term of address. **3** [1910s–50s] (*US*) a sheep-herder. **4** [1940s+] (*Aus.*) a baby.

snoozer *n.*[2] [SNOOZE *n.*] **1** [mid–late 19C] a thief who steals from the hotel or house in which they are staying. **2** [mid-19C–1930s] (*US Und.*) one who is asleep and thus a potential victim of crime. **3** [1900s–10s] a fool. **4** [1910s] a bedroom. **5** [1930s–60s] (*US*) a pullman sleeping car. **6** see SLEEPER *n.* (1a).

snoozing and snoring *adj.* [rhy. sl.] [20C+] boring.

snoozing ken *n.* [SNOOZE *v.* (2) + KEN *n.*[1] (1)] **1** [late 18C–mid-19C] (*also* **snooze-ken**) a brothel. **2** [early–mid-19C] (*also* **snuskin**) a bedroom, a bed. **3** [19C] (*also* **snoozing-crib, snoozing jug**) a lodging house [CRIB *n.*[1] (1)].

snoozy *n.* [SNOOZE *v.* (2)] [early 19C] a night constable.

snop *n.* [? borrowing f. SNOPS *n.*] [1960s–70s] (*drugs*) marijuana.

snops *n.* (*also* **snaps, snopsy**) [SE *Schnapps*, the drink] [late 19C] (*US*) gin.

(DERIVATIVES)

❑ **snopsy** *adj.* [19C] (*US*) drunk.

snora *v.* [joc. var. on SE *snort*] [2000s] (*S.Afr. gay*) to sniff cocaine.

Snor City *n.* [Afk. *snor*, a moustache + SE *city*; many male Pretorians supposedly wear moustaches] [1980s+] (*S.Afr.*) Pretoria.

snore *n.* **1** [20C+] a sleep or sleep in general. **2** [1950s–80s] (*Aus./UK*) a sleeping place, esp. a hostel for tramps and vagrants; a bed. **3** [1950s+] a boring person or thing.

(DERIVATIVES)

❑ **snoreville** *n.* (*also* **snoresville**) [SE *snore(s)* + -VILLE *sfx*[1]] **1** [1960s] bedtime; sleep. **2** [2000s] (*orig. US*) anything or anywhere considered tedious, boring; thus adj. *snore-/snoresville*, boring.

(IN PHRASES)

❑ **in the snore** [2000s] **1** in bed. **2** in fig. use, friendly with, 'in bed with'.

snore-off *n.* [SNORE OFF *v.*] [1940s–60s] (*Aus./N.Z.*) a sleep or nap, esp. after a drinking session.

snore off *v.* [ext. of SE *snore*] [1920s–60s] (*Aus.*) to go to sleep.

snorer *n.*[1] [SE *snore*] [mid-19C–1950s] the nose.

snorer *n.*[2] *see* SNORRER *n.*

snoresville *n. see* SNOREVILLE *under* SNORE *n.*

snore through (it) *v.* [early 19C] to glide along, to move easily.

snoring kennel *n. see under* KENNEL *n.*[2].

snork *n.* [SE *snork*, a piglet] (*Aus./N.Z.*) **1** [1940s+] a baby **2** [1960s+] a young man, a boy.

snorker *n.* [SAusE *snork*, a piglet] (*Aus.*) **1** [1940s+] a sausage **2** [1960s–70s] the penis.

snorky *n.* (*also* **snork**) [ety. unknown] [1950s] (*US*) a Swede.

snorrer *n.* (*also* **snorer**) [SCHNORRER *n.*] [20C+] **1** a scrounger a beggar. **2** a difficult customer.

snort *n.* **1** [mid-19C+] a gulp or single shot of alcohol. **2** [late 19C+] (*Aus.*) a pot of tea. **3** [1920s] a large glass of beer **4** [1940s+] (*drugs*) a dose or measure of a powdered narcotic **5** [1970s+] (*drugs*) cocaine.

snort *v.* (*also* **snort up**) (*drugs*) **1** [1930s+] to inhale narcotics usu. cocaine or heroin, through the nostrils; thus adj. *snorted* under the influence of the drug [SE *snort*]. **2** [1960s+] to inhale glue etc [SE *snort*]. **3** [1970s+] to drink alcohol [SNORT *n.* (1)].

snorter *n.*[1] **1** [early 19C] a blow on the nose. **2** [early 19C+ the nose. **3** [1940s+] (*drugs*) one who inhales (rather than injects) narcotics [SNORT *v.* (1)].

snorter *n.*[2] [fig. uses of SE *snort*] **1** [mid-19C] (*US*) 'a dashing riotous fellow' (Bartlett, *Dict. Americanisms*). **2** [mid–late 19C a gale, a stiff breeze. **3** [mid-19C+] anything or anyone exceptionally large, strong, violent etc. **4** [late 19C] a difficulty **5** [1910s] a severe reprimand. **6** [1920s] (*N.Z.*) an ill-tempered tetchy person. **7** [1950s] a sausage.

snorter *n.*[3] [SNORT *n.* (1)] **1** [late 19C+] a drink of alcohol. **2** [1910s] a drunkard.

snorting *adj.* (*also* **hellsnorting**) [SNORTER *n.*[2] (3)] [mid-19C+] a general intensifier, excellent, first-rate, very large, very unpleasant etc.

snort out *v.* [SE *snort*; i.e. the noise one makes while eating] [1980s+] (*US campus*) to overeat, to eat voraciously.

snorts *n.* [? play on HOG *n.* (7)] [1970s] (*drugs*) phencyclidine.

snort up *v. see* SNORT *V.*

snorty *adj.* [SE *snort*] [late 19C] bad-tempered, disagreeable.

snossidge *n.* [joc. mispron.] [late 19C] a sausage.

snot *n.*[1] (*also* **snotters**) [MDu. *snotte*; SE in 15C–17C but was generally seen as sl. by 18C; cognate with 14C SE *snite*, to wipe mucus from the nose and thus ult. to SE *snout*] **1** [18C+] nasal mucus. **2** [mid-19C+] a pej. term for a person, the usual implication being of their arrogance or, in the case of women, their promiscuity. **3** [late 19C+] the nose. **4** [1920s] (*US tramp*) an oyster. **5** [1930s+] semen; thus *snotty-nosed*, of the head of the penis, covered with semen. **6** [1970s] arrogance, verbal unpleasantness. **7** [1980s+] (*drugs*) residue produced from smoking amphetamine. **8** [2000s] the essence, the 'daylights'. **9** *see* SNOTNOSE *n.* (1). **10** *see* SNOTNOSE *n.* (3).

IN COMPOUNDS

□ **snot and tears** *n.* [synon. Afk. phr. *snot en trane*] [1960s+] (*S.Afr.*) misery, wretchedness. □ **snot-arse** *n.* [-ARSE *sfx*] [1970s] (*Aus.*) a contemptible person. □ **snotbag** *n.* (*also* **snotball**) [2000s] (*US*) an arrogant, pompous individual. □ **snotball** *n.* [1980s+] (*drugs*) rubber cement rolled into a ball and burned so that the fumes can be inhaled; usu. in pl. □ **snotbox** *n.* (*also* **snotter box, snotty-box**) [SE *box*] [early 19C; 20C+] the nose. □ **snotface** *n.* [1950s] (*US*) a derog. term of address. □ **snotgobbler** *n.* [SE *gobbler*] [1990s+] a general term of derision. □ **snothead** *n.* [2000s] (*N.Z.*) a general derog. term. □ **snot horn** *n.* [late 18C+] the nose. □ **snotkop** *n.* [Du. *kop*, head] [1990s+] (*S.Afr.*) a term of abuse. □ **snot-locker** *n.* [SE *locker*] [1970s+] (*US*) **1** the nose. **2** the vagina. □ **snotnose/-nosed** *see* separate entries. □ **snotrag** *n. see* separate entry. □ **snot sjambok** *n.* [Afk. *sjambok*, a whip] [20C+] (*S.Afr.*) a penis. □ **snot-poor** *n.* [1960s] (*US*) impoverished.

IN PHRASES

□ **blow snot-rockets** *v.* [1990s+] (*US campus*) to blow one's nose without the use of a tissue, by blocking one nostril and blowing hard through the other nostril. □ **bucket of snots** *n.* [2000s] (*Irish*) an unattractive person. □ **scare the snot out of** *v.* [1980s] to terrify. □ **sling a snot** *v.* [late 19C–1900s] to blow one's nose with one's fingers. □ **throw snot about** *v.* [mid-17C] to weep.

snot *n.*[2] [he is seen as SNOTTY *adj.* (1)] [mid-19C] (*UK Und.*) a gentleman.

snot *adj. see* SNOTTY *adj.* (1).

snot *v.* **1** [early 19C+] (*US*) to treat disdainfully [SNOT *n.*[1] (2)]. **2** [1990s+] to hit in the nose [SNOT *n.*[1] (3)]. **3** [2000s] to weep.

snotnose *n.* [SNOT *n.*[1] + SE *nose*] [1920s+] (*orig. US*) **1** (*also* **snot**) an arrogant, snobbish person. **2** a small child with a running nose, a grubby child; also in fig. use. **3** (*also* **snot, snothole**) a young person.

snot-nosed *adj.* (*also* **snotnose**) [SNOTNOSE *n.*] **1** [1910s+] of a person, with a runny nose. **2** [1940s+] in fig. use, of a young or immature person. **3** [1940s+] arrogant, snobbish.

snotrag *n.* [SNOT *n.*[1] (1) + SE *rag*] [late 19C+] a handkerchief; a paper tissue.

snotter *n.* [SNOT *n.*[1] (1)] **1** [mid-19C] the nose. **2** [mid-19C] a pickpocket who specializes in stealing handkerchiefs. **3** [mid-19C+] a (dirty, ragged) handkerchief; thus *snotter-hauling*, stealing handkerchiefs; a paper handkerchief. **4** [20C+] (*Ulster*) a dirty, unpleasant person.

snotter *v.* [ext. of Scot. *snotter*, to hit on the nose] [1910s] (*Aus.*) to kill.

snotter box *n.* **1** *see* SNOTBOX *under* SNOT *n.*[1]. **2** *see* SNOTTLE-BOX *n.*

snotters *n. see* SNOT *n.*[1].

snottery *adj.* [? var. on SNOTTY *adj.* (2)] [20C+] unpleasant, arrogantly annoyed.

snottinger *n.* [SNOT *n.*[1] (1)] [mid-19C] a pocket handkerchief.

snottle-box *n.* (*also* **snotter-box**) [SNOT *n.*[1] (1) + SE *box*] [late 18C–1950s] the nose.

snotty *adj.* [orig. late 17C SE] **1** [mid-19C+] (*also* **snot**) superior, snobbish, stuck-up. **2** [1910s+] (*Aus./US*) angry, irritated; thus *snottiness*, ill-temper, irritation. **3** [1950s+] dirty, paltry, contemptible.

snotty *adv.* [SNOTTY *adj.* (1)] [1930s+] arrogantly, in a domineering manner.

snotty-box *n. see* SNOTBOX *under* SNOT *n.*[1].

snotty-nose *n.* [SE until 19C] [19C+] **1** a dirty, contemptible, grubby person [SNOT *n.*[1] (1)]. **2** an arrogant, snobbish person [SNOTTY *adj.* (1)].

snotty-nosed *adj.* [SE] **1** [20C+] lit. having a runny nose. **2** [1940s–80s] young, immature, childish. **3** [1950s+] arrogant, snobbish.

'snouns! *excl.* (*also* **cat's nouns! cox-nowns! nouns! 'snowns!**) [mid-16C–18C] a mild, blasphemous oath, a euph. for *God's wounds*.

snout *n.*[1] [play on SE *hogshead*, i.e. a 'pig's nose'] [late 18C–early 19C] (*UK Und.*) a hogshead.

snout *n.*[2] [SE *snout*; when tobacco was barred from prisons, a prisoner would mask his smoking by pretending to rub his nose] **1** [late 19C+] tobacco; thus (*UK prison*) *snout day*, the weekly issue of tobacco. **2** [1950s+] a cigarette.

IN COMPOUNDS

□ **snout baron** *n. see* BARON *n.* (3). □ **snout china** *n.* [CHINA (PLATE) *n.* (1)] [1940s–50s] (*UK prison*) an intimate friend, lit. one with whom one shares tobacco; the opposite of a GRAFT CHINA *under* GRAFT *n.*[2].

snout *n.*[3] [SE *snout*, nose; the person gets 'up one's nose'] [late 19C+] (*Aus./N.Z.*) a grudge.

IN PHRASES

□ **have a snout on someone** *v.* (*also* **take a snout on someone**) [20C+] to bear a grudge against someone, to take offence.

snout *n.*[4] [SNOUT *v.*[2] (1)] [1920s+] an informer; thus *snouting*, passing on information to the police.

snout *v.*[1] [SE *snout*; to 'stick one's nose in the air'] [1910s] (*Aus./N.Z.*) to bear ill-will towards, to treat with disfavour, to rebuff; thus *snouted*, rebuffed, jilted.

DERIVATIVES

□ **snouted** *adj.* [1910s+] (*Aus.*) in trouble, out of favour; thus *snouted on*, bearing ill will towards.

snout *v.*[2] **1** [1920s+] to act as a police informer [SE *snout*, i.e. one who 'pokes their nose in']. **2** [1960s+] (*also* **snout around, snout about**) to search [SE *snout*, i.e. one who 'roots around'].

snouter *n.* [SNOUT *n.*[2] (1)] [1940s–70s] a tobacconist; thus *snoutery*, a tobacco wholesaler.

snout-piece *n.* [SE *snout*] [17C–19C] the nose, the face.

snouty *n.* [var. on SNOUT *n.*[2] (1)] [1930s] (*UK Und.*) tobacco.

snouty *adj.* [having one's 'snout' or nose in the air] [mid-19C] overbearing, insolent.

snow *n.*[1] [the colour and consistency; the usu. ref. is to cocaine] **1** in senses of colour, i.e. whiteness. **(a)** [19C] (*UK Und.*) (wet) linen [it 'falls' on the hedges where it is left to dry]. **(b)** [1910s+] money, silver coins, small silver change. **(c)** [1940s+] (*Aus.*) (*also* **snowy**) a blond-haired person. **(d)** [1950s–60s] (*US black*) a white woman. **(e)** [1950s+] any white person. **(f)** [1960s+] (*Aus. juv.*) a blond-haired weakling. **2** in drug uses. **(a)** [1910s+] cocaine; thus *snow party*, a party where the guests take cocaine. **(b)** [1920s+] heroin; *snowey*, a heroin addiction. **(c)** [1930s–80s] morphine. **(d)** [1990s+] crack cocaine. **(e)** [2000s] amphetamine.

pertaining to linen

IN COMPOUNDS

□ **snow-birding** *n.* [1970s+] (*Aus./N.Z.*) stealing washing, usu. women's underwear, from clothes-lines. □ **snow-drop/**

-dropper/-dropping *see* separate entries. ❑ **snow-gatherer** *n.* [mid-19C] (*UK Und.*) one who who steals clean clothes off the hedges. ❑ **snow-hunting** *n. see* SNOW-DROPPING *n.* ❑ **snow lay** *n.* [LAY *n.*[3] (1)] [mid-19C] (*UK Und.*) the practice of stealing laundry from clothes-lines. ❑ **snow rig** *n.* [RIG *n.*[2] (1)] [late 18C] (*US Und.*) stealing clothes hanging in the open air.

pertaining to drugs

IN COMPOUNDS

❑ **snowbank** *n.* [1920s–50s] (*US drugs*) a place where cocaine users gather to take their drug. ❑ **snowball** *n. see* separate entry. ❑ **snow bird** *n. see* separate entry. ❑ **snow-cap** *n.* [SE *cap*] [1980s] (*drugs*) cocaine sprinkled onto a pipe of marijuana and smoked. ❑ **snowcones** *n.* [play on US ice-cream brand] [1980s+] (*drugs*) cocaine. ❑ **snowfall** *n. see* separate entry. ❑ **snowflake** *n. see* separate entry. ❑ **snow flower** *n.* [literary synon. for woman] [1920s–50s] (*US drugs*) a female cocaine addict. ❑ **snow pallets** *n.* [1980s+] (*drugs*) amphetamine. ❑ **snow seals** *n.* **1** [1980s] a kind of waterproof packet used to package cocaine. **2** [2000s] (*drugs*) a mix of cocaine and amphetamine. ❑ **snowstorm** *n. see* SNOWFALL *n.* ❑ **snow toke** *n.* [TOKE *n.*[2] (1)] [1980s+] (*drugs*) crack cocaine. ❑ **snow white** *n.* [1950s+] (*drugs*) cocaine.

IN PHRASES

❑ **blow snow** *v.* [1950s–70s] (*drugs*) to inhale cocaine. ❑ **caught in a snowstorm** *adj.* **1** [1920s–50s] (*US drugs*) under the influence of cocaine, esp. when experiencing extreme effects. **2** [1930s] experiencing the hallucinations which accompany an overdose of morphine. ❑ **snow powder and rocks** *n.* [1980s+] (*Aus. prison*) a specific grade of heroin.

based on colour

IN COMPOUNDS

❑ **snowball** *see* separate entries. ❑ **snowdrop** *n. see* separate entry. ❑ **snowflake** *n. see* separate entry. ❑ **snow job** *n. see* separate entry. ❑ **snow queen** *n.* (*also* **snow shoveller**) [QUEEN *n.* (2)] [1970s+] (*US black/gay*) a homosexual, whether black or white, who prefers blond, 'Nordic' partners. ❑ **snow storm** *n.* **1** [1970s+] (*US gay*) a heavy ejaculation of semen. **2** *see* SNOWFALL *n.* ❑ **snow top** *n.* [1950s] (*US*) a white-haired person.

IN PHRASES

❑ **put snow in one's game** *v.* [GAME *n.* (6)] [1960s+] (*US black*) to ensnare a white person for financial gain.

SE in slang uses

IN COMPOUNDS

❑ **snowball** *v. see* separate entry. ❑ **snow bird** *n. see* separate entry. ❑ **snowbound** *adj. see* SNOWED *adj.* ❑ **snow broth** *n.* [SE *snow-broth*, water produced or obtained by the melting of snow, esp. from natural causes] [late 19C–1910s] cold tea. ❑ **snow bunny** *n.* [BUNNY *n.*[1] (1b)] **1** [1950s+] (*orig. US*) a woman who frequents the ski slopes as much for the sex as for the sport [note WW2 US milit. *snow bunny*, a novice skier]. **2** [2000s] (*US black*) a white woman. ❑ **snowfall** *n. see* SNOW JOB *n.*[1]. ❑ **snow job** *see* separate entries. ❑ **snowman** *n. see* separate entry. ❑ **snow shoe** *n.* [1930s] (*US tramp*) hot chocolate.

IN PHRASES

❑ **roast snow in a furnace** *v.* [19C+] to attempt the impossible. ❑ **snow again** [pun] [1930s–50s] a phr. used to request someone to repeat an ill-heard statement; often ext. as *snow again, I didn't catch your drift*.

snow *n.*[2] [abbr. SNOW JOB *n.*[1]] [1950s+] (*orig. US*) smooth talk, bluff, bluster, lies.

snow *adj.* [SNOW *n.*[1] (1e)] [1970s] (*US black*) white.

snow *v.* (*also* **snow under, snow up**) [fig. use of SE *snow*] [late 19C+] (*US*) to confuse with a deluge of smooth, if insincere, talk.

snow and ice *n.* [rhy. sl.] [20C+] the price.

snow and slushed *adj.* [rhy. sl.] [2000s] flushed.

snowball *n.*[1] [? SE *snowball*, a cocktail orig. based on crème de menthe, now on advocaat] **1** [late 17C] an ejaculation. **2** [1990s+] semen that has been ejaculated in a partner's mouth and that is then returned via a passionate kiss [SNOWBALL *v.*[2]].

snowball *n.*[2] (*also* **snowdrop**) **1** [late 18C–early 19C] a black person [a humourless joc. reversal]. **2** [1930s+] (*US/W.I.*) an ice-cream cornet or an iced confection. **3** [1940s+] (*US black/W.I.*) a white person. **4** [1980s] (*US gay*) a black homosexual. **5** [1990s+] (*drugs*) MDMA [the white pill].

SE in slang uses

IN PHRASES

❑ **eat snowballs** *v.* [1930s] (*US tramp*) to stay in the north during the winter (many tramps wintered in the warmer south).

snowball *n.*[3] [SNOW *n.*[1] (2a)] (*US drugs*) **1** [1930s+] cocaine. **2** [1940s] a narcotic drug addict.

snowball *v.*[1] [? weather forecasting] [1900s–10s] (*US*) to predict.

snowball *v.*[2] [1970s+] to fellate and then spit the ejaculated semen back into one's partner's mouth.

snow bird *n.*[1] [SE *snow* + BIRD *n.*[1] (3a)] **1** [1900s–30s] (*US*) an impoverished tramp who enlists in the forces as the winter arrives in order to get food and shelter for the next few months then deserts when the warmer weather returns. **2** [1920s–40s] (*US tramp*) a tramp who goes south for the winter. **3** [1920s+] (*US, Florida and other Southern states*) a winter tourist who travels south to avoid the chilly weather. **4** [1920s+] a fan of winter weather and/or winter sports. **5** [1990s+] (*US gay*) a wealthy gay man who moves to Miami, Florida, one of the US's gay capitals, to enjoy sun and sex.

snow bird *n.*[2] [SNOW *n.*[1] (2) + BIRD *n.*[1] (3a)] (*drugs*) **1** [1910s–60s] a cocaine user. **2** [1920s+] (*US Und.*) a heroin or morphine addict. **3** [1930s] a woman involved in the cocaine trade [BIRD *n.*[1] (1b)].

snowdrop *n.* **1** [1940s+] a military police officer [the distinctive white caps]. **2** *see* SNOWBALL *n.*[2].

snow-drop *v.* [SNOW-DROPPING *n.*] [late 19C+] to steal clothes from a washing line.

snow-dropper *n.* [SNOW-DROP *v.*] [mid-19C+] (*Aus./UK Und.*) a person who steals washing from clothes-lines.

snow-dropping *n.* (*also* **snow-hunting**) [SNOW *n.*[1]] [mid-19C+] (*Aus./UK Und.*) the stealing of washing, usu. women's underwear, from unguarded clothes-lines.

snowed *adj.* (*also* **snowbound**) [SNOW *n.*[1] (2)] [1920s+] (*drugs*) under the influence of heroin or cocaine; thus punning synon. *snowed in, snowed up*.

snowed over *adj.* [play on SE *snowed under*, overburdened] [1970s+] (*US campus*) obsessively in love, infatuated.

snowfall *n.* (*also* **snow-storm**) [SNOW *n.*[1] (2)] [1950s] (*US drugs*) the using of cocaine or morphine.

snowflake *n.*[1] [SNOW *n.*[1] (2a) + FLAKE *n.*[1]] **1** [1950s] cocaine. **2** [1980s+] (*drugs*) crack cocaine.

snowflake *n.*[2] [SNOW *n.*[1] (1e) + SE *flake*/FLAKE *n.*[2] (1)] [1970s+] (*US black*) a white; or a black person who apes whites.

snowing *n.* [abbr. SNOW-DROPPING *n.*] [mid–late 19C] the stealing of linen from the drying grounds.

snowing down below! *excl.* [1930s–40s] (*N.Z.*) an excl. to a woman that her petticoat is showing.

snow job *n.*[1] (*also* **snowfall**) [SNOW *v.* + JOB *n.*[2] (2)/JOB *n.*[2] (1b)] [1940s+] (*US*) an untrue but totally convincing story, a con man's patter; also as v.

snow job *n.*[2] [the 'snow-whiteness' of semen + JOB *n.*[2] (2)] [1960s] (*US gay*) fellatio.

snowjob *v.* [SNOW JOB *n.*[1]] [1950s] (*US*) to flatter, to confuse.

snowman *n.* [SNOW *v.*] [1960s+] (*US*) anyone who has a smooth, seductive line of talk.

'snowns! *excl. see* 'SNOUNS! *excl.*

snow whites *n.* [rhy. sl.] [1970s+] tights.

snowy *n.* **1** [late 19C] linen [SNOW *n.*[1] (1a)]. **2** *see* SNOW *n.*[1] (1c).

snozzle *n.* (*also* **snoz, snoozle**) [var. on SCHNOZZLE *n.*] [1930s+] the nose.

snozzle *v.* [SNOZZLE *n.*] **1** [1920s] (*US*) to drink. **2** [1930s] (*US drugs*) to inhale cocaine or heroin.

snozzled *adj.* [SNOZZLE *v.* (1)] [1920s+] (*US*) drunk.

snozzler *n.* [1930s+] (*Aus./N.Z.*) anything or anyone considered excellent or attractive.

snozzy *adj. see* SNAZZY *adj.*

snubbed *adj.* [mid-19C] (*US*) drunk.

snubby *n.* (*also* **snubbie**) [SE *snub-nosed*] [1960s+] (*US*) a cheap, short-barrelled revolver.

snub devil *n.* [SE *snub*, to reject; i.e. he 'renounces the Devil and all his works'] [late 18C–late 19C] a parson.

snubs! *excl.* [SE *snub*; ult. Scand. *snubba*, to cut short] [1930s–40s] (*mainly teen*) used to indicate one's complete contempt for the subject of the excl.; usu. as *snubs to him/her.*

snucks *n.*

IN PHRASES

❑ **go snucks** *v.* [var. on *GO SNACKS under* SNACK *n.*[1]] [1910s] to divide up, to hand over a share of the profit.

snudge *n.* (*also* **smoudge, smudge**) [? SNEAK *n.*[1] (1) + BUDGE *n.*[1] (1); Nares defines it as 'a miser, or curmudgeon; a sneaking fellow'] [mid-17C–early 18C] (*UK Und.*) a thief who first enters a house, then hides, and emerges when the coast is clear to effect the robbery; also a mean, miserly person.

snuff *n.*[1] [SE *snuff*, a fit of temper, emotion]

IN PHRASES

❑ **in high snuff** *adj.* (*also* **in great snuff, in mighty snuff**) **1** [late 17C; mid-19C–1930s] elated, very happy. **2** [early 19C] of dress, showy, stylish. **3** [mid-19C–1930s] healthy, in good shape.

snuff *n.*[2] [SNUFF *v.*[2] (2)] **1** [1930s+] a murder. **2** *see* SNUFF MOVIE *under* SNUFF *v.*[2].

snuff *n.*[3] [SE *snuff*, a preparation of powdered tobacco] [1950s] (*US teen*) heroin; thus *snuff-peddler*, a heroin seller.

SE in slang uses

IN COMPOUNDS

❑ **snuff-box** *n.* **1** [early–mid-19C] the nose. **2** [mid-19C] a coffin [visual resemblance]. **3** [1940s] a gas mask. **4** [1980s] a short person. ❑ **snuff-dipper** *n.* [? play on SE *snuff-dipper*, a snuff-chewer, i.e. a ref. to the provision of oral sex or SNUFF *v.*[2] (2), i.e. the possibility of her being killed while working] [1970s] (*US*) a prostitute working from a car. ❑ **snuff-lurker** *n. see* SNEEZE-LURKER *under* SNEEZE *n.* ❑ **snuff racket** *n.* [RACKET *n.*[1] (1)] [early 19C] (*UK Und.*) temporarily blinding a shopkeeper with a handful of snuff, then seizing his money or stock. ❑ **snuff stick** *n.* [SE *snuff-stick*, an implement for dipping snuff] [1970s] (*N.Z.*) a cigarette.

IN PHRASES

❑ **give someone snuff** *v.* [SE *snuff*; the image is of beating someone to powder] [late 19C–1920s] to punish, to reprimand. ❑ **like snuff at a wake** *adv.* [20C+] (*Irish*) **1** very quickly. **2** in large amounts. ❑ **take snuff** *v.* (*also* **take in snuff**) [SE *snuff*, the unpleasant smell of a snuffed candle, thus one fig. 'turns up one's nose'] [late 16C–mid-19C] to be offended; thus *in snuff*, offended.

snuff *adj.* [1980s] (*orig. US*) pertaining to a SNUFF MOVIE *under* SNUFF *v.*[2].

snuff *v.*[1] [early 19C] (*UK Und.*) to throw snuff into a victim's face, rendering them temporarily blind and thus easier to rob.

snuff *v.*[2] [SE *snuff out*] **1** [late 19C] to stop doing something. **2** [1960s+] to murder, to kill. **3** [1970s+] (*US black*) to knock someone down.

IN COMPOUNDS

❑ **snuff powder** *n.* [1960s] (*US drugs*) a poisoned injection, a 'hot shot'. ❑ **snuff movie** *n.* (*also* **snuff, snuffer, snuff film**) [1980s+] (*orig. US*) a film, usu. pornographic, that climaxes in the actual death of one of the participants, usu. an actress or, if paedophiliac, a child.

IN PHRASES

❑ **snuff (it)** *v.* [mid-19C+] to die. ❑ **snuff out** *v.* **1** [mid-19C–1940s] to die. **2** [mid-19C–1940s] to kill. **3** [1900s] to dismiss or reject someone. ❑ **snuff someone's candle** *v.* (*also* **snuff someone's light, snuff the wick**) **1** [20C+] to kill, to murder. **2** [1910s] (*Aus.*) to die.

snuff *v.*[3] [SE *snuff*, to sniff] [1910s–50s] (*US drugs*) to sniff cocaine or similar drug.

snuff *v.*[4] [SE *snuffle up*] [1930s] to eat.

snuffer *n.*[1] [SE *snuff*, to sniff/SNUFF *v.*[3]] **1** [1910s] (*US drugs*) a cocaine user. **2** [1910s–40s] (*US black*) the nose.

snuffer *n.*[2] *see* SNUFF MOVIE *under* SNUFF *v.*[2].

snuffers *n.* [SE *snuff*, to sniffle or *snuffer*, a cone-shaped implement for extinguishing candles; orig. of SNUFFER *n.*[1] (2)] [mid-17C–early 18C] the nostrils.

snuffers! *excl.* [? the insubstantiality of SE *snuff*] [late 19C] a mild excl.

snuffer-tray *n.* [it 'carries' the SNUFFERS *n.*] [mid-19C–1900s] in boxing, the nose.

snuffle *n.* **1** [early–mid-19C] the nose [SE *snuff*, to sniffle or *snuffer*, a cone-shaped implement for extinguishing candles]. **2** [mid-19C+] (*Aus./N.Z*) pious cant, humbug.; thus phr. *on the snuffle*, canting, uttering sanctimonious pieties; thus a nickname for a puritan [the SE *snuffling* tones of the self-appointed moralist].

IN COMPOUNDS

❑ **snuffle-buster** *n.* (*also* **snufflebody**) [late 19C–1900s] (*Aus./N.Z.*) a puritan; thus *snuffle-busting, snufflebustious*, puritanical.

snuffling community *n.* [ety. unknown; ? SE *snuffle*, as ? to sniff, to talk through the nose was a characteristic of contemporary prostitutes] [early 18C] prostitutes, seen collectively.

snuffy *n.*[1] [SNUFF *v.*[3]] [1950s] (*US drugs*) one who inhales (rather than injects) a narcotic.

snuffy *n.*[2] [ety. unknown] [1960s–70s] (*US*) a combat infantryman; a Marine.

snuffy *adj.* [*OED* links this to SE *snuff*, but no real relevance] [mid-18C–mid-19C] tipsy, drunk.

snug *n.* [SE *snug*, comfortable, cosy] **1** [early 19C+] the bar-parlour of a public house or inn. **2** [20C+] (*US Und.*) a small revolver that can be concealed easily.

snug *adj.* [SE *snug*, comfortable, cosy] [19C] drunk.

SE in slang uses

IN PHRASES

❑ **all's snug** [early 18C–early 19C] all is quiet.

snug *v.*[1] [SE *snug*, to snuggle] [19C] to have sexual intercourse with.

IN PHRASES

❑ **bit of snug** *n.* [late 19C] sexual intercourse.

snug *v.*[2] [SE *snug*, to place neatly] [mid-19C] (*US*) to steal, to conceal from the proper owner.

snuggies *n.* [despite the root in SE *snug*, i.e. cosy, not necessarily of winter thickness] [1970s] (*US campus*) women's underwear.

snuggle-pup *n.* [1920s–30s] (*US teen*) a young man or woman who enjoys partying; one's boyfriend or girlfriend.

snuggy *n.* [SE *snug/snuggle*] **1** [1940s–50s] a woman's muff. **2** [1990s+] (*US*) a sexually attractive woman who is looking for sexual liaisons. **3** *see* WEDGIE *n.*

snug's the word! *excl.* [SE *snug*, i.e. covered up] [18C–mid-19C] say nothing about this!

snurge *n.* [ety. unknown] **1** [1920s–40s] a Poor Law Institution. **2** [1930s–50s] a tattle-tale, a sycophant. **3** [1930s+] a generally contemptible person (reputed to sniff women's bicycle seats).

snurge *v.* [ety. unknown; ? link to SNEAK *n.*[1] (2)] [1930s+] to sneak off to avoid work or responsibilities.

snuskin *n. see* SNOOZING KEN *n.* (2).

snyde *n. see* SNIDE *n.*

snyde-pitcher *n. see* SNIDE PITCHER *under* SNIDE *n.*

snyder *n.* (*also* **snider**) [Ger. *schneider*, a tailor] [17C–mid-19C] a tailor.

snydey *adj. see* SNIDE *adj.*

so *adj.* [euph.] **1** [19C] drunk. **2** [mid-19C] flustered, overcome emotionally. **3** [mid-19C+] menstruating. **4** [late 19C] pregnant. **5** [late 19C–1950s] homosexual.

so *adv.* [1970s+] (*US campus/teen*) completely, utterly.

so! *excl.* [1910s+] used to add emphasis to a statement contradicting a negative assertion made by the previous speaker, e.g. 'No you didn't.' 'I did so!'.

s.o.a.b. *n. see* S.O.B. *n.*

soak *n.*[1] [SOAK *v.*[1] (1)] **1** [late 18C+] a drunkard, usu. with *old*; note earlier SOAKER *n.*[1] (1). **2** [mid-19C] (*US*) a drink. **3** [mid-19C+] a heavy drinking session. **4** [1900s–50s] a despised person.

IN COMPOUNDS

❑ **soakapee** *n.* [SE *soak* + PEE *n.*[1] (1); such drunkards may well foul their clothes] [1940s] (*W.I.*) a habitual drunkard, an alcoholic. ❑ **soakpot** *n.* [early 18C] a drunkard.

IN PHRASES

❑ **get a soak on** *v.* [late 19C] (*US*) to drink heavily.

soak *n.*[2] [SOAK *v.*[2]] [1900s] (*US*) a blow.

soak *v.*[1] **1** in context of alcohol. (**a**) [17C+] to drink heavily; thus (late 19C) *come out of soak*, to get over one's hangover; adj., *soaky*, drunk. (**b**) [19C] to ply with liquor. (**c**) [1900s] to spend money on drink. **2** in monetary senses. (**a**) [mid-19C–1920s] (*also* **put into soak**) to pawn; to give as collateral. (**b**) [1910s–40s] (*US campus*) to borrow [one leaves one's possession 'to soak'].

IN PHRASES

❑ **in soak** **1** [mid–late 19C] in prison. **2** [mid-19C+] in pawn. **3** [late 19C] (*Aus.*) drunk. ❑ **put into soak** *v. see* sense 2a above. ❑ **soak it** *v.* (*also* **let it soak**) [late 19C+] of a man, to linger before withdrawing one's penis after intercourse.

SE in slang uses

IN PHRASES

❑ **soak one's clay** *v. see* MOISTEN THE CLAY *under* CLAY *n.* ❑ **soak one's face** *v.* (*also* **soak the face**) [SE *face*] [late 18C+] to drink, to quench one's thirst. ❑ **soak the chaffer** *v. see under* CHAFFER *n.*[2]. ❑ **soak the mill** *v.* [SE *mill*, used as generic for one's property] [late 19C] (*US*) to drink away one's possessions.

IN EXCLAMATIONS

❑ **go soak your head!** (*also* **go soap your ear!**) [late 19C+] an abusive, dismissive remark.

soak *v.*[2] (*also* **soak it to**) [var. on SOCK *v.*[1] (1)] [late 19C+] **1** (*US*) to hit; also in fig. use. **2** (*US*) in fig. use, to give, to punish, to criticize. **3** (*orig. US*) to overcharge or charge a high price, to tax heavily, to extort money from, to cheat. **4** (*US*) to win money from; thus in passive, to lose.

soak away *v. see* SOCK *v.*[2] (2).

soaked *adj.* [SOAK *v.*[1] (1)] **1** [late 16C; mid-19C+] (*also* **soakful**) drunk. **2** [1910s+] (*US*) intoxicated by a drug.

soaked bum *n.* [1900s] (*US short order*) a portion of beets.

soaker *n.*[1] [SOAK *v.*[1] (1)] **1** [late 16C+] (*also* **soker**) a drunkard, a drinker. **2** [1910s] a drunken spree.

soaker *n.*[2] **1** [mid-19C–1910s] very wet weather; a very wet day. **2** [late 19C–1920s] (*US tramp*) a sickening experience.

soaker *n.*[3] [? SOAK *v.*[2] (1)] [1940s–50s] (*US prison*) a warder.

soakful *adj. see* SOAKED *adj.* (1).

soak it to *v. see* SOAK *v.*[2].

so-and-so *n.* **1** [mid-19C+] (*also* **so-and-such**) an unspecified object, person or place. **2** [late 19C+] a euph. for any derog. name, esp. SONOFABITCH *n.*

so-and-so *adj.* **1** [mid-18C; 1920s+] a euph. for any obscenity. **2** [1910s–20s] in a given manner.

soap *n.*[1] **1** [19C] a thick soup. **2** [mid-19C–1930s] (*US*) money, esp. corruption money. **3** [mid-19C+] flattery; the act of flattering someone [abbr. SOFT SOAP *n.*]. **4** [late 19C–1900s] (*also* **bit of soap**) women, esp. promiscuous ones or prostitutes. **5** [late 19C+] (*Aus.*) processed cheese. **6** [1980s+] (*Aus. prison*) a prisoner who does not wash. **7** [2000s] (*US drugs*) gamma hydroxybutyrate (GHB).

IN COMPOUNDS

❑ **soap-crawler** *n.* [mid-19C–1900s] a toady. ❑ **soap dope** *n.* [2000s] (*US drugs*) methamphetamine with a pinkish tint.

IN PHRASES

❑ **bit of soap** *n. see* sense 4 above. ❑ **lump of soap** *n.* [late 19C–1900s] a woman. ❑ **no soap** *see* separate entry. ❑ **out of soap** *adj.* (*US*) impoverished, bankrupt.

SE in slang uses

IN COMPOUNDS

❑ **soap dodger** *n.* [the supposed dirtiness of those concerned] [1990s+] **1** a Protestant, as used in Scotland and Northern Ireland; thus adj. *soapdodging*. **2** (*UK prison*) a prisoner who chooses to avoid showering. **3** anyone seen as dirty, e.g. a 'New Age' traveller. **4** (*Aus.*) a newly arrived British immigrant. ❑ **soap game** *n.* [1930s–40s] (*US Und.*) a form of confidence trick that involves the apparent wrapping of bars of soap in $20 bills; the bars are then sold to victims. ❑ **soap-locked/locks** *see* separate entries. ❑ **soap-suds** *n.* [early 19C] hot gin and water, with lemon and lump sugar.

IN PHRASES

❑ **drop the soap** *v. see* separate entry. ❑ **how are you off for soap?** [mid–late 19C; 1990s] a general phr. of greeting, i.e. *how are things? how are you doing?*

soap *n.*[2] [? JOE SOAP *n.* (2)] [1950s+] (*Aus.*) a fool, a simpleton.

soap *n.*[3] [rhy. sl. = DOPE *n.*[1] (6)] [2000s] (*drugs*) cannabis.

soap *n.*[4] *see* SOAP OPERA *n.*

soap *v.* [SOAP *n.*[1] (3)] [mid-19C+] to flatter.

IN PHRASES

❑ **soap over** *v.* [mid-19C] to humbug. ❑ **soap the geyser** *v.* [the addition of special *soap* to a geyser to improve its spouting] [1940s+] (*N.Z.*) to get started, to set off. ❑ **soap up** *v.* [1950s] (*US*) to act kindly, to ingratiate oneself.

IN EXCLAMATIONS

❑ **go soap your ear!** *see* GO SOAK YOUR HEAD! *under* SOAK *v.*[1].

soap and flannel *n.* [rhy. sl. = SE *the panel*, those doctors who accepted patients under the National Health Insurance Act (1913)] [1910s–40s] the drawing of sickness benefit.

soap and lather *n.* [rhy. sl.] [late 19C+] a father.

soap and water *n.* [rhy. sl.] [20C+] a daughter.

soapbox artist *n.* [-ARTIST *sfx*] [1930s] (*N.Z.*) a public orator, esp. an extremist or rabble-rouser.

soapboxer *n.* [early 20C] (*US*) a public orator, a rabble-rouser.

soaped *adj.* [SOAP *n.*[3]] [1940s] (*S.Afr. drugs*) under the influence of marijuana.

soaper *n.*[1] *see* SOAP OPERA *n.*

soaper *n.*[2] *see* SOPOR *n.*

soap-freak *n. see under* SOAP OPERA *n.*

soapie *n.* [1980s+] (*Aus./N.Z./S.Afr.*) a radio or TV soap opera.

soap-locked *adj.* [SOAP LOCKS *n.*] [mid-19C] wearing SOAP LOCKS *n.*

soap locks *n.* [mid-19C] (*US*) **1** a hairstyle favoured by the New York gangs of the period, a lock of hair was carefully curled then covered with soap to make it lie flat; thus the rowdy young men who adopted the style. **2** in sing., one who wears this hairstyle, thus a gang member, a thug.

soap opera *n.* (*also* **soap, soaper**) [the original 1920s radio show, *The Goldbergs*, was sponsored by US soap manufacturer Proctor & Gamble] [1930s+] (*orig. US*) **1** a radio or TV drama series, e.g. *The Archers*, *Coronation Street*, which tells the interminable tale of supposedly 'ordinary life'; also as v., to watch a soap opera. **2** also in fig. use, of anything endlessly repetitive, albeit melodramatic.

IN COMPOUNDS

❑ **soap-freak** *n.* [-FREAK *sfx*] [2000s] (*US*) a fan or devotee of radio or TV drama series.

soap opera *adj.* [SOAP OPERA *n.*] [1930s+] (*US*) typical of family and social life as it is portrayed in radio or TV drama series, e.g. *soap opera mentality*.

soaps, the *n.* [1940s+] (*orig. US*) a generic term for radio and TV drama series.

soapy *adj.* **1** [mid-19C+] ingratiating, unctuous, smoothly insincere [? originated in the nickname '*Soapy* Sam', used of Bishop Wilberforce (1805–73)]. **2** [1930s+] (*Aus.*) foolish, silly, effeminate. **3** [1990s+] typical of family and social life as portrayed in radio and TV drama series [SOAP OPERA *n.*].

IN COMPOUNDS

❑ **soapy fits** *n.* [late 19C] (*UK Und.*) a fake fit used to obtain sympathetically donated alms, created by chewing a small piece of soap, thus creating 'foam' at the mouth.

soapy bubble *n.* [rhy. sl.] [1990s+] trouble.

soapy Isaac *n. see* SUETY ISAAC *n.*

soar *v.* [i.e. up to heaven] [late 19C] (*Aus.*) to die.

s.o.b. *n.* (*also* **s.o.a.b., sob, s. of b.**) [abbr.] **1** [1910s+] a general term of abuse, i.e. *s*on *o*f a *b*itch. **2** [1910s+] silly old *b*ugger/*b*astard. **3** [1920s+] *s*hit *o*r *b*ust. **4** [1940s+] an unspecified object or person, without pej. overtones.

sob *n.*[1] **1** [1900s] (*Aus.*) talk; conversation. **2** [20C+] a pitiful, if dubious tale, a 'sob-story'; thus adj. *sobby*.

IN COMPOUNDS

❑ **sob act** *n.* [1950s+] (*US*) a pretence of emotion, an appeal to someone's sympathies. ❑ **sob book** *n.* [early 1900s] (*US*) any form of mawkish, sentimental fiction, aimed at a female market. ❑ **sob brother** *n.* [play on SOB SISTER below] [1910s] (*US*) a sentimental man. ❑ **sob-raiser** *n.* (*also* **sob specialist**) [1910s–1930s] (*US*) one who plays on the public's emotion to elicit sympathy for a cause. ❑ **sob-reporter** *n.* [1920s] (*US*) a journalist specializing in 'human interest' stories. ❑ **sob sister** *n.* (*US*) **1** [1910s+] an advice columnist, usu. a woman; a woman journalist. **2** [1920s+] by ext. of sense 1, a liberal, a 'do-gooder'. **3** [1920s+] a woman, occas. a man, given to tearfulness. **4** [1940s] (*US Und.*) a beggar (of either sex) who attempts to play on people's emotions to elicit money. ❑ **sob squad** *n.* [1910s] (*US*) a generic term for journalists specializing in 'human interest' stories. ❑ **sob story** *n.* (*also* **sob music**) [1910s+] a pitiful tale, which may reduce the listener to tears whether it has any basis in truth or is designed merely for felonious purposes. ❑ **sob stuff** *n.* [1910s+] distressing facts, stories etc, often used to obtain sympathy and poss. money too.

sob *n.*[2] *see* SOV *n.*

SoBe *n.* [abbr.] [1990s+] (*US gay*) *So*uth *Be*ach Miami, Florida, popular among gay men.

sober-water *n.* [the pun reflects its use as a partial cure for hangovers] [mid-19C] soda water.

sob the blues *v. see under* BLUES *n.*[1] (1).

soc *n.* (*also* **soch, sosh**) [abbr. SE *social*] **1** [1900s–70s] one who behaves in a socially acceptable manner, usu. in a negative sense, ie lacking in anything other than polish. **2** [1960s+] (*US teen*) a social climber.

socdol(l)ager *n. see* SOCKDOLAGER *n.*

Social, the *n.* [1970s+] the local office of the Department of Health and Social Security, from where one gets unemployment and other benefits.

social *adj.*

IN PHRASES

❑ **go social** *v.* [1960s] (*US teen gangs*) to maintain a truce.

social dandruff *n.* [they spread through physical proximity] [1970s+] (*US gay*) a pubic louse.

social donut (hole) *n.* [i.e. an 'empty space'] [1980s+] (*US campus*) a socially inept person.

social E *n.* [late 19C] (*middle class*) a euph. for *social* evil, itself coined in 1857 as a euph. for prostitution.

social work *n.*

IN PHRASES

❑ **do social work** *v. see under* DO *v.*[1].

social worker *n.* [1960s–70s] (*US gay*) a homosexual who finds partners among homeless and destitute men.

society *n.* [late 19C] the workhouse.

socio *n.* [abbr.] [1970s] (*US/P.R.*) a social worker.

sock *n.*[1] **1** [late 17C; mid–late 19C] credit, esp. as *on sock*, on credit. **2** [late 17C–18C] a pocket. **3** [1920s–50s] a sock used as a receptacle for money. **4** [1930s–50s] the store of money itself, as in a bag, safe etc. **5** [1970s] a filthy, messy room, i.e. as used by a student, young man etc [coined by UK novelist Martin Amis (b.1949) and enjoyed brief popularity].

SE in slang uses

IN PHRASES

❑ **gamble one's socks** *v. see* BET ONE'S BOOTS *under* BET *v.* ❑ **— one's socks off** *v.* (*also* **— the socks off**) [mid-19C+] used as an intensifier, e.g. BLOW THE SOCKS OFF *v.*; *KNOCK THE SOCKS OFF under* KNOCK *v.*; *ROT THE SOCKS OFF under* ROT *v.*; *see also* synons. at FUCK *v.*, POP *v.*[1] (1), SCREW *v.* ❑ **put a sock in it** *v.* (*also* **shove a sock in it, stick..., stuff...**) [it gags the mouth] [1910s+] to stop talking, to be quiet; esp. as imper. *put a sock in it!* ❑ **something in socks** *n.* [1910s+] a bachelor, a single man, supposedly what 'every woman wants'.

sock *n.*[2] [late 17C; 1900s–50s] a farthing or any small coin.

sock *n.*[3] [SOCK *v.*[1] (1)] **1** [late 17C+] a blow. **2** [1900s–10s] a shock. **3** [1930s] (*US*) a thrill, excitement, a 'kick'. **4** [1930s+] in show business, a success. **5** [1950s] (*US*) marijuana, a marijuana cigarette.

sock *n.*[4] [1990s+] (*US black/juv.*) a penis.

sock *adj.* [fig. use of SOCK *n.*[3] (1)] [20C+] excellent, first-rate.

IN COMPOUNDS

❑ **sock frock** *n.* [joc./assonant use of SE *frock*] [1940s] (*US black*) one's best suit.

sock *v.*[1] (*also* **sock up**) [ety. unknown] **1** [late 17C+] to hit, to punch; thus *sock into*, to assault, to beat; *give someone sock(s)*, to give someone a thrashing. **2** [mid-19C] (*US*) to knock someone's hat over their head. **3** [late 19C] (*US*) to throw. **4** [late 19C–1900s] (*US*) (*also* **sock down**) to pay. **5** [late 19C–1970s] to thrust an object. **6** [20C+] in fig. use, to 'hit'. **7** [1900s] (*US*) to give. **8** [1910s–60s] (*Aus.*) (*also* **sock away, sock down**) to drink (alcohol). **9** [1920s+] as *sock for*, to demand, to extort.

IN PHRASES

❑ **sock it on** *v.* [20C+] to wager money. ❑ **sock it to** *v. see* separate entry. ❑ **sock the clock** *v.* [1930s+] to register on the time clock.

sock *v.*[2] (*also* **sock away, sock in, soak away**) [SOCK *n.*[1]] **1** [mid–late 19C] to obtain credit. **2** [late 19C–1950s] (*orig. US*) to set aside money for savings. **3** [1900s] (*Aus.*) to pocket.

sockdolager *n.* (*also* **slockdolager, slockdologer, socdol(l)ager, sockdologer, sogdologer, stockdolager**) [SOCK *v.*[1] (1) + ? Irish *dallacher*, the act of blinding or dazing or UK dial. *dallack*, to dress gaudily. The adj. form, *sockdolagizing*, was among the last words that President Abraham Lincoln heard: it is used in the play *Our American Cousin* in a line that was spoken by the cousin himself (Asa Trenchard) at the very moment when Lincoln's assassin fired the fatal shot] **1** [early 19C+] (*orig. US*) a knock-down blow, a heavy blow; thus fig., something conclusive. **2** [mid-19C+] a exceptional person or thing, esp. if large.

socked *adj.* [fig. use of SOCK *v.*[1] (1)] [2000s] intoxicated by drink or drugs.

socked in *adv.* **1** [1950s] (*Irish*) joined up with, as in having sexual relations. **2** [1980s] isolated, cut off.

socker *n.* [SOCK *v.*[1] (1)] **1** [late 18C] a thug, a lout. **2** [late 18C] a simpleton, a fool. **3** [late 19C+] a heavy blow. **4** [1920s+] one who hits powerfully.

sockeroo *n.* (*also* **sockerino**) [SOCK *n.*[3] (5) + -EROO *sfx*] [20C+] (*orig. US*) something very successful, a hit.

socket *n.* [mid-15C–19C] the vagina.

IN COMPOUNDS

❑ **socket-money** *n.* **1** [late 17C–mid-19C] a dowry. **2** [18C–19C] money paid by a man to his wife to placate her after he has been caught in an adulterous affair. **3** [early 19C] the payment given to a prostitute. **4** [mid-19C] hush-money.

IN PHRASES

❑ **on the socket** [1930s] practising blackmail.

socketer *n.* [SOCKET-MONEY *under* SOCKET *n.*] [mid-19C] a blackmailer.

sockful *n.* [1940s] (*US*) a large amount, usu. of money.

socking *n.* [SOCK *v.*[1] (1)] [20C+] a beating.

socking *adj.* [late 19C+] very great, enormous.

sock it to *v.* [fig. use of SOCK *v.*[1] (1); *sock it to me!* was popularized on TV's *Rowan & Martin's Laugh-In* (1967–73)] **1** [mid-19C+] (*also* **sock it in, sock it into**) to hit hard, lit. or fig., e.g. to charge someone a high price. **2** [late 19C–1900s] to reprimand. **3** [late 19C–1900s] in fig. sense, to 'hit', e.g. in playing an instrument. **4** [1910s+] an excl. of exhortation. **5** [1950s] to cuddle, to embrace. **6** [1950s+] to shock, to surprise; thus excl. *sock it to me!* amaze me! surprise me! **7** [1960s] (*orig. US black*) to have sexual intercourse. **8** [1960s] to explain.

socko *n.* [SOCKO *adj.*] [1930s+] a major success, a show business 'hit'.

socko *adj.* [SOCK *n.*[3] (5)] [1930s+] (*esp. show business*) wonderful, excellent.

socko *adv.* [1930s+] directly, forcefully.

so cool *n.* [COOL *adj.* (2); a play on the area's self-image] [1980s+] (*US campus*) southern California.

Sod *n.* [rhy. sl. = MOD *n.*[2] (1)] [1960s] (*Scot.*) a member of a teenage cult, the mods, orig. *c.*1961, who wore specific distinguishing clothes, rode motor scooters and fought their main rivals, the motorcycle-riding, leather-clad 'rockers'.

sod *n.*[1] [abbr. SE *sodomite*, but, except in sense 2, the sexual ref. is coincidental] **1** [early 19C+] an unpleasant person. **2** [late 19C+] a sodomite, a male homosexual. **3** [1910s+] a person, either pej., neutral or affectionate. **4** [1930s+] an animal, an object. **5** [1940s+] anything categorized as difficult or annoying to perform. **6** [1950s+] a general term of address, not necessarily pej.

IN COMPOUNDS

❑ **sod-all** *n.* [1940s+] absolutely nothing. ❑ **sod's law** *n.* [1970s+] a metaphorical 'law' of human experience, in this case the belief that 'if anything can go wrong in any situation, it will'.

IN PHRASES

❑ **sod about** *v.* [1950s+] to mess around, to waste time.

sod *n.*[2] [abbr. SE *sodden*] [20C+] (*Aus.*) a wet damper, i.e. a flour and water pancake.

sod *n.*[3] [SE *sot*] [1920s+] (*US campus*) a drunkard.

sod *n.*[4] *see* OLD SOD *n.*

SE, meaning a lump of earth, in slang uses

IN COMPOUNDS

❑ **sod-buster** *n.* [BUST *v.*[1] (1)] **1** [1910s+] a peasant, a farmer, an unsophisticated rural person. **2** [1920s] (*US*) an undertaker. ❑ **sod widow** *n.* [the corpse is 'under the sod'] [1900s–30s] an actual widow, whose husband has died.

sod *v.* [abbr.] **1** [late 19C; 1930s+] lit. to *sod*omize; thus fig. use, synon. with 'to hell with'. **2** [1950s] to butt in.

IN PHRASES

❑ **sod off** *v.* [SOD OFF! below] [1980s+] to go away, to leave.

IN EXCLAMATIONS

❑ **sod it!** (*also* **sod!**) [1940s+] a general excl. of exasperation, resignation, annoyance etc. ❑ **sod off!** [semi-euph. for FUCK OFF! *excl.*] [1940s+] go away! ❑ **sod that/this for a game of soldiers!** *see* FUCK THAT/THIS FOR A GAME OF SOLDIERS! *under* FUCK *v.* ❑ **sod you!** [semi-euph. for FUCK YOU! *excl.*] [late 19C+] a general excl. of hostility, dismissal.

soda *n.*[1] [? faro jargon *soda*, the top card that is exposed before the start of the game; this card is not counted for betting; see Asbury *Sucker's Progress* (1938) 16: 'An extraordinary number of the terms, technical and otherwise, which were employed by Faro players in the palmy days of the game have passed into the language [...] and are commonly used by millions who never heard of Faro. Here are some of them: [...] *Soda* — The first card, exposed face up before bets were made. Said to have been a corruption of zodiac'] [1930s+] (*Aus.*) something easy to accomplish, a simple task, an easy victim.

soda *n.*[2] [play on SE *baking soda*] [1980s+] (*US drugs*) a form of injectable cocaine used in Hispanic communities.

soda and B *n.* [late 19C] a drink of brandy and soda.

soda cracker *n.* (*also* **soda biscuit**) [such *crackers* or (UK) water biscuits are light in colour] [1960s+] (*US campus*) a white person.

soda-jerker/-juggler *n. see* JERKER *n.*[1] (1).

sodden *adj.* [note Shakespearian use of *sodden*, heavy, dull, stupefied] [late 19C+] drunk.

sodding *adj.* [SOD *n.*[1] (1)] [late 19C+] a derog. intensifier.

sodgeries *n.* [mispron. of SE *soldier*] [late 19C] a military exhibition, held in 1890 at the Chelsea Barracks.

Sodom and Gomorrah *v.* [rhy. sl.] [1990s+] to borrow.

sodomite *n.* [1990s+] (*W.I./Rasta*) a lesbian.

soetgirl *n.* [Afk. *soet*, sweet] [1980s] (*S.Afr.*) a prostitute.

sofa-pounder *n.* [1900s] (*US*) an observer, a non-participant.

sofa spud *n.* (*also* **sofa yam**) [SPUD *n.*[3] (1); var. on COUCH POTATO *under* COUCH *n.*] [1980s+] (*US campus*) someone who lies around doing nothing.

soft *n.* **1** [mid-19C–1900s] a weakling. **2** [20C+] a male homosexual. **3** [1930s] (*US black*) a woman, a girlfriend. **4** *see* SOFT MONEY *n.*

IN PHRASES

❑ **do the soft (on)** *v.* **1** [late 19C] to make love. **2** [1910s–20s] to flatter.

soft *adj.* **1** [late 17C; 19C+] stupid, dull, foolish; also in phr. *soft as shite*. **2** [mid-18C; 1920s] (*US campus*) partially or totally intoxicated by drink or drugs. **3** [19C+] overly kind, easily imposed upon; insufficiently ruthless; vulnerable. **4** [mid-19C+] easy, comfortable, requiring no effort. **5** [20C+] (*US campus*) weak, timid, not able to defend oneself. **6** [1940s] (*US Und.*) of a place, vulnerable. **7** [1950s] constr. with *on*, attracted to, in love with. **8** [1980s+] (*W.I. Rasta*) (*also* **soff**) unable to cope, impoverished. **9** [1980s+] (*W.I. Rasta*) not well done, amateurish. **10** [2000s] (*W.I. Rasta*) effeminate, homosexual; thus n. *softman*.

IN COMPOUNDS

❑ **soft bit** *n. see under* BIT *n.*[1]. ❑ **soft cop** *n.* **1** *see under* COP *n.*[1]. **2** *see under* COP *n.*[2]. ❑ **soft ha'porth** *n.* (*also* **daft ha'porth**) [20C+] a weakling, a simpleton. ❑ **soft-headed** *adj. see* SOFT IN THE HEAD below. ❑ **soft mark** *n. see under* MARK *n.*[1]. ❑ **soft number** *n. see under* NUMBER *n.* ❑ **soft one** *n.* **1** [early 19C+] (*UK Und.*) a gullible, easily fooled victim. **2** [1900s] in betting, a certainty. ❑ **soft roll** *n.* [ROLL IN THE HAY *n.* + play on SE] [1940s–50s] a woman who is easy to seduce. ❑ **soft snap** *n. see under* SNAP *n.*[1]. ❑ **soft stuff** *n.* **1** [late 19C+] (*Aus.*) 'soft', i.e. non-alcoholic or weak drinks. **2** [1920s] (*US Und.*) (*also* **soft sugar**) paper money, notes [var. on SOFT MONEY *n.* (1)]. **3** [1960s] (*drugs*) 'soft' drugs, e.g. cannabis, amphetamines rather than narcotics [STUFF *n.* (5)]. ❑ **soft sucker** *n. see* SISSY SOFT SUCKER *under* SISSY *n.* ❑ **soft teat** *n.* [1960s] (*US*) an easy job. ❑ **soft touch** *n. see under* TOUCH *n.*[1].

IN PHRASES

❑ **in soft** [1910s] (*US*) enjoying a comfortable situation. ❑ **soft in the head** *adj.* (*also* **soft-headed, soft in the shell, soft in the upper story**) [mid-17C+] stupid, poss. insane; thus n. *softhead*, a fool.

SE in slang uses

IN COMPOUNDS

❑ **soft ass** *see* separate entries. ❑ **soft-arsed** *adj.* [1990s+] foolish. ❑ **softball** *adj. see* separate entry. ❑ **soft butch** *n. see under* BUTCH *n.*[1]. ❑ **soft clothes** *n.* [1940s+] (*US*) civilian clothes, plain clothes. ❑ **soft collar** *n. see under* COLLAR *n.* ❑ **soft con** *n. see under* CON *n.*[1]. ❑ **softcore** *adj.* [on model of SE *softcore* pornography, titillating but not legally 'obscene'] [1970s+] (*orig. US*) mild, not extreme. ❑ **soft corn** *n. see* SOFT SAWDER *n.* ❑ **soft dough** *n. see* SOFT MONEY *n.* (3). ❑ **soft gut** *n.* [1910s] (*US*) something unexceptional. ❑ **soft heel** *n. see* RUBBER HEEL *n.* (1). ❑ **soft horn/-horned** *see* separate entries.

❑ **soft-leg** *n.* (*also* **soft legs**) [1950s–70s] (*US black*) a woman, esp. an attractive woman. ❑ **soft-mash** *n.* (*also* **soft-shoes**) [SE *mash*, to crush] [20C+] (*W.I.*) a pair of rubber-soled, canvas sneakers. ❑ **soft money** *n. see* separate entry. ❑ **soft pedal** *v.* (*also* **put the soft pedal on, work the soft pedal**) [piano imagery] [1910s+] to play down, to diminish, to keep a low profile, to act in a restrained manner. ❑ **soft-roed** *adj.* [SE *soft roe*, the sperm of a male fish] [late 19C–1900s] kind-hearted; weak. ❑ **soft salve** *n. see* SOFT SOAP *n.* (1). ❑ **soft sawder/-sawderer** *see* separate entries. ❑ **soft-shoe** *adj.* [20C+] restrained; of talk, as in *give the soft-shoe*, to be unforthcoming. ❑ **soft song man** *n.* [1920s–60s] (*S.Afr./US Und.*) a confidence trickster. ❑ **soft soap** *see* separate entries. ❑ **soft sodda** *n. see* SOFT SAWDER *n.* ❑ **soft spot** *n.* **1** [mid-19C+] a feeling of kindness, sympathy. **2** [late 19C+] anything, esp. a job, considered easy and enjoyable, undemanding. **3** [1900s–50s] a weakness. ❑ **soft swinging** *n. see under* SWINGING *n.*². ❑ **soft tack** *n. see under* TACK *n.*¹. ❑ **soft thing** *n. see* separate entry. ❑ **soft tommy** *n. see under* TOMMY *n.*². ❑ **soft-top** *n.* [1940s] (*US black*) a padded stool, esp. as found in a bar.

IN PHRASES

❑ **put the soft pedal on/work the soft pedal** *v. see* SOFT PEDAL above.

soft *adv.* **1** [mid-19C+] foolishly, stupidly. **2** [1930s] comfortably. **3** [1940s] (*W.I.*) absolutely overcome, defeated.

soft ass *n.* (*also* **soft arse**) [-ASS *sfx*] [1960s] a weak, ineffectual man, a coward.

soft-ass *adj.* [-ASS *sfx*] [1970s+] (*US*) weak, ineffectual.

soft as silk *n.* [rhy. sl.] [20C+] (*Aus.*) milk.

softball *adj.* [SAmE *softball* rather than baseball] [1970s+] (*US*) trivial, not worthy of consideration, easy.

softballs *n.* [var. on GOOFBALL *n.*¹ (2)] [1970s] (*drugs*) barbiturates.

soften the cough *v.* [1990s+] (*Irish*) to reduce, to 'take down a peg'.

softhorn *n.* [a donkey has soft ears rather than horns] **1** [19C] a donkey, an ass. **2** [mid-19C] a simpleton, a fool.

IN PHRASES

❑ **soft is your horn** [Bee cites a supposed Irishman who mistook a jackass – with its soft ears – for a bull – with hard horns] [early–mid-19C] you're mistaken, lit. 'you're an ass'.

soft-horned *adj.* [SOFTHORN *n.* (2)] [mid-19C] stupid.

softie *n. see* SOFTY *n.*¹.

softing loose *n.* [one is living a *soft, loose* life] [1990s+] taking things easy and not doing anything.

soft money *n.* (*also* **soft**) **1** [mid-19C+] notes, bills, paper money. **2** [mid-19C+] (*US*) currency that is likely to lose its value. **3** [1910s+] (*also* **soft dough**) money that is easily earned or otherwise gained.

IN PHRASES

❑ **do some soft** *v.* [mid-19C] to pass counterfeit notes.

soft sawder *n.* (*also* **sawder, sawder to order, soft corn, soft sodda**) [SE (*soft*) *solder*, a pliable form of solder, made of tin and lead] [mid-19C+] flattery.

soft sawder *v.* (*also* **sawder**) [SOFT SAWDER *n.*] [mid-19C–1900s] to flatter.

soft-sawderer *n.* [SOFT SAWDER *n.*] [mid–late 19C] a flatterer.

soft soap *n.* [mid-19C+] (*orig. US*) **1** (*also* **soft salve, olive oil**) flattery. **2** an act of flattering someone. **3** kindness.

soft soap *v.* [SOFT SOAP *n.*] [mid-19C+] (*orig. US*) to flatter, to charm.

soft thing *n.* **1** [mid-19C+] an easily duped simpleton. **2** [late 19C+] an easy job, an easy win etc.

IN PHRASES

❑ **have a soft thing on** *v.* [late 19C] (*US campus*) to be in an advantageous position.

softy *n.*¹ (*also* **softie**) **1** [mid-19C+] a foolish weakling; the image is of unnecessary kindliness. **2** [1970s] an impotent man, i.e. one whose penis is soft.

softy *n.*² **1** [1940s] (*US black*) a bed. **2** [2000s] (*Aus.*) a roll of banknotes.

sogdologer *n. see* SOCKDOLAGER *n.*

soggy *adj.* [late 19C–1920s] (*US*) drunken; initiated by drunkenness; thus *sogged*, drunk; *sog*, drunkenness.

soggy biscuit *n.* (*also* **soggy Saos**) [Aus. brandname *Sao*] [1960s+] (*orig. Aus.*) a masturbation game, popular among schoolboys, whereby the participants masturbate and then ejaculate onto a biscuit; the last to reach orgasm must eat the semen-covered biscuit.

sogs *n.* [1960s] (*Aus.*) sausages.

so help me...! *excl. see under* S'ELP ME...!

s.o.h.f. *n.* [abbr. Often discerned in someone who fails to appreciate the throwing of bread rolls, baiting of minorities etc] [1970s+] (*UK society*) sense of humour failure.

so hoe *n.* [abbr. SE *sorority* + HO *n.* (2)] [1990s+] (*US campus*) a member of a sorority.

soil *n.* [rhy. sl.] [1980s+] (*Aus. prison*) hashish oil.

soiled dove *n.* (*also* **dove of the roost**) [literary euph.] [mid-19C–1920s] (*Aus./US*) a prostitute; thus *dovecotery*, prostitution.

so is your old man! *excl.* (*also* **so's your old man!**) [1910s+] (*orig. US*) an excl. used as a retort to an insult or slur.

soixante-neuf *n. see* SIXTY-NINE *n.*

s.o.l. *n.* [abbr. *s*hit *o*n one's *l*iver] [1930s+] (*Aus.*) a bad temper.

s.o.l. *adj.* [abbr. *s*hit *o*ut of *l*uck] [1910s+] (*US*) unfortunate, unlucky, in a difficult situation.

sol *adj.* [abbr.] [20C+] (*US Und.*) in *sol*itary confinement; also as n., *Old Sol*.

sold *adj.* [SELL *v.* (1); Partridge notes phr. *sold again and got the money* as 'a costermonger's catch-phrase on having successfully "done" someone in a bargain'] **1** [early 19C+] tricked, fooled. **2** [late 19C+] convinced, successfully persuaded.

IN PHRASES

❑ **sold like a bullock in Smithfield** *adj.* [Smithfield (founded in the 12C) remains London's main wholesale meat-market, although live animals have not been brought there since 1855] [early–mid-19C] badly cheated; utterly betrayed. ❑ **sold on** *adj.* [1920s+] convinced, fascinated by.

soldi *n. see* SALTEE *n.*

soldier *n.* **1** [early–mid-19C] in plays on the 'red coat'. (**a**) a red herring. (**b**) a boiled lobster. (**c**) (*W.I.*) a crayfish. **2** [1930s] (*US*) a term of address, usu. to one whose name one does not know. **3** in prison/Und. uses. (**a**) [1930s] (*US prison*) a lookout man during a burglary. (**b**) [1960s+] (*US Mafia*) a lower echelon member of a Mafia family, the run-of-the-mill gangsters who fight the gang wars. (**c**) [1990s+] (*Aus./US prison/Und.*) a member of a prison gang. **4** [1940s] (*US*) a dollar. **5** [1970s+] (*UK black*) a member of a (teen) gang.

SE in slang uses

IN COMPOUNDS

❑ **soldier's bottle** *n.* [orig. naut. jargon; the presumption being that soldiers either drink excessively or need alcohol to fortify their courage] [late 17C–early 19C] a very large bottle. ❑ **soldier's farewell** *n.* (*also* **lag's farewell**) [late 19C+] 'goodbye, good luck and fuck you!'; 'hello, how are you and fuck you!'. ❑ **soldier's joy** *n.* [note naut. jargon *soldier's joy*, pease pudding] [mid-19C–1900s; 2000s] masturbation. ❑ **soldier's maund** *n. see under* MAUND *n.* ❑ **soldiers on horseback** *n.* [late 19C] (*US short-order*) fishballs and dropped eggs. ❑ **soldier's pomatum** *n.* [*pomatum*, pomade; thus a sneer at soldiers who cannot afford to dress their hair with anything better than tallow] [late 18C–mid-19C] a piece of tallow or animal-fat candle. ❑ **soldier's supper** *n.* [the soldier's last meal of the day was tea; there was no supper] [late 19C] nothing; a drink of water and a cigarette or pipe. ❑ **soldier's thigh** *n.* [military poverty] [mid–late 19C] an empty pocket. ❑ **soldier's wash** *n.* [the privations of the battlefield] [20C+] the washing of one's face with a scoop of water in cupped hands rather than using a flannel.

IN PHRASES

❑ **come the old soldier** *v. see under* COME THE... *v.* ❑ **dead**

soldier *n.* (*also* **fallen soldier**) [late 19C+] an empty bottle; thus *half-dead soldier*, a partially empty bottle.

soldier ants *n.* [rhy. sl.] [20C+] pants.

soldier bold *n.* [rhy. sl.] [20C+] (*Aus.*) a (head) cold.

soldiers bold *adj.* [rhy. sl.] [20C+] cold.

sold out *adj.*[1] (*also* **sold up**) **1** [mid-19C] bankrupt. **2** [mid-19C–1930s] defeated, beaten.

sold out *adj.*[2] [SELL OUT v. (1b)] [1930s+] (*US*) corrupted, susceptible to bribery.

soles *n.* [the piece of hashish is approx. shaped like a sole; or the smuggling of hashish in the soles of purpose-built shoes] [1970s] (*drugs*) hashish.

sol-fa *n.* [SE *sol-fa man*, a music teacher; thus f. the clerk's leading of the sung responses in church] [late 18C–early 19C] a parish clerk.

solicitor general *n.* [SAmE; a pun on SE *solicit*] [19C] the penis.

solid *n.* [someone or something that has substance, thus dependable, trustworthy] **1** [20C+] (*UK tramp*) the road. **2** [1920s] (*US Und.*) a trustworthy fellow criminal or prison inmate. **3** [1950s+] (*US black*) a favour.

IN PHRASES

❑ **do (someone) a solid** *v.* [1920s+] (*US*) to perform a great favour.

solid *adj.* [SE *solid*, thorough, downright, vigorous; note Mezzrow & Wolfe, *Really the Blues* (1946): '*Solid*, which is short for *solid as the Rock of Gibraltar* and describes a man who isn't going to be washed away so easy'] **1** [mid-19C+] full, complete, entire, esp. of time, e.g. *a solid month*. **2** [late 19C] as *solid on*, devoted to. **3** [late 19C+] (*orig. jazz*) trustworthy, dependable, exciting, outstanding. **4** [late 19C+] trusted; usu. in comb. *solid with*. **5** [late 19C+] definite. **6** [1910s–60s] (*Aus./N.Z.*) severe, difficult, unfair, unreasonable. **7** [1920s–50s] (*US*) secure, free of problems.

IN COMPOUNDS

❑ **solid con** *n. see under* CON *n.*[1]. ❑ **solid man** *n.* [late 19C] (*US Und.*) a woman's long-term male lover (as opposed to any transient entanglements). ❑ **solid sender** *n.* [SEND *v.*] [1920s+] (*US black*) **1** an admirable person, esp. a jazz or swing musician. **2** a real, genuine, amazing thing.

SE in slang uses

IN COMPOUNDS

❑ **solid ivory** *adj.* [IVORY *n.*] [1910s–30s] (*US*) stupid. ❑ **solid shot** *n.* [late 19C] (*US short order*) an apple dumpling.

solid *adv.*[1] [SOLID *adj.*] [late 19C] (*orig. US black*) trustworthily, dependably, excitingly, outstandingly.

IN PHRASES

❑ **stick solid** *v.* [1990s+] (*Aus. Und.*) to remain silent under interrogation.

solid *adv.*[2] [late 19C+] completely, unreservedly.

solid! *excl.* [SOLID *adj.*] [1910s+] (*orig. US*) a general excl. of approbation, implying a firm bond, honesty, excellence etc.

solidment! *excl.* [Fr. *solidement*, solidly] [1990s+] (*US campus*) an affirmative response.

solitaire *n.* [SE *solitaire*, a game played by oneself] **1** [1900s] (*US prison*) a solitary confinement cell. **2** [1940s] (*US black*) suicide.

solitary *n.* [abbr.] **1** [mid-19C+] *solitary* confinement in prison; also used fig. **2** [1900s] (*Aus. Und.*) an act of crime performed without an accomplice.

solitary as a bastard on Father's Day *adj. see* LONELY AS A BASTARD ON FATHER'S DAY *under* LONELY *adj.*

sollicker *n.* [? SOCKDOLAGER *n.* or dial. *sollock*, impetus, force] (*Aus.*) **1** [late 19C+] something notably large, 'a whopper'. **2** [1940s–50s] a large penis.

Solly *n.* [the once-popular Jewish given name *Solomon*] [late 19C–1950s] a generic term for any Jew.

solly *n.* [Lat. *sol*, the sun] [1910s] (*Aus.*) the sun.

Solly Isaacs *n. see* SOLOMON ISAAC *n.*

solo *n.* [1940s] (*US black*) the number one.

SE in slang uses

IN PHRASES

❑ **do a solo** *v.* [1930s–40s] (*US prison*) to confess, to turn State's evidence.

solomon *n.*[1] (*also* **saloman, salmon**) [the biblical king, *Solomon*, or Fr. *serment*, an oath. Rowlands, *Martin-Mark-all* (1610), notes that while *solomon/salomon* duly means Mass, 'Many men I have heard take this word Solomon to be the chief commander among the beggars. But to put them out of doubt, this is not he. Marry, there was one Solomon in King Henry the Eighth's time that was a jolly fellow among them, who kept his court [...] at Foxhall (Vauxhall) [...] who was successor to Cock Lorel'] [mid-16C–mid-19C] (*UK Und.*) an altar or mass; thus *by the solomon! by the saloman!* by the Mass!

solomon *n.*[2] [? rhy. sl. but on what?] [late 19C] a job.

Solomon Isaac *n.* (*also* **Solly Isaacs**) [late 19C–1910s] a Jew.

so long *phr.* [? Heb. *shalom*, peace, and used as a basic word of greeting and farewell or Heb. *selah*, God be with you] [mid-19C+] (*orig. mainly US*) goodbye.

solo player *n.* [pun on SE use, in this case the soloist performs alone whether they wish it or not] [late 18C–early 19C] a poor player of any instrument, whose musicianship immediately empties a room of listeners and leaves them playing without an audience.

soma *n.* [Skrt *soma*, a drug used in Vedic rituals. Note *Soma*, Aldous Huxley's name for the 'happiness' drug used in his novel *Brave New World* (1932) + SOMA, the Society of Mental Awareness, formed in 1967 to campaign for the legalization of cannabis in the UK] [1970s] (*drugs*) phencyclidine.

sombitch *n. see* SONOFABITCH *n.* (1).

some *n.* **1** [mid-19C+] (*US*) violence, physical hurt. **2** [20C+] sexual intercourse; esp. in phr. *give me some*; thus antonym *none*. **3** [1960s] (*US campus*) sexual caresses short of intercourse. **4** [1970s] (*US campus*) an attractive, alluring person. **5** [2000s] energy, spirit, commitment.

IN PHRASES

❑ **get some** *v.* [euph.] (*orig. US*) **1** [mid-19C+] to have sexual intercourse; thus *get none*, to be deprived of sex. **2** [1970s] to be physically beaten. **3** [1970s+] to fight hard; to kill. ❑ **want some** *v.* [1970s+] (*US campus*) to search for sex. ❑ **want some?** [1970s+] a form of verbal challenge that may lead on to a fight.

IN EXCLAMATIONS

❑ **get some!** [as used in by US troops in the Vietnam War (1964–75)] [1960s+] (*US*) a cry of encouragement, esp. to one participant in a fight or firefight.

some *adj.* [mid-19C+] (*orig. US*) **1** of an object, or situation, great, splendid; also used ironically. **2** of a person, exceptional; also used ironically.

IN PHRASES

❑ **some pumpkins** *n. see under* PUMPKIN *n.* ❑ **some shakes** *n. see under* SHAKE *n.*[1]. ❑ **some stuff** *adj.* [late 19C+] (*US*) impressive, outstanding.

IN EXCLAMATIONS

❑ **some people!** *see under* PEOPLE *n.*

some *adv.* (*also* **any**) [mid-18C+] to a great extent, very well or much.

IN PHRASES

❑ **go some** *v.* [20C+] (*orig. US*) **1** to go fast, to work hard, to do well. **2** to be excessive.

so mean... *phr.* [20C+] (*Aus./N.Z.*) a phr. denoting an individual's meanness, and prefaced by *they're so mean they wouldn't...*; combs. include *...give a dog a drink at their mirage, ...give a rat a railway pie, ...give a shout if a shark bit them, ...give a wave if they owned the ocean, ...give you a fright if they were a ghost, ...give you a light for your pipe at a bushfire, ...give you a shock if they owned the powerhouse, ...give you their cold, ...spit in your mouth if your throat was on fire, and so mean they still have their lunch money from school.*

some kind of *adv.* [20C+] (*US*) extremely, very, as an intensifier; usu. positive with words like *wonderful* or *fine*.

someone blew out his/her pilot light *phr.* [1970s+] (*US campus*) referring to anyone considered somewhat odd, intoxicated on drugs etc.

someone's ass, to be *v.* [ASS *n.* (4)] [1980s+] (*US campus*) to cause someone's downfall, to destroy someone.

somersault *v.* [1980s+] (*Aus. prison/Und.*) **1** to reverse one's plea in court. **2** to happily take both the passive and active roles in homosexual relationships.

Somerset (Maugham) *adj.* [rhy. sl.; ult. UK writer William Somerset Maugham (1874–1965)] [1920s+] warm.

something *n.* **1** [mid-19C+] a euph. for the obscenity or oath of the speaker's choice; e.g. 'I don't give a something', i.e. a FUCK *n.* (2a) or a DAMN *n.* (1). **2** [1920s+] (*orig. US*) a remarkable thing or person, e.g. *She's really something!*

IN EXCLAMATIONS

❑ **something else!** [20C+] an excl. or description of approval or wonder; also as n.

SE in slang uses

IN COMPOUNDS

❑ **something damp** *n.* [mid-19C–1900s] a drink. ❑ **something good** *n.* [late 19C+] a good racing tip.

IN PHRASES

❑ **father something on someone** *v.* [20C+] to put the blame for something on someone else, to 'pass the buck'. ❑ **get something from someone** *v.* [1940s] (*US black*) to attack someone physically, esp. with a knife. ❑ **get something on someone** *v.* [1910s+] (*orig. US*) to find out incriminating or otherwise negative information about someone, to gain an advantage over someone. ❑ **give someone something for themselves** *v.* [ironic] [late 19C] to thrash, to beat. ❑ **have something on someone** *v.* [20C+] (*orig. US Und.*) **1** to have someone at a disadvantage, usu. through incriminating or negative information. **2** to be popular with. **3** to be better than, although usu. in negative. ❑ **something in socks** *n.* see *under* SOCK *n.*[1]. ❑ **something in the City** *n.* [ironic play on SE] [late 19C] a dubious figure, prob. a fraudster or even a burglar. ❑ **something on the ball** *n.* [baseball imagery] [1910s+] (*US*) skill, talent, great ability. ❑ **something's rotten in Denmark** [*Hamlet* I:iv: 'Something is rotten in the state of Denmark' + ref. to the pioneering operation undergone in Denmark by Christine (formerly George) Jorgensen] [1950s+] (*gay*) referring to someone who is presumed to have had a sex-change. ❑ **something the cat brought in** *n.* (*also* **something the cat dragged in**) [20C+] a distasteful, prob. dirty or unkempt, object or person. ❑ **that's another something** [1970s] (*US black*) that's a different matter.

something *adj.* **1** [late 18C+] a general intensifier, usu. negative, e.g. *something cruel, something dreadful*. **2** [mid-19C+] a euph. for *damn well* or *bloody (well)*, e.g. *I'll do as I something well please*.

something *adv.* [1910s] exceedingly.

-something *sfx* [the popular 1980s TV show *Thirty-something*] [1980s+] of age, within a specified decade, e.g. *thirty-something*; thus used in pl. to categorize a generation, *thirty-somethings, twenty-somethings*.

sometime *n.* [? the excuse, 'I'll do it sometime, I'll get round to it sometime'; cf. Sp. *mañana*, lit. tomorrow] [1960s+] (*US prison*) one who cannot be depended upon.

DERIVATIVES

❑ **sometimey** *adj.* [i.e. *sometimes* they are this, *sometimes* that] [mid-19C+] (*US black*) moody, changeable, inconsistent.

somnambulance *n.* [play on SE *somnambulance*, sleep-walking] [1980s+] (*US campus*) someone who is amusing, likeable, eccentric.

son *n.*[1] (*also* **sonnie, sonny, sonny boy, sonny jim**) [mid-19C+] a general term of address to a man or boy.

son *n.*[2] [2000s] (*US prison*) the passive partner in a homosexual couple.

son *n.*[3] *see* SONOFABITCH *n.*

sonabitch *n. see* SONOFABITCH *n.*

son and daughter *n.* [rhy. sl.] [1940s] water.

son and daughter *v.* [rhy. sl. = SE *slaughter*] [2000s] to murder.

sonbitchery *n.* [SONOFABITCH *n.* (1)] [1960s] (*US*) cruelty, underhand behaviour.

soncy *adj. see* SONSY *adj.*

song *n.* **1** [late 16C; 18C+] a small amount of money. **2** [1990s+] usu. of money, a large amount. **3** *see* SONG AND DANCE *n.*[1] (3).

SE in slang uses

IN COMPOUNDS

❑ **songbird** *n.* [SING *v.* (4)] [1970s] (*US Und.*) an informer. ❑ **song factory** *n.* [play on BIRD *n.*[1] (2) + SE *factory*] [1910s] (*US Und.*) a prison.

IN PHRASES

❑ **change one's song** *v.* [musical imagery; var. on next] [mid-17C–early 19C] to alter one's opinions or statements. ❑ **off song** [one is not 'in tune' or is 'off key'] [late 19C+] not working well, in bad condition. ❑ **on song** [one is 'in tune'] [1960s+] working well, in prime condition. ❑ **sing a song** *v.* [late 19C] (*US*) to ask for credit. ❑ **what's your song, King Kong?** [assonance] [1940s] (*US black*) how are you? how do you feel?

song and dance *n.*[1] [late 19C+] **1** an elaborate excuse or account of a situation aimed at persuading or manipulating the listener. **2** a fuss. **3** (*also* **song**) anything (over-)elaborate.

IN PHRASES

❑ **give someone a song and dance** *v.* [late 19C+] (*orig. US*) to tell fanciful tales for the purpose of confusing or tricking the listener. ❑ **make a song and dance (about)** *v.* [late 19C+] to make a fuss.

song and dance *n.*[2] [rhy. sl. = NANCE *n.* (1)] [1910s–30s] a male homosexual.

song-and-dance *v.* [SONG AND DANCE *n.*[1] (1)] [1990s+] (*US*) to use an elaborate strategem to persuade someone.

songs and sighs *n.* [rhy. sl.] [1920s] (*US*) thighs.

sonk *n.* [backform. f. SONK(E)Y *n.*] [1950s–60s] (*Aus.*) an ungainly, clownish figure.

sonk *v.* [SOCK *v.*[1] (1) or SONK(E)Y *n.* (1)] [1950s] (*N.Z.*) to hit, to thump.

sonk(e)y *n.* [dial. *sonkie*, a man like a sackful of straw] **1** [mid-19C+] a thug. **2** [mid-19C+] a foolish, clumsy person. **3** [1910s] (*Aus.*) an upper-class weakling.

sonk(e)y *adj.* [SONK(E)Y *n.* (2)] [20C+] (*Aus.*) stupid, foolish.

son lo *n. see* SAN LO *n.*

sonnie *n. see* SON *n.*[1].

sonno *n.* [SE *son*/SON *n.*[1] + -O *sfx* (3)] [1910s+] (*Aus.*) a general form of address to a man or boy.

sonny (boy/jim) *n. see* SON *n.*[1].

sonny Jim *n. see* SUNNY JIM *n.*

sonobitch *n. see* SONOFABITCH *n.*

son of a... *n.*

euphs. for SONOFABITCH *n.*

IN COMPOUNDS

❑ **sonofabiscuit** *n.* (*also* **sonofabiscuit eater**) [1950s] (*US black*) ❑ **sonofagun** *n. see* separate entry.

IN PHRASES

❑ **son of a sea-cook** *n.* (*also* **son of a cook, ...custard-maker, ...hickory, ...hoss thief, ...sand turtle, ...sawbuck, ...sea-calf, ...sea-sarpint, ...sheep-stealer, ...shite-breeks, ...shotten herring, ...skunk, ...rip, ...tinker, ...toad**) [mid-18C; mid-19C+] ❑ **son of a sheep** *n.* (*also* **son of an ape, son of a fox, ...mule, ...she-dawg, ...skunk, ...slug, son-of-a-woodlouse**) [1910s–30s] ❑ **son of a son** *n.* [1940s] ❑ **son of a sow (gelder)** *n.* (*also* **son of a horned cow, ...corby-crow**) [17C+] ❑ **son of nobody out of nothing** *n.* [mid-19C] ❑ **son of your mother** *n.* (*also* **mother's son, son-of-one's-mother's-misbehaviour**) [1930s–60s] (*US*)

sonofa *n.* (*also* **sonova**) [1930s+] abbr. of SONOFABITCH *n.*

sonofabitch *n.* (*also* **sombitch, son, sonabitch, sonbitch, sonobitch, son of a bastard, sonofabastard, sonofabee, son of a big-shoe, son of a bitch, son-of-a-bitch, son of a dog, son of a two-legged dog, sonofawhore, sonovabitch, sonumbitch, sonuvabit, sonuvabitch, sumbitch, sumph, sunabitch**) [coined *c.*1330 in the form *Biche-sone* and in its current form in Shakespeare's *King Lear* (1605). Like a number of otherwise derog. terms (cf. BASTARD *n.*; MOTHERFUCKER *n.*), it can be used affectionately and of a woman, albeit rarely, as well as of a man. It can also be used as a general non-specific referent meaning 'thing', e.g. *pass the sonofabitch over here*] **1** [17C+] a derog. general term of abuse. **2** [late 19C] (*Aus.*) a moustache, as worn by cattle-buyers and wool inspectors. **3** [1910s] (*US*) a stew. **4** [1920s+] an affectionate term of address. **5** [1930s+] something or someone exceptional. **6** [1950s+] a thing, 'it'.

IN PHRASES

❑ **like a sonofabitch** *adv.* [var. on *LIKE A BASTARD under* BASTARD *n.*] [1940s+] very hard, with absolute commitment, to a very great extent.

IN EXCLAMATIONS

❑ **I'll be a sonofabitch!** [20C+] a general excl. of surprise or annoyance.

sonofabitch *adj. see* SONOFABITCHING *adj.*

sonofabitch! *excl.* [1940s+] a general excl. of frustration, annoyance, surprise, affirmation.

sonofabitchbastard! *excl.* [1950s+] a general excl. of annoyance, surprise etc.

sonofabitching *adj.* (*also* **sonofabitch, sonofabitchy, sonsabitching, sumbitching**) [mid-18C; 20C+] a general term of abuse.

son of a dog *n. see* SONOFABITCH *n.*

sonofagun *n.* (*also* **son of a wooden gun, sonsagun**) [SE *son* + *gun*/GONNOF *n.*] [19C+] euph. for SONOFABITCH *n.*

sonofagun! *excl.* [SONOFAGUN *n.*] [20C+] a general excl.

son of a two-legged dog/sonofawhore *n. see* SONOFABITCH *n.*

son of a wooden gun *n. see* SONOFAGUN *n.*

son of ebony *n. see* EBONY *n.*

son of prattlement *n.* [early 18C–early 19C] a lawyer.

son of the brush *n. see BROTHER OF THE BRUSH under* BROTHER (OF THE)... *n.*

sonova *n. see* SONOFA *n.*

sonovabitch *n. see* SONOFABITCH *n.*

sonsabitching *adj. see* SONOFABITCHING *adj.*

sonsagun *n. see* SONOFAGUN *n.*

sonsy *adj.* (*also* **sancy, sauncy, soncy, sonsie, sunsey**) [early 18C; mid-19C+] (*Irish/Scot.*) lively, fun; of a woman, buxom; thus *unsonsey*, dull, staid.

sonuvabitch *n. see* SONOFABITCH *n.*

soogan *n. see* SUGAN *n.*

sook *n.* (*also* **sookey, sookie, sooky**) [? dial. *suck*, a stupid fellow] [1930s+] (*Aus./N.Z.*) a coward, a crybaby.

sook *v.* [SOOK *n.*] [1990s+] (*Aus./N.Z.*) to make a fuss, to whinge.

sooky *adj.* (*also* **sucky**) [SOOK *n.* (1)] [1950s] (*usu. Aus./N.Z.*) cowardly, weak, sentimental.

sool *v.* [? dial. *sowl*, to handle roughly or *sowl into*, to attack fiercely] (*Aus./N.Z.*) **1** [late 19C+] to set a dog on. **2** [late 19C+] to persuade someone to attack a third party. **3** [late 19C+] of a dog, to worry. **4** [20C+] to confuse, to fool; thus *soolin' sod*, a hypocrite. **5** [1900s–10s] lit. and fig., to chase. **6** [1930s] (*Aus.*) to dismiss. **7** [1940s–50s] to run.

Sooner *n.* [SE *sooner than*; used of those who attempted to take over a territory before official permission, the main example was in Oklahoma] [late 19C+] (*US*) an Oklahoman.

sooner *n.* [all ref. to something or someone that would 'soon as be/sooner do one thing as another'] **1** [late 19C+] (*Aus.*) a lazy person, one who would 'sooner' loaf around than work or, in context, fight. **2** [20C+] a mongrel or any dog that would 'rather feed than fight'; the same applies to cats. **3** [20C+] (*US*) an illegitimate child [born too *soon* for the wedding]. **4** [1900s] (*US Und.*) one who takes things for granted; a mistaken optimist [they feel optimistic too *soon*]. **5** [1920s+] (*Aus.*) a confidence trickster. **6** [1930s–40s] (*US black*) a dirty, unkempt person. **7** [1930s–40s] (*US black*) dirty, ragged clothes. **8** [1950s] (*US*) a choice. **9** [1980s] (*N.Z.*) an ill-behaved, lazy horse.

soon-man *n.* (*also* **soon-woman**) [late 19C–1930s] (*US black*) a smart, alert, intelligent man or woman.

sooper-dooper *adj. see* SUPER-DUPER *adj.*

soor *n.*[1] [Hind. *soor*, a pig; pron. 'sewer' and used famously as such by Nancy Mitford's fictional Uncle Matthew (in *The Pursuit of Love*, 1945 *et al.*), although he confuses matters by spelling it 'sewer'] [mid-19C–1930s] a general pej. term.

soor *n.*[2] [? SE *swear*, i.e. 'I swear this is true...'] [20C+] (*W.I., Guyn.*) a useful piece of confidential information, esp. when passed on to ingratiate or flatter.

soot-bag *n.* [mid–late 19C] a reticule or small basket.

soother *n.* [its positive effects] [late 19C] a drink.

sooty *n.* [mid-19C+] a derog. term for a black person.

sooty *adj.* **1** [18C–19C] (*US*) black, in the context of a person. **2** [1900s] black, in the context of a general negative, despondent, depressed.

sooty jimmy *n. see under* JIMMY *n.*[4] (1).

sop *n.* [abbr. SE *milksop*, a weakling, a spiritless person, lit. a piece of bread soaked in milk] **1** [mid-19C+] a fool, a simpleton. **2** [1900s] a drunkard.

IN COMPOUNDS

❑ **sop-can** *n.* [1950s+] a simpleton, a weakling. ❑ **sophead** *n.* [-HEAD *sfx* (1)] [19C] a fool, a simpleton.

soper *n. see* SOPOR *n.*

soph *n.* [abbr.] **1** [late 17C–mid-19C] (*UK campus*) a *soph*ister, a student in their second or third year. **2** [late 18C+] (*US*) a *soph*omore.

sophisticated lady *n.* [play on GIRL *n.*[2] (1) + the 'smart' image of the drug] [1970s+] (*US black*) cocaine.

sop joint *n.* [SE *sop*, liquid + JOINT *n.* (1)] [1960s] (*US black*) the bath-house and masseur's salon.

sopor *n.* (*also* **soaper, soper**) [brandname of *Sopor*, a form of methaqualone, but note SE *soporific*] [1970s+] (*drugs*) any form of barbiturate drug, usu. methaqualone.

soppie *n.* (*also* **soppies**) [ety. unknown; ? one can SE *sop up* food or drink] [1960s–70s] (*S.Afr.*) a cinema tea-room or bio-café, a form of cinema at which one can eat snacks while watching a film.

soppings *n.* [1920s] (*US tramp*) gravy.

soppy *adj.* [? joc. use of SE *sopping wet*] **1** [late 19C+] (*UK teen*) vapid, naïve, esp. romantic; thus *soppy date*, a sentimentalist, a romantic. **2** [1940s] drunk.

IN COMPOUNDS

❑ **soppyballs** *n.* [1980s] a general derog.; the implication is of stupidity. ❑ **soppy ha'porth** *n.* [1930s+] a fool, often used affectionately.

IN PHRASES

❑ **soppy on** *adj.* [1920s+] obsessed with to a foolish extent.

soppy *adv.* [SOPPY *adj.* (1)] [1940s] vapidly, sentimentally, stupidly.

sordid *n.* [1950s] an unpleasant person.

sore *adj.*[1] [mid-19C+] (*mainly US*) angry, irritated.

IN PHRASES

❑ **sore as...** [20C+] (*orig. Aus.*) very angry, annoyed, in various comparative phrs., incl. *sore as a boil, ...boiled owl, ...gum boil, ...pup, sore as sox, sorer than a mashed thumb.*

SE in slang uses

IN COMPOUNDS

❑ **soreback** *n.* [the supposed hospitality of Virginians, an attitude that is underlined by their constantly slapping one another's backs in camaraderie] [20C+] (*US*) a native of Virginia. ❑ **sore-foot** *n.* [20C+] (*W.I.*) any unsightly, continually bandaged sore, irrespective of its position on the body. ❑ **sorefoot** *n.*

[1990s+] a derog. term for an British Asian. ❑ **sore hand** *n.* [resemblance to a cut hand] [1980s+] (*Ulster*) a very thick sandwich of bread and jam. ❑ **sore leg** *n.* [the supposed resemblance] [late 19C] **1** a sausage. **2** plum pudding. ❑ **sore piece** *n.* [SE *piece*, a person] [20C+] (*Ulster*) a troublesome person. ❑ **sore-rump** *n.* [1900s] (*US milit.*) a cavalryman.

IN PHRASES

❑ **dressed up like a sore finger/thumb/toe** *adj. see under* DRESSED *adj.* ❑ **have a sore eye** *v.* [one's eyes weep with laughter] [mid-19C] (*US Und.*) to have a good time. ❑ **stick out like a sore thumb** *v. see* separate entry.

sore *adj.*[2] [mid-19C+] **1** (*Irish*) as an intensifier, complete, utter. **2** (*Irish/juv.*) good, great.

sore *adv.* [mid-19C+] (*Irish*) as an intensifier, absolutely, utterly.

sorehead *n.* [mid-19C+] (*US*) a grumpy, irritable person.

soreheaded *adj.* (*also* **sorehead**) [SOREHEAD *n.*] [mid-19C+] (*US*) bad-tempered, grumpy.

sore up *v.* [SORE *adj.*[1]] [1920s+] (*US*) to annoy, to irritate.

IN PHRASES

❑ **sored up** *adj.* [1930s–40s] angry.

sorghum *n.* [the racist response to the replacement of such offensive terms as 'kaffir beer' or 'kaffir corn' by 'sorghum beer' and 'sorghum corn'] [1970s] (*S.Afr.*) a derog. term for a black person.

soro *n. see* SUE *n.*

sorority house *n.* [1940s] (*US Und.*) a women's prison.

sorrel-pate *n.* [the reddish colour of SE *sorrel*] [late 17C–early 19C] a red-headed person.

sorrel-top *n.* [the reddish colour of SE *sorrel*] [mid-19C–1930s] (*US*) a red-headed person.

sorrel-topped *adj.* [SORREL-TOP *n.*] [1930s] having red hair.

sorrowful tale *n.* [rhy. sl. = SE *gaol*] [mid-19C–1940s] three months in prison.

sorry *n.* [late 19C] (*US*) the remorse that can accompany a serious hangover.

sorry and sad *n.* [rhy. sl.] [20C+] a father, i.e. 'dad'.

sorry and sad *adj.* [rhy. sl.] [1950s+] bad.

sorry-ass *adj.* (*also* **sorry-assed**) [SE *sorry*, worthless + -ASS *sfx*] [1960s+] (*orig. US black*) unfortunate, despicable; as n., a pathetic person, oneself.

sort *n.* **1** [mid-19C+] a person, a type; usu. as *bad sort*, *good sort*. **2** [1910s+] (*orig. Aus.*) a woman; very occas. applied also to men.

IN PHRASES

❑ **that's your sort** [late 18C–mid-19C] a general term of approval, agreement.

sort *v.* (*also* **sort out**) **1** [20C+] to tease, to 'pull someone's leg'. **2** [1940s+] (*orig. Aus.*) to deal with, esp. violently. **3** [1950s] (*UK prison*) of a warder, to harass an inmate. **4** [1970s+] to arrange, to organize. **5** [1990s+] to provide someone with drugs. **6** [1990s+] to pay one's debts. **7** [2000s] to provide with sexual pleasure or satisfaction.

sorted *adj.* [1980s+] an all-purpose term of approval, worked out, content, satisfactory, supplied with drugs etc.

sort of *phr.* (*also* **sorta, sorter**) [mid-19C+] to an extent, in a way.

sort out *v. see* SORT *v.*

s.o.s. *n.*[1] [abbr. *s*ame *o*ld *s*hit] [1920s+] (*US*) the same thing as usual.

s.o.s. *n.*[2] [abbr.; *s*mash *o*n *s*ight or *s*hoot *o*n *s*ight] [1990s+] (*US gang*) a contract to murder.

s.o.s. *n.*[3] *see* SHIT ON A SHINGLE *under* SHIT *n.*

sosh *n.*[1] [? SLOSHED *adj.*] [late 19C] (*US*) a state of drunkenness.

IN PHRASES

❑ **have a sosh on** *v.* [1900s] to be drunk.

sosh *n.*[2] *see* SOC *n.*

soshed *adj. see* SLOSHED *adj.*

so-so *adj.*[1] [euph.] **1** [mid-18C–early 19C] drunk. **2** [mid–late 19C] menstruating.

so-so *adj.*[2] [1910s+] (*US black*) important, special, superior; usu. in derog. contexts.

so-so *adv.* [? SE *solo* + redup.] [1940s+] (*W.I. Rasta*) only, solely, unaccompanied.

so-so *phr.* [1900s] (*US Und.*) goodbye.

soss-brangle *n.* [SE *soss*, a muddy puddle; a sloppy mess of food; + *brangle*, a muddle] [late 18C–mid-19C] a slatternly woman.

sosselled *adj. see* SOZZLED *adj.*

sossie *n. see* SAUSIE *n.*

sossinger *n. see* SASSIGER *n.*

sossled *adj. see* SOZZLED *adj.*

sossselled/sossled *adj. see* SOZZLED *adj.*

so's your old man! *excl. see* SO IS YOUR OLD MAN! *excl.*

sot *adj.* [Fr. *sotte*, foolish + UK dial. *sot*, a fool] [20C+] stupid, silly, foolish.

sothead *n.* [dial. *sot*, a fool + -HEAD *sfx* (1)] [20C+] a fool, a simpleton.

sot-weed *n.* [SE *sot*, a fool or a drunkard + *weed*; the implication being that only such figures smoked] [late 17C–early 19C] tobacco.

sou *n.* (*also* **sou-markee, sous, souse**) [late 17C+] an extremely small amount of money.

IN PHRASES

❑ **not a sou** *n.* (*also* **not a sous, …souse**) [Fr. *sou*, a coin of very low value (one twentieth of a livre, later five centimes) generally trans. as 'a penny'] [mid-18C–1900s] not a penny, nothing at all.

sougan *n. see* SUGAN *n.*

soul *n.*[1] **1** [late 17C–mid-18C] a drunkard, esp. on brandy. **2** [1950s] (*US black/drugs*) marijuana.

SE in slang uses

IN PHRASES

❑ **get one's soul in soak** *v.* [early 19C] to become very drunk. ❑ **have a soul above buttons** *v.* (*also* **have a soul above socks**) [late 18C–1900s] to see oneself realistically or otherwise as superior to the situation in which one currently exists.

soul *n.*[2] **1** [1910s+] (*W.I.*) (*also* **souley, soulie**) as a term of address to a fellow black. **2** [1940s+] (*orig. US black*) the essential quality of black being, unavailable, however much aped and pirated, to anyone who is not black (and American). **3** *see* SOUL FOOD *n.*

IN PHRASES

❑ **go for soul** *v.* [1930s–40s] (*US black*) to be deeply moved.

soul *adj.*[1] [SOUL *n.*[2]] [1940s+] (*orig. US black*) black, used in a variety of combs. for which see below.

DERIVATIVES

❑ **souling** *n.* [1960s] (*US black*) doing anything well, esp. when playing jazz. ❑ **Soulville** *n.* [-VILLE *sfx*[1] (1)] [1950s+] (*US black*) **1** the black area of a city or town. **2** thus fig., any black place or situation. **3** Africa.

IN COMPOUNDS

❑ **soul brother** *n.* [1930s+] (*orig. US black*) a (fellow) black man; also attrib. ❑ **soul brother number one** *n.* (*also* **soul sister number one**) [NUMBER ONE *adj.*] (*US black*) a black person who epitomizes everything positive in the black experience; thus *soul brother/sister number two*, a lesser version, or a sympathetic white person. ❑ **soul child** *n.* [1970s] (*US campus*) of black students, anyone with conspicuous black pride and identity. ❑ **Soul City** *n.* [-CITY *sfx* (1)] [1960s+] (*US*) Harlem, New York, the centre of black America. ❑ **soul dancing** *n.* [1950s+] (*US black*) dancing in accordance with the current dance style favoured in the black community. ❑ **soul folks** *n.* [1960s] (*US black*) black people. ❑ **soul food** *n.* see separate entry. ❑ **soul kiss** *n.* [1900s; 1950s+] a deep kiss, involving putting one's tongue into one's partner's mouth; thus as v., to kiss in this way. ❑ **soul language** *n.* [1940s+] (*US black/W.I., Jam.*) black American slang. ❑ **soul minority** *n.* [1960s–70s] (*US black*) African Americans considered collectively. ▫ **soul patch** *n.* [1990s+] (*orig. US black*) a single tuft of hair worn beneath the lower lip. ▫ **soul power** *n.* [1960s–70s] (*US black*) the political and cultural influence wielded by the black community. ▫ **soul sauce** *n.* **1** [1970s+] (*US gay*) a black man's semen, or, by metonymy, the man himself. **2** [1990s+] (*US*) blood. ▫ **soul session** *n.* [1960s–70s] (*US black*) a gathering of black people. ▫ **soul shake** *n.* [1960s+] (*orig. US black*) the ritualized shaking and slapping of hands. ▫ **soul sister** *n.* **1** [1900s] (*US*) a girlfriend. **2** [1960s+] (*orig. US black*) a black woman. ▫ **soul sister number one** *n. see* SOUL BROTHER NUMBER ONE above. ▫ **soul sounds** *n.* [1950s–70s] (*US black*) music. ▫ **soul talk** *n.* [1950s–70s] (*US black*) a conversation between two or more black people.

IN PHRASES

▫ **soul on** [1960s–70s] (*US black*) do your best, keep your black identity.

soul *adj.*[2]

SE in slang uses, pertaining to religion

IN COMPOUNDS

▫ **soul aviator** *n. see* SKYPILOT *under* SKY *n.*[2]. ▫ **soul-bolt** *n.* [mid-19C–1900s] (*Aus./US*) a metaphorical 'bolt' that holds the soul, and thus the person, together; esp. in phr. *knock/shake the soul-bolts out of*, to disturb or worry to a substantial degree; *start my soul-bolts!* an excl. of alarm. ▫ **soul-butter** *n.* [*see* BUTTER *n.*[1] (2)] [mid–late 19C] (*US*) moralizing drivel. ▫ **soul-case** *n. see* separate entry. ▫ **soul-doctor** *n.* **1** [late 18C–19C] a clergyman. **2** [1950s] a psychiatrist. ▫ **soul-driver** *n.* [late 17C–mid-19C] a clergyman, or one who acts as such. ▫ **soul-faker** *n.* [FAKER *n.*] [late 19C] a member of the Salvation Army. ▫ **soul-snatcher** *n.* (*also* **soul-snaveller**) [late 19C–1900s] a preacher, a missionary. ▫ **soul swaddler** *n.* [mid-19C] (*UK Und.*) a Methodist minister.

soul-case *n.* **1** [late 18C–early 19C] the body; thus *make a hole in one's soul-case*, to wound. **2** [late 19C+] (*US/Aus.*) one's spirit, usu. in the context of worry, suffering or oppression; thus *worry/belt/sweat the soul-case out of*, to annoy, to drive, to punish.

IN PHRASES

▫ **burst one's soul-case** *v.* (*also* **bother one's soul-case, rack..., wear out..., work out...**) [late 19C+] (*W.I.*) to wear oneself out with hard work.

souley *n. see* SOUL *n.*[2] (1).

soul food *n.* (*also* **soul**) [SOUL *adj.*[1] (1) + SE *food*] **1** [1960s+] (*US black*) food prepared and preferred by the black community. **2** [1970s] thus, by extension, any nationally preferred food.

soulie *n. see* SOUL *n.*[2] (1).

sou-markee *n. see* SOU *n.*

sound *n.* **1** [1940s–50s] (*US black*) one's point of view. **2** [1950s] (*US street gang*) conversation, talk. **3** [1980s+] (*UK/US black/W.I.*) a group of reggae or rap artists.

IN COMPOUNDS

▫ **sound boy** *n.* (*also* **sound man**) [1970s+] (*W.I./UK black teen*) a sound system operator.

sound *adj.* (*also* **sound on**) **1** [mid-17C–early 18C] healthy, esp. free of venereal disease. **2** [19C+] excellent, first-rate, totally satisfactory, admirable, dependable. **3** [mid-19C+] (*orig. US*) knowledgeable about, expert in. **4** [mid-19C+] dependable, trustworthy, of sober judgement (in the view of the speaker). **5** [2000s] safe.

IN COMPOUNDS

▫ **sound egg** *n.* [EGG *n.*[2] (1)] [1920s–30s] a 'good chap', a 'decent fellow'.

sound *v.* (*UK Und.*) **1** [early 19C+] to elicit information from a person. **2** [early 19C+] to check out, to check over. **3** [1920s+] fig., to work something out, to ascertain. **4** [1930s] to knock on a door to see if the occupants are at home. **5** [1940s–50s] (*US black/teen*) to inform, to tell. **6** [1950s] (*street gang*) to tease, to taunt, to joke with. **7** [1950s] to listen. **8** *see* SOUND ON below.

IN PHRASES

▫ **sound on** *v.* [1950s–80s] **1** (*US*) to flirt, to seduce. **2** (*US*) to criticize. **3** (*US*) (*also* **sound**) to compete in ritualized mutual insults. **4** (*US prison*) to speak to, to make a request to.

sound! *excl.* [1960s+] a general excl. of approval, i.e. excellent! fine! no problems!

sounder *n.* [SOUND *v.* (2)] [1910s] a person who checks a place out in advance, esp. in preparation for a burglary.

sound on *adj. see* SOUND *adj.*

sounds *n.* [1950s+] (*orig. US*) music, spec. records; occas. sing.

IN COMPOUNDS

▫ **sounds and tunes** *n.* [1970s] (*US campus*) songs.

sounds! *excl. see* ZOUNDS! *excl.*

soup *n.* **1** [mid–late 19C] (*Aus./UK Und.*) *white soup*, melted silver plate; thus *soup-shop*, a place where such plate is melted down and disposed of. **2** [20C+] (*orig. US Und.*) gelignite, nitroglycerine, as used in the blowing open of a safe; thus *cook soup*, to dissolve a stick of dynamite in hot water to extract crude nitroglycerine; as v., to use the above. **3** [1940s] (*US*) insecticide. **4** [1940s+] (*US*) gasoline, petrol, esp. high-performance fuel used in customized cars. **5** [1970s] (*US gay*) sweat; anal juices; fecal matter. **6** [1990s+] (*Aus.*) electricity. **7** *see* SUPER *n.*[1] (5). **8** *see* SUPER *n.*[2].

IN COMPOUNDS

▫ **soup and peter man** *n.* [PETER *n.*[2] (2)] [1940s] (*US Und.*) a safe breaker. ▫ **soup and peter work** *n.* [1940s] (*US Und.*) safe breaking with nitroglycerine. ▫ **soup man** *n.* **1** [1910s+] a professional villain who specializes in handling nitroglycerine to blow open safes. **2** [1950s] a person who mixes their own high-performance petrol for customized cars.

IN PHRASES

▫ **on the soup** *adj.* [1990s+] (*Aus.*) drinking. ▫ **scare the soup out of** *v.* [1920s] to terrify.

SE in slang uses

IN COMPOUNDS

▫ **soup and fish** *n.* (*also* **soup and fish clothes, ...outfit**) [the food one eats when wearing it] [1910s+] a dinner jacket. ▫ **soup house** *n.* [1920s–30s] (*US tramp*) a cheap restaurant. ▫ **soup jockey** *n.* [see JOCKEY *n.*[2] (3b)] [1930s] (*US*) a waiter or waitress. ▫ **soup-plate (track)** *n.* [it is fig. no bigger than the circumference of a *soup-plate*] (*Aus.*) **1** [1900s–50s] a small racecourse. **2** [1910s] a soldier's round hat. ▫ **soup strainer** *n.* [1910s+] a large moustache.

IN PHRASES

▫ **drink soup off someone's head** *v.* (*also* **drink soup over someone's head**) [20C+] (*W.I.*) to be taller than someone. ▫ **take the soup** *v.* (*also* **drink soup off**) [for ety. *see* SOUPER *n.*[1]] [mid-19C+] to convert from Catholicism to Protestantism.

soup *v.* [SE colloq. phr. *in the soup*] **1** [late 19C+] to cause someone to fail. **2** [1920s] to fail, to get into trouble.

soup and gravy *n.* [rhy. sl.] [20C+] the Royal Navy.

soupbone *n.* (*also* **super**) **1** [1900s–10s] (*US*) an arm. **2** [1920s–50s] the penis. **3** [1930s] (*US*) the tongue.

SE in slang uses

IN COMPOUNDS

▫ **soupbone bitch** *n.* [BITCH *n.*[1] (1)] [her role as a cook] [2000s] (*US black*) a regular, long-term female partner.

souped *adj.* [SE colloq. phr. *in the soup*] [late 19C+] (*Anglo-Irish*) in trouble.

souped-up *adj.*[1] [ety. unknown, SOUP UP *v.* is later; perhaps fig. use of SE *soup*, for alcohol] [late 19C] (*Aus.*) drunk.

souped-up *adj.*[2] (*also* **souped, suped-up**) [SOUP *n.* (4), or racing use *soup*, anything injected into a horse to alter its speed or temperament] **1** [1940s+] intensified, accelerated, usu. of a car that has been modified by its owner to exceed the basic factory-created performance. **2** [1980s+] in fig. use, of a person.

souper *n.*[1] [such conversions, however nominal, were often achieved by the appeal of Protestant missionaries handing out free soup, orig. at the time of the great famine of 1845–7] **1** [mid-19C+] (*orig. Irish*) a convert from Roman Catholicism to Protestantism; thus any Protestant. **2** [late 19C] one who scrounges free soup tickets.

souper *n.*[2] *see* PEASOUP *n.*[1] (2).

souper *n.*[3] *see* SUPER *n.*[2].

soup up *v.* [SOUP *n.* (4)] **1** [1940s] to accelerate. **2** [1940s+] (*orig. of engines*) to increase in power, to aggrandize in some manner. **3** [1950s+] (*US*) in fig. use, to stimulate a woman's vagina.

IN COMPOUNDS

❑ **soup job** *n.* [JOB *n.*[2] (2)] [1940s+] (*US*) anything (orig. a car) that is increased, heightened in value, competence or attractiveness.

soupy *adj.*[1] [SE *soup*, i.e. the vomit] [late 19C] extremely drunk, usu. to the point of vomiting.

soupy *adj.*[2] [var. on SOPPY *adj.*] [1910s–20s] vapid, naïve, esp. romantic.

sour *n.* (*also* **sour dough, sour paper**) [fig. use of SE *sour* + DOUGH *n.* (1)/PAPER *n.* (2)] **1** [late 19C–1930s] counterfeit money, apparently silver but made from pewter; or forged cheques. **2** [1920s–40s] (*US Und.*) a bad cheque.

IN COMPOUNDS

❑ **sourplanter** *n.* [PLANT *v.*[1] (6)] [19C] a distributor of counterfeit money; thus *plant the sour*, to spread around such 'money'.

sour *adj.*

SE in slang uses

IN COMPOUNDS

❑ **sour-apple quickstep** *n.* [1990s+] diarrhoea. ❑ **sourball/-balled** *see* separate entries. ❑ **sour belly** *n. see* SOW-BELLY *n.* ❑ **sour cudgel** *n.* [early 17C] a severe thrashing. ❑ **sour dough** *n.* **1** [late 19C+] (*orig. Can.*) an experienced prospector in Alaska, the Yukon or the Northwest Territories [the use of sourdough (fermenting dough, esp. that left over from a previous baking, used as leaven) in the making of bread in mining camps. Allegedly, the need to keep this warm meant that, on cold nights, the miners would sleep with a lump]. **2** *see* SOUR *n.* ❑ **sour paper** *n. see* SOUR *n.* ❑ **sourpuss** *n. see* separate entry.

sour *v.*[1] [? SE *sour*, to cause fermentation] [18C] (*UK Und.*) to beat.

sour *v.*[2] *see* CURDLE *v.*

sourball *n.* (*also* **sourbelly**) [1900s–50s] (*US*) **1** a grumpy person. **2** ill temper.

sour-balled *adj.* [SOURBALL *n.* (1)] [1900s–30s] grumpy.

sourcrout *n. see* SAUERKRAUT *n.*

soured on *adj. see* SOUR ON *adj.*

sour grape *n.* [rhy. sl.] [1980s+] (*Aus./N.Z. Und.*) a rape; also as v.

sourkrout *n. see* SAUERKRAUT *n.*

sour on *adj.* (*also* **soured on**) [20C+] (*orig. Aus./US*) hostile towards.

sour on *v.* [mid-19C+] (*orig. US*) to become hostile towards.

sourpuss *n.* [PUSS *n.*[2] (1)] [1930s+] (*orig. US*) **1** a sour-faced person, a grumbler, a killjoy. **2** a grumpy expression.

DERIVATIVES

❑ **sourpussed** *adj.* [1950s+] (*orig. US*) **1** mean, puritanical. **2** sour-featured.

sous/souse *n. see* SOU *n.*

souse *n.* [? backform. f. SOUSED *adj.* (1)] **1** [18C; 20C+] a drunkard. **2** [1900s] a state of drunkenness. **3** [1900s–50s] a drinking bout.

IN COMPOUNDS

❑ **souse-pot** *n.* [-POT *sfx*] (*orig. US black*) a drunkard.

souse *v.* [*see* prev.] **1** [mid-19C] (*US*) to eat. **2** [20C+] to drink heavily, to become drunk.

IN COMPOUNDS

❑ **souse-crown** *n.* [SE *souse* + *crown*, lit. a 'drunken head'] [late 17C–18C] a fool.

soused *adj.* (*also* **soused-up**) [SOUSE *n.* (1)] [17C+] drunk.

IN PHRASES

❑ **soused to the gills** *adj.* (*also* **soused to the guards, ... (head and) ears**) [*TO THE GILLS under* GILLS *n.*] [mid-17C; 20C+] (*UK/US*) very drunk.

souse me! *excl.* [late 18C] an excl. of denial, or refusal.

sousch *n.* [backsl.] [mid-19C] a house.

soustannie *n.* [Afk., lit. 'salt-auntie'] [1990s+] (*S.Afr.*) a well-built woman.

sousy *adj.* [SOUSE *v.* (2)] [1950s] drunken.

south *adj.* [SOUTH *adv.*] **1** [19C+] used in var. phrs. to mean down, e.g. SOUTH POLE *n.* (2) and phrs. below. **2** [1930s] morally 'down', i.e. racy, sexy, pornographic. **3** [1990s+] less than.

IN COMPOUNDS

❑ **south end** *n.* [mid-19C+] (*US*) the buttocks (cf. ARSE-END *n.*). ❑ **southpaw** *see* separate entries. ❑ **south pole** *n. see* separate entry.

IN PHRASES

❑ **down south** *adj.* **1** [1910s+] (*Aus./N.Z.*) hidden, buried; in one's pocket; thus *put down south*, to pocket. **2** [2000s] (*N.Z.*) below the hem, where a slip is showing. ❑ **south of the border** [1970s+] (*US*) below the waist, usu. referring to the vagina. ❑ **way down south in Dixie** *n.* [1980s] fellatio.

south *v.* (*also* **put down south**) **1** [1940s+] to pocket. **2** (*US Und.*) to hold out.

south *adv.* [19C+] used in var. phrs. to mean downwards, *see* below.

IN PHRASES

❑ **dip south** *v.* [1940s+] (*Aus./N.Z.*) to put one's hand in one's pocket, esp. when one's funds are running low. ❑ **go south** *v.* (*also* **go down south, go way down south in Dixie**) [DIXIE *n.*] [1930s+] (*US*) to perform cunnilingus or anilingus.

SE in slang terms

IN PHRASES

❑ **go south** *v.* (*orig. US*) **1** [20C+] to abscond with, to run off. **2** [1910s] of a person, to exhaust. **3** [1970s+] to collapse, to malfunction, to break down; of events, to go wrong. **4** [1970s+] to be killed. **5** [1980s+] to be defeated, to lose. **6** [1990s+] to lose interest. **7** [2000s] to squander, waste.

South County Indian *n.* [South County, Rhode Island, where such immigrants have congregated] [20C+] a Portuguese immigrant to the US.

Southend-on-Sea *n.* [rhy. sl. = PEE *n.*[1]] [20C+] urination.

Southend pier *n.* [rhy. sl.] [20C+] an ear.

southerly buster *n.* (*also* **southerly burster**) **1** [mid-19C+] (*Aus.*) the cool, gusty wind that springs up at the end of a hot day, sometimes accompanied by a shower. **2** [1940s] a cocktail.

southern can *n.* [SE *southern*, thus SOUTH *adj.* (1) + CAN *n.*[1] (1c)] [1930s+] (*US black*) the buttocks.

south gate discharge *n. see* BACK-GATE EXIT *under* BACK *adj.*[2].

southie *n.* [SOUTHPAW *n.* (1)] [1970s] (*US*) a left-hander.

south of France *n.* [rhy. sl.] [20C+] a dance.

southpaw *n.* [SOUTH *adj.* (1), i.e. the image of the left hand as being 'beneath' the right + PAW *n.* (1)] (*orig. US baseball*) **1** [late 19C+] a left-hander, esp. in boxing. **2** [late 19C+] the left hand. **3** [1920s] a blow with the left hand.

southpaw *adj.* [SOUTHPAW *n.* (1)] **1** [late 19C+] left-handed. **2** [1920s–60s] in fig. use, eccentric, odd.

south pole *n.* [rhy. sl. = HOLE *n.*[1] (1); + also SOUTH *adj.*] **1** [19C] the vagina. **2** [20C+] the anus.

South Sea (Mountain) *n.* (*also* **south-sea sherry**) [? the *South Sea Bubble*, a financial scandal of 1727; the effects of gin, like that of the Bubble, are to promote deleterious fantasies] [early 18C–mid-19C] gin, or any other strong liquor.

south Sydney *n.* [rhy. sl.] [20C+] (*Aus.*) a kidney (cf. NORTH SYDNEY *n.*).

soutie *n.* [abbr. SOUTPIEL *n.*] [1940s+] (*S.Afr.*) an Englishman who retains his colonialist mentality; also attrib.

soutpiel *n.* [Afk. *sout*, salt + *piel*, penis; thus lit. 'salt-dick', because he has one foot in South Africa, one in England and his penis dangling in the ocean in between. Despite the date, as cited in *DSAE*, it must be assumed that the term is much older, but left unprinted through taboo; thus Namibian synon. *sandpiele*, in this case the penis rests on the burning sands of the Kalahari desert] [1970s+] (*S.Afr.*) an Englishman, esp. one who has a notably colonialist mentality; also attrib.

souvenir *n.* (*also* **souvy**) [1910s] a trophy; something that has been found, thus a euph. for something stolen.

souvenir *v.* [SOUVENIR *n.*; orig. WW1 milit. use] **1** [1910s+] to steal. **2** [1970s+] (*US*) to give, to hand over; usu. as phr. *souvenir me*.

souvenir egg *n.* [late 19C–1930s] (*US*) an old, rotten egg.

souvy *n. see* SOUVENIR *n.*

sov *n.* (*also* **sob**) [abbr.; *sob* is mispron.] **1** [early 19C+] a sovereign, £1 sterling; thus *half-sov*, half a sovereign, ten shillings (50p). **2** [2000s] a ring made out of an old gold sovereign.

sovvy *n.* [SOV *n.* (1)] **1** [1960s] (*Aus.*) £1; A$2.00. **2** [2000s] a sovereign ring.

sow *n.*[1] **1** [mid-16C; early 18C+] derog. term for a (fat) woman. **2** [1910s+] a general term of abuse, irrespective of gender.

(IN COMPOUNDS)

❑ **sowface** *n.* [1950s] a derog. term applied to an ugly woman. ❑ **sow-pen** *n.* [1960s] (*Aus.*) any area of a hotel (i.e. public house) reserved for women only.

sow *n.*[2] [on pattern of UK GRUNTER *n.* (2); HOG *n.* (1); SOW'S BABY *n.* (2), but no apparent connection] [1930s–40s] (*US black*) any coin, esp. a nickel (5 cents).

sow-belly *n.* (*also* **hog bosom, sour belly, sow bosom**) (*US*) **1** [mid-19C+] a side of salted pork; bacon. **2** [1960s] a fat person.

sower *n.* [? it is full of fig. seeds, note later SEED *n.* (1a)] [mid-18C] (*UK Und*) a purse.

so what? *phr.* [1930s+] a widely used term of disinterest or defiance, a rejoinder to the previous speaker's announcement, revelation etc.

So-where-to *n.* [1970s] (*S.Afr.*) Soweto.

sowkins *n.*

(IN EXCLAMATIONS)

❑ **by my sowkins!** [1900s] (*Aus.*) an excl. of asseveration.

sowns! *excl. see* ZOUNDS! *excl.*

sow's baby *n.* **1** [late 17C–18C] a sucking pig [euph.]. **2** [mid-19C] sixpence (2½p), occas. a shilling (5p) [sixpence is smaller than a HOG *n.* (1a), i.e. a shilling].

soy pucks *n.* [their constituent and their resemblance to an ice-hockey *puck*] [20C+] (*US prison*) prison-cooked hamburgers.

sozzle *n.* [backform. SOZZLED *adj.* (1)] [late 19C–1900s] (*US*) the act of drinking; thus *sozzle session*, a drunken spree.

sozzle *v.* [backform. f. SOZZLED *adj.* (1)] [1930s–50s] **1** to drink heavily. **2** (*US*) to walk unsteadily, as if drunk.

sozzled *adj.* (*also* **sizzled, sosselled, sossled, sozzle-eyed**) [? US *sozzle*, to splash; ult. dial. *sozzle*, to mix or mingle in a sloppy manner] [mid-19C+] drunk.

s.p. *n.* [orig. racing jargon starting *price*] [1970s+] basic information, facts.

spa *n.* [abbr. *spastic*] [1980s+] (*Irish*) a general derog., an incompetent.

spa *adj.* [SPA *n.*] [1980s+] (*Irish*) crazy, inept, socially unacceptable.

spa bar *v.* [rhy. sl. = *IRON BAR under* IRON *adj.*] [1980s+] (*Aus. prison*) to beat up.

space *n.* [SE *space of time*/TIME *n.* (1)] [1900s–40s] (*US Und.*) a jail sentence.

SE in slang uses

based on being 'high' on drugs

(IN COMPOUNDS)

❑ **space base** *n.* (*also* **space ball, ...cadet, ...dust**) [BASE *n.*[1] (4)/ SE *cadet/dust* + play on the 1980s sweet Space Dust] [1990s+] (*drugs*) a cigar stuffed with a mixture of phencyclidine and crack cocaine. ❑ **space cadet** *n.* (*also* **space cowboy**) [SPACED (OUT) *adj.* (1) + SE *cadet*] **1** [1970s+] (*drugs*) (*also* **cadet**) any heavy user of drugs, esp. cannabis or hallucinogens. who is continually 'flying'. **2** [1970s+] (*US*) (*also* **space queen**) a mad or eccentric person. **3** [1980s] (*US campus*) (*also* **cadet**) a misfit, an unappealing person. ❑ **space cake** *n.* [1990s+] (*drugs*) a cake which is baked with cannabis as an extra ingredient. ❑ **space case** *n.* (*also* **space cookie, space ghost**) [1980s+] a crazy person. ❑ **spaceman** *n.* [1940s+] (*Aus. prison/ US*) one who is intoxicated on drugs; a madman. ❑ **space pill** *n.* (*also* **space biscuit**) [2000s] (*drugs*) MDMA. ❑ **space ship** *n.* [1980s+] (*drugs*) a glass pipe used to smoke crack cocaine.

(IN PHRASES)

❑ **sergeant space** *n.* [1980s+] (*US campus*) someone who is out of touch with reality.

general uses

(IN COMPOUNDS)

❑ **space opera** *n.* [on model of SOAP OPERA *n.* or *HORSE OPERA under* HORSE *n.*] [1940s+] (*US*) an SF or outer space drama film.

space *v.* [1980s+] (*US black gang*) to travel, to move.

spaced (out) *adj.* [the image of 'flying'] [1960s+] (*orig. drugs*) **1** intoxicated by a drug, esp. a hallucinogen. **2** generally disorientated, with or without drugs.

space (out) *v.*[1] [one 'flies' into space] [1960s+] (*US*) to daydream, to drift off, esp. when under the influence of drugs.

space (out) *v.*[2] [SE *make a space*] [1970s] (*US black*) to leave, to depart.

spacer *n.*[1] [SPACE *n.*] [1920s] (*US Und.*) a convicted criminal.

spacer *n.*[2] [SPACED (OUT) *adj.* (1); the underlying implication is of their probable drug-taking] [1980s+] (*Irish*) **1** a streetwise young person. **2** a crazy person.

spacey *adj.* (*also* **spacy**) [SPACED (OUT) *adj.*] [1960s+] **1** of a person, disorientated, whether through drug use or not. **2** exhibiting characteristics actually or fig. reminiscent of those experienced when taking a hallucinogen. **3** (*drugs*) of an experience or event, generally disorientating, with or without drugs. **4** edgy, nervous.

spacies *n.* [abbr.] [1980s+] (*N.Z.*) the video/computer game *Space Invaders*; thus generically for other electronic games.

spacka *n.* (*also* **spack, spacker, spacko**) [abbr. SPASTIC *n.*] [1990s+] a general term of abuse.

spackhead *n.* [SPACKA *n.* + -HEAD *sfx* (1)] [1990s+] a fool, an eccentric.

spackle-filler *n.* [proprietary name *Spackle*, a compound used to fill cracks in plaster and produce a smooth surface before decoration] [1980s] (*Aus.*) foundation make-up.

spacko *n. see* SPACKA *n.*

spacy *adj. see* SPACEY *adj.*

spade *n.* [SE phr. *black as the ace of spades*; *spadelet*, a nonce-word, found only in Colin MacInnes, *Absolute Beginners* (1959); poss. derog. in the US, it is seen as a neutral/affectionate term in the UK; Kuethe, 'Prison Parlance', *American Speech* IX:1 (1934) defines as 'a very dark Negro'] [1910s+] (*orig. US*) a black person, esp. West Indian or African; thus *spadelet*, a black child; *Spadesville*, the black area of a city.

(IN PHRASES)

❑ **queen of spades** *n.* [QUEEN *n.* (2)] (*US gay*) a respected black homosexual.

SE in slang uses

(IN COMPOUNDS)

❑ **spadework** *n.* [1980s] (*S.Afr. campus*) flirtation.

(IN PHRASES)

❑ **call a spade a (bloody) shovel** *v.* [a play on the usu. phr. *call* *a spade a spade*] [1910s+] to speak aggressively or vehemently. ❑ **in spades** *adv.* (*also* **in chunks**) [SE *spade*, i.e. 'spadefuls'; note in cards *spades* are the highest suit] [1920s+] (*orig. US*) to the greatest extent, very much, extremely, any form of intensifier; thus *you can say that in spades*, you couldn't be more right.

spade *adj.* [SPADE *n.*] [20C+] referring or pertaining to the black community or black culture.

spadet *n.* [? SPACE CADET *under* SPACE *n.*] [1980s+] (*US campus*) a student who is preoccupied with studies.

spadge *n.* [SPASTIC *n.*] [1990s+] (*UK juv.*) a general term of abuse.

spadger *n.* [dial. *spadger*, a sparrow] **1** [late 19C] a boy. **2** [1990s+] (*Aus.*) the vagina.

spaff *v.* [echoic] [1990s+] to ejaculate.

spag *n.*[1] [dial. *spadger*] [1950s+] (*Aus.*) a sparrow.

spag *n.*[2] [abbr. SE *spaghetti*, a staple Italian food] **1** [1960s+] (*Aus.*) (*also* **spaggie**) an Italian. **2** [1960s+] (*society*) spaghetti; thus *spag bol, spag bog*, spaghetti bolognese (usu. in some adulterated British version). **3** *see* SPAGHETTI WESTERN *under* SPAGHETTI *n.*

IN COMPOUNDS

❑ **spag fag** *n.* [FAG *n.*[5] (1); play on FAG-HAG *n.*[2]] [1990s+] (*gay*) one who prefers Italian partners.

spag *n.*[3] (*also* **spagga**) [SPASTIC *n.*] [1980s+] (*US campus/UK juv.*) an unpleasant, stupid person; can be used affectionately.

spa-gag-me *n.* [abbr. SE *spaghetti* + *gag*, to choke] [1990s+] (*US prison*) prison-cooked spaghetti.

spaggie *n. see* SPAG *n.*[2] (1).

spaghetti *n.* (*also* **spaghetti eater**) [stereotyping] [1910s+] (*orig. US*) an Italian.

SE in slang uses

IN COMPOUNDS

❑ **spaghetti bender** *n.* (*also* **spaghetti eater, spaghetti twister**) [1930s+] an Italian. ❑ **spaghetti corner** *n.* [1950s+] (*US*) an Italian community within an urban area. ❑ **spaghetti head** *n.* [-HEAD *sfx* (1)] [20C+] **1** (*US*) an Italian. **2** a stupid person. ❑ **spaghetti junction** *n.* (*also* **spaghetti bowl**) [1960s] a complex of motorways forming a multi-levelled interchange, esp. the Gravelly Hill interchange between the M1 and M6 outside Birmingham, UK. ❑ **spaghetti western** *n.* (*also* **spag**) [1970s+] (*orig. US*) a cowboy film, usu. made in Europe by Italian directors. ❑ **spaghetti works** *n.* [1900s] (*US*) an Italian restaurant.

spagingy-spagade *n.* (*also* **spaginzy**) [pig Lat. for SPADE *n.* (1)] [1920s+] (*US black*) a black person; thus *spaggot*, a black homosexual.

spalpeen *n.* (*also* **spalpean**) [Irish *spailpín*, a low or mean fellow, orig. a casual farm labourer] [mid-18C+] a rogue, a rascal; also attrib.

spam *n.* [SE *Spam*, proprietary name for a brand of pork luncheon meat] [2000s] the penis.

IN COMPOUNDS

❑ **spam alley** *n.* (*also* **spam purse**) [1990s+] the vagina. ❑ **spam chasm** *n.* [1990s+] the vagina. ❑ **spamjagger** *n.* [2000s] the penis. ❑ **spam javelin** *n.* (*also* **spam lance**) [1990s+] the penis. ❑ **spam juice** *n.* [JUICE *n.*[1] (2)] [2000s] semen. ❑ **spam sceptre** *n.* [SCEPTRE *n.* (1)] [1990s+] the penis. ❑ **spam supper** *n.* [2000s] fellatio.

SE in slang uses

IN COMPOUNDS

❑ **spamhead** *n.* [1990s+] (*UK juv.*) one who has a notably large forehead.

spam *adv.* [1940s] (*US*) echoic of the sound of a sudden blow.

spam fritter *n.* [rhy. sl. = SHITTER *n.*[1] (1)] [2000s] the anus.

span *adj.* [abbr. SE *spic and span*; ult. ON *spán-nýr*, chip-new] [mid-19C; 1980s+] (*UK/Irish*) brand new.

span *adv.* [fig. use of S.Afr.E. *span*, a team of oxen] [1960s+] (*S.Afr., mainly teen*) a lot, very much.

spang *adv.* [? SPANK *v.*[2] (2)] [late 18C+] (*orig. US*) absolutely, entirely, e.g. *right spang in the middle.*

spangle *n.*[1] [SE *spangle*, i.e. its glitter and shininess] **1** [19C] a seven-shilling piece; thus used fig. for a pound. **2** [late 19C] generic for money.

spangle *n.*[2] [1990s+] **1** semen. **2** (*Scot. juv.*) a fool.

spangles *n.* [late 17C–mid-18C] (*UK Und.*) off-cuts of gold or silver.

IN PHRASES

❑ **with spangles** *adj. see* WITH BELLS ON *under* BELL *n.*[1].

spaniard *n.* [? negative stereotyping] [1940s–50s] (*Can.*) a louse, a flea.

Spanish *n.* **1** [late 18C–early 19C] sack, a type of white wine produced in Spain and the Canary Islands. **2** [late 18C–mid-19C] constr. with *the*, cash, ready money [? the association of Spain with bullion fleets]. **3** [mid–late 19C] a Spanish onion. **4** [1900s] (*US campus*) nonsense [negative stereotyping, the language being supposedly incomprehensible]. **5** [1980s] (*US*) intercourse whereby the man reaches orgasm by rubbing his penis between a woman's breasts.

IN PHRASES

❑ **speak Spanish** *v.* [the *Spanish dollar*, the basic currency of the early years of the Australian colony, worth five shillings (25p); other contemporary coins were the *colonial dollar*, worth 75% of the Spanish one, and the *dump*, worth 25%] [early–mid-19C] (*Aus.*) to have money.

Spanish *adj.* [the role of Spain as England's primary national enemy during 16C–17C; these stereotypes, presumably encouraged by the late 19C Spanish-American War, persist in 20C+ US use] used in combs. below to denote arrogance, duplicitousness, treachery, sexual corruption etc.

IN COMPOUNDS

❑ **Spanish archer** *n.* (*also* **Spanish fiddle**) [pun on cod Spanish *el bow* i.e. ELBOW *n.* (4)] [1980s+] dismissal, rejection. ❑ **Spanish athlete** *n.* [play on *throw the bull* (*see* THROW IT *v.*)] [1930s] (*US campus*) a braggart, a boaster. ❑ **Spanish buttons** *n.* [late 16C] syphilitic sores. ❑ **Spanish coin** *n.* [stereotyping of the Spanish as impeccably courteous but deeply untrustworthy] [late 18C–mid-19C] empty compliments and meaningless courtesies. ❑ **Spanish cure** *n.* [? as used in Spain] [20C+] treatment of drug addiction by forced total abstinence. ❑ **Spanish faggot** *n.* [SE *faggot*, a piece of kindling wood; the stereotype of the Spanish Inquisition; the sun burns, as did the Inquisition] [late 18C–mid-19C] the sun. ❑ **Spanish fiddle** *n. see* SPANISH ARCHER above. ❑ **Spanish gout** *n.* (*also* **Spanish needle**) [reflecting the contemporary role of Spain as the national enemy. This was soon replaced by France (cf. FRENCH CROWN *under* FRENCH *adj.* etc), although the old term lingered into 19C] [late 17C–early 19C] venereal disease, syphilis. ❑ **Spanish machete** *n.* [the Spanish machete has a two-edged blade and thus 'cuts both ways'] [late 19C+] (*W.I.*) a hypocrite. ❑ **Spanish padlock** *n.* (*also* **Italian lock, Italian padlock**) [16C–early 19C] a chastity belt. ❑ **Spanish pip** *n.* [PIP *n.*[1] (2)] [late 16C–early 17C] venereal disease. ❑ **Spanish pox** *n.* [POX *n.*[1] (1)] [16C–early 18C] venereal disease, syphilis. ❑ **Spanish rice** *n.* [1970s] (*gay*) lumpy semen. ❑ **Spanish supper** *n.* [1940s–50s] (*US*) no supper at all or very little supper. ❑ **Spanish time** *n.* [the Spanish, stereotypically, are reputed to maintain a flexible attitude to appointments] [1990s+] (*Aus.*) unpunctuality. ❑ **Spanish trick** *n.* [Williams (1994) suggests additional ety. of conventional or 'missionary position' intercourse] [early 17C–early 18C] sexual intercourse. ❑ **Spanish trumpeter** *n.* [pun on SE *Don Key/donkey*] [late 18C–mid-19C] a (braying) donkey. ❑ **Spanish tummy** *n.* [1960s+] diarrhoea or any form of stomach upset experienced by tourists to Spain. ❑ **Spanish walk** *n.* [? the way Spanish pirates supposedly forced their prisoners to walk on tiptoes while they were held by the scruff of the neck, or the tip-toeing gait of flamenco dancers] [mid-19C–1940s] (*US*) a constrained style of walking assumed, willy-nilly, by those who are being ejected from a bar or saloon; thus v. *walk Spanish*. ❑ **Spanish worm** *n.* [contemporary dislike of Spain] [late 18C–early 19C] a nail found embedded in a piece of wood that one is sawing.

Spanish guitar *n.* [rhy. sl.] [20C+] (*US*) a cigar.

Spanish main *n.* [rhy. sl.] [20C+] a drain.

Spanish onion *n.* [rhy. sl.] [20C+] a bunion.

Spanish waiter *n.* [rhy. sl. (Cockney pron. 'potater')] [20C+] a potato.

spank *n.*[1] [SPANKER *n.*[1] (2)] [early 18C–mid-19C] a coin.

IN PHRASES

❑ **up the spank** [? var. *UP THE SPOUT under* SPOUT *n.*[2]] [late 19C] at the pawnbroker's.

spank *n.*[2] **1** [late 18C] a slap with an open hand [later use is SE]. **2** [early 19C] the breaking of a shop window before grabbing whatever can be reached.

IN PHRASES

❑ **do the spank** *v.* [1990s+] (*US black*) to have sexual intercourse.

spank *v.*[1] **1** [early 18C] to slap [later use is SE]. **2** [early 19C] (*UK Und.*) to rob a shop by breaking its window and grabbing whatever is within reach. **3** [late 19C] to play at. **4** [late 19C–1940s] (*N.Z.*) to milk a cow. **5** [20C+] in var. combs. meaning, of a man, to masturbate; thus *spank frank, …one's little boy, …one's monkey, …the bishop, …the carrot, …the donkey, … the plank, …the salami, …the tank, …the turkey, …wank.* **6** [1940s] to criticize, to make fun of. **7** [1960s] (*US*) to imprison. **8** [1960s+] to beat up. **9** [1960s+] to beat comprehensively in a sport or game. **10** [2000s] (*US black*) to buy an item of clothing.

IN PHRASES

❑ **spank a/the glaze** *v. see under* GLAZE *n.* ❑ **spank the monkey** *v.* [MONKEY *n.* (9b)] [1980s+] to masturbate.

spank *v.*[2] **1** [late 18C–1900s] to move smartly, briskly and stylishly, esp. when seated on horseback; also as adv. phr. *full spank*, quickly. **2** [mid-19C] to crack a whip. **3** [1980s+] (*US teen*) to masturbate. **4** [1990s+] (*US campus*) to beat decisively.

spank *adv.* [mid-19C–1940s] a general intensifier, completely, entirely, absolutely, quite.

spanked *adj.* [fig. use of SE *spank*] **1** [1920s+] intoxicated. **2** [1990s+] (*US campus*) defeated, worn out.

spanker *n.*[1] [dial. *spank*, to sparkle] **1** [mid-17C–late 18C] a gold coin. **2** [late 18C–early 19C] money in general.

spanker *n.*[2] **1** [mid-18C–1920s] anything exceptional or particularly admirable of its type. **2** [late 18C–1900s] a fast horse or ship, any creature.

spanker *n.*[3] [late 18C–late 19C] a hard, resounding slap or blow.

spanker *adj.* [mid-17C] large, first-class, showy.

spanking *n.* [SPANK *v.*[1] (1); modern use is of adults, usu. as ironic euph. for serious harm, thus in a criminal context] [mid-19C+] a beating.

spanking *adj.* **1** [late 17C+] large, first-class, showy. **2** [mid-18C–late 19C] of horse or vehicular movement, moving fast or vigorously. **3** [early 19C] of people, dashing, lively. **4** [1990s+] (*US campus*) exciting.

spanking *adv.* [late 19C+] very, exceedingly; thus *brand spanking new.*

spanky *adj.* [SPANKING *adj.* (1)] [late 19C–1930s] smart, esp. when overly so.

spanner *n.* (*also* **spanner-head**) [1980s+] **1** a fool; an unpleasant person. **2** a physically handicapped person.

SE in slang uses

IN PHRASES

❑ **drop a spanner** *v. see under* DROP *v.*[1]. ❑ **throw a spanner in(to) the works** *v.* (*also* **put a spanner in the works**) [var. on *THROW A MONKEY WRENCH INTO THE MACHINERY under* MONKEY *n.*)] [1920s+] to destroy or disable something that had hitherto been working perfectly, to ruin someone else's plans or system.

spanners *n.* [she 'tightens your NUTS *n.*[2] (1)'] [1950s+] (*Aus.*) a sexually provocative woman.

spar *n.* [SE *sparring partner*] [1970s+] (*orig. W.I.*) a friend.

spar *v.*[1] [late 19C] (*US*) to ask for credit.

spar *v.*[2] [SPAR *n.*] [1970s+] (*W.I./UK black*) to befriend, to associate with.

sparagrass *n. see* SPARROW-GRASS *n.*

sparaser *n. see* SPRARSER *n.*

spare *n.*[1] [dial. *spare*, a slit in the front of a garment] [1900s–60s] the buttoned fly of a man's trousers.

spare *n.*[2] [SE *spare*] **1** [1930s] a married man's mistress, a wife's lover. **2** [1940s] (*US black*) a friend. **3** [1960s+] (*also* **bit of spare**) an unattached woman, considered to be open to male sexual advances; esp. as *bit of spare*; thus *have a bit of spare*, to commit adultery. **4** [1990s+] an idiot, a boring person. **5** [2000s] an unattached person.

spare, the *n.* [1980s] cash, money to spend.

spare *adj.* **1** [20C+] idle, useless, superfluous. **2** [1940s+] (*orig. milit.*) overwrought, distraught.

IN PHRASES

❑ **go spare** *v.* [1940s+] to lose one's temper, to act crazily.

SE in slang uses

IN COMPOUNDS

❑ **spare boy** *n.* [ety. unknown; ? the sugar gives one extra energy, the equivalent of an assistant] [1920s+] (*Aus. rural*) treacle, golden syrup. ❑ **spareribs** *n.* [1930s–50s] (*US black*) a very thin person. ❑ **spare tyre** *n.* (*also* **rubber tyre, spare tire**) **1** [1920s+] the roll of flesh that surrounds an overweight stomach. **2** [1940s+] (*US*) an unwelcome or irrelevant person, a boring person.

spare my days! *excl.* (*also* **spare me (dinkum) days!**) [late 19C+] (*mainly Aus./N.Z.*) a mild excl.

spare my grief! *excl. see GOOD GRIEF! under* GOOD *adj.*[1].

spare rib *n.* [rhy. sl. = FIB *n.*] [1990s+] a lie.

sparesie *n. see* SPRARSER *n.*

spark *n.* **1** [mid-18C–1950s] (*orig. UK Und.*) (*also* **sparker**) a diamond; a diamond pin. **2** [1940s] (*US black*) a light. **3** [1940s] (*US black*) a marijuana cigarette.

IN COMPOUNDS

❑ **spark fawney** *n.* [FAWNEY *n.* (1)] [mid-19C–1910s] (*UK/US Und.*) a diamond ring. ❑ **spark grafter** *n.* [GRAFTER *n.*[1] (1)] [1900s] (*US Und.*) a jewel-thief. ❑ **spark prop** *n.* [PROP *n.*[3] (1)] [mid-19C–1920s] (*UK Und.*) a diamond pin or tie-pin.

SE in slang uses

IN COMPOUNDS

❑ **spark jiver** *n.* [1950s] (*US black*) an electric organ. ❑ **spark plug** *n.* **1** [1920s+] (*US*) one who sets events or plans in motion, a facilitator; thus as v., to initiate, to spur on. **2** [1990s+] (*US campus*) a sanitary tampon [resemblance]. ❑ **spark wagon** *n.* [1900s] a motor-car.

IN PHRASES

❑ **bright spark** *n.* (*also* **clever spark**) [20C+] a lively, energetic person, but often used ironically as a derog. ❑ **get a spark up** *v.* [1930s+] (*N.Z.*) to strengthen one's spirits by taking a drink. ❑ **have a spark in one's throat** *v.* [early 18C–early 19C] **1** to be continually thirsty. **2** to be keen on, to be enthusiastic. ❑ **old sparky** *n.* (*also* **sparkie, sparky chair**) [1970s+] (*US prison*) the electric chair.

spark *v.*[1] (*also* **spark it**) [SE *spark*, a beau, lover or suitor] [late 18C+] (*US*) to pay court to, to make love to, to play the suitor.

SE in slang uses

IN PHRASES

❑ **spark (it) (up)** *v.* [the *spark* of one's lighter flint] [1980s+] (*orig. UK/US black*) to light a tobacco or cannabis cigarette.

spark *v.*[2] [? SE *spark*, a beau, i.e. a womanizer, who watches women intently] [1900s–50s] (*Aus. Und.*) to watch carefully.

sparker *n. see* SPARK *n.*

sparkers *adj.* [SPARK OUT *adj.* + -ER *sfx*] [1930s+] asleep, exhausted.

sparkie *n.*[1] *see OLD SPARKY under* SPARK *n.*

sparkie *n.*[2] *see* SPARKS *n.*[2].

spark it *v. see* SPARK *v.*[1].

sparkle *n.* [appearances notwithstanding, this use has no link other than homonymic with the mid-15C–late 17C SE *sparkle*, a small ruby or diamond] [1930s+] (*UK Und.*) **1** a diamond, a diamond ring. **2** jewels.

sparkle plenty *n.* [*Sparkle Plenty*, a character in the *Dick Tracy* comic strip by Chester Gould (1900–85)] [1960s–70s] (*drugs*) amphetamine.

sparkler *n.* **1** [mid-18C–1900s] usu. as pl., a bright or sparkling eye. **2** [late 18C+] usu. in pl., jewellery, spec. diamonds. **3** [early–mid-19C] a drink of liquor. **4** [late 19C] (*UK Und.*) a match. **5** [late 19C] an admirable person. **6** [1970s] (*drugs*) amphetamine.

sparkle up *v.* [mid–late 19C] to hurry up, to 'get on with' things.

sparkling *adv.* [late 19C] lavishly.

sparkly *n.* [2000s] champagne.

sparko *adj.* [var. on SPARKERS *adj.*] [1970s+] asleep, exhausted; unconscious.

spark out *adj.* [electrical imagery] **1** [1920s+] asleep, unconscious, exhausted; dead. **2** [2000s] rendered incapable by drug use.

spark out *v.* [SPARK OUT *adj.* (1)] **1** [1930s+] to fall fast asleep. **2** [1970s+] to be knocked unconscious.

sparks *n.*[1] [SPARK *n.* (1)] **1** [mid-19C–1930s] diamonds, precious stones in general. **2** [1970s] (*US gay*) imitation jewels.

sparks *n.*[2] (*also* **sparkie, sparky**) [1910s+] **1** (*US milit.*) a radio operator. **2** an electrician, usu. theatrical and film use.

sparky chair *n. see* OLD SPARKY *under* SPARK *n.*

sparring bloke *n.* (*also* **sparring gill**) [SE *spar* + BLOKE *n.*] [mid–late 19C] a boxer, usu. a sparring partner.

sparring partner *n.* [SPAR *n.* + play on SE] [1990s+] (*W.I.*) a friend.

sparrow *n.* **1** in senses of a 'lustful' woman [classical and later writers believed that sparrows had sex up to seven times every hour, thus symbolizing lust (and shortening their lives); the orig. 17C use of the Cockney cliché 'cock-sparrow' as a term of address, was invariably linked to the addressee's sexlife]. (**a**) [early 18C] a prostitute. (**b**) [1940s] (*US Und.*) a young woman who moves from one lover to the next. **2** [late 19C] a tip, as given to a dustman or milkman or any regular provider of services to one's door [its monetary insignificance; note dustman's jargon *sparrow*, anything saleable, e.g. a silver spoon or thimble, found in a dustbin]. **3** [late 19C–1940s] (*Aus./US*) a physically weak individual [the image of the small bird]. **4** [1960s] money, a dollar bill.

SE in slang uses

IN COMPOUNDS

▫ **sparrow-brain** *n.* (*also* **sparrowhead**) [1930s+] a person of little or no intelligence. ▫ **sparrow-cheater** *n.* [late 19C–1900s] a boy who cleans horse-dung from the streets with a brush and dustpan [the bird's appetite for horse-dung]. ▫ **sparrow chirp** *n. see* SPARROW-FART *n.*[1]. ▫ **sparrow cop** *n.* [COP *n.*[1] (1); a duty often allotted officers currently out of favour with their superiors] [late 19C–1960s] (*US*) a park police officer. ▫ **sparrow-fart** *n. see* separate entries. ▫ **sparrow-grass** *n. see* separate entry. ▫ **sparrow-hawk** *v.* [var. CHICKEN-HAWK *n.*] [1990s+] to pick up homeless youngsters of either sex for sexual exploitation, esp. runaways who have just arrived at rail or bus stations. ▫ **sparrow-mouth** *n.* [the bird's anatomy] [early 17C–1920s] a very large mouth; thus *sparrow-mouthed*, wide mouthed. ▫ **sparrow's chirp** *n. see* BEE'S KNEES *n.* ▫ **sparrow-starver** *n.* [1900s–20s] (*Aus./UK*) a street-cleaner [sparrows peck at garbage]. ▫ **sparrow tail** *n.* [the shape of the tails] [mid-19C] a tail-coat, as worn as part of full evening dress.

IN PHRASES

▫ **at sparrow crow** [euph. for *AT SPARROW'S FART* below] [1940s] (*Aus.*) at dawn. ▫ **at sparrow's fart** [the dawn chorus; note synon. use by British Army in North Africa during WW2, *crow-pee*] [late 19C+] at dawn, early in the morning; usu. *up at …* ▫ **flock of sparrows flying out of one's backside** (*also* **nest of sparrows flying out of one's backside**) [1950s+] (*Aus.*) a phr. used to describe the sensation of the male orgasm; also as *flock/nest of geese/peacocks/swallows flying out…*

sparrow-fart *n.*[1] (*also* **sparrow's fart, sparrow chirp, sparrow's**) [the dawn chorus] [20C+] dawn.

sparrow-fart *n.*[2] [its insignificance] [1920s+] (*Irish*) **1** an unimportant person. **2** an irritable child.

sparrow-grass *n.* (*also* **sparagrass**) [the word, based on the 16C–18C *sparagus*, was SE mid-17C–mid-19C, but dropped into sl. thereafter] [late 19C+] asparagus.

sparrow's (fart) *n. see* SPARROW-FART *n.*[1].

sparrow's knees *n.* [rhy. sl.] [1940s] the number three.

spar up *v.* [? SPAR *v.*[1]] [1930s] (*Aus.*) to hand over.

sparzer *n. see* SPRARSER *n.*

spas *see under* SPAZ.

spasm band *n.* [the jerky, arhythmical sounds of the makeshift instruments; orig. by Emile 'Stale Bread' Lacoume, a white race-track tout] [1900s–20s] (*US black*) a spontaneously assembled musical group, playing on homemade instruments (washtubs, washboards etc); the precursors of the skiffle groups of the 1950s.

spasm chasm *n.* [the SE *spasm* is that of orgasm] [1990s+] the vagina.

spaso *n.* [SPAZ *n.* + -O *sfx* (3)] [1980s+] (*Aus.*) a spastic, either actual or fig. as a derog. term.

spas out *v. see* SPAZ *v.* (2).

spass *n. see* SPAZ *n.*

spastic *n.* [1960s+] a general derog., an incompetent.

spastic *adj.* [SE *spastic*, afflicted by spastic paralysis, characterized by sudden muscle spasm] [1960s+] **1** convulsed with laughter and thus incapable of coherent mental or physical activity. **2** uncoordinated, socially unacceptable [generally considered unacceptable since it is, in effect, a derog. attack on those who suffer this paralysis]. **3** dull, foolish.

DERIVATIVES

▫ **spastically** *adv.* [1960s] (*US*) helplessly. ▫ **spasticated** *adj.* [1990s+] a general term of derision, implying physical inadequacy.

spat *n.* [echoic] (*orig. US*) **1** [19C+] a tiff, a dispute, a quarrel. **2** [1900s] a smart blow, smack or slap; also the sound thereof.

spat *v.* [SPAT *n.* (1)] [19C+] to fight, esp. in the context of a lover's tiff.

spatter *v.* [1940s+] to beat up severely.

spawny *adj.* [ety. unknown. ? link to Scot. game *spawnie*, played with buttons, in which one player throws a button, the others attempt to throw theirs nearest to it, and the button that comes within a *spawn* (SE *span*) is the winner] [1990s+] lucky.

spaz *n.* (*also* **spas, spass, spazz, spazzer, spazzo**) [SE *spastic*, one who suffers from spastic paralysis, i.e. 'a condition in which some muscles undergo tonic spasm (sometimes resulting in abnormal posture) [...] so that voluntary movement of the part affected is difficult and poorly co-ordinated' (*OED*)] [1960s+] **1** a spastic. **2** (*student/school*) one who is useless, clumsy, incompetent and is thus socially unacceptable; thus *spaz attack*, a state of excitement; also as adj. **3** (*US campus*) a general pej.; no physical incompetence is implied.

DERIVATIVES

▫ **spazzy** *adj.* [SPAZ *n.*] **1** [1920s+] (*also* **spazzed, spazzled**) stupid, uncontrolled, bizarre, intense, nervous. **2** [1950s] good, wonderful. **3** [1990s+] physically un-co-ordinated, spastic.

IN COMPOUNDS

▫ **spaz cut** *n.* [1990s+] (*UK juv.*) an unflattering haircut. ▫ **spaz pads** *n.* [1970s+] orthopaedic shoes. ▫ **spazwheels** *n.* [WHEELS *n.* (1b)] [1990s+] a wheelchair. ▫ **spaz-wit** *n.* [1980s+] a fool, an idiot.

IN PHRASES

▫ **chuck a spaz** *v.* (*also* **chuck a spas**) [1990s+] (*Aus.*) to lose one's temper.

spaz *adj.* [SPAZ *n.*] [1980s+] uncoordinated.

spaz *v.* (*also* **spas, spazz**) [SPAZ *n.*] [1960s+] **1** to make twitch. **2** (*also* **spas out, spaz out**) to act foolishly, to lose control, to act in an uncoordinated manner – either mentally or physically.

3 to surprise, and thus render the third party momentarily unable to respond.

spaza *n.* (*also* **spaza shop, sphaza, sphaza shop**) [Ngwenya *spaza*, camouflaged] [1980s+] (*S.Afr. township*) an illicit (thus 'camouflaged') or latterly informal grocery or general store.

spazmo *n.* [SPASTIC *n.* + SE *spasmodic*] [1970s+] a general term of abuse; an incompetent, an inadequate.

spaz out *v. see* SPAZ *v.* (2).

spazz *see under* SPAZ.

spazzed *adj. see* SPAZZY *under* SPAZ *n.*

spazzer *n. see* SPAZ *n.*

spazzled *adj. see* SPAZZY *under* SPAZ *n.*

spazzo *n. see* SPAZ *n.*

speak *n.*[1] [SPEAK *v.*] [early 19C] (*UK Und.*) a stolen item, a robbery.

IN PHRASES

❑ **make a speak** *v.* [early 19C] (*UK Und.*) to commit a robbery.

speak *n.*[2] [abbr. SPEAKEASY *n.*] [1920s–30s] (*US*) an illicit drinking establishment.

speak *v.* (*also* **speak to, speak with**) [ironic euph.] [early 18C–mid-19C] (*UK Und.*) to hold up; to rob.

SE in slang uses

IN PHRASES

❑ **on speakers** (*also* **on speaks**) [1900s–20s] (*UK society*) on speaking terms. ❑ **speak a mouthful** *v. see* SAY A MOUTHFUL *under* SAY *v.* ❑ **speak bandog and Bedlam** *v. see under* BANDOG *n.* ❑ **speak brown tomorrow** *v.* [late 19C] to get sunburned. ❑ **speak French** *v. see under* FRENCH *n.* ❑ **speak holiday** *v.* [SE *holiday*; thus the image of one's 'best' language] [late 16C–early 17C] to speak elegant, formal English. ❑ **speak like a mouse in cheese** *v.* [late 17C–early 19C] to speak quietly or indistinctly. ❑ **speak on the big white telephone** *v. see under* TELEPHONE *n.* ❑ **speak pound notes** *v.* [the assumed correspondence of wealth and 'good' English] [1980s] (*Irish*) to speak Standard English. ❑ **speak pretty** *v. see* TALK PRETTY *under* TALK *v.* ❑ **speak proper** *v.* [abbr. *speak proper English* or, thus ironically, misusing *proper* in place of *properly*] [20C+] to talk in Standard English, rather than in colloq., dial. or sl., often as an imper. ❑ **speak Welsh** *v.* [echoic] [1990s+] to vomit. ❑ **speak white** *v.* [1960s+] (*Can.*) used by English speakers, to speak English (as opposed to French, which is the first language of many Canadians, esp. the Québecois).

speakeasy *n.* (*also* **speakie**) [SE *speak* + *easy*, speak softly, e.g. the tone of voice in which one addressed the lookout or in which the patrons were urged to talk in case the police were at the door; the *speakeasy* appeared *c.*1890, when it meant an illicit liquor shop or an unlicensed bar. The advent of Prohibition (1920–33) elevated the once-marginal institution into the mainstream of US life] [late 19C+] (*US*) an illicit drinking establishment.

speaker *n.* [SPEAK *v.*] [mid-19C] (*UK Und.*) a thief.

speako *n.* [abbr. SPEAKEASY *n.* + -O *sfx* (6)] [1920s–30s] (*US*) an illicit drinking establishment.

speaky *n.*[1] [SPEAK *v.*] [late 19C] the proceeds of a robbery.

speaky *n.*[2] [abbr.] [1930s] (*US Und.*) a speakeasy.

spear *n.* **1** [20C+] (*Aus.*) as *the spear*, dismissal from a job. **2** in US drug uses. (**a**) [1930s+] a hypodermic syringe. (**b**) [1980s+] a branch of marijuana, 15–35cm (6–14in) long, weighing several ounces. **3** [1980s] (*US Und.*) a pickpocket.

IN PHRASES

❑ **get the spear** *v.* (*also* **get the harpoon**) [late 19C–1960s] (*Aus.*) to be dismissed from a job. ❑ **toss the spear** *v. see* SPEAR *v.* (3).

SE in slang uses

DERIVATIVES

❑ **spearo** *n.* [-O *sfx* (3)] [1960s–70s] (*Aus.*) a spear-fisherman.

IN COMPOUNDS

❑ **spearchucker** *n.* [1950s+] (*US*) **1** a derog. term for a black person [the image of the African tribesman as a 'primitive']. **2** (*US campus*) a college student, a young adult [the image of the African tribesman as a young warrior].

spear *v.* **1** [20C+] (*Aus.*) to dismiss from a job. **2** [20C+] (*Aus.*) to throw out of a pub, dancehall etc. **3** [1910s–60s] (*US*) (*also* **toss the spear**) to beg, to obtain through begging. **4** [1930s–40s] (*US prison*) to arrest. **5** [1980s] (*US Und.*) to pickpocket. **6** [1980s+] (*Aus. prison*) to put something somebody's way.

IN PHRASES

❑ **spear a job** *v.* [1940s+] (*Aus.*) to get a job. ❑ **spear the bearded clam** *v. see under* BEARDED CLAM *n.*

spec *n.* [SE *speculation*] **1** [late 18C–1900s] (*also* **speck**) a business, a commercial enterprise. **2** [mid-19C] a lottery. **3** [1930s–60s] a speculator.

spec *adj.* [abbr.] [1960s+] *spec*ulative.

spechie *n.* [SE *special*] [1980s+] (*W.I./UK black teen*) a gun, particularly a .38 special.

special *n.* **1** [1970s+] a prostitute's client who has any particular tastes, costumes, bondage, fetishes etc. **2** [1990s+] (*UK juv.*) a pupil requiring special needs.

special *adj.* **1** [early–mid-19C] especially interested or informed. **2** [1980s] (*US campus*) unpleasant. **3** [2000s] (*US teen*) odd and slightly interesting.

Special K *n.* (*also* **super K, vitamin K**) [the breakfast cereal *Special K*, supposedly an adjunct to better health] **1** [1970s+] (*drugs*) ketamine. **2** [1980s+] a heroin-based hallucinogen.

specimen *n.* [mid-19C+] a human being, esp. in pej. use, e.g. a *queer specimen, an odd specimen*.

Speck, the *n.* [its relatively small (to mainland Aus.) size] [1910s+] (*Aus.*) Tasmania.

speck *n.*[1] **1** [mid-19C–1910s; 1950s] (*costermonger/Aus.*) a decaying orange with *specks* of mould; any spotted or damaged fruit or vegetable; thus adj. *specky, specked*, rotten. **2** [1970s] (*US black*) a black person [? abbr. SE *speck of dirt*; if so then used ironically].

SE in slang uses

IN COMPOUNDS

❑ **speck bum** *n.* [SE *speck*, a contemptible person + BUM *n.*[3] (1)] [1920s–40s] (*US tramp*) a very decrepit, alcoholic tramp.

speck *n.*[2] *see* SPEC *n.* (1).

specked wiper *n.* (*also* **speckled wipe**) [SE *speckled* + WIPER *n.* (1)] [late 17C–early 19C] (*UK Und.*) a coloured handkerchief, presumably with spots.

specker *n.* [abbr.] [1910s] (*Aus.*) a financial *spec*ulator.

speckle *n.* [their complexion] [1950s] (*W.I.*) an albino.

speckle-belly *n.* [? a distinctive style of garment, presumably a waistcoat, sported by such figures, but note also northeastern US dial. *speckle-belly*, a grey duck. Nonconformist clergymen were more likely to dress in muted than colourful tones] [late 19C] (*US*) a dissenter, a nonconformist.

speckled birds *n.* [? packaging + they make one FLY *v.* (3)] [1970s–80s] (*US drugs*) amphetamines.

speckled wipe *n. see* SPECKED WIPER *n.*

specky *adj.* [SPECS *n.*] **1** [1910s+] wearing spectacles. **2** [1990s+] thus fig., weak, inadequate.

specs *n.* (*also* **specks**) [abbr.] **1** [early 19C+] glasses, *spec*tacles. **2** [1930s+] a nickname for one who wears glasses.

spectacles-seat *n.* (*also* **spectacle-beam**) [late 19C–1900s] the nose.

spectrum *n. see* NEXUS *n.*

sped *n.* [abbr. *sp*ecial *ed*ucation] [1980s+] (*US campus*) a slow or stupid person.

spee *n.* [var. SPAR *n.*] [1990s+] (*black*) a friend.

speech *n.* [mid–late 19C] a horseracing tip; esp. in phrs. *get the speech*, to receive a tip; *give the speech*, to pass on information.

speech *v.* [SE *speech*] [1980s+] (*UK black*) **1** to argue. **2** to persuade.

speeching *n.* [SPEECH *v.*] [1980s+] (*UK black*) **1** talking seductively to a woman. **2** talking fluently and well. **3** defeating in an argument.

speechless *adj.* [late 19C+] euph. for drunk.

speed *n.* **1** [1910s+] metaphorical for style, way of life or action. **2** [1910s+] energy. **3** [1920s–30s] (*US*) a fast liver, a hedonist. **4** [1930s] of a man, an affectionate term of address. **5** [1930s] a good time. **6** [1960s+] (*drugs*) any amphetamine-based stimulant drug [its effect on the heart and brain].

pertaining to drugs

DERIVATIVES

❑ **speeder** *n.* [1960s] (*drugs*) an amphetamine user. ❑ **speedy** *adj.* [2000s] under the influence of amphetamines.

IN COMPOUNDS

❑ **speedball** *see* separate entries. ❑ **speed boat** *n.* [1980s+] (*drugs*) marijuana, phencyclidine and crack cocaine combined and smoked. ❑ **speedcoke** *n.* [COKE *n.*[1] (1)] [1990s+] (*drugs*) a mixture of amphetamine and heroin, seen and experienced as a potent rival/replacement for crack cocaine. ❑ **speed freak** *n.* [-FREAK *sfx*] **1** [1960s+] (*drugs*) a regular user of amphetamines. **2** *see also* SE compounds below.

IN PHRASES

❑ **bathtub speed** *n.* [artificial amphetamine, on pattern of *bathtub gin/whisky* etc, i.e. home-produced liquor] [1960s+] (*drugs*) methcathinone, a form of amphetamine that produces a more intense and longer lasting 'high' than does cocaine. ❑ **speed for lovers** *n.* (*also* **lover's speed**) [its aphrodisiac or at least affection-enhancing effects] [1980s+] (*drugs*) MDMA. ❑ **speedrap** *v.* [RAP *v.*[1] (1e)] [1970s] to talk fast, usu. under the influence of amphetamine.

pertaining to a style or way of life

IN PHRASES

❑ **about one's speed** (*also* **just one's speed**) [1930s–70s] (*orig. US*) suitable, to one's own taste. ❑ **not one's speed** [1960s+] (*orig. US*) unsuited to one's taste.

SE in slang uses

DERIVATIVES

❑ **speedo** *n.* [abbr.] [1930s+] a *speedo*meter.

IN COMPOUNDS

❑ **speedball** *see* separate entries. ❑ **speed bug** *n.* [BUG *n.*[4] (3b)] [1910s–20s] (*US*) a fan of travelling at high speed. ❑ **speed bump** *n. see under* BUMP *n.*[1]. ❑ **speed cop** *n.* [COP *n.*[1] (1)] [1920s+] (*orig. US*) a motorcycle-mounted police officer, charged with enforcing speed limits. ❑ **speed freak** *n.* [-FREAK *sfx*] **1** [1980s] a very fast runner. **2** [1990s+] (*US black*) one who enjoys driving or being driven at high speed. **3** *see also* drug uses above. ❑ **speed hog** *n.* [HOG *n.* (2)] [1910s+] one who consistently ignores speed limits when driving. ❑ **speed king** *n.* [1910s+] (*US*) a motor-racing champion. ❑ **speed limit** *n.* [the urban speed limit, 30mph (48kph)] [1940s+] (*bingo*) the number 30. ❑ **speed merchant** *n.* [MERCHANT *n.*] [1910s+] (*orig. US*) one who drives excessively fast. ❑ **speed shop** *n.* [1950s+] (*US*) an automobile supplier specializing in the parts for (and sometimes building) modified cars. ❑ **speed trap** *n.* [ety. unknown] [1930s+] (*S.Afr.*) methylated spirits, as drunk by alcoholics and tramps. ❑ **speed wagon** *n.* [WAGON *n.* (1a)] [1940s] (*US Und.*) a police patrol car.

IN PHRASES

❑ **more speed to your elbow** *see* MORE POWER TO YOUR ELBOW *under* POWER *n.*

speed *v.* **1** [1960s+] (*drugs*) to use amphetamines [SPEED *n.* (6)]. **2** [1980s] (*US campus*) to work very hard, esp. when preparing for a test or examination [SE *speed*].

DERIVATIVES

❑ **speeding** *n.* **1** [1960s+] (*drugs*) the taking of or experiencing amphetamines or a similar 'go-faster' drug. **2** [1990s+] fig. use of sense 1; an energized experience similar to the above, but without the use of drugs.

IN EXCLAMATIONS

❑ **speed the wombats!** [1920s+] (*Aus.*) a general excl. of surprise, alarm, fascination etc.

speedball *n.*[1] [SPEED *n.* (6)] **1** [20C+] (*drugs*) a mixture of cocaine and heroin and/or morphine, either injected or sniffed by the user, occas. Methedrine and heroin; also a ball of opium placed beneath the tongue. **2** [1920s–30s] (*US*) a glass of wine, strengthened by a shot of spirits. **3** [1930s] (*drugs*) a dose of a narcotic. **4** [1950s–60s] a mixture of valium and marijuana. **5** [1970s] (*drugs*) amphetamine.

speedball *n.*[2] [? the speed with which it is cooked or passes through the eater's stomach] [1960s+] (*Aus.*) a rissole, esp. as cooked for shearers.

speedball *v.*[1] [1950s] to run off fast.

speedball *v.*[2] [SPEEDBALL *n.*[1] (1)] [1960s+] (*drugs*) to smoke, sniff or inject a mixture of heroin and cocaine or morphine and cocaine.

DERIVATIVES

❑ **speedballer** *n.* [1990s+] (*drugs*) one who injects or sniffs a mixture of heroin and cocaine.

speedos *n.* [the brandname *Speedo*] [1990s+] (*Aus.*) tight-fitting male swimming briefs.

speedy *n.* [2000s] (*Irish*) a police motorbike.

speedy *adj.* [play on FAST *adj.*[1] (2)] [1910s–20s] living a pleasure-seeking, hedonistic life.

speedy Gonzales *n.* [the old joke about *Speedy Gonzales*, a quick and eager fornicator] [20C+] (*US*) a person who moves, works or operates very fast; as adj., quick.

speel *v.*[1] [Scot. *speel*, to clamber] [mid–late 19C] to run away, to decamp.

speel *v.*[2] *see* SPIEL *v.*[1] (1).

speeler *n. see* SPIELER *n.*

speelken *n. see* SPELLKEN *n.*

speel (on) the drum *v. see under* DRUM *n.*[3].

speewa *n. see* SPEWAH *n.*

speil *see under* SPIEL.

speler *n. see* SPIELER *n.*

spell *n.*[1] [Ger. *spiel*, to play] [mid-18C–mid-19C] a theatre.

IN PHRASES

❑ **breaking up of the spell** *n.* [19C] the end of the nightly performance at the Theatres-Royal, London; as the crowds disperse pickpockets move among them looking for valuables.

spell *n.*[2] [SE *spell*, a short time] [late 19C–1910s] a sentence of three months' imprisonment.

SE in slang uses

IN COMPOUNDS

❑ **spell job** *n.* [1980s+] (*Ulster*) a job of uncertain or indefinite duration.

spell *v.* [SE *spell out*] [mid-19C] to advertise, to put into print.

SE in slang uses

IN PHRASES

❑ **spell baker** *v.* [ety. unknown; ? ironic, since *baker* is easily spelled; ? *baker* was the first word of two syllables in Webster's 'Blue-back Speller'] [mid-19C] (*US*) to perform a difficult or challenging task, to be up to the mark.

spell for *v.* [SE *spell*, to engage in study or contemplation of something] **1** [mid–late 19C] to long for. **2** [20C+] (*W.I.*) to wait for, with the intention of attacking verbally or physically. **3** [1940s] (*US*) to take over, to relieve.

spellken *n.* (*also* **speelken, spiel-ken**) [Ger. *spiel*, to play + KEN *n.*[1] (1)] **1** [late 18C–mid-19C] a theatre. **2** [early–mid-19C] (*UK Und.*) a cockpit.

spell-o *n.* [SAus.E *spell*, to relieve by an interval of rest; to rest + -O *sfx* (3)] [late 19C+] (*Aus.*) a rest; also as v.

spence *n.* [obs. SE *spend(ings)*, semen] [20C+] (*W.I.*) ejaculated semen.

spencer *n.* [ety. unknown; ? a local landlord or well-known drinker] [early–mid-19C] a small glass of gin.

spend *n.* [SPEND *v.*] [late 19C] **1** semen. **2** an orgasm.

spend *v.* [mid-17C–late 19C] to have an orgasm, to ejaculate.

spends *n.* [1990s+] spending money.

speng *n.* [? Carib.E. *spengle*, a fighting cock] [1980s+] (*W.I./UK black teen*) **1** a gun. **2** a form of strutting walk. **3** an urban gangster. **4** a slut. **5** a fool.

sperm *n.*

SE in slang uses

IN COMPOUNDS

❑ **sperm-bucket** *n.* [1980s] an ageing prostitute. ❑ **sperm-burper** *n.* [1990s+] **1** a person who performs fellatio. **2** spec. a male homosexual. **3** an insult. ❑ **sperm spouter** *n. see* SPOUTER *n.*[3]. ❑ **sperm-sucker** *n.* [late 19C] the vagina.

IN PHRASES

❑ **sperm the worm** *v.* [1990s+] to masturbate.

sperrib *n.* [SE *spare rib*, that bone from which the Bible claimed Eve was created] [late 19C] (*middle class*) a wife.

spesh *n.* [abbr. of pron.] **1** [1900s] a *spec*ialist. **2** [1990s+] Carlsberg *Spec*ial Brew, a strong beer popular with alcoholic tramps.

spew *n.* [SE *spew*, vomit] [1980s+] (*orig. US campus*) semen.

IN COMPOUNDS

❑ **spew alley** *n.* **1** [19C] the vagina. **2** [mid-19C–1900s] the throat.

SE in slang uses

DERIVATIVES

❑ **spewsome** *adj.* [on model of AWESOME *adj.*; lit. enough to make one vomit] [late 19C; 1990s+] of food, drink, objects, events or people, disgusting, repellent. ❑ **spewy** *adj.* [SPEW *v.* (4)] [1980s] (*Aus.*) angry.

IN PHRASES

❑ **have a spew** *v.* [2000s] (*N.Z.*) to have an emotional outburst.

spew *v.* [SE *spew*, to vomit] **1** [late 17C; late 19C; 1980s] (*US campus*) to ejaculate. **2** [late 18C; mid-19C+] to speak, esp. to confess. **3** [1970s–80s] (*N.Z. prison*) to inform on, to betray. **4** [1980s+] (*Aus./N.Z./US black*) to argue angrily, to let loose a diatribe.

IN PHRASES

❑ **spew chunks** *v. see BLOW CHUNKS under* BLOW *v.*[1]. ❑ **spew one's goo** *v.* [GOO *n.*[1] (1)] [1990s+] to ejaculate. ❑ **spew one's guts** *v.* [1930s+] **1** to vomit violently. **2** to make a full confession of crimes. ❑ **spew one's ring** *v. see under* RING *n.*

IN EXCLAMATIONS

❑ **spew it out!** [20C+] say your piece! make your point!

spewah *n.* (*also* **speewa**) [David Mulhallen, 'A Swag of Yarns', Internet, (2002): 'The stories of Speewah and Crooked Mick first came to notice in the *Australian Worker* in the early 1920s, when a writer named Julian Stuart started writing some articles. Stuart was an ex-shearer who had been at the 1891 Shearers' Strike and he reckoned that these stories had been very popular in the shearing sheds throughout the 1880's.'] [late 19C+] (*Aus.*) a fantasy outback station, used as a site for a variety of far-fetched tales; thus the tale itself.

spewing *adj.* [fig. use of SE *spew*] [1980s+] (*Aus. teen*) in a furious temper.

sphaza (shop) *n. see* SPAZA *n.*

sphinc *n.* [abbr.] [2000s] the anal *sphinc*ter.

sphukupuk *n.* (*also* **sphukupuku**) [used in Fanagalo, a Zulu/English/Nguni pidgin spoken in the mines; this pidgin, created by whites, is generally disliked by black miners] [20C+] (*S.Afr.*) a fool, a dunce, a blockhead.

spic *n.* (*also* **spick, spig, spik**) [abbr. SPIGGOTY *n.*; orig. an Italian, when seen as a mispron. of *spaghetti* or 'no spicka da English'] [1910s+] (*US*) **1** a derog. name for an Italian. **2** a derog. term for a Puerto Rican, a Mexican, a Cuban; thus *Spicsville*, the Puerto Rican etc area of a town. **3** any Spanish language. **4** (*US campus*) a course in Spanish. **5** Spanish; Spanish-American.

spic *adj.* (*also* **spick, spicky, spik**) [SPIC *n.* (2)] **1** [1930s+] (*orig. US*) pertaining to Latin American or Puerto Rican people or culture. **2** [1980s] Spanish.

IN COMPOUNDS

❑ **Spic town** *n.* (*also* **Spicktown**) [1950s–60s] (*US*) a derog. term for the Puerto Rican or Mexican area of a town.

spic and span *n.* [play on SE phr. + SPIC *n.* (2) + *Span(ish)*, although both refer only to the Hispanic partner] [1950s+] (*US black*) a mixed Puerto Rican and black couple.

spice *n.*[1] [SPICE *v.*[2]] [early 19C] (*UK Und.*) mugging, footpad robbery.

IN COMPOUNDS

❑ **spice gloak** *n.* [GLOAK *n.*] [early–mid-19C] a footpad, a highwayman, a mugger.

spice *n.*[2] [SPICY *adj.* (3)] [late 19C+] sexual provocativeness; in anecdotes, jokes etc, smuttiness.

spice *v.*[1] **1** [mid–late 17C] to infect with venereal disease [play on SE, presumably the spice would be HOT *adj.* (1a)]. **2** [late 18C] to adulterate [ext. of SE].

spice *v.*[2] [? Ger. *speissen*, to eat or SPEAK *v.*] [early 19C] (*UK Und.*) to rob; thus *spice the swell*, to rob the gentleman; *spicing*, a street robbery.

spice island *n.* [pun] [early 19C] **1** the anus. **2** a privy. **3** any dirty, stinking place.

spice of life *n. see SLICE OF LIFE under* SLICE *n.*

spicer *n.* [SPICE *v.*[2]] [late 18C–mid-19C] (*UK Und.*) a robber, a footpad.

spick *see under* SPIC.

spicket *n.* [SE *spicket*, a spigot, a tap] [late 17C–early 18C] the penis.

Spicktown *n. see Spic TOWN under* SPIC *adj.*

spicky *adj. see* SPIC *adj.*

spicy *adj.* **1** [19C+] smart, spirited; thus n. *the spicy*. **2** [mid–late 19C] smart-looking, neat. **3** [mid-19C+] sexually provocative [may have started out as a genuine euph. but invariably carries slightly ludicrous 'dirty old man' overtones].

IN PHRASES

❑ **cut it spicy** *v.* (*also* **cut it fat**) [late 19C] to have a good, if vulgar time.

spicy *adv.* [mid-19C] civilly, politely.

spider *n.* **1** in context of alcohol [? it 'creeps up' on the drinker]. (**a**) [mid-19C+] (*Aus.*) a drink composed of brandy and lemonade or of brandy and beer or of sherry and lemonade. (**b**) [late 19C] claret and lemonade. (**c**) [1940s] (*US*) the dregs of a bottle. **2** [late 19C–1930s] (*US*) a wire picklock, a skeleton key. **3** as a vehicle. (**a**) [late 19C–1940s] (*Aus.*) a light gig or two-wheeled, one-horse carriage. (**b**) [1900s] a bicycle. (**c**) [1930s] (*US tramp*) a Ford automobile. (**d**) [1940s] (*US Und.*) a stripped down automobile. **4** [1920s] (*US*) a term of abuse. **5** [1970s] (*US campus*) a hard worker [the industrious arachnid]. **6** *see* ROCK SPIDER *n.*

SE in slang uses

IN COMPOUNDS

❑ **spider-brusher** *n.* [their housework] [mid-19C] a domestic servant. ❑ **spider-catcher** *n.* [in SE *spider-catcher* is a general, if vague, term of abuse, referring not to anatomy but propensity] **1** [late 16C; mid-19C] a monkey. **2** [late 17C–early 18C] an extremely thin man. ❑ **spider-claw** *v.* [the clawing movements of one's hand, reminiscent of a spider's scrabbling legs] [late 19C] of a man, to play with one's testicles. ❑ **spiderman** *n.* [1950s] (*US*) a steel erector. ❑ **spider monkey** *n.* [they are 'climbing the walls'] [2000s] (*US prison*) a prisoner who is finding it hard to do their sentence. ❑ **spider-shanked** *adj.* [late 18C–early 19C] used to describe a man with very thin legs. ❑ **spider's legs** *n.* **1** [1960s] (*Scot.*) very thin hand-rolled cigarettes. **2** [1990s+] (*UK teen*) pubic hairs that protrude beyond a woman's panties or bikini.

spiel *n.* (*also* **speil**) [SPIEL *v.*[1]] **1** [late 19C–1900s] (*US*) a drinking spree. **2** [late 19C–1920s] (*US tramp*) the commodity that a pedlar is selling. **3** [late 19C–1930s] (*US*) a dance, as found in New York dance-halls; thus as v., to dance. **4** [late 19C+] patter, speech, esp. of a salesman or market stall-holder, fairground stall-holder or confidence trickster. **5** [late 19C+] a verbose, 'wordy' explanation. **6** [late 19C+] a conversation, a chat. **7** [20C+] a situation. **8** [1900s] (*US campus*) an eloquent passage in an oration or essay. **9** [1900s] (*US campus*) a failure at recitation. **10** [1930s] lies, deceit. **11** [1930s+] (*orig. Aus.*)

formal advice, a set of instructions. **12** [1940s] a letter. **13** [1990s+] a drinking club.

IN PHRASES

❑ **hard spiel** *n.* [1930s–40s] (*US black*) **1** black slang, jive talk. **2** interesting, persuasive patter.

spiel *v.*[1] [Ger. *spielen*, to play] **1** [mid-19C+] (*also* **speel**) to gamble. **2** [late 19C] to pose. **3** [late 19C–1900s] (*US campus*) to play, to dance. **4** [late 19C+] (*also* **speil**) to talk. **5** [late 19C+] to patter, to talk glibly. **6** [late 19C+] to 'shoot a line', to tell a tale; to perform a confidence trick.

IN PHRASES

❑ **spiel the nuts** *v.* [NUTS *n.*[2] (3)] [1910s–40s] (*US Und.*) to play the 'shell game', using a good deal of talk to disguise the cheating.

spiel *v.*[2] [dial. *speel*, to move fast] **1** [late 19C–1910s] (*Aus.*) to gallop; thus *spieler* n. a good horseman. **2** [1910s] (*US*) to dance.

spieler *n.* (*also* **shpeiler, shpieler, speeler, speiler, speler**) [SPIEL *v.*[1]] **1** [mid-19C+] a swindler, a fraud, a card-sharp, a crooked gambler [briefly US, Matsell includes it in *Vocabulum* (1859); the underlying implication is a sense of humour behind the cheating; thus Henry Lawson (1895): 'He was [...] good-natured in his way; he was a "spieler" pure and simple, and did things in humorous style']. **2** [late 19C] (*Aus.*) a bookmaker. **3** [late 19C–1950s] a shop tout or fairground stall-holder. **4** [late 19C+] (*Aus./US prison*) a fluent talker; a plausible, 'sharp' individual. **5** [20C+] a persuasive talker, e.g. an evangelical preacher. **6** [1900s–40s] (*US*) a young, lower-class single woman, esp. as found frequenting dance-halls; also applied to male dancers. **7** [1920s+] an illegal gambling club. **8** [1930s] (*US Und.*) a corrupt lawyer. **9** [1930s+] a street seller, e.g. of perfumes. **10** [1940s–50s] (*Aus.*) a fast horse.

spieling *n.* [SPIEL *v.*[1] (1)] **1** [mid–late 19C] (*UK Und.*) gambling. **2** [late 19C+] (*Aus./N.Z./UK*) card-sharping, swindling.

IN COMPOUNDS

❑ **spieling club** *n.* [late 19C–1920s] a gambling club where the innocent patrons are swindled.

spiel-ken *n.* see SPELLKEN *n.*

spiff *n.* [SPIFFY *adj.*; note drapery jargon *spiff*, a percentage allowed to salesmen when they sell off old or unfashionable stock, thus 'Mr. Spiffs, the linendraper' in James Greenwood, *Dick Temple* (1877)] **1** [mid-19C+] a dandy. **2** [late 19C] something first-rate, exciting, stimulating.

spiff *adj.* (*also* **spif, spifly**) [? echoic of a sharp sound and thus fig. exciting, important, astonishing (cf. SPANG *adv.*; SPANK *n.*[2])] **1** [mid-19C+] smartly dressed, dandified. **2** [late 19C+] first-rate, excellent.

spiffed *adj.* [play on SE *spiffed*, neat, smart] [mid-19C–1960s] (*orig. Scot.*) tipsy, slightly drunk.

spiffical *adj.* see SPIFFY *adj.*

spiffing *adj.* [? Derby dial. *spiffyn*, work well done or *spiffer*, anything exceptional in quality or size] [mid-19C+] excellent, first-rate.

spiffingly *adv.* (*also* **spiffing, spifflingly**) [SPIFFING *adj.*] [late 19C+] extremely well.

spifflicate see *under* SPLIFICATE.

spiffs *n.* [note drapery jargon *spiff*, a percentage allowed to salesmen when they sell off old or unfashionable stock] [1930s–40s] (*US Und.*) bonus money, extras.

spiff up *v.* (*also* **spiff out**) [SPIFF *adj.* (1)] [1970s+] to smarten up.

spiffy *adj.* (*also* **spiffical, spifly, spivish, spivvish, spivvy**) [SPIFF *adj.*] [mid-19C+] excellent, wonderful, neatly dressed.

spiffy *adv.* [SPIFFY *adj.*] [1970s+] smartly, neatly, esp. of dress.

spiflicate *v.* (*also* **smifligate, spifflicate**) [ety. unknown; ? 'fanciful' (*OED*); SE *stifle* + *suffocate* (Hotten, 1864); SE *suffocate* or dial. *smothercate* (Ware); SE *spill* + *stifle*/dial. *stiffle* (Partridge)] **1** [late 18C–mid-19C] to confound, to silence, to dumbfound. **2** [late 18C+] to thrash, to beat, to overcome completely. **3** [early 19C] to betray to the authorities. **4** [1900s] to cause pain or unhappiness, in some unspecified manner. **5** [1900s] to be killed.

spiflicated *adj.* (*also* **smificated, smifligated; spifflicated**) [SPIFLICATE *v.*] **1** [mid-19C] unkempt, messy. **2** [20C+] (*orig. US*) drunk.

spiflicating *n.* (*also* **spifflicating**) [SPIFLICATE *v.*] [mid-19C] aggressive, crushing.

spiflication *n.* (*also* **spifflication, spiflification**) [SPIFLICATE *v.*] [mid–late 19C] absolute destruction.

spifly *adj.* **1** *see* SPIFF *adj.* **2** *see* SPIFFY *adj.*

spig *n. see* SPIC *n.*

spig *adj.* [SPIGGOTY *n.*] [1910s–1940s] (*US*) pertaining to Central or South America.

spiggoty *n.* (*also* **spig**) [? broken English 'spikka da English'] **1** [1900s–40s] (*US*) a Spanish-speaking native of Central or South America. **2** [1910s] the Spanish language. **3** [1940s–80s] an Italian [SE *spaghetti*].

spigot *n.* [SE *spigot*, a tap] [mid-17C–19C] the penis; thus *spiggot-hole*, the vagina.

IN COMPOUNDS

❑ **spigot-sucker** *n.* [SUCK *v.*[1] (1)] [19C] a fellator or fellatrix.

spij *n.* [? SE *spit*] [1990s+] (*UK juv.*) chewing gum.

spik *see under* SPIC.

spike *n.*[1] **1** [mid–late 19C] the erect penis. **2** [1920s] a needle, a nail. **3** [1920s] (*US Und.*) a lock. **4** [1930s+] a needle; a hypodermic syringe. **5** [1940s+] the act of injecting a narcotic drug. **6** [1990s+] a style of haircut.

IN PHRASES

pertaining to drugs

❑ **hit the spike** *v.* [2000s] to inject a narcotic drug. ❑ **on the spike** [1930s–50s] (*US drugs*) using or addicted to narcotics.

pertaining to irritation or annoyance

❑ **get the spike** *v.* [late 19C+] to be extremely annoyed. ❑ **give someone the spike** *v.* [1910s] to irritate. ❑ **have one's spike up** *v.* [1940s] to be in a bad temper. ❑ **have the spike** *v.* [1950s] to be angry, irritated.

SE in slang uses

IN COMPOUNDS

❑ **spike-faggot** *n.* [FAGGOT *n.*[3]] [17C] the penis. ❑ **spike hotel** *n.* [the metal *spikes* on the walls] [early–mid-19C] a prison. ❑ **Spike Park** *n.* [mid-19C] the Queen's Bench prison; thus *spike park*, the grounds of a prison. ❑ **spike team** *n.* [the lead horse represents the *spike*] [mid–late 19C] (*US*) a coach drawn by three horses, two abreast and one in the lead.

IN PHRASES

❑ **look over the spikes** *v.* [the spikes that top the front edge of the dock] [late 19C] (*Aus.*) to appear in court as a defendant. ❑ **Spikes, the** *n.* [early 19C] the King's Bench Prison, London.

spike *n.*[2] [the lack of comfort] **1** [mid-19C+] a lodging house, orig. a local authority workhouse or lodging house; thus *spike-ranger*, a tramp who wanders from one such place to another. **2** [1960s+] (*Irish*) a maternity hospital.

spike *n.*[3] [SPIKE *v.*[2] (1)] [1900s] (*US*) a shot of alcohol (when added to an otherwise non-alcoholic drink).

spike *v.*[1] [? SE *spike a gun*, to immobilize a cannon by driving a spike into the touchhole, or *spike*, a pointed stick for holding papers, bills etc] **1** [late 19C–1900s] (*US campus*) to get possession of; thus, to convict. **2** [late 19C+] to harm, to undermine; also as phr. *spike someone's guns*. **3** [20C+] (*US*) to reject, to quash, to delete.

spike *v.*[2] [such adulteration adds 'sharpness'] **1** [late 19C+] to add alcohol (clandestinely) to an ostensibly non-alcoholic drink. **2** [1920s–30s] to adulterate 'near-beer' (brewed during Prohibition) with a mixture of ginger beer and pure alcohol. **3** [1920s+] to adulterate a drink, alcoholic or otherwise, or food, with a knockout drug. **4** [1960s] to add a stronger drug to another, less potent one. **5** [1960s+] to dose someone with a hallucinogenic drug (usu. LSD) without their knowing (usu. by putting it into a drink or, occas., food). **6** [2000s] to adulterate food or drink with a foreign substance other than a drug, i.e. ground glass.

spike *v.*^{3} **1** [late 19C+] to have sexual intercourse [SPIKE *n.*^{1} (1)]. **2** [1930s+] (*Aus.*) to hit someone hard, to knock someone down [SE *spike*, to pierce].

spike *v.*^{4} (*also* **spike up**) [SPIKE *n.*^{1} (4)] [1930s+] (*drugs*) to inject a drug with a hypodermic syringe.

spiked *adj.* **1** [late 19C–1920s] upset. **2** [1930s+] of an ostensibly non-alcoholic drink, having had alcohol added to it [SPIKE *v.*^{2} (1)].

spiker *n.* [SPIKE *v.*^{2}] [1930s] (*US*) lemon phosphate.

spikes *n.*^{1} [ety. unknown] [1930s] (*US black*) a dollar; in pl., used generically for money.

spikes *n.*^{2} [the spikes used on running and other sports shoes] [1980s+] **1** stiletto or 'spike' heeled shoes. **2** (*N.Z./US campus*) shoes, for either sex and of any kind.

spiky *n.* **1** [late 19C+] in religious terms, extremely ritualistic or High Church Anglican [the SE *spike* or spire of a trad. church]. **2** [1950s+] aggressive, harsh, unsympathetic, uncompromising.

spill *n.*^{1} [? SE *spill*, to pour out a small amount] **1** [late 17C–early 19C; 1940s] a small gift of money or reward. **2** [late 19C–1910s] a drink.

spill *n.*^{2} [*SPILL ONE'S GUTS under* SPILL *v.*] [1910s–40s] (*US Und.*) a betrayal, a confession.

spill *n.*^{3} [ety. unknown; ? SE *spill*, either of blood or semen] [1940s–50s] (*US black*) a person of mixed US black and Puerto Rican blood; a Puerto Rican; a black person.

spill *v.* [fig. uses of SE] **1** [late 18C–1910s] to drink. **2** in the context of falling or knocking. (**a**) [late 18C+] to cause to fall. (**b**) [mid-19C–1920s] to knock down in a fight. (**c**) [1910s] to crash. (**d**) [1930s] (*US Und.*) to take advantage of, to 'knock over'. (**e**) [1980s+] (*US campus*) to fall. **3** (*also* **spill it**) in the context of speech. (**a**) [early 19C] (*UK Und.*) to betray a confederate. (**b**) [20C+] (*orig. US*) (*also* **spill out**) to confess. (**c**) [20C+] (*also* **spill off**) to tell, to recount. **4** [1920s] (*US Und.*) to release from prison.

IN PHRASES

❑ **spill a line** *v.* (*also* **spill a bibful, spill some gab**) [LINE *n.*^{1} (2b)/GAB *n.*^{2} (2)] [1920s+] to concoct a smooth patter with the specific aim of seduction; also ironic use. ❑ **spill one's guts** *v.* (*also* **spill one's insides**) [GUT *n.* (1b)] **1** [1910s+] (*orig. US*) to confess one's crimes in full; to tell all. **2** [1940s] (*US*) to shoot dead. **3** [1940s] to vomit. **4** [1950s+] to speak out, forcefully; to lose one's temper. **5** [1950s+] to divulge intimacies of one's personal life. ❑ **spill one's nut** *v.* (*also* **spill one's brains**) [NUT *n.*^{1} (1b)] [1930s+] to confess, to make an admission. ❑ **spill the beans** *v.* (*also* **spill the dice, ...the dirt, ...the dope, ...the gravy, ...the works, ...someone's tea**) [fig. use of SE] **1** [1900s–10s] to cause a disaster. **2** [1910s+] (*orig. US*) to confess, to let out a secret, to talk unguardedly.

SE in slang uses

IN PHRASES

❑ **spill ink** *v. see SLING INK under* INK *n.*

spillin' *n.* [SE *spill blood*] [1980s+] (*US black*) a gunfight in which quantities of bullets are fired and wounds inflicted.

spin *n.*^{1} [late 19C] (*Aus. Und.*) a jail sentence.

spin *n.*^{2} [abbr. SE *spinster*] [late 19C–1910s] a poor, unmarried young woman who travels to India in the hope of finding a husband.

spin *n.*^{3} [? a spin of the dice or coin] **1** [late 19C+] a try, a chance. **2** [1910s+] (*Aus./N.Z.*) an experience, a piece of luck, whether good or bad.

IN PHRASES

❑ **do the spin** *v.* [late 19C+] (*Aus.*) to toss the coins in a game of two-up. ❑ **fair spin** *n.* [mid-19C+] fair treatment, a reasonable chance. ❑ **give it a spin** *v.* [1980s] to have a go. ❑ **rough spin** *n.* [ROUGH *adj.* (2)] [1910s+] (*Aus.*) **1** bad luck; a (period of) ill fortune. **2** unfair treatment.

spin *n.*^{4} [SPINNAKER *n.*] [1940s+] (*Aus.*) five in various contexts, e.g. £5 sterling, five ounces weight, a five-year prison sentence.

spin *n.*^{5} [SPIN *v.*^{2} (2)] [1970s+] **1** (*UK Und./police*) any form of search or interrogation. **2** (*UK prison*) a search of a cell.

spin *v.*^{1} [mid-19C–1920s] to fail a candidate for a military or university examination; esp. in passive use, *spun*.

SE in slang uses

IN COMPOUNDS

❑ **spin-house** *n. see* SPINNING HOUSE *n.*

IN PHRASES

❑ **make someone spin** *v.* [20C+] (*W.I.*) to give someone a hard time, to 'lead someone a dance'. ❑ **spin a dit** *v.* [SE *ditty*] [1940s] (*Aus.*) to tell a story. ❑ **spin a hen** *v. see under* HEN *n.* ❑ **spin at the track with a fool's dim** *v.* [1940s] (*US black*) to go out dancing with a maid-servant on her night off. ❑ **spin a wren** *v. see under* WREN *n.* ❑ **spin crooked spindles** *v. see MAKE CROOKED SPINDLES under* SPINDLE *n.*^{1}. ❑ **spin for** *v.* [the game of two-up or fishing imagery] [1940s+] (*Aus.*) to court a woman. ❑ **spin it out of one's ass** *v.* [ASS *n.* (2)] [1970s] (*US*) to lie, to brag. ❑ **spin off** *v.* [late 16C–early 17C] of a woman, to bring a man to orgasm. ❑ **spin one's wheels** *v.* **1** [1970s+] (*US*) to waste time or work fruitlessly. **2** [1990s+] (*US campus*) to excite, esp. sexually. ❑ **spin out** *v.* **1** [1950s+] (*orig. US*) of a vehicle, to go out of control. **2** [1980s+] (*Aus. prison*) to suffer the effects of prison life. ❑ **spin round on one's ear** *v. see GET (UP) ON ONE'S EAR under* EAR *n.*^{1}. ❑ **spin street-yarn** *v.* [note SE *spin a yarn*] [mid-19C–1920s] (*orig. US*) to wander from house to house, chatting and exchanging gossip. ❑ **spin the bat** *v. see under* BAT *n.*^{4}. ❑ **spin the bull** *v. see SHOOT THE BULL under* BULL *n.*^{6}. ❑ **spin the dope** *v. see under* DOPE *n.*^{3}. ❑ **spin top in the mud** *v.* [20C+] (*W.I.*) to waste one's time attempting a frustrating task.

spin *v.*^{2} [SE *spin*] **1** [late 19C–1900s] (*US*) to wager. **2** [1970s+] (*UK Und.*) to search; usu. in *spin a drum*, to search a house, also a prison cell. **3** [2000s] (*UK Und.*) of money, to take illegally earned money and pass it through a legitimate business to render it free of criminal taint; to 'launder' [? the illegal money is made to 'turn around' + play on the *spin*-dryer in a launderette].

spinach *n.*^{1} [the drinker's head *spins*] [mid-19C] (*UK Und.*) gin.

spinach *n.*^{2} (*US*) **1** [20C+] a beard. **2** [1910s–40s] a moustache. **3** [1920s–40s] pubic hair. **4** [1920s–60s] money; dollar bills [like the vegetable, it is green].

spinach *n.*^{3} [*see gammon and spinach* at GAMMON AND PICKLES *under* GAMMON *n.*^{2}] **1** [1900s–40s] (*US*) rubbish, nonsense. **2** [1940s] a term of contempt.

spinach *n.*^{4} *see* CABBAGE *n.*^{2} (2a).

spindle *n.*^{1} **1** [mid-16C–19C] the penis. **2** [1900s] a leg.

IN PHRASES

❑ **make crooked spindles** *v.* (*also* **spin crooked spindles**) [the abandonment of proper wifely tasks] [late 16C–early 17C] of a woman, to commit adultery, to cuckold one's husband.

spindle *n.*^{2} [? the *spindle* of a key] [1920s–40s] (*US prison*) a guard.

spindle-assed *adj.* [1950s] (*US*) a general derog. epithet.

spindleshanks *n.* [mid-16C+] a long, thin person, lit. 'thin legs'; thus adj. *spindle-shanked*.

spinebasher *n.* [SE *spine* + BASH *v.* (1); i.e. the hitting of the back against a chair] [1940s+] (*Aus.*) an idler, a loafer; thus *spinebashing*, loafing; *spinebash*, a rest, time off from work; also sleeping.

spiney biff *n.* [SE *spina bifida*, 'a congenital malformation of widely varying severity in which there is a failure of one or more vertebræ to surround completely the meninges and spinal cord, usu. with effects on spinal cord function' (*OED*)] [1990s+] (*UK juv.*) a physically unco-ordinated person.

spinifex wire *n.* [SE *Spinifex*, 'One or other of a number of coarse grasses [...] which grow in dense masses on the sand-hills of the Australian deserts, and are characterized by their sharp-pointed, spiny leaves' (*OED*) + *wire*, a telegraph] [1930s+] (*Aus.*) the outback version of the 'bush telegraph'; thus, a rumour.

spinikin *n. see* SPINNIKEN *n.*

spinnaker *n.* [SE *spinnaker*, a large three-cornered sail carried by racing-yachts] [late 19C–1950s] (*Aus.*) a £5 note, a $5 bill.

spinner *n.*[1] [late 19C] (*Aus.*) a fast horse.

spinner *n.*[2] [SPINNAKER *n.*] [1910s–60s] (*Aus.*) £5.

spinner *n.*[3] **1** [1910s+] (*Aus.*) (*also* **nob-spinner**) in two-up, the man who is tossing, i.e. *spinning* the coins. **2** [1970s] a coarse reference to a fantasized female [the image of the woman spinning like the propellor on a *propeller-beanie* hat]. **3** [1980s+] (*Aus. prison*) an eccentric [their brain is *spinning*].

spinner-up *n.* [SE *spin a yarn*] [1900s] (*Aus.*) a teller of 'tall tales'.

spinniken *n.* (*also* **spinikin, spinnick, spinning ken**) [Du. *spinnhuis*, a women's house of correction; presumably the inmates were forced to spin thread + KEN *n.*[1] (1)] [18C–19C] a workhouse, esp. the St Giles's workhouse.

spinning *adj.* [late 19C] speedy, quick.

spinning house *n.* (*also* **spin-house**) [for ety. *see* SPINNIKEN *n.*] [mid-17C; mid-19C] a workhouse.

spinning jenny *n.* [SE *spinning jenny*, a prototype spinning machine] [19C] the vagina.

spinning jinny *n.* (*also* **spinning jenny**) [resemblance to naut. *spinning jenny*, a prismatic compass] [mid-19C–1930s] a roulette table.

spinning ken *n. see* SPINNIKEN *n.*

spinning top *n.* [rhy. sl. = COP *n.*[1] (1)] [1930s+] a police officer.

spinny *adj.* [their head is 'in a spin'] [1970s] (*Can.*) insane, eccentric.

spinsrap *n.* [backsl.] [mid-19C] parsnips.

spinster *n.* [SE *spinster*, an unmarried woman, irrespective of age] [early 17C–early 18C] a prostitute.

spintry *n.* [? Lat. *spinter*, a bracelet; thus those men who wear them and the image of male homosexual sex as having bodies linked together like the links of a bracelet] [late 16C–mid-17C] a male homosexual prostitute; thus adj. *spintrian*.

spire and steeple *n.* [rhy. sl.] [20C+] (*Aus.*) people.

spirit *n.* [1970s+] (*US black*) jazz or blues music.

spiritsuiper *n.* [Afk. *suip*, to 'swill'] [2000s] (*S.Afr.*) a drinker of methylated spirits.

spiritual flesh-broker *n.* [late 17C–18C] a parson.

spiry *adj.* [fig. resembling a tall spire] [early 19C] highly distinguished.

spit *n.*[1] [SE *spit*, a sharpened rod used to roast meat] [17C–early 19C] a sword.

SE in slang uses

IN COMPOUNDS

❑ **spit roast** *n.* (*also* **roast**) [1990s+] a woman or homosexual man who is simultaneously fellating one man while having intercourse, from the rear, with a second.

IN PHRASES

❑ **on the spit** [visual resemblance] [1970s+] of a woman, having vaginal or anal intercourse with one man and fellating another; of a man, to be sodomized and simultaneously to be fellating another man. ❑ **put four quarters on the spit** *v.* [cooking imagery; the *quarters* are the couple's legs] [18C] to have sexual intercourse.

spit *n.*[2] [earlier phr. 'as like his father as if he had been spit out of his mouth'] [18C+] identity, similarity, esp. in familial resemblance; thus in phrs. *the spit of, the dead spit of, the very spit of.*

spit *n.*[3] [? SPIT AND A DRAG *n.*] [1940s–50s] a cigarette; a puff of a cigarette.

SE in slang uses

DERIVATIVES

❑ **spitless** *adj. see* separate entry.

IN COMPOUNDS

❑ **spitball** see separate entries. ❑ **spit-cat** *n.* (*also* **spit-kitten**) [cf. SE *spitfire*] [late 19C–1910s] a termagant, one who has a very short temper. ❑ **spitfire** *n.* **1** [mid-17C] the vagina. **2** [1980s] a prostitute. ❑ **spit-fire machine** *n. see under* MACHINE *n.* ❑ **spit-fuck** *n.* [FUCK *n.* (1a); thus the saying 'If spit doesn't work, it isn't love'] [1990s+] (*gay*) anal intercourse or penetration of the anus by the fingers or fist where the only lubricant is spit. ❑ **spithead** *n.* [-HEAD *sfx* (1)] [1940s] (*US*) a general term of abuse. ❑ **spit meth** *n.* [1990s+] regurgitated *meth*adone.

IN PHRASES

❑ **exchange spit** *v.* [1970s] (*US*) **1** to have sexual intercourse. **2** to kiss. ❑ **like spit on a hot griddle** *adv. see* LIKE SHIT OFF A SHOVEL *under* SHIT *n.* ❑ **swallow one's spit** *v. see under* SWALLOW *v.*

spit *v.* **1** [late 18C–19C] of a man, to have sexual intercourse [SE *spit*, to pierce]. **2** [1970s] to ejaculate. **3** [1990s+] (*US black*) to write and perform hip-hop or rap lyrics; unlike these, however, there is no necessity to produce rhyming lines.

IN PHRASES

❑ **ready to spit** [20C+] on the verge of ejaculation.

SE in slang uses

IN COMPOUNDS

❑ **spit-bit** *n. see under* BIT *n.*[1].

IN PHRASES

❑ **spit amber** *v.* [the colour of the spittle] [late 19C] (*US*) to spit while chewing tobacco. ❑ **spit-and-scratch game** *n.* [women supposedly do not use their fists] [1910s–20s] a fight, usu. between women. ❑ **spit beef** *v.* [1970s] (*US campus*) to vomit. ❑ **spit cards** *v.* [late 18C–1920s] to leave visiting cards on one's social round. ❑ **spit chips** *v.* [*chips* of wood] (*orig. Aus.*) **1** [late 19C+] to feel extreme thirst. **2** [1960s+] to manifest acute anger or vexation. ❑ **spit cotton** *v.* **1** [mid-19C–1940s] (*US*) to be very thirsty, to have a dry mouth. **2** [1940s] to be very angry. **3** [1950s] (*drugs*) to spit white balls of spittle while under the influence of amphetamines. ❑ **spit game** *v. see* TALK GAME *under* GAME *n.* ❑ **spit one's death** *v.* [the practice of spitting to confirm the sincerity of one's oath] [1900s–10s] to swear one's honesty. ❑ **spit one's guts** *v.* [1930s] (*US*) to confess one's crimes in full. ❑ **spit out of the window** *v.* [1930s+] (*gay*) to spit out one's partner's semen after fellatio. ❑ **spit (out) the dummy** *v.* [the image of a furious baby] [1980s+] (*Aus.*) to lose one's temper badly. ❑ **spitting at the tongs** *adj.* [ety. unknown; ? a folk saying] [20C+] (*Ulster*) pregnant. ❑ **spitting on the sidewalk** *n.* [tramp jargon for police harassment, an arrest for no other reason than that one is a vagrant] [20C+] any trivial offence for which one still faces prosecution. ❑ **spit sixpences** *v.* (*also* **spit white (broth)**) [late 16C–late 18C] to spit out small gobbets of white mucus. ❑ **spit tacks** *v.* [note synon. UK milit. *spit button-sticks*] [1950s+] (*Aus./US*) to be irate, furious. ❑ **spit up** *v.* **1** [1940s] (*Aus.*) to vomit. **2** [1940s–60s] to confess.

IN EXCLAMATIONS

❑ **spit it out!** [mid-19C+] speak up! confess! explain yourself! ❑ **spit me death!** [SPIT ONE'S DEATH above] [1940s–50s] (*Aus.*) a defensive retort, meaning that one's last statement is absolutely true. ❑ **spit o' my hand!** [the spitting on one's hand that seals a bargain] [late 19C–1920s] used to emphasize whatever it is one has said, e.g. *spit o' my hand, you know it's the truth.*

Spitalfields' breakfast *n.* [*Spitalfields*, in the East End of London and, as such, an impoverished area] [mid-19C] a tight necktie and a short pipe, i.e. no breakfast.

Spitalfields crawl *n.* [the insanitary condition of housing in Spitalfields, East London] [1900s–10s] (*UK tramp*) the squirming action of someone who is covered in lice.

Spital whore *n.* (*also* **Spital lady, Spittle sinner**) [*Spitalfields*, a tough East End area of London + SE *spital*, a hospital (and origin of the district's name), thus underlining the physical perils of being a prostitute] [mid-16C–early 17C] a prostitute.

spit and a drag *n.* (*also* **spit and a draw**) [? rhy. sl. = FAG *n.*[4] (2), or the result of a badly rolled cigarette, from which one spits out the odd strand of tobacco, while dragging or drawing down the smoke] **1** [late 19C+] (*orig. RN*) a surreptitious smoke. **2** [1930s–70s] a cigarette.

spitball *n.* [SE *spitball*, a small saliva-soaked ball of paper] [20C+] (*US*) an insult, a jibe.

spitball *v.* [SPITBALL *n.*] (*US*) **1** [20C+] to accuse or taunt. **2** [1950s+] to suggest, to hypothesize.

spitless *adj.*

IN PHRASES

❑ **scared spitless** *adj.* [euph. for *SCARED SHITLESS under* SCARE *v.*] [1920s+] absolutely terrified.

spitter *n.*[1] [1970s] (*US Und.*) a hoodlum, a thug, a gangster.

spitter *n.*[2] [she spits out the semen after performing fellatio] [1980s] (*Aus.*) a derog. term for a female.

Spittleonian *n.* [its manufacture in Spitalfields] [mid-19C] (*UK Und.*) a yellow (silk) handkerchief.

Spittle sinner *n. see* SPITAL WHORE *n.*

spitz poodle *n.* [ety. unknown; the variety of dog seems to have no relevance] [late 19C] (*US*) a mild degree of drunkenness.

spiv *n.* (*also* **spive**) [? Rom. *spiv*, sparrow, used by gypsies as a derog. ref. to those who existed by picking up the leavings of their betters, criminal or legitimate; alternative theories include the reverse of *V.I.P.s* or police abbr. *s*uspected *p*ersons and *i*tinerant *v*agrants; note also SPIFF *n.* (1)] [1920s+] a flashy, sharp individual who exists on the fringes of real criminality, living by their wits rather than a regular job.

DERIVATIVES

❑ **spivmobile** *n.* [-MOBILE *sfx*] [1980s+] an exceptionally ostentatious and flashy car, such as might be driven by a spiv or their successors.

spiv *v.* [SPIV *n.*] [1940s+] to work as a street trader, esp. with overtones of illegality.

spivish *adj.* **1** [1940s+] exhibiting the characteristics and/or lifestyle of a SPIV *n.* **2** *see* SPIFFY *adj.*

spivot *n.* [ety. unknown] [1930s–40s] (*US*) a young woman.

spivvish *adj. see* SPIFFY *adj.*

spivvy *adj.* (*also* **spivy**) **1** [1940s+] one who has the characteristics and lifestyle of a SPIV *n.* **2** *see* SPIFFY *adj.*

spizz *n.* [? var. on SPIKE *n.*[1] (4)] [1960s] (*US drugs*) a hypodermic syringe.

spizzerinktum *n.* (*US*) **1** [mid-19C] a dollar; money in general [SE *specie*]. **2** [1940s] vigour, zest [nonce-word, reminiscent of *fizz, pizzazz* etc].

S.P. joint *n.* (*also* **S.P. shop, S.P. money**) [SE *s*tarting *p*rice + JOINT *n.* (3b)] [1920s–50s] (*Aus.*) a betting shop, offering only starting prices.

splag *v.* [? echoic] [1980s+] (*US campus*) to vomit.

splang *n.* [? echoic] [1970s] (*US black*) sharp words; thus as v., to curse.

splash *adj.* [SE *splash*, style or dash] [mid-19C–1930s] elegant, fashionable, distinguished.

splash *v.* **1** [late 19C+] to spend money extravagantly. **2** [1930s+] to masturbate. **3** [1940s] (*US*) for a boxer to lose a fight voluntarily, usu. in return for payment [play on *TAKE A DIVE under* DIVE *n.*[1]].

SE in slang uses

IN PHRASES

❑ **splash (on)** *v.* [the *splash* of blood] [1990s+] (*US black gang*) to shoot. ❑ **splash one's boots** *v.* (*also* **splash the boots**) [1960s+] to urinate. ❑ **splash out (on)** *v.* [1970s+] to spend money unrestrainedly; thus *splash*, a spending spree. ❑ **splash the salties** *v.* [i.e. *salt* tears] [1940s] (*US black*) to weep.

splashing *n.* [late 19C–1900s] garrulous or foolish chatter.

splashing *adj.* (*also* **splashy**) [SE *splash*, a striking or ostentatious display, appearance or effect] [late 19C–1910s] fine, excellent, first-rate; also as adv.

splash-up *adj.* [late 19C+] first-rate, excellent.

splashy *adj. see* SPLASHING *adj.*

splat *v.* [SPLAT! *excl.*] [1920s+] to hit a hard surface, with a slapping or splashing noise.

splat *adv.* [echoic] [mid-19C+] evocative of a solid but soft body hitting a hard surface.

splat! *excl.* [echoic] [late 19C+] the slapping or splashing noise of something that hits a hard surface.

splatter *n.*

SE in slang uses

IN COMPOUNDS

❑ **splatter dabs** *n.* [1940s] (*US*) pancakes. ❑ **splatterdash** *n.* [synon. Yorks. dial.] [late 19C] an uproar. ❑ **splatter face** *n.* [Northumberland/Oxon. dial. *splatter-faced*, broad-faced, 'platter-faced'] [mid-19C] a broad face. ❑ **splatter movie** *n.* (*also* **splat movie, splatter film**) [1970s+] a genre of ultra-violent films, coined as a name by director George Romero (b.1939), e.g. *The Texas Chainsaw Massacre* (1974), *The Driller Killer* (1979); thus *splatterpunk*, a similarly violent genre of fiction; *splatterporn*, violent pornography.

splatter one's batter *v. see under* BATTER *n.*[1].

splaw *n.* [ety. unknown] [1900s–1910s] (*Aus.*) one who lives/works in the bush.

splay head *n.* [1980s] (*US campus*) a fool.

spleef *n. see* SPLIFF *n.* (1).

spleefer *n.* [SPLIFF *n.* (1) + REEFER *n.*[1] (2)] [1990s+] (*drugs*) a cannabis cigarette.

splendacious *adj.* (*also* **splendidious, splendidous**) [intensifier of SE *splendid*] [17C; late 19C–1910s] splendid, excellent, first-rate.

splendiferous *adj.* [intensifier of SE *splendid*] [mid-19C+] wonderful, perfect.

spleuchan *n.* [Gael. *spliùchan*, a tobacco pouch, a purse] [late 18C] the vagina.

splib *n.* (*also* **splid**) [ety. unknown] **1** [1960s+] (*US black*) a fellow black person. **2** [1970s] 'a liberal black who looks angry but will not upset the status quo' (*American Speech* XLIX, 1976); i.e. a derog. term for a black person. **3** [1970s] a drunkard.

splice *n.* [SPLICE *v.* (1)] **1** [early 19C–1920s] one's wife. **2** [mid–late 19C] the act or institution of marriage.

IN PHRASES

❑ **do a splice** *v.* [late 19C] to get married.

splice *v.* (*also* **splice up**) [SE *splice*, to join, orig. of ropes] **1** [mid-18C+] to marry; thus *spliced*, married. **2** [late 19C] to have sexual intercourse. **3** [1900s] to perform the marriage ceremony.

splid *n. see* SPLIB *n.*

spliff *n.* (*also* **splif**) **1** [1930s+] (*orig. W.I., esp. Rasta*) (*also* **spleef**) a marijuana or hashish cigarette [SPIFLICATE *v.*; i.e. the effects]. **2** [1980s] (*US campus*) a particle of food lodged between teeth [ety. unknown]. **3** [1980s] (*UK prison*) a hand-rolled cigarette; a cigarette-paper. **4** [2000s] cannabis. **5** [2000s] (*US black*) a male companion or friend [ety. unknown].

DERIVATIVES

❑ **spliffed** *adj.* [2000s] intoxicated by cannabis.

IN COMPOUNDS

❑ **spliffhead** *n.* (*also* **spliff-man**) [-HEAD *sfx* (4)] [1990s+] (*drugs*) a smoker of cannabis.

IN PHRASES

❑ **build a spliff** *v.* [1980s+] to roll a cannabis cigarette.

spliff *v.* [SPLIFF *n.* (1)] [2000s] to smoke a marijuana or hashish cigarette.

spliggaty-splack *v.* [2000s] (*US black*) to ejaculate.

splinter *n.* [1910s–50s] (*US*) a notably thin person.

splinter belly *n.* [1920s–40s] (*US tramp*) a tramp who works as a part-time carpenter.

splish and splash *v.* [1970s+] (*US black*) to debate a topic, to ponder without coming to a decision.

split *n.* **1** in senses of division. (**a**) [mid-19C] (*UK Und.*) the parting of a group of criminals. (**b**) [late 19C+] the division of criminal spoils, or of any sum of money. **2** in senses of informing, betrayal [SPLIT *v.* (3a)]. (**a**) [mid-19C+] (*also* **splitter**) an informer. (**b**) [late 19C+] a detective or police officer. (**c**)

[1950s] (*US Und.*) an act of betrayal. **3** in senses of physiology. (**a**) [mid-19C+] the vagina. (**b**) [1930s+] (*also* **split end, split stuff, split tail**) a female, women, esp. as viewed as sex objects. **4** [late 19C] small change. **5** [late 19C] a pimp, a procurer [he *splits* the woman's earnings with her]. **6** in senses of liquid measurement. (**a**) [late 19C–1900s] a drink composed of two different alcoholic liquors. (**b**) [late 19C–1900s] a half-glass of spirits. (**c**) [late 19C–1910s] (*US*) a drink composed of half water/half alcohol. (**d**) [late 19C+] a small bottle of mineral water. (**e**) [late 19C+] a half-bottle of champagne. **7** [1930s–50s] (*Aus./US*) a safety match. **8** [1960s–70s] (*US drugs*) any pill – an amphetamine or barbiturate – that has a groove embedded in its surface.

split *v.* **1** [mid-17C; 19C+] to have sexual intercourse. **2** in lit. or fig. senses of departure [the fig. *split* or 'tear' in a group that such a departure makes]. (**a**) [late 18C–mid-19C] to walk or run at great speed. (**b**) [mid-19C+] to leave, to depart. (**c**) [1960s] (*US black*) to die. **3** in senses of disclosure [to *split* or break a confidence]. (**a**) [late 18C+] to betray, to inform against; usu. *split on*. (**b**) [early 19C] to believe. (**c**) [mid-19C+] to disclose, to reveal secrets. **4** [mid-19C+] to quarrel with someone, to break off relations, to reject. **5** [1940s+] (*orig. US*) (*also* **split the blanket, ...sheets**) to divorce. **6** [20C+] to share out profits or proceeds. **7** *see* SPLIT A GUT below.

DERIVATIVES

❑ **splitsville** *n.* [-VILLE *sfx*[1]] **1** [1960s+] (*orig. US*) the end of a relationship, a divorce etc. **2** [2000s] the state of departure.

IN PHRASES

❑ **split about** *v.* [mid-19C] to inform, to betray, esp. to the police. ❑ **split a gut** *v.* [var. on *BUST A GUT under* GUT *n.*] **1** [late 17C; 1950s] to vomit. **2** [mid-19C+] (*also* **split**) to laugh hysterically. **3** [1940s+] to become very angry. **4** [1950s+] (*US*) to exert maximum effort. ❑ **split fair** *v.* [mid–late 19C] to tell the truth. ❑ **split out** *v.* **1** [late 19C+] to separate. **2** [1930s+] (*US*) to part company, to take one's leave. **3** [1970s] (*US prison*) to escape. ❑ **split the beard** *v. see under* BEARD *n.* ❑ **split the blanket** *v. see* sense 5 above. ❑ **split the breeze** *v.* [1950s+] to depart, to travel, to run fast. ❑ **split the cup** *v.* [1970s] (*US black*) to deflower a virgin. ❑ **split the peach** *v.* [PEACH *n.*[1] (5e)] [1990s+] to sodomize. ❑ **split the scene** *v. see under* SCENE *n.* ❑ **split the sheets** *v. see* sense 5 above. ❑ **split up** *v.* [1940s+] (*orig. US*) to become divorced. ❑ **turn split** *v.* [sense 3a above] [early 19C] to become an informer, to inform against someone.

SE in slang uses

IN COMPOUNDS

❑ **split apricot** *n.* [late 17C–19C] the vagina. ❑ **split arse/-arsed** *see* separate entries. ❑ **split-ass** *adj. see* separate entry. ❑ **split beaver** *n. see under* BEAVER *n.*[1]. ❑ **split bit** *n. see under* BIT *n.*[1]. ❑ **split-cause** *n.* [the profession's reputation as splitters of legal hairs] [late 18C–early 19C] a lawyer. ❑ **split crow** *n.* [supposed resemblance] [late 18C–early 19C] the public-house sign of the spread eagle. ❑ **split end** *n. see* sense 3b above. ❑ **split fig** *n.* **1** [late 17C–early 19C] a grocer. **2** [late 19C–1940s] the vagina [note synon. Ital. *fica*]. ❑ **split finger** *n.* [1930s–40s] (*US prison/Und.*) a (prison) clerk. ❑ **split kipper** *n.* [1990s+] the vagina. ❑ **split mutton** *n. see* separate entry. ❑ **split rump** *n. see RUMP-SPLITTER under* RUMP *n.* ❑ **split stuff/tail** *n. see* sense 3b above. ❑ **split 'un** *n.* [1930s+] (*Aus.*) a banknote that has been divided in halves. ❑ **split-whisker** *n.* [WHISKERS *n.*[1] (4)] [1940s+] (*Aus.*) women, viewed sexually. ❑ **split wig** *n.* [*SPLIT ONE'S WIG under* WIG *n.*[2]] [1960s] a lunatic.

IN PHRASES

❑ **make all split** *v.* [late 16C–early 17C] to cause a disturbance, to make a commotion. ❑ **split-arsed one** *n. see* separate entry. ❑ **split-arse mechanic** *n. see* separate entry.

IN EXCLAMATIONS

❑ **split me!** (*also* **split my wig! ...my windpipe!**) [late 17C–mid-19C] an oath used by contemporary upper-class dandies.

split arse *n.* [SE *split* + ARSE *n.* (1)] **1** [1970s+] a woman. **2** [2000s] (*US*) a male homosexual.

split-arse *adj.* [1920s–40s] daring; thus *splitassing*, acting recklessly.

split-arse *adv.* [SE *split* + ARSE *n.* (1); the movement of one's legs and buttocks] [1910s–20s] very quickly; as *v.*, to move quickly.

split-arsed *adj.* [SPLIT ARSE *n.* (1)] [1980s] of a man, cowardly, effeminate.

split-arsed one *n.* [SPLIT ARSE *n.* (1)] [late 19C] a woman, esp. a baby girl.

split-arse mechanic *n.* [SPLIT ARSE *n.* (1) + SE *mechanic*; note RAF jargon *split-arse merchant*, a reckless, showy or daring airman; *split-arse cap*, the Royal Flying Corps cap, similar to a Glengarry] [late 19C] a prostitute.

IN PHRASES

❑ **take on a split-arse mechanic** *v.* [late 19C–1910s] to have sexual intercourse.

split-ass *adj.* [ety. unknown] [1910s] (*Aus.*) unusual.

split asunder *n.* [rhy. sl.] [mid–late 19C] a costermonger.

split mutton *n.* [SE *split* + MUTTON *n.* (1c)] **1** [17C–19C] the penis. **2** [18C–1900s] the vagina. **3** [18C–1900s] a derog. generic term for womankind.

IN PHRASES

❑ **have a bit of split mutton** *v.* [18C–1900s] to have sexual intercourse.

split pea *n.* [rhy. sl.] [mid-19C] tea.

splitter *n. see* SPLIT *n.* (2a).

splitter (of causes) *n.* [the profession's reputation as splitters of legal hairs] [late 17C–19C] a lawyer.

spliv *n.* [SPLIB *n.* (1)] [1960s–70s] (*US black*) a fellow black person.

splivins *n.* [ety. unknown] [1960s–70s] (*drugs*) amphetamine.

splodger *n.*[1] [dial. *splodge*, to wade through mud] [mid-19C] **1** a lout, a rough countryman. **2** a grave-robber.

splodger *n.*[2] (*also* **sploger, splojer**) [rhy. sl. = SE *codger*] [mid-19C] an old man.

splooge *n.* (*also* **sploodge**) [SPLOOGE *v.*] [1980s+] (*US campus*) semen.

splooge *v.* [var. on SE *splurge*] [1980s+] (*US campus*) to ejaculate.

splorger *n.* [? var. on SPLODGER *n.*[2]; but note Cohen *Comments on Etymology* XIII:1 (1/10/83): 'Webster III under *splodge* — says "splash, slosh", e.g. "splodged about the streets". Maybe *splodger* "fellow" derived directly from this meaning of *splodge*, i.e. the reference was merely to someone walking through the snow or rain-soaked streets'] [mid-19C] (*UK Und.*) a fellow, a person.

splosh *n.*[1] (*also* **sploosh**) [? SPLASH *v.* (1)] [late 19C+] money.

splosh *n.*[2] [SE *splosh*, the sound of a liquid falling or having something dropped into it] [1940s–70s] tea.

splosher *n.* [? var. on SLAPPER *n.*[2] (1)] [2000s] a young woman.

splosh it on *v.* [ext./var. SPLASH *v.* (1)] [1920s+] to bet heavily, esp. at race-tracks.

splow *n.* [? echoic] [1960s] (*US black*) ritual handslapping that signifies a greeting or farewell.

splurge *n.* [SE *splurge*, an ostentatious display or effort] [mid-19C] a rush, a sudden movement.

splush! *excl.* [1920s] (*US*) nonsense! rubbish!

splutter *n.* [dial. *splutter*, a fuss, a disturbance] [1910s–20s] a scandal.

S.P. money *n. see* S.P. JOINT *n.*

spod *n.* [? Scot. *spodlin*, a child who is just learning to walk] [1990s+] (*UK teen*) an unpopular schoolchild.

spod *v.* [ety. unknown] [1990s+] **1** to engage in meaningless activities whether or not there is work to do. **2** to spend time on newsgroups on the Internet.

spoda *n.* [ety. unknown; ? link to SPORT *n.* (2)] [2000s] (*US black*) a white person who attempts (unsuccessfully) to adopt black culture and style.

spodiodi *n.* [ety. unknown, the wine is seen as a 'jacket' for the rough whisky; noted as a song lyric, 'Drink wine spodiodi', in Jack Kerouac, *On the Road* (1957); ? the rhythmic sound of the word is echoic of the mixing of the drinks; Décharné, *Straight from the Fridge* (2000), suggests McGhee's lyrics were a bowdlerized version of 'an obscene US army drinking song' which ran 'Drinking wine, motherfucker, drinking wine'] [1940s+] (*orig. US*) a mixture of cheap port and generic bar whisky, much loved by jazz musicians and beatniks.

spoffish *adj.* [? SE *officious*] [mid-19C] interfering, meddlesome.

spoffskins *n.* [ety. unknown] [late 19C–1900s] a prostitute, esp. one who poses as her regular client's 'wife'.

spoffy *adj.* [var. SPOFFISH *adj.*] [mid-19C] interfering, meddlesome, acting like a busybody.

spog *v.* (*also* **spogh**) [Du. *spochen*, to boast] [mid-19C+] (*S.Afr.*) to boast, to brag.

spoil *v.* **1** [early 19C] to stop someone else achieving their object. **2** [early–mid-19C] to hurt, to bruise. **3** [mid-19C] (*US*) to kill. **4** [mid-19C] in fig. use of sense 3, to finish (a drink).

SE in slang uses

IN COMPOUNDS

❑ **spoil-iron** *n.* [late 18C–early 19C] a blacksmith. ❑ **spoil-pudding** *n.* [a long-winded parson keeps his congregation in church so long that their cooking spoils] [late 18C–early 19C] a parson.

IN PHRASES

❑ **spoil (a woman's shape)** *v.* [late 17C–early 18C] to make pregnant. ❑ **spoil someone's dough** *v.* [late 19C] (*US*) to sabotage someone's plans.

spoilers *n.* [proper name *Spoilers*, a leading gang in the 1940s, then applied to all such young men, gang members or not; ult. title of a popular film] [1940s+] (*S.Afr.*) a township thug or criminal.

spoke-box *n.* [the 'spokes' are the teeth] [19C] the mouth.

spoken to *adj.* [SPEAK *v.*] [mid-19C] deceived, tricked.

spoke to *adj.* [? SPEAK *v.*] (*UK Und.*) **1** [late 18C–early 19C] suffering a great misfortune, beyond help [? a message from the deity]. **2** [late 18C–early 19C] arrested, sentenced to death. **3** [early 19C] (*also* **spoke with**) robbed; the type of robbery can be added; thus *spoke to upon the screw/crack/sneak/hoist/buz*.

spon *n.* (*also* **spondos, sponds, spons**) [abbr. SPONDULICS *n.*] [late 19C+] money.

sponditious *adj.* [coined by UK comedian Lenny Henry (b.1958); ? SE *spon*taneous + de*licious*] [1980s] excellent.

spondulics *n.* (*also* **spondulacks, spondulicks, sponduliks, spondooli, sponds, spondulix**) [? Gk *spondulikos*, the adjectival form of *spondulox*, a type of shell used as early 'money'; or corruption of GREENBACK *n.* (1); note Michael Quinion, *World Wide Words* (Internet, 29/9/01): 'Doug Wilson pointed out that the Greek stem suggested as the origin of this term in last week's Weird Words piece is also the source of various English words beginning in "spondylo-" that refer to the spine or vertebrae. He suggested that a stack of coins may have been likened to the spine, with each coin a vertebra. He found a supporting reference in an 1867 book, "A Manual of the Art of Prose Composition: for the Use of Colleges and Schools", by John Mitchell Bonnell. A list of provincialisms included: "Spondulics – coin piled for counting".'] [mid-19C+] money.

sponge *n.* (*also* **spunge**) [their absorption, whether of alcohol, knowledge or another's favours] **1** [late 16C+] a heavy drinker; thus adj. *spongy*. **2** [17C] a dedicated scholar. **3** [17C+] someone who lives through cadging off others. **4** [mid-19C] (*UK Und.*) a fool, a naïve countryman. **5** [mid-19C] (*US Und.*) a miser. **6** [1920s–30s] (*US Und.*) a prohibition officer. **7** [1960s] a hollow sponge that is placed inside the mouth of the vagina by a prostitute as protection against disease and accidental pregnancy; thus as v., to use such a sponge; *sponge tricks*, to deceive clients by using a sponge.

IN PHRASES

❑ **chuck up the sponge** *v.* (*also* **chuck in the sponge, fling up..., throw in..., throw up..., toss in...**) [boxing imagery] **1** [mid-19C+] to give in, to surrender. **2** [1910s–30s] to die.

sponge *v.* (*also* **spunge**) [SE from mid-19C] **1** [late 17C+] to live on others in a parasitic manner; to obtain assistance or maintenance by mean arts; thus *sponger*, one who sponges. **2** [mid-19C] (*US Und.*) to steal.

sponge cake *n.* [var. on PIECE OF CAKE *under* PIECE *n.*; i.e. it is SOFT *adj.* (4)] [late 19C–1940s] (*US*) anything simple, ridiculously easy.

sponging-house *n.* (*also* **sponge house, spunging-house**) ['to which persons arrested are taken, till they find bail, or have spent all their money; a house where every species of fraud and extortion is practised, under the protection of the law' (Grose, 1785). The corrupt bailiff's officers 'sponge up' their victims' money] [late 17C–1960s] a bailiff's lock-up.

spons *n. see* SPON *n.*

sponsor *n.* **1** [1950s] (*US black*) a man who is conned into paying in general. **2** [1970s] (*US black*) a man who 'keeps' a woman, in return for sexual favours. **3** [1970s+] (*US gay*) an older homosexual man who supports his young lover. **4** [1990s+] (*US prison*) (*also* **financier**) a man who sends money and gifts in to a female inmate.

sponsor *v.* [1970s–80s] (*UK black*) to lend or give money.

spoo *n.* [SPEW *n.*] [1980s+] (*US campus*) semen; thus as v., to ejaculate.

spooch *n.* [ext. of SPOO *n.*/SPEW *n.*] [1980s+] (*US campus*) semen; thus as v., to ejaculate.

spoof *n.*[1] [SE *spoof*, a game, involving hoaxing one's rival players, invented by the comedian Arthur Roberts (1852–1933)] [late 19C+] a hoax, a confidence trick; thus *spoofer*, one who practises such trickery.

spoof *n.*[2] [? *spit* + *poof!*, onomat. noise of a small explosion] [1910s+] (*Aus.*) semen; thus as v., to ejaculate.

spoof *adj.* [SPOOF *n.*[1]] [late 19C+] fake, spurious, sham.

spoof *v.* [SPOOF *n.*[1]] **1** [late 19C+] to hoax, to fool, to trick. **2** [1910s–40s] (*US*) make fun of. **3** [1940s] (*UK prison*) of an informer, to be looking for information; usu. as *on the spoof*. **4** [1980s] (*US campus*) to engage in sexual activity short of intercourse [link to SPOOF *n.*[2]]. **5** [1990s+] (*US campus*) to blunder.

DERIVATIVES

❑ **spoofery** *n.* [late 19C] trickery, hoaxing.

spoofer *n.* [SPOOF *v.* (1)] [1910s+] a trickster.

spooferies *n.* [the orig. *Spooferies* seems to have been the Trafalgar Club in Maiden Lane near the Strand, but the term was generic and the card-game *spoof* (in which the appearance of certain cards at the same time is called a 'spoof') was invented at the Adelphi Club; for details see Binstead, *Pitcher in Paradise* (1903), pp. 227 ff. and Binstead & Wells, *A Pink 'Un and a Pelican* (1898), p. 56] [late 19C–1900s] a second-rate sporting club.

spoofie *n.* [? SPOOF *v.* (4)] [1970s] (*Aus.*) an attractive young woman.

spoof tube *n.* [SPOOF *n.*[1]/SE *puff*] [2000s] (*US drugs*) an empty toilet paper roll stuffed with sheets of fabric softener; this works as a 'filter' for telltale smoke when smoking marijuana surreptitiously.

spooge *n.* [? ext. SPOO *n.*] **1** [1980s+] (*US*) semen. **2** [2000s] (*US black*) a verbal explosion.

spooge *v.* [ext. of SPOO *n.*] [1990s+] **1** to explode or splurge out; thus adj. *spooged*. **2** to ejaculate.

spook *n.* [SE *spook*, a ghost] **1** [1930s–70s] (*US black*) a white person. **2** [1940s] a derog. term for an Italian. **3** [1940s+] a derog. term for a black person. **4** [1940s+] (*US*) an intelligence agent, esp. CIA; thus *spookic/spookical*, *spookish*, *spookism*, *spookological*, *spookology* [Yale University secret society Skull & Bones, from among whose members were recruited the personnel of the OSS, the WW2 predecessor of the CIA]. **5** [1960s–70s] a derog. term for a Chinese or Vietnamese person. **6** [1960s–80s] (*US black*) used to describe a fellow black person. **7** [1970s] (*drugs*) a heroin addict. **8** [1970s] (*Aus.*) a derog. term for a native Australian. **9** [1980s+] (*S.Afr.*) a fright, a scare.

IN COMPOUNDS

❑ **spook juke** *n.* [JUKE *v.*[2] (3), i.e. one who has sex with blacks] [1980s] (*US prison*) a white inmate who is seen as overly friendly to black ones.

spook *adj.*[1] [SPOOK *n.* (3)] [1950s+] (*US*) relevant to black people or black culture or lifestyle.

spook *adj.*[2] [SPOOK *n.* (4)] [1960s+] (*US*) pertaining to undercover/intelligence operations.

spook *v.* [SE *spook*] (*orig. US*) **1** [mid-19C+] to scare, to unnerve. **2** [1930s+] to take fright, to become scared. **3** [1950s] to steal.

spooked *adj.* [SE *spook*/SPOOK *v.*] **1** [1920s+] under the influence of a malign spirit. **2** [1950s+] frightened, alarmed. **3** [1950s+] annoyed; disgusted.

spooks, the *n.* [1950s+] (*US/Aus.*) a sense of terror, of emotional uneasiness.

spooky *adj.*[1] [note surfing jargon *spooky*, of a dangerous or frightening wave] **1** [mid-19C+] (*orig. US*) frightening, eerie, pertaining to the 'spirit world'. **2** [1920s+] (*US*) nervous, easily frightened, superstitious. **3** [1950s+] of a person, frightening, menacing.

spooky *adj.*[2] [SPOOK *n.* (3)] [1950s] pertaining to black people or black culture.

spoon *n.* [SE *spoon*, which is 'open' and 'shallow'. 'A spoon has been defined to be "a thing that touches a lady's lips without kissing them"' (Hotten, 1860)] **1** [late 18C–19C; 1980s+] a fool, a simpleton [note *Online Dict. of Playground Slang* (2001) defines a spoon as as 'a person so dense they were not allowed to use a sharp object, they could only have a spoon']. **2** [mid-19C–1910s] a foolishly infatuated lover. **3** [late 19C] a foolish, sentimental affection. **4** [late 19C; 2000s] a flirt; thus *do spoons, come the spoon*, to offer sentimental and ridiculous protestations of love; *at spoons with*, sentimentally in love with. **5** [1910s] an act of flirtation. **6** [1920s] (*US*) a shovel. **7** [1950s+] (*also* **spoonful**) 2g ($^1/_{16}$ oz) of heroin or cocaine [approx. 1 teaspoonful]. **8** [1970s+] enough heroin to provide a single injection [the contents of the spoon that is used to heat the drug].

DERIVATIVES

❑ **spoonified** *adj.* **1** [mid-19C] tricked, deceived. **2** [1910s] sentimental. ❑ **spooniness** *n.* [mid-19C] sentimentality.

IN PHRASES

❑ **come the spoon** *v.* [mid–late 19C] to court, to make love. ❑ **in the spoon** [1970s+] (*drugs*) using narcotics. ❑ **it's a case of spoons with them** [mid-19C–1920s] a phr. used of a couple who are obviously in love. ❑ **out of the spoon** [1950s+] (*drugs*) not using drugs. ❑ **spoons on** *adj.* [mid–late 19C] **1** sentimentally in love with. **2** courting; also as *spoons about, spoons with.*

spoon *v.*[1] [SPOON *n.*] [mid-19C+] to flirt with, esp. in a foolish or sentimental manner; thus *spooning*, flirtation.

IN PHRASES

❑ **spoon the burick** *v.* [BURICK *n.* (2)] [late 19C] to pay attentions to one's best friend's wife or girlfriend.

spoon *v.*[2] [SE *spoon*] [1960s] (*US campus*) to eat together.

spoon and gravy *n.* [20C+] a dinner jacket.

spooner *n.* [SPOON *v.*[1]] [mid-19C–1930s] a flirt.

spooney *see under* SPOONY.

spoonful *n. see* SPOON *n.* (7).

spoony *n.* (*also* **spooney, spooneymouth**) [SPOON *n.*] **1** [late 18C–1900s] a fool, a simpleton; thus used as a derog. term of address. **2** [early–mid-19C] one who is in sentimental love. **3** [early–mid-19C] a coward. **4** [1900s–60s] an effeminate young man, poss. homosexual.

spoony *adj.* (*also* **spooney**) [SPOON *n.*] **1** [19C] very drunk. **2** [early 19C] greedy, avaricious. **3** [early 19C–1900s] weak minded, simple. **4** [mid-19C] effeminate. **5** [mid-19C–1960s] besotted with a member of the opposite sex.

spoops *n.* (*also* **spoopsey**) [? echoic of an insignificant noise] [mid-19C] (*US campus*) an insignificant person, a weakling.

spoopsy *adj.* [SPOOPS *n.*] [mid-19C] (*US campus*) foolish.

spooran *n. see* SPORRAN *n.*

spoorie *n.* [Afk. *spoor(weg)*, railway + sfx *-ie*; lit. a railway worker, the term is used as generic for all artisans] [20C+] (*S.Afr.*) a black artisan.

spoot *n.* [var. on SPOOGE *n.* (1)] [2000s] (*US black*) semen.

spoot-canned *adj.* [var. on SHITCAN *v.* (2)] [2000s] (*US*) dismissed from a job.

spores *n.* (*drugs*) **1** [1960s] a psilocybe or 'magic' mushroom. **2** [1970s+] phencyclidine.

sporran *n.* (*also* **spooran**) [Gael. *sporan*, a purse, worn in front of the kilt by Scottish Highlanders] [19C] the pubic hair.

sport *n.* [SPORT *v.*] **1** [16C+] sexual intercourse. **2** [mid-19C+] a playboy, a man-about-town, with the accent on gambling, womanizing and other areas of the 'fast' life. **3** [late 19C] an eccentric. **4** [late 19C+] (*esp. Aus.*) a man; thus a general term of address to a man. **5** [late 19C+] in weaker use of sense 4, a general term of approbation, 'a good chap'; esp. in phr. *be a sport*. **6** [1970s+] (*US gay*) a male prostitute.

IN COMPOUNDS

❑ **sport house** *n.* [HOUSE *n.*[1] (1)] [20C+] (*W.I.*) a brothel.

IN PHRASES

❑ **old sport** *n.* [mid-19C+] a general greeting or form of address given to a man (usu. one whom one knows).

SE in slang uses

IN COMPOUNDS

❑ **sportfuck** *v.* [FUCK *v.* (1)] [1960s+] to have spontaneous, casual sexual intercourse; thus n. *sportfucking*.

sport *v.* **1** [16C+] to have sexual intercourse; thus (W.I.) *sporter, sportgirl*, a prostitute. **2** [mid-17C–1940s] to behave showily or ostentatiously in public. **3** [late 17C–early 18C; mid-19C] to read an author for amusement (rather than instruction). **4** [early 18C–mid-19C] to make a speculative investment in sport or business, to wager, to make a bet. **5** [early–mid-19C] to treat, usu. to food and/or drink. **6** [mid–late 19C] to spend money freely or extravagantly. **7** [mid-19C; 1920s+] (*US black/campus*) to wear stylish clothes. **8** [1930s–40s] to live the 'fast' life of a gambler, a pimp and other underworld figures. **9** [1980s+] (*US campus*) to give. **10** [1980s+] (*US black*) to spend money, usu. on a woman.

IN COMPOUNDS

❑ **sports king** *n.* [1930s] (*Irish*) a noisy, drunken, hedonistic individual. ❑ **sportsman** *n. see* separate entry. ❑ **sportswoman** *n. see* SPORTING LADY *under* SPORTING *adj.*

IN PHRASES

❑ **sport a toe** *v.* [early–mid-19C] to dance. ❑ **sport (away) money** *v.* [mid-19C] to spend money freely on a hedonistic lifestyle. ❑ **sport a woodie** *v. see under* WOODIE *n.*[2]. ❑ **sport blubber** *v. see under* BLUBBER *n.*[2]. ❑ **sport off** *v.* [1960s–70s] to show off, to display. ❑ **sport one's ivory** *v. see under* IVORY *n.* ❑ **sport one's wood** *v. see under* WOOD *n.*[1]. ❑ **sport out** *v.* [1980s] (*W.I.*) to go out spending money, enjoying oneself, usu. in pursuit of/accompanied by a woman. ❑ **sport the dairy** *v. see under* DAIRY *n.*[1].

sportify *v.* [1950s] (*W.I.*) to make people laugh, to amuse.

sporting *adj.* **1** [early 19C] promiscuous. **2** [1980s+] (*US black/campus*) well-dressed, looking good [SPORT *v.* (7)]. **3** [2000s] pertaining to SPORT *n.* (1).

IN COMPOUNDS

❑ **sporting equipment** *n.* [1990s+] (*Aus.*) a contraceptive sheath, a condom. ❑ **sporting goods** *n.* (*also* **dealer in sporting goods**) [ext. of SPORT *n.* (6)] [1970s+] a male homosexual prostitute. ❑ **sporting house** *n.* (*also* **sporting crib, ...mansion, ...resort, ...room**) [SPORT *v.* (1) + SE *house*/HOUSE *n.*[1] (1)] [mid-19C–1970s] (*US*) a brothel or a gambling den. ❑ **sporting lady** *n.* (*also* **sporting girl, ...woman, sportswoman**) [SPORT *v.* (1) + *SPORTING HOUSE* above] [18C–1950s] (*US*) a prostitute, esp. when employed in a brothel. ❑ **sporting life** *n. see* separate entry. ❑ **sporting man** *n.* **1** [19C+] one who lives a hedonistic, enjoyable life. **2** [mid-19C–1920s] (*also* **sporting gent**) a genteel term for a gambler.

sporting life *n.*[1] [SPORT *v.*] **1** [20C+] the 'good' life, i.e. money, liquor, women, all the desired pleasures of the flesh; the term is particularly popular as a description of the lifestyle of a US pimp. **2** [1950s] a term of address, usu. ironic, to one who sets themselves up as a pimp, gambler etc [use may be a specific ref. to the 1951 George Gershwin musical *Porgy & Bess* and its eponymous 'city slicker' character]. **3** [1970s] (*drugs*) cocaine [its prominence in the lifestyle described in sense 1].

sporting life *n.*^{2} [rhy. sl.] [20C+] a wife.

sportsman *n.* **1** [mid-16C–19C] (*also* **sportster**) a womanizer, a promiscuous man [SPORT *v.*; note Ned Ward, *The London Spy* (1699), referring to the prostitutes available at the Bedlam Hospital, ''Tis a new *Whetstone's Park* [...] where a *Sportsman*, at any Hour in the Day, may meet with *Game* for his purpose']. **2** [mid-18C–19C] a genteel term for a gambler [SPORT *v.*]. **3** [late 19C–1910s] a person; no sporting prowess is suggested. **4** [1900s] a general term of familiar address. **5** [1900s–30s] an admirable human being [the English fantasy of 'good sportsmanship'].

IN COMPOUNDS

▫ **sportsman for liquor** *n.* [late 19C–1900s] a dedicated drinker (but not, in this context, a drunkard). ▫ **sportsman's gap** *n.* (*also* **sportsman's hole**) [19C] the vagina.

sporty *adj.* [SPORT *n.*] **1** [late 19C–1940s] sexy, provocative, 'fast'. **2** [1910s+] (*US black/campus*) attractive, good-looking. **3** [1950s–60s] (*US*) accomplished.

spot *n.*^{1} [omnibus jargon *spot*, a plain-clothes official, employed by the company to oversee drivers and conductors; ult. SE *spot*, to notice] **1** [mid-19C–1910s] a detective. **2** [1930s–40s] a guess, a gamble.

IN PHRASES

▫ **get a spot on** *v.* [late 19C] to make a surveillance of. ▫ **put a spot on** *v.* [1970s] (*US black*) to focus on, to stare at.

spot *n.*^{2} [-SPOT *sfx*] **1** [mid-19C+] (*orig. US*) a term of imprisonment, usu. one year; usu. with a preceding number as -SPOT *sfx* (1). **2** [mid-19C+] a dollar or pound sterling, usu. with a number sfx but not a specific denomination of a note, which is -SPOT *sfx* (2). **3** [1940s–50s] (*Aus./N.Z.*) a ten-pound note. **4** [1960s] (*US black*) a ten-dollar note. **5** [1960s+] (*Aus./N.Z.*) £100; latterly A$100 or NZ$100.

spot *n.*^{3} [late 19C] a cake; thus *spot and scalder*, cake and tea.

spot *n.*^{4} [abbr. SE *in a spot of bother*] [1920s+] difficulties, trouble; usu. in phr. *in a spot*.

IN COMPOUNDS

▫ **spot killer** *n.* [1930s] (*US Und.*) a hired assassin.

IN PHRASES

▫ **put on the spot** *v.* (*orig. US*) **1** [1920s] (*US tramp*) to leave waiting at an appointed meeting place. **2** [1920s–50s] to arrange to have someone killed; to put someone in the position of being killed. **3** [1920s+] (*also* **put in a spot, put the spot on**) to place in a difficult or disadvantageous position.

spot *n.*^{5} [SE *spot*, a place/abbr. SE *night spot*] **1** [1920s+] (*US Und.*) anywhere seen as a potential site for a robbery, e.g. a jewellery store, wealthy apartment etc. **2** [1930s+] (*orig. US black*) a nightclub. **3** [1930s+] a restaurant. **4** [1930s+] (*orig. US black*) an after-hours club. **5** [1970s+] (*S.Afr.*) an illicit bar, a shebeen. **6** [1970s+] (*US gay*) any homosexual gathering place other than a gay bar. **7** [1990s+] (*US*) an apartment used spec. for the sale of drugs. **8** [1990s+] (*US black/drugs*) anywhere in the street that drug dealers congregate.

SE in slang uses

IN PHRASES

▫ **have a vacant spot** *v.* [late 19C–1900s] to be stupid, i.e. 'not all there'. ▫ **spot in the road** *n.* *see* BAD PLACE IN THE ROAD *under* BAD *adj.*

SE, meaning a small mark or dot, in slang uses

IN COMPOUNDS

▫ **spotlight** *n.* [1960s–70s] (*US black*) a light-skinned black woman. ▫ **spot on** *adj.* [1950s+] perfect, exactly right, accurate.

IN PHRASES

▫ **off the spot** *adj.* [reverse of ON THE SPOT below] [late 19C–1900s] uncertain, lacking in awareness. ▫ **on the spot** *adj.* [metaphorical, but note *Saturday Evening Post* 13/4/29: '*Spot*, the, n. A piece of carpet eight inches square on which an offending prisoner must stand for two days. In some prisons the Spot is a painted mark on the wall against which the prison must hold his nose'] **1** [late 19C–1930s] alert, aware. **2** [1930s+] (*US Und.*) marked for death, facing assassination. **3** [1930s+] (*also* **on a spot**) in trouble, facing problems. ▫ **spot on burnt** *n.* [1920s] a poached egg on toast; often in pl. with pfx *two, three* etc.

spot *v.*^{1} **1** [early 18C; mid-19C] to mark or note as a criminal or suspected person. **2** [mid-19C] to inform against. **3** [mid-19C–1960s] to place a watch, to observe, to spy on. **4** [mid-19C+] (*UK Und.*) (*also* **spot off, spot out**) to reconnoitre possible sites for future burglary or look over victims for pickpocketing. **5** [late 19C–1930s] (*US*) to kill, to murder.

IN PHRASES

▫ **on the spot** [mid-19C] (*UK Und.*) looking for places that can be broken into and robbed. ▫ **spot someone out** *v.* [1970s] (*US black*) to ascertain the characteristics, hidden or otherwise, of a person.

SE in slang uses

IN PHRASES

▫ **spot one's pants** *v.* *see* WET ONE'S PANTS *under* PANTS *n.*

IN EXCLAMATIONS

▫ **spot your dot!** *see under* DOT *n.*^{2}.

spot *v.*^{2} [*spotting* winners] [late 19C] to gamble.

spot *v.*^{3} [? to place a mark or 'spot' on a ledger] **1** [20C+] to advance on credit. **2** [1920s+] to offer an advantage to.

spot *v.*^{4} [SE colloq. *spot*, a small drink] [1920s+] (*Aus./N.Z.*) to treat (others or oneself) to a drink; thus *spotting*, occasional drinking.

-spot *sfx* [the number of pips on a playing-card was described in this way] **1** [mid-19C; 20C+] (*orig. US*) a term of imprisonment, usu. one year; thus usu. preceded by the number of years. **2** [mid-19C+] a dollar, a pound, as a denomination of a note; note also SPOT *n.*^{2}.

IN PHRASES

▫ **five-spot** *n.* **1** [late 19C+] (*also* **V-spot**) a $5 or £5 note. **2** [1900s–60s] (*US*) a five-year prison sentence. **3** [1910s] (*US*) a five-dollar gold piece. **4** [1980s] (*N.Z.*) NZ$500. ▫ **one-spot** *n.* **1** [late 19C+] (*US*) a $1 bill. **2** [1940s] (*US Und.*) (*also* **one-spot sleep**) a one-year prison sentence. **3** [1990s+] (*Aus. drugs*) A$100 worth of heroin. ▫ **ten-spot** *n.* **1** [mid-19C+] (*US*) a $10 bill or £10 note. **2** [1900s] (*US campus*) (*also* **ten-strike**) a perfect recitation [from sense 1, but also the idea of ten out of ten]. **3** [1900s–60s] (*US prison*) a ten-year prison sentence. ▫ **twenty-spot** *n.* [mid-19C+] a £20 note or $20 bill. ▫ **two-spot** *n.* **1** [mid-19C+] (*US*) a $2 bill. **2** [late 19C–1930s] any low-value playing card. **3** [late 19C–1930s] thus in fig. use, an insignificant person. **4** [1900s–40s] (*US prison/Und.*) (*also* **two-spotter**) a two-year sentence. **5** [1970s–80s] (*Aus. Und.*) A$200. **6** [1990s+] (*Aus. drugs*) A$200 worth of heroin.

SE in slang uses

IN PHRASES

▫ **nine-spot** *n.* [card imagery: the relative low ranking of nine, compared to the court cards] [late 19C–1900s] (*US*) a nonentity.

spotted *adj.* [SPOT *v.*^{1}] [mid-19C] known by the police, under surveillance.

SE in slang uses

IN COMPOUNDS

▫ **spotted dog** *n.* [joc. pron. of SE *spotted dough*, the 'spots' are plums] **1** [mid–late 19C] (*also* **spotted duff**) a plum pudding. **2** [20C+] a currant loaf. **3** [1920s] a sailor's stew. ▫ **spotted donkey** *n.* [19C] a plum pudding. ▫ **spotted leopard** *n.* [late 19C] a plum pudding.

spotted dick *adj.* [rhy. sl.] [20C+] sick.

spotter *n.*^{1} [SPOT *v.*^{1}/SE *spot*] **1** [mid-19C–1950s] a detective. **2** [mid-19C+] (*US Und.*) one who searches for suitable places or victims to rob. **3** [20C+] (*drugs*) a lookout. **4** [1910s–60s] an informer.

spotter *n.*^{2} [the stereotype of the SE *trainspotter*] [1990s+] an insignificant weakling.

spotters *n.* [SPOT *v.*[1]] [1940s] (*US black*) the eyes.

spotty *adj.* [1960s] inferior.

spotty dog *n.* [rhy. sl. = WOG *n.*[1] (3)] [1970s] a derog. term for any foreigner, irrespective of colour or race.

spounce *n.* (*also* **spunks**) [SPUNK *n.* (1) + SE *bounce*] [20C+] (*W.I.*) brashness, sauciness, courage, esp. of a young woman.

spouse *n.* [1980s+] (*US campus*) one's regular boy- or girlfriend.

spout *n.*[1] [SPOUT *v.*[1]] **1** [early 17C; late 19C] a religious or political orator. **2** [late 19C] speechifying, haranguing. **3** [1900s] a large and ever-open mouth.

spout *n.*[2] [SE *spout*, a lift formerly in use in pawnbrokers' shops, up which pawned articles were taken for storage; note Egan, *Life in London* (1821): 'It was a *long narrow spout*, which reached from the top of the house of the *Money-Lender* down to his counter, and through which articles of property when *redeemed*, were conveyed, in order to facilitate business'] **1** [19C] a pawnbroker's shop. **2** [early 19C] as ext. of sense 1, a police cell, a prison.

IN PHRASES

❑ **down the spout** [antonym of UP THE SPOUT below] [mid-19C] out of pawn. ❑ **up the spout** **1** [early 19C–1920s] hospitalized, imprisoned. **2** [early 19C+] in the pawnshop. **3** [early 19C+] having problems, 'in a bad way'. **4** [mid-19C+] (*orig. US*) gone to waste, ruined. **5** [late 19C+] dead. **6** [1900s–10s] (*also* **up the gargoyle**) bankrupt. **7** [1940s+] (*also* **up the shoot**) pregnant. **8** [1960s] wrong, incorrect. ❑ **up the spout and Charley-Wag** [CHARLEY WAG *n.*] [late 19C] a general phr. used of something that has gone to waste, been squandered or lost.

spout *n.*[3] [SE *spout*] **1** [mid-19C] the vagina. **2** [mid-19C; 1940s+] the penis.

SE in slang uses

IN PHRASES

❑ **get it down the spout** *v. see* HAVE ONE'S TEAPOT MENDED *under* TEAPOT *n.*

spout *v.*[1] [early 17C+] to talk effusively.

IN PHRASES

❑ **spout Billy** *v.* [William, *i.e. Billy* Shakespeare] [19C] to make one's living by reciting portions of Shakespeare in public houses. ❑ **spout ink** *v.* [late 16C; late 19C–1920s] to write for a living. ❑ **spout off** *v.* (*also* **spout on**) [mid-19C+] to gabble on.

spout *v.*[2] [the pawnbroker's SE *spout*] [early 19C–1910s] to pawn.

spouter *n.*[1] [SPOUT *v.*[1]] **1** [mid-18C–1920s] a verbose, effusive speaker; a preacher or lecturer. **2** [mid-19C–1900s] (*Aus.*) spec. a 'soap-box' orator.

spouter *n.*[2] [SPOUT *n.*[2] (1)] [early 19C] one who places items in pawn.

spouter *n.*[3] (*also* **sperm spouter**) [late 19C] the penis.

spouting *n.* [SPOUT *v.*[1]] [mid-18C–19C] oratory, speechifying; in weak sense, talking loud.

spow *n.* [? SE *spew*, vomit] [1940s–50s] (*US prison*) prison-made coffee.

spraff *v.* [ety. unknown] [20C+] to talk, to chat.

sprag *n.* [SE *sprag*, a sprightly young fellow, ? ult. SE *sprig*] [early 18C] a fop, a dandy.

sprag *v.* [SE *sprag*, a piece of wood used to check the revolution of a wheel or roller, usu. by inserting it between two of the spokes; a rod or bar used to prevent a vehicle from running backwards; fig., to arrest a person's progress] **1** [1910s] to accost truculently. **2** [1910s] to persuade. **3** [1910s–30s] (*Aus.*) to meddle in someone's plans, to thwart. **4** [1990s+] (*UK juv.*) (*also* **spragg**) to inform on another pupil.

sprain one's ankle *v. see* BREAK ONE'S ANKLE *under* BREAK *v.*[1].

sprang *adj.* [var. on PRANG *adj.*] [1990s+] (*US black*) extremely intoxicated, esp. by crack cocaine.

sprarser *n.* (*also* **sparaser, sparesie, sparzer, sprarzer, sprarzy, sprasey, sprasy, sprazey Anna, sprowsie**) [? SPRAT *n.*] [1900s–70s] a sixpence.

sprat *n.* (*also* **sprazi, sprazzy**) [its diminutive size, like that of the fish] [mid-19C–1950s] a sixpence.

sprat day *n.* [the arrival of *sprats* in the market at approx. the same time, i.e. early Sept.] [mid–late 19C] the Lord Mayor's Day in London.

sprats *n.* [ety. unknown; ? fig. use of SPRAT *n.*] [late 19C] one's possessions.

sprauncy *adj.* [? dial. *sprouncey*, cheerful] [1950s+] smart or showy in appearance or sound of voice.

spray *n.* [1990s+] (*Aus.*) a voluble (and boring) conversation.

SE in slang uses

IN COMPOUNDS

❑ **sprayhead** *n.* [-HEAD *sfx* (4)] [1990s+] (*US teen*) one who inhales the fumes of spray paint. ❑ **spray starch** *n.* [1960s+] (*US gay*) a fig. substance that keeps heterosexual wrists from drooping.

spray *v.*

SE in slang uses

IN PHRASES

❑ **spray and pray** *n.* [1990s+] an Ingram MAC 10 sub-machine gun. ❑ **spray someone's tonsils** *v.* [1940s+] (*gay*) to ejaculate in one's fellator's mouth.

sprazey Anna *n. see* SPRARSER *n.*

sprazi/sprazzy *n. see* SPRAT *n.*

spread *n.* **1** [late 18C–mid-19C] a saddle [SE *spread*, a coverlet; the saddle also *spreads* the rider's legs]. **2** [late 18C–mid-19C] (*UK/US Und.*) butter. **3** [early–mid-19C] jam, marmalade or any similar addition to bread and butter. **4** [early 19C+] a meal, esp. a sumptuous one; sometimes further defined as *morning spread*, breakfast etc; also as v. [by 20C the term was mainly facet./archaic, classically found in the children's stories of Enid Blyton (1897–1968)]. **5** [mid-19C] an umbrella. **6** [mid-19C] a lady's shawl. **7** [mid-19C+] (*US*) a newspaper; thus a page, as in coverage of a news article or advertisement in a paper or magazine, e.g. a *two-page spread*; thus *spread-crib*, a printer's or newspaper office. **8** [1930s+] the thickening of one's waistline; esp. in *middle-aged spread*, the onset of fat in middle age.

IN PHRASES

❑ **do a spread** *v.* [SPREAD (FOR) *under* SPREAD *v.*] [mid-19C] of a woman, to offer oneself for sexual intercourse. ❑ **make a spread** *v.* [1930s–50s] (*drugs*) to lay out the equipment used for giving oneself an injection.

spread *v.* **1** [1900s] (*Aus.*) to hit. **2** [1940s] (*UK Und.*) to accelerate a car.

IN PHRASES

❑ **spread one's jenk** *v.* [ety. unknown but note SE (*high*) *jinks* or dial. *jannock*, liberal, hospitable, one who pays their share] [1920s–30s] (*US black*) to have a good time, to celebrate, to have sex.

SE in slang uses

IN COMPOUNDS

❑ **spread beaver** *n. see* SPLIT BEAVER *under* BEAVER *n.*[1]. ❑ **spread city** *n.* [the SE *spread* of such real estate developments + -CITY *sfx*] [1960s+] (*US*) the dormitory suburbs of a big city. ❑ **spread eagle** *see* separate entries.

IN PHRASES

❑ **spread (for)** *v.* [the man *spreads* and the woman *spreads for*] **1** [mid-19C+] to have sexual intercourse. **2** [1970s+] (*US gay*) to sodomize or to be sodomized. ❑ **spread it thick** *v.* **1** [mid-19C+] (*US*) to exaggerate or elaborate. **2** [1920s] to live well; thus *spread it thin*, to live in poverty. ❑ **spread one's shots** *v.* [2000s] (*US prison*) to borrow from a number of people. ❑ **spread out** *v.* [1990s+] (*W.I.*) to relax, to 'let off steam'. ❑ **spread the...** *v. see under* relevant n.

spread eagle *n.* [20C+] a position of heterosexual intercourse.

spreadeagle *adj.* [SE *spreadeagle*, a boastful or self-assertive person, ult. the image of the bird's wide-spread wings] [mid-19C–1920s] (*US*) pompous, verbose; also as v.

spreader *n.* (*also* **spreadum**) [its properties] **1** [17C–mid-18C] (*UK Und.*) butter. **2** [2000s] (*N.Z.*) a blanket.

spreck up *v.* [SE *spray*] [1990s+] to ejaculate.

spree *n.*[1] [? SE *spray*, a drinking bout, but ? dial. *spreagh/spreath*, a cattle raid, ult. Gaelic *spréidh*, cattle (Partridge); Hotten (1860) suggests Fr. *ésprit*, spirit or Du. root, as do B&L] [early 19C+] **1** a hearty, boisterous good time. **2** a prolonged bout of drinking; thus [mid-19C+] *on a/the spree*, out on a party; *spreeing it*, drinking excessively.

DERIVATIVES

□ **spreeish** *adj.* [19C] tipsy, drunk.

IN COMPOUNDS

□ **spree-boy** *n.* [1950s] (*W.I.*) **1** a very well-dressed man, a dandy. **2** one who prefers pursuing pleasure to working hard; thus *spree-girl/-man/-master/-woman*. □ **spree-child** *n.* [1950s] (*W.I.*) a very well-dressed, stylish woman.

spree *n.*[2] [? fig. ext. of SPREE *n.*[1] (1)] [1940s] (*W.I.*) a girlfriend.

spree *v.* [SPREE *n.*[1] (1)] **1** [early 19C+] to go out on a party, to take it easy; ext. to any form of spree, i.e. serial robberies; thus n. *spreer*, one who goes on a spree. **2** [1900s] to treat someone else to a party.

sprig *n.* [? SE *sprig*, a young descendant] [late 18C+] a show-off.

spring *n.* [SPRING *v.* (8)/SPRING *v.* (9)] [1900s–50s] an escape or release from prison; thus *make a spring*, to escape, to cause to be released.

SE in slang uses

IN COMPOUNDS

□ **springbutt** *n.* [BUTT *n.*[1] (1a)] [1960s+] (*US*) a keen, eager person. □ **spring cleaning** *n.* [1990s+] (*US Und.*) cleaning up, hiding or getting rid of evidence. □ **spring-sides** *n.* [20C+] (*Aus.*) elastic-sided boots.

IN PHRASES

□ **spring ankle warehouse** *n.* [SE *spring*, i.e. sprain an *ankle* + *warehouse*; once confined in such a place, the inmates are unable to run off] [late 18C–early 19C] a prison (cf. *ANKLE SPRING WAREHOUSE* under ANKLE *n.*).

spring *v.* [SE *spring*, to cause to appear] **1** [17C+] to make something appear or happen suddenly. **2** [19C+] (*orig. UK Und.*) of both persons and objects, to discover, to come upon [late 19C+ use is Aus.]. **3** [mid-19C] to appear suddenly, e.g. *where did you spring from?* **4** [mid-19C] to offer a higher price. **5** [mid-19C+] (*also* **spring for**) to pay over a sum of money, to buy a certain amount; to produce; to pay for, to treat. **6** [late 19C–1910s] to afford. **7** [1900s] (*US Und.*) to open (a lock). **8** [20C+] (*orig. US*) (*also* **spring out**) to escape from prison. **9** [20C+] to get a person out of prison, to have someone released, to release. **10** [1940s] to alter. **11** [1940s] as sense 9 in a non-prison context. **12** [1970s] (*US prison*) to leave prison after completing one's sentence. **13** [1980s+] (*Aus. prison*) to catch someone engaged in an illicit activity.

IN PHRASES

□ **spring a leak** *v. see TAKE A LEAK under* LEAK *n.* □ **spring a partridge** *v.* [sporting jargon *spring a partridge*, of a beater to cause a partridge to rise from cover] [17C–18C] of a confidence trickster, to entrap a victim and then rob or otherwise defraud them. □ **spring a plant** *v. see under* PLANT *n.* □ **spring for** *v. see* sense 5 above. □ **spring in** *v.* [1920s] (*US tramp*) to break into a loaded boxcar. □ **spring it** *v.* (*also* **spring on**) **1** [late 19C+] to reveal a plan or idea, with some element of surprise. **2** [1920s] to pull a joke. □ **spring out** *v. see* sense 8 above. □ **spring to** *v.* **1** [late 19C–1900s] to afford, to come up with sufficient money for. **2** [late 19C–1900s] to achieve, to manage. **3** [20C+] to treat, e.g. to a free meal.

springer *n.* [SPRING *v.* (9)] [1940s–50s] (*US Und.*) a bail bondsman.

springer-up *n.* [the clothes 'spring up' without much art] [mid-19C] **1** a cheap tailor, selling off-the-peg clothing. **2** a tailor who pays his employees the lowest possible wages.

Springs, the *n.* [the running springs found on Blackwell's Island in 18C] [mid-19C] (*US Und.*) Blackwell's Island prison, New York City.

springs *n.*[1] [? the dampness of such cells, situated below ground-level] [1910s–50s] (*US Und.*) a small, solitary cell; thus phr. *at the springs*, confined in a strait-jacket.

springs *n.*[2] [1990s+] (*US black*) the ability to jump high during a game of basketball.

sprinkle *v.*[1] [the application of holy water] [mid-19C+] to christen.

sprinkle *v.*[2] [1990s+] (*US black teen*) to tell a story, to lay out a situation.

spritz *n.* [Yid. *spritz*, spray] [1910s+] (*US*) **1** carbonated water as a mixer for drinks. **2** a light shower of rain. **3** any form of spray, e.g. of blood. **4** a spontaneous stage performance.

spritz *v.* [Yid. *spritz*, to spray] [1950s+] (*US*) **1** to perform a stage monologue with much impromptu ad libbing, free-associating etc. **2** to air one's feelings, to emote. **3** of an object, e.g. a gun, to spray.

sprog *n.* (*also* **sproglet, sprogster**) [18C *sprag*, a lively young fellow; note milit. *sprog*, a recruit] [1940s+] a child; thus *sprog*, to have a child.

sprout *n.*[1] [SE *sprout*, an offshoot] [early 18C+] a child, a youngster.

sprout *n.*[2] [fig. use of SE in some way] [mid-19C–1910s] (*US*) a beating; thus *put through a course of sprouts*, to beat, to flog, to subject to intense, harsh discipline.

sproutsy *adj.* [? the HIPPIE *n.*[2] (3) diet of bean *sprouts* etc] [1970s+] (*US*) unconventional, HIPPIE *adj.*

sprowsie *n. see* SPRARSER *n.*

spruce *n.* [1920s] (*US black*) a gullible individual.

spruce *v.* [SE *spruce up*, i.e. the facts, or SPRUIK *v.* (1)] [20C+] to tell lies, 'stories'; thus n. *sprucer*, a liar or one who exaggerates.

spruicher *n. see* SPRUIKER *n.*

spruik *n.* [SPRUIK *v.*] **1** [1910s] (*Aus./N.Z.*) a rant; an oration; a showman's or other salesman's patter. **2** [1950s] (*Aus.*) a chat, a visit.

spruik *v.* [? Yid. *shpruch*, saying, charm, incantation or Du. *spreken*, to talk] [1910s+] (*Aus./N.Z.*) **1** to speak in a way that resembles a showman; thus to speak in an insincere manner. **2** to chatter (about).

spruiker *n.* (*also* **spruicher**) [SPRUIK *v.*] [1910s+] (*Aus.*) **1** a barker for a fairground or carnival sideshow or a cinema, theatre or similar entertainment, who stands on the street to promote the show and attract an audience. **2** a loud and continual talker. **3** a platform speaker, an orator. **4** a barrister.

sprung *adj.* [? one bounces along] **1** [early 19C–1920s] drunk; also fig. use. **2** [late 19C; 1990s+] of the mind, unstable [later use US gang]. **3** [1950s+] (*US teen*) (*also* **sprung on**) sexually obsessed, romantically besotted.

IN PHRASES

□ **sprung on** *adj.* **1** [2000s] (*US black teen*) having an erection [one's penis *springs up*]. **2** *see* sense 3 above. □ **sprung on the cat** *adj.* [CAT *n.*[1] (2a)] [2000s] (*US black*) of a man, addicted to sex.

S.P. shop *n. see* S.P. JOINT *n.*

spud *n.*[1] [ety. unknown; ? the low value of the SPUD *n.*[3] (1)] **1** [mid-19C] (*US Und.*) counterfeit money. **2** [1910s–40s] (*US Und.*) a swindle in which the con men convince the victim that he can buy real money from a man who has stolen plates from the government but it is, in fact, counterfeit money.

IN PHRASES

□ **on the spud** *adj.* [1920s] (*US Und.*) practising swindling.

spud *n.*[2] [SE *pudgy* or dial. *spud*, a short, stumpy person] [mid–late 19C] a baby's hand.

spud *n.*[3] [? SE *spud*, a digging fork with three broad prongs or dial. *spud*, a stumpy thing] **1** [mid-19C+] a potato. **2** [20C+] (*W.I.*) a ripe banana. **3** [1910s–30s] nickname for an Irishman [note 19C US *little potato skin*, an Irish child]. **4** [1930s] any person. **5** [1940s] (*US Und.*) a revolver; a pistol. **6** [1980s+] (*N.Z. teen/US*) a general term of abuse. **7** [1990s+] (*US*) a child, a young person. **8** *see* POTATO *n.* (3).

IN COMPOUNDS

□ **spud barber** *n.* [1930s–40s] one who peels potatoes.

▫ **spud-bashing** *n.* [BASH *v.* (1); orig. milit. use, when the job was compulsory and part of kitchen fatigues] [1940s+] the activity of peeling potatoes. ▫ **spud-eater** *n. see* POTATO-EATER *under* POTATO *n.* ▫ **spud face** *n. see* POTATO-FACE *under* POTATO *n.* ▫ **spud-islander** *n.* [the high quality of its potatoes] [1950s+] a native or inhabitant of Prince Edward Island, Canada. ▫ **spud juice** *n.* **1** [1960s] (*US prison*) illegally distilled alcohol, based on potatoes [JUICE *n.*[1] (3a)]. **2** [1990s+] semen [JUICE *n.*[1] (2)]. ▫ **spud-miner** *n.* [late 19C] (*Aus.*) a peasant. ▫ **spudsacked** *adj.* [1990s+] passed out in a heap. ▫ **spuds and swimmers** *n.* [1900s] fish and chips. ▫ **spudwater** *n.* [1990s+] thin, watery semen.

(IN PHRASES)

▫ **in the spud line** *adj.* [1930s+] pregnant. ▫ **love spuds** *n.* [1990s+] the testicles.

spud *v.* [? dial. *spud*, to muddle, to be uselessly busy] [1920s–30s] (*US black*) to play cards for low stakes.

spuddy *n.* [SPUD *n.*[3] (1)] [mid-19C] **1** a seller of bad potatoes. **2** a seller of hot baked potatoes.

spudge around *v.* (*also* **spudge up**) [? var. on SE *push*] [late 19C–1920s] (*US*) to exert oneself, to apply oneself.

spuff *n.* [SPUFF *v.*] [1990s+] semen.

spuff *v.* ['echoic' of the ejaculation] [1990s+] to ejaculate.

(IN PHRASES)

▫ **spuff up** *v.* [1990s+] to masturbate.

spug *n.* [dial. *spadger*, a sparrow] [1920s+] (*Aus./N.Z.*) a sparrow.

spum *v.* [SE *sperm* + CUM *v.*] [2000s] (*US black*) to ejaculate.

spume *n.* [SE *spume*, foam] [1990s+] semen.

spumoni *adj.* [SAmE *spumoni*, a variety of ice-cream; ult. synon. Ital. *spumone*] [1990s+] (*US campus*) excellent, first-rate.

spun *adj.* **1** [20C+] defeated, lost for ideas. **2** [1920s] exhausted, drained of energy. **3** [1980s] exhilarated, stimulated. **4** [1990s+] drunk. **5** [1990s+] intoxicated by drugs. **6** [1990s+] confused, stressed.

spunge *see under* SPONGE.

spunging-house *n. see* SPONGING-HOUSE *n.*

spunk *n.* [? fig. use of Scot./dial. *spunk*, a spark] **1** [late 18C+] courage, bravery. **2** [late 18C+] in fig. use, spirit. **3** [early 19C] (*Scot. Und.*) life. **4** [mid–late 19C] a match; usu. in phrs. below [dial. *spunk*, spark, tinder, ult. dial. *spunk* a dried fungus used as tinder; note dial. *spunks*, lucifer matches]. **5** [mid-19C+] semen. **6** [1960s+] (*also* **spunky**) (*Aus.*) someone seen as sexually attractive.

(IN COMPOUNDS)

pertaining to sex

▫ **spunk-bag** *n.* [SE *bag*/BAG *n.*[1] (1f)] [1990s+] **1** a condom. **2** a general term of abuse. ▫ **spunkbone** *n. see* separate entry. ▫ **spunk-bubble** *n.* **1** [1970s] (*Aus.*) an attractive young woman, a nubile teenager. **2** [1990s+] a term of abuse. ▫ **spunk bucket** *n.* (*also* **spunk-dustbin**) [1990s+] a promiscuous woman or one who is branded as such. ▫ **spunk-gobbed** *adj.* [GOB *n.*[1] (1); the image is of a man fellating another] [1990s+] a general term of abuse; lit. 'semen-mouthed'. ▫ **spunk-gullet** *n.* [2000s] a general term of abuse, lit. a fellator. ▫ **spunkhammer** *n.* [HAMMER *n.*[1] (1)] [2000s] the penis. ▫ **spunk-head** *n.* [-HEAD *sfx* (1)] [1990s+] a general term of abuse. ▫ **spunk-pot** *n.* [note Rochester c.1673: 'To be a Whore, understanding, / A Passive *Pot* for *Fools* to spend in'] [1990s+] the vagina. ▫ **spunk-rat** *n.* [1980s+] (*Aus.*) a sexually attractive person. ▫ **spunk-trumpet** *n.* (*also* **junket trumpet**) [1990s+] the penis.

pertaining to match-selling

▫ **spunk-faker** *n.* [FAKER *n.* (4)] [mid-19C] (*US*) an ostensible match-seller, whose outwardly respectable, if impoverished profession often hides less reputable, and usu. fraudulent, pursuits. ▫ **spunk-fencer** *n.* [-FENCER *sfx*] [mid–late 19C] (*Aus./UK Und.*) a match-seller.

spunk *v.* [lit./fig. uses of SPUNK *n.* (5)] **1** [late 19C+] (*also* **spunk off**) to ejaculate. **2** [1950s] as sense 1, of a woman. **3** [1990s+] to consume, to use up.

(IN PHRASES)

▫ **spunk off** *v. see* sense 1 above. ▫ **spunk up** *v.* [SPUNK *n.* (1)] **1** [mid-19C+] (*US*) to act aggressively, courageously. **2** [mid-19C+] (*US*) to encourage someone to be courageous. **3** [1940s] (*US black*) to speak out.

spunkbone *n.* [SPUNK *n.* (5) + BONE *n.*[1] (1)] [2000s] the penis.

(IN COMPOUNDS)

▫ **spunkbone jockey** *n.* [2000s] a male homosexual.

spunker *n.*[1] [SPUNK *n.* (5)] [1990s+] **1** a cheerful, happy person. **2** a general term of abuse, usu. aimed at a male. **3** a sexually provocative person. **4** an affectionate man-to-man term of address. **5** one who ejaculates.

spunker *n.*[2] [SPUNK *v.* (3)] [2000s] a spendthrift.

spunkie *n.* [SPUNK *n.* (2)] [19C–1900s] (*Irish*) a lively young man.

spunking *adj.* [SPUNK *n.* (5)] [1920s] used as a negative intensifier.

spunks *n. see* SPOUNCE *n.*

spunky *n. see* SPUNK *n.* (6).

spunky *adj.* [SPUNK *n.*] **1** [late 18C+] courageous, brave, plucky; usu. of young people and applied equally to either gender. **2** [mid-19C–1910s] (*US*) angry. **3** [late 19C+] pertaining to semen. **4** [1980s] as a term of address. **5** [1980s+] (*Aus.*) sexy. **6** [1990s+] of an object, smart and showy.

spun out *adj.* [motor-racing imagery] [1990s+] of a person, out of control, crazy.

spur *n.*

SE in slang uses

(IN PHRASES)

▫ **have a spur in one's head** *v.* [late 18C] of a fellow jockey, to be an honest person, to be no coward.

spur *v.* (*also* **give someone the spur**) [late 19C–1900s] to irritate, to annoy.

spurge *n.* [SE *spurge*, one or other of several species of the genus *Euphorbia*, some of which are considered near weeds; thus a pun on WEEDY *adj.* (2)] [1920s+] (*Aus.*) an effeminate young man.

spurt *n.* [mid-19C] a small amount, a small quantity, esp. of alcohol.

sputnik *n.* [SE *sputnik*, the Russian spacecraft (lit., 'travelling companion', 'fellow traveller') launched in 1957; it puts you 'into orbit'] [1980s+] (*drugs*) a mixture of Pakistani cannabis and opium.

sputterbudget *n.* [SE *sputter* + *budget*, one who has certain characteristics] [1910s] (*US*) one who chatters on to excess.

sputterer *n.* [? the *sputtering* pipe] [1930s] (*US drugs*) a novice opium smoker, still assured that they will never become addicted.

sputumnal *adj.* [SE *sputum*, 'saliva or spittle mixed with mucus or purulent matter, and expectorated in certain diseased states of the lungs, chest, or throat' (*OED*)] [1990s+] (*Aus.*) weird, unpleasant.

spuzz *n.* [SE *sperm* + JIZZ *n.*] [1990s+] semen.

spy *n.* [late 16C–early 17C] the eye.

spy-smashers *n.* [1970s+] (*US gay*) wrap-around sunglasses.

squab *n.*[1] [? SE *squab*, a fat cushion or a well-upholstered sofa] **1** [late 17C–early 19C; 1920s] a very fat person. **2** [mid-19C] a short person.

squab *n.*[2] [SE *squab*, a raw, inexperienced person + later uses as a young, unfledged bird or animal; ult. play on CHICKEN *n.* (1a)] (*US*) **1** [19C+] a fool, an unsophisticated person, a peasant. **2** [1910s–60s] a young woman.

(IN COMPOUNDS)

▫ **squab job** *n.* [1910s] a job that suits a young woman.

squab *n.*[3] [abbr. SE *squabble*] [1990s+] (*US gang*) an argument or fight.

squab *v.* [? abbr. SE *squabble*] [1990s+] (*US black*) to confront.

squabby *adj.* (*also* **squab, squobby**) [SQUAB *n.*[1] (1)] [mid-17C–1950s] squat, short and thick.

Squad, the *n.* [abbr.] [1920s+] (*UK Und.*) the Flying *Squad*.

squad *n.*[1] [late 18C] a group of prostitutes.

squad *n.*[2] [1990s+] (*US black*) a gang or group of friends.

squaddie *n.* (*also* **squaddy, squatti, swaddie**) [SE *squad*] [1920s+] a regular private soldier.

squadrol *n.* [SE *squad* + pat*rol*] [1940s–70s] (*US*) a small police van.

squaggy *adj.* [ety. unknown] [mid-19C] (*UK Und.*) ill-tempered.

squail *n.* [? Scot. *squeal*, a spree] [late 18C–mid-19C] a glass of liquor, a dram.

squalino *v.* [SE *squall*, to scream loudly or discordantly] [early 19C] to squeal or squall.

squall *n.*[1] [SE *squall*, an insignificant person] [late 16C–mid-17C] an up-market whore, kept by a rich gallant; also used as an endearment.

squall *n.*[2] (*also* **squawl**) [weak use of SE] [early 18C–mid-19C] (*UK Und.*) a voice.

square *n.* **1** in senses of respectability [fig. rectilinearity; American Dialect Soc. (Nov. 1958) suggests the steady 1-2-3-4 rhythm played without variation]. (**a**) [mid-19C] (*UK Und.*) a respectable pose; an excuse, thus a shield from arrest. (**b**) [late 19C+] (*Aus.*) a respectable woman; thus expanded as *square Jane and no nonsense*. (**c**) [20C+] (*orig. US*) a regular working man or woman; usu. pej., implying a tedious conventional person. **2** [mid-19C–1960s] (*Aus.*) gin, a bottle of gin; also as *square cut* [the shape of the bottle]. **3** [mid-19C+] (*US*) a proper or *square* meal [abbr.]. **4** [1920s+] (*US, usu. prison*) a factory-made cigarette, whether prison-issue or commercially produced [SQUARE *adj.* (1)]. **5** in senses of gullibility, innocence. (**a**) [1930s+] (*orig. US black*) a naïve person, one who believes in white America's promises, one who has little sexual sophistication; the use has a similar pej. implication to sense 1c. (**b**) [1940s–60s] (*US drugs*) one who eschews drugs. (**c**) [1940s+] (*US black*) a man who pursues women and is thus tricked out his money. (**d**) [1950s+] (*gay*) a heterosexual, or a gay man who is not used to the gay scene. **6** [1970s] (*US black*) a sexual deviant.

IN PHRASES

❑ **half-square** *n.* (*also* **half-squarie**) [1920s–60s] (*Aus.*) a sexually experienced woman, positioned in the contemporary moral spectrum between an all-out prostitute and a respectable woman; an 'amateur' prostitute.

SE in slang uses

IN COMPOUNDS

❑ **square-bashing** *n.* [SE *square*, the parade ground + BASH *v.* (1)] [1950s+] military drill; thus *square-basher*, a private soldier. ❑ **square one** *n.* [the image of children's board-games, e.g. snakes and ladders] [1960s+] (*orig. US*) the starting point, the beginning.

IN PHRASES

❑ **catch a square** *v.* [the corners in a boxing ring] [2000s] (*US prison*) to prepare for a fight. ❑ **in the square** [1960s] (*US*) in the respectable world. ❑ **square in a social circle** *n.* [var. on SE *square peg in a round hole*] [1930s–40s] (*US black*) a misfit. ❑ **take it to the square** *v.* [a square boxing ring] [2000s] (*US prison*) to call out for a fight.

square, the *n.* [SQUARE *adj.*] **1** [mid-19C] (*UK Und.*) the laws and customs of the underworld, by which all criminals should abide. **2** [mid-19C+] a respectable way of life. **3** [1930s] (*US black*) a trustworthy individual.

square *adj.* **1** [mid-17C+] of a thing, honest, truthful, fair; thus *squareness*, honesty [prior use SE from 16C]. **2** [19C+] of a person, honest, respectable, upright. **3** [mid-19C] (*US*) substantial. **4** [mid-19C] (*US*) of a drink, unadulterated by water. **5** [mid-19C–1910s] (*Aus.*) safe. **6** [mid-19C+] (*UK/US Und.*) dependable; as sense 1 but from a criminal standpoint. **7** [mid-19C+] sorted out, dealt with, even. **8** [late 19C+] sober. **9** [1930s+] correct, real. **10** [1930s+] (*orig. US black*) conventional, conservative, naïve, dull; thus n. *squareness*, conventionality. **11** [1940s] (*US black campus*) cheap. **12** [1960s] heterosexual.

DERIVATIVES

❑ **squaredom** *n.* [1950s+] (*orig. US*) the world of the unsophisticated, the unworldly. ❑ **squaresville** *n.* (*also* **squareville**) [SQUARE *n.* (1c) + -VILLE *sfx*[1]] [1950s+] (*US black/teen*) a conventional and thus boring place, person or event.

IN COMPOUNDS

❑ **square affair** *n.* (*also* **square bit, square piece**) [SE *affair*/BIT *n.*[1] (2a)/PIECE *n.* (1a)] [late 19C–1910s] one's regular girlfriend. ❑ **square apple** *n. see under* APPLE *n.*[1]. ❑ **square article** *n.* [early 19C] (*UK Und.*) anything one has purchased or otherwise acquired honestly. ❑ **square-ass** *adj.* (*also* **square-assed**) [-ASS *sfx*/-ASSED *sfx*] [1940s+] (*US black*) unsophisticated, naïve, 'straight'. ❑ **square-ball** *adj.* [1950s] (*US*) conventional. ❑ **squarebrain** *n.* [sfx *-brain*] **1** [20C+] a fool. **2** [1940s–50s] (*US black*) a conventional person, a fool, a dullard, with overtones of conservatism. ❑ **square broad** *n. see under* BROAD *n.*[2]. ❑ **square business** *n.* [1970s+] (*US black/prison*) honesty, truth; often affixed to a declaratory sentence as a means of emphasizing the speaker's sincerity. ❑ **square concern** *n.* [early 19C] (*UK Und.*) anything one has purchased or otherwise acquired honestly. ❑ **square cove** *n. see under* COVE *n.* ❑ **square crib** *n. see under* CRIB *n.*[1]. ❑ **square deal** *n.* [SE *deal*; see Asbury *Sucker's Progress* (1938): 'An extraordinary number of the terms, technical and otherwise, which were employed by Faro players in the palmy days of the game have passed into the language [...] *Square deal* — Twenty-five turns in which the dealer used a pack with squared edges. With these cards the chances of a crooked deal were minimized'] [mid-19C+] (*orig. US*) honest treatment, a proper business deal, a good bargain etc. ❑ **square dinkum** *adj. see* FAIR DINKUM *adj.* ❑ **square go** *n. see under* GO *n.*[1]. ❑ **square-goods** *adj. see* SQUARE-JOHN *adj.* ❑ **squarehead** *see* separate entries. ❑ **square john** *see* separate entries. ❑ **square moll** *n. see under* MOLL *n.* ❑ **square paper** *n. see under* PAPER *n.* ❑ **square piece** *n. see* SQUARE AFFAIR above. ❑ **square plug** *n.* [SE *plug*, which does not 'fit in the round hole' of criminality] **1** [1910s–40s] (*US Und.*) a 'civilian' who admires and mingles with criminals but lacks the courage or desire actually to commit a crime. **2** [1920s+] (*US Und.*) a prisoner who is not a professional criminal. ❑ **square pusher** *n. see under* PUSHER *n.* ❑ **square rigger/-rigged** *see* separate entries. ❑ **square setting** *n.* [SET *n.*[2] (1b)] [1950s–60s] (*US black*) a respectable party, without drugs, loud music etc. ❑ **square shake** *n.* [SE *shake* (of the dice)] [1930s+] (*US*) a fair deal, honest treatment. ❑ **square shooter/-shooting** *see* separate entries.

IN PHRASES

❑ **get square (with)** *v.* [late 19C] to get even (with). ❑ **on the square** (*also* **upon the square**) [? Masonic jargon] **1** [mid-17C+] in an honest manner, truthfully. **2** [late 17C–early 19C] having revenged oneself, 'even' with someone. **3** [late 17C+] living an honest, law-abiding (and tedious) life. **4** [early 19C] having settled all debts with someone. **5** [mid-19C+] (*US Und.*) trustworthy (to condone or perform illegal acts). **6** [mid-19C+] honest, truthful. **7** [1920s] accurate. **8** [1930s+] (*Aus.*) conducting a regular monogamous relationship. ❑ **square as a billiard ball** *adj.* (*also* **square as a golf ball, ...a tennis ball**) [1940s–50s] (*Aus.*) anything but honest or 'square', whether morally, sexually or otherwise. ❑ **square to the wood** *adj.* [1940s+] (*US black*) extremely respectable, conservative, naïve. ❑ **square with** *adj.* [19C+] **1** in an honest, honourable manner. **2** making amends with, made up with, even with. ❑ **turn square** *v.* (*also* **turn square-guy**) [mid-19C–1940s] of a criminal, to reform, to join the world of the law-abiding.

IN EXCLAMATIONS

❑ **square dinkum!** *see* FAIR DINKUM! *excl.*

SE in slang uses

IN COMPOUNDS

❑ **square eyes** *n.* [1960s+] one who watches an excess of TV and who, supposedly, develops eyes the same shape as the screen; thus *square-eyed*, obsessed with watching television. ❑ **square face** *n.* [the shape of the bottle] [late 19C–1920s] gin. ❑ **squarehead/-headed** *see* separate entries. ❑ **square**

mackerel *n.* [sea-borne smuggling of marijuana] [1980s+] (*drugs*) marijuana. ❑ **square pair** *n.* (*also* **windows**) [i.e. 'four by four'] [2000s] (*US*) the throw of double-four (eight) in craps dice. ❑ **square party** *n.* [the four sides of the 'square'] [1920s] two pairs of married people indulging in a wife-swapping party. ❑ **square rigger** *n.* *see* separate entry. ❑ **square toes** *n.* [his chosen, old-fashioned style of footwear] [mid-18C–mid-19C] an old man; a father.

square *v.* [SQUARE *adj.*] **1** [early 19C+] (*also* **square up**) to settle, to put right, spec. to deal with problems, often by using influence, bribes, threats etc; thus *square his nibs*, to pay off a policeman. **2** [mid-19C–1930s] to pay one's debts; to pay a bill. **3** [mid-19C+] (*UK Und.*) to sort things out with another person. **4** [late 19C] to murder, to kill. **5** [late 19C–1920s] to give or lend money. **6** [late 19C+] to make things equal. **7** [1920s] (*US Und.*) to gain a pardon. **8** [1920s–40s] to take up a respectable, honest life. **9** [1970s+] (*US gay*) to have heterosexual intercourse. **10** [1980s] (*Aus.*) to bribe. **11** *see* SQUARE OFF *v.*[1].

IN COMPOUNDS

❑ **square-off** *n.* *see* separate entry.

IN PHRASES

❑ **square a rap** *v.* *see under* RAP *n.*[1]. ❑ **square away** *v.* [milit. jargon *square away*, to put in proper order] **1** [20C+] to deal with, to settle. **2** [20C+] to sort out, to put away, to put in order, whether emotionally or physically; usu. as *squared away*. **3** [1920s] to explain, to put in the picture. ❑ **square it** *v.* **1** [mid-19C+] to live or act honestly. **2** [mid-19C+] to explain, to make excuses. **3** [late 19C] to render acceptable, appealing; to make things right. ❑ **square off** *v.* *see* separate entries. ❑ **square one's circle** *v.* [1980s+] (*US campus*) to have sexual intercourse with someone. ❑ **square out** *v.* [SQUARE OFF *v.*[1]/ SQUARE UP *v.*[1]] [1960s+] (*US black*) **1** to ridicule, to tease. **2** of two people, to indulge in a series of ritual insults. ❑ **square the beef** *v.* *see under* BEEF *n.*[2]. ❑ **square up** *v.* **1** *see* sense 1 above. **2** *see* separate entries.

square *adv.* [SQUARE *adj.*] [mid-19C+] (*US*) **1** completely, unreservedly. **2** fairly, honestly, straightforwardly. **3** (*US*) completely, exactly. **4** properly, correctly.

IN PHRASES

❑ **live square** *v.* [1950s+] (*Aus.*) to lead a respectable life. ❑ **play square (with)** *v.* [1900s–50s] to behave in a decent manner, to treat someone honestly. ❑ **square an' all** *adv.* [20C+] (*Aus.*) absolutely, honestly, truly.

square at *v.* *see* SQUARE UP *v.*[1].

square for *v.* *see* SQUARE UP *v.*[1].

squarehead *n.*[1] [SQUARE *adj.* (1) + -HEAD *sfx* (1)] **1** [mid-19C+] an honest person, a respectable person. **2** [1910s+] a stupid person. **3** [1920s+] (*Aus.*) a timid or conscience-ridden thief. **4** [1930s+] (*Aus.*) one who has no previous criminal convictions.

squarehead *n.*[2] **1** [20C+] a German or one of German origins [SE *square* + *head*; ? the severe 'Prussian' haircuts]. **2** [20C+] (*Aus./US*) a Scandinavian. **3** [1930s] (*US*) a Pole [SE *square* + *head*; ? the severe 'Prussian' haircuts]. **4** [1970s] (*Can.*) an Anglophone Canadian.

squarehead *adj.*[1] **1** [1910s] (*US*) Scandinavian. **2** [1930s] German.

squarehead *adj.*[2] [SQUAREHEAD *n.*[1] (2)] [1920s+] (*US*) stupid.

squareheaded *adj.* [SQUAREHEAD *n.*[1]/SQUAREHEAD *n.*[2]] [1910s+] **1** stupid. **2** Swedish. **3** German.

square john *n.* [SQUARE *adj.* (1) + JOHN *n.* (1)] **1** [1920s+] a respectable member of society. **2** [1920s+] (*US Und.*) a prisoner who is not a professional criminal. **3** [1930s–50s] (*drugs*) one who eschews drugs. **4** [1940s–60s] (*US Und.*) in criminal terms, a dependable, reliable person. **5** [1970s+] (*US gay*) a heterosexual man who enjoys the company of lesbians.

square-john *adj.* (*also* **square-goods**) [SQUARE JOHN *n.*] [1940s+] (*US*) respectable, upright; esp. when pertaining to a non-criminal world or sensibility.

square-off *n.* [SQUARE OFF *v.*[2] (1)] [1920s+] (*Aus.*) an excuse.

square off *v.*[1] [SE *square*] [mid-19C+] (*US*) (*also* **square**) to prepare for a fight, to adopt an aggressive posture.

square off *v.*[2] [SQUARE *v.*] [1920s+] (*Aus./N.Z.*) **1** to placate or conciliate someone, to apologize. **2** to pay; can be used quite legitimately, but often carries a sense of corruption, bribery etc. **3** to pay off, e.g. a debt.

squarer *n.* [SQUARE *v.* (1)] **1** [late 19C–1900s] (*Aus.*) one who 'fixes' a situation, usu. through bribery (however well disguised). **2** [1900s] something that helps sort out a problem.

square-rigged *adj.* [naut. jargon] [mid-19C–1920s] well-dressed, smart, respectable.

square rigger *n.*[1] (*N.Z.*) **1** [20C+] a square gin bottle, often used to hold beer. **2** [1980s] a half-gallon (3 litre) flagon of beer.

square rigger *n.*[2] [rhy. sl. = NIGGER *n.*[1] (1)] [20C+] a derog., euph. term for a black person.

square shooter *n.* [SQUARE *adj.* (1) + SE *shooter*] [1910s+] (*US*) **1** an honest, trustworthy person. **2** one who espouses a respectable (as opposed to criminal) life.

square-shooting *adj.* [SQUARE SHOOTER *n.* (1)] [1920s–30s] (*US*) honest.

square up *v.*[1] (*also* **square at, square for, square up to**) [the head-on postures of the opponents] [late 18C+] to challenge, usu. preparatory to a fight; often in fig. use.

square up *v.*[2] [SQUARE *v.* (1)] [mid-19C+] to pay off one's debts, whether financial or otherwise; thus *squaring-up*, the settlement of debts.

square up *v.*[3] [SQUARE *adj.* (2)] (*orig. US black*) **1** [1940s+] to leave the underworld, whether of pimping, drug sales and use or general criminality and devote oneself to a conventional lifestyle. **2** [1960s] to persuade someone to take up a respectable lifestyle. **3** [1960s] to betray. **4** [1990s+] to calm down.

square up to *v.* *see* SQUARE UP *v.*[1].

squarie *n.*[1] (*also* **squarey**) [SQUARE *n.* (1b)] [1910s+] (*Aus. navy*) a young woman, a girlfriend.

IN PHRASES

❑ **half-squarie** *n.* *see* *HALF-SQUARE under* SQUARE *n.*

squarie *n.*[2] (*also* **squarey**) [abbr. SQUAREHEAD *n.*[1]] (*Aus.*) **1** [1920s+] a timid or conscience-ridden thief. **2** [1930s+] one who has no previous criminal convictions.

squash *n.* (*also* **squash-head, squashie**) [SE *squash*, the vegetable] **1** [late 19C–1960s] (*US campus*) a fool. **2** [1930s+] (*US*) the head, face.

squash *v.* [20C+] **1** to crush verbally. **2** to argue, to fight. **3** (*US*) to sort out a problem.

IN PHRASES

❑ **get off the squash** *v.* [1930s] (*US*) to have sexual intercourse.

squashed *adj.* [1970s+] very drunk.

squashed flies *n.* (*also* **dead-fly cake, fly pies, squashed fly**) [late 19C+] biscuits containing currants, Garibaldi biscuits.

squash-head *n.* *see* SQUASH *n.*

squasho *n.* ['the negro's love of melons, pumpkins, squashes etc' (Ware) but more likely QUASHIE *n.*] [late 19C+] (*US*) a derog. term for a black person.

squashy *adj.* [1930s–50s] (*US black*) dumpy.

squat *n.*[1] **1** [late 19C–1910s] a seat, a chair. **2** [1970s] (*US*) an act of defecation; of females, also urination. **3** [1970s+] (*US*) excrement. **4** [1990s+] (*US prison*) the electric chair; electrocution.

IN PHRASES

❑ **take a squat** *v.* [1970s+] to defecate.

squat *n.*[2] [abbr. DIDDLY-SQUAT *n.*[1]] [1950s+] (*US*) nothing, zero.

squat *v.* (*also* **squat the blot**) **1** [mid-19C+] (*US*) to sit down, usu. to do nothing is implied. **2** [1930s–40s] (*US prison*) to be executed in the electric chair; to execute. **3** [1960s] (*US*) to defecate.

IN COMPOUNDS

❑ **squat pad** *n.* *see under* PAD *n.*[2].

IN PHRASES

❑ **squat hot** *v.* [*hot squat* at HOT SEAT *n.* (1)] [1940s] (*US*) to be executed in the electric chair. ❑ **squat on** *v.* [late 19C] (*US*) to oppose.

squativoo *n.* [SQUATTEZ-VOUS *phr.* + *hot squat* at HOT SEAT *n.* (1)] [1930s] (*US*) the electric chair.

squattage *n.* [SE *squatter* + -AGE *sfx*, implying a sphere of action] [1930s+] (*Aus.*) a farmer's home and the land they own.

squatter *n.* **1** [20C+] the buttocks. **2** [1930s+] (*Ulster*) a voyeur. **3** [1940s] (*US black*) a stool, a chair.

squatter's daughter *n.* [rhy. sl.] [1960s+] (*Aus.*) water.

squattez-vous *n.* [SQUATTEZ-VOUS *phr.*] [1900s] an act of sitting down.

squattez-vous *phr.* [cod Fr.] [late 19C–1930s] sit down.

squatti *n. see* SQUADDIE *n.*

squattocracy *n.* (*also* **squattocrasy**) [SE *squatter* + sfx *-ocracy*] [mid-19C+] (*Aus.*) the élite of the country's farming magnates, viewed as an Australian aristocracy; thus *squattocrat*, a member of the group; adj. *squattocratic*.

squatty *adj.* [mid-19C–1960s] of a person, squat, thickset, thus as a nickname for such a person; also used of a small object.

squaver *v.* [SE *quaver*] [20C+] (*Ulster*) to wave one's arms, to direct vehicles (as in parking), to square up to.

squaw *n.* **1** [mid-19C+] (*US*) a woman. **2** [late 19C–1950s] a subservient woman, occas. man. **3** [20C+] a wife. **4** [1990s+] (*US prison*) a passive homosexual.

squawk *n.* [SQUAWK *v.*] **1** [20C+] (*US*) a complaint. **2** [1920s+] a verbal betrayal. **3** [1930s–40s] (*US*) a complainer. **4** [1940s–50s] (*UK prison*) any form of petition, to the governor or to the Home Secretary. **5** [1950s+] (*US black*) a comment.

IN COMPOUNDS

❑ **squawk-box** *n.* [1940s+] (*orig. US*) an internal communication system; usu. in the context of an office or similar business. ❑ **squawk buggy** *n.* [1960s] a vehicle with a loudspeaker.

IN PHRASES

❑ **put up a squawk** *v.* [1900s–50s] to make a fuss.

squawk *v.* **1** [late 19C+] (*US*) to complain, to make a fuss. **2** [1920s+] to inform, to betray.

squawker *n.* [SQUAWK *v.*/SE *squawk*] **1** [1920s] (*US*) one who makes a complaint, esp. a victim of crime. **2** [1920s–40s] an informer. **3** [1950s] (*US teen*) a parent. **4** [1950s] (*US teen*) a record-player.

squawl *n. see* SQUALL *n.*[2].

squawman *n.* [1900s–1930s] (*US*) a white man living with a native woman.

squeak *n.* [SQUEAK *v.*] **1** [late 18C–mid-19C; 1950s+] (*also* **squeek**) an informer, esp. one who turns informer to save themselves after being arrested. **2** [20C+] a piece of information passed over to the police. **3** [1910s] (*US*) a remark, a comment. **4** [1940s] (*US police*) a complaint.

IN PHRASES

❑ **put the squeak in** *v. see* SQUEAK *v.* (1).

SE in slang uses

IN COMPOUNDS

❑ **squeak box** *n.* [1940s–50s] (*US black*) a violin.

squeak *v.* **1** [late 17C+] (*UK Und.*) to inform, to confess; thus [20C+] *squeak on*, to betray, to inform against; [1930s+] *put the squeak in*, to turn informer, to inform. **2** [1910s] to complain; to make a noisy fuss.

squeak beef *v. see under* BEEF *n.*[2].

squeaker *n.* **1** [late 17C–18C] a child, esp. an illegitimate child [note Hay, *The Lighter Side of School Life*, (1914): 'Lastly, comes the little boy — the Squeaker, the Tadpole, the Nipper, what you will']. **2** [late 17C–mid-19C] a pot-boy. **3** [late 18C–early 19C] an organ pipe. **4** [early 19C] a foxhound. **5** [mid-late 19C] a young pig. **6** [late 19C] a heavy blow which makes the recipient 'squeak'. **7** [late 19C–1900s] a general insult; the image is of one who complains. **8** [late 19C+] an informer. **9** [1930s–40s] a violinist.

IN PHRASES

❑ **stifle the squeaker** *v.* (*also* **stifle a squeaker**) [SE *stifle*] **1** [late 17C–1900s] to murder a child 'and throw it into a House of Office [privy]' (B.E.). **2** [19C–1900s] to procure an abortion.

squeakers *n.* [SE *squeak*] [20C+] (*Aus.*) boots, shoes.

squeaky *adj.* [2000s] nervous, cowardly.

squeaky shoe *n.* **1** [1940s] a plain-clothes police officer. **2** [1960s] a private detective.

squeal *n.*[1] [SQUEAL (ON) *v.*] **1** [early 19C] an informer. **2** [mid-19C–1950s] a complaint; a fuss. **3** [mid-19C+] (*Und.*) the report of a crime by a member of the public, or an informer; thus *squeal mama*, a female informer. **4** [1940s] (*US black campus*) talk. **5** [1950s+] (*US*) the investigation by police of a crime, using an informer.

IN PHRASES

❑ **put the squeal on** *v.* [1970s+] to betray, to inform against.

squeal *n.*[2] (*US, esp. short order*) **1** [1900s] boiled meal served with molasses. **2** [1930s–40s] bacon; ham.

squeal copper *v. see* HOLLER COPPER *v.*

squealer *n.*[1] (*also* **squeeler**) [SQUEAL *n.*[1]] **1** [mid-19C+] an informer. **2** [late 19C–1910s] a complainer. **3** [1930s] (*US Und.*) a pack of *Jack Rose* cigars [after the witness of the same name who acted as informer in the Rosenthal case].

squealer *n.*[2] **1** [mid-19C+] (*US*) a child. **2** [1980s] (*Aus.*) a promiscuous young girl.

squealer *n.*[3] [SE *squeal*] [1930s] (*UK tramp*) a pork sausage.

squeal (on) *v.* [late 19C+ use mainly US, but note Edgar Wallace title, *The Squealer* (1927)] **1** [mid-19C–1920s] to complain. **2** [mid-19C–1940s] to own up. **3** [mid-19C+] to inform against one's partners, esp. partners in crime. **4** [20C+] to report a crime to the police or any other authority.

IN COMPOUNDS

❑ **squeal rule** *n.* (*also* **squeal law**) [1960s+] (*US*) the law requiring parental notification when an underage girl applies for a prescription for contraceptives.

squeeg *n. see* SQUEEZE *n.*[1] (2a).

squeegee *n.*[1] [1920s] (*UK Und.*) a homemade cosh.

squeegee *n.*[2] *see* SQUEEZE *n.*[1] (7).

squeek *n. see* SQUEAK *n.* (1).

squeek *v.* [? play on SE *squeak*] [1980s] (*US campus*) to have sexual intercourse.

squeeler *n. see* SQUEALER *n.*[1].

squeench-eye *n. see* SQUINT-EYE *under* SQUINT *n.*

squeezable *adj.* [SQUEEZE *v.* (2)] [1910s–20s] used of one whom it is easy to make speak (and reveal information).

squeeze *n.*[1] **1** [late 18C–mid-19C] a crowded social gathering. **2** uses based on the idea of squeezing the body. (**a**) [late 18C–19C] (*also* **squeeg**) the neck [i.e. that which is squeezed]. (**b**) [mid-19C] the rope used for a hanging [i.e. that which squeezes]. (**c**) [1940s] (*Aus.*) the female waist [it is squeezed]. **3** [19C–1900s] a hard bargain. **4** [19C+] an escape; thus *narrow squeeze*, a lucky escape. **5** [mid-19C] (*UK Und.*) a break-in for the purpose of robbery. **6** [mid-19C–1900s] a plan, an occupation [? one 'squeezes' the brain]. **7** [mid-19C+] (*also* **squeegee**) silk, and any garment made of it, e.g. a silk tie, a silk handkerchief [the quality of the fabric that will squeeze into a minuscule space]. **8** [late 19C–1940s] (*orig. Aus.*) an impression of a key made for criminal purposes. **9** [20C+] a difficult situation; trouble with the police. **10** uses based on financial pressure [SQUEEZE *v.*; but note 18C use of SE to mean the same thing]. (**a**) [1900s] financial stress. (**b**) [1930s–40s] (*US Und.*) extortion money. (**c**) [1930s+] (*US*) an act of blackmail or extortion. (**d**) [1930s+] pressure, emotional stress. **11** uses based on physical affection. (**a**) [1910s] (*US Und.*) the head of an institution or an undertaking. (**b**) [1910s+] a girl- or boyfriend. (**c**) [1970s+] (*orig. US black*) a close friend. (**d**) [2000s] something very special. **12** [1940s] (*US Und.*) a dishonest device for controlling a mechanical gambling game.

13 [1970s–80s] (*UK black*) a discount; something free or cut-price. **14** [1990s+] (*UK Und.*) a short prison sentence.

IN PHRASES

❑ **give someone the squeeze** *v.* [1920s–30s] to blackmail. ❑ **home squeeze** *n.* [SE *home*] **1** [1970s+] (*orig. US*) one's most favourite person, usu. a lover. **2** [1970s+] (*orig. US black*) one's wife or regular partner. ❑ **main squeeze** *n.* [SE *main*] **1** [late 19C+] (*US*) the boss, the foreman, any important person. **2** [1920s+] (*orig. US*) (*also* **main mellow, main piece, number-one squeeze**) one's most favoured person, usu. a lover or most intimate same-sex friend. ❑ **put the squeeze on** *v.* (*also* **put the squeeze to**) [SQUEEZE *v.*; but note 18C use of SE *squeeze* to mean the same thing] [1920s+] (*orig. US*) to pressurize, to extort, to blackmail.

SE in slang uses

IN COMPOUNDS

❑ **squeeze-box** *n.* **1** [late 19C–1900s] a harmonium [the pressing of feet on the pedals]. **2** [1930s+] an accordion or concertina [the pressing together of the two sides of the instrument]. ❑ **squeeze crab** *n. see under* CRAB *n.*[1]. ❑ **squeeze-clout** *n.* [SE *clout*] [late 18C] a neck-cloth, a (silk) handkerchief. ❑ **squeeze-eye** *n.* [the supposed 'squeezed' shape of their eyes] [1940s–60s] (*W.I.*) a derog. term for a Chinese person. ❑ **squeeze-pidgin** *n.* [SE *pidgin*, language (here of corruption); but note PIGEON *n.*[1] (2a)] [late 19C] a bribe. ❑ **squeeze-wax** *n.* [late 17C–early 19C] a surety for a loan; 'a good-natured foolish fellow, ready to become security for another, under hand and seal' (Grose, 1785).

IN PHRASES

❑ **squeeze and a squirt** *n. see* SQUIRT AND A SQUEEZE *under* SQUIRT *n.* ❑ **squeeze-'em-close** *n.* [late 19C] sexual intercourse.

squeeze *n.*[2] **1** [1970s] (*US black*) liquor [ety. unknown; ? the *squeezing* of grapes]. **2** [1990s+] (*drugs*) phencyclidine [ety. unknown].

squeeze *adj.* [events, objects that *squeeze through*] [1980s+] (*US campus*) **1** accidental, fortunate. **2** of poor quality, second-rate.

squeeze *v.* **1** [19C–1910s] to bring in trouble, to cause difficulties for. **2** [late 19C+] (*orig. US*) to pressurize, to blackmail. **3** [1940s+] (*orig. US*) to inform, to pass on information.

IN COMPOUNDS

❑ **squeeze-play** *n.* [PLAY *n.* (2) + pun on baseball jargon *squeeze play*, 'a tactic whereby the batter bunts so that a runner at third base can attempt to reach home safely and score' (*OED*)] **1** [1910s+] (*US*) the application of force or pressure to get what one wants. **2** [1940s] pickpocketing.

SE in slang uses

IN PHRASES

❑ **squeeze a kidney** *v. see* TAP A KIDNEY *under* TAP *v.*[2]. ❑ **squeeze off (on)** *v.* [SE *squeeze* the trigger] [1950s+] to fire a gun, to fire a gun at someone. ❑ **squeeze one off** *v.* [1990s+] to masturbate. ❑ **squeeze one's lemon** *v. see under* LEMON *n.* ❑ **squeeze (the) cheese** *v.* [the smell] [2000s] to break wind. ❑ **squeeze the lizard** *v. see under* LIZARD *n.*

IN EXCLAMATIONS

❑ **squeeze me!** [pron.] [1990s+] (*US campus*) excuse me! ❑ **squeeze me gently!** [1950s] an excl. of pleasure.

squeezer *n.* **1** [late 18C–19C] the gallows. **2** [mid-19C] the neck. **3** [20C+] (*W.I.*) a pair of pince-nez spectacles. **4** [1940s] (*US black*) a belt. **5** [1970s] (*UK Und.*) a blackmailer [SQUEEZE *v.* (2)]. **6** [1990s+] (*US campus*) an untrustworthy person.

IN PHRASES

❑ **put squeezers on** *v.* [1960s] (*US*) to pressurize.

squelch *v.* [SQUELCHER *n.*] [early 17C+] to deal a crushing blow; also fig.

squelcher *n.* [SE *squelch*] [mid–late 19C] a crushing blow.

squelch-gutted *adj.* [late 18C–early 19C] fat-bellied.

squelching *n.* [note former punk star Johnny Rotten (John Lydon; b.1957): 'Love is two minutes fifty-two seconds of squishing noises. It shows your mind isn't clicking right'] [1950s–80s] (*gay*) sex without any pretence at affection.

squib *n.*[1] [SE *squib*, an unpleasant person] [mid-18C] a casino employee who checks on the activities of the house players.

squib *n.*[2] **1** [mid-19C] a gun; thus *double-tongued squib*, a double-barrelled gun [SE *squib*, a small firework]. **2** [mid-19C] a paintbrush [resemblance]. **3** [mid-19C] (*costermonger*) a head of asparagus [resemblance]. **4** [mid-19C] a form of sweet made from treacle [resemblance]. **5** [1930s+] a plan that fails to work [a 'damp squib'].

squib *n.*[3] [dial. *squib*, to run away] (*Aus.*) **1** [20C+] a coward, one who backs down or loses popularity. **2** [1910s+] a weakling, a small person.

squib *v.* [late 18C–mid-19C] to fire a gun; also in fig. use.

IN PHRASES

❑ **squibbed off** *adj.* [1930s] (*US*) shot, murdered. ❑ **squib off** *v.* [mid-19C] (*Aus.*) to explode.

squib (it) *v.* [UK dial. *squib*, to run away] [1910s+] (*Aus.*) **1** to behave in a cowardly manner, to back down, to squirm. **2** to evade a responsibility, to shirk a duty, to betray, to let down.

IN PHRASES

❑ **squib on** *v.* [SQUIB *n.*[3] (1)] [1930s+] (*Aus.*) to betray; to back down; to surrender.

squid *n.*[1] **1** [20C+] (*Can.*) (*also* **squidjigger**) any resident of the Maritime provinces [fishing jargon *squidjigging*, fishing for squid with a baited hook that one 'jigs' in the hope of luring one's target]. **2** [1970s] (*US*) a member of the US Navy. **3** [1970s+] (*US campus*) (*also* **squidbrain**) a fool, an incompetent. **4** [1980s+] (*Aus. teen/US campus*) a particularly hard worker. **5** [1990s+] a fast, dangerous driver.

squid *n.*[2] [ext. of QUID *n.*] [1900s; 1990s+] one pound sterling.

squiff *n.* [SQUIFFY *adj.*] **1** [1900s] (*Aus.*) a drunkard. **2** [1930s] a contemptible person. **3** [1950s] menstruation.

squiff *v.*[1] [? SE *quaff*] [19C] to drink.

DERIVATIVES

❑ **squiffed** *adj.* [late 19C+] drunk.

IN PHRASES

❑ **squiff out** *v.* [1950s] to collapse through drunkenness.

squiff *v.*[2] [? QUIFF *n.*[1] (1)] [1950s] to menstruate.

squiffer *n.* [? SE *squeezer*] [late 19C–1910s] a concertina.

squiffy *adj.* [SQUIFF *v.*[1]; ? underpinned by SE colloq. *skew-whiff*, crooked, aslant; note dial. *squiffy*, left-handed] **1** [mid-19C+] drunk. **2** [1930s+] (*UK teen*) menstruating. **3** [1940s+] (*Aus.*) foolish, silly. **4** [1940s+] askew, unbalanced. **5** [1950s] malfunctioning.

IN COMPOUNDS

❑ **squiffy-eyed** *adj.* [late 19C+] drunk.

squigger *n.* [the script of Asian languages, e.g. Hindi or Urdu, seen as 'squiggles' + WIGGER *n.*[3]] [2000s] (*US black*) an Asian who attempts to adopt black style and culture.

squilde *n.* [the name in question being *Oscar Wilde* (1854–1900), then facing his rapid fall from grace] [late 19C] 'a term of street chaff. Word designed from a Christian name and a surname coalesced' (Ware).

squillion *n.* [1940s+] a hypothetical and enormous number, a multiple of many millions.

squills *n.* [ety. unknown] [mid-19C] (*US Und.*) boots.

squinny-eyes *n.* [17C; mid–late 19C] squinting eyes; thus *squinny-eyed*, squinting.

squint *n.* **1** [late 18C+] a glance, a look. **2** [1900s–20s] (*Aus.*) an eye.

IN COMPOUNDS

❑ **squint-a-pipes** *n.* ['Said to be born in the middle of the week, and looking both ways for Sunday' (Grose, 1796)] [late 18C–mid-19C] a squinting man or woman. ❑ **squint-eye** *n.* (*also* **squeench-eye**) [derog. physiological stereotyping] [1960s–70s]

(*US*) a derog. term for an Asian, esp. a Japanese or Vietnamese person.

squinter *n.* **1** [early 19C] a monocle. **2** [mid-19C] a squinting eye.

squint-fuego *n.* [Sp. *fuego*, fire] [late 17C–18C] one who squints badly.

squint like a bag of nails *v.* [the squinter's eyes point in as many directions as nails dropped into a bag] [late 18C–early 19C] to squint in a noticeable manner.

squire *n.* [SE *squire*, a title orig. used to denote an esquire, a young man of good birth, attendant upon a knight, but by 17C referring mainly to a country gentleman] **1** [17C] a fool [one who is foolish enough to serve another]. **2** [17C–1900s] a general title used ironically in a number of contexts, e.g. *APPLE SQUIRE under* APPLE *n.*[1]; *see also* phrs. below. **3** [early 19C+] a general term of address, no particular rank or intimacy indicated. **4** [mid-19C] (*UK Und.*) a successful criminal. **5** [mid-19C] (*US*) a magistrate.

DERIVATIVES

□ **squirish** *adj.* [late 18C–early 19C] foolish.

IN PHRASES

□ **squire of Alsatia** *n.* [ALSATIA *n.*; best known as the title of Thomas Shadwell's play, first staged in 1688] **1** [late 17C] a gentleman who has been drawn to the criminal world and there found himself fleeced, robbed and generally rendered destitute by its denizens. **2** [late 17C] an overly generous man. **3** [late 17C–early 19C] a rich fool. □ **squire of the body** *n.* [mocking the SE *esquire* or the 'country squire' + SE *body*; cf. KNIGHT OF THE… *n.* and its combs.] [17C–early 18C] a pimp, or a term of abuse. □ **squire of the company** *n.* [late 18C] one who treats the rest of the company. □ **squire of the cross** *n.* [CROSS *n.*[1] (1)] [mid-19C] (*UK Und.*) a thief. □ **squire of the gimlet** *n.* [SE *gimlet*, used as a corkscrew] [late 17C–late 18C] a publican, a tapster. □ **squire of the gusset** *n. see BROTHER OF THE GUSSET under* BROTHER (OF THE)… *n.* □ **squire of the pad** *n.* [PAD *n.*[1] (1)] [early 18C] a highwayman. □ **squire of the petticoat** *n.* (*also* **petticoat-peer**) [metonymic use of SE *petticoat* = women] [late 17C] a pimp; as a term of abuse. □ **squire of the placket** *n.* [PLACKET *n.*] [17C] a pimp. □ **stand squire** *v.* [late 18C–early 19C] to treat the company.

squirish *adj.* [? he poses as a SE *squire*] [late 17C–18C] used of 'One that pretends to Pay all Reckonings, and is not strong enough in the Pocket' (B.E.).

squirly *adj.* [SQUIRRELY *adj.*] (*US campus*) **1** [1960s] sexually frustrated. **2** [1990s+] emotionally unrestrained.

squirm, the *n.* [the curves and curlicues that typified it] [1900s–10s] the art nouveau style.

squirrel *n.* **1** in senses pertaining to a woman. (**a**) [early 17C–early 19C] a prostitute ['like that animal she covers her back with her tail' (Grose, 1796)]. (**b**) [early 18C] the vagina [coined independently of sense 1a]. (**c**) [1910s+] a woman, usu. as a sex object [coined independently of sense 1a]. (**d**) [1970s] (*US campus*) the female pubic hair [coined independently of sense 1a]. **2** [mid-19C–1930s] (*US*) illicitly distilled liquor [its woodland orgins]. **3** in senses punning on NUTS *adj.* (2). (**a**) [1910s+] (*US*) an eccentric person. (**b**) [1930s] a psychoanalyst. (**c**) [1940s] (*US*) a stupid, shortsighted person. (**d**) [1970s] (*US campus*) one who is slow on the uptake. (**e**) [1970s+] a mentally ill person, a psychopath; thus adjs. *squirrel, squirrelly*, unstable, neurotic. (**f**) [2000s] (*US prison*) a mentally ill prisoner. **4** [1950s] (*US drugs*) a careful heroin user, who always hides away some drugs for an emergency [i.e. he 'squirrels it away']. **5** [1970s+] (*drugs*) a mixture of LSD and some other drug, or of cocaine, marijuana and phencyclidine [the effects are to make one SQUIRRELY *adj.*].

IN COMPOUNDS

□ **squirrel covers** *n.* [1990s+] knickers, panties. □ **squirrel-dodger** *n.* [1920s] (*US*) an eccentric. □ **squirrel food** *n.* **1** [1910s–60s] (*US*) one who appeals to women. **2** [1920s] (*US*) (*also* **squirrel-feed, squirrel-fodder**) one who is crazy or eccentric. □ **squirrel hunting** *n. see* HUNTING *n.* □ **squirrel ranch** *n.* (*also* **squirrel cage, squirrel pen**) [1930s–40s] (*US prison*) the prison mental ward. □ **squirrel-shit** *adj. see* SQUIRRELY *adj.* (1).

IN PHRASES

□ **shoot the squirrel** *v.* [1970s+] (*US campus*) to catch a glimpse of a woman's panties or pubic hair.

SE in slang uses

IN COMPOUNDS

□ **squirrel-kisser** *n.* [1990s+] (*US campus*) an environmentalist. □ **squirrel-shooter** *n.* (*also* **squirrel hunter, squirrel-popper**) [1900s–40s] (*US*) a farmer, a rustic; thus a novice or inexperienced person.

squirrely *adj.* (*also* **squirrelly**) [pun on NUTS *adj.* (2)] **1** [1930s+] (*orig. US campus*) (*also* **squirrel-shit**) eccentric, odd, insane. **2** [1960s] (*US*) reckless. **3** [1980s+] nervous.

squirt *n.* **1** as a bodily function. (**a**) [late 16C–mid-18C] as *the squirt, squirts*, diarrhoea. (**b**) [1940s+] (*orig. US*) ejaculation; semen. (**c**) [1960s] (*Aus.*) an act of vomiting. (**d**) [1960s+] an act of urination. (**e**) [1980s+] (*US campus*) a faecal stain on one's underwear due to liquid emitted when breaking wind or through a badly cleaned anus. **2** as a person, usu. derog. (**a**) [early 18C; mid-19C+] (*orig. US*) a dandy, a fop. (**b**) [mid-19C+] (*also* **pop-squirt**) a small, insignificant person or, occas., place or thing; thus adj. *squirty*. (**c**) [1920s] a general insult, irrespective of size. **3** [mid-19C] (*US campus*) a showy recitation. **4** [mid-19C] champagne [it *squirts* from the bottle]. **5** [mid–late 19C] a doctor, a chemist [their use of syringes]. **6** in context of weaponry. (**a**) [late 19C–1950s] (*mainly Aus.*) a revolver [it *squirts* bullets]. (**b**) [1910s] (*Aus.*) a bayonet. (**c**) [1950s] gunfire. **7** [1920s+] very cheap but still effective beer [it *squirts* from the beer-tap]. **8** [1960s] (*N.Z.*) petrol [it *squirts* from the pump]. **9** [2000s] (*US drugs*) an injectable narcotic.

DERIVATIVES

□ **squirtish** *adj.* [mid-19C] (*US campus*) ostentatious.

IN COMPOUNDS

□ **squirt game** *n.* [1920s+] drinking the cheapest forms of alcohol for intoxication's sake alone. □ **squirt gun** *n.* [1980s] a water pistol.

IN PHRASES

□ **head squirt** *n.* [1910s] (*US*) an important figure, a manager. □ **on the squirt** *adj.* [2000s] (*Aus.*) out drinking. □ **squirt and a squeeze** *n.* (*also* **squeeze and a squirt**) [note Williams for 17C/18C use of *squirt* to mean ejaculate] [late 19C] sexual intercourse; thus *do a squirt and a squeeze*, to have intercourse. □ **squirt 'n' spurt** *n.* [1990s+] (*US*) masturbation; thus *play squirt 'n' spurt*, to masturbate. □ **wild squirt** *n.* [late l7C–early 19C] diarrhoea.

squirter *n.* [ext. of SQUIRT *n.* (6a)] [1900s–30s] a pistol.

squirt (off) *v.* **1** [late 17C; 1930s+] to ejaculate. **2** [mid-19C] (*US campus*) to make a showy recitation. **3** [1970s] to confess, to give away secrets.

IN PHRASES

□ **squirt one off** *v.* [1990s+] to masturbate. □ **squirt one's juice** *v.* [JUICE *n.*[1] (2a)] [late 19C] of a man, to ejaculate.

squirts *n. see* SQUIRT *n.* (1a).

squirty *adj.* [SQUIRT *n.* (3)] [mid-19C] (*US campus*) ostentatious.

squish *adj.* [? var. on SWISH *adj.*] [2000s] (*US black*) a general term of approval: attractive, sophisticated.

squish *v.* [echoic] **1** [mid-19C; 1950s+] to squash, to squeeze. **2** [1990s+] to destroy, to spoil.

squishy *adj.* [fig. use of SE *squish*, to move through soft substances with a 'squishy' sound] [1950s+] (*US*) sentimental, mawkish.

squit *n.*[1] [SQUIRT *n.* (2b)] **1** [mid-19C+] a worthless, contemptible person. **2** [1950s+] (*juv.*) a short person.

squit *n.*[2] [fig. use of SQUITTERS, THE *n.*] [1950s] sentimental nonsense.

squitters, the *n.* (*also* **squits, squitter**) [SHIT *n.* (1a)/ME *scite*; prior use f. 17C is SE; also as SE v., thus D'Urfey, *Pills to Purge Melancholy* (1719), 'And here be de Mob make 'em squitter and tremble'] [late 19C+] diarrhoea; also as v.

squivalens *n.* [? SE *equivalents*] [late 19C–1900s] (*Aus.*) extras, 'perks'.

squiz *n.* (*also* **squizz**) [SE *quiz*, to look at + ? *squint* or Devon dial. *squiz*, to examine critically] [1910s+] (*Aus./N.Z.*) a look, a glance; thus *squiz, take a squiz*, to inspect, to peep at surreptitiously.

squizz *v.* (*also* **squiz**) [SQUIZ *n.*] [1930s+] (*Aus.*) to look at.

squobby *adj. see* SQUABBY *adj.*

squooshy *adj.* (*also* **squoo, squoodgy, squshy**) [SE *squashy/squishy*] [late 19C+] (*US*) soft and insubstantial.

sres-wort *n.* [backsl.] [mid-19C] trousers.

sret-sio *n.* (*also* **swret-sio**) [backsl.] [mid-19C] oysters.

s.r.h. *n.* [*s*perm *r*etention *h*eadache] [2000s] (*S.Afr. gay*) a supposed headache that indicates the desire to have sex.

Sri Lanka *n.* [rhy. sl. = WANKER *n.* (2)] [1990s+] a general term of abuse.

Sri Lankan brown *n.* [1990s+] (*Aus. drugs*) a variety of heroin refined in Sri Lanka.

s.r.o. *n.*[1] [abbr. *s*tanding *r*oom *o*nly] [20C+] (*orig. entertainment use*) **1** a full house. **2** anything that sells out or is very popular.

s.r.o. *n.*[2] [abbr.] [1990s+] (*US*) a hotel offering *s*ingle *r*ooms *o*ccupancy.

s.s. *n.*[1] [abbr. SAMMY (SOFT) *n.* (1)] [early 19C–1930s] a fool.

s.s. *n.*[2] [abbr.] [1930s] (*drugs*) a *s*kin *s*hot, i.e. one that does not hit a vein.

s.s. *n.*[3] [abbr.] [1940s–70s] (*US Und.*) a *s*uspended *s*entence.

s/s *n.* [abbr.] [1980s+] used in contact advertisements, safe sex; either condoms are used or the sex is non-penetrative.

s.s.d.d. *phr. see* SAME SHIT, DIFFERENT DAY *under* SAME *adj.*

stab *n.*[1] **1** [late 19C+] (*orig. US*) a try, an attempt; thus *have/make a stab at*, to try. **2** [1980s] (*US black*) one's style, type of behaviour.

stab *n.*[2] [STAB *v.*] **1** [1910s+] a female, esp. in the context of sexual intercourse. **2** [1950s+] (*Aus./US*) sexual intercourse.

stab *v.* (*also* **stob**) [the image of the penis as a weapon] [late 16C–early 17C] to have sexual intercourse.

IN PHRASES

▫ **stabbed with a Bridport dagger** *adj.* [the best variety of British hemp (used for the noose) was grown near Bridport, Dorset] [mid-17C–early 19C] hanged. ▫ **stab in the main vein** *v.* [mid-17C] of a man, to have sexual intercourse. ▫ **stab in the thigh** *v.* [late 19C] to have sexual intercourse. ▫ **stab oneself and pass the dagger** *v.* [mid-19C] to take a glassful then circulate the bottle.

stabber *n.*[1] [SE *stub out*] [1930s+] (*Irish*) the butt end of a cigarette.

stabber *n.*[2] [1940s] (*US*) a knife.

stable *n.* (*US*) **1** [20C+] any group of people working under one manager. **2** [1920s+] a group of prostitutes working for a pimp; occas. referring to heterosexual males. **3** [1960s] (*US*) a group of regular prostitute's clients.

IN COMPOUNDS

▫ **stable boss** *n.* [BOSS *n.*[2] (1)] [1930s–40s] (*US Und.*) a pimp who runs a string of prostitutes. ▫ **stable sister** *n.* [1970s] (*US black*) one of a group of prostitutes working for a single pimp.

IN PHRASES

▫ **stable up** *v.* [1960s] (*US black*) of a prostitute, to join those girls working for a given pimp.

stable *v.* [STABLE *n.* (2)] **1** [1940s–50s] (*Aus.*) to be having an affair. **2** [1960s] (*US*) for a pimp to enroll a prostitute in his 'team'.

stach *see under* STASH.

stach *v. see* STASH *v.*[1].

stache *n.* [abbr.] [1970s] (*US*) a mou*stache*.

stache *v. see* STASH *v.*[1].

stack *n.*[1] **1** [late 19C+] (*orig. US*) a large amount of money; something valuable, e.g. a piece of jewellery. **2** [1910s] (*US*) a large amount. **3** [1950s–70s] (*drugs*) a pack of marijuana cigarettes.

SE in slang uses

IN PHRASES

▫ **blow one's stack** *v.* [the image of a release of smoke through a smokestack] [1940s+] (*US*) **1** (*also* **flip one's stack, snap...**) to lose control, to lose one's temper. **2** to make someone lose their temper. **3** to be emotionally overwhelmed. **4** to achieve orgasm. ▫ **swear on a stack of Bibles (a mile high)** *v. see under* SWEAR *v.*

stack *n.*[2] [1960s+] (*US*) a 'stacked', i.e. prepared, deck of cards; also in fig. use.

stack *n.*[3] [STACKED *adj.*[1] (2)] [1960s+] (*US*) a well-built woman, esp. with large breasts.

stack *v.* **1** [late 19C] (*also* **stack it**) to cease from an action [SE *stack*, to pile up one's chips in a casino]. **2** [1900s] (*US campus*) to break up a college room [one 'stacks' the furniture]. **3** [1930s–60s] to hide away. **4** [1980s] to put to one side. **5** [1990s+] (*US black gang/campus*) (*also* **stack chips, stack paper**) to accumulate and/or save money.

IN PHRASES

▫ **stack it** *v. see* sense 1 above. ▫ **stack chips/paper** *v. see* sense 5 above.

SE in slang uses

IN PHRASES

▫ **stack asses** *v.* [ASS *n.* (2)] [1970s] (*US*) to defeat heavily, to thrash. ▫ **stack it** *v.* [one *stacks* up fantasies] [1970s+] (*N.Z. prison*) to boast, to exaggerate. ▫ **stack it up** *v.* [late 19C] (*US*) to charge exorbitant prices. ▫ **stack (on)** *v.* [1940s+] (*Aus.*) to contrive, to produce. ▫ **stack on an act** *v.* [1940s+] (*Aus.*) to lose one's temper and deliver a stream of obscenities/oaths. ▫ **stack on a turn** *v.* [1940s+] (*Aus.*) to make a fuss. ▫ **stack one's drapery** *v.* (*also* **stack one's apparel**) [1910s+] (*Aus.*) to put one's jacket (and at one time hat) on the ground before starting a fight. ▫ **stack the deck** *v.* (*also* **stack the cards**) [poker imagery] [20C+] (*US*) to arrange things in one's favour, usu. dishonestly. ▫ **stack up/stack up to** *v. see* separate entries. ▫ **stack Zs** *v. see under* Z *n.*[1].

stacked *adj.*[1] (*also* **stacked up**) **1** [1920s+] wealthy; sometimes ext. as *well-stacked*. **2** [1930s+] of a woman, attractively well-built, esp. with large breasts. **3** [1950s] of a man, muscular. **4** [1960s+] (*Irish*) drunk. **5** [1970s+] (*US gay*) having a large penis.

IN PHRASES

▫ **well-stacked** *adj.* [1950s+] (*orig. US*) of a woman, attractive, esp. having a good figure, spec. large breasts and buttocks.

stacked *adj.*[2] [1970s+] (*US prison*) of sentences, served consecutively.

stackel-flim *n.* [ety. unknown] [mid-19C] (*UK Und.*) a cheque.

stacking *n.* [STACK *v.* (5)] [1990s+] (*US black teen*) making money.

stackola *n.* [STACK *n.*[1] (1) + -OLA *sfx*] [1990s+] (*US black*) a large amount of money, a pile of money.

stacks *n.*[1] [late 19C+] (*orig. US*) a great many, a good deal, a large amount; often of money.

stacks *n.*[2] [1970s] (*US*) stack- or high-heeled shoes.

stack up *v.*[1] **1** [late 19C] to challenge. **2** [late 19C–1900s] to meet. **3** [late 19C+] to emerge, to develop, to maintain, to appear as it should; also in negative phr. *that doesn't/don't stack up*, that isn't logical, that fails to reach a standard. **4** [20C+] to compare with; usu. as *stack up against*.

stack up *v.*[2] [STACKED *adj.*[1] (2)] [1940s–60s] of a woman, to look attractive.

stack up *v.*[3] [1950s–60s] (*US teen*) to crash a car.

stack up (to) *v.* [1920s] (*US tramp*) to give, to provide.

stadsjapie *n.* [Afk. *stad*, city + JAAP *n.*] [1970s+] (*S.Afr.*) a city-dweller, esp. when ignorant of country ways.

staff *n.*

SE in slang uses

IN COMPOUNDS

▫ **staff breaker** *n.* (*also* **staff climber**) [19C] the vagina; thus a woman.

IN PHRASES

▫ **staff of life** *n.* [punning on SE *staff of life*, bread or any other staple] [mid-17C–1900s] the penis. ▫ **staff of love** *n.* [mid-17C–mid-18C] the penis.

staff-naked *n.* [? a misprint of the synon. STARK-NAKED *n.*] [mid-19C] gin.

Stafford Court *n.*

SE in slang uses

IN PHRASES

▫ **have a trial at Stafford Court** *v.* [pun on SE *staff*] [early 17C] to be beaten, to be thrashed.

stafford law *n.* [pun on SE *staff*, a stick] [late 16C–mid-17C] a beating, often in the context of a punishment.

staffrider *n.* [*see* RIDE STAFF *under* RIDE *v.*] [1960s+] (*S.Afr.*) one who clings to the outside (or stands on the roof) of a moving train, having boarded it while it is in motion.

stag *n.*[1] [orig. dial.; deer supposedly turn on any one of their number that is being hunted] **1** [early 18C–1950s] a pursuer, an informer. **2** [early–mid-19C] a man who attends courts in order to hire himself out as a defence witness, usu. to provide an alibi for an otherwise guilty defendant. **3** [1930s–50s] (*US*) a detective.

IN PHRASES

▫ **stand stag** *v.* [mid-18C] (*UK Und.*) to keep watch. ▫ **turn stag** *v.* [late 18C–mid-19C] to betray someone, to inform against someone.

stag *n.*[2] [mid-19C] (*UK Und.*) a flea.

stag *n.*[3] [? play on HOG *n.* (1)] [mid–late 19C] a shilling.

stag *n.*[4] [20C+] (*orig. US*) **1** an unaccompanied man at a dance or similar gathering; thus *go stag*, to attend a social event without a female partner. **2** any form of party or similar entertainment attended only by men; also adv. use. **3** *see* STAG MOVIE below.

IN COMPOUNDS

▫ **stag dance** *n.* [mid-19C–1910s] (*US*) a men-only dance, usu. performed in bar-rooms or taverns. ▫ **stag line** *n.* **1** [1920s+] (*US*) a number of unescorted men at a dance, who usu. stand in line eyeing the women. **2** [1960s] (*US gay*) a gathering of gay male prostitutes in a park or similarly well-known area. ▫ **stag month** *n.* [at such a time a man's infidelities were considered acceptable] [late 19C] the first month that follows childbirth. ▫ **stag movie** *n.* (*also* **stag, stag film, stag flick, stag show**) [1950s+] a pornographic film. ▫ **stag night** *n.* [1960s+] **1** any social event from which women are excluded. **2** the trad. uproarious eve-of-wedding party held by the groom and his male cronies. ▫ **stag party** *n.* [mid-19C+] (*orig. US*) an all-male party, esp. on the night preceding the wedding of one of the men. ▫ **stag widow** *n.* [late 19C] a man whose wife has just given birth.

IN PHRASES

▫ **make a stag** *v.* (*also* **make someone wear the stag's crest**) [punning use of the stag's horns/HORNS *n.*] [late 16C–mid-17C] of a woman, to cuckold one's husband. ▫ **stag or shag?** [SHAG *n.*[1] (1)] [1940s+] (*orig. US*) will you be coming, usu. to a party, alone or with a female companion?

stag *n.*[5] **1** [late 19C–1910s] (*Irish*) a cruel, selfish woman. **2** [1920s] a large, energetic woman [orig. Yorks. dial.].

stag *n.*[6] [2000s] (*N.Z.*) a terrible example of something, a bad representative of something, anything useless; usu. as *she's a stag of a…*

stag *adj.* (*also* **staggish**) [STAG *n.*[4]] (*orig. US*) **1** [mid-19C+] of a man, by oneself in a social situation, e.g a dance, where other men have partners. **2** [mid-19C+] pertaining to men, usu. in a sexual context. **3** [late 19C+] for men only, in a non-sexual context.

stag *v.*[1] [STAG *n.*[1] (1)] **1** [mid-18C–19C] to find, to observe. **2** [early 19C+] to inform against.

stag *v.*[2] [early–mid-19C] **1** to refuse a request for a loan. **2** to demand money, to cadge, to trick.

stag *v.*[3] [STAG *n.*[4] (1)] **1** [20C+] (*US*) of a man, to attend a social function without a female companion. **2** [1920s] to be a bachelor. **3** [1960s] (*US campus*) to reject a request for a date.

stage-door johnnie *n.* (*also* **stage-door johnny, johnnie**) [SE *stage-door* + JOHNNY *n.*[1]] [late 19C+] a man, poss. rich, who hangs around theatre stage doors hoping to meet his female idols.

stage fright *n.*[1] [rhy. sl.] [1970s] light (ale).

stage fright *n.*[2] [2000s] (*S.Afr. gay*) **1** inability to maintain an erection during sex. **2** inability to urinate at a public urinal when other men are present.

stagger *n.*[1] [STAG *v.*[1] (1)] [mid-19C] a watcher, a lookout.

stagger *n.*[2] [mid-19C–1930s] (*orig. US*) an effort, a try.

SE in slang uses

IN COMPOUNDS

▫ **stagger-back** *n.* [1950s] (*W.I.*) a form of toffee that is so tough that one 'staggers back' as one attempts to chew it. ▫ **stagger juice** *n.* [JUICE *n.*[1] (3a); note Dickens *Martin Chuzzlewit* (1843–44): 'A pint of the the celebrated staggering ale, or Real Old Brighton Tipper'] [late 19C+] alcohol; thus *stagger juicery*, a public house. ▫ **stagger-soup** *n.* [1930s–40s] (*US*) strong, if not very high-quality whisky.

staggering bob *n.* [meat trade jargon *bob, bobby*, inedible meat, esp. that taken from animals that have died rather than been slaughtered; note dial. *staggering bob* (*with his yellow pumps*), a new-born calf (with yellow hooves) that is killed for veal] [19C+] meat declared unfit to eat.

staggers *n.* (*also* **blind staggers**) [SE *stagger*, note also the SE *hungry staggers*, suffered by those weakened by starvation] [17C; mid-19C+] extreme drunkenness.

staggish *adj. see* STAG *adj.*

staggle-dick *n.* [ety. unknown] [mid-19C] (*UK Und.*) a horse-pistol, i.e. 'a large pistol carried on the pommel of the saddle while on horseback' (*OED*).

stag-traps *n.* [STAG *n.*[2]] [mid-19C] blankets.

stain *n.* [1990s+] (*US campus*) **1** a dislikeable, unsuccessful person. **2** a drunk.

stained *adj.* [early 17C] drunk.

Staines *n. see* AT THE BUSH *under* BUSH, THE *n.*[1].

stainless steel ride *n. see* BIG JAB *under* JAB *n.*

stair *n.*

SE in slang uses

IN COMPOUNDS

▫ **stair-dancer** *n.* [DANCER *n.*] [1950s+] a thief who steals from buildings, e.g. offices, that have not been properly secured. ▫ **stair-steps** *n.* (*also* **stair-steppers**) [their respective heights resemble a flight of stairs] [1920s–50s] a family with children ranged at equal intervals. ▫ **stair-work** *n.* [late 16C–early 17C] casual or clandestine sexual intercourse.

IN PHRASES

▫ **come down stair-rods** *v.* (*also* **come down curtain-rods, rain curtain-rods, rain stair-rods**) [20C+] to rain very heavily. ▫ **dance the stairs** *v. see* DANCE *v.* (3). ▫ **get up stairs** *v.* [mid-19C] (*UK prison*) to work on the treadmill. ▫ **stairs without a landing** *n.* [mid-19C] a prison treadmill. ▫ **stairway to heaven** *n.* **1** [1960s] (*US black*) the female thighs. **2** [1980s] (*Aus./N.Z.*) a ladder in a stocking. **3** [2000s] the vagina.

Stait, the *n. see* START, THE *n.* (2).

stake *n.* **1** [mid-18C; late 19C+] a large sum of money. **2** [early 19C] the booty gained in a robbery. **3** [early 19C] gambling winnings. **4** [late 19C+] money saved up for future use.

IN COMPOUNDS

▫ **stake-man** *n.* [their need of money] [late 19C–1930s] (*US*) a hobo, a tramp.

stake *v.* (*also* **stake to**) [STAKE *n.*] [mid-19C+] to lend money, to put up funds for someone's enterprise.

IN PHRASES

❑ **stake one's bottom dollar** *v. see* BET ONE'S BOTTOM DOLLAR *under* BET *v.*

stake-out *n.* (*also* **stake**) [STAKE OUT *v.*] **1** [1930s+] (*orig. US*) the surveillance of a suspect by police stationed in clandestine hiding places. **2** [1960s] (*US*) one who conducts such a surveillance. **3** [1960s–70s] (*US Und.*) the preparatory surveillance of the target of a robbery, e.g. a bank or diamond merchant.

stake out *v.* (*also* **stake**) [the placing of *stakes* to mark out a piece of land, e.g. a mining claim] (*orig. US*) **1** [1900s] to subject to preliminary analysis; to target. **2** [1930s+] to conduct a surveillance. **3** [1990s+] to wait in a place in the hope of making an encounter, e.g. of the media.

stakes *n.* [racing jargon *stakes*, a race for money, usu. defined by a specific name, e.g. St Leger Stakes] [late 19C+] used fig. to indicate some form of profession or occupation in which there is an implication of challenges that must be overcome, e.g. the *matrimonial stakes*, the *novel-writing stakes*.

stakey *adj.* [STAKE *n.* (4)] [1950s] (*US*) in possession of money.

staky *n.* [STAKE *n.* (4)] [1940s] (*US Und.*) one who has made enough money to retire.

stale *n.*[1] [15C–18C SE *stale*, a 'decoy-bird'] **1** [mid-16C] a prostitute. **2** *see* STALL *n.*[1] (1).

stale *n.*[2] [1980s+] (*US drugs*) a cannabis hangover.

stale drunk *adj.* [SE *stale*] [late 19C] hungover.

stale fish *n.* [mid-19C] (*US prison*) a veteran prisoner.

stale mutton *n.* [SE *stale* + MUTTON *n.* (1a)] [17C] a prostitute.

stalewhimper *n. see* STALL-WHIMPER *n.*

stalk *n.* **1** [17C–mid-18C; 1920s+] the erect penis. **2** [mid-19C] the gallows. **3** [late 19C] (*UK Und.*) a policeman. **4** [1930s] a tie-pin [resemblance]. **5** [1970s] in fig. use of sense 1, cheek. **6** [1970s] (*US black*) in pl., the human legs.

IN COMPOUNDS

❑ **stalk-fever** *n.* [1970s] priapism.

IN PHRASES

❑ **climb the stalk** *v.* [mid-19C] to be hanged.

stalk a judy *v. see under* JUDY *n.*[1].

stall *n.*[1] [SE *stall*, a decoy bird] **1** [late 16C–mid-17C; mid-19C+] (*also* **stale**) a pickpocket's helper who distracts the attention of the victim whose pocket is being emptied or purse cut. **2** [17C+] any form of decoy who works with a criminal gang. **3** [late 18C] (*UK Und.*) a pickpocket's manoeuvre whereby a target is pinioned and rendered open to theft. **4** [late 18C+] a pretext, which offers an opportunity to steal. **5** [mid-19C] (*UK Und.*) the act of rendering a victim vulnerable to a pickpocket. **6** [mid-19C+] an act of time-wasting or prevarication, an excuse. **7** [1910s] (*Aus./US*) a hoax; a disappointment. **8** [1920s] (*US Und.*) a fraudulent alibi. **9** [1920s] a misdirection.

IN COMPOUNDS

❑ **stallsman** *n.* (*also* **stalsman**) [mid–late 19C] a pickpocket's or other thief's assistant.

IN PHRASES

❑ **chuck a stall** *v.* [mid-19C] (*UK Und.*) to carry out a pickpocketing technique in which one member of the team walks in front of the victim, slowing him or her down while another picks the pocket. ❑ **put up a stall** *v.* [1910s] to act in a deceptive, misleading manner.

stall *n.*[2] [? Irish *stail*, a stallion] [20C+] (*Irish*) an act of sexual intercourse.

stall *n.*[3] [1900s] (*US*) a walk.

stall *n.*[4] [1930s] (*US*) the head.

stall *v.*[1] [SE *stall*, to set in a place, itself the root of *install*] (*UK Und.*) **1** [mid-16C–early 19C] to apprentice or to work with, i.e. 'to stall a beggar to a rogue'. **2** [mid-19C] to attach oneself (to a criminal gang).

IN PHRASES

❑ **stall to the rogue** *v.* (*also* **stall to the order of rogues**) [mid-16C–early 19C] to enlist a beggar as a full member of the underworld; thus *stalling*, the enlistment or 'ordaining' process.

stall *v.*[2] [STALL *n.*[1]] **1** [late 16C+] (*UK Und.*) to shield a pickpocket, confidence trickster or thief. **2** [17C–early 18C] (*UK Und.*) to steal, to pick a pocket. **3** [mid-18C+] (*US*) to loiter or linger around. **4** [mid-19C] (*UK Und.*) to use something to shield one's face. **5** [late 19C+] to play for time, to make excuses, to delay; thus (US) *quit stalling*, stop wasting time, stop making excuses. **6** [1900s] (*UK Und.*) to jostle and distract one whose pocket is about to be picked. **7** [1940s+] to make someone wait. **8** [1970s] (*Aus. Und.*) to abandon an attempt, to give up.

IN PHRASES

❑ **stalling (for a dip)** *n.* [STALL *v.*[2] + DIP *n.*[1] (3)] [19C] (*UK Und.*) the shielding of a pickpocket by an accomplice. ❑ **stall out** *v.* **1** [1910s] (*US*) to make one's excuses. **2** [1980s+] (*US black gang*) to leave alone. ❑ **stall up** *v.* [early 19C] (*UK Und.*) to surround a person, forcing them to hold their hands in the air while they are stripped of their possessions.

stall *v.*[3] [mid-19C] (*UK Und.*) to frighten, to discourage.

stall *v.*[4] [SE *stall*, to live with] **1** [mid–late 19C] to spend the night in a room provided by a public house. **2** [mid-19C–1950s] to travel about. **3** [mid-19C+] (*also* **stall off**) to walk off.

IN PHRASES

❑ **stall one's mug** *v. see under* MUG *n.*[1].

staller *n.* (*also* **staller-up**) [late 18C–mid-19C] (*UK Und.*) a pickpocket's accomplice.

stall-fed *adj.* [synon. dial.; the image is of an indulged horse] [early 17C; 20C+] (*Irish*) pampered.

stalling-ken *n.* (*also* **stauling-ken**) [SE (*in*)*stall*, to put in place + KEN *n.*[1] (1)] [mid-16C–mid-19C] (*UK Und.*) a depository for stolen goods, esp. as used by the RUFFLER *n.* to hide his booty.

stallion *n.* **1** [mid-16C+] a sexual athlete; a womanizer. **2** [late 16C–17C] a courtesan, a kept woman [? Fr. *estalon*, a decoy, an enticement, or *stale*, the lowest class of prostitute]. **3** [17C–early 19C] a heterosexual male prostitute or kept man. **4** [late 17C–18C] (*UK Und.*) a pimp. **5** [mid-18C+] the penis. **6** [1950s+] (*US black*) a tall, good-looking woman, poss. highly sexed. **7** [1970s] (*US black/Und.*) a female prostitute. **8** [1970s+] (*US gay*) a 'masculine' lesbian with a large clitoris.

stall off *n.* [STALL OFF *v.* (4)] **1** [early–mid-19C] one who gets away with a successful ruse for a friend. **2** [early 19C+] any form of evasive story or trick.

stall off *v.* [ext. of STALL *v.*[2]] **1** [mid-18C+] to impede, to get in the way of, to hinder; thus one who gets away with a successful ruse for a friend, has *stalled him off in prime twig*; also phr. *stall someone out* as an imper., to leave someone alone. **2** [early 19C] (*UK Und.*) to save an accomplice from arrest or disgrace. **3** [early 19C] (*UK Und.*) to avoid a person or place. **4** [early–mid-19C] (*UK Und.*) of a villain's accomplice, to screen or disguise a robbery. **5** [early 19C; 1950s] to use artifice to avoid punishment or problems. **6** [1920s–50s] to defer, to postpone. **7** *see* STALL *v.*[4] (3).

stall-whimper *n.* (*also* **stalewhimper**) [late 17C–mid-19C] (*UK Und.*) an illegitimate child.

stalsman *n. see* STALLSMAN *under* STALL *n.*[1].

stamer-strap *n.* [ety. unknown] [mid-19C] (*UK Und.*) a beefsteak.

stam flash *v. see under* FLASH *n.*[1] (1).

stamina daddy *n.* (*also* **stamina mummy**) [1980s+] (*W.I./UK black teen*) a man or woman known for their powers of sexual endurance.

stammel *n.* (*also* **strammel**) [SE *stammel*, a coarse woollen petticoat] [late 17C–early 19C] 'a brawny, lusty, strapping Wench' (B.E.).

stammer *n.* [early 19C] (*Scot. Und.*) an indictment.

stammer and stutter *n.* [rhy. sl.] [20C+] butter.

stammer-hankey *n.* [mid-19C] (*UK Und.*) a lawyer.

stammery *n.* [mid-19C] (*UK Und.*) a trial; thus *stammerydictus*, an indictment.

stamp *n.*[1] [1980s] (*UK Und.*) the post office.

stamp *n.*[2] [STAMP v.] [1990s+] (*Aus. Und.*) of the police, an attempt to extort a bribe.

stamp *v.* [SE *stamp*] [1990s+] (*Aus. Und.*) of a police officer, to extort a bribe.

SE in slang uses

IN COMPOUNDS

❑ **stamp-crab** *n. see under* CRABS *n.*[2].

IN PHRASES

❑ **stamp a bitch** *v. see under* BITCH *n.*[1].

stamped paper *n.* [early–mid-19C] a promissory note.

stamper *n.* [late 17C–19C] (*UK Und.*) a carrier.

stampers *n.* **1** [mid-16C–mid-19C] boots or shoes. **2** [mid-18C] (*UK Und.*) feet or legs. **3** [late 18C–mid-19C] stairs.

stamping ground *n.*[1] (*also* **stomping ground**) [18C SE, a place frequented by animals] [mid-19C+] one's home territory, one's area of operation.

stamping ground *n.*[2] [the stamping of a stallion in rut] [1900s] anywhere known as a 'lover's lane'.

stamp-picker *n.* [printers' jargon *stamp*, a piece of type] [late 19C] a typographer, a compositor.

stamps *n.*[1] [SE *stamp*] (*UK Und.*) **1** [mid-16C–mid-19C] legs, feet. **2** [mid-18C–19C] boots or shoes.

IN COMPOUNDS

❑ **stamp-drawers** *n.* [DRAWERS *n.* (1)] [17C–early 19C] stockings.

stamps *n.*[2] [the stamping of money-orders and similar documents] [mid-19C+] (*US*) money.

stan *n.* [negative stereotyping of 'common' name] [1970s] (*Aus. teen*) a fool, an insignificant, socially inept individual.

Stan and Ollie *n.* [rhy. sl. = BROLLY *n.* (1)] [1990s+] an umbrella.

stanch (out) *v.* [? SE *start out*] [1930s–40s] (*US black*) to begin.

stand *n.* **1** [late 16C–mid-17C] (*UK Und.*) a lookout, spec. for a team of lock-pickers. **2** [17C+] (*also* **standing**) an erection [COCKSTAND *n.*]. **3** [early 19C; 1920s] (*UK/US Und.*) a hold-up. **4** [late 19C] a prostitute who specializes in fellatio. **5** [1950s] (*US teen*) a single-combat fight.

IN COMPOUNDS

❑ **standpipe** *n. see* PIPE *n.*[1] (2a).

IN PHRASES

❑ **make standing room for** *v.* [late 19C] of a woman, to permit sexual intercourse.

stand *v.*[1] [mid-16C+] of a man, to have an erection.

stand *v.*[2] [abbr. SE *stand treat*] **1** [early 18C+] (*also* **stand up**) to cost, to be charged. **2** [mid-18C+] to bear the company's expenses, to pay for everyone with whom one is eating or drinking. **3** [mid–late 19C] to make an investment; to wager. **4** [mid-19C+] to give as a present.

IN PHRASES

❑ **stand ben** *v. see under* BEN *n.*[2]. ❑ **stand for** *v.* [mid-19C] (*UK Und.*) to pay for. ❑ **stand in** *see* separate entries. ❑ **stand on** *v. see* separate entry. ❑ **stand one's hand** *v.* [late 19C–1950s] (*Aus.*) to treat the assembled company. ❑ **stand sam** *v.* (*also* **stand sammy**) [? generic use of proper name *Sam*(*uel*); US icon *Uncle Sam*, and the letters 'US' stencilled on US Army knapsacks; he 'pays for all'] **1** [mid-18C–1900s] (*orig. US*) to pay for, to pick up a bill. **2** [19C] to buy a drink or round of drinks. ❑ **stand the huff** *v.* [SE *huff*/HUFF *n.*; the image is of the boastfulness that can underpin the gesture] *see under* HUFF *v.* ❑ **stand (the) shot (to)** *v.* [SHOT *n.*[1]] [19C] to pay the bill for everyone else. ❑ **stand up** *v. see* sense 1 above.

SE in slang uses

IN COMPOUNDS

❑ **stand-on** *n. see* separate entry. ❑ **stand-out** *see* separate entries. ❑ **standstill** *n. see* separate entry.

IN PHRASES

❑ **do something standing on one's head** *v.* (*also* **do something on one's nob, do something standing up**) [late 19C+] to accomplish something with the minimum of effort, to endure any challenging situation, often used of serving a jail sentence. ❑ **stand ace (with)** *v. see under* ACE *n.* ❑ **stand a good fag** *v. see under* FAG *n.*[2] (1). ❑ **stand a rap for** *v.* [1940s] (*US Und.*) to resemble someone closely. ❑ **stand around with one's finger up one's ass** *v. see* SIT THERE WITH ONE'S FINGER UP ONE'S ASS *under* ASS *n.* ❑ **stand bitch** *v. see under* BITCH *n.*[1]. ❑ **stand bluff** *v.* [SE *bluff*, rough, abrupt, blunt] [late 18C] to swear, to be adamant. ❑ **stand buff** *v.* **1** [late 17C–mid-19C] to suffer without complaining, to bear the brunt. **2** [late 17C+] to swear, to be adamant. ❑ **stand chickie** *v. see under* CHICKEE! *excl.* ❑ **stand dixie** *v.* [? DICK *n.*[5] (1)] [1990s+] to keep guard, to keep a lookout. ❑ **stand down** *v.* [1970s] (*US*) to humiliate. ❑ **stand for** *v.* **1** [mid-19C] to hold back. **2** [mid-19C+] (*orig. US*) to tolerate, to put up with. ❑ **stand frisk** *v. see under* FRISK *n.*[1]. ❑ **stand hitched** *v.* (*also* **stay hitched**) [20C+] (*US*) to be trustworthy, to keep a secret. ❑ **standing on one's head** *adv. see* DO SOMETHING STANDING ON ONE'S HEAD above. ❑ **standing on the top step** [1940s–50s] (*UK Und.*) a phr. used of a man on trial who is facing the likely prospect of a maximum sentence. ❑ **standing there like a tit in a trance** *see under* TIT *n.*[3]. ❑ **stand jiggers** *v.* (*also* **hold jiggers**) [SE *stand* + JIGGER! *excl.*] [1950s–70s] (*US prison*) to keep a lookout. ❑ **stand Miss Slang** *v.* [mid-18C] (*UK Und.*) of a member of a pickpocket team, to stand to one side, ready to be passed whatever has been stolen. ❑ **stand Moses** *v.* [biblical myth] **1** [17C–early 19C] to have another man's illegitimate child fathered upon one's wife; one is obliged by the parish to maintain it. **2** [mid-19C] (*US*) to act as a surrogate father and, for money, impregnate another man's wife. **3** [mid-19C–1930s] to adopt a child. ❑ **stand off** *see* separate entries. ❑ **stand on** *v. see* separate entry. ❑ **stand one's corner** *v.* [late 19C+] to take or pay for one's share of anything, to do one's share. ❑ **stand on one's joint** *v. see under* JOINT *n.* ❑ **stand on one's own bottom** *v.* (*also* **stand on one's own pantofles**) [later use SE; BOTTOM *n.*[1] (2)/SE *pantofles*, high-corked shoes] [16C–18C] to act in an independent manner. ❑ **stand on velvet** *v. see under* VELVET *n.* ❑ **stand out like...** *v. see* separate entry. ❑ **stand over** *see* separate entries. ❑ **stand pad** *v. see under* PAD *n.*[1]. ❑ **stand pat** *v.* (*also* **sit pat, stand peter**) [poker jargon] [late 19C+] to stay as one is, to refuse to move, to refuse to speak or betray someone. ❑ **stand point** *v.* [milit. *point*, the lead man of a patrol] [1960s+] (*Can. prison*) to be on the alert. ❑ **stand Sam** *v.* [? the common-ness of the name *Sam*] [early 19C] to be likened to. ❑ **stand someone on their ear** *v.* (*also* **stand someone on their head**) [20C+] (*US*) to knock down, to defeat. ❑ **stand squire** *v. see under* SQUIRE *n.* ❑ **stand still for** *v.* (*also* **hold still for**) [1950s+] to tolerate, to permit, to accept. ❑ **stand the...** *v. see also under* relevant n. ❑ **stand the patter** *v.* (*also* **patter**) [PATTER *n.* (1)] [late 18C–early 19C] (*UK Und.*) to be tried in a court. ❑ **stand there like a tit in a trance** *v. see under* TIT *n.*[3]. ❑ **stand to attention** *v.* [1990s+] to have an erection. ❑ **stand to pan-pudding** *v.* [SE *pan-pudding*, a heavy pudding made of flour, with small pieces of bacon in it, baked in a pan] [late 17C–early 18C] to stand one's ground, in lit. or fig. use. ❑ **stand up** *see* separate entries.

IN EXCLAMATIONS

❑ **stand on me!** [1950s+] believe me!

stand and shiver *n. see* SHAKE AND SHIVER *n.*

standard *n.* [2000s] (*UK black/teen*) something unexciting.

stand at ease *n.* [rhy. sl.] **1** [20C+] fleas. **2** [1910s+] (*orig. milit.*) cheese.

stand-by guy *n. see* STAND-UP GUY *n.*

stander *n.* **1** [early 17C] a lookout for a criminal gang [he *stands* and watches]. **2** [1920s] (*US*) the victim of a confidence trickster [he 'stands for' the trick].

stander-up *n.* [19C] a street thief who robs drunks under the pretence of helping them up from the gutter into which they have fallen (or been pushed).

stand from under *n.* [rhy. sl.] [20C+] thunder.

stand-in *n.* [late 19C–1920s] (*US*) a friendly or profitable arrangement; a corrupt arrangement, a 'put-up job'.

stand in *v.*[1] **1** [mid-19C–1910s] to go shares with, to join, to be a partner with. **2** [late 19C+] to have a friendly or profitable understanding with, to be in league with, to be on good terms with.

stand in *v.*[2] [SE mid-15C–mid-19C] **1** [mid-19C+] (*orig. UK society*) to cost, e.g. *it stands me in £10*. **2** [1910s] (*Aus.*) to hand over (money).

standing *n.*[1] [mid-19C] (*US Und.*) buying stolen property.

standing *n.*[2] *see* STAND *n.* (2).

standing ague *n.* [STAND *v.*[1] + SE *ague*, the 'shaking sickness', i.e. the erect penis is lit. shaking with lust] [mid-17C] the state of erection.

standing budge *n.* [SE *stand* + BUDGE *n.*[1] (1)] [late 17C] a thief's accomplice or a lookout.

standing patterer *n.* [SE *stand* + PATTERER *n.*] [mid-19C] a man who takes 'a stand on the curb of a public thoroughfare, and deliver[s] prepared speeches to effect a sale of any articles [he has] to vend' (Hotten, 1859).

standing room for one *n.* [pun on SE/STAND *v.*[1]] [19C] the vagina.

IN PHRASES

❑ **give standing room for one** *v.* [late 19C] of a woman, to have sexual intercourse.

standings *n.* [? the stallholder *stands* behind it] [1930s–40s] (*Irish*) a second-hand clothes stall.

standing ware *n.* [STAND *v.*[1] + SE *ware*, goods] [early 18C–late 19C] the erect penis.

stand-off *n.* [STAND OFF *v.*] **1** [mid-19C+] a deadlock, a stalemate. **2** [late 19C–1900s] (*US*) an extension of credit, a postponement of payment. **3** [late 19C–1910s] aloofness.

stand-off *adj.* [abbr. SE *standoffish*] [late 19C–1920s] (*Aus./Irish*) haughty, unfriendly.

stand off *v.* **1** [late 19C–1900s] to put off, to evade (a creditor, a questioner). **2** [late 19C+] (*US*) to keep at a distance, to repel, to hold at bay. **3** [1910s–20s] to gain or extend credit.

stand-on *n.* **1** [1900s] (*US*) a leg [SE]. **2** [1940s+] an erection [STAND *v.*[1] on model of HARD-ON *n.*].

stand on *v.* **1** [late 19C] to wager on. **2** [late 19C+] to trust, to rely on.

stand-out *n.* [1920s+] (*US/Can.*) one who distinguishes themselves from a crowd.

stand-out *adj.* [STAND-OUT *n.*] [1930s+] (*orig. US*) conspicuous, better than average.

stand out like... *v.* [20C+] a phr. appearing in various combs., meaning to be very obvious, very large, e.g. *stand out like chapel hatpegs* (usu. of erect nipples), *...cod's ballocks*, *...dog's ballocks*, *...a sore thumb*, *...a shit-house in the fog*.

standover *n.*[1] [one 'stands over' the sole] [1900s] (*Aus.*) a shoe.

standover *n.*[2] [STAND OVER *v.*] [1930s+] (*Aus.*) **1** a threat, an act of intimidation. **2** one who engages in intimdatory actions or words.

stand over *v.* [the menacing position the demander adopts] [1930s+] (*Aus./N.Z.*) to intimidate, spec. to demand money with menaces.

stand-over man *n.* (*also* **stand-over merchant**) [STAND OVER *v.*] [1930s+] (*Aus.*) a bully; esp. one who demands money with menaces.

standstill *n.* [mid-19C] (*UK Und.*) a table.

stand to (attention) *n.* [rhy. sl.] [20C+] a pension.

stand-up *n.* **1** [mid-19C] a dance. **2** [mid-19C] a seatless carriage used on the early railways. **3** [late 19C] a snack taken standing up; the snack bar where this takes place. **4** [late 19C+] (*also* **stand-up job**) sexual intercourse when both partners are standing up. **5** [1900s–40s] (*US*) a police identification parade. **6** [1930s+] (*orig. US*) the act of 'standing someone up', i.e. breaking an appointment; thus *give the stand-up*, to miss a scheduled meeting, esp. to break a date. **7** [1990s+] (*US prison*) a loyal, dependable friend.

stand-up *adj.* [f. *stand up and be counted*, to make one's presence felt] [1940s+] (*US Und.*) honest, trustworthy, dependable; esp. in phr. *stand-up guy*.

SE in slang uses

IN COMPOUNDS

❑ **stand-up job** *n. see* STAND-UP *n.* (4). ❑ **stand-up supper** *n.* [SE *stand-up supper*, a late supper at which those invited ate while on their feet; such a supper was, *de facto*, less grand (and less expensive to cater) than a full-scale sit-down meal] [late 19C] (*UK society*) anything mean or niggardly.

stand up *v.* **1** in senses of 'leaving someone standing'. (**a**) [20C+] (*orig. US*) to fail to keep an appointment with someone. (**b**) [1930s–40s] (*US black*) to treat someone as second-rate, unimportant. (**c**) [1940s] to keep someone waiting. **2** in senses of 'standing up tall'. (**a**) [1910s] (*US*) to hold out for, to exert pressure on. (**b**) [1920s+] (*orig. US*) to withstand pressure, esp. police questioning or criminal intimidation. **3** [1970s] (*orig. US*) to confess.

SE in slang uses

IN PHRASES

❑ **stand (up) to one's lick-log, salt or no salt** *v.* [SAmE *lick-log*, a notched log (occas. a wooden trough) used to hold salt for livestock] [mid-19C+] (*US*) to stand by one's decision come what may; thus *come to the lick-log*, to face up to a tough decision. ❑ **stand up drinks** *v.* [20C+] (*Aus.*) to set out drinks. ❑ **stand upon one's pantables** *v.* (*also* **stand upon one's pantacles, ...pantap, ...pantaphels, ...pantofles**) [SE *pantofle* (ult. Fr. *pantoufle*), a slipper, esp. one with a high heel and a built-up sole to make the wearer appear taller and more imposing] [late 16C–mid-18C] to stand upon ceremony, to act in a dignified manner.

stand-up guy *n.* (*also* **stand-by guy, stand-up boy, stand-up dude**) [STAND-UP *adj.* (1) + GUY *n.*[2] (1)] [1920s+] (*US*) an honest, dependable person, one who 'stands up to be counted'.

stand up to the rack *v. see* COME UP TO THE RACK (OR JUMP THE FENCE) *under* COME UP *v.*[1].

'Stang *n.* [abbr.] [1990s+] (*US*) a Ford Mus*tang* automobile.

stangey *n.*[1] (*also* **stangy**) [SE *stang*, a sting or prick; i.e. the needle] [late 18C–mid-19C] a tailor.

stangey *n.*[2] (*also* **stangy**) [phr. *ride the stang*, 'to be mounted astride of a pole borne on the shoulders of two men, and carried through the streets for the derision of the spectators' (*OED*). This custom, however, once popular in Scotland and the north, focused on unpopular, rather than spec. wife-dominated men, but the implication is that he has to ride a pole, since he cannot 'ride' his wife] [mid-19C] a man who is dominated by his wife.

stank *n.* [SE *stink*] [1980s+] **1** (*US black*) the anus. **2** (*US black*) (*also* **stank-stank**) the vagina. **3** (*US campus*) an ugly woman. **4** (*US black*) the smell of sex. **5** (*US campus*) any form of unpleasant smell.

stank *adj.* (*also* **stanking**) [STANK *n.*] [1980s+] **1** (*US black*) foul-smelling. **2** (*US campus*) ugly. **3** (*US campus*) extremely unpleasant.

IN COMPOUNDS

❑ **stank ho** *n.* (*also* **stank bitch**) [HO *n.* (1)] [1970s+] (*US black/campus*) an ugly woman, with suggestions of promiscuity.

stanky *adj.* (*also* **stank**) [STANK *n.*] [1960s+] (*orig. US*) **1** smelly, dirty, unattractive. **2** in fig. use, a general negative: useless, disgusting etc.

Stanley facial *n.* [2000s] slashing the face with a Stanley knife.

Stanley knife *n.* [rhy. sl.] [1990s+] one's wife.

staph *n.* [abbr.] [1930s+] *staph*ylococcus, a genus of disease-inducing bacteria.

stapled down *adj.* [2000s] (*US black*) of a man, dominated by his female partner.

stap me! *excl.* [despite STAP MY VITALS! *excl.*, based on a mispron., more likely SE *stab*] [18C+] an oath orig. popular among upper-class dandies.

stap my vitals! *excl.* (*also* **stap my breath! stop my vitals!**) [SE *stop*; the first printed use as 'stap' appears in the play *The Relapse, or, Virtue in Danger* (1697), by John Vanbrugh; it is spoken by Lord Foppington, among whose affectations is the consistent pron. of 'o' as 'a'] [late 17C+] an oath popular among upper-class dandies.

Star, the *n.* [mid-19C] the Star and Garter public house, in Richmond, south of London.

star *n.*[1] [the theatrical/film/sports/rock use of *star*, while obviously linked, has been SE since its early 19C coinage] **1** [19C] a conspicuous member of society, who shines out among their peers. **2** [mid-19C] one who is exceptional within their own world. **3** [mid-19C] (*US*) a police officer, esp. in New York. **4** [1950s+] (*US black*) a man's favourite woman, a very attractive woman. **5** [1960s+] the most favoured/successful prostitute in a pimp's string of girls. **6** [1970s] (*US black*) a top-level pimp. **7** [1980s+] (*W.I./UK black*) (*also* **star-bwai, star-boy**) an attractive, sophisticated, articulate, brave, well-dressed man; esp. as extended to a leading gangster. **8** [1980s+] (*UK black*) a term of address between black people, esp. friends. **9** [1990s+] a very unpleasant person, e.g. *what a fucking star!*

IN COMPOUNDS

□ **star boarder** *n.* [1930s] (*US Und.*) the best-performing prostitute in a brothel. □ **star-bwai/-boy** *n. see* sense 7 above. □ **star-fucker/-fucking** *n. see* separate entries.

IN PHRASES

□ **star of the line** *n.* [LINE *n.*[1] (4)] [1960s+] (*US black*) a pimp's favourite prostitute.

SE in slang uses

IN COMPOUNDS

□ **stardust** *n. see* separate entry. □ **starfish** *n. see* BROWN STAR *under* BROWN *adj.*[2]. □ **star-gazer** *n.* **1** [17C–18C] the erect penis. **2** [mid-17C–early 19C] a horse that persistently throws its head up. **3** [late 18C–mid-19C] a country prostitute who plies her trade in the open air or under hedges. □ **star-gazing** *adj.* [1900s] unconscious. □ **star hotel** *n.* (*also* **starlight hotel**) [1930s–50s] the open air; esp. in phr. *sleep/doss in the star hotel*, to sleep in the open air. □ **star pitch** *n.* [late 19C] (*UK/US tramp*) sleeping in the open air.

IN PHRASES

□ **go star-gazing (on one's back)** *v.* [the earlier use, which had languished, has recently reappeared, although without any 'open air' implication] **1** [late 18C–mid-19C] (*also* **study astronomy**) of a woman, to have sex in the open air. **2** [1990s+] of a woman, to have sexual intercourse. □ **shoot stars** *v.* [var. of SEE STARS *under* SEE *v.*] [mid-19C] to experience dizziness as a result of a blow to the head. □ **star in the east** *n.* [1990s+] used to refer to someone's flies being undone. □ **stars and stripes** *n. see* separate entry. □ **stars for studs** *n.* [STUD *n.* (1)] [1970s+] (*US campus*) a course in basic astronomy.

star *n.*[2] (*also* **star man**) [abbr. prison jargon *star prisoner*, a star is affixed to their name in the prison records] [late 19C+] (*UK prison*) a first offender.

star *n.*[3] [1980s+] (*W.I./UK black teen*) **1** a term of respect, synon. with SE *sir*. **2** a general term of address, synon. with MAN *n.*[1], e.g. *Wha' apen star?* What's up man?

star, the *n.* [*see* STAR THE GLAZE *under* GLAZE *n.*] [early 19C] (*UK Und.*) the practice of cutting a hole in a shop's window, then extracting such items as can be reached.

IN COMPOUNDS

□ **star-glazer/-glazing** *n. see* separate entries. □ **star lay** *n.* [LAY *n.*[3] (1)] [early 19C] robbery by breaking shop or house windows.

IN PHRASES

□ **star the glaze** *v. see under* GLAZE *n.*

star *adv.* [i.e. like an SE *star*] [1990s+] (*UK black*) proudly, e.g. *walk star*.

starbolic (naked) *adj. see* STARK BALLOCK NAKED *adj.*

starch *n.* **1** [mid-19C+] courage, well being. **2** [late 19C+] semen. **3** [1900s] (*US*) face powder.

IN PHRASES

□ **put on starch** *v.* [1900s] (*Aus.*) to act in an arrogant manner. □ **take the starch out of** *v.* **1** [mid-19C–1920s] of a woman, to have sexual intercourse with [the wilted post-orgasmic penis]. **2** [mid-19C+] to break the spirit of someone or something, to make weary or less arrogant.

starch *v.* **1** [mid-19C–1910s] (*UK Und.*) to smarten oneself up. **2** [1940s+] to kill, to die.

starched *adj.* [late 17C–mid-19C] affected, stand-offish, snobbish.

starcher *n.* [late 19C–1900s] a starched cravat; a stiff white tie.

starchy *n.* [STARCHY *adj.* (3)] [2000s] a snob, a stiff, unfriendly person.

starchy *adj.* **1** [mid-19C] of clothes, showy, fashionable. **2** [mid-19C+] drunk. **3** [mid-19C+] stiff, unbending, reserved, lacking in social warmth.

starder *n.* [mid-19C] (*US Und.*) a receiver.

stardust *n.* [ext. of DUST *n.* (6), underpinned in sense 1 by the popularity of cocaine among rock and film stars] (*drugs*) **1** [1950s+] cocaine. **2** [1980s+] phencyclidine.

stare-cat *n.* [SE *stare* + CAT *n.*[1] (1c)] [mid-19C+] (*orig. US*) an inquisitive neighbour, usu. a woman.

stare like a dead pig *v.* (*also* **stare like a stuck pig**) [late 17C–early 18C] to gape, to stare at fixedly.

star-fucker *n.* [SE *star* + FUCKER *n.*] [1960s+] a sycophant, a hanger-on, esp. of celebrities.

star-fucking *n.* [STAR-FUCKER *n.*] [1960s+] **1** acting as a toady, a parasite. **2** living as a GROUPIE *n.*[2] (1).

star-glazer *n.* [mid-19C] (*UK Und.*) one who cuts the panes out of shop-windows.

star-glazing *n.* [the star-shaped hole in the glass + play on SE *star-gazing*] [mid–late 19C] smashing and removing a pane of glass in order to steal items from a shop display or to break onto a house.

stariben *n. see* STURRABIN *n.*

staring quarter *n.* [note dial. *staring-quarter*, a laughing-stock] [late 18C–early 19C] an ox-cheek.

stark *adj. see* STARK STARING BONKERS *adj.*

stark ballock naked *adj.* (*also* **starbolic (naked), stark bollick naked, stark bollock-naked, stark bollux naked, starko-bollocko, stark rollock naked**) [SE *stark naked* + BALLOCK *n.*] [late 19C+] absolutely naked.

starkers *adj.*[1] (*also* **starko**) [SE *stark naked* + -ER *sfx*/-O *sfx* (5)] [1910s+] nude.

starkers *adj.*[2] *see* STARK STARING BONKERS *adj.* (1).

stark-naked *n.* [the neat alcohol comes without 'clothing' + the poverty that results from excessive consumption] [early–mid-19C] neat, undiluted gin.

stark-naked *adj.* [STARK-NAKED *n.*] [mid–late 19C] unadulterated, esp. of drinks.

starko *adj. see* STARKERS *adj.*[1].

starko-bollocko/stark rollock naked *adj. see* STARK BALLOCK NAKED *adj.*

stark staring bonkers *adj.* (*also* **stark, starkers, stark raving bats, stark raving bonkers, stark raving loony, stark staring, stark staring crackers, stark staring dippy**) [ext. of BONKERS *adj.*] [1910s+] absolutely crazy.

star man *n. see* STAR *n.*[2].

starn *n.* [SE *stern*] [late 19C+] the buttocks.

starps *n.* [backsl.] [mid-19C] sprats.

starrer *n. see* ANGLER *n.* (1).

starry *n.*

IN PHRASES

□ **do a starry** *v.* [SE *star*] [1920s–30s] (*UK Und.*) to sleep in the open air.

stars and stripes *n.* **1** [late 19C] Bostonians, esp. the more puritanically religious of them, seen as eaters of sense 2. **2** [late 19C–1950s] (*US*) a dish of pork (belly) and baked beans; frankfurters and baked beans [the baked beans resemble stars and the pork belly/frankfurters resemble stripes].

Starsky and Hutch *n.* [rhy. sl.] [1980s+] the crotch.

Star's Nap *n.* [rhy. sl. = TAP *n.*[2] (3)] [1990s+] a loan; the act of borrowing.

Start, the *n.* [? SE *start*, a shock, a surprise; thus the effect of entering prison + a new *start* to one's life, whether good or bad] **1** [mid-18C–early 19C] a prison, esp. Newgate [? Newgate as the start of one's journey along Holborn towards Tyburn]. **2** [mid-18C–19C] (*UK Und.*) (*also* **Stait, the**) London; (*US*) New York [because London is the starting point for a tramp's journeying round Britain]. **3** [mid-19C] (*UK Und.*) attrib., pertaining to or from London. **4** [mid-19C] the Old Bailey.

start *n.*[1] [SE *start*, a shock] [mid-19C–1900s] an odd circumstance, a surprise; often as *rum* or *rummy start*.

start *n.*[2] [? a lit. or fig. SE *start* on a project, an activity] **1** [late 19C+] (*Aus.*) a job. **2** [1960s+] (*S.Afr.*) money.

start *v.* [SE *start*, to begin; *nagging* etc are assumed] [20C+] to commence complaining, nagging, being a nuisance etc.

IN PHRASES

❑ **don't (you) start** [late 19C+] a phr. used to indicate that one is already sufficiently displeased or annoyed by statements that have been made and that one does not need the irritation that their repetition would cause; or, usu. to a child, meaning, 'I'm annoyed already, don't start behaving badly and make things worse.' ❑ **start on** *v.* (*also* **start in on, start up on**) (*orig. US*) **1** [late 19C+] to nag, to assail verbally; to criticize. **2** [20C+] to attack physically. **3** [1960s–70s] to seduce, to have sexual intercourse with.

SE in slang uses

IN PHRASES

❑ **start a fowl-roost** *v.* [ety. unknown] [20C+] (*Aus.*) to take on a 'double-barrelled' surname.

starter *n.*[1] [SE *start*, to jump in surprise; a question, esp. as to one's clandestine activities, may cause one to do this] **1** [late 17C–18C] (*UK Und.*) a question. **2** [late 17C–early 19C] a restless person, one who leaves a convivial company.

starter *n.*[2] [all senses of SE *start*, to begin, to initiate] **1** [late 19C–1920s] a laxative. **2** [1940s] (*US Und.*) a crooked dealer in a gambling house. **3** [1940s–50s] (*Aus.*) one who makes a brave attempt. **4** [1960s+] (*N.Z.*) one who is keen to initiate a new activity. **5** [1980s+] (*Aus. prison*) any form of lubricant used to facilitate anal intercourse.

starters *n.* [1960s+] initial actions, plans etc.

starvation *adv.* [late 19C+] a negative intensifier, excessively, extremely; lit. 'productive of starvation', e.g. *starvation cruel*, very cruel.

starve *n.*

IN PHRASES

❑ **do a starve** *v.* [1910s+] (*Aus.*) to go hungry.

starver *n.* [1900s–50s] (*Aus.*) **1** a roll. **2** a saveloy [a large sausage, it fills the stomach of a starving person].

starve the...! *excl.*

SE in Aus. slang uses

IN EXCLAMATIONS

❑ **starve the bardies!** [SE *bardy*, an edible Australian wood-boring grub (*Bardistus cibarius*) or its larva] [1940s+] (*W. Aus.*) a general excl. ❑ **starve the crows!** [1910s+] a general excl. ❑ **starve the lizards!** (*also* **starve the mopokes! ...ninnies! ...rats! ...roan bullocks! ...wombats!**) [1910s+] a general excl.

stash *n.*[1] [? SE *ostentatious*] [20C+] (*W.I., Guyn.*) a woman who dresses flashily; thus *stash*, to dress showily.

stash *n.*[2] **1** [1910s+] any form of cache. **2** [1920s+] (*US*) money. **3** [1920s+] (*orig. US*) (*also* **stach**) a hiding place. **4** [1930s+] (*drugs*) (*also* **sach, stasch**) a hiding place for drugs. **5** [1930s+] (*drugs*) a cache of any drug, esp. cannabis. **6** [1940s+] a place (to stay).

IN COMPOUNDS

❑ **stash catcher** *n.* (*also* **catcher**) [1980s+] (*drugs*) one who stands outside a window to catch drugs that are thrown out during a police raid. ❑ **stash-house** *n.* [1990s+] (*US drugs*) a place where a drug dealer can store a cache of drugs. ❑ **stash pad** *n.* [PAD *n.*[2] (2)] [1980s+] (*drugs*) a room, apartment or house where drugs are stored.

IN PHRASES

❑ **make for a stash** *v. see under* MAKE *v.* (1d).

stash *n.*[3] [abbr.] [1940s+] (*US*) a moustache.

stash *v.*[1] (*also* **stach, stache**) [18C Und. *stash*, put a stop to + influences f. SE *stop, stow, squash* + Fr. *cacher*, to hide; orig. cant, the term was dormant during 19C but has been revived, mainly among drug users, since mid-20C+] **1** [late 18C–1910s] (*UK Und.*) to stop, to refrain, to give up; esp. in excl. *stash it!* stop that!, *stash the glim*, douse the light. **2** [late 18C+] to hide, esp. since 1930s, drugs. **3** [1930s–40s] (*US black*) to go to sleep. **4** [1930s+] to place, whether clandestinely or in view.

IN PHRASES

❑ **stash it** *v.* **1** [early-19C–1920s] to give up one's bad habits. **2** [mid-19C+] (*US*) to stop doing something; also as imper. ❑ **stash up** *v.* [1900s] to stop doing something instantly, abruptly.

IN EXCLAMATIONS

❑ **stash me!** an excl. of surprise.

stash *v.*[2] **1** [late 19C] to leave, to go, to accompany. **2** [1940s–80s] (*US black*) to stand around, to stay. **3** [1970s] (*US*) to walk in, to enter; to visit, to arrive at.

stashed *adj.* **1** [1920s+] hidden [STASH *v.*[1] (2)]. **2** [1930s–40s] (*US black*) standing; remaining [STASH *v.*[2] (2)].

stashie *adj.* (*also* **stashy, stashied up**) [STASH *n.*[1]] [20C+] (*W.I./Irish*) smartly or showily dressed.

stat *n.* [abbr.] **1** [1940s+] usu. pl., a *stat*istic, *stat*istics. **2** [1950s+] a photo*stat*, a Xerox copy.

statch *n.* [abbr./mispron. of SE] [1950s+] (*US*) statutory rape.

state *n.* **1** [mid-19C+] a condition of emotional distress or mental agitation. **2** [late 19C+] an unkempt, dirty condition of dress or cleanliness. **3** [1980s] a state of drunkeness.

IN PHRASES

❑ **state of you** [1980s+] a phr. used to express disgust or disbelief at the way somebody is behaving, or at something they have said.

SE in slang uses

IN PHRASES

❑ **lying in state** *adj.* [1920s+] (*US prison*) serving time in jail. ❑ **out of state** *adj.* [pun on OUT OF SIGHT *adj.* (2)] [1970s+] (*US campus*) excellent, first-rate.

state *adj.* used in combs. pertaining to US institutions, esp. prison.

DERIVATIVES

❑ **state-o** *n.* [1950s+] (*US prison*) **1** a prisoner's official prison clothing. **2** anything to do with prison.

IN COMPOUNDS

❑ **state college** *n.* [COLLEGE *n.* (3)] [1940s] (*US prison/Und.*) a state prison. ❑ **state con** *n.* (*also* **state man**) [mid-19C; 1990s+] (*US Und.*) a prisoner who is seen as overly friendly with the authorities. ❑ **state grad** *n.* [1940s] a former prisoner. ❑ **state holiday** *n.* [1990s+] (*US*) a prison sentence. ❑ **state house** *n.* [1900s] (*US Und.*) a public lavatory. ❑ **state-raised** *adj.* [1970s+] (*US*) used of one who has been brought up in institutions.

Stateside *n.* [1940s+] (*US*) the USA, as opposed to foreign countries; thus attrib., of or pertaining to the USA.

static *n.* [SE *static*, atmospherics, radio noise] [1920s+] (*orig. US*) difficulties, aggravation, impudent or argumentative talk.

static! *excl.* [STATIC *n.*] [1980s+] a cry of warning, e.g. from a street dealer's lookout at the approach of the police.

Statie *n.* [1940s+] (*US Und.*) a *State* police officer.

station-jack *n.* [ety. unknown] [mid-19C] (*Aus.*) a boiled meat pudding, usu. cooked in the bush or at a sheep station.

statue act *n.* [1950s] (*US black*) standing still.

stauling-ken *n. see* STALLING-KEN *n.*

stavel *v.* [mid-19C] (*UK Und.*) to lay down money, to pay.

stavin chain *n.* [the mythical hero of the ballad 'Wining Boy Blues' by Jellyroll Morton (1890–1941), Stavin Chain's prowess was sexual] [1900s–40s] (*US black*) a ladies' man, a wanderer.

staving *adj.* [SE *stave*, to go with a rush or dash] [mid-19C–1910s] big, excessive; thus *staver*, someone or something exceptional.

staving *adv.* [SE *stave*, to go with a rush or dash] [mid-19C–1900s] (*US*) very, excessively.

stay *n.* [? SE *stays*, which the errant wife might also discard for the pleasures of sex] [early 19C] a cuckold.

stay *v.*

SE in slang uses

IN COMPOUNDS

❑ **stay-awake** *n.* [1960s+] (*drugs*) any form of stimulant and amphetamine. ❑ **stay-home sauce** *n.* (*also* **stay-home soup, ...tea**) [20C+] (*W.I.*) food that supposedly contains 'magic' ingredients that will influence a man to choose a particular woman.

IN PHRASES

❑ **stay down** *v.* [1990s+] (*US prison*) to maintain one's role as a professional criminal/gangster. ❑ **stay down low** *v.* (*also* **stay down**) [1970s+] (*US black*) to remain inconspicuous, to behave normally; also as a parting expression. ❑ **stay hitched** *v. see* STAND HITCHED *under* STAND *v.*[2]. ❑ **stay loose** *see* separate entries. ❑ **stay up** [1990s+] (*US teen*) goodbye, see you later. ❑ **stay with** *v.* [euph.] **1** [late 19C] (*US*) to court. **2** [late 19C] (*US*) of food, to assuage or satisfy one's hunger. **3** [late 19C+] to keep up with, to persist in an endeavour. **4** [1930s+] to have sexual intercourse.

stay loose *v.* (*orig. US*) [SE *loose*/LOOSE *adj.* (5)] **1** [1950s+] to relax, to remain calm. **2** [1980s] to keep an open mind.

stay loose *phr.* [STAY LOOSE *v.*] [1960s+] goodbye, esp. in communities influenced by California's post-HIPPIE *n.*[2] (3) era 'new therapies'.

staytape *n.* [SE *staytape*, material used for binding the edges of fabric] **1** [late 18C–early 19C] a tailor. **2** [mid-19C] (*US Und.*) a clerk in a dry-goods store.

s.t.b. *n.* [abbr. *s*traight *t*o *b*ed] [2000s] (*S.Afr. gay*) a sexually desirable man.

steady *n.* (*also* **steady company**) **1** [late 19C+] (*orig. US*) a regular girl- or boyfriend. **2** [1950s] (*US*) a regular customer. **3** [1960s+] (*US*) a prostitute's regular customer.

steady lapper *n.* [1910s] (*Aus.*) an inveterate drunkard.

steady on the case *phr.* [ON THE CASE *under* CASE *n.*[1]] [1950s–60s] (*US black*) persistent, unremitting.

steak *n.* [var. on BEEF *n.*[1] (4)] [1970s–80s] (*S.Afr./UK black*) a young woman, usu. attractive.

SE in slang uses

IN COMPOUNDS

❑ **steak and bull's eyes** *n.* [1930s] steak-and-kidney pudding. ❑ **steakdahoyst** *n.* (*also* **steaka-da-oyst**) [the 'Italian' pronunciation] [1910s–20s] (*Aus.*) an Italian restaurant specializing in *steak* and *oysters*. ❑ **steak drapes** *n.* [1990s+] the labia majora.

IN PHRASES

❑ **round steak** *n.* **1** [1970s] (*US prison*) bologna sausage. **2** [2000s] (*US black*) the penis.

steak and ale *n. see* GINGER ALE *n.* (2).

steak and kidney *n.* [rhy. sl.] **1** [20C+] the proper name Sidney. **2** [1940s+] (*Aus.*) Sydney.

steal *n.* **1** [late 19C–1960s] an act of theft. **2** [1930s+] (*orig. US*) a bargain; esp. in phr. *it's a steal*, often + *at...* (a sum of money).

steal *v.* (*also* **steal on**) [SE *steal up on*] [1980s+] (*US prison*) to attack without warning.

SE in slang uses

IN PHRASES

❑ **steal a shive of a cut loaf** *v.* [SE *shive*, a slice of bread] [late 16C–early 17C] of a man, to have adulterous intercourse with a married woman. ❑ **steal blind** *v.* [BLIND *adv.*[1] (1)] [1920s+] (*US*) to rob or cheat to an extreme extent.

stealers *n.* (*also* **ten stealers**) [20C+ use is US black] [mid-17C; 1940s] the fingers.

stealth *n.* [1990s+] (*US black*) self-possession; character.

stealth *adj.* [1990s+] (*US campus*) underhand, deceitful.

steam *n.* **1** [late 19C–1970s] (*US black*) beer, wine; a glass of beer [it 'gets one's steam up'; but note late 19C US proprietory *steam beer* (*pump*)]. **2** [1910s] (*US*) a temper. **3** [1930s+] (*Aus./N.Z.*) (*also* **steamboats**) cheap wine, esp. if laced with methylated spirits; methylated spirits drunk by itself. **4** [1960s] (*US*) blame, sarcasm, intense criticism. **5** [1970s] (*drugs*) phencyclidine. **6** [1970s] (*US*) problems, difficulties, trouble.

SE in slang uses

IN COMPOUNDS

❑ **steam-and-cream** *n.* [SE *steam*, i.e. of the sauna + CREAM *v.*] [1970s] (*US*) a brothel, masquerading/doubling as a sauna. ❑ **steamboat/steamboated** *see* separate entries. ❑ **steam clean** *n.* [1980s] (*US black*) an act of fellatio. ❑ **steam daddy** *n.* (*also* **steam queen**) [DADDY *n.* (8)/QUEEN *n.* (2)] [1970s] (*US gay*) 'a middle-aged homosexual spending most of his time in the cloudy steamroom of a bath' (Rodgers, *The Queens' Vernacular*, 1972). ❑ **steam engine** *n.* [? the steam that emanates from the hot potatoes] [1930s] (*US prison*) a potato pie, a cooked potato. ❑ **steamroll/steamroller** *see* separate entries.

IN PHRASES

❑ **blow off steam** *v.* (*also* **get off steam, let off..., shoot off..., let off wind**) [early 19C+] to release one's (pent-up) emotions, to become angry or noisy and excited. ❑ **blow steam** *v.* [1950s] (*US*) to chatter aimlessly and pointlessly. ❑ **get someone's steam up** *v. see* STEAM *v.*[1] (2). ❑ **like steam** *adv.* [20C+ use (Aus.)] [mid-19C+] very quickly, very easily, energetically. ❑ **like steam on piss** *adv. see* LIKE SHIT OFF A SHOVEL *under* SHIT *n.* ❑ **not give someone the steam off one's turds** *v.* [1970s+] to be very mean. ❑ **not give someone the steam on one's piss** *v.* [1980s+] to hold in absolute contempt. ❑ **put on the steam** *v.* [railroad or factory whistle imagery] [1950s] (*US*) to whistle.

steam *adj.* [the obsolete railway *steam* engines, long displaced by diesel] [1970s+] old-fashioned.

steam *v.*[1] **1** [mid-19C; 1910s+] (*orig. US*) to be annoyed, to be angry, to talk aggressively. **2** [mid-19C; 1990s+] (*also* **get someone's steam up**) to annoy, infuriate. **3** [1960s] to make someone amorous.

IN COMPOUNDS

❑ **steam-up man** *n.* [1960s] (*S.Afr.*) a person who incites another to commit a crime.

IN PHRASES

❑ **steam up** *v.* **1** [1910s+] to stimulate emotionally, to arouse; to infuriate. **2** [1940s] to speak emotionally. **3** [1950s] to get oneself drunk.

steam *v.*[2] (*also* **steam ahead, steam away**) **1** [mid-19C+] to work vigorously, to make great progress. **2** [1940s+] to go fast in a vehicle.

IN PHRASES

❑ **steam in** *v.* **1** [1940s+] (*also* **steam up**) to arrive in an energetic manner. **2** [1960s+] (*also* **steam, steam into**) to attack; to commit oneself completely, esp. in a fight. ❑ **steam into** *v.* [2000s] to approach, e.g. sexually. ❑ **steam the socks off** *v. see* KNOCK THE SOCKS OFF *under* KNOCK *v.*

steamboat *v.* [1960s] (*drugs*) 'to inhale the butt of a marijuana cigarette stuck in a hole in a toilet roll, the hand enclosing one end, the mouth on the other end' (Lingeman, *Drugs from A to Z*, 1969).

steamboated *adj.* (*also* **steamboats**) [? STEAMED (UP) *adj.*] [1970s+] very drunk.

steamboats *n.* [STEAM *n.* (3)] **1** [2000s] (*N.Z.*) methylated spirits mixed with tea. **2** *see* STEAM *n.* (3).

steamed (up) *adj.* **1** [1910s+] fighting drunk. **2** [1920s+] tense, annoyed. **3** [1920s+] excited. **4** [1930s+] sexually excited. **5** [1940s] (*drugs*) under the effects of narcotics.

steamer *n.*[1] [the smoke or SE *steam* produced] **1** [early 19C] a tobacco pipe. **2** [1950s+] (*W.I.*) a form of hookah or water-pipe used for smoking marijuana. **3** [1990s+] a cigarette. **4** [2000s] a piece of excrement [semantically linked to TURD *n.*[1], with its root in SE *torn*, the image is of a piece of excrement which, in the cold, might steam with body heat].

IN PHRASES

❑ **clip a steamer** *v.* [1990s+] (*UK juv.*) to defecate.

steamer *n.*[2] [1930s] (*US*) an attractive woman.

steamer *n.*[3] [rhy. sl. *steam tug* = MUG *n.*[1] (2)] **1** [1930s+] a fool, a gullible person. **2** [1960s+] (*gay*) a male homosexual, esp. the client of a male prostitute.

steaming *n.*[1] [late 19C] any form of steamed pudding.

steaming *n.*[2] [? *STEAM IN under* STEAM *v.*[2]] [1980s+] the act of mugging, esp. when performed *en masse* against a 'captive audience' by a gang on a bus or, more likely, an underground train.

steaming *adj.*[1] [1950s+] a general intensifier with euph. overtones, since usu. in negative use, e.g. *steaming hangover.*

steaming *adj.*[2] [STEAM *n.*] [1960s+] drunk.

steaming *adv.* [1940s+] a general intensifier, completely, very.

steam-packet *n.* [rhy. sl.] [mid–late 19C] a jacket.

steamroll *v.* [1920s] (*US black*) to commit adultery, to deceive a lover.

steamroller *n.*[1] [rhy. sl.] [20C+] a bowler hat.

steamroller *n.*[2] [2000s] (*N.Z.*) a roll-your-own cigarette that uses a large amount of tobacco.

steam tug *n.* [rhy. sl.] **1** [1930s+] a fool, a gullible person [MUG *n.*[1] (2a)]. **2** [1930s+] a bug. **3** [2000s] (*Aus.*) a pug, i.e. a prize-fighter.

steamy *adj.* [euph.] **1** [1910s] angry. **2** [1960s] sweaty. **3** [1960s+] (*orig. US*) sexually arousing, erotic, salacious. **4** [1970s+] (*US gay*) sexually excited.

steeazick *n.* [*STICK OF GAGE under* STICK *n.* + -IZ- *infix*] [1940s] (*US drugs*) a cannabis cigarette.

steed *n.* [SE *steed*, a horse, although he does the 'riding'] [1970s] a sexual expert.

Steel, the *n.* [abbr. BASTILLE *n.*] **1** [19C] Coldbath Fields Prison. **2** [early 19C–1950s] a prison. **3** [mid-19C] a treadmill.

IN PHRASES

❑ **on the steel** *adj.* [mid-19C] (*Aus./UK Und.*) imprisoned, thus forced to be on the treadmill.

steel *n.* **1** [late 19C+] (*US Und.*) a knife. **2** [20C+] (*US black*) a gun.

SE in slang uses

IN PHRASES

❑ **pink steel** *n.* [metonymy] [1990s+] the erect penis.

steel *adj.*

SE in slang uses

IN COMPOUNDS

❑ **steel balls** *n. see* BRASS BALLS *n.* ❑ **steel bar** *n. see* separate entry. ❑ **steel bottom** *n.* [? the need for a SE *steel bottom* in one's stomach to drink such a thing] (*W.I.*) **1** [1950s] an alcoholic cocktail that mixes gin and wine. **2** [1970s] a drink of white rum with a beer chaser. ❑ **steel jockey** *n.* [SE *steel*, i.e. the railway + JOCKEY *n.*[2] (3)] [1940s] (*Aus.*) one who rides a train without paying. ❑ **steel-nose** *n.* [? it gives one a red nose that 'glows' like molten steel] [mid-17C] a form of strong drink. ❑ **steel pen** *n.* [the resemblance of the tail to a *steelpen* nib] [late 19C] (*US*) a 'swallow-tail' or tail-coat, worn for formal evening wear.

IN PHRASES

❑ **steel and concrete cure** *n. see IRON CURE under* IRON *adj.*

steel *v.* [20C+] (*US*) to stab.

steel bar *n.* [late 18C–early 19C] a needle.

IN COMPOUNDS

❑ **steel bar flinger** *n.* (*also* **steel bar driver**) [late 18C–early 19C] a tailor.

Steele Rudds *n.* [rhy. sl.; ult. author *Steele Rudd* (pseud. of Arthur Hoey Davis) (1868–1935)] [20C+] (*Aus.*) spuds, potatoes.

steelie *n.* [2000s] a steel-toe-capped boot.

steen *adj.* [1900s] (*US*) an indefinite or large amount of; also as n.

steep *adj.* [mid-19C+] (*orig. US*) **1** over-priced, exorbitant, excessive, exaggerated. **2** extreme, beyond the limit; esp. in phr. *a bit steep.*

steeples *n.* [1910s] (*Aus.*) steeplechasing.

steer *n.* [SE *steer*, to direct] **1** [late 19C+] (*US*) facts, a useful piece of information. **2** [1900s–40s] (*US/UK Und.*) someone who gives directions or information. **3** [1910s] (*US*) an inaccurate piece of information.

steer *v.* [late 19C+] (*orig. US Und.*) to decoy someone into a place, activity or situation.

IN COMPOUNDS

❑ **steer joint** *n.* (*also* **steering joint**) [JOINT *n.* (1)] [1930s+] (*orig. US*) a nightclub to which patrons are directed by a cab-driver, doorman etc, who is paid by the establishment.

steerer *n.* [STEER *v.*] **1** [mid-19C+] (*US Und.*) that member of a confidence trick team who engages the prospective victim and lures him into the con. **2** [late 19C+] (*US Und.*) anyone, e.g. a cab driver, hotel doorman or similar figure, who points a searcher towards the variety of self-indulgence they seek, e.g. sex, drugs, gambling. **3** [1920s–40s] a crooked lawyer; an agent who supplies such a lawyer with clients. **4** [1950s] (*US gay*) a man who runs a string of homosexual male prostitutes.

steer the ship *v. see under* SHIP *n.*[1].

steeven *n.* [STIVER *n.* (1); although here the coins are presumably far from worthless] [early–mid-19C] money.

steever *n.*[1] [2000s] (*Irish*) a kick in the buttocks.

steever *n.*[2] *see* STIVER *n.*

steez *n.* [SE *style* + -IZ- *infix*] [1990s+] (*US black*) one's personal style.

Steffie Graf *n.* [rhy. sl.; ult. Ger. tennis player *Steffi Graf* (b.1969)] [1990s+] **1** a laugh. **2** a bath.

Steffi Graf *v.* [rhy. sl.; see prev.] [2000s] to laugh.

Steinie *n.* [abbr.] [2000s] (*N.Z.*) a small bottle of Steinlager beer.

steiver *n. see* STIVER *n.*

stella *v.* [initial letter of SE *steal*] [2000s] (*S.Afr. gay*) to steal; thus as n., a thief.

stella dallas *n.* [film title *Stella Dallas* (1937), a celebrated tear-jerker starring Barbara Stanwyck] [1930s+] (*camp gay*) a loser, an unfortunate.

stellar *adj.* [1980s+] excellent, wonderful, 'out of this world'.

stem *n.* (*also* **the stem**) **1** [late 19C+] (*US, orig. tramp*) a street; usu. as MAIN STEM *n.* **2** in drug uses. (**a**) [1900s–1950s] an opium pipe. (**b**) [1970s] in pl., marijuana stems, as unsmokeable debris. (**c**) [1970s+] a marijuana/hashish pipe. (**d**) [1980s+] a crack cocaine pipe (laboratory pipette). **3** [1910s–40s] (*US Und.*) a drill, used in safebreaking. **4** [1920s] the area where tramps beg. **5** [1920s–30s] (*US tramp*) an act of begging. **6** [1930s+] (*US black*) the world of the street, as a generic.

IN PHRASES

❑ **hit the stem** *v.* **1** [1920s–50s] (*US tramp*) to beg on the main street. **2** [1930s–40s] (*US drugs*) to smoke opium. ❑ **mooch the stem** *v. see under* MOOCH *v.*[1]. ❑ **on the stem** [1990s+] smoking crack cocaine. ❑ **up against the stem** [1900s] (*US drugs*) smoking opium.

stem *v.*[1] [STEM *n.* (5)] (*US*) **1** [1920s] to grab, to get hold of. **2** [1920s–60s] to beg (from).

stem *v.*[2] [STEM *n.* (3)] [1920s–40s] (*US Und.*) to drill a safe as part of breaking it open.

stemmer *n.* [STEM *n.*] [1920s–60s] (*US tramp*) a tramp who begs on a main street.

stemming *n.* [STEM *v.*[1]] [1920s–30s] (*US*) begging.

stems *n.*[1] [mid-19C+] the legs, esp. of an attractive woman.

stems *n.*[2] *see* STEM *n.* (2b).

stem-wheeler *n.* [play on SE *stern-wheeler*, a truck powered from *behind*] [20C+] (*US*) a homosexual man.

stem-winder *n.* [the then newly invented *stem-winding* watch, which, with its rejection of any need for the usual key, was seen as the finest example of state-of-the-art technology. The term currently exists only in US political speech, meaning a rousing speech] **1** [late 19C+] (*US*) anything, or anybody, considered excellent, first-rate; thus *stem-winding*, persuasive, powerful. **2** [1940s] a battered old car [with ref. to the 'historical' image of such watches]. **3** *see* KEY WINDER *under* KEY *n.*[1].

stench-trench *n.* [1990s+] **1** the anus. **2** the vagina.

stencil *n.* [? play on SE *pencil*] [1970s–80s] (*drugs*) an extra-long marijuana cigarette.

stenner *n.* [abbr. Franken*stein*, whose monster had such a forehead] [1990s+] (*UK juv.*) a person who has a larger than average forehead.

steno *n.* [abbr.] [20C+] (*US*) a *steno*grapher, a typist.

stenog *n.* [abbr.] [1900s–60s] (*US*) a (shorthand) typist, a *stenog*rapher.

stenog *v.* [STENOG *n.*] [1900s–1940s] (*US*) to work as a (shorthand) typist.

step *n.*[1] [abbr. DOORSTEP *n.* (1)] **1** [late 19C–1900s] a slice of bread. **2** *see* DOORSTEP *n.*

SE in slang uses

IN PHRASES

□ **all the steps** *n.* [the WW1 thriller *The Thirty Nine Steps* (1915) by John Buchan] [20C+] (*bingo*) the number 39. □ **eleven steps** *n.* [the eleven steps that led to the front door of a well-known court house] [1950s] (*W.I.*) an arrest, a trial. □ **up the steps** (*also* **down the steps, up the road, ...stairs**) [the steps that lead from the cells beneath the Old Bailey up into the dock] **1** [1930s+] on trial; thus *go up the stairs/steps*, to be tried at the Old Bailey, to be sent to the Old Bailey from a lower court. **2** [1950s] to be sent to prison.

step *n.*[2] STEP-ON *n.*

step *v.* (*also* **step it**) **1** [mid-19C+] to leave. **2** [20C+] (*US campus/black*) to dance. **3** [1900s] to exist. **4** [1960s+] to start a fight. **5** [1970s–80s] (*orig. US black*) to work as a prostitute [? *stepney*, a white-slaver's current top woman; more simply her 'street-walking']. **6** [1970s+] to carry on with one's life.

IN PHRASES

□ **step around** *v. see* STEP OUT *v.* (3). □ **step fast** *v.* [1960s+] (*US black*) to do what is necessary to survive in a harsh world. □ **step it up** *v. see* STEP ON IT *under* STEP ON *v.* □ **step off** see separate entries. □ **step on** see separate entries. □ **step out** *v.* see separate entry. □ **step to** *v.* (*also* **step up**) [SE *step towards* or *step up to*] [1980s+] (*US black*) **1** to challenge. **2** to make sexual advances towards. □ **step up** *v.* [1980s+] (*drugs*) to move from selling drugs retail to distributing larger quantities wholesale.

stephen *n.* (*also* **steven**) [? STIVER *n.*; STEEVEN *n.*] [late 18C–mid-19C] money; thus *Steven's at home*, one has money.

Stephenson's Rocket *n.* [rhy. sl.] [1990s+] a pocket.

stepinfetchit *n.* **1** [1900s] (*US*) an old man with a lively step [lit. 'step and fetch it']. **2** [1930s+] (*US black*) a subservient black person, fitting willingly into the stereotyped and inferior image refined by generations of white supremacy [nickname of Lincoln Perry (1892–1985), who specialized in playing stereotypical 'dumb nigger' roles for Hollywood; he chose the nickname after a winning racehorse].

stepmother's breath *n.* [the trad. negative image of the 'wicked stepmother'] [20C+] (*Ulster*) a sudden draught of cold air.

step-off *n.* [1940s] (*US black*) a street curb.

step off *v.* **1** [1900s–20s] (*US*) to get married. **2** [1920s–40s] (*US*) to be executed. **3** [1920s+] (*US*) to die. **4** [1990s+] (*US black*) to leave. **5** [1990s+] (*US teen*) to leave alone, to stop interfering.

IN EXCLAMATIONS

□ **step off!** [1990s+] (*US black /campus/teen*) go away! leave me alone!

step-on *n.* (*also* **step**) [STEP ON *v.* (1)] [1970s+] (*drugs*) the adulteration of a narcotic drug.

step on *v.* (*also* **jump on**) [the image of lit. squashing something and thus making it appear larger than it is] [1970s+] (*drugs*) to adulterate narcotics for more profitable sales.

SE in slang uses

IN PHRASES

□ **step on it** *v.* (*also* **step it up, step on her**) ['it' being the accelerator] [1920s+] (*orig. US*) to move or drive faster, esp. as an imper.; also sometimes in fig. use. □ **step on one's cock** *v. see under* COCK *n.*[3]. □ **step on one's dick** *v. see under* DICK *n.*[1]. □ **step on one's motor** *v.* [1950s] (*US black*) to boast, to make (empty) threats. □ **step on one's tongue** *v.* [1970s] to say something one will regret. □ **step on someone's toes** *v.* (*also* **tread on someone's toes**) [mid-19C+] to annoy, to give offence to. □ **step on the gas** *v.* [1920s+] (*orig. US*) **1** to accelerate a motorcar. **2** to go faster, esp. in imper. **3** to liven up, to take action.

step out *v.* **1** [mid-19C–1900s] (*US*) to die or disappear. **2** [20C+] (*orig. US black*) to go to a party, dance or some form of entertainment. **3** [1920s+] (*US*) (*also* **step around**) to escort or go out with someone socially; usu. as *step out with*.

IN PHRASES

□ **step out on** *v.* [1950s+] (*orig. US black*) to cuckold, to commit adultery. □ **step (someone) out** *v.* [the challenging phr. 'do you want to step outside?'] [1970s–80s] (*N.Z.*) to challenge someone to a fight. □ **step someone out on the green** *v.* [the image of 'going outside' to some supposed turf] [1940s+] (*US black*) to challenge someone to a fight.

stepper *n.* **1** [mid–late 19C] the treadmill. **2** [mid-19C–1900s] a trotting-horse. **3** [late 19C] a door-step cleaner, a 'step-girl'. **4** [1910s+] (*US*) a good dancer. **5** [1920s+] (*US*) a promiscuous woman [a judgmental use of STEP OUT *v.* (2)]. **6** [1920s+] an ambitious man [he takes *steps* for self-advancement]. **7** [1980s] (*US black*) a prostitute [STEP *v.* (5)].

steppers *n.* [mid-19C] the feet.

stepping *n.* **1** [1950s+] (*US black*) working as a prostitute [STEP *v.* (5)]. **2** [2000s] (*US black*) pursuing the opposite (or same) sex [SE *step out with*].

stepping ken *n.* [SE *step*, to dance + KEN *n.*[1] (1)] [mid-19C] (*US*) a cheap dancehall.

-ster *sfx* [ult. ME, where it represents nouns of action; in SE such terms include *jokester, trickster, punster* etc. Recent sl. uses have adopted the sfx, adding it to a surname or nickname and prefixing that with *the*, e.g. the US wrestler 'Hulk' Hogan is *The Hulkster* etc] [late 17C+] a sfx implying agency.

sterics *n.* [abbr. SE *hysterics*] [mid–late 18C] hysteria.

sterks *n.* (*also* **sturks**) [abbr. SE *hysterics*] [1930s+] (*Aus.*) a fit of anger or exasperation; thus *give one the sterks*, to aggravate, to irritate.

sterky *adj.* [STERKS *n.*, but note SE *stercoraceous*, consisting of, containing, or pertaining to faeces] [1930s+] (*Aus.*) frightened, terrified; thus suffering a bout of diarrhoea, engendered by fear.

sterling *n.* [play on SE (pound) *sterling/sterling* of high quality] [19C+] (*Aus.*) one born in Britain who has emigrated to Australia.

stern *n.* **1** [late 16C+] the buttocks. **2** [1940s–50s] thus punning phr. *stern approach*, buggery or intercourse from the rear.

IN COMPOUNDS

□ **sternpost** *n.* [naut. imagery] **1** [early 19C] the buttocks. **2** [mid–late 19C] the penis. □ **sternwheeler** *n.* [play on SE *sternwheeler*, a boat propelled by a wheel at its *rear*] [1940s–70s] (*US gay*) a passive male homosexual.

IN PHRASES

□ **stern over appetite** [euph. ARSE OVER APPETITE *under* ARSE *n.*] [1930s+] (*Aus.*) head over heels.

Sterno Hilton *n.* [the use of Sterno ('canned heat') to power a camping stove] [1990s+] (*US*) a campsite.

sterrika *n.* [? Yid.] [1980s] a hard case.

stetson *adj.* [the perceived excellence of the *Stetson* hat] [1920s] (*US tramp*) of a person or thing, the very best.

steve *n.* [1910s+] (*Aus.*) a generic term of address to a man.

steve hart *v.* [rhy. sl.] **1** [1940s–50s] (*US Und.*) to start; esp. of a horserace. **2** [1980s] (*Aus.*) to fart.

Steve McQueens *n.* [rhy. sl.; ult. US movie star *Steve McQueen* (1930–80)] [2000s] jeans.

steven *n. see* STEPHEN *n.*

steve's mission *n.* [OLD STEVE *under* OLD *adj.*] [1950s] (*US drugs*) a place where a narcotics addict may buy and/or use drugs.

Stevie Wonder *n.* [rhy. sl.; ult. US singer *Stevie Wonder* (b.1950)] [1990s+] thunder.

stew *n.*[1] (*also* **stue**) **1** [19C+] a mess, a troublesome situation. **2** [1940s] (*US Und.*) nitroglycerine [var. SOUP *n.* (2)]. **3** [1980s+] (*Aus. prison*) a prearranged fight.

IN PHRASES

❑ **in a stew** [20C+ use is SE] [late 19C] sweating heavily, bathed in perspiration.

stew *n.*[2] [STEWED *adj.*[1] (1)] **1** [mid-19C+] (*US*) a drunkard. **2** [1900s–60s] a drunken carouse.

stew *n.*[3] (*also* **stewie**) [abbr.] [1960s+] a stewardess, an air hostess.

stew *v.*[1] **1** [mid-19C–1950s] to study hard. **2** [1940s] (*US Und.*) to be executed in the electric chair. **3** [1950s+] (*US*) to be irritated, concerned, worried.

stew *v.*[2] [? obs. SE *stew*, to check, to restrain] [20C+] (*W.I.*) to abort a pregnancy.

stew and blue *v.* [1980s] (*Aus.*) to look round at the wrong time.

Stewart Granger *n.* [rhy. sl.; ult. film actor Stewart Granger (1913–93)] [1980s+] **1** danger. **2** a chance, an opportunity [fig. use of danger (cf. NO DANGER *under* DANGER *n.*)].

stew bum *n.* **1** [late 19C+] a down-and-out alcoholic, the most deprived of vagrants [STEW *n.*[2] (1)]. **2** [1920s] (*US tramp*) one who eats only cheap foods [SE *stew* + BUM *n.*[3] (1)]. **3** [1920s+] a term of abuse [STEW *n.*[2] (1)].

stewed *adj.*[1] (*also* **stewed up**) **1** [mid-17C+] drunk. **2** [1920s+] crazy, or easily fooled. **3** [2000s] (*drugs*) intoxicated by a drug.

IN PHRASES

❑ **stewed as a prune** *adj.* (*also* **stewed as a goat**) [1910s+] extremely drunk. ❑ **stewed to the gills** *adj.* (*also* **stewed to the ears, ...eyeballs, ...eyebrows**) [GILLS *n.*] [1920s+] extremely drunk.

stewed *adj.*[2] [STEW *n.*[1]] [1980s+] (*US campus*) in trouble.

stewed Quaker *n.* [? its brown colour, the *Quaker* colour; or the use of such a remedy among Quakers] [late 18C–early 19C] (*US*) burnt rum with a piece of butter, 'an American remedy for a cold' (Grose 1785).

stewed, screwed and tattooed *adj. see* SCREWED, BLUED AND TATTOOED *under* SCREWED *adj.*

stewed up *adj. see* STEWED *adj.*[1].

stewer *n.* [her *stewing* up of gossip, rumours, slander etc or play on OLD HEN *under* OLD *adj.*/SE *old hen*, which would be stewed] [1940s] (*US black*) a malicious, gossiping old woman.

stew-for-beans *adj.* [1950s] (*US Und.*) equal, 'fifty-fifty'.

stewie *n.*[1] [STEWED *adj.*[1] (1)] [1940s+] (*US black*) a drunkard.

stewie *n.*[2] *see* STEW *n.*[3] (1).

stew-pit *n.* [1990s+] (*Irish*) an idiot.

stewpot *n.* [SE *stew*, a brothel + *pot*] [early–mid-17C] the vagina, spec. of a prostitute.

S.T.F.O.! *excl.* [abbr.] [1980s] (*US black*) Step The Fuck Off! an excl. denoting that someone has said something offensive or behaved unacceptably.

S the spot *v.* [1990s+] (*W.I.*) to leave.

stibber-gibber *n.* [Beale (*DSUE*, 1984) suggests a corruption of two typical contemporary names, *Stephen* and *Gilbert*, generic for lying clerks] [mid-16C] a habitual liar.

Stick, the *n.* [abbr.] [1990s+] (*US black teen*) Candlestick Park, in San Francisco.

stick *n.* **1** pertaining to the shape. (**a**) [18C+] the penis; thus (*US gay*) *bent stick, dead stick*, an impotent penis. (**b**) [mid-19C] (*UK Und.*) a breast-pin. (**c**) [mid-19C+] (*US*) a baseball bat. (**d**) [late 19C–1960s] (*UK Und.*) a crowbar, a jemmy. (**e**) [late 19C+] a police truncheon. (**f**) [1920s–40s] (*US Und./prison*) a blackjack. (**g**) [1930s–40s] a clarinet. (**h**) [1930s+] (*US gambling*) a croupier [the croupier's rake or *stick*]. (**i**) [1940s+] (*US*) a billiard or pool cue; thus *stick hall*, a poolroom. (**j**) [1980s+] (*US black*) a knife. (**k**) [1990s+] (*US campus*) a surfboard. (**l**) [2000s] (*US*) a manual gear lever, thus a car with manual gears. **2** in senses of solidity, of being 'wooden' or 'cross-grained'. (**a**) [early 18C] as *stick of wood*, a fool. (**b**) [mid–late 18C] a sermon [? the 'wooden' delivery of some sermons or the wooden pulpit]. (**c**) [19C+] an awkward or dull person; since 1950s also used affectionately, e.g. *not a bad old stick*. (**d**) [2000s] (*N.Z.*) a friend, esp. as a term of address. **3** [late 18C+] (*UK Und.*) (*also* **candy stick**) a pistol, usu. pl.; thus *stow your sticks!* hide your pistols!; *flash one's sticks*, to draw but not (yet) fire one's pistols [abbr. *shooting stick*]. **4** in context of alcohol. (**a**) [19C–1950s] a shot of spirits, usu. rum or brandy added to coffee or tea; usu. in phr. *with a stick in it* [? Ger. schtuck, a piece]. (**b**) [1930s] (*US*) one who deals in illicit liquor. (**c**) [1940s] (*US black*) a drunkard. **5** [19C+] a piece of furniture; usu. in pl. **6** pertaining to shape, in senses of smoking/drugs. (**a**) [late 19C+] a cigarette. (**b**) [1910s] a quantity of opium. (**c**) [1930s–40s] an opium pipe. (**d**) [1930s+] a marijuana cigarette; ext. as *stick of pot, stick of tea, stick of weed*; thus *stick man*, a marijuana smoker. (**e**) [1940s] (*US drug*) a very thinly rolled marijuana cigarette. (**f**) [1990s+] (*US drug*) an injection of heroin. (**g**) *see* SHERM STICK *under* SHERM *n.* **7** a decoy or accomplice. (**a**) [1920s+] (*US Und.*) a criminal's accomplice who poses as an ordinary person to distract or influence the victims of an intended crime or swindle. (**b**) [1920s+] (*US Und./gambling*) an accomplice who loses deliberately so as to encourage the victim to continue playing. (**c**) [2000s] (*US prison*) a close friend. **8** [1940s+] (*US*) (*also* **plank**) a bar; thus *behind the stick*, working as a bartender. **9** [1960s–70s] (*UK/US black*) a prostitute [her role as a *stick*, i.e. tool, who solves a pimp's financial problems]. **10** [1960s+] a reprimand, a criticism; verbal aggression in general; usu. as *get stick*, to be on the receiving end of these attacks; also in *give someone stick*. **11** [1970s] violence. **12** [1990s+] (*US prison*) (*also* **long stick, sharp stick**) influence, 'clout'. **13** [1990s+] (*US black*) an act of sexual intercourse. **14** *see* SCHTICK *n.*

pertaining to drugs

IN PHRASES

❑ **blast a stick** *v.* [1960s+] (*drugs*) to smoke marijuana. ❑ **blow a stick** *v.* [1950s+] (*drugs*) to smoke cannabis. ❑ **break a stick** *v.* [1950s+] to smoke a marijuana cigarette. ❑ **hot stick** *n.* [HOT *adj.* (5)] [1950s+] (*drugs*) a marijuana cigarette. ❑ **stick of gage** *n.* (*also* **stick of dynamite, ...pot, ...tea, ...weed**) [GAGE *n.*[2]/POT *n.*[3]] [1940s–60s] a marijuana cigarette.

pertaining to the penis

IN COMPOUNDS

❑ **stick book** *n.* [1980s] (*Aus.*) a pornographic book or magazine. ❑ **stickman** *n. see* separate entry. ❑ **stick pussy** *n.* [PUSSY *n.* (1)] [1970s+] (*US gay/prison*) **1** the penis, in a homosexual context. **2** a young inmate, forced into homosexuality. ❑ **sticksman** *n. see* separate entry.

IN PHRASES

❑ **bash the stick** *v.* [1950s+] (*Aus.*) to masturbate. ❑ **beat the stick** *v.* [1990s+] to masturbate. ❑ **blow stick** *n.* [BLOW *v.*[2]] [1960s+] the penis. ❑ **dip one's stick** *v.* [1970s] of a man, to have sexual intercourse. ❑ **play with one's stick** *v.* [1970s] to masturbate.

general uses

IN PHRASES

❑ **dry stick** *n.* [SE *dry*] [20C+] an unpleasant, humourless person. ❑ **give someone stick** *v.* [1960s+] to threaten, to criticize roughly, to beat up.

SE in slang uses

IN COMPOUNDS

❑ **stick and bangers** *n.* [SE *banger*, that which bangs together] [late 19C] **1** a billiard cue and the balls with which one plays. **2** the penis and testes. ❑ **stickman** *n. see* separate entry. ❑ **stick slinger** *n.* [mid-19C] **1** (*Aus.*) a pimp. **2** a violent thief.

IN PHRASES

❑ **big stick** *n.* [? their real or fig. truncheon or similar badge of office/chastisement. Note Theodore Roosevelt's dictum: 'Speak softly and carry a big stick'] [20C+] (*orig. US*) **1** an important person. **2** a figure of authority, esp. a policeman or foreman. **3** fig., authority, violence. **4** [1930s] (*US*) dynamite. ❑ **carry the stick** *v. see* CARRY THE BANNER *under* BANNER *n.* ❑ **drop sticks** *v.* [1960s+] (*UK/W.I. Und.*) to work as a pickpocket. ❑ **give (some) stick** *v.* [1960s+] to hit, to assault, both lit. and fig. ❑ **have the stick** *v.* [1950s+] (*Aus.*) to be finished, to be permanently damaged. ❑ **keep at the stick's end** *v.* [late 19C–1920s] to snub, to keep 'at arm's length'. ❑ **off one's stick** *adj.* [1960s] mad, crazy. ❑ **on the stick** *adj.* **1** [1950s+] efficient, aware, in control; thus *get on the stick*, to get down to work [the gearstick of a car or joystick of an aircraft, both of which exert control]. **2** *see* UP THE STICK below. ❑ **put the stick about** *v.* [1960s+] to use violence, usu. in a criminal context. ❑ **short end (of the stick)** *n.* (*also* **dirty end (of the stick), raw end (of the stick), shitty end (of the stick), shitten end of a brick, short end of the funnel, short end of the shitstick**) [the *funnel* is that which feeds meat into a mincing machine] [mid-19C+] (*orig. US*) unfair treatment, deliberately engineered bad luck. ❑ **sticks and stones** *n. see* separate entry. ❑ **swinging the stick** *n. see under* SWING *v.* ❑ **up the stick** *adj.* (*also* **on the stick**) [var. UP THE POLE *adj.*[2]] [1930s+] (*orig. Aus.*) pregnant.

IN EXCLAMATIONS

❑ **strike me up a stick!** *see under* STRIKE ME…! *excl.*

stick, the *n.* [? the *sticky* discharge of gonorrhoea] [late 19C+] venereal disease.

stick *adj.* [mid-19C+] a synon. of SE *stark*, as in phr. *stick staring wild.*

stick *v.* **1** in sexual senses. (**a**) [17C+] (*also* **stick up**) of a man, to have heterosexual sexual intercourse; thus *double stick*, two bouts of intercourse in succession. (**b**) [1960s] to sodomize another man. **2** in the context of extortion. (**a**) [late 17C+] to cheat or swindle, esp. to overcharge. (**b**) [mid-19C+] to take in, to impose upon. (**c**) [1910s+] (*also* **stick for**) to demand money from. **3** to attack, lit. or fig. (**a**) [mid-18C–mid-19C; 1950s+] (*US*) to hit; thus *stuck*. (**b**) [20C+] (*US/UK prison*) to charge with a crime. (**c**) [1900s] to amaze. (**d**) [1920s+] (*US black*) to attack, verbally or physically. (**e**) [1920s+] (*US*) to defeat. (**f**) [1950s] to punish. **4** to pierce the flesh. (**a**) [mid-18C+] to stab with a knife. (**b**) [late 19C] to bayonet. (**c**) [1940s+] (*US*) to inject with a hypodermic syringe. **5** to render lit. or fig. immobile. (**a**) [mid–late 19C] to stymie, to bring or come to a stop, to render or become unable to move. (**b**) [late 19C+] to nonplus; thus *stuck for*, bereft of ideas. **6** [late 19C+] (*also* **stick out**) to tolerate, to put up with. **7** [1940s–60s] (*drugs*) to supply or use marijuana; esp. in phr. *are you sticking?* **8** [1940s+] fig. to dump something in the rubbish, to throw it away; usu. used in a hostile conversation [abbr. of *stick it up your arse!* at SHOVE IT UP YOUR ARSE! *excl.*]. **9** [1950s] to give to, to pass over. **10** [1950s] to link one to. **11** *see* STICK AROUND below.

IN PHRASES

❑ **stick a bust** *v. see under* BUST *n.*

SE in slang uses

IN COMPOUNDS

❑ **stick-flams** *n.* (*also* **stick famms, stickhams**) [FAM *n.*[1], for which *flams* is prob. a misprint; thus lit. 'stick [to hands']] [late 17C–mid-19C] gloves. ❑ **stick-jaw** *n.* **1** [early 19C–1950s] any sweet food, e.g. a pudding, a sweet, e.g. toffee, that is hard to chew. **2** [1910s–20s] anything seen as extremely tedious. ❑ **stickman/sticksman** *n. see* separate entries. ❑ **stick partner** *n. see* separate entry. ❑ **stick-ups** *n. see* separate entry.

IN PHRASES

❑ **stick a fork in them, they're done** [1940s+] (*US*) a phr. of condemnatory dismissal. ❑ **stick and lift** *v.* [the actions of digging] [late 19C–1920s] to eke out an impoverished life. ❑ **stick a point** *v.* [mid-17C; late 19C–1920s] to settle an argument. ❑ **stick around** *v.* (*also* **stick on, stick**) [late 19C+] (*orig. Can./US*) to stay close by; often as imper. ❑ **stick as close as shit on a blanket** *v.* [1930s+] to stay very close. ❑ **stick a tail on** *v.* [TAIL *n.* (3)] [1960s+] to admire sexually; usu. in phr. *I could stick a tail on that.* ❑ **stick-at-it** *n.* [1900s] a persistent, dedicated person. ❑ **stick away** *v.* [20C+] to hide something or someone away. ❑ **stick fat** *v.* [1980s+] **1** (*Aus. Und.*) to maintain silence rather than betraying one's peers. **2** (*Aus.*) to maintain one's loyalty. ❑ **stick for** *v.* **1** *see* sense 2c above. **2** *see* STICK UP FOR *v.* ❑ **stick for drinks** *v.* [late 19C] to play and win a toss of the dice (occas. turn of cards) to determine who pays for the next round of drinks. ❑ **stick in for** *v. see* STICK SOMEONE FOR below. ❑ **stick in one's gizzard** *v.* [late 17C+] to be unpalatable, to infuriate, to be unacceptable. ❑ **stick in one's throat** *v.* (*also* **stick in one's craw, ...crop, ...neck**) [20C+] to be unpalatable, to infuriate, to be unacceptable. ❑ **stick-in-the-middle** *n.* [although the dumpling is shaped like a doughnut and might have had a stick pushed through its centre to make the requisite hole, the term more likely refers to the way the heavy dumpling *sticks to* one's stomach] [1950s] (*W.I.*) a form of dumpling. ❑ **stick-in-the-mud** *n. see* separate entry. ❑ **stick in the ribs** *n.* [19C] a thick soup. ❑ **stick it** *v. see* separate entries. ❑ **stick on** *v. see* STICK AROUND above. ❑ **stick one on** *v. see under* ONE *n.*[1]. ❑ **stick one's bib in** *v. see under* BIB *n.* ❑ **stick one's duck in the mud** *v.* (*also* **get some mud for the duck**) **1** [1970s] (*US*) of a man, to have sexual intercourse. **2** [1980s+] (*US gay*) to have anal intercourse. ❑ **stick oneself up (to be)** *v.* [late 19C] to claim, to make oneself out to be. ❑ **stick one's oar in** *v. see* SHOVE ONE'S OAR IN *under* SHOVE *v.* ❑ **stick one's spoon in the wall** *v.* [mid–late 19C] to die. ❑ **stick on (the price)** *v.* [mid-19C+] to overcharge. ❑ **stick out/stick out for** *see* separate entries. ❑ **stick out like a sore thumb** *v. see* separate entry. ❑ **stick solid** *v. see under* SOLID *adv.*[1]. ❑ **stick someone for** *v.* **1** [late 19C+] (*also* **stick in for**) to take from someone, usu. but invariably money. **2** [1910s+] (*also* **stick someone with**) to make someone pay a bill; to borrow money without repaying it. **3** [1920s+] (*also* **stick someone with**) fig. to burden someone with something, e.g. a jail sentence. ❑ **stick someone with** *v.* [1950s+] to make responsible for a usu. unpleasant responsibility or something unpleasant, e.g. a faulty computer. ❑ **stick (the) dick to** *v. see under* DICK *n.*[1]. ❑ **stick to** *v. see* separate entry. ❑ **stick up** *v.* **1** *see* sense 1a above. **2** *see* separate entries.

IN EXCLAMATIONS

❑ **stick a pin in there!** **1** [early–mid-18C] wait! hold it! **2** [mid-19C–1940s] note carefully! bear in mind! ❑ **stick 'em up!** [the first-use date reflects the probable creation of the phr. for the Western film, rather than in the 19C world that such films claimed to portray] [1930s+] put your hands up! a robber's trad. order to their victim to raise their hands above their head. ❑ **stick it!** *see* separate entry. ❑ **stick that/this for a game of soldiers!** *see* FUCK THAT/THIS FOR A GAME OF SOLDIERS! *under* FUCK *v.* ❑ **stick with it!** [1960s+] a general excl. of farewell.

stickability *n.* [STICK *v.* (6)] [late 19C+] the ability to endure or preserve.

stick-em-up kid *n. see* STICK-UP MAN *under* STICK-UP *n.*

sticker *n.*[1] **1** [mid-19C] (*UK Und.*) a lengthy period, a stay. **2** [mid-19C–1900s] a guest who overstays their welcome. **3** [mid-19C–1910s] a commodity that does not find a ready sale [it SE *sticks* in the shop]. **4** [late 19C–1950s] one who 'sticks to' his beliefs, job etc. **5** [1970s] (*UK police/Und.*) a prisoner who does not get bail but stays on remand until their trial.

sticker *n.*[2] [SE *stick*, to pierce] **1** [mid–late 19C] a butcher. **2** [mid-19C+] a pointed, stabbing weapon, e.g. a knife, rather than one that is used to slash. **3** [1920s–60s] (*US tramp*) a scarf pin. **4** [1960s] the penis. **5** [1960s] a narcotics addict.

sticker *n.*[3] [one is *stuck* for a response] [mid-19C–1950s] a difficult, surprising, embarrassing or pointed question.

sticker *n.*[4] **1** [late 19C–1940s] (*US*) a thorn, a burr [it SE *sticks* to one's clothes]. **2** [1900s–40s] (*US*) a postage stamp. **3** [1990s+] (*Aus./N.Z.*) a traffic ticket, which was orig. stuck to one's windscreen.

IN COMPOUNDS

❑ **sticker-licker** *n.* [the SE *stickers* they affix to cars] **1** [1960s+] (*S.Afr.*) a judge. **2** [1980s] (*Aus., South*) a parking police officer. ❑ **sticker shock** *n.* [the price sticker] [1970s+] (*US*) a shock from learning the price of something.

stickers *n.* [1910s] (*US tramp*) beggars who pretend to be selling sticking plaster to gain an approach to a possible donor.

sticker-up *n.* [STICK UP *v.*[1] (1)] [late 19C] (*Aus.*) one who stages hold-ups and robberies.

Stickeys, the *n. see* STICKIES, THE *n.*

stickhams *n. see* STICK-FLAMS *under* STICK *n.*

Stickies, the *n.* (*also* **Stickeys, the**) [? the Officials *stick to* trad. IRA policies or they *stick on* their Easter lilies while the Provisionals use pins. Share suggests 'adhesive employed on identity badge'] [1960s+] the Official Irish Republican Army.

stickies *n.* [play on SE *sticky-buds*] [1980s+] (*N.Z. drugs*) the potent flowering tops of marijuana plants.

sticking *adj.* (*US black*) **1** [1960s–70s] of a person, attractive. **2** [2000s] of clothes, looking good on the wearer.

sticking-plaster *n.* **1** [1910s–20s] a very boring visit, made by an acquaintance [the visitor *sticks around*]. **2** [1940s] (*UK Und.*) a (lengthy) prison sentence [the criminal *sticks* in prison]. **3** *see* PLASTER *n.* (3c).

stickings *n.* [mid–late 19C] butcher's off-cuts laid out on the chopping board, to which they stick.

stick-in-the-mud *n.* (*also* **stick-in-the-ditcher**) [early 19C+] an old-fashioned, conservative person.

stick it *v.* (*also* **stick in**) **1** [mid-19C+] to persist, to continue in something, esp. a job. **2** [2000s] (*US teen*) to succeed in an achievement or trick.

IN PHRASES

❑ **stick it in** *v.* (*also* **stick it on**) **1** [early 19C+] to charge extortionately. **2** [20C+] (*Aus.*) to work hard. ❑ **stick it into** *v.* **1** [mid-19C] to victimize. **2** [20C+] (*Aus.*) to beg for a loan. **3** [20C+] (*Irish*) (*also* **stick it off**) to have sexual intercourse. ❑ **stick it on** *v.* **1** [1950s] to accuse unfairly, to 'frame up'. **2** [1950s+] to hit, to beat. **3** [1980s] (*N.Z.*) to have sexual intercourse. **4** *see* STICK IT IN above. **5** *see* STICK IT UP below. ❑ **stick it off** *v. see* STICK IT INTO above. ❑ **stick it out** *v.* [mid-19C+] to persist, to tolerate a situation (esp. an unpleasant one). ❑ **stick it to** *v.* **1** [1940s+] (*US*) to treat harshly; to assault violently. **2** [1970s+] to defraud; to take advantage of. **3** [1970s+] (*US*) to copulate. **4** [1990s+] to tease, to malign, to attack. **5** [2000s] in fig. use, to consume. ❑ **stick it up** *v.* (*also* **stick it on**) **1** [mid-19C+] to leave a bill unpaid; to place a purchase on account [i.e. to *stick it* on the running bill]. **2** [mid-19C+] to take advantage of, esp. financially [the image is of *sticking* something sharp *up* the victim]. **3** [1990s+] to act uncompromisingly in pursuit of victory. ❑ **stick it up someone's ass** *v.* (*also* **tuck it up someone's ass**) [1980s+] **1** (*US*) to betray, to let down. **2** to humiliate. ❑ **stick it up to** *v.* [early 19C+] to charge to, to give responsibility to.

IN EXCLAMATIONS

❑ **stick it up your...!** *see* SHOVE IT UP YOUR ARSE! *excl.*

stick it! *excl.* [*up your arse/ass* is assumed] [1920s+] (*orig. US*) a derog. reply to a question, i.e. 'What shall I do with this?', or in response to an opinion with which one disagrees.

IN EXCLAMATIONS

❑ **stick it in your ear!** (*also* **stick it in your eye! ...up the sewer! ...up your chimney!**) [1920s+] a general dismissive excl. ❑ **stick it up your arse!/butt!** *see* SHOVE IT UP YOUR ARSE! *excl.* ❑ **stick it up your arse sideways!** [1990s+] a general excl. of dismissal, abuse. ❑ **stick it up your cunt!** [CUNT *n.* (1)] [1930s+] (*Aus.*) a general expression of disdain, dismissal, rejecting the previous speaker's idea, opinion, insult etc. ❑ **stick it up your jacksy!** *see under* JACKSIE *n.*[1]. ❑ **stick it up your jumper!** (*also* **stuff it up your jumper**) [1930s+] (*usu. teen*) an excl. rejecting the previous speaker's idea, opinion, insult etc. ❑ **stick it up your nose!** *see* SHOVE IT UP YOUR NOSE! *excl.*

stickman *n.*[1] **1** [mid-19C+] the member of a pickpocket gang who is handed the stolen goods by the actual pickpocket and who must also try to hinder any attempts to capture their confederate by police or public. **2** [1970s+] a store detective.

stickman *n.*[2] **1** [1910s+] (*US*) a croupier [the rake or *stick* with which they collect and distribute chips]. **2** [1950s+] a good lover, a potent, experienced man [STICK *n.* (1)]. **3** [1960s–70s] (*US black*) a police officer.

stickman *n.*[3] [he *sticks with* his friends] [1990s+] (*US black*) a close ally, a backup, a lookout.

stick of chalk *n.* [rhy. sl.] [20C+] (*Aus./UK*) a walk.

stick of rock *n.* [rhy. sl. = COCK *n.*[3]] [1990s+] the penis.

stick-out *n.* [1930s+] (*US*) **1** (*also* **standout**) a horse that seems a certain winner. **2** an outstanding sportsman.

stick out (for) *v.* **1** [mid-19C+] to persist in one's demand. **2** [late 19C] to argue with.

stick out like a sore thumb *v.* (*also* **stick out a mile, ...a foot, ...like a fly on a wedding cake, ...like a wart on a hebrew's nose, stick up like a sore thumb**) [late 19C+] to be very conspicuous or obvious.

stick partner *n.* [var. STICKMAN *n.*[3] (1)] [1990s+] (*US black*) a close friend, a fellow member of a street gang.

sticks *n.*[1] **1** [early 19C+] the legs. **2** [1910s] a thin person. **3** [1910s–40s] a person missing one or both legs. **4** [1930s+] (*US black*) matches.

sticks *n.*[2] [they both SE *stick in their heels*] (*S.Afr.*) **1** [late 19C] an obstinate horse. **2** [20C+] an obstinate person.

sticks *n.*[3] [SE *stick*, as a generic for the world of trees and nature + theatrical jargon *stick*, a town outside the regular touring circuits and far beyond New York City] [20C+] (*orig. US*) the world beyond the big cities, esp. small towns and hamlets.

sticks and stones *n.*[1] [ext. STICK *n.* (5)] [mid–late 19C] furniture.

sticks and stones *n.*[2] [rhy. sl.] [20C+] bones.

sticksing *n.* [STICKSMAN *n.*[1] (1)] [1970s+] (*UK black*) the practice of picking pockets.

sticksman *n.*[1] [? one *sticks* one's hand in another's pocket] [1970s+] (*UK black*) a pickpocket.

sticksman *n.*[2] [STICK *n.* (1)] [1980s] a womanizer.

stick to *v.* [17C+] **1** to remain loyal. **2** to maintain a position or opinion.

DERIVATIVES

❑ **stick-to-it-iveness** *n.* [mid-19C+] persistence, determination.

IN PHRASES

❑ **stick to one's knitting** *v.* (*also* **mind one's knitting, 'tend one's own knitting**) [mid-18C; late 19C+] (*US*) to mind one's own business; to get down to the task in hand.

stickum *n.* (*US*) **1** [20C+] glue, cement. **2** [1960s+] any viscous substance.

stick-up *n.* **1** [mid-19C+] a hold-up, an armed robbery. **2** [20C+] an armed robber. **3** [1980s] (*Aus./N.Z.*) a hold-up, a delay, a problem; thus as v.

IN COMPOUNDS

❑ **stick-up man** *n.* (*also* **stick-up artist, ...boy, ...guy, ...kid, stick-em-up kid**) [STICK UP *v.*[1] (1) + ARTIST *n.* (1)/GUY *n.*[2] (1)/KID *n.*[1] (4)] [1910s+] an armed robber.

stick up *v.*[1] [the shout of 'stick up your hands!'; senses 2–6 are fig./ext. uses of sense 1] **1** [mid-19C+] (*orig. Aus.*) to rob, to hold up. **2** [late 19C+] to blackmail, to extort from; to beg. **3** [1900s] (*Aus.*) to summon, e.g. a bus to stop. **4** [1910s] to take money from legally, e.g. through gambling. **5** [1930s+] in fig. use, to cost money. **6** [1940s] (*US/N.Z. Und.*) of the police, to hold for questioning.

stick up *v.*[2] [the sum is *stuck on* a running account] **1** [mid-19C+] to place on account. **2** [late 19C] (*UK Und.*) to leave a companion with an undue share of a tavern bill.

stick up *v.*[3] [late 19C] to hold one's ground in an argument.

IN PHRASES

□ **stick up to** *v.* [mid-19C+] to challenge, to oppose, esp. when one is ostensibly at a disadvantage.

stick up *v.*[4] **1** [late 19C] (*UK Und.*) to keep someone waiting. **2** [late 19C–1950s] (*Aus./N.Z.*) to hinder, to impede, to puzzle, to confuse. **3** [late 19C+] (*US*) to break an appointment; to abscond.

stick up *v.*[5] [1920s+] (*UK Und.*) to put forward, usu. to offer a name to the police.

stick up for *v.* (*also* **stick for**) [STICK UP *v.*[3] (1)] [mid-19C+] to defend, to champion.

stick up like a sore thumb *v.* *see* STICK OUT LIKE A SORE THUMB *V.*

stick-ups *n.* [mid-19C] stiff shirt collars.

stick up to *v.* [mid-19C; 1900s] to court, to pursue sexually.

stickville *n.* [STICKS *n.*[3] (1) + -VILLE *sfx*[1] (1)] [20C+] the world beyond the big cities.

sticky *n.* **1** [mid-19C] sealing wax. **2** [late 19C+] sticking plaster. **3** [1920s–60s] sticky buns. **4** [1930s+] sticky tape. **5** [1970s+] (*US gay*) semen. **6** [1980s+] a cannabis cigarette [one *sticks* two or more cigarette papers together].

sticky *adj.*[1] **1** [mid-19C+] (*US*) mawkish, sentimental. **2** [late 19C+] of weather, muggy. **3** [late 19C+] of a person, awkward, uncooperative, punctilious, prone to cause trouble. **4** [1910s+] of circumstances, awkward, presenting great difficulty, disagreeable because of hardship or danger. **5** [1930s+] of a social function, slow to start, stiff, uncomfortable. **6** [1930s+] unpleasant. **7** [2000s] pertaining to (commercial) sex.

SE in slang uses

IN COMPOUNDS

□ **sticky spud gun** *n.* [the ejaculated semen] [1990s+] the penis.

sticky *adj.*[2] [STICKYBEAK *n.*] [1940s+] (*Aus./N.Z.*) inquisitive, curious.

stickybeak *n.* [1920s+] (*Aus./N.Z.*) **1** an inquisitive person, one who *sticks* in their BEAK *n.*[2]. **2** an inquisitive look; thus *have a sticky*, have a look around.

stickybeak *v.* [STICKYBEAK *n.*] [1930s+] (*Aus./N.Z.*) to pry, to snoop; thus *stickybeaking*, prying, 'poking one's nose in'.

sticky bun *n.* [rhy. sl.] [20C+] a son.

sticky fingers *n.* [1940s+] a thief.

IN COMPOUNDS

□ **sticky-fingered** *adj.* [1940s+] larcenous.

IN PHRASES

□ **play sticky fingers** *v.* [1960s] to rob.

sticky toffee *n.* [rhy. sl.] [1970s] coffee.

stiff *n.*[1] **1** [late 18C+] an erection; thus [1970s+] (*US black*) *sport a stiff*, to have an erection. **2** [late 18C+] a corpse, also used fig. **3** pertaining to any form of document. (**a**) [early 19C–1930s] (*also* **cross-stiff**) paper, a document, esp. a promissory note or bill of exchange, a clandestine letter. (**b**) [mid-19C] attrib., pertaining to a bill as opposed to cash. (**c**) [mid-19C–1900s] (*US Und.*) a newspaper. (**d**) [mid-19C–1930s] a currency note or cheque, whether genuine or forged. (**e**) [mid-19C+] (*Aus./N.Z./US/UK Und.*) a note, usu. between prisoners or passed illicitly into a prison by a relation etc. (**f**) [late 19C] a poster. (**g**) [late 19C–1910s] a hawker's licence, or similar licence. (**h**) [late 19C–1930s] paper money. (**i**) [late 19C–1940s] (*US Und.*) a piece of counterfeit money. (**j**) [late 19C–1960s] a letter. (**k**) [20C+] (*Aus./N.Z.*) a summons from the police. (**l**) [1910s] the identification of a person targeted to be murdered. (**m**) [1910s] (*US Und.*) a prescription. **4** in fig./ext. uses of sense 2. (**a**) [late 19C+] (*US*) a penniless man, a wastrel, a tramp, a migratory or unskilled worker. (**b**) [late 19C+] (*orig. N.Z./US*) a disagreeable, or contemptible person; also used joc./affectionately. (**c**) [late 19C+] (*US*) a mean, grasping person. (**d**) [late 19C+] an average person, often with a description, e.g. WORKING STIFF *n.* (**e**) [20C+] (*US Und.*) a funeral. (**f**) [20C+] a drunkard. (**g**) [20C+] (*horseracing*) a useless, losing horse [abbr. STIFF 'UN *n.*]. (**h**) [20C+] (*US*) any failure, a flop; in sport, a second-rater. (**i**) [1900s–40s] (*US tramp*) a tramp that has a job or occupation.

IN COMPOUNDS

□ **stiff dealer** *n.* [early 19C] a dealer in promissory notes. □ **stiff dodger** *n.* [late 19C] one who borrows against fraudulent promissory notes. □ **stiff-fencer** *n.* [-FENCER *sfx* (1)] [mid-19C] a street-seller of writing paper. □ **stiff wagon** *n.* [1910s] (*US Und.*) a hearse.

IN PHRASES

□ **big stiff** *n.* [20C+] (*orig. US*) a general term of abuse, a fool; often as direct address, *you big stiff!* □ **bit of stiff** *n.* **1** [late 19C] an erection. **2** [mid-19C–1900s] money as notes or bills of exchange; thus *do/take a/the bit of stiff*, to accept a post-dated cheque or promissory note. □ **board stiff** *n.* [1900s–40s] (*US*) a 'sandwich man'. □ **cattle stiff** *n.* [1910s–20s] (*US tramp*) a cowboy. □ **governor's stiff** *n.* [late 19C] (*US*) a pardon. □ **line stiff** *n.* [1930s] (*US tramp*) a tramp who spends all day in different bread lines. □ **pencil stiff** *n.* [1960s] (*US*) a clerk. □ **proper stiff** *n.* [PROPER *adj.* (2)] [1910s–20s] (*US tramp*) a tramp who refuses to perform manual labour. □ **pub stiff** *n.* [1940s] (*N.Z.*) a lookout or sentinel acting on behalf of a licensee selling alcoholic drinks after the legal closing time. □ **ring stiff** *n.* [1920s] (*US tramp*) an itinerant seller of worthless jewellery at fraudulently inflated prices.

stiff *n.*[2] [1900s] (*US*) a lie.

stiff *adj.*[1] [SE *stiff*, rigid] **1** [mid-18C+] (*orig. US*) drunk; esp. very drunk and passed out cold; thus ext. *stiff as a board*. **2** [mid-18C+] dead. **3** [late 19C] unconscious. **4** [1910s] (*Aus.*) uncompetitive. **5** [1960s] (*US*) (*also* **stiffened**) intoxicated by a drug.

IN PHRASES

□ **bore stiff** *v.* [var. on SE *bore rigid* + SE *stiff*, corpse-like; one is rendered virtually dead by tedium] [20C+] (*orig. US*) to bore completely. □ **go stiff** *v.* [late 19C] (*Aus.*) to lose (a race) deliberately. □ **knock-'em-stiff** *n.* [mid-19C–1900s] (*US*) strong whisky. □ **knock stiff** *v.* [mid-19C–1920s] (*US*) **1** to knock unconscious or to shoot. **2** to amaze or impress.

stiff *adj.*[2] [fig. uses of SE] **1** [early 19C+] strong, usu. of liquor, e.g. *a stiff drink, a stiff one, stiff 'un*. **2** [early 19C+] demanding, difficult. **3** [mid-19C] (*UK Und.*) reliable, staunch. **4** [mid-19C+] (*US*) expensive; thus adv. *stiffish*, expensively. **5** [1920s+] of a blow, hard, painful. **6** [1950s] (*US prison*) of a sentence, long.

IN COMPOUNDS

□ **stiff lad** *n.* [mid-19C] (*UK Und.*) someone who is dependable, whether as a source of money or support.

SE in slang uses

pertaining to an erection

IN COMPOUNDS

□ **stiff and stout** *n.* [mid-17C–19C] the erect penis. □ **stiff deity** *n.* [late 17C–19C] the erect penis. □ **stiff lock** *n.* [rhy. sl. on COCK *n.*[3] (1)] [1990s+] a morning erection, experienced on waking up. □ **stiff stander** *n.* [mid-17C–19C] an erection; the erect penis; thus adj. *stiff-standing*.

general uses

IN COMPOUNDS

□ **stiff-arm** *v.* [1940s+] (*US*) to mistreat, to snub, to push aside. □ **stiff-arsed** *adj.* (*also* **stiffassed**) [-ARSED *sfx*/-ASSED *sfx*] [1930s+] supercilious, arrogant, standoffish. □ **stiff-ass** *adj.* [-ASS *sfx*] [1960s–70s] a general term of derision. □ **stiff bikkies** *n.* (*also* **stiff biccies, ...bickies, tough biccies, ...bickies, ...bickkies**) [STIFF *adj.*[2] (2)/TOUGH *adj.* (1) + BIKKIES *n.*] [1970s+] (*Aus./N.Z.*) tough luck; the inference is that the speaker has very little actual sympathy. □ **stiff cheddar** *n.* (*also* **stiff cheese, ...luck, ...turps**) [play on *HARD CHEESE under* HARD *adj.*] [1910s+] (*N.Z./Aus.*) bad luck. □ **stiff one** *n.* **1** *see* STIFF

'UN *n.* (2). **2** *see* STIFF 'UN *n.* (3). ❑ **stiff rump** *n.* [early 18C–early 19C] a pompous, arrogant person; thus *stiff-rumped*, arrogant, pompous. ❑ **stiff shirt** *n. see* STUFFED SHIRT *n.* ❑ **stiff shit** *n.* [fig. use of SHIT *n.* (1)] [1980s+] (*Aus.*) hard luck; the inference is that the speaker has very little actual sympathy. ❑ **stiff 'un** *n. see* separate entry.

IN PHRASES

❑ **get on some stiff time** *v.* [ety. unknown] [1930s–70s] (*US black*) to succeed, esp. in an illicit, but profitable, occupation. ❑ **stiff as a crutch** *adj.* [late 19C+] (*Aus./N.Z.*) **1** physically stiff. **2** completely penniless. ❑ **stiff as a poker** *adj.* (*also* **stiff as a beaver board, ...pike-staff, ...ramrod, ...starfish**) [mid-18C+] very stiff. ❑ **stiff in the back** *adj.* [i.e. SE *unbending*] [late 19C] resolute, determined. ❑ **stiff on** *adj.* [1910s] (*Aus.*) keen on. ❑ **stiff out** *v.* [1990s+] to die.

stiff *adj.*[3] [late 19C–1930s] **1** of a competitor, certain to win. **2** of a competition, a certainty.

stiff *adj.*[4] [late 19C+] (*orig. Aus./N.Z.*) **1** impoverished; thus *stiff and swagless*, with neither money nor possessions. **2** unlucky, unfortunate. **3** unacceptable. **4** as excl.

stiff *adj.*[5] [1950s] (*US*) of a cheque, counterfeit, fraudulent.

stiff *v.*[1] [? the response, 'I say, that's a bit stiff,' to such an outburst] [late 19C–1960s] to curse, to swear.

stiff *v.*[2] [i.e. to treat as a form of STIFF *n.*[1] (4f)] (*orig. US*) **1** [20C+] to lie, to mislead. **2** [1950s+] to cheat, to swindle, to rob. **3** [1950s+] to fail to tip a waiter, doorman etc [to become a STIFF *n.*[1] (4c)]. **4** [1960s] to transmit misleading or lying information. **5** [1970s+] (*US*) to mistreat, to snub, to push aside. **6** [2000s] to fail, e.g. of a film release.

DERIVATIVES

❑ **stiffing** *n.* [1990s+] robbery, swindling.

IN PHRASES

❑ **stiffin' and jivin'** *n.* [JIVE *v.*[1] (2); note jazz use *stiff and jive*, to play flashily but with little genuine skill] [1930s–50s] (*US black*) making unreal, empty conversation.

SE in slang uses

IN PHRASES

❑ **stiff (on) the stroll** *v.* [one stands *stiff*, i.e. upright + STROLL *n.*] [1930s–40s] (*US black*) to stand on the corner.

stiff *v.*[3] [STIFF *n.*[1] (2)] **1** [1910s+] to cause death, to kill, to murder. **2** [1990s+] to destroy.

stiff *v.*[4] [STIFF *n.*[1] (1)] [1930s+] of a man, to have sexual intercourse with.

stiff *adv.* [mid-19C+] to a great (and unpleasant) extent.

stiffen *v.*[1] [ext. STIFF *v.*[3] (1)] **1** [late 19C] (*Aus.*) (*also* **stiffen out**) to die. **2** [late 19C] (*Aus.*) in fig. use, to punish. **3** [late 19C–1900s] to kill, to murder; lit. or fig. **4** [late 19C+] (*Aus.*) to knock someone unconscious. **5** [1900s] (*Aus.*) in fig. use, to ruin, to undermine, to 'put paid to'.

SE in slang uses

IN EXCLAMATIONS

❑ **stiffen the lizards!** (*also* **stiffen me! ...the crows! ...the rooks! ...the snakes! ...the wombats!**) [1910s+] (*orig. Aus.*) an excl. of surprise, shock etc.

stiffen *v.*[2] [STIFF *v.*[2] (2)] **1** [late 19C–1930s] to bribe, to corrupt; of a player, to lose a game; of a horse, to interfere with its ability to win a race. **2** [late 19C+] to swindle, usu. in passive.

stiffened *adj. see* STIFF *adj.*[1] (5).

stiffener *n.*[1] (*also* **stiffner**) [early–mid-19C] (*UK Und.*) a letter.

stiffener *n.*[2] **1** [mid-19C+] (*orig. US*) a fortifying alcoholic drink. **2** [1900s] (*Aus.*) a knockout punch. **3** [2000s] as sense 1, but with reference to cannabis.

stiffener *n.*[3] *see* DOG-STIFFENER *under* DOG *n.*[2].

stiffen out *v. see* STIFFEN *v.*[1] (1).

stiffer *n.* [STIFF *n.*[1]] [1990s+] an erection.

stiffie *n.* (*also* **stiffy**) [STIFF *n.*[1]] **1** [1960s+] an erection. **2** [1980s+] an invitation. **3** *see* STIFFY *n.*[1] (1).

IN PHRASES

❑ **crack a stiffie** *v.* [1940s+] to get an erection.

stiffner *n. see* STIFFENER *n.*[1].

stiff 'un *n.* **1** [early 19C+] (*also* **stiff one**) a corpse [ext. STIFF *n.*[1] (2)]. **2** [mid–late 19C] a heavy drinker. **3** [mid-19C+] (*also* **stiff one**) a strong alcoholic drink [STIFF *adj.*[2]]. **4** [late 19C] a difficult racecourse [STIFF *adj.*[2] (2)]. **5** [late 19C] (*Aus.*) a general term of abuse [SE *stiff* formal + ext. STIFF *n.*[1] (2)]. **6** [late 19C–1950s] a forgery [STIFF *n.*[1] (3d)]. **7** [late 19C+] (*horseracing*) a useless, losing horse and thus an erroneous, losing wager [fig. use of STIFF *n.*[1] (2)].

stiffy *n.*[1] [STIFF *n.*[1] (2)] **1** [late 19C–1980s] (*also* **stiffie**) a corpse. **2** [1910s–20s] (*US tramp*) a tramp who poses as being paralyzed. **3** [1960s] (*S.Afr.*) a paralytic.

stiffy *n.*[2] [STIFF *n.*[1] (4b)] [1950s–60s] a fool, an irritating person.

stiffy *n.*[3] *see* STIFFIE *n.*

stifle *v.* [SE *stifle*, to conceal] [early 17C] to slip money surreptitiously into another person's hand.

stifler *n.* [all 'take one's breath away'] **1** [early 19C] the gallows. **2** [early 19C] a dram of spirits. **3** [late 19C] a severe blow.

stifle the squeaker *v. see under* SQUEAKER *n.*

stig *n.* [the book/TV series *Stig of the Dump*] [1990s+] (*UK juv.*) an impoverished person, resembling a vagrant.

still *n.*[1] [abbr.] [mid–late 19C] a *still*-born child.

still *n.*[2] [pun on SE *still*, quiet/*still*, a distillery] [late 19C–1920s] (*US*) a quiet drunkard.

still *v.* [late 18C] to silence, by murdering or knocking out.

stillie *n.* [abbr.] [2000s] a stiletto heeled shoe.

still-screw *n. see under* SCREW *n.*[1].

still sow *n.* [pvb 'the still sow eats up half the draff', i.e. the quiet pig eats more than its share of fodder] **1** [late 16C–early 17C] 'a close, slie lurking knave' (Florio, *World of Wordes*, 1598). **2** [early 18C] a prostitute.

stilly *n.* [? they are *still there*] [1940s] (*W.I.*) a faithful lover.

stilo *n. see* STYLE *n.*

stilting *n.* [mid-19C] (*UK Und.*) the highest level of pick-pocketing.

Stilton, the *n.* [play on CHEESE, THE *n.* (2)/CHESHIRE, THE *n.* (1)] [mid–late 19C] of people, objects, experiences: the best of a type or style, the superlative.

stilts *n.* **1** [late 18C+] (*US black*) the human legs. **2** [1920s–60s] crutches. **3** [1960s] as *stilt-heels*, high heeled shoes.

stimulate *v.* [mid-19C–1910s] (*US*) to drink alcohol.

DERIVATIVES

❑ **stimulated** *adj.* [mid-19C] (*US*) euph. for drunk.

stina *n. see* STINNIE *n.*

sting *n.* **1** [17C–early 18C] the penis, esp. in context of impotence. **2** [20C+] any form of robbery, esp. as a complex fraud planned well in advance. **3** [1910s+] (*Aus.*) strong (cheap) drink; occas. methylated spirits. **4** [1930s–40s] (*US black*) a wallet. **5** [1930s+] (*US Und.*) a reasonably large sum of money ($500 average) obtained by some form of deception or trickery. **6** [1940s–50s] (*Aus.*) a drug, esp. as given to a racehorse. **7** [1970s+] a police undercover operation designed to entrap alleged criminals. **8** [1990s+] (*W.I.*) the currently favoured object, person, experience.

IN PHRASES

❑ **put in the stings** *v.* [1910s+] (*Aus.*) to demand a loan or a gift. ❑ **put the sting on** *v.* [1940s+] (*US Und.*) to cheat, to swindle, to defraud.

sting *v.* **1** [early 19C+] (*orig. UK Und.*) to steal, to cheat, both in fact and as merely overcharging. **2** [20C+] (*US*) to levy a charge upon, usu. financial but also fig., e.g. a prison sentence. **3** [1900s] to equal. **4** [1900s–30s] (*US*) to unmask, to reveal. **5** [1910s+] to demand or beg for something. **6** [1920s+] (*US Und.*) to make a successful coup as a confidence trickster. **7** [1930s] (*US prison*) to report a convict for a disciplinary offence. **8** [1940s] (*US Und.*) to arrest.

IN PHRASES

❑ **sting for** *v.* [20C+] (*orig. US*) to extort money from someone by begging or borrowing it in a demanding manner.

stingaree *n.*[1] [STING *v.* (1)] **1** [1900s–20s] (*US Und.*) a swindle based on short-changing a cashier. **2** [1920s] (*US*) a mean person.

stingaree *n.*[2] [? link to STING *n.* (1) but prob. SE *stinger*] [1920s+] (*US black*) the penis.

sting-bum *n.* [SE *sting* + BUM *n.*[1] (1); poss. earlier use of STING *v.* (1)] [late 17C–early 19C] a miser, a mean person.

stinger *n.* **1** [17C+] 'something that stings or smarts, e.g. a sharp blow, or the hand that delivers it; something that causes sharp distress, a pungent speech or crushing argument; a sharp frost' (*OED*). **2** [mid-19C] a swig of alcohol. **3** [mid-19C; 1940s] something noteworthy. **4** [mid-19C+] (*Aus./US*) any period of extreme weather, hot or cold. **5** [1930s–40s] (*US prison*) a disciplinary report. **6** [1950s] (*US drugs*) a hypodermic syringe. **7** [1970s] (*US*) the penis. **8** [1970s+] (*US black/prison*) (*also* **stringer**) a hotplate that is run from two wires attached to a light socket [STING *v.* (2) or SE *string*, i.e. the wires; note Maledicta V:1+2 267: 'The stinger consists of wires with both ends exposed. One end is inserted into an electrical socket and the other is placed in the water to heat it, to prepare coffee'].

stingo *n.*[1] [it *stings* the drinker] [mid-17C+] very strong ale.

stingo *n.*[2] [STING *n.* (7)] [1900s] (*Aus. Und.*) an arrest.

stingo *adj.* [SE *sting*/fig. use of STINGO *n.*[1]] [late 19C] energetic, spirited, lively.

stingtail *n.* [the *sting* in a scorpion's *tail*/a whore's TAIL *n.* (4), in this context venereal disease; note Ned Ward, *Hudibras Redivivus* (1705–07): 'For am'rous Joys, we alays find, / Leave a repenting Sting behind'] [17C] a prostitute.

stingy-brim *n.* (*also* **short-brim, stingy-rim**) [lit. a 'mean brim'] [1930s–80s] (*orig. US black*) a hat with a narrow brim.

stink *n.* **1** [early 19C+] a fuss, a furore, a scandal; esp. in phr. *kick up a stink*, *raise a stink*, to make a fuss. **2** [1910s+] a contemptible person. **3** [1940s+] a fight. **4** [1980s] (*US black*) the vagina.

SE in slang uses

IN COMPOUNDS

❑ **stink bomb** *n.* [1930s–50s] (*US*) something, or someone, disgusting or deplorable. ❑ **stinkbone** *n. see* STINKPOT *n.* (2). ❑ **stink-car** *n.* **1** [1900s–10s] (*also* **stink engine**) a motorcar [also pun on STINKER *n.*[1] (3)]. **2** [1910s] a motorbike. ❑ **stink-eye** *see* separate entries. ❑ **stink-finger** *see* separate entries. ❑ **stinkgat** *n.* [1990s+] (*S.Afr.*) a lavatory. ❑ **stink-hole** *n.* [1940s–50s] a lavatory. ❑ **stinkpot** *n. see* separate entry. ❑ **stink weed** *n.* **1** [1940s+] (*drugs*) marijuana. **2** [1950s] a smoker of marijuana.

IN PHRASES

❑ **a stink of a…** *n.* [1970s+] a great deal of, a large amount of. ❑ **get on stink** *v.* [20C+] (*W.I.*) to behave badly, to start a noisy argument. ❑ **kick up a stink** *v.* [19C+] to cause trouble, to create a disturbance. ❑ **like stink** *adv.* (*also* **to stink**) [? euph.] [1920s+] intensely, furiously. ❑ **stink-hole bay** *n.* [early 19C] the anus. ❑ **take a stink for a nosegay** *v.* [a *nosegay* smells sweet, a *stink* does not] [late 18C–mid-19C] to make a foolish blunder, to be very gullible.

stink *adj.* [1940s+] (*US*) good, fine.

stink *v.* **1** [mid-19C] (*US Und.*) to publish an account of a robbery. **2** [mid-19C+] to behave offensively, to appear offensive to someone. **3** [1910s+] (*orig. US*) to be morally inadequate or physically incompetent; generally to be rubbish. **4** [1930s] to fail, in a monetary sense. **5** [1930s+] in ironic use, to be full of, redolent of. **6** [1930s+] to be highly improbable, to lack verisimiltude.

IN PHRASES

❑ **stink of** *v.* (*also* **stink with**) [20C+] (*orig. US*) to be full of, characterized by, e.g. *stink of success*, *stink with money*. ❑ **stink on ice** *v.* [1930s+] (*US*) to be disgusting or deplorable. ❑ **stink to high heaven** *v.* [TO HIGH HEAVEN *under* HIGH *adj.*[1]] [1970s+] (*orig. US*) to be very disgusting and unpleasant. ❑ **stink up** *v.* [1930s+] (*US*) **1** to soil, to sully. **2** to 'smell' suspicious.

stinka *n. see* STINKER *n.*[2].

stinkard *n. see* STINKER *n.*[1].

stinkaroo *n.* [late 19C–1930s] a cigar or pipe.

stinkarooed *adj.* [var. STINKING *adj.*[2] (3)] [1940s] (*US*) drunk.

stinker *n.*[1] (*also* **stinkard**) [SE *stink*] **1** [17C+] a loathsome, unpleasant person or object; occas. used teasingly/affectionately. **2** [early 19C–1950s] a black eye [20C+ use is Aus.]. **3** [mid-19C+] anything that emits an offensive smell, orig. aimed at cigars and cigarettes. **4** [20C+] (*Aus.*) a very hot or humid day. **5** [1900s] (*Aus.*) a Chinese person. **6** [1900s] a brandy-ball sweet. **7** [1910s+] a strongly-worded letter; a disagreeable review or other communication. **8** [1910s+] anything considered unpleasant because of the difficulty in accomplishing it, e.g. a school essay; thus [1920s+] *come a stinker*, to fall into difficulties. **9** [1910s+] an exceptional example of, e.g. a cold in the head. **10** [1930s] an unfunny 'joke'. **11** [1940s+] a failure. **12** [1990s+] a promiscuous woman. **13** [1990s+] a bad mood.

IN PHRASES

❑ **penny stinker** *n.* [late 19C–1930s] a cheap cigar.

stinker *n.*[2] (*also* **stinka**) [the wholly negative image it enjoyed in the black community; such passes were scrapped in 1985] [1970s+] (*S.Afr. black*) a passbook.

stinkeroo *n.* [STINKER *n.*[1] (1) + -EROO *sfx*] [1930s+] (*Aus./US*) something disgusting or deplorable.

stink-eye *n.* [1990s+] (*US*) an aggressive, hostile look.

IN PHRASES

❑ **give someone the stink-eye** *v.* [1990s+] to stare at someone in a hostile manner.

stink-eye *v.* [2000s] to stare at in a hostile manner.

stink-finger *n.* (*also* **stinky-finger, stinky-pinky**) [late 19C+] **1** the middle finger [its use in sexual foreplay]. **2** manual stimulation of the female genitals.

IN PHRASES

❑ **play (at) stink-finger** *v.* [mid-19C–1970s] to manually stimulate a woman's genitals.

stink-finger *v.* [late 19C+] to manipulate a woman's genitals.

stinkibus *n.* [SE *stink*; note smugglers' use, a case of liquor that has been left under the water so long as to be undrinkable] [early 18C] bad beer or liquor, esp. when adulterated.

stinkies *n.* [2000s] (*Irish*) excrement.

stinking *adj.*[1] [prior use from 13C is SE] **1** [early 17C+] (*also* **stinking-ass**) a general negative intensifier, disgusting, repellent, odious. **2** [20C+] a general intensifier, euph. for DAMNED *adj.*, FUCKING *adj.* etc.

stinking *adj.*[2] **1** [late 19C+] very drunk. **2** [1940s] under the influence of drugs. **3** [1940s+] as abbr. of *stinking rich*, very well-off.

stinkingly *adv.* (*also* **stinking**) [20C+] excessively, extraordinarily.

stinking with *adj.* [1910s+] in possession of a large amount of something, usu. money.

stinkious *n.* [? a misprint for STINKIBUS *n.*] [18C] gin.

stinko *n.* [STINKO *adj.* (2)] **1** [1920s+] (*Aus.*) wine. **2** [1930s–40s] (*US*) an alcoholic tramp [ref. to *Sterno* or 'canned heat', i.e. solidified alcohol consumed by down-and-outs]. **3** [1940s–60s] (*Aus.*) a drunk.

stinko *adj.* [1920s+] **1** very poor, less than mediocre. **2** (*also* **stinky**) very drunk.

Stinkomalee *n.* [coined by the Tory wit and writer Theodore Hook (1788–1841) with ref. to contemporary concerns over Trincomalee, to the fact that the university, founded in 1836, allowed in nonconformists (Oxford and Cambridge did not), and to the farms and their animals that formerly occupied the site] [mid-19C] London University.

stinkpot *n.* **1** [18C] a chamberpot. **2** [20C+] (*also* **stinkbone**) a general term of abuse, aimed usu. at people rather than things [esp. refers in N.Z. to a child who wets themselves]. **3** [20C+] (*Aus.*) a small firework. **4** [20C+] an engine that emits foul fumes; thus a vehicle with such an engine. **5** [1910s] a large cap, called a mushroom. **6** [1910s] a stink-bomb. **7** [1950s–70s] (*US black*) the vagina.

stinks *n.* [mid-19C+] (*mainly UK public school*) chemistry, as a subject.

stinky *adj.*[1] [STINK v.] [1910s+] (*orig. US*) disgusting, nasty, inferior; dangerous.

stinky *adj.*[2] *see* STINKO *adj.* (2).

stinky *adv.* [1940s] badly.

stinky-butt *adj.* [1960s] (*US black*) a general term of abuse, lit. 'stinking anus'.

stinky-finger *n. see* STINK-FINGER *n.*

stinky-pie rich *adj.* [var. on STINKING *adj.*[2] (3) + SE *rich*] [1990s+] (*US black*) extremely rich.

stinky-pinky *n. see* STINK-FINGER *n.*

stinnie *n.* (*also* **stina**) [2000s] (*S.Afr. gay*) a smell, a stink.

stipe *n.* [abbr.] **1** [mid-19C+] *stip*endiary magistrate. **2** [1940s+] (*Aus.*) a *stip*endiary racing steward.

stir *n.*[1] (*also* **stur**) [abbr. Rom. *sturiben*, a prison, *staripen*, to imprison; ult. *śtar*, to imprison] [mid-19C+] prison.

IN COMPOUNDS

❑ **stir-batty** *adj. see* STIR-CRAZY below. ❑ **stir belly** *n.* [1940s+] (*US prison*) indigestion caused by tension or fear. ❑ **stir-bug** *n.* (*also* **stir-nut**) [BUG *n.*[4] (3d); NUT *n.*[2] (1)] [1920s+] (*US prison*) one who has gone mad due to the pressures of incarceration. ❑ **stir-bugs** *adj.* (*also* **stir-nuts, stir-psycho, stirry, stir-simple, stir-wacky**) [BUGS *adj.*] [20C+] (*Can./US prison*) insane from too long a confinement in prison. ❑ **stirbum** *n.* [1930s] (*US Und.*) a jailbird. ❑ **stir cramps** *n.* [1970s] (*US prison*) psychological/physical problems that come with a jail sentence. ❑ **stir-crazy** *adj.* (*also* **stir-batty, stir-happy, stir-looney**) [SE *crazy/happy*] [1930s+] (*orig. US*) used of a prisoner who has succumbed to prison-induced insanity; thus *stir-craziness*, psychosis induced by imprisonment; ext. to non-prison use. ❑ **stir croaker** *n.* [CROAKER *n.*[5] (1)] [1950s] (*US prison*) a second-rate, barely qualified doctor, assigned to prison work. ❑ **stir fries** *n.* [2000s] (*S.Afr. gay*) underage boys. ❑ **stir hustler** *n.* [HUSTLER *n.* (4)] [1940s+] (*US prison*) one who has mastered the 'art' of incarceration. ❑ **stir lawyer** *n.* [1950s] (*US prison*) a fellow prisoner who offers advice based on his own purported legal expertise. ❑ **stir nut** *n. see STIR-BUG* above. ❑ **stir-nuts/-psycho/-simple/-wacky** *adj. see STIR-BUGS* above. ❑ **stirwise** *adj.* [-WISE *sfx*] [1930s–50s] (*US Und.*) well-adjusted to prison life, capable of sustaining one's existence in prison.

IN PHRASES

❑ **big stir** *n.* [1910s] (*US Und.*) a Federal prison. ❑ **crush the stir** *v.* [CRUSH *v.*[1] (1)] [late 19C] (*UK Und.*) to break out of prison.

stir *n.*[2] [SE *stir*, movement] **1** [late 19C] a crowd. **2** [1940s+] (*Ulster*) a plan, a scheme. **3** [1940s+] (*orig. Ulster*) fun, enjoyment, a party. **4** [1970s+] (*N.Z.*) a bout of troublemaking.

stir *adj.* [STIR *n.*[1] (1)] [1930s+] pertaining to prison.

stir *v.* [abbr. SE *stir up trouble*] [1960s+] **1** to gossip maliciously, to cause trouble deliberately by so doing. **2** (*orig. Aus.*) to tease, to provoke; thus *for a stir*, for trouble's sake. **3** (*Aus.*) to cause trouble (other than through gossip etc).

SE in slang uses

IN COMPOUNDS

❑ **stir-about** *n.* **1** [late 18C+] porridge. **2** [late 19C] any pudding that requires stirring. **3** [1910s] prison. ❑ **stir-shit** *n.* [SHIT *n.*] [late 19C–1900s] a sodomite, a male homosexual.

IN PHRASES

❑ **stir it up** *v.* [1950s+] of a woman, to masturbate. ❑ **stir one's stew** *v.* (*also* **stir the batter, stir the sauce**) [1950s+] to masturbate, usu. of a woman. ❑ **stir one's stumps** *v.* (*also* **start one's stumps, stir a peg, ...one's pins, ...one's shanks**) [SE *stir* + *stump*, a leg, STUMPS *n.* (1)] [late 16C+] to get a move on; to dance; to do one's duty keenly. ❑ **stir shit out of** *v.* [SHIT *n.*] [1940s+] (*N.Z.*) to criticize harshly, to reprimand severely. ❑ **stir the possum** *v. see under* POSSUM *n.* ❑ **stir the porridge** *v. see under* PORRIDGE *n.* ❑ **stir the pot** *v.* [2000s] (*N.Z.*) to deliberately cause trouble. ❑ **stir the sauce** *v. see STIR ONE'S STEW* above. ❑ **stir (the) shit** *v.* (*also* **disturb (the) shit**) [SHIT *n.*] [1950s+] to go out of one's way to make trouble, esp. by gossiping or telling tales. ❑ **stir up** *v.* [late 19C] to visit without any previous announcement. ❑ **stir-up Sunday** *n.* [the collect for that day begins with the words 'Stir up ...'] [mid-19C+] the Sunday before Advent.

Stirling Moss *n.* [rhy. sl. = TOSS *n.*[1] (1); ult. UK racing driver *Stirling Moss* (b.1929)] [20C+] a damn, a curse; usu. in phr. *I don't give a stirling.*

stirred *adj.* [STIR v.] [1940s+] provoked, incited to violence or action, gone crazy.

stirrer *n.*[1] [1940s] (*US*) a penis.

stirrer *n.*[2] [STIR v.] [1960s+] (*Aus.*) one who stirs up trouble or discontent, an agitator, a trouble-maker; an unpleasant, malicious gossip.

stirrup *v.* [early–mid-18C] to thrash someone with a shoemaker's *stirrup*.

stirry *adj. see STIR-BUGS under* STIR *n.*[1].

stitch *n.*[1] [metonymy] [mid-17C–early 19C] a tailor.

IN COMPOUNDS

❑ **stitch-back** *n.* [? its back-strengthening properties. Note early 17C SE *steelback*, Alicante wine, which was supposed to help back problems] [late 17C–early 19C] very strong ale. ❑ **stitch-louse** *n.* [mid-19C] a tailor.

stitch *n.*[2] [the physical SE *stitch* that can accompany laughter] [1960s+] (*US campus/teen*) anything or anyone seen as amusing; intensified as *stitch and a half.*

stitch *v.* (*also* **go upon the stitch**) [the in and out SE *stitching* movement of the penis or of the fists] **1** [18C–mid-19C] to have sexual intercourse. **2** [1930s+] to beat in a fight or contest. **3** [1960s] (*US*) to shoot dead, to kill.

stitched *adj.* **1** [mid-18C+] drunk [f. *STITCH-BACK under* STITCH *n.*[1]]. **2** [1920s+] (*Aus.*) defeated [STITCH *v.* (2)].

stitched up *adj.* [2000s] (*US prison*) of a problem, dealt with, usu. after a fight.

stitch-up *n.* [STITCH UP *v.* (1)] [1970s+] a false arrest, based on concocted or fraudulent evidence; also in non-police contexts.

stitch up *v.* [sewing up a garment neatly and conclusively] **1** [1970s+] (*UK Und./police*) of the police, to ensure a conviction by planting evidence, faking confessions etc; also in non-police use. **2** [1970s+] to complete a task to one's complete satisfaction. **3** [1980s+] to cheat someone. **4** [2000s] to place in one's power.

stiver *n.* (*also* **steever, steiver, stuiver, stuyver**) [Du. *stiver*, a low-valued coin, the smallest monetary unit in use at the Cape under the Dutch East India Co., one-twentieth of a florin or gulden, worth a little more than one (old) penny; Nares (1822) suggests 'an inhabitant of the stews' i.e, a whore] [mid-17C+] **1** something of little value; thus in cash terms, a penny. **2** in pl., money.

IN COMPOUNDS

❑ **stiver-cramped** *adj.* [late 18C–early 19C] impoverished.

stoag *n. see* STOGIE *n.*

stoat *n. see* STOAT-THE-BAW *n.*

stoater *n.* (*also* **stoter**) [Du. *stooter*, *stooten*, to knock, to push] **1** [17C–late 18C] a violent blow; thus *tip someone a stoater*, give someone a blow. **2** [20C+] a bruise.

stoater *v.* (*also* **stoter**) [STOATER *n.*] [17C–early 18C] to hit.

stoat-the-baw *n.* (*also* **stoat**) [? Scot. *stoat/stot*, a bullock or SE *stoat*; but *stoat* = *hit*, and lit. 'translation' is 'bounce-the-ball' (poss. associated with the image of patting the young person reassuringly on the head) so poss. just a fool, cognate with *head-the-ball*] [1990s+] (*Scot.*) a statutory rapist or paedophile; a man who has intercourse with a girl below the legal age of consent.

stoat-the-baw *adj.* [STOAT-THE-BAW *n.*] [1990s+] pertaining to statutory rape and those who commit it.

stoat-the-baw *v.* [STOAT-THE-BAW *n.*] [1990s+] to commit statutory rape.

stob *v. see* STAB *v.*

stocious *adj.*[1] (*also* **stotious**) [? Scot. *stot*, staggering] [1930s+] (*Irish/Scot.*) drunken.

stocious *adj.*[2] (*also* **stoosh, stoshious, stoshus, stotious**) [? SE *ostentatious*] [1950s+] (*W.I.*) **1** well-dressed, stylish, high-class. **2** good-looking. **3** snobbish.

stock *n.*[1] [abbr. SE *stock of impudence*] [late 18C–early 19C] cheek; often as *good stock*.

SE in slang uses

IN COMPOUNDS

□ **stockbanger** *n.* [1930s] (*Aus.*) a stockman; thus *stockbanging*, working on a cattle farm. □ **stockholder** *n.* [ironic use of SE] [1930s–40s] (*US prison*) a convict who curries favour with the authorities.

IN PHRASES

□ **stock-in-trade** *n.* [SE *stock-in-trade*, a workman's tools] [late 19C–1900s] the genitals.

stock *n.*[2] [? Du. *stok*, a piece; thus cognate with PIECE *n.* (1a)] [2000s] (*S.Afr.*) a young woman.

stock *n.*[3] *see* STOOK *n.*

stock *v.* [mid–late 19C] in card-games, to *stack* the cards in a certain way to facilitate cheating; also fig. use.

stockdolager *n. see* SOCKDOLAGER *n.*

stock-drawers *n.* (*also* **stock-draers**) [? the *stockings* are *drawn* on] [mid-17C–early 19C] (*UK Und.*) stockings.

stocker *n.* [1970s+] (*US*) a stock-car racer.

stocking *n.*[1] (*also* **stocking stuffer**) [mid-19C+] (*UK Und.*) money.

stocking *n.*[2] [2000s] (*N.Z.*) bullying or extortion by youths on younger children.

stockings *n.* [1970s] (*US black*) the female legs.

stocking stuffer *n. see* STOCKING *n.*[1].

stoddle *v.* [mid-19C] (*UK Und.*) to halt proceedings.

stodge *n.* [SE *stodge*, thick, liquid, viscous mud] **1** [mid-19C+] heavy, filling, nutritionless food; thus *stodegepot*, a container of such food. **2** [mid-19C+] heavy, demanding but relatively unrewarding work. **3** [mid-19C+] heavy, tedious writing or speech. **4** [late 19C–1940s] food in general. **5** [1900s] a snack. **6** [1980s] (*Aus.*) a cake.

stodge *v.* [STODGE *n.*] **1** [mid-19C+] to gorge, to eat to excess; thus *stodging*, eating heavily, gorging. **2** [1900s–50s] to work steadily at something tedious.

stodger *n.* [STODGE *v.*] **1** [late 19C] an old -fashioned person. **2** [late 19C–1920s] a glutton. **3** [1900s–20s] (*also* **stodge, stodgie, stodgy**) a dull, spiritless person; thus *stodgery*, the manner in which such a person behaves. **4** [1910s] (*US*) a cook with slovenly habits.

stoepkakker *n.* [Afk. *stoep*, porch, veranda + *kakker*, SHITTER *n.*[1]] **1** [1980s+] (*S.Afr.*) 'a small, fat and old dog of the spoiled rotten variety which has found its sunny spot on the stoep (veranda) and refuses, with miniature fangs at full snarl, to budge for anyone or anything, not even to take care of its bodily functions' (*Cyberbraai*, Internet, 1997). **2** [2000s] (*S.Afr.*) in fig. use, an 'attack dog', any person who never gives up.

stoep-sitter *n.* [Afk. *stoep*, veranda + SE *sitter*] [1930s+] (*S.Afr.*) a farmer who is not primarily dependent on agriculture for their income.

stog *n.* (*also* **stogarette**) [STOGIE *n.*] [1990s+] (*US black*) a cigarette.

stogey *n. see* STOGIE *n.*

stogger *n.* [mid-19C] (*US Und.*) a pickpocket.

stoggs *n.* [dial. *stog*, a sharp-pointed instrument] [1990s+] the male genitals.

stogie *n.* (*also* **stoag, stogey, stogy**) [abbr. *Conestoga*; supposedly smoked by the 'stoga drivers', i.e. the drivers of the Conestoga wagons plying between Wheeling and Pittsburgh, Pennsylvania] **1** [late 19C+] (*US*) a cigar. **2** [1980s] (*US drugs*) an over-sized marijuana cigarette.

stoinker *n.* [STINKER *n.*[1]] [1990s+] a malodorous (whether lit. or fig.) and promiscuous woman.

stoke *adj. see* STOKE ON TRENT *adj.*

stoke *v.*[1] [? obs. SE *stoke*, to make a thrust at] [20C+] (*W.I.*) to humiliate, to treat badly.

stoke *v.*[2] [1970s+] (*Aus./US*) of a person, to have a good time; of an object, to prove first-rate; to please or impress someone.

IN PHRASES

□ **stoke up** *v.* [1980s+] (*US campus*) to please, to encourage.

IN EXCLAMATIONS

□ **stoke me!** (*also* **stoke me up!**) [1980s+] (*US campus*) a general excl. of approval, that's wonderful! I'm so happy! great!

stoked *adj.* (*also* **stoked on, stoked up**) [SE *stoke*, to build up and stir a furnace] **1** [1910s] (*Aus.*) full (of food). **2** [1960s+] (*orig. Aus.*) drunk. **3** [1960s+] (*US campus/teen, esp. California*) elated, delighted, thrilled. **4** [1960s+] (*also* **stoked in**) sexually excited, lustful. **5** [1970s+] intoxicated by a drug. **6** [1980s] (*also* **stoked out**) tired out. **7** [1980s] (*US campus*) fully prepared. **8** [1990s+] (*US campus*) surprised, amazed.

stoke on trent *n.* [rhy. sl. = BENT *n.*] [1970s+] a male homosexual.

stoke on trent *adj.* (*also* **stoke**) [BENT *adj.* (4) and BENT *adj.* (5)] [1980s+] **1** illegal. **2** homosexual.

stoke-up *n.* [STOKE UP *v.*] [1950s] a large, sustaining meal.

stoke up *v.* [late 19C+] to eat.

stokkies *n.* [? Afk. *stok*, the stocks] [20C+] (*S.Afr. Und.*) **1** a prison. **2** in sing. *stokkie*, a prisoner.

stolen a manchet out of the brewer's basket *phr.* (*also* **stolen a roll out of the brewer's basket**) [SE *manchet*, a small loaf or roll made from the finest wheat flour] [late 17C–early 19C] tipsy.

stole (on) *v.* [? SE *steal a march*] [1990s+] (*US black*) to hit with a surprise punch.

Stoli *n.* (*also* **Stoly**) [abbr.] [1970s+] *Stoli*chnaya vodka.

stoll *v.*[1] [SE *stall*, to put in place] [mid-19C] (*Ulster*) to understand.

stoll *v.*[2] [? Norfolk dial. *stole*, to drink, to swallow] [late 19C] to drink; thus *stolled*, tipsy.

Stoly *n. see* STOLI *n.*

stomach *n.*

IN COMPOUNDS

□ **stomach habit** *n. see under* HABIT *n.* □ **stomach robber** *n. see* BELLY BURGLAR *under* BELLY *n.* □ **stomach Steinway** *n.* (*also* **stomach pump**) [SE *stomach*, against which it is held + *Steinway*, a piano] [1930s] (*US*) a piano accordion.

stomach ache *n.* [rhy. sl.] [1990s+] a steak.

stomp *n.* [SAmE *stomp*, to stamp] (*US black*) **1** [1940s] a foot. **2** [1940s+] a shoe. **3** *see* STOMPING *n.*

stomp *v.* (*also* **stomp on, stomp out**) [SE *stamp*/SAmE *stomp*] **1** [1940s+] (*US*) to beat up, to defeat. **2** [1950s] (*US teen*) to dance. **3** [1950s+] (*Aus. teen*) to dance. **4** [1980s] (*US black*) to use language that is likely to cause a fight.

IN COMPOUNDS

□ **stomp-ass** *adj.* [-ASS *sfx*] [1940s+] (*US*) violent, aggressive.

IN PHRASES

□ **stomp it** *v.* [one 'stomps' on the accelerator] [1930s] to hurry, to go fast, esp. in a vehicle. □ **stomp someone's buzz** *v. see* KILL SOMEONE'S BUZZ *under* BUZZ *n.*

stomp-down *adj.* [1950s+] a general intensifer, complete, utter.

IN COMPOUNDS

□ **stomp-down woman** *n.* (*also* **stomp-down whore**) [1950s–70s] (*US black*) the hardest working woman in a pimp's 'stable' of prostitutes. □ **stomp-down and drag-out** *adj. see* KNOCK-DOWN-(AND)-DRAG-OUT *adj.*

stompers *n.* (*also* **stumpers, stomps**) [SAmE *stomp*, to stamp] **1** [mid-18C; late 19C+] (*US*) large, heavy boots, esp. cowboy boots. **2** [1940s+] (*UK Und./US black*) shoes.

stompie *n.* [Afk. *stomp*, stump] [1940s+] (*S.Afr.*) a cigarette butt, a partially smoked cigarette, esp. one stubbed out and kept for relighting later; thus a worthless remnant.

stomping *n.* (*also* **stomp**) [STOMP *v.* (1)] [1940s+] (*orig. US*) a beating, esp. one in which the victim is kicked or trampled on.

stomping ground *n. see* STAMPING GROUND *n.*[1].

stomp on/out *v. see* STOMP *v.*

stomps *n. see* STOMPERS *n.*

stoms *n. see* STUMBLERS *n.*

stone *n.*[1] **1** [mid-16C+] a testicle [SE mid-12C–early 18C]. **2** [20C+] (*US Und.*) a diamond, or jewel. **3** [1960s+] in fig. use of sense 1, courage, bravery; usu. in pl. **4** [1990s+] (*drugs*) crack cocaine.

IN COMPOUNDS

□ **stone-getter** *n. see* PROP-GETTER *under* PROP *n.*[3].

IN PHRASES

□ **take a stone in the ear** *v.* [ety. unknown; ? link to SE *stone*, a testicle; or to the *stoning* of adulteresses in some cultures] [late 17C–early 18C] of a woman, to fall into an immoral lifestyle. □ **white stone** *n.* **1** [1910s] (*US Und.*) a diamond. **2** [1940s–50s] (*US black*) a fake diamond, esp. as used in a confidence trick.

stone *n.*[2] [1950s–60s] (*US black*) a dollar.

stone *n.*[3] [STONED *adj.*] [1950s+] a state of drunken or drugged intoxication.

stone *n.*[4] [? imperial weight: 14 pounds = one *stone*] [1970s] (*US Und.*) a prison sentence (?) of 14 days.

stone *adj.* [STONE *adv.*] [1950s+] complete, absolute, e.g. *stone addict*, one who is deeply addicted to a drug.

IN COMPOUNDS

□ **stone butch** *n.* [note 'The term comes from African American slang, in which "stone" means "very." It has come to have other meanings as well. A butch can be sexually stone, as in, not being able to permit herself to be touched on the genitals for sex; emotionally stone, meaning that she has locked away her emotions and has trouble acknowledging or expressing them; or physically stone, having trouble being touched at all. A stone butch is usually some combination of all of these' (Scott, *Rebecca's Dict. of Queer Sl.*,1998)] [1960s+] (*US gay*) a very masculine lesbian. □ **stone cold** *n.* [1930s+] (*Aus. Und.*) a villain who would never betray their fellows whatever the circumstances. □ **stone end** *n.* (*also* **stone finish**) [1950s+] (*Aus.*) the absolute end, an intolerable situation. □ **stone femme** *n.* [FEMME *n.* (3); *see* STONE BUTCH above] [1990s+] (*US gay*) a lesbian who invariably accepts a passive role; a lesbian who does not wish to be touched. □ **stone fox** *n.* (*also* **stone-cold fox**) [FOX *n.*[1] (6)] [1970s+] (*US black/campus*) a beautiful woman. □ **stone ginger** *n.* [the N.Z. racehorse *Stone Ginger*, known as phenomenally successful; ult. racing *ginger*, a showy, fast horse] [1910s+] an absolute certainty. □ **stone killer** *n.* [1970s] (*US*) an outstanding example of a person or thing.

IN PHRASES

□ **stone to the bone** *adj.* [TO THE BONE *under* BONE *n.*[1])] [1950s+] (*US black*) said of one who is considered wholly admirable in every respect.

SE in slang uses

denoting a prison

IN COMPOUNDS

□ **stone college** *n.* [1940s–60s] (*US Und.*) a prison. □ **stone crock** *n.* [SE *crock*, a jug, thus play on STONE JUG *n.*[1]] [1920s–30s] (*US tramp*) a state prison; orig. Sing Sing, New York. □ **stone doublet** *n.* [SE *doublet*, tight-fitting body armour] [late 17C–18C] a prison, esp. Newgate prison. □ **stone dump** *n.* [DUMP *n.*[3] (2)] [20C+] (*US Und.*) a prison. □ **stone hotel** *n.* [1970s] (*US*) a prison. □ **stone house** *n.* [1930s–60s] a prison. □ **stone jacket** *n.* [late 18C] (*US*) a prison. □ **stone jug** *n. see* separate entry. □ **stone mansion** *n.* [1920s] (*US Und.*) a prison. □ **stone tavern** *n.* [late 18C–early 19C] a prison.

IN PHRASES

□ **rocked in a stone cradle** *adj.* [late 19C] (*US*) to have been born in prison.

general uses

IN COMPOUNDS

□ **stoneface** *n.* [the first (SE) use of the phr. is in Nathaniel Hawthorne's story 'The Great Stone Face' (*National Era*, 16 January 1850), in which it referred to a natural rock formation. The unsmiling silent era comedian Buster Keaton (1898–1966) was known as the 'Great Stone Face'] [1940s+] a totally unemotional person. □ **stone fence** *n.* [ety. unknown] (*US*) **1** [19C–1940s] whisky or another spirit mixed with cider. **2** [mid-19C–1900s] ginger-beer and brandy. □ **stonehead** *n.* [1920s] (*US*) a fool. □ **stonewall** *v. see* separate entry.

stone *v.* [the image of throwing or knocking down with a rock] [1940s+] **1** (*drugs*) (*also* **stone up**) to render intoxicated with a drug, usu. marijuana or hashish. **2** in fig. use, to create the same effect without drugs. **3** (*US*) to criticize, to upbraid.

IN PHRASES

□ **stone out** *v.* [1940s–50s] (*drugs*) to become over-intoxicated by a drug, usu. marijuana or hashish. □ **stone up** *v. see* sense 1 above.

SE in slang uses

IN EXCLAMATIONS

□ **stone me!** (*also* **god stone me! stone me up a gum tree!**) [SE *stone*, to throw stones at] [1930s+] an excl. of surprise. □ **stone the crows!** [1920s+] (*orig. Aus./N.Z.*) an excl. of surprise, wonder, alarm.

stone *adv.* (*also* **stone-cold, stony**) [i.e. the solidity of a stone] [17C+] absolutely, purely, completely, to the highest degree, e.g. *stone bonkers*, absolutely crazy etc.

IN COMPOUNDS

□ **stone-blind** *adj.* [STONED *adj.* (2) + BLIND *adj.*[1]] [1950s] extremely intoxicated with a drug. □ **stone broke** *adj. see* separate entry.

stone broke *adj.* (*also* **stone motherless broke, stony broke**) [STONE *adv.* + BROKE *adj.*[1] (1)] [late 19C+] penniless, absolutely impoverished; thus *stone-broke, stone-broker, stony-broke, stony-broker*, one who is impoverished.

stoned *adj.* (*also* **stoned out**) [1950s+] **1** drunk. **2** intoxicated with some form of drug; thus *stoned out of one's brain/gourd/head/mind/skull*, very intoxicated, on drink or, more usu., drugs. **3** ecstatic, without drink or drugs.

IN PHRASES

□ **stoned over** *adj.* [1980s+] (*US drugs*) lethargic after smoking cannabis. □ **stoned to the eyes** *adj.* (*also* **stoned to the eyeballs**) [1950s+] (*orig. US*) very intoxicated from drugs or alcohol.

stone jug *n.*[1] (*also* **stone pitcher**) [JUG *n.*[1] (1); note synon. US Navy 1900s *stone frigate*] **1** [17C+] (*also* **stone john**) generic for any prison. **2** [late 18C–mid-19C] Newgate prison, the main criminal prison in London. **3** [mid-19C] (*US Und.*) Sing Sing prison, New York.

stone jug *n.*[2] [rhy. sl. = MUG *n.*[1] (2a)] [1920s+] a fool, a dupe.

stone motherless broke *adj. see* STONE BROKE *adj.*

stoner *n.* [STONED *adj.*] **1** [1970s+] a drug user, spec. of marijuana. **2** [1990s+] (*US teen*) a delinquent.

stones, the *n.* [abbr. SE *cobblestones*] [mid-19C] the streets (of London).

IN PHRASES

□ **off the stones** [mid-19C+] outside London. □ **on the stones** **1** [early 19C+] in the open air, usu. referring to a fight, often with sidebets and between local champions, arranged outside the normal boxing world. **2** [mid-19C] unemployed. **3** [mid-19C+] in London. **4** [20C+] homeless; living on the street. **5** [20C+] selling goods laid out on the pavement rather than on a stall.

stones and bones *n.* [1970s+] (*US campus*) a course in prehistory.

stonewall *v.* [the earliest cited use is late 19C cricket jargon, thence to political use and thence to general, but note US General Thomas 'Stonewall' Jackson, nicknamed for the implacable stand he conducted during the US Civil War Battle of Bull Run, 21 July 1861] [late 19C+] (*orig. Aus.*) to put up barriers, to obfuscate, to prevaricate; thus *stonewall*, a person or thing that obstructs.

stoney *adj. see* STONY *adj.*

stonicky *n.* [naut. *stonicky*, a rope's end, used for punishment] [1970s] (*UK Und.*) a cosh.

stonk *n.* [1960s] (*N.Z.*) a bombardment.

stonk *v.* [milit. term for bombarding a target] [1980s] to hurl abuse.

stonker *n.* [STONKER *v.*] [1980s+] **1** anything large, or impressive of its type. **2** (*also* **stonk, stonk-on**) an erection.

stonker *v.* [echoic; orig. milit. use; ? link to dial. *stonk*, the game of marbles, echoic of the click of one marble on another] [1910s+] (*Aus.*) **1** to render useless, to put out of action, to thwart. **2** to kill, to destroy. **3** to defeat, to outwit.

stonkered *adj.* [STONKER *v.*] [1910s+] (*orig. Aus.*) **1** drunk; thus *stonkering*, drinking. **2** satiated. **3** beaten, defeated, in serious trouble. **4** exhausted. **5** dead.

stonking *adj.* [STONKER *n.* (1)] [1980s+] a general term of approval, enormous, excellent etc, esp. as *stonking great…*

stonk-on *n. see* STONKER *n.* (2).

stony *adj.* (*also* **stoney**) [abbr. STONE BROKE *adj.*] [late 19C+] absolutely penniless.

stony *adv. see* STONE *adv.*

stony blind *adj.* [STONE *adv.* + BLIND *adj.*[1] (1)] [1920s–30s] (*Aus.*) absolutely drunk.

stony broke *adj. see* STONE BROKE *adj.*

stoob *n.* [backsl.] [mid-19C] boots.

stoock *n. see* STOOK *n.*

stood *adj.* [1920s] (*US*) drunk.

stooge *n.* [? SE *student*; orig. show business, a comedian's assistant or 'straight man'] **1** [1910s+] (*orig. US*) any despised underling. **2** [1940s–60s] (*US Und.*) an informer. **3** [1960s+] (*US campus*) a general term of abuse.

stooge *adj.* [STOOGE *v.* (4)] [1990s+] (*Aus.*) hoaxing, deceitful.

stooge *v.* [STOOGE *n.*] **1** [1930s+] (*orig. US*) to work as an assistant or underling. **2** [1940s] to idle, to wait around. **3** [1940s–60s] to inform against someone. **4** [1950s+] (*Aus./US*) to fool, to deceive.

stook *n.* (*also* **stock, stoock, stookey, stuke**) [? Ger. *Stück*, a piece of cloth] [mid-19C–1910s] a pocket handkerchief.

IN COMPOUNDS

❑ **stook buzzing** *n.* [mid-19C] (*UK Und.*) pickpocketing handkerchiefs. ❑ **stook hauler** *n.* (*also* **stook buzzer**) [mid-19C] (*UK Und.*) a thief specializing in taking pocket handkerchiefs.

stook *v.* [S.Afr.E. *stook*, to distil spirits] [20C+] (*S.Afr.*) to stir up trouble.

stooked *adj.* [mid-19C+] of stolen goods or money, hidden.

stookey *n. see* STOOK *n.*

stool *n.* [abbr. STOOL-PIGEON *n.*[1] (1)] **1** [1910s+] (*also* **stooler**) an informer. **2** [1920s] a plainclothes detective.

stool *v.* (*also* **stool on**) [abbr. STOOL-PIGEON *n.*[1] (1)] **1** [20C+] (*US*) to act as an informer. **2** [1920s] (*US Und.*) to search premises for drugs.

stoolie *n.* (*also* **stooley, stoolo, stooly**) [abbr. STOOL-PIGEON *n.*[1] (1)] [1920s+] (*orig. US*) an informer.

stooling *n.* [abbr. STOOL-PIGEON *v.*] [1920s+] (*US*) acting as an informer.

stoolo *n. see* STOOLIE *n.*

stool on *v. see* STOOL *v.*

stool-pigeon *n.*[1] [SE *stool-pigeon*, a bird that is tied to a stool in order to lure other birds towards the waiting hunter. In this case the 'stool' is that in a police station; apparently coined for the fame of faro – see Asbury *Sucker's Progress* (1938) 16: '*Stool-pigeon*—Originally this word meant a pigeon used to decoy others into a trap. A few years before the turn of the nineteenth century it came into general use among American gamblers to designate a capper or a hustler for a Faro bank, and was still used as late as 1915'] (*orig. US*) **1** [mid-19C+] an informer, one who makes a confession implicating others. **2** [1920s] a time-and-motion overseer. **3** [1920s] (*US Und.*) an 'inside man' who takes a job to gain information about the proposed site of a robbery. **4** [1920s–50s] in fig. use, any person or thing that shows another person up.

stool-pigeon *n.*[2] [he is stting on a bar-*stool*; play on STOOL-PIGEON *n.*[1] (1)] [1900s] (*Aus.*) a drinker in a public house.

stool-pigeon *n.*[3] [SE *stool*, excrement or seat + pun on STOOL-PIGEON *n.*[1] (1)] [1980s+] (*US gay*) one who loiters in men's lavatories in order to offer fellatio.

stool-pigeon *v.* (*US*) **1** [mid-19C] to make a false arrest; the victim is then released on payment of a bribe and all records are expunged. **2** [mid-19C+] of one villain, to inform on another; esp. as n. *stool-pigeoning*.

stooly *n. see* STOOLIE *n.*

stoomer *n. see* STUMER *n.*[1].

stoom out *v.* [SHTUM *adj.* (1)] [1900s] (*Aus.*) to render someone silent; thus to to kill.

stoop *n.*[1] **1** [mid-18C–early 19C] the pillory; thus *stooped*, placed in the pillory [the position one adopts while thus confined]. **2** [1940s+] (*Aus.*) a petty thief [he *stoops* to pick up things].

IN COMPOUNDS

❑ **stoop-buzzing** *n.* [mid-19C] (*UK Und.*) the robbery of a man she has picked up by a woman (? a prostitute). ❑ **stooping-match** *n.* [early 19C] the placing of a number of people in the pillory at the same time. ❑ **stoop-napper** *n.* [NAPPER *n.*[1] (1)] [late 18C–early 19C] (*UK Und.*) a man standing in a pillory.

stoop *n.*[2] *see* STUPE *n.* (1).

stoop *v.*[1] **1** [late 16C] to be ensnared by a confidence trickster or a thief. **2** [1980s] (*US black*) to have sexual intercourse.

stoop *v.*[2] [STOOP *n.*[1] (1)] [early 19C] to put someone in the pillory.

stooper *n.* [SE *stoop*, to bend down] **1** [1920s–30s] (*tramp*) (*also* **stoop tobacco**) a cigarette stub, picked up in the street. **2** [1960s] (*US*) a person who forages for betting tickets on the ground at racetracks.

stoosh *adj. see* STOCIOUS *adj.*[2].

stop *n.*[1] [he *stops* malefactors] [mid-19C] a detective.

stop *n.*[2] [play on FENCE *n.*[1] (1)] [1930s–40s] (*US Und.*) a receiver of stolen goods.

stop *n.*[3] [Afk. *stop*, a plug or fill of tobacco] [1940s+] (*S.Afr. drugs*) **1** marijuana. **2** a single pipeful of marijuana or enough to roll a single cigarette. **3** the smallest measure of marijuana sold.

stop *v.* [1920s+] (*Aus.*) **1** in a fight, to knock one's opponent down or knock them out. **2** in fig. use, to defeat. **3** to consume, e.g. a drink.

SE in slang uses

IN COMPOUNDS

❑ **stop-gap** *n.* [1910s–20s] the last child born to a family. ❑ **stop-lay** *n.* [mid-19C] (*UK Und.*) a method of picking pockets in which one criminal stops a likely pedestrian ostensibly to ask directions while an accomplice does the thieving. ❑ **stop-out** *n.* [20C+] one who stays out enjoying themselves longer than the speaker considers respectable; usu. as *dirty stop-out*. ❑ **stop work** *n.* [the male retirement age] [1940s+] (*bingo*) the number 65.

IN PHRASES

❑ **stop a packet** *v. see* COP A PACKET *under* PACKET *n.* ❑ **stop a pot** *v.* (*also* **stop a pint**) [SE *pot* (of ale)/*pint*] [1910s–40s] (*Aus.*) to have a drink. ❑ **stop a slug** *v.* (*also* **stop a bullet, stop lead**) [SLUG *n.*[1] (1a)/*bullet*/LEAD *n.* (1)] [1930s–50s] (*US*) to be shot (dead). ❑ **stop-hole abbey** *n.* [SE *stophole*, a plug; presumably some large if otherwise abandoned and decaying building, poss. in the criminal zone of ALSATIA *n.*, to which easy entrance, i.e. by the authorities, was barred] [late 17C–early 19C] (*UK Und.*) the headquarters of the contemporary London underworld. ❑ **stop off** *v.* [late 19C–1900s] (*N.Z.*) to stop doing something, often as imper. ❑ **stop one** *v. see under* ONE *n.*[1]. ❑ **stop someone's blubber** *v. see under* BLUBBER *n.*[1]. ❑ **stop someone's clock** *v.* **1** [20C+] to defeat heavily. **2** [1950s+] to kill. ❑ **stop-the-clock** *n.* [the custom of stopping the clocks following a death in the house] [20C+] (*Ulster*) a pessimist. ❑ **stop two gaps with one bush** *v.* [later use is SE] [16C] to accomplish two tasks simultaneously.

IN EXCLAMATIONS

❑ **stop my vitals!** *see* STAP MY VITALS! *excl.* ❑ **stop your gab!** *see under* GAB *n.*[1]. ❑ **stop your gap!** *see under* GAP *n.*[1]. ❑ **stop your jaw!** *see* HOLD ONE'S JAW *under* JAW *n.*

stop and go *n.* [rhy. sl.] [20C+] a toe.

stop and start *n.* [rhy. sl.] [20C+] the heart.

stople *v.* [SE *stopple*, to close with a bung] [1990s+] (*Irish*) to have sexual intercourse.

stopper *n.* **1** [early 19C] (*boxing*) a heavy blow. **2** [early 19C+] anything that causes events to come to a halt; esp. in phr. *put a stopper on*, to bring to a halt. **3** [mid-19C] (*UK Und.*) a policeman.

stoppers *n.* [they SE *stop* one moving] [1970s] (*drugs*) depressants, barbiturates.

stopping oyster *n. see* CHOKING OYSTER *n.*

stoppo *n.* [SE *stop* + -O *sfx* (1)] **1** [1930s] a break from work. **2** [1930s+] an escape, a getaway; thus *stoppo driver*, a getaway driver; *stoppo car*, the car in which criminals escape.

IN PHRASES

❑ **take stoppo** *v.* [1950s] to make a getaway.

stoppo *v.* [1950s] (*UK Und.*) to make an escape.

stoppo! *excl.* [1950s] stop what you are doing!

stop thief *n.* [rhy. sl.; note HOT BEEF! *excl.* = stop thief!] [mid-19C+] **1** beef. **2** stolen meat.

store *n.* [note US carnival use *store*, any form of carnival concession] [1900s–40s] (*US Und.*) anywhere that provides the site for a confidence trick.

SE in slang uses

IN PHRASES

❑ **give up the store** *v.* [20C+] to surrender, to give in.

store-bought hair *n.* [1900s–30s] (*US black*) a wig, a hairpiece.

stored away *adj.* [1940s–50s] (*US Und.*) in prison.

storefront preacher *n.* [1950s+] (*US black*) a local gossip, who 'preaches' only to those who idle away their days outside the general store of some small town.

storekeeper *n.* [late 19C] (*US*) an article that has remained unsold for so long that it may never leave the shop.

stork *v.* [the myth of storks bringing babies] [1970s] (*US campus*) to make pregnant.

storm and strife *n.* [rhy. sl.] [late 19C+] (*mainly US*) one's wife.

storm-buzzard *n. see under* BUZZARD *n.*

stormer *n.* **1** [mid-19C] (*US gambling*) a heavy winner. **2** [1920s+] a success.

storm-stick *n.* [1930s+] (*Aus.*) an umbrella.

stormy dick *n.* [rhy. sl. = PRICK *n.* (1)] [20C+] (*US*) the penis.

stormy end *n.* [1920s] (*US tramp*) the windowless or 'blind' baggage car of a passenger train.

storrac *n.* [backsl.] [mid-19C] carrots.

story *n.* ['a Puritanism that came into fashion with the trade against romances, all novels and stories being considered as dangerous and false' (Hotten, 1864)] **1** [late 17C+] euph. for a lie; thus [mid-18C+] *story-teller*, a liar; *story-telling*, lying; also v. *story along*, to deceive, to tell a false tale. **2** [1900s] (*W.I.*) a row. **3** [1900s–20s] a liar. **4** [1950s] (*US*) a fuss. **5** [1970s] (*US campus*) an afternoon television soap opera. **6** [2000s] (*N.Z.*) a term of acknowledgment or approval (sometimes *the story*).

IN PHRASES

❑ **do the story with** *v.* [SE *the old, old story*, the basic falsehood underlying the exchange of counterfeit affection for money] [18C] of a prostitute, to have sex with. ❑ **what's the story (morning glory)?** *see* separate entry.

IN EXCLAMATIONS

❑ **look story!** [20C+] (*W.I.*) a general excl. of dismissal or contempt, how absurd! ❑ **that's the story!** [1940s+] (*N.Z.*) a general excl. of encouragement.

story *v.* [1950s] (*US*) to tell a lying to story to.

stoshious/stoshus *adj. see* STOCIOUS *adj.*[2].

stoshy *n.* [? STOCIOUS *adj.*[2]; but note UK dial. *stoushie*, a stout and healthy child] [1940s–50s] (*W.I.*) a boyfriend.

stoter *see under* STOATER.

stotious *adj. see under* STOCIOUS.

stotor *n.* [for ety. *see* STOATER *n.*] [mid-19C] (*UK Und.*) a heavy blow, a 'settler'.

stott-on *n.* [1990s+] (*UK juv.*) the erect penis.

stoush *n.* (*also* **stouch, stoush-up**) [STOUSH *v.*] **1** [20C+] (*Aus./N.Z.*) a fight, fighting; thus *stoush-artist/-merchant*, a habitual and competent fighter, a bully; *deal out stoush, put in the stoush*, to attack violently, to fight enthusiastically; *take stoush*, to take a beating; *the Big Stoush*, WW1; *reinstoushments*, reinforcements. **2** [1910s] a beating.

IN PHRASES

❑ **drop stoush** *v.* [2000s] (*UK black*) to act aggressively.

stoush *adj.* (*also* **stush**) [? STOUSH *n.* (1); poss. indep. origin] [1990s+] (*W.I./UK black teen*) arrogant, stuck-up.

stoush *v.* (*also* **stouch, stoush up**) [? UK dial. *stashie*, a quarrel, an uproar] **1** [late 19C+] (*Aus./N.Z.*) to have a fight; to beat, to hit. **2** [1900s] to stop, to cease. **3** [1900s–30s] in fig. uses, e.g. to steal; *stoushed*, beaten (in a race). **4** [1910s] to wound.

stousher *n.* [STOUSH *v.* (1)] [20C+] (*Aus./N.Z.*) a fighter; thus *stoushie*, a soldier; *stoushing*, fighting, beating up.

stoush-up *n. see* STOUSH *n.*

stoush up *v. see* STOUSH *v.*

stout *n.* [the modern use, as a synon. for SE *porter* emerged *c.*1750] [late 17C–mid-18C] (*UK Und.*) strong beer.

stout house *n.* [1960s] (*US*) a local gaol.

stove *n.* [SE *stove*, to fumigate with sulphur] [20C+] (*Ulster*) a strong or unpleasant smell, esp. that of drink; thus *stoving*, drunk.

stoved-up *adj. see* STOVE-UP *adj.*

stove lid *n.* [the blackening of the utensil] [1930s+] a derog. term for a black person.

stove-pipe *n.* **1** [mid-19C–1950s] (*US*) (*also* **stove-pipe hat**) a tall hat, a top hat. **2** [mid-19C; 1960s+] (*also* **stovies, trouser-pipe**) tight, narrow trousers.

stove-up *adj.* (*also* **stoved up**) [SE *stave*, to smash] [1930s–60s] (*US*) usu. of people, run-down, exhausted, worn-out.

stow *v.* [SE *stow*, to put away, to put on one side] **1** [mid-16C–mid-19C] to stop talking; esp. in phrs. *stow it! stow you!* shut up! *stow that!* that's not true! *stow your noise! stow your yap!* be quiet! **2** [18C+] to stop, to desist (other than speech).

IN PHRASES

❑ **stow one's whids** *v. see under* WHID *n.*

IN EXCLAMATIONS

❑ **stow faking!** [FAKE *v.*[1] (3)] [mid-19C] stop that! ❑ **stow magging!** (*also* **stow mangling!**) [MAG *v.* (2)] [early 19C] be quiet! stop talking! ❑ **stow your jabber!** (*also* **stow your racket!**) [early 19C] be quiet! stop talking!

stowed *adj.* [dial. *stow*, to fill up] [1980s+] packed closely, very full.

s.t.p. *n.* (*drugs*) **1** [1960s+] a form of hallucinogen [abbr. of either *s*erenity, *t*ranquillity and *p*eace, or play on *s*cientifically *t*reated *p*etroleum, a gasoline additive]. **2** [1980s+] phencyclidine [a mistaken use of sense 1].

stract *adj.* [orig. synon. US milit. *strac*; note Dave Wilton (American Dialect Society List 10 Aug. 2002): '"STRAC." Originally an 1950s acronym for Strategic Army Corps, a group of four elite divisions maintained at a high readiness for overseas deployment. It began to be used as an adjective, to be "STRAC" was to be prepared [...] After the demise of the Corps, the adjectival use hung on. A new, unofficial backronym was formed for it, "Skilled, Tough, Ready, Around the Clock." It was very common in the US Army of the 1980s.'] [1990s+] (*US prison*) neat and clean in appearance and dress.

straddle *v.* [early–mid-18C] to draw lots or throw dice to determine who shall pay a bill.

straddle a chamberpot *v. see* PEE BETWEEN TWO HEELS *under* PEE *v.*

straight *n.*[1] **1** [mid-19C–1950s] (*US*) unadulterated or very strong whisky. **2** [1950s+] (*S.Afr. black*) a 750ml (26fl oz) bottle of spirits or beer. **3** [1950s+] (*drugs*) a tobacco cigarette. **4** [1960s+] an unfiltered cigarette.

straight *n.*[2] **1** [late 19C] (*UK Und.*) someone one can trust, and thus, usu. not at all 'straight'. **2** [1910s+] (*also* **straight-head**) a conventional, respectable person; by ext. one who does not use drugs. **3** [1930s+] (*orig. gay*) a heterosexual person. **4** [1930s+] conventional heterosexual intercourse in the face to-face 'missionary position'; thus pornography featuring this. **5** [1990s+] (*US campus*) one who stands outside the current social norms.

DERIVATIVES

❑ **straightnik** *n.* [-NIK *sfx*; but note *STRAIGHT NECK under* STRAIGHT *adj.*[1]] [1970s] (*US gay*) a heterosexual male.

IN PHRASES

❑ **run off the straight** *v.* [i.e. the 'straight and narrow'] [late 19C] to abandon a respectable life for criminality.

straight *n.*[3] *see* STRAIGHT SHOOTER *n.*[2] (2).

straight, the *n.* [mid-19C–1940s] (*US*) the facts, the truth, trustworthy information.

straight *adj.*[1] **1** [early 17C+] of accounts, satisfactorily settled, balanced; also in fig. use. **2** [mid-19C+] esp. of language, unadorned, undiluted, expressed in a straightforward manner. **3** [mid-19C+] of a woman, chaste; of a man, honest. **4** [mid-19C+] of a situation, honest, satisfactory, as one desires. **5** [mid-19C+] respectable, law-abiding, honest. **6** [late 19C] of a wager, definite. **7** [late 19C+] of information, etc, trustworthy, undisputable. **8** [late 19C+] in criminal terms, trustworthy. **9** [20C+] synon. for *right*. **10** [1920s+] aware, understanding, comprehending. **11** [1930s+] in the sex industry, normal heterosexual intercourse, with no 'perversions', e.g. flagellation or bestiality. **12** [1940s+] heterosexual. **13** [1960s+] conventional, as opposed to the values of the 'counterculture'. **14** [1990s+] (*US campus*) likeable. **15** [2000s] successful.

IN COMPOUNDS

❑ **straight bogy** *n. see STRAIGHT BOGEY under* BOGEY *n.*[1]. ❑ **straight crip** *n. see under* CRIP *n.* ❑ **straight goer** *n. see under* GOER *n.* ❑ **straight going** *n.* [? *STRAIGHT GOER under* GOER *n.*] [late 18C] (*Aus.*) honest behaviour. ❑ **straight goods** *n.* (*also* **straight stuff**) [late 19C+] (*US*) **1** the absolute truth. **2** a person who tells the truth. **3** undiluted spirits. ❑ **straight oil** *n. see under* OIL *n.* ❑ **straight pitching** *n. see under* PITCH *v.* ❑ **straight poop** *n. see* POOP *n.*[4] (2). ❑ **straight skinny** *n. see under* SKINNY *n.*[3]. ❑ **straight stuff** *n. see STRAIGHT GOODS* above. ❑ **straight tip** *n. see under* TIP *n.*[5]. ❑ **straight trick** *n. see under* TRICK *n.*[1]. ❑ **straight wire** *n. see under* WIRE *n.*[1].

IN PHRASES

❑ **on the straight** [late 19C–1910s] behaving respectably and honestly. ❑ **run straight** *v.* **1** [late 19C] (*UK society*) to remain faithful to one's husband. **2** [1900s] (*UK Und.*) of a criminal, to lead a law-abiding life. ❑ **straight and narrow** *n.* [Matt. 7:14: 'Because strait is the gate, and narrow is the way which leadeth unto life, and few there be that find it.' Note the mid-19C hymn: 'Loving Shepherd, ever near,/Teach Thy lamb Thy voice to hear;/ Suffer not my steps to stray/From the straight and narrow way'] [1910s+] conventionally moral and law-abiding behaviour; thus *keep on the straight and narrow*, to maintain a regular, law-abiding life. ❑ **you straight?** (*US campus*) a greeting, 'how are you?'

IN EXCLAMATIONS

❑ **straight dinkum!** *see* FAIR DINKUM! *excl.*

SE in slang uses

IN COMPOUNDS

❑ **straight ahead** *see* separate entries. ❑ **straight arrow** *see* separate entries. ❑ **straight drinking** *n.* [late 19C] drinking while upright, i.e. standing at a bar rather than sitting at a table. ❑ **straight-hair** *n.* [the convict crop; thus derog. ref. to Western Australia] (*Aus.*) **1** [mid-19C] a convict. **2** [late 19C+] a Western Australian. ❑ **straight-head** *n. see* STRAIGHT *n.*[2] (2). ❑ **straight neck** *n.* [1960s] (*US*) a conventional, disapproving person. ❑ **straight off** *adv.* [1930s+] immediately. ❑ **straight out** *see* separate entries. ❑ **straight peg** *n.* [1980s+] a law-abiding person. ❑ **straight shit** *n.* [STRAIGHT *adj.*[1] (2)] [1960s+] **1** the truth. **2** utter lies. ❑ **straight shooter** *n. see* separate entries. ❑ **straight shot** *n. see under* SHOT *n.*[1]. ❑ **straight up** *see* separate entries. ❑ **straight walk-in** *n.* [i.e. one needs only walk in and introduce oneself] [1920s–30s] a woman who is seen as easy to seduce.

IN PHRASES

❑ **dry straight** *v.* [woodworking imagery, of wood that dries without warping] [late 19C–1930s] to work out in time. ❑ **get one's head (on) straight** *v.* [1970s+] (*US*) to think clearly; to sort oneself out. ❑ **straight as a dog's leg** *adj.* (*also* **straight as a loon's leg, ...a butcher's hook**) [mid-19C–1940s] crooked. ❑ **straight bit of goods** *n. see* separate entry.

straight *adj.*[2] (*drugs*) **1** [mid-19C+] unadulterated, of liquor; subseq. or of a powdered narcotic. **2** [mid-19C+] sober; emotionally stable. **3** [1950s+] not currently using drugs; orig. of narcotics but extended to any drug. **4** [1950s+] cured of one's withdrawal pains by an injection of heroin. **5** [1950s+] of an addict, having had the first dose of the day. **6** [1950s+] in possession of drugs. **7** [1950s+] (*US*) under the influence of drugs, thus free of withdrawal symptoms. **8** [1970s] of marijuana, of average quality.

IN PHRASES

❑ **get straight** *v.* **1** [1940s+] (*US campus*) to sober up, from either drink or drugs, esp. when overcoming an addiction; also in fig. use. **2** [1960s+] (*drugs*) of a heroin addict, to inject the drug, thus relieving the pain of withdrawal symptoms. **3** [1960s+] (*drugs*) to consume a narcotic, whether or not one is addicted/suffering withdrawal. ❑ **put (someone) straight** *v.* [1950s+] to sell drugs to an addict; to give an addict their injection of drugs.

straight *adj.*[3] [1970s+] (*orig. US black*) a general intensifier, e.g. *straight chilling* (lit. unadulterated).

IN COMPOUNDS

❑ **straight flounging** *n.* [SE *lounge*] [1990s+] (*US teen*) acting in whatever manner is dictated by one's current circumstances.

straight *adj.*[4] (*also* **strizzy**) [1990s+] (*US teen*) cheerful, satisfied.

straight *adv.* **1** [late 16C–late 17C; late 19C+] without any reservations. **2** [mid-19C] (*US*) properly, efficiently. **3** [mid-19C+] honestly, really. **4** [late 19C+] (*orig. US*) consecutively, in a row. **5** [1950s+] sensibly. **6** [2000s] (*US black*) very well.

IN PHRASES

❑ **play it straight** *v.* [the warning used to actors not to overact] [1920s+] (*orig. theatre*) to behave in an honest manner, to resist embellishing one's actions with artifice.

SE in slang uses

IN PHRASES

implying (rustic) naivete

❑ **straight from the bog** [late 19C+] a derog. term used of an Irish immigrant to the UK. ❑ **straight off the banana boat** **1** [1970s] (*US campus*) strange. **2** [2000s] naive. ❑ **straight off the turnips** [1930s+] (*Aus./N.Z.*) used of a country bumpkin. ❑ **straight out of the trees** [1950s+] a derog. phr. used of black immigrants, irrespective of background, to the UK.

general uses

❑ **straight down the pike** [1990s+] (*US*) a general intensifier, indicating a supreme example of the preceding n. ❑ **straight from the feed box** *adj.* (*also* **straight from the nosebag**) [earlier var. on *STRAIGHT FROM THE HORSE'S MOUTH* below] [1900s–30s] of news, information, absolutely reliable, from 'inside' sources. ❑ **straight from the fridge** *adj.* [i.e. COOL *adj.* (5)] [1960s] (*US black/teen*) excellent, first-rate. ❑ **straight from the horse's mouth** *adj.* [1920s+] (*orig. racing jargon*) of news or information, absolutely reliable, gleaned from 'inside' sources. ❑ **straight from the shoulder** *adv.* *see* separate entry.

straight! *excl.* **1** [late 19C+] an excl. of affirmation, honestly! really! **2** [1990s+] (*US black*) a general term of agreement.

straight-ahead *adj.* [late 19C+] (*Aus./US*) committed, reliable, e.g. *a straight-ahead guy*.

straight ahead! *excl.* [1960s] (*US black*) an excl. of encouragement, support, affirmation.

straight arrow *n.* **1** [1960s+] (*US*) an honest, clean-living, clean-cut, upright, if naïve and unsophisticated person. **2** [1970s] (*US gay*) a heterosexual male.

straight-arrow *adj.* [STRAIGHT ARROW *n.* (1)] [1960s+] honest, upright, respectable, clean-living.

straight-arrow *adv.* [STRAIGHT-ARROW *adj.*] [1960s] (*US*) honestly.

straight bit of goods *n.* [STRAIGHT *adj.*[1] (3) + BIT OF GOODS *n.*] [late 19C] a respectable young woman.

straighten *v.*[1] **1** [late 19C–1900s] (*Aus.*) to defeat, to overcome; to beat up. **2** [20C+] (*UK Und.*) (*also* **straighten out, straighten up**) to bribe, usu. to bribe a police officer [i.e. to make STRAIGHT *adj.*[1] (8)]. **3** [20C+] (*also* **straighten out**) to sort a person out, to make them aware, to initiate them. **4** [1910s+] (*also* **straighten out, straighten up**) to settle an account or debt. **5** [1910s+] to settle an argument or a grudge by fighting [SE *straighten things out*]. **6** [1940s+] to look after. **7** [1950s–60s] to calm down, to defuse a situation. **8** *see* STRAIGHTEN OUT *v.* (1).

IN PHRASES

❑ **straighten up** *v.* [i.e. to make oneself STRAIGHT *adj.*[1] (5)] [20C+] to take up, or encourage to take up, an honest, respectable life. ❑ **straighten up and fly right** *v.* [orig. used in folktale, recorded by Joel Chandler Harris in *Short Stories Told After Dark* (1889)] [late 19C+] (*orig. US black*) to behave oneself, to mend one's ways and live a sensible, respectable life.

straighten *v.*[2] (*also* **straighten out**) [STRAIGHT *adj.*[2]] **1** [1920s+] (*drugs*) to give an injection of narcotics to relieve someone's withdrawal symptoms. **2** [1930s+] (*also* **straighten up**) to stop (someone) taking addictive drugs. **3** [1960s] in general sense, to give or sell drugs. **4** [1970s] of non-addictive drugs, to intoxicate pleasantly.

straightener *n.* **1** [1900s] (*Aus.*) a reviving drink; a drink that renders an alcoholic 'normal'. **2** [1950s+] an argument that may escalate into an physical fight. **3** [1950s+] an act of punishment, retribution. **4** [1950s+] a bribe.

straighten out *v.* **1** [late 19C+] (*also* **straighten**) to teach someone manners, to make them socially acceptable within a context. **2** [1920s+] to 'teach someone a lesson', to punish. **3** [1920s+] (*US*) to give an explanation; to sort a situation out. **4** [1920s+] to act in an acceptable manner, to remedy one's mistakes. **5** [1940s+] to soothe one's emotions; to cheer someone up. **6** [1950s] (*US Und.*) to introduce. **7** *see* STRAIGHTEN *v.*[1]. **8** see STRAIGHTEN *v.*[2].

straighten up *v.* **1** *see* STRAIGHTEN *v.*[1]. **2** *see* STRAIGHTEN *v.*[2] (2).

straight from the shoulder *adv.* (*also* **square from the shoulder**) [1910s+] openly, honestly, in a straightforward manner.

straight-out *adj.* [20C+] (*US*) uncompromising, absolute.

straight out *adv.* [1980s] (*US black*) honestly.

Straights, the *n.* [17C] a network of alleyways and small courts in an area bounded by St Martin's Lane, Half Moon Street and Chandos Street, all in Covent Garden, London; the haunt of pimps, thugs and similar unsavoury characters.

straight shooter *n.*[1] [fig. use of SE] [1920s+] (*US*) an honest, dependable, trustworthy person; thus adj. *straight-shooting*.

straight shooter *n.*[2] **1** [1970s] one who injects narcotics. **2** [1990s+] (*also* **straight**) a hypodermic, a syringe.

IN PHRASES

❑ **straight line shooter** *n.* [1930s] (*US drugs*) a drug addict who injects into the vein.

straight up *adj.*[1] [ext. of SE *straight*, undiluted] **1** [late 19C] (*US short order*) of eggs, 'sunny-side up'. **2** [1960s] (*US prison*) of a sentence, served without parole. **3** [1960s+] simple. **4** [1970s+] (*US*) of drinks, served without ice cubes.

straight up *adj.*[2] **1** [late 19C+] a general term of emphasis, implying honesty and genuineness; thus excl. *straight up!* honestly! really! **2** [20C+] respectable. **3** [1930s+] honest, trustworthy. **4** [1970s+] undeniable. **5** [1990s+] (*US black*) rigid, strict.

SE in slang uses

IN PHRASES

❑ **straight up six o'clock girl** *n.* [the position of the clock's hands] [1940s] (*US black*) a very thin woman.

straight up *adv.* [STRAIGHT UP *adj.*[2] (3)] **1** [late 19C+] (*US*) honestly. **2** [1990s+] completely, unreservedly.

strain *v.*

SE in slang uses

IN PHRASES

❑ **strain hard** *v.* [ext. use of SE] [late 17C–18C] to tell a substantial lie. ❑ **strain off** *v.* [20C+] to urinate. ❑ **strain one's greens** *v.* [pun on *greens*/GREENS *n.*[1]] **1** [1900s–30s] of a man, to have sexual intercourse. **2** [1980s+] to urinate. ❑ **strain one's milk** *v.* (*also* **strain the milk**) [20C+] (*US*) to strain oneself. ❑ **strain the main vein** *v.* [1950s+] to masturbate. ❑ **strain the potatoes** *v.* (*also* **strain the spuds, strain the taters**) [mid-19C+] to urinate.

strained out *adj.* [1960s] (*US drugs*) experiencing a drug's maximum effect.

stram, the *n.* (*also* **stramm, the**) [? SE *strumpet*, or US *stram*, to walk some distance or dial. *stram*, to bang, to strike and the widespread equation of sexual intercourse with 'banging'] [late 19C] the profession of street-walking.

stramel *n.* *see* STROMMEL *n.*

strammel *n.*[1] *see* STAMMEL *n.*

strammel *n.*[2] *see* STROMMEL *n.*

strammer *n.* [fig. use of dial. *stram*, to bang] [mid–late 19C] anything exceptional, whether in size or effect.

strange *n.* [1960s+] an unknown woman, usu. in a sexual context; thus a *bit of strange*.

strange *adj.*[1] [note *Leaves from the Diary of a Celebrated Burglar and Pickpocket* (1865): 'Jimmy Glindon [...] had left her because of her great relish for strange "blokes" during Jimmy's absence on the "dip".'] [20C+] of women, unknown, hitherto unencountered.

strange *adj.*[2] [1990s+] (*US campus*) on the bad=good pattern, excellent, first-rate.

strange fruit *n.* [1940s–60s] (*US black*) an odd, unpredictable person.

strangely weird *n.* [rhy. sl.] [20C+] a beard.

strange-o *n.* [SE *strange* + -O *sfx* (1)] [1950s–60s] an eccentric, a madman.

stranger *n.* **1** [late 18C–19C] (*usu. tramp*) a guinea [to encounter so large a sum is a rare event]. **2** [19C+] (*orig. US*) a term of address to one whose name is unknown. **3** [mid-19C] (*US*) a barrel of whisky [in a 'dry' county the whisky has to be imported from a distance]. **4** [1900s–30s] a sovereign [to encounter so large a sum is a rare event]. **5** [1930s+] anyone one knows but has not seen for some time; thus *hello stranger*, a greeting to a long-absent friend.

strangle and smother *n.* [rhy. sl.] [20C+] (*Aus.*) a mother.

strangle a parrot *v.* *see* SMOTHER A PARROT *v.*

strangle-goose *n.* [late 18C–late 19C] a poulterer.

strangler *n.* [? SE + pun on *choker*] [1920s–30s] a necktie.

strangle the goose *v.* **1** [1940s] (*N.Z.*) (*also* **strangle the gander**) to urinate. **2** [1970s+] (*also* **strangle the snake, strangle the stogie**) to masturbate.

strap *n.*[1] (*also* **streepach, streepo**) [Irish *straip*, a whore] [mid–late 17C; mid-19C+] (*Irish*) a whore; thus fig., an unpleasant woman.

strap *n.*[2] [late 17C] (*UK Und.*) a scheme, a plan.

strap *n.*[3] [early 19C] (*UK Und.*) an officer.

strap *n.*[4] [the SE *strop* used to sharpen razors. Note Hugh *Strap*, a barber, in Tobias Smollett's *Roderick Random* (1748)] [mid-19C] a barber.

strap *n.*[5] **1** [mid-19C+] credit; thus *on strap*, on credit [? it 'holds one together']. **2** [1900s–40s] (*US Und.*) 'a short-con game played with a coiled strap, one coil of which the mark tries to catch with a pencil' (Maurer, *The Big Con* 1940). **3** [1940s] (*US Und.*) a cosh, a blackjack. **4** [1970s] (*Can.*) a thug. **5** [1980s+] (*US black*) a gun; thus *strap me*, give me a gun [one 'straps' it to one's waist or into a holster].

IN PHRASES

❑ **strap up** *v.* [1990s+] (*US*) to carry a gun.

strap *v.*[1] **1** [early 19C] (*also* **strap at, strap to**) to work hard, to get on with, to buckle down to [one applies the fig. strap to one's own back]. **2** [1980s] to interrogate [one applies the fig. strap to another's back].

strap *v.*[2] [STRAP *n.*[5]] [mid–late 19C] to give credit.

IN PHRASES

❑ **strap up** *v.* [20C+] (*Aus.*) to obtain on credit; to offer credit.

strap *v.*[3] *see under* STRAPPING *n.*

strap at *v. see* STRAP *v.*[1] (1).

strap-oil *n.* (*also* **oil of strap'em, ...strappem**) [thus the popular April Fool's joke of sending a boy for 'a pennyworth of strap-oil'] [mid-19C–1930s] a flogging with a strap.

strap-on *n.* [1950s+] a dildo, with straps that anchor it to the user's body.

strap on *v.* [coarse use of SE] [1960s+] to have sexual intercourse.

strapped *adj.* (*also* **strapped down, strapping**) [STRAP *n.*[5] (5)] [1980s+] carrying a gun.

strapped (for cash) *adj.* [? the consequent 'tightening of one's belt', usu. a leather strap; or dial. *strap*, to drain dry, esp. of a cow's udder; ? STRAP *n.*[5]] [mid-19C+] (*orig. US*) **1** impoverished, poor. **2** in non-monetary contexts, e.g. *strapped for time*.

IN PHRASES

❑ **on the strap** *adj.* [1910s+] (*Aus.*) impoverished.

strapper *n.* [one who is fig. 'bound together with straps'] **1** [late 17C–mid-19C] a big, strong person, a notably hard worker; thus 19C *strapping-shop*, any workplace where an especially large volume of work is required of the employees. **2** [mid-19C] (*UK Und.*) an attractive woman.

strapping *n.* [SE *strapping*, a beating; i.e. image of intercourse as violence] [late 17C–early 19C] sexual intercourse.

strapping *adj. see* STRAPPED *adj.*

strapponia *n.* [SE *strap*] [mid-19C] (*US*) a physical beating.

straps *n.*[1] [joc. mispron.] [late 19C] sprats.

straps *n.*[2] [1940s] (*US black*) suspenders (UK, braces).

strap to *v. see* STRAP *v.*[1] (1).

strat *n.* [abbr.] [1960s+] a *Strat*ocaster guitar.

stratocruiser *n.* [1980s] (*W.I. drugs*) a large marijuana/tobacco cigarette.

straw *n.* [abbr. SE *straw blond(e)*] **1** [20C+] a person with light blond hair. **2** [1900s–60s] (*US black*) a hat, although not necessarily a straw hat [note 19C SE use, a straw hat]. **3** in drug uses [senses a and b from the shape, sense c from the colour]. (**a**) [1940s–50s] an opium pipe. (**b**) [1960s] a marijuana cigarette or marijuana. (**c**) [1960s] rolling papers. **4** *see* STRAWING *n.* **5** *see* STRAW BOSS below.

IN PHRASES

❑ **in the straw** *adj.* (*also* **in the strummel**) [18C SE *straw* as the stuffing of a bed, but note the defunct practice of laying straw in the street outside the house of a woman in labour in order to quieten the passing traffic; 20C+ use mainly Aus.] [mid-17C+] pregnant, in labour, giving birth.

SE in slang uses

IN COMPOUNDS

❑ **straw boss** *n.* (*also* **straw**) [orig. a threshing crew hierarchy in which the chief deals with the grain, the subordinate with the straw] **1** [late 19C+] (*US*) a person who is second-in-command, assistant to the boss. **2** [1920s+] (*US tramp*) the foreman of a work crew. ❑ **straw chipper** *n.* **1** [early–mid-19C] a barber. **2** [mid-19C] a straw bonnet maker. ❑ **straw hat** *n.* [metonymy] **1** [early 18C] a Billingsgate fish-wife. **2** [1900s–30s] (*Aus.*) a dandy, a fashionable person; thus *straw hat push*, the social élite. ❑ **strawhead** *n.* [1950s–60s] (*US*) a derog. term for an immigrant, lit. one, i.e. a peasant, with straw in their hair. ❑ **straw house** *n.* [late 19C] (*US*) a home for destitute seamen. ❑ **straw yard** *n.* [the straw laid down for bedding] **1** [early 19C] (*Anglo-Irish*) (*also* **straw hall**) a debtor's prison. **2** [mid-19C] a night-shelter or casual ward, occupied by the impoverished street-dwellers.

IN PHRASES

❑ **bang-straw** *n.* [what his job entails] [late 18C] a farm-worker, esp. a thresher. ❑ **whopstraw** *n.* (*also* **Johnny Whopstraw, Whipstraw**) [his SE *whopping* or threshing straw] [mid–late 19C] a countryman, a peasant. ❑ **draw straws** *v.* (*also* **gather straws, pick straws**) [pvb *one eye draws straw, t'other serves the thatcher*; Grose (1796) has the single *straw*] [mid-18C–mid-19C] to show signs of sleep; esp. as *one's eyes draw straws*. ❑ **wear a straw in one's ear** *v.* [? the custom of standing with a straw in one's mouth, which indicates one's desire to find a new job; + ? dial. *draw a straw across*, to beguile] [1910s–20s] of a woman, to seek a new husband.

strawb *n. see* STRAWBERRY (RIPPLE) *n.*

strawberry *n.* [the colour] **1** [late 19C] a broken-veined, bloated nose that exhibits signs of its possessor's heavy drinking. **2** [20C+] a red nose. **3** [1920s+] a bruise, esp. a graze or sore that results from friction with the ground. **4** in drug uses [the colour of the tablets]. (**a**) [1970s] amphetamines. (**b**) [1970s] mescaline. (**c**) [1970s+] LSD [the Beatles' song 'Strawberry Fields Forever' (1967)]. **5** [1980s+] (*US teen*) a promiscuous woman, esp. one who barters sex for drugs [? the woman spends so much time on her knees (for fellatio) or on her back (for intercourse) that she gets scars]. **6** [1990s+] (*US campus*) a good-looking woman.

SE in slang uses

IN COMPOUNDS

❑ **strawberries and cream** *n.* [1950s] (*UK prison*) the punishment diet of bread and water. ❑ **strawberry kiss** *n.* (*also* **strawberry Sunday**) [2000s] cunnilingus or intercourse with a menstruating woman.

strawberry box *n.* [1930s+] (*Aus./N.Z.*) a receptacle used for vomit on ships and aeroplanes.

strawberry dip *n.* [rhy. sl. = TRIP *n.*[4] (1)] [1980s+] (*Aus. prison*) LSD.

strawberry (ripple) *n.* (*also* **strawb**) [rhy. sl.; var. on RASPBERRY (RIPPLE) *n.* (2)] [1980s+] a disabled person.

strawberry tart *n. see* RASPBERRY TART *n.*

strawbug *n.* [joc. mispron.] [1950s] (*juv.*) a strawberry.

strawer *n. see under* STRAWING *n.*

strawing *n.* (*also* **straw**) [Ebsworth (intro to *Bagford Ballads*, 1880) notes '"Jack Straw" selling [...] single straws, "a penny a piece, choice from the corn-stack;" while to each winking purchaser he gave, with a rich leer, "gratooitously," a copy of the ditty he was singing'] [mid-19C] a form of illicit street-selling by which the buyer purchases a straw, usu. for one penny, and is given, as a 'free gift', a pamphlet (either pornographic or political) or a gold ring, neither of which items, the seller claims, are they allowed to sell; thus *strawer*, the seller.

stray *n.*[1] (*also* **stray bit, stray piece**) [SE *stray* + BIT *n.*[1] (2a)/PIECE *n.* (1a)] [1920s+] a pick-up, a casual sexual partner; thus casual sexual intercourse.

stray *n.*[2] [STRAIGHT *adj.*[1] (12) + GAY *adj.* (6)] [2000s] a heterosexual man with homosexual tendencies.

strayway *adj.* [SE *stray away*] [20C+] (*W.I., Gren.*) **1** given to wandering the streets. **2** undisciplined, unsettled.

streak *n.* **1** [mid-19C+] (*orig. US*) a rapid journey or rapid move; usu. in phr. *make a streak for*. **2** [1910s] (*US*) a fast runner. **3** [1940s+] (*orig. Aus.*) a tall, lean person [abbr. SE *long thin streak*]. **4** [1970s] (*US campus*) an exciting time, esp. at a party. **5** [1970s+] an act of discarding one's clothes in public, usu. at a sporting occasion, and disporting oneself in front of the crowd.

(IN PHRASES)

❑ **blue streak** *n.* [SE *blue streak*, that which resembles a flash of lightning] [late 19C+] (*orig. US*) that which is fast and at great length; usu. of speech. ❑ **long streak of misery** *n.* (*also* **lanky fathom of misery, long slab of misery, long streak (of gnat's piss)**) [late 19C+] a very tall person, esp. one with a mournful, depressed air. ❑ **long (thin) streak of piss** *n.* (*also* **long (thin) streak of pee**) **1** [20C+] (*also* **long thin streak of pelican shit**) an unflattering description of a tall, thin person. **2** [1900s–10s] one who over-estimates their own importance or abilities. ❑ **on a streak** [1990s+] (*US*) menstruating. ❑ **put a streak into it** *v.* [20C+] (*Anglo-Irish*) to hurry up, to 'get a move on'; esp. as excl. *put a streak into it!* ❑ **streak of lavender** *n. see under* LAVENDER *adj.* ❑ **streak of lightning** *n. see under* LIGHTNING *n.* ❑ **streak of weasel shit** *n.* [1960s] (*N.Z.*) a very fast runner.

streak *v.* **1** [mid-19C–1950s] (*also* **streak it, make streaks**) to run [SE *streak*]. **2** [1900s] (*also* **streak it**) to go, to walk [SE *streak*]. **3** [1970s+] to strip in public and run naked in front of a crowd; thus *streaking*, performing this exhibition [STREAKER *n.*].

streaked *adj.* [early–mid-19C] (*US*) irritable, irascible, ill-tempered, embarrassed.

streaker *n.* [originated on US campuses, where it amounted to the trad. *mooning* (cf. MOON *n.* (1d)), writ much larger, then transferred into a variety of larger arenas, notably the venues of major sporting events around the world] [1970s+] (*orig. US*) one who runs naked through a public place.

streak it *v.* **1** *see* STREAK *v.* (1). **2** *see* STREAK *v.* (2).

streaky *adj.* [one is neither one emotional 'colour' nor another] **1** [mid-19C] irritable, irascible. **2** [late 19C–1900s] (*also* **stripy**) variable in character, unstable, changeable.

strealy *adj. see under* STREELER *n.*

stream *n.*

(IN PHRASES)

❑ **up the big stream** *adj. see* UP THE RIVER *under* RIVER *n.*

streamer issue *n.* [1930s–40s] (*US black*) a necktie.

streamline *v.* [1980s+] (*Aus. prison*) to endure one's sentence with a minimum of problems.

stream's town *n. see* TIPPERARY FORTUNE *n.*

streeler *n.* (*also* **streel, strool**) [Irish *straoill*, a slattern] [mid-19C+] (*Irish*) of women, a slattern; of men, a slovenly, lazy person, also as adj., *streely, strealy, streelishness*.

streepach *n. see* STRAP *n.*[1].

streepo *n. see* STRAP *n.*[1].

Street, The *n.* **1** [19C+] (*US*) Wall Street, New York City. **2** [19C+] (*US*) Madison Avenue, New York City. **3** [20C+] Fleet Street, London EC, until 1990s home to the main newspaper offices. **4** [1900s–10s] (*US*) Broadway, New York City. **5** [1930s–40s] (*US*) 52nd Street, between 5th and 6th Avenues, then the centre of New York City jazz clubs.

street, the *n.* (*also* **the streets, street**) (*orig. US*) **1** [20C+] the mythical world of 'real life', which exists on the streets, rather than in the protected environments of home, office, family etc. **2** [1940s+] (*orig. US Und.*) the world of freedom, as opposed to that of prison; thus *on the street*, at liberty; *street time*, time on parole or between prison sentences. **3** [1960s] the world of commercial homosexual encounters.

(DERIVATIVES)

❑ **streetified** *adj.* [1970s+] (*US black*) well-versed in the ways of the urban lifestyle as seen on the inner-city streets.

(IN COMPOUNDS)

❑ **street beef** *n. see under* BEEF *n.*[2]. ❑ **street cred** *n.* [abbr. SE *credibility/credible*. Coined in the rock business and subseq. popular in any industries targeting the young consumer, it is based on the belief that the 'artist' must relate genuinely to the 'people', i.e. the working-class youth of the streets and housing estates and thus, sincerely or otherwise, offer an air of rebellion and informality] [1980s+] acceptability on a mass cultural level. ❑ **street legal** *adj.* [1990s+] (*US*) illegal, but acceptable in the 'real life' context of the street. ❑ **streetman** *n.* **1** [20C+] a petty criminal who 'works' on the street, usu. as a drug dealer or pickpocket. **2** [1980s] (*US black*) a person who is wise in the ways of the street. ❑ **street money** *n.* [1960s+] (*US*) money earned on the street, usu. through drug-dealing, pickpocketing or prostitution. ❑ **street nigger** *n. see under* NIGGER *n.*[1]. ❑ **streetside** *n.* [SIDE *n.* (2c)] [2000s] (*UK black*) the street; the world of the street. ❑ **street smart/smarts** *see* separate entries. ❑ **streetwise** *see* separate entries.

(IN PHRASES)

❑ **go street** *v.* [1990s+] (*US black/drugs*) to be involved in the use of and selling of crack cocaine. ❑ **run the street(s)** *v.* [1930s+] (*US black*) to spend one's time in self-indulgence, partying, drinking and enjoying the freedoms of a non-domestic life.

SE in slang uses

(IN COMPOUNDS)

❑ **street Arab** *n.* [the Black Muslims' identification with (mainly Arabic) Islam + play on SE *street Arab*, a homeless urchin] [1940s–50s] (*US black*) a member of the Black Muslims. ❑ **street-corner cowboy** *n. see* CORNER COWBOY *under* CORNER *n.*[2]. ❑ **street grizzling** *n. see under* GRIZZLE (ONE'S GUTS) *v.* ❑ **street people** *n.* [1960s–70s] a form of HIPPIE *n.*[2] (3), who wears the clothes but espouses more of a trad. begging ethic than that of the 'love and peace' generation. ❑ **street pitcher** *n. see under* PITCHER *n.*[2]. ❑ **street pizza** *n.* [1990s+] (*US black*) debris, a smashed-up mess. ❑ **street rat** *n. see under* RAT *n.*[1]. ❑ **street talk** *n.* [such information, the product of the *street* culture of petty crime, is considered valueless] [1940s+] gossip, rumour.

(IN PHRASES)

❑ **by a street** *adv.* [20C+] by a long way. ❑ **hit the street(s)** *v.* **1** [1950s+] (*orig. US*) to leave, to go out for the night. **2** [1960s+] (*US prison*) to return to free society. ❑ **hold court in the street** *v.* [1960s+] (*US*) to engage in a gun battle on the street (with the implication that one would rather die than face prison). ❑ **in the same street** *adv. see* IN THE SAME BOX *under* BOX *n.*[1]. ❑ **in the street** *adv.* [1960s+] (*US black*) openly, publicly. ❑ **play the streets** *v.* [1940s] (*US*) to work as a street prostitute. ❑ **put it on the street** *v.* [1950s+] (*orig. US*) to make gossip, information etc available for general consumption. ❑ **take it to the street** *v.* [20C+] (*US*) to take a private conflict or issue into the public arena.

street *adj.* [STREET, THE *n.*] [1970s+] (*orig. US black*) used of people believed to be of the 'real life', of the world which exists on the streets; sophisticated and aware, trendy.

street *v.* **1** [1920s] (*US Und.*) to throw someone out, e.g. of a bar. **2** [1940s] (*US Und.*) to guide a victim away from the site of a confidence trick. **3** [1950s+] (*drugs*) of a prisoner, to send out money so that a confederate can buy and smuggle back in some drugs. **4** [1960s] (*US Und.*) to release a prisoner.

street *adv.* [STREET *adj.* (1)] [1980s+] (*orig. US black*) in a manner typical of the STREET, THE *n.*

-street *sfx* [1960s+] (*orig. US*) a general sfx meaning place or situation, whether concrete or abstract.

streeter *n.* [1960s] one who lives in the streets or regularly frequents a given street.

street smart *adj.* [STREET, THE *n.* (1) + SE *smart*] [1970s+] (*orig. US*) able to survive in the inner city or the ghetto streets, despite a lack of material, bourgeois advantages.

street smarts *n.* [STREET, THE *n.* (1) + SMARTS *n.*] [1970s+] instinctive knowledge as opposed to learned knowledge.

streetwise *adj.* [STREET, THE *n.* (1) + -WISE *sfx* (1)] [1960s+] (*orig. US*) able to survive in the inner city or the ghetto streets despite a lack of material, bourgeois advantages.

streetwise *adv.* [1970s] (*US*) in the style of the streets.

strel *n.* (*also* **strell**) [Ital. *strillare*, to shriek] [late 19C+] (*Polari*) a banjo; thus *strel/strell-homey*, a banjo-player.

strength *n.* [note 'Get with the Strength', the advertising slogan of the Commonwealth Bank of Australia, whose emblem is an elephant] [20C+] (*orig. Aus./N.Z.*) the facts, the details of a situation; usu. as *the strength of*; thus *get the strength of*, to understand.

IN PHRASES

❑ **on the strength** *adv.* [SE *strong*, important, vital] [1990s+] (*US black*) used to underline the importance and seriousness of the subject under discussion.

strengthening-plaster *n.* [mid-19C] (*UK Und.*) a reprieve.

strep *n.* [abbr.] **1** [1920s+] *strep*tococcus, a form of bacterium, esp. in comb. *strep throat*. **2** [1950s+] *strep*tomycin, an antibiotic orig. used to combat tuberculosis, but now usu. used in combination with other drugs because of its toxicity.

stress *n.* [2000s] (*US black*) weak, second-rate marijuana.

SE in slang uses

IN COMPOUNDS

❑ **stress-case** *n.* [1980s+] (*US campus*) a very nervous, tense person. ❑ **stress-monger** *n.* (*also* **stress-monster**) [-MONGER *sfx*/-MONSTER *sfx*] [1980s+] (*US campus*) a very stressed, nervous person.

stress *v.* [1980s+] **1** to worry, to panic, to lose control; also as excl.; also adj. *stressy*. **2** (*US campus*) to work hard. **3** to challenge, to cause irritation for someone.

IN PHRASES

❑ **stress out** *v.* [1980s+] **1** to become stressed. **2** to cause someone to become stressed.

stretch *n.* **1** in prison/Und. uses [abbr. SE *stretch of time*]. (**a**) [19C] a year. (**b**) [early 19C+] (*also* **stretcher**) a twelve-month sentence; thus *two stretch*, two years; *three stretch*, three years etc. (**c**) [mid-19C+] a sentence of undetermined length. **2** [early 19C] a yard (3ft/91cm). **3** [mid-19C] a march, a long journey. **4** [1940s] (*US*) a general term of address, usu. to a tall thin person. **5** [1950s] a long time. **6** [1980s] (*US*) a period of enlistment in the armed forces. **7** [1980s+] a *stretch* limousine.

IN PHRASES

❑ **half a stretch** *n.* (*also* **half stretch**) [mid-19C+] (*UK Und.*) six months' imprisonment; also used by criminals for any period of six months. ❑ **in the stretch** [horseracing term *the stretch*, the last part of the course] [20C+] almost complete, near the end.

stretch *v.* **1** [17C–1960s] to hang, to be hanged; thus *stretcher*, a hangman; *stretched*, hanged [abbr. SE *stretch one's neck*]. **2** [late 19C+] (*also* **stretch out**) to knock down, to kill [SE *stretch (someone) out* on the ground]. **3** [1940s+] of a man, to have sexual intercourse [? link to *STRETCH LEATHER* ***under*** LEATHER *n.*].

IN PHRASES

❑ **stretch someone's neck** *v.* [mid-19C–1950s] to hang. ❑ **stretch (the) hemp** *v.* (*also* **pull hemp, stretch a line**) [the hempen noose] [mid-19C–1950s] to be hanged or to hang oneself.

SE in slang uses

IN COMPOUNDS

❑ **stretch one** *n.* [1930s] (*US*) a large glass of Coca-Cola.

IN PHRASES

❑ **stretch a pipe** *v. see under* PIPES *n.*[1]. ❑ **stretch (it)** *v.* [SE *stretch the truth*] [late 17C+] to exaggerate, to lie. ❑ **stretch out** *v.* [jazz use *stretch out*, to play to one's limits, with no restraints other than one's stamina and skill] **1** [1950s–60s] (*US black*) to live one's life without restraint, to act uninhibitedly. **2** *see* sense 2 above. ❑ **stretch some jeans** *v.* [the removal of one's jeans or trousers] [1980s+] (*US prison, esp. homosexual*) to have sexual intercourse. ❑ **stretch someone's breeches** *v.* [the bent-over buttocks tighten the cloth that covers them] [late 19C] to administer a thrashing; thus *have one's breeches stretched*, to suffer a beating.

stretched *adj.*[1] [the fabric of one's trousers is SE *stretched* over the tightened buttocks] [late 19C] whipped.

stretched *adj.*[2] *see under* STRETCH *v.*

stretcher *n.* **1** [late 17C–late 19C] a lie [it SE *stretches* the truth]. **2** [mid-18C–late 19C] a large penis. **3** [mid-19C] (*US Und.*) a racehorse [SAmE *stretch*, the final run-in of a horserace]. **4** [late 19C] (*Anglo-Irish*) a layer-out of the dead. **5** [1920s] a long stretch of road, the journey taken upon it. **6** [1930s–40s] (*US black*) a necktie. **7** [1930s–40s] (*US black*) a belt. **8** [1940s] (*US Und.*) a sodomite. **9** [1960s] (*S.Afr. Und.*) a judge. **10** see STRETCH *n.* (1b).

SE in slang uses

IN EXCLAMATIONS

❑ **get the stretcher!** (*also* **get the ambulance!**) [late 19C] an excl. used when seeing someone who is falling down drunk.

stretcher case *n.*[1] [STRETCHER *n.* (1) + play on SE] [1940s+] a liar.

stretcher case *n.*[2] [2000s] (*N.Z.*) an extremely crazy person.

stretcher-fencer *n.* [STRETCHERS *n.* (1) + -FENCER *sfx*] [mid-19C] a street-seller of braces (suspenders, US).

stretchers *n.* **1** [mid-19C+] braces (suspenders US). **2** [1900s–60s] shoelaces.

stretching *n.* [late 17C–mid-19C] (*UK Und.*) a judicial hanging.

IN COMPOUNDS

❑ **stretching match** *n.* **1** [mid-19C] a judicial hanging. **2** [1930s] a double hanging. **3** [1940s] (*US*) a lynching.

'strewth! *excl.* (*also* **'stroof! strufe! struth! 'struth!**) [mid-19C+] a mild, euph. oath; lit. 'God's truth!'.

strib *n.* [? fig. use of dial. *strib*, to drain] [20C+] (*US Und.*) a prison warden.

stricsies *n.* [? SE *restrict*] [mid-19C] (*UK Und.*) handcuffs.

strictly *adv.* [1930s+] (*orig. US*) totally, entirely.

IN PHRASES

❑ **strictly from** [1930s+] in the style of, derivative of, exactly like. ❑ **strictly from hunger** [1930s+] **1** driven by dire necessity, usu. financial. **2** emptily, foolishly, to a distressing degree. **3** most unsatisfactorily.

strictly! *excl.* [1970s+] (*US campus*) really! honestly! absolutely!

stride *v.* [1970s] (*US black*) to perform with great skill.

striders *n.* [var. on STRIDES *n.* (1)] [1940s] (*US black*) trousers.

strides *n.* **1** [mid-19C+] (*now mainly Aus.*) trousers. **2** [1910s+] (*Aus.*) knickers, panties. **3** [1960s] (*US*) shoes.

stride-wide *n.* [? its effects] [late 16C] a strong beer.

strife *n.* [weak use of SE] **1** [1910s+] (*Aus.*) trouble, disgrace, difficulties; esp. as *in strife*. **2** [1950s–60s] (*UK Und.*) a life sentence.

strike *n.* **1** [early 18C–mid-19C] (*UK Und.*) a sovereign, a guinea [SE *strike*, to mint a coin]. **2** [late 19C–1900s] a watch [SE *strike*, to ring the time]. **3** [1900s–50s] (*US*) a failure to seduce [baseball imagery]. **4** [1910s+] (*US Und.*) an arrest and the prison sentence that follows; thus *two strikes*, two terms in prison; *three strikes*, three arrests and the mandatory life sentence that follows in many states [baseball imagery, *three strikes and you're out*]. **5** [1930s–50s] (*US*) any position of weakness [baseball imagery]. **6** [1970s] (*US prison*) a disciplinary charge [baseball imagery].

SE in slang uses

IN COMPOUNDS

❑ **strike breaker** *n.* [1920s] (*US*) a woman who takes advantage of a temporary estrangement to date the male of a couple.

IN PHRASES

❑ **make a strike** *v.* [skittles/bowling imagery] [mid-19C+] to be lucky, to be successful. ❑ **make a ten-strike** *v.* [bowling use *ten-strike*, the knocking over of all ten pins] [late 19C–1940s] (*US*) to do well, to succeed.

strike *v.* **1** [mid-16C–mid-18C] to steal goods, to rob a person. **2** [17C] to borrow money. **3** [mid-18C–19C] to make a sudden and pressing demand upon someone for money; to beg. **4** [late 19C–1900s] to get money suddenly. **5** [late 19C–1920s] to ask for, e.g. food. **6** [1910s] to persuade someone to spend money.

IN PHRASES

❑ **strike a jigger** *v. see under* JIGGER *n.*[1].

SE in slang uses

IN COMPOUNDS

❑ **strikefire** *n.* [? play on LIGHTNING *n.* (1)] [early 18C] gin.

(IN PHRASES)

□ **strike a blow for liberty** *v.* [1920s–30s] (*US*) in the Prohibition era, to take a clandestine drink. □ **strike a bright** *v.* [SE *bright thought*] [late 19C–1900s] to have a sudden, pleasant thought, to have a piece of good luck. □ **strike a light** *v.* [fig. use of SE] **1** [early 19C] to pull oneself together. **2** [mid-19C] to run up credit at a public house. □ **strike for tall timber** *v. see* TAKE TO THE TALL TIMBER(S) *under* TALL TIMBERS *n.* □ **strike (it) lucky** *v.* [1930s+] to become lucky. □ **strike it rich** *v.* [orig. used in oil-/goldfields] [mid-19C+] to gain sudden wealth. □ **strike-me-blind** *n.* [the belief that rice would make one blind; thus naut. jargon *strike-me-blind*, rice] [late 19C] boiled rice and black-strap molasses. □ **strike me dead** *n. see* separate entries. □ **strike oil** *v.* (*also* **strike ile**) [mid-19C+] (*orig. US*) to do well, to prosper. □ **strike one's breath** *v.* [late 19C+] (*Aus.*) to 'cross one's heart and hope to die', as part of an assurance of one's honesty. □ **strike out** *v.* [baseball jargon *strike out*, of the batter to fail to make legal contact with the ball in four attempts] [20C+] (*US*) **1** to die. **2** to fail, esp. in an attempt to seduce a woman or man or trick a potential victim for a confidence trick. □ **strike the gag** *v. see under* GAG *n.* □ **strike the gig** *v. see under* GIG *n.*[3]. □ **strike up** *v.* [1980s+] (*US black gang*) to inscribe a wall with a gang name.

(IN EXCLAMATIONS)

□ **strike a light!** [20C+] (*orig. Aus.*) a general excl. of surprise, shock, amazement etc.

strike! *excl.* [1910s+] (*Aus.*) an excl. of amazement, irritation etc; usu. ext. to *STRIKE ME BLIND! under* STRIKE ME...! *excl.*; *STRIKE ME PINK! under* STRIKE ME...! *excl.*

strike-me *n.* [rhy. sl. *strike me dead*] [20C+] bread.

strike me...! *excl.*

(IN EXCLAMATIONS)

□ **strike me!** [abbr. next] [mid-19C+] a mild excl. □ **strike me balmy!** *see STRIKE ME SILLY!* below. □ **strike me blind!** (*also* **strike me bandy! ...bob! ...down! ...dumb! ...lame! ...paraytic! ...ugly!**) [18C+] a general excl. of surprise, amazement; implies calling on God/the gods to make some concomitant gesture. □ **strike me blue!** (*also* **strike me bloody! ...hooray! ...horray!**) [late 19C+] (*Aus./N.Z.*) a mild oath. □ **strike me dead!** (*also* **strike me stiff!**) [late 18C+] a mild oath. □ **strike me dilly!** *see STRIKE ME SILLY!* below. □ **strike me doleful!** [early 19C] (*US*) a mild excl. □ **strike me fat!** [late 19C+] (*Aus./N.Z.*) a mild excl. □ **strike me funny!** [early 19C] a mild excl. □ **strike me handsome!** (*also* **strike me pretty!**) [1910s+] (*Aus./N.Z.*) a mild excl. □ **strike me holy!** [1900s] (*Aus.*) a mild oath. □ **strike me hooray!/horray!** *see STRIKE ME BLUE!* above. □ **strike me lame!** *see STRIKE ME BLIND!* above. □ **strike me lucky!** [UK in 19C, it re-emerged in mid-20C+ Aus. use; Nares (1882) notes earlier 17C *strike me luck*, 'a familiar phrase, which seems to have arisen from striking a bargain, and giving earnest upon it', i.e. by shaking or striking each other's palm] [early 19C+] a general oath, esp. on the sealing of a bargain by slapping hands together. □ **strike me moral!** [late 18C] a mild excl. □ **strike me paralytic!** *see STRIKE ME BLIND!* above. □ **strike me perp(endicular)!** [var. on *STRIKE ME DEAD!* above] [late 19C–1900s] a general excl. of surprise, alarm, shock etc. □ **strike me pink!** (*also* **do me pink! strike me purple!**) **1** [late 19C+] a mild excl. of surprise, irritation etc. **2** [1910s] as v., to render someone foolish. □ **strike me pretty!** *see STRIKE ME HANDSOME!* above. □ **strike me roan!** [1910s+] (*Aus./N.Z.*) a mild excl. □ **strike me silly!** (*also* **strike me balmy! ...dilly! ...sensible! ...stupid!**) [early 18C; 1910s–20s] a mild excl. of surprise, irritation etc. □ **strike me sober!** [1900s] (*Aus.*) a mild excl. □ **strike me stiff!** *see STRIKE ME DEAD!* above. □ **strike me sunburnt!** [var. on *STRIKE ME PINK!* above] [late 19C] a mild excl. of surprise, irritation etc. □ **strike me ugly!** *see STRIKE ME BLIND!* above. □ **strike me up a pipe!** [1910s] (*Aus.*) an excl. of annoyance, frustration. □ **strike me up a stick!** [1910s] (*Aus.*) a mild excl. of annoyance, frustration. □ **strike me up a tree!** (*also* **strike me up a gum (tree)!**) an excl. of astonishment.

strike-me-dead *n.*[1] [joc. ref. to its effects – it is relatively weak] [mid-19C] small beer.

strike-me-dead *n.*[2] [rhy. sl.] [late 19C+] bread.

striker *n.*[1] [the equation of sex and violence] **1** [late 16C–mid-17C] a womanizer, a pimp. **2** [late 16C–mid-17C] a prostitute. **3** [19C] the penis. **4** [mid-19C] (*US Und.*) a street tout who entices players into a gambling club; he doubles as a thug in the case of complaints. **5** [1910s] (*US prison*) a home-made device used to light cigarettes. **6** [1950s+] a match.

striker *n.*[2] **1** [1900s] (*US milit.*) an officer's servant. **2** [1980s] (*US Und.*) a recruit for a motorcycle gang.

striking *adj.* [linked to such excl. as *STRIKE ME DEAD! under* STRIKE ME...! *excl.*] [1950s] (*W.I.*) a general intensifier.

strill *n.* [Ital. *strillare*, to shriek, to cry out] [late 19C+] (*Ling. Fr./Polari*) a musical instrument, esp. a portable harmonium or a piano; thus *strill-homey*, a male pianist; *strill-polone*, a female pianist.

strilla *adj.* [? SE *real*/REAL *adj.*] [2000s] (*US black*) good, satisfactory.

string *n.* **1** [early 19C–1910s] a hoax, a fraud [STRING (ALONG) *v.* (1a)]. **2** [early 19C+] a condition, restriction; usu. in phr. *no strings*. **3** [late 19C–1920s] (*US Und.*) a form of confidence trick. **4** [1910s–40s] (*US Und.*) a fuse, as used for detonation when 'blowing' a safe. **5** [1920s+] (*also* **string of ponies**) a group of prostitutes working for a single pimp [SE *string*, a set or stud of horses]. **6** [1950s+] (*US*) the penis; thus *string and nuggets*, the penis and testicles.

(IN COMPOUNDS)

□ **stringbean** *n. see* separate entry. □ **string city** *n. see* separate entry.

(IN PHRASES)

□ **off the string** *adv. see OFF THE CHAIN under* CHAIN *n.* □ **string of ponies** *n. see* sense 5 above.

string *v.* [STRING *n.* (5)] [1960s] (*US Und.*) to work as a pimp, i.e. to run a string of prostitutes.

string (along) *v.* **1** in senses of persuasion [the image of dragging someone along on the end of a string]. (**a**) [early 19C+] (*also* **string on**) to fool, to deceive someone, esp. over a drawn-out period of time; to tease. (**b**) [late 19C+] (*Aus./N.Z./US*) to encourage, to egg on. **2** in senses of movement. (**a**) [mid-19C] (*US*) to progress, to walk along. (**b**) [20C+] to accompany. **3** [1960s] (*US Und.*) to 'fix' horseraces.

(DERIVATIVES)

□ **stringing** *n.* [1900s] (*US*) teasing, deceiving.

(IN PHRASES)

□ **string (along) with** *v.* [1910s+] (*orig. US*) **1** to accompany; to associate with. **2** to agree with. **3** to support. □ **string on** *v.* **1** [late 19C+] (*Aus./N.Z.*) to deceive; in a relationship, to lead someone on. **2** *see* sense 1a above. □ **string (someone) out** *v.* [1960s+] **1** to keep someone in suspense. **2** to deceive someone over a period of time.

string and top *n.* (*also* **silk and top**) [rhy. sl. = COP *n.*[1] (1)] [1920s–50s] (*US*) a police officer.

stringbean *n.* (*also* **piece of string**) **1** [1910s+] a tall, skinny person; thus as a nickname; also attrib. [note D'Urfey, *Pills to Purge Melancholy* (1719): (of a woman) 'The one thin and lean, As a Garden French Bean']. **2** [1970s] (*US black*) a very thin, long penis.

string beans *n.* [rhy. sl.] [1970s+] jeans.

string city *n.* [it is 'strung out' along the road] [2000s] a suburban ribbon development.

stringer *n.*[1] **1** [17C; 1910s+] (*US*) a pimp [? *string* of prostitutes/STRING *n.* (6)]. **2** [early–mid-19C] (*UK Und.*) a confidence trickster, a swindler [STRING *n.* (1)]. **3** [mid-19C] a hoax, a trick [STRING *n.* (1)]. **4** [late 19C–1910s] (*N.Z.*) a woman who works in a public house or bar encouraging the patrons to drink [STRING (ALONG) *v.* (1b)].

stringer *n.*[2] *see* STINGER *n.* (8).

stringers *n.* [late 19C–1900s] handcuffs.

string oneself out *v.* [20C+] (*US*) to be disturbed, upset or worried.

string out *v.* [STRUNG OUT *adj.*] [1960s+] **1** (*drugs*) to use and be addicted to narcotic drugs. **2** (*US campus*) suffering from some minor ailment.

string the fives on *v. see under* BUNCH OF FIVES *n.*

string up *v.* [*string up*, to hang is SE] [late 19C–1910s] to garrotte.

string vest *n.* [rhy. sl.] [1990s+] a pest, an annoying person.

stringybark *n.* [for ety. *see* STRINGYBARK *adj.*] **1** [late 19C] beer. **2** [late 19C–1950s] (*Aus.*) a supposed 'whisky', actually made of turpentine and fuel oil; thus bad liquor in general. **3** *see* STRINGYBARKER *under* STRINGYBARK *adj.*

stringybark *adj.* [SE *stringybark*, one of many trees, typically the eucalyptus, that has a thick, rough and fibrous bark and is found in the bush of southeast Aus.] **1** [mid–late 19C] (*Aus.*) unsophisticated, rural, remote. **2** [1950s] tough, brave, hardy.

DERIVATIVES

❑ **stringybarker** *n.* (*also* **stringy-bark**) [late 19C–1950s] (*Aus.*) one who lives in the outback.

IN COMPOUNDS

❑ **stringybark cockatoo** *n.* [COCKATOO *n.*² (3)] [20C+] (*Aus.*) a small farmer, often a failed prospector forced to turn to farming in order to survive.

Strip, the *n.* [1930s+] (*US*) any main street or central area of a city devoted to entertainment, esp. Las Vegas.

strip *v.* **1** [late 17C–18C] (*UK Und.*) to rob a house, esp. when the thieves empty it of all moveable contents. **2** [late 17C+] to rob a person. **3** [1980s] (*US campus*) to upset or harm a person.

SE in slang uses

IN COMPOUNDS

❑ **strip act** *n.* (*also* **strip**) [1930s+] (*orig. US*) a striptease show; similarly *strip club, strip dancer, strip show.* ❑ **strip-bush** *n.* [laundry was orig. laid out on hedges to dry] [mid-19C] one who steals washing from its drying lines. ❑ **strip-down** *n.* [1950s] (*US*) an automobile that has been modified to improve its performance. ❑ **strip-eel** *n.* [one of his jobs] [early 18C] a fishmonger. ❑ **strip joint** *n.* [JOINT *n.* (3b)] [1950s+] (*US*) a bar or club that offers striptease shows.

IN PHRASES

❑ **strip a peg (in Plunket Street)** *v.* [*Plunket Street*, the old-clothes market in Dublin] [late 18C] (*Irish*) to dress in second-hand clothes. ❑ **strip-me-naked** *n. see* separate entries. ❑ **strip teeth and bite** *v.* [1900s] (*Aus.*) to become fiercely argumentative.

IN EXCLAMATIONS

❑ **strip me!** [mid-18C] a general excl. of imprecation.

stripe *n.* **1** [1950s+] a scar, usu. the result of being slashed with an open razor. **2** [1990s+] a police patrol car, carrying some form of fluorescent stripe on its sides. **3** [2000s] (*W.I.*) abbr. Red Stripe beer brand.

stripe *v.* [STRIPE *n.* (1)] **1** [1950s+] to slash with a cut-throat razor or other edged weapon. **2** [1970s] thus fig., to harm (in a non-physical manner). **3** [1970s] to defraud.

striped *adj.* [mid-19C] (*US*) drunk.

stripes *n.*¹ (*US*) **1** [mid-19C–1940s] a prison uniform; thus *wear the stripes*, to serve a prison sentence. **2** [1990s+] a referee.

IN PHRASES

❑ **take stripes** *v.* [the old striped uniforms] [late 19C–1940s] (*US*) to be sent to prison.

stripes *n.*² *see* OLD STRIPES *under* OLD *adj.*

strip(e)y *adj.* [? fig. use of SE *stripey*, i.e. not plain (and simple)] **1** [1900s] difficult. **2** [2000s] (*N.Z.*) unconvincing, dubious.

stripey fat *v.* [rhy. sl. = *GO OFF THE BAT under* BAT *n.*²] [1980s+] (*Aus. prison*) to masturbate.

striping *n.* [STRIPE *v.* (2)] [2000s] a reprimand.

strip-me-naked *n.*¹ [mid-18C–mid-19C] a fiery drink, esp. raw gin.

strip-me-naked *n.*² [? the quantity of the food fills one up and one gets relief by taking off one's clothes, or the expense involved in purchasing the food leaves one 'naked' of cash] [1950s] (*W.I.*) any form of food made from flour, e.g. biscuits, cake.

stripped *adj.* [mid-19C–1900s] of spirits, neat.

stripper *n.*¹ **1** [mid–late 19C] a thief, usu. a woman, who specializes in luring young children into secluded places, where they are stripped of their clothes, which are later sold, and left naked in the street. **2** [1920s] (*US Und.*) a thief who removes all valuable parts from a car.

stripper *n.*² [abbr. SE *striptease*] [1930s+] (*orig. US*) a striptease performer.

strippers *n.* (*also* **belly strippers, low belly strippers**) [mid-19C+] (*US gambling*) playing cards of which the sides and/or ends have been slightly trimmed to help cheating.

IN PHRASES

❑ **play strippers on** *v.* [late 19C+] (*US gambling*) to cheat at cards by using a deck in which the sides of certain cards have been microscopically shaved or 'stripped'.

stripping law *n.* [LAW *n.* (1)] [late 16C–early 17C] (*UK Und.*) the practice of stripping prisoners of their valuable possessions as carried out by prison staff.

stripy *adj.*¹ *see* STREAKY *adj.* (2).

stripy *adj.*² *see* STRIP(E)Y *adj.*

strizzy *adj. see* STRAIGHT *adj.*⁴.

strobe-light honey *n. see under* HONEY *n.*¹.

stroke *n.*¹ [late 16C+] (*20C+ mainly US black*) sexual intercourse; thus *take a stroke*, to have sexual intercourse; *strokability*, sexual potential.

stroke *n.*² **1** [19C+] (*UK Und./police*) an action considered audacious or daring; sometimes criminal activity. **2** [1920s] (*US*) a monopoly; rights to do something.

IN PHRASES

❑ **pull a stroke** *v.* [SE *stroke*, 'a vigorous attempt to gain or do something' (*OED*); a suggested link with rowing strokes seems implausible] [1910s+] to attempt and/or get away with anything outrageous or daring.

stroke *v.*¹ [20C+ use is mainly US black] **1** [mid-17C+] to have sexual intercourse. **2** [1960s+] to masturbate.

IN COMPOUNDS

❑ **stroke book** *n.* (*also* **stroke mag, stroke magazine, stroke rag**) [1960s+] a pornographic book or magazine. ❑ **stroke house** *n.* [1970s] a cinema showing pornographic films.

IN PHRASES

❑ **stroke it off** *v.* [1950s+] to masturbate; *stroke* is used in a number of combs. to mean masturbate, e.g. *stroke one's beef, …one's ego, …one's poker, …one's steven, …the bloke, … the dog, …the goat, …the trumpet.* ❑ **stroke one's lizard** *v. see under* LIZARD *n.* ❑ **stroke the beaver** *v. see under* BEAVER *n.*¹.

SE in slang uses

IN PHRASES

❑ **stroked out** *adj.* [fig. use of sense 2 above] [1960s] exhausted. ❑ **stroke out** *v.* [i.e. to suffer a stroke] [1970s+] to die.

stroke *v.*² [fig. use of SE *stroke*] **1** [1960s+] (*US prison*) to curry favour with a more powerful inmate or with the authorities. **2** [1980s] (*US campus*) to trick, to deceive. **3** [1990s+] (*UK juv.*) to steal [the thief's hands run gently over the desired object].

Stroke City *n.* [SE *stroke*, a solidus + -CITY *sfx* (1); the dual names of the city, claimed respectively by Catholics/Protestants and the futile attempt to rename it 'Londonderry/Derry'] [1960s+] (*Ulster*) Derry/Londonderry, Ireland.

stroker *n.* [STROKE *v.*¹ (2)] [1960s+] a masturbator; also fig. use, a loser.

stroll *n.* [SE *stroll*, to wander along; usu. US; the original *stroll* was situated between 26th and 63rd Streets on New York's West Side, the mid–late 19C centre of the black population. During the 1890s the stroll moved to Seventh Avenue between 23rd to 34th Streets and when the focus of black life moved again, to Harlem (*c.*1920) the stroll moved up-town on Seventh Avenue between 131st and 132nd Streets] **1** [mid-19C; 1920s+] (*mainly US black*) the main street, esp. when used as a social centre. **2** [1930s+] (*US*) anything requiring only minimal effort, an easy task. **3** [1950s+] (*US pimp*) those streets or blocks on which prostitutes ply their trade; thus a prostitute; thus as v., to work as a street prostitute. **4** [2000s] (*US black*) a place where drugs are sold.

SE in slang uses

IN PHRASES

❑ **take the morning stroll** *v.* [1940s] (*Belfast*) to be hanged.

stroll *v.* [to walk away with something] [1940s+] to get away with something, to go free, to do well.

stroller *n.* [note SE *stroll*] **1** [1950s] (*US*) an automobile. **2** [1980s+] (*S.Afr.*) a homeless young street beggar; thus v. *stroll* [Scot. *stroller*, a vagabond].

strollers *n.* [1940s] (*US black*) trousers.

strolling mort *n.* (*also* **strowling mort, ... punk**) [SE *stroll* + MORT *n.* (1)/PUNK *n.*[1]] [mid-17C–early 19C] (*UK Und.*) an unmarried female beggar, often accompanied by a child, who claims to be widowed and begs for her and her offspring's keep.

stroll on! *excl.* [1950s+] a general excl. of dismissal or disbelief, 'you must be joking!'.

strommel *n.* (*also* **stramel, strammel, stromell, strumil, strummel**) [? OF *estramer*, to spread with straw or rushes] **1** [mid-16C–1900s] (*UK Und.*) straw. **2** [mid-17C–mid-19C] hair; thus *strummolo*, false pubic hair.

IN COMPOUNDS

❑ **strommel-faker** *n.* [FAKER *n.* (1)] [late 18C–early 19C] a barber. ❑ **strommel-patch** *n.* [late 16C–early 17C] a pej. name for a person.

strong *n.* [var. STRENGTH *n.*] [20C+] (*Aus.*) the truth, the facts, the essential information; thus *what's the strong of it?* what is the truth? what are the precise facts?

strong *adj.* **1** [mid-17C; mid-19C+] extreme, excessive. **2** [mid-19C+] of people, uncompromising, zealous. **3** [late 19C–1900s] competent, able, well-versed. **4** [late 19C–1950s] in funds, rich; thus phr. of enquiry: *how strong are you?* how much money do you have? **5** [1900s–50s] as *strong for*, keen on. **6** [1910s] (*US*) popular. **7** [1960s+] pornographic, usu. found in advertisements in such magazines.

SE in slang uses

IN COMPOUNDS

❑ **strongarm/armer/arming** *see* separate entries. ❑ **strong box** *n.* [1930s+] (*UK prison*) a prison, a punishment cell. ❑ **strong-eye** *see* separate entries. ❑ **strong game** *n. see* HEAVY GAME *under* GAME *n.* ❑ **strong joint** *n.* [JOINT *n.* (3b)] [1910s+] **1** (*US*) a crooked or cheating gambling game. **2** (*US*) a crooked casino or gambling house. **3** (*Aus. Und.*) a swindler. ❑ **strong man** *n.* [he 'pushes through' one's resistance] [1930s+] (*Aus.*) a confidence trickster. ❑ **strong-mouth** *n. see* separate entry. ❑ **strong-physic** *see* separate entries.

IN PHRASES

❑ **strong it** *v.* [i.e. to pose as a SE *strong man*] [1960s+] to act in an aggressive or extreme manner.

strong *adv.* **1** [early 19C+] keenly, enthusiastically. **2** [1910s] intimately.

IN PHRASES

❑ **come it strong** *v. see under* COME IT *v.*[1]. ❑ **come on strong** *v. see under* COME ON *v.*[1]. ❑ **come out strong** *v.* **1** [mid-19C+] to speak emphatically and frankly. **2** [late 19C] to act generously. ❑ **draw it strong** *v.* [mid–late 19C] to exaggerate. ❑ **go it strong** *v.* (*also* **go it thick**) [GO IT *v.* (2)] [mid-19C+] to speak frankly, to act forcefully. ❑ **pitch it strong** *v. see under* PITCH *v.* ❑ **play (it) strong** *v.* [1950s–70s] (*US black*) to act in an aggressive, determined manner.

strong and thin *n.* [rhy. sl.] **1** [1930s–40s] (*US*) gin. **2** [1940s] (*US*) a hand [FIN *n.*[1] (1)].

strongarm *n.* **1** [mid-19C+] violence. **2** [late 19C] (*US tramp*) the act of throttling a victim so as to immobilize them for theft. **3** [20C+] a thug, a bodyguard. **4** [1960s] strength.

strong-arm *adj.* **1** [late 19C+] violent, used of a person who gets things done through threats of, as well as actual, physical violence. **2** [1930s] physical effort, other than in the context of violence.

IN COMPOUNDS

❑ **strong-arm man** *n.* (*also* **strong-arm artist, ...boy, ...guy, strongarmer**) [20C+] a thug, a hoodlum, a gangster. ❑ **strong-arm woman** *n.* [late 19C] (*US Und.*) a thuggish, violent woman, very often a street thief or the madame of a brothel.

strong-arm *v.* [STRONGARM *n.*] [20C+] (*orig. US*) to rob or otherwise influence someone through threats and potential, rather than actual, violence.

strongarming *n.* [STRONG-ARM *v.*] [1930s–40s] **1** violence, esp. when allied to robbery or extortion. **2** (*US Und.*) a form of robbery whereby a woman, posing as a whore, lures a man into a dark alleyway or similar space; she then puts a stranglehold around his neck and her male partner(s) rob(s) the victim, who is thus held captive.

strong-eye *n.* [1900s] (*W.I.*) covetousness.

strong-eye *adj.* [STRONG-EYE *n.*] [1900s–10s] (*W.I.*) **1** covetous, greedy. **2** selfish, domineering. **3** determined.

strong-mouth *n.* [mid–late 19C] (*W.I.*) bullying, brow-beating.

strong-physic *n.* [lit. 'strong medicine'] [mid–late 19C] (*W.I.*) a self-willed person.

strong-physic *adj.* [STRONG-PHYSIC *n.*] [mid–late 19C] (*W.I.*) hot-tempered, irascible.

'stroof! *excl. see* 'STREWTH! *excl.*

strool *n. see* STREELER *n.*

strop *n.* [STROP *v.*[1]] [1970s+] **1** (*S.Afr.*) trouble, 'backchat', obstreperous behaviour. **2** a bad temper.

strop *v.*[1] [? backform. f. STROPPY *adj.*] [1970s+] to display one's bad temper; thus *strop around*, to wander about in a bad mood.

strop *v.*[2] [SE *strop*, to sharpen a razor] [1990s+] (*Aus.*) to masturbate.

strop one's beak *v. see under* BEAK *n.*[2].

stropper *n.* [fig. use of SE *strop*, to sharpen a razor] [1910s] (*US*) a large, husky man.

stroppy *adj.* [mispron. OBSTROPOLOUS *adj.*, i.e. SE *obstreperous*; note naut. jargon *jack strop*, a know-it-all, a braggart] [1950s+] bad-tempered, irritable.

strowling mort/punk *n. see* STROLLING MORT *n.*

struck *adj.* [abbr. STRUCK ON *adj.*] [20C+] (*W.I.*) greedy, gluttonous.

struck on *adj.* (*also* **struck, struck upon, struck with**) [mid-19C+] obsessed with, esp. in a sexual sense.

structure *n.* [1950s+] (*W.I. Rasta*) the body, health.

strudel *n.* [2000s] (*Aus.*) a plump or well-built female.

struesbob! *excl.* (*also* **'strue as Bob! struse Bob!**) [lit. *it's true as Bob*, i.e. God] [1970s+] (*S.Afr.*) a general excl. of assertion.

'strufe! *excl. see* 'STREWTH! *excl.*

struggle *n.* [STRUGGLE *v.*] [1920s–30s] (*US*) a party or dance.

SE in slang uses

IN COMPOUNDS

❑ **struggle-buggy** *n.* [it 'struggles along'] [1920s–60s] (*US*) a run-down old car, esp. an early model Ford. ❑ **struggle-town** *n.* [1990s+] (*Aus.*) a state of penury and/or unemployment. ❑ **struggle valley** *n.* [the SE *struggle* to survive] [1930s+] (*Aus.*) a tramps' encampment.

struggle *v.* [1920s–60s] (*US*) to dance.

struggle and strain *n.* [rhy. sl.] [1910s+] a railway train.

struggle and strainers *n.* [rhy. sl.] [1980s+] trainers.

struggle and strife *n.* [rhy. sl.] [20C+] **1** one's wife. **2** life.

strum *n.*[1] (*also* **strump**) [abbr. SE *strumpet*] [late 17C+] a sexually available (young) woman; a prostitute.

strum *n.*[2] [STROMMEL *n.* (2)] [late 17C–early 19C] a wig.

strum *v.* (*also* **strump**) **1** [late 18C+] to have sexual intercourse. **2** [1960s+] (*US*) (*also* **strum heads**) to hit; to fight. **3** [1990s+] to masturbate.

IN PHRASES

❑ **go strumming** *v.* [SE *strum*, to play on a stringed instrument] [19C] to have sexual intercourse.

strum and stroll *n.* [rhy. sl.] [20C+] (*Aus.*) the dole.

strumil/strummel *n.* see STROMMEL *n.*

strummond *n.* [? STRAMMER *n.*] [mid-19C] a pot of liquor, a 'bumper'.

strump *see under* STRUM.

strung out *adj.* **1** [late 19C+] obsessively in love, infatuated with someone. **2** [1930s+] (*also* **strung-up**) nervous, unhappy, depressed. **3** [1940s+] obsessed with a topic or activity. **4** [1950s+] (*drugs*) (*also* **strung, strung up**) addicted to narcotics, esp. when suffering the pain of withdrawal. **5** [1980s+] (*drugs*) under the influence of any drug (with no suggestion of actual addiction).

strunt *n.* [SE *strunt*, the fleshy part of an animal's tail] [early 17C] the penis.

struse Bob! *excl. see* STRUESBOB! *excl.*

strut *n.* [SE *strut*] [1930s+] (*orig. US black*) a party where the guests buy their refreshments to help pay the rent.

'struth! *excl.* (*also* **struth!**) *see* 'STREWTH! *excl.*

strut-noddy *n.* [SE *strut* + NODDY *n.* (1)] [19C] an arrogant fool with no idea of their own stupidity.

strut one's stuff *v.* (*also* **strut it, strut some**) [SE *strut* + STUFF *n.* (1)] **1** [1920s] (*US*) to act on stage. **2** [1920s+] (*orig. US black*) to act proudly, uninhibitedly.

strychnine *n.* **1** [mid-19C] (*US*) whisky. **2** *see* QUININE *n.*

stu *n.* [abbr.] [1990s+] a *stu*pid person.

stub *n.* **1** [19C] a short person. **2** [1940s] a child.

stubbie *n.* (*Aus./N.Z.*) **1** [1950s+] a short, squat beer bottle holding 375ml (13fl oz). **2** [1970s+] shorts [underpinned by brandname *Stubbies*].

IN PHRASES

❑ **one stubbie short of a six-pack** *n.* [2000s] (*N.Z.*) used of one who is eccentric, 'not all there'.

stubble *n.* [SE *stubble*] [late 18C–1900s] a woman's pubic hair.

IN PHRASES

❑ **take a turn in the stubble** *v.* (*also* **take a turn through the stubble**) [18C–19C] to have sexual intercourse.

stubble it! *excl.* [SE *stubble*, to clear the land of stubble, to cut it short] [late 17C–19C] (*UK Und.*) hold your tongue! be quiet!

stubble-jumper *n.* [1920s+] (*Can./US*) a poor farmer.

stubbs *n.* [SE *stub*, the end of a cigar or cigarette] [19C] nothing.

stub-faced *adj.* [SE *horse stubs*, horse nails; thus 'the devil run over his face with horse stubs in his shoes' (Grose, 1796)] [late 18C–19C] having one's face pitted with the scars of smallpox.

stuccoed *adj.* [play on PLASTERED *adj.*[1] (1)] [1920s–30s] (*US*) drunk.

stuck *adj.* [fig. uses of SE, but note SHTUCK *n.*] **1** [mid-19C+] left in an impossible position, deceived, completely mistaken. **2** [mid-19C+] out of money, impoverished. **3** [1990s+] (*US black*) killed. **4** *see* STUCK ON below.

IN COMPOUNDS

❑ **stuck out** *adj.* [1970s+] (*US prison*) lazy, forgetful; deprived. ❑ **stuck-up** *n.* [colloq. *stuck up*, arrogant] [late 19C–1940s] an arrogant, snobbish or reserved person. ❑ **stuck up** *adj.* [late 19C] penniless.

IN PHRASES

❑ **get stuck in** *v.* [1930s+] **1** to begin, esp. of a meal or a job. **2** to fight; to act in an aggressive manner, esp. in a sporting context. ❑ **get stuck into** *v.* [1910s+] (*orig. Aus./N.Z.*) **1** to start any form of activity; the implication is one of enthusiasm and activity. **2** to start a fight. **3** to abuse verbally. ❑ **stuck for** *adj.* [1930s] owing, in debt. ❑ **stuck on** *adj.* (*also* **stuck, stuck after**) (*orig. US*) **1** [mid-19C+] obsessed with, devoted to. **2** [late 19C+] in love with, pleased with. **3** [1910s] (*US*) hostile towards. ❑ **stuck with** *adj.* [mid-19C+] (*orig. US*) saddled with, unable to get rid of either a person or an object.

stuckadee *n.* (*also* **stuckedee**) [ext. of STUCKY *n.*] [1940s] (*W.I.*) a faithful lover.

stucky *n.* [? STUCK ON *under* STUCK *adj.*] [1930s–50s] (*W.I.*) a faithful lover.

stud *n.* [SE *stud*, a stallion or mare kept for breeding] **1** [late 19C+] (*US white*) a man, not invariably but usu. sexually successful. **2** [20C+] a general form of address, usu. congratulatory. **3** [1920s+] a man, irrespective of race or colour. **4** [1930s+] (*US black*) a sophisticated man, but with no sexual connotation. **5** [1940s+] (*US*) a masculine lesbian. **6** [1950s–60s] (*Aus.*) a mixed-race Aboriginal woman, used for sexual pleasure. **7** [1960s+] a male prostitute catering to either sex. **8** [1960s+] a man as a sexual performer. **9** [1960s+] a 'masculine' male homosexual. **10** [1960s+] (*US prison*) a 'masculine' jail homosexual (who usu. reverts to heterosexuality on release). **11** [1970s+] (*US gay*) the penis. **12** [1980s+] (*US campus*) a physically strong or athletically powerful man or woman.

DERIVATIVES

❑ **studette** *n.* [sfx *-ette*] [1980s+] (*US teen*) a sexually and socially successful, physically attractive woman. ❑ **studly** *adj.* [1960s+] (*US campus*) displaying the characteristics of a sexually successful man. ❑ **studola** *n.* [-OLA *sfx*] [1980s+] (*US campus*) a concentration of sexually successful men.

IN COMPOUNDS

❑ **stud broad** *n.* [BROAD *n.*[2] (3)] [1960s+] (*US*) a masculine lesbian. ❑ **stud dog** *n.* [1960s] (*US*) a male sexual predator. ❑ **stud (gin)** *n.* [GIN *n.*[1] (1)] [1910s+] (*Aus.*) an Aboriginal woman seen as an object of sexual pleasure for a white man. ❑ **stud horse** *n.* (*also* **stud hoss**) [1940s+] a man with sexual and/or athletic prowess, usu. as a term of address whether self-referentially or to a friend. ❑ **studhunk** *n.* [HUNK *n.*[1] (6)] [1980s] a 'masculine' man, a 'ladykiller'. ❑ **stud hustler** *n.* [HUSTLER *n.* (7)] [1960s–70s] (*US gay*) a male prostitute. ❑ **stud-muffin** *n.* [MUFFIN *n.*[1] (8)] [1980s] (*orig. US campus*) an exceptionally successful and attractive person; occas. of an animal. ❑ **stud-up** *n.* [1970s] (*US prison*) a homosexual male who tries to change to being heterosexual.

IN PHRASES

❑ **old stud** *n.* [mid–late 19C] (*US*) a familiar term of address. ❑ **stud out** *v.* (*US campus*) **1** [1960s] to play a good-natured practical joke. **2** [1980s+] to achieve something, to do well; usu. in past tense, referring to a proven success.

IN EXCLAMATIONS

❑ **stud horse!** (*also* **stud hoss!**) [20C+] (*US*) a general form of greeting between men.

stud *adj.* [STUD *n.*] **1** [1940s+] (*US*) fine, excellent, outstanding. **2** [1960s] (*also* **studdish**) aggressive. **3** [1970s] of homosexuals, overtly masculine.

stud *v.*[1] [STUD *n.*] [1940s+] (*US*) **1** to pursue sexually. **2** to work as a pimp. **3** to work as a heterosexual male prostitute.

stud *v.*[2] [SE *study*] [2000s] (*US black*) to listen to; to learn.

studdish *adj. see* STUD *adj.* (2).

studdy *n.* [STUD *n.* (4)] [1940s] (*US black*) a general term of address: friend, 'old boy'.

stude *n.* [abbr.] (*US*) **1** [1910s–30s] a *stud*ent. **2** [1960s–70s] a *Stude*baker.

student *n.* **1** [1930s–50s] (*drugs*) an inexperienced or novice drug-taker. **2** [1940s] (*US Und.*) a political heeler, living off the city payroll.

SE in slang uses

IN COMPOUNDS

❑ **student's lamp** *n.* [1900s] (*US*) a cigarette.

Studie *n.* (*also* **Studey**) [abbr.] [1930s+] (*US*) a *Stude*baker automobile.

studio gangsta *n.* [1990s+] (*US black teen*) one who poses as a GANGSTA *n.* purely for the purpose of making records; their experience of street life, however, is marginal.

study *n.* [SE *study*, a portrait] [mid-19C+] an expression of incredulity, shock; usu. in phr. *You should have seen your face – it was a study!*

study *v.* **1** [late 19C+] (*W.I./UK black*) (*also* **study on**) to think about. **2** [1950s+] (*gay*) to appraise a potential sexual conquest or partner. **3** [1960s] (*US campus*) to indulge in sexual caresses short of intercourse.

SE in slang uses

IN COMPOUNDS

❑ **study mongrel** *n.* (*also* **study hog**) [1990s+] (*US campus*) someone who studies hard.

IN PHRASES

❑ **study astronomy** *v. see* GO STAR-GAZING (ON ONE'S BACK) *under* STAR *n.*[1].

stue *n. see* STEW *n.*[1].

stuff *n.* **1** [late 16C+] things or activities in general, varying as to context. **2** [17C+] semen. **3** [mid-17C+] anything that has no proper name, things that one cannot be bothered to describe properly. **4** [late 17C+] nonsense; lies. **5** as euph. for drink or drugs. (**a**) [18C+] (*also* **liquid stuff**) alcohol, esp. bootleg liquor. (**b**) [20C+] (*drugs*) (*also* **needle-stuff**) drugs, esp. heroin, morphine ['William Lee', *Junkie* (1953): 'General terms for opium and all derivatives of opium: morphine, heroin, Delaudid [*sic*], pantopon, codeine, dionine']. (**c**) [1940s] marijuana. **6** [mid-18C+] money. **7** [mid-19C] (*US Und.*) a copper watch which has been galvanized and is sold as 'gold'. **8** in sexual contexts [20C+ use is usu. US black]. (**a**) [mid-19C+] the vagina, the buttocks; fig. used as female sexuality. (**b**) [late 19C+] a woman, usu. attractive and often out, enjoying herself. (**c**) [1960s+] (*US prison*) a male homosexual. **9** [late 19C+] arguments. **10** [late 19C+] a person. **11** [late 19C+] (*US*) personality, character; ability. **12** [20C+] (*US*) something important, meaningful. **13** [20C+] (*US prison*) someone, or something, of value. **14** [1900s] (*US Und.*) an unappealing person. **15** [1900s–30s] stolen goods. **16** [1960s+] (*US prison*) a knife or gun. **17** [1980s] a term of address. **18** [1980s] constr. with *the*, euph. for FUCK *n.*, HELL, THE *phr.* etc.

IN COMPOUNDS

❑ **stuff-all** *n.* [var. on FUCK ALL *n.*] [1980s+] nothing at all.

IN PHRASES

❑ **do one's stuff** *v.* **1** [mid-17C+] to perform as one is expected to. **2** [1920s–70s] to show off a speciality. ❑ **feel one's stuff** *v.* [1930s–50s] (*US black*) to base one's actions or speech on one's most intense and sincere emotions. ❑ **give a stuff** *v.* [backform. f. NOT GIVE A STUFF below] [1990s+] (*Aus./N.Z.*) to care; usu. in negative use, e.g. *who gives a stuff?* ❑ **hit the stuff** *v.* **1** [1910s+] (*US*) to drink alcohol. **2** [1930s–50s] (*drugs*) to smoke opium. **3** [1950s] to use narcotics. ❑ **no stuff** [1920s–60s] (*US black*) no fooling, no lies, absolutely honest and sincere. ❑ **not give a stuff** *v.* (*also* **not give a gippo's stuff**) [i.e. euph. for NOT GIVE A FUCK *v.*] [1960s+] to not care whatsoever. ❑ **on the stuff** [1920s+] (*drugs*) using a narcotic drug, esp. heroin. ❑ **peddle one's stuff** *v. see* PEDDLE ONE'S ASS *under* PEDDLE *v.* ❑ **play stuff** *v.* [1960s+] (*US black*) to deceive or defraud by a smart line of verbal patter. ❑ **put someone's stuff down** *v.* [PUT DOWN *v.*[1] (2a) + sense 1 above] [1970s+] (*US black*) to disparage, to ridicule. ❑ **sit on one's stuff** *v.* [1970s] (*US black*) to work as a prostitute. ❑ **sweet stuff** *n. see under* SWEET *adj.*[1].

SE in slang uses

IN PHRASES

❑ **and stuff** [late 17C+] a meaningless addition to the end of a sentence, the implication is that the 'stuff' is essentially meaningless, irrelevant. ❑ **play with one's stuff out of the window** *v.* (*also* **have one's stuff out the window**) [? image of one who, planning an escape, has already placed their possessions outside the house] [1900s–40s] (*US black*) to act with caution, e.g., when playing cards; esp. to act carefully when conducting a love affair. ❑ **that's the stuff** (*also* **that's the style**) [20C+] a general term of approval.

stuff, the *n.* **1** [mid-18C+] what one wants, the ideal; usu. in phr. *THAT'S THE STUFF under* STUFF *n.* **2** [1990s+] an important (or self-important) person.

stuff *v.*[1] [SE *stuff*, to fill up but increasingly seen as euph. for FUCK *v.* (1); note *double entendre* in D'Urfey, *Pills to Purge Melancholy* (1719): 'Three things must be stuffed, I'll tell you if I can; / A pudding, a cushion, and a Woman'] **1** [18C+] to have sexual intercourse; also anal intercourse. **2** [mid-19C+] (*also* **stuff up**) to tease, to tell lies, to fool, to hoax. **3** [1900s] to place a false name on a payroll so as to draw the salary illegally. **4** [1940s+] as a general euph. for FUCK *v.* (1). **5** [1940s+] to defeat, to outwit. **6** [1980s] (*US black*) to attack, verbally or physically. **7** [1990s+] to cause trouble for.

IN PHRASES

❑ **stuff about** *v.* [2000s] (*N.Z.*) a euph. for FUCK ABOUT *v.* (1). ❑ **stuff a fat pig in the arse** *v. see* GREASE A FAT SOW IN THE ARSE *under* GREASE *v.*[1]. ❑ **stuff up** *v.* **1** [2000s] to ruin, to make a mess of. **2** *see* sense 2 above.

IN EXCLAMATIONS

❑ **stuff and butter it!** [2000s] (*N.Z.*) an excl. of annoyance; as *stuff and butter me!*, an excl. of surprise. ❑ **stuff it up and break it off!/stuff it up your ...!** *see* SHOVE IT UP YOUR ARSE! *excl.* ❑ **stuff me!** (*also* **stuff me sideways! stuff my old boots!**) [euph. for FUCK ME! *excl.*] [1950s+] an excl. of surprise, astonishment. ❑ **stuff off!** (*N.Z./S.Afr.*) a euph. for FUCK OFF! *excl.* (1).

stuff *v.*[2] [STUFF *n.* (7)] [mid-19C] (*US Und.*) to sell brass or galvanized copper watches as 'gold' ones; often as *watch-stuffing* or *watch-stuffer*; thus *stuffer*, a person who does this; *stuff cover*, his assistant.

stuff *v.*[3] [SE *stuffy*] [late 19C] to sit indoors when one could/should be out enjoying the fresh air.

stuff! *excl.* [late 17C–1940s] nonsense! rubbish!

stuff-cover *n. see* STUFFER *n.*[1].

stuff cuff *n.* [1940s] (*US black*) the padded cuff of a draped suit.

stuffed *adj.*[1] **1** [mid–late 19C] put-down, mocked, denigrated. **2** [1940s+] defeated, ruined, exhausted; drunk [STUFF *v.*[1] (5)].

stuffed *adj.*[2] [euph. synon. for FUCKED *adj.*[1] (9)] [1930s+] bothered, concerned; usu. in phr. *can't/won't be stuffed.*

IN EXCLAMATIONS

❑ **get stuffed!** [1940s+] a general excl. of dismissal.

stuffed *adj.*[3] *see* STUFFED SHIRT *adj.*

stuffed eel-skin *n.* [mid-19C] an old, prob. impotent, man.

stuffed monkey *n.* [late 19C] (*East London Jewish*) 'a very pleasant close almond biscuit' (Ware).

stuffed rat *n.* [1930s+] (*Aus.*) a loaded die.

stuffed shirt *n.* (*also* **stiff shirt, stuffed polony, stuffed suit**) [i.e. the shirt is there, but there is no one inside it] [late 16C; 20C+] (*orig. US*) a pompous, aristocratic but ineffectual person, a bore.

stuffed shirt *adj.* (*also* **stuffed**) [STUFFED SHIRT *n.*] [1920s+] pompous, self-satisfied.

stuffer *n.*[1] (*also* **stuff-cover**) [mid-19C] (*UK Und.*) one who passes off inferior goods as being of higher worth.

stuffer *n.*[2] [the active/passive 'stuffing' of the anus] **1** [1940s] (*US Und.*) a male homosexual. **2** [1970s] a term of abuse. **3** [1970s+] (*drugs*) a smuggler who hides drugs in the anus or vagina.

stuffer *n.*[3] [STUFF *n.* (5)] [1970s+] (*drugs*) a drug addict; as v., to take drugs.

stuffer *n.*[4] [thy are *stuffed full* of ego] [1990s+] (*UK juv.*) one who is very pleased with themselves.

stuffing *n.*[1] (*also* **stuffings**) [late 19C+] (*orig. US*) the essence, the 'daylights', as in phrs. below; also used fig.

IN PHRASES

❑ **beat the stuffing out of** *v.* [late 19C+] to beat up thoroughly. ❑ **knock the stuffing out of** *v.* [late 19C+] to beat up thoroughly, to defeat comprehensively.

stuffing *n.*[2] [STUFF *v.*[1] (2)] [1970s] (*US black*) the practice of tricking or conning a victim.

stuff it! *excl.* [1940s+] a euph. excl. for FUCK IT! *excl.*

stuff-up *n.* [2000s] (*N.Z.*) a euph. for FUCK-UP *n.* (1).

stuff up *v.*[1] [var. of *STUMP UP under* STUMP *v.*[3]; note STUFF *n.* (6)] [1900s] (*Aus.*) to hand over money, to pay a bill.

stuff up *v.*[2] *see* STUFF *v.*[1] (2).

stuffy *n.* [STUFF *n.* (8b)] [mid-19C–1900s] a woman.

stuffy *adj.*[1] **1** [19C–1920s] angry, sulky. **2** [late 19C+] (*also* **stuffy-nosed**) pompous, snobbish.

stuffy *adj.*[2] [STUFF *n.* (6)] [1930s+] (*orig. US*) wealthy, rich.

stug *n.* [backsl. GUT *n.* (2a)] [late 19C–1930s] courage, bravery, staying power.

stuiver *n.* SEE STIVER *n.*

stuk *n.* [Afk. *stuk*, a piece, a part] [1940s] (*S.Afr.*) a (promiscuous) woman.

stuke *n.* SEE STOOK *n.*

stuling-ken *n.* SEE STALLING-KEN *n.*

stum *v.* [abbr. SE *stumble*] [1970s+] (*drugs*) to be intoxicated by a drug.

stuma *n.* SEE STUMER *n.*[1].

stumble *v.* [SE *stumble*] [1940s] (*US black*) to suffer serious problems and misfortunes.

IN PHRASES

▫ **stumble and fall** *v.* [FALL *v.*[1]] [1940s] **1** (*US black*) to suffer serious misfortunes. **2** to be arrested. **3** to be killed.

stumblebum *n.* [SE *stumble* + BUM *n.*[3] (1)] [1930s+] (*US*) **1** a shambling, useless, foolish person. **2** a third-rate boxer. **3** a drunk, a homeless drifter; also attrib.

stumble bumble *n.* [play on STUMBLEBUM *n.*] [1970s+] (*drugs*) a barbituate.

stumblers *n.* (*also* **stoms, stums**) [their effects] [1960s+] (*drugs*) barbiturates.

stumer *n.*[1] (*also* **schtumer, shtoomer, stewmer, stoomer, stuma**) [ety. unknown; ? fig. use of SHTUM *adj.*; northeast dial. *stumor*, n. a 'difficult person to handle', adj. stupid; note WW1 milit. *stumer*, a dud shell that fails to explode] **1** [late 19C+] a dud cheque or other fraudulent monetary draft, a counterfeit banknote. **2** [late 19C+] (*Aus./N.Z.*) a person without money, a defaulter, a bankrupt; thus *stumered*, bankrupt. **3** [late 19C+] something or someone worthless, useless, a 'flop'. **4** [1910s–20s] (*UK Und.*) a certainty. **5** [1920s+] a fool. **6** [1930s] a state of agitation. **7** [1960s+] a blunder, a mistake.

IN PHRASES

▫ **come a stumer** *v.* [1910s] (*Aus.*) to be financially ruined. ▫ **in a stumer** [1980s+] (*Aus./N.Z.*) in a (financial) mess.

stumer *n.*[2] [SHTUM *adj.*] [1910s+] a deaf-mute.

stumm *adj.* SEE SHTUM *adj.*

stumm and crum *adj.* [ext. of SHTUM *adj.*] [1970s+] extremely quiet, 'silent as the grave'.

stump *n.* **1** [17C; late 19C+] the penis; thus as v., to enter, to have intercourse. **2** [early–mid-19C] money [it is 'stumped up']. **3** [mid–late 19C] (*US*) a dare, a challenge to do something difficult or dangerous. **4** [late 19C] a fool [one who is short and THICK *adj.* (1a)]. **5** [1910s] (*US prison*) a sentence of less than one year. **6** [1960s] an old woman.

IN COMPOUNDS

▫ **stump-break** *v.* [1970s+] (*US*) to commit bestiality with an animal. ▫ **stump-chubby** *v.* [mid-19C] (*UK Und.*) one who clips coins.

SE in slang uses

IN COMPOUNDS

▫ **stump-glim** *n.* [mid-19C] (*US Und.*) a lamp-post. ▫ **stump-jumper** *n.* [stereotyping] [1930s+] (*US*) **1** a rural person, a yokel, a farmer. **2** an unsophisticated person. ▫ **stump-knocker** *n.* (*also* **stump orator**) [he jumps up on a *tree stump* to preach] [mid-19C+] (*US*) an unprofessional, part-time lay preacher; also *stump-speech* n., a preacher's sermonizing.

IN PHRASES

▫ **find a stump to fit your rump** (*also* **find a stump to rest your rump, grab a stump...**) [1960s] (*US black*) an invitation to sit down. ▫ **up a stump** [orig. UK but almost immediately taken over by US] **1** [early 19C+] in difficulties, perplexed. **2** [1950s] (*US*) as *up the stump*, pregnant. ▫ **up to the stump** [? var. on UP A STUMP above] [mid-19C] (*US*) out of money, impoverished.

stump *v.*[1] [late 18C–1940s] (*Can.*) to challenge (usu. to a fight), to dare.

stump *v.*[2] [SE *stump*, to walk clumsily] [19C+] to go on foot, to be off, to leave; esp. as *stump it*.

stump *v.*[3] (*also* **stump down**) [STUMP *n.* (2)] [early 19C] to pay.

IN PHRASES

▫ **stump the pew** *v.* [? abbr. PEWTER *n.*] [early–mid-19C] to pay up. ▫ **stump up** *v.* [early 19C+] to hand over, esp. of money; thus *stumped up*, impoverished.

stump *v.*[4] [mid-19C] (*UK Und.*) to boast, to lie.

stump *v.*[5] [? SE *stump*, to confuse or to reduce to a fig. *stump* of wood] [mid-19C–1900s] to ruin economically, usu. in pass. *stumped*, ruined.

stump *v.*[6] [? SE *stomp*] [1970s] (*US black*) to rob or mug a person.

stump down *v.* SEE STUMP *v.*[3].

stumped *adj.* (*also* **stumped up**) [STUMP *v.*[5]] [mid-19C+] **1** ruined, impoverished. **2** lost for ideas.

stumpers *n.* SEE STOMPERS *n.*

stumpf *adj.* SEE SHTUM *adj.*

stumps *n.* [SE *stump*, something broken off; only the pl. is sl.] **1** [17C+] the legs; esp. in phr. *STIR ONE'S STUMPS under* STIR *v.* **2** [early 18C] the teeth. **3** [mid-18C] (*UK Und.*) shoes.

stumpy *n.*[1] [STUMP *n.* (2)] [early–mid-19C] money.

stumpy *n.*[2] [SE *stump* of a tree/of a leg] **1** [mid-19C] (*US*) a short person; later use as adj. **2** [late 19C+] (*US*) a crippled beggar, esp. one with a leg missing; also as adj.

stums *n.* SEE STUMBLERS *n.*

stun *n.* [backsl.] [mid–late 19C] nuts.

stun *v.* [mid-19C] (*UK Und.*) to cheat, to swindle; esp. in phr. *stun out of*, to defraud.

IN PHRASES

▫ **put the stuns on** *v.* [late 19C] (*Aus.*) to amaze, to astound.

stun! *excl.* (*also* **stunner!**) [1980s+] (*UK juv.*) an excl. used to underline the amusement one derives from another's misfortune.

stung *adj.*[1] **1** [late 19C+] (*also* **stung for**) tricked out of money (or some other commodity) [STING *v.* (1)]. **2** [1900s] enamoured of [fig. use of SE]. **3** [1910s+] (*orig. Aus.*) persuaded to lend money [STING *v.* (1)]. **4** [1910s+] subjected to some form of problem [STING *v.* (1)].

stung *adj.*[2] [STING *n.* (3)] [1910s+] (*Aus.*) drunk.

stunlaws *n.* [backsl.] [mid-19C] walnuts.

stunned *adj.* **1** [1910s–30s] (*Aus./N.Z.*) drunk. **2** [1970s] (*US gay*) intoxicated by a drug.

stunned on skilly *phr.* [SE *stun* + SKILLY *n.* (1)] [mid-19C] (*UK Und.*) sent to prison and thus forced to endure a diet of gruel.

stunner *n.* [SE *stun*] **1** [mid–late 19C] an expert in their own job or profession. **2** [mid-19C+] a first-rate person or object. **3** [mid-19C+] a notably attractive young woman, revived in the late 1980s+ to describe a woman posing as a pin-up for the tabloid press or for softcore pornographic magazines; often spelled *stunna/stunnah*. **4** [mid-19C+] a stunning blow. **5** [late 19C] (*US*) an unusually good story or anecdote. **6** [late 19C+] a surprise, something that 'stuns'.

IN PHRASES

▫ **put the stunners on** *v.* [mid-19C] to astonish, to amaze, to surprise.

stunner! *excl.* SEE STUN! *excl.*

stunning *adj.* (*also* **stunny**) **1** [mid-19C] clever, knowing. **2** [mid-19C+] excellent, first-rate. **3** [mid-19C+] very attractive.

stunning *adv.* [STUNNING *adj.* (2)] [mid-19C] excellently, wonderfully.

stunning joe banks *adj.* [STUNNING *adj.* (2) + proper name *Joe Banks*, a contemporary publican–cum–receiver, based in Dyott Street, Seven Dials, London, and later in the Cranbourne Street ROOKERY *n.* (2), who always gave a fair price to the thieves with whom he dealt. Like many receivers, he added to his income by returning, for a price, the stolen goods to their original owners. His neckties, adds Hotten (1860), were as *stunning* as his character and the aristocracy, as well as the underworld, patronized his after-hours drinking club] [mid–late 19C] excellent to the highest degree.

stunny *adj. see* STUNNING *adj.*

stunt *n.* [orig. US campus sports use, 'an act which is striking for the skill, strength, or the like, required to do it; a feat' (*Webster* Supplement, 1900)] [late 19C+] **1** anything done with the intention of improving or advertising one's image or gaining an advantage over rivals, a gimmick or device for attracting attention. **2** a scheme, a plan. **3** (*US Und.*) a criminal scheme.

IN COMPOUNDS

❑ **stunt cock** *n.* [COCK *n.*[3] (1)] [1990s+] in pornographic film-making, a stand-by who can achieve an erection on demand.

IN PHRASES

❑ **big stunt** *n.* [1910s] the First World War. ❑ **put up a stunt** *v.* [1910s] (*Aus.*) to make something happen.

stunt *v.* [2000s] **1** (*US prison*) to lie, or to pretend to have knowledge of something. **2** (*US black*) to show off.

stunty *adj.* [STUNT *n.* (1)] [1920s] (*US*) ostentatious.

stup *v. see* SCHTUP *v.*

stupe *n.* (*also* **stoop**) [abbr. SE *stupid*] [mid-18C+] a fool, an idiot.

stupe-head *n.* [STUPE *n.* + -HEAD *sfx* (1)] [1950s+] (*US*) a fool.

stupid *n.* (*also* **stupido**) [early 18C+] a fool.

stupid *adj.* **1** [early 19C+] drunk. **2** [20C+] (*W.I.*) insignificant, small, contemptible. **3** [1980s+] (*US campus*) crazy, insane, absurd. **4** [1980s+] (*US campus*) pleasant, popular, excellent.

IN PHRASES

❑ **get stupid** *v.* [as sense 1 above] [1990s+] (*US black/teen*) **1** to attend a party. **2** to become drunk or intoxicated by drugs.

SE in slang uses

IN COMPOUNDS

❑ **stupid-head** *n.* [-HEAD *sfx* (1)] [mid-19C] a fool.

IN PHRASES

❑ **stupid as arseholes** *adj. see* under ARSEHOLE *n.*

stupid *adv.* **1** [1960s+] (*US*) extremely, very. **2** [1990s+] (*US teen*) used of a large quantity of something.

stupidie *n.* [SE *stupid*] [20C+] (*W.I.*) a fool, an idiot.

stupidie *adj.* [STUPIDIE *n.*] [20C+] (*W.I.*) stupid, idiotic.

stupido *n. see* STUPID *n.*

stupo *n.* [SE *stup(id)* + -O *sfx* (2)] [1920s] (*Anglo-Irish*) a fool.

stupp *v. see* SCHTUP *v.*

stur *n. see* STIR *n.*[1].

sturks *n. see* STERKS *n.*

sturrabin *n.* (*also* **stariben, sturaban, sturbin, sturbon**) [Rom. *sturiben*, a prison, *staripen*, to imprison] [mid-19C–1900s] a prison.

stush *adj. see* STOUSH *adj.*

stutter and stammer *n.* [rhy. sl.] [20C+] a hammer.

stuyver *n. see* STIVER *n.*

style *n.* (*also* **stilo**) **1** [1910s+] (*US black*) anything one needs (fancy clothes, a clever line of patter, a personal style, a mental attitude) for the successful promotion of one's schemes; thus n. *styler*, a person preoccupied with appearance. **2** [1940s] (*S.Afr.*) a form of dance music.

IN PHRASES

❑ **drop off a style** *v. see under* DROP OFF *v.*[1]. ❑ **make style** *v.* [20C+] (*W.I.*) **1** to behave in an exhibitionist manner to attract attention. **2** to be overly fussy, fastidious. ❑ **sweat someone's style** *v. see under* SWEAT *v.*[2]. ❑ **that's the style** *see* *THAT'S THE STUFF under* STUFF *n.*

-style *sfx* (*also* **-stylee**) [1960s+] used in comb. with a n. to create an adv. meaning 'in that manner', e.g. *disco-style*.

style (off) *v.* [STYLE *n.* (1)] [1960s+] (*orig. US black*) to show off, to strut around.

styles *n.* [1980s] (*US black*) clothing.

stylie *n.* [1980s+] a white person wearing trad. black dreadlocks.

stylie! *excl.* [2000s] (*N.Z. teen*) an excl. of approval.

styling *n.* [STYLE (OFF) *v.*] **1** [1960s+] showing off, acting ostentatiously. **2** [1980s+] (*US campus*) doing well, succeeding, academically as well as socially.

IN PHRASES

❑ **styling and profiling** *n.* [PROFILE *v.*] [1980s+] (*US black/campus*) posing as a cool, sophisticated individual, and backing that image with smart, fashionable clothes.

styling *adj.* [STYLE *n.* (1)] [1990s+] (*US black*) ostentatious, fashionable.

stymie *v.* [STYMIED *adj.*] **1** [1920s+] to frustrate, to destroy. **2** [1980s] (*US campus*) to deprive others by taking the last of anything.

stymied *adj.* [golfing imagery; SE *stymie*, 'an opponent's ball which lies on the putting green in a line between the ball of the player and the hole he is playing for, if the distance between the balls is not less than six inches' (*OED*)] [20C+] (*orig. US*) confused, frustrated, in difficulties.

Styx *n.*

IN PHRASES

❑ **go over the Styx** *v. see* *GO ACROSS THE RIVER under* RIVER *n.*

suave *n.* (*also* **swave**) [SE *suave*, soothingly agreeable; ult. Lat. *suavis*, sweet] [1980s+] (*US campus/teen*) smooth style, charm; as v., to be charming.

suavo *n.* [SE *suave* + -O *sfx* (1)] [1970s] a sophisticate.

sub *n.*[1] [abbr.] **1** [mid-18C–1910s] a *sub*altern. **2** [mid-19C] a *sub*ject of the monarch. **3** [mid-19C] a *sub*scriber. **4** [mid-19C+] (*also* **subbie**) a loan, esp. an advance on wages; thus *do a sub*, to borrow money. **5** [mid-19C+] a *sub*stitute. **6** [late 19C] (*US*) a *sub*ject, e.g. of conversation. **7** [late 19C+] a *sub*scription. **8** [1910s+] a *sub*marine.

sub *n.*[2] [Hind. *sab*, all] [mid-19C–1940s] everything, all, the lot.

sub *n.*[3] (*also* **subbie**) [SE *sub-human*] [late 19C; 1990s+] a general term of abuse, denoting a despised, poverty-stricken or otherwise inadequate person.

sub *n.*[4] *see* SUBMARINE *n.*[1] (2).

sub *v.*[1] [SE *subsistence money*] **1** [mid-19C+] (*also* **sub up**) to give or get an advance on wages, a loan. **2** [1900s] to hand over money (e.g., as a bet). **3** [1960s] to hand over money as a bribe.

sub *v.*[2] [abbr. SE *substitute*] [mid-19C+] to fill in for (on a job), to deputize for; in sport, to substitute for or to be substituted.

subaltern's butter *n.* [the officer's preference] [late 19C–1920s] the flesh of an avocado pear.

subaltern's luncheon *n.* [late 19C–1900s] a glass of water and the tightening of one's belt.

sub-beau *n. see under* BEAU *n.*[1].

subbie *n.*[1] *see* SUB *n.*[1] (4).

subbie *n.*[2] *see* SUB *n.*[3].

subbie *n.*[3] *see* SUBBY *n.*

subbies *n.* [abbr.] [2000s] (*UK drugs*) *Sub*utex, a form of synthetic heroin.

subby *n.* (*also* **subbie**) [abbr.] [1950s+] a *sub*-contractor.

sub-chaser *n.* [? SUB-DEB *n.*] [1920s] (*US teen*) a man who attempts to pick up girls in the street.

sub-cheese *n.* [SE *sub*, inferior + CHEESE, THE *n.*] [mid-19C+] (*mainly Anglo-Ind.*) everything, the lot, all there is.

sub-deb *n.* [1910s–40s] (*US*) a girl who is on the verge of 'coming out' as a debutante.

sub-human *n.* [1980s+] (*US campus*) a socially unacceptable person; thus as adj., distasteful, gross, stupid.

sublime rascal *n.* [mid-19C] a lawyer.

submarine *n.*[1] [resemblance] **1** [1930s–40s] (*US Und.*) a doughnut. **2** [1940s+] (*US*) (*also* **sub**) a type of large, over-filled sandwich; thus *super-sub*. **3** [1980s+] (*US campus*) a tampon.

SE in slang uses

IN COMPOUNDS

❑ **submarine races** *n.* [1960s–70s] (*US teen*) petting.

submarine *n.*[2] [rhy. sl. = QUEEN *n.* (2) + ? ref. to GO DOWN *v.* (6)] [1990s+] (*Aus.*) a male homosexual.

submarine turkey *n. see* DEEP SEA TURKEY *under* DEEP SEA *n.*

submerged *adj.* [1910s] drunk.

subs *n.* [abbr. SE *submarine*] [2000s] (*N.Z. teen*) crumbs found in a shared drink.

sub up *v. see* SUB *v.*[1] (1).

suburb *n.* [the 17C suburbs – Holborn, Wapping, Mile End, Bermondsey, Clerkenwell – are now parts of central London; then, however, they were beyond the City proper, and were home to various 'stink' industries, e.g. tanning, leper hospitals, playhouses and brothels] [late 16C–early 19C] used in a variety of phrs., all denigrating suburban life and poss. near-SE, e.g. *suburb-garden*, a house in which one installs a mistress; *suburb-humour*, unpleasant humour, usu. at another's expense; *suburb justice*, corrupt justice, easily amenable to bribes; *suburb-trade*, prostitution; *suburb tricks*, sexual amusements; *suburb sinner*, a prostitute; *aunt of the suburbs*, a prostitute; *suburban roarer*, a pimp or male 'heavy' in a brothel; *house in the suburbs*, a brothel; *minion of the suburbs*, a male prostitute.

IN COMPOUNDS

❑ **suburban (wench)** *n.* (*also* **suburban roarer, suburb lady, ...whore**) [17C–early 18C] a prostitute who works in the suburbs rather than the West End of London. ❑ **suburb trade** *n.* [late 17C] the world of suburban prostitution; thus *suburbian-trader*, a prostitute's client.

suburbian *n.* [SUBURB *n.*] [17C–early 18C] a prostitute; thus as adj.

suburbicarian *n.* [SUBURBIAN *n.*] [17C] one who lives in the suburbs, i.e. those areas immediately outside London's city walls, and is, as such, considered socially dubious.

subway alumni *n.* [they turn up at the college by *subway*] [1940s+] (*US*) supporters of college sports teams who are not actually *alumni*, i.e. members or former members of the college.

subway dealer *n.* [SE *subway* as 'underground'] [20C+] (*US Und.*) a card-sharp who deals from the bottom of the pack.

subway silver *n.* [1980s] (*US drugs*) a (mythical) form of marijuana growing in the New York subways, the result of the drug being flushed away to avoid police raids.

succory-seed *n.* [SE *succour*, help] [mid-19C] (*UK Und.*) money.

such-a-much *adj.* **1** [20C+] (*US*) of a thing, important. **2** [1960s] (*US black*) of a person, (self-)important.

suck *n.*[1] (*also* **sucky**) [SE *suck*, a small measure or glass of liquid] [late 17C–mid-19C] (*UK Und.*) wine or strong drink.

IN COMPOUNDS

❑ **suck casa** *n.* [CASA *n.*[1] (1)] [mid-19C] a public house, a tavern. ❑ **suck crib** *n.* [CRIB *n.*[1] (3)] [late 19C] a public house, a tavern.

suck *n.*[2] [play on SE *breast*, which gives *suck*] [early–mid-19C] (*UK Und.*) the breast pocket.

suck *n.*[3] **1** [mid-19C–1950s] some form of suckable sweetmeat. **2** [1940s+] the act of fellatio.

IN COMPOUNDS

❑ **suck job** *n.* [JOB *n.*[2] (2)] [2000s] fellatio. ❑ **suck queen** *n.* [1970s+] (*US gay*) one who enjoys man-to-man fellatio.

suck *n.*[4] (*also* **suckie**) [SUCK UP *v.*] **1** [mid-19C–1950s] a parasite, a toady, a sycophant. **2** [1910s+] (*Irish*) a first-year school boy. **3** [1970s+] (*Can.*) a worthless, contemptible person.

IN COMPOUNDS

❑ **suck-around** *n.* [1950s] (*US*) a toady, a parasite.

suck *n.*[5] [SUCK *v.*[1] (5)] **1** [mid-19C+] (*orig. US*) a disappointment. **2** [20C+] (*US black*) empty words, nagging, pointless arguments.

IN PHRASES

❑ **shut one's suck** *v.* [1980s] (*US*) to stop talking.

suck *n.*[6] *see* SUCKER *n.*[1] (3a).

suck *adj.* [SUCK *v.*[1] (5)] [1970s] worthless, second-rate.

suck *v.*[1] **1** [mid-17C+] (*also* **suck-a-butt**) to perform fellatio or cunnilingus. **2** [19C] to pump someone for information. **3** [1940s+] in dismissive/challenging phr. *(go) suck (on) this*. **4** [1950s] (*W.I.*) to nag. **5** [1960s+] (*also* **suck out loud, suck a big dog's dick**) to be worthless, contemptible, pointless, objectionable. **6** [1970s+] (*US campus*) to be on one's last legs, to be struggling [i.e. to suck for air]. **7** *see* SUCK UP *v.* (1).

IN COMPOUNDS

❑ **suck-prick** *n.* [late 17C] a homosexual fellator.

IN PHRASES

❑ **suck a big dog's dick** *v. see* sense 5 above. ❑ **suck-a-butt** *v. see* sense 1 above. ❑ **suck a dog's dick** *v.* [1960s+] (*orig. US black*) to perform the lowest act of which one is capable. ❑ **suck dick** *v. see under* DICK *n.*[1]. ❑ **suck out loud** *v. see* sense 5 above. ❑ **suck someone's dick** *v. see under* DICK *n.*[1].

IN EXCLAMATIONS

❑ **suck a fatty!** [lit. *go and suck a fat penis!*] [1990s+] (*US*) a general excl. of dismissal, aggression. ❑ **suck my dick!** (*also* **suck my cock!**) [lit. 'perform an act of fellatio!'] [1970s+] (*orig. US*) a general excl. of contempt, dismissal; often ext.

SE in slang uses

IN COMPOUNDS

❑ **suck and swallow** *n.* [the role of the vagina as a predator] [19C] the vagina. ❑ **suck-ass** *see* separate entries. ❑ **suck-back** *n.* [one who should have been *sucked back* into the womb at birth] [1990s+] (*Aus.*) an extremely obnoxious person. ❑ **suck-bottle** *n.* [mid-17C–mid-18C] a drinker. ❑ **suck-egg** *see* separate entries. ❑ **suck-(h)arse** *n. see* KISS-ARSE *n.* ❑ **suck-hole** *n. see* separate entry. ❑ **suck-in** *n. see* separate entry. ❑ **suck-off** *n. see* separate entry. ❑ **suck-pint** *n.* [early 17C] a drinker. ❑ **suck-pot** *n.* [18C; 19C] a drinker. ❑ **suck-silly** *adj.* [1940s] (*US*) deranged. ❑ **suck-spigot** *n.* [late 16C–early 17C] a drinker. ❑ **suck-up** *n. see* separate entry.

IN PHRASES

❑ **suck (a)round** *v.* [var. SUCK UP *v.* (1)] [1910s+] (*US*) to act in a toadying manner. ❑ **suck air** *v.* [var. on SUCK WIND *v.*] **1** [1950s+] (*US*) to be fearful; to encounter problems. **2** [1980s] (*US campus*) to laugh. ❑ **suck a kumara** *v.* [Maori *kumara*, a sweet potato] [1980s] (*N.Z.*) of a machine, to break down, to crash. ❑ **suck ass/arse** *v. see* SUCK SOMEONE'S ASS/ARSE *under* ASS *n.* ❑ **suck diesel** *v.* [2000s] (*Irish*) to enjoy oneself. ❑ **suck eggs** *v. see* separate entry. ❑ **suck face** *v.* (*also* **suck heads**) [note synon. 18C *suck one's jowl*] [1970s+] (*orig. US campus*) to kiss. ❑ **suck hind tit** *v. see under* TIT *n.*[2]. ❑ **suck hole** *v. see* separate entry. ❑ **suck in** *v. see* separate entry. ❑ **suck in on** *v.* [1950s] (*US drugs*) to smoke marijuana. ❑ **suck it and see** *v.* [the image of sucking a lollipop to taste it] [late 19C+] a phr. aimed derisively at someone who has asked what is considered a stupid or impudent question. ❑ **suck it easy** *v.* [the image of lying peacefully sucking on a cool drink] [1980s+] (*US campus*) to relax, to lie around. ❑ **suck it up** *v.* [1970s+] (*US campus*) to tolerate, to endure, to deal with. ❑ **suck lemons** *v. see under* LEMON *n.* ❑ **suck off** *v. see* separate entry. ❑ **suck one's face** *v.* (*also* **suck one's guts, suck one's muns**) [17C–mid-18C] to drink. ❑ **suck salt** *v. see under* SALT *n.*[3]. ❑ **suck shit** *v.* [1970s] (*US*) to suffer, to endure hardship. ❑ **suck someone's ass/arse** *v. see under* ASS *n.* ❑ **suck someone's titty** *v. see under* TITTY *n.* ❑ **suck spit** *v. see* SWAP SPIT(S) *under* SWAP *v.* ❑ **suck suds** *v. see under* SUDS *n.*[1]. ❑ **suck teeth** *v. see* KISS TEETH *under* KISS *v.* ❑ **suck the bag** *v.* [early 19C] to spend money. ❑ **suck (the) bamboo** *v. see under* BAMBOO *n.* ❑ **suck the monkey** *v.* [note Hotten 1873: 'Originally, as Captain Marryatt [*sic*] states, to SUCK THE MONKEY, was to suck rum from the cocoa-nuts, which spirit had been inserted in place of the milk, for the private use of the sailors'] **1** [late 18C–late 19C] to suck liquor through a straw from the ship's barrel, which has been bored with a gimlet. **2** [mid-19C] to replace the milk of a coconut with rum, and consume it through a straw. **3** [mid-19C] to drink from the bottle. ❑ **suck the mop** *v.* [play on NURSE *v.* (2); SE *mop*, a baby's dummy] [mid–late 19C] for one omnibus to lose its passengers to those of a rival firm, which has boxed it in; thus *left sucking the mop*, rendered impotent and beyond hope, put at an utter disadvantage. ▫ **suck the sugar-stick** *v. see under* SUGAR-STICK *n.* ▫ **suck tonsils** *v.* [1990s+] (*US campus*) to kiss passionately. ▫ **suck up** *v. see* separate entry. ▫ **suck wind** *v. see* separate entry.

IN EXCLAMATIONS

▫ **suck eggs!** *see* separate entry. ▫ **suck gas!** [1950s] (*US*) a dismissive excl. ▫ **suck my ass!/arse!** *see under* ASS *n.* ▫ **sucks to be you!** *see* separate entry. ▫ **sucks (to you)!** see separate entry.

suck *v.*[2] [? backform. f. SUCKER *n.*[1] (3b)] [1970s+] (*US campus*) to make someone into a victim of one's plans, tricks etc.

suck! *excl.* [1980s+] (*US campus*) a general excl., a euph. for FUCK! *excl.*

sucka *n.* [deliberate mis-spelling of SUCKER *n.*[1] (3b)] [1990s+] **1** (*orig. US black teen*) a foolish, gullible person. **2** (*orig. US black teen*) a general term of abuse. **3** (*US campus*) redup. as a term of affectionate address.

Sucka Free *n.* [SUCKA *n.* (2) + SE *free*] [1990s+] (*US black teen*) San Francisco.

suck-ass *n.* [*SUCK SOMEONE'S ASS/ARSE under* ASS *n.*] [20C+] (*US*) a toady.

suck-ass *adj.* (*also* **suck-arse**) [*SUCK SOMEONE'S ASS/ARSE under* ASS *n.*] [1970s+] useless, pointless, unpleasant – all deriving from the need to be obsequious.

sucked *adj.* [early–mid-19C] (*UK Und.*) (very) drunk.

suck-egg *n.* [17C SE *suck-egg*, a young man] [mid-19C] a foolish person.

suck-egg *adj.* [SUCK-EGG *n.*] [mid-19C+] (*US*) despicable, foolish.

suck eggs *v.* [20C+] **1** (*US, esp. Southern*) to be mean and irritable; to be overbearing and unpleasant. **2** (*US*) of a person, thing or situation, to behave in a disgusting manner, to be reprehensible, e.g. *that sucks eggs*.

suck eggs! *excl.* [abbr. colloq. phr. *teach one's grandmother to suck eggs*] [20C+] (*US*) a general excl. of hostility or dismissal.

sucker *n.*[1] **1** [early 17C; mid-19C; 1980s] a parasite [SE *sucker*, one who sucks, in this case money and favours]. **2** as a part of the body. (**a**) [mid-18C] the vagina. (**b**) [late 19C] the penis. (**c**) [1940s] (*N.Z.*) the buttocks. (**d**) [1970s] (*Irish*) a woman's breast. **3** (*orig. US*) pertaining to people, esp. when innocent [14C *sucker*, an animal before it is weaned, a child at the breast; thus the innocence of both; the term was popularized by New York nightclub hostess Texas Guinan whose celebrated greeting was 'Hello sucker!']. (**a**) [mid-18C+] (*also* **suck**) an innocent, a dupe. (**b**) [mid-19C+] the victim of any kind of crooked plan. (**c**) [mid-19C+] a person (occas. animal) or object, irrespective of status. (**d**) [mid-19C+] an unpleasant, mean person. (**e**) [1910s+] a general term of address, either derog. or teasing. (**f**) [1940s+] an enthusiast, a 'pushover'. (**g**) [1950s] (*US*) a fan. **4** [mid-19C] (*US*) a drunkard. **5** [late 19C+] people who SUCK *v.*[1] (1). (**a**) a fellatrix. (**b**) a lesbian. (**c**) (*US Und.*) a male homosexual. **6** [1950s] (*W.I.*) a nagging old woman [note dial. *old suck*, a blood-sucking demon in the shape of an old woman].

IN COMPOUNDS

▫ **sucker-ass** *n.* [-ASS *sfx*] [1990s+] (*US black*) a general term of abuse. ▫ **sucker-bait** *n.* [1940s+] (*US Und.*) **1** young women hired by casinos to appear available and thus lure and distract gamblers. **2** any form of fraudulent enticement. ▫ **sucker list** *n.* [note WW2 US milit. *sucker list*, duty roster] [1930s+] (*US*) a client list, a mailing list. ▫ **sucker play** *n.* [PLAY *n.* (2)] **1** [late 19C–1950s] (*US*) any form of scheme intended to trap a gullible victim. **2** [1910s] a foolish action. ▫ **sucker-punch** see separate entries. ▫ **sucker snow** *n.* [SNOW *n.*[1] (2a)] [1950s+] (*drugs*) second-rate, over-adulterated cocaine, esp. as sold to gullible consumers. ▫ **sucker stroking** *n.* [2000s] (*US prison*) becoming tearful at the thought of one's absent girlfriend. ▫ **sucker town** *n.* [the inference is that the populace are too innocent to accept bribes] [1940s] (*US Und.*) a town or city in which any criminal activity is unwise – the authorities have proved impervious to corruption. ▫ **sucker weed** *n.* [SUCKER *n.*[1] (3b) + WEED *n.*[1] (4)] [1950s+] (*US black/drugs*) poor-quality marijuana, esp. as sold to gullible consumers.

IN PHRASES

▫ **sucker out** *v.* [1960s] (*US*) to act like a fool; to make a mistake.

sucker *n.*[2] [? the state fish (*Catostomus commersoni*), the sucker; the sucking of much-needed water from the natural artesian wells; the gullibility of the early settlers in the hands of unscrupulous land speculators; for detailed discussion see R. H. Thornton, *An American Glossary*, I pp.32–3 (1912)] [mid-19C+] (*US*) an inhabitant of Illinois.

sucker *n.*[3] [? euph. for FUCKER *n.*, abbr. COCKSUCKER *n.*] **1** [1930s+] a generally pej. description. **2** [1980s+] an object, irrespective of quality.

sucker *adj.* [SUCKER *n.*[1] (3a)] **1** [mid-19C] mean, untrustworthy. **2** [1910s+] (*orig. US*) foolish, naïve.

sucker *v.* [SUCKER *n.*[1] (3a)] [1930s+] (*orig. US*) (*also* **suckerize**) **1** to cheat, to trick; thus *sucker in*, to ensnare, to entrap. **2** to be deceived, to 'fall for'. **3** to behave stupidly.

sucker-punch *n.* [SUCKER *n.*[1] (3a) + SE *punch*] [1940s+] a surprise punch.

sucker-punch *v.* [SUCKER-PUNCH *n.*] [1960s+] (*US*) **1** to hit when the victim is not looking or is otherwise unprepared. **2** in fig. use, to shock. **3** to fool, to trick.

suck-hole *n.* **1** [late 19C+] (*orig. Aus./Can.*) (*also* **suckholer**) a toady, a flatterer [SUCK UP *v.* (1) + HOLE *n.*[1] (1a)]. **2** [1970s+] (*US gay*) a hole drilled or carved between the partitions of two toilet stalls in a men's room and used for sex [SUCK *v.*[1] (1) + SE *hole*]. **3** [2000s] an unpleasant place.

suck hole *v.* [SUCK-HOLE *n.*] [1960s+] (*Aus./Can./US*) to toady, to curry favour.

suckie *n. see* SUCK *n.*[4].

suck-in *n.* [SUCK IN *v.*] **1** [mid-19C–1920s] a disappointment. **2** [1910s] (*Aus.*) sharp practice; a cunning scheme; deceit. **3** [1940s] (*US Und.*) a swindler.

suck in *v.* **1** [mid-19C] to accept, to believe. **2** [mid-19C+] to deceive, to cheat.

sucking *n.* [abbr. COCKSUCKING *n.*] [1920s+] (*orig. US*) fellatio.

sucking *adj.*[1] [SE *suck*, i.e. at the maternal breast] [mid-19C] ripe for duping; thus naut. jargon *sucking Nelson*, a midshipman.

sucking *adj.*[2] [despite synonymity, chronology appears to eliminate a link to SUCK *v.*[1] (5)] [mid-19C+] (*US*) worthless, useless, contemptible.

sucking duppy *n.* [SE *sucking* + dial. *duppy*, a ghost, a malevolent spirit (allegedly of the dead)] [1940s] (*W.I.*) tuberculosis.

suck-o! *excl.* [SUCK *v.*[1] (5) + -O *sfx* (3)] [1980s+] (*Aus. prison*) an excl. of satisfaction at someone else's misfortune.

suck-off *n.* [SUCK OFF *v.*] **1** [1920s+] (*US*) a despicable person, esp. a toady; thus *suck-off*, repellent, contemptible. **2** [1930s] an act of oral sex.

suck off *v.* [the *off* (cf. COME OFF *v.*[3]) implies orgasm] **1** [20C+] to fellate [SUCK *v.*[1] (1)]. **2** [1920s+] (*US*) to toady to [SUCK UP *v.* (1)]. **3** [1930s+] to perform cunnilingus. **4** [1960s+] to act as a parasite. **5** [1980s] to make a fool of. **6** [2000s] (*N.Z.*) as a dismissive excl.: go away!

suckster/suckstress *n.* [SUCKER *n.*[1] (5a)] [late 19C+] a fellator, a fellatrix.

sucks to be you *phr.* [SUCK *v.*[1] (5)] [1990s+] (*US campus*) an expression of commiseration.

sucks (to you)! *excl.* (*also* **sucks yourself**) [? euph. for FUCK! *excl.*] [1910s+] (*usu. teen*) a disdainful, dismissive excl.

suck-up *n.* [SUCK UP *v.* (1)] [1960s+] one who curries favour with others, a toady, a parasite; also attrib.

suck up *v.* **1** [mid-19C+] (*also* **suck, suck up to**) to curry favour, to be obsequious, to grovel shamelessly in return for favours, esteem etc. **2** [1950s+] to drink.

suck wind *v.* **1** [1960s+] (*US*) to be on one's last legs, to be struggling. **2** [1970s] (*US teen*) a dismissive retort to someone who is showing off.

IN PHRASES

▫ **have one's face out a yard and sucking wind** *v.* [one fig. gasps for air] [1970s] (*US*) to be a braggart.

sucky *n. see* SUCK *n.*[1].

sucky *adj.*[1] [SUCK *n.*[1] (1)] [late 17C–18C] tipsy, slightly drunk.

sucky *adj.*[2] (*US campus*) **1** [1910s+] awful, terrible, unpleasant [link to SUCK *v.*[1] (5) but chronology appears to negate this; *OED*, quoting Paul Beale in *DSUE* (1984) suggests that which makes one *suck* in one's cheeks with pain]. **2** [1960s+] toadying, sycophantic [SUCK UP *v.* (1)].

sucky-sucky *n.* (*also* **sucky-fucky**) [SUCK *v.*[1] (1)] [1970s+] fellatio.

suction *n.*[1] [early 19C–1910s] the heavy drinking of alcohol; thus [mid-19C] *power of suction*, one's drinking capacity; [1900s] *live on suction*, to drink heavily.

suction *n.*[2] [? fig. use of SE or play on SUCK WIND *v.*] [1950s–70s] (*US black*) empty words, nagging, pointless arguments.

sud-buster *n.* [1920s–40s] (*US black*) a cleaner.

sudden *adj.* [1900s–20s] **1** (*Aus.*) fast, efficient, keen. **2** (*orig. Aus.*) brutal, ruthless, drastic; of clothes, garish.

sudden death *n.*[1] **1** [mid-19C] (*Anglo-Ind.*) a spatch-cocked fowl [the bird was caught and killed as the putative eater dismounted from his horse and by the time he had washed and dressed was ready for the table]. **2** [mid-19C–1910s] (*US*) a strong alcoholic drink, esp. cheap whisky. **3** [mid-19C+] (*sporting*) in a variety of games (orig. coin-tossing), a way of deciding the victor in a tied contest by giving the judgement to the next individual or team to score; thus [20C+] *sudden-death play-off*. **4** [late 19C] a plain boiled pudding. **5** [late 19C–1900s] coffee. **6** [late 19C+] a crumpet or bun. **7** [1950s] (*Aus.*) one who is overwhelmed or infatuated, impulsively.

sudden death *n.*[2] [rhy. sl.] [1970s+] (*Aus.*) breath.

sudden death on *phr.* [ext. SUDDEN *adj.*] [1920s+] (*Aus.*) **1** expert, skilled at. **2** unnecessarily cruel or harsh towards.

suds *n.*[1] [the product's intense soap-suds-like fizziness and (to UK palates) taste. The 18C phr. *little in the suds*, drunk, is presumably coincidental] **1** [late 19C+] (*US*) beer; thus *suds slinger/jerker*, a bartender; (*Aus.*) *suds shop*, a hotel (i.e. public house). **2** [1900s] drink in general. **3** [1920s+] coffee.

IN PHRASES

❑ **crack some suds** *v.* [1940s–70s] (*orig. US black*) to open and drink a can of beer. ❑ **in the suds** **1** [17C–mid-19C] in trouble, in a disagreeable situation [SE *suds*, filth, muck]. **2** [mid-18C–early 19C] tipsy. ❑ **little in the suds** *adj.* [18C] drunk. ❑ **suck suds** *v.* [1940s+] (*US*) to drink beer.

SE in slang uses

IN PHRASES

❑ **bust suds** *v.* [1950s+] (*US black*) to work as a washer-up. ❑ **lost in the suds** *adj.* [1930s] (*US black*) unaware, unsophisticated.

suds *n.*[2] [? fig. use of SE *suds*, froth, i.e. that which money brings to life] [1910s] (*US campus*) money.

sudsday *n.* [mid-19C] (*US*) washday.

sudser *n.* [SE *soap suds*] [1950s+] (*US*) a soap opera.

sud-up *adj.* [1990s+] (*W.I.*) referring to the mix of vaginal secretions/semen that follows intercourse.

sue *n.* (*also* **soro, susie, susy, suzi, suzy**) [generic use of the proper name] [1980s+] (*US campus*) a usu. derog. term for a stereotypical sorority member; thus *sue out*, to dress, look and act like a sorority member.

sue city *n.* [SE *sue* + -CITY *sfx* + pun on *Sioux City*] [1960s+] (*US*) involvement in a court case or similar legal situation.

suede *n.* **1** [1940s–70s] (*black*) a dark-skinned black person. **2** *see* SUEDEHEAD *n.*

suede *adj.* [SUEDE *n.* (1)] [1960s–70s] (*US black*) dark-skinned.

suedehead *n.* (*also* **suede**) [1970s+] a form of SKINHEAD *n.* (3) whose hair is grown slightly longer than the usual absolute bald look and thus presents a slight fuzz, somewhat reminiscent of suede.

suet *n.* [mid-19C] (*US Und.*) liquor.

suet-headed *adj.* [along the lines of PUDDING-HEADED *adj.*] [late 19C] foolish, stupid.

suety Isaac *n.* (*also* **soapy Isaac**) [? its sallow 'complexion', supposedly reminiscent of a Jew; i.e. the 'Jewish' proper name *Isaac*] [1900s–20s] a suet pudding.

suey bowl *n.* [1940s–50s] (*US Und.*) an opium den.

suey pow *n.* (*also* **sui gow**) [ety. unknown; ? presumably transliteration of Chinese] [1900s–50s] (*drugs*) a cloth or sponge used to cool or clean an opium pipe or bowl.

suff *adj.* (*also* **suffish**) [abbr.] [late 19C–1910s] (*N.Z./UK*) sufficient.

suffer *n.* [the listeners 'suffer' through it] [1940s] (*US black*) a lengthy story, tediously recounted.

suffer a recovery *v.* [joc. euph.] [1910s–40s] to have a hangover.

sufferer *n.*[1] [? his professional problems, usu. poverty] [mid-19C] a tailor.

sufferer *n.*[2] ['Cockney' mispron.] [mid–late 19C] a sovereign.

suffering —! *excl.* [mid-19C+] used with suitable n. to create a mild oath.

suffer with the shorts *v. see under* SHORT *adj.*[1].

suffier *n.* [? Netherlands High Ger. *suff*, drink] [late 16C] (*UK Und.*) that member of a team of confidence tricksters passing off fake gold who poses as a drunk.

suffish *adj. see* SUFF *adj.*

sug *n.*[1] [Du. *zuchten*, to sigh, to groan] [20C+] (*S.Afr.*) a moan, a whinge; thus as v., to whinge.

sug *n.*[2] *see* SHUG *n.*

sug *n.*[3] *see* SUGAR *n.*[4] (2).

sugan *n.* (*also* **soogan, sougan, suggan**) [1900s–40s] (*US tramp*) a quilt.

sugar *n.*[1] [fig., but note SUGAR AND HONEY *n.*; Cohen (ed.), *Studies in Slang II* (1989), suggests that on the basis of *honey* = gold, *sugar* = silver as well as the plain generic] **1** [mid-19C+] money. **2** [late 19C] a premium, an unexpected bonus. **3** [late 19C+] monetary gifts or bribes.

IN COMPOUNDS

❑ **sugar bag** *see* separate entries. ❑ **sugar daddy** *n. see* separate entry. ❑ **Sugar Hill** *n. see* separate entry. ❑ **sugar mama** *n. see* separate entry. ❑ **sugar mummy** *n. see* separate entry. ❑ **sugar papa/pops** *n. see* SUGAR DADDY *n.*

IN PHRASES

❑ **big sugar** *n.* [1920s] (*Aus.*) a large amount of money. ❑ **heavy sugar** *n.* [HEAVY *adj.* (2a)] **1** [1920s+] (*orig. US*) a large amount of money; thus *heavy sugar guy*, a big spender; *heavy sugar papa*, a sweet old man with a fat purse. **2** *see* SUGAR DADDY *n.*

sugar *n.*[2] **1** [late 19C+] a euph. for SHIT *n.* (1). **2** [1910s] a contemptible person, a euph. for SHIT *n.* (2a).

sugar *n.*[3] [*double entendre*, e.g. Bessie Smith, 'Want Some Sugar in My Bowl'] [late 19C+] (*US black*) semen.

IN COMPOUNDS

❑ **sugar basin** *n.* [19C] the vagina.

sugar *n.*[4] **1** [1920s+] a general term of endearment, can be used of and to either sex. **2** [1930s+] (*orig. US*) (*also* **sug**) an attractive female. **3** [1930s+] (*US black*) (*also* **sugar lump, sugarpie**) an attractive male. **4** [1960s+] (*US black*) a kiss. **5** [1970s–80s] (*US black*) diabetes. **6** [1990s+] (*US black*) homosexuality [? the 'sweetness' of gay men].

IN COMPOUNDS

❑ **sugar-baby** *n.* (*also* **sugar-doll, sugar puss**) [BABY *n.* (4)/PUSS *n.*[2] (1)] [1920s+] (*US*) anyone or anything attractive, pleasing; also a direct term of address. ❑ **Sugar Hill** *n. see* separate entry. ❑ **sugar lump** *n. see* sense 3 above. ❑ **sugar man** *n. see* SWEETBACK (MAN) *n.* ❑ **sugarpie** *n. see* sense 3 above. ❑ **sugar report** *n.* [orig. milit. WW2] [1940s+] (*US campus*) a letter from one's sweetheart. ❑ **sugar scoop** *n.* (*also* **sugar walls**) [1950s] the vagina. ❑ **sugar shack** *n.* **1** [1960s] (*US black*) spare space used for putting up a temporary guest. **2** [1990s+] somewhere a couple go to have sex. ❑ **sugar-stick** *n. see* separate entry.

(IN PHRASES)

❑ **deep sugar** *n.* [its 'sweetness'] [1940s] (*US black*) sweet talk. ❑ **sugar on** *adj.* [var. on SWEET ON *under* SWEET *adj.*[1]] [late 19C] in love with, infatuated with. ❑ **sweet sugar** *n.* [1980s] (*US black*) an attractive male.

SE in slang uses

(IN COMPOUNDS)

❑ **sugar-bag** *adj. see* separate entry. ❑ **sugar-bush** *n.* [2000s] (*S.Afr. gay*) the pubic hair [resemblance]. ❑ **sugar cubes** *n.* [1940s] dice [resemblance]. ❑ **sugar pimp** see separate entries. ❑ **sugar tit** *n. see under* TIT *n.*[2]. ❑ **sugar weed** *n. see under* WEED *n.*[1].

sugar *n.*[5] (*drugs*) **1** [1930s+] morphine or heroin; thus [1970s] *sugar people*, rich young heroin addicts [note that *sugar people* is also influenced by SUGAR DADDY *n.*]. **2** [1930s+] (*also* **booger sugar**) cocaine [BOOGER *n.*[1]]. **3** [1960s+] LSD.

(IN COMPOUNDS)

❑ **sugar and salt** *n.* [1930s] (*US drugs*) any powdered narcotic. ❑ **sugar block** *n.* [1980s+] (*drugs*) crack cocaine. ❑ **sugar cubes** *n.* (*also* **sugar lumps**) [early doses of LSD came on *sugar cubes/lumps*] [1960s+] (*drugs*) LSD.

sugar *adj.* [mid-19C] easy, comfortable.

sugar *v.*[1] [fig. uses of SE *sweeten* or phr. *sugar the pill*] **1** [late 16C; 1930s] to flatter, to pander to. **2** [late 19C–1900s] to bribe. **3** [late 19C–1950s] to present a fake appearance, to 'cook the books', to pose as something one is not.

(IN PHRASES)

❑ **sugar up** *v.* [1910s–20s] to flatter, to toady to.

sugar *v.*[2] [late 19C+] a euph. for SHIT *v.* or BUGGER *v.*[1] in various uses.

sugar! *excl.* **1** [mid-19C] a cry of exultation after a victory, supposedly given as one stands on one leg and waves the other about. **2** [mid-19C+] (*also* **ginger!**) a euph. for SHIT! *excl.* or BUGGER! *excl.* **3** [late 19C] a euph. for *the hell with*.

sugar and honey *n.* [rhy. sl.] [mid-19C–mid-20C] money.

sugar and spice *n.* [rhy. sl.] [20C+] ice.

sugar and spice *adj.* [rhy. sl.] [20C+] nice.

sugar-bag *n.* [they are willing to take a SE *sweetener*] [late 19C+] (*Aus.*) one who accepts bribes.

sugar-bag *adj.* [the Depression-era use of *sugar bags* (made of fine sacking) for a variety of makeshift and do-it-yourself tasks] [1970s] (*Aus./N.Z.*) second-rate, cheap, impoverished.

sugar-bag *v.* [1980s] (*Aus.*) to bribe.

sugar-candy *n.* [rhy. sl.] [mid-19C+] brandy.

sugar candy *adj.* [rhy. sl.] [20C+] handy.

sugar daddy *n.* (*also* **sugar, sugar papa, sugar-pops, sweet sugar**) [1920s+] (*orig. US*) an older man who is willing to provide the various material wants of a younger mistress or, if gay, a younger male lover.

sugared *adj.* [late 19C+] euph. for BUGGERED *adj.*[1] etc; usu. in phrs. *I'll be sugared! I'm sugared!*

Sugar Hill *n.* [note Lincoln U. (Oxford, Penn.) use *c.*1934: 'Sugar Hill. The newest dormitory, where rentals and appointments are relatively high] (*US black*) **1** [1920s–40s] that area of Harlem otherwise known as Coogan's Bluff, between Amsterdam and Edgecombe Avenues, between 138th and 155th Streets. As well as the rich, many black intellectuals and artists chose to live in the area, known for its grand apartment houses, once the original white population had moved out during the 1920s [SUGAR *n.*[1] (1)]. **2** [1930s–50s] the brothel and 'red-light' area of the black part of any southern town [SUGAR *n.*[4] (1)].

sugar mama *n.* [feminization of SUGAR DADDY *n.*] **1** [1970s+] (*US*) an older woman who keeps a (usu.) younger lover. **2** [1970s–80s] (*US gay*) an effeminate older gay man providing material support for his younger lover.

sugar mummy *n.* [on the model of SUGAR DADDY *n.*] **1** [1950s+] an older woman who provides for the material wants of a younger male or female lover. **2** [1980s+] (*S.Afr. township*) a wealthy white woman who pays for the companionship of attractive, younger black men.

sugar pimp *n.* (*also* **sweet pimp**) [SE *sugar* + *pimp*] [1970s] a pimp who prefers charm and persuasion to threats and violence when dealing with his women.

sugar pimp *v.* [SE *sugar* + *pimp*] [1950s–70s] to be a pimp who treat one's prostitutes with charm and persuasion rather than threats and violence.

sugar ray *v.* [rhy. sl.] [1980s] (*Aus.*) to pay.

sugar-stick *n.* [mid-17C+] the penis.

(IN PHRASES)

❑ **have a bit of sugar-stick** *v.* [Puxley, *Cockney Rabbit: A Dick 'n' Arry of Rhyming Slang* (1992) suggests rhy. sl. on PRICK *n.* (1), but rhy. sl. tends to be coined later] [19C] of a woman, to have sexual intercourse. ❑ **suck the sugar-stick** *v.* [19C] **1** of a woman, to have sexual intercourse. **2** usu. of a woman, to fellate.

suggan *n. see* SUGAN *n.*

suicide *n.* **1** [mid-19C] four horses driven in a line. **2** [1940s+] (*Aus.*) a punning ref., used by motorists, to the 'side' of a vehicle on which one should not attempt to pass. **3** [1970s+] (*Aus.*) used in Northern Territory to refer to the rainy season or 'wet', considered unendurable by many people.

suicide blonde *n.* [? she drives men to *suicide*; or ? pun on 'dyed by her own hand'] [1930s+] (*orig. US*) a woman with dyed blonde or peroxide blonde hair.

suicide seat *n.* [1980s] the seat beside the driver, considered to be more vulnerable in a crash.

sui gow *n. see* SUEY POW *n.*

suit *n.*[1] [SE *suit*, a full set of clothes] **1** [early 18C–mid-19C] a gold watch and seals. **2** [1940s] (*US*) a plainclothes detective. **3** [1950s+] (*also* **gray-suit, three-piece suit**) a member of management, a businessman, anyone who has to wear a suit for their daily work, as opposed to more casually dressed creative or freelance workers, or those in jobs that in any case have no need for suits; thus an uncreative, authoritarian person.

(IN PHRASES)

❑ **suit up** *v.* [1980s+] to dress oneself in a suit or uniform.

suit *n.*[2] [SE *suit*, a pursuit] [early–mid-19C] a trick, a scheme.

suit and cloak *n.* [? the liquor warms one up] [late 17C–19C] a drink, esp. brandy.

suitcase *n.* **1** [1930s–40s] (*US black*) a drum kit. **2** [1990s+] (*US*) the anus. **3** see BRIXTON SUITCASE *n.*

suitcase *v.* [SUITCASE *n.* (2)] [2000s] (*US prison*) to hide drugs or other contraband in the rectum and thus carry it around a prison.

sukey *n.* [*Sukey*, a dimin. of proper name *Susan*, but ? Welsh Gypsy *sukar*, to hum, to whisper (cf. BLACK SAL *under* BLACK *adj.*; the immediate root was presumably mid-18C+ nursery rhyme 'Polly put the kettle on'] **1** [early 18C] a male homosexual. **2** [mid-18C] a lower servant girl. **3** [19C–1950s] a kettle. **4** [mid–late 19C] a fool.

sukey-tawdry *n.* [SUKEY *n.* (2) + SE *tawdry*] [mid-19C] a slatternly woman, dressed in a flashy, vulgar style.

sulph *n.* [abbr.] [1980s+] (*drugs*) amphetamine *sulph*ate.

sulphate *n.* [abbr.] [1970s+] amphetamine *sulphate*.

sultry *adj.* [late 19C–1900s] of language, writing or pictures, coarse, obscene, vulgar, 'smutty'.

sumbitch *n. see* SONOFABITCH *n.*

sumbitching *adj. see* SONOFABITCHING *adj.*

summer bird *n.* [play on SE *cuckoo*, which appears in summer] [mid-16C–early 17C] a cuckold.

summer cabbage *n.* **1** *see under* CABBAGE *n.*[2]. **2** *see* HAVE A BIT OF SUMMER CABBAGE *under* CABBAGE *n.*[6].

summer teeth *n.* [i.e. *some are...some are...*] [2000s] (*US black*) crooked or missing teeth.

summertime *n.* [late 19C] (*US*) **1** oatmeal. **2** bread and milk.

summertime ho *n.* [HO *n.* (1)] [1970s+] an occasional prostitute who works, not necessarily in summer, but only when she needs the money or the mood takes her; often incl. high school girls, who turn to whoring in the summer holidays.

sumph *n. see* SONOFABITCH *n.*

sun *n.*

SE in slang uses

IN COMPOUNDS

❑ **sunbake** *see* separate entries. ❑ **sunbeam** *n. see* separate entry. ❑ **sunburned** *adj. see* separate entries. ❑ **Sun City** *n. see* separate entry. ❑ **sundodger** *n. see* separate entry. ❑ **sundown/sundowner** *see* separate entries. ❑ **sunrise** *v. see* separate entry. ❑ **sunshades** *n. see* SHADE *n.*[1] (7). ❑ **sunshine** *v. see* separate entry. ❑ **sunspecs** *v. see* separate entry.

IN PHRASES

❑ **have the sun in one's eyes** *v.* (*also* **have been in the sunshine, have been standing too long in the sun**) [mid–late 19C] to be drunk.

sunabitch *n. see* SONOFABITCH *n.*

sunbake *n.* [SUNBAKE *v.*] [1950s] a sunbathe.

sunbake *v.* (*also* **sun off**) [1910s+] (*Aus.*) to sunbathe.

sunbeam *n.* [*as bright as a sunbeam*] **1** [1950s+] (*Aus.*) an item of crockery or cutlery laid out on the table but still unused. **2** *see* SUNSHINE *n.* (3).

sunburned *adj.*[1] (*also* **sunburnt**) **1** [late 16C–late 19C] infected with a venereal disease [pun on SE *burned*/BURNED *adj.*[1] (1)]. **2** [early 17C] drunk.

sunburned *adj.*[2] (*also* **sunburnt**) [pun on SE *son*] [late 17C–early 19C] having too many male children.

sunburned Irishman *n.* (*also* **smoked Irishman**) [immigrant blacks and Irish occupy the same low social position in the UK] [20C+] a derog. term for a black person.

sunburnt *adj. see under* SUNBURNED.

Sun City *n.* [*Sun City*, the luxury hotel and entertainment complex near Rustenberg, North-West Province] [1980s+] (*S.Afr.*) an ironic nickname for Diepkloof Prison, Gauteng Province.

Sunday *n.*[1] (*N.Z.*) used in combs. to imply laziness, inactivity.

IN COMPOUNDS

❑ **Sunday face** *n.* [play on SE *Sunday face*, a sanctimonious expression] **1** [19C] the backside. **2** [20C+] (*US black*) a very attractive face. ❑ **Sunday flash togs** *n.* [FLASH *adj.* (1) + TOGS *n.* (1)] [late 19C–1900s] one's best clothes. ❑ **Sunday jinal** *n.* [dial. *jinal*, a clever person; thus a con-man, a crook; ult. pron. of SE *general*] [1950s] (*W.I.*) any variety of clergyman or preacher. ❑ **Sunday man** *n.* **1** [late 18C–early 19C] a criminal or debtor who only dares go out on Sunday, when the police are inactive. **2** [late 19C] a pimp [Sunday is the only day he can go out with his woman; the remainder of the time she will be working]. ❑ **Sunday morning quarterback** *n. see* MONDAY MORNING QUARTERBACK *n.* ❑ **Sunday promenader** *n.* [early 19C] a debtor, one who risks going out on Sundays only. ❑ **Sunday saint** *n.* [late 19C+] one whose degenerate weekday behaviour is replaced every Sunday by an air of sanctimonious and ultimately hypocritical piety. ❑ **Sunday-school story** *n.* [1920s] (*US*) a fantasy, a lie. ❑ **Sunday-school words** *n.* [1900s] (*US*) curses, swearing.

IN PHRASES

❑ **in one's Sunday** *see* OLD MAN HAS HIS SUNDAY CLOTHES ON *under* OLD MAN *n.* ❑ **six ways from Sunday** (*also* **all ways to Sunday, eight ways from Tuesday, every which way from Sunday, six sides of Sunday, six ways for Sunday, six ways to Sunday**) [ety. unknown] [mid-19C+] askew, at an angle.

Sunday *n.*[2] *see* SUNDAY (PUNCH) *n.*

Sunday *v.* [late 19C] (*UK society*) to spend Sunday with a person or persons.

Sunday best *n.* [rhy. sl.] [1920s] a vest (undershirt).

Sunday go-to-meeting *adj.* [mid-19C+] (*US*) of clothes and other things, the best.

IN COMPOUNDS

❑ **Sunday-go-to-meeting clothes** *n.* (*also* **Sunday-go-to-Church, Sunday-go-to-meeting outfit, Sunday-go-to-meeting(s)**) [one dresses for church] [mid-19C+] (*orig. US*) one's best clothes.

Sunday morn *n.* (*also* **early morn**) [rhy. sl. = HORN *n.*[2] (1c)] [20C+] an erection.

Sunday (punch) *n.* [on the pattern of *Sunday*, therefore best, suit] [1910s+] (*orig. US*) a very hard or knockout blow.

IN PHRASES

❑ **cop a Sunday** *v.* [1920s+] (*US*) to hit someone very hard.

sundodger *n.* [since their likely job would be on a farm, such indolence keeps them out of the sun] [1910s–40s] (*Aus./US*) one who loiters around in the hope of hand-outs, which will save them from having to earn a living.

sundown *n. see* SUNSHINE *n.* (3).

sundown *adj.* [late 19C–1940s] (*US*) used of one who works outside their normal hours of practice, e.g. lawyers, doctors.

sundown *v.* [SUNDOWNER *n.* (1)] [late 19C–1920s] (*Aus.*) to beg someone for food and drink.

sundowner *n.* **1** [mid-19C+] (*Aus./N.Z.*) a tramp or vagrant who arrives at a station about sundown under the pretence of seeking work, but really, since work stops at dusk, to obtain food and a night's lodging. **2** [late 19C–1900s] (*US*) a professional who takes on extra work outside their normal hours of practice. **3** [1940s] an evening drink. **4** [1940s] (*Aus.*) a lazy sheepdog or cattle-dog.

sunk *adj.* [naut. imagery] **1** [1920s+] hopeless, finished, no chance. **2** [1980s+] (*Aus. prison*) found guilty in court.

sunnies *n.* [abbr.] [1990s+] (*Aus./N.Z.*) *sun*glasses.

sunning *n.* [? the patronizing use of SE *son* as a term of address in such a context] [1990s+] (*US black*) taking orders.

sunny bank *n.* [pun on SE *banking*, a fire] [late 17C–early 19C] a good fire in winter.

Sunny Jim *n.* (*also* **sonny Jim**) [the slogan for Force breakfast food: 'High o'er the fence leaps Sunny Jim / "Force" is the food that raises him' coined 1903] [1910s+] a general term of address, esp. affectionate.

sunny side *n.* [the *sunny side of the street*] [20C+] the good, easy, materially satisfying life.

sunny south *n.* [rhy. sl.] [late 19C] the mouth.

sun off *v. see* SUNBAKE *v.*

sunrise *v.* [1940s] (*US Und.*) to jail a tramp overnight, prior to expelling him from town in the morning.

sunsey *adj. see* SONSY *adj.*

sunshine *n.* **1** [late 18C] prosperity. **2** [1930s] (*US Und.*) gold. **3** [1950s+] (*also* **sunbeam, sundown**) a general form of address, e.g. *Oi! sunshine!* **4** [1960s–70s] (*drugs*) a variety of LSD [abbr. ORANGE SUNSHINE *n.*; i.e. the orange-coloured pills containing the drug].

IN PHRASES

❑ **let sunshine through** *v. see* LET THE DAYLIGHT INTO/THROUGH *under* DAYLIGHT *n.*[1] .

sunspecs *n.* [abbr. SPECS *n.* (1)] [1970s+] *sun*glasses.

suntans *n.* [1960s] **1** (*US*) shorts. **2** a military tan shirt.

sup *n.*[1] (*also* **supp**) [abbr.; note mid-19C theatre jargon *sup*, a supernumerary or extra] **1** [1920s+] a *sup*plement. **2** [1960s+] a newspaper colour *sup*plement and spelled with double *p*, often as *colour supp*.

sup *n.*[2] *see* SUPER *n.*[1] (5).

sup *v.*

IN PHRASES

❑ **sup with Sir Thomas Gresham** *v. see* DINE WITH SIR THOMAS GRESHAM *under* DINE *v.*

's up *phr.* [contraction of *what's up?*] [1980s+] (*US black/campus/teen*) a greeting.

'sup *excl. see* WHAT'S UP? *phr.*

supe *see also under* SUPER.

supe *n.* [abbr. SE *supernumerary*] **1** [early 19C–1910s] a minor stage character, a 'walk-on'. **2** [late 19C] (*US campus*) a toady, a sycophant.

supe *v.* [SUPE *n.*] [mid–late 19C] (*US campus*) to act as a toady.

suped-up *adj. see* SOUPED-UP *adj.*[2].

super *n.*[1] **1** [mid-19C–1920s] (*US*) a theatrical understudy. **2** [mid-19C+] (*Aus.*) the *super*intendent of a sheep station. **3** [late 19C+] (*also* **supe**) a police or prison *super*intendent. **4** [1900s–30s] (*US*) a film extra. **5** [1910s+] (*US*) (*also* **soup, sup, supe**) a *super*intendent, e.g. of a work crew. **6** [1930s+] (*orig. US*) a building *super*intendent, a janitor. **7** [1970s+] (*Aus.*) a *super*annuation pension. **8** [2000s] a *super*market.

super *n.*[2] (*also* **soup, souper**) [? SE *soup-plate*; i.e. the size and shape of a watch] [mid-19C+] (*UK Und.*) **1** a watch; thus *super/souper and slang*, a watch and chain. **2** the ring that secures a watch-chain to one's garment.

IN COMPOUNDS

❑ **super-screwing** *n. see under* SCREW *v.* ❑ **super twister** *n. see* THIMBLE-TWISTER *under* THIMBLE *n.*

super *n.*[3] [1980s+] (*UK black*) **1** a star, an important figure. **2** thus a form of respectful address.

super *n.*[4] *see* SOUPBONE *n.*

super *adj.* (*also* **supe**) [Lat. *super*, above] **1** [mid-19C+] very good or pleasant, first-rate, excellent. **2** [1930s+] as an intensifier, complete, utter.

super *v.* [1970s+] (*Aus.*) to dismiss, to superannuate.

super *adv.* [early 19C+] (*US*) as an intensifier, extremely, very.

IN COMPOUNDS

❑ **supercolossal** *adj.* [1930s+] extremely large, outsized; remarkable, stupendous. ❑ **supercool** *adj.* [COOL *adj.* (2)] [1960s+] extremely relaxed, sophisticated. ❑ **superfatted** *adj.* [1920s–40s] very fat. ❑ **super saucy** *adj.* [2000s] (*US black*) excellent, first-rate. ❑ **supersnagative** *adj.* [late 19C] (*Aus./N.Z.*) excellent, wonderful, superb.

super- *pfx*

SE in slang uses

IN COMPOUNDS

❑ **superbad** *adj. see* SUPERFLY *adj.* ❑ **super buick** *n.* [BUICK *v.*; the effects are unpleasant and poss. nauseating] [1990s+] (*US drugs*) a cocktail of heroin and/or cocaine plus various prescription drugs, incl. scopolamine. ❑ **super c** *n.* [1980s+] (*drugs*) ketamine. ❑ **super charge** *n.* [its effects] [1980s+] (*drugs*) crack cocaine. ❑ **super cloud** *n.* [the clouds of smoke that accompany its use] [1980s+] (*drugs*) crack cocaine. ❑ **super-duper** *adj. see* separate entry. ❑ **super duck** *n.* [2000s] (*S.Afr.*) an inflatable boat with a powerful outboard motor used by poachers and smugglers. ❑ **super ecstasy** *n.* [1990s+] (*drugs*) a far stronger form of MDMA known as DOB *n.* ❑ **superfly** *see* separate entries. ❑ **supergrass** *n. see* separate entries. ❑ **super honkie** *n.* [HONKIE *n.*] [1960s–80s] (*US black*) an exceptionally authoritarian or otherwise powerful white person. ❑ **super K** *n. see* SPECIAL K *n.* ❑ **supermax** *n.* [1990s+] (*US prison*) extreme lockdown. ❑ **super pot** *n. see* SUPERGRASS *n.*[2]. ❑ **superscrew** *n. see under* SCREW *n.*[1]. ❑ **super skunk** *n.* [SKUNK *n.* (4a)] [1990s+] (*drugs*) an extremely potent form of marijuana. ❑ **supertoke** *v.* [TOKE *v.*] [1980s+] (*US drugs*) to inhale a cannabis cigarette from both ends. ❑ **supersoul** *n.* [SOUL *n.*[2] (2)] [1970s] (*US campus*) of black students, an exceptionally sophisticated individual. ❑ **superstud** *n.* [STUD *n.* (1)] [1970s+] a man who is obsessed with and notably successful at sex. ❑ **superweed** *n. see* SUPERGRASS *n.*[2].

super-duper *n.* [abbr. SE *superannuation*] [1960s] (*N.Z.*) a state pension.

super-duper *adj.* (*also* **sooper-dooper**) [SE pfx *super-* + redup.] [1950s+] (*juv.*) excellent, first-rate, wonderful.

superfly *n.* [SUPERFLY *adj.* + play on FLY *v.* (3)] [1970s+] cocaine, usu. of high quality.

superfly *adj.* (*also* **superbad**) [SE pfx *super-* + FLY *adj.* (7)/BAD *adj.* (3)] [1970s+] (*US black*) of people, situations, drugs etc, excellent, first-rate.

superfly *adv.* [SUPERFLY *adj.*] [1960s+] excellently.

supergrass *n.*[1] [SE pfx *super-* + GRASS *n.*[3]] [1970s+] (*UK Und.*) an informer who betrays a large number of important fellow criminals, thus helping solve many hitherto unresolved crimes.

supergrass *n.*[2] (*also* **super pot, superweed**) [SE pfx *super-* + GRASS *n.*[4]] **1** [1960s+] (*drugs*) especially strong marijuana. **2** [1970s+] phencyclidine.

superintendent of the pavement *n. see under* PAVEMENT *n.*

supermarket conversation *n.* [with no more intrinsic quality than the Muzak played in supermarkets] [1990s+] (*US black*) empty, meaningless chatter.

supernaculum *n.* (*also* **supernagulum**) [Lat. *supernaculum*, over the nail. The tradition of upending one's emptied glass onto the left thumbnail, thus proving that one had drunk every drop] **1** [late 16C–mid-19C] exceptionally good liquor; thus as adv., to the last drop, to the bottom. **2** [early 19C] any first-rate commodity.

supersonic *adj.* [1940s+] (*juv.*) absolutely wonderful.

superstitious pie *n.* [late 17C–early 18C] a mince pie or Christmas pie, as made by Puritans or Precisians sometime before Christmas.

supervisor of the pavement *n. see under* PAVEMENT *n.*

supouch *n.* [? SE *sup*, to drink] [late 17C–18C] a hostess or landlady.

supp *n. see* SUP *n.*[1].

suppelar *n.* [Ital. *suppelettile*, household fittings] [mid-19C+] (*Ling. Fr./Polari*) a hat.

supper sneak *n.* (*also* **supper man**) [1900s–50s] (*US Und.*) a robbery that takes place while the occupants of a house are gathered together eating.

suppose *n.* [rhy. sl.] [mid-19C+] a nose.

surat *n.* [textile jargon *surat*, second-rate cotton made from a mix of US (good) cotton and *surat* (bad) cotton] [mid-19C] any article of inferior quality, made from a mix of first- and second-rate materials.

sure *adj.*

SE in slang uses

IN COMPOUNDS

❑ **sure card** *n. see under* CARD *n.*[2]. ❑ **sure cop** *n. see under* COP *n.*[2]. ❑ **sure-enough** *adj.* [SE phr. *sure enough*, definitely] [late 19C+] (*US*) definite, absolute, certain, genuine. ❑ **sure-fire** *n.* [SURE-FIRE below] [1910s] (*US*) an unassailable person. ❑ **sure-fire** *adj.* [the image of an efficient firearm] [20C+] (*orig. US*) certain, definite, unassailable. ❑ **sure-God** *adv.* [1920s] (*US*) definitely. ❑ **sure model** *n. see* SURE THING *n.* ❑ **sure nuff** *adv. see* SHO' 'NUFF *adv.* ❑ **sure pop** *n. see under* POP *n.*[1]. ❑ **sure-shot** *adj.* [var. on SURE-FIRE above] [1910s+] (*US*) successful, influential. ❑ **sure thing** *see* separate entries.

IN PHRASES

❑ **for sure** *see* separate entries. ❑ **I am sure** [1990s+] (*US teen*) a phr. meaning 'I am sure that you are wrong/that I don't want to do what you suggest' etc; intensified as *I am so sure*, a phr. used at the end of a sentence to imply either 'I don't know' or 'I am sure of that'. ❑ **sure as...** *see* separate entry. ❑ **sure to hell** *see* SURE AS HELL *under* SURE AS... *phr.*

IN EXCLAMATIONS

❑ **sure-shootin'!** *see* SURE THING! *excl.*

sure *adv.* [mid-19C+] a general intensifier, definitely, absolutely.

sure! *excl.* [coined in the UK, the term moved to the US by the mid-19C, although it returned to the UK in the early 20C+] [early 18C+] definitely! absolutely!

sure as... *phr.*

IN PHRASES

❑ **sure as fuck** [1990s+] definitely, without the slightest doubt. ❑ **sure as God made little (green) apples** (*also* **sure as Christ made/put worms in sour apples, sure as God made daisies, sure as God made/put worms in sour apples**) [late 19C+] (*UK/US*) definitely, for sure. ❑ **sure as hell** (*also* **sure as heck, ...heaven's happy, ...hell's hell, ...hell's hot, sure hell, sure in hell, sure to hell**) [20C+] without a doubt, certainly. ❑ **sure as hogs are made of bacon** (*also* **sure as beans is beans, ...eggs ain't chicken, ...eggs is eggs, ...mutton's mutton, true as eggs is bacon**) [mid-19C] certain. ❑ **sure as**

shit (*also* **shure as shit, sure as cowflops, ...shit and taxes, ...shite on your shoe, ...shit rolls downhill from a privy**) [SHIT *n.* (1a)] **1** [1950s+] certainly; definitely. **2** [1970s+] (*US*) used as an affirmation. ▫ **sure as shooting** (*also* **sure as pop**) [mid-19C+] (*US*) definitely, for sure. ▫ **sure as shucks** [1930s] (*US*) for certain. ▫ **sure as the devil's in London** [mid-19C] (*UK Und.*) without doubt. ▫ **sure as twopence** [mid-18C] undoubtedly. ▫ **sure as you're a foot high** (*also* **sure as I'm a foot high, ...I'm a man fit to wear britches, ...the day is long, ...you live, ...you're alive, ...you're born**) [mid-19C–1950s] (*US*) absolutely, without a doubt.

sure thing *n.* (*also* **sure shot, sure model**) [mid-19C+] (*US*) an absolute certainty, a guarantee; also attrib.

sure-thing *adj.* [SURE THING *n.* (1)] [late 19C+] **1** definite, certain, regular. **2** (*US Und.*) major and extremely lucrative, of a situation or deal.

sure thing! *excl.* (*also* **sure-shootin'!**) [SURE THING *n.*] an affirmative excl., absolutely! certainly! I agree!

surf and turf *n.* [1960s+] (*orig. US*) **1** a restaurant specializing in seafood and steak. **2** a meal of seafood and steak.

surf bum *n. see* BUM *n.*^{3} (10).

surf bunny *n. see under* BUNNY *n.*^{1}.

surfer *n.* [? one *surfs* inner space] [1970s+] (*drugs*) phencyclidine.

surfie *n.* [1960s+] (*Aus.*) a surfer; thus *surfie chick*, a woman who associates with surfers.

surfoholic *n.* [SE *surf*, to browse the Internet] [1990s+] (*US teen*) one who is addicted to browsing the Internet.

surf the crimson wave *v.* [1990s+] (*US teen*) to menstruate.

surgical truss *n.* [rhy. sl.] [1990s+] a bus.

surly-boots *n.* (*also* **surly-chops**) [SE *surly* + sfx *-boots/-chops*] [early 18C–mid-19C] a surly, morose person.

surprise package *n.* [SE *surprise* + PACKAGE *n.* (8)] [1970s] (*US gay*) a penis that is substantially larger than expected when erect.

surprise pie *n.* [2000s] a pie served in prison, with dubious or unknown contents.

surprise, surprise! *excl.* [1960s+] an ironic or sarcastic rejoinder to a piece of supposedly revelatory information.

surreverence *n. see* SIR-REVERENCE *n.*

Surrey docks *n.* [rhy. sl. = POX *n.*^{1} (3)] [1970s] venereal disease.

Surro *n.* [*Surry* + -O *sfx* (3)] [1940s] (*Aus.*) Surry Hills, a run-down district of Sydney (latterly gentrified).

surround *v.* [? 'get your mouth around that'] [late 19C–1910s] (*Aus.*) to drink or eat.

surveyor of the highways *n.* [the drunkard's frequent falling over] [late 18C–early 19C] a drunkard.

surveyor of the pavement *n. see under* PAVEMENT *n.*

sus *n.* (*also* **suss**) [abbr.] [1930s+] **1** a *sus*pected person. **2** a *sus*picion. **3** an inkling [SE *suspect/suspicion*].

sus *adj.* (*also* **suss**) [abbr.] [1950s+] *sus*picious; thus the *sus laws*, controversial powers that permitted the police to stop and search persons allegedly suspected of a crime and that were considered as racist by the black and Asian communities.

sus *v.* (*also* **suss**) [abbr.] [1950s+] to *sus*pect.

sus *adv.* (*also* **suss**) [abbr.] [1950s] *sus*piciously.

susancide *n.* [joc. blend of SE *Susan* + *suicide*] [late 19C] suicide.

susan saliva *n.* ['he lives by his spits'] [1950s–70s] (*camp gay*) a fellator, esp. one who works as a male prostitute.

s.u.s.f.u. *phr.* [abbr.] [1940s+] (*orig. milit.*) situation unchanged, still fucked up.

sushi *n.*

IN COMPOUNDS

▫ **sushi nigger** *n.* [*sushi*, the popular Japanese dish + NIGGER *n.*^{1} (1)] [2000s] (*US black*) a derog. term for an East Asian person. ▫ **sushi socialist** *n. see* CHAMPAGNE SOCIALIST *under* CHAMPAGNE *n.* ▫ **sushi taco** *n.* [mix of popular Japanese (*sushi*, i.e. raw fish) and Mexican (*taco*) dishes] [1990s+] the labia majora.

IN PHRASES

▫ **go for sushi** *v.* [1990s+] (*US campus*) to kiss passionately. ▫ **tongue sushi** *n.* [SE *tongue* + *sushi*, a form of Japanese snack, usu. based on rice and raw fish] [1980s+] (*US campus*) deep kissing with tongues.

susie *n.*^{1} *see* SUE *n.*

susie *n.*^{2} *see* SUSY *n.*^{1}.

Susie-Q wagon *n.* [ety. unknown] [1940s] (*US prison*) a small cart carrying cleaning equipment.

susie (sorority) *n. see* SUZI (SORORITY) *n.*

sus out *v. see* SUSS OUT *v.*

suspended *n.* [abbr.] [1970s+] a *suspended* sentence.

sus. per coll. *adj.* [Lat. *suspensus per collum*, hanged by the neck; this notation is entered in the prison ledger] [late 18C–early 19C] hanged.

suspish *n.* [abbr.] [1900s–10s] a suspicion.

suspish *adj.* [abbr.] [1940s+] from the authority's point of view, *suspicious*; thus adv. *suspishly*.

suss *see also under* SUS.

suss *n.* [backform. f. SUSS OUT *v.*] **1** [1970s+] natural intelligence, instinctive knowledge, esp. as used in petty crime or other marginal occupations. **2** [2000s] a piece of information.

suss *v. see* SUSS OUT *v.*

sussed *adj.* (*also* **suss, sussed out**) [1970s+] **1** worked out. **2** clever, sophisticated, aware. **3** (*UK Und.*) arrested.

sussies *n.* [1990s+] suspenders.

susso *n.* [abbr. SE *sustenance* + -O *sfx* (3)] [1930s] (*Aus.*) **1** state government relief paid to the unemployed, esp. during the 1930s depression. **2** one who is receiving the relief; thus *on the susso*, receiving state benefits.

suss out *v.* (*also* **suss, suss on, sus out**) [SE *suspicious/suspect*] [1960s+] **1** to understand, to work out. **2** to discover.

sussy *adj.* [SUSS OUT *v.*] [1970s+] of a situation/person, suspicious, dubious.

su-su *n.* [SUSU *v.*] [1950s+] (*W.I. Rasta*) gossip, the sound of whispering.

susu *v.* [? echoic or Twi *susuw ka*, to utter a suspicion + SE *sussurate*, to whisper] [1950s+] (*W.I.*) to gossip, to malign.

susy *n.*^{1} (*also* **susie**) [rhy. sl. *Susy Anna* = TANNER *n.* (1)] [1930s+] sixpence.

susy *n.*^{2} *see* SUE *n.*

sutler *n.* [SE *sutler*, one who sells provisions to soldiers, whether in the garrison or in camp] [late 17C–early 19C] 'He that Pockets up, Gloves, Knives, Handkerchiefs, Snuff and Tobacco-boxes, and all the lesser Moveables' (B.E.).

suz *n. see* SIS *n.*

suzi *n. see* SUE *n.*

suzie (sorority) *n. see* SUZI (SORORITY) *n.*

suzie wang *n.* (*also* **suzie wong**) [the musical/film *The World of Suzie Wong* (1960) + pun on WANG *n.*^{2} (1)] [1960s] (*camp gay*) an East Asian homosexual.

Suzie Wong *n.* [ult. fr. novel and film *The World of Suzie Wong* (1960) by Richard Mason (1919–97)] [1980s+] **1** a smell [rhy. sl. = PONG *n.*^{1}]. **2** a song [rhy. sl.]. **3** (*Aus. prison*) a cannabis pipe [rhy. sl. = BONG *n.*^{1} (1)].

suzi (sorority) *n.* (*also* **susie (sorority), suzie (sorority)**) [play on proper name] [1970s+] (*US campus*) a stereotypical sorority member.

suzy *n. see* SUE *n.*

Suzy Slut *n.* [1970s] (*US teen*) a promiscuous young woman.

swab *n.*^{1} (*also* **swob, swobber**) [SE *swab*, a washcloth or mop] **1** [late 17C+] an unpleasant person. **2** [1920s] (*Aus.*) a derog. term for an Aboriginal woman.

swab *n.*^{2} [SE *swab*, a washcloth or mop, used to clean the decks] **1** [late 18C–mid-19C] a naval officer. **2** [mid-19C] the epaulette worn by a naval officer. **3** [20C+] (*US*) a merchant seaman, a sailor in the US Navy.

swab *v.* [fig. use of SE *swab*, to wipe up] [1910s] to grab, to steal.

swabber *n.* [SE *swabber*, one of a ship's crew whose business it was to swab the decks etc; thus one who behaves like a sailor of low rank] **1** [late 16C–early 19C] a general term of abuse. **2** [mid-17C] a promiscuous woman.

swabbers *n.* [? SE *swab*, to mop up. In the variety of whist known as *whisk and swabbers* a player that held these cards was automatically entitled to a share of the pot] [late 17C–early 19C] in cards, the ace of hearts, the knave of clubs, the ace and deuce of trumps.

swabble *v.* (*also* **swobble**) [? SE *swill* + *gobble*] [1920s–40s] (*US black/Harlem*) to eat fast and greedily.

swabby *n.* (*also* **swabbie**) [SWAB *n.*[2] (3)] [20C+] (*US*) a sailor.

swab jockey *n.* [SWAB *n.*[2] (3) + JOCKEY *n.*[2] (3b)] [1940s+] (*US*) a merchant seaman, a sailor in the US Navy.

swack *n.* [? dial. *swack*, a blow] [1970s+] (*US black*) the penis.

swacked (up) *adj.* [dial. *swack*, a blow, but note Scot. *swack*, to drink deeply] [1930s+] very drunk.

swacko *adj.* [SWACKED (UP) *adj.*] [1930s+] very drunk.

swack-up *n.* [fig. use of SE *swack*, to hit] [mid-19C] a lie.

swad *n.* [SE *swad*, a country bumpkin] [mid-17C–mid-19C; 1910s] (*UK Und.*) a soldier.

swadder *n.* (*also* **swaddler**) [SWADDLE *v.*. Harman claims they are 'not at all evil, but of an indifferent behaviour' but by 1725 the *New Canting Dict.* condemns them as 'not content to rob and plunder, but beat and barbarously abuse, and often murder the Passengers'] [mid-16C–early 19C] (*UK Und.*) a criminal pedlar.

swaddie *n.*[1] *see* SQUADDIE *n.*

swaddie *n.*[2] *see* SWADDY *n.*

swaddle *v.* [SE *swaddle*, to wrap up, to restrict movement] [mid-16C–mid-19C] to beat up, to assault.

swaddler *n.*[1] [Charles Wesley, *Journal*, 10 September 1747: 'We dined with a gentleman, who explained our name to us. It seems we are beholden to Mr Cennick for it, who abounds in such like expressions as, "I curse and blaspheme all the gods in heaven, but the babe that lay in the manger, the babe that lay in Mary's lap, the babe that lay in swaddling clouts", &c. Hence they nicknamed him, "Swaddler, or Swaddling John"; and the word sticks to us all, not excepting the Clergy.' Hotten (1860) adds that during the sermon, 'an ignorant Romanist, to whom the words of the English Bible were a novelty [...] shouted out in derision "A swaddler! a swaddler!", as if the whole story were the preacher's invention'] **1** [mid-18C–19C] (*also* **swadler**) a Methodist; thus *swaddling*, Methodism. **2** [mid–late 19C] any type of Protestant.

swaddler *n.*[2] *see* SWADDER *n.*

swaddy *n.* (*also* **swoddy, swaddie**) [SWAD *n.*] [early 19C+] a soldier.

swad-gill *n.* (*also* **swod-gill**) [dial. *swad* + GILL *n.*[1] (2)] [early 18C–early 19C] a soldier.

swadkin *n.* [dial. *swad* + dimin. sfx *-kin*] [early 18C–mid-19C] (*UK Und.*) a newly enlisted soldier.

swadler *n. see* SWADDLER *n.*[1] (1).

swag *n.*[1] [14C SE *swag*, a bulgy bag] **1** [mid-17C–early 19C] (*UK Und.*) a shop (and its contents) viewed as booty. **2** [mid-18C+] (*orig. UK Und.*) a thief's booty (esp. linen or clothes as opposed to jewels or plate) or a pedlar's wares. **3** [mid-18C+] any form of goods. **4** [early 19C–1920s] money. **5** [mid-19C] (*UK Und.*) a share in booty. **6** [mid-19C] a trader in small articles, the keeper of a *SWAG SHOP* below. **7** [mid-19C] the trade in small, second-rate articles. **8** [mid-19C+] a lot or plenty of anything. **9** [mid-19C+] (*UK/Aus./N.Z.*) the pack carried by an itinerant or vagrant. **10** [mid-19C+] paper money, currency. **11** [1990s+] (*drugs*) cannabis. **12** *see SWAG SHOP* below.

IN COMPOUNDS

▫ **swag-barrow man** *n.* [mid-19C] a street-seller of miscellaneous goods; thus *swag-barrow*, his cart. ▫ **swag chovey** *n.* [CHOVEY *n.*] [mid–late 19C] (*UK Und.*) a criminal receiver's shop or store; thus *swag-chovey bloke*, a marine store dealer. ▫ **swag-cove** *n.* [COVE *n.* (1)] [mid-19C] (*UK Und.*) a receiver of stolen goods. ▫ **swagman** *n. see* separate entries. ▫ **swag shop** *n.* (*also* **swag**) [early 19C–1920s] a shop that deals the wholesale of cheap articles. ▫ **swagsman** *n. see* separate entry. ▫ **swag-woman** *n. see* SWAGMAN *n.*[1].

IN PHRASES

▫ **dead swag** *n.* [mid-19C] (*US Und.*) a disappointing haul from a robbery. ▫ **gentleman of the swag** *n.* [1940s–50s] (*N.Z.*) a tramp. ▫ **go on the swag** *v.* [1980s+] (*Aus./N.Z.*) to travel as an itinerant. ▫ **hump one's swag** *v.* [HUMP *v.*[1] (2d)] [mid-19C+] to carry a pack. ▫ **look for one's swag straps** *v.* [one is about to strap on one's *swag* and get moving] [late 19C+] (*Aus./N.Z.*) to start thinking of leaving one job and going in search of another. ▫ **penny swag** *n.* [mid-19C] a seller of penny lots. ▫ **swag it** *v.* [mid-19C–1910s] (*Aus.*) to live as a tramp, or itinerant worker.

swag *n.*[2] [? SE *swig* or Scot. *swag*, a deep draught of liquid] [1970s+] (*US black*) hard liquor.

swag *n.*[3] [abbr. scientific *w*ild-*a*ss *g*uess] [1980s] (*US campus*) a wild guess, used to answer homework or examination questions.

swag *v.* [SWAG *n.*[1] (2)] **1** [mid-19C+] to steal, to take forcibly. **2** [mid-19C+] to drag away, to arrest. **3** [mid-19C+] to place, to put, to carry. **4** [1930s+] to hustle along, to hurry. **5** [1950s+] to smuggle. **6** [1980s] (*UK Und.*) to sell stolen property.

IN PHRASES

▫ **swag away** *v.* [1950s+] to abduct, to kidnap; thus in fig. use.

swagger *n.* **1** *see* SWAGMAN *n.*[1]. **2** *see* SWAGMAN *n.*[2]. **3** *see* SWAGSMAN *n.* (2).

swagger *adj.* [SE *swagger*, to flaunt oneself] [late 19C–1930s] (*UK society*) smart, fashionable.

swaggery *adj.* [lower-class version of SWAGGER *adj.*] [late 19C] smart, fashionable.

swaggie *n.* (*also* **swagg(e)y**) [abbr. SWAGMAN *n.*[2]] [late 19C+] (*Aus./N.Z.*) a vagrant, a tramp.

swagging *n.* [SWAG *n.*[1] (9)] **1** [mid-19C+] (*N.Z.*) walking in the mountains with a pack. **2** [late 19C+] (*Aus./N.Z.*) living as a tramp, esp. in the outback.

swaggish *adj.* [2000s] (*UK black*) second-rate.

swag in *v.* [SE *swag*, to make someone sway or sag] [1910s–20s] to cause someone to enter surreptitiously.

swagman *n.*[1] (*also* **swagger, swag-woman**) [SWAG *n.*[1] (7)] [mid-19C–1930s] a man in the *SWAG SHOP under* SWAG *n.*[1] trade, and street-seller of miscellaneous goods.

swagman *n.*[2] (*also* **swagger, swag seller, swagsman**) [SWAG *n.*[1] (9) + sfx *-man*] [late 19C+] (*Aus./N.Z.*) an itinerant worker, who travels with his pack on his back while looking for employment.

swagsman *n.* [SWAG *n.*[1] (2)] (*UK Und.*) **1** [mid-19C] (*also* **swagman**) one who takes the booty away after a successful burglary. **2** [late 19C–1940s] (*also* **swagger**) a receiver of stolen goods.

swailer *n.* [? dial. *swail*, to swing the arms while walking; thus to swing the cosh] [1970s] (*UK Und.*) a cosh.

swain *v.* [1990s+] (*US*) spontaneously to revoke or take back, as in words or actions.

swak *adj.* [Du. *zwak*, feeble] [20C+] (*S.Afr.*) weak, feeble.

swaler *n.* [ety. unknown] [mid-19C] (*UK Und.*) a grave-robber.

S.W.A.L.K. *phr.* (*also* **S.W.A.K.**) [abbr.] [1910s+] *s*ealed *w*ith *a* *l*oving *k*iss; usu. found on the back of envelopes; other versions include *s.w.a.k.*, *sealed with a kiss*; *s.w.a.n.k.*, *sealed with a nice kiss*; and *s.w.a.l.c.a.k.w.s.*, *sealed with a lick 'cos a kiss won't stick*.

swallow *n.* **1** [late 18C–1910s] the throat. **2** [late 19C] a mouthful. **3** [1980s+] a puff of a cigarette.

swallow *v.* (*also* **gulp, swallow it, swallow it whole**) **1** [17C+] to accept, esp. a false story that one is told. **2** [mid-19C] to be accepted. **3** [20C+] to abandon life as a professional criminal, to 'go straight'. **4** [20C+] to accept defeat, i.e. in a game.

SE in slang uses

IN COMPOUNDS

▫ **swallow-pipe** *n.* [18C+] (*W.I., Bdos*) the throat.

IN PHRASES

▫ **swallow a hair** *v.* [SE *hair*, which must be washed down the throat] [mid-17C] to be drunk. □ **swallow a hare** *v.* [? the drunkard may leap around like the animal] [late 17C–early 19C] to become very drunk. □ **swallow a sailor** *v.* [the naval predilection for rum] [late 19C] (*UK port/harbour*) to get drunk on rum. □ **swallow a tavern token** *v.* [SE *tavern token*, a token given as part of one's change; it can be used in payment for subsequent drinks] [late 16C–mid-18C] to become drunk. □ **swallow one's spit** *v.* (*also* **swallow one's neck, ...toad**) [1920s+] (*W.I.*) to keep quiet, to hold one's tongue. □ **swallow the anchor** *v. see under* ANCHOR *n.*

IN EXCLAMATIONS

□ **oh swallow yourself!** [late 19C] an excl. of dismissal, go to hell!

swallower *n.* [1980s+] **1** (*drugs*) a drug smuggler who swallows carefully wrapped drugs to take them through customs. **2** (*Aus.*) a derog. term for a woman [she swallows the semen after performing fellatio].

swallow tail *n.* [mid-19C–1930s] a swallow-tailed coat; thus *swallow-tailed*, dressed in such a coat.

swally *n.* [SE *swallow*] **1** [1950s+] (*Scot./Irish*) alcohol, a drink. **2** [1990s+] a drinking binge.

swally *v.* [SE *swallow*] [late 19C+] (*Irish*) to drink, to eat.

Swamp, the *n.* [late 19C] (*US*) a rough area of New Orleans comprising several blocks from the river.

swamp *n.*

SE in slang uses

IN COMPOUNDS

□ **swamp-angel** *n. see* SWAMP-RAT below. □ **swamp ass** *n.* [1990s+] (*US teen*) sweat gathering between the cleft of the buttocks. □ **swamp breath** *n.* [1980s] a contemptible person. □ **swamp donkey** *n.* [1990s+] a very unattractive woman; occas. man. □ **swamp guinea** *n.* [GUINEA *n.*[1] (1)] [1960s–70s] a derog. name for an Italian; the inference is of utter stupidity. □ **swamp-hog** *n.* [1980s+] (*Aus.*) a general term of abuse, usu. aimed at girls or women. □ **swamp-rat** *n.* **1** [mid-19C+] (*US*) (*also* **swamp-angel, swamp fox, swamp-rabbit**) a rural Southerner from the southern coastal states; a Cajun. **2** [1990s+] (*Aus.*) a general term of abuse.

swamp *v.*[1] [? SE *swap*] **1** [mid-19C–1910s] to spend one's entire earnings, usu. on alcohol; ext. as *swamp a cheque*. **2** [20C+] (*Aus.*) to exchange, to barter.

IN PHRASES

□ **swamp down** *v.* [mid-19C–1920s] (*Aus.*) to drink.

swamp *v.*[2] [SWAMPER *n.*] **1** [late 19C+] to work as a bullock driver's or truck driver's assistant, or to help in another occupation. **2** [1950s+] (*Aus.*) to travel, to travel with.

swamp *v.*[3] [Scot. *swamped*, arrested] [1930s+] (*US prison*) to arrest.

swamper *n.* [? logging jargon *swamper*, one who clears a way for the loggers to move through the woods] **1** [mid-19C+] (*orig. US*) an assistant to a driver of horses, mules or bullocks. **2** [1900s–40s] (*US tramp*) a bar room cleaner. **3** [1920s+] a truck- or van-driver's assistant. **4** [1920s+] (*Aus.*) one who travels on foot but has his pack carried on a wagon. **5** [1920s+] (*Aus.*) one who obtains a lift. **6** [1950s–60s] (*US prison*) a cleaner, esp. a prisoner working as a cleaner.

Swamps, the *n.* [1990s+] (*US*) a derog. term for the Sunnydale projects in the southern part of San Francisco.

swan *n.* [1980s] (*US*) a swan-dive.

swan *v.* [the image of a swan gliding over water] [late 19C+] to wander, to drift, to amble.

IN PHRASES

□ **swan about** *v.* (*also* **swan around**) [1940s+] (*orig. milit.*) to wander blithely and carelessly without a care in the world.

Swanee *n.*

IN PHRASES

□ **up the Swanee** *adj.* [generic use of *UP THE RIVER under* RIVER *n.* to imply any form of trouble + ref. to the Al Jolson song 'Swanee'; ? ult. *Suwannee River*, Georgia/Florida, USA] [1970s+] ruined, destroyed, broken, out of order. □ **go up the Swanee** *v.* [1970s+] to be ruined, to become bankrupt.

swanger *n.* [ety. unknown] [mid-19C] (*US*) a dandy.

swank *n.*[1] [mid-19C] (*UK Und.*) a fine; thus *muzz-swanked*, fined for drunkenness.

swank *n.*[2] [SWANK *v.*] **1** [mid-19C+] arrogant, showing-off behaviour. **2** [late 19C–1910s] insincere flattery. **3** [1920s+] an aristocrat, a member of the upper classes. **4** [1990s+] (*US black*) stolen goods. **5** *see* SWANKER *n.*

swank *adj.* [SWANK *v.* (1)] **1** [1910s+] showy, vulgar, arrogant. **2** [1920s+] classy, sophisticated.

swank *v.* [? OHG *swanc*, swing the body; orig. use as Midlands dial., then general sl. c.1900] **1** [early 18C; 1910s+] to swagger. **2** [late 19C–1910s] to work hard at school or university. **3** [late 19C+] to pretend, to make as if. **4** [1910s+] to show someone or something off. **5** [1910s+] to boast.

swankee *adj. see* SWANKY *adj.*

swanker *n.* (*also* **swank**) [SWANK *v.* (1)] [mid-19C–1950s] a braggart, a show-off.

swankest *adj. see* SWANKY *adj.*

swankey *n. see under* SWANKY.

swank(e)y (swipes) *n.* [SWANKY *n.*[2] + SWIPES *n.* (1)] [mid-19C] weak beer.

swanking *n.* [SWANK *v.* (1)] [20C+] showing off, acting in an arrogant or vulgar manner.

swankpot *n.* [SWANK *v.* (5) + -POT *sfx* (1)] [20C+] a boaster, a braggart.

swank-pot *adj.* [SWANKPOT *n.*] [1950s] showy, ostentatious.

swanky *n.*[1] (*also* **swankey**) [SWANK *v.* (1)] [mid–late 19C] an arrogant, showy, vulgar person.

swanky *n.*[2] (*also* **swankey**) [? Essex dial. *swank*, the last portion of liquor/beer in a glass, enough for a single draught] [mid-19C–1900s] table beer, weak beer.

swanky *adj.* (*also* **swankee, swankest**) [SWANK *v.*] **1** [late 19C+] smart, sophisticated, chic. **2** [1900s–50s] of a person, conceited, arrogant, vulgar. **3** [2000s] of an object, vulgar, showy.

swan lake *n.* [rhy. sl.] [20C+] a cake.

Swannee River *n.* [rhy. sl.; ult. *Suwannee River*, Florida/Georgia, USA] [20C+] the liver, whether human or animal.

Swannee Rivers *n.* (*also* **Swannees**) [rhy. sl.] [20C+] (*Aus.*) the shivers.

swannie *n.* [proprietary name *Swanndri*] [1980s+] (*N.Z.*) a large woollen bush shirt-cum-coat.

Swanny *n.*

IN PHRASES

□ **down the Swanny** *adj. see DOWN THE RIVER under* RIVER *n.*

Swan Stream *n.* [the city is on the Swan River] [mid-19C] Perth, Australia.

swap *n.* (*also* **swop**) [SWAP *v.*; Grose (1785) suggests 'Irish cant'] [late 18C+] an act of exchange.

IN PHRASES

□ **get/have the swap** *v.* [late 19C–1900s] to be dismissed from one's employment.

swap *v.* (*also* **swop**) [echoic *swap*, the sound of a slap; thus the slaps exchanged on sealing a bargain. Orig. Irish tinker's/horse-dealer's term, to *swap a bargain*, to strike a deal. Despite these origins, sense 1 is now effectively SE] **1** [late 16C+] to exchange. **2** [mid-19C–1900s] to dismiss from a job. **3** [late 19C] (*US*) to cheat, to take in. **4** [1900s] to change one's clothes.

SE in slang uses

IN PHRASES

□ **swap cans** *v.* [CAN *n.*[1] (1b)] [1940s+] (*US prison*) to take alternate active/passive roles in anal intercourse. □ **swap dandruff** *v.* [1930s] to talk confidentially. □ **swap gravy** *v.* [GRAVY *n.* (1)] [2000s] (*US black*) to have sexual intercourse. □ **swap lead** *v.* [1940s] to engage in a shooting match. □ **swap spit(s)** *v.* **1** [1930s+] to perform oral intercourse. **2** [1940s+] (*also* **suck spit, swap chews, ...tongues**) to kiss, usu. a French kiss. **3** [1970s+] in joc./fig. use, to become intimate, to bond.

swap-out *n.* [SWAP *v.* (1)] [1990s+] (*Aus. Und*) an act of barter whereby one criminal offers the police an alternative victim in order to evade his own prosecution for a crime.

swap out *v.*[1] [1970s] (*US prison*) to take alternate active/passive roles in anal intercourse.

swap out *v.*[2] [SWAP-OUT *n.*] [1990s+] (*Aus. Und.*) to betray a fellow criminal in order to escape one's own prosecution for a crime.

swapper *n.*[1] (*also* **swopper**) [SWAP *v.* (1)] [late 17C–late 19C] one who effects swaps or exchanges.

swapper *n.*[2] (*also* **swopper**) [SE *swap/swop*, to hit] [early 18C–early 19C] something large of its type, e.g. a barefaced lie.

swapperchop *n.* [ety. unknown] [mid-19C] (*UK Und.*) a banker; thus *swapperchop-brammums*, a bank.

swapping *n.* (*also* **swopping**) [SWAP *v.* (1)] [late 17C+] exchanging one thing for another, bartering.

swapping *adj.* (*also* **swooping, swopping**) [SWAPPER *n.*[2]] [mid-15C–19C] very big, enormous, huge.

swarry *n.* (*also* **sworray**) [joc. mispron. of SE *soiree*] [mid-19C+] an evening party, gathering, or social meeting.

swartgat *n.* [Afk. 'black arse'] [1960s–70s] (*S.Afr.*) a term of abuse.

swart varkie *n.* [Afk. *swart*, black + *varkie*, a piglet; such bulk purchases were banned in July 1982] [1970s+] (*S.Afr.*) a 20-litre (35-pint) black plastic container, used for buying wine in bulk.

swartzer *n. see* SCHWARTZE *n.*

swash-bucket *n.* [SE *swash-bucket*, a receptacle for household rubbish; orig. dial.] [late 19C] a slatternly woman.

swassle-box *n. see* SWATCHEL-BOX *n.*

swat *n.*[1] [northern dial.; the term had faded in UK before re-appearing in the US, most noticeably in the nickname of the big-hitting 1920s baseball star 'Babe' Ruth (1895–1948), the 'Sultan of Swat'] [20C+] (*US*) a heavy blow; also in fig. use.

swat *n.*[2] *see* SWOT *n.*

swat *v.*[1] [SWAT *n.*[1]] [mid-19C+] to hit.

swat *v.*[2] *see* SWOT *v.*

swatched *adj.* [? Warwickshire dial. *swatched*, of a woman, untidily dressed] [1950s] tipsy.

swatchel-box *n.* (*also* **schwassle-box, swassle-box**) [showman's jargon *Swatchel*, Mr Punch; ult. *swatchel*, the distorting instrument a puppeteer holds in his mouth in order to produce Punch's characteristic squeaky tones or Ger. *schwätzeln*, usual form of *schwatzen*, to chatter, to tattle] [mid-19C] a Punch and Judy show, esp. the booth in which it is performed.

swatchel-cove *n.* [for ety. *see* SWATCHEL-BOX *n.* + COVE *n.* (1)] [mid–late 19C+] a Punch and Judy man.

swat flies *v.* [1920s+] (*US tramp*) to beg from a person who is standing on the curb or in front of a shop window.

swattled *adj.* [SE *swat*] [late 19C] drunk.

swatty-blouse *n.* [2000s] (*N.Z.*) a weakling, a 'wimp'.

swave *n. see* SUAVE *n.*

swave and blaze *adj.* [1960s+] deliberate mispron. of *suave* and *blasé*.

sway *n. see* SWY *n.*

sway away on all top ropes *v.* (*also* **carry on top-ropes**) [early 19C] to live in a hedonistic, self-indulgent manner.

swazzled *adj. see* SWIZZLED *adj.*

swear *n.* [SE *swear*] [mid-17C–late 19C] an oath.

swear *v.*

SE in slang uses

IN PHRASES

❑ **swear blind** *v.* [BLIND *adv.*[1]] [1930s+] to affirm emphatically and without qualification. ❑ **swear by** *v.* [mid-18C+] to accept as the truth, to have complete faith in. ❑ **swear off** *v.* [? one's oath of self-denial] [late 19C+] to give up, to abandon, to renounce. ❑ **swear on a stack of Bibles (a mile high)** *v.* (*also* **swear on a truckload of Bibles**) [mid-19C+] (*orig. US*) to make an elaborate or exaggerated oath, usu. in the face of another's disbelief. ❑ **swear to beef** [2000s] (*US black*) a general interrogatory phr.

swear and curse *n.* (*also* **swear and cuss**) [rhy. sl.] [20C+] a bus.

sweat *n.* **1** [late 18C] a form of amusement practised by such street gangs as the Mohocks, who surrounded a victim, pricking him with their swords and thus keeping him 'dancing' until through his exertions he had sweated sufficiently; thus *sweater*, one who practised this urban terrorism. **2** [late 18C+] a problem, a worry, a struggle, anything that works up real or fig. sweat. **3** [1960s–70s] an occupation, job. **4** *see* OLD SWEAT below.

SE in slang uses

IN COMPOUNDS

❑ **sweat back** *n.* [? he sweats during intercourse] [1940s] (*US Und.*) a womanizer; a dandy. ❑ **sweat board** *n.* (*also* **sweat cloth, sweat table**) [mid–late 19C] (*UK/US Und.*) the board or cloth upon which THREE-CARD MONTE *n.* is played. ❑ **sweat-box** *n. see* separate entry. ❑ **sweat cure** *n.* **1** [1940s] (*US Und.*) the THIRD DEGREE *n.* **2** [1940s–50s] (*US drugs*) withdrawal from narcotics by simple abstinence. ❑ **sweat drink** *n.* [one is still sweating from one's labours] [1960s+] (*Irish*) a trad. 'after-work' drink. ❑ **sweat hog** *n.* [1970s+] (*US campus*) **1** an exceptionally difficult student, singled out at school or college for special attention [SE *hog*]. **2** an exceptionally unattractive woman [HOG *n.* (5b)]. **3** a sexually promiscuous woman [HOG *n.* (5b)]. ❑ **sweat pads** *n.* [resemblance] [1930s–40s] (*Can./US*) pancakes. ❑ **sweat rag** *n.* [mid-19C+] (*US*) a rag used for wiping the sweat from one's eyes; thus, a handkerchief. ❑ **sweat-room** *n.* **1** [1940s–50s] (*US drugs*) a room (in jail or hospital) in which a narcotic addict is confined during withdrawal [SE *sweat* + *room*]. **2** [1960s+] (*US Und.*) a room in a police station where suspects are interrogated and/or beaten up [SWEAT *v.*[2] (2) + SE *room*]. ❑ **sweat table** *n. see* SWEAT BOARD above. ❑ **sweat thing** *n.* [1960s] a stressful situation.

IN PHRASES

❑ **bust a sweat** *v.* [BUST *v.*[1]] [1980s+] (*US black*) to be sexually excited. ❑ **neversweat** *n.* **1** [mid-19C+] a lazy person, an idler, one whose job requires little effort [20C+ use is US; note naut. jargon *do a never*, to shirk, to idle]. **2** [1970s] (*Aus.*) a council worker. ❑ **no sweat off one's balls** (*also* **no sweat off one's arse**) [1930s+] (*orig. US*) no problem, no worries; of no importance. ❑ **old sweat** *n.* (*also* **sweat**) [? the *sweat* of battle and thus of one's labours. The British philologist Ernest Weekley has suggested, in *Xenophobia* (1932), that it may have originated during the Thirty Years' War as the German *alter Schweele*, old Swede, but its first appearance c.1919 militates against the theory] **1** [1910s+] (*orig. milit.*) any veteran. **2** [1990s+] (*Irish*) an old friend.

sweat *v.*[1] [fig. uses of SE] **1** [late 16C] to spend money. **2** [late 18C–late 1900s] (*UK Und.*) to lighten gold coins by immersing them in acid; thus *sweater*, one who practises such deception. **3** [early 19C] to pawn. **4** [early 19C] to remove some of the contents of. **5** [early 19C–1930s] to deprive someone of something. **6** [mid-19C] (*UK Und.*) of pickpockets etc, to subject a person or place to criminal activities. **7** [mid–late 19C] to extract money, usu. through menaces or violence. **8** [mid–late 19C] to squander money, whether one's own or someone else's. **9** [late 19C] (*UK Und.*) to melt down the solder that holds together an otherwise impenetrable strong-box. **10** [1950s] (*US Und.*) to break up stolen high denomination notes into smaller, legal bills. **11** [1950s] (*Aus.*) to borrow (usu. a horse) without its owner's permission.

IN PHRASES

❑ **sweat a cheque** *v.* [late 19C] (*Aus./N.Z.*) to spend all one's pay on drink.

sweat *v.*[2] **1** [early 17C; mid-19C+] to suffer, esp. in the context of an interrogation. **2** [mid-18C+] to put someone, esp. a prisoner, under pressure. **3** [late 18C] (*Irish*) to deprive of. **4** [late 18C–early 19C] to intimidate. **5** [late 19C+] to work very hard. **6** [late 19C+] to make someone work hard. **7** [1910s] to travel with difficulty. **8** [1920s+] (*also* **sweat it**) (*orig. US*) to worry about, to take trouble over. **9** [1920s] to wait for. **10** [1960s] to need, to be deprived of. **11** [1970s+] (*US black*) to proposition. **12** [1990s+] (*US black*) to get involved in someone's business. **13** [1990s+] (*US black*) to be obsessed with someone to the extent of sweating in their presence; to like something very much. **14** [1990s+] (*US prison*) to cause trouble for, to annoy. **15** [1990s+] to enthuse over (to an excessive extent), to flirt eagerly.

SE in slang uses

(IN PHRASES)

❑ **don't sweat it** [1950s+] (*orig. US black*) don't worry. ❑ **let it sweat** *v.* [1920s+] to stop worrying or interfering, to just let things turn out as they will. ❑ **no sweat** [i.e. there is no need to make an effort that might produce sweat] [1950s+] (*orig. US*) no problem; don't worry; it's all right. ❑ **sweat bird turds** *v.* [1960s] (*US*) to work hard. ❑ **sweat bricks** *v.* **1** [1990s+] to work very hard. **2** *see* SHIT A BRICK *V.* ❑ **sweat bullets** *v.* [1950s+] (*US*) **1** to worry excessively; to be terrified. **2** to work very hard. ❑ **sweat cobs** *v.* (*also* **sweat neaters**) [SE *cob*, a rounded lump, but note *HAVE A COB ON under* COB *n.*[5]] [1950s+] to perspire very heavily. ❑ **sweat duds** *v. see under* DUDS *n.*[1]. ❑ **sweat it** *v. see* sense 8 above. ❑ **sweat (it) out** *v.* **1** [1920s+] (*orig. US*) to endure hardships and difficulties in the hope of achieving solutions or successes in the end. **2** [1940s–50s] (*US drugs*) to withdraw from narcotic addiction. **3** [1940s+] to worry. **4** [1950s] to work out, to elucidate. ❑ **sweat like a nigger (at election)** *v.* [NIGGER *n.*[1] (1)] [1900s–50s] (*US*) **1** to sweat profusely. **2** to work very hard. ❑ **sweat (on)** *v.* **1** [1910s+] (*US*) to be near to attaining, to wait for. **2** [1990s+] (*US campus*) to focus on, to stare at. ❑ **sweat one's arse off** *v.* (*also* **sweat one's balls (off), ...bollocks off, ...butt off, ...can off**) [ARSE *n.* (1)/BALLS *n.* (1)/BOLLOCK *n.*/BUTT *n.*[1] (1a)/CAN *n.*[1] (1b)] [1920s+] to work extremely hard. ❑ **sweat one's guts out** *v. see under* GUT *n.* ❑ **sweat one's tail off** *v. see WORK ONE'S TAIL OFF under* WORK *V.* ❑ **sweat on the top line** *v.* [the 'lines' that must be filled in the game of lotto or bingo] [1910s+] (*Aus.*) to be within a touch of obtaining what one desires. ❑ **sweat out of** *v.* [late 19C+] (*US*) to extract information from someone, usu. by intimidation. ❑ **sweat someone's style** *v.* [1980s] (*US black*) to harass, to bother another person. ❑ **sweat the fence** *v.* [1990s+] (*US prison*) to fantasize about escape. ❑ **sweat up** *v.* [1910s] to learn, to commit to memory.

sweat-box *n.* [note 'The original "sweat box" used during the period following the (US) Civil War [...] was a cell in close proximity to a stove, in which a scorching fire was built and fed with old bones, pieces of rubber shoes etc, all to make great heat and offensive smells, until the sickened and perspiring inmate of the cell confessed in order to get released' (deposition to the Rep. Nat. Comm. Law Observance & Enforcement, 1931)] **1** [mid-19C–1950s] any small, hot room, or place. **2** [mid-19C+] (*orig. US*) an oppressively small cell; a punishment cell. **3** [late 19C] (*US*) the upper gallery of a theatre. **4** [late 19C+] a cell for prisoners waiting to appear in a magistrate's court. **5** [20C+] a room, usu. in a police station, in which prisoners undergo interrogation. **6** [1950s] (*US*) one who is sweating heavily. **7** [1970s] (*US black*) a crowded party. **8** [1970s+] a prison van, used to transport prisoners from court to prison etc.

sweater *n.*[1] [SWEAT *v.*[2]] **1** [mid-19C] a hard, demanding job. **2** [mid-19C–1900s] a harsh, demanding employer. **3** [1960s] (*US campus*) a worrier.

sweater *n.*[2] [SE *sweater*] **1** [1940s] (*US Und.*) a strait jacket. **2** [1990s+] a condom.

sweating *n.* [SWEAT *v.*[2] (2)] [early 19C+] (*US*) an interrogation.

sweats *n.* [1930s+] (*drugs*) **1** the sweating that is one of a heroin addict's withdrawal symptoms; thus *sweat cure*, the sudden and unsupported withdrawal from drugs. **2** sweating that accompanies excessive use of cocaine.

sweaty *adj.* **1** [1910s+] of a task, harsh, demanding; also in fig. use. **2** [1990s+] (*UK juv.*) of a person, very unpleasant or unattractive.

sweaty sock *n.* [rhy. sl. = JOCK *n.* (2)] [20C+] a Scot.

sweave *v.* [1980s+] (*US campus*) to *swerve* and *weave* when drunk or drugged.

Swede *n.* [the stereotype of Swedish immigrants as strong but stupid] [20C+] (*US*) a blunderer.

swede *n.* [SE *swede* (US rutabaga). The urban conception of the country's main product, foodstuff etc; thus *Swedey*, Metropolitan Police nickname (punning on SWEENEY (TODD), THE *n.*) for Operation Countryman, an investigation into corruption carried out by officers of rural and provincial forces] **1** [1910s+] the head; thus *crash/crash down the swede, set the swede down*, to go to sleep. **2** [1940s+] an ignorant country person, thus *swedeland*, the countryside; *swede language/talk*, rural talk; also adj. *swede-eating/gnawing*. **3** [1990s+] a haircut.

swede *adj.* [SWEDE *n.* (2)] [1950s+] rural, unsophisticated.

swede-basher *n.* [ext. of SWEDE *n.* (2)] [1930s+] a country bumpkin, an unsophisticated peasant.

swede-bashing *adj.* [SWEDE-BASHER *n.*] [1930s+] unsophisticated, rustic and peasantlike.

swedge *n.* [? SE *swedge*, a type of chisel with a bevelled edge, orig. used for making a groove around a horseshoe and latterly for various jobs requiring the bending of cold metal] [20C+] (*Scot.*) a fight.

swedge *v.* [SWEDGE *n.*] [20C+] (*Scot.*) to fight.

Swedish *n.* [the companionship and the sweating one experiences in a Swedish sauna bath] [1960s+] **1** masturbation or mutual masturbation. **2** the use of rubber garments in sex.

Swedish *adj.* [? misreading of the sex-change operations carried out in Denmark] [1990s+] (*US*) homosexual.

SE in slang uses

(IN COMPOUNDS)

❑ **Swedish culture** *n.* [1960s+] the use of rubber, PVC etc in sex. ❑ **Swedish fiddle** *n.* [its popularity among Swedish immigrants] [late 19C+] (*US*) an accordion. ❑ **Swedish headache** *n.* [? a problem of Swedish immigrants] [1930s+] (*US*) intense sexual frustration.

sweedle *v.* [SE *swindle* + *wheedle*] [1910s–30s] to trick with flattery, to 'sweet-talk'.

sweeney *n.* [the fictional *Sweeney Todd*, the 'demon barber' of Fleet Street, who sold 'golopshious' pies made from the flesh of those he had murdered] [1920s+] a barber.

(IN PHRASES)

❑ **that'll do for Sweeney** [var. on *TELL IT TO SWEENEY!* below] [1910s] (*US*) a phr. used in response to a piece of information that is considered unreliable, nonsensical.

(IN EXCLAMATIONS)

❑ **tell it to Sweeney!** (*also* **save it for Sweeney!**) [? anecdotal or *Sweeney* as generic] [20C+] (*US*) a dismissive excl. of disbelief in a previous far-fetched statement.

Sweeney (Todd), the *n.* [rhy. sl.; ult. *Sweeney Todd*, the musical] [1930s+] the Flying Squad; thus *sweenies*, members of the Flying Squad.

(IN PHRASES)

❑ **on one's sweeney** [backform f. *ON ONE'S TOD (SLOAN) under* TOD (SLOAN) *adj.*] [1990s+] (*Irish*) alone.

sweenies *n.* [TV police series *The Sweeney*, in which such sideboards were displayed by stars John Thaw and Dennis Waterman] [1980s+] (*UK juv.*) large sideboards (US sideburns).

sweep *n.* [SE *chimney sweep* whose job, if not person, is regarded as unpleasant] [mid-19C–1960s] an unpleasant person.

SE in slang uses

(IN COMPOUNDS)

❑ **sweep's frill** *n.* [such facial hair was typical of a sweep] [late 19C] a beard and whiskers that run round the line of the chin, leaving the rest of the face clean-shaven. ❑ **sweep's trot** *n.* [mid-19C] a high-stepping form of amble, the best way to carry the sweep's load of brushes etc.

(IN PHRASES)

❑ **take a sweep (with both barrels)** *v.* [1930s–50s] (*US drugs*) to inhale cocaine (through both nostrils).

sweep *v.* [play on BROOM *v.*] [1930s] (*US prison*) to disappear quickly.

sweet *n.* **1** [mid-19C–1940s] (*also* **confectionery**) a pretty young girl [SE *sweet*]. **2** [1920s] (*US black*) money [play on SUGAR *n.*[1] (1)]. **3** [1960s–80s] (*US black*) (*also* **sweet boy**) a male homosexual [SE *sweet*]. **4** [1980s] (*US black*) an attractive heterosexual male [SE *sweet*]. **5** [1990s+] (*US drugs*) a cigar hollowed out and filled with marijuana [abbr. *swisher sweet*].

(DERIVATIVES)

❑ **sweeted** *adj.* [1990s+] intoxicated by marijuana.

(IN PHRASES)

❑ **get some sweet** *v.* [1980s] (*US black*) of a woman, to have sexual intercourse.

sweet *adj.*[1] **1** [early 17C+] (*orig. Aus.*) excellent, perfect, simple, correct, in order; also used negatively, e.g. a *sweet mess*. **2** of human characteristics. (**a**) [late 17C–early 19C] gullible. (**b**) [early 18C+] dextrous, expert. (**c**) [mid-19C+] amenable; usu. in phr. *keep/have someone sweet*, to keep someone well-disposed towards oneself, esp. by complaisance or bribery. (**d**) [1930s+] (*Aus.*) affectionate, amorous towards. (**e**) [1950s–70s] effeminate. (**f**) [2000s] intimate with (in a non-sexual context). **3** [19C+] a general term of approval, applicable to people, objects, actions and events. **4** [late 19C] (*UK Und.*) not suspicious. **5** [1910s–50s] substantial. **6** [1940s+] (*Aus.*) ready, prepared. **7** [1940s+] safe, devoid of problems. **8** [1980s+] (*US campus*) easy.

(IN COMPOUNDS)

❑ **sweet-arse** *adj.* [1990s+] excellent, wonderful. ❑ **sweet cop** *n.* [COP *n.*[2] (2)] [20C+] **1** (*Aus.*) a pleasant, enviable situation. **2** (*Aus. Und.*) a successful scheme or criminal enterprise. ❑ **sweet go** *n. see under* GO *n.*[1]. ❑ **sweet kid** *n.* (*also* **sweet girl, sweetmeat**) [KID *n.*[1] (10)/MEAT *n.* (1)] [1960s+] (*Can./US prison*) a younger prisoner who joins up with an older man. ❑ **sweet lady** *n.* [1950s] (*US gay*) a woman who runs a string of homosexual male prostitutes.

(IN PHRASES)

❑ **she's sweet** (*also* **she'll be sweet**) [1940s+] (*Aus.*) everything is satisfactory. ❑ **sweet as (a) nut** *adj.* (*also* **sweet as a button, ...clock, ...lolly**) [mid-17C+] (*orig. UK Und.*) easy, simple, no problems, delightful, esp. of a robbery or other 'job'. ❑ **sweet on** *adj.* **1** [late 17C+] (*also* **sweet upon**) in love with, infatuated by; very fond of, in non-amatory sense. **2** [mid-19C+] in a non-sexual context, satisfied with, happy about.

SE in slang uses

(IN COMPOUNDS)

drug uses

❑ **sweet air** *n.* [1980s+] nitrous oxide. ❑ **sweet dreams** *n.* [the comatose state it induces] [1980s+] (*drugs*) heroin. ❑ **sweet Lucy** *n.* **1** [1950s+] hashish dissolved into wine. **2** [1960s] marijuana. **3** [1960s] barbiturates dissolved into muscatel wine. **4** [1960s+] a variety of cheap, sweet wine. ❑ **sweet Morpheus** *n.* [*Morpheus*, the Greek god of dreams; the root of *morphine*] [1970s+] (*drugs*) morphine. ❑ **sweet stuff** *n.* [1930s–50s] (*drugs*) **1** heroin or morphine. **2** cocaine. ❑ **sweet tooth** *n.* [1960s] (*US drugs*) a craving for, or addiction to, narcotics.

general uses

❑ **sweet b.a.** *n.* [abbr. *sweet bugger all*] [1940s+] nothing at all. ❑ **sweetback** *n. see* separate entry. ❑ **sweetback (man)** *n. see* separate entry. ❑ **sweet boy** *n. see* SWEET *n.* (3). ❑ **sweetbread** *n. see* separate entry. ❑ **sweet briar** *n.* [17C] the female pubic hair. ❑ **sweet bugger all** *n. see* BUGGER ALL *n.* ❑ **sweet but-all** *n. see* SWEET FUCK ALL below. ❑ **sweetcakes** *n.* **1** [1960s+] (*also* **sweet chips**) a term of affection. **2** [1980s+] (*US gay*) the buttocks. ❑ **sweetcheeks** *n.* [1980s+] (*US gay*) the buttocks. ❑ **sweet con** *n. see under* CON *n.*[1]. ❑ **sweet daddy** *n. see under* DADDY *n.* ❑ **sweet damn-all** *n.* [1920s+] nothing whatsoever. ❑ **sweet-eye** *n.* [20C+] (*W.I.*) a lustful glance or wink; thus *make sweet-eye*, to glance in this way; *get sweet-eye*, of a woman, to receive such a glance. ❑ **sweet Fanny Adams** *n. see* separate entry. ❑ **sweet fuck all** *n.* (*also* **sweet but-all, sweet eff-ay**) [1910s+] absolutely nothing. ❑ **sweetheart** *see* separate entries. ❑ **sweet jesus** *n.* [the addict's 'saviour'] [1960s+] (*drugs*) morphine; heroin. ❑ **sweet-lick** *v. see under* LICK *v.*[1]. ❑ **sweet-lips** *n.* [late 19C–1900s] a glutton. ❑ **sweet mack** *n. see under* MACK *n.*[2]. ❑ **sweet mama** *n.* **1** [1920s] an excl. of praise. **2** [1920s+] (*US black*) (*also* **sweet momma**) a black man's female lover. ❑ **sweetman** *n. see* separate entry. ❑ **sweetmeat** *n. see* separate entry. ❑ **sweet Miss Adams** *n. see* SWEET FANNY ADAMS *n.* ❑ **sweetmouth** *see* separate entries. ❑ **sweetmouth man** *n. see* SWEETMOUTH *n.* (1). ❑ **sweet papa** *n.* (*also* **sweet poppa**) [1920s+] (*US black*) a man who provides for the material wants of his lover. ❑ **sweet patootie** *n. see under* PATOOTIE *n.* ❑ **sweet pea** *n. see* separate entries. ❑ **sweet-pie** *n. see* SWEETIE-PIE *under* SWEETIE *n.* ❑ **sweet pimp** *n. see* SUGAR PIMP *n.* ❑ **sweet potato pie** *n.* [the common equation of sex and food] **1** [1920s+] (*US black*) an attractive young man or woman. **2** [1920s+] (*also* **sweet potato**) male or female genitals. **3** [1980s] sexual intercourse. **4** [1980s] a general term of endearment. ❑ **sweet sugar** *n. see* SUGAR PIMP *n.* ❑ **sweet talk** *see* separate entries. ❑ **Sweet Willie** *n.* [1970s] (*US black*) a kindly, attentive man; esp. as a pose practised by a pimp when 'catching' a new whore.

(IN EXCLAMATIONS)

❑ **sweet bleeding Jesus!** (*also* **sweet jeez!**) [20C+] a general excl. ❑ **sweet fucking Jesus!** [20C+] (*US*) an expletive with no particular meaning, conveying annoyance and surprise. ❑ **sweet Jesus!** (*also* **sweet Christ!**) [late 18C+] a mild, if blasphemous, oath. ❑ **sweet papa!** [1920s] (*US*) a general excl. ❑ **sweet patootie!** *see* separate entry.

sweet *adj.*[2] (*W.I.*) **1** [1940s] tipsy, slightly drunk. **2** [1950s] of a man, fashionably dressed, smart.

sweet *v.* **1** [late 18C+] (*W.I.*) to please. **2** [late 19C] (*US Und.*) to lose.

sweet *adv.*[1] [mid-19C] amorously.

sweet *adv.*[2] **1** [mid-19C+] without any problems, easily. **2** [1920s] of a man, living off the wages of a woman, for example, as a pimp.

sweet! *excl.* [1920s+] excellent! wonderful!

sweetback *n.* [1930s] **1** (*US tramp*) a 'part-time' tramp, who can and will opt out of the lifestyle when he wishes. **2** in fig. use, someone who poses as having 'dropped out' of conventional society or as being unsuccessful.

sweetback (man) *n.* [his physique, which women like to touch] **1** [1920s–40s] (*US Und.*) a pimp. **2** [1920s+] (*US black*) (*also* **pie-back, sugar-man**) a womanizer, a ladies' man.

sweetbread *n.* [SE *sweetbread*, the pancreas, or thymus gland, of an animal, a delicacy] [mid–late 17C] a bribe.

sweetcorn shiner *n.* [coarse ref. to sodomy] [1990s+] a male homosexual.

sweeten *v.* **1** [late 17C+] (*UK Und.*) to lure, to decoy, to swindle, to flatter. **2** [early 19C+] to bribe; to corrupt. **3** [mid-19C–1930s] to calm down, to assuage someone's worries; in criminal contexts, to calm a suspicious victim. **4** [1930s] to add alcohol to a non-alcoholic drink.

(IN PHRASES)

❑ **sweeten a grawler** *v.* [early 19C] (*UK Und.*) to give money to a beggar. ❑ **sweeten (the pot)** *v.* [poker jargon: to add money to a pot, to raise the betting] [1920s+] to make a proposition more alluring, to improve a situation.

sweetener *n.*[1] (*also* **sweetner**) (*UK Und.*) **1** [late 17C–mid-19C] a rogue who specializes in dropping something supposedly valuable where it will be found by a potential victim, who is either lured into a game or persuaded to buy the 'valuable', while the con-man claims that although they should, by rights, share the profits, he will sell his share and let the victim have the whole benefit. **2** [late 19C] one who poses as an innocent player in order to ensnare a genuine innocent into playing a game in which he will invariably find himself the defrauded loser.

sweetener *n.*[2] **1** [early 19C+] something pleasant; something encouraging; a bribe. **2** [mid-19C] (*US*) a drink. **3** [mid-19C] a hard blow. **4** [late 19C] (*UK Und.*) in pl., the lips. **5** [1900s] the penis.

sweetening *n.* (*also* **sweetening lay**) [ext. of SWEETENER *n.*[1] (1) + LAY *n.*[3] (1)] [late 17C–mid-18C] a confidence trick based on deliberately dropping a guinea and swindling the dupe who picks it up.

sweet Fanny Adams *n.* (*also* **Miss Adams, S.F.A., sweet F.A., sweet Fatty Arbuckle, sweet Miss Adams**) [euph. for *SWEET FUCK ALL under* SWEET *adj.*[1]; the identity of Fanny Adams remains a mystery and is presumably based only on the initial letters] [1910s+] **1** absolutely nothing at all. **2** as excl.: rubbish! piffle!

sweetheart *n.* [ext. of SE, often ironic] **1** [20C+] as a term of address; no affection is implied. **2** [1920s+] a person, usu. used in a derog. sense. **3** [1930s–40s] anything considered good. **4** [1940s] (*US Und.*) a stolen automobile in good condition.

IN COMPOUNDS

❑ **sweetheart life** *n.* [1950s] (*W.I.*) the state of living together but not being married.

sweetheart *adj.* [1970s] (*US*) easy, simple.

IN COMPOUNDS

❑ **sweetheart contract** *n.* (*also* **sweetheart deal**) [1950s+] (*orig. US*) a union-employer contract that favours the company over its employees; a union-employer contract that favours all those negotiating, but not the workers the union supposedly represents.

sweetheart *v.* **1** [mid–late 19C] to make advances to, to 'chat up.'. **2** [1960s] (*US black*) to have a (sexual) relationship with.

sweetie *n.* (*also* **sweety**) **1** [late 19C+] an attractive young woman. **2** [20C+] a beloved child. **3** [1910s+] (*orig. US*) (*also* **sweetie-man**) a boy- or girlfriend. **4** [1920s+] a term of address, not necessarily implying intimacy. **5** [1920s+] used ironically to mean an unpleasant person, e.g. *He's a real sweetie*. **6** [1930s+] a pleasant person. **7** [1960s–70s] an effeminate homosexual.

IN COMPOUNDS

❑ **sweetie-pie** *n.* (*also* **sweetie-pops, sweet-pie, sweety pie, twinklepie**) [praising the beloved as 'good enough to eat'] [1920s+] a general term of affection; a girlfriend.

sweeties *n. see* SWEETS *n.*[2].

sweetman *n.* **1** [1920s–60s] (*US black*) (*also* **sweetie-man**) a male lover. **2** [1920s+] (*UK Und.*) a pimp who runs only one prostitute and lives off her earnings alone. **3** [1970s+] (*W.I.*) a (married) woman's lover, to whom she gives money and presents.

sweetmeat *n.* [SE *sweet* + MEAT *n.* (1)/SE *sweetmeat*, which is 'good enough to eat'] **1** [mid–late 19C] an underage or child prostitute. **2** [mid–late 19C] a mistress. **3** [late 19C; 1970s+] the penis [SE *sweet* + MEAT *n.* (2) + pun; 1970s+ use is US gay]. **4** [1940s+] (*US Und.*) a young woman. **5** [1960s+] a general term of affectionate address. **6** *see SWEET KID under* SWEET *adj.*[1].

sweetmouth *n.* [mid-19C+] (*W.I.*) **1** (*also* **sweet-mouth man**) a flatterer, a persuasive person. **2** flattery, persuasiveness.

sweetmouth *adj.* [SWEETMOUTH *n.*] (*W.I.*) **1** [1920s] flattering. **2** [1950s] greedy, gluttonous.

sweetmouth *v.* [SWEETMOUTH *n.*] [1940s+] (*orig. US black*) to flatter.

sweetner *n. see* SWEETENER *n.*[1].

sweetness and light *n.* [1950s] (*Aus.*) whisky.

sweet pea *n.*[1] [rhy. sl.] **1** [early 19C] whisky [PEE *n.*[1] (1); note Partridge suggests 'the colour of the resulting urine']. **2** [late 19C] urine [PEE *n.*[1] (1)]. **3** [1960s+] tea. **4** [1970s] LSD.

sweet pea *n.*[2] [1930s–40s] (*US Und.*) **1** anything easy. **2** a gullible, vulnerable individual.

sweet pea *n.*[3] [1930s+] **1** a girl- or boyfriend. **2** a term of affection; also in ironic use.

sweets *n.*[1] [1920s+] (*US/W.I.*) a general term of address, both friendly and otherwise.

sweets *n.*[2] (*also* **sweeties**) [resemblance] [1960s+] (*drugs*) amphetamines.

sweet talk *n.* (*also* **sweet talking**) [late 19C+] persuasive, seductive talk.

sweet talk *v.* [1930s+] (*orig. US black*) **1** to persuade, to charm, to lull into false confidence. **2** spec. to seduce.

sweety *n. see* SWEETIE *n.*

IN PHRASES

❑ **sweety pie** *n. see SWEETIE-PIE under* SWEETIE *n.*

swell *n.*[1] [for the connoisseur of such gradations, the *swell* differed from the older aristocracy in the need and capacity for display; the aristocracy had position but no fashion, the swell had fashion and used it to win position, but his social position might be fractionally less grand. In time he, or at least his children, might attain the absolute social peaks] **1** [late 18C+] an aristocrat, a sophisticated, stylish, rich person; fem. *swelless*; thus *swellism*, the world of a 'swell'; *swellness*, being a 'swell'. **2** [early 19C] a good time, a spree. **3** [early 19C–1910s] the outstanding member of any profession or occupation. **4** [mid-19C–1900s] used ironically as one who unsuccessfully emulates the style and manners of sense 1. **5** [1920s] (*US*) a good-looking young woman.

DERIVATIVES

❑ **swellish** *adj.* **1** [mid-19C] gentlemanly. **2** [mid-19C–1910s] fashionably dressed.

IN COMPOUNDS

❑ **swell's lush** *n.* [LUSH *n.*[1] (1)] [mid–late 19C] (*Aus.*) champagne. ❑ **Swell Street** *n. see* separate entry.

IN PHRASES

❑ **chuck a swell** *v.* [1930s] to spend extravagantly. ❑ **cut a swell** *v.* (*also* **do the swell**) [19C] to swagger. ❑ **swell hung in chains** *n.* [mid-19C] a rich or ostentatious man given to wearing quantities of jewellery. ❑ **swell it** *v.* [late 19C] to behave or pose as an aristocrat or a rich man.

swell *n.*[2] [abbr.] [2000s] (*N.Z.*) a female yuppie, i.e. single woman earning lots of lolly.

swell *adj.* (*also* **swellified**) [SWELL *n.*[1]; 20C+ use mainly US] [early 19C+] (*orig. US Und.*) **1** excellent, wonderful, delightful; thus *swell article*, anything of high quality; *swell crib*, a genteel house; also ironic use. **2** pertaining to the upper classes. **3** showy, ostentatious, fashionable, usu. as regards dress; thus *swell mollisher*, a very well-dressed woman etc.

IN COMPOUNDS

❑ **swell cove** *n.* (*also* **swell kidder**) [COVE *n.* (1)] a gentleman, a dandy. ❑ **swell dona** *n.* [DONA *n.* (1)] [late 19C] a lower-class woman affecting airs of grandeur. ❑ **swell fencer** *n.* [-FENCER *sfx*; needles are required for the tailoring that garbs a swell] [mid-19C] a street-seller of needles. ❑ **swell mob** *n. see* separate entry. ❑ **swell woman** *n.* [late 19C] an élite prostitute; a woman kept by a rich lover.

swell *v.* [SWELL *n.*[1] (1)] **1** [early 19C–1920s] to act in an aristocratic, ostentatious manner. **2** [late 19C] to exaggerate.

SE in slang uses

IN COMPOUNDS

❑ **swellhead** *n. see* separate entries. ❑ **swell-headed** *adj. see* separate entry. ❑ **swell-nose** *n.* [its effects] [early 16C–18C] strong beer. ❑ **swell-skull** *n. see BUSTSKULL under* BUST *v.*[1].

swell *adv.* [mid-19C+] (*US*) very well, excellently, kindly.

swell! *excl.* [1930s+] (*US*) excellent! wonderful!

swelled *adj.* (*also* **swelled up**) [SWELL *n.*[1] (1)] [mid-19C–1920s] (*US*) snobbish, pleased with oneself.

swelled-headed *adj. see* SWELL-HEADED *adj.*

sweller *n.* [1900s] (*US*) a braggart, one who 'swells' the truth.

swellhead *n.*[1] [SE *swell* + *head*] **1** [mid-19C] a drunkard. **2** [1960s+] (*US black*) one who has passed out through drug use. **3** *see BUSTSKULL under* BUST *v.*[1].

IN PHRASES

❑ **have a swelled head** *v.* [late 19C] to feel tipsy, drunk.

swellhead *n.*[2] [backform. f. SWELL-HEADED *adj.*] [mid-19C+] **1** (*also* **swelled-head, swelled nut**) a braggart, a boaster, a show-off. **2** (*also* **swelled bean**) conceit, arrogance; also as phr. *have the swell-head*.

IN PHRASES

❑ **have a swelled head** *v.* (*also* **get one's skull swelled**) [late 19C–1950s] to be arrogant, conceited.

swell-headed *adj.* (*also* **swell-head, swelled-headed**) [SE *swell + head*] [early 19C+] arrogant, conceited.

swelling *n.* [1900s] an erection.

swellish *adj. see* SWELL *n.*[1] (1).

swell mob *n.* [SWELL *adj.* (1) + MOB *n.*[2] (3)] (*UK Und.*) **1** [mid-19C–1920s] leading pickpockets whose dress reflects their success (as well as facilitating their entry into the wealthy world on which they prey). **2** [mid-19C–1940s; 2000s] a major criminal gang, irrespective of their specialities; also attrib.

IN COMPOUNDS

❑ **swell mobsman** *n.* [mid-19C–1920s] a leading pickpocket.

Swell Street *n.* [SWELL *n.*[1] (1) + SE *street*] [19C] the West End of London.

IN PHRASES

❑ **in swell street** [early 19C] well-off. ❑ **live in swell street** *v.* [early 19C] (*UK Und.*) to live a prosperous, respectable, secure life.

swelp me davy! *excl. see* S'ELP ME BOB! *excl.*

swelp me lucky! *excl. see* SWOP ME BOB! *excl.*

swelp me taters! *excl. see* S'ELP MY TATER! *excl.*

swelp me ten men! *excl. see* S'ELP ME BOB! *excl.*

swelter *n.* [late 19C] hot, hard work.

swep' *adj.* (*also* **swept**) [abbr. SE phr. *swept off one's feet*] [1980s+] (*US black/campus*) sexually or emotionally obsessed with, or overwhelmed by.

swept *adj.* [it has been *swept away*] [1910s+] (*N.Z.*) totally without money.

swept up *adj.* [1980s] (*N.Z.*) smart, wealthy.

swerve *n.* [SWERVE *v.* (2)] [1980s+] (*N.Z.*) an act of avoidance.

SE in slang uses

IN PHRASES

❑ **get one's swerve on** *v.* [1990s+] **1** (*US black*) to dance. **2** (*US black*) to have sexual intercourse. **3** to do something well, to be in the swing of things. **4** (*US black*) to send a prostitute out to work. **5** (*US teen*) to drink. ❑ **get the swerve** *v.* [baseball imagery] [1970s] (*US*) to be deceived, to be let down. ❑ **put the swerve on** *v.* [1930s] (*US Und.*) to deceive (with a confidence trick).

swerve *v.* **1** [1950s+] (*Aus.*) to practise coitus interruptus [motoring imagery: one 'avoids a child']. **2** [1980s+] (*N.Z./US*) to avoid.

swi *n. see* SWY *n.*

swift *n.* [1920s] (*US Und./Aus.*) a fast horse, used for getaways in the pre-motorcar era; or in horseracing.

SE in slang uses

IN PHRASES

❑ **dull swift** *n.* [lit. a stupid messenger] [late 18C–early 19C] a stupid, sluggish person.

swift *adj.* **1** [late 19C–1900s] exciting. **2** [late 19C+] sexually forward. **3** [1ate 19C+] smart, clever, cunning. **4** [1960s–70s] (*US campus*) dull, stupid, ignorant. **5** [1970s+] of a police officer, carrying out any illegal activities, esp. during an arrest. **6** [1980s] (*US campus*) good, excellent. **7** [1990s+] healthy.

IN COMPOUNDS

❑ **swift 'un** *n.* [1970s+] (*UK Und.*) corrupt police procedure when arresting a suspect.

IN PHRASES

❑ **a bit swift** [1970s+] (*UK police/Und.*) describing the taking of unfair advantage, usu. the complaint is made by the villain against the arresting officer.

SE in slang uses

IN COMPOUNDS

❑ **swift one** *n.* (*also* **swifter**) [mid-19C+] a quick drink.

swiftie *n.*[1] (*also* **swifty**) [1940s+] (*Aus./N.Z.*) a hoax, a fraud, a deception; esp. in phr. *pull/work a swiftie*, to deceive.

swiftie *n.*[2] (*also* **swifty**) **1** [1940s+] (*US*) one who moves fast, either physically or mentally; also in ironic use. **2** [1970s] a quick blow.

swiftly flow *v.* [rhy. sl.] [late 19C–1900s] (*Aus.*) to go.

swigman *n.* [? unrecorded early use of SWAG *n.*[1] (2)] [mid-16C–mid-19C] (*UK Und.*) a criminal beggar, posing as a legitimate pedlar.

swill *n.* [? SE *swill*, kitchen refuse] **1** [mid-19C+] unpleasant food or drink. **2** [late 19C–1950s] alcohol. **3** [1930s+] in fig. use, anything disgusting, second-rate, distasteful. **4** [1940s–60s] a cup of tea.

IN COMPOUNDS

❑ **swill-tub** *n.* (*also* **swill-belly, swill bowl, swill pail**) [SE *swill tub*, a refuse container] [mid-16C–early 19C; 1970s] a drunkard.

swill *v.* (*also* **swill one's guts**) [SE *swill*, to drink heavily; from 1916 to 1955 New South Wales pubs took 'last orders' at 6 p.m. and the resultant rush of the all-male drinkers was termed the *SIX O'CLOCK SWILL under* SIX *adj.*; other states maintained the law for longer] [mid-16C+] to drink heavily; thus as n., a drink.

swillery *n.* (*also* **swill pot**) [SWILL *v.*] [1940s+] (*Aus.*) a hotel with a bar, a pub.

swim *n.* [SE *swim*, a section of river well stocked with fish] [mid-19C–1900s] a scheme, a plan; thus *in a good swim*, having a spell of good luck.

swim *v.* [1980s] (*US prison*) to conform to prison society.

IN PHRASES

❑ **make someone swim for it** *v.* [mid-19C] (*UK Und.*) to cheat an accomplice out of his share of the proceeds. ❑ **swim in golden grease** *v.* (*also* **swim in golden lard, ...oil**) [17C] to be offered and to take an abundance of bribes.

swimmer *n.*[1] **1** [late 17C–18C] (*UK Und.*) a counterfeit coin [? the metal used was light enough to float]. **2** [early 19C] a tender or guard-ship. **3** [early 19C] a thief who escapes a prison sentence by enlisting in the Royal Navy. **4** [1980s] one who retrieves drug packages which have been purposely dropped into the sea during importation.

swimmer *n.*[2] (*also* **swimmers, swimmies**) [1920s+] a bathing costume.

swindging *adj. see* SWINGEING *under* SWINGE *v.*

swindle *n.* **1** [19C] tossing to decide who pays for the next round of drinks. **2** [mid-19C] (*US*) the cost, the bill; esp. in phr. *what's the swindle?* **3** [mid-19C–1910s] a disappointment, something that proves to be a fraud and not what it was advertised as being. **4** [late 19C] a lottery. **5** [2000s] (*UK Und.*) any form of criminal activity, e.g. drug dealing; there is no necessary implication of confidence trickery.

IN COMPOUNDS

❑ **swindle sheet** *n.* [orig. boxing use, the accounts made up by a manager and shown to his fighter. Bitter fighters felt that these were rarely relevant to the actual money involved] [1910s+] (*orig. US*) an expense account; any form of charges.

swindle *v.* [1990s+] (*US prison*) to fight with one's fists.

swindlecat *n. see* SHINDYKIT *n.*

swindler *n.* [Yid. *schwindeln*, to be giddy, to act thoughtlessly or extravagantly, to swindle. Orig. Und. and supposedly imported to the UK by German Jewish immigrants c.1762, it entered SE during the 19C] [mid-18C–mid-19C] (*UK Und.*) a trickster, a fraud.

swindling gloak *n.* [mid-19C] (*UK Und.*) a confidence trickster.

swine *n.* **1** [late 19C+] anything considered as difficult or exhausting to achieve. **2** [1940s] (*UK prison*) prison guards. **3** [1970s+] (*US black*) constr. with *the*, the police [PIG *n.* (2a)]. **4** [1980s+] (*Aus. prison*) the police [var. on PIG *n.* (2a)]. **5** *see* SWINE-EATER below.

SE in slang uses

IN COMPOUNDS

❑ **swine-eater** *n.* (*also* **swine**) [the Muslim prohibition on pig products] [1980s+] (*US black Muslim*) **1** a white person. **2** a police officer [PIG *n.* (2a)]. ❑ **swine-up** *n.* [pigs are supposedly ill-tempered] [early 19C–1900s] (*orig. US*) an argument.

IN PHRASES

❑ **go the complete swine** *v.* (*also* **go the entire swine**) [var. on

GO THE WHOLE HOG *under* WHOLE HOG *n.*] [late 19C–1920s] to do thoroughly, to go all the way, to commit oneself unreservedly.

swing *n.*[1] [1910s+] (*US*) a rest period between two shifts.

swing *n.*[2] [1970s+] (*US black*) stimulation, excitement, something that makes things 'go with a swing'.

swing, the *n.* [SWING *v.* (1)] [late 18C–mid-19C] the gallows.

swing *v.* **1** [mid-16C+] to hang. **2** [early 18C+] to have someone hanged. **3** [mid-19C+] (*also* **swing it**) to arrange, to achieve. **4** [1900s] (*US Und.*) of a crime, to be remunerative. **5** [1920s+] to make a sneering remark. **6** [1930s+] (*US*) to act or live in a given manner. **7** [1930s+] to cope, to deal with a situation, to make sure that things work out as one desires, often through trickery/deception/manipulation. **8** in terms pertaining to sex. (**a**) [1930s+] to enjoy an active and varied sex life, to have sexual intercourse. (**b**) [1940s+] (*gay*) to fellate. (**c**) [1950s] (*US*) to work as a prostitute. (**d**) [1960s] to carry on an affair with someone. (**e**) [1960s] of a place, to be devoted to sex. **9** in terms describing a positive experience. (**a**) [1930s+] to enjoy oneself, to have a good time. (**b**) [1950s] (*US drugs*) to experience the effects of a drug. (**c**) [1950s+] (*orig. gay*) to achieve the supreme level of well-being and satisfaction. (**d**) [1960s] of anything, to work out well, as planned. (**e**) [1960s+] of a party, a club, a place of entertainment, to go well, to be enjoyable. (**f**) [1970s+] to arrange and participate in husband-and-wife swapping parties. **10** [1950s] (*US teen*) to leave, to go. **11** in terms pertaining to crime. (**a**) [1950s] (*US Und.*) of a pimp, to run a prostitute. (**b**) [1950s–60s] (*US drugs*) to cheat. (**c**) [1950s+] (*US*) to be a member of a teenage street gang; to fight as a member of a teenage street gang. (**d**) [1960s] to involve oneself in corruption or illegality. (**e**) [1960s–70s] (*US black*) to be dealing narcotics. **12** [2000s] (*US*) to give, to hand over, to pay. **13** *see* SWING BOTH WAYS below. **14** *see* SWING THE LEAD below.

pertaining to hanging

IN PHRASES

❑ **big swing** *n.* [1960s+] (*US*) the prison gallows. ❑ **swing for** *v.* [the implication is that the speaker is willing to commit murder to get what they want and thus face the gallows] [mid-19C+] a general threat. ❑ **swing in a halter** *v.* [mid–late 16C] to be hanged.

pertaining to deception

IN PHRASES

❑ **swing it on** *v.* (*also* **swing it across**) [20C+] (*mainly Aus./N.Z.*) to deceive, to impose on, to do a bad turn. ❑ **swing (with)** *v.* [1950s–70s] (*US*) to steal.

pertaining to sex

IN COMPOUNDS

❑ **swing daddy** *n. see under* DADDY *n.* ❑ **swing (party)** *n.* [1970s+] (*orig. US*) an orgy, esp. when the participants are husband-and-wife swapping couples.

IN PHRASES

❑ **swing both ways** *v.* (*also* **swing, swing either way, ...three-sixty**) [1960s+] to practise bisexuality. ❑ **swing low** *v.* [sense 8a above + SE *low*] [1990s+] (*US black teen*) to have oral sex. ❑ **swing to the left** *v.* [1970s] (*US*) to be a homosexual. ❑ **swing with** *v.* [sense 8 above] **1** [1950s+] to associate with [may be SE *swing*, i.e. on buses or other public transport]. **2** [1960s] to have a relationship with, to have sex with. **3** [1960s+] to ally oneself to a group, or individual, to agree with a concept. **4** [1960s+] to enjoy, to appreciate.

other senses

IN COMPOUNDS

❑ **swingdog** *n.* [sense 9a above + DOG *n.*[2] (2a)] [1990s+] (*US teen*) a fashionable dresser. ❑ **swing man** *n.* [? he makes things go *with a swing* or ? sense 9 above] [1950s–60s] a drug dealer.

SE in slang uses

IN COMPOUNDS

❑ **swing-out** *n. see* separate entry. ❑ **swing-tail** *n.* [late 18C–early 19C] a hog.

IN PHRASES

❑ **swing a bag** *v.* [the prostitute's inevitable handbag] [1940s+] (*Aus.*) to work as a street-walker. ❑ **swing by** *v.* (*also* **swing around**) [SE *swing*, a trip] [1980s+] (*orig. US*) to visit. ❑ **swinging on the meat** *adj.* [1940s] (*US*) overly anxious to please. ❑ **swinging the stick** *n.* [the physical action of the bludgeoner] [mid-19C] robbery with violence. ❑ **swing into** *v.* [1960s] (*US*) to arrive. ❑ **swing it** *v.* **1** *see* SWING *v.* (3). **2** *see* SWING THE LEAD below. ❑ **swing like sixty** *v. see under* LIKE SIXTY *adv.* ❑ **swing of the door** *n.* [1930s] the seventh drink of a session, supposedly the very last one has before leaving the pub. ❑ **swing on** *v.* **1** [1910s+] (*US*) to hit or punch. **2** [1960s] in fig. use, to talk forcefully. **3** [1960s] (*Aus.*) to keep, to take. ❑ **swing out** *v. see* separate entry. ❑ **swing the bag** *v. see under* BAG *n.*[1]. ❑ **swing the billy** *v. see* SLING THE BILLY *under* SLING *v.* ❑ **swing the cuff** *v. see under* CUFF *n.*[2]. ❑ **swing the dice** *v.* [1990s+] (*US black*) to accept that much of life is a matter of luck and to live it accordingly. ❑ **swing the gate** *v.* [sheep-shearing jargon, used of a fast and expert shearer] [1930s+] (*Aus.*) to work hard, to do well, to win in a contest. ❑ **swing the lead** *v.* (*also* **swing (it), swing the hammer**) [the image is of a leadsman, taking soundings from a ship, but that job is skilful rather than easy] [1910s+] (*orig. milit.*) **1** to malinger, to avoid one's duties. **2** to brag, to boast.

swinge *v.* [SE *swinge*, to beat, to castigate] **1** [16C–17C] to drink up, to drink off. **2** [17C] (*also* **switch, switchel**) to have sexual intercourse.

DERIVATIVES

❑ **swingeing** *adj.* (*also* **swindging**) [SE *swinge*, to beat; SE in 20C+, typically as *swingeing cuts* in the health budget] [late 17C+] a general intensifier, very large, very forceful, very powerful; 17C use often describing venereal disease.

IN PHRASES

❑ **swinged off** *adj.* [late 17C–early 18C] suffering from venereal disease. ❑ **swinge off** *v.* (*also* **swinge up**) **1** [early 16C–mid-17C] to toss down a drink. **2** [17C–18C] to infect with a bad case of venereal disease. ❑ **swinge someone's jacket** *v. see* TRIM SOMEONE'S JACKET *under* TRIM *v.*

swinger *n.*[1] **1** [late 16C–late 19C] anything notably large or forceful of its type. **2** [late 17C–early 18C] an outrageous lie. **3** [1920s+] (*Aus.*) an admirable person. **4** [1960s–70s] an exciting, lively place (usu. a club or bar).

swinger *n.*[2] **1** [17C; 1920s+] (*Aus.*) in pl., the female breasts, esp. when unsupported but still firm. **2** [19C+] in pl., the testicles. **3** [mid-19C] (*UK Und.*) a lame leg. **4** [2000s] (*UK prison*) a prisoner who has committed suicide by hanging.

swinger *n.*[3] [SWING *v.* (8)] **1** [mid–late 17C; 1960s+] one who leads an active and varied sex life (modern use orig. US). **2** [1950s+] one who leads an active and sophisticated social life. **3** [1960s+] one who participates in husband-and-wife swapping parties.

swinging *n.*[1] [SWING *v.* (1)] [mid-17C–late 19C] hanging; a hanging.

swinging *n.*[2] [SWING *v.* (9f)] [1960s+] indulging in husband-and-wife swapping parties; thus *closed swinging*, swapping parties in which only husband-and-wife partnerships take part, no singles are allowed to unbalance the situation; as opposed to *open swinging*, in which all-comers – married or single – are welcome and all end up in the same bed.

IN PHRASES

❑ **soft swinging** *n.* [1970s+] a partner-swapping party where the only intercourse is performed by couples who arrived together; non-penetrative sex, however, is enjoyed at random.

swinging *adj.*[1] [var. SWINGEING *under* SWINGE *v.*] [late 16C+] a general intensifier, e.g. *swinging fellow*, a very large man; *swinging lie*, an outrageous lie.

DERIVATIVES

❑ **swingingly** *adv.* [late 17C–late 18C] very much, extensively.

swinging *adj.*[2] [SE *swing* + SWING *v.* (8)] [1950s+] (*orig. US*) **1** uninhibited, lively, fashionable; esp. in phrs. *swinging London*, *swinging '60s*. **2** a general term of approval. **3** pertaining to drug use and culture. **4** aware, 'on the ball'.

SE in slang uses

IN COMPOUNDS

❑ **swinging dick** *n.* (*also* **swinging Richard**) [SE *swinging* + DICK *n.*[1] (5). Popularized in Tom Wolfe's novel *Bonfire of the Vanities* (1987) where *big swinging dicks* was used to characterize the most successful of Wall Street's financial wheeler-dealers] [1970s+] (*US*) **1** a person; usu. in phr. *every swinging dick*. **2** an aggressive person.

swinging *adj.*[3] [SWING *v.* (8)] [1960s+] **1** referring to those who participate in husband-and-wife swapping parties or those who enjoy a promiscuous sex life. **2** sexually active; used for sexual contacts.

IN COMPOUNDS

❑ **swinging single** *n.* (*also* **swingle**) [1960s+] (*US*) a sexually promiscuous unmarried person.

swinging *adj.*[4] [i.e. in motion] [1970s] (*Aus. Und.*) of a court case, adjourned.

swinging! *excl.* [SWING *v.* (8); the term migrated to UK as the catchphrase of entertainer Norman Vaughan, compere of television's *Sunday Night at the London Palladium*, who alternated the positive *swinging* with the negative *dodgy*; it was further associated with the image of 'swinging London' and the 'swinging Sixties'] [1950s–80s] (*orig. US black*) a general term of approval.

swinging door *n.* [rhy. sl. = whore] [1930s] a prostitute.

swingle *n. see* SWINGING SINGLE *under* SWINGING *adj.*[3].

swing-out *n.* [SWING OUT *v.*] [1950s–70s] (*US black/PR*) a violent street fight between rival urban gangs.

swing out *v.* (*US*) **1** [1950s–70s] to fight. **2** [1960s] (*US campus*) to lose emotional control. **3** [1960s] to associate with. **4** [1990s+] to absent oneself.

swingy *adj.* [SWING *v.* (8); SWING BOTH WAYS *under* SWING *v.*] [1970s+] (*US gay*) **1** bisexual. **2** enjoyable.

swinjer *n.* [? SWINGEING *under* SWINGE *v.*] [1940s–50s] (*Aus.*) something excellent; also as adv.

swinny *adj.* [dial. *swinny*, giddy] [19C] drunk.

swipe *n.*[1] **1** [mid-19C+] cheap, inferior, home-brewed alcohol. **2** [mid-19C+] a heavy drinker.

swipe *n.*[2] [? obs. SE *swip*, to hit, to slip away] **1** [1900s–50s] (*US*) an unpleasant, objectionable person. **2** [1920s] objectionable people considered collectively.

swipe *n.*[3] [1910s–50s] (*US*) a stable-boy.

swipe *n.*[4] (*also* **swipestake**) [? SE *swipe*, to hit, or abbr. KIDNEY-WIPER *under* KIDNEY *n.*] [1950s–80s] (*US black*) the penis.

swipe *v.*[1] [orig. northern dial.] [early 19C–1900s] to drink (hastily and copiously).

swipe *v.*[2] [SE *swipe*, to strike] **1** [late 19C–1900s] (*US campus*) to defeat. **2** [late 19C–1940s] (*US Und.*) to assault. **3** [late 19C+] (*orig. US*) to steal.

swiped *adj. see* SWIPEY *adj.*

swipe me! *excl.* [? S'ELP ME BOB! *excl.* or SE *swipe*] [1970s+] an excl. of surprise.

swiper *n.* [SWIPE *v.*[1]] [early–mid-19C] a heavy drinker.

swipes *n.* [naut. jargon *swipes*, weak or 'small' beer furnished by the purser; a sailor was allowed four quarts (five litres) a day, but the quality was atrocious; ult. SWIPE *v.*[1]] **1** [late 18C–late 19C] weak beer; sour beer. **2** [late 18C–1920s] any beer. **3** [early–mid-19C] a public-house potman.

swipestake *n. see* SWIPE *n.*[4].

swipey *n.* [SWIPES *n.*] [mid-19C] a brewery drayman.

swipey *adj.* (*also* **swiped**) [SWIPES *n.*] [19C] drunk, tipsy.

swipington *n.* (*also* **swippington**) [SWIPES *n.* + LUSHINGTON *n.*] [1930s+] (*Aus.*) a drunkard.

swips *v.* [SWIPE *v.*[1]] [1950s] (*W.I.*) to drink off at a single draught, to 'knock back'.

swirly *n.* (*also* **swirlie**) [1980s+] (*US campus*) a ducking of someone's head in a toilet bowl.

swish *n.* (*also* **swishy**) **1** [1920s–80s] (*orig. US*) an effeminate style [SWISH *v.*[1] (2)]. **2** [1930s] (*orig. US*) (*also* **swisher**) a homosexual man [SWISH *v.*[1] (2)]. **3** [1930s] soda water, e.g. *Scotch and swish*. **4** [1950s] (*N.Z.*) (*also* **swisher**) any dispenser worked by a pump. **5** [1960s+] (*Aus.*) (*also* **swisho**) physical violence [SE *swish*, echoic of cane used in corporal punishment]. **6** [1980s+] (*N.Z. prison*) abuse, harassment, heckling.

swish *adj.* (*also* **swishy**) **1** [20C+] fancy, elegant, 'posh' [? the SE *swishing* of a fashionable woman's dress]. **2** [1940s+] effeminate, homosexual [SWISH *n.*].

swish *v.*[1] **1** [mid-19C–1950s] (*UK juv.*) to cane; thus *swishing*, a caning [the sound of the cane]. **2** [1940s+] of a man, to act in an effeminate manner [SE *swish*, to move with a swish]. **3** [1970s–80s] (*N.Z. prison*) to hit, to punch.

IN COMPOUNDS

❑ **swish-tail** *n. see* separate entry.

swish *v.*[2] [ety. unknown] [1980s+] (*N.Z. drugs*) to distribute or sell drugs; esp. in phr. *swish on luckies*, to distribute or sell LSD or MDMA (a designer hallucinogen).

swish! *excl.* [1920s] a disdainful, ironic excl., is that it? is that all?

Swish Alps *n.* [play on SWISH *n.* (2)/*Swiss*] [1950s–60s] (*US gay*) a gay area in the Hollywood Hills.

swished *adj.* (*also* **switched**) [? one is *switched* from the single to the marital state] [mid-19C] married.

swisher *n.*[1] [? SE *switch*] [1990s+] (*drugs*) a cigar in which tobacco is replaced with marijuana.

swisher *n.*[2] **1** *see* SWISH *n.* (2). **2** *see* SWISH *n.* (4).

swishiness *n.* [SWISHY *adj.*] [1940s+] effeminacy.

swishing *adj.* [SWISH *v.*[1] (2)] [1970s] of a (usu. gay) man, openly and extremely effeminate.

swisho *n. see* SWISH *n.* (5).

swish-tail *n.* **1** [late 18C–mid-19C] a pheasant [SE]. **2** [mid-19C] a school-master [SWISH *v.*[1] (1) + TAIL *n.* (2)]. **3** [late 19C] a horse with an undocked tail [SE].

swishy *n. see* SWISH *n.*

swishy *adj.* [SWISH *n.* (1)] **1** [1930s+] effeminate, exhibiting the supposed characteristics of a male homosexual. **2** [1990s+] (*US gay*) sexually enjoyable. **3** *see* SWISH *adj.*

Swiss *adj.* [negative stereotyping] **1** [1970s+] (*US teen*) neutral, of no specific opinion. **2** [1990s+] unimpressive, second-rate.

IN COMPOUNDS

❑ **Swiss itch** *n. see* separate entry.

Swiss Army (knife) *n.* [rhy. sl.] [1990s+] one's wife.

Swiss banker *n. see* MERCHANT BANKER *n.* (1).

Swiss itch *n.* [ety. unknown; ? anecdotal] [1920s–60s] a popular method of drinking tequila, one places a pinch of salt on the back of the hand, licks it off, drinks down a shot of tequila and immediately bites into a segment or a slice of lime.

swiss-roll *n.* [rhy. sl.] [2000s] **1** (*Irish*) the anus [HOLE *n.*[1] (1)]. **2** sexual intercourse [HOLE *n.*[1] (1)].

swissy *adj.* [1990s+] (*US teen*) bizarre, fashionable, daring.

switch *n.*[1] **1** [20C+] an exchange, esp. when it involves criminal deception. **2** [1920s–40s] (*US Und.*) substituting one thing, e.g. a deck of cards or pair of dice, for another to facilitate cheating. **3** [1940s] (*US Und.*) in a confidence trick, the transfer of the victim's trust from the man who first befriended him to the principal trickster, to whom he has been introduced. **4** in sexual contexts. (**a**) [1960s] (*US Und.*) one who enjoys non-standard sexual activity, e.g. flagellation. (**b**) [1990s+] (*US gay*) one who varies their sexual preferences, i.e. masculine to feminine, sadist to masochist. (**c**) [1990s+] (*W.I.*) a heterosexual who has become homosexual; as phr. *make the switch*. **5** [2000s] (*US*) a change.

IN COMPOUNDS

❑ **switch-hitter** *n.* [baseball jargon *switch-hitter*, an ambidextrous batter] **1** [1960s+] (*orig. US*) a bisexual. **2** [1980s] one who changes their religion.

IN PHRASES

❑ **in the switches** *adj.* [SE *switch*, to change or transfer, i.e. an image of indecision] [1940s–50s] (*US*) confused, undecided.

❑ **pull a switch** *v.* [SE *switch*, to swop] **1** [1950s] (*US*) to change sides. **2** [1980s] to act deceitfully.

switch *n.*[2] [SE *switch*, to flourish] [1930s–50s] (*US black*) the movement of a woman's hips as she walks, also of a man; thus as v., to walk with a sway of the hips.

IN PHRASES

❑ **hit switches** *v.* (*also* **hit a switch, hit the switch**) [2000s] (*US black*) to have sexual intercourse.

switch *n.*[3] [abbr.] **1** [1940s–60s] (*US*) a *switch*-blade knife. **2** [1940s+] (*Aus.*) a telephone *switch*board.

switch *v.*[1] **1** [late 18C; late 19C–1930s] to have sexual intercourse. **2** [2000s] (*UK black*) to lose one's temper.

SE in slang uses

IN PHRASES

❑ **switch on** *v.* [1960s+] **1** (*US drugs*) to become intoxicated by drugs. **2** (*US*) to excite, to arouse sexually. **3** (*US*) to participate in the latest cultural trends. ❑ **switch up** *v.* [1910s+] to fail, to malfunction.

IN EXCLAMATIONS

❑ **I'll be switched!** [SE *switch*, to whip] [mid-19C–1940s] an excl. of irritation, surprise, denial. ❑ **switch off!** [electrical imagery] [1900s–20s] shut up! be quiet!

switch *v.*[2] *see* SWINGE *v.* (2).

switch and bone *n.* [rhy. sl.] [1930s–40s] a telephone.

switched *adj. see* SWISHED *adj.*

switched off *adj.* [1960s+] (*orig. US*) unfashionable.

switched on *adj.* [SWITCH ON *under* SWITCH *v.*[1]] [1960s+] (*orig. US*) **1** intoxicated by drugs. **2** sexually stimulated. **3** aware, sophisticated, up to the minute.

switched out *adj.* [on pattern of SWITCHED ON *adj.* (3)] [1970s] alienated.

switchel *v. see* SWINGE *v.* (2).

switcher *n.* [early 19C] (*UK Und.*) **1** a hangman [he *switches* his victim from life to death]. **2** a confidence trickster [one who *switches* 'good' things for 'bad' ones].

switcheroo *n.* [SE *switch* + -EROO *sfx*] [1930s+] (*US*) the opposite, the reverse, an exchange.

switching *n.* [SWISHED *adj.*] [mid–late 19C] a marriage.

swive *v.* [OE *swífan*, to move in a course + ON *svífa*, to rove, to ramble, to drift. Coined *c.*1440, *swive* was SE until *c.*1700. Like a number of 'obscenities' it is not genuine sl., but was for many years excluded from SE dictionaries as a taboo vulgarism] **1** [mid-16C+] to have sexual intercourse. **2** [mid-18C] to have anal intercourse.

swivel *n.* [the head *swivels*] [1910s–40s] a glance, a look at.

SE in slang uses

IN COMPOUNDS

❑ **swivel-eye/-eyed** *see* separate entries. ❑ **swivel-neck** *n. see* separate entry.

IN PHRASES

❑ **on the swivel** *adj.* [late 19C] active, showing one's paces.

swivel *v.* [2000s] (*S.Afr. gay*) to mingle socially.

swivel-eye *n.* [backform. f. SWIVEL-EYED *adj.*] **1** [mid-19C] a squint. **2** [late 19C] a swindler, a term of abuse.

swivel-eyed *adj.* **1** [late 18C+] squint-eyed. **2** [late 19C] a general term of abuse.

swivelly *adj.* [late 19C] drunk.

swivel-neck *n.* [the head swivels up and down when giving oral sex] [1970s–80s] (*N.Z. prison*) a passive male homosexual.

swivet *n.* [dial. *swivet*, haste, hurry, passion] [late 19C+] (*US*) an irritable mood.

swiz *n.*[1] (*also* **swizz**) [abbr. SWIZZLE *n.* (1)] [19C] intoxicating liquor.

swiz *n.*[2] (*also* **swizz, swizzle**) [SE *swindle*] [1910s+] (*mainly teen*) a fraud, a hoax, a disappointment.

swiz *n.*[3] (*also* **swizz**) [SWINJER *n.*] [1930s–50s] (*Aus.*) an excellent, first-rate thing.

swiz *v.* (*also* **swizz**) [SWIZ *n.*[2] (1)] [1950s] (*mainly juv.*) to cheat, to swindle.

swizzle *n.* [echoic of its fizziness] [mid-18C–mid-19C] **1** any form of intoxicating liquor. **2** (*US*) a mix of spruce ('Prussian') beer, rum and sugar.

swizzle *v.*[1] [SWIZZLE *n.* (1)] [mid–late 19C] to drink.

swizzle *v.*[2] [SWIZ *v.*] [1930s] to hoax, to trick.

swizzled *adj.* (*also* **swazzled, swozzled**) [SWIZZLE *v.*[1]] **1** [mid-19C+] drunk. **2** [20C+] (*US*) obsessed, infatuated.

swizzler *n.* [SWIZZLE *v.*[2]] [1930s+] a cheater, a swindler.

swizzy *n.* [var. on SWIZZLE *n.* (1)] [late 18C] any form of intoxicating drink.

swizzy *v.* [var. on SWIZZLE *v.*[1]] [mid–late 19C] to drink.

swob! *excl.* [var. on S'ELP ME BOB! *excl.*] [1910s–20s] a general excl. of intensification and affirmation.

swob(ber) *n. see* SWAB *n.*[1].

swobble *v. see* SWABBLE *v.*

swock *v.* [dial. *swack*, a blow] [1960s] (*US*) to hit, to attack.

swoddy *n. see* SWADDY *n.*

swod-gill *n. see* SWAD-GILL *n.*

swole *adj.* [SE *swollen*] **1** [1990s+] (*US campus*) muscled. **2** [2000s] in fig. use, successful.

'swolks! *excl. see* 'SWOUNDS! *excl.*

swoll *adj.* (*also* **swole**) [1990s+] (*US prison*) angry.

swonie *n. see* SWOON UNIT *n.*

swoon! *excl.* [1980s+] (*US campus*) an excl. of approval used by a woman on seeing an attractive man.

swooner *n.* [he causes girls to *swoon*] [1950s] (*US black*) a very attractive person.

swoon time *n.* [1950s] (*US black*) a time of day when young people meet to chat and enjoy themselves.

swoon unit *n.* (*also* **swonie**) [SE *swoon*, to faint] [1990s+] (*US teen*) a particularly attractive woman.

swoony *adj.* [lit. inducing a *swoon*] [1930s+] distractingly attractive, delightful.

swoop *v.* **1** [1920s+] (*US black*) to move fast, to approach or leave quickly. **2** [1950s+] (*US black*) to steal someone else's lover, esp. when the manoeuvre is conducted quickly. **3** [1960s+] (*US campus*) to overtake in a car. **4** [1960s+] (*US black/N.Z. prison*) to steal, to take; to arrest. **5** [1970s+] (*US black*) to assault in a group. **6** [1970s+] (*US black/campus*) to make a pass at, to make sexual advances towards.

swooper *n.* [1990s+] (*UK prison*) a prisoner who is constantly swooping down to pick up discarded cigarette ends.

swooping *adj. see* SWAPPING *adj.*

swop *see under* SWAP.

swop me bob! *excl.* (*also* **swelp me lucky! swop me dicky! swop my greens!**) [all vars. on S'ELP ME BOB! *excl.*/S'ELP ME GREENS! *excl.*] [mid-19C–1910s] a general excl. of intensification and affirmation.

swop slob *v.* [abbr. SE *swap slobber*] [1940s] (*US black/campus*) to kiss.

sword *n.* [note D'Urfey, *Pills to Purge Melancholy* (1719): 'Brave Carpet Knights in *Cupid*'s Fights, their milk-white Rapiers drew'] [mid-15C–mid-19C; 1970s+] the penis.

IN COMPOUNDS

❑ **sword fight** *n.* [1990s+] a primarily male party. ❑ **sword-fighter** *n.* [1970s+] (*UK juv.*) a male homosexual; thus *swordfighting*, mutual masturbation. ❑ **swordsman** *n.* [Williams notes a similar 17C use of *fencer*] [1950s+] a male sexual athlete. ❑ **sword-swallower** *n.* [1960s+] (*orig. Aus.*) a fellator or fellatrix; thus *swallow a sword*, to fellate.

SE in slang uses

IN COMPOUNDS

❑ **sword racket** *n.* [RACKET *n.*[1] (1)] [early 19C] a means of making money by enlisting in a regiment, taking the bounty, deserting and moving on to a new regiment. ❑ **sword-swallower** *n.* [1940s] (*Aus.*) one who eats from his knife. ❑ **sword-swallowing** *n.* [1910s] (*US*) eating.

IN PHRASES

❑ **have the sword** *v.* [1960s+] (*Aus.*) to be finished or exhausted, to be irreparably damaged.

swordfish *n.* [mid-19C] (*US*) a form of liquor (whisky?).

sworn at Highgate *phr.* ['a ridiculous custom formerly prevailed at the public houses in Highgate (then a village north of London), to administer a ludicrous oath to all travellers of the middling rank who stopped there. The party was sworn on a pair of horns, fastened on a stick, the substance of the oath was never to kiss the maid when he could kiss the mistress, never to drink small beer when he could get strong, with many other injunctions of the like kind to all of which was added the saving clause of "unless you like it best"' (Grose, 1785)] [late 18C–early 19C] clever, smart.

sworray *n.* see SWARRY *n.*

swosh *n.* [abbr. HOGWASH *n.*] [late 19C–1920s] rubbish, nonsense.

swot *n.* (*also* **swat**) [SWOT *v.* (1)] **1** [mid-19C+] a hard worker. **2** [1960s–70s] hard work, revision.

swot *v.* (*also* **do some swat, swat (up)**) [supposedly via Dr William Wallace, an instructor at the Royal Military College, Sandhurst c. 1800, whose Scot. pron. turned the word 'sweat' (as in work that is so hard as to make one sweat) into *swot*. The 20C+ implication is slightly derog. – to work harder than seen as necessary by your peers] [mid-19C+] to work extremely hard, esp. on the eve of examinations or tests; thus *swot up*, to learn intensely.

swotter *n.* [SWOT *v.*] [1900s–10s] a very hard worker.

'swounds! *excl.* (*also* **'dswounds! 'swolks! 'swouns! 'zwouns!**) [mid-16C–early 19C] a mild oath, lit. 'God's wounds'.

swozzled *adj.* see SWIZZLED *adj.*

swret-sio *n.* see SRET-SIO *n.*

swuft *adj.* [var. on SWIFT *adj.* (3)] [1970s] (*US campus*) smart, clever, cunning.

swy *n.* (*also* **sway, swi**) [Ger. *zwei*, two] [1920s+] **1** two, esp. a two-shilling (10p) coin or a two-year prison sentence. **2** (*Aus.*) the game of two-up; also as *swy-up*, the *swy game*, a game of two-up; *swy school*, a group of people who have gathered to play two-up.

sycher *n.* (*also* **zoucher**) [dial. *sycher*, a bad man] [late 19C] an objectionable, unpleasant person.

Sydney *adj.*

proper name in slang uses

IN COMPOUNDS

❑ **Sydney bird** *n.* [mid–late 19C] a convict. ❑ **Sydney blanket** *n.* [late 19C+] (*Aus.*) a rough blanket, used by vagrants and tramps and made of a sack or bag. ❑ **Sydney duck** *n.* [mid-19C] (*US*) (*also* **Sydney cove**) an Australian who joined the Californian Gold Rush of 1849; thus a former Aus. convict who pursued his villainies in San Francisco.

IN PHRASES

❑ **Sydney or the bush** [the comparison between making a fast fortune in the big city or eking out a much harder life in the outback] [20C+] (*Aus.*) all or nothing.

Sydney Harbour *n.* (*also* **coff's harbour, Dover harbour**) [rhy. sl.] [1920s+] (*Aus./US*) a barber.

Sydneysider *n.* [*Sydney*, the state capital] (*Aus.*) **1** [mid–late 19C] a convict. **2** [mid-19C+] a native of New South Wales; thus adj. *Sydneyside.*

syebuck *n.* (*also* **si-buxom**) [Hotten (1859) has *fye-buck* but this is a misreading of an 18C long 's'] [mid-18C–mid-19C] a sixpence.

syff *n.* see SYPH *n.*

Sylvester (Stallone) *adj.* [rhy. sl.; ult. *Sylvester Stallone*, US film actor (b.1946)] [1990s+] alone.

sympathy *n.* [a pun on 'a fellow feeling'] [20C+] sexual caresses.

sympathy sticks *n.* [1940s] (*US Und.*) a beggar's crutches.

synagogue *n.* [by late 19C, Covent Garden market was very much a Jewish enterprise] [late 19C] a shed – its use is not specified – standing at that time in the northeast corner of Covent Garden, London.

synagogue twins *n.* [mocking the Jewish prohibition of pork] [1930s] (*US*) ham and eggs.

synch *n.*

IN PHRASES

❑ **in synch** (*also* **in sync**) [SE phr. *in synchronization*, of sound, usu. in films] [1970s+] fig., in tune with.

syntax *n.* [SE; popularized through *The Tour of Dr Syntax* (1813) by William Combe] [late 18C–early 19C] a schoolmaster.

synth *n.* [abbr.] [1970s+] a *synth*esiser.

syph *n.* (*also* **sif, siph, syff, the syph(s)**) [abbr.] [late 19C+] *syph*ilis; also attrib.; thus adjs. *syphy, siffed up.*

sypho *n.* [abbr. SE *syphilis* + -O *sfx* (3)] **1** [1910s+] (*Aus.*) syphilis. **2** [1970s+] (*US gay*) a syphilitic.

syphon the python *v.* see SIPHON THE PYTHON *v.*

syrup *n.* **1** [1900s] alcohol; a drink. **2** [1930s] (*US*) nitroglycerin, as used as an explosive. **3** [2000s] (*US drugs*) a codeine-based prescription cough syrup.

syrup (of figs) *n.* [rhy. sl.] **1** [1970s+] a wig. **2** [1980s] (*Aus.*) an eavesdropper [rhy. sl. = FIZGIG *n.*^{2}].

IN EXCLAMATIONS

❑ **keep your syrup on!** (*also* **keep your wig on!**) [1980s+] relax! calm down!

S.Y.T. *n.* [*s*weet *y*oung *t*hing] [1970s] (*US gay*) a teenage male homosexual.

T *n.*[1] [abbr. TEA *n.* (4a)] [1950s+] (*drugs*) marijuana.

T *n.*[2] [abbr.] **1** [1960s+] (*US drugs*) a gram of methamphetamine. **2** [1970s] phencyclidine [PCP which is misreading of THC, i.e. *tetrahydrocannabinol*]. **3** [1970s+] (*also* **tee**) Tuinal.

T *n.*[3] [1970s] (*US*) Tijuana, Mexico.

T *n.*[4] (*also* **tee**) [1970s+] (*orig. US*) a T-shirt.

T *n.*[5]

IN PHRASES

❑ **on T** *see* ON *TIME under* TIME *n.*

t.a. *see under* TITS AND ASS.

ta! *excl.* [orig. juv.; 'Ex a young child's difficulty with *th* and *nks*' (*DSUE*)] [late 18C+] thank you.

IN EXCLAMATIONS

❑ **no ta hey!** [late 18C+] (*S.Afr.*) absolutely not, thank you very much! ❑ **ta for niks!** [late 18C+] (*S.Afr.*) thanks for nothing! ❑ **ta, hey!** [late 18C+] (*S.Afr.*) thank you very much!

tab *n.*[1] (*also* **tabhole**) [dial.] [mid-19C+] the human ear.

tab *n.*[2] [TABBY *n.*] **1** [late 19C–1910s] an elderly woman. **2** [1910s+] (*Aus.*) a young woman.

tab *n.*[3] [abbr. SE *table*; *see* Asbury, *Sucker's Progress* (1938) 14–15: An extraordinary number of the terms, technical and otherwise, which were employed by Faro players in the palmy days of the game have passed into the language [...] and are commonly used by millions who never heard of Faro. Here are some of them: [...] *Tabs* – Printed sheets on which the players noted the cards as they won or lost. *Keeping tabs* – Making this record] **1** [late 19C+] (*US*) the bill, credit, an IOU, used fig. to imply that an action, good or bad, will be paid for later. **2** [20C+] (*US prison*) any form of prison documentation, esp. reports on prisoners that are submitted to the parole board. **3** [1930s–40s] (*US prison*) letters passed between inmates; a letter smuggled out of prison.

IN COMPOUNDS

❑ **tab action** *n.* (*also* **tab issue**) [ACTION *n.* (3)/SE *issue*] [1930s–40s] (*US black*) a line of credit at a bar or any other type of business.

IN PHRASES

❑ **keep tabs on** *v.* (*also* **keep (a) tab on**) [late 19C+] (*orig. US*) to keep under surveillance, to take note of. ❑ **pick up the tab** *v.* [1930s+] (*orig. US*) **1** to pay a bill, usu. in a restaurant; the implication is one of treating one's fellow eaters. **2** to take responsibility, to accept the consequences, esp. if financial.

tab *n.*[4] [dial. *tab*, the pointed end of anything] [1910s+] a cigarette.

tab *n.*[5] [abbr.] [1920s+] a *tab*loid newspaper.

tab *n.*[6]

IN PHRASES

❑ **ain't coming on that tab** [1930s–40s] (*US black*) a phr. rejecting another person's suggestion.

tab *n.*[7] [abbr.] (*drugs*) **1** [1950s+] a *tab*let, esp. one containing a hallucinogenic drug. **2** [1980s] a dose of LSD in non-tablet form.

tab, the *n.* [abbr.] [1980s] (*Aus./N.Z.*) the Totalizator Agency Board.

tab *v.*[1] (*also* **tab up**) [abbr. SE *tabulate*] (*US*) **1** [late 19C–1940s] to charge with a crime. **2** [1910s+] to identify, to categorize. **3** [1920s] to survey a place prior to robbing it. **4** [1930s] to name, to nickname. **5** [1970s] to obtain credit.

tab *v.*[2] [*keep tabs on* under TAB *n.*[3]] [1920s–40s] to follow a person, to place someone under surveillance.

tab *v.*[3] [1930s–40s] (*US black*) to hit someone.

tabankca *n.* (*also* **tabanka**) [? Fr. *t'as bon ça*, you are good] [20C+] (*W.I.*) love-sickness, sexual obsession.

tabankca *adj.* [TABANKCA *n.*] [20C+] (*W.I.*) passionate, obsessed.

tabasco *n.* [play on *Tabasco* hot sauce] [1920s] spirit.

tabasco *adj.* [play on *Tabasco* hot sauce] [1920s] excited, dramatic, 'hot'.

tabbed *adj.* [? SE *tab*, a label] [1970s+] (*US black*) well-dressed.

IN PHRASES

❑ **tabbed to the bone** *adj.* [*to the bone* under BONE *n.*[1]] [1970s+] (*US black*) dressed in one's very best, most fashionable clothes.

tabber *n.* [mid-19C] (*UK Und.*) to beat; to knock on a door.

tabbing *n. see* TRIPPING *n.*

tabby *n.* [SE *tabby cat*, ult. *tabby*, striped or watered silk (orig. produced in the Baghdad suburb of Attabiy), and thus applied to the colouring of the cat; thus theatrical jargon *tabs*, an old woman; note Aus. WW1 milit. *tabby*, a woman (irrespective of age)] **1** [late 17C+] an old lady, usu. as pej. **2** [early 19C; 1910s–50s] a young woman, esp. an attractive one. **3** [1910s–30s] (*Aus./US Und.*) a prostitute.

DERIVATIVES

❑ **tabbyism** *n.* [late 17C+] the tendency to act as a querulous, interfering old woman.

IN COMPOUNDS

❑ **tabby meeting** *n.* [note proper name *Tabitha*, a typically 'religious' name] [late 19C–1900s] a meeting of evangelists and their congregations at Exeter Hall, London. ❑ **tabby party** *n.* [19C] a party consisting only of women.

tabby *adj.* [TABBY *n.* (1)] [1920s] (*US*) **1** interfering, inquisitive, judgmental. **2** like an old woman.

tabitha *n.* [initial letter] [2000s] (*S.Afr. gay*) a tooth.

table *n.*

SE in slang uses

IN COMPOUNDS

❑ **table bird** *n.* [CHICKEN *n.* (1b)] [1960s] (*Aus.*) a sexually attractive woman. ❑ **table-end man** *n.* [late 19C+] a man whose sexual desire is so intense that he makes love to his partner over the dining/kitchen table rather than waiting until they reach the bedroom. ❑ **table-hop** *v.* [1950s+] (*orig. US*) to circulate among the tables at a restaurant, greeting and chatting with friends and acquaintances. ❑ **table-tapper** *n.* [their thumping of the *table* as they preach] [20C+] (*US*) an unprofessional, part-time lay preacher. ❑ **table-topper** *n.* (*also* **table hopper**) [the mortuary *table* or slab] [1980s+] a necrophile.

IN PHRASES

❑ **get one's feet under the table** *v.* **1** [1920s+] to establish friendly relations with someone, to start to settle in. **2** [1980s+] of a man, to start living with a woman (occas. vice versa). ❑ **under the table** *see* separate entry.

tablet *n.* [1990s+] an MDMA tablet.

t.a.b.u. *n. see* S.A.B.U. *n.*

tac *n.* [PCP is a misappropriation of initials *THC*, i.e. *tetrahydrocannabinol*] [1960s+] (*drugs*) phencyclidine.

tach *n.*[1] [backsl.] [mid-19C] a hat.

tach *n.*[2] (*also* **tacho, tack**) [abbr.] [1960s+] a *tach*ometer, an instrument that measures the velocity of machines.

tache *n. see* TASH *n.*

tack *n.*[1] [SE *tack*, solidity or *tackle*, food] **1** [mid-19C] (*UK Und.*) in pl., money, either notes or coins. **2** [mid-19C+] (*orig. naut.*) food, ship's biscuit. **3** [late 19C+] drink. **4** [1950s] money [separate development to sense 1].

IN PHRASES

▫ **break the tack** *v.* [1910s] to drink after a period of abstinence. ▫**go on the tack** *v.* [1910s] to abstain from alcohol [? SE *tackle*]. ▫**soft tack** *n.* **1** [mid–late 19C] (*orig. naut.*) bread as opposed to biscuits or *hard tack*. **2** [1900s] (*Aus.*) a soft drink, as opposed to hard liquor.

tack *n.*[2] [SE *tack*, an alien, odd or unpleasant flavour; ? ult. Lat. *tactus*, infection] [mid-19C+] (*later Irish*) anything mouldy or sour, esp. a taste (in food or drink) that is other than one expects.

tack *n.*[3] **1** [1930s–60s] (*US black*) a nickel, five cents. **2** [1950s+] (*W.I. Rasta*) a bullet.

tack *n.*[4] [? SE *tacit*, silent] (*US black*) **1** [1950s–60s] a fool. **2** [1950s–60s] a conservative. **3** [1950s+] an unsophisticated person. **4** [1960s–70s] a clever person [phr. *smart as a tack*].

tack *n.*[5] [TACKY *adj.*[1]] [1980s+] (*orig. US*) bad taste.

IN PHRASES

▫ **tack attack** *n.* [1990s+] (*orig. US*) a rush of bad taste or an experience of bad taste.

tack *n.*[6] [1990s+] (*US Und.*) a (prison-created) tattoo.

tack *n.*[7] *see* TACH *n.*[2].

tack *v.* (*also* **tackle**) [late 17C–19C] to join in marriage.

IN PHRASES

▫ **tack up** *v.* [SE *tackle*] [2000s] (*US prison*) to approach someone in a confrontational manner.

tacked down *adj.* [SE *tack*, to join] [1960s–70s] (*US black*) well-dressed.

tacker *n.* [dial. *tacker*, a child] [1940s+] (*Aus.*) a small boy.

tackery *n.* [TACK *n.*[1] (1)] [mid-19C] (*UK Und.*) credit.

tackhead *n.* (*also* **tackey, tacky, tackyhead**) [TACKY *adj.*[1] + -HEAD *sfx* (1)] **1** [20C+] (*US*) a stupid person, a rural farmer. **2** [20C+] (*US*) an overdressed or excessively stylish person. **3** [1960s+] (*US black*) an unattractive, unkempt woman [equating ill-kempt or unfashionable hair with an unappetizing person]. **4** [1990s+] (*US*) a troublemaker.

tackie *n. see* TAKKIE *n.*

tackie *v.* [S.Afr.E. *fat tackie*, a large tyre, used for racing or beach-driving] [1990s+] (*S.Afr.*) to drive fast, to accelerate.

tackle *n.*[1] [SE *tackle*, equipment, appliances etc] **1** [mid-16C–19C; 1980s+] the male genitals. **2** [early 17C–mid-19C] one's best clothes. **3** [late 17C–mid-19C] a prostitute, a mistress. **4** [19C+] any clothes. **5** [mid-19C–1900s] food or drink. **6** [late 19C–1940s] a watch chain. **7** [1980s+] (*Ulster*) a showily or bizarrely dressed woman. **8** [2000s] drugs.

IN PHRASES

▫**red tackle** *n.* [late 19C–1940s] a gold watch chain. ▫**toy and tackle** *n.* [late 19C–1940s] a watch and chain.

tackle *n.*[2] [SE *tackle*, to handle; here one who is 'hard to tackle'] [1980s+] (*Ulster*) **1** a cantankerous, verbally abusive woman. **2** a difficult child.

tackle *v.* **1** [early 19C–1910s] to grip, to lay hold of. **2** [mid-19C–1910s] to attack. **3** [mid-19C–1920s] to take in hand, to deal with. **4** [mid-19C–1960s] to enter into a discussion with, to approach or question some subject. **5** [mid-19C+] to grapple with, to attempt to deal with. **6** [late 19C–1910s] to fall upon (food), to eat. **7** [1950s+] (*W.I.*) to get to know someone with the specific aim of initiating an affair. **8** *see* TACK *v.*

tacks *n.*

IN PHRASES

▫ **get/come down to (brass) tacks** *v. see under* BRASS TACKS *n.*

tacky *n. see* TACKHEAD *n.*

tacky *adj.*[1] [ety. unknown; ? link to SAmE *tack*, a run-down horse, a poor Southern white] **1** [mid-19C+] (*orig. US*) unattractive, second-rate. **2** [late 19C+] off-putting, in poor taste. **3** [1900s] (*US campus*) drunk. **4** [1900s] (*US campus*) untidy, unkempt.

tacky *adj.*[2] [SE *tack*, a new or altered course or line of action, endurance, stability, strength] [1950s] (*W.I.*) **1** tricky, hard to beat, cunning. **2** good, skilled, clever.

tackyhead *n. see* TACKHEAD *n.*

taco *n.* [Sp. *taco*, a fried, unleavened cornmeal pancake or tortilla holding a variety of seasoned fillings, a popular Mexican food] **1** [1960s+] (*US*) a derog. term for a Mexican; thus used adj. to stereotype anything 'Mexican', i.e. cheap, stupid and/or lazy. **2** [1980s] (*US black/L.A.*) used as a derog. to a fellow black; the premise being one is no better than a Mexican.

IN COMPOUNDS

▫ **taco (bell)** *n.* [play on *Taco Bell*, chain of US restaurants selling Mexican fast food/BELL END *n.* (1)] [1990s+] (*US teen*) the penis. ▫ **taco belle** *n.* [see prev.] [1980s+] a Latin American woman. ▫ **taco-bender** *n.* [1960s+] (*US*) a derog. term for a Mexican, a Chicano; also as adj. ▫ **taco-breath** *adj.* [1970s] (*US*) Mexican. ▫ **taco-eater** *n.* [1960s+] (*US*) a derog. term for a Mexican, a Chicano. ▫ **taco-head** *n.* [+ -HEAD *sfx* (2)] [1960s+] (*US*) a derog. term for a Mexican or a Chicano. ▫ **tacoland** *n.* [1960s+] a derog. name for that part of a town in which the Mexicans live. ▫ **taco queen** *n.* [QUEEN *n.* (2)] [1970s+] (*US gay*) an anglo homosexual who prefers Hispanic partners. ▫ **Taco Town** *n.* (*also* **Tamaleville**) [SE *town*, the Mexican population/SAmE *tamale*, a Mexican dish consisting of corn husks wrapped around a variety of fillings + SE sfx *-ville*] [1960s+] (*US*) a derog. term for San José, US. ▫ **taco wagon** *n.* [SE *wagon*, such cars are popular among Mexican youths] [1960s+] (*US*) a derog. term for a car with its rear end lowered.

SE in slang uses

IN PHRASES

▫ **go for a taco** *v.* [the shape of the thighs] [1990s+] (*US teen*) to move one's face between a woman's thighs preparatory to performing cunnilingus. ▫ **toss one's tacos** *v. see* TOSS ONE'S COOKIES *under* COOKIE *n.*[1]. ▫ **two tacos short of a combination plate** *see under* …SHORT OF… *adj.*

tacou *adj.* [ety. unknown] [20C+] (*W.I.*) foolish, stupid.

tad *n.*[1] [ety. unknown; ? SE *tadpole*] **1** [mid-19C–1900s] (*US*) one who attempts to avoid paying a bill. **2** [mid-19C+] (*US*) a person, esp. a young boy. **3** [1940s+] (*orig. US*) a small amount, usu. as *a tad*, slightly.

tad *n.*[2] [*Thaddeus*, a popular Irish name] [20C+] (*US*) an Irish Catholic.

tad blame it! *excl.* [1950s] (*US*) a euph. for GOD-DAMN IT! *excl.*

taddler *n.* [? link to TADGER *n.*] [1900s–20s] **1** a large sausage. **2** the penis.

tadger *n.* (*also* **todger, togger**) [northern UK dial.] [late 19C+] the penis.

tad-larruping *adj. see* LARRUPING *adj.*

tadpole *n.* **1** [mid-19C–1940s] (*US*) a native of Mississippi. **2** [1990s+] (*US black*) a young inexperienced boy.

tadpole carrier *n.* [sperm's resemblance to tadpoles] [1990s+] the scrotum.

taepo *n. see* TAIPO *n.*

taf *adj.* (*also* **taff, taffy**) [backsl.] [mid–late 19C] fat.

ta fearfully! *excl. see* TA MUCHLY! *excl.*

Tafee *n. see* TAFFY *n.*

Taff *n.* [abbr. TAFFY *n.*] [mid-17C; mid-19C+] a Welshman, also as a direct term of address.

taffeta girl *n. see* TIFFITY-TAFFETY *n.*

Taffy *n.* (*also* **Tafee, Taffie**) [Welsh *Dafydd*, David] [early 17C+] a Welshman or a nickname for a Welshman.

IN COMPOUNDS

❑ **Taffyland** *n.* [early 17C+] Wales. ❑ **Taffy's day** *n.* [early 17C+] St David's Day.

Taffy *adj.* [TAFFY *n.*] [1970s+] Welsh.

taffy *n.*[1] [SE *taffy*, toffee] [late 19C–1920s] (*US*) insincere and obvious flattery; deceptive and deluding talk.

IN COMPOUNDS

❑ **taffy-head** *n.* [-HEAD *sfx* (1)] [1970s] a braggart, a boaster, a 'big-head'.

taffy *n.*[2] (*also* **taffy goat, taffy ram**) [? the white ram that is the regimental symbol of the Royal Welch Fusiliers regiment, which has been stationed in Jamaica. This use, lit. an 'old goat', is used respectfully] [1900s–50s] (*W.I.*) an old person.

taffy *adj. see* TAF *adj.*

taffy *v.* [TAFFY *n.*[1]] [late 19C] (*US*) to tease.

taffy-tugger *n.* [*TUG ONE'S TAFFY under* TUG *v.*] [1990s+] a masturbator.

tag *n.*[1] [SE *tag along*] **1** [mid-19C] a servant, esp. an under-servant who assists another. **2** [1960s+] one who 'tags along' behind another person, esp. for detective or spying purposes.

tag *n.*[2] [the SE *tag* or 'moral' added to the end of a play] [mid–late 19C] an actor.

tag *n.*[3] [SE *tag*, a label] **1** [1920s+] (*UK/US black*) a name. **2** [1930s] (*US prison*) a letter smuggled out of prison. **3** [1930s] (*US*) a parking ticket conviction. **4** [1930s+] a vehicle number-plate. **5** [1930s+] (*US Und.*) an arrest warrant. **6** [1940s] a car licence. **7** [1960s+] a label commonly given to a person or thing. **8** [1980s+] the 'signature' used by a graffiti artist, spraying their name on walls, subway trains etc. **9** [2000s] (*US prison*) a piece of information.

IN PHRASES

❑ **catch tags** *v.* [2000s] to leave one's graffiti tag in various places. ❑ **run someone's tags** *v.* [one reads their notional *dogtags*] [2000s] (*US prison*) to discover information about a fellow inmate.

tag *v.*[1] [SE *tag*, to label] **1** [1910s+] to punch. **2** [1930s+] to arrest. **3** [1950s] to imprison. **4** [1950s+] to blame, to accuse. **5** [1960s+] to identify. **6** [1970s] in fig. use, to suffer, to be punished. **7** [1980s] to give a parking ticket. **8** [2000s] (*US black*) of a man, to have sexual intercourse.

tag *v.*[2] (*also* **tag up**) [TAG *n.*[3] (8)] [1980s+] (*orig. US*) of graffiti artists, to affix one's name to a picture, a wall etc, thus n. *tagging.*

tag-a-long *n.* [1950s–60s] (*Aus.*) a girl- or boyfriend.

tagger *n.* [TAG *v.*[2]] [1980s+] one who writes their tag or personal label on walls and other visible sites; a graffiti artist.

taggy *n.* [mid-19C] (*UK Und.*) an accuser, a hostile witness.

tagnuts *n.* [1990s+] small pieces of excrement adhering to the anal hairs.

tag, rag and bobtail/longtail *n. see* RAG, TAG AND BOBTAIL *n.*

Taig *n.* (*also* **Tague, Teague, Teg, Tege, Tegue, Teig**) [Irish name *Tadhg*, usu. rendered as Thaddeus in English] [mid-17C+] **1** a Roman Catholic, spec. as used by Protestants in Northern Ireland. **2** a generic term for an Irishman; thus *Taig/Teague-land*, Ireland.

tail *n.* [SE *tail*, of an animal] **1** as items of clothing [SE until 18C]. (**a**) [late 13C–19C] the train attached to a woman's dress, usu. for formal use only. (**b**) [16C–19C] (*UK Und.*) the tail of a man's coat; in the context of pickpocketing; thus *tail kick*, the pocket in a tailcoat. **2** [14C+] the posterior, the buttocks; thus fig. use synon. with *arse/ass*; as oneself [SE until 1750]. **3** [mid-14C–1940s] the penis; thus synons. *tail-pike, tail-pin, tail-tackle, tail-trimmers* [SE until 18C]. **4** [mid-15C+] (*also* **tale**) the vagina; thus synons. *tail-gap, tail-gate, tail-hole*; similarly used in homosexual contexts for the anus [SE until 18C]. **5** [late 17C–mid-19C] (*UK Und.*) (*also* **tale**) a sword; thus *TAIL-DRAWER* below [the way it projects beyond the wearer's body]. **6** [late 18C+] a prostitute. **7** [1910s+] women viewed collectively and as sex objects; thus *PIECE OF TAIL under* PIECE *n.* **8** [1930s+] sexual intercourse. **9** [1940s] young boys suitable for homosexual relationships. **10** in senses of surveillance. (**a**) [20C+] (*orig. US*) one who carries out a surveillance, esp. when following the target in the street. (**b**) [1910s+] (*also* **tail job**) an act of surveillance. (**c**) [1970s] (*US prison*) an infomer. **11** [1990s+] (*drugs*) the long-term effect of a drug, as opposed to the initial RUSH *n.* (4a). **12** [1990s+] (*US prison*) parole.

IN COMPOUNDS

❑ **tailbone** *n.* [20C+] (*US*) the buttocks. ❑ **tail-buzzer** *n.* (*also* **tail-dip, tail-diver**) [BUZZER *n.*[1]/DIP *n.*[1] (3)/DIVE *v.*] [mid–late 19C] (*UK Und.*) a thief who specializes in the picking of coat pockets. ❑ **tail-buzzing** *n.* [mid–late 19C] (*UK Und.*) stealing a wallet from a tailcoat pocket. ❑ **tail-chaser** *n.* [1940s+] (*US*) a womanizer. ❑ **tail-drawer** *n.* [late 17C–early 19C] (*UK Und.*) a thief who steals gentlemen's swords from their sides. ❑ **tail-feathers** *n.* [mid-15C+] pubic hair. ❑ **tail-fodder** *n. see BUM-FODDER under* BUM *n.*[1]. ❑ **tail-fruit** *n.* [mid-15C+] children. ❑ **tail-gunner** *n.* [1940s+] (*US*) a male homosexual. ❑ **tail-juice** *n.* [mid-15C+] urine. ❑ **tailman** *n.* [1960s] (*US campus*) a womanizer, a sexual athlete. ❑ **tail-pit** *n.* [1900s–30s] (*US Und.*) a side pocket. ❑ **tail tea** *n.* [Once Queen Victoria had died, her son Edward VII (r.1901–10) moved the 'drawing rooms' to the evening, a time more congenial to his own lifestyle] [late 19C] (*UK society*) an afternoon tea attended by aristocratic ladies who had already been at the day's 'royal drawing room' (Queen Victoria's formal receptions) where trains were a part of formal dress. ❑ **tail timber** *n.* [late 19C] lavatory paper. ❑ **tail-trader** *n.* [19C] a prostitute. ❑ **tail-trading** *n.* [mid-15C+] prostitution. ❑ **tail tree** *n.* [mid-18C–19C] the penis. ❑ **tail-wagging** *n.* (*also* **tail-work**) [mid-15C+] sexual intercourse. ❑ **tail water** *n.* [18C] urine. ❑ **tail worker** *n.* [SE *worker*/WORKER *n.*[1] (1)] [19C] a prostitute. ❑ **tale-bearer** *n.* [mid-15C+] a prostitute.

IN PHRASES

❑ **back a tail** *v.* [1960s+] (*Aus.*) to sodomize. ❑ **bit of tail** *n.* [SE *bit* + BIT *n.*[1] (2c)/ TAIL *n.* (8)] [1920s+] a young woman, the vagina, thus sexual intercourse. ❑ **break one's tail** *v. see BUST ONE'S ASS under* BUST *v.*[1]. ❑ **carry one's tail** *v.* [20C+] (*W.I.*) to leave, to run off. ❑ **chew someone's tail** *n. see CHEW (ON) SOMEONE'S ASS under* CHEW *v.* ❑ **cut tail** *v.* [1950s–60s] (*US*) to run away. ❑ **drag one's tail** *v.* **1** [1920s+] (*US*) to mope around, to look miserable. **2** [1950s] to move. ❑ **get one's tail in a crack/trap** *v. see GET ONE'S ASS IN A CRACK under* ASS *n.* ❑ **get on someone's tail** *v. see GET (ON) SOMEONE'S ASS under* ASS *n.* ❑ **get shot in the tail** *v.* [late 17C–early 18C] of a woman, to have sexual intercourse. ❑ **get some tail** *v.* [1970s+] (*US*) of a man, to have sexual intercourse. ❑ **give her a tail** *v.* [1960s+] of a man, to have sexual intercourse. ❑ **go tail-tickling** *v.* (*also* **go tail-twitching**) [late 17C–early 18C] of a man, to have sexual intercourse. ❑ **have a maggot in one's tail** *v.* [late 17C–early 18C] of a woman, to be venereally diseased. ❑ **have one's tail in a crack** *v. see GET ONE'S ASS IN A CRACK under* ASS *n.* ❑ **hoist tail** *v.* [1940s] (*US*) to get going, to set off. ❑ **hot in the tail** *adj.* (*also* **light..., warm...**) [HOT *adj.* (1a)/LIGHT *adj.* (1)/WARM *adj.* (14)] **1** [late 17C–early 18C] wanton, promiscuous. **2** [1930s–50s] (*also* **hot in the pants**) zealous; sexually eager. ❑ **hot-tailed** *adj. see under* HOT *adj.* ❑ **let the tail go with the hide** *v.* (*also* **let the hide go with the tallow**) [butchers'/slaughterhouse jargon; it implies the throwing in of the relatively worthless tail with the valuable hide] [20C+] (*US*) to ignore small details while concentrating on the overall picture. ❑ **on someone's tail** [1930s+] harassing, pursuing. ❑ **play at up-tails all** *v.* [SE *uptails-all*, the name of a song; ult. SE *up* + TAIL *n.* (2)/TAIL *n.* (3)/TAIL *n.* (4) (which are all 'up' during sexual intercourse)] [17C–mid-18C] of a man, to have sexual intercourse. ❑ **put someone's tail in a crack** *v.* [1980s] (*US*) to cause trouble for someone. ❑ **tail out** *v.* [SE *tail*; TAIL *n.* (2), i.e. one 'moves one's arse'] [late 19C] (*US*) to run away, to make one's escape. ❑ **with one's tail on fire** *adj.* [mid-18C] infected with venereal disease.

IN EXCLAMATIONS

❑ **my tail!** [late 17C+] a general excl. of disdain, dismissal, arrogant contempt.

SE in slang uses

IN COMPOUNDS

❑ **taildraft** *n.* [SE *draught/draft*, the act of pulling] [20C+]

(*Ulster*) an idler, one who holds back. ❑ **tail-piece** *n.* [mid-19C] (*UK Und.*) three months' imprisonment. ❑ **tailshred** *v.* ['adapted from fowlyard behaviour involving pecking out tail feathers. 1990s' (McGill, *Dict. N.Z. Slang*, 2003)] [2000s] (*N.Z.*) to drive a car closely (too closely) behind the one in front. ❑ **tail-wagger** *n.* [1940s+] **1** a dog. **2** a general insult [the pej. use of SE *cur*].

IN PHRASES

❑ **get on one's own tail** *v.* **1** [1910s+] (*Aus.*) **2** to become angry. **3** to become scared. ❑ **keep one's tail quiet** *v.* [20C+] (*W.I.*) to stay where one is, to keep quiet, to stay out of trouble. ❑ **tail-end Charlie** *n.* [RAF jargon *tail-end charlie*, a tail-gunner, the last aircraft in a flying formation] [1940s+] the person or vehicle that comes last in a queue.

tail *v.* **1** [late 18C+] to have sexual intercourse with, to work as a prostitute. **2** [20C+] to follow, to keep under (police) surveillance. **3** [1930s] to make the object of a criminal plan.

tailgate *v.* [SAmE *tailgate*, the tailboard of a truck or wagon] **1** [1950s+] to drive a car closely (too closely) behind the one in front. **2** [1970s+] also in fig. use, to follow, esp. of things that are endlessly repetitive. **3** [1990s+] (*US campus*) to watch women passing by.

tailgater *n.* [the hijacker stops the truck, lowers the *tailgate* and removes the load; TAILGATE *v.* (1)] [1960s+] (*US*) **1** a hijacker. **2** one who drives too close to the car in front.

tailie *n.* [SE *tail*, of a coin] [1910s+] (*Aus.*) in the game of two-up, one who favours betting on 'tails'.

tailing *n.* [TAIL *v.* (1)] [late 19C+] sexual intercourse.

tailor *n.* [abbr. TAILOR-MADE *n.* (2)] [1920s+] (*US prison/Aus.*) a factory-made cigarette, whether prison-issue or commercially produced.

SE in slang uses

IN COMPOUNDS

❑ **tailor's helper** *n.* [1930s] (*US tramp*) a vicious dog. ❑ **tailor's ragout** *n.* [? its popularity with tailors; they could not afford a proper meat ragout] [late 18C–early 19C] bread soaked in the dressing in which cucumbers have stood.

tailor *v.* [? snobbish dismissal of 'trade' shooters; or one 'cuts them up'] [late 19C–1900s] to shoot badly at birds so as to wound rather than actually kill them.

tailor-made *n.* **1** [late 19C–1900s] (*US*) a personally tailored garment. **2** [1910s+] (*usu. prison*) (*also* **tailor job**) a factory-produced cigarette.

tailpipe *n.* [SE *tailpipe* + pun on TAIL *n.* (2)] [1990s+] (*US*) the anus.

tail-pipe *v.* [1970s] (*US*) to follow closely.

tails *n.* [abbr.; note TAIL *n.* (1b)] [late 19C+] a formal *tail*coat; thus *white tie and tails*.

t'aint *n.* (*also* **taint, taintmeat, tent**) [i.e. *t'aint pussy and t'aint asshole*] [1970s+] (*orig. US*) the perineum, the space between the vagina and the anus.

taipo *n.* (*also* **taepo**) [? Maori *taepo*, the devil, but ? pidgin rom Maori pron. of SE *devil*] [mid-19C+] (*N.Z.*) a vicious horse, often used as the name for a dog.

taj *adj.* [proper name *Taj Mahal*, synon. with fabulous luxury] [late 19C–1910s] (*UK teen*) excellent, wonderful, luscious.

take *n.* **1** [late 19C+] money acquired by theft or fraud. **2** [1930s+] (*US*) a share of money that is deducted for tax or some other form of levy. **3** [1930s+] (*US*) a portion, an extract, a bit. **4** [1930s+] (*US*) profits, e.g. the entrance money taken at a musical, sporting or gambling event. **5** [1930s+] (*orig. US*) bribery. **6** [1930s+] (*Aus.*) a thief, a villain, esp. a cheat at cards. **7** [1930s+] (*Aus.*) a swindle. **8** [1930s+] (*Aus./US*) a theft; a robbery. **9** [1990s+] wages.

IN COMPOUNDS

❑ **take-artist** *n.* [-ARTIST *sfx*] [1950s] (*US*) one who regularly gains income from the taking of bribes, illicit 'commissions' etc.

IN PHRASES

❑ **on the take** [1930s+] of an official, typically a politician or police officer, accepting bribes.

take *v.* **1** [mid-19C+] to swindle, to cheat, to extort money from, often ext. as TAKE SOMEONE FOR below. **2** [late 19C+] to overcome, to defeat, to kill. **3** [1920s+] to accept bribery. **4** [1920s+] to break in, to rob. **5** [1920s+] to confront, to attack.

IN COMPOUNDS

❑ **take man** *n.* [1970s] (*Aus. Und.*) in a shoplifting team, the member who actually steals the targeted object.

IN PHRASES

❑ **take it** *v.* [1920s] (*US Und.*) to accept a bribe. ❑ **take someone for** *v.* [1930s+] to trick, to deceive, to obtain from one who is unwilling otherwise to give, esp. in the extraction of money, e.g. *I took him for a tenner.*

SE in slang uses

IN PHRASES

❑ **don't take me there** [1990s+] (*US teen*) I am not interested, I don't want to hear it. ❑ **take...** *v. see also under* relevant n. or adj. ❑ **take a course with** *v.* [early 17C–early 19C] **1** to cause problems for, to interfere with. **2** to follow closely. ❑ **take a flourish** *v.* [late 18C–early 19C] to have swift and spontaneous sexual intercourse, usu. when both parties are wholly or partially dressed. ❑ **take a leap at Tyburn** *v. see under* TYBURN *n.* ❑ **take a leap in the dark** *v.* [note T. Brown (1702): 'A brother player, who pretends he received all his memoirs from your own mouth, a little before you made a leap into the dark', where the phr. simply means 'to die'] [17C–early 18C] to be hanged. ❑ **take an application** *v.* (*also* **take a test drive**) [1960s–80s] (*US*) to interview a woman as a prospective prostitute. ❑ **take an oath** *v.* (*also* **take the oath**) [late 19C–1900s] to have a drink. ❑ **take a turn among her frills** *v.* (*also* **...up her petticoats**) [19C] to have sexual intercourse. ❑ **take a turn on one's back** *v.* [19C] to have sexual intercourse. ❑ **take into the woodshed** *v.* [the practice of taking an errant child into the woodshed for a thrashing] [20C+] (*US*) to scold, to punish. ❑ **take low** *v.* [late 19C+] (*W.I./US black*) to adopt a humble attitude in order to forward one's aims. ❑ **take one's degrees** *v.* [play on ACADEMY *n.* (4)] [early–mid-19C] to be imprisoned, to serve a sentence. ❑ **take one's end** *v.* [SE *end*, death, i.e. 'to laugh oneself to death'] [20C+] (*Irish*) to be convulsed with laughter. ❑ **take outdoors on someone** *v.* [1930s] to leave alone, to avoid someone. ❑ **take over the hurdles** *v.* [horseracing imagery] [1940s–50s] (*US prison*) to attack in a group. ❑ **take (someone) apart** *v.* **1** [20C+] to beat severely. **2** [1950s] to reprimand someone. ❑ **take someone out of winding** *v.* [SE *wind*, breath] [1920s+] (*Aus.*) to silence someone, to leave someone 'at a loss for words'. ❑ **take someone's pulse** *v.* [1970s] (*gay*) to fondle someone's genitals. ❑ **take the burnt chops** *v.* [the campfire meals musterers eat] [late 19C–1940s] (*N.Z.*) to take up work as a musterer or drover. ❑ **take the cure** *v.* [SE *take the cure*, to withdraw from alcohol/drug addiction] [20C+] (*US*) to give up something or refrain from doing something. ❑ **take the electric cure** *v.* [1920s] (*US prison/Und.*) to be executed in the electric chair. ❑ **take the dairy off** *v.* [corruption of SE *direction*, i.e. redirect attention] [1910s+] to divert suspicion. ❑ **take the Michael** *v. see* EXTRACT THE MICHAEL *v.* ❑ **take the scenic route** *v.* [1960s+] (*orig. US teen*) **1** to concentrate on pleasure at the expense of efficiency or speed. **2** to do things 'the hard way'. ❑ **take the veil** *v.* [1940s–70s] (*US gay*) to abandon the homosexual lifestyle. ❑ **take to the fair** *v.* [the excitements of a *fair*] [1940s+] (*Irish*) to amaze, to astonish; thus *take things to the fair*, to exaggerate. ❑ **what it takes** *n.* [the centrality of money to daily life] [1920s–30s] (*orig. US*) money.

IN EXCLAMATIONS

❑ **take it!** [1930s–60s] (*gay*) an excl. used by one demanding fellatio.

take a fright *n.* [rhy. sl.] [mid–late 19C] the night.

take and give *v.* [rhy. sl.] [late 19C–1900s] to live, esp. as man and wife.

take care of *v.* [euphs.] **1** [late 19C–1910s] to arrest. **2** [20C+] to beat up; to kill. **3** [1920s+] to bribe; to exert (political) pressure on. **4** [1940s+] to have sexual intercourse with. **5** [1950s+] to cause trouble for. **6** [1970s] to pay, to give a tip.

take-care-of-business *adj.* [TAKE CARE OF BUSINESS v.] [1970s] efficient.

take care of business *v.* (*also* **t.c.b.**) [1950s+] (*orig. US black*) to deal efficiently with matters in hand; to have sexual intercourse.

take care of number one *v.* (*also* **take care of numero uno**) [NUMBER ONE *n.* (1)] [mid-19C+] to put oneself first, no matter what the situation.

take-down *n.* [TAKE DOWN v. (3)] [late 19C–1930s] **1** a swindle, a deception. **2** a deceiver, a swindler, a cheat. **3** (*US*) a win, e.g. in gambling.

take down *v.* **1** [17C] to abuse. **2** [mid-18C+] to challenge, to overcome, to surpass; to kill. **3** [mid-19C+] (*orig. Aus.*) to cheat, to swindle, to rob. **4** [late 19C+] to destroy, to dispose of. **5** [1940s+] (*US Und./police*) to arrest. **6** [1960s] (*US prison*) to have homosexual sexual intercourse.

(IN PHRASES)

❑ **take someone down (a buttonhole)** *v.* (*also* **let someone down a buttonhole, take someone a buttonhole lower**) [the image of humiliating someone by undressing them in public] [late 16C–1920s] to humiliate someone, to deflate someone.

take-in *n.* [TAKE IN v. (2)] **1** [late 18C–1920s] a hoax, a swindle. **2** [early 19C] a swindler.

take-in *adj.* [TAKE-IN *n.* (1)] [early 19C] deceptive, swindling.

take in *v.* **1** [late 17C–early 18C] to take hold of someone in order to rob them. **2** [mid-18C+] to hoax, to cheat, to deceive. **3** [late 19C+] (*US*) to arrest.

SE in slang uses

(IN PHRASES)

❑ **take in and do for** *v.* [pun on the same phr. used in lodging house advertisements, 'Single men taken in and done for', note DO v.[1] (1a)] [19C] of women, to have sexual intercourse.

take it *v.* [1910s+] to have sexual intercourse.

(IN PHRASES)

❑ **take it any way** *v.* [1930s–40s] (*gay*) to enjoy fellatio.

SE in slang uses

(IN PHRASES)

❑ **take it easy** [SE colloq. v. *take it easy*, to relax] **1** [mid-19C+] as imper.: a phr. meaning relax, don't worry, calm down, be careful. **2** [1950s+] (*US*) a phr. meaning goodbye, see you later. ❑ **take it from the head** *v.* [the gunshot to the head] [1990s+] (*US gang*) to be murdered. ❑ **take it from the top** *v.* [jazz use, i.e. *the top* of the score] [1930s+] (*US*) to start at the beginning. ❑ **take it in the blind** *v.* [i.e. no one else is aware of the activity] [20C+] (*US prison*) to fight in private to settle a score. ❑ **take it light** *v.* [var. on SE colloq. v. *take it easy*, to relax] [1960s+] (*US black*) to act in a restrained manner, to resist excess, to go slowly. ❑ **take it on one's toes** *v.* see HAVE IT AWAY v. ❑ **take it on the run** *v.* [1900s–30s] (*US*) to run away. ❑ **take it out** *v.* [late 19C+] (*Aus.*) to serve a prison term rather than pay a fine. ❑ **take it slow** [1930s+] (*orig. US black*) **1** goodbye, see you later. **2** calm down, quieten down, relax. **3** be careful.

take it! *excl. see under* TAKE V.

take it on the Arthur Duffy *v.* (*also* **...the Dan O'Leary, ...the Jesse Owens**) [proper name *Arthur F. Duffy*, (US world record-holder of the 100-yard (100m) dash (1902–5); *Jesse Owens*, (1913–80) winner of four Olympic gold medals, 1930s; *Dan O'Leary* 'the champion long distance walker of the world' fl. 1900s] [1900s–50s] (*US*) to run, run off, to escape.

taken short *adv. see* CAUGHT SHORT *adj.* (1).

take-off *n.*[1] [1940s] (*US black*) the hips.

take-off *n.*[2] [TAKE OFF v.[2] (1)] [1940s–50s] (*US prison*) an escape.

take-off *n.*[3] [TAKE OFF v.[1] (4)] [1940s+] (*US Und.*) an armed street robbery or mugging.

(IN COMPOUNDS)

❑ **take-off artist** *n.* [ARTIST *n.* (1)] [1940s+] (*US Und.*) a robber, rapist or killer.

take off *v.*[1] [SE *take off*, to remove] (*US black/Und.*) **1** [mid–late 19C] to execute. **2** [late 19C–1900s] to deprive of money. **3** [late 19C+] to hurt, to kill. **4** [20C+] to rob. **5** [1960s+] to obtain, e.g. money. **6** [1970s] to make a raid on.

SE in slang uses

(IN PHRASES)

❑ **take someone off the calendar** *v.* [1980s] (*US*) to kill, to murder. ❑ **take someone off the count** *v.* [milit./prison imagery: to remove from the roster of personnel or inmates] [1980s] to murder, to kill.

take off *v.*[2] [the sl. use derives immediately from aircraft imagery, but *take off*, to go off, to start off, to run away, has been SE since early 19C] **1** [20C+] to die. **2** [1940s] (*US black*) to start talking. **3** [1940s+] in drug uses [i.e. to get HIGH *adj.*[1] (2)]. (**a**) to take narcotics. (**b**) to feel the effects of a drug. **4** [1950s–60s] to go to, to visit.

(IN PHRASES)

❑ **take off like a big-assed bird** *v.* (*also* **...like a bat out of hell, ...like a cut cat**) [sense 1 above + SE + -ARSED *sfx*] [1940s+] (*US*) to leave very quickly.

take off *v.*[3] [1960s] (*US black*) to engage in sexual behaviour.

take-on *n.* [TAKE ON v. (2)] [1920s+] (*Aus.*) a fight, usu. with the fists.

take on *v.* **1** [1910s+] (*US police*) to stop and search. **2** [1930s+] (*US*) to have sexual intercourse with.

take out *v.* [abbr. SE *take out of the picture*] **1** [late 19C+] to knock out. **2** [1930s+] (*orig. US*) to kill, to destroy (a specific target).

(IN COMPOUNDS)

❑ **take-out guy** *n.* [1950s+] (*US Und.*) the man in a crooked card-game who always wins and as such attracts attention away from the real cheat who is manipulating all winning and losing cards.

(IN PHRASES)

❑ **take oneself out** *v.* [1960s+] (*US*) to commit suicide.

taker *n.* **1** [mid-16C–18C] (*also* **taker-up**) the member of a criminal gang who keeps watch or entices a victim into a crooked gambling game; spec. part of a *barnard's law* team *see under* BARNARD *n.* **2** [mid-19C+] (*US*) a person who accepts an offer or challenge. **3** [1940s+] (*UK Und.*) a receiver of stolen goods. **4** [1950s+] (*US gay/prison*) a passive prison homosexual.

take the cake *v.* (*also* **capture the crumb, cop the cake, take the baker's shop, ...the bakery, ...the beer, ...the duff, ...the gingerbread, ...the pastry**) [the perceived 'tastiness' of the *cake*] **1** [mid-19C+] to surpass, to outdo, esp. in excessive or extreme behaviour or of a near-intolerable situation or happening. **2** [1960s+] to be highly improbable.

take the mickey (out of) *v.* (*also* **take a mike, take the mick, ...the mic-mac, ...the mike (out of)**) [the assumed ety. is rhy. sl.: *take the mickey bliss* = TAKE THE PISS (OUT OF) *under* PISS *n.*; however, note that citations for the non-rhyming *take a/the mike* exist from 1920s, while those for *take the mickey* begin only in mid-1950s] [1920s+] to tease; thus *mickey-take, mickey-taking*.

take to *v.* [abbr. SE *take one's fists to*] [20C+] (*Aus./N.Z.*) to attack, usu. with the fists.

take up *v.* (*also* **tuck up**) [early 18C+] to arrest.

take your pick *adj.* [rhy. sl. = THICK *adj.*] [1990s+] stupid, foolish.

Taki-Taki *n.* [i.e. 'talky-talky'] [20C+] (*W.I.*) Sranan, the Surinamese Creole language.

takkie *n.* (*also* **tackie**) [SE *tacky*, sticky] [1910s+] (*S.Afr.*) a rubber-soled, laced canvas shoe.

(IN PHRASES)

❑ **piece of (old) takkie** *n.* [1970s] something easy.

talcum queen *n.* [SE *talcum* (*powder*, usu. white) + -QUEEN *sfx*] [1980s+] (*US black*) a black homosexual who prefers white partners.

tale *n.*[1] **1** [20C+] any form of words designed to ensnare the listener for commercial purposes, e.g. the story told by a confidence trickster to ensnare the victim. **2** [20C+] a womanizer's 'line'. **3** [1940s] (*UK Und.*) a specific con where someone is persuaded to pay the con-man, who is posing as a bookmaker, for a lost bet that he did not ask to be made.

IN COMPOUNDS

❑ **tale-pitcher** *n.* [thus the popular nickname of the racing journalist, raconteur and bon viveur Arthur Binstead (1861–1914), 'The Pitcher', best known to the readers of the *Sporting Times*] [late 19C–1900s] one who tells a good story, a romantic. ❑ **tale-teller** *n.* [1940s] (*UK Und.*) a confidence trickster.

IN PHRASES

❑ **ain't got no tale** *v.* (*also* **have no tale**) [1940s] (*US black campus*) to feel bad. ❑ **cop the tale** *v.* [20C+] to be fooled by a confidence trickster. ❑ **pitch a tale** *v. see* PITCH A YARN *under* YARN *n.* ❑ **tell the tale** *v.* [ext. use of SE] [20C+] **1** to deceive, to hoax, to cheat through verbal dexterity. **2** to engage in amorous talk. **3** to tell a story designed to elicit a loan or a monetary gift. **4** to tell any kind of unbelievable or pathetic story. ❑ **what's your tale?** (*also* **what's your jive?, what's your lick?**) [SE *tale*/JIVE *n.*[1] (3)/LICK *n.*[2] (8)] [1940s] (*US black campus*) a greeting, how are you?

tale *n.*[2] **1** *see* TAIL *n.* (4). **2** *see* TAIL *n.* (5).

tale *n.*[3] *see* TOL *n.*[1].

talent *n.* **1** [mid-19C+] attractive young women, esp. those standing around at a party, in a club or dancehall etc. **2** [late 19C–1940s] (*Aus.*) a LARRIKIN *n.* (1). **3** [late 19C–1960s] (*orig. Aus.*) a generic term for the criminal underworld. **4** [1950s+] attractive young men. **5** [1960s+] in police terms, a suspect.

IN COMPOUNDS

❑ **talent scout** *n.* [mid-19C+] a pimp.

tale of two cities *n.* [rhy. sl. = *titties* (TITTY *n.* (1))] [1950s–70s] the female breasts.

talk *n.* [late 19C+] a seducer's 'line' of conversation; nonsense.

IN PHRASES

❑ **talk that talk** *v.* [1930s+] (*US black*) **1** to chatter inconsequentially; to make empty promises. **2** to indulge in ritual name-calling, esp. based on insulting one's opponent's mother. ❑ **talk that talk and walk that walk** [1960s+] (*US black*) a phr. of encouragement for one's verbal skills.

talk *v.* **1** [1920s+] (*UK Und.*) to confess or turn informer to the police or similar authority. **2** [1990s+] (*US campus*) to have a relationship with someone.

SE in slang uses

IN COMPOUNDS

❑ **talk doctor** *n.* [1990s+] (*US*) a psychoanalyst, a psychotherapist. ❑ **talk trap** *n.* [TRAP *n.*[1] (4)] [20C+] (*US*) the mouth.

IN PHRASES

❑ **all talk and no cider** [supposedly orig. at a party in Buck County, PA, which had been arranged to enjoy a particularly good barrel of cider; a political argument began and emotions became so heated that half the guests left, claiming that the 'party' had been merely an excuse to wrangle, rather than drink] [19C] (*US*) all theory and no practice, all proposals and no concrete results. ❑ **it's the beer talking** (*also* **beer's talking, booze talking, drink's talking, grog talking, liquor's talking, whisky's talking**) [20C+] an excuse for any excessive talk or actions when drunk, either at the time or when sober on reflection; thus *beer/whisky talk*, such talk itself. ❑ **now you're talking** [late 19C+] a phr. stating that the speaker is (finally) dealing with pertinent topics or talking to some purpose. ❑ **talk...** *v. see also under* relevant n. or adj. ❑ **talk braille** *v.* [2000s] (*N.Z.*) to be drunk. ❑ **talk crisp** *v.* [note SE *talk sharply*] [1910s–20s] to say unpleasant things. ❑ **talking to Jamie Moore** *adj.* [? anecdotal] [late 19C–1930s] (*Scot.*) drunk. ❑ **talk like pound notes** *v.* [1950s] to talk in an affected, supposedly 'classy' manner. ❑ **talk one's head off** *v.* (*also* **gab one's head off, gas one's head off, talk one's ass off, talk one's leg off, talk the leg off an iron pot**) [SE *talk*/GAS *v.*[1] (1)] [1910s+] (*orig. US*) to talk incessantly. ❑ **talk one's mouth off** *v. see* SHOOT ONE'S MOUTH OFF *under* SHOOT *v.* ❑ **talk out of school** *v.* [20C+] to tell tales, to talk unguardedly. ❑ **talk out of one's head** *v.* (*also* **...one's hat**) [var. on SE *talk out of one's hat*] [20C+] (*US black*) to talk nonsense. ❑ **talk out of the other side of one's mouth** *v.* [mid-19C+] to change one's mind, to contradict an earlier statement. ❑ **talk out of the wrong end** *v.* [euph. for *TALK OUT OF ONE'S ARSEHOLE under* ARSEHOLE *n.*] [1990s+] to talk nonsense. ❑ **talk packthread** *v.* ['to use indecent language, well wrapt up' (Grose 1796). SE *packthread*, heavyweight cord or twine used for tying bundles] [late 18C–early 19C] to talk in double entendres. ❑ **talk pretty** *v.* (*also* **speak pretty**) [late 19C–1910s] (*mainly Aus.*) to speak in an affectionate, friendly manner. ❑ **talk sideways** *v.* [1910s+] (*US prison*) to talk disrespectfully, to talk 'clever'. ❑ **talk someone down** *v.* [the comforter brings them down from the 'high' and back to normality] [1960s+] (*drugs*) to comfort a person who is having a bad experience, usu. after taking drugs, esp. LSD. ❑ **talk someone's ear off** *v.* [1930s] (*orig. US*) to talk incessantly at someone. ❑ **talk someone's head off** *v.* (*also* **jaw someone's head off**) [SE *talk*/JAW *v.*[1] (1); ext. of prev., but also note *TALK ONE'S HEAD OFF* above] [1920s+] (*orig. US*) to talk incessantly at someone. ❑ **talk thirty bob to the pound** *v.* [var. on FORTY TO THE DOZEN *adv.*] [1950s] to talk very fast and unintelligibly. ❑ **talk through one's socks** *v.* [1900s] (*Aus.*) to talk nonsense. ❑ **talk through the top of one's skull** *v.* [1950s] to talk nonsense. ❑ **talk to the canoe-driver** *v.* [play on SE *canoe/cunnilingus* + play on LITTLE MAN (IN THE BOAT) *n.*] [1960s+] (*US*) to perform cunnilingus. ❑ **talk up a breeze** *v.* [var. on *TALK UP A STORM* below] [1940s+] to talk in a fluent, persuasive manner. ❑ **talk up a storm** *v.* (*also* **beg up a storm**) [1940s+] (*US*) to talk loudly, at length and impressively. ❑ **talk up at the big gate** *v.* [1950s] (*US black*) to threaten to leave.

talk-down *n.* [*talk someone down* under TALK *v.*] [1960s+] the comforting of someone who is having a bad experience, usu. through injudicious use of drugs, esp. a hallucinogen.

talkee-talkee *n.* [fake pidgin, to underpin the image of empty chatter] **1** [early 19C–1900s] chatter, conversation. **2** [late 19C] a talkative person.

talkfest *n. see* BLABFEST *under* BLAB *n.*

talking *n.* [euph.] **1** [1950s+] (*US black/campus*) being involved in a relationship, dating. **2** [1960s+] a use of SE *talking* with the word 'about' unstated, implying not so much person-to-person communication, but as a way of emphasizing the importance and immediacy of the topic in hand, e.g. *we're talking telephone numbers*, this will be a very large sum of money [originated in Hollywood where hyperbole is dominant, the implication is often one of slight reproof, i.e. don't forget, we are not discussing any old topic, sum of money etc but something quite exceptional or startling]. **3** [1970s+] (*lesbian*) having a relationship with another woman while in prison.

talking iron *n. see* SHOOTING IRON *n.* (1).

talkorexia *n.* [SE *talk* + -OREXIA *sfx*] [1980s+] (*US campus*) a state of talking incessantly (and thus irritating others).

talk to *v.* [note TALKING *n.* (1)] [1990s+] (*US campus*) to date.

SE in slang uses

IN PHRASES

❑ **talk to the engineer, not the oily rag** *v.* (*also* **talk to the butcher, not the block**) [1940s+] to deal with the boss, not an assistant. ❑ **talk to the hand** *v.* [1990s+] (*US teen*) a dismissive phrase: 'don't waste my time'; often ext. with *because the face don't understand* or other vars. ❑ **talk to the mike** *v.* [SE *microphone*] [1980s+] (*US teen*) to perform fellatio.

talky *adj.* [late 19C–1900s] (*US*) chatty, verbose; self-opinionated.

talky-talk *n.* (*also* **talky-talky**) [late 19C+] idle, futile, empty talk; thus adj. *talky-talky*.

talky-talky boots *n.* [late 19C] (*W.I.*) squeaky shoes or boots.

tall *adj.* **1** [mid-17C–19C] of speech, boastful, high-flown. **2** [mid-19C] of speech, intense, melodramatic. **3** [mid-19C] of dress or appearance, flashy. **4** in senses of quantity, measure. (**a**) [mid-19C] (*UK Und.*) well-supplied. (**b**) [mid-19C] (*UK Und.*) many, numerous. (**c**) [mid-19C+] (*orig. US*) large, esp. in quantity, eg of money; also in phr. *tall order* under ORDER *n.* (**d**) [mid-19C+] serious, substantial; usu. in comb. with a v., such as *tall drinking* or *tall weeping*. **5** [mid-19C+] of speech, extravagant, untrue; esp. in phr. TALL STORY below. **6** [mid-19C+] (*orig. US*) excellent in quality; thus *tallest*, the best. **7** in senses of intoxication [play on HIGH *adj.*[1] (1)]. (**a**) [mid-19C+] (*orig. UK Und.*) drunk [20C+ use of is US black]. (**b**) [1930s–60s] (*US drugs*) intoxicated by marijuana.

IN COMPOUNDS

❑ **tall money** *n.* [1940s+] (*US black*) a large amount of money, substantial wealth. ❑ **tall story** *n.* (*also* **tall tale**) [mid-19C+] an extravagant, boastful story, a lie. ❑ **tall talk** *n.* [mid-19C+] (*orig. US*) boasting, bragging, the telling of far-fetched stories and anecdotes. ❑ **tall talker** *n.* [mid–late 19C] a braggart, a boaster. ❑ **tall timbers** *n. see* separate entry.

SE in slang uses

IN COMPOUNDS

❑ **tall boy** *n.* **1** [late 17C–early 19C] (*also* **tallen**) a large wine glass. **2** [late 17C–early 19C] a 3-litre (2-quart) pot filled with wine. **3** [1970s+] (*US*) a tall glass or can of beer. ❑ **tall cotton** *n. see* HIGH COTTON *n.* ❑ **tall order** *n. see under* ORDER *n.* ❑ **tall paper** *n. see* BIG PAPER *under* PAPER *n.* ❑ **tall poppy** *n.* [1930s+] (*Aus./N.Z.*) a conspicuously high earner or other VIP. ❑ **tall 'un** *n.* [late 19C–1900s] a pint of coffee.

tallawah *adj.* [synon. Ewe *talala*] [1950s+] (*W.I.*) **1** honest, honourable, decent. **2** sturdy, fearless, physically capable.

talley-wagger *n. see* TALLYWHACKER *n.*

tallie *n.* [TALL *adj.* (5)] [1930s+] (*Aus.*) an extravagant boastful story.

tallow *n.* [resemblance] [19C] semen.

IN PHRASES

❑ **tallow up one's pole** *v.* [the image is of a saddle that becomes dried out with inactivity and needs rubbing with tallow soap, in this case sense 1 above] [19C–1950s] to have sexual intercourse, esp. after a period of abstinence.

SE in slang uses

IN COMPOUNDS

❑ **tallow-breeched** *adj.* [18C–19C] having fat buttocks. ❑ **tallow-gutted** *adj.* [18C–19C] pot-bellied. ❑ **tallow pot** *n.* [1910s–40s] (*US tramp/railroad*) a locomotive fire man.

tall timbers *n.* (*also* **tall pines, tall timber**) **1** [mid-19C+] (*US*) the rural areas, the backwoods, lit. and fig. **2** [1920s] (*US*) the gallows.

IN PHRASES

❑ **take to the tall timber(s)** *v.* (*also* **break for tall timber, put for…, pull for…, strike for…**) [mid-19C+] to run off.

tally *n.*[1]

IN PHRASES

❑ **live tally** *v.* [SE *tally*, one of two corresponding parts; compare earlier TALLY-HUSBAND *n.*] [mid-19C+] (*mainly north*) to cohabit, to live as man and wife without an actual marriage; thus *tally-ho*, living in this manner.

tally *n.*[2] [abbr.] [1950s+] an Italian; also as adj.

tally-boy *n. see* TARRY-BOY *n.*

tally ho *n.*[1] [SE excl. *tally ho!*, esp. in foxhunting] [20C+] (*Irish*) confusion, fuss.

tally ho *n.*[2] [2000s] (*US prison*) rubber cement found in prison shoes, used as an inhalant.

tally-husband *n.* (*also* **tally-man**) [LIVE TALLY *under* TALLY *n.*[1] although this seems to predate it; cf. TALLY-WIFE *n.*] [late 17C–19C] the man with whom a woman cohabits.

tallywag *n.* (*also* **tallywock, tollewag, tooleywag**) [TALLYWAGS *n.*] [late 18C–19C] the penis.

tallywagger *n. see* TALLYWHACKER *n.*

tallywags *n.* (*also* **tarrywags**) [? SE *tally*, a notched stick or TAIL *n.* (3)] [late 17C–early 19C] the testicles; the male genitals.

tally water *n.* [2000s] (*US prison*) an intoxicant that is inhaled.

tallywhacker *n.* (*also* **talley-wagger, tallywagger, tillywhacker**) [later ext. of TALLYWAG *n.*] [20C+] the penis.

tally-wife *n.* (*also* **tally-woman**) [LIVE TALLY *under* TALLY *n.*[1] although this seems to predate it; cf. TALLY-HUSBAND *n.*] [early 18C–19C] the woman with whom a man cohabits.

tallywock *n. see* TALLYWAG *n.*

t.a.l.o.i.a. *phr.* [abbr.] [1950s+] there's *a*lot *o*f *i*t *a*bout.

tam *n.* [abbr. SE *tam o'shanter*] **1** [1930s+] (*US, latterly gay*) any form of hat. **2** [1950s+] (*W.I. Rasta*) the large woollen hat used by Rastafarians to cover their dreadlocks.

tamale *n.* [Sp. *tamale*, a Mexican dish consisting of corn husks wrapped around a variety of fillings] **1** [1960s+] (*US gay*) gaudy ceramic crockery typical of that sold to tourists in Mexico. **2** *see* HOT TAMALE *n.*

IN COMPOUNDS

❑ **tamale-eater** *n.* [used adj. to denote alleged Mexican stereotypes] [1900s] (*US*) a Mexican.

Tamaleville *n. see* TACO TOWN *under* TACO *n.*

tamarind *n.* [mid-19C] (*UK Und.*) a woman's watch.

Tambaroora *n.* [*Tambaroora*, a town in New South Wales, home of the game] [late 19C–1940s] (*Aus.*) a bar game in which the winner buys drinks for the players.

IN COMPOUNDS

❑ **Tambaroora muster** *n.* [late 19C–1940s] (*Aus.*) a group of drinkers pooling their money and buying one 'wholesale' round, since in this way more alcohol can be purchased.

tambourine man *n.* [? the Bob Dylan song 'Mr Tambourine Man' (1964)] [1960s+] (*US drugs*) a drug dealer.

tame the shrew *v. see* TAME THE BEEF WEASEL *under* BEEF *n.*[1].

tamp *v.* [SE *tamp*, to ram down hard] **1** [1920s–60s] (*US Und.*) to beat up. **2** [1940s+] (*US black*) to walk, to go. **3** [1940s+] (*US black*) to pump, to fill.

IN PHRASES

❑ **tamp someone up** *v.* [1920s–60s] (*US*) to beat someone up.

tampax *n.* [*Tampax*, a proprietory brand of tampons] [1990s+] (*UK juv.*) a general term of abuse.

tamp braces *n. see* TAMPON BRACES *n.*

tampi *n.* [ety. unknown] [1970s+] marijuana.

tamping *n.* [*tamp someone up* under TAMP *v.*] [1960s] (*US prison*) a beating.

tampon *n.*[1] [they are both 'stuck up'] [2000s] a snobbish person.

tampon *n.*[2] [2000s] (*S.Afr.*) a doctor.

tampon braces *n.* (*also* **tamp braces**) [1930s–40s] (*US black*) a derog. term for unattractive legs on a woman.

tamtaffeta *n.* [mid-19C] (*UK Und.*) stolen goods.

ta muchly! *excl.* (*also* **ta fearfully!**) [late 19C+] thank you very much!

Tan *n.* [*Black and Tans*, pro-Ulster Protestants] [2000s] (*Irish*) an English person.

t.a.n. *adj.* [abbr. *t*ough *a*s *n*ails] [1980s+] (*US campus*) aggressively masculine.

tan *v.*[1] [SE *tan*, to process skins into leather] **1** [17C+] to hit, to attack; thus *tanning*, a beating; usu. in phr. TAN SOMEONE'S HIDE *under* HIDE *n.* **2** [1970s+] (*also* **tan it**) used fig. meaning to do something aggressively or to extreme, e.g. *tan the bevvy*, to drink heavily.

tan *v.*[2]

W.I. pron. of SE *stand*, in slang uses

IN PHRASES

❑ **tan pon it long** *n.* [lit. 'stand up on it for a long time'] [1980s+] (*W.I./UK black teen*) sexual stamina. ❑ **tan so back** [lit. 'stand back'] [1990s+] (*W.I.*) calm down, stop being aggressive. ❑ **tan-study** [lit. 'stand steady'] [1990s+] (*W.I.*) calm down, relax.

tancy lee *n. see* NANCY LEE *n.* (2).

tand *n.* [? fig. use of Du. *tand*, a tooth, thus the chewing of the tough food] [2000s] (*S.Afr. prison*) food, prison rations.

T & A *n. see under* TITS AND ASS.

tang *n.*[1] [SE *tangy*] [1960s] (*US*) the vagina.

tang *n.*[2] [SE *tang*, a flavour; such a person gives the situation an 'unpleasant flavour'] [1970s+] (*US campus*) someone who puts a damper on things.

tangerines *n.* [shape] [1930s] (*US*) the buttocks.

tangi *n.* [Maori *tangi*, a tribal gathering at a funeral] [20C+] (*N.Z.*) a party or wake, involving (heavy) drinking.

IN PHRASES

❑ **hold a tangi** *v.* [20C+] (*N.Z.*) to dispute. ❑ **on the tangi** [20C+] (*N.Z.*) celebrating.

Tangier *n.* [the sufferings imposed on the victims of the contemporary Tangiers pirates] [18C–19C] a room in Newgate gaol, dedicated to the imprisonment of debtors, who were known as *tangerines*.

tangle *n.* [its effects] [late 19C–1900s] (*Aus.*) alcoholic liquor.

tangle *v.* [TANGLE *n.*] [mid–late 19C] to add alcohol to a drink.

IN COMPOUNDS

❑ **tangle-monger** *n.* [SE *tangle*, a knotted mess + -MONGER *sfx*] [late 19C] (*UK society*) a woman scandalmonger.

IN PHRASES

❑ **tangle assholes** *v.* (*also* **tangle-ass, tangle holes**) [ASSHOLE *n.*/ASS *n.* (2)/HOLE *n.*[1] (1a)] [1920s+] (*US*) to fight. ❑ **tangle with** *v.* **1** [1910s+] to fight with; lit. or fig. **2** [1940s+] (*also* **tangle up with**) to become involved with. **3** [1970s] to meet.

tangled *adj.* [TANGLE *n.*] [late 19C–1910s] (*Aus.*) drunk.

tangle-foot *n.* (*also* **tanglehoof**) [its effects] **1** [mid-19C–1930s] whisky. **2** [1910s–50s] (*Aus.*) second-rate liquor; occas. beer.

DERIVATIVES

❑ **tangle-footed** *adj.* [mid-19C–1940s] drunk.

tangle-leg *n.* [its effects] [mid-19C–1900s] whisky.

DERIVATIVES

❑ **tangle-legged** *adj.* [mid-19C] drunk.

tangler *n.* [SE *tangle*, a mess] [1940s] a small-time crook who deals in smuggled or stolen property.

tango & cash *n.* [film title *Tango & Cash*, 1989; ? rhy. sl. = HASH *n.*[2]] [1980s+] (*drugs*) fentanyl.

tango pirate *n.* (*also* **tango-lizard**) [such men took advantage of the tango craze of the early 20C to meet, seduce and even live off the affluent women they met at tea-dances] [20C+] (*US*) a gigolo.

tang out *v.* [TANG *n.*[2]] [1970s+] (*US campus*) to abandon, to put an end to.

tank *n.*[1] [TANK (UP) *v.*] **1** [late 19C–1940s] (*also* **beer-tank**) a drinker, a drunkard. **2** [1930s–50s] (*Aus./US*) a pint of beer [? influenced by SE *tankard*].

IN PHRASES

❑ **daddy tank** *n.* [DADDY *n.* (14)] [1970s+] (*US Und.*) an area set aside to provide protective custody for effeminate homosexuals. ❑ **drunk tank** *n.* [1940s+] (*Can./US*) a short-term lock-up for a night's drunk arrests before sending them to court. ❑ **go in the tank** *v.* (*also* **go in the water**) [fig. use of boxing jargon *go in the tank*, to lose a fight deliberately; ult. SE *tank*, a swimming pool, thus synon. with *TAKE A DIVE under* DIVE *n.*[1]] [1910s+] **1** to surrender, to give up, esp. when such a surrender is by no means necessary. **2** to collapse, to go badly wrong. ❑ **in the tank** *adj.* [SE *tank*, a swimming pool; one is 'sodden' with liquor] [1970s+] drunk.

SE in slang uses

IN PHRASES

❑ **get one's tank filled** *v.* [late 19C] (*US*) to become drunk. ❑ **wash one's foot in the tank** *v.* [1940s] (*US black*) to drive a car very fast.

tank *n.*[2] [SE *tank*, a storage receptacle] **1** [late 19C+] (*Aus./US prison*) a cell. **2** [1910s+] (*Can./US prison*) (*also* **drunk tank**) a holding cell. **3** [1910s+] (*Aus./N.Z. Und.*) a safe. **4** [1950s+] (*Can./US prison*) a prison, a prison wing. **5** [1960s] an isolation cell. **6** [1970s+] a bank. **7** [2000s] money. **8** see TANK TOWN *n.*

IN COMPOUNDS

❑ **tank artist** *n.* (*also* **tankblower, tankman**) [1910s+] (*Aus./N.Z. Und.*) a safe-cracker.

tank *n.*[3] [the then newly invented SE *tank*, a bulky and misshapen form of weapon] **1** [1910s+] a worn-out old prostitute. **2** [1930s–40s] (*US Und.*) a bulletproof car. **3** [1960s–70s] (*US campus*) an unattractive female.

tank *v.*[1] [SE *tank*, a swimming pool, thus the boxer 'takes a dive'] [1920s+] **1** (*also* **go in the tank**) to abandon deliberately, to give up, poss. for illicit monetary gain, esp. in boxing. **2** to fail.

DERIVATIVES

❑ **tanking** *n.* [1920s+] the deliberate losing of matches.

IN COMPOUNDS

❑ **tank fight** *n.* [1920s+] a contest in which one fighter has been bribed to lose. ❑ **tank job** *n.* (*also* **tank act**) [1930s] a corrupt sporting contest with a pre-arranged result.

tank *v.*[2] **1** [1940s+] (*US*) to beat up [also linked to TANK *v.*[1]]. **2** [1990s+] (*Ulster*) to administer a paramilitary 'punishment beating'.

tank *v.*[3] *see* TANK (UP) *v.*

tanka *n.* [SE *tanker*, i.e. a large receptacle] [1980s+] (*US campus*) a large container of soft drink.

tanked (up) *adj.* (*also* **fuelled**) [TANK (UP) *v.*] **1** [late 19C+] drunk; thus intensified in phr. *tanked to the wide*. **2** [1960s] intoxicated by a drug. **3** [1960s] in fig. use, i.e. satiated, filled up with.

tanker *n.*[1] [TANK (UP) *v.* (1)] [1910s–30s] a heavy drinker.

tanker *n.*[2] [TANK *v.*[1] (1)] [1920s+] **1** a prize-fighter who has agreed to accept cash in return for losing a fight. **2** in fig. use, a second rate person.

tankie *n.* [they are 'built like a tank'] [1990s+] (*UK juv.*) a very fat person.

tanking *n.* [1980s] (*UK tramp*) the act of concealing money on one's person.

IN PHRASES

❑ **deep tanking** *n.* concealing money deep within one's clothing.

tank (into) *v.* [1990s+] to rush towards, to attack.

tank town *n.* (*also* **tank, tank station**) [the positioning of water tanks at such railway stops, the only reason why a train might stop there; note late 19C US theatrical *water tank show*, a small touring company] [20C+] (*US*) a small, insignificant town.

tank town *adj.* [TANK TOWN *n.*] [1930s+] (*US*) insignificant, petty.

tank-up *n.* [TANK (UP) *v.*] [1950s] a heavy drinking session.

tank (up) *v.* [SE *tank*, a cistern] **1** [late 19C+] to drink heavily. **2** [1970s+] thus fig., to satisfy one's appetite, to fill up with food.

IN COMPOUNDS

❑ **tank time** *n.* [1980s+] (*US campus*) time to start drinking.

tanky *adj.*[1] [TANK (UP) *v.*] [1930s+] (*US*) drunk.

tanky *adj.*[2] [1980s] (*US*) physically large.

tanna *n.* see TOMMY TANA *n.*

tanner *n.* [Rom. *tawno*, small or f. a ponderous Biblical joke about St Peter's supposed banking transaction when he 'lodged with one Simon a tanner'] [early 19C–1970s] sixpence, thus post-metrication 2½p.

IN COMPOUNDS

❑ **tannercab** *n.* [1900s–10s] a sixpenny cab. ❑ **tanner case** *n.* [early 19C] a pocket. ❑ **tannergram** *n.* [19C–1910s] a sixpenny telegram.

tannery *n.* **1** [late 19C] (*US*) a pair of outsize boots or shoes [SE *tannery*, a leather-maker's]. **2** [1910s] (*Aus.*) a school [errant pupils will receive a TANNING *n.*].

tannie *n.* [Afk. *tante*, aunt; used affectionately or respectfully the word means simply 'auntie'] **1** [1950s+] (*S.Afr.*) an old(er) woman of pronounced and vocal moral values; in derog. use, a narrow-minded, puritan, small-town woman. **2** [1970s+] a term of respect and/or affection.

tanning *n.* [mid-19C+] a beating, a thrashing.

tan-pan-mi *n.* [lit. 'stand upon me', the clothing has become stiffened through the accretion of dirt] [1950s] (*W.I.*) ragged old work-clothes, esp. when very filthy.

tantadlin *n. see* TANTOBLIN *n.*

tantany *n. see* ANTHONY *n.*

tantaria *n.* [? SE *tantara*, imitation word for the sound of a trumpet or drum] [20C+] (*W.I.*) an abusive, loud, shrewish woman.

tante *n. see* AUNTIE *n.*[2] (1).

tantivy *n.* [SE *tantivy*, a gallop at full tilt. The nickname use arose *c.*1680, when a caricature was published in which a number of High Church clergymen were represented as mounted upon the Church of England and 'riding tantivy' to Rome, behind the Duke of York] **1** [mid-17C–18C] (*also* **tantwivy**) imitative of the sound of a hunting horn. **2** [late 17C–mid-18C] (*also* **tantivy boy**) a nickname given to the post-Restoration High Churchmen and Tories, esp. in the reigns of Charles II (1660–85) and James II (1685–8).

tantoblin *n.* (*also* **tantadlin, tantoblin tart**) [SE *tantoblin*, a large, round sweet tart and dial. *tantablin tart*, cow dung] [mid-17C–early 19C] a piece of excrement.

tantony *n. see* ANTHONY *n.*

tan track *n.* [Rodgers, *The Queen's Vernacular* (1972), suggests an origin in hobo use] [late 19C+] the anus.

tan-tracker *n.* (*also* **tan-track rider**) [TAN TRACK *n.*] [1930s+] (*orig. Aus.*) a homosexual man.

tantrems *n.* [var. on TANTRUM *n.*[2] + dial. *tantrum*, a freak, a whimsy] [mid–late 19C] pranks, games, jollification.

tantrum *n.*[1] [northern dial. *tantril*, a wanderer] [late 17C–late 18C] the penis.

tantrum *n.*[2] [SE by 20C+, ? Ital. *tarantella*, a whirling dance which may reduce the dancers to near- or apparent hysteria; Hotten (1860) adds 'the involuntary phrenzy and motions caused by the bite of the tarantula'] [early 18C+] a burst of petulant ill-temper, seen as childish or actually produced by a child.

tantwivy *n. see* TANTIVY *n.* (1).

tanty *n.* [abbr.] [1980s+] Aus. a temper tantrum.

tanyok *n.* [Shelta] [18C+] a halfpenny.

taoc *n.* [backsl.] [mid–late 19C] a coat, and thus its wearer.

taoc-tisaw *n.* [backsl.] [mid-19C] a waistcoat.

tap *n.*[1] [late 19C+] (*US*) a very small amount.

tap *n.*[2] [TAP *v.*[2] (3b)] **1** [1920s] (*US Und.*) a person likely to give a donation to a charitable cause. **2** [1930s] (*US tramp*) a house known to be a good place to beg. **3** [1990s+] a loan; an act of requesting a loan.

tap *n.*[3] [TAP *v.*[2] (2)] [1930s–60s] (*US*) a robbery; a confidence trick.

tap *v.*[1] [the image is of 'turning on a *tap*' of gifts etc] [early 18C; 1930s] to spend freely and generously.

tap *v.*[2] **1** in senses of SE *tap*, to hit + *tap*, a valve. (**a**) [mid-18C–19C] to hit and thus draw blood from a victim's nose. (**b**) [1910s] (*US*) to exhaust one's finances. (**c**) [1920s+] (*US Und.*) to hit on the head. (**d**) [1940s+] to have sexual intercourse. (**e**) [1960s–70s] (*drugs*) to inject oneself with a hypodermic syringe. (**f**) [2000s] to shoot (dead). **2** [mid-19C+] (*US Und.*) to rob, to steal from. **3** in senses of the lit. or fig. *tap* on the shoulder. (**a**) [mid-19C–1940s] to arrest. (**b**) [late 19C+] (*also* **tap for, tap up**) to beg for, to accost someone for something, to ask for a loan, whether of money or fig.; often in phr. *tap someone for*. (**c**) [20C+] to obtain money (other than as a loan). (**d**) [1920s+] to select, to 'line up'. (**e**) [1920s+] (*US*) to select for a college fraternity or society. **4** [1920s+] (*also* **tap up**) to defraud, to cheat.

(IN PHRASES)

▫ **on the tap** [1930s+] attempting to beg money. ▫ **tap a judy** *v. see under* JUDY *n.*[1]. ▫ **tap a till** *v.* (*also* **tap a damper, till-tap**) [sense 2 + SE *till*] [mid-19C+] to rob, to steal, usu. from a cash register; thus *TILL-TAPPER under* TILL *n.* ▫ **tap off** *v.* [on model of COP OFF *v.*[3] (1)] [1990s+] to pick up or seduce. ▫ **tap someone's claret** *v. see under* CLARET *n.*

SE in slang uses

(IN COMPOUNDS)

▫ **tap-lash** *n.* [lit. 'beat the tap', i.e. thump it in order to extract the very last drips from the cask or barrel] **1** [17C–early 19C] inferior liquor, esp. its dregs. **2** [mid-17C–early 18C] a publican. ▫ **tap-tub** *n.* [early–mid-19C] the *Morning Advertiser* newspaper, also known as the *Gin and Gospel Gazette*.

(IN PHRASES)

▫ **tap a girl** *v.* [late 17C–early 19C] to deflower a woman [note sense 1d]. ▫ **tap a house** *v.* [late 19C] to burgle a house. ▫ **tap a kidney** *v.* (*also* **squeeze a kidney, tilt a kidney**) [1970s+] (*US*) to urinate. ▫ **tap the admiral** *v.* [according to Hotten (1864), the practice originated when sailors sucked out the liquor from the barrel in which Admiral Horatio Nelson's body had been preserved on the journey home after his death at the battle of Trafalgar, 'to such an extent as to leave the gallant Admiral high and dry'] [mid–late 19C] to suck liquor through a straw from the ship's barrel which has been bored with a gimlet. ▫ **tap up** *v.* [2000s] (*drugs*) to tap a vein in order to make it stand out from the surrounding flesh preparatory to an injection of narcotics.

tap city *n.* [SE *tap*, f. the tradition of tapping the table to signify passing in poker/TAP *v.*[2] (3b)/TAP OUT *v.* (1) + -CITY *sfx*] **1** [1920s+] the state of being unable to raise a stake for further betting. **2** [1920s+] a metaphorical place devoted to borrowing or begging money. **3** [1930s+] (*also* **tapsville**) state of poverty [-VILLE *sfx*[1]].

tapdance *v.* **1** [1920s+] (*orig. US*) to wriggle out of trouble, to evade something cleverly. **2** [1940s] (*US gay*) to masturbate.

(DERIVATIVES)

▫ **tapdancer** *n.* [1940s] (*US gay*) a masturbator (of others).

tap dancer *n.* [rhy. sl.] [1980s] (*Aus.*) cancer.

tape *n.* [ety. unknown; ? link to SE *taphouse*] [early 18C–19C] a fiery drink, spirits, usu. gin.

taped *adv.* [the use of a fig. *tape measure*] [1910s+] (*US*) sized up, fully understood.

taped-up *adj.* [1970s–80s] (*US black*) of a woman, already with a boyfriend, thus secured from other admirers.

tape off *v.* [SE *tape measure*] [1920s+] (*Aus.*) **1** to prepare, to get ready, to put into place. **2** to reprimand. **3** to measure out correctly.

taper *adj.* [SE *taper off*] [mid-19C] of money or supplies, diminishing, running out.

taper (off) *v.* **1** [late 19C] to gradually diminish the quantity or potency of one's drink. **2** [1910s–40s] (*drugs*) to withdraw from narcotics by gradual reduction of dosage. **3** [1940s] (*drugs*) to force someone to withdraw from narcotics by reducing their dose.

tape the gerbil *v.* [ety. unknown] [1990s+] (*US teen*) to study hard.

tapioca *adj.*[1] [TAP OUT *v.* (1)] [1930s–70s] (*US*) absolutely penniless.

tapioca *adj.*[2] [TAPPED-OUT *adj.* (3)] [1950s] (*US*) asleep, exhausted.

tap (on the shoulder) *n.* [late 18C–early 19C] an arrest.

tap out *v.* [SE *tap* running out, also gambling use of tapping on the table to signify passing] **1** [1930s+] (*orig. US*) to come to the end of one's finances. **2** [1960s] to fail, to 'draw a blank'. **3** [1960s–70s] to relieve someone of their last money. **4** [1970s] (*Aus.*) in a fight, to give in, to surrender by indicating with a tap on the ground. **5** [1980s+] (*US campus*) to be exhausted [fig. use of sense 1]. **6** [2000s] to reach a conclusion.

tapped *adj.* [DOOLALLY TAP *n.*] [1910s+] insane, crazy.

tapped-out *adj.* (*also* **tapped**) [TAP OUT *v.*] **1** [1930s+] drunk. **2** [1950s+] out of money, having nothing to use for further betting. **3** [1950s+] (*US*) exhausted. **4** [1970s+] emotionally or mentally destroyed. **5** [1990s+] intoxicated by a drug, usu. crack cocaine.

tapper *n.*[1] **1** [late 18C–early 19C] a bailiff [SE *tap* on the shoulder]. **2** [mid-19C] (*US Und.*) a policeman [TAP *v.*[2] (3)]. **3** [20C+] a cadger, a beggar.

tapper *n.*[2] [SE *tap*, to broach a cask] [1910s–30s] one who cuts into casks of wine or spirits and uses a straw to drink the contents.

tapper and sucker racket *n.* [1940s–50s] (*UK Und*) a scheme to arrange for typewriters and vacuum cleaners to be left on approval at a residence, the goods would then be sold and the premises quickly vacated by the con man and his partner.

tappie *n.* [2000s] (*S.Afr.*) a cigarette end.

taps *n.* [because they tap conversations] [mid-18C–19C] the ears.

tapsville *n. see* TAP CITY *n.* (3).

tar *n.*[1] **1** [late 17C+] (*also* **tar-jacket, tarr**) a sailor [the use of tar on board ship]. **2** [1930s+] (*drugs*) opium, heroin [colour and consistency of Mexican heroin].

IN PHRASES

□ **black tar** *n.* (*also* **coal tar**) [1980s+] (*drugs*) heroin processed in Mexico.

SE in slang uses

IN COMPOUNDS

□ **tar-boiler/-burner** *n. see* TARHEEL *n.* □ **tar bucket** *n.* [1920s] (*US*) coffee. □ **tar pit** *n.* [the resemblance of *tar* to excrement] [1970s] (*US*) the anus. □ **Tartown** *n.* [1980s] (*US black*) a black neighbourhood.

IN PHRASES

□ **like tar** *adv.* [1900s] very keenly, very quickly.

tar *n.*[2] [appearance] [1900s] (*US*) money.

tar *n.*[3] [fig. use of SE *tar* = essence, 'daylights']

IN PHRASES

□ **kick the tar out of** *v.* (*also* **batter..., knock..., lick..., pound..., whale...**) [20C+] (*US*) to beat someone up very badly. □ **tar out** *v.* [i.e. *to beat the tar out of*] [mid-19C–1900s] to punish, to beat.

ta-ra *n.* [TA-RA *phr.*] [1970s+] a goodbye, the act of saying goodbye.

ta-ra *phr.* [1950s+] (*mainly north*) goodbye.

taradiddle *n.* (*also* **tarradiddle**) [DIDDLE *v.*[2] (2)] [late 18C–1970s] a petty lie; as v., to lie.

DERIVATIVES

□ **taradiddler** *n.* [late 18C–1970s] a petty liar.

taradiddle! *excl.* [TARADIDDLE *n.*] [mid-19C] rubbish! nonsense!

Taranaki *adj.* [*Taranaki*, an area of the South Island, which has many dairy herds] (*N.Z.*) used in combs. (*see* below) to imply backwardness, rurality.

IN COMPOUNDS

□ **Taranaki bullshit** *n.* [BULLSHIT *n.* (1) + *Taranaki*, an area of the South Island, has many dairy herds] [1940s+] (*N.Z.*) excessive boasting. □ **Taranaki cow** *n.* [1940s+] (*N.Z.*) a nondescript, inferior cow. □ **Taranaki drive** *n.* [2000s] (*N.Z.*) an unsalubrious road. □ **Taranaki gate** *n.* [20C+] (*N.Z.*) a gate made of strands of barbed wire interwoven with palings for strength. □ **Taranaki spanner** *n.* [2000s] (*N.Z.*) a bottle opener. □ **Taranaki sunshine** *n.* [1990s+] (*N.Z.*) rain or drizzle. □ **Taranaki violin** *n.* [2000s] (*N.Z.*) cowbells.

IN PHRASES

□ **Taranaki top dressing** *n.* [1940s+] (*N.Z.*) cattle dung.

tar and feather *n.* [rhy. sl.] [20C+] **1** leather, usu. a leather jacket. **2** weather.

tar and ouns!/taranouns! *excl. see* TARE AN' OUNS! *excl.*

tarantula-juice *n.* [its alcoholic 'bite'] [mid-19C–1930s] inferior whisky.

tar baby *n.* [the *Tar Baby*, created by Joel Chandler Harris in 1881, when in one of his 'Uncle Remus' tales the scheming Br'er Fox, determined to catch Harris's lapine hero Brer Rabbit, 'got im some tar, en mix it wid some turkentime, en fix up a contrapshun what he call a Tar-Baby'] **1** [20C+] (*US*) a 'sticky' problem. **2** [1940s+] (*US*) a black person. **3** [1950s] (*N.Z.*) a derog. term for a Maori.

tard *n.* [abbr. RETARD *n.*] [1970s+] (*US*) a fool.

tare an' ages! *excl.* (*also* **blur-an-agers! tear and ages!**) [SE *tears and aches* (*of Christ*); *blur* = blood] [mid-19C–1950s] (*Irish*) a euph. oath.

tare an' ouns! *excl.* (*also* **blur an' ouns! tar and ouns! taranouns! tear and wounds!**) [SE *tears and wounds* (*of Christ*)] [mid-19C–1920s] (*Irish*) a euph. oath.

t.a.r.f.u. *phr.* [abbr.] [1940s+] (*orig. US milit.*) things are really fucked-up.

target *n.* **1** [late 17C–19C] the vagina [coined by John Wilmot, Earl of Rochester (1642–80)]. **2** [1920s–40s] (*US Und.*) a lookout man [his vulnerability to police or by-standers]. **3** [1970s–80s] (*S.Afr. township*) anything, esp. a motor vehicle owned by a white-run company, seen as symbolic of apartheid and as such liable to criminal and violent acts.

tarheel *n.* (*also* **tar-boiler, tar-burner, tar-heeler**) [SE *tar* as a principal product of the state] [late 18C+] a native of North Carolina.

tarheel *adj.* [mid-19C+] (*US*) pertaining to North Carolina or the state's culture.

tariff *n.* [2000s] a prison sentence.

taring *adj. see* TEARING *adj.*

tarleather *n.* [SE *tarleather*, a strip of leather used in a flail. The women thus described are presumably seen as 'scolds' and, given that *leather* means vagina, the word is a distant precursor of *pussy-whipped* under PUSSY *n.*] [16C–17C] a general term of abuse directed at women.

tarman *n.* [ety. unknown; ? pron.] [1990s+] (*UK juv.*) a tampon.

tarnal *adj.* (*also* **etarnal**) [SE *eternal*] [late 18C+] (*US*) used as a usu. negative intensifier, cussed, damned.

tarnation *n.* (*also* **the nation**) [lit. *damnation*; note 18C abbr. dial./SE *nation*, damnation] [late 18C+] (*US*) a euph. for hell.

tarnation *adj.* (*also* **dingnation**) [TARNATION *n.*] [late 18C+] (*US*) hellish, damnable.

tarnation *adv.* (*also* **nation**) [TARNATION *n.*] [late 18C+] (*US*) damnably.

tarnation! *excl.* (*also* **blarnation! carnation! darnation! hell and tarnation!**) [TARNATION *n.*] [late 18C+] (*US*) a euph. substitute for DAMNATION! *excl.*

tarp *n.* [abbr.] [20C+] a *tarpaulin*.

tarpaulin *n.* [use of SE *tarpaulin* on ships] [mid-17C–1920s] a sailor, esp. (in the days when appointments were made as much on connections as on ability) a sailor with practical experience of seamanship.

tarpaulin *adj.* [TARPAULIN *n.*] [late 17C] pertaining to sailors or sea-travel.

IN COMPOUNDS

□ **tarpaulin muster** *n.* (*also* **blanket muster, calico muster, canvas muster**) [naut. jargon *tarpaulin muster*, a collection or pooling of money among seamen] [late 19C+] (*Aus./N.Z.*) a collection of money, either for a round of drinks or for donation to a third party or a cause.

tarpot *n.* [SE *tar* is black] **1** [1930s+] (*Aus/N.Z.*) a derog. term for a Maori or Aborigine. **2** [1980s] (*US*) a black child.

IN PHRASES

□ **hit the tarpot** *v.* [1930s+] (*N.Z.*) to pursue a Maori woman.

tarradiddle *n. see* TARADIDDLE *n.*

tarra-warra *n.* (*also* **warra-warra**) [? echoic of the hesitation over or mumbling of 'bad' words] [1950s+] (*W.I. Rasta*) a polite way of expressing omitted bad words, a verbal asterisk.

tarrel *n.* [mid-19C] (*US Und.*) a skeleton key.

tarry-boy *n.* (*also* **tally-boy**) [Scot. *tarry-fingers*, dishonest person] [1970s] (*Irish*) a dishonest, dubious person, also a randy individual.

tarry-breeks *n.* (*also* **tarry brecks, tarry jacket, tarry John**) [lit. 'tarry breeches'; TAR *n.*[1] (1)] [late 18C–mid-19C] a sailor.

tarry rope *n.* **1** [1940s] (*US*) a fool [rhy. sl. = *dope*]. **2** [1940s–60s] (*Aus.*) a woman, poss. a prostitute, who associates with sailors [SE *tarry*, covered in tar + *rope*].

tarrywags *n.* see TALLYWAGS *n.*

tart *n.* [Aus./N.Z. uses remain positive or neutral in spite of earlier shift to derog. meaning] **1** [mid-19C+] a woman, a girlfriend; thus dimin. *tartlet* [usu. only in dialect]. **2** [late 19C+] a promiscuous woman, a prostitute; also of heterosexual men since 1960s [dominating use since early 20C]. **3** [1920s] (*Aus.*) an attractive young woman. **4** [1930s+] (*gay*) an older man's young male lover. **5** [1930s+] (*gay*) a gay prostitute. **6** [1990s+] a promiscuous homosexual. **7** [2000s] a fool, irrespective of gender.

IN COMPOUNDS

❑ **tart fuel** *n.* [2000s] alcopops.

IN PHRASES

❑ **queen of tarts** *n.* [QUEEN *n.* (2)] [1970s] (*US gay*) a pimp for homosexuals.

tart *adj.* [late 19C] (*US*) mediocre, second-rate.

tart *v.* [TART *n.* (1)] [1940s] (*Aus./N.Z.*) to pursue women.

IN PHRASES

❑ **tart (around)** *v.* (*also* **tart about**) [1930s+] of a woman, to act in a promiscuous manner. ❑ **tarted (up)** *adj.* [*TART UP* below] **1** [1930s+] usu. of women, flashily overdressed. **2** [1950s+] applied to anything overdecorated, e.g. a 'theme pub'. ❑ **tart up** *v.* **1** [1930s+] of a person, to dress up. **2** [1950s+] of an object, to be decorated, to be ornamented. ❑ **tart with** *v.* [1940s] to flirt with.

tartan *n.* [? rhy. sl.] [2000s] (*UK Und*) cocaine.

tartar *n.* [proper name *Tartar*, an inhabitant of the region of Central Asia extending east from the Caspian Sea, and formerly known as Independent and Chinese Tartary; ult. Persian *Tatar*, but linked in Western ears and superstitions with Lat. *tartarus*, hell] **1** [late 16C–18C] a strolling vagabond, a beggar, a criminal mendicant. **2** [late 16C–1940s] (*also* **tart**) a general derog. description. **3** [late 18C–19C] a champion, an expert.

IN PHRASES

❑ **catch a tartar** *v.* [late 17C+] to encounter an apparent victim or weakling who turns out to be much stronger than suspected.

tartarian *n.* [ext. of TARTAR *n.* (1)] [early–mid-17C] a thief.

tarty *adj.* [TART *n.* (2)] [1910s+] cheap, gaudy, vulgar, thus fig. reminiscent of a prostitute.

Tas *adj.* (*also* **Tassie**) [abbr.] [late 19C+] (*Aus.*) *Tas*manian.

tash *n.* (*also* **tache, tasche, tush**) [abbr.] [mid-19C+] mous*tache*.

taste *n.* **1** [late 19C+] (*UK Und.*) a share of, e.g. a bribe, the proceeds of a robbery. **2** [late 19C+] a very small amount, an almost imperceptible degree, a little. **3** [1920s+] a sample, a piece. **4** [1930s+] a drink, alcohol. **5** [1950s–60s] a sum of money. **6** [1950s+] sexual intercourse. **7** [1960s+] (*drugs*) a sample of drugs; a small measure of drugs. **8** [1980s+] (*Aus./US*) an injection of heroin.

IN COMPOUNDS

❑ **taste face** *n.* [1960s] (*US drugs*) a heroin addict who rents out his drugs equipment in exchange for small amounts of the drug.

taste *adj.* [backform. f. TASTY *adj.* (2)] [1980s] (*US campus*) enviable, appealing, attractive.

taste *v.* [17C–19C] to have sexual intercourse.

taste bud *n.* [esp. in the context of cunnilingus] [1960s+] the clitoris.

-tastic *sfx* [1990s+] (*orig. US*) a qualitative intensifier, e.g. *craptastic*.

tasty *adj.* **1** [late 18C+] pleasant, admirable, well-dressed. **2** [late 19C+] sexually alluring, attractive. **3** [1940s+] of a thing (usu. some form of criminal plan), valuable, worthwhile. **4** [1970s+] of a person, smart, sharp, often as 'tasty geezer'; or prob. criminal; thus *tasty villain*, a known criminal.

Taswegian *n.* [abbr. + play on SE *Glaswegian*] [1930s+] (*Aus.*) a person from *Tas*mania.

tat *n.*[1] [Hind. *tat*, a strip of coarse canvas, used to make mats or screens; thus as SE, coarse canvas made esp. of jute and used for sacking] **1** [mid–late 19C] (*also* **tatter**) an old rag. **2** [1920s+] anything seen as mediocre, vulgar, rubbishy.

IN PHRASES

❑ **milky tats** *n.* [mid–late 19C] linen or otherwise white cloth rags.

tat *n.*[2] [TATS *n.* (1)] [20C+] (*US*) any confidence trick; usu. performed with dice.

IN PHRASES

❑ **ring a tat into** *v.* [1900s] (*Aus.*) to fool, to play a confidence trick on.

tat *n.*[3] (*also* **tatt**) [abbr.] [1960s+] (*orig. US prison*) a *tat*too.

tat *n.*[4] and combs. *see* TATS *n.*

tat *adj.* [TAT *n.*[1] (2)] [1950s+] second-rate.

tat *v.*[1] [Hampshire dial. *tat*, to pat] [early–mid-19C] to flog, to thrash.

tat *v.*[2] [TAT *n.*[1] (1)] **1** [mid-19C] to gather rags for a living. **2** [1970s+] (*US gay*) to piece together, to create something out of left-over bits and pieces.

ta-ta *n.* [TA-TA *phr.*] **1** [late 19C+] (*also* **da-da**) a goodbye, an act of farewell. **2** [1930s] a hat.

IN PHRASES

❑ **give someone the ta-tas** *v.* [1960s+] (*N.Z.*) to make a derisive gesture, to 'give the finger'.

tata *n.*[1] [infant mispron. but note its use in many African languages, e.g. Ewe, Ge, N'gombe] [early 19C+] (*W.I.*) father, an affectionate and respectful title for an old man.

tata *n.*[2] [such a person tends to use baby talk, e.g. *go for a tata*, go for a walk] [1920s+] a foolish person.

ta-ta *v.* [TA-TA *n.*] [1910s–30s] to say goodbye, to leave.

ta-ta *phr.* (*also* **tat-ta**) [earlier use in nursery context] [mid-19C+] goodbye!

tataram *n.* [TATA *n.*[1] + RAM *n.*[1] (2)] [1930s+] (*W.I.*) a foolish old man, esp. one with sex on his mind.

ta-tas *n.*[1] [1960s] (*Aus.*) delirium tremens.

ta-tas *n.*[2] [TITTY *n.* (1)] [1980s+] (*US*) the female breasts.

tate *n.* [rhy. sl. = DATE *n.*[3] (2)] [1950s] buttocks.

Tate and Lyle *n.* [rhy. sl.; ult. a well-known brand of sugar] [20C+] style, i.e. cheek, audacity.

tater *n.* (*also* **'tatur**) **1** [mid-18C+] a po*tato*; often in pl. [abbr.]. **2** [late 19C+] a hole in one's sock [fig. use of sense 1, i.e. the exposed, dirty flesh resembles the vegetable]. **3** [1980s+] (*US*) the penis.

IN COMPOUNDS

❑ **tater and point** *n.* [dial. *taties and point*, potatoes plus a small piece of fish or meat, so tiny as only to be pointed at, rather than providing any nutrition] [mid–late 19C] a meal made up almost entirely of potatoes. ❑ **tater-eater** *n. see POTATO-EATER under* POTATO *n.* ❑ **tatur-headed** *adj. see POTATO-HEADED under* POTATO-HEAD *n.* ❑ **tater-trap** *n.* (*also* **tatoe-trap, tattie-trap, tatur-trap**) [sense 1 / TATIE *n.* + SE *trap*/TRAP *n.*[1] (4); var. on *POTATO-TRAP under* POTATO *n.*] [early 19C–1910s] the mouth.

IN PHRASES

❑ **settle someone's tater** *v.* [late 19C+] to beat someone up.

IN EXCLAMATIONS

❑ **that's the tatur!** [mid-19C] (*US*) an excl. of affirmation.

tater-pillin' *n.* [rhy. sl.; TATER *n.* (1) + pron. of SE *peeling*] [20C+] a shilling (5p).

taters (in the mould) *adj.* (*also* **taties, tatters in the mold**) [rhy. sl. = cold; ult. TATER *n.* (1)] [20C+] cold.

tatie *n.* (*also* **tato, tattie**) [abbr.] [19C+] a po*tato*.

tatler *n.* (*also* **tattle, tattler**) [SE *tattler*, one who tattles or gossips, use revived by US blacks] (*UK Und.*) [late 17C–mid-19C] a watch, esp. a striking watch or a repeater.

IN PHRASES

❑ **flash a tatler** *v.* (*also* **...tattler**) [late 18C–late 19C] to wear a watch.

tatlers *n.* [unknown; ? the noise of money rattling in the pocket] [early 19C] money.

tato *n. see* TATIE *n.*

tatoe-trap *n. see* TATER-TRAP *under* TATER *n.*

tats *n.* (*also* **tatts**) [ety. unknown; ? the rattle of dice as they hit the table] **1** [late 17C+] dice, esp. crooked dice. **2** [1910s+] (*Aus./N.Z.*) teeth [refers to the ivory in dice and teeth]. **3** [1960s+] (*Aus./N.Z.*) a set of false teeth [refers to the ivory in dice and teeth].

IN COMPOUNDS

❑ **tat-box** *n.* (*also* **tatt-box**) [mid–late 19C] a dice-box. ❑ **tat-man** *n.* (*also* **tatt-man**) [late 18C–mid-19C] a professional dice cheat. ❑ **tat-monger** *n.* (*also* **tattmonger**) [-MONGER *sfx*] [late 17C–early 19C] a professional dice-cheat. ❑ **tat-shop** *n.* [SHOP *n.*[1] (3)] [early 19C] (*UK Und.*) a gambling den.

IN EXCLAMATIONS

❑ **tats and all!** [early 19C] nonsense! rubbish! humbug!

tatt *n. see* TAT *n.*[3].

tatter *n.* [SE *tatter*] **1** [17C] a beggar. **2** *see* TAT *n.*[1] (1).

tatter a kip *v. see under* KIP *n.*[1].

tatterdemallion *n.* [SE *tatterdemallion*, a person in ragged clothing] [17C–1920s] **1** (*UK Und.*) a wandering beggar who deliberately adopts ragged, filthy clothes in the hope of extracting more money from the kind-hearted. **2** a rascal.

tatters in the mold *adj. see* TATERS (IN THE MOULD) *adj.*

tattie *n. see* TATIE *n.*

tattie short, a *phr.* [1960s] (*Scot.*) to be crazy.

tattie-trap *n. see* TATER-TRAP *under* TATER *n.*

tatting *n.* [TAT *n.*[1] (1)] **1** [mid-19C–1930s] gathering old rags. **2** [1990s+] collecting scrap iron.

tattler *n.*[1] [its light 'tells tales' on criminal activity] [18C] (*UK Und.*) the moon.

tattler *n.*[2] *see* TATLER *n.*

tattogey *n.* [elision of TATTY TOG *n.*] [mid-18C] **1** a dice-cloth, onto which one tosses the dice. **2** one who cheats by using loaded dice.

tattoo *n.* **1** [1960s] (*US drugs*) the mark of a narcotics injection. **2** *see* DEVIL'S TATTOO *under* DEVIL *n.*

Tatt's *n.* [abbr.] **1** [mid-19C–1900s] (*also* **Tat's**) *Tattersall's* horse market in London. **2** [late 19C–1960s] (*Aus.*) (*also* **Tatt**) *Tatt's* sweep, a lottery established in 1881 on that year's Sydney Gold Cup by George Adams (1839–1904), licensee of Tattersall's Hotel, Sydney.

IN PHRASES

❑ **fair as Tatt's** *adv.* (*also* **square as Tatt's**) [late 19C–1960s] (*Aus.*) absolutely honest.

tatts *n. see* TATS *n.*

tatty *adj.* [TAT *n.*[1]] [1930s+] **1** inferior, cheap, badly-made, shabby. **2** unkempt, untidy, dishevelled.

tatty muncher *n.* [TATIE *n.*; stereotyping of the Irish, seen as Catholics, on a diet of potatoes] [1980s+] a derog. term for a Roman Catholic.

tatty tog *n.* [TATS *n.* (1) + TOG *n.*] [early–mid-19C] a gaming cloth.

'tatur *n. see* TATER *n.*

tatur-trap *n. see* TATER-TRAP *under* TATER *n.*

Taunton turkey *n.* [the trade in such herrings in the town] [mid-19C–1950s] a salt herring.

tavern treat *n.* [the physical and metaphorical proximity of taverns to brothels] [early 18C] sexual intercourse.

taw *n.* [? SE *taw*, the large marble with which a player shoots] **1** [1910s] (*Aus.*) a first-rate person. **2** [1920s+] (*US Und*) cash in hand; funds.

tax *n.* **1** [1970s+] (*UK black*) any form of entry charge, e.g. to a dance. **2** [1990s+] (*drugs*) (*also* **taxing**) a charge paid to enter a building where crack cocaine is sold. The charge is based either on the race of the customer (whites pay more) or on the frequency of their custom. **3** [2000s] a stolen item, an act of theft.

SE in slang uses

IN COMPOUNDS

❑ **tax-collector** *n.* [mid–late 19C] a highwayman. ❑ **tax-fencer** *n.* [-FENCER *sfx*] [late 19C] a disreputable shopkeeper, whose prices are set extortionately high.

tax *v.* **1** [mid-19C–1900s] (*US, esp. New England*) to set a price on, to charge. **2** [1980s+] to extort, to demand money with menaces. **3** [1980s+] to rob; to steal.

taxi *n.*[1] [1910s+] a small passenger aeroplane.

IN COMPOUNDS

❑ **taxi-driver** *n.* [1910s+] the pilot of a small passenger aeroplane.

taxi *n.*[2] [New York cabs which displayed these figures, indicating their rates per mile, on the side] [1930s+] (*US*) a sentence of 5 to 15 years.

taxicabs *n.* [rhy. sl. = SE colloq. *crabs*] [20C+] body lice.

taxi eleven *n.* [the supposed similarity of shape] [1950s+] (*W.I.*) one's legs.

IN PHRASES

❑ **catch taxi eleven** *v.* [1950s+] (*W.I.*) to walk.

taxing *n.*[1] [TAX *v.* (2)] [1980s+] (*drugs*) the robbery by small-time dealers of their more successful peers.

taxing *n.*[2] *see* TAX *n.* (2).

taxi rank *n.* [rhy. sl.] [1990s+] a bank.

taxi-rank *v.* [rhy. sl. = WANK *v.* (1)] [1970s+] to masturbate.

taz *n.* [var. on TASH *n.*] [1920s+] **1** a beard. **2** a moustache. **3** light adolescent facial hair.

taz *adj.* [contraction of swee*t as*] [2000s] (*N.Z. teen*) first-rate, excellent.

t.b. *n.*[1] [abbr. *TB*, tuberculosis] **1** [1920s–40s] (*US*) a sufferer from tuberculosis. **2** [1930s–40s] (*US*) a confidence trickster [tuberculosis = consumption, abbr. = *con* = *confidence-man*].

t.b. *n.*[2] [abbr. *two beauts*] [1920s+] (*Aus.*) a pair of large and shapely breasts.

t.b. *n.*[3] [TIDY *adj.* (1) + BOILER *n.*[2] (2)] [1990s+] (*UK juv.*) a good-looking young woman.

t-bagging *n. see* TEABAGGING *n.*

t.b.h. *n.* [abbr. *to be had/too bloody hot*] [1970s+] (*gay*) a potential sexual conquest.

T-bird *n.* [abbr.] **1** [1950s+] a Ford *Thunderbird*. **2** [1980s+] *Thunderbird* wine, a cheap wine drunk primarily by alcoholics.

T-bone *n.* [? SE *T-bone steak*, thus implying virility; however, Major, *Juba to Jive: A Dict. of Afro-American Sl.* (1994), associates the term with blues musician Aaron 'T-bone' Walker (1910–75), who took the name from his own middle name, Thibeaux, thus implying that the man, not the meat, was the paradigm] [1950s+] (*US black*) a common black nickname.

T-bone *v.* [1990s+] (*US*) to crash into a car at a right angle, usu. by going over a red light at a junction.

T-buzz *n.* [T *n.*[2] +BUZZ *n.* (3c)] [1970s+] (*drugs*) phencyclidine.

TCB *phr.* [abbr. *typical cracker behaviour*; CRACKER *n.*[3] (4)] [2000s] (*US black*) behaviour seen as stereotypically white.

t.c.b. *v. see* TAKE CARE OF BUSINESS *v.*

tchatchka *n. see* TCHOTCHKE *n.*

tchi *v.* (*also* **chy**) [? SE *Chinese*] [late 19C–1950s] (*US drugs*) to roll an opium pellet preparatory to smoking.

tcho! *excl. see* CHA! *excl.*

tchotchke *n.* (*also* **chotchkie, tchatchka, tchotzke, tsatske**) [Yid. *tsatske*, Slav *shaleh*, a plaything] [1960s+] (*US*) **1** any small decorative thing. **2** an adorable person, esp. a small child. **3** a woman considered as a plaything.

t.d.f. *phr. see* TO DIE (FOR) *phr.*

t'd off *adj. see* TEED OFF *adj.*

tea *n.* [reflecting the colour of tea without milk] **1** [late 17C–18C] strong liquor; often as COLD TEA *under* COLD *adj.*, brandy. **2** [18C–early 19C; 1970s+] urine [1970s+ use is gay]. **3** [late

19C+] (*US*) whisky. **4** in drug uses [the *OED* citation from the *Boston Sunday Herald* (26 March 1967), 'Marijuana...when brewed with hot water' is prob. a teasing HIPPIE *n.*[2] (3) gulling a foolish journalist]. (**a**) [1930s+] marijuana. (**b**) [1930s+] a marijuana cigarette. (**c**) [1970s+] phencyclidine.

IN COMPOUNDS

□ **tea-canister** *n.* [mid-19C] a brandy flask.

pertaining to marijuana

□ **tea-head** *n.* [-HEAD *sfx* (4)] [1940s+] (*drugs*) a marijuana smoker. □ **tea-hound** *n.* [-HOUND *sfx*] [1930s+] (*orig. US black*) a marijuana smoker. □ **tea-joint** *n.* [sense 3a above + JOINT *n.* (3b)] [1940s] (*US*) a place, e.g. a bar or club, where marijuana can be smoked. □ **tea man** *n.* (*also* **T-man**) [1930s–50s] (*US*) a smoker of marijuana. □ **tea pad** *n.* [PAD *n.*[2] (2)] [1930s–60s] (*drugs*) a place for smoking marijuana. □ **tea party** *n.* **1** [1920s] a drinking binge. **2** [1930s–60s] (*drugs*) a gathering of people for the purpose of communal smoking of marijuana. □ **tea stick** *n.* [STICK *n.* (6)] [1930s–50s] (*US drugs*) a marijuana cigarette. □ **tea-timers** *n.* [the need to wear sunglasses to hide one's marijuana-affected pupils] [1970s+] (*US gay*) dark glasses.

IN PHRASES

□ **read the tea leaves** *v.* [1970s] (*drugs*) to smoke marijuana.
□ **tea up** *v.* [SE *tea*/sense 3 above] [1910s–20s] to get drunk.

SE in slang uses

IN COMPOUNDS

□ **tea fight** *n.* **1** [mid-19C] an evening party. **2** [mid-19C–1920s] a tea party. □ **tea fighter** *n.* [late 19C] (*Aus.*) one who attends a tea party (and by implication dislikes alcohol). □ **tea-hound** *n.* [1920s] (*US*) **1** a man who frequents tea parties. **2** a womanizer. □ **tea scramble** *n.* *see* BUN-STRUGGLE *under* BUN *n.*[3]. □ **tea squall** *n.* [early–mid-19C] (*US*) a tea party. □ **tea-towel holder** *n.* [the small round plastic holder that a teatowel is pushed into resembles the anus] [1990s+] the anus. □ **tea voider** *n.* [late 18C–early 19C] a chamberpot.

IN PHRASES

□ **give them away with a pound of tea** [late 19C+] **1** a phr. used to deride something, or someone, considered of little or no value; e.g. 'Expensive? He gives them away...'. **2** an ironic reply by a criminal to questions referring to the origins of obviously stolen goods in his possession. 'Stolen goods, officer? No. Give them away...'. □ **go for one's tea** *v.* [20C+] to die. □ **have a cup of tea** *v.* [1970s+] (*US gay*) to have sex in a public lavatory. □ **not for all the tea in China** (*also* **not for all the rice in China, ...meat in China, not for King Dick, ...mink, not for a tinker's**) [late 19C+] (*orig. Aus.*) on no account, no chance whatsoever; occas. in positive use. □ **take tea with** *v.* [orig. colonial phr. *take tea with*, to associate with, esp. when the relations are mainly hostile] **1** [late 19C+] (*Aus.*) to consort with someone, to associate with someone. **2** [1970s+] (*UK Und.*) to outsmart a clever person or to defeat someone in authority. □ **tea and sugar burglar** *n.* (*also* **tea and sugar bandit**) **1** [late 19C–1900s] (*Aus.*) a vagrant [the fig. 'theft' of the commodities, which are more likely offered free]. **2** [1960s+] a petty thief [the smallness of the objects that are stolen]. □ **tea and sugar man** *n.* [1930s] (*UK tramp*) a casual labourer, who works for as long as it takes him to supply himself with his basic needs, before moving on. □ **tea and tattle** *n.* [1920s+] (*Aus.*) a formal afternoon tea for a number of guests, a minor social get-together. □ **tea and turn out** [19C] a phr. used to indicate that there is no tea; i.e. one is simply SE *turned out*. □ **wet the tea leaves** *v.* (*also* **wet the tea**) [mid-19C+] to make tea.

IN EXCLAMATIONS

□ **tea-oh!** [1940s+] (*N.Z.*) a call to indicate that it is time for a tea-break.

tea and cocoa *n.* [rhy. sl.] [20C+] say-so.

tea-and-toast *n.* [rhy. sl.] [20C+] the post, the mail.

tea and toast *v.* [rhy. sl. = ROAST *v.* (3)] [1980s] (*Aus.*) to scold, to reprimand.

teabag *n.* [rhy. sl. = SLAG *n.*[1] (1)] [2000s] a general term of abuse, a worthless, irrelevant person.

teabag *adj.* [1990s+] tear-jerking.

teabagging *n.* (*also* **t-bagging**) [the dipping action] [1990s+] the sucking of a man's testicles by his partner.

tea caddy *n.* [rhy. sl. = PADDY *n.* (1)] [2000s] an Irish person.

teach *n.* [abbr. SE *teacher*] [1940s+] **1** (*US*) (*also* **teech**) teacher. **2** (*US black*) anyone considered intelligent or intellectual.

teach school *v.* *see under* SCHOOL *n.*

teach someone a thing or two *v.* *see* KNOW A THING OR TWO *v.*

tead/tea'd/teaed (up) *adj.* *see* TEED UP *adj.*

tea-for-two and a bloater *n.* [rhy. sl. = MOTOR *n.* (2)] [1900s–50s] a car.

tea grout *n.* [rhy. sl.] [20C+] a Boy Scout.

Teague *n.* *see* TAIG *n.*

Teagueland *n.* [TEAGUE *n.* + SE *land*] [late 17C–mid-19C] Ireland.

DERIVATIVES

□ **Teaguelander** *n.* [late 17C–mid-19C] an Irishman.

teahouse *n.* *see* TEAROOM *n.*

teaich gens *n.* *see* THEG GENS *n.*

teaich-gir *adj.* (*also* **teatchgir**) [backsl., pron. 'tadger'] [mid-19C–1900s] right (quality, not direction).

teaich guy *n.* [backsl.] [mid-19C] eight shillings (40p).

teaich-yenneps *n.* [backsl.] [mid-19C] eight pence.

teakettle purger *n.* [? one who *purges*, i.e. cleans *teakettles* or uses tea to purge out alcohol; note Ducange Anglicus, *The Vulgar Tongue* (1857), definition: 'men who exchange their old clothes'] [mid-19C–1900s] a total abstainer.

tea leaf *n.* (*also* **tealeaf**) [rhy. sl.] [late 19C+] a thief.

IN PHRASES

□ **on the tealeaf** [1950s+] working as a thief.

tealeaf *v.* [TEA LEAF *n.*] **1** [late 19C+] (*orig. UK Und.*) to work as a thief. **2** [1990s+] to rob.

DERIVATIVES

□ **tea-leafing** *n.* [late 19C+] (*orig. UK Und.*) thieving.

team *n.* **1** [1930s+] a gang of criminals. **2** [1950s+] a squad of police. **3** [1980s+] (*Aus. prison*) a group of inmates.

IN COMPOUNDS

□ **team-handed** *adv.* [1950s+] (*Und.*) working in a group.

SE in slang uses

IN COMPOUNDS

□ **team cream** *n.* [SE *team* + CREAM *v.* (1a)] [1960s+] (*orig. gay*) an orgy. □ **team player** *n.* [2000s] (*S.Afr. gay*) a homosexual male; he in turn is *on the team*.

IN PHRASES

□ **double-team** *v.* [farming jargon *double-team*, to employ two teams of animals to haul heavy weights through difficult terrain; subseq. adopted in football use] [mid-19C+] (*US*) **1** to gang up on, to use extra force against. **2** to work as a pair. □ **whole team (and the dog under the wagon)** (*also* **full team**) [mid-19C–1910s] (*US*) a phr. used to indicate one's own or another's importance, energy etc, usu. as *ain't I/he/she/they the whole team* .

team *adv.* [1980s+] (*US campus*) wearing clothes or accessories that brand one as part of an identifiable subculture.

teameo *n.* (*also* **teamio**) [1920s–30s] (*US*) a member of the Teamsters' Union.

team Xerox *n.* [TEAM XEROX *v.*] [1980s+] (*US campus*) cheating.

team Xerox *v.* [*Xerox*, generic for 'to photocopy'] [1980s+] (*US campus*) to cheat.

teapot *n.* **1** [mid-19C] a black person [the colour of the typical brown/black *teapot*]. **2** [late 19C–1900s] a total abstainer. **3** [late 19C+] one who drinks an excessive amount of tea, often as *old teapot, regular teapot*. **4** [1990s+] (*UK juv.*) a male homosexual [the children's song 'I'm a little teapot, short and stout...' and the gestures that accompany it; while designed to represent the teapot's handle and spout, they can also be interpreted as those of the stereotyped camp gay man with a 'broken', drooping wrist].

SE in slang uses

IN COMPOUNDS

❑ **teapot sucker** *n.* [20C+] a tee-totaller or other spoilsport.

IN PHRASES

❑ **have one's teapot mended** *v.* (*also* **get it down the spout**) [late 19C] (*UK prison*) to regain the privilege – earned by good behaviour – of replacing the usual gruel with tea.

teapot (lid) *n.* [rhy. sl.] [1920s+] **1** a Jew [= YID *n.*[1]]. **2** a child [= KID *n.*[1] (1)]. **3** £1 sterling [= QUID *n.* (1)].

tear *n.* [SE *tear*, to go at full tilt] **1** [mid-19C–1900s] (*US campus*) a perfect recitation. **2** [mid-19C+] (*orig. US*) a spree, a jollification. **3** [1990s+] a state of excitement.

IN PHRASES

❑ **go (out) on a tear** *v.* (*also* **go out on the rip**) [mid-19C+] (*orig. US*) to go out on a spree. ❑ **hit up a tear** *v.* [1900s] (*Aus.*) to get drunk.

tear *v.* [late 16C+] to rush around excitedly, energetically.

IN PHRASES

❑ **tear out** *v.* [20C+] (*US black*) to rush away, to leave fast.

SE in slang uses

IN COMPOUNDS

❑ **tearcat** *n.* (*also* **tearer**) [SE *tear*, to rip apart; note Nares: 'To TEAR A CAT. To rant, and behave with violence; probably from a cruel act of that kind having been performed by some daring ruffian, to excite surprise and alarm'] [17C–early 18C] a thug, a bully.

IN PHRASES

❑ **tear arse** *see* separate entries. ❑ **tear down** *v.* [the victim's confidence is *torn down*] **1** [late 19C+] (*US*) to reprimand severely, to attack verbally. **2** [1940s+] (*also* **tear the place down**) to demonstrate great emotion, to act intensely and wildly. **3** [1950s–60s] to depress. **4** [1970s+] to destroy. ❑ **tear into** *v. see* separate entry. ❑ **tear it** *v.* [20C+] to spoil one's chances, to put an end to one's plans etc; esp. in phr. *THAT'S TORN IT* below. ❑ **tear-it-down** *n.* [1990s+] (*W.I.*) a fantastic performance. ❑ **tear loose** *v.* [1910s+] (*US black*) to escape from a person or situation. ❑ **tear off** *v. see* separate entries. ❑ **tear one's ass** *v.* (*also* **tear one's pants**) [SE *tear* + ARSE *n.* (1)/ASS *n.* (2)/SE *pants*] [1930s+] (*US*) to injure oneself, thus fig. to get into trouble. ❑ **tear open** *v.* [1900s–50s] (*US Und.*) to rob extensively. ❑ **tear someone a new ass** *v. see* separate entry. ❑ **tear someone's ass** *v. see* separate entry. ❑ **tear someone's meat-house down** *v.* [SE *meat-house*, a larder, here meaning one's body] [20C+] (*US*) to defeat, to thrash. ❑ **tear someone's playhouse down** *v.* [1950s] (*US black*) to render someone's life unhappy or unpleasant. ❑ **tear someone up for arse-paper** *v. see* separate entry. ❑ **tear the arse out of** *v.* (*also* **tear the bollocks off**) [1940s+] to destroy completely, to render useless. ❑ **tear the doors off** *v. see BLOW THE DOORS OFF under* BLOW *v.*[1]. ❑ **tear the end off** *v.* [1920s] to finish with a person or thing. ❑ **tear up** *see* separate entries. ❑ **that's torn it** [*TEAR IT* above] [20C+] that has ruined it, spoiled it.

tear and ages! *excl. see* TARE AN' AGES! *excl.*

tear and wounds! *excl. see* TARE AN' OUNS! *excl.*

tear-arse *n.*[1] (*also* **tear-ass**) [their effect on the stomach; ARSE *n.* (1)/ASS *n.* (2)] **1** [20C+] cheese. **2** [1920s+] (*Aus./N.Z.*) treacle, golden syrup.

tear-arse *n.*[2] (*also* **tear-ass**) [TEAR ARSE *v.*] [1920s+] a very busy, energetic person.

tear arse *v.* (*also* **tear ass**) [TEAR *v.* (1) + ARSE *n.* (1)/ASS *n.* (2)] **1** [1920s+] to leave very quickly, to rush off; to rush around; often with prep. eg *...about*, *...away*. **2** [1950s] to attack violently.

tear-ass *adj.* [TEAR ARSE *v.*] [1950s+] agitated and angry.

tearaway *n.* [SE *tearaway*, an unruly person] [1930s+] a minor gangster, a small-time villain.

tearing *adj.* (*also* **taring**) [TEAR *v.*] **1** [mid-17C–1900s] impressive, splendid, first-rate. **2** [mid-17C–1920s] violent, rowdy or reckless in behaviour. **3** [1920s] of work, exhausting.

tear into *v.* [20C+] **1** (*also* **tear in**) to throw oneself enthusiastically into a task. **2** to attack physically, or verbally.

IN PHRASES

❑ **get tore in** *v.* [1940s+] (*Scot.*) to fight vigorously.

tearjerker *n.* [1910s+] (*orig. US*) **1** a heavily romantic film with either a sad or happy conclusion, either of which should guarantee a weeping audience. Similarly used to describe mawkish ballads and love-songs, or a sad situation. **2** one who creates such material.

tearjerking *n.* [backform. TEARJERKER *n.*] [1940s+] an act of inducing sentimental feelings in someone.

tearjerking *adj.* (*also* **tearjerker, tear-yanking**) [backf. TEARJERKER *n.*] [1930s+] maudlin, sentimental.

tear off *v.*[1] [TEAR *v.*] [mid-19C+] to rush away, to leave at speed.

tear off *v.*[2] [SE *tear off*, to rip off a piece] **1** [late 19C+] (*US*) to perform an action or activity. **2** [20C+] (*US Und.*) to steal. **3** [1940s] (*US Und.*) to cheat one's partner of their share of criminal profits.

IN PHRASES

❑ **tear off a lump** *v.* [1910s] (*Aus.*) to succeed, to accomplish something. ❑ **tear off a piece** *v.* (*also* **...a bit, ...a chunk, ...a piece of ass, ...a piece of tail**) [SE *tear off* + PIECE *n.* (6)/BIT *n.*[1] (2c)/SE *chunk*] [1930s+] (*orig. Aus.*) of a man, to have sexual intercourse. ❑ **tear off a strip** *v.* (*also* **tear a strip off, tear strips off**) [the fig. removal of a *strip*(e) of rank] [1940s+] (*orig. RAF/milit.*) to criticize severely, to reprimand.

tear off *v.*[3] **1** [1910s] (*US*) to speak in an aggressive manner. **2** [1940s] to snore.

tearoom *n.* (*also* **teahouse, t-room**) [SE *toilet* + *room* + play on *tearoom*] [1920s+] (*US gay*) a public lavatory popular for casual sex and assignations.

IN COMPOUNDS

❑ **tearoom queen** *n.* (*also* **tearoom cruiser, T-room queen**) [-QUEEN *sfx*] [1960s+] (*US gay*) a homosexual who hangs around public lavatories for sex. ❑ **tearoom trade** *n.* (*also* **tea trade**) [TRADE *n.* (3)] [1950s+] (*US gay*) **1** the world of sexual assignations, pick-ups and consummation practised in public lavatories. **2** men who enjoy being fellated in public lavatories.

tears *n.*[1] [1920s] (*US*) onions.

tears *n.*[2] [resemblance] [1930s–40s] (*US*) pearls.

tears and cheers *n.* [rhy. sl.] [1920s–40s] (*US*) ears.

tears of the tankard *n.* [late 17C–mid-19C] drops of liquor that fall onto the careless drinker's clothing.

tear someone a new ass *v.* (*also* **cut someone..., rip..., tear someone a new asshole, tear someone a new one**) [ASS *n.* (2)/ASSHOLE *n.* (1)] [1960s+] (*US*) to attack someone savagely, either physically or verbally.

tear someone's ass *v.* (*also* **rip..., cut..., ...asshole**) [SE *tear* + ASS *n.* (2)/ASSHOLE *n.* (1)] **1** [1930s+] (*US*) to criticize someone severely. **2** [1930s+] (*W.I., Guyn.*) to thrash severely, to flog, usu. with *out* or *up*. **3** [1960s+] (*US*) in fig. use, e.g, to lose when gambling.

tear someone up for arse-paper *v.* (*also* **chew someone up for arse-paper, rip..., tear someone up for dunny paper**) [SE *tear up* + ARSE *n.* (1)/DUNNY *n.*[2] + SE *paper*] [1910s+] (*mainly N.Z.*) to scold, to reprimand, to attack and totally overcome in an argument; thus ext. as *well, I'll be torn up for arse-paper!*, an excl. of surprise or disbelief.

tear-up *n.*[1] [mid-19C+] a commotion, esp. as [1950s+] (*US jazz*), a spell of wild, destructive behaviour, a mêlée.

tear-up *n.*[2] [late 19C] (*UK tramp*) a rag, ragged clothing.

tear up *v.* **1** [1920s+] (*also* **tear it up, tear up shit**) (*US black*) to enjoy oneself, to do something with relish or well. **2** [1930s–80s] (*US black*) to have sexual intercourse. **3** [1940s+] to criticize, to attack verbally. **4** [1940s+] to make a great impression (on). **5** [1950s+] (*US*) to distress, to upset; often in ironic use. **6** [1950s+] to destroy, lit. and fig., occas. to beat up. **7** [1960s+] (*US gang*) to cry [ext. of sense 5].

IN PHRASES

❑ **tear up jack** *v. see* CUT UP JACK *v.*

tear up the pea patch *v.* [1910s+] (*US*) to go on a rampage.

tease *n.* **1** [late 18C–mid-19C] a menial servant. **2** [mid-19C] one who can easily be teased. **3** [mid-19C+] (*also* **teaze**) one who likes to tease. **4** [1920s+] a woman or homosexual man who provokes a man sexually but then resists intercourse; also used of men. **5** [1920s+] the act of teasing somebody else sexually.

tease *v.*[1] (*also* **teaze**) [SE *tease*, to 'thrash' out the fibres of wool, flax etc, before spinning] [late 18C–mid-19C] to flog, to whip (esp. of convicted villains who were secured to a cart for their punishment).

tease *v.*[2] [SE *tease*/abbr. COCKTEASE *v.*] [1920s+] of a woman, to provoke a man sexually but to refuse him actual intercourse.

IN PHRASES

❑ **tease someone's cock** *v. see* COCKTEASE *v.*

teaser *n.*[1] (*also* **teazer**) [boxing jargon *teaser*, a tricky opponent, hard to beat] [mid-18C–1930s] something that causes annoyance or is difficult or hard to deal with.

teaser *n.*[2] (*also* **teazer**) [? TIZZY *n.*[1]] [mid-19C] a sixpence (2½p).

teaser *n.*[3] [abbr. COCKTEASER *n.*] [late 19C+] a woman who allows, even encourages some physical intimacies but, however daring, will always stop short of intercourse.

teaser *n.*[4] [20C+] (*orig. US*) a sample of something to arouse or whet one's appetite, a taste.

teaser *n.*[5] [1900s] a small patch of hair grown beneath the lower lip.

teaser of (the) catgut *n.* (*also* **teazer of the catgut**) [early–mid-19C] a violinist, a fiddler.

teaspoon *n.*[1] [mid-19C] (*UK Und.*) £5000.

teaspoon *n.*[2] [it is half a SPOON *n.* (7)] [1950s+] (*drugs*) a measure of narcotic drugs.

teaster *n. see* TESTER *n.*[1].

tea strainers *n.* [rhy. sl.] [1980s+] trainers.

teat *n.*

IN PHRASES

❑ **get on someone's teats** *v. see* GET ON SOMEONE'S TITS *under* TIT *n.*[2].

teatchgir *adj. see* TEAICH-GIR *adj.*

teatowel-head *n. see* TOWEL-HEAD *under* TOWEL *n.*

tea trade *n. see* TEAROOM TRADE *under* TEAROOM *n.*

teatree *n.*

IN PHRASES

❑ **away in the teatree** *adj.* (*also* **up in the teatree**) [2000s] (*N.Z.*) living in a remote area.

teaze *v. see* TEASE *v.*[1].

teazer *n.* **1** *see* TEASER *n.*[1]. **2** *see* TEASER *n.*[2].

IN PHRASES

❑ **teazer of (the) catgut** *n. see* TEASER OF (THE) CATGUT *n.*

teazle *n.* [SE *teasel*, a plant with prickly leaves and flower-heads; + ? pun on sexual teasing] [19C] the vagina.

tec *n.* [abbr.] **1** [mid-19C+] (*also* **teck, tect**) a detective. **2** [1930s–70s] a detective story.

tec- *pfx see* TECHNO- *pfx.*

tecata *n.* [synon. Sp.] [1960s+] (*US drugs*) heroin.

tecato *n.* [TECATA *n.*] [1960s+] (*US drugs*) **1** a heavy user of marijuana. **2** a morphine or heroin addict.

tech *n.* [abbr.] [1940s+] (*orig. US*) a technician.

techie *n.* (*also* **teckie, technico**) [abbr.] **1** [1960s+] a technician. **2** [2000s] a computer enthusiast or expert. **3** [2000s] technology. **4** [2000s] (*US black*) someone who first steals one's possessions and then displays them openly.

technicolour yawn *n.* (*also* **living color yawn, technicolor cough, ...laugh, ...spit, ...yodel**) [the multicoloured effluvia so produced] [1960s+] (*orig. Aus.*) the act of vomiting.

techno- *pfx* (*also* **tech-**) [1980s+] (*US*) a comb. form used to indicate technological expertise or involvement, esp. as regards computing, e.g. *technofreak*.

teck *n. see* TEC *n.* (1).

teckie *n. see* TECHIE *n.*

tect *n. see* TEC *n.* (1).

Ted *n.*[1] [Ital. *tedesco*, German] [1940s–50s] (*N.Z. milit.*) a German soldier.

Ted *n.*[2] **1** [1950s+] a *teddy* boy [abbr.; the youth cult orig. known as 'Edwardians' and named for their sartorial style, borrowed from the contemporary upper-class dandies who in turn had recreated the fashions of their own grandfathers]. **2** [1990s+] a person [from sense 1].

ted *adj.* [abbr. WASTED *adj.* (4)] [1980s+] (*US campus*) drunk.

teddy bear *n.*[1] [rhy. sl.] **1** [20C+] a pear. **2** [1930s+] (*Aus.*) a show-off, esp. a cricketer who jokes around on the field and plays to the crowd [= LAIR *n.* (1)].

teddy bear *n.*[2] **1** [20C+] (*Irish*) a large, brown shawl. **2** [1940s–50s] (*Aus.*) a koala. **3** [1950s+] (*US black*) a plump, sexy woman. **4** [1990s+] a sanitary towel [euph.]. **5** [2000s] (*S.Afr. gay*) a hirsute, usu. plump, man.

ted frazer *n.* [rhy. sl.] [1960s+] a razor, always a cut-throat, 'open' model.

Ted Heath *n.* [rhy. sl.; pron. 'heef', ult. *Edward Heath* (1916–2005), British prime minister 1970–74] [1970s+] **1** a thief. **2** teeth.

tee *n.* **1** *see* T *n.*[2] (3). **2** *see* T *n.*[4].

teed off *adj.* (*also* **t'd off**) [TEE OFF *v.*] [1950s+] (*US*) annoyed, irritated, upset.

teed up *adj.* (*also* **tea'd, tead up, teaed up, tee'd, teed out, t-oed**) [TEA *n.* (3)/TEA *n.* (4a)] **1** [late 19C+] (*US*) drunk; ext. as *teed up to the tits*. **2** [1930s+] (*US drugs*) intoxicated by marijuana. **3** [1940s] in a state of tense excitement due to circumstances [fig. use of sense 2].

teef *see under* T'IEF.

tee-hee *n.*

IN PHRASES

❑ **give someone the big tee-hee** *v.* [1900s] (*US*) to laugh at.

teen- *pfx* [1950s+] (*orig. US*) a comb. form for anything applicable to or enjoyed by teenagers, e.g. *teenflick, teenzine*, a magazine for teenagers.

teenchy weenchy/teencie-weencie *adj. see* TEENSIE-WEENSIE *adj.*

teener *n.*[1] (*also* **teen, teenie, teeny**) [abbr.] [1950s+] (*US*) a teenager.

teener *n.*[2] [abbr.] [1990s+] (*US drugs*) a sixteenth of an ounce of a given (powdered) drug.

teenie *n. see* TEENER *n.*[1].

teenie weenie *n.* [*teenie* (see TEENER *n.*[1]) + WEENIE *n.*[1] (4)] [1970s+] (*US gay*) a teenager available for being fellated.

teensie-weensie *adj.* (*also* **eensie-teensie, eensy-beensy, eensy-weensy, eentsy-weentsy, teenchy weenchy, teencie-weencie, teensy, teensy-weensy, teentsy-weentsy, teeny-weeny, tintsy-wintsy, weeny teeny**) [infant pron. of SE *tiny*] [late 19C+] (*orig. US juv.*) very small, minuscule.

teenth *n.* [abbr. SE a *sixteenth* of an ounce (2g)] [1990s+] (*drugs*) a very small amount of cannabis.

teeny *n. see* TEENER *n.*[1].

teeny *adj.* [SE *teen*] [1960s+] pertaining to a teenager, usu. a girl.

teenybopper *n.* (*also* **teenybobber, teeny-bop, teenboppette, teenyrocker**) [TEENY *n.* + BOP *v.* (5)] **1** [1960s+] a young girl, usu. in very early teens, with a predilection for rock music and the boys who play it; occas. used of a trend-obsessed boy. **2** [1960s+] anybody teenage or considered too young for the situation. **3** [1960s+] (*US black*) a young, inexperienced (and as such unpopular) person. **4** [1970s+] (*US gay*) an underage boy.

teenybopper *adj.* (*also* **teenybop**) [TEENYBOPPER *n.*] **1** [1960s+] pertaining to a teenager, usu. a young girl. **2** [1990s+] in fig. use insignificant, 'lightweight'.

teeny-weeny *adj. see* TEENSIE-WEENSIE *adj.*

tee off *v.* (*also* **tee off on**) [? fig. use of golfing jargon *tee off* + euph. for *pee off* under PEE *v.*/PISS OFF *v.* or ? var. on TICK OFF *v.*[1]] [1950s+] (*US*) **1** to criticize, to reprimand, to attack verbally, to irritate or anger someone. **2** to feel anger or irritation. **3** to hit very hard.

tee (something) up *v.* [golfing jargon] [1930s+] to get (something) ready, to prepare (something).

tee-tee *n. see* TITTY *n.*

tee-tee *adj. see* TI-TI *adj.*

teeth *n.* **1** [1950s] (*W.I. Rasta*) bullets [similarity in shape]. **2** [1980s+] (*drugs*) cocaine, crack cocaine [similarity in colour/size].

(IN PHRASES)

❑ **chip one's teeth** *v.* [one's fury fig. damages one's teeth] [1940s+] (*US, orig. milit.*) to talk, esp. to excess or angrily. ❑ **draw teeth** *v.* [Hotten (1864) cites it as 'Medical Student slang'] [mid–late 19C] (*UK Und.*) to wrench off door-knockers. ❑ **give skin-teeth** *v.* [fig. use of 'the skin of one's teeth' to mean superficiality] [20C+] (*W.I.*) **1** to smile falsely when one actually feels furious or embittered. **2** to laugh cynically. ❑ **give teeth** *v.* [1990s+] to smile. ❑ **have one's back teeth afloat** *v.* (*also* **have one's back teeth awash, have one's back teeth under, have one's teeth swimming**) (*orig. US*) **1** [late 19C+] to be very drunk. **2** [20C+] (*also* **have one's kidneys afloat**) to be desperate to urinate. ❑ **have one's back teeth underground** *v.* [1900s–10s] to have eaten to satiation or excess. ❑ **not pick one's teeth** *v.* (*also* **unpick one's teeth**) [20C+] (*W.I.*) to make no comment, to stay absolutely silent, to say nothing. ❑ **punish one's teeth** *v. see under* PUNISH *v.* ❑ **scribble one's teeth** *v.* [2000s] (*US black*) to talk; to preach. ❑ **strip teeth and bite** *v. see under* STRIP *v.* ❑ **throw one's teeth** *v.* [mid-19C] to speak.

(IN EXCLAMATIONS)

❑ **in your teeth!** [late 17C–mid-18C] a dismissive rejoinder. ❑ **keep your teeth!** [mid-19C] calm down!

teether *n.* [1960s] an immature person, a 'baby'.

teetotal hotel *n.* [where there would be absolutely no liquor] [late 19C] **1** a workhouse. **2** a prison.

teetotally *adv.* [early 19C–1930s] completely.

tee up *v. see* TEE (SOMETHING) UP *v.*

teevee *n. see* T.V. *n.*

Tefal *n.* [a series of advertisements for Tefal non-stick pans in which such individuals featured] [1990s+] (*UK juv.*) one who has a notably large forehead.

Teflon kid *n.* [nothing 'sticks' to him, ult. the advert for the Teflon brand] [1980s+] (*Aus. prison*) a tough young person.

Teg/Tege *n. see* TAIG *n.*

tegebreg *n.* (*also* **teggereg**) [1950s+] (*W.I.*) a loud-mouthed domineering person.

Tegue/Teig *n. see* TAIG *n.*

tekeesha *n.* [W.I. pron. of SE *take*, + ?] [1990s+] (*W.I.*) a woman who bases her relationships on the partner's wealth.

tek life *n.* [W.I. pron. of SE *take*, i.e. one who 'takes hold of' life] [1980s+] (*W.I./UK black teen*) a fashionable, popular person, a fashionable thing or place.

tekram *n.* [backsl.] [mid-19C+] market, esp. Covent Garden; thus *ogging ot tekram*, going to market.

Tel *n.* [1970s+] the almost invariable nickname for working-class Londoners called Terry.

tele *n. see* TELLY *n.*

telegram carrier *n.* [he 'comes fast'] [1990s+] (*W.I.*) a man who prematurely ejaculates.

telegraph *n.* **1** [early 19C–1900s] a scout or spy. **2** [mid-19C–1900s] (*Aus.*) a member of a bushranging gang whose task is to keep the others informed of the whereabouts of potential victims or efforts to capture them. **3** [mid-19C+] a network of gossip and rumour that brings news (often inaccurate) before the official sources. **4** [1960s+] (*UK prison*) a means of inter-cell communication in prison, by tapping mutually understood codes on the walls.

telegraph *v.* [1920s+] (*US*) to communicate one's intentions, usu. inadvertently.

telephone *n.* **1** [1950s+] (*Can.*) a bilingual or multilingual Canadian who moves between the two national groups – Anglo*phone* and Franco*phone* – and is generally despised by both. **2** [1970s+] (*US campus*) a euph. for toilet; e.g. *I have to use the men's telephone.* **3** [1980s+] (*Aus. prison*) a means of inter-cell communication in prison by tapping on the plumbing pipes. **4** [1990s+] (*UK Und.*) a scar in the form of a curving line from the corner of the mouth to the earlobe, inflicted on an informer's face.

(IN PHRASES)

❑ **big white telephone** *n.* [1970s+] the lavatory. ❑ **speak on the big white telephone** *v.* (*also* **talk on the..., talk to God on the..., ...great white telephone**) [1960s+] (*orig. US*) to vomit. ❑ **talk to Ralph on the big white telephone** *v.* [RALPH *v.*] [1970s+] (*orig. US campus*) to vomit. ❑ **talk to the big telephone** *v.* (*also* **talk into a porcelain telephone**) [1970s+] (*orig. US campus*) to vomit.

telephone number *n.* [the digits used in big city exchanges] [1940s+] extremely large sums of money; recent use is pl.; also in phr., *talking telephone numbers*.

telephone number bit *n. see* BIT *n.*[1].

telephone pole *n. see* BEANPOLE *n.*

telescope *n.* [1930s] (*US tramp*) a nested set of tin cans used for cooking.

telescope *v.* [late 19C–1950s] (*Aus.*) to silence, to suppress.

teletubby *n.* [rhy. sl. = HUBBY *n.*; ult. *Teletubbies*, the children's TV programme] [1990s+] one's husband.

tell *v.*

SE in slang uses

(IN PHRASES)

❑ **get one told** *v.* [1930s–50s] (*US black*) to reprimand someone, to upbraid someone, to tell someone off. ❑ **tell...** *v. see also under* relevant n. ❑ **tell a thing or two** *v. see* KNOW A THING OR TWO *v.* ❑ **tell it like it is** *v.* (*also* **say it like it is, t.i.l.i.s.**) [1940s+] (*orig. US black/hippie*) to be absolutely honest, to reject dissembling; often as an exhortatory imperative.

teller *n.* [mid-18C–mid-19C] (*boxing*) a heavy, telling blow.

tell-tale *n.*[1] [mid-19C] the mouth.

tell-tale *n.*[2] [it shows where one/the car is] [1950s+] (*Aus.*) a motor vehicle's indicator light.

telly *n.* (*also* **tele**) [abbr.] **1** [1930s+] *tele*vision [TELE *n.*]. **2** [1990s+] (*US black*) a hotel [SE ho*tel*].

temazzy *n.* (*also* **mazzy**) [abbr.] [1990s+] (*UK drugs*) temazepam.

temmies *n.* (*also* **temazies, tems**) [abbr.] [1980s+] (*drugs*) *tem*azepam (a tranquillizer and short-acting hypnotic).

temp *n.*[1] [abbr.] [late 19C+] *temp*erature.

temp *n.*[2] [abbr.] [1930s+] a *temp*orary worker; usu. a secretary.

temp *v.* [TEMP *n.*[2]] [1970s+] to take on a job as a temporary worker, usu. a secretary.

temple *n.* **1** [late 18C] a brothel. **2** [mid-19C+] the lavatory.

temple balls *n.* [1960s+] (*drugs*) strong Nepalese hashish, sold in small balls and allegedly manufactured in Buddhist temples.

temple-pickling *n.* [proper name *the Temple*, two of the Inns of Court (the Inner and Middle Temple) + SE *pickle*, i.e. to 'bathe' in liquid. During 17C any bailiff caught within the limits of the temple was automatically thus punished] [late 17C–early 19C] (*UK Und.*) the ducking of court officials beneath a pump.

tempus-map *n.* [Lat. *tempus*, time + SE *map*] [mid-19C] (*UK Und.*) a watch.

tems *n. see* TEMMIES *n.*

Ten *n.* [1990s+] (*US black*) a Mac-10 automatic pistol.

Ten, the *n.* [established as a publicity stunt in 1930s by J. Edgar Hoover (1895–1972), head of the FBI] [1930s+] (*US Und.*) the Ten Most Wanted Criminals List.

ten *n.* **1** [1940s] (*US black*) the human toes. **2** [1980s+] the ideal woman or man [the 'perfect' score of 10 out of 10, reinforced by the film *10* (1979)]. **3** *see* TEN BONES *n.*

SE in slang uses

(IN PHRASES)

❑ **ten and two** *n.* (*also* **ten-two**) [1940s+] (*US Und.*) a prostitute's charge: $10 for herself plus $2 for a hotel room. ▫ **ten in the hundred** *n.* [interest of 10% was considered extortionate] [17C–early 19C] a usurer. ▫ **ten o'clock girl** *n.* [they had to surrender to their bail at the Magistrates' Court at that time in the morning] [1930s–50s] a London prostitute. ▫ **ten, ten, two and a quarter** (*also* **ten, eight, two and a quarter; ten, twelve...**) [10lb (54kg) of flour, (10lb/8lb/12lb of meat,) 2lb (9kg) of sugar and ¼lb (113g) of tea] [mid-19C–1910s] (*Aus.*) the regular weekly ration of food, as issued to hands on a rural property. ▫ **ten times ten** *n.* [mid-19C] (*US*) $100. ▫ **ten-twenty-thirty joint** *n.* [the seat prices: 10¢, 20¢, 30¢ + JOINT *n.* (1)] [1900s–40s] (*US*) a cheap theatre.

ten *adj.*

SE in slang uses

IN COMPOUNDS

▫ **ten-bob squats** *n.* [the price (ten shillings/50p) of the seats] [late 19C] the stalls in a theatre. ▫ **ten-bob taxi** *n.* [1960s–80s] (*Aus.*) a police car. ▫ **ten-cent** *adj.* see TWO-CENT *adj.* ▫ **ten-cent bag** *n.* (*also* **ten cents**) [BAG *n.*[1] (7)] [1950s+] (*drugs*) a $10 bag of marijuana or any other drug, e.g. crack cocaine. ▫ **ten commandments** *n.* [stereotyping of a domineering wife or an aggressive woman] [mid-16C–1910s] a woman's fingernails, esp. in the context of scratching someone's face. ▫ **ten-dollar word** *n.* [1940s+] (*US*) any form of writing or speech seen as exceeding the style or vocabulary limits of a 'normal' person; the number of dollars is variable. ▫ **ten inches** *n.* see *TWELVE INCHES under* TWELVE *adj.* ▫ **ten-letter word** *n.* see FOUR-LETTER WORD *n.* ▫ **tenpenny** *n.* [? size of tenpenny piece, an obsolete coin since 18C, or SE *tenpenny nail*, a large (5cm/3in) nail] [1940s] (*W.I.*) a bloated, fat stomach. ▫ **ten yards** *n.* [SE ten + YARD *n.*[3] (1)] [1940s] (*US Und.*) $1000.

IN PHRASES

▫ **ten miles of bad road** *n.* (*also* **five miles of bad road**) **1** [1960s+] (*US black*) bad luck, esp. if it persists. **2** [2000s] (*Aus.*) something particularly unattractive. ▫ **tenpence to the shilling** *adj.* [a shilling had twelve pence] [mid-19C+] not very intelligent, slightly eccentric, odd. ▫ **ten pounds of shit in a five-pound bag** [20C+] (*US*) anything considered ugly, esp. someone obese or overweight.

tenant *n.*

SE, based on old legal jargon, in slang uses

IN PHRASES

▫ **tenant at will** *n.* [*tenant at will*, one whose tenancy only exists according to the will of the landlord] **1** [mid-17C–early 19C] one whose wife arrives at the alehouse to make him come home. **2** [early 19C] a male lover [also note APARTMENT TO LET *n.*]. ▫ **tenant for life** *n.* [early 19C] a married man. ▫ **tenant in tail** *n.* [*tenant in tail*, a tenancy held under certain specific limitations + note TAIL *n.* (3)] **1** [mid-17C] one whose drunkenness promotes indiscriminate displays of affection. **2** [18C–19C] the penis. **3** [late 18C–early 19C] one whose wife arrives at the alehouse to make him come home.

ten bones *n.* (*also* **ten**) [late 15C–mid-16C; 1940s] (*later use is US black*) the fingers of both hands; thus excl. *by these ten bones!* a mild oath.

tench *n.*[1] [? image of the vagina as a prison (TENCH *n.*[2]), or SE *tench*, and thus another term that equates the vagina with fish] [mid–late 19C] the vagina.

tench *n.*[2] [abbr. SE *penitentiary*] **1** [mid-19C] (*Aus.*) the convict prison in Hobart, Tasmania; thus *tenchman*, an inmate of that prison. **2** [mid–late 19C] Millbank Prison.

tender *adj.*

SE in slang uses

DERIVATIVES

▫ **tenderoni** *n.* [SE *tender* + cod Ital.] [1980s+] (*US black teen*) a sweet young woman.

IN COMPOUNDS

▫ **tender box** *n.* [BOX *n.*[1] (1)] [1970s+] (*gay*) a young boy with alluring buttocks. ▫ **tender dick** *n.* [DICK *n.*[1] (5)] [1960s+] (*US black*) the sexual equivalent of a soft heart: one's actions are dictated by sexual rather than emotional/intellectual feelings. ▫ **tenderfoot** *n.* [orig. used of the new arrivals in the mining or ranching areas of the Western US] [mid-19C+] (*orig. US*) a novice, an inexperienced person. ▫ **tender parnel** *n.* [ironic uses of SE *tender parnel*, a tenderly educated and gently brought-up woman, but note 'Tender Parnell, who broke her finger in a posset drink' (Grose, 1785)] [late 17C–early 19C] **1** a squeamish, oversensitive person. **2** a prostitute who works in a brothel.

tenderloin *n.* [SE *tenderloin*, a tender cut of beef, pork etc. Coined for an area of New York City, the term was extended to cover similar areas of other major US cities, notably San Francisco, where it is still in use. The concept was linked to police corruption and so great were the bribes and pay-offs available to officers of the 29th Precinct, who administered the area, that they termed it 'the juicy part of the service'. First used in 1876 by a notably corrupt policeman, Alexander S. 'Clubber' Williams (nicknamed for his propensity for violence rather than any love of nightspots), who had just moved to the 29th Precinct. 'I have been living on rump steak in the Fourth District,' he remarked, 'I will have some tenderloin now'] [late 19C+] (*US*) **1** the area of a city devoted to pleasure and entertainment, typically containing restaurants, theatres, gambling houses and brothels. **2** an area where the homeless gather.

tenement house in Greenwich Village *n.* [play on SE *greens/Greenwich*] [late 19C] (*US*) an order of soup with greens in it.

tenements to let *n.* see APARTMENT TO LET *n.*

ten-four *phr.* (*also* **10-4, Ten Four**) [US police '10 codes', e.g. 10–15 civil disturbance, 10–31 crime in progress] **1** [1960s+] message received and understood. **2** [1990s+] thus, fig. ready, prepared.

ten furlongs *n.* [rhy. sl. = *a mile and a quarter*] [20C+] (*Aus.*) a daughter.

ten-hut *n.* [milit. order *ten-hut*, stand to attention] [1970s] (*US*) an erection.

tenip *n.* [backsl.] [mid–late 19C] a pint.

Tennant creek *n.* [rhy. sl.] [1980s+] (*Aus.*) a Greek.

tenner *n.* **1** [mid-19C+] (*Aus./UK*) £10, a £10 note. **2** [late 19C+] (*US*) a $10 bill. **3** [late 19C+] (*UK/US prison*) a ten-year prison sentence.

Tennessee *n.* [stereotyping of Southern food] [mid-19C] (*US*) hot corned bread.

tennies *n.* (*also* **tenners, tenny pumps, tenny runners, tennys**) [abbr.] [1960s+] (*US*) tennis shoes or trainers.

tennis fan *n.* [a variety of 'out' modern lesbian tennis stars] [1990s+] a lesbian.

tennis racket *n.* [rhy. sl.] [20C+] a jacket.

tenny pumps/runners *n.* see TENNIES *n.*

tennys *n.* see TENNIES *n.*

ten-per-cent *adj.* [TEN-PER-CENTER *n.* (2)] [1940s+] inadequate, useless.

10% *n.* [for ety. *see* 5% NATION *n.*] [1990s+] (*US black*) that percentage of (black) people who are rich, are only interested in personal gain and material wealth and who exploit the poor.

ten-per-center *n.* (*also* **ten per cent man**) **1** [1920s+] (*orig. US*) an agent who takes 'ten per cent' of one's earnings. **2** [1940s+] an inadequate, a failure [their success rate/popularity].

DERIVATIVES

▫ **ten-percenterie** *n.* [1920s+] (*orig. US*) an agency.

ten per cent house *n.* [mid-19C] (*US*) a cheap, poss. crooked, casino.

tenpin *v.* (*also* **do the bowling hold, hold a bowling ball**) [simulating the effect of holding a bowling ball] [1970s+] to insert the thumb into a woman's anus and the middle finger into her vagina simultaneously, doing a rhythmic swinging motion of the arm to provide sexual stimulation.

tens *n.* [the 10mg tablets] [1960s+] (*US drugs*) amphetamine.

tens and twos *n.* [rhy. sl.] [20C+] (*Aus.*) shoes.

tense *adj.* [on bad = good pattern] [1990s+] a general term of approval.

tenski *n.* (*also* **tensky**) [SE *ten* + 'Slav' sfx *-ski*] [1950s+] (*US*) **1** 10%. **2** a $10 bill.

tent *n.*[1] **1** [1900s] (*Anglo-Irish*) an umbrella. **2** [1910s] (*US Und.*) a prison cell. **3** [1920s–40s] (*US prison*) prison uniform; civilian clothes. **4** [1950s] any form of ill-fitting garment. **5** [1970s] a fat woman dressed in a kaftan or similarly voluminous garment.

tent *n.*[2] *see* T'AINT *n.*

Tenterden Park *n.* [ety. unknown] [mid-19C] (*UK Und.*) the King's Bench prison for debtors.

tenth part of a man *n. see* NINTH PART OF A MAN *n.*

Tenth Street *n.* [1940s] (*US black*) $10.

ten to two *n.* [rhy. sl.] [1930s+] a Jew.

tent peg *n.*[1] [the shape, but note the Biblical story of Jael and Sisera, i.e. the penis as a weapon (cf. AXE *n.* (2))] [19C] the penis.

tent peg *n.*[2] [rhy. sl.] [late 19C+] an egg.

tenuc *n.* [backsl. = CUNT *n.* (1)] [late 19C] the vagina.

ter *n. see* TERR *n.*

tercel-gentle *n.* [SE *tercel-gentle*, a male falcon] [late 16C–early 19C] (*UK Und.*) a well-off knight or any rich gentleman.

termage *n.* [SE *term*, a limit, a full extent] [late 16C–early 17C] (*UK Und.*) winnings at crooked gambling, esp. through cheating at bowls and later cards.

terminal *n.* [1990s+] death, murder.

terminal *adj.* [SE *terminal*, used of disease that will kill the sufferer] [1970s+] extreme, total.

term of endearment among sailors *phr.* [20C+] a euph. for BUGGER *n.*[1] (1).

terps *n. see* TURPS *n.*

terr *n.* (*also* **ter, terro**) [abbr./pron.] **1** [1930s+] (*Irish*) an ignorant but provocative individual. **2** [1970s+] (*S.Afr.*) a terrorist. **3** [1980s+] a tourist, esp. from Transvaal.

terrace *n.* [rhy. sl.; *terrace of houses* = trousers] [1940s+] (*Aus.*) trousers.

terra firma *n.* [Lat. *terra firma*, land, as opposed to sea] [late 17C–early 19C] a landed estate.

terrible *adj.* [on bad = good model] [early 19C+] (*Irish;US black/teen*) wonderful, admirable, first-rate.

terrible Turk *n.* [rhy. sl.] [20C+] work; as v., also as *slave and Turk*.

terrier crop *n.* [resemblance to a short-haired breed of dog] [mid–late 19C] a bristly haircut, denoting a person's recent stay in prison, where hair is cropped short.

Terries *n.* [abbr.] [1930s–50s] (*N.Z.*) the Territorial Army.

terrif *adj.* [abbr. TERRIFIC *adj.* (2)] [1970s+] wonderful, marvellous.

terrific *adj.* [SE *terrific*, terrifying] **1** [19C] very severe, excessive. **2** [late 19C+] a general term of approval, wonderful, very good indeed, 'great'.

terro *n. see* TERR *n.*

terrorist *n.* [joc. mispron.] [1980s+] (*S.Afr., W. and S.W. Cape*) a tourist, usu. from Transvaal.

terror to cats *n.* [late 19C] an ill-behaved small boy.

terry toon *n.* [rhy. sl.] **1** [1970s+] (*Aus.*) a pimp, one who lives off a prostitute [HOON *n.* (2)]. **2** [1980s+] (*Aus. prison*) derog. term for a black person [COON *n.* (5)].

Terry Waite *adj.* [rhy. sl.; ult. *Terry Waite* (b.1939), British humanitarian, also a famous hostage in Lebanon] [1990s+] late.

test *n.* (*also* **tess**) [? obs. SE *test*, a witness] [20C+] (*UK W.I.*) a person, a fellow.

tester *n.*[1] (*also* **teaster, testern, teston, testone**) [Fr. *teston*, a silver coin struck at Milan by Duke Galeazzo Sforza (1468–76). It had his own head on it, as did similar testons coined by Louis XII (r.1498–1515) and his successor François I (r.1515–47) of France and by Henry VIII (r.1509–47) of England] **1** [late 16C–1920s] sixpence. **2** [mid-19C–1940s] (*Aus.*) 25 strokes of the lash [reflects the association of numbers of lashes with denominations of coins].

tester *n.*[2] [1990s+] (*US drugs*) a free sample of a given drug, given out so as to encourage word-of-mouth reports that the dealer's stock is worth buying.

testoed *adj.* [SE *testosterone*] [2000s] macho, invigorated.

teston(e) *n. see* TESTER *n.*[1].

Tetbury portion *n.* [the poor image of the town of *Tetbury* in Gloucestershire] [late 18C–early 19C] sexual intercourse that is followed by a dose of venereal disease; 'A **** [CUNT *n.*] and a clap' (Grose, 1788).

tetched *adj.* [SE *touched*] [1930s+] (*US*) eccentric.

tete *n.* [? SE *tetter*, any pustule that erupts on the skin] [20C+] (*W.I.*) a bacterial skin disease, usu. attacking the feet.

tetes *n.* [TITTY *n.* (1)] [1960s] (*W.I.*) a large-breasted woman.

tet-galaxy *n.* [mid-19C] (*UK Und.*) the female breasts.

tether one's nags on *v. see under* NAG *n.*

tetra *n.* [SE *tetrahydrocannabinol*, the active ingredient of cannabis] [2000s] (*US black/drugs*) cannabis, usu. marijuana.

teuf-teuf *phr.* [synon. Fr. *teuf-teuf*, echoic of the sound of an early automobile motor, hence the automobile itself; the UK use suggests the departure of the (human) vehicle] [1900s–20s] goodbye.

teviss *n.* [backsl. form of Du. *stiver*, a small coin] [mid–late 19C] **1** a shilling. **2** a sixpence.

tew *v.* [SE *tew*, to beat, flog, belabour] [late 17C] of a man, to have sexual intercourse.

texan rude *adv.* [backsl.] [mid-19C+] next door.

(IN PHRASES)

❑ **texan rude nam** *n.* [mid-19C+] lit. 'next-door man', thus neighbour.

Texas *adj.*

(IN COMPOUNDS)

❑ **Texas-league** *adj.* [the stereotyping of the ostentatious taste of Texan millionaires; note earlier baseball jargon *Texas league*, second-rate] [1940s] (*US*) nouveau riche, vulgar. ❑ **Texas mickey** *n.* [1930s+] (*Can.*) a 84l cc. (130fl oz) bottle of rye whisky. ❑ **Texas roll** *n.* [ROLL *n.* (2)] [1970s+] (*US*) a fake bankroll, a note of a high denomination around a large number of notes of smaller denomination. ❑ **Texas shoe-shine** *n.* [2000s] (*US drugs*) inhalants. ❑ **Texas steel** *n.* [1970s+] (*US prison*) a prison. ❑ **Texas tea** *n.* (*also* **Texas pot**) [TEA *n.* (4a); the easy availability of wild marijuana in the state] [1930s+] (*drugs*) marijuana. ❑ **Texas turkey** *n.* [the armadillo is common in the state] [20C+] (*US*) an armadillo, as eaten *faute de mieux* during the Great Depression.

Tex Ritter *n.* [rhy. sl.; ult. Country and Western star *Tex Ritter* (1905–74); note THELMA (RITTER) *n.*] [1990s+] **1** bitter (beer). **2** the lavatory [SHITTER *n.*[1] (4)].

textiles *n.* [the opposite of a SE *naturist*] [1990s+] a person who frequents a beach with clothes on.

t.f.a. *adj.* [abbr. *too fucking awesome*] [1980s+] (*US campus*) wonderful, exceptional, very good.

t.g. *n.* [abbr. *tiny gangsta*] [1990s+] (*US black gang*) a junior member of a gang, under the age of ten.

t.g.i.f. *phr.* [abbr.] [1930s+] (*orig. US*) thank God it's Friday.

Thai *adj.*

SE used as a drug 'brandname'

(IN COMPOUNDS)

❑ **Thai (stick)** *n.* (*also* **ti-stick**) [1960s+] (*drugs*) a form of marijuana grown in Thailand, soaked in hashish oil and sold tied around a thin stick resembling a satay skewer. ❑ **Thai tabs** *n.* [2000s] (*US drugs*) dianabol, a form of methamphetamine. ❑ **Thai white** *n.* [1990s+] (*drugs*) a variety of heroin, refined in Thailand.

Thames butter *n.* [the '*South London Press* ...published a paragraph to the effect that a Frenchman was making butter out of Thames mud at Battersea. In truth this chemist was extracting yellow grease from Thames mud-worms' (Ware)] [late 19C–1900s] totally rancid butter.

thang *n.* [pron.] [1960s+] (*US black teen*) thing, esp. in phr. *do your own thang* etc.

IN PHRASES

❑ **dick thang** *n.* see DICK *n.*[1].

thank Christ *phr.* (*also* **thank fuck**) [1930s+] ext. of thank God.

thanks... *phr.*

SE in slang uses

IN PHRASES

❑ **thanks a bunch** (*also* **thanks a bundle, ...heap**) [? ironic use of SE *bunch* as many, thus 'many thanks'] [1950s+] thank you very much, often ironic. ❑ **thanks a million** [1950s+] thank you very much, often ironic. ❑ **thanks a pile** (*also* **...shitpotful**) [1990s+] (*Irish*) thank you very much, often in ironic use. ❑ **thanks for nothing** [late 19C+] a phr. of annoyance and contempt. ❑ **thanks for the buggy-ride** [1920s–30s] (*US*) thank you.

thank you and good night *phr.* [1970s+] a dismissive, sarcastic phr., 'what a load of nonsense', 'is that the best you can offer?'.

that *n.* [euph.] **1** [mid-17C; 1940s] sexual intercourse. **2** [19C] the penis. **3** [19C] the vagina.

that *adj.* [mid-19C+] a mildly derog. use of 'that' to imply one's disapproval, e.g. *Are you seeing that Terry tonight?*

thataboy! *excl.* see ATTABOY! *excl.*

that accounts for the milk in the coconut *phr.* see MILK IN THE COCONUT *under* MILK *n.*

that ain't hay *phr.* (*also* **that ain't chopped liver, that ain't/isn't peanuts, that isn't hay, there ain't no persimmons**) [the perceived insignificance of the various items] [1930s+] (*US*) a phr. used to mean that something is a large and/or significant amount.

that and a dime will get you a cup of coffee *phr.* (*also* **that and a nickel..., that and a quarter...**) [1950s+] (*US*) used of something considered unimportant or worthless.

that and this *n.* [rhy. sl. = PISS *n.* (2)] [20C+] urination.

thatch *n.* **1** [17C+] (*also* **top thatch**) the human hair. **2** [mid-19C+] a woman's pubic hair.

IN PHRASES

❑ **off one's thatch** *adj.* see OFF ONE'S HEAD *adj.*

-thatched *sfx* [THATCH *n.* (1)] [late 19C+] describing a person's hair, e.g. *well-thatched*, having a good growth of hair.

thatched head *n.* [his stereotyped unkempt appearance] [early 17C] an Irishman.

thatched house (under the hill) *n.* (*also* **reed-roof'd-cot**) [THATCH *n.* (2), but note *Thatched House* Lodge, Surrey, built for the keepers of Richmond Park in 1673 and subseq. owned by prime minister Sir Robert Walpole (1676–1745)] [late 18C–19C] the vagina.

thatch-gallows *n.* [all they are good for] [late 18C–mid-19C] a worthless person.

that's quacked! *excl.* [play on SE *cracked*] [1980s+] (*US campus*) that's unfair.

that's the way it goes *phr.* (*also* **that's the way the shit goes**) [late 19C+] that is the way things work out and one must accept the facts, like it or not.

thatta baby! *excl.* see ATTABOY! *excl.*

that there *n.* [euph.] [20C+] the vagina.

IN PHRASES

❑ **a bit of that there** *n.* [20C+] sexual intercourse.

that way *adj.* [euphs.] **1** [late 19C+] (*US*) pregnant. **2** [1910s+] (*also* **this way**) engaged in crime. **3** [1920s] drunk. **4** [1920s+] homosexual. **5** [1930s+] in love. **6** [1930s+] of a given character, e.g. voyeuristic.

THC *n.* [misreading of *t*etra*h*ydro*c*annabinnol, the active ingredient of cannabis] [1970s+] (*drugs*) phencyclidine.

the *adj.* [in imitation of a similar practice with the definite article in Fr. and Ital.] [mid-18C+] used before the names of certain well-known figures, esp. singers and actresses.

theatre *n.* [the accused, whether guilty or not, will 'act' their role, also the ironic acceptance that justice often depends more on image than facts] [mid-19C–1900s] a police court.

theg gens *n.* (*also* **teaich gens**) [backsl.; GEN *n.*[1]] [mid–late 19C] eight shillings (40p).

theg yeneps *n.* [backsl.; YENNEP *n.*] [mid-19C] eight pence.

Thelma (Ritter) *n.* [rhy. sl.; ult. *Thelma Ritter* (1905–69), US actress; note TEX RITTER *n.*] [1990s+] **1** the anus [SHITTER *n.*[1] (1)]. **2** a lavatory [SHITTER *n.*[1] (4)].

Thelonius Monk *n.* [rhy. sl. = SPUNK *n.* (5); ult. jazz pianist *Thelonius Monk* (1917–82)] [1940s+] semen.

them things *n. see under* THINGS *n.*

the rabbit died *phr.* [the test formerly used to determine pregnancy] [1940s+] I am pregnant.

therapy *n.* [1980s+] (*Aus. prison*) a beating by prison guards.

there *adj.* **1** [late 19C] (*Aus.*) of a person, attractive. **2** [20C+] (*US*) of a person, well informed; empathetic. **3** [1930s] (*US*) drunk. **4** [1930s–40s] (*US Und.*) reliable, trustworthy. **5** [1960s+] (*drugs*) intoxicated by drugs.

Theresa *n.* [initial letter] [2000s] (*S.Afr. gay*) **1** a traffic police officer, usu. male. **2** a tampon.

there's 'air! *excl.* (*also* **there's air! there's hair!**) [ref. is to a hairstyle featuring the side hair being pulled up and then shaped] [late 19C–1920s] a general excl., lit. there's a woman with a lot of *hair*.

there you are *n.* [rhy. sl.] **1** [late 19C+] a bar. **2** [20C+] tea [CHA *n.*[1]].

there you go *phr.* [1950s+] (*orig. US*) **1** a general phr. of agreement and approval. **2** a usu. negative phr. implying that the person is acting in their own particular way (yet) again.

these and those *n.* [rhy. sl.] [20C+] **1** a suit of clothes. **2** toes. **3** the nose.

thesp *n.* [abbr. SE *thespian*] [1960s+] an actor.

thespian *n.* (*also* **West End thespian**) [pun on SE + ? alleged prevalence of homosexual men in theatre] [1970s+] a lesbian.

thesping *adj.* [THESP *n.*] [1990s+] acting, e.g. *thesping business*.

they *n.* **1** [late 19C+] those in authority or power, the Establishment. **2** [1940s] (*US black*) a wife or mistress.

theydon bois *n.* [rhy. sl., pron. 'boyze'; ult. *Theydon Bois*, a town in Essex] [20C+] noise.

they're off, Mr Cutts! *excl.* [the racehorse trainer *Mr* E. *Cutts*, starter of the Auckland races] [1940s+] (*N.Z.*) things have started! now we're getting down to business!

thick *n.* [SE *thick*] **1** [mid-19C–1940s] any drink having a dense consistency, e.g. porter, cocoa, coffee. **2** [mid-19C+] (*orig./mainly juv.*) (*also* **thickwit**) a fool, an ignoramus. **3** [late 19C] mud. **4** [late 19C–1910s] a thick slice of buttered bread. **5** [1930s–60s] a thick fog. **6** [1990s+] (*US black*) one who has a muscular, well-developed physique.

IN PHRASES

❑ **fall in the thick** *v.* [late 19C] to become very drunk.

thick *adj.* **1** in senses of SE *thick-headed*. (**a**) [late 16C+] stupid, dull, foolish; often as THICK AS... *adj.* (1). (**b**) [late 19C–1950s] drunken. **2** in senses of lit. or fig. closeness. (**a**) [mid-18C+] close, intimate; also as THICK AS... *adj.* (2). (**b**) [1930s+] (*US campus*) emotionally involved, romantically attached. **3** [late 19C+] unacceptable due to its excess, too much to handle; usu. in phr. *a bit thick*. **4** [late 19C+] intense. **5** [1990s+] (*US black*) in senses of density, weight. (**a**) of money, plentiful [i.e. a thick roll of cash]. (**b**) thus ext. use of objects or people, displaying wealth. (**c**) (*UK/US black*) of a woman, physically attractive. (**d**) of a man, having a large penis. (**e**) (*US campus*) overweight.

IN PHRASES

❑ **thick in the clear** *adj.* [mid–late 19C] confused, at a loss for coherence.

SE in slang uses

IN COMPOUNDS

❑ **thick ear** *n.* (*also* **thick earhole**) **1** [late 19C+] an ear that has swollen up after a blow; usu. in phr. *give one a thick ear*.

2 [1970s] in fig. use, a thug. ❑ **thick end** *n.* [mid-19C+] the larger portion. ❑ **thick-leg** *n.* [his physique] [late 19C–1900s] a navvy. ❑ **thick lip** *n.* [var. on THICK EAR above] [1930s+] a minor beating, lit. a lip that has swollen up after receiving a blow. ❑ **thicklugged** *adj.* [1920s] very stupid. ❑ **thickneck** *n.* [1900s–50s] a large, thuggish person. ❑ **thick shins** *n.* [late 19C–1900s] (*UK prison*) food. ❑ **thick-skulled** *adj.* (*also* **thick-sculled, thickskin**) [late 17C–18C; 1940s] stupid, foolish.

IN PHRASES

❑ **thick 'n' thins** *n.* [? the pattern which may include stripes of varying widths] [1950s–70s] (*US black*) stylish nylon socks, usu. black or brown.

thick *adv.* **1** [late 16C; 19C] heavily. **2** [mid-19C+] intensely, severely. **3** [late 19C+] densely. **4** [late 19C+] intimately.

thick and dense *n.* [rhy. sl.] [1920s–40s] (*US*) expenses.

thick and thin *n.* [rhy. sl.] [20C+] **1** the chin. **2** gin. **3** (*Aus.*) the skin.

thick as... *adj.* **1** [late 16C+] stupid; used in a variety of combs, for the best-known of which see below. **2** [mid-18C+] very close, extremely intimate; used in a variety of combs, for the best-known of which see below.

IN PHRASES

❑ **...fiddlers in hell** (*also* **thick as flies round a treacle pot**) [20C+] (*US*) plentiful, numerous. ❑ **...poundies** [late 19C–1900s] (*Irish*) very stupid [Irish *poundies*, mashed potato mixed with onion and milk]. ❑ **...thieves** [mid-19C+] very intimate. ❑ **...three in a bed** [early 19C–1930s] very intimate. ❑ **...two inkle-weavers** [mid-18C–early 19C] very close [SE *inkle*, linen tape]. ❑ **...two short planks** (*also* **thick as eight short planks, ...two bricks**) [1970s+] very stupid.

thicker *n.* [? THICK 'UN *n.* (1)] [mid–late 19C] £1.

thicket *n.* [late 19C+] pubic hair, usu. female.

thick head *n.* [20C+] a hangover.

thickhead *n.* [THICK-HEADED *adj.*] [late 18C+] a fool, a simpleton; also as a term of address.

thick-headed *adj.* (*also* **clumpheaded**) [mid-18C+] stupid, foolish.

thickie *n.* [THICK *adj.*] [1960s+] a fool.

thicko *n.* [THICK *adj.*] [1970s+] a fool.

thick 'un *n.* (*also* **thick one**) [the dimensions of the coin/foodstuff] **1** [mid-19C–1950s] a sovereign (£1). **2** [1900s] five shillings, a crown (25p). **3** [1900s–40s] a slice of bread and butter. **4** [1930s] a silver dollar.

IN PHRASES

❑ **do someone a thick 'un** *v.* [1920s+] to play a 'dirty trick' on someone. ❑ **half-thick ('un)** *n.* (*also* **half-a-thick**) [late 19C–1900s] (*N.Z.*) a half-sovereign, ten shillings.

thickwit *n.* see THICK *n.* (2).

thief *n.*

IN PHRASES

❑ **you are a thief and a murderer and you have killed a baboon and stole his face** see under BABOON *n.*

thief *v.* [1950s+] (*W.I.*) to steal.

thief and robber *n.* [rhy. sl. = COBBER *n.*^{2} (1)] [20C+] (*Aus.*) a friend.

thieftaker *n.* [mid-18C] a man who hires himself out to swear on oath.

thieves' kitchen *n.* [ironic ref. to the supposed respectability and actual venality of such places] **1** [late 19C] the Law Courts in the Strand, London. **2** [1910s–20s] the Athenaeum Club, London. **3** [1920s+] the Stock Exchange.

thieving hooks *n.* [HOOK *n.*^{1} (1)] [early 19C] the fingers.

thieving irons *n.* [? their use in cutting purses] **1** [early 19C] scissors. **2** [early 19C–1910s] (*Aus.*) hands.

thigh-slapper *n.* [the exaggerated slapping of one's thighs to intimate the intensity of one's hilarity] [1960s+] (often used ironically) a supposedly very amusing joke.

thimble *n.* (*also* **thim**) [naut. *thimble*, a thick ring of metal, through which a rope can be pushed; thus the similarity in shape] [late 18C–1940s] (*UK Und.*) a watch.

IN COMPOUNDS

❑ **thimble-crib** *n.* [CRIB *n.*^{1} (1)] [early–mid-19C] (*UK Und*) a watchmaker's or jeweller's shop. ❑ **thimble-twister** *n.* (*also* **super twister, thimble-screwer**) [mid-19C–1930s] (*UK Und.*) a thief who specializes in stealing watches from their wearers.

IN PHRASES

❑ **draw a thimble** *n.* [late 18C–mid-19C] (*UK Und.*) to steal a pocket watch.

thimble cove *n.* [mid-19C+] (*UK Und*) one who operates a game of THIMBLE-RIG *n.*

thimble-crib *n.* [THIMBLE *n.* + CRIB *n.*^{1} (1)] [early–mid-19C] (*UK Und*) a watchmaker's or jeweller's shop.

thimbled *adj.*^{1} [THIMBLE *n.*] [early 19C] wearing a watch.

thimbled *adj.*^{2} [pun on THIMBLED *adj.*^{1} = wearing a watch, i.e. the police watching someone] [early 19C] arrested.

thimble-rig *n.* [SE *thimble* + RIG *n.*^{2} (1). Sante, *Low Life* (1991), suggests this to be one of 'the only major gambling games actually invented in the United States'. However, neither *DSUE* nor the *OED*'s first citation (*Hone's Every-day Book*, 1825) mentions this and Sante himself places its US appearance around 1860] [mid-19C–1930s] a version of the three-card trick, in which punters are asked to bet on which of three rapidly manipulated thimbles contains a pea; it is very rare that anyone other than the sharper's accomplice manages to bet correctly.

thimble-rigger *n.* (*also* **thimblerig**) [THIMBLE-RIG *n.*] [mid-19C+] one who operates a game of THIMBLE-RIG *n.*

thin *n.* **1** [mid-19C–1910s] a *thin* slice of bread and butter. **2** [1920s–40s] (*US*) ten cents [thin dime].

thin *adj.* [backform. f. *THIN DIME* below] **1** [1920s+] (*US tramp*) without money, broke. **2** [1970s+] (*US black*) of money, insubstantial.

SE in slang uses

IN COMPOUNDS

❑ **thin city** *n.* [antonym of FAT CITY *n.*^{1}] [1960s+] (*US campus*) a problematic or unpleasant situation. ❑ **thin dime** *n.* [the dime (ten cents) is the thinnest coin, as well as the smallest] [1920s–60s] (*US*) a tiny amount of money. ❑ **thin-gut** *n.* [17C] a very thin, starving person. ❑ **thin-hips** *n.* [1930s–40s] (*US drugs*) a veteran opium smoker who has lain on one hip for so long that it is misshapen. ❑ **thin one** *n.* (*also* **thin 'un**) [the coin's dimensions] [1920s–60s] (*US black/tramp*) a dime, ten cents. ❑ **thin time** *n.* [1920s+] a period of suffering or discomfiture. ❑ **thin 'un** *n.* [the coin's dimensions] [mid-19C–1920s] a half-sovereign (50p).

thin and thick *n.* [rhy. sl. = DICK *n.*^{1} (5)] [1980s] (*Aus.*) the penis.

Thing *n.* (*also* **thing**) [THING *n.* (1)] [20C+] used when one cannot remember a person's actual surname, e.g. *Mr Thing, Lady Thing.*

thing *n.* **1** [late 13C+] a person; esp. someone whose name one does not know or who is unimportant. **2** in sexual senses. (**a**) [early 16C+] seduction, sexual intercourse. (**b**) [late 16C+] the vagina; a prostitute. (**c**) [17C+] (*also* **something**) the penis. (**d**) [1920s+] the buttocks; usu. in phr. *shake that thing.* (**e**) [1940s] in pl. the testicles. (**f**) [1950s] (*US*) menstruation. **3** [20C+] (*US*) a non-specific descriptor, used when one either cannot or does not wish to use the correct term, e.g. *Shall we do the coffee shop thing? I have to do the work thing.* **4** in derog. uses. (**a**) [1920s–30s] (*US campus*) a male homosexual. (**b**) [1980s+] (*Aus. prison*) a term of abuse for an informer. **5** [1920s+] anything to which one cannot or does not wish to give a name. **6** [1930s+] an obsession, a preoccupation with (whether negative or positive), e.g. *I have a thing about...* **7** [1930s+] one's lifestyle, one's opinion, personal stance etc; usu. as *one's own thing* and in the phr. DO ONE'S (OWN) THING below. **8** [1930s+] an argument, a fuss. **9** [1940s+] a relationship, usu. sexual. **10** [1960s+] in drug uses. (**a**) heroin, cocaine, marijuana, whatever is one's current drug of choice. (**b**) an addiction to heroin or another narcotic. (**c**) a portion – a capsule, a bag – of a narcotic. (**d**) marijuana. **11** [1970s] (*US black*) a party. **12** [1970s+] any activity one enjoys. **13** [1980s+] (*US black*) a thing of importance; usu. as *it ain't* *no thing*, it is not important. **14** [1990s+] (*W.I.*) a girlfriend.

IN PHRASES

pertaining to the body and sex

❑ **do a thing** *v.* (*also* **do the thing**) [1970s+] **1** (*US*) to have sexual intercourse. **2** (*W.I., Jam.*) to get married. ❑ **do the natural thing** *v.* (*also* **...nasty thing, ...pussy thing, get down to the natural thing**) ['just as nature intended'] [1970s–80s] (*US black*) to have sexual intercourse. ❑ **get one's things** *v.* [1970s–80s] (*UK black*) of a man, to have sexual intercourse. ❑ **one thing** *n.* [abbr. *the one thing men desire*] [20C+] (*Irish*) sexual intercourse. ❑ **skin one's thing** *v.* [1970s] (*US*) to masturbate. ❑ **that thing** *n.* (*orig. US black*) **1** [1900s–40s] sexual intercourse. **2** [1900s–40s] the vagina. **3** [1960s+] the penis.

pertaining to one's lifestyle

❑ **dick thing** *n. see under* DICK *n.*[1]. ❑ **do one's (own) thing** *v.* [1950s+] (*orig. US black*) **1** to behave as dictated by one's personal beliefs, wishes, idiosyncrasies etc. **2** to put on an act. **3** (*W.I.*) to dance in an uninhibited manner, to enjoy oneself to the full. **4** to perform an action. ❑ **do one's things** *v. see* DO ONE'S BUSINESS *under* BUSINESS *n.* ❑ **do the thing** *v.* [1970s+] (*US gay*) to pursue a homosexual lifestyle. ❑ **get one's thing off** *v.* **1** [1970s+] (*US black*) to gain pleasure from any act. **2** [1980s+] (*drugs*) to inject oneself with heroin. ❑ **get one's thing together** *v.* [1970s+] to sort out one's way of life, one's business. ❑ **ghetto thing** *n.* [1990s+] (*US black*) anything pertaining to black cultural identity. ❑ **whole 'nother thing** *n.* [1960s+] (*US*) a totally different situation; something else completely. ❑ **your thing** *n.* (*also* **yo thang**) [1960s+] (*orig. US black*) one's preference, one's own style, one's role within the group.

other uses

❑ **have a thing about** *v.* (*also* **have a thing for**) [1930s+] (*orig. US*) **1** to be obsessed with, esp. to be sexually obsessed. **2** to dislike intensely. ❑ **have a thing with** *v.* (*also* **have a thing going, have something going**) **1** [1940s+] to have a love affair with. **2** [1960s+] (*US*) to have a complaint, a criticism of someone.

SE in slang uses

IN PHRASES

❑ **any old thing** *n.* [late-19C+] (*US*) any thing whatever. ❑ **do the — thing** *v.* [all such terms have a slight air of insincerity or at least of calculated performance, although they may equally well be quite genuine] [19C+] to perform a particular action, as defined by the missing adj. and the word *thing*; thus *do the amiable* (*thing*), *do the charming* (*thing*), *do the civil* (*thing*) etc. ❑ **do things to** *v.* (*also* **do things for**) [1930s+] to excite, usu. sexually. ❑ **up/down to a thing or two** *see* KNOW A THING OR TWO *v.* ❑ **you'll have to do the other thing** [i.e. *go to hell*] [mid-19C+] a phr. meaning if you don't like it this way, then…

thing, the *n.* **1** [18C+] whatever is correct or fashionable within the context; thus *un-thing*, unfashionable. **2** [1940s] in good health.

thingahoochie *n.* [1970s] anything otherwise unnamed, whether through choice or one's inability to recall the correct title.

thing-a-ling *n. see* DINGALING *n.*[2].

thingamadoodle *n. see* THINGUM *n.*

thingamadoodles *n. see* THINGUMABOB *n.*

thingamajig/thingamajigger *n. see* THINGUMAJIG *n.*

thingamerry *n.* (*also* **thingamerrybob, thingumsmeribob**) [20C+] (*W.I.*) anything otherwise unnamed, whether through choice or one's inability to recall the correct title.

thingamy/thingammy *n. see* THINGUMMY *n.*

thingembob/thinggumjybob *n. see* THINGUMABOB *n.*

thingie *n. see* THINGY *n.*

thingio *n. see* THINGY *n.* (1).

thingmadodger *n. see* THINGUMABOB *n.*

thingmegig *n. see* THINGUMAJIG *n.*

thingmy *n. see* THINGY *n.* (1).

thingmybob *n. see* THINGUMABOB *n.*

thingo *n.* [abbr. THINGUMABOB *n.*] [20C+] (*Aus.*) a nameless object.

thing-o-me *n. see* THINGUMMY *n.*

things *n.* **1** [late 16C+] clothes in general, esp. those that women put on to go out, in addition to their indoor dress. **2** [17C+] one's possessions carried at a particular time, eg on a journey. **3** [late 17C–19C] implements or equipment for some special use, utensils. **4** [early 19C] (*UK Und.*) stolen goods. **5** [mid-19C] (*UK Und.*) counterfeit money.

IN PHRASES

❑ **things and stuff** *adj.* [1930s] (*US black*) well-dressed; sophisticated.

SE in slang uses

IN PHRASES

❑ **them things** *n.* [20C+] (*drugs*) marijuana cigarettes. ❑ **things are brown** [1950s] (*W.I./UK black*) 'there is little money in hand and none coming' (Allsopp, *Dict. Caribbean English Usage*, 1996). ❑ **things are crook in Misclebrook** (*also* **things are crook at Musselbrook, things are crook in Tallarook, things are weak at Julia Creek, things is weak in Werris Creek**) [1960s+] (*Aus.*) various assonant/rhyming phrs. used to denote an unsatisfactory situation. ❑ **things curry** [? rhy. sl.; *curry and rice* = nice] [1990s+] (*W.I.*) everything is great, satisfactory.

things, the *n.* [mid-19C] (*UK Und.*) counterfeit money.

thingstable *n.* [i.e. to avoid saying CUNT *n.* (1)] [late 18C–early 19C] a constable; 'Mr Thingstable, Mr Constable, a ludicrous affectation of delicacy in avoiding the first syllable in the title of that officer, which in sound has some similarity to an indecent monosyllable' (Grose, 1785).

thingum *n.* (*also* **thingamadoodle**) [late 17C–1900s] an unnamed object or person; often used euph.

thingumabob *n.* (*also* **thingamerry, thingamadoodles, thingembob, thingmadodger, thingmybob, thingumbee, thingumbob, thingumjybob, thingummibob, thingumydoochy**) [late 17C+] anything, often small, to which one cannot put a name, also an unnamed person or place; often used euph.

thingumabobs *n.* (*also* **thingumbobs**) [euph. of THINGUMABOB *n.*] **1** [mid-18C+] the testicles. **2** [late 19C–1900s] trousers. **3** [1940s] the female breasts.

thingumajig *n.* (*also* **thingamajig, thingamajigger, thingmegig, thingummijig, thingummyjib, thingummyjig**) [mid-19C+] a nameless object, or person.

thingummies *n.* [euph.] **1** [early 19C+] the testicles. **2** [late 19C–1900s] trousers.

thingummy *n.* (*also* **thingamy, thingammy, thing-o-me, thingumme**) **1** [late 18C+] any nameless object, or person, or situation. **2** [late 19C+] the penis [euph. use of sense 1].

thingumsmeribob *n. see* THINGAMERRY *n.*

thingumydoochy *n. see* THINGUMABOB *n.*

thingy *n.* (*also* **thingie**) **1** [1930s+] (*also* **thingmy, thingio**) an unnamed object or person. **2** [1930s+] the penis. **3** [1950s] a woman's breasts; in pl. **4** [2000s] the vagina.

think *v.*

SE in slang uses

DERIVATIVES

❑ **thinker** *n.* (*also* **thinky**) [mid-19C+] the mind, the brain.

IN COMPOUNDS

❑ **thinkbox** *n.* (*also* **thinkpad, thoughtbox**) **1** [late 19C–1940s] (*Aus.*) the head. **2** [1910s+] (*US*) the brain. ❑ **think factory** *n.* **1** [1900s] the brain. **2** [1950s+] (*US*) a research institution. ❑ **thinking box** *n.* (*also* **thinking apparatus**) **1** [mid-19C+] (*Aus./US*) (*also* **thinking stall**) the brain. **2** [1900s] the head. **3** [20C+] a study. ❑ **thinkpiece** *n.* [1970s] (*US black*) the brain; the mind. ❑ **think-tank** *n.* **1** [20C+] the brain. **2** [1990s+] (*US campus*) a toilet.

IN PHRASES

❑ **think one has sugar on one's dick** *v. see under* DICK *n.*[1].

❑ **think one's penny silver** *v.* [late 16C–early 18C] to have a good opinion of oneself.

third *adj.*

SE in slang uses

IN COMPOUNDS

❑ **third base** *n.* [baseball imagery] [1940s+] (*US*) contact with the vagina or penis, in the context of sexual exploration (cf. FIRST BASE *n.* (1); *SECOND BASE under* SECOND *adj.*; HOME RUN *n.* (3)). ❑ **third beer** *n.* [2000s] (*N.Z.*) a woman, generally, a girlfriend, who is considered plain and unexciting. ❑ **third eye** *n.* [-EYE *sfx*] [20C+] (*US*) the anus. ❑ **third leg** *n.* [1970s+] the penis. ❑ **third sexer** *n.* [SE *third sex*, homosexuality, coined by sexologist Magnus Hirschfeld (1868–1935)] [20C+] (*US*) a homosexual. ❑ **third-world briefcase** *n.* [SE *third-world*, i.e. non-white] [1980s+] a large portable stereophonic tape deck/radio, particularly popular among black youths in the US and UK.

IN PHRASES

❑ **need like a third nut** *v. see* NEED LIKE A HOLE IN THE HEAD *under* HOLE IN ONE'S HEAD *n.*

third degree *n.* [the *first* and *second* degrees of interrogation are never specified] (*orig. US Und.*) **1** [late 19C+] the beating up and similar physical abuse of suspects by policemen in order to extract confessions; although allegedly outlawed in the last couple of decades reality proves otherwise. **2** [1910s+] used fig., referring to intense questioning but devoid of physical abuse.

third degree *v.* (*also* **put on the third degree**) [THIRD DEGREE *n.*] [1910s+] to interrogate forcefully and/or violently.

third rail *n.*[1] [like the subway's electrified third rail, such liquor 'gives you a jolt'] [1910s–60s] (*US*) extremely strong liquor.

third rail *n.*[2] [play on 'untouchable'/TOUCH *v.*[1]] [1930s–40s] (*US Und.*) one who cannot be bribed.

third-rail *adj.* [*see* THIRD RAIL *n.*[1]] [1900s] (*US*) dangerous.

thirst *n.* [1980s+] (*drugs*) the need for crack cocaine.

IN COMPOUNDS

❑ **thirst monster** *n.* [1980s+] (*drugs*) one who smokes crack cocaine to excess.

thirst bazaar *n.* (*also* **thirst emporium, thirst parlor**) [1900s] (*US*) a bar; a tavern.

thirsty *adj.* [1980s+] (*US drugs*) in desperate need of drugs.

thirteen *n.* (*also* **13**) [the initial letter *M*, 13th in the alphabet] [1960s+] (*drugs*) marijuana.

SE in slang uses

IN PHRASES

❑ **thirteen and a wash-out** *n.* [the supposed unluckiness of *thirteen*; the WASH-OUT *n.* (1) is death; some prisons, using hanging, have thirteen steps onto the gallows] [1930s–40s] (*US prison*) the execution chamber. ❑ **thirteen and the odd** *n.* [ety. unknown] [1910s–30s] a tail-coat, as worn with 'white tie and tails'. ❑ **thirteen to the dozen** *n. see* FORTY TO THE DOZEN *adv.*

13 *n.* [the initial letter of *M*exican is 13th in the alphabet] [1990s+] (*US prison*) a symbol showing affiliation to a Mexican gang.

thirteen *adj.*

IN COMPOUNDS

❑ **thirteen inches** *n. see* TWELVE INCHES *under* TWELVE *adj.*

IN PHRASES

❑ **thirteen clean shirts** *n.* [prisoners were allotted one clean shirt every week] [late 19C–1950s] (*UK prison*) a three-month sentence.

13 ½ *n.* [2000s] (*US prison*) '12 jurors, one judge, and one half-chance, often featured in tattoos'.

thirteence *n.* [there were twelve pence in a shilling; presumably a child could count 'elevenpence, twelvepence, one shilling', the 13 number] [1920s–40s] one shilling (5p).

thirteener *n.* (*also* **thirteen**) [late 18C–19C] a shilling.

thirty *n.*[1] [the notation – *30* – used orig. by printers and telegraphers to indicate the end of a story or despatch] [late 19C+] (*US*) the end.

thirty *n.*[2] [1940s] (*US black*) one month, i.e. 30 days.

IN PHRASES

❑ **first thirty** *n.* [although January has 31 days] [1940s] (*US black*) January.

thirty cents (shy of a quarter) *adj.* (*also* **twenty-four cents shy of a quarter**) [a quarter is 25¢, thus lit. '–5¢'] [20C+] (*US black*) very poor.

IN PHRASES

❑ **like thirty cents** *adj.* [pun on *feel like a million dollars* (*see under* MILLION *n.*] [late 19C+] (*US*) cheap, worthless, esp. as *feel like/look like thirty cents.*

thirty-eight *n.* (*also* **tray eight**) [abbr.; note TWENTY-TWO *n.*] **1** [1920s+] (*orig. US*) a *.38* calibre pistol. **2** [1930s+] (*orig. US*) a bullet from a .38 pistol.

thirty-eight and/plus two *adj. see* FORTY *adj.*[2].

thirty-first of May *n.* [rhy. sl. = GAY *n.*[2] (1)] [1920s+] (*Aus.*) a fool, a simpleton.

thirty-one *n.* [a short order code] [1930s] (*US*) lemonade.

thirty-three-oh-five *n.* [the statute number of the New York penal code] [1950s–60s] (*US drugs/New York*) an arrest for possession of drugs.

thirty-two *n.* [1920s+] (*US*) a *.32* calibre pistol.

— this! *excl.* [euph. for *fuck this*] [1980s+] (*US campus*) used in comb. with a n. to negate the previous speaker's suggestion, e.g. 'Let's play pool.' 'Pool this! I've got work to do.'.

this and that *n.* [rhy. sl.] **1** [20C+] a hat. **2** [1900s] (*also* **thises and thats**) spats. **3** [2000s] a cricket bat. **4** [2000s] a cat.

this is an A and B conversation, C yourself out *phr.* [pun on SE phr. *see yourself out*] [1990s+] (*US black*) a phr. used to dismiss a third party who butts into a private conversation.

this is protected by the red, the black and the green (with a key) [the colours of black nationalism; play on the minatory signs that indicate a building's security system] [1990s+] (*US black teen*) **1** keep out, this is none of your business. **2** this is for blacks only, you couldn't understand, optionally ext. by *sisseeeee*, i.e. SISSY *n.* (1).

this, that and the other *n.* [late 19C+] a euph. for any form of obscenity.

thistledown *n.* [like blowing *thistledown*, they wander. Note Devon dial. *thistleseed*, gypsies] [late 19C–1900s] (*Anglo-Irish*) children, esp. those of 'a wandering nature' (Ware).

thistledown *adj.* [THISTLEDOWN *n.*] [late 19C–1910s] young, unsophisticated, childish.

this way *adj. see* THAT WAY *adj.* (2).

T.H. Lowry *n.* [rhy. sl.; ult. N.Z. farmer and racehorse breeder *T.H. Lowry*, owner of horse *Desert Gold*, famous in the 1910s] [2000s] (*N.Z.*) a Maori.

Thomas *n.*[1] [biblical figure Doubting *Thomas*] [1950s] (*W.I.*) a stubborn, conceited man.

Thomas *n.*[2] *see* TOMMY ATKINS *n.*

thomas *n.* [abbr. JOHN THOMAS *n.*] **1** [mid-18C–mid-19C] the penis. **2** [mid-19C] a liveried servant.

Thomas Atkins *n. see* TOMMY ATKINS *n.*

Thomas Cook *n.* [rhy. sl.; ult. *Thomas Cook*, the UK travel agents] [1990s+] a look, a glance.

thomas tilling *n.* [rhy. sl.; ult. 19C haulier *Thomas Tilling* (1825–93)] [late 19C–1930s] a shilling (5p).

thornback *n.* [SE *thornback*, a ray or stickleback. The usage puns on the female child of a stickleback, a *maid* or (Scot.) *maiden-skate*] [late 17C–early 19C] an old maid.

thorough *adj.* **1** [20C+] (*US campus*) of a person, admirable. **2** [1980s+] (*US campus*) used of one who is acting arrogantly or cheekily. **3** [1990s+] (*US teen*) in absolute and complete control of a situation.

playing on SE *through*

IN COMPOUNDS

❑ **thorough churchman** *n.* [late 18C–early 19C] one who

goes in at one door of a church and out of the other without stopping for prayer. ▫ **thorough cough** *n.* [the wind goes 'through' the body] [late 17C–mid-19C] a cough accompanied by a simultaneous breaking of wind. ▫ **thorough passage** *n.* [late 17C–early 19C] the going 'in one ear and out the other'.

IN PHRASES

▫ **thorough-go-nimble** *n.* [late 17C–early 19C] **1** diarrhoea. **2** sour or second-rate beer.

SE in slang uses

IN PHRASES

▫ **thorough good-natured wench** *n.* ['one who being asked to sit down, will lie down' (Grose, 1785)] [late 18C–early 19C] a promiscuous woman. ▫ **thorough-handed man** *n.* [late 19C–1900s] (*US*) a generous person.

thoroughbred *n.* [horseracing imagery] **1** [20C+] an admirable person, a dependable person. **2** [1950s+] (*drugs*) a dealer who sells pure or high quality narcotics. **3** [1960s] (*US black*) a male sexual athlete. **4** [1960s+] (*US black*) a sophisticated hustler. **5** [1960s+] (*UK Und.*) a successful, trustworthy villain. **6** [1960s+] a prostitute with style, sophistication and knowledge, generally considered among the élite of her profession [note Cleland, *Memoirs of a Woman of Pleasure* (1748–9): '*Phoebe* herself, that hackney'd, thorough-bred *Phoebe*, to whom all modes and devices of pleasure were known'].

thoroughbred *adj.* **1** [late 19C] sophisticated, upper-class. **2** [20C+] admirable, dependable, trustworthy.

IN COMPOUNDS

▫ **thoroughbred black** *n.* [1950s+] (*US black*) the ideal black woman.

thoroughfare *n.* [orig. W.I. use, many men have 'ridden' down her] [1930s] (*US black*) a promiscuous woman.

thorough-stitch *n.*

IN PHRASES

▫ **go thorough-stitch (with)** *v.* [tailors' jargon *go thorough-stitch*, to finish a job that has been begun] [late 18C–1900s] to perform something thoroughly, to carry it out completely.

thou *n.* [abbr. SE *thousand*] [mid-19C+] (*orig. US*) 1,000, esp. dollars.

thoughtbox *n. see thinkbox* under THINK *v.*

thought foundry *n.* [1900s] (*US*) the brain.

thousand eyes *n.* [1980s] (*US black*) brogues.

thousand-miler *n.* (*also* **one thousand miles, thousand-mile shirt**) [orig. naut., its being washed after every 1,000 miles of a voyage] [1910s+] a dark shirt, made of black or navy twill, that does not show dirt.

thousand-on-a-plate *n.* [late 19C–1950s] (*US*) a dish of peas or beans.

thousand pities *n.* [rhy. sl. = TITTY *n.* (1)] [late 19C–1900s] a woman's breasts.

thrap *v.* (*also* **throp**) [dial. *threap*, to beat, to flog] [1990s+] to masturbate.

thrash *n.* **1** [1930s+] a rumbustious, uninhibited party. **2** [1950s+] a drinking spree. **3** [1980s+] any form of fast, loud and harsh-sounding music.

thrash *v.* **1** [1960s+] (*Aus./N.Z.*) to overwork a piece of machinery, e.g. an automobile. **2** [1960s+] (*orig. Aus./N.Z.*) to drive at great speed. **3** [1980s+] (*US campus*) to wreck, to make a mess of.

SE in slang uses

IN PHRASES

▫ **thrash the daylights out of** *v. see* BEAT THE (LIVING) DAYLIGHTS OUT OF *under* DAYLIGHTS *n.* ▫ **thrash on** *v.* [1980s+] (*US campus*) to criticize negatively.

thrashed *adj.* [1980s+] (*US campus*) **1** worn out, broken, exhausted. **2** drunk, intoxicated by a drug.

thrasher *n.* [THRASH *v.* (3)] [1990s+] **1** (*orig. surfing use*) a show-off. **2** (*US campus*) a destructive person. **3** (*US campus*) a skateboarder. **4** (*US campus*) a wild party at which there are breakages.

thrattle-pipe *n.* see THROTTLE *n.*

thray *n.* [TREY-BIT *n.*] [1900s–70s] (*N.Z.*) a threepenny piece.

thread *v.*[1] [*play at thread the needle* (*see* PLAY (AT)... *v.* (1))] **1** [1940s–50s] of a man, to have sexual intercourse. **2** [1960s+] (*US gay*) to have anal intercourse.

thread *v.*[2] [1960s] (*US*) to dress oneself, to wear.

threaded (down) *adj.* [THREADS *n.*] [1950s] (*US black*) dressed up.

threads *n.* [metonymy] [1920s+] (*orig. US*) clothes; occas. in sing.

threateners *n.* [1990s+] breasts, usu. large.

three *n.* **1** [1950s–70s] (*drugs*) a $3 bag of heroin. **2** see FINGER *n.* (1b).

SE in slang uses

DERIVATIVES

▫ **three-er** *n.* [1940s] a three-year prison sentence. ▫ **threesome** *n.* [1970s+] group sex involving three people of the same or mixed sexes.

IN PHRASES

▫ **three-a-dayer** *n.* [1930s] (*US drugs*) one who smokes opium three times a day; thus multiples, i.e. *four-a-dayer*.

three *adj.*

SE in slang uses

IN COMPOUNDS

▫ **three balls** *adj. see* separate entry. ▫ **three Bs** *n.* **1** [late 19C–1900s] as used by churchmen, *b*right, *b*rief and *b*rotherly, three precepts for a good service, in all of which the younger clergy felt that the very conservative contemporary church was distinctly lacking. **2** [1920s+] (*Aus.*) *b*urn, *b*ash and *b*ury, what should be done with rubbish that accumulates in the outback. **3** [1960s+] (*US gay*) *b*low job, *b*ed and *b*reakfast [BLOW JOB *n.* (1)]. ▫ **three-bulb plant** *n.* [late 19C–1900s] (*US*) a pawnbroker. ▫ **three-bullet Joey** *n.* [their being armed + generic use of proper name *Joey*] [1960s–80s] (*US black*) the police. ▫ **three-card monte** *n. see* separate entry. ▫ **three-cents** *adj.* [the tiny sum] [20C+] (*W.I.*) insignificant, unimportant, worthless. ▫ **three-chinned dame** *n.* [the three chins that come with age and loss of looks] [17C] a procuress, a bawd. ▫ **three cold Irish** *n. see* FENIAN *n.* ▫ **three-cornered** *adj.* **1** [mid-19C+] (*Aus.*) of a quadruped, usu. a horse, awkwardly shaped, scraggy, weak. **2** [1940s] of anything, misshapen, ill-fitting; fig. use naive, stupid. ▫ **three-cornered scraper** *n. see* SCRAPER *n.* (1). ▫ **three-cornered tree** *n.* (*also* **tree with three corners**) [mid-17C–18C] the gallows, esp. the great 'triple tree' at Tyburn. ▫ **three Cs** *n.* **1** [late 19C] the Central Criminal Court, London, i.e. the Old Bailey, technically the main court for the County of Middlesex, but acknowledged as the most important court in the UK. **2** [1910s] (*UK public school*) Christianity, Cold bath and Cricket. ▫ **three-d masher** *n.* [SE *three d*, i.e. 3d. or three old pence + MASHER *n.* (2)] [late 19C–1900s] a young man who poses as a gentleman but lacks the savoir-faire, not to mention the funds. ▫ **three-dollar bill** *n.* [no such currency exists] [1960s+] (*US campus*) anyone or anything eccentric or odd. ▫ **three eyes** *n.* [? they have an eye in the back of their heads] [1980s] (*US black*) the police. ▫ **three-inch fool** *n.* [late 16C] one who has a short penis. ▫ **three-legged beaver** *n.* [*THIRD LEG under* THIRD *adj.* + BEAVER *n.*[1] (5)] [1970s+] a male homosexual. ▫ **three-legged instrument** *n.* [17C] the gallows. ▫ **three-legged mare** *n.* (*also* **three-legged stool**) [late 17C–early 19C] the gallows, esp. the 'triple tree' at Tyburn. ▫ **three-letter man** *n.* [note O. Henry *An Unfinished Story* (1906): 'The words-of-three-letters lesson in the old blue spelling book begins with Piggy's biography. He was fat; he had the soul of a rat, the habits of a bat, and the magnanimity of a cat'] [1930s+] **1** (*orig. RN*) an unpleasant person [the letters were *c-a-d*]. **2** (*orig. US campus*) euph. for a homosexual [the letters were orig. *f-a-g*, now *g-a-y*]. ▫ **three Ms** *n.* [*M*ulga *M*adness *M*ixture] [1900s] (*Aus.*) rough liquor, drunk in the Australian outback. ▫ **three on** *n.* [late 19C] (*US short order*) three butter cakes. ▫ **three-out** *see* separate entries. ▫ **three-piece suit** *n. see* SUIT *n.*[1] (3). ▫ **three-piece suite** *n.* (*also* **three-piece set, ...suit**) [furnishing/tailoring imagery] [1920s+] **1** the male genitals. **2** thus a term of abuse. ❑ **three planks** *n.* [late 19C–1900s] a coffin. ❑ **three-point drinker** *n.* [the three additives] [1920s–40s] one who drinks sixpennyworth of gin, with bitters, a shot of lime juice and soda. ❑ **three-pointer** *n.* [1940s–60s] (*US black*) an urban street corner; thus *three-pointer of the ace trill in the twirling top*, any corner of 7th Avenue in Harlem. ❑ **three-ring circus** *n.* [the *three rings* = the anus, mouth, vagina] [1970s+] (*US gay*) a heterosexual woman. ❑ **three-rounder** *n.* [junior or amateur boxing matches are restricted to three rounds, professional bouts run to 12 or (formerly) 15] [1950s–60s] a petty criminal. ❑ **three screws** *n. see under* SCREW *n.*[1]. ❑ **three sheet...** *see* separate entries. ❑ **three square** *n.* [mid-19C] a penis. ❑ **three squares** *n.* [abbr.] [20C+] *three square* meals, regular eating. ❑ **threeswins** *n.* (*also* **treewins, treswins**) [SE *three* + WIN *n.*] [late 17C–early 19C] (*UK Und.*) threepence; (*US*) three cents. ❑ **three threads** *n.* [late 18C–early 19C] 'half common ale, mixed with stale and double beer' (Grose). ❑ **three-time loser** *n.* [LOSER *n.* (2)] **1** [20C+] (*orig. US Und.*) a prisoner who has been convicted of two crimes worthy of a prison sentence and faces a life sentence or execution if convicted a third time; also occas. *two-time, four-time, five-time*, etc. **2** [1980s+] a failure, a social inadequate [fig. use of sense 1 + ext. of LOSER *n.* (1)]. ❑ **three-time winner** *n.* [gambling imagery] [1900s] (*US*) a lucky person or thing. ❑ **three trees** *n.* [the early gallows was made of three vertical posts joined by a long horizontal bar] [late 16C–mid-17C] the gallows. ❑ **threeway** *see* separate entries. ❑ **three weeks** *n.* [the title of the then 'sexy' novel by Elinor Glyn, *Three Weeks* (1907)] [1900s–10s] an intense but brief sexual relationship. ❑ **three-year-old** *n.* [the three-pound weight] [early–mid-19C] (*Anglo-Irish*) a stone weighing approx. 36kg (3lb), used as a weapon.

IN PHRASES

❑ **three bricks shy of a load** *adj.* [20C+] (*US*) not very intelligent, slightly eccentric, odd. One of a number of phrs. meaning stupid or eccentric. ❑ **three blue beans in a blue bladder** *n.* (*also* **three blue beans in one blue bladder**) [the image of a jester and his trad. bladder on a stick, made noisier by the dried beans it contains] [late 16C–early 18C] futile, pointless (if noisy) talk. ❑ **three draws and a spit** *n.* (*also* **two draws and a spit**) [SE *draw*, a puff] [late 19C–1910s] a cigarette. ❑ **three-ed up** *adv.* [1960s+] (*UK prison*) living three to a cell. ❑ **three halfporth of gawdelpus** *n.* [GAWDELPUS *n.* (2)] [late 19C+] a street urchin. ❑ **three hots and a cot** *n. see under* HOT *n.* ❑ **three jerks of a lamb's/dead lamb's/sheep's tail** *see* TWO SHAKES OF A LAMB'S TAIL *phr.* ❑ **three links of the Atlantic cable** *n.* [late 19C] (*US*) sausage. ❑ **three of the best** *n.* [1920s+] (*Aus.*) a packet of condoms, usu. containing three. ❑ **three shakes of a lamb's/dead lamb's/sheep's tail** *see* TWO SHAKES OF A LAMB'S TAIL *phr.* ❑ **three tears and a bucket** [the insignificant effect of *three tears* in *a bucket*] [1970s–80s] (*US black*) a phr. of dismissal, disinterest. ❑ **three times as queer as a three-dollar bill** *n.* [QUEER *adj.* (4) + *THREE-DOLLAR BILL* above; NINE-DOLLAR BILL *n.* (2)] [1960s+] homosexual, in the eyes of the speaker, exceptionally or ostentatiously so. ❑ **three-times-seven** [late 19C–1950s] (*US black*) 21, i.e. legally adult in USA.

three and sixpenny thoughtful *n.* [play on *PENNY DREADFUL under* PENNY *n.*; *SHILLING SHOCKER under* SHILLING *n.*] [late 19C] (*UK society*) 'a feminine theory novel' (Ware), e.g. those of Mrs Craik (1826–87) or Mrs Humphry Ward (1851–1920), who wrote on social and religious themes, often dealing with women (but never suffragism).

three bags *v.* [rhy. sl.; *three bags full* = PULL *v.* (6)] [1980s] (*Aus.*) to masturbate.

three bags full *n.* [rhy. sl.] **1** [20C+] (*Aus.*) a pack of lies [a load of BULL *n.*[6] (1)]. **2** [1980s+] (*Aus. prison*) an act of masturbation [PULL *v.* (6)].

three balls *n.* [the trad. three brass balls that hang outside a pawnshop. The stereotypical pawnbroker was Jewish. The three balls themselves supposedly come from the arms of the Medicis (although these were 6 red balls, rather than the three gold ones of pawnbroking) and were imported to London by the Lombard bankers and thence to the US] **1** [mid-19C+] (*also* **Mr Three Balls, three-ball exchange, three ball joint, three-ball man**) a pawnbroker or pawnbroker's shop. **2** [1930s+] (*US black*) a Jew.

three blind mice *n.* [rhy. sl.; ult. the nursery rhyme] [20C+] (a sack of) rice.

three-card monte *n.* (*also* **three-card molly**) [Sp. *monte*, a 19C game of chance, played with 45 cards. The modern game is played only by confidence tricksters. There is no gambling and unless the trickster desires otherwise – to entice a new victim – the house invariably wins; however, note Asbury *Sucker's Progress* (1938): 'Three-Card Monte was a Mexican invention, and a misnomer if ever there was one, for it had no more actual relationship to *Monte* than to Old Maid.'] [late 19C+] (*orig. US*) the three-card trick; thus *three-card man*, one who runs such a game.

three-card trick *n.* [rhy. sl. = PRICK *n.* (1)] [2000s] the penis.

311 *phr.* (*also* **three-eleven**) [? police code] [1990s+] (*US campus*) happy, keen, enthusiastic.

365 *n.* [the inevitable appearance of the dish on a café menu every day of the year] [19C–1950s] any frequently served dish, e.g. ham and eggs, bacon and eggs, mutton.

3M *n.* [abbr.] [2000s] (*Irish*) a young man who only cares for his *ma*, his MOTH *n.* (2) and his *m*oustache.

Three Ones Hotel *n.* [a popular meeting place for Australians in London at the time. Downing, *Digger Dialects*(1919), suggests 'i.e. "one arm, one eye and one pedestal"', but the un-bowdlerized appendage is 'one arsehole'] [1910s] (*Aus.*) Nelson's Column, Trafalgar Square, London.

three-out *n.* [early 19C–1900s] a glass that holds one third of a quart (of beer).

three-out *adj.* [1970s] (*S.Afr. drugs*) large, of a marijuana cigarette.

threepenny *adj.*

SE in slang uses

IN COMPOUNDS

❑ **threepenny dodger** *n.* (*also* **threepenny Johnnie**) [SE *dodge*, i.e. one is hard to get hold of/generic use of proper name] [1900s–10s] a silver threepenny bit. ❑ **threepenny shot** *n.* [late 19C–1900s] a round steak and kidney pudding, sold at threepence a portion. ❑ **threepenny upright** *n.* (*also* **threepenny ordinary, twopenny upright, twopenny uprighter**) [her fee of 3d/2d + SE *upright*] [mid-17C–early 19C; 2000s] a cheap prostitute who has no room of her own and must stand against a wall for intercourse; thus the intercourse itself.

threepenny bits *n.* [rhy. sl.] **1** [20C+] diarrhoea [SHITS, THE *n.* (1)]. **2** [1970s+] a woman's breasts [TIT *n.*[2] (1)].

IN PHRASES

❑ **give someone the threepennies** *v.* [fig. use of sense 1] [late 19C+] to annoy, to irritate someone.

threepen'orth *n.* [1930s] (*UK Und.*) a three year prison sentence.

three quarters of a peck *n.* (*also* ¾ of a neck) [rhy. sl.] [mid-19C–1940s] the neck.

three-sheet *v.* [carnival/theatre use, a three-sheet poster is larger than usual; note Philipp *Vaudeville* (FWP ms. 1939): 'When an egotistic performer loitered about the lobby, or the sidewalk in front of the theatre, – perhaps to "date up a town gal" or merely to let the natives know he was an actor, – this was called "three-sheeting." (A three-sheet is a poster measuring 44 by 84 inches.) Managers generally frowned upon this practise, for to permit the public to view the performers in their private characters was supposed to detract from the mystery and glamour of the stage. And so the managers regarded with disfavor certain actors who were addicted to the debunking proclivities known as "three-sheeting in front of the theatre."'] [20C+] (*US*) to advertise, thus to boast, to brag.

three sheets in the wind *phr.* (*also* **a few sheets in the wind, a sheet in the wind's eye, three sheets before the breeze, ...in the breeze, ...to the wind, ...over, ...spread**) [naval imagery, a ship carrying 'three sheets (sails) to the wind' is 'top-heavy'] [early 19C+] drunk, also as *one/two/four/six/seven* *sheets to the wind*; abbr. as *three sheets* etc; occas. intoxicated by a drug.

three-way *n.* [1970s+] sexual activity involving three people.

three-way *adj.* [1930s+] (*US*) of a prostitute, willing to offer her vagina, anus and mouth to clients; usu. as *THREE-WAY GIRL* below.

IN COMPOUNDS

❑ **three-way deal** *n.* [1960s+] sex involving three partners at once; thus *four-way deal* etc. ❑ **three-way girl** *n.* (*also* **...bitch, ...broad, ...doll, ...wench**) [1930s+] a prostitute (or woman) who will offer her vagina, anus and mouth to clients.

three ways (and Sunday) *adv. see nine ways from breakfast under* NINE *n.*

three-wheeled trike *n.* [rhy. sl. = DYKE *n.* (1)] [1990s+] a lesbian.

three-wheeler *n.* [rhy. sl. = SHEILA *n.*[1] (1)] [1980s+] (*Aus. prison*) a woman.

threp *n.* (*also* **threps, thrip, thrips, thrups**) [colloq. pron.] [late 17C–1910s] threepence; the smallest coin.

thresh *n.* (*also* **thresh-up**) [? SE *thrash/thresh*] [1930s+] (*Aus.*) a fight.

thrifty *n.* [the twelve-sided coin, minted only 1937–52, carried a picture of the plant *thrift* on its reverse + play on SE] [1930s–50s] a threepenny bit.

thrill *n.* [ext. uses of SE] **1** [late 19C] a sensational story, a 'thriller'. **2** [1920s+] an orgasm. **3** [1950s+] (*Irish*) a promiscuous woman.

IN COMPOUNDS

❑ **thrill and chill** *n.* [1970s+] (*US black*) a sexual experience so wonderful it 'sends chills up one's spine'.

IN PHRASES

❑ **give someone a thrill** *v.* [1920s+] **1** to bring to orgasm. **2** of a man, to have sexual intercourse.

thrilled skinny *adj. see under* SKINNY *adj.*

thriller *n.* **1** [late 19C+] a sensational play, film or story. **2** [1900s] a company of actors, specializing in melodrama. **3** [1950s+] a sensational person.

thriller-diller *adj. see* KILLER-DILLER *adj.*

thrip/thrips *n. see* THREP *n.*

throat *n.* [SE *cut-throat*] [1960s+] (*US campus*) someone who works harder than average, and enjoys it.

SE in slang uses

IN COMPOUNDS

❑ **throat burner** *n.* [1900s] (*US*) a drink of spirits. ❑ **throat latch** *n.* [late 19C–1920s] (*US*) the Adam's apple. ❑ **throat oil** *n.* [1990s+] (*Aus.*) beer or alcohol generally. ❑ **throatwash** *n.* [1900s] (*US*) bourbon whisky.

IN PHRASES

❑ **have by the throat** *v.* [1940s+] (*Aus.*) to have the situation under control; often as *get the game by the throat*.

throat *adj.* [THROAT *n.*] [1990s+] (*US campus*) fiercely competitive.

throat *v.* [THROAT *n.*] [1960s] (*US campus*) to work very hard.

throbbing gristle *n.* [GRISTLE *n.*] [1990s+] the penis.

throg *v.* [? THROW DOWN *v.* (5) + GROG *n.*[1] (1)] [1980s+] (*US campus*) to drink.

throne *n.* (*also* **king's throne, throne room**) [1920s+] a lavatory.

IN PHRASES

❑ **hug the throne** *v. see KISS THE PORCELAIN GOD under* PORCELAIN GOD *n.* ❑ **pretender to the throne** *n.* [1950s–60s] (*US gay*) **1** a heterosexual who poses as gay for the purposes of avoiding the draft. **2** a vice squad policeman who poses as gay to entrap genuine homosexuals. ❑ **sit on the throne** *v.* [1920s+] to use a lavatory. ❑ **throne up** *v.* [1920s] to use the lavatory. ❑ **worship the throne** *v. see KISS THE PORCELAIN GOD under* PORCELAIN GOD *n.*

SE in slang uses

IN PHRASES

❑ **throne of love** *n. see* ALTAR OF HYMEN *n.*

throp *v. see* THRAP *v.*

throttle *n.* (*also* **thrattle-pipe**) [northern UK dial.] [mid-16C+] the throat.

throttle-box *n.* [1940s] (*Aus.*) the throat.

throttle-jockey *n.* [SE *throttle* + JOCKEY *n.*[2] (3b)] [1940s–60s] (*US*) **1** a pilot. **2** a hot-rodder.

throttle one *v.* [play on *CHOKE A DARKIE under* DARKIE *n.*] [1960s] (*Aus.*) to defecate.

throttling pit *n.* [play on *CHOKE A DARKIE under* DARKIE *n.*] [1960s+] the lavatory.

through *adj.* [SE *through*, exhausted] [1990s+] **1** (*US black/teen*) drunk or intoxicated by drugs to the point of virtual collapse. **2** (*US campus*) annoyed, disgusted. **3** (*US campus*) ugly. **4** (*US campus*) unpleasant.

through *v.* [mid-19C] (*US Und.*) to search.

through and through *n.* [ext. of SE use] [1970s+] (*US black*) a wholly admirable (black) person.

througher *n.* [2000s] a day's unbroken drinking.

through oneself *adj.* [20C+] (*Ulster*) confused.

throw *n.* [late 19C+] a go, each, usu. in comb. with a sum of money, e.g. *10 pence a throw*.

throw *v.* **1** [19C+] to vomit. **2** in transitive senses. (**a**) [mid-19C] (*US Und.*) to cheat, to rob. (**b**) [late 19C+] (*US*) to do, to perform, to put across. (**c**) [1900s] (*US Und.*) to send to prison. (**d**) [1930s] (*US black*) to cast a spell. (**e**) [1940s–50s] (*US Und.*) to rob at gunpoint. (**f**) [1940s+] (*US*) to shoot a bullet. (**g**) [1980s+] (*US*) to sell, e.g. *throw joints*, to sell marijuana cigarettes. **3** [mid-19C+] (*orig. US*) to disconcert, to surprise, to worry. **4** in senses of SE *throw away*. (**a**) [mid-19C+] to lose deliberately, esp. in sports. (**b**) [20C+] (*US*) to get rid of, to overcome; of a police officer, to drop a charge. **5** [1920s+] (*US*) to host a party or social event. **6** [1930s] to go out on a spree. **7** [1970s+] to have sexual intercourse.

SE in slang uses

IN PHRASES

❑ **throw...** *v. see also under* relevant n. ❑ **throw a benny** *v.* [1990s+] (*UK juv.*) to lose one's temper, to throw a tantrum. ❑ **throw a brick** *v.* [the *throwing of a brick* through a shop window] **1** [1950s–60s] (*US black*) to act violently, to kill someone. **2** [1960s–70s] (*US*) to commit a minor crime. **3** [2000s] in a ball game, to blunder, to fail. ❑ **throw a buttonhole on** *v.* [pun on BUTT *n.*[1] (1a) + HOLE *n.*[1] (1a)] [1960s+] (*US black*) to have anal intercourse. ❑ **throw a maddie** *v.* [SE *mad*] [1960s+] to go mad, to go crazy. ❑ **throw a punch** *v.* [boxing imagery] [1950s+] to defend oneself, verbally as well as physically. ❑ **throw a scare into** *v.* [20C+] to terrorize, to intimidate. ❑ **throw a thing in someone's dish** *v.* [? the image of tossing something other than money into a beggar's dish] [late 18C–19C] to tease, to reproach. ❑ **throwaway** *see* separate entries. ❑ **throw back** *v.* [1940s+] (*US*) to eat or drink, esp. in quantity. ❑ **throw bouqets at** *v.* [20C+] (*US*) to praise. ❑ **throw bricks at the jailhouse** *v.* [1960s] to take foolish chances, to tempt fate. ❑ **throw craps** *v.* [craps jargon *craps*, a losing throw] [20C+] (*US*) **1** to fail. **2** to experience bad luck. ❑ **throw donuts** *v. see BLOW ONE'S DOUGHNUTS under* BLOW *v.*[1]. ❑ **throw down** *see* separate entries. ❑ **throw 'em** *v. see THROW HANDS under* HAND *n.*[1]. ❑ **throw in and in** *v. see PLAY (AT) IN AND IN under* PLAY (AT)... *v.* ❑ **throw iron** *v. see PUMP IRON under* IRON *n.* ❑ **throw one's science about** *v.* [1900s] (*Aus.*) var. on SE *throw one's weight about*. ❑ **throw one's voice** *v.* [1960s+] (*Aus.*) to vomit. ❑ **throw over the bridge** *v.* [the image is of two confederates getting together to throw a third party from a (metaphorical) bridge] [19C] (*UK Und.*) to double-cross, to betray (a confidence); in gambling to deceive one's backer by deliberately losing the game. ❑ **throw shade** *v.* (*also* **shade**) [? to 'put in the shade'] [1990s+] (*US campus*) to humiliate (someone) exceedingly. ❑ **throw sixes** *v.* [craps dice, a throw of twelve (double six) is a losing throw] [20C+] to die. ❑ **throw someone for** *v.* [1940s–50s] (*Aus.*) to cheat, to swindle; to persuade someone to give up something. ❑ **throw someone out on their ass** *v.* (*also* **throw someone out on their ear**) [20C+] (*Aus./US*) to eject someone forcibly. ❑ **throw**

something at *v.* [1970s+] (*US*) to attempt to solve or dismiss a problem with an excess of some resource.

throwaway *n.* **1** [1980s+] (*US Und.*) a garment, e.g. a shirt, which is worn for a street crime, then immediately discarded so as to alter one's identity. **2** [1990s+] (*US*) a homeless outcast.

throwaway *adj.* [1950s+] (*US*) useless, hopeless, e.g. a *throwaway man*.

throw-down *n.* [wrestling jargon *throw-down*, a fall] [late 19C–1900s] **1** a defeat. **2** a rejection.

throwdown *n.* [THROW DOWN *v.* (4b)] **1** [late 19C] (*US*) a comeuppance, a punishment. **2** [1980s+] (*US campus*) (*also* **shakedown**) a party. **3** [1990s+] (*US black*) a (gang) fight.

throw down *v.* **1** [late 19C] to overcome, to prove too much for [wrestling imagery]. **2** [late 19C+] (*US*) to discard, to abandon. **3** [1900s–20s] (*US*) to get someone into trouble, to betray. **4** in senses of SE *throw down the gauntlet*. (**a**) [1910s+] (*US*) to challenge, in an aggressive manner. (**b**) [1980s+] (*US black*) to get into a fight with. (**c**) [1980s+] (*US teen*) to challenge a rival breakdancer. **5** [1930s+] (*US campus*) to eat or drink voraciously. **6** [1960s+] to blame. **7** [1980s+] (*US black/campus*) to enjoy oneself vigorously, to dance. **8** [1980s+] (*US black/campus*) to perform well; to work hard on a major project. **9** [1980s+] (*US campus*) to have sexual intercourse. **10** [1980s+] (*US drugs*) to give someone some drugs, usu. pills.

IN PHRASES

❑ **throw down (on)** *v.* **1** [late 19C+] (*US Und.*) to hold a gun on. **2** [1960s+] to blame. ❑ **throw down one's cards** *v.* (*also* **throw up one's cards**) [late 17C+] to give up a project, a way of life.

throwed *adj.* [SE *thrown*] [1990s+] (*US campus*) defeated, humiliated.

throw-in *n.* [SE *throw in*, to add (something) on for free, esp. in a transaction] [late 19C–1900s] (*Aus.*) an unexpected piece of good luck.

throw it *v.* (*also* **throw the bull**) [20C+] (*US*) to brag, to boast, to claim what one cannot achieve.

SE in slang uses

IN PHRASES

❑ **throw it up against someone** *v.* (*also* **throw it into someone's teeth, throw it at/to someone, throw it at/to/in someone's face**) [late 19C+] (*US*) to criticize someone, to hold someone up as an object of reproach.

throw it in *v.* [abbr. colloq. *throw in the towel*] [1910s+] (*Aus.*) to stop doing something.

throw (it) into *v.* **1** [late 19C] to tease. **2** [late 19C–1950s] (*US*) (*also* **chuck into, shoot into**) to impose upon. **3** [1920s] (*US tramp*) to talk in slang. **4** [1930s] as *throw a — into*, to force something upon someone. **5** [1950s] to assault, to kill. **6** [1970s] (*US gay*) to sodomize. **7** [2000s] to have sexual intercourse.

throw me in the dirt *n.* [rhy. sl.] [mid-19C+] a shirt.

throw-off *n.* [THROW OFF *v.*] [1900s–30s] **1** a hostile or critical remark or allusion. **2** an illusion, a disguise. **3** (*US Und.*) a supposedly legitimate business which in fact masks a criminal one.

throw off *v.* **1** in forms of speech. (**a**) [late 18C+] (*orig. Und.*) to deride, to ridicule, esp. under the guise of apparent pleasantry. (**b**) [early–mid-19C] (*UK Und.*) to boast of one's successful crimes. **2** [mid-19C] (*UK Und.*) to (break) open. **3** [mid–late 19C] (*US*) to abandon, to neglect; to cease from an action. **4** [1980s+] (*Aus. prison*) to avoid an issue.

throw off (upon) *v.* [1940s+] (*W.I.*) to give away things one no longer needs to a poorer person.

throw-up *n.* [THROW UP *v.* (2)] [1980s+] (*orig. US*) a simple piece of graffiti art, using only two colours; e.g. the artist's own name.

throw up *v.* [abbr. *THROW UP ONE'S ACCOUNTS* below] **1** [mid-18C+] (*also* **throw up one's guts**) to vomit. **2** [1980s+] to express one's allegiance to a gang; to make the crew's hand sign or to place one's name on a piece of graffiti.

IN PHRASES

❑ **throw up at (someone)** *v.* [1930s–50s] (*Aus.*) to criticize someone. ❑ **throw up one's accounts** *v.* [var. on *CAST UP ONE'S ACCOUNTS under* CAST *v.*] [mid–late 18C] to vomit. ❑ **throw up one's boots** *v.* [mid-19C+] (*US*) to vomit intensely. ❑ **throw up one's heels** *v.* (*also* **...one's heel taps, ...one's toes**) [VOMIT UP ONE'S TOENAILS *v.*] [20C+] (*US*) to vomit copiously. ❑ **throw up one's ring** *v. see SPEW ONE'S RING under* RING *n.*

thruff *n.* [ety. unknown] [early 19C] (*US Und.*) a pickpocket.

thrum *n.* [THRUM *v.* (1)] [early 18C] a prostitute.

thrum *v.* [SE *thrum*, to play on a stringed instrument] **1** [mid-16C–19C] (*also* **thrum one's jacket**) to have sexual intercourse. **2** [17C–early 19C] to thrash.

thrumbuskins *n. see* THRUMS *n.* (1).

thrum-cap *n.* [SE *thrum*, a short piece of waste thread or yarn] [17C–19C] any form of roughly made or improvised headgear.

thrums *n.* (*also* **thrum, thrumbuskins, thrummer, thrum-mop, thrumms, thrummup, thrum wins**) (*UK Und.*) **1** [late 17C–1950s] *threepence*. **2** [late 18C] ? the shell game, the 'three-card trick'.

thrups *n.*[1] (*also* **thrupennies**) [play on THRUPS *n.*[2]; ult. rhy. sl. on THREEPENNY BITS *n.* (2) = TIT *n.*[2] (1)] [late 19C+] the breasts.

thrups *n.*[2] *see* THREP *n.*

thrush *n.* (*US*) **1** [1920s–50s] a woman singer. **2** [1940s+] the female pubic hair.

thrush *v.* [THRUSH *n.* (1)] [1920s–50s] (*US*) to sing.

thrust *n.* [late 18C] (*UK Und.*) an apparently luxurious and expensive waistcoat used by a confidence trickster to obtain money from a landlord.

thrusters *n.* [the effects; it makes the user 'go faster'] [1960s+] (*drugs*) amphetamine.

thud *n.* [1910s] (*Aus.*) a bad fall (usu. in fig. contexts).

IN PHRASES

❑ **come a thud** *v.* [2000s] (*N.Z.*) to fall from grace; to meet disaster.

thud *v.* [SE *thud*, onomat. for an object hitting something hard] [1910s+] (*Aus.*) to hit someone.

thug *n.* [the image of the successful SE *thug* as a cool role model; note *The Source* Oct. 1998: 'See a thug doesn't mean anything bad. All a thug means is you're doing something that one particular group doesn't agree with'] [1990s+] (*US black*) a ghetto black male.

thugette *n.* [1990s+] (*US black*) a female THUG *n.*

thugged out *adj.* [THUG *n.*] [1990s+] (*US black*) of a young man, adopting the hyper-macho gangsta style (e.g. tattoos, carrying weapons, gang colours).

thugging *n.* [THUG *n.*] [1990s+] (*US black*) relaxing, acting in a cool manner.

thumb *n.* [one sucks it] [1960s+] (*drugs*) marijuana, a marijuana cigarette.

SE in slang uses

IN COMPOUNDS

❑ **thumb-snag** *v.* [1950s] (*US*) to hitchhike.

IN PHRASES

❑ **get one's thumb out of one's ass** *v. see GET ONE'S FINGER OUT under* FINGER *n.* ❑ **give someone the rub of the thumb** *v.* [the gesture of rubbing one's thumb against the forefinger] [mid–late 19C] to impart information to someone. ❑ **sit there/stand around with one's thumb up one's ass** *see SIT THERE WITH ONE'S FINGER UP ONE'S ASS under* ASS *n.* ❑ **thumb in bum and mind in neutral** [BUM *n.*[1] (1)] [1960s+] (*orig. Aus.*) a phr. used of one who seems to have fallen into a vacant reverie. ❑ **thumb in one's eye** *n.* [20C+] (*US*) an irritation, an annoyance. ❑ **thumb of love** *n.* [late 19C+] the penis. ❑ **weigh one's thumb** *v.* [the age-old practice of a shopkeeper keeping his thumb pressing on the scales when weighing goods] [late 19C] to give short measure.

thumb *v.* [SE *thumb*, to riffle through, to press or soil with the thumb] **1** [late 18C–19C] of a man, to have sexual intercourse;

thus *well-thumbed girl*, a worn-out prostitute. **2** [20C+] (*Irish*) of a woman, to masturbate.

thumber *n.*[1] [1950s] one shilling.

thumber *n.*[2] [SE *thumb*, to put up one's thumb in the hope of getting a free ride] [1980s+] (*US campus*) a beggar, a borrower, someone constantly scrounging from their friends.

thumb in *v.* [the individual is given the 'thumbs-up'] [1950s] (*US*) to be included, to be given a job.

thump *n.* [SE *thump*, a blow, to hit] [1970s+] **1** (*US black*) a street-fight, esp. with fists or knives. **2** (*US teen*) sexual intercourse.

thump *v.* **1** [late 16C–early 18C] to have sexual intercourse. **2** [late 16C; late 18C+] to defeat heavily, esp. in battle or, more recently, in sport. **3** [1960s+] (*US black*) to fight, usu. of a gang. **4** [1980s+] (*US teen*) of a man, to have sexual intercourse.

SE in slang uses

IN COMPOUNDS

❑ **thump-(the-)cushion** *n. see* CUSHION-THUMPER *under* CUSHION *n.*

IN PHRASES

❑ **thump seven kinds of shit out of** *v. see under* SHIT *n.* ❑ **thump the shit out of** *v. see* BEAT THE SHIT OUT OF V.

thump! *excl.* [THUMP V. (1); euph. for FUCK! *excl.*] [20C+] used to accentuate one's rejection of a statement or idea, e.g. *do I thump! is she thump!* etc.

thumper *n.* **1** [early–mid-16C] a rank of villain [the details are unknown, presumably the 16C equivalent of a mugger: 'Tynckers... tryfullers, turners, and trumpers, Tempters, traytoures, trauaylers, and thumpers' (Anon., *A New Interlude called Thersites*, *c*.1537)]. **2** [early 17C] a coin [one thumps it on the counter or table]. **3** [mid-17C–19C] anything, occas. anyone, notably large as to type. **4** [late 17C–1900s] a major lie. **5** [late 19C–1900s] (*US*) a dedicated liar. **6** a large or tough individual. (**a**) [1960s] (*Aus.*) a large out-door labouring man. (**b**) [1990s+] (*US black*) a street gangster, a thug.

IN PHRASES

❑ **double-thumper** *n.* [mid–late 19C] an especially audacious lie. ❑ **drop a thumper** *v.* [1960s+] to break wind loudly.

thumping *adj.* [late 16C+] enormous, very large.

thumping *adv.* [THUMPING *adj.*] [mid-19C+] very, extremely, often as *thumping great*.

thumpingly *adv.* [THUMPING *adj.*] [late 17C+] very, exceedingly; to a very great extent.

thunder *n.* **1** [18C+] (*US*) euph, for hell or the 'daylights'. **2** [mid-19C] (*UK Und.*) a glass of brandy. **3** [2000s] (*US drugs*) heroin.

IN PHRASES

❑ **all to thunder** *adv.* [late 19C] (*US*) completely, comprehensively. ❑ **knock thunder out of** *v. see* KNOCK SEVEN BELLS OUT OF *under* BELL *n.*[1].

SE in slang uses

IN COMPOUNDS

❑ **thunderbags** *n.* [SE *thunder* + SE *bags*/ BAGS *n.*[1] (2); i.e. the noise of breaking wind] [20C+] (*Aus.*) men's underpants. ❑ **thunderbox** *n.* **1** with ref. to (the noise of) defecation. (**a**) [20C+] (*US*) the buttocks. (**b**) [1930s+] (*also* **thunder bowl**) a lavatory. (**c**) [1930s+] a portable commode. **2** [1960s] (*Aus.*) a double bass. **3** [1980s+] (*US*) a portable tape deck or radio. ❑ **thunder chicken** *n.* (*also* **thunder chick**) [1970s+] (*US black*) an unkempt, unattractive woman, esp. with messy hair. ❑ **thundergob** *n.* [1990s+] (*Irish*) a loud talkative person. ❑ **thundermug** *n.* (*also* **thunder jug**) [SE *thunder* MUG *n.*[1] (3b) + / SE *jug*; i.e. the noise of defecation/urination] [mid-19C+] a chamberpot. ❑ **thunder-thighs** *n.* [1980s+] an overweight person, esp. a woman with fat thighs.

IN PHRASES

❑ **raise thunder and tommy** *v. see* PLAY HELL AND TOMMY *under* HELL *n.*

IN EXCLAMATIONS

❑ **thunder and ouns!** (*also* **oons and thunder!**) [var. on Ger. *donner und blitzen!* thunder and lightning! + *ouns*, (Christ's) wounds] [mid-19C+] (*Irish*) a mild excl. ❑ **thunder and turf!** [19C] a general excl. of fury, surprise, indignation etc.

thunder *v.* [i.e. to 'make a noise'] [1980s+] (*US campus*) to succeed, to do well.

thunder! *excl.* [18C+] euph. for FUCK! *excl.*, HELL! *excl.* or DAMN! *excl.* or in a variety of phrs., e.g. *for thunder's sake, by thunder, like thunder, what in thunder, why in thunder, who the thunder, go to thunder.*

thunder and lightning *n.* [LIGHTNING *n.*] **1** [19C] gin and bitters. **2** [early 19C+] (*Irish*) a mixture of shrub and whisky. **3** [late 19C–1900s] treacle and clotted cream. **4** [1900s] brandy sauce when ignited.

thunder and lightning *adj.* [mid-18C–19C] 'applied to articles of apparel of a 'loud' or 'flashy' style, or combining two strongly contrasted colours.' (*OED*); also as n.

thunder and lightning! *excl.* (*also* **thunder and blazes! thunder and blue lightning! thunder and damnation!**) [var. on synon. Ger. *Donner und Blitzen!*] [mid-19C+] a general excl. of fury, surprise, indignation etc.

thunder and rain *n.* [rhy. sl.] [20C+] (*Aus.*) a train.

thunderation! *excl.* (*also* **great thunderation!**) [SE *thunder* + sfx *-ation*; var. on DAMNATION! *excl.*] [mid-19C+] (*orig. US*) a mild expletive.

thundering *adj.* [17C+] a general intensifier, excessive, immense, also in phrs. e.g. *thundering cats!*

thundering *adv.* [mid-18C+] a general intensifier, excessively, immensely, greatly.

thunk *v.* [joc. past tense of SE *think*] [late 19C+] (*US*) I/you/he/she/we/they thought.

thusly *adv.* [mid-19C–1900s] (*US*) thus, to sum things up.

thuzzy-muzzy *n.* [mispron. of SE] [late 19C–1910s] enthusiasm.

T.I. *n.* [1970s] (*Aus.*) a Thursday Islander.

tib *n.*[1] [SE *tib*, 'a typical name for a woman of the lower classes' (*OED*)] [mid-16C–17C] a prostitute.

tib *n.*[2] [backsl.] [mid–late 19C] a bit, a piece.

tib *n.*[3] [2000s] (*US prison*) a cell.

tibby *n.*[1] [SE *tib*, a female cat] [late 18C–mid-19C] a cat.

tibby *n.*[2] [Fr. *tête*, the head] [19C–1900s] the head.

tibby *n.*[3] [? SE *tabloid*] [1930s+] (*Aus.*) a tabloid newspaper.

tibby drop *n.* [rhy. sl.] [mid-19C+] hop.

IN PHRASES

❑ **on one's tibby drop** [rhy. sl. = ON THE HOP *under* HOP *v.*[1]] [mid–late 19C] unawares.

tib (of the buttery) *n.* [SE *tib*, a young woman or a cat, presumably the femininity is the point rather than the specific animal] [mid-16C–mid-19C] a goose.

tib's eve *n. see* ST TIBB'S EVE *n.* (1).

tic *n.* [misreading of *THC*, i.e. *tetrahydrocannabinol*; like TAC *n.* or *tic-tac*] [1970s+] (*drugs*) phencyclidine.

tical *n.* [? abbr. SE *practical*] [1990s+] (*orig. US black*) marijuana.

tick *n.*[1] [17C–early 18C] a signature.

tick *n.*[2] [SE *tick*, a parasitical mite] **1** [17C+] an unpleasant, insignificant person, usu. male. **2** [1970s+] (*US campus*) an overweight person. **3** [1970s+] (*US campus*) a greedy or selfish person.

tick *n.*[3] (*also* **tik**) [abbr. SE *ticket*, the writing down of one's debt] **1** [17C+] credit. **2** [early 19C] a creditor. **3** [mid-19C–1910s] a dunning letter, a bill.

DERIVATIVES

❑ **ticking** *n.* [1990s+] the obtaining of goods on credit.

IN COMPOUNDS

❑ **tick list** *n.* [1990s+] a large number of debts.

IN PHRASES

❑ **buy on the never tick** *v.* [1920s] to buy on credit. ❑ **River Tick** *n.* [early 19C] debtors' prison. ❑ **run on tick** *v.* [mid-17C–

early 18C] to set up a line of credit, to get into debt. ▫ **turn ticks on** *v.* [? TICK *n.*[3] (1)] [1950s] (*W.I.*) to beg from.

tick *n.*[4] [the sound and thus its minimal duration] **1** [late 18C–early 19C] a watch. **2** [early 19C+] (*also* **tick-tack**) a second; thus [20C+] *two ticks*. **3** [1930s–40s] (*US black*) used to indicate time, usu. with the number doubled as means of confusing outsiders, e.g. *tick twenty*, ten o'clock. **4** [20C+] (*US*) a small degree or amount, usu. an increase.

IN PHRASES

▫ **on the tick** *adv.* (*also* **to the tick**) [19C] precisely on time.

tick *n.*[5] [mid-19C] (*US campus*) a recitation by a student who is ignorant of what the text actually means.

tick *v.*[1] [TICK *n.*[3] (1)] **1** [late 17C+] to obtain or place on credit. **2** [19C+] to grant someone credit; to place a debt on credit.

tick *v.*[2] [image of a clock which *ticks* mindlessly on] [1980s+] (*US campus*) **1** to talk in class without having prepared the assignment. **2** to talk nonsense.

IN PHRASES

▫ **make one tick** *v.* [1930s+] to stimulate, to motivate one.

tickaddyboo *adj. see* TICKETTY-BOO *adj.*

ticked (off) *adj.* [TICK OFF *v.*[1] (1)] [1950s+] (*orig. US*) irritated, annoyed.

ticker *n.*[1] [the regular *ticking* or beating] **1** [early 19C+] a watch. **2** [mid-19C] (*US campus*) one who recites by rote, but with no knowledge of the text. **3** [1930s+] the human heart. **4** [1930s+] (*Aus./US*) courage.

IN PHRASES

▫ **flash one's ticker** *v.* [mid–late 19C] to take one's watch out frequently. ▫ **mug's ticker** *n.* [1970s+] (*UK Und.*) a piece of worthless jewellery or a fake Swiss watch.

ticker *n.*[2] [SE *tick off*, they tick off sums of money] [1970s+] an accountant.

ticket *n.* **1** [early 19C] a blow, a punch. **2** in lit. senses. (**a**) [mid–late 19C] (*UK Und.*) a ticket of leave, parole. (**b**) [late 19C–1930s] (*US*) a playing card, as used in three-card monte. (**c**) [1900s] a prescription. (**d**) [1910s] (*UK Und.*) probation. (**e**) [1920s–40s] (*US*) a betting slip. (**f**) [1920s–40s] (*US Und.*) a prison sentence. (**g**) [1930s] track record, history. (**h**) [1930s+] (*US prison*) a disciplinary record. (**i**) [1940s] (*US prison*) a certificate of release. (**j**) [1940s] a certificate of demobilization from the armed forces [note WW1 Aus. milit. *ticket*, a discharge from the Army]. (**k**) [1940s–70s] (*UK Und.*) an arrest warrant. (**l**) [1950s+] (*US*) a licence. (**m**) [1960s–70s] a pass or passport, whether valid or counterfeit. (**n**) [2000s] (*US black*) a lottery ticket, usu. in pl. **3** in fig. use, as an ideal [? SE *winning ticket* or Fr. *etiquette* (suggested by Hotten, 1867)]. (**a**) [mid-19C+] the right, proper, best or fashionable thing to do. (**b**) [mid-19C+] the task in hand, the relevant procedure. **4** [mid-19C–1900s] the facts, the truth [? Fr. *etiquette* (suggested by Hotten, 1867) or SE *ticket*, a bill or invoice]. **5** [1930s+] a person (as used esp. by a MOD *n.*[2] (1) in the early 1960s). **6** [1960s+] (*Aus. drugs*) a single dose of LSD, dripped onto a small piece of absorbent paper [resemblance to a SE *ticket* or TICKET *n.* (3), i.e. its positive effects; note Beatles title 'Ticket To Ride']. **7** [1990s+] (*US*) the ideal person [? SE *winning ticket*].

IN PHRASES

▫ **buy a ticket** *v.* (*US*) **1** [late 19C+] to die. **2** [1970s] to trust, to tolerate, to accept someone's statements. **3** [1980s] to call someone's bluff. ▫ **cancel someone's ticket** *v.* [1960s+] to murder, to assassinate. ▫ **come in on a sparrow's ticket** *v.* [one has 'flown over the wall'] [20C+] (*Aus.*) to gain admission to a sporting event or other entertainment without paying. ▫ **draw a good ticket** *v.* [lottery imagery] [1910s] to have good luck, to be successful. ▫ **have tickets on** *v.* [i.e. one would pay to see them/oneself] [20C+] (*Aus.*) to be very fond of someone; thus *have tickets on oneself*, to be vain, to be conceited. ▫ **just the ticket** (*also* **just the job**) [? a winning lottery ticket, or SE *ticket*, the list of candidates put forward by a political party/SE *job*] [mid-19C+] perfect, ideal, exactly as desired and required. ▫ **not the ticket** *adj.* [20C+] physically or more usu. mentally 'below par'. ▫ **one-way ticket** *n.* [1930s] (*US Und.*) a life sentence. ▫ **private ticket** *n.* [1980s] (*US*) a private detective. ▫ **speeding ticket** *n.* [2000s] (*US prison*) a rules violation notice for inappropriate behaviour in the visiting room. ▫ **ticket of leave** *n.* [SE *ticket of leave*, a parole licence] [late 19C] a holiday. ▫ **ticket-skinner** *n.* [play on SE *mule-skinner*, a mule-driver] [late 19C] (*US*) a ticket tout. ▫ **traffic ticket** *n.* [2000s] (*US prison*) a minor disciplinary offence. ▫ **universal ticket** *n.* [late 19C] (*US tramp*) a notched board cut to fit on the iron bars that support a passenger coach and which can thus be used to support a tramp. ▫ **walking ticket** *n.* **1** [mid-19C–1900s] (*US*) a notice of dismissal. **2** [1950s+] (*Aus./US prison*) an official notice to inform a prisoner that they have finished their sentence. ▫ **work one's ticket** *v.* [orig. Br. Army use, obtaining a discharge through faking illness] [1910s+] to malinger, to escape onerous duties by shamming illness or similar unsuitability. ▫ **write one's own ticket** *v.* [late 19C+] to be able to stipulate one's own conditions, to be in an advantageous position.

IN EXCLAMATIONS

▫ **that's the ticket!** [mid-19C+] just what is wanted, the ideal thing; occas. as *that's the ticket for soup*.

ticket *v.* [SE *ticket*, a written pass] [late 19C–1940s] to sentence to prison.

tickets *n.* [? the tearing up of betting slips or tickets after one's choice has failed to win] [1960s+] (*S.Afr.*) the end, the finish.

ticketty-boo *adj.* (*also* **tickadyboo, tickety-boo, tiggerty-boo**) [? TICKET *n.* (3a) or Hind. *tikai babu*, it's all right, sir] [1910s+] (*orig. services*) fine, wonderful, all in order.

tickey *n.* (*also* **tickie, ticky**) [? dial. *ticky*, small, or Du. *stukje*, a little bit, or Hind. *taka*, a stamped silver coin] [mid-19C+] (*S.Afr.*) **1** a threepenny piece (2½ cents post-decimalization). **2** anything or anyone very small; thus phrs. *half a brick/two bricks and a tickey high*, very small.

IN COMPOUNDS

▫ **tickey box** *n.* [1950s+] (*S.Afr.*) a telephone kiosk. ▫ **tickey-line** *n.* [1960s] (*S.Afr.*) a term of abuse; also as adj., cheap, second-rate. ▫ **tickey-phone** *n.* [1960s] (*S.Afr.*) a pay-phone. ▫ **tickey-snatching** (*S.Afr.*) *n.* [1920s+] making quick profits; also as adj., close-fisted, mean. ▫ **tickey wire** *n. see* LONG TICKEY below.

IN PHRASES

▫ **long tickey** *n.* (*also* **long tickey-wire**) [1970s] (*S.Afr.*) a coin on a thread that can be used to operate a telephone kiosk, then retrieved and used again.

tickieman *n.* (*also* **tickman, tick-merchant**) [one gets the goods 'on tick'] [1960s+] (*Ulster*) a doorstep salesman.

tickle *n.* (*also* **tickler**) [? it *tickles one's fancy* or the image of SE *tickling* trout] **1** [1930s+] (*UK Und.*) a robbery or other crime, esp. a successful and lucrative one. **2** [1930s+] a piece of information. **3** [1970s+] a success in gambling.

tickle *v.* **1** [late 16C+] to amuse, to make laugh, thus *tickle it*, enjoy oneself. **2** [late 19C–1910s] to puzzle, to confuse. **3** [1920s+] to rob, to steal from. **4** [1920s+] (*Aus.*) to ask someone for a loan.

IN COMPOUNDS

▫ **tickle-faggot** *n.* [SE *faggot*, a woman] [19C] the penis. ▫ **tickle-gizzard** *n.* [it tickles the woman's GIZZARD *n.* (1)] [mid-17C–19C] the penis. ▫ **tickle-pitcher** *n.* [PITCHER *n.*[1] (1)] **1** [late 17C–early 19C] a drunkard. **2** [mid-18C] a promiscuous person of either sex. ▫ **tickle-text** *n.* [early 18C–1900s] a parson. ▫ **tickle-thomas** *n.* [THOMAS *n.* (1)] [19C] the vagina. ▫ **tickle-toby** *n.* [TOBY *n.*[1]] **1** [late 17C–19C] a sword. **2** [late 17C–19C] the penis. **3** [late 17C–19C] the vagina. **4** [late 17C–19C] a promiscuous woman. **5** [mid-19C] a rod or birch.

IN PHRASES

▫ **tickle one's fancy** *v.* [mid-19C+] to gain sexual pleasure. ▫ **tickle one's innards** *v.* [late 19C+] (*US*) to take a drink. ▫ **tickle one's pickle** *v.* [1970s+] to masturbate. ▫ **tickle someone's back** *v.* [late 19C] (*Aus. Und.*) to inflict a judicial lashing. ▫ **tickle someone's ears** *v.* [1900s–20s] to flatter. ▫ **tickle someone's hole** *v.* [1920s–50s] to masturbate a woman, usu. performed by someone else. ▫ **tickle**

someone's liver *v.* [late 19C] (*Aus.*) to stab. ▫ **tickle someone's mutton** *v.* [early 19C] to thrash, to beat. ▫ **tickle someone's ribs** *v.* *see* RIB TICKLE *under* RIB *n.*[1]. ▫ **tickle someone's toby** *v.* [TOBY *n.*[1]] [late 17C–19C] **1** to thrash, to beat. **2** to have sexual intercourse. ▫ **tickle the ivories** *v.* (*also* **bang the ivories, tickle the keys**) [the ivory keys] [1920s+] to play the piano; thus *ivory-tickler*, a pianist. ▫ **tickle the minikin** *v.* [usu. used with sexual innuendo, thus John Marston (?), *The Comedie of Pasquil & Katherine/Jacke Drums Entertainment* (1601), 'When I was a yong man and could tickle the Minikin, I had the best stroke, the sweetest touch, but now I am falne from the Fidle, and betooke me to thee (the Pipe)'] [17C] to play the lute or fiddle. ▫ **tickle the peter** *v.* [PETER *n.*[2] (2)] [1940s+] (*mainly Aus./N.Z.*) to rob a safe, till or cashbox. ▫ **tickle the shit out of** *v.* [SHIT *n.* (5)] [1950s+] (*US*) to please or amuse someone.

tickled *adj.* [TICKLE *v.*] [late 16C+] amused, pleased.

tickler *n.* **1** [17C] a sword [it 'tickles the ribs]. **2** [late 18C–1900s] a puzzle, something or someone that is hard to deal with or understand [it *tickles* one's brain]. **3** [19C] (*US*) a small knife or pistol. **4** [19C–1920s] (*US*) a small measure of spirits (approx. 300ml/½ pint), a hip flask [it *tickles* the palate]. **5** [mid-19C] (*US*) a blow; also fig. use. **6** [mid-19C] a knowing individual. **7** [mid–late 19C] a whip or cane. **8** [late 19C] a short poker used to preserve the smarter, 'best' one. **9** [late 19C+] the penis. **10** [late 19C+] the vagina. **11** [1920s–40s] (*US*) a moustache. **12** [1930s] (*Aus.*) an electric battery. **13** [1950s+] (*US*) a pianist [*TICKLE THE IVORIES under* TICKLE *v.*; note Ward, *The dancing School* (1700): 'the Ticklers of Cat-Guts' i.e. violinists]. **14** [1970s+] a junior official or assistant who is used by their superior(s) to pass on policies etc to still lower ranks, so that the superiors don't have to make face-to-face contact themselves. **15** *see* *FRENCH TICKLER under* FRENCH *adj.*

ticklers *n.* [20C+] the fingers.

tickle-tail *n.* [SE *tickle* +] **1** [mid-15C–19C] a prostitute, a promiscuous woman [TAIL *n.* (3)]. **2** [late 17C–early 19C] a schoolmaster [TAIL *n.* (2)]. **3** [late 18C–19C] a cane [TAIL *n.* (2)]. **4** [early 19C] the penis [TAIL *n.* (4)].

tickle-tail function *n.* [ext. of TICKLE-TAIL *n.* (1)] [late 17C–early 18C] a prostitute.

tickle your fancy *n.* [rhy. sl. = NANCY *n.* (2a)] [20C+] a homosexual.

tickman *n.* *see* TICKIEMAN *n.*

tick-merchant *n.* *see* TICKIEMAN *n.*

tick off *v.*[1] **1** [late 19C+] (*orig. milit.*) to scold, to reprimand; thus *tick-off, ticking-off*, a scolding. **2** [1910s+] to identify, to mark.

tick off *v.*[2] [? euph. TICK OFF *v.*[1] (1) or PISS OFF *v.* (2)] [1950s+] (*US*) to irritate, to annoy.

tickrum *n.* (*also* **tick-rome**) [SE *ticket*] [mid-17C–early 19C] (*UK Und.*) a licence.

tick-tack *n.*[1] (*also* **trick-track**) [SE *ticktack*, 'an old variety of backgammon, played on a board with holes along the edge, in which pegs were placed for scoring' (*OED*) + the rhythmical movements] [mid-16C+] sexual intercourse.

tick-tack *n.*[2] (*also* **tic-tac**) [TIC-TAC *n.*] [late 19C+] a system of telegraphy used on racecourses to keep the bookmakers abreast of the changing odds; thus *tick-tack man* or *ticktacker*, one who performs such telegraphy (by using a 'vocabulary' of hand and arm movements and signals).

tick-tack *n.*[3] *see* TICK *n.*[4] (2).

tick-tock *n.* [its regular beating] **1** [1940s] (*US black*) (*also* **tick**) the heart, the heartbeat. **2** [1950s] (*Aus. Und.*) a clock or watch.

ticky *n.* *see* TICKEY *n.*

ticky-tacky *n.* [coined by American folksong writer Malvina Reynolds (1900–1978); redup. TACKY *adj.*[1]] [1960s+] cheap or inferior quality material, which is used to build houses.

ticky-tacky *adj.* [TICKY-TACKY *n.*] [1960s+] vulgar and banal, unsophisticated, corny.

ticky-ticky *adj.* [1990s+] (*W.I.*) insignificant, worthless.

Tico-tico Land *n.* [1970s] (*US*) Brazil.

tic-tac *n.* [rhy. sl.] [20C+] a fact.

tid *n.* [abbr. TIDDLY *adj.*] [1920s+] (*Aus.*) a drunkard.

tid-bit *n.* *see* *TIT-BIT under* TIT *n.*[1].

tiddivate *v.* *see* TITIVATE *v.*

tiddle *v.*[1] [? SE *tid*, to move forward in slow stages, Norfolk dial. *tid*, of a boat, to drift with the tide] **1** [mid-16C–19C] to fondle or indulge to excess, to tend carefully, to cherish. **2** [mid-18C–1940s] to fidget, to 'mess around', to play with trifles. **3** [mid-19C+] to move forward in slow stages.

tiddle *v.*[2] [var. on PIDDLE *v.* (1)] [20C+] to urinate.

tiddle-a-wink *n.* [var. on TIDDLEYWINK *n.*[1] (1)] [mid-19C] an unlicensed beerhouse.

tiddled *adj.* [TIDDLY *adj.*] [1920s+] slightly drunk, tipsy.

tiddler *n.* **1** [late 19C+] anything small, esp. a small fish. **2** [20C+] a penis, usu. that of a small boy. **3** [1920s–60s] (*Aus.*) £1 sterling.

tiddler's bait *adj.* [rhy. sl.] [20C+] late.

tiddley *n.* **1** [1920s–30s] (*Aus.*) a small glass of beer. **2** [1920s–60s] (*Aus.*) a threepenny bit [the smallness of the coin]. **3** *see* TIDDLEYWINK *n.*[2]. **4** *see* TIDDLY *n.*

tiddley *adj.* *see* TIDDLY *adj.*

tiddleywink *n.*[1] (*also* **tiddlywink**) [? TITLEY *n.* + (*on the*) *wink*, surreptitiously] **1** [mid–late 19C] an unlicensed establishment (e.g. a beerhouse, pawnbroker's or brothel). **2** [late 19C] a snack, a bite of food.

tiddleywink *n.*[2] (*also* **tiddley, tiddlywink**) [rhy. sl.] **1** [late 19C+] a drink, usu. a spirit rather than beer or wine. **2** [1970s+] a Chinese person [CHINK *n.* (1)].

tiddleywink *v.* (*also* **tiddlywink**) [? the relative triviality of the game of *tiddlywinks*] [late 19C–1900s] to potter about, to fiddle.

DERIVATIVES

▫ **tiddlywinking** *adj.* [late 19C–1900s] insignificant, unimportant.

tiddly *n.* (*also* **tiddley**) [abbr. TIDDLEYWINK *n.*[2] (1)] [20C+] a drink.

tiddly *adj.* (*also* **tiddy, tiddley**) [TIDDLY *n.* (+ ? SE *tiddly*, small); ? earlier ref. in play *Everyone Has His Fault* (1793): 'Lady Doll Primrose says to Lady Sly, "You know, Miss Tiddlikins? Yes – looks awry –."'] [20C+] slightly drunk, tipsy.

tiddly-push *n.* [1930s] (*Irish*) the male genitals.

tiddlywink *n.* **1** *see* TIDDLEYWINK *n.*[1]. **2** *see* TIDDLEYWINK *n.*[2].

tiddlywink *adj.* [? the dimensions of a SE *tiddlywink*] [mid-19C–1920s] slim, thin, puny.

tiddlywink *v.* *see* TIDDLEYWINK *v.*

tiddy *n.* *see* TITTY *n.*

tiddy *adj.* *see* TIDDLY *adj.*

tiddy umpty *adv.* *see* UMPTY *adv.*

tiddyvate *v.* *see* TITIVATE *v.*

tide *n.*

SE in slang uses

IN PHRASES

▫ **get under the tide** *v.* (*also* **get under**) [late 19C–1900s] (*US/Aus.*) to become very drunk.

tidgen *n.* [backsl.] [1930s] night-time; thus *on tidgen*, on night-work.

tidy *adj.* **1** [mid-17C; mid-19C+] usu. of a woman, attractive. **2** [early 19C+] (*also* **tidyish**) good, satisfactory. **3** [early 19C+] substantial; usu. of money, e.g. *a tidy sum*. **4** [late 19C] in good health. **5** [20C+] competent., e.g. in a fight. **6** [1990s+] smart, clever.

tidy *adv.* [TIDY *adj.* (2)] [early 19C+] a general intensifier, usu. satisfactorily or very.

tidy! *excl.* [TIDY *adj.* (2)] [20C+] a general excl. of agreement or admiration.

tidy and neat *v.* [rhy. sl.] [20C+] to eat.

tie *n.* (*also* **tie-off**) [1960s+] (*drugs*) any form of tourniquet, e.g. a belt or bandanna, used to isolate the vein into which a drug is to be injected.

tie *v.*

SE in slang uses

(IN COMPOUNDS)

❑ **tie-head** *n.* [they *tie* their *heads* in white scarves] [20C+] (*W.I.*) a member of the Spiritual Baptist Church.

(IN PHRASES)

❑ **can you tie that?** (*also* **...tie him? ...tie it?**) [SE *tie*, to equal, thus lit. 'can you equal that'] [late 19C–1930s] (*US*) an excl. of surprise or amazement; would you believe it? ❑ **tie...** *v. see also under* relevant n. ❑ **tie a knot with the tongue that cannot be undone with the teeth** *v.* [late 16C–19C] to get married. ❑ **tie into** *v.* [20C+] (*US*) **1** to assault, to attack. **2** to get to work on someone or something. **3** to start eating voraciously, to 'tuck into'. ❑ **tie it** *see* separate entries. ❑ **tie off** *v.* **1** [1960s+] (*drugs*) to tie up a vein and isolate it before injecting narcotic drugs. **2** [1990s+] in fig. use, to postpone. ❑ **tie on** *v.* [abbr. *TIE ONE ON* below] [1950s+] **1** (*orig. US black*) to fight. **2** (*US*) to be drunk. ❑ **tie one on** *v.* (*also* **tye one on**) [1950s+] **1** (*UK/US*) to be drunk. **2** (*Aus.*) to provoke a fight. **3** (*Ulster*) to get dressed. ❑ **tie that bull to outside** (*also* **tie that bull to another ashcan, tie the animal outside**) [BULL *n.*[6] (1)] [1920s] (*US*) stop talking nonsense. ❑ **tie the knot** *v.* **1** [late16C+] (*also* **knit the knot**) to get married; thus *knot-tying*, a wedding. **2** [late 19C] of a clergyman, to marry a couple. ❑ **tie the noose** *v.* [NOOSE *v.* (2)] [mid-18C+] to marry. ❑ **tie to** *v.* (*also* **tie up to**) [mid-19C–1940s] (*US*) to trust to something or someone, to seek support in (someone). ❑ **tie up** *see* separate entries. ❑ **tie up a dog** *v.* [DOG *n.*[6]] [20C+] (*Aus.*) to get credit at a public house or hotel. ❑ **tie with St Mary's knot** *v.* [Scot.; ult. ety. unknown] [17C–18C] to hamstring.

(IN EXCLAMATIONS)

❑ **tie a loop in your chin!** [1910s] (*US*) stop talking!

tied up *adj.*[1] **1** [early 17C; mid-19C+] (*also* **tied**) married. **2** [early 19C+] (*orig. boxing jargon*) finished, completed. **3** [late 19C] constipated. **4** [20C+] busy, involved with.

tied up *adj.*[2] [1920s–30s] **1** hanged. **2** dressed.

t'ief *n.* (*also* **teef, tief**) [W.I. pron. of SE *thief*] [late 19C+] (*orig. UK black*) a thief.

t'ief *v.* (*also* **teef, tief**) [W.I. pron. of SE *thieve*] [mid-19C+] (*UK black*) to steal.

tiefiness *n.* (*also* **tiefness**) [T'IEF *v.*] [1950s+] (*W.I.*) theft, thieving.

tiefin tief *n.* [W.I. pron.; lit. 'a thieving thief'] [1950s] (*W.I.*) an absolute, uncompromising thief.

tief-tief *v.* [T'IEF *v.* + redup.] [1950s] (*W.I.*) to steal continually.

tie it *v.* [the railroad ties and tracks that one follows] [late 19C] (*US*) to walk (from town to town).

tie it! *excl.* ['it' is the mouth; note *TIE A LOOP IN YOUR CHIN! under* TIE *v.*] [1930s] shut up!

tiersman *n.* [abbr. SE *frontiersman*] [1940s] (*Aus.*) one who lives in the mountains of Tasmania.

tie-up *n.*[1] [TIE UP *v.*[1] (4)] [1920s+] (*US Und.*) connection, association.

tie-up *n.*[2] [TIE UP *v.*[4]] [1950s+] (*drugs*) the rubber tube, handkerchief, string or other object used for tying off a vein before injecting narcotics.

tie-up *n.*[3] [1990s+] (*UK Und.*) an act of burglary during the day that requires tying up the occupants.

tie up *v.*[1] **1** [19C–1900s] to get a woman pregnant. **2** [late 19C–1900s] to perform a marriage ceremony, to join in marriage. **3** [late 19C–1950s] to get married; to cohabit. **4** [late 19C+] to associate with, to join in partnership. **5** [20C+] (*W.I.*) to secure a (usu. male) partner's affections, to make infatuated. **6** [1920s–40s] to link two people, ideas, etc together. **7** [1920s–50s] to have a relationship with.

tie up *v.*[2] [the image of *tying up* one's villainy and putting it away] [early 19C–1900s] (*UK Und.*) to abandon, to give up, e.g. *tie up prigging*, to give up one's criminal life, to become honest.

tie up *v.*[3] **1** [early 19C–1900s] to defeat or disable in a contest, to finish. **2** [1920s] to fight.

tie up *v.*[4] [1950s+] (*US drugs*) to tie a rubber tube or similar ligature around the arm in order to make a vein prominent prior to injecting a narcotic.

tiff *n.*[1] [? SE *tipple*] **1** [mid-17C–mid-19C] a drink, esp. a thin or diluted one. **2** [early 18C–early 19C] a small bowl (of liquor).

tiff *n.*[2] [? echoic of an exhalation of gas or breath, as in shouting] **1** [early 18C–19C] a fit of temper. **2** [mid-18C+] (*also* **tift**) a petty quarrel, esp. an argument between lovers.

tiff *v.*[1] [? TIFFITY-TAFFETY *n.* or 15C SE *tiff*, to be busy with trifles] [late 17C–early 19C] (*UK Und.*) to have sexual intercourse.

tiff *v.*[2] [TIFF *n.*[1]] [mid-18C–early 19C] to drink, esp. in small sips.

tiff *v.*[3] [TIFF *n.*[2] (2)] [mid-18C+] to have a petty argument.

tiffing *n.* [TIFF *v.*[2]] [18C–early 19C] snacking, eating or drinking other than at mealtimes.

tiffity-taffety *n.* (*also* **taffeta girl, tiffany trader**) [SE *tiffany* + *taffeta*, transparent silks used for dresses] [late 16C–17C] a prostitute.

tiffle up *v.* [SE *tiff*, to adorn oneself, to dress up] [early 18C] to dress oneself up.

tiffy *adj.* [TIFF *n.*[2] (2)] [mid–late 19C] **1** quick to take offence; overly particular, petty. **2** angry, irritated, 'tetchy'.

tift *n. see* TIFF *n.*[2] (2).

tig *v.* [1910s] (*Aus.*) to obtain a loan.

tiger *n.* **1** with ref. to individuals. (**a**) [19C] (*Aus.*) a menial outdoor worker. (**b**) [19C] an overdressed, showy man. (**c**) [early 19C–1930s] a smartly dressed manservant, esp. a boy who accompanies his master in his coach; (*Aus.*) a groom (often black). (**d**) [mid-19C] an omnibus conductor. (**e**) [mid-19C] a parasite, a sponger, a rake. (**f**) [mid-19C] a ferocious woman. (**g**) [mid–late 19C] any male servant. (**h**) [late 19C] (*US*) a 'bouncer' in a casino. (**i**) [late 19C+] (*Aus.*) a (hard) worker in a shearing shed. **2** [mid-19C–1940s] (*US*) a form of college cheer, esp. in phr. *three cheers and a tiger*, the three usual 'hip-hip-hoorays' plus a long-drawn-out shriek, often of the word 'tiger'. **3** [mid-19C+] (*US*) the game of faro; a faro table [the card-game faro itself originated in mid-17C France, moving thence via Fr. immigrants to New Orleans and thus across the US. It takes its name f. the Egyptian *Pharaoh*, for unknown reasons, although it has been claimed that the early faro decks had a card with a picture of the Egyptian monarch]. **4** [late 19C–1900s] (*US*) a prostitute [? she claws her partner + play on CAT *n.*[1] (1a)]. **5** [late 19C–1900s] (*US*) a wife. **6** [late 19C–1900s] streaky bacon [its stripes]. **7** [late 19C–1900s] (*UK juv.*) bread with a tough crust. **8** [20C+] (*Aus.*) with ref. to alcohol [its 'bite']. (**a**) alcoholic liquor. (**b**) a heavy drinker. **9** [1920s+] an outstanding sportsman. **10** [1920s+] any outstanding individual. **11** [1940s] (*US black*) the worst hand in poker. **12** [1970s] (*US/P.R.*) a newly arrived Puerto Rican immigrant [the ship *Marine Tiger*, which brought many Puerto Ricans to the US]. **13** [1980s+] (*drugs*) heroin [its 'bite']. **14** [1980s+] (*S.Afr. black*) a ten-rand note; thus *five tiger*, 50 rand, *half tiger*, five rand [its design]. **15** [1990s+] as a term of address. **16** *see* BLIND TIGER *n.*

(DERIVATIVES)

❑ **tigerish** [19C] flashily dressed.

(IN COMPOUNDS)

❑ **tiger cage** *n.* [1930s] (*US black*) cheap, homemade gin or whisky. ❑ **tiger den** *n.* [mid-19C–1940s] (*US*) a gambling house that specializes in the game of faro. ❑ **tiger-hunter** *n.* [late 19C–1930s] a gambler. ❑ **tiger piss** *n.* [1970s] (*US*) beer. ❑ **tiger's milk** *n.* [SE *tiger milk*/Afk. *tiermelk*, liquor] [mid-19C–1910s] (*US/S.Afr.*) **1** gin. **2** (*also* **tiger snake**) any form of strong liquor. ❑ **tiger sweat** *n.* [1930s] (*US black*) cheap, homemade gin or whisky.

(IN PHRASES)

❑ **buck the tiger** *v.* (*also* **buck, fight the tiger, whip the tiger**) [mid-19C+] (*US*) **1** to play the game of faro; thus fig. *buck against the tiger*, to face overwhelming odds. **2** to gamble. ❑ **fight the tiger** *v.* (*also* **hit..., hunt..., spread..., tackle..., twist the tiger's tail**) [mid-19C+] (*US*) to play the game of faro. ❑ **on the tiger** [20C+] (*Aus.*) out on a serious drinking-bout. ❑ **tiger bit them hard** [mid–late 19C] (*US*) said of one who loses heavily in a casino, esp. when playing faro. □ **tiger for** *n.* [late 19C+] (*Aus.*) an enthusiast for a task. □ **toss the tiger** *v.* [echoic of vomiting] [1960s+] (*N.Z.*) to vomit. □ **whip the tiger** *v.* [mid-19C+] (*US*) to play the game of faro.

tiger *v.* [TIGER *n.* (1)] [1950s+] (*Aus.*) to work hard, to labour.

tiger (tim) *n.* [rhy. sl.] [20C+] (*Aus.*) a swim.

tiggerty-boo *adj. see* TICKETTY-BOO *adj.*

tiggy *n.* [? TEC *n.* (1) or game of *tig*, a juv. catching game] [late 19C–1910s] a detective.

tight *n.*[1] **1** [mid-19C] (*US*) alcohol; a drunken spree. **2** [1920s] a drunkard.

tight *n.*[2] [TIGHT *adj.* (9)] [1960s+] (*US black gang*) one's intimate friend.

tight *adj.* **1** in positive senses. (**a**) [late 16C+] a general positive epithet, meaning competent, skilful, admirable etc; thus *tight-cock*, a skilful fellow. (**b**) [late 17C+] (*later use US black*) spruce, neat; well-dressed, fashionable; dressed up. (**c**) [1920s+] (*US black*) of circumstances, secure, properly worked out, organized. (**d**) [1970s+] (*US campus*) good-looking, well-built. (**e**) [1990s+] (*US teen*) used of something that one likes very much. **2** in negative senses. (**a**) [mid-18C+] of a situation or thing, hard to deal with, difficult, tough; thus *tight corner*. (**b**) [early 19C+] of a contest, one in which the contestants are evenly matched. **3** pertaining to an individual. (**a**) [19C+] of an individual, mean, avaricious, ungenerous. (**b**) [1910s+] (*US*) of an individual, tough, unyielding, aggressive. **4** in financial senses. (**a**) [19C+] impoverished, in financial difficulties. (**b**) [mid-19C] of a sale, offering very little profit. (**c**) [mid-19C+] hard to obtain, usu. of money; thus *tight money*. **5** [early 19C+] (mildly) drunk. **6** [1910s+] very close, friendly, intimate. **7** [1970s] (*Aus. teen*) sexually unresponsive, frigid. **8** [1990s+] (*US*) very unfair. **9** *see* UPTIGHT *adj.*[2].

SE in slang uses

IN COMPOUNDS

□ **tight cravat** *n.* (*also* **cravat**) [late 18C–19C] a hangman's noose. □ **tight (eyes)** *n.* [1980s+] (*US black*) a pej. term for an Asian, usu. a Japanese. □ **tight hand** *n.* [1950s] (*W.I.*) a miser. □ **tight head** *n.* [1930s–40s] (*US black*) a head of kinky black hair. □ **tight house** *n.* [SE *women's tights* + HOUSE *n.*[1] (1)] [1890s] (*US*) a drinking club or house where young scantily dressed women entertain the customers. □ **tight jaws** *n.* (*also* **tight cheeks**) [a grimace of fury] [1960s–70s] (*US black*) intense anger; usu. as *have tight jaws/cheeks*, to get angry, to be angry; thus *TIGHTEN SOMEONE'S JAW under* JAW *n.* □ **tight-wad** *n. see* separate entries. □ **tight-wadded** *adj.* [1980s+] (*US campus*) drunk.

IN PHRASES

□ **get one's head tight** *v.* [var. on *GET ONE'S HEAD RIGHT under* RIGHT *adj.* but note TIGHT *adj.* (7)] [1940s–60s] (*US black*) to take drugs. □ **give someone it tight** *v.* [1990s+] to constrain someone, to limit someone's freedom. □ **lay tight** *v.* [1940s+] (*US black*) to stay calm, to retain one's grip of a situation. □ **not wrapped too tight** *adj.* [one is 'coming apart at the seams'] [1960s+] (*US*) **1** unstable, eccentric. **2** unsophisticated. □ **packed tight** *adj.* [i.e. 'constipated'] [1970s] (*US*) nervous, unhappy, worried. □ **wrapped tight** *adj.* [the image of a neatly *wrapped* package] [1960s+] (*US campus/teen*) **1** sane, balanced, esp. in negative uses, e.g. *he's not wrapped too tight*. **2** feeling fine, happy.

comparatives based on either SE or slang uses above

IN PHRASES

□ **tight as a boiled owl** *adj. see* DRUNK AS A BOILED OWL *adj.* □ **tight as a coot** *adj. see* DRUNK AS A COOTIE *adj.* □ **tight as a crab's arse** *adj.* **1** [1940s+] (*also* **...a budgie's bum, ...a bull's arse, ...a crow's arse, ...a duck's arse, ...a fish's arse(hole), tighter than a bull's ass in fly time, tighter than a clam's ass**) very tight [SE *tight*/TIGHT *adj.* (6a) + ARSE *n.* (1)]. **2** [1960s] very mean. □ **tight as a gnat's twat** *adj.* [2000s] very mean. □ **tight as a lord** *adj.* [1910s–20s] very drunk. □ **tight as a mouse's earhole** *adj.* [1950s+] of a vagina, very tight. □ **tight as an owl** *adj. see* DRUNK AS A BOILED OWL *adj.* □ **tight as a tick** *adj.* (*also* **...drum, ...handcart, ...mink, ...pup**) **1** [20C+] drunk. **2** [1960s] (*US gang*) well prepared. □ **tight as Chloe** *adj. see* DRUNK AS CHLOE *adj.* □ **tight as Dick's hatband** *adj.* (*also* **...Jimmy's hatband, tighter than...**) [SE *tight*/TIGHT *adj.* (8a) + DICK'S HATBAND *n.*] **1** [early 19C+] (*US*) extremely tight. **2** [1980s] of one's finances, impoverished. □ **tight as Kelsey's nuts** *adj. see under* KELSEY'S NUTS *n.* □ **tight as O'Reilley's balls** *adj.* [unlike prev., for which this is merely synon., there is no brandname identification] [20C+] (*US*) very mean, stingy. □ **tight as peep** *adj.* (*also* **drunk as (a) peep**) [mid–late 19C] very drunk. □ **tighter than a gnat's nuts** *adj.* [NUTS *n.*[2] (1)] [1980s] (*US*) very close, very intimate. □ **tighter than a turtle's snatch** *adj.* [1990s+] very tight. □ **tighter than a witch's cunt** *adj.* (*also* **...a nun's cunt**) [CUNT *n.* (1)] [20C+] extremely tight-fitting. □ **tight with** *adj. see* separate entries.

tight-arse *n.* (*also* **tight-ass, tight-butt**) [SE *tight* +ARSE *n.* (1)] **1** [1960s+] (*orig. US*) a mean person, a skinflint. **2** [1970s+] a puritan, a moral conservative [from sense 1]. **3** [2000s] (*Aus.*) an irritating parent [from sense 1]. **4** [2000s] a sexually attractive woman.

tight-arse *adj.* (*also* **tight-arsed, tight-ass, tight-assed**) [TIGHT-ARSE *n.*] **1** [late 19C+] of a woman, chaste [lit. image]. **2** [1930s] smartly dressed (the image is of well-cut clothes). **3** [1960s+] mean. **4** [1970s+] repressed, self-denying, puritanical.

tighten *v.* **1** [mid-19C+] (*Irish*) to drink heavily. **2** [late 19C] to wear a tight corset or stays.

SE in slang uses

IN PHRASES

□ **tighten someone's jaws** *v. see under* JAW *n.*

tightener *n.* (*also* **tightner**) [mid-19C–1950s] a large, heavy meal.

IN PHRASES

□ **do the tightener** *v.* (*also* **...tightner**) [its effects on one's stomach] [mid-19C] (*coster*) to have dinner.

tighten (up) *v.* **1** [1940s+] to persuade, to make someone do what one desires, esp. in the context of a confidence game. **2** [1970s+] (*drugs*) to give or sell narcotics (to a desperate addict). **3** [1970s+] (*US drugs*) to take another dose of a drug, to maintain a state of intoxication. **4** [1990s+] (*US black*) to criticize, to urge someone to a better life.

IN PHRASES

□ **tighten someone up** *v.* [1980s+] (*US*) to repay a debt. □ **tighten up one's game** *v.* [1950s+] (*US black*) **1** to take control of one's life or of a situation in which one is interested. **2** (*also* **keep one's game tight**) to behave in a sensible, positive manner, to maintain one's image, to act in a self-beneficial manner.

tightie whities *n. see* TIGHTY WHITIES *n.*

tightner *n. see* TIGHTENER *n.*

tightwad *n.* [SE *tight* + WAD *n.*[1] (1)] [late 19C+] an ungenerous, mean person.

tightwad *adj.* [TIGHTWAD *n.*] [20C+] miserly.

tight with *phr.* [TIGHT *adj.* (9)] [1950s+] very friendly with.

tighty whities *n.* (*also* **tightie whities**) **1** [1980s+] (*US campus*) men's briefs. **2** [2000s] (*US*) a tight, white T-shirt.

tigress *n.* [TIGER *n.* (1)] [mid–late 19C] a flashily overdressed woman.

Tijuana *adj.* used in combs. to imply negative Mexican stereotypes, spec. the era when US citizens saw Tijuana, Mexico, as the vice capital of Central America.

IN COMPOUNDS

□ **Tijuana bible** *n.* [1940s+] a small, illustrated pornographic book. □ **Tijuana cha-cha** *n.* [1990s+] diarrhoea, esp. when contracted on holiday. □ **Tijuana queen** *n.* [1970s+] (*US gay*) a Hispanic homosexual. □ **Tijuana racetrack** *n.* [1950s+] (*US*) stains on the underwear that result from an attack of diarrhoea. □ **Tijuana taxi** *n.* [1970s] (*US*) a police car.

Tijuanero *n.* (*also* **Tijuanera**) [Sp., a citizen of Tijuana, the border town through which legal immigrants often pass] [1960s+] (*US*) a newly arrived immigrant from Mexico.

tik *n.*[1] [? SE *tick*, one ticks them off as a potential victim] [1990s+] (*UK black*) a prospective victim.

tik *n.*[2] [2000s] (*S.Afr. drugs*) methamphetamine.

tik *n.*[3] *see* TICK *n.*[3].

tike-lurking *n. see* BUFFER-LURKING *under* BUFFER *n.*[1].

Tilbury *n.* [the fare charged by the trans-Thames ferry from Gravesend to *Tilbury* Fort] [late 18C–mid-19C] sixpence (2½p).

Tilbury docker *n.* [rhy. sl. = KNOCKER *n.*[1] (7); ult. *Tilbury docks* (in East London)] [1970s] (*UK prison*) a prisoner who does not pay his debts.

Tilbury docks *n.* [rhy. sl.; ult. the docks in East London] [late 19C+] **1** (*orig. navy*) socks. **2** venereal disease [= POX *n.*[1] (3)].

'tilda *n.* (*also* **tilder**) [abbr. MATILDA *n.*] [late 19C–1950s] (*Aus.*) a vagrant's pack.

tile *n.* [it sits on top of one's ROOF *n.* (2)] [early 19C–1910s] a hat.

IN PHRASES

❑ **fly a tile** *v.* [early 19C] to knock off a man's hat as a form of practical joke. ❑ **have a tile loose** *v.* (*also* **...a slate loose, ...a tile off**) **1** [mid-19C+] to be eccentric or foolish. **2** [1910s] (*US*) to be drunk. ❑ **loose in the tiles** *adj. see* LOOSE IN THE BEAN *under* BEAN *n.*[1]. ❑ **off one's tile** *adj.* [1910s] (*Aus.*) mad, angry. ❑ **take the tiles off** *v.* [? one's fig. disposal of all one's assets, up to the house tiles] [late 19C] (*UK society*) to live in an extremely extravagant manner.

tiled *adj.* [having a (*tiled*) roof over one's head] [early–mid-19C] **1** snug, comfortable. **2** arrested, locked up, confined.

t.i.l.i.s. *v. see tell it like it is* under TELL *v.*

till *n.* [19C] the vagina [its commercial potential/one puts 'money', i.e. the penis, into it].

SE in slang uses

IN COMPOUNDS

❑ **till-boy** *n.* [mid-19C] a shop assistant who steals from the shop till. ❑ **till diving** *n.* [early 18C] (*UK Und*) an act of theft from a shop till; thus *till-diver*, one who carries out such a theft. ❑ **till frisker** *n.* [FRISK *v.*[2] (2)] [mid-19C] (*UK Und.*) a person who steals from a shop cash register. ❑ **till lifting** *n.* [LIFT *v.* (1a)] [late 19C] (*UK Und.*) the robbery of a shop cash register. ❑ **till-tapper** *n.* [mid-19C+] (*US Und.*) one who steals from a cash register, esp. when employed as the cashier. ❑ **till-tilting** *n.* [the tilting of the till until it opens] [mid-19C] (*US Und.*) the robbery of shop cash registers.

till *v.* [1970s+ use is US black] [late 16C–mid-18C; 1970s+] to have sexual intercourse.

till all is blue *phr.* [the effect of the alcohol on one's eyesight. According to Smyth, *Sailor's Wordbook* (1867), 'a phrase borrowed from the idea of a vessel making out of port, and getting into blue water'] **1** [17C–19C] to the extreme, esp. used of excessive drinking. **2** [19C–1900s] (*US*) to the very end, the 'bitter' end.

tilley-vally/tillie vallie *n. see* TILLY-VALLY *n.*

till-tap *v. see* TAP A TILL *under* TAP *v.*[2].

till the last dog is hung *phr.* [mid-19C+] to the very end, until everything is resolved.

tilly *n.*[1] [abbr. MATILDA *n.*] [1900s–20s] (*Aus./N.Z.*) a vagrant's swag or pack.

tilly *n.*[2] [abbr. SE *utility*] [1950s+] (*Aus.*) a utility vehicle.

tilly *n.*[3] (*also* **Tilly law**) [the use of a woman's name to 'feminize' the force] [1960s+] (*gay*) the police.

tilly *v.* [2000s] (*S.Afr. gay*) to masturbate.

tilly-vally *n.* (*also* **tilley-vally, tillie vallie, tully-vally**) [ety. unknown] [late 15C–19C] piffle, rubbish, nonsense.

tillywhacker *n. see* TALLYWHACKER *n.*

tillywhiz *n.* [var. on TALLYWHACKER *n.*] [1970s] (*US*) the penis.

tilt *n.* (*also* **tylt**) [early–mid-18C] (*UK Und.*) a picklock key.

tilt *v.* [1910s] (*US*) in cards, to raise the bet.

tilt a kidney *v. see* TAP A KIDNEY *under* TAP *v.*[2].

tilt-boat *n.* [SE *tilt-boat*, 'a large rowing boat having a tilt or awning, formerly used on the Thames, esp. as a passenger boat between London and Gravesend' (*OED*)] [17C] a promiscuous woman; a prostitute.

tilter *n.* [SE *tilter*, one who takes part in a joust or tournament] [late 17C–early 18C] a rapier, a sword.

Tim *n.* [the proper name *Tim Malloy*, stereotyped as Catholic] [1960s+] (*Scot.*) a derog. term for a Roman Catholic.

timber *n.* **1** [early 19C] (*US*) a thrashing. **2** [early 19C] (*Anglo-Irish*) a wooden leg. **3** [early 19C–1960s] a match, also as *small timber*. **4** [mid-19C] the stocks. **5** [late 19C] a clubbing at the hands of the toughs of a town unfriendly to tramps. **6** [1930s–40s] (*US black*) a toothpick. **7** [1930s–40s] (*US Und.*) a police nightstick. **8** [1970s] (*drugs*) stems and stalks found in a batch of marijuana.

IN COMPOUNDS

❑ **timber-doodle** *n.* [mid–late 19C] (*US*) any form of spirituous liquor. ❑ **timber-merchant** *n.* [MERCHANT *n.*] [early 19C–1930s] a match-seller.

SE in slang uses

IN COMPOUNDS

❑ **timber-head** *n.* [+ -HEAD *sfx* (1)] [mid–late 17C; mid-19C] a fool. ❑ **timber stairs** *n.* [its wooden construction; logic would suggest the treadmill or 'everlasting staircase', but this was not invented until the early 19C] [mid-18C] the pillory.

IN EXCLAMATIONS

❑ **saw your timbers!** [mid-19C] go way! be off!

timbers *n.* [SE *timber*, a wooden foundation] **1** [late 16C+] the legs. **2** [1910s–40s] (*US tramp*) a beggar who poses as a pencil-seller. **3** [1930s] (*US tramp*) one who has a wooden leg.

IN EXCLAMATIONS

❑ **dash my timbers!** *see* DASH MY BUTTONS! *under* DASH! *excl.*

timber-toe *n.* [late 18C–1900s] **1** a wooden leg. **2** a person who has a wooden leg.

timber-toed *adj.* [TIMBER-TOE *n.*] **1** [late 18C+] having a wooden leg. **2** [late 19C] (*US Und.*) cowardly, easily scared [? fig. use of sense 1].

Timbucktoo *n.* [the perceived distance] [1980s+] a euph. for SE *hell*; usu. in phr. *go to Timbucktoo*.

time *n.* **1** [mid-19C+] a prison sentence; thus *do time*, to serve a sentence. **2** [late 19C; 1970s] (*US*) (*also* **times**) a good time, a drinking spree [backform. f. SE phr. *a good time was had by all*]. **3** [20C+] (*Irish/US*) credit.

IN COMPOUNDS

❑ **time drunk** *adj.* [1970s] (*US prison/Und.*) intellectually depleted after a long jail sentence.

IN PHRASES

❑ **build time** *v.* [1960s] (*US prison/Und.*) to serve a jail sentence. ❑ **copper time** *n.* [COPPER *n.* (5)] [1940s+] (*US Und.*) time off for good behaviour in prison. ❑ **dance to the time of shaking the sheets (without music)** *v. see under* DANCE *v.* ❑ **dead time** *n. see under* DEAD *adj.* ❑ **do one's own time** *v.* [20C+] (*US prison/Und.*) to serve a prison sentence without becoming involved in any of the prison gangs, illicit business etc. ❑ **do time** *v.* **1** [19C+] to serve a prison sentence. **2** [20C+] in ext. use, irrespective of the institution. ❑ **easy time** *n.* [20C+] (*US Und.*) an uneventful time in prison. ❑ **full time** *n.* [1940s] (*US Und./prison*) a life sentence. ❑ **good time** *n. see* separate entry. ❑ **hard time** *n. see* separate entry. ❑ **have oneself a time** *v.* [1930s+] to enjoy onself, to go out on a spree. ❑ **if you can't do the time, don't do the crime** [1960s+] (*orig. Und.*) don't take an action if you cannot deal with the concomitant responsibilities. ❑ **light time** *n.* [1940s–50s] (*US Und.*) an uneventful time in prison. ❑ **make a time** *v.* **1** [late 19C–1900s] (*US*) to make a fuss [? SE *difficult/hard time*]. **2** [1910s] to enjoy oneself, celebrate. ❑ **make time with** *v.* (*US*) **1** [1930s+] to make advances, to court, to flirt. **2** [1950s] to associate with. ❑ **pull time** *v.* **1** [1940s+] (*US prison*) to be sentenced to/serve a term of imprisonment. **2** [1980s] (*US*) spend time in a place. ❑ **sleeping time** *n.* [TIME *n.* (1), var. on SLEEP *n.* (1); one could sleep it away] [1920s–60s] (*US Und.*) a short prison sentence. ❑ **wino time** *n.* [WINO *n.* (1); habitual drunkards generally receive short sentences, i.e. days rather than years in prison] [1940s+] (*US Und.*) a short sentence.

IN EXCLAMATIONS

□ **do your own time!** [1970s] imper., mind your own business!

SE in slang uses

IN COMPOUNDS

□ **time bandit** *n.* [-BANDIT *sfx* (1); ult. Terry Gilliam's 1981 film *Time Bandits*] [1990s+] a thief who specializes in snatching expensive watches.

IN PHRASES

□ **bowl me the time** [SE *bowl*, to deliver (a ball); orig. milit. use] [1950s–80s] (*S.Afr.*) what's the time? □ **by the new time** *adv.* [Irish *the new time*, popular name for daylight saving time] [1910s+] very quickly. □ **give her the time** *v.* [euph.] [1950s] of a man, to have sexual intercourse. □ **give someone a hot time** *v.* [mid-19C+] to make someone unhappy, to punish, to reprimand; to cause problems for. □ **I've got the time if you've got the money** [the supposed conversation between a streetwalker and her client who has asked, as a way of initiating their relationship, 'Do you have the time?'] [1910s+] a joc. phr. delivered to one who asks 'Have you got the time?'. □ **know the time of day** *v.* (*also* **know what day it is**) [early 19C+] to be well aware of what is going on. □ **know what time of day it is** *v.* (*also* **know the right time, know what o'clock it is, know what's o'clock, see what o'clock it is**) [early 19C+] to be aware, to know what is going on; often in neg. □ **more time** [1950s+] (*W.I. Rasta*) see you later. □ **on time** (*also* **on T**) [1940s+] (*US black*) at the emotionally or psychologically apposite moment (rather than the chronologically prompt one); of good quality; also as phr. *get on time*, to have fun. □ **put one's time in** *v.* [late 19C+] to spend time, to occupy one's time. □ **show (someone) what time it is** *v.* (*also* **tell someone...**) [1980s+] (*orig. US black*) to explain, to 'put someone in the picture', to 'teach someone a lesson'. □ **time of day** *n.* (*also* **time o' day**) **1** [late 17C; early 19C+] the current situation, what is going on; thus *put one up to the time of day*, explain the situation to one. **2** [19C] a trick, a ruse, the practice of theft. **3** [mid-19C] the correct or pertinent thing or situation. □ **what in time?** (*also* **why in time?**) [mid-19C–1920s] (*US*) a question, often deriving from one's incomprehension or surprise, 'what on earth', 'what in the world' etc.

time *prep.* [1910s+] at the time, by the time, once, e.g. *Time the day be done.*

timer *n.* [TIME *n.*] [late 19C+] (*UK Und.*) a criminal who has served time in jail; often in combs, e.g. *FIRST-TIMER under* FIRST *adj.*, SHORT-TIMER *n.* (1).

times *n.*[1] [mid-19C] multiples of one shilling (5p), e.g. *nine times*, nine shillings (45p).

times *n.*[2] *see* TIME *n.* (2).

timothy *n.* [? rhy. sl.; *timothy grass* = ARSE *n.* (1) or *timothy titmouse* = HOUSE *n.*[1] (1)] [1940s+] (*Aus.*) a brothel.

timothy-tool *n.* [TOOL *n.*[1] (1)] [late 19C] the penis.

Tims *n.* [abbr.] [1990s+] *Tim*berland boots.

tim-tim *n.* [Carib.E. excl. *tim-tim!* used by a story-teller to indicate that he/she is about to tell a folk-tale. ? ult. Fr. *tiens*, hello! look! or SE (*it's*) *time*] [20C+] (*W.I.*) an unreliable story, a fantasy.

tin *n.* **1** in context of its metallic qualities. (**a**) [mid-19C–1960s] money, esp. silver. (**b**) [1920s–30s] (*US*) a trifling amount of money. (**c**) [1920s+] (*US*) a police officer's or sheriff's badge [its main component; thus those gifts and favours – free meals, drinks – obtained by showing one's official badge]. **2** in senses of a container, i.e. a SE *tin can*. (**a**) [1900s] (*US*) a drink. (**b**) [1910s–60s] (*US*) a small container of opium. (**c**) [1930s] a one-gallon can of alcohol. (**d**) [1950s+] (*drugs*) 28g (1oz) of marijuana [the selling of marijuana in measures based on the size of a popular brand tobacco tin; the use for cocaine may be a misinterpretation]. (**e**) [1960s–70s] (*US*) a few grains of cocaine. (**f**) [1980s+] (*US campus*) beer.

IN COMPOUNDS

□ **tinman** *n.* [TIN *n.* (1) + SE *man*] [mid–late 19C] (*UK sporting*) a very rich man, a millionaire. □ **tin roofer** *n.* [1900s; 2000s] (*US*) a confidence trickster. □ **tin soldier** *n.* [1970s+] a prostitute's client, usu. middle- or upper-class, who doesn't want sex but only to act as a servant or 'slave' to the prostitute. □ **tin wife** *n.* [1920s] (*US*) a police officer's wife.

IN PHRASES

□ **clippings of tin** *n.* [1910s+] (*Irish*) a trifling, worthless quantity. □ **do one's tin** *v.* [1920s] (*Aus.*) to spend all, one's money. □ **have a bun in one's tin** *v. see HAVE A BUN IN THE OVEN under* OVEN *n.* □ **in the tin** [1940s–50s] (*Aus.*) in trouble, in a tight spot. □ **jink one's tin** *v.* [SE *jink*, to rattle with a metallic sound] [mid-19C–1900s] **1** to pay out money. **2** to rattle one's change. □ **kick the tin** *v.* [1960s+] (*Aus.*) to make a financial contribution, esp. to buying a round of drinks. □ **yard of tin** *n.* [mid-19C] a horn, esp. in hunting or coaching.

tin, the *n.* [20C+] (*Aus.*) tin-mining country.

tin *adj.* **1** [1900s–10s] (*US campus*) best, admirable. **2** *see* TIN-POT *adj.*

IN COMPOUNDS

□ **tin-arse(d)** *see* separate entries. □ **tin-back/-bum** *n. see* TIN-ARSE *n.*

SE in slang uses

IN COMPOUNDS

□ **tin-badge** *n.* (*also* **tin cop**) [1950s] **1** (*US*) an auxiliary or volunteer police officer. **2** a private detective. □ **tin-can** *see* separate entries. □ **tin cow** *n.* [note synon. WW2 US Army *armored cow/city cow*] [1920s–40s] (*US tramp*) tinned milk. □ **tin derby** *n. see* TIN HAT *n.*[1] (1). □ **tin dog** *n.* (*also* **tinned dog**) [note WW1 milit. *corned dog*, canned beef] [20C+] (*Aus./N.Z.*) canned meat. □ **tin-ear(ed)** *see* separate entries. □ **tin grin** *n.* [1970s+] (*US campus/UK teen*) a person wearing orthodontic braces. □ **tin hare** *n.* **1** [1920s+] (*mainly Aus.*) the electric hare used for greyhound racing. **2** [1930s+] a train, esp. a rail-motor, i.e. a small passenger train consisting of the engine and one coach. □ **tin hat** *see* separate entries. □ **tinhorn** *see* separate entries. □ **tin lizzie** *n.* (*also* **tin lizard, Liz, lizzie**) [affectionate nickname] **1** [1910s+] (*orig. US*) a Model T Ford. **2** [1920s+] (*orig. Aus.*) any kind of ageing, broken-down vehicle. □ **tin mittens** *n.* [MITTEN *n.* (1)] [1930s–40s] (*US Und.*) a person who arranges something at a high price. □ **tin-pot** *adj. see* separate entries. □ **tin ribs** *n.* [late 19C] (*UK Und.*) a policeman. □ **tin shield** *n.* [metonymy] [1990s+] (*US*) a police officer. □ **tin shirt** *n.* [1920s] (*US Und.*) a bullet-proof vest. □ **tin star** *n.* [20C+] (*US*) a private detective; a country police officer. □ **tin teller** *n.* [2000s] (*N.Z.*) an ATM. □ **tin throne** *n.* [SE *throne*/THRONE *n.*] [1930s–40s] (*US prison*) a cell latrine.

tina *n.* [abbr. CHRISTINA *n.*] [2000s] crystal meth(amphetamine).

tina *adj.* [initial letter of SE *tiny*] [2000s] (*S.Afr. gay*) very small, usu. with reference to the penis.

tin and tap *n.* (*also* **tip and tap**) [rhy. sl.] [1930s–50s] (*US Und.*) a cap.

tin-arse *n.* (*also* **tin-back, tin-bum**) [TIN *n.* (1)+ ARSE *n.* (1)/SE *back*/BUM *n.*[1] (1)] [late 19C+] (*Aus./N.Z.*) an extremely lucky person.

tin-arsed *adj.* (*also* **tin-arse**) [TIN-ARSE *n.*] [1930s+] (*Aus./N.Z.*) thick-skinned, impervious to pain, lucky.

tin bath *n.* [rhy. sl., pron. 'barf'] [20C+] scarf.

tin can *n.* **1** [1910s+] a dilapidated old car; or aeroplane, or ship. **2** [1920s–50s] (*US milit.*) a destroyer. **3** [1920s–60s] (*US Und.*) a safe; thus *tin-opener*, an implement for opening a safe. **4** [1950s] a tank.

tin-can *v.* [the image of a dog with a tin can tied to its tail] **1** [1900s–20s] (*US*) to retreat, to runaway. **2** [1920s] (*US Und.*) to cheat, to deceive.

tin can cop *n.* [TIN CAN *n.* (1) + COP *n.*[1] (1)] [1970s+] (*US*) a rural sheriff.

tincture *n.* [hugely popularized by the'Dear Bill' column in the magazine *Private Eye*, lampooning Denis Thatcher, husband of prime minister Margaret Thatcher (b.1925)] [1910s+] a drink.

tinder-box *n. see FIRELOCK under* FIRE *n.*

tin derby *n. see* TIN HAT *n.*[1] (1).

tin ear *n.* (*Aus./US*) **1** [1910s+] an eavesdropper. **2** [1930s+] a fool, simpleton.

IN PHRASES

❑ **put a tin ear on** *v.* [1920s+] (*US*) to batter the head and ears, giving the victim a 'cauliflower' ear.

tin-ear *v.* [TIN EAR *n.* (1)] [1910s+] (*Aus./US*) to eavesdrop.

tin-eared *adj.* [TIN EAR *n.* (2)] [1930s+] foolish.

tin flute *n.* [rhy. sl.] [20C+] a suit.

ting-a-ling *n.* [rhy. sl.] [1940s–80s] (*Aus.*) a ring.

tingle *n.* [1940s+] (*Aus.*) a call on the telephone.

tin hat *n.*[1] **1** [20C+] (*also* **tin derby**) a helmet. **2** [1910s] a senior officer [rare var. on *BRASS HAT under* BRASS *adj.*[1]].

IN PHRASES

❑ **put the tin hat on** *v.* (*also* **put the brass hat on, put the tin lid on**) [WW1 milit. *tin hat*, a steel helmet] [1910s+] to finish off for good.

tin hat *n.*[2] [rhy. sl. = PRAT *n.*[1] (6)] [1960s+] a fool.

tin hat *adj.* [? abbr. *PUT THE TIN HAT ON under* TIN HAT *n.*[1]] [late 19C–1910s] drunk; thus *two tin hats*, very drunk, *three tin hats*, incapably drunk.

tin hat *v.* [TIN HAT *n.*[1] (2)] [1910s–40s] (*Aus.*) to indicate one's contempt; to patronize, to talk down to.

tinhorn *n.* [late 19C+] a contemptible person, esp. if superficially flashy; a fool; usu. referring to a smalltime gambler.

tinhorn *adj.* [abbr. gambling use *tinhorn gambler*, a second-rate class of gambler: 'Chuck-a-luck operators shake their dice in a "small churn-like affair of metal" – hence the expression, "tinhorn gambler", for the game is rather looked down upon as one for "chubbers" and chuck-a-luck gamblers are never admitted within the aristocratic circle of faro-dealers.' G.F. Willison, *Here They Dug Gold* (1931)] [late 19C+] second-rate, inferior, superficially flashy.

tink *n.* [mid-19C+] **1** a *tinker* [abbr.]. **2** a foul-mouthed, obstreperous person [? the stereotype of sense 1].

tinkard *n.* [SE *tinker*; '[He leaveth his bag a sweating at the ale house...and in the mean season goeth abroad begging' (Awdeley)]] [16C] (*UK Und.*) a tinker who alternates legitimate work with begging.

tinker *n.*[1] [mid-19C] (*UK Und.*) sixpence.

tinker *n.*[2] [SE *tinker*, a pedlar/'a clumsy or inefficient mender' (*OED*)] **1** [20C+] an affectionate term usu. used to a child by an exasperated parent, a rascal. **2** [1920s] (*US Und.*) a novice burglar.

SE in slang uses

IN COMPOUNDS

❑ **tinker's budget** *n.* (*also* **tinker's news**) [SE *tinker* + *budget*, a long letter full of news/*news*; a tinker, being on the move, would catch up with news late] [mid–late 19C] stale news. ❑ **tinker's (cuss)** *n.* **1** *see* NOT CARE A TINKER'S (CURSE) *v.* **2** *see* NOT WORTH A CURSE *phr.* ❑ **tinker's time** *n.* [the slow progress and unreliability of the SE *tinker*] [20C+] (*Irish*) unpunctuality.

IN PHRASES

❑ **not for a tinker's** *see NOT FOR ALL THE TEA IN CHINA under* TEA *n.*

tinker *n.*[3] [var. on *tinkle*] [1950s–60s] (*Can.*) the penis.

Tinker Bell *n.* [the character *Tinker Bell* the fairy in J.M. Barrie's *Peter Pan* (1904)] [1950s–70s] (*camp gay*) a pleasingly plump person.

tinkerty-tonk *phr.* [1920s–30s] a nonsense term used for goodbye.

tinkle *n.* [the sounds involved] **1** [1930s+] a ring on the telephone, usu. in phr. *give one a tinkle*. **2** [1940s] (*US black*) a doorbell. **3** [1960s] money. **4** [1960s+] an act of urination.

IN COMPOUNDS

❑ **tinklebox** *n.* (*also* **tinkler**) [1900s–40s] (*US*) a piano.

tinkle *v.* [TINKLE *n.* (4)] [1960s+] (*usu. juv.*) to urinate.

tinkle box *n.* [TINKLE *v.* + SE *box*] [1960s] (*US campus*) a lavatory.

tinkler *n.*[1] [? his bell or SE *tinker*] [18C–19C] a mendicant tramp.

tinkler *n.*[2] [20C+ use is US black] [mid-19C; 1930s–40s] a (front-door) bell.

IN PHRASES

❑ **ring the tinkler on** *v. see RING THE BELL ON under* BELL *n.*[1]. ❑ **sling a tinkler** *v.* [late 19C–1920s] to ring a bell.

tinkle-tinkle *n.* [1910s] (*Aus.*) an effeminate man.

tin lid *n.*[1] [rhy. sl.] **1** [20C+] (*Aus.*) a child [KID *n.*[1] (1)]. **2** [1940s–70s] a Jew [YID *n.*[1]].

tin lid *n.*[2]

IN PHRASES

❑ **put the tin lid on** *v. see PUT THE TIN HAT ON under* TIN HAT *n.*[1].

tinned *adj.* [tin beer cans] [1940s+] drunk.

tinned dog *n. see TIN DOG under* TIN *adj.*

tinner *n.* [1910s] (*US Und.*) a police officer, by metonymy from their tin badge.

tinnie *n.* (*also* **tinny**) **1** [1960s+] (*orig. Aus. surfer*) a can of beer. **2** [1960s+] (*Aus.*) a small aluminium boat. **3** [1980s+] (*N.Z. drugs*) . (**a**) silver foil, as used in smoking heroin. (**b**) silver foil, used for wrapping measures of cannabis; thus the measure of cannabis as sold as a single unit.

tinny *n.*[1] [? Gaelic/Erse *teine*, fire, Shelta *tini*, fire or SE *tinder*, use in lighting fires] **1** [mid-18C–early 19C] a fire. **2** [early 19C] (*UK Und.*) a discovery, by the police.

IN COMPOUNDS

❑ **tinny-hunter** *n.* ['No beast of prey is so noxious to Society, or so destitute of feeling, as these wretches' (George Parker, *A View of Society*, 1781)] [late 18C–early 19C] a thief who robs people whose homes are burning down, while pretending to give assistance.

tinny *n.*[2] [? TIN *n.* (1)] [1930s] (*US Und*) a thief.

tinny *n.*[3] *see* TINNIE *n.*

tinny *adj.*[1] [TIN *n.* (1)] **1** [mid–late 19C] wealthy, rich. **2** [1910s+] (*Aus./N.Z.*) lucky. **3** [1930s+] (*Aus./N.Z.*) mean, grasping.

IN PHRASES

❑ **on the tinny luck** [1910s+] (*Aus./N.Z.*) by a fortunate chance.

tinny *adj.*[2] [SE *tin*] [1920s+] cheap, second-rate.

tinny house *n. see BULLET HOUSE under* BULLET *n.*[5].

tin of beans *n.* [rhy. sl.] [1960s+] jeans.

tin of fruit *n. see* BAG (OF FRUIT) *n.*

tin plate *n.* [rhy. sl. = MATE *n.* (1)] [20C+] a friend.

tin-pot *adj.* (*also* **tin, tin-pan**) [note naut. jargon *tin-potter*, an idler, one who shirks their duties by claiming to be ill. The use of *tin-pot* as cheap, inferior is SE] [mid-19C+] of a place, small, insignificant; of a person, mediocre, second-rate; of an event, irrelevant.

tinsel teeth *n.* [1970s+] (*US campus*) a person wearing orthodontic braces.

Tinsel Town *n.* (*also* **Tinseltown**) [the towns' glittering images] **1** [1930s+] Hollywood, California. **2** [1960s] Manhattan, N.Y. **3** [1980s+] (*Aus.*) Sydney.

tint *n.* [abbr. SE *tincture*] [20C+] (*Irish*) a measure of liquor.

tin-tack *n.* [rhy. sl.] **1** [1930s–50s] dismissal from a job [SACK *n.* (2a)]. **2** [1940s+] a bed [SACK *n.* (4)].

tin tacks *n.* [rhy. sl.; phr. allegedly coined by the critic and playwright George Bernard Shaw (1856–1950)] [20C+] facts, usu. in phr. *GET DOWN TO TIN TACKS* below; also the basics, the smallest components.

IN PHRASES

❑ **get down to tin tacks** *v.* (*also* **come down to tin tacks**) [1920s–40s] to approach and deal with the central issues of a situation.

tin tank *n.* [rhy. sl.] [20C+] a bank.

tints *n.* [they are SE *tinted*] [1970s+] (*US black*) **1** tinted or dark glasses. **2** tinted windows in an automobile.

tintsy-wintsy *adj. see* TEENSIE-WEENSIE *adj.*

tiny tim *n.* [rhy. sl. = FLIM *n.*[1] (1)] [20C+] a £5 note.

Tío Taco *n.* (*also* **Tío Tomás**) [Mex. *tío*, uncle + *taco*, the foodstuff; ult. a play on UNCLE TOM *n.* (1)] [1970s+] (*US*) a derog. term for a Mexican who is considered insufficiently nationalistic by others.

tip *n.*[1] [SE *tip a glass* or abbr. TIPPLE *n.* (1)] [early 17C–mid-19C] a draught of liquor; thus drink in general.

IN PHRASES

❑ **have a tip on** *v.* [1900s–20s] to be drunk.

tip *n.*[2] [SE *tip*, a gratuity] **1** [19C] money as used in any form of contract. **2** [early–mid-19C] a bribe.

IN COMPOUNDS

❑ **tip street** *n.* [early–mid-19C] a state of wealth, thus *in tip street*, well-off.

tip *n.*[3] [ety. unknown] **1** [mid-19C; 1930s+] (*orig. US Und.*) a crowd of people. **2** [1990s+] (*US Und.*) a prison gang.

IN PHRASES

❑ **working the tip** [mid-19C] working as a pickpocket.

tip *n.*[4] [proper name *Tipperary*] [mid–late 19C] (*Aus.*) an Irishman, esp. a gold-miner.

tip *n.*[5] **1** [mid-19C+] a piece of 'inside' information, esp. as regards a sporting contest, usu. racing or boxing. **2** [late 19C] the subject of the tip, usu. a horse. **3** [late 19C] one's point, one's intention. **4** [late 19C+] a special hint or trick. **5** [20C+] a tip-off, but used as any reason for an arrest, not simply information given to the police. **6** [1900s] (*US Und.*) a warning. **7** [1910s–40s] (*US Und.*) a confidence trick in cards where the victim is lured with the offer of being given information about another player's hand.

IN COMPOUNDS

❑ **tip sheet** *n.* [1930s] (*US Und.*) a fake financial guide used in swindles.

IN PHRASES

❑ **miss one's tip** *v.* [mid–late 19C] (*orig. circus*) to fail in one's aim or objective. ❑ **sling the tip** *v.* [mid–late 19C] to warn, to provide with information. ❑ **straight tip** *n.* [STRAIGHT *adj.*[1] (2)] [mid–late 19C] honest advice.

tip *n.*[6] [SE *tip*, the point] **1** [late 19C+] the end, the ultimate. **2** [1960s] (*US*) the female nipple.

IN PHRASES

❑ **on someone's tip** [? the tip of the penis; note *ON THE DICK under* DICK *n.*[1]] [1980s] (*US black*) of a woman, to be ready for sexual activity, to be (sexually) interested in.

tip *n.*[7] [SE *tip*, advice, guidance] [1940s+] (*US black*) the aspect, the point of view, the angle, e.g. *on the art tip*, from the artistic point of view; *on the sales tip*, from the aspect of sales; ult. synon. with SE *thing*.

IN PHRASES

❑ **get off someone's tip** *v.* [1980s] to stop being irritating. ❑ **hipped to the tip** *adj.* [1940s] (*US black campus*) very knowledgeable.

tip *n.*[8] [abbr. SE *rubbish tip*] [1970s+] a very untidy, messy place, e.g. a child's bedroom.

tip *v.*[1] [? SE *tip*, to touch lightly, orig. Und., but sl. by mid-18C] **1** [early 17C+] to give, to hand over, to lend. **2** [18C+] to give a monetary gratuity. **3** [late 18C–1910s] to pay. **4** [early–mid-19C] to bribe.

IN PHRASES

❑ **tip the brads** *v.* [BRAD *n.*[1] (2)] [19C] **1** to be generous. **2** to be a gentleman. ❑ **tip the cole** *v. see under* COLE *n.* ❑ **tip up** *v.* [mid-19C+] to hand over (money), usu. as imper.

tip *v.*[2] [abbr. SE *tipple*, to drink] **1** [mid-17C–mid-19C] to drink, to toast. **2** [1970s] (*US campus*) to drink heavily.

tip *v.*[3] [late 17C+] to do, to make, to perform, usu. in phrs., e.g. *TIP A DADDLE under* DADDLE *n.*

IN PHRASES

❑ **tip...** *v. see also under* relevant n. ❑ **tip a hint** *v.* [late 18C] to warn, to inform. ❑ **tip a nod** *v.* **1** [late 18C+] to warn, to signal. **2** [mid–late 19C] to recognize someone. ❑ **tip a pike** *v.* [PIKE *v.*[1] (1)] [early 18C–mid-19C] to run off, to make an escape. ❑ **tip a settler** *v.* [SETTLER *n.* (2)] [early 19C] to hit hard, to knock out. ❑ **tip a slang** *v.* [SLANG *n.*[1]] [late 18C] (*UK Und.*) to raise the forefinger of the right hand to one's nose as a sign of understanding. ❑ **tip a snitch** *v.* [SNITCH *n.*[1] (2)] [mid-18C] (*UK Und.*) to give someone a blow, to punch. ❑ **tip a sock** *v.* [SOCK *n.*[3] (1)] [late 17C–19C] to hit hard, to knock out. ❑ **tip a yarn** *v.* [YARN *n.* (1)] [19C] to tell a story. ❑ **tip one's ditto** *v.* [late 19C] to agree. ❑ **tip one's fin** *v.* (*also* **tip one's flipper**) [FIN *n.*[1] (1)/FLIPPER *n.*[1] (2)] [19C–1940s] to shake hands; usu. in phr. *tip us your fin/flipper.* ❑ **tip one's mitt** *v.* (*also* **tip one's hand, ...duke**) [MITT *n.* (3)/MITT *n.* (2)] **1** [early 19C+] (*also* **...fist, ...mauley, ...mauns, ...mawley**) to shake hands. **2** [late 19C+] (*US*) to disclose one's plans inadvertently; to inform. ❑ **tip one's rags a gallop** *v.* (*also* **tip the...**) [SE *rags* as fig. for clothes; RAGS *n.* (1) is a later development] [19C] to leave, to depart. ❑ **tip someone a queer one** *v.* [mid-18C] UK Und. to use sleight of hand to pass over a fake. ❑ **tip someone the gum** *v.* [mid-18C] (*UK Und.*) to smile, to chat pleasantly. ❑ **tip someone the office** *v.* [late 19C] to warn someone. ❑ **tip someone the token** *v.* [TOKEN *n.* (2)] [late 18C–early 19C] to give a partner a venereal disease. ❑ **tip someone the turnips** *v.* [late 18C] to jilt, to 'chuck'. ❑ **tip the bucket on** *v. see DROP THE BUCKET ON under* DROP *v.*[1]. ❑ **tip the chaff** *v.* [early 19C] to tease, to banter with. ❑ **tip the claws (for breakfast)** *v.* [SE *claws*, those of the cat-o'-nine-tails] [18C] to be whipped, as a judicial punishment. ❑ **tip the go-by** *v.* [var. on *GIVE SOMEONE THE GO under* GO-BY *n.*] [late 18C–early 19C] **1** to avoid, to disregard deliberately. **2** to allow, to turn a blind eye to. **3** to dismiss, to get rid of. **4** to go fast. ❑ **tip the gripes in a dangle** *v.* (*also* **...in a tangle**) [SE *gripe*, to grasp] [late 18C] to shake hands. ❑ **tip the lag** *v.* [LAG *n.*[2] (1)] [mid-18C] (*UK Und*) to have someone transported. ❑ **tip the lion** *v.* [the expression this hostile gesture produces is supposedly similar to that of a lion] [late 18C–mid-19C] to squeeze someone's nose flat against their face and either poke their eyes with one's extended fingers or place them in the person's mouth, thus extending it. ❑ **tip the long 'un** *v.* [SE *long one*] [late 19C–1900s] of a man, to have sexual intercourse. ❑ **tip the queer on** *v.* [QUEER *adj.* (1)] [early 19C–1900s] to pass a sentence of imprisonment on. ❑ **tip the quids** *v.* [QUID *n.* (2)] [late 17C–early 19C] **1** (*also* **tip the lowyer**) to spend money. **2** to lend money. ❑ **tip the scroby (for breakfast)** *v.* [? SE *scrub*] [late 18C–mid-19C] to be whipped, as a judicial punishment. ❑ **tip the velvet** *v.* [VELVET *n.* (1)] **1** [late 17C–1900s] to kiss with the tongue [this has subseq. been interpreted as cunnilingus, notably in Sarah Waters' novel, *Tipping the Velvet* (1999), but other than in a single 1684 ref. to 'kissing and tonguing' the vagina, *tonguing* did not mean cunnilingus until c.1890]. **2** [early–mid-19C] to tell off, to scold. **3** [early–mid-19C] to use flowery language in hopes of a seduction. ❑ **tip the whistle** *v.* [SE *whistle*] [late 19C] to warn. ❑ **tip us the monish** [? mockery of the immigrant Jewish pron. of SE *money*] [mid-19C] give us the money.

tip *v.*[4] **1** [mid-18C–mid-19C] to indicate surreptitiously by a wink or similar gesture. **2** [late 19C+] to give information, esp. secret, privileged, 'inside' information; to warn. **3** [1900s] (*US Und.*) to introduce. **4** [1910s] (*Aus.*) to plan. **5** [1910s–40s] (*Aus.*) to guess, to recognize. **6** [1950s+] (*US black*) to gain knowledge of, to understand.

IN PHRASES

❑ **tip in** *v.* [1960s+] to inform against. ❑ **tip into** *v.* [1960s–70s] (*US*) to visit briefly; to arrive at. ❑ **tip the pot** *v.* [1950s] (*US*) to inform. ❑ **tip to** *v.* [1950s] (*US*) to discover, to find out about.

tip *v.*[5] [abbr. TIP OFF *v.*[1]] [19C] to die.

tip *v.*[6] [? SE *tip*, to knock over, to tilt] **1** [1920s+] (*US black*) to cheat on one's lover or mate. **2** [1980s+] to perform an illicit act. **3** [1980s+] to be in a place where one should not be.

IN PHRASES

❑ **tip out** *v.* (*also* **tip over**) [1920s+] (*US black*) to have sex with someone other than one's spouse or regular lover.

SE in slang uses

IN PHRASES

❑ **tip the bucket on** *v. see DROP THE BUCKET ON under* DROP *v.*[1]. ❑ **tip the (little) finger** *v.* [late 19C+] (*Aus.*) to have a drink.

tip *v.*[7] (*also* **tip out**) [SE *tip*, to move lightly or tiptoe] **1** [1930s+] (*US black*) to leave. **2** [1980s+] (*Aus. prison*) to forcibly transfer.

IN PHRASES

❑ **tip grand** *v.* [1930s] (*US Und.*) to leave quickly, to run away.

tip and tap *n. see* TIN AND TAP *n.*

tip-an-pawn *n.* [dial. *tip*, to strike lightly + *pawn*, to grasp, to pick up. The image is of the jerky movement of the legs] [1950s] (*W.I.*) one who limps.

tip-merry *adj.* [TIP *n.*[1] + sfx *-merry*] [17C] tipsy.

tip-off *n.* [TIP OFF *v.*[2]] **1** [20C+] a piece of information, esp. concerning criminal activity. **2** [1940s+] (*also* **tip off man**) an informer, an 'inside man'. **3** [1950s] the trigger for action.

tip off *v.*[1] (*also* **tip off the perch**) [late 17C–early 19C] to die.

tip off *v.*[2] [ext. of TIP *v.*[4] (2)] **1** [late 19C+] to warn. **2** [late 19C+] (*also* **tip**) to provide with information. **3** [1910s–20s] to expose someone.

IN PHRASES

❑ **tip off the blarney** *v. see under* BLARNEY *n.*[1].

tip over *v.*[1] [SE *tip over*] [1910s–30s] (*US*) to drink.

tip over *v.*[2] [? ext. of TIP *v.*[6] (2)] **1** [1920s] (*US Und.*) to raid; also as n., a police raid. **2** [1940s+] (*US*) to rob.

tip-over-charley *phr.* [1910s] (*Aus.*) head-over-heels.

tipped *adj.* [TIP *v.*[2] (1)] [early 17C–early 18C] drunk.

tipped up *adj.* [TIP *n.*[3] (2)] [2000s] (*US prison*) having a membership in a prison gang or clique.

tipper *n.* [proper name of the brewer *Thomas Tipper*. It was brewed from notably brackish water from one specific well.] [mid–late 19C] a beer brewed in Brighton, with a nationwide reputation.

Tipperary *adj.* [one 'tips' over] [late 18C] drunk, tipsy.

Tipperary fortune *n.* ['Two *town lands* (the breasts), *stream's town* (the pudenda) and *ballinocack* (the anus) (Grose 1785)] [late 18C–early 19C] **1** an Irish woman with no fortune other than her body. **2** the breasts, vagina and anus.

Tipperary lawyer *n.* [racial stereotyping] [mid–late 19C] a cudgel.

Tipper Gore *n.* [*Tipper Gore*, wife of politician Al Gore (b.1948), apostrophized by her critics as a byword for narrow-minded stupidity] [1990s+] (*US teen*) one who is narrow-minded, puritanical, repressive.

tippery *n.* [SE *tip*/TIP *v.*[1] (3)] [early 19C–1900s] payment, i.e. the 'world of tips'.

tippet *n.*[1] [pun on TIP *v.*[1]] [16C; 19C] a generous person, someone who treats their companions.

tippet *n.*[2] *see* ST JOHNSTONE'S TIPPET *n.*

tippet-de-witchet *n.* [? SE *tippet*, 'a long narrow slip of cloth or hanging part of dress, formerly worn, either attached to and forming part of the hood, head-dress, or sleeve, or loose, as a scarf or the like' (*OED*)] [early 18C] the vagina.

tippin' *adj.* [TIP-TOP *adj.* (1)] [1970s+] (*US black*) in full control, on top of one's game.

tipple *n.* [SE *tipple*, to drink] **1** [late 16C+] any alcoholic drink. **2** [late 17C+] any drink, esp. that which one prefers, i.e. *one's tipple*. **3** [1920s] in fig. use of sense 2, any form of preference.

IN PHRASES

❑ **on a tipple** [late 18C+] very drunk.

tipple *v.* [i.e. they 'get a tip'] [1990s+] appreciate, understand, work out.

tippling-ken *n.* (*also* **...house, ...office, ...school, ...shop, ... tenement, typling house**) [SE *tipple* + KEN *n.*[1] (1)/OFFICE *n.*] [late 16C–mid-19C] a public house, a tavern.

tipply *adj.* [SE *tipple over*/TIPPLE *n.* (1)] **1** [1900s] unsteady. **2** [1910s–30s] drunk.

tippy *n.* [TIP-TOP *n.* + ? TIP *n.*[2] (1)] [late 18C–mid-19C] **1** as *the tippy*, the height of fashion. **2** thus a dandy or a smart young woman.

IN COMPOUNDS

❑ **tippybob** *n.* **1** [late 18C–19C] a dandy. **2** [late 19C] (*US*) by ext., a derog. name for a member of the social élite.

tippy *adj.* [TIPPY *n.*] [19C] **1** in the height of fashion, smart, fine. **2** clever, ingenious.

tippy toe *n.* [1980s] (*Aus.*) dismissal from a job.

tips *n.* [1950s] filter-*tipped* cigarettes.

tip-slang *adj.* [? *TIP A SLANG under* TIP *v.*[3]] [mid-19C] abusive, foul-mouthed.

tipslinger *n.* [TIP *n.*[5] (1) + SE *slinger*, lit. 'thrower'] [1920s+] (*Aus.*) a racecourse tipster.

tipster *n.* [TIP *n.*[5]] **1** [mid-19C+] one who gives out or sells advice on horseracing, dog-racing [SE from 1900]. **2** [late 19C] one who gives monetary tips to servants, employees etc [SE *tip*]. **3** [20C+] one who gives out any form of 'inside' information; spec. (*US Und.*) a 'civilian' who alerts criminals to potential victims, places to rob, etc.

tip-toe *adj.* [1950s] (*US black*) excellent, first rate.

tip-top *n.* (*also* **tip-topper**) [SE *tip* + *top*, i.e. the top of the top] **1** [18C–19C] the very best, the ultimate, the epitome. **2** [mid-18C–mid-19C] a collective n. for the cream of society; also in pl. as swells.

tip-top *adj.* [TIP-TOP *n.*] **1** [early 18C+] excellent, supreme, ultimate; with the superlative *tip-toppest*, *tippest-toppest*. **2** [late 19C] snobbish.

tip-top *adv.* [TIP-TOP *adj.* (1)] [late 19C–1920s] excellently, superbly.

tip-topmost *adj.* [TIP-TOP *adj.* (1)] [1930s+] very good, excellent, the best.

tip-topper *n.* [TIP-TOP *n.*] **1** [mid-19C–1910s] anything, or anybody, excellent, first-rate. **2** [mid-19C–1940s] a dandy, a fashionable man.

tired *adj.* **1** [mid-19C+] drunk. **2** [late 19C–1940s] extremely lazy. **3** [late 19C+] of people, things or events, tedious, dull, hackneyed; usu. in phr. *to make someone tired*, to bore someone.

IN COMPOUNDS

❑ **tired people** *n.* [1930s+] (*orig. US black*) weak or displeasing people. ❑ **tired woman** *n.* [1970s+] (*US black*) a woman who lacks sophistication.

IN PHRASES

❑ **make one tired** *v.* [late 19C+] (*orig. US*) to irritate someone, to bore. ❑ **that tired feeling** *n.* [1900s] (*Aus.*) a joc. euph. for a state of drunkenness.

SE in slang uses

IN COMPOUNDS

❑ **tired-ass** *adj.* [-ASS *sfx*] [1960s+] (*US*) tedious, clichéd. ❑ **tired blood** *n. see under* BLOOD *n.*[1].

IN PHRASES

❑ **born a bit tired** *adj.* [late 19C–1940s] a sarcastic description of a congenitally lazy person, e.g. *you have to forgive him, he was born tired.* ❑ **tired and emotional** *adj.* (*also* **tired and overwrought**) [coined as 'tired and overwrought' in the magazine *Private Eye* f. the popular euph. to mask the activities of the famous. The orig. citation read: 'Mr George Brown [MP] had been tired and overwrought on many occasions' (*Private Eye*, 29 September 1967)] [1960s+] (*euph.*) extremely drunk. ❑ **too tired to pull a greased stick out of a dog's arse** *adj.* [1980s+] (*Aus.*) exhausted. ❑ **you make me tired** (*also* **you make my butt tired**) [supposedly imported to UK by the contemporary Duchess of Marlborough, a fashion leader] [late 19C+] (*orig. US*) you bore me.

tirliry-pufkin *n.* [nonsense words used to suggest the 'flightiness' of her behaviour] [17C] a promiscuous woman.

tirly-whirly *n.* [coined by Robert Burns (1759–96); SE *tirly-whirly*, a whirligig or, Scot. *tirly-whirly*, winding, intricate] [late 18C–19C] the vagina.

tirret *n.* (*also* **tirrit**) [? SE *tirl*, St Vitus's Dance] [late 16C] a fit of temper.

tish *n.* (*also* **titch**) [var. on TIC *n.*] [1970s+] (*drugs*) phencyclidine.

tish *v.* [abbr. SE *tissue paper*, used as a protective wadding] **1** [1950s] (*US*) to pad or enhance something. **2** *see* TISSUE *v.*

tishy *n. see* TISSUE *n.*

tishy *adj.* ['drunken' mispron. of *tipsy*] [1910s–30s] drunk.

tisket *n.* [song lyric 'A tisket, a tasket, a little yellow basket', thus BASKET *n.*[2]] [1940s] a bastard.

tissfatart around *v. see* TIT ABOUT *under* TIT *n.*[3].

tissick *n.* (*also* **tissic**) [SE *phthisis*] [20C+] (*Irish*) a cough; thus *tizicky*, fastidious about one's food, self-conscious.

tissied up *adj.* [TIZ UP v.] [1960s+] (*Aus.*) dressed up.

tissue *n.* (*also* **tishy**) [1950s+] (*Aus./N.Z.*) a cigarette paper.

tissue *v.* (*also* **tish**) [SE *tissue*/abbr.] [1920s–40s] (*US Und.*) of a con man, to perform a practical joke where he pretends to place a large denomination bill in a woman's stocking, promising her that if she removes it before morning it will turn into tissue paper. Inevitably she cannot wait – and invariably it is indeed tissue paper.

ti-stick *n. see Thai* (*stick*) *under* THAI *adj.*

tit *n.*[1] [despite SE *teat*/TIT *n.*[2] (1), ety. is onomat. term meaning anything small + Scand. dial. terms *titta*, a little girl, *tita*, a small fish etc] **1** with ref. to horses. (**a**) [mid-16C–1910s] a small or half-grown horse [SE until *c.*1800]. (**b**) [19C] a coach horse. **2** [late 16C+] a girl or woman, esp. in derog. or generic use, e.g. *a tasty bit of tit*, but also as a term of affection, often as *little tit*. **3** [18C+] generic for a person of either sex. **4** [early 18C–1900s] the vagina.

IN COMPOUNDS

❑ **tit-bit** *n.* [mid-17C–early 19C] **1** the vagina. **2** the penis. **3** (*also* **tid-bit**) a young woman. **4** (*US*) an ineffectual person.

IN PHRASES

❑ **jackel-tit** *n.* [mid-19C] (*UK Und.*) a stolen horse. ❑ **jolly tit** *n.* [early 18C] a pleasant companion. ❑ **willing tit** *n.* [note B.E.: 'Willing-Tit, a little horse that Travels chearfully'] [18C–early 19C] a complaisant woman.

tit *n.*[2] [SE *tit* is an archaic var. sp. of *teat*] **1** [late 19C+] a breast, usu. a woman's; usu. in pl. **2** [1910s+] (*orig. milit.*) anything considered to resemble a breast or, more often, the nipple, e.g. a button or a small switch etc. **3** [1950s+] (*also* **nipple**) in fig. use, something on which one 'feeds', e.g. a hand-out, a government grant [suggests the simplicity of a child's finding its mother's breast]. **4** [1960s+] something extremely simple and usu. rewarding, esp. a criminal scheme. **5** [1970s+] the nipple. **6** [2000s] (*also* **bluetit**) an English police helmet [resemblance].

DERIVATIVES

❑ **titsy** *adj.* [1970s+] (*US*) featuring bare-breasted women; having attractive breasts.

IN COMPOUNDS

❑ **tit and bum** *adj. see* TITS AND ASS *adj.* ❑ **tit-and-pussy** *n. see* TITS AND ASS *n.* ❑ **tit-bag** *n.* [SE *bag*. Note synon. naut. use *tit-hammock*] **1** [1940s+] a brassiere. **2** [2000s] a term of abuse. ❑ **tit fuck** see separate entries. ❑ **tithead** *n.* [TIT *n.*[2] (1)/TIT *n.*[2] (6)] [1980s+] **1** a general term of abuse. **2** a weakling. **3** an English policeman. ❑ **tit job** *n. see* BOOB JOB *under* BOOB *n.*[3]. ❑ **tit-kisser** *n.* [1970s] (*US*) a womanizer. ❑ **titless wonder** *n.* [1930s+] (*orig. RAF*) a flat-chested woman. ❑ **tit man** *n.* (*also* **tits man**) [1950s+] a man who finds a woman's breasts her most appealing feature; as opposed to an *ASS-MAN under* ASS *n.* ❑ **tit-off** *n.* [1970s] (*Aus.*) the caressing of a woman's breasts. ❑ **tit pants** *n.* [1990s+] a brassiere. ❑ **tit-proud** *adj.* [1950s] (*N.Z.*) of a woman, proud of one's breasts. ❑ **tit-puller** *n.* [2000s] (*N.Z.*) a dairy farmer. ❑ **tits and ass** see separate entries. ❑ **tits deep** *adj.* [var. on *ASS DEEP under* ASS *n.*] [2000s] totally involved with, with an excessive amount of. ❑ **tit show** *n.* [1960s+] a burlesque or striptease show. ❑ **tit spanners** *n.* [the image of a man groping a woman's breasts in an ungainly fashion] [1970s+] (*S.Afr.*) the hands, not necessarily in a sexual context. ❑ **tit-sucker** *n.* [1940s] (*US*) a weak, babyish person. ❑ **tit-wank** *n.* [WANK *n.* (1)] **1** [1990s+] an act of intercourse in which the man rubs his penis between the woman's breasts. **2** [1990s+] a general term of abuse. ❑ **tit-wrench** *n.* [1990s+] an extremely foolish or misguided person, usu. male.

IN PHRASES

❑ **all tits and teeth** *adj.* [1910s+] a woman who capitalizes on her physical charms, esp. her smile and (presumably) large breasts, to make up for the lack of more subtle attractions; sometimes expanded by *...like a third-row chorus-girl*. ❑ **bit of tit** *n.* [SE *bit*] **1** [1920s+] a woman regarded as a sex object. **2** [1980s] sexual intercourse. ❑ **bushel of tits** *n.* [1970s] (*US*) a woman with large breasts. ❑ **full tit** *n.* [i.e. the image of pressing hard on a button or switch] [1950s+] (*N.Z.*) the greatest possible effort. ❑ **get one's tits in a twist** *v.* (*also* **...in a knot, get one's tit in a wringer, put one's tits in a tangle**) [1990s+] (*US*) to be upset, to be in a frightening situation. ❑ **get one's tits out** *v.* [the image of a woman revealing her breasts both as a gesture of her own lack of inhibition and as a display for male delectation, esp. in phr. 'get your tits out for the lads!'] [1990s+] to act in an uninhibited manner; usu. of a woman, but not necessarily so. ❑ **get on someone's tits** *v.* (*also* **...teats, ... tit, ...tit-ends**) [1930s+] **1** to infuriate, to annoy. **2** (*US*) to pursue sexually (used by a woman of a pursuing man). ❑ **have one's tit in a tight crack** *v.* [1920s+] (*Can.*) to find oneself in trouble, in an unpleasant situation. ❑ **have one's tit in a wringer** *v.* (*also* **have one's tit caught in a wringer**) [1960s+] (*US*) to be in difficulties, to be foolish. ❑ **have someone/something by the left tit** *v. see HAVE SOMEONE BY THE BALLS under* BALLS *n.* ❑ **keep one's tits on** *v.* [var. on KEEP ONE'S HAIR ON v.] [1990s+] (*US*) to be patient. ❑ **lick tits** *v.* [1990s+] (*UK black*) to run errands and perform small tasks. ❑ **living off the tit** [1960s+] living in luxury, overly protected. ❑ **not give a fish's tit** *v.* (*also* **not give a rat's tit**) [1940s–50s] not to care in the slightest. ❑ **off (of) one's tits** *adj.* (*also* **out of one's tits**) **1** [1970s+] intoxicated by drugs. **2** [1990s+] very drunk. **3** [1990s+] an intensifier, meaning extremely bored. ❑ **...one's tits off** *adv.* [1990s+] a general intensifer. ❑ **on someone's tit** *adv.* [1980s] (*US campus*) pursuing, lit. or fig, thus being annoying. ❑ **on the hind tit** *adj.* [1940s] feeling angry, aggrieved. ❑ **pull someone's tit** *v.* [1910s+] (*Aus./N.Z.*) to tease. ❑ **put someone's tits in a tangle** *v.* [1930s+] (*Aus.*) to discomfit, to embarrass, to irritate someone. ❑ **set of tits** *n.* [1970s] a sexually attractive woman. ❑ **suck hind tit** *v.* (*also* **suck hind titty**) [1920s+] (*US*) **1** to be inferior, to take a secondary role; thus as n. *hind tit*, bad, unfair treatment. **2** [1960s–80s] to curry favour. ❑ **sugar tit** *n.* [1910s+] (*US*) something comforting, someone desirable. ❑ **sweet tits** *n.* [1990s+] a male-to-female term of affection. ❑ **tit off** *v.* [on the model of JERK OFF v. (1)] [1970s] (*Aus.*) to caress a woman's breasts. ❑ **tits and zits** *adj.* [ZIT *n.*[2] (1)] [1970s+] (*US*) pertaining to teenage love and sex. ❑ **tits on a bull** (*also* **...boar, ...canary**) [1940s+] something utterly useless, usu. in phr. *no more use than tits on a bull* etc. ❑ **tits on toast** *n.* [the belly-pork often has nipples still attached] [1900s–50s] (*N.Z.*) belly-pickled pork on toast. ❑ **tits-up** *adj.* [1970s+] (*orig. Can. prison*) dead, i.e. laid out on one's back; thus in fig. use, ruined, destroyed, esp. in phr. *go/gone tits-up*. ❑ **tit up** *v.* [1960s] to fondle a woman's breasts. ❑ **to the tits** *adv.* [1970s+] completely; esp. in *RIPPED TO THE TITS under* RIPPED *adj.*[1]. ❑ **tough tit(s)** *see TOUGH TITTY under* TITTY *n.* ❑ **up to one's tits** *see UP TO ONE'S ARMPITS under* ARMPIT *n.* ❑ **useless as tits on a nun** *adj.* (*also* **...a tit on a hand, ...tits on a boar (hog), ...on a bull, ...on a gumdigger's dog**) [1930s+] (*US/Aus.*) utterly useless. ❑ **with tits on** *adj. see WITH BELLS ON under* BELL *n.*[1].

IN EXCLAMATIONS

❑ **my tit!** [1950s] a semi-euph. var. on *MY ARSE! under* ARSE *n.*

tit *n.*[3] (*also* **tit-end**) [? TIT *n.*[1] (2) or TIT *n.*[2] (1)] [1940s+] a fool; thus *look an absolute tit*, *look a right tit*, to appear a total fool, thus the school 'witticism', *I feel a right tit*.

IN PHRASES

❑ **big tit** *n.* [1960s–70s] (*US*) an important person; or one who thinks they are. ❑ **make a tit of oneself** *v.* [2000s] to make a fool of oneself. ❑ **stand there like a tit in a trance** [20C+] said of one who is lost in thought, abstracted. ❑ **tit about** *v.* (*also* **tissfatart about, tit around**) [1940s+] to play around, to waste time, to act in a trivial, pointless manner.

tit *n.*[4] [2000s] (*US prison*) heroin.

tit *adj.*[1] [TIT *n.*[2] (1)] [1950s+] pertaining to the female breast, usu. in context of pornography, e.g. in phrs. below.

IN COMPOUNDS

❑ **tit art** *n.* [1950s+] (*US*) pictures of attractive young women. ❑ **tit book** *n.* [1970s] a softcore pornographic magazine. ❑ **tit**

mag *n.* (*also* **tit magazine**) [MAG *n.*[4] (1)] [1960s+] a magazine which features scantily clad women. The pictures are interspersed with varying amounts of prose, reviews etc but despite all other pretensions, they are in the end an aid to masturbation.

tit *adj.*[2] [ext. of TIT *n.*[2] (4)] **1** [1960s+] (*S.Afr.*) a general term of approval meaning excellent, wonderful, good-looking. **2** [1990s+] (*US campus*) easy.

titch *n. see* TISH *n.*

titchy *adj.* [according to *OED* the nickname preceded the wider use: 'The stage name Little Tich of the dwarfish music-hall comedian Harry Relph (1868–1928), who was given the nickname as a child because of a resemblance to the Tichborne claimant.' The claimant was Arthur Orton (1834–98), who claimed in 1866 to be Roger Charles Tichborne (1829–54), the heir to an English baronetcy, who was lost at sea. Orton was finally discredited and imprisoned in 1874] [1950s+] (*mainly juv.*) small, tiny, undersized; thus *Tich* or *Titch*, popular nickname for a short person (and, with heavy humour, for an exceptionally tall one).

tit-end *n. see* TIT *n.*[3].

IN PHRASES

❑ **get on someone's tit-ends** *v. see* GET ON SOMEONE'S TITS *under* TIT *n.*[2].

titfer *n.* (*also* **titfa, tit-for**) [abbr. TIT FOR TAT *n.* (1)] **1** [1910s+] a hat. **2** [1960s] as excl. of surprise or pleasure.

tit for tat *n.* [rhy. sl.] **1** [1910s+] a hat. **2** [2000s] (*Aus.*) a rat, i.e. a non-trade unionist.

tit for tats *n.* [1940s+] (*Aus.*) the female breasts.

tit fuck *n.* (*also* **titty fuck**) [TIT *n.*[2] (1)/TITTY *n.* (1) + FUCK *n.* (1)] [1970s+] (*orig. US*) intercourse in which the man rubs his penis between the woman's breasts.

tit-fuck *v.* (*also* **titty-fuck**) [TIT FUCK *n.*] [1990s+] to have intercourse or masturbate between the breasts.

ti-ti *adj.* (*also* **tee-tee**) [2000s] (*US black*) small, little.

titire-tu *n. see* TITTERY-TU *n.*

titivate *v.* (*also* **tiddivate, tiddyvate, tittivate**) [? SE *tidy*] **1** [19C–1910s] to smarten oneself up, to put the finishing touches to. **2** [1920s] to treat kindly or gently.

title page *n.* [mid-19C] the face.

titley *n.* [? dial. *titley* tickle; i.e. one's palate or SE *tiddly*, small, i.e. a small portion; var. on TIDDLY *n.*] [mid-19C–1930s] a drink.

IN PHRASES

❑ **titley and binder** *n.* [mid-19C–1930s] a glass of beer and a piece of bread and cheese.

titley *adj.* [TITLEY *n.*] [mid-19C+] slightly drunk, tipsy.

titmouse *n.* [joc. use of SE] [mid-17C–19C] the vagina.

tits *n.*[1] [abbr.] [1980s] (*US campus*) two *i*ncomes, *t*wo *s*tinkers: a working couple with two children.

tits *n.*[2] *see* TIT *n.*[2] (1).

tits, the *n.* [fig. use of TIT *n.*[2] (1)] [1950s+] perfection, excellence, an ideal situation.

tits *adj.* [TIT *n.*[2] (4)] **1** [1960s+] (*US*) wonderful, excellent. **2** [1990s+] (*US campus*) easy, simple.

tits! *excl.* [TIT *n.*[2] (1); on model of BALLS! *excl.*] [mid-19C+] nonsense! rubbish!

tits and ass *n.* (*also* **t.a., T & A, tit-and-pussy, tits and arse, tits and bums, T 'n' A**) [TIT *n.*[2] (1) + ASS *n.* (2)/ARSE *n.* (1)] [1950s+] (*orig. US*) **1** a burlesque show, cheap sex-orientated entertainment which features strippers etc. **2** any softcore pornography. **3** sex appeal; women viewed as nothing more than sex objects.

tits and ass *adj.* (*also* **t.a., T & A, tits and arse, tit and bum, titties and cans**) [TITS AND ASS *n.*] [1950s+] (*orig. US*) relating to sex-orientated entertainment or softcore pornography.

titsun *n.* see DITSOON *n.*

titted *adj.* [var. on CUNTED *adj.*[2] + fig. use of TIT *n.*[3]] [1990s+] drunk.

titter *n.*[1] [SE *titter*, to giggle, or TITTY *n.* (1)] [19C] a young woman.

titter *n.*[2] [TIT *n.*[2] (1)] [1940s] (*US*) a close fitting woman's sweater.

tittery *n.* [dial. *tittery*, unstable, on the verge of falling, i.e. its effects] [early–mid-18C] gin.

tittery-tu *n.* (*also* **titire-tu, tityre-tu, tytere-tu**) [the first words of Virgil's first eclogue, '*Tityre, tu patulae recubans sub tegmine fagi*'. The Lat. tag implied that these privileged rogues were men of leisure and fortune, who 'lay at ease under their patrimonial beech trees'] [early 17C–19C] a street gang, esp. of well-to-do roughs who infested the London streets, committing their crimes for amusement rather than gain.

titties and cans *adj. see* TITS AND ASS *adj.*

tittivate *v. see* TITIVATE *v.*

tittle *v.* [? SE *teeter* or dial. *tittle*, very lightly] [20C+] (*Ulster*) to walk in a mincing manner.

tittle-tat *n.* [abbr. SE *tittle-tattle*] [1950s+] **1** (*Aus.*) a gossip. **2** (*juv.*) a piece of gossip.

tittup *n. see* TITUP *n.*

titty *n.* (*also* **tee-tee, tiddy**) [dimin. of TIT *n.*[2] (1); note earlier use as dimin. of SE *tit*, var. sp. of SE *teat*, meaning the nipple only] **1** [late 19C+] a woman's breast; usu. in pl. **2** [20C+] milk. **3** [1920s] (*W.I.*) a woman, as term of address, lit. 'sister'. **4** [1930s+] in fig. use, a source of nourishment. **5** [1940s] (*US*) a woman.

IN COMPOUNDS

❑ **titty bar** *n.* (*also* **tittie bar**) [1980s+] (*US*) a striptease or lap-dancing bar. ❑ **titty fuck** *n. see* TIT FUCK *n.* ❑ **titty girl** *n.* (*also* **titty**) [2000s] (*UK black*) a consciously sexy young woman. ❑ **titty magazine** *n.* [1990s+] (*US*) a (softcore) pornographic magazine. ❑ **titty oggy** *n.* [1960s] (*US*) intercourse in which the man rubs his penis between the woman's breasts.

IN PHRASES

❑ **bump titties** *v.* [1990s+] (*US black*) to fight. ❑ **on someone's titty** (*also* **at...**) [1970s+] (*US*) dependent on someone (for money, work, protection, etc); thus *off someone's titty*. ❑ **suck someone's titty** *v.* [SE *suck*; the image of dependency implicit in breastfeeding] [1970s] (*US*) to depend on, to act as a parasite towards. ❑ **tough titty** (*also* **hard titty, tough tiddy, tough tit, tough titties, tough tits,**) [var. on *TOUGH LUCK under* TOUGH *adj.*] [1920s+] bad luck; thus *tough tits, toots*, a phr. of dismissal.

titup *n.* (*also* **tittup**) [SE *tittup*, a horse's canter] [late 19C–1930s] the correct or fashionable thing.

tit willow *n.* [rhy. sl.; ult. f. *The Mikado* (1885) opera] [1930s+] a pillow.

tityre-tu *n. see* TITTERY-TU *n.*

tius *n.* [backsl.] [late 19C–1900s] a suit of clothes.

Tiv, the *n.* [abbr.] **1** [late 19C–1910s] the *Tiv*oli Music Hall, London. **2** [1910s–50s] the *Tiv*oli Music Hall, Sydney.

tives *n.* [abbr.] [1970s+] (*US campus*) one's rela*tives*.

tivvy *n.* [SE *activity*] [19C] the vagina.

'Tizer, the *n.* [abbr.] [mid-19C] the *Morning Advertiser* newspaper.

tiz up *v.* [? TITIVATE *v.*] [1930s+] (*Aus.*) to dress up.

tizzy *n.*[1] (*also* **tizzie**) [? TILBURY *n.* or TESTER *n.*[1] (1); note WW1 RN *tizzy snatcher*, an Assistant Paymaster] [late 18C–1910s] a sixpence.

tizzy *n.*[2] (*also* **tiz-wizz, tizz**) [ety. unknown; ? echoic of one's rushing around, whether lit. or fig.] **1** [1930s+] (*orig. US*) a panic, a 'state', a flap. **2** [1960s] (*US*) a party, a get-together.

tizzy *adj.*[1] [TIZ UP *v.*] [1930s+] (*Aus.*) **1** showily or flashily overdressed. **2** of a person, ostentatious, showy, vulgar. **3** of an object, flashy but cheaply manufactured.

tizzy *adj.*[2] [? ext. of TIGHT *adj.* (4)] [2000s] (*US black*) a general term of approval.

tizzy *v.* (*also* **tizzy up**) [TIZ UP *v.*] [1960s+] (*Aus.*) to titivate, to dress up in one's finery.

T.J. *n.* [abbr.] [1960s+] (*US*) *T*ijuana, Mexico.

tjeers *phr.* [1950s+] (*S.Afr.*) goodbye.

tjommie *n. see* CHOMMIE *n.*

T-Jones *n.* [ety. unknown] [1970s+] (*US prison*) the mother of a prisoner.

tjorie/tjorrie *n. see* CHORRIE *n.*

t.k.o. *v.* [boxing jargon *t.k.o.*, a technical knock-out] [1950s+] (*orig. US*) to defeat in theory, if not in practice.

T.L. *n.* [SAmE *trade last*, 'a compliment offered in exchange for one that is directed towards the speaker; also, in weakened sense, a compliment, whether reciprocal or not' (*OED*)] [1920s+] (*US*) a compliment, esp. one given in return for a previous compliment paid to onseself; also a compliment passed onto its subject by an intermediary, when the original speaker is too shy to speak themselves.

TL *n.* [abbr. TENDERLOIN *n.* (1)] [1990s+] (*US*) the Tenderloin district of San Francisco.

t.l. *n.* [abbr. Yid. *toches lecher*, arse-licker] [1950s+] (*US*) a toady, a sycophant.

t.l.c. *n.* [abbr. *tender loving care*] [1960s+] (*orig. US*) kindness, consideration etc.

t.m. *n.* [abbr. TAILOR-MADE *n.* (2)] [1930s+] (*Aus./Can.*) a factory-made cigarette.

T-man *n.*[1] [lit. *Treasury-man*] [1920s+] (*US*) a law enforcement officer of the US Treasury Department.

T-man *n.*[2] [TIT *n.*[2] (1) + SE *man*] [1960s] (*US*) a man who likes (large) breasts.

T-man *n.*[3] *see* TEA MAN *under* TEA *n.*

T'n'A *n. see* TITS AND ASS *n.*

t.n.t. *n.*[1] [abbr. *two nifty tits*; TIT *n.*[2] (1)] [1950s+] the female breasts.

t.n.t. *n.*[2] [SE *TNT*, trinitrotoluene] **1** [1960s+] (*US black*) anyone or anything that is metaphorically 'dynamite', wonderful, exceptional etc. **2** [1980s+] in drug uses. (**a**) heroin. (**b**) fentanyl.

T.O. *n.* [abbr.] [1950s+] (*US*) *Toronto, Ontario.*

toac *n.* [backsl.] [mid-19C] a coat.

toac-tisaw *n.* [backsl.] [mid-19C] a waistcoat.

toad *n.* **1** [early 17C+] an unpleasant or unattractive person. **2** [mid-19C] the penis [pun on SE *toad in the hole*/HOLE *n.*[1] (1b)]. **3** [1970s+] (*US*) a black person. **4** [1980s] (*US gay*) an unattractive middle-aged gay man.

SE in slang uses

IN COMPOUNDS

❑ **toadmuffin** *n.* [1990s+] (*US campus*) a man who treats women badly. ❑ **toadskin** *n.* [play on FROG *n.*[3] (1)] **1** [mid-19C] (*US*) a five-cent stamp; thus *his purse is made of toadskin*, he is a mean, grasping person. **2** [1900s–40s] (*also* **toad**) (*US/Aus.*) a banknote. ❑ **toad-stabber** *n.* [note synon. army jargon *cat-stabber*] [late 19C–1960s] (*US*) a large pocketknife or jackknife. ❑ **toad-sticker** *n.* (*US*) **1** [mid–late 19C] a sword. **2** [20C+] a large knife; a bayonet.

IN PHRASES

❑ **biggest toad in the puddle** *n.* [mid-19C–1910s] (*US*) a leader, a chief, the most important person in a situation. ❑ **swallow one's toad** *v. see* SWALLOW ONE'S SPIT *under* SWALLOW *v.* ❑ **toad in the hole** *n.* [SE *toad-in-the-hole*, meat surrounded with batter and baked] **1** [mid–late 19C] a 'sandwich man' who carries four, rather than the usual two boards. He is thus completely surrounded by advertising displays. **2** [1930s–40s] a bankroll [rhy. sl.].

to a fare-thee-well *phr.* (*also* **to a fare-ye-well, to a fare-you-well**) [20C+] (*US*) thoroughly, completely.

toak *n. see* TOKE *n.*[2].

to and fro *n.* [rhy. sl.] **1** [20C+] snow. **2** [1960s–80s] (*Aus.*) a moustache [= MO *n.*[1] (1)].

to and fro *v.* [rhy. sl.] [1960s–80s] (*Aus.*) to leave, to go.

to-and-from *n.*[1] [the movements of the player's arms] [1910s+] a concertina.

to-and-from *n.*[2] [rhy. sl. = *pom* (see POMMIE *n.*)] [1940s+] (*Aus.*) a British immigrant to Australia.

toast *n.*[1] [abbr. OLD TOAST *n.*] [late 17C–19C] **1** the Devil. **2** a lively old man. **3** a drunkard.

toast *n.*[2] [SE *toast*, a dedicatory remark prefacing the taking of a drink] **1** [1950s+] (*US Und.*) a long and epic poem, often trad. in prisons. **2** [1950s+] (*US*) the best, the finest, anything outstanding [i.e. that which deserves a SE *toast*].

toast *n.*[3] (*also* **toaster**) [it turns people into SE *toast*] [2000s] (*US black*) a gun.

toast *adj.*[1] [TOAST *n.*[2] (2)] **1** [1950s+] (*US black/teen*) excellent, wonderful. **2** [1970s] in phr. *on toast*, an intensifier.

toast *adj.*[2] [SE *toast*] [1980s+] **1** useless, finished. **2** (*US campus*) (*also* **french toast, toasty**) tipsy or hungover. **3** dead.

toast *v.* [SE *toast*, to make a speech when drinking someone's health] **1** [1950s+] (*US black*) to recount a lengthy epic poem, usu. based in the pimping or underworld experience. **2** [1960s+] (*W.I.*) of a disc jockey, to perform one's own lyrics to the background of a reggae song, usu. in a dub (no lyrics, only bass and rhythm lines) version.

toast *adv.* [SE *toast*] [1980s+] (*US campus*) in big trouble, the victim of misfortune, esp. in phr. *you're toast*.

toasted *adj.* [SE *toast*] **1** [1940s] (*US Und.*) executed in the electric chair. **2** [1980s+] (*US*) physically or mentally exhausted. **3** [1980s+] tipsy, either slightly or extremely drunk. **4** [1980s+] (*drugs*) intensely intoxicated by a drug.

toasted bread *adj.* [rhy. sl.] [1990s+] dead.

toaster *n.*[1] [it turns things into SE *toast*] **1** [1960s] (*US*) a flamethrower. **2** *see* TOAST *n.*[3].

toaster *n.*[2] [TOAST *v.* (2)] [1960s+] (*US black*) a singer of reggae rap music.

toasting fork *n.* (*also* **toaster, toasting iron**) [note WW1 milit. *toasting fork*, a bayonet] [late 16C–1900s] a sword.

toast rack *n.* [supposed resemblance] **1** [20C+] a horse-drawn tram as found at Douglas, Isle of Man. **2** [1920s–50s] (*Aus.*) a footboard tram in Sydney.

toasty *adj. see* TOAST *adj.*[2] (2).

toat *v. see* TOTE *v.*[1].

tobacco baron *n. see* BARON *n.* (3).

Tobacco Road *n.* [Erskine Caldwell's novel *Tobacco Road* (1932)] [1930s+] (*US*) any primitive rural area; thus used pej. of those who live there.

tobacco worm *n.* [state known for its tobacco crops] [mid-19C] (*US*) a person from Virginia.

tobe *v.* [? SE *top* (of the head)] [mid-19C] (*UK Und.*) to rob with violence.

tober gloak *n.* [late 18C–early 19C] a highwayman.

tober omee *n.* [Rom. *tober*, road + OMEE *n.*] [late 19C+] (*Ling. Fr./Polari*) a toll collector, e.g. a fairground or market stall superintendant.

toboggan *n.* [play on ON THE SKIDS *under* SKIDS *n.*] [late 19C+] (*US*) a rapid decline, usu. towards ultimate disaster, esp. in phr. *on the toboggan*.

toby *n.*[1] [*Toby*, dimin. of proper name Tobias; thus euph.] **1** [late 17C–mid-19C] the posterior, the buttocks. **2** [late 17C–1920s] a woman's genitals.

toby *n.*[2] [Shelta *tobar* or Rom. *tober*, the road, ? ult. Irish *bothar*, road. Note police jargon *toby*, an area, a police division] **1** [19C–1940s] (*US Und.*) highway robbery; as *low toby*, on foot, and *high toby*, mounted robbery. **2** [19C–1950s] the road, the highway, esp. as a place where robbers and highwaymen can find their victims. **3** [1930s] (*also* **tobyman**) a tramp; the life of tramping.

IN COMPOUNDS

❑ **toby-cove** *n.* [mid-19C] (*US Und.*) a street robber. ❑ **toby-gill** *n.* [GILL *n.*[1] (2)] [early–mid-19C] a highwayman. ❑ **toby-gloak** *n.* (*also* **tobyman**) [GLOAK *n.*/SE *man*] [19C–1900s] a highwayman. ❑ **toby lay** *n.* (*also* **toby concern**) [LAY *n.*[3] (1)/SE *concern*] [19C] highway robbery. ❑ **tobyman** [mid-19C] a street or house robber.

toby *n.*[3] [the style of collar trad. worn in Punch and Judy shows by the dog *Toby*] [late 19C] (*UK society*) a frilled collar worn by women.

toby *n.*[4] [abbr. brandname *Conestoga*; STOGIE *n.* (1)] [late 19C–1940s] (*US*) a second-rate brand of cigar.

toby *n.*[5] [proper name *Tobias*, + ref. to *Toby*, Mr Punch's dog] [1920s+] (*Aus.*) **1** a simple, foolish man, but one who is kind and amenable and thus popular. **2** an expert.

IN PHRASES

❑ **have a toby on** *v.* [1920s+] to feel kindly or friendly towards.

toby *n.*[6] [the presumed 'poshness' and thus effeminacy of the name] [1990s+] (*UK juv.*) a male homosexual.

toby *v.* [TOBY *n.*[2]] **1** [19C] (*also* **ply the toby**) to rob someone on the highway. **2** [1930s–50s] (*UK tramp*) to walk the roads as a tramp; thus *on the toby*, tramping.

toby jug *n.* [rhy. sl.] [20C+] **1** a fool [= MUG *n.*[1] (2a)]. **2** an ear [= LUG *n.*[1]].

toby-lifting *n.* [? ext. use of TOBY *n.*[1] (1) on model of KEISTER *n.*] [1900s–30s] (*UK Und.*) luggage stealing at railway stations.

toch eno! *excl.* [backsl. *hot one!*] [mid-19C+] look out! take care! etc.

toches *n.* (*also* **dokus, tochus, tocus, tokis, tokus, tookus, tooky, tuchas, tuches, tuchis, tuckus, tukkis**) [synon. Yid. *toches*] **1** [late 19C+] posterior, buttocks. **2** [1900s] the vagina.

IN COMPOUNDS

❑ **toches-licker** *n.* (*also* **tokus-licker**) [i.e. *ARSE-LICKER under* ARSE-LICK *v.*] [1950s+] (*orig. US*) a toady, a sycophant.

tockley *n.* [ety. unknown; ? link to SE *tag*] [1990s+] (*Aus.*) the penis.

toco *n.* (*also* **toko**) [? Gk *tokoz*, interest (*OED*), Hind. *tokna*, to censure (Y&B), Maori *toko*, a rod (Partridge)] [early 19C–1940s] punishment.

IN PHRASES

❑ **get toco for yam** *v.* (*also* **nap...**) [*for* in this context equals 'instead of'] [19C] to be punished; opposite of *GIVE COCO FOR YAM under* COCO *n.*[1]. ❑ **give someone toco** *v.* [early 19C–1940s] to beat someone, to thrash someone.

tocus *n. see* TOCHES *n.*

tod *n.* [abbr. SE *toddy*] [late 18C–1910s] (*US*) a drink; a heavy drinker.

IN PHRASES

❑ **will you tod?** [mid-19C] an invitation to drink.

today *adj.* [1960s+] (*orig. US*) fashionable, up-to-the-minute.

toddle *v.* (*also* **toddle along, toddle off**) [Vaux cites *toddle* as 'Und.' in 1812, but *OED* says SE. Partridge suggests that only upper-class 20C+ use is colloq.] [early 18C+] to move, to walk, to go or leave.

IN PHRASES

❑ **on the toddle** [early 19C] on the move; walking along.

toddler *n.* [TODDLE *v.*; note *toddler*, 'one who toddles', e.g. a child or an infirm old person, is UK Und. in Vaux but is SE in the *OED*] **1** [late 18C–1920s] a walker. **2** [early 19C] a foot.

toddlers *n.* (*also* **toddles**) [TODDLE *v.*] [mid-19C] the legs.

toddles *n.* [SE *toddles*, an infant] [mid-19C] a pretty young woman.

toddy blossom *n. see under* BLOSSOM *n.*[2].

toddy-stick *n.* [SE *toddy-stick*, a spatula, usu. of glass or metal, for stirring toddy] [mid–late 19C] a muddler, one who 'messes (things) around'.

todge *v.* [dial. *todge*, a very thick soup, spoon-meat, i.e. meat boiled almost to paste] [late 18C–early 19C] to beat, to thrash.

todger *n. see* TADGER *n.*

to die (for) *phr.* (*also* **t.d.f.**) [note *OED* cites a single late 19C use, but then nothing until 1980s] [late 19C; 1950s+] (*US*) excellent, wonderful, perfect, e.g. *that boy is to die pretty*.

to-do *n.* [one who makes a SE *to-do*] [1990s+] (*US*) an important person.

todoment *n.* [SE *to-do* + sfx *-ment*] [20C+] (*W.I., Bdos*) **1** noise, confusion. **2** open-air fun and excitement.

tod (sloan) *adj.*

IN PHRASES

❑ **on one's tod (sloan)** *adj.* [rhy. sl.; ult. the US jockey James Forman *'Tod' Sloan* (1874–1933)] [1930s+] alone.

toe *n.* [the use of the *toe*, i.e. the foot, in running] [late 19C+] (*Aus./N.Z.*) strength, speed.

SE in slang uses

DERIVATIVES

❑ **toeology** *n.* [1950s] (*US black*) dancing, esp. of a high standard.

IN COMPOUNDS

❑ **toecutter** *n.* [1980s+] **1** (*Aus Und.*) a criminal who specializes in preying on other successful, and thus wealthy, criminals. **2** (*US*) an aggressively selfish and single-minded individual. ❑ **toeface** *n.* [1910s–20s] an unpleasant or dirty person. ❑ **toe-jam (queen)** *n. see* separate entries. ❑ **toe party** *n.* [1920s–30s] (*US black*) a party game whereby all the women present line up behind a sheet with nothing visible but their toes. The men then take turns to choose their preferred toes and pair off accordingly. ❑ **toe queen** *n.* [-QUEEN *sfx* (3)] [1950s+] (*gay*) a foot fetishist. ❑ **toerag/-ragger** *n. see* separate entries. ❑ **toe soldier** *n.* [play on SE *foot soldier*] [1900s] (*Aus.*) an infantryman.

IN PHRASES

❑ **cock up one's toes** *v.* [mid-19C+] to die. ❑ **give it toes** *v.* [1990s+] to run away, to escape. ❑ **have it on one's toes** *v.* [1950s+] (*UK Und.*) to run away, to escape. ❑ **on one's toes** **1** [20C+] ready and alert. **2** [1910s] quickly. **3** [1950s+] on the run, fleeing justice. **4** [1970s] in the process of leaving. ❑ **on the toe** [1900s] (*tramp*) travelling as a beggar. ❑ **raddle someone's toe** *v.* [shearing jargon *raddle*, to mark a sheep as imperfectly shorn] [late 19C] (*Aus.*) to request someone to buy a round of drinks. ❑ **take one's toe** *v.* [20C+] (*Ulster*) to affect, to 'get into'. ❑ **take to the toe** *v.* (*also* **get on the toe, hit the toe**) [1950s+] (*Aus./N.Z.*) to leave quickly, to run off. ❑ **throw in one's toe** *v.* [1900s] (*Aus.*) to die. ❑ **toe it away** *v.* [1970s+] (*UK Und.*) to escape. ❑ **toe to toe** *see* separate entries. ❑ **toes lively** *adv.* [1970s+] very fast. ❑ **toes up** *adj.* [abbr. SE *turn one's toes up*] **1** [mid-19C–1950s] lying dead. **2** [late 19C] ill, indisposed.

toe *adj.*[1] [Afk. *toe*, closed] [1970s+] (*S.Afr.*) very stupid.

toe *adj.*[2] (*also* **toe up**) [US black pron. of TORE UP *adj.*] [1970s+] (*US black/campus*) **1** drunk; hungover. **2** emotionally shattered. **3** (*US campus/teen*) unfashionable, badly dressed.

toe *v.* **1** [mid–late 19C] to dance. **2** [1950s] (*US*) to kick.

IN PHRASES

❑ **toe the chalk/crack/mark** *v. see* WALK THE CHALK *v.* (2).

t-oed *adj. see* TEED UP *adj.*

toe-jam *n.* (*also* **toe-cheese**) [1930s+] (*US*) dead skin and dirt found between unwashed toes; thus also a term of abuse.

toe-jam queen *n.* [TOE-JAM *n.* + -QUEEN *sfx* (3)] [1960s–70s] (*US gay*) a male homosexual foot-fetishist.

toerag *n.*[1] (*also* **towrag**) [SE *toerag*, the foot-bindings used by tramps.] **1** [late 19C] a second-rate, inferior newspaper [RAG *n.*[1] (4)]. **2** [late 19C] (*Aus.*) a £1 note. **3** [late 19C] (*N.Z.*) a handkerchief. **4** [late 19C+] a general term of abuse [Puxley, *Cockney Rabbit: A Dick' n' Arry of Rhyming Slang* (1992), suggests rhy. sl. = SLAG *n.*[1] (1)]. **5** [20C+] a tramp.

IN COMPOUNDS

❑ **toerag tommy** *n.* [late 19C] (*Aus.*) a small bookmaker.

toerag *n.*[2] [rhy. sl. = FAG *n.*[4] (2)] [1930s–70s] a cigarette.

toe-ragger *n.* (*also* **toe-rigger**) [TOERAG *n.*[1]] (*Aus./N.Z.*) **1** [late 19C+] a down-and-out vagrant. **2** [late 19C+] a general term of contemptuous abuse. **3** [1910s+] one who is given a short prison sentence.

toet *n.* [TWAT *n.* (1)] [1950s+] (*S.Afr.*) the vagina.

toe-tee *n.* [ety. unknown] [2000s] (*W.I.*) the penis.

toe to toe *n.* [SE *toe to toe*, in close combat] [1980s+] a fight, a brawl.

toe-to-toe *v.* [TOE TO TOE *n.*] [1990s+] (*US*) to fight.

toe up *adj. see* TOE *adj.*[2].

toey *n.*[1] [? fig. use of TOE *n.*] (*Aus./N.Z.*) **1** [late 19C–1900s] a fashionable, smart person, a sophisticate. **2** [1900s] (*Aus.*) an infantryman. **3** [1970s+] an alert person; one who is watchful and prepared.

toey *n.*[2] *see* TOY *n.*[2] (1).

toey *adj.* [SE *toe* n.] [1930s+] **1** (*Aus./N.Z.*) nervous, touchy. **2** (*Aus. prison*) liable to attempt an escape. **3** (*Aus./N.Z.*) of a horse or person, fast.

toff *n.* [? SE *tuft* as in TUFT-HUNTER *n.* (any link to *TOFFEE-NOSED under* TOFFEE *n.* is invalidated by chronology)] **1** [mid-19C] a male house-owner. **2** [mid-19C+] (*also* **toft**) an aristocrat, an upper-class person in general. **3** [late 19C+] anyone considered either to be or to be posing as a superior person. **4** [late 19C+] one who acts bravely or 'nobly'. **5** [late 19C+] one who behaves kindly, generously; thus in phr. *you're a toff*, you're very kind, thank you very much. **6** [2000s] (*Aus.*) an expert.

DERIVATIVES

❑ **toffish** *adj.* (*also* **toffy**) [mid-19C+] aristocratic, stylish, sophisticated.

IN COMPOUNDS

❑ **toff-ken** *n.* (*also* **tuff ken**) [KEN *n.*[1] (1)] [mid–late 19C] the house of prosperous owners. ❑ **toff-omee** *n.* [OMEE *n.* (3)] [late 19C–1900s] a very fine gentleman. ❑ **toff-shoving** *n.* [late 19C] (*UK Und.*) pushing about well-dressed gentlemen in a crowd, presumably to facilitate picking their pockets.

IN PHRASES

❑ **penny toff** *n.* [late 19C] a lower-class dandy who can only imitate the richer, genuine article.

toffed-up *adj.* [TOFF *n.* (2)] [late 19C+] dressed up, esp. showily; as v. to *toff-up*.

toffee *n.* **1** [20C+] nonsense, flattery [? its 'sweetness]. **2** [1930s] tobacco [the colour]. **3** [1940s+] gelignite [the colour].

SE in slang uses

IN COMPOUNDS

❑ **toffee-nose** *n.* [1940s+] (*orig. milit.*) a snobbish or supercilious person. ❑ **toffee-nosed** *adj.* (*also* **toffee, toffy-nosed**) [TOFF *n.* (2) + a nose fig. stuck in the air to avoid the noxious smells of everyday life] [1910s+] snobbish, arrogant.

IN PHRASES

❑ **for toffee** *adv.* [late 19C+] at all, in the slightest; usu. in negative phrs., often as *can't — for toffee*, a phr. said of a particularly incompetent person where 'it' varies as to context.

toffee wrapper *n.* [rhy. sl. = NAPPER *n.*[2] (2)] [1990s+] the head.

toffer *n.* [TOFF *n.* (2)] [mid–late 19C] a well-dressed prostitute, catering for rich clients.

tofficky *adj.* [TOFF *n.* (2)] [mid–late 19C] showily or ostentatiously dressed.

toffish *adj. see under* TOFF *n.*

toffishness *n.* [TOFFISH *adj.*] [mid–late 19C] affectation, 'putting on airs'.

toffy *adj.*

IN PHRASES

❑ **toffy-nosed** *adj. see TOFFEE-NOSED under* TOFFEE *n.*

toft *n. see* TOFF *n.* (2).

tog *n.* (*also* **toge, togee, togg, togge, togger, toggy, tugg**) [OE *toge*, a toga; ult. Lat. *toga*, a toga or cloak. As toga, it dates back to c.1400, as found in the line 'Alle with taghte mene and towne in togers fulle ryche' (Sir Thomas Malory, *Morte d'Arthur*] **1** [18C–1960s] an outer garment, a coat; thus, *upper tog*. **2** [1910s] (*US Und.*) among pickpockets, an overcoat used as a shield.

DERIVATIVES

❑ **toggish** *adj.* [mid-19C] fashionable, smart in appearance.

IN COMPOUNDS

❑ **tog and kicks** *n.* [18C–1960s] coat and trousers. ❑ **tog-bound** *adj.* [late 19C–1900s] lacking decent or fashionable clothes. ❑ **tog-fencer** *n.* [-FENCER *sfx*] **1** [late 19C–1910s] a tailor. **2** [1930s] (*UK tramp*) a market seller of secondhand clothes.

IN PHRASES

❑ **long tog** *n.* (*also* **long togs**) [early 19C] (*US Und.*) an overcoat; a suit? ❑ **outside tog(e)** *n.* [18C–1960s] a cloak. ❑ **simp togs** *n.* [1960s] best clothes, smart clothes. ❑ **top tog** *n.* [mid-19C] (*UK Und.*) an overcoat. ❑ **under tog** *n.* [18C–1960s] an under petticoat. ❑ **waist tog** *n.* [mid-19C–1900s] a waistcoat.

tog *v.* [TOG *n.* (1)] **1** [19C] to supply someone with clothing. **2** [early 19C–1960s] to dress up, to get dressed.

IN PHRASES

❑ **togged to the bricks** *adj.* [1930s–60s] (*US black*) dressed in style.

togemans *n.* (*also* **togamans, togeman, togman**) [Fr. *toge* or Lat. *toga*, toga + -MANS *sfx*] [mid-16C–mid-19C] a coat or cloak.

together *adj.* [1960s+] **1** aware, in control, self-assured, au fait, sophisticated. **2** of a place or situation, excellent, first-rate. **3** united. **4** happy. **5** prepared, organized.

IN PHRASES

❑ **get it together** *v.* [1960s+] (*orig. US black*) **1** to start a sexual relationship. **2** to make a decision, to take action. **3** to pull oneself together, to stop vacillating etc. ❑ **get one's act together** *v. see under* ACT *n.* ❑ **get oneself together** *v.* [1960s+] (*orig. US*) **1** to dress oneself well. **2** to mend one's ways; to pull oneself together. **3** to amass a sum of money. **4** to sort out one's emotions. ❑ **get one's eyes together** *v. see under* EYES *n.*[1]. ❑ **get one's game together** *v. see under* GAME *n.* ❑ **get one's head together** *v. see under* HEAD *n.* ❑ **get together** *v.* **1** [1950s+] (*US campus*) to have sexual relations, with or without intercourse. **2** [1970s] (*US black*) to improve one's appearance. ❑ **hang together** *v.* [1990s+] (*US black*) to survive. ❑ **keep it together** *v.* (*also* **have it together**) [1980s+] (*orig. US black*) **1** to maintain a satisfactory lifestyle. **2** to keep emotional control. ❑ **that's together** [1970s] (*US black/campus*) an expression of approval.

together *adv.* [1960s+] competently, in an emotionally worked-out manner.

togg/togge *n. see* TOG *n.*

togged *adj.* [TOG *v.* (2)] [19C+] dressed; thus *rum togged*, well dressed.

IN PHRASES

❑ **togged down** *adj.* [1930s–60s] (*US black*) very well dressed. ❑ **togged out (to the nines)** *adj.* [UP TO THE NINES *phr.*] **1** [early 19C+] dressed up, usu. in one's finest clothes; of a place, decorated. **2** [1910s] equipped with a wardrobe. ❑ **togged to the knocker** *adj.* [1910s] (*Aus.*) well-dressed. ❑ **togged to the teeth** *adj.* [1970s] (*US black*) very well dresed. ❑ **togged up** *adj.* (*also* **togged out**) [mid-19C+] dressed up.

togger *n.*[1] *see* TADGER *n.*

togger *n.*[2] *see* TOG *n.*

toggery *n.* [ext. of TOG *n.* (1)] **1** [early 19C–1940s] clothing, harness, 'domestic paraphernalia of any kind' (Hotten). **2** [late 19C–1940s] any variety of official or vocational dress.

togging *n. see* TOGS *n.* (1).

toggs *n. see* TOGS *n.*

toggy *n. see* TOG *n.*

tog it *v. see* TOG UP *v.*

togman *n. see* TOGEMANS *n.*

tog out *v. see* TOG UP *v.*

togs *n.* (*also* **toggs**) [TOG *n.* (1)] **1** [mid-18C+] (*also* **tuggs, togging**) clothes, often in combs., e.g. *long togs, sporting togs, Sunday togs*. **2** [1940s+] (*Aus./N.Z.*) a swimming costume.

tog-up *n.* (*also* **tog-out**) [TOG UP *v.*] [late 19C] a suit of clothes.

tog up *v.* (*also* **tog it, tog out**) [TOG *v.* (2)] **1** [early 19C–1960s] to get dressed up, esp. in preparation for a night out, a party or similar event. **2** [mid-19C–1900s] to dress someone up (in their best clothes).

toilet *n.* **1** [1930s] (*US*) the buttocks, as in phr. *kick one's toilet around the block*, to be angry with oneself. **2** [1930s+] (*also* **toilet paper**) an incompetent, undesirable person or thing. **3** [1950s] (*US*) of a woman, a good figure. **4** [1950s+] (*orig.*

US) anywhere considered disgusting, esp. (show business) a third-rate venue. **5** [1960s+] a position of complete failure. **6** [1970s+] (*US gay*) the anus.

(IN COMPOUNDS)

❑ **toilet-mouthed** *adj.* [2000s] using obscene language. ❑ **toilet talk** *n.* [1950s+] obscenities, coarse language.

(IN PHRASES)

❑ **go down the toilet** *v.* (*also* **...crapper, ...pan, ...sewer**) [1960s+] to collapse, to end in failure. ❑ **go in the toilet** *v.* [1960s+] (*US*) to fail, usu. in show business context. ❑ **in the toilet** [1980s+] (*US*) in difficulties, undergoing problems, in debt.

toilet roll *n.* [rhy. sl.] [20C+] the dole.

toit *n.* [1960s] (*S.Afr.*) a woman.

to it *v.* [1950s] (*UK prison*) to run off, to abscond, to escape.

toity *n.* [1980s+] (*N.Z.*) a lavatory.

Tojo *n.* [proper name *Hideki Tojo* (1884–1948), Japanese general and milit. dictator during WW2] [1940s–60s] (*Aus./US*) the Japanese nation, esp. its armed forces.

(IN COMPOUNDS)

❑ **Tojoland** *n.* [1940s–60s] (*Aus./US*) Japan.

toke *n.*[1] [ety. unknown; ? link to Scot. *token*, a small quantity] **1** [mid-19C] a lump, a chunk, a portion. **2** [mid-19C–1950s] dry bread, esp. in comb. *skilly and toke*, gruel and dry bread, as served in prisons and workhouses. **3** [late 19C–1910s] bread. **4** [late 19C–1910s] food in general.

(IN COMPOUNDS)

❑ **toke-and-streamy** *n.* [late 19C–1900s] a period of time in prison.

toke *n.*[2] (*also* **toak**) [TOKE *v.*] [1950s+] (*orig. US black*) **1** a puff or drag of any kind of cigarette (usu. cannabis), or a pipe. **2** a marijuana cigarette; a pipeful of marijuana.

(IN PHRASES)

❑ **sink tokes** *n.* [1980s+] (*US drugs*) a gravity pipe, made with 2-litre (3½-pint) bottle and pipe bowl. ❑ **smoke a toke** *v.* [1980s+] (*US*) to smoke marijuana; lit. 'smoke a smoke' thus as much f. assonance as accuracy. ❑ **sneak-a-toke** *n.* [1980s+] (*US drugs*) a hand-held smokeless pipe.

toke *n.*[3] [abbr. SE *token*] [1970s+] **1** (*US gambling*) a gambling chip, esp. one given to a dealer as a gratuity. **2** (*US*) a tip given to a cab-driver for bringing clients to a gambling establishment, brothel etc.

toke *v.* (*also* **toke up**) [? ext. of TOKE *n.*[1] (1); i.e. a portion of the drug] **1** [1950s+] (*drugs*) to take a puff on a (usu. cannabis) cigarette or a pipe of crack cocaine. **2** [2000s] (*US*) to drink alcohol.

token *n.* [SE *token*, a sign] **1** [early 16C] the vagina. **2** [17C–early 19C] (signs of) venereal disease [sign of disease, i.e. a discharge or gangrenous spots]. **3** [mid-17C–early 18C] the plague [sign of disease, i.e. a discharge or gangrenous spots].

tokis *n. see* TOCHES *n.*

toko *n.*[1] [fig. use of TOCO *n.*] [1920s+] (*Aus.*) praise, esp. if 'laid on with a trowel'.

toko *n.*[2] *see* TOCO *n.*

tokoloshes *n.* [1970s] (*S.Afr Und.*) the police.

tokus *n. see* TOCHES *n.*

Tokyo rose *n.* (*also* **Tokyos**) [rhy. sl.; ult. WW2 pro-Japanese propagandist *Tokyo Rose* (Iva Toguri D'Aquino, 1916–2006)] [1940s–50s] the nose.

tol *n.*[1] (*also* **tale**) [abbr. proper name *Toledo*, from where the best swords came; thus note Ward, *Writings* (1704): 'I have a long Sword; you may tak't on my Word, / For the blade is a Toledo Trusty'] [late 17C–early 19C] (*UK Und.*) a sword.

tol *n.*[2] [backsl.] [mid–late 19C] a lot, a share.

told out *adj.* [SE *tell*, to count, to enumerate; lit. counted out] [mid-19C] exhausted, run down, 'finished'.

tole-dish *n. see* TOLL DISH *n.*

toley *n. see* TOLY *n.*

toliban rig *n.* (*also* **tolliban rig**) [? *toloben* f. Rom. *tullipen*, lard, grease + RIG *n.*[2] (1), but note *toliban*, a turban, emphasizing the 'Oriental' exoticism of conjurers] [late 18C–mid-19C] a confidence trick carried out by a woman who poses as a deaf and dumb conjurer.

toll dish *n.* (*also* **tole-dish**) [SE *toll dish*, a vessel used to measure the grain ground at a mill; thus added inferences of *grinding* etc] [18C–19C] the vagina.

toller *n.* (*also* **rifler**) [SE *toller*, tax gatherer] [late 16C–early 17C] (*UK Und.*) a horse-stealer.

tollewag *n. see* TALLYWAG *n.*

tolliban rig *n. see* TOLIBAN RIG *n.*

tollie-lekker *n.* [Afk; lit. 'penis-licker'] [2000s] (*S.Afr.*) a woman who performs fellatio.

tol-lol *adj.* (*also* **toll-loll, tollollish**) [SE *tolerable*] **1** [19C–1900s] tolerable, bearable. **2** [late 19C+] (*Aus.*) overbearing. **3** [late 19C+] (*Aus.*) foppish.

tol-lollish *adv.* [TOL-LOL *adj.*] [mid-19C] tolerably.

tollywhacker *n.* [juv. *tolly*, a candle (the similarity in shape) + WHACK *v.*[1] (1)] [1920s+] a roll of paper used as a club in children's play.

toly *n.* (*also* **toley**) [? Scot. *toalie*, a small round cake] [1960s+] a piece of excrement.

Tom *n.*[1] *see* TOM (THUMB) *n.*

Tom *n.*[2] *see* UNCLE TOM *n.*

Tom *adv.* [UNCLE TOM *n.*] [1960s] (*US black*) in a subservient, white-pleasing manner.

tom *n.*[1] [abbr. SE *tom fool*] **1** [mid-16C–mid-19C] (*also* **tommy**) a generic term for a man, esp. a foolish one; often used in combs. (see below) denoting one's occupation. **2** [early 18C] a generic for a waiter, a servant. **3** [1960s] (*US black*) a white man.

(IN COMPOUNDS)

❑ **Tom coney** *n.* (*also* **Tom conney, Tom cony**) [CONY *n.* (3)] [late 17C–early 19C] a fool, the victim of a confidence trick. ❑ **tom double** *n.* [DOUBLE *n.*[1]] [18C–mid-19C] an equivocator, a cheat, a 'double-dealer'. ❑ **tom essence** *n.* [SE *essence*, perfume] [late 17C–early 18C] a fop, a dandy. ❑ **tom farthing** *n.* [FARTHING *n.*] [late 17C–19C] a fool. ❑ **tom long** *n.* [the proverbial figure, *John Long* (16C) or *Tom Long* (17C), 'the carrier who will never do his errand'; or simply SE *long*] [17C–early 19C] a bore, a teller of long and tedious stories with neither end nor point. ❑ **tom pepper** *n.* [orig. naut., a mythical sailor ejected from Hell for lying; note WW1 RN *tom pepper*, a proverbial storyteller] [early 19C+] a liar. ❑ **tom tell-troth** *n.* [ext. of 14C SE *Tom True-Tongue*] [mid-17C–19C] an honest man. ❑ **tom tiler** *n.* (*also* **tom tyler**) [SE *tier*, used as generic for any ordinary job; assonant here] [late 16C–19C] **1** an ordinary man, 'Mr Average'. **2** a henpecked husband. ❑ **tom todger** *n.* [1990s+] (*Irish*) a small cheeky boy. ❑ **tom topper** *n.* (*also* **tom tug**) [popular song] [late 18C–19C] a ferryman, a waterman. ❑ **tom turdman** *n.* [TURD *n.*[1] (1)] [late 17C–early 19C] a nightsoil cleaner; thus *tom turdman's fields, tom turdman's hole*, the dump where the nightsoil is deposited. ❑ **tom wallager** *n.* [1950s] (*US*) an outstanding example of something.

tom *n.*[2] (*also* **tommy, tom-tom**) [mid–late 19C; 1960s+] the penis.

tom *n.*[3] [abbr. TOMMY *n.*[1] (3)] **1** [late 19C] (*S.Afr.*) a barmaid. **2** [1940s+] a prostitute, esp. one working in Mayfair.

(IN COMPOUNDS)

❑ **tom-carding** *n.* [1990s+] the distribution of cards advertising prostitute's services, thus *tom-carder*. ❑ **tom patrol** *n.* (*also* **toms patrol, tom squad**) [1940s+] (*UK Und./police*) the vice squad, esp. as regards prostitution.

tom *n.*[4] [the masculine name; euphemized by Ware as 'one who does not care for the society of others than of her own sex'] [late 19C; 1970s+] (*UK society/US gay*) a lesbian.

(IN PHRASES)

❑ **old tom** *n.* **1** [1960s] (*US*) a lesbian. **2** [1960s] (*US*) a prostitute catering to lesbians. **3** [1970s+] (*US gay*) an old lesbian.

tom *n.*[5] [abbr. TOM-TART *n.*] [20C+] (*Aus.*) a woman; also a generic term for women in general.

IN COMPOUNDS

❑ **tom rig** *n.* (*also* **tomrigg**) [SE *rig*, a wanton woman] [late 17C–early 19C] a promiscuous young woman; also a tomboy.

tom *n.*[6] [abbr. TOMMY ATKINS *n.*] [20C+] a British soldier.

tom *n.*[7] [abbr.] [1920s+] a *tomato*.

tom *n.*[8] [rhy. sl.; abbr. *tomfoolery*] **1** [1950s+] jewellery. **2** [1950s+] (*S.Afr.*) money.

tom *n.*[9] [abbr. *t*otally *o*bedient *m*oron] [1990s+] (*US campus*) a computer.

tom *n.*[10] *see* TOM MIX *n.*

tom *n.*[11] *see* TOMTIT *n.*

tom *adj.* [TOM *v.*[2] (1)] [1950s+] **1** of a black person, acting subserviently towards white society. **2** (*US*) admirable, trustworthy. **3** second-rate, unpleasant. **4** insane, eccentric.

tom *v.*[1] [SE *tom-cat*] [19C] of a man, to have sexual intercourse.

tom *v.*[2] [UNCLE TOM *n.*] (*mainly US black*) [1960s+] **1** (*also* **tom it (up), tom slick**) of a black person, to act in an inferior and obsequious manner to whites, to act as a black stereotype; thus *tomming*. **2** to toady. **3** (*also* **tom out**) to betray, to inform.

IN PHRASES

❑ **tom-and-try** *v.* [TOM *v.*[2] (1) + SE *try*] [1960s–70s] (*US black*) to advance oneself professionally by conforming to white stereotypes of black behaviour.

Tom a Doodle *n. see* TOM DOODLE *n.*

tomahawk *n.* [late 19C] a policeman's truncheon.

tomahawk *v.* (*also* **tommyhawk**) [mid-19C+] (*Aus.*) to shear incompetently.

tomahawker *n.* (*also* **tommyhawker**) [TOMAHAWK *v.*] [20C+] (*Aus.*) a rough, incompetent shearer.

tomale *n. see* HOT TAMALE *n.*

tom-a-lee *n.* [a black subservient enough to have worked for the Confederate general Robert E. Lee (1807–70)] [1940s–80s] (*US black*) a subservient black.

Tom and Dick *n. see* TOM, DICK AND HARRY *n.*

tom and dick *n.* [TOM AND DICK *adj.*] [2000s] one who is sick.

tom and dick *adj.* [rhy. sl.] [1970s+] sick, ill.

tom (and funny) *n.* [rhy. sl., 20C+ use as *tom* in S.Afr. only, the rhy. sl. origin has presumably been forgotten] [late 19C+] money.

tom and jerry *n.* [*Tom* and *Jerry*, two fictional men-about-town created by Pierce Egan in *Life in London, or Days and Nights of Jerry Hawthorne and his elegant friend Corinthian Tom* (1821), who lent their name to a low inn (note synon. JERRY SHOP *n.*, with no bearing on the book and found a year earlier), and to a drink (which is still being drunk in Damon Runyon's short stories more than a century later); to Warner Bros. cartoon cat and mouse, and to the protagonists of the hit BBC TV sit-com *The Good Life* (1975–8)] **1** [19C–1900s] a hard round hat. **2** [early 19C] (*US*) a rowdy celebrant. **3** [mid-19C–1940s] a highly spiced punch.

DERIVATIVES

❑ **tom-and-jerryism** *n.* [early–mid-19C] rowdiness.

IN COMPOUNDS

❑ **tom and jerry days** *n.* [19C] the Regency, the reign of George IV. ❑ **tom and jerry gang** *n.* [early–mid-19C] a gang of rowdy men, devoted to womanizing, drinking, gaming and other pleasures. ❑ **tom-and-jerry (shop)** *n.* [mid–late 19C] a cheap tavern.

tom and jerry *adj.* [rhy. sl.; note also TOM AND JERRY *n.*] [19C] merry.

tom and jerry *v.* [for ety. see TOM AND JERRY *n.*] [early–mid-19C] to indulge in drinking, to go on a spree.

tom and sam *n.* [rhy. sl.] [20C+] (*Aus.*) jam.

tomasso di rotto *n.* [cod Ital. 'translation' of TOMMYROT *n.*] [late 19C–1900s] (*middle-class youth*) nonsense, rubbish.

tomato *n.* [the luscious ripeness of the fruit] **1** [1920s–30s] (*US*) the buttocks, the posterior. **2** [1920s–30s] (*US*) a fool. **3** [1920s+] (*orig. US*) an attractive woman. **4** [1930s] (*US*) an attractive (effeminate) young man. **5** [1930s] (*US Und.*) a pimp. **6** [1930s] (*US Und.*) a prostitute. **7** [1930s] (*US Und.*) a stolen car. **8** [1930s+] (*US*) a woman. **9** [1990s+] (*US*) the vagina. **10** (*N.Z.*) NZ$100 bill.

IN PHRASES

❑ **hot tomato** *n.* **1** [1920s–30s] (*US*) a clever person. **2** [1950s] (*US Und.*) a passionate or tough woman. ❑ **ripe tomato** *n.* [1920s+] a woman who is ready for seduction or even marriage.

SE in slang uses

IN COMPOUNDS

❑ **tomato-picker** *n.* [their employment as farm labourers] [1960s–70s] (*US*) a derog. term for a Puerto Rican or Mexican.

tomato can *n.* **1** [1920s–40s] (*US*) the badge worn by a local or small-town police officer [the cheapness of its manufacture]. **2** [1970s] a second rate boxer [he is easily crushed].

IN COMPOUNDS

❑ **tomato-can vag** *n.* (*also* **can moocher, tomato can stiff, tomato-can tramp**) [late 19C–1940s] (*US tramp*) the lowest rank of vagrant.

tomato purée *n.* [rhy. sl.] [1990s+] a jury.

tomato sauce *n.* [rhy. sl.] [20C+] (*Aus./N.Z.*) a horse; thus *tomato sauces*, the horses, i.e. horseraces.

tomb *n.* [i.e. it is 'deep and dark'] [20C+] (*US*) the anus.

tombhead *n.* [the rounded top of the head supposedly resembles a tombstone] [1960s] (*W.I.*) **1** a large head. **2** a person who has such a head.

Tom Bray's bilk *n.* [? anecdotal] [early–mid-19C] (gaming) laying out the ace and deuce when playing cribbage.

Tom Brown *n.* [? anecdotal] [early–mid-19C] in gaming, the game of 'twelve in hand', generally known as cribbage.

Tombs, the *n.* [one is 'buried' there] [mid-19C+] (*US*) New York City prison.

IN EXCLAMATIONS

❑ **by the Tombs!** [late 19C] (*US*) an excl. of irritation.

tombstone *n.* **1** [mid-19C–1900s] a pawn ticket [the inscription 'in memory of' and the implication that once pawned, items are rarely possessed again]. **2** [mid-19C–1930s] a snaggle- or crooked tooth [resemblance]. **3** [1980s+] (*drugs*) a capsule or pill of amphetamine.

tomcat *n.*[1] [rhy. sl.] [20C+] a doormat.

tomcat *n.*[2] [reverse anthropomorphism] **1** [1920s+] (*orig. US*) a womanizer, a philanderer. **2** [1940s] (*US*) a promiscuous woman.

IN COMPOUNDS

❑ **tomcat's delight** *n.* [1960s] (*Aus.*) a free drink from a publican.

tomcat *n.*[3] **1** [1930s] (*US Und.*) a machine gun. **2** [1930s–50s] (*US drugs/prison*) an improvised hypodermic needle made from a sewing-machine needle.

tom cat *v.* [TOMCAT *n.*[2] (1)] [1920s+] (*orig. US*) to strut around looking for sexual conquests.

Tom Collins *n.* [the mythical figure Tom Collins, fl. 1890 in south-eastern states, to whom rumours and dubious information was attributed; the name was subseq. adopted as pseudonym by the writer Joseph Furphy (1843–1912), brother to John (1842–1920), the creator of FURPHY *n.*] [1940s] (*Aus.*) a rumour.

Tom Cruise *n.* [rhy. sl. = BOOZE *n.* (1); ult. US film star *Tom Cruise* (b.1962)] [1990s+] drink, a drink.

Tom, Dick and Harry *n.* (*also* **Bill, Tom and Harry; Dick and Harry; Dick, Tom and Joe; Jack, Tom and Harry; Tom and Dick; Tom, Dick and Jerry**) [orig. sl. but SE by mid-19C] [mid-17C+] any men, young or old, irrespective of given names.

tom doodle *n.* (*also* **Tom a Doodle**) [BOOZE *n.* (1) + DOODLE *n.*[1]] [18C] a fool.

tom doolies *n.* [rhy. sl. = GOOLIE *n.* (1); ult. the popular song 'Hang Down Your Head, Tom Dooley' by the Kingston Trio, 1958] [1950s+] the testicles.

Tom Drum's entertainment *n.* see JACK DRUM'S ENTERTAINMENT *n.*

Tom Finney *adj.* [rhy. sl.; ult. UK footballer *Tom Finney* (b.1922)] [1990s+] skinny.

tomfoolery *n.* [rhy. sl.] [20C+] jewellery, often imitation.

tom, harry and dick *adj.* [rhy. sl.] [20C+] sick.

tom it (up) *v.* see TOM *v.*[2] (1).

tom long *n.* [the proverbial figure, *John Long* (16C) or *Tom Long* (17C), 'the carrier who will never do his errand'; or simply SE *long*] [17C–early 19C] a bore, a teller of long and tedious stories with neither end nor point.

tommie *n.* see TOMMY ATKINS *n.*

tom mix *n.* (*also* **tom**) [rhy. sl.; ult. US film cowboy *Tom Mix* (1880–1940)] **1** [1930s+] the number six. **2** [1940s+] a problem, a predicament [SE *fix*, a dilemma]. **3** [1970s+] an injection of heroin [FIX *n.*[3] (1)].

Tom Molly *n.* see MOLLY *n.*[1].

tommy *n.*[1] [? TOM-TART *n.*] **1** [18C] a lesbian. **2** [early 19C] a male homosexual. **3** [late 19C+] (*US*) a prostitute, or promiscuous young woman.

(IN COMPOUNDS)

▫ **tommy buster** *n.* [BUST *v.*[1] (1)] [1940s] (*US Und.*) a rapist; one who physically abuses women.

tommy *n.*[2] [orig. milit. jargon *tommy*, the bread supplied as part of rations. This in turn had evolved from orig. 18C *brown george* to *brown tommy* to *tommy brown* and thence to its abbr. Note that St Thomas' Day, on which bread was distributed by charities, preceded the milit. coinage] **1** [late 18C–1930s] (a loaf of) bread. **2** [mid-19C–1940s] solid food in general. **3** [late 19C+] (*Aus.*) bread baked with sugar and currants.

(IN COMPOUNDS)

▫ **tommy shop** *n.* [mid-19C] a bakery.

(IN PHRASES)

▫ **brown tommy** *n.* [late 18C–19C] brown bread. ▫ **soft tommy** *n.* [late 18C–19C] white bread. ▫ **tommy and exes** *n.* [late 19C–1900s] bread, beer and tobacco.

(IN EXCLAMATIONS)

▫ **that's the tommy!** [late 19C] that's right!

tommy *n.*[3] [Gk *tomé*, a section; orig. Trinity College, Dublin] [mid-19C] a worn-out shirt.

tommy *n.*[4] [abbr.] [late 19C] **1** a *tomato*. **2** (*US*) *tomato* soup.

tommy *n.*[5] **1** [late 19C–1910s] used as a term of address to a young boy whose real name is unknown. **2** [1910s–20s] a pimp [? generic use of proper name].

tommy *n.*[6] [SE *tomahawk*] [late 19C–1930s] (*Aus/N.Z.*) an axe.

tommy *n.*[7] [euph.] [late 19C+] menstruation.

tommy *n.*[8] [ety. unknown; unless a derog. ref. to TOMMY *n.*[5] (2); *DNZE* suggests rhy. sl. on SE *book* or *Tommy Rook*] [1920s+] (*Aus./N.Z.*) **1** a bookmaker. **2** a bookmaker's ledger.

tommy *n.*[9] see TOM *n.*[1] (1).

tommy *n.*[10] see TOM *n.*[2].

tommy *n.*[11] see TOMMY ATKINS *n.*

tommy *n.*[12] see TOMMY GUN *n.*

tommy *n.*[13] see TOMMYROT *n.*

tommy *n.*[14] see TOMMY TANA *n.*

tommy *n.*[15] see UNCLE TOM *n.*

tommy *v.*[1] [ety. unknown] [20C+] (*Aus.*) to leave.

tommy *v.*[2] see TOMMY TRIPE *v.*

Tommy Atkins *n.* (*also* **Thomas, Thomas Atkins, tom, tommie, tommy**) ['arising out of the casual use of this name in the specimen forms given in the official regulations from 1815 onward...In some of the specimen forms other names are used; but "Thomas Atkins" being that used in all the forms for privates in the Cavalry or Infantry, is by far the most frequent, and thus became the most familiar; thus 1815 (Aug. 31) War Office, Collection of Orders, Regulations etc 75 (Form of a Soldier's Book in the Cavalry when filled up). Description, Service, &c. of Thomas Atkins, Private, No. 6 Troop, 6th Regt. of Dragoons. Where Born...Parish of Odiham, Hants...Bounty, £ Received, Thomas Atkins, his x mark' (*OED*); thus WW1 milit. *Thomasina Atkins*, a WAAC] **1** [late 19C+] a generic for a typical private soldier in the British army. **2** [1980s] an Englishman.

tommy dod *n.* see TOMMY DODD *n.*[3] (1).

tommy dodd *n.*[1] [rhy. sl. = odd] [mid–late 19C] **1** in coin-tossing, the 'odd man' who goes out. **2** the game of coin-tossing itself. **3** the winner or loser in coin-tossing, the choice for the name allotted by previous agreement.

tommy dodd *n.*[2] [rhy. sl.] **1** [late 19C] a sodomite [= *sod*]. **2** [late 19C–1950s] God. **3** [1920s+] (*US*) a gun [= ROD *n.* (2)].

tommy dodd *n.*[3] [? anecdotal] **1** [late 19C–1910s] (*Aus.*) (*also* **tommy dod**) a style of hat. **2** [late 19C+] (*Aus./N.Z.*) a small glass of beer, approx. one quarter-pint. **3** [1910s] a walking stick.

Tommy Farr *n.* [rhy. sl.; ult. UK boxer *Tommy Farr* (1913–1986)] [20C+] a bar.

Tommy get out, and let your father in *n.* see LET YOUR FATHER IN *n.*

tommy gun *n.* (*also* **tommy**) [one of the earliest brands, the .45 calibre *Thomson*] [1920s+] (*orig. US Und.*) a sub-machine gun.

(IN COMPOUNDS)

▫ **tommy gee** *n.* [1930s] (*US Und./prison*) a machine-gunner. ▫ **tommy man** *n.* [1920s–30s] (*US Und.*) an armed gangster.

tommy-gun *v.* [TOMMY GUN *n.*] [1960s] to blast with a sub-machine gun.

tommy-gunner *n.* [TOMMY GUN *n.*] [1940s+] (*orig. US Und.*) someone bearing a sub-machine gun.

tommy guns *n.* [rhy. sl. = RUNS, THE *n.* (1); ult. TOMMY GUN *n.*] [1990s+] diarrhoea.

tommyhawk *v.* see TOMAHAWK *v.*

tommyhawker *n.* see TOMAHAWKER *n.*

tommy kiki *n.* see TOMMY TANA *n.*

tommy nonsense *n.* see TOMMYROT *n.*

Tommy O'Rann *n.* [rhy. sl. = SCRAN *n.* (2)] [mid-19C+] food.

tommy rabbit *n.* [rhy. sl., if weak] [late 19C–1900s] a pomegranate.

tommy rocks *n.* see JOE ROCKS *n.*

tommy roller *n.* (*also* **charley roller**) [rhy. sl.] [late 19C+] a collar.

tommy rollocks *n.* (*also* **jimmy rollocks, rollock**) [rhy. sl. = BALLOCKS *n.* (2)] [20C+] the testicles.

tommyrot *n.* (*also* **tommy, tommy nonsense, tommy tripe**) [? the red coat of a TOMMY ATKINS *n.* (1), thus euph. for BLOODY *adj.* (1)] [late 19C+] absolute nonsense.

tommyrot *v.* [TOMMYROT *n.*] [late 19C+] **1** to fool around. **2** to hoax, to deceive, to humbug.

(DERIVATIVES)

▫ **tommyrotter** *n.* [late 19C+] a confidence trickster.

tommy steeles *n.* [rhy. sl.; ult. UK pop star *Tommy Steele* (b.1936)] [20C+] eels.

tommy talker *n.* [generic/assonant use of proper name *tommy* + its sound] [1930s+] **1** a kazoo. **2** a ventriloquist's dummy with a pull string.

Tommy Tana *n.* (*also* **tanna, tommy, tommy kiki, Tommy Tanna, Tommy Tanner**) [generic use of proper name *Tommy* + *Tanna*, an island near Vanuatu (the Near Hebrides)] [1900s–10s] (*Aus.*) a nickname for a Pacific Islander imported as a labourer.

tommy tit *n.* [generic/assonant use of proper name *tommy* + SE *tit*, a person] [18C–early 19C] a smart young fellow.

Tommy Trinder *n.* [rhy. sl.; Cockney pron. 'winder'; ult. UK comedian *Tommy Trinder* (1909–89)] [1990s+] a window.

tommy tripe *n.*[1] [rhy. sl.] [20C+] a (tobacco) pipe.

tommy tripe *n.*[2] see TOMMYROT *n.*

tommy tripe *v.* (*also* **tommy**) [rhy. sl. = PIPE *v.*[3] (2)] [mid-19C–1900s] to examine, to survey, to keep a watch.

tommy tucker *n.* [rhy. sl. + ref. to the nursery rhyme] **1** [1930s+] (*also* **Tom Tucker**) supper. **2** [1990s+] a person [FUCKER *n.* (6)]. **3** [1990s+] (*UK Und.*) a gullible individual [SUCKER *n.*[1] (3a)].

tommy tupper *n.* [rhy. sl.] [20C+] supper.

tom noddy *n.* [rhy. sl.] [20C+] (*US*) a body, i.e. a corpse.

Tom of Bedlam *n.* [proper name *Bedlam*, by the 16C a generic term for lunatic asylums, but orig. applied spec. to the Hospital of St Mary of Bethlehem in London. A general hospital by 1330, in 1402 it became a hospital for the insane] [17C–19C] a genuine (rather than criminal and thus fake) beggar.

tomorrow *v.* [rhy. sl.] [20C+] to borrow; usu. in abbr. phr. *on the tommy*, looking for a loan.

tom pat *n.*[1] [abbr. PATRICO *n.* (1)] [late 17C–18C] a parson.

tom pat *n.*[2] [Rom. *tom pat*, a foot] [19C] a shoe.

tom right *n.* [rhy. sl.] [mid-19C] the night.

toms *n. see* TOM-TITS *n.*

Tom Sawyer *n.* [rhy. sl.; ult. *Tom Sawyer*, novel (1876) by US writer Mark Twain (Samuel Langhorne Clemens, 1835–1910)] [late 19C+] a lawyer.

tom slick *n.* [TOM *n.*[2] + SLICK *n.*[1] (2); i.e. they charm their friends and inform on them to the police] [1960s+] (*US black*) a black police informer.

tom slick *v. see* TOM *v.*[2] (1).

tom-tart *n.* [rhy. sl.] **1** [late 19C–1950s] (*Aus.*) a woman [? = sweetheart]. **2** [1940s+] (*US*) a breaking of wind [= FART *n.* (1)].

Tom (Thumb) *n.* [rhy. sl.] **1** [late 19C+] (*orig. Aus.*) rum. **2** [20C+] the buttocks [BUM *n.*[1] (1)]. **3** [1940s+] (*Aus.*) inside information [DRUM *n.*[6] (1)].

Tom Thumb (queen) *n.* [2000s] (*S.Afr. gay*) a man with a small penis.

tom tiddler's ground *n.* [the children's game *Tom Tiddler's ground*, in which one player is 'Tom', who stands behind a 'land' which marks the 'ground'. The other players dash forward over the ground, singing 'We're on Tom Tiddler's ground, picking up gold and silver', and the first or sometimes last child caught becomes Tom; Brewer, *Dict. of Phrase and Fable* (1894), suggests that *Tiddler* is an elision of *t'idler*] **1** [mid-19C–1940s] anywhere that money or other items can be obtained easily. **2** [late 19C] a no-man's-land, a debatable territory.

tomtit *n.* (*also* **tom**) [rhy. sl. = SHIT *n.* (1a)/SHIT *n.* (2a)] [20C+] **1** an act of defecation. **2** a piece of excrement. **3** a contemptible person.

tomtit *v.* [rhy. sl. = SHIT *v.* (1a)] [late 19C+] to defecate.

tom-tits *n.* (*also* **toms**) [rhy. sl. = SHITS, THE *n.* (1)] [1940s+] (*Aus.*) diarrhoea.

(IN PHRASES)

□ **get the tom-tits** *v.* (*also* **have the tom-tits**) [1950s+] to become annoyed. □ **give someone the tom-tits** *v.* [1950s+] to annoy someone.

tom-tom *n. see* TOM *n.*[2].

tom tripe *n.* [rhy. sl.] [mid-19C] a pipe.

Tom Tucker *n. see* TOMMY TUCKER *n.* (1).

tom tug *n.*[1] [rhy. sl.] **1** [late 19C] a bedbug. **2** [late 19C–1940s] a fool, a victim [MUG *n.*[1] (2a)]. **3** [1950s] (*US*) a thug.

tom tug *n.*[2] *see* TOM TOPPER *under* TOM *n.*[1].

ton *n.*[1] [SE *ton*, 100 cubic feet] **1** [late 18C+] a very large (unspecified) amount; thus TONS *n.* **2** [1940s+] £100. **3** [1950s+] 100 miles per hour. **4** [1960s+] any unit of 100, e.g. 100 years, 100 runs (in cricket).

(IN PHRASES)

□ **do a ton** *v.* [1960s+] to drive a motorcycle or car at 100 mph. □ **half-a-ton** *n.* **1** [1940s+] £50. **2** [1960s+] (*bingo*) the number ten [the 'half' is visual, 10 has only one of the two 0s of 100].

ton *n.*[2] [abbr.] [1960s] tonic water.

tondalayo *n.* [proper name of any 'African queen'/QUEEN *n.* (2a)] [1950s–70s] (*camp gay*) an ostentatious, flagrant homosexual.

tondo *n.* [1970s] (*S.Afr.*) the penis.

tone *n.* [1950s] (*W.I./UK black*) to tease.

tone/toney *adj. see* TONY *adj.*

tongue *n.* [metonymy] [1930s+] (*US Und.*) a public defender, a lawyer.

SE in slang uses

(IN COMPOUNDS)

□ **tongue bath** *n.* [1940s] the licking and sucking of the partner's body, incl. the genitals and sometimes the anus. □ **tongue-diving** *n.* [1970s] (*US*) kissing. □ **tongue-job** *n.* [JOB *n.*[2] (2)] [1960s+] (*orig. US*) oral sex, whether fellatio or cunnilingus. □ **tongue lash** *v.* [1930s+] (*US gay*) to perform fellatio or anilingus. □ **tongue pad** *n. see* separate entries. □ **tongue party** *n.* [1940s] (*US*) mutual oral-genital intercourse. □ **tongue pie** *n. see* separate entry. □ **tongue plating** *n. see* PLATING *n.* □ **tongue sandwich** *n.* **1** [1970s+] (*US gay*) anilingus. **2** [1980s+] a deep kiss. □ **tongue wang** *v.* [? SE *wag* or WANGLE *v.*] [1900s] (*Aus.*) to harangue, to berate. □ **tongue wrestle** *v.* [1980s+] to kiss deeply, using the tongues.

(IN PHRASES)

□ **give someone (a lick with) the rough side of one's tongue** *v.* [pun on SE *lick*, a blow/*lick*, an act of licking] [late 19C+] to attack verbally. □ **give someone the length of one's tongue** *v.* [late 19C+] to attack verbally. □ **swap tongues** *v. see* SWAP SPIT(S) *under* SWAP *v.* □ **tonguing for** *adj.* [1990s+] (*Aus.*) desperate for, usu. alcohol. □ **walk on one's tongue** *v.* [1900s] (*Aus.*) to have one's tongue hanging out with thirst. □ **wash one's tongue on** *v.* [20C+] (*W.I.*) to malign.

tongue *v.* **1** [mid-19C] to talk down. **2** [late 19C] to fellate. **3** [late 19C+] (*also* **tongue fuck**) to perform cunnilingus. **4** [late 19C+] to kiss with tongues in each other's mouth. **5** [20C+] (*Ulster*) to scold.

(IN PHRASES)

□ **tongue for** *v.* [2000s] to be desperate for.

tongued *adj.* (*also* **tonguey**) [TONGUE *v.*] [mid-19C] talkative; impertinent.

tongue pad *n.* [SE *tongue* + PAD *n.*[1], on model of SE *footpad*] [late 17C–early 19C] a talkative person, esp. one who persuades one to act foolishly or against one's will; by ext., a confidence trickster.

tongue pad *v.* [TONGUE PAD *n.*] [late 17C–early 19C] **1** to scold, to tell off, to reprimand. **2** to persuade, to talk someone into something.

tongue pie *n.* **1** [mid-19C–1920s] a scolding, a telling off. **2** [1980s+] cunnilingus.

(IN PHRASES)

□ **get tongue pie (with chin sauce)** *v.* (*also* **get tongue**) [1900s–20s] to receive a scolding. □ **give tongue pie** *v.* [1900s–20s] to give a scolding, to harangue.

tongue-plating *n. see* PLATING *n.*

tonguey *n.* [1970s+] (*Aus. teen*) a kiss with the tongue.

tonguey *adj. see* TONGUED *adj.*

tonic *n.*[1] (*also* **thonic**) [ety. unknown; ? link to TANNER *n.*] [19C] a halfpenny.

tonic *n.*[2] [late 19C+] alcohol.

(DERIVATIVES)

□ **tonicked** *adj.* [late 19C+] (*Aus.*) drunk.

tonish *adj. see* TONY *adj.*

tonk *n.*[1] [1930s+] (*US/N.Z.*) a seedy, 'lowlife' bar.

tonk *n.*[2] [ety. unknown, ? link to TONKY *adj.*] [1940s+] (*Aus.*) **1** a male homosexual, or an effeminate heterosexual man. **2** a fool. **3** someone whose speech appears to set them above their peers.

tonk *adj.* [2000s] (*UK teen*) very large.

(IN COMPOUNDS)

□ **tonked up** *adj.* muscled.

tonk *v.* [echoic] [1910s+] **1** to hit. **2** in fig. use, to defeat, overcome. **3** to have sexual intercourse. **4** to punish. **5** to masturbate. **6** to run.

tonkie *n.* [ety. unknown] [1980s] a condom.

tonky *adj.* [? TONY *adj.* + SWANKY *adj.* (1) or Fr. (*bon*) *ton*] **1** [1930s+] (*N.Z.*) smart, fashionable. **2** *see* TONY *adj.*

ton o' my rocks *n.* [rhy. sl.] [20C+] (*Aus.*) socks.

tons *n.* [TON *n.*[1] (1)] [late 19C+] a very large amount, a great deal.

tons *adv.* [TONS *n.*] [20C+] (*US campus*) very, extremely, really etc, e.g. *I feel tons better now.*

tonsil *n.*

SE in slang uses

IN COMPOUNDS

❑ **tonsil hockey** *n.* (*also* **tonsil tennis**) [1980s+] kissing. ❑ **tonsil polish** *n.* (*also* **tonsil bath, tonsil lubricator, tonsil paint, tonsil varnish**) [20C+] alcohol or tea. ❑ **tonsil-tickler** *n.* [1930s] (*US*) a (large) penis.

IN PHRASES

❑ **box the tonsils** *v.* [1980s+] to kiss with the tongue, to French kiss. ❑ **play tonsil hockey** *v.* (*also* **play tonsil tennis**) [1980s+] (*US campus*) to kiss deeply. ❑ **suck tonsils** *v. see under* SUCK *v.*[1]. ❑ **swab someone's tonsils** *v.* [1920s+] to kiss.

tons of fun *n.* [TONS *n.* + SE *fun*] [1980s+] (*US*) a cynical term of address.

Tonto *n.* [the character *Tonto*, the 'Red Indian' sidekick, played by Jay Silverheels (1919–80), who rode with TV's *Lone Ranger* (1952–6)] [1950s+] a Native American who is considered insufficiently nationalistic and overly subservient to the white man by other Native Americans; occas. of blacks.

tonto *adj.* [Sp. *tonto*, stupid] [1980s+] crazy.

Tonto no go to town *phr.* [for ety. *see* TONTO *n.*, the line was a catchphrase of the TV show] [1990s+] (*US black teen*) it wouldn't be prudent at this juncture.

ton-up boy *n.* [TON *n.*[1] (3)] [1960s+] a member of a motorcycle gang.

tony *n.* [abbr. of proper name; coined in Middleton & Rowley's play *The Changeling* (1653)] [mid-17C–mid-19C; 1960s] a fool.

tony *adj.* (*also* **tone, toney, tonish, tonky**) [SE *tone*, style] [late 18C+] (*orig. US*) classy, sophisticated, chic.

Tony Benn *n.* [rhy. sl.; ult. UK politician *Tony Benn* (b.1925)] [1990s+] £10 (cf. AYRTON (SENNA) *n.*).

Tony Blair *n.* [rhy. sl.; ult. *Tony Blair*, (b.1953) UK prime minister (1997–2007)] [1990s+] **1** hair. **2** a nightmare.

tonygle *v. see* ety. at NIGGLE *v.*

Tony Hatch *n.* [rhy. sl.; ult. UK pop composer *Tony Hatch* (b.1939)] [1990s+] **1** the vagina [SNATCH *n.* (1)]. **2** a (young) woman [SNATCH *n.* (1)]. **3** a match.

Tony's den *n. see* WILSON'S DEN *n.*

tony (whitemeat) *n.* [2000s] a white woman who associates with Asian men.

too-a-roo *phr. see* TOOROO *phr.*

too-bad-Jim *adj.* [1950s] (*US black*) serious, with no leniency.

toodle *n.* [TOODLE *v.*] [early 19C] a walk.

toodle *v.* [TODDLE *v.*] [early 19C+] to move, to go, to wander.

toodle-oo *phr.* (*also* **tootle-oo**) [? SE *toot*, the tooting of a horn, in this case as a coach moves off or Fr. *à tout à l'heure*, goodbye] [20C+] goodbye, occas. hello.

toodle-pip *phr.* (*also* **tootle-pip**) [var. on TOODLE-OO *phr.*] [1970s+] a nonsense word used to say goodbye.

toodley-oodley *adj.* [nonsense word] [mid–late 19C] satisfactory.

tooeys *n. see* TOOIES *n.*

toofah/toofer *n. see* TWOFER *n.* (2).

tooies *n.* (*also* **tooeys, tooles, toolies, tuies**) [abbr. proprietory name *Tuinal*] [1960s+] (*drugs*) barbiturates, esp. Tuinal.

tookus/tooky *n. see* TOCHES *n.*

tool *n.*[1] **1** as a lit. or fig. bodily organ (but primarily the penis) was SE mid-16C–mid-19C; sense 1c from sense 1a on model of PRICK *n.* (3). (**a**) [mid-16C+] the penis. (**b**) [late 17C] the vagina. (**c**) [late 17C+] a stupid, useless, socially inept person. **2** in senses of that which is used [SE *tool*, an instrument of manual operation, ult. ON *tol*, to prepare or make]. (**a**) [late 17C–mid-19C] an unskilful workman; usu. as *dull tool, poor tool.* (**b**) [19C] a whip. (**c**) [mid-19C] (*UK Und.*) a small boy who is put through a window that is too small for the adult members of that gang to enter and who then opens the door to admit them. (**d**) [mid-19C–1960s] (*UK/US Und.*) that member of the pickpocket team who does the actual stealing; the WIRE *n.*[2]. (**e**) [mid-19C+] a weapon, usu. a gun, knife or razor. (**f**) [late 19C+] a burglar's implement, spec. a jemmy. (**g**) [1960s+] (*also* **power tool**) (*US campus*) a very hard worker. (**h**) [1990s+] (*US drugs*) a hypodermic syringe.

IN COMPOUNDS

❑ **toolbox** *n.* **1** [19C+] the vagina. **2** [1990s+] (*also* **toolshed**) a group of idiots, or just a very extreme idiot. ❑ **tool chest** *n.* [19C] the vagina. ❑ **toolhead** *n.* [-HEAD *sfx*] [1970s+] (*US campus*) a fool, an idiot. ❑ **tool house** *n.* [1960s] (*Irish*) a urinal. ❑ **toolman** *n.* [sense 2e/2f + SE *man*] **1** [1940s+] a lock-picker; one who deals with alarms etc. **2** [1940s+] (*US*) a safe-breaker. **3** [2000s] a gun-carrying robber.

IN PHRASES

❑ **have broken tools in one's garage** *v.* [1970s] (*US*) to be foolish or crazy. ❑ **lawful tool** *n.* [1950s] (*UK Und.*) a tool used for committing a burglary. ❑ **tool of generation** *n. see* GENERATING TOOL *n.*

tool *n.*[2] [TOOL *v.* (2b)] [late 19C] a drive (in a horse-drawn vehicle).

tool *n.*[3] [abbr. *GARDEN TOOL under* GARDEN *n.*] [1990s+] **1** (*US*) a promiscuous woman. **2** (*US campus*) a despicable person.

tool *v.* **1** [mid-18C–19C] of a man, to have sexual intercourse. **2** to move, to drive. (**a**) [early 19C–1930s] to drive a mail coach or any other horse-drawn vehicle. (**b**) [mid-19C+] to be driven in a horse-drawn vehicle; thus to drive or travel in a car or any other vehicle; usu. as *TOOL ALONG under* TOOL *v.* (**c**) [mid-19C+] to proceed in a leisurely, aimless way; usu. as *TOOL ALONG under* TOOL *v.* (**d**) [late 19C+] to leave at speed; usu. as *TOOL ALONG under* TOOL *v.* **3** [mid-19C] to pick pockets. **4** to attack with a weapon [coined by Thomas De Quincey (1785–1859), punning on SE *tool*, a dagger + the decoration or 'tooling' of a blade]. (**a**) [mid–late 19C] to murder, usu. with a knife. (**b**) [1940s+] to stab; to slash with a razor [underpinned by TOOL *n.*[1] (2e)]. **5** [1960s+] (*US campus*) to study.

tool *v.*

IN PHRASES

❑ **tool along** *v.* (*also* **...about, ...around**) [mid-19C+] **1** to drive around, esp. to drive fast. **2** to walk or travel leisurely. **3** to walk off fast. **4** to walk with, to guide. ❑ **tool in** *v.* [1960s+] (*US campus*) to arrive, usu. at speed. ❑ **tool off** *v.* (*also* **...out**) [late 19C–1960s] to leave, to go away; to abandon, to desert. ❑ **tool up** *v.* [TOOL *n.*[1] (2e)/TOOL *n.*[1] (2f)] **1** [1940s+] to arm oneself; thus phr. *tool up on*, to shoot someone. **2** [1970s+] to carry housebreaking implements.

based on SE *tool*/TOOL *n.*[1] (1)

IN PHRASES

❑ **tool (around)** *v.* [1960s+] (*US campus*) to mistreat someone. ❑ **tool about** *v.* (*also* **...around**) [1920s+] to behave in an aimless, irresponsible manner, to waste time.

tooled (up) *adj.* [*TOOL UP under* TOOL *v.*] **1** [1940s+] carrying a weapon. **2** [1970s+] carrying housebreaking implements. **3** [1990s+] in fig. use, kitted out with something.

tooler *n.* [TOOL *v.* (3)] [mid-19C] a pickpocket.

Tooleries *n.* [late 19C–1900s] Toole's Theatre, sited in William IV Street, London WC.

tooles *n. see* TOOIES *n.*

Tooley Street tailor *n.* [the three tailors of Tooley St (SE1) who supposedly put together a petition to Parliament. It carried none but their own signatures but was headed grandiosely, 'We the people of England...'] [late 19C–1900s] a braggart, a boaster.

tooleywag *n. see* TALLYWAG *n.*

toolie *n.* [SE *tool*] [1970s+] (*US campus*) an engineering student.

toolies *n. see* TOOIES *n.*

tooling *n.* [TOOL *v.* (3)] [mid-19C–1910s] skilful pickpocketing.

tools *n.* **1** [early 19C+] (*UK Und.*) any implements used in the commission of crime, e.g. housebreaking implements, guns, pistols or other weapons. **2** [mid-19C–1900s] the human hands. **3** [late 19C+] (*US*) eating utensils. **4** [1960s+] (*drugs*) equipment used for injecting drugs.

too many *adj.* [mid-19C–1920s] (*US*) overwhelming.

too much *adj.* [abbr. SE *too much to take*] [late 19C+] (*orig. US*) **1** wonderful, excellent, the very best; sometimes ext. as *too fucking much*. **2** unpleasant, disgusting or overwhelming. **3** extreme, with an inference of absurd, ludicrous.

too much! *excl.* [TOO MUCH *adj.*] [1930s+] **1** an excl. of surprise or shock. **2** an excl. of pleasure, satisfaction, excitement.

too numerous to mention *phr.* [euph.] [late 19C] extremely and angrily drunk.

tooraladi *phr. see* TOOROO *phr.*

tooraloorals *n.* [SE *tooralooralay*, a popular, often ribald, song chorus] [late 19C–1900s] (*orig. theatre*) a woman's breasts, esp. as exposed by a notably decolleté dress.

too right! *excl.* (*also* **two eyes right**) [1910s+] (*orig. Aus.*) a general excl. of agreement.

tooroo *phr.* (*also* **tooraladi, too-a-roo,**) [TOODLE-OO *phr.*] [1910s+] (*Aus.*) goodbye.

toosh *n.* [TOCHES *n.* (1)] [1990s+] a girl, a woman.

tooshie *n.* [TOCHES *n.* (1)] [1930s+] (*US*) the buttocks.

tooshy *n. see* TUSH *n.*[2].

toot *n.*[1] [Scot. *tout*, to drink copiously, to take a large draught, thus ext. to drug use] **1** [late 18C] (*also* **tout**) a drinking match. **2** [late 18C+] (*also* **tout**) a drunken binge or spree, usu. in phr. *on a/the toot*, also in fig. use. **3** [late 18C+] a tea party. **4** [late 18C+] (*also* **tout**) a swallow of a drink, a drink. **5** [1970s+] cocaine. **6** [1970s+] a device for inhaling cocaine. **7** [1970s+] a measure of a narcotic, usu. cocaine, enough for a single inhalation; thus an inhalation.

(IN PHRASES)

❑ **toot up** *v.* [1930s] (*US*) to go on a drunken spree.

toot *n.*[2] [? rhy. sl. = LOOT *n.*[1] (2)] [late 19C–1960s] money.

toot *n.*[3] [? dial. *tut*, a small seat or TOOT *v.*[2]] [1960s+] **1** excrement. **2** (*Aus.*) a lavatory.

(IN PHRASES)

❑ **in the toot** *adv.* [1960s+] in trouble, facing problems.

toot *n.*[4] [Ital. *tutti*, Fr. *tout*, everything, all] [1970s+] (*S.Afr.*) the whole thing, the lot.

toot *n.*[5] [2000s] (*N.Z.*) the buttocks; the anus.

(IN PHRASES)

❑ **a root up the toot** *n.* [2000s] a kick in the behind; an act of sodomy.

toot *adj.* [? 'not worth a toot'] [1910s] insignificant, no good.

toot *v.*[1] [Fr. *tout suite*, immediately] [1910s–50s] (*Aus./US*) to hurry along.

toot *v.*[2] [the noise] [1940s+] to break wind.

SE in slang uses

(DERIVATIVES)

❑ **tootmobile** *n.* [the 'toot-toot' of its horn] [1960s–70s] (*US black*) a car.

(IN PHRASES)

❑ **toot the ringer** *v.* (*also* **toot the ding-dong**) [late 19C–1940s] (*US tramp*) to ring a doorbell.

toot *v.*[3] (*also* **toot up**) [TOOT *n.*[1] (7)] **1** [1950s–60s] to smoke marijuana. **2** [1970s+] (*orig. US drugs*) to inhale cocaine; occas. heroin.

tooted *adj.* [TOOT *n.*[1] (4)] [1960s] (*US campus*) drunk.

tooter *n.*[1] [the noise it makes when blown] [1910s] (*US*) the nose.

tooter *n.*[2] [TOOT *v.*[3] (2)] [2000s] (*UK drugs*) a thin tube of kitchen foil, used when smoking heroin.

tooth *n.*

SE in slang uses

(IN COMPOUNDS)

❑ **tooth booth** *n.* [1940s] (*US black*) a dentist's surgery. ❑ **tooth box** *n.* [1900s] (*Aus.*) the mouth. ❑ **tooth carpenter** *n.* [mid-19C–1940s] (*US*) a dentist. ❑ **tooth harp** *n.* [1960s] (*Aus.*) a mouth organ. ❑ **toothman** *n.* [1950s–60s] (*Aus.*) a hearty eater. ❑ **tooth music** *n.* [late 18C–early 19C] chewing.

(IN PHRASES)

❑ **have an aching tooth** *v.* [pun; note TOOTHACHE *n.*] **1** [16C] to desire, usu. sexually. **2** [mid-18C] to be angry with. ❑ **put a tooth in it** *v.* [one starts 'chewing' immediately] [1930s+] to come straight to the point; also in negative, *not put a tooth in it*. ❑ **put a tooth on it** *v.* [1940s] (*Aus.*) to refrain from criticism. ❑ **sweet tooth** *n. see under* SWEET *adj.*[1]. ❑ **toothless gibbon** *n.* [1990s+] the vagina.

toothache *n.* [euph.] [19C] an erection.

(IN PHRASES)

❑ **give someone a toothache** *v.* [pun on SE; but note sense above] [1990s+] to be 'sweet', e.g. *he said you gave him the toothache*.

toothful *n.* [Scot. *toothful*, to tipple] **1** [early 19C–1930s] a measure of alcohol, a dram. **2** [1910s] in fig. use.

(IN PHRASES)

❑ **do a toothful** *v.* [late 19C] (*Aus.*) to have a drink.

toothpick *n.* [note WW1 milit. *toothpick*, a bayonet; an entrenching tool] **1** [19C] (*also* **tooth picker**) a heavy club, a shillelagh, a watchman's stick. **2** [mid-19C+] (*orig. US*) a pocketknife. **3** [late 19C–1900s] a narrow, pointed boat. **4** [late 19C–1910s] (*US*) a long, narrow shoe. **5** [late 19C–1940s] (*US*) a native of Arkansas [generic use of *ARKANSAS TOOTHPICK under* ARKANSAS *adj.*]. **6** [1900s] (*UK Und.*) a house-breaker's short crowbar. **7** [1930–50s] (*US black*) a thin leg. **8** [1930s–60s] a derog. term for something small and insignificant. **9** [1960s+] (*US black*) a thin marijuana cigarette.

toothpicker *n.* [*CRUTCH-AND-TOOTHPICK BRIGADE under* CRUTCH *n.*[1]] [late 19C] a fashionable man about town and/or a man who hangs around theatre stage doors (to meet female performers), with a uniform of crutch-handled walking-stick and a *toothpick*.

toothy *adj.* [2000s] (*US*) smiling.

toothy-pegs *n.* (*also* **tooty**) [SE *tooth*] [early 19C+] (*usu. juv.*) the teeth.

tootie *n.* **1** *see* PATOOTIE *n.* (3). **2** *see* TOOTSIE *n.*

tooti-frooti *n.* (*also* **tootie fruitie**) [play on FRUIT *n.* (2) + lit. Ital. *tutti-frutti*, 'all the fruits', a type of ice-cream filled with chopped preserved fruits, nuts etc] [1960s+] (*US black*) a homosexual man.

tooting *n.* [? abbr. ROOTING-TOOTING *adj.*] [1980s] (*US black*) the trade of prostitution.

tooting *adj.* [SE *toot*, to make a noise (of e.g. a siren or horn). The image is the intensity of one's statement having a 'noisy' impact] [1910s+] (*orig. US/US black*) **1** a general intensifier, usu. in combs., e.g. *darn/durn tooting, plumb tooting, too damn tooting*. **2** correct.

(IN PHRASES)

❑ **you're darn tootin'** (*also* **darn tootin', you're damn tootin', you're durn tootin'**) [abbr. *you're darn tootin' right*] [1930s+] (*orig. US*) you're absolutely right.

Tooting (Bec) *n.* [rhy. sl; ult. *Tooting Bec* (a London suburb)] [20C+] **1** a light kiss [= SE *peck*]. **2** food [= PECK *n.*[1] (1)].

tooting-ken *n. see* TOUTING-KEN *n.*

tooting stomps *n.* [SE *toot* + STOMP *n.* (2)] [1940s] (*US black*) a fashionable style of shoe.

tootle *n.* [SE *tootle*, to blow a wind instrument (thus punning on BLOW *v.*[2] (1))] [1990s+] the penis, thus fig. a male homosexual.

(IN COMPOUNDS)

❑ **tootle-merchant** *n.* [MERCHANT *n.*] [1990s+] a male homosexual.

tootle *v.*[1] [TODDLE *v.*] [late 19C+] to walk, to wander casually or aimlessly.

tootle *v.*[2] [TOOTLE *n.*] [1990s+] to fellate, usu. in a homosexual context.

tootledum-pattick *n.* [Cornish dial.] [19C] a fool.

tootle-oo *phr. see* TOODLE-OO *phr.*

tootle-pip *phr. see* TOODLE-PIP *phr.*

tootling stick *n.* [SE *tootle* + STICK *n.* (1a)/ play on FLUTE *n.*[1] (2)] [1990s+] the penis.

too-too *adj.* (*also* **tutu**) [redup. of SE *too*, which emphasizes the adj.] [late 19C+] a general term of approval, usu. regarded as somewhat affected.

toots *n.* (*also* **tots**) [abbr. TOOTSIE *n.* (2)] **1** [1910s+] a general form of address, usu. to a woman. **2** [1930s–40s] a girl or girlfriend.

tootsie *n.* (*also* **toots(e)y-woots(e)y, tootsie-wootsie, tootie**) [development of baby talk] (*orig. US*) **1** [mid-19C+] a playful or affectionate name for a foot, usu. a child's foot; thus also toes; mostly in pl. [created from baby-talk]. **2** [late 19C+] (*also* **tootsie doll**) an affectionate name, usu. for a woman or girl, occas. a male lover. **3** [1910s] a baby. **4** [1960s+] (*Aus.*) a lesbian.

Tootsie Roll *n.* [brandname of a small chocolate cake + ref. to JELLY ROLL *n.*] **1** [1920s] (*US*) the penis. **2** in drug uses. (**a**) [1960s+] a marijuana cigarette [play on SE *roll*]. (**b**) [1970s+] Mexican heroin [the consistency and colour of Mexican heroin and *CHOCOLATE (STUFF) under* CHOCOLATE *adj.*]. (**c**) [1970s+] methadone [the image is of 'fake' heroin of no more worth to an addict than a *Tootsie Roll*]. (**d**) [2000s] opium. **3** [1970s+] (*US black*) an attractive woman. **4** [1990s+] (*US black teen*) a dance in which the knees are moved inwards and outwards, supposedly showing off one's buttocks [? TOCHES *n.* (1) + SE *roll*].

tooty *n. see* TOOTHY-PEGS *n.*

tooty fruity *adj.* [TOOTI-FROOTI *n.*] [1970s] (*US black*) effeminate, poss. homosexual.

too utterly too *adj.* [TOO-TOO *adj.*] [late 19C] a general term of approval, usu. regarded as somewhat affected.

top *n.* **1** [mid-19C] a dying speech on the gallows. **2** [1930s+] (*US black*) the head; as phr. *on top*, intelligence. **3** [1950s+] (*US Und.*) a maximum prison sentence. **4** [1970s+] in a sado-masochistic relationship, the dominant partner [as opposed to a BOTTOM *n.*[3]]. **5** [1980s+] (*US drugs*) a vial of crack cocaine [different varieties are indicated by the variously coloured plastic tops of the vial].

IN PHRASES

❑ **slip one's top** *v.* [SE *top*, i.e. the head/brain] [1960s] (*US*) to go mad.

SE in slang uses

IN COMPOUNDS

❑ **top-heavy** *adj.* [mid-17C–1910s] drunk. ❑ **topknot** *n.* (*also* **topknob**) [SE *topknot*, a tuft of hair or ribbon on top of the head] [early 19C–1950s] the head; the scalp.

IN PHRASES

❑ **deal one off the top** *v. see* DEAL *v.* ❑ **go on the top** *v.* [early 18C] (*UK Und.*) to break into houses using entry via an upper window. ❑ **go over the top** *v.* [WW1 imagery; the 'top' was that of a trench] [1920s+] to do something dangerous or remarkable, esp. to get over excited or angry. ❑ **go upon the top** *v.* [18C] (*UK Und.*) for one thief to jump onto a partner's shoulders to climb through a window. ❑ **knock the top off** *v.* (*also* **knock the head off**) [1980s+] (*Aus. prison*) to masturbate. ❑ **little bit off the top** *adj.* [pun on hairdressing use] [1910s+] (*Aus.*) slightly insane. ❑ **off the top** *adv.* **1** [20C+] taken first, esp. when sharing out money, legally or otherwise, e.g. expenses come *off the top*. **2** [1990s+] (*US*) from the beginning, immediately [musical imagery, one reads a score from the top]. ❑ **over the top** *adj.* **1** [1960s+] beyond the usual bounds of taste, behaviour, credibility etc. **2** [1980s+] very drunk. ❑ **top of the bill** *n.* (*also* **top of the pork barrel, top of the pot**) [theatrical/culinary imagery] [20C+] the best, the ultimate. ❑ **top of the house** *n.* (*also* **top of the shop**) [the highest numbers on a card] [20C+] (*bingo*) the number 99 or 100. ❑ **top of the joint/score** *n. see* JOINT *n.* (4c). ❑ **top of the tree** *adj.* [late 18C+] upper-class, superior, aristocratic. ❑ **top-storey worker** *n.* [SE *top storey* + SE *worker*/WORKER *n.*[1] (1)] [1930s–40s] (*UK Und.*) a cat burglar.

top *adj.* **1** [1920s+] excellent, first-rate. **2** [1960s] extreme.

SE in slang uses

IN COMPOUNDS

❑ **top...** *n. see also under* relevant n. ❑ **top ballocks** *n.* (*also* **top bollocks, top buttocks**) [BALLOCKS *n.* (2) / SE *buttocks*] **1** [late 19C+] a woman's breasts. **2** [2000s] the best or most popular of it's kind [+ var. on DOG'S BALLOCKS *n.*]. ❑ **top banana** *n.* [show business *top banana*, the leading comic in a burlesque show] [1950s+] (*orig. US*) the chief, the boss, the president. ❑ **top brass** *n.* [BRASS *n.*[1] (3a)] **1** [1940s+] (*orig. US*) in the services or the police, the most senior officers. **2** [1950s+] (*orig. US*) in business or industry, the highest executive manager. **3** [1960s+] a leader, chief, someone or something of importance. ❑ **top cat** *n.* [1950s+] (*orig. US black*) the leader of a group, esp. of a clique of down-and-outs. ❑ **top deck** *n.* [1920s+] (*Aus.*) the head. ❑ **top diver** *n.* [SE *dive on top (of)*] **1** [late 17C–early 19C] a lecher, a womanizer. **2** [1970s+] (*US gay*) a lesbian. ❑ **top dog** *n.* (*also* **topdog**) [20C+] a dominant figure; usu. in an institution – the boss, a senior member of an organization, a leader. ❑ **top drawing-room** *n.* [late 19C–1900s] a garret. ❑ **top dressing** *n.* **1** [19C] the hair. **2** [2000s] (*N.Z.*) deception. ❑ **top end** *n.* **1** [late 19C] the head. **2** [1910s+] (*Aus.*) (*also* **top, top half**) northern Australia; thus *top-ender*, *topsider*, one who lives there. ❑ **top flat** *n.* [late 19C; 1940s] the head. ❑ **top floor** *n. see* separate entry. ❑ **top hamper** *n.* [1900s] (*US*) the head, the brain. ❑ **top hat** *n.* [? their 19C attire] [1930s] (*UK Und.*) a detective. ❑ **top-hole** *adj. see* separate entry. ❑ **top kick** *n.* (*also* **top kicker**) [US army jargon *top kick*, a first sergeant] [1910s–40s] (*orig. US*) the boss, the head of a group, whether legal or criminal ❑ **top man** *n.* **1** [late 18C+] a leading villain. **2** [late 19C+] a police superintendent. **3** [1930s+] the dominant partner in a homosexual (sado-masochistic) couple. **4** *see under* TOP *v.*[3]. ❑ **topnobber** *n.* [SE *top* + NOB *n.*[2] (1)] [1900s–20s] (*Anglo-Irish*) an important person. ❑ **top piece** *n.* **1** [mid-19C–1920s] a hat. **2** [mid-19C+] (*also* **top storey**) the head, the brain. ❑ **top-ropes** *adv.* [1990s+] (*Aus.*) stylishly. ❑ **top sawyer** *n. see* separate entry. ❑ **top sergeant** *n.* ['she takes command of the girls' privates'] [1940s–70s] (*gay*) a masculine lesbian. ❑ **top set** *n.* [1970s+] a woman's breasts. ❑ **top-shackled** *adj.* [early 17C] drunk, fuddled, confused in the head. ❑ **top shelf(er)** *see* separate entries. ❑ **top side(r)** *see* separate entries. ❑ **top storey** *n. see TOP PIECE* above. ❑ **top thatch** *n. see* THATCH *n.* (1). ❑ **top 'uns** *n.* [1940s–50s] a woman's breasts. ❑ **top whack** *see* separate entries. ❑ **top woman** *n.* [1940s+] a senior or most favoured prostitute among a group working for a given pimp.

IN PHRASES

❑ **carry on top-ropes** *v. see* SWAY AWAY ON ALL TOP ROPES *v.* ❑ **off one's top traverse** *adj.* [20C+] (*Aus.*) mad, eccentric. ❑ **on top** [1970s+] discovered, unmasked, found out; usu. as *come on top*. ❑ **sway away on all top ropes** *v. see* separate entry.

top *v.*[1] [i.e. one places oneself 'on top' of the other person] **1** [17C; 1920s+] to have sexual intercourse with. **2** [mid-17C] to oppose. **3** [late 17C–mid-18C] to impose upon, to intrude. **4** [late 17C–early 19C] to insult. **5** [2000s] (*gay*) to take the role of the dominant or sadistic partner; thus *topped*, subjected to sadistic sex. **6** [2000s] (*UK teen*) of a boy, to caress a girl's breasts.

SE in slang uses

IN PHRASES

❑ **top...** *v. see also under* relevant n. ❑ **top off** *v. see KNOCK THE TOP OFF under* TOP *n.* ❑ **top out** *v.* [building trade jargon *top out*, to finish off a high building, to construct the very top floor] [1950s+] to reach a limit. ❑ **top the house** *v.* [HOUSE *n.*[1] (1)] [1930s] (*US Und.*) of a brothel prostitute, to make the most money during a given evening or night. ❑ **top up** *v.* [to place a fig. *top* on] [mid-19C+] to end up, to conclude.

top *v.*[2] [SE *top*, the required card is made to appear at the top of the deck] [mid-17C–early 19C] (*UK Und.*) to cheat, esp. at dice or cards.

IN PHRASES

❑ **top the deck** *v.* [late 19C] to use a mechanical device hidden beneath one's cuff to hold a card until it is required, when it is slipped surreptitiously onto the deck.

top *v.*^{3} **1** [mid-17C+] to execute by hanging, thus as excl. *top me!* **2** [late 19C+] to kill, to murder. **3** [1910s] as an excl. or mild oath.

IN COMPOUNDS

❑ **topman** *n.* [early 17C] a hangman. ❑ **topsman** *n.* [18C–mid-19C] a hangman.

IN PHRASES

❑ **top oneself** *v.* [1930s+] to commit suicide.

topanaris *n.* [? SE *top* + *nara*, i.e. another (person)] [1980s+] (*W.I.*) an excellent person; an upper-class person.

toper *n.* [Rom. *tober*, the road] [mid–late 19C] the road.

top floor *n.*

SE in slang uses

IN PHRASES

❑ **have a vacancy on the top floor** *v.* [1970s+] (*US*) to be stupid, i.e. 'not all there'.

top gun *n.* [rhy. sl. = TON *n.*^{1} (2)] [1990s+] £100.

top hat *n.* [rhy. sl.] [20C+] **1** a fool [= PRAT *n.*^{1} (6)]. **2** a cat. **3** a rat (the rodent). **4** a chat.

topher *adj.* [2000s] (*US black*) unable to achieve an erection, impotent.

top-hole *adj.* [synon. with SE *top notch*, i.e. the *top hole* in any measure] [20C+] excellent, first-rate, the best.

DERIVATIVES

❑ **top-holer** *n.* [20C+] an excellent person or object.

IN EXCLAMATIONS

❑ **top-hole!** [20C+] excellent! wonderful! perfect!

topi *n.* (*also* **tops**) [? the top of the peyote cactus] [1960s+] (*drugs*) **1** peyote. **2** mescaline.

topital *adj.* [1990s+] (*US teen*) excellent, first-rate.

top joint *n.* [rhy. sl.; *joint* pron. *jint*] [mid-19C] a pint (590ml) of beer.

toplights *n.* [18C–19C] the eyes.

IN EXCLAMATIONS

❑ **douse my toplights!** a mild oath, synon. for DAMN ONE'S EYES! *under* DAMN! *excl.*

top-loft *n. see* ATTIC *n.* (1).

top-loftical *adj.* [SE *top* + *lofty*] [19C–1920s] haughty, arrogant.

top-lofty *adj.* [SE *top* + *lofty*] [mid-19C–1930s] haughty, arrogant.

top-off *n.* (*also* **top-off man, top-off merchant**) [TOP (OFF) *v.*] [1930s+] (*Aus.*) an informer.

top (off) *v.* (*also* **top on**) [? TIP OFF *v.*^{2} (2) or fig. use of TOP OFF *v.*] [1930s+] (*Aus./N.Z.*) to inform against.

top off *v.* **1** [mid-19C+] to finish off, to put the finishing touch to. **2** [1910s] (*Aus.*) to kill. **3** [1910s] (*Aus.*) (*also* **top on, top up**) to beat up. **4** [1930s] (*US Und*) to cheat at a dice game. **5** [1930s+] to fill up, to complete a cargo. **6** [1940s+] to fill up a petrol tank.

top-off man/merchant *n. see* TOP-OFF *n.*

top of Rome *n.* (*also* **top o' Rome**) [rhy. sl.] [mid-19C–1920s] home.

top on *v. see* TOP OFF *v.* (3).

top o' reeb *n.* [backsl.] [mid–late 19C] a pot of beer.

top o' Rome *n. see* TOP OF ROME *n.*

topped *adj.* [TOP *v.*^{3}] **1** [early 18C+] hanged. **2** [late 19C+] killed, murdered.

topped up *adj.* **1** [1960s+] drunk. **2** *see* TOP OFF *v.* (3).

topper *n.*^{1} **1** [late 17C+] an outstanding person or thing of its kind. **2** [18C] the boss, the master. **3** [mid-19C–1900s] in context of smoking, the 'top' of a cigar, cigarette or pipe. **4** [mid-19C+] the final word in an argument. (**a**) the stub of a cigar or cigarette. (**b**) the remains of burnt tobacco left in a pipe; thus *topper-hunter*, one who scavenges for cigar or cigarette stubs. **5** [late 19C] as *my topper*, a term of affectionate address. **6** [late 19C] in pl. with *the*, the upper classes. **7** [1910s] (*US milit.*) the top sergeant. **8** [1930s+] a supposedly (but prob. not very) funny story or joke; a punchline [it 'tops' or surpasses all others]. **9** [1950s+] the last in a series, the 'last straw'.

topper *n.*^{2} [late 18C–19C] a blow to the head, either with a fist or a weapon.

topper *n.*^{3} **1** [19C] (*UK Und.*) a hat (but not a 'top hat'). **2** [early 19C+] a top hat. **3** [late 19C–1900s] a tall, thin person. **4** [late 19C–1950s] (*usu. US*) a loosely cut jacket or coat, generally worn by women and children.

topper *n.*^{4} [TOP *v.*^{3}] **1** [1920s–30s] a hangman. **2** [1940s+] (*UK/US prison*) someone who has attempted suicide.

topper *n.*^{5} [1940s–50s] (*UK Und.*) a man who acts as a lookout man or a diversion for a DROPPER *n.*^{1} (1).

topper *n.*^{6} [TOP (OFF) *v.*] [1940s+] (*Aus./N.Z.*) an informer.

topper *v.* [TOPPER *n.*^{2}] [19C] to kill with a blow on the head.

topper-off *n.* [TOP (OFF) *v.*] [1950s] (*Aus. prison*) an informer.

topper-toodle *n.* [mid-19C] (*UK Und.*) a gullible fool, esp. as prey to crooked gamblers.

toppie *n.* [? Zulu *thopi*, growing sparsely (e.g. of hair) or Hind. *topi*, a hat] [1960s+] **1** (*S.Afr.*) an old person of either sex. **2** a father.

topping *n.*^{1} [late 17C–early 18C] (*UK gambling*) a form of cheating with dice.

topping *n.*^{2} [TOP *v.*^{3}] **1** [late 18C+] execution by hanging. **2** [1990s+] suicide.

IN COMPOUNDS

❑ **topping cheat** *n.* [CHEAT *n.* (1); lit. 'hanging thing'] [late 17C–mid-19C] (*UK Und.*) the gallows. ❑ **topping cove** *n.* [COVE *n.* (1)] [mid-17C–mid-19C] (*UK Und.*) a hangman. ❑ **topping fellow** *n.* [pun on SE *topping fellow*, an admirable man; Partridge implies that the inclusion of the term in B.E. and Grose is in fact a heavy-handed pun; but neither author, both of whom define *topping cove* as a hangman, and *topping fellow* as an expert or pre-eminent individual, appear to be joking] [mid-17C–mid-19C] a hangman. ❑ **topping shed** *n.* [mid-19C–1950s] that part of a prison in which the gallows is kept.

topping *adj.* [SE *top*, 20C+ use is either ironic or consciously archaic] [late 16C+] excellent, enjoyable, first-rate; occas. as adv.

topping man *n.* [TOPPING *adj.* + SE *man*] [late 18C–early 19C] a superior, rich man.

toppings *n.* [1920s+] (*US tramp*) something sweet, esp. old cakes.

topping school *n.* [TOP *v.*^{1} (1)] [mid-17C–early 18C] a brothel.

toppy *adj.* **1** [20C+] excessive. **2** [1900s] (*US*) upper-class.

top-row *adj.* [late 19C] aristocratic, socially superior.

top-row *adv.* [late 19C] in a superior position; successfully.

top-rung *adj. see* TOP-SHELF *adj.* (2).

tops *n.*^{1} [TOP *n.* (1)] [mid–late 19C] pamphlets and broadsheets that purport to detail last words from the gallows, deathbed confessions etc.

tops *n.*^{2} [the predicted side rolls to the *top*] [1920s+] (*gambling*) doctored dice used for cheating purposes.

IN COMPOUNDS

❑ **tops and bottoms** *n.* [1930s+] **1** a roll of notes in which only those on the very top and bottom are genuine, the rest being paper trimmed to fit and to bulk out the roll; also of precious stones. **2** (*US gambling*) crooked dice.

tops *n.*^{3} **1** [1930s] (*US black*) as an admiring form of address. **2** [1930s+] (*orig. US*) the best, the ultimate, the winner.

tops *n.*^{4} *see* TOPI *n.*

tops *adj.* [TOPS *n.*^{3} (2)] [1940s+] excellent.

tops *adv.* [SE *at a top estimate*] [1930s+] at the most, at the top estimate, e.g. *five years tops, ten quid tops.*

top sawyer *n.* [timber trade: 'It is a piece of Norfolk slang and took its rise from Norfolk being a great timber country, where the top sawyers get double the wages of those beneath them' (Egan's Grose)] [early 19C–1910s] **1** the leader in any profession, job, occupation. **2** the best of its kind.

IN PHRASES

□ **play at top sawyer** *v.* [late 19C–1900s] to have sexual intercourse.

top shelf *n.* [as stored in a bar] [1950s+] (*Aus./N.Z.*) spirits.

top-shelf *adj.* **1** [late 19C] upper-class. **2** [20C+] (*also* **top-rung**) excellent, first-class, the best public service; as *adv.*, top quality. **3** [20C+] usu. of magazines, pornographic [euph.; the positioning of such material in a newsagent's].

top-shelfer *n.* [TOP-SHELF *adj.*] [late 19C] an upper-class person.

top shot *n. see* BIG SHOT *n.*

topside *adj.* [? pidgin use] [mid–late 19C] in charge, in control.

topsider *n.* [? TOPSIDE *adj.*; the image is that such a dog controls the master rather than vice versa] [1910s+] (*Aus.*) a lazy dog.

topsy boozy *adj.* [TOPSY FRIZY *adj.* + BOOZY *adj.* (1)] [late 19C] tipsy, half-drunk.

topsy frizy *adj.* [one's *top* is SE *frizy*, curled] [late 18C–19C] tipsy, drunk.

topsy-versy *adv.* [SE *topsy-turvy* + ARSEY-VARSEY *phr.* (1)] [mid-18C–1910s] upside down.

top tens *n.* [rhy. sl.; *top ten hit* = TIT *n.*[2] (1)] [2000s] (*Irish*) the breasts.

top up *v. see* TOP OFF *v.* (3).

to put it mildly *v.* [1910s+] to downplay one's feelings, usu. ironic, i.e. to put it very strongly.

top whack *n.* [TOP WHACK *adv.*] [1970s+] the highest price or rate possible.

top whack *adv.* (*also* **top wack**) [WHACK *n.*[1] (1)] [1950s+] at the most.

top-yob *n.* [backsl.] [mid-19C] a pot-boy.

t.o.q. *n.* [tatty/tired old queen] [2000s] (*S.Afr. gay*) an old but still lecherous homosexual.

to raas *phr.* [1980s] (*W.I.*) a general intensifier, absolutely, to the utmost extent, 'to a T'.

torah *n. see* BIBLE *n.* (3a).

torbo *n.* [abbr. tradenames *Torbutrol* and *Torbugesic*] [2000s] (*US drugs*) butorphanol.

torch *n.* **1** [1900s] (*US*) a large cigar. **2** [1920s+] (*orig. US*) an arsonist. **3** [1920s+] (*orig. US*) an act of arson. **4** [1920s+] (*orig. US*) in fig. combs. (see below), referring to lost or unrequired love [the 'light of love' is still burning, even if it is unreciprocated]. **5** [1930s–60s] (*US tramp*) a revolver, a pistol. **6** [1960s–70s] (*US black*) an oversized cigarette lighter. **7** [1960s+] (*US prison*) the murder of a fellow inmate by tossing a Molotov cocktail or petrol bomb into the cell. **8** [1970s+] (*drugs*) a marijuana cigarette. **9** [1980s+] (*drugs*) a butane lighter used to ignite a crack cocaine pipe; thus *torch cooking*, using such a lighter and pipe.

IN COMPOUNDS

□ **torch job** *n.* [JOB *n.*[2] (1a)] [1930s+] (*US*) an act of arson. □ **torch man** *n.* [1940s] (*US Und.*) an expert in the use of an oxy-acetylene torch. □ **torch song** *n.* (*also* **torch ballad**) [1920s+] a song that focuses on unrequited or lost love, thus a singer of such songs, a *torch singer*.

IN PHRASES

□ **carry a torch** *v.* (*also* **...the torch**) [1930s+] (*orig. US*) to mourn a dead love affair, to feel love without its being returned; thus *torch-carrier*, one who is suffering such pain. □ **torch (for)** *v.* **1** [1930s+] (*orig. US*) to mourn a dead love-affair; to offer unrequited love. **2** [1960s+] to lust after.

torch *v.* **1** [1930s+] (*orig. US*) to commit arson; to set on fire. **2** [1980s+] to light a cigarette. **3** [1990s+] (*US prison*) to throw a Molotov cocktail into an inmate's cell.

IN PHRASES

□ **torch up** *v.* **1** [1910s–20s] (*US*) to get drunk. **2** [1950s+] (*drugs*) to light a cannabis cigarette or pipe; thus to smoke marijuana. **3** [1990s+] to light a cigarette.

torch-cul *n.* (*also* **torchecul**) [synon. Fr. sl. *torchecul*, lit. 'give one's arse a quick smack'] [mid-17C–early 19C] lavatory paper.

torched *adj.* [TORCH v. (1)] [1960s+] (*US*) submitted to an arson attack, burned out.

torcher *n.* [1940s+] (*US*) a 'torch' singer, a singer of maudlin, romantic songs.

torchy *n.* [TORCH v. (1)] [1930s–70s] (*US Und.*) a professional, criminal arsonist.

torchy *adj.* [*TORCH (FOR) under* TORCH *n.*] [1930s+] (*US*) suffering unrequited love; thus painful emotionally.

torcida, la *n.* [Sp.] [1980s+] (*US teen gang*) prison.

tore down *adj.* (*also* **tore, torn down**) **1** [1940s+] (*US black*) depressed, miserable [DOWN *adj.*[2] (1)]. **2** [1940s+] (*US black*) unattractive, ugly. **3** [1950s+] (*drugs*) (*also* **tore back**) drunk or intoxicated by a drug.

tore out of the frame *phr.* **1** [1970s+] (*US campus*) drunk. **2** [1980s] (*US campus*) shocked.

tore up *adj.* (*also* **all tore up, all torn up, torn up**) [TEAR UP v. (6)] **1** [late 19C; 1950s+] (*US black/campus*) miserable, depressed. **2** [1950s] physically exhausted, very tired. **3** [1950s+] (*US black/campus*) drunk or intoxicated by a drug. **4** [1970s] physically beaten. **5** [1990s+] broken, wrecked, in a mess. **6** [2000s] ugly. **7** [2000s] overwhelmed, e.g. by a performance.

to rights *adv.* [legal jargon *to be to rights*, to have a legal case against someone; note Bartlett, *Dict. of Americanisms* (1848), 'to rights, directly; soon'] **1** [early 19C–1900s] first-rate, excellent; also as excl. of approval. **2** [mid-19C+] completely. **3** [mid-19C+] as required/desired.

IN PHRASES

□ **do to rights** *v.* [late 19C] to perform satisfactorily, to do properly. □ **have to rights** *v.* [mid-19C+] to settle with, to get even with, to conquer.

tormented *adj.* [19C–1930s] (*US*) a mild synon. for DAMNED *adj.*

tormentor *n.* **1** [early 19C] a large meat fork. **2** [19C–1900s] a water-squirter. **3** [late 19C–1910s] a back-scratcher.

tormentor of catgut *n.* [late 18C–early 19C] a fiddle player, a violinist.

tormentor of sheepskin *n.* [early 19C] a drummer.

tormentors *n.* [mid–late 19C] riding spurs.

torn down *adj. see* TORE DOWN *adj.*

torn up *adj. see* TORE UP *adj.*

torp *n. see* *TORPEDO JUICE under* TORPEDO *n.*[2].

torpedo *n.*[1] [mid-19C] (*UK Und.*) a Bow Street runner.

torpedo *n.*[2] **1** it's shape. (**a**) [1910s] (*US*) a pointed woman's shoe. (**b**) [1940s] a fat marijuana cigarette. (**c**) [1960s] (*US teen*) a large breast. (**d**) [1980s+] (*drugs*) a cigarette made of crack cocaine and marijuana. (**e**) [1980s] (*US*) a large, well-filled sandwich. (**f**) [1990s+] (*US teen*) a penis that is wide at the base but grows narrower as it reaches the head. **2** its 'explosiveness'. (**a**) [1920s+] (*US*) a thug, a hoodlum, the 'weapon' used by a gang boss and sent out to destroy enemies. (**b**) [1930s–60s] a drink containing chloral hydrate.

IN COMPOUNDS

□ **torpedo juice** *n.* (*also* **torp**) ['a combination of bush beer and toddy and acquires its name from its lethal effect. The original torpedo juice was the neat alcohol extracted from torpedoes during the war by American servicemen and sometimes mixed with local bush beers' (*The Guardian*, 26 September 1961)] [1940s+] (*orig. milit.*) extremely strong, home-distilled liquor.

torpedo *v.*[1] [TORPEDO *n.*[2] (2b)] **1** [1930s–60s] to drug with chloral. **2** [1940s] to make drunk.

torpedo *v.*[2] [1960s] (*Aus.*) of a man, to have sexual intercourse.

torque *v.* [1980s] **1** (*US campus*) to try to seduce someone. **2** to annoy, to 'wind up'.

torqued *adj.* **1** [1960s+] (*US*) angry. **2** [1980s+] (*US campus*) drunk, intoxicated by a drug.

torrac *n.* [backsl.] [mid–late 19C] **1** a carrot. **2** the penis; thus a phr. of dismissal *ekat a torrac*, take a carrot (presumably + *and shove it…*).

torrid *adj.* [late 18C–1900s] drunk.

torril *n.* [dial.] [19C] a general insult referring to a woman or a horse.

torso-tosser *n.* [1920s–50s] an erotic dancer.

Tortoise Town *n.* [? its slow pace in comparison to Sydney] [1900s] (*Aus.*) Adelaide.

tory rory *n.* [*Tory*, a late 17C nickname for one opposed to the exclusion of James, Duke of York (a Roman Catholic) from the succession to the British crown + proper name *Rory*] [mid-18C–mid-19C] one who wears their hat cocked distinctly to one side.

tory-rory *adv.* [TORY RORY *n.*] [late 18C] lop-sided, all over the place.

tosh *n.*[1] [Fr. *poche*, a pocket] [19C] (*UK Und.*) a pocket.

tosh *n.*[2] [backsl.] [late 19C–1900s] a hat.

tosh *n.*[3] [? BOSH *n.*[1] or dial. *toshy*, muddy; Puxley, *Fresh Rabbit: A Dick 'n' Arry of Rhyming Slang* (1998), suggests a link to the items scavenged by a TOSHER *n.* (1)] [late 19C+] (*orig. Oxford Univ.*) nonsense, rubbish.

tosh *n.*[4] [abbr. SE *mackintosh*] [1900s] (*Aus.*) a raincoat.

tosh *n.*[5] [? Scot. *tosh*, smart, neat or dial. *toshy*, of masculine appearance, hairy-faced] [1940s+] a form of familiar address to someone whose name one does not know.

tosh *n.*[6] *see* TOSHEROON *n.*

tosh! *excl.* [TOSH *n.*[3]] [1910s] rubbish! nonsense!

toshed-out *adj.* [1970s] (*N.Z.*) exhausted.

tosher *n.* [dial. *toshy*, muddy] **1** [mid-19C] one who scavenges copper from ships' bottoms, items from the Thames mud, the sewers, etc. **2** [1970s+] a painter and decorator.

tosheroon *n.* (*also* **tosh, tosher, tush, tusheroon, tusseroon**) [? mispron. of Polari *MADZA CAROON under* MADZA *n.*; Hotten (1859) claims definition of 'a crown', which appears to be a misreading] [mid-19C–1980s] (*orig. Ling. Fr./Polari*) half-a-crown, 2s 6d (12½p).

IN PHRASES

❑ **half-a-tosheroon** *n.* (*also* **half-a-tusheroon**) [*see* comment in ety. above about Hotten misreading *tosheroon* and thus creating this meaning] [mid–late 19C] half-a-crown, 2s 6d (12½p).

toshy *adj.* [TOSH *n.*[3]] [1900s] trashy, rubbishy.

toss *n.*[1] [TOSS (OFF) *v.*] **1** [late 19C+] in fig. use, something of infinitesimal or zero importance; usu. in phr. *not give a toss*. **2** [1940s+] nonsense. **3** *see* TOSS-OFF *n.* (1).

IN PHRASES

❑ **give a toss** *v.* (*also* **care a toss**) [1990s+] (*orig. US*) to care, usu. in negative use, e.g. *who gives a toss*.

toss *n.*[2] [TOSS *v.* (7)] [1950s+] (*orig. US prison*) a search, esp. one carried out by police.

toss *n.*[3]

IN PHRASES

❑ **give someone the toss** *v.* [1900s] to dismiss, usu. from a job. ❑ **toss in the hay** *n. see* ROLL IN THE HAY *n.*

toss *n.*[4] *see* TOSSER *n.*[1] (4).

toss *n.*[5] *see* TOSS-UP *n.* (1).

toss *v.* [SE *toss*, to throw] **1** [1920s] (*US Und.*) to desert a partner, sexual or professional. **2** [1920s; 2000s] (*US black*) to beat up. **3** [1940s] to overcome. **4** [1950s] (*Aus.*) to criticize harshly, to assault verbally. **5** [1950s+] (*US campus*) to vomit. **6** [1950s+] to throw out. **7** [1950s+] (*orig. US prison*) to search an apartment, car or person, esp. for weapons etc. **8** [1980s] (*US*) to bribe. **9** [1980s] to take money from. **10** [1990s+] (*US*) to expose someone as a homosexual against their will.

IN PHRASES

❑ **toss a reverse lunch** *v.* [the regurgitation of food] [1970s+] (*N.Z.*) to vomit.

SE in slang uses

IN PHRASES

❑ **toss…** *v. see also under* relevant n. ❑ **toss in one's agate** *v.* [SE *agate*, a type of marble] [1900s] (*Aus.*) to die; lit. or fig. ❑ **toss in one's jock** *v.* (*also* **…the jock**) [1950s+] (*US*) to give up, to quit. ❑ **toss in the alley** *v.* [1960s] (*Aus.*) to die. ❑ **toss (it) in** *v.* [1940s–60s] (*Aus./N.Z./US*) to give up, to finish. ❑ **toss it to** *v.* [1960s+] (*US*) of a man, to have sexual intercourse. ❑ **toss it up airy** *v.* [1920s] to put on airs. ❑ **toss one's lollies** *v.* (*also* **chuck…, lose…**) [N.Z. *lolly*, any form of sweet] [1980s+] (*N.Z.*) to vomit. ❑ **toss someone across** *v.* (*also* **…around**) [1910s–30s] (*US*) to deceive, to cheat. ❑ **toss (someone) around** *v.* [1930s] (*US Und.*) to mistreat, to swindle.

toss-bottle *n. see* TOSSPOT *n.*

tossed salad *n. see under* SALAD *n.*

tossel *n.* (*also* **tossle**) [? SE *tassel*] [1980s+] (*Aus.*) a penis, usu. a child's penis.

tosser *n.*[1] [TOSS (OFF) *v.*] **1** [late 19C] a (large) penis. **2** [late 19C+] (*Aus.*) an affectionate term of address. **3** [1970s+] a masturbator [the chronology of sense 2 suggests a much earlier if uncited use]. **4** [1970s+] (*also* **toss**) a despicable, worthless person [the chronology of sense 2 suggests a much earlier if uncited use].

tosser *n.*[2] [SE *toss*, to throw] **1** [1900s–50s] (*also* **tosseroon**) any coin, esp. a sovereign. **2** [1930s+] (*Irish*) a low-value coin.

tosser *adj.* [TOSSER *n.*[1] (3)] [2000s] of a person, despicable, second-rate, unimportant.

tosser sign *n.* [TOSSER *n.*[1] (3)] [1990s+] a coarse gesture whereby the hand is moved up and down, imitating the action of masturbation.

tossicate *v.* [SE *intoxication* + *toss*] [20C+] (*Ulster*) to disturb, to worry.

tossing *adj.* [TOSS (OFF) *v.*] [1930s+] useless, worthless, euph. for FUCKING *adj.*

tossle *n. see* TOSSEL *n.*

toss-off *n.* [TOSS (OFF) *v.*] **1** [mid-18C+] (*also* **toss**) an act of masturbation. **2** [20C+] a worthless, unpleasant person.

toss (off) *v.* **1** [mid-17C; mid-18C+] to masturbate; often as *toss oneself off*. **2** [mid-19C+] to get rid of, to discard. **3** [1910s+] to give up, to abandon (a task), to lose.

IN COMPOUNDS

❑ **toss-arse** *n.* [1990s+] (*UK juv.*) a habitual masturbator. ❑ **toss-bag** *n.* (*also* **toss-bags**) [1990s+] an unpleasant, worthless person. ❑ **toss parlour** *n.* [1990s+] a brothel. ❑ **toss-rag** *n.* [1950s] a piece of tissue that has been or will be used to wipe the penis after masturbation.

toss off! *excl.* [TOSS (OFF) *v.*] [1980s+] euph. for FUCK OFF! *excl.*

tossout *n.*[1] [1930s] (*US Und.*) a beggar who specializes in throwing their limbs out of joint in order to excite pity.

tossout *n.*[2] [TOSS OUT *v.*] [1940s] (*US drugs*) an addict who feigns fits.

toss out *v.* [1930s–70s] (*US drugs*) of a drug addict, to fake a fit.

tosspot *n.* (*also* **toss-bottle**) [TOSS (OFF) *v.* but note earlier SE *tosspot*, a drunkard] [1940s+] a fool.

tossprick *n.* [TOSS (OFF) *v.* + PRICK *n.* (1)] [20C+] a general term of abuse.

toss-up *n.* **1** [late 18C+] (*also* **toss**) a wager (esp. fig.) in which chances are even and either eventuality is equally likely [SE *toss up coins*]. **2** [1980s+] (*drugs*) a woman who trades sex for crack cocaine or for money to buy crack cocaine. **3** [1990s+] (*Aus.*) a promiscuous woman [SE *toss*, to throw; she throws herself 'up to' the man].

tossy *adj.*[1] [SE *tossy*, contemptuous] [1910s–20s] arrogant, supercilious, conceited.

tossy *adj.*[2] [TOSS *n.*[1] (1)] [1940s] second-rate, useless, inferior.

tostado *n.* [Mex. *tostado*, a popular toasted snack composed of a deep-fried cornmeal pancake topped with a seasoned mixture of beans, mincemeat and vegetables] [1960s–80s] (*US black*) a derog. term for a Latino or Chicano.

tot *n.*[1] [ety. unknown] **1** [early 18C+] a very small or tiny child, an infant. **2** [19C] a very small drinking vessel. **3** [early 19C+] a small glass of alcohol, e.g. a *tot of rum*. **4** [early 19C+] a very small quantity of anything. **5** [mid-19C–1910s] (*also* **tote**) a very heavy drinker.

tot *n.*[2] (*also* **tote**) [abbr. + ? joc. ref. to TOT *n.*[1] (3)] [late 19C] a *tot*al abstainer from alcohol.

tot *n.*[3] [Ger. *tod*, dead] [late 19C+] a rag or bone.

IN COMPOUNDS

❑ **tot-hunter** *n.* [late 19C–1900s] lit. a collector of bones, which were recycled in a variety of manufacturing processes; used as a term of abuse. ❑ **tot-picker** *n.* (*also* **tot-raker**) [late 19C+] a scavenger, a 'rag-and-bone man'.

tot *n.*[4] [1960s] (*S.Afr.*) a Hottentot.

tot *n.*[5] (*also* **tott**) [dimin. TOTTIE *n.*[2] (2)] [1990s+] a young woman.

IN COMPOUNDS

❑ **tot hunting** *n.* [late 19C–1900s] the pursuit of wandering the streets in search of pretty women. ❑ **tot-teaser** *n.* [1970s] (*US gay*) a pederast.

tot *v.*[1] [TOT *n.*[1] (3)] [mid-19C–1930s] to drink a dram.

tot *v.*[2] [TOT *n.*[3]] [mid-19C+] to go rag-picking or scavenging.

totacho *n.* [1960s+] (*US/Hisp.*) the slang used in the barrio.

total *adj.* [1950s+] (*orig. US teen*) a general intensifier; absolute, complete.

IN COMPOUNDS

❑ **total blowchoice** *n.* [BLOW *v.*[2] (2b) + SE *choice*; i.e. it would be a wasted choice] [1980s+] (*US teen*) something appealing but essentially irrelevant. ❑ **total lame-out** *n.* [LAME *adj.* (2)] [1990s+] (*US teen*) that which is very stupid or tedious.

total *v.* [i.e. to destroy *totally*] [1950s+] (*orig. US*) **1** to crash a vehicle so badly as to render it beyond repair. **2** to destroy, kill or maim anything or anyone.

total *adv.* [1960s+] (*US teen/campus*) utterly, completely, totally.

totalled *adj.* (*also* **totaled, totalled out**) [TOTAL *v.*] [1960s+] (*orig. US*) **1** unattractive. **2** wrecked. **3** drunk or drugged. **4** physically or emotionally exhausted. **5** of a person, absolutely destroyed, defeated.

totally! *excl.* [SE *totally*] [1980s+] (*orig. US campus*) a general excl. of approval or enthusiasm, absolutely! exactly! really!

totally clueless *adj.* [note orig. but poss. distinct 1930s RAF use] [1950s+] (*orig. US teen*) ignorant, unaware.

total swine *n. see* WHOLE HOG *n.*

total wreck *n. see* NERVOUS WRECK *n.*

Tote *n.* [abbr.] [late 19C+] (*orig. Aus.*) **1** the *Tot*alizator, a machine that calculates the number of tickets sold to betters on each horse/greyhound in a race. **2** the system of betting based on these calculations.

tote *n.* **1** *see* TOT *n.*[1] (5). **2** *see* TOT *n.*[2].

tote *v.*[1] (*also* **toat**) [the *OED* dismisses either black or Ind. origins, but Farmer, *Americanisms Old New* (1889), suggests OE *totian*, to lift up, to elevate and legal jargon *tolt*, a writ by which a cause was removed from a court baron to the county court, itself f. Lat. *tolle*, to lift or remove] **1** [late 17C+] (*US*) to carry, to haul a load; also fig. to carry around, not lit. a load. **2** [mid-18C+] to take someone, to lead or conduct someone; thus reflexively, to take oneself, to go.

IN COMPOUNDS

❑ **tote load** *n.* [late 17C+] (*US*) as much as one can carry.

IN PHRASES

❑ **big toter** *n.* [1970s] (*US*) a shotgun. ❑ **tote fair** *v.* [late 17C+] (*US*) to carry one's fair share. ❑ **tote the mail** *v. see* HAUL THE MAIL *under* HAUL *v.*

tote *v.*[2] [SE *total*] [1930s+] (*US*) to add up.

tother side *n.* [SE *the other side*] [mid-19C+] (*Aus.*) **1** used in West Australia to refer to the eastern states. **2** used in Tasmania to refer to the Australian mainland.

t'other sider *n.* (*also* **othersider**) [they have come from 'the other side of the world'] (*Aus.*) **1** [19C] a transported felon. **2** [late 19C+] a Western Australian [note TOTHER SIDE *n.*]. **3** [1900s] an Australian from the eastern part of the country [note TOTHER SIDE *n.*].

tots *n. see* TOOTS *n.*

totsi *n. see* TSOTSI *n.*

totsie *n.* [var. on TOTTIE *n.*[2] (2)] [1930s–40s] a young woman, usu. one who is sexually available.

tott *n. see* TOT *n.*[5].

totter *n.* [TOT *v.*[2]] [late 19C+] a 'rag-and-bone' man, a scavenger.

tottie *n.*[1] (*also* **totty**) [abbr. (*Hotten*)*tot*, the orig. and derog. name for the Khoikhoi] [early 19C–1930s] (*S.Afr.*) **1** a Khoikhoi. **2** any black or esp. 'coloured' person.

tottie *n.*[2] (*also* **totty**) [TOT *n.*[1] (1)] **1** [late 19C–1920s] a high-class prostitute. **2** [late 19C+] a young woman, or boy, usu. one who is sexually available; also collectively. **3** [1900s] (*Aus.*) a chorus-girl (the inference is of on-stage vulgarity and off-stage promiscuity).

IN PHRASES

❑ **tottie all-colours** *n.* [late 19C–1900s] a woman whose dress resembles a 'coat of many colours'. ❑ **tottie one-lung** *n.* [late 19C–1900s] an asthmatic or a sufferer from tuberculosis who still manages to muster some degree of style.

tottie *adj.* [TOTTIE *n.*[1]] [19C–1930s] (*S.Afr.*) unpopular, vulgar, unfashionable.

tottie fie *n.* (*also* **tottie fay, tottie hardbake**) [TOTTIE *n.*[2] (2) + SE *fie!*; SE *hardbake*, almond toffee, which is 'hard' albeit sweet] [late 19C+] a woman, usu. a prostitute or at least an 'enthusiastic amateur', who dominates her surroundings.

tot-tots *n.* [2000s] (*W.I.*) a woman's breasts.

totty *n.*[1] *see* TOTTIE *n.*[1].

totty *n.*[2] *see* TOTTIE *n.*[2].

totty-headed *adj.* [SE *totty*, unsteady, dizzy, befuddled] [late 17C–early 19C] **1** foolish, giddy. **2** drunk.

touch *n.*[1] **1** [16C] a trick, a dodge. **2** [18C–1920s] any item that will persuade purchasers to buy, albeit within certain price limits; thus a *sixpence touch, a guinea touch*. **3** [19C+] (*also* **touch-off**) an act of stealing or theft, esp. of pocket-picking. **4** [mid-19C] (*UK Und.*) an arrest. **5** [late 19C+] (*also* **the touch**) the act of cadging a loan, usu. small; thus the loan. **6** [20C+] (*US Und.*) the money gained illegally, e.g. that which is 'stolen' by a confidence trickster's scheme; also in fig. use. **7** [1900s] (*US Und.*) the climax of a confidence trick, when the victim hands over their money. **8** [1930s] one from whom one obtains a loan or a monetary gift. **9** [1930s] the victim of a confidence trick. **10** [1930s+] a piece of good fortune; e.g. an acquittal. **11** [1950s+] a woman who can be easily picked up. **12** [1980s+] (*N.Z.*) one's turn to buy a round of drinks, the round itself.

IN COMPOUNDS

❑ **touch artist** *n.* [1940s–60s] (*US*) a beggar, one who is always asking for a loan. ❑ **touch game** *n.* [mid-19C] (*US Und.*) synon. for the MURPHY (GAME), THE *n.* (1). ❑ **touch guy** *n.* [GUY *n.*[2] (1)] [1970s] (*US*) one who is constantly scrounging. ❑ **touch house** *n.* [mid-19C] (*US Und.*) any tavern or similar establishment where victims are robbed, beaten and even killed; they may also be subjected to the MURPHY (GAME), THE *n.* (1). ❑ **touch merchant** *n.* [early 19C+] a petty thief.

IN PHRASES

❑ **chew up old touches** *v.* [1950s] (*US*) to reminisce. ❑ **cut up (old) touches** *v.* [CUT UP *v.*[2] (2)] [1920s+] (*US Und.*) **1** (*also* **cut up old dough**) to reminisce over old successes, villainies etc. **2** to share out the spoils of criminal acts. ❑ **easy touch** *n.* **1** [1930s+] one who can be easily solicited for money or favours. **2** [1970s] (*UK Und.*) a robbery that can be carried out without difficulty. **3** [1990s+] a situation which is easily exploitable. ❑ **make a touch** *v.* [late 19C+] (*orig. US*) **1** to borrow money, esp. when the donor is less than enthusiastic. **2** to pickpocket. ❑ **on the touch** [late 19C] begging. ❑ **put the touch on** *v.* [mid-19C+] to (attempt to) borrow or extort money. ❑ **soft touch** *n.* [SOFT *adj.* (3)] **1** [1920s] one who is easily beaten. **2** [1920s–70s] an easy job or sinecure; thus an easily achieved robbery or similar crime. **3** [1930s+] one who can easily be solicited for money, or goods or favours. **4** [1990s+] a sympathetic person, one who is easily persuaded.

SE in slang uses

IN COMPOUNDS

❑ **touch crib** *n.* [CRIB *n.*[1] (3)] [19C] a brothel. ❑ **touch-trap** *n.* [SE *touch-trap*, a contrivance that operates when *touched*] [17C–19C] the penis. ❑ **touch-tripe** *n.* [late 17C] the penis.

IN PHRASES

❑ **give someone a touch of them** *v.* [fig. use of *TOUCH OF 'EM* below] [1920s+] (*Aus.*) to infuriate. ❑ **touch of 'em** *n.* [euph.] **1** [late 19C–1900s] (*Aus.*) delirium tremens. **2** [1920s–60s] diarrhoea. ❑ **touch of the...** *n.* (*also* **case of the...**) [adapted from SE phr. *touch of the...* but always used with a pl. n.] [1970s+] used with pl. (often proper) nouns to imply a condition that is seen as typical of the n., e.g. *touch of the New Labours, case of the Princess Di's*. ❑ **touch of the holy bone** *n.* [ironic ref. to the supposed power of holy 'relics', but note BONE *n.*[1] (1)] [19C+] (*orig. Irish, then US*) sexual intercourse. ❑ **touch of the seconds** *n.* [abbr. SE *second thoughts*] [1950s+] last minute hesitation. ❑ **touch of the tarbrush** *n.* (*also* **dash..., lick..., touch of the tar**) [SE f. 1900; note Haliburton *Sam Slick in England* (1843): (to a black slave) 'You one werry good nigger [...] I make a man of you, you dam old tarbrush'] [late 18C+] a derog. term used to described someone who supposedly has a degree of black ancestry; thus *tar-brush*, black or coloured; as *n.* a black person.

touch *n.*[2] [SE *touch*, ability, esp. of a performer] [1910s] (*Aus.*) style, fashion, manner.

IN PHRASES

❑ **come the touch on** *v.* [20C+] (*Aus.*) to adopt a manner or attitude.

touch *n.*[3] [SE *touched*, eccentric, mad] [1910s+] (*Aus.*) a simpleton.

touch *v.*[1] **1** [early 17C+] to take money into one's own hands, to steal; often as *touch (someone) for*, see below. **2** [mid-18C] to offer a loan. **3** [mid-18C+] to borrow something, usu. money, from, to cadge; often as *touch (someone) for*, see below. **4** [late 18C] to inherit money. **5** [mid-19C–1930s] to pick someone's pocket. **6** [late 19C] (*US*) to defeat a bookmaker; to win a bet. **7** [late 19C+] (*Aus.*) to swindle, to cheat; usu. as *touch (someone) for*, see below. **8** [1910s–40s] to ask for a favour.

IN PHRASES

❑ **touch lucky** *v.* [late 19C–1950s] to experience good fortune. ❑ **touch one's kick** *v.* (*also* **touch one's pants, ...strides, ... tweeds**) [SE *touch* + KICK *n.*[4] (1)/ SE *pants*/STRIDES *n.* (1)/SE *tweeds*] [1950s+] (*N.Z.*) **1** to pay for a round of drinks. **2** to make a small loan. ❑ **touch (someone) for** *v.* **1** [mid-18C+] to cadge. **2** [19C+] to remove, to take, to steal. **3** [late 19C+] (*Aus.*) to swindle, to cheat.

SE in slang uses

IN PHRASES

❑ **can't touch the sides** [1970s+] a coarse joke referring to a large, and thus loose, vagina or anus, used by both hetero- and homosexuals. ❑ **couldn't touch someone with a ten-foot pole** *v.* [1970s] (*US*) to be inferior to someone. ❑ **never touch it** *n.* ['it' being alcohol] [late 19C–1900s] (*Aus.*) a teetotaller. ❑ **touch all bases** *v.* [baseball imagery] [20C+] (*US*) to be very thorough, or adaptable and versatile. ❑ **touch base** *v.* (*also* **touch ground**) [baseball imagery] [1960s+] to communicate with, to make contact. ❑ **touch 'em up** *n.* [19C] the vagina. ❑ **touching the dog's arse** *n.* [the initials *t*aking and *d*riving *a*way] [1980s] (*UK Und*) the act of stealing a car. ❑ **touch-off man** *n.* [he *touches off* the fire] [1920s–40s] (*US Und.*) a professional, criminal arsonist. ❑ **wouldn't touch it with a (barge-)pole** (*also* **....with a ten-foot/forty-foot (barge-)pole, ...with the end of a barge-pole, ...with mine**) **1** [mid-19C+] an expression of a lack of interest in something. **2** [20C+] a phr. used by one man to another to express his lack of interest in a woman they are observing. ❑ **wouldn't touch it with a dog's prick** [1960s] a general phr. of aversion, esp. in a sexual context. ❑ **wouldn't touch it with a hoppole** [mid-17C] a phr. indicating aversion or uninterest. ❑ **wouldn't touch it with a pair of tongs** [mid–late 17C; late 19C] a phr. indicating aversion or uninterest. ❑ **wouldn't touch it with a red-hot poker** [1930s+] (*Aus.*) a phr. indicating one's absolute aversion. ❑ **wouldn't touch it with a rotten stick** [mid-19C] a phr. indicating one's absolute aversion. ❑ **wouldn't touch it with yours** [late 19C+] a popular phrase between two men observing a woman when the speaker finds her unattractive – *yours* is the penis. ❑ **wouldn't touch it with a pitchfork** [late 19C] used by one man to another to express his lack of interest in a woman they are observing.

IN EXCLAMATIONS

❑ **touch bone and whistle!** ['Anyone having broken wind backwards, according to the vulgar law, may be pinched by any of the company till he has touched bone (i.e. his teeth) and whistled', Grose (1788)] [late 18C–early 19C] usu. as an imper.

touch *v.*[2] (*also* **get a touch on**) [late 18C+] (*UK Und./Aus.*) to arrest.

touchable *adj.* [? TOUCH *v.*[1] (1)] [1940s] (*US Und.*) susceptible to corruption.

touch and tap *n.* [rhy. sl.] [20C+] a cap.

touched *adj.* [SE *touched*, mentally unstable] [19C] tipsy.

toucher *n.*[1] [SE *touch*] **1** [early 19C] a very tight fit, an instance of very close contact. **2** [early 19C] a blow. **3** [early 19C+] a near thing. **4** [1980s+] (*US black/drugs*) one who becomes physically affectionate after smoking crack cocaine [note NON-TOUCHER *n.*].

toucher *n.*[2] [TOUCH *v.*[1]] **1** [mid-19C] (*US Und.*) a pickpocket. **2** [mid-19C–1900s] one who practises the *TOUCH GAME under* TOUCH *n.*[1]. **3** [mid-19C–1950s] (*US*) a thief. **4** [mid-19C+] a cadger, one who solicits small loans.

touch-hole *n.* [SE *touch-hole*, the vent of a firearm, through which the charge is ignited] **1** [17C–early 18C] the anus. **2** [17C–19C] the vagina.

touchie-feelie *adj.* (*also* **touchy-feely**) [1970s+] (*US*) pertaining to therapies and sensitivity training which encourage people to touch, hug and support one another physically.

touching *n.* [TOUCH *v.*[1] (3)] [mid-18C–19C] **1** obtaining money through theft or pocket-picking. **2** bribery.

touching-up *n. see* TOUCH UP *n.*[1].

touch-me *n.* [rhy. sl.; *touch-me-on-the-nob* = BOB *n.*[3] (2)] [late 19C–1930s] one shilling (5p).

touch-my-nob *n.* [var. on TOUCH-ME *n.*] [late 19C] one shilling (5p).

touch of the hairy heel *phr. see HAIR ABOUT THE HEELS under* HAIR *n.*

touch up *n.*[1] (*also* **touching-up**) [TOUCH UP *v.*[1] (2)] [1950s+] an act of sexual fondling.

touch up *n.*[2] [SE *touch up*, to strike with a whip] [1990s+] (*Aus. Und.*) a beating.

touch up *v.*[1] **1** [late 18C–19C] of a man, to have sexual intercourse. **2** [late 18C+] to fondle or molest sexually.

IN PHRASES

❑ **touch oneself up** *v.* [1960s+] to masturbate.

SE in slang uses

IN PHRASES

❑ **touch someone up** *v.* [SE *touch up*, to tap (a horse) with a whip] **1** [late 18C–mid-19C] to urge someone into action, to exert influence on. **2** [19C] to jog the memory. **3** [late 19C] to stimulate, to interest.

touch up *v.*[2] **1** [late 19C–1900s] (*US*) to approach for a loan or a favour. **2** [1900s] to win money.

IN PHRASES

❑ **touch someone up** *v.* **1** [early 19C–1900s] to rob someone. **2** [mid-19C] to blackmail someone.

touchy-feely *adj. see* TOUCHIE-FEELIE *adj.*

tough *n.* [TOUGH *adj.*] **1** [1960s] (*US black*) an attractive or admirable person. **2** [1970s] (*US black*) money gained from theft or confidence tricks that is used for buying drugs.

tough *adj.* [SE *tough*, capable of great physical or moral endurance] **1** [late 19C+] unfair, 'mean', difficult. **2** [20C+] (*orig. US*) resolute, vigorously uncompromising, severe. **3** [20C+] (*orig. US*) aggressive, menacing. **4** [1920s+] unfortunate, pertaining to hard luck usu. as *that's tough* [backform. f. *TOUGH LUCK* below]. **5** [1930s] bad, depressed. **6** [1930s+] (*US black/campus*) admirable, excellent [on bad = good model]. **7** [1950s–90s] of clothes or their wearer, fashionable [on bad = good model]. **8** [1960s+] attractive, of objects or people [on bad = good model].

IN COMPOUNDS

❑ **tough baby** *n.* [BABY *n.* (7)] **1** [1910s+] a thug, a violent, lawless person. **2** [1920s–40s] (*US gang*) a young woman who associates with gang members. **3** [1960s] a challenging proposition, a problem. ❑ **tough bickkies/biccies/bickies** *n. see STIFF BIKKIES under* STIFF *adj.*[2]. ❑ **tough boy** *n.* [1920s+] a thug, a violent, lawless person. ❑ **tough cat** *n.* [1950s+] (*US black*) a man who is a successful womanizer. ❑ **tough cheese** *adj.* (*also* **tough Cheddar**) [var. on *HARD CHEESE under* HARD *adj.*] [1970s+] bad luck. ❑ **tough cookie** *n.* [COOKIE *n.*[1] (2)] [1950s+] (*US*) a survivor, an emotionally, or physically, strong person. ❑ **tough dancing** *n.* [the term and style originated in the brothels of San Francisco's BARBARY COAST *n.* and spread into the mainstream dancehalls, or their less salubrious counterparts] [20C+] physically close dancing, emphasizing (and offering an opportunity for) sexual intimacy. ❑ **tough egg** *n.* (*also* **hard egg**) [senses 2 and 3 above + play on HARD-BOILED *adj.*] **1** [1910s+] a thug, a violent person. **2** [1920s] an uncompromising individual. ❑ **tough fit** *n.* [1950s–70s] (*US black*) a well-cut suit or other garment. ❑ **tough guy** *see* separate entries. ❑ **tough luck** *n.* [late 19C+] bad luck, esp. as excl. *tough luck!* ❑ **tough monkey** *n. see* TOUGH GUY *n.* (1). ❑ **tough nut** *see* separate entries. ❑ **tough shit** *see* separate entries. ❑ **tough sledding** *n.* (*also* **hard sledding, heavy sledding**) [1920s+] (*US*) a problematic, demanding situation; hard times. ❑ **tough stuff** *n.* **1** [1950s] bad luck. **2** [1970s–80s] (*US black*) anything appealing or pleasing in the realms of sex or drugs. ❑ **tough takkie** *n.* [fig. use of TAKKIE *n.*] [1910s+] (*S.Afr.*) hard luck. ❑ **tough toenails** *n.* [euph. var. on *TOUGH TITTY under* TITTY *n.*] [1950s] bad luck. ❑ **tough turkey** *n.* [? euph. *TOUGH TITTY under* TITTY *n.*] [1900s] (*US*) bad lack. ❑ **tough 'un** *n.* **1** [late 19C] a very great lie. **2** [20C+] an aggressive person.

IN PHRASES

❑ **tough as shoe-leather** *adj.* (*also* **...as a biled owl, ...as fencing wire, ...as old boots**) [mid-19C+] used of one who is considered 'hard' or 'tough'. ❑ **tough on** *adj.* [late 19C+] (*orig. US*) hostile towards, making life hard for someone.

IN EXCLAMATIONS

❑ **tough apples!** *see under* APPLE *n.*[1]. ❑ **tough beans!** [1960s+] (*US*) bad luck (not that I care). ❑ **tough darts!** [euph. for *TOUGH TITTY under* TITTY *n.*] [1960s+] (*US*) a phr. of dismissal, uninterest, 'that's your bad luck'. ❑ **tough noogies!** [fig. use of NOOGIE *n.*] [1970s+] (*US*) (that's) bad luck!

tough *adv.* [TOUGH *adj.*] **1** [1920s+] intensely, enthusiastically, commitedly. **2** [1930s+] in an aggressive manner. **3** [1950s–60s] attractively. **4** [1990s+] resolutely.

IN PHRASES

❑ **ride tough** *v.* [1970s+] (*US black*) **1** to be intoxicated by a drug. **2** to be riding in a noteworthy car.

toughed up *adj.* [TOUGH *adj.* (3)] [1950s] (*US*) aggressive.

tough guy *n.* [TOUGH *adj.* (3)/TOUGH *adj.* (2) + GUY *n.*[2] (1)] **1** [1920s+] (*orig. US*) (*also* **tough monkey**) a thug. **2** [1930s+] someone who cannot easily be checked or thwarted.

tough-guy *adj.* [TOUGH GUY *n.*] [1950s+] aggressive, uncompromising.

toughie *n.* [TOUGH *adj.* + sfx *-ie*] **1** [1920s] (*US*) an attractive young woman. **2** [1920s–60s] one who enjoys playing very 'rough' sports. **3** [1930s+] a 'hard', ruthless, callous person. **4** [1940s+] a thug. **5** [1960s+] (*also* **toughy**) something that one finds 'tough' to do, understand, accept etc.

tough (it) (out) *v.* [mid-19C+] to withstand abuse or a bad situation; most commonly as *tough it out*.

tough nut *n.* (*also* **tough cud, rough nut**) [TOUGH *adj.* (2) + NUT *n.*[1] (1)] [mid-19C+] (*orig. US*) a person difficult, obstinate or dangerous to deal with; also of a place.

tough-nut *adj.* [TOUGH NUT *n.*] [1990s+] aggressive, macho, obstinate.

tough shit *n.* [var. on *TOUGH LUCK under* TOUGH *adj.*] **1** [1940s+] (*orig. US*) unfortunate or unpleasant circumstances. **2** [1970s] of drink, powerful.

tough shit *adj.* (*also* **tough-sheiss**) [TOUGH SHIT *n.*] **1** [1940s+] unfortunate. **2** [1970s] essential, basic.

tough shit! *excl.* (*also* **tough, tough shitski**) [TOUGH SHIT *n.*] [1950s+] so what! see if I care! a response indicating little or no sympathy with the first speaker.

toughy *n. see* TOUGHIE *n.* (5).

toup *n.* [abbr. SE *toupee*] [1950s+] a wig.

toupee *n.* [SE *toupee*, a wig] [mid-18C–19C] **1** a woman's pubic hair. **2** a pubic wig or merkin.

tour *v.* (*also* **toure, towre**) [? SE *tower*, to stand high above (so as to look down on); Ribton-Turner, *A History of Vagrants* (1887), suggests Erse *tòirigh*, Gaelic *tòirich*, to search after, pursue] [mid-16C–1900s] (*UK Und.*) to see, to survey, to spy on.

tour guide *n.* [play on TRIP *n.*[4] (1)] [1960s+] (*US drugs*) a person who aids and supports someone having a psychedelic drug experience.

tourist *n.* **1** [1920s–40s] (*US tramp*) a hobo who travels south to avoid the cold northern winters. **2** [1940s+] (*gay*) one who occas. enjoys homosexual sex, but is not a member of the subculture.

touristas *n.* (*also* **turistas**) [Sp., lit. 'tourists'] [1950s+] diarrhoea or any form of stomach upset contracted on a foreign holiday.

touse *v. see* TOUZLE *v.*

tousle *n.* (*also* **touzle**) [mid–late 19C] bushy whiskers.

tout *n.*[1] [TOUT *v.*; note *tout*, a person who solicits custom, is SE] **1** [18C–early 19C] a thief's lookout; thus *strong tout*, a very observant eye. **2** [late 18C–early 19C] a 'lookout house' (Grose 1785). **3** [early–mid-19C] the act of spying or surveying; thus *keep tout*, see below. **4** [mid-19C+] (*US*) a person who sells betting advice. **5** [mid-19C] (*UK prison*) a despised policeman. **6** [late 19C] a lookout for a criminal gang. **7** [1900s] (*Aus.*) one who spies for the purpose of blackmail. **8** [1940s] a spy working for a casino owner, checking the honesty of the dealers. **9** [1950s+] (*Irish/Scot.*) an informer. **10** [1980s+] (*drugs*) an assistant to a street drug dealer, directing buyers to the seller.

IN PHRASES

❑ **keep tout** *v.* [early–mid-19C] to spy on, to keep a lookout. ❑ **pushing tout** *n.* [early 18C] (*UK Und.*) a thief's watchman or scout.

tout *n.*[2] *see* TOOT *n.*[1].

tout *v.* [SE *tout*, to peep, to peer; note *tout*, to solicit for custom, is SE] **1** [late 17C–19C] to watch, to spy on. **2** [late 17C–19C] (*UK Und.*) to keep a careful lookout, to be on one's guard. **3** [1990s+] (*US drugs*) to work as an assistant to a drug dealer.

touted *adj.* [late 18C–mid-19C] (*UK Und.*) followed, pursued.

touter *n.* [TOUT *v.* + sfx *-er*] **1** [early–mid-19C] in horseracing, one who keeps an eye on horses when training, the health of jockeys, the orders given by owners, etc. **2** [mid-19C] (*UK Und.*) a thief's lookout.

touting *n.* **1** [late 18C–early 19C] (*UK Und.*) acting as a lookout. **2** [early 19C] eyeing up women.

touting-ken *n.* (*also* **tooting-ken**) [Scot. *tout*, the act of drinking a large draught, a large draught of liquor + KEN *n.*[1] (1)] [late 17C–early 19C] (*UK Und.*) a tavern, an alehouse or the bar within.

touze *v. see* TOUZLE *v.*

touzery gang *n.* (*also* **towzery gang**) [? SE *touse*, to pull about, to abuse] [mid–late 19C] mock-auction swindlers.

touzle *n. see* TOUSLE *n.*

touzle *v.* (*also* **touse, touze, towzle**) [Scot. *touzle*, to handle (esp. a woman) rudely or indelicately] [late 18C–19C] of a man, to fondle intimately; to have sexual intercourse.

tow *n.* [SE *tow*, strands of flax used for a light (money, like tow, 'burns' fast)] [mid–late 19C] money.

towel *n.* [abbr. OAKEN TOWEL *n.*] [mid-18C–mid-19C] a cudgel.

SE in slang uses

IN COMPOUNDS

❑ **towel-head** *n.* (*also* **teatowel-head, towlie**) [SE *towel* + -HEAD *sfx* (2)/SE *head*; the term became particularly popular during and after the Gulf War of 1991] [1980s+] a derog. term for an Arab from the Middle East. ❑ **towel-tugger** *n.* [1990s+] (*Aus.*) a childish person, weakling?

IN PHRASES

❑ **throw in the towel** *v.* (*also* **chuck in…, sling in…, shoot in…, throw the towel in**) [boxing use, whereby a towel or sponge thrown into the ring indicates the retirement of a fighter who is losing badly; note earlier at *CHUCK UP THE SPONGE under* SPONGE *n.*] **1** [20C+] to give in, to capitulate. **2** [1900s] (*also* **throw the handkerchief**) to resign. **3** [1910s–30s] to die.

towel *v.* [OAKEN TOWEL *n.*] [18C+] to beat, to cudgel, to thrash.

IN PHRASES

❑ **towel up** *v.* [1910s+] (*Aus.*) to beat, to thrash.

towelling *n.* [TOWEL *v.*] [mid-19C–1900s] a thrashing, a beating.

tower *n.*[1] [SE *tower*, a very high head-dress worn by women late 17C–early 18C] [late 17C–early 18C] false hair.

tower *n.*[2] [*Tower Hill*, London, a centre of contemporary criminality] [late 18C–early 19C] (*UK Und.*) clipped money.

IN PHRASES

❑ **go around the tower** *v.* (*also* **go round…**) [play on the *Tower* of London, where money was minted, and a *tour* around the circumference of the coin] [late 17C–early 19C] (*UK Und.*) to clip money.

tower *v.* [SE *tower*, to rise to a great height (and thus be able to spy on the surrounding area)] [late 18C–early 19C] to spy upon.

tower bridge *n.* [rhy. sl.; ult. London's *Tower Bridge*] [20C+] a fridge.

tower bridge *phr.* [*Tower Bridge* in London goes 'up and down'] [1930s] a phr. used in reply to 'How are you?', meaning 'up and down', 'so-so'.

tower dock *n.* [rhy. sl. = COCK *n.*[3] (1)] [2000s] the penis.

Tower Hill *v.* [rhy. sl.; ult. the area in London] [1990s+] to kill.

Tower Hill play *n.* [the criminal environs of *Tower Hill* where such rough-housing would have been common] [late 17C–early 19C] 'A slap on the face and a kick on the breech' (Grose 1785).

Tower Hill vinegar *n.* [the sword preceded the noose as a means of execution; criminals, esp. political ones, were executed at the Tower of London] [16C–17C] the swordsman's block.

Tower of Babel *n.* [derog. ref. to the meaningless chatter therein] [mid-19C] (*UK Und.*) the Mansion House, the official residence of the Lord Mayor of London.

towhead *n.* [SE *tow-head*, a light-haired boy, from SE *tow*, flax] [mid–late 19C] (*US, West*) one who is considered effeminate, a smartly presented city type.

towie *n.* [abbr.] [1970s+] (*Aus.*) the driver of a *tow*-truck.

towlie *n. see TOWEL-HEAD under* TOWEL *n.*

towline *v. see* TOW OUT *v.*

town *n.*[1] [rhy. sl. = BROWN *n.* (2b)] [late 19C–1900s] a halfpenny.

town *n.*[2]

SE in slang uses

IN COMPOUNDS

❑ **town-crack** *n. see* CRACK *n.*[3] (2).

IN PHRASES

❑ **go all over town with** *v.* [the tongue 'travels' around the body. Usu. used by a prostitute as part of the 'menu' of paid services she can offer; a 'localized' var. of AROUND THE WORLD *n.*] [1940s+] to lick and suck the partner's body, incl. the genitals and sometimes the anus. ❑ **in town** *adj.* **1** [early 19C] well-off, having plenty of money. **2** [1960s] (*US campus*) acceptable. ❑ **on the town** [18C SE *on the town*, in the swing of fashionable life; 19C use implies that those so occupied are not fashionable, merely dedicated to urban pleasures, smart or not] **1** [early 18C–1950s] working as a prostitute; thus *take to the town*, to work as a prostitute. **2** [early–mid-19C] living as a professional criminal. **3** [early–mid-19C] living as a sophisticate, a man of the world. ❑ **out of town** [i.e. lit. or fig. absent] **1** [early 19C] in prison for debt. **2** [early–late 19C] hard up, penniless. **3** [mid-19C] unexcited, unstimulated. **4** [1920s–60s] (*US Und.*) in prison. **5** [1940s–60s] (*US*) crazy. **6** [1960s] (*US black*) unacceptable, unfashionable.

IN EXCLAMATIONS

❑ **fire down town!** [1950s] (*W.I.*) a call for speedy and generous service, esp. on arriving at a bar and calling for a quick round of drinks. ❑ **get out of town!** [1980s+] (*orig. US black/campus*) a general excl. of disbelief, dismissal.

SE in slang uses

IN COMPOUNDS

❑ **town bull** *n.* [SE *town bull*, a bull housed in turn by the cow-keepers of a village] **1** [late 17C–18C] a promiscuous man. **2** [late 17C–early 19C; 1910s–20s] a 'whoremaster', i.e. a pimp or procurer. ❑ **town clown** *n.* (*also* **clown**) [1920s–60s] (*US*) a police officer working in a village or small town. ❑ **town lands** *n. see* ety. at TIPPERARY FORTUNE *n.* ❑ **town pump** *n.* (*also* **town punch**) [PUMP *n.* (1f)/PUNCH *n.*] [1970s+] a very promiscuous woman. ❑ **town shift** *n. see under* SHIFT *n.* ❑ **town stallion** *n.* [STALLION *n.* (1)] [late 17C–18C] a womanizer, a lecher. ❑ **town tabby** *n.* [colloq. *Town*, London + TABBY *n.* (1)] [mid-19C] a smart dowager. ❑ **town toddler** *n.* [TODDLER *n.* (1), i.e. one who wanders around open to exploitation] [late 18C–mid-19C] (*UK Und.*) a gullible person, prey to confidence tricksters. ❑ **town trap** *n.* [pun on SE trap, to ensnare / TRAP *n.*[1] (2)] [late 17C–early 18C] a pimp. ❑ **town-went** *adj.* [1990s+] (*US campus*) used of something that is/has been done to excess.

IN PHRASES

❑ **lawless as a town bull** *adj.* [late 17C–early 19C] of a man, extremely promiscuous. ❑ **Town of the Wind** *see* WINDY CITY *n.* (1).

-town *sfx see* -CITY *sfx.*

town halls *n.* [rhy. sl. = BALLS *n.* (1)] [2000s] the testicles.

townie *n.* [abbr.] **1** [early 19C–1950s] a fellow *towns*man. **2** [early 19C+] a *town*-dweller, esp. a Londoner. **3** [mid-19C+] (*usu. campus/private school*) an inhabitant of the *town* rather than of the campus/school. **4** [2000s] a working-class 'lad', dressed in sportswear.

townie *adj.* [as seen by a peasant, the supposed characteristics of a TOWNIE *n.* (2)] [early 19C] cunning, duplicitous.

towns *n.* [rhy. sl.; *town halls* = BALLS *n.* (1)] [2000s] the testicles.

towns and cities *n.* [rhy. sl. = TITTY *n.* (1)] [1900s–40s] a woman's breasts.

towny *n. see* TOWNIE *n.*

tow out *v.* (*also* **towline**) [naut. imagery] [early–mid-19C] (*UK Und.*) to decoy a potential victim away from the victim's premises so that one's accomplice can enter and rob them.

towrag *n. see* TOERAG *n.*[1].

towre *v. see* TOUR *v.*

tow row *adj.* [SE *tow row*, a hubbub, a din. Note milit. jargon *tow row*, a grenadier] [18C–19C] drunk (and disorderly).

Tow Street *n.* [SE *tow*, to drag] [19C] a fig. 'street' in which one is decoyed.

IN PHRASES

❑ **be in Tow Street** *v.* [19C] to be decoyed, to be persuaded (against one's will).

tow-wow *n.* [? TOWZE *v.*] [mid-18C] the vagina.

towze *v.* [Scot. *touse*, to pull (a woman) about rudely or indelicately] [17C–mid-18C] to have sexual intercourse.

towzery gang *n. see* TOUZERY GANG *n.*

towzle *v. see* TOUZLE *v.*

tox *v.* [abbr.] [mid-17C] to intoxicate.

DERIVATIVES

❑ **toxed** *adj.* (*also* **toxt**) [mid-17C] intoxicated, drunk.

toxic waste dump *n.* [1980s+] (*US campus*) a person who uses drugs or drink to excess.

toxy *n.* [? mis-reading of TOY *n.*[2] (1)] [1960s+] (*drugs*) a small container of opium.

toy *n.*[1] **1** [17C–19C] the penis. **2** [mid-17C] a mistress. **3** [mid-17C–19C] the vagina. **4** [early 19C] a prostitute. **5** [early 19C+] a watch; thus *toy and tackle*, a watch and chain. **6** [1910s+] (*US black teen*) a gullible person, a fool; a novice. **7** [1980s+] in graffiti, anything or anyone second-rate.

IN COMPOUNDS

❑ **toy-getter** *n.* [late 19C] a thief specializing in stealing watches.

SE in slang uses

IN COMPOUNDS

❑ **toy boy** *n.* (*also* **boy toy**) [i.e. his role as a plaything] [1950s+] a young attractive man popular among older, richer women (or homosexual men); thus *boy toy*, which can mean the same or a young attractive woman, popular among older men. ❑ **toy soldier** *n.* [derisive use of SE] [1940s] (*US black*) an officer cadet.

toy *n.*[2] (*drugs*) **1** [1910s–60s] (*also* **pin-yen toy, toey**) a small container, approx. 54 cm (1in) diam., used to hold prepared opium. **2** [1930s–60s] a measure of opium, a small ball, approx. the size of a pea. **3** [1960s–80s] a hypodermic syringe.

toy *v.* [? SE *toy*, to play with, to tease + implication of acting childishly] [1990s+] (*US black/teen*) to destroy another graffiti artist's work by drawing over it; thus *toy someone out*; as *n.*, one who is inferior in the hierarchy of graffiti artists.

toys *n.* **1** [early 18C] fig. use meaning sexual 'wares'. **2** [1960s+] (*drugs*) equipment for injecting narcotics. **3** [1970s+] any appliances designed to increase sexual pleasure or fantasies.

t.p.t. *n.* [abbr.] [1990s+] (*US teen*) trailer park trash.

trac *n.* [abbr. SE *intractable*] [1960s+] (*Aus.*) a prisoner who refuses to accept the rules.

trace (off) *v.* [? link to UK dial. *trace*, to tell stories of old times or SE *trace*, to track, to pursue] [1950s+] (*W.I. Rasta*) to curse or speak abusively to someone.

Tracey *n. see* SHARON *n.*

Track, the *n.* (*also* **the Bitumen**) [1930s+] (*Aus.*) the Stuart Highway running from Darwin to the south.

track *n.*[1] (*also* **trag**) [backsl.] [mid-19C] one quart (757ml).

track *n.*[2] **1** [mid-19C+] the highway or street as the home of tramps, prostitutes, pickpockets etc. **2** [late 19C–1950s] (*Aus.*) any outback road. **3** [1940s–70s] (*US black*) a dancehall, a ballroom, esp. the Savoy Ballroom in Harlem. **4** [1940s–70s] (*US black*) the world of pimping, hustling, confidence tricks etc; the Eastern cities are the *fast track*, California and the West are the *slow track* or *soft track*. **5** [1960s+] (*US black*) that area of a street where a prostitute works.

IN COMPOUNDS

❑ **track dolie** *n.* (*also* **track man**) [DOLIE *n.* (1). During the Depression itinerants were issued with food ration cards, but were not allowed to remain in any one place] [1940s] (*Aus.*) an itinerant. ❑ **track pizza** *n.* [2000s] (*US*) one who throws themselves in front of a subway train. ❑ **track thirteen** *n.* (*also* **track 13**) [the trad. unlucky number] [1910s–40s] (*US Und.*) a life sentence.

IN PHRASES

❑ **(been) around the track** *adj.* [1950s+] (being) experienced, usu. spec. sexually experienced; if used of a woman (the usu. form) derog. ❑ **down the track** *adj.* [1980s+] **1** experienced. **2** referring to the passage of time. ❑ **fly the track** *v.* [horseracing imagery] [19C+] (*US*) to abandon one's duties, to depart from an expected course of action. ❑ **grub track** *n.* [1900s] the search for food. ❑ **off (the) track** [20C+] behaving badly, making mistakes, being inconsistent. ❑ **on the track** [late 19C+] the world of the outback, thus used of a person to imply a vagrant's life. ❑ **take the track** *v.* [1910s+] (*N.Z.*) to be dismissed from a job.

track *n.*[3] [TRACK *v.*[2]] [1960s+] (*Aus. prison*) a warder who is bribed to smuggle items for the inmates.

track, the *n. see* TURF *n.* (2).

track *v.*[1] **1** [late 17C–19C] (*UK Und.*) to go; thus *track the dancers*, to go upstairs. **2** [late 19C–1920s] (*US*) to wander aimlessly. **3** [1910s–50s] to leave, to run off. **4** [1970s+] to maintain emotional or verbal stability, to 'keep on the right track'; to understand. **5** [1990s+] (*US black*) to talk.

IN PHRASES

❑ **track square** *v.* (*also* **track straight**) [SQUARE *adv.* (2)/STRAIGHT *adv.* (3)] [1910s] (*Aus.*) to pursue a love affair with honourable intentions (i.e. eventual marriage rather than short-term sex). ❑ **track with** *v.* [1910s+] (*Aus.*) to associate with someone of the opposite sex.

track *v.*[2] [1960s+] (*N.Z. prison*) to smuggle goods into/out of prison.

trackie *n.* (*also* **trackies, tracky dacks**) [abbr.] [1990s+] a tracksuit.

tracks *n.* (*also* **track, track marks, marks**) [1960s+] (*drugs*) punctures and scar tissue that accumulate along the veins of a regular drug addict.

IN PHRASES

❑ **tracked up** *adj.* [1960s+] (*drugs*) of a narcotics addict, having one's arms (and other parts of the body) covered in scars from injections. ❑ **run a railroad** *v.* [pun] [1960s] (*drugs*) to be addicted to narcotics.

tracky dacks *n. see* TRACKIE *n.*

trade *n.* **1** [late 16C+] (*also* **trading**) prostitution, sexual intercourse. **2** [1920s+] a prostitute's client. **3** [1920s+] (*gay*) a man with whom one has (commercial) sex, a male prostitute; a male prostitute's customer. **4** [1940s] one who works as a prostitute.

IN PHRASES

❑ **do for trade** *v.* [1940s+] (*gay*) to perform fellatio without reciprocation; note GAY TRADE *under* GAY *adj.* ❑ **take it out in trade** *v.* [1940s+] (*Can./US*) to have sexual intercourse as the 'price' of taking a woman out.

trade, the *n.* (*UK Und.*) **1** [early 19C] (*also* **fair trade, free trade**) smuggling. **2** [mid–late 19C] burglary.

trade *adj.* [TRADE *n.* (3)] [1930s+] (*gay*) used of someone involved in commercial sex.

trade *v.* [TRADE *n.*] **1** [17C–early 18C; 1950s] to work as a prostitute; to run a brothel. **2** [late 18C] to go looking for sexual partners. **3** [1990s+] of a heterosexual man, to have sex with a homosexual partner.

trademark *n.* [late 19C] a scratch on the face.

trader *n.* [TRADE *n.*] **1** [17C–early 19C] a prostitute, a promiscuous woman. **2** [mid-17C–early 18C] an adulterer; a womanizer. **3** [1970s+] (*US gay*) a male homosexual prostitute.

tradesman *n.* [joc. euph.] [mid-18C–early 19C] a thief.

tradesman's (entrance) *n.* [a pun on *back passage*] [1990s+] the anus; thus *go in by/up the tradesman's*, to have anal intercourse.

IN PHRASES

❑ **he doesn't mind if he uses the front door or the tradesman's entrance** [1990s+] a phr. used to denote someone is bisexual.

tradey *adj.* [TRADE *n.* (3)] [1950s] (*gay*) pertaining to commercial sex.

trading *n. see* TRADE *n.* (1).

trading dame *n.* (*also* **...lady, ...woman**) [TRADE *n.* + SE *dame*] [17C–early 19C] a prostitute.

trading justices *n.* [late 18C–early 19C] 'Broken mechanics, discharged footmen, and other low fellows, smuggled into the commission of the peace, who subsist by fomenting disputes, granting warrants, and otherwise retailing justice' (Grose 1796).

Trafalgar Square *n.* [rhy. sl.; ult. the London square] [1990s+] a chair.

traffic *n.* (*also* **traffick, trafficker, traffique**) [SE *traffic*, the buying and selling of goods or the goods themselves] **1** [late 16C–18C] (*UK Und.*) a prostitute, esp. one working as a confidence trickster. **2** [1930s] (*US prison*) a male homosexual (poss. a prostitute).

trag *n. see* TRACK *n.*[1].

tragic *adj.* [1970s+] an all-purpose negative meaning disastrous, appalling, very bad; as *n.*, a hopeless or unpopular person.

tragic magic *n. see under* MAGIC *n.*

trago *n.* [Sp.] [1960s+] (*US*) a drink.

trail *n.* [TRAIL *v.*] [mid-19C–1900s] a hoax.

trail *v.* [18C SE *trail*, to persuade, to seduce (non-sexually)] [mid-19C–1900s] to hoax, to fool.

trailer *n.*[1] (*also* **traylor**) [they *trail* their victims] **1** [late 16C] a highway robber, usu. on foot. **2** [late 16C–early 17C] a horse thief.

trailer *n.*[2] **1** [1900s–20s] a helper. **2** [1920s–40s] (*US tramp*) a tramp who follows the circus.

trailer *n.*[3] [the SE *trailer* where such visits take place] [1990s+] (*US prison*) a conjugal visit.

SE in slang uses

IN COMPOUNDS

❑ **trailer-load** *n.* [1990s+] (*W.I.*) a large quantity. ❑ **trailer trash** *n.* (*also* **trash**) [SE *trailer* + WHITE TRASH *n.*] [1990s+] (*US*) poor whites living in trailers (large, static caravans), exhibiting a lack of sophistication and enjoying what is seen as a distasteful lifestyle.

trail muffin *n. see* MEADOW MUFFIN *n.*

trails *n.* [the SE *vapour trails* produced by jet aircraft] [1980s+] (*drugs*) colourful incandescent paths in the air, 'seen' in the wake of moving objects by those who have taken hallucinogens such as LSD.

trail the wing *v.* [ornithological imagery] [20C+] (*Ulster*) to seek sympathy.

train *n.*[1] (*also* **choo choo**) [1940s+] (*orig. US*) group sex, usu. involving a single woman and a number of men; it can be voluntary or not.

IN PHRASES

❑ **pull a train** *v.* (*also* **run a train**) [the woman is the 'engine', her assailants/partners are the 'rolling-stock'] **1** [1940s+] to participate in a gang rape. **2** [1960s+] to be the victim of a gang rape. **3** [1960s+] of a woman, to have sex voluntarily with a number of partners in quick succession. ❑ **run a double train** *v.* (*also* **pull a double train**) [1980s+] (*US black*) of two men, to penetrate a woman simultaneously by the vagina and the anus. ❑ **run a train** *v.* [the victim is the 'engine'; the attackers the 'passengers'] [1970s+] (*orig. US*) to gang rape.

SE in slang uses

IN COMPOUNDS

❑ **train jockey** *n.* [1930s] (*Aus.*) an unemployed vagrant. ❑ **trainspotter** *n.* [generic use of SE] [1980s+] an obsessive, one who specializes in the collection of trivia, the knowledge of minutiae etc.

IN PHRASES

❑ **go like a train** *v.* [20C+] **1** to go very fast. **2** of a woman, to be a very enthusiastic sexual partner [GO *v.* (1)].

train *n.*[2] [1960s+] (*US Und.*) transportation from one prison to another, the mode of transport is irrelevant.

train *v.*[1] [pun on CARRY ON *v.* /SE *carry on*, to keep going] [late 19C] (*US, mainly New England*) to romp, to play around, to behave obstreperously.

train *v.*[2] [*PULL A TRAIN under* TRAIN *n.*[1] + an undertone of SE *train*, to teach (one) disciplined behaviour. This is not gang rape as such, since the woman is ostensibly willing, but she may in reality have little option but to accede. Originated during a well-publicized incident at Ingham, N. Queensland in 1977; but note TRAIN *n.*[1] which predates it] **1** [1970s+] (*Aus./US*) of a woman, to have sex with several men in a single session. **2** [1990s+] of a man or men, to indulge in group sex with a single woman.

trained nurse *n.* [1930s–50s] (*US drugs/prison*) narcotics smuggled into jail.

trainies *n.* [abbr.] [1990s+] a trainer, a training shoe.

train (with) *v.* [late 19C–1940s] (*US*) to associate with, to cooperate with.

train wreck *n.* [rhy. sl.] [1920s] (*US*) the neck.

traipse *see under* TRAPES.

trake *n.* [SE *tracheostomy*, the operation of making an opening in the trachea (the windpipe) near its upper end, so that the patient can breathe through it] [1990s+] (*US black teen*) a general term of abuse, lit. somebody down whose throat you want to thrust your fingers.

tra-la-la *phr.* [late 19C–1900s] goodbye.

tra-la-las *n.* [? his ability to say 'Tra-la-la!' to cares and problems that might cause trouble for less wealthy or dissipated people] [late 19C] 'one of the wealthiest and most dissipated class of dissipated men' (B&L).

trallywagger *n.* [SE *trail*, to drag behind + *wag*] [20C+] (*Irish*) a loose thread hanging from the hemline of one's clothing.

tram fare *n.* [late 19C] twopence, esp. as a euph. used by the lowest ranks of prostitutes.

tramline *n.* **1** [1940s+] a scar. **2** [1990s+] a thin shaved line in an eyebrow, or a thin line of short hair on a shaved head; usu. in pl.

trammie *n.* (*also* **trammy**) [abbr.] [1940s+] (*Aus./N.Z.*) the driver or conductor of a *tram*.

tramp *n.* (*also* **trampie**) **1** [20C+] (*orig. US*) a general term of abuse, esp. of someone incompetent, second-rate. **2** [1910s+] (*orig. US*) a promiscuous woman; occas. used of a man [her 'wandering' from man to man]. **3** [1960s] (*US gay*) a male prostitute. **4** [1980s] (*US campus*) an affectionate term of address.

SE in slang uses

IN COMPOUNDS

❑ **tramp-ass** *adj.* (*also* **trampish-ass**) [-ASS *sfx*] [1970s] (*US black*) of a woman, promiscuous. ❑ **tramp's lagging** *n.* [LAGGING *n.* (2)] [1940s+] (*UK Und*) a sentence of 90 days imprisonment, commonly that meted out for vagrancy.

tramp *adj.* [TRAMP *n.* (1)] [1910s+] (*US black*) second-rate, inferior.

tramp *v.* [SE *tramp*, to stamp on, to crush] [1940s+] (*Aus.*) to dismiss (from a job).

SE in slang uses

IN PHRASES

❑ **tramp on the gas** *v.* [1940s] to accelerate.

IN EXCLAMATIONS

❑ **tramp on it!** [1940s] (*US*) hurry up!

tramped *adj.* [TRAMP *v.*] [1920s+] (*Aus.*) dismissed from one's job.

trampers *n.* [SE *tramp*] [late 18C–19C] the feet or shoes.

trampie *n. see* TRAMP *n.*

trampish-ass *adj. see TRAMP-ASS under* TRAMP *n.*

tramp (it) *v.* [SE *tramp*, to stride] **1** [mid–late 19C] to cure one's feeling ill or 'out of sorts' by walking it off. **2** [mid-19C+] to travel or wander, esp. as a beggar.

IN PHRASES

❑ **on the tramp** *adv.* [mid-19C] on a thieving expedition, pickpocketing.

trample *v.* [1990s+] (*W.I.*) to have sexual intercourse.

trampler *n.* [they *trample* the path] [early–mid-17C] a go-between, an intermediary, a lawyer.

trampo *n.* [TRAMP *n.* (1) + -O *sfx* (1)] [1940s] (*US*) a good-for-nothing.

trampooze *v.* (*also* **trampoose**) **1** [late 18C–1930s] (*US*) to wander around. **2** [1920s+] (*W.I.*) to go out on the town.

trampy *adj.* [TRAMP *n.* (2)] [1980s] (*orig. US*) promiscuous, usu. but not invariably of women.

tram troub/trube *n. see* TROUB *n.*

trank *n.* [abbr.] (*drugs*) **1** [1960s+] (*also* **tranc, tranq, tranx**) any type of *tranq*uillizer. **2** [1980s+] phencyclidine [used non-recreationally as an animal tranquillizer].

DERIVATIVES

❑ **tranked (out)** *adj.* [1960s+] drugged by tranquillizers.

tranklement *n.* [ety. unknown, logically SE *tracklement*, a jelly to accompany meat, but this was unknown until its coinage in 1954] [19C] the stomach, the intestines.

tranny *n.* (*also* **trannie**) [abbr.] **1** [1960s+] a *trans*istor radio. **2** [1960s+] an automobile *trans*mission. **3** [1960s+] a Ford *Trans*it van. **4** [1980s+] a *trans*vestite. **5** [1980s+] a *trans*sexual.

tranq *n. see* TRANK *n.* (1).

tranquillo *v.* [SE *tranquil*] [1990s+] (*US black/W.I.*) calm, relaxed, COOL *adj.* (2).

Trans, the *n.* [SE *trans*, across] [1920s+] (*Aus.*) the train that runs from Adelaide to Perth across the Nullarbor Plain.

trans *n.* [abbr. SE *transsexual*] [1990s+] (*gay*) a transgender, transsexual or transvestite person.

transfag *n.* [1990s+] (*US gay*) a female to male transsexual who becomes a homosexual man.

transfer *v.* [euph.] [late 19C–1900s] (*UK society*) to steal.

transformer *n.* [the toy *Transformers*, popular in the 1980s, which appear to be one thing, e.g. a car, but can be changed into another, e.g. a robot] [1990s+] (*US black gang*) a spy.

translated *adj.* [satirical play on SE *translate*, to be taken to heaven] [late 19C–1900s] (*UK society*) very drunk, poss. to the extent of passing out.

translate the truth *v.* [euph.] [late 19C] (*UK society*) to lie.

translators *n.* [SE *translate*, i.e. from old to new] **1** [late 17C–mid-19C] shoemakers specializing in the sale of mended footwear. **2** [mid-19C] second-hand shoes that have been rebuilt by the shoemaker and then resold.

transmogrify *v.* (*also* **transmigrafy, transmogriphy, transmugrify**) [subseq. SE, *OED* suggests orig. version was *transmigrafy* and links it to illiterate corruption of SE *transmigure* or *transmigrate*, to move from one place to another] [mid-17C–19C] to metamorphose, to alter.

DERIVATIVES

❑ **transmogrifier** *n.* [mid-17C–19C] (*UK Und.*) one who disguises stolen watches for resale.

transnear *v.* [? 17C SE *transnear*, to cross a street so as to meet] [late 17C–early 19C] (*UK Und.*) to come up with or draw level with (a person).

transporter *n.* [the sentence of *transportation* that comes from a judge's *mouth*] [mid-19C] (*UK Und.*) the mouth.

transy *n.* [1970s+] (*US*) a transvestite.

tranx *n. see* TRANK *n.* (1).

trap *n.*[1] **1** [late 17C–19C] trickery, fraud; thus *trap is down*, the trick has failed. **2** [18C–early 19C] one who blackmails a prostitute's client. **3** [18C+] usu. in pl., a policeman or similar agent of the law [metonymy]. **4** [late 18C+] the mouth; esp. in phrs. *KEEP ONE'S TRAP SHUT* below, *SHUT ONE'S TRAP* below [it is a 'trap' for food, often used in combs., e.g. *BREAD TRAP under* BREAD *n.*[1], *MEAT TRAP under* MEAT *n.*]. **5** [1920s+] a place, a house or apartment, a nightclub. **6** [1930s] (*US tramp*) a hiding-place for liquor or other illegal goods. **7** [1940s] (*US black*) the military draft during WW2. **8** [1960s] (*drugs*) a hiding place for drugs. **9** [1970s] a cubicle or stall in a public lavatory. **10** [1970s+] (*US black*) the number of customers a prostitute is assigned as a daily tally by her pimp to reach a financial target [i.e. those whom she SE *traps*]. **11** [2000s] the vagina. **12** *see WOLF-TRAP under* WOLF *n.*

IN PHRASES

❑ **keep one's trap shut** *v.* [20C+] to be quiet. ❑ **shoot off one's trap** *v.* [SHOOT *v.* (4c)] [1930s–40s] to talk injudiciously, to boast. ❑ **shut one's trap** *v.* (*also* **close one's trap, hush one's trap**) [late 18C+] to be quiet, usu. as imper. *shut your trap!*

SE in slang uses

IN COMPOUNDS

❑ **trap house** *n.* [HOUSE *n.*[1] (1)] [mid-19C] (*US Und.*) a brothel where clients are robbed while in flagrante by an accomplice who reaches in through a concealed panel. ❑ **trap money** *n.* [1970s+] (*US black*) a prostitute's daily earnings. ❑ **trap (number) two** *n.* [joc. use of greyhound terminology] [1990s+] the anus; thus *take it up trap two*, to submit to anal intercourse. ❑ **trap-stronghold** *n.* [18C+] (*Aus.*) a police station.

IN PHRASES

❑ **check a trap** *v.* (*also* **check one's trap**) [play on SE *check one's trap*, but note CHECK *v.* (1)] [1990s+] (*US black*) **1** to monitor a given situation, to oversee one's business, esp. when it is illicit. **2** to spend time with a lover, esp. one with whom one is having an affair. ❑ **go round the traps** *v.* [the image is of a farmer, gamekeeper or poacher touring the traps set to catch game] [1930s–60s] (*Aus.*) to make a tour of inspection. ❑ **understand trap** *v.* [late 17C–19C] to be aware, to know what is in one's interest. ❑ **up to trap** *adj.* [late 17C–19C] aware.

trap *n.*[2] [abbr. RATTLETRAP *n.* (2)] **1** [19C] a small, sprung, two-wheeled carriage, a gig. **2** [1930s–60s] (*US*) a dilapidated old car.

IN PHRASES

❑ **hot trap** *n.* [HOT *adj.* (1d)] [1930s–50s] (*US Und.*) a stolen car.

trapan *n.* (*also* **trepan**) [SE *trap*] [mid-17C–18C] (*UK Und.*) **1** a person who benefits by ensnaring other people into actions that will harm them. **2** a trick or snare.

trapan *v.* (*also* **trappan, trepan, treypan**) [TRAPAN *n.*] [mid-17C–mid-19C] (*UK Und.*) to ensnare, to deceive.

trapanner *n.* (*also* **trappanner, trepanner**) [TRAPAN *v.*] [mid-17C–mid-18C] a cheat, a deceiver.

trapes *n.* (*also* **traipse, trapse**) [TRAPES *v.*] **1** [late 17C–19C] a slatternly woman. **2** [mid-19c] a tedious, laborious task.

IN COMPOUNDS

❑ **trapish** *adj.* [18C] slovenly, aimless, dawdling.

trapes *v.* (*also* **traipse**) [? synon. SE *trape*, but chronology is dubious (one citation 1440, then none until 1706, after coinage of *traipse*). ? OFr. *trapasser, trepasser*, to pass over or beyond] [late 16C+] to trudge about, to walk in a slovenly, aimless manner (with the image or actuality of one's clothes dragging on the ground).

trapeze artist *n.* [ARTIST *n.* (1)] **1** [1930s+] a sexual contortionist. **2** [1930s–40s] (*US tramp*) a tramp who rides the trains. **3** [1940s] a woman who enjoys cunnilingus, esp. as part of sex exhibitions. **4** [1940s] (*US gay*) a fellator.

trapish *adj. see under* TRAPES *n.*

trappan *v. see* TRAPAN *v.*

trappanner *n. see* TRAPANNER *n.*

trapper *n.* [ext. of TRAP *n.*[2] (1)] [late 19C] a horse that draws a small two-wheeled carriage.

trapping *n.* [2000s] (*S.Afr.*) walking.

traps *n.*[1] [SE *trappings*] **1** [early 19C+] one's personal effects. **2** [mid-19C] (*UK Und.*) clothes. **3** [mid–late 19C] (*Aus.*) a pack. **4** [late 19C] tools, equipment. **5** [1970s] (*gay*) men's underwear.

traps *n.*[2] [ety. unknown, ? visual resemblance to animal traps] [20C+] drums or other percussion devices.

trapse *n. see* TRAPES *n.*

trapstick *n.* [SE *trapstick*, a stick used in the game of trap or trap-ball] **1** [mid-17C–18C] the penis, thus *well-trapped*, well-endowed. **2** [18C–mid-19C; 1950s] usu. in pl., legs, esp. thin legs.

trash *n.* **1** [late 16C–19C] money [the identification of money and dirt]. **2** [1950s+] (*US black*) loose talk, banter, teasing [note Joyce, *Ulysses* (1922): 'He was going about with some of them Sinner Fein lately or whatever they call themselves talking his usual trash and nonsense']. **3** [1980s] (*US drugs*) heroin [i.e. DIRT *n.* (10b)]. **4** *see TRAILER TRASH under* TRAILER *n.*[3]. **5** *see* WHITE TRASH *n.*

IN COMPOUNDS

❑ **trashmouth** *n.* [1970s+] (*US campus*) one who regularly uses profanity or obscenity; slanderous talk. ❑ **trash talk** *n.* *see* separate entries.

IN PHRASES

❑ **let's talk trash** [1950s] (*US*) a phr. of greeting. ❑ **talk trash** *v.* [1950s+] (*US black*) to talk insincerely, to boast, to lie, esp. when pursuing sex. ❑ **talking trash** *n.* [1940s+] (*US black*) any verbal by-play, banter between men, flirtation between a man and a woman etc.

SE in slang uses

IN COMPOUNDS

❑ **trashcan** *n.* [1970s] (*US*) a ricketty old truck.

IN PHRASES

❑ **empty one's trash** *v.* [1970s] (*US black*) to have sexual intercourse; usu. to ejaculate.

trash *adj.* [1990s+] (*US campus/gay*) sexually promiscuous.

IN PHRASES

❑ **trash (an' ready)** *adj.* [1990s+] (*W.I./UK black teen*) attractive, fashionable, trendy.

trash *v.* [SAmE *trash*, rubbish, garbage] **1** [1960s+] (*orig. US*) to break windows, destroy appliances etc as part of a demonstration, a prison search, a robbery, etc; thus *trasher*, a (political) vandal, *trashing*, the action of political vandalism [coined by the radical Weatherman movement. Note the 1960s 'underground' revolutionary cartoon hero 'Trashman', created by Spain Rodriguez]. **2** [1970s+] (*orig. US*) to beat up, to injure badly. **3** [1970s+] (*orig. US*) to criticize (a work of art or similar creative effort) so as to undermine its validity, to malign. **4** [1970s+] (*US*) to scavenge discarded goods, other people's rubbish. **5** [1970s+] (*US*) to go out to find casual sex. **6** [1970s+] (*orig. US*) to vandalize, to destroy, to render a mess (with no political overtones).

IN PHRASES

❑ **trash one's act** *v.* [1970s] (*US campus*) to cease what one is doing, usu. as imper.

trashed *adj.* (*also* **trashed-out**) [fig. use of TRASH *v.* (2)] **1** [1960s+] very drunk. **2** [1980s+] very intoxicated by a drug. **3** [1980s+] extremely ill or emotionally disturbed. **4** [1980s+] exhausted, tired, overworked. **5** [1980s+] of an object, wrecked, ruined, destroyed.

trash talk *n.* [TRASH TALK *v.*] [1990s+] (*US black*) nonsense.

trash talk *v.* [TRASH TALK *n.*] [1960s+] (*orig. US black*) **1** to talk nonsense, to lie. **2** to talk insultingly, disparagingly.

trashy *adj.* [SE *trashy*, of objects, worthless] **1** [mid-19C+] of people, worthless, disreputable. **2** [1930s+] (*US*) characteristic of poor WHITE TRASH *n.* **3** [1970s+] sluttish, tarty.

trasseno *n.* *see* TROSSENO *n.*

trat *n.* [backsl. = TART *n.* (2)] [late 19C–1900s] a young and attractive prostitute.

tratt *n.* (*also* **trat**) [abbr.] [1960s+] a *tratt*oria or small, Italianate restaurant, esp. fashionable in 1960s.

travel *v.* **1** [early 19C] (*UK Und.*) to be transported. **2** [mid-19C+] to move quickly, to leave, depart.

SE in slang uses

IN PHRASES

❑ **it's a fine day for travelling** [ironic use of SE] [1950s+] (*Aus.*) a phr. used in the outback to signify that one has received notice to quit. ❑ **travel by Harry Pannell** *v.* [*H*(*arry*) *Pannell* & Co; makers of stout walking boots] [1920s+] (*N.Z.*) to go by foot, to walk. ❑ **travel by Mr Foot's horse** *v.* *see under* MR FOOT'S HORSE *n.* ❑ **travel by rail** *v.* [1930s+] (*Aus.*) to be so drunk that one can only proceed by hanging onto things. ❑ **travel on one's thumb** *v.* [the raising of one's thumb in hope of a lift] [1920s+] to hitchhike.

travel agent *n.* [play on TRIP *n.*[4] (1a)] **1** [1960s] (*drugs*) LSD. **2** [1960s] an LSD guide. **3** [1960s+] an LSD supplier.

traveller *n.* **1** [18C–mid-19C] a highwayman. **2** [mid-18C] one shilling [? it travels about from person to person or it enables one to travel]. **3** [mid-18C–1900s] (*chiefly Aus.*) a tramp. **4** [19C] an itinerant pedlar. **5** [19C] (*UK Und.*) a thief who moves from town to town. **6** [mid-19C+] a gypsy. **7** [late 19C–1900s] a sermon which can be delivered by the same preacher on different occasions and in different places. **8** [1980s+] a young itinerant who travels the UK by car or caravan but has no Romany connections and is often from a HIPPIE *n.*[2] (3), punk or similar youth subculture and is often interested in a variety of 'green' or allied issues. **9** [2000s] (*Aus.*) alcohol that is bought in a public house for consumption elsewhere.

SE in slang uses

IN PHRASES

❑ **tip the traveller** *v.* (*also* **play the traveller**) [TIP *v.*[1] (1), the association of gypsies with telling a *TALL STORY under* TALL *adj.*] [mid-18C–19C] to boast, to exaggerate, also as phr. *tip the traveller upon*, to fool, to deceive with 'tall tales'. ❑ **traveller at Her Majesty's expense** *n.* [mid-19C–1900s] a convict condemned to be transported.

trawler *n.* [it *trawls* the streets looking for suspects] [1920s+] (*Aus.*) a police car or van; a 'Black Maria'.

tray *n.*[1] (*also* **dray, tre, trey,**) [Ital. *tre*, three] **1** [late 15C+] three, whether as a digit or a set of three. **2** [late 19C+] (*also* **treemoon, treyer**) a three-month or three-year prison sentence. **3** [1950s] £3. **4** [1950s+] (*also* **treyer**) $3. **5** [1960s+] (*US black/drugs*) (*also* **trey bag**) a $3 packet of heroin. **6** [1970s+] a $3 packet of marijuana.

IN COMPOUNDS

❑ **tray eight** *n.* *see* THIRTY-EIGHT *n.*

IN PHRASES

❑ **trey of knockers** *n.* [the three balls hanging above such shops] [1940s] (*US black*) a pawnbroker's shop.

tray *n.*[2] *see* TREY-BIT *n.*

traylor *n.* *see* TRAILER *n.*[1].

trayning cheat *n.* *see TRINING CHEAT under* TRINING *n.*

tray-trapper *n.* [TREY-BIT *n.* + SE *trapper*] [1900s–50s] (*Aus.*) one who takes round a collection, 'passes round the hat'.

treach *adj.* (*also* **treacherous**) [abbr./ext. of SE *treacherous*, on bad = good model] [1980s+] (*US black/teen*) very good, excellent.

treacle *n.* **1** [late 18C+] inferior port. **2** [early 19C+] glutinously sentimental love-making. **3** [mid-19C] (*UK Und.*) bribe money [+ play on SWEETEN *v.* (2)]. **4** [late 19C] (*Aus. drugs*) opium. **5** [late 19C–1930s] insincere, empty talk, typically that of a politician.

SE in slang uses

IN COMPOUNDS

❑ **treacle-arse** *n.* [ARSE] **1** [1940s–50s] (*Aus.*) a passive homosexual. **2** [2000s] (*N.Z.*) an unlikeable and/or sycophantic person. ❑ **treacle-billy** *n.* [20C+] (*Irish*) a lodging house. ❑ **treacle-man** *n.* [the stickiness and sweetness of SE *treacle*] [late 19C–1900s] **1** a good-looking man who works as a decoy for burglars by charming the housemaid while the gang slip in unnoticed. **2** a smooth-talking, good-looking travelling salesman, who uses his charms to persuade the 'lady of the house' to buy his wares. **3** a shop assistant, esp. in a draper's, who has the same effect on customers. ❑ **treacle-miner** *n.* [1910s] (*Aus.*) a man who boasts of his wealth or position. ❑ **treacle plaster** *n.* [1920s–30s] (*UK Und.*) a sticky piece of brown paper used by a thief to remove glass carefully; also as a form of gag. ❑ **treacle sleep** *n.* [the slow pouring of thick SE *treacle*] [mid-19C] deep, uninterrupted sleep.

IN EXCLAMATIONS

❑ **treacle(-trousers)!** [? they stick to the wearer's legs] [1920s–40s] (*Aus.*) a jibe aimed at one whose trousers are too short.

treacle tart *n.* [rhy. sl. = FART *n.* (1)] [1990s+] an act of breaking wind.

Treacle Town *n.* [late 19C] **1** Bristol [its treacle refineries]. **2** Macclesfield [F&H posit an unlikely story of a treacle hogshead bursting and inundating the town's gutters].

tread *v.* [SE *tread*, of the male bird, to copulate with] [mid-16C–17C; late 19C–1950s] of a man, to have sexual intercourse.

treaders *n.* [late 19C; 1940s] (*later US black*) shoes.

tread on someone's toes *v. see* STEP ON SOMEONE'S TOES *under* STEP ON *v.*

treads *n.* [1960s] (*US campus*) trainers.

treasure *n.*[1] **1** [mid-16C+] an admirable person. **2** [1920s+] (*also* **treas**) an affectionate term of address.

SE in slang uses

IN COMPOUNDS

❑ **Treasure State** *n.* [its reserves of precious metals] [1930s–50s] (*US*) Montana. ❑ **treasure trail** *n. see* HAPPY TRAIL *under* HAPPY *adj.*

IN PHRASES

❑ **treasure of love** *n.* [mid–late 18C] the vagina.

treasure *n.*[2] **1** [late 16C–19C; 1980s+] the vagina [a relatively rare positive image, also *see* TREASURE OF LOVE *under* TREASURE *n.*[1]]. **2** [18C–19C] the penis.

treasure hunt *n.* [rhy. sl. = CUNT *n.* (1)] [1990s+] the vagina.

treasury of love *n. see nature's treasury* under NATURE *n.*

treat *n.* **1** [19C+] anything (or occas. anyone) admirable, enjoyable or pleasurable, also used ironically. **2** [1980s] (*US campus*) a good-looking woman.

IN PHRASES

❑ **give the boys a treat** *v.* [late 19C+] of a girl or woman, to reveal inadvertently more of her body than you would otherwise see, such as cleavage by leaning over or upper thighs or underwear when getting out of a vehicle or bending down to pick something up.

treat *v.* [2000s] (*US teen*) to teach someone, to correct someone's behaviour, to punish.

treat, a *adv.* (*also* **treato**) [late 19C+] wonderfully, extremely, excessively, e.g. *that'll go down a treat.*

IN PHRASES

❑ **do one a treat** *v.* [late 19C+] to suit one absolutely.

treat like shit *v. see under* SHIT *n.*

treatment *n.*

SE in slang uses

IN PHRASES

❑ **give someone the treatment** *v.* **1** [1960s+] to have sexual intercourse with. **2** [1970s+] to beat up, to torture, usu. in order to elicit information. **3** [1970s+] to submit someone to some form of verbal interrogation or telling-off.

treato *adv. see* TREAT, A *adv.*

treble chance *n.* [rhy. sl.] [20C+] a dance.

treddlie *n.* [SE *treadle*, 'A lever worked by the foot in machines and mechanical contrivances' (*OED*)] [2000s] (*Aus.*) a child's bicycle.

tree *n.* [the characteristics of a tree] **1** [1960s] (*US black, Los Angeles*) a police officer who is susceptible to bribery [its colour SE *green* of a tree and GREEN *n.*[2] (1)]. **2** [1960s+] (*US campus*) a very tall woman – 6ft (180cm) or more; thus *CHERRY TREE under* CHERRY *n.*[its height]. **3** [2000s] (*US*) a gearstick [its shape]. **4** [2000s] (*US drugs*) a marijuana cigarette. **5** *see* TRIPLE TREE *n.* **6** *see* WOOD *n.*[1] (5).

IN PHRASES

❑ **go up a tree** *v.* **1** [mid-19C] to be hanged. **2** [1910s+] (*Aus.*) to fall off one's horse. ❑ **kill a tree** *v. see* KILL A SNAKE *under* SNAKE *n.*[1]. ❑ **off one's tree** *adj.* [2000s] mad, eccentric. ❑ **out of one's tree** *adj.* (*also* **off one's tree, out of one's bush**) [the sufferer has fig. fallen out of a tree] **1** [1960s+] crazy, insane. **2** [1990s+] totally intoxicated by drugs. **3** [2000s] utterly bored.

SE in slang uses

IN COMPOUNDS

❑ **tree-dweller** *n.* [1990s+] a fool, a peasant. ❑ **tree-hugger** *n.* (*also* **hugger, tree nymph**) [1960s+] (*US campus*) an environmentalist; thus adj. *tree-hugging.* ❑ **tree-jumper** *n.* (*also* **tree-bagger, tree-chopper**) [his jumping out of trees to attack a victim] [1970s+] (*US prison*) a rapist or sexual molester. ❑ **tree suit** *n.* [i.e. wood] [1940s–70s] (*US black*) a coffin.

IN PHRASES

❑ **tree of knowledge** *n.* [1940s+] (*S.Afr. drugs*) marijuana. ❑ **tree of the triple crook** *n.* (*also* **crooked tree**) [17C–19C] the gallows. ❑ **tree that bears fruit all the year round** *n.* (*also* **...bears twelve times a year**) [mid-17C–mid-19C] the gallows. ❑ **tree with three corners** *n. see* THREE-CORNERED TREE *under* THREE *adj.* ❑ **up a tree** see separate entries.

tree and sap *n.* [rhy. sl.] [20C+] (*Aus.*) a tap (faucet).

treed *adj.* [1980s+] **1** (*US drugs*) extremely intoxicated by a drug. **2** (*US campus*) thrilled.

treemoon *n. see* TRAY *n.*[1] (2).

trees *n.* [pun on GREEN *n.*[2] (3)] [1990s+] (*US black/drugs*) marijuana.

treewins *n. see THREESWINS under* THREE *adj.*

tremblers *n.*[1] **1** [19C] (*Anglo-Irish*) the stairs. **2** [1960s+] a woman's breasts, esp. when large, thus able to tremble.

tremblers *n.*[2] [1970s] (*drugs*) the shakes that accompany heroin withdrawal.

trembles *n.* [19C] delirium tremens.

tremendous *adj.* (*also* **tremenjous**) [early 19C+] extraordinary, esp. admirable, remarkable.

trench *n.*[1] [late 15C+] the vagina.

trench *n.*[2] [abbr.] [1970s+] (*orig. US black*) a *trench*coat.

trenches *n.* [1990s+] (*US black teen*) any impoverished area.

trendoid *n.* [SE *trend*; on pattern of SF *android*, a human-like robot] [1980s+] one who is slavishly devoted to following the latest trends (but never quite achieves the correct effect).

trendy *n.* (*also* **trend**) [SE *trend*] [1960s+] a devoted, if not always wholly successful, trend-follower.

trendy *adj.* [SE *trendy*, fashionable] [1980s] (*US campus*) excellent.

trepan *see under* TRAPAN.

trepanner *n. see* TRAPANNER *n.*

très *adj.* [synon. Fr.] [1920s+] very.

treswins *n. see THREESWINS under* THREE *adj.*

Trev *n.* [abbr. the stereotyped 'proletarian' name *Trevor*] [1990s+] (*UK juv.*) generic for any stupid, working-class teenager.

t. rex *n.* [rhy. sl.; ult. *T. Rex*, a pop group of the early 1970s] [1970s+] sex.

trey *n. see* TRAY *n.*[1].

trey bag *n. see* TRAY *n.*[1] (5).

trey-bit *n.* (*also* **tray bit, tray, trey, tray-piece**) [late 19C+] (*orig. Aus./N.Z.*) **1** a threepenny piece. **2** a term of contempt for an insignificant person.

trey-bits *n.* [rhy. sl.; ult. TREY-BIT *n.* (1)] [1950s+] (*Aus./N.Z.*) **1** the female breasts [= TIT *n.*[2] (1)]. **2** diarrhoea [= SHITS, THE *n.* (1)].

trey eight *n.* [TREY *n.* + SE *eight*] [1980s+] (*US black*) a .38 calibre gun.

treyer *n. see various under* TRAY *n.*[1].

treyning *n. see* TRINING *n.*

treyning cheat *n. see TRINING CHEAT under* TRINING *n.*

trey of sous *n.* [TREY *n.* + SOU *n.* (+ RUFF *n.*)] [1940s] (*US black*) three dimes, 30 cents; thus *trey of sous and a double ruff*, four nickels, 40 cents.

treypan *v. see* TRAPAN *v.*

trezzie *n. see* TRIZZIE *n.*

triangle *n.* [1930s+] a three-way relationship, in any combination of sexes and sexualities.

triangles *n.* [due to the hallucinations, nothing is 'on the square'] [mid-19C] delirium tremens.

trib *n.* [SE *tribulation*] [late 17C–1910s] (*UK Und.*) a prison.

tribe *n.* [late 19C+] (*US Und.*) a gang; a given group of criminal specialists.

trichi *n.* [abbr.] [mid–late 19C] (*Anglo-Ind.*) a *Trichi*nopoly cigar.

trick *n.*[1] [note Dillard, *Lexicon of Black English* (1977): 'The term *trick* for the sexual performance of a prostitute probably comes, ultimately, from the voodoo term for achieving control (often sexual control), possibly reinforced by the nautical term meaning "a task"' i.e, TRICK *n.*[4] (1)] **1** [late 16C+] sexual intercourse, occas. other forms of sexual encounter, esp. a prostitute's intercourse (or other activity) with a client. **2** [20C+] a girl, a young woman. **3** [1920s+] (*also* **trip**) a prostitute's client, whether hetero- or homosexual, the implication being of deceiving any such client into parting with money. **4** [1920s+] any casual sex partner. **5** [1950s+] a general term of abuse, equating the subject with a whore's client. **6** [1970s+] (*US black*) one who can be easily manipulated, e.g. a longterm admirer who is never allowed sex, but merely kept in tow for the material pleasures they offer. **7** [1970s+] a boyfriend; hetero- or homosexual. **8** [1990s+] (*US prison*) a prisoner who can be easily exploited for money or presents.

pertaining to commercial sex

IN COMPOUNDS

❑ **trick-ass** *adj.* [-ASS *sfx*] [1960s+] (*US black*) a general derog. term, the implication is of sexual inadequacy (for a man) or promiscuity (for a woman). ❑ **trick baby** *n.* [given no positive evidence to the contrary, the prostitute-mother assumes the father to have been one of the paying customers; note *TRICK DADDY* below] [1960s+] (*orig. US black*) an illegitimate child born to a prostitute. ❑ **trick bag** *n.* [on model of SCUMBAG *under* SCUM *n.*; the pimp assumption that only victims pay for sex and that such a victim deserves whatever happens to him] **1** [1960s+] (*US black*) an unpleasant and disadvantaged position, a no-win situation. **2** [1980s+] a fool, one who thinks they are better than they are. ❑ **trick broad** *n.* [BROAD *n.*[2] (3)] [1970s] (*US black*) a prostitute. ❑ **trick bunk** *n.* [1990s+] (*US prison*) that bunk in a convict dormitory which is used for clandestine sex. ❑ **trick daddy** *n.* [2000s] (*US black*) the father of a prostitute's child. ❑ **trick dough** *n.* [DOUGH *n.* (1)] [1960s] (*US Und.*) money earned by a prostitute. ❑ **trick flick** *n.* [1950s+] (*gay*) a pornographic film. ❑ **trick house** *n.* [HOUSE *n.*[1] (1)] [1930s+] (*US black*) a brothel. ❑ **trick money** *n.* [1940s+] (*US black*) the money a prostitute earns and hands over to her pimp. ❑ **trick pad** *n.* [PAD *n.*[2] (2)] [1990s+] (*US Und.*) an apartment, room or hotel room used by prostitutes to entertain their clients. ❑ **trick rider** *n.* [TRICK *n.*[1] (7) + RIDE *v.* (1)] [1980s] (*US*) a homosexual man. ❑ **trick room** *n.* [1920s+] a room, in a hotel or motel, where a prostitute can take clients. ❑ **trick suit** *n.* [1950s+] a prostitute's dress that can be removed easily and is thus suitable for business. ❑ **trick towel** *n.* [1950s+] (*gay*) a towel for wiping oneself after intercourse. ❑ **trick willy** *n.* [generic *Willy*] [1950s+] (*US black*) a gullible black man.

IN PHRASES

❑ **beat a trick** *v.* [1970s+] (*US Und.*) of a prostitute, to rob a client. ❑ **boss trick** *n.* [BOSS *adj.* (1)] [1960s+] in prostitution, a good customer. ❑ **champagne trick** *n.* [2000s] a particularly wealthy or generous client for a prostitute. ❑ **cheap-trick** *adj.* [1960s] pertaining to the poorer of a prostitute's clients. ❑ **do the trick** *v.* **1** [late 17C; mid-19C+] of a man, to have sexual intercourse; also in homosexual use. **2** [early 19C] (*UK Und.*) to blunder. **3** [early 19C+] (*orig. UK Und.*) to get what one wants, to succeed, e.g. to perform a successful robbery, to achieve a seduction [SE from mid-19C]. **4** [late 19C] of a woman, to lose one's virginity, to be deflowered. **5** [late 19C] to impregnate a woman. **6** [1910s] (*Aus.*) to get married. ❑ **do the trick of the loop** *v.* [Gifford, *Ulysses Annotated* (1988) '"the trick of the loop", a carnival game in which the contestants try to win prizes by pitching small wooden hoops at a group of upright stakes.'] [1920s] to have sexual intercourse. ❑ **freak trick** *n.* [FREAK *n.*[1] (7)] [1960s+] (*US prostitute*) any customer who requires out-of-the-way sex or who attacks the woman physically. ❑ **get up to tricks** *v.* [late 19C] to work as a prostitute. ❑ **pull a trick** *v.* [1950s] (*US Und.*) to perform male homosexual fellatio. ❑ **straight trick** *n.* [STRAIGHT *adj.*[1] (11)] [1970s+] a prostitute's client who requires no 'extras' beyond normal intercourse. ❑ **turn a trick** *v.* *see* separate entry.

general uses

IN COMPOUNDS

❑ **trick-acting** *n.* [20C+] (*Irish*) showing off. ❑ **trick-bag** *n.* [1970s] (*US*) a fig. respository of secrets and surprises. ❑ **trick roll** *n.* [1910s] (*Aus. Und.*) a roll of money in which low-value notes or even sheets of blank paper are wrapped in single high-denomination bill.

SE in slang uses

DERIVATIVES

❑ **trickology** *n.* [SE *trick* + -OLOGY *n.*] [1970s] subterfuge, deception.

IN PHRASES

❑ **catamaran trick** *n.* [? early 19C SE *catamaran*, an ill-tempered person] [early 19C] a practical joke. ❑ **cross-road trick** *n.* [the trad. burying of suicides at a crossroads] [late 19C] (*Aus. prison*) suicide. ❑ **can't take a trick** *v.* [card-game imagery] [1940s+] (*Aus.*) to be consistently unlucky. ❑ **take a trick** *v.* [card imagery] [late 19C] (*Aus.*) to show promise; to be successful. ❑ **whole bag of tricks** *n.* *see* separate entry.

trick *n.*[2] **1** [early 18C+] (*UK/US Und.*) a crime, esp. a robbery or theft; thus *pull a trick*, TURN A TRICK *v.*[1]. **2** [mid-19C] (*UK Und.*) any article stolen by a pickpocket.

trick *n.*[3] [mid-18C–early 19C] (*US Und.*) a watch.

trick *n.*[4] [naut. use *trick*, a turn at the wheel] **1** [mid-19C+] a period of work, usu. one that is physically demanding or unpleasant. **2** [late 19C–1900s] any period spent within an institution, e.g. a hospital. **3** [late 19C+] (*US*) a prison sentence. **4** [1900s–50s] (*US*) a term of service, e.g. in the army, on a ship. **5** [1910s] a situation one dislikes. **6** [1920s] an organization.

trick *n.*[5] **1** [late 19C+] (*US/Aus.*) (*also* **tricksie**) a small or amusing adult, animal or child. **2** [20C+] a clever person, also used sarcastically.

trick *adj.*[1] **1** [1950s+] relating to commercial or casual sex. **2** [1970s+] used lit. or fig. to imply the foolish gullibility of anyone who is, or might as well be a prostitute's client.

trick *adj.*[2] (*also* **tricked out**) [SE *tricky*, *tricksy*] [1980s+] (*US campus*) **1** interesting, pleasing. **2** technologically sophisticated.

trick *v.* [TRICK *n.*[1] (3)] (*US*) **1** [1930s+] to work as a prostitute, to have sex with a client; thus TRICKING *n.*[note Milner & Milner, *Black Players* (1972): 'By implication, one is literally tricking a man by taking money for doing what women should do for free.']. **2** [1960s+] to have casual sex. **3** [1960s+] (*gay*) to pick up a partner for casual, unpaid sex. **4** [1960s+] (*US black*) of a man, to spend money on a woman other than one's regular partner. **5** [1960s+] of a man, to pay for sex with a prostitute. **6** [1990s+] of a man, to spend money on a woman in the hope of being repaid with sex.

SE in slang uses

IN PHRASES

❑ **trick (on)** *v.* [1970s] (*US black*) to inform on; to betray. ❑ **trick the books** *v.* [1910s] (*Aus.*) to deceive a bookmaker. ❑ **trick up** *v.* [1920s+] (*Aus.*) to take advantage of, to confuse, to outwit.

trick cyclist *n.* [joc. derog. mispron.] [1950s+] (*orig. milit.*) psychiatrist.

tricker *n.* [SE *trick*, some form of pincers or expandable wedge; 'engines of Iron so cunningly wrought, that he wil cut a barre of Iron in two with them' (Greene, *The Blacke Bookes Messenger*, 1592)] [late 16C–early 17C] (*UK Und.*) a burglar's tool, spec. a gadget used to force open a window.

trickeration *n.* [SE *trick* + sfx *-eration*] **1** [1930s–40s] (*US black*) showing off, boasting, flaunting oneself or one's possessions. **2** [1940s–60s] (*US black/prison*) the act of fooling, deceiving and otherwise manipulating someone.

trickett *n.* [the New South Wales champion sculler Edward *Trickett* (1851–1916), who stated, for advertising purposes, that 'beer's best for an A1 nation'] [late 19C–1900s] (*Aus., New South Wales*) a long drink of beer.

trickie *n.* [TRICK *n.*[5] (1)] [20C+] (*Irish*) an amusing person.

DERIVATIVES

□ **trickified** *adj.* [20C+] (*Irish*) aware.

tricking *n.* [TRICK *v.* (1)] [1930s+] (*orig. US black*) having sex for money.

trickle *n.* [2000s] (*US juv.*) the vagina.

tricks *n.* [backform. f. colloq. greeting *how's tricks?*] [1930s+] circumstances, one's life.

tricksie *n. see* TRICK *n.*[5] (1).

trick-track *n. see* TICK-TACK *n.*[1].

trickum legis *n.* [pig Lat.; 'trick of the law'] [late 18C–early 19C] a legal trick.

tricky bits *n.* [1990s+] (*Aus.*) the male genitals.

tried at Stafford Court, be *v.* [pun on SE *staff*] [early 17C] to be beaten, to be thrashed.

trif *adj.* (*also* **trife**) [SE *triffling*] [1990s+] worthless, disgusting.

trifecta *n.* [gambling *trifecta*, a bet on the first three places in a horserace] [1960s+] (*US*) any chance situation involving three components.

triff *n.* [abbr.] [1900s] a *trif*le.

trifle *n.* [euph.] [late 19C] the penis.

triflin' *n.* [SE *trifling*] [1950s+] (*US black*) acting irresponsibly, esp. as a parasite, e.g. *Don't trust a word he says, that boy is just triflin'*.

trig *n.*[1] [late 18C–early 19C] (*UK Und.*) a piece of paper that is left to mark a door for the purpose of robbing an empty house, thus phr. *trigging the jigger*, the placing of such a marker.

trig *n.*[2] [abbr.] [mid-19C+] *trig*onometry.

trig *n.*[3] [17C SE *trig*, to go in a hurry] [late 19C] a trot, a hurried walk, a trip.

trigger *n.*[1] (*also* **triggerboy, trigger guy, triggerman**) **1** [1930s] the index finger. **2** [1930s+] (*US*) a gunman, esp. one working for organized crime. **3** [1940s–50s] an armed bodyguard. **4** [1950s+] that member of a criminal gang who uses a gun. **5** [1990s+] (*US prison*) an armed prison guard.

trigger *n.*[2] [on model of GUN *n.*[1] (2)] [1940s] the penis.

trigger happy *adj.* [SE *trigger happy*, over-eager to use a gun] [1940s+] (*orig. US*) overemotional, keen to put action before thought.

triggerman *n. see* TRIGGER *n.*[1].

trig it *v.* [SE *trig*, to walk off quickly] [late 18C–19C] to play truant.

trigry-mate *n.* [SE *trig*, to walk briskly + SE *mate*; they are both people with whom one walks around] **1** [late 17C–1900s] an idle woman companion. **2** [late 19C] an intimate friend.

trig up *v. see* RIG *v.*[1].

trike *n.* [abbr.] [late 19C+] a *tri*cycle.

tril *n.* [Afk. *dril/tril*, shiver, vibrate] [2000s] (*S.Afr.*) a penis.

trilby *n.* [the heroine of the novel *Trilby* (1894) by George du Maurier, whose feet were particularly attractive. Note SE *trilby*, a type of shoe fashionable in US *c.*1900] [late 19C–1930s] (*US*) a foot.

trilby hat *n.* [rhy. sl. = PRAT *n.*[1] (6)] [1960s+] a fool.

trill *n.*[1] [? punning Lat. *ars musica*, the musical art] [late 17C–19C] the anus.

trill *n.*[2] [TRILBY *n.*] [1930s–40s] (*US black*) **1** departure. **2** an affected way of walking.

IN PHRASES

□ **knock one's trill** *v.* [1940s] to walk (in an affected manner).

trill *adj.* (*also* **trill-ass**) [2000s] (*US black*) excellent, admirable.

trill *v.* (*also* **trilly, trilly-walk**) [? SE *trill*, to trundle, to move on wheels or TRILBY *n.*] **1** [1930s–40s] (*US black/P.R.*) to leave, to walk off. **2** [1970s] to arrive, to enter.

trill like a canary *v. see* SING LIKE A CANARY *under* SING *v.*

trim *n.* [? SE *trim*, neat, attractive, pretty] (*orig. US black*) **1** [1930s+] a woman's genitalia; the female pubic hair. **2** [1930s+] (*also* **trimming**) a woman, always in a sexual context; thus GET SOME TRIM below. **3** [1950s+] cunnilingus.

IN PHRASES

□ **get some trim** *v.* [1980s+] of a man, to seduce, to have sexual intercourse.

trim *v.* [SE *trim*, to cut the hair, thus to 'fleece'] **1** [early 16C+] (*also* **trim up**) to beat, to trounce, to defeat; also fig. use. **2** [early 16C+] to reprimand, to scold. **3** [17C–18C; 1960s+] to have sexual intercourse. **4** [late 17C+] to cheat of money or possessions.

IN PHRASES

□ **trim someone's jacket** *v.* (*also* **swinge someone's jacket**) [cf. SE *dress*, *array*, to beat/*swinge*, to trash] [mid-18C–early 19C] to beat, to thrash someone. □ **trim someone's rim** *v.* [assonance] [1970s] (*US*) to have anal intercourse. □ **trim the buff** *v.* [SE *trim*, to clip + *buff*, bare skin] [late 18C] to deflower a woman.

trimble *adj.* [? SE *tremble*] [20C+] (*W.I., Gren.*) selfish, greedy, fearful of sharing what one has.

trimmer *n.*[1] [TRIM *v.*] **1** [early 18C] a self-serving, braggart and cheat. **2** [mid-18C–19C] a thing that defeats another, e.g. a blow, a stiff letter etc. **3** [19C–1930s] a person who beats, scolds, reprimands etc. **4** [late 19C–1900s] a thieving prostitute. **5** [late 19C+] (*US Und.*) a swindler; a confidence trickster; also crooked lawyer. **6** [1900s] (*US*) a dice cheat. **7** [2000s] (*N.Z.*) a spoilsport, a disappointment.

trimmer *n.*[2] [SE *trimming*, excellent, first-rate] [1940s+] (*Aus./N.Z.*) something or someone that is excellent, wonderful, approved of.

trimming *n.*[1] [SE *trim*, to cut the hair, thus to 'fleece'] **1** [early 16C; late 17C+] a beating; a defeat. **2** [17C] (*UK Und.*) sleight-of-hand used by a confidence trickster. **3** [late 17C+] a reprimand, a dressing down, a verbal beating. **4** [1910s–40s] (*UK Und.*) the final stage of a confidence game, in which the victim loses his money.

trimming *n.*[2] *see* TRIM *n.* (2).

trimmings *n.* [a period when shops (as opposed to 'sinful' public houses) were allowed to sell alcohol. Shopkeepers, typically drapers and silk-merchants, thus itemized as 'trimmings' the drinks their female customers consumed, on the bills that were sent to their husbands] [late 19C–1940s] secretly drunk alcohol, usu. consumed by a woman.

trindle-tail *n. see* TRUNDLE-TAIL *n.*

trine *n.* [TRINE *v.*[1], Tyburn's 'occupation'] [mid-17C–mid-19C] the gallows, thus Tyburn.

trine *v.*[1] [synon. 14C–16C SE *trine*, ult. OSwed. *trina*, to go] [17C–mid-18C] to go, to step.

IN PHRASES

□ **trine to the cheats** *v.* [CHEAT *n.* (3)] [17C–18C] to go to the gallows, to be hanged, lit. 'walk to the things'.

trine *v.*[2] [? abbr. *TRINE TO THE CHEATS under* TRINE *v.*[1] or TRINING *n.*] [17C–19C] (*UK Und.*) to hang.

tringham-trangham/tringum-trangum *n. see* TRINKUM-TRANKUM *n.*

trining *n.* (*also* **treyning, tryning**) [prob. SE *trine*, threefold. The ref. is to the three-part Tyburn gallows. For alt. ety. see *TRINE TO THE CHEATS under* TRINE *v.*[1]] [mid-16C–early 19C] (*UK Und.*) a hanging.

IN COMPOUNDS

□ **trining cheat** *n.* (*also* **trayning cheat, treyning cheat**) [CHEAT *n.* (3)] [early 17C] the gallows.

trinity kiss *n.* [late 19C] (*UK society*) a triple kiss given to children at bedtime by their parents.

trinket *n.* [SE *trinket*] **1** [17C–early 18C] the vagina. **2** [mid-19C–1910s] a baby's or small boy's penis [note TRINKETS *n.* (1)].

trinkets *n.* **1** [mid-17C; 19C] the male genitals [note TRINKET *n.* (2)]. **2** [mid-19C] (*US Und.*) personal weaponry, i.e. a knife and revolver.

trinkum-trankum *n.* (*also* **tringham-trangham, tringum-trangum**) [SE *trinket*] **1** [late 17C–1900s] a whim or fancy. **2** [18C–1900s] a trifle.

trip *n.*[1] [? SE *trip*, to cause to fall over] **1** [mid-19C–1930s] a prostitute or a thief's female companion, esp. one who decoys and then robs drunks. **2** *see* TRICK *n.*[1] (3).

trip *n.*[2] **1** [1900s–50s] (*US Und.*) a prison sentence. **2** [1920s+] (*US Und.*) an arrest. **3** [1930s] (*US prison*) a transfer from one prison to another.

trip *n.*[3] [neutral form of TRIP *n.*[1] (1)] [1910s–20s] an affectionate term of address.

trip *n.*[4] **1** in the context of hallucinogenic or other drugs. (**a**) [1950s+] the experience that follows the ingestion of LSD or another hallucinogenic. (**b**) [1960s+] a dose of a hallucinogenic drug, usu. LSD. (**c**) [1970s+] any form of drug experience. **2** in fig./ext. uses of sense 1. (**a**) [1960s+] any form of experience, event, lifestyle or attitude. (**b**) [1960s+] a challenging, surprising or otherwise out of the ordinary experience, often as *it's a trip*. (**c**) [1970s] anything considered simple. (**d**) [1970s+] (*US campus*) an odd, eccentric person; a funny person. (**e**) [1980s] an argument, a lecture, a story. (**f**) [1980s+] (*US campus*) a cheering, pleasing event.

DERIVATIVES

❑ **tripper** *n. see* separate entry.

IN COMPOUNDS

❑ **triphead** *n.* [sense 1 above + -HEAD *sfx* (4)] [1990s+] (*drugs*) a regular consumer of LSD.

IN PHRASES

❑ **businessman's trip** *n.* (*also* **businessman's lunchtime high, businessman's special**) [unlike the eight-hour duration of a 'normal' LSD *trip*, sense 1a above, this vastly intensified experience lasts only a few minutes, leaving the user free to get on with other things] [1960s+] (*drugs*) dimethyltryptamine. ❑ **Cambodian trip** *n.* (*also* **Cam trip**) [*Cam*bodian + sense 1a above] [1960s+] (*drugs*) a very potent, almost hallucinogenic variety of marijuana. ❑ **death trip** *n.* [1960s+] a fantasy about death, often stimulated by (hallucinogenic) drugs. ❑ **down trip** *n.* [DOWN *adj.*[2]] [1960s+] (*drugs*) **1** an unpleasant experience induced after taking LSD. **2** in fig. use., anything unpleasant, tedious, depressing. ❑ **freak trip** *n.* [1960s] (*US drugs*) an unpleasant experience following the taking of LSD. ❑ **natch trips** *n.* [abbr. SE *natural*] [1960s] (*drugs*) a variety of quasi-drug experiences gained from smoking such natural substances as nutmeg, banana, mace, etc. ❑ **on an ay yo trip** *adj.* [the cry of *Ay! Yo!*] [1980s+] (*W.I./UK black teen*) used of one who is forever demanding attention, making themselves conspicuous. ❑ **on a trip** *adj.* [1960s+] (*drugs*) **1** under the influence of drugs. **2** disorientated, seemingly 'in another world'. **3** crazy, temporarily insane.

SE in slang uses

IN PHRASES

❑ **make a trip** *v.* [play on *BREAK ONE'S ANKLE under* BREAK *v.*[1]] [late 18C–early 19C] to be mother to an illegitimate child. ❑ **take a trip to the West Indies** *v.* [early 19C] (*UK Und.*) of a suspect criminal, to leave a town or place to avoid arrest. ❑ **take for a trip** *v. see TAKE FOR A RIDE under* RIDE *n.* ❑ **trip to the moon** *n.* [MOON *n.* (1a)] [1940s+] (*orig. gay*) anal intercourse.

trip *v.*[1] [TRIP *n.*[4] (1)] **1** with ref. to hallucinogenic drugs. (**a**) [1960s+] (*drugs*) to take LSD. (**b**) [1960s+] (*drugs*) to take any hallucinogenic drug. **2** in fig./ext. uses of sense 1. (**a**) [1960s+] to play around, to 'mess about'. (**b**) [1970s+] to be delighted, to be ecstatic; often as *trip for, trip over*; thus *TRIP OFF (OF)* below. (**c**) [1980s+] (*US black*) to lose control, to go mad, to act under a misapprehension, to overreact. (**d**) [1980s+] to be passionately interested or involved in; thus *TRIP OFF* below. (**e**) [1990s+] to worry. (**f**) [1990s+] to be surprised. (**g**) [1990s+] to suffer.

IN PHRASES

❑ **trip off** *v.* [1980s+] (*US*) to turn against, to become emotionally distanced. ❑ **trip off (of)** *v.* [the image is of an experience so intense that it replicates the effects of LSD] [1960s+] (*orig. US*) to enjoy. ❑ **trip out** *v. see* separate entry. ❑ **tripped-out** *adj. see* separate entry.

SE in slang uses

IN PHRASES

❑ **trip down** *v.* [SE *trip*, to walk lightly] [1960s–80s] (*US*) to go to, to leave. ❑ **trip in** *v.* [1960s–80s] (*US*) to arrive, to enter. ❑ **tripped up** *adj.* [var. on TRIPPED-OUT *adj.* with the added image of falling over] [1980s] (*US campus*) experiencing the effects of excessive drinking. ❑ **trip up on** *v.* [1980s] (*US black*) to betray a lover, to commit adultery.

trip *v.*[2] **1** [1980s+] (*US black gang/campus*) to make an error, to blunder. **2** [1990s+] (*US*) to lie.

tripe *n.*[1] (*also* **tripes**) [SE mid-15C–mid-18C] [mid-18C+] the guts, the intestines, thus DOUBLE TRIPE *n.*[1].

IN COMPOUNDS

❑ **tripe-hound** *n.* [SE *tripe*/TRIPE *n.*[2] + -HOUND *sfx* (1)] **1** [20C+] an unpleasant or contemptible person. **2** [20C+] (*Aus./N.Z. derog*) a dog, esp. a sheepdog. **3** [1920s] a newspaper reporter or an informant. ❑ **tripe-shop** *n.* [early 19C] the stomach.

IN PHRASES

❑ **don't bust your tripes** [1980s+] (*N.Z.*) don't get over-excited; don't overdo things. ❑ **have someone by the tripes** *v.* [1900s] to have someone at a disadvantage. ❑ **tripe and trillibub** *n.* (*also* **tripes and trullibubs**) [SE *tripes and trillibubs*, animal intestines] [17C–early 19C] a nickname for a fat person.

tripe *n.*[2] [virtually SE by 20C] [late 19C+] nonsense, utter rubbish.

IN COMPOUNDS

❑ **tripe merchant** *n.* [late 19C+] a purveyor of nonsense.

IN PHRASES

❑ **up to tripe** *adj.* [1900s–10s] worthless, unpleasant, distasteful.

tripey *adj.* [TRIPE *n.*[2]] [1940s+] rubbishy.

triple *n.* [1980s+] a sexual act involving three particpants.

triple *adj.*

SE in slang uses

IN COMPOUNDS

❑ **triple-clutcher** *n.* [1950s+] a euph. for MOTHERFUCKER *n.* ❑ **triple-decker sandwich** *n. see* SANDWICH *n.* (2). ❑ **triple-hip** *adj.* [SE *triple* + HIP *adj.* (1)] [1940s+] (*US black*) extra smart, very wise. ❑ **triple master blaster** *n.* [SE *triple* + *MASTER BLASTER under* MASTER *n.*] [1980s+] (*drugs*) a situation in which one smokes crack cocaine while simultaneously being fellated and sodomized. ❑ **triple nine** *v.* [the UK emergency phone number: 999] [2000s] to call the police. ❑ **triple-threat queen** *n.* [-QUEEN *sfx* (3)] [1960s+] (*US gay*) a gay man who is happy to put his penis into a mouth, an anus or an armpit. ❑ **triple W** *n.* [i.e. a warm, wet, womb] [1970s] (*US black*) a very sexy and accommodating woman. ❑ **triple whammy** *n.* [ext. of *DOUBLE WHAMMY under* DOUBLE *adj.*] [1950s+] (*US*) a three-part attack, threat or difficulty.

triple tree *n.* (*also* **gallus tree, fatal tree, tree, triple trestle, woody**) [this giant three-cornered gallows, capable of dispatching 21 villains at a time, stands menacingly in the background of Hogarth's 1747 engraving of a public hanging] [late 16C–1930s] the gallows, orig. that sited at Tyburn, London; thus ext. to other gallows.

IN PHRASES

❑ **climb the triple tree** *v.* [18C] to be hanged.

trip out *v.*[1] [ext. of TRIP *v.*[1] (1)] **1** [1960s+] to experience a hallucinogenic drug or a simulacrum thereof; also fig. use. **2** in fig. or ext. uses of sense 1. (**a**) [1960s+] to lose control, to leave normality. (**b**) [1960s+] to strike one as funny, crazy, extraordinary or amazing. (**c**) [1970s+] to obsess or fantasize about. (**d**) [1980s+] to be amazed, delighted. (**e**) [1990s+] to feel confused. (**f**) [1990s+] to confuse, to render emotionally unstable, to worry.

trip out *v.*[2] (*US black/campus*) **1** [1960s+] to leave. **2** [1980s] to fool, to trick, to dupe.

tripped-out *adj.* [TRIP OUT *v.*[1]] **1** [1960s+] (*drugs*) under the influence of LSD or another hallucinogen. **2** [1970s+] disorientated, confused, upset.

tripper *n.* [TRIP *v.*[1] (1)] **1** [1960s+] (*drugs*) one who takes LSD or similar hallucinogens. **2** [1980s+] in fig. use, one who leads a surreal life.

tripper-up *n.* (*also* **tripper**) [SE *trip*] [19C] a thief who robs innocent pedestrians who have been deliberately tripped up by a confederate; often a woman who preys on drunken seamen.

trippet *n.*

IN PHRASES

❑ **down as a trippet** *see* DOWN AS A HAMMER/NAIL/TRIPPET *under* DOWN *adj.*[1].

tripping *n.* (*also* **tabbing**) [TRIP *v.*[1] (1)] **1** [1960s+] taking a drug, usu. LSD. **2** in fig. or ext. uses of sense 1. (**a**) [1960s+] fantasizing, acting in an irrational manner. (**b**) [1960s+] (*US black*) doing something beyond the norm, in a positive way. (**c**) [1960s+] daydreaming. (**d**) [1990s+] (*US black*) becoming angry; overreacting. **3** [1990s+] (*US black*) responding to the effects of narcotics.

tripping *adj.* [TRIP *v.*[1] (2b)] **1** [1980s+] (*US campus*) excellent, admirable. **2** [1990s+] crazy.

-tripping *sfx* [TRIPPING *n.* (2)] [1960s+] a general sfx denoting a style of action or opinion, e.g. *power-tripping*, asserting oneself over others; *head-tripping*, thinking.

trippy *adj.* [TRIP *n.*[4]/TRIP *n.*[4] (2c)] **1** [1960s+] (*orig. US*) bizarre, strange, disturbing (fig. approximating the sensation of taking a hallucinogen). **2** [1960s+] (*drugs*) characteristic of an LSD-taking HIPPIE *n.*[2] (3). **3** [1990s+] (*US teen*) excellent, first-rate. **4** [1990s+] (*drugs*) pertaining to MDMA.

IN COMPOUNDS

❑ **trippy-hippie** *adj. see* HIPPY-TRIPPY *adj.*

triss *n.*[1] (*also* **trizz**) [abbr. TRIZZIE *n.*] [1920s+] (*Aus.*) a threepenny bit.

triss *n.*[2] (*also* **trizz**) [TRISS ABOUT *v.*] [1950s+] (*Aus.*) an effeminate male homosexual.

triss about *v.* [synon. with SWISH *v.*[1] (2)] [1940s+] (*Aus.*) to act in an effeminate manner.

trissy *adj.* (*also* **trizzy**) [TRISS ABOUT *v.*] [1950s+] (*Aus.*) homosexual, effeminate.

trixie *n.* [shares initial letter with TRADE *n.* (3)] [2000s] (*S.Afr. gay*) **1** a man with whom one has a fleeting sexual contact. **2** an insatiably promiscuous gay man.

triznann *n.* [? TRIM *n.* (2)+ -IZ- *infix*] [2000s] (*US black*) sexual intercourse; also as v.

trizz *n.* **1** *see* TRISS *n.*[1]. **2** *see* TRISS *n.*[2].

trizzer *n.* [a time when the charge for a 'wash-and-brush-up' was three pence, i.e. a TRIZZIE *n.*] [1920s+] (*Aus.*) a public lavatory.

trizzie *n.* (*also* **trezzie**) [TRAY *n.*[1] (1) or SE *three*] [1920s–60s] (*orig. Aus.*) a threepenny piece.

trizzoe *n.* [TRICK *n.*[1] (2) + HO *n.*] [2000s] (*US black*) a derog. term for a woman.

trizzy *adj. see* TRISSY *adj.*

Troc, the *n.* [abbr.; now recreated as a vast amusement arcade] **1** [late 19C+] the *Tro*cadero Music Hall, Piccadilly Circus, London. **2** [1920s] the *Tro*cadero Dance Hall, New York. **3** [1940s] the*Tro*cadero Music Hall, Sydney, Australia; or the Brisbane dancehall.

trod *n.* [1970s–80s] (*UK black*) a journey on foot.

trod *v.* [1970s–80s] (*UK black*) to walk.

DERIVATIVES

❑ **trodder** *n.* [1970s–80s] (*UK black*) a pedestrian.

trodder boots *n.* [TROD *v.*+ SE *boots*] [1980s] (*UK black*) heavy boots.

trods *n.* [SE *tread*] [1940s] (*US black*) the feet.

troepie *n. see* TROOPIE *n.*

trog *n.* [SE *troglodyte*, a prehistoric cave dweller, loosely defined in sl. contexts as 'the lowest form of human life'] [1950s+] (*orig. naut.*) a general term of disdain.

Trojan *n.* (*also* **trusty Trojan**) [proper name *Trojan*, a brave or plucky person, a person of great energy or endurance, ult. the Homeric legends] **1** [17C–19C] an intimate companion, esp. as a fellow drinker and roisterer. **2** [17C–1910s] a generally good fellow. **3** [early–mid-19C] a professional gambler.

IN PHRASES

❑ **like a Trojan** *adv.* (*also* **like a turk**) [mid-19C+] in a staunch, determined manner (although moral excellence is not indispensable, as one can *lie like a Trojan*).

Trojan horse *n.* [the Homeric myth of deception] [1960s+] (*US gay*) a gay man who poses as a 'straight' masculine person.

troll *n.*[1] (*also* **trol, trollocks**) [abbr. SE *trollop*; 20C+ use is N.Z.] [mid-19C+] a sluttish, idling woman.

troll *n.*[2] [SE *troll*, a monster] **1** [1940s+] (*US campus*) an ugly man or woman. **2** [1960s] (*US campus*) a notably hard worker. **3** [1980s] (*US campus*) a small girl or woman, i.e. under six feet (in contrast to a tall one – *Munro*). **4** [1980s] (*US campus*) a lecherous older man. **5** [1980s+] (*US gay*) an unattractive middle-aged gay man.

troll *v.* (*also* **troll about, ...around**) [ult. OF *troller*, to search for game (without purpose) of Fr. *trôler*, to ramble] **1** [late 14C+] to wander around, to saunter; also fig. **2** [1950s+] of a prostitute, to look for clients. **3** [1950s+] (*gay*) to walk the streets in search of a sexual partner. **4** [1960s+] to search, to root around for. **5** [1980s] (*US campus*) to go drinking in a succession of bars.

IN PHRASES

❑ **troll for faggots** *v.* [FAGGOT *n.*[1] (3)] [1970s] (*gay*) to search the streets for a sexual partner. ❑ **troll hazard of race** *n.* [sense 1 above + *trace*, a track or line of footprints] [mid-16C] (*UK Und.*) someone who follows their master as far as the master can be seen. ❑ **troll hazard of titrace** *n.* [sense 1 + *tritrace*, an unknown word which ? linked to *treytrace*, itself another mystery] [mid-16C] (*UK Und.*) one who 'goeth gaping after his master' (Awdeley, *Fraternitie of Vagabondes*, c.1561). ❑ **troll with** *n.* [mid-16C] (*UK Und.*) a servant who walks alongside his master; 'he that no man shall know the seruaunt from ye Maister' (Awdeley, *op cit*).

troll and troll by *n.* [? TROLL *v.* (1)] [mid-16C] (*UK Und.*) one who is esteemed by no one and esteems no one.

trolley *n.* [1900s–50s] (*US drugs/prison*) any means of moving illegal drugs or other commodities around a jail.

SE in slang uses

IN COMPOUNDS

❑ **trolley-dolly** *n.* **1** [1980s+] (*orig. gay*) an air steward. **2** [2000s] an air hostess.

fig. uses, esp. denoting the mind

IN PHRASES

❑ **knock off one's trolley** *v.* [1900s] to knock down. ❑ **off one's trolley** *adj.* [SE *trolley-car*, a electric-powered coach running along metal tracks set into the roadway. The Manhattan trolleys, which were not allowed overhead cables (as were those in Brooklyn) after so many came down in the hurricane of 1888, picked up their supply from an electrified third rail and so if the car became derailed, its power was lost] **1** [late 19C+] crazy, eccentric. **2** [1900s] physically unbalanced. **3** [2000s] drunk. ❑ **slip one's trolley** *v.* (*also* **slip one's gears**) [late 19C+] to lose emotional control, to go mad.

trolley *v.* **1** [20C+] (*US*) of a person, to move (fast). **2** [1910s] (*US*) to travel by tram or trolleybus.

trolley and tram *n.* [rhy. sl.] [20C+] ham.

trolley (and truck) *n.* [rhy. sl. = FUCK *n.* (1). Note naval use *trolley-oggling*, acting as a voyeur] [1910s+] an act of sexual intercourse.

trolley (and truck) *v.* [TROLLEY (AND TRUCK) *n.*] [1910s+] to have sexual intercourse.

trolleyed *adj.* [*OFF ONE'S TROLLEY under* TROLLEY *n.*] [1990s+] drunk or under the influence of drugs.

trolleys *n. see* TROLLIES *n.*

trollied *adj.* [2000s] (*N.Z.*) suffering from an excess of drink and/or drugs.

trollies *n.* (*also* **trolleys, trollys**) [Lancashire dial. *trollys*, a woman's drawers, itself linked to Scot. *trolly*, any object with its length disproportionate to its width, ? ult. SE *trail*] **1** [1950s+] underpants. **2** [1990s+] trousers.

trolling *n.* [TROLL *v.*] **1** [mid-19C+] the pursuit of idling or sauntering. **2** [1930s+] the pursuit of working as a prostitute.

3 [1960s+] (*gay*) the pursuit of strolling the streets looking for possible partners.

trollocks *n. see* TROLL *n.*[1].

trollop *n.* [SE *trollop*, but without the sexual implications] [20C+] (*US black*) an unattractive, ugly woman.

trollopee *n.* [? pun on SE *trollop*, i.e. 'loose'] [mid-18C] a loose dress.

trollopping *adj.* [SE *trollop*] [mid-18C–early 19C] **1** like a trollop. **2** ungainly, gauche.

trolly lolly *n.* [Flem. *tralje/traalj*, trellis, lattice, mesh] [late 17C–early 19C] a type of lace, coarsely made but once very fashionable.

trollys *n. see* TROLLIES *n.*

trolly-wags *n.* [? rhy. sl. = BAGS *n.*[1] (2)] [19C] trousers.

trom *n.* [ironic abbr. of SE *traumatize*, to damage psychologically] [1990s+] (*drugs*) marijuana.

trombone *n.* [partial rhy. sl., i.e. only one element rather than the usual two] [1930s+] a telephone.

trombone *v.* [1990s+] to rack the slide of a shotgun, loading a cartridge into the breech.

tromboning *n.* **1** [late 19C] sexual intercourse. **2** [1990s+] a sex act in which a woman or gay man licks their partner's anus while simultaneously masturbating him.

tromp *adj.* (*also* **trueing, trong, trung**) [2000s] (*UK black*) attractive.

trompie *n.* [Afk. *trompie*, a trumpet, a jew's harp] [1970s+] (*S.Afr. drugs*) a long, conically-shaped marijuana cigarette.

tron *n.* [abbr. SE *waitron*, preferred non-sexist term] [2000s] (*US*) a waitress or waiter; also as v.

trong *adj. see* TROMP *adj.*

tronk *n.* [Fr. *tronc*, box, Du. *tronk* or Buganese *tarunka*, a prison. The word could have been imported by Buganese and Balinese slaves; also used in mid-20C Pennsylvania as n., a prison and v., to imprison] [late 18C–1900s] (*S.Afr.*) prison.

t-room *n. see* TEAROOM *n.*

T-room queen *n. see* TEAROOM QUEEN *under* TEAROOM *n.*

troop *n.*[1] [2000s] (*US teen*) a long walk.

troop *n.*[2] *see* TROUPE *n.*

trooper *n.*[1] [milit. *trooper*, but note theatrical/SE *trouper*, a veteran, stalwart actor] **1** [mid-17C; mid-19C] a prostitute. **2** [mid-17C] a prostitute's customer. **3** [1930s+] (*also* **trouper**) a brave or stalwart person [backform. f. *like a trooper*, see below].

(IN PHRASES)

▫ **like a trooper** *adv.* [SE *trooper*] [18C+] vigorously, energetically; thus *swear like a trooper, eat like a trooper, lie like a trooper*.

trooper *n.*[2] [? its making up part of an SE *trooper's* pay] [late 17C–18C] (*UK Und.*) half-a-crown, 2s 6d (12.5p).

troopie *n.* (*also* **troepie**) [SE *trooper*] [1970s+] (*S.Afr.*) a soldier, esp. the lowest rank of national serviceman.

troop (off) *v.* (*also* **troop out**) [SE *troop*, to walk; late 20C+ use is mainly US campus] [early 18C+] to leave, to go off.

troops *n.* [1930s+] (*US*) a gang, a mob.

trophy *n.* [1970s] (*US campus*) 200ml (half a gallon) of alcohol.

tropical *adj.* [fig. uses of HOT *adj.*] **1** [late 19C+] of language, obscene. **2** [1940s+] (*Aus.*) of stolen goods, illegal, dishonest. **3** [1990s+] (*Aus.*) intense. **4** [1990s+] (*Aus. Und.*) highly suspicious; very dangerous for criminal activity.

tropical fish *n.* [half rhy. sl. = PISS *n.* (2)] [2000s] an act of urination.

troppo *adj.* [SE *tropical*, i.e. the effects of the heat, + -O *sfx* (4)] [1940s+] (*Aus./N.Z.*) mad, insane.

(IN PHRASES)

▫ **go troppo** *v.* [1940s+] (*Aus./N.Z.*) to go mad.

tross *n.* (*also* **tros**) [backsl.] [mid–late 19C] a sort.

(IN EXCLAMATIONS)

▫ **sling your tross!** [late 19C] go away! be off!

trosseno *n.* (*also* **trasseno, troseno**) [backsl., lit. 'one sort'] [mid–late 19C] anything that is bad.

trossy *adj.* [? dial. *make a trossle of oneself*, to be slatternly] [late 19C–1910s] dirty, unkempt.

Trot *n.* [abbr.] [1960s+] a *Trots*kyite, used indiscriminately for any hard-left group in the UKs.

(IN COMPOUNDS)

▫ **trot-slot** *n.* [1960s+] in media use, a programme that concerns itself with, or apparently propagandizes for, such groups.

trot *n.*[1] [SE *trot*, a hag, an old woman] **1** [16C–mid-18C] a prostitute. **2** [18C–19C] the vagina. **3** [1910s–30s] a fellow, esp. as *old trot*. **4** [1920s+] (*N.Z.*) a woman. **5** *see* TROTS *n.* (1).

trot *n.*[2] [SE *trot*, the horse's gait] **1** [mid-19C–1920s] a child just learning to walk or run. **2** [late 19C] a baby animal. **3** [late 19C+] a walk, a journey. **4** [1910s+] (*Aus.*) a sequence of consecutive events, a run of good or bad luck; thus phrs. *good/bad/lean/tough trot*. **5** [1950s] an escape (from prison).

(IN PHRASES)

▫ **cop a trot** *v.* [1940s] (*US black*) to walk, to move. ▫ **long trot** *n.* [1910s] (*Aus.*) a winning streak. ▫ **rough trot** *n.* (*also* **stiff trot**) [ROUGH *adj.* (2)] [1960s] (*Aus.*) a period of bad luck. ▫ **take for a trot** *v. see* TAKE FOR A RIDE *under* RIDE *n.*

trot *n.*[3] [play on HORSE *n.* (5a) or PONY *n.* (3a)] [late 19C+] (*US campus*) a translation, a study aid.

trot (out) *v.* (*also* **trot along, trot off**) [SE *trot*, to go or move quickly; ult. from the horse's gait] **1** [early 19C+] to leave, to move off. **2** [late 19C] to steal openly, in broad daylight. **3** [late 19C–1960s] to take out (a woman), to 'walk out with'. **4** [1950s] to escape (from prison).

(IN COMPOUNDS)

▫ **trot palace** *n.* [1910s] a dancehall, a nightclub.

(IN PHRASES)

▫ **how trots it?** [late 19C] how are you? ▫ **on the trot** **1** [late 19C] on holiday. **2** [late 19C] walking around. **3** [late 19C+] hiding away (usu. from the police or other authorities) to avoid an arrest, usu. by leaving one's home, town etc. ▫ **take it on the trot** *v.* [1930s] to run off, to leave at speed. ▫ **trot in** *v.* [late 19C] to arrest and take to trial. ▫ **trot out** *v.* [horseracing jargon *trot out*, to exhibit, to display a horse] **1** [mid–late 19C] to spend one's money; usu. as *trot out the pieces* [f. sense 3 above]. **2** [mid-19C+] to produce, esp. of an excuse or a lie [f. sense 3 above]. **3** [mid-19C+] (*trot up*) to exhibit (someone or something), to put on display. ▫ **trout round** *v.* [mid-19C+] to go round (to), to pay a call (on). ▫ **trot someone round** *v.* [late 19C+] to show someone around a place.

trots *n.* **1** [early 19C+] (*also* **trot**) usu. constr. with *the*, diarrhoea [note synon. US Appalachian use *johnny trots*]. **2** [mid-19C–1900s] policemen [this must be ext. of next, but cites predate]. **3** [late 19C–1900s] feet. **4** [late 19C+] (*Aus.*) constr. with *the*, trotting races.

trotter *n.* [SE *trot*] **1** [late 17C+] a foot, usu. in pl. **2** [late 18C+] (*also* **trotler**) a racehorse; usu. in pl. meaning horseracing in general. **3** [1920s] a dancing person. **4** [1960s+] (*UK Und.*) a deserter from the armed forces.

(IN COMPOUNDS)

▫ **trotter-box** *n.* (*also* **trotter-case**) [early–mid-19C] a shoe.

(IN PHRASES)

▫ **jab trotters** *v.* [1900s] (*Aus.*) to travel with a pack. ▫ **shake one's trotters** *v.* [early–mid-19C] to move, to dance, thus *trotter-shaking*, dancing.

(IN EXCLAMATIONS)

▫ **box your trotters!** [early 19C] go away!

trottery *n.* [SE *trot*] [1920s–60s] (*US*) a dancehall.

trottie *adj. see* TROTTY *adj.*

trotting-cases *n.* [SE *trot*] [mid-19C] shoes.

trotty *adj.* (*also* **trottie**) [TROT *n.*[2] (1)] [late 19C] of a person's figure, small, dainty; of clothes neat, fashionable.

trou *n.*

(IN PHRASES)

▫ **down trou** *v. see* DROP TROU *under* DROP *v.*[1]. ▫ **drop trou** *v. see* DROP *v.*[1].

troub *n.* (*also* **tram troub, tram trube**) [SE *troubador*, a wandering singer, i.e. the conductor 'sings out' the stops] [1910s+] (*Aus.*) a tram conductor.

trouble *n.* [euph.] [late 19C] **1** (*US*) a day of public festivity. **2** (*US*) any interruption of ordinary work. **3** (*Aus.*) a criminal conviction.

IN PHRASES

❑ **get into trouble** *v.* **1** [mid-19C+] a euph. phr. for suffering a variety of legal penalties, being arrested, imprisoned, fined etc. **2** [1930s+] to get pregnant. ❑ **in trouble** *adv.* [euph.] **1** [mid-16C; late 19C–1900s] serving a sentence in prison. **2** [late 19C+] of a woman, pregnant and unmarried.

IN EXCLAMATIONS

❑ **my troubles!** (*also* **my troubs! my trubs!**) [late 19C+] (*Aus.*) a dismissive excl., 'don't worry about me', 'I don't care'; also *his troubles*, *her troubles*, etc.

trouble *v.* [late 19C+] to bother, to worry (about).

IN COMPOUNDS

❑ **trouble-giblets** *n.* [late 19C] the penis. ❑ **trouble-gusset** *n.* [mid-17C] the penis. ❑ **trouble-monkey** *n.* [MONKEY *n.* (9b)] [2000s] the penis.

trouble and fuss *n.* [rhy. sl.] [1960s+] a bus.

trouble and strife *n.* [rhy. sl.] **1** [1900s] life. **2** [20C+] one's wife.

troubles and cares *n.* [rhy. sl.] [20C+] stairs.

trough *n.* **1** [mid-19C+] eating. **2** [20C+] the place at which one eats.

trough (out) *v.* [1980s+] (*US campus*) to eat voraciously.

trounce *v.* [SE *trounce*, to beat, to overcome] [mid-19C–1900s] to have sexual intercourse.

trouncer *n.* **1** [19C] a strong drink. **2** [20C+] a highly capable or expert individual. **3** [20C+] something amazing or astounding. **4** [20C+] (*Ulster*) an attractive woman.

troupe *n.* (*also* **troop**) [1930s–50s] (*US Und.*) a gang of thieves.

trouper *n. see* TROOPER *n.*[1] (3).

troused *adj. see* TROUSERED *adj.*

trouser *n.* (*also* **trowser**) [? he will turn his hand to anything so long as he *trousers* his payment] [late 19C] a jack of all trades, an odd-job man.

SE in slang uses

IN COMPOUNDS

❑ **trouser bandit** *n.* [1990s+] a male homosexual. ❑ **trouser cakes** *n.* [CAKES *n.* (2)] [1990s+] buttocks. ❑ **trouser chuff** *n.* (*also* **trouser cough**) [CHUFF *n.*[3]; note synon. 17C *cough in the breech*, i.e. buttocks] [1980s+] a fart. ❑ **trouser department** *n.* [1990s+] the male genital area. ❑ **trouser pipe** *n. see* STOVE-PIPE *n.* (2). ❑ **trouser snake** *n.* [2000s] the penis. ❑ **trouser trout** *n.* (*also* **trouser mouse**) [1980s+] (*US*) the penis.

IN PHRASES

❑ **wear the trousers** *v.* [1930s+] to dominate, usu. implying that the woman in a relationship is the one who dictates the rules.

trouser *v.* [late 19C+] to pocket.

IN PHRASES

❑ **trouser off** *v.* [1920s+] (*Irish*) to ejaculate.

trousered *adj.* (*also* **troused**) [1990s+] drunk.

trout *n.*[1] [? on pattern of FISH *n.*[1] (5); note SE *trow*, faith, trust, belief] [17C–early 19C] a boon companion, a true friend, a trusted servant; often as TRUSTY TROUT *n.*

trout *n.*[2] [the identification of women and fish; note FISH *n.*[1] (1)] **1** [mid–late 17C; mid-19C+] a woman; often as *OLD TROUT* below. **2** [1950s–60s] (*US black*) the vagina.

IN COMPOUNDS

❑ **trout-fishing** *n.* [1960s+] (*US gay*) of a gay man, seeking out rich old women who offer money in return for companionship.

IN PHRASES

❑ **old trout** *n.* [late 19C+] an older person, usu. a woman and usu. used as a pej.

SE in slang uses

IN COMPOUNDS

❑ **trout's ankles** *n. see* *EEL'S ANKLE under* EEL *n.*[2].

IN PHRASES

❑ **have a trout in the well** *v.* [1940s+] (*Irish*) to be pregnant.

trout *n.*[3] [mid-18C] a Catholic priest.

trowser *n. see* TROUSER *n.*

troy (school) *n.* [ety. unknown] [1940s–60s] (*Aus.*) a gambling game.

trubs *n.* [abbr.] [20C+] (*Aus.*) troubles, problems.

trucha *v.* [Sp.] [1960s+] (*US*) to be alert, to watch out.

truck *n.*[1] [naut. jargon *truck*, the 'cap' on the very top of a mast] [mid–late 19C] a hat.

SE in slang uses

DERIVATIVES

❑ **truckie** *n.* [var. on SAmE *trucker*] [1950s+] (*Aus./N.Z.*) a long distance truck-driver, or his lorry.

IN COMPOUNDS

❑ **truck driver** *n.* [1950s+] (*US black*) an ostentatiously 'masculine' homosexual, poss. dressed as a trucker or in similar macho clothes. ❑ **truck drivers** *n.* [their use by *truck-drivers* and others in staying awake] [1970s+] (*drugs*) amphetamines. ❑ **truck jewellery** *n.* [? one needs a SE *truck* to carry it or SE *truck*, miscellaneous articles suitable for barter] [1990s+] (*US black teen*) items of large, gold jewellery. ❑ **truckload** *n.* [1980s+] a large amount.

truck *n.*[2] [TRUCK *v.*[1] (5)] [1980s+] (*US campus*) someone who moves very slowly.

truck *v.*[1] [? 17C truck, to trudge, ult. synon. Ital. *truccare*] **1** [mid-17C; 1930s] (*US black*) to have sexual intercourse. **2** [1930s–70s] to dance the truck, a contemporary popular dance ['that jerky yet rhythmic dance which combines a bend of the body, a tightening of the hand muscles and a slight strut with the legs' (Baltimore *Sun*, 15 November 1935)]. **3** [1930s+] to move, to travel; often in comb, with *along*, *around*, etc. **4** [1930s+] (*US black*) to leave, to depart. **5** [1980s+] (*US campus*) to move slowly. **6** [1990s+] (*also* **truck it**) (*US campus*) to hurry.

truck *v.*[2] [SE *truck*, to give (a commodity) in exchange] [mid-19C] (*UK Und.*) to steal money by confusing the shopkeeper who is giving change.

trucking *n.* [TRUCK *v.*[1]] **1** [1930s+] (*US black*) strutting, strolling. **2** [1930s+] dancing the truck. **3** [1960s+] moving, struggling along, getting on with it; esp. as in HIPPIE *n.*[2] (3) slogan *keep on trucking*, an exhortation to continue with one's life.

trucks *n.* [? TROLLY-WAGS *n.* or SE *trucks*, odds and ends] [mid-19C–1900s] trousers.

trudge the streets *v. see* *POUND THE PAVEMENT under* POUND *v.*[2].

trudging house *n. see* TRUGGING HOUSE *n.*

true *adj.* [revival of 11C–19C SE] [1990s+] (*US black teen*) loyal, faithful, dependable.

SE in slang uses

IN COMPOUNDS

❑ **true blue** *n.* [early 19C] gin. ❑ **true blue** *adj.* [play on SE *true blue*, orig. the colour of 17C Scot. Covenanters (the reversal of the monarchy's red), subseq. of 19C+ Tories] [mid–late 17C] describing a regular, dedicated drinker. ❑ **true dat** [pron. of SE *true that*] [1990s+] (*US black*) an affirmative phr. ❑ **true dinkum** *n.* (*also* **true dink, true dinks**) [SE *true* + DINKUM *adj.*] [1900s–40s] (*Aus./N.Z.*) the absolute truth. ❑ **truepenny** *n.* [the image of a sound coin] [late 16C–17C; 19C–1900s] a trusty, honest person. ❑ **true trout** *n. see* TRUSTY TROUT *n.*

IN PHRASES

❑ **for true** *adj.* [late 19C] (*US*) genuine. ❑ **for true** [20C+] (*orig. W.I.*) a general intensifying phr., in all honesty, without a doubt. ❑ **true as eggs is bacon** *see* *SURE AS HOGS ARE MADE OF BACON under* SURE AS… *phr.*

trueing *adj. see* TROMP *adj.*

truff *n.* [SE *truffle*] [18C] a purse.

truff *v.* [Scot. *truff*, to pilfer, to obtain by deceit] [mid-19C+] (*northern*) to steal, to pilfer, thus (*Irish*) *truff.*, stolen goods.

trug *n.* [It. *trucca*, 'a fustian or rogish word for a trull, a whore, or a wench' (Florio 1598). ? cognate with SE *truck*, to barter or exchange commodities] (*UK Und.*) **1** [late 16C–18C] (*also* **trugmallion**) a prostitute, a mistress. **2** [17C] a catamite or young homosexual boy.

trugging house *n.* (*also* **trudging house, trugging ken, trugging place**) [TRUG *n.* (1) + HOUSE *n.*[1] (1)/KEN *n.*[1] (1)/SE *place*] [late 16C–early 17C] a brothel.

trugmoldy *n.* [? var. on *trugmallion*] [mid-17C–early 19C] a prostitute.

trull *n.* [Ger. *Trulle*, a prostitute] (*UK Und.*) **1** [early 16C–1950s] a prostitute. **2** [mid-17C–early 19C] a tinker's or soldier's companion.

IN PHRASES

❑ **go trulling** *v.* [early 16C–1950s] to go whoring.

truly *n.*

IN EXCLAMATIONS

❑ **by my truly!** (*also* **upon my truly!**) [late 16C–late 18C] a mild oath, used to underpin the veracity of one's statement.

trump *n.*[1] [TRUMP *v.*] [18C–1900s] an act of breaking wind audibly; occas. also a similar sound emitted from the vagina during intercourse.

trump *n.*[2] [card-playing imagery] **1** [early 19C+] an admirable person, an excellent fellow. **2** [mid-19C] an excellent thing; a stroke of luck. **3** [1910s–60s] (*also* **trump of the dump**) (*Aus./N.Z.*) a person in charge.

IN PHRASES

❑ **put to one's trumps** *v.* [SE *put to one's trumps*, of a card-player, to be forced to play one's trumps, since no alternative cards are available] [mid-17C–19C] to be in an extreme situation, to be in great difficulties. ❑ **trump tight** *adj.* [letter to American Dialect Society List 27/1/06: 'Probable origin: In the card game of bid whist – the social card game of choice in Afrite America – when a player has a hand that consists entirely of trumps, he/she is said to be "trump-tight." The person who is trump-tight turns the rest of the tricks [...] and thereby wins the deal and, under the right circumstances, also wins the game.'] [1990s+] (*US black*) first class, fully worked out.

trump *adj.* [millionaire property developer, Donald *Trump* (b.1946)] [1990s+] (*US black*) rich and successful, with overtones of flashiness.

trump *v.* [SE *trump*, to trumpet] [mid-17C+] to break wind loudly; occas. also of the vagina, to make a similar noise during intercourse.

trumper *n.* [TRUMP *v.*] [early–mid-19C] one who breaks wind loudly.

trumpery *n.* [SE *trumpery*, valueless goods] [mid-18C–early 19C] a worn-out old prostitute.

trumpet *n.* **1** [19C] the nose. **2** [mid-19C] (*UK Und.*) a vain man. **3** [late 19C; 1990s+] an act of breaking wind. **4** [1970s+] the telephone. **5** [1990s+] (*US teen*) one who has an extremely large ego.

SE in slang uses

IN PHRASES

❑ **go trumpet-cleaning** *v.* [the trumpeter in question being the angel Gabriel] [late 19C–1910s] to die.

trumpet *v.* [1920s+] to break wind.

trumpeter *n.* **1** [mid-17C–early 18C] one who belches or breaks wind. **2** [late 18C–early 19C] one who has bad breath [to play the trumpet one needs 'strong', here 'bad' breath]. **3** [late 19C] a general term of affectionate address.

SE in slang uses

IN PHRASES

❑ **one's trumpeter is dead** ['He is therefore forced to sound his own trumpet' (Grose, 1796)] [late 18C–early 19C] said of a braggart, a self-advertiser.

trumpeters *n.* [? the noise of the chains] [late 19C] (*Aus. Und.*) 'irons which connect…ordinary leg-chains with a bazil [bezel] riveted around each leg immediately below the knees' (P. Warung, *Tales of the Early Days*, 1894).

trumpie *v.* [1970s] a braggart, a boaster.

trump the hump *v.* [SE *tramp*] [1930s–40s] (*US black*) to climb a hill.

trumpy *adj.* [TRUMP *n.*[2] (1)] [early 19C] of a person, admirable, first-rate.

truncheon *n.* **1** [18C–19C] the penis. **2** [2000s] an erection.

IN PHRASES

❑ **punching the truncheon** *n.* [1990s+] masturbation.

trundlers *n.* [SE *trundle*, to roll along (around one's plate)] [late 17C–early 19C] (*UK Und.*) peas.

trundle-tail *n.* (*also* **trindle-tail**) [SE *trundle-tail*, a cur, a mongrel, lit. a dog with a curly tail] [17C] a derog. description of a person.

trundling-cheat *n.* [SE *trundle* + CHEAT *n.* (1)] [17C] any form of wheeled vehicle.

trung *adj. see* TROMP *adj.*

trunk *n.*[1] [idea of it being a chest filled with treasure] [17C–mid-19C] the vagina.

IN COMPOUNDS

❑ **trunk-muncher** *n.* [2000s] (*N.Z.*) one who practises cunnilingus. ❑ **trunk work** *n.* [early 17C] casual or clandestine sexual intercourse.

trunk *n.*[2] [SE *trunk*, the body, bereft of the head] [19C] a fool.

trunk *v.* [1960s] of a man, to have sexual intercourse.

trunk and tree *n.* [rhy. sl.] [1990s+] the human knee.

trunkmaker-like *adj.* [SE *trunkmaker*, one who makes trunks or boxes; thus the noise so created] [late 18C–early 19C] used of someone who makes more noise than they do real work.

trus mi *phr. see* TRUS WI *phr.*

trustafarian *n.* [SE *trust* (*fund*) + joc. abbr. (*Rasta*)*farian*] [1980s+] someone fortunate enough to have a trust fund to insulate them from work or 'real life', esp. if they emulate the lifestyle and image of a Rastafarian.

trust-buster *n.* [SE *trust* + BUST *v.*[1] (1)] [20C+] (*US*) a campaigner against the power of monopolistic industrial or business trusts.

trusty *n.*[1] [it can be trusted to keep one warm/dry] [19C] (*Anglo-Irish*) an overcoat.

trusty *n.*[2] (*also* **trustee, trustie**) [early 19C+] (*Aus./UK/US prison*) a convict who on the grounds of good behaviour and trustworthiness is allotted a privileged position in the jail; may also be an informer on other prisoners.

trusty Trojan *n. see* TROJAN *n.*

trusty trout *n.* (*also* **true trout**) [TROUT *n.*[1]] [mid-17C–early 19C] a boon companion, a true friend.

trus wi *phr.* (*also* **trus mi**) [pron. SE *trust we/me*] [1980s+] (*W.I./UK black teen*) believe (in) us/me, trust (in) us/me.

trut *n.* [SE *thruppence/threepence*] [1930s–60s] (*Aus.*) a threepenny bit.

try *v.*

SE in slang uses

IN COMPOUNDS

❑ **try-hard** *n.* [i.e. the person is trying too hard to be liked or accepted] [1990s+] (*Aus. teen*) a general term of abuse. ❑ **try-on** *n.* [early 19C+] **1** an attempt at imposition or deceit. **2** the subject of the attempt. **3** any form of attempt at something. ❑ **try-out** *n.* [20C+] a trial run, a trial period, an experimental attempt.

IN PHRASES

❑ **don't even try it** [1980s+] (*US campus*) a warning or a response to deter someone. ❑ **try for white** *v.* [1940s+] (*S.Afr.*) to attempt to pass oneself off as white; less common are *try for black, try for coloured.* ❑ **try it on** *v.* **1** [19C] (*also* **try on**) to live by thieving. **2** [early 19C+] to attempt to get away with something, usu. that which one is not entitled to have. **3** [early 19C+] to make a sexual pass (at someone). ❑ **try it on for size** *v.* [1940s+] (*orig. US*) to try out, to see if something (often fig.)

will work. ❑ **try it on the dog** *v.* [the testing of possibly poisoned meat by giving it to an unfortunate dog; or ? theatre jargon *try it on the matinée dog*, the implication being that a matinée performance or audience is less important those of the evening] [late 19C+] usu. of a play or film, to experiment with, to try out. ❑ **try it on with** *v.* [early 19C+] to attempt to persuade someone who is otherwise unwilling. ❑ **try to front** *v.* (*also* **want to front**) [1980s] (*US campus*) to denigrate, to make negative comments about.

tryke *n.* [SE *transsexual* + DYKE *n.* (1)] [1990s+] (*US gay*) a female transsexual lesbian.

tryning *n. see* TRINING *n.*

t.s. *n.* [abbr. TOUGH SHIT *n.*] **1** [1940s+] (*orig. US milit.*) tough shit, often used ironically or mockingly as well as sympathetically. **2** [1960s] (*US Und.*) Times Square.

t/s *n.* (*also* **t.s.**) [abbr.] [1970s+] a transsexual.

Ts and Blues *n.* [abbr. *T*alwin + BLUE *n.*[1] (4b)] [1980s] (*US drugs*) a combination of Talwin and PBZ (an anti-histamine), used as a cheap substitute for heroin.

tsang *n.* [ety. unknown; ? echoic of chinking coins] [1960s–70s] (*S.Afr. township*) money.

tsatske *n. see* TCHOTCHKE *n.*

t.s.h. *phr.* [abbr. *t*hat *s*hit *h*appens] [1980s+] (*US campus*) an expression of commiseration or resignation.

tsooris/tsoris *n. see* TSURIS *n.*

tsotsi *n.* (*also* **totsi**) [Sotho pron. of ZOOT SUIT *n.*; note *Johannesburg Star* , 22/2/62: 'The term "tsotsi", meaning a criminal tough, came into use in Johannesburg in 1946 following the exhibition of a film entitled "Stormy Weather" in which the all-Negro caste [*sic*] wore stove-pipe trousers, wide-brimmed hats, and massive watch-chains which dangled from their gaudy vests. African youths, who adopted this kind of dress as something which was symbolic of derring-do, became known as tsotsis, the name being derived from the actual Sotho word, tsotsi meaning stovepipe trousers'] [1940s+] (*S.Afr.*) **1** a flashily dressed township thug or gangster. **2** the tight trousers worn by such gangsters.

IN COMPOUNDS

❑ **tsotsi-taal** *n.* [1940s+] (*S.Afr.*) the slang used by tsotsis.

tsuris *n.* (*also* **tsooris, tsoris, tsouris, tzuris**) [Yid. *tsuris*, ult. Heb. *tsarah*, trouble] [20C+] troubles, worries, suffering.

t.t. *n.* [abbr.] [1910s+] a *t*ee*t*otaller, thus adj. teetotal.

t/t *phr.* [abbr.] [1970s+] used in sex contact advertisements, *t*it *t*orture.

T-tab *n.* [ety. unknown, but note SE colloq. phr. *T-zone*, a state of transcendental bliss] [1960s–70s] (*drugs*) phencyclidine.

t.t.f.n. *phr.* [*t*a-*t*a *f*or *n*ow, orig. created and popularized on comedian Tommy Handley's BBC Radio show *ITMA* (*It's That Man Again*, 1939–49). Dorothy Summers, as 'Mrs Mopp' (the comic charlady) actually used the phr., which was revived by BBC Radio 2 disc jockey Jimmy Young (b.1923)] [1940s+] goodbye.

tub *n.*[1] (*also* **bathtub**) **1** [17C+] a boat; thus [1920s–40s] transatlantic liners, esp. as venues for crime, thus *WORK THE TUBS under* WORK *v.* **2** [mid-17C–1910s] a pulpit. **3** [late 17C–mid-19C] a coach, esp. a form of covered carriage known as a 'chariot'. **4** [mid–late 19C] a seatless carriage used on the early railways. **5** [mid-19C–1900s] (*US*) a fire engine. **6** [1900s] a glass containing approx. one pint. **7** [1910s–50s] a car. **8** [1920s–80s] (*UK Und.*) an omnibus, a bus; thus *WORK THE TUBS under* WORK *v.* **9** [1930s] a truck. **10** [1960s] (*Aus. prison*) a sanitary bucket.

IN COMPOUNDS

❑ **tub-drubber** *n. see* TUB-THUMPER *n.* ❑ **tub house** *n.* [1900s] (*US*) a mission. ❑ **tub-hunter** *n. see* TUB-THUMPER *n.* ❑ **tub-man** *n.* (*also* **tub-preacher**) [mid-17C–early 18C] a preacher, a parson. ❑ **tub-pounder** *n. see* TUB-THUMPER *n.* ❑ **tub-thumper/-thumping** *see* separate entries.

SE in slang uses

IN PHRASES

❑ **tub of blood** *n. see BLOODY BUCKET under* BLOODY *adj.* ❑ **tub of lard** *n.* (*also* **bundle of lard, butter tub, gourd of hog's lard, lump of lard, sack of lard, tub of blubber, tub of butter, tub of 'gator guts, tub of guts, tub of hog fat, tub of soapgrease**) [mid-19C+] a fat person. ❑ **tub of shit** *n.* [1980s] (*US*) a term of abuse for a fat person. ❑ **tub of turds** *n.* [TURD *n.*[1] (1)] [mid-17C] (*UK Und*) an ugly fat person.

tub *n.*[2] (*also* **tubbo**) [abbr. SE *tubby*] [late 19C+] a fat person.

tub *n.*[3] [? rhy. sl.; ? simple image of quantity] [1980s] £100.

tub *v.* [SE *tub*, a bath] [early 17C; mid-19C+] to wash oneself (in a bath or *tub*).

tubbichon *n.* [Fr. *tirebuchon*, corkscrew, a term used to describe this hairstyle, popularized *c.*1860 by the Empress Eugénie] [mid–late 19C] a single curled lock of back hair, worn pulled forwards over the left shoulder.

tubbing *n.* **1** [19C] (*UK prison*) a prison sentence [one is placed inside a *tub*, i.e. a cell]. **2** [late 19C] an act of washing (in a bath).

tubbo *n. see* TUB *n.*[2].

tubby *n.* [SE *tubby* adj.] [late 19C+] (*US*) a fat person, often used as a (usu.) affectionate nickname.

tube *n.*[1] [SE *tube*] **1** [mid-18C+] the penis. **2** [late 19C–1950s] a telephone [the telephone's short-range predecessor, the SE *speaking tube*]. **3** [20C+] the London Underground, orig. the *TWOPENNY TUBE under* TWOPENNY *adj.* **4** [1920s–50s] (*US*) the New York Subway. **5** [1940s–70s] a cigarette. **6** [1940s+] (*UK prison*) a prison officer who makes a habit of listening for information from prison informers. **7** [1950s+] (*orig. US*) television, as a medium, the industry [abbr. cathode ray *tube*, a basic component of the TV]. **8** [1950s+] (*orig. US*) a television set. **9** [1960s] (*US prison*) a Benzedrine inhaler, esp. used recreationally. **10** [1960s] (*US campus*) a very promiscuous young woman. **11** [1960s] (*US campus*) an easy course [? surfing imagery]. **12** [1960s+] (*orig. Aus.*) a bottle or can of beer. **13** [1980s+] (*US drugs*) a large water pipe.

IN PHRASES

❑ **crack a tube** *v.* [1950s+] (*Aus.*) to open a can of beer. ❑ **go down the tubes** *v.* (*also* **...the tube**) [1960s+] (*orig. US*) to fail badly, to collapse completely. ❑ **line one's tubes** *v.* [1950s] (*Aus.*) to eat. ❑ **tube it** *v.* **1** [1910s+] to travel on the London Underground. **2** [1950s+] to watch television.

tube *n.*[2] [ety. unknown] [1980s+] (*Scot.*) a person, usu. with derog. overtones.

tube *v.* [*GO DOWN THE TUBES under* TUBE *n.*[1]] [1960s+] (*US campus*) to do badly at work.

tubed *adj.* (*also* **tubed out**) [*GO DOWN THE TUBES under* TUBE *n.*[1] + TUBE *n.*[1] (12)] **1** [1960s+] very drunk. **2** [1990s+] (*Irish*) worn out, useless.

tubesteak *n.* **1** [1960s+] (*US*) a hot dog, a frankfurter; bologna. **2** [1970s+] (*orig. US*) the penis [f. sense 1].

IN COMPOUNDS

❑ **tubesteak tarzan** *n.* [1990s+] a homosexual.

IN PHRASES

❑ **hide the tubesteak** *v.* [1990s+] to have sexual intercourse.

tubs *n.* **1** [mid–late 19C] a butter seller [the butter *tubs*]. **2** [1940s–60s] (*orig. US*) drums [the shape]. **3** [1960s+] (*US gay*) a gay bathhouse [SE *tub*, a bath].

tubster *n.* [TUB *n.*[1] (2) + sfx *-ster*] [early 18C] a parson.

tub-thumper *n.* (*also* **tub-drubber, -hunter, -pounder**) [TUB *n.*[1] (2) + SE *thumper/drubber*; 'from the old Puritan fashion of "holding forth" from a tub, or beer barrel, as a mark of their contempt for decorated pulpits' Hotten (1864)] [18C+] a vehement preacher or orator, either clerical or secular.

tub-thumping *n.* [TUB-THUMPER *n.*] [mid-19C+] preaching or speechifying, whether or not on religious topics.

tubular *adj.* [? surfer jargon *tube*, the inside curve of a good wave] [1980s+] (*US teen*) the ultimate in perfection.

tuchas/tuches/tuchis *n. see* TOCHES *n.*

tuck *n.*[1] [TUCK *v.*[2] (1); + ? ref. to the strain placed on the tucks in one's garments] **1** [early–mid-19C] a hearty meal; more usu. TUCK-IN *n.* or TUCK-OUT *n.*[1]. **2** [mid-19C] a hearty appetite. **3** [mid-19C+] (*mainly juv.*) food, esp. sweet cakes and pastries. **4** [1970s] (*UK Und.*) a successful robbery.

tuck *n.*[2] *see* TUX *n.* (1).

tuck *v.*[1] [SE *tuck*, to tug or snatch] [late 17C–early 19C] to hang; usu. as TUCK UP *v.* (1).

tuck *v.*[2] [late 18C+] to eat, esp. heartily or greedily; usu. with a prep.; thus TUCK IN *v.*

tuck *v.*[3] [one 'tucks it away'] [1960s+] to tape the penis to the groin (usu. in the context of transvestism).

Tuckahoe *n.* [mid-19C–1950s] (*US*) an inhabitant of Virginia.

tucked away *adj.* (*also* **tucked under**) [20C+] (*Aus./US*) dead and buried.

tucked up *adj.*[1] [TUCK UP *v.* (1)] [late 17C–mid-19C] hanged.

tucked up *adj.*[2] [? TUCKED UP *adj.*[1]] **1** [mid-19C] dazed, unconscious. **2** [mid-19C] (*UK Und.*) married. **3** [late 19C–1910s] worn down, deprived, exhausted. **4** [20C+] (*UK Und.*) captured without any chance of escape. **5** [1990s+] under control.

tucked up *adj.*[3] [TUCKER *v.*] [1920s] well fed.

tuck 'em fair *n.* [TUCK *v.*[1] + SE *fair*] [18C] a judicial hanging.

IN PHRASES

❑ **dance at tuck 'em fair** *v.* [18C] to be hanged.

tucker *n.* [ext. of TUCK *n.*[1] (3), orig. rations of 19C gold-diggers] [mid-19C+] (*Aus./N.Z.*) food, rations.

IN COMPOUNDS

❑ **tucker chute** *n.* [mid-19C+] (*Aus./N.Z.*) the anus (occas. the mouth). ❑ **tucker-fucker** *n.* [1980s+] (*Aus.*) **1** a cook, esp. institutional. **2** a microwave. **3** tomato sauce. ❑ **tucker job** *n.* [mid-19C+] (*Aus./N.Z.*) a poorly paid job (which just covers the cost of one's rations). ❑ **tucker money** *n.* [mid-19C+] (*Aus./N.Z.*) a pittance.

IN PHRASES

❑ **earn one's tucker** *v.* (*also* **earn one's peasoup, make one's tucker**) [late 19C] to earn (at least enough for) one's bed and board.

tucker *v.* [TUCKER *n.*] **1** [late 19C+] to provide someone with food. **2** [20C+] to eat a meal.

tuckerbox *n.* [Jack Moses poem (*c.*1920s) 'The dog sat on the tuckerbox/Nine miles from Gundagai', usu. recited as '*shat* on...' thus the derog. term] [1970s+] an informer.

tuckered (out) *adj.* [TUCKER OUT *v.*] [mid-19C+] (*Aus./US*) exhausted, worn out.

tucker out *v.* [9C–13C SE *tuck*, to punish, to ill-treat] [mid-19C+] (*orig. US*) to become exhausted, to collapse.

Tuckie *n.* (*also* **Tuk, Tukkie**) [initials *T.U.C.* + dimin. *-kie*] [1910s–30s] (*S.Afr.*) a student of the *T*ransvaal *U*niversity *C*ollege, since 1930 renamed University of Pretoria.

tuck-in *n.* [TUCK IN *v.* or ext. of TUCK *n.*[1] (1)] [mid-19C+] a good meal.

tuck in *v.* [SE *tuck in*, in the sense of 'put away'] [early 19C+] to eat, or drink, heartily or greedily.

tuck-out *n.*[1] [ext. of TUCK *n.*[1] (1)] [early 19C+] a feast, a hearty meal.

tuck-out *n.*[2] [9C–13C SE *tuck*, to punish, to ill-treat] [mid-19C] (*Aus.*) a fight, a beating.

tucks of time *n.* [20C+] (*Irish*) plenty of time.

tuck up *v.* [TUCK *v.*[1]] **1** [early 18C–19C] to hang. **2** [1940s–80s] to defraud, to steal from. **3** *see* TAKE UP *v.*

tuck up fair *n.* [TUCK *v.*[1] + SE *fair*, note TUCK 'EM FAIR *n.*] [mid-19C] the gallows.

tuckus *n. see* TOCHES *n.*

Tucson blanket *n. see* CALIFORNIA BLANKET *under* CALIFORNIA *adj.*

'tude *n. see* ATTITUDE *n.*

tuff *adj.* [mis-sp. SE *tough*] [1960s+] (*US teen*) good or cool.

tuff ken *n. see* TOFF-KEN *under* TOFF *n.*

Tufnell Park *n.* [rhy. sl. = LARK *n.*[3]; ult. the area of north London] [1990s+] a game, an amusing episode.

tuft *n.* **1** [mid-17C–mid-18C; 1970s+] female pubic hair, by ext. the vagina. **2** [mid-18C–19C] an aristocratic, titled undergraduate [the *tuft* was that adorning the mortarboards of titled students – of gold threads rather than the usual black].

tuft-hunter *n.* [TUFT *n.* (2)] **1** [mid–late 18C] an undergraduate who pursues the acquaintance of rich or titled students. **2** [mid-19C+] a snob, a toady, a social climber. **3** [1960s] (*US black*) a womanizer.

tuft-hunting *n.* [TUFT-HUNTER *n.* (2)] [late 18C–19C] social climbing, pursuing aristocratic connections.

tuft-hunting *adj.* [TUFT-HUNTER *n.* (2)] [mid-19C+] socially aspirant.

tug *n.* **1** (*Aus.*) with (derog.) ref. to a person. (**a**) [late 19C–1930s] a card-sharp [? they *tug* cards from the bottom of the pack]. (**b**) [late 19C–1930s] a confidence trickster. (**c**) [late 19C–1940s] (*chiefly Aus.*) a dirty, uncouth, repellent person [? generalized use of Etonian public school jargon *tug*, a scholar, a clever person, a (too) hard worker; itself abbr. SE *tug-mutton*, a ref. to their meals but ? also to masturbation. Such figures are disdained by their aristocratic peers]. **2** as a physical act. (**a**) [1940s–60s] (*Irish*) the breaking out of someone from prison. (**b**) [1960s+] an arrest. (**c**) [1970s] the act of picking up, meeting, introducing oneself. (**d**) [1970s+] a warning. (**e**) [1950s+] an act of masturbation.

IN COMPOUNDS

❑ **tug job** *n.* [2000s] (*US*) the masturbation of a partner.

IN PHRASES

❑ **have a tug** *v.* [1950s+] to masturbate.

tug *v.* [SE *tug*] **1** [17C; 2000s] of a man, to have sexual intercourse [2000s use, US black]. **2** [1950s+] (*orig. Aus.*) to masturbate.

IN COMPOUNDS

❑ **tug-mutton** *n.* [MUTTON *n.* (1)/MUTTON *n.* (3)] **1** [17C] a pimp. **2** [late 19C] the penis.

IN PHRASES

❑ **tug one's slug** *n. see under* SLUG *n.*[3]. ❑ **tug one's taffy** *n.* (*also* **pull one's taffy**) [1990s+] (*US*) to masturbate.

SE in slang uses

IN PHRASES

❑ **tug (a head)** *v.* [1970s] (*Aus. Und.*) to distract someone's attention while a crime is being committed. ❑ **tug-button Tuesday** *n.* [mid-19C] the Tuesday before Advent. ❑ **tug someone's coat** *v. see* PULL SOMEONE'S COAT *under* PULL *v.*

tugg *n. see* TOG *n.*

tugger *n.*[1] [the wicker boxcar in which she collects her stock and which she tugs around the streets] [20C+] (*Irish*) a woman who deals in old clothes.

tugger *n.*[2] [TUG *v.* (2)] **1** [2000s] a male masturbator. **2** [2000s] (*N.Z.*) a term of abuse.

tuggs *n. see* TOGS *n.* (1).

tug o' war *n.* [rhy. sl.] [20C+] a prostitute.

tuies *n. see* TOOIES *n.*

t.u.i.f.u. *n.* [orig. usage, abbr. *t*he *u*ltimate *i*n *f*uck *u*ps] [1940s+] (*US*) a terrible blunder.

Tuk/Tukkie *n. see* TUCKIE *n.*

tukkis *n. see* TOCHES *n.*

tulip *n.* **1** [late 18C] a beauty. **2** [early–mid-19C] a dandy. **3** [mid-19C] a bishop's mitre. **4** [mid-19C] the penis. **5** [mid-19C] as *my tulip*, a person, used affectionately. **6** [mid-19C–1910s] the female genitals. **7** [1910s] (*Aus.*) an attractive young woman. **8** [1950s+] (*Irish*) a fool, usu. a funny one.

IN PHRASES

❑ **tulips of the goes** *n.* [GO *n.*[1] (2a)] [early–mid-19C] the cream of the fashionable world.

tulips *n.* [rhy. sl.; ult. *tulips and roses*] [2000s] multiple sclerosis.

tulip-sauce *n.* [pun on 'two lips'] [late 19C–1900s] a kiss, the act of kissing.

tully-vally *n. see* TILLY-VALLY *n.*

tum *n.* (*also* **tum-tum**) [abbr.; redup.] [mid-19C+] (*usu. juv.*) the stomach.

tumbe *n.* [Sp. *tumbar*, to knock down] [1970s] (*US/P.R. Und.*) a swindle, a confidence trick.

tumble *n.* **1** in senses of understanding, apprehension. (**a**) [mid-19C–1930s] (*UK Und.*) an act of discovery. (**b**) [late 19C+] (*US*) a sign of recognition, a response. (**c**) [20C+] (*US Und.*) an arrest. **2** [late 19C+] an act of sexual intercourse. **3** [1920s] (*US Und.*) a chance, an opportunity.

IN PHRASES

❑ **do a tumble** *v.* [1900s] of a woman, to have sexual intercourse with a man. ❑ **give someone a tumble** *v.* **1** [late 19C+] to have sexual intercourse. **2** [1920s] in fig. use of sense 1, to do someone a favour, to give a present. **3** [1920s+] (*US*) to recognize, to acknowledge. ❑ **take a tumble** *v.* [late 19C+] (*orig. Aus.*) to come to a realization, to work something out. ❑ **tumble in the hay** *n. see* ROLL IN THE HAY *n.*

SE in slang uses

IN PHRASES

❑ **give it a tumble** *v.* [1910s+] to try out, to experiment. ❑ **take a tumble** *v.* **1** [1900s] (*US Und.*) to 'fall for' a confidence trick. **2** [1930s–50s] (*US Und.*) to be arrested and jailed.

tumble *v.*[1] [SE *tumble*, to cause to fall] **1** [early 16C+] to seduce, to have sexual intercourse. **2** [1960s] to murder. **3** [1960s+] (*Aus.*) to confuse, to throw off balance.

SE in slang uses

IN COMPOUNDS

❑ **tumble-a-bed** *n.* [her stereotypical availability] [late 18C–19C] a chambermaid. ❑ **tumble-turd** *n.* [18C US regional dial. *tumble-turd*, a large black beetle that rolls and buries pieces of dung] [1940s–50s] (*W.I.*) a short, stocky person.

IN PHRASES

❑ **tumble down to grass** *v.* [the image of once cultivated fields returning to grass] [late 19C–1900s] to go to rack and ruin. ❑ **tumble out** *v. see* TURN OUT *v.*[1]. ❑ **tumble to pieces** *v.* [the *pieces* are the mother and newborn child] [mid–late 19C] to go successfully through childbirth. ❑ **tumble up** *v.* [19C] (*orig. nautical*) **1** to rush, to hurry. **2** to rise from bed.

tumble *v.*[2] [fig. uses of SE *tumble on*, chance on] **1** [mid-19C+] to realize, to notice, to recognize; thus *TUMBLE TO* below. **2** [mid-19C+] to agree (to), to take a liking (to). **3** [mid-19C+] (*UK Und.*) to understand. **4** [mid-19C+] (*UK Und.*) to alert, to make someone suspicious. **5** [20C+] (*US Und.*) to be arrested. **6** [1950s+] to unmask, to recognize as fake.

IN PHRASES

❑ **tumble to** *v.* **1** [mid–late 19C] to involve oneself energetically or enthusiastically. **2** [mid-19C+] (*US*) to discover, to become aware of.

tumble and trip *n.* [rhy. sl. = WHIP *n.*[1] (1)] [20C+] a collection of money.

tumble and trips *n.* [rhy. sl.] [1920s] (*US*) lips.

tumbledown *n.* (*also* **tumble-down-the-sink**) [rhy. sl. = drink] **1** [early–mid-19C] grog. **2** [1910s+] any form of alcohol.

tumble (down the sink) *n.* [rhy. sl.] [1910s+] a drink.

tumble-in *n.* [TUMBLE IN *v.*] [mid–late 19C] an act of sexual intercourse.

tumble in *v.* [mid-19C+] **1** to have sexual intercourse. **2** to go to bed [ext. of sense 1].

tumbler *n.*[1] [SE *tumbler*, a dog like a small greyhound, formerly used to catch rabbits (i.e. CONY *n.* (3))] [17C–mid-19C] the member of a confidence tricking team who searches out and ensnares a suitable victim.

tumbler *n.*[2] [SE *tumbler*, a tumbril] [late 17C–mid-19C] a cart.

IN PHRASES

❑ **nap the flog at the tumbler** *v.* [mid–late 18C] to be whipped at the cart's tail. ❑ **shove the tumbler** *v.* (*also* **...the flogging tumbler, shove-tumrill**) [late 17C–mid-19C] (*UK Und.*) to be whipped at the cart's tail.

tumblers *n.* [cf. BANGERS *n.*] [early–mid-17C] the testicles.

tumblings and blanket *n. see* BLANKET *n.* (6).

tummler *n.* (*also* **tumler**) [Yid./Ger. *Tummel*, disorder] [1960s+] **1** (*US*) the 'life and soul of the party', a person who talks a great deal but accomplishes little. **2** (*US, show business*) the MC of a (Jewish) hotel in Catskill Mts, NY.

tummy *n.* [abbr.] [mid-19C+] (*usu. juv.*) the stomach.

IN COMPOUNDS

❑ **tummy-timber** *n. see BELLY TIMBER under* BELLY *n.*

tummy banana *n. see under* BANANA *n.*

tump *v.* [SE *tump*, to strike] [19C] to have sexual intercourse.

tumpa *adj.* [1940s+] (*W.I. Rasta*) a stump.

IN PHRASES

❑ **tumpa-foot man** *n.* [1940s+] (*W.I. Rasta*) a one-footed man.

tum-tum *n. see* TUM *n.*

tun *n.* [abbr. LUSHINGTON *n.* + pun on SE *tun*, a large barrel] [mid-19C–1900s] a drunkard.

tuna *n.* [1970s] **1** (*US*) one who believes themselves to be far more sophisticated than is the reality. **2** (*US gay*) a homosexual sailor who only takes the passive role in fellatio. **3** (*US campus/gay*) an attractive man; thus *hot tuna!* an excl. said on seeing a sexy man.

IN COMPOUNDS

❑ **tuna (fish)** *n.* [1960s+] **1** (*US campus/black*) a girlfriend, a woman. **2** (*orig. US black*) the vagina, both positive and negative.

SE in slang uses

IN COMPOUNDS

❑ **tuna taco** *n.* [*taco*, a Mexican cornmeal pancake] [1990s+] a woman's genitals; esp. in the context of cunnilingus. ❑ **tuna wagon** *n.* [its only use would be to convey fish] [1970s+] (*US*) an old, decrepit car.

tune *n.*

IN PHRASES

❑ **dance to the tune of shaking the sheets (without music)** *v. see under* DANCE *v.* ❑ **do a tune** *v. see BLOW SOME TUNES under* BLOW *v.*[2].

tune *v.* [? to get a fig. *tune* – positive or otherwise – from one's target] **1** [late 18C+] to beat, to thrash. **2** [1960s+] (*US teen*) to talk to, esp. flirtatiously. **3** [1970s+] (*S.Afr.*) take notice, to look. **4** [1980s] (*S.Afr.*) to enjoy life. **5** [1980s+] (*S.Afr.*) to tease, to hoax, to deceive.

IN PHRASES

❑ **tune one's pipes** *v.* [pun on SE *pipe one's eye*] [18C] to cry. ❑ **tune out** *v.* [radio imagery] [1920s+] **1** to lose concentration, deliberately or otherwise. **2** to dismiss a topic or person from one's mind. ❑ **tune someone grief** *v.* (*also* **tune someone skeef**) [SE *grief*/S.Afr. *skeef*, disapprovingly, ult. Afk. *skeef*, askew, crooked] [1970s+] (*S.Afr.*) to abuse someone verbally, to give someone trouble. ❑ **tune up** *v.* [fig. use of SE *tune up*, of musical instruments] **1** [1920s+] to get drunk. **2** [1960s] (*US campus*) to become intoxicated by drugs. **3** [1970s+] to beat, to thrash.

tuned in *adj.* [TUNE IN *v.*] [1950s+] aware of what is going on, at one with the nuances and niceties of a situation or conversation.

tuned out *adj.* [radio imagery] [1950s+] **1** out of touch, unaware. **2** daydreaming, inattentive.

tuned (up) *adj.* (*also* **tuned in**) [TUNE IN *v.*] [1920s+] (*US*) stimulated by alcohol but not drunk.

tune in *v.* [radio imagery] [1920s+] **1** (*orig. US*) to be aware, culturally sophisticated; thus 1960s HIPPIE *n.*[2] (3) slogan 'turn on, *tune in*, drop out'. **2** to make someone aware, to explain.

IN PHRASES

❑ **tune in one's mike** *v.* [1940s] (*US black*) to listen.

tunes *n.* [1980s+] (*US campus*) music.

tune the old cow died of *n.* (*also* **...on**) **1** [early 19C–1910s] (*also* **tune the old cat died of**) a discordant or unpleasant piece of music. **2** [late 19C+] a lecture or homily delivered to a beggar instead of money.

tunker *n.* [Penn. Du. *dunken*, a Baptist, lit. 'dipped'] [late 18C–1900s] a street preacher.

tunnel *n.* **1** [1970s] (*US*) the mouth. **2** [1970s+] (*US gay*) the anus. **3** [1980s+] (*Aus. prison*) a woman.

SE in slang uses

IN COMPOUNDS

❑ **tunnel-grunters** *n.* [dial.] [19C] potatoes. ❑ **tunnel rat** *n.* [note Vietnam era milit. *tunnel rat*, a soldier who entered – and fought in – the extensive enemy tunnel system] **1** [20C+] (*US prison*) one who escapes by digging their way out of prison. **2** [1990s+] (*US, NY*) a transit police officer. ❑ **tunnel stiff** *n.* [SE *tunnel* + STIFF *n.*[1] (4d)] [20C+] (*US*) an underground tunnel worker.

IN PHRASES

❑ **tunnel (of love)** *n.* [19C] the vagina.

Tunnels *n.* [this London theatre, which was demolished in 1899 during the building of the Aldwych, was built largely underground and featured a number of subterranean passages, leading patrons from the street to the auditorium] [late 19C] the Opera Comique in the Strand.

tun of grease *n.* (*also* **tun of fat**) [early 18C] a fat person.

tunti *n.* [? Afr. langs. Kissi: *tumta* or Songhay: *tunde*, backside] [1950s+] (*W.I. Rasta*) the vagina.

tun-tun *n.* [suggested links to DUNDUS *n.* or Carib.E. *tun-tun*, turned cornmeal, are unlikely; ? SE *turn* + redup., the movements of intercourse] [1950s+] (*W.I., USVI*) **1** the vagina. **2** a term of affection.

tup *n.*[1] [TUP v.] **1** [early 17C] a lecher. **2** [17C–early 19C] a cuckold.

tup *n.*[2] [abbr. SE *tuppence*] [late 19C–1950s] (*W.I.*) **1** 1½ (old) pence. **2** a very small amount.

IN PHRASES

❑ **tup-an-gill** *n.* [GILL *n.*[3] (1)] [mid-19C+] (*W.I.*) 2½ (old) pence.

tup *adj.* [pron. SE (*locke*)*d up*] [late 19C] arrested.

tup *v.* [SE *tup*, a ram; thus Shakespeare's *Othello* (1604), when Iago informs Brabantio that: 'An old Blacke Ram Is tupping your White Ewe'] **1** [late 16C+] to have sexual intercourse. **2** [early 17C] to render a cuckold [the ram's HORNS *n.*].

tuppence *n.* [phr. '(only) *tuppence* in the quid'] [1940s+] (*Aus.*) a fool, a halfwit.

tuppence coloured *adj.* [from toy theatres, advertised as 'penny plain, tuppence coloured'] **1** [late 19C] exciting. **2** [1910s] upper-class.

tuppenny damn *n.* see DAMN *n.*

tuppenny halfpenny *adj.* (*also* **tuppence ha'penny, tuppenny ha'penny**) [the low value of the sum] [mid-19C+] cheap, second-rate, inferior.

tupper *n.* ['takes its rise from Mr Martin *Tupper* who wrote a phenomenally successful book called *Proverbial Philosophy* – composed entirely of self-evident propositions' (Ware)] [late 19C–1900s] (*UK society*) a bore.

tupperware *n.* [2000s] (*N.Z.*) a dismissive term for any ostentatious external embellishments of an automobile.

tuppy *adj.* [? SE *tupped*, used for breeding; also Abor. use *tuppy*, vagina] [late 19C–1950s] (*Aus.*) of an animal, worn out, thus worthless.

tu quoque *n.* [lit. Lat. 'you also', ? play on QUIM *n.* (1) and similar terms for the vagina beginning with *q*; Williams suggests it began as a Lat. rejoinder to the insult 'You're a cunt'] [17C–19C] the vagina.

turbo *n.* [SE *turbo*-charged] **1** [1980s+] (*drugs*) crack cocaine and marijuana smoked together. **2** [1990s+] (*US campus*) a very energetic, 'speedy' person; as *adj.*, slightly crazy.

turbobitch *n.* [SE *turbo* + BITCH *n.*[1] (1)/SE *slut*] [1980s+] (*US campus*) an unpleasant, irritable, negative woman.

turbo-charged *adj.* [1990s+] (*W.I.*) of a woman, very attractive.

turboslut *n.* [1980s] (*US campus*) a notably promiscuous woman.

turd *n.*[1] [OE *tord*, ult. presumed Indo-Eur. root *der, tear or split. Orig. use, *c.*1000, was simply excrement, the additional pej. meaning was added mid-15C. Thus Harman's *Caveat* (1567) translates the Und. phrase 'Gerry gan the Ruffian cly thee' as 'A torde in thy mouth, the deuill take thee' (*Gerry*, JERE *n.*). As with many similar terms, vulgar rather than actual sl., *turd* was excluded from polite speech (and dictionaries) by late 18C. It has remained off-limits, although like many of the 'milder' obscenities, it has crept gradually into spoken, if not written English, esp. where, like its cognate SHIT *n.* (1) it refers not to excrement, but to a human object of derision or dislike] **1** [11C+] a piece of excrement. **2** [mid-15C+] (*also* **bugturd, turdball**) an unappealing person, or object.

DERIVATIVES

❑ **turdish** *adj.* [1930s+] unpleasant, obnoxious. ❑ **turdy** *adj.* [early 17C] covered in excrement, or generally disgusting.

IN COMPOUNDS

❑ **turdburger** *n.* [2000s] (*Aus.*) a term of abuse. ❑ **turd-burglar** *n.* (*also* **turd bandit, ...puncher, ...tapper**) [SHIT *n.* (1) + SE *burglar*, his predilection for anal intercourse] [1960s+] (*orig. Aus.*) a homosexual man. ❑ **turd cutter** *n.* [1990s+] (*US campus*) the buttocks. ❑ **turd-eating** *adj.* see TURD-STRANGLING *adj.* ❑ **turdhead** *n.* [-HEAD *sfx* (1)] [1940s+] a term of abuse. ❑ **turdkicker** *n.* [1960s] (*US*) a yokel, a peasant. ❑ **turd-packer** *n.* (*also* **shit-packer, turd-tapper**) [1930s+] (*orig. US*) a homosexual. ❑ **turd-poodle** *n.* [1980s] (*US campus*) an unappealing and stupid person. ❑ **turd-puncher** *n.* [1970s+] a homosexual. ❑ **turd strangler/strangling** *see* separate entries.

IN PHRASES

❑ **all honey or all turd with them** [late 18C–mid-19C] said of those whose relationship fluctuates violently, they are either the closest of friends or the deepest of enemies. ❑ **as popular as a turd in a fruit salad** [1990s+] (*Aus.*) extremely unpopular. ❑ **chuck a turd** *v.* [19C+] to excrete. ❑ **fine as a cow turd stuck with primroses** [late 18C–early 19C] excellent, first-rate, very fine. ❑ **he would skin a turd** [late 19C+] (*Can.*) said of particularly mean person. ❑ **not give someone the steam off one's turds** *v. see under* STEAM *n.* ❑ **not worth a turd** *adj.* [late 15C+] worthless, useless. ❑ **push a turd uphill (with a toothpick)** *v.* [1980s+] to work, talk etc, unsuccessfully, against the odds. ❑ **scare bird turds out of** *v.* [1920s+] (*orig. US*) to terrify. ❑ **turd for..., a** [mid-17C–19C] a general phr. of dismissal, i.e. *go to hell*. ❑ **turd in the punchbowl** *n.* [1990s+] (*US*) a general term of abuse.

IN EXCLAMATIONS

❑ **turd in your teeth!** [mid-16C–mid-17C] go to hell! (and stay there).

turd *n.*[2] *see* DOG TURD *n.*

turdbird *v.* [1950s–60s] (*US*) to lie, to exaggerate.

turd strangler *n.* [2000s] (*N.Z.*) a plumber.

turd-strangling *adj.* (*also* **turd-eating**) [1970s] (*US/Aus.*) a generally derog. adj.

turf *n.* [note SE *turf*, as a general noun for the world of horseracing] **1** [mid-19C+] the highway or street as the home of tramps and the criminal underworld; thus spec. *the turf*. **2** [mid-19C+] (*also* **the track**) constr. with *the*, the occupation of prostitution; thus *ON THE TURF* below. **3** [1940s+] the area with which one is familiar and where one is recognized as a regular figure. **4** [1950s+] (*US Und.*) the area controlled by a street or prison gang. **5** [1960s] (*US Und.*) the ground. **6** [1960s+] that area of life, work or other activity in which a person's authority or influence is recognized.

IN PHRASES

❑ **hit the turf** *v.* [1950s+] (*US Und.*) to resume a criminal career after leaving prison. ❑ **on the turf** **1** [mid-19C–1930s] working as a prostitute. **2** [1900s] (*US campus*) calling on a young woman. **3** [1900s–60s] (*US Und.*) living as a vagrant. **4** [1950s] (*US Und.*) engaged in regular criminal activity.

SE in slang uses

IN COMPOUNDS

❑ **turf patrol** *n.* [play on GRASS *n.*[4]] [1980s+] (*Irish*) a session of smoking marijuana.

IN PHRASES

❑ **hit the turf** *v. see HIT THE GRIT under* GRIT *n.*[2].

turf *v.* [SE *turf*, the grass] [1940s–50s] (*Aus.*) to have sexual intercourse in the open air.

IN PHRASES

▫ **turf it** *v.* **1** [mid-19C] to work as a prostitute. **2** [late 19C–1930s] to sleep outdoors, usu. under a tent. **3** [late 19C–1940s] to live as a tramp. ▫ **turf out** *v.* (*also* **turf off**) **1** [late 19C+] to eject, to throw out, supposedly on to some grass; to dismiss from a job. **2** [1950s] (*N.Z.*) (*also* **turf**) to reject a lover. ▫ **turf up** *v.* [1920s+] (*Aus.*) to abandon, to leave a job.

turfer *n.* [TURF *n.* (2)] [late 19C] a prostitute.

turfite *n.* [SE *turf*, as a general noun for the world of horseracing] **1** [mid-19C–1900s] a gambler. **2** [1990s+] (*W.I.*) a veteran.

turistas *n. see* TOURISTAS *n.*

turk *n.*[1] [racist stereotyping] **1** [late 16C–17C] (*also* **mahomet**) a low-class prostitute. **2** [late 17C+] a boorish, unpleasant person [prob. underpinned by Irish *torc*, a boar or hog]. **3** [early 18C; 1930s+] (*gay*) one who enjoys anal intercourse. **4** [late 19C+] (*US*) an Irish immigrant. **5** [1910s+] (*US prison*) a 'masculine', predatory prison homosexual. **6** [1970s+] a sexually active man.

IN PHRASES

▫ **like a turk** *adv. see* LIKE A TROJAN *under* TROJAN *n.* ▫ **turn Turk** *v.* [racial stereotyping] [late 16C–17C; 20C+] to become a renegade, a rebel.

turk *n.*[2] [abbr.] **1** [late 19C+] (*Aus.*) a *turkey*. **2** [1910s–60s] a Turkish cigarette.

turk *v.* [racial stereotyping] [20C+] of a man, to have sexual intercourse, esp. with a degree of brutality.

turkey *n.*[1] **1** [mid-19C] a state of drunkenness [DRIVE TURKEYS TO MARKET below; ? one walks like the bird]. **2** [1900s–40s] (*Aus./US*) a vagrant's pack, a lumberman's kit pack [resemblance to the bulky bird which has been 'stuffed']. **3** [1910s–40s] (*US Und.*) a suitcase; a large traveling bag [resemblance to the bulky bird which has been 'stuffed']. **4** in senses of failure, weakness [according to Cohen (ed.) *Studies in Slang* IV (1995) pp.100–119, originating in the theatrical *turkey show*, a touring show, usu. burlesque, mounted at a moment's notice and staffed by a third-rate cast, even stage-struck amateurs]. (**a**) [1920s+] a failure, an incompetent, a dull person. (**b**) [1930s+] (*drugs*) inferior quality or even fake drugs. (**c**) [1940s] (*US gang*) a gang member who won't or can't fight, but runs messages etc. (**d**) [1940s+] an unappealing or worthless thing, a disappointment. (**e**) [1950s+] a general derog. term of address. (**f**) [1950s+] an unattractive man or woman. (**g**) [1970s+] (*US Und./teen*) a victim, e.g. of a mugging or shooting.

IN COMPOUNDS

▫ **turkey neck** *n.* [1950s+] the penis.

IN PHRASES

▫ **bleed one's turkey** *v.* [1920s+] to urinate. ▫ **catch a turkey** *v.* [mid-19C] (*US*) to get drunk. ▫ **come one's turkey** *v.* [late 19C+] to masturbate. ▫ **have a turkey on one's back** *v.* (*also* **carry...**) [mid-19C–early 20C] to be in a state of drunkenness. ▫ **not say turkey** *v.* (*also* **not say pea-turkey**) [mid-19C–1900s] (*US*) to say nothing, to stay silent. ▫ **turkey on a string** *n.* [1970s+] (*US black*) one who is infatuated and thus easily led and controlled. ▫ **turkey out** *v.* [1950s] (*US*) to run off, to act in a cowardly manner.

SE in slang uses

IN COMPOUNDS

▫ **turkey buyer** *n.* [orig. use is Leadenhall Market; turkeys were beyond the pockets of the poor] [late 19C–1900s] a rich person. ▫ **turkey-buzzard** *n.* [20C+] (*US black*) a white man, usu. derog. ▫ **Turkey Day** *n.* [the trad. dish] [1910s–40s] (*US black*) Thanksgiving. ▫ **turkey gobble** *n.* [1980s+] (*Aus. prison*) fellatio; thus *turkey gobbler*, a fellator/fellatrix. ▫ **turkey merchant** *n.* [puns on SE *Turkey merchant*] **1** [late 17C–mid-19C] one who buys and sells turkeys, a poulterer [allegedly credited to Horne Tooke (1736–1812), when questioned by fellow Etonians as to his father's occupation]. **2** [mid-19C] (*UK Und.*) a dealer in smuggled silk [the play was on *merchant*, i.e. a legitimate dealer]. ▫ **turkey's elbow** *n. see* BEE'S KNEES *n.* ▫ **turkey shoot** *n.* [the large SE *turkey* presents an easy target; SAmE *turkey shoot*, a shooting match at which turkeys are the targets and the prizes] [1940s+] **1** (*US*) a combat in which one's own side wins without any difficulty, killing and destroying on a large scale; also in fig. use. **2** anything exceptionally easy. ▫ **turkey tail** *n.* (*also* **turkey turd**) [1980s] (*US*) a term of abuse.

IN PHRASES

▫ **dead turkey** *n. see under* DEAD *adj.* ▫ **drive turkeys to market** *v.* [the turkey-driver is forced to follow the birds' meandering course along the road] [mid–late 19C] to walk in a drunken, unsteady manner. ▫ **eat turkey** *v.* [var. EAT *(BOILED)* CROW *under* EAT *v.*] [1960s–70s] (*US*) **1** to suffer humiliation and insult without reciprocating. **2** to take second best, to accept an inferior role. ▫ **head over turkey** *adv.* (*also* **head over tuck**) [SE *turkey*, the plucked bird here seen as resembling the shape of the buttocks] [20C+] (*Aus./N.Z.*) head-over-heels. ▫ **turkey off** *v.* [20C+] (*Aus./N.Z.*) to leave in a hurry, to run off.

turkey *n.*[2] [TURK *n.*[1] (4)] [20C+] (*US*) an Irish immigrant.

turkey *n.*[3] [ety. unknown] **1** [1970s+] amphetamine. **2** [1980s+] (*drugs*) cocaine.

turkey *n.*[4] *see* PLAIN-TURKEY *n.*

turkey *adj.* [? TURKEY *n.*[1] (4a)] **1** [1910s] (*US*) easily accomplished and enjoyed or desired. **2** [1950s] (*US gang*) cowardly.

IN PHRASES

▫ **turn turkey** *v.* [1950s] (*US gang*) to back down through fear.

turkey *v.*[1] [1910s] to strut around.

turkey *v.*[2] [resemblance to a puffed up SE *turkey*] [1960s] (*US campus/drugs*) to breathe marijuana smoke through the nose.

Turkey puddle *n.* [early 18C] coffee.

Turkey trot *n.* [1960s] diarrhoea suffered by tourists.

turking *n.* [TURK *v.*] [20C+] sexual intercourse, copulating.

Turkish (bath) *n.* [rhy. sl.; Cockney pron. 'barf'] [1990s+] a laugh.

Turkish (delight) *adj.* [rhy. sl.] **1** [1990s+] mean, grasping [= TIGHT *adj.* (6a)]. **2** [2000s] rubbishy [= SHITE *adj.* (1)].

Turk McGurk *n.* [1970s] (*US*) a deceitful, untrustworthy person.

turn *n.*[1] [SE *turn off*, to kill] [17C–18C] a judicial hanging.

turn *n.*[2] [SE *turn-up*, a prostitute + *turn*, an act, a performance] [17C–19C; 2000s] an act of sexual intercourse.

IN PHRASES

▫ **do a turn on one's back** *v.* [for the woman to *turn* over onto her back + pun on theatrical use] [late 19C+] of a woman, to make herself available for sexual intercourse.

turn *n.*[3] [SE *turn*, a go] [1900s–10s] a robbery.

SE in slang uses

IN PHRASES

▫ **have a turn** *v.* [late 19C] to fight.

turn *n.*[4] [TURN IT ON *v.*] [1950s+] (*Aus., usu. teen*) a party.

turn *v.*[1] **1** [17C–19C] to deceive or rob [? SE *turn against/on*]. **2** [1910s+] US Und. uses [SE *turn round*]. (**a**) to betray to the authorities. (**b**) to give state's evidence. (**c**) of a police officer, to become corrupt. (**d**) to persuade a villain to give evidence against, or spy on, fellow criminals. **3** [1970s] to distract someone's attention [they are *turned* away]. **4** *see* TURN A TRICK *v.*[2] (2).

IN PHRASES

▫ **on the turn** [1930s] (*US*) out on a spree. ▫ **turn around** *v.* [1960s+] (*US*) to change someone's attitude or behaviour, esp. to persuade a criminal to turn informer; also to disorientate.

SE in slang uses

IN COMPOUNDS

▫ **turn-tongue** *adj.* [20C+] (*W.I.*) duplicitous, hypocritical, lying.

IN PHRASES

▫ **don't turn that side to London** [the idea that only the best is good enough for display in the metropolis] [late 19C] a phr. used to condemn whatever object is under discussion. ▫ **turn...** *v. see also under* relevant n. or adj. ▫ **turn a date** *v. see* TURN A TRICK *v.*^{2} (2). ▫ **turn and wind the penny** *v.* [late 17C–early 18C] to spend one's money judiciously. ▫ **turn every which way but loose** *v. see* CUT EVERY WHICH WAY BUT LOOSE *under* CUT *v.*^{2}. ▫ **turn funny** *v. see* GET FUNNY WITH *under* FUNNY *adj.*^{2}. ▫ **turn in one's dinner pail** *v. see* HAND IN ONE'S DINNER-PAIL *under* HAND *v.* ▫ **turn into fish food** *v.* [20C+] to drown. ▫ **turn it down** *v.* [radio/TV imagery] [1960s+] (*gay*) to moderate one's more flagrantly homosexual behaviour. ▫ **turn one's crank** *v.* [1940s+] of something, to give a person pleasure. ▫ **turn one's damper down** *v.* [SE *damper*, a device to slow down machinery, lower the heat in fires, etc] **1** [1900s–30s] (*US black*) to calm down, to relax, esp. as imper. *turn your damper down!* **2** [1920s–50s] (*US black*) to satisfy sexually, also fig. use. ▫ **turn on one's lights** *v.* [1990s+] to start thinking, to act sensibly. ▫ **turn on the fan** *v.* [FAN *v.*^{2} (1)] [20C+] (*US*) to hurry, to move quickly. ▫ **turn on the (tear) tap** *v.* (*also* **turn the tap(s) on**) [the implication is of a lack of sincerity] [late 19C+] to start crying, thus *turn off the tap*, to stop crying. ▫ **turn on the toe** *v.* [a ladder was employed before the early 19C development of the drop] [late 16C–early 17C] to push (the victim) off the ladder at the climax of a judicial hanging. ▫ **turn someone's mouth behind their back** *v.* [to 'knock someone's face through the back of their neck'] [20C+] (*W.I.*) to beat one up severely. ▫ **turn state** *v.* (*also* **...state's**) [abbr.] [20C+] (*US Und.*) to give state's evidence. ▫ **turn the bucket on** *v. see* DROP THE BUCKET ON *under* DROP *v.*^{1}. ▫ **turn the corner** *v.* [1970s+] of a man, to become homosexual or acknowledge one's homosexuality. ▫ **turn the corner of Bolt Street** *v.* [play on BOLT *v.* (1)] [19C] to escape, to run off. ▫ **turn the key on** *v.* [1930s] (*UK Und.*) to give a life sentence. ▫ **turn the set/shit out** *v. see* TURN OUT THE SET *under* TURN OUT *v.*^{3}. ▫ **turn the tables** *v.* [SE *turn the tables*, to reverse the relations between two parties] [1930s+] (*gay*) of a male homosexual prostitute, to blackmail a client. ▫ **turn the trick** *v. see* TURN A TRICK *v.*^{1}. ▫ **turn to custard** *v.* [2000s] (*N.Z.*) to malfunction, go wrong. ▫ **turn tricks** *v. see* TURN A TRICK *v.*^{2} (2).

IN EXCLAMATIONS

▫ **turn blue!** [1950s–60s] a euph. version of FUCK OFF *v.* (1).

turn *v.*^{2} **1** [1930s] (*US drugs*) to sell drugs; of a doctor or dentist, to write prescriptions for narcotics. **2** [1960s] (*US Und.*) to sell, usu. stolen goods.

turnabout *n.*^{1} [the turning to present one's buttocks] **1** [20C+] (*Aus.*) sodomy. **2** [1960s+] (*US black*) sexual intercourse. **3** [1960s+] (*US black*) a male homosexual.

turnabout *n.*^{2} [the drug's effects] [1980s+] (*drugs*) amphetamine.

turn a trick *v.*^{1} (*also* **turn the trick**) [TRICK *n.*^{2}] **1** [late 19C+] (*US*) to carry out a successful robbery, theft or confidence trick. **2** [early 20C] to perform any action successfully.

turn a trick *v.*^{2} [TRICK *n.*^{1} (1)] (*orig. and chiefly US*) **1** [late 19C+] to make something happen as required or desired. **2** [1920s+] (*also* **do a trick, turn, turn a date, turn tricks**) to be paid for sexual intercourse, either as a professional prostitute or on a one-off or occasional basis in between working as a student, actress or model; thus n. *trickster*, a prostitute. **3** [1920s+] to have sexual intercourse.

Turnbull Street bee *n.* [Turnbull Street was a well-known centre of whoring] [early 17C] a venereally diseased prostitute.

Turnbull Street flea *n.* [for ety. *see* TURNBULL STREET BEE *n.*] [early–mid-17C] a crab-louse.

Turnbull Street rogue *n.* [for ety. *see* TURNBULL STREET BEE *n.*] [early 17C] a dissipated villain, a pimp.

turn down *v.*^{1} [the tilting of the glass or bottle] [mid-18C–1930s] to drink down, to 'toss back' a drink.

turn down *v.*^{2} [20C+ use is SE] [early 19C+] (*orig. US*) to reject, to snub, to rebuke.

-turned *sfx* [1930s+] (*US*) of a certain type, disposed, natured, always in combs., e.g. *nice-turned, mild-turned*.

turned around *adj.* [1960s+] (*US*) confused, disorientated.

turned off *adj.*^{1} [mid-19C–1910s] (*UK society*) married.

turned off *adj.*^{2} [TURN OFF *v.*^{4}] **1** [1950s+] unexcited (in a sexual context). **2** [1960s+] out of touch, unaware, daydreaming. **3** [1960s+] (*US campus*) unenthusiastic.

turned on *adj.* [TURN ON *v.*] **1** [1950s+] (*US*) intoxicated, esp. by drugs. **2** [1960s+] sexually stimulated. **3** [1960s+] aware, sophisticated, up-to-the-minute.

turned over *adj.* [? *turned over* to the authorities] [mid-19C] **1** remanded in custody pending one's trial. **2** stopped and searched by the police.

turned up *adj.*^{1} [early 19C] ruined.

turned up *adj.*^{2} [early–mid-19C] **1** stopped and searched by the police. **2** acquitted of a crime in court, esp. through lack of evidence.

turned up *adj.*^{3} [? turn up one's nose] [1980s] disgusted.

turner out *n.* [SE *turn out*, to manufacture] [mid-19C] (*UK Und.*) a counterfeiter.

turnie *n.* [abbr.] [1990s+] a turnstile.

turn-in *n.*^{1} [TURN IN *v.*^{1} (1)] [late 19C] a bed.

turn-in *n.*^{2} *see* TURN-UP *n.* (3).

turn in *v.*^{1} **1** [late 17C+] to go to bed. **2** [1910s+] to stop doing something, to abandon. **3** [1920s] to die.

turn in *v.*^{2} (*also* **turn up**) [1920s+] to betray; to give up someone to the authorities.

turning joint *n.* [JOINT *n.* (1)] [late 19C] (*US Und*) a place where innocent people were brought to be swindled out of their legitimate money in exchange for counterfeit notes.

turning over *n.* [late 19C–1900s] (*US*) a reprimand, a telling-off.

turning-tree *n.* [SE *turn off*, to hang + TRIPLE TREE *n.*; also an image of the turning, hanging corpse] [mid-16C–mid-17C] the gallows.

turnip *n.* **1** [early 19C+] (*also* **turnup**) an old-fashioned watch; thus *cut turnip-tops*, to steal a watch, chain and seals [its rotundity and thickness]. **2** [mid-19C+] (*also* **turnip-eater, turnip-head**) a simpleton, a fool, a naive country fellow; as adj., *turnip-faced*. **3** [mid-19C+] the head. **4** [1910s–20s] a term of affectionate address; usu. as *old turnip*.

DERIVATIVES

▫ **turnipy** *adj.* [mid-19C+] foolish.

SE in slang uses

IN COMPOUNDS

▫ **turnip greens** *n.* (*also* **collard greens**) [play on the popular soul food] [1970s–80s] (*US black*) marijuana. ▫ **turnip-pate** *n.* [late 17C–early 19C] a very fair head of hair; thus *turnip-pated*, having white hair or very light blond hair. ▫ **turnip-snagger** *n.* (*also* **turnip-sucker**) [SE *turnip* + *snag*, to snatch] [20C+] (*Irish*) a peasant, a country person.

IN PHRASES

▫ **give someone turnips** *v.* [pun on TURN UP *v.*^{2} (3)/SE *turnip*; note Suffolk dial. *give someone cold turnips*, to turn down a proposal of marriage/love] [early–mid-19C] to abandon or jilt, esp. heartlessly, ruthlessly.

turnipes *n.* [early 19C] a symbol of cuckoldry.

turnips *n.* [? joc. pron. of *turn up*] [late 18C] (*US Und.*) acquitted.

turn it in! *excl. see* TURN IT UP! *excl.*

turn it on *v.* **1** [1920s+] to make things happen, to intensify things, to spice things up. **2** [1940s+] (*Aus.*) to start a fight. **3** [1940s+] (*Aus.*) to provide food and drink, to host a party. **4** [1940s+] (*Aus.*) to allow or offer sex, often with more than one partner.

turn it up *v.*^{1} [TURN UP *v.*^{2} (6)] **1** [early 19C+] (*also* **turn it off**) to stop doing something. **2** [1900s–10s] (*Aus.*) in ext. use, to die.

turn it up *v.*^{2} [1980s+] (*N.Z.*) of a female, to offer oneself for sex.

turn it up! *excl.* (*also* **turn it in!**) [TURN IT UP *v.*^{1} (1)] [late 19C+] stop doing that!, don't exaggerate!

turnkey *n.* [i.e. no more than open and shut the doors] [2000s] (*US prison*) a guard who does the bare minimum required for their shift.

turn-off *n.* [TURN OFF *v.*[4]] [1960s+] anything or anyone repellent, whether physically (esp. sexually) or emotionally.

turn off *v.*[1] **1** [late 16C–1930s] to execute by hanging. **2** [mid-18C] to dismiss from a job. **3** [mid-18C–1920s] (*US Und.*) to break open; often when using some form of picklock; to rob.

turn off *v.*[2] [late 19C–1900s] (*Aus.*) to marry, or be married.

turn off *v.*[3] [1920s] of a man, to have sexual intercourse.

turn off *v.*[4] **1** [1950s+] to alienate. **2** [1960s] (*drugs*) to deprive of a supply of drugs. **3** [1960s+] to repel sexually. **4** [1960s+] to lose interest in, esp. sexually.

IN PHRASES

❑ **make the turn** *v.* [1980s+] (*drugs*) to withdraw from drug use.

turn off (the gas) *v.* (*also* **...the alarm clock, ...the tap**) [SE *turn off* + GAS *n.*[1]] [late 19C–1960s] to stop bragging or boasting.

turn-on *n.* [TURN ON *v.*] **1** [1950s–60s] (*Can.*) something done by an 'in-group' to provoke outsiders. **2** [1960s+] of objects or people, a thrill, sexual or otherwise. **3** [1960s+] (*drugs*) enough of a drug to produce its desired effects.

turn on *v.* **1** [late 19C–1920s] to persuade someone to do something. **2** [1930–50s] (*US black*) to explain. **3** [1940s–60s] (*US black*) to render angry. **4** [1940s+] (*Aus./N.Z.*) to provide liquor, etc, e.g. for a party. **5** [1950s+] (*orig. US*) to take drugs, esp. heroin, morphine or cannabis [note exhortation by Timothy Leary (1920–96) to '*turn on*, tune in and drop out']. **6** [1950s+] (*orig. US*) to offer, or introduce drugs to another person. **7** [1950s+] (*orig. US*) to introduce someone or something (non-drugs) to someone. **8** [1950s+] (*orig. US*) to stimulate, usu. sexually, to appeal to someone. **9** [1960s+] (*orig. US*) to become stimulated. **10** [1970s] (*US*) to drink liquor.

IN PHRASES

❑ **whatever turns you on** [1970s+] whatever you like, esp. as slightly sarcastic response to a revelation of an especially bizarre or distasteful pleasure (usu. sexual).

turn-out *n.*[1] [the participants *turn out* to fight] [early 19C+] a fist-fight.

turn-out *n.*[2] **1** [late 19C+] any kind of activity. **2** [1900s–50s] a resolution, a solution.

turn-out *n.*[3] [TURN OUT *v.*[2] (2)] [1950s] (*US Und.*) a discharge from prison.

turn-out *n.*[4] [TURN OUT *v.*[4]] [1960s–70s] **1** (*US*) a novice, a recent initiate, e.g. a new whore. **2** (*US prison*) (*also* **penitentiary turn-out**) a young prisoner who is forced into life as homosexual.

turn out *v.*[1] (*also* **tumble out**) [SE *turn-out*, a getting up from one's bed] [19C+] to get out of bed.

turn out *v.*[2] [SE *turn out*, to leave home and start work] **1** [late 19C–1900s] (*Aus.*) to leave home and become a bushranger. **2** [1910s] (*US Und.*) to free a criminal from arrest. **3** [1960s] (*US Und.*) to become a professional thief.

turn out *v.*[3] [? TURN-OUT *n.*[1]] **1** [20C+] to beat up. **2** [1930s+] (*US black*) to cause trouble, e.g. at a party, in school, to turn a place over. **3** [1950s+] (*US black*) to dominate, to take over.

IN PHRASES

❑ **turn out the set** *v.* (*also* **turn out a set, turn the set out, turn the shit out**) [sense 2 + SET *n.*[2] (1b)/SHIT *n.* (3h)] [1970s+] (*US black*) to disrupt a situation or occasion, esp. permanently.

turn out *v.*[4] **1** [1920s–40s] (*US Und.*) of a young confidence trickster, to commence one's career. **2** [1940s+] (*orig. US black*) to initiate a newcomer in a variety of situations, e.g. *pimp* to run a prostitute on the streets; *Hell's Angels* to use a woman for multiple sex; (*US Und.*) to make a new inmate into a prison homosexual (usu. only for the duration of their sentence). **3** [1960s] to start using a drug. **4** [1960s+] (*US Und.*) to work as a prostitute. **5** [1970s+] (*US black*) to use unconventional means to introduce someone to any important first experience. **6** [1980s] (*US black*) to start living/working on the streets. **7** [1990s+] to take someone's virginity.

turn over *n.* **1** [early 19C] (*UK Und.*) a fight. **2** [mid–late 19C] (*UK Und.*) a body search. **3** [1930s] (*US prison*) a transfer between prisons. **4** [1940s] (*US prison*) the last night of a sentence. **5** [1950s+] (*UK prison*) a search of a prisoner's cell.

turnover *n.* [*TURN OVER ON under* TURN OVER *v.*[1]] [1980s+] (*US*) one who is seen as betraying their race, usu. black or Puerto Rican, by assimilating into or at least succeeding in the white society.

turn over *v.*[1] **1** [mid-19C+] (*UK Und.*) to search a house or apartment or prison cell, usu. with the maximum of damage and mess. **2** [mid-19C+] to search a person. **3** [late 19C–1910s] to rob. **4** [1950s+] (*also* **turn up**) to beat up, to attack. **5** [1980s+] to destroy a place.

SE in slang uses

IN PHRASES

❑ **turn over on** *v.* [late 19C+] (*UK/US Und.*) **1** to inform on (a fellow inmate). **2** to cheat, to defraud.

turn over *v.*[2] (*also* **turn up**) [turns one's stomach over or up] [mid-19C+] to distress, to make nauseous.

turn over *v.*[3] [the physical act that may precede the intercourse] [1930s+] (*gay*) to allow anal intercourse.

turnpike *n.* [cf. ALLEY *n.*[1] (1)] [mid-17C–19C] the vagina.

turnpike man *n.* [from the fees or tolls the clergy collect for christenings and funerals: 'our entrance into and exit from the world' (Grose 1785)] [late 18C–mid-19C] a parson.

turnpike sailor *n.* [mid–late 19C] a wandering beggar who poses as the victim of a shipwreck.

turn-up *n.* [SE *turn up*, to throw into disorder] **1** [19C–1900s] a boxing or wrestling match or contest. **2** [19C–1900s] a street fight. **3** [19C+] (*also* **turn-in**) any form of argument, altercation. **4** [late 19C–1910s] (*society*) a minor quarrel, a tiff.

turnup *n. see* TURNIP *n.*

turn up *v.*[1] [SE *turn up*; note *TURN UP ONE'S TAIL* below] **1** [17C–early 18C] to prostitute oneself or another [*OED* cites it only as 'apparently']. **2** [19C] of a woman, to have sexual intercourse. **3** *see* TURN OVER *v.*[2].

SE in slang uses

IN PHRASES

❑ **turn up jack** *v. see* CUT UP JACK *v.* ❑ **turn up one's guts** *v.* [1910s] (*Aus.*) to vomit. ❑ **turn up one's tail** *v.* [TAIL *n.* (4)/TAIL *n.* (2)] [mid-17C–early 18C] of a woman, to have sexual intercourse. ❑ **turn up the heat (on)** *v. see TURN ON THE HEAT under* HEAT *n.*

turn up *v.*[2] [SE *turn up*, to turn a horse loose] **1** [late 18C] (*UK Und.*) to cheat. **2** [early 19C] to remove one's custom. **3** [19C–1900s] to ignore a former friend or end a sexual relationship. **4** [19C] to run away. **5** [early 19C–1930s] to set free, to release (a prisoner), to acquit. **6** [early 19C+] to abandon. **7** [mid-19C] to dismiss from a job. **8** [mid–late 19C] to alter, to change. **9** [mid-19C+] (*UK Und.*) to inform against someone, to turn someone over to the police. **10** [late 19C] (*US*) to rob. **11** [1920s] (*US*) to give up, to weaken. **12** [1960s] (*Aus. Und/*) to take the blame for someone else's crime. **13** [2000s] to annoy. **14** *see* TURN IN *v.*[2]. **15** *see* TURN OVER *v.*[1] (4).

IN PHRASES

❑ **turn up sweet** *v.* [early 19C] (*UK Und.*) to abandon somebody but leave them unaware or happy.

turn up *v.*[3] [mid–late 19C] (*UK Und.*) to hand (something) over.

turn up *v.*[4] [? SE *turn upside down*] [mid-19C–1920s] (*UK/US*) to search.

turn-ups *n.* [TURN UP *v.*[2] (3)] [late 19C–1900s] the rejection of a suitor.

Turpentine, the *n. see* SERPS, THE *n.*

turps *n.* (*also* **terps**) [abbr. SE *turpentine*] **1** [mid-19C+] any form of alcohol. **2** [late 19C+] (*Aus.*) beer.

IN COMPOUNDS

❑ **turps nudger** *n.* [1990s+] a heavy drinker.

IN PHRASES

❑ **on the turps** [mid-19C+] drinking (heavily).

turret *n.* **1** [mid-19C] (*boxing*) the face. **2** [1910s] (*Aus.*) the head.

turrl *n. see* TWIRL *n.*

turtle *n.* **1** [1900s] (*US*) a racehorse (presumably slow). **2** [20C+] (*orig. Aus.*) a promiscuous woman [i.e. 'once she's on her back, she's fucked'].

SE in slang uses

IN COMPOUNDS

□ **turtle shit** *n.* [SHIT *n.* (4a)/SHIT *n.* (3d)] (*US*) **1** [1950s+] (*also* **cat shit**) nonsense, rubbish [var. on BULLSHIT *n.* (1)]. **2** [1990s+] stuffing, the daylights, the insides.

IN PHRASES

□ **go like a herd of turtles** *v. see* GO LIKE A RABBIT *under* RABBIT *n.*[1].

turtle *v.* [1940s] (*US black*) to turn.

turtle (dove) *n.*[1] [15C+] a lover, a term of affection.

IN PHRASES

□ **go turtles over** *v.* [1970s] to fall in love with, to become sexually obsessed with.

turtle (dove) *n.*[2] [rhy. sl.] [mid-19C+] usu. in pl., a glove, esp. those worn by housebreakers to hide fingerprints.

turtle (dove) *v.* [TURTLE (DOVE) *n.*[1]] [mid-19C+] to love, to be in a romantic state.

turtlehead *n.* (*also* **turtle's head**) [1990s+] a piece of excrement poking out of the anus, due to the urgent need to defecate.

turtleneck (sweater) *n.* (*also* **winter wear**) [resemblance] [1970s+] (*US campus/gay*) an uncircumcised penis.

tush *n.*[1] [Djerma *tosi*, excrement; but note TUSH *n.*[2] (1)] [1940s] (*W.I.*) human excrement.

tush *n.*[2] (*also* **tooshy, tushie, tushy, tussy**) [TOCHES *n.*] **1** [1950s+] the buttocks. **2** [1970s+] (*US gay*) the vagina.

IN EXCLAMATIONS

□ **my tush!** [late 17C+] a general excl. of disdain, dismissal, arrogant contempt.

tush *n.*[3] *see* TOSHEROON *n.*

tush *n.*[4] *see* TASH *n.*

tush *adj.* [SE colloq. use of *tush*, as n., meaning a wealthy light-skinned black person] [1930s–50s] (*US black*) **1** classy, well-mannered, sophisticated. **2** aggressive, threatening.

tush *v.* [TUSH *n.*[1]] [1910s] (*W.I.*) to excrete.

tusheroon *n.* **1** [mid–late 19C] a crown piece, five shillings [*OED* suggests that this is 'erroneous']. **2** *see* TOSHEROON *n.*

tush hog *n.* [ety. unknown; note Lincoln U. (Oxford, Penn.) use c.1934: 'TUSH-HAWK (or TUSH-HAWG). A city slicker; a big shot; a sophisticated person with money, clothes, and a line'] (*US*) **1** [1930s+] a bully, an aggressive person. **2** [1940s] (*US black*) an aggressive sexual athlete. **3** [1950s+] an aggressive homosexual.

tushie *n. see* TUSH *n.*[2].

tushroon *n.* [var. on TOSHEROON *n.*] [1900s–50s] (*US black*) money.

tush-teeth *n.* [SE *tusk*] [20C+] (*W.I.*) buckteeth, protruding teeth.

tushy *n. see* TUSH *n.*[2].

tusk *n.* [SE *elephant's tusk*] [1910s] (*US Und.*) a tooth.

tuskee *n.* (*also* **tuskie**) [? resemblance to an elephant's *tusk*] [1970s–80s] (*US black*) a large marijuana cigarette.

tuskin *n.* [? dial. *tush*, the broad part of a ploughshare, ult. *tusk*, tooth] [late 18C–early 19C] a country carter or ploughman.

tuss *n.* [abbr.] [1990s+] (*US drugs*) Robotussin; also as v., to take Robotussin for its narcotic effects.

tusseroon *n. see* TOSHEROON *n.*

tussle *n.* [TUSSLE *v.* (3)] [1960s+] (*US*) sexual intercourse.

tussle *v.* [SE post-1890, Scot. *tousle*, to push around roughly, to struggle or contend with] **1** [mid–late 19C] to argue. **2** [1950s+] (*US black*) to fight. **3** [1960s+] (*US*) to engage in sexual activity.

tussocker *n.* [Aus./N.Z. *tussock land*, uncultivated grassland used for sheep-grazing, across which he has travelled] [late 19C+] (*Aus.*) a tramp or vagrant pretending to seek work but actually keener on board and lodging.

tussock-jumper *n.* [for ety. *see* TUSSOCKER *n.*] [1960s+] (*N.Z.*) a musterer.

tussy *n.*[1] [abbr. SE *intoxicated*] [19C] a drunkard.

tussy *n.*[2] *see* TUSH *n.*[2].

tussy-mussy *n. see* TUZZY-MUZZY *n.*

tute *n.* [abbr.] [mid-19C+] **1** a *tutor*. **2** a *tutorial*.

tutti-frutti *n.* [SE *tutti-frutti*, a multicoloured ice-cream] [1980s+] **1** (*drugs*) a variety of flavoured cocaine. **2** (*US*) a male homosexual [a play on FRUIT *n.* (2)].

IN PHRASES

□ **go tutti-frutti** *v.* [1970s] (*US*) to act crazily, to get angry.

Tuttle Nask *n.* [*Tuttle*, i.e. Tothill + NASK *n.*] [late 17C–18C] the Tothill house of correction in Tothill Fields, London.

tut-tut-tut *n.* [rhy. sl.] [1900s] (*Aus.*) a hut.

tutu *adj. see* TOO-TOO *adj.*

tutus *n.* [Carib.E. *tutu*, a conch shell] [1940s] (*W.I.*) the male genitals.

tux *n.* [abbr. SE *tuxedo*, a dinner jacket, named for Tuxedo Park, N.Y., where the jacket was first introduced at the country club in 1886] **1** [1910s+] (*also* **tuck**) (*US*) a dinner jacket. **2** [1940s] (*US Und.*) a straitjacket.

tuxed up *adj.* [TUX UP *v.*] [1990s+] (*orig. US*) wearing a dinner jacket.

tux up *v.* [TUX *n.* (1)] [1930s+] to put on a dinner jacket.

tuzzy-muzzy *n.* (*also* **tussy-mussy, tuz, tuzimuzzy, tuzzy**) [dial. *tuzzy-muzzy*, dishevelled, ragged, rough; alternative definition as a nosegay or bouquet garni and for 'old man's beard' (i.e. clematis)] [late 17C–19C] the vagina.

t.v. *n.* (*also* **teevee**) [1970s+] a *transvestite*.

t.v. *adj.* [T.V. *n.*] [1980s+] pertaining to transvestism.

TV style *n.* [*TV*, television, which can optionally be watched when adopting this position for sex] [1950s–70s] (*gay*) anal intercourse with one partner on his knees.

twachel *n. see* TWATCHEL *n.*

twack *n.* [*tw*elve + p*ack*] [1980s+] (*US campus*) a twelve-pack of beer.

twaddle *n.* ['a fashionable term that for a while succeeded that of *bore*' (Grose 1785). SE *twaddle*, idle talk, nonsense, itself f. synon. *twattle*, ? ult. *tattle*] [late 18C–early 19C] a bore.

twaddle *v.* [SE *twaddle*] [late 18C–19C] to trifle, to 'mess around'.

twag *v.* [? abbr. HOP THE WAG *under* HOP *v.*[1]] [1990s+] (*UK juv.*) to play truant.

IN COMPOUNDS

□ **twag man** *n.* (*also* **...lady**) [1990s+] (*UK juv.*) an official who searches out truants.

twak *n.* [Afk. *twak*, nonsense] [1950s+] (*S.Afr.*) nonsense, rubbish.

twam *n.* (*also* **twammy, twim**) [? TWAT *n.* (1) + QUIM *n.* (1)] [20C+] the vagina.

twamp *n.* [1980s] (*US drugs*) a 20 dollar rock of cocaine.

twang *n.*[1] [TWANG *v.*[1]] **1** [late 17C–18C] a thieving prostitute. **2** [18C] a pimp or a prostitute's male accomplice, who arrives to beat up victims whom she has robbed, under the guise of offering them intercourse.

IN COMPOUNDS

□ **twangman** *n.* [sense 2 + sfx *-man*] [20C+] (*Irish*) a pimp.

SE in slang uses

IN PHRASES

□ **twang one's wire** *v. see under* WIRE *n.*[1].

twang *n.*[2] [Chinese or cod Chinese, ? f. *twankay*, green tea] [late 19C–1930s] (*Aus.*) opium.

twang *v.*[1] (*also* **twangle**) [? SE *twang*, to fire an arrow; note D'Urfey, *Pills to Purge Melancholy* (1719): 'Twangdillo, A New Ballad', which deals with the many female pursuers of one 'Roger Twangdillo'] [mid-16C–18C; 1980s+] to engage in spontaneous sexual intercourse.

IN PHRASES

❑ **as good as ever twanged** **1** [late 16C–early 17C] as good as possible, in any context. **2** [17C] of the male genitals, in prime condition, esp. in the sexual context. **3** [17C–early 18C] of women, as good as one might wish, esp. in the sexual context.

twang *v.*[2] [1940s+] (*UK black*) to persuade, to sweet-talk.

twang adam cove *n.* [? SE *twang* + ? ADAM *n.*[1] + COVE *n.* (1)] [mid-18C] (*UK Und.*) the act – through plausible, beguiling speech – of luring victims into the hands of a team of confidence tricksters.

twange *n.* [? revival of TWANG *n.*[1] (1) + MINGE *n.* (2)] [1990s+] the vagina.

twanger *n.* [fig. uses of SE *twang*, to reverberate] **1** [late 16C–mid-17C; late 19C] the penis. **2** [late 19C] something very large or fine of its kind.

twanging *adj.* [SE *twang*, to give off a ringing note] [early 17C] excellent, first-rate.

IN PHRASES

❑ **go off twanging** *v.* [early 17C] to turn out very well.

twangy *adj.* [TWANG *v.*[1]] [1980s+] (*US*) pertaining to male prostitution.

twangy boy *n.* [TWANGY *adj.*] [1980s+] (*US*) a young male prostitute.

twank *n.* [? the pantomime 'dame' *Widow Twankey* or WANK *n.* (1)] [1960s+] **1** (*gay*) an older man. **2** in prostitute usage, an older man who enjoys watching young women at work but has no personal interest in sex.

twankay *n.* (*also* **twankey**) [tea trade jargon *twankey*, green tea, thus ? the root of the pantomime dame Widow Twankey] [1900s] gin.

twanky *n.* [pron.] [2000s] (*US black*) twenty.

twasted *adj.* [TWATTED *adj.* + WASTED *adj.* (4)] [2000s] intoxicated by drink or drugs.

twat *n.* [? dial. *twitchel*, a narrow passage] **1** [mid-17C+] (*also* **twat-hole, twattle, twit-twat, twoit, twot, twotch**) the vagina; in pl. the labia [twit-twat is lit. abbr. SE *twittle-twattle*, idle talk]. **2** [20C+] (*also* **twotface**) a derog. term for a woman. **3** [1910s+] (*also* **twatt, twot**) a term of abuse, irrespective of gender. **4** [1950s+] (*US*) the buttocks. **5** [1970s+] (*US gay*) the anus. **6** [1980s+] something unpleasant, second-rate. **7** [2000s] (*US black*) used as a deliberately coarse substitute for SE *what?* **8** [2000s] a neutral term for a person.

IN COMPOUNDS

❑ **twat-faker** *n.* [FAKER *n.* (6)] [1900–20s] a pimp. ❑ **twathead** *n.* [-HEAD *sfx* (1)] [2000s] a general term of abuse. ❑ **twathole** *n.* see sense 1 above. ❑ **twat-hooks** *n. see* CUNT-HOOKS *under* CUNT *n.* ❑ **twat-mag** *n.* [1990s+] a pornographic magazine. ❑ **twatman** *n.* [play on the superhero Batman] [1990s+] (*UK juv.*) a general term of abuse. ❑ **twat-masher** *n.* [MASH *v.* (1)] [1900–20s] a pimp, a procurer. ❑ **twatmaster** *n.* [1990s+] a term of abuse or hostility. ❑ **twat-rug** *n.* [late 19C–1900s] a woman's pubic hair.

IN PHRASES

❑ **bag of smacked twats** *n.* [1990s+] a general derog. description of an unattractive woman. ❑ **go twat-faking** *v.* (*also* **go twat-raking**) [FAKE *v.*[1] (3)/RAKE *v.*[1] (1)] [1900s–20s] of a man, to have sexual intercourse. ❑ **go twatting** *v.* [1900s–20s] of a man, to have sexual intercourse.

twat *v.* [TWAT *n.* (3)] **1** [1980s+] to hit someone. **2** [1990s+] to behave in an unsophisticated manner. **3** [1990s+] to waste time.

IN PHRASES

❑ **twat on** *v.* [1990s+] to talk inconsequentially, to chatter.

twatchel *n.* (*also* **twachel, twatchil, twatchylle**) [dimin. of TWAT *n.* (1) + dial. *twitchel*, a passage] [mid-17C–early 19C] the vagina.

twatling-strings *n. see* TWATTLING-STRINGS *n.*

twat-scourer *n.* [TWAT *n.* (1) + SE *scourer*, a cleaner, a polisher] **1** [late 17C] a general term of abuse. **2** [early 18C] a surgeon, a doctor.

twat-scouring *adj.* [TWAT-SCOURER *n.* (1)] [late 17C] a general term of abuse.

twatted *adj.* [fig. use of TWAT *v.* (1)] [1990s+] intoxicated by drink or drugs.

twatting *n.* [TWAT *v.* (1)] **1** [19C] sexual intercourse. **2** [1980s+] a beating.

twatting *adj.* [TWATTING *n.* (1), i.e. a euph. for FUCKING *adj.*] [2000s] a general negative intensifier.

twattle *n. see* TWAT *n.* (1).

twattling-strings *n.* (*also* **twatling-strings, twiddling-strings**) [joc. use of dial. *twattle*, to chatter, to talk idly] [late 16C–early 19C] the anal sphincter, esp. in the context of breaking wind.

twatty *adj.* [TWAT *n.* (3)] [1970s+] stupid.

twaxy *n.* [SE *twist*, 'a beverage consisting of a mixture of two liquors or ingredients' (*OED*)] [mid-19C] (*UK Und.*) rum and milk.

tweague *n.* (*also* **tweak**) [SE *tweak*, a wrench, a sharp tug] [late 17C–mid-19C] a state of excitement or agitation.

tweaguey *adj.* [TWEAGUE *n.*] [late 18C–early 19C] angry, irritated.

tweak *n.*[1] (*also* **tweake**) [? SE *tweak*, the act of tugging, thus fig. sexual intercourse] **1** [17C–early 18C] a prostitute. **2** [18C–early 19C] a whoremonger.

tweak *n.*[2] *see* TWEAGUE *n.*

tweak *n.*[3] *see* TWEAKS *n.*

tweak *v.*[1] [TWEAKER *n.*[1]] [late 19C] to hit a target with a missile from a catapult.

IN PHRASES

❑ **tweak on** *v.* [2000s] (*US*) to attack. ❑ **tweak out** *v.* (*also* **twig out**) [1980s+] (*US campus*) to hurt, to damage.

tweak *v.*[2] [SE *tweak*, to wrench, to pull sharply] **1** [1970s] (*drugs*) to inject narcotics. **2** [1980s+] (*drugs*) to be intoxicated with heroin or crack cocaine. **3** [1980s+] to suffer heroin or crack cocaine withdrawal. **4** [1980s+] (*US black/campus*) to act as if one were intoxicated by drugs, to act energetically or strangely.

IN PHRASES

❑ **tweak out** *v.* (*also* **twig out**) [1980s+] (*US campus*) to lose control, to act eccentrically.

tweake *n. see* TWEAK *n.*[1].

tweaked *adj.* [TWEAK *v.*[2]] [1980s+] (*US, chiefly campus/black*) **1** drunk or under the influence of a drug. **2** (*also* **tweaked out**) experiencing the effects of methamphetamine, crack cocaine. **3** mad. **4** broken, out of order, messy. **5** exhausted. **6** on edge, tense, nervous, upset.

tweaker *n.*[1] [SE *tweak*, to pinch] [late 19C] a catapult.

tweaker *n.*[2] [TWEAK *v.*[2] (2)] [1980s+] (*drugs*) **1** a drug user, usu. of some form of amphetmaine. **2** a crack cocaine user.

tweakified *adj.* [TWEAK *v.*[2] (2)] [1990s+] (*US drugs*) suffering the paranoia-inducing effects of smoking crack cocaine.

tweaking *n.* [SE *tweak*, i.e. to 'pinch' someone's sensibilities] (*US black*) **1** [1990s+] talking inappropriately or tactlessly. **2** [2000s] angry.

tweaking *adj.* [TWEAK *v.*[2]] [1990s+] **1** (*US black/drugs*) intoxicated by drugs. **2** (*US campus*) tense, emotional, hyperactive.

tweaks *n.* (*also* **tweak**) [TWEAK *v.*[2] (2)] **1** [1980s] methamphetamine. **2** [1980s] a single puff of crack/ inhalation of cocaine. **3** [2000s] (*US drugs*) crack cocaine.

IN COMPOUNDS

❑ **tweak freak** *n.* [1980s] a regular user of methamphetamine.

tweaky *adj.* [TWEAKS *n.*] [2000s] **1** (*US drugs*) exhibiting the signs of addiction to crack cocaine. **2** nerve-racking, suspenseful.

tweed *n.* [*the* WEED *n.*[1] (4)] [1950s+] (*US black/drugs*) marijuana.

tweed-capper *n.* [the headgear worn] [1910s] (*Aus.*) an immigrant from the UK.

tweedle, the *n.* [SE *twiddle*, to twist] **1** [late 19C+] (*UK Und.*) the substitution of fake jewellery for the real thing, usu. by sleight of hand in a jewellery store, esp. in the form of a *tweedle*, a fake ring studded with paste diamonds. **2** [1910s+] the sale of any dubious goods.

tweedledum sir *n.* [late 19C–1900s] (*UK society*) usu. in pl., a baronet or knight who is given his honours for 'services to music', e.g. Sir Arthur Sullivan (1842–1900).

tweedler *n.* [TWEEDLE, THE *n.*] (*UK Und.*) **1** [1920s+] a small-time confidence trickster. **2** [1970s] a stolen vehicle which is passed off as perfectly legitimate.

tweedling *n.* [TWEEDLE, THE *n.*] [1920s+] (*UK Und.*) selling stolen property or even non-existent property to innocent purchasers who assume the goods are legitimate.

tweeds *n.* **1** [1950s+] (*Aus./N.Z.*) trousers. **2** [1960s] (*US campus*) a suit.

IN PHRASES

❑ **drop one's tweeds** *v.* [1960s] to have sexual intercourse, lit. to remove one's trousers/underwear.

tweegat jakkals *n.* [Afk. *twee gat jakkals*, a jackal with two anuses] [1990s+] (*S.Afr.*) a term of extreme vilification.

tweek *n.* (*also* **tweeker**) [SE *tweak*; i.e. its effects] [1980s+] (*drugs*) methcathinone.

tween *n.* (*also* **tweenie**) [on model of SE *teen*; ? ult. from the children's TV programme, *The Tweenies*] [1990s+] a sophisticated pre-teenager.

tweenie *n.* [? they are 'between' the sexes] [2000s] (*Aus.*) a male homosexual.

tweer *n.* see TWIRE *n.*

tweezer-lipped *adj.* [2000s] (*S.Afr. gay*) angry.

twelve *adj.*

SE in slang uses

IN COMPOUNDS

❑ **twelve godfathers** *n.* (*also* **the twelve**) [they 'give a name' to one's crime] [18C–mid-19C] the jury; thus *you will be christened by twelve godfathers someday before long*. ❑ **twelve inches** *n.* (*also* **one foot, ten inches, thirteen inches, twelve incher**) [mid-18C; 1960s+] a (large) penis.

1200 *n.* [1990s+] in rap music, the Technics SL *1200* turntable, regarded as the best turntable for DJ'ing.

twelve-inch rule *n.* [rhy. sl.] [20C+] a fool.

12:01 *n.* [? the time] [2000s] (*US prison*) a discharge.

twelver *n.* **1** [late 17C–19C] (*UK Und.*) (*also* **twelve**) one shilling (5p) [the twelve pennies it represented, use after 1730s mainly Aus.]. **2** [late 19C] (*Aus. Und.*) a twelve-month sentence.

twelves *n.*

IN PHRASES

❑ **slip in the twelves** *v.* see *PLAY THE DOZENS* under DOZENS *n.*

12/12 *v.* [2000s] (*US prison*) to serve the whole of one's sentence without parole.

twenty *n.* (*also* **twennie**) [1980s+] (*US drugs*) $20 worth of crack cocaine.

IN PHRASES

❑ **twenty and forty** *n.* [2000s] (*US black*) $20 worth of marijuana and a 40oz. bottle of malt liquor.

SE in slang uses

IN PHRASES

❑ **twenty and a ten** *n.* see FIVE AND TWO *n.* ❑ **twenty in the pounder** *n.* [i.e. twenty shillings to a (pre-decimal) pound] [late 19C–1900s] one who pays their debts in full rather than opting to pay in instalments.

twenty *adj.*

SE in slang uses

IN COMPOUNDS

❑ **twenty-carat** *adj.* see TWENTY-FOUR CARAT *adj.* ❑ **twenty cents** *n.* [1930s–70s] (*US black*) **1** $2; $20. **2** a $20 bag of marijuana. ❑ **twenty sack** *n.* [1990s+] (*US*) $20 worth of drugs, usu. marijuana or crack cocaine.

IN PHRASES

❑ **twenty-minute man** *n.* [his con-man persona only lasts 20 minutes] [1900s] (*US Und.*) a con-man who is unable to keep the victim from complaining after he has lost his money. ❑ **twenty-percent man** *n.* [note TEN-PER-CENTER *n.*] [1950s] a money lender. ❑ **twenty-twenty vision** *n.* [ophthalmic jargon *20/20*, perfect vision] [20C+] perfect vision, in a fig. sense; thus *twenty-twenty hindsight*, a fig. perfect understanding or appreciation of what has already been seen.

twenty-five *n.*[1] [its chemical name, *d-lysergic acid diethylamide-25*] [1960s+] (*drugs*) LSD.

twenty-five *n.*[2] [1980s+] (*US drugs*) a $25 bag of cocaine.

twenty-five, the *n.* [2000s] the M25 motorway, encircling Greater London and the adjacent home counties.

twenty-five cent word *n.* see FIFTY-CENT WORD *n.*

25 with an izl *n.* [SE *izl*, i.e. the * notation next to the years of one's sentence, denoting 'life'] [1990s+] (*US*) a prison sentence of 25 years to life.

twenty-four carat *adj.* (*also* **twenty-carat, twenty-two (carat), forty-eight carat**) [fig. use of the SE descriptions of the purity of gold] **1** [20C+] complete, authentic. **2** [1900s–50s] very wealthy. **3** [1960s] totally reliable, wholly trustworthy.

twenty-four cents shy of a quarter *phr.* see THIRTY CENTS (SHY OF A QUARTER) *adj.*

24/24 *adv.* [24 hours out of the daily 24] [1980s+] (*orig. US prison*) all day, continually.

twenty-nine and a wake-up *n.* [29 whole days and the WAKE-UP *n.* (2); i.e. the last, on which one only wakes up in prison] [1960s+] (*US prison*) the period between receiving a notice of parole and one's actual release, i.e. one month.

20 on the hype *n.* (*also* **30 on the hype**) [the number of mililitres on the HYPE *n.*[2] (1)] [1950s+] (*drugs*) a very heavy intake of heroin.

twenty-six girl *n.* (*also* **26 girl**) [1940s] a young woman who runs a dice game played in a bar.

twenty-three skidoo! *excl.* (*also* **twenty-three! 23! 23 skidoo! twenty-three skiddoo!**) [ety. unknown, theories include: downdraughts created by the Flatiron Building at the corner of Broadway and 23rd St, NYC, which would blow up women's skirts to the delight of male observers – the phr. developed f. the police who saw these men at *23* (the corner) and shooed them away with a shout of *skiddoo*; railway telegraph jargon *23*, a message of the greatest urgency (however as listed in the generally used *Phillips Code* [1925 edn] 23 does not mean this – rather 'all copy'); or a number signifying finality or completion; *skid* from SKID ROW *n.*, *23* from NYC's 23rd St which once had the ferries and depots for 80% of those – including the skid row tramps – who wished to leave the city; note SKIDOO *v.*] [late 19C+] (*US*) go away! get out!

twenty-two *n.* [abbr.; note THIRTY-EIGHT *n.* (1)] [1920s+] (*US*) a .22 calibre pistol.

twenty-two carat *n.* [TWENTY-TWO CARAT *adj.*] [1940s] (*UK drugs*) high-quality, pure cocaine.

twenty-two carat *adj.* see TWENTY-FOUR CARAT *adj.*

twerp *n.* (*also* **twirp**) [ety. unknown, J.R.R. Tolkien (letter, 6 October 1944) suggests an early 20C+ Oxford contemporary *T.W. Earp*] [1910s+] an idiot, a nincompoop.

DERIVATIVES

❑ **twerpy** *adj.* [1960s+] foolish, idiotic.

t.w.i. *phr.* [*t*otally *w*ith *i*t] [2000s] absolutely committed.

twibill *n.* [SE *twibill*, a two-edged axe] [17C; late 19C] a thug, a bully.

twice *v.* [TWO-TIME *v.*] [late 19C–1940s] to cheat, to deceive.

twice laid *n.* [i.e. the remains of a previous meal] **1** [mid–late 19C] a dish of cold fried fish and potatoes. **2** [20C+] (*US*) a dish of minced meat on toast.

twicer *n.* [SE *twice*] **1** [late 17C; late 19C–1900s] one who attends church twice on a Sunday. **2** [mid-19C] (*Aus. Und.*) one who has twice been convicted of a criminal offence. **3** [mid–late 19C] something or someone very important, i.e. doubly valuable, relevant, forceful etc. **4** [late 19C+] (*Aus.*) a sycophant [SE *two-faced*]. **5** [20C+] a widow or widower who marries for the second time. **6** [1910s+] (*orig. Aus.*) a confidence trickster, one who engages in any form of 'double-dealing'. **7** [1910s+] (*Aus.*) a very demanding person, lit. one who asks for two helpings of food. **8** [1910s+] two of something; e.g. a whipping, a two-year prison sentence. **9** [1940s] (*UK Und.*) two shilling pieces.

twicers *n.* [late 19C–1900s] twins.

twice-twenty *adj. see* FORTY *adj.*[2].

twiddle *n.* [1950s] (*UK prison*) the practice of letting a warder suspect one of holding contraband, only to reveal that one is holding something completely innocuous; once suspicions have been allayed, one can then reveal or pass on the actual contraband, e.g. tobacco.

twiddle-diddles *n.* [SE *twiddle*, to play with + redup.] [late 18C–early 19C] the testicles.

twiddlepoop *n.* [SE *twiddle*, to twirl around + POOP *n.*[1] (3)] [late 18C–early 19C] an effeminate-looking man.

twiddling-strings *n. see* TWATTLING-STRINGS *n.*

twig *n.*[1] [ety. unknown, ? TWIG *v.*[2]] **1** [late 18C–mid-19C] style, fashion; usu. as *in twig*, smartly or fashionably dressed. **2** [early–mid-19C] (*orig. boxing*) condition, fettle, spirits; often as *IN FINE TWIG* below. **3** [early–mid-19C] a stylish (young) man.

IN PHRASES

❑ **in fine twig** *adv.* (*also* **in good twig, in prime twig**) [SE *fine/good*/PRIME *adj.*] [19C] splendidly, admirably, stylishly; in high spirits or good order. ❑ **in full twig** *adv.* [early 19C] dressed up.

twig *n.*[2] [TWIG *v.*[2] (1)] [mid–late 19C] (*UK Und.*) a look.

twig *n.*[3] **1** [1940s] (*US black*) a tree. **2** [1930s–40s] (*US black*) a human leg. **3** [1960s–70s] a marijuana cigarette. **4** [1980s+] (*US campus*) a notably thin person. **5** [2000s] (*US drugs*) a very small piece of crack cocaine. **6** [2000s] the penis.

IN COMPOUNDS

❑ **twig and berries** *n.* [20C+] a young boy's penis and testes.

SE in slang uses

IN PHRASES

❑ **drop off the twig** *v.* [1960s+] to die, as if one were a bird. ❑ **fall off the twig** *v.* [2000s] to die. ❑ **hop the twig** *v. see* separate entry. ❑ **jump the twig** *v. see* HOP THE TWIG *v.* (1). ❑ **leap the twig** *v. see* HOP THE TWIG *v.* (2). ❑ **snap one's twig** *v.* [1980s] (*Aus.*) to lose emotional control.

twig *v.*[1] [? SE *tweak* or *twitch*] [18C–19C] to disengage, to break off.

IN PHRASES

❑ **twig the darbies** *v.* [18C–19C] (*UK Und.*) to knock off the handcuffs or irons.

twig *v.*[2] [? fig. uses of dial. *twick*, to jerk] **1** [mid-18C–1910s] to observe, to watch. **2** [late 18C+] to understand, to work out. **3** [late 18C+] to recognize, to expose. **4** [19C–1930s] to catch sight of, to become aware of.

IN PHRASES

❑ **out of twig** *adj.* [mid-18C–mid-19C] (*UK Und.*) **1** disguised in order to evade arrest. **2** wearing shabby clothes, reduced to that state through poverty. **3** of a stolen article, altered to make the article unrecognizable.

twigged *adj.* [TWIG *n.*[3] (3)] [1980s+] (*US drugs*) intoxicated by drugs.

twigger *n.* [SE *twigger*, a ewe that is a prolific breeder] [late 16C–17C] **1** a promiscuous woman, a prostitute. **2** a womanizer.

twiggez-vous (the chose)? *phr.* (*also* **twiggy-vous...**) [a 'macaronic' or mixed-language phr. based on a Frenchified form of TWIG *v.*[2] (2) + Fr. *vous*, you + *chose*, thing] [late 19C–1950s] do you understand (what this is/what's happening)?

twig out *v.* **1** *see* TWEAK OUT *under* TWEAK *v.*[1]. **2** *see* TWEAK OUT *under* TWEAK *v.*[2].

twillip *n.* [TWERP *n.* + ?] [1940s] a general term of abuse.

twim *n. see* TWAM *n.*

twin-coat *n.* [i.e. one who has two fig. *coats*] [1970s] (*W.I.*) a hypocrite.

twine *n.* [TWINE *v.*] [1960s] (*Aus. Und.*) a confidence trick.

IN PHRASES

❑ **draw the twine** *v. see under* DRAW *v.*[4].

twine *v.* [? SE *twine*] [mid-19C; 1980s+] (*Aus. prison*) to trick, to deceive; as in passing a counterfeit coin for a good one.

twink *n.*[1] (*also* **twinkle, twinky**) [SE *twinkling* (of a star)] [17C–19C] a moment, a very brief period of time; usu. as *in a twink*, in a very short time.

twink *n.*[2] (*also* **twinkle toes**) [? the SE *twinkle* in his eye; according to Cage, *Gayle* (2003): 'from the sponge cake, Twinkie, which is soft, brown and filled with cream.'] **1** [1960s] (*US campus*) a male homosexual, or one who is suspected as being such. **2** [1960s+] (*US gay*) an available attractive young boy, whether working for money or not.

twink *n.*[3] [1960s+] (*US campus*) someone unusual, crazy or stupid.

Twinkie *n.* [a *Twinkie* biscuit, which is 'brown on the outside and white inside'] [1990s+] (*US campus*) an Asian who identifies with Caucasians.

twinkie *n.* (*also* **twinky, twink**) [? fig. use of *Twinkie*, a variety of sweet biscuit; or ? ext. of TWINK *n.*[2]/TWINK *n.*[3]] **1** [1970s+] (*US gay*) a young, inexperienced homosexual man. **2** [1980s+] a young (underage) sex object, whether male or female and seen as suitable for exploitation. **3** [1980s+] anyone considered odd or eccentric. **4** [1990s+] the penis.

twinkies *n.* [2000s] (*US black*) chrome car wheels.

twinkle *n. see* TWINK *n.*[1].

twinklepie *n. see* SWEETIE-PIE *under* SWEETIE *n.*

twinklers *n.* [SE *twinkle*, to sparkle] **1** [mid-17C–mid-19C; 1940s] the eyes [1940s use is US black]. **2** [18C+] the stars. **3** [1900s–20s] diamonds.

twinkle toes *n. see* TWINK *n.*[2].

twinky *n.* **1** *see* TWINK *n.*[1]. **2** *see* TWINKIE *n.*

twinkydink *adj.* [play on RINKY-DINK *adj.*[2]] [1990s+] (*US*) crazy.

twin-mouth *n.* [i.e. one who speaks with two fig. mouths] [1970s] (*W.I.*) a hypocrite.

twire *n.* (*also* **tweer**) [dial. *twire*, to look covertly, to peer, to peep] [late 17C–early 18C] a glance, esp. a leer.

twirl *n.* (*also* **turrl**) [late 19C+] **1** (*UK/US Und.*) a key, esp. a skeleton or duplicate key. **2** (*UK prison*) a prison officer.

SE in slang uses

IN PHRASES

❑ **give it a twirl** *v. see GIVE SOMETHING A WHIRL under* WHIRL *n.*

twirl, the *n.* [1950s–60s] **1** (*UK Und.*) working as a fraudulent bookmaker, typically taking large bets but putting them down on a less popular horse – if the originally betted horse wins, the bookmaker simply claims the bettor was mistaken. **2** a confidence trick that involves the substitution of a fake jewel for a real one.

IN PHRASES

❑ **on the twirl** *adv.* [1930s] working as a professional thief.

twirl *v.* [1980s+] (*US campus*) to party, to dance.

IN PHRASES

❑ **twirl the pearls** *v.* [1960s+] (*US camp gay*) to dance.

twirler *n.*[1] [they wave the clothes in the air to attract attention] [late 18C–mid-19C] (*UK Und.*) a seller of (old) clothes.

twirler *n.*[2] [TWIRL *n.* (1)] [1920s+] a key, esp. a skeleton or duplicate key.

twirp *n. see* TWERP *n.*

twiss *n.* [an attack on the English writer Richard *Twiss* (1747–1821), who had published the highly critical 'Tour in Ireland'. To take their revenge the Irish produced a chamberpot with a picture of Richard Twiss inside it, beneath which was inscribed the rhyme 'Let everyone piss/On lying Dick Twiss'] [late 18C–early 19C] (*Irish*) a chamberpot.

twist *n.*[1] **1** [late 17C–early 19C] a drink of tea and coffee mixed together. **2** [late 18C–mid-19C] any mixed alcoholic drink, typically brandy and eggs or brandy, beer and eggs, brandy and gin or a *gin twist*, gin and hot water. **3** [early 19C] the hangman's noose. **4** [mid-19C+] the arm lock forced on a person who is being arrested. **5** [late 19C] (*UK Und.*) a hold on something or someone. **6** [20C+] (*Irish*) a quarrel, an argument; thus phrs. *in good twist*, on good terms; *in bad twist*, on bad terms, *in twist*, in agreement. **7** [20C+] cheating, dishonesty, treachery; thus *at the twist*, double-crossing, *on the twist*, thieving. **8** [1910s+] (*Aus.*) a professional criminal [abbr. TWISTER *n.* (3) or ? not being STRAIGHT *adj.*[1] (5)]. **9** [1930s+] (*drugs*) a marijuana cigarette [it is *twisted* into shape]. **10** [1960s] (*US Und.*) a sexual eccentric. **11** [1970s+] (*Irish*) a turn. **12** [1980s] (*Aus.*) a key. **13** [2000s] (*drugs*) a small bag of heroin secured with a twist tie.

twist *n.*[2] [*TWIST (DOWN) (APACE) under* TWIST *v.*] [late 18C–1950s] an appetite, a capacity for eating.

twist *n.*[3] [abbr. TWIST AND TWIRL *n.*] **1** [1920s+] (*US Und.*) a girl, a woman. **2** [1950s+] the passive member of a lesbian relationship. **3** [1960s] (*US*) a sexual pervert. **4** [1960s] a male homosexual. **5** [1970s] (*US prison*) a prostitute.

twist *v.* **1** [18C–mid-19C] to hang, to be hanged; thus as excl. *twist me!* [lit./fig. twisting on the rope]. **2** in senses of 'twisting the rules'. (**a**) [mid–late 19C] to steal. (**b**) [20C+] to cheat, to defraud. (**c**) [1920s] to lie. **3** [mid-19C–1900s] (*UK Und.*) to steal a watch by first snapping and twisting off its ring. **4** [20C+] (*Aus.*) to be convicted of a crime. **5** [1910s+] (*also* **twist a burn**) (*US*) to roll a cigarette. **6** [1940s+] (*drugs*) to roll a marijuana cigarette. **7** [1950s] to leave.

IN PHRASES

❑ **twist (down) (apace)** *v.* [? the twisting of the wrist in eating or tearing pieces of bread from a loaf; note Worcestershire dial. *twist something down one*, to eat heartily] [late 17C–early 19C] to eat, esp. to eat heartily.

SE in slang uses

IN PHRASES

❑ **twist hay** *v.* [2000s] (*Irish*) to start trouble, usu. playfully. ❑ **twist it, choke it, and make it scream** [1930s] (*US/NY short order*) an order for an egg malted milk. ❑ **twist one's wig** *v.* [WIG *n.*[2] (1)] [1960s] (*orig. US black*) to make the utmost effort, to stretch one's mind. ❑ **twist someone's arm** *v. see under* ARM *n.* ❑ **twist someone's cap** *v.* [2000s] (*US prison*) to shoot, to kill. ❑ **twist the tiger's tail** *v. see FIGHT THE TIGER under* TIGER *n.*

twist and twine *v.* [rhy. sl.] [20C+] (*Irish*) to whine.

twist and twirl *n.* [rhy. sl.] [20C+] a girl.

twisted *adj.*[1] [TWIST *v.* (1)] [late 18C–early 19C] hanged.

twisted *adj.*[2] **1** [20C+] annoyed, out of emotional control. **2** [20C+] odd, bizarre, extraordinary. **3** [20C+] confused. **4** [1930s+] (*orig. US*) (*also* **twister**) very drunk. **5** [1960s+] (*orig. US*) extremely intoxicated by a drug, esp. the hallucinogens or cannabis. **6** [1960s+] cynical, disenchanted. **7** [1990s+] (*US campus*) of a female, bisexual.

twisted *adj.*[3] [1950s–70s] (*US*) **1** arrested. **2** serving time in jail.

twister *n.* **1** [late 17C] a voracious eater [*TWIST (DOWN) (APACE) under* TWIST *v.*]. **2** [mid-19C] (*US*) a spree. **3** in senses of 'twisting the rules'. (**a**) [mid-19C] (*UK Und.*) an informer. (**b**) [mid-19C+] (*US Und.*) a pickpocket, a thief. (**c**) [late 19C] as a term of address, with no negative implication. (**d**) [1910s+] an untrustworthy person, a crook, a liar. (**e**) [1910s+] a homosexual. (**f**) [1920s–30s] one who, through their own corruption, is impervious to the cheating and trickery of others. **4** [mid–late 19C] (*US*) a story, an extravagant, boastful tale. **5** [mid-19C–1950s] (*US*) something that causes a person to go into fig. contortions; thus *knock a twister*, to disconcert very much. **6** [20C+] (*US prison*) a prison guard [they 'twist' or turn a key]. **7** [1930s–50s] drug uses. [one is SE *twisted* up by the drugs or their effects] (**a**) a user of marijuana. (**b**) an injection of mixed narcotic drugs. (**c**) violent retching or vomiting of blood or mucus during withdrawal sickness. (**d**) fake withdrawal symptoms; one who is exhibiting them. (**e**) a ration of narcotics. **8** [1930s–70s] (*US black*) a front-door key; thus *twister to the slammer*, the door key. **9** [1950s] (*US Und.*) a beggar or drug addict who can fake convincing fits in order to obtain money or drugs.

IN PHRASES

❑ **cut back a twister** *v.* [1930s] to perform in an outstanding manner. ❑ **frame a twister** *v.* [1930s] (*US drugs*) to throw a fake withdrawal fit in the hope of obtaining narcotics from a doctor.

twistical *adj.* [SE *twisted*] [19C] crooked, morally ambiguous.

twistie *n.* [one *twists* it up] [2000s] (*US drugs*) a marijuana cigarette.

twisting *n.* [one's emotions are *twisted*] **1** [mid-19C–1900s] a scolding, a telling-off. **2** [1910s–20s] a cause of anxiety or unhappiness.

twisto *n.* (*also* **twisty**) [TWISTED *adj.*[2] (2)] [1990s+] (*US*) a sexual pervert.

twit *n.* [TWERP *n.* + TWAT *n.* (3)] **1** [1920s+] (*also* **twitface**) a fool, an idiot. **2** [1940s] a state of excitement or anxiety. **3** [1960s–70s] (*gay*) an effeminate male homosexual.

twit *v.* [ult. AS *wītan*, to blame, to reproach] [late 16C+] to tease, to make fun of.

twitch *n.*[1] [SE *twitch*: 'a noose or loop; spec. a noose which may be tightened by twisting the stick to the end of which it is attached, used to compress the lip or muzzle of a horse to restrain him during a painful operation' *OED*] [1930s] (*US Und*) an instrument of torture.

twitch *n.*[2] [1950s] (*US*) a young woman.

twitch, the *n.* (*also* **the twitchers, the twitches**) [1980s+] (*drugs*) a nervous mannerism that afflicts regular users of crack cocaine.

twitched *adj.* [SE *twitch*] [late 19C+] nervous, irritable.

twitcher *n.* [SE *twitch*/TWITCH, THE *n.*] **1** [1950s] (*US drugs*) a drug addict. **2** [1980s+] a crack cocaine addict who is afflicted by nervous twitching.

twitchers/twitches *n. see* TWITCH, THE *n.*

twitchet *n.* [1920s–50s] (*US*) the vagina.

twitchety *adj.* (*also* **twitchetty**) [SE *twitch*] [mid–late 19C] nervous, fidgety.

twitching *n.* [early 19C] (*Scot. Und.*) stealing shawls from women wearing them in the street.

twitface *n. see* TWIT *n.* (1).

twitter *n.* [1900s] either an effeminate man or masculine woman.

twitting *adj.* [TWIT *n.* (1)] [1920s+] foolish, stupid.

twittoc *n.* [corruption of SE *two*] [late 18C–mid-19C] (*UK Und.*) two.

twit-twat *n. see* TWAT *n.* (1).

twitty *adj.* [TWIT *n.* (1)] [1980s+] (*US campus*) silly, foolish, ineffectual.

twize *n.* [abbr./pron.] [1970s+] (*US campus*) Budweiser beer.

t.w.k. *adj.* [abbr.] [mid–late 19C] (*Anglo-Ind.*) ? of a woman, too well known.

two *n.* **1** [late 19C–1930s] two pennyworth (of spirits). **2** [20C+] (*UK Und.*) a two-year sentence.

IN PHRASES

❑ **know two of that** *v.* [late 19C+] to know something much better. ❑ **two-and-over** *n.* [1920s–40s] (*US Und.*) very cheap whisky, as manufactured during Prohibition. ❑ **two for nine** *n.* [1980s+] (*US drugs*) two $5 vials or bags of crack cocaine for $9. ❑ **two in a bowl** *n.* [late 19C] (*US short order*) a plate of oyster stew. ❑ **two in one** *n.* [1960s] (*US drugs*) cocaine and heroin injected together. ❑ **two in the air** *n.* [late 19C] (*US short order*) two fried eggs. ❑ **two looking at you** *n.* (*also* **two looking up**) [20C+] (*orig. US short order*) two fried eggs 'sunny-side up'. ❑ **two with their eyes closed** *n.* [20C+] (*US short order*) two fried eggs turned over in the pan. ❑ **two with their eyes open** *n.* [1940s] (*US*) two eggs fried on one side only. ❑ **two with you** [late 19C] let's have a (twopenny) drink.

two *adj.*

SE in slang uses

IN COMPOUNDS

❑ **two-bagger** *n. see DOUBLE-BAGGER under* DOUBLE *adj.* ❑ **two bit** *see* separate entries. ❑ **two-blink** *adj. see under* BLINK *n.*[1].

❑ **two-bob** *see* separate entries. ❑ **two-bulb** *n.* [the two flashing lights on roof] [2000s] (*Irish*) a police car. ❑ **two camels** *n.* [? the time needed to smoke two *Camel* cigarettes] [1940s] (*US black*) ten minutes. ❑ **two-cards** *adj.* [1920s] second-rate, despicable. ❑ **two cent(s)** *see* separate entries. ❑ **two dicks** *n.* [the image of one who is such a WANKER *n.* (2) that he requires two penises] [1990s+] (*UK juv.*) a general term of abuse. ❑ **two-dog night** *n.* [orig. aboriginal term, the need to sleep between a pair of dogs to batten onto their warmth] [1970s+] (*Aus./US*) a very cold night. ❑ **two dollar** *adj. see* separate entry. ❑ **two dozen** *n.* [late 19C] (*Aus. Und.*) a punishment of 25 lashes. ❑ **two-ender** *n.* [1930s] (*tramp*) a two-shilling piece (10p). ❑ **two-eyed steak** *n.* (*also* **two-eyed beefsteak**) [its flatness] [late 19C–1930s] a kipper, a salted herring or cod. ❑ **twoface** *v.* [SE *two-faced*] [1930s+] (*Can./US*) to treat in a duplicitous manner. ❑ **two-finger/-fingered shuffle** *see* separate entries. ❑ **two-fingered salute** *n.* [1960s+] an obscene gesture of dismissal; a 'V-sign'. ❑ **two-fisted** *adj.* **1** [late 18C+] good at fist-fighting, thus tough, manly. **2** [early–mid-19C] clumsy. **3** [20C+] sense 1 extended to inanimate objects, e.g. *two-fisted yarn*, a tough, male-orientated story. ❑ **two-gun man** *n.* [1970s] (*Aus.*) a person who drinks both rum and beer, one being a chaser. ❑ **two-hand bracelet** *n. see* BRACELETS *n.* ❑ **two-handed** *adj. see* separate entry. ❑ **two-inched** *adj.* [the lit./fig. dimensions of the man's penis] [1990s+] (*US black*) of a woman, given insufficient sexual gratification. ❑ **two Jews** *n.* [1940s] the number two. ❑ **two-leaved book** *n.* [late 16C–17C] the vagina. ❑ **two-legged mare** *n.* [mid-16C–17C; late 19C] the gallows. ❑ **two-legged tree** *n.* [19C] the gallows. ❑ **two-legged tympany** *n. see* separate entry. ❑ **two-mac** *n.* [SE *two* + MAC *n.*[1] (1)] [1950s+] (*W.I.*) two shillings (post-1969 value 20 cents). ❑ **two-mouth** *n.* [dial. *two-mouth*, a double-edged machete] [1950s] (*W.I.*) a hypocrite. ❑ **two-out** *see* separate entries. ❑ **two-peg** *n.* [PEG *n.*[3]] [1900s–60s] (*Aus.*) a florin, a two-shilling piece (10p). ❑ **twopenny...** *see* separate entries. ❑ **two-pipe** *n.* [1940s] (*US Und.*) a double-barrelled shotgun. ❑ **two-pot screamer** *n. see* ONE-POT SCREAMER *n.* ❑ **two Ps** *see* MAY YOUR PRICK AND PURSE NEVER FAIL YOU *under* PRICK *n.* ❑ **two-quidder** *n.* [late 19C] one who earns two pounds per week, thus a member of the lower middle classes. ❑ **two spaces** *n.* [i.e. two year-long spaces in one's life] [20C+] (*US Und.*) a two-year prison sentence. ❑ **two-stemmer** *n.* [on pattern of MAIN STEM *n.* (2); i.e. the two major streets that such a town could boast] [19C] (*US*) a small town. ❑ **two-step** *n.* [1920s–40s] (*US tramp*) a chicken. ❑ **twos up** *see* separate entries. ❑ **two-time/-timer/-timey/-timing** *see* separate entries. ❑ **twotone** *n.* [1940s+] (*US gay*) sex between black and white men. ❑ **two-upper** *n.* [1910s+] (*Aus.*) a player of the gambling game of 'two-up'; thus *two-up school*, on the model of SE *card-school*, the place where the game is carried on. ❑ **two-way** *adj. see* separate entry. ❑ **two years** *n.* [1940s] (*US Und.*) a two-dollar bill.

IN PHRASES

❑ **two bad boys from Illinois** *n.* [20C+] (*US*) in craps dice, the roll of two. ❑ **two bastards on bikes** *n.* [2000s] (*Aus./N.Z.*) in the gambling game of two-up, a throw in which two coins come up 'tails'. ❑ **two bowers and an ace** *n.* [euchre terminology: *bowers*, the name of the two highest cards – the knave of trumps, and the knave of the same colour, called right and left bower respectively] [late 19C] (*US*) something excellent; an advantage. ❑ **two bricks short of a load** *adj. see under* ...SHORT OF... *adj.* ❑ **two by four** *n. see* separate entry. ❑ **two draws and a spit** *n. see* THREE DRAWS AND A SPIT *under* THREE *adj.* ❑ **two drinks and a sandwich** *n. see* COFFEE AND CAKES *under* COFFEE *n.* ❑ **two dots and a dash** *n.* [visual likeness] **1** [1910s–20s] fried eggs and bacon. **2** [1960s+] (*US gay*) the male genitals. ❑ **two-faced as a Methodist axe** *adj.* (*also* **two-faced as a cod**) [US regional *Methodist axe*, a double-bladed axe] [1960s+] (*US*) duplicitous, deceitful, untrustworthy. ❑ **two faces under one hood** *n.* [i.e. SE *two-faced*] [late 16C–early 19C] double-dealing, cheating, duplicity; a deceitful person. ❑ **two fat cheeks (and ne'er a nose)** *n.* [18C–19C] the posterior, the buttocks. ❑ **two fat ladies** *n.* (*also* **two fat women, two old ladies**) [the supposedly similar shapes] [1940s+] (*bingo*) the number 88. ❑ **two flips of a humming-bird's tail** *see* TWO SHAKES OF A LAMB'S TAIL *phr.* ❑ **two-for-a-nickel** *adj.* (*also* **two for a cent**) [1920s–60s] (*US*) cheap, second-rate. ❑ **two jerks of a lamb's tail** *see* TWO SHAKES OF A LAMB'S TAIL *phr.* ❑ **two ladies on bikes** *n.* [the image on the coin of Britannia's shield, which could be seen as resembling a bicycle wheel] [2000s] (*Aus./N.Z.*) in the gambling game of two-up, a throw in which two coins come up 'tails'. ❑ **two little crutches** *n.* [the supposedly similar shapes] [1940s+] (*bingo*) the number 77. ❑ **two (little) ducks** *n.* [the supposedly similar shapes] [late 19C+] (*bingo*) the number 22. ❑ **two pence short of a bob** *n. see under* ...SHORT OF... *adj.* ❑ **two pence wet and two pence dry** *n.* [? a 'low' gambling game, *see* C. Johnson, *History of Highwaymen*, p.59: 'Come, said he, what shall we do with all this Drink? We will play Two pence wet, and Fourpence dry [...] at at this low Gaming Rumbold had, in short, won of his Confederate ten shillings'] [18C] a brief act of intercourse with a prostitute, either vaginal, i.e. *wet*, or anal, i.e. *dry*, or masturbation. ❑ **two sandwiches short of a picnic** *adj. see* ONE SANDWICH SHORT OF A PICNIC *under* ...SHORT OF... *adj.* ❑ **two shakes of a lamb's tail** *n. see* separate entry. ❑ **two snaps up** [referring to the snapping of one's fingers, and a play on the phr. 'two thumbs up' used by US TV film critics Roger Ebert and Gene Siskel] [1990s+] (*US campus*) an expression of approval. ❑ **two stone underweight** *adj.* (*also* **two stone wanting**) [pun on STONE *n.*[1] (1)] [late 18C–1900s] castrated, thus a eunuch. ❑ **two tacos short of a combination plate** *adj. see under* ...SHORT OF... *adj.* ❑ **two thieves beating a rogue** [late 18C–early 19C] a phr. said of a person beating their hands against their sides to get warm on a cold day. ❑ **two-to-one** *n.* [either the arrangement of the trad. three balls hanging outside the pawnbroker's (one above, two below) or the popular belief that it was two-to-one odds that one's pledge would never be redeemed] [19C] (*US*) a pawnbroker. ❑ **two-to-one shop** *n.* [for ety. *see* prev.] [late 18C–early 19C] a pawnbroker's shop. ❑ **two twists of a lamb's tail** *see* TWO SHAKES OF A LAMB'S TAIL *phr.* ❑ **two ways from the jack** *adv. see* FORTY WAYS FROM THE JACK *under* FORTY *adj.*[1]. ❑ **two winks of a mole's eye** *see* TWO SHAKES OF A LAMB'S TAIL *phr.*

IN EXCLAMATIONS

❑ **two to one against you!** [for ety. *see* TWO-TO-ONE above] [late 19C–1900s] you have no hope, the odds are stacked against you.

two and eight *n.* [rhy. sl.] [1910s+] a state, a panic.

two bit *n.* [mid-19C+] (*W.I.*) ninepence (post-1969 value, five cents).

two-bit *adj.* (*also* **two-bits**) [SE *two* +BIT *n.*[1] (1), lit. worth 25 cents] [20C+] (*US*) second-rate, inferior.

IN COMPOUNDS

❑ **Two-bit Annie** *n.* (*also* **two-bit Sadie**) [+ proper name] [1940s] (*US*) a cheap prostitute. ❑ **two-bit hustler** *n.* [HUSTLER *n.*] [1940s–50s] (*US Und.*) **1** a promiscuous woman; a low-priced prostitute. **2** a second-rate confidence trickster. **3** a passive homosexual or low-priced male homosexual prostitute.

two bits *n.* [BIT *n.*[1] (1d)] **1** [mid-19C+] 25 cents. **2** [1940s–60s] (*US Und.*) $25.

two-bitty *adj.* [TWO-BIT *adj.*] [1940s] (*W.I.*) feeling poorly, not up to much.

two-bob *adj.* [BOB *n.*[3] (2); lit. worth two shillings (10p)] [1940s+] (*orig. Aus.*) inferior, useless, second-rate.

two-bob bit *n.* (*also* **two-bob bits**) [rhy. sl.] [1930s+] **1** an act of defecation [= SHIT *n.* (1)]. **2** diarrhoea [= SHITS, THE *n.*]. **3** breasts [= TIT *n.*[2] (1)]. **4** a contemptible person [= SHIT *n.* (2a)].

two-bob each way *phr.* [the cheapness of such a bet] [1960s+] (*Aus.*) uncommitted.

two-bob watch *n.* [2000s] used in phrs. to imply intensity, excess, speed e.g. *my heart was racing like a two-bob watch*.

two by four *n.*[1] [1910s] (*US*) an insignificant person.

two by four *n.*[2] (*also* **five to four, six to four, sixty-four**) [rhy. sl. = SE *whore*] [1930s+] a prostitute.

two-by-four *adj.* (*also* **two-by-nothing**) [the minimal dimensions] [late 19C+] (*US*) small, insignificant.

twoc *n. see* TWOCKER *n.*

2CB *n. see* NEXUS *n.*

two-cent *adj.* (*also* **ten-cent**) [var. on TWO-BIT *adj.*; worth only 2¢] [late 19C+] inferior, second-rate.

IN COMPOUNDS

□ **two-cent dosser** *n.* [DOSSER *n.* (1); note UK, despite US denomination] [late 19C] a man who lives in stale-beer shops, which specialized in stale or old and strong beer.

two cents *n.* [1930s–40s] (*US black*) $2.

two cents' worth *n.* (*also* **two cents**) **1** [1900s–50s] (*US*) a little, a trivial amount. **2** [1910s+] one's personal opinion, a remark about a topic.

IN PHRASES

□ **put in one's two cents' worth** *v.* (*also* **...three cent's worth,** *UK:* **...twopennorth, ...two bobs**) [1910s+] (*US*) to make a contribution, usu. gratuitous and/or malicious, to an argument or conversation.

twocer *n. see* TWOCKER *n.*

twock *n.* [TWOCK *v.*] [2000s] a vehicle that has stolen and been driven illegally.

twock *v.* (*also* **twoc**) [take without owner's consent] **1** [1990s+] to steal cars, usu. for joy-riding. **2** [2000s] to steal, other than cars.

twocker *n.* (*also* **twoc, twocer, twok**) [TWOCK *v.*] [1990s+] a youth who steals cars to use in a crime or for amusement; developed into a non-specific term of abuse.

two-dollar *adj.* **1** [1900s] expensive. **2** [1960s+] (*US*) second-rate [var. on TWO-CENT *adj.*].

IN COMPOUNDS

□ **two-dollar words** *n.* (*also* **five-dollar words, ...expression, six-bit words**) [20C+] (*US*) any language considered 'difficult' or 'intellectual', most likely by a speaker who claims to despise such locutions.

twoed-up *adv.* (*also* **two'd up**) [1960s+] (*UK prison*) having two prisoners sharing a cell; thus *threed-up* etc.

twoer *n.* **1** [late 19C] a two-wheeled cab. **2** [late 19C] a two-shilling (10p) piece. **3** [1930s] a two-year prison sentence. **4** [1940s+] £20; £200.

two eyes of blue! *excl.* [rhy. sl.] [1920s+] too true!

two eyes right! *excl. see* TOO RIGHT! *excl.*

twofer *n.* [? 'two for the price of one'] **1** [late 19C] a harlot. **2** [late 19C–1930s] (*US*) (*also* **toofah, toofer**) a cheap cigar. **3** [20C+] a prostitute who is amenable to vaginal and/or anal intercourse. **4** [1940s–50s] (*US*) a theatre ticket sold at half price, or similar offer; a sandwich man sells such tickets.

two-fifth *n.* [2000s] (*US*) a .25 calibre pistol.

two-finger *v.* [1940s] (*US police*) to pickpocket.

two-fingered shuffle *n.*

IN PHRASES

□ **do the two-fingered shuffle** *v.* (*also* **...two-fingered tango**) [1990s+] of a woman, to masturbate.

two-foot rule *n.* [rhy. sl.] [mid–late 19C] a fool.

two-handed *adj.* **1** [late 17C–1920s] usu. of people, large, strapping; thus *two handed fellow, two-handed wench.* **2** [mid-19C–1920s] clumsy, maladroit. **3** [1910s–30s] (*US*) dedicated, committed; generous.

IN PHRASES

□ **two-handed put** *n.* [SE *two-handed*, whole-hearted + *put*, an act of thrusting or pushing] [late 18C–19C] sexual intercourse.

200 on a plate *n.* [1940s] (*US*) pork and beans.

twoit *n. see* TWAT *n.* (1).

twok *n. see* TWOCKER *n.*

two-legged tympany *n.* (*also* **tympany with two heels**) [SE *tympany*, a morbid swelling or tumour] [mid-16C–early 18C] a baby, esp. in embryonic stage.

IN PHRASES

□ **cured of a tympany with two heels** *v.* [mid-17C] to give birth. □ **have a two-legged tympany** *v.* [mid-16C–early 18C] to be pregnant.

twonk *n.* [TWAT *n.* (3) + PLONKER *n.* (3)] [1980s] a fool.

211 *n.* [California police code number] [1990s+] (*US black*) an armed robbery; thus as v.

213 *n.* [the telephone area code] [1990s+] (*US black*) Los Angeles.

twoonie *n.* [SE *two* + LOONIE *n.*[1]] [1990s+] (*Can.*) a two-dollar coin.

twoosie(-woosie) *n.* [? play on FLOOZY *n.*] [1940s] an attractive young woman.

two-out *n.* [mid-19C] a small measure or glass of gin, prob. 2d. worth.

two out *adv.* [TWOED-UP *adv.*] [1980s+] (*Aus. prison*) having two prisoners sharing a cell.

twopenny *n.*[1] [rhy. sl.; *twopenny loaf = loaf of bread*; note the later LOAF (OF BREAD) *n.*] [mid-19C–1930s] the head.

twopenny *n.*[2] [late-19C–1910s] a pawnbroker's professional go-between, who charges twopence to take one's goods to the pawnshop and negotiate a deal.

twopenny *n.*[3] [1910s–20s] a general term of affection.

twopenny *adj. see* TWOPENNY-HALFPENNY *adj.*

SE in slang uses

IN COMPOUNDS

□ **twopenny burster** *n.* [its price and its effect on the stomach] [early 19C] a loaf of bread. □ **twopenny damn** *n. see* DAMN *n.* □ **twopenny hop** *n.* [the 2d. price of admission + HOP *n.*[1] (1): 'the clog hornpipe, the pipe dance, flash jigs, and horn pipes in fetters, à la Jack Sheppard, are the favourite movements' (Hotten 1867)] [mid–late 19C] cheap dancehalls and the dances held at them. □ **twopenny rope** *n.* [orig. two ropes strung across a room, with rough bedding (usu. sacking) strung between them, on which bedless tramps could lean and fitfully sleep for a 2d. payment; note Dickens *Pickwick Papers* (1836–7): ''Ven the lady and gen'lm'n as keeps the Hot-el, first begun business, they used to make the beds on the floor; but this wouldn't do at no price, 'cos instead o' taking a moderate twopenn'orth o' sleep, the lodgers used to lie there half the day. So now they has two ropes, 'bout six foot apart, and three from the floor, which goes right down the room; and the beds are made of slips of coarse sacking, stretched across em.'] [mid-19C–1930s] (*UK tramp*) a hostel, a casual ward. □ **twopenny tube** *n.* [the original fare of 2d. + TUBE *n.*[1] (3)] [1900s–30s] the London Underground. □ **twopenny upright** *n. see* THREEPENNY UPRIGHT *under* THREEPENNY *adj.*

twopenny-halfpenny *adj.* (*also* **twopence-halfpenny, twopenny-ha'penny**) [the value; Williams notes a *twopenny whore* as the cheapest 17C prostitute] [early 19C+] virtually worthless, insignificant, paltry.

twos *n.* [1970s+] (*UK prison*) the second landing of cells in a prison block; similarly *threes, fours*, etc.

two's and fews *phr.* [orig. of prostitutes who charge two dollars, but often have to take less, i.e. whatever they can get] [1940s–50s] having no or very little money.

twos and threes *n.* [rhy. sl.] [1960s–80s] **1** keys. **2** knees.

two shakes of a lamb's tail *phr.* (*also* **fling of a cow's tail, two flips of a humming-bird's tail, two shakes of a (dead) sheep's tail, ...of a donkey's tail, ...of a duck's tail, ...of a frog's whisker, ...of the mainbrace, two jerks of a lamb's tail, two twists..., two winks of a mole's eye, three jerks of a lamb's tail, three shakes of a..., whisk of a...**) [mid-19C+] a very short time, usu. with *in a...*, meaning extremely quickly, at once.

two-slice *n.* [rhy. sl.] [1990s+] an office.

twos up *n.* **1** [1960s+] sexual intercourse involving two men and one woman. **2** [2000s] spec. when a woman has two men simultaneously penetrating her anus and her vagina.

two's up! *excl.* [1970s] an excl. used to denote one's desire to share a cigarette.

twot *n.* **1** *see* TWAT *n.* (1). **2** *see* TWAT *n.* (3).

IN COMPOUNDS

□ **twotface** *n. see* TWAT *n.* (2).

twotch *n. see* TWAT *n.* (1).

two-thirty *adj.* [rhy. sl.] [late 19C+] dirty.

two-time *v.* **1** [1910s+] (*also* **five-time**) to deceive sexually. **2** [1920s+] (*orig. US*) to cheat, esp. to double-cross.

two-time loser *n.* **1** [1910s+] (*US Und.*) a person who already has two convictions and so risks a higher sentence the third time. **2** [1950s+] (*US*) a person who has been divorced twice.

two-timer *n.* [TWO-TIME *v.*] [1920s+] (*orig. US*) a cheat, a double-crosser.

two-timey *adj.* [1940s] (*US*) indecisive.

two-timing *adj.* (*also* **two-time**) [TWO-TIME *v.* (1)] [1920s+] (*orig. US*) duplicitous, esp. in a sexual context.

two UEs *n.* (*also* **2 UEs**) [rhy. sl.] [20C+] (*Aus.*) fleas.

two-way *adj.* [1960s] (*US*) duplicitous.

pertaining to sexuality

(IN COMPOUNDS)

❑ **two-way baby** *n.* [1960s+] (*US*) a bisexual. ❑ **two-way girl** *n.* (*also* **two-way bitch, two-wayer**) [1930s+] a woman who is amenable to vaginal and anal intercourse. ❑ **two-way man** *n.* [1930s+] a male prostitute who is willing to act as passive or active partner in sodomy or fellatio.

two-wheeler *n.* [rhy. sl. = SHEILA *n.*[1]] [20C+] (*Aus.*) a woman.

twunt *n.* [TWAT *n.* (3) + CUNT *n.* (4)] [1990s+] a despicable person.

ty *n.* [abbr.] [1920s] (*Aus.*) typhoid fever.

Tyburn *n.* [later use is historical] [16C–19C] sited near what is now Marble Arch, the village of Paddington, the principal site of public executions in London between 1388–1783, when it was replaced by Newgate; not sl. as such but occurring in many combs. below.

(IN COMPOUNDS)

❑ **Tyburn bird** *n.* [late 17C] a criminal, destined to be hanged at Tyburn. ❑ **Tyburn blossom** *n.* ['who in time will ripen unto fruit born by the DEADLY NEVERGREEN *n.*' (Grose, 1796)] [late 18C–early 19C] a young thief or pickpocket. ❑ **Tyburn check** *n.* [16C–early 19C] a hangman's noose. ❑ **Tyburn collar** *n.* [mid-19C] a fringe of beard worn under the chin. ❑ **Tyburn collop** *n.* [16C] a miserable face. ❑ **Tyburn face** *n.* [late 17C–18C] a miserable, down-in-the-mouth look. ❑ **Tyburn foretop** *n.* (*also* **Tyburn top**) [late 18C–early 19C] **1** a wig with its foretop combed forward over the eyes. Such wigs were esp. popular among the underworld. **2** a hairstyle associated with criminals. ❑ **Tyburn piccadill** *n.* (*also* **piccadill**) [*Tyburn*, generic for the execution ground + SE *piccadill*, an ornamented collar fashionable in the early 17C. The term comes from the Sp. *picadillo*, the dimin. of *picado*, meaning pricked, pierced, punctured, slashed or minced (thus *picada*, a puncture and *picadillo*, minced meat). The piccadill was brought to the UK either by Robert Baker (*The London Encyclopedia*, 1983) or by 'one Higgins' (*The Atheneum*, 1901). Whatever the name, the individual in question made a fortune from his import, sufficient to buy land around what is now Piccadilly Circus and to erect, *c.*1622, a large mansion which was promptly and irreverently christened Piccadilly Hall. The surrounding area soon became known as Piccadilly. However, the *OED* cites a source writing in 1656 who claimed that the house was thus named because, being at the furthest edge of the parish of St Martin in the Fields, in which it lay, it was therefore serving as a 'collar', or outer edge of the area] [mid-17C–early 19C] a hangman's noose; thus *put on a Tyburn piccadill*, to be hanged. ❑ **Tyburn stretch** *n.* [SE *stretch* one's neck] [mid-16C–early 19C] a hanging. ❑ **Tyburn string** *n.* [mid-17C–18C] a hangman's noose. ❑ **Tyburn tiffany** *n.* [SE *tiffany*, a transparent gauze muslin, often used as a headcover] [17–18C] a hangman's noose. ❑ **Tyburn tippet** *n.* [SE *tippet*, a scarf, a band of silk or fur worn around the neck] [mid-16C–early 19C] a hangman's noose. ❑ **Tyburn tree** *n.* (*also* **Tyburnian tree**) [The best-known *Tyburn tree*, a great triple gallows on which 21 malefactors could be 'turned off' simultaneously, was erected in June 1751. Its first victim was 'Romish Canonical Doctor' John Story; although this gallows was the first permanent such structure on the site, hangings had taken place at Tyburn since 1388. Tyburn was in the then village of Paddington, thus synon. 'Paddington-tree', e.g. in broadside 'Cromwell's Coronation' c.1656; later use is historical] [mid-17C+] the gallows sited at Tyburn.

(IN PHRASES)

❑ **dance the Tyburn hornpipe on nothing** *v. see under* DANCE *v.* ❑ **dance/do the Tyburn jig** *v. see under* DANCE *v.* ❑ **dangle in a Tyburn string** *v. see under* DANGLE *v.* ❑ **fetch a Tyburn stretch** *v.* [late 18C–early 19C] to be hanged. ❑ **make a Tyburn show** *v.* [late 18C–early 19C] to be hanged. ❑ **preach at Tyburn cross** *v.* [mid-16C–18C] to be hanged. ❑ **take a leap at Tyburn** *v.* [17C–early 19C] to be hanged.

tyee *n.* (*also* **tyhee**) [Chinook jargon *tyee*, a chief] [late 18C+] (*US*) an important person.

tye one on *v. see* TIE ONE ON *under* TIE *v.*

tying-up *n.* [TIE UP *v.*[1] (2)] [1900s] (*Aus.*) a marriage ceremony, a wedding.

tyke *n.* [TEAGUE *n.*] [20C+] (*Aus./N.Z.*) a Roman Catholic, thus *Tykeland*, Ireland.

tyke-boy *n.* [SE *tyke*, dog] [19C] a dog fancier; one who supports dog fights.

tylt *n. see* TILT *n.*

tympany with two heels *n. see* TWO-LEGGED TYMPANY *n.*

typer *n.* [1930s–50s] **1** (*orig. US*) a typewriter. **2** (*US Und.*) a machinegun.

typewriter *n.*[1] **1** [1900s] (*US*) the queen in cards. **2** [1910s+] a machinegun or sub-machinegun [its 'tapping' noise].

typewriter *n.*[2] [rhy. sl.] [1930s+] a boxer, a fighter (lit. or fig.).

typling house *n. see* TIPPLING-KEN *n.*

tyrekicker *n.* [car sales use *tyrekicker*, one who examines a car at length, then does not buy it] [1980s+] (*N.Z.*) of a politician or other decision-maker, one who discusses and debates, but fails to act.

Tyrone Power *n.* [rhy. sl.; ult. real name US actor *Tyrone Power* (1914–58)] [1940s+] (*Aus.*) a shower.

tyrooger *n.* [nonsense word] [1960s] (*US*) the penis.

tytere-tu *n. see* TITTERY-TU *n.*

tzing-tzing *adj.* [? CHIN-CHIN! *excl.*] [late 19C] excellent, first-rate.

tzuris *n. see* TSURIS *n.*

Ubangi *n.* [1980s] (*US*) a black person.

u.b.d.'d! *excl.* [abbr.] [1910s–20s] *you be damned!*

ubrown *n.* [the colour] [1980s+] (*S.Afr. township*) brandy.

u.b.s *n.* [abbr. *underbodies*] [1970s] (*US campus*) underwear, usu. female use.

u.c. *n.* [abbr.] [1980s] (*US*) an undercover agent.

u.c. *adj.* [abbr.] [2000s] (*US Und./police*) undercover.

u/c *adj.* [abbr. *uncut*] [1970s+] used in contact advertisements, uncircumcised.

ucky *adj. see* YUCKY *adj.*

u-clever *n. see* CLEVER *n.*

ud *n.* (*also* **cud**) [17C–mid-18C] euph. for *God*, used in a variety of oaths.

udders *n.* [early 18C; 1930s+] the female breasts.

udsnigs! *excl. see* 'SNIGGERS! *excl.*

U-ey *n. see* U-IE *n.*

uff *n. see* OOF *n.*

U4euh *n.* (*also* **euphoria**) [SE *euphoria*] [2000s] (*US drugs*) a term for the drug 4-methylaminorex.

ug *n.* [2000s] an *ugly* woman.

Ugandan discussion *n.* [originated in the UK satirical magazine *Private Eye*, following the catching *in flagrante* of a Ugandan diplomat who excused herself by claiming that she and her partner had been 'talking about Uganda'] [1970s+] sexual intercourse; plus vars., such as *talk about Uganda, Ugandan affairs*.

uggies *n.* (*also* **ugg boots**) [SE *ugly*] [1990s+] (*Aus.*) sheepskin boots or slippers.

uglies, the *n.* **1** [mid-19C+] a fit of depression or bad temper. **2** [late 19C] delirium tremens. **3** [1910s] (*S.Afr.*) a type of eyeshade worn by women [UGLY *n.* (2)]. **4** [1950s+] the state of being unattractive. **5** [1970s] nitrogen narcosis, 'rapture of the deep'.

ugly *n.* **1** [mid–late 19C] a derog. term of address, also as *Mr Ugly*. **2** [mid–late 19C] (*UK society*) a bonnet shade [what was generally seen as its lack of style or taste]. **3** [1950s+] (*also* **uglee**) an unattractive person, usu. female.

ugly *adj.* [1990s+] (*US campus*) difficult, unpleasant.

SE in slang uses

IN COMPOUNDS

□ **ugly customer** *n.* [the format dates to 16C *lewd customer*] **1** [early 19C] a black eye. **2** [early 19C+] an unpleasant, menacing individual. □ **uglyman** *n.* [mid–late 19C] that member of the garrotting team who actually does the choking.

IN PHRASES

□ **have taken ugly pills** *v.* [1950s+] (*Can.*) to be unpleasant, aggressive, unattractive etc.

ugly as... *adj.* (*also* **(so) ugly that...**) [early 19C+] (*US*) used in combs. meaning very ugly or unwell-looking.

IN PHRASES

□ **...a hatful of arseholes** (*also* **ugly as a bagful of busted arseholes, ...bagful of bums, ...bagful of busted boils**) [ARSEHOLE *n.* (1)] [1950s+] (*Aus./N.Z./US*) very ugly. □ **...a hatful of bronzas** *see under* BRONZE *n.*^{2}. □ **...a shithouse rat** *see under* SHITHOUSE RAT *n.* □ **...a tarantula** [late 19C] very angry, unpleasant. □ **...bull-beef** [mid-19C] a general term of contempt; thus *go to the billy-fencer and sell yourself for bull-beef*.

ugly sister *n.* [rhy. sl.; note SKIN-AND-BLISTER *n.* = sister] [20C+] a blister.

ugly stick *n.* [often cited as a supposed reason for the lack of good looks] [1960s+] (*US*) the state of being unattractive.

IN PHRASES

□ **beat with an ugly stick** *v.* (*also* **hit over the head with the ugly stick**) **1** [1960s+] (*Aus./US*) to cause to be unattractive; often as a supposed reason for one's lack of good looks, *he was beat with an ugly stick*. **2** [1980s+] (*US campus*) of a man, to have sexual intercourse. □ **slapped with an ugly stick** *adj.* [1960s–80s] (*US*) unattractive. □ **whipped with an ugly stick** *adj.* [1960s–80s] unattractive.

U-haul *n.* [the US truck rental company U-Haul] [1990s+] (*US gay*) a lesbian who fall in love at first sight and moves in right away with a new lover.

U-ie *n.* (*also* **U, U-ey, yewie, yoo-ee, youee**) [1960s+] (*orig. Aus.*) a U-turn; thus *do/chuck/bang a U-ie*, to make a U-turn.

IN PHRASES

□ **cut a U** *v.* [1980s] (*US*) to make a U-turn. □ **hang a U-ie** *v.* (*also* **hang a U-ey, ...Ulysses, ...yewie, ...youee**) [HANG *v.*^{7} + U-IE *n.*] **1** [1960s+] (*orig. Aus.*) to make a U-turn. **2** [1990s+] to urinate [pun on sense 1 as well as initial letter of SE *urinate*].

uke *n.* [abbr.] [1920s+] (*orig. US*) *ukelele*.

ullage *n.* [SE *ullage*, the amount of wine or other liquor by which a cask or bottle falls short of being quite full; note WW1 RN *ullage*, an incompetent] [late 19C] the dregs in the bottom of wine glasses or casks.

ultimate *n.* [the potency and effects] (*drugs*) [1980s+] **1** cocaine. **2** crack cocaine.

ultimatum *n.* [SE *ultimatum*, the final point, extreme limit] [early 19C] the buttocks, the posterior.

ultra! *excl.* [SE *ultra*, on pattern of MEGA *adj.*, but note Polari *ultra*, very] [1980s+] excellent! first-rate! wonderful!

ultracool *adj.* [SE *ultra* + COOL *adj.* (5)] [1960s+] (*orig. US*) extremely sophisticated.

ultramarine *adj.* [play on BLUE *adj.*^{3}] [late 19C–1910s] obscene, 'smutty'.

ultraswoopy *adj.* [2000s] (*US*) very stylish, streamlined.

umac *n.* [? MACK *n.*^{2} (3)] [1960s+] (*S.Afr. black*) a young man about town.

umberstick *n.* [SE *umbrella* + *stick*] [20C+] (*Ulster*) an umbrella.

umble-cum-stumble *v.* [late 19C] to understand comprehensively.

umbrella *n.*^{1} **1** [1930s] a cowardly boxer, one who cannot take the punches [he 'folds up', thus FOLD *v.*]. **2** [1930s] cowardice. **3** [1960s–70s] (*US*) police protection, obtained through bribery [it keeps one from being 'rained on' – see *RAIN ON under* RAIN *v.*].

SE in slang uses

IN COMPOUNDS

□ **umbrella branch** *n.* (*also* **umbrella brigade**) [they may dress in the bowler hat and rolled umbrella uniform of their bureaucratic masters in Whitehall] [1970s+] the Special Branch.

umbrella *n.*[2] [rhy. sl.; Cockney pron. 'fella'] [1990s+] a fellow, usu. a husband, boyfriend or lover.

ump *n.* [20C+] (*US*) an umpire.

umpchay *n.* (*also* **umpcha**) [pig Lat. = CHUMP *n.*[1]] [1900s–30s] a fool.

umph *n. see* OOMPH *n.*

umpteen *n.* [orig. WW1 milit. use, deliberately replacing a specific number with a noncommittal *um* for communications secrecy] [1910s+] an unspecified large number or amount; thus adj. use *umpteenth*.

umpty *adj.* (*also* **umpty-umph**) (*orig. milit.*) **1** [1910s+] of an indefinite number, usu. a large one, in combs. e.g. *umpty-nine, umpty-eleven*; thus *umptieth* [UMPTEEN *n.*]. **2** [1910s+] unpleasant, difficult [? *GET THE HUMP under* HUMP *n.*[1]].

umpty *adv.* [1930s] (*US black*) (*also* **tiddy umpty**) completely, entirely.

umpty-doo *adj.* (*also* **humpty-doo**) [the nursery rhyme *Humpty-Dumpty*, who 'fell off a wall'] [1910s+] (*Aus.*) **1** drunk. **2** in fig. uses, extreme, excessive, whether positive or negative; first-rate.

u.m.s. *phr.* [abbr. *u*gly *m*ood *s*wing] [1980s+] (*US campus*) a sudden, unpredictable change of mood.

un *n.* [negative SE pfx *un-*] [1990s+] (*US campus*) an outsider, someone who does not fit in.

una *n.* [Ital. *uno*, one] [mid-19C+] (*Ling. Fr./Polari*) the number one.

un-ass *v.* [SE pfx *un-* + ASS *n.* (2)] [1960s+] **1** (*US black*) to hand over, to give up. **2** to leave, to abandon.

unavoidable circumstances *n.* [late 19C] (*US*) formal dress breeches worn for Court appearances.

unavoidable wreck *n.* [rhy. sl.] [1930s] the neck.

unbelt *v. see under* BELT *n.*

unbenefit *v.* [lit. 'to withdraw one's benefits from'] [1990s+] (*US teen*) to disassociate oneself from someone after a disagreement or an unpleasant occurrence.

unbetty *v.* [BETTY *v.*] **1** [early–mid-19C] to unlock. **2** [1930s] (*US Und.*) of a prostitute, to unbutton the customer's trousers.

unbleached American *n. see under* BLEACH *v.*

unbleached Australian *n. see under* BLEACH *v.*

unboiled lobster *n.* [the uncooked lobster is blue, like a police uniform. The cooked lobster has turned red/pink, like a soldier's] [mid-19C] a policeman.

unbooted *adj.* [a country person, who does not wear shoes] [1940s–50s] (*US black*) naïve, ignorant.

unbreech *v. see* UNRIG *v.* (1).

unc *n.* [abbr.] [20C+] (*US*) uncle.

unchummy *adj.* [SE pfx *un-* + CHUMMY *adj.*] [1920s] unfriendly.

Uncle *n.* (*also* **my uncle, our uncle**) [abbr. UNCLE SAM *n.*] [mid-19C+] the USA, esp. the US armed forces or other federal/national authorities.

IN PHRASES

❑ **duck Uncle** *v.* [1940s] (*US black*) to avoid the draft.

uncle *n.* **1** [mid-18C+] (*also* **mine uncle, mine uncle's, my uncle, my uncle's, uncle sam**) a pawnbroker [the avuncular help he gives 'relatives' in temporary financial distress]. **2** [late 18C–early 19C] a privy. **3** [mid-19C–1960s] (*US*) (*also* **unkey, unky**) a form of address to a black male whose name one does not know or ignores. **4** [late 19C–1910s] as *your uncle*, oneself. **5** [20C+] (*also* **unkey, unky**) a general term of address to a man; there need be neither prior acquaintance or any form of relationship. **6** [1920s–40s] (*US*) (*also* **auntie**) a receiver of stolen goods. **7** [1940s–70s] (*US gay/prison*) an older homosexual male with a taste for young men or boys. **8** *see* DUTCH UNCLE *n.*

IN PHRASES

❑ **cry uncle** *v.* (*also* **holler..., say...**) ['"uncle" in this expression is surely a folk etymology, and the Irish original of the word is *anacol* (*anacal, anacul*) "act of protecting; deliverance; mercy, quarter, safety", a verbal noun from the Old Irish verb *aingid* "protects"' (*American Speech* LI, 1976)] [1910s+] (*US*) to beg someone to stop an action, to surrender; also fig. ❑ **go to visit one's uncle** *v.* [euph; but note RAF jargon *go uncling*, to pursue a married woman; her children call the suitor 'uncle'] [late 18C–early 19C] to abandon one's wife shortly after the marriage ceremony. ❑ **send to uncle's** *v.* [19C] to pawn. ❑ **where uncle's doodle goes** *adv.* [mid–late 19C] the vagina, thus *be where uncle's doodle goes*, to have sexual intercourse.

uncle! *excl.* [*CRY UNCLE under* UNCLE *n.*] [1910s+] (*US*) an excl. used to signify one's surrender, usu. in a physical confrontation.

Uncle Arthur *n.* (*also* **Arthurs**) [founder Arthur Guinness (1725–1803)] [20C+] (*Irish*) generic for Guinness and the family who own it, thus phr. *Arthur Guinness talk*, drunken language.

Uncle Ben *n.*[1] [rhy. sl.] [1940s+] (*bingo*) the number ten.

Uncle Ben *n.*[2] [play on UNCLE TOM *n.* + whiteness of *Uncle Ben's* brand of rice] [1970s+] (*US gay*) a homosexual black man who prefers white men; thus a term of abuse.

Uncle-Ben Black *n.* [*Uncle Ben's rice*, a staple black food] [1960s] (*US black*) a deep sense of one's blackness.

Uncle Benny *n.* (*also* **Uncle Ben**) [typical Jewish name *Benjamin*; pawnbroking is seen as a 'Jewish' occupation] [1920s–40s] (*US Und.*) a pawnbroker.

Uncle Bert *n.* [rhy. sl.] [20C+] a shirt.

Uncle Bill *n.* [OLD BILL *n.*] [1930s–50s] a police officer, the police.

Uncle Bob *n.*[1] [rhy. sl. = KNOB *n.* (1c)] [20C+] the penis.

Uncle Bob *n.*[2] [BOBBY *n.* (1)] [1940s] a police officer.

Uncle Bob *n.*[3] [rhy. sl.] [1990s+] a job.

Uncle Dick *n.* [rhy. sl. = PRICK *n.* (1)] [1950s+] the penis.

Uncle Dick *adj.* [rhy. sl.] [1940s+] ill, sick.

Uncle Dick *v.* [rhy. sl. = SE *sick*] [1970s+] to be ill.

Uncle Fred *n.* [rhy. sl.] [1930s+] bread.

Uncle Gus *n.* [rhy. sl.] [1960s] (*Aus.*) a bus.

Uncle Guvvie *n.* [2000s] (*S.Afr.*) the government.

Uncle Joe *n.* [? anecdotal] [1940s] (*W.I.*) a large, dense cake.

Uncle John *n.* **1** [1990s+] (*US campus*) mens' lavatory. **2** [2000s] a penis.

Uncle Lester *n.* [rhy. sl.] [1990s+] a child molester.

Uncle Mac *n.* [rhy. sl. = SMACK *n.*[2] (1)] [1980s+] (*drugs*) heroin.

Uncle Melvin *n. see* MELVIN *n.*

Uncle Merv *v.* [rhy. sl. = PERV *v.*] [1990s+] (*Aus.*) of a man, to ogle, to leer.

Uncle Nabs *n.* [NAB *n.*[2] (1)] [1970s+] (*US black*) the police.

Uncle Ned *n.*[1] [rhy. sl.] **1** [20C+] (*Aus.*) bread. **2** [1910s+] a bed. **3** [1930s+] (*also* **old ned**) the head. **4** [1960s] (*Aus.*) dead.

Uncle Ned *n.*[2] [1900s] (*Aus.*) a black South African.

Uncle Payther *n.* [the characteristics of Uncle *Payther* (Peter Flynn) a character in *The Plough and the Stars* (1926) by Sean O'Casey] [20C+] (*Irish*) a whingeing complainer.

Uncle Sam *n.* (*also* **aunt Sam, Sam, Sammy, Uncle Sambo, Uncle Sammy, Uncle Samuel, Uncle Samwell, Uncle Sugar**) [created during the War of 1812 as the equivalent symbol to UK's John Bull. 'He' is always pictured as a bewhiskered, high-hatted old gentleman, garbed in red, white and blue. The figure is supposed to have been based on a Samuel Wilson, an inspector of provisions based in Troy, NY. The symbol gained further currency during WW1 when he was painted by James Montgomery Flagg as a stern figure pointing a finger at passers-by in a celebrated recruiting poster; note Bartlett, *Dict. Americanisms* 1848: 'Immediately after the last declaration of war with England, Elbert Anderson of New York, then a contractor, visited Troy, on the Hudson; where was concentrated, and where he purchased, a large quantity of provisions, beef, pork, &c. The inspectors of these articles at that place were Messrs. Ebenezer and Samuel Wilson. The latter gentleman (invariably known as '*Uncle Sam*') generally superintended in person a large number of workmen, who, on this occasion, were employed in overhauling the provisions purchased by the contractor for the army. The casks were marked 'E. A.–U. S.' This work fell to the lot of a facetious fellow in the employ of the Messrs. Wilson, who, on being asked by some of his fellow-workmen the meaning of the mark (for the letters U. S. for United

States, were then almost entirely new to them), said, 'he did not know, unless it meant *Elbert Anderson* and *Uncle Sam'*–alluding exclusively, then, to the said *'Uncle Sam' Wilson.* The joke took among the workmen, and passed currently; and *'Uncle Sam'* himself being present, was occasionally rallied by them on the increasing extent of his possessions'] **1** [19C+] a generic term for the USA and American culture; esp. the armed forces or federal agencies of the USA. **2** [1970s+] (*drugs*) a Federal narcotics agent.

(IN COMPOUNDS)

❑ **Uncle Sam's action** *n.* [ACTION *n.* (4)] [1940s] (*US black*) induction into one of the services (after being drafted). ❑ **Uncle Sam's I.O.U.** *n.* [1940s] money, a note. ❑ **Uncle Sam's pets** *n.* [1940s] (*US black campus*) soldiers. ❑ **Uncle Sam's sheep** *n.* [20C+] (*US*) deer that has been illegally shot by poachers.

uncle sam *n.* [rhy. sl.] [20C+] a cut of lamb.

Uncle Samantha *n.* [a camp feminization of UNCLE SAM *n.*] [1950s–60s] (*camp gay*) the United States government.

uncles and aunts *n.* [rhy. sl.] [1920s–40s] pants.

Uncle Sham *n.* [SE *sham*, fake; coined by the US protest movement to ridicule the hollowness at the heart of the so-called 'American dream'] [1960s–70s] (*US black*) a derog. version of UNCLE SAM *n.*

Uncle Sugar *n. see* UNCLE SAM *n.*

Uncle Thomas *n.* [JOHN THOMAS *n.*] [1920s] (*US*) the penis.

uncle three balls *n.* [UNCLE *n.* (1) + the three golden balls that trad. indicate a pawnshop] [late 19C] a pawnbroker.

Uncle Tom *n.* (*also* **Doctor Thomas, Doctor Tom, Dr Thomas, Mr Thomas, Mr Tom, Tom, Uncle George, Uncle Thomas**) [*Uncle Tom*, the hero of Harriet Beecher Stowe's (1811–96) anti-slavery novel *Uncle Tom's Cabin* (1852)] (*orig. US black*) **1** [20C+] a subservient black person, fitting willingly into the stereotyped and inferior image refined by generations of white supremacy; a middle-class black who wishes to distance themsleves from the ghetto; an affected or pretentious black person. **2** [1940s+] a tattle-tale, a person who befriends another, usu. in the workplace, only to deceive them.

(IN PHRASES)

❑ **play the tom** *v.* [late 19C+] (*US black*) to pretend to a fawning stupidity, in order to fool a gullible or self-important white person.

Uncle Tom *adj.* (*also* **Tom, uncle, Uncle Tomish**) [UNCLE TOM *n.*] [20C+] (*orig. US black*) outwardly subservient, in the context of black/white relations; sometimes extended to any relationship between unequals.

Uncle Tom *v.* (*also* **uncle**) [UNCLE TOM *n.* (1)] [1940s+] (*US black*) to act in a subservient, obsequious manner to whites.

Uncle Tomahawk *n.* [play on UNCLE TOM *n.* + SE *tomahawk*, the trad. 'Red Indian' weapon] [1970s+] (*US*) a Native American, who is condemned as insufficiently nationalistic.

Uncle Whiskers *n.* [the facial hair trad. adorning images of UNCLE SAM *n.*] [1920s+] (*US Und.*) a Federal agent or agency.

Uncle Wilf *n.* [rhy. sl. = FILTH *n.* (3), pron. 'filf'] [20C+] the police.

Uncle Willie *adj.* [rhy. sl.] **1** [1920s+] chilly. **2** [1930s+] (*also* **Auntie Willy**) silly.

unco *adj.* [abbr. SE *uncoordinated*] [1990s+] (*Aus. teen*) of a person or object, unco-ordinated.

unconscious *n.* [1920s–30s] **1** a day-dreamer. **2** (*US campus*) a fool.

unconscious *adj.* [1990s+] (*US campus*) performing instinctively (and successfully).

uncool *adj.* [SE pfx *un-* + COOL *adj.*] [1950s+] (*orig. US*) unpleasant, emotional, rude, tactless, unsophisticated, unfair; various negative meanings as to a particular context.

uncunt *v.* (*also* **decunt**) [late 19C] **1** for a man to withdraw the penis from the vagina. **2** for a woman to remove the penis from the vagina.

uncunty *adj.* [SE *un-* + *cunty*, sexy, attractive] [1970s] unattractive, lacking sex appeal.

uncut *adj.* **1** [1930s+] (*usu. drugs*) pure, unadulterated. **2** [1970s+] (*US gay*) uncircumcised.

undeniable *n.* [19C] the vagina.

under *n.* [i.e. the place of the genitals *under* the body] [1930s–50s] sexual intercourse.

(IN PHRASES)

❑ **bit of under** *n.* [BIT *n.*[1]] [1930s–50s] sexual intercourse.

under *adj.* [abbr. *under the influence*] [1930s+] drunk, thus *put under*, to render drunk.

under and over *n.* [late 19C] sexual intercourse.

under-arm *adj.* [? UNDER THE ARM *under* ARM *n.*] [1950s–70s] pornographic.

under-belongings *n.* [19C] the vagina.

underbeneaths *n.* [rhy. sl.] [1920s] (*US*) teeth.

under board *adj. see* ABOVE BOARD *adj.*

undercarriage *n.* [1990s+] the penis.

underchunders *n.* [1990s+] (*Aus.*) underpants.

undercomestumble *v.* (*also* **undercumestumble, understumble**) [play on SE *stumble upon*] [mid-19C] to understand.

undercover *n.*[1] [abbr.] [1930s+] a plain-clothes detective or *undercover* agent.

undercover *n.*[2] [1950s+] (*US black*) sexual intercourse.

undercover man *n.* [play on UNDERCOVER *n.*[1] (1)] [1940s–60s] a male homosexual.

undercrackers *n.* [1990s+] male underwear.

undercumestumble *v. see* UNDERCOMESTUMBLE *v.*

underdaks *n.* [SE *under* + DAKS *n.*] [1940s+] (*Aus.*) male underpants.

underdig *v.* [SE *understand* + DIG *v.*[3]] [2000s] (*US black*) to understand fully.

under-dimple *n.* [19C] the vagina.

underdone *adj.* [cooking imagery] [late 19C–1900s] said of one who has a pale complexion.

underdubber *n.* [DUB *v.*[1] (1)] [early 19C] (*UK prison*) a turnkey.

underdungers *n.* [SE *under* + *dungarees* + play on *dung*] [1980s+] (*N.Z.*) underpants.

under-entrance *n.* [19C] the vagina.

underfugs *n.* [1910s] underpants.

under full sail *adj.* [like a ship, one is heeling from side to side] [1930s] (*US*) drunk.

underground jungle *n.* [1920s] (*US tramp*) a graveyard.

underground mutton *n.* (*also* **underground chicken**) [the animal's habitat and edibility] [1930s+] (*Aus.*) rabbit.

underhung *adj. see* HUNG *adj.* (1a).

underpinners *n.* [mid-19C] (*US*) the legs.

underpinnings *n.* [mid-19C+] the legs.

underput *n.* [SE *put under*; i.e. the position of sexual intercourse] [early 17C] a mistress.

under rations *n.* [ext. of UNDER *n.*; note *GROUND RATIONS under* GROUND *n.*] [1930s–40s] (*US black*) sexual intercourse.

under-rigging *n.* **1** *see* RIGGING *n.*[1] (1). **2** *see* UNDER-WORKS *n.*

undershell *n.* [19C] a waistcoat.

understanding *n.* [1970s] (*US black*) the buttocks.

understandings *n.*[1] [puns] **1** [late 18C–19C] boots or shoes. **2** [early 19C–1920s] the legs.

understandings *n.*[2] [pun + play on SE *understanding*, a relationship + STAND *n.* (2), an erection] [late 19C] of a woman, sexual conquests.

undertaker *n.* [17C use of SE *undertake* as euph./pun for copulate with] [19C] the vagina.

undertaker's job *n.* [SE *undertaker* + JOB *n.*[2]] **1** [1930s+] (*orig. US*) a hopeless proposition; thus 'dead'. **2** [1970s+] (*gambling*) a horse or greyhound which is deliberately – for the sake of the odds – not meant to win, whatever legitimate gamblers may presume.

under the arm *adj. see under* ARM *n.*

under the hatches *adj.* [mid-16C–1910s] in trouble, dead, in jail.

under the table *adj.* **1** [19C+] drunk, one has fallen there; thus *drink under the table*, to outdrink a fellow-drinker [popularized by George Washington 'Chuck' Connors, a New York character known as 'the Bowery philosopher']. **2** [mid-19C+] (*also* **under the bed**) clandestine, secret, corrupt.

IN PHRASES

❑ **put someone under the table** *v.* [1920s+] to make someone insensibly drunk, usu. by outdrinking them.

undertog *n.* [mid–late 18C] a petticoat.

underwear *n.* [1960s+] (*US gay*) an unshaven chin; thus *your underwear is showing*, you need a shave.

SE in slang uses

IN PHRASES

❑ **get one's underwear in a twist** *v. see* GET ONE'S KNICKERS IN A TWIST *under* KNICKERS *n.*

under-works *n.* (*also* **under-rigging**) [early 19C] the male genitalia.

underworld *n.* [late 19C] the vagina.

under wraps *adv.* [20C+] restrainedly.

undies *n.* [abbr. SE *underwear, under-garments*] [20C+] underwear, usu. women's.

undigested Ananias *n.* [the biblical figure *Ananias*, one who, 'with Sapphira his wife, sold a possession and kept back part of the price' (*Acts* v. 1, 2); used allusively for a liar] [late 19C] a triumphant liar.

undress *v.* [1950s+] (*Aus.*) of a sheep, to steal.

undub *v.* [DUB *v.*[1] (1)] [mid-18C–early 19C] (*UK Und.*) to unlock.

IN PHRASES

❑ **undub the qua** *v.* [early 19C] (*US Und.*) to escape from prison.

undue perversity *n.* [joc. reversal] [1980s+] (*US campus*) Purdue University, West Lafayette, Indiana.

uneat *v.* [1980s–90s] (*US campus*) to vomit.

unfair shake *n. see under* SHAKE *n.*[1].

unfledged *adj.* [lit. 'featherless'] [1910s–20s] naked.

unfortunate *n.* [euph. SE *unfortunate woman*] [late 18C–1900s] a prostitute, a 'fallen woman'.

unfuckingbelievable *adj.* (*also* **unfucking real**) [1960s+] an intensified form of SE *unbelievable/unreal*.

unglued *adj.* [1950s+] unstable, emotional, lacking control.

ungodly *adj.* (*also* **ungoddamly**) **1** [late 19C+] appalling, awful, esp. as *ungodly hour*, very late. **2** [1970s] (*US campus*) extremely good.

ungodly *adv.* [UNGODLY *adj.*] [1960s+] (*US*) extremely.

ungood *adj.* (*also* **double plus ungood**) [part of the basic lexicon of Newspeak, the lang. of Orwell's *1984*] [1980s] (*US*) bad.

ungrateful man *n.* [late 18C–early 19C] a parson, 'who at least once a week abuses his best benefactor, i.e. the devil' (Grose 1785).

ungroovy *adj.* [GROOVY *adj.*[2]] [1940s] (*US black*) unsophisticated; unaware.

unguentum aureum *n.* [Lat. 'golden ointment'] **1** [late 16C–early 19C] a bribe. **2** [early 19C] an advance payment.

unhip *adj.* (*also* **unhep, unhipped**) [HIP *adj.* (1)] [1930s+] (*orig. US*) unaware, unsophisticated, ignorant.

unhook *v.* **1** [1950s] released from being arrested, in prison [fig. use of SE]. **2** [1950s–60s] (*drugs*) to stop taking narcotics [HOOKED *adj.*[3]].

uni *n.* [abbr.] **1** [late 19C+] (*orig. Aus.*) university. **2** [1960s] (*US campus*) a uniform.

unicorn *n.* [the image of the *unicorn's* protruding horn] **1** [17C] a cuckold [play on HORN *n.*[1] (1)]. **2** [late 18C–mid-19C] a coach drawn by three horses, two abreast and one in the lead. **3** [late 19C] a woman and two men/two women and a man in league for criminal purposes.

SE in slang uses

IN PHRASES

❑ **go the complete unicorn** *v.* [mid-19C] to make a display of oneself.

uniform *n.* (*also* **uniforms**) [metonymy] **1** [1920s+] a uniformed police officer. **2** [1940s+] (*gay*) a member/members of the armed or uniformed services. **3** [1970s] (*gay*) a gay man who dresses in some form of uniform, e.g. military or police. **4** [1970s] a prison officer.

Union, the *n.* [*Union House*] [late 19C+] the workhouse.

union card *n.* [its use in gaining work] [1970s] (*US campus*) a university degree certificate.

union jack *n.*[1] ['Cut it where you will when it's cooked it's red, white and blue' (Binstead, *Pitcher in Paradise* 1903)] [1900s] Argentine frozen beef.

union jack *n.*[2] [rhy. sl.] [1990s+] the human back.

union wage *n.* [? the primary motivation for their activities] [1970s+] (*US black*) the police.

unit *n.* **1** [1960s+] (*US campus*) a person; a thing. **2** [1970s] the vagina. **3** [1970s+] the penis. **4** [1980s+] (*US campus*) (*also* **female unit**) a girl, a woman.

units *n. see* RENTAL UNITS *n.*

universal staircase *n.* [19C] a prison treadmill.

university of hard knocks *n. see* SCHOOL OF HARD KNOCKS *n.*

university of life *n.* (*also* **university of coffee-houses**) [20C+] the fig. 'college' attended by those who claim personal experience as infinitely superior to academic knowledge.

unk *n.* (*also* **unkie**) [abbr.] [20C+] uncle.

unkey *n. see* UNCLE *n.* (3).

unkie *n.* [abbr. JUNKIE *n.*] [1950s–70s] (*drugs*) morphine.

unkjay *n.* [pig Lat. for JUNKIE *n.*] [1940s–50s] a heroin addict.

unlaid *adj.* [LAY *v.*[1] (1)] [1960s+] of a woman or man, virgin.

unlax *v.* [popularized by the 1930s–40s US radio series *Amos and Andy*] [1920s–30s] (*US*) to relax, unwind.

unload *v.* **1** [mid-18C; late 19C–1930s] to take someone's money or possessions. **2** [mid-19C; 1930s+] to ejaculate. **3** [mid-19C+] to drop, to dispose of, get rid of. **4** [20C+] (*US*) to get off or out of a vehicle. **5** [20C+] to throw a punch, to beat up. **6** [1900s] to offer one's opinion; to give orders. **7** [1910s+] (*US*) to fire one's gun. **8** [1940s] to defecate. **9** [1960s+] (*Aus.*) to vomit.

SE in slang uses

IN PHRASES

❑ **unload pewter** *v.* [mid-19C] to drink from a quart pot.

unloading *n.* [UNLOAD *v.* (2)] [1990s+] masturbation.

unlucky for some *n.* [the number most prone to superstitious interpretation] **1** [1940s+] (*bingo*) the number 13. **2** [1950s+] £13.00.

unmarked *n.* [1950s+] (*US police*) an unmarked police car.

unmentionable *n.* [1950s] a euph. for a variety of negative personal descriptions.

unmentionables *n.* (*also* **don't name 'ems, mustn't-mention'ems, unspeakables, untalkaboutables, unutterables, unwhisperables**) [the supposed 'obscenity' of the garment] **1** [mid-19C–1920s] trousers. **2** [2000s] underwear.

unmonkeyable *adj.* [MONKEY *v.* (1)] [1910s–20s] of a person, impervious to trickery.

unnecessary *adj.* [1930s+] excited, usu. sexually.

unoofy *adj.* [OOF *n.* (1)] [late 19C] impoverished, poor.

unpalled *adj.* [PAL *n.* (1)] [early 19C] (*UK Und.*) of a thief, whose gang has been arrested and is thus forced to work solo.

unparliamentary *adj.* [SE *unparliamentary language*, as laid down in *Erskine May*, which covers all Parliamentary procedure] [mid-19C] obscene.

unpaved *adj.* **1** [early 17C] castrated [one has 'lost one's stones', i.e. STONE *n.*[1] (1)]. **2** [late 19C] aggressively drunk.

unpin one's back hair *v.* **1** [mid-19C+] (*orig. US*) to relax one's inhibitions. **2** [1930s+] to admit to being homosexual.

unreal *adj.* (*also* **not real**) **1** [1960s+] (*Aus./US*) unbelievable, unacceptable, unpleasant, an all-purpose negative that depends for precise meaning on context. **2** [1970s+] (*Aus./N.Z./US campus*) a term of all-encompassing approbation, esp. as used by teenage girls.

unrig *v.* [RIG *v.*[1] (1)] **1** [late 17C–early 19C] (*also* **unbreech**) to strip someone of their clothes, thus *unrigged*, stripped. **2** [late 17C–mid-19C] to get undressed.

unruly member *n. see under* MEMBER *n.*[1].

unscrew *v. see under* SCREW *v.*

unsheik *v.* [brandname *Sheik*, a popular US condom] [1920s] (*US black*) to divorce.

unshingle *v.* [SE *shingle*, a roof tile] [early–mid-19C] (*Aus.*) to knock off someone's hat.

unshop *v. see under* SHOP *n.*[1].

unsliced *adj.* [var. UNCUT *adj.* (2)] [1970s+] (*US gay*) uncircumcised.

unslough *v. see under* SLOUGH *v.*

unslour *v.* [*pfx. un-* + SLOUR (UP) *v.*] [early 19C] (*UK Und.*) to unlock.

unspeakables *n. see* UNMENTIONABLES *n.*

unspit *v.* [late 19C] to vomit.

unswallow *v.* [1930s] to vomit.

unsweetened *n.* [late 19C–1910s] gin.

untalkaboutables *n. see* UNMENTIONABLES *n.*

unthimble *v.* [THIMBLE *n.*] [early 19C] (*UK Und.*) to rob a man of his watch.

untie *v.* [1960s+] (*drugs*) to remove the tourniquet – a belt, a shoelace – used to isolate a vein for injecting narcotics.

until the last dog dies *phr.* (*also* **...last dog is hung, ...eagle screams**) [note UK proverb 'give a dog a bad name and hang him'] [20C+] (*US*) till the very end.

untogether *adj.* [antonym of TOGETHER *adj.*] [1960s+] **1** a general negative, of a person, not in full possession of their faculties; of a situation, less than satisfactorily under control. **2** (*US*) unstylish, lacking social awareness.

untwisted *adj.* [late 17C–18C] ruined, 'undone'.

unutterables/unwhisperables *n. see* UNMENTIONABLES *n.*

unwind *v.* [1910s] (*Aus.*) to cheat, to deceive.

u.p. *adv.* [spelling out of SE *up*] [early 19C–1930s] up, usu. in phr. *it's all u.p. for him.*

up *n.*[1] **1** [mid-18C+] an excited mood, a feeling of stimulation, intoxication. **2** [1940s+] a prospective purchaser in a store [? they pick things *up*].

IN PHRASES

❑ **have the ups** *v.* [abbr. of SE *upper hand*] [1940s] (*US black*) to have an advantage over. ❑ **in two ups** *adv.* [1930s+] (*Aus.*) very quickly.

up *n.*[2] *see* UPPER *n.*[2].

up *adj.* **1** [late 18C] drunk. **2** [1940s+] (*orig. US*) mentally stimulated, excited, hopeful. **3** [1940s+] (*also* **up on**) intoxicated by a drug. **4** [1950s+] (*US black*) of a person, ready, prepared. **5** [1960s+] (*US campus*) sexually aroused. **6** [1970s] intoxicating. **7** [1970s] (*US*) upset; bothered. **8** [1970s+] stimulating, uplifting. **9** [1980s] mentally stimulated in a negative way, stressed. **10** [1990s+] (*US black*) tense, nervous.

IN PHRASES

❑ **up on it** *adj.* [SE *up on*, adept] [1980s+] (*US black*) aware, knowledgeable. ❑ **up on the stickers** *adj.* [1940s] (*US black*) aware, appreciative of what is important.

up *v.* **1** [17C+] to begin, to push oneself forward, to say or do something, usu. in phr. *ups and ...*, e.g. *he ups and starts saying.* **2** fig. senses of to increase. (**a**) [mid-18C–late 19C] of mood or spirits, to raise, to pick up, to lift. (**b**) [1930s+] (*orig. US*) to raise, to increase prices, charges etc. (**c**) [1950s+] (*orig. US*) to improve, to boost; to promote. (**d**) [1960s] (*US black*) to be better, to beat. **3** [late 19C] to have sexual intercourse with [the man puts his penis *up* the vagina]. **4** [1940s] (*US*) to enlist, i.e. join *up*. **5** [1950s] (*US black*) to play music. **6** [1950s+] in terms of contempt or dismissal; usu. as *up yours*. **7** [1960s–70s] (*US*) to hand over, to produce [SE *come up with*]. **8** [2000s] (*UK Und.*) to beat up. **9** [2000s] to mock [to 'put two fingers *up* to].

IN PHRASES

❑ **up and dust** *v.* [DUST *v.*[2] (1)] [20C+] (*US black*) to leave in a hurry, to run away.

up *adv.* **1** [late 19C+] having sexual relations with. **2** [late 19C+] (*orig. UK Und.*) arrested; in prison. **3** [1900s] of an object, offered, put in place.

IN PHRASES

❑ **up above** [1910s] (*Aus.*) in prison. ❑ **have (someone) up** *v.* [1980s+] to bring someone before the courts. ❑ **up each other** *adj.* [1940s+] (*Aus.*) indulging in mutual flattery. ❑ **up her like a rat up a drain(pipe)** (*also* **...a rhododendron**) [1960s+] (*orig. Aus.*) **1** immediately involved in sexual intercourse, based on the assumption that a woman will be freely, easily and speedily sexually available to the speaker. **2** in non-sexual contexts, suggesting speed. ❑ **up in the tooth** *adj. see* OLD IN THE TOOTH *under* OLD *adj.* ❑ **up oneself** *adj.* [image of auto-sodomy] [1940s+] (*orig. Aus.*) arrogant, self-satisfied, full of oneself. ❑ **wouldn't know if someone was up one** [1910s+] (*Aus.*) a phr. used of a very stupid person, usu. a woman, as *she wouldn't know if someone was up her.*

IN EXCLAMATIONS

❑ **up a flume!** [mid-19C] (*US*) a dismissive, insulting excl. ❑ **up you!/your arse!/yours!** *see* separate entries.

up *prep.* **1** [mid-19C] in possession of. **2** [1930s+] at, e.g. *up the market.*

up against *phr.* **1** [late 19C+] (*orig. US*) facing problems, in difficulties; esp. in phr. *up against it.* **2** [1900s] to the responsibility of. **3** [1930s+] (*US prison*) addicted to drugs.

IN PHRASES

❑ **up against one's duckhouse** (*also* **...one's fowlhouse**) [1930s+] (*Aus.*) denoting a setback, a problem; usu. in phr. *that's one up against your duckhouse.* ❑ **up against the eightball** *see* BEHIND THE EIGHT BALL *phr.* ❑ **up against the stem** [STEM *n.*] [1970s+] (*drugs*) addicted to smoking marijuana. ❑ **up against the wall** (*also* **...the bit, ...the gun, ...the push, ...the ropes, ...the wire**) [the putting of prisoners against a wall to face a firing squad] (*orig. milit.*) **1** [1910s+] facing serious problems. **2** [1960s+] (*US campus*) foolish, stupid [reinforced by 1960's radical slogan, *Up against the wall, motherfucker!*].

up-and-down *n.*[1] **1** [early 17C; 1970s] sexual intercourse. **2** [1900s] a housemaid [her running up- and downstairs]. **3** [1970s+] (*US gay*) mutual oral-genital stimulation.

up-and-down *n.*[2] [rhy. sl.] [20C+] brown, usu. brown ale.

up-and-down *n.*[3] [rhy. sl.] [1930s] a town.

up-and-down, the *n.* [the movement of one's eyes] **1** [1910s+] a look, a scrutiny, usu. in phr. *give [...] an/the up-and-down.* **2** [1920s] an official investigation.

up-and-down *adj.* **1** [mid–late 19C] (*also* **up-and-downstairs**) absolute, complete. **2** [mid-19C+] honest, law-abiding, straightforward.

up-and-down *adv.* **1** [mid-19C] (*US*) in a straightforward, open and honest manner. **2** [late 19C+] unrestrainedly, often as *swear up and down.*

up-and-downer *n.* [the fluctuating fortunes of the fighters] [1910s+] a fight, a tussle.

up and under *n.* [rhy. sl.] [1990s+] thunder.

up and under *v.* [rhy. sl. = CHUNDER *v.*] [1950s+] (*Aus.*) to vomit.

up-and-up *n.* [1950s] an aristocrat, an upper-class person.

SE in slang uses

IN PHRASES

❑ **on the up and up** *adj.* **1** [mid-19C+] (*orig. US*) honest, legitimate. **2** [1910s+] (*orig. US*) in an increasingly favourable, lucky, pleasant situation. **3** [1930s–50s] (*US drugs*) taking a narcotics cure. **4** [2000s] (*N.Z.*) recovering one's health after injury or illness.

up and up *adj.* [ON THE UP AND UP *under* UP-AND-UP *n.*] **1** [1900s] (*Aus.*) evenly matched. **2** [1920s+] (*orig. US*) fair, honest, straightforward.

(IN COMPOUNDS)

❑ **up-and-up gee** *n.* [UP AND UP *adj.* (2) + GEE *n.*[3] (1)] [20C+] (*US Und.*) an inmate who has not properly learned prison survival.

up a tree *n.* [rhy. sl.] [1980s+] (*bingo*) the number three.

up a tree *phr.* **1** [1910s+] annoyed, emotionally unstable. **2** [1930s+] drunk.

upbeat *adj.* [orig. jazz use] [1940s+] (*orig. US*) optimistic, positive.

upchuck *v.* [CHUCK *v.*[2] (14)] [1920s+] (*orig. US*) to vomit; thus *upchucking*, the act of vomiting, *upchuck*, vomit.

upcited *adj.* [1960s] Aus. upset.

up-crop *n.* [mid-19C] (*UK Und.*) an insolent upstart.

up-foot *v.* [late 19C] to get to one's feet.

up front *adj.* (*also* **in front, out front, upfront**) **1** [1950s+] (*orig. US*) open, honest. **2** [1970s] in the foreground; foremost.

up front *adv.* (*also* **in front, out front**) [SE/FRONT *v.*[3] (1)] **1** [1950s+] in advance, esp. of money paid for illegal activities, e.g. drug purchases. **2** [1950s+] openly, without deception. **3** [1970s] fig., in the foreground. **4** [1970s+] (*orig. US black*) first, at the start.

upful *adj.* (*also* **uphill**) [SE *hopeful*] [1950s+] (*W.I./Rasta*) positive, encouraging.

uphill gardener *n.* [the ref. is to anal intercourse] [1980s] a male homosexual; thus *uphill gardening*, homosexual anal intercourse.

uphills *n.* [late 17C–early 19C] (*UK Und.*) fixed dice that will always show high numbers.

up in G *phr.* (*also* **up to G**) [? play on the musical note G] **1** [late 19C–1920s] (*US*) very best, superlative. **2** [1900s] with a loud voice.

up in the boughs *adj.* [late 17C+] angry, irritated.

up in the stirrups *adj.* [riding imagery] [early–mid-19C] prospering, doing well.

up in the tea-tree *adj.* (*also* **away in...**) [SE *tea-tree*, the manuka or kanuka tree] [20C+] (*N.Z.*) in the deep countryside; in a very remote area.

upjump *n.* [SE *jumped up*] [1910s] (*Aus.*) an upstart, a nouveau riche, a general term of abuse.

upon my sam! *excl.* [? SALAMON *n.*] [late 19C+] a general excl. of emphasis, thus ext. as *...sacred Sam! ...sainted Sam!*

upon my sivvy! *excl.* (*also* **'pon my...! upon my civey! ... sivey! ...sivy!**) [? SE *asseveration*, keeping one's word. *DSUE* (1984) rejects this, opting for SE *affidavit* or *soul*] [mid-19C–1910s] a mild oath, on my soul!, on my oath!

upon my truly! *excl. see under* TRULY *n.*

upped *adj.* [UP *adv.*] [1930s] raped.

upper *n.*[1] [abbr.] [1940s+] a member of the *upper* classes.

upper *n.*[2] (*also* **up, uppie, ups**) **1** [1960s+] (*drugs*) amphetamine or a similar form of drug, e.g. Methedrine; often in pl. **2** [1960s+] (*US*) a state of optimistic excitement (poss. the result of ingesting amphetamines).

upper *adj.*

SE in slang uses

(IN COMPOUNDS)

❑ **upper apartment** *n.* [19C] the head. ❑ **upper benjamin** *n.* (*also* **upper ben**) [according to Hotten (1873) an acknowledgement of the large number of (? Jewish) tailors called *Benjamin*] **1** [late 18C–late 19C] (*orig. UK Und.*) an overcoat, a greatcoat. **2** [mid-19C] in pl., a pair of trousers. ❑ **upper deck** *n. see separate entry* . ❑ **upper garret** *n. see* UPPER STOREY below. ❑ **upper Holloway** *n.* [HOLLOWAY *n.* (1)] [19C] the vagina. ❑ **upper miserys** *n.* [2000s] (*US black*) the state of feeling physically sick. ❑ **upper shell** *n.* [mid-18C–19C] an overcoat. ❑ **upper stock** *n.* [SE *upper stock*, the upper part of the stockings] [late 18C–early 19C] breeches. ❑ **upper storey** *n.* (*also* **upper extremity, ...garret, ...loft, ...works**) **1** [mid-18C+] the head, the brain, the mental capacity that resides within it; thus *his upper storey/garret is unfurnished*, he is a foolish or 'empty' person, he is 'not all there' (cf. GARRET *n.* (1)). **2** [late 19C+] (*US*) the female breasts. ❑ **upper tog** *n.* (*also* **upper togger**) [SE *upper* + TOGS *n.*] [early–mid-19C] a greatcoat, an overcoat.

(IN PHRASES)

❑ **have one's upper storey unfurnished** *v.* [late 18C] to be a fool.

upper and downer *n.* **1** [late 19C] a form of wrestling match in which the opponents attempt to throw each other, but do not use blows; thus any form of physical fight. **2** [1990s+] an argument.

upper crust *n.* **1** [early–mid-19C] the head, esp. in boxing use. **2** [mid-19C] a hat. **3** [mid-19C+] the social élite, the aristocracy; thus adj. *upper-crusted*, aristocratic. **4** [1950s] any form of élite, e.g. criminal, but with no aristocratic implications.

upper crust *adj.* (*also* **pan-loaf**) [UPPER CRUST *n.* (3)] [mid-19C+] conceited, snobbish; upper class.

upper deck *n.*[1] [rhy. sl.] [1930s–40s] the neck.

upper deck *n.*[2] [1940s+] (*Aus.*) the female breasts.

uppers and beneath *n.* [1920s–40s] (*US Und.*) the teeth.

uppers and downers *n.* (*also* **uppers and unders**) [1910s–60s] the teeth.

upper ten *n.* [abbr. SE *upper ten thousand*, coined by the journalist Nathaniel Parker Willis (1806–67) in a piece entitled 'Necessity for a Promenade Drive' (1848) in which he stated 'At present there is no distinction among the upper ten thousand of the city.'] [mid-19C–1950s] (*orig. US*) **1** the social élite; thus *uppertendom*, the world of the social élite. **2** in fig. use, any superior group.

upper ten *adj.* [UPPER TEN *n.*] [mid–late 19C] socially elite, of or pertaining to the social elite.

(IN COMPOUNDS)

❑ **upper ten push** *n.* [PUSH *n.* (1)] [late 19C] (*Aus. prison*) upper-class prisoners. ❑ **upper ten set** *n.* [late 19C] those servants who work for the 'upper ten thousand'.

uppie *n.*[1] [*U*niversity of *P*ort *E*lizabeth] [1970s+] (*S.Afr.*) a student of the University of Port Elizabeth.

uppie *n.*[2] *see* UPPER *n.*[2].

uppish *adj.* **1** [late 17C–mid-19C] well-off, provided with sufficient money. **2** [late 17C+] proud, arrogant [Johnson terms this a 'low word', thus its inclusion here, but *OED* lists as SE]. **3** [early 18C] tipsy. **4** [late 19C–early 19C] irritable, easily offended.

uppities *n.* [UPPITY *adj.* (1)] [late 19C–1950s] (*US*) social climbers.

uppity *n.* [1940s+] arrogance, nerve, gall.

uppity *adj.* (*also* **uppity-ass**) [SE *up*] **1** [late 19C+] (*orig. US*) cheeky, arrogant, one who refuses to 'know their place', esp. in phr. *uppity nigger*, a black person who refuses to accept his or her second-class status. **2** [1910s+] (*also* **uppity-up, upty-up**) snobbish, elitist. **3** [1980s] promiscuous in a fig. sense, generalized, merchandised.

upright *n.* **1** [late 18C–mid-19C] a pint or quart measure of liquor, thus a pot of that size. **2** [late 18C+] (*also* **uprighter**) sexual intercourse performed while standing up. **3** [early 19C] a cheap bed, rented out for 3d or 4d.

(IN COMPOUNDS)

❑ **upright grand** *n.* [pun on SE *upright grand* piano] [1920s+] (*Aus.*) sexual intercourse while standing up.

upright grin *n.* (*also* **upright wink**) [physiognomy] [late 19C] the vagina.

(IN PHRASES)

❑ **flash the upright grin** *v.* [mid-19C–1920s] to expose one's vagina.

upright man *n.* (*also* **upright cove**) [his stance. He adopted no form of counterfeit physical deformity, as did many of his peers, in his pose as a solid citizen. As such he both gulled the public and commanded loyalty and financial dues from lesser thieves] [mid-16C–early 19C] (*UK Und.*) a senior criminal beggar, outranked, if at all, only by the RUFFLER *n.*. Such a villain held absolute power, demanding and receiving both cash and kind, including their women, from his inferiors and beating them without fear of revenge.

uprights *n.* [late 19C–1940s] (*US black*) the legs.

upright sneak *n.* [SE *upright* + SNEAK *n.*[1] (1)] [late 18C–early 19C] (*UK Und.*) one who steals pewter pots from the boys employed by taverns to collect them.

IN PHRASES

❑ **go on the upright** *v.* [early 19C] to steal pewter pots.

uproar *n.* [a heavy pun] [mid-18C–mid-19C] an opera.

SE in slang uses

IN PHRASES

❑ **get one's ass in an uproar** *v.* (*also* **get it in an uproar**) [1950s+] to get excited, to become emotionally overwrought. ❑ **get one's bowels in an uproar** *v.* (*also* **...pants..., ... balls...**) [20C+] to become excited or agitated.

ups *n. see* UPPER *n.*[2] (1).

upsadaisy *adv.* [20C+] head-over-heels, upside down [SE *upside down*].

upsadaisy! *excl.* (*also* **oops-a-daisy! upsidaisy! upsydaisy!**) [mid-19C+] a soothing excl. offered to a fallen child as one picks them up; a cry for anything about to rise up, e.g., a plane [? the image of plucking a daisy from a lawn].

up-say *n.* [1960s] (*S.Afr.*) self-importance.

upsee *adj.* (*also* **upsey, upsie**) [Du. *op zijn*, on his. A second ety. suggests Du. *op zee*, overseas or imported, and thus refers to the drink itself, whether English, Dutch or whatever, rather than the manner of drinking; Nares (1822) sees this as 'near to another English phrase for drunkenness, being *half-seas over*'; note Ebsworth (*Roxburghe Ballads*, 1876): 'Like "Wassael" and "Trinkael" the phrase upsie-friese, or vrijster, seems to have been used as a toast, perhaps for "To your sweetheart."'] [late 16C–17C] in the manner/style of, esp. as applied to drinking habits; thus *upsee-Dutch*, in the Dutch manner; *upsee-English*, in the English manner; *upsee-Freeze* either, in the Friesian manner or, strong drink; to drink; *upsee-freeze cross*, to drink with arms intertwined.

upset *v.*

SE in slang uses

IN PHRASES

❑ **upset Mrs Jones** *v. see* MRS JONES *under* MRS *n.* ❑ **upset the lobster cart** *v.* [early 19C] (*mainly US*) to knock a person down. ❑ **upset the shopping cart** *v.* [1980s–90s] (*US campus*) to vomit.

upshot *n.* [dial. *upshot*, a feast, a celebration] [early 19C] a riotous frolic.

upside *adj.* [1960s+] (*US black*) next to, up against; thus *upside one's head*, of a blow, against the head.

up South *n.* [the implication is that racism and prejudice is just as widespread as it is 'down South'] [1950s–60s] (*US black*) the Northern states.

upstage *adj.* (*also* **upstageish**) [theatre jargon] [1900s–30s] (*US*) conceited, snobbish.

upstage *v.* [theatrical jargon] [late 19C+] (*US*) to outwit, to win or be superior to another person.

upstairs *n.* **1** [late 19C] the best brands of spirits [kept on a special high shelf in the public house]. **2** [1910s+] (*US*) heaven. **3** [1930s] (*US prison*) the gallows. **4** [1930s–40s] (*US Und.*) an inside breast pocket. **5** [1930s+] (*US*) the mind, esp. as regards its intelligence. **6** [1950s+] a higher authority, a senior position. **7** [1970s] a lavatory. **8** [2000s] (*UK Und.*) the Crown Court.

IN PHRASES

❑ **go upstairs out of the world** *v.* [? the steps to mount the gallows] [late 17C–early 18C] to be hanged.

upstairs *adj.*[1] [1920s+] in the mind, intellectually.

upstairs *adj.*[2] [1950s] (*US black*) superior.

upstairs *adv.* [1990s+] into a senior position.

upstate *n.* [the main New York state prisons are upstate] [1930s+] (*New York Und.*) prison.

SE in slang uses

IN PHRASES

❑ **go upstate** *v.* [euph.] [2000s] (*US Und.*) to die by assassination.

upstate *adj.* [SE *upscale*] [1950s] (*US black*) socially or economically superior.

upstocks *n.* [mid-19C] (*UK Und.*) plenty of money.

upstooled *adj.* [mid-19C] (*UK Und.*) defeated; discovered.

upta *adj.* (*also* **upter, up to shit**) [f. *up to putty*, as worthless as putty] [20C+] (*Aus.*) useless, no use whatsoever.

up the pole *adj.*[1] [note late 19C US milit. *up the pole*, sober, 'military' and within regulation; the *pole* was the flagpole bearing the nation's emblem] **1** [late 19C–1900s] (*US*) teetotal. **2** [late 19C–1920s] drunk, thus *half up the pole*, tipsy. **3** [late 19C+] wrong, in error, in trouble, facing difficulties. **4** [late 19C+] insane, eccentric. **5** [1910s] bankrupt.

IN PHRASES

❑ **get up the pole** *v.* [late 19C–1900s] to be approaching drunkenness.

up the pole *adj.*[2] (*also* **up the chute**) [20C+] pregnant.

up there Cazaly! *excl.* [Australian rules football player Roy *Cazaly* (1893–1963), star of the South Melbourne team and noted for his leaps into the air for a 'mark'] [1940s+] (*Aus.*) a cry of encouragement.

up the way *adj.* [f. *in the family way*] [1930s+] (*Aus.*) pregnant.

uptight *adj.*[1] **1** [1930s+] in difficulties. **2** [1940s+] (*US black*) trapped, in a position from which there is no escape. **3** [1960s–70s] addicted.

uptight *adj.*[2] (*also* **tight**) [SE *tight*, tense] **1** [1930s+] tense, nervous, annoyed. **2** [1960s+] formal, unbending, strait-laced. **3** [1960s+] under emotional control.

uptight *adj.*[3] [SE *tight*, faithful] **1** [1950s+] close, friendly. **2** [1960s] (*US campus*) very attractive. **3** [1960s+] satisfactory, good. **4** [1960s+] having sexual intercourse.

uptight *adj.*[4] (*also* **up tight**) [f. *tight*, impoverished] [1960s–70s] out of money, impoverished.

up to *adv.* (*also* **up**) [20C+ use is SE] [late 18C+] aware of, knowledgeable about.

up to G *phr. see* UP IN G *phr.* (1).

up to here *phr.* [HAVE HAD IT UP TO HERE *under* HAVE HAD IT *v.*] **1** [late 19C+] bored, disgusted, utterly intolerant of an event, someone's statements, actions etc. **2** [1900s] full, usu. of food and/or drink.

up to no good *phr.* [1980s+] having sexual intercourse with someone.

up top *n.* [1950s+] (*Aus.*) northern Australia; thus *uptoppers*, those who live there.

up to shit *adj. see* UPTA *adj.*

up to the nines *phr.* (*also* **to the nines**) [ety. unknown; ? the numerologistic attribution of nine as a mystic number or (according to Ware) a corruption of an older phr. *up to the eyen*, up to the eyes, i.e. the satisfaction of the eyes] **1** [late 18C+] to the highest degree, to perfection; usu. as DRESSED (UP) TO THE NINES *phr.* **2** [mid-19C] aware, alert, knowledgeable.

uptown *n.* [UPTOWN *adj.* (1)] **1** [1950s+] (*W.I./Rasta*) the upper classes. **2** [1970s] (*US drugs*) cocaine, always considered the drug of the more affluent.

uptown *adj.* [SE *uptown*, the residential area of a US city] [1920s+] (*US*) sophisticated, worldly, rich.

IN PHRASES

❑ **go uptown (on)** *v.* [1960s] (*US*) to act in a snobbish manner (towards).

uptown *v.* [1920s] (*US Und.*) to act or treat in an arrogant manner.

uptucker *n.* [TUCK *v.*[1]] **1** [mid-19C] the hangman. **2** [1930s] (*US prison*) the noose.

upty-up *adj. see* UPPITY *adj.* (2).

upways *n.* [SE *upways*, in an upward direction] [1970s+] (*US black*) a snobbish, stand-offish person.

upya! *excl.* [UP YOU! *excl.*] [1940s+] (*Aus.*) a dismissive, contemptuous excl., lit. *up you!*

up you! *excl.* [*euph. of* FUCK YOU! *excl.*, esp. when accompanied by the (orig. US) raised middle-finger gesture] [late 19C+] a dismissive, contemptuous excl.

IN EXCLAMATIONS

❑ **up you for the rent!** [1940s+] (*Aus.*) a dismissive, contemptuous excl.

up your arse! *excl.* (*also* **up your ass! ...back! ...bum! ... buns! ...butt! ...date! ...dinger! ...hole!**) [a preceding 'stick it ...' is taken as read] [1920s+] a dismissive, insulting excl.

IN PHRASES

❑ **up your bum to the neck** *adj.* [2000s] (*N.Z.*) self-important.

up your jumper! *excl.* (*also* **...gumboots! ...jersey!**) [1920s+] (*Aus.*) a euph. synon. of UP YOUR ARSE! *excl.*

up yours! *excl.* (*also* **up yours with a lawnmower! ...for the rent!**) [euph. abbr. of UP YOUR ARSE! *excl.*] [1930s+] (*orig. US*) an excl. of contempt.

urban surfing *n.* [1970s+] riding on the outside of moving vehicles.

urger *n.* **1** [1910s+] (*Aus.*) a man who obtains money illegally or dishonourably, esp. as a tipster at a racecourse. **2** [1920s–60s] a sponger or idler.

uriah heep *n.* [rhy. sl. = CREEP *n.* (3); ult. *Uriah Heep*, a villain in Dickens' *David Copperfield* (1849–50)] [20C+] an unpleasant person.

urinal *n.* [1960s] (*US*) a penis.

urinal of the planets *n.* [a literary usage that reflects the country's high rainfall] [late 17C–early 19C] Ireland.

u.s. *adj.* (*also* **u/s**) [abbr. SE *unserviceable*] [1940s+] (*orig. RAF*) useless.

u.s.a. *n.* [*u*nder *s*kirt *a*rea] [1990s+] (*UK juv.*) a girl's upper thighs and genital area.

use *v.*[1] (*also* **use up**) [abbr. of SE *abuse*] **1** [mid-19C; 1970s+] (*US*) to criticize or abuse [20C+ use is US campus]. **2** [1910s] (*US prison*) to submit someone to anal intercourse.

use *v.*[2] **1** [1910s+] to need, to desire, 'do with', e.g. *I could use a decent meal.* **2** [1920s+] (*drugs*) to take narcotic drugs, esp. heroin. **3** [1940s] to consume a drink.

SE in slang uses

IN PHRASES

❑ **use one's...** *v. see also under* relevant n. ❑ **use one's head** *v.* [1930s+] to think, to act intelligently, to work things out.

use at *v.* [late 19C] to frequent, to visit.

used-beer department *n.* [1920s+] (*Aus./Can.*) the lavatory in a bar.

used food tube *n.* [1980s] (*Aus.*) the anus.

used fruit chute *n.* [1990s+] (*Aus.*) the anus, esp. in homosexual context.

used-to-be *n.* [1920s–60s] (*US black*) an ex-lover.

used up *adj.* [a message sent by Gen. John Guise during his attack on Cartagena during the war with Spain *c.*1740 when he requested that he be sent more grenadiers because of the 1200 he already had, 50% were killed or wounded, in other words 'used up'] **1** [mid-18C–mid-19C] dead, killed in battle; murdered. **2** [mid-19C] beaten up. **3** [mid-19C] bankrupt. **4** [mid-19C] broken-hearted. **5** [mid-19C+] exhausted, whether of a person, a vehicle, a place.

useful *n.* [SE *general/generally useful*] [mid-19C+] (*Aus.*) a general helper, esp. in a public house.

useful *adj.* [2000s] sexually attractive.

useless as... *adj.*

SE in slang uses

IN PHRASES

❑ **...a one-legged man in an ass-kicking contest** [1960s+] (*US*) absolutely worthless. ❑ **...a pork chop at a Jewish wedding** (*also* **...slice of bacon at a Jewish wedding**) *see under* PORK CHOP AT A JEWISH WEDDING *phr.* ❑ **...a spare prick at a lesbian wedding** [1960s+] totally useless.

user *n.* [USE *v.*[2] (2)] [1920s+] a drug addict.

u.s.g. *n.* [abbr. *U*nited *S*tates *g*hettos] [1990s+] (*US black*) the American black community, i.e. the status of blacks, governmental statements of equal rights notwithstanding, as regards the larger US world.

usher! *excl.* [? Yid. *user*, it is so] [late 19C–1920s] yes!

usher of the back door *n. see* GENTLEMAN OF THE BACK DOOR *under* GENTLEMAN OF... *n.*

usher of the hall *n.* [late 19C] (*UK society*) the odd-job man in a great house.

usual, the *n.* **1** [mid-19C+] one's habitual choice of drink or beverage. **2** [1990s+] sexual intercourse.

U.T.B.N.B. *phr.* [*U*p *T*he *B*um, *N*o *B*abies] [1990s+] anal intercourse as a means of contraception.

ute *n.* [abbr.] [1940s+] (*Aus./N.Z.*) a *ut*ility vehicle, a small truck.

utopiate *n.* [pun on SE *opiates* + *Utopia*] [1970s] (*US drugs*) a hallucinogen.

utsnay *n.* [pig Lat. for NUTS *n.*[2] (1)] [1970s] (*US*) the testicles.

utzpay *n.* [Pig Lat.: PUTZ *n.* (2)] [1930s] a fool, an idiot.

UVs *n.* [abbr. *u*ltra-*v*iolet rays] [1960s+] (*US teen*) sunshine; thus *soak up UVs*, to get a tan.

uxter *n.* [dial. *uxter/oxter*, an armpit or armhole of a jacket, thus the wallet that is carried in an inside pocket; note dial. *come with a crooked oxter*, to bring a present, to come with a good dowry] [late 19C] money.

u.y.b. *n.* [UPPITY *adj.* (1)] [1980s] (*US campus*) uppity yankee bitch.

V *n.*[1] [Lat. numeral *V*, five] **1** [mid-19C–1960s] (*also* **V-spot**) (*US*) a five-dollar bill. **2** [1930s–60s] (*US prison*) a five-year jail sentence.

V *n.*[2] [1930s–40s] (*US Und.*) a bank vault.

V *n.*[3] [1950s–80s] (*UK black*) the crotch; the genitals.

V *n.*[4] [VINE *n.*[1] (1)] [1960s] (*US Und.*) a suit.

V *n.*[5] [1970s] (*US black/campus*) television.

V *n.*[6] [abbr.] [1970s] (*US*) volume, e.g. on a stereo.

V *n.*[7] [abbr.] [1980s+] (*drugs*) the mild tranquillizer Valium.

V *n.*[8] [abbr. SE *V-sign*] [2000s] a V-sign, the waving of the index and second finger as a sign of contempt, meaning 'fuck off'.

IN PHRASES

❑ **give someone the V** *v.* (*also* **give something the V**) [2000s] to the make obscene gesture known as 'V-sign'.

v *v.* [SE *veto*] [1990s+] (*US campus*) to reject.

v *adv.* [abbr.] [late 19C+] very.

Vaalie *n.* (*also* **Vaaljapie**) [*Transvaal* + JAAP *n.*] [1970s+] (*S.Afr.*) a native of the Transvaal, generally looked down upon by the citizens of Cape Town, esp. when they appear there on holiday.

vacant lot *n.* [1980s] (*US campus*) a person who is not in touch with reality.

vacation *n.* **1** [late 19C] the period a criminal spends out of prison. **2** [1920s+] (*US*) time spent in prison.

vacuum *n.* [both 'suck'] **1** [19C] the vagina. **2** [1980s+] (*US campus*) a hearty eater.

vacuum cleaner *n.* [it helps one 'pick up bits of fluff'] [1940s–50s] a sports car.

vacuum cleaners *n.* [1940s] (*US black*) the human lungs.

vada *v. see* VARDA *v.*

vade-mecum *n.* [Lat. *vade mecum*, lit. 'come with me', fig. 'a useful thing'] [19C] the vagina.

vag *n.*[1] [abbr.] [mid-19C+] (*Aus./N.Z./US*) **1** a vagrant. **2** a charge of vagrancy; thus *vag-lewd*, vagrancy and lewd behaviour.

IN PHRASES

❑ **on the vag** [mid-19C+] (*Aus./N.Z.*) living as a tramp, homeless.

vag *n.*[2] (*also* **vadge**) [1980s+] **1** the vagina. **2** thus, a general term of abuse.

vag *v.* [VAG *n.*[1]] [mid-19C+] (*Aus./US*) to charge and/or arrest someone for vagrancy.

vagabond *n.* (*also* **vagabone, vargybin', vargybun', wagabone**) **1** [mid-19C–1920s] a lazy but inoffensive young man. **2** [20C+] (*W.I.*) a lecherous old man.

vaggerie *v.* [Ital. *viaggiare*, to travel] [mid-19C+] (*Ling. Fr./Polari*) to go, to leave.

vagina little-finger *n.* [*vagina* puns on Virginia, seen as a typical upper-class name. *Little-finger* refers to the affected crooking of the little finger when drinking] [1960s–70s] (*camp gay*) a snob.

vagitarian *n.* [play on *vagina/vegetarian* although she too will EAT *v.* someone's MEAT *n.* (3)] [1990s+] (*US gay*) a lesbian.

vague *v.* [coined in late 1990s US TV show *Buffy the Vampire Slayer*] [1990s+] to be more precise.

Val *n.* [1980s+] (*US*) **1** a *Val*ley Girl. **2** San Fernando *Val*ley, California.

val *n.* [abbr.] [2000s] value.

valentine *n.* [ironic uses of SE] [1920s–40s] **1** (*US prison*) a short sentence, max. one year. **2** (*US police*) a reprimand, a punishment.

Valentine Dyalls *n.* [rhy. sl.; ult. UK movie actor Valentine Dyall (1908–85)] [1990s+] piles.

valentino *v.* [film star *Rudolph Valentino* 1895–1926] [1960s] to make love.

Vallie *n.* (*also* **vally, vals**) [abbr.] [1990s+] *Val*ium, a mild tranquillizer.

vamoose *v.* (*also* **vam, vamoose the ranch, vamos, vamose**) [Sp. *vamos*!, let's go!] [mid-19C+] (*orig. US*) to go away, leave; esp. as imper. *vamoose!*, go away! be off!; thus *vamoosed*, missing, lost.

vamoosing *n.* [VAMOOSE *v.*] [mid-19C] flight.

vamp *n.*[1] [SE *vamp*, that part of the stocking that covers the ankle and foot] [late 17C–mid-19C] an old stocking that has had the foot repaired.

vamp *n.*[2] [VAMP *v.*[1] (1)] **1** [mid–late 19C] a robbery. **2** [1900s] a robber.

vamp *v.*[1] [SE *vamp*, to repair, to patch up; 20C+ is US black] **1** [mid-17C–19C; 1990s+] to pawn, to steal. **2** [1990s+] to beg (from).

vamp *v.*[2] **1** [20C+] (*US*) to vanish, to disappear; to travel. **2** [1920s+] to play the seductress. **3** [1950s] to walk.

vamper *n.* (*also* **vampire**) [SE *vamp*, to improvise + VAMP *v.*[1] (1)] [mid-19C–1920s] a thief, esp. one who deliberately starts fights between others in order to rob them in the confusion.

vampers *n.* [SE *vamp*] [late 17C–18C] (*UK Und.*) stockings.

vampire's teabag *n.* (*also* **vampire-bag**) [coarse use of SE] [1990s+] (*US black*) a sanitary napkin.

vamp on *v.* [? SE *vampire*] [1970s+] (*US black*) **1** to make an unjust attack, to arrest. **2** when aimed at the oppressor, to correct; to force him to mend his ways [esp. popular with 1960s–70s radicals].

Van *n. see* VAN DER MERWE *n.*

vancouver *n.* [rhy. sl.] [1990s+] a vacuum cleaner, a hoover.

vandemonianism *n.* [the one-time prison colony of Van Dieman's Land or Tasmania + ref. to SE *pandemonium*] [mid–late 19C] (*Aus.*) rowdyism, riotousness, thus adj. *vandemonian*, rowdy.

Vanderbilt *n.* [New York's multi-millionaire *Vanderbilt* family] [late 19C] (*US*) a very rich man.

Van der Merwe *n.* (*also* **Van**) [the common Afrikaner surname] [1960s+] (*S.Afr.*) the generic, stereotypical Afrikaner, the subject of a wide range of 'Van der Merwe' jokes characterizing him as loutish, bigoted and stupid; thus the *real Van der Merwe*, synon. with REAL MCCOY, THE *n.* (1); *meet one's Van der Merwe*, meet one's Waterloo.

van dragger *n.* [20C+] a thief who specializes in stealing goods from the back of vans and carts; thus *van-dragging*.

V and V *n.* [abbr.] [1970s] (*US*) a combination of Valium and Vermouth.

V and X (store) *n.* [Lat. *V*, five + *X*, ten, i.e. a 'five and ten cent' store] [1940s] (*US black*) a corner store.

van dyke *n.* [1960s+] (*US gay*) **1** a lesbian with a trace of a moustache on her upper lip [pun on DYKE *n.* (1) + portraitist Anthony *Van Dyke* (1599–1641) who was thus bearded]. **2** a lesbian truck driver [puns on SE *van*, a truck + proper name Anthony *Van Dyke*].

vanilla *n.* [for ety. *see* VANILLA *adj.*] **1** [1930s+] (*US black*) (*also* **vanilla malt**) a white person, esp. a female. **2** [1980s+] (*US*) a heterosexual who practises normal sexual behaviour. **3** [1980s+] (*US gay*) non-penetrative sex: cuddling and mutual masturbation.

vanilla *adj.* (*also* **plain vanilla**) [the plainest ice-cream flavour. The term was popularized in the 1980s+ but ? coined by the saxophonist Lester Young (1909–59) *c.*1935] [1970s+] plain, simple; bereft of authenticity.

IN COMPOUNDS

❑ **vanilla dinge** *n.* [DINGE *n.*] [1960s] (*US*) a coloured man who prefers white women. ❑ **vanilla queen** *n.* [-QUEEN *sfx* (3)] **1** [1980s+] (*US black*) a gay black male who prefers white partners. **2** [2000s] a gay man who practises 'tame', non-experimental sex. ❑ **vanilla sex** *n.* [1990s+] (*gay*) a phr. for relatively conventional forms of sexual activity, usu. in contrast to sado-masochistic sex.

vanilla fudge *n.* [rhy. sl.] [1980s] (*Aus.*) a judge.

vanilla ripple *n. see* RASPBERRY (RIPPLE) *n.* (2).

vanity *n.* [SE *vanity*, a thing of which one is vain] [late 19C] one's favourite liquor.

vanity fair *n.* [rhy. sl.] [20C+] a chair.

van John *n.* [Fr. *vingt-et-un*, (the game of) 21] [mid-19C] in cards, the game of pontoon or 21.

vank *v.* [? SE *vanquish*] **1** [1990s+] (*W.I.*) to dismiss someone. **2** [1990s+] (*W.I.*) to die.

vanny *n.* [2000s] a van-driver.

vantage loaf *n.* [SE *vantage*, an advantage, in this case to the buyer; note synon. 17C SE *vantage of bread*] [19C] the 13th loaf in a 'baker's dozen'.

vap *n.* [? Fr. *vapeur*, dizziness, light-headedness + obs. SE *the vapours*] [20C+] (*W.I./UK black*) **1** a bad mood. **2** an impulse.

IN PHRASES

❑ **catch a vap** *v.* (*also* **...vapse**) [20C+] (*W.I.*) to be suddenly inspired to do something, to do something on the spur of the moment.

vapors *n.*[1] [1980s+] (*US drugs*) the smoke issuing from a crack pipe.

vapors *n.*[2] [? obs. SE *vapours*, a fantasy, a foolish boast] [1990s+] (*US black*) **1** a newly realized desire for an individual who, once shunned, has now gained status/material possessions and is thus suddenly alluring. **2** jealousy.

varda *v.* (*also* **vada, varder, vardi, vardo, vardy, verda**) [Venetian *vardia*, a look; however note Polari etymologist WS Wilcox in a letter 25/11/99: 'Partridge and others derive the word *varder* from Italian *vedere*, but *guardare* (look, regard) fits the form better. *Guarda*, *guardare* tend to sound *warda*, *wardare* (and indeed are pronounced so in some Italian dialects) and given the well-attested wavering between *v*- and *w*- in 19th Century English the progression to *varder* is predictable, (no doubt reinforced by *vedere*)'] [mid-19C+] (*Ling. Fr./Polari*) to look at; thus *varda d'amour*, a loving look; esp. in imper., e.g. *varda the riah!* look at that hair!; *bona vardering*, good-looking.

IN PHRASES

❑ **have a varda** *v.* [1960s] to have a look.

vardo *n.* [Rom. *vardo*; *wardo*, a cart] [early 19C+] a gypsy wagon; thus *vardo-gill*, a waggoner.

vardy *n.* [SE *verdit*, obs. form of *verdict*] [late 18C–mid-19C] an opinion, a viewpoint.

varicose-vein flat *n.* [the cracked plaster is reminiscent of varicose veins] [1990s+] a flat in poor maintenance.

vark *n.* [Afk. *vark*, pig, thus PIG *n.* (2a)] [1950s+] (*S.Afr.*) a general term of abuse, esp. of a police officer.

varment *n.* (*also* **varmint**) [? *DSUE* (1984) suggests dial. *varment/vermin*, any animal destructive of game, but *OED* disputes this, rejecting any such link] [late 18C–early 19C] an amateur sportsman who has the skill of a professional.

varmint *adj.* (*also* **varment**) [VARMENT *n.*] **1** [19C] shrewd, knowing, 'au fait'. **2** [early–mid-19C] fashionable, 'swell', dashing.

varnish *n.* **1** [late 19C] (*UK society*) second-rate champagne. **2** [1900s] (*UK society*) a second-rate person, an inadequate. **3** [1900s] sauce offered with food sold from a coffee-stall. **4** [1920s] (*US Und.*) bootleg liquor, esp. 'rye' whisky.

varnisher *n.* [mid-19C] a counterfeiter of fake sovereigns.

varnish remover *n.* [1940s+] (*US*) cheap, inferior whisky.

varnish the cane *v. see under* CANE *n.*[1].

varoom *v. see* VROOM *v.*

vasbyt *v.* [Afk. *vasbyt*, to bite hard, to seize with the jaws] [1960s+] (*S.Afr.*) (orig. milit. use.) to keep going, to 'tough it out', 'bite the bullet'.

Vaseline *n.* [1910s; 1970s] (*Aus./US*) butter or margarine.

brandname in slang uses

IN COMPOUNDS

❑ **Vaseline brown** *n. see* HIGH BROWN *n.* ❑ **vaseline valley** *n.* [the use of Vaseline to ease anal intercourse + ? pun on California's Silicon Valley] **1** [1940s] (*US gay*) used of the gay cruising aea of Central Park in NYC. **2** [1980s+] (*Aus.*) a stretch of Oxford Street, Sydney acknowledged as the city's gay centre. ❑ **vaseline villa** *n.* (*also* **vaseline alley**) [*see* prev.] [1960s+] (*US gay*) a YMCA frequented by gay men; and thus any such rendezvous.

v.a.t. *n.* [abbr. from the TV series *Minder* (1979–81); a pun on *Value Added Tax*] [1980s+] vodka and tonic.

vat en sit *n.* [Afk. *vat en sit*, stay put, lit. take and sit] [1950s+] (*S.Afr. township*) a 'live-in lover', a common-law partner, an unsolemnnized marriage, also as adj.

vat hom Fluffie! *excl.* [Afk. lit. 'go get him Fluffie'; no record exists of the original Fluffie (a dog, presumably)] [1970s+] (*S.Afr.*) an exhortation, esp. in the context of sports events or business meetings when the subject(s) of the cry has to pull something special out of the hat.

vatican roulette *n.* [the only form permitted by the Catholic Church] [1960s+] the notoriously undependable rhythm method of contraception.

vato *n.* [1970s+] **1** a member of a Mexican teen gang; thus *vato loco*, a gang member with a reputation for extra violence, poise, courage and other attributes of street life. **2** in Chicano use, a man, irrespective of race.

vato loco *n. see* BATO LOCO *n.*

vatterig *adj.* [Du. *vatten*, to take, to catch] [1970s+] (*S.Afr.*) used of one who has 'wandering' hands.

vaughn *n.* [VONCE *n.* (1)?] [1950s–60s] (*US black*) a marijuana cigarette.

vault *v.* [SE *vault*, to jump, leap] [late 16C–17C] to have sexual intercourse.

vaulter *n.* (*also* **vawter**) [VAULT *v.*] [late 16C–17C] a prostitute.

vaulting house *n.* (*also* **vaulting school**) [VAULT *v.* (1) + HOUSE *n.*[1] (1)] [late 16C–early 19C] a brothel.

vawter *n. see* VAULTER *n.*

vaykay *n.* [1970s] (*US*) a holiday, a vacation.

vay-ki-vay *adj.* [Fr. *vaille que vaille*, come what may, any old how] [20C+] (*W.I.*) unplanned, haphazard.

vay-ki-vay *adv.* [VAY-KI-VAY *adj.*] [20C+] (*W.I.*) carelessly, shabbily.

vazey *adj.* [mid-19C] (*UK Und.*) stupid.

v.b.c. *phr.* [abbr. *v*isible *b*utt *c*rack] [1980s+] (*US campus*) having the outline of one's buttocks showing through tight trousers; or revealing the top of one's buttocks due to wearing one's trousers lower than the waist.

v.b.d. *n.* [abbr. *v*ery *b*ad *d*ate] [1960s] (*US black*) an unsatisfactory evening with a member of the opposite sex.

v.c. *adj.* [abbr. *Victoria Cross*] [late 19C] plucky, courageous.

veal *n.*[1] [1920s] (*US*) a young woman who flirts maliciously.

veal *n.*[2] *see* CALF *n.*[1] (1).

veal will be cheap – calves fall! *excl.* [late 17C–late 19C] a mocking cry aimed at one who has very thin legs.

vee-dub *n.*[1] [abbr. for *vee-double-you*] [1970s+] (*Aus.*) a Volkswagen.

vee-dub *n.*[2] [the shaved genital area supposedly resembles the bonnet of a Volkswagen VW] [1990s+] (*US teen*) the shaved female genitals.

vee-in *n.* [? VAMP ON *v.*/SE *violence*] [1980s+] (*US black gang*) an initiation ritual whereby the new member is beaten by other gang members for an allotted time, e.g. one minute.

veejay *n. see* V.J. *n.*

veeno *n. see* VINO *n.*

veep *n.* [pron. of initial letters] [1940s+] (*US*) a vice-president.

vees *n.* [1930s+] (*N.Z.*) minimal male swimming trunks, little more than a thong.

vee-wee *n.* [pron. of initial letters] [1960s+] a Volkswagen car.

veg *n.* (*also* **veges, veggies**) [abbr.] **1** [late 19C+] vegetables. **2** [1980s+] in fig. use, a moron, a madman.

IN PHRASES

❑ **go for veg** *v.* [i.e. to enter a *vegetative* state] [1970s] (*US campus*) to become drunk.

veg *v.* (*also* **veg out**) [abbr. SE *vegetate*] [1960s+] to do nothing, to lapse into a totally apathetic and passive state.

vega *n.* [the cigar brand Garcia y *Vega*, the West Coast version of Phillies Blunts] [1990s+] (*US black teen*) a marijuana cigarette rolled inside the outer leaves of a cigar.

Vegemite *n.*

IN PHRASES

❑ **drill for Vegemite** *v. see under* DRILL *v.*[1].

Vegemite Valley *n.* [the Aus. brown yeast spread *Vegemite*, equivalent to UK *Marmite*] [1990s+] (*Aus./N.Z.*) the anus or rectum, in the context of (homosexual) anal intercourse.

vegetable *n.* **1** [1960s+] a stupid person. **2** [1970s+] (*US gay*) a lesbian [FRUIT *n.* (2)].

vegetable *adj.* [1970s] **1** (*US campus*) very drunk. **2** brainless, very stupid.

vegetable John *n.* [SE *vegetable* + JOHN CHINAMAN *n.* (1)] [1920s] (*Aus.*) a Chinese greengrocer.

vegetarian *n.* [1960s+] (*US*) a female prostitute or male homosexual who will not perform fellatio, i.e. will not EAT *v.* (4) MEAT *n.*

vegged (out) *adj.* [VEG *v.*] [1980s+] (*US campus*) **1** heavily intoxicated by drugs. **2** exhausted.

veggie *n.* (*also* **vege, veggy, vegie, vegy**) [abbr.] **1** [1950s+] a vegetable. **2** [1970s+] a vegetarian. **3** [1980s+] a person reduced to a vegetative state. **4** [1980s+] (*Irish*) a derog. term for a physically or mentally disabled child.

veggie *adj.* [1980s+] vegetarian.

veggie-meat *n.* [1990s+] (*W.I.*) an available young woman; a virgin.

veggies *n. see* VEG *n.*

veg out *v. see* VEG *v.*

V-8 *n.* [? abbr. SE *deviate*, i.e. she 'must be' a lesbian] [1940s] (*US black*) a solitary woman who prefers her own company to that of others, esp. of men.

veil up *v.* [1930s–40s] (*US*) to get married.

vein *n.*

IN PHRASES

❑ **drain the (main) vein** *v. see under* DRAIN *v.*

vein shooter *n.* [VEIN SHOT *n.*] [1930s–50s] (*US drugs*) one who injects into the vein, thus a veteran addict.

vein shot *n.* [SE *vein* + *shot*, injection] [1930s–50s] (*US drugs*) an injection of narcotics directly into a vein.

veiny bang-stick *n.* (*also* **veiny love-stalk**) [BANG *n.*[1] (2b) + STICK *n.* (1)] [1990s+] a penis.

velcro grin *n.* [1990s+] (*US*) a false rigid smile.

velcro head *n.* [*Velcro* + -HEAD *sfx* (1) the supposed resemblance of the material to tightly curled hair] [1970s+] (*US*) a derog. term for a black person.

velveeta *adj.* [*Velveeta*, a processed cheese spread, thus play on CHEESY *adj.*[2] (1)] [1980s+] (*US campus*) unappealing or unpleasant.

velvet *n.* **1** [late 17C–19C] the tongue. **2** [late 19C+] in fig. use, gain, profit, winnings; thus *to the velvet*, to the good [*see* Asbury, *Sucker's Progress* (1938) 17: An extraordinary number of the terms, technical and otherwise, which were employed by Faro players in the palmy days of the game have passed into the language [...] and are commonly used by millions who never heard of Faro. Here are some of them: [...] *Velvet*—The bank's money]. **3** [1950s] (*Aus./N.Z.*) any dark-skinned woman; thus *a bit of velvet* [abbr. BLACK VELVET *under* BLACK *adj.*]. **4** [1980s] the female pubic hair.

IN PHRASES

❑ **on velvet** *adj.* (*also* **on the velvet**) [late 18C+] secure, cheerful, enjoying a life without problems. ❑ **stand on velvet** *v.* [mid-19C–1920s] to be in a financially advantageous position, esp. following successful gambling. ❑ **velvet-lined meat grinder** *n.* (*also* **velvet cone**) [1940s–70s] (*US*) the vagina.

velvet *adj.*

SE in slang uses

IN COMPOUNDS

❑ **velvet orbs** *n.* (*also* **orbs**) [the shape; and the 'feel'] [1970s] (*US gay*) the testicles. ❑ **velvet room** *n.* [mid-19C] (*US*) the back room of a saloon where patrons might enjoy a slightly quieter and more salubrious atmosphere than in the rowdier front.

venerable monosyllable *n. see* MONOSYLLABLE *n.*

venison out of Tup Park *n.* [SE *tup*, a ram] [late 17C–mid-18C] mutton.

ventilate *v.* [i.e. to 'let air into'] **1** [late 19C] to stab. **2** [late 19C+] (*orig. US*) to shoot, to kill with a bullet.

vent man *n.* [their sleeping over warm subway air vents] [2000s] (*US*) a tramp, a street person.

venture girl *n.* [mid-19C] a single woman sent out to India in the hope of winning herself a husband.

Venus's curse *n.* [early 19C] venereal disease.

Venus's game *n.* [GAME *n.* (1)] **1** [late 17C–early 18C] prostitution. **2** [late 18C] sexual intercourse.

Venus's glove *n.* [late 16C–early 17C] the vagina.

Venus's highway *n.* (*also* **Venus's anvil, ...cave, ...court, ...cup, ...field, ...garden, ...hall, ...highway, ...honeypot, ...mark, ...secret cell, grove of Venus, gulf of..., hill of..., shrine of..., temple of...**) [lit. euph.] [late 16C–1900s] the vagina.

vep *n.* [Fr. *vêpres*, vespers, a service at which there is no collection and is thus 'free'] [20C+] (*W.I.*) a lift, a free ride.

Vera *n.* [initial letters] [2000s] (*S.Afr. gay*) valium.

Vera *v.* [2000s] (*S Afr gay*) to vomit.

Vera Lynn *n.* (*also* **vera**) [rhy. sl.; ult. UK singer *Vera Lynn* (b.1917)] [1940s+] **1** gin; thus a gin-drinker. **2** skin. **3** (*UK/Aus.*) the chin. **4** (*Irish*) in pl., cigarette papers [= SKIN *n.*[1] (2c)].

verandah *n.* **1** [late 19C] the gallery of the Old Vic Theatre, London. **2** [20C+] (*Aus./US*) a pot belly.

SE in slang uses

IN PHRASES

❑ **on the verandah** *adj.* [i.e. not in the house proper] [1980s+] (*N.Z.*) marginal, peripheral.

vera vice *n.* (*also* **victoria vice**) [joc. 'feminization' of the squad] [1950s+] (*gay*) the police vice-squad.

verbal *n.* (*also* **verbals**) [1960s+] **1** a statement (usu. untrue), by a police officer, designed to ensure the conviction of a suspect. **2** (*UK Und.*) a statement, often self-incriminatory, to the police either voluntarily or during and after interrogation. **3** insults, abuse, 'backchat'; thus *give one the verbals*, to abuse; *give it the verbal*, to talk aggressively. **4** a conversation.

verbal *v.* [VERBAL *n.*] [1960s+] (*UK/Aus. Und.*) **1** of the police, to fake a confession by claiming that one's statement under interrogation admitted the crimes for which in court one is pleading not guilty. **2** to talk. **3** to confess under interrogation. **4** to talk aggressively, to abuse.

verbal diarrhoea *n.* [note late 17C–late 19C fig. use of SE *diarrhoea*, an excessive flow of words etc] [1940s+] excessive talk, esp. when meaningless, pointless and irritating to the hearer.

verb-grinder *n.* [early 19C] a nit-picking school master.

verda *v. see* VARDA *v.*

verdomde *adj.* [Du. *verdoemd*, damned] [mid-19C+] (*S.Afr.*) damned, infernal.

verge *n.* [mid-19C] (*US Und.*) a gold watch.

verification shot *n.* [SE *shot*, injection] [1930s–50s] (*US drugs*) the drawing of blood back into the syringe to make sure that one has hit a vein.

vermilion *adj.* [late 19C] (*Aus.*) euph. for BLOODY *adj.* (1).

vermilion *v.* [early 19C] to cover or smear someone with blood.

Vermont charity *n.* [? the meanness of that state's authorities] [1910s–40s] (*US tramp*) sympathy.

verneuk *v.* [Du. sl. *verneuken*] [late 19C+] (*S.Afr.*) to cheat, to swindle.

(DERIVATIVES)

❑ **verneukery** *n.* [1900s] cunning.

Veronica Lake *n.* [rhy. sl.; ult. the film star *Veronica Lake* (1919–73)] [1950s+] a steak.

versatile *adj.* [euph.] [1950s–60s] **1** bisexual. **2** (*US gay*) able to enjoy both active and passive sexual roles.

verse *v.* [SE *verse*, to pour out the voice] [16C] (*UK Und.*) to practise a fraud or deceit by verbal means.

verser *n.* (*also* **retriever**) [VERSE *v.*] [mid-16C–early 17C] (*UK Und.*) that member of a confidence trickster team who actually plays the game of chance through which a victim is defrauded and who would often claim to be a friend of one of the victim's friends.

versing law *n.* [VERSE *v.* + LAW *n.* (1)] [16C] (*UK Und.*) those confidence tricks that focus on the use of counterfeit gold to entrap the victim.

vertical *adj.*

SE in slang uses

(IN COMPOUNDS)

❑ **vertical care-grinder** *n.* [mid–late 19C] the prison treadmill. ❑ **vertical drinking** *n.* [1950s+] (*N.Z.*) drinking while standing at the bar, esp. in a crowd. ❑ **vertical smile** *n.* [20C+] the vagina.

vertical bacon sandwich *n. see under* BACON *n.*[1].

very best *n.* [rhy. sl.] [1960s] (*S.Afr.*) the human chest.

very famillionaire *adj.* [play on SE *very familiar*] [mid-19C] (*UK society*) typical of a nouveau riche.

very froncey *adj.* [Fr. *très français*, very French] [late 19C] (*UK society*) vulgar.

very well *adj.* [lit. an intensifier of *well*] [mid-19C+] acceptable; thus *that's all very well ...*

vessel *n.* [when 'tapped' it 'overflows' with blood] [early 19C] the nose.

vest *n.* **1** [1930s+] (*US*) a bullet-proof vest. **2** [1950s] (*US Und.*) watches and/or jewellery worn on the waistcoat.

SE in slang uses

(IN PHRASES)

❑ **lose one's vest** *v.* [19C] to lose one's temper.

vestal *n.* [SE *vestal virgin*, a Roman priestess supposedly dedicated to absolute chastity] [early 19C] a sexually unrestrained person.

vestry *n.* [19C] the vagina.

vestryman *n.* [VESTRY *n.*] [19C] the penis.

vet *n.* [abbr. SE *veteran*] **1** [mid-19C+] an ex-serviceman. **2** [1910s+] an old-timer, an ageing or experienced person. **3** [1960s+] an ageing, experienced or worn-out prostitute.

vet, the *n.* [SE *vet*, a veterinary surgeon] [1930s+] (*orig. milit.*) a doctor, thus (*S.Afr.*) a prison doctor.

vet *adj.* [VET *n.*] [1930s–50s] (*US*) veteran, experienced.

veterano *n.* [Sp.] [1980s] (*US*) a veteran of gang life.

Vette *n.* [abbr.] [1950s+] a Cor*vette* automobile.

vex *adj.* (*also* **vexed, vexed up**) [SE *vexed*] [1920s+] (*orig. W.I.*) annoyed, angry; thus *vex*, to annoy, *vexness*, bad temper.

vex-money *n.* [Carib.E. *vex*, irritating, annoying + SE *money*] [20C+] (*W.I., Trin.*) money a woman carries with her on a date. If, for whatever reason (usu. the denial of sex), she is forced to make her own way home, she has some funds.

v.g. *adj.* [abbr.] [1940s+] very good.

V-girl *n.* [abbr. *Victory-girl* + play on B-GIRL *n.*] [1940s] (*US*) a woman willing to have sex (or at least go out) with servicemen for patriotic reasons.

vibe *n.* (*also* **vibes**) [abbr. SE *vibrations*] [1960s+] **1** atmosphere; thus *good vibes, bad vibes*. **2** feelings, intuitions. **3** of a person, personality, style.

vibe *v.* [VIBE *n.*] **1** [1960s+] (*US*) to experience, enjoy. **2** [1960s+] to give off an atmosphere. **3** [1980s+] (*US black*) to carry on a relationship, usu. sexual. **4** [1990s+] to create a pleasant, exciting atmosphere.

(IN PHRASES)

❑ **vibe out** *v.* [1990s+] (*W.I.*) to relax, to take a break.

vibes *n.*[1] [abbr.] [1930s+] a *vib*raphone or *vib*raharp.

vibes *n.*[2] *see* VIBE *n.*

vibe someone out *v.* [VIBE *n.*] [1960s+] to produce emotional effects, usu. negative and confusing, in someone.

Vic *n.* [abbr.] **1** [mid–late 19C] the *Vic*toria Theatre, London. **2** [mid-19C+] (*also* **Viccy**) Queen *Vic*toria; also as name of public house. **3** [late 19C] *Vic*toria railway station, London. **4** [late 19C] (*Aus.*) the *Vic*toria Theatre, Sydney. **5** [1910s–1940s] (*US*) a *Vic*trola brand phonograph. **6** [1930s+] (*Aus.*) the state of *Vic*toria; a *Vic*torian. **7** [2000s] (*S.Afr.*) the *Vic*toria Falls.

vic *n.* [abbr.] (*US Und.*) **1** [1910s–40s] a convict, i.e. a self-styled *vic*tim of justice. **2** [1930s+] (*also* **vick**) a *vic*tim of crime. **3** [1990s+] a prostitute's client.

vic *v.* [abbr.] [1990s+] to *vic*timize, to make the subject of a crime.

vicar of Bray *n.* [rhy. sl. = TRAY *n.*[1] (1)] [20C+] in cards, a three.

Viccy *n. see* VIC *n.* (2).

vice *n.* [abbr.] [1950s+] the *vice* squad.

vice *v.* [SE *vice*, to force, to strain, but note 15C *vice*, to treat arrogantly or oppressively] [1950s+] (*US black*) to do harm, to cheat, steal, to cause physical pain.

vice-admiral (of the narrow seas) *n.* [mid-17C–early 19C] 'A drunken man that pisses under the table into his companions' shoes' (Grose 1796).

vicer *n.* [1960s] (*US*) a member of the vice squad.

vice versa *n.* [1960s] (*US gay*) mutual cunnilingus or fellatio.

vice-whipper *n.* [late 17C] a clergyman; a pious person.

vicey-versey *adv.* (*also* **vicky-verky, wisey warcy**) [deliberate joc. mispron.] [mid-19C+] vice versa.

vicious *adj.* [on bad = good model] (*US black/teen*) **1** [1980s] serious. **2** [1980s+] wonderful, excellent, admirable.

viciously *adv.* [1950s+] (*US*) seriously, very much.

vick *n. see* VIC *n.* (2).

vicky *n.*[1] [the initial 'V'] **1** [1960s] a dismissive 'V' hand sign. **2** [1990s+] a virgin.

vicky *n.*[2] [2000s] (*S.Afr. gay*) a pornographic video.

vicky-verky *adv. see* VICEY-VERSEY *adv.*

vict *n.* [abbr.] [1930s–60s] (*US black*) a crime *vict*im.

victoria monk *n.* [rhy. sl. = SPUNK *n.* (5), ult. music-hall star *Victoria Monks* (1884–1972), best known for her version of 'Won't you come home, Bill Bailey?'] [late 19C–1900s] semen.

victoria vice *n. see* VERA VICE *n.*

Victor Trumper *n.* [rhy. sl. = BUMPER *n.*[4]; ult. Aus. cricketer *Victor Trumper* (1877–1915)] [20C+] (*Aus.*) a cigarette butt.

victory *n.* [the 'V for Victory' campaign of WW2] [1940s–50s] (*W.I.*) a style of haircut that gave a man's hair a V-shape at the back.

victory V *n.* [rhy. sl. = PEE *n.*[1] (2)/WEE *n.*] [1990s+] an act of urination.

victualler *n.* [innkeepers who doubled as pimps] [late 16C–early 17C] a pimp; thus *victualling-house*, a brothel.

victualling department *n.* (*also* **victualling office**) [SE *victuals*, food] [late 17C–1900s] the stomach.

vid *n.* **1** [1980s+] videotape [abbr.]. **2** [1990s+] a hallucination, presumably drug-induced. **3** [1990s+] a situation.

vidaholic *n.* [SE *video* + -AHOLIC *sfx*] [1980s+] (*US*) a TV/video addict.

viddle-de-vop *n.* [? echoic] [1940s] (*US black*) a low whistle.

vide-ho *n.* [play on SE *video* + HO *n.* (2)] [1990s+] an attractive (young) woman, who dances on TV shows.

vietas *n. see* FIETAS *n.*

Vietnik *n.* [*Viet*(nam) + -NIK *sfx*] [1960s–70s] (*US*) an active protester against the US involvement in the Vietnam War (1964–75).

viewy *adj.* [it/one becomes a SE *view*] [early–mid-19C] flashy, showy, attractive.

vigorish *n.* (*also* **vig, vigerage, viggerish, viggresh**) [? Yid./Rus. *vyigrysh*, profit, winnings] **1** [1910s+] (*US*) interest on a loan, or debt. **2** [2000s] profit.

vig ounce *n.* [VIGORISH *n.* (1)] [1970s+] (*US drugs*) an ounce (28g) of narcotics.

Viking *n.* [2000s] (*US prison*) an inmate who has an untidy, dirty cell.

Viking *v.* [2000s] (*US prison*) to live a good life, with plenty of material comforts, despite being incarcerated.

Viking cheat *n.* [1990s+] (*W.I.*) a member of the Establishment, an authority, thus an oppressor.

Viking queen *n.* [*Viking* + SE *queen*/-QUEEN *sfx*] [1960s+] (*gay*) **1** a (dyed) blond male. **2** one who prefers Nordic partners.

vile *n.* (*also* **vil, vill, ville, voil, vyle**) [Fr. *ville*, town; before late 17C only in combs., i.e. as -VILE *sfx*] [late 17C+] a town or village.

-vile *sfx* (*also* **-ville**) [Fr. *ville*, town] [mid-16C–19C] used in combs. to mean town or village; thus DEUSEAVILLE *n.*; RUM VILLE *n.*

Village, the *n.* [abbr.] **1** [19C] mainly hunting/horseracing, London. **2** [late 19C–1900s] (*US*) the Lower East Side, NYC. **3** [1910s+] (*US*) Greenwich Village, NYC.

village *adj.*

SE in slang uses

IN COMPOUNDS

❑ **village bike** *n. see* RALEIGH BIKE *n.* ❑ **village butler** *n.* (*also* **village bustler**) [late 18C] 'old thieves, that would rather steal a dishclout than discontinue the practice of thieving' (Potter, *Dict. Cant*, 1795). ❑ **village ram** *n.* [RAM *n.*[1] (2)] [1930s+] (*W.I.*) a local philanderer and ladies' man.

villain *n.* [specific use of SE] [1960s+] a professional criminal.

Ville, the *n.* [abbr.] **1** [1920s+] Penton*ville* prison, London. **2** [2000s] (*US*) Greenwich Village, NYC.

ville *n. see* VILE *n.*

-ville *sfx*[1] [first use is UK, but popularized by 1950s US beatniks; *Storyville* in New Orleans has been suggested as poss. ety.] [mid-19C+] (*mainly US*) used to emphasize a particular characteristic, e.g. *dragsville*, very boring, *sticksville*, very rural or suburban.

-ville *sfx*[2] *see* -VILE *sfx*.

villecat *n.* [mid-19C] (*UK Und.*) an old brothel-keeper.

vim-man *n.* [SE *vim* = strength] [mid-19C] a coal seller's assistant.

vin blong *n.* (*also* **vin blank, vin blinc, ving blong, von blink, vonblong**) [mispron. of Fr. *vin blanc*/*vin rouge*, white wine/red wine] [1910s] (*orig. milit.*) cheap white wine; thus *vongrooge*, cheap red wine; *vinblanced*, drunk.

vincent *n.* [VINCENT'S LAW *n.*] [late 16C–early 17C] (*UK Und.*) the victim of a crooked gambling game.

Vincent Price *n.* [rhy. sl., ult. film star *Vincent Price* (1911–93)] [1990s+] ice.

vincent's law *n.* [Lat. *vincens*, victorious; the use is ironic + LAW *n.* (1)] [late 16C–early 19C] (*UK Und.*) cheating for profit at bowls and later cards.

vine *n.*[1] (*also* **vines**) [SE *vine*; i.e. a well-cut suit clings to the figure as does the plant to a tree] [1930s+] (*orig. US black*) a suit; usu. male; often in pl.

vine *n.*[2] [GRAPEVINE *n.*[1]] [1960s] (*orig. UK Und.*) any unofficial underground network of information.

vine, the *n.* [1970s+] (*US black*) wine.

vine-bud-nipper *n.* [mid-19C] (*UK Und.*) an older woman who entices young virgins into prostitution.

vined *adj.* [VINE *n.*[1]] [1960s] dressed.

vinegar *n.* **1** [late 17C–early 19C] (*UK Und.*) a cloak, an overcoat. **2** [2000s] semen.

IN COMPOUNDS

❑ **vinegar stick** *n.* **1** [1930s] (*US Und.*) a thin, stiletto-like knife. **2** [2000s] the penis [STICK *n.* (1)].

SE in slang uses

IN COMPOUNDS

❑ **vinegar pisser** *n.* [PISS *v.* (2)] [early 17C] a miser, a mean person. ❑ **vinegar strokes** *n.* (*also* **gravy strokes**) [? one 'puts a bit of vinegar' into them; note Barry Humphries, *The Traveller's Tool* (1985) in 'Les's Large Appendix': 'The penultimate phase in sexual connection when the active partner experiences a facial rictus similar to that produced by drinking vinegar (information supplied by a doctor)'] [1970s+] the final thrusts of sexual intercourse.

vineyard *n.* [1970s+] (*US black*) ironic ref. to anywhere that alcoholics congregate.

ving blong *n. see* VIN BLONG *n.*

vinnecky-vasky *n.* [mid-19C] (*UK Und.*) suffering from and complaining of a hangover.

vinnies *n.* [abbr.] [1980s+] (*Aus./N.Z.*) the Society of St *Vincent* de Paul.

vinny's *n.* [abbr.] [1980s] (*Aus./N.Z.*) the second-hand clothes shops run by the Society of St *Vincent* de Paul.

vino *n.* (*also* **veeno**) [Ital. *vino*, wine] **1** [late 19C+] wine, usu. cheap. **2** [1990s+] (*Aus.*) a glass of wine.

vintage *n.* [SE *vintage*, the year of a wine's creation] [late 19C] (*orig. US*) the year of one's birth.

vintner *n.* [play on SE] [early 18C] a heavy drinker.

vinyl *n.* [1970s+] records, (as opposed to tapes or CDs); thus *vinyl junkie*, one who is obsessed by records, rejecting all other forms of recorded music.

violate *v.* [1960s+] (*US*) to forfeit one's parole for a violation of the rules and to be returned to prison.

violet *n.* (*also* **garden violet**) [although the terms are found in several dicts., none, incl. *OED*, provides an actual citation] **1** [late 19C–1940s] an onion, but in pl. spring onions or sage and onion stuffing. **2** [1920s–30s] cabbage.

violet crumble *v.* [rhy. sl. = TUMBLE *v.*[2]; ult. an Aus. sweet] [1990s+] (*Aus.*) to understand.

violin *n.* [1980s+] (*Aus. drugs/prison*) a hypodermic syringe, thus *play the violin*, to inject oneself.

violin-case *n.* [1910s–40s] (*US*) an oversized shoe.

vip *n.* [? SE *viper*] [1930s–50s] (*Aus.*) a miser.

vipe *v.* [VIPER *n.*] [1930s–60s] (*drugs*) to smoke marijuana.

viper *n.* [ety. unknown; obviously f. SE *viper*, but which characteristics?] (*drugs*) **1** [1930s+] a regular user of marijuana. **2** [1970s] a regular user of heroin. **3** [1980s] an injection of morphine and heroin.

DERIVATIVES

❑ **viperish** *adj.* [1950s] (*drugs*) regularly using marijuana.

IN COMPOUNDS

❑ **viperland** *n.* [1940s] the world of marijuana smokers. ❑ **viper's drag** *n.* [1930s] a marijuana cigarette. ❑ **viper's weed** *n.* [WEED *n.*[1] (4)] [1930s–50s] marijuana.

virgie *n.* (*also* **virg**) [abbr.] [1930s–60s] a *virgin*, also as adj. virginal.

virgin *n.*[1] [abbr.] [1910s–20s] **1** a cigarette made of *Virgin*ia tobacco. **2** (*US*) a martini, i.e. a mix of *v*ermouth and *gin*.

virgin *n.*[2] [note 1940s US Army *virgin*, a soldier who has yet to contract venereal disease] [1970s] (*US Und.*) a criminal with no convictions.

SE in slang uses

(IN COMPOUNDS)

❑ **virgin pullet** *n.* [PULLET *n.* (1)] [early 19C] 'a young woman who though often trod has never laid' (Jon Bee), i.e. no longer a virgin but not yet a mother. ❑ **virgin vault** *n.* [1990s+] (*US campus*) residence hall for females.

(IN PHRASES)

❑ **born-again virgin** *n.* [1980s+] (*US gay*) a celibate homosexual man. ❑ **virgins' bus** *n.* ['so named satirically in reference of the chief patronesses at that late hour' (Ware), i.e. girls who have resisted male advances] [late 19C] the last bus to run westward from Piccadilly Circus.

virgin bride *n.* [rhy. sl.] [20C+] (*Aus.*) a ride.

virginia *n.* [joc. misprons] **1** [1990s+] (*US*) the vagina. **2** [2000s] (*S.Afr. gay*) a male virgin.

virtue rewarded *n.* [the initials *V.R.*, i.e. *Victoria Regina*, on the side of the prison van] [late 19C] prison.

virtuoso of the skin flute *n.* [SKIN FLUTE *n.*] [20C+] a masturbator.

virus, the *n.* [euph.] [1980s+] (*orig. US*) HIV, the virus that causes AIDS.

vi's *n.* [abbr.] [1960s] (*US campus*) Levi–Strauss jeans.

visa-body *n.* [1990s+] (*W.I.*) a human object of desire.

vision *n.* [abbr.] [1970s] tele*vision*.

visit *v.*

SE in slang uses

(IN PHRASES)

❑ **visit cafe la mamma** *v.* [play on SE *mama*, a mother/the NYC theatre group *Café la Mama* (founded 1961)] [1990s+] (*US*) to feed at one's mother's breast. ❑ **visit Miss Murphy** *v.* [euph.] [20C+] to visit the lavatory. ❑ **visit Mrs Jones** *v. see* MRS JONES *under* MRS *n.* ❑ **visit Mrs White** *v.* [? the white lavatory bowl] [1920s] to visit the lavatory. ❑ **visit one's Indian cousin** *v.* [Indian hair is straight] [1940s+] (*W.I.*) to have one's hair straightened. ❑ **visit Rosy Palm and her five daughters** *v. see* HAVE A BIG DATE WITH ROSY PALM *under* ROSY PALM AND HER FIVE (LITTLE) SISTERS *n.* ❑ **visit Sir Harry** *v.* [euph.] [mid-19C] to visit the lavatory. ❑ **visit the sandbox** *v.* [SE *sandbox*, a pet's litter tray] [1960s] (*US campus*) to visit the lavatory.

visiting fireman *n.* [orig. 1855 when the Baltimore *Sun* reported that 'A company of firemen from Rochester, N.Y. ... continue to receive the attentions of their brother firemen of Baltimore ... This evening the visiting firemen will be the guests of the Washington Hose Company' (25 October 1855)] [1920s+] (*orig. US*) **1** a person or group who are especially well looked after when visiting an organization of kindred spirits. **2** tourists who are expected to spend freely. **3** parasites, hangers-on.

visitor *n.* [euph.] [1940s+] a menstrual period.

SE in slang uses

(IN PHRASES)

❑ **visitor to Vegemite valley** *n.* [VEGEMITE VALLEY *n.*] [1990s+] a male homosexual.

vitamin *n.*

SE in slang uses

(IN COMPOUNDS)

❑ **vitamin A** *n.* [1980s+] **1** LSD [ACID *n.*[1] (2)]. **2** MDMA [ACID *n.*[1] (3)]. ❑ **vitamin C** *n.* [C *n.*[3] (1)] [1980s+] cocaine. ❑ **vitamin DB** *n.* [2000s] (*N.Z.*) draught bitter from the *D*ominion *B*reweries. ❑ **vitamin E** *n.* [ECSTASY *n.*] [1980s+] MDMA. ❑ **vitamin G** *n.* [its pharmaceutical name *G*-abapentin] [2000s] (*US drugs*) Neurontin. ❑ **vitamin H** *n.* [1980s+] (*Aus. drugs/prison*) heroin. ❑ **vitamin K** *n.* [abbr. SE *k*etamine] **1** [1980s+] (*drugs*) a synthetic hallucinogen, allegedly 5000 times stronger than LSD; according to researchers, it takes the user to subatomic reality and one can experience the consciousness of inanimate objects. **2** *see* SPECIAL K *n.* ❑ **vitamin M** *n.* [1970s] (*US drugs*) Methedrine, methamphetamine. ❑ **vitamin S** *n.* [2000s] (*W.I.*) semen. ❑ **vitamin T** *n.* [f. *tea*, marijuana] [1980s+] (*drugs*) marijuana. ❑ **vitamin V** *n.* [initial letter of *vodka*] [2000s] vodka. ❑ **vitamin X** *n.* [pron. of ECSTASY *n.*] [1980s+] MDMA. ❑ **vitamin XXX** *n.* [*XXX*, a mark of a beer's strength] [1980s+] alcohol.

vitamins *n.* [play on the supposedly health-giving properties of SE *vitamins*] **1** [1950s] money. **2** [1980s+] (*drugs*) any drugs available in pill or capsule form.

Vivian *n.* [initial letters] [2000s] (*S.Afr. gay*) a vibrator, or a man who uses one.

viz *n.* [abbr. SE *visage*] [1990s+] a face.

v.j. *n.* (*also* **veejay**) [abbr.; on pattern of D.J.] [1980s+] (*US*) video jockey, a TV presenter of music videos.

vlam *n.* [Afk. *vlam*, flame] [1970s+] (*S.Afr.*) methylated spirits (as drunk by alcoholics); thus *vlam-drinker*.

vlam *v.* [1980s] (*S.Afr.*) to drink methylated spirits.

voce *n.* (*also* **voche, votch**) [Ital. *voce*, a voice] [mid-19C+] (*Ling. Fr./Polari*) the voice.

vodders *n.* (*also* **vod**) [1990s+] vodka.

voddy *n.* (*also* **voddies**) [abbr.] [1980s+] *vod*ka.

vodeodo *n.* [play on musical *vo-do-deo-do*, a meaningless refrain used to produce rhythm + DOUGH *n.* (1)] [1930s] plunder, booty, cash.

voetjie-voetjie *n.* [Afk. *voet*, foot; FOOTSIE-FOOTSIE *n.*] (*S.Afr.*) **1** [1910s+] the surreptitious nudging of someone's foot out of sight of anyone else, typically beneath a table; the contact is usu. a prelude to greater intimacy. **2** [1980s+] in fig. uses, implying non-sexual flirtation.

voetsak *n.* [Afk. *voertsek*, forward, more usu. found as a dismissive command, be off! go away!] **1** [1970s+] (*S.Afr.*) an infinite, non-specific number, e.g. *straight from the year voetsek*, the equivalent of 'God knows when' or 'the year dot'. **2** [1980s] a shoe with soles made from rubber car tyres.

voetsak! *excl.* (*also* **voetsek!**) [Du. *voort seg ik*, be off, I say!] [mid-19C+] (*S.Afr.*) a general excl. of dismissal, go away! be off! get out!

vogel grafter *n.* [Ger. *vogel*, a bird or FOGLE *n.* (1) + GRAFTER *n.*[1] (1)] [1900s] (*US Und.*) one who robs young children.

vogue *n.* [? its fashionability] [1960s–70s] (*gay*) a cigarette.

voil *n. see* VILE *n.*

voker *v.* [Lat. *vocare*, to speak] [mid-19C+] **1** to speak. **2** to understand.

volkie *n.* [Du. *volk*, people] [1940s+] (*S.Afr.*) a derog. term for a coloured farm labourer.

Volks *n.* [abbr.] [1950s+] a *Volks*wagen car.

Volksie *n.* [abbr.] [1960s+] (*Aus./S.Afr.*) a *Volks*wagen 'Beetle' car or camper van.

voluntary knee drill *n.* [the subject throws themselves to their knees] [late 19C] abject adulation.

vom *n.* [VOM *v.*] [1990s+] **1** vomit. **2** bad, disgusting food.

(DERIVATIVES)

❑ **vomatose** *adj.* [SE *vomit* + *comatose*] [1980s+] (*US campus*) disgusting.

vom *v.* [abbr. SE *vomit*] [1990s+] to be sick.

vomit up one's toenails *v.* [2000s] (*US*) to vomit copiously.

vomity *adj.* (*also* **vomitrocious**) [SE *vomit*] [1970s–80s] (*orig. US*) very disgusting, thus as *n.*, a disgusting person.

von blink *n. see* VIN BLONG *n.*

von-blinked *adj.* [? rhy. sl. = drink] [1910s] (*Aus.*) drunk.

vonblong *n. see* VIN BLONG *n.*

vonce *n.* **1** [1950s] (*US black/jazz*) marijuana [Yid. *vonce*, a bedbug, thus = ROACH *n.* (2)]. **2** [1960s] (*US*) a term of abuse [? abbr. of SCHWANTZ *n.* (2)].

(IN PHRASES)

❑ **do the vonce** *v.* [1950s] (*US black/jazz*) to have sexual intercourse.

Von Trappe *n.* [rhy. sl. = CRAP *n.*[1]] [2000s] trouble, difficulties.

voom *v. see* VROOM *v.*

voompse *v.* (*also* **vumpse**) [ety. unknown] [20C+] (*W.I.*) to pay attention to; usu. in negative, thus *not even voompse at/upon*, to ignore, to cut dead.

vot *n.* [1950s+] (*US prison*) a masculine lesbian.

votch *n. see* VOCE *n.*

vote for the alderman *v.* [joc. ref. to ALDERMAN LUSHINGTON *n.*] [early–mid-19C] to take a drink.

voucher *n.* [he *vouches* for its authenticity] [late 17C–mid-18C] (*UK Und.*) an accomplice who passes the counterfeit money produced by the coiner.

vowel *v.* [the *vowels* IOU] [early 18C–mid-19C] of a losing gamester, to pay off his debts with an IOU.

voyager *n.* [they are on a TRIP *n.*[4] (1)] [1960s] one who is under the influence of LSD.

v.p.l. *n.* [abbr. *v*isible *p*antie *l*ine] [1980s+] of a female, having the line of one's underwear visible through a tight outer garment.

v.r. *n.* [the monarch's initials (for *V*ictoria *R*egina), painted on its sides; also joc. abbr. *v*agabonds *r*emoved] [mid–late 19C] a prison van.

vreet *v.* [Du. *vreten*, to eat; usu. of an animal and thus sl. when used of a person] [1970s+] (*S.Afr.*) to devour, to gobble up.

vrek *n.* (*also* **vrekker**) [1970s+] (*S.Afr.*) a conservative, a reactionary.

vrek *v.* [Afk. *vrek*, to die, usu. of animals] [1910s+] (*S.Afr.*) to die; thus *gaan vrek*, drop dead.

vrij *v. see* VRY *v.*

vroom *v.* (*also* **varoom, voom**) [echoic of the sound of an engine] [1950s+] (*US*) to go fast, esp. to drive a vehicle at speed.

vrot *adj.* [fig. use of Du. *verotten*, to rot] (*S.Afr.*) **1** [1910s+] rotten, lousy, esp. as a catch-all negative or intensifier, i.e. very much. **2** [1990s+] drunk.

vrow-case *n.* [Du. *vrouw*, a woman + CASA *n.*[1]; CASE *n.*[3] (3)] [late 17C–mid-19C] a brothel.

vry *v.* (*also* **fraai, fray, frey, vrij**) [synon. Afk. *vry*] [late 19C+] (*S.Afr.*) to caress amorously, to pet; to court, to woo.

DERIVATIVES

❑ **vrytijie** *n.* [1970s] love-making.

v.s. *n.* [1930s–50s] (*US drugs*) a vein shot, i.e. an intravenous injection of narcotics; a VEIN SHOOTER *n.*

V-spot *n. see FIVE-SPOT under* -SPOT *sfx.*

V-town *n.* [abbr.] [1990s+] (*US black teen*) Vallejo, California.

vuilgat *n.* (*also* **vuilgoed**) [Afk. *vuil*, foul + GAT *n.*[2] (1)] [1910s+] (*S.Afr.*) a general term of abuse, esp. to an extremely dirty person.

vu ja de *phr.* [inverse of Fr. *déjà vu*, already seen, the sense that one has been somewhere before, seen or done something previously] [1980s+] (*US campus*) I have never done anything of this sort before; this is a complete novelty.

vulture *n.* [1960s] (*S.Afr.*) a loafer.

vumpse *v. see* VOOMPSE *v.*

vut *n.* [? PHUT *adv.* (1)] [1990s+] (*UK juv.*) a failure, an inadequate.

v. w/e (*also* **v.w.e.**) [abbr. *v*ery WELL-ENDOWED *adj.*] [1960s+] used in sex contact advertisements, having notably large genitals.

vyle *n. see* VILE *n.*

W *n.*[1] [abbr. SE *W.C.*] [1910s+] (*orig. N.Z.*) a lavatory.

W *n.*[2] [abbr.] [1950s+] (*UK Und.*) a warrant for arrest, search etc.

w *v.* [WELCH *v.*] [1900s] to cheat, to swindle.

waai *v.* [Afk. *waai,* to blow] [1960s+] (*S.Afr.*) to leave.

wabbler *n.* (*also* **wobbler**) [SE *wobble*] **1** [19C] a boiled leg of mutton. **2** *see* FOOT-WABBLER *under* FOOT *n.*

wabbly *adj. see* WOBBLY *adj.*[2].

wack *see also under* WHACK and combs.

wack *n.* [1980s] (*US drugs*) phencyclidine; n., *wack back,* a user of phencyclidine who becomes violent.

wack *adj.* (*also* **the wack, wack-ass, wacked, wak, whack**) [orig. popularized in 1986 through the anti-CRACK *n.*[7] mural by Keith Haring (1958–90), which bore the slogan: 'Crack is wack.' Note W.I. *wacka-tac,* a disagreeable person] **1** [1980s+] (*also* **whacked**) (*US black*) second-rate, phoney, unsatisfactory; a general term of opprobrium; thus *wack-ass* (intensifier). **2** [1990s+] positive, extremely good.

(IN COMPOUNDS)

❑ **wack-ass** *adj.* [1990s+] (*US black*) second-rate, inferior.

(IN PHRASES)

❑ **wack around** *v.* [1980s] (*US campus*) to act lazily.

wack! *excl.* (*also* **wacker!**) [? dial. *wacker,* active, lively] [1960s+] (*orig./mainly Merseyside*) a term of address to a man.

wacker *n.* [WHACK *v.*[1] (8)] [1990s+] a penis.

wacker *adj.* (*also* **wacka, whacker**) [WHACK *v.*[1] (1)] [1940s+] (*Aus.*) excellent, wonderful.

wackey dust *n. see* WHACKY BACCY *under* WHACKY *adj.*

wack job *n. see under* WHACKO *n.*

wackness *n.* [WACK *adj.* (1)] [2000s] (*US black*) mediocrity.

wacko *see under* WHACKO.

wacky *adj. see* WHACKY *adj.*

wacky dust *n.* [WHACKY *adj.*] [1930s] (*US drugs*) cocaine.

wacky house *n.* [WHACKY *adj.*] [1930s] (*US Und.*) a psychiatric institution.

waco! *excl. see* WHACKO! *excl.*

wad *n.*[1] [SE *wad,* a bundle; Irish *wad,* a lump of bread (Holinshed's *Irish Chronicle*); repopularized *c.*1985 by UK comedian Harry Enfield's character 'Loadsamoney', with his Thatcherite credo, 'Wad is God'] **1** [early 19C+] a roll of money or money in general; thus *wadded,* possessing a good deal of money. **2** [late 19C+] (*Aus./US*) a large quantity of a commodity. **3** [1910s–30s] a drink of alcohol. **4** [1910s+] (*orig. milit.*) food, esp. a bun, cake or sandwich. In all cases its filling qualities are more important than taste etc; thus *char and wads,* tea and buns. **5** [2000s] (*drugs*) a bag of tobacco or marijuana.

(IN COMPOUNDS)

❑ **wad-shifter** *n.* [1910s–30s] a teetotaller.

(IN PHRASES)

❑ **blow one's wad** *v.* [1940s+] (*US*) to spend all one's money. ❑ **buy the wad** *v.* [1960s] (*US*) to suffer whatever is worst. ❑ **wad that would choke a wombat** *n.* (*also* **wad that would choke a coal chute, ...a donkey**) [20C+] (*Aus./US*) an exceptionally impressive roll of cash.

wad *n.*[2] [abbr. SE *wadding*] [mid–late 19C] straw used for bedding.

wad *n.*[3] [SE *wad,* a bundle] [late 19C+] semen, esp. an ejaculation of semen.

(IN COMPOUNDS)

❑ **wad-waste** *n.* [1960s] a term of abuse.

(IN PHRASES)

❑ **blow one's wad** *v.* **1** [1970s+] to indicate surprise or excitement. **2** [1990s+] to speak one's mind. **3** [2000s] to ejaculate. ❑ **pop one's wad** *v.* [1970s] (*US*) of a man, to achieve orgasm. ❑ **shoot one's wad** *v.* **1** [late 19C+] (*orig. US*) to ejaculate. **2** [late 19C+] (*orig. US*) to exhaust oneself, or one's possibilities; to speak out forcefully and finally [SE *wad,* a plug that holds in the powder in a cartridge]. **3** [1950s+] (*US*) to commit or bet everything one has, to say all one has to say [WAD *n.*[1] (1)]. **4** [1960s+] (*US*) to break down emotionally.

wad *n.*[4] [WAD *n.*[3]/ abbr. TIGHTWAD *n.*] **1** [20C+] (*orig. US campus*) (*also* **wad-waste**) a fool, an idiot, an unpleasant person. **2** [1970s] (*US campus*) a sexually aggressive man.

wad *n.*[5] [ety. unknown] [1900s] (*US campus*) the mouth.

-wad *sfx* [? WAD *n.*[4] (1)] [1980s+] (*US campus*) an all-purpose usu. negative sfx that can be added freely to any word to mean a fool, e.g. *asswad, stainwad.*

waddie *n.* (*also* **waddy**) [SE *wadding,* something that 'fills in'] (*US, West*) **1** [late 19C–1900s] a cow-rustler, a person who steals or rebrands cattle. **2** [1900s–1950s] a cowboy, esp. a temporary cowhand.

waddy *n.* [Dharuk *wadi,* a tree, a stick] [early 19C+] (*Aus.*) (*also* **waddie**) a club or cudgel.

waddy *v.* [WADDY *n.* (1)] (*Aus.*) **1** [mid-19C+] to hit someone, usu. with a club or cudgel. **2** [late 19C] to beg, to implore.

wade *n.* [SE *wade,* to step through water] [19C] a ford.

wade in *v.* (*also* **wade into**) [mid-19C+] **1** to commit oneself whole-heartedly, esp. to a fight. **2** to commence an action.

waders *n.* [1940s] (*US black*) boots (there is no suggestion of water as in SE *waders*).

wadge *n.* (*also* **wodge**) [orig. synon. dial.] **1** [mid-19C+] a thick, chunky, dense lump. **2** [1990s+] (*Irish*) a thick slice of bread.

wad-jank *n.* [Carib. *wajang,* a prostitute or promiscuous woman] [2000s] (*W.I.*) a self-important man.

wafer-woman *n.* [? her posing as a legitimate maker of *wafers,* i.e. filigree] [17C–mid-18C] a madame.

waffle *n.*[1] [SE *waffle,* a form of batter-cake; ? play on SE *waffle iron* and IRON n.] **1** [1930s+] (*US Und.*) a male homosexual. **2** [1940s] a woman.

waffle *n.*[2] [orig. late 19C printers' jargon. 'Twaddle, gossip, or "jaw"' (*OED*)] [1930s+] nonsense, rubbish.

waffle *v.*[1] (*also* **whaffle, woffle**) [orig. Scot./northern dial.; ult. *waff,* to yelp] [late 19C+] to dither, to talk nonsense.

waffle *v.*[2] [play on WAFFLE STOMPERS *n.*] [1950s+] (*US*) to tread or trample; to beat up.

waffle iron *n.* [resemblance] [1910s] (*US*) a sidewalk or pavement grating.

waffles *n.* [WAFFLE *v.*[1] (1)] [mid-19C] an idler, a loafer.

waffle stompers *n.* [1970s+] (*US campus*) heavy boots with thick cleated soles that resemble a waffle iron.

wag *n.*[1]

(IN PHRASES)

□ **play the wag** *v.* [SE *wag*, a mischievous boy; ult. ? SE *waghalter*, one likely to end up 'wagging a halter', i.e. being hanged] [mid-19C+] to play truant.

wag *n.*[2] [abbr./pron.] [late 19C–1950s] (*Aus./US*) a vagrant.

wag *n.*[3] [their wagging head, whether through stupidity or the desire to affirm whatever has been sad] [late 19C+] **1** a general term of contempt. **2** anyone without firm opinions, a 'yes-man'.

wag *n.*[4] *see* WAG-AT-THE-WALL *n.*

wag *v.* [SE *vagrant*] **1** [late 17C+] (*also* **wag off**) to leave, to walk slowly. **2** [mid-19C+] (*Aus.*) (*also* **wag it, wag off**) to play truant. **3** [19C+] (*US black*) to procrastinate, to find it hard to make any decisions.

SE in slang uses

(IN PHRASES)

□ **wag hemp in the wind** *v.* [the hempen rope] [mid-16C–early 17C] to be hanged. □ **wag one's chin** *v.* (*also* **...jaw, ... tongue**) [early 18C; late 19C+] to talk, to gossip. □ **wag one's chops** *v. see under* CHOPS *n.*[1]. □ **wag one's tail** *v.* [TAIL *n.* (4)] [late 17C–19C] of a woman, to act in a promiscuous manner; to be a prostitute.

wagabone *n. see* VAGABOND *n.*

wag-at-the-wall *n.* (*also* **wag**) [20C+] (*Irish*) a clock.

wage *n. see* WEDGE *n.*[1] (1).

wages *n.* [1920s+] any form of illicit earnings.

wagga *n.* (*also* **wagga blanket, wagga rug, wagga-wagga rug**) [*Wagga Wagga*, a town in New South Wales; ult. Abor. phr. *many crows*] [20C+] (*Aus.*) an improvised covering, made by stitching together a pair of chaff bags, sacks etc.

wagga-wagga *adj.* [Yoruba *waga-waga*, bundled together] [1970s+] (*W.I.*) plentiful, abundant.

wagger *n.* [*HOP THE WAG under* HOP *v.*[1]] [late 19C] a truant.

waggle *n.*

(IN PHRASES)

□ **get a waggle on** *v. see GET A WIGGLE ON under* WIGGLE *n.*

waggon *n.* [? brandname] [1900s–40s] (*S.Afr.*) a cigarette.

waggon lay *n.* [SE *waggon* + LAY *n.*[3] (1)] [18C] (*UK Und.*) waiting in the street to waylay and rob waggons; thus *waggon-layer*, a waggon thief.

wagh! *excl. see* FAUGH! *excl.*

wag off *v.* **1** *see* WAG *v.* (1). **2** *see* WAG *v.* (2).

wagon *n.* **1** as an official vehicle. (**a**) [late 19C+] (*US*) a police patrol *wagon*. (**b**) [20C+] an ambulance. (**c**) [20C+] an automobile. (**d**) [1950s] a hearse. **2** [1920s+] (*Irish/US*) a derog. name for a woman. **3** [1920s+] (*Irish/US*) a prostitute [she gives you a RIDE *n.* (1a)]. **4** [1930s] (*US Und.*) a revolver [? the revolving chamber resembles a wagon wheel].

(IN COMPOUNDS)

□ **wagon-chasing** *adj.* [1950s] of a lawyer, one who fig. pursues the police wagon in the hope of picking up otherwise unrepresented cases.

(IN PHRASES)

□ **black wagon** *n.* (*US*) **1** [mid-19C+] a hearse. **2** [late 19C] a police car.

SE in slang uses

(IN COMPOUNDS)

□ **wagon-hunter** *n.* [mid-18C] a brothel-keeper's agent who solicited for customers at coaching inns.

(IN PHRASES)

□ **on the wagon** see separate entry.

wagoning *n.* [mid–late 19C] coach-driving.

wagonish *adj.* [*see WATER WAGON under* WATER *n.*[1]] [late 19C–1950s] (*US*) slow.

wagon-wheel *n. see* WHEEL *n.* (1).

wagtail *n.* (*also* **water-wagtail**) [SE *wag* + TAIL *n.* (4)] [late 16C–early 19C] (*also* **wag**) a promiscuous woman, a prostitute; occas. a dissolute man; also attrib.

wagtailed *adj.* [WAGTAIL *n.*] [mid-17C] promiscuous.

wail *n.* [SE wail, i.e the unhappiness occasioned] [1930s] (*US Und.*) a legal trial.

wail *v.* **1** [1950s+] (*orig. US black*) to abandon one's inhibitions, to lose oneself in an activity, esp. of musicians during an improvised solo, or of sexual pleasure. **2** [1960s–70s] (*W.I.*) to behave badly, aggressively; thus *wail down the place*, to dance and sing with utter abandon. **3** [1960s+] (*orig. US black*) to sing, to play a musical instrument. **4** see WHALE *v.*[1].

wailing *adj.* (*also* **whaling**) [WAIL *v.* (1)] [1950s+] (*US black/campus*) excellent, wonderful.

wail on *v. see* WHALE *v.*[1].

waistcoateer *n.* (*also* **wastcotier**) [the *waistcoat* that served her as a 'badge of office'; 20C use historical] [17C–1920s] a prostitute.

waistcoat piece *n.* [its supposed resemblance to that part of a suit] [late 19C] the breast and neck of mutton.

wait and linger *n.* [rhy. sl.] [20C+] a finger.

waiter *n.* [it 'waits' for the rest of the field to finish; Stephens & O'Brien, *Materials for a Dict. of Aus. Slang* (ms.; 1900–10), suggest that the owner is waiting for a more profitable race or deliberately running the horse badly so as to improve its handicapping in another race] [late 19C] (*Aus.*) a losing horse.

wait for dead men's shoes *v.* [mid-17C–1900s] to expect an inheritance, to hope to succeed to someone else's job.

wajan *n.* (*also* **wajang, wajank**) [ety. unknown; ? pron. of SE *wait, John*] [20C+] (*W.I., Trin.*) **1** a prostitute, a promiscuous woman esp. from the slums. **2** an expert.

wak *adj. see* WACK *adj.*

waka blonde *n.* ['the reference derives from Whakarewarewa wahines, the Rotorua Maori women observed by tourists'] [1980s+] (*N.Z.*) derog. term for a Maori woman.

wake *n. see* WIDE-AWAKE *n.*

wake *v. see* WISE UP *v.*

SE in slang uses

(IN COMPOUNDS)

□ **wake-amine** *n.* [it 'wakes one up'] [1990s+] (*drugs*) amphetamine.

(IN PHRASES)

□ **don't wake it up** [cf. SE *let sleeping dogs lie*] [1920s+] (*Aus.*) don't talk about it. □ **wake 'n' bake** *v.* [1990s+] (*US drugs*) to smoke marijuana upon waking. □ **wake snakes** *v. see under* SNAKE *n.*[1]. □ **wake the dead** *v.* [the 'resurrection' of one's flaccid penis] [1990s+] to masturbate.

(IN EXCLAMATIONS)

□ **wake it!** [1980s+] (*US campus*) an exhortation to action, get with it!

wake-up *n.* **1** [1930s+] (*Aus.*) an alert and resourceful person, always aware of the possibilities of a situation, thus v. *to be a (full) wake-up(s)*. **2** [1940s+] (*US prison*) the last day of one's sentence or term of milit. service [the days left are calculated as 'X and a wake-up'; thus one 'wakes up' in an institution, but goes to bed in freedom; similarly used in US milit. for the final morning of one's service]. **3** [1940s+] (*also* **wake-me-up**) the first drink of the day. **4** [1950s+] (*also* **wake-up boost, wake-up hit, wake-up shot**) a narcotics user's first injection of the day; a crack cocaine user's first pipe. **5** [1960s+] any form of stimulant and amphetamine, also as *waker, wake-up pill*.

wake up *v. see* WISE UP *v.*

SE in slang uses

(IN PHRASES)

□ **wake up and smell the coffee** *v.* [1980s+] to come to one's senses.

(IN EXCLAMATIONS)

□ **wake it up!** [1950s+] (*Aus./N/Z.*) hurry up! get on with it!

wakey-wakey *v.* [WAKEY, WAKEY! *excl.*] [1980s] to awaken, to get up.

wakey, wakey! *excl.* [orig. milit. use; the *locus classicus* was as used on the 1950s radio show the *Billy Cotton Bandshow*, where the eponymous bandleader adopted it as a catchphrase] [1940s+] **1** up you get! **2** get a move on! stop day-dreaming!

wakker *adj.* [Du. *wakker*, to wake, thus fig. lively] [1960s+] lively, noisy, energetic; 'on the ball'.

wal *n.* [abbr. WALLOPER *n.*[1] (6)] [1940s–60s] (*Aus.*) a police officer.

wale *v. see* WHALE *v.*[1].

Waler *n.* (*also* **whaler**) [abbr.] (*Aus.*) **1** [mid–late 19C] a horse reared in the colony and exported to India. **2** [late 19C+] a native of New South Wales.

waler *n.* **1** *see* WHALER *n.*[1]. **2** *see* WHALER *n.*[2].

walk *n.* **1** in senses of a regular 'beat'. (**a**) [mid-19C; 1970s] the area walked by a street prostitute. (**b**) [1990s+] (*US prison*) the regular patrol route of a prison warder. **2** [1950s+] a release from a charge. **3** [1980s] (*US campus*) a release from a class.

IN PHRASES

❑ **give someone a walk** *v.* [1990s+] (*US*) to ignore, to abandon. ❑ **go for a walk** *v.* [euph.] [1950s+] to be stolen. ❑ **take a walk** *v.* (*orig. US*) **1** [late 19C+] to leave, to be dismissed, esp. as imper. *take a walk!* go away! **2** [1910s+] to escape criminal proceedings. **3** [1930s+] to run off. **4** [1930s+] of a group of workers, to resign. ❑ **take a walk up back** *v.* [1920s–30s] (*US prison*) to be moved from one's cell to the execution chamber. ❑ **take for a walk** *v. see TAKE FOR A RIDE under* RIDE *n.*

walk *v.* **1** [mid-19C] to die. **2** [late 19C–1900s] (*US campus*) to take an examination without using any form of cheating aid. **3** [late 19C+] of objects, to go missing (presumed stolen) [SE *walk off*]. **4** [1940s] (*US tramp*) to banish, to eject from a place [SE *walk away, walk off*]. **5** [1950s] (*US*) to beat up [i.e. to 'walk all over']. **6** [1950s+] in senses of 'walking away'. (**a**) (*UK Und.*) to be found not guilty. (**b**) (*US prison/Und.*) to be released from prison or arrest. (**c**) (*US prison*) to release someone from prison. **7** [1960s+] to leave, to walk off; to resign.

IN PHRASES

❑ **walk (all) over** *v.* [mid-19C+] **1** to defeat someone comprehensively. **2** to treat someone with contempt. ❑ **walk around** *v.* (*also* **walk round**) **1** [mid-19C] (*US*) to cheat. **2** [1900s] to defeat easily. ❑ **walk it** *v.* (*also* **walk in**) [the relative lack of effort put out] [1930s+] to win easily, usu. in a sporting context. ❑ **walk the check** *v.* [abbr. SE *walk away from the check*] [1970s+] (*US campus*) to walk deliberately out of a restaurant without paying the bill. ❑ **walk up (against) the wall** *v.* [the landlord chalks one's running debts on the wall] [late 18C–early 19C] to run up credit at a public house.

SE in slang uses

IN COMPOUNDS

❑ **walkalone** *n.* [2000s] (*US prison*) a prisoner who has to exercise alone. ❑ **walkback** *n.* [1940s] (*US black*) an apartment at the rear of the block. ❑ **walkboy** *n.* [they *walk* together] [1980s+] (*US black*) a close male friend. ❑ **walk-by** *n.* [on model of DRIVE-BY *n.*] [1990s+] (*US black gang*) a shooting in which the attacker walks past the victim or their home and fires. ❑ **walk-foot** *n.* [any white who walks rather than rides is assumed to be poor] [1900s] (*W.I.*) **1** a poor white. **2** a beggar. ❑ **walktalk** *n.* [1910s+] (*Aus.*) a stroll on which the walkers chatter together.

IN PHRASES

❑ **walk...** *v. see also under* relevant n. ❑ **walk a chalk line/crack** *v. see* WALK THE CHALK *v.* ❑ **walk and nyam** *n.* [NYAM *v.* (1)] [early 19C+] (*W.I.*) a poor white; thus a sponger of any race. ❑ **walk both sides of the street** *v. see WORK BOTH SIDES OF THE STREET under* WORK *v.* ❑ **walk cool** *v.* [COOL *adv.* (1)] [1960s] (*US black*) to act in an unconcerned, relaxed manner, esp. in the face of problems or menaces. ❑ **walk dandy-dude** *v.* [SE *dandy* + DUDE *n.*[1] (1)] [1940s] (*W.I.*) to kick out one's legs when walking, the result of a deformity. ❑ **walk down someone's throat** *v.* [late 19C+] to tell off, to scold, to reprimand. ❑ **walked off** *adj.* [the condemned person is escorted from court] [1910s–20s] taken off to prison. ❑ **walk heavy** *v.* [1960s] (*US black*) to impose oneself on the world, to walk about in a deliberately self-assured manner. ❑ **walk like she can't mash ants** *v.* [note SE phr. *butter wouldn't melt in their mouth*] [20C+] (*W.I.*) used of a woman, implying that she appears far more innocent than her behaviour would reveal. ❑ **walk Matilda** *v. see* WALTZ MATILDA *v.* ❑ **walk of shame** *n.* **1** [1990s+] (*orig. US campus*) a woman's public appearance after spending the night with a new lover. **2** [2000s] of a man, the walk back to one's friends, e.g. in a bar, after failing to pick up a woman. ❑ **walk one's chalks** *v. see under* CHALKS *n.* ❑ **walk on rocky socks** *v.* [20C+] (*US*) to walk unsteadily owing to an excess of drink. ❑ **walk soft** *v.* [1970s+] (*US black*) to behave modestly. ❑ **walk someone's log** *v.* [late 19C] (*US campus*) to hurt someone. ❑ **walk the carpet** *v.* [such errant servants were summoned into the carpeted parlour to be told off by the master or mistress] [early 19C] to receive a reprimand, esp. of household servants. ❑ **walk the dog** *v.* **1** [1910s+] (*US*) to show off by driving or walking at speed. **2** *see FUCK THE DOG (AND SELL THE PUPS) under* DOG *n.*[2]. ❑ **walk the pavement** *v. see POUND THE PAVEMENT under* POUND *v.*[2]. ❑ **walk the piazzas** *v.* [the *piazzas* of Covent Garden were popular among prostitutes] [early 19C] to (start) work as a prostitute. ❑ **walk the plank** *v.* [the trad. (if mythical) punishment of Caribbean pirates] [late 19C+] (*US*) to be dismissed from a job. ❑ **walk the way of a trollop** *v.* [a play on the more usu. *walk the way of the warrior*, much loved by martial arts films, etc] [1990s+] (*US campus*) of a woman, to signal sexual availability. ❑ **walk up ladder Lane and down Hemp Street** *v.* [orig. naut. jargon] [19C] to be hanged.

walk-about *n.* (*also* **walk-a-leg, walk-a-picky, walker-leg, walker-picky**) [her tale-telling perambulations] [20C+] (*W.I.*) of a woman, a busybody, a gossip.

walk-about money *n.* [1930s+] daily expenses, petty cash rather than a large amount that needs investing or depositing.

walker *n.* **1** [mid-19C] a postman, a courier. **2** [mid-19C] (*UK und.*) a street-walker, a prostitute. **3** [1980s+] a man, often rich, invariably personable and socially acceptable, who accompanies the wives of prominent men to parties, on shopping expeditions, to the theatre etc.

walker *v.* [ety. unknown] [late 19C] to pawn.

walker! *excl.* [abbr. HOOKEY WALKER! *excl.*] [19C] an all-purpose teasing, dismissive excl.; nonsense! humbug! rubbish!

Walker & Co. *n.* [one *walks* around searching for work] [20C+] (*W.I.*) a notional place used fig. to mean a state of unemployment.

walker-leg/walker-picky *n. see* WALK-ABOUT *n.*

walkers *n.* [early 17C–mid-19C] the feet.

walkie-talkie *n.* [he *walks* and *talks* to the guards] [1990s+] (*Aus./US prison*) a prisoner who is overly friendly towards the authorities.

walk-in *n.* **1** [1920s] (*US*) one who gatecrashes parties. **2** [1960s] (*US*) a sexually available female; thus by ext., a prostitute.

walking *n.*

IN COMPOUNDS

❑ **walking orders** *n.* [var. WALKING PAPERS below] [early–mid-19C] a notice of dismissal. ❑ **walking papers** *n.* **1** [early 19C+] (*US*) a notice of dismissal. **2** [early 19C+] (*also* **papers**) an announcement that a relationship is over; divorce papers. **3** [1960s+] (*US prison*) an official notice to inform a prisoner that they have finished their sentence.

walking *adj.*

SE in slang uses

IN COMPOUNDS

❑ **walking dandruff** *n. see GALLOPING DANDRUFF under* GALLOPING *adj.* ❑ **walking distiller** *n.* [CARRY THE KEG *under* KEG *n.*] [early 19C] one who is easily annoyed, unable to take a joke. ❑ **walking gentleman** *n.* [orig. theatre *walking gentleman*, 'walking gentleman: an actor playing a part requiring gentlemanlike appearance, but with little or nothing to say' OED] [late 19C] one who poses as something but lacks the expertise to back the image. ❑ **walking mort** *n.* [MORT *n.* (1)]

[mid-16C–17C] (*UK Und.*) an unmarried female beggar, often accompanied by a child, who claimed to be widowed and begged for her and her offspring's keep. ❑ **walking poulterer** *n.* [late 18C–early 19C] a rural thief who steals fowls, then hawks them from door to door. ❑ **walking stationer** *n.* [ext. of SE *walking stationer*, a bookseller; cf. early 17C SE *standing stationer*, one who has a stall in a market] [late 18C–mid-19C] a hawker of pamphlets, gallows confessions, popular songs and similar materials. ❑ **walking train** *n.* [its lack of velocity] [1920s+] (*W.I.*) a local train. ❑ **walking tree** *n.* [1960s] (*S.Afr. prison*) a warder. ❑ **walking wounded** *n.* [orig. WW1 milit.] [1960s+] (*US*) anyone who, despite substantial problems in their life, is still able to function.

IN EXCLAMATIONS

❑ **walking Moses!** [1910s–20s] a general excl. of surprise, excitement, alarm etc.

walking the line *phr.* [rhy. sl. = DO *TIME under* TIME *n.*] [1980s+] (*Aus. prison*) serving a jail sentence.

walk into *v.* [all come from image of making a space or hole, whether in a meal, a purse or a person and *walking into it*] **1** [mid-19C] in fig. use, to approach aggressively, to concentrate on. **2** [mid-19C] to be indebted to, e.g. a tradesman. **3** [mid-19C] to defeat in a game of chance; to win money from. **4** [mid-19C] to spend money freely. **5** [mid-19C] (*US Und.*) to cheat, to defraud. **6** [mid-19C–1900s] to scold, to reprimand. **7** [mid-19C+] to attack, to overcome, to demolish. **8** [mid-19C+] to eat or drink to excess.

IN PHRASES

❑ **walk into somone's affections** *v.* [ironic uses of SE, to gain someone's love effortlessly] [mid-19C] **1** to beat, to scold. **2** to run up debts.

walk the chalk *v.* (*also* **walk a chalk line, ...crack**) **1** [early 19C+] to walk along a chalked line in order to prove one's sobriety. **2** [mid-19C+] (*also* **toe the chalk, ...crack, ...mark**) to behave in a sober, respectable manner.

walk-up fuck *n.* [SE *walk up* + FUCK *n.* (1); one needs only to *walk up and ask*] [20C+] (*Aus.*) a woman who is readily available for sex.

wall *n.*

SE in slang uses

IN COMPOUNDS

❑ **Wall City** *n.* [the prison wall + -CITY *sfx*] [1930s] (*US Und.*) San Quentin prison, California. ❑ **wall-eyed** *adj.* [SE *wall-eyed*, squinting] **1** [mid–late 19C] of any work badly done. **2** [20C+] of any odd or irregular action. **3** [1910s+] (*US*) drunk. **4** [2000s] under the influence of marijuana. ❑ **wall-falling** *adj.* [1970s+] (*Irish*) exhausted, tired out. ❑ **wall fruit** *n.* [mid-19C] kissing up against a wall. ❑ **wall-hugger** *n.* [1980s+] an eccentric, a mad person; thus *wall-hugging*, crazed. ❑ **wall job** *n.* [1950s] (*US gay*) anal entry done in a standing position. ❑ **wall queen** *n.* [1970s] (*US gay*) **1** a man who leans against a wall while he has sex. **2** a gay man who enjoys reading the inscriptions on public lavatory walls.

IN PHRASES

❑ **go over the wall** *v.* [lit. and fig. uses of SE] **1** [1910s] to go to prison. **2** [1910s+] (*orig. US*) to escape from prison. **3** [1940s+] to leave a religious order also as *jump over the wall, leap over the wall.*; in army context, *go over the wire*; also in fig. use, to gain sexual experience. **4** [1960s+] to go mad. **5** [1970s] to defect to another country. ❑ **go up the wall** *v.* [1950s+] **1** to lose one's temper. **2** to be terrified. ❑ **hang someone to the wall** *v.* [SE *hang*, the victim is tied against a wall for a beating; also HANG *v.*[6] (2)] [20C+] to punish severely. ❑ **hit the wall** *v.* (*also* **hit the hump**) **1** [1940s+] (*US prison*) to make an escape. **2** [1980s+] (*Aus. prison*) to make an unsuccessful escape. ❑ **inside the walls** *see* BEHIND THE WALLS *under* BEHIND *prep.* ❑ **off the wall** *see* separate entries. ❑ **over the wall** **1** [1930s+] escaped from prison. **2** [1950s] stolen. **3** [1970s] in prison. **4** [1980s] (*US*) (*also* **over the blue wall**) in a hospital for the criminally insane. ❑ **up the wall** *adj.* (*also* **up the walls**) [1940s+] (*US*) crazy, eccentric or over-excited, anxious. ❑ **wall it** *v.* [late 18C–mid-19C] to chalk up a debt on the wall of a public house. ❑ **wall-to-wall** *adj.* [abbr. SE *wall-to-wall carpet*] [1960s+] everywhere, all over.

wallaby *n.* [his nomadic life] **1** [mid-19C] (*Aus.*) a swagman's pack. **2** [mid-19C+] (*Aus.*) a vagrant; a swagman; usu. attrib.

IN PHRASES

❑ **on the wallaby** [mid-19C+] (*Aus.*) **1** on a spree. **2** on the move, tramping. **3** travelling to search for work. **4** impoverished. ❑ **wallaby track** *n.* [mid-19C+] (*Aus.*) the route followed by an itinerant moving from station to station in search of work; thus phr. *hit the wallaby*, to set off down the road, as a tramp.

wallaby *v.* [WALLABY *n.* (2)] [1900s] (*Aus.*) to wander around.

Wallace and Gromit *v.* [rhy. sl.] [2000s] to vomit.

Wallace Beery *n.* [rhy. sl.; ult. US movie star *Wallace Beery* (1885–1949)] [1990s+] a query, a question.

wallah *n.* [Hind. sfx *wala*, pertaining to or connected with, and comes in turn from the Arabic *wal*, proximity. It is the equivalent, therefore, of the Lat. *-arius*. Although found today as a single term, its 19C uses tended to be in combinations, such as *Agra wallah*, a native of Agra, *banghy-wallah*, a porter who carries loads with a banghy, or shoulder-yoke, *howdah-wallah*, an elephant accustomed to carry a howdah, and the Anglo-Indian *competition wallah*, those who entered the Civil Service competitive exams, established in 1856 to replace the old system of personal patronage] **1** [mid-18C+] a man, esp. in sense of a man who is pertaining to or connected with something, usu. a job. **2** [1910s] an Indian soldier. **3** [1960s+] a bureaucrat, an administrator. **4** [1970s] a thing.

wall-banger *n.* [the effect of methaqualone is to slow and 'soften' one's movements] [1960s+] (*US teen/drugs*) **1** a Quaalude or methaqualone capsule. **2** anyone who is so intoxicated by drugs that they cannot walk straight.

wallbanging *n.* [SE *bang*, i.e. one 'hits' a wall] [1980s+] (*US gang*) painting graffiti, esp. gang slogans or gang nicknames on walls.

waller *n.* [ety. unknown] [2000s] (*US black*) a general derog. term.

wallflower *n.* **1** [19C+] a woman (occas. a man) who does not join in dancing at a ball or dance, either through her inability to find a partner or through her desire to remain solo; thus a retiring, shy person [fig. use of SE]. **2** [1910s] (*US Und.*) a scrounger. **3** [1980s] (*UK prison*) a prisoner obsessed with the possibility of escape [fig. use of sense 1].

wallflowers *n.* [joc. use of prev.] [early–mid-19C] old or second-hand clothes hanging up for sale.

wallflower week *n.* [WALLFLOWER *n.* (1)] [20C+] those days during which a woman is menstruating and is, trad., sexually inactive.

wallio *n. see* WALYO *n.*

wallop *n.*[1] [WALLOP *v.* (2)] **1** [early 19C+] (*orig. boxing*) (*also* **whollop, wollop**) a resounding blow; lit. or fig. **2** [1910s] a time, a share, a go. **3** [1910s+] a try. **4** [1930s] a success. **5** [1950s] a severe punishment or prison sentence.

IN PHRASES

❑ **get the wallop** *v.* [1900s] (*Aus.*) to be dismissed. ❑ **pack a wallop** *v.* [1920s] to deliver a heavy blow. ❑ **come a wallop** *v.* [1920s–60s] to take a fall.

wallop *n.*[2] [ext. of WALLOP *n.*[1] (1), i.e. its strength; in WW2 beer only] [late 19C+] (*orig. Aus.*) beer, alcohol in general.

wallop *v.* [? Walloon *waloper*, to beat linen in water or Fr. *galoper*/Ital. *gallopare*, to gallop] **1** [18C–1910s] to make violent, noisy movements, to move clumsily or convulsively, to flounder. **2** [19C+] (*also* **whollop, wollop**) to beat, to thrash, to hit hard. **3** [late 19C+] to overcome, to surpass, to defeat. **4** [1990s+] to have sexual intercourse. **5** [2000s] (*S.Afr.*) to leave, to run away.

IN PHRASES

❑ **wallop it in** *v.* [late 19C+] to penetrate sexually, therefore to have sexual intercourse. ❑ **wallop the flint** *v. see* HIT THE GRIT *under* GRIT *n.*[2].

wallop! *excl.* [20C+] an excl. indicative of a sudden action.

walloper *n.*[1] [WALLOP *v.* (2)] **1** [early 19C] a blow. **2** [early 19C+] anyone who beats up their victims with a cudgel or stick. **3** [late 19C+] (*US*) anything or anyone exceptional in quality, size, character etc. **4** [1910s+] one who beats, e.g. hitting a child. **5** [1910s+] (*Aus./N.Z. milit.*) a worker, e.g. *base walloper*, a clerk; *security walloper*, a guard [influenced by WALLAH *n.*]. **6** [1930s+] (*Aus.*) a police officer. **7** [1940s] a clumsy fellow. **8** [1980s+] (*Aus.*) the penis. **9** [2000s] (*N.Z.*) a masturbator.

walloper *n.*[2] [WALLOP *n.*[2]] [1930s] a hotel, a bar.

wallopies *n.* [Scot. *wallop*, to dangle, to flop about] [1970s+] (*US campus*) female breasts, esp. large ones.

walloping *n.* [WALLOP v. (4)] [1990s+] an act of sexual intercourse.

walloping *adj.* [WALLOP *v.*] **1** [early 19C] clumsy, awkward. **2** [early 19C+] (*also* **wholloping, wolloping**) a general intensifier, usu. as to size and often ext. as *walloping great*. **3** [late 19C+] in fig. use, powerful.

wallop someone's block off *v. see* KNOCK SOMEONE'S BLOCK OFF *under* BLOCK *n.*[1].

wallpaper *n.* **1** [1940s+] (*US*) worthless paper money such as counterfeit notes [it has no monetary use]. **2** [1980s+] (*drugs*) money [one has enough to use it as wallpaper].

wally *n.*[1] [late 19C+] a pickled cucumber.

wally *n.*[2] (*also* **wolly**) [ety. unknown. ? abbr. Scot. *wally-drag*, a feeble, ill-grown or worthless person. The proper name *Walter* is sometimes categorized as a 'silly' name. In police jargon, a *wally* is a trainee and thus incompetent police officer: ext. of WALLY *n.*[1]; note Newman (1970) 'He would resign rather than return to being a wolly'] **1** [1920s+] an unfashionable, unintelligent, 'suburban' person, lacking in taste and sophistication. **2** [1930s] (*US tramp*) a tramp who stays within radius of his home town. **3** [1970s] a person with learning difficulties. **4** [1970s+] (*Aus.*) a bungler. **5** [1990s+] (*US campus*) an otherwise socially unacceptable person who is accepted into a social group because they are needed for their intelligence, athletic ability or good looks.

wally *n.*[3] [the older-brother character *Wally* in US TV show *Leave It to Beaver*] [1980s+] (*US campus*) used of someone seen as acting like a big brother or sister.

Wally Grout *n.* [rhy. sl. = SHOUT *n.* (1a); ult. Aus. wicket keeper *Wally Grout* (1927–68)] [1990s+] (*Aus.*) one's turn to buy a round of drinks.

Wally-O *n. see* WALYO *n.*

wally the monk *adj.* [rhy. sl.] [1980s] (*Aus.*) drunk.

walnut-shell *n.* [resemblance] [early 19C] a very light carriage.

walnut whip *n.* [rhy. sl.] [1990s+] **1** a sleep [= KIP *n.*[1] (4)]. **2** a *nipple*. **3** a vasectomy [= SE *snip*].

walrus *n.* **1** [1910s–60s] a large, bushy moustache, supposedly reminiscent of the animal. **2** [1920s+] (*US*) a short, fat person. **3** [2000s] (*Irish*) £50.

walter joyce *n.* [rhy. sl.] [late 19C] the voice.

Walter Mitty *n.* [rhy. sl. = TITTY *n.* (1)] [1980s+] (*Aus.*) the female breast.

Walter Scott *n.* [rhy. sl.; ult. novelist Sir *Walter Scott* (1771–1832)] [1950s+] a pot (of beer).

waltz *n.* [WALTZ v. (4)] [1920s+] **1** anything that can be accomplished with minimum effort. **2** an easy success; esp. in sporting use, e.g. a boxing match in which neither fighter makes much effort.

IN PHRASES

□ **do a dry waltz with oneself** *v.* [1940s+] to masturbate.

waltz *v.* (*also* **waltz along, ...around, ...in, ...into, ...off, ...up**) **1** [late 19C+] to move lightly, blithely, unconcernedly. **2** [late 19C+] to move or to take someone. **3** [late 19C+] to persuade someone. **4** [20C+] to achieve something easily, esp. in sporting use. **5** [1970s] (*US*) to evade or deceive someone.

IN PHRASES

□ **waltz into** *v.* [1910s+] to attack.

waltz Matilda *v.* (*also* **walk Matilda**) [SE *waltz* + MATILDA *n.*] [late 19C+] (*Aus.*) to go on the tramp, carrying one's pack; thus *Matilda-waltzer*, a tramp.

waltz me around *n.* [rhy. sl.] [1980s] (*Aus.*) a pound.

walyo *n.* (*also* **wallio, Wally-O, wallyo**) [? Ital. dial. *uaglio*, a young one] [20C+] (*US*) **1** a young man, often used affectionately by an older man to a younger one. **2** an Italian man.

wamba *n. see* WONGA *n.*

wamble *n.* [SE *wamble*, to feel queasy, to walk unsteadily, ? ult. Dan. *vamle*, to feel nausea + Norw. *vamla*, to stagger] [late 16C–17C] a feeling of nausea, queasiness, often as *the wambles*; thus *wamble-cropped*, *wamble-stomached*, feeling nauseous, sick; thus adj. *wambling*.

wamblety-cropped *adj.* (*also* **wamble-cropped, womblescropt, womblety-cropped**) [SE *wamble-cropped*, sick in the stomach] [late 17C–mid-19C] suffering from an upset stomach due to excessive drinking.

wame *n.* [Scot. *wame*, the womb; the stomach] [late 18C–early 19C] the vagina.

wampo *n.* [? RAF sl. *wampo*, intoxicating liquor; ? note *Wampole*, a preparation of alcohol, quinine, and strychnine sold by an eponymous US drug firm c. 1910] [1940s+] beer slops or overflow, recycled and served as fresh beer.

wampum *n.* [Algonquin *wampumpeag*, beads made from quahog shells and used as money; often abbr. to *wampum* itself] [mid-19C+] (*orig. US*) money.

SE in slang uses

IN PHRASES

□ **wampum and warpaint** *n.* [*wampum*, beads, worn as ornamental garments or jewellery + WARPAINT *under* WAR *n.*] [late 19C] evening dress.

wampus *n.* [? abbr. CATAWAMPUS *n.* (2)] [1950s] (*W.I.*) a large man.

wampy *adj.* [? WAMPO *n.*] [1950s–70s] (*N.Z.*) mad, insane.

wana *n.* [abbr./pron.] [1970s+] (*drugs*) marijuana.

wan and wan *n. see* ONE-AND-ONE *n.*[1].

wand *n.* [17C+] the penis.

IN PHRASES

□ **wave the (magic) wand** *v.* [1970s+] to masturbate.

Wanda Wandwaver *n.* [WAND *n.* (1) + SE *waver*] [1960s–70s] (*camp gay*) an exhibitionist.

wander! *excl.* [late 19C] go away!

wandering star *n.* [mid-19C] a woman who coyly seduces men in the street in order to rob them.

Wandering Willie *n.* [1910s–30s] (*US*) a vagrant, a tramp.

wang *n.*[1] [1920s–40s] a notable person.

wang *n.*[2] (*also* **wanger, wang-wang, wing-wang**) **1** [1930s+] (*orig. US*) the penis [WHANG *n.*[1] (4)]. **2** [1990s+] (*S.Afr.*) a cigarette [resembles the shape of sense 1].

wanga *n. see* WONGA *n.*

wanga gut *n.* (*also* **wonga-gut**) [? WONGA *n.* + SE *gut*, i.e. one is 'hungry' for cash] [1980s+] (*W.I./UK black teen*) greediness or jealousy.

wangdoodle *n.* **1** *see* WHANGDOODLE *n.*[1]. **2** *see* WHANGDOODLE *n.*[2].

wanger *n. see* WANG *n.*[2].

wangle *n.* [dial. *wangling*, sickly, weak, delicate] [late 19C–1910s] (*Irish*) a thin, tall, weak young man.

wangle *v.* [late 19C+] to obtain what one wants, often through a degree of manipulation or cunning.

wangled *adj.* [WANGLE *v.*] [1940s] stolen.

wangler *n.* [WANGLE *v.*] [1910s–20s] one who uses a variety of irregular means to accomplish a purpose.

wanglo-saxon *n.* [1970s] (*US*) a white *Anglo-Saxon*.

wang-tang *n.* [? fig. use of WANG *n.*[2] (1) + SE *tang*, a flavour] [1970s+] (*US black*) anything, esp. on a sexual level, that is especially desirable.

wang-wang *n. see* WANG *n.*[2].

wangy *n.* [1910s] (*US tramp*) a beggar who sells bootlaces as a front for his basic trade of begging.

wank *n.* [WANK *v.*] **1** [1940s+] masturbation. **2** [1970s+] in fig. use, self-indulgence. **3** [1980s] (*US campus*) a person who is logged on to a computer (usu. the Internet or involved in hacking) for a long time. **4** [1990s+] nonsense. **5** [2000s] something worthless. **6** see WANKER *n.* (2).

IN PHRASES

❑ **not worth a wank** *adj.* [1970s+] worthless, useless. ❑ **posh wank** *n.* [POSH *adj.* (1)] [1990s+] an act of masturbation while wearing a condom. ❑ **yank one's wank** *v.* [YANK *v.*[1] (1)] [20C+] to masturbate.

wank *adj.* [1990s+] a general pej.; unpleasant, distasteful, useless, etc.

wank *v.* [ety. unknown, but note the many 'beating' synons, the orig. sp. *whank* and late 18C Scot./dial. *whank*, to beat, to thrash] [1940s+] **1** to masturbate. **2** in fig. use, to waste time. **3** in fig. use, to abuse someone else. **4** to be logged on to a computer for a long time.

DERIVATIVES

❑ **wankily** *adv.* [1990s+] in a second-rate manner.

IN COMPOUNDS

❑ **wank-bag** *n.* [1990s+] a general term of abuse. ❑ **wank mag** *n.* [MAG *n.*[4] (1)] [1960s+] a pornographic magazine. ❑ **wank tank** *n.* [2000s] a large, ostentatious car, purchased for the enhancement of it's owner's ego and the display of his material success.

IN PHRASES

❑ **wanked out** *adj.* [1970s+] exhausted. ❑ **wank off** *v.* (*also* **whank off**) [1940s+] **1** to masturbate. **2** to masturbate another person, usu, male. ❑ **wank on** *v.* [1980s+] to bore, to talk nonsense for a long time. ❑ **wank the crank** *v.* [CRANK *n.*[3] (1)] [1960s+] to masturbate.

wank! *excl.* [WANK *v.*] [1970s+] (*US campus*) a general negative retort.

wanker *n.* [WANK *v.* (1), note late 19C Yorks./Norfolk dial. *wanker*, a simpleton; Partridge suggests origin in 'late C.19' but offers no evidence] [1940s+] **1** a masturbator. **2** (*also* **wank**) a general derog. description of a lazy, incompetent, unpleasant person. **3** (*US campus*) an undesirable situation or thing. **4** the penis.

IN COMPOUNDS

❑ **wanker's doom** *n.* [1940s+] (*orig. RAF*) a fig. unpleasant fate.

IN PHRASES

❑ **go like a wanker's elbow** *v.* [1990s+] to be extremely busy.

wankered *adj.* (*also* **wanked**) [WANK *v.* (1)] [1990s+] **1** exhausted, worn out. **2** having consumed a large quantity of alcohol or drugs.

wanking *n.* [WANK *v.* (1)] **1** [1940s+] masturbation. **2** [1990s+] in fig. sense, doing something repetitive or mundane.

IN COMPOUNDS

❑ **wanking spanners** *n.* [1940s+] the hands.

wankshaft *n.* [WANK *v.* (1)] [1990s+] (*UK juv.*) the penis.

wanksta *n.* [WACK *adj.*/WANNABE *adj.*/WANKER *n.* (2) + GANGSTA *n.* (2)] [2000s] **1** a white person espousing black gangster culture. **2** a would-be gangster.

wankstain *n.* [WANK *n.* + SE *stain*] [1990s+] an ineffectual person.

wankstain *adj.* [WANKSTAIN *n.*] [2000s] ineffectual, worthless.

wanky *adj.* [fig./lit. uses of WANK *v.* (1)] **1** [1920s+] pretentious. **2** [1940s+] covered in post-masturbatory semen. **3** [1970s+] inferior, second-rate. **4** [1970s+] sexually titillating, conducive to masturbation. **5** [1980s] (*US juv.*) crazy.

wannabe *n.* [SE *I want to be ...*, orig. US black, where the term simply meant a fantasist and latterly a white person wishing to be black + from surfing jargon a learner. Popularized with the rise of the pop star Madonna (Madonna Louise Veronica Ciccone, b.1958), whose fans declared, either verbally or in the way they dressed, *I wanna be like Madonna*] **1** [1970s+] an aspirant, one who yearns to be a certain individual, usu. more talented and famous than they are; of an object, a copy, something second-best. **2** [1990s+] (*US prison*) a young prisoner who poses as a prison-wise veteran.

IN PHRASES

❑ **Woodstock wannabe** *n.* [the *Woodstock* Festival of 1969 (seen as the high-watermark of hippiedom) + WANNABE *n.*] [1990s+] (*US campus*) one whose lifestyle and attitudes are reminiscent of the HIPPIE *adj.* Sixties.

wannabe *adj.* [WANNABE *n.* (1)] [1980s+] aspirant.

wannabe raped look *n.* [ext. of SE *want to be raped*] [1980s+] of a woman, a sluttish, provocative style of dressing.

wanna do a thing? *phr.* [SE *want* + DO A THING *under* THING *n.*] [1960s+] (*US black*) asking a passing woman if she fancies intercourse.

Wanno *n.* [1990s+] (*UK Und.*) HMP Wandsworth, in south London.

wansteads *n.* [rhy. sl.; ult. East London area *Wanstead Flats*] [1920s–30s] spats.

want *n.* [such a person is *in want* of some brains] **1** [20C+] (*Irish*) any form of mental deficiency. **2** [1940s–70s] (*US police*) a charge, a 'wanted' notice.

want *v.*

SE in slang uses

IN PHRASES

❑ **want portholes in one's coffin** *v.* [1910s] (*Aus.*) to be hard to please. ❑ **want to front** *v. see* TRY TO FRONT *under* TRY *v.* ❑ **want to make something of it?** (*also* **want to do something about it?**) [1920s+] (*orig. US*) a ritual request that may well herald a fight, but still gives the other person the chance to back down.

wanting *adj.* [SE *wanting* intelligence, brains etc] [mid-19C] mentally unbalanced, insane.

wantz *n.* [abbr. of SCHWANTZ *n.* (1)] [1970s] (*US*) the penis.

wap *n.* [WAP *v.*] **1** [early 18C] the act of copulation. **2** *see* WOP *n.*[1] (1).

wap *v.* [SE *wap*, to throw violently, to pull down; Hencke suggests link to *wap*, a mongrel and thence to BITCH *n.*[1] (1)] [mid-16C–early 19C] to have sex, usu. used of a woman.

wapi *n.* [? WAP *n.* + familiarizing sfx *-i/-y*] [1950s] (*W.I.*) sexual intercourse.

wap-john *n.* [SE *wap*, to hit + JOHN *n.* (1)] [mid-19C] a gentleman's coachman.

wappen-bappen *n.* [echoic of hammering such a shack together] [1930s+] (*W.I.*) a tumbledown, slum shed or shanty made of old tins, bits of wood, discarded packaging and similar found objects.

wapper-eyed *adj.* [dial. *wapper*, to have sore eyes, to blink] [17C–early 19C] sore-eyed, squinting.

wapper-jawed *adj. see* WHOPPER-JAWED *adj.*

wapping *n.* [WAP *v.* (1)] [mid-16C–18C] sexual intercourse.

IN COMPOUNDS

❑ **wapping cove** *n.* [COVE *n.* (1)] [mid-18C] (*UK Und.*) a frequenter of prostitutes. ❑ **wapping dell** *n.* (*also* **wapping-mort**) [DELL *n.* (2) /MORT *n.*] [17C–mid-18C] a prostitute. ❑ **wapping ken** *n.* [KEN *n.*[1] (1)] [mid-18C] (*UK Und.*) a brothel.

wapping *adj. see* WHOPPING *adj.*

wappy *adj.* [? SE *wet* + *soppy*] [1950s–60s] sentimental, idealistic, 'soft'.

waps *n.* (*also* **wap-waps**) [SE *wap*, to move, to shake] [1990s+] the female breasts.

war *n.*

SE in slang uses

IN COMPOUNDS

❑ **war baby** *n.* **1** [1910s–20s] (*UK/Aus.*) a young or newly conscripted soldier. **2** [1920s] (*US Und.*) money gained through the successful hoaxing of a man who had made his money in the (still-recent) World War I. **3** [1920s; 1940s] an illegitimate child, conceived and born while the mother's husband is away on active service. **4** [1920s–40s] (*US*) a bond that is sold during wartime with the presumption that it will 'grow' in value. ❑ **war club** *n.* [20C+] (*US*) a baseball bat. ❑ **war cry** *n.* [a satire on the Salvation Army newspaper *The War Cry* and the belief that while the Army spoke 'stoutly' it used only 'mild' terms] [late 19C] a mixture of stout and mild ale. ❑ **war daddy** *n.* [2000s] (*US prison*) an inmate who protects another from problems while incarcerated; the protected inmate will be expected to offer homosexual services. ❑ **warhorse** *n.* **1** [late 19C+] (*US*) a veteran, an old-timer. **2** [1930s] (*US campus*) an uncompromising, determined woman. ❑ **warlord** *n.* [1950s+] **1** (*US black/teen*) a street-gang leader. **2** (*US prison*) a gang leader, who takes control of gang fights and killings, although not the absolute head of a gang. ❑ **warpaint** *n.* **1** [mid-19C] military uniform. **2** [mid-19C–1920s] court dress, formal dress. **3** [mid-19C+] cosmetics, make-up. ❑ **war stories** *n.* [1960s+] (*US*) stories of one's adventurous exploits, e.g. in a street gang; real war plays no part.

warahoon *n.* [? name of a tribe of (unidentified) S. American coastal Amerindians, poss. the Warrau of the Orinoco Delta and northwest Guyana] [1960s+] (*W.I.*) a noisy ill-bred person.

war and strife *n.* [rhy. sl.] [1900s–70s] one's wife.

warap *n.* [Carib.E. *warap*, a drink made from fermented sugar cane, drunk by poor peasants] [20C+] (*W.I.*) **1** a cheap, tasteless meal, esp. a soup. **2** a cheap meal made of fish or meat and 'ground-provisions', i.e. locally available starchy roots, all boiled up together.

wara-wara *n.* [WARA-WARA *adj.* (1)] [20C+] (*W.I., Jam.*) bits and pieces.

wara-wara *adj.* [Yoruba *wara-wara*, half done, in a hurry] [20C+] (*W.I., Guyn.*) cheap, of inferior quality, esp. of clothing.

warb *n.* [? SE *warble*, the maggot of a warble-fly] [1930s+] **1** (*Aus.*) a fool, a simpleton. **2** (*Aus.*) a dirty, unkempt person; a loafer. **3** (*UK Und.*) a drunkard, a down-and-out. **4** (*Aus.*) a low-paid manual worker.

warbag *n.* [1930s+] (*US*) a bag for one's belongings.

warble *v.* [late 19C+] to talk in a pleasant manner.

warbler *n.* **1** [mid-18C; late 19C–1920s] a male singer. **2** [early 19C] '*Warblers*, singers who go about to 'free and easy' meetings, to chaunt for pay, for grog, or for the purpose of putting off benefit-tickets' (Jon Bee). **3** [early 19C; 1920s+] a female singer. **4** [1970s+] a telephone whose bell *warbles* rather than rings. **5** [1940s–50s] (*US Und.*) a public defender.

warby *adj.* [WARB *n.*] [1940s+] (*Aus.*) **1** unprepossessing in appearance or disposition, unkempt, disreputable, decrepit. **2** insecure, unwell.

warden *n.* [1950s–60s] (*US teen*) a parent or any other authority figure.

ware *n.* [SE *ware*, goods on sale, thus the commercial potential of sex] **1** [late 16C–early 19C] the vagina; the maidenhead; thus generic for a woman. **2** [late 18C] the penis.

warehouse *n.* **1** [1900s–1920s] (*UK society*) a large, fashionable pawn shop. **2** [1930s] (*US*) a bank. **3** [1960s+] a large and impersonal institution offering shelter to the mentally ill, the old or the poor. **4** [2000] (*US prison*) an overcrowded prison.

warehouse *v.* [WAREHOUSE *n.*] **1** [late 19C] to imprison (for a long time). **2** [1900s–20s] (*UK society*) to place in pawn. **3** [1970s+] (*US*) to place an individual, usu. a mental patient, in a large and impersonal institution, i.e. to 'put them away'.

ware (the) hawk! *excl.* (*also* **ware the bull!**) [hunting jargon *ware hawk!*, a warning cry either to or of animals. The *hawk* personifies any 'grasping' person, whether working for or against the law] [17C–1900s] a warning cry, orig. indicating that a bailiff or constable is approaching, thus n. *war-hawk*, a bailiff.

warm *adj.* **1** [17C–1900s] rich, well-off. **2** [mid-18C] infected with a venereal disease. **3** [mid-18C] enthusiastic, zealous. **4** [mid-18C] slightly drunk. **5** [mid-18C+] sharp-tempered. **6** [early 19C–1920s] suggestive, esp. of speech. **7** [mid-19C–1920s] unpleasant, uncomfortable. **8** [mid-19C–1950s] (*Und.*) under suspicion; of a place, dangerous for criminal activity. **9** [mid-19C+] of a situation or place, exciting, active. **10** [late 19C] of a bill, large, poss. exorbitant. **11** [late 19C] (*US*) fast or powerful. **12** [late 19C] of a picture, smutty. **13** [late 19C–1910s] (*US*) able, competent. **14** [late 19C+] of a woman, sexy, provocative. **15** [1910s–30s] (*Aus.*) intimate. **16** [1990s+] (*US black*) human, affectionate, the opposite of COOL *adj.* (1).

(IN COMPOUNDS)

❑ **warm baby** *n.* [late 19C–1920s] (*US*) a fashionable, exciting individual. ❑ **warm britches** *n.* *see* HOT PANTS *n.* ❑ **warm corner** *n.* [mid-19C–1900s] anywhere frequented by prostitutes. ❑ **warm member** *n.* [SE *member*, a participant/MEMBER *n.*[1] (1)] [late 19C–1920s] (*US*) a promiscuous man, a philanderer. ❑ **warm shop** *n.* (*also* **warm show**) [1910s–20s] a brothel. ❑ **warm 'un** *n.* [late 19C] a prostitute.

(IN PHRASES)

❑ **play the warm for** *v.* [1930s] (*US*) to make advances towards, to ingratiate with. ❑ **warm as they make them** *adj.* [late 19C] of a woman, very sexy.

SE in slang uses

(IN COMPOUNDS)

❑ **warm beer** *n.* [its colour] [1970s+] urine. ❑ **warm body** *n.* [20C+] (*US*) an insignificant person, someone who is present but does not participate. ❑ **warm flannel** *n.* *see* HOT FLANNEL *under* HOT *adj.* ❑ **warm-mouth** *n.* [1950s] (*W.I.*) the very first meal of the day, eaten between 4 and 6 a.m. and preceding a proper breakfast. ❑ **warm water** *n.* *see* HOT WATER *n.* ❑ **warm weather** *n.* [1900s] (*US*) a (self-)important person. ❑ **warm with** *n.* [mid–late 19C] a drink of *warm* spirits *with* water or sugar.

(IN PHRASES)

❑ **make it warm for** *v.* *see* MAKE IT HOT FOR *under* HOT *adj.* ❑ **warm in the tail** *adj.* *see* HOT IN THE TAIL *under* TAIL *n.*

warm *v.* **1** [late 18C+] to thrash, to beat, esp. in descriptive combs., such as *warm one's arse*, *warm one's jacket*, to thrash. **2** [mid-19C] to abuse, to scold.

(IN PHRASES)

❑ **warm someone's behind** *v.* *see under* BEHIND *n.* ❑ **warm someone's ear** *v.* **1** [20C+] (*Ulster*) (*also* **warm someone's lug**) to hit someone across the ear; usu. in unexecuted threat, *I'll warm your ear (for you!)*. **2** [1920s–30s] (*US*) to chatter and gossip incessantly. ❑ **warm someone's jacket** *v.* [late 18C–1930s] to thrash, esp. on context of school beatings. ❑ **warm the wax of someone's ear** *v.* [mid-19C–1910s] to box someone's ears.

SE in slang uses

(IN PHRASES)

❑ **warm the husband's supper** *v.* (*also* **...husband's dinner, ...old man's supper**) [19C] to stand in front of the fire with lifted skirts. ❑ **warm the oven** *v.* [mid-19C] to drink, to get drunk. ❑ **warm the whole of one's body** *v.* [pun on *whole/hole*, i.e. the anus] [20C+] to stand with one's back to the fire.

warm *adv.* [20C+] (*Aus./W.I.*) a great deal, much.

warm bit *n.* *see under* BIT *n.*[1].

warmed over *adj.* [SE *warm over*, of food, to reheat, to warm up] [late 19C+] (*US*) derivative, unimaginative.

warming pan *n.*[1] **1** [17C] the vagina. **2** [mid-17C–mid-18C] a female bed companion. **3** [mid-19C–1900s] a place-holder, a deputy, used orig. of clergy.

warming pan *n.*[2] [the shape] [late 17C–19C] a large, gold pocket watch.

warm up *n.* [1970s+] **1** sexual foreplay [WARM UP *v.*]. **2** a wash before intercourse [sporting imagery, i.e. exercising to preparing oneself for the match].

warm up *v.* [WARM *adj.* (14)] [1900s–70s] to indulge in sexual foreplay.

warp *n.* (*also* **warpe**) [? SE *ward*, to watch] [late 16C–mid-17C] (*UK Und.*) the lookout man for a team of thieves who steal by hooking objects from stalls or shop windows.

warpe *n.* *see* WARP *n.*

warped *adj.* [2000s] (*Irish*) drunk.

warp out *v.* (*also* **warp away**) [the use of *warpspeed* in the *Star Trek* TV series (from 1966) and films (from 1980)] [1990s+] (*US*) to leave hastily.

warp-seven *adj.* [*see* WARP OUT *v.*] [1990s+] (*US black*) very fast.

warrab *n.* [backsl.] [mid-19C] a barrow.

warra-warra *n. see* TARRA-WARRA *n.*

warren *n.*[1] [abbr. *CUNNY WARREN under* CUNNY *n.*] **1** [late 16C–early 19C] a brothel. **2** [late 17C–early 19C] a boarding school.

warren *n.*[2] [? SE *warrant*] [17C–early 19C] a creditor, part of a confidence team, who encourage rich young men to run up large bills and then dun them.

warrior bold *adj.* (*also* **warrior's hold**) [rhy. sl.] [20C+] cold; as n., a cold in the head.

warrocks! *excl.* [SE *war hawks!* i.e. tomahawks, and presumably referring to a Native American attack] [late 19C] (*US*) beware! look out!

wart *n.* [note milit. use *wart*, (RN) a junior midshipman, (Br. Army) a young subaltern] [late 19C+] (*orig. US*) an unpleasant, obnoxious person.

warts and all *phr.* [the story of Oliver Cromwell (1599–1658) ordering the painter Sir Peter Lely (1618–1680) to 'use all your skill to paint my picture truly like me, and not flatter me at all; but remark all these roughnesses, pimples, warts and everything as you see me, otherwise I will never pay a farthing for it'] [1910s+] not excluding any deficiencies or negative characteristics.

Warwick Farm *n.* [rhy. sl.; ult. *Warwick Farm*, a Sydney racecourse] [1940s+] (*Aus.*) an arm.

waser *n.* (*also* **wasser**) [Fr. *oiseau*, a bird] [1900s–10s] a young woman.

wash *n.*[1] **1** [early 18C; mid-19C] tea. **2** [mid-19C+] beer, also as an accompaniment to a spirit. **3** [late 19C] (*Aus.*) a tea-party. **4** [1940s] (*US*) soda water. **5** [1940s+] (*US*) a second drink, one to wash down the first. **6** [1960s+] (*W.I.*) the mash of cheap grain and sugar that is distilled to produce the homemade spirit sold in illicit drinking clubs [SE *wash*, malt, etc steeped in water to undergo fermentation]. **7** [1970s] (*US drugs*) a mix of heroin, water and blood that is injected by the user. **8** [1980s+] crack cocaine [the process of chemical purification, known as 'washing', that is used when making the drug]. **9** *see* WHITEWASH *n.* (2).

IN PHRASES

❑ **black wash** *n.* [1940s+] (*W.I.*) coffee.

wash *n.*[2] [abbr. of *EYEWASH under* EYE *n.*] [1910s] verbal nonsense.

wash *v.* **1** [1930s–70s] (*US Und.*) to kill, to murder, to assassinate; thus n., *wash day* (prison), execution day [fig. use of SE *wash out*]. **2** [1970s+] to 'de-criminalize' corruptly or illegally gained money by 'washing' it through a casino till or bank [var. LAUNDER *v.*]. **3** [1980s+] (*drugs*) to alter the properties of cocaine base by a chemical process.

IN PHRASES

❑ **wash away** *v.* [1940s+] (*US*) **1** to kill, to murder. **2** in fig. use. to overwhelm.

SE in slang uses

IN COMPOUNDS

❑ **wash-and-go** *n.* [play on the brandname shampoo] [1990s+] (*gay*) one who leaves immediately after sex. ❑ **wash-belly** *n.* [the image of finally 'cleaning out' the womb] [1950s] (*W.I.*) a woman's last child. ❑ **wash-mouth** *n.* [late 19C] liquor. ❑ **washpot** *n. see* MOAB *n.* ❑ **washrock** *n.* [WASH *n.*[1] (8) + ROCK *n.* (4c)] [1990s+] (*drugs*) crack cocaine. ❑ **washtub** *n.* [1970s] (*US*) a boat.

IN PHRASES

❑ **wash one's brain** *v.* (*also* **wash one's head**) [early 19C] to drink wine. ❑ **wash one's foot in the tank** *v. see under* TANK *n.*[1]. ❑ **wash one's liver with milk** *v.* [the idea that *milk* rather than blood is running through one's veins] [late 17C–mid-18C] to stop behaving in a cowardly manner. ❑ **wash one's mouth** *v.* [late 19C–1910s] to have a drink. ❑ **wash one's mouth upon** *v.* [1940s] (*W.I.*) to gossip about, to denigrate behind someone's back. ❑ **wash one's neck** *v.* (*also* **put it down one's neck, wash it down...**) [late 19C–1920s] to drink. ❑ **wash one's skin** *v.* [20C+] (*W.I.*) to beat, to thrash, to defeat comprehensively. ❑ **wash the ivories** *v. see under* IVORY *n.* ❑ **wash-your-foot-and-come** *n.* [20C+] (*W.I.*) an impromptu dance, with no special dressing-up required.

washed rock *n.* [WASH *v.* (3)+ ROCK *n.* (4c)] [1980s+] (*drugs*) crack cocaine.

washed up *adj.*[1] [theatrical use *washed up*, finished for the night] **1** [20C+] (*orig. US*) useless, exhausted, failed. **2** [1920s+] of a relationship, ended. **3** [1930s] of a person, finished doing something; of an event, concluded. **4** [1930s–40s] upset, depressed.

washed up *adj.*[2] [i.e. one is CLEAN *adj.* (11)] [1930s+] (*drugs*) no longer using drugs.

washer *n.*[1] **1** [1900s–10s; 1970s] (*US*) a dollar [SE *washer*, a small metal disk]. **2** [1970s+] (*US gay*) a condom [its being placed between two surfaces to relieve friction].

washer *n.*[2] [? BELLY WASH *n.* (2)] [1940s] (*US black*) a tavern, a bar, a fast-food restaurant.

washer-dona *n.* (*also* **water-dona**) [SE *washer/water* + DONA *n.* (1)] [late 19C] a washerwoman.

washer-dryer *n.* [1980s] (*US black*) a douche-bag and towel.

washer-upper *n.* [1960s+] one who washes dishes, usu. in a restaurant, hotel etc.

washicong(s) *n.* (*also* **watchekong(s)**) [Chi. *hua xie kong hong*, lit. 'flower shoes (which are) full of holes'; 'this cheap footwear was most popular among the chinese indentured labourers in Trin. in the late 19C' (Allsopp, *Dict. Caribbean English Usage*, 1996)] [1950s] (*W.I., Gren./Trin.*) sandals, plimsolls; spec. sandals with open-work in the pattern of a flower.

washing *n.*[1]

SE in slang uses

IN PHRASES

❑ **don't hang dirty washing in my backyard** [1940s] (*US black*) don't lie to me; don't tell me stories.

washing *n.*[2] [WASH *v.* (3)] [1980s+] (*drugs*) preparing crack cocaine.

washing powder *n.* [1970s+] (*US black*) a douching solution.

washman *n.* [mid-16C] (*UK Und.*) a criminal mendicant sporting fake sores and wounds. Their superior in the criminal hierarchy, the PALLIARD *n.*, saw them as inferior rivals and would treat them accordingly.

wash-out *n.* **1** [20C+] a disappointment, a failure. **2** [1910s] (*US prison*) a life sentence. **3** [1910s+] a useless or unsuccessful person; also as adj., *washed-out*.

wash out *v.* **1** [1910s+] (*orig. milit.*) to remove, to cancel, to dismiss (e.g. from a course). **2** [1910s+] to fail, e.g. a course. **3** [1930s] (*US*) to lose all one's money, esp. from gambling. **4** [1940s] to lose or spoil anything.

wash-up *n.* [WASH UP *v.* (1)] [1900s–50s] (*usu. Aus.*) the final assessment, the outcome, the 'bottom line'.

wash up *adj. see* WASHED UP *adj.*[1].

wash up *v.* [supposedly coined thus: 'That guy might be all right if he washed up [washed, cleaned himself],' commented Buck ... Just then the stage manager called out, 'What will I do with this act, Mr. Ziegfeld?' 'Wash up him and the bird,' said Flo [Ziegfeld] and that was the last of the Italian and his trained canary ... Hype Igoe, the World's sporting writer, heard of the incident ... and in commenting ... upon Frank Moran, heavy weight pugilist, advised that matchmakers 'wash him up'. The phrase ... has become a colloquial fixture ... as a meaty synonym for finals and farewell' (N.Y. *World*, 25 October 1925); however note date of WASH-UP *n.*] **1** [1900s–50s] (*US*) to bring to a conclusion, to end. **2** [1930s] to finish a relationship. **3** [1950s] (*US drugs*) to withdraw from narcotics addiction. **4** [1980s] to render a failure, to destroy hopes.

was my face red! *excl.* [1930s+] an excl. of embarrassed regret, usu. when recounting some shameful solecism.

WASP *n.* [abbr. orig. Chicago sl./Ohio Valley social workers' jargon *WASP*, White Appalachian Southern Protestants] [1950s+]

White Anglo-Saxon Protestant, the predominant racial group in the USA; thus *wasp, waspish, waspy*, characteristic of this social grouping.

wasp *n.*[1] ['she carries a sting in her tail'] [late 18C–early 19C] a diseased prostitute.

wasp *n.*[2] [the black and yellow colours of the uniform] [1960s+] (*Irish*) a traffic warden.

wasp v. [1940s] (*US*) to tease maliciously; thus adj. *waspish*.

wasp and bee *n.* [rhy. sl.] [20C+] (*Aus.*) tea.

wasser *n. see* WASER *n.*

was she worth it? *n.* (*also* **seven and six**) [the then price of a UK marriage licence, 7s 6d (37½ pence)] [1940s+] (*bingo*) the number 76.

wassock *n. see* WAZZOCK *n.*

wassup? *phr. see* WHAT'S UP? *phr.*

wassy *adj. see* WAXY *adj.*[2].

waste *n.*

SE in slang uses

(IN COMPOUNDS)

❑ **waste-butt** *n.* **1** [early 19C] a landlord, a publican. **2** [early–mid-19C] a drunkard. **3** [late 19C] an eating-house. ❑ **waste case** *n.* (*also* **waste machine**) [WASTED *adj.* (8) + SE *case*] **1** [1980s+] (*US campus*) a drunkard. **2** [1990s+] an outcast. ❑ **wastepipe** *n.* [late 18C–19C] the vagina. ❑ **waste product** *n.* **1** [1960s+] a general term of abuse. **2** [1980s+] (*US campus*) a drunkard.

waste v. **1** [1940s+] (*orig. US milit.*) to kill, to beat up. **2** [1960s+] (*US teen/street gang*) to defeat, to trounce. **3** [1960s+] to get drunk or intoxicated by a drug. **4** [1960s+] to smash, to destroy.

wasted *adj.* [WASTE v.] **1** [1950s+] (*orig. US*) killed. **2** [1950s+] (*US*) ruined, destroyed. **3** [1950s+] (*US*) penniless. **4** [1950s+] utterly overcome by a drug. **5** [1950s+] feeling very ill. **6** [1950s+] exhausted. **7** [1960s–70s] badly beaten up. **8** [1960s+] very drunk. **9** [1970s] in serious trouble. **10** [1980s] (*US black*) of a woman, unattractive.

waster *n.* [WASTE v. (1)] [1980s] (*UK black*) a gun.

wat *n.* [dial.] [16C–17C] a hare.

watch *n.* [perhaps the image is of the idea of a person being synon. with one who is watching, i.e. is alive] [mid-16C–early 18C] self, usu. as *my watch, his watch* etc.

watch v.

SE in slang uses

(IN COMPOUNDS)

❑ **watchpot** *n.* [they *watch* the cooking *pot*] [late 19C–1910s] (*Irish*) one who hangs around at mealtimes in the hope of being offered a meal. ❑ **watch queen** *n.* [SE *watch* + -QUEEN *sfx* (3)] [1970s+] a male homosexual voyeur.

(IN PHRASES)

❑ **watch it** v. [late 19C+] to look out, to be careful, esp. in imper. *watch it!* used as a warning or a threat. ❑ **watch one's ass** v. (*also* **watch one's arse**) [SE *watch* + ASS *n.* (2)/ARSE *n.* (1)] [1960s+] (*orig. US*) **1** to take care, to take note, to be warned; usu. as *watch your arse*. **2** to behave, mind one's manners; usu. as *watch your arse*. ❑ **watch one's back** v. [1950s+] to take care of oneself. ❑ **watch oneself** v. [1950s+] to take care; esp. as an imper. when the implication is of a threat from the speaker. ❑ **watch one's lip** v. (*also* **...mouth, ...tongue**) [LIP *n.*[1] (1a)/MOUTH *n.* (3)/SE *tongue*] [1950s+] to mind one's manners, to talk politely; also as imper. ❑ **watch someone's back** v. (*also* **get..., take...**) [1950s+] **1** to look after or protect someone else. **2** to take care of someone else. ❑ **watch someone's waters** v. [SE *hold one's water*, to delay urination] [18C–early 19C] to keep a close watch on someone's actions. ❑ **watch the ant races** v. [the image of having collapsed on the floor] [1970s+] to be excessively drunk. ❑ **watch (the) submarines (race)** v. [1960s+] (*US*) to indulge in sexual by-play.

(IN EXCLAMATIONS)

❑ **watch my dust!** [the SE *dust* of departure; note DUST v.[2] (1)] [1910s+] (*US*) see me go! ❑ **watch your hip!** [euph. *hip*, the buttocks, the backside] [1950s+] (*W.I.*) watch your manners!

watch and chain *n.* [rhy. sl.] [20C+] the brain.

watch (chain) and seals *n.* **1** [early–mid-19C] a sheep's head and pluck, i.e. heart, liver and lungs. **2** [late 19C] the male genitals.

watchekong(s) *n. see* WASHICONG(S) *n.*

watchie *n.* (*also* **watchy**) [abbr.] [early–mid-19C; 2000s] a *watch*man.

watch-maker *n.* [mid-19C] a pickpocket, esp. one who specializes in stealing watches.

water *n.*[1] [early version of WATERWORKS *n.*] [late 18C] tears.

(IN PHRASES)

❑ **pump water** v. [mid-19C–1900s] to cry.

SE in slang uses

(IN COMPOUNDS)

❑ **water bag** *n.* [1930s+] (*Aus.*) a fanatical teetotaller. ❑ **water barrel** *n. see* WATER-BUTT below. ❑ **water bewitched** *n.* [late 17C–1900s] weak tea, punch or any other liquor. ❑ **water-bobby** *n.* [BOBBY *n.* (1)] [late 19C] a river policeman. ❑ **water-bonse** *n.* [SE *water* + BONCE *n.* (1), lit. *water-head*] [late 19C–1910s] a 'cry-baby'. ❑ **water-bottle** *n.* **1** [mid-17C] the penis [its urinary function]. **2** [late 19C] a total abstainer, a teetotaller. ❑ **waterbox** *n.* (*also* **watercourse, watergap**) [note D'Urfey, *Pills to Purge Melancholy* (1719): 'She knew him for a Workman that had the ready skill / To open well her Water-gate, and best supply her Mill'] [mid-17C–early 18C] the vagina. ❑ **waterboy** *n.* (*also* **waterman**) [play on *TAKE A DIVE under* DIVE *n.*[1]] **1** [1930s+] (*US*) a useless boxer who accepts money to lose fights. **2** [1950s] by ext., an informer. ❑ **water buffalo** v. [? echoic] [1980s+] (*US campus*) to vomit. ❑ **water burner** *n.* [1950s+] (*Aus.*) a cook. ❑ **water-butt** *n.* (*also* **water-barrel**) [mid-19C] the stomach. ❑ **water-cart** v. [mid-19C–1920s] to weep, to cry. ❑ **water-crockery** *n.* [mid-19C] (*UK Und.*) girls' virginities, maidenheads. ❑ **water-dog** *n.* [the ref. is to *Norfolk Broads*; note a *Norfolk dumpling* also means a native of Norfolk] [mid-19C–1900s] a Norfolk dumpling, a plain dumpling made from bread dough. ❑ **water-dona** *n. see* WASHER-DONA *n.* ❑ **water-engine** *n.* [late 19C] the urinary organs, irrespective of gender. ❑ **waterfall** *n.* [resemblance] **1** [19C] a handkerchief worn in the top pocket. **2** [mid-19C] pubic hair. **3** [mid-19C] a neckcloth, scarf or tie with long pendant ends. **4** [mid-19C–1920s] false hair. ❑ **water-funk** *n.* [FUNK *n.*[2] (3)] [late 19C] one who is afraid to go into water. ❑ **watergap** *n. see* WATERBOX above. ❑ **watergate** *n.* [mid-16C] the vagina when wet with sexual excitement. ❑ **waterhead** *n.* [lit. one who has 'water on the brain'] [1960s+] a foolish person. ❑ **water-lily** *n.* [mid-19C] (*UK Und.*) an oyster. ❑ **waterlogged** *adj.* [1910s–20s] very drunk. ❑ **waterman** *n. see* WATERBOY above. ❑ **watermill** *adj.* [mid-17C–early 19C] the vagina. ❑ **water pad** *n.* [PAD *n.*[1] (3)] [late 17C–mid-19C] a thief who specializes in robbing ships on the River Thames. ❑ **water pistol** *n.* [1970s] the penis. ❑ **water plant** *n.* [joc. resemblance] [early–mid-19C] an umbrella. ❑ **water rat** *n.* **1** [late 16C] a pirate. **2** [late 19C–1930s] a sergeant in the Thames River Police. **3** [1950s+] (*Ulster*) a customs officer. ❑ **water scriger** *n.* [? corruption of *scriver*, a scribe] [late 18C–early 19C] a doctor who diagnoses on the basis of a patient's urine. ❑ **water sneak** *n.* (*also* **water sneaksman**) [SNEAK *n.*[1] (1b)] [late 18C–early 19C] a thief who works on a river. ❑ **water sports** *n.* (*also* **w.s.**) [1970s+] urolagnia, urinating on a partner for sexual stimulation. ❑ **water sprinkler** *n.* [the act of christening with holy water] [1900s] (*Aus.*) a priest; a clergyman. ❑ **water wagon** *n.* (*also* **ice wagon**) [late 19C+] a fig. state of sobriety; usu. in phr. ON THE WAGON *phr.*; also attrib.

(IN PHRASES)

❑ **blow someone out of the water** v. [1950s+] (*orig. US*) to defeat comprehensively, to overwhelm. ❑ **draw water** v. *see under* DRAW v.[4]. ❑ **get one's water hot** v. [1940s] (*US*) to get over-excited, to lose one's temper. ❑ **go in the water** v. *see* GO IN THE TANK *under* TANK *n.*[1]. ❑ **go through without a water-bag** v. [1940s–50s] (*Aus.*) to rush, to be in a very great hurry. ❑ **hold one's water** v. [fig. ref. to restraining oneself from urinating] (*also* **hold one's urine**) [20C+] to be patient, to remain calm, esp. in imper. *hold your water!* calm down! ▫ **out in the water** [20C+] (*US*) in debt. ▫ **take water** *v.* **1** [late 19C–1910s] (*US*) to back down. **2** [20C+] (*Aus.*) to leave a bar or public house after spending all one's cash on drink. ▫ **water of life** *n.* **1** [early–mid-19C] gin. **2** [mid-19C] whisky. **3** [1930s] (*US drugs*) any drug. **4** [1950s+] (*US black*) semen.

water *n.*[2] [ety. unknown] (*drugs*) **1** [1960s+] injectable amphetamine. **2** [1970s+] phencyclidine. **3** [1990s+] furanon di-hydro, used medically to encourage sleep and assist muscle recovery and growth. **4** [2000s] gamma hydroxybutyrate.

water, the *n.* **1** [17C+] the River Thames in London; thus *over the water*, south of the Thames, or vice versa. **2** [18C–1930s] (*also* **big water, the wave**) the Atlantic Ocean, thus *over the water*, in America / Britain / Europe / Australia. **3** [19C] the English Channel. **4** [1950s–80s] (*UK black*) Bayswater, London W2. **5** [1980s+] the River Mersey in Liverpool.

IN PHRASES

▫ **over the water** [Southwark being south of the Thames] [early 19C] (*UK Und.*) in the King's Bench Prison, Southwark.

water *v.* **1** [mid-18C] to stand treat, to entertain [SE *water*, to provide water for, usu., a horse]. **2** [late 18C] (*US*) to 'pack' a jury with members who are likely to deliver a biased verdict [SE *water*, to dilute]. **3** [1970s] (*US*) to drink (alcohol).

SE in slang uses

IN PHRASES

▫ **water one's cheeks** *v.* [1990s+] (*US black*) to cry. ▫ **water one's horse/pony** *v. see* WATER THE MULE *under* MULE *n.* ▫ **water one's nag** *v.* [mid-19C] to urinate. ▫ **water one's plants** *v.* [late 16C] to weep. ▫ **water the dragon** *v.* [euph.; ? long antedating of DRAGON *n.*[4] (1)] [mid-19C] to urinate. ▫ **water the flowers** *v.* (*also* **water the wisteria**) [euph.] [1980s] to urinate. ▫ **water the horses** *v.* [euph. but note *WATER ONE'S HORSE/PONY* above] [1960s–70s] to urinate. ▫ **water the mule** *v. see under* MULE *n.*

water-blister *n. see* SKIN-AND-BLISTER *n.*

waterbury watch *n.* [rhy. sl.; the popular watches made in Waterbury, Conn.] [1930s] Scotch whisky.

watercress *n.* [rhy. sl.] [1970s+] a dress; as adj., *dressed*.

water (hen) *n.* [rhy. sl.] [1960s+] the number ten.

watering hole *n.* (*also* **water hole**) [SE *water-hole*, a pool or reservoir, esp. as used by animals for drinking] **1** [1950s+] a restaurant, a bar, anywhere where alcoholic refreshment is available. **2** [1970s] (*gay*) an area where one can wander in search of sexual partners, usu. a park or a bar.

watering place *n.* **1** [early 18C] the vagina. **2** [late 18C–1900s] (*also* **watering-house**) any place where alcohol is available. **3** [late 19C–1930s] (*US*) a restaurant or similar place of entertainment for public drinking favoured by the rich.

waterloo *n.*[1] [the halfpenny toll to cross *Waterloo* Bridge] [late 19C] a halfpenny.

waterloo *n.*[2] [rhy. sl.] [20C+] stew.

waterman *n.*[1] [SE *water*, euph. for white rum] [1950s] (*W.I.*) a heavy drinker, an alcoholic.

waterman *n.*[2] *see* WATER'S MAN *n.*

watermelon *n.*

IN PHRASES

▫ **drop one's watermelon** *v. see DROP ONE'S CANDY under* DROP *v.*[1].

watermelon man *n.* [euph.; stereotyped association of *watermelons* and US blacks] [1970s] (*US black*) a drug seller.

watermelons *n.* [ext. of MELON *n.* (4)] [1960s+] (*orig. US campus*) large female breasts.

waters *n.* [their use on wet days] [1940s] (*US black*) wellington boots, galoshes.

water's man *n.* (*also* **waterman**) [the light and dark blue colours sported by Cambridge and Oxford university oarsmen] [mid–late 19C] a costermonger's handkerchief, coloured light or dark blue.

water-wagtail *n. see* WAGTAIL *n.*

waterworks *n.* **1** [mid-19C+] tears. **2** [late 19C+] the urinary organs. **3** [1910s] the vagina. **4** [1930s] rain. **5** [2000s] one who weeps, a 'crybaby'.

IN PHRASES

▫ **turn on the waterworks** *v.* (*also* **turn on the main**) [mid-19C+] to start crying; *to turn off the…*, to stop crying; also var. *turn off the faucet*.

watery-headed *adj.* [late 18C–19C] tearful, prone to crying; thus n. *watery head*, one who cries.

wattle *n.* [rhy. sl.; *wattle and daub* = WARB *n.* (2)] [1940s–50s] (*Aus.*) a dirty, grubby person.

wattles *n.* [SE *wattles*, the 'ears' of a turkey or cock] [late 17C–mid-19C] (*orig. UK Und.*) ears.

waunds!/wauns! *excl. see* WOUNDS! *excl.*

wave, the *n. see* WATER, THE *n.* (2).

wave *v.*

SE in slang uses

IN PHRASES

▫ **wave a flag of defiance** *v.* [one's temporary boldness] [late 19C–1910s] to be drunk. ▫ **wave one's willy** *v. see under* WILLIE *n.*[4]. ▫ **wave the lily** *v. see under* LILY *n.* ▫ **wave the magic wand** *v. see under* WAND *n.*

Wavy Navy *n.* [the *wavy* braid worn by its officers on their uniform sleeves until 1956] [1910s+] the Royal Naval Volunteer Reserve.

wax *n.*[1] [arch. SE *wax wrath*, to become angry; WAX *v.*[2]] **1** [mid-19C–1910s] a temper, state of anger; thus *on the wax*, *waxy*, angry, *waxiness*, fury. **2** [1990s+] (*US black*) sexual intercourse.

IN COMPOUNDS

▫ **wax-pot** *n.* [-POT *sfx*; on pattern of SE *fusspot*] [1910s–20s] an ill-tempered person.

wax *n.*[2] **1** [20C+] (*US black*) chewing gum. **2** [1920s+] (*orig. US*) a gramophone record; thus *put on wax*, to record [the *wax* master discs in which the recording stylus cuts its groove]. **3** [2000s] (*US black*) a deposit of dried, shiny vaginal secretions on the buttocks and/or thighs. **4** *see BODY WAX under* BODY *n.*

IN COMPOUNDS

▫ **wax pilot** *n.* [2000s] (*US black*) a highly talented disk jockey.

IN PHRASES

▫ **melt the wax** *v.* [1950s] (*US drugs*) to smoke opium.

SE in slang uses

IN COMPOUNDS

▫ **wax borer** *n.* [i.e. they 'bore' through one's ear *wax*] [1950s+] (*Aus.*) a talkative bore, thus v., *wax-bore*, to talk tediously at someone. ▫ **waxhead** *n.* [SE *wax*, as used on surfboards + -HEAD *sfx* (3)] [1980s+] (*Aus.*) a surfer. ▫ **waxworks** *n.* **1** [1960s] (*US*) a record company [WAX *n.*[2] (2) + SE *works*]. **2** [1980s+] (*US gay*) anywhere, e.g. a bar, mainly frequented by older, less attractive gay men [derog. use of SE].

IN PHRASES

▫ **the whole ball of wax** *n.* [mid-19C+] (*US*) absolutely everything.

wax *v.*[1] [late 19C–1900s] **1** to mark down. **2** (*UK Und.*) to remember clearly.

wax *v.*[2] [SE *wax*, to grow in intensity + WHACK *v.*[1] (1)] **1** [late 19C+] to defeat in competition. **2** [late 19C+] to beat up, to thrash. **3** [1960s+] to kill. **4** [1990s+] to have sexual intercourse. **5** [1990s+] to fellate. **6** [2000s] (*US black*) to leak vaginal secretions onto the buttocks and/or thighs.

IN PHRASES

▫ **wax ass** *v.* [ASS *n.* (3)] [1970s+] (*US black*) to have sexual intercourse. ▫ **waxed, buffed and simonized** *adj.* [car valeting imagery] [1980s+] (*US black*) **1** comprehensively defeated, beaten up. **2** describing something that is superlative, impressive. ▫ **wax someone's ass** *v.* (*also* **wax someone's head, …plow, …tail**) [ASS *n.* (2)/SE *head*/TAIL *n.* (2)] [1960s+] (*US*) to beat up, to thrash; ult. to kill. ▫ **wax**

something up *v.* [late 19C] to ruin, to make a mess of; to cause trouble.

SE in slang uses

IN PHRASES

▫ **go wax a gaza** [lit. 'go climb a gas lamp'] [20C+] (*Irish*) a dismissive phr. ▫ **wax one's carrot** *v.* [1980s+] to masturbate. ▫ **wax the buick** *v.* (*also* **wax the candle-stick, ...car, ...carrot, ...dolphin, ...surfboard, ...womb**) [1980s+] to masturbate. ▫ **wax up** *v.* [SE *wax*, to polish] [1970s+] (*US black*) **1** to propitiate someone whom one has insulted or annoyed. **2** to hide evidence [suggests making things look better].

wax *v.*[3] [WAX *n.*[2] (2)] [1930s+] (*orig. US*) to make a record.

wax *v.*[4] [? WHACK *n.*[1] (1)] [1980s+] (*Aus. prison*) to share; thus *waxer*, who who is entitled to a share.

waxed *adj.* [? SE *wax*, to polish, i.e. they 'shine' in a crowd] **1** [1900s–70s] having a personality and characteristics that are known well. **2** [1960s+] (*US campus*) drunk.

IN PHRASES

▫ **have someone waxed** *v.* [1910s] to have someone at a disadvantage.

waxie *n.* (*also* **waxey**) [late 19C] (*UK Und.*) a 'nigger minstrel', a burnt cork artiste, who works on the street.

waxy *n.* [the *waxed* thread he uses] [mid-19C–1900s] a cobbler.

waxy *adj.*[1] [WAX *n.*[1] (1)] [mid-19C–1950s] angry.

waxy *adj.*[2] (*also* **wassy**) [SE *waxy*, i.e. an image of 'shininess'] [1940s+] (*W.I.*) **1** lively, exciting, enjoyable. **2** of a person, attractive.

way *adv.* [SE *a long way*, reinforced by WAY-OUT *adj.*[1] (2), WAY TO GO! *excl.*; but note W.I. *waay! waay-ou!* an excl. of great amusement, excitement, exultation] [late 19C+] (*US*) very, extremely, a general intensifier.

way! *excl.* [1990s+] the affirmative response to the negative NO WAY! *excl.* (2).

wayback *n.* **1** [late 19C–1910s] (*US*) an old-fashioned person. **2** [late 19C–1930s] (*Aus./N.Z./US*) the outback or the West or any rural nowhere. **3** [1900s–30s] (*also* **waybacker**) a person or animal from the outback. **4** [1970s] (*US black*) an old person.

way back *phr.* [SE *from way back*, from a long time ago] [1940s–60s] (*US black*) well-established, traditional, tried and tested.

way down south in Dixie *n. see under* SOUTH *adj.*

way-in *n.* [SE *way in*, an entry] [late 19C] the vagina.

way in *adj.* [1970s] fashionable, chic.

way of all flesh *phr.* [var. on orig. Bible phr. *go the way of all the earth*; popularized in trans. of Douay Bible (1609)] [19C] dead.

IN PHRASES

▫ **go the way of all flesh** *v.* [19C+] to die.

way of life *n. see under* LIFE *n.*

way-oh! *excl.* [late 19C] a dismissive excl. not likely!

way-out *n.* [WAY-OUT *adj.*[1] (1)] [1960s–70s] (*US*) an unconventional or eccentric person; thus *way-outness*, unconventionality.

way-out *adj.*[1] [orig. jazz use] [1950s+] (*orig. US*) **1** bizarre. **2** fantastic, exceptional.

way-out *adj.*[2] [abbr. *way out of line*] [1950s+] (*US*) wholly wrong, greatly mistaken.

way out *adv.* [1950s] in possession of a large amount.

way past *adv.* [lit. 'beyond'] [1980s+] (*orig. US black*) a general intensifier, e.g. *way past bad, way past cool*.

way poo cow! *excl.* [Fr. *voir pour corps-vous*, lit. 'see for your body', hence look out for yourself] [20C+] (*W.I., Gren.*) watch out for yourself! look out for the consequences!

wayside ditch *n.* (*also* **wayside fountain**) [late 19C] the vagina.

way to go! *excl.* (*also* **how to go! way to be!**) [allegedly coined for the 1940 film *Knute Rockne*] [1940s+] excl. of approval, i.e. *that's the right way to go*.

way-up *adj.* **1** [late 19C–1900s] (*US*) top-rank, first-class, socially and otherwise superior. **2** [1940s–50s] (*US drugs*) in a very positive mood, poss. drink or drug-induced [play on HIGH *adj.*[1]].

way up! *excl.* [late 19C] (*US*) definitely! very much so!

waz *n.* (*also* **wazz**) [WAZ *v.*] [1990s+] **1** urination. **2** masturbation.

waz *v.* (*also* **wazz**) [dial. *wass*, to urinate] [1990s+] **1** of a man, to urinate. **2** of a woman, to masturbate. **3** to waste.

wazoo *n.* [? var. GAZOO *n.*/KAZOO *n.*] **1** [1960s+] the vagina. **2** [1970s+] (*US*) the buttocks, the anus.

IN PHRASES

▫ **up the wazoo** [1980s+] (*orig. US*) full up, as much as one can handle, to excess.

wazz *see under* WAZ *n.*

wazzed *adj.* [1990s+] drunk [play on PISSED *adj.*[1] (1)].

wazzock *n.* (*also* **wassock**) [? WAZOO *n.*] [1990s+] a fool.

wazzocked *adj.* [var. on WAZZOOED *adj.*] [1980s+] drunk or intoxicated by a drug.

wazzooed *adj.* [echoic or play on WAZZED *adj.* (1)] [1970s+] (*drugs*) extremely intoxicated by a drug.

wazzup? *phr. see* WHAT'S UP? *phr.*

w/e *adj.* [abbr. WELL-ENDOWED *adj.*] [1960s+] used in sex contact advertisements, having notably large genitals.

weak *n.* [as opposed to coffee] [late 19C] tea.

weak *adj.* **1** [1950s] lacking in funds, poor. **2** [1950s+] poor, disappointing, ineffectual. **3** [1970s+] stupid. **4** [1990s+] (*US campus*) frustrated.

IN COMPOUNDS

▫ **weak-ass** *adj.* [-ASS *sfx*] [1980s+] a derog. term for second-rate, unimpressive, powerless. ▫ **weak shit** *n.* [1960s+] **1** (*drugs*) second-rate, relatively ineffective drugs [SHIT *n.* (6c)]. **2** second-rate, weak, inadequate words or actions [SHIT *n.* (3e)].

SE in slang uses

DERIVATIVES

▫ **weakie** *n.* [WEAK *adj.* (2) + sfx *-ie*] [1940s+] (*Aus.*) an unreliable, untrustworthy person.

IN COMPOUNDS

▫ **weakheart** *n.* [1970s] (*UK/W.I.*) a derog. term for a police officer. ▫ **weak-jointed** *adj.* [mid-19C] (*US*) euph. for drunk. ▫ **weaksauce** *n.* [2000s] (*US teen*) an unfunny joke. ▫ **weak tap** *n.* [TAP *v.*[2] (3b)] [1950s] one who has a low income. ▫ **weak-wristed** *adj. see* LIMP-WRISTED *adj.*

IN PHRASES

▫ **weak as gin's piss** *adj.* (*also* **...cat breath, ...nun's piss, ... puppy's piss, ...a pygmy maiden's piss, ...weasel's piss**) [GIN *n.*[1] (1) + PISS *n.* (1)] [1940s+] (*orig. Aus.*) extremely weak, thus adj. *pissweak*. ▫ **weak in the arm** *n. see under* ARM *n.*

weapon *n.*[1] [first cited in an 11C glossary and in Langland's *Piers Plowman* (1377), 'While thou art young and thy weapon keen ...'. It was used more widely from the mid-18C] [late 16C+] the penis.

weapon *n.*[2] [2000s] (*Irish*) a good and positive thing, as in phr. *it's a weapon*.

weaponhead *n.* [? WEAPON *n.*[1] + -HEAD *sfx* (1); thus play on DICKHEAD *n.*] [1980s+] (*Aus. prison*) a foolish person.

wear *n.* [the two mouths are so entwined that it appears that one is 'wearing' the other] [1950s+] (*Irish*) an open-mouthed kiss; thus the person who gives one.

wear *v.* [1910s+] to tolerate, to stand, to believe.

SE in slang uses

IN COMPOUNDS

▫ **wear-arse** *n.* [SE *wear out* + ARSE *n.* (1); from the jolting] [late 18C–early 19C] a one-horse chaise or light, open carriage.

IN PHRASES

▫ **wear...** *v. see also under* relevant n. ▫ **wear a cut-glass veil** *v.* (*also* **wear a crystal veil**) [such a transparent 'veil' hides nothing] [1940s–70s] (*US gay*) to attempt unsuccessfully to hide one's homosexual preferences. ▫ **wear a fork** *v.* [SE *fork*, i.e. the 'horns' that a cuckold wears] [early 17C] to be cuckolded.

□ **wear a hat** *v.* [the once universal hat was seen as a badge of dull respectability in 1960s] [1960s] (*US teen*) **1** to have a steady girlfriend; to be married; to bring one's partner to a party. **2** to lead a respectable life. □ **wear a head** *v.* [early 19C] to be intelligent. □ **wear a mourning veil** *v.* [such a 'veil' is black and thus impenetrable] [1940s–70s] (*US gay*) to attempt to hide one's homosexual proclivities. □ **wear a red sweater** *v.* (*also* **wear a red tie, ...a green sweater, ...a green tie**) [? the brightness of the colours; i.e. one cannot hide one's sexuality; or the belief that such clothes denote a homosexual wearer (red was a stereotypical 'queer' colour)] [1960s+] (*US gay*) to act in an obviously homosexual manner. □ **wear a smile** *v.* [1900s–70s] (*US black*) to be naked. □ **wear bifocals** *v.* [1970s+] (*US gay*) to be bisexual. □ **wear iron boots** *v.* [1950s] (*US black*) to be very well-off. □ **wear one's badge** *v.* [formerly this was a red tie, now obs.] [1940s–60s] (*US gay*) to wear an outward sign of being a homosexual. □ **wear one's business** *v.* [+ BUSINESS *n.* (7); var. on SE *to wear one's heart on one's sleeve*] [1990s+] (*US Und.*) to act in an obvious manner, to betray one's secrets. □ **wear one's lunch** *v.* [1980s–90s] (*US campus*) to vomit. □ **wear someone's face off** *v.* [2000s] (*Irish*) to kiss intensely. □ **wear the bands** *v.* [BANDED *adj.*] [early 19C] (*mainly UK Und.*) to be hungry. □ **wear the blue and buttons** *v.* [the uniform] [late 19C] (*US*) to be a member of the police. □ **wear the blues** *v.* (*also* **wear the stripes**) [the colour/pattern of prison uniforms] [1900s] (*US*) to be in prison. □ **wear the bull's feather** *v.* [pun on the bull's 'feather', i.e. its SE *horn*/HORN *n.*[1]] [mid-16C–early 19C] to be a cuckold; to be cuckolded, to be betrayed by one's lover or spouse. □ **wear the dog** *v.* [SE *hangdog* look] [1970s] (*US black*) to go around looking deeply depressed. □ **wear the leek** *v.* [SE *leek*, the national emblem] [late 19C] to be Welsh. □ **wear the rag** *v. see RIDE THE RAG under* RIDE *v.* □ **wear the ring** *v.* [the wedding *ring* + the image of a *ring* through a bull's nose] [1970s+] (*US black*) to be in a regular relationship, whether actually married or not, and thus to reject any alternative entanglements. □ **wear the vine leaf** *v.* [1900s] (*Aus.*) to be drunk. □ **wear the willow** *v.* [abbr. SE *wear the willow garland*; the symbolic role of the weeping *willow*] [late 16C–1900s] to have been abandoned by one's mistress or lover. □ **wear two pairs of shoes** *v.* [1970s+] (*US gay*) to be bisexual. □ **wear yellow hose** *v.* (*also* **wear yellow stockings**) [play on YELLOW *adj.* (1); thus the character of Malvolio in Shakespeare's *Twelfth Night* (1599)] [17C] to be jealous.

Wearie *n.* (*also* **Weary**) [SE *weary* but note OE *wearg*, the accursed one] [20C+] (*Ulster*) the Devil.

wearies, the *n.* [1950s] (*US*) tiredness, boredom, apathy.

wear it *v.* [WEAR *v.* (1)] **1** [early–mid-19C] (*UK Und.*) to be accused of becoming an informer. **2** [20C+] (*US Und.*) to take the blame for a crime even when not actually guilty.

IN PHRASES

□ **wear it upon** *v.* ['it' is the nose, i.e. NOSE *n.* (1)] [early 19C] (*UK Und.*) to inform against.

Weary *n. see* WEARIE *n.*

weary *adj.* [euph.] [late 17C–1900s] drunk.

weary willie *n.* [SE *weary* + assonant/generic *Willie*] [20C+] (*US*) a tramp, a migrant worker.

weary willie and tired tim *n.* (*also* **weary willie and tired thomas**) [the cartoon tramps created in *Illustrated Chips* in April 1898 by Tom Browne (1870–1910)] [1900s–30s] a pair of idling, loafing individuals.

weasel *n.* **1** [mid-17C; 20C+] (*also* **weasle**) a general derog. term; also as adj. *weasel-assed*, *weasily* [reverse anthropomorphism; Williams has 17C use of *weasel*, a lecher]. **2** [mid-19C+] (*US*) a native of South Carolina [the state has a large population of the animal]. **3** [1920s+] (*US*) an informer. **4** [1920s+] (*orig. US*) the penis [it 'burrows']. **5** [1930s] (*US Und.*) a private detective. **6** [1940s+] (*N.Z.*) a sly or devious person.

IN PHRASES

□ **grease the weasel** *v.* [1990s+] (*US teen*) to have sexual intercourse.

weasel (and stoat) *n.* [rhy. sl. = coat] [1950s+] an overcoat.

weasel (out) *v.* (*also* **weasel-word**) [reverse anthropomorphism] (*orig. US*) **1** [20C+] to evade, to equivocate. **2** [1940s+] to wriggle out of a promise or duty.

weasle *n. see* WEASEL *n.* (1).

weathercock *n.* [late 19C] the head.

weather gig *n.* [SE *wether*, a castrated ram + GIG *n.*[1] (1)] [late 17C–early 18C] the vagina.

weatherhead *n.* [SE *weather* + -HEAD *sfx* (1); the image is of the fool's head turning like that of a *weathercock*; Hotten prefers SE *wether*, a ram, thus the person has a 'sheepish' look] [late 17C–mid-19C] a fool, a simpleton, also as adj., *weatherheaded*.

weather-sharp *n. see under* SHARP *n.*[1].

weave *n.* (*US black*) **1** [1970s] clothing. **2** [1970s] a trick. **3** [1980s+] false hair; hair extensions.

IN PHRASES

□ **put the weave on** *v.* [1970s] to deceive, to trick. □ **weave hustling** *n.* [1930s] (*US Und.*) selling spurious cloth.

weaver *n.* [1950s+] (*US*) a poor driver who *weaves* from lane to lane along the road.

weavers' claret *n.* [mid-19C] (*UK Und.*) porter.

weave the four F's *v.* [i.e. *f*ind 'em, *f*eel 'em, *f*uck 'em and *f*orget 'em] [1940s] (*orig. US black*) of a man, to seduce.

weaving *n.* [19C] in cards, cheating by secreting a number of cards on one's knee, or wedged between a knee and the underside of the table. These cards can be brought into the hand, swapping them for those one has been dealt, as and when required.

webbed up *adj.* [SE (spider's) *web*] [1980s+] **1** involved or caught up in. **2** having a relationship (with).

web-foot *n.* [they all encounter wet paths etc] **1** [mid-19C–1910s] (*US*) an infantryman. **2** [mid-19C+] (*US*) a native of Oregon, the state of Oregon. **3** [late 19C] a native of Lincolnshire. **4** [1970s+] (*US*) an environmentalist.

Webster Avenue walking stick *n.* [1960s] (*US teen gang*) a baseball bat studded with razorblades.

wedded to the Duke of Exeter's daughter *phr.* [the rack had been introduced into England by John Holland, 4th *Duke of Exeter* in 1447] [late 16C] suffering the torture of the rack.

wedding *n.*[1] [? SE *weeding*] [late 18C] the emptying of a privy.

wedding *n.*[2] *see IRISH WEDDING under* IRISH *adj.*

wedding bells *n.* [ety. unknown; ? it 'rings' in one's skull] [1970s] (*drugs*) LSD.

wedding kit *n.* (*also* **wedding gear, wedding tackle**) [SE *wedding* + *kit*/TACKLE *n.*[1] (1)] [1910s+] the male genitals.

wedge *n.*[1] **1** [18C+] (*also* **wage**) silver, money in general. **2** [18C–1910s] silver plate. **3** [mid-18C] (*UK Und.*) a silver buckle. **4** [late 19C] (*UK Und.*) a receiver [the silver plate was melted down into *wedges* by receivers]. **5** [1970s+] a thick, chunky roll of banknotes, usu. folded in half; thus a large amount of money or wealth in general.

IN COMPOUNDS

□ **wedge-hunter** *n.* [mid-19C–1900s] (*UK Und.*) a thief specializing in silver plate and silver watches. □ **wedge-hunting** *n.* [late 19C] (*UK Und.*) stealing silver-plate or silver watches.

IN PHRASES

□ **flash the wedge** *v.* [19C] (*UK Und.*) to dispose of one's 'swag' or booty. □ **wedged (up)** *adj.* [1990s+] well-off, rich. □ **wedge up** *v.* [2000s] to amass money.

SE in slang uses

IN COMPOUNDS

□ **wedgeass** *n.* [SE *wedge* + -ASS *sfx*] [1940s–50s] (*US*) a general term of abuse; thus adj. *wedge-assed*. □ **wedgehead** *n.* [1990s+] one who has a 'wedge' haircut.

wedge *n.*[2] **1** [18C+] the penis [it *wedges* open the vagina]. **2** [1960s] (*US campus*) in fig. use, derog. term for a hard worker.

wedge *n.*[3] (*also* **wej**) [backsl.] [mid-19C] a Jew.

wedge *n.*[4] (*also* **wedges, wedgies**) [? the shape of the pill] [1960s+] (*drugs*) LSD.

wedge *adj.* [WEDGE *n.*[1] (2)] [mid-19C] silver, silver-plated.

IN COMPOUNDS

❑ **wedge-bob** *n.* [*RUM BOB under* RUM *adj.*, as generic for a box] [mid-19C] (*UK Und.*) a silver snuff-box. ❑ **wedge-feeder** *n.* [WEDGE *adj.*+ FEEDER *n.* (1)] [late 18C–mid-19C] a silver spoon. ❑ **wedge-lobb** *n.* [LOB *n.*[1] (1)] [early 19C] a silver snuff-box. ❑ **wedge-super** *n.* [SUPER *n.*[2] (1)] [mid-19C] (*UK Und.*) a silver watch.

wedges *n.* *see* WEDGE *n.*[4].

wedgie *n.* (*also* **snuggy, wedgy**) [SE *wedge*, to stick or thrust between] [1970s+] a trick whereby one pulls an unsuspecting victim's underpants up between their buttocks.

wedgies *n.*[1] [abbr.] [1940s+] women's *wedge*-heeled shoes.

wedgies *n.*[2] *see* WEDGE *n.*[4].

wedgy *n.* *see* WEDGIE *n.*

wee *n.* (*also* **wee-wee**) [? juv. mispron. of 'u-ween' (urine) or var. PEE *n.*[1] (1)] [late 19C+] (*mainly juv.*) urine, urination.

IN PHRASES

❑ **poor as wee-wee** *adj.* [var. *PISS-POOR under* PISS- *pfx*] [1960s] (*N.Z.*) unacceptable, second rate.

wee *adj.*

SE in slang uses

IN COMPOUNDS

❑ **wee man** *n.* [1990s+] (*Irish*) the penis. ❑ **wee small hours** *n.* [mid-19C+] the very early morning.

IN EXCLAMATIONS

❑ **wee buns!** (*also* **onions!**) [20C+] (*Ulster*) no problem!

wee *v.* (*also* **go wee-wee, make wee-wee, wee-wee**) [WEE *n.*] [late 19C+] (*mainly juv.*) to urinate.

weed *n.*[1] [ext. uses of SE] **1** [17C+] tobacco. **2** [mid-19C–1940s] a cigar. **3** [late 19C+] a cigarette. **4** [1920s+] (*also* **weeds**) (*drugs*) marijuana. **5** [1930s] (*US*) a green vegetable. **6** [1930s+] a marijuana cigarette.

IN COMPOUNDS

❑ **weed-hound** *n.* [-HOUND *sfx*] [1940s–50s] (*US*) a marijuana user. ❑ **weed house** *n.* [1980s] (*US drugs*) a family home from which marijuana is sold. ❑ **weed tea** *n.* [1960s–70s] (*drugs*) marijuana tea.

IN PHRASES

❑ **sugar weed** *n.* [1960s–80s] (*drugs*) second-rate, adulterated marijuana.

weed *n.*[2] [SE *weed*, a mourning garment, often a black hatband] [mid-19C] a hatband.

SE in slang uses

IN PHRASES

❑ **have a weed on** *v.* [1920s] to be in a bad temper.

weed *n.*[3] **1** [mid–late 19C] an ill-conditioned, weak horse. **2** [20C+] a weakling, a feeble and thus contemptible person. **3** [1930s–60s] (*also* **weed in the garden**) (*US Und/black/teen*) a stranger, an ousider.

weed *v.*[1] [late 18C] (*US Und.*) to speak.

weed *v.*[2] **1** [early 19C] (*UK Und.*) to steal small amounts, e.g from a warehouse, so as not to alert the victim. **2** [early 19C–1930s] (*orig. UK Und.*) to steal part rather than all of a potential booty. **3** [mid-19C+] to take, to steal; thus *weed a leather*, to steal a wallet and strip out its contents.

IN PHRASES

❑ **weed the swag** *v.* [SWAG *n.*[1] (2)] [early 19C] (*UK Und.*) to embezzle part of the booty before dividing what remains with one's gang.

weed *v.*[3] [1930s–40s] (*US black/Und.*) **1** to lend, esp. money; thus *weed a holler note until mother comes in*, to lend someone $100 until their gambling luck changes. **2** to give, to hand.

weed *v.*[4] [WEED *n.*[1] (4)] [1990s+] (*US drugs*) to smoke marijuana.

weeder *n.* [WEED *v.*[2]] **1** [early–mid-19C] (*UK Und.*) a villain who steals a proportion of the gang's joint booty. **2** [1900s] (*US Und.*) a thief. **3** [1940s+] (*US Und.*) one who steals in small amounts to avoid detection.

Weedgie *n.* *see* WEEDJIE *n.*

weedhead *n.* [WEED *n.*[1] (4) + -HEAD *sfx* (4)] [1930s+] (*drugs*) a marijuana smoker.

weedheaded *adj.* [WEEDHEAD *n.*] [1940s] (*US black/drugs*) intoxicated by marijuana.

weeding dues *n.* [WEED *v.*[2] (2)] [early 19C] (*UK Und.*) 'Speaking of any person, place, or property, that has been weeded [i.e. robbed], it is said "weeding dues have been concerned"' (Vaux).

Weedjie *n.* (*also* **Weedgie**) [a Glas*wegi*an] [1990s+] (*Scot.*) a native of Glasgow.

weed out *v.* [WEED *n.*[1] (4)] [1950s+] (*drugs*) to smoke marijuana to excess.

weeds *n.* **1** [16C+] clothes. **2** *see* WEED *n.*[1] (4).

weeds, the *n.* [its position on the edge of town] **1** [1920s–30s] (*US tramp*) a hobo camp. **2** [1950s] (*US Und.*) the outskirts, the suburbs.

weedy *adj.* [WEED *n.*[3]] **1** [19C] of a horse, weak-legged, lacking strength. **2** [mid-19C+] of humans, weak, cowardly, spineless. **3** [1920s+] of things, boring, troublesome, small, insignificant.

weedy-weedy *v.* [? echoic of whispering] [2000s] (*US prison*) to inform.

wee georgie wood *adj.* [rhy. sl.; the epon. musical hall star, popular 1920s–30s] [1930s+] (*Aus.*) good.

weejee *n.* (*also* **wejee**) [ety. unknown] [mid-19C] **1** a chimneypot. **2** a chimneypot hat. **3** anything outstanding of its type, esp. an invention.

weejuns *n.* [brandname, *Weejuns*] [1950s+] (*US teen*) moccasins, loafers.

weekend *n.* [1940s–50s] (*UK prison*) a very short period of imprisonment.

SE in slang uses

IN PHRASES

❑ **in town for the weekend** *adj.* [1970s] (*US campus*) homosexual. ❑ **it looks like a wet weekend** (*also* **...season**) [1930s+] (*orig. Aus.*) used by a woman announcing, or registering, the onset of a menstrual period.

weekend *adj.* [1960s+] part-time, infrequent, irregular, usu. in combs.

IN COMPOUNDS

❑ **weekend habit** *n.* [HABIT *n.* (1)] [1930s+] (*drugs*) the occasional use of drugs. ❑ **weekend ho** *n.* [HO *n.* (1)] [1970s+] (*US black*) **1** a part-time prostitute, often without a pimp but poss. helping out her boyfriend with cash. **2** (*also* **weekend warrior**) an underage prostitute. ❑ **weekend man** *n.* [1970s+] (*US black*) a family man who can only manage the street life at weekends. ❑ **weekend pussy** *n.* [PUSSY *n.* (2)] [1990s+] (*US black*) an adulterous female lover, lit. one whom one only visits at the weekend. ❑ **weekend warrior** *n.* **1** [1960s+] (*US*) members of the National Guard. **2** [1970s+] anyone deemed to be insufficently dedicated to a given activity or occupation. **3** [1980s] (*Aus.*) a member of the Australian Army's Reservist units. **4** [1980s] (*US drugs*) one who takes potentially addictive narcotic drugs on weekends (or similarly special occasions) only. **5** *see* WEEKEND HO above.

weekender *n.* **1** [19C] a prostitute who only works at the weekend. **2** [1940s+] a weekend cottage. **3** [1950s+] (*drugs*) someone who is not a serious drug taker, thus not addicted. **4** [1960s+] a suitcase suitable for packing those items needed for a weekend's trip or holiday. **5** [1970s] (*US prison*) a person who serves their prison sentence at weekends only. **6** [2000s] (*N.Z.*) a temporary resident, rather than a permanent one.

ween *n.* (*also* **weenie, weeny, wiener**) [WEENIE *n.*[1] (5)] [1950s+] (*US campus*) **1** (*also* **ween bucket**) a boring, socially unappealing or unacceptable person. **2** a hard-working student.

IN PHRASES

❑ **queen ween** *n.* [1990s+] (*US campus*) someone who backs out of a commitment.

weenchy *adj.* [WEENY *adj.*] [20C+] (*US*) tiny, very little.

weenie *n.*[1] (*also* **weener, weeney, weeny, wiener, wienie, winnie**) [SAmE *wiener*, a Vienna sausage; ult. Ger. *Wienenwurst*] (*US*) **1** [late 19C+] (*US*) a frankfurter sausage; a HOT DOG *n.*[1] (1). **2** [1900s] (*US Und.*) bread. **3** [1920s+] (*US*) a young woman, an effeminate man. **4** [1930s+] (*US, usu. juv.*) the penis. **5** [1950s+] (*US*) a general derog. **6** *see* WEEN *n.*

IN COMPOUNDS

❑ **weenie bin** *n.* [1970s+] (*US campus*) a library carrel. ❑ **weenie waver** *n.* (*also* **weenie wagger, weinie wiggler**) [1970s+] an exhibitionist. ❑ **weenie woman** *n.* [1990s+] (*US*) an effeminate homosexual.

IN PHRASES

❑ **bite the weenie** *v.* [1950s+] (*US*) a general derog. expression. ❑ **dip the weenie** *v.* [1950s+] (*US*) of a man, to have sexual intercourse. ❑ **hide the weenie** *v.* [1910s+] to have sexual intercourse. ❑ **sink the weenie** *v. see* SINK THE SAUSAGE *under* SINK *v.*

weenie *n.*[2] **1** [1940s–60s] (*US*) a good idea, a scheme. **2** [1970s] a hidden catch.

weenie *adj.* [WEENIE *n.*[1] (5)] **1** [1960s–80s] (*US campus*) second-rate, insignificant. **2** *see* WEENY *adj.*

weenie (out) *v.* [WEENIE *n.*[1] (5)] [1990s+] (*US*) to act cowardly, wimpishly.

weeny *n.*[1] *see* WEEN *n.*

weeny *n.*[2] *see* WEENIE *n.*[1].

weeny *adj.* (*also* **weenie**) [infant pron.] [late 18C+] tiny.

weeny-bopper *n.* [WEENY *adj.* + BOP *v.* (5) on pattern of TEENYBOPPER *n.* (1)] [1970s+] a very young pop fan.

weeny teeny *adj. see* TEENSIE-WEENSIE *adj.*

weep and wail *n.* [rhy. sl.] [late 19C–1950s] a tale, esp. a beggar's tale of woe.

weep city *n.* [SE *weep* + -CITY *sfx*] [1940s] (*US black*) crying, tearfulness.

weeper *n.*[1] [? long sideburns or *payes* as worn by orthodox Jews] [mid-17C] (*UK Und.*) a Jew.

weeper *n.*[2] [? the trailing ends of crepe once worn at funerals – where mourners wept] **1** [mid–late 19C] a piece of black crepe worn around the hat of a mourner or undertaker. **2** [late 19C–1910s] usu. in pl.; a long, sweeping moustache, long sidewhiskers.

weeper *n.*[3] [1930s] (*US prison*) a pistol.

weeper *n.*[4] *see* WEEPIE *n.*

weepers *n.* [mid-19C–1940s] (*US*) one's best clothes; thus those one wears to funerals.

weepie *n.* (*also* **weeper**) [1920s+] a film, or story, whose main effect is to reduce its audience to tears, usu. consciously romantic; thus *three-handkerchief weepie*, a very emotional film.

Weeping Jesus! *excl. see* JESUS! *excl.*

weeping willow *n.*[1] [rhy. sl.] [late 19C+] a pillow.

weeping willow *n.*[2] [1920s] (*US*) a pessimist, a killjoy.

weep Irish *v.* [racial stereotyping] [mid-17C–early 18C] to talk nonsense, to shed crocodile tears.

weeps, the *n.* [late 19C+] **1** (*US*) tears. **2** as *the weeps*, tearfulness, crying. **3** (*US tramp*) a hard-luck story.

wee-wee *n.*[1] (*also* **oui-oui, wewi, wi-wi**) [the excl. *oui oui!*, yes, yes! + derog. pun on WEE *n.*] **1** [mid-19C] (*orig. Aus./N.Z.*) a French person. **2** the French language.

wee-wee *n.*[2] **1** [1970s+] the penis. **2** see WEE *n.*

IN PHRASES

❑ **go/make wee-wee** *v. see* WEE *v.*

wee-wee *v. see* WEE *v.*

wee-wee off *v.* [euph. for PISS OFF *v.* (2)] [1960s] (*N.Z.*) to annoy, infuriate.

Wee Willie Winky *n.* [rhy. sl. = CHINKY *n.* (1)] [1990s+] a derog. term for a Chinese person.

weezo *n.* [? play on SE *wheeze*] [2000s] (*US prison*) and informer.

wegro *n.* [SE *white* + *negro*] [2000s] (*US black*) a white person who takes on black culture and style.

we here *phr.* [US black var. of SE *we are here*] [1990s+] (*US campus*) expression of support.

weigh *v.*

SE in slang uses

IN PHRASES

❑ **weigh forty** *v.* [the £40 cash bonus awarded to any policeman who secured a 'Tyburn ticket', i.e. captured a murderer] [early 19C] (*UK Und.*) of a thief, to have moved into serious crimes, which will make it worth his arrest. ❑ **weigh into** *v.* [1930s+] (*orig. Aus.*) to attack verbally or physically, to criticize. ❑ **weigh off** *v.* [orig. milit.] **1** [1910s+] (*UK Und.*) to sentence a convicted prisoner; thus *weighed off*, sent off to prison. **2** [1930s+] to get one's own back, to take revenge on. **3** [2000s] to estimate, to consider as. **4** [2000s] to injure, to hurt. **5** [2000s] to deal with. ❑ **weigh on** *v.* [i.e. add some fig. 'weight' to a relationship] [2000s] to repay a favour. ❑ **weigh one's weight** *v.* [under an act of William and Mary the reward for the capture of a highwayman or coiner had been set at £40] [19C] to commit a capital offence. ❑ **weigh out** *v.* **1** [late 19C] to apportion shares. **2** [late 19C+] to hand over money.

weigh in *v.* [horseracing use, i.e. the pre-race *weigh-in*] **1** [late 19C+] (*US*) to assert oneself. **2** [late 19C+] to pay or give one's share. **3** [20C+] to join in, esp. in an argument. **4** [1910s+] to play one's part. **5** [1920s+] to arrive.

IN PHRASES

❑ **weigh in the sacks on** *v.* [1930s–40s] (*US*) to criticize.

weigh-meat *n.* [late 19C+] (*W.I.*) bones that are weighed up by the butcher and charged for along with the meat that accompanies them.

weight *n.* (*orig. US*) **1** in fig. senses. (**a**) [late 18C+] influence, importance. (**b**) [1940s+] blame, emotional or psychological pressure. (**c**) [1950s–70s] responsibility, obligation, duty; thus CARRY WEIGHT *under* CARRY *v.* **2** as a weapon. (**a**) [1940s] (*US Und.*) a police truncheon. (**b**) [1960s+] (*US black*) a gun, a pistol. **3** in drug uses. (**a**) [1960s+] a large quantity of drugs (esp. pounds of hashish/marijuana, kilos of cocaine/heroin). (**b**) [1960s+] 1lb of marijuana, cannabis; may be qualified by number, e.g. *five weight of hash*, 5lb of hashish. (**c**) [1990s+] 1oz of heroin. (**d**) [1990s+] a measure of a given drug, differing as to the drug in question.

IN PHRASES

❑ **have someone's weights up** *v.* [horseracing imagery] [1970s+] (*N.Z.*) to have the measure of a person. ❑ **hold no weight** *v.* [1980s] (*US black*) to be lacking in the attributes required for 'street credibility'. ❑ **pull the weight** *v.* [1910s+] (*Aus.*) to deal with a sudden financial problem. ❑ **put one's weight on it** *v.* [2000s] (*US black*) to dance energetically. ❑ **put one's weights up** *v.* [1920s] (*N.Z.*) to cause trouble deliberately. ❑ **take the weight** *v.* [1950s+] (*US*) to take responsibility. ❑ **that's your weight** [1970s] (*US black*) a phr. meaning that something is somebody else's responsibility or duty. ❑ **worth one's weight in burnt copper** [var. on the SE phr. *worth one's weight in gold*; copper has little value compared with gold] [late 19C] worthless, worth very little.

weight pile *n. see* IRON PILE *under* IRON *adj.*

weighty *adj.* [2000s] (*UK teen*) good.

weigh (up) *v.* [late 19C+] to appraise, to assess.

weinie wiggler *n. see* WEENIE WAVER *under* WEENIE *n.*[1].

weird *adj.* [20C+] (*orig. UK society*) wonderful, excellent.

SE in slang uses

IN COMPOUNDS

❑ **weird-ass** *adj.* [-ASS *sfx*] [1960s+] (*US*) strange, eccentric, mad. ❑ **weird beard** *n.* (*also* **weirdie-beardie, weirdo beardo**) [1960s+] (*UK juv.*) a derog. term for one who looks like a beatnik, an eco activist, anti-nuclear protestor, etc.

weirdie *n.* (*also* **weird-ball, weirdy**) [SE *weird* + sfx *-ie*] **1** [late 19C+] an eccentric person, esp. as *bearded weirdie/beardy-weirdy*, a man with long hair and/or a beard and as such negatively stereotyped as an 'intellectual'. **2** [1940s+]

anything, typically a book or film, that is considered fantastic, bizarre or grotesque. **3** [1960s] a male homosexual. **4** [1960s] (*US campus*) an unattractive female.

weirdie *adj.* (*also* **weirdy**) [1950s+] odd, eccentric, peculiar.

IN COMPOUNDS

❑ **weirdie-beardie** *n. see* WEIRD BEARD *under* WEIRD *adj.*

weirdo *n.* [SE *weird* + -O *sfx* (7)] **1** [1950s+] an eccentric, a peculiar person. **2** [1960s+] one who enjoys non-standard sexual practices.

weirdo *adj.* [WEIRDO *n.* (1)] [1960s+] eccentric, odd, bizarre, out of the ordinary.

IN COMPOUNDS

❑ **weirdo beardo** *n. see* WEIRD BEARD *under* WEIRD *adj.*

weird out *v.* [1970s+] **1** to horrify, to play mental games. **2** (*drugs*) to experience hallucinations from intoxication by narcotics. **3** to feel confused or at a loss.

weirdsville *n.* [SE *weird* + -VILLE *sfx*[1]] [1950s+] (*US*) anywhere considered off or out of the ordinary; a bizarre situation.

weirdy *see under* WEIRDIE.

weisenheimer *n. see* WISENHEIMER *n.*

wej *n. see* WEDGE *n.*[3].

wejee *n. see* WEEJEE *n.*

welch *n.* [WELCH *v.* (1)] [late 19C–1900s] (*US*) the act of defrauding a bettor.

welch *v.* (*also* **welsh**) [racist stereotyping, but note Ger. *Welsch*, foreigner] **1** [mid-19C+] to refuse to pay a gambling debt or other bill; refuse to hand over any sum of money. **2** [late 19C+] in fig. use, to let down, to disappoint. **3** [1920s+] (*US campus*) to reject, to stand aside from, to turn down (all relate to a social engagement). **4** [1920s+] to renege on one's words or on a promised action.

IN PHRASES

❑ **welch out** *v.* [1980s] (*US campus*) to opt out of an activity.

Welch comb *n.* (*also* **Welsh comb**) [racial stereotyping] [mid-17C–early 19C] the thumb and four fingers, used to smooth one's hair.

welcher *n.* (*also* **welsher**) [WELCH *v.*] **1** [mid-19C+] anyone who refuses to pay their debts, gambling or otherwise. **2** [1900s] in fig. use, one who disappoints, lets down. **3** [1920s–60s] an informer.

welcome green *n. see* GREEN *n.*[2] (1).

welcome, I'm sure! *excl.* [an equivalent to the various European forms of acknowledgement that greet 'please', e.g. Ital. *prego*. In the UK, however, the form is strictly lower-/lower-middle-class] [late 19C+] you're welcome to it!

welcome wagon *n.* [1970s+] (*US gay/prison*) the man who is first in line in a gang-rape.

welfare mother *n.* [ironic use of SE] [1970s+] (*US black*) any woman, irrespective of status vis-à-vis welfare, who is poorly dressed and unkempt.

welfare pimp *n.* [2000s] (*US black*) a pimp who collects the welfare checks due to his prostitutes.

welk! *excl.* [abbr.] [1980s+] (*US campus*) you're *wel*come!

well *adj.*

SE in slang uses

IN PHRASES

❑ **get well** *v.* **1** [20C+] (*US Und.*) to improve one's financial position; to amass money. **2** [2000s] (*US drugs*) to inject narcotics to stop feeling 'sick'.

well *v.* **1** [early 19C] (*UK Und.*) to defraud one's criminal confederates, to divide booty unfairly. **2** [mid-19C] to pocket; thus *well it*, to be well-off, to make a good income. **3** [late 19C+] to conceal a proportion of one's income or estate from one's creditors.

well *adv.*[1] [Ware labels late 19C use 'society' but earlier general use] [mid-19C+] a general intensifier, very, definitely, extremely etc; thus *well tasty*, *well sus* etc.

well *adv.*[2] [late 19C] used as an intensifier in such combs. as *bloody well*, *damn well*, *jolly well* etc.

well away *adj.* **1** [1920s+] (*also* **well on**) drunk or on one's way towards being so. **2** [1940s] asleep. **3** [1960s+] making headway in a seduction.

well-breeched *adj. see* WELL-HEELED *adj.*[1].

well-bushed *adj.* [BUSH *n.*[1] (1)] [20C+] of a man, having notably large genitals; of a woman, having plentiful pubic hair.

well-cemented *adj.* [1950s] (*Aus.*) rich.

well-covered *adj. see* WELL-UPHOLSTERED *adj.*

well, duh! *excl. see* DUH! *excl.*

well-endowed *adj.* [euph.] **1** [1950s+] (*also* **well-end**) of a man, having notably large genitals. **2** [1960s+] of a woman, having notably large breasts.

well-fixed *adj.* (*also* **well-got**) [SE *fixed*, sorted out] [early 19C+] (*US*) reasonably affluent, comfortable.

well fucked and far from home *phr.* [20C+] of a man, conducting an adulterous relationship.

well-furnished *adj.* [euph.] [mid-18C] of a man, having notably large genitals.

well-got *adj. see* WELL-FIXED *adj.*

well-heeled *adj.*[1] (*also* **all-heeled, well-breeched**) [the quality of a rich person's footwear] [mid-19C+] rich; financially secure.

well-heeled *adj.*[2] *see* HEELED *adj.* (1).

well hove! *excl.* [SE *hove*, past tense of *heave*] [1910s–20s] well done! well played!

well-hung *adj.*[1] [late 17C+] of a man, having notably large genitals.

well-hung *adj.*[2] [rhy. sl.] [20C+] young.

wellie *n.* (*also* **welly**) [1950s+] a *well*ington boot.

IN PHRASES

❑ **give it some welly** *v.* [abbr.; phr. underlined by an extra image of the 'wellie-chucking' contests that have become popular] [1970s+] **1** to apply more force, energy or effort. **2** to reject, to get rid of.

wellied *n.* [WELLY *v.* (2)] [1990s+] drunk.

wellies *n.* (*also* **green wellies**) [SE *wealthy* + the green wellington boots that such students wear for various rural pleasures] [1980s+] public-school educated, upper-middle and upper-class students, who are seen as playing rather than working their way through university.

well, I'll be dipped in shit! *excl.* [SHIT *n.* (1a)] [1960s+] (*US*) a general. excl. of surprise, amazement.

well-in *adj.* **1** [mid-19C+] (*Aus.*) well-off, affluent. **2** [late 19C+] popular, secure, entrenched. **3** [20C+] successfully ingratiated, on the way to a successful seduction.

wellington *n.* [rhy. sl.; *wellington boot* = ROOT *n.*[1] (1d)] [1960s+] (*Aus.*) sexual intercourse.

well-inlaid/-inlayed *adj. see* INLAID *adj.*

well-lined *adj.* [one *lines one's pockets*] [late 19C] rich, prosperous.

well-mended *adj.* [20C+] (*Irish*) of an ill person, improved in health.

well-oiled *adj.* [SE *well* + OIL UP *under* OIL *v.*] [late 19C+] very drunk.

well on *adj. see* WELL AWAY *adj.* (1).

well put-on *adj.* [1920s+] (*Scot./Ulster*) well-dressed.

well-shod *adj.* [fig., but also, no doubt, lit. 'wearing good shoes'] [late 19C] (*US*) rich.

well-sprung *adj.* [one is 'bouncing up and down'] [1910s–30s] drunk.

well to live *phr. see under* LIVE *v.*

well under way *adj.* [mid-19C] (*US*) drunk.

well up *adj.* [1990s+] (*Irish*) very tall.

well-upholstered *adj.* (*also* **well-covered**) [1930s+] plump, fleshy, fat.

welly *n.*[1] [WELLY *v.* (2)] [2000s] a beating.

welly *n.*[2] *see* WELLIE *n.*

welly *v.* [the use of a WELLIE *n.* to kick] [1980s+] **1** to kick, to trip up. **2** to beat up, to assault.

Welsh *adj.*

IN COMPOUNDS

❑ **Welsh bait** *n. see* SCOTCH BAIT *under* SCOTCH *adj.* ❑ **Welsh comb** *n. see* WELCH COMB *n.* ❑ **Welsh cricket** *n.* [negative stereotyping] [late 16C–early 17C] a louse. ❑ **Welsh ejectment** *n.* [the stereotyped meanness of the Welsh] [early 19C] removing the roof of a tenant's house, with the purpose of making the house uninhabitable. ❑ **Welsh fiddle** *n. see* SCOTCH FIDDLE *under* SCOTCH *adj.* ❑ **Welsh parsley** *n.* [early–mid-17C] hemp, as used in the hangman's rope. ❑ **Welsh pineapple** *n.* [mid-19C] (*UK Und.*) bread and toasted cheese sopped in small beer. ❑ **Welsh turkey** *n.* [mid-19C] (*UK Und.*) a leek.

welsh *v. see* WELCH *v.*

welsher *n. see* WELCHER *n.*

Welshie *n.* (*also* **Welshy**) **1** [1920s] (*Aus.*) a native of New South Wales. **2** [1950s+] a Welshman.

welt *n.* [dial. *welter*, something large or heavy of its type] [2000s] (*Scot.*) the penis.

welter *n.*

IN PHRASES

❑ **make a welter** *v.* [dial. *welter*, something exceptionally big or heavy of its kind] [1910s+] (*Aus.*) to make a fuss, to make an issue out of something.

wem *n.* [SE *wem*, a blemish, a defilement or by confusion with *wen*, a protruberance] [mid-17C–early 17C] the vagina.

wembleys *n.* [SE *w*obble + *t*r*emble*] [1960s] (*US campus*) the female breasts.

wem-wadding *n.* [fig. use of SE *wem*, a scar, thus the mouth + SE *wadding*] [mid-19C] (*UK Und.*) food and drink.

wen *adj.* [backsl.] [mid-19C+] new; thus, *teg a wen eno*, get a new one.

wench *n.* [SE use, coined *c.*1290, is archaic] **1** [late 14C+] a woman. **2** [16C+] a promiscuous woman, a prostitute. **3** [1940s+] (*US campus*) an unpleasant or unattractive woman.

wendy *n.*[1] [? *Wendy*, the 'goody-goody' daughter in J.M. Barrie's *Peter Pan* (1904)] [1980s+] (*juv.*) a school child (of either sex) who has been rejected by their fellows.

wendy *n.*[2] [2000s] (*S.Afr. gay*) a white man.

wentworth falls *n.* (*also* **wentworth's balls**) [rhy. sl. = BALLS *n.* (1); ult. the *Wentworth Falls*, near Katoomba in the Blue Mountains of New South Wales] [1920s+] (*Aus.*) the testicles.

werris *n.* [rhy. sl.; abbr. *Werris Creek*, a small 'railway town' in New South Wales] [1960s+] (*Aus.*) a Greek.

Wessi *n.* [Ger. sl.; ult. from *Westdeutsche*, West German] [1990s+] an occupant of the former West Germany; as opposed to OSSI.

West *n.*

IN PHRASES

❑ **up West** [late 19C+] the West End of London, as seen either from the East End or from the further western or suburban areas.

west *adj.*

SE in slang uses

IN COMPOUNDS

❑ **Westbound, the** *n.* [1930s] (*US tramp*) death. ❑ **West Broadway** *n.* [ety. unknown] [mid-19C] (*US*) hash, stew. ❑ **West Buttfuck** *n. see* BUMFUCK, EGYPT *n.* ❑ **west central** *n.* [a pun on SE *WC*/the *W.C.* (west central) London postal district] [mid-19C] a water closet. ❑ **west coast turnarounds** *n.* [their use in keeping long distance drivers awake] [1980s+] (*drugs*) amphetamines; MDMA. ❑ **West End thespian** *n. see* THESPIAN *n.* ❑ **western guy** *n.* [1930s–40s] (*US Und.*) an out-of-town thief. ❑ **West Hell** *n.* (*also* **East Hell**) [1930s+] (*US*) anywhere considered as far away, unpleasant and culturally alien.

IN PHRASES

❑ **go west** *v.* [the image of the setting sun, going down in the west + the drive west that took a condemned criminal along Holborn from Newgate prison to the 'triple tree' at Tyburn (today's Marble Arch); note 'A Budg and Snug Song' (1676): 'With a kiss we part, and westward part, / To the nubbing cheat in a cart'] [1910s+] to die, to end, to collapse; thus *gone west*, dead; of objects, worn out; *send west*, to kill.

West Ham(s) (Reserves) *n.* [rhy. sl.; fr. *West Ham* United, London football team] [1970s+] nerves.

westie *n.* **1** [1980s+] (*Aus.*) one who lives in the *western* suburbs of Sydney. **2** [2000s] (*Aus.*) one who totally lacks fashion sense. **3** [2000s] (*N.Z.*) one who lives in the *western* suburbs of Auckland.

Westminster abbey *n.* [rhy. sl.] [20C+] a cabbie.

Westminster brougham *n. see* WHITECHAPEL BROUGHAM *under* WHITECHAPEL *adj.*

Westminster wedding *n.* [the contemporary negative reputation of Westminster; thus the pvb 'Who goes to Westminster for a wife, to Paul's for a man, and to Smithfield for a horse may meet with a whore, a knave, and a jade.'] [mid-17C–early 19C] 'A Whore and a Rogue Married together' (B.E.); a visit to a prostitute.

Westphalia *n.* [pun on *Westphalia* ham/SE *ham*, the back of the thigh and buttock] [late 19C–1920s] the posterior, the buttocks.

Westralia *n.* [abbr.] [late 19C+] (*Aus.*) *Western Australia*; thus *Westralian*, *Westralienne*, a Western Australian.

wet *n.* **1** with ref. to liquids. (**a**) [late 17C+] (*also* **whet**) a drink; thus *wet stuff*, alcohol. (**b**) [late 19C–1930s] (*US*) an anti-Prohibitionist, who wants alcohol to remain legal. (**c**) [1920s+] the act of urination. (**d**) [1960s] (*US campus*) a drinking party. **2** [1930s+] (*orig. juv.*) (*also* **wet end, wetso**) an ineffectual, weak, foolish person. **3** *see* WETBACK *n.*

IN PHRASES

❑ **light wet** *n.* [19C] gin.

wet, the *n.* [late 19C+] (*Aus./N.Z.*) the rainy season.

wet *adj.*[1] **1** [late 17C; late 19C+] of a woman, sexually excited, 'secreting lech-water'. **2** with ref. to alcohol. (**a**) [early 18C+] drunk; sometimes *all wet*. (**b**) [mid-19C–1920s] drunken; often as *wet night*. (**c**) [mid-19C+] (*US*) permitting the sale of alcohol; thus a *wet state*. (**d**) [1900s] (*US Und.*) of alcohol, diluted. **3** in fig. senses. (**a**) [1910s+] (*usu. upper-middle-/upper-class*) weak, spineless; thus *wetness*, weakness, ineffectuality, spinelessness. (**b**) [1920s+] incorrect, mistaken, no good; usu. in phr. *all wet*.

pertaining to alcohol

IN COMPOUNDS

❑ **wet bargain** *n.* [early 19C] a deal concluded over drinks. ❑ **wetbrain** *n.* [note SE *water on the brain*, encephalitis] [1950s+] a state of stupidity induced by alcoholism; thus an alcoholic; in general use, a fool. ❑ **wet food** *n.* [1900s] (*US*) alcohol. ❑ **wet goods** *n.* [opposite of SE *dry goods*, groceries etc] [late 18C; mid-19C–1940s] alcohol. ❑ **wet hand** *n.* [late 19C] a drunkard, a heavy drinker. ❑ **wet one** *n.* (*also* **wet daddy**) [WET *adj.*[1] (1)] **1** [early 19C] a drinker. **2** [1980s] (*US drugs*) a cigarette saturated with phencyclidine; thus as adj., *wetted-up*, intoxicated with phencyclidine. ❑ **wet parson** *n.* [late 18C–early 19C] a parson with a taste for liquor. ❑ **wet Quaker** *n.* **1** [late 17C–mid-19C] one who pretends to be religious and abjure alcohol, but in fact drinks regularly in secret. **2** in fig. use, any hypocritical person. ❑ **wet-see-through** *n.* [early 19C] gin. ❑ **wet soul** *n.* [early 19C] a regular, and reasonably heavy drinker. ❑ **wetworks** *n.* [1900s] (*US*) a bar.

IN PHRASES

❑ **get wet** *v.* [1960s] (*US*) to have a drink.

pertaining to sex

IN COMPOUNDS

❑ **wetbox** *n.* [WET *adj.*[1] (1) + BOX *n.*[1] (1)] [2000s] (*US*) the vagina. ❑ **wet check** *n.* [1990s+] (*Aus.*) a contraceptive sheath, a condom. ❑ **wet deck** *n.* [the accumulation of sexual fluids] **1** [late 19C+] (*Can./US*) a woman or prostitute who performs serial sex acts. **2** [1970s] ejaculation without penetration, e.g. after mutual male masturbation. ❑ **wet hen** *n.* [? HEN *n.* (1)] [late 19C] (*US*) a prostitute. ❑ **wet suit** *n.* [1990s+] (*Aus.*) a contraceptive sheath, a condom.

IN PHRASES

❑ **get it wet** *v.* **1** [1950s+] (*also* **get one's dick wet, get wet**) of a man, to have sexual intercourse. **2** [1960s] to be fellated. ❑ **leave it wet for** *v.* [1990s+] (*US black*) to have sexual intercourse; the idea being with someone else's partner.

general uses

IN COMPOUNDS

❑ **wet end** *n.* see WET *n.* (2). ❑ **wet goose** *n.* [GOOSE *n.*[4] (1)] [late 19C] a foolish, naïve person. ❑ **wet smack** *n.* [fig. use of SE *smack*] [1920s+] (*US*) a weakling, an ineffectual person; a disappointment. ❑ **wet work** *n.* (*also* **wet affairs, wet arts**) [trans. KGB sl. *Mokryye Dela*, the department of wet affairs] [1960s+] murder; assassination, esp. as carried out by secret services.

IN PHRASES

❑ **all wet** [1920s+] **1** (*orig. US*) silly, foolish. **2** (*orig. US black*) useless, worthless, wrong. ❑ **get wet** *v.* [the blood that, figuratively at least, gets on one's hands; thus KGB, CIA, MI6 jargon *get wet*, to kill] [1970s+] **1** to murder, to kill. **2** to be wounded, to be stabbed.

SE in slang uses

IN COMPOUNDS

❑ **wetback** see separate entries. ❑ **wet bottom** *n.* see separate entry. ❑ **wet day** *n.* see WET WEEK below. ❑ **wet dream** *n.* see separate entry. ❑ **wet foot** *n.* [1970s] a naïve, inexperienced, innocent person, also as adj. ❑ **wethead** *n.* [SE *wet* + -HEAD *sfx* (1)] [1970s+] (*US black*) a simpleton, an innocent, a novice. ❑ **wet leg** *n.* [? they are fig. urinating down their own leg] [1920s–30s] a self-pitying person. ❑ **wet-nosed** *adj.* [1960s] (*US*) innocent, naïve. ❑ **wet rag** *n.* [1940s+] **1** an emotional, sentimental person. **2** (*US campus*) an unpleasant, unpopular person. ❑ **wet 'un** *n.* see separate entries. ❑ **wet 'uns** *n.* [late 19C] tears. ❑ **wet week** *n.* (*also* **wet day**) [? being *wet* it 'shrinks'] [20C+] (*Irish*) a short time.

IN PHRASES

❑ **get someone wet** *v.* [the image of dunking them in water] [1920+] (*N.Z.*) to gain an advantage over someone. ❑ **get wet** *v.* [? one gets wet with sweat] **1** [late 19C–1950s] (*Aus.*) to lose one's temper, to become angry. **2** [1900s–40s] (*Aus./N.Z.*) to gain the upper hand over, to have at one's mercy.

wet *adj.*[2] [1910s–50s] (*Aus.*) angry.

wet *adj.*[3] [WET *n.* (3)] [1920s–40s] a horse stolen and smuggled from Mexico.

wet *adj.*[4] [play on FISHY *adj.*[2] (1)] [1970s] (*US black*) suspicious.

wet *adj.*[5] [2000s] (*US black teen*) first-rate, excellent.

wet *v.* **1** [late 17C+] (*also* **wet it, wet one's nose, wet up, whet**) to drink. **2** [mid-19C] (*US campus*) to 'christen' new clothes by treating one's friends to a drink on the first occasion of wearing them. **3** [mid–late 19C] to treat to a drink for any form of celebration. **4** [1970s–80s] (*UK black*) (*also* **wet up**) to slash or stab with a knife [blood is *wet*]. **5** [1990s+] (*US black*) to excite a woman.

IN PHRASES

❑ **wet someone's ass** *v.* [2000s] (*US black*) to shoot someone.

SE in slang uses

IN PHRASES

pertaining to drinking

❑ **wet in** *v.* [1970s] to celebrate a promotion by drinking (to excess). ❑ **wet it** *v.* see sense 1 above. ❑ **wet one's goozle** *v.* [GOOZLE *n.*] [1920s] (*US*) to have a drink. ❑ **wet one's luck** *v.* [1900s] (*Aus.*) to drink in celebration of one's good fortune. ❑ **wet one's neck** *v.* **1** [early–mid-19C] to get drunk. **2** [early 19C; 1910s] to have a drink. ❑ **wet one's nose** *v.* see sense 1 above. ❑ **wet one's stripes** *v.* [1920s] to drink in celebration of a promotion. ❑ **wet one's tonsils** *v.* [1940s–60s] (*US*) to drink. ❑ **wet one's whistle** *v.* (*also* **wet one's pipe, ...throttle**) **1** [late 14C+] to take a drink; thus *whistle-wetter*, a drink. **2** [17C–early 18C; 1960s] to give someone a drink. ❑ **wet the deal** *v.* (*also* **wet the bargain, ...coat**) [mid-19C+] to seal a deal with a drink. ❑ **wet the other eye** *v.* (*also* **wet both eyes, ... t'other eye**) [mid-18C–19C] to follow one drink immediately by another. ❑ **wet up** *v.* **1** *see* sense 1 above. **2** *see* sense 4 above.

general uses

❑ **wet oneself** *v.* [i.e. WET ONE'S PANTS *under* PANTS *n.*] [1930s+] to become overexcited.

wet *adv.* [1910s+] foolishly, weakly.

IN PHRASES

❑ **talk wet** *v.* [1910s+] to talk in a sentimental, 'soft' manner; to talk stupidly.

wet and damp *n.* [rhy. sl. = CAMP *n.*[2] (1)] [1980s+] (*Aus. prison*) a homosexual.

wetback *n.* (*also* **wet**) [the condition of the immigrants who trad. swim the Rio Grande as the best means of beating border checks. Despite its reputation as a racist slur, Hispanics accept it; thus Mex.Am. self-description *los mojados*, the wet ones] [1920s+] a derog. term for an illegal Mexican immigrant to the USA; thus for Mexicans and so Hispanics in general.

wetback *adj.* [WETBACK *n.*] [1940s+] (*US*) pertaining to illegal Mexican immigrants.

wetback *v.* [1970s+] (*US*) to gain illegal entry to the US by swimming the Rio Grande.

wet bottom *n.*

IN PHRASES

❑ **do a wet bottom** *v.* (*also* **get a wet bottom**) [the result of male ejaculation and vaginal secretions] [19C] of a woman, to have sexual intercourse.

wet dream *n.* [ext. uses of SE] **1** [1910s–40s] something pathetic. **2** [1920s+] a fantasy, esp. a particularly optimistic one. **3** [1980s+] a daydreamer, one who lacks concentration.

SE in slang uses

IN PHRASES

❑ **could fuck up a wet dream** (*also* **would fuck up a wet dream**) [1960s+] referring to one who is exceptionally incompetent, stupid or clumsy.

wetso *n.* see WET *n.* (2).

wettie *n.* [abbr.] [1990s+] (*Aus./N.Z.*) a wet suit.

wetty *n.* [1960s] (*Aus.*) a disappointment.

IN PHRASES

❑ **have a wetty** *v.* [1960s] (*Aus.*) to work oneself up into a rage.

wet 'un *n.*[1]

IN PHRASES

❑ **do a wet 'un** *v.* [for ety. *see* WET BOTTOM *n.*] [19C] of a woman, to have sexual intercourse.

wet 'un *n.*[2] [*wet 'un* presumably means 'wet brain' and the disease must have been the same as, or at least similar to, the late-20C+ BSE, 'mad cow disease'] [mid-19C] a diseased cow, technically unfit for human consumption, but often sold for conversion into sausages.

wet 'un *n.*[3] *see* WET HAND *under* WET *adj.*[1].

wewi *n.* see WEE-WEE *n.*[1].

we wuz robbed! *excl.* [coined by US boxing Manager Joe Jacobs, manager in 1932 of the German world heavyweight champion Max Schmeling (1905–2005). Defending his title in America, Schmeling systematically destroyed his opponent but was still declared the loser, outpointed by the challenger, local boy Jack Sharkey (1902–94). Jacobs' phrase made his feelings plain] [1930s+] we were cheated!

WGB *n.* [abbr.] [2000s] (*US black*) a white girl's buttocks.

w.g.f. *phr.* [abbr.] [1960s+] used by transsexuals to mean whole girl fantasy or fetish.

whack *n.*[1] (*also* **wack**) [ext. uses of WHACK *v.*[1] (1)] **1** [late 18C+] a share, a portion. **2** [early 19C+] a swig of a drink, a gulp of food. **3** [late 19C] (*US*) a bargain. **4** [late 19C+] (*US*) a try, an attempt. **5** [late 19C+] a 'go', a time. **6** [1950s] (*US*) an aspect. **7** [1980s+] (*W.I.*) a large sum of money. **8** [1990s+] (*drugs*) a portion of a drug, e.g. a 'line' of a narcotic, a puff of cannabis. **9** [2000s] income. **10** *see* WHACKER *n.*[1].

IN PHRASES

❑ **get a whack at** *v.* [1900s] (*US*) to gain access to. ❑ **go whack** *v.* [mid-19C–1940s] to take or offer a share. ❑ **have a whack at** *v.* (*also* **take a whack at, ...whang at**) [mid-19C+] (*orig. US*) to make an attempt or attack upon. ▫ **have one's whack** *v.* (*also* **take one's whack**) [mid-19C+] to have or take one's share. ▫ **into whack** [SE *whack*, to hit a blow, i.e. ref. to that which has been knocked home properly] [1930s] into order.

whack *n.*^{2} (*also* **wack**) [WHACK *v.*^{1}] **1** [late 18C+] a blow, usu. with some form of stick. **2** [1940s] (*US Und.*) a prison sentence. **3** [1960s+] (*Scot./Aus.*) a punishment, one's desserts. **4** [1980s+] (*drugs*) the act of diluting bulk drugs, e.g. heroin, for retail sale.

IN PHRASES

▫ **black whack** *n.* [1980s+] (*drugs*) phencyclidine. ▫ **cop one's whack** *v.* [1970s+] (*Scot./Aus.*) to get one's deserts. ▫ **go to whack** *v.* [1910s+] to collapse, to break down (lit. and fig.). ▫ **out of whack** [late 19C+] lit. or fig. off-centre, out of true, out of order, feeling unwell.

whack *n.*^{3} [early 19C] (*Anglo-Irish*) a pickpocket.

whack *n.*^{4} (*also* **wack**) [Scot. *whack*, a slice, appetite] [mid-19C–1910s] (*Anglo-Irish*) food, sustenance.

whack *n.*^{5} (*also* **wack**) [abbr. WHACKO *n.*] **1** [1940s+] (*US*) a mad or eccentric person; occas. of a place. **2** [1980s+] (*US campus*) (*also* **wack, whacker**) a fool.

IN COMPOUNDS

▫ **whack attack** *n.* (*also* **wack attack**) [1980s+] (*US black*) the onset of apparent insanity, usu. through the use of drugs. ▫ **whack job** *n.* [JOB *n.*^{2} (4a)] [1970s+] (*US*) an insane person, a madman.

whack *adj.* **1** *see* WACK *adj.* **2** *see* WHACKY *adj.*

whack *v.*^{1} (*also* **wack**) **1** [late 18C+] to hit. **2** [1900s] (*US*) to lie. **3** [1900s] to criticize. **4** [20C+] to hit in fig. sense, e.g. to sentence to prison. **5** [20C+] (*also* **whack out**) to defeat in a competition, to outdo. **6** [1930s+] (*also* **wack out, whack out**) to murder, to kill; also fig. **7** [1930s+] (*US*) to cut or chop. **8** [1950s+] (*also* **wack off, whack off**) to masturbate. **9** [1970s+] (*also* **bang out, whack up**) (*US drugs*) to dilute or 'cut' a narcotic.

IN PHRASES

▫ **whack into** *v.* [fig. use of WHACK *v.*^{1}] [2000s] (*N.Z.*) to set to on a task enthusiastically. ▫ **whack it** *v.* (*also* **wack it**) [fig. use of WHACK *v.*^{1}] [1960s+] to masturbate. ▫ **whack it in** *v.* (*also* **wack it in, wack it up, whack it up**) [1960s+] to masturbate. ▫ **whack it out** *v.* (*also* **wack it out**) [1910s–20s] to defend or support successfully. ▫ **whack it up** *v.* [1910s] (*Aus.*) to do something energetically. ▫ **whack something out of** *v.* **1** [1960s] of objects, to destroy. **2** [1990s+] to render unconscious. ▫ **whack the crap out of** *v.* [1960s] (*orig. US*) to beat hard. ▫ **whack the one-eyed worm** *v.* (*also* **...weasel, wack the one-eyed worm, ...weasel**) [*ONE-EYED (WONDER) WORM under* ONE-EYED *adj.*/WEASEL *n.* (4)] [1960s+] to masturbate.

whack *v.*^{2} (*also* **wack**) [WHACK *n.*^{1}] **1** [early 19C] (*also* **whack out, whack up**) to share or divide equally, thus *whack the blunt*, share out the money. **2** [1960s+] to charge money, usu. *whack for*.

IN PHRASES

▫ **whack the grievances** *v.* [mid-19C] (*UK Und.*) to share expenses.

whack-a-doo *n.* [ext. of WHACKO *n.*] [20C+] a lunatic, an eccentric.

whackadoo *adj.* [WHACK-A-DOO *n.*] [1980s] (*US*) mad, eccentric.

whackatabacky *n. see WHACKY BACCY under* WHACKY *adj.*

whackdoodle *n. see* WHACKO *n.*

whack down *v.* **1** [20C+] (*also* **wack down, whack on**) to lay down money, to wager; to write down notes. **2** [1960s+] (*also* **whack off**) to consume, to eat or drink. **3** [2000s] to inhale.

whacked *adj.* (*also* **wacked, whacked to the wide**) [WHACK *v.*^{1}] **1** [20C+] completely shocked, overcome. **2** [20C+] beaten, defeated. **3** [1910s+] absolutely exhausted. **4** [1940s+] (*US campus*) eccentric. **5** [1990s+] overcome by an excess of drink or drugs. **6** [1990s+] (*US campus*) stupid. **7** [2000s] ruined, in disrepair. **8** *see* WACK *adj.* (1).

whacked out *adj.*^{1} (*also* **wacked, wacked out, whacked**) [WHACK *v.*^{1}] [1960s+] **1** (*orig. US*) murdered. **2** exhausted. **3** having lost all one's money gambling. **4** (*also* **whacked**) under the influence of a drug or of alcohol. **5** emotionally drained. **6** unstable, eccentric.

whacked out *adj.*^{2} (*also* **wacked out**) [WHACKO *n.*] [1960s+] crazy, insane, eccentric.

whacked to the wide *adj. see* WHACKED *adj.*

whacked-up *adj.* (*also* **wacked-up**) [1940s+] (*US*) **1** absurd, ludicrous, crazy [WHACKED *adj.* (4)]. **2** badly injured [WHACK *v.*^{1} (1)].

whacker *n.*^{1} (*also* **whack**) [WHACK *v.*^{1} (1)] [late 18C+] anything especially large or notable, e.g. a lie.

whacker *n.*^{2} [WHACK *v.*^{1} (1)] [1910s] (*UK Und.*) a police truncheon.

whacker *n.*^{3} [WHACK *n.*^{1} (2)] [1930s] (*Irish*) a small glass of brandy.

whacker *n.*^{4} (*also* **wacker**) [WHACK OFF *v.*] [1940s+] (*US*) a masturbator, lit. and fig.

whacker *n.*^{5} (*also* **wacker**) [WHACKY *adj.* but note WHACK OFF *v.*, i.e. the mythical links of masturbation and insanity] **1** [1960s] (*Aus.*) a fool. **2** [1960s] a person who is seriously mentally unstable. **3** *see* WHACK *n.*^{5} (2).

whacker *adj. see* WACKER *adj.*

whacking *n.* [WHACK *v.*^{1}] **1** [mid-19C+] a blow, a beating. **2** [2000s] a murder.

whacking *adj.* (*also* **wacking**) [WHACKER *n.*^{1}] [early 19C+] a general intensifier, usu. in *whacking great, whacking horrible* etc.

whackle out *v.* [fig. use of WHACK *v.*^{1} (1) + SE fidd*le*] [1910s] (*Aus.*) to consider deeply.

whacko *n.* (*also* **wack, wacko, whackdoodle**) [WHACKO *adj.*^{1}] [1960s+] **1** an unstable or mentally ill person. **2** a crazy, eccentric, or extreme person.

IN COMPOUNDS

▫ **wack job** *n.* [1980s+] (*US*) an eccentric or insane person.

whacko *adj.*^{1} (*also* **wacko**) [WHACKY *adj.*] [1940s+] crazy, insane, eccentric.

whacko *adj.*^{2} [WHACKO! *excl.*] [1950s–60s] (*Aus.*) exciting, pleasurable.

whacko! *excl.* (*also* **wacko! waco!**) [1910s+] (*Aus.*) a general excl. of pleasure.

IN EXCLAMATIONS

▫ **whacko the chook!** (*also* **whacko the goose!**) [WHACKO! *excl.* + CHOOK *n.* (1)/*goose*] [1970s+] (*Aus.*) excellent! first-rate! absolutely wonderful!

whack off *v.* (*also* **wack off**) [WHACK *v.*^{1}] **1** [1950s+] to masturbate; thus *whack-silly*, addicted to masturbation and as such, mad. **2** *see* WHACK DOWN *v.* (2).

IN COMPOUNDS

▫ **whack attack** *n.* (*also* **wack attack**) [play on McDonalds' hamburger's coinage, *Mac attack*, a sudden craving for a hamburger] [1980s+] an act of masturbation; often as *have a whack attack*.

whack on *v. see* WHACK DOWN *v.* (1).

whacko the diddle-oh *adj.* [WHACKO THE DIDDLE-OH! *excl.*] [1940s+] (*Aus.*) excellent, splendid, first-rate.

whacko the diddle-oh! *excl.* (*also* **whacko the did!**) [ext. WHACKO! *excl.*] [1940s+] (*Aus.*) a general excl. of pleasure, esp. on seeing an attractive woman.

whack-out *n.* [WHACK *v.*^{1} (6); i.e. one is 'dead'] [1960s] (*US*) an absolute failure.

whack out *v.* (*also* **wack out**) [fig. uses of WHACK *v.*^{1}] **1** [20C+] to create, to make. **2** [1910s+] to play (music), to 'knock out' (a tune). **3** *see* WHACK *v.*^{1} (5). **4** *see* WHACK *v.*^{1} (6). **5** *see* WHACK *v.*^{2} (1).

whack-up *n.*^{1} [late 19C+] a division of the spoils.

whack-up *n.*^{2} [2000s] (*N.Z.*) a quick 'cheap and cheerful' act of building or construction.

whack up *v.*[1] [WHACK *n.*[1]] **1** [late 19C+] (*US*) to make a contribution, a donation. **2** [late 19C+] to come up with, to create. **3** [1980s+] (*US*) to acquire money, esp. by bribery.

whack up *v.*[2] [ext. WHACK *v.*[2] (1)] **1** [late 19C+] (*orig. US*) to divide (loot). **2** [1990s+] (*US drugs*) to dilute drugs by adding a WHACK *n.*[2] (4), thus increasing the weight and potential profits. **3** *see* WHACK *v.*[2] (1).

whack up *v.*[3] [ext. use of WHACK *v.*[1]] **1** [20C+] of an engine, a vehicle, to accelerate. **2** [1980s+] (*Aus. prison*) to inject narcotics.

whacky *adj.* (*also* **wack, wacky, whack**) [Yorks. dial. *whacky*, a fool, a simpleton, a blockhead; also Warwickshire dial. *whacky*, left-handed] **1** [1930s+] (*orig. US*) eccentric. **2** [1940s+] obsessed, passionate about.

DERIVATIVES

❑ **whackiness** *n.* (*also* **wackiness**) [1930s+] eccentricity.

IN COMPOUNDS

❑ **whacky baccy** *n.* (*also* **wackey dust, wacky weed, ...baccy, whackatabacky, whacky weed**) [WHACKY *adj.* + abbr. SE *tobacco*/WEED *n.*[1] (4)/DUST *n.* (6d)] [1930s; 1980s+] (*drugs*) marijuana.

IN PHRASES

❑ **do the whacky** *v.* [coined in late 1990s US TV show *Buffy the Vampire Slayer*] [1990s+] to lose emotional control. ❑ **whacky for** *adj.* [1960s] (*US*) keen on, fascinated by.

-whacky *sfx* (*also* **-wacky**) [WHACKY *adj.*] [1930s+] (*US*) comb. adj. to describe an enthusiasm or habit e.g. *car-wacky*, car crazy.

whaddaya know? *phr. see* WHAT DO YOU KNOW? *phr.*

whaddaya whaddaya? *phr.* [1950s+] a general interrog. phr.; lit. what do you?

whaddup? *phr.* [var. WHAT'S UP? *phr.* (1)] [1990s+] (*US black*) a phr. of greeting.

whaffle *v. see* WAFFLE *v.*[1].

wha' gwaan *phr. see* WHAT A GWAAN? *phr.*

whail *v.* (*also* **whale**) [1940s–60s] (*US black*) to do something especially well or efficiently.

whale *n.* [joc. uses of SE, the size of the creature] **1** [mid-19C–1920s] (*US, orig. campus*) an exceptionally brilliant scholar, thus in general a very competent person. **2** [late 19C–1910s] (*Aus.*) an exceptional performer in a given discipline; thus phr. *be a whale on*; also ironic use. **3** [late 19C+] (*US*) an exceptionally large or fat person. **4** [late 19C+] (*also* **gale**) a large quantity; a general intensifier. **5** [1900s–10s] a fanatic, an obsessive.

IN PHRASES

❑ **whale of a...** *n.* [1910s+] someone or something exceptional. ❑ **whale in the bay** *n.* (*Aus.*) **1** [1930s] someone who has money to spend and uses it on the assembled company. **2** [1980s+] 'a major influence at work behind the scenes' (Wilkes).

SE in slang uses

IN COMPOUNDS

❑ **whale and whitewash** *n.* [1930s] (*UK tramp*) fish in white sauce. ❑ **whale belly** *n.* [1930s] (*US tramp*) a steel coal-car.

IN PHRASES

❑ **play the whale** *v.* [echoic + ? the biblical story of Jonah, who was vomited up by a whale] [1960s–70s] (*Aus.*) to vomit.

whale *v.*[1] (*also* **wail, wail on, wale, whale on**) [? SE *wale*, to mark the flesh with wales (weals), or a *whale*bone whip] **1** [mid-19C+] (*US*) to hit, thrash or trounce; also fig. use. **2** [1950s+] (*US black/campus*) to act or do well. **3** [1950s+] (*US*) to attack. **4** [1950s+] to act aggressively, fast.

IN PHRASES

❑ **whale down** *v.* [1950s+] to eat furiously. ❑ **whale the — out of someone** *v.* [1970s+] to beat viciously.

whale *v.*[2] **1** [1900s–40s] (*Aus.*) to live as a vagrant [WHALER *n.*[2]]. **2** *see* WHAIL *v.*

IN PHRASES

❑ **whale up the Lachlan** *v.* [1950s] (*Aus.*) to live as a tramp.

whale away *v.* (*also* **whale into, whale it**) [ext. of WHALE *v.*[1] (1)] [mid-19C+] (*US*) to attack or work at something vigorously, esp. when vocalizing a point; usu. as *whale away at*.

whalebone lay *n.* [SE *whalebone* + LAY *n.*[3] (1)] [early 18C] (*UK Und.*) using a piece of whalebone daubed with an adhesive to rob a shop till.

whaled *adj.* [fig. use of WHALE *v.*[1] (1)] [1980s–90s] (*US campus*) drunk.

whale into/it *v. see* WHALE AWAY *v.*

whale on *v. see* WHALE *v.*[1].

whaler *n.*[1] (*also* **waler**) [SE *whale*] [mid-19C–1960s] (*US*) anything considered large of its kind.

whaler *n.*[2] (*also* **waler**) [late 19C–1940s] (*Aus.*) a tramp, a vagrant.

IN PHRASES

❑ **whaler's delight** *n.* [1900s–20s] (*Aus.*) brown sugar mixed with cold tea to make a thick paste.

whaler *n.*[3] *see* WALER *n.*

whales on *adj.* [WHALE *n.* (5)] [late 19C] (*US*) obsessed with, devoted to.

whaling *n.* [WHALE *v.*[1] (1)] [mid-19C+] a beating.

whaling *adj.*[1] [SE *whale*] [1900s–10s] (*US*) as an intensive, enormous.

whaling *adj.*[2] *see* WAILING *adj.*

wham *n.* [WHAM *v.* (1)] **1** [1910s+] a blow, usu. from a fist; also fig. use. **2** [1980s] (*US black*) a large, aggressive man. **3** [1980s] an unpleasant woman.

wham *v.* [echoic] **1** [1910s+] (*orig. US*) to hit or strike; also fig. use. **2** [1920s+] to throw hard.

wham! *excl.* (*also* **whammo!**) [echoic] [1920s+] **1** (*US*) used to express surprise or convey the impact of a sudden violent attack or blow. **2** attrib., resounding, making an impact.

wham bam! *excl.* [1950s+] (*orig. US*) used to express sudden or speedy movement.

wham-bam-thank-you-ma'am *phr.* (*also* **gangbang, thank you ma'am; ram, bam, thank you ma'am; slam-bam-thank-you-ma'am; whambam; wham-wham-wham**) [echoic] [1940s+] **1** epitomizing brief sexual intercourse intended on the whole for male satisfaction only; similarly used in homosexual context. **2** anything, in a non-sexual sense, that has to be done quickly and perfunctorily. **3** thank you, usu. cynical.

whambang *adj.* [1950s+] (*US*) loud, large and impressive.

whamdanglers *n.* [WHAM *v.* + SE *dangle*] [1990s+] an extremely large pair of breasts.

whammer *n.* [WHAM *v.* (1)] [1990s+] the penis.

whammo! *excl. see* WHAM! *excl.*

whammy *n.* [WHAM *v.*; note *Whammy*, a character who can paralyze with a stare in comic strip *Li'l Abner*] **1** [1930s+] a 'hex', an evil influence, the evil eye. **2** [1950s+] a punchline, anything devastating and beyond a similarly powerful response. **3** [1960s] spiritual or positive force. **4** [1960s] (*US drugs*) (*also* **whammie**) a portion of a given drug that will induce the desired level of intoxication. **5** [1980s+] (*US campus*) an extremely unattractive woman.

IN PHRASES

❑ **double whammy** *n.* [best known as the title of US thriller-writer Carl Hiaasen's 1988 novel, the term (attempting to point up the UK Labour Party threats to the UK economy) was central to the rival Conservative Party's advertising campaign in the general election of 1992] [1950s+] a double blow, an extreme problem; an intensifier of WHAMMY *n.* (2). ❑ **put the whammy on** *v.* [1930s–50s] **1** to cause problems for; to condemn. **2** (*US*) to influence, to 'hex'. **3** (*US black*) to hit hard.

wham-wham-wham *phr. see* WHAM-BAM-THANK-YOU-MA'AM *phr.*

whang *n.*[1] [WHANG *v.* (1)] **1** [late 18C+] a reverberating blow. **2** [1910s+] (*Aus.*) a large piece, a share, a portion. **3** [1930s–

40s] (*US*) (*also* **whangdanger**) an excellent thing. **4** [1930s+] (*orig. US*) the penis, usu. large [the aggressive image of the penis as that which 'hits' the vagina].

IN PHRASES

❑ **step over one's whang** *v. see* STEP ON ONE'S DICK *under* DICK *n.*[1]. ❑ **take a whang at** *v. see* HAVE A WHACK AT *under* WHACK *n.*[1].

whang *n.*[2] [Scot. *whang*, a bootlace] [20C+] (*Irish*) a thin, lanky person.

whang *n.*[3] [1920s–30s] (*US Und.*) a stupid person.

whang *v.* [SE *thong*, to flog or lash with a thong, ult. f. ON *þvengja*, to secure or fasten with a thong] **1** [late 18C+] to hit. **2** [19C+] to throw, drive, pull, shoot etc with force or with violent impact.

whangdanger *n. see* WHANG *n.*[1] (3).

whangdoodle *n.*[1] (*also* **wangdoodle, wingdoodle**) [nonsense word] (*US*) **1** [mid-19C] a mythical beast of uncertain character. **2** [late 19C+] an unspecified object, something one does not know the name of [fig. use of sense 1]. **3** [1920s] nonsense. **4** [1920s] jazz music.

whangdoodle *n.*[2] (*also* **wangdoodle, wingdoodle**) [WHANGDOODLE *n.*[1] (2) + ext. of WHANG *n.*[1] (4); note DOODLE *n.*[2] (1) although the link is unlikely] [1970s+] (*US*) the penis.

whangee *n.* [Chinese *huang*, bamboo sprouts that were too old for eating; thus the *whangee* was a cane made from the stem of one or other species of *Phyllostachys*, Chinese and Japanese plants allied to and resembling bamboos; 20C use is historical and joc.] [1900s–60s] a cane.

whanger *n.* [WHANG *v.* (1)] **1** [late 19C] anything large or unusual of its kind. **2** [1910s+] the penis, usu. larger than average.

whank (off) *v. see* WANK *v.*

whap *n.* [WHAP *v.*] [1920s–60s] a hit, a blow.

whap *v. see* WHOP *v.*

whap! *excl. see* WHOP! *excl.*

whap bang! *excl.* (*also* **whap! wop bang!**) [mid-19C] echoic of a sudden, violent action.

wha'ppen? *phr. see* WHAT'S HAPPENING? *under* HAPPEN *v.*

whapper *n. see* WHOPPER *n.*

whapping *adj. see* WHOPPING *adj.*

wharfie *n.* [SE *wharf*, the usu. Aus./N.Z. term for SE *dock*] [1910s+] (*Aus./N.Z.*) docker.

wharf-rat *n.* [SE *wharf* + RAT *n.*[1] (1)] [mid-19C–1940s] (*orig. US*) anyone who hangs around wharfs, looking out for an opportunity to steal from a cargo.

what? *phr.* **1** [mid-16C+] used as an affirmative at the end of a statement, isn't it/he/etc, e.g. *That's a nasty fellow, what?* **2** [early 19C+] short for *What did you say?* or *What is it?* **3** [mid-18C+] (*also* **eh, what?**) an expletive tacked on to the end of a sentence to give it greater emphasis but of no actual meaning.

what about it? *phr.* [1910s] (*Aus.*) an invitation to drink.

what a gwaan? *phr.* (*also* **wha' gwaan**) [1970s+] (*W.I./UK black teen*) what is going on? what's happening? how are things?

what-all *n.* [1940s+] anything for which one has no proper name, often as *I don't know what all*.

what can I do you for? *phr.* [DO *v.*[1] (2a)] [1920s+] a facetious reversal of SE *what can I do for you?*

whatchamacallit *n.* (*also* **whatchacallem, whatchacallit, whatchamahoosis, whatchie, watchumajigger, what-sha-call-him, what-you-call-it, what-you-may-call-'ems**) [late 16C; mid-19C+] anything to which one cannot give a name when required; also used euph.

whatdayacallit *n. see* WHAT-D'YOU-CALL-IT *n.*

what-do-you-call-it *n.* (*also* **what d'ye callum**) [euph.] **1** [17C–18C] the male or female genitals. **2** *see* WHAT-D'YOU-CALL-IT *n.*

what do you know? *phr.* (*also* **whaddaya know? what do you think?**) **1** [20C+] an excl. of surprise, usu. ironic. **2** [1910s+] a greeting, 'hello and how are you?', 'what are you/have you been doing?'.

whatd'youcallhim *n.* (*also* **what-d'ye-call'em, whatd'youcallher**) [late 16C+] anyone for whom one cannot provide the name.

what-d'you-call-it *n.* (*also* **whatdayacallit, what-do-you-call-it, whatdyecall, whatd'yecall'em, whatd'yecallum, whatyermecallems, whatyermycalit**) [late 16C+] anything for which one has no precise name.

what-er? *n.* (*also* **what-y?**) [late 19C] a form of 'what' used when questioning the previous speaker's self-description, e.g. *'I'm a butcher.' – 'A what-er?'*.

whatever *adv.* **1** [20C+] whatever happens, at all events. **2** [1970s+] (*orig. US back/teen*) a general expression of dismissal, disinterest.

whatever bakes one's biscuit *phr.* [2000s] (*US*) whatever makes one happy, satisfied.

whatever blows your dress up *phr. see under* BLOW *v.*[1].

what-for *n.* (*also* **what-sort**) [? abbr. of the question 'what are you doing this to me/is this happening for?'] [late 19C+] a punishment, trouble, a fuss.

IN PHRASES

❑ **give someone what-for** *v.* [a response to presumed SE *query* 'what is that for?'] **1** [late 19C+] (*also* **give someone what's what**) to reprimand severely, to inflict severe pain or chastisement, esp. of an errant child. **2** [late 19C+] to beat up. **3** [1950s+] of a man, to have sexual intercourse. ❑ **give — what-for** *v.* [20C+] to talk eloquently about a given topic.

what Harry gave Doll *n.* (*also* **what Robin gave Nell**) [generic use of proper names] [late 17C–19C] sexual intercourse.

IN PHRASES

❑ **get what Harry gave Doll** *v.* [late 19C–early 20C] of a woman, to have sexual intercourse.

what-have-you *n.* [1960s+] something which the speaker cannot precisely name.

what-ho *adj.* [WHAT HO! *excl.*] [1930s] (*US*) enjoyable, fun.

what ho! *excl.* (*also* **what oh!**) [late 17C; early 19C+] a general excl., usu. of greeting.

IN PHRASES

❑ **get what-ho** *v.* [1910s+] to be punished, treated badly. ❑ **give what-ho** *v.* [1910s+] to punish, to treat badly.

what ho, she bumps! *excl.* [orig. used of a boat moving through choppy seas] [late 19C+] an excl. used on seeing a special display of energy, esp. by a woman.

what-I-might-say *n. see under* SAY *v.*

what in Cain? *phr.* [euph. for WHAT IS IT? *phr.*] [mid-19C] a general intensifier of a question.

whatisit *n. see* WHATSIT *n.*

what is it? *phr.* (*also* **what is?**) [the usual response is 'What it was'] [1970s+] (*US black/campus*) a greeting.

what it is? *phr.* [1970s+] (*US black*) a friendly greeting, hello, how are you?

what-nosed *adj.* [play on 'what do they know?', being so drunk + the swollen/red *nose* of drunkenness] [19C] drunk.

what-not *n.* **1** [late 16C+] used when the correct description or name eludes the speaker; also of an un-named action. **2** [1930s] the penis.

what odds? *phr.* (*also* **what's the odds?**) [mid-19C+] what's the difference?

what-oh *n.* [the appreciative *what, oh* remark of a watching male] [1910s–20s] a 'fast' young woman.

what oh! *excl. see* WHAT HO! *excl.*

what price (the) – ? *phr.* [racing use *price*, the odds] [late 19C+] what do you think of (something/someone) now?

what Robin gave Nell *n. see* WHAT HARRY GAVE DOLL *n.*

whatsamajig *n.* [1990s+] (*Aus.*) something the name of which one does not know or has forgotten.

what's crackulatin'? *phr. see* WHAT'S KRACKALACKIN? *phr.*

what's doing? *phr.* [20C+] (*Aus./US*) a greeting; an inquiry as to what is happening.

what's going on? *phr.* (*also* **what's going?**) [1950s+] a common greeting.

what-sha-call-him *n. see* WHATCHAMACALLIT *n.*

what-shall-call-um *n.* [euph.] **1** [early 17C] a need to urinate. **2** [mid-17C] anyone for whom one cannot provide the name. **3** [early–mid-19C] a prostitute, a promiscuous woman.

what's hanging? *phr. see* HOW'S IT HANGING? *phr.*

whatshername *n. see* WHATSHISNAME *n.*

whatshisface *n.* (*also* **whatsherass, whatsherface, whats-her-head, whatshisass, whatzerface**) [1960s+] used for a name one has temporarily forgotten.

what's-his-fuck *n.* [2000s] (*US*) someone whose name cannot be recalled.

whatshisname *n.* (*also* **whatshername, whatsiname, whatsisname, whatsoname, what's-their-names, what's your name, whatzername, whatzisname, whatzizname, wotsaname**) [mid-17C+] any person or thing to which one cannot give a proper name.

whatsie *n.* [abbr. WHATSHISNAME *n.*] [1950s+] (*Aus.*) any person or thing to which one cannot give a proper name.

whatsit *n.* (*also* **whatisit, whatsis, what's it, what's-oh, whatzis, wotsit**) **1** [late 19C+] (*US*) an unspecified or unspecifiable person or object. **2** [1980s] a homosexual or lesbian.

what's itching you? *phr. see WHAT'S BITING YOU? under* BITE *v.*

what's it going to be? *phr. see* WHAT WILL YOU HAVE? *phr.*

whatsits *n.* **1** [1950s+] (*also* **wotsit**) the male genitals. **2** [1960s] the menstrual period.

what's its name *n.* (*also* **whatsitsname**) [euph.] **1** [mid-19C+] (*also* **whatsyname**) an unspecified object. **2** [late 19C] the penis. **3** [late 19C] the vagina.

what's it to you? *phr.* (*also* **what's that to you?**) [early 18C; mid-19C+] an aggressive reply to a questioner implying that whatever the answer may be, it is none of their business.

what's krackalackin? *phr.* (*also* **what's crackulatin'?**) [2000s] (*US black*) a greeting.

whatsname *n. see* WHATSHISNAME *n.*

what's-oh *n. see* WHATSIT *n.*

whatsoname *n. see* WHATSHISNAME *n.*

what-sort *n. see* WHAT-FOR *n.*

what's the (big) idea? *phr.* [1910s+] (*orig. US*) more a threat than a question, usu. asked when someone is doing or saying something of which the speaker disapproves.

what's the deal? *phr.* (*also* **what's the dealie yo?**) **1** [1940s+] (*US*) what's happening? what's going on? **2** [1990s+] what's the problem?

what's the dilly? *phr.* (*also* **what's the dills? ...dilly-o?**) [? DILLY *n.*[3]; pron. of *deal/dealie* in WHAT'S THE DEAL? *phr.*] [1990s+] (*US black*) a phr. of greeting.

what's the good word? *phr.* **1** [1910s+] what are the facts? **2** [1940s+] (*US*) a cordial greeting, how are you?

what's-their-names *n. see* WHATSHISNAME *n.*

what's the odds? *phr. see* WHAT ODDS? *phr.*

what's the story (morning glory)? *phr.* (*also* **what's your story (morning glory?)**) **1** [1930s+] (*US black*) explain yourself, what are you up to? **2** [1940s+] (*orig. US black*) a general greeting: how are you? [grew in popularity in the UK after the 1995 release of (*What's the Story*) *Morning Glory?* by Oasis].

what's the verdict? *phr.* [1990s+] (*US black*) what's happening?, what's going on?

what's the word? *phr.* [assonance + ref. to *Thunderbird*, a sweet, fortified wine] [1950s–80s] (*US black*) a greeting; usu. with the response *Thunderbird!* (also *Johannesburg!*).

what's-this *n.* [1930s] (*US*) euph. for hell.

what's to it? *phr.* [1940s–50s] (*US black/teen*) a phr. of greeting.

what's up, G? *phr.* (*also* **what up toe?**) [WHAT'S UP? *phr.* + G *n.* (7)] [1990s+] (*orig. US black*) a greeting.

what's up? *phr.* (*also* **'sup? wassup? wazzup? what up? 'zup?**) **1** [mid-19C+] a general enquiry or greeting. **2** [mid-19C+] what's the matter? esp. in *what's up with you/her? etc.* **3** [1910s+] what is happening?, what is going on?

what's what *n.*

IN PHRASES

□ **give someone what's what** *see GIVE SOMEONE WHAT-FOR under* WHAT-FOR *n.*

what's with —? *phr.* [1930s+] (*US*) what's the meaning of —?, what's the matter with —?

whatsyname *n. see* WHAT'S ITS NAME *n.* (1).

what's your name *n. see* WHATSHISNAME *n.*

what's your poison? *phr.* (*also* **what's your medicine? ... nourishment?**) [POISON *n.*/MEDICINE *n.* (1)] [mid-19C+] a general invitation to have a drink.

what's yours? *phr.* [late 19C+] an invitation to take a drink.

what's your story (morning glory)? *phr. see* WHAT'S THE STORY (MORNING GLORY)? *phr.*

what the Connaught man shot at *n.* [negative stereotyping] [late 19C] (*Anglo-Irish*) nothing.

what the crap! *excl. see* WHAT THE FUCK! *excl.*

what the devil! *excl.* (*also* **how the devil! where the devil! who the devil!**) [mid-14C+] a general interrogatory intensifier, euph., for what the hell! why the hell! etc.

what the dickens! *excl.* (*also* **what the diggings!**) [euph.] [late 16C+] a euph. for WHAT THE DEVIL! *excl.*; also used as an intensifier.

what the dogs! *excl.* [late 18C–mid-19C] a mild oath, euph. of WHAT THE HELL!

what-the-fuck *adj.* [2000s] incomprehending.

what the fuck! *excl.* (*also* **what the crap! what the shit! W.T.F!**) [FUCK *n.* (1)/ CRAP *n.*[1] (2)/ SHIT *n.* (1a)] [1960s+] **1** an excl. of shock, surprise. **2** an excl. of resignation, acceptance, disinterest.

what the fuck...? *phr.* (*also* **what the blue fuck? ...fock? ... frig? ...fug? ...funk? ...piss? ...shit?**) [FUCK *n.* (1)/SHIT *n.* (1a)/ PISS *n.* (1)] [1940s+] (*orig. US*) a phr. used to indicate one's incomprehension.

what the Hanover! *excl.* (*also* **what the Hampton Court!**) [euph., via the initial 'h', for WHAT THE HELL!] [late 19C] an excl. of surprise, shock, alarm or resignation etc.

what up? *phr. see* WHAT'S UP? *phr.*

what up dog? *phr.* (*also* **what up?**) [WHAT'S UP? *phr.* + DOG *n.*[2] (1)] [1990s+] (*US black teen*) a general greeting.

what up toe? *phr. see* WHAT'S UP, G? *phr.*

what will you have? *phr.* (*also* **what's it going to be?**) [mid-19C+] a general invitation to have a drink.

what-y? *n. see* WHAT-ER? *n.*

whatyermecallems *n. see* WHAT-D'YOU-CALL-IT *n.*

whatyermycalit *n. see* WHAT-D'YOU-CALL-IT *n.*

what-you-call-it *n. see* WHATCHAMACALLIT *n.*

what you know *n. see* YOU KNOW WHAT *n.* (4).

what you know? *phr.* (*also* **what you know, Joe? what you say? what you saying?**) [1940s+] (*US campus*) a greeting, hello.

what-you-may-call-'ems *n. see* WHATCHAMACALLIT *n.*

whatzerface *n. see* WHATSHISFACE *n.*

whatzername *n. see* WHATSHISNAME *n.*

whatzis *n. see* WHATSIT *n.*

whatzizname *n. see* WHATSHISNAME *n.*

whazood *adj.* [var. on WAZZOCKED *adj.*] [1970s+] (*US campus*) drunk.

w.h.b. *n.* [abbr. *w*andering *h*and *b*rigade] [late 19C–1900s] a collective term for men who take unwanted liberties with women, 'gropers'.

wheadle *n.* (*also* **wheedle, wheedler**) [WHEADLE *v.*] [late 17C–mid-19C] (*UK Und.*) a sharper, a confidence trickster.

IN PHRASES

□ **cut a wheedle** *v.* [late 18C–early 19C] (*UK Und.*) to deceive by flattery.

wheadle *v.* (*also* **wheedle**) [SE *wheedle*, to flatter] [mid-17C–late 19C] (*UK Und.*) to cheat.

Wheadler *n.* (*also* **whiddler**) [see OLIVER WIDDLES *under* OLIVER *n.*] [early 18C] (*UK Und.*) the Moon.

wheat *n.*[1] [1900s] (*US*) a rustic, a peasant.

wheat *n.*[2] [1960s+] (*drugs*) marijuana.

wheat belt *n.* [? pun on OATS *n.*[2]] [1920s+] (*Aus.*) a prostitute.

Wheatlander *n.* [1900s] (*Aus.*) a South Australian.

wheedle *n. see* WHEADLE *n.*

wheedle *v.*[1] *see* WHEADLE *V.*

wheedle *v.*[2] *see* WHIDDLE *V.*

wheedler *n. see* WHEADLE *n.*

wheek *v.* [Antrim dial. *wheek*, to snatch away] [20C+] (*Ulster*) to steal.

wheeker *n.* [WHEEK *V.*, i.e. something worth stealing] [20C+] (*Ulster*) anything exceptionally good.

wheel *n.* **1** in context of coinage [abbr. CARTWHEEL *n.*[1] (1)]. (**a**) [late 18C–1930s] (*US*) (*also* **wagon-wheel**) a $1 coin. (**b**) [19C] a five shilling coin; thus *half-a-wheel*, 2s 6d (12½p.). (**c**) [1940s] coins in general, money. **2** [late 19C–1940s] (*orig. Aus./US*) a bicycle. **3** [1980s+] (*also* **wheels, wheels of steel**) the record turntable or turntables as used by hip-hop and rap DJs [the circular shape of the turntable, usu. used in pl. The DJ manipulates two turntables (some use three), simultaneously, selecting the portions of records and mixing them together]. **4** *see* BIG WHEEL *under* BIG *adj.*

IN PHRASES

□ **half-wheel** *n.* [1960s] (*N.Z.*) half-a-crown, 2s 6d (12½p).

SE in slang uses

IN PHRASES

□ **get on someone's wheel** *v.* [1950s+] (*Aus/US*) to irritate, to pester someone. □ **go around the wheel** *v. see* GO AROUND THE BLOCK *under* BLOCK *n.*[8]. □ **on someone's wheel** [cycling imagery] [1920s+] (*Aus.*) close behind, in pursuit; putting pressure on someone to do something. □ **on wheels** [mid-19C+] (*orig. US*) used as an intensifier, e.g. SHIT ON WHEELS *under* SHIT *n.* □ **we had one but the wheels came off** [1910s+] a phr. used to indicate that the speaker has not understood the subject of the conversation in which they had been involved. □ **wheel of life** *n.* [pun on SE *life*, existence/*life sentence*] [19C] a prison treadmill. □ **wheels came off** [automobile imagery] [1960s+] events went wrong, plans did not turn out as expected. □ **when the wheels come off** [1990s+] (*US*) of a situation, to deteriorate.

wheel *v.* **1** [mid-19C+] (*US*) to drive fast, to ride fast. **2** [late 19C–1900s] to ride a bicycle or similar pedal-powered vehicle. **3** [1930s+] (*US black*) to drive an automobile. **4** [1940s+] to drive someone, as in a taxi. **5** [1980s] (*US campus*) (*also* **wheel on over**) to make a visit, to travel.

IN PHRASES

□ **wheel a spiel** *v.* [SPIEL *n.* (4), although it suggests earlier use of colloq. *wheel and deal*] [1950s] (*US black*) to talk, esp. in a persuasive, fluent manner. □ **wheel in** *v.* (*also* **wheel out, ...up**) [1910s+] (*orig. US*) of a person or an object, to bring in to or remove from a meeting, an interview etc, esp. in imper. *wheel one in*, bring one in!

wheel! *excl.* [? WHEEL *n.* (3)] [1980s+] (*W.I./UK black teen*) a demand that a DJ replay a favourite song; thus phr. *wheel and come again*.

wheel-band in the nick *phr.* [SE *wheelband in the nick*, a tyre that runs along a regular groove] [late 17C–early 19C] drinking in the normal fashion, tilting the glass over the left thumb.

wheelchair *n.* [1940s] (*US black*) a motor vehicle.

wheelchair set *n.* [1970s] (*US gay*) old homosexuals, considered as a group.

wheeled *adj.* [WHEEL *V.* (4); i.e. one who goes about in a *wheeled* cab] **1** [late 19C] conveyed in a cab. **2** [late 19C] successful, rich, important.

wheeler *n.* [WHEEL *V.* (2)] **1** [late 19C–1910s] a cyclist. **2** [1940s] (*US Und.*) a motorcycle police officer. **3** [1950s+] a driver.

wheeler-dealer *n.* (*also* **wheeler and dealer**) [SE *wheel and deal*] **1** [1950s+] an entrepreneur, an 'operator'; also attrib. **2** [1960s] (*Aus.*) a petty confidence trickster.

wheelie *n.*[1] [1960s+] the stunt of riding on the back wheel only of a motorcycle or bicycle.

wheelie *n.*[2] [abbr.] [1990s+] a *wheel*chair.

wheelie *v.* [WHEELIE *n.*[1]] **1** [1960s+] to perform the stunt of riding on the back wheel only of a motorcycle or bicycle. **2** [1970s] (*US campus*) to drive a car fast and recklessly causing the tyres to screech.

wheelman *n.* [WHEELS *n.* (1b)] **1** [late 19C] (*US*) a cyclist. **2** [1930s+] (*orig. UK Und.*) an expert car driver, either for the police or for criminals.

wheels *n.* **1** as vehicles. (**a**) [late 19C] a bicycle. (**b**) [1930s+] a car; thus phr. *on wheels*, driving a car. (**c**) [1960s–70s] a truck. (**d**) [1990s+] a motorcycle. **2** [1910s+] (*US*) the legs. **3** [1940s] influence [the image is of machinery working in the head/government, etc]. **4** [1970s] (*US*) brains. **5** [2000s] (*US*) female breasts. **6** *see* WHEEL *n.* (3).

IN PHRASES

□ **set of wheels** *n.* [metonymy] [1950s+] (*orig. US*) a car.

SE in slang uses

IN PHRASES

□ **have wheels in one's head** *v.* [fig. use of SE *ride*, e.g. an eccentric idea] [late 19C–1930s] (*US*) to be insane, eccentric.

wheels of steel *n. see* WHEEL *n.* (3).

wheen *n.* [Anglo Saxon *hwaene*, few] [1910s+] (*Irish*) a small or large number.

wheesh!/wheesht! *excl. see* WHISHT! *excl.*

whee up *v.* [echoic excl. *whee!*, inferring speediness + GEE UP *n.*] [1940s] (*US*) to excite, to stimulate.

wheeze *n.* [orig. theatre use, a joke or comic gag introduced into the performance by a clown or comedian, esp. a constantly repeated catchphrase] **1** [late 19C] (*orig. theatre*) a joke, a catch-phrase. **2** [late 19C–1930s] a piece of special information, a 'tip'. **3** [late 19C+] a trick or dodge frequently used. **4** [1910s] a simpleton. **5** [1960s] a theory, a concept.

wheeze *v.* [late 19C–1900s] to pass on information, to betray.

wheezer *n.* **1** [1900s] (*US Und.*) a beggar who backs their entreaties with the playing of a patriotic tune on an accordion or portable organ. **2** [1970s] the penis. **3** [2000s] a cigar.

wheezy anna *n.* [rhy. sl.] [20C+] a spanner.

Whelan the Wrecker *n.* [the name of a demolition firm, *Whelan the Wrecker*, Sydney Road, Coburg, Melbourne] [1930s+] (*Aus.*) a vandal.

whelk *n.* [equation of the vagina with fish (FISH *n.*[1] (1a))] [mid–late 19C] the vagina; thus the fake-threatening phr. *I'll have your whelk*.

whelp *n.* [mid-19C+] a native of Tennessee.

whelp *v.* [SE *whelp*, of a dog, to give birth] [late 19C–1940s] to give birth.

when cock get teeth *phr.* (*also* **when cock make teeth, when fowl cut..., when fowl get...**) [20C+] (*W.I.*) absolutely never.

when-shee *n. see* YEN-SHEE *n.* (1).

when the red is over the pink, go for the brown *phr. see under* BROWN *n.*

when the road runs red, hit the dirt track *phr. see under* DIRT TRACK *n.*

when-we *n.* [the common use of *when we were in* ... to start a bitterly nostalgic sentence] [1980s+] (*S.Afr.*) an immigrant from a country once part of the British Empire who maintains their old beliefs, including feelings of racial superiority. Such figures, who were often middle-ranking administrators, also despise the South Africans among whom they have been forced to live. The type, drawn to S. Africa by apartheid, have presumably all but died out since majority rule.

when you were... *phr.* [1920s+] a phr. based on one's childhood, or even earlier life, all of which mean a very long time ago: (*Aus.*) *...just a dirty look, ...just a gleam/twinkle in* *your father's eye, ...still in/wearing short pants, ...running up and down your father's backbone, (Aus.) when your mother was cutting bread on you.*

whereabouts *n.* [pun on SE *wear-abouts*] [1930s+] (*Aus.*) male underpants.

where do we go from here? (*also* **...there?**) [1920s+] what happens now/next?

where it's at *phr.* (*also* **where it is, where it's happening**) **1** [mid-19C+] the truth, the right place, the ideal situation, opinion, experience, an expression of approval/affirmation. **2** [1970s+] (*also* **where are you at?**) as a greeting.

where-me-and-the-chair-come-together *n.* [1970s–80s] (*US black*) a euph. for the buttocks.

where one is at *phr.* (*also* **where one is coming from, where one is coming out, where one's head is at**) [1940s+] (*orig. US black*) one's lifestyle, attitudes, philosophy, mood or overall emotional state.

wheresis *n.* [1930s] (*US*) an otherwise unidentified place.

where the devil! *excl. see* WHAT THE DEVIL! *excl.*

where the five'n'arf? *phr.* [rhy. sl.; 5½ yards = one rod (unit of measurement) = God] [1920s–30s] where in God's name?

where the sun doesn't shine *phr.* (*also* **where the skin turns pink**) [20C+] (*US*) a euph. for the anus.

wherewith *n.* (*also* **wherewithal**) [the role of money in sustaining life] [19C] money.

where you at? *phr.* [WHERE ONE IS AT *phr.*] [2000s] (*US black*) a phr. of greeting.

wherry-go-nimble *n.* [? SE *where he go nimbly*] [20C+] **1** the lavatory. **2** diarrhoea.

whet *see under* WET.

whetshire cully *n.* [mid-18C] (*UK Und.*) a goldsmith.

Whetstone Park deer *n.* (*also* **Whetstone, Whetstone Park lady, Whetstone park mutton**) [proper name *Whetstone Park*, a lane between Holborn and Lincoln's Inn Fields, well known for its 'nest of wenches' (B.E.) + SE *deer*/MUTTON *n.* (1a); thus Wycherley (1672) attacking a loose woman: 'If I had met you in *Wheatstones*-Park with a drunken Foot-Soldier, I should not have been jealous of you' and Ward (1699) on the prostitutes available in the women's section of Bedlam Hospital: ''Tis a new *Whetstone's Park* [...] where a *Sports-man*, at any Hour in the Day, may meet with *Game* for his purpose'] [17C–18C] prostitutes.

whetting corn *n.* (*also* **whetting stone**) [lit. a 'grindstone'] [17C–mid-19C] the vagina.

whib-bob *n.* (*also* **whibb-bob**) [Hencke suggests that the term exists only in the five *Wandering Whore* pamphlets] [mid-17C] the female genitals.

whiblin *n.* [ety. unknown] [early–mid-17C] **1** anything for which one has no proper name. **2** the testicles.

whid *n.* (*also* **whidd**) [SE *word* and OE *cwide*, a statement] **1** [mid-16C–mid-19C] (*UK Und.*) a word, usu. in pl. **2** [mid-19C] a salesman's patter. **3** [mid-19C] a lie.

IN PHRASES

❑ **crack a whid** *v.* [19C] to speak; thus *crack some queer whids*, to speak badly, to use coarse expressions. ❑ **hold one's whid** *v.* [mid-19C] to be quiet. ❑ **stow one's whid** *v.* [STOW *v.* (1)] [17C–mid-19C] (*UK Und.*) to be quiet, to stop talking, to be careful. ❑ **stubble one's whids** *v.* [STUBBLE IT! *excl.*] [late 17C–mid-19C] (*UK Und.*) to be quiet, to stop talking.

whid *v.* (*also* **whiddy**) [WHID *n.* (1)] [17C–early 19C] to talk criminal jargon, to lie.

whidding cheat *n.* [WHID *v.*+ CHEAT *n.* (1)] [mid-18C] (*UK Und.*) the tongue.

whiddle *n.* [WHIDDLE *v.*] [early 19C] a trial, an interrogation.

whiddle *v.* (*also* **wheedle**) [? WHID *v.*] [late 17C–mid-19C] (*UK Und.*) **1** to tell, to recount. **2** to inform against, to raise a hue and cry. **3** to bribe.

IN PHRASES

❑ **whiddle beef** *v. see under* HOT BEEF! *excl.*

whiddler *n.* [WHIDDLE *v.*] **1** [late 17C–mid-19C] an informer. **2** [late 18C–mid-19C] a talkative individual. **3** *see* WHEADLER *n.*

whiddy *v. see* WHID *v.*

whidgey *n.* (*also* **widgey**) [ety. unknown] [1990s+] (*Irish*) the vagina.

whiff *n.* (*also* **wif, wiff**) [SE *whiff*, to inhale, to sniff; note 17C SE *take the whiff*, to smoke] **1** [mid-19C–1910s] a cigar, or tobacco. **2** [1900s–60s] an inhalation of marijuana or cocaine. **3** [1970s+] (*US drugs*) cocaine. **4** [1980s] a puff of cannabis.

IN PHRASES

❑ **do a whiff** *v.* [late 19C] to have a smoke.

whiff *adj. see* WHIFFY *adj.*

whiff *v.* **1** [late 19C+] to smell unpleasantly; thus *whiff out*, to 'stink out' a room [ME *weffe*, an offensive odour or taste]. **2** [late 19C+] (*US drugs*) to inhale a drug, orig. opium, usu. cocaine [SE *whiff*, to inhale, to sniff]. **3** [1910s+] (*US*) to miss a ball; thus *whiff*, a miss [SE *whiff*, to move as a puff of air, and so one hits air rather than the ball]. **4** [1910s+] to make someone miss. **5** [1930s] (*US*) to kill, to murder [play on SE *whiff*, to blow away].

whiffed *adj.* [WHIFF *v.* (2)] [1910s] (*US drugs*) incapacitated from an excess of a drug, marijuana or cocaine.

whiffer *n.* [? used to take drugs in] [1970s] (*US*) a lavatory.

whiffet *n.* [SE *whiffet*, a small dog] [mid-19C–1920s] (*US*) an insignificant person, a whippersnapper.

whiffle *n.* [SE *whiffle*, to blow on, as with a puff of air] [early 19C] a blow.

whiffle *v.* [SE *whiffle*, to talk idly] [20C+] (*Ulster*) to make an evasive answer.

whiffled *adj.* [? SE *whiffle*, to move lightly as if blown by a puff of air] [1920s–30s] drunk.

whifflegig *adj.* [SE *whiffle*, to talk idly + GIG *n.*[1] (2)] [mid-19C] trivial, trifling.

whiffles *n.* [SE *whiffle*, to move lightly] [late 18C–early 19C] 'a relaxation of the scrotum' (Grose 1785).

whiffmagig *n.* [SE *whiff*, a puff of wind] [mid-19C] a trifler, an insignificant or contemptible fellow.

whiffy *adj.* (*also* **whiff, wiffy**) [SE *whiff*, an unpleasant smell] [late 19C+] smelly; also fig. use.

whigger *n. see* WIGGA *n.*

Whigland *n.* [its being a centre of *Whig* politics] [late 17C–mid-19C] Scotland; thus *Whiglander*, a Scot.

whig out *v. see* WIG OUT *under* WIG *v.*[1].

whillikins! *excl. see* GEE WHILLIKINS! *excl.*

whim *n. see* WHIM-WHAM *n.* (1).

whimble-wambles *n.* [redup. WAMBLE *n.*] [mid-19C] stomach cramps.

whimp *n. see* WIMP *n.*[1].

whimsy *n.* [like WHIM-WHAM *n.* (1), a play on a SE term for 'trifle'] [early 17C] a promiscuous woman.

whim-wham *n.* [SE *whim-wham*, a trifle, a trinket] **1** [17C–18C] (*also* **whim**) the vagina [+ link to QUIM *n.*]. **2** [17C; mid-19C] the penis. **3** [early–mid-19C] nonsense, rubbish. **4** [1950s+] (*US*) in pl., anxiety, nervousness.

whin-bush *n.* [SE *whin-bush*, a furze-bush + BUSH *n.*[1] (1)] [late 19C] the pubic hair.

whiners *n.* [note B.E.: 'To Whine, to cry squeekingly, as at Conventicles'] [late 17C–mid-19C] prayers.

IN PHRASES

❑ **chop (up) the whiners** *v.* [18C–mid-19C] to mumble one's prayers speedily and with no interest in their meaning.

whingding *n. see* WING-DING *n.*

whings *n. see* WINGS *n.*

whing-whang *n.* [late 19C] something, typically a small gadget, for which one has no specific name.

whip *n.*[1] [abbr. SE *whip-round*] **1** [mid-19C+] a collection of money, an appeal for money. **2** [1940s] (*US Und.*) a bail bond.

whip *n.*[2] **1** [late 19C+] (*Aus./N/Z.*) an abundance [play on SE *lashings*]. **2** [1960s+] (*Aus.*) rum, esp. in phr. *crack of the whip* [its effects; i.e. one is 'whipped' into action].

SE in slang uses

IN PHRASES

❑ **drink on the whip** *v. see under* DRINK *v.* ❑ **lick on the whip**

v. see DRINK ON THE WHIP under DRINK v. ❑ **under the whip** [1900s] (*Aus.*) at a disadvantage. ❑ **when the whips are cracking** [20C+] (*Aus.*) when the action begins.

whip *n.*[3] [? SE *whiplash*] [1990s+] (*US black*) an automobile.

whip *v.*[1] [SE *whip*, to take briskly, suddenly] **1** [mid-17C+] (*orig. US*) to steal, to make off with. **2** [mid-19C] (*orig. US*) to swindle; thus *whipped*, cheated of one's share. **3** [mid-19C] to drag someone, to force someone to do something, usu. comb. with prep. e.g. *in, along, up*. **4** [mid-19C+] to place, to move.

whip *v.*[2] [late 17C; mid-19C+] (*US Und.*) to walk, to travel, to go.

whip *v.*[3] [ext. of SE *whip*] **1** [19C+] (*US*) to defeat. **2** [1930s+] to beat up.

IN COMPOUNDS

❑ **whip-shack** *n.* [1970s+] (*US black*) anywhere one can have sexual intercourse.

IN PHRASES

❑ **whip it** *v.* **1** [18C; 1970s+] (*also* **whip it in**) to have sexual intercourse, esp. in modern phr. *whip it in, whip it out and wipe it*. **2** [20C+] to masturbate. ❑ **whip it on** *v.* [1950s+] (*US street gang*) to attack, to start a fight. ❑ **whip it on someone** *v.* (*US*) **1** [1940s+] (*drugs*) to inject someone other than oneself with narcotics. **2** [1970s] of a man, to have sexual intercourse. ❑ **whip on** *v.* **1** [mid-19C] (*UK Und.*) to lay (the blame) on. **2** [1960s] (*US*) to beat up. **3** [1970s+] (*US*) to subject to. ❑ **whip one's/the lizard** *v. see* CHOKE THE LIZARD *under* LIZARD *n.* ❑ **whip one's dummy** *v. see* BEAT ONE'S/THE DUMMY *under* DUMMY *n.*[3]. ❑ **whip some skull on** *v. see under* SKULL *n.*[1]. ❑ **whip someone's ass** *v.* (*also* **whip someone's arse, whip someone's fanny, whoop someone's ass, whup somone's ass**) [ARSE *n.* (1)/ASS *n.* (2)] [1950s+] (*orig. US*) to beat completely and comprehensively, whether or not with violence. ❑ **whip someone's head to the red** *v.* [1930s–40s] (*US black*) to threaten injury or retaliation (whether genuinely or as a bluff). ❑ **whip the baloney pony** *v.* (*also* **whip the dummy, ...lizard, ...pony, ...weasel, ...wire**) [BALONEY *n.* (2)/DUMMY *n.*[3]/LIZARD *n.* (7)/SE *pony*/WEASEL *n.* (4)/WIRE *n.*[1] (12)] [1990s+] to masturbate.

SE in slang uses

IN COMPOUNDS

❑ **whip-arse** *n.* [ARSE *n.* (1)] [early 17C] a schoolmaster. ❑ **whip-belly (vengeance)** *n.* [its unpleasant effects] [18C–early 19C] very thin beer. ❑ **whip boss** *n. see under* BOSS *n.*[2]. ❑ **whip-jack** *n.* [SE *whip*, to beat + *Jack*, a general nickname. An alt. ety., WHIP *v.*[1] (1) + JACK *n.*[2] (1), requires a substantially later coinage] **1** [16C–l19C] (*UK Und.*) a mendicant villain who poses as a discharged mariner, backed by a counterfeit licence, suitably adorned with fake seals, he also specialized in robbing stalls, fairground booths and similar open displays of goods. **2** [early 19C] as a general derog.

IN PHRASES

❑ **whip a game on** *v. see under* GAME *n.* ❑ **whip off** *v. see* separate entry. ❑ **whip out** *see* separate entries. ❑ **whip the cat** *v. see* separate entry. ❑ **whip the dog** *v.* [euph. var. on FUCK THE DOG (AND SELL THE PUPS) *under* DOG *n.*[2]] [1910s+] (*US*) **1** to waste time and loaf on the job. **2** to bungle, to blunder. ❑ **whip up** *see* separate entries.

whip *v.*[4] [1980s+] (*US*) to give.

IN PHRASES

❑ **whip it on someone** *v.* [1960s+] (*US*) **1** to explain and inform someone of facts and events. **2** to give, to hand over. ❑ **whip (something) on** *v.* [1970s] (*US*) to give, to hand over.

whip *v.*[5] [? SE *whiplash*, the way in which one's head slumps suddenly onto one's shoulder] [1990s+] (*US campus*) to fall asleep while sitting up.

whip *v.*[6] [WHIP *n.*[3]] [2000s] (*US black*) to drive an automobile.

whip and lash *n.* (*also* **whip and slash**) [rhy. sl.] [20C+] a moustache.

whip and top *v.* [rhy. sl. = STROP *v.*[2]] [20C+] to masturbate.

whipass *n.* (*also* **whoop-ass**) (*US*) energy, determination, aggression; also attrib.

IN PHRASES

❑ **open a can of whoop-ass on** *v.* [1990s+] to assault, to beat up.

whip-cat *n.* [WHIP THE CAT *v.* (5)] [mid-19C] a tailor.

whip-cat *adj.* [WHIP THE CAT *v.* (2)] [late 16C–early 17C] drunken.

whip her Ginny/whip-her-ginny/whip-her-jenny *n. see* WHIPPERGINNIE *n.*

whip off *v.* [SE *whip*, to move suddenly, to take briskly] **1** [17C–early 19C] to drink greedily. **2** [late 17C–18C] (*UK Und.*) to steal. **3** [late 18C+] to run off. **4** [20C+] (*US campus*) to masturbate.

whip-out *n.* [WHIP OUT *v.*] [1970s+] (*US*) money, esp. a first payment or investment.

whip out *v.* [early 18C; late 19C+] to produce, usu. quickly.

IN COMPOUNDS

❑ **whip-out man** *n.* [1960s] (*US*) an exhibitionist.

IN PHRASES

❑ **excuse me while I whip this out** [*this* is one's fist or poss. a weapon] (*US black teen*) **1** [1970s] one's last words before commencing a fight. **2** [2000s] a phr. said before exposing one's penis.

whipped *adj.* [WHIP *v.*[3]] **1** [mid-19C+] defeated. **2** [mid-19C+] (*US*) drunk, intoxicated. **3** [1920s+] dominated, subservient, meek [fig. use of SE]. **4** [1940s] (*US black*) hungover. **5** [1950s+] (*US*) exhausted. **6** [1960s+] willing to do anything one's partner demands [fig. use of SE underlined by abbr. PUSSY-WHIPPED *under* PUSSY *n.*]. **7** [1980s+] (*US campus/teen*) in love, infatuated.

IN PHRASES

❑ **get whipped** *v.* [1970s+] (*US campus*) to get married.

whipped cream *n.* [resemblance] [1970s+] (*US black*) semen.

whipped up *adj.* [WHIPPED *adj.* (5)] [1930s–50s] (*US black*) exhausted, worn out, physically wrecked.

whipper *n.* [WHIP *v.*[5]] [1980s] (*US campus*) a very tedious class.

whipperginnie *n.* (*also* **whip-her-Ginny, whip-her-ginny, whip-her-jenny**) [lit. *whip her, Jenny*] [late 16C–early 17C] a term of abuse for a woman.

whippets *n.* (*also* **whippet**) [as dispensed from a can of *whipped cream*] [1970s] (*drugs*) nitrous oxide.

whipping *n.* [WHIP *v.*[3] (1)] **1** [mid-19C+] (*US*) a sound, comprehensive beating or defeat. **2** [1900s–60s] punishment, physical discipline.

whippit quick *n.* [rhy. sl. = PRICK *n.* (1)] [1990s+] the penis.

whippy *n.* [WHIP *v.*[1]] [1960s+] (*Aus.*) **1** a pocket. **2** a hiding place, esp. for money. **3** a wallet.

whippy *adj.* [smart as a whip] [1960s–70s] **1** (*US*) smart, well-dressed. **2** cheeky, mocking. **3** (*US campus*) intelligent, clever.

whips *n.*[1] [dial. *whips*, plenty] [20C+] (*orig. Aus.*) a great deal, an abundance; usu. as *whips of*.

whips *n.*[2] [the repressive imagery of their institutions] [1970s+] (*US black*) **1** the white establishment. **2** the police.

whip saw *v.* (*also* **whipsaw**) [SE *whip-saw*, something that is disadvantageous in two ways; *see* Asbury, *Sucker's Progress* (1938) 17: An extraordinary number of the terms, technical and otherwise, which were employed by Faro players in the palmy days of the game have passed into the language [...] and are commonly used by millions who never heard of Faro. Here are some of them: [...] *Whipsawed*—Losing two different bets on the same turn] **1** [late 19C+] (*US*) to have at a complete disadvantage, to overcome completely; to benefit or win by manipulating a situation so that one's rivals attack one another. **2** [1900s] to attack, assault.

whipsey *adj.* [? WHIPPED *adj.* (2)] [1920s] (*US*) tipsy.

Whipshire *n.* [? the hunting gentry who live there] [late 17C–early 19C] Yorkshire.

whipster *n.* **1** [17C–early 19C] a clever, cunning person [they are 'sharp as a whip']. **2** [20C+] (*Irish*) a forward, impudent woman, also occas. a man [WHIP *v.*[1] (1) as they are inclined to steal].

whip-stitch! *excl.* [note SAmE phr. *every whip-stitch*, at short or frequent intervals] [late 17C–early 18C] an excl. used to indicate a sudden movement or action.

whip-the-cat *n.* [WHIP THE CAT *v.* (5)] [mid–late 19C] an itinerant tailor.

whip the cat *v.* **1** [early 17C+] to play a practical joke ['A trick often practised on ignorant country fellows, by laying a wager with them that they may be pulled through a pond by a cat; the bet being made, a rope is fastened round the waist of the person to be catted and the end thrown across the pond, to which the cat is also fastened by a pack-thread, and three or four sturdy fellows are appointed to lead and whip the cat; these on a signal given, seize the end of the cord, and pretending to whip the cat, haul the astonished booby through the water' (Grose 1785)]. **2** [mid-17C–mid-18C] to get drunk. **3** [mid-17C–19C] to vomit through excessive drinking. **4** in senses of blame, complaint [i.e. *whip the cat* that has spilt the milk over which one is crying]. (**a**) [late 18C] to lay the blame of one's offences on someone else. (**b**) [late 19C+] (*Aus./N.Z.*) to suffer guilt and remorse for past errors, to worry about something about which one can do nothing. (**c**) [20C+] (*Aus.*) to complain *ad nauseam*, to whinge at length. **5** [late 18C+] to work as an itinerant tailor, carpenter, locksmith, knife-grinder etc [dial. *whip the cat*, to go from house to house as an itinerant tailor, such a job was unlikely to reap very rich rewards]. **6** [19C+] to shirk work on Mondays. **7** [early 19C] to idle on the job.

whip-up *n.* [WHIP UP *v.* (1)] [1920s] a monetary collection.

whip (up) *v.* [17C–early 19C] to drink greedily, quickly.

whip up *v.* **1** [early 18C+] to collect, to organize. **2** [1930s+] to create, e.g. a suit of clothes.

whirl *n.* **1** [20C+] (*US*) a chance, an opportunity, a 'go'. **2** [1910s] an outing.

IN PHRASES

❑ **give something a whirl** *v.* (*also* **give it a whirl, ...twirl, take a whirl**) [late 19C+] (*orig. US*) to try something out.

whirligig *n.* **1** [late 18C–mid-19C] (*UK Und.*) the pillory. **2** [1910s+] an unspecified gadget.

whirligigs *n.* [SE *whirligig*, a variety of toy that is whirled or spun around] [late 17C–early 19C] the testicles.

whirlpit *n.* [mid-17C] the vagina.

whirlybird *n.* [1950s+] (*US*) a helicopter.

whisht! *excl.* (*also* **wheesh! wheesht! whist!**) [late 16C+] be quiet!, also as n., silence; phr. *hold one's whist*.

whisk *n.* [they make no more impression on the world than does a quick *whisk* on dirt] [late 17C–early 19C] an insignificant person, a whippersnapper.

whiskbroom 'with' *n.* [an anecdote of late-19C Prohibition (then restricted to certain states rather than the nationwide version of 1920–33), a temperance campaigner, on entering a haberdasher's to buy a whiskbroom was offered one 'with' and one 'without'. On asking what this meant she was shown that a broom 'with' had a small bottle of whisky hidden amid its bristles] [late 19C] (*US*) drunkenness.

whisker *n.*[1] [SE *whisk*, to move briskly] [late 17C–early 19C] anything excessive, esp. a great lie.

whisker *n.*[2] **1** [1910s] (*US*) a country dweller. **2** [1910s+] (*orig. US*) a very small, infinitesimal amount or distance. **3** [1920s–60s] a young woman. **4** [1930s+] (*Aus.*) the pubic hair. **5** [1990s+] the penis.

IN COMPOUNDS

❑ **whisker splitter** *n.* [late 18C–early 19C] a womanizer.

whiskerando *n.* [the character Don Ferolo *Whiskerandos* in R.B. Sheridan's play *The Critic* (1779)] [mid-19C] a man who is heavily whiskered.

whisker-bed *n.* [mid-19C] the jaw; the face.

Whiskeries *n.* (*also* **Whiskyries**) [Irish *whisky*] [late 19C] the Irish Exhibition held in London in 1888.

whiskers *n.*[1] **1** [mid-19C+] (*US*) an old man, thus *his whiskers*, the head of the household; also as term of address. **2** [1920s] (*US*) the chin. **3** [1930s+] (*US Und.*) the US government, Army, or any other institution [the bewhiskered UNCLE SAM *n.*]. **4** [1940s] (*US*) pubic hair. **5** [1940s–50s] (*US Und.*) of a woman, a lesbian; of a man a homosexual. **6** [1980s] (*US*) courage.

IN PHRASES

❑ **part the whiskers** *v. see SPLIT THE BEARD under* BEARD *n.* ❑ **take the whiskers off** *v.* [1920s] (*US tramp*) to work for a farmer gathering the harvest.

whiskers *n.*[2] [late 19C] (*US short-order*) mutton chops.

whiskin *n.* [abbr. *pimp-whiskin* (*see* PIMP WHISK *under* PIMP *n.*)] [mid-17C] a pimp.

whisking *adj.* [SE *whisk*, to move briskly] **1** [17C–mid-19C] brisk, lively, smart. **2** [late 17C–early 18C] great, excessive.

whisk of a lamb's tail *phr. see* TWO SHAKES OF A LAMB'S TAIL *phr.*

whisky *n.*

SE in slang uses

IN COMPOUNDS

❑ **whisky bottle** *n.* [stereotyping] [late 19C] a Scottish drunkard. ❑ **whiskyhead** *n.* (*also* **whiskey-leg**) [1930s+] (*US*) **1** one who drinks a great deal of whisky [-HEAD *sfx* (4)]. **2** delirium tremens [HEAD *n.* (4a)]. ❑ **whisky-skin** *n.* [mid–late 19C] (*US*) a mixed drink containing a large proportion of whisky.

IN PHRASES

❑ **whisky's talking** *see IT'S THE BEER TALKING under* TALK *v.*

whisky-frisky *adj.* [SE *whisk* + *frisk*] [late 18C; 1910s] flighty.

Whiskyries *n. see* WHISKERIES *n.*

whisper *n.*[1] [the surreptitious tones of the request] [mid-19C+] (*UK Und.*) a request for money.

IN PHRASES

❑ **sling the whisper** *v.* **1** [mid-19C+] (*UK Und.*) (*also* **give the whisper**) to ask for a loan. **2** [20C+] (*Aus./US*) (*also* **chuck (someone) the whisper**) to inform, to impart information.

whisper *n.*[2] **1** [late 19C; 1970s] a criminal's lookout man or tipster. **2** [late 19C+] a rumour, usu. of impending crimes, a tip.

whisper *n.*[3] [rhy. sl.; *whisper and talk* = walk] [late 19C+] a walk.

whisper *n.*[4] **1** [1900s] (*US Und.*) a sentence of 15–30 days. **2** [1930s] (*US prison*) the final portion of a sentence.

whisper *v.* [WHISPER *n.*[1]] [mid–late 19C] **1** to borrow money from. **2** to persuade someone to give money.

IN PHRASES

❑ **on the whisper** [late 19C] (*Aus.*) using influence (to gain admission) rather than paying.

whisperer *n.* [1900s] (*Aus.*) **1** a racehorse tipster, who expects a share of the supposed winnings. **2** a cadger.

whispering dudder *n. see* DUDDER *n.*[1].

whispering gallery *n.* [a play on the more respectable *Whispering Gallery* encircling the dome of St Paul's Cathedral, and from the less well-off patrons whispering 'Can you lend me...?'] [late 19C] the bar of the Gaiety Theatre.

whist! *excl. see* WHISHT! *excl.*

whister-clister *n.* (*also* **whisterpoop**) [dial. *whister*, whisper + SE *clyster*, an enema] [late 18C–mid-19C] a blow on the ear.

whister-snefet *n.* (*also* **whister-snivit**) [dial. *whister*, whisper + SE/dial. *snite*, to wipe/SE *snivel*, nasal mucus] [mid-16C] a blow on the ear.

whisticaster *n.* [dial. *whister*, whisper + SE *cast*, to throw] [early 19C] a blow on the ear.

whistle *n.* [? the sounds] **1** [late 14C–mid-19C] the mouth, the throat; for subseq. uses *see WET ONE'S WHISTLE under* WET *v.* **2** [mid-18C] a eunuch. **3** [late 19C] the penis [resemblance; Williams notes the 'lascivious' 17C stories/ballads of the 'Carman's whistle'; note earlier *WHISTLE AND BELLS* below]. **4** [1910s] the lungs.

IN COMPOUNDS

❑ **whistle and bells** *n.* [late 18C] the penis and testes.

IN PHRASES

❑ **blow someone's whistle** *v.* [1970s+] (*US gay*) to fellate.

SE in slang uses

IN COMPOUNDS

❑ **whistle bait** *n.* [one at whom men *whistle*] [1940s–50s] (*US*) an attractive woman. ❑ **whistle-belly thumps** *n.* [rumbling and the pain in the stomach] [1990s+] stomach aches associated with diarrhoea. ❑ **whistle-belly vengeance** *n.* [var. on WHIP-BELLY (VENGEANCE) *under* WHIP *v.*[3]; the rumbling it produces in the drinker's stomach] [mid-19C] bad or thin beer. ❑ **whistle-drunk** *adj.* [despite appearances, there seems to be no connection between this and WHISTLED *adj.*] [mid-18C] very drunk.

IN PHRASES

❑ **blow the whistle on** *v.* **1** [1920s+] to bring to an end. **2** [1930s+] to inform against someone. **3** [1960s+] to moralize.

whistle *v.* [it makes a 'noise'] [1930s+] to smell unpleasantly.

SE in slang uses

IN PHRASES

❑ **whistle Dixie** *v. see under* DIXIE *n.* ❑ **whistle in the cage** *v.* [fig. use of SE *whistle* +CAGE *n.* (8)] [early 19C] for a villain, on being arrested, to betray his accomplices. ❑ **whistle in the dark** *v.* [1960s–70s] (*US*) to perform cunnilingus. ❑ **whistle up a breeze** *v. see* RAISE THE WIND *under* RAISE *v.*

whistle (and flute) *n.* [rhy. sl.] **1** [1910s+] a suit of clothes. **2** [1960s] (*Aus.*) in pl., boots. **3** [2000s] cocaine [= TOOT *n.*[1] (5)].

whistle and toot *n.* [rhy. sl. = LOOT *n.*[1] (2)] [1910s+] money.

whistlecock *n.* (*also* **whistleprick**) [an initiation ritual-cum-prophylactic whereby the underside of the penis is slit to make a permanent incision in the urethra; the effect is to prevent the normal ejaculation of semen into one's partner] [late 19C+] (*Aus.*) a derog. name for a Native Australian, an Aborigine.

whistled *adj.* [1930s–40s] (*orig. milit.*) drunk.

whistler *n.*[1] **1** [19C] a broken-down horse, whose breath whistles in his lungs. **2** [early 19C] (*UK Und.*) a counterfeit halfpenny or farthing [the false ring when tapped]. **3** [early–mid-19C] the proprietor of an unlicensed spirit-shop in a prison [his drinks are kept hidden so that when the police raid they can *whistle for them*]. **4** [mid-19C] a bullet [abbr. BLUE WHISTLER *under* BLUE *adj.*[1]]. **5** [1910s–20s] a revolver. **6** [1910s–20s] anything especially large. **7** [1930s] (*US Und.*) a police car. **8** [1940s] a female railway porter. **9** [1940s+] (*US Und.*) an informer.

whistler *n.*[2] **1** [early–mid-19C] the mouth. **2** [1970s] an audible breaking of wind. **3** [1970s+] (*US gay*) a fellator. **4** [1980s+] (*drugs*) a nasal hole resulting from excessive cocaine use.

whistle stop *n.* [orig. railroad jargon *whistlestop town*, trains do not halt at such a town unless a passenger informs the conductor who then signals the fact by pulling on the signal cord and the engineer acknowledges the request by two whistles. The derog. sl. use led to the abandoning of the term by the railroads, who substituted *flag stop* or *flag station* to spare local feelings] [1930s+] (*US*) a small town; also attrib.

whistling berries *n.* [their effect on breaking wind] [1930s] (*US*) beans.

whistling-breeches *n.* (*also* **whistlers**) [the swishing noise the material makes as the legs brush together] [late 19C–1930s] corduroy trousers.

whistling shop *n.* [WHISTLE *n.* (1)/WHISTLER *n.*[1] (3)+ SHOP *n.*[1] (3)] **1** [late 18C–mid-19C] a room in the King's Bench (or any other) prison where one could buy drink illicitly. **2** [mid-19C] any illicit drinking house.

Whit *n.* (*also* **Whitt, the**) [abbr. WHITTINGTON('S) COLLEGE *n.*] [late 17C–early 19C] (*UK Und.*) Newgate prison, Tothill prison.

white *n.* **1** with ref. to intoxicating drinks. (**a**) [19C–1920s] gin. (**b**) [1930s] (*US*) any form of alcohol. (**c**) [1950s] (*Aus.*) methylated spirits. **2** [late 19C+] (*Aus.*) a shilling. **3** with ref. to the colour of various drugs. (**a**) [20C+] morphine, heroin. (**b**) [1930s+] (*orig. UK Und.*) cocaine. (**c**) [1960s+] amphetamine. (**d**) [1980s+] crack cocaine.

SE in slang uses

IN PHRASES

❑ **hit the white** *v.* [1950s] (*Aus.*) to succeed.

white *adj.* **1** [late 16C–1940s] silver. **2** [mid-19C+] honest, upright, fair-dealing [coined without any consciously negative overtones and representing a rare (if unsurprisingly) positive racial stereotype, the term has been used in an increasingly ironic manner, esp. since 1960s]. **3** [1960s] (*US black*) patronizing, exploitative (but not necessarily white-skinned). **4** [1970s+] (*S.Afr.*) cheeky, insubordinate [used of a black person 'getting above themselves' and thus trespassing on perceived white prerogatives].

IN COMPOUNDS

pertaining to silver

❑ **white-bait** *n.* [early 19C] (*UK Und.*) silver. ❑ **white broth ken** *n.* [SE *broth* (as precursor of SOUP *n.* (1)) + KEN *n.*[1] (1)] [mid-19C] (*UK/US Und.*) a place where stolen silver is melted down. ❑ **white buzman** *n.* [BUZMAN *under* BUZ *n.*] [mid-19C] (*UK Und.*) a pickpocket, esp. one who steals silver, white handerchiefs. ❑ **white fish** *n.* [mid-19C] a silver dollar. ❑ **white george** *n.* [mid-19C] (*UK Und.*) a (silver) half-crown piece (2/6d = 12½p). ❑ **white jenny** *n.* [? abbr. SE *engine*] [18C–19C] a watch made of foreign silver. ❑ **white lot** *n.* [SE *lot*, an article] [19C] a silver watch. ❑ **white money** *n.* **1** [mid-16C–early 17C; mid-19C+] silver coins. **2** [20C+] (*US*) an illegal political contribution [it is seen as 'invisible', unlike green dollars]. **3** [1940s] large banknotes [the old large 'white' £5 note]. ❑ **white one** *n.* **1** [1920s] (*US Und.*) a diamond. **2** [1920s–40s] (*US Und.*) a silver watch [WHITE *adj.* (1)]. **3** [1940s] (*US black*) a white shirt. ❑ **white prop** *n.* [PROP *n.*[3] (1)] [mid-19C] a diamond stickpin. ❑ **white slang** *n.* [SLANG *n.*[2] (2)] [1910s] (*US Und.*) a silver watch chain. ❑ **white soup** *n.* [SOUP *n.* (1)] [late 18C–19C] (*UK Und.*) silver that has been melted down from the original, stolen plate. ❑ **white swelling** *n.* **1** [early 19C] (*UK Und.*) a large quanitity of silver. **2** *see also* SE compounds below. ❑ **white toy** *n.* [TOY *n.*[1] (5)] [mid–late 19C] a silver watch. ❑ **white 'un** *n.* [mid–late 19C] a silver watch. ❑ **white wool** *n.* **1** [early 17C] (*UK Und.*) the silver pieces that are left with the victim of a substitution fraud. **2** [late 17C–mid-19C] silver in general.

SE in slang uses

IN COMPOUNDS

❑ **white...** *n.* **1** *see also under* relevant n. **2** *see also* separate entries.

pertaining to alcohol, esp. gin

❑ **white coffee** *n.* [1920s] (*US Und.*) bootleg whisky. ❑ **white eye** *n.* [its alleged effect; one's eyes apparently roll up in their sockets, exposing the whites] [19C–1910s] cheap, rough whisky. ❑ **white horse** *n.* [its translucency and its effects] [1900s–30s] (*US*) pure alcohol, diluted for drinking. ❑ **white lady** *n.* [SE *white lady*, a cocktail made of two parts of dry gin, one of orange liqueur and one of lemon juice] [1930s+] (*Aus.*) methylated spirits. ❑ **white lightning** *n.* [the effects] [1920s+] (*US*) illicit home-brewed whisky or poteen. ❑ **white line** *n.* [ety. unknown] **1** [late 19C–1920s] (*US tramp*) alcohol that has been diluted. **2** [1910s] a drinker. **3** [1910s–30s] (*also* **white lime**) alcohol; thus *white-liner*, a dealer in or drinker of alcohol. ❑ **white mule** *n.* [it has a 'kick like a mule'] [1900s–60s] (*US*) homemade whisky made from grain alcohol. ❑ **white port** *n.* [mid-18C–mid-19C] (*UK Und.*) gin. ❑ **white ribbon** (*also* **white ribbin**) [RIBBON *n.*[1]] [early 19C] gin. ❑ **white satin** *n.* [the term is still in use as a proprietory name for a brand of gin, *Sir Robert Burnett's White Satin Gin*] [mid-19C–1900s] gin, esp. as a euph. used by women. ❑ **white tape** *n.* (*also* **white wool**) [TAPE *n.*] [18C–mid-19C] gin or genever. ❑ **white velvet** *n.* [mid-19C] (*UK Und.*) gin. ❑ **white wine** *n.* [euph.; gin was seen as a degenerate drink] [early–mid-19C] gin.

pertaining to drugs

❑ **white bag** *n.* [BAG *n.*[1] (7); the colour of the drug; cheaper Mexican heroin is brown] [1970s] (*US black/drugs*) high-quality heroin. ❑ **white brick** *n.* [BRICK *n.* (2c)] [1980s+] (*drugs*) cocaine (in bulk). ❑ **white cloud** *n.* [var. WHITE GHOST below] [1980s+] (*drugs*) crack cocaine smoke. ❑ **white cross** *n.* (*drugs*) **1** [1900s–20s] cocaine. **2** [1940s–50s] morphine; heroin. **3** [1970s] amphetamine pills with a white cross cut into one surface. ❑ **white-cut** *n.* [CUT *n.* (11b)] [1950s] (*US drugs*) heroin. ❑ **white devil** *n.* [2000s] (*UK black*) crack cocaine.

❑ **white dust** *n.* [the form in which the drug is sometimes sold] [1970s] (*drugs*) **1** phencyclidine. **2** LSD. ❑ **white dynamite** *n.* [its colour and effects] [1990s+] (*drugs*) heroin. ❑ **white ghost** *n.* [the white smoke it exudes] [1980s+] (*drugs*) crack cocaine. ❑ **white girl** *n.* [GIRL *n.*[2]] [1970s+] (*drugs*) cocaine, heroin. ❑ **white goods** *n.* [1920s] (*US Und.*) narcotics. ❑ **white horse** *n.* [HORSE *n.* (7); heroin is usu. brown, cocaine is white] [1950s+] **1** (*drugs*) cocaine; occas. heroin; thus *RIDE THE WHITE HORSE under* RIDE *v.* **2** heroin. ❑ **white lady** *n.* [its colour, although the bulk of late-20C+ heroin is light brown; note cocaine is a 'feminine' drug, see GIRL *n.*[2]] [1960s+] (*drugs*) **1** cocaine. **2** heroin, thus good quality heroin, *white queen*. ❑ **white lightning** *n.* [1970s+] (*drugs*) (*also* **white light**) LSD. ❑ **white line fever** *n.* [the LINE *n.*[1] (5d) of the powdered drug that is inhaled by users] **1** [1970s+] the obsessive use of cocaine. **2** *see also* SE compounds below. ❑ **white mosquitoes** *n.* [the mosquito-bite-like mark left after an injection] [1940s–50s] cocaine or any powdered drug. ❑ **white-out** *n.* [1980s+] (*US drugs*) a momentary loss of consciousness while taking cocaine. ❑ **white pipe** *n.* [PIPE *n.*[1] (3d)] [1990s+] (*S.Afr.*) a mixture of marijuana, tobacco and a crushed tablet of Mandrax (the brandname of methaqualone). ❑ **white powder** *n.* [1940s+] any form of narcotic or other drug that comes in the form of white powder. ❑ **white serpent** *n.* [1990s+] heroin. ❑ **white shit** *n.* [SHIT *n.* (6)] **1** [1970s+] heroin. **2** [1990s+] cocaine. ❑ **white silk** *n.* [1930s–50s] (*US drugs*) morphine crystals. ❑ **white widow** *n.* [1990s+] (*drugs*) a form of marijuana (i.e. super-compacted SKUNK *n.* (4a)) that is so dense as to exude white crystals.

general uses

❑ **white alley** *n.* [marbles imagery] [late 19C–1930s] (*US*) an opportunity, one's 'best shot'. ❑ **white-arsed** *adj.* (*also* **white-ass**) [ARSE *n.* (1)/ASS *n.* (2)] **1** [1920s+] a general term of abuse. **2** [1990s+] (*US black/campus*) a derog. ref. to third-rate white American culture; used by both whites and blacks. ❑ **whitebait** *n.* [2000s] (*N.Z.*) a thin person. ❑ **white-bag man** *n.* [early 19C] a pickpocket. ❑ **white-belly rat** *n.* [this variety of rat supposedly blows on the thing it bites to minimize the pain] [1920s–50s] (*W.I.*) a hypocrite. ❑ **white cow** *n.* [COW *n.*[1] (5)] (*US*) **1** [1920s+] a vanilla milkshake. **2** [1940s+] a vanilla ice-cream soda. ❑ **white ewe** *n.* [late 17C–18C] a beautiful and important woman in a band of villains. ❑ **white eyes** *n.* [the term *paleface* is generally fictional and invariably used by whites rather than the 'Red Indians' to whom they attribute it] **1** [20C+] (*Native American*) white people. **2** [1960s+] (*S.Afr./US black*) a white person. ❑ **white fever** *n. see PADDY FEVER under* PADDY *n.* ❑ **white hat** *n.* [*white hats* were worn by the heroes and black hats by the villains in the old, silent Western films] **1** [1960s+] a hero, a 'good' character (as opposed to a 'bad' one) in any fictional medium. **2** [1990s+] (*US campus*) a wealthy, smug, white male. ❑ **white homie** *n.* [HOMIE *n.*[3] (1)] [2000s] (*N.Z.*) middle-class children aping the lifestyle of working-class children. ❑ **white house** *n.* [underpinned by a ref. to the *White House*, home of the US presidency] [1950s–70s] (*US black*) the world of white society. ❑ **white lilies** *n.* [1940s] (*US black*) bed linen. ❑ **white line fever** *n.* [the *white lines* that divide traffic lanes] **1** [1970s+] (*US*) an obsessive driver. **2** *see also* drug uses above. ❑ **white mouse** *n.* [1900s] (*Aus.*) a gullible person. ❑ **white mouth** *v.* **1** [1930s] (*US black*) to pretend servility in one's conversations with whites [one 'talks their language']. **2** [2000s] to fellate [the white semen]. ❑ **white nigga** *n. see* WIGGA *n.* ❑ **white-on-white** *n.* **1** [1940s+] (*US black*) a white Cadillac with white interior finish and white upholstery; thus *white-on-white-in-white*, a black person who seeks the supposed status of association with white people, esp. through a white girlfriend and a white Cadillac. **2** [1950s+] a white shirt. ❑ **whiteout** *n.* **1** [1980s+] (*drugs*) isobutyl nitrite [its effect on the brain]. **2** [2000s] (*US*) a temporary loss of consciousness [as opposed to a fullscale SE *blackout*]. ❑ **white owl** *n.* **1** [1900s] (*US*) a chamberpot. **2** [1970s] a white penis. ❑ **white pointer** *n.* [SAusE *white pointer* shark, aka 'Great White Shark'] [1990s+] (*Aus.*) a highway patrolman. ❑ **white pudding** *n. see* PUDDING *n.* (2). ❑ **white quarter** *n. see* RED CENT *n.* ❑ **white rat** *n.* [1980s+] (*Aus. prison*) an albino prisoner. ❑ **white Russian** *n.* [the similarity of white semen to the colour of a *white Russian* cocktail] [1960s+] (*gay*) the oral exchange of semen. ❑ **white satin** *n.* [play on *BLACK VELVET under* BLACK *adj.*] [1950s] (*Aus.*) a white woman, considered sexually. ❑ **white serjeant** *n.* [late 18C–19C] a wife who dominates her husband. ❑ **white shirt** *n.* [1950s+] (*UK/US prison*) a senior prison officer, who (in UK) wears a white rather than the blue of the junior ranks. ❑ **white sidewall** *n. see* WHITEWALL below. ❑ **white sneaker set** *n.* [1960s] (*US gay*) homosexual society. ❑ **white-staff** *n.* [SE *white staff*, 'a white rod or wand carried as a symbol of office by certain officials, e.g. the steward of the king's household and the lord high treasurer' *OED*] [mid-18C] the penis. ❑ **white swallow** *n.* [1990s+] (*US, mainly West Coast*) semen, usu. in the context of fellatio. ❑ **white swelling** *n.* **1** [late 18C–mid-19C] pregnancy; a pregnant woman. **2** [mid–late 19C] a suet dumpling. **3** *see also* silver compounds above. ❑ **white top** *n.* **1** [1950s] (*US*) a police patrol car. **2** [1990s+] (*US campus*) an old (white-haired) person. ❑ **whitewall** *n.* (*also* **white sidewall**) [1970s+] (*orig. US milit.*) a very severe 'short back and sides' haircut, orig. in the US Marines.

IN PHRASES

❑ **white it out** *v.* [? one SE *whites out*, i.e. erases, that period of one's life] [late 19C–1950s] (*Aus.*) to serve a jail sentence.

white *adv.* [WHITE *adj.* (2)] [late 19C+] honestly, fairly, use in comb. with *treat*.

white about the gills *phr.* (*also* **pale about the gills**) [GILLS *n.* (1)] **1** [mid-19C+] frightened. **2** *see GREEN ABOUT THE GILLS under* GILLS *n.*

white-ant *v.* [reverse anthropomorphism] **1** [1930s+] (*Aus./N.Z.*) to sabotage, during a labour dispute; thus *white-anter*, a saboteur, *white-anting*, sabotage. **2** [1980s] to slander; to verbally pressurize.

white ants *n.* [the supposed eating away of one's brain by white ants] [1900s–50s] (*Aus.*) eccentricity, insanity; thus *have white ants*, to be crazy.

white bread *n.* **1** [1980s] (*US black*) a derog. term for a black person with a light complexion. **2** [1990s+] a pasty, unhealthy complexion.

white bread *adj.* **1** [1970s+] (*US*) used of anything pertaining to white, middle-class, mainstream styles: bland, unexciting, suburban. **2** [1980s] (*US campus*) used of anything good, admirable.

Whitechapel *n.*[1] [mid-19C] **1** in coin-tossing, a score of two out of three wins [presumably popular in this area of London's East End]. **2** an upper-cut [? a blow favoured by East Enders].

Whitechapel *n.*[2] [rhy. sl.] [20C+] an apple.

Whitechapel *adj.* [*Whitechapel*, the home of Cockney London and the heart of London's impoverished and thus often criminal East End] [late 18C–19C] not sl. as such but used in the following combs. to denote poverty, roughness and criminality.

IN COMPOUNDS

❑ **Whitechapel beau** *n.* [ironic use of SE *beau*] [late 18C] one 'who dresses with a needle and thread, and undresses with a knife' (Grose, 1785). ❑ **Whitechapel breed** *n.* [late 18C] a woman who is 'fat, ragged and saucy' (Grose, 1785). ❑ **Whitechapel brougham** *n.* (*also* **Westminster brougham**) [the closed carriage known as a *brougham* was beyond the income of the average Whitechapel costermonger] [mid-19C] a costermonger's donkey-barrow. ❑ **Whitechapel oner** *n.* [ONER *n.* (1); i.e. he is *number one* in local estimation] [late 19C] a fashionable young man-about-Whitechapel, an East End dandy. ❑ **Whitechapel play** *n.* [both uses stress the snobbish assumption that East Enders are unable to play ostensibly patrician games with the correct skill and subtlety] **1** [mid-18C–early 19C] in whist, the leading of all one's best cards, with no attempt to finesse the opponent. **2** [mid-19C+] in billiards, to pot an opponent's ball. ❑ **Whitechapel portion** *n.* (*also* **Whitechapel fortune**) **1** [late 17C–18C] the vagina, 'two torn smocks and what Nature gives' (B.E.). **2** [19C] 'a clean gown and a pair of pattens' (Hotten 1864). ❑ **Whitechapel shave** *n.* [the poor cannot afford a barber to shave them] [mid-19C] whitening applied to the face to lighten the 'five o'clock shadow'.

white-choker *n.* [the white bands that are part of his dress] [late 19C–1910s] a clergyman; also attrib.

DERIVATIVES

❑ **white-chokery** *n.* [i.e. those who wear a *white choker* or large white neckerchief as part of their evening dress] [late 19C] the upper classes.

White Cliffs (of Dover) *adv.* [rhy. sl.] [20C+] over, usu. in phr. *all White Cliffs*.

Whitehall warrior *n.* [*Whitehall*, the home of the UK government] [1960s+] **1** a civil servant. **2** an officer in the services who has been seconded to administrative rather than active duties.

Whitehaven docks *n.* [rhy. sl. = POX *n.*[1] (3)] [1970s] venereal disease.

whitehead *n.* [2000s] (*UK drugs*) a cocaine user.

white-headed *adj.* [1900s] (*Aus.*) angry, indignant.

white-knuckle *adj.* [the *whitening* of one's *knuckles* as one grips onto something to control one's emotions] [1970s+] (*orig. US*) terrifying, very frightening, often of a fairground ride or horror film.

white-knuckle *v.* [1990s+] to suffer bravely, irrespective of the pain.

white-knuckler *n.* [WHITE-KNUCKLE *adj.*] [1970s+] (*US*) **1** an aeroplane flight. **2** a tense, anxious person.

white liver *n.* [SE *white*, pure] **1** [1930s–60s] a homosexual who has no interest whatsoever in women. **2** [1960s] a lesbian with no interest whatsoever in men. **3** [1990s+] (*US/W.I.*) nyphomania.

white-livered *adj.* **1** [mid-16C+] (*also* **liver-faced, yellow-livered**) cowardly [the assumption that a coward has insufficient bile or 'choler' in his liver, so rendering it white and him weak]. **2** [1950s] (*US black/W.I.*) promiscuous.

white man *n.* [SE *white*/WHITE *adj.* (2); modern use usu. ironic] **1** [mid-19C+] (*UK/US*) (*also* **white guy**) an honourable person. **2** [1950s] (*W.I.*) an albino.

SE in slang uses

IN PHRASES

❑ **white man's burden** *n.* [Kipling's poem 'The White Man's Burden', in which the task was the ruling of the 'new-caught sullen peoples/Half-devil and half-child'] [1940s–50s] work; the matter in hand. ❑ **white man's chance** *n.* [as opposed to the treatment of non-whites] [mid–late 19C] (*US*) a fair chance. ❑ **white man's disease** *n.* [1980s+] (*US black*) the relative inability of Caucasians to jump, a term of derision almost exclusively used in a basketball context.

white meat *n.* (*also* **light meat**) **1** [1930s] (*US*) an easy target; something desirable [SE *white* + MEAT *n.* (1), pun on the genteel euph. for the 'breast' of a chicken]. **2** [1930s+] (*US black/W.I.*) a white person, usu. a woman and in a sexual context [the tenderness of young SE *chicken*; note printers' jargon *white meat*, an actress]. **3** [1970s] (*gay*) young (underage) boys [the tenderness of CHICKEN *n.* (4d)]. **4** [1970s+] a white penis [MEAT *n.* (2)]. **5** [1980s+] the vagina.

white mice *n.* [rhy. sl.] **1** [1930s] (*Aus.*) lice. **2** [1940s–50s] dice.

white mouth *v.* **1** [1930s] (*US black*) to pretend servility in one's conversations with whites [one 'talks their language']. **2** [2000s] to fellate [the white semen].

white nigger *n.* [SE *white* + NIGGER *n.*[1] (1)] **1** [mid–late 19C] a derog. term for a white person who does menial labour [note *Ward* (1700) '[The Irishman is] a Valuable Slave in our *Western-Plantations*, where they are distinguish'd by the Ignominious Epithet of *White-Negroes*']. **2** [mid-19C; 1960s+] a black person who is regarded as deferring to white people or accepting a role prescribed by them. **3** [late 19C] (*Sierra Leone*) a European. **4** [1930s] (*US*) a Jew. **5** [1940s+] a Mediterranean and thus relatively dark-skinned immigrant to the US, e.g. a Greek or Italian. **6** [1950s–70s] beatniks, hippies and other counter-cultural groups who see their alienation from mainstream culture as analogous with the everyday role of any black person [note Norman Mailer *The White Negro* (1957): 'The hipster had absorbed the existentialist synapses of the Negro, and for practical purposes could be considered a White Negro']. **7** [1960s+] (*Can.*) self-description by embittered French Canadians who see themselves as second-class citizens in a primarily British country.

white nurse *n.* [the 'health-giving' effects; note Rolling Stones' song 'Sister Morphine' (1969)] [1930s+] (*drugs*) any form of powdered white drugs.

IN PHRASES

❑ **chase the (white) nurse** *v.* [1950s] to be addicted to morphine.

white Owsley's *n.* *see* OWSLEY ACID *n.*

whites *n.* **1** [late 17C–mid-18C; late 19C+] venereal disease, spec. a vaginal discharge, gonorrhoea [the colour of the discharge; 20C+ use is Aus.]. **2** [19C–1900s] silver coins; thus in counterfeiters' jargon *large whites*, half-crowns, *small whites*, shillings. **3** [1960s] (*W.I.*) a drink of white rum. **4** [1960s+] (*drugs*) amphetamines.

white-shoe *adj.* **1** [1950s+] (*US*) immature, effeminate. **2** [1960s+] of the US establishment, e.g. a *white-shoe law firm*. **3** [1990s+] (*Aus.*) describing businessmen who prefer casual clothes to the trad. 'uniform' of black shoes and dark suits.

white stuff *n.* **1** [mid–late 19C] anything made of silver [WHITE *adj.* (1)]. **2** [20C+] (*drugs*) morphine or heroin [STUFF *n.* (5)]. **3** [1920s] (*US*) grain alcohol used for making illicit liquor. **4** [1920s+] (*drugs*) cocaine [STUFF *n.* (5)]. **5** [1930s] (*also* **white slufe**) opium [STUFF *n.* (5)]. **6** [1940s] diamonds. **7** [1950s] large denomination notes [large 'white' £5 notes]. **8** [1980s] (*drugs*) Demerol [STUFF *n.* (5)]. **9** [1980s+] (*US*) any clear coloured alcohol.

white trash *n.* (*also* **ofay trash, trash**) [lit. 'white rubbish'] [mid-19C+] (*orig. US black*) a derog. term for the poor white population of the Southern states; thus extended to non-US contexts; occas. sing..

white trash *adj.* [WHITE TRASH *n.*] [1940s+] (*orig. US*) pertaining to the culture and mores of the white underclass; occas. ext. as *brown trash*, with ref. to an equivalent black community.

whitewash *n.* **1** [mid-19C–1900s] a glass of sherry taken as the finale after a meal spent drinking port and claret [its relatively 'white' colour and its 'washing' away of the red wines]. **2** [mid-19C+] (*also* **wash**) in sport, the complete defeat of one team by another; thus any crushing defeat. **3** [1940s] (*US*) milk.

whitewash *v.* **1** [mid-18C–1900s] to free oneself of debts by becoming a bankrupt. **2** [mid-19C+] (*US*) to win or defeat decisively. **3** [1960s+] in sexual contexts [the whiteness of the semen]. (**a**) to have sexual intercourse. (**b**) to ejaculate. (**c**) (*US gay*) to lick the anus.

IN PHRASES

❑ **whitewash someone's kidneys** *v.* [1950s+] (*Aus.*) to have anal intercourse. ❑ **whitewash someone's tonsils** *v.* [1960s+] (*US*) to ejaculate in someone's mouth, following fellatio.

whitewashed *adj.* [WHITEWASH *v.* (1)] [mid-18C–1900s] freed of one's debts by becoming a bankrupt.

whitewasher *n.* [var. WHITEWASH *n.* (1); one 'cleans up' the palate] [late 19C] a glass of white wine taken at the end of dinner.

whitewashing *n.* **1** [mid-18C] ((*W.I.*) insincerely accepting religious conversion when the alternative is to be killed [the black man or woman is 'washed white' through baptism]. **2** [early 19C] declaring oneself bankrupt (and serving the concomitant prison sentence) to nullify one's debts; thus a *whitewashing buck*, one who makes such a declaration.

white wing *n.* [SE, the *locus classicus* was the nickname of the New York City street sweepers, who wore white uniforms after the reforms of the city's street cleaning by Col. George F. Waring in 1895] [late 19C–1950s] (*US*) any wearer of a white uniform.

white wings *n.* **1** [late 19C–1900s] (*US*) eggs [those of the hens that lay them]. **2** [1900s–10s] (*US*) a New York City street cleaner [their white uniform and 'angelic' occupation].

whitey *n.* **1** [early 19C; 1930s+] (*US/UK black*) any white individual; occas. ext. to Latinos and Chicanos. **2** [mid-19C+] (*US/UK black*) the white race in general. **3** [1950s] (*US black*) a nickname for a very dark-skinned black person. **4** [1990s+] (*Aus.*) Carlton draft beer. **5** [1990s+] (*UK juv.*) a short-term attack of panic and increased heart-rate caused by an excess of cannabis [the white pallor of the victim's skin].

whitey cockroach *n.* [1950s+] (*W.I.*) a term of abuse for a white person.

whitey mcfly *n.* [WHITEY *n.* (1) + MCFLY *n.*] (*US black*) a white person attempting to adopt black culture and style.

whitey-whitey *n.* [1950s] (*W.I.*) an albino.

whither-go-ye *n.* (*also* **whither-do-go**) [the question asked by a stereotypically nagging, over-inquisitive wife] [late 17C–early 19C] a wife.

Whit's Palace *n.* [late 19C] Newgate Prison.

Whitt *n. see* WHIT *n.*

Whittington priory *n.* [its association with Dick *Whittington* (*c.*1358–1423), who 'turned again' at nearby Highgate] [late 19C] Holloway Prison.

Whittington('s) college *n.* [the name of a Warden or the rebuilding of Newgate in 1423 by the executors of Richard ('Dick') Whittington, the former Lord Mayor + COLLEGE *n.* (2)] [late 16C–early 19C] (*UK Und.*) Newgate prison.

whittle *v.* [WHIDDLE *v.* (2)] [early 18C] to confess, to betray one's confederates.

whittled as a penguin *adj.* [16C–17C SE *whittled*, drunk] [1960s] (*Aus.*) extremely drunk.

whittler *n.* [lacking big-city crimes, he sits *whittling* a piece of wood] [1920s–40s] (*US tramp*) a small-town sheriff or constable.

whittle the stick *v.* (*also* **whittle one's tool**) [play on SE *stick/tool* + STICK *n.* (1)/TOOL *n.*[1] (1)] [1960s] to masturbate.

whit-whit *n.* [? WHITES *n.* (1)] [2000s] (*US black*) an untrustworthy woman; a woman whose vagina smells and is poss. infected.

whiz *n.*[1] [echoic] **1** [late 18C–early 19C] noise, commotion, a 'buzz'. **2** [1900s] (*US*) a spree. **3** [1910s+] (*Aus.*) energy, spirit.

IN COMPOUNDS

❑ **whiz pop** *n.* [they emulate a dud firework, which *whizzes* then sputters out with an anti-climactic *pop*] [1970s] (*US campus*) a stupid person. ❑ **whiz wagon** *n.* [1900s] (*US*) an automobile.

IN EXCLAMATIONS

❑ **hold your whiz!** [late 19C–1920s] be quiet! shut up!

whiz *n.*[2] [ety. unknown; ? the speed i.e. SE *whiz* of its conclusion] [mid-19C] (*US*) a deal, a bargain.

whiz *n.*[3] (*also* **whizz, wiz**) [SE *wizard*] **1** [late 19C+] a general term of approbation, esp. of a highly satisfying thing or event. **2** [20C+] a general term of approbation, esp. of a very skilful or talented person.

whiz *n.*[4] (*also* **whizz, wiz, wizz**) [SE *whiz*, to move fast] **1** [1920s+] a pickpocket. **2** [1930s+] thus *whiz artist*, *whiz-boy*, *whizman*, a pickpocket. **3** [1990s+] amphetamine, amphetamine sulphate.

IN COMPOUNDS

❑ **whiz mob** *n.* (*also* **whiz gang, whizz mob, whizzmob**) [MOB *n.*[2] (3)] [1920s+] the world of pickpockets; a gang of pickpockets.

whiz *n.*[5] [abbr.] [1950s–60s] (*US*) *whiskey*.

whiz *n.*[6] (*also* **whizz, wizz**) [WHIZ *v.*[2]] [1960s+] an act of urination.

IN PHRASES

❑ **take the wizz** *v.* [var. on *TAKE THE PISS (OUT OF)* *under* PISS *n.*] [2000s] to tease.

whiz *adj.* [WHIZ *n.*[3]] [1910s+] a general term of admiration.

whiz *v.*[1] (*also* **whizz, wizz**) [WHIZ *n.*[4] (1)] **1** [1920s+] (*US Und.*) to pickpocket. **2** [1960s+] to steal. **3** [2000s] (*UK drugs*) to take any form of amphetamine drug.

IN PHRASES

❑ **on the whiz** [1920s+] working as a pickpocket.

whiz *v.*[2] (*also* **whizz**) [echoic of urine hitting the lavatory bowl] [1920s+] to urinate.

IN PHRASES

❑ **whiz jizzum** *v.* [JISM *n.* (2)] [20C+] to masturbate.

whiz! *excl.* [mid-18C–mid-19C] a general excl.

whiz bang *n.*[1] [WHIZ *n.*[3] (2) + SE *bang*] [1910s+] (*US*) any person or thing that is impressive or successful.

whiz bang *n.*[2] [the *whiz* of the cocaine + the *bang* of the opiate] [1930s–50s] (*drugs*) an injection of cocaine plus heroin or morphine.

whiz bang *adj.* [WHIZ BANG *n.*[1]] [1910s+] (*US*) describing a person or thing that is impressive or successful.

whiz off *v. see* RACE OFF *v.*

whizz *see also under* WHIZ.

whizz-bomb *n.* [2000s] (*drugs*) MDMA.

whizzer *n.*[1] [WHIZ *n.*[3]] [late 19C+] something or someone extraordinary or wonderful.

whizzer *n.*[2] (*also* **wizzer**) [WHIZ *n.*[4] (1)] [20C+] a pickpocket.

whizzer *n.*[3] [SE *whiz*] [1960s] a spree, a drinking bout.

whizzing *n.* [WHIZ *v.*[1] (1)] [1920s–40s] working as a pickpocket.

whizzing *adj.* [WHIZ *n.*[3] (1)] [1900s–50s] (*mainly juv.*) wonderful, first-rate, and as a positive intensifier.

whizzo *adj.* (*also* **wizz, wizzo**) [WHIZ *n.*[3] (1)] [1940s+] (*usu. juv., except when ironic*) wonderful, brilliant, amazing; also as excl.

whizz off *v. see* RACE OFF *v.*

whizzy-whizzy *v. see* WIZZY-WIZZY *v.*

whoaball *n.* (*also* **whoa-ball, whoball, whow-ball, woball**) [SE *whoa*, stop + *Ball*, a common name for a cow] [late 17C–mid-19C] a milkmaid.

whoa, bust me! *excl.* [BUST *v.*[1] (5c)] [19C] a general excl. of anger, amazement.

whoady *n.* [2000s] (*US black*) a friend, a partner.

whoa, Emma (mind the paint) *phr.* [an inquest on one *Emma* who had died suddenly and whose husband had attempted to revive her with this phrase] [late 19C] a phr. used to a woman who either looks odd or is behaving strangely or excessively in public.

whoa, Jameson! *excl.* [the audacious but politically disastrous *Jameson* Raid, 1896] [late 19C] an excl. used, with a certain degree of admiration, to restrain one that the speaker feels is 'going too far'.

who are you? *phr.* **1** [mid–late 19C] an aggressive phr. used in London streets, usu. greeted with the equally aggressive rejoinder 'Who are *you*?'. **2** [1980s+] (*US campus*) what's the matter, what's your problem? **3** [1980s+] (*US campus*) as excl., be quiet!

whoball *n. see* WHOABALL *n.*

who cares? [mid-19C+] a dismissive phr. indicating one's lack of concern.

whocker-jawed *adj. see* WHOPPER-JAWED *adj.*

whocko *v.* [echoic] [1950s] (*US teen*) to vomit.

who cut the cheese? *phr.* [the smell associated with some soft cheeses] [1950s+] (*orig. US, usu. juv.*) who broke wind?

whodunnit *n.* [SE *whodunnit*, a murder mystery; the 'murder victim' is the prison cat] [1940s–50s] (*UK prison*) meat pie.

whodyamaflick *n.* [2000s] used for a name one has temporarily forgotten.

whole... *n.* in combs. meaning everything, the whole lot; as well as combs. below and separate entries, *see also under* relevant nouns.

IN COMPOUNDS

❑ **whole box and dice** [late 19C+] (*Aus.*) ❑ **whole caboodle** *n. see* *WHOLE KIT AND CABOODLE* *under* WHOLE KIT *n.* ❑ **whole caboose** [late 19C+] (*Aus./Irish*) ❑ **whole circus** [1910s+] (*Aus.*) ❑ **whole cooloo** [1930s] ❑ **whole enchilada** (*also* **full enchilada**) [1930s] ❑ **whole gimbang** *see* WHOLE SHEBANG *n.* (1). ❑ **whole jingbang** [Scot., ? echoic of people moving] [late 19C+] ❑ **whole route** [1900s] (*US*) ❑ **whole shool and biling** *see* *WHOLE KIT AND BILING* *under* WHOLE KIT *n.* ❑ **whole shoot** *see* WHOLE BANG SHOOT *n.*

whole bag of tricks, the *n.* (*also* **whole box of tricks**) [mid-19C+] everything necessary to deal with a situation.

whole bang shoot *n.* (*also* **bang shoot, entire shoot, whole bang lot, whole shoot(ing), whole shot**) [late 19C+] everything or everybody, relevant and involved.

IN PHRASES

❑ **go for the whole shot** *v.* [20C+] to make an absolute commitment, to indulge oneself completely. ❑ **go the whole shoot** *v.* (*also* **go the whole shot**) [mid-19C+] to commit oneself wholeheartedly.

whole boiling lot *n.* (*also* **whole biling, ...boiling, ...boiling bunch**) [19C+] absolutely everything, absolutely everyone.

whole cheese *n.* (*US*) **1** [1900s] everything. **2** [1900s–30s] an important person.

whole famn damily, the *n.* (*also* **whole famdamily**) [2000s] (*US*) a euph. for the *whole damn family*.

whole-footed *adj.* [SE *whole-footed*, treading with one's whole foot, not just the toes] [mid-18C–mid-19C] unreserved, frank, free and easy.

whole ghesabo *n. see* WHOLE SHEBANG *n.*

whole hog *n.* [mid-19C+] absolutely everything, the very best of something; usu. in phr. below.

IN PHRASES

❑ **go the whole hog** *v.* (*also* **cut the whole hog, play..., go the total swine**) [? to eat a complete pig; for suggestions based on sense 1 above, i.e. 'going' or wagering money, *see* Schele de Vere, *Americanisms* (1872), 606: 'Some seek its source in the fact that in vernacular English *hog* was for many centuries the name of a piece of money; first of a shilling or six pence [...] and now of a five shilling-piece in England, but only of a shilling in Ireland. It is but fair to presume that one gambler would go, as their slang suggests, a shilling, another half a crown, and a third would say, 'I'll go the whole hog,' the whole piece of five shillings. Another explanation is suggested by the fact that the collections of coin-dealers contain numbers of large silver coins, on which the figure of a hog was stamped. These coins were frequently crossed deeply on the reverse for the convenience of breaking them into two or four pieces (fourth thing — farthing) should the bargain require it, and the parties have no small change. Persons who were willing to spend the whole coin would very naturally say, 'I'll go the whole hog.' Either of these derivations is more probable than the suggestion made recently that hog might be, not the name of the animal, but an abbreviation of the Jewish word *hoger*, a ducat.'] [mid-19C+] (*orig. US*) to do thoroughly, to go all the way; thus various derivs., *whole-hogger, -hoggery, -hoggism, -hoggite, whole-hogging*; also attrib.

whole-hog *adj.* [WHOLE HOG *n.*] [mid-19C+] complete, absolute, unswerving, devoted, usu. with regard to politics.

whole kit *n.* [late 18C–mid-19C] (*also* **whole kip**) the entire lot, the full collection.

IN PHRASES

❑ **whole kit and biling** *n.* (*also* **kit and boiling, whole shool and boiling**) [mid-19C–1940s] (*US*) absolutely everything and everyone, the lot. ❑ **whole kit and caboodle** *n.* (*also* **kit and caboodle, whole kit and boodle, whole kit-and-kaboodle**) [CABOODLE *n.*] [mid-19C+] (*orig. US*) the lot, everything there is. ❑ **whole kit and cargo** *n.* (*also* **whole kit and crew, ...and killybang, ...and parcel, ...and posse, ...and tolic, ...and tuck**) [mid-19C+] (*US*) the lot.

whole nine yards *n.* (*also* **whole nine**) [ety. unknown, but most of the many suggestions involve supposed standards of measurement, from the dimensions of a nun's habit to the capacity of a cement truck and the length of an ammunition clip to that of a hangman's rope. However, few, when checked, actually run to nine yards. It is most likely to be the use of nine as a form of 'mystic' number] [1960s+] everything, the complete package.

whole 'nother thing *n. see under* THING *n.*

whole shebang *n.* (*also* **whole gimbang, ...ghesabo**) [US milit. jargon *shebang*, a soldier's tent, where his possessions were kept, ult. SE *shebang*, a hut, a dwelling] **1** [mid-19C+] absolutely everything. **2** [1950s] of a person, the best, the ultimate.

whole shoot(ing) *n. see* WHOLE BANG SHOOT *n.*

whole shooting match, the *phr.* (*also* **whole shooting gallery, ...shooting lot**) [late 19C+] (*orig. US*) absolutely everything.

whole shot *n. see* WHOLE BANG SHOOT *n.*

who let you out? *phr.* [one has been released from an asylum] [late 19C–1940s] a deliberately deflating response to someone who is behaving far too self-confidently.

wholewheat bread *n.* [1970s+] (*US black*) a light-skinned person.

whole works, the *n. see* WORKS, THE *n.*

whollop *n. see* WALLOP *n.*[1] (1).

whollop *v. see* WALLOP *v.* (2).

wholloping *adj. see* WALLOPING *adj.* (2).

whomp *n.* (*also* **whump, wump**) [echoic] (*US*) **1** [1920s+] a heavy, low sound. **2** [1950s] a spree. **3** [1970s+] a heavy blow.

whomp *v.* (*also* **give someone a whomping, whomp on, whump, womp**) [WHOMP *n.*] **1** [1930s+] to hit; also fig. use. **2** [1950s+] (*US*) to defeat, trounce. **3** [1980s+] to have sexual intercourse.

IN PHRASES

❑ **whomp out** *v.* [1970s] (*US teen*) to have an enjoyable time. ❑ **whomp up** *v.* (*also* **whump up**) [1950s+] (*US*) **1** to create, devise or make up. **2** to stimulate, to stir up.

whomp! *excl.* (*also* **whump!**) [WHOMP *n.*] [1950s+] echoic of the sound of a sudden blow, used to indicate suddenness, immediacy.

whonk *v.* [var. on WHACK *v.*[1] (1)] [1950s] (*US*) to hit hard.

whoobang *v.* [? HO *n.* + 'bang on about'] [2000s] (*US teen*) to gossip maliciously; to talk nonsense.

whoof it in *v.* (*also* **whoomf**) [echoic] [1950s+] to push something in(to).

whoogie *n.* [SE *white* + BOOGIE *n.*[2] (1)] [20C+] (*US black*) a derog. term for a white person.

whoop *v.* **1** *see* WHOP *v.* **2** *see* WHUP *v.* (3).

whoop and a holler *n.* [SE *whoop* + *holler*, both meaning shout, and so the distance such cries would carry] [early 19C+] (*US*) a short distance, also *two whoops and a holler*.

whoop-de-do *n.* (*also* **whoop-de-doodle**) (*US*) **1** [1920s+] an uproar, noisy celebration, a significant event. **2** [1940s] praise.

whoop-de-do *adj.* (*also* **whoop-de-doodle**) [WHOOP-DE-DO *n.* (1)] [1940s+] (*US*) uproarious, noisy.

whoop-de-do! *excl.* (*also* **whoop-dee-doo! whoop gee wo! whoopty-woo! woopty-woo!**) [ext. of WHOOPEE! *excl.*] [late 19C+] an excl. of joy, excitement; often ironic.

whooped *adj.* (*also* **whupped**) [WHOP *v.* (1)] [1980s] (*US campus*) drunk; also fig. use as in infatuated, in love.

whoopee *n.* [WHOOPEE! *excl.*] [1920s+] (*US*) a wild party; self-indulgence of any sort; also attrib.

IN COMPOUNDS

❑ **whoopee mama** *n.* [MAMA *n.* (1)] [1920s–30s] a flighty young woman, usu. middle class, in her late teens or very early 20s, pursuing a lifestyle as far as possible removed from that desired by her parents. ❑ **whoopee water** *n.* [1940s] (*US*) alcohol.

IN PHRASES

❑ **make whoopee** *v.* [the coinage seems to have been in G. Kahn's 1928 song '*Makin' Whoopee*', 'Another bride, another June, Another sunny honeymoon, Another season, another reason for making whoopee!'] [1920s+] **1** to go out on a spree, to enjoy oneself uproariously. **2** to have sexual intercourse.

whoopee! *excl.* (*also* **hoopee! whoopie!**) [SE *whoop*, a cry + sfx -*ee*] [mid-19C+] (*orig. US*) a cry of intense delight.

whoop 'em up Liza Jane *v. see* WHOOP IT UP *v.*

who opened their lunch? *phr. see under* LUNCH *n.*

whooper-dooper *n.* [SE *whoop* + redup.] [1930s+] (*US*) a wild celebration, a carouse.

whooperup *n.* [SE *whoop*] [late 19C] a second-rate singer who produces noise rather than music.

whoop gee wo! *excl. see* WHOOP-DE-DO! *excl.*

whoopie! *excl.* see WHOOPEE! *excl.*

whooping *adj.* [mid-19C+] very large of its type.

whoop it up *v.* (*also* **hoop up, whoop 'em up Liza Jane, whoop her up, whoop things up, whoop up**) [SE *whoop*, a cry] **1** [late 19C+] (*orig. US*) to have a noisy, ostentatious good time; thus *whooper-up*, one who acts in this way. **2** [late 19C+] (*also* **whoop on**) to stir things up, to create excitement, to praise something and thus arouse support for it. **3** [1910s] (*US*) to vomit. **4** [1940s] (*US*) to raise, increase.

whoops *v.* (*also* **whoopsie**) [SE *whoops!*, an excl. of apology + echoic] [1920s+] (*US*) to vomit.

whoopsie *n.* (*also* **whoopsie-boy, whoops-m'dear**) [1940s+] a homosexual.

whoopsie *adj.* (*also* **whoopsy**) [WHOOPSIE *n.*] [1940s–50s] (*US*) homosexual, effeminate.

whoopsie-doodle *adj.* [1950s] eccentric.

whoop someone's ass *v.* see *WHIP SOMEONE'S ASS under* WHIP *v.*[3].

whoopsy *adj.* see WHOOPSIE *adj.*

whoop the ante *v.* see *UP THE ANTE under* ANTE *n.*

whoop things up *v.* see WHOOP IT UP *v.*

whoopty-woo! *excl.* see WHOOP-DE-DO! *excl.*

whoop-up *n.* [WHOOP IT UP *v.* (2)] **1** [1900s] (*Aus.*) praise, support. **2** [1950s] a plan, a scheme.

whoop up *v.* see WHOOP IT UP *v.*

whooray *n.* see HOORAY (HENRY) *n.*

whoosh *v.* [1910s] (*Aus.*) to hit.

whooshed *adj.* [the world 'whooshes' around the drinker's head] [1960s] (*US campus*) drunk.

whoosis/whoozit *n.* see WHOSIS *n.*

whoozis *n.* (*also* **whoosis, whoozit**) [SE *who's this/it*] **1** [1920s+] (*US*) an unknown or unspecifiable thing or person. **2** [2000s] a penis.

whooziz *n.* see WHOSIS *n.*

whoozy *adj.* see WOOZY *adj.*

whop *n.* [WHOP *v.* (1)] **1** [mid-19C–1960s] (*UK juv.*) a beating, a caning. **2** [1900s] (*US Und.*) a sentence of 15–30 days. **3** [1920s] a fine example. **4** [1940s] (*US black campus*) (*also* **whupp**) a hangover. **5** [1950s+] (*US*) an attempt, a try. **6** [1990s+] (*US drugs*) a go, a time.

whop *v.* (*also* **whap, whoop, wop**) [? SE *quap*, to beat, to throb, ult. Ger. *quappen*, to flop, *quappeln*, to quiver] **1** [late 16C+] to hit, to beat, to flog. **2** [mid-17C] to have sexual intercourse. **3** [mid-19C+] to overcome, to surpass, to defeat. **4** [1910s] (*US*) to shoot.

(IN PHRASES)

❑ **whop it up** *v.* (*also* **whop it in**) [1960s+] of a man, to have sexual intercourse, esp. in *I could whop it up her/that*, I would like to have sex with that woman.

whop! *excl.* (*also* **whap!**) [mid-19C+] echoic of the sound of a sudden blow.

whopcacker *n.* (*also* **wopcacker**) [? WOOPKNACKER *n.*] [1920s+] (*Aus.*) anything notable, amazing etc.

whopper *n.* (*also* **whapper, wopper**) [fig. use of WHOP *v.* (1)] **1** [18C+] a notably large object, or creature. **2** [late 18C+] a notably large person. **3** [mid-19C+] a notably large blow. **4** [mid-19C+] a particularly gross lie; also a lying person. **5** [1960s+] a large or erect penis. **6** [1960s+] in pl., exceptionally large breasts. **7** [1990s+] a very stupid person.

whopper-jawed *adj.* (*also* **wapper-jawed, whocker-jawed, womper-jawed**) [WHOP *v.* (1) + SE *jaw*] **1** [1910s+] (*US*) crooked, out of place, damaged, broken. **2** [1920s] crazy.

whoppie *n.* [*WHOP IT UP under* WHOP *v.*] [1970s] (*US*) sexual intercourse.

whopping *n.* [WHOP *v.* (1)] [mid-19C–1960s] a beating, a thrashing.

whopping *adj.* (*also* **wapping, whapping, wopping**) [WHOP *v.* (1)] [early 17C+] enormous, very large; esp. ext. as *whopping great*.

whop-straw *n.* see *under* STRAW *n.*

who pulled your chain? *phr.* [1910s+] a derisive phr. to one who has 'butted in' to a private conversation, who asked you to make a comment?

who put the quarter in your slot? *phr.* see *under* QUARTER *n.*

whore *n.* [rooted in SE *whore*, but carrying no commercial overtones] **1** [20C+] a general derog. term of address, irrespective of sex. **2** [1950s] in cards, the queen. **3** [1950s] (*US prison*) a passive male homosexual, a catamite. **4** [1950s+] a promiscuous woman, but not necessarily, and not even usu., an actual prostitute; also of homosexual men. **5** [1960s] (*US black*) a girlfriend.

SE in slang uses

(IN COMPOUNDS)

❑ **whorebag** *n.* [2000s] an unattractive woman, poss. a prostitute. ❑ **whore car** *n.* [1960s] (*US*) an unmarked car used by police to patrol street prostitutes. ❑ **whore-chaser** *n.* [1960s] (*US black*) a womanizer, whether pursuing actual prostitutes or merely available women. ❑ **whoredog** *n.* [1980s+] (*US campus*) **1** an unrespectable or criminal person. **2** a promiscuous woman. ❑ **whore-eater** *n.* [early 18C] a pimp. ❑ **whore-hopper** *n.* (*also* **whore-fucker**) [HOP *v.*[1] (8)] [1940s+] (*US*) a sexually voracious man who frequently visits prostitutes. ❑ **whorehound** *n.* [-HOUND *sfx*] [1940s+] a man who enjoys sex with prostitutes. ❑ **whore-pipe** *n.* [PIPE *n.*[1] (2a)] [late 18C–early 19C] the penis. ❑ **whore's bath** *n.* see *WHORE SPLASH* below. ❑ **whore's bird** *n.* [BIRD *n.*[1]] [mid-16C–early 19C] a term of abuse; a debauchee. ❑ **whore scars** *n.* see SCARS *n.* ❑ **whore's curse** *n.* [the going rate for a prostitute's favours was half a guinea (10s 6d), the gold coin worth 5s 3d was substituted by mean customers who liked to be seen giving the woman gold, but saw no reason to be over-generous] [late 18C–early 19C] 5s 3d (26p), thus presumably the telling-off one received for offering only 5s 3d. ❑ **whore's get** see *under* GET *n.*[1]. ❑ **whore's ghost** *n.* (*Irish*) **1** [1970s+] anything seen as intractable or obnoxious. **2** [1990s+] a child of a prostitute. ❑ **whore splash** *n.* (*also* **whore's bath**) [1950s+] a brief, cursory wash, often a quick shower, as taken by a prostitute between clients; also in non-prostitution use.

(IN PHRASES)

❑ **cry whore** *v.* [lit. to accuse someone of being a prostitute] [mid-17C–18C] to put the blame on. ❑ **demure as a whore at a christening** *adj.* (*also* **...as a harlot..., ...as an old whore...**) [early 18C+] extremely demure and well-behaved. ❑ **sings more like a whore's bird than a canary bird** [late 18C–early 19C] a phr. said of one who has a strong, manly voice.

-whore *sfx* [1980s+] (*US campus*) used in a comb. with a noun to denote a fanatic, someone who is obsessed by the noun in question, e.g. *bookwhore, partywhore*.

whorehouse *adj.* [SE *whorehouse*] [1940s+] (*US*) cheap, tawdry, in bad taste.

whorehouse broad *n.* (*also* **whorehouse chick, ...girl, ... woman**) [BROAD *n.*[2] (2)/CHICK *n.*[1] (2)/SE *girl*/SE *woman*] [1970s+] (*US black*) a prostitute who works in a brothel rather than on the streets.

whoride *n.* [WHORIDE *v.*] [1990s+] (*US black*) any form of extreme activity, a shooting, a riot etc.

whoride *v.* [ety. unknown] [1990s+] (*US black*) to mock; to be noisy.

whosamajig *n.* [1990s+] (*Aus.*) a generic name for someone whose name one either does not know or has forgotten.

whosermybob (*also* **whosemawhat, whosemyjig, whosermyjig**) [vars. on THINGUMABOB *n.*; THINGUMAJIG *n.*] [1930s+] (*Aus.*) anything or anyone that one has forgotten the name of.

who-shot-John *n.* see HE-SAY-SHE-SAY *n.*

whosis *n.* [SE *who is this?*] (*also* **whoosis, whoozit, whooziz, whosit, whosthis, whozis**) [20C+] (*US*) a generic name for someone whose real name one does not know.

(IN PHRASES)

❑ **scare the whosis out of** *v.* [euph. for *SCARE THE (LIVING) SHIT(S) OUT OF under* SHIT *n.*] [1950s] (*US*) to terrify.

who struck Buckley? *phr.* [ety. unknown; presumably anecdotal, although poss. merely assonant] [mid-19C] 'a common phrase used to irritate Irishmen' (Hotten 1864).

who the devil! *excl. see* WHAT THE DEVIL! *excl.*

whow-ball *n. see* WHOABALL *n.*

whozis *n. see* WHOSIS *n.*

whump *see under* WHOMP.

whup *v.* [SE *whip*] [20C+] (*US*) **1** to defeat, e.g. in a competition. **2** to make someone suffer, i.e. to beat fig. **3** (*also* **whoop**) to attack, to beat up. **4** to punch.

IN COMPOUNDS

❑ **whup-a-child** *n.* [1970s+] (*US black*) the police, a police officer.

IN PHRASES

❑ **whup someone's ass** *v. see* WHIP SOMEONE'S ASS *under* WHIP *v.*[3]. ❑ **whup the game** *v.* [GAME *n.* (6)] [1970s+] (*US black*) to succeed in life.

whupp *n. see* WHOP *n.* (4).

whupped *adj.* **1** [1980s] (*US campus*) henpecked [WHUP *v.* (3)]. **2** *see* WHOOPED *adj.*

IN PHRASES

❑ **dick-whupped** *adj.* (*also* **d-whupped**) *see under* DICK *n.*[1].

why buy a cow when milk is so cheap? *phr.* [late 17C+] why get married when sexually permissive women are so available?

whyms *n.* [a supposed 'telescoping' of the initials] [late 19C] members of the Y.M.C.A.

why the arse! *excl. see* WHAT THE ARSE! *under* ARSE *n.*

why the devil! *excl.* (*also* **why the fuck! why the hell! why the shit!**) [all intensified forms of SE *why?* + SE *devil*/FUCK *n.* (1)/SE *hell*/SHIT *n.* (1a)] [18C+] an exclamatory query of amazement, annoyance etc.

wibble *n.*[1] [it makes one's stomach *wibble*, i.e. wobble] [18C–early 19C] any form of weak or bad drink.

wibble *n.*[2] [SE *whibble*, to rock backwards and forwards] [early 19C] (*US Und.*) an auger.

wibble-wobble *adv.* (*also* **wibblety-wobblety, wibbly-wobbly**) [SE *wobbly*] [mid-19C+] unsteadily; thus as n., an old and unsteady person.

wibbly-wobbly *adj.* [WIBBLE-WOBBLE *adv.*] [1910s+] uneven.

wibling's witch *n.* (*also* **w.w.**) [the gambler James *Wibling* (*fl.* early 17C) who made a fortune from gambling and whose lucky card was supposedly the four of clubs] [late 18C–19C] the four of clubs.

wicher *adj. see* WITCHER *adj.*

wicher-cully *n.* [WITCHER *adj.* + CULLY *n.*[1] (4)] [mid-17C–18C] (*UK Und.*) a silversmith.

wick *n.*[1] [mid-19C+] a penis.

IN COMPOUNDS

❑ **wick-dipping** *n.* [1970s] sexual intercourse.

IN PHRASES

❑ **dip one's wick** *v.* (*also* **dip one's dick, dip the wick**) [mid-19C+] of a man, to have sexual intercourse. ❑ **moisten one's wick** *v.* [1970s] of a man, to have sexual intercourse [phr. reinforced by HAMPTON (WICK) *n.* (1)].

wick *n.*[2]

IN PHRASES

❑ **get on someone's wick** *v.* [rhy. sl.; *Hampton Wick* = PRICK *n.* (1); a link to WICK *n.*[1] would appear coincidental] [1930s+] to irritate, to annoy.

wicked *adj.* [although the modern bad = good model properly dates f. 1970s US black vocab. the *OED*'s first cited use is in F. Scott Fitzgerald's *This Side of Paradise* (1920): 'Phoebe and I are going to shake a wicked calf'] **1** [mid-17C; late 19C+] unpleasant, terrible, awful. **2** [mid-19C+] (*orig. US*) (*also* **wikid**) excellent, wonderful.

IN COMPOUNDS

❑ **wicked awesome** *adj.* [AWESOME *adj.* (2)] [1990s+] (*US teen*) used of anything especially excellent. ❑ **wicked pisser** *n.* [PISSER *n.* (2a)] [1990s+] (*US, mainly northeast*) something very good or very bad. When used without an article, e.g. *This food is wicked pisser*, it is taken to mean very good; when used with an article, e.g. *This job is a wicked pisser*, it is taken to mean something very bad. ❑ **wicked thing** *n.* [1970s+] (*US black*) an extraordinary event or situation.

IN PHRASES

❑ **wicked, wassy and wild** *adj.* [1990s+] (*W.I.*) extraordinary.

SE in slang uses

IN COMPOUNDS

❑ **wicked loser** *n.* [LOSER *n.* (1)] [1980s+] (*US campus*) a failure, esp. one who could equally well have succeeded had they so decided.

wicked *adv.* [19C+] very, really.

wicked! *excl.* [WICKED *adj.* (2)] [1950s+] general excl. of affirmation, approval: excellent, wonderful.

wicked rumours *n.* [rhy. sl.] [20C+] bloomers.

wicked witch *n.* [rhy. sl. = BITCH *n.*[1] (1)] [1990s+] an unpleasant, malicious woman.

wicket *n.* [SE *wicket*, a gate] **1** [late 16C] the mouth or throat. **2** [late 19C] the vagina.

wick-wack *adj.* [redup. WACK *adj.* (1)] [1990s+] (*US black*) inferior, second-rate.

widdle *n.* [WIDDLE *v.*] [1950s+] (*mainly juv.*) an act of urination.

widdle *v.* [? WEE *v.*+ PIDDLE *v.* (1)] [1950s+] to urinate.

widdy *n.* [abbr.] [late 18C+] a widow.

wide *adj.* [SE *wide* (*of the mark*), going astray, deviating from the proper course (of life/action); prior use f. 16C is SE] **1** [mid-19C+] (*also* **wide-o, wide-oh**) 'sharp'. **2** [late 19C] lax, loose, immoral. **3** [1930s+] aware of.

DERIVATIVES

❑ **wideness** *n.* **1** [late 19C+] perspicacity, intelligence. **2** [2000s] audacity.

IN COMPOUNDS

❑ **wide-boy** *n.* [1930s+] a minor villain, often dabbling in 'get-rich-quick' schemes. ❑ **wide man** *n.* **1** [1930s–40s] (*also* **wide chump, wide con**) a swindler, a con-man. **2** [1950s] (*UK Und.*) a professional thief.

IN PHRASES

❑ **come wide** *v.* [1960s] to get the better of. ❑ **half-wide** *adj.* **1** [16C] immoral. **2** [19C+] reasonably intelligent, aware of what goes on and thus, in certain contexts, corruptible.

SE in slang uses

IN COMPOUNDS

❑ **wide C** *n. see* OPEN CHARMS *under* OPEN *adj.* ❑ **wide load** *n.* [1990s+] (*US campus*) someone with large hips and buttocks. ❑ **wide-on** *n.* [on the pattern of the male HARD-ON *n.* (1), the image is of a gaping vagina] [1960s+] of a woman, sexual excitement.

IN PHRASES

❑ **give someone a wide** *v.* [SE *give a wide berth*] [20C+] to avoid. ❑ **wide place in the road** *n.* (*also* **broad place in the road**) [its unimportance in the eyes of those who drive through] [20C+] (*US*) a derog. phr. for a small town or hamlet.

wide-awake *n.* (*also* **wake**) [a pun on the material, which lacked a 'nap'] [mid-19C–1930s] a soft felt hat with broad brim and low crown.

wide-awake *adj.* **1** [19C] vigilant, aware, knowing; thus as n., a knowing person. **2** [mid-19C] (*UK Und.*) pertaining to the underworld. **3** [1900s] of a garment, flashy, ostentatious, i.e. as worn by a 'wide boy'.

widen *v.* [Mezzrow & Wolfe (1946) 'To widen means to widen the gap between you and the other person – in other words, to leave'] [1940s] (*US black*) to leave.

wide-o *n.* [WIDE *adj.* (1); on the pattern of RAPE-O *n.*] [1920s+] a minor villain, a 'spiv'.

wide-o *adj.* [SE *wide-open*] **1** [1930s] vulnerable. **2** *see* WIDE *adj.* (1).

wide-oh *adj. see* WIDE *adj.* (1).

wide-oh! *excl.* [WIDE *adj.* (1)] [late 19C] look out! take care! be on your guard!

wide-open *adj.* [boxing imagery] **1** [mid-19C+] morally and legally unconstrained. **2** [late 19C+] vulnerable, undefended. **3** [1950s+] (*US*) of driving, very fast [the throttle is 'wide open']. **4** in fig. senses. (**a**) [1950s+] (*US black*) sexually excited [*HAVE ONE'S NOSE OPEN under* NOSE *n.*]. (**b**) [1980s] (*US campus*) drunk [fig. use of WIDE-OPEN *adj.* (1)]. (**c**) [1980s] (*US campus*) wild [fig. use of WIDE-OPEN *adj.* (1)].

wide open *adv.* [WIDE-OPEN *adj.* (1)] **1** [late 19C+] of an illegal business, without constraint from the authorities. **2** [20C+] (*US*) of driving, at full speed.

wide-open beaver *n. see under* BEAVER *n.*[1].

widgeon *n.* [note Freddie *Widgeon*, one of P.G. Wodehouse's (1881–1975) foolish members of the Drones Club] [17C–mid-18C] a fool.

widgey *n. see* WHIDGEY *n.*

widgie *n.* [post-1960s use historical only; ? RIDGIE-DIDGIE *adj.*] [1950s+] (*Aus.*) the female counterpart of a BODGIE *n.* (2).

wido *n.* [WIDE *adj.* (1) + ? earliest use of -O *sfx* (7)] [mid-19C] an alert, aware person, one who is 'no fool'.

Widow, the *n.* [Fr. *veuve*, a widow] [late 18C+] a nickname for Veuve Cliquot champagne, therefore champagne in general.

widow *n.*[1] **1** [early 18C] an expiring fire. **2** [mid–late 19C] an extra hand dealt to the table in certain card-games.

SE in slang uses

IN COMPOUNDS

▫ **widow-bewitched** *n.* [early 18C–mid-19C] a woman whose husband is temporarily absent. ▫ **widow five-finger** *n. see FIVE-FINGERED WIDOW under* FIVE-FINGER(ED) *adj.* ▫ **Widow Jones** *n.* (*also* **Widow Jones's house**) [var. on *MRS JONES under* MRS *n.*] [1900s] the lavatory. ▫ **widow-maker** *n.* [1940s+] (*Can./US*) a dead branch caught high in a tree which may fall and kill or injure someone below.

widow *n.*[2] [1930s] (*US*) a condom.

widow *n.*[3] [abbr. *BLACK WIDOW under* BLACK *adj.*] [1970s] (*drugs*) any black capsule that contains amphetamine.

-widow *sfx* [20C+] of a woman who is left behind while her husband devotes himself to an obsession, usu. sport or a hobby; e.g. *golf-widow*, *cricket-widow* etc.

-widower *n.* [1960s+] the male version of the more common -WIDOW *sfx.*

widower bewitched *n.* [masculine var. on *WIDOW-BEWITCHED under* WIDOW *n.*[1]] [early 18C] a husband separated from or deserted by his wife.

widow's mite *n.* [rhy. sl.] [1910s–70s] a light, usu. for a cigarette.

widow's wink *n.* [rhy. sl. = CHINK *n.* (1)] [1970s] a Chinese person.

widow twankey *n.* [rhy. sl.] [20C+] **1** a handkerchief, i.e. a *hankie*. **2** an American [= *yankee*].

wiener *n.* **1** *see* WEEN *n.* **2** *see* WEENIE *n.*[1].

wienie *n. see* WEENIE *n.*[1].

wif *n.* (*also* **wiff**) **1** [1920s] (*US*) a wife. **2** *see* WHIFF *n.*

wife *n.* **1** in senses of 'locking up' her husband. (**a**) [mid-19C] (*UK prison*) a key. (**b**) [19C–1930s] a fetter fixed to one leg. **2** [1920s–30s] (*US campus*) one's roommate. **3** [1920s+] the supposedly subservient, 'female' partner in a gay couple. **4** [1930s+] (*US black/UK Und.*) a pimp's favoured prostitute, or one of group working for a pimp. **5** [1940s+] (*US gang*) the steady girlfriend of a gang member. **6** [1980s+] (*US campus*) a regular girlfriend.

SE in slang uses

IN COMPOUNDS

▫ **wife-beater** *n.* [the association of such singlets with men who are prone to domestic violence] [1990s+] (*US*) a sleeveless singlet. ▫ **wife-in-law** *n.* (*also* **in-law**) [1960s+] (*US black*) any woman in a pimp's group of prostitutes, other than his favourite and thus most privileged woman. ▫ **wife's dream** *n.* [1900s] (*Aus.*) a racing tip, the inference is of its unlikeliness. ▫ **wife-starver** *n.* [1960s+] (*Aus.*) a man who defaults on his maintenance payments.

IN PHRASES

▫ **go to Westminster for a wife** *v.* (*also* **go to Paul's for a wife, go to St. Paul's for a wife**) [16C proverb: 'Who goes to Westminster for a wife, to St Paul's for a man or to Smithfield for a horse, may meet with a horse, a knave and a jade.' Despite the supposed difference indicated in the proverb, Old St Paul's Cathedral was also well-known for the raffish individuals who frequented its purlieus] [late 16C–early 19C] to visit a brothel. ▫ **wife in watercolours** *n.* [the image of colours fading as do the passions of the newly married or the idea that the loving (if essentially hired) mistress was less strident than an intolerant harridan of a wife. Watercolours, suggests Grose 1785, are, like mistresses, 'easily effaced, or dissolved'] [late 18C–early 19C] a mistress. ▫ **wife out of Westminster** *n.* [WESTMINSTER WEDDING *n.*] [18C–19C] a wife unconstrained by monogamy. ▫ **wife's best friend** *n. see under* BEST FRIEND *n.*

wifey *n.* (*also* **wifie**) [mid-19C+] **1** a wife or regular girlfriend. **2** attrib., pertaining to a wife, the implication is of respectable behaviour. **3** (*US prison*) a male inmate's male lover.

wiff *n.* **1** *see* WHIFF *n.* **2** *see* WIF *n.*

wiffle-woffle *n.* [? WIFFLE-WOFFLES *n.*; i.e. a fig. stomach-ache renders them ill-humoured] [1910s–20s] an arrogant person.

wiffle-woffles *n.* [mid-19C] **1** stomach-ache. **2** a state of depression.

wiffy *adj. see* WHIFFY *adj.*

wifie *n. see* WIFEY *n.*

wig *n.*[1] [WIG *v.*[2]] **1** [late 18C–1900s] a severe scolding, a telling-off. **2** [late 18C+] a dignitary, lit. one who wears a wig for professional reasons, usu. a judge or barrister.

wig *n.*[2] **1** [mid-19C; 1940s+] (*later use US black*) the head, the brain or its functions. **2** [mid-19C+] the pubic hair of either sex. **3** [20C+] the hair. **4** [1930s+] (*US black*) hair that has been artificially straightened. **5** [1950s] (*W.I.*) a male haircutting style that supposedly resembles a judge's wig. The hair is cut into a peak at the front and there is no sharp razor line at the back. Those requesting such a cut would tell the barber, 'Try me'. **6** [1950s–70s] (*US black*) (*also* **wigger**) an eccentric, a mad person. **7** [1970s] (*US*) something of importance.

IN COMPOUNDS

▫ **wig-block** *n.* **1** [late 18C] a fool. **2** [late 18C–1970s] (*also* **wig box, wig stand**) the head. ▫ **wig bust** *n.* [fig. use of BUST *v.*[1] (5b)] [1940s+] (*US black*) the altering of a natural crinkly black head of hair into a straight PROCESS *n.* (1) style. ▫ **wig city** *adj.* [-CITY *sfx*] [1960s+] (*US teen*) eccentric, unbalanced. ▫ **wig hat** *n.* [1950s+] (*orig. US black*) a wig; a hairpiece. ▫ **wig-picker** *n.* [1960s+] (*US*) a psychiatrist. ▫ **wig tightener** *n.* [1950s] (*US black*) a wonderful, admirable individual. ▫ **wig trig** *n.* [1940s] (*US*) an idea.

IN PHRASES

▫ **blow one's wig** *v.* **1** [1930s–40s] (*US black*) (*also* **fracture one's wig**) to feel excited, enthusiastic or furious. **2** [1950s] to lose one's mind. ▫ **crack one's wig** *v.* [1950s] to go mad. ▫ **flip one's wig** *v.* [1930s+] (*orig. US*) **1** to lose one's temper. **2** to lose one's sanity; in weak use, to become emotional, e.g. through love. ▫ **have a tight wig** *v.* [1970s] (*US black*) to be drunk. ▫ **keep one's wig cool** *v.* (*also* **keep one's wig on**) [1910s+] to remain calm. ▫ **knock one's wig** *v.* [1940s] (*US black*) to comb one's hair. ▫ **lift the wig** *v.* [1940s] (*US black*) to amaze, to delight, to thrill. ▫ **loose wig** *n.* [1950s] (*orig. US black*) one who is without inhibitions; open to new ideas; as v., *loosen one's wig*, to behave crazily. ▫ **lose one's wig** *v.* [1960s] (*drugs*) to lose one's mind from drug intoxication. ▫ **lower wig** *n.* [19C] the pubic hair. ▫ **slip one's wig** *v.* [1940s] (*US*) to go mad. ▫ **snap one's wig** *v.* [1950s–70s] to lose emotional control. ▫ **split one's wig** *v.* **1** [1950s–60s] (*US*) to suffer pain, to feel depressed, to be at the end of one's tether. **2** [2000s] (*US prison*) to hit someone quickly and hard in the head. **3** [2000s] (*US black*) to hit hard; to kill. ▫ **tighten one's wig** *v.* [1940s+] **1** to smoke marijuana. **2** to give someone else marijuana. **3** to delight. ❑ **trig one's wig** *v.* [SE *trig(ger)*, to set off, to launch] [1940s] (*US black*) to think fast.

IN EXCLAMATIONS

❑ **blow my wig!** [early–mid-19C] a mild excl. ❑ **dash my wig(s)!** (*also* **burn my old wig!**) *see under* DASH! *excl.* ❑ **keep your wig on!** *see* KEEP YOUR SYRUP ON! *under* SYRUP (OF FIGS) *n.* ❑ **my wig!** (*also* **my wig and whiskers! my wigs!**) [19C–1900s] a mild excl. of surprise, irritation etc.

SE in slang uses

IN COMPOUNDS

❑ **wig-faker** *n.* [FAKER *n.* (1)] [18C–19C] a wig-maker, a hairdresser.

IN PHRASES

❑ **wigs on the green** *n.* (*also* **jigs on the green, mill on the green**) [if one has not already removed it, one's wig is likely to fall or be knocked off in such a fight] [19C+] (*orig. Irish*) an argument, a fight.

wig *v.*[1] [fig. uses of WIG *n.*[2] (1)] **1** [late 18C; 1950s] (*US black*) to inform, to explain. **2** [1930s+] (*US*) to talk, chatter. **3** [1930s+] to annoy, to irritate. **4** [1950s] (*US black*) to delight, to impress. **5** [1950s] to understand, to approve. **6** [1950s+] (*US*) to play cerebral, intellectual jazz music. **7** [1950s+] (*US*) to be in good spirits, to enjoy. **8** [1950s+] (*US*) to become or render nervous, hysterical, overly stressed, mentally unbalanced. **9** [1960s+] (*US*) to reach a different state through drugs.

IN PHRASES

❑ **wig out** *v.* **1** [1950s+] (*US*) (*also* **whig out, wig**) to lose control, to have a breakdown; thus *wigged out*, eccentric, over-emotional. **2** [1950s+] (*orig. jazz*) to enjoy oneself, lose one's inhibitions. **3** [1960s+] (*US campus*) to shock or be shocked; to excite, to thrill.

wig *v.*[2] [a judge's *wig*, i.e. the scolder uses quasi-judicial authority] [19C+] to scold, to reprimand.

wiganowns *n.* [? ext. of SE *wig*] [late 18C–early 19C] a man wearing a notably large wig.

wigeon *n.* [SE *widgeon*; *wigeon*, a wild duck, thus DUCK *n.*[1] (1)] [1940s+] (*Aus.*) an affectionate term for a young woman.

wigga *n.* (*also* **whigger, white nigga, wigger**) [SE *white* + NIGGA *n.*, invariably derog. term used by blacks to sneer at those who ape their culture and by whites in a generally racist sense] [1990s+] **1** (*orig. US*) a white person who adopts a black, spec. *hip-hop/rap*, lifestyle and is not merely a consumer of the records, but attempts to emulate what is otherwise an autonomous black culture. **2** (*US campus*) an African American who identifies with whites.

wigga-wagga *n.* [SE *wiggle/waggle*] **1** [late 19C–1910s] a walking stick. **2** [1900s–70s] (*also* **wigger-wagger**) the penis.

wigged (out) *adj.* [WIG OUT *under* WIG *v.*[1]] (*orig. US*) **1** [1950s–60s] (*drugs*) intoxicated by a drug. **2** [1960s] inspired or intoxicated by an idea. **3** [1970s+] eccentric, insane, deluded, out of touch.

wiggen *n.* [mid-19C] (*UK Und.*) the neck.

wigger *n.*[1] [WHIDGEY *n.*] [1990s+] (*Irish*) a derog. term for a woman.

wigger *n.*[2] [WIG *n.*[2] (6)] **1** [1990s+] (*US campus*) an unstable, eccentric person. **2** *see* WIG *n.*[2] (6).

wigger *n.*[3] *see* WIGGA *n.*

wigger-wagger *n. see* WIGGA-WAGGA *n.* (2).

wigging *n.* [WIG *v.*[2]; note Hotten (1860): 'If the head of a firm calls a clerk into the parlour, and rebukes him, it is an EAR-WIGGING; if done before the other clerks it is a WIGGING'] [mid-19C+] a reprimand, a telling off.

wiggins *n. see* EARWIG *n.* (6).

wiggins, the *n.* [1990s+] (*US campus*) feelings of unease.

wiggle *n.*

IN PHRASES

❑ **get a wiggle on** *v.* (*also* **do a wiggle, get a waggle on, get a wriggle on**) [late 19C+] to bustle, to hurry, to 'look lively'.

wigglers *n.* [SE *wiggle*] [1940s] (*US black*) the fingers; the toes.

wigglestick *n.* [1970s] the penis.

wiggy *adj.* [WIG *n.*[2] (6)] [1960s+] **1** eccentric, bizarre, unpleasant, disturbing. **2** confused. **3** pleasing, enjoyable, exciting and up to date. **4** (*US drugs*) intoxicated with narcotics.

wigsby/wigster *n. see* MR WICSBY *under* MR *n.*

wig-wag *n.* [1900] (*US*) a wave.

wig-wag *v.* [SE *wiggle* + *wag*] [20C+] to wave or move with a writhing movement; thus *wig-wagger*, one who *wig-wags*, *wig-waggy*, tortuous, winding.

wikid *adj. see* WICKED *adj.* (2).

wilbur *n.* [rhy. sl.; ult. air pioneer *Wilbur* Wright (1867–1912)] [20C+] a flight.

wild *n.* [SE *wild*, a wild or waste place] **1** [mid-19C] (*UK tramp*) a village. **2** [1950s] in pl., the suburbs.

wild *adj.* **1** [1920s+] (*US*) exciting, wonderful. **2** [1940s] (*US*) enthusiastic. **3** [1940s+] eccentric, bizarre, weird, odd. **4** [1960s+] (*US Und.*) consecutive, referring to prison sentences. **5** [1990s+] (*W.I.*) philandering.

IN COMPOUNDS

❑ **wild-ass** *adj.* (*also* **wild-assed**) [WILD *adj.* (3) + -ASS *sfx*] [1960s+] (*US*) crazy, insane, unbalanced.

SE in slang uses

IN COMPOUNDS

❑ **wild-buck** *adj.* [1950s] uncontrolled, unrestrained. ❑ **wild card** *n.* [poker imagery] [1920s+] (*US*) something or someone unknown or unpredictable, also as adj. ❑ **wildcat/catter** *see* separate entries. ❑ **wildfire** *n.* [its taste and effects] [mid-18C] a fiery drink. ❑ **wild hair** *n.* [1950s] (*US*) a theory, poss. extravagant; as adj., *wild-haired*. ❑ **wild oats** *n.* [SE *sow one's wild oats*] [mid-16C–early 17C] a dissolute young man, a rake. ❑ **wild rogue** *n.* [ext. of ROGUE *n.* (1)] [16C–early 19C] (*UK Und.*) a dedicated professional villain. ❑ **wild squirt** *n. see under* SQUIRT *n.* ❑ **wild thing, the** *see* separate entry. ❑ **wild Willy** *n.* [late 19C] (*US campus*) a dedicated hedonist.

wild *v.* [popularized through media reports of the savage rape and beating of New York's 'Central Park jogger' in 1989. According to the accused, 'wild', like its noun form 'wilding', is a nonce word, used by them alone and meaning simply going wild. It was elevated to a slang term after a report in the *New York Times* on 22 April 1989. However, the term is used, in the criminal sense and earlier, by the rapper Ice T on his album *Rhyme Pays* (1987); note also BUCK-WILD *adj.*] (*US black*) **1** [1980s+] to go out looking for victims to mug and attack; usu. as noun *wilding* or pron. *wilin'*. **2** [2000s] to have sexual intercourse.

IN PHRASES

❑ **wild out** *v.* [poss. equally linked to WILD *adj.* (1)] [2000s] to party, to act crazily.

wild! *excl.* [WILD *adj.* (1)] [1950s–60s] wonderful! fabulous! the best!

wildcat *n.* **1** in financial contexts [wildcat banks existed in the western US before the National Bank Act of 1863 and were virtually unregulated. The notes they issued were essentially worthless]. (**a**) [mid-19C–1900s] the notes issued by a wildcat bank; thus any worthless money. (**b**) [mid-19C–1920s] (*US*) an unsound, dubious business, esp. a 'wildcat bank'. **2** pertaining to intoxicants. (**a**) [late 19C–1940s] (*US*) illicitly distilled whisky. (**b**) [1920s] (*US Und.*) an illicit brewery. (**c**) [1980s+] (*drugs*) methcathinone. (**d**) [1980s+] (*drugs*) cocaine. **3** [1970s+] (*US black*) someone who participates intensely and also to his own advantage in street life [SE *wildcat/wild*/WILD *adj.* (2) + CAT *n.*[5] (1)].

wildcat *adj.* [WILDCAT *n.* (1)] **1** [mid–late 19C] describing the notes issued by a wildcat bank, thus of any money or finances, worthless, fraudulent. **2** [mid-19C–1930s] fraudulent, highly speculative. **3** [mid-19C–1940s] (*orig. US*) of a business practice, unsound, dubious, esp. in phr. *wildcat bank*.

wildcatter *n.* [SAmE *wildcatter*, a prospector who sinks wildcat wells] [late 19C+] a freelance bootlegger.

wild duck *n.* [? rhy. sl. = FUCK *n.* (4)] [1980s+] (*Aus. prison*) a prisoner who does not pay his debts.

wilding *n. see* WILD *v.* (1).

wilds, the *n.* [WILD *adj.* (3)] [late 19C–1900s] (*Aus.*) a fit of depression, a temper tantrum; thus *give one the wilds*, to depress, to 'bring down', to annoy.

wild thing, the *n.* [1980s+] (*orig. US black/campus*) **1** sexual intercourse. **2** rape.

IN PHRASES

❑ **do the wild thing** *v.* [1980s+] (*US black/campus*) to have sexual intercourse.

wild west *n.* [rhy. sl.] [20C+] a vest or undershirt.

Wilkie Bards *n.* [rhy. sl.; ult. music-hall comedy star *Wilkie Bard* (1874–1944)] [1910s+] playing cards.

Wilkinson sword *adj.* [rhy. sl.] [1990s+] bald.

willamakanka *n. see* BULLAMAKANKA *n.*

will do *phr.* [1950s+] a general affirmative, OK, I'll do it.

willeys *n. see* WILLIES *n.*

will I...! *excl. see* DID I...! *excl.*

william *n.*[1] [? abbr. of *William* = bill] [mid-19C–1920s] **1** a bill, esp. in phr. *meet sweet William*, to pay off a bill as soon as it is presented. **2** (*US*) a dollar bill.

william *n.*[2] [proper name, on pattern of JOHN THOMAS *n.*] [mid-19C+] the penis.

william *n.*[3] [rhy. sl.; *william pitt* = SHIT *n.* (1a); ult. UK politician *William* Pitt the Younger (1759–1806)] [1950s+] **1** excrement. **2** an act of defecation.

William Pitts *n.* [rhy. sl. = SHITS, THE *n.* (1); ult. *see* WILLIAM *n.*[3]] [1990s+] diarrhoea.

William Powell *n.* [rhy. sl.; ult. film star *William Powell* (1892–1984)] [1930s+] a towel.

William Tell *n.* [rhy. sl.; ult. the 15C Swiss hero *William Tell*] [20C+] a smell.

William the Third *n.* [rhy. sl. = TURD *n.*[1] (1)] [1960s–70s] (*Aus.*) a piece of excrement, a stool.

willie *n.*[1] [? generic uses of proper name] **1** [late 19C–1900s] (*US tramp*) a tramp. **2** [late 19C–1940s] a weak, cowardly or frightened man. **3** [late 19C+] (*also* **willy, willie-boy, willie watcher**) a male homosexual [? link to then dial. use of WILLIE *n.*[4] (1)]. **4** [1900s] an affected, effeminate (but not homosexual) man. **5** *see* WILLY *n.*[1].

IN PHRASES

❑ **Sweet Willie** *n. see under* SWEET *adj.*[1].

willie *n.*[2] [? WILLIES *n.* or abbr. SAusE *willy*, a whirlwind or link to SE *willy-nilly*] [1940s+] (*orig. Aus.*) a tantrum.

IN PHRASES

❑ **chuck a willie** *v.* (*also* **chuck a willy, throw a willy**) [1940s+] (*Aus.*) to throw a fit, lit. or fig.

willie *n.*[3] (*also* **willy**) [ety. unknown; ? given the context of betting, SE *will he...won't he* (and should I bet on it)] (*Aus.*) **1** [1940s+] money, esp. money set aside for use in betting. **2** [1960s+] a wallet.

willie *n.*[4] (*also* **willy**) [orig. in northern but non-dial. use] [1960s+] the penis.

IN COMPOUNDS

❑ **willie-waving** *n.* (*also* **willy-waving**) [1970s+] acting, speaking or posing in an exaggeratedly macho fashion.

IN PHRASES

❑ **wave one's willie** *v.* [1960s+] of a man, to act in an exaggeratedly macho manner.

Willie boy *n. see* WILLIE *n.*[1] (3).

willie lump-lump *n. see* WILLIE LUNCHMEAT *under* WILLY *n.*[1].

Willies, the *n.* [play on name; ? influenced by HOLY WILLIE *under* HOLY *adj.*] [1920s–30s] (*US tramp*) the Good Will Industries of the Methodist Church.

willies *n.* (*also* **willeys**) [ety. unknown, ? link to fig. use of dial. *willy-wambles*, stomach-rumbling] [late 19C+] nerves, worries, tension, esp. in phr. *give (someone) the willies*, to unnerve.

willie watcher *n. see* WILLIE *n.*[1] (3).

willing *adj.* [20C+] (*Aus./N.Z.*) pugnacious, aggressive, violent; thus *willing go*, a tough boxing match with both fighters exerting their utmost.

IN COMPOUNDS

❑ **willing winchell** *n. see* WINCHELL *n.*

will o'the wisps *n.* [rhy. sl.] [20C+] crisps.

willow *adj.* [SE *willowy*, slim] [late 17C–18C] (*UK Und.*) poor, of no reputation.

will's whiff *n.* [rhy. sl. = abbr. *syph*; ult. brandname of *Will's Whiff*, a small cigar] [20C+] syphilis.

willy *n.*[1] (*also* **willie**) **1** [1910s] (*US*) lunchmeat. **2** *see also under* WILLIE.

IN PHRASES

❑ **willie lunchmeat** *n.* (*also* **sammy lunchmeat, willie lump-lump**) [generic use of proper name + the stolidity and density of SE *lunchmeat/lump*; note the US comedian Red Skelton's 'character', the drunken *Willie Lump-Lump*] [1980s+] (*US Und.*) a fool; also attrib.

willy *n.*[2] [? earlier ref. to WILLIE *n.*[4] (1)] [1930s] (*US*) physical effort.

willy lees *n.* [rhy. sl.] [1940s+] (*Aus.*) a flea, fleas.

willy wacht *n.* [Scot.; *Willy* Arnot (a distiller? a landlord?), good whisky + *wacht/waught*, to drink deeply] [late 19C] a drink, esp. of whisky.

willy wag *n.* [rhy. sl. = SWAG *n.*[1] (9)] [20C+] (*Aus.*) a pack.

willy-welly *n.* [WILLIE *n.*[4] (1)+ WELLIE *n.*] [1990s+] a condom.

willy-willy *n.* [20C+] (*Aus.*) a violent wind storm.

Willy Wonka *n.* [rhy. sl.] **1** [1970s+] the penis [= PLONKER *n.* (2)]. **2** [1990s+] a fool [= PLONKER *n.* (3)].

willy woofter *n. see* WOOFTER *n.*

wilma *n.* [the character *Wilma* in the cartoon (1960s) and film (1994) *The Flintstones*] [1980s+] (*US campus*) an ugly, stupid woman.

Wilson Pickett *n.* [rhy. sl.; ult. soul star *Wilson Pickett* (1941–2006)] [1970s] a ticket.

Wilson's den *n.* (*also* **Tony's den**) [10 Downing Street, then home to Prime Minister Harold *Wilson* (1916–95), presumably the name can be altered to fit the current incumbent] [1960s+] (*bingo*) the number ten.

wilt *v.* [late 19C] to fade, i.e. to run off, to bolt.

wimble *n.* [SE *wimble*, a gimlet, an instrument for boring into soft ground] [mid-17C–18C] the penis.

wimble *v.* [WIMBLE *n.*; lit. to pierce with a gimlet] [mid–late 17C] of a man, to have sexual intercourse.

wimp *n.*[1] (*also* **whimp**) [? ext. WIMP *n.*[2] + note Wellington *Wimpy* a character in the cartoon film *Popeye*] **1** [1910s–20s] a fellow, a man, no pej. implications. **2** [1910s+] a weakling, an indecisive person.

DERIVATIVES

❑ **wimpish** *adj.* [1920s+] (*orig. US*) ineffectual and/or effeminate.

IN COMPOUNDS

❑ **wimp-dog** *n.* [DOG *n.*[2] (2a)] [1980s+] (*US campus*) a male with little personality or assertiveness. ❑ **wimp-guts** *n.* [1980s+] a coward, a weakling.

IN PHRASES

❑ **wimp out** *v.* [1960s+] (*orig. US*) to act in a cowardly manner, to let someone down, to fail to live up to a commitment.

wimp *n.*[2] [note 1910s Oxford University sl. *go wimping*, for a male undergraduate to go out looking for women] [1920s–40s] a woman.

wimp *adj.* [WIMP *n.*[1] (2)] [1980s] unimportant, insignificant, irrelevant.

wimpette *n.* [WIMP *n.*[1] (2) + fem. sfx *-ette*] [1980s] an insignificant, cowardly female.

wimpish *adj. see under* WIMP *n.*[1].

wimpo *n.* (*also* **wimpoid**) [WIMP *n.*[1] (2)+ -O *sfx* (1)/*-oid*] [1980s+] a weakling, an ineffective person.

wimpy *adj.* [WIMP *n.*[1] (2)] [1960s+] (*orig. US*) weak, ineffective, cowardly.

win *n.* (*also* **winn, wyn**) [origin unknown, but Vaux suggests, without further explanation, an abbr. of *Winchester*; Ribton-Turner, *A History of Vagrants* (1887), suggests synon. Erse *pinghin*, Manx *ping*] [mid-16C–mid-19C] a penny.

win *v.* [euph.] [late 17C–1940s] to steal.

SE in slang uses

IN PHRASES

❑ **win a pair of gloves** *v.* [the woman who does so was trad. rewarded with a pair of gloves] [late 18C–early 19C] to kiss a sleeping man. ❑ **win on** *v.* [1940s+] (*Aus.*) to seduce a woman. ❑ **win the shine-rag** *v.* (*also* **win the shiny rag**) [? one is thus reduced to cleaning shoes for a living] [mid–late 19C] to lose one's money by gambling.

Winchcombe Carson *n.* [rhy. sl.] [20C+] (*Aus.*) a parson.

winchell *n.* (*also* **willing winchell, winning winchell**) [gossip columnist Walter *Winchell* (1897–1972)] [1930s–40s] **1** (*US Und.*) a confidence trickster's victim, a sucker [? the image of the gossipy writer as 'swallowing' any story]. **2** a generic term for a gossip columnist.

winchester *n.* [WIN *n.*] [early 19C] a penny.

Winchester goose *n.* (*also* **goose, Winchester pigeon**) [the popular brothels of Southwark came under the jurisdiction of the Bishop of *Winchester*; thus 17 pvb referring to a well-known whore: 'No Goose bit so sore as Bess Broughton's'] [mid-16C–17C] venereal disease.

wind *n.*[1] [it catches one's breath] [early–mid-18C] strong liquor, esp. gin.

wind *n.*[2] [SE *wind*, the breath of life] **1** [early 19C] life; thus (*UK Und.*) *lagged for one's wind*, transported for one's natural life. **2** [mid-19C] (*UK Und.*) courage.

SE in slang uses

IN COMPOUNDS

❑ **windbag(s)** *see* separate entries. ❑ **wind-cutter** *n.* [its shape] [19C] a cocked hat. ❑ **wind instrument** *n.* [SE *break wind*] [early 17C] the anus. ❑ **windmill** *see* separate entries. ❑ **wind-pies** *n.* (*also* **wind-pies and air sausages, ...nutten-chops, wind-sandwich and breeze-pie**) [20C+] (*W.I., Bdos/Trin.*) no food, nothing to eat. ❑ **wind pudding** *n. see* AIR PUDDING *under* AIR *n.* ❑ **windpumps** *n. see* WINDBAGS *n.* ❑ **wind-settled** *adj. see* SETTLED *adj.* ❑ **windsheet** *n.* [1970s+] (*US black*) a thin overcoat. ❑ **windshield** *n.* [1910s] (*US*) a table napkin. ❑ **wind-stopper** *n.* [mid–late 19C] a garrotter. ❑ **wind-sucker** *n.* **1** [mid-19C] a worn-out horse, fit only for slaughter [its heavy breathing]. **2** [1920s] (*US*) a braggart [the expulsion of *wind*, i.e. breath]. ❑ **wind tormentors** *n.* (*also* **wind-teasers**) [1900s–20s] extremely long sideburns, eg. the *paies* as worn by an orthodox Jew, occas. also other facial hair. ❑ **wind vertical** *n. see* DRAFT UP *n.*

IN PHRASES

❑ **get in the wind** *v.* [1950s–70s] (*orig. US black*) **1** to leave, to depart quickly. **2** as imper., go away! ❑ **get the wind up** *v.* (*also* **get wind up, get the breeze up, have the..., have the wind up**) [abbr. *get the wind up one's trousers*] **1** [mid-19C; 1910s+] to become nervous. **2** [1910s] to make others nervous. ❑ **give someone the wind** *v.* [1930s] to get rid of someone. ❑ **have wind in one's jaws** *v.* [1950s–70s] (*US black*) to be extremely annoyed. ❑ **in the wind** [1970s+] (*orig. US prison*) **1** freed from prison; absenting oneself. **2** of money, being used for a transaction, rather than held in a wallet, bank etc. ❑ **I'm in the wind** [1970s] goodbye. ❑ **put it in the wind** *v.* [1970s+] (*US black*) to leave. ❑ **put the wind up** *v.* (*also* **poke the wind up**) **1** [1910s+] to worry, to frighten; thus *wind-up*, a state of worry. **2** [1970s+] become scared.

wind *v.* [SE *wind*, to writhe, to wriggle] [late 18C+] (*W.I.*) of a woman, to move in a provocative manner, with much swishing of the hips.

SE in slang uses

IN PHRASES

❑ **wind one's ball of yarn** *v.* (*also* **ravel up one's ball of yarn**) [1930s–50s] (*US*) of a man, to have sexual intercourse. ❑ **wind one's clock** *v.* [1970s] (*US*) of a woman, to be excited sexually, to have sexual intercourse. ❑ **wind someone's cotton** *v.* [mid-19C–1900s] to cause someone trouble, to create difficulties for someone. ❑ **wind the horn** *v.* [17C] to break wind. ❑ **wind up the clock** *v.* [based on a mildly coarse scene in Laurence Sterne's novel *Tristram Shandy* (1759–67)] [late 18C] to have sexual intercourse.

wind and kite *n.* [rhy. sl.] [2000s] a website.

wind and rain *n.* [rhy. sl.] (*Aus.*) **1** [1960s+] a train. **2** [1980s] an airplane.

windbag *n.* **1** [mid-19C+] a braggart, a boaster, a 'loudmouth'; thus v. *windbag*, to boast. **2** [1930s] (*UK Und.*) a confidence trick, based on selling envelopes that are apparently filled with valuables; in the event they contain only rubbish.

windbags *n.* (*also* **wind-pumps**) [their role in one's body] [mid-18C; 1900s–40s] (*US black*) the lungs.

wind do twirl *n.* [rhy. sl. = girl] [mid-19C] a woman.

winded-settled *adj. see* SETTLED *adj.*

winder *n.*[1] [WIND *n.*[2] (1)] [early–mid-19C] a sentence of transportation for life.

winder *n.*[2] [SE *wind*, to deprive of breath, usu. through a blow] [mid-19C] something so astounding that it 'takes one's breath away'.

windgat *n.* [SE *wind* + Afk. *gat*; lit. 'windy-arse'] [1980s+] (*S.Afr.*) a braggart, a boaster, a 'blowhard'.

windgat *adj.* [WINDGAT *n.*] [1980s+] (*S.Afr.*) cocky, self-opinionated.

windgat *v.* [WINDGAT *n.*] [1990s+] (*S.Afr.*) to brag, to boast.

windie *n.* [abbr.] [1980s+] (*N.Z.*) a *wind*-surfer.

Windies *n.* [elision] [1960s+] (*orig. Aus.*) the *West Indies* cricket team; thus *Windie*, a member of the team.

winding boy *n.* (*also* **winding ball**) [he can 'wind up' his sexual 'machinery'] [1930s–40s] (*US black*) a sexual athlete.

windjammer *n.*[1] [SE *wind*, i.e. 'hot air' + *jam*, to force; note late 19C US army *windjammer*, a trumpeter] [late 19C–1950s] (*orig. US*) a talkative, loquacious person, thus a liar; thus *windjamming*, loquacity.

windjammer *n.*[2] [rhy. sl.] [20C+] (*Aus.*) a hammer.

windjammer *n.*[3] [play on SE *jam*, to force + (the source of) *wind*, i.e. the anus] [1980s+] (*Aus.*) a male homosexual.

windmill *n.* [SE *wind* + *mill*, i.e. the unpleasant odours] [early 19C] the anus; thus *she has no fortune but her mills*, i.e. the WINDMILL *n.* and *WATERMILL under* WATER *n.*[1].

SE in slang uses

IN PHRASES

❑ **have windmills in the head** *v.* [Don Quixote's 'tilting at windmills'] [17C–early 19C] to entertain crazy notions, to fantasize.

windmill cocktail *n.* [the stream that runs by a mill] [20C+] (*US*) **1** rainwater. **2** glass of water.

window *n.* (*also* **pane of glass, windowpane**) **1** [late 19C–1920s] a monocle. **2** *see* WINDOWS *n.*[1].

SE in slang uses

IN COMPOUNDS

❑ **window-blind** *n.* [late 19C] a sanitary towel. ❑ **window climber** *n. see PORCH CLIMBER under* PORCH *n.* ❑ **window-licker** *n.* ['Comes from the 'special' people who ride on 'special' buses, sitting on the bus, face leant against the glass, tongue hanging out' *Dict. Playground Sl.*] [1990s+] (*UK juv.*) a mentally handicapped person. ❑ **window-man** *n.* [Afk. *vensterkies*, a little window or *vensterjies kyk*, to look at little windows, i.e. one who pretends to be gazing into shop windows when embarrassing friends appear] [1950s+] (*S.Afr.*) a coloured person who is trying to pass as white and thus cuts their darker friends or relatives when they see them in public. ❑ **window-peeper** *n.* [he 'peeps' at the number of windows a house has] [late 18C–early 19C] a collector of the window tax. ❑ **window shop** *v.* [play on SE] [1970s+] (*US campus*) to go out looking for desirable members of the opposite sex. ❑ **window warrior** *n.* [2000s] (*UK prison*) a prisoner who shouts from his cell window.

windowpane *n.*[1] (*also* **pane, window glass**) [a small square of gelatine impregnated with LSD] [1970s+] (*drugs*) a variety of LSD.

windowpane *n.*[2] *see* WINDOW *n.*

windows *n.*[1] **1** [mid-19C+] the eyes. **2** [1900s–10s] (*US*) spectacles.

windows *n.*[2] *see* SQUARE PAIR *under* SQUARE *adj.*

windsheet *n.* [1970s+] (*US black*) a thin overcoat.

windshield *n.* **1** [1910s] (*US*) a table napkin. **2** [1970s+] (*US black*) a thin overcoat.

windsor castle *n.* [rhy. sl. = ARSEHOLE *n.*] [20C+] the anus.

Windsor Group hotel *n.* [play on Windsor, the surname of the Royal Family, and the legal phr. 'detained at Her Majesty's Pleasure'] [1990s+] a prison.

Windtown *n. see* WINDY CITY *n.* (1).

wind-trap *n.* [rhy. sl.] [20C+] a flap, esp. of hair.

wind-up *n.*[1] [SE *wind up*/WIND UP *v.*] **1** [early 19C+] conclusion, end; death. **2** [1930s] (*US*) promotion, praise. **3** [1940s] (*US*) a fight. **4** [1980s+] a practical joke. **5** [1980s+] a deliberate attempt to worry, to render unhappy. **6** [1980s+] a deliberate attempt to mislead.

IN COMPOUNDS

❑ **wind-up artist** *n.* (*also* **wind-up merchant**) [-ARTIST *sfx*/ MERCHANT *n.*] [1980s+] someone who specializes in teasing, poss. to the point of at least verbal retaliation.

IN PHRASES

❑ **in the wind** [1960s] in the end.

wind-up *n.*[2] [SE *wind* n.] [1910s–20s] anxiety, nerves.

wind up *v.* **1** in senses of SE *wind up*, i.e. the winding up of something that has been extended while in use. (**a**) [early 17C; 19C+] to end up, to find oneself somewhere. (**b**) [early 18C+] to bring to a conclusion. (**c**) [mid-19C+] to result; to come to a conclusion. **2** in senses of SE *wind up*, i.e. winding up a clock to 'make it go'. (**a**) [20C+] to cause someone to become annoyed. (**b**) [1960s+] to tease, to misinform, usu. maliciously.

Windville *n. see* WINDY CITY *n.* (1).

windward passage *n.* [late 18C] the anus.

IN PHRASES

❑ **navigator of the windward passage** *n.* [late 18C+] a sodomite, a male homosexual. ❑ **use the windward passage** *v.* (*also* **navigate the windward passage**) [late 18C–early 19C] to sodomize.

Windy, the *n. see* WINDY CITY *n.* (1).

windy *adj.*[1] [SE *wind*, i.e. 'hot air'] **1** [late 17C–19C] foolish. **2** [mid-19C+] conceited, boastful [prior use is SE].

IN COMPOUNDS

❑ **windy wallets** *n.* [i.e. a WINDBAG *n.*] [late 19C–1900s] a loquacious, talkative self-aggrandizing person.

windy *adj.*[2] [GET THE WIND UP *under* WIND *n.*[2]] [late 19C+] (*usu. juv.*) cowardly, scared.

Windy City *n.* [the climate; note B. Popik (American Dialect Society List 22/8/01): 'Troy was first known as the "windy city." Later, Siena, Italy, was called the "city of winds" (*Citta dei Venti*). In the early 1880s, the Chicago Tribune wanted to promote Chicago as a summer resort. An attraction was the cool breeze off the lake. By 1885, Chicago was the "city of winds" and "windy city."'] **1** [late 19C+] (*US*) (*also* **Town of the Wind, the Windy, Windtown, Windville**) Chicago, Illinois. **2** [1980s+] (*S.Afr.*) Port Elizabeth.

wine *n.*[1] [mid–late 19C] (*orig. university*) a party at which those assembled drink wine; thus *wine and dine*, to entertain others.

SE in slang uses

IN COMPOUNDS

❑ **wine bag** *n.* [late 19C] a drunkard who prefers wine to beer or spirits. ❑ **wine bum** *n.* [BUM *n.*[3] (1)] [1920s] (*US Und.*) a wine-drinking alcoholic. ❑ **wine-dot** *n.* [a pun on SE *Wyandotte*, a breed of medium-sized domestic fowls, orig. found in US] [1950s+] (*Aus.*) a drinker of cheap wine. ❑ **wine dump** *n.* [DUMP *n.*[3] (2)] [1920s] (*US Und.*) a cheap bar, frequented by wine-drinking alcoholics. ❑ **winegut** *n.* [1950s] (*US*) an alcoholic for whom wine is the intoxicant of choice. ❑ **winehead** *n.* [SE *wine* + -HEAD *sfx* (4)] [1950s+] (*US*) an alcoholic who opts for wine as their preferred intoxicant; also attrib.

wine *n.*[2] [? the turning of one into the other] [1930s–60s] (*US black*) money.

wine *n.*[3] (*also* **wining**) [W.I. pron. of SE *wind*; i.e. the partners would *wind* round each other] [1990s+] (*W.I.*) a form of highly erotic dancing, esp. as seen at carnivals; thus *wine*, to dance in this manner.

wine *v.* [WINE *n.*[1]] [19C] to give or attend a party where wine is drunk.

wined *adj.* [late 19C] (*Aus.*) drunk.

winey *adj.* [mid-19C–1910s] tipsy, slightly drunk.

wing *n.*[1] **1** [mid–late 18C] an oar; often as *pair of wings*. **2** [19C+] an arm. **3** [late 19C] (*UK prison*) a single leaf of rolling tobacco. **4** [1970s] (*US*) a car door.

SE in slang uses

IN PHRASES

❑ **wings over Sing-Sing** [? the result of statutory rape is that one will 'fly' into prison] [1940s] (*US black*) a girl who is under the age of consent, and with whom intercourse may lead to imprisonment for statutory rape.

wing *n.*[2] [WIN *n.*] [late 19C–1940s] (*Aus./Irish*) a pre-decimalization penny.

wing *n.*[3] *see* WING-DING *n.* (1).

wing *adj.* [mid-19C] (*UK Und.*) alert, knowing.

wing *v.* [lit. 'to hit in the SE *wing*'] **1** [late 18C+] to shoot but not kill; to wound. **2** [mid-19C+] to hit with a ball, or missile.

SE in slang uses

IN PHRASES

❑ **wing (it)** *v.* [one fig. 'takes wing'] **1** [late 19C+] to improvise, to ad lib, to play a situation by ear without practice or rehearsal. **2** [1900s–70s] to move fast, to 'fly'. ❑ **wing out** *v.* [1990s+] (*UK black*) to leave, to go away.

wing'd *adj. see* WINGED *adj.*[1].

wing-ding *n.* (*also* **whing-ding**) [redup. of WING *n.*[1] (2), i.e. the image of waving one's arms in a frenzy] **1** [1920s+] (*also* **wing**) a fit, esp. as suffered by a withdrawing narcotics user. **2** [1930s+] a fake fit, 'thrown' by a prisoner in the hope of convincing authorities that he should be placed in the more comfortable surroundings of a mental ward. **3** [1940s+] (*orig. US*) a boisterous, noisy party. **4** [1950s–60s] an outburst of emotion or temper. **5** [1950s+] a dramatic, noisy event. **6** [1960s] an unstable, crazy person. **7** [1960s+] a sexual encounter.

IN PHRASES

❑ **throw a wing-ding** *v.* [1930s–60s] **1** (*drugs*) to pretend to be suffering severe withdrawal pains in order to persuade a doctor to give one some heroin. **2** (*US prison*) to fake illness to gain leniency or to avoid a work detail.

wing-dinger *n.* [WING-DING *n.*] **1** [1930s] a withdrawing narcotics user who throws a fake fit, in order to convince a doctor of the need for a supply of drugs. **2** [1940s] a fake fit. **3** [1970s] an outburst of emotion.

wingdinging *adj.* [1960s] (*US black*) splendid.

wingdoodle *n.* **1** *see* WHANGDOODLE *n.*[1]. **2** *see* WHANGDOODLE *n.*[2].

winged *adj.*[1] (*also* **wing'd**) **1** [mid-19C] tipsy, slightly drunk [HIT UNDER THE WING *under* HIT *adj.*]. **2** [1950s–70s] (*US drugs*) addicted to cocaine [? play on FLY *v.* (3)].

winged *adj.*[2] [WING *v.* (1)] [mid-19C+] wounded.

winger *n.* [SE *wing*] [mid-19C] long, bushy sideburns growing beyond the edge of the chin.

wingers *n.* [mid-19C] long whiskers.

wingey *n. see* WINGY *n.*

winging *adj.* [1900s] **1** (*US drugs*) suffering from withdrawal of a narcotic drug. **2** anxious.

wingless wonder *n. see* CHINLESS WONDER *n.*

wingnut *n.*[1] [ext. of NUT *n.*[2] (1)] [1980s+] an eccentric, a fool; also as adj.

wingnut *n.*[2] [SE *wingnut*, i.e. the shape] [1990s+] (*UK juv.*) a person with large, protruding ears.

wings *n.* (*also* **whings**) [one becomes HIGH *adj.*[1] but also play on US Air Force/RAF jargon *get one's wings*, to be commissioned as a pilot] [1930s+] (*US drugs*) any powdered narcotic.

IN PHRASES

❑ **get one's wings** *v.* [1960s+] (*drugs*) to start using heroin. ❑ **give someone wings** *v.* [1960s+] (*drugs*) to inject someone or teach someone to inject heroin.

wing-wang *n.* **1** [1970s+] (*US gay*) the anus. **2** *see* WANG *n.*[2].

wingy *n.* (*also* **wingey**) [WING *n.*[1] (2)] [late 19C+] (*Aus./US*) the 'automatic' nickname of any one-armed man.

wining *n. see* WINE *n.*[3].

winji *adj.* [UK dial. *winge*, to shrivel, as in fruit that is drying out] [1940s+] (*W.I.*) sickly, frail, weak, puny.

wink *n.*[1] [? WIN *n.*: or resemblance to a *tiddlywink*] [1920s–60s] (*Aus.*) a sixpence.

wink *n.*[2] [the glans 'winks' from within the foreskin] [1980s+] (*US gay*) an uncircumcised penis.

wink *n.*[3]

IN PHRASES

❑ **catch some winks** *v. see* CATCH A FEW *Z's under* Z *n.*[1].

winker *n.* [its supposed resemblance to a vertical 'eye'] [1970s] the vagina.

winkers *n.* **1** [late 18C+] usu. of a horse, blinkers. **2** [early 19C; 20C+] (*Aus.*) spectacles. **3** [early 19C+] (*also* **winklers**) the eyes or eyelashes. **4** [1950s+] vehicle indicators.

IN PHRASES

❑ **put the winkers on** *v.* [SE *winker*, a horse's blinker] [mid-19C] to deceive, to hoodwink.

winker-stinker *n.* [the shape and the odour] [1960s+] (*US prison*) the anus.

winkie *n. see* WINKY *n.*

winkle *n.*[1] [late 19C+] (*usu. juv.*) the penis.

IN PHRASES

❑ **have (something) on the winkle** *v.* [1920s+] to be obsessed by something. ❑ **spit the winkle** *v.* [1980s+] (*Aus.*) to squirt water from one's anus (a surfer's 'party trick').

winkle *n.*[2] *see* WRINKLE *n.* (1).

winklebag *n.* (*also* **winkle**) [rhy. sl. = FAG *n.*[4] (2)] [1970s+] cigarette.

winkle-fishing *n.* [1910s–20s] picking one's nose.

winklepickers *n.* [orig. favoured by Teddy Boys in the 1950s, but latterly absorbed into the wide variety of teen fashions] [1960s+] highly pointed-toed boots or shoes.

winkler *n.* [SE *winkle out*] [1970s] one who assists in the eviction of tenants, usu. by means of threats and pressure.

winklers *n. see* WINKERS *n.* (3).

wink out *v.* [late 19C–1920s] (*US*) to die.

winks *n.* [abbr.] [mid-19C] periwinkles.

wink the other eye *v.* (*also* **wink the off eye**) [late 19C–1900s] to disregard and dismiss what has just been said.

winky *n.* (*also* **winkie**) [dimin. of WINKLE *n.*[1]] [late 19C+] a very small or a child's penis; thus excl. *my winky!*

winn *n. see* WIN *n.*

winner *n.* **1** [20C+] a person or project that is a potential success. **2** [1960s] (*US campus*) used ironically, a social outcast, i.e. a LOSER *n.* (1).

winner *adj.* [WINNER *n.* (1)] [1960s+] first-rate, excellent.

winners *n. see* WINNINGS *n.*

winnet *n. see* WINNIT *n.*

winnick *adj.* [the asylum at *Winnick*, Lancashire] [1910s] crazy, eccentric.

winnie *n.*[1] [the bear *Winnie*-the-Pooh who 'licks the honeypot', i.e. HONEYPOT *n.* (1)] [1990s+] a lesbian.

winnie *n.*[2] *see* WEENIE *n.*[1].

winnings *n.* (*also* **winners**) [WIN *v.*] [late 17C–early 19C] (*UK Und.*) booty, plunder; payment for criminal activity.

winning winchell *n. see* WINCHELL *n.*

winnit *n.* (*also* **winnet**) [ety. unknown] [1990s+] a piece of excrement adhering to the anal hairs.

winny-popper *n.* [WINKLE *n.*[1] + POP *v.*[1] (7a)] [1950s+] (*Can. juv.*) the penis.

wino *n.* [SE *wine* + -O *sfx* (1)] **1** [late 19C+] (*orig. US*) an alcoholic, usu. living in poverty; also attrib. **2** [2000s] (*US campus*) a wine connisseur.

Winona Ryder *n.* [rhy. sl.] [2000s] cider.

win or lose *n.* [rhy. sl. = BOOZE *n.* (1)] [20C+] alcohol, liquor.

win-out *n.* [late 19C–1900s] (*US*) a success, esp. against the odds; also attrib.

winry *n.* [1990s+] (*W.I.*) sexual prowess.

winter *adj.*

SE in slang uses

IN COMPOUNDS

❑ **winter bush** *n.* [BUSH *n.*[1] (2a)] [2000s] (*US black*) a pronounced growth of a woman's pubic hair; shaved in the summer it is allowed to grow in the winter. ❑ **winter cricket** *n.* [the 'sewing' motions of the insect's legs] [late 18C–early 19C] a tailor. ❑ **winter Friday** *n.* [20C+] (*Irish*) a chilly looking, impoverished individual. ❑ **winter-hedge** *n.* [the way a full clothes-horse 'hedges off' a portion of the room; summer washing is dried out of doors] [late 19C–1920s] a clothes-horse. ❑ **winter palace** *n.* [impoverished criminals or tramps deliberately have themselves jailed during the cold winter months] [late 19C] a prison. ❑ **winter rat** *n.* [1970s+] (*US*) an old car, driven in bad weather. ❑ **winter tread** *n.* [i.e. a winter tread tyre, thus play on TREAD *v.* (1)] [1990s+] (*Aus.*) a condom, a contraceptive sheath. ❑ **winter wear** *n. see* TURTLENECK (SWEATER) *n.*

wipe *n.* **1** [late 16C–early 17C] the act of drinking [? one 'wipes' the glass with one's lips]. **2** [late 16C+] (*UK Und.*) a blow, also in fig. use, a reflection, a pause for thought. **3** [18C+] a handkerchief; thus *the wipe lay*, stealing handkerchiefs. **4** [1900s–40s] (*US Und.*) a form of confidence trick based on persuading the victim that money can be raised to higher denomination; it is first secreted in a handkerchief. **5** *see* ASS-WIPE *n.*

IN COMPOUNDS

❑ **wipe-drawer/-hauler** *n. see* WIPER-DRAWER *under* WIPER *n.* ❑ **wipe-prigging** [late 18C] (*UK Und.*) stealing handkerchiefs.

IN PHRASES

❑ **sleek wipe** *n.* [19C] a silk handkerchief.

wipe *v.* [SE *wipe out*] **1** [19C+] to attack, whether physically or verbally. **2** [1900s] (*Aus.*) to give in, to give up. **3** [1920s+] to destroy, defeat. **4** [1930s] (*Aus./N.Z.*) to refuse to grant a loan or any other form of gift, e.g. food for a beggar; to render bankrupt. **5** [1940s–60s] (*Aus./N.Z.*) to repudiate, to forget, to dismiss from one's mind. **6** [1940s+] (*also* **wipe out**) to murder. **7** [1980s] (*US*) to throw.

IN PHRASES

❑ **wipe down** *v.* **1** [mid-19C] to flatter, to pacify. **2** [1930s] (*Aus.*) in gambling, to win and take another person's money. **3** *see* WIPE OFF *v.* ❑ **wipe one's eye** *v.* [mid-19C] to take a drink, esp. to offer or to accept another drink. ❑ **wipe round** *v.* [late 19C] to hit, usu. in phr. *wipe one round the face/mouth/head.* ❑ **wipe someone's ass** *v.* [1970s] (*US*) to defeat comprehensively. ❑ **wipe someone's eye** *v.* [sporting use *wipe one's eye*, to shoot someone else's bird] **1** [mid-19C+] to get the better of, to defeat. **2** [1920s+] to discomfit, to 'give someone a black eye'. ❑ **wipe someone up** *v.* [1930s] (*UK Und.*) to be picked up or arrested by the police. ❑ **wipe the smile off someone's face** *v.* (*also* **wipe that smile off someone's face, wipe the look off one's face**) [1920s+] to disappoint, to render a formerly cheerful person unhappy; the converse phr. is *wipe the/that scowl...*

IN EXCLAMATIONS

❑ **wipe your chin!** (*also* **wipe your eye!**) [? thus removing the 'shit' they are talking] [1900s] (*Aus.*) an excl. used to upbraid one who is presumed to be lying.

wiped out *adj.* [SE *wipe out*, to erase] **1** [20C+] (*US*) financially ruined. **2** [1950s+] exhausted. **3** [1950s+] (*also* **wiped**) drunk, intoxicated by drugs.

wipe-off *n.* [WIPE *v.* (5)] [1930s+] (*Aus.*) a rejection, a dismissal.

wipe off *v.* (*also* **wipe down**) **1** [mid-19C+] to get rid of, to remove [*wipe off*, to erase]. **2** [1920s+] (*Aus.*) to bid a last farewell, esp. to a place [WIPE *v.* (5)].

wipe-out *n.* [orig. ski/surf jargon *wipe-out*, a spectacular fall] **1** [1960s+] (*US*) a major failure; a crushing defeat, annihilation. **2** [1970s] (*US*) an overwhelming experience, esp. as the result of an excess of drugs and/or drink. **3** [1980s] (*US*) a killing. **4** [1990s+] (*Aus.*) a general term of abuse.

wipe-out *adj.* [1970s] (*US*) exhausting, physically draining.

wipe out *v.* **1** [mid-19C+] to beat up. **2** [mid-19C+] to kill. **3** [mid-19C+] to ruin financially. **4** [20C+] (*US*) to defeat, to destroy. **5** [1960s] (*US campus*) to destroy something, e.g. an automobile; to harm oneself. **6** [1960s] to incapacitate. **7** [1960s+] to astonish. **8** [1960s+] (*US campus*) to fail. **9** [2000s] to exhaust one's stocks, supplies. **10** *see* WIPE *v.* (6).

IN PHRASES

❑ **wipe oneself out** *v.* [20C+] to commit suicide.

wiper *n.* **1** [17C–19C] a handkerchief. **2** [late 19C] a severe physical blow, a harsh verbal attack, anything that will overwhelm an opponent. **3** [late 19C] an impudent boy. **4** [late 19C] a thug, a person who delivers physical blows. **5** [1930s+] (*US Und.*) a hired killer.

IN COMPOUNDS

❑ **wiper-drawer** *n.* (*also* **wipe-drawer, wipe-hauler, wiper**) [late 17C–18C] (*UK Und.*) a stealer of handkerchiefs; thus *wipe-drawing, wipe-hauling*.

IN PHRASES

❑ **draw a wiper** *v.* (*also* **nap the wiper, nim a wiper**) (*UK Und.*) to steal a pocket handkerchief.

wipe the floor (with) *v.* (*also* **clean the floor with, dust..., ... the furniture with, wipe the earth with, ...ground with, ...street with, ...dirt**) [note synon. RN *wipe the deck with*] [late 19C+] to beat decisively, to thrash.

wire *n.*[1] **1** [mid-19C] (*US campus*) a trick, a hoax, a strategem. **2** [mid-19C–1960s] a telegram [SE in 20C+]. **3** [20C+] a private warning; thus *get/give the wire*, get/give a warning or message [note Papua New Guinea Tok Pisin *wialis*, a gossip, a matchmaker a psychic, f. SE *wireless*]. **4** [1910s] (*US tramp*) articles constructed of stolen telegraph wire and sold in the street. **5** [1920s–50s] (*US Und.*) 'a racing swindle in which the con men convinced the victim that with the connivance of a corrupt Western Union official they could delay the race results long enough for him to place a bet after the race had been run, but before the bookmakers received the results.' (Maurer, 1940). **6** [1920s+] (*US*) a telephone. **7** [1930s] (*US prison*) a guard who does favours for the inmates. **8** [1940s] (*Aus.*) a scolding, a reprimand. **9** [1940s+] (*US black*) the gossip circuit, the 'grapevine'; usu. in phr. *ON THE WIRE* below. **10** [1960s] (*US black*) a 'line' of talk. **11** [1960s+] any form of electronic eavesdropping device [abbr. SE *wire-tapping*]. **12** [1960s+] the penis. **13** [1990s+] (*US*) the Internet, connected by a modem. **14** [1990s+] (*drugs*) a vein used for the injection of drugs. **15** [2000s] (*US prison*) a message, a phonecall.

IN PHRASES

pertaining to information

❑ **get the wire** *v.* [1910s+] (*US*) to find out, to be informed. ❑ **have the wire on** *v.* [1960s] (*US*) to keep under surveillance. ❑ **hot wire** *n.* [1900s–50s] (*US prison*) information. ❑ **on the wire** (*also* **over the wire**) [1930s+] generally known, going the rounds of gossip and rumour. ❑ **pull wires** *v.* (*also* **pull a wire, pull the wires**) [19C+] to exert influence, esp. behind the scenes. ❑ **put it on the wire** *v.* [1960s+] (*US black*) to circulate gossip or other information. ❑ **straight wire** *n.* [STRAIGHT *adj.*[1] (2)] [late 19C+] (*Aus./N.Z.*) the honest truth; also used without an article to emphasize the truth of an assertion.

pertaining to masturbation

❑ **pull one's wire** *v.* **1** [1940s+] (*also* **pull one's wood**) to masturbate. **2** [1950s+] (*Irish*) to provoke, to fool someone. ❑ **twang one's wire** *v.* (*also* **twang the wire**) [1950s+] to masturbate.

SE in slang uses

IN COMPOUNDS

❑ **wire-draw** *n.* [SE *wire-draw*, to draw out, to persuade by subtle arguing] [late 16C–18C] (*UK Und.*) a trick that ensnares a victim; thus *wire-drawn*, tricked in this way; *wiredrawer*, a trickster. ❑ **wire-inspector** *n.* [i.e. SE *wire*, fencing] [1900s–30s] (*Aus.*) a boundary rider. ❑ **wire parlour** *n.* [1910s] (*US Und.*) an execution chamber, using the electric chair. ❑ **wire-tapper** *n.* [late 19C–1930s] (*US*) a confidence trickster who claims that he can intercept the wire bringing racecourse results and thus cheat the bookmakers; thus *wire-tapping*, the swindle itelf.

IN PHRASES

❑ **down to the wire** [horseracing imagery] [20C+] approaching the crux, the climax; to the very limit. ❑ **get under the wire** *v.* [1940s] (*US black*) to obtain something, e.g. money. ❑ **go off the wire** *v.* [1990s+] (*US*) to lose control. ❑ **under the wire** [horse-racing imagery] [1930s+] at the very last minute.

wire *n.*[2] [the SE *wire* used as an adjunct to the fingers] [mid-19C–1960s] the pickpocket who actively steals from his victim, rather than the various accomplices on his team; thus as *v.*, to pickpocket.

IN PHRASES

❑ **on the wire** [1940s–60s] (*US Und.*) working as a pickpocket. ❑ **sling the wire** *v.* [mid-19C] (*UK Und.*) to pickpocket.

wire *v.* **1** [mid-19C+] to send a telegram. **2** [mid-19C+] to trick, to swindle. **3** [late 19C] (*Aus.*) to hurry. **4** [1900s] (*Aus.*) to suggest, to instruct. **5** [1950s+] (*US*) to place an eavesdropping device in a room, 'to bug', or to conceal on one's person [WIRE *n.*[1] (11)]. **6** [1980s] (*US*) to stimulate, to excite. **7** *see* HOT-WIRE *v.* (1).

IN PHRASES

❑ **wire up** *v.* [1970s+] (*US black*) to explain the current situation, to tell what has been or is happening.

wire chair *n. see* CHAIR, THE *n.*

wired *adj.*[1] (*also* **wired up**) [SE *wired*, carrying electricity] **1** [late 19C] (*US*) irritated, provoked. **2** [1960s+] (*orig. US drugs*) addicted to heroin. **3** [1960s+] using cocaine or some form of amphetamines or caffeine. **4** [1960s+] tense, nervous, irritable, full of 'electricity'. **5** [1960s+] in fig. use, addicted to a person, an activity. **6** [1970s] (*US prison*) having a homosexual lifestyle prior to entering prison. **7** [1970s] (*US gay*) sexually excited. **8** [1970s+] drunk. **9** [1970s+] highly stimulated, excited, eager. **10** [1980s+] crazy. **11** [1980s+] affected by cannabis.

IN PHRASES

❑ **wired for sound** *adj.* [1990s+] (*drugs*) experiencing the most extreme effects of cocaine or amphetamines. ❑ **wired in** *adj.* [1930s+] (*US*) **1** well connected in political or business circles. **2** in control, secure and assured. ❑ **wired into** *adj.* [SE *wired together*] [1960s+] (*US*) intimately involved in or with. ❑ **wired up to the moon** *adj.* [1990s+] (*Irish*) crazy.

wired *adj.*[2] [SE *wired together*] **1** [1940s+] (*gambling*) of cards, back to back. **2** [1950s+] satisfactory, ideal, as one desires.

wire in *v.* (*also* **wire into**) [fig. use of SE *wire*, to join together with wires] **1** [mid–late 19C] to set about one's work enthusiastically, to set about a meal and start eating heartily; to attack physically. **2** [late 19C] to criticize.

IN PHRASES

❑ **wire in and get one's name up** *v.* [orig. used as an invitation to enter a boxing ring and prepare for a contest] [mid–late 19C] **1** to seduce. **2** to attempt success.

wireless *n.* [WIRE *n.*[1] (3) + pun on SE] [1920s–30s] a baseless rumour.

wire-puller *n.*[1] (*also* **wire-worker**) [PULL WIRES *under* WIRE *n.*[1]] [mid-19C+] a person who exerts influence or manipulates, esp. in politics.

wire-puller *n.*[2] [WIRE *n.*[1] (12) + SE *pull*] [late 19C+] a male masturbator.

wirer *n.* [WIRE *n.*[2]] [mid-19C] an expert pickpocket who uses a wire to remove objects from his victims.

IN PHRASES

▫ **fine wirer** *n.* (*also* **fine worker**) [mid-19C–1900s] the most skilful grade of pickpocket, esp. one who steals from women.

wires *n.* [1920s] the electric chair.

wire-worker *n. see* WIRE-PULLER *n.*[1].

wiring *n.* [WIRE *n.*[2]] [mid–late 19C] (*UK Und.*) working as a professional pickpocket.

Wisacres Hall *n.* [SE *wiseacre*, one who thinks himself, or wishes to be thought, wise; thus a sneer at the Society's intellectual membership] [mid-18C–mid-19C] Gresham College, London, esp. as home of the Royal Society.

wisdom-weed *n.* [SE *wisdom* + *weed*/WEED *n.*[1] (4)] [1950s+] (*US black/W.I.*) any herb that is seen as having the effect of making one wiser, esp. marijuana.

wise *adj.* **1** [late 19C+] (*orig. US*) shrewd, cunning, knowing, aware. **2** [late 19C+] stupid, foolish, in ironic use, i.e. one who believes themselves shrewd. **3** [1940s–60s] homosexually experienced.

IN COMPOUNDS

▫ **wise-aleck** *n. see* SMART ALECK *n.* ▫ **wise apple** *n. see* APPLE *n.*[1]. ▫ **wise-ass** *see* separate entries. ▫ **wise boy** *n. see* WISE GUY *n.* ▫ **wisecrack/cracker/cracking** *see* separate entries. ▫ **wiseguy** *see* separate entries. ▫ **wise-head** *n.* **1** [mid-19C] an ironic ref. to one who sees themselves as clever. **2** [1910s–30s] (*Aus./US*) a clever, cunning person. ▫ **wise hombre** *n.* [HOMBRE *n.* (1)] [20C+] (*US*) a shrewd, clever person. ▫ **wise Injun** *n.* [INJUN *n.*] [1910s] (*US*) an expert. ▫ **wise money** *n.* (*also* **smart money**) [1930s–40s] (*US*) in betting, the opinion of the experienced bettor. ▫ **wisemouth** *n.* [1970s+] (*US*) cruel teasing, impudence; also as adj. ▫ **wise punk** *n. see* WISE GUY *n.* ▫ **wise puss** *n. see* WISE-ASS *n.*

IN PHRASES

▫ **blow wise** *v.* [BLOW *v.*[1]] [late 19C+] (*US*) **1** to see one's own interest. **2** to understand, to work out a deception. ▫ **catch wise** *v.* [1930s–70s] (*US*) to understand, to grasp. ▫ **get wise (to)** *v.* (*also* **get wise on**) [late 19C+] (*orig. US*) **1** to become aware, to learn about. **2** to come to one's senses. ▫ **get wise (with)** *v.* [1930s+] **1** (*also* **act wise**) to act in a cheeky, 'smart' manner. **2** to make a sexual pass (at someone). ▫ **not so wise** [1910s] not very well. ▫ **put wise** *v.* [20C+] (*orig. US*) **1** to explain, to tell about. **2** to pass on information. ▫ **wise off** *v.* [note also WISECRACK *v.*] [1950s+] (*US*) **1** to make jokes at someone's expense. **2** to boast, to brag. ▫ **wise to** [late 19C+] aware of what is going on, 'in the know'.

wise *v.* **1** [1970s] (*US black*) to agree with; to understand. **2** *see* WISE UP *v.*

wise *adv.* [WISE *adj.* (1)] [1940s+] (*US*) in a sophisticated manner.

-wise *sfx* (*orig. US*) **1** [1930s+] aware of, in the know. **2** [1940s+] with reference to, as regards, e.g. *job-wise, success-wise.*

wise-ass *n.* (*also* **wise-arse, wisepuss**) [WISE *adj.* (2) + -ASS *sfx*] [1950s+] (*US*) one who sees themselves as cleverer than they really are.

wise-ass *adj.* (*also* **wise-assed**) [WISE-ASS *n.*] [1950s+] self-opinionated, self-aggrandizing.

wise-ass *v.* [WISE-ASS *n.*] [1950s+] (*US*) to act in a 'smart' manner.

wisecrack *n.* (*also* **wise crack, wisecracker**) [WISE *adj.* (1) + CRACK *n.*[1] (1)] [1910s+] (*orig. US*) a witty retort, a smart comment, a joke at someone else's expense.

wisecrack *v.* [WISECRACK *n.*] [1910s+] (*orig. US*) to make a witty retort or a smart comment, to make a joke at someone else's expense.

wisecracker *n.* [WISECRACK *v.*] [1920s+] a person who makes a witty retort or smart comment, or a joke at someone else's expense.

wisecracking *adj.* [WISECRACK *v.*] [1910s+] describing a person who makes smart retorts.

wised(-up) *adj.* [WISE *adj.* (1)/WISE UP *v.*] [20C+] (*US*) aware, knowledgeable.

wise guy *n.* (*also* **smart guy, wise boy, wise punk**) [WISE *adj.* (1) + GUY *n.*[2] (1)] **1** [late 19C+] (*gambling*) gamblers who are first to favour a particular line of betting, which influences the changing odds. **2** [late 19C+] (*US*) a shrewd person. **3** [20C+] (*US*) anyone who thinks they are particularly knowing or clever; a general derog. description: the implication being that the person is too clever for their own good. **4** [1910s] (*US*) a criminal. **5** [1940s+] (*US*) as a form of personal address. **6** [1970s+] (*orig. US*) a member of an organized crime syndicate, usu. the US Mafia.

wise-guy *adj.* (*also* **smart-guy**) [WISE GUY *n.*] **1** [1920s+] (*US*) clever in a showy kind of way. **2** [1950s+] (*US*) related to the US Mafia or its culture and lifestyle.

wise monkey *n.* [rhy. sl. = FLUNKY *n.*[3]] [20C+] a condom.

wisenheimer *n.* (*also* **weisenheimer, wisenstein**) [WISE *adj.* (1) + Ger./Jewish sfx *-heimer*, usu. part of a surname] [20C+] a know-it-all, a self-appointed smart fellow.

wise-up *n.* [1980s] (*US*) understanding, comprehension.

wise up *v.* (*also* **wake, wake up, wise**) [WISE *adj.* (1)] [late 19C+] (*orig. US*) **1** to inform, to explain to someone. **2** to (begin to) understand, appreciate; also to start acting sensibly, to cease being stupid; often as imper. *wise up.*

wisey *n.* [1940s] (*US*) a WISE GUY *n.* (3).

wisey warcy *adv. see* VICEY-VERSEY *adv.*

wishbone *n.* [SE *wish* (for sex) + BONE *n.*[1] (1)] [1970s] the penis.

wish book *n.* [1920s+] (*Can./US*) a mail-order catalogue.

wish to hell *v.* (*also* **hope to hell, wish to Christ, wish to hell and little centipedes, wish to jiminy, wish to Pete**) [late 19C+] (*orig. US*) to desire intensely.

wisty-castor *n.* (*also* **wistycastor**) [var. on WHISTER-CLISTER *n.*] [early 19C] a punch, a blow.

witboernaaier *n.* [lit. 'white Afrikaaner fucker', i.e. FUCKER *n.* (3)] [2000s] (*S.Afr.*) a white racist Afrikaner.

witch *n.* **1** [1940s–50s] a girlfriend. **2** [1950s] an ugly woman. **3** [1950s–70s] (*US black*) a prostitute.

witch, the *n.* [? it 'bewitches' the user] [1940s–60s] (*drugs*) heroin, cocaine, morphine.

witcher *adj.* (*also* **wicher**) [? WHITE *adj.* (1)+ SE *silver*] [late 17C–early 19C] (*UK Und.*) silver.

IN COMPOUNDS

▫ **witcher(-bubber)** *n.* (*also* **witcher-cheat**) [BUBBER *n.*[1] (2)] [late 17C–early 19C] (*UK Und.*) a silver bowl. ▫ **witcher-cully** *n.* [CULLY *n.*[1] (4)] [mid-17C–early 19C] (*UK Und.*) a silversmith. ▫ **witcher-tilter** *n.* [TILTER *n.*] [late 17C–early 19C] (*UK Und.*) a silver-hilted sword.

witchetty grub *n.* [rhy. sl.] [20C+] (*Aus.*) a cub scout.

witch-hazel *n.* [ext. of WITCH, THE *n.*+ ref. to the light brown colour of much heroin; note HAZEL *n.*[1]] [1930s–50s] (*drugs*) heroin.

witgat *n.* [1970s+] (*S.Afr.*) an abusive term for a white person; lit. 'white-arse'.

with/without *prep.* [mid-19C] of a mix of warmed or chilled alcohol, i.e. *with/without sugar.*

within (a) cooee of *phr.* [Abor. *cooee*, a bush call later adopted by the colonists and thence by UK English-speakers] [late 19C+] (*Aus./N.Z.*) within hailing distance, within easy reach, near; thus *out of cooee*, at a distance.

within an ass's roar (of) *phr.* (*also* **within a bull's roar, within the bawl of an ass**) [20C+] (*Irish*) **1** very near. **2** a short time.

with it *adj.* [esp. popular during the Beatnik era of the 1950s + 'Swinging London' period of the 1960s] **1** [1940s+] *au fait*, aware, knowledgeable, fashionable, up-to-date; thus *get with* *it*, to get oneself informed or up-to-date. **2** [1960s] (*US gay*) as interj., yes.

without dip or derry *phr. see under* DERRY *n.*[1].

with the birdies *adj.* [1990s+] (*Aus.*) eccentric, insane.

with tits on *phr. see* WITH BELLS ON *under* BELL *n.*[1].

wit ou *n.* (*also* **witman**) [Afk. *wit*, white + OU *n.*] [1970s+] (*S.Afr. Indian*) a white person.

witpyp *v.* [Afk. 'white pipe'; the capsules of Mandrax are white] [1960s+] (*S.Afr.*) to smoke a mixture of marijuana and powdered methaqualone (Mandrax).

Wits *n.* [abbr.] [1990s+] (*S.Afr.*) Witwatersrand University.

witter *v.* [? Scot. *whitter*, to twitter] [1950s+] to chatter on pointlessly.

wittol *n.* (*also* **wittal**) [SE *woodwale*, a bird that is often the target of a cuckoo, who lays its egg in the woodwale's nest] [late 16C–early 18C] a complaisant husband who makes no effort to discourage his wife's adventuring; thus adj. *wittoly*.

wi-wi *n. see* WEE-WEE *n.*[1].

wix *adj.* [WICKED *adj.* (2)] [2000s] (*UK teen*) good, excellent.

wiz *n.*[1] [SE *whiz*, to move fast] [1940s] (*US drugs*) cocaine.

wiz *n.*[2] **1** *see* WHIZ *n.*[3]. **2** *see* WHIZ *n.*[4].

wizard *adj.* [despite US origin, the main use has been UK society, esp. by those who attended prep schools] [1920s+] (*orig. US*) a general term of approval, excellent, wonderful.

wizz *see also under* WHIZZ.

wizzy *adj.* [1900s] (*US*) strange, bizarre.

wizzy-wizzy *v.* (*also* **whizzy-whizzy**) [SE *whisper*] [20C+] (*W.I., Bdos*) to whisper together.

wob *n.* [abbr. WOBBLY *n.*[1]] [1910s–30s] (*US*) the trade union Industrial Workers of the World or IWW, their collective members.

woball *n. see* WHOABALL *n.*

wobbegong *n.* [? Abor. *wobbegong*, a carpet-shark + play on SE *wobegone*] [1920s+] (*Aus.*) anything excellent or outstanding.

wobble *n.* **1** [20C+] (*Irish*) shaving lather [the stirring of the lather before its use]. **2** [1980s+] (*US drugs*) (*also* **wobble-weed**) phencyclidine [its effects].

IN COMPOUNDS

❑ **wobble-shop** *n.* [the effects of the liquor one buys there] [mid-19C] an unlicensed liquor store.

wobbler *n.*[1] *see* FOOT-WABBLER *under* FOOT *n.*

wobbler *n.*[2] *see* WABBLER *n.*

wobbler *n.*[3] *see* WOBBLY *n.*[2].

wobblers *n.* **1** [late 19C] eggs. **2** [1980s] pills, usu. amphetamine. **3** [1990s+] the female breasts.

wobble-weed *n. see* WOBBLE *n.* (2).

wobbly *n.*[1] [1910s+] (*US*) a member of the trade union Industrial Workers of the World or IWW.

wobbly *n.*[2] (*also* **wobbler**) [1930s+] a fit of nerves, of panic, of bad temper; thus one who has such attacks.

IN PHRASES

❑ **chuck a wobbly** *v.* (*also* **chuck a wobbler**) [1960s+] (*Aus./N.Z.*) to tell a dubious story. ❑ **throw a wobbly** *v.* [1970s+] of people, to panic, to suffer a fit of nerves; also used fig. of things.

wobbly *adj.*[1] [WOBBLY *n.*[1]] [1910s+] (*US*) pertaining to the trade union Industrial Workers of the World.

wobbly *adj.*[2] (*also* **wabbly**) [1920s+] unlikely, 'shaky', e.g. of plans or prospects.

IN COMPOUNDS

❑ **wobbly eggs** *n.* [the oval shape + the effect on the user] [1990s+] Temazepam. ❑ **wobbly pop** *n.* [1990s+] (*US*) beer.

wodge *n. see* WADGE *n.*

woejus *adj. see* WOJUS *adj.*

woema *n.* [? Zulu *vuma*, to thrive] [1970s+] (*S.Afr.*) energy, power.

woes *adj.* [Du. *woest*, fierce] [1970s+] (*S.Afr., usu. juv.*) furious, ill-tempered.

woffle *v.* [? dial. *woffle*, to chew] **1** [early 19C] to eat. **2** *see* WAFFLE *v.*[1].

woffle dust *n.* [? nonce word] [20C+] (*Aus.*) a fig. term for luck, esp. if gambling when one *puts a bit of woffle dust* on the cards/dice.

wog *n.*[1] [ety. unknown; it appears to have been used in East End of London from c. 1910; suggestions include that of F.C. Bowen in *Sea Slang* (1929), who includes 'Wogs, lower class Babu shipping clerks on the Indian coast', but provides no further detail. Popular belief has always chosen the acronym *w*esternized *o*riental *g*entleman or *w*ily *o*riental *g*entleman, while Partridge opts for abbr. of SE *golliwog*, and certainly this once-popular doll, with its caricatured 'black' features, has long since been marginalized as politically incorrect] **1** [1910s+] (*also* **woggy, woggo**) a derog. term for any non-white, esp. an Indian or Pakistani and latterly, in the UK, Bangladeshi. **2** [1920s+] (*Aus. juv.*) a very young child. **3** [1940s+] any foreigner, esp. in the phr. *the wogs begin at Calais*. **4** [1960s] (*N.Z.*) a Maori. **5** [1960s+] a black person. **6** [1970s] (*US*) as *white wog*, an Irishman. **7** [1970s+] an Indian meal, an Indian restaurant. **8** [1980s+] (*Aus.*) a Mediterranean immigrant, e.g. a Greek or Yugoslav.

DERIVATIVES

❑ **woggish** *adj.* [2000s] (*Aus.*) characteristic of immigrants.

IN COMPOUNDS

❑ **wog-bashing** *n.* [1980s+] the unprovoked, racist assault on those of a different colour. ❑ **wog chariot** *n.* [1980s+] (*Aus.*) a vehicle seen as esp. popular among immigrants. ❑ **wogland** *n.* [2000s] any country whose natives are seen to qualify as 'wogs', e.g. India, Pakistan.

IN PHRASES

❑ **wog it** *v.* [1940s] of a westerner, to adopt the lifestyle of a poor Asian worker; synon. with 'go native'.

wog *n.*[2] [1920s+] (*Aus.*) **1** a germ or parasite, an insect [ety. unknown; ? link to dial. *wog*, to twitch, to move]. **2** an illness, usu. influenza; a disease, a 'bug' [fig. use of sense 1]. **3** a tiny fragment.

wog *adj.* (*also* **woggy**) [WOG *n.*[1] (1)] [1940s+] pertaining to an Indian, Arab, etc; extended to anyone with a dark complexion; of food, anything foreign.

IN COMPOUNDS

❑ **wog box** *n.* [1980s+] a large, portable stereo tape-recorder-cum-radio, particularly beloved of ghetto youths. ❑ **wog gut** *n.* [1940s] diarrhoea or any stomach upset that assails a tourist in any exotic part of the world.

wog *v.* [1950s] (*Aus.*) of a white male, to have sexual intercourse with a black woman.

woggie *adj.* [WOG *n.*[1] (1)] [1940s+] foreign, esp. Asian.

woggo *n. see* WOG *n.*[1] (1).

woggy *n. see* WOG *n.*[1] (1).

woggy *adj.* **1** [1960s+] (*Aus.*) pertaining to immigrants. **2** *see* WOG *adj.* (1).

wojus *adj.* (*also* **woejus, wojious**) [SE *woeful* + *atrocious*] [1980s+] (*Irish*) bad, terrible.

wok *v.* [? WHACK IT IN *under* WHACK *v.*[1]] [1990s+] (*UK black/teen*) to have sexual intercourse; thus as n., sexual intercourse.

DERIVATIVES

❑ **wokable** *adj.* [2000s] sexy, lit. 'fuckable'.

wolf *n.* **1** [mid-19C+] a male overtly pursuing women for sex. **2** [1910s] (*US*) an obsessive, one who is very keen. **3** [1910s] (*US Und.*) a tramp who rides on passenger trains by virtue of strength rather than cunning. **4** [1910s+] (*US gay*) a predatory male or female homosexual; esp. in context of prison. **5** [1920s+] (*US*) an older, usu. homosexual, tramp who travels with a young boy. **6** [1930s] (*US Und.*) a criminal who works alone [SE *lone wolf*]. **7** [1950s+] (*W.I. Rasta*) one who is not a Rastafarian but wears their hair in dreadlocks. **8** [1970s] (*drugs*) phencyclidine [its non-recreational use as an animal tranquillizer]. **9** [1970s] (*US prison*) a 15-year sentence. **10** [1990s+] a professional poker player.

IN COMPOUNDS

❑ **wolf-call** *v.* [1940s+] to whistle at a passing woman in an admiring, lustful way; also as n. ❑ **wolf's handshake** *n.* [1970s] (*US gay/prison*) the tweaking of a new inmate's cheek by a veteran homosexual.

SE in slang uses

IN COMPOUNDS

❑ **wolf-trap** *n.* (*also* **trap**) [mid–late 19C] (*US*) a cheap, poss. crooked casino.

IN PHRASES

❑ **wolf in the breast** *n.* [mid-18C–19C] (*UK Und.*) a trick practised by strolling beggar women, who ask for alms to obtain medicine to deal with a gnawing pain in their breast.

wolf *v.*[1] [? SE *woof*/WOOF *v.*[1]] **1** [1910s] (*US*) to complain, to criticize. **2** [1960s+] (*US prison*) to banter.

wolf *v.*[2] [WOLF *n.* (1)] **1** [1920s–40s] (*US*) to pursue women. **2** *see* WOLF-WHISTLE *v.*

wolfess *n.* [WOLF *n.* (1) + sfx *-ess*] [1940s+] a sexually aggressive woman, both hetero- and homosexual.

Wolfe (Tone) *n.* [rhy. sl.; ult. *Wolfe Tone* (1763–1798), leading founder of Irish republicanism] [2000s] (*Irish*) a telephone.

wolfies *n. see* ROOFIE *n.*[2].

wolfing *n.* (*also* **wolfing it**) [WOOF *v.*[1]] [1920s+] (*US black*) talking grandiloquently, but not always backing up one's words with action.

wolf pack *n.* [1950s+] (*US*) a juvenile or prison gang.

wolf pack *v.* **1** [1960s] (*US black/gang*) to fight. **2** *see* RAT PACK *v.*

wolf-pussy *n.* [? SE *whiff* + PUSSY *n.* (1)] [1970s] (*US black*) unpleasant vaginal odours.

wolf ticket *n.* [WOOF *v.*[1]] [1970s+] (*US black*) a threat; an empty boast.

wolf-whistle *n.* [WOLF *n.* (1) + SE *whistle*] [1950s+] a two-note whistle aimed at a passing woman by an admiring, lustful man; or vice versa.

wolf-whistle *v.* (*also* **wolf**) [WOLF-WHISTLE *n.*] [1950s+] to whistle at a passing woman in an admiring, lustful way.

wollapalooza *n. see* LALLAPALOOSA *n.*

wollie *n.* (*also* **woola, woolah, woolas, woolie, woolies, wooly**) [1980s+] (*drugs*) a cigarette of crack or base cocaine, mixed with marijuana and wrapped in a cigar leaf.

wollied *adj.* [WALLY *n.*[2] (1); i.e. one is rendered stupid] [1980s] drunk.

wollies *n.* [? joc. excl. *oh olive!*] [late 19C] olives.

wollop *n. see* WALLOP *n.*[1] (1).

wollop *v. see* WALLOP *v.* (2).

wolloping *adj. see* WALLOPING *adj.* (2).

wolly *n. see* WALLY *n.*[2].

Wolverine *n.* [mid-19C+] (*US*) an inhabitant of Michigan.

wolverine *n.* [fem. of WOLF *n.* (1)] [1930s–50s] (*US black*) a sexually aggressive woman.

woman *n.* **1** [late 18C–1900s] in coin-tossing, the reverse of a coin [the engraving of Britannia; the face of the coin had the then male monarch's head]. **2** in senses of effeminacy. (**a**) [1920s] a tramp's young boy companion. (**b**) [1960s+] (*US prison*) a prisoner's male lover; the homosexuality may only exist for the length of the sentence. (**c**) [1980s+] (*US juv.*) an effeminate boy, an unpopular boy.

SE in slang uses

IN COMPOUNDS

❑ **woman-be-damned** *n.* [1940s–50s] (*W.I.*) any form of cooking that is done by men only, e.g. a labouring gang. ❑ **woman-drawer** *n.* [SE *woman drawer*, a barmaid; what the whore 'draws' is semen] [early 17C] prostitutes. ❑ **woman-lover** *n. see* LADY LOVER *under* LADY *n.* ❑ **woman-man** *n.* [20C+] (*US/W.I., Gren.*) an effeminate male homosexual. ❑ **woman trouble** *n.* [1950s+] **1** from a female point of view, gynaecological problems. **2** from a male point of view, problems in a relationship.

IN PHRASES

❑ **woman about town** *n.* (*also* **girl about town, ...of the town, lady..., woman...**) [as opposed to a *man about town* or *man of the town*, a generally congratulatory phr., these female counterparts were invariably condemnatory, however much of a euph. the term might be] [late 17C–1900s] a prostitute. ❑ **woman and her husband** *n.* [reverse of usual order, SE *man and wife*] [late 18C–early 19C] a married couple where the wife is larger than the husband. ❑ **woman in comfortable shoes** *n.* [1990s+] a lesbian. ❑ **woman of all work** *n.* [pun on SE *maid of all work*] [late 18C–early 19C] a maidservant 'who refuses none of her master's commands' (Grose 1796), i.e. who not only waits upon but sleeps with her master. ❑ **woman of pleasure** *n. see* LADY OF PLEASURE *under* LADY *n.*

womba *n. see* WONGA *n.*

wombat *n.*[1] **1** [20C+] (*Aus./US*) a fool, an eccentric [SE *wombat*, a burrowing marsupial resembling a small bear]. **2** [1980s] (*US campus*) an ugly person. **3** [2000s] a pointless occupation, i.e. *w*aste *o*f *m*oney, *b*rains *a*nd *t*ime.

IN PHRASES

❑ **in the wombats** [1960s] (*Aus.*) having hallucinations, seeing things which are not there.

wombat *n.*[2] [pun on he 'eats roots and leaves'/*eats*, ROOT *v.* (5a) and leaves] [1980s+] an unappreciative male.

wombat *adj.* [rhy. sl. = *hors de combat*] [20C+] (*Aus.*) dead.

womb-beater *n.* (*also* **womb-sweeper**) [1960s–70s] (*US black*) a man with a large penis.

womb broom *n. see* BROOM *n.*[1] (1).

womble *n.* [the *Wombles*, puppet stars of a 1970s UK children's TV series] [1970s+] a fool, a socially unacceptable individual.

womblescropt/womblety-cropped *adj. see* WAMBLETY-CROPPED *adj.*

wombo *n.* [1990s+] (*US*) the female breast.

womb sweeper *n.* see WOMB-BEATER *n.*

womp *adj.* [WHOMP *v.* (1)] [1990s+] (*US*) of a situation, bad, problematic.

womp *v.* [WOMP *adj.*] **1** [1990s+] to be second-rate. **2** *see* WHOMP *v.*

womper-jawed *adj. see* WHOPPER-JAWED *adj.*

won *adj.* [WIN *v.*] [late 17C–19C] stolen.

wong *n.*[1] (*also* **Mr Wong**) [var. on WANG *n.*[2] (1)] [1940s+] (*US*) the penis.

wong *n.*[2] [abbr. WONGA *n.*] [1990s+] (*UK black*) money.

wonga *n.* (*also* **wamba, wanga, womba, wongur**) [Rom. *wanger*, coal, fig. money; thus Rom. *wongar-camming mush*, a miser, lit. 'one who loves coal' + ? pun on COLE *n.* (1)] [late 19C+] money.

wonga gut *n. see* WANGA GUT *n.*

wonk *n.*[1] [? WONKY *adj.* (1); note political jargon *policy wonk*, an expert in the minutiae of policy; Martin Amis (2000) suggests backslang from S.E. *know*] **1** [1910s–40s] a weak-looking, ungainly person [note Hong Kong *wonk*, a scruffy mongrel, lit. a 'yellow dog' (from Ning Po pron. of letters y.d.]. **2** [1930s–60s] (*Aus.*) a white person, usu. as an insult. **3** [1940s+] (*Aus.*) an effeminate or homosexual male. **4** [1950s+] (*US campus*) anyone who works harder than the rest of the students see fit.

wonk *n.*[2] [1940s] echoic of an explosion, a hit, a loud noise.

wonk one's conker *v.* [assonance, but note WANK *v.*] [1990s+] to masturbate.

wonky *adj.* [ety. unknown, note synon. Ger. *wankel*] [1910s+] **1** (*also* **on a wonk**) of a person or object, unsteady, unstable, out of kilter. **2** (*Aus.*) mad; thus *wonkite*, a mad person. **3** nervous.

IN PHRASES

❑ **all of a wonk** *adj.* [1910s] jumpy, nervous, tense.

woo *n.* [SE *woo*, to court] [1930s+] (*N.Z./US*) a petting session.

IN COMPOUNDS

❑ **woo number** *n.* [NUMBER *n.* (1)] [1950s] (*US black*) a girlfriend or boyfriend.

wood *n.*[1] **1** [early 19C; 1940s+] money [ref. to the barrels in which valuable liquor is stored]. **2** [mid–late 19C] the pulpit.

3 [1920s] (*US Und.*) a beer keg, holding bootleg alcohol. **4** [1940s] a police truncheon. **5** [1950s+] (*also* **tree**) the penis. **6** [1980s+] an erection; thus *get good wood*, to have a strong erection, *give/slip someone wood*, of a man, to have sexual intercourse [the solidity of the erection].

sexual terms

IN PHRASES

❑ **buff the wood** *v.* [1990s+] to masturbate. ❑ **catch wood** *v.* [1980s+] (*US*) to get an erection; thus in fig. use, to become extremely excited. ❑ **get wood** *v.* [1990s+] to achieve an erection. ❑ **give wood** *v.* [1990s+] to render erect. ❑ **morning wood** *n.* [1990s+] (*US*) an erection of the penis first thing in the morning. ❑ **pull one's wood** *v. see* PULL ONE'S WIRE *under* WIRE *n.*[1]. ❑ **put the wood to** *v.* [1970s+] (*US*) of a man, to have sexual intercourse. ❑ **sport a wood** *v. see* SPORT A WOODIE *under* WOODIE *n.*[2]. ❑ **sport one's wood** *v.* [2000s] to display an erection.

general uses

IN COMPOUNDS

❑ **wood rash** *n.* [1970s–80s] (*N.Z. prison*) an injury inflicted by a truncheon.

IN PHRASES

❑ **have the wood on** *v. see* HAVE THE DEADWOOD ON *under* DEADWOOD *n.* ❑ **lay the wood to** *v.* [1970s] (*US*) to beat severely. ❑ **look over the wood** *v.* [late 18C–early 19C] to mount the pulpit, to preach. ❑ **put the wood to** *v.* [image of hitting with a wooden club or truncheon] [1970s+] (*US*) **1** to punish, to coerce by threats. **2** to cause serious trouble for.

SE in slang uses

IN COMPOUNDS

❑ **wood butcher** *n.* [19C+] a carpenter. ❑ **wood duck** *n.* [Aus. *wood duck*, technically classified as a *maned goose*, thus pun on SE *goose*, a fool] [1980s+] **1** (*Aus.*) a fool. **2** (*Aus. prison*) an inexperienced prisoner. ❑ **woodheap** *v.* [SE *woodheap*, a stack of firewood] (*Aus.*) [1910s+] **1** to ostracize a fellow worker. **2** to force an itinerant to chop firewood in return for food and accommodation. ❑ **wood hick** *n.* [SE *wood(land)* + HICK *n.*[1] (1)] [19C] (*US*) a derog. term for a rustic, a peasant. ❑ **wood merchant** *n.* [late 19C–1910s] a street seller of matches. ❑ **wood-pussy** *n.* (*also* **woods-pussy**) [lit. 'wood-cat'] [late 19C+] (*Can./US*) a skunk, a polecat.

IN PHRASES

❑ **look through the wood** *v.* [late 18C–mid-19C] to stand in the pillory. ❑ **poor as wood** *adj.* (*also* **poor as mud**) [20C+] (*Aus.*) second-rate. ❑ **put the wood in the hole** *v.* (*also* **put a piece of wood in it**) [1910s+] to shut the door; usu. as imper. ❑ **take in wood** *v.* (*also* **wood up**) [? the *wooden* barrels that hold liquor] [mid-19C] (*US*) to drink, usu. in question *Do you take in wood?* Will you have a drink? ❑ **wood-and-water joey** *n.* [JOEY *n.*[1] (2a), they run for firewood, drinking water etc] [late 19C+] (*Aus.*) **1** a general labourer. **2** a sycophant, a hanger-on. ❑ **up to the arms in wood** [early 19C] standing in the pillory.

wood *n.*[2] [abbr. PECKERWOOD *n.*] [1960s+] **1** (*US black*) a derog. term for a white person. **2** (*US prison*) a term of address between white males.

wood *n.*[3] *see* WOODIE *n.*[1].

wood *v.* [1960s] (*Aus.*) to hit.

woodbine *n.* [Wills' *Woodbine* cigarettes, a cheap UK brand and as such popular among WW1 troops] **1** [1910s] any cheap cigarette, irrespective of brand. **2** [1910s; 1940s] (*Aus.*) an Englishman, esp. a soldier.

woodcock *n.* [the ease with which the SE *woodcock* can be caught in a snare] **1** [16C–mid-18C] a fool, a gullible person. **2** [late 18C–early 19C] a tailor who has presented a substantial bill [pun on the bird's long *bill*]. **3** [mid-19C] (*US*) pork and beans [? mis-reading of *Scotch Woodcock*: hard boiled eggs chopped up with anchovy sauce, and then laid on slices of buttered toast].

woodcock's head *n.* [the shape] [late 16C] a pipe.

wooden *adj.*

SE in slang uses

IN COMPOUNDS

❑ **wooden aspro** *n.* [*Aspro*, a painkiller] [1970s+] (*N.Z. prison*) a blow on the head with a truncheon; the truncheon itself. ❑ **wooden casement** *n.* (*also* **wooden cravat**) [late 17C] the pillory. ❑ **wooden coat** *n. see* WOODEN OVERCOAT below. ❑ **wooden doublet** *n.* [mid-18C] a coffin. ❑ **wooden fit** *n.* [one drops 'like wood' to the ground] [late 19C–1900s] a fainting fit. ❑ **wooden habeas** *n.* [SE *wooden* + pun on *habeas corpus*, lit. 'thou shalt have the body', a writ whereby an accused and jailed person must be brought before the court and the reason for their imprisonment justified] [late 18C–early 19C] a coffin; thus *go out with a wooden habeas*, to die in prison. ❑ **wooden horse** *n.* [mid-16C–17C] the gallows. ❑ **wooden kimono** *n.* (*also* **...kimino, ...kimona**) [1910s+] a coffin. ❑ **wooden nickel** *n.* (*also* **copper nickel, wooden money**) [a non-existent and undoubtedly worthless coin] [1920s+] (*orig. US*) something worthless, thus in phr. 'don't take any wooden nickels,' meaning be watchful. ❑ **wooden nutmeg** *n.* [the use of such 'nutmegs' in confidence trickery; thus the negative image of such individuals] [mid–late 19C] (*US*) **1** a native of Connecticut. **2** a confidence trickster. **3** a trick. ❑ **wooden overcoat** *n.* (*also* **wooden coat, ...suit, ...uniform**) [mid-19C+] a coffin, often used in fictional versions of organized crime; thus *wooden overcoat man*, an undertaker. ❑ **wooden parenthesis** *n.* [the sides of the pillory supposedly resemble the curves of a *parenthesis*, i.e. ( )] [early 19C] the pillory. ❑ **wooden ruff** *n.* (*also* **wooden shoes**) [like the SE *ruff* it encircles the neck] [late 17C–mid-19C] (*UK Und.*) a pillory or the stocks; thus *wear the wooden ruff*, to stand in the pillory. ❑ **wooden shoes** *n.* **1** [late 17C–mid-18C] the supporters of the Old Pretender, James Stuart (1688–1766) [the wearing of wooden *sabots* by the French]. **2** [mid-18C] the French, France; thus foreigners in general. **3** [1940s] (*US Und.*) a Dutchman. ❑ **wooden spoon** *n.* [the actual *wooden spoon* trad. awarded to that Cambridge undergraduate unfortunate enough to come bottom in the year's mathematical tripos. Note the synon. *wooden wedge*, named after the philologist Hensleigh Wedgwood, who took last place in the Cambridge classical tripos of 1824] **1** [mid-19C] (*US campus*) at Yale, a prize conferred at the end of the junior year for the 'most popular man in class'. **2** [late 19C] a fool. **3** [20C+] (*orig. sports*) a metaphorical prize for the competitor or team who comes last in a sporting contest. ❑ **wooden surtout** *n.* [SE *surtout*, an overcoat] [late 18C–mid-19C] a coffin. ❑ **woodentop** *n.* [the UK children's TV series] [1970s+] **1** a uniformed police officer. **2** a simpleton. ❑ **wooden ulster** *n.* [SE *ulster*, a long, loose overcoat] [late 19C] a coffin. ❑ **wooden uniform** *n. see* WOODEN OVERCOAT above.

IN PHRASES

❑ **wooden (out)** *v.* [WOODENER *n.*[1] (1)] [20C+] (*Aus./N.Z.*) to knock down, knock out.

woodener *n.*[1] [it renders the recipient 'dead wood'] [late 19C–1920s] (*Aus./N.Z.*) **1** a staggering blow; a knockout punch. **2** in fig. use, something, e.g. an excess of drink, that 'knocks one out'.

woodener *n.*[2] [1920s–60s] (*Irish*) a cheap wooden seat at the cinema.

woodener *n.*[3] [the *wooden* spoon once issued + rhy. sl. *wooden spoon* = MOON *n.* (2a)] [1940s–50s] (*UK prison*) a one-month sentence.

wooden leg *n.* [rhy. sl.] [1990s+] an egg.

wooden-legged mare *n.* [18C–mid-19C] the gallows.

wooden pegs *n.* [rhy. sl.] [20C+] the legs.

wooden plank *n.* [rhy. sl. = YANK *n.* (1)] [1980s+] an American.

wooden (spoon) *n.* [rhy. sl.; wooden spoon = MOON *n.* (2a)] [1930s–50s] (*UK prison*) a one-month sentence.

woodie *n.*[1] (*also* **wood, woods, woody**) [abbr.] [20C+] **1** a Wills *Wood*bine cigarette. **2** any cheap cigarette [fig. use of sense 1].

woodie *n.*[2] (*also* **woody**) [ext. of WOOD *n.*[1] (6)] [1940s+] (*orig. US*) an erection; the erect penis; also in fig. use, as a thrill.

IN PHRASES

❑ **juice a woodie** *v.* [1990s+] to masturbate. ❑ **sport a woodie** *v.* (*also* **sport a wood**) [1980s+] (*US teen*) to have an erection.

woodie *n.*[3] [abbr.] **1** [1960s+] (*orig. US surfer*) (*also* **woody**) a *wood*-panelled station wagon. **2** [2000s] (*N.Z.*) a woodsman. **3** [2000s] (*N.Z.*) a wood-burning stove.

woodpecker *n.* [SE *woodpecker*, which takes repeated small pecks at a tree, gradually creating a substantial hole] **1** [17C–early 19C] (*UK Und.*) in a crooked gambling game, the accomplice who urges on the victim, helping him by providing a succession of small stakes. **2** [1940s–50s] (*US Und.*) a typist. **3** [1940s+] (*US/Aus.*) a machine-gun [adds the tapping noise]. **4** [1950s] (*W.I.*) a district police officer [the red stripes on their uniform, reminiscent of the bird's colouring]. **5** *see* PECKERWOOD *n.*

woodpile *n.* [its manufacture] [1930s] (*US*) a xylophone.

woodpile cousin *n.* [the sharing of a common woodpile] [20C+] (*US*) a distant relation, e.g. a third or fourth cousin, a family friend.

woodrow *n.* [ext. of WOOD *n.*[1] (6)] [1990s+] an erection, usu. in phr. *to slip her the woodrow*.

Woods *n.* [1950s] a Wills Woodbine cigarette.

woods *n.* **1** [1900s] (*US Und.*) whiskers. **2** [1960s] (*US campus*) female pubic area. **3** *see* WOODIE *n.*[1].

SE in slang uses

IN PHRASES

❑ **go to the woods** *v.* [1910s] (*Aus.*) to get drunk. ❑ **put it in the woods** *v.* [1970s] (*US prison*) to escape.

woods colt *n.* [SAmE, *woods colt*, a horse of unknown paternity; such a *colt* is conceived and/or reared in the *woods*, rather than in a stable] [late 19C+] (*US*) an illegitimate child.

woodser *n. see* JIMMY WOODSER *n.*

woodsman *n.* [WOOD *n.*[1] (5) + sfx *-man*] [1960s+] a sexual athlete.

wood up *v. see* TAKE IN WOOD *under* WOOD *n.*[1].

woody *n.*[1] *see* TRIPLE TREE *n.*

woody *n.*[2] **1** *see* WOODIE *n.*[1]. **2** *see* WOODIE *n.*[3] (1).

woof *n.* [fig. use of WOOF *v.*[1] (1)] [1990s+] (*US black*) a criminal.

woof *v.*[1] [US black pron. of SE *wolf* + SE *woof*, the sound of barking] [1910s+] (*mainly US*) to speak in a variety of ways, the meaning differs as to context: flirtatious, aggressive, meaningless, threatening, bullying, bluffing, joking.

IN PHRASES

❑ **woof on someone** *v.* [1980s] **1** (*US black*) to brag, to boast; to trick, to lie; to play the DOZENS *n.* **2** (*US campus*) to be irritatingly curious.

woof *v.*[2] [1940s] (*Aus.*) to poke.

woof *v.*[3] [echoic] [1970s+] (*US campus*) to vomit.

woof! *excl.* **1** [1920s+] used by a man on seeing a passing attractive young woman; or vice versa [? an imitation of the howl of a lovesick dog]. **2** a non-sexual excl. of appreciation.

woof (down) *v.* [SE *wolf*] [1920s+] to consume voraciously.

woofer *n.* [WOOF *v.*[1]] [1930s+] (*US black*) a loud, loquacious talker who says a good deal, but with little actual meaning.

woofer coon *n.* [a COON *n.* (5) who makes one WOOF *v.*[3]] [1980s] (*US black*) an extremely ugly woman.

woofers *n.* [1980s] (*Aus.*) greyhounds.

woofing *n.* [WOOF *v.*[1]] [1920s+] (*US black*) speaking in a variety of ways, the meaning differs as to context, e.g. flirtatiously, aggressively, meaninglessly, threateningly, in a bullying or bluffing manner.

IN COMPOUNDS

❑ **woofing session** *n.* (*also* **lugging session**) [1980s] (*US black*) a session of amicable chatter, of joking.

woof it *v.* [SE *wolf*, to eat ravenously/play on EAT *v.* (4)] [1980s+] (*US gay*) to perform fellatio energetically and voraciously.

woofits *n.* [ety. unknown; ? link to SE *fit*, a seizure] [1910s–20s] nerves, tension; thus *get the woofits*, to become tense, nervous; a hangover.

woofled *adj.* [1930s] (*US*) drunk.

woofter *n.* (*also* **willy woofter**) [var. on POOFTER *n.*] [1980s+] a male homosexual.

IN COMPOUNDS

❑ **woofterish** *adj.* (*also* **woolly-woofterish**) [1980s+] (*Aus./N.Z.*) of an argument, indecisive, unconvincing.

woof-woof *n.* [1990s+] a dog.

woof! woof! *excl.* [1920s] (*US*) an excl. of ridicule or indignation.

woogie *n.* [var. BOOGIE *n.*[2] (1) + SE *boogie-woogie* music] [1960s] (*US black*) a black person.

woo-hah! *excl.* [1990s+] (*US black teen*) an excl. implying one's domination of a situation.

wook *n.* [the *wookie*, the hair-covered quasi-ape who co-pilots the space ship *Millennium Falcon*, in the *Star Wars* films] [1980s+] an individual who is completely committed to an alternative lifestyle, living far outside mainstream society.

wool *n.*[1] **1** [mid-19C–1910s] courage, fortitude, 'character' [orig. boxing jargon]. **2** [mid-19C+] hair. **3** [1960s+] (female) pubic hair and by extension, a woman as a sex object [metonymic use of sense 2].

IN PHRASES

❑ **all wool** *adj.* [mid-19C–1900s] (*Aus./US*) excellent, first-class. ❑ **all wool and a yard wide** *adj.* [advertising copy for clothing trade promotions, orig. by the J O Ballard woollen mill at Malone, NY] **1** [late 19C+] of people, excellent, dependable. **2** [2000s] (*N.Z.*) fat. ❑ **knock the wool out of one's head** *v.* [1900s] (*N.Z.*) to wake up; to think (or make someone else think) clearly. ❑ **lose one's wool** *v.* (*also* **get one's wool off**) [19C–1940s] to lose one's temper. ❑ **pull one's wool** *v.* **1** [late 19C] (*US*) to get angry with. **2** [1920s] (*Aus.*) to annoy, to drive into a temper.

IN EXCLAMATIONS

❑ **keep your wool on!** (*also* **hold your wool on!**) [20C+] calm down! don't lose (emotional) control!

SE in slang uses

IN COMPOUNDS

❑ **wool barber** *n.* (*also* **wool-chopper**) [late 19C+] (*Aus.*) a sheep-shearer. ❑ **wool-bird** *n.* (*also* **woolly bird**) [late 18C–mid-19C] (*UK Und.*) a sheep. lamb; thus *wing of a woolbird*, a shoulder of lamb. ❑ **wool-bug** *n.* [BUG *n.*[1] (1)/ BUG *n.*[4] (3b)] [late 19C–1930s] (*N.Z.*) a sheep-shearer. ❑ **wool-grower** *n.* **1** [mid-18C] in boxing, the head. **2** [1960s] (*Aus.*) a sheep farmer. ❑ **wool hat** *n.* (*also* **wool-hat boy**) [their stereotypical headgear; urbanites wear silk hats] [mid-19C–1950s] (*US*) a rural person. ❑ **wool-hawk** *n.* [20C+] (*Aus.*) a skilful shearer. ❑ **wool-hole** *n.* [orig. printers' jargon, an old or unemployed printer described himself as being *in the wool-hole*, a fig. use of wool-hole, defined in Savage's *Dict. of Printing* (1841) as 'a place boxed off sometimes under a stair case, or in any situation where the dust will not affect the press room, in which the wool is carded wherewith to make the balls'] [mid-19C–1900s] the workhouse. ❑ **woolworm** *n.* [1940s] (*US Und.*) a shoplifter specializing in woolen garments.

wool *n.*[2] [abbr. WOOLLY-BACK *under* WOOLLY *adj.*[2]] [1990s+] an unsophisticated person, peasant.

wool *v.* **1** [mid-19C] to confuse, to discomfit [SE *pull the wool over someone's eyes*]. **2** [1930–50s] (*US*) to pull someone's hair in play or anger [WOOL *n.*[1] (2)].

woola/woolah/woolas/woolie *n. see* WOLLIE *n.*

Woolies *n.* [abbr.] [1930s+] a nickname for F.W. *Wool*worth's (1852–1919) department stores.

woolies *n.*[1] [late 19C+] long woollen underwear.

woolies *n.*[2] *see* WOLLIE *n.*

woollies, the *n.* [mid-18C] (*US*) the police.

woolloomooloo *adj.* [*Woolloomooloo*, a waterside suburb in Sydney] [late 19C+] (*Aus.*) rough, unsophisticated, thuggish;

thus *Woolloomooloo bushman*, one who rides a horse badly, *Woolloomooloo upper-cut*, kick to the groin.

(IN COMPOUNDS)

❑ **woolloomooloo Yank** *n.* (*also* **woolloomooloo Frenchman**) [YANK *n.* (1)/SE *Frenchman*] [1940s] (*Aus.*) a relatively unsophisticated person who attempts to ape the supposedly more sophisticated style of an American or Frenchman.

woolly *n.* **1** [late 19C–1900s] (*Aus./US*) a blanket. **2** [20C+] (*Aus./US*) a sheep. **3** [1900s] (*US*) a cigarette or cigar end. **4** [1960s+] (*Aus./US*) a farmer.

woolly *adj.*[1] **1** [mid-19C] ill-tempered [given WOOL *n.*[1] (2), ? link to KEEP ONE'S HAIR ON *v.*]. **2** [1930s] tipsy, a little drunk.

(IN PHRASES)

❑ **get the woollies** *v.* [1980s] (*US*) to become bored, nervous.

woolly *adj.*[2] [SE *wool*/WOOL *n.*[2]] [late 19C+] pertaining to a country person, a peasant.

SE in slang uses

(IN COMPOUNDS)

❑ **woolly-back** *n.* [the resemblance to their sheep; esp. used by Liverpudlians] [1960s+] an unsophisticated, country person. ❑ **woolly bird** *n. see* WOOL-BIRD *under* WOOL *n.*[1]. ❑ **woolly crown** *n.* [late 17C–mid-19C] a fool, i.e. a 'soft-headed fellow' (Grose 1785). ❑ **woolly dog** *n.* [1910s] (*Aus.*) a term of abuse. ❑ **woolly woofter** *n.* (*also* **woolly woof**) [WOOFTER *n.* + assonance] [1980s+] a male homosexual.

woolly hoof *n.* [rhy. sl. = POOF *n.* (1)] [1980s] (*Aus.*) a male homosexual.

woolly vest *n.* [rhy. sl.] [1990s+] a pest, an irritating person.

Woolwich and Greenwich *n.* [rhy. sl., pop. with cockney greengrocers] [20C+] spinach.

Woolwich ferry *n.* [rhy. sl.] [20C+] sherry.

Woolwich pier *n.* [rhy. sl.] [20C+] an ear.

Woolworth marriage *n.* (*also* **Woolworth wedding**) [an era when hoteliers looked askance if a couple had no visible proof of their wedded status] [1920s–60s] a 'marriage' that exists only in the cheap Woolworths' ring purchased for the occasion.

wooly *n. see* WOLLIE *n.*

wooly scarf *n.* [rhy. sl.] [2000s] a laugh.

wooly west *n.* [rhy. sl.] [1920s] (*US*) the breast, the chest.

woop *n.* [WOOP-WOOP *n.*] [1920s+] (*Aus./N.Z.*) **1** a tough, but isolated and backward country-dweller. **2** a simpleton, a 'hayseed'.

woopknacker *n.* (*also* **wopcacker**) [? WOOP *n.* (1)+ SE *knacker*, a horse-slaughterer] [1920s+] (*N.Z.*) a very tough, recalcitrant person, a 'hard case'.

woopty-woo! *excl. see* WHOOP-DE-DO! *excl.*

Woop-Woop *n.* (*also* **Woo Poo**) [? redup. based on the style of Aborigine language] [1910s+] (*Aus.*) **1** an imaginary place that is a byword for backwardness and remoteness. **2** an unsophisticated rural person.

(IN COMPOUNDS)

❑ **Woop-Woop pigeon** *n.* [1930s+] (*Aus.*) **1** a kookaburra. **2** a swamp pheasant.

woosey *adj. see* WOOZY *adj.*

wooz *n.* [1910s] (*US*) an expert.

woozie *adj. see* WOOZY *adj.*

woozily *adv.* [WOOZY *adj.* (1)] [late 19C+] (*orig. US*) vaguely or unsteadily.

woozled *adj.* (*also* **woozed, woozed up**) [WOOZY *adj.* (5)] [late 19C–1920s] tipsy, drunk; thus *wooze*, drunkenness.

woozy *adj.* (*also* **hoozy, whoozy, woosey, woozie, wuzzy**) [? echoic of one's blurred mumblings] [late 19C+] **1** (*orig. US*) vague, befuddled, dizzy or unwell. **2** (*orig. US*) sentimental, affectionate, thus *wooziness*, sentimentality. **3** (*US campus*) pleasant, enjoyable. **4** (*US*) keen on, interested in (other than romantically). **5** (*orig. US*) under the influence of drugs or drink, poss. of a blow on the head; thus backform, *wooze*, *woozishness*, drunkenness(*orig. US*) . **6** mad, eccentric.

wop *n.*[1] [Sp. *guapo*, a dandy, which was taken up in Sicily during an occupation by Spain and thus imported to the US by 19C immigrants; note Torres, *After Hours* (1979): 'Plenty of the *guapi* (pretty ones), Neapolitan and Sicilian, around in those days. But they wasn't all pretty, at least to the Irish, who tagged them "wops" '; note Tosches, *Where Dead Voices Gather* (2001): 'The probable root of "wop" is the Latin *uappu*, which was used literally to describe wine gone bad, but which was also used figuratively as early as the first century B.C., by Horace, to describe a good-for-nothing, a worthless character. From *uappu* came the Sicilian *vappu* and *guappu*, which connoted arrogance, bluster, and maleficence entwined. It was these Sicilian words that were commonly used to describe the work-bosses who lured their greenhorn *paesani* into servitude in New York City in the early years of the twentieth century. In New York and other American seaports, the lowly labor of the Italian immigrants' servitude-the dockside toil and offal-hauling that others shunned came to be called, after the work-bosses, *guappu* work; and eventually the laborer himself, and not the boss, was known as *guappu*. The peasant immigrants' tendency to clip the final vowels from standard Italian and Sicilian [...] rendered *guappu* as *guapp'*, which was pronounced, more or less, as *wop*'] **1** [20C+] (*also* **wap, woppe**) a derog. term for an Italian; thus *wopalina*, an Italian girl or woman. **2** [1900s] (*US*) a peasant, a country-dweller. **3** [1910s] (*US*) a manual labourer. **4** [1910s–40s] any non-specific foreigner. **5** [1910s+] the Italian language.

(IN PHRASES)

❑ **work like a wop** *v.* [var. on WORK LIKE A NIGGER *under* WORK *v.*] [1920s] (*US black*) to work very hard.

wop *n.*[2] [ety. unknown] [1910s–40s] (*US prison*) **1** the very last few weeks or days of one's sentence. **2** a short sentence.

wop *n.*[3] [? var. on POP *n.*[1] (3a)] [1950s] a 'go', a time.

wop *n.*[4]

(IN PHRASES)

❑ **up the wop** [ety. unknown] [1980s+] (*N.Z.*) **1** pregnant. **2** broken, out of order.

wop *n.*[5] [2000s] (*S.Afr.*) the penis.

wop *adj.* [WOP *n.*[1]] **1** [1910s+] referring to an Italian person or to Italian culture; as a nickname for an Italian; thus *wop joint*, an Italian restaurant. **2** [2000s] referring to a Spaniard or South American or to their culture.

(IN COMPOUNDS)

❑ **wop stick** *n.* [STICK *n.* (1g)] [1930s–40s] (*US*) a clarinet. ❑ **wop town** *n.* (*also* **wop flat**) [1930s+] (*US*) that part of a town in which the Italian community lives.

wop *v.* [var. on WHOP *v.* (1)] **1** [mid-19C] to beat, to overcome. **2** [mid-19C+] to hit; also fig. **3** *see* WHOP *v.*

wop bang *excl. see* WHAP BANG *excl.*

wopcacker *n.* **1** *see* WHOPCACKER *n.* **2** *see* WOOPKNACKER *n.*

woppe *n. see* WOP *n.*[1] (1).

wopper *n. see* WHOPPER *n.*

woppidown *n.* [? WHOP *v.* (1) *it down* on the plate] [1910s+] (*Aus.*) a damper.

wopping *adj. see* WHOPPING *adj.*

wop-wop *n.* [?, WHOP *v.* (1) i.e. the noise of the man running up and down the shearing shed carrying fleeces to the wool tables] **1** [1900s–1950s] (*Aus.*) a roustabout, a handyman, a casual labourer. **2** [1950s+] (*N.Z.*) a sheep farm, thus the country as opposed to the town.

word *n.*

SE in slang uses

(IN COMPOUNDS)

❑ **wordhole** *n.* [1990s+] (*US*) the mouth. ❑ **word-grubber** *n.* [SE *grub up*] [late 18C–early 19C] a critic; one who deliberately uses hard words in their conversation. ❑ **word-pecker** *n.* [pun on SE *woodpecker*] [late 17C–mid-19C] a punster. ❑ **word-slinger** *n.* [1930s] (*US*) a newspaper reporter.

(IN PHRASES)

❑ **drink by word of mouth** *v. see under* DRINK *v.* ❑ **drop word(s)** *v. see under* DROP *v.*[4]. ❑ **give the good word** *v.*

[2000s] to pass on information, to 'tip off'. ❑ **know the words and music** *v.* [1940s+] (*gay*) to understand and partake in the gay sub-culture. ❑ **word is bond** (*also* **word is born**) [SE phr. *my word is my bond*] [1990s+] (*orig. US black*) a general term of affirmation, I mean it, I promise.

(IN EXCLAMATIONS)

❑ **I'll be a dirty word!** *see under* DIRTY *adj.* ❑ **word booty!/word life!** *see* WORD! *excl.* ❑ **word to the mother!** (*also* **word to the mother bird!**) [1980s+] (*US black*) an excl. of approval, admiration etc.

word, the *n.* [late 19C+] (advance) information.

(IN PHRASES)

❑ **put the word out (on)** *v.* [1910s–60s] (*US Und.*) to mark for assassination or arrest.

word *adj.* [phr. *the last word in...*, ult. Fr. *le dernier cri*] [1980s+] (*US campus*) fashionable; a term of general approval.

word *v.* **1** [late 19C+] to tip off, to warn, to inform. **2** [20C+] (*Aus.*) to speak to, accost, to tell, pass word to, to rebuke or tell off. **3** [1910s] to make sexual advances, to 'chat up'. **4** [2000s] (*US black*) to swear (an oath).

word! *excl.* (*also* **word booty! word life!**) [abbr. WORD UP! *excl.* + ? SE *the last word in, that's my last word*] [1980s+] (*orig. US black*) **1** (*also* **that's word**) an excl. of approval, admiration, agreement etc. **2** an expression of greeting or farewell. **3** used to signify that one is having the final say in an argument.

-word *sfx* [1980s+] a euph. sfx used, with a single initial letter, to denote a variety of 'unsayable' synons., e.g. the *C–word*, CUNT *n.*; the *F-word*, FUCK *n.*; also, often in a newspaper context, to denote a topic of importance, which has become so over-used as to become tediously clichéd, e.g. the *M-word*, Maastricht etc.

word up *v.* [WORD UP! *excl.*] [1990s+] (*US black*) to speak plainly, openly.

word up! *excl.* (*also* **say word!**) [1980s+] (*orig. US back*) an excl. of approval, admiration, agreement etc.

work *n.* **1** [mid-18C+] (*also* **piece of work**) the criminal life or a criminal act; thus *work clothes*, clothes used for committing a crime. **2** [20C+] (*US Und.*) the written records held by illegal bookmakers. **3** [1920s] (*US tramp*) begging. **4** [1920s+] (*US Und.*) the marking of cards by a cardsharp. **5** [1920s+] (*US Und.*) some form of weight used to make 'loaded' dice. **6** [1990s+] (*W.I.*) a sexual relationship; usu. in *lose the work*, to lose one's girlfriend. **7** [2000s] (*US drugs*) a supply or consignment of a given drug.

(IN PHRASES)

❑ **get one's work in** *v.* [late 19C] (*US*) to succeed in a course of (criminal) action. ❑ **go to work on** *v.* [mid-19C+] to attack. ❑ **put in work** *v.* [1990s+] (*US black gang*) to get busy, esp. in the performance of any dangerous and/or illegal act, e.g. theft or murder. ❑ **put work in** *v.* **1** [1980s+] (*US gang*) to take part in an attack on a rival gang. **2** [2000s] to murder. ❑ **put work on** *v.* [1960s–70s] (*Aus.*) to attempt the verbal stages of seduction, to 'chat up'.

SE in slang uses

(IN COMPOUNDS)

❑ **work plug/stiff** *n. see* WORKING STIFF *n.*

work *v.* **1** [17C+] to have sexual intercourse. **2** [late 18C+] to do, to perform, to carry through a plan of action, usu. in combs. such as *WORK THE BULLS* below, *WORK THE ORACLE* below etc. **3** [late 18C+] to exploit. **4** [late 18C+] to practise one's occupation as a criminal, e.g. a thief, confidence trickster or beggar. **5** [late 19C+] (*US*) to charm or enthral, esp. an audience. **6** [late 19C+] to get or to get rid of, esp. by artifice. **7** [late 19C+] of an object, to be in active use, e.g. *here's a dollar that's not working*. **8** [1930s+] to work as a street prostitute. **9** [1960s–70s] (*orig. US black*) to exchange sexual favours for money; thus to work as a call-girl, 'escort' or prostitute. **10** [1960s+] (*US*) to place under pressure; to interrogate; to cause strong feelings. **11** [1960s+] to deal with in some way. **12** [1980s+] (*US campus*) to beat up. **13** [1990s+] to stimulate sexually. **14** [1990s+] to work as a street seller.

(IN COMPOUNDS)

❑ **workbench** *n.* [WORK *v.* (1)] [early 19C; 1960s] a bedstead.

(IN PHRASES)

❑ **work a clout** *v.* [late 18C] to steal a handkerchief. ❑ **work a crowd** *v.* (*also* **work a room**) **1** [late 19C] of a pickpocket, to make one's way through a crowd, robbing opportunistically. **2** [1930s+] to ply one's trade to an audience, begging, preaching, entertaining etc. ❑ **work a door** *v.* (*also* **work a house**) [*SE* door/HOUSE *n.*[1] (1)] [1920s+] to work as a prostitute, standing or sitting in one's own doorway; thus *door*, a brothel; or from a whore-house. ❑ **work a game** *v.* [GAME *n.* (6)] [1950s] to pursue a (usu. criminal) scheme or plan. ❑ **work a joint** *v.* [1900s] (*Aus.*) to carry off some form of swindle. ❑ **work a point** *v. see under* POINT *n.* ❑ **work a ready** *v.* [1910s+] (*Aus.*) to concoct a swindle or fraud. ❑ **work a spot** *v.* [1990s+] (*US black*) to sell drugs or sex from a specific location. ❑ **work from a book** *v.* (*US black*) **1** [1940s+] for a pimp, to run his professional life by the recognized 'rules and regulations' of the pimping life, supposedly enshrined in an authoritative *Book* [BOOK, THE *n.* (2)]. **2** [1960s+] to conduct business through an address book, so eliminating many of the problems (esp. police interference) that are met in street prostitution [BOOK *n.* (1b)]. ❑ **work high** *v.* [1930s] (*US Und.*) **1** to rob in broad daylight. **2** to work out of one's criminal class. ❑ **work hot** *v.* [HOT *adj.* (1a)] [1980s+] (*Aus. prison*) to do something illegal. ❑ **work it** *v.* [late 19C+] to arrange, often by underhand or duplicitous methods. ❑ **work low** *v.* [anton. of *WORK HIGH* above] [1930s] (*US Und.*) to take on a less prestigious criminal job than usual. ❑ **work off** *v.* **1** [mid–late 19C] to hang; to execute. **2** [late 19C] (*UK Und.*) to pass a forged bank note into general circulation. ❑ **work on** *v.* [SE/var. WORK OVER *v.* (2)] [1930s–60s] (*US prison*) to beat up. ❑ **work one's nut** *v.* (*also* **work one's head, ...loaf, ...skull**) [NUT *n.*[1] (1b)/LOAF (OF BREAD) *n.*] [1910s+] to scheme, to plot, to use one's brains to avoid work. ❑ **work one's points** *v.* [1940s] (*US*) to get on with something, to do or perform. ❑ **work on shorts** *v.* [the pickpocketing team is *short*, i.e. composed of just one person] [1920s] (*US Und.*) to work as a pickpocket by oneself. ❑ **work the boards** *v.* [BOARDS *n.*] [1970s] (*UK Und.*) to run the 'three-card trick'. ❑ **work the bulls** *v.* [BULL *n.*[3] (3)] [mid-19C] (*Aus./UK Und.*) to pass counterfeit crown coins. ❑ **work the hole** *v.* (*also* **make the hole**) [1940s–50s] (*US Und.*) to rob drunks who have passed out in the subway. ❑ **work the knocker** *v.* [1950s–60s] (*UK Und.*) touring houses, ostensibly to buy or sell goods, but spec. to trick or bully people into selling heirlooms, antiques etc for minimal prices. ❑ **work the noble** *v.* [late 19C] (*UK tramp*) to beg as an impoverished clergyman or upperclass person. ❑ **work the oracle** *v.* [SE *oracle*, a prophet] **1** [19C] to raise money by fraud or deceit. **2** [19C] to raise money. **3** [mid-19C] (*US Und.*) to plan a robbery. **4** [mid-19C+] to plan, to manoeuvre, to succeed through cunning. **5** [1910s] (*Aus.*) to reach a satisfactory conclusion. ❑ **work the rattlers** *v.* [RATTLER *n.* (1d)] **1** [1900s] (*Aus. Und.*) to hang around railway stations looking for a chance to pick pockets or work a confidence trick. **2** [1920s] (*US Und.*) to rob freight trains or the passengers on subway trains. ❑ **work the stem** *v.* [STEM *n.*] [1910s+] (*US tramp*) to beg on the streets; also n., *stemwinder*, a tramp who goes begging. ❑ **work the tubs** *v.* [1920s–40s] (*UK Und.*) **1** (*also* **ride the tubs**) to commit crimes, usu. card-sharping, on board transatlantic liners; thus *tub worker*, a confidence trickster who focusses on the passengers of such boats [TUB *n.*[1] (1)]. **2** to pickpocket on the buses or at bus-stops [TUB *n.*[1] (8)]. ❑ **work the wires** *v.* [SE *wires*, i.e. the connections] [late 19C] (*US*) to engage in political chicanery. ❑ **work with the bogies** *v.* [BOGEY *n.*[1] (3)] [late 19C–1930s] to act as an informant.

(IN EXCLAMATIONS)

❑ **get worked!** [20C+] (*Aus.*) a general excl. of dismissal or contempt.

SE in slang uses

(IN PHRASES)

❑ **he wouldn't work in an iron lung** [the purpose of an iron lung is to perform the patient's breathing for them] [1940s+]

(*Aus.*) a phr. said of someone who is totally lazy. ▫ **work...** *v. see also under* relevant n. ▫ **work both sides of the street** *v.* (*also* **play both ends in the middle, ...sides of the street, ... game**) **1** [20C+] to ally oneself to both sides in a dispute or division, to behave in an opportunistic manner. **2** [1960s+] (*also* **play both sides of the fence, walk both sides of the street**) to be a bisexual. **3** [1990s+] (*US*) to work exceptionally hard. ▫ **work for Street and Walker** *v.* [puns] [1900s–50s] (*Aus.*) to be unemployed and walking the streets in search of a job. ▫ **work like a kaffir** *v.* [KAFFIR *n.*[1] (1)] [1970s+] (*S.Afr.*) to work very hard. ▫ **work like a nigger** *v.* (*also* **work like a black, ...Chinaman, ...nig**) [NIGGER *n.*[1] (1)] [mid-19C+] (*orig. US*) to work very hard. ▫ **work one's arse off** *v.* (*also* **work one's ass off, ...balls off, ...bollocks off, ...can off, ...fanny off, ...nuts off, ...pants off, ...tits off**) [ARSE *n.* (1)/ASS *n.* (2)/BALLS *n.* (1)/BALLOCKS *n.* (2)/CAN *n.*[1] (1b)/FANNY *n.*[1] (3)/NUTS *n.*[2] (1)/TIT *n.*[2] (1)] **1** [1920s+] to work extremely hard. **2** [1950s+] to make another person work hard. ▫ **work one's butt off** *v.* (*also* **act one's butt off, battle..., work one's buns off**) [BUTT *n.*[1] (1a); var. on *WORK ONE'S ARSE OFF* above] [1960s+] (*orig. US*) to work very hard. ▫ **work oneself off** *v.* (*also* **work it**) [16C+] to masturbate. ▫ **work one's mealie off** *v.* [euph. var. on *WORK ONE'S ARSE OFF* above] [1990s+] (*S.Afr.*) to work very hard. ▫ **work one's nerves** *v.* (*also* **work one's last nerve**) [1990s+] (*US black/campus*) **1** to annoy, to irritate. **2** to exert emotional pressure upon someone. ▫ **work one's tail off** *v.* (*also* **sweat one's tail off**) [fig. use of TAIL *n.* (2)] [1920s+] (*orig. US*) to work very hard. ▫ **work out** *see* separate entries. ▫ **work out of one's hat** *v.* [the wearing of a *hat* as one travels around] [1990s+] (*US*) to freelance; to work independently of a specific organization. ▫ **work over** *v. see* separate entry. ▫ **work the tear-pump** *v.* [late 19C–1900s] to burst, prob. insincerely, into tears. ▫ **work up** *v.* [mid-19C] (*US*) of a detective, to follow a suspect.

workaholic *n.* (*also* **workoholic**) [SE *work* + -AHOLIC *sfx*/-OHOLIC *sfx*] [1960s+] anyone who is obsessed by working and thus very rarely stops.

worker *n.*[1] [WORK *v.*] **1** [mid-19C+] a criminal, usu. in combs. such as *BADGER WORKER under* BADGER *n.*[1], *CHARITY WORKER under* CHARITY *n.*, *DUNNIGAN WORKER under* DUNNAKEN *n.*, *LUSH WORKER under* LUSH *n.*[1], *SKIN WORKER under* SKIN *n.*[1], *TAIL WORKER under* TAIL *n.* **2** [1910s] in a pickpocket team, the member who actually picks the victim's pocket.

IN PHRASES

▫ **fine worker** *n. see FINE WIRER under* WIRER *n.*

worker *n.*[2] [WORK *v.* (8)] [1970s+] (*Aus.*) a prostitute.

workie *n.*[1] [abbr.] [1930s–40s] (*US*) the workhouse.

workie *n.*[2] *see* WORKY *n.*

working *n.* [WORK *v.* (4)] **1** [mid-19C] (*UK Und.*) shoplifting. **2** [1900s] (*US Und.*) stealing. **3** [1980s+] (*drugs*) selling crack cocaine.

working classes *n.* [rhy. sl.] [20C+] glasses.

working girl *n.* [WORK *v.* (8)] **1** [1930s+] (*also* **working broad, ...chick, ...woman**) (*US*) a prostitute [BROAD *n.*[2] (2)/CHICK *n.*[1] (2)]. **2** [1970s+] an effeminate male prostitute.

working-john *n. see* WORKING STIFF *n.*

working-man's smile *n.* [1980s+] (*US*) the top of the crevice between a man's buttocks, visible when he bends over and the waist of his low-cut trousers is forced downwards.

working-over *n.* [WORK OVER *v.* (2)] [1920s+] **1** a beating. **2** a search. **3** in fig. use, non-physical harsh treatment.

working stiff *n.* (*also* **working joe, ...john, ...plug, work plug, ...stiff**) [SE *work* + STIFF *n.*[1] (4d)/JOE *n.*[1] (1b)/JOHN *n.* (1)/PLUG *n.*[3] (5)] [20C+] an average, unexceptional working man; also attrib.

working the cuts *phr.* [WORK *v.* (8) +SE *cut*, a passage, a route] [20C+] used of a prostitute who works on the street rather than in a brothel.

working woman *n. see* WORKING GIRL *n.*

workman *n.* [WORK *v.* (4)] **1** [16C] a dice cheat. **2** [mid-19C–1900s] a card-sharp. **3** [1910s] (*UK Und*) a pickpocket.

workman's entrance *n.* [i.e. 'the back door'] [1990s+] the anus.

workoholic *n. see* WORKAHOLIC *n.*

work-out *n.* [SE *work out*, to loosen, to get rid of] **1** [1900s–30s] the simultaneous sacking or dismissal of a large number of a firm's workers. **2** [1930s+] (*US*) a beating.

work out *v.* [SE *work out*, to exercise] **1** [1940s–50s] (*US Und.*) to beat up; to give the 'third degree'. **2** [1960s+] (*US black*) to have sexual intercourse.

work out! *excl.* [1970s] (*US black*) an excl. of exhortation.

work over *v.* **1** [1910s] to search and steal from somebody's clothes. **2** [1920s+] (*orig. US*) to beat up, to hurt to any extent short of murder; thus *work-over*; *working over*, a thrashing, a beating; also in fig. use.

Works, the *n.* [late 19C] (*UK prison*) any of the convict prisons at Chatham, Portsmouth, Portland, or Dartmoor.

works *n.* [SE *works*, the internal parts of a machine] **1** [1900s] (*Aus./US*) the intestines of an animal. **2** [1910s] (*Aus./US*) the brain. **3** [1910s+] (*Aus./US*) the human stomach or its contents. **4** in drug uses. (**a**) [1930s+] (*drugs*) the equipment used by a narcotics user for injecting themself. (**b**) [1990s+] the equipment used for smoking crack cocaine, heroin etc.

IN PHRASES

▫ **get on someone's works** *v.* [1940s+] (*Aus.*) to annoy.

works, the *n.* (*also* **the whole works**) **1** [late 19C+] everything, the lot. **2** [1900s–20s] the leader, the 'boss'. **3** [1920s] the situation. **4** [1920s+] the finest example. **5** [1930s–40s] a beating; the 'third degree'; murder. **6** [1930s–40s] (*US Und.*) an informer; a confession. **7** [1930s–50s] (*US gay*) a passive homosexual. **8** [1930s+] sexual intercourse. **9** [1950s] (*US teen*) a machine. **10** [1980s+] in prostitution, the full range of a prostitute's services.

IN PHRASES

▫ **big works** *n.* [1910s] (*US*) an important person. ▫ **get the works** *v.* **1** [1920s–50s] to suffer, to be punished, to be killed. **2** [1920s+] (*US prison*) to receive a death sentence, to receive a very long sentence. **3** [1990s+] (*US prison*) to serve one's entire sentence, without deductions for good behaviour. ▫ **give someone the works** *v.* **1** [1920s–40s] (*also* **tell the works**) to reveal everything. **2** [1920s+] (*also* **put the works on**) to harm, ranging from beating up to actual murder. **3** [1920s+] to put all one's efforts into communicating something, typically a sermon or political oration, or doing something, criticizing or selling something etc. **4** [1930s+] (*US tramp*) to be given a job by a social agency. **5** [1930s+] to make sexual advances towards. **6** [1930s+] to engage in sexual intercourse. **7** [1940s] (*also* **hand the works to**) to spoil someone's chances. **8** [1950s] to make a thorough medical inspection. ▫ **put the works on** *v.* **1** [1900s] (*US Und.*) to beat up. **2** [1920s] (*US*) to direct one's energies towards, e.g. in order to deceive or seduce.

workus *n.* [mid–late 19C] **1** a workhouse [Cockney pron.]. **2** a derog. term for a Methodist chapel [from its deliberate plainness].

worky *n.* (*also* **workie**) [SE *work*] [mid-19C+] an employed person.

world *n.* **1** [late 18C] (*UK society*) a knowledge of the fashionable world, the *beau monde*. **2** *see* FREE WORLD *n.* (2).

IN PHRASES

▫ **done to the wide world** *adj. see under* DONE *adj.*

world, the *n.* **1** [1960s] (*US gay*) the world of homosexuality. **2** [1960s+] (*US*) the world as lived outside an institution, e.g. the army, a prison. **3** [1990s+] (*US*) everything.

worm *n.* **1** [17C–early 18C; 1940s+] the penis [note ? predating in Oxford Jests (1712): A little slender Northern lass was ask'd, How she durst venture on so big Man? Oh, says she, a little Worm may lie under a great Stone; if stone = STONE *n.*[1] (1), then contextually worm may mean penis]. **2** [mid-19C] a policeman [? SE *worm*, an unpleasant, despicable person]. **3** [1910s–40s] (*US Und.*) silk; thus *worm-worker*, a thief who specializes in stealing silk [play on SE *silkworm*]. **4** [1920s–40s] (*US*) in pl., spaghetti, thus *worms in blood*, spaghetti in tomato sauce. **5** [1960s] (*US campus*) a notably hard worker. **6** [1980s+] (*drugs*) phencyclidine [ety. unknown].

IN COMPOUNDS

❑ **worm farm** *n.* [1960s+] (*orig. US*) an eccentric, one whose mind is 'full of worms'; thus *living on a worm farm*, crazy, eccentric. ❑ **worm hustling** *n.* (*also* **worm work**) [HUSTLE v. (2)] [1930s–40s] (*US Und.*) selling fake silk.

IN PHRASES

❑ **burp the worm** *v.* (*also* **burp the snake**) [1990s+] to masturbate.

SE in slang uses

IN COMPOUNDS

❑ **wormbait** *n.* (*also* **worm food, worm meat**) [1940s+] a corpse. ❑ **worm-crusher** *n.* [mid-19C] (*US*) a foot soldier. ❑ **wormrod** *n.* (*also* **wormdick**) [ROD *n.* (1)/DICK *n.*[1] (5)] [1990s+] a very unpleasant person; thus a general term of abuse.

IN PHRASES

❑ **are you saving it for the worms?** (*also* **are you keeping it for the worms?**) [SE *worm's meat*, a corpse] [1940s+] (*orig. US*) addressed to a supposed virgin, this phr. is intended to shame or bluster her into intercourse. ❑ **take one for the worms** *v.* [the assumption that drinking will, eventually, prove fatal] [late 19C–1930s] to have a drink of alcohol.

worm *v.* [SE *worm*, to remove intestinal worms from an animal] [mid-19C] to remove the beard from an oyster or mussel.

worms and snails *n.* [rhy. sl.] [20C+] fingernails.

worrab *n.* [backsl.] [mid-19C+] (*coster*) a barrow.

worrit *n.* [WORRIT v. (2)] [mid-19C–1910s] anxiety, worry; thus a person suffering from such problems.

worrit *v.* [orig. dial.] [early–mid-19C] **1** to worry someone, to nag. **2** to be worried, anxious.

worry and strife *n.* [rhy. sl., var. on TROUBLE AND STRIFE *n.* (2)] [1930s+] one's wife.

worryguts *n.* (*also* **worry puss**) [-GUTS *sfx*] [1930s+] a pathological worrier, esp. as a term of address.

worry wart *n.* [SE *worry* + WART *n.*] [1930s+] (*US*) a pathological worrier.

worse for wear *adj.* [mid-19C+] drunk, intoxicated by drugs.

worse half *n. see* BETTER HALF *n.*

worse than a fart/two-bob fart in a bottle *see* NOT WORTH A FART *phr.*

worship at the altar *v.* [1970s+] (*US gay*) to fellate.

worship the porcelain god/goddess *v. see* KISS THE PORCELAIN GOD *under* PORCELAIN GOD *n.*

worship the white god *n.* [1950s] (*US*) to inject oneself with a narcotic drug.

worst *adj.* [mid-19C] (*US campus*) a general superlative, used sarcastically.

worst kind, the *phr.* [mid-19C+] (*US*) to the greatest extent, extremely, very badly.

worst (of it) *phr.* (*also* **worst, the**) [mid-19C+] a disadvantage, unfair treatment.

worst part *n.* [16C] the vagina.

worth a... *phr. see also under* relevant n.

IN PHRASES

❑ **worth a cent** *adv.* (*also* **worth a busted nickel, ...a copper, ...twopence**) [late 19C+] (*Aus./US*) to the least amount, e.g. *you ain't helping your Mom worth a cent.* ❑ **worth a whoop** *adj.* [SE *whoop*, a shout] [1900s] (*US*) valuable.

wossname *n.* [20C+] popular mis-sp. of WHATSHISNAME *n.*

wotcher! *excl.* (*also* **wotcha!**) [elision of 16C+ SE *what cheer*, the trad. response to the extended *wotcher, cock!* is 'How's yer mother off for dripping?'] [mid-19C+] a stereotypical Cockney greeting.

wotchero! *excl.* [ext. of WOTCHER! *excl.*] [late 19C] hello!

wotsaname *n. see* WHATSHISNAME *n.*

wotsit *n.* **1** *see* WHATSIT *n.* **2** *see* WHATSITS *n.* (1).

would I had Kemp's shoes to throw after you *phr.* [William *Kemp* (*fl.* 1600), who had played the original Dogberry in the first performance of *Much Ado About Nothing.* In 1600 he was thrown out of Shakespeare's troupe at the Globe, and to restore his image and win some needed publicity, he danced his way from London to Norwich in nine days. The account he then printed and circulated was entitled *Kemp's Nine Days Wonder*] [late 16C–early 19C] a phr. used to wish someone good luck.

wouldn't it! *excl.* [abbr. *wouldn't it make you sick, wouldn't it root you, wouldn't it make you spit chips* and similar phrs.] [1940s+] (*Aus./N.Z.*) a general excl. of dismay, exasperation or disgust.

wouldn't it rotate you? *phr.* (*also* **wouldn't it rip yer? ...rock yer? ...root you? ...rot yer sock?**) [1940s+] (*Aus./N.Z.*) a general excl. of dismay, exasperation or disgust.

wounded *adj.* [2000s] (*US campus*) exhausted; hungover.

wounded soldier *n.* [play on *DEAD SOLDIER under* SOLDIER *n.*, which is completely empty] [1990s+] (*US campus*) a partially empty beer container.

wounds! *excl.* (*also* **waunds! wauns!**) [mid-16C–mid-19C] a euph. excl., lit. 'God's wounds!'.

wound-up *adj.* **1** [mid-19C] drunk. **2** [1910s+] (*also* **wound up like an eight-day clock, woundy**) annoyed, tense and irritated.

woundy *adv.* (*also* **woundey, woundily**) [18C–19C] general intensifier, very, extremely; also as adj. very great.

wow *n.* [SE excl. *wow!*] [1910s+] (*US*) an exciting, admirable or astonishing thing or person.

wow, the *n.* [*Whaw*, a local nickname for an area of Avondale, Auckland, associated with such institutions since mid-19C] [1940s+] (*N.Z.*) a psychiatric institution.

wow *v.* [SE excl. *wow!*] [1920s+] to delight, to enthral, to please very much.

wowse *v.* [backform. f. WOWSER *n.*[1] (1)] [1900s–10s] (*Aus.*) to behave as a puritan and/or censor; thus n. *wowsing*, prudishness, religiosity.

wowser *n.*[1] [UK dial. *wow*, to howl like a dog, to grumble, to complain. Claimed by John Norton (1858–1916), editor of the Sydney *Truth*, as his coinage. However, a correspondent (5 June 1910) cited him as the popularizer but not the coiner of a term that 'in the ordinary parlance of the proletariat ... signifies a "bald-headed, bad-breathed, bible-banging bummer, who ought to be banged with a bowser"'; Norton, as noted by Seal (1999; who declares it a FURPHY *n.*, i.e. a fantasy) claimed the term was an acronym for 'We Only Want Social Evils Righted/Rectified/Removed'] **1** [late 19C+] (*Aus./N.Z.*) a puritan, a self-appointed censor, a 'Mrs Grundy'; thus *wowserdom, wowserism*, the world of puritanism, *wowserish*, puritanical, *wowseristic*, prudish, *wowserly*, puritanically. **2** [1900s–10s] a general term of abuse. **3** [1950s] a bluestocking. **4** [1950s] a teetotaller.

wowser *n.*[2] (*also* **wowzer**) [SE *wow!*] [1910s+] (*US*) something, or somebody, impressive, sensational, successful.

wowzers! *excl.* [ext. SE *wow!*] [1990s+] (*US teen*) a general excl. of approval.

wozzed *adj.* [2000s] (*N.Z.*) exhausted.

wozzle *n.* [2000s] (*N.Z.*) a radio.

w.p. *n.* [abbr. WARMING PAN *n.*[1] (3)] [mid-19C–1900s] a place-holder, a deputy, used orig. of a clergyman who holds a living *pro tempore.*

w.p.b. *n.* [abbr.] [late 19C+] *waste paper basket.*

wragtig *excl.* [1930s+] (*S.Afr.*) affirmative excl.

wrap *n.*[1] [RAP *n.*[1] (3h)] [1950s+] (*Aus./N.Z.*) a boost, a commendation.

wrap *n.*[2] **1** [1970s+] a conclusion, something over and done with, finished [movie jargon *wrap*, the end of a day's filming; *WRAP (IT) UP under* WRAP *v.*]. **2** [1980s+] (*US campus*) a girlfriend [? SE *wrap* around each other or ? SE *rapture*]. **3** [1990s+] (*drugs*) a small quantity of powder-based drugs, e.g. heroin, cocaine, folded into a small square of paper.

IN COMPOUNDS

❑ **wrap-up** *n.* **1** [1930s] (*US Und.*) a gullible person who has been successfully tricked. **2** [1940s–50s] (*US Und.*) a promising deal or plan. **3** [1960s] (*Irish*) a parcel of scraps from the butcher. **4** [1960s+] the end, conclusion.

wrap *v.* **1** [mid-18C] of a man, to have sexual intercourse. **2** *see* RAP *v.*[1] (2f).

SE in slang uses

IN COMPOUNDS

❑ **wrap-rascal** *n.* [despite SE origin, not necessarily worn by criminals] **1** [18C–late 19C] a loose overcoat or greatcoat, worn mainly in the 18C. **2** [late 18C–early 19C] a red greatcoat.

IN PHRASES

❑ **wrap around** *v.* (*also* **wrap round, wrap up**) [1950s+] (*orig. US*) to crash one's car. ❑ **wrap (it) up** *v.* (*also* **wrap**) **1** [1930s+] to bring to an end, to conclude, to stop doing something, esp. as imper. *wrap it up!*, stop! **2** [1940s–50s] (*N.Z./US Und.*) to win. ❑ **wrap oneself around** *v.* (*also* **get around**) [late 19C+] (*orig. US*) to eat and drink, often as imper, *wrap yourself around that.* ❑ **wrapt up in the tail of his mother's smock** [late 18C–early 19C] said of one who has notable success with women. ❑ **wrapt up in warm flannel** [ref. to such terms as WHITE RIBBON *under* WHITE *adj.*; WHITE SATIN *under* WHITE *adj.* that, like flannel, are 'textiles' that describe gin] [late 18C–early 19C] drunk on spirits, esp. gin. ❑ **wrap up** *v.* **1** [1940s+] to stop talking, esp. as a command, *wrap up!* **2** *see* RAP *v.*[1] (2f). **3** *see* WRAP AROUND above.

wrapped *adj.* [abbr. SE *wrapped up in*] [1960s+] (*orig. Aus./US campus*) **1** besotted with, infatuated by, in love with. **2** fascinated by, enthused with.

IN PHRASES

❑ **wrapped up** *adj.* **1** [1900s–40s] (*US*) aware, 'in tune', sophisticated. **2** [1910s+] affected, in love with. **3** [1930s+] (*also* **wrapped**) sorted out.

wrapped tight *adj. see under* TIGHT *adj.*

wrapper *n.* [note US *wrapper*, a woman's loose robe or gown] **1** [early–mid-19C] an overcoat. **2** [1910s+] (*Aus./US prison*) a cigarette paper. **3** [1930s] (*US Und.*) a large-denomination bill that encloses a roll of lesser denominations; the intention is to appear well-off. **4** [1970s] (*US*) an unmarked police car.

IN PHRASES

❑ **in the wrapper** *see* IN THE BAG *under* BAG *n.*[1].

wrapping *n.* [1920s–70s] (*US teen*) clothes, esp. female.

wraps *n.*[1] [RAPT *adj.*]

IN PHRASES

❑ **be big wraps on** *v.* (*also* **have big wraps on**) [1990s+] (*N.Z.*) to be very impressed (by).

wraps *n.*[2] [they 'wrap around' the face] [2000s] (*UK black*) dark glasses.

wrap-up *n.* [RAP *v.*[1] (2f) + image of SE *wrapping* the subject in fine words] [1940s+] (*Aus.*) a flattering account.

wrap up *v.* [WRAP-UP *n.*] [1950s+] (*Aus.*) to praise, to flatter; thus *wrapped*, overjoyed.

wrated *adj. see* RAATID *adj.*

wreath of roses *n.* [the ring of ulcers that surrounds the diseased genitals] [1900s–30s] a venereal ulcer.

wreck *n. see* SHIPWRECK *under* SHIP *n.*[1].

wreck *v.* [1960s–70s] (*gay*) **1** to degrade a fellow homosexual when he is not expecting it. **2** to deliberately exaggerate one's effeminacy as a shock tactic.

SE in slang uses

IN PHRASES

❑ **wreck a bed** *v. see under* BED *n.* ❑ **wreck someone's beads** *v. see under* BEADS *n.*[2]. ❑ **wreck the head** *n.* [2000s] (*Irish*) one who is highly infuriating.

wrecked *adj.* **1** [1960s+] very drunk. **2** [1970s+] (*drugs*) heavily affected by a drug. **3** [1980s] (*US campus*) very upset. **4** [2000s] exhausted.

wren *n.* **1** [mid-19C] a prostitute who specialized in army camps. **2** [1910s–60s] (*US*) an attractive woman.

IN PHRASES

❑ **spin a wren** *v.* [1940s] (*US black*) to dance with a (pretty) woman.

wrester *n.* [SE *wrest*, to twist] [late 16C–early 17C] (*UK Und.*) a pick-lock.

wrestle one's chuck *v. see under* CHUCK *n.*[3].

wrestle one's hash *v. see under* HASH *n.*[1].

wretch *n.* [SE *wretch*, a miserable, wretched person] [1980s+] (*US campus*) an involuntary celibate, someone unable to find a sexual partner despite their best efforts.

wretch-claat *n.* (*also* **wretch-claht**) [SE *wretch* + Jamaican *claat* or *cloth*] [1980s] (*UK black*) a term of abuse.

wriggle *n.*

IN PHRASES

❑ **get a wriggle on** *v. see* GET A WIGGLE ON *under* WIGGLE *n.*

wriggle *v.*

SE in slang uses

IN PHRASES

❑ **wriggle like a cut snake** *v.* [1940s+] (*Aus.*) **1** to act the toady. **2** to be evasive. ❑ **wriggle navels** *v.* (*also* **wriggle your navels**) [note Williams 17C ref. '*wriggle*, allusive of copulatory motion'] [18C] to have sexual intercourse. ❑ **wriggle off** *v.* [late 19C] to leave.

wriggle-diggle *n.* [the woman SE *wriggles*, the man SE *digs*] [1960s+] petting, mutual fondling; thus sexual intercourse.

wriggling pole *n.* (*also* **wriggling stick**) [POLE *n.*] [early 18C] the penis.

wrinch *v.* [1990s+] (*W.I.*) to scowl.

wring *v.* [SE *wring*, to press or squeeze, to clasp] [late 19C] (*US*) to pick someone's pocket.

IN PHRASES

❑ **wring in** *v.* [? prior use of RING IN *v.*[2] (2)] [mid-19C] (*US Und.*) to include, to pay for.

SE in slang uses

IN COMPOUNDS

❑ **wring-jaw** *n.* [its effects] [late 18C–mid-19C] (*US*) rough cider.

IN PHRASES

❑ **wring oneself** *v.* [late 19C] (*UK Und.*) to change clothes. ❑ **wring out one's sock** *v.* [1980s+] of a man, to urinate. ❑ **wring the dew off the branch** *v.* [2000s] to urinate. ❑ **wring out the rattlesnake** *v.* [1960s–70s] to urinate.

wringer *n.*

IN PHRASES

❑ **catch one's balls in a wringer** *v.* (*also* **catch oneself in a wringer, catch one's tit in a wringer**) [1970s+] to find oneself in trouble, in an unpleasant situation. ❑ **put through a/the wringer** *v.* (*also* **run through the wringer**) [1940s+] (*orig. US*) to pressurize, to subject to severe interrogation, to enforce harsh treatment.

wringer *n.*[2] **1** *see* RINGER *n.* (1a). **2** *see* RINGER *n.* (2a).

wringing and twisting *n.* [i.e. the SE *wringing* and *twisting* is of other people's heads or one's own hands] [1940s] (*US black*) suffering racial discrimination and dealing with it either by rebellion or acquiescence.

wring neck *n. see* RING NECK *n.*

wrinkle *n.* [? 14C–16C SE *wrinkle*, a tortuous, sinuous movement] **1** [late 16C+] (*also* **rinkle, winkle**) an idea, device or trick, esp. a new one. **2** [early 19C] a lie. **3** [mid-19C] (*US*) a bit, a small amount. **4** [mid-19C+] a useful piece of information. **5** *see* WRINKLY *n.*

SE in slang uses

IN COMPOUNDS

❑ **wrinkle-bellied** *adj.* [her stretch-marks] [late 18C–20C] having had a number of children, usu. used of a prostitute, i.e. *wrinkle-bellied whore.* ❑ **wrinkle ranch** *n.* [1990s+] (*US campus*) a retirement or old people's home. ❑ **wrinkle room** *n.* [1970s+] (*gay*) a bar, a club or that area of a club where older gay men gather.

IN PHRASES

❑ **have more than one wrinkle in one's arse** *v.* ['Every fresh piece of knowledge being supposed by the vulgar naturalists to add a wrinkle to that part' (Grose, 1796); note WRINKLE *n.* (1)] [late 18C–mid-19C] to have gained a fresh piece of knowledge.

wrinkle *v.* [WRINKLE *n.* (2)] [early 19C] to lie; thus *wrinkler*, a habitual liar.

wrinkles *n.* [? resemblance] [1970s] (*US black*) chitterlings.

wrinkly *n.* (*also* **wrinkle, wrinklies**) **1** [1920s+] (*mainly UK upper/upper-middle-class juv.*) an old person, the old. **2** [1980s+] (*Aus. prison*) an old prisoner.

wrist *n.* (*also* **wristjob**) [the movement of the wrist in masturbation, usu. accompanied by using the forefinger of one hand to point to the wrist of the other] [1990s+] an unpleasant person.

wristy *adj. see* LIMP-WRISTED *adj.*

writ bug *n.* (*also* **writ writer**) [BUG *n.*[4] (3b)] [1940s–70s] (*US prison*) a prison inmate who has made themselves into a self-taught lawyer, either to pursue their own case, combat prison corruption or help their fellow inmates.

write *v.* **1** [1940s–60s] (*drugs*) of a doctor, to write prescriptions for narcotics. **2** [1960s] to pass dud cheques.

SE in slang uses

IN PHRASES

❑ **that's all she wrote** (*also* **that's what she wrote**) [? the unhappy man's remark on reaching the terminal statements of a DEAR JOHN *n.* letter] [1940s+] (*orig. US milit.*) a general term of finality, that's all there is. ❑ **write one's name above another's** *v.* [late 19C] (*orig. sporting*) to hit in the face. ❑ **write one's name on** *v.* [mid-19C+] to reserve for oneself, to have the first go at. ❑ **write out** *v.* [fig. a role *written out* of of a script] [1930s] (*US Und.*) to order to be killed. ❑ **write scrip** *v.* (*also* **write script**) [SCRIP *n.*[2]/SCRIPT *n.* (1)] [1930s+] (*drugs*) to give out prescriptions for narcotics.

write-off *n.* [in orig. service use, it is *written off* the inventory] (*orig. milit.*) **1** [1910s+] anything or anyone that is completely destroyed, beyond all hope of repair. **2** [1970s] a farewell, a termination.

write off *v.* **1** [1910s+] (*orig. RAF*) to completely destroy something, so that it is beyond all hope of repair. **2** [1940s+] to give up on.

writer *n.* **1** [1930s+] (*drugs*) a doctor who will write prescriptions for narcotics and ask no questions about the user [WRITE *v.* (1)]. **2** [1980s+] (*orig. US*) a graffiti artist.

write-up *n.* [1920s+] (*US prison*) a disciplinary report.

write up *v.* [WRITE-UP *n.*] [1920s+] **1** (*US prison*) to report a convict for misconduct. **2** (*US*) to report a worker for inadequate work or a misdemeanor.

writing *n.* **1** [1930s–50s] (*US drugs/prison*) a means of smuggling drugs into prison: a letter is soaked in some form of narcotized solution and the text of the letter makes it clear, with simple codes, that this has been done [WRITE *v.* (1)]. **2** [1930s–50s] (*US drugs*) a narcotics prescription [WRITE *v.* (1)]. **3** [1990s+] graffiti [WRITER *n.* (2)].

IN COMPOUNDS

❑ **writing doctor** *n.* (*also* **writing croaker**) [CROAKER *n.*[5] (1)] [1930s+] (*drugs*) a doctor who will write prescriptions for narcotics and ask no questions about the user.

writ writer *n. see* WRIT BUG *n.*

wrokin *n.* [? Du. *vrouw*, a woman + dimin. sfx *-kin*] [17C–19C] a Dutch woman.

wrong *adj.* **1** [mid-19C] (*UK Und.*) unsafe (for criminal activity). **2** [mid-19C] (*UK Und.*) of money, counterfeit. **3** [20C+] (*US Und.*) untrustworthy (in criminal terms), too close to the authorities; thus honest. **4** [1900s–50s] in respectable terms, corrupt. **5** [1920s] false, concocted, e.g. of a criminal charge. **6** [1940s–50s] (*Aus.*) eccentric, insane [note earlier use in SE phrs. below]. **7** [1960s] (*US black/campus*) irritating, contrary. **8** [1980s] (*US campus*) grumpy, unfriendly. **9** [1990s+] right, good.

IN PHRASES

❑ **go wrong** *v.* [1940s] (*US Und.*) to turn informer. ❑ **in wrong** (*US*) **1** [1900s–50s] in trouble, unpopular. **2** [1910s–20s] wrong, erroneous. **3** [1920s] wronged.

SE in slang uses

IN COMPOUNDS

❑ **wrong number** *n.* [1920s+] (*US*) **1** a mistaken idea. **2** a dangerous person. **3** a dishonest, untrustworthy person. ❑ **wrong riff** *n.* [orig. jazz use] [1930s–40s] (*US black*) a mistake, a blunder. ❑ **wrong steer** *n.* [1900s–60s] (*US*) misdirection, both lit. and fig. ❑ **wrong tree** *n. see* BARK UP THE WRONG TREE *v.*

IN PHRASES

❑ **all wrong** *adj.* [1910s] (*Aus.*) drunk. ❑ **wrong end of the pineapple** *n. see* ROUGH END OF THE PINEAPPLE *under* ROUGH *adj.* ❑ **wrong in one's garret** *adj.* [GARRET *n.* (1)] [mid-19C] insane, eccentric. ❑ **wrong in one's nut** *adj.* [NUT *n.*[1] (1b)] [late 19C] mad, eccentric. ❑ **wrong in one's upper storey** *adj.* [UPPER STOREY *under* UPPER *adj.*] [mid-19C+] insane. ❑ **wrong in the bellows** *adj.* [1900s] insane.

wrong *adv.* [mid-19C] in a criminal or socially unacceptable manner.

IN PHRASES

❑ **get down wrong** *v.* [1970s] (*US black*) to misbehave. ❑ **get in wrong** *v.* **1** [1910s–50s] to blunder, to get oneself into trouble. **2** [1910s+] to irritate, to annoy.

wrong for *adj.* [WRONG *adj.* (3)] [1970s] (*US Und.*) biased against.

wrong guy *n.* (*also* **wrong gee, wrong Injun**) [WRONG *adj.* (3) + GUY *n.*[2] (1) / GEE *n.*[3] (1) / INJUN *n.* (1)] [1920s+] (*US Und.*) **1** an incompetent, an untrustworthy person; a criminal. **2** an informer [spec. use of sense 1].

wrongo *n.* (*also* **wronggo, wrong-o**) [-O *sfx* (2)] [1930s+] (*orig. US*) **1** a criminal; in weak use, an undesirable person. **2** a mistake, error or lie.

wrongo *adj.* [WRONGO *n.*] [1950s+] (*US*) **1** mistaken, inept, prone to error. **2** unpleasant, undesirable.

wrong 'un *n.* [racing jargon *wrong 'un*, a horse that had been deliberately pulled up during a race; ult. SE *wrong one*] [late 19C+] **1** an untrustworthy, incompetent person, animal, action, circumstance, event. **2** a piece of counterfeit money. **3** a prostitute. **4** a law-breaker, a criminal.

wrought *see* RORT and its combs.

wrought iron! *excl.* [joc. var. on the excl. RIGHT ON! *excl.*] [1970s] (*US campus*) an excl. of approval.

wrung out (like a dishcloth) *adj.* [1950s+] (*orig. US*) exhausted.

wrung-up *adj.* [play on UPTIGHT *adj.*[2] (1)] [1980s] (*US campus*) over excited, out of control.

wry mouth and a pissen pair of breeches *n.* [SE *wry*, contorted, twisted + *pissen*, pissed upon; i.e. the effect on the victim's bodily functions] [late 18C–early 19C] a hanging.

wry neck day *n.* [for ety. *see* WRY MOUTH AND A PISSEN PAIR OF BREECHES *n.*] [late 18C–early 19C] the hanging day.

w.s. *n. see* WATER SPORTS *under* WATER *n.*[1].

w/s *n.* (*also* **w.s.**) [abbr. *water sports*] [1960s+] used in sex contact advertisements, urolagnia.

w.t. *n.* [abbr. WHITE TRASH *n.*] [2000s] (*UK juv.*) a derog. ref. to poor, working-class/underclass pupils.

W.T.F! *excl. see* WHAT THE FUCK! *excl.*

W2 *n.* [the signature affixed to his telegram sent to Paul Kruger (1825–1904), president of the South African Republic and leader of the Boers, on New Year's day 1896] [late 19C] the German Kaiser Wilhelm II (r.1888–1918); thus ext. to any military-looking man.

wuckless *adj.* [ety. unknown] [1990s+] (*UK juv.*) homosexual.

wuk *v.* [pron. of/var. on WORK *v.* (1)/WHACK IT IN *under* WHACK *v.*[1]/ WAX *v.*[2] (4)] [1990s+] (*UK black*) to have sexual intercourse.

wukka *n.* [? WICKED *adj.* (2) + PUKKA *adj.*] [1980s+] (*US campus*) a very good-looking man or woman.

wump *n. see* WHOMP *n.*

wuppie *n.* [initial letter of SE *w*ebsite + YUPPIE *n.*] [1990s+] a young urban professional who has made money via the Internet.

wurp *n.* [? abbr. of TWERP *n.*] [1920s] (*US*) a social inadequate.

wuss *n.* (*also* **wuss bag, wussette, wussy**) [WIMP *n.*[1] (2) + PUSSY *n.* (10); note Eble (1996) gives first use as 1976] [1970s+] (*orig. US teen*) a weakling, someone who cannot be depended on.

IN PHRASES

□ **wuss out** *v.* [1970s+] to lose courage, to backdown.

wusser *n.* [? play on Ger. *wasser*, water] [late 19C] a canal boat.

wussify *v.* [1990s+] to render weak.

wussy *adj.* [WUSS *n.*] [1970s+] cowardly, weak, effeminate.

wuzzy *adj.* see WOOZY *adj.*

w.w. *n.* see WIBLING'S WITCH *n.*

Wyatt Earp *n.*[1] [rhy. sl. = CURP *n.*, backsl. PRICK *n.* (1); ult. US lawman *Wyatt Earp* (1848–1929)] [1970s] the penis.

Wyatt Earp *n.*[2] [rhy. sl.; ult. US lawman *Wyatt Earp* (1848–1929)] [2000s] a burp.

wylin' *adj.* [ext. WILD *adj.* (1)] [2000s] (*US teen*) excellent.

wylo *v.* [orig. Anglo-Chinese] [late 19C] (*UK Und.*) to run away.

wyn *n.* see WIN *n.*

Wyoming ketchup *n.* **1** [1920s] opium. **2** [1930s] (*US*) alcohol.

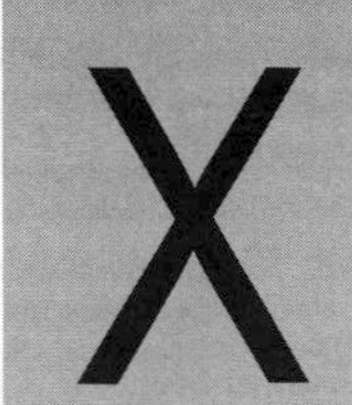

X *n.*[1] [Roman numeral *X*, ten] [mid-19C+] (*US*) a $10 bill, $10 cash.

X *n.*[2]

IN PHRASES

❑ **have the X on** *v.* [note US carnival use *X*, the exclusive right to work a particular novelty or type of concession] [1920s] (*US*) to prove superior to; to place at a disadvantage.

X *n.*[3] [image is that *X* 'marks the spot'] [1950s] (*US drugs*) a narcotic injection.

X *n.*[4] *see* EX *n.*[1].

x *n.*[1] [the crossed position of the arm] [mid-19C] a method of arrest whereby a policeman grasps the villain's collar and holds their arm in such a way that the more they struggle, the more likely it is for the arm to be broken.

x *n.*[2] [pron.] [1950s+] (*W.I.*) the accelerator on a car.

x *n.*[3] [the use of *x* as a code, i.e. because drugs are prohibited] (*drugs*) **1** [1950s+] an injection. **2** [1980s+] (*US drugs*) MDMA [pron. of ECSTASY *n.*]. **3** [1990s+] marijuana.

x *adj.* (*also* **ex**) [*x* = lit. 'cross'] [1950s+] angry.

x *v.*[1] (*also* **ex**) [*x*, a cross, thus cross out] [1950s+] (*Aus./US campus*) to stop, to eliminate.

x *v.*[2] (*also* **x out**) [x *n.*[3] (2)] [1980s+] (*US drugs*) to experience MDMA; usu. as *x-ing*.

X amount *n.* [algebra, where *x* is used for an unknown number] [1980s+] (*US*) a very large amount.

X-cat *n.* [abbr. *category X*] [2000s] (*US prison*) an inmate who is in need of mental health care.

x'ed out *adj.* [X OUT *v.*[1]] [1970s] (*US black*) used of something that, while once important, is no longer relevant.

Xerox *v.* [brandname of Rank *Xerox* Corp., leading copier manufacturers] **1** [1960s–70s] (*US campus*) to cheat in a test. **2** [1990s+] (*US black*) to copy, to imitate.

Xerox copy *n.* [rhy. sl.; *see* XEROX *v.*] [1950s+] (*Aus.*) a Remembrance Day poppy.

Xerox queen *n.* [*Xerox* (see XEROX *v.*) + -QUEEN *sfx* (3)] [1960s+] (*US gay*) a man who prefers all his sexual partners to resemble each other.

X Files *n.* [rhy. sl. = piles; ult. US TV show *X Files*, aired 1993–2002] [1990s+] haemorrhoids.

xippie *n.* [the *X* of Douglas Coupland's *Generation X* + HIPPIE *n.*[2] (3)] [1990s+] a modern young person who wishes to adopt the lifestyle of the hippies of the 1960s.

xis *n. see* EXIS *n.*

X kegger *n. see* KEGGER *n.*

X-man *n.* [such men are not 'real' men but '(e)x-men'; note also *X-Men* Marvel comic book series (f. 1963), made into a film in 2000, where the eponymous heroes are mutants] [1990s+] (*UK juv.*) a male homosexual.

x out *v.*[1] [the use of an 'X' to cross out text] [1970s+] (*US black*) to dismiss something as no longer important or relevant.

x out *v.*[2] *see* X *v.*[2].

x-rated *adj.*

SE in slang uses

IN PHRASES

❑ **get x-rated** *v.* [2000s] (*US black*) to have sexual intercourse.

x-ray *v.* [1950s] (*US black*) to watch closely, to stare at.

X-ray dress *n.* [1920s] (*US*) a see-through dress.

x-row *n.* [fig. use of *x* as 'nameless', or the inmates are the *ex-living*, i.e. looking forward only to execution; note also EX *v.*] [1990s+] (*US prison*) the condemned cells.

x's *n.* (*also* **x.s.**) [abbr./pron.] [mid-19C+] expenses.

X's hall *n.* [*X*, one Hicks, a notoriously punitive judge] [late 19C] the London session house.

XTC *n.* [pron. of ECSTASY *n.*] [1980s+] (*drugs*) MDMA.

XX *n. see* DOUBLE-X *n.*[2].

xyz *n.* [x *n.*[3] (1)] **1** [1950s] (*US drugs*) an infected lesion that results from injecting with an improvised syringe. **2** [1990s+] (*US campus*) a warning to someone whose trousers are unzipped.

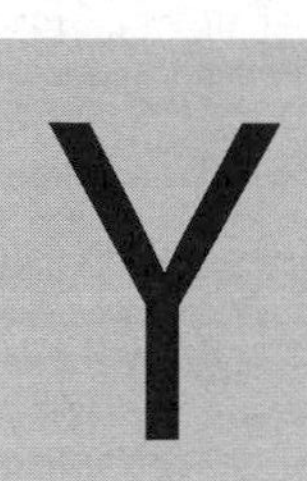

Y *n.* [abbr.] [1910s+] (*orig. US*) the Young Men's Christian Association (YMCA), often as *the Y*.

yaba *n.* (*also* **ya ba**) [Thai *ya ba*, crazy medicine/drug] [1990s+] a form of methamphetamine, orig. created by Nazi chemists during WW2, but particularly popular in Thailand.

yabber *n.* [? pidgin; ult. Wuiwurung *yaba*, to speak, but note SE *jabber*] [mid-19C+] (*Aus.*) talk, chatter.

yabber *v.* [YABBER *n.*] [mid-19C+] (*Aus./N.Z.*) to talk, to chatter; thus n., *yabberer*, a talkative, loquacious person.

yabbos *n.* (*also* **yarbos**) [1980s] (*US campus*) breasts.

yabby *n.* [SAusE *yabby*, a crayfish; the crouching, padded and gauntleted keeper supposedly resembles one] [1980s+] (*Aus.*) in cricket, a wicket-keeper.

yachtie *n.* [abbr.] [1940s+] (*Aus./N.Z.*) a *yacht*ing enthusiast.

yack *n.*[1] [? Welsh gypsy *yakengeri*, a clock, lit. 'a thing of the eyes'] [late 18C–19C] a watch.

yack *n.*[2] (*also* **yak**) [echoic] **1** [1940s+] (*orig. US*) (*also* **yack-yack**) empty, tedious, trivial talk. **2** [1950s] (*US, Western*) a fool. **3** [1950s+] (*US*) a laugh, a joke. **4** [1980s+] (*US campus*) vomit.

yack *adj.* [YUCK *adj.*] [2000s] disgusting.

yack *v.* (*also* **yak**) [YACK *n.*[2]] **1** [1940s+] (*also* **yak it up**) to chatter tediously. **2** [1950s] to laugh. **3** [1950s] to render humorous. **4** [1960s] to fellate someone. **5** [1980s] to make a sharp noise. **6** [1980s+] (*US campus*) (*also* **yag**) to vomit.

yacker *n.*[1] (*also* **yakker**) [YAKKA *n.*, i.e. the result of work is money to buy food] [late 19C+] (*Aus.*) food.

yacker *n.*[2] (*also* **yakkapukee, yakker**) [ext. YACK *n.*[2] (1)] [1950s+] (*Aus.*) **1** talk, chatter. **2** a gossip, one who talks too much.

yacker *n.*[3] *see* YAKKA *n.*

yacker *v.* (*also* **yakker**) [YACK *v.* (1)] [1950s+] (*Aus.*) to talk, to chatter, to gossip.

yackety-yak *n.* (*also* **yackety-yack, yacky-yak, yakety-yack/-yak, yakkety-yack/-yak, yak-yak**) [early 18C use presumably echoic; later use YACK *n.*[2] (1) + redup.] [early 18C; 1940s+] aimless chatter.

yackety-yak *v.* (*also* **yackety-yack, yakety-yack/-yak, yakkety-yack/yak**) [YACKETY-YAK *n.*] [1940s+] to chatter aimlessly.

yacking *n.* (*also* **yakking**) [YACK *v.* (1)] [1950s+] inconsequential chatter.

yack-yack *n. see* YACK *n.*[2] (1).

yacky-yak *n. see* YACKETY-YAK *n.*

yacoo *n.* (*also* **yakoo**) [*Yacub*, the white devil-figure of black Muslim theology] [1960s+] (*US black*) a white racist bigot.

yad *n.* [backsl.] [mid-19C] a day.

yadda yadda yadda *phr.* (*also* **yada yada yada**) [YATTER *n.* + redup.] [1990s+] predictable, repetitive, essentially meaningless chatter.

yadnab *n.* (*also* **yadnarb**) [backsl.] [mid-19C] brandy.

yaffle *v.*[1] [? Yorks. dial. *yaffle*, to mumble or yelp (like a dog)] [late 18C–1930s] (*orig. UK Und.*) to eat or drink, esp. noisily or greedily.

yaffle *v.*[2] [? SNAFFLE *v.* (1)] [1910s–50s] (*US Und.*) to arrest, to snatch, to take.

yaffner *n.* [ety. unknown] [late 19C–1930s] (*US black*) an untrustworthy person, a tell-tale.

yag *v. see* YACK *v.* (6).

yaga yaga *n.* [YAGA-YAGA! *excl.*] [1980s+] (*W.I. Rasta*) a friend, an intimate.

yaga-yaga! *excl.* [fig. use of RAGA-RAGA *adj.*; the 'y' substitution comes from the folk-tales of Anansi the spider, whose 'Bungo talk' uses 'y' for 'r'] [1980s+] (*W.I./UK black teen*) a greeting, a means of attracting attention to oneself.

yagga-yagga *n.* [Cassidy & LePage, *Dict. Jam. English* (1980), suggest 'Bungo talk' substitution of *y* for *r*, thus ref. to *rags* and the person that wears them] [1990s+] (*W.I.*) unmannerly behaviour.

yahoo *n.*[1] [Jonathan Swift's *Gulliver's Travels* (1727), in which the *Yahoos* were an imaginary race of brutes having the form of men; note Aus. *yahoo*, a prob. mythical creature resembling a large hairy man, said to haunt eastern Australia] **1** [18C+] a person lacking cultivation or sensibility, a philistine, a hooligan. **2** [1970s+] a person.

yahoo *n.*[2] *see* YEYO *n.*

yahoo *v.* [YAHOO *n.*[1] (1)] [late 19C+] to behave in a loutish manner.

Yah-yah *n.* [Ger. *ja, ja*, yes, yes] [late 19C] **1** a German. **2** the German language.

yak *see under* YACK.

yak *n.*[1] [YACK *v.* (1); i.e. one who talks rubbish all the time; and/or someone who looks like a SE *yak*] [1980s+] (*US*) a general term of abuse.

yak *n.*[2] *see* 'GNAC *n.*

yakety-yack/-yak *see under* YACKETY-YAK.

yakka *n.* (*also* **yacker, yakker**) [Jagara *yaga*, work; but note Ulster *yokkin*, a spell of work, lit. the 'yoking' of horses] [late 19C+] (*Aus.*) exhausting work.

yakka *v.* (*also* **yakker**) [YAKKA *n.*; note J.D. Lang, *Cooksland* (1847) 447: 'The word *yacca* in the Moreton Bay dialect of the Aboriginal language, is one of those unfortunate words that has more than double duty to perform. It signifies everything in the shape of service or performance from the first incipient attempts at motion, to the most violent exertion, and it usually takes its signification from the noun to which it is appended, as in the instance [...] mooyoom yacca, to read, to write, or to cast accounts.'] [late 19C+] (*Aus.*) to work hard, to labour.

yakkapukee *n. see* YACKER *n.*[2].

yakker *see under* YACKER.

yakkety-yack/-yak *see under* YACKETY-YAK.

yakking *n. see* YACKING *n.*

yak off *v.* [? joc. pron. of JACK OFF *v.*[1] (2)] [1960s] (*US Und.*) to masturbate someone.

yakoo *n. see* YACOO *n.*

yaks *n. see* YOKS *n.*

yak-yak *n. see* YACKETY-YAK *n.*

yale *n.* [brandname of the syringe] **1** [1960s–70s] (*US drugs*) a hypodermic syringe. **2** [1980s+] (*drugs*) crack cocaine [misreading of sense 1].

yaller-boy *n. see* YELLOW BOY *under* YELLOW *adj.*

yaller gal *n. see* YELLOW GIRL *under* YELLOW *adj.*

yally-molly *n.* [MOLL *n.* (1) + ety. unknown] [mid-19C] (*UK Und.*) a quarrelsome woman.

yam *n.* [West African words such as Hausa *nama*, flesh, meat; Swahili *nyama*, meat; Fulah *nyama*, to eat; all these in turn based on SE *yam*, a variety of edible tuber] **1** [early 18C+] food; 'this word is used by the lowest class all over the world; by the Wapping sailor, West India negro, or Chinese coolie' (Hotten, 1867). **2** [mid-19C–1920s] (*US black*) a West Indian.

yam *v.* [YAM *n.* (1)] [early 18C+] to eat.

ya mamma! *excl. see* YO' MAMA! *excl.*

yamneck *n.* (*also* **yamhead**) [1920s–40s] (*US*) a person, a fellow, usu. foolish.

yanepatine *n. see* YENNEPATINE *n.*

yang *n.* [var. on WANG *n.*[2] (1)] [1960s+] the penis.

IN PHRASES

❑ **out the yang** *see* UP THE YING-YANG *under* YING-YANG *n.*

yanga *n. see* NYANGA *n.*

yang yang *n.* [nonsense word + ? play on YANG *n.* on pattern of COCK *n.*[5] (2)] [1980s+] (*Aus./US campus*) nonsense, rubbish.

Yank *n.* [abbr. SE *Yankee*; ult. Du. *Janke*, a dimin. of Jan (John) and coined as a derisive nickname by either the Dutch or the English in the New England states. Substantial documentary evidence bears this out, with many late 18C–early 19C records of sailors, pirates and one black slave nicknamed *yankey, yanky or yankee*. The term is most likely an elision of *Jan Kees* (Kees being a dimin. of Cornelius), the Dutch equivalent of 'Joe Doakes' or 'John Doe' and based in its turn on *Jan Kaas*, lit. 'John Cheese'. It seems to have been coined as a nickname for the Dutch settlers, then, with the appearance of the English in Connecticut, used on the newcomers by the Dutch and then ext. to the whole of New England] **1** [late 18C+] a usu. derog. term for an American. **2** [mid-19C–1920s] (*also* **Yanky**) a Northerner, a New Englander; a Union soldier.

Yank *adj.* [YANK *n.* (1)] [mid-19C+] American.

IN COMPOUNDS

❑ **Yank tank** *n.* [1980s+] (*N.Z.*) a large US car.

Yank *v.* [YANK *n.* (1)] [1940s] of British women, to pick up American servicemen during WW2.

yank *n.*[1] [YANK *v.*[1] (1)] **1** [early 19C+] a tug, a pull, a wrench. **2** [1940s] (*US*) a hurry. **3** [2000s] an act of masturbation.

yank *n.*[2] *see* YANKEE *n.*[1] (3).

yank *v.*[1] [ety. unknown] (*orig. US*) **1** [mid-19C+] to drag, to pull. **2** [late 19C–1900s] to earn, to win money; thus n. *yank-down*, a profit, a commission [var. on PULL DOWN *v.* (3)]. **3** [late 19C+] to arrest. **4** [1900s] (*US*) to victimize, to harass, to dupe. **5** [1910s+] to masturbate; in phrs. below. **6** [1940s+] to remove. **7** [1990s+] (*US campus*) (*also* **yoink**) to steal.

IN PHRASES

❑ **yank (off)** *v.* [1910s+] to masturbate. ❑ **yank one's crank** *v.* [CRANK *n.*[3] (1)] [1970s+] (*US*) to masturbate. ❑ **yank one's meat** *v.* [MEAT *n.* (2)] [1970s+] to masturbate. ❑ **yank someone's chain** *v.* (*also* **yank someone's crank**) [1960s+] to irritate someone, to annoy someone, to remind or distract someone forcibly. ❑ **yank someone's coat** *v.* [ext. of *PULL SOMEONE'S COAT under* PULL *v.*] [2000s] (*US prison*) to confront a fellow-inmate with a secret they do not wish to be revealed. ❑ **yank the plank** *v.* [PLANK *n.*[3] + assonance; or poss. rhy. sl. = WANK *v.* (1)] [1990s+] to masturbate. ❑ **yank up** *v.* [1930s+] to bring up or educate a child roughly, without controls, manners or discipline.

yank *v.*[2] [echoic] [1980s] (*US campus*) to vomit.

yankee *n.*[1] [SE *Yankee*] **1** [19C] (*US*) a glass of whisky sweetened with molasses. **2** [mid-19C] (*UK Und.*) a black man. **3** [mid-19C–1900s] (*also* **yank**) a cheater, a swindler. **4** [1900s] (*also* **yankee-trick**) an act of cheating.

SE in slang uses

IN COMPOUNDS

❑ **Yankee heaven** *n.* (*also* **Yankee paradise**) [the dictum 'When good Americans die, they go to Paris', coined c.1860 by Thomas G. Appleton (1812–84)] [late 19C] Paris. ❑ **Yankee shout** *n.* (*also* **Scotch shout, Scotchman's shout**) [stereotyping of SE *Yankees* or *Scots* as miserly + SHOUT *n.* (1b); such individual payments run contrary to the Aus. tradition of buying rounds for one's whole company] [1940s–60s] (*Aus./N.Z.*) a round of drinks where each individual buys their own drink; anything where people pay for themselves. ❑ **Yankee's yawn** *n.* [1950s–60s] (*US gay*) the open mouth of a climaxing male.

yankee *n.*[2] [YANK (OFF) *under* YANK *v.*[1]] [1970s–80s] (*gay*) masturbation; a masturbator.

yankee *v.* (*also* **come yankee over/with, play yankee over/with**) [SE *Yankee*, i.e. the poor reputation of New England businessmen and lawyers + COME OVER *v.*[1]/SE *play*] [19C+] to cheat, to drive a hard bargain.

Yankee Doodle *n.* [SE *Yankee*] [early 19C] spec. a New-Englander.

Yankee Doodles *n.* [rhy. sl.] [1990s+] noodles.

Yankeeland *n.* (*also* **Yankieland, Yankland**) [SE *Yankee*/YANK *n.*] [early 19C+] America.

yankeeries *n.* [SE *Yankee*] [late 19C] Buffalo Bill's Wild West Show, which arrived in London in 1887 (and was seen at Earl's Court by Queen Victoria).

yanker *n.* [YANK (OFF) *under* YANK *v.*[1]] [1930s+] (*US*) a masturbator.

Yankieland/Yankland *n. see* YANKEELAND *n.*

Yank mag *n.* [play on YANK *n.* (1)/YANK *v.*[1] (5) + MAG *n.*[4] (1)] [1960s] American pulp magazines, as distributed in the UK.

Yanky *n. see* YANK *n.* (2).

yannep/yannup *n. see* YENNEP *n.*

yanta *n.* [ety. unknown; ? link to YENTA *n.*] [1990s+] (*US*) a derog. term for a black person.

yaoh *n. see* YEYO *n.*

y.a.p. *n.* [abbr.] [1980s] (*US*) a young aspiring professional.

yap *n.*[1] [SE *yap*, a yelping dog; or its bark] **1** pertaining to speech. (**a**) [mid-19C+] (*US*) (*also* **yapper, yop**) the mouth, usu. in derog. sense, e.g. *shut your yap!* etc. (**b**) [mid-19C+] (*orig. US*) (*also* **yop**) idle, trivial chatter. (**c**) [20C+] (*Irish*) (*also* **yerp**) a whining, complaining person. (**d**) [20C+] (*also* **yapper, yap yap**) (*US*) a chatterer. (**e**) [1910s–20s] (*US*) a tell-tale, an informer. (**f**) [1950s] a sound. (**g**) [1950s+] (*orig. US*) a chat, a conversation. (**h**) [1980s] a petty swindler. **2** fig., derog. uses. (**a**) [late 19C–1940s] (*US*) a contemptible person, irrespective of class or background. (**b**) [late 19C+] (*US*) (*also* **yawp**) a derog. term for a peasant, a rustic simpleton. (**c**) [20C+] (*US Und.*) a criminal's victim. (**d**) [1920s] (*US tramp*) a novice within the hobo community.

IN COMPOUNDS

❑ **yap-bean** *n.* [BEAN *n.*[1] (3)] [1920s] (*US*) a rustic. ❑ **yap wagon** *n.* [1920s] (*US*) a vehicle taking tourists on sightseeing tours.

IN PHRASES

❑ **clap one's yap** *v.* [1950s] (*US*) to be quiet.

yap *n.*[2] [? Chinese surname] [1950s] (*W.I.*) a Chinese person.

yap *v.*[1] [dial. *yap*, to talk loudly, foolishly] **1** [early 19C+] (*also* **yap it up**) to talk, to make a noise, esp. to shout at, like a dog. **2** [20C+] (*US*) to complain, to nag.

yap *v.*[2] [backsl.] [mid–late 19C] to pay back; thus *yap-poo, yap-pu*, pay up.

yapper *n. see* YAP *n.*[1].

yappies, the *n.* [SE *yap*, to bark] [1940s+] (*Aus.*) 'the dogs', i.e. greyhound racing, coursing.

yap-poo/-pu *v. see* YAP *v.*[2].

yappy *adj.* [YAP *n.*[1]] **1** [mid-19C+] foolish, soft. **2** [20C+] (*Ulster*) thin, hungry-looking [one's mouth is fig. open with hunger]. **3** [1930s+] (*orig. US*) noisy, talkative; thus *yappiness*, verbosity. **4** [1990s+] (*US campus*) over-generous.

yapster *n.* [SE *yap*, to bark + sfx *-ster*] [late 18C–19C] a dog.

yap yap *n. see* YAP *n.*[1] (1d).

yap-yap *v.* [YAP *n.*[1] (1a) + redup.] [1950s] (*W.I.*) to open one's mouth wide through hunger.

yar *adj.* [ety. unknown] [1960s] (*US*) in love.

yaram *n. see* YARRUM *n.*

yarbles *n.* [? link to dial. *yarb*, 'an opprobrious epithet' (*EDD*) + BALLS *n.*; popularized by the film *A Clockwork Orange* (1971)] [1970s+] **1** testicles. **2** courage, guts.

yarbos *n. see* YABBOS *n.*

Yard *n.* [1980s+] Jamaica, often as *the Yard;* thus YARDIE *n.*

DERIVATIVES

❑ **yardie** *n. see* separate entry.

IN COMPOUNDS

❑ **yardman** *n.* [1980s+] (*W.I./UK black teen*) a Jamaican, a Jamaican gangster.

Yard, the *n.* [20C+] Scotland Yard; later New Scotland Yard, the headquarters of London's Metropolitan Police.

yard *n.*[1] (*also* **yeard**) [prior use SE f. late 14C; Old Teutonic *gazdjo*, a thin pole + ? link to Lat. *hasta*, a spear + Ital. *cazzo*, penis; note *double entendre* in D'Urfey, *Pills to Purge Melancholy* (1719): 'A fine dapper Taylor, with a Yard in his hand, / Did profer his Service to be at Command'] [19C] the penis.

yard *n.*[2] **1** [20C+] (*W.I./UK black*) one's home; one's community. **2** [1910s+] (*US prison*) the recreation area of a prison. **3** [1920s+] a house or other dwelling place. **4** [1970s] (*S.Afr.*) a brothel. **5** [1980s+] (*US campus*) the campus. **6** [1990s+] (*Irish*) a toilet.

IN COMPOUNDS

❑ **yard bull** *n.* [BULL *n.*[5]] **1** [1910s+] (*US*) (*also* **railroad dick, yard dick**) a railroad police officer, guard or detective [SE *marshalling yard*]. **2** [1930s+] a prison guard. ❑ **yard hack** *n.* [HACK *n.*[3] (4)] [1960s+] (*US*) a prison guard. ❑ **yard patrol** *n.* [20C+] (*US prison*) **1** a group of convicts. **2** a prison guard. ❑ **yard queen** *n.* [-QUEEN *sfx* (3)] [2000s] (*US prison*) a prison homosexual. ❑ **yard rat** *n.* [RAT *n.*[1] (1h)] **1** [1990s+] (*US prison*) a prisoner who frequents the prison yard, socializing with friends. **2** [2000s] in a non-prison context.

IN PHRASES

❑ **on the yard** [1980s+] (*US prison*) of a prisoner, associating with the general population (rather than in solitary confinement or protective custody). ❑ **play in someone else's yard** *v.* [1950s+] (*US black*) to have an adulterous affair.

SE in slang uses

IN COMPOUNDS

❑ **yard boy** *n.* [1990s+] (*US gay*) one who prefers sex outdoors. ❑ **yard dog** *n.* [1930s–40s] (*US black*) **1** a fool, a gullible person. **2** an ill-dressed, badly behaved individual. **3** a loyal but mediocre companion. ❑ **yard fowl** *n.* [1970s+] (*W.I.*) a term of abuse. ❑ **yard nigger** *n.* [NIGGER *n.*[1] (1); the differentiation under slavery between the 'domesticated' blacks who worked as house servants and those who, seen as more rebellious, merely toiled in the plantation fields] [20C+] a subservient, acquiescent black.

IN EXCLAMATIONS

❑ **get up the yard!** [20C+] (*Irish*) **1** an invitation to have sexual intercourse. **2** a general dismissive excl.

yard *n.*[3] **1** [1920s+] (*US*) 100, usu. of dollars. **2** [1930s+] (*US prison*) a year, thus a sentence of one year. **3** [1960s] (*drugs*) $100 worth of heroin. **4** [1990s+] (*US Und.*) a sentence of 100 years.

IN PHRASES

❑ **half-a-yard** *n.* (*also* **half-yard**) **1** [1920s+] (*US*) $5. **2** [1960s] $50 (in drugs, $50 worth of heroin).

yard *n.*[4]

SE in slang uses

IN PHRASES

❑ **yard of clay** *n.* [19C] a clay pipe with a notably long stem. ❑ **yard of pump water** *n.* [late 19C] a tall, thin person. ❑ **yard of satin** *n.* [SE *yard*, a glass + SATIN *n.* (1a)] [early 19C–1920s] a glass of gin. ❑ **yard of tape** *n.* [SE *yard*, a glass + TAPE *n.*] [mid-19C] (*UK Und.*) a glass of gin.

yard *adj.* [YARD *n.*] [1990s+] (*W.I./UK black*) Jamaican.

yard *v.*[1] [YARD *n.*[1]] [mid-18C] (*UK Und.*) of man, to have sexual intercourse.

yard *v.*[2] **1** [1900s] (*Aus.*) to marry. **2** [1910s–40s] to round up; to imprison.

yard *v.*[3] [fig. uses of SE *yard*] **1** [1950s+] (*US black*) (*also* **yard on**) to be sexually unfaithful [note *PLAY IN SOMEONE ELSE'S YARD under* YARD *n.*[2]]. **2** [1960s] (*US black*) to chat, to make small talk [image of chatting over the fence between two backyards].

yardbird *n.*[1] [SE *yard* + BIRD *n.*[1] (3a)/BIRD *n.*[1] (2b)] [1940s+] (*US*) **1** a civilian dock worker in a military institution, e.g. a naval dockyard. **2** anyone confined by authority to a restricted area, usu. prison.

IN COMPOUNDS

❑ **yardbird lawyer** *n.* [1940s+] (*US Und.*) a prison inmate who has become a self-taught lawyer, either to pursue his own case, to combat prison corruption or to help fellow inmates.

yardbird *n.*[2] (*also* **pigeon**) [1990s+] (*US prison*) fried chicken.

yardie *n.* [YARD *n.*] [1980s+] (*orig. W.I.*) **1** a Jamaican [Francis-Jackson, *Official Dancehall Dict.* (1995), defines this as 'a Jamaican residing overseas']. **2** one of a gang of Jamaican organized criminals who specialize in purveying drugs and violence on an international level.

yardnarb *n.* [backsl.] [late 19C] brandy.

yard of tripe *n.* [rhy. sl.] [mid-19C] a pipe.

yarf *v.* [echoic] [1990s+] (*US campus*) to vomit.

yarm *n. see* YARRUM *n.*

Yarmouth bloater *n.*[1] [the town's main occupation: fishing] [mid-19C] an inhabitant of Yarmouth.

Yarmouth bloater *n.*[2] [rhy. sl. = MOTOR *n.* (2)] [1910s+] an automobile.

Yarmouth capon *n.* (*also* **Norfolk capon**) [the local fishing industry] **1** [mid-17C–1900s] a red herring. **2** [early 19C] a soldier, i.e. his red coat. **3** [mid-19C] a bloater.

yarn *n.* [the stories told by sailors during the lengthy processes of making ropes; note Hall Caine, *The Deemster* (1897): 'Without motive a story is not a novel, but only a yarn': in other words, a *yarn* implies the dichotomy between 'literary' and 'popular' writing] (*orig. naut.*) **1** [early 19C+] a story, esp. a long and poss. implausibly wonderful one. **2** [1910s+] a chat, a conversation.

IN COMPOUNDS

❑ **yarn-chopper** *n.* (*also* **yarn-slinger, yarn-spinner**) [late 19C–1920s] a story-teller, a chatterer.

IN PHRASES

❑ **pitch a yarn** *v.* (*also* **pitch a tale**) [mid-19C+] to recount a story. ❑ **sling a yarn** *v.* [SLING *v.* (2a)] [late 19C+] to tell a story.

yarn *v.* [YARN *n.*] **1** [early 19C+] to tell tales, prob. implausible or far-fetched ones. **2** [mid-19C+] to talk to, to chatter with.

yarpie *n.* [JAAP *n.*] [1980s+] (*Aus.*) a South African; thus *Yarpieland*, South Africa.

yarra *adj.* [the psychiatric hospital at *Yarra* Bend, Victoria] [late 19C+] (*Aus.*) insane; thus *yarra*, n. a stupid person.

Yarra banker *n.* [the *banks* of the *Yarra* are the equivalent of London's Hyde Park Corner] [late 19C–1940s] (*Aus.*) **1** (*also* **Yarra-sider**) a soap-box orator. **2** (*also* **Yarra bender**) an idler, a loafer found on the banks of Melbourne's Yarra River.

yarrum *n.* (*also* **yaram, yarm, yarrim, yarum**) [? a corruption of SE *yellow* or *yallow*; 1573 edn of Harman has *param*; Ribton-Turner, *A History of Vagrants* (1887), suggests Gaelic *uaram*, fresh water] [mid-16C–mid-19C] (*UK Und.*) milk; thus *poplars of yarrum*, milk porridge.

yasha *n.* [Rus. *yasha*, a peasant] [1970s] (*camp gay*) an idiot, a fool.

yassas! *excl. see* YISSUS! *excl.*

yasser *n.* [*CRACK A FAT under* FAT *n.*, i.e. a pun on PLO leader *Yasser Arafat* (1929–2004)] [1990s+] (*US*) an erection.

yat *n. see* YATTY *n.*

yatata *n.* [YATTER *v.*] [1940s–50s] (*US*) talk, chatter; also as v., to talk montonously, tediously.

yattaboy! *excl. see* ATTABOY! *excl.*

yatter *n.* [orig. Scot.] [early 19C+] talk, chatter, gabble.

yatter *v.* [YATTER *n.*] [early 19C+] to talk, to chatter, to gabble.

yatty *n.* [ety. unknown] [2000s] (*UK black*) **1** (*also* **yat**) a young woman, a girlfriend; esp. derog., i.e. a promiscous woman, a prostitute. **2** a cowardly man.

yaup *v. see* YAWP *v.*

yaupy *adj.* (*also* **yaupish**) [YAWP v. (1); note SE *yawpish*, hungry] [19C] drunk.

yawn *n.* [late 19C+] anything or anyone considered tedious, boring and thus productive of *yawns*.

yawner *n.* [YAWN *n.* + sfx *-er*] [1940s+] (*US*) anything boring, yawn-producing.

yawney *n.* (*also* **yawny**) [dial.; their mouth *yawns* open in stupidity] [19C; 1950s] a fool, a simpleton; also as adj., simple.

yawn graveyards *v.* [late 19C] (*US campus*) to yawn excessively.

yawp *n.*[1] [YAWP v.] (*US*) **1** [1910s–20s] the mouth. **2** [1970s+] loud or foolish chatter.

yawp *n.*[2] *see* YAP *n.*[1] (2b).

yawp *v.* (*also* **yaup**) [dial./YAP *v.*[1] (1)] **1** [late 19C+] (*orig. US*) to talk loudly or foolishly, to nag. **2** [1940s] to vomit.

yay *n. see* YEYO *n.*

yay *adv. see* YEA *adv.*

ya-ya *n.* [their use of Ger. *ja*, yes] [2000s] (*N.Z.*) a German tourist.

yay-nay *n.* [bereft of communicative powers, they can only answer 'yea' or 'nay' to any question] [mid-19C] a simpleton, an unsophisticated person.

yayo *n.* [? YEYO *n.*] [2000s] (*US black*) **1** marijuana. **2** money.

yayo/yayoo *n. see* YEYO *n.*

y-bone steak *n.* [the fork of the thighs + play on SE *T-bone steak*] [1970s] the female genitals.

yea *adv.* (*also* **yay**) [1950s+] (*orig. US black*) this, e.g. *yea big*, this big; *yea high*, this high.

yea and nay (man) *n.* [the Quakers' supposed predilection for simple, black and white answers; the simpleton's inability to deal in complexities] [late 17C–early 19C] **1** a Quaker. **2** a simpleton, capable of answering only 'yes' or 'no'; thus a poor conversationalist, a monosyllabic person.

yeah *adv.* (*also* **yeh**) [pron.] [late 19C+] (*orig. US*) yes.

yeah man *n.* [such a person chatters on; one intersperses their monologue by saying 'Yeah, man' occasionally] [1980s+] (*US campus*) a boring person.

yeaho *n. see* YEYO *n.*

yeah, right *phr. see* RIGHT *phr.*

year *n.* [1940s–50s] (*US Und.*) $1; thus *five years*, $5 etc.

yeard *n. see* YARD *n.*[1].

year dot *n. see under* DOT *n.*[2].

yearn *n.* [1970s] (*drugs*) an obsession with and desire for narcotic drugs that precedes a full-blown physical addiction.

year one *n. see* YEAR DOT *under* DOT *n.*[2].

yeasting *n.* [the way in which yeast makes otherwise flat dough rise] [1940s–60s] (*US black*) exaggerating, boasting.

yecch/yech *see under* YUCK.

yecchy *adj. see* YUCKY *adj.*

yeck!/yeech! *excl. see* YUCK! *excl.*

yeeick! *excl. see* YIKES! *excl.*

yegg *n.* (*also* **johnny yeg, john yegg, yegger, yeggman**) [? John *Yegg*, a contemporary villain and the first safe-breaker to use nitroglycerine; however, Cohen (ed.), *Studies in Slang* VI (1999) 22–6, notes article in *S.F Chronicle* 6/3/1904 citing criminal John Yeager who led a gang of tramps who robbed the Reading railroad; his name was the basis of generic 'John Yegg', the notional leader of all similar gangs; note also Jack Black, *You Can't Win* (1926): 'Yegg [...] is a corruption of "yekk", a word from one of the many dialects spoken in Chinatown, and it means beggar. When a hypo or beggar approached a Chinaman to ask for something to eat, he was greeted with the exclamation, "yekk man, yekk man." The underworld is quick to seize upon strange words, and the bums and hypos in Chinatown were calling themselves yeggmen years before the term was taken out on the road and given currency by eastbound beggars. In no time it had a verb hung on it, and to yegg meant to beg. The late William A. Pinkerton was responsible for its changed meaning [...] A burglar with some humor fell into Pinkerton's hands and when asked who was breaking open the country "jugs" he whispered to the detective that it was the yeggs. Investigation convinced Pinkerton that there were a lot of men drifting about the country who called themselves yeggs. The word went into a series of magazine articles Pinkerton was writing at the time and was fastened upon the "box" men. Its meaning has since widened until now the term "yegg" includes all criminals whose work is "heavy"'; Irwin, *American Tramp and Und. Slang* (1931), suggests: 'Originally a man too wise, too cautious, too old or too cowardly to risk crime in a city, where police and private detectives were alert, and who took to "the road" for easier "graft" and "pickings"'] (*US Und.*) **1** [20C+] a thief, spec. a safe-cracker; thus *yegg mob*, a gang of safe-breakers. **2** [20C+] any variety of criminal. **3** [1900s] a beggar. **4** [1910s–20s] a hold-up man, a robber with violence. **5** [1910s–30s] (*also* **yeg**) a beggar.

yegg *v.* [YEGG *n.*] [1900s–30s] (*US Und.*) **1** to hold up and rob. **2** to break open a safe.

ye gods (and little fishes)! *excl.* [early 18C–1950s] a mild oath.

yeh *adv. see* YEAH *adv.*

Yehudi *n.* [Heb. *yehudi*, a Jew] [20C+] (*US*) a Jew.

yeknod *n.* (*also* **jerk-nod**) [backsl.] [mid-19C] a donkey.

yell *n.*[1] [its *yell*ow colour] [mid–late 19C] beer; thus *yell-house*, ale house.

yell *n.*[2] **1** [1920s+] (*also* **yells**) something or someone hilarious. **2** [1950s] (*US Und.*) the betrayal of one's confederates. **3** [1950s] (*US black*) someone considered excellent, attractive. **4** [1960s+] an act of vomiting.

yell *v.* [1940s–50s] (*US Und.*) to confess; to betray and/or testify against an accomplice; to register a complaint.

(IN PHRASES)

❑ **yell calf-rope** *v. see* HOLLER CALF-ROPE *under* HOLLER *v.* ❑ **yell copper** *v. see* HOLLER COPPER *v.*

yeller *n.* [SE *yell*, i.e. his verbosity] [1950s] (*US Und.*) a lawyer.

yeller feller *n. see* YELLOW FELLOW *under* YELLOW *adj.*

yellow *n.* **1** [mid-17C] in pl., constr. with *the*, a venereal infection, esp. gonorrhoea [the pus-filled discharge]. **2** [late 19C+] cowardice; often as *streak of yellow*. **3** as gold. (**a**) [1910s] a sovereign, £1 sterling. (**b**) [1920s] (*US tramp*) a gold watch. **4** as skin tone. (**a**) [1910s–20s] an Asian. (**b**) [1920s+] a light-skinned black person. **5** [1930s] a coward. **6** [1940s] (*US Und.*) a (fake) telegram used in confidence tricks. **7** in drug uses. (**a**) [1960s+] (*drugs*) a Nembutal, a depressant [the colour of the pills]. (**b**) *see* MELLOW YELLOW *n.* (2). **8** [1970s] (*US*) a taxi [colour of New York City taxis].

yellow *adj.* **1** [early 17C+] jealous; thus *yellows*, jealousy. **2** pertaining to skin tone. (**a**) [late 18C+] (*US*) of a black person, light-skinned. (**b**) [late 18C+] of a person, of mixed race, half-white, half-black. (**c**) [mid-19C+] pertaining to East Asia, e.g. Japan or China. **3** [mid-19C–1930s] gold, golden. **4** [mid-19C+] cowardly; thus *yellowness*, cowardice [the negative image of the colour; ? reinforced, even subconsciously, by the widespread use of some form of identification, usu. yellow, forced on European Jews by the Catholic Church; the stereotypical Jew is not a hero]. **5** [late 19C–1970s] (*orig. US*) unsatisfactory, second-rate, of dubious quality.

(IN COMPOUNDS)

pertaining to race, usu. East Asian or mixed-race

❑ **yellow agony** *n.* [generic use of SE *yellow* for Chinese; the *agony* was that of Aus. workers, esp. sailors, who saw their jobs threatened by such immigrants] [late 19C–1910s] (*Aus.*) **1** (*also* **agony**) a generic term for Chinese immigrants to Australia. **2** a single immigrant. ❑ **yellow and black** *n.* [late 19C] (*Aus.*) an Aboriginal. ❑ **yellow-ass** *n.* [-ASS *sfx*] [1930s–60s] (*US*) a light-coloured black woman. ❑ **yellow-black** *n.* [1940s] (*US Und.*) a mulatto. ❑ **yellow boy** *n.* [mid-19C–1900s] (*US*) a mulatto. ❑ **yellow face** *n.* [late 19C–1900s] a Chinese person, usu. derog. ❑ **yellow fellow** *n.* (*also* **yeller feller**) [20C+] (*US/Aus.*) a mulatto, a half-white, half-Aborigine man. ❑ **yellow fever** *n.* [1950s–60s] (*orig. US gay*) an obsession, either hetero- or homosexual, with having East Asian lovers. ❑ **yellow fish** *n.* [20C+] (*US*) an illegal Chinese immigrant. ❑ **yellow girl** *n.* (*also* **yaller gal**) [mid-19C+] a mulatto, a half-white, half-

Aborigine woman. ❑ **yellow goods** *n.* [1940s] (*US Und.*) smuggled Chinese immigrants. ❑ **yellow head** *n.* [-HEAD *sfx* (2)] [1960s] (*US*) a Viet Cong soldier. ❑ **yellow nigger** *n.* (*also* **yellow nig**) [NIGGER *n.*[1] (1)] **1** [mid-19C–1940s] (*US*) a derog. term for a mulatto. **2** [1960s+] an Asian. ❑ **yellow snake** *n.* [late 18C] (*W.I.*) a mulatto. ❑ **yellow tail** *n.* [TAIL *n.* (2)] **1** [1920s] (*US*) a Japanese person. **2** [1970s] (*Aus.*) a person from New South Wales. ❑ **yellow velvet** *n.* [var. on *BLACK VELVET under* BLACK *adj.*] [1970s–80s] an Asiatic woman, esp. in the context of sex.

pertaining to the colour gold or coins

❑ **yellow and white** *n.* [WHITE *adj.* (1)] [late 19C] (*US Und.*) a watch. ❑ **yellow bird** *n.* [the eagle engraved upon these coins] [mid-19C] (*US*) a dollar. ❑ **yellow boy** *n.* **1** [mid-17C–19C] (*also* **yaller-boy**) a sovereign; a guinea (£1.05) or a golden guinea. **2** [1910s–30s] (*US*) money [note *YELLOW BACK* below]. ❑ **yellow dust** *n.* [late 18C] gold, money. ❑ **yellow george** *n.* [GEORGE *n.*[1] (3)] [18C–19C] a guinea. ❑ **yellow jacket** *n.* [mid-19C] (*US*) a gold piece. ❑ **yellow kelter** *n.* [KELTER *n.*] [20C+] (*Irish*) a gold coin. ❑ **yellow one** *n.* **1** [mid-19C] a gold coin. **2** [late 19C–1920s] a gold watch. ❑ **yellow stuff** *n.* [early 19C–1910s] gold; thus money, wealth.

pertaining to cowardice

❑ **yellow back** *n.* **1** [1920s] a coward; thus *yellow-backed*, cowardly. **2** *see also* SE compounds below. ❑ **yellow-bellied** *adj.* (*also* **yellow-ass, -assed, -belly**) [1910s+] cowardly. ❑ **yellow-born** *adj.* [1940s] cowardly. ❑ **yellow guts** *n. see* YELLOW BELLY *n.* (6). ❑ **yellow gutted** *adj.* [GUT *n.* (1a)] [1940s+] cowardly. ❑ **yellow heel** *n. see* YELLOW BELLY *n.* (6). ❑ **yellow leg** *n.* [1900s–10s] (*US*) a strikebreaker [pattern of SE *blackleg*]. ❑ **yellow-livered** *adj. see* WHITE-LIVERED *adj.* (1). ❑ **yellow route** *n.* [1980s] (*S.Afr.*) the departure of white South Africans in the face of the imminent take-over by a multiracial government.

other uses

❑ **yellow gloak** *n.* [GLOAK *n.*] [early–mid-19C] a jealous man, esp. a jealous husband.

SE in slang uses

IN COMPOUNDS

❑ **yellow back** *n.* **1** as a banknote [the former printing of certain denominations of US dollar bills in yellow rather than the usual green]. (**a**) [1900s] a $10 note. (**b**) [1900s–10s] a $500 dollar note. (**c**) [1900s–40s] (*US*) a $20 note. (**d**) [1920s] a $1,000 note. **2** [1940s+] (*Aus.*) a gob of phlegm. **3** *see also* sl. compounds above. ❑ **yellow dimples** *n.* [1970s] (*drugs*) LSD, esp. when combined with another drug. ❑ **yellow eye** *n.* [1940s] (*US black*) an egg. ❑ **yellow fancy** *n.* [mid–late 19C] a costermonger's handkerchief, yellow with white spots. ❑ **yellow jack** *n.* (*also* **yellow johnnies**) [mid-19C+] yellow fever. ❑ **yellow jacket** *n.* **1** [mid-19C] (*Aus.*) a convict [the yellow uniform]. **2** [1950s+] (*orig. US black*) (*also* **jacket, yellow jack**) usu. in pl., Nembutal, a proprietary brand of pentobarbital sodium [the packaging]. ❑ **yellow Jesus** *n.* [its light-brown colour] [1990s+] (*Aus. drugs*) home-manufactured heroin. ❑ **yellow leg** *n.* **1** [mid-19C] (*US*) an East Tennessean. **2** pertaining to a uniform, i.e. the yellow stripe running down the trousers. (**a**) [late 19C] (*US*) a US cavalryman. (**b**) [1940s+] (*Can.*) a member of the Royal Canadian Mounted Police. ❑ **yellow man** *n.* **1** [early–mid-19C] a costermonger's handkerchief, coloured plain yellow. **2** [mid-19C] (*Scot.*) lemonade. ❑ **yellow pack** *n.* [the yellow packaging of the 'own-brand' goods sold by the Quinnsworth chain of supermarkets] [1990s+] (*Irish*) low-paid employment of young people and the concomitant dismissal of more expensive senior employees. ❑ **yellow packet** *adj.* [in 1980s Fine Fare supermarkets offered a range of 'Yellow Packet' goods, generally seen as second-rate and good only for the very poor] [1980s+] (*UK juv.*) cheap, indicative of poverty. ❑ **yellow punk** *n. see* PUNK *n.*[3]. ❑ **yellow sheet** *n.* [SHEET *n.* (4)] [1950s+] (*US Und.*) a criminal's record of arrests. ❑ **yellow sunshine** *n.* [var. on ORANGE SUNSHINE *n.*] [1970s+] (*drugs*) a form of LSD.

IN PHRASES

❑ **yellow brick road** *n.* [ref. to the Yellow Brick Road of the book/movie *The Wizard of Oz*] [2000s] (*US prison*) yellow lines on the ground that indicate areas beyond which prisoners are forbidden to step.

yellow *v.* [YELLOW *adj.* (4)] [1930s–50s] (*US Und.*) to turn cowardly.

IN PHRASES

❑ **do a yellow** *v.* [1960s] to run off in a cowardly fashion. ❑ **yellow up** *v.* [1930s] (*US*) to turn cowardly.

yellow *adv.* [YELLOW *adj.* (4)] [1920s] in a cowardly manner.

yellow belly *n.* **1** [late 18C+] a native of Lincolnshire, esp. of the southern or fenland part of the county [the yellow-stomached frogs and/or the eels that abound there]. **2** [mid-19C] (*US*) a low denomination coin, poss. 25 cents [ety. unknown]. **3** [mid-19C–1910s] (*US*) a Mexican, esp. a soldier [the colour of their uniforms and stereotyping of Mexicans as YELLOW *adj.* (4)]. **4** senses based on the 'yellow' complexion. (**a**) [mid-19C–1930s] a Chinese person; thus *yellow-bellied*, Chinese. (**b**) [late 19C–1930s] (*UK/US*) a half-caste; a Eurasian. (**c**) [1940s] (*Aus.*) a Japanese person. **5** [late 19C] (*US*) a Dutchman [the link of the Dutch to butter]. **6** [1920s+] (*also* **yellow guts, yellow heel**) a coward [*YELLOW-BELLIED under* YELLOW *adj.*].

yellow dog *n.* (*also* **yellow pup**) [late 19C+] (*US*) a general term of contempt for a person or thing.

IN COMPOUNDS

❑ **yellow dog contract** *n.* [1920s+] (*US*) an employee's work contract forbidding union membership.

yellowhammer *n.* [SAmE *yellowhammer*, the golden-winged woodpecker] **1** [early–mid-17C] a golden guinea [the colour of the golden coin]. **2** [mid-19C–1930s] (*US*) an unsophisticated rustic [synon. for PECKERWOOD *n.*]. **3** [late 19C] (*US*) an Alabamian [f. sense 2]. **4** [1900s] (*US*) a Chinese person [YELLOW *adj.* (2c)]. **5** [1910s] (*US*) a coward [YELLOW *adj.* (4)].

yellow peril *n.* [SE *yellow*/YELLOW *adj.* (2c)] **1** [20C+] a derog. term for any East Asian person; the concept that such 'teeming' races are poised to overtake white 'civilization'. **2** in joc. uses. (**a**) [1910s+] a Gold Flake cigarette. (**b**) [1980s] (*UK prison*) vegetable soup. **3** [1960s+] the Communist Chinese.

yellow silk *n.* [rhy. sl.] [late 19C–1900s] milk.

yells *n. see* YELL *n.*[2] (1).

yelper *n.* **1** [early 18C–early 19C] (*also* **yelp**) a town crier. **2** [late 18C] (*UK Und.*) a town clerk. **3** [early 19C] a wild beast. **4** [early–mid-19C] a whiner, a complainer. **5** [1930s–40s] (*US Und.*) an informer. **6** [1950s+] (*US*) a police car or emergency vehicle siren.

yen *n.*[1] (*also* **yin**) [Beijing dial. Chinese *yen*, smoke, poss. reinforced by SE *yearn* (cf. YEARN *n.*)] **1** [late 19C+] (*drugs*) a desperate desire for a narcotic drug, usu. heroin. **2** [20C+] in non-drug contexts, a craving, an intense desire. **3** [1920s–40s] opium.

IN COMPOUNDS

❑ **yen chee** *n. see* YEN-SHEE *n.* (1). ❑ **yen chiang** *n. see YEN TSIANG* below. ❑ **yen dong** *n.* [late 19C–1930s] (*US drugs*) the lamp used to heat 'pills' of opium. ❑ **yen hock** *n.* (*also* **yen hauck, ...hawk, ...hok, ...hoke, ...nock**) **1** [late 19C–1960s] (*US drugs*) the needle used to prepare a pipe of opium. **2** [1910s] attrib., pertaining to a thin object or person. ❑ **yen hop** *n.* [late 19C–1930s] (*US drugs*) the box that contains opium paraphernalia. ❑ **yen on** *n.* [1940s] (*US drugs*) withdrawal from opium addiction. ❑ **yen pok** *n.* [late 19C–1930s] (*US drugs*) a pill of opium. ❑ **yen pop** *n.* [1930s–50s] (*US drugs*) marijuana. ❑ **yen pox** *n.* [1940s–60s] (*drugs*) pills of opium; Burroughs *Junkie* (1953) prefers opium ashes/residue (which can still be recycled when desperate). ❑ **yen-shee** *n. see* separate entry. ❑ **yen-shi** *n. see* YEN-SHEE *n.* (1). ❑ **yen sleep** *n.* [1970s+] (*drugs*) a restless, drowsy sleep that accompanies opiate withdrawal. ❑ **yen tsiang** *n.* (*also* **yen chiang**) [Chinese *yen tsiang*, 'opium pistol'] [mid-19C–1930s] (*US drugs*) an opium pipe. ❑ **yen yen** *n.* [the term uses both the orig. Chinese and the derived SE term; however, note Cantonese *yinyan*, craving for opium] [late 19C–1950s] (*US drugs*) a craving for opium.

IN PHRASES

□ **get one's yen off** *v.* [1930s] (*US drugs*) to satisfy one's need for narcotics when suffering withdrawal symptoms.

yen *n.*[2] [adoption of Jap. *yen*, a gold or silver coin orig. valued at $1 in the mid-19C] [1900s–20s] (*US Und.*) money; a dollar.

yen *v.* [YEN *n.*[1]] **1** [1920s–60s] (*drugs*) to desire narcotics. **2** [1930s–50s] to desire someone or something.

yenams *n.* (*also* **yenems, yenhams**) [synon. Yid. *yenams*, lit. 'his'] [1920s–70s] someone else's property, cigarettes etc.

yenep *n. see* YENNEP *n.*

yeng *n.* [? echoic of a shot] [1970s] (*US black*) a gun.

yenhams *n. see* YENAMS *n.*

yennep *n.* (*also* **yannep, yannup, yenep, yennap, yennop**) [backsl.] [mid-19C+] a penny.

yennepatine *n.* (*also* **yanepatine**) [backsl.; YENNEP *n.*] [mid-19C] a penny a time.

yennep flatch *n.* [backsl.; YENNEP *n.* + FLATCH *n.*] [mid-19C] three halfpence.

yennop *n. see* YENNEP *n.*

yenom *n.* [backsl.] [mid-19C] money.

yenork *n.* (*also* **yennork**) [backsl.] [mid-19C–1930s] a crown, five shillings (25p).

IN PHRASES

□ **half-yennork** *n.* (*also* **flatch-enorc, -yennork, -ynork**) [FLATCH *n.*] [mid-19C–1930s] half-a-crown, 2s 6d (12½p).

yen-shee *n.* [Chinese or mock-Chinese; note Irwin, *American Tramp and Underworld Slang* (1931): 'Despite the declaration of several educated Chinese that they know of no word in their own language anything like the preceding as representing opium, it is easy to see that the underworld has taken the term from some Chinese root word or sentence'] (*drugs*) **1** [late 19C+] (*also* **when-shee, yen-chee, yen-she, yen-shi**) opium. **2** [late 19C+] opium residue; thus *yen-shee hop*, the box used to hold opium ashes, sold to impoverished users, *yen-shee gow*, an implement to clean out an opium pipe. **3** [1910s–40s] tincture of opium, sometimes mixed with whisky. **4** [1950s] heroin.

IN COMPOUNDS

□ **yen-shee baby** *n.* [one effect of addiction is long-term constipation] [1930s+] (*drugs*) hard impacted faeces produced, often painfully, by a heroin addict during a period of withdrawal. □ **yen-shee boy** *n.* [1930s–50s] (*US drugs*) an opium addict. □ **yen-shee gow** *n.* [late 19C–1950s] (*US drugs*) the tool used to remove opium residue from a pipe. □ **yen-shee quay** *n.* (*also* **yen-shee-kwoi**) [late 19C–1950s] (*US drugs*) an opium addict. □ **yen-shee suey** *n.* [SE (*chop*) *suey*] [1930s–50s] (*drugs*) opium residue dissolved into wine.

IN PHRASES

□ **shoot yenshee** *v.* [1930s] to inject oneself with a solution based on opium or, usu., opium residue.

yenta *n.* [Ital. *gentile*, a lady; thence adopted by Yid. speakers and popularized through the fictional *Yenta Telebende*, created in the Jewish New York press by the humourist 'B. Kovner' (Jacob Adler)] [1920s+] (*orig. US*) a nagging, whining person, usu. female.

yentz *v.* [*see* YENTZER *n.*] **1** [1930s] to cheat, to swindle, to deceive. **2** [1930s–70s] to have sexual intercourse.

yentzer *n.* [Yid. *yenzter*, synon. with FUCKER *n.* (3) but lit. f. contrived euph. *yents*, trans. as 'that' or 'the other'] [1930s+] (*US*) a cheat, a deceiver, a liar.

yeo *n. see* YEYO *n.*

yeoman of the vinegar bottle *n.* [the use of vinegar as a 'cure' for such a disease; as well as internal or external use some doctors suggested that the mercury used in the treatment of syphilis should first be boiled in vinegar] [late 16C] a sufferer from venereal disease.

yep *adv.* (*also* **yump, yup**) [pron.] [late 19C+] (*orig. US*) yes.

yer actual *adj. see* YOUR ACTUAL *adj.*

yerba *n.* [Sp. *yerba*, herb] [1960s+] (*drugs*) marijuana; thus *yerba buena/mala*, good/bad marijuana.

yerknod *n.* (*also* **jerk-nod, jirk-nod, keynod**) [backsl.] [mid-19C] a donkey.

yernt *n.* [? YENTA *n.*] [1980s] (*US campus*) a socially inept person.

yerp *n. see* YAP *n.*[1] (1c).

yerquick *n.* [*you're quick*, i.e. sarcastic use of SE *quick*, intelligent] [2000s] (*Aus.*) an absolute fool.

yerriso *n.* [pron. of SE *I hear so*] [20C+] (*W.I.*) gossip, rumour.

yes *v.* [20C+] to act in an obsequious manner.

yes-baas *n.* [lit. 'yes, boss'] [1960s+] (*S.Afr.*) a servile, subservient black person.

yesca *n.* (*also* **llesca, yesco**) [Sp. *llesca*, tinder, fuel; pron. 'yesca'] [1940s+] (*US drugs*) marijuana.

yes sir! *excl.* (*also* **yes siree!**) [late 18C+] (*orig. US*) an emphatic assertion.

yes siree bob! *excl.* [mid-19C+] a general excl. of affirmation: definitely! certainly! absolutely!

yessus! *excl. see* YISSUS! *excl.*

yest *n.* [abbr.] [early 18C–early 19C] yesterday.

yestergay *n.* [SE *yesterday* + *gay*] [2000s] a former homosexual man who has (re-)adopted heterosexuality.

yesty *n.* [abbr.] [1950s] (*Aus.*) yesterday.

yet *adv.* [Yid. *noch*, another] [1930s+] (*orig. US*) an ironic intensive placed at the end of a sentence.

yet to be *adj.* [rhy. sl.] [1950s+] free (both of behaviour and of cost).

yew-crib *n.* [SE *yew* tree + CRIB *n.*[1] (1)] [mid-19C] a carpenter's shop; thus *yewman*, a carpenter.

yewie *n. see* U-IE *n.* (1).

yeyo *n.* (*also* **jejo, yahoo, yaoh, yay, yayo, yayoo, yeaho, yeo**) [synon. Sp. *llello*, pron. 'yeayo'] [1990s+] (*drugs*) **1** cocaine. **2** crack cocaine.

yfeck! *excl. see* I'FECKS! *excl.*

yick! *excl. see* YUCK! *excl.*

yicky *adj. see* ICKY *adj.* (3).

Yid *n.*[1] (*also* **Yiddo, Yit, Yitt**) [Ger. *Jude*, Jew; ult. Yehuda or Judah, one of the biblical Jacob's sons. The term, as Rosten, *The Joys of Yiddish* (1968), points out, is neutral if pronounced 'yeed' as it would be by Jews speaking the Judaeo-German language Yiddish, but unashamedly offensive if pronounced 'yid'] [mid-19C+] a Jew; both derog. and general use, depending on context; thus pl. *Yidden*.

Yid *n.*[2] (*also* **Yit, Yitt**) [rhy. sl. = QUID *n.* (3) but note stereotyped link of Jews and money] [1950s–70s] (*Aus.*) a sovereign; thus *half a Yid*, a half sovereign, ten shillings (50p).

Yiddel *n. see* YIDDLE *n.*

Yiddish *adj.* (*also* **Yid**) [YID *n.*[1]] [late 19C+] Jewish.

IN COMPOUNDS

□ **Yiddish highway** *n.* [New York Jews trad. move to Miami for their retirement; the relatives use the highway for visits] [20C+] (*US*) US301, the route from New York City to Miami. □ **Yiddish Renaissance** *n.* [1950s+] over-elaborate furniture in doubtful taste. □ **Yiddish screwdriver** *n. see* JEWISH SCREWDRIVER *under* JEWISH *adj.*

Yiddisher *n.* [late 19C–1910s] a Jew.

Yiddisher *adj.* [Yid. *yiddishe*, Jewish] [late 19C+] Jewish.

IN COMPOUNDS

□ **Yiddisher fiddle** *n.* [pun on SE *fiddle*/FIDDLE *n.*[3] (2)] [1920s–50s] minor cheating or other illegality. □ **Yiddisher piano** *n.* [negative stereotyping] [1910s+] a cash register.

Yiddle *n.* (*also* **Yiddel**) [dimin. of YID *n.*[1]] [1940s+] a Jew.

Yiddo *n. see* YID *n.*[1].

yield the crow a pudding *v. see* GIVE THE CROW A PUDDING *under* CROW *n.*[2].

yike *n.* [ety. unknown; ? echoic or dial. *yike*, the call of the woodpecker] (*Aus.*) **1** [1930s–60s] an argument, a dispute, a fight, a brawl. **2** [1940s] a boxing match.

yikes *n.* [? backform. f. YIKES! *excl.*] [1970s+] worries, nervousness.

yikes! *excl.* (*also* **yeeick! yipe! yipes!**) [? link to SE *yoicks!* or CRIKEY! *excl.*] [1940s+] an excl. of surprise or shock.

Yim, Yoe and Yesus *n.* [? ref. to disciples James (Jim) and Joseph (Joe) and Jesus, in a cod-'Scandinavian' accent] [1930s+] (*Aus.*) in cards, three knaves or jacks.

yin *n. see* YEN *n.*[1].

ying-yang *n.* (*also* **yin-yang**) [? var. on WANG *n.*[2] (1); *HDAS*'s link to 'Hindu' *yin* and *yang* seems spurious] **1** [1950s] (*US*) sexual intercourse. **2** [1950s+] the penis. **3** [1960s+] the anus; esp. in phr. *UP THE YING-YANG* below. **4** [1970s] the testicles. **5** [1970s+] in fig. use, nonsense. **6** [2000s] (*US drugs*) LSD.

(IN PHRASES)

❑ **up the ying-yang** (*also* **out the yang**) [sense 3 above] [1960s+] to an excess, to the extreme.

yip *n.* [SE *yip*, a short, sharp bark] **1** [1910s] (*US*) talk. **2** [1920s] (*US Und.*) a dog. **3** [1930s+] (*US Und.*) a complaint.

yip *v.* [SE *yip*, to yelp] [1910s+] (*US*) to talk in a petulant or irritating manner.

yipe(s)! *excl. see* YIKES! *excl.*

yippee bean *n.* [rhy. sl.] [1960s] (*Aus.*) an amphetamine.

yips *n.* [popularly linked to golf use; coined by the golfer T.D. Armour, according to a citation in P. Davies' *Dict. of Golfing Terms* (1980)] [1930s+] nerves; thus as v., to feel nervous, twitchy.

yip-yap drug *n.* [YIP *v.* + YAP *v.*[1] (1)] [1990s+] (*Aus. drugs*) any drug that makes one talk fast and usu. meaninglessly, e.g. amphetamines, cocaine.

yissus! *excl.* (*also* **shassas! yassas! yessus!**) [JESUS! *excl.*] [1940s+] (*S.Afr.*) a general excl.

yit *n.* [ety. unknown] [1970s–80s] (*UK juv.*) a general term of abuse.

Yit/Yitt *n. see under* YID.

yi-yen *n. see* GEE YEN *n.*

Y.M./Y.W. *n.* [abbr.] [1910s+] (*orig. US*) the Young Men's Christian Association; the Young Women's Christian Association.

Y.M.C.A. *adj.*[1] [the religiously based organization] [late 19C–1930s] priggish, puritan, 'goody-goody'.

Y.M.C.A. *adj.*[2] [*y*esterday's *m*uck *c*ooked *a*gain] [1950s] of food, disgusting, unappetizing.

yo *n.* [YO! *excl.* (2)] [1990s+] (*US*) a young black man, esp. one who deals drugs on the street; thus fem. *yoette*.

yo *v.* [YO! *excl.* (2)] [1980s+] (*UK black*) to greet with a shout of 'Yo!'.

yo! *excl.* [orig. used in 15C as interj. of warning; ? abbr. US black/ Southern *y'all*] **1** [1910s+] yes! **2** [1960s+] (*US*) a general term of address. **3** [1990s+] used to add emphasis to a statement.

yob *n.* [backsl.; note WW1 milit. use, *yob*, a young, gullible officer] **1** [mid-19C–1900s] a boy. **2** [mid-19C+] an uncouth, vulgar youth; thus the fem. *yobette*. **3** [1910s] a man. **4** [1910s–50s] (*Aus.*) a man, with derog. implications.

yobbo *n.* [ext. of YOB *n.* (2)] [1920s+] a lout, a hooligan; a general derog. term used of working-class youths.

yobby *adj.* [YOB *n.* (2)] [1960s+] loutish.

yobette *n. see* YOB *n.* (2).

yo-boy *n.* [his use of the common black greeting YO! *excl.* (2)] [1980s+] (*US black*) a white youth who apes his black contemporaries.

yock *n.* (*also* **yockele, yok**) [backsl. for GOY *n.*] **1** [20C+] a gentile. **2** [1930s+] a fool.

yock *v.* **1** [1950s+] to laugh or shout loudly; thus adj. *yocky*, hilarious [YOKS *n.*]. **2** [1990s+] to spit [SE *hawk*].

yocker *n.* **1** [1990s+] (*UK juv.*) a lump of spit [YOCK *v.* (2)]. **2** [2000s] (*Irish*) a testicle [in ext. sense of 'lump'].

yocks *n. see* YOKS *n.*

yocky *adj. see* YOCK *v.* (1).

yodel *v.* (*also* **yodel over the mahogany**) [1960s+] (*Aus./N.Z.*) to vomit.

yodeler *n.* [YODEL IN THE CANYON (OF LOVE) *v.* (1)] [1920s] (*US Und.*) a derog. term for a male homosexual.

yodel in the canyon (of love) *v.* (*also* **grin in the canyon (of love), yodel from the highest tower, yodel in/up the valley**) **1** [1920s] (*US*) to fellate. **2** [1930s+] to perform cunnilingus. **3** [1970s] (*Aus.*) to vomit.

yoette *n. see* YO *n.*

yoghurt *n.*

(IN PHRASES)

❑ **cough one's yoghurt** *v.* [1990s+] to ejaculate.

Yogi Bear *n.* [rhy. sl. = LAIR *n.*; ult. US cartoon character *Yogi Bear*] [1960s+] (*Aus.*) a prison dandy.

yo-ho! *v. see* YOO-HOO! *excl.*

yoink *v. see* YANK *v.*[1] (7).

yok *n. see* YOCK *n.*

yoke *n.*[1] (*Irish*) **1** [mid-19C–1940s] a horse-drawn carriage. **2** [late 19C–1900s] a riding horse, as opposed to a racehorse. **3** [20C+] any form of unspecified gadget or object. **4** [1910s+] a car, a vehicle, e.g. a police wagon, a boat. **5** [1930s+] a person. **6** [1960s+] a (young) woman.

yoke *n.*[2] [SE *yoke*, a form of collar] **1** [1940s–50s] (*US black/ teen*) a job. **2** [1980s+] the act of grabbing someone around the neck as part of a mugging.

yoke *v.* [SE *yoke*, a collar placed across the neck] **1** [mid-19C+] (*US*) to murder by strangulation or by cutting someone's throat from behind. **2** [1940s+] to rob while choking or strangling the victim, either with a rope or stick; one person does the *yoking*, the other rifles the victim's pockets.

yoked *adj.* [? one's shoulders resemble a SE *yoke*] [1980s+] (*US campus*) muscular, well-built.

yoks *n.* (*also* **yaks, yocks, yuks**) [echoic] [1940s+] (*US*) laughs.

(IN PHRASES)

❑ **get one's yuks** *v.* [1970s] (*US*) to derive pleasure. ❑ **yuck up** *v.* [1980s+] (*US*) to laugh.

yokuff *n.* [SE *coffer*] [mid-19C] a large box, a chest.

yola *n.* [? Sp.] [1900s–40s] (*US black*) a light-skinned young woman.

yold *n.* (*also* **yuld**) [Heb. *yeled*, a boy] [1940s–50s] (*US*) a gullible victim.

yom *n.* (*also* **yomo**) [their common use of YO' MAMA! *excl.*] [1970s+] (*US*) **1** a black street boy. **2** a black woman.

yom *adj.* [YOM *n.*] [1970s] pertaining to black and Puerto Rican culture, lifestyle.

yo' mama! *excl.* (*also* **ya mamma! yo' Momma! your mama! your mammy!**) [US black pron. of YOUR MOTHER! *excl.*] [1940s+] (*US black*) a general excl. which, like MOTHERFUCKER *n.*, varies as to context, from the jovially teasing to the deliberately insulting; usu. used as a retort.

yomo *n. see* YOM *n.*

yomp *v.* [orig. Royal Marine term for marching with weapons and a 120lb pack across appalling terrain in extremely hostile conditions on the premise that once this ultimate in route marches is concluded, the troops will be prepared to fight a battle at the other end; poss. Norwegian word used by skiers to describe the crossing of obstacles. The term gained widespread currency during the Falklands War of 1982] [1980s+] to march, to walk (in difficult conditions).

yonker *n. see* YOUNKER *n.*

yonks *n.* [ety. unknown; ? SE *donkey's years*] [1960s+] a long time; esp. in phr. *for yonks*.

yonnie *n.* [ety. unknown; ? Abor. language] [1940s+] (*Aus.*) a small stone, a pebble.

yoo-ee *n. see* U-IE *n.*

yoof *adj.* [deliberate mispron. of SE *youth* + mimicry of the 'street-cred' London accents of presenters of such programmes and of their doyenne, the then TV executive Janet Street-Porter] [1980s+] used of anything – esp. TV programmes – high on pop gossip and fashion, low (in critical eyes) on intelligence, that is aimed at the young.

yoo-hoo *v.* [YOO-HOO! *excl.*] [1940s+] to shout 'hello', to attract someone's attention.

yoo-hoo! *excl.* (*also* **yo-ho!**) [1940s+] hello!

IN COMPOUNDS

❑ **yoo-hoo boy** *n.* [his camp shrieks of YOO-HOO! *excl.*] [1940s–70s] (*US*) an effeminate homosexual.

yook *n.* [ety. unknown] [mid-19C] (*UK Und.*) venereal disease.

yoot *n. see* YOUT *n.*

yop *n.*[1] [YOB *n.* (2)] [late 19C] (*US*) a lout.

yop *n.*[2] *see* YAP *n.*[1].

York *n.* [abbr.] [mid-19C–1960s] (*US tramp*) New *York* City.

York *adj.* [YORK *n.*] [early 18C; 19C] (*US*) of or pertaining to New York City.

york *n.* [YORK v.] [early 19C] a stare, a glance.

york *v.* [? Cheshire dial. *york*, to pierce, or the stereotyped Yorkshireman's shrewd appraisal] [early 19C] to stare at.

Yorker *n.* [YORK *n.*] [mid-18C–1940s] a New Yorker.

Yorkie *n.* (*also* **Yorky**) [abbr.] **1** [mid-19C+] a *York*shireman; also in direct address. **2** [1950s+] a *York*shire terrier.

York Minster to a brass farthing *phr.* [early–mid-19C] the longest posible odds.

Yorkshire *n.* [Ware defines as 'fair and square payments', but this may be ironic] [mid-19C–1900s] sharp practice.

Yorkshire *adj.* [stereotyping of Yorkshire people as mean, thus also in combs. that follow] [early 17C; late 18C–mid-19C] mean, grasping.

IN COMPOUNDS

❑ **Yorkshire bite** *n.* **1** [late 18C–mid-19C] over-reaching, greediness. **2** [mid-19C] a grasping person. ❑ **Yorkshire compliment** *n.* [mid-19C–1900s] a gift that means nothing to the donor and is useless to the recipient. ❑ **Yorkshire cravat** *n.* [mid-19C] (*UK Und.*) the hangman's noose. ❑ **Yorkshire estate** *n.* [negative stereotyping of Yorks. business or legal methods] [mid-19C–1900s] money that is in prospect but not yet handed over; thus *when I come into my Yorkshire estates*, when I finally have some money. ❑ **Yorkshire hog** *n.* [SE *Yorkshire hog*, a very large pig, but 'The Old Yorkshire Pig is by some considered as the very worst of the large varieties, very long legged, weak loined, not of strong constitution, nor good stye pigs, but yet quicker feeders' (*Encycl. Metrop.* 1845)] [late 18C] a fat wether or castrated ram. ❑ **Yorkshire reckoning** *n.* [COME (THE) YORKSHIRE OVER below] [mid-19C] a situation where every member of the company pays for themselves.

IN PHRASES

❑ **come (the) Yorkshire over** *v.* (*also* **put (the) Yorkshire on**) [local stereotyping] [18C–mid-19C] to cheat.

Yorkshire *v.* [negative stereotyping] [late 19C] to defraud, to deceive.

Yorkshire penny bank *n.* [rhy. sl. = WANK *n.* (1)] [20C+] masturbation; usu. in phr. *not worth a Yorkshire penny bank*.

Yorkshire rippers *n.* [rhy. sl.] [1980s+] slippers.

Yorkshire tyke *n.* [rhy. sl.] [1940s+] a mike, i.e. microphone.

York Street *n.*

IN PHRASES

❑ **there is York Street concerned** (*also* **there York Street is concerned**) [YORK v.] [19C] a phr. meaning that someone is staring.

Yorky *n. see* YORKIE *n.*

you ain't know *phr.* [i.e. you didn't know that already?] [1990s+] (*US black/ campus*) a phr. of affirmation, esp. when confirming what the speaker seems only to be questioning.

you and me *n.* [rhy. sl.] **1** [20C+] tea. **2** [20C+] urination, urine [= PEE *n.*[1]]. **3** [1910s–30s] a flea. **4** [1940s+] (*bingo*) the number three. **5** [1960s+] (*Aus.*) a pea.

you and whose army? *phr.* (*also* **you and who else?**) [1930s+] (*usu. teen*) a phr. addressed to anyone who is threatening violence.

you be hanged! *excl.* (*also* **you be shot!**) [17C–1900s] a general excl. of dismissal, contempt.

you can have it! *excl.* (*also* **you can keep it!**) [1930s+] no thanks! it's all yours! I don't want it!

youee *n. see* U-IE *n.*

you got it! *excl.* **1** [1960s–70s] a phr. implying that nothing new has happened, there is no information to pass on; usu. as response to the query *what's happening?* **2** [1970s+] (*orig. US esp. black*) a general affirmative reply, usu. to a yes/no question.

you know *n.*[1] [euph.] [1920s–30s] (*US*) the posterior, the buttocks.

you know *n.*[2] [rhy. sl. = SNOW *n.*[1] (2a)] [1930s+] (*drugs*) cocaine.

you know *phr.* [abbr. earlier *don't you know*] [late 19C+] a verbal punctuation, with no real meaning.

you-know-his-name *n. see* YOU KNOW WHO *n.*

you know it (is) *phr.* [late 19C; 1960s+] (*orig. US*) any form of emphatic agreement, yes indeed, you're right etc.

you know what *n.* **1** [17C] the vagina. **2** [mid-17C–mid-18C] the penis. **3** [late 17C–early 18C; 1950s+] sexual intercourse. **4** [late 17C+] (*also* **what you know**) anything the speaker does not wish to name specifically; often used euph. **5** [2000s] the buttocks.

you know what you can do with... *phr.* [the implication being SHOVE IT UP YOUR ARSE! *excl.*] [1920s+] a dismissive phr. used to counter a suggestion, an unacceptable offer etc.

you know where *n.* **1** [mid-18C+] a euph. depending on context; if sexual, ref. to the vagina or penis; if hostile, the anus or the testicles. **2** [mid-19C+] hell. **3** [1920s] the lavatory.

you know who *n.* (*also* **you-know-his-name**) [late 17C+] used of a person whose name one knows, but prefers not to mention.

You Must Come Across *n.* [COME ACROSS v. (1)] [1930s] (*US tramp*) the YMCA.

young *adj.* **1** [mid-19C+] diminutive, miniature, a small version of. **2** [1930s+] (*US black*) immature, unversed in street life. **3** [1940s] (*Irish*) tipsy.

IN COMPOUNDS

❑ **young kipper** *n.* [a pun on the Jewish festival of *Yom Kippur*, the Day of Atonement, at which time it is customary to spend the day fasting] [20C+] an inadequate meal. ❑ **young suit** *n.* [1930s–40s] (*US black*) a suit which is badly fitting or too small.

IN PHRASES

❑ **young in the head** *adj.* [1970s+] (*US black*) childish, immature.

SE in slang uses

IN COMPOUNDS

❑ **young-ass** *adj.* [-ASS *sfx*] [1950s+] (*US black*) immature. ❑ **young bantam** *n.* [BANTAM *n.* (4)] [1940s] (*US black*) a very young girl. ❑ **young hemp** *n.* [? link to HEMPEN *adj.*, i.e. a candidate for the gallows] [late 18C–early 19C] an ill-behaved young man or boy. ❑ **young horse** *n.* [1930s] (*US prison*) roast beef. ❑ **young 'un** *n.* [mid-19C+] a young person, often as a direct term of address.

IN PHRASES

❑ **young, dumb, and full of come** [CUM *n.* (1)] [1970s+] (*US*) used of a teenager or young person whose enthusiasm for life (and esp. sex) outweighs their intelligence; usu. of a man, but occas. of a woman.

young and frisky *n.* [rhy. sl.] [20C+] (*Aus.*) whisky.

youngie *n.* [SE *young* + dimin./affectionate sfx *-ie*; on pattern of OLDIE *n.* (1)] **1** [1960s+] (*Aus.*) a young woman. **2** [1990s+] a young person.

younker *n.* (*also* **yonker, yunker**) [Du. *jonker, jonkheer*, young master] [mid-16C–1960s] a lad, a boy; sometimes a female child.

your actual *adj.* (*also* **yer actual**) [coined by Barry Took and Marty Feldman for the 1950s–60s BBC radio show *Round the Horne*] [1960s+] an emphatic intensifier of a person or object, e.g. *your actual Rolls Royce*.

you're another! *excl.* [mid-18C+] a meaningless or vaguely contemptuous and ultimately childish retort, responding to a speaker who has made the offensive comment, 'You're a...'.

you're it *phr.* [1970s] (*US campus*) used as a response to the greeting 'What's happening (man)?'.

you're so tan I hate you *phr.* [1990s+] (*US campus*) goodbye.

you're telling me! *excl.* [? Gus Kahn song-title 'You're Telling Me' (1932): the first *OED* citation] [1930s+] that's absolutely right; I don't disagree at all, I know only too well.

your face and my ass/butt! *excl. see* KISS MY ARSE! *excl.*

your mama!/mammy! *excl. see* YO' MAMA! *excl.*

your man *n.* (*also* **your woman**) [1930s+] (*Irish*) **1** an unnamed, although quite poss. specified, individual. **2** a specific thing, a good thing. **3** the devil.

Your Man Upstairs *n.* [YOUR MAN *n.* (1) + UPSTAIRS *n.* (2)] [1990s+] (*Irish*) God.

your mother! *excl.* (*also* **your mom! your momma!**) [euph. for *GO FUCK YOUR MOTHER! under* FUCK *v.*] [1940s+] (*orig. US, mainly teen*) a rejoinder to an insult, implying that whatever that insult is, it applies most to the speaker's own mother; see also YO' MAMA! *excl.*

(IN EXCLAMATIONS)

❑ **your mother's cunt!** (*also* **your mother's box! ...twat!**) [CUNT *n.* (1)/BOX *n.*[1] (1a)/TWAT *n.* (1)] [1950s+] a derisive, dismissive excl.

yours and ours *n.* (*also* **yours and hours**) [rhy. sl., used by Covent Garden Market porters and street vendors] [20C+] flowers.

— yourself *phr.* [late 19C+] used as a retort, mocking or rebutting what has just been said, e.g. *'Hello', 'Hello yourself'*.

yours truly *n.* (*also* **yours faithfully, ...sincerely**) [mid-19C+] a joc. ref. by a speaker to themselves.

your woman *n. see* YOUR MAN *n.*

yout *n.* (*also* **yoot**) [SE *youth*; the deliberate mispron. accentuates the oppositional stance of such young men] (*W.I./UK black*) [1970s+] **1** a child, a young man, an immature man. **2** rebellious, politically active young people.

yout'man *n.* [YOUT *n.* + sfx *-man*] [1980s+] (*W.I./UK black teen*) a young person, man or woman.

you've got a nerve *phr.* [? orig. US (the *OED* citation is three years before), although B&L credit Eton College sl. *nerve*, impudence, cheek] [late 19C+] how dare you.

you what? *excl.* [SE *what?*, the speaker pretends not to have heard what has been said] [1920s+] an excl. spoken as a challenge, say that again!

yowl-box *n.* [SE *yowl*, to make a noise] [1920s] (*US*) a radio.

yowza! *excl.* [YES SIR! *excl.*] [1930s+] (*US teen*) a general excl., either of approval or of vaguely non-committal agreement.

yoxter *n.* [ety. unknown; ? link to Scot./dial. *yox*, to vomit, to cough up, i.e. the convict has 'come up again'] [mid-19C] a convict who has returned from transportation before the full expiry of their sentence.

yoyo *n.*[1] [all go 'up and down'] **1** [1920s+] the penis, esp. when small. **2** [1940s+] (*US*) an unpredictable or inconsistent person whose moods and actions go up and down, thus a fool; also as adj. **3** [1980s] (*US campus*) a bisexual person.

yoyo *n.*[2] (*also* **yoyo boy**) [YO! *excl.*] [1980s+] (*US black*) a street youth.

Y.T. *n.* [1940s+] oneself, i.e. YOURS TRULY *n.*

yuck *see also under* YUK.

yuck *n.* (*also* **yecch, yech, yuck-a-buck, yuk**) [YUCK! *excl.*] [1940s+] (*US*) anything or anyone seen as disgusting or repulsive; a fool.

(IN COMPOUNDS)

❑ **yuck mouth** *n.* [2000s] (*US black*) an extremely proficient fellatrix.

yuck *adj.* (*also* **yucko**) [YUCK *n.*] [1970s+] disgusting, repulsive.

yuck *v.* [echoic] [1960s+] (*US campus/teen*) to vomit.

(IN PHRASES)

❑ **yuck up** *v.* [1960s+] **1** (*W.I.*) to annoy, to irritate. **2** (*also* **yurk**) to vomit. **3** *see under* YOKS *n.*

yuck! *excl.* (*also* **yecch! yech! yeck! yeech! yick! yuk!**) [echoic] [1960s+] (*mainly juv.*) an all-purpose excl. of distaste.

yucko *adj. see* YUCK *adj.*

yucky *n.* [YUCK *n.*] [1980s] an act of defecation.

yucky *adj.* (*also* **ucky, yecchy, yukky**) [YUCK! *excl.*] [1960s+] (*usu. juv.*) unpleasant, disgusting, with overtones of stickiness or smelliness.

Yug *n.* (*also* **Jug, Yugo**) [abbr.] [1950s+] **1** a *Yugoslav*. **2** (*Aus.*) an immigrant from former *Yugoslavia*.

yuk *see also under* YUCK.

yuk *n.*[1] [ety. unknown] [1930s] (*US prison*) a friend.

yuk *n.*[2] (*also* **yuck, yukyuk**) [YUK *v.* (1)] [1960s+] (*US*) a laugh, the sound of laughter; thus *yuck it up*, to laugh.

yuk *v.* (*also* **yuck, yukyuk**) **1** [1960s+] (*US*) to laugh. **2** [1970s+] (*US gay*) to be excited.

(IN PHRASES)

❑ **yuck up** *v.* [1980s+] (*US*) to laugh.

yuke *v.* [echoic] [1980s+] (*US campus*) to vomit.

yukker *n.* [YUCK *n.*] [1990s+] (*UK juv.*) a baby, a toddler.

yukky *adj. see* YUCKY *adj.*

yuks *n. see* YOKS *n.*

yukyuk *see under* YUK.

yuld *n. see* YOLD *n.*

Yuletide log *n.* [rhy. sl.] [1970s] a dog.

yum! *excl.* (*also* **yum-yum!**) [echoic] [late 19C+] an expression of praise for anything delightful, usu. delicious food.

yummies *n.* [YUMMY *adj.* (2), i.e. 'good enough to eat'/EAT *v.* (4)] [1970s+] (*US gay*) the male genitalia.

(IN PHRASES)

❑ **get some yummies** *v.* [1970s+] (*US gay*) to have anal intercourse.

yummy *n.* [YUMMY *adj.* (2), i.e. 'good enough to eat'] [1960s+] **1** an attractive teenage girl. **2** an attractive young man.

yummy *adj.* [YUM! *excl.*] [late 19C+] **1** tasty, delicious, flavoursome. **2** used similarly of people, objects, experiences etc.

yummy *v.* [YUMMY *adj.* (2)] [1950s] to have sexual intercourse.

yump *adv. see* YEP *adv.*

yumpie *n.* [abbr.] [1980s] (*US*) a young, *upwardly-mobile professional*.

yum-yum *n.* [YUM! *excl.*; note naut. jargon *yum-yum*, a love letter] **1** [late 19C] a pretty young woman. **2** [late 19C] the vagina. **3** [late 19C–1920s] anything deliciously pleasurable, esp. love-making; thus *yum-yum girl*, a prostitute. **4** [1970s+] (*drugs*) any drug in pill or capsule form.

yum-yum *adj.* **1** [late 19C] of a woman, very attractive. **2** [late 19C] sexually provocative. **3** [late 19C–1920s] deliciously pleasurable.

yum-yum! *excl. see* YUM! *excl.*

yunk *n.* [? SE *hunk*] [1910s+] (*Aus.*) a lump, a chunk; thus *yunk of dodger*, a slice of bread (cf. DODGER *n.*[2]).

yunker *n. see* YOUNKER *n.*

yuntry *adj.* [Carib. pron. of SE] [1990s+] (*W.I.*) countrified, rural, as a derog.

yup *adv. see* YEP *adv.*

yuppie *n.* (*also* **yup, yuppy**) [abbr.; the term created a variety of often one-off derivations, e.g. *pumpie*, *previously upwardly-mobile prat*, i.e. a failed or former yuppie] [1980s+] (*orig. US*) a young, *upwardly-mobile professional*; thus v. *yuppify*, *yuppification*.

(IN COMPOUNDS)

❑ **yuppie flu** *n.* (*also* **yuppie disease**) [the condition appeared to become more prevalent during the 1980s and resembled the most deleterious form of 'flu. It was often dismissed by doctors as no more than hypochondria, although its sufferers were able to demonstrate a variety of definite symptoms] [1980s+] ME, myalgic encephalomyelitis. ❑ **yuppie puppie** *n.* [1990s+] a child of a *yuppie*, for whom children were seen as something of a fashion accessory in the early 1990s.

yuppie *v.* [echoic of straining, plus derog. ref. to social type, i.e. *PIECE OF SHIT under* PIECE *n.*] [1980s] (*US campus*) to defecate.

yupster *n.* [YUPPIE *n.* + -STER *sfx*] [1990s+] a synon. of YUPPIE *n.*

yurk *v. see YUCK UP under* YUCK *v.*

yush! *excl.* [1980s+] (*W.I./UK black teen*) a general expression of greeting.

yutz *n.* [US Yid. *yutz*, a penis] [1980s+] **1** a penis. **2** a fool, an idiot.

Y.W. *see* Y.M./Y.W. *n.*

Z

Z *n.* [abbr.] **1** [1980s] (*US*) a Mercedes model 300Z. **2** [1990s+] a Datsun 280Z. **3** *see* ZIP (GUN) *n.*

z *n.*[1] (*also* **Z, zed, zee, z's, zzz**) [echoic of the sound of one's breathing] [1960s+] (*orig. US*) in pl., sleep in general, esp. in phrs. below.

IN COMPOUNDS

❑ **z-head** *n.* [-HEAD *sfx* (1)] [1980s] (*US campus*) a stupid person.

IN PHRASES

❑ **bag Z's** *v.* (*also* **bag zeds**) [1960s+] (*US campus*) to nap, to sleep. ❑ **blow Z's** *v.* (*also* **hit some Zs**) [1960s+] (*US*) to sleep; also to snore. ❑ **bust some Z's** *v.* (*also* **cut (some) Z's, pick up some Z's, pile up some Z's**) [1960s+] (*US*) to have a nap; to sleep. ❑ **catch a few Z's** *v.* (*also* **catch some winks**) [1960s+] (*US*) to have a nap. ❑ **clock Z's** *v.* [1990s+] (*US black*) to sleep. ❑ **cop some Z's** *v.* (*also* **count (some) Z's**) [1960s+] (*US*) to sleep, to have a nap). ❑ **stack Zs** *v.* [1960s+] (*US*) to have a sleep, to nap.

z *n.*[2] (*also* **zee**) [abbr. *oz.*] [1970s+] (*US drugs*) **1** 1oz (28g) of cannabis. **2** 1oz (28g) of heroin.

z *v.* (*also* **ze, z-out, z's, zzz**) [z *n.*[1]] [1960s+] (*US black/teen*) to sleep.

IN PHRASES

❑ **z'd out** *adj.* [1960s+] (*US teen*) unable to wake up properly, still sleepy.

'z *abbr. see 's abbr.*

za *n.* [abbr.] [1960s+] (*US teen/campus*) pizza; thus *do a za*, to buy or eat a pizza.

zac *n.* (*also* **zack, zack-bit, sac**) [? SE *six* or Scot. *saxpence*] (*Aus./N.Z.*) **1** [late 19C+] a sixpence, a very small sum of money; A5$. **2** [1930s+] a six-month prison sentence.

Zacatecas purple *n.* [the town of *Zacatecas*, Mexico, near which the marijuana is assumed to have been grown; the buds are coloured *purple*] [1960s+] (*drugs*) a variety of marijuana from Mexico.

zachary scotts *n.* [rhy. sl. = TROTS *n.*; ult. film star *Zachary Scott* (1914–65)] [1940s–50s] diarrhoea.

'zack *n. see* BOZACK *n.*

zack(-bit) *n. see* ZAC *n.*

zad *n.* [the crooked shape of the letter Z] [early 18C–early 19C] a crooked person or thing.

zaftig *adj.* (*also* **zoftick, zoftig**) [Ger. *zaftig*, juicy] [1920s+] usu. of a woman, plump, buxom.

zak *n.* [? ZAC *n.*] [1960s–70s] (*S.Afr. township*) money.

zambo *n. see* SAMBO *n.*[1].

Zambuck *n.* (*also* **Zambuk**) [name of *Zam-buk*, a proprietary antiseptic ointment; Zambuk website: 'The word Zam-Buk originated in New Zealand, and was used to describe someone who administered first aid to wounded sportsmen. A "Zambuck" was a member of the Order of St. John, which was established at the time of the Crusades to care for the injured'] [1920s+] (*Aus.*) a St John's Ambulance man.

zamie (girl) *n.* [? Fr. *les amies*, female friends] [1950s+] (*W.I.*) a lesbian; thus *make zamie*, to have a relationship with another woman.

zamietess *n.* [ZAMIE (GIRL) *n.* + sfx *-ess*] [1950s+] (*W.I.*) a tough, brawling, noisy woman.

zane *n.*[1] [ety. unknown] [mid-19C–1960s] (*US gay*) a male homosexual.

zane *n.*[2] [Ger. *zehn*, ten] [1910s] (*US*) ten cents, a dime.

Zane Grey *n.* [rhy. sl.; ult. Western writer *Zane Grey* (1872–1939)] [1930s+] (*Aus.*) pay, wages.

zang *v. see* ZING *v.* (2).

zanzy *adj.* [*Zanzibar*, a part of Africa and thus viewed positively] [1960s] (*US black*) attractive, first-rate.

zap *n.* [ZAP! *excl.*] [1960s+] (*orig. US*) energy, enthusiasm.

zap *v.* [ZAP! *excl.*] **1** [1940s+] (*orig. US milit.*) to kill. **2** [1950s+] (*US black*) to move quickly. **3** [1960s+] to put an end to, to do away with. **4** [1960s+] to attack, to criticize. **5** [1960s+] (*US campus*) to fail someone in a test or examination. **6** [1960s+] to overwhelm emotionally; to shock, to alarm. **7** [1960s+] to send, to put or to hit forcefully; also fig. use. **8** [1960s+] to engage in sexual relations. **9** [1960s+] to encounter problems; of a criminal, to get arrested, imprisoned. **10** [1960s+] to shoot. **11** [1980s] to dismiss from a job. **12** [1980s+] (*US campus*) to cook in a microwave. **13** [1980s+] to steal.

zap! *excl.* [? echoic of the noise of a speeding bullet] [1920s+] (*orig. US*) an excl. used to describe the force of a sudden impact.

zapped *adj.* [ZAP *v.*] **1** [1950s+] killed, destroyed; exhausted; overhwelmed. **2** [1970s+] intoxicated by drink and/or drugs.

zappy *adj.* [ZAP *v.*] [1960s+] (*US*) energetic, spirited, amusing.

zar *n.* [? SE *it's there*] [1900s–50s] (*US black*) anywhere considered far away, unpleasant and culturally alien.

zarndrer *n.* [its originator, Princess, later Queen *Alexandra*, wife of King Edward VII] [mid-19C] a long, single curl brought from the back hair over the left shoulder and allowed to fall on the breast.

zarp *n.* [abbr. Zuid Afrikaansche Republik Politie, Republic of South Africa Police] [late 19C–1900s] (*S.Afr.*) a police officer.

zasu pitts *n.* [rhy. sl. = SHITS, THE *n.* (1); ult. film star *Zasu Pitts* (1894–1963)] [1930s–50s] diarrhoea.

zat *n. see* ZIT *n.*[2] (1).

zatch *v.* [? echoic] [1990s+] to have sexual intercourse.

zazzle *n.* [? abbr. of PIZZAZZ *n.*] [1950s] (*US black*) sexual desire or sensuality.

zazzy *adj.* [ZAZZLE *n.*] [1930s–60s] (*US black*) sexy, sensuous, erotic.

'zblood!/'zbud! *excl. see* 'SBLOOD! *excl.*

'zdeath! *excl. see* 'SDEATH! *excl.*

z'd out *adj. see under* Z *v.*

ze *v. see* Z *v.*

zeb *adj.* [backsl.] [mid–late 19C] best; thus *zeb taoc*, best coat.

zebbled *adj.* [ety. unknown] [1990s+] (*UK juv.*) circumcised.

zebra *n.* [in all cases, the image is of a mixture of black and white] **1** [late 19C–1920s] (*US*) a striped prison uniform. **2** [late 19C–1920s] (*US*) (*also* **zebu**) a convict. **3** [1970s–80s] (*UK black*) a half-caste. **4** [1970s+] (*US*) (*also* **zebe**) a stripe-shirted sports umpire. **5** [1990s+] (*US black teen*) a white person who poses as black.

SE in slang uses

IN PHRASES

❑ **get zebras** *v. see* HAVE KITTENS *under* KITTEN *n.*

zed *n.* [Z *v.*/Z *n.*[1]] **1** [1960s] (*Aus.*) a snore. **2** [1980s+] (*orig. US black*) a sleep, a nap. **3** *see* Z *n.*[1].

zed about *v.* [the shape of the letter *Z*] [late 19C] (*UK society*) to wander about in a zigzag manner.

Zedland *n.* [the local dials. in which 's' tends to be pronounced as 'z'] [late 18C–19C] the southwestern counties of England: Somerset, Devon, Cornwall, Dorset.

zee *see under* Z n.

zeek out *v.* (*also* **zoom out**) [nonsense word *zeek* (the image is of going to extremes, in this case the last letter of the alphabet)/fig. use of SE *zoom*] [1980s+] (*US teen*) to act outrageously, to lose control, esp. through drugs or drink; thus adj. *zeeked out*, exhausted, stupid, a general negative.

zees *n.* [*Zig-Zag* rolling papers] [2000s] (*US black/drugs*) a pack of cigarette papers.

zef *n.* [1970s+] (*S.Afr. teen*) a member of the lower classes.

zelda *n.*[1] [? the 'old-fashioned' name, (*pace* Zelda Fitzgerald)] [1950s+] (*US teen*) a dull, uninteresting young woman.

zelda *n.*[2] [initial letters] [1970s] (*S.Afr. gay*) a pure blooded Zulu.

zelda gooch *n.* [? anecdotal; note late 1970s erotic gay male oriented 'Zelda Gooch' colouring book, created by Wilton David] [1970s] (*camp gay*) anyone considered unfashionable.

zen *n.* [SE *Zen* Buddhism, i.e. its spiritual effects] [1960s+] (*drugs*) LSD.

Zep *n.* (*also* **Zepp**) [abbr.] [1910s+] a *Zeppelin* airship.

IN PHRASES

❑ **Zepps in a cloud** *n.* [visual resemblance] [1910s–20s] sausage and mash.

zerked (out) *adj.* [? abbr. SE *berserk*] [1980s] (*drugs*) completely intoxicated on a drug.

zero *n.* [1920s+] **1** [1920s+] (*also* **double zero**) a nobody, a totally useless and insignificant person. **2** [1920s+] nothing. **3** [1980s] (*US black*) the vagina, sexual intercourse [the 0 shape, or misogyny]. **4** [1990s+] an insignificant, unimpressive place.

IN COMPOUNDS

❑ **zero minus** *adj.* [i.e. 'less than nothing'] [1970s+] (*US campus*) utterly, completely impossible, unacceptable.

IN PHRASES

❑ **deal in zeroes** *v. see under* DEAL *v.* ❑ **take the zero** *v.* [1980s+] (*US campus*) to pass something by, to turn down an offer, to reject.

zero *adj.* [1970s] useless, worthless.

SE in slang uses

IN COMPOUNDS

❑ **zero cool** *adj.* [COOL *adj.* (3)/SE *cool*, i.e. 'no heat whatsoever'] [1950s–60s] (*US campus*) extremely aware, sophisticated. ❑ **zero-hero** *n.* [their alcohol consumption is *zero*] [1990s+] (*UK teen*) the designated non-drinking driver escorting their drinking friends for a night out.

zero *v.* [i.e. to reduce to zero, or nothing] **1** [1980s] to render incompetent, to knock out lit. or fig. **2** [1990s+] (*US/W.I*) to kill, to murder; of an object, to destroy.

zeroed *adj.* [i.e. reduced to a ZERO *n.* (1)] [1960s] (*US campus*) drunk to unconsciousness.

zetz *n.* [synon. Yid.; ult. Ger. *Zurücksetzung*, a setting back] [1970s+] (*US*) a blow or punch, often fig.

z'foot! *excl. see* 'SFOOT! *excl.*

zhlob/zhlub *n. see* SCHLUB *n.*

zhlubby *adj.* [SCHLUB *n.*] [1960s+] (*US*) coarse, boorish.

zhoosh *v.* [echoic of one's rushing about] [mid-19C+] (*Polari*) to fix, to tidy.

zhwah *adj. see* SCHWAH *adj.*

zib *n.* [ety. unknown; ? ZIP *n.*[1] (1), i.e. a human *zero*] [1910s–50s] (*US*) an eccentric person.

ziff *n.*[1] [? SE *thief*] [mid-19C] a young thief.

ziff *n.*[2] [ety. unknown] [1910s+] (*Aus./N.Z.*) a beard.

zig *n.* [var. on JIG *n.*[4] (1)] [1920s–60s] (*US*) a derog. name for a black person.

zigabo/zigaboo/ziggerboo *n. see* JIGABOO *n.*

ziggy *n. see* ZOOK *n.*

zigzagged *adj.* (*also* **zig-a-zag, zigzag**) [one's unsteady gait; reinforced in sense 2 by *Zig-Zag* rolling papers] **1** [1910s–20s] drunk. **2** [1950s] (*drugs*) intoxicated by a drug.

zig-zig *n.* (*also* **zig-zag, ziggy-zig**) [var. on JIG-A-JIG *n.*] [1910s+] sexual intercourse; often found in pidgin slangs.

IN PHRASES

❑ **get the zig** *v.* [? fig. use of ZIG-ZIG *n.*, i.e. 'fucked (off)'] [2000s] to become angry.

zilch *n.*[1] [? US campus *Joe Zilsch*, an insignificant person, popularized in 1930s magazine *Ballyhoo* as Joe Zilch] (*orig. US campus/teen*) **1** [1940s+] zero, nothing, unimportant; also as adj. **2** [1960s] an ordinary or insignificant person.

zilch *n.*[2] [? var. on ZIT *n.*[2] (1)] [1960s+] (*US teen*) a spot or skin blemish.

zilch *v.* [ZILCH *n.*[1] (1)] [1960s+] **1** (*US campus*) to fail or do badly on an examination. **2** to make into nothing.

zillion *n.* (*also* **b'zillion, gajillion, kerzillion**) [1930s+] (*orig. US*) an unspecified, very large number.

zillion, a *adv.* [ZILLION *n.*] [1970s] to a very great extent, very successfully.

zillionaire *n.* [ZILLION *n.*] [1940s+] an uncountably rich person.

zim-zim *n.* [SE *-ism*, i.e. shorthand for politico-ideological beliefs] [1980s] (*S.Afr.*) a member of a politically orientated black youth gang.

zinc *n.*[1] [common metal used as bar surface in France] [1910s] (*Can.*) a bar.

zinc *n.*[2] [1990s+] (*UK juv.*) something extremely unfashionable.

'zine *n.* [abbr.] [1970s] (*US drugs*) Thorazine or Stelazine.

-zine *sfx* [abbr. SE *magazine*] [1960s+] (*US*) used to describe a type of magazine, e.g. *fanzine*, *teenzine*.

zing *n.* [echoic] **1** [1910s+] (*orig. US*) a high-pitched noise. **2** [1910s+] energy, enthusiasm. **3** [1920s] in pl. a state of drunkenness.

IN PHRASES

❑ **put the zing on** *v.* [1930s–40s] **1** to subject someone to one's emotions, whether positive or negative. **2** to ask for money.

zing *v.* [ZING *n.*] (*orig. US*) **1** [1920s+] to rush around energetically or at high-speed. **2** [1930s+] (*also* **zang**) to throw. **3** [1940s+] to make a high-pitched noise. **4** [1960s+] to insult, to tease. **5** [1960s+] to make a snappy delivery of a witticism. **6** [1960s+] to shock with an unforeseen revelation. **7** [1960s+] to bet heavily, usu. at dice.

IN PHRASES

❑ **zing up** *v.* [i.e. to impart ZING *n.* (2)] [1970s] (*orig. US*) to enliven something, e.g. food.

zinger *n.* [ZING *v.* (5)] **1** [1940s+] (*also* **zingie**) something exceptional, whether good or bad. **2** [1940s+] a witty line, a one-line joke or repartee; a slanderous or disparaging comment. **3** [1970s+] a surprise question, an unexpected turn of events.

zingo! *excl. see* BINGO! *excl.* (1).

zingy *adj.* [ZING *n.* (2)] [1930s+] (*orig. US*) enthusiastic, energetic.

Zinski *n.* [the *-zinski* ending of many Polish surnames] [1910s] (*US*) a generic name for a Polish immigrant.

zip *n.*[1] (*also* **zippo**) [SE *zero*] **1** [late 19C+] (*orig. US campus*) a grade or mark of zero. **2** [1950s+] (*US*) nothing. **3** [1960s+] (*US prison*) zero, used in specifying the maximum length of a sentence, e.g. *zip-five*, from 0–5 years; *zip-ten*, 0–10 years etc. **4** [1970s+] (*also* **zip sack**) an insignificant person; an unpleasant person with no good qualities.

IN COMPOUNDS

❑ **zip squat** *n.* [SQUAT *n.*[2]] [1990s+] (*US campus*) a very small amount, nothing.

zip *n.*[2] (*also* **zipp, zippo**) **1** [20C+] energy, a stimulus. **2** [1960s] a highly energetic person.

zip *n.*[3] [SE *sip*] [1950s] a sip of a drink; a single measure of alcohol.

zip *n.*[4] [ZIP *n.*[1] (1), i.e. their alleged lack of intelligence or abbr. ZIPPERHEAD *under* ZIPPER *n.*] [1960s+] (*US*) a derog. term for a Vietnamese (or other Indo-Chinese) person.

zip *n.*[5] [ext. of Z *n.*[2]] [2000s] (*US drugs*) one ounce of a given drug.

zip *adj.* [ZIP *n.*[1] (1)] **1** [1970s+] zero, none. **2** [1980s] (*US campus*) unpleasant, bad, generally negative.

zip *v.*[1] [echoic, esp. of a speeding bullet] (*orig. US*) **1** [mid-19C+] of a vehicle or driver, or an object, to move fast. **2** [late 19C+] of a person, to run around energetically, to be highly energetic; to do something energetically. **3** [1920s+] of a situation, e.g. a stage performance, to move fast. **4** [1970s+] (*orig. US*) to engage in sexual relations [note also SE *zip(per)*].

zip *v.*[2] (*also* **zip up**) [var. on ZIP ONE'S LIP *v.*] [1930s+] to be quiet, to shut up.

(IN EXCLAMATIONS)

□ **zip it (up)!** [1930s+] be quiet! shut up!

zip *v.*[3] [echoic of the *zip* sound of a bullet but note ZIP *n.*[1], i.e. one renders the target 'nothing'] [1960s+] (*US*) to shoot (dead).

zipalid *n.* (*also* **zipperhead, zipperlid**) [i.e. one whose head has been 'unzipped' and the brain removed] [1970s+] a complete fool.

zip coon *n.* [song 'Ole Zip Coon'; ult. COON *n.* (5); defined here as in Major, *Juba to Jive: A Dict. of Afro-American Slang* (1994), but note Tosches, *Where Dead Voices Gather* (2001): 'The figure of the black dandy, the Northern zip coon'] [mid-19C–1920s; 1980s] (*US black*) a subservient black person.

zip (gun) *n.* (*also* **Z**) [SE *zip*, the noise of a fired bullet. To make a *zip gun*, one takes a short length of pipe, 4–10 ins. long, with its inside diameter the same as that of a bullet; a bullet is placed at one end and detonated by a sharp tap from a pointed steel rod which is hit by the heel of one's hand or by a small object] [1940s+] (*US*) a homemade firearm capable of firing single bullets.

ziphead *n. see* ZIPPERHEAD *under* ZIPPER *n.*

zip one's lip *v.* (*also* **zip one's mouth, zipper one's mug, … trap**) [SE *zip* + *lip/mouth*/MUG *n.*[1] (1d)/TRAP *n.*[1] (4)] [1930s+] (*orig. US*) to stop talking, esp. in imper.

zipp *n. see* ZIP *n.*[2].

zipped up *adj. see* ZIPPY *adj.*

zipper *n.* [? such a woman is full of ZIP *n.*[2] (1) or ? the SE *zipper* of the men's trousers] [1920s–30s] a promiscuous woman.

SE in slang uses

(IN COMPOUNDS)

□ **zipper club** *n.* [the lowering of the *zipper* of one's fly] [1970s+] (*US gay*) anywhere that plays host to repeated oral sex, e.g. a lavatory or bath-house. □ **zipperfish** *n.* [1990s+] **1** the penis. **2** the female genitals. □ **zipperhead** *n.* (*also* **ziphead**) **1** [1960s+] (*US*) a Vietnamese, any Asian person. **2** *see* ZIPALID *n.* □ **zipper pockets** *n.* [1970s] (*US*) a mean, grasping person. □ **zipper sex** *n.* (*also* **zipper dinner**) [1970s+] (*US gay*) quick, spontaneous fellatio without even dropping one's trousers, just unzipping and pulling out the penis.

(IN PHRASES)

□ **quick on the zipper** [1960s] (*Aus.*) sexually eager.

zippered *adj.* [? ZAP *v.* or ZIP *n.*[2] (1)] [1940s+] drunk.

zipperlid *n. see* ZIPALID *n.*

zippo *n.*[1] *see* ZIP *n.*[1].

zippo *n.*[2] *see* ZIP *n.*[2].

zippy *n.* [ZIPPY *adj.*] [1910s] (*US*) an exceptional, attractive person.

zippy *adj.* (*also* **zipped up**) [ZIP *n.*[2] (1)] **1** [20C+] energetic, full of 'pep'. **2** [1920s] (*US*) fashionable. **3** [1920s+] fast, speedy. **4** [1990s+] (*drugs*) containing amphetamine or similar stimulant.

zip sack *n. see* ZIP *n.*[1] (4).

zircon *n.* [SE *zircon*, a fake diamond] [1960s] (*US*) a fool.

zit *n.*[1] [1920s] (*US*) facial hair.

zit *n.*[2] [ety. unknown] **1** [1950s+] (*orig. US teen*) (*also* **zat, zitz, zort**) a spot, pimple or blackhead; thus adj. *zitty*, spotty; n., *zitty*, a person with acne. **2** [1960s] (*US campus*) any form of mark. **3** [1960s] (*US campus*) a general insult. **4** [1960s] (*US gay*) an underage boy. **5** [1970s+] a skin blemish left by a lovebite.

(IN COMPOUNDS)

□ **zit doctor** *n.* [1980s] (*US teen*) a dermatologist. □ **zit features** *n.* [1990s+] a general term of abuse, delivered to one who has acne. □ **zithead** *n.* [-HEAD *sfx* (1)] [1990s+] (*US*) a teenager, the image is of acned mediocrity.

zitz *n.* [? ZIT *n.*[1]] [1980s] the vagina, esp. when glimpsed beneath clothes.

zizz *n.*[1] [abbr. PIZZAZZ *n.*] [1940s+] (*US*) gaiety, liveliness.

zizz *n.*[2] (*also* **ziz**) [ZIZZ *v.* (1)] [1940s+] (*orig. milit.*) a nap, a snooze, a brief sleep.

zizz *v.* [echoic] [1930s+] **1** to have a nap or snooze; thus *zizzing*, dozing, napping. **2** (*US*) to move fast. **3** (*US*) to make a sizzling noise.

zizzy *adj.* [the image of an insect buzzing around the eccentric's brain] [1900s] (*US*) crazy.

'zlead!/'zleads!/'zlid! *excl. see* 'SLID! *excl.*

znees *n.* (*also* **znus, znuz**) [? SE *sneeze*, the product of such weather] [18C–mid-19C] frost; thus *zneesy*, frosty (weather).

zo *n.* [abbr.] [1960s] (*US campus*) zoology.

zob *n.* [note Jan Ivarsson on *American Dialect Society-List* 23/3/03: '"Zob" with the variants "zobi", "zeb" or "zébi" is well established in French slang since at least 1870 [...] It comes from maghrebin Arabic "zebbi" or classical Arabic "zubb". The sense of the word is "penis", and it is very often used pejoratively about a person.'] [1900s–40s] (*US*) a good-for-nothing, a weak person.

zod *n.* [SE *he's odd*] [1980s+] (*US campus/teen*) an eccentric, a strange person.

zoftick/zoftig *adj. see* ZAFTIG *adj.*

zogs *n.* [1960s] (*US campus*) the female breasts.

zoid *n.* [-ZOID *sfx*] [1980s+] **1** a school child who has been rejected by their fellows. **2** (*US campus*) a fan of punk rock and its attendant styles.

-zoid *sfx* [1980s+] (*orig. US*) used to invest a variety of terms, usu. negative and derog. descriptions of people, with a 'space-age', SF aura.

zol *n.* [ety. unknown; *zol* is recorded as 1950s US/Mex. border drug use, but no provable link exists; Branford, *Dict. of South African English* (4th edn, 1993) notes the obs. trade name of miniature cheroots but gives no date; if it precedes drug use it would be an obvious root] [1940s+] (*S.Afr. drugs*) **1** a hand-rolled cigarette. **2** a marijuana cigarette; thus *zol-rooker* a marijuana smoker. **3** a measure of marijuana, enough to make a single cigarette. **4** cannabis.

Zola Budd *n.* [the S.Afr. runner *Zola Budd* Pieterse (b.1966) was permitted to represent England after a lengthy press campaign; she ran against the US champion Mary Decker Slaney and stepped on her foot; Decker was considered the superior athlete; thus Budd is equated with the slow vehicles] [1980s+] (*S.Afr.*) **1** a black taxi. **2** a slow armoured police vehicle.

zombie *n.* [SE *zombie*, 'a soulless corpse said to have been revived by witchcraft; formerly, the name of a snake-deity in voodoo cults of or deriving from West Africa and Haiti' (*OED*); ult. Kongo *nzambi*, god, *zumbi*, fetish] **1** [1930s+] (*US black/campus*) a bizarre-looking person. **2** [1940s+] a dullard, a slow-witted person; thus *zombied out*, slow-witted; *zombie up*, to 'freeze'; *zombie off*, to lose consciousness. **3** [1940s+] (*US/UK black*) (*also* **zom box**) a radio or television [radio/television renders its listener/watcher a *zombie*]. **4** [1980s+] (*UK prison*) a prison officer who looks permanently miserable and humourless. **5** [1980s+] a policewoman. **6** [1980s+] (*US black*) a very African-looking person, short of stature, with a dark complexion and broad features. **7** [1980s+] a crack addict.

(IN COMPOUNDS)

□ **zombie (weed)** *n.* (*also* **zombie buzz**) [its effects render one zombie-like] [1970s+] (*drugs*) phencyclidine.

zombied *adj.* (*also* **zombified**) [1980s+] (*US campus*) drunk.

zonched *adj. see* ZORCHED *adj.*

zone *n.* (*also* **zoner**) [ZONE *v.* (3)] [1990s+] (*US drugs*) **1** a habitual drug user. **2** an ounce of crack cocaine.

zone *v.* (*also* **zone out**) [one is in one's own private SE *zone*] **1** [1970s+] to lose consciousness or concentration. **2** [1990s+] to relax. **3** [1990s+] to be intoxicated by a hallucinogenic drug.

IN PHRASES

❑ **in a zone** [1980s+] (*US campus*) out of touch with reality, daydreaming or drunk.

zoned *adj.* (*also* **zoned out**) [ZONE *v.*] [1970s+] **1** (*US*) drunk or intoxicated by a given drug. **2** exhausted, burned out. **3** disorientated.

zoner *n. see* ZONE *n.*

zonk *n.*[1] [ety. unknown] [1940s+] (*S.Afr.*) a sandwich.

zonk *n.*[2] [ZONK *v.*, i.e. one's foolishness is the result of a lit. or fig. blow to the head] [2000s] (*N.Z.*) a fool.

zonk *v.* (*also* **zonk out**) [SE *zonk*, echoic of a blow or solid impact] **1** [1950s+] to hit or strike. **2** [1960s] to fail. **3** [1960s+] to fall asleep. **4** [1970s+] (*US*) to die, to lose consciousness, esp. from alcohol or drugs. **5** [1970s+] to overcome, to knock out, lit. or fig.

zonked (out) *adj.* (*also* **zonkers**) [ZONK *v.*] **1** [1950s+] intoxicated by a given drug or by drink. **2** [1960s+] (*also* **zonky**) confused, mentally impaired. **3** [1960s+] completely exhausted. **4** [1970s+] (*US*) enthusiastic or excited.

zonker *n.* [ZONK *v.*] **1** [1960s] (*US campus*) an unpleasant or unpopular person. **2** [1970s+] anyone who takes drugs to excess.

zonko *n.* [ZONK *v.* + -O *sfx*] [1970s+] (*US campus*) a boring, dull thus socially unacceptable person.

zonk out *v. see* ZONK *v.*

zonky *adj. see* ZONKED (OUT) *adj.* (2).

zoo *n.*[1] [fig. uses of SE *zoo*] **1** [1900s] a bug. **2** [1920s–60s] a jail; a brothel whose workers come from 'all nations'. **3** [1960s+] (*US campus*) a wild party; thus as v., to be noisy and rowdy. **4** [1970s] (*US*) a police station. **5** in personifications [the senses suggest antithetical images of such a place]. (**a**) [1980s] (*US campus*) an amusing person. (**b**) [1990s+] (*W.I.*) a very unattractive person.

zoo *n.*[2] [in a scale where A is best, Z is worst] [1970s+] (*US campus*) the lowest grade possible; thus as v., to fail an exam.

zoodikers! *excl. see* ZOOKS! *excl.*

zooed *adj.* [i.e. reduced to animal-like inarticulacy] **1** [1960s+] (*US campus*) drunk. **2** [1980s+] (*US drugs*) highly intoxicated by a drug.

zooey! *excl. see* ZOWIE! *excl.*

zooie *n.* [ety. unknown] [1960s–70s] (*drugs*) an implement that holds the butt of a marijuana cigarette.

zooie! *excl. see* ZOWIE! *excl.*

zook *n.* **1** [1920s–70s] (*UK black*) a veteran prostitute [ety. unknown]. **2** [1990s+] (*also* **ziggy**) a marijuana cigarette, esp. when laced with crack cocaine [var. on ZOOM *n.*[1] (4)/pron. of SE *cigarette*].

zooks! *excl.* (*also* **zoodikers! zookers!**) [abbr. *GADZOOKS! under* GAD *n.*[1]; 20C+ use is historical/joc.] [17C+] a general excl.

zool *v.* [echoic] [1980s+] (*US campus*) to vomit.

zoolooed *adj.* [? *Zulu*; the image is of a charging warrior as portrayed in the 1964 film] [1970s+] (*US campus*) drunk.

zooly *adj.* [ety. unknown] [1960s] (*US teen*) fine, good, exciting.

zoom *n.*[1] [ZOOM *v.* (1)] **1** [1930s] (*US Und.*) a police raid. **2** [1960s+] zest, vivacity, enthusiasm. **3** [1970s] (*drugs*) amphetamine [the effects]. **4** [1980s+] (*drugs*) phencyclidine; marijuana laced with phencyclidine.

zoom *n.*[2] [abbr. BAZOOM *n.*] [1960s] (*US campus*) the female breast; usu. in pl.

zoom *v.* (*also* **zoom around, zoom off**) [SE *zoom*, echoic of moving at speed] **1** [1910s+] to rush, to move fast. **2** [1930s] to drag someone off quickly. **3** [1930s–40s] (*US black*) to get something without paying for it, e.g. a ticket to a show [i.e. one 'zooms off' with it/'zooms' it away]. **4** [1950s+] (*drugs*) to start to feel a drug working; to exhibit (drug-fuelled) energy.

IN COMPOUNDS

❑ **zoom in** *n.* [1990s+] (*US*) a sudden, unexpected and sometimes unwanted kiss.

IN PHRASES

❑ **on a zoom** [1940s] (*US black*) for free. ❑ **zoom someone off** *v.* [1970s] (*US black*) to deceive, to betray someone emotionally. ❑ **zoom someone out** *v.* [1970s–80s] (*US black*) **1** to amaze, to fascinate, to surprise. **2** to overwhelm someone by the force of one's speech, to take over someone's mind.

zoomer *n.* [abbr. BAZOOM *n.*] [2000s] a female breast.

zoom out *v. see* ZEEK OUT *v.*

zoomy *adj.* [ZOOM *v.* (1)] [1940s+] (*US*) fast, stylish, high-flying.

zoons! *excl. see* ZOUNDS! *excl.*

zoosed *adj. see* ZOTZED *adj.*

zoot *n.*[1] **1** [1940s] (*US*) a member of a teenage gang who wears a ZOOT SUIT *n.* (2). **2** *see* ZOOT SUIT *n.* (2).

zoot *n.*[2] (*also* **zootie, zut**) [ety. unknown] [1970s+] (*UK black*) a cannabis cigarette.

zoot *adj.* [1930s+] (*US black*) over-exaggerated, as applied to clothes.

zoot *v.* [ZOOT SUIT *n.*] [1930s–40s] (*US black*) to dress flashily or vulgarly.

zooted (up) *adj.* (*also* **zootied**) [ZOOT *n.*[2]] [1980s+] (*US black/campus*) under the influence of drink or drugs.

zootie *n.* [ety. unknown] **1** [1980s+] (*US drugs*) phencyclidine. **2** *see* ZOOT *n.*[2].

zoot suit *n.* (*also* **zoot**) [? New Orleans patois *zoot*, cute] **1** [1930s–40s] (*US black*) overexaggerated clothes. **2** [1940s+] (*orig. US black*) a style of suit worn in the 1940s and 1950s, characterized by a long, draped jacket with padded shoulders and high-waisted tapering trousers; thus *zoot-shirt*, a brightly coloured shirt designed to be worn with a zoot suit; *zoot pants*, trousers designed like those of a zoot suit; *zoot suit action*, a fashion competition in which a wearer of a zoot suit attempts to outdo their rivals. **3** [1970s+] (*UK prison*) prison clothing worn in the punishment cell.

DERIVATIVES

❑ **zoot-suiter** *n.* [1930s–60s] (*US*) **1** a wearer of a zoot-suit, thus a fashionable person. **2** in derog. use, a foolish, arrogant, vulgar young man, esp. when his image is boosted by flashy clothes.

IN PHRASES

❑ **zooted up** *adj.* [1940s] (*US*) wearing a *zoot suit*.

zooty *adj.* [ZOOT SUIT *n.*] [1940s–60s] (*US*) flashily dressed, smart.

zoo-zoos and wham-whams *n. see* ZUUZUUS AND WHAMWHAMS *n.*

zorba *n.* [*Zorba the Greek* (1952), the novel and later film by Nikos Kazantakis] [1980s] (*Aus.*) a Greek.

zorba *v.* [rhy. sl.; *Zorba the Greek* = LEAK *v.* (1); ult. *see* ZORBA *n.*] [1950s+] to urinate.

zorba'd *adj.* [rhy. sl.; *Zorba the Greeked* = *leaked* = pissed, i.e. PISSED OFF *adj.*: ult. *see* ZORBA *n.*] [1990s+] annoyed, angry.

zorch *v.* [representative of speed] [1960s] (*Aus.*) to go at speed.

zorch! *excl.* [1970s] an excl. of admiration.

zorched *adj.* (*also* **zonched**) [? ZONKED (OUT) *adj.* + SE *torched*, set on fire] [1960s] experiencing the effects of an excess of drink or drugs; thus *zorch out*, to drink heavily, to take drugs.

zort *n.*[1] [ety. unknown] [1970s] (*US*) a dollar.

zort *n.*[2] *see* ZIT *n.*[2] (1).

zortch *n.* [? ZOT *v.*] [1970s] (*US*) sex.

zot *n.*[1] (*also* **zotz**) [SE *zero* + ? SQUAT *n.*[2]] [1960s+] (*US campus*) zero, e.g. as in an examination.

zot *n.*[2] [ZOT *v.*] **1** [1970s] (*Aus.*) an act of sexual intercourse. **2** [1990s+] (*S.Afr.*) a term of abuse.

zot *n.*[3] [var. on ZIT *n.*[2] (1)] [2000s] (*N.Z.*) a pimple.

zot *v.* [ety. unknown; ? use of initial 'z' to denote speed] **1** [1960s] (*Aus./US*) to hit. **2** [1960s+] (*orig. US*) to move quickly; thus *zot* *along, zot down* etc. **3** [1970s] (*Aus.*) to act in a speedy manner, to do something abruptly, e.g. down a drink.

zot! *excl.* [echoic] [1960s–70s] (*Aus.*) an excl. denoting suddenness.

zotz *n.* see ZOT *n.*[1].

zotz *v.* [ZETZ *n.*] [1990s+] (*US*) to kill, to murder.

zotzed *adj.* (*also* **zoosed**) [fig. use of ZOTZ *v.*] [1990s+] (*US*) drunk, intoxicated by drugs.

zouch *n.* [? SE *slouch*, 'an awkward, slovenly, or ungainly man; a lubber, lout, clown; also, a lazy, idle fellow' (*OED*)] [18C] a slovenly, ungenteel man, one who walks with a slouch.

zoucher *n. see* SYCHER *n.*

zounds! *excl.* (*also* **sowns! sounds! zoons! zouns!**) [late 16C+] a euph. excl., lit. 'God's wounds!'; sometimes intensified to *zounds and blood!* or *zounds and death!*

z-out *v. see* Z *v.*

zowie *n.* [ZOWIE! *excl.*] [1910s+] keenness, enthusiasm, energy.

zowie! *excl.* (*also* **zooey! zooie! zowy!**) [echoic of speed] [20C+] (*orig. US*) an excl. used to describe a sudden impact, or fig. amazement.

z's *see under* Z.

zubrick *n.* [Arabic *zubrak*, the penis] [1960s+] (*Aus./US gay*) the penis.

zuch *n.* [? ZOUCH *n.*] [1940s+] (*US Und.*) an informer.

zuche *n.* [obs. SE *zuche*, a withered tree-stump] [mid-19C] (*UK Und.*) an ageing, run-down prostitute.

zug up *v.* [ety. unknown; ? the shape of the letter 'Z' implies raggedness] [20C+] (*W.I., Gren.*) to cut a man's or boy's hair in an amateurish, raggedy manner.

zuke *v.* [echoic] [1980s+] (*US campus*) to vomit.

Zulu *n.* [SE *Zulu*, a member of a Bantu people inhabiting Zululand or Natal] [late 19C+] (*US*) a derog. term for a black person.

IN PHRASES

❑ **Zulu princess** *n.* [1960s–70s] (*US gay*) a young, handsome black man.

zulu *n.* [derog. stereotyping of aggressive, violent blacks (since Zulus have a reputation as fighters)] [1920s] (*US*) a thug.

zum-zum *n.* [? var. on PUM-PUM *n.*[2]] [2000s] (*W.I*) the vagina.

zup *n.* [ZUP *v.*] [2000s] (*UK black*) an escape.

zup *v.* [one 'ups and' leaves] [2000s] (*UK black*) to make an escape.

'zup? *phr. see* WHAT'S UP? *phr.*

zurucker *n.* [Ger. *zurück*, backwards; thus ? detectives follow a line of clues *backwards* to the perpetrator] [1940s] (*Aus.*) a police trooper.

zut *n. see* ZOOT *n.*[2].

zutt *n.* [? play on BUTT *n.*[1] (2a)] [1950s] (*UK black*) a cigarette end.

zutupeck *n.* [ety. unknown] [1990s+] (*W.I.*) an unattractive woman.

zuuzuus and whamwhams *n.* (*also* **zoo-zoos and wham-whams**) [ety. unknown; but SAmE *Zu-Zu* or *Zou-Zou*, a nickname for the Zouaves in the Union Army] [1960s+] (*US prison*) confectionery sold to the prisoners.

zybo-fucker *n.* [ety. unknown] [2000s] (*US black*) a white man who seduces a black man's woman, esp. by force or greater material wealth.

zzz *see under* Z.

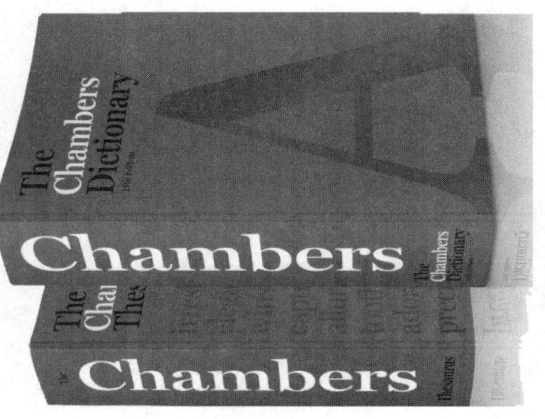